ST. JAMES GUIDE TO
CHILDREN'S *Writers*

St. James Guide to Writers Series
(formerly Twentieth-Century Writers Series)

St. James Guide to Children's Writers
St. James Guide to Crime & Mystery Writers
St. James Guide to Fantasy Writers
St. James Guide to Horror, Ghost & Gothic Writers
St. James Guide to Science Fiction Writers
St. James Guide to Young Adult Writers

Twentieth-Century Romance & Historical Writers
Twentieth-Century Western Writers

ST. JAMES GUIDE TO

CHILDREN'S *Writers*

FIFTH EDITION

WITH A PREFACE BY
MARGARET MAHY

EDITORS
SARA PENDERGAST
&
TOM PENDERGAST

ST. JAMES PRESS
AN IMPRINT OF GALE

DETROIT • LONDON

Sara Pendergast & Tom Pendergast, *Editors*

Laura Standley Berger and David Collins, *Project Coordinators*

Joann Cerrito, Nicolet V. Elert, Miranda Ferrara,
Kristin Hart, Margaret Mazurkiewicz, Michael J. Tyrkus,
St. James Press Staff

Peter M. Gareffa, *Managing Editor, St. James Press*

Mary Beth Trimper, *Production Director*
Cindy Range, *Production Assistant*

Cynthia Baldwin, *Product Design Manager*
Pamela Galbreath, *MacIntosh Artist*

The paper used in this publication meets the minimum
requirements of American National Standard for Information Sciences—
Permanence Paper for Printed Library Materials, ANSI Z39.48-1984.

This book is printed on recycled paper that meets Environmental Protection Agency Standards.

ISBN 1-55862-369-8

Printed in the United States of America
Published simultaneously in the United Kingdom

St. James Press is an imprint of Gale

10 9 8 7 6 5 4 3 2 1

CONTENTS

PREFACE

Out on the Edge

by Margaret Mahy

Instruction is part of the traditional function of children's stories, though that instruction takes many forms. There is the sort of instruction which can be described as "moral" or "politically correct" and which compels the story to set a good example according to the perceptions of the time. There is an ancient expectation that a child will be a better and brighter child as a result of listening to such tales. But there is also in children's stories an older and less self-conscious tradition. Once upon a time adults and children listened to the same stories; there was no such category as children's literature. The storyteller told, and the listeners, regardless of age, listened and were accordingly terrified or mystified or transformed with satisfaction as the good ended happily and the bad unhappily. All the same these stories have mysterious and implicit instructions of their own, for they knot listeners or readers into a network of fellowship, allowing them to recognise their own idiom, and to see their own faces reflected in the storyteller's eyes or, perhaps, looking back at them from behind the lines on the page. "This is who you are," the story tells us, secretly reinforcing familiar actions, scenes, and language, vindicating our existences and completing the world out there by giving it internal existence as well.

Like most writers for children I began as a listener, progressed to being a reader, and grew determined to make myself as much a part of the story as possible, by pushing my way into it and sometimes telling it what to do. I loved stories for their clarity of event, and their games with words, for their jokes, for the sympathy and alarm they aroused in me and for their energetic drive to a conclusion. I loved them because, through the exciting lives of the characters inside the stories, my own life was fulfilled. However, the internal reality the stories created within me was always a little at odds with my outer world.

My situation, first as reader and later as writer, was both commonplace and peculiar. Like many older people in Australia and New Zealand I grew up hearing stories that were, almost without exception, stories from another place. My parents, along with most European New Zealanders of the time, thought of England as the cradle of civilisation and of ourselves as exemplifying, through inheritance, all the English virtues. The first stories they read to me were tales from their own childhoods—folk and fairy tales, Beatrix Potter, A. A. Milne—and were overwhelmingly English. Later I was read Ballentyne, Marryatt, and Rider Haggard as my parents continued to share their own childhood favourites with me. But the country in which they were reading me these stories lay on the opposite side of the world from the counties in which the stories originated, and the stories in which I most closely recognised the mood of my own community tended to be Australian ones. So my absorption in story did not tie me into my own country, but set up a disjunction between real and imaginative life which, though largely eliminated by now, I still detect from time to time as a primitive belief that true story-life belongs in some zone where lions, children, cowboys, crocodiles, explorers, and winged horses, along with various magical identities, are glimpsed in the shadows of fantastic forests, forests that never quite coincide with the forests of New Zealand.

There were books produced in New Zealand of course. They tended to be despised for their crude production and illustration, but they were around if you knew where to look for them. Some of them were so imitative of their British models they might almost have been British, and their local reference seemed irrelevant. Some of these titles were good books, written in New Zealand but published in the United Kingdom, and enjoyed a reasonably extended life. Others vanished, virtually unread and remembered by no one. Locally produced children's books were not easy to find in our bookshops. They tended to be overwhelmed by more elegantly produced British books, and the necessarily small size of each print run meant that they were not necessarily cheaper than books imported from half way around the world. They were not displayed in any significant way. Indeed they tended to have an embarrassed and accidental appearance on bookshop shelves.

From the time I began writing at the age of seven I had all the ambitions of a hardworking tradesperson: I wanted not only to tell a story, but to publish a book, and to make a living as a writer. I went in for competitions, sent stories and poems to children's pages in papers and magazines with some success, and to publishers in Australia and New Zealand with no success at all. The paradox was that in order to compete with the books coming in from overseas these publishers needed to concentrate on stories with local themes—the very books I found myself incapable of writing with any ease. In 1960, when I was about twenty four, I sent several stories to the *New Zealand School Journal,* a particularly successful literary magazine (though, since it is aimed at children, it has never really been acknowledged as such). These stories included at least one which was set rather self-consciously in New Zealand. The editors, recognising my lack of ease with local reference, ignored the story which had been particularly included to please them and chose those set in that other unclassifiable domain, storyland itself. I continued to write industriously and prolifically for the *New Zealand School Journal* and the *New South Wales School Magazine* and to submit stories for possible publication in both Australia and New Zealand, though still without any great success.

In or about 1967 copies of the *New Zealand School Journal* were sent to the United States as part of an international printing exhibition, and one of my stories, *A Lion In the Meadow,* was noticed by an editor working for Franklin Watts Incorporated. This editor wrote to me, suggesting that I might like to have the story published as a book, a proposal which transformed me with astonishment and delight. I responded with predictable enthusiasm, completely unaware of just how lucky I was. In those halcyon days, I was told some years later, there was a federal grant available to many schools in the United States, a grant which was to be spent on books, and only on books. Authors and illustrators of children's books, along with their publishers, were enjoying a boom time, and, sliding around on the uneasy edges, I profited from it. Asked if I had other stories to show I responded by sending everything that seemed remotely possible, over a hundred stories and poems I was later told. Mrs. Helen Hoke Watts, an editor and director of Franklin Watts Inc., actually came to New Zealand to see me. "The wonderful thing about your stories," she told me, "is that no one could tell they were written in New Zealand." She believed herself to be paying me a compliment but there was a degree of uneasiness mixed in with the pleasure with which I received her praise. Predictably enough perhaps, though my stories were launched with an incredible ebullience—five picture books came out in 1969, along with a colour brochure recommending them to librarians and parents—my books, for many years, did better in the United Kingdom than in the United States. And in my own country I profited from a false psychological advantage. Being published overseas, back then, suggested that a writer must be a better writer than if he or she were simply published locally. Stories were admired for international success at least much as for the quality of the writing. Besides, there were still not many children's books published in New Zealand. In 1969 local bibliography records twenty-two new titles, five of them, if I may boast a little, by me.

All the same, there were many aspects of my stories which were far more local than I had realised, and editors in the United Kingdom and the United States detected these elements with professional precision, generally requesting me to discard them. British editors suggested I cut out any mention of yellow leaves in May or of roses in November, since it was felt that such references would confuse British children. New Zealanders and Australians still point out rather self-righteously that they have never demanded such alterations in stories coming from the United Kingdom and the United States. Antipodean children cope with such confusions quite cheerfully. Nevertheless even Australia, that bigger market across the Tasman, sometimes demands alterations in New Zealand texts. In the end it becomes a question of the power of the market making the demands. Publishers in the United States want their own vocabularies to be used. Not all authors hasten to go along with them, though I certainly did. It is not always a question of substituting, say, "sidewalk" for "footpath" either. All sorts of small moral judgements have tended to intrude over the years. In my picture book *Jam,* Mr. Castle offers Mrs. Castle a sherry when she comes home at night after a hard day's work. While British publishers accepted this as a civilized act of adult consideration, editors in the United States did not want the story corrupted by any mention of alcohol. In the United States, Mr. Castle simply offers Mrs. Castle a drink. When editors in the United States wanted a pirate to drink passionfruit juice rather than rum, however, I found myself insisting that rum was basic to piratical cuisine, and I wanted it kept that way in my story. The editors indulged me, though commenting plaintively that it would affect the book's sales—and perhaps it did. I am sure there are people who scan children's stories hoping to detect such moral aberration. However this was one of the cases where I felt one had to be true to the underlying archetype—that I must not allow the pirate to become too wholesome. Once again I was made aware of the clash between the two systems—the one that recognises the story as art and the one that tries to make the book profitable (to the benefit of both author and publisher) by responding to perceived public morality.

By now I have written many books, and some of them have done well. The picture book stories are illustrated by people who, with one exception, have never seen the place in which I live—but the illustrator's images do not have to match up with the author's provided they are true to the story itself. I have had two books illustrated by Steven Kellogg, who creates in his pictures a storybook land that is all its own, yet which is co-existent with mine. His visual stories and my verbal ones sit together on the page and, in spite of the distance between us, seem to make a satisfactory whole. I love the way he extends my story with his own pictorial narratives. Yet *The Rattlebang Picnic,* which features a volcano, seems to me to be a New Zealand story, though secretly so. There is a reference at the end of the story, to a place of possible future adventure: Tornado Valley. Originally this place was named Earthquake Valley, but the name was changed because the book was to be launched at a Bookseller's Conference in Los Angeles, a city which had recently suffered a very bad earthquake of its own, and it was felt that any light-hearted reference to earthquakes would be in doubtful taste. I certainly do not wish to joke about anyone else's misfortunes, and I do not underestimate the ferocity of earthquakes (of which I have felt many). However, when I read the story to children in New Zealand I find myself correcting the text on the page. "Earthquake Valley," I find myself saying, because, deep down I believe that this is its true name. The alteration of that one word makes a New Zealand story of *The Rattlebang Picnic*. We do not, on the whole, have tornadoes here, but we do have earthquakes just as we have volcanoes. Steven's picture land, complete with vultures, is not a New Zealand landscape, but the underlying voice telling the story becomes, in my ears at least, a New Zealand voice.

I have frequently thought about my own disjunction. By now I have worked my way to a point where I can write naturally about my own country, though many of my simpler stories are still set in that story country where children can quite readily consort with crocodiles. I don't regret any of my childhood reading. Even if there were disadvantages in my displacement there were advantages too, for I think my reading made me a citizen of the world in many important ways. I think of stories as setting up networks of imaginative connection, and in certain stories written for older children, I make reference, through quotation and allusion, to the existence of this network. Some people object to this, feeling it is not quite democratic, that there is something of elitism in this appeal to unnaturally well read children. I was asked at one stage to take references to *The Jungle Book* out of my novel *The Other Side of Silence,* since (I was told) "nobody reads *The Jungle Book* any more." The publishers were probably right. I must say I don't know of any children who read it but the central situation of the story lives on, (though altered and distorted) in film. Reference and association is still legitimate, and I do not think the good reader should be denied these satisfactions, which constantly knit and re-knit meaning.

Still, we live in a changing world. The federal funding of books for schools in the United States has, I gather, long since disappeared. In New Zealand businesses will sponsor computers for schools but schools struggle to provide their own books. They have had "responsibility for their own libraries restored to them." (I quote a piece of Government jargon, which heralded a cut in school library services). Libraries in the United Kingdom, the United States, and in New Zealand too, suffer from reduced funding. Yet children's books are being produced in greater numbers.

When I go to Australia I am astonished by the authors and illustrators of whom I was unaware, similarly in the United States and Canada. Australians coming to New Zealand are surprised in turn to find how many children's books we publish these days. And these days books by New Zealand writers are now prominently displayed in local book shops and most children can read accounts of lives and events that readily link into their own. The landscapes, sunrises, city monuments, motorways, the plumes of lazy smoke over distant volcanoes—all these are referred to with a new ease, and have indeed become part of the imagination of the community. Maori tales are available in both languages. People are proud of our local literature, and what was once an advantage to me—the advantage of being recognised internationally—is no longer anything like the same advantage. Books brought in from abroad are very expensive, and New Zealanders, let alone Australians, are much more confident of their own excellence. And I, well, I have written so very much. A few years ago this was an advantage, but now my books tend to compete with one another in local bookshops.

The advantage of all this is finding our own place recognised and celebrated in stories for children. The danger, since there are always dangers, is the growth of a new insularity. England finds it harder to sell its books here than formerly, for now we have so many of our own. The number of books being published world-wide is huge (between seven and eight thousand new titles for children every year in the United Kingdom alone, I am told) and all at a time when a book's power to confer status is lessening relative to the glory inherent in a whole range of other objects and activities: computer games, organised sport, and television watching. Many books are not kept in print long enough to establish themselves in the traditional way. The necessities of the publishing industry and the cost of books may cause us to retreat into our own culturally fortified castles, looking out nervously at a changing world. I do want to see countries like New Zealand developing their own literature ... but I do not want my grandchildren to lose what I once had: access to stories of the world, stories in print, stories for the voice. Images dominate so much story-telling these days, and I do not want the narrative power and poetry of language to be ignored. As for life on the edge, I don't know that it exists any more, since systems like the Internet ensure that everyone who is on the edge can simultaneously be in the centre too. Sometimes it seems that, in spite of that old imaginative dislocation, I am having the best of several worlds, and, in greedy moments, I'm sure I hope so.

EDITOR'S NOTE

The *St. James Guide to Children's Writers* is a new edition of *Twentieth-Century Children's Writers*. The book includes English-language authors and illustrators of fiction, nonfiction, poetry, and drama for children. An expert advisory board selected the entrant list.

The majority of the book focuses on authors whose work was published after 1900. For your convenience, an appendix contains information on some important 19th century authors. Since some children's books translated from other languages have had an important impact in English-speaking countries, information on selected foreign-language writers is included in the back of the book.

Entries include a biography, a complete list of published works, and a signed critical essay. Critical essays were written especially for this book by professors of English and children's literature, librarians, teachers, book reviewers, critics, and other individuals knowledgeable in the field. All living authors were encouraged to submit a personal comment on their books for children.

Original English-language, British, and U.S. editions of all works have been listed; revised editions have been included as well. The "Publications for Children" rubric lists titles that at some time since their publication have been considered children's books.

This book's companion volume, the *St. James Guide to Young Adult Writers,* contains authors considered primarily writers for young adults. Some authors found previously in *Twentieth-Century Children's Writers* can now be found in the *St. James Guide to Young Adult Writers.*

ADVISERS

Pat Donlon
Barbara Elleman
Betty Gilderdale
David H. Jenkinson
Fiona Lafferty
Donnarae MacCann
Amy McClure
Peter F. Neumeyer
Jon C. Stott

CONTRIBUTORS

Lucien L. Agosta
Janice M. Alberghene
William D. Anderson
Marilyn F. Apseloff
Fran Ashdown
Judith Atkinson
Gillian Avery

Janet E. Baker
Jan Bakker
Keith Barker
Ann Bartholomew
Juliana Bayfield
Anthea Bell
Linda Benson
Valerie Bierman
Betty Boegehold
Freida Bostian
Bill Boyle
Patricia Bradley
J. S. Bratton
Julia Briggs
Valerie Brinkley-Willsher
Angela Bull
Mary Mehlman Burns
Dorothy Butler
Francelia Butler
Dennis Butts

Mary Cadogan
Alasdair K.D. Campbell
Margaret Campbell
Humphrey Carpenter
Michael Cart
Anne Carter
Charity Chang
Joel Chaston
Mary Blount Christian
John Churcher
Berna C. Clark
Pamela Cleaver
Ilene L. Cooper
Frank Corbett
Mary Silva Cosgrave
Patricia Craig
Anne Drolett Creany
Hilary S. Crew
Marcus Crouch
Mary Croxson
Norman Culpan

Alan Edwin Day
Rosanne Fraine Donahue
Pat Donlon
Jane Doonan
Brain Doyle
Robert Dunbar
Peter du Sautoy

Audrey Eaglen
Judith Elkin
Barbara Elleman
Anne W. Ellis
Sarah Ellis
A.W. England
Clarie England
Fred Erisman
Gwyneth Evans

Ellen G. Fader
Adele M. Fasick
Martha J. Fick
Tom Fitzgibbon
Sheila Flanagan
Rachel Fordyce
Geoff Fox
Gillian Freeman
Norma R. Fryatt

Marcia G. Fuchs

James Cross Giblin
Lois Rauch Gibson
Betty Gilderdale
Michael Glover
Jacqueline L. Gmuca
Cecilia Gordon
John Gough
Margaret Greaves
Roger Lancelyn Green
Lucille Gregory
Patrick Groff

Irene Haas
Eric Hadley
Dennis Hall
Dennis Hamley
Graham Hammond
Nancy C. Hammond
Jane Anne Hannigan
Anne Harvey
Ann G. Hay
Renee Haynes
Diane Hebley
Peggy Heeks
Ravenna Helson
Linnea Hendrickson
James E. Higgins
Elbert R. Hill
Martha Hixon
Peter Hollidale
Jackie Horne
Karen Nelson Hoyle
Caroline C. Hunt
Peter Hunt

Fred Inglis

Clara O. Jackson
David H. Jenkinson
Coleman A. Jennings
Patrick Jones
Raymond E. Jones
Ursula M. Jones
Nels Juleus

Marilyn Kaye
Hugh T. Keenan
Gordon R. Kelly
Edward Kemp
Meena Khorana
Eric A. Kimmel
Lee Kingman
Carolyn T. Kingston
Gillian Klein
Judson Knight

Fiona Lafferty
Selma G. Lanes
Keith Lawrence
Anne Lazim
Robert Leeson
Linda S. Levstik
Claudia Lewis
Naomi Lewis
Mary J. Lickteig
Myra Cohn Livingston
Rebecca J. Lukens
Mary Lystad

Donnarae MacCann
Alexandra MacLennan
Anne Scott MacLeod
Gertrud Mander
Gwen Marsh
Margaret R. Marshall
Janelle Mathis
Margaret F. Maxwell
Jill P. May
David McCord
Christine McDonnell
Myles McDowell
Joan McGrath
Walter McVitty
Margaret Meek
Leonard R. Mendelsohn
Cathryn M. Mercier
Jean F. Mercier
Susan Meyers
Christine Miller
Colin Mills
Joan Mills
Irma McDonough Milnes
Noami Mitchison
Christian H. Moe
Francis J. Molson
Doris Langley Moore
Caroline Moorehead
Anita Moss
Elaine Moss
Marcie Muir

Stephanie Nettell
Mary Nettleford
Peter F. Neumeyer
Vivien Noakes

Osayimwense Osa
Ruth Osler

Jill Paton Walsh
Lissa Paul
Kit Pearson
Pat Pflieger
Kathy Piehl
Reba Pinney
Robert Protherough

Eric Quayle

Sheila G. Ray
Mary Raynor
David Rees
James Reeves
Selma K. Richardson
Mae Durham Roger
Jim Roginski
Nancy Tillman Romalov
Gerald J. Rubio
Mary Rubio
Jean Russell

Glen Edward Sadler
Allison Sage
Lance Salway
Rebecca Saulsbury
Maurice Saxby
Elizabeth Schafer
Nancy J. Schmidt
Mabel D. Segun
Richard D. Seiter
Nancy Shepherdson
Carolyn Shute
Dorothy D. Siles
Sanjay Sircar
Sarah M. Smedman
Karen Patricia Smith
John Robert Sorfleet
John D. Stahl
Susan B. Steffel
Kenneth J. Sterck
Madeleine B. Stern
Rosemary Stones
Christine Doyle Stott
Jon C. Stott

Zena Sutherland

Gwen Athene Tarbox
Jennifer Taylor
Joyce Thomas
Ann Thwaite
John Rowe Townsend
Geoffrey Trease
Felicity Trotman
Margaret M. Tye

Kay E. Vandergrift
Peter Vansittart

Margaret Walker
Aidan Warlow
Fiona Waters
Marcia Welsh
Joyce Irene Whalley
Joy Whitby
Kerry White
Frank Whitehead
Winifred Whitehead
Angela Wigan
Martin Williams
Denise Murcko Wilms
Barbara Ker Wilson
Lisa A. Wroble

Jessica Yates
Linda Yeatman
Jane Yolen

Laura Zaidman
Linda Zoppa

ST. JAMES GUIDE TO
CHILDREN'S *Writers*

LIST OF ENTRANTS

Verna Aardema
Chester Aaron
Chinua Achebe
Jeanie Adams
Arnold Adoff
John Agard
Allan and Janet Ahlberg
Ruth Ainsworth
Sue Ann Alderson
Lloyd Alexander
Aliki
Mabel Esther Allan
Eric Allen
Jonathan Allen
Pamela Allen
George Ancona
C. W. Anderson
Prudence Andrew
J. S. Andrews
Peggy Appiah
Edward Ardizzone
Ronda Armitage
Richard Armstrong
Ruth Arthur
Honor Arundel
Meshack Asare
Frank Asch
Richard Atwater
Esther Averill
Gillian Avery
W. V. Awdry
Jim Aylesworth

Natalie Babbitt
Martha Bacon
R. L. Bacon
Enid Bagnold
Carolyn Sherwin Bailey
Betty Baker
Jeannie Baker
Molly Garrett Bang
Angela Banner
Helen Bannerman
Cicely Mary Barker
Kitty Barne
J. M. Barrie
Margaret Stuart Barry
Graeme Base
Leonard Baskin
L. Frank Baum
Nina Beachcroft
John and Patricia Beatty
Ian Beck
Michael Bedard
Shonto Begay
Harry Behn
Hilaire Belloc
Ludwig Bemelmans
Rex Benedict
Stan and Jan Berenstain
Elisabeth Beresford
Leila Berg
James Berry
Bettina
Margery Williams Bianco
Val Biro
Claire Huchet Bishop
Donald Bisset
Malorie Blackman
Ann Blades
Quentin Blake
Erik Blegvad
Joan W. Blos
Judy Blume
Enid Blyton
N. M. Bodecker
Michael Bond
Ruskin Bond
Crosby Bonsall
Arna Bontemps
Lucy Boston
Helen Dore Boylston
Tony Bradman
Christianna Brand
John Branfield
Angela Brazil
Elinor M. Brent-Dyer
Teresa Breslin
Jan Brett
Norman Bridwell
K. M. Briggs
Raymond Briggs
Robert Bright
Carol Ryrie Brink
Hesba Brinsmead
Joyce Lankester Brisley
Bill Brittain
L. Leslie Brooke
William Brooke
Walter R. Brooks
Marc Brown
Marcia Brown
Margaret Wise Brown
Pamela Brown
Roy Brown
Ruth Brown
Anthony Browne
Dorita Fairlie Bruce
Mary Grant Bruce
Joseph Bruchac
Ashley Bryan
Margaret Buffie
Angela Bull
Clyde Robert Bulla
Thornton Waldo Burgess
Ben Lucien Burman

Frances Hodgson Burnett
Sheila Burnford
John Burningham
Virginia Lee Burton
Nick Butterworth
Oliver Butterworth

Joanna Cannan
Eric Carle
Natalie Savage Carlson
Bruce Carter
Peter Carter
Sylvia Cassedy
Arthur Catherall
Charles Causley
Mary Chalmers
Nan Chauncy
Christine Chaundler
Joseph E. Chipperfield
Charlotte Chorpenning
Richard Church
John Ciardi
Ann Nolan Clark
Catherine Anthony Clark
Emma Chichester Clark
Leonard Clark
Mavis Thorpe Clark
Gus Clarke
Pauline Clarke
Beverly Cleary
Dorothy Clewes
Lucille Clifton
Shirley Climo
Eleanor Clymer
Elizabeth Coatsworth
Mary Cockett
Eleanor Coerr
Barbara Cohen
Babette Cole
Brock Cole
Padraic Colum
Marita Conlon-McKenna
Barbara Cooney
Lettice Cooper
Scott Corbett
W. J. Corbett
William Corlett
Joy Cowley
Helen Cresswell
Donald Crews
Samuel Rutherford Crockett
Richmal Crompton
Margrit Cruickshank
Pat Cummings
John Cunliffe
Julia Cunningham
Jane Louise Curry

Penny Dale
Alice Dalgliesh
Ruth Dallas
Annie Dalton
Niki Daly
David Scott Daniell
Marjorie Darke
James Daugherty
Edgar and Ingri Parin d'Aulaire
Andrew Davies
Peter Dawlish
C. Day Lewis
Marguerite de Angeli
J. O. de Graft-Hanson
Joan de Hamel
Meindert De Jong
Walter de la Mare
Demi
Tomie dePaola
Beatrice Schenk de Regniers
Anne de Roo
Anita Desai
Elizabeth Borton de Treviño
Lynley Dodd
Mary Alice Downie
V. H. Drummond
William Pène du Bois
Maurice Duggan
Jane Duncan
Norman Duncan
Mary Durack
Roger Duvoisin

Edward Eager
Walter D. Edmonds
Dorothy Edwards
Monica Edwards
Lois Ehlert
Cyprian Ekwensi
E. M. Ellin
Buchi Emecheta
Elizabeth Enright
Eleanor Estes
Marie Hall Ets
Hubert Evans

Eleanor Farjeon
G. E. Farrow
Max Fatchen
Louise Fatio
Edward Fenton
Kathleen Fidler
Rachel Field
Anna Fienberg
Anne Fine
George Finkel
Winifred Finlay
Aileen Fisher
Dorothy Canfield Fisher
Leonard Everett Fisher
Sheree Fitch
John D. Fitzgerald
Louise Fitzhugh
Marjorie Flack
Sid Fleischman
James Flora
Dennis Foon
Michael Foreman

Antonia Forest
Mem Fox
Barbara C. Freeman
Bill Freeman
Don Freeman
Fiona French
Maeve Friel
Jean Fritz
Gyo Fujikawa
Roy Fuller
Rose Fyleman
J. G. Fyson

Wanda Gág
Laszlo Gal
Ruth Stiles Gannett
Joyce Gard
Patricia Gauch
Maria Louise Gay
Maurice Gee
Gail Gibbons
May Gibbs
Phoebe Gilman
Nikki Giovanni
Libby Gleeson
Morris Gleitzman
Paul Goble
Martyn Godfrey
Rumer Godden
Gaelyn Gordon
John Gordon
Edward Gorey
Elizabeth Goudge
Bob Graham
Eleanor Graham
Harry Graham
Kenneth Grahame
Hardie Gramatky
Nicholas Stuart Gray
Margaret Greaves
Roger Lancelyn Green
Bette Greene
Constance C. Greene
Eloise Greenfield
Ted Greenwood
Frederick Grice
Helen V. Griffith
G. D. Griffiths
Helen Griffiths
Nikki Grimes
Johnny Gruelle

Berta and Elmer Hader
Roderick Haig-Brown
J. B. S. Haldane
Kathleen Hale
Joyce Hansen
Michael Hardcastle
Lee Harding
Aurand Harris
Geraldine Harris
Mary K. Harris
Rosemary Harris

Libby Hathorn
Erik Haugaard
Charles Boardman Hawes
John F. Hayes
Carolyn Haywood
Mairi Hedderwick
Florence Parry Heide
Marguerite Henry
Constance Heward
Anita Hewett
Florence Hightower
Jamake Highwater
E. W. Hildick
David Hill
Lorna Hill
Russell Hoban
Mary Ann Hoberman
C. Walter Hodges
Margaret Hodges
Syd Hoff
Mary Hoffman
Grace Hogarth
Isabelle Holland
Holling C. Holling
William Hooks
Jacynth Hope-Simpson
Charlotte Hough
Gloria Houston
James Howe
Edith Howes
Jan Hudson
Shirley Hughes
Katharine Hull and Pamela Whitlock
Mabel Leigh Hunt
Peter Hunt
Bernice Thurman Hunter
Norman Hunter
Thatcher Hurd
Johanna Hurwitz
Hazel Hutchins
Pat Hutchins
Trina Schart Hyman

Rachel Isadora
Sulamith Ish-Kishor

Jesse Jackson
Will James
Randall Jarrell
Ann Jellicoe
W. E. Johns
Angela Johnson
Crockett Johnson
Ann Jonas
Sherryl Jordan
William Joyce
Aaron Judah
Mavis Jukes

Virginia Kahl
Elijah Kariuki
Geraldine Kaye
Ezra Jack Keats

Charles Keeping
Steven Kellogg
Eric Kelly
Gene Kemp
Richard Kennedy
X. J. Kennedy
Tim Kennemore
Judith Kerr
Dayal Kaur Khalsa
Barbara Kimenye
Lee Kingman
Dick King-Smith
Rudyard Kipling
Jim Kjelgaard
Eric Knight
E. L. Konigsburg
Gordon Korman
Phyllis Krasilovsky
Joanna Halpert Kraus
Robert Kraus
Ruth Krauss
William Kurelek
Don Kushner
Karla Kuskin
Michael Kusugak
Elisabeth Kyle

Lois Lamplugh
Evelyn Sibley Lampman
Jack Lasenby
Deborah Nourse Lattimore
Eleanor Lattimore
Ann Lawrence
Robert Lawson
Munro Leaf
Dennis Lee
Amy Le Feuvre
Madeleine L'Engle
Lois Lenski
Betty Levin
Elizabeth Levy
C. S. Lewis
Hilda Lewis
Joan M. Lexau
Betty Jean Lifton
Norman Lindsay
David Line
Eric Linklater
Leo Lionni
William Lipkind
Janet Taylor Lisle
Jean Little
Lessie Jones Little
Penelope Lively
Myra Cohn Livingston
Anita Lobel
Arnold Lobel
Elsie Locke
Hugh Lofting
Maud Hart Lovelace
Janet Lunn
Patricia Lynch
Mary E. Lyons

David Macaulay
Caroline Macdonald
Elisabeth MacIntyre
Claire Mackay
Constance D'Arcy Mackay
Walter Macken
Patricia MacLachlan
Angus MacVicar
Gregory Maguire
Margaret Mahy
Rosemary Manning
Ruth Manning-Sanders
Bessie Marchant
Markoosie
James Marshall
David Martin
Petra Mathers
Christobel Mattingley
Mercer Mayer
Sam McBratney
Tom McCaughren
Robert McCloskey
David McCord
Emily Arnold McCully
Gerald McDermont
Sheryl McFarlane
Phyllis McGinley
Roger McGough
Iona McGregor
Hilary McKay
David McKee
Patricia and Frederick McKissack
Allan Campbell McLean
Janet McNeill
Stephen W. Meader
Mary Melwood
Jean Merrill
Laurence Meynell
A. A. Milne
Else Minarik
Wendell Minor
Elyne Mitchell
Naomi Mitchison
Tololwa M. Mollel
F. N. Monjo
L. M. Montgomery
Dorothea Moore
Ursula Moray Williams
Walt Morey
Alison Morgan
Helen Morgan
Jean Morris
Dhan Gopal Mukerji
Michael Mullen
Robin Muller
Robert Munsch
Jill Murphy
Jim Murphy

Bill Naughton
Phyllis Reynolds Naylor
Violet Needham
E. Nesbit

Evaline Ness
Robert Newman
Ruth Nichols
William Nicholson
Sorche Nic Leodhas
Helen Nicoll
Éilís Ní Dhuibhne
Jenny Nimmo
Diana Noonan
Lilith Norman
Sterling North
Mary Norton
Flora Nwapa
Robert Nye

Graham Oakley
Asenath Odaga
Eileen O'Folain
Mary O'Hara
sean o huigan
Anezi Okoro
Pamela Oldfield
Iona and Peter Opie
Edward Ormondroyd
Pat O'Shea
Jenny Overton
Gareth Owen
Helen Oxenbury

C. Everard Palmer
M. Pardoe
Peggy Parish
Richard Parker
Siobhan Parkinson
Anne Parrish
Mary Elwyn Patchett
Katherine Paterson
Brian Patten
Gary Paulsen
Philippa Pearce
Howard Pease
Bill Peet
Maud and Miska Petersham
Stella Pevsner
Barbara Leonie Picard
Ann Pilling
Andrea Pinkney
Brian Pinkney
Stephanie Plowman
Patricia Polacco
Marguerite Poland
Madeleine A. Polland
Charlotte Pomerantz
Josephine Poole
Gene Stratton Porter
Sheena Porter
Beatrix Potter
Rhoda Power
Chris Powling
Terry Pratchett
Jack Prelutsky
Evadne Price
Susan Price

Willard Price
Alison Prince
Laurence Pringle
Christine Pullein-Thompson
Diana Pullein-Thompson
Josephine Pullein-Thompson
Virginia Pye

John Quinn

Gwynedd Rae
Arthur Ransome
Peggy Rathmann
Mary Ray
Mary Rayner
David Rees
Leslie Rees
James Reeves
Meta Mayne Reid
H. A. and Margret Rey
Alice Hegan Rice
Frank Richards
Laura E. Richards
M. Richler
Antonia Ridge
Philip Ridley
E. V. Rieu
Faith Ringgold
Charles G. D. Roberts
Elizabeth Madox Roberts
Keith Robertson
Joan G. Robinson
Anne Rockwell
Mary Rodgers
Michael Rosen
Michael J. Rosen
Tony Ross
Dick Roughsey
Glen Rounds
Philip Rush
Joanne Ryder
Cynthia Rylant

Louis Sachar
Julia Sauer
Ruth Sawyer
Allen Say
Vernon Scannell
Richard Scarry
Jack Schaefer
Miriam Schlein
Jon Scieszka
Bill Scott
Jenny Seed
Mabel D. Segun
George Selden
Maurice Sendak
Kate Seredy
Dr. Seuss
David Severn
Helen Sewell
Monica Shannon
Marjorie Weinman Sharmat

Bill Scott
Jenny Seed
Mabel D. Segun
George Selden
Maurice Sendak
Kate Seredy
Dr. Seuss
David Severn
Helen Sewell
Monica Shannon
Marjorie Weinman Sharmat
Margery Sharp
Sylvia Sherry
Uri Shulevitz
Shel Silverstein
Isaac Bashevis Singer
Barbara Sleigh
Louis Slobodkin
Esphyr Slobodkina
Alfred Slote
William Jay Smith
Barbara Claassen Smucker
Donald J. Sobol
Barbara Softly
Virginia Sorensen
Armstrong Sperry
Peter Spier
Gennedy Spirin
E. C. Spykman
Diane Stanley
Mary Q. Steele
William O. Steele
William Steig
John Steptoe
James Stevenson
A. C. Stewart
Margaret Storey
Catherine Storr
Herbert Strang
Joyce Stranger
Noel Streatfeild
Rodie Sudbery
Eve Sutton
Matthew Sweeney
Ronald Syme
John Symonds
Geraldine Symons
Cyndy Szekeres

Nancy Tafuri
Shizuye Takashima
Ethel Talbot
Booth Tarkington
Joan Tate
Cora Taylor
Sydney Taylor
William Taylor
Albert Payson Terhune
James Thurber
Ann Thwaite
Eve Titus
Barbara Euphan Todd
J. R. R. Tolkien
Ruth Tomalin
Katharine Tozer
P. L. Travers
Mary Treadgold
Alvin Tresselt
Meriol Trevor
Percy Trezise
Brinton Turkle
Ann Turner
Philip Turner

Yoshiko Uchida
Tomi Ungerer
Alison Uttley

Chris Van Allsburg
Hilda Van Stockum
John Verney
Judith Viorst
Elfrida Vipont

Bernard Waber
Martin Waddell
Jenny Wagner
Jan Wahl
David Walker
Stuart Walker
Dorothy Wall
Ian Wallace
Mildred Pitts Walter
Phyl Wardell
D. J. Watkins-Pitchford
Clyde Watson
James Watson
Sylvia Waugh
Jenifer Wayne
Jean Webster
Rosemary Weir
David Weisner
Ronald Welch
Rosemary Wells
Joyce West
Percy Westerman
Nadia Wheatley
E. B. White
Eliza Orne White
Ester Wier
Kate Douglas Wiggin
Laura Ingalls Wilder
Nancy Willard
Vera B. Williams
Henry Williamson
Barbara Ker Wilson
Gina Wilson
Jacqueline Wilson
David Wisniewski
David Wood
Valerie Worth
Kit Wright
Olwen Wymark
May Wynne

APPENDIX

FOREIGN-LANGUAGE WRITERS

A

AARDEMA, Verna

Nationality: American. **Born:** 6 June 1911, New Era, Michigan. **Education:** Michigan State College of Agriculture and Applied Science (now Michigan State University), B.A., 1934. **Family:** Married Albert Aardema, May 29, 1936 (died in 1974); married Joel Vugteveen, 1975; one son and one daughter (first marriage). **Career:** Grade school teacher in Pentwater, Michigan, 1934-35, in Muskegon, Michigan, 1935-36 and 1945-46, and at Lincoln School, Mona Shores, 1951-73; Muskegon Chronicle, Muskegon, staff correspondent, 1951-72; writer. Sunday school teacher for twelve years. Frequent guest at book fairs held throughout the United States. **Member:** National Education Association, Juvenile Writers' Workshop (publicity chair, 1955-65), Michigan Education Association, Mona Shores Education Association (corresponding secretary, 1965-70). **Awards:** American Library Association notable book, 1975, 1977, 1994; Randolph Caldecott Medal, 1976; Lewis Carroll Shelf Award, 1978; Redbook Best Children's Book, 1991, for *Borreguita and the Coyote*; Junior Library Guild selection, 1991, 1995, 1997; Parents' Choice, 1996, 1997. **Address:** 36 Barkley Circle, Apt. 124, Fort Myers, Florida 33907, U.S.A.

PUBLICATIONS FOR CHILDREN

Fiction (retold African and Mexican folktales)

Tales from the Story Hatitali, illustrated by Elton Fax. New York, Coward, 1960.
Otwe, illustrated by Elton Fax. New York, Coward, 1960.
The Na of Wa, illustrated by Elton Fax. New York, Coward, 1960.
The Sky-God Stories, illustrated by Elton Fax. New York, Coward, 1960.
More Tales from the Story Hat, illustrated by Elton Fax. New York, Coward, 1966.
Tales for the Third Ear: From Equatorial Africa, illustrated by Ib Ohlsson. New York, Dutton, 1969.
Behind the Back of the Mountain: Black Folk Tales from Southern Africa, illustrated by Leo Dillon and Diane Dillon. New York, Dial, 1973.
Why Mosquitoes Buzz in People's Ears: A West African Tale, illustrated by Leo Dillon and Diane Dillon. New York, Dial, 1975.
Who's in Rabbit's House?: A Masai Tale, illustrated by Leo Dillon and Diane Dillon. New York, Dial, 1977.
Ji-Nongo-Nongo Means Riddles, illustrated by Jerry Pinkney. New York, Four Winds, 1978.
The Riddle of the Drum: A Tale from Tizapan, Mexico, illustrated by Tony Chen. New York, Four Winds, 1979.
Half-a-Ball-of-Kenki: An Ashanti Tale, illustrated by Diane Stanley Zuromskis. New York, Warne, 1979.
Bringing the Rain to Kapiti Plain, illustrated by Beatriz Vidal. New York, Dial, 1981.
What's So Funny, Ketu?, illustrated by Marc Brown. New York, Dial, 1982.
The Vingananee and the Tree Toad: A Liberian Tale, illustrated by Ellen Weiss. New York, Warne, 1983.
Oh, Kojo! How Could You!: An Ashanti Tale, illustrated by Marc Brown. New York, Dial, 1984.
Bimwili and the Zimwi: A Tale from Zanzibar, illustrated by Susan Meddaugh. New York, Dial, 1985.
Princess Gorilla and a New Kind of Water: A Mpongwe Tale, illustrated by Victoria Chess. New York, Dial, 1988.
Rabbit Makes a Monkey of Lion: A Swahili Tale, illustrated by Jerry Pinkney. New York, Dial, 1989.
Pedro and the Padre, illustrated by Friso Henstra. New York, Dial, 1991.
Traveling to Tondo: A Tale of the Nkundo of Zaire, illustrated by Will Hillenbrand. New York, Knopf, 1991.
Borreguita and the Coyote, illustrated by Petra Mathers. New York, Knopf, 1991.
Anansi Finds a Fool, illustrated by Bryna Waldman. New York, Dial, 1992.
Sebgugu the Glutton, illustrated by Nancy L. Close. New York, Eerdmans, 1993.
A Bookworm Who Hatched. New York, Owen, 1993
Misos, illustrated by Reynold Ruffins. New York, Knopf, 1994.
How the Ostrich Got a Long Neck: A Tale from the Akamba of Kenya, illustrated by Marcia Brown. New York, Scholastic, 1995.
Jackal's Flying Lesson, illustrated by Dale Gottlieb. New York, Knopf, 1995.
The Lonely Lioness and the Ostrich Chicks: a Masai Tale, illustrated by Yumi Heo. New York, Knopf, 1996.
Anansi Does the Impossible, illustrated by Lisa Desimini. New York, Atheneum, 1997.
This for That: A Tonga Tale, illustrated by Victoria Chess. New York, Dial, 1997.

*

Manuscript Collections: University of South Florida, Fort Myers.

Verna Aardema comments:

My mother read a poem I had written when I was 11 years old; she said, "Why, Verna, you're going to be a writer"—just like my grandfather. At once I decided that's what I wanted to do."

* * *

Beginning with *Tales from the Story Hititali* in 1960, Verna Aardema has provided English-speaking readers with a treasury of African and Mexican folktales and has secured her reputation as an author who, in the retelling of her source material, maintains the integrity of the original tales by refusing to alter them in order to shield her young audience from the often violent or psychologically complex resolutions that are common traits of traditional folklore. Aardema's *Sebgugugu the Glutton* is a Bantu tale from Rwanda which explores the nature of greed and disobedience when Sebgugugu tries the patience of Imana who finally takes away everything. *Misoso: Once Upon a Time Tales from Africa* contains twelve tales retold by Aardema that include stories of revenge, justice, silliness, greed, and trickery. As always in her books, Aardema provides full source notes and, in this instance, a map showing the places of origin for each story. Moreover, by emphasizing the idea that retribution—often in the form of death—comes to those who are wicked or selfish, Aardema preserves the spirit of the orginals.

What's So Funny, Ketu? is a humorous retelling of an old Nuer tale that tells of a reward given young Ketu for saving the life of a snake. Ketu is allowed to hear the animals think, but this gets him into great trouble with his wife for he laughs at the comments of the animals he alone hears. The condition of his gift is to keep it secret, but the town leaders demand that he tell his secret or lose his wife and baby. *Traveling to Tondo* is a tale of the Nkundo of Zaire in which Bowane the civet cat is on his way to Tondo to marry a beautiful cat, but he requires his friends to accompany him on the journey. On the way, each friend delays him and all wait in great patience; but, alas, they wait far too long, only to discover that the cat has married and Bowane and his friends run, fly, scurry, and streak home when the new husband, an even larger civet cat, bares his teeth.

Who's In Rabbit's House? is a Masai tale in which Aardema has skillfully combined repetition of key phrases with authentic African ideophones to produce a rhythmic read-aloud text which preserves the essential flavor of an African tale. Poor rabbit is frightened by someone who is in her house, and it takes a clever frog and a frightened caterpillar to solve the situation. *Bringing the Rain to Kapiti Plain,* a Nandi tale, is a rhythmic and cumulative version relating how Ki-pat brought rain to the drought-stricken plain. The language is a perfect match to the tale: "This was the shot/that pierced the cloud/And loosed the rain/with thunder LOUD!" In another Masai tale dealing with a mother bird's attempts to retrieve her lost babies, *The Lonely Lioness and the Ostrich Chicks,* Aardema shows the way a crafty mongoose manages a rescue by playing to the lioness' weakness, her sense of pride.

The first of Aardema's Ashanti tales, *Anansi Finds a Fool,* is a funny story of Anansi being out-maneuvered by his friend Bonsu in trying to catch fish. Perhaps the best sequence is the finding of the python stuffed with the fish trapped in their basket. In *Anansi Does the Impossible,* the spider protagonist and his clever wife win back their culture's folktales by completing three seemingly impossible tasks, thus outsmarting the vengeful Sky God.

Featuring the Caldecott-winning illustrations by the Dillons, *Why Mosquitoes Buzz in People's Ears,* is West African in origin and explores Mosquito telling Iguana a fib about yams, thus beginning a series of cumulative events that lead to a serious conclusion: "And now Mother Owl won't wake the sun/so that the day can come." *Borreguita and the Coyote* is a tale from Ayutla, Mexico, that tells of the clever sheep that outwit the naive coyote. When sheep run into coyote's mouth, it is the final blow and coyote gives up for good. Versions of this tale appear in other cultures, but this is a particularly clear and funny version.

In the *Jackal's Flying Lesson,* Aardema retells a Khoikhoi tale of mother dove who believes the a trickster Jackal when he threatens to climb up to her nest and eat her babies if she refuses to send them down to him. After he eats both of the babies and disappears, the dove is comforted by her friend the blue crane, who says: "Jackal made you believe he could climb a tree.... I'll make him believe he can learn to fly." After winning the trust of the Jackal, the blue crane, with the aid of tree gum and feathers, convinces the trickster that with these additions to his coat, he is ready to fly. She lifts him off high into the sky, releases him, and instructs him to flap his "wings." Of course, the Jackal plummets to the ground and vows "never to get involved with blue cranes, or baby birds and their mothers ... again." Upon impact, the two baby doves are released unharmed from the Jackal's stomach and are returned to their mother by the blue crane, who "wisely observes, 'it is a true saying: whoever sows evil will see it come forth in his own garden.'"

Aardema is an extraordinary teller of tales who does careful research to find appropriate tales and to provide her readers with a quality adaptation. In her photo-autobiography, *A Bookworm Who Hatched,* Aardema writes: "Being an author involves more than just writing the books. For me, it also means speaking and telling stories." Indeed, her life has been devoted to providing another generation with the timeless tales of Africa and Mexico.

—Kay E. Vandergrift, updated by Gwen Athene Tarbox

AARON, Chester

Nationality: American. **Born:** Butler, Pennsylvania, 9 May 1923. **Education:** Butler High School, graduated 1941; University of California, Los Angeles, 1945-48, and Berkeley, 1954-56, B.A. 1956; San Francisco State University, 1974-77, M.A. 1977. **Military Service:** United States Army Armored Infantry, 1943-45. **Family:** Married Marguarite Kelly in 1954 (divorced 1973); one stepson. **Career:** X-ray technician, Kaiser Permanente, San Francisco, 1957-58; chief X-ray technician, Alta Bates Hospital, Berkeley, 1958-71; technical writer, MKI Engineering, San Francisco, 1971-72. Assistant Professor, 1972-82, and since 1983 Professor of English, Saint Mary's College, Moraga, California. **Awards:** Huntington Hartford Foundation fellowship, 1950, 1951; Chapelbrook Foundation grant, 1970; National Endowment for the Arts grant, 1976. **Address:** P.O. Box 388, Occidental, California 95465, U.S.A.

Publications for Children

Fiction

Better Than Laughter. New York, Harcourt Brace, 1972; London, Gollancz, 1973.
An American Ghost, illustrated by David Lemon. New York, Harcourt Brace, 1973; London, Gollancz, 1974.
Hello to Bodega. New York, Atheneum, 1975.
Spill. New York, Atheneum, 1977.
Catch Calico! New York, Dutton, 1979.
Gideon. New York, Lippincott, 1982.
Duchess. New York, Lippincott, 1982.
Out of Sight, Out of Mind. New York, Lippincott, 1985.
Lackawanna. New York, Lippincott, 1986.
Alex, Who Won His War. New York, Walker, 1991.

Publications for Adults

The Cowbank (play; produced Berkeley, California, 1955).
About Us (novel). New York, McGraw Hill, 1967.

Contributor of short stories to periodicals.

*

Chester Aaron comments:

I have always liked to read stories. That means, to me, a series of events connected by growing excitement and continuing pleasure. With characters I could not necessarily admire but respect, almost envy. E.M. Forster's rule—the urge to know what happens next, the breathless need to keep turning pages—is always hovering in my mind somewhere, when I write. This is true whether I write for adults or young adults. I respect passion in people, and so my characters are usually committed to a certain behavior passionately. I even try to develop a prose that is impassioned as it moves the story forward. My love for animals often interferes with my love for people, and I am always on the alert for stories that will include both animals and humans. I am concerned with characters and families in conflict: often with themselves but always with their societies.

* * *

Chester Aaron, who "likes to read stories," is himself an excellent storyteller, with good plots, action, continual points of tension, and a special rapport with his teenage or younger central characters. His expertise on whatever may be his theme of the moment—oil spillage, sheep dog training, rivers in flood—is a further fictional asset.

Aaron's books belong in kind to the sterling old adventure genre, though with more inner subtleties. They are also allied to the novel of ideas, and this is both a merit and the reverse. The problem is not so much the ideas themselves as their narrative presentation. In the best of Aaron's books—notably *An American Ghost*—narrative and polemic are totally fused. In *Out of Sight, Out of Mind,* highly readable though it is, they are not fused at all.

A quick survey of Aaron's books shows something of his range of theme and treatment. *Spill* has an increasingly topical subject: an oil spill and its effects on the seabirds and creatures and on their would-be rescuers. A collision of tankers off the coast of northern California results in devastating pollution, threatening both a noted bird sanctuary, where migrating birds are just due to arrive, and an offshore area of unique marine life. Deeply involved in the emergency are members of a family whose home already serves as an unofficial animal hospital. Judy (14) is totally dedicated to the cause. Her older brother Jeff has begun to taste the illicit pleasures of independence; but he is still concerned about his secret find—a rare giant sea anemone living in an offshore reef. Has it survived? Judy sets out to discover the answer.

In *Catch Calico!* a 14-year-old boy, alone with a sick grandfather in their holiday mountain cabin, has to take on the responsibility of dealing with a much-loved cat with rabies. A further shock to separate fact and dream is the unravelling of a mystery linking the boy's father, dead in battle, with his grandfather's tales of his own heroic war days, which really never existed at all. Marty, the main character in *Duchess,* is a New York delinquent and gang leader. As an alternative to custody, he is sent to his uncle's remote sheep ranch in California. His plans of escape come to nothing (the uncle is no fool), but his surly interest is roused at last by watching the prowess of Princess, a border collie sheep dog. The real awakening comes when Marty finds and feeds a starving pup and is allowed to keep and train it. Duchess becomes a winner—so does Marty, both at school and on the farm. He has found where his future lies.

Gideon is a powerful and important book, the story of a 14-year-old boy in the Warsaw ghetto who is determined to be a survivor. His Aryan looks and reckless temperament are a help (he starts by slipping out to join smuggling gangs in the city), but the price will be almost intolerably high. He is to lose every member of his family and every close companion of his journey. He will know the sewers and the barbed wire whip; he will escape from the crammed and waterless cattle truck—and be recaptured; he will be made to undress the victims of the gas chambers: he is one of the very few survivors of the rising at Treblinka. Gideon has had to change his whole identity, even to himself. It is what he seeks to reclaim, his lost Jewishness especially, when he sets down the tale for his own descendants.

Out of Sight, Out of Mind, with its touch of the supernatural—or should it be supranormal?—differs again from the rest. Young teenage twins, with a worldwide reputation for their miraculous extrasensory powers (not only can they read thoughts, they can move distant vehicles), are orphaned when their mother and father are killed in a plane crash. The parents were on their way to speak at a major international conference on psychic phenomena; the text of their speech ("Extrasensory Perception: A Key to World Peace") survives, and the twins plan to travel to Berkeley to deliver it themselves. But a certain foreign government wishes to capture the gifted pair; the hunt is on, and they have the terrible problem of finding shelter without endangering their hosts. What's more, adolescence is daily weakening their childhood powers. A thriller indeed!—fast-paced and gripping: you gladly suspend disbelief. The weakness of the book is its message itself, which could be replaced without changing the structure at all.

Lackawanna is less convincing. In the Depression years, around 1930 and 1931, a group of orphaned children turn themselves into a kind of family; they live by begging, street singing, whatever each day offers. When the youngest (Herbie, aged nine) disappears during one of their freight car-jumping expeditions, a cross-country search begins. Eventful, poignant (poverty, like other extremes, is an effective fictional motif), the book is a real adventure yarn for juniors—though adults might puzzle here and there over detail. Had Aaron in mind Brecht's poem "The Children's Crusade?"

All of the best elements in Aaron's fiction meet in *An American Ghost.* Albie is a boy in pioneer Wisconsin of the 1850s. He loves his family and accepts their beliefs and values. Thus, in the brief prelude, when two ragged boys (Indians?, runaway slaves?) are casually shot dead by Albie's father and their neighbour Sam, it does not occur to him to question this, any more than he questioned the killing that same day of a cougar (panther, puma, "American ghost—the name depending on who might be cursing it"). But Albie chances to be alone at home when the nearby river floods and the little white house is sent racing down toward the Mississippi, among the debris of drowned animals and wrecked dwellings. A great tree halts its course, which allows a cougar to enter the house: a female, about to give birth to cubs. Gradually boy and beast become allies. The real danger comes from a passing boat of drunken thieves, their vessel stuffed with loot and a sad mass of dying animals. The thieves capture Albie: maybe he'll fetch a ransom. He escapes. Finally, when land is sighted, the cougar takes each cub in turn to safety, and returns for the boy. Albie and his family are reunited. But the end, though enigmatic, is startling, even brilliant. In a moment of truth Albie confronts in himself his family's rooted values. True, it is hardly likely that a boy on his own so long ago could resist for long the mores, codes, and conventions of an entire people—but some readers today may feel themselves to be in a different position.

However harsh its theme, every Aaron book has an unquenchable spark of optimism, a hopeful energy, always to be found in the central youthful characters. His novels may not reach the bestseller lists, but the best of them have a lasting quality. This is true of *Gideon* and of *Spill*—and most of all of *An American Ghost,* which should never be allowed to go out of print.

—Naomi Lewis

ACHEBE, Chinua

Nationality: Nigerian. **Born:** Albert Chinualumogu in Ogidi, 16 November 1930. **Education:** Government College, Umuahia, 1944-47; University College, Ibadan, 1948-53, B.A. (London) 1953. **Family:** Married Christiana Okoli in 1961; two sons and two daughters. **Career:** Talks producer, Lagos, 1954-57, controller, Enugu, 1958-61, and director, Lagos, 1961-66, Nigerian Broadcasting Corporation; chairman, Citadel Books Ltd., Enugu, 1967; Senior Research Fellow, 1967-73, Professor of English, 1973-81, and since 1984 Professor Emeritus, University of Nigeria, Nsukka. Visiting Professor, 1972-75, and Fulbright Professor, 1987-88, University of Massachusetts, Amherst; Visiting Professor, University of Connecticut, Storrs, 1975-76; Regents' Lecturer, University of California, Los Angeles, 1984. Founding editor, Heinemann African Writers series, 1962-72 and since 1970 director, Heinemann Educational Books (Nigeria) Ltd., and Nwankwo-Ifejika Ltd. (later Nwamife), publishers, Enugu; since 1971 editor, *Okike: An African Journal of New Writing,* Nsukka. Member, University of Lagos Council, 1966; chairman, Society of Nigerian Authors, 1966, and Association of Nigerian Authors, 1982-86; Pro-Chancellor and Chairman of Council, Anambra State University of Technology, Enugu, 1986-88. **Awards:** Margaret Wrong Memorial prize, 1959; Nigerian National trophy, 1960; Rockefeller fellowship, 1960; Unesco fellowship, 1963; Jock Campbell award (*New Statesman*), 1965; Commonwealth Poetry prize, 1973; Neil Gunn International fellowship, 1974; Honorary Fellow, Modern Language Association (USA), 1975; Nigerian National Merit award, 1979; Order of the Federal Republic of Nigeria, 1979; Honorary Member, American Academy, 1982; Fellow, Royal Society of Literature, 1983; Commonwealth Foundation award, 1983. Litt.D.: Dartmouth College, Hanover, New Hampshire, 1972; University of Southampton, 1975; University of Ife, 1978; University of Nigeria, 1981; University of Kent, Canterbury, 1982; University of Guelph, Ontario, 1984; Mount Allison University, Sackville, New Brunswick, 1984; Franklin Pierce College, Rindge, New Hampshire, 1985; D. Univ.: University of Stirling, 1975; LL.D.: University of Prince Edward Island, Charlottetown, 1976; D.H.L.: University of Massachusetts, 1977. **Address:** P.O. Box 53, University of Nigeria, Nsukka, Anambra State, Nigeria.

PUBLICATIONS FOR CHILDREN

Fiction

Chike and the River, illustrated by Prue Theobalds. London and New York, Cambridge University Press, 1966.
How the Leopard Got His Claws, with John Iroaganachi, illustrated by Per Christiansen. Enugu, Nwamife, 1972; New York, Third Press, 1973.
The Flute, illustrated by Tayo Adenaike. Enugu, Fourth Dimension, 1977.
The Drum, illustrated by John Roper. Enugu, Fourth Dimension, 1977.

PUBLICATIONS FOR ADULTS

Novels

Things Fall Apart. London, Heinemann, 1958; New York, McDowell Obolensky, 1959; with an introduction by Kwame Anthony Appiah; New York, Knopf, 1992.
No Longer at Ease. London, Heinemann, 1960; New York, Obolensky, 1961.
Arrow of God. London, Heinemann, 1964; New York, Day, 1967; adapted by Emeka Nwabueze as *When the Arrow Rebounds,* Enugu, Nigeria, ABIC Publishers, 1991.
A Man of the People. London, Heinemann, and New York, Day, 1966.
Anthills of the Savannah. London, Heinemann, 1987; New York, Doubleday, 1988.

Short Stories

The Sacrificial Egg and Other Stories. Onitsha, Etudo, 1962.
Girls at War. London, Heinemann, and New York, Doubleday, 1972.

Poetry

Beware, Soul-Brother and Other Poems. Enugu, Nwankwo-Ifejika, 1971; revised edition, Enugu, Nwamife, and London, Heinemann, 1972.
Christmas in Biafra and Other Poems. New York, Doubleday, 1973.

Other

Morning Yet on Creation Day: Essays. London, Heinemann, and New York, Doubleday, 1975.
In Person: Achebe, Awoonor, and Soyinka at the University of Washington. Seattle, University of Washington African Studies Program, 1975.
The Trouble with Nigeria. Enugu, Fourth Dimension, 1983; London, Heinemann, 1984.
The World of the Ogbanje. Enugu, Fourth Dimension, 1986.
Hopes and Impediments: Selected Essays 1965-1987. London, Heinemann, 1988.
The University and the Leadership Factor in Nigerian Politics. Enugu, ABIC, 1988.
The African Trilogy (fiction). London, Picador, 1988.
The Voter, adapted by Ivan Vladislavic, illustrated by Renee Koch. Johannesburg, Viva Books, 1994.
Another Africa (essay and poems), photographs by Robert Lyons. New York, Anchor Books, 1997.
Conversations with Chinua Achebe, edited by Bernth Lindfors. Jackson, University Press of Mississippi, 1997.

Editor, with Dubem Okafor, *Don't Let Him Die: An Anthology of Memorial Poems for Christopher Okigbo.* Enugu, Fourth Dimension, 1978.
Editor, with C.L. Innes, *African Short Stories.* London, Heinemann, 1985.
Editor, with others, *Beyond Hunger in Africa: Conventional Wisdom and a Vision of Africa in 2057.* London, Currey, 1990.
Editor, with C.L. Innes, *The Heinemann Book of Contemporary African Short Stories.* London, Heinemann, 1992.

*

Biography: *Chinua Achebe: A Biography* by Ezenwa-Ohaeto, Bloomington, Indiana University Press, 1997.

Bibliography: In *Africana Library Journal* (New York), Spring 1970; *Chinua Achebe: A Bio-bibliography,* Nnamdi Azikiwe Library, University of Nigeria, 1990.

Critical Studies: *The Novels of Chinua Achebe* by G.D. Killam, London, Heinemann, and New York, Africana, 1969, revised edition, as *The Writings of Chinua Achebe,* Heinemann, 1977; *Chinua Achebe* by Arthur Ravenscroft, London, Longman, 1969, revised edition, 1977; *Chinua Achebe* by David Carroll, New York, Twayne, 1970, revised edition, London, Macmillan, 1980; *Chinua Achebe et la tragédie de l'histoire* by Thomas Melone, Paris, Présence Africaine, 1973; *Chinua Achebe* by Kate Turkington, London, Arnold, 1977; *Critical Perspectives on Chinua Achebe* edited by Bernth Lindfors and C.L. Innes, London, Heinemann, and Washington, D.C., Three Continents, 1978; *Achebe's World: The Historical and Cultural Context of the Novels of Chinua Achebe* by Robert M. Wren, Washington, D.C., Three Continents, 1980, London, Longman, 1981; *The Four Novels of Chinua Achebe: A Critical Study* by Benedict C. Njoku, Bern, Switzerland, Lang, 1984; *L'Oeuvre de Chinua Achebe* by Denise Coussy, Paris, Présence Africaine, 1985; *Chinua Achebe: A Celebration* edited by Kirsten Holt Petersen and Anna Rutherford, London, Heinemann, 1991; *Reading Chinua Achebe: Language and Ideology in Fiction* by Simon Gikandi, London, Currey, 1991; *Chinua Achebe: New Perspectives* by Umelo Ojinmah, Ibadan, Spectrum Books Limited, 1991; *Chinua Achebe: A Celebration,* edited by Kirsten Holst Petersen and Anna Rutherford, Oxford and Portsmouth, New Hampshire, Heinemann, 1991; *Challenging Hierarchies: Issues and Themes in Colonial and Postcolonial African Literature,* edited by Leonard A. Podis and Yakubu Saaka, New York, P. Lang, 1998.

* * *

Chinua Achebe's fiction is well-known to secondary school children in English-speaking Africa because some of his novels written for adults are included in school syllabuses. But Achebe also writes fiction especially for children that he hopes will entertain, excite, educate, and retrieve "our valid culture," e.g., Nigerian and Igbo culture, as he noted in *New Culture 1* in 1979.

The hero of *Chike and the River* comes from Umuofia, the same village depicted in *Things Fall Apart.* Like Achebe's novels for adults, *Chike and the River* includes proverbs, folk tales, dialogue appropriate to the status of the speakers, and cultural details that are unobtrusively woven into the story. Chike goes to the city of Onitsha to live with his uncle and learns that Onitsha is different from Umuofia, but not necessarily better. Chike wants to cross the Niger River from Onitsha to Asaba in a ferry, but he has no money to pay the fare. In his efforts to obtain money, the hero learns that one must not write dishonest letters to British pen pals, has an encounter with a money doubler, narrowly escapes paying for a bicycle he accidentally damages, and washes cars. Although all ends well, Chike's ferry trip nearly turns into a disaster when he misses the return ferry and the lorry in which he is sleeping is stolen by cloth thieves. This fast-moving adventure story emphasizes "good" values which are both implicit in the action and explicitly stated in proverbs.

Achebe's other children's books are Igbo folk tales from which he has created adventure stories. Achebe aims to create fictional situations in which children can identify themselves. In *How the Leopard Got His Claws,* written with John Iroaganachi, the explanatory tale of the title is greatly elaborated to include the story of how dog became man's "slave," why animals are no longer friends, and why hunter is the enemy of all animals. The story includes praise songs, folk tales, and a deer's song, which is a poem "The Lament of the Deer" by the late Nigerian poet Christopher Okigbo.

The Drum and *The Flute* are also written in Igbo as *Igba* and *Oja. The Drum* is based on a widespread West African folk tale about tortoise's magic drum which he uses to feed other animals during a drought. Achebe has created a situation in which the drum is obtained from spirits in the underworld after tortoise threatens to kill a spirit boy who eats a fruit that tortoise lost. Tortoise's desire for power and aristocratic privileges leads to the drum being broken when he appoints elephant as his drumbeater. After the drum is repaired and produces too little food to satisfy the animal's greed, tortoise returns to the underworld and again tricks the spirits into giving him a drum. But this time the drum produces whips, wasps, and bees, which explains why animals have been running in all directions ever since. The story is told in contemporary language, and includes songs, "traditional" rituals, and ideophones, such as "Aja mbene, Mbe mbene, aja mbene" for tortoise's footsteps. Stylistically, *The Flute* is a similar story. It is based on a widespread folk tale theme of a woman who is jealous of gifts that her co-wife's son obtains from spirits with a magic flute. She sends her own ill-mannered son to obtain similar gifts, but is rewarded with death in the form of leprosy, smallpox, and yaws.

Achebe's children's fiction is characterized by the same creative imagination and writing skill as his fiction for adults. Although it is based on Nigerian and Igbo cultural traditions, its universal themes make it understandable to children throughout Africa and the world.

—Nancy J. Schmidt

ADAMS, Jeanie

Nationality: Australian. **Awards:** Crichton award, 1990; Children's Book Council of Australia Book of the Year, younger, 1990. **Address:** Albert Whitman & Company, 6340 Oakton St., Morton Grove, Illinois 60053-2723, U.S.A.

Publications for Children

Fiction

Pigs and Honey. Adelaide, Omnibus, 1989;
Going for Oysters. Norwood, Omnibus, 1991; Morton Grove, Illinois, A. Whitman, 1994.

Publications for Adults

Crafts from Aurukun: Design for a Local Environment. Aurukun Community Incorporated, 1983.

*

Illustrator: With Rachel Tonkin, *Biaga and Lagi: Five Stories* by Jack Goodluck, 1976; *Dictionary and Sourcebook of the Wik-Mungkan Language* (for adults), compiled by Christine Kilham et al, 1986; *Tucker's Mob* by Christobel Mattingley, 1992.

* * *

It is significant that the acknowledgment included at the beginning of Jeanie Adams's second book, *Going for Oysters,* should record her "thanks to all the people at Aurukun who have shared their lives and stories with me." No other non-aboriginal author or artist has more sympathetically or convincingly portrayed the family and community life of contemporary "outback" Australian aborigines.

Her first book, *Pigs and Honey,* won the Crichton award for a first-time illustrator as well as the Children's Book Council of Australia Younger Readers award for 1990. The motivation for *Pigs and Honey* and *Going for Oysters* grew out of Adams's empathy with the aboriginal people at Aurukun, a town on Cape York Peninsula in Far North Queensland. She drew on that same deeply felt experience and her keen and perceptive observation to illustrate *Tucker's Mob,* Christobel Mattingley's story of black family life that was dedicated to "aboriginal people everywhere."

Through their pastor and the elders of their church, members of the community that gave *Pigs and Honey* its birth endorsed its publication. Permission for *Going for Oysters* was granted by the clan leader of the aboriginal custodians of Love River—or Thuukul, as the local people call it—where the story is set. The aboriginal people whose lives and experiences are celebrated in the stories and illustrations have rightly expressed their approval of and pleasure in the work of Jeanie Adams. And the judges of the 1990 Australian Book of the Year awards reported that *Pigs and Honey,* "in its unself-conscious acceptance of the characters and their way of life, marks another step toward the accurate and natural representation of the aboriginal people in Australian children's literature." They praised the book for its "cultural and artistic integrity."

Both *Pigs and Honey* and *Going for Oysters* are authentic accounts of an aboriginal family's weekend expeditions into the bush around Aurukun. In the first story, Granny says she is hungry for meat, so the entire family leaves on Saturday morning to hunt wild pigs and gather honeycomb. Later they make a ground oven to cook the pig, Mum bakes a damper, and the extended family gathers around the fire to "eat until they are full." Then it is time for Granny's stories and a night of dreaming under the stars. In *Going for Oysters,* "the milky-pine flowers are in bloom, and that means the oysters are fat and juicy and going to waste," inspiring yet another camping expedition. This time, however, Grandad warns of Yaatamay, the Carpet Snake, who is the guardian of Thuukul. Grandad is prevailed upon to anoint the youngest children "with an underarm smell" so that "the spirits of the Old People will recognise them and keep them safe." Nevertheless the children who disregard Grandad's warning are taught a salutary lesson.

In both books, the voice of the narrator, belonging to a youthful member of the clan, has both immediacy and conviction. Here is genuine family "gossip," the sort of anecdote which belongs to the folk and the community. One can almost smell and feel the earth and the bush, taste the sweetness of the honeycomb. The "oystery, smoky smell drifting under the casuarina trees" tantalises the taste buds. These stories recount the realities of bush life in matter-of-fact and unself-conscious prose, yet they also celebrate the joy of living and convey a deep sense of spirituality.

Adams successfully evokes the spirit of aboriginal art through her own illustrations, not only with her wax crayon drawings and use of watercolours, but especially through her technique of introducing a white outline to her figures. Yet her work is not derivative, for her style is unique. Her scenes are never static, as in much aboriginal art. She depicts the exuberance with which the clan interacts with their environment as well as with one another; she not only creates a feeling of family solidarity and warmth but also one of dynamic energy. Yet when Granny tells her campfire story in *Pigs and Honey,* there are mysterious depths to the blues and night shades of the illustrations that denote the eternal inscrutability of the past, mingling with the present to produce a latter-day Dreamtime. Adams lyrically confirms the reality, permanence, and joy of a life lived in harmony with the earth and its creatures.

—Maurice Saxby

ADLER, Irene. See **STORR, Catherine.**

ADOFF, Arnold

Nationality: American. **Born:** New York City, 16 July 1935. **Education:** City College of New York, B.A. 1956; Columbia University, New York, 1956-58; New School for Social Research, New York, 1965-67. **Military Service:** New York National Guard. **Family:** Married Virginia Hamilton, *q.v.*, in 1960; one daughter and one son. **Career:** Teacher in public schools, New York, 1957-69. Since 1977 literary agent, Yellow Springs, Ohio. Visiting Professor, Queens College, Flushing, New York, 1986-87. **Award:** National Council of Teachers of English award, for poetry, 1988. **Address:** Box 293, Yellow Springs, Ohio 45387, U.S.A.

Publications for Children

Poetry

Ma nda lA, illustrated by Emily McCully. New York, Harper, 1971.
Black Is Brown Is Tan, illustrated by Emily McCully. New York, Harper, 1973.
Make a Circle, Keep Us In: Poems for a Good Day, illustrated by Ronald Himler. New York, Delacorte Press, 1975.
Big Sister Tells Me That I'm Black, illustrated by Lorenzo Lynch. New York, Holt Rinehart, 1976.
Tornado!, illustrated by Ronald Himler. New York, Delacorte Press, 1977.
Under the Early Morning Trees, illustrated by Ronald Himler. New York, Dutton, 1978.
Where Wild Willy, illustrated by Emily McCully. New York, Harper, 1978.
Eats, illustrated by Susan Russo. New York, Lothrop, 1979.
I Am the Running Girl, illustrated by Ronald Himler. New York, Harper, 1979.
Friend Dog, illustrated by Troy Howell. New York, Lippincott, 1980.
Today We Are Brother and Sister, illustrated by Glo Coalson. New York, Lothrop, 1981.
OUTside INside Poems, illustrated by John Steptoe. New York, Lothrop, 1981.
Birds, illustrated by Troy Howell. New York, Lippincott, 1982.
All the Colors of the Race, illustrated by John Steptoe. New York, Lothrop, 1982.
The Cabbages Are Chasing the Rabbits, illustrated by Janet Stevens. San Diego, Harcourt Brace, 1985.
Sports Pages, illustrated by Steven Kuzma. New York, Lippincott, 1986.
Flamboyan, illustrated by Karen Barbour. San Diego, Harcourt Brace, 1988.
Greens, illustrated by Betsy Lewin. New York, Lothrop, 1988.
In for Winter, Out for Spring, illustrations by Jerry Pinkney. San Diego, Harcourt Brace Jovanovich, 1991.
Hard to Be Six, illustrated by Cheryl Hanna. New York, Lothrop, Lee & Shepard Books, 1991.
Slow Dance Heartbreak Blues, illustrated by William Cotton. New York, Lothrop, Lee & Shepard Books, 1995.
Street Music: City Poems, illustrated by Karen Barbour. New York, HarperCollins, 1995.
The Return of Rex and Ethel, illustrated by Catherine Deeter. San Diego, Harcourt Brace Jovanovich, 1996.
Touch the Poem, illustrated by Bill Creevy. New York, Scholastic, 1996.
Love Letters, illustrated by Lisa Desimini. New York, Blue Sky Press, 1997.

Other

Malcolm X, illustrated by John Wilson. New York, Crowell, 1970.

Editor, *I Am the Darker Brother: An Anthology of Modern Poems by Negro Americans.* New York, Macmillan, 1968; revised and expanded, New York, Simon & Schuster, 1997.
Editor, *Black on Black: Commentaries by Negro Americans.* New York, Macmillan, 1968.
Editor, *City in All Directions: An Anthology of Modern Poems,* illustrated by Donald Carrick. New York, Macmillan, 1969.
Editor, *Black Out Loud: An Anthology of Modern Poems by Black Americans,* illustrated by Alvin Hollingsworth. New York, Macmillan, 1970.
Editor, *Brothers and Sisters: Modern Stories by Black Americans.* New York, Macmillan, 1970.
Editor, *It Is the Poem Singing into Your Eyes: An Anthology of New Young Poets.* New York, Harper, 1971.
Editor, *The Poetry of Black America: An Anthology of the 20th Century.* New York, Harper, 1973.
Editor, *My Black Me: A Beginning Book of Black Poetry.* New York, Dutton, 1974.
Editor, *Celebrations: A New Anthology of Black American Poetry.* Chicago, Follett, 1977.

* * *

Arnold Adoff has distinguished himself as a poet, anthologist, and biographer. His poetry is notable for its pungent musical quality, best appreciated when read aloud. Unusual word, phrase, and sentence configurations, which may appear arbitrary on the page, take on a rhythmic logic when spoken. His poems range in tone and mood from the festive to the meditative, but a common element is a sense of gentle warmth. This warmth is most clearly evident in his affectionate family portraits. *Make a Circle, Keep Us In* follows one day in a family's life, with the family portrayed as a strong unit that nurtures and protects itself. *Black Is Brown Is Tan* describes the everyday experiences of an interracial family. It begins by focussing on the wide spectrum of colors apparent in family members: for mother,

i am black
i am a brown sugar gown
a tasty tan and coffee pumpkin pie
with dark brown eyes and almond ears
and my face gets ginger red
when i puff and yell you into bed

for father,

i am white i am white
i am light
with pinks and tiny tans
dark hair growing on my arms
that darken in the summer sun
brown eyes big yellow ears

and for the children,

black is brown is tan
is girl is boy
is nose is face
is all the colors
of the race

For every hue there is an expression of delight, and the description of family life extends the focus beyond color to encompass a family's delight in each other.

Ma nda lA displays through colorful illustrations by Emily McCully an African family's activities, accompanied by Adoff's sing-song verse, a simple compilation of sounds that evoke a sense of celebration.

Adoff's sensitive and understated expressions of feelings are particularly evident in his poems that center on an individual child's thoughts. The young daughter of a black mother and white father explores her own sense of identity in *All the Colors of the Race,* a series of related poems. The poems contain a variety of emotions; the young girl expresses pride in her varied ancestry, and a sense of affiliation with all the colors, religions, and cultures that have contributed to create her unique self. There is humor in her perception of her racial make-up:

At the meeting
they said they wanted to send
one white
and one black kid to the celebration,
to make it even and equal.
So
I said to just send me and it would still be
fair,
and we could still
save one round-trip fare.
Then they waited to see if I was smiling
before they laughed,
and my motion lost because I forgot
I couldn't be a boy.

But there is also a melancholy tone in a description of a family outing as she shows her awareness of potential prejudice:

We live the same: our way,
and walk
the same;
and talk,
no matter where we live
and go.
And most people
smile at us on sunny Ohio afternoons
in parks and restaurants.
But
while we talk and smile
and eat
our way through
Sundays, we keep a corner
of our eyes for
any
bad guys.

OUTside INside Poems is the introspective yet simply expressed going on outside himself with what he's actually feeling. In *Big Sister Tells Me That I'm Black,* a small boy offers a rousing cheer for himself and all who are like him.

Eats celebrates one of life's more carnal pleasures; it's a lively ode to good food and the joys of eating. *The Cabbages Are Chasing the Rabbits* is an energetic romp in which cabbages turn the tables on the rabbits who have been nibbling on them. The result is a wild and crazy pursuit. With lyrical blank verse, *Sports Pages* extolls the thrill of victory and the agony of defeat in 37 poems celebrating young athletes, while *Greens* is an exuberant collection that presents imaginative observations on things that are the color green, from grasshoppers to pea soup.

Adoff captures the spirit of a growing child in *Flamboyan.* Set on the island of Puerto Rico, this is a rhythmic melange of poetry and prose that describes the days and dreams of a young girl whose hair is the color of the Flamboyan tree blossoms.

As an anthologist, Adoff is noted especially for his thoughtfully selected collections of black poetry that center on uplifting themes of hope, survival, and triumph. *My Black Me: A Beginning Book of Black Poetry* contains poems accessible to younger children by such poets as Langston Hughes, Nikki Giovanni, and Lucille Clifton. *I Am the Darker Brother: An Anthology of Modern Poems by Negro Americans* is a collection of more complex and sophisticated poems suitable for older children. *Malcolm X* is a forthright account of major events in the life of the controversial black leader. While limited in scope, the biography nonetheless offers a solid, general overview of the man and his mission.

A constant factor in Adoff's work is the imaginative expression of faith in people and their spirit. Each work, in its own way, salutes the human condition and its ability to triumph.

—Marilyn Kaye

AGARD, John

Nationality: British (emigrated to England, 1977). **Born:** British Guiana (now Guyana), 1949. **Career:** Has worked as an actor and a performer with a jazz group. **Awards:** Casa de las Américas Poetry prize (Cuba), 1982; Children's Rights Workshop other award, 1986.

Publications for Children

Fiction

Letters for Lettie and Other Stories, illustrated by Errol Lloyd. London, Bodley Head, 1979.

Dig Away Two-Hole Tim, illustrated by Jennifer Northway. London, Bodley Head, 1981.

Poetry

I Din Do Nuttin and Other Poems, illustrated by Susanna Gretz. London, Bodley Head, 1983.

Say It Again, Granny!: Twenty Poems from Caribbean Proverbs, illustrated by Susanna Gretz. London, Bodley Head, 1986.

Lend Me Your Wings, illustrated by Adrienne Kennaway. London, Hodder and Stoughton, 1987.

The Calypso Alphabet, illustrated by Jennifer Bent. New York, Holt, 1989.

Go Noah, Go! Hodder and Stoughton, 1990.

Laughter Is an Egg, illustrated by Alan Rowe. London, Viking, 1990.

The Emperor's Dan-Dan. Hodder and Stoughton, 1992.

Other

Wake Up, Stir About: Songs for Assembly (traditional tunes arranged by Barrie Carson Turner), with others, illustrated by Peter Kent. Cambridge, Massachusetts, Unwin Hyman, 1989.

Editor, with Grace Nichols, *A Caribbean Dozen,* illustrated by Cathie Felstead. Cambridge, Massachusetts, Candlewick Press, 1994.

Editor, with Grace Nichols, *No Hickory, No Dickory, No Dock: A Collection of Nursery Rhymes,* illustrated by Cynthia Jabar. Cambridge, Massachusetts, Candlewick Press, 1994.

PUBLICATIONS FOR YOUNG ADULTS

Poetry

Life Doesn't Frighten Me At All. New York, Holt, 1990.

PUBLICATIONS FOR ADULTS

Poetry

Shoot Me with Flowers. Privately printed, 1973.
Man to Pan. Havana, Casa de las Américas, 1982.
Limbo Dancer in the Dark. Privately printed, 1983.
Mangoes and Bullets: Selected and New Poems 1972-84. London, Pluto, 1985.
Lovelines for a Goat-born Lady. London, Serpent's Tail, 1991.

* * *

Try the best with what you have right now
If you don't have horse, then ride cow.

John Agard is a lively and original poet who combines a shrewd understanding of children with an ability to speak directly to them and to their concerns. He writes in vivid, particular images drawn from the Caribbean and Britain, but the experiences he describes are universal ones of family, the land, and the elements. Agard's early prose work for children is set in the Guyana he knew when young, and it places young people firmly within a well-realised family and village life. As the titles suggest, *Letters for Lettie and Other Poems* centres on a cheerful girl who loves to write letters and *Dig Away Two-Hole Tim* on a boy fascinated by holes, both of them causing problems for the adults around them. Their anecdotal adventures are economically conveyed by an effective combination of words and pictures. However, it is through his poetry rather than his fiction that Agard has made his major contribution to children's literature.

Agard is an extremely effective performance poet, and his work requires the speaking voice to convey its catchy rhythms and lively turning upside-down of conventional phrases. His intention of using speech styles is clear in the title poem of *I Din Do Nuttin and Other Poems,* a collection of poems empathising with children's views of the adult world. He has a gift for raising everyday spoken language into poetic form and significance; the poems shuttle between page and performance. Elements of creole suggest the rhythms and intonation, but there are few words or phrases that create any real barrier to understanding. As in his political or love poems for adults (notably *Mangoes and Bullets: Selected and New Poems 1972-84* and *Lovelines for a Goat-born Lady*) there is always a sense of dance and physical movement in words on the page, "So I reached for my hip-hop cap/ got into my egg-leg tap/ broke into my laughing rap."

Two volumes in the mid-1980s made serious points with a wry humour and an undertone of personal feelings. *Say it Again, Granny!: Twenty Poems from Caribbean Proverbs,* drew on the same fund of traditional wisdom that James Berry used in "Jamaican Caribbean Proverbs" and embodied it in the salty life experience of Granny. *Lend Me Your Wings,* with its delightful illustrations, tells a fable of how Sister Fish and Brother Bird each envy the other's environment. They exchange wings and fins so that they can explore sky and river, but after some dangerous encounters, they are happy enough to return to their own worlds.

Of Agard's more recent work, *Laughter Is an Egg* is a volume in which all of the poems revolve around one or both of the two terms in the title. Dracula is transmuted into Count Laughula, "Plastic Town" is marked by its lack of laughter, and even the Bogeyman Headmaster has his own "bogeyman joke." There are some amusing or challenging juxtapositions ("Why not start your day with scrambled jokes on toast?") but the ideas seem rather overstretched by the end of the volume. *No Hickory, No Dickory, No Dock: A Collection of Nursery Rhymes,* a gathering of Caribbean nursery rhymes written jointly with Grace Nichols (also from Guyana), is an enjoyable mixture of traditional rhymes and new poems. "London Bridge" is juxtaposed with "This Old Lady from Caribee." Anancy is celebrated alongside the feats of the cricketer, Garfield Sobers: "Six six in a row/ Licks-o licks-o!/ Sir Garfield on de go." Some of the rhymes challenge the conventional version, like the title poem in which the little mouse admits eating the bread and the cheese, but protests "I didn't run up no clock." "Pussycat, pussycat" modulates into "Pumpkin, pumpkin"; and "Tom Tom the piper's son" is revised by "what my teacher say." Others encourage a healthy skepticism about authority, like the children's down-to-earth parody of "Onward, Upward," a pompously patriotic Guayanan national song. The liveliness, the empathy, and the feeling for language are the qualities to which young people respond with pleasure.

—Robert Protherough

AHLBERG, Allan and Janet

Nationality: British. **AHLBERG, Allan: Born:** 5 June 1938. **Education:** Sunderland College of Education, 1963-66. **Family:** Married the illustrator Janet Ahlberg (née Hall) in 1969 (died 1994); one daughter. **Career:** Has had various jobs, including postman, soldier, schoolteacher, grave digger, and plumber's mate. **Awards:** Kate Greenaway medal, 1978 and 1991; Children's Rights Workshop Other award, 1980; *Parents* magazine Best Book for Babies award, 1985; Maschler award, 1986; Federation of Children's Book Groups award, 1987.

Publications for Children

Fiction

Brick Street Boys (*Here Are the Brick Street Boys, A Place to Play, Sam the Referee, Fred's Dream, The Great Marathon Football Match*), illustrated by Janet Ahlberg. London, Collins, 5 vols., 1975-76.
Burglar Bill, illustrated by Janet Ahlberg. London, Heinemann, and New York, Greenwillow, 1977.
Jeremiah in the Dark Woods, illustrated by Janet Ahlberg. London, Kestrel, 1977; New York, Viking, 1978.
The Vanishment of Thomas Tull, illustrated by Janet Ahlberg. London, A. and C. Black, and New York, Scribner, 1977.
The One and Only Two Heads, illustrated by Janet Ahlberg. London, Collins, 1979.
Son of a Gun, illustrated by Janet Ahlberg. London, Heinemann, 1979.
The Little Worm Book, illustrated by Janet Ahlberg. London, Granada, 1979; New York, Viking, 1980.
Two Wheels, Two Heads, illustrated by Janet Ahlberg. London, Collins, 1979.
Funnybones, illustrated by Janet Ahlberg. London, Heinemann, and New York, Greenwillow, 1980.
The History of a Pair of Sinners, illustrated by John Lawrence. London, Granada, 1980.
The Baby's Catalogue, illustrated by Janet Ahlberg. London, Kestrel, and Boston, Little Brown, 1982.
Ten in a Bed, illustrated by André Amstutz. London, Granada, 1983.
The Cinderella Show, illustrated by Janet Ahlberg. London and New York, Viking Kestrel, 1986.
The Jolly Postman, illustrated by Janet Ahlberg. London, Heinemann, and Boston, Little Brown, 1986.
Woof!, illustrated by Fritz Wegner. London, Viking Kestrel, 1986.
The Clothes Horse and Other Stories, illustrated by Janet Ahlberg. London, Viking Kestrel, 1987; New York, Viking Kestrel, 1988.
Bye Bye Baby, illustrated by Janet Ahlberg. London, Heinemann, 1989.
The Worm Book, illustrated by Janet Ahlberg. London, Collins, 1989.
The Jolly Christmas Postman, illustrated by Janet Ahlberg. London, Heinemann, 1991.
The Bear Nobody Wanted, illustrated by Janet Ahlberg. New York, Viking, 1992.
It Was a Dark and Stormy Night, illustrated by Janet Ahlberg. London, Viking, 1993; New York, Viking, 1994.
Funnybones:
The Black Cat, illustrated by André Amstutz. London, Heinemann, 1990; New York, Mulberry, 1993.
The Pet Shop, illustrated by André Amstutz. London, Heinemann, 1990; New York, Mulberry, 1993.
Dinosaur Dreams, illustrated by André Amstutz. London, Heinemann, 1991.
Mystery Tour, illustrated by André Amstutz. London, Heinemann, 1991.
Bumps in the Night, illustrated by André Amstutz. London, Heinemann, 1991.
Give the Dog a Bone, illustrated by André Amstutz. London, Heinemann, 1991.
Skeleton Crew, illustrated by André Amstutz. London, Heinemann, and New York, Greenwillow, 1992.
The Ghost Train, illustrated by André Amstutz. London, Heinemann, and New York, Greenwillow, 1992.
The Giant Baby, illustrated by Fritz Wegner. London, Viking Kestrel, 1994.
The Jolly Pocket Postman, illustrated by Janet Ahlberg. London, Heinemann, 1995.
The Better Brown Stories, illustrated by Fritz Wegner. London, Viking Kestrel, 1995.
The Mysteries of Zigomar, illustrated by John Lawrence. London, Walker, 1997.

Poetry

Cops and Robbers, illustrated by Janet Ahlberg. London, Heinemann, and New York, Greenwillow, 1978.
Each Peach Pear Plum, illustrated by Janet Ahlberg. London, Kestrel, 1978; New York, Viking, 1979.
Peepo!, illustrated by Janet Ahlberg. London, Kestrel, 1981; as *Peek-a-Boo!*, New York, Viking, 1981.
Please, Mrs. Butler, illustrated by Fritz Wegner. London, Kestrel, 1983.
Daisychains (*That's My Baby!, Summer Snowmen, Which Witch?, Ready Teddy Go, Monster Munch, The Good Old Dolls, Rent-a-Robot, Clowning About, One True Santa*), illustrated by Janet Ahlberg and André Amstutz. London, Heinemann, 9 vols., 1983-85.
The Mighty Slide, illustrated by Charlotte Voake. London and New York, Viking Kestrel, 1988.
Heard It in the Playground, illustrated by Fritz Wegner. Viking Kestrel, 1989.
Mrs. Butler's Songbook (based on poems from *Please Mrs. Butler* and *Heard It in the Playground*), music by Colin Matthews, illustrated by Fritz Wegner. London, Viking, 1992.

Other

The Old Joke Book, illustrated by Janet Ahlberg. London, Kestrel, 1976; New York, Viking, 1977.
Happy Families (readers; U.S. editions as *Wacky Families*):
Mr. Biff the Boxer, illustrated by Janet Ahlberg. London, Kestrel, 1980; New York, Golden Press, 1982.
Mrs. Plug the Plumber, illustrated by Joe Wright. London, Kestrel, 1980; New York, Golden Press, 1982.
Mrs. Wobble the Waitress, illustrated by Janet Ahlberg. London, Kestrel, 1980; New York, Golden Press, 1982.
Master Salt the Sailor's Son, illustrated by André Amstutz. London, Kestrel, 1980; New York, Golden Press, 1982.
Miss Jump the Jockey, illustrated by André Amstutz. London, Kestrel, 1980.
Mr. Cosmo the Conjuror, illustrated by Joe Wright. London, Kestrel, 1980.
Miss Brick the Builder's Baby, illustrated by Colin McNaughton. London, Penguin, 1981; New York, Golden Press, 1982.
Mr. Buzz the Beeman, illustrated by Faith Jaques. London, Penguin, 1981; New York, Golden Press, 1982.
Mr. and Mrs. Hay the Horse, illustrated by Colin McNaughton. London, Penguin, 1981; New York, Golden Press, 1982.
Mrs. Lather's Laundry, illustrated by André Amstutz. London, Penguin, 1981; New York, Golden Press, 1982.
Master Money the Millionaire, illustrated by André Amstutz. London, Penguin, 1981.

Mr. Tick the Teacher, illustrated by Faith Jaques. London, Penguin, 1981.
Miss Dose the Doctors' Daughter, illustrated by Fritz Wegner. London, Viking Kestrel, 1988.
Master Bun the Bakers' Boy, illustrated by Fritz Wegner. London, Viking Kestrel, 1988.
Mrs. Jolly's Joke Shop, illustrated by Colin McNaughton. London, Viking Kestrel, 1988.
Mr. Creep the Crook, illustrated by André Amstutz. London, Viking Kestrel, 1988.
The Ha Ha Bonk Book (joke book), illustrated by Janet Ahlberg. London, Kestrel, and New York, Penguin, 1982.
Help Your Child to Read (*Fast Frog, Silly Sheep, Double Ducks, Bad Bear, Poorly Pig, Rubber Rabbit, Hip-Hippo-Ray, King Kangaroo, Mister Wolf, Spider Spy, Tell-Tale Tiger, Travelling Moose*), illustrated by Eric Hill and André Amstutz. London, Granada, 12 vols., 1982-83.
Foldaways (*Circus, Families, Monsters, Zoo*), illustrated by Colin McNaughton. London, Granada, 4 vols., 1984.
Slot Books (*Yum Yum, Playmates*), illustrated by Janet Ahlberg. London, Viking Kestrel, 2 vols., 1984-85; New York, Viking Kestrel, 2 vols., 1985.
Red Nose Readers (*Help!, Big Bad Pig, Happy Worm, Fee Fi Fo Fum, Make a Face, So Can I, Jumping, Bear's Birthday, Me and My Friend, Shirley's Shops, Push the Dog, Crash! Bang! Wallop!, Blow Me Down!, Look Out for the Seals!, One Two Flea!, Tell Us a Story*), illustrated by Colin McNaughton. London, Walker, 16 vols., 1985-86; first 4 vols. published New York, Random House, 1985.
Starting School, illustrated by Janet Ahlberg. London and New York, Viking Kestrel, 1988.
Miss Dirt the Dustman's Daughter, illustrated by Tony Ross. London, Viking Kestrel, 1996.
Mrs. Vole the Vet, illustrated by Emma Chichester Clark. London, Viking Kestrel, 1996.
Master Track's Train, illustrated by André Amstutz. London, Viking Kestrel, 1997.
Ms. Cliff the Climber, illustrated by Fritz Wegner. London, Viking Kestrel, 1997.

*

Critical Studies: "More than words" by Elaine Williams, in *The Times Educational Supplement*, vol. 4212, 21 March 1997, 8; *Children's Books and Their Creators*, edited by Anita Silvey, Boston, Houghton Mifflin, 1995, 8; *Major Authors and Illustrators for Children and Young Adults*, edited by Collier & Nakamura, Detroit, Michigan, vols. 6, 1993, 2609.

Allan Ahlberg comments:

Janet and I made books for our own pleasure and to earn a living. How we worked: I wrote, Janet illustrated, together we designed. We were book makers rather than author and illustrator. What mattered to us was the printed bound object: the whole book, cover to cover. Janet died in 1994. Presently (1997), I am attempting to make books without her. A difficult business.

* * *

Janet and Allan Ahlberg worked in perfect tandem for twenty years, creating captivating books about childhood and families. The Ahlbergs' books are seamless—a blend of text, illustration and design so perfectly interwoven that readers cannot distinguish the individual impact of any of those factors. Allan stated in *The Times Educational Supplement* that he and Janet would follow a typical pattern when creating their books. Allan would propose a story line and share his writing with Janet, who he described as his first critic. She, in turn, would produce drawings to which Allan would respond. For several months they would work back and forth, providing each other with feedback until they created a mock-up to show a publisher. Janet and Allan were involved with every aspect of a book's production: size, layout, typeset, cover, endpapers and even blurbs. For this inventive couple, creating a book involved far more than combining words and illustrations. The Ahlbergs' books are complete entities, charming children and adults alike with neat plots that frequently focus on family life. The book, *Peek-a-boo*, is an example of this emphasis, with its cut-out holes for young readers to peep through and witness British family life of the 1940s as seen through a baby's eyes.

Another typical theme in Janet and Allan Ahlbergs' books is their playful reference to traditional literature. The enormously successful design of *The Jolly Postman* book, which combines pages of verse and envelopes containing correspondence addressed to folklore characters, is repeated in *The Jolly Christmas Postman* and in *The Jolly Pocket Postman.* The latter weaves together figures from folktales and nursery rhymes with figures from classic fantasy, such as *Alice in Wonderland* and *The Wizard of Oz.* In *The Jolly Pocket Postman*, the improbable chain of events that befall the now familiar postman begin when a giant baby rattle falls from the sky just as the hapless postal worker walks beneath a beanstalk. Children who explore the intricacies of this book will certainly appreciate the minuscule postman's efforts to survive in a giant's world. On the other hand, adult readers are likely to recognize the veracity of the Ahlbergs' statements about the role of coincidence in our lives. Both adults and children will be amused by the hero's close escapes and the appearance of a classic cast of literary celebrities. The inclusion of a pocket lens for magnifying small details makes Janet's intricate, delicate illustrations even more accessible to readers who will revel in the opportunity to find the hidden bits. *The Jolly Pocket Postman* is an ideal showcase for the considerable talents of Janet and Allan Ahlberg. This outstanding book was also their final collaboration.

Janet Ahlberg died in November 1994, and Allan experienced a devastating loss on both a personal and professional level. In an interview with Elaine Williams, Allan acknowledged that after Janet's death, he did little but sit around for nearly a year until he realized that he had to try to start over. Since 1995, in collaboration with other illustrators, Allan has written collections of poetry, short stories and fiction. An example of his fiction is *The Better Brown Stories*, a chapter book that describes an extraordinary collaboration between the Brown family, who decide that whoever is writing the script of their life is producing rubbish, and the writer they confront, who attempts to satisfy their demands. This slim volume is ingeniously crafted, filled with droll humor and subtle references to literary classics.

The Mysteries of Zigomar is a collection of short stories and poems that feature Ahlberg's characteristic wry humor, parodies of folklore and sardonic accounts of school days. One of the poems, "The Vampire and the Hound" is rather macabre, but most of the entries sport a typically subtle and frequently silly British humor. "The Paper Boy" is an inventive tale of a boy made of paper who tires of being persecuted by bullies and determines to make something of his life. "Snow White Lies" is an acerbic account of what really happened in the dwarfs' cottage. This short story is classic Ahlberg with its blend of folklore characters and sarcastic commentary that has tremendous appeal to readers who appreciate poking fun at the tales of their long-ago youth. American children may have to work to understand some of the British allusions. Nevertheless, older elementary children will appreciate Ahlberg's tongue in cheek style and his obvious recognition of their status as mature readers.

—Anne Drolett Creany

AINSWORTH, Ruth (Gallard)

Nationality: British. **Born:** Manchester, Lancashire, 16 October 1908. **Education:** Ipswich High School; Froebel Training Centre, Leicester. **Family:** Married Frank L. Gilbert in 1935; three sons. **Career:** Scriptwriter, *Listen with Mother* and *English for Schools* series, BBC, London. **Address:** Field End, Corbridge, Northumberland NE45 5JP, England.

Publications for Children

Fiction

Tales about Tony, illustrated by Cora E.M. Paterson. London, Epworth Press, 1936.
Mr. Popcorn's Friends. London, Epworth Press, 1938.
The Gingerbread House. London, Epworth Press, 1938.
The Ragamuffins. London, Epworth Press, 1939.
Richard's First Term. London, Epworth Press, 1940.
Five and a Dog. London, Epworth Press, 1949.
"Listen with Mother" Tales, illustrated by Astrid Walford. London, Heinemann, 1951.
Rufty Tufty the Golliwog, illustrated by Dorothy Craigie. London, Heinemann, 1952.
Rufty Tufty at the Seaside, illustrated by Dorothy Craigie. London, Heinemann, 1954.
Charles Stories and Others, from "Listen with Mother," illustrated by Sheila Hawkins. London, Heinemann, 1954.
More about Charles and Other Stories, from "Listen with Mother," illustrated by Sheila Hawkins. London, Heinemann, 1954.
The Snow Bear, illustrated by Rosemary Trew. London, Heinemann, 1956.
Rufty Tufty Goes Camping, illustrated by Dorothy Craigie. London, Heinemann, 1956.
Rufty Tufty Runs Away, illustrated by Dorothy Craigie. London, Heinemann, 1957.
Five "Listen with Mother" Tales about Charles, illustrated by Matvyn Wright. London, Adprint, 1957.
Nine Drummers Drumming, illustrated by John Mackay. London, Heinemann, 1958.
Rufty Tufty Flies High, illustrated by D.G. Valentine. London, Heinemann, 1959.
Cherry Stones: A Book of Fairy Stories, illustrated by Pat Humphreys. London, Heinemann, 1960.
Rufty Tufty's Island, illustrated by D.G. Valentine. London, Heinemann, 1960.
Lucky Dip: A Selection of Stories and Verses, illustrated by Geraldine Spence. London, Penguin, 1961.
Rufty Tufty and Hattie, illustrated by D.G. Valentine. London, Heinemann, 1962.
Far-Away Children, illustrated by Felice Trentin. London, Heinemann, 1963; New York, Roy, 1968.
The Ten Tales of Shellover, illustrated by Antony Maitland. London, Deutsch, 1963; New York, Roy, 1968.
The Wolf Who Was Sorry, illustrated by Doritie Kettlewell. London, Heinemann, 1964; New York, Roy, 1968.
Rufty Tufty Makes a House, illustrated by D.G. Valentine. London, Heinemann, 1965.
Daisy the Cow, illustrated by Sarah Garland. London, Hamish Hamilton, 1966.
Horse on Wheels, illustrated by Janet Duchesne. London, Hamish Hamilton, 1966.
Jack Frost, illustrated by Jane Paton. London, Heinemann, 1966.
Roly the Railway Mouse, illustrated by Leslie Atkinson. London, Heinemann, 1967; as *Roly the Railroad Mouse,* New York, Watts, 1969.
The Aeroplane Who Wanted to See the Sea. London, Bancroft, 1968.
Boris the Teddy Bear. London, Bancroft, 1968.
Dougal the Donkey. London, Bancroft, 1968.
More Tales of Shellover, illustrated by Antony Maitland. London, Deutsch, and New York, Roy, 1968.
Mungo the Monkey. London, Bancroft, 1968.
The Old Fashioned Car. London, Bancroft, 1968.
The Rabbit and His Shadow. London, Bancroft, 1968.
The Noah's Ark, illustrated by Elsie Wrigley. London, Lutterworth Press, 1969.
The Bicycle Wheel, illustrated by Shirley Hughes. London, Hamish Hamilton, 1969.
Look, Do and Listen, illustrated by Bernadette Watts. London, Heinemann, and New York, Watts, 1969.
The Phantom Cyclist and Other Stories, illustrated by Antony Maitland. London, Deutsch, 1971; Chicago, Follett, 1974.
The Phantom Fisherboy: Tales of Mystery and Magic, illustrated by Shirley Hughes. London, Deutsch, 1974.
Bedtime Book. Maidenhead, Berkshire, Purnell, 1974.
Three's Company, illustrated by Prudence Seward. Guildford, Surrey, Lutterworth Press, 1974.
The Bear Who Liked Hugging People and Other Stories, illustrated by Antony Maitland. London, Heinemann, 1976; New York, Crane Russak, 1978.
The Phantom Roundabout and Other Ghostly Tales, illustrated by Shirley Hughes. London, Deutsch, 1977; as *The Phantom Carousel,* Chicago, Follett, 1978.
Up the Airy Mountain: Stories of Magic, illustrated by Eileen Browne. London, Heinemann, 1977.
Mr. Jumble's Toy Shop, illustrated by Paul Wrigley. Guildford, Surrey, Lutterworth Press, 1978.
The Talking Rock, illustrated by Joanna Stubbs. London, Deutsch, 1979.
The Mysterious Baba and Her Magic Caravan: Two Stories, illustrated by Joan Hickson. London, Deutsch, 1980.
The Pirate Ship and Other Stories, illustrated by Shirley Hughes. London, Heinemann, 1980.
Mermaids' Tales, illustrated by Dandi Palmer. Guildford, Surrey, Lutterworth Press, 1980.

The Little Yellow Taxi and His Friends, illustrated by Gary Inwood. Guildford, Surrey, Lutterworth Press, 1982.

Plays

Three Little Mushrooms: Four Puppet Plays (includes *Here We Go round the Buttercups, Lob's Silver Spoon, Hide-and-Seek, Hay-Making*). London, Heinemann, 1955.

More Little Mushrooms: Four Puppet Plays (includes *Three Clever Mushrooms, Tick-Tock, Christmas Eve, The White Stranger*). London, Heinemann, 1955.

Poetry

All Different, illustrated by Linda Bramley. London, Heinemann, 1947.

The Evening Listens. London, Heinemann, 1953.

Other

The Ruth Ainsworth Readers (*The Cottage by the Sea; Little Wife Goody; The Robber; The Wild Boy; A Comfort for Owl; Sugar and Spice; Fun, Fires and Friends; Black Bill; A Pill for Owl; Tortoise in Trouble; The Pirate Ship; Hob the Dwarf*). London, Heinemann, 12 vols., 1953-55.

Look Ahead Readers, with Ronald Ridout, illustrated by John Mackay. London, Heinemann, 8 vols., 1956-57.

Books for Me to Read, with Ronald Ridout:

Red Books (*Jill and Peter; The House of Hay; Come and Play; A Name of My Own; The Duck That Ran Away; Tim's Hoop*), illustrated by Ingeborg Meyer-Rey. London, Bancroft, 6 vols., 1964.

Blue Books (*At the Zoo; What Are They?; Colours; Silly Billy; A Pram and a Bicycle; Pony, Pony*), illustrated by Gwyneth Mamlock. London, Bancroft, 6 vols., 1965.

Yellow Books (*David's Picture, Andrew's Engine, Hunt the Thimble, Something Alive, The Singing Grasshopper, A Little Black Lamb*), illustrated by Susan Bailey. London, Bancroft, 6 vols., 1967.

Green Books (*Susan's House; What Can You Hear?; Tim's Kite; Flippy the Frog; Huff the Hedgehog; A House for a Mouse*), illustrated by William Robert Shaw. London, Bancroft, 6 vols., 1968.

The Look about You Books (*In Woods and Fields, Down the Lane, Beside the Sea, By Pond and Stream, In Your Garden, In the Park*), illustrated by Jennie Corbett. London, Heinemann, 6 vols., 1967-69.

The Ruth Ainsworth Book, illustrated by Shirley Hughes. London, Heinemann, and New York, Watts, 1970.

Dandy the Donkey (reader). London, Bancroft, 1971.

The Wild Wood (reader). London, Bancroft, 1971.

Fairy Gold: Favourite Fairy Tales Retold for the Very Young, illustrated by Barbara Hope Steinberg. London, Heinemann, 1972.

Editor, *Book of Colours and Sounds.* London, Purnell, 1968.

*

Ruth Ainsworth comments:

I had a quiet childhood by the sea in Suffolk. Many of my stories have a background of lonely beaches, sand dunes, marram grass, and small prints of bare feet. Mermaids occur as well as shrimps and anemones.

My father died when I was a baby. I started writing as soon as I could use a pencil and published poems in periodicals in my teens. I won a Gold Medal for poetry.

I love reading biography, letters, novels, and poetry. I especially enjoy Jane Austen and Ivy Compton-Burnett. I like walking, architecture, looking at paintings, and listening to music. My chief joy is seeing my family and my friends informally and often. Life in this small Northumberland town suits me pretty well, though I still feel that Suffolk is my native home.

* * *

When reading is new to children, stories are inextricably linked with their play. The fantastic has its roots in the workaday and the domestic. Playthings, toys, and animals are anthropomorphised as friends. Ruth Ainsworth's books reflect this special time. Her external world is that of nurseries, gardens, and play places. Novice readers (and listeners) learn to understand stories as a particular kind of imaginative activity—and also as statements about what the world could be like. It pays to be kind; disobedience usually brings disaster.

Ainsworth's early work showed that she could engage her audience without patronising or trivialising. *"Listen with Mother" Tales* and *Charles Stories* had uncluttered plots, and their origin as radio scripts made them—like all her work—perfect for reading aloud. The Rufty Tufty books, about "the happiest little golliwog in Golliwog Village," may now have been made unpalatable by a heightened social sensitivity, but were well-meaning at the time.

The 1960s showed a new vibrancy in Ainsworth's writing: *Roly the Railway Mouse* has an endearing central character, lively pace, and skilled use of background. In *The Noah's Ark,* the pairs of creatures inside George's toy ark come to life when he is asleep. The important business of "let's pretend" that is the plot of early childhood is cleverly realised. The best-rounded of her works are the Shellover Tales. An affable tortoise spins stories for the animals in Mrs. Candy's garden. The sharing of stories is a recurrent activity in Ainsworth's books: a natural mode of depicting justice, retribution, good deserts, and commonsense.

The Phantom stories show increased stealth in dealing with the unfamiliar (even the frightening). Realistic adventure is handled more acutely than in earlier books in *Three's Company,* a matter-of-fact telling of the close friendship between two girls and a boy. A story such as *Mr. Jumble's Toy Shop* from the late 1970s encapsulates this author's attraction for the very young. The frightened and lonely are comforted. Predators (horrid children with names like Basil and Edwina) are kept at bay. Problems are shared and solved in bedtime-story length episodes under the benevolent paternalism of the proprietor.

Children are not disturbed, puzzled, or challenged by Ruth Ainsworth's books, but some lessons about the sophisticated play that is reading are well taught. Most important, the magical thinking in the stories and the timeless camaraderie between children, animals, and toys are confirmed, extended, and supported by the grown-ups. She also knows well the important driving power of "that's just like me" (and of "what happens next?") when one is new to the game.

—Colin Mills

ALDERSON, Sue Ann

Nationality: American; Canadian landed immigrant. **Born:** New York City, 11 September 1940. **Education:** Antioch College, Yellow Springs, Ohio, 1957-62, B.A. in literature 1962; Ohio State University, Columbus, 1962-64, M.A. in English 1964; University of California, Berkeley, 1964-67. **Family:** Married Evan Alderson in 1965 (divorced 1986); one daughter and one son. **Career:** Instructor, Simon Fraser University, 1967-71, and Capilano College, 1972-80, both Vancouver, British Columbia. assistant professor, 1980-84; associate professor of creative writing, 1984-90, and professor since 1991, University of British Columbia, Vancouver. **Address:** 4004 West 32nd Avenue, Vancouver, British Columbia V6S 1Z6, Canada.

PUBLICATIONS FOR CHILDREN

Fiction

Bonnie McSmithers You're Driving Me Dithers, illustrated by Fiona Garrick. Edmonton, Tree Frog Press, 1974.
Hurry Up, Bonnie!, illustrated by Fiona Garrick. Edmonton, Tree Frog Press, 1976.
The Adventures of Prince Paul, illustrated by Jane Walsack. Vancouver, Fforbez, 1977.
The Finding Princess, illustrated by Jane Walsack. Vancouver, Fforbez, 1977.
Bonnie McSmithers Is at It Again!, illustrated by Fiona Garrick. Edmonton, Tree Frog Press, 1979.
Comet's Tale, illustrated by Georgia Pow Graham. Edmonton, Tree Frog Press, 1983.
The Not Impossible Summer, illustrated by C. Rother. Toronto, Irwin, 1983.
The Something in Thurlo Darby's House, illustrated by Deborah Drew-Brook-Cormack. Toronto, Ginn, 1984; Huddersfield, Yorkshire, Schofield and Sims, 1985.
Ida and the Wool Smugglers, illustrated by Ann Blades. Toronto, Groundwood, 1987; New York, McElderry, 1988.
Maybe You Had to Be There, by Duncan. Vancouver, Polestar Press, 1989.
Chapter One. Toronto, General Publishing, 1990.
Sure As Strawberries, illustrated by Karen Reczuch. Red Deer, Alberta, Red Deer College Press, 1992.
A Ride for Martha, illustrated by Ann Blades. Toronto, Groundwood, 1993.
Ten Mondays for Lots of Boxes, illustrated by C. T'Kenye. Vancouver, Ronsdale Press, 1995.
Pond Seasons, illustrated by Ann Blades. Toronto, Groundwood, 1996.

PUBLICATIONS FOR ADULTS

Other

Editor, *Explorations 1* (poetry) by Betty Coombs and Lalie Harcourt. Don Mills, Ontario, Addison Wesley, 1986.
Editor, *Explorations 2* (poetry) by Betty Coombs. Don Mills, Ontario, Addison Wesley, 1987.

*

Sue Ann Alderson comments:

My first book, *Bonnie McSmithers You're Driving Me Dithers,* grew from a story I made for my young daughter, in which I tried to explore our relationship and resolve our discord. Desires to explore feelings and relationships, and to resolve discord, have continued to inform all of my writing. I would like my books to empower the children they come to, enlarging their view of their worlds (inner as well as outer) and providing what insights I can that may enable them better to resolve the discords they encounter. I have been fortunate to be able to travel through three childhoods: my own (in New York, with my younger sister and psychologist-parents), my daughter's, and my son's (both in Canada). All three journeys have included side-trips, not only to what-is, but also to what-could-be, and lots to look at—and write about—along the way!

* * *

Sue Ann Alderson is a versatile writer who works in several genres for a variety of ages. Common to all her stories, from picture book texts to novels, are recurring themes of the empowerment of children, the joys of animals and nature, the pleasures of cooperative projects, and the value of individuality and imagination.

Two of Alderson's early works for children, a pair of fairytale-like stories, *The Finding Princess* and *The Adventures of Prince Paul,* are basically apprentice works. Although somewhat derivative they do show Alderson's talent for shaping a story, her quirky humour, and her interest in the natural world.

Best known of her works is a trio of picture books featuring a small heroine named Bonnie McSmithers who exasperates her mother and delights her readers with her vagueness, tardiness, eccentricity, and irrepressible confidence and energy. The texts move along with bouncing rhythms, and each has a refrain that makes it perfect for reading aloud. In *Bonnie McSmithers You're Driving Me Dithers, Hurry Up, Bonnie!,* and *Bonnie McSmithers Is at It Again!,* Alderson artfully captures the personality and viewpoint of the preschool child.

In two novels for older children, *Comet's Tale* and *Maybe You Had to Be There, by Duncan,* Alderson deals, in a wider-ranging format, with the theme of a child's growing confidence. *Comet's Tale* is a madcap fantasy of a family that pulls together to help save a threatened animal shelter. With its cartoon-like pace and crowded cast, it tends to collapse under the weight of its own wackiness, and its final effect is somewhat diffuse. *Maybe You Had to Be There, by Duncan,* written as a sixth grader's English project turned autobiographical novel, recounts a week's zany adventures in which Duncan discovers self-worth while thwarting a dentist who has developed a futuristic machine for stealing objects.

The Not Impossible Summer, the story of a summer vacation on a west coast island, deals with a strained mother-daughter relationship and its resolution sparked by an heroic act by the protagonist, Jenny, who rescues a lost and injured boy. Alderson leavens the seriousness of the theme with a restrained use of mayhem, as when Jenny smuggles a cow into the basement, and with touches of pawky humour as when we are privy to the heroic exploits of Jenny's daring and splendid alter-ego. In *Chapter One,* a teenager living with her mother discovers the difference between true and false friends, her love of her dying grandmother, and the limitations of her distant father. Written in a limited vocabulary format, the novel includes some cliched teenage situations but presents a clear picture of the girl's growing confidence.

The most accomplished of Alderson's works is *Ida and the Wool Smugglers,* about a middle child in a turn-of-the-century farming family The heroine is frustrated by being told she is too small to take on the responsibilities she longs for. One day, while delivering bread to a neighbouring family, she surprises a pair of sheep smugglers and in an act of bravery herds a ewe and two lambs to safety. Based on the history of Salt Spring Island off the coast of British Columbia, the story is spare, plausible, and has the rhythm and energy of the truly accomplished picture book. In a sequel, *A Ride for Martha,* the heroine, annoyed that she must bring her little sister on an expedition she and her friends are making, learns the value of friendship when the other girls help her to rescue Martha from a boat that has been set adrift by the rising tide. Alderson deals with the multicultural nature of this turn of the century society and the important roles that all its members play.

—Sarah Ellis, updated by Jon C. Stott

ALEXANDER, Lloyd (Chudley)

Nationality: American. **Born:** Philadelphia, Pennsylvania, 30 January 1924. **Education:** West Chester State College and Lafayette College, Pennsylvania, 1942-43; the Sorbonne, Paris, 1946. **Family:** Married Janine Denni in 1946; one daughter. **Career:** Since 1946, writer and translator. Author-in-residence, schools in Springfield, Pennsylvania, 1967-68, and Temple University, 1970-74. Cartoonist, layout artist, advertising copywriter, and editor of industrial magazine, 1947-70. Since 1970 director, Carpenter Lane Chamber Music Society, Philadelphia; since 1973 member of the Editorial Advisory Board, *Cricket* magazine, Peru, Illinois. **Military Service:** Served in the U.S. Army Combat Intelligence and Counter-Intelligence corps, 1942-46: Staff Sergeant. **Awards:** Isaac Siegel Memorial Juvenile award, 1959, for *Border Hawk: August Bondi;* ALA notable book citation, 1964, for *The Book of Three;* Newbery Honor Book, 1965, for *The Black Cauldron;* "Best Books" citations, *School Library Journal,* 1967, for *Taran Wanderer,* 1971, for *The King's Fountain,* and 1982, for *Westmark;* citation from American Institute of Graphic Arts Children's Books, 1967- 68, for *The Truthful Harp;* "Children's Book of the Year" citation, Child Study Association of America, 1968, for *The High King,* 1971, for *The King's Fountain,* 1973, for *The Cat Who Wished to Be A Man,* 1974, for *The Foundling and Other Tales of Prydain,* 1975, for *The Wizard in the Tree,* 1982, for *The Kestrel,* and 1985, for *The Black Cauldron* and *Time Cat;* Newbery Medal, National Book award nomination, both 1969, both for *The High King;* "Best Books of the Year" citation, Library of Congress, 1970, and National Book Award, 1971, both for *The Marvelous Misadventures of Sebastian;* Drexel award, 1972 and 1976, for outstanding contributions to literature for children; *Boston Globe-Horn Book* award, 1973, for *The Cat Who Wished to Be a Man;* "Outstanding Books of the Year" citation, *New York Times,* 1973, for *The Foundling and Other Tales of Prydain;* Laura Ingalls Wilder award nomination, 1975; CRABbery award, Oxon Hill Branch of Prince George's County Library (Maryland), 1979, National Book award nomination, 1979, Silver Pencil award, 1981, and Austrian Children's Book award, 1984, all for *The First Two Lives of Lukas-Kasha;* American Book Award nomination, 1980, for *The High King,* and 1982, for *The Wizard in the Tree;* ALA "Best Books for Young Adults" citation, 1981, for *Westmark,* 1982, for *The Kestrel,* and 1984, for *The Beggar Queen;* American Book award, 1982, for *Westmark;* Parents' Choice award, 1982, for *The Kestrel,* 1984, for *The Beggar Queen,* and 1986, for *The Illyrian Adventure;* Golden Cat award, Sjoestrands Foerlag (Sweden), 1984, for excellence in children's literature; Regina Medal, Catholic Library Association, 1986; Church and Synagogue Library Association award, 1987; Field award, Pennsylvania Library Association, 1987, for *The Illyrian Adventure;* Lifetime Achievement award, Pennsylvania Center for The Book in Philadelphia, 1991; "Best Book" Citations from *Booklist, School Library Journal,* and Parents' Choice award, all 1991, all for *The Remarkable Journey of Prince Jen;* Parents' Choice award, *Parenting* award, both 1992, both for *The Fortune-Tellers; Boston Globe-Horn Book* award for *The Fortune-Tellers,* 1993. **Agent:** Brandt & Brandt, 1501 Broadway, New York, New York 10036. **Address:** 1005 Drexel Ave., Drexel Hill, Pennsylvania 19026, U.S.A.

Publications for Children

Fiction

Time Cat: The Remarkable Journeys of Jason and Gareth, illustrated by Bill Sokol. New York, Holt Rinehart, 1963; as *Nine Lives,* London, Cassell, 1963.

Coll and His White Pig, illustrated by Evaline Ness. New York, Holt Rinehart, 1965.

The Truthful Harp, illustrated by Evaline Ness. New York, Holt Rinehart, 1967.

The King's Fountain, illustrated by Ezra Jack Keats. New York, Dutton, 1971.

The Four Donkeys, illustrated by Lester Abrams. New York, Holt Rinehart, 1972; Kingswood, Surrey, World's Work, 1974.

The Foundling and Other Tales of Prydain, illustrated by Margot Zemach. New York, Holt Rinehart, 1973.

The Cat Who Wished to Be a Man. New York, Dutton, 1973.

The Wizard in the Tree, illustrated by Laszlo Kubinyi. New York, Dutton, 1975.

The Town Cats and Other Tales, illustrated by Laszlo Kubinyi. New York, Dutton, 1977.

The Fortune-Tellers, illustrated by Trina Schart Hyman. New York, Dutton, 1992.

Publications for Young Adults

Fiction

The Marvelous Misadventures of Sebastian. New York, Dutton, 1970.

The First Two Lives of Lukas-Kasha. New York, Dutton, 1978.

The Remarkable Journey of Prince Jen. New York, Dutton, 1991.

The Iron Ring. New York, Dutton, 1997.

***Prydain* series:**

The Book of Three. New York, Holt Rinehart, 1964; London, Heinemann, 1966.

The Black Cauldron. New York, Holt Rinehart, 1965; London, Heinemann, 1967.
The Castle of Llyr. New York, Holt Rinehart, 1966; London, Heinemann, 1968.
Taran Wanderer. New York, Holt Rinehart, 1967; London, Fontana, 1979.
The High King. New York, Holt Rinehart, 1968; London, Fontana, 1979.

The Westmark Trilogy:

Westmark. New York, Dutton, 1981.
The Kestrel. New York, Dutton, 1982.
The Beggar Queen. New York, Dutton, 1984.

The Vesper Holly Adventures:

The Illyrian Adventure. New York, Dutton, 1986.
The El Dorado Adventure. New York, Dutton, 1987.
The Drackenberg Adventure. New York, Dutton, 1988.
The Jedera Adventure. New York, Dutton, 1989.
The Philadelphia Adventure. New York, Dutton, 1990.

Biographies

Border Hawk: August Bondi, illustrated by Bernard Krigstein. New York, Farrar, Straus, 1958.
The Flagship Hope: Aaron Lopez, illustrated by Bernard Krigstein. Philadelphia, Jewish Publication Society, 1960.

PUBLICATIONS FOR ADULTS

And Let the Credit Go (novel). New York, Crowell, 1955.
My Five Tigers. New York, Crowell, and London, Cassell, 1956.
Janine Is French. New York, Crowell, 1958; London, Cassell, 1960.
My Love Affair with Music. New York, Crowell, 1960; London, Cassell, 1961.
Park Avenue Vet, with Dr. Louis Camuti. New York, Holt Rinehart, and London, Deutsch, 1962.
Fifty Years in the Doghouse. New York, Putnam, 1963; as *Send for Ryan!,* London, W. H. Allen, 1965.
My Cats and Me: The Story of an Understanding. Philadelphia, Running Press, 1989.

Translator from the French

The Wall and Other Stories, by Jean-Paul Sartre. New York, New Directions, 1948; as *Intimacy and Other Stories,* London, Peter Nevill, 1949.
Nausea, by Jean-Paul Sartre. New York, New Directions, 1949; as *The Diary of Antoine Roquentin,* London, Lehmann, 1949.
Selected Writings, by Paul Eluard. New York, New Directions, 1951; as *Uninterrupted Poetry: Selected Writings,* New York, New Directions, 1975.
The Sea Rose, by Paul Vialar. London and New York, Neville Spearman, 1951.

Contributor

Horn Book Reflections on Children's Books and Reading, edited by Elinor Whitney Field. Boston, Horn Book, 1969.
Cricket's Choice. Chicago, Open Court, 1974.
Celebrating Children's Books, edited by Betsy Hearne and Marilyn Kaye. New York, Lothrop, 1981.
Innocence and Experience, edited by Barbara Harrison and Gregory Macguire. New York, Lothrop, 1987.
The Voice of the Narrator in Children's Literature, edited by Charlotte F. Otten and Gary D. Schmidt. Westport, Connecticut, Greenwood, 1989.
The Big Book for Peace, edited by Ann Durell and Margaret Sachs. New York, Dutton, 1990.
The Cat on My Shoulder, edited by Lisa Angowski. Stamford, Connecticut, 1993.
The Zena Sutherland Lectures, 1983-1992, edited by Betsy Hearne. New York, Clarion, 1993.

*

Media Adaptations: Stage versions of *The Cat Who Wished to Be a Man* and *The Wizard in the Tree.* produced in Japan; television serial version of *The Marvelous Misadventures of Sebastian.* produced in Japan; *The Black Cauldron* (film based on the Prydain novels), Walt Disney Productions, 1985.

Biography: Entry in *Third Book of Junior Authors,* New York, H.W. Wilson, 1972; entry in *Dictionary of Literary Biography,* Volume 52, Detroit, Gale, 1986; essay in *Authors and Artists for Young Adults,* Volume 1, Detroit, Gale, 1989; essay in *Speaking for Ourselves: Autobiographical Sketches by Notable Authors of Books for Young Adults,* Volume 1, compiled and edited by Donald R. Gallo, National Council of Teachers of English, 1990; *Lloyd Alexander* by Jill P. May, Boston, Twayne, 1991.

Bibliography: *Lloyd Alexander, Evangeline Walton Ensley, Kenneth Morris: A Primary and Secondary Bibliography* by Kenneth J. Zahorski, Boston, Hall, 1981; *Lloyd Alexander: A Bio-Bibliography* by James S. Jacobs and Michael O. Tunnell, Westport, Connecticut, Greenwood, 1991.

Critical Studies: *A Tribute to Lloyd Alexander* by Myra Cohn Livingston, Philadelphia, Drexel Institute, 1976; *Lloyd Alexander: A Critical Biography* by James S. Jacobs, unpublished dissertation, University of Georgia, 1978; *Children's Literature Review,* Detroit, Gale, Volume 1, 1976, Volume 5, 1983; *The Prydain Companion* by Michael O. Tunnell, Westport, Greenwood, 1989; *Lloyd Alexander* by Jill P. May, Boston, Twayne, 1991.

Lloyd Alexander comments:

After writing some dozen years for adults, writing for young people was the most creative and liberating experience of my life. In books for young people, I was able to express my own deepest feelings far more than I could ever do in writing for adults. Though most of my books have been in the form of fantasy, I believe that is merely one of the many ways to express attitudes about real human relationships and problems.

* * *

Although he first wrote and translated adult literature, Lloyd Alexander turned to children's literature in the early 1960s when he sensed a feeling of despair in adult fiction and began to believe that there was little future in writing it. Since the publication of his first children's book in 1958, Alexander has been recognized as an outstanding 20th-century American author of children's literature. Since he does not write in one genre alone, he is difficult to categorize. His overall contribution to children's literature reflects the diversity to be found in the field today. His tone, choice of subjects, and writing style suggest that Alexander understands today's society, children, and their reading interests.

In researching *Time Cat,* his first children's novel, Alexander returned to the Welsh legends he had read as a youth. Unwilling to use the legends as backdrop for just part of *Time Cat,* Alexander determined to write a full-length fantasy series based on Celtic myth.

Alexander's *Prydain* series begins with the established body of legends, literary patterns, and character types found in the *Mabinogion,* but it becomes a modern fantasy series early on, centering on 20th-century problems. Written during the United States' involvement in Vietnam, the series sees Taran, the youthful protagonist, move from a lowly assistant pig keeper to the ruler of a newly formed kingdom and, in the process, learn to savor home and seek harmony among all people rather than enjoy the victories of war. In the end, he seeks peace for all and hopes to rule democratically by fostering better lives for the poorest as well as the richest. Designed with a youthful audience in mind, the books replace the *Mabinogion*'s emphasis on legendary adult personalities with new young heroes. The series is not a simple recounting of Celtic legend, but rather an extension of old myths in a modern retelling. Alexander's story contains heroes that the child reader can identify with, an active plot based on the typical pattern of the circular journey, and resolutions that fit the standards of contemporary children's literature.

Because the old rulers disappear at the end of the series and Taran begins his reign without the help of the supernatural, the story becomes more American than Celtic in its overall tone. American critics have credited Alexander with a believable series that is contemporary in its tone and compelling in its lively characterizations, well-defined fantasy world, and adventurous plots. British critics, however, have looked upon the series with less regard. The stories have been unfavorably compared to the original *Mabinogion* and the books of Tolkien. While British critics attest to Alexander's skill as a writer, they disdain his "flippancy" and "pedestrian" adventures. Nevertheless, the books are favorites among children in several countries.

Alexander's second major contribution to children's literature is the *Westmark* series, a three-book set depicting the horrors of revolution and unrest and the conflicts caused by corrupt leadership. These books are quite different in tone and setting than the *Prydain* series. Written with an older audience in mind, the *Westmark* series is not based upon any earlier legends, but the story has events and characters reminiscent of the French Revolution. The main protagonist is a young orphan who rises to power through his friendship with the young princess of the kingdom. When a democratic government is formed at the end, the "hero" and his young princess must go into exile. In the series, Alexander successfully combines sub-plots, writes realistic dialogue, and exposes the inhumanities that leaders inflict upon those they rule. He makes it clear that his is a story about the need for freedom and democracy.

Alexander's next series, the Vesper books, is much more lighthearted. It contains a great deal of action and seems to be designed with a different audience in mind. The plots are fast-moving, the characters seem rather one-dimensional, and the settings too exotic. The action centers on the deeds of an independent and highly intelligent young heroine. Set in a four-year span during the 1800s, the adventures begin in Philadelphia where Vesper, a wealthy orphan, and her male guardian, Professor Brinton Garrett, live. Vesper's inheritance triggers each adventure in one way or another, and she and Professor Garrett set forth to a distant land. The books are shorter in length and are dominated by action rather than conversation. Because the episodes are narrated by Professor Garrett, the heroine appears to be always in control, always self-confident. The reader watches an adventuresome young woman interact with those around her without getting a sense of her changing attitudes. The situations encountered always involve injustices against a minority, with Vesper helping the minority gain respectability. Swashbuckling adventure stories, the Vesper books contain enough action in their plots and exoticism in their settings to appeal to the typical teenager who watches adventure films or reads today's popular fiction. However, the books' adventures imply that something is wrong with the early colonialism of the western world, that people have sometimes been forced to abandon their cultural heritages in underdeveloped countries. In all of Vesper's adventures, justice restores the rights of the natives, suggesting that large, highly industrialized governments have no right to inflict their values on others. Once again, Alexander is placing modern day concerns in historical situations.

Alexander's short fairytales contain moral lessons, much as La Fontaine's fables did. Stories such as those found in *The Town Cats and Other Tales* appeal to dual audiences—adults can see the satires while children can enjoy the adventures. These tales provide a link between the writings of earlier fairytale authors such as Hans Christian Andersen and Oscar Wilde and 20th-century political social fantasy.

The diversity in Alexander's style and in his intended audience suggests that he is a serious writer who tries to keep in touch with his audience while implanting cultural ideals and exploring moral values in his stories. His body of work shows how modern storytelling can be accomplished using traditional literary patterns.

—Jill P. May

ALGER, Leclaire. See **NIC LEODHAS, Sorche.**

ALIKI

Full name is Aliki Liacouras Brandenberg. **Nationality:** Greek American. **Born:** Wildwood Crest, New Jersey. **Education:** Graduated from Philadelphia Museum School of Art (now Philadelphia College of Art), Philadelphia, Pennsylvania, 1951. **Family:** Married Franz Brandenberg, 1957; one daughter and one son. **Career:** Muralist, commercial and display artist, and designer, Philadelphia, Pennsylvania, and New York, New York, 1951-1957, and Zurich, Switzerland, 1957-1960; writer and illustrator of children's books, New York, New York, 1960-1977, and in London, England, since 1977. **Awards:** Junior Literary Guild author, 1963,1964, and 1976; Boys' Clubs of America Junior Book Award, 1968; American Institute of Graphic Arts Children's Book Show, 1976; Children's Book Council Children's Book Showcase, 1977; New York Academy of Sciences Children's Science Book Award, 1977; Dutch Children's Book Council Silver Slate Pencil Award, 1981, and Garden State (New Jersey) Children's Book Award, 1981 and 1996; Omar's Book Award, 1986; Prix du Livre pour enfants (Geneva), 1987; World Reading Readers' Choice Award (Silver Burdett & Ginn), 1989; Drexel University/Free Library of Philadelphia citation, 1991; Pennsylvania School Librarians Association Award, 1991. **Address:** 17 Regent's Park Terrace, London NW1 7ED, England.

PUBLICATIONS FOR CHILDREN (ILLUSTRATED BY THE AUTHOR)

Fiction

The Wish Workers. New York, Dial, 1962.
Keep Your Mouth Closed, Dear. New York, Dial, 1966.
June 7! New York, Macmillan, 1972.
At Mary Bloom's. New York, Greenwillow, 1976.
The Two of Them. New York, Greenwillow, 1979; New York, Morrow, 1987.
We Are Best Friends. New York, Greenwillow, 1982.
Use Your Head, Dear. New York, Greenwillow, 1983.
Jack and Jake. New York, Greenwillow, 1986.
Overnight at Mary Bloom's. New York, Greenwillow, 1987.
Welcome, Little Baby. New York, Greenwillow, 1987.
Christmas Tree Memories. New York, HarperCollins, 1991.
Tabby: A Story in Pictures. New York, HarperCollins, 1995.
Best Friends Together Again. New York, Greenwillow, 1995.
Those Summers. New York, HarperCollins, 1997.
Marianthe's Story: Painted Words & Spoken Memories. New York, Greenwillow, 1998.

Folktales

Three Gold Pieces: A Greek Folk Tale. New York, Pantheon, 1967; New York, HarperCollins, 1994.
(Editor) *Hush Little Baby: A Folk Lullaby.* New York, Prentice-Hall, 1968.
The Eggs: A Greek Folk Tale. New York, Pantheon, 1969.
Go Tell Aunt Rhody. New York, Macmillan, 1974.
The Twelve Months: A Greek Folktale. New York, Greenwillow, 1978.
The Gods and Goddesses of Olympus. New York, HarperCollins, 1994.

Nonfiction

My Five Senses. New York, Crowell, 1962; New York, HarperCollins, 1989.
My Hands. New York, Crowell, 1962; revised, New York, HarperCollins, 1990.
New Year's Day. New York, Crowell, 1967.
My Visit to the Dinosaurs. New York, Crowell, 1969; revised edition, 1985.
Fossils Tell of Long Ago. New York, Crowell, 1972; revised edition, 1990.
The Long Lost Coelacanth and Other Living Fossils. New York, Crowell, 1973.
Green Grass and White Milk. New York, Crowell, 1974.
Corn Is Maize: The Gift of the Indians. New York, Crowell, 1976.
Wild and Woolly Mammoths, New York, Crowell, 1977; revised edition, New York, HarperCollins, 1996.
Mummies Made in Egypt. New York, Crowell, 1979.
Digging up Dinosaurs. New York, Crowell, 1981; revised edition, New York, HarperCollins, 1988.
A Medieval Feast. New York, HarperCollins, 1983.
Feelings. New York, Greenwillow, 1984.
Dinosaurs Are Different. New York, Crowell, 1985.
How a Book Is Made. New York, Crowell, 1986.
Dinosaur Bones. New York, Crowell, 1988.
My Feet. New York, Crowell, 1990.
Manners. New York, Greenwillow, 1990.
I'm Growing! New York, HarperCollins, 1992.
Milk: From Cow to Carton. New York, HarperCollins, 1992.
Aliki's Dinosaur Dig: A Book and Card Game. New York, HarperCollins, 1992.
My Visit to the Aquarium. New York, HarperCollins, 1993.
Communication. New York, Greenwillow, 1993.
My Visit to the Dinosaurs. New York, HarperCollins, 1994.
My Visit to the Zoo. New York, HarperCollins, 1997.
Hello! Good-bye! New York, HarperCollins, 1997.

Biography

The Story of William Tell. New York, A.S. Barnes, 1960.
The Story of Johnny Appleseed. New York, Prentice-Hall, 1963; New York, Simon & Schuster, 1971.
George and the Cherry Tree. New York, Dial, 1964.
The Story of William Penn. New York, Prentice-Hall, 1964; New York, Simon & Schuster, 1994.
A Weed Is a Flower: The Life of George Washington Carver. New York, Prentice-Hall, 1965; New York, Simon & Schuster, 1988.
Diogenes: The Story of the Greek Philosopher. New York, Prentice-Hall, 1969.
The Many Lives of Benjamin Franklin. New York, Prentice-Hall, 1977; New York, Simon & Schuster, 1988.
King's Day: Louis XIV of France. New York, Crowell, 1989.
Aliki's Americans, New York. Simon & Schuster, forthcoming.
William Shakespeare and the Globe. New York, HarperCollins, forthcoming.

*

Illustrator of Books by Franz Brandenberg: *I Once Knew a Man,* 1970; *Fresh Cider and Pie,* 1973; *No School Today!,* 1975; *A Secret for Grandmother's Birthday,* 1975; *A Robber! A Robber!,* 1976; *I Wish I Was Sick, Too!,* 1976; *What Can You Make of It?,* 1977; *Nice New Neighbors,* 1977; *A Picnic, Hurrah!,* 1978; *Six New Students,* 1978; *Everyone Ready?,* 1979; *It's Not My Fault!,* 1980; *Leo and Emily,* 1981; *Leo and Emily's Big Idea,* 1982; *Aunt Nina and Her Nephews and Nieces,* 1983; *Aunt Nina's Visit,* 1984; *Leo and Emily and the Dragon,* 1984; *The Hit of the Party,* 1985; *Cock-a-Doodle-Doo,* 1986; *What's Wrong with a Van?,* 1987; *Aunt Nina, Good Night!,* 1989.

Illustrator: *Who Lives Here?* by Pat Witte and Eve Witte, 1961; *Cathy is Company,* 1961, and *That's Good, That's Bad,* 1963, both by Joan M. Lexau; *Listening Walk* by Paul Showers, 1961; *What's for Lunch, Charley?* by Margaret Hodges, 1961; *What Can I Buy?* by Mickey Marks, 1962; *A Book to Begin On: Alaska* by Dorothy Les Tina, 1962; *The Lazy Little Zulu,* 1962, *Mister Moonlight and Omar,* 1963, *Sherlock on the Trail,* 1964, all by James Holding; *This Is the House Where Jack Lives* by Joan M. Heilbronner, 1962; *The Horse That Liked Sandwiches* by Vivian L. Thompson, 1962; *Archimedes and His Wonderful Discoveries,* 1962, and *New Ways in Math,* 1962, both by Arthur Jonas; *Computers at Your Service,* 1962, *Everything Has a Size,* 1964, *Everything Has a Shape,* 1964, *One Day It Rained Cats and Dogs,* 1965, all by Bernice Kohn; *Television and How It Works,* 1962, and *Electricity in Your Life,* 1963, both by Eugene David; *Mister Moonlight and Omar,* 1963; *Bees and Beelines* by Judy Hawes, 1964; *Five Dolls in a House,* 1965, *Five Dolls in the Snow,* 1967, *Five Dolls and the Monkey,* 1967, *Five Dolls and Their Friends,* 1968, *Five Dolls and the Duke,* 1968, all by Helen Clare; *Is It Blue as a Butterfly?* by Rebecca Kalusky, 1965; *Mother's Day* by Mark K. Phelan, 1965; *I Want to Read!* by Betty Ren Wright, 1965; *Is That a Happy Hippopotamus?* by Sean Morrison, 1966; *Mrs. Neverbody's Recipes* by Wilma Yeo, 1968; *At Home: A Visit in Four Languages* by Esther R. Hautzig, 1968; *Oh Lord, I Wish I Was a Buzzard* by Polly Greenberg, 1968; *Birds at Night* by Roma Gans, 1968; *Weighing and Balancing,* 1970, and *Averages,* 1975, both by Jane Jonas Srivastava; *On the Other Side of the River* by Joanne Oppenheim, 1972; *Ears and Tails and Common Sense: More Stories from the Caribbean* by Philip M. Sherlock and Hilary Sherlock, 1974; *Evolution* by Joanna Cole, 1987; *Mommy's Briefcase* by Alice Low, 1995.

Critical Sources: Entry in *Something About the Author,* Vol. 75, Detroit, Gale, 1985, 13-18; entry in *Children's Literature Review,* Vol. 9, Detroit, Gale, 1984, 15-32; "Cover Artist—Aliki" by Margaret Carter, in *Books for Your Children,* Vol. 19, No. 1, 1984, 9.

Aliki comments:

I started to walk, draw, sing and play tunes on the piano all around the same time. Since kindergarten, I've wanted to be an artist. I thank my parents, my family, and my teachers (and librarians) for their constant encouragement.

In the third grade I began a lifelong habit: writing my feelings in poems or journals. But I never knew I would be a writer until I wrote my first book. All that early writing gave me the practice of putting words together, I guess.

Much of my work involves intricate and time-consuming research—made doubly difficult because I both write and illustrate. I spend long hours at my desk. Some books take three years to complete. That is why I call what I do "hard fun". But I love the challenge of a new idea, and finding out something I don't know about a subject—or even myself.

I travel a lot, work in my garden, enjoy theater, films, music, and do it all on very little sleep. There aren't enough hours in one day, so I have invented double-days.

* * *

When Aliki was a young child, her artistic ability was already evident to those around her. Perhaps this early focus on her talent helped her maintain a child-like simplicity in explaining complex topics. Her work is known for its attention to detail and unique and humorous presentation—as one might find in the fresh perspectives of a child. Her artistic talent continued to develop through childhood art lessons, a degree from Philadelphia College of Art, and working in various aspects of the artistic field, and so did her natural desire to investigate and write about a diversity of topics in many genres. As a result, Aliki's books reflect the most essential criteria of a picture book—a book in which the illustrations and the text work together to tell the story. As Aliki herself said in *Something About the Author,* "I have to find the right way to express the words in pictures. The words and the pictures should blend so that the pictures add to the words and make them more important."

After graduating from college and working for four years as a display artist, free-lance advertiser, art and ceramics teacher, and a creator of murals and greeting cards, Aliki decided in 1956 to visit the native country of her parents, Greece, and other European cities. While on this self-directed tour, she met Franz Brandenberg and they married the next year and settled in his native Switzerland. While in Switzerland, she wrote her first picture book, *The Story of William Tell.* Soon thereafter, Aliki and Franz moved to New York City and, while illustrating children's books for others, she wrote *My Five Senses.* Since then, her diverse interests in topics and artistic styles have created a significant body of children's literature that crosses genre and age levels.

Aliki's work reflects her own interests and experiences. She has written biographies of people, such as George Washington Carver and William Penn, that are simple and yet reveal the significant contributions of these people to young readers. Likewise, she selects topics to write about which she personally has always wanted to investigate. Aliki's diverse artistic style is determined by the particular book she is writing. *Mummies Made in Egypt* is presented frieze style with captions under the illustrations. *A Medieval Feast* is illustrated in the style of illuminated manuscripts and tapestries. Both *Mummies Made In Egypt* and *A Medieval Feast* provide detailed information in simple terms and the illustrations illuminate the text.

Corn Is Maize combines science and history in telling the story of corn, its significance in the life of the American Indian, and its eventual important role in other societies. As this book looks at both ancient and modern people and those of diverse ethnic backgrounds, it exemplifies approaching culture within a meaningful context. As well as using a diversity of illustration styles—including cartoons or paintings in mediums of watercolor, pen and ink, and gouache—Aliki also provides commentaries on the main text in a number of ways. *Corn Is Maize* represents one example of the "text-within-text" format that Aliki uses to include all the information she wishes to portray in an easily understood manner. Other commentaries come in the form of bubbles, as in *My Visit to the Dinosaurs,* in which the perspectives of young museum visitors highlight information about dinosaurs. In *Digging Up Dinosaurs,* the reader also gets perspectives from paleontologists, geologists, and photographers. Sometimes labels and added facts within the illustrations provide the extra insight to the researched topic, as in *My Visit to the Zoo.* Her unique approaches to text format reflect the vast amount of information she has discovered and discerningly selected while researching a topic. In an interview by Margaret Carter in *Books for Your Children,* Aliki said "It's best for me to know nothing about a subject when I begin, that way I have to get it right. Because I am not a scientist I can perhaps approach the subject with fresh eyes." The research she has invested in each of her books makes them valuable resources to use across the curriculum.

As a writer of fiction, Aliki has entertained with refreshingly light-hearted stories. She has provided intense emotional experiences in stories that touch on generational relationships, such as *The Two of Them, At Mary Bloom's,* and *Marianthe's Story: Painted Words & Spoken Memories. We Are Best Friends* and *Hello! Goodbye!* both center on feelings children experience in various life situations. In *Christmas Tree Memories, Those Days,* and *Those Summers* Aliki has focused on family memories, filling each story with personal connections for many readers of all ages. In addition to the warm illustrations evoking each memory is imagery well suited to each text.

Aliki also has retold folktales from her Greek heritage. *Three Gold Pieces: A Greek Folk Tale* and *The Gods and Goddesses of Olympus* are told in a "teller's" style and are supported with rich illustrations. All of her folktales are retold with a freshness that holds the readers' attention.

Aliki's contribution to the field of children's literature is manyfold. As an illustrator and author she has provided books that are examples of text and illustration collaboratively telling the story. Additionally her books nurture visual literacy among readers by inviting attention to detail and integrating picture and print in a meaningful manner. She has also contributed to the need for authentic literature to support learning across the curriculum, providing well-researched perspectives on a variety of topics. Her books span across many cultural groups represented by ethnicity, gender, and geography. They do not isolate a group but place it in a meaningful context within society. Finally, Aliki has used many shared human experiences dealing with emotions, memories, and communication to invite readers to realize the common nature through their personal connections.

—Janelle B. Mathis

ALLAN, Mabel Esther

Pseudonyms: Jean Estoril; Priscilla Hagon; Anne Pilgrim. **Nationality:** British. **Born:** Wallasey, Cheshire, 11 February 1915. **Education:** Private schools. **Military Service:** Served in the British Women's Land Army during World War II. **Address:** 11 Oldfield Way, Heswall, Wirral, L60 6RQ, England.

PUBLICATIONS FOR CHILDREN

Fiction

The Glen Castle Mystery. London, Warne, 1948.
The Adventurous Summer, illustrated by Isabel Veevers. London, Museum Press, 1948.
The Wyndhams Went to Wales, illustrated by Beryl Thornborough. London, Sylvan Press, 1948.
Mullion, illustrated by R. Walter Hall. London, Hutchinson, 1949.
Cilia of Chiltern's Edge, illustrated by Betty Ladler. London, Museum Press, 1949.
Trouble at Melville Manor, illustrated by Isabel Veevers. London, Museum Press, 1949.
Holiday at Arnriggs. London, Warne, 1949.
Chiltern Adventure, illustrated by T.R. Freeman. London, Blackie, 1950.
Jimmy John's Journey. London, Dean, 1949.
Over the Sea to School, illustrated by W. Mackinlay. London, Blackie, 1950.
School under Snowdon. London, Hutchinson, 1950.
Everyday Island. London, Museum Press. 1950.
Seven in Switzerland, illustrated by Isabel Veever. London, Blackie, 1950.
The Exciting River, illustrated by Helen Jacobs. London, Nelson, 1951.
Clues to Connemara, illustrated by Philip. London, Blackie, 1952.
The Maclains of Glen Gillean. London, Hutchinson, 1952.
Return to Derrykereen. London, Ward Lock, 1952.
A School in Danger, illustrated by Eric Winter. London, Blackie, 1952.
The School on Cloud Ridge. London, Hutchinson, 1952.
The School on North Barrule. London, Museum Press, 1952.
The Secret Valley, illustrated by C. Instrell. Leeds, E.J. Arnold, 1953.
Room for the Cuckoo: The Story of a Farming Year. London, Dent, 1953.
Three Go to Switzerland, illustrated by Isabel Veevers. London, Blackie, 1953.
Lucia Comes to School. London, Hutchinson, 1953.
Strangers at Brongwerne. London, Museum Press, 1953.
Meric's Secret Cottage. London, Blackie, 1954.
Adventure Royal, illustrated by C.W. Bacon. London, Blackie, 1954.
Here We Go Round: A Career Story for Girls. London, Heinemann, 1954.
Margaret Finds a Future. London, Hutchinson, 1954.
New Schools for Old. London, Hutchinson, 1954.
The Summer at Town's End, illustrated by Iris Weller. London, Harrap, 1954.
Adventures in Switzerland. London, Pickering and Inglis, 1955.
The Mystery of Derrydane, illustrated by Vera Chadwick. Huddersfield, Yorkshire, Schofield and Sims, 1955.
Changes for the Challoners. London, Ward Lock, 1955.
Glenvara. London, Hutchinson, 1955; as *Summer of Decision,* New York, Abelard Schuman, 1957.
Judith Teachers. London, Lane, 1955.
Swiss School. London, Hutchinson, 1955.
Adventure in Mayo. London, Ward Lock, 1956.
Balconies and Blue Nets: The Story of a Holiday in Brittany, illustrated by Peggy Beetles. London, Harrap, 1956.
Lost Lorrenden, illustrated by Shirley Hughes. London, Blackie, 1956.
Strangers in Skye. London, Heinemann, 1956; New York, Criterion, 1958.
Two in the Western Isles. London, Hutchinson, 1956.
The Vine-Clad Hill, illustrated by T.R. Freeman. London, Lane, 1956; as *Swiss Holiday,* New York, Vanguard Press, 1957.
Flora at Kilroinn. London, Blackie, 1956.
The Amber House. London, Hutchinson, 1956.
Ann's Alpine Adventure. London, Hutchinson, 1956.
At School in Skye, illustrated by Constance Marshall. London, Blackie, 1957.
Black Forest Summer. London, Bodley Head, 1957; New York, Vanguard Press, 1959.
Sara Goes to Germany. London, Hutchinson, 1957.

Blue Dragon Days. London, Heinemann, 1958; as *Romance in Italy,* New York, Vanguard Press, 1962.
The Conch Shell, illustrated by T.R. Freeman. London, Blackie, 1958.
The House by the Marsh, illustrated by Sheila Rose. London, Dent, 1958.
Rachel Tandy. London, Hutchinson, 1958.
Amanda Goes to Italy. London, Hutchinson, 1959.
Catrin in Wales. London, Bodley Head, 1959; New York, Vanguard Press, 1961.
A Play to the Festival. London, Heinemann, 1959; as *On Stage, Flory,* New York, Watts, 1961.
Shadow over the Alps. London, Hutchinson, 1960.
A Summer in Brittany. London, Dent, 1960; as *Hilary's Summer on Her Own,* New York, Watts, 1961.
Tansy of Tring Street, illustrated by Sally Holliday. London, Heinemann, 1960.
Holiday of Endurance. London, Dent, 1961.
Bluegate Girl. London, Hutchinson, 1961.
Pendron under the Water, illustrated by T.R. Freeman. London, Harrap, 1961.
Home to the Island, illustrated by Geoffrey Whittam. London, Dent, 1962; New York, Vanguard Press, 1966.
Signpost to Switzerland. London, Heinemann, 1962; New York, Criterion, 1964.
The Ballet Family, illustrated by A.R. Whitear. London, Methuen, 1963; New York, Criterion, 1966.
Kate Comes to England. London, Heinemann, 1963.
New York for Nicola. New York, Vanguard Press, 1963; London, White Lion, 1977.
The Sign of the Unicorn: A Thriller for Young People, illustrated by Shirley Hughes. London, Dent, and New York, Criterion, 1963.
It Happened in Arles. London, Heinemann, 1964; as *Mystery in Arles,* New York, Vanguard Press, 1964.
The Ballet Family Again, illustrated by A.R. Whitear. London, Methuen, 1964; as *The Dancing Garlands,* New York, Criterion, 1968.
Fiona on the Fourteenth Floor, illustrated by Shirley Hughes. London, Dent, 1964; as *Mystery on the Fourteenth Floor,* New York, Criterion, 1965.
A Summer at Sea, illustrated by Geoffrey Whittam. London, Dent, 1965; New York, Vanguard Press, 1967.
The Way over Windle, illustrated by Raymond Briggs. London, Methuen, 1966.
Skiing to Danger. London, Heinemann, 1966; as *Mystery of the Ski Slopes,* New York, Criterion, 1966.
In Pursuit of Clarinda, illustrated by Margaret Wetherbee. London, Dent, 1966.
It Started in Madeira. London, Heinemann, 1967; as *The Mystery Began in Madeira,* New York, Criterion, 1967.
Missing in Manhattan, illustrated by Margaret Wetherbee. London, Dent, 1967; as *Mystery in Manhattan,* New York, Vanguard Press, 1968.
The Wood Street Secret, illustrated by Shirley Hughes. London, Methuen, 1968; New York, Abelard Schuman, 1970.
The Kraymer Mystery. New York, Criterion, 1969; London, Abelard Schuman, 1973.
Climbing to Danger. London, Heinemann, 1969; as *Mystery in Wales,* New York, Vanguard Press, 1971.
Dangerous Inheritance. London, Heinemann, 1970.
The Wood Street Group, illustrated by Shirley Hughes. London, Methuen, 1970.
Christmas at Spindle Bottom, illustrated by Lynette Hemmant. London, Dent, 1970.
The Secret Dancer, illustrated by Juliet Mozley. London, Dent, 1971.
The May Day Mystery. New York, Criterion, 1971; London, Severn House, 1980.
The Wood Street Rivals, illustrated by Shirley Hughes. London, Methuen, 1971.
An Island in a Green Sea, illustrated by Charles Robinson. New York, Atheneum, 1972; London, Dent, 1973.
Behind the Blue Gates. London, Heinemann, 1972.
Time to Go Back. London, Abelard Schuman, 1972; New York, Criterion, 1974.
The Wood Street Helpers, illustrated by Shirley Hughes. London, Methuen, 1973.
A Formidable Enemy. London, Heinemann, 1973; Nashville, Nelson, 1975.
Mystery in Rome. New York, Vanguard Press, 1974; as *The Bells of Rome,* London, Heinemann, 1975.
Crow's Nest. London, Abelard Schuman, 1974.
A Chill in the Lane. Nashville, Nelson, 1974.
The Night Wind, illustrated by Charles Robinson. New York, Atheneum, 1974; London, Severn House, 1982.
Ship of Danger. London, Heinemann, and New York, Criterion, 1974.
The Secret Players, illustrated by James Russell. Leicester, Brockhampton Press, 1974.
Bridge of Friendship. London, Dent, 1975; New York, Dodd Mead, 1977.
Romansgrove, illustrated by Gail Owens. New York, Atheneum, 1975.
The Flash Children, illustrated by Gavin Rowe. Leicester, Brockhampton Press, and New York, Dodd Mead, 1975.
Away from Wood Street, illustrated by Shirley Hughes. London, Methuen, 1975.
Trouble in the Glen, illustrated by Jutta Ash. London, Abelard Schuman, 1976.
The Rising Tide. London, Heinemann, 1976; New York, Walker, 1978.
My Family's Not Forever. London, Abelard Schuman, 1977.
The View Beyond My Father. London, Abelard Schuman, 1977; New York, Dodd Mead, 1978.
The Pine Street Pageant, illustrated by Rosemary Chanter. London, Abelard Schuman, 1978.
Wood Street and Mary Ellen, illustrated by Lesley Smith. London, Methuen, 1979.
Tomorrow Is a Lovely Day. London, Abelard Schuman, 1979; as *A Lovely Tomorrow,* New York, Dodd Mead, 1980.
Pine Street Goes Camping, illustrated by Patricia Drew. London, Abelard Schuman, 1980.
The Mills Down Below. London, Abelard Schuman, 1980; New York, Dodd Mead, 1981.
Strangers in Wood Street, illustrated by Lesley Smith. London, Methuen, 1981.
The Horns of Danger. New York, Dodd Mead, 1981.
The Pine Street Problem, illustrated by Patricia Drew. London, Abelard Schuman, 1981.
A Strange Enchantment. London, Abelard Schuman, 1981; New York, Dodd Mead, 1982.

Goodbye to Pine Street, illustrated by Patricia Drew. London, Abelard Schuman, 1982.
Growing Up in Wood Street, illustrated by Lesley Smith. London, Methuen, 1982.
Alone at Pine Street, illustrated by Patricia Drew. London, Abelard Schuman, 1983.
The Crumble Lane Adventure, illustrated by Nola Edwards. London, Methuen, 1983.
A Dream of Hunger Moss. New York, Dodd Mead, 1983; London, Severn House, 1985.
Friends at Pine Street, illustrated by Patricia Drew. London, Abelard Schuman, 1984.
A Secret in Spindle Bottom, illustrated by David Leeming. London, Abelard Schuman, 1984.
Trouble in Crumble Lane, illustrated by Jane Bottomley. London, Methuen, 1984.
The Flash Children in Winter, illustrated by Doreen Caldwell. London, Hodder and Stoughton, 1985.
The Pride of Pine Street, illustrated by Patricia Drew. London, Blackie, 1985.
The Crumble Lane Captives, illustrated by Jane Bottomley. London, Methuen, 1986.
A Mystery in Spindle Bottom, illustrated by Patricia MacCarthy. London, Blackie, 1986.
The Road to Huntingland. London, Severn House, 1986.
The Crumble Lane Mystery, illustrated by Jane Bottomley. London, Methuen, 1987.
Up the Victorian Staircase: A London Mystery. London, Severn House, 1987.
First Term at Ash Grove, illustrated by Liz Roberts. London, Blackie, 1988.
The Mystery of Serafina. Chester, Bemrose Shafron, 1990.
Chiltern School. Chester, Bemrose Shafron, 1990.
Queen Rita at the High School and Other School Stories. Chester, Bemrose Shafron, 1991.
The Two Head Girls and Other School Stories. Chester, Bemrose Shafron, 1992.
The Way to Glen Bradan and Other Scottish, Welsh, and Irish Stories. Chester, Bemrose Shafron, 1993.

Other

Ragged Robin Began It and Other Articles About Old Girls' Books. Chester, Bemrose Shafron, 1993.

Fiction as Jean Estoril

Ballet for Drina, illustrated by Eve Guthrie and M.P. Steedman Davies. London, Hodder and Stoughton, 1957; New York, Vanguard Press, 1958.
Drina's Dancing Year. London, Hodder and Stoughton, 1958.
Drina Dances in Exile. London, Hodder and Stoughton, 1959.
Drina Dances in Italy, illustrated by Eve Guthrie and M.P. Steedman Davies. London, Hodder and Stoughton, 1959; New York, Vanguard Press, 1962.
Drina Dances Again. London, Hodder and Stoughton, 1960.
Drina Dances in New York. London, Hodder and Stoughton, 1961.
Drina Dances in Paris. London, Hodder and Stoughton, 1962.
Drina Dances in Madeira. London, Hodder and Stoughton, 1963.
Drina Dances in Switzerland. London, Hodder and Stoughton, 1964.
Drina Goes on Tour. Leicester, Brockhampton Press, 1965.
We Danced in Bloomsbury Square. London, Heinemann, 1967; Chicago, Follett, 1970; as *The Ballet Twins,* London, Macdonald, 1989; London, Simon and Schuster, 1991.
Drina Ballerina. London, Simon and Schuster, 1991.

Fiction as Anne Pilgrim

The First Time I Saw Paris. New York and London, Abelard Schuman, 1961.
Clare Goes to Holland. New York and London, Abelard Schuman, 1962.
A Summer in Provence. New York and London, Abelard Schuman, 1963.
Strangers in New York. New York and London, Abelard Schuman, 1964.
Selina's New Family, illustrated by Graham Byfield. New York and London, Abelard Schuman, 1967.

Fiction as Priscilla Hagon

Cruising to Danger, illustrated by William Plummer. Cleveland, World, 1966; London, Harrap, 1968.
Dancing to Danger, illustrated by Susanne Suba. Cleveland, World, 1967.
Mystery at Saint-Hilaire, illustrated by William Plummer. Cleveland, World, 1968.
Mystery at the Villa Bianca, illustrated by William Plummer. New York, World, 1969.
The Mystery of the Secret Square, illustrated by Ray Abel. New York, World, 1970.

PUBLICATIONS FOR ADULTS

Novel

Murder at the Flood. London, Stanley Paul, 1957.

Poetry

The Haunted Valley and Other Poems. Privately printed, 1981.

Other

To Be an Author: A Short Autobiography. Privately printed, 1982.
More About Being an Author. Privately printed, 1985.
The Background Came First: My Books and Places. Privately printed, 2 vols., 1988.
The Road to the Isles and Other Places: Some Journeys with a Rucksack. Privately printed, 1989.

*

Manuscript Collections: University of Southern Mississippi, Hattiesburg.

Mabel Esther Allan comments:
I am a collector of old girls' books and I soon found that, with a few exceptions, most authors had left little personal record. That was why I wrote two autobiographies, *To Be an Author* and *More*

About Being an Author, and had them printed privately. I felt it was time to set the record straight. I also brought my poems together in a privately printed booklet, for they tell a good deal about me, and where I was living, and writing, at different times.

I have had a long writing life. But, though I wrote many, I didn't publish a book until 1948. Until then, as well as writing all those unpublished novels and children's books, I sold short stories, articles, and, during the war, poetry. In so many years my work has often changed: I feel I have done a great deal more than create "dream worlds." In the middle years I did certainly write a number of books for older girls that had "romantic" endings. But they *were* largely written between certain dates, and even then, I was writing other books.

In the early years I wrote for rather younger readers, and some of the books were fairly original. *Holiday at Arnriggs,* for instance, was about a group of Yorkshire boys, and one girl, who tried to make the long and complicated North Skelton sword dance a perfect thing. All my school stories were far ahead of their time, as even the *Times Literary Supplement* admitted when they based a front page article on one of them. My schools were all progressive and often coeducational. I believed that young people had the right to run their own affairs. I believed in self-discipline, rather than in imposed discipline. And my views haven't changed.

In the early 1970s there was a very great change. I wrote *An Island in a Green Sea, Time to Go Back,* and a number of others that had an autobiographical basis. One of the pleasures of being older, or old, is that one can look back and form early experiences into stories. *The Mills Down Below* was different. In that book I wrote about women's rights. I wish I had done more books on that theme.

From now on it is possible that I will write only for younger readers. I seem to be obsessed with the poorer streeets of Liverpool and with the Lancashire towns and moors. Gone are the days when I only wanted to write about New York.

My early books are eagerly collected by adults of all ages. In a way it makes me feel dead already, but, unlike most authors who are collected, I can still speak for myself.

(1994) It is now about five years since I wrote the above. During the intervening years, some things have surprised and pleased me. The main happening has been the amazing revival of my Jean Estoril pen name and all my ballet stories, including the two "Ballet Family" stories originally published under my own name thirty years ago by Methuen. It was Macdonald that first took up these books and started to publish them in hardback and paperback. This was around 1986. Then Simon and Schuster bought the list and the "Drina" books went from strength to strength, with several reprints. They are still in the S. and S. catalogue this year, with the addition of the eleventh in the series, *Drina Ballerina.* This is the book I longed to write nearly thirty years ago, but publishing changes made it impossible then.

Drina Ballerina will remain my last commercially published book. I updated all the books myself. People who are convinced that the Sixties were a different world may be surprised to learn that it wasn't attitudes that I had to change, apart from taking out several references to gloves! It was purely practical things, mainly buildings and money in different countries as well as here. So many London stores had gone, that I simply put "a West End store." The saddest thing was the loss of the vegetable market around the Royal Opera House in Covent Garden. I simply cut out references to it. In the original Hodder edition of *Drina Dances in New York* she went (as I did) to the old Metropolitan Opera House. In the recent version she went, of course, to Lincoln Center. As a matter of interest I saw the whole of that great complex rise from the Manhattan mud.

Another thing that surprises and pleases me is the way my long ago wartime poetry won't die. Some of the early ones appeared in the prestigious monthly *The National Review,* and in other good magazines. "I Saw a Broken Town" was, at the time, in an anthology here, and the first thing I ever had published in the U.S.A. was a poem called "I Looked at England" in a Houghton Mifflin anthology of war poetry. I used single poems in many of my books, and many were in "Time to Go Back." In 1984 "I Saw a Broken Town" (Wallasey) and "Immensity" were included in Virago's "Chaos of the Night," and the second one was read on the BBC the same year. In 1989 Oxford University Press used "I Saw a Broken Town" in "Peace and War." I have just heard that "Immensity" will appear in *Women, War and Poetry,* being planned for private publication by the University of Delaware Press. No one thinks of me as a poet, but it seems that I am, among many other things. If one lives long enough many things come full circle.

One strange thing is that my early school stories, published forty and more years ago, are still largely ahead of their time. School Councils, when the boys and girls make the rules and therefore try to keep them, are still rare, and my violent belief in self-discipline rather than imposed discipline still holds. A. S. Neill's words: "There are no problem children, only problem parents" are quoted by me frequently still. I have had a lot to do with children and young people of all classes in my time, and during the war I became convinced that a child is ruined by the time it is two.

So...I have a long and, I think, precise memory. I remember the day when I was about four when I realized that I couldn't see like other people. That day was born pride as well as fear that has never left me. I never admitted to being "different." Born also then was a passionate joy in the visual, especially in the printed word, even though the book was held near my nose. I don't remember learning to read—it seems I always could. "Look Your Last on All Things Lovely Every Hour" was, I suppose the crowning theme of my life. Alas, all my pleasures have been visual, or pretty nearly all. Maybe, if it hadn't been for a lifetime of terrible eye trouble I would never have become an author. I might be an ordinary woman with six grandchildren.

As I have said in my autobiography, I never wanted a baby, only a *book.* I never became the "great novelist" I imagined as a child, but I've kept going in a difficult world for a very long time, and, over the books at least, always pleased myself and then prayed that someone would like the result. I don't think I every really thought of readers, except that of course an author must have them to survive. Over the 330 short stories I sold between early 1936 and 1957 that was largely different. They were tossed off to make a quick guinea, or, if I was lucky, five pounds or so. I was middle aged before the books really began to pay off, when they started to be sold in America, and in a large number of other countries...Poland, France, Holland, Italy, Portugal and several more.

Today the "Drinas" are currently appearing here, and in Finland and Germany. And in the U.S.A. Scholastic has done the first five in their Apple paperbacks. I get a lot of mail from many states, mainly from young fans who are learning ballet.

But the most satisfying thing is that I am in touch with adults in many parts of the world. My name was in the National Library of Tallinn before Estonia was free, and in Samarkand; Uzbekistan, too. Samarkand! I thought it was a dream place in poetry. But, not surprisingly, it seems very real now.

I have few regrets. I've done what I wanted to do. Being an author is a lonely, hardworking life, unless you are in the top five percent or so. I was always disciplined. I sat at a typewriter after school from the age of twelve. It was worth it.

* * *

Mabel Esther Allan's long writing career cannot easily be summarized. Her books vary in theme, have no settled pattern, and are directed at no one single age-group. In other words, she defies that peculiarly English trait of classifying and labelling authors into clearly defined categories. Only since the early 1960s can a developing theme be noticed, and even then it is not exclusively consistent. The book that marked this switch in emphasis, *The Sign of the Unicorn,* first appeared in 1963. The themes developed here—personal unhappiness, unsettling and disturbing changes in home environment, sometimes voluntary but more often forced by circumstances, homesickness for the old, apprehension and fear at the new, a gradual change in attitude, helped in most cases by meeting new friends, and the cumulative effect they have on a teenage heroine on the verge of womanhood—are all conspicuous in later books like *Dangerous Inheritance* and *A Formidable Enemy,* and many others, usually set either in Paris or New York.

More recently Allan has taken up the challenge presented by the inner cities in an honest attempt to relate literature to the lives of working-class children who might otherwise find books wholly reflecting middle-class mores in situations and surroundings completely alien to their own. The Wood Street Gang series, rumbustious and fast-moving episodes from life in Liverpool, is concerned not with ponies, hilltrekking in the Scottish Highlands, ballet, or summer holidays in Brittany, but with encounters with the police, the formation of a pop group and the antagonism it meets when it needs to practice, and the inevitable hostility with rival gangs. It provides a splendid example, if example were necessary, of Allan's vitality, exuberance, and versatility.

—Alan Edwin Day

ALLEN, Alex B. See **HEIDE, Florence Parry.**

ALLEN, Eric

Pseudonym for Eric Allen Ballard. **Other Pseudonyms:** Paul Dallas; Edwin Harrison. **Nationality:** British. **Born:** London, 25 February 1908. **Family:** Married Janet Ballard. **Career:** Jazz promoter in the 1930s and founder of *Hot News* jazz magazine, London, 1932; freelance writer in the Middle East, 1946-48, South Africa, 1948-52, Spain, Morocco, and Italy, 1952-59, and London, from 1959. **Died:** 2 March 1968.

PUBLICATIONS FOR CHILDREN

Fiction

How Many Miles to Cyprus, illustrated by Janet Allen Ballard. London, Methuen, 1955.

Pepe Moreno, illustrated by Hazel Cook. London, Faber, 1955; New York, A.S. Barnes, 1960.

Pepe Moreno and the Roller Skates, illustrated by David Knight. London, Faber, 1958; New York, A.S. Barnes, 1959.

Pepe on the Run, illustrated by David Knight. London, Faber, 1959; New York, A.S. Barnes, 1960.

Pepe Moreno and the Dilapidated Donkey, illustrated by David Knight. London, Faber, 1960; New York, A.S. Barnes, 1961.

The Story of Lorenzo the Magnificent, illustrated by David Knight. London, Faber, 1961.

Pepe Moreno's Quixotic Adventure, illustrated by David Knight. London, Faber, 1963.

The Latchkey Children, illustrated by Charles Keeping. London, Oxford University Press, 1963.

Smitty and the Plural of Cactus [Egyptian Cat], illustrated by Andrew Dodds. London, Nelson, 2 vols., 1965-66.

Plays

Television Series: *Pepe Moreno,* 1958.

Other

The Incredible Adventures of Don Quixote: A Retelling, illustrated by David Knight. London, Faber, 1958.

PUBLICATIONS FOR ADULTS

Novels

Into My Parlour (as Paul Dallas). London, Methuen, 1940.

Prayer Is Better Than Sleep. London, Wells Gardner, 1946.

Death on Delivery. London, Hammond, 1958.

Perilous Passport. London, Hammond, 1958; as *Passport to Murder,* London, Corgi, 1959.

The Man Who Chose Death. London, Hammond, 1959.

Canaries Also Sing. London, Hammond, 1960.

Novels as Edwin Harrison

Diamonds Can Be Trouble. London, Amalgamated Press, 1958.

The Fatal Hour. London, Amalgamated Press, 1958.

Killer's Playground. London, Amalgamated Press, 1959.

Witness to Murder. London, Amalgamated Press, 1959.

Short Stories

Eric Allen's Broadcast Stories. London, Rich and Cowan, 1947.

Plays

Television Plays: *The Pen of My Aunt* series, 1959; *Front Page* series, 1961; *Brother for Joe* series, 1961; *Bad Company,* 1962; *The Young Troubadour,* 1963.

* * *

Eric Allen particularly deserves recognition for *The Latchkey Children,* a runner-up for the Carnegie Medal in 1963. This novel was applauded as a worthy addition to the limited number of stories for children of the calibre of *The Family from One End Street* by Eve Garnett and *Magnolia Buildings* by Elizabeth Stucley. *The Latchkey Children* is competently constructed with a convincing portrayal of everyday life and its problems combined with a satisfying element of adventure.

The author leaves at least two definite impressions with his readers: a strong sense of place and a vivid picture of the humdrum daily lives of the five children who are the central characters in the story. The impression of place is achieved by the writer choosing a London council estate for the background to his plot, a setting ensuring appeal to a wide readership. The detail of the lives of "the latchkey children" is most painstakingly done and wholly authentic. It is a realistic picture of children with mothers at work: chores have to be performed, often reluctantly; meals have to be produced; agreements have to be made to stay at home to deal with tradesmen; money is in short supply.

To this down-to-earth setting is added a plausible degree of excitement and adventure with gang forays, a dog incident, and *the* tree issue. These adventure elements are credible—a difficult feat to achieve. The author also appeals to children's interests with the introduction of a television personality and film crew into the plot. The four children, who consider themselves friends and not a gang, form a lively group in the reader's mind rather than clear-cut individuals, and the West Indian boy Duke who joins the group is portrayed as a sympathetic character. The adult characters in the story are described, however small their roles in the plot, with an acute understanding of human weaknesses.

Although *The Latchkey Children* is probably Allen's best-known novel for children, he also wrote fiction for the younger 8-10 age group. The Pepe Moreno books set in Spain and the Smitty books about a lively schoolboy offer much needed material of a high standard for an age group less well provided for than its older counterparts. Allen has made a worthwhile contribution to children's fiction, and although less prolific than similar writers such as E. W. Hildick and A. Stephen Tring, he is another writer who appears to have made a serious attempt to cater for children's varying reading needs—a task only a small number of writers are willing to attempt.

—Anne W. Ellis

ALLEN, Jonathan B(urgess)

Nationality: British. **Born:** Luton, 17 February 1957. **Education:** Denbigh High, Luton; Impington Village College, Cambridge; Cambridge College of Arts and Technology, Art Foundation year; St. Martin's College of Art, London, B.A. in Graphic Design. **Family:** Married; two children. **Career:** Children's book illustrator and writer. **Address:** Acorn Cottage, South Street, Lillington, NR Royston, Herts SG8 0QR, England.

PUBLICATIONS FOR CHILDREN (ILLUSTRATED BY THE AUTHOR)

Fiction

Guthrie Comes Clean. London, Dent, 1984.
My Cat. London, Macmillan, 1986.
My Dog. London, Macmillan, 1987.
Who's at the Door? London, Orchard Books, 1992.
Keep Fit Canaries. London, Orchard Books, 1993.
Mucky Moose. London, Macmillan, 1990; New York, Alladin, 1996.
Two by Two by Two. London, Orion Children's Books, 1994; New York, Dial, 1995.
Sweetie. London, Macmillan, 1994.
Chicken Licken. London, Doubleday, 1996.
Fowl Play. London, Orion Children's Books, 1996.
Wake Up, Sleeping Beauty! London, Tango Books, 1997; New York, Dial, 1997.
Wolf Academy. London, Orchard Books, 1997.
Jonathan Allen Picture Book. London, Orchard Books, 1997.
Flying Squad. London, Yearling, 1998.

"Wizard Grimweed" Series

B. I. G. Trouble. London, Orchard Books, 1993.
Potion Commotion. London, Orchard Books, 1993.
The Funniest Man in the World. London, Orchard Books, 1994.
Nose Grows. London, Orchard Books, 1994.
The Witch Who Couldn't Spell. London, Orchard Books, 1996.
Dragon Dramatics. London, Orchard Books, 1996.

"Fred Cat Board Books" Series

Dressing Up. London, Orchard Books, 1997.
My Noisy Toys. London, Orchard Books, 1997.
Weather and Me. London, Orchard Books, 1997.
What My Friends Say. London, Orchard Books, 1997.

"Jonathan Allen Board Books" Series

Purple Sock, Pink Sock. London, Orchard Books, 1992.
Big Owl, Little Towel. London, Orchard Books, 1997.
One with a Bun. London, Orchard Books, 1997.
Up the Steps, Down the Slide. London, Orchard Books, 1997.

Poetry

A Bad Case of Animal Nonsense. London, Dent, 1981; Boston, Godine, 1997.
A Pocketful of Painful Puns and Poems. London, Dent, 1983.

*

Illustrator: *There's a Wolf in My Pudding,* 1986, *Yucky Ducky,* 1988, *Gander of the Yard,* 1989, *Gideon Gander Solves the World's Greatest Mysteries,* 1993, all by David Henry Wilson; *The Great White Man-Eating Shark,* 1989, *The Three-Legged Cat,* 1993, and *Beaten by a Balloon,* 1997, all by Margaret Mahy; *Burton and Stanley* by Frank O'Rourke, 1993; *Nonsense Songs* by Edward Lear, 1993; *Red Dragon,* 1993, and *Bear Buys a Car,* 1995, both by Stephen Wyllie; *Clark the Toothless Shark,* 1994, and *Bruce the Balding Moose,* 1996, both by Corinne Mellor; *Monster and Frog Get Fit, Monster's Terrible Toothache, Monster and Frog Mind the Baby,* and *Monster and Frog at Sea,* all 1994, all by Rose Impey; *The Bear Whose Bones Were Jezebel Jones* by Bill Grossman, 1997.

* * *

Jonathan Allen's trademark is his zany sense of humour, which is instantly recognisable in his quirky illustrations and in his marvelously inventive and mildly eccentric stories. He writes about and draws animal characters with instinctive humour. Two of his early books, *My Dog* and *My Cat,* are good examples of how his illustrations complement the text. In both the text gives straightforward information about cats or dogs, focusing on the characteristics of one particular animal. The illustrations, however, show the animals with wonderfully apt expressions, injecting immediate humour.

Allen has used his ability to give expression to animals to impart messages that would perhaps seem heavy handed using real people. For example, in *Guthrie Comes Clean* Guthrie is a panda who would rather be "tall and sleek and white like a polar bear" than "small, podgy and patchy." He tries everything from scrubbing to dressing up and finally manages to convince himself he looks like a polar bear. However, his friends are not fooled and show they like him just the way he is. The underlying moral, that everyone should be proud of who they are, whatever their size or colour of their skin, is deftly got across.

In other books Allen enjoys a joke by turning something on its head. In *Mucky Moose* a distinctly anti-social moose offends all the other animals, which are forever complaining about his dreadful smell. In the end, though, it is a positive advantage as the terrible smell puts the hungry wolf off eating him. In similar vein is *Sweetie,* about a family of skunks who, when they get to a certain age, practise making nasty smells. Sweetie, however, is sweet smelling and the other skunks make fun of her. However, when Great Big Hairy Smelly Bear is looking for something to eat, Sweetie's delicate smell puts him off and inadvertently saves the others. Much of the attraction of these books for children is the delight in the unsavoury smells and the language used to describe them.

Allen delights in playing with language and ideas, sometimes offering a different perspective on something familiar. In *Who's at the Door?* he plays around with the nursery story of the three little pigs. The wolf comes to the pigs' door in different disguises, but they always spot that it is him. Finally they give him the fright of his life by dressing up as an old lady. In *Chicken Licken* he adapts the familiar story, introducing new characters like Funny Bunny and Lovey Dovey and changing the ending. In *Two by Two by Two* he takes the familiar story of Noah's ark and imagines what might have happened. Humour abounds in the illustrations and the animals indulge in non-stop banter in speech bubbles. The sloths and bats formed an Upside Down Society, the skunks and polecats formed the Smelly Society. On a serious note, there are over a hundred animals all correctly named.

In *Fowl Play* Jonathan Allen uses speech bubbles to excellent effect in the pictures. When six of Farmer Pugh's prize chickens go missing, Hubert Hound and his assistant Reg are called to investigate. The style of questioning and responses of the suspects are straight out of a detective film and appeal to older children and adults reading to them.

Jonathan Allen has also written some longer stories, which demonstrate further his wacky ideas and allow his imagination fuller reign. His Wizard Grimweed stories are about a wizard famed for his potions. They centre round something going wrong and a farcical situation arising. For example, in the first story *B.I.G. Trouble,* some of the wizard's potion for turning "babies into giants" spills and a mouse drinks it. Before he can do anything a gigantic mouse has burst through the roof of his laboratory. The antidote is buried somewhere in the rubble and he throws all sorts of potions at the mouse before getting the right one. The mouse ends up with green, shaggy fur impersonating Elvis! The others in the series have equally amusing plots that make them entertaining and satisfying for children beginning to read on their own.

In *Keep-Fit Canaries* and its sequel *Flying Squad* he has created another set of wonderfully quirky characters in some canaries that are desperate for freedom. They break out of their cage after keep-fit training and form themselves into a terrifying formation team that swoop on unsuspecting people and steal their sandwiches. The plots are cleverly constructed and puns and jokes abound, and this longer format allows him to develop an idea in more depth. He has illustrated these longer stories in black and white with his distinctive characters with slightly off-centre features.

Allen's style of illustration has worked particularly well in novelty books, some of which have been collaborations with other authors. *Wake Up, Sleeping Beauty!* is another example of having fun with a well-known source. Prince Eggbert sets out, with his assistant Kelvin, to wake the Sleeping Beauty and win her hand in marriage. Each pop-up is accompanied by a spectacular sound. After an ear-splitting whistle, crashing cymbals, and electric guitar full volume, a brass gong, and a pneumatic drill, Eggbert is ready to give in. What happens next is not quite what Prince Eggbert had in mind, but once again it shows Allen's irrepressible sense of humour and penchant for the unexpected ending!

Allen has successfully illustrated many books by other authors, most notable with Margaret Mahy and novelty books with Stephen Wyllie and Corinne Mellor. In these, as in his own books, his humorous illustrations interpret the text admirably and add substantially to the books as a whole.

—Fiona Lafferty

ALLEN, Pamela (Kay)

Nationality: New Zealander. **Born:** 3 April 1934, Devonport, Auckland. **Education:** Elam School of Art (now Auckland University), diploma of fine art 1954; Auckland Teachers Training College, 1955-56. **Family:** Married William Robert Allen, 12 December 1964; one son and one daughter. **Career:** Art teacher, Pio Pio District High School, New Zealand, 1956, and Rangitoto College, Auckland, 1957-58, 1960-64; writer and illustrator, since 1979. **Awards:** New South Wales Premier's Literary award, 1980, 1981, 1983; Australian Book Publishers Association Book Design award, 1981; Children's Book Council of Australia Picture Book of the Year, 1983, 1984; Russell Clark Award, New Zealand Library Association, 1986; Helen Paul Encouragement Award, 1989; New Zealand Aim Children's Book award, 1991. **Agent:** Curtis Brown Ltd., 27 Union Street, Paddington, Sydney, New South Wales 2021, Australia.

PUBLICATIONS FOR CHILDREN (ILLUSTRATED BY THE AUTHOR)

Fiction

Mr. Archimedes' Bath. Sydney, Collins, London, Bodley Head, and New York, Lothrop, 1980.

Who Sank the Boat? Melbourne, Thomas Nelson, Auckland, Hodder & Stoughton, and London, Hamish Hamilton, 1982; New York, Coward, 1983.
Bertie and the Bear. Melbourne, Thomas Nelson, Auckland, Hodder & Stoughton, and London, Hamish Hamilton, 1983; New York, Coward, 1984.
A Lion in the Night. Melbourne, Thomas Nelson, Auckland, Hodder & Stoughton, and London, Hamish Hamilton, 1985; New York, Putnam, 1986.
Simon Said. Melbourne, Thomas Nelson, and Auckland, Hodder & Stoughton, 1985.
Watch Me. Melbourne, Thomas Nelson, and Auckland, Hodder & Stoughton, 1985.
Herbert and Harry. Melbourne, Thomas Nelson, Auckland, Hodder & Stoughton, and London, Hamish Hamilton, 1986; as *Hidden Treasure,* New York, Putnam, 1987.
Mr. McGee. Melbourne, Thomas Nelson, Auckland, Hodder & Stoughton, and London, Hamish Hamilton, 1987.
Fancy That! Melbourne, Thomas Nelson, Auckland, Hodder & Stoughton, London, Hamish Hamilton, and New York, Orchard Books, 1988.
Simon Did. Ringwood, Victoria, Viking Kestrel, and Auckland, Hodder & Stoughton, 1988.
Watch Me Now. Ringwood, Victoria, Viking Kestrel, and Auckland, Hodder & Stoughton, 1988.
I Wish I Had a Pirate Suit. Ringwood, Victoria, Viking Kestrel, Auckland, Hodder and Stoughton, and London, Hamish Hamilton, 1989; New York, Viking, 1990.
My Cat Maisie. Ringwood, Victoria, Viking, Auckland, Hodder and Stoughton, London, Hamish Hamilton, and New York, Viking, 1990.
Black Dog. Ringwood, Victoria, Viking, 1991, and Auckland, Hodder and Stoughton, 1991; London, Hamish Hamilton, 1992.
Belinda. Ringwood, Victoria, Auckland, Hodder and Stoughton, and New York, Viking, 1992; London, Hamish Hamilton, 1993.
Mr. McGee Goes to Sea. Ringwood, Victoria, Viking, Auckland, Hodder & Stoughton, and London, Hamish Hamilton, 1992.
Alexander's Outing. Ringwood, Victoria, Viking, 1993; London, Hodder & Stoughton, 1994.
Mr. McGee and the Blackberry Jam. Ringwood, Victoria, Viking, Auckland, Hodder and Stoughton, and London, Hamish Hamilton, 1993.
Clippity Clop. Ringwood, Victoria, Viking, and Auckland, Hodder and Stoughton, 1994.
Waddle Giggle Gargle! Ringwood, Victoria, Puffin Books, 1996.
The Bear's Lunch. Ringwood, Victoria, Viking, 1997.
Mr. McGee and the Biting Flea. Ringwood, Victoria, Viking, 1998.

*

Illustrator: *Mummy, Do Monsters Clean Their Teeth?,* 1975, *Mummy, How Cold Is a Witch's Nose?,* 1976, *Big Sloppy Dinosaur Socks,* 1977, and *Mummy, Are Monsters Too Big for Their Boots?,* 1977, all by Jan Farr; *Three Cheers for McGinty, McGinty Goes to School, McGinty the Ghost,* and *McGinty in Space,* all by T.E. Wilson, all 1976; *The Pow Toe* by N.L. Ray, 1979; *A Tall Story* by Sally Fitzgerald, 1981; *There's a Bunyip Under the Bed* by Marcia Vaughan, 1989; *Ordinary Albert* by Nancy Antel, 1996.

* * *

Pamela Allen's award winning children's book *Who Sank the Boat?* is regarded as a modern classic, and with many other fine titles almost as popular, she is the best known picture book creator for the very young in Australia. The combination of vigorous, jaunty texts with bold, spare illustrations that emphasise movement and expression make her books read-aloud favourites with preschoolers. Recurring subjects are water, chases, sounds, and cows—and many of the books invite problem solving in delightful cumulative scenarios that reward participation: "You DO know who sank the boat."

The concept of displacement is at the core of *Mr Archimedes' Bath, Who Sank the Boat?* and *Alexander's Outing.* When pinkly naked Mr. Archimedes is joined in his bath by a wombat, a goat, and a kangaroo the water overflows. Who is too blame? Mr. Archimedes solves the problem ("Eureka!") and the four enjoy a wild night jumping in and out of the bath. In *Who Sank the Boat?* an involuntary wetting awaits a donkey, a cow, a pig, a sheep, and a tiny little mouse, five friends who decide to go for a row on the bay. One by one the fat animals with their knitting and umbrellas squeeze into the small row boat; last of all, with the boat listing dangerously and appearing ready to burst at the seams, the mouse makes a leap from the jetty. The animals' various expressions of anticipation as the mouse is airborne makes for one of the funniest illustrations in children's picture book history. In *Alexander's Outing,* a wayward duckling is rescued from a deep, narrow hole by the simple expedient of filling the hole with water. Of course from the crowd of would-be rescuers, it is a little boy who prompts this solution.

The chase central to the humour and action of *Bertie and the Bear* begins without any preamble: "Because a bear was chasing Bertie, the Queen shouted, 'Shoo, shooo you monster YOU!'" The Queen is joined by the King blowing a trumpet, the Admiral with a gong, and so on, to culminate in a munificent cacophony which so flatters the bear that he stops chasing rotund Bertie to bow and dance for his pursuers. Similarly, a night time chase after a royal baby, found riding on a lion's back in *A Lion in the Night,* combines text and illustration to lead the reader to replicate the action as we "pursue" the characters through field, forest, and river. Chaplin-like Mr. McGee also travels in the four tales of his eccentric adventures, in *Mr. McGee and the Blackberry Jam,* this being a short and sudden flight over a fence when butted by an angry bull! And recalcitrant cattle are central to the hilarious romp, *Belinda,* where cross-dressing is farmer Tom's solution to milking the stubborn cow Belinda, who is accustomed to the feminine presence of Bessie, away visiting her daughter in the city. Another farmyard is the setting for *Fancy That!,* a cumulative tale for the very young incorporating concepts of colour, number, place, and sound. Little red hen is sitting on six brown eggs. "Took" she says to a white leghorn. Soon a noisy chorus welcomes six cheeping chicks and the hen house chorus ends with a "cock-a-doodle-doo" from the rooster.

Allen has written a number of cautionary tales. Four of these are wordless texts, light-hearted depictions of a boastful and greedy boy who comes to grief in *Simon Said, Watch Me,* and *Simon Did,* but who fortunately heeds good advice in *Watch Me Now. My Cat Maisie* and *Black Dog* are both about relationships between animals and humans. Maisie the cat comes back to lonely Andrew after he learns a lesson about the unpleasantness of rough treatment. In *Black Dog,* however, rejection almost leads to tragedy when Christina's obsession with a blue bird (which might not exist) leads her to neglect everything, including Black Dog, who, in desperation, tries to fly from a high tree. The protagonists of *Herbert and Harry* are brothers who share and do everything together, until the day they find a treasure box. Herbert takes the treasure and the guarding of it occupies the rest of his life. Meanwhile Harry, who has no treasure, marries and has children. Brothers also feature in *I Wish I Had a Pirate Suit.* A little boy wishes he had a pirate suit like his brother Peter. In all their games the little brother gets the inferior role, and even when he does finally get the suit, the game has changed. Characteristically there is much humour, but despite this, one is left with a rather depressing depiction of sibling relationships.

In 1996 an illustration from *Who Sank the Boat?* was reproduced as an Australia Post stamp, one of a set of four postage stamps (the others were illustrations from books by Ron Brooks, Bob Graham, and Graeme Base) to mark the fiftieth anniversary of the Australian Children's Book Council awards, an acknowledgement of Allen's pre-eminence in her field and the classic status of that particular book. Three picture books published in the late 1990s remind of the skill of her illustrative technique—the way a reader's eye is drawn to what is important, her use of colour, the telling details usually only noticed on later readings—and are a return to the style of *Bertie and the Bear,* where interaction between people and animals is central to the plot and a noisy and exuberant reading is essential. In *Clippity-Clop* a "little old woman" and a "little old man" try to move two stubborn donkeys, they both succeed but only one does it cleverly! The events depicted in *Waddle Giggle Gargle,* where Jonathan, Grandma, and Grandpa attempt to outwit an aggressive nesting magpie, are familiar to most Australians and resourcefulness is also required by Wendy and Oliver in *The Bear's Lunch* when a huge, hungry bear is out looking for a meal and finds their picnic. Eating that "little lunch" he looks around for more—to the children cowering on the end of a jetty! Fortunately Oliver saves them by growling back at the bear. *The Bear's Lunch,* with a chase, a tense situation to be resolved, eating, and a text that will inspire and flatter the read-aloud abilities of any parent or teacher, showcases Allen's motifs and strengths.

—Kerry White

ANCONA, George

Nationality: American. **Born:** New York, New York, 4 December 1929. **Education:** Academia San Carlos, 1949-1950, Art Students League, 1950-51, and Cooper Union, 1950-51 (all New York City). **Family:** Married 1) Patricia Apatow, 1951 (divorced, 1966); two daughters and one son; 2) journalist Helga Von Sydow, 1968; two daughters and one son. **Career:** Art director, *Esquire* magazine, New York City, 1951-53; promotion department director, *Seventeen* magazine, New York City, 1953-54; art director, Grey Advertising, New York City, 1954-57; art director, Daniel & Charles, New York City, 1957-61; photographer and film maker, George Ancona Inc., New York City, from 1961; instructor, Rockland Community College and School of Visual Arts, New York; lecturer on film, design, photography, and books. **Awards:** Art Director's Show awards, 1959, 1960, 1967; Council on Non-Theatrical Events Cine Golden Eagle Awards, 1967 and 1972; American Institute of Graphic Arts awards in 1967, 1968, 1974; Industry Film Producers Association Cindy Award, 1967; New York Academy of Sciences Nonfiction Younger Honor Science Book Award, 1975; Golden Kite Award, 1980; Junior Literary Guild Selection, 1984; American Library Association Notable Book and Notable Children's Book in the Field of Social Studies, 1986; New York Times Best Illustrated Children's Books of the Year citation, 1987; Carter G. Woodson Book Award for Outstanding Merit, National Council for the Social Studies, 1987; Junior Literary Guild selection and New York Academy of Sciences Children's Science Book Award, 1988; Notable Trade Book in the Field of Social Studies, 1989; Texas Blue Bonnet Award, 1989; Notable Children's Book in the Field of Social Studies, 1990; American Booksellers Association Pick of the Lists citation, 1991; Bank Street College Children's Book of the Year citation, 1993; New York Times Public Library Best 100 children's books citation, 1993; Parents' Choice Award, 1994; Child Study Children's Book Committee Children's Book of the Year award, 1994; Golden Duck Award, 1994; National Science Teachers Association and Children's Book Council Outstanding Science Trade Book for Children citation, 1994.

PUBLICATIONS FOR CHILDREN (ILLUSTRATED BY THE AUTHOR)

Nonfiction

Handtalk. New York, Parents Magazine Press, 1974.
Monsters on Wheels. New York, Dutton Children's Books, 1974.
And What Do You Do? New York, Dutton Children's Books, 1975.
I Feel: A Picture Book of Emotions. New York, Dutton, 1977.
Growing Older. New York, Dutton, 1978.
It's a Baby! New York, Dutton, 1979.
Dancing Is. New York, Dutton, 1981.
Bananas: From Manolo to Margie. Boston, Houghton Mifflin Company, 1982.
Monster Movers. New York, Dutton, 1983.
Team Work: A Picture Essay About Crews and Teams at Work. New York, Crowell, 1983.
With Remy Charlip and Mary B. Miller, *Handtalk: An ABC of Finger Spelling & Sign Language.* New York, Simon & Schuster, 1984.
Freighters: Cargo Ships and the People Who Work Them. New York, Crowell, 1985.
Sheep Dog. New York, Lothrop, Lee & Shepard, 1985.
Turtle Watch. New York, Macmillan, 1987.
With Remy Charlip and Mary B. Miller, *Handtalk Birthday: A Number & Story Book in Sign Language.* New York, Simon & Schuster, 1987.
With Mary Beth Miller, *Handtalk Zoo.* New York, Simon & Schuster, 1989.
Bananas. Boston, Houghton Mifflin, 1990.
Riverkeeper. New York, Macmillan, 1990.
The Aquarium Book. Boston, Houghton Mifflin Company, 1991.
With Mary Beth Miller, *Handtalk School.* New York, Simon & Schuster, 1991.

Helping Out. New York, Clarion Books, 1985; Boston, Houghton Mifflin, 1991.
Man & Mustang. New York, Simon & Schuster Children's, 1992.
My Camera. New York, Crown Publishers, 1992.
Pablo Remembers: The Fiesta of the Day of the Dead. New York, Lothrop, Lee & Shepard, 1993.
Powwow. San Diego, Harcourt Brace & Company, 1993.
The Golden Lion Tamarin Comes Home. New York, Simon & Schuster, 1994.
The Piñata Maker—El Piñatero. San Diego, Harcourt Brace & Company, 1994.
Ricardo's Day. New York, Scholastic, 1994.
Cutters, Carvers & the Cathedral. New York, Lothrop, Lee & Shepard, 1995.
Earth Daughter: Alicia of Acoma Pueblo. New York, Simon & Schuster, 1995.
Fiesta U.S.A. New York, Dutton Children's Books, 1995.
Mayeros: A Yucatec Maya Family. New York, Lothrop, Lee & Shepard, 1997.
Let's Dance. New York, Dutton Children's Books, 1998.
Fiesta Fireworks. New York, Lothrop, Lee & Shepard, 1998.
Let's Eat. New York, William Morrow & Company, 1999.

Other

Also author of film scripts, including "Doctor" and "Dentist," *Sesame Street*; "Getting It Together"; "Cities of the Web," Macmillan; "Looking for Pictures," "Looking for Color," "Seeing Rhythm," "Faces," and "The River"; "Reflections," American Crafts Council; "The Link," Orba Coporation; and "Expansion," Diamond International Corporation.

*

Biography: Entry in *Something About the Author Autobiography Series,* Vol. 18, Detroit, Gale, 1994, 1-18; entry in *Something About the Author,* Vol. 85, Detroit, Gale, 1995, 5-13.

Illustrator: *A Snake-Lover's Diary,* 1970, *Faces,* 1970, *Bodies,* 1973, all by Barbara Brenner; *Grandpa Had A Windmill, Grandma Had A Churn,* 1977, *Over on the River,* 1980, both by Louise A. Jackson; *My Feet Do* by Jean Holzenthaler, 1979; *Finding Your First Job* by Sue Alexander, 1980; (with A. Eisenstaedt) *Your Future in Art* by the Design School Staff, 1981; *The First Thanksgiving Feast* by Joan Anderson, 1984; *Being Adopted,* 1984, *Being A Twin, Having A Twin,* 1985, *Making A New Home in America,* 1986, *Artists of Handcrafted Furniture at Work,* 1988, and *Brothers and Sisters,* 1991, all by Maxine B. Rosenberg; *Christmas on the Prairie,* 1985, *The Glorious Fourth at Prairietown,* 1986, *Pioneer Children of Appalachia,* 1986, *Joshua's Westward Journal,* 1987, *A Williamsburg Household,* 1988, *From Map to Museum: Uncovering Mysteries of the Past,* 1988, *Spanish Pioneers of the Southwest,* 1989, *Harry's Helicopter,* 1990, *Pioneer Settlers of New France,* 1990, *Christopher Columbus: From Vision to Voyage,* 1991, *The American Family Farm: A Photo Essay,* 1993, *Earth Keepers,* 1993, *Richie's Rocket,* 1993, *Twins on Toes: A Ballet Debut,* 1993, *Sally's Submarine,* 1995, and *Cowboys: Roundup on an American Ranch,* 1996, all by Joan Anderson; *Jackpot of the Beagle Brigade* by Sam Epstein and Beryl Epstein, 1987; *The American Family Farm: A Photo Essay* by Joan Anderson, 1989; *Mom Can't See Me,* 1990, and *Mom's Best Friend,* 1992, by Sally Hobart Alexander; *City! New York,* 1990, *City! San Francisco,* 1990, and *City! Washington, D. C.,* 1991, all by Shirley Climo; *My New Baby-Sitter* by Christine Loomis, 1991; *Just Beyond Reach and Other Riddle Poems* by Bonnie Larkin Nims, 1992; *Over Here It's Different: Carolina's Story* by Mildred Leinweber Dawson, 1993.

* * *

George Ancona believes that as a photographer he can participate in other people's lives. He commented in *Something About the Author Autobiography Series* "...I think people are fascinating and I love to find myself in strange places, meeting people, getting to know them and learning about them. This helps me to learn about myself. Photographing, filming, or writing about someone or someplace is my way of feeling alive and in touch with the world around me...." Within the children's books he has created, George Ancona has celebrated the lives of people both in ordinary circumstances and amidst the color and significance of cultural events.

Born in New York to Mexican parents, Ancona grew up experiencing the crowds and excitement on the summer beaches of Coney Island. Aware of his artistic abilities at a young age, he found support for his work in junior high and high school art teachers. Painting signs for vendors in the summer and participating in special projects in high school gave Ancona the opportunity for early authentic experiences focusing on his art. During high school he won a scholarship to the Art Students League in New York City, and about the same time he met Rufino Tamayo, who invited Ancona to visit him in Mexico. Ancona accepted the invitation and while in Mexico also met other renowned Mexican artists, such as Jose Clemente Orozco, Igor Stravinsky, Diego Rivera, and Frida Kahlo. He also visited his extended family during a trip to Yucatan. After returning to New York and attending the Art Students League, he held several jobs, such as staff designer and art director for several prominent magazines, and he married his first wife. As his artistic ability began to mature, a job with NBC led him in the direction of film. At the age of thirty, Ancona decided to become a freelance photographer and film-maker and the following years involved time spent in travel, a second marriage, and six children.

With so many life experiences behind him and people around him, Ancona was well able to capture the needed images when a friend asked him to illustrate with photography one of her books. After creating illustrations for three books, Ancona was then asked to write and illustrate his own book. His creation was based on the fascination he held as a child for huge machinery. *Monsters on Wheels* describes a variety of construction machinery and was followed by *Monster Movers,* a book focusing on machinery that moves cargo across land and onto ships. Ancona's entry into the world of children's literature was a natural extension of his artistic abilities. He explains on his publisher's internet site, "For me, a children's book is a series of images strung together to tell a story. As far back as I can remember, I have always been creating images: by drawing, painting, cutting and pasting, and finally by shooting photographs. The words came later. They filled in what the pictures couldn't convey."

Ancona's celebration of people through children's books begins with *Freighters,* in which he describes the people who operate machines. These everyday occupations are treated as anything but ordinary in the text and photographs within this book. *And What*

Do You Do and *Teamwork: A Picture Essay About Crews and Teams at Work* also celebrate a diversity of people working together.

The Sheep Dog and *Riverkeeper* extend the celebrations to our environment in black-and-white photographs and simple but comprehensive text. *The Sheep Dog* considers the role of sheep dogs in protecting and herding and how the various breeds accomplish their tasks. The environmental issues surrounding protecting sheep with the use of traps and poisons are seen in light of the various European breeds of guard dogs that could be more effective against natural predators. *Riverkeeper* explores the life of one whose job is to protect the Hudson River and its animals and vegetation from polluters such as factories and people. *Riverkeeper* emphasizes the need for public knowledge and education about keeping the river clean for all. *Turtle Watch* and *The Golden Lion Tamarin Comes Home* are other works that celebrate our environment through expressive photographs and explanatory text.

Ancona has worked with Mary Beth Miller in a series of books that focus on sign language. *Handtalk Zoo* contains color photographs that captures the spirit of the children using sign language. Other books focusing on challenges people face include *Mom Can't See Me* and *Mom's Best Friend,* illustrated by Ancona and written by Sally Hobart.

It is only natural that Ancona's tacit celebrations of the many people he has observed and lived around should lead to books that describe actual celebrations. Within these books, he continues to be fascinated with a diversity of people, such as in *Powwow. Powwow* invites the reader to explore an American Indian celebration. The focus for this particular book is the Crow Fair in Montana. Known as the largest powwow in the United States, the illustrations depict contemporary American Indians as they prepare for and participate in traditional dances with elaborate symbolic costuming. Young and old individuals from various tribes are illuminated in Ancona's photographs as they recreate significant stories, characters, and symbols from their heritage.

Perhaps, though, Ancona should be most noted for bringing to life celebrations of his own heritage as he captures special events in the lives of Hispanic people. *Fiesta USA* focuses on four major Hispanic celebrations as they are observed in four different areas of our country. Colorful costumes, decorations, and the faces of people glowing with excitement are all well framed within the photographs that tell the story with well chosen text. The narrative both tells what the participants in the fiestas are doing as well as the story behind each celebration. A glossary with pronunciation of Spanish words adds to the authenticity of the text. Several books take place in Mexico. *Pablo Remembers: The Fiesta of the Day of the Dead* focuses on the celebration of The Day of the Dead in Mexico. The three days of the celebration are seen through Pablo's family's experiences. *The Piñata Maker* combines photographs and text in both English and Spanish to investigate pinatas from the beginnings of its construction to its use. The personal artistry described in this craft emphasizes the time and care involved as this man creates puppets, masks, and pinatas. *Fiesta Fireworks* describes an artist in the town of Tultepec, Mexico, as they prepare for the fiesta of the town's patron saint. Again, Spanish words are emphasized and the focus on the young girl Caren attracts children as well as other readers who have experienced this yearly event.

Building on his life experiences and those of his earlier years in art, publishing, and film, Ancona's contributions to children's literature brings into perspective that which seems to be distant and illuminates what might be considered ordinary. He has authentically created cultural insights through his photography and carefully selected text that accompanies the illustrations in telling a story. His love of people is evident in each of his books as he celebrates with them many aspects of their lives and shares this celebration with his readers.

—Janelle B. Mathis

ANDERSON, C(larence) W(illiam)

Nationality: American. **Born:** Wahoo, Nebraska, 12 April 1891. **Education:** Wahoo High School; Art Institute, Chicago, three years. **Family:** Married Madalena Paltenghi. **Career:** Freelance artist and illustrator. Judge for American Horse Shows Association. **Member:** Society of American Graphic Artists. **Died:** 26 March 1971.

PUBLICATIONS FOR CHILDREN (ILLUSTRATED BY THE AUTHOR)

Fiction

Billy and Blaze. New York, Macmillan, 1936.
Blaze and the Gypsies. New York, Macmillan, 1937; London, Country Life, 1939.
Blaze and the Forest Fire. New York, Macmillan, 1938.
Salute. New York, Macmillan, 1940.
High Courage. New York, Macmillan, 1941.
Bobcat. New York, Macmillan, 1949.
Blaze Finds the Trail. New York, Macmillan, 1950.
A Pony for Linda. New York, Macmillan, 1951.
Linda and the Indians. New York, Macmillan, 1952.
The Crooked Colt. New York, Macmillan, 1954.
Blaze and Thunderbolt. New York, Macmillan, 1955.
The Horse of Hurricane Hill. New York, Macmillan, 1956; Leicester, Brockhampton Press, 1958.
Afraid to Ride. New York, Macmillan, 1957; Leicester, Brockhampton Press, 1959.
Pony for Three. New York, Macmillan, 1958.
Blaze and the Mountain Lion. New York, Macmillan, 1959.
A Filly for Joan. New York, Macmillan, 1960.
Lonesome Little Colt. New York, Macmillan, 1961.
Great Heart. New York, Macmillan, 1962.
Blaze and the Indian Cave. New York, Macmillan, and London, Collier Macmillan, 1964.
Another Man o' War. New York, Macmillan, 1966; London, Collier Macmillan, 1967.
Blaze and the Lost Quarry. New York, Macmillan, and London, Collier Macmillan, 1966.
The Outlaw. New York, Macmillan, and London, Collier Macmillan, 1967.
Blaze and the Gray Spotted Pony. New York, Macmillan, and London, Collier Macmillan, 1968.
Blaze Shows the Way. New York, Macmillan, and London, Collier Macmillan, 1969.
Phantom, Son of the Gray Ghost. New York, Macmillan, and London, Collier Macmillan, 1969.
Blaze Finds Forgotten Roads. New York, Macmillan, and London, Collier Macmillan, 1970.

The Blind Connemara. New York, Macmillan, and London, Collier Macmillan, 1971.
The Rumble Seat Pony. New York, Macmillan, and London, Collier Macmillan, 1971.

Other

Twenty Gallant Horses. New York, Macmillan, 1965.

Editor, *C.W. Anderson's Favorite Horse Stories.* New York, Dutton, 1967.

Publications for Adults

Other

And So to Bed: Seventy-Six Drawings. New York, Loring and Mussey, 1935.
Black, Bay, and Chestnut: Profiles of Twenty Favorite Horses. New York, Macmillan, 1939.
Deep Through the Heart: Profiles of Twenty Valiant Horses. New York, Macmillan, 1940.
Thoroughbreds. New York, Macmillan, 1942.
Big Red. New York, Macmillan, 1943.
Heads Up, Heels Down: A Handbook of Horsemanship and Riding. New York, Macmillan, 1944.
A Touch of Greatness. New York, Macmillan, 1945.
Tomorrow's Champion. New York, Macmillan, 1946.
Sketchbook. New York, Macmillan, 1948.
All Thoroughbreds. New York, Harper, 1948.
Post Parade. New York, Harper, 1949.
Horses Are Folks. New York, Harper, 1950.
Horse Show. New York, Harper, 1951.
Turf and Bluegrass. New York, Harper, 1952.
The Smashers. New York, Harper, 1954.
Grey, Bay, and Chestnut. New York, Harper, 1955.
Colts and Champions. New York, Harper, 1956.
Accent on Youth. New York, Harper, 1958.
Bred to Run. New York, Harper, 1960.
Complete Book of Horses and Horsemanship. New York, Macmillan, and London, Collier Macmillan, 1963.
The Look of a Thoroughbred. New York, Harper, 1963.
The World of Horses. New York, Harper, 1965.
Before the Bugle. New York, Macmillan, 1968.
Horse of the Century: Man o' War. New York, Macmillan, 1970.
The Miracle of Greek Sculpture. New York, Dutton, 1970.

*

Manuscript Collections: Kerlan Collection, University of Minnesota, Minneapolis; University of Oregon Library, Eugene.

Illustrator: *Honey, The City Bear,* 1937, *Remus Goes to Town,* 1938, *Rumpus Rabbit,* 1939, and *Honey on a Raft,* 1941, all by Madalena Paltenghi; *A Pony Called Lightning* by Miriam Mason, 1948; *Midnight, Rodeo Champion,* 1951, and *A Horse Named Joe,* 1956, both by Robert Edward Gard.

* * *

All young readers who love horses know Billy and Blaze. If they remain devoted to horses, they come to know C.W. Anderson's books for older children. For these deal, too, with horses whether in fiction or nonfiction. Nonfiction writing gave Anderson a means of sharing his vast knowledge gained from experience and research, while his fiction for older readers provided stories about children who love horses and who learn about horse care, breeding, raising, training, and racing—this information generally imparted by a groom, trainer, or other older person.

Anderson thought of himself as an artist only, but the editor who discovered Anderson as artist and illustrator, Doris Patee, provoked and encouraged the early texts which Anderson wrote to accompany his illustrations in *Billy and Blaze, Blaze and the Gypsies,* and *Blaze and the Forest Fire.* From these brief stories concerning young Billy and his horse Blaze (each book is basically an adventure story about Blaze) grew Anderson's writing ability.

Anderson's own enthusiasm for things equestrian permeates all his books. His observations and thoughts about horses for the cowboy, huntsperson, or jockey are detailed as the trainer or groom, often Black, explains to the young boy or girl in the story what makes a good horse, a courageous horse, a fast horse, and so on, as well as what constitutes a good owner. These are elements that Anderson's illustrations alone cannot capture, and thus, his simple text is essential, and well-written. Perhaps the best among this second group of Anderson's books are *Salute, High Courage, The Horse of Hurricane Hill,* and *A Filly for Joan.* Each contains a sense of action, represented by words such as "shining," "brushing," "polishing," "cleaning," "rubbing," all perhaps routine to someone whose living is made grooming a horse, but exciting to the reader. Pictures of horses often fill the stable wall or the young owner's room. Long talks with the groom or trainer, that embodiment of Anderson as horse lover and authority, may conclude at chapter's end with the senior's apology for having become enthused and having talked too much. It may represent an apology to the reader, a device to end a chapter, but to the horse fan the clever conclusion leads quickly to the next chapter.

Most chapters in these books tend to cover a single element in breeding, care, or racing, or one episode in what becomes little more than a collected series of horse stories. Anderson applied the same technique to his non-fiction when he gathered individual stories to create the collections *Black, Bay, and Chestnut* and *Deep Through the Heart.* His best nonfiction efforts are *Complete Book of Horses and Horsemanship* and *Big Red,* the latter being the story of Man o' War, introduced by the "softly slurred Negro voice" of Man o' War's trainer and exercise boy. Anderson may be criticized in the future for his rendition of the Black American dialect, but his depiction is never derogatory; often it is the Black groom who is dearly loved by the children and respected for his knowledge as the story unfolds.

Anderson has few rivals within his chosen field of writing and illustration. He combined a magnificent talent for illustrating all kinds of horses with an ability to write clearly and to convey to all ages his love and knowledge of horses.

—Edward Kemp

ANDREW, Prudence (Hastings)

Nationality: British. **Born:** Prudence Hastings Petch, London, 23 May 1924. **Education:** St. Anne's College, Oxford, B.A. (honours) in history, 1946. **Family:** Married G.H.L. Andrew in 1946; two daughters. **Career:** Worked in the personnel department, Joseph Lucas Ltd., Birmingham, 1944-45; staff member, Nuffield Institute of Colonial Affairs, Oxford, 1945-47; history teacher, St. Michael's Convent School, Monmouthshire, 1956-60. **Address:** c/o Heinemann Ltd., 81 Fulham Rd., London SW3 6RB, England.

Publications for Children

Fiction

Ginger over the Wall, illustrated by Charles Mozley. London, Lutterworth Press, 1962.
Ginger and Batty Bill, illustrated by Charles Mozley. London, Lutterworth Press, 1963.
Ginger and Number 10, illustrated by Charles Mozley. London, Lutterworth Press, 1964.
The Christmas Card, illustrated by Mary Russon. London, Hamish Hamilton, 1966.
Ginger among the Pigeons, illustrated by Charles Mozley. London, Lutterworth Press, 1966.
Mr. Morgan's Marrow, illustrated by Janet Duchesne. London, Hamish Hamilton, 1967.
A New Creature. London, Hutchinson, and New York, Putnam, 1968.
Dog!, illustrated by Trevor Stubley. London, Hamish Hamilton, 1968; Nashville, Nelson, 1973.
A Man with Your Advantages. London, Hutchinson, 1970.
Mister O'Brien. London, Heinemann, 1972; Nashville, Nelson, 1973.
Una and Grubstreet. London, Heinemann, 1972; as *Una and the Heaven Baby,* Nashville, Nelson, 1975.
Rodge, Silvie, and Munch, illustrated by Jael Jordan. London, Heinemann, 1973.
Goodbye to the Rat. London, Heinemann, 1974.
The Heroic Deeds of Jason Jones, illustrated by Jael Jordan. London, Heinemann, 1975.
Where Are You Going To, My Pretty Maid? London, Heinemann, 1977.
Robinson Daniel Crusoe. London, Heinemann, 1978; as *Close Within My Own Circle,* New York, Elsevier Nelson, 1980.
The Other Side of the Park. London, Heinemann, 1984.

Publications for Adults

Novels

The Hooded Falcon. London, Hutchinson, 1960; New York, Putnam, 1961.
Ordeal by Silence: A Story of Medieval Times. London, Hutchinson, and New York, Putnam, 1961.
A Question of Choice. London, Hutchinson, and New York, Putnam, 1962.
The Earthworms. London, Hutchinson, 1963; as *The Constant Star,* New York, Putnam, 1964.
A Sparkle from the Coal. London, Hutchinson, 1964.
A New Creature. London, Hutchinson, and New York, Putnam, 1968.
A Man with Your Advantages. London, Hutchinson, 1970.

* * *

Prudence Andrew made a notable contribution to children's literature between 1962 and 1984, reflecting some of the key points in its development in Britain during that period.

In the 1960s, her four books about Ginger and his gang attracted attention; she had updated the popular "William" figure and placed him in an urban setting which also portrayed the newly emergent multi-cultural society. Andrew was one of the first children's writers to include black characters as an integral part of the story, and although *Ginger and Number 10* was criticised for her descriptions of these characters, it also won praise for its clear condemnation of racial prejudice.

Mister O'Brien and *Una and Grubstreet* are both mainstream children's novels, published in the early 1970s when teachers and librarians were looking for stories about what were seen as young people's problems. Mister O'Brien, a colourfully dressed, one-legged man, is a figment of handicapped Christopher's imagination, who makes his appearance whenever Christopher has to decide between two courses of action. It is Mister O'Brien who is responsible for his friendship with Penny and for his consequent decision to accomplish the difficult feat of walking ten miles in a sponsored charity walk. Motherless Una seeks comfort and support in conversations with Grubstreet, a small toy bear, who represents her more responsible, sensible self in their imaginary exchanges. Both Christopher and Una learn to come to terms with their respective circumstances—Christopher with his handicap, Una with her father's remarriage.

Both of these books are concerned with the parent-child relationship, but this theme is taken a stage further in her two latest books. *Robinson Daniel Crusoe* is about a teenager whose loneliness arises largely from the pressures put upon him by his father who is trying to compensate, through his gifted son, for his own lack of success. In the end Daniel commits suicide, sailing off down the Mersey—several of Andrew's books have a Liverpool setting—on a raft in imitation of his hero Robinson Crusoe. In *The Other Side of the Park,* the central character is a girl; she too is moving toward independence after the unexplained death of her much-loved great-grandmother provides a reason for her to crystallise her attitudes toward her father's apparent greed for money and her mother's need for help. Here, the support of her sensible boyfriend brings about a happier solution.

Andrew also contributed to several publishers' series which were aimed at groups recognised as having special reading needs. *The Christmas Card* and *Dog!* are two of her books written for younger children who need a short, readable story with a few clearly defined characters, with which to practise their newly acquired reading skills. *Goodbye to the Rat* and *Where Are You Going To, My Pretty Maid?,* on the other hand, are short novels for teenagers, both of them about groups of young people leaving school without qualifications and trying to find their feet in the adult world.

Andrew writes well-constructed, entertaining stories about both boys and girls; although she tackles unusual themes and gives the reader an insight into the characters, there is plenty of action and humour to keep the story moving at a steady pace. From the point of view of style, *Robinson Daniel Crusoe* represents her most interesting work. The story is told by Daniel's younger brother, Jimmy, who, being a football-oriented extrovert, is a complete contrast to the serious and ultimately tragic Daniel; his account of events is interspersed with extracts from Daniel's diaries, which enable the reader to understand Daniel's inner feelings, while Jimmy's comments help to lighten the story.

Andrew's gifts for reproducing conversation, for accurate observation, and for creating plausible characters are apparent throughout her work, even when she is writing to a formula. In *Mr. Morgan's Marrow,* one of her books for younger children, the Welsh setting comes out clearly through the characters' names and their turns of speech. In the two short books for teenagers, she economises by giving each of the characters a rather stereotyped background, but nevertheless manages to achieve documentary realism and plausibility of character. She is good on relationships—between children and parents, between children and their friends. In *Mister O'Brien,* Christopher's overprotective mother and his newfound friend Penny both come clearly from the page. Marion, the encouraging and supportive friend of Jason Jones, is another minor character who lives on in the reader's mind. These very rounded supporting characters contribute to the humour that is an important feature of Andrew's work.

Equally important is the fact that her characters achieve success, however modest. Handicapped Christopher, buoyed up by his wish to help Penny and his admiration for Scott of the Antarctic, walks his ten miles for charity, Una is left with her wish for a baby brother likely to be fulfilled, Jason Jones, weedy and unsuccessful, wins newspaper glory almost involuntarily. Through their experiences, Andrew's heroes and heroines develop and grow and, in doing so, provide a rewarding and enriching reading experience.

—Sheila G. Ray

ANDREWS, J(ames) S(ydney)

Also writes as Jim Andrews. **Nationality:** British. **Born:** Belfast, Northern Ireland, 14 December 1934. **Education:** Rossall School, Fleetwood, Lancashire. **Family:** Married Judith Ann McCartan in 1962; three daughters. **Career:** Until 1987 director, Isaac Andrews and Sons, Belfast. **Address:** c/o David and Charles Publishers, Brunel House, Newton Abbot, Devon TQ12 4PU, England.

Publications for Children

Fiction

The Bell of Nendrum. London, Bodley Head, 1969; as *The Green Hill of Nendrum,* New York, Hawthorn, 1970.

The Man from the Sea. London, Bodley Head, 1970; New York, Dutton, 1971.

Cargo for a King. London, Bodley Head, 1972; New York, Dutton, 1973.

Publications for Adults as Jim Andrews

Other

Catamarans for Cruising. London, Hollis and Carter, 1974.

Simple Sailing. Kingswood, Surrey, World's Work, 1975.

Family Boating. London, Hollis and Carter, 1982.

Food for Arthritics, Based on Dr. Dong's Diet, with Judy Andrews. London, Faber, 1982.

Twelve Ships A-Sailing: Thirty-Five Years of Home-Water Cruising. Newton Abbot, Devon, David and Charles, 1986.

* * *

The novels of J.S. Andrews share a number of features: a fascination with sailing and the sea, an awareness of the savagery of Ulster's history, and a central role for young male heroes. They belong to the genre usually designated "historical fiction," of the kind which favours colour, action, and confrontation rather than totally convincing characterization or stylistic subtlety. Placed beside the work of a Rosemary Sutcliff or a Leon Garfield, they have an old-fashioned feel, particularly in their no-nonsense emphasis on simplified notions of moral and physical courage. They have, however, the merit of strong storylines; and, even more interestingly, their depictions of earlier Irish conflicts provide many illuminating parallels with what in recent years we have come to call the Ulster "troubles." As Andrews says in a prefatory note to *The Bell of Nendrum,* "the story is one of life a thousand years ago—toward the end of the so-called 'Dark Ages'. And in seeing this, we hold up a mirror, which in some way reflects our own astonishing existence..."

The hero of *The Bell of Nendrum* is Nial Ross, a 15-year-old obsessed with sailing, especially around the islands in Strangford Lough. He finds himself, as the result of a time slip, drawn backward to the 10th century, when a monastic settlement on the island of Mahee is being ravaged by the Vikings. His stay with the welcoming and bemused monks is a tranquil prelude to the violence of the attack with which the book ends—a violence that is graphically and horrifically described. It is, however, Nial's knowledge that such violence will still be widespread in his own far-off century that gives the story its special frisson. He is a serious, sensible youth, cleancut and resilient, the type of whom Henty would have been proud; he does, though, retain a rather stolid sense of his Ulster-Scottish origins and values.

For the setting of *The Man from the Sea,* Andrews chooses Ireland of the Early Bronze Age and, as his locality, the coastal landscape of Donaghadee Sound at the outer end of Belfast Lough. Here the hardships of a small fishing community, aggravated by the disappearance of its men on a fishing expedition, are temporarily eased by the sudden arrival of the charismatic and quasi-mystical figure of Hadra. Hadra's journey to "Albin" (southwest Scotland) to find the lost fishermen constitutes the central chapters of the novel, a journey which will end in his own death but, simultaneously, in the return to life of others. The young hero, Euan, one of those accompanying Hadra, learns principally of the need to accept hardship and loss, developing an earnest stoicism in the process.

Ragnor MacHelli, the 17-year-old hero of *Cargo for a King,* is the most immediately likeable of Andrews's characters. Following his father's murder, he decides to carry on his business as a trader plying the pirate-infested waters between his native Isle of

Man and Ireland's east coast. The year is 1210 and in power in Ulster is the treacherous Hugh de Lacy, whose machinations have earlier displaced the highly regarded Sir John de Courcy. Ragnor throws his weight behind Sir John and in the ensuing maritime confrontations manages to assist in his restoration, avenge his father's death, and meet and fall in love with Afrin, a former slave girl. This last element of the book is treated with considerable good humour, and the portrayal of the young people's growing sexual awareness provides a refreshing diversion from the cut-and-thrust of successive sea-battles.

The topographical and historical precision of Andrews's stories evinces his respect for his native province and its inhabitants, past and present. One senses, beneath the muscular prose and the occasional moments of overt moralizing, a deep concern for the destinies of those whom one of the characters in *Cargo for a King* describes as "a strange, mountainy people, with a hardness and closeness resembling the granite rocks of their land."

—Robert Dunbar

ANDREWS, Wendy. See **SHARMAT, Marjorie Weinman.**

APPIAH, Peggy

Nationality: British. **Born:** Filkins, Gloucestershire, 21 May 1921; daughter of the politician Sir Stafford Cripps. **Education:** Norland Place and Queen's College, London; Maltman's Green, Buckinghamshire; Whitehall Secretarial College. **Family:** Married Joe E. Appiah in 1953; one son and three daughters. **Career:** Formerly research assistant, Ministry of Information, London; secretary, Racial Unity, London. From 1968 chairman of the Advisory Committee, Kumasi Children's Home. **Awards:** M.B.E. (Member, Order of the British Empire), 1996. **Agent:** David Higham Associates Ltd., 5-8 Lower John Street, London WIR 4HA, England. **Address:** P.O. Box 829, Kumasi, Ashanti, Ghana.

Publications for Children

Fiction

The Children of Ananse, illustrated by Mora Dickson. London, Evans, 1968.
Gift of the Mmoatia, illustrated by Nii O. Quao. Tema, Ghana Publishing Corporation, 1972.
Ring of Gold, illustrated by Laszlo Acs. London, Deutsch, 1976.
Kofi and the Crow. Accra-North, Ghana, Quick Service Books, 1991.
Afua and the Mouse. Accra-North, Ghana, Quick Service Books, 1991.
Abena and the Python. Accra-North, Ghana, Quick Service Books, 1991.
Kyekyekulee: Grandmother's Tales. Accra-North, Ghana, Quick Service Books, 1992.
Rattletat, illustrated by schoolchildren. Windhock, New Namibia Books, 1995.
Busy Body. Accra, Ghana, Asempa, 1996.
Deserted Village. Accra, Ghana, Asempa, forthcoming.
Rubbish Heap. Accra, Ghana, Asempa, forthcoming.

Other

Ananse the Spider: Tales from an Ashanti Village, illustrated by Peggy Wilson. New York, Pantheon, 1966.
Tales of an Ashanti Father, illustrated by Mora Dickson. London, Deutsch, 1967; Boston, Beacon Press, 1989.
The Pineapple Child and Other Tales from Ashanti, illustrated by Mora Dickson. London, Deutsch, 1969.
The Lost Earring (reader), illustrated by J. Jarvis. London, Evans, 1971.
Yao and the Python (reader), illustrated by J. Jarvis. London, Evans, 1971.
Why There Are So Many Roads (folktales), illustrated by A.A. Teye. Lagos, African Universities Press, 1972.
Why the Hyena Does Not Care for Fish and Other Tales from the Ashanti Gold Weights, illustrated by Joanna Stubbs. London, Deutsch, 1977.

Publications for Adults

Novels

A Smell of Onions. London, Longman, 1971.
A Dirge Too Soon. Tema, Ghana Publishing Corporation, 1976.
The Ring of Justice (for all ages). Lagos, Nigeria, Malthouse Press, forthcoming.

Poetry

Poems of Three Generations. Kumasi, Ghana, University of Science and Technology, 1978.

*

Biography: "The Attic of My Mind" (autobiography), in *Something about the Author,* Detroit, Gale Research, 1995.

Peggy Appiah comments:

All the books I have so far published have been about Ashanti, where I live. The country is full of stories, and I find the atmosphere conducive to writing. Life in Africa has much of the unexpected, and people are closely involved in each other's lives. I have tried to project its liveliness and interest in my books and to give children in other parts of the world some idea of the life of those in Ghana. I have also tried to write for Ghanaian children about themselves, as in the past they have had to depend on books with foreign backgrounds. Most of the books are about village and forest life, animals and birds. I was brought up in the country, and it is there my main interests lie. Kwaku Ananse the Spider is the Brer Rabbit of Ghana: *Aesop's Fables* are so like the Spider stories that Ghanaian children read them as such. The wind in the willows is the same one that breathes through the palm fronds. It is this universality of children's lore that I try to promote through my writing, hoping it will help to promote mutual understanding in this troubled world.

More recently I have been writing short children's books with African backgrounds and in simple English for publication in Ghana, Nigeria, and Namibia. The cost of books is so high now that African countries cannot afford to import many books from outside Africa. I have also collected and translated some 7,000 Ashanti proverbs which will be printed in the States. A book on Ashanti Goldweights is under publication with the State Publishing Corporation in Ghana.

* * *

Peggy Appiah, first English, then, through her marriage, Ashanti, is in a singularly good position to write stories in English about Ashanti. Other parts of Ghana barely appear, but then why should they? Ashanti itself has an old and complex culture and enough stories to last a few lifetimes. People who live sociably in family and village groups without television and newspapers are apt to be good storytellers, and when one lives among them one can't help picking up the story habit. Appiah has done just that for a double audience in two countries: her stories must be as acceptable in Ghana as they are in England. By now there are thousands of children out there speaking and reading English as their second language but probably finding most English children's books a bit boring and unintelligible—nothing they can connect with.

They must enjoy Appiah's books and so will children who are at all interested in other countries. Her stories often have an element of folklorist fantasy, though *A Smell of Onions* (originally published for adults) is amusingly factual, a tangled tale of village life, very much as it is elsewhere and as it might be told. *Gift of the Mmoatia* in which two little girls, one Ghanaian, the other British, make friends and share joys and troubles, shows both Appiah's gifts and her limitations. In Ghana the wee folk of the deep forest are plausible, but the English fairies are booksy. This is surely because the author doesn't believe in them whereas she can at least suspend disbelief in the strange little Mmoatia who helped the children! Abena's reactions and puzzlements during her English visit are charmingly and beautifully observed, especially her astonishment at the long English evenings. Appiah is very happy with the children in her stories as also with the animals and insects, including Ananse, the important spider who comes into so many West Coast stories, and into her book *Tales of an Ashanti Father,* for people live close to them and would not find it strange to speak their language—nor I think would Peggy Appiah.

—Naomi Mitchison

ARDIZZONE, Edward (Jeffrey Irving)

Nationality: British (originally French; moved to England 1905, became British citizen 1921). **Born:** Haiphong, Ton Kin, French Indo-China (now Vietnam), 16 October 1900. **Education:** Clayesmore School, Iwerne Minster, Dorset, 1913-17; Westminster School of Art, London, 1922-27. **Military Service:** Served in the Royal Artillery, 1939-40; official war artist, 1940-45. **Family:** Married Catherine Anderson in 1929; one daughter and two sons. **Career:** Clerk, Eastern Telegraph Company and other firms, London, 1920-26; instructor in graphic design, Camberwell School of Art, London, 1948-52; instructor in audio-visual aids, UNESCO, Southern India, 1952-53; visiting tutor in etching and lithography, Royal College of Art, London, 1953-60. Individual shows: Bloomsbury Gallery, 1930, Leger Gallery, 1931-36, Nicholson Gallery, 1939, Leicester Galleries, 1948, Mayor Gallery, 1962, Victoria and Albert Museum, 1973, New Grafton Gallery 1975, Illustrator's Art, 1982, and Hunter and Seale Gallery, 1986, all in London; Scottish Arts Council Gallery, Edinburgh, 1979; group shows: London Group, 1935, New English Group, 1936, Royal Society of Painters in Water Colours, 1954, and Royal Academy Summer Exhibition from 1964, all in London. **Awards:** Recipient (for illustration): Library Association Kate Greenaway Medal, 1957. **Member:** Fellow, Society of Industrial Artists; Associate, 1962, and Member, 1970, Royal Academy; Honorary Associate, Royal College of Art; Royal Designer in Industry, Royal Society of Arts, 1974. C.B.E. (Commander, Order of the British Empire), 1971. **Died:** 8 November 1979.

Publications for Children (illustrated by the author)

Fiction

Little Tim and the Brave Sea Captain. London and New York, Oxford University Press, 1936; revised edition, London, Oxford University Press, and New York, Walck, 1955.

Lucy Brown and Mr. Grimes. London and New York, Oxford University Press, 1937; revised edition, London, Bodley Head, 1970; New York, Walck, 1971.

Tim and Lucy Go to Sea. London and New York, Oxford University Press, 1938; revised edition, London, Oxford University Press, and New York, Walck, 1958.

Nicholas and the Fast-Moving Diesel. London, Eyre and Spottiswoode, 1947; New York, Walck, 1959.

Paul, The Hero of the Fire. London, Penguin, 1948; Boston, Houghton Mifflin, 1949; revised edition, London, Constable, 1962; New York, Walck, 1963.

Tim to the Rescue. London and New York, Oxford University Press, 1949.

Tim and Charlotte. London and New York, Oxford University Press, 1951.

Tim in Danger. London and New York, Oxford University Press, 1953.

Tim All Alone. London, Oxford University Press, 1956; New York, Walck, 1961.

Johnny the Clockmaker. London, Oxford University Press, and New York, Walck, 1960.

Tim's Friend Towser. London, Oxford University Press, and New York, Walck, 1962.

Peter the Wanderer. London, Oxford University Press, 1963; New York, Walck, 1964.

Diana and Her Rhinoceros. London, Bodley Head, and New York, Walck, 1964.

Sarah and Simon and No Red Paint. London, Constable, 1965; New York, Delacorte Press, 1966.

Tim and Ginger. London, Oxford University Press, and New York, Walck, 1965.

Tim to the Lighthouse. London, Oxford University Press, and New York, Walck, 1968.

Johnny's Bad Day. London, Bodley Head, 1970; as *The Wrong Side of the Bed,* New York, Doubleday, 1970.
Tim's Last Voyage. London, Bodley Head, 1972; New York, Walck, 1973.
Ship's Cook Ginger. London, Bodley Head, 1977; New York, Macmillan, 1978.

Other

Editor, *Ardizzone's Hans Andersen: Fourteen Classic Tales,* translated by Stephen Corrin. London, Deutsch, 1978; New York, Atheneum, 1979.
Editor, *Ardizzone's English Fairy Tales: Twelve Classic Tales.* London, Deutsch, 1980.

Publications for Adults

Other

Baggage to the Enemy. London, Murray, 1941.
The Young Ardizzone: An Autobiographical Fragment. London, Studio Vista, and New York, Macmillan, 1970.
Diary of a War Artist. London, Bodley Head, 1974.
Visiting Dieppe. London, Warren, 1981.
Indian Diary 1952-53. London, Bodley Head, 1984.

* * *

Bibliography: "Edward Ardizzone: A Preliminary Hand-List of His Illustrated Books, 1929-1970" by Brian Alderson, in *The Private Library* (Pinner, Middlesex), Spring 1972.

Critical Studies: *Edward Ardizzone, Artist and Illustrator* by Gabriel White, London, Bodley Head, 1979, New York, Schocken, 1980; *Edward Ardizzone* (exhibition catalogue), Edinburgh, Scottish Arts Council, 1979; *My Father and Edward Ardizzone: A Lasting Friendship* by Edward Booth-Clibborn, London, Hardy, 1983.

Illustrator: *In a Glass Darkly* by Sheridan Le Fanu, 1929; *The Library* by George Crabbe, 1930; *The Mediterranean* edited by Paul Bloomfield, 1935; *Tom, Dick, and Harriet* by A. Neil Lyons, 1937; *Great Expectations,* 1939, *Bleak House,* 1955, *David Copperfield,* 1955, and *Short Stories,* 1971, all by Charles Dickens; *The Local,* 1939, *Back to the Local,* 1949, *Londoners,* 1951, and *Showmen and Suckers,* 1951, all by Maurice Gorham; *Mimff,* 1939, *Mimff in Charge,* 1949, *Mimff Takes Over,* 1954, and *Mimff-Robinson,* 1958, all by H.J. Kaeser; *My Uncle Silas,* 1939, and *Sugar for the Horse,* 1957, both by H.E. Bates; *The Battle of France* by André Maurois, 1940; *The Road to Bordeaux* by C. Denis Freeman and Douglas Cooper, 1940; *Peacock Pie,* 1946, *The Story of Joseph,* 1958, *The Story of Moses,* 1959, *The Story of Samuel,* 1960, and *Stories from the Bible,* 1961, all by Walter de la Mare; *The Poems of François Villon,* 1946; *Hey Nonny Yes* edited by Hallam Fordham, 1947; *The Pilgrim's Progress* by John Bunyan, 1947; *Three Brothers and a Lady* by Margaret Black, 1947; *The True and Pathetic History of Desbarollda the Waltzing Mouse,* 1947, and *The Land of Green Ginger,* 1966, both by Noel Langley; *Camberwell School of Arts and Crafts Jubilee,* 1948; *Charles Dickens Birthday Book* edited by Enid Dickens Hawksley, 1948; *The Otterbury Incident,* 1948, and *Christmas Eve,* 1954, both by C. Day Lewis; *Somebody's Rocking My Dreamboat* by Noel Langley and Hazel Pynegar, 1949; *The Tale of Ali Baba* translated by J.C. Mardrus and E. Powys, 1949; *The Comedies* by Shakespeare, 1951; *The Blackbird in the Lilac,* 1952, *Pigeons and Princesses,* 1956, *Prefabulous Animiles,* 1957, *The Wandering Moon,* 1957, *Exploits of Don Quixote, Retold,* 1959, *Titus in Trouble,* 1959, *Hurdy-Gurdy,* 1961, *Sailor Rumbelow and Britannia,* 1962, *Sailor Rumbelow and Other Stories,* 1962, *The Story of Jackie Thimble,* 1964, *Three Tall Tales,* 1964, *The Secret Shoemakers,* 1966, *Rhyming Will,* 1967, *The Angel and the Donkey,* 1969, *How the Moon Began,* 1971, *Complete Poems for Children,* 1973, *The Lion That Flew,* 1974, *More Prefabulous Animiles,* 1975, *Arcadian Ballads,* 1977, and *The James Reeves Story Book,* 1978, all by James Reeves; *The Modern Prometheus* by Zareh Nubar, 1952; *The Warden,* 1952, and *Barchester Towers,* 1953, both by Anthony Trollope; *The Fantastic Tale of the Plucky Sailor and the Postage Stamp* by Stephen Corrin, 1954; *The Newcomes,* 1954, and *Henry Esmond,* 1956, both by W.M. Thackeray; *The Little Bookroom,* 1955, *Jim at the Corner,* 1958, *Eleanor Farjeon's Book,* 1960, *Italian Peepshow,* 1960, *Mrs. Malone,* 1962, *Kaleidoscope,* 1963, and *The Old Nurse's Stocking-Basket,* 1965, all by Eleanor Farjeon; *The Minnow on the Say* by Philippa Pearce, 1955; *Pictures on the Pavement* by G.W. Stonier, 1955; *The Suburban Child* by James Kenward, 1955; *Sun Slower Sun Faster* by Meriol Trevor, 1955; *Marshmallow* by Clare Newberry, 1956; *Hunting with Mr. Jorrocks* by R.S. Surtees, edited by Lionel Gough, 1956; *St. Luke's Life of Christ* translated by J.B. Phillips, 1956; *A Stickful of Nonpareil* by George Scurfield, 1956; *Ding Dong Bell* by Peter Young, 1957; *Lottie,* 1957, *Elfrida and the Pig,* 1959, and *The Stuffed Dog,* 1967, all by John Symonds; *The School in Our Village* by Joan M. Goldman, 1957; *Brief to Counsel,* 1958, *Know about English Law,* 1965, and *Learn about English Law,* 1974, all by Henry Cecil; *Pinky-Pye,* 1958, *The Witch Family,* 1960, *The Alley,* 1964, *Miranda the Great,* 1967, and *The Tunnel of Hugsy Goode,* 1972, all by Eleanor Estes; *Father Brown Stories* by G.K. Chesterton, 1959; *The Godstone and the Blackymor* by T.H. White, 1959; *Holiday Trench,* 1959, and *Kidnappers at Coombe,* 1960, both by Joan Ballantyne; *The Nine Lives of Island Mackenzie* by Ursula Moray Williams, 1959; *Boyhoods of Great Composers* by Catherine Gough, 2 vols., 1960, 1963; *Merry England* by Cyril Ray, 1960; *The Penny Fiddle,* 1960, and *Ann at Highwood Hall,* 1964, both by Robert Graves; *The Rib of the Green Umbrella* by Naomi Mitchison, 1960; *The Adventures of Huckleberry Finn,* 1961, and *The Adventures of Tom Sawyer,* 1961, both by Mark Twain; *Down in the Cellar* by Nicholas Stuart Gray, 1961; *Folk Songs of England, Ireland, Scotland, and Wales* edited by William Cole, 1961; *The Island of Fish in the Trees,* 1962, *The Land of Right Up and Down,* 1964, and *Kali and the Golden Mirror,* 1967, all by Eva-Lis Wuorio; *J.M. Barrie's Peter Pan* by Eleanor Graham, 1962; *London since 1912* by John Hayes, 1962; *Naughty Children* edited by Christianna Brand, 1962, and *Nurse Matilda,* 1964, *Nurse Matilda Goes to Town,* 1967, and *Nurse Matilda Goes to Hospital,* 1974, all by Brand; *A Ring of Bells* by John Betjeman, 1962; *The Singing Cupboard,* 1962, and *Swanhilda-of-the-Swans,* 1964, both by Dana Faralla; *The Story of Let's Make an Opera!* by Eric Crozier, 1962; *Stig of the Dump* by Clive King, 1963; *Hello, Elephant,* 1964, and *The Muffletumps,* 1966, both by Jan Wahl; *The Thirty-Nine Steps* by John Buchan, 1964; *The Milldale Riot* by Freda P. Nichols, 1965; *Old Perisher* by Diana Ross, 1965; *Timothy's Song* by William J. Lederer, 1965; *The Truants and Other Poems* by John Walsh, 1965; *The Year Round* by

Leonard Clark, 1965; *Daddy-Long-Legs* by Jean Webster, 1966; *The Little Girl and the Tiny Doll,* 1966, and *The Night Ride,* 1973, both by Aingelda Ardizzone; *The Dragon* by Archibald Marshall, 1966; *The Eleanor Farjeon Book: A Tribute,* 1966; *The Growing Summer* by Noel Streatfeild, 1966; *Long Ago When I Was Young* by E. Nesbit, 1966; *In Search of Elsie Piddock* by Denys Blakelock, 1967; *A Likely Place* by Paula Fox, 1967; *Travels with a Donkey in the Cevennes,* 1967, and *Home from Sea,* 1970, both by Robert Louis Stevenson; *Robinson Crusoe* by Daniel Defoe, 1968; *Upsidedown Willie,* 1968, *Special Branch Willie,* 1969, and *Fire-Brigade Willie,* 1970, all by Dorothy Clewes; *Do You Remember What Happened* by Jean Chapman, 1969; *A Riot of Quiet* by Virginia Sicotte, 1969; *Dick Whittington, Retold* by Kathleen Lines, 1970; *The Old Ballad of the Babes in the Wood,* 1972; *Rain, Rain Don't Go Away* by Shirley Morgan, 1972; *The Second-Best Children in the World* by Mary Lavin, 1972; *The Little Fire Engine,* 1973, *The Little Train,* 1973, *The Little Steam Roller,* 1974, and *The Little Horse Bus,* 1974, all by Graham Greene; *Ardizzone's Kilvert* edited by William Plomer, abridged by Elizabeth Divine, 1976; *A Child's Christmas in Wales* by Dylan Thomas, 1978; *Twelve Fairy Tales from the Collection of Joseph Jacobs,* 1986.

* * *

For more than 50 years, Edward Ardizzone's books have been loved by succeeding generations of children all over the world. One of the most attractive aspects of his work is its presentation of an idiosyncratic, and instantly recognizable, view of life, always affectionate and sympathetic without ever lapsing into sentimentality. This sympathetic vision springs from Ardizzone's readiness to enter into the texture of his characters' experience—a readiness exemplified in the precise observation of apparently casual detail which authenticates his draughtsmanship. The purity and directness of his vision and insight reveal something childlike in his own nature.

His writing is similarly perceptive and authentic. The seagoing adventures of Tim, his most famous creation, have many elements of romance—storm, shipwreck, last-minute rescue. At the same time, however, they are full of the homely detail of shipboard life. Tim may be the hero, but he is not immune from sea sickness, and we see him peeling potatoes and scrubbing floors as well as detecting fires and saving the ship's cat. The narrative is always strong and economical; the illustrations, with their comic-strip captions, are never merely ornamental, and the writing always carries the story forward. This is clearly an important factor in the popularity of the tales.

But Ardizzone did not simply tell tales. His work is an unpretentious celebration of certain human qualities and moral values. Most children find it easy to identify with the heroes and heroines, who are all (especially the boys) characterised by self-reliance, courage, and fortitude in adversity. They are often lonely and far from home. Their plans and hopes are threatened, whether by natural disaster or by the scorn and bullying of hostile figures (such as the taunting schoolboys in *Johnny the Clockmaker*). But they have perseverance and self-confidence, and there are always allies as well as enemies. The hero triumphs through his own doggedness and through the loyalty and affection that bind him to his friends. After the wildest exploits, he returns to the familiarity of home, and the young reader, having lived through perilous voyages, is left with a reassuring sense of warmth and companionship. It is as if we are told: Life starts at home and, after a journey of adventure, conflict, and reconciliation, ends there.

—James Reeves

ARMITAGE, Ronda (Jacqueline)

Nationality: New Zealander. **Born:** Ronda Jacqueline Minnitt, Kaikoura, 11 March 1943. **Education:** St. Cuthbert's College, Auckland; University of Auckland, 1963, 1969; Massey University, Palmerston North, 1965; Hamilton Teachers College, Diploma of Teaching, 1963. **Family:** Married the artist David Armitage in 1966; one son and one daughter. **Career:** Infant teacher, Duvauchelles, 1964-66, and Auckland, 1968-69; supply teacher, London, 1966; adviser on children's books, Dorothy Butler Ltd., booksellers, Auckland, 1970-71; moved to Britain, 1974; assistant librarian, Lewes Priory Comprehensive School, Sussex, 1976-77; member of the supply teaching staff, East Sussex County Council, from 1978. Working as a family therpaist. **Award:** New Zealand Library Association Esther Glen award, 1978. **Address:** Old Tiles Cottage, Church Lane, Hellingly, East Sussex BN27 4HA, England.

PUBLICATIONS FOR CHILDREN (ILLUSTRATED BY DAVID ARMITAGE)

Fiction

The Lighthouse Keeper's Lunch. London, Deutsch, 1977.
The Trouble with Mr. Harris. London, Deutsch, 1978.
Don't Forget Matilda. London, Deutsch, 1979.
The Bossing of Josie. London, Deutsch, 1980; as *The Birthday Spell,* London, Hippo, 1981.
Ice Creams for Rosie. London, Deutsch, 1981.
One Moonlit Night. London, Deutsch, 1983.
Grandma Goes Shopping. London, Deutsch, 1984.
The Lighthouse Keeper's Catastrophe. London, Deutsch, 1986.
The Lighthouse Keeper's Rescue. London, Deutsch, 1989.
When Dad Did the Washing. London, Deutsch, 1990; New York, Puffin, 1992.
Looking After Chocolates. London, Deutsch, 1992.
A Quarrel of Koalas. London, Deutsch, 1992; as *Harry Hates Shopping,* New York, Scholastic, 1993.
The Lighthouse Keeper's Picnic. London, Scholastic, 1994.
The Lighthouse Keeper's Cat. London, Scholastic, 1995.
Flora and the Strawberry Red Birthday Party. New Zealand, Penguin, 1997.

Other

Drinking. Hove, Sussex, Wayland, 1987.
New Zealand. Hove, Sussex, Wayland, 1988.

*

Ronda Armitage comments:

To me, the fascination of creating a picture book lies in making something that will work in several different ways. I need to enjoy writing it, but, equally, the story needs to work in terms of the young child's experience. Unlike books for older children, picture books are for reading aloud, so the story must flow smoothly and each sentence needs to be rhythmic. This form of writing is perhaps more akin to poetry than to prose in the sense that each word has to play its part—after all, there aren't very many of them. And then there is that other vital ingredient—that other half—the illustrations. Ideally these should complement the text, filling it out, adding those essential details that, if included in the text, would make the story too unwieldy for the young.

* * *

Ronda Armitage has the knack of being able to write simple and enjoyable picture book texts, which are illustrated with matching ingenuous charm by her husband, David. The essential quality of these books is their focus on the child reader. In an age when so much in this genre seems calculated to impress sophisticated adults, it is refreshing to encounter books that are so clearly intended for young children and that keep this focus always in mind.

In each of Armitage's amusing stories, a problem is posed and then solved. In *The Lighthouse Keeper's Lunch,* seagulls steal food from the picnic basket that Mrs. Grinling sends daily to her husband along a high wire suspended between her mainland cottage and the lighthouse on the rocks. Knowing how interested children are in food, the author is careful to specify the contents each day, and the joke is that every meal is a gourmet's delight—a banquet, indeed, for a solo diner—rather than mere sandwiches. Particularly droll is her attempt to send her pet cat, Hamish, along the wire in another basket as a deterrent to the marauding gulls: "Sadly, flying did not agree with Hamish. His fur stood on end when the basket swayed, his whiskers drooped when he peered down at the wet, blue sea and he felt much too sick even to notice the seagulls, let alone scare them away from the lunch."

In an equally droll sequel, *The Lighthouse Keeper's Catastrophe* (itself a pun, Hamish the cat being the cause of the problem) a nervous Mr. Grinling is forced to take a ride on a precarious high wire himself to reach the lighthouse in stormy weather. He is getting old and is almost forced to retire, but manages to keep his job after saving a beached whale in *The Lighthouse Keeper's Rescue.*

In *The Trouble with Mr. Harris,* the problem is the impatient new postmaster who seems unfriendly toward the people of Hogeton. A little girl shows her fellow townsfolk that he is really a shy person, unused to slow village ways. The story ends, typically, with a tea party.

Grandma Goes Shopping is a cumulative tale, curiously redolent of some of Pat Hutchins' work, with lots of repetition and an ending ("...and then she set off for home...through the forest...down the hill...into the pond...and got home in time for tea") reminiscent of *Rosie's Walk.*

Some of Armitage's stories deal with comical family situations. Matilda, the subject of *Don't Forget Matilda,* is a baby bear of ebullient personality in a family given to forgetting things—even her name. Harry and Matilda, two young koalas who misbehave in public while out shopping with their mother in *A Quarrel of Koalas,* soon find that she is able to play that game too, embarrassing them even more. In *Watch the Baby, Daisy,* Mum tells her literal-minded daughter to do just that: Daisy *does* watch the baby, Amy, doing everything she shouldn't. *When Dad Did the Washing* shows how incompetent the father is when left in charge while Mum is out.

Although texts by Ronda Armitage are simple, they are never simplistic. Her style is distinguished by fluid, literate sentences that, rather than condescend, happily include words like "brusque" or "irascible" when these are ones that best suit their context. While being entertaining and child-centered, her stories still manage to enrich and delight.

—Walter McVitty

ARMSTRONG, Richard

Pseudonym: Cam Renton. **Nationality:** British. **Born:** Northumberland, 18 June 1903. **Education:** Walbottle Primary School, 1908-16. **Family:** Married in 1926; one son. **Career:** Worked as an errand boy, labourer, greaser, and crane driver in steelworks, Tyneside, 1916-19, typist, secretary, architect's assistant, and undertaker's labourer, 1937-54. **Military Service:** Sailor and radio operator, Merchant Navy, 1920-37; **Awards:** Library Association Carnegie Medal, 1949. **Died:** 1986.

Publications for Children

Fiction

The Mystery of Obadiah, illustrated by Marjorie Sankey. London, Dent, 1943.

Sabotage at the Forge, illustrated by L.P. Lupton. London, Dent, 1946.

Sea Change, illustrated by M. Leszczynski. London, Dent, 1948.

The Whinstone Drift, illustrated by Michael A. Charlton. London, Dent, 1951.

Wanderlust: Voyage of a Little White Monkey, illustrated by Frederick K. Crooke. London, Faber, 1952.

Danger Rock, illustrated by M. Leszczynski. London, Dent, 1955; as *Cold Hazard,* Boston, Houghton Mifflin, 1956.

The Lost Ship: A Caribbean Adventure, illustrated by Edward Osmond. London, Dent, 1956; New York, Day, 1958.

No Time for Tankers, illustrated by Reg Gray. London, Dent, 1958; New York, Day, 1959.

Another Six. Oxford, Blackwell, 1959.

The Lame Duck, illustrated by D.G. Valentine. London, Dent, 1959; as *Ship Afire!,* New York, Day, 1961.

Before the Wind. Oxford, Blackwell, 1959.

Horseshoe Reef, illustrated by D.G. Valentine. London, Dent, 1960; New York, Duell, 1961.

Out of the Shallows, illustrated by D.G. Valentine. London, Dent, 1961.

Trial Trip, illustrated by D.G. Valentine. London, Dent, 1962; New York, Criterion, 1963.

The Ship Stealers (as Cam Renton), illustrated by Val Biro. Penshurst, Kent, Friday Press, 1963.

Island Odyssey, illustrated by Andrew Dodds. London, Dent, 1963; as *Fight for Freedom: An Adventure of World War II,* New York, McKay, 1966.

Big-Head (as Cam Renton), illustrated by Val Biro. Penshurst, Kent, Friday Press, 1964.

The Big Sea, illustrated by Andrew Dodds. London, Dent, 1964; New York, McKay, 1965.
The Greenhorn, illustrated by Roger Payne. London, Nelson, 1965.
The Secret Sea, illustrated by Roger Payne. London, Dent, and New York, McKay, 1966.
The Mutineers, illustrated by Gareth Floyd. London, Dent, and New York, McKay, 1968.
The Albatross, illustrated by Graham Humphreys. London, Dent, and New York, McKay, 1970.

Other

A History of Seafaring:
1. *The Early Mariners.* London, Benn, 1967; New York, Praeger, 1968.
2. *The Discoverers.* London, Benn, 1968; New York, Praeger, 1969.
3. *The Merchantmen.* London, Benn, and New York, Praeger, 1969.

Themselves Alone: The Story of Men in Empty Places. London, Benn, and Boston, Houghton Mifflin, 1972.
Powered Ships: The Beginnings. London, Benn, 1975.

Editor, *Treasure and Treasure Hunters.* London, Hamish Hamilton, and New York, David White, 1969.

Publications for Adults

Novels

The Northern Maid. London, Dent, 1947.
Passage Home. London, Dent, 1952.
Sailor's Luck. London, Dent, 1959.
Storm Path. London, Dent, 1964.

Other

Grace Darling, Maid and Myth. London, Dent, 1965.

*

Richard Armstrong commented:

(1978) My ambition was to be a school teacher, but poverty and the First World War denied me the necessary education, and when the dust settled I did the next best thing and became a writer. This accounts for the didactic element in my books. My aim has been to tell young people groping through the fantasies of adolescence (and anyone else who wants to know) what the real world looks like to me and perhaps a little something of what life is all about. But first I had to provide my family with a roof overhead and three squares a day, so the main body of my work is a compromise between what I wanted to say in it and what my publishers would accept and pay for. From time to time I chanced my arm and wrote a book regardless, but the end result was always another pile of rejection slips, an increase in my overdraft and a frosty letter from my bank manager. Consequently what is considered by competent commentators, unconnected with the publishing trade, to be my best work to date—a novel on faith and three books for boys—remains unpublished and up for grabs.

* * *

The best writers of adventure stories for young people have three particular things to offer: their own experience of action, a straightforward style full of vitality, and a positive attitude to life in general. These qualities are abundantly present in the work of Richard Armstrong. You could add a talent for exciting plots, but these seem to grow naturally from his own experience of action and men.

Some of his early books were about boys in heavy industry, notably *Sabotage at the Forge* and *The Whinstone Drift,* but most of his books concern the sea and ships. Everything he wrote is authentic, based on his knowledge of ships and the men who sail them—as exciting as real-life adventure. Early in his writing career, it was Armstrong's avowed intention to teach young readers something of the crafts and skills of steel workers, miners, and seamen, but the effect is far from didactic; he made all the details so fascinating that one's understanding of them enhances the drama of his stories. One appreciates how much depends on a man's skill and judgment, with moral issues and conflicts of temperament contributing to the tension.

His style makes sensible use of colloquial speech; it is vigorous and descriptive. His strength lay in his complete knowledge of the scene: he was not painting for effect; he was telling it as it is and with a rare feeling for words and the rhythms of language. He credited his readers with intellect as well as feeling, but he was no mandarin writer.

Nor do his plots follow a formula. The plot line emerges from situation and character; no two are the same. Wreckers, salvage, whaling, and war are only a few of his themes. Several books concern youths for whom a voyage full of natural hazards and human conflicts marks an important stage in growing up. There is often an older man, captain or mate perhaps, who wins the boy's respect. Such men are imaginative and humane; their senses and intuition are alert to the pulse of communal feeling on board ship, and they never act without regard to this. They take life and death decisions without any illusions—men of ideals, but realists too.

Often the adventure is shared by two boys of contrasting temperaments, linked by friendship, as in *Horseshoe Reef* and *The Big Sea* (though these are otherwise quite different stories). Others concern the interplay of personalities in a group of young people trapped and held under pressure, as in *Danger Rock;* in *The Mutineers* where they are marooned by choice in what should have been an island paradise; in *The Albatross* where they steal a ketch and make off with treasure trove but cannot land anywhere because of the law—a tragic adventure in which only one survives.

The 15 boys of *The Mutineers* are also fleeing the law. They are all 16 or 17, emigrating to Australia under a training scheme. Having taken over the ship at gunpoint for kicks, they escape the consequences by sailing away in one of the boats. Bo-bo Bolton has the know-how to sail and to find the island, but it is Chick Hinshelwood who emerges as the leader. He is a good organiser, but he imposes his authority brutally and soon shows his appetite for power. Stubby, who could have stood up to him at the beginning, refuses the responsibility of leadership. This is an awesome story of brutalized human beings in a "prison" of their own making.

This book bears striking similarities to William Golding's *Lord of the Flies.* Both books say something of deep interest about human nature and about fear and the lust for power. But their messages are quite different: Armstrong's is positive, Golding's pessimistic. The contrast highlights an essential ingredient in a book for young readers if it is to appeal to them. However sad or horrifying the story, there must be characters with inner strength to identify with. We leave Stubby, Bo-bo, and Jake wiser and stronger for their appalling experiences.

Sea stories used to be a distinct category of fiction and one of the most popular, its readers not confined to the young only. But, regrettably, this is no longer so. Richard Armstrong was undoubtedly one of the masters of the genre (writing for adults as well as young people) and served it well for 20 years. Gradually, though, times and tastes change; he sensed this and reflected these changes. There is nothing old-fashioned about the youths in his later novels. They are less naive, more of a problem to themselves than his early heroes. It is characteristic of Armstrong that he never ceased to respond to each younger generation as it came. This sensitive rapport with his fellow men is at the heart of all his work.

—Gwen Marsh

ARTHUR, Ruth (Mabel)

Nationality: British. **Born:** Glasgow, Scotland, 26 May 1905. **Education:** St. Columbus School, Kilmacolm, Renfrewshire; Froebel Educational Institute, Roehampton, London, Froebel certificate 1926. **Family:** Married Frederick N. Huggins in 1932; two sons and four daughters. **Career:** Froebel kindergarten teacher, Laurel Bank School, Glasgow, 1927-30, and High School, Loughton, Essex, 1930-32. **Died:** 6 March 1979.

Publications for Children

Fiction

Friendly Stories, illustrated by C.F. Christie. London, Harrap, 1932.

The Crooked Brownie [*in Town, at the Seaside*], illustrated by R.M. Turvey. London, Harrap, 3 vols., 1936-42.

Pumpkin Pie. London, Collins, 1938.

Cowslip Mollie. London, Hutchinson, 1949.

Carolina's Holiday and Other Stories, illustrated by Dodie Masterman. London, Harrap, 1957.

The Daisy Cow and Other Stories of the Channel Islands, illustrated by Lucien Lowen. London, Harrap, 1958.

Carolina's Golden Bird and Other Stories, illustrated by Lucien Lowen. London, Harrap, 1958.

A Cottage for Rosemary, illustrated by M. Whitaker. London, Harrap, 1960.

Carolina and Roberto, illustrated by Lucien Lowen. London, Harrap, 1961.

Dragon Summer, illustrated by Margery Gill. London, Hutchinson, 1962; New York, Atheneum, 1963.

Carolina and the Sea Horse, and Other Stories, illustrated by Lucien Lowen. London, Harrap, 1964.

My Daughter Nicola, illustrated by Fermin Rocker. New York, Atheneum, 1965; London, Gollancz, 1966.

A Candle in Her Room, illustrated by Margery Gill. London, Gollancz, and New York, Atheneum, 1966.

Requiem for a Princess, illustrated by Margery Gill. London, Gollancz, and New York, Atheneum, 1967.

Portrait of Margarita, illustrated by Margery Gill. London, Gollancz, and New York, Atheneum, 1968.

The Whistling Boy, illustrated by Margery Gill. London, Gollancz, and New York, Atheneum, 1969.

The Saracen Lamp, illustrated by Margery Gill. London, Gollancz, and New York, Atheneum, 1970.

The Little Dark Thorn, illustrated by Margery Gill. London, Gollancz, and New York, Atheneum, 1971.

The Autumn People, illustrated by Margery Gill. London, Gollancz, and New York, Atheneum, 1973; as *The Autumn Ghosts,* London, Target, 1976.

After Candlemas, illustrated by Margery Gill. London, Gollancz, and New York, Atheneum, 1974; as *Candlemas Mystery,* London, Target, 1976.

On the Wasteland, illustrated by Margery Gill. London, Gollancz, and New York, Atheneum, 1975.

An Old Magic, illustrated by Margery Gill. London, Gollancz, and New York, Atheneum, 1977.

Miss Ghost. London, Gollancz, and New York, Atheneum, 1979.

Other

Mother Goose Stories. London, Collins, 1938.

*

Ruth Arthur commented:

(1978) I write about the intricacies of human relationships and the difficulties of adolescence. In my stories I try to introduce children of 11 and 12 upwards to some of the universal problems of the grown-up world such as adoption, divorce, loneliness, delinquency.

* * *

"I am rather an odd person," confesses Elspeth, the heroine-narrator of Ruth Arthur's *Miss Ghost,* published posthumously. One might say the same about the others. Her heroines are all, if not odd, highly sensitive, unconventional, and often unhappy. Arthur deals in human problems, especially those of adolescent girls. In less skillful hands, her stories might have seemed too much alike. To her concern for the distressed or deprived child, however, the writer added great understanding of the human heart, a strong sense of place, and, above all, exceptional skill in storytelling. Very quietly, avoiding publicity, without subscribing to any contemporary theory, and indeed going against the stream of the literary fashions of her day, she nevertheless made a place for herself among the very best of those writing for the older girl.

Each of Arthur's novels has a girl for the central character who also tells the story. Often the girl is by choice a loner, but in each the solution of her problem lies in involvement with others. Far from showing the child in isolation, the writer always shows the value of the community, whether of a family or a village. Adults play a significant role in each story. Sometimes, in the most successful novels, the action spans several generations. The books deal with social problems, like adoption, broken marriages and the re-marriage of parents, fostering and children in care, but they must be seen as psychological, not sociological novels. Their object is to show the heroine working out her own salvation by discovering herself and others.

Next to the heroine, the most important element in each book is the setting. It may be the Cumbrian mountains—*The Little Dark Thorn*—or Cornwall—*Requiem for a Princess*—or East Anglia—*The Whistling Boy*—or Wales—*A Candle in Her Room;* always the spirit of place exerts a powerful influence. With this concern for places is often associated a feeling for the past which may manifest itself in the supernatural. So Willow in *Requiem for a Princess,* working out her personal problem while staying in an ancient Cornish house, finds herself caught up in the tragedy of a Spanish girl shipwrecked in Elizabethan times. By a neat reversal of the conventional ghost story, *The Saracen Lamp* shows the Lady Melisande, a grass-widow of the Hundred Years War, taking comfort in the visits of Perdita, a ghost from the 20th century.

The reader's involvement in these stories is ensured by Arthur's own concern and by her passionate writing—perhaps one must at times say over-writing. They are stories that demand the closest cooperation from the reader; without this they may become what indeed they may superficially appear to be, "magazine fiction."

Arthur was at her best in two stories with similar settings—west Wales—and similar constructions. *A Candle in Her Room* spans three generations and shows, with great subtlety and delicacy, a conflict of good and evil forces. Three sisters go to live in Pembrokeshire. The eldest, Melissa, gives herself joyously to her new life. The youngest is tolerant and easy-going. The middle girl, Judith, is a malcontent who hates the new life. Her discontent is focused by Dido, a wooden doll found in the house. Dido, one must assume, had belonged to a witch and she is impregnated with evil. Melissa is crippled in an accident, and Judith takes advantage of this to steal her lover, having a child by him. This girl, Dilys, grows up, hated by her mother and father and fostered by Melissa, until, at the beginning of the Second World War, she travels to Poland with her Polish lover. They disappear. Melissa lives on in the big house, alone. After the war she finds herself haunted by dreams of a child. This is Nina, Dilys's daughter, now an orphan living in a refugee camp somewhere in Europe. Her wish to find the child forces Melissa to conquer her disability; she goes to find her grand-niece and brings her home. Back in Wales, Nina finds the wooden doll. Dido's instinct for evil is as strong as ever, but Nina, who has lived through war and its aftermath, is made of tougher stuff than her mother and grandmother. She destroys the doll. Good triumphs! This story, so melodramatic in this summary, is written with deep conviction. It is tightly knit, and the inter-relationship of characters and their commitment to the country in which they live give it great strength. On the right reader it can make a lasting impression.

An Old Magic has a comparable setting and pattern. Again the scene is Wales, and the story links three generations. But the working-out is very different. The writing is atmospheric, but there is less sharpness in the delineation of character. One consequently feels rather less concern for the fortunes of the principals.

Whether the theme is historical or the mechanics supernatural, the essential matter of each of Arthur's novels is self-discovery. Her attractive, wayward, sometimes willful heroines are, each in her own way, learning to distinguish between reality and fantasy. Their problems and their solutions must strike a chord of recognition in many young readers.

—Marcus Crouch

ARUNDEL, Honor (Morfydd)

Nationality: British. **Born:** Llanarmon, Gwynedd, 15 August 1919. **Education:** Hayes Court, Kent; Somerville College, Oxford, 1938-39. **Family:** Married Alex McCrindle in 1952; three daughters and one stepdaughter. **Career:** Worked as a typist, journalist, engineer, and film, radio and theatre critic. **Died:** 8 June 1973.

Publications for Children

Fiction

Green Street, illustrated by Eileen Armitage. London, Hamish Hamilton, 1966; New York, Hawthorn, 1970.

The High House, illustrated by Eileen Armitage. London, Hamish Hamilton, 1966; New York, Meredith Press, 1968.

Emma's Island. London, Hamish Hamilton, 1968; New York, Hawthorn, 1970.

The Two Sisters. London, Heinemann, 1968; New York, Meredith Press, 1969.

The Amazing Mr. Prothero, illustrated by Jane Paton. London, Hamish Hamilton, 1968; Nashville, Nelson, 1972.

The Longest Weekend. London, Hamish Hamilton, 1969; New York, Nelson, 1970.

The Girl in the Opposite Bed. London, Hamish Hamilton, 1970; New York, Nelson, 1971.

Emma in Love. London, Hamish Hamilton, 1970; Nashville, Nelson, 1972.

The Terrible Temptation. London, Hamish Hamilton, and New York, Nelson, 1971.

A Family Failing. London, Hamish Hamilton, and Nashville, Nelson, 1972.

The Blanket Word. London, Hamish Hamilton, and Nashville, Nelson, 1973; as *Love Is a Blanket Word,* New York, Scholastic, 1976.

Publications for Adults

Play

Radio Play: *The Home Game,* 1960.

Other

The Freedom of Art. London, Lawrence and Wishart, 1965.

Editor, with Maurice Carpenter and Jack Lindsay, *New Lyrical Ballads.* London, Editions Poetry, 1945.

* * *

In the late 1960s and early 1970s, books for adolescents or "new adults" were finding their bearings in the gap between "popular" fiction—chiefly magazine stories for girls—and novels that laid claim to the high seriousness of "literature." There was a potential readership of competent, wordly-wise yet sensitive teenagers (again, mostly girls), who needed variety in their reading matter.

They wanted books that took seriously their growing awareness of the complexities of emotions and events and that did not give them moral instruction but, instead, sympathetic understanding of the predicaments that come with new freedoms. In this mid-20th-century development in writing for the young, Honor Arundel's novels are something of a landmark. They can be linked, in theme and treatment, to the kinds of writing that the women's movement in publishing has brought into prominence. They also show many of the preoccupations and much of the feeling tone of the 1960s.

Arundel's response to the demand for "realistic" stories was to avoid the mawkishness of formula fiction while using some of its oldest scenes: sick beds, family failings, and amorous encounters. She explores the ambivalences and ambiguities of moral dilemmas, especially those that arise in near-adult personal relationships. She exploits, with sensibility and good sense, new pains and awarenesses. She links adolescence and early childhood, which it resembles (the stories all have young children too), the pains of parenthood and the loss of innocence (and virginity). The heroines and their consorts have their families whose goodness is crushing or whose dependability is uncertain, but all are recognisable. Somehow the girls must spring the family trap until they are released by self-knowledge and less self-absorbed loving and caring. The seriousness and depth of the author's motivations are balanced by a wise good humour that constantly treads through the inevitable dumps that attend adolescent egocentrism. A preponderance of older Scottish worthies is offset by a number of unconventional artists who are seen as hardworking and hungry. The young stand poised in the middle, tugged by loyalties and attractions, by ideals and the inevitable realism of having to earn a living.

The plots move at a brisk pace and are conspicuously circumstantial so as to pack in enough significant details of contemporary living. Foreign holidays with music festivals, Highland jaunts and long train journeys, unexpected lavish generosity—all can be accounted for by the providentiality of rich and generous friends. Yet the heroines experience the common hazards of their generation, with examinations and first love vying for attention, despair and delight alternating over a weekend. Eileen (*The Longest Weekend*) has most to cope with: too-understanding parents and a three-year-old daughter. Jan (*The Terrible Temptation; The Blanket Word*) longs for order, calm, detachment, but is shaken by family demand and uncertainty. Emma, the best-known, has a bumpy course with her artist aunt and gifted brother. All of them long to be petted and indulged as the teenage culture suggests they should be. They want to bend others to their will and the world to their desires. But they are saved by a core of inner strength that grows out of their very female resilience that enables them to resist the seduction of males whose ambitions do not include them and still be able to come to understand the need for collaborative partnership.

It is now possible to see more clearly the social criticism in these novels and to appreciate a quite clean break in style with much writing for the young in the previous decade. The text on the page is "readerly" with its untagged dialogue and first-person narration which gives the teller full egotistical scope. Yet Honor Arundel's authorial ease is deceptive, as many imitators have discovered, and re-readings re-establish the regard with which these stories may still be held.

—Margaret Meek

ASARE, Meshack (Yaw)

Nationality: Ghanaian. **Born:** Nyankumasi, 18 September 1945. **Education:** University of Science and Technology, Kumasi; University of Wisconsin, Madison; School of Journalism and Television, Berkshire, England. **Family:** Married Rose Tachie Menson in 1969; four children. **Career:** Teacher in elementary school, Tema, 1966-68, and at Lincoln Community School, Accra, 1969-79. From 1979 art director and illustrator, Educational Press and Manufacturers, Accra. **Awards:** National Book award (Ghana), 1980; Noma award, 1982. **Address:** c/o Educational Press and Manufacturers, P.O. Box 9184, Airport, Accra, Ghana.

Publications for Children (illustrated by the author)

Fiction

Tawia Goes to Sea. Accra, Ghana Publishing, 1970.
I Am Kofi. Accra, Ghana Publishing, 1972.
Mansa Helps at Home. Accra, Ghana Publishing, 1972.
The Brassman's Secret. Accra, Educational Press, 1981.
The Canoe's Story. Accra, Three Brothers and Cousins, 1982.
Chipo and the Bird on the Hill: A Tale of Ancient Zimbabwe. Harare, Zimbabwe Publishing House, 1984.
Cat in Search of a Friend. Brooklyn, Kane Miller, 1986.
Halima. London, Macmillan, 1992.
The Frightened Thief. London, Heinemann, 1993.

*

Illustrator: *Akousa in Brazil* by Alero and Cecile McHardy, 1970; *Bury My Bones but Keep My Words: African Tales for Retelling* by Tony Fairman, 1992.

* * *

Meshack Asare is an imaginative storyteller and talented artist who skillfully weaves cultural traditions and daily realities of life into picture stories for African children.

Some of Asare's earliest stories are school books for younger children about commonplace daily activities in which the illustrations provide the African context. *I Am Kofi* focuses on a boy's household chores, such as carrying water, sweeping the floor, and fanning a fire, while *Mansa Helps at Home* focuses on a girl's activities, including cooking, washing clothes, and feeding a younger sibling.

Asare illustrated *Cat in Search of a Friend,* his picture story for younger children, in the distinctive style that he had developed over the last two decades. This story, based on oral tradition, tells how cat sought protection from many animals, including monkey, lion, elephant, and rhino, as well as man, only to find that she is capable of being her own master.

The Brassman's Secret received the Noma award for African writing, the only children's book to receive this honor. In this highly original story, the boy hero helps his father make goldweights, a process depicted in both words and detailed illustrations. During a celebration, the hero falls asleep and in his dream asks a goldweight to tell its secret. When it does so, it reveals its historical significance and symbolism. The dream is both exciting and frightening and teaches the hero the lesson "Learn from the past."

A similar blend of cultural history and contemporary reality is found in *Chipo and the Bird on the Hill,* a book about Zimbabwe. The story focuses on a girl who listens to tales of the past about Zimbabwe and wants to learn where the Great Bird of legend went. The heroine finds a young boy to take her to see the stone bird and in the process sees weaving and iron smelting. She also witnesses ceremonies—imaginatively reconstructed in the story and illustrations—associated with Zimbabwe. Like Asare's other books published in Africa, this one demonstrates that excellent illustrations in picture books do not need to be in color.

Tawia Goes to Sea and *The Canoe's Story* are about fishing in southern Ghana. *The Canoe's Story* is a first-person narrative by a Wawa tree about its life in the forest; its feelings of pride and pleasure about the way it was cut down, carved into a canoe and transported to the sea; and its response to a new life among its canoe neighbors and the men and boys who use it for work and give it the new name "Never leave me." The canoe likes its life at the sea coast because in the forest no one ever liked and cared for it as do the people at the coast, who help it travel with sails and a motor and bring it many offerings. The illustrations complement the text, providing the coastal setting of the action.

Tawia Goes to Sea is located more specifically in a fishing village near Accra. The hero is too young to go to sea, but he carefully observes the fishermen and their boats and the women who collect fish to sell. Using knowledge acquired from these observations Tawia makes a toy canoe of coconuts and launches it in the sea, only to have it swamped by a wave. The fishermen think Tawia is clever and promise to take him with them, and Tawia goes home and dreams of riding out to sea.

Asare's picture stories skillfully incorporate the cultural content of specific African settings in a manner that makes them widespread in their appeal to African children regardless of their cultural background. Moreover, his original and effective style of illustration can be reproduced on equipment available in Africa, thus serving as a model for illustrators of African-published children's books.

—Nancy J. Schmidt

ASCH, Frank

Nationality: American. **Born:** Somerville, New Jersey, 6 August 1946. **Education:** Cooper Union, New York, B.A. 1968. **Career:** Has worked as a Montessori school teacher and in children's theatre.

Publications for Children (illustrated by the author)

Fiction

George's Store. New York, McGraw Hill, 1969.
Linda. New York, McGraw Hill, 1969.
Elvira Everything. New York, Harper, 1970.
The Blue Balloon. New York, McGraw Hill, 1971.
Yellow, Yellow, illustrated by Mark Alan Stamaty. New York, McGraw Hill, 1971.
Rebecka. New York, Harper, 1971.
I Met a Penguin. New York, McGraw Hill, 1972.
In the Eye of the Teddy. New York, Harper, 1973.
Gia and the Hundred Dollars' Worth of Bubble Gum. New York, McGraw Hill, 1974.
Good Lemonade, illustrated by Marie Zimmerman. New York and London, Watts, 1976.
Monkey Face. New York, Parents' Magazine Press, 1977; revised edition as *Bread and Honey,* 1981.
MacGoose's Grocery, illustrated by James Marshall. New York, Dial Press, 1978; London, Kestrel, 1979.
Moon Bear. New York, Scribner, 1978.
Turtle Tale. New York, Dial Press, 1978.
Popcorn. New York, Parents' Magazine Press, 1979.
Running with Rachel, with Jan Asch, photographs by Jan Asch and Robert Michael Buslow. New York, Dial Press, 1979.
Sand Cake. New York, Parents' Magazine Press, 1979; London, Viking Kestrel, 1980.
The Last Puppy. Englewood Cliffs, New Jersey, Prentice Hall, 1980; London, Evans, 1981; New York, Little Simon, 1989.
Starbaby. New York, Scribner, 1980.
Goodnight, Horsey. Englewood Cliffs, New Jersey, Prentice Hall, 1981.
Just Like Daddy. Englewood Cliffs, New Jersey, Prentice Hall, 1981; London, Transworld, 1984.
Happy Birthday Moon. Englewood Cliffs, New Jersey, Prentice Hall, 1982; London, Hodder and Stoughton, 1984.
Milk and Cookies. New York, Parents' Magazine Press, 1982.
Moon Cake. Englewood Cliffs, New Jersey, Prentice Hall, 1983; London, Hodder and Stoughton, 1984.
Moongame. Englewood Cliffs, New Jersey, Prentice Hall, 1984; London, Hodder and Stoughton, 1985.
Pearl's Promise. New York, Delacorte Press, 1984; London, Corgi, 1988.
Skyfire. Englewood Cliffs, New Jersey, Prentice Hall, 1984; London, Hodder and Stoughton, 1985.
Bear Shadow. Englewood Cliffs, New Jersey, Prentice Hall, 1985; London, Hodder and Stoughton, 1986.
Bear's Bargain. Englewood Cliffs, New Jersey, Prentice Hall, 1985; London, Hodder and Stoughton, 1986.
Goodbye House. Englewood Cliffs, New Jersey, Prentice Hall, 1986; London, Hodder and Stoughton, 1987.
I Can Blink. New York, Crown, 1986; London, Picture Corgi, 1989.
I Can Roar. New York, Crown, 1986; London, Picture Corgi, 1989.
Pearl's Pirates. New York, Delacorte Press, 1987.
Oats and Wild Apples. New York, Holiday House, 1988.
Journey to Terezor. New York, Holiday House, 1989.
Baby in the Box. New York, Holiday House, 1989.
Here Comes the Cat! = Siuda idet kot!, with Vladimir Vagin. New York, Scholastic, 1989.
Dear Brother, with Vladimir Vagin. New York, Scholastic, 1991.
Little Fish, Big Fish. New York, Scholastic, 1992.
Short Train, Long Train. New York, Scholastic, 1992.
Moondance. New York, Scholastic, 1993.
The Flower Faerie, with Vladimir Vagin. New York, Scholastic, 1993.
Moonbear's Books. New York, Simon & Schuster, 1993.
Moonbear's Canoe. New York, Simon & Schuster, 1993.
Moonbear's Friend. New York, Simon Schuster, 1993.
Moonbear. New York, Simon Schuster, 1993.
Insects from Outer Space, with Vladimir Vagin, illustrated by Vladimir Vagin. New York, Scholastic, 1994.

The Earth and I. San Diego, California, Gulliver, 1994.
Hands Around Lincoln School. New York, Scholastic, 1994.
Water. San Diego, Harcourt Brace, 1995.
Up River, photographs by Ted Levin and Steve Lehmer. New York, Simon & Schuster, 1995.
Moonbear's Pet. New York, Simon & Schuster, 1997.
Barnyard Lullaby. New York, Simon & Schuster, 1998.
Good Night, Baby Bear. San Diego, Harcourt Brace, 1998.
Baby Bird's First Nest. San Diego, Harcourt Brace, 1999.

Poetry

City Sandwich. New York, Greenwillow, 1978.
Country Pie. New York, Greenwillow, 1979.
The Alphabet Zoo, illustrated by Lee Lee Brazeal. Illinois, Scott Foresman, 1989.
Sawgrass Poems: A View of the Everglades, photographs by Ted Levin. San Diego, Harcourt Brace, 1996.
Cactus Poems, photographs by Ted Levin. San Diego, Harcourt Brace, 1998.

Other

Little Devil's ABC [*1,2,3*] (readers). New York, Scribner, 2 vols., 1979.
One Man Show (autobiography), photographs by Jan Asch. Katonah, New York, R.C. Owen, 1997.

* * *

To Frank Asch, childhood and literature are equivalents. Like the age group that supports his expansive output, the writings manifest an aspiring restlessness, abrupt changes of direction, and an acute, if brief, fascination with a variety of ventures. There are realms of revelation and worlds of concealment, areas of enchantment alongside oodles of the ordinary. Asch is distinguished for the brevity of his texts, but he has shown himself capable of composing novels as well.

One recent undertaking, *Oats and Wild Apples,* balances the delights of the familiar with those that dwell among the shadows. A playful calf is coaxed by a fawn to try those pleasures that lie beyond the pasture fence. Nudging frogs and feasting upon wild apples prove blissful ventures, but the dark side of the forest, particularly the predators ("terrible only if they catch you"), is the source of a discomfiting awareness. Besides, the familiarity of the farm provides a security that quite offsets the sameness that the child-spirit tries to go beyond. The anxious calf returns to his mother, whom the approaching darkness has driven into the barn where light and the farmer-supplied oats provide solace from the shadows.

Even Fawn, child of the forest, enjoys the oats and the rest of what to him is altogether unfamiliar. He is offered the opportunity to dwell forever with his newfound friend, but he has no chance to ponder the invitation, as Mother Deer summons him at the barn door, and the two disappear into the shadows which for them contain all the delights of the ordinary. Light and dark, sun and shade hold treasures for discovery, and the contrast itself underlies the appealing entities that emerge from each of the opposites. But their dominion must be supreme and separate. The subjects of their respective realms have, however, the right from time to time to move from one to the other. And it appears to be the restless heritage of the childlike to exercise this privilege with rash frequency. Security can be confining, novelty devastating; oats are tasty, wild apples exotic. The playful spirit, the childlike quest, finds allurement both in novelty and in sameness. With the courtship of one, however, comes the relinquishing of the other.

Yellow, Yellow, a tale in less than 100 words, features immediate importance, enchantment, and enhanced self-image endowed upon a young boy by nothing more than finding a bright yellow construction hat. Acquisition of object and attributes prove temporary, however. The young finder is soon confronted by the original owner. Shadowing despair is in turn countered by youthful ingenuity. The key components of delight, "yellow" and "hat" can be revived by nothing more than a pair of scissors and a few sheets of construction paper to provide an oversized cap with the appropriate colour. Treasures are discovered then lost, but inventive desire can often reclaim what seems to have vanished for good. Astute insight probes the basics of desire, among them shape, colour and texture—each every bit as important to fancy as utility. Asch's unqualified popularity must derive in part from his own capability to sense those shifting but all too real fundamentals of delight.

Wherever it is that fancy is bred, it is probably not a near neighbor of novelty. Novelty either fizzles or proves to have questionable consequences. The appetite for novelty, that questing for the unnecessary, underlay the fall of man, and it too is a theme Asch touches upon. Eden-like joys of an enclosed, seemingly self-sufficient world provoke their own dissolution. Lion (*I Met a Penguin*) lives on an ocean islet with numerous friends, animal and human. Each day provides an unchanging ritual of pleasurable forgetfulness. They play in the morning, fish each afternoon, and cook their catch in the evening in a large communal pot. Apparently everyone is content with the routine until a serpent figure remarks on lion's incapacity as a fisherman. All agree with the assessment, and the pensive lion sets out to sea in order to ponder the consensus. Intemperate weather drives lion from the tropical isle all the way to the South Pole. Here, however, he establishes another utopian existence with a penguin who quickly becomes the love of his life. Contentment is curtailed when he brings up the bothersome question about his capacity as an angler. Her reply assures lion that he is competent. But assurance cannot still the meditative mode. Lion sets out to sea to reflect and a storm banishes him from an Antarctic bower. He is driven back to the original idyllic spot, but is now permanently subjected to memories of paradise lost. The inability to endure without reflection taints the most ideal of circumstances. And it is in this moment of sad reflection that the reader takes leave of lion—the creature of loving capacity whose awareness separates him from the bliss he is so capable of creating.

Certainly the children's tale does not of itself undertake philosophical consideration. Still, Asch's narratives contain an irresistible lure for entertaining certain questions. Does childhood cease with the onset of contemplation? Could it be that meditation forfeits more than it redeems? Seated as they are in that magical glade presided over by an innocent audience of children, Asch's picture books play with notions that innocence and unbridled pleasure are incompatible with reflection. Is the story destroying the aura it is created to sustain? Perhaps such queries are as unnecessary as they are threatening. Asch's books are fun, to be sure, but throughout there are signs that the author is fully aware of the fragility of the world he addresses.

Such restless reflection is apparently a condition shared by the author-artist with both his audience and his character creations. Shadows loom ominously, and they do block the light—but besides concealing, they project new forms, new narratives, and with these emerging tales, new possibilities and renewed relationships. Such is the case with his full-length novel, *Pearl's Promise,* where imminent death at any moment confronts a hapless mouse—and the victim's plight is effectively sustained for almost half of the book without any damage to the child world. Ingenuity might have its ingenuous qualities after all. The mouse characters share something with the total realism of a book like *Running with Rachel* where photographs replace drawings, and the endeavours follow the development of a young girl's commitment to running. Here too the seeds of discipline and achievement rise out of the dark side. "I looked down at my shadow. It seemed alive to me."

There seems to be salvation in shadows. In the incessant variated restlessness of the world of Frank Asch, there is the snaring and taming of those innumerable intriguing moments one might think are destined to vanish into thin air. His effort to capture the poetry of the urban mode (*City Sandwich*) assures us that "the subway always gives you more than just a ride." The tracks are fixed, etched as they are in bedrock. The path pursued is hidden from the sun. The stops are preset, the direction only to and fro. But for the ever-responsive rider, novelty, even enlightenment, are in the offing. So prodigious an output on the part of any author is certain to make many of the same stops, some to places forever unburnished and uninviting. Sometimes there is discovery, sometimes unwanted repetition. But the celebration of the moment endures. In such expectancy the spirit rightly associated with childhood lives on.

—Leonard R. Mendelsohn

ATWATER, Richard (Tupper)

Nationality: American. **Born:** Frederick Mund Atwater in Chicago, Illinois, 20 December 1892. **Education:** University of Chicago, 1907-17, Associate in Arts 1909, B.A. (honors) in Greek 1910. **Family:** Married Florence H. Carroll; two daughters. **Career:** Taught at the University of Chicago; columnist, *Tribune, Evening Post* (as "Riq"), and *Daily News,* all Chicago. **Died:** 1938.

PUBLICATIONS FOR CHILDREN

Fiction

Doris and the Trolls, illustrated by John Gee. Chicago, Rand McNally, 1931.

Mr. Popper's Penguins, completed by Florence Atwater, illustrated by Robert Lawson. Boston, Little Brown, 1938; London, Harrap, 1939.

PUBLICATIONS FOR ADULTS

Poetry

Rickety Rimes of Riq. Chicago, Ballou, 1925.

Other

Translator, *Secret History of Procopius.* New York, Covici Friede, 1934.

* * *

Penguins are engaging creatures. With their black and white "tuxedos," dignified, upright demeanor, and short, Chaplinesque steps, they are especially amusing to children. And when the penguins are *Mr. Popper's Penguins* (alliteration, assonance, and a sing-song beat), they are very funny, indeed.

Mr. Popper is a mild house painter. We meet him on his way home from work, clumsy and bungling, "spattered with paint and calcimine," with "bits of wallpaper clinging to his hair and whiskers": Mr. Popper is "rather an untidy man." Much to the chagrin of his tidy and practical wife, he is also absent-minded and quite a dreamer. He likes to sit with his pipe and read about faraway places—especially the North and South Poles. In fact, he is quite an authority on the subject.

Mr. Popper is particularly fond of penguins. Describing to his wife a movie he has seen about the Drake Expedition to the Antarctic, Mr. Popper concludes:

> I think the nicest part of all is the penguins. No wonder all the men on that expedition had such a good time playing with them. They are the funniest birds in the world. They don't fly like other birds. They walk erect like little men. When they get tired of walking they just lie down on their stomachs and slide. It would be very nice to have one as a pet.

One evening, as Mr. Popper is reading a new book from the library, *Antarctic Adventures,* listening to a radio-broadcast of Admiral Drake—direct (with static) from the South Pole—he suddenly hears Drake say: "Hello, Mr. Popper, up there in Stillwater. Thanks for your nice letter about the pictures of our last expedition. Watch for an answer. But not by letter, Mr. Popper. Watch for a surprise. Signing off. Signing off."

The "surprise" arrives at 432 Proudfoot Avenue the next day. Inside the large package, marked UNPACK AT ONCE and KEEP COOL and punched with air holes, is a live *penguin!* "Ork! Ork!" it squeals. "Gook! Gook!" And his name is Captain Cook. The fun begins! As if one penguin weren't fun enough, another—Greta—soon arrives from the Aquarium in Mammoth City. Ten baby penguins soon follow. 432 Proudfoot Avenue becomes a penguin paradise as Mr. Popper transforms first the living room, then the basement into an Arctic adventureland.

But pragmatic demands of the real world intervene. Money. It takes a lot of it to feed 12 hungry penguins. Mr. Popper's solution: train the penguins, build up an act, hit the Big Time. The story slides along from there on its stomach, through many adventures, until finally Mr. Popper is confronted with a serious dilemma: sign a movie contract and take the troupe to Hollywood (not a very wholesome place to bring up penguins), or let Admiral Drake take them on an expedition to the North Pole (where there are as yet no penguins). He makes his sad decision. What a surprise when Drake invites Mr. Popper to come too!

Atwater's *Mr. Popper's Penguins* (lovingly completed by Atwater's wife Florence after his death) has been a favorite with younger children for over 50 years, with its perfect interplay of wild hilarity and dead-pan seriousness, its smoothly sliding, adventure-filled plot, its charming and lovable characters (gaily depicted by illustrator Robert Lawson) and vivid detail; and its portrayal of an ordinary man—"just a house painter"—who has his happiest dreams come true.

—Marcia G. Fuchs

AVERILL, Esther (Holden)

Pseudonym: John Domino. **Nationality:** American. **Born:** Bridgeport, Connecticut, 24 July 1902. **Education:** Vassar College, Poughkeepsie, New York, B.A. 1923; Brooklyn Museum Art School. **Career:** Editor for *Women's Wear Daily,* New York, 1923-25; freelance journalist/photographer in field of fashion and decorative arts, Paris, 1925-31; founding publisher, Domino Press, Paris, 1931-34, and New York 1935-38; worked in the children's section of the New York Public Library. **Awards:** *Cartier Sails the St. Lawrence* was selected as an American Library Association Notable Book. **Died:** 1992.

Publications for Children

Fiction (illustrated by the author)

Powder: The Story of a Colt, The Duchess, and a Circus, with Lila Stanley, illustrated by Feodor Rojankovsky. Paris, Domino Press, New York, Smith and Haas, and London, Faber, 1933.
Flash: The Story of a Horse, A Coach-Dog, and the Gypsies, with Stanley, illustrated by Feodor Rojankovsky. Paris, Domino Press, New York, Smith and Haas, and London, Faber, 1934.
Fable of a Proud Poppy (as John Domino), illustrated by Emile Lahner. Paris, Domino Press, 1934.
The Cat Club; or, The Life and Times of Jenny Linsky. New York, Harper, 1944.
The Adventures of Jack Ninepins. New York, Harper, 1944.
The School for Cats. New York, Harper, 1947.
Jenny's First Party. New York, Harper, 1948.
Jenny's Moonlight Adventure. New York, Harper, 1949.
When Jenny Lost Her Scarf. New York, Harper, 1951.
Jenny's Adopted Brothers. New York, Harper, 1952.
How the Brothers Joined the Cat Club. New York, Harper, 1953; Kingswood, Surrey, World's Work, 1959.
Jenny's Birthday Book. New York, Harper, 1954.
Jenny Goes to Sea. New York, Harper, 1957.
Jenny's Bedside Book. New York, Harper, 1959.
The Fire Cat. New York, Harper, 1960; Kingswood, Surrey, World's Work, 1961.
The Hotel Cat. New York, Harper, 1969.
Captains of the City Streets. New York, Harper, 1972.
Jenny and the Cat Club (*The Cat Club, Jenny's First Party, When Jenny Lost Her Scarf, Jenny's Adopted Brothers, How the Brothers Joined the Cat Club*). New York, Harper, 1973; London, Fontana, 1976.

Other

The Voyages of Jacques Cartier, illustrated by Feodor Rojankovsky. New York, Domino Press, 1937; revised edition, as *Cartier Sails the St. Lawrence,* New York, Harper, 1956.
King Philip: The Indian Chief, illustrated by Vera Belsky. New York, Harper, 1950.
Eyes on the World: The Story and Work of Jacques Callot. New York, Funk and Wagnalls, 1969.

Editor, with Lila Stanley, *Daniel Boone: Historic Adventures of an American Hunter among the Indians,* illustrated by Feodor Rojankovsky. Paris, Domino Press, and London, Faber, 1931; revised edition, New York, Harper, 1945.

Translator, *Tales of Poindi,* by Jean Mariotti, illustrated by Feodor Rojankovsky. New York, Domino Press, 1938.

* * *

Jenny Linsky is undoubtedly Esther Averill's most famous and enduring character. Over a dozen books for younger readers have been written about this shy, orphan cat with the engaging personality. Most of the stories are short enough to be read comfortably in one sitting and concern the various adventures of Jenny and her fellow members of the Cat Club.

Averill's descriptive prose is characterized by a light, delicate touch. With deft strokes of the pen she endows Jenny and her companions with distinct personalities which are in keeping with their physical appearance. Jenny's quiet courage is sympathetically and humorously portrayed in *Jenny's Moonlight Adventure.* Her agonizing decision to rescue a friend's prize possession is realistically explored as she wavers from a firm decision not to help, to shame that she hasn't the courage to act, and finally to the conviction that she must help her friend.

Averill's world is black and white—good deeds are rewarded, bad deeds are punished, and transgressors of the Cat Club rules are made to see the error of their ways. Moral overtones are evident throughout Averill's fiction. There is an emphasis, for example, on the praiseworthiness of facing up to one's problems, admitting guilt when one has done wrong, and treating one's fellows properly. Jenny's initial encounter with the Cat Club teaches her that shyness is a handicap which may be overcome. Likewise, fear of the unknown in *Jenny's Moonlight Adventure* is shown to be diminished by a direct stand against those fears.

The understated style of Averill's writing makes her books a delight to read. She uses words sparingly to provide a setting, describe the characters and get the story under way. Her sure sense of story is evident—even in *Jenny's Bedside Book,* which lacks any action at all, the story-within-a-story technique holds the reader's attention.

The humor of Averill's work is derived from her straightforward tongue-in-cheek descriptions and the exaggerated dignity that she invests in her animal characters. Relationships between the characters are almost always positive. The books are full of tenderness and warm, loving friendships; with their gaiety and charm they have made an important contribution to the genre of children's fantasy, confirmed by their continuing popularity.

—Fran Ashdown

AVERY, Gillian (Elise)

Nationality: British. **Born:** Reigate, Surrey, 30 September 1926. **Education:** Dunottar School, Reigate. **Family:** Married A.O.J. Cockshut in 1952; one daughter. **Career:** Junior reporter, *Surrey Mirror,* Redhill, 1944-47; staff member, *Chambers Encyclopaedia,* London, 1947-50; assistant illustrations editor, Clarendon Press, Oxford, 1950-54. Chairman, Children's Books History Society, 1987-89. **Awards:** *Guardian* award, 1972. **Address:** 32 Charlbury Road, Oxford OX2 6UU, England.

Publications for Children

Fiction

The Warden's Niece, illustrated by Dick Hart. London, Collins, 1957; as *Maria Escapes,* illustrated by Scott Snow, Simon, 1992.
Trespassers at Charlcote, illustrated by Dick Hart. London, Collins, 1958.
James without Thomas, illustrated by John Verney. London, Collins, 1959.
The Elephant War, illustrated by John Verney. London, Collins, 1960; New York, Holt Rinehart, 1971.
To Tame a Sister, illustrated by John Verney. London, Collins, 1961; Princeton, New Jersey, Van Nostrand, 1964.
The Greatest Gresham, illustrated by John Verney. London, Collins, 1962.
The Peacock House, illustrated by John Verney. London, Collins, 1963.
The Italian Spring, illustrated by John Verney. London, Collins, 1964; New York, Holt Rinehart, 1972; as *Maria's Italian Spring,* New York, Simon and Schuster, 1993.
Call of the Valley, illustrated by Laszlo Acs. London, Collins, 1966; New York, Holt Rinehart, 1968.
A Likely Lad, illustrated by Faith Jaques. London, Collins, and New York, Holt Rinehart, 1971.
Ellen's Birthday, illustrated by Krystyna Turska. London, Hamish Hamilton, 1971.
Ellen and the Queen, illustrated by Krystyna Turska. London, Hamish Hamilton, 1972; Nashville, Nelson, 1974.
Jemima and the Welsh Rabbit, illustrated by John Lawrence. London, Hamish Hamilton, 1972.
Freddie's Feet, illustrated by Krystyna Turska. London, Hamish Hamilton, 1976.
Huck and Her Time Machine. London, Collins, 1977.
Mouldy's Orphan, illustrated by Faith Jaques. London, Collins, 1978.
Sixpence!, illustrated by Antony Maitland. London, Collins, 1979.

Other

Gillian Avery's Book of the Strange and Odd (nonfiction), illustrated by Michael Jackson. London, Kestrel, 1975.
Authors' Choice: Stories, with others, illustrated by Krystyna Turska. London, Hamish Hamilton, 1970.

Editor, *A Flat Iron for a Farthing,* by Juliana Horatia Ewing. London, Faith Press, 1959.
Editor, *Jan of the Windmill,* by Juliana Horatia Ewing. London, Faith Press, 1960.
Editor, *The Sapphire Treasury of Stories for Boys and Girls.* London, Gollancz, 1960.
Editor, *In the Window Seat: A Selection of Victorian Stories,* illustrated by Susan Einzig. London, Oxford University Press, 1960; Princeton, New Jersey, Van Nostrand, 1965.
Editor, *Father Phim,* by Annie Keary. London, Faith Press, 1962.
Editor, *Unforgettable Journeys,* illustrated by John Verney. London, Gollancz, 1965.
Editor, *School Remembered,* illustrated by John Verney. London, Gollancz, 1967; New York, Funk and Wagnalls, 1968.
Editor, *A Great Emergency, and A Very Ill-Tempered Family,* by Juliana Horatia Ewing. London, Gollancz, 1967.
Editor, *The Gold of Fairnilee and Other Stories,* by Andrew Lang. London, Gollancz, 1967.
Editor, *Village Children,* by Charlotte Yonge. London, Gollancz, 1967.
Editor, *Banning and Blessing,* by Margaret Roberts. London, Gollancz, 1967.
Editor, *Gollancz Revivals* (twelve reissued volumes of nineteenth-century children's books), Gollancz, 1967-70.
Editor, *The Hole in the Wall and Other Stories,* illustrated by Doreen Roberts. London, Oxford University Press, 1968.
Editor, *Victoria-Bess and Others,* by Brenda, Mrs. Gatty, and Frances Hodgson Burnett. London, Gollancz, 1968; as *Victorian Doll Stories,* New York, Schocken, 1969.
Editor, *The Wallypug of Why,* by G.E. Farrow, illustrated by Harry Furniss. London, Gollancz, 1968.
Editor, *Froggy's Little Brother,* by Brenda. London, Gollancz, 1968.
Editor, *My New Home,* by Mary Louisa Molesworth, illustrated by L. Leslie Brooke. London, Gollancz, 1968.
Editor, *The Life and Adventures of Lady Anne* (anonymous), illustrated by F.D. Bedford. London, Gollancz, 1969.
Editor, *Stephanie's Children,* by Margaret Roberts. London, Gollancz, 1969.
Editor, *Anne's Terrible Good Nature and Other Stories for Children,* by E.V. Lucas. London, Gollancz, 1970.
Editor, *The Rival Kings,* by Annie Keary. London, Gollancz, 1970.
Editor, *Red Letter Days,* illustrated by Krystyna Turska. London, Hamish Hamilton, 1971.
Editor, *The Everyman Anthology of Poetry for Children.* London, Everyman's Library, 1994.
Editor, *Russian Fairy Tales.* London, Everyman's Library, 1995.

Publications for Adults

Novels

The Lost Railway. London, Collins, 1980.
Onlookers. London, Collins, 1983.

Other

Mrs. Ewing. London, Bodley Head, 1961; New York, Walck, 1964.
Nineteenth Century Children: Heroes and Heroines in English Children's Stories 1780-1900, with Angela Bull. London, Hodder and Stoughton, 1965.
Victorian People in Life and Literature. London, Collins, and New York, Holt Rinehart, 1970.

The Echoing Green: Memories of Victorian and Regency Youth. London, Collins, and New York, Viking Press, 1974.
Childhood's Pattern: A Study of the Heroes and Heroines of Children's Fiction 1770-1950. London, Hodder and Stoughton, 1975.
The Best Type of Girl: A History of the Girls' Independent Schools, Deutsch, 1991.
Behold the Child: A History of American Children and Their Books 1621-1922. London, Bodley Head, and Baltimore, Johns Hopkins University Press, 1994.

Editor, *Children and Their Books: A Celebration of the Work of Iona and Peter Opie,* with Julia Briggs. London, Oxford University Press, 1989.

* * *

For over two decades, Gillian Avery has been producing extremely believable children's stories set in the late Victorian era. She has a sympathetic understanding of her chosen period which is evoked without sentimental inflation or a retrospective smoothness. She manages to express the past *as* the present by underlining its unevenness and normality. Stringent observation of character and manners, and a flair for humorous incident, enhance the realism of her stories.

Avery recalls that when she wrote her first book she seemed to know more about the feelings of the children of 1875 than the self-assured attitudes of young people in the 1950s. She felt that there was an affinity between her own pre-war generation with its "meek acceptance of the power of the adult world" and the Victorian child who had always been accustomed to authoritarian treatment. However, the objective of her fictional children—even the most diffident—is usually to assert themselves in some particular way. This often involves a flouting of the restraining conventions of the time, with consequent conflict or social unease. Avery makes this type of embarrassment acutely credible to readers brought up in today's more liberal environment. She also makes the most of the humorous elements which occur in these situations—especially when they arise from confrontations between children and adults. Her stories, despite their serious moments, are really domestic or social comedies.

The Warden's Niece was Avery's first book and it is still one of the most popular. She started writing it one winter as "an escape from the weeping ... skies and raw fogs" of Manchester, where she was then living; appropriately the book begins with an escape of a different kind. Maria runs away from her dispiriting boarding school to her uncle, the Warden of an Oxford college. Although she has shown no sign of academic distinction, she hopes one day to become a lecturer in Latin and Greek. Her uncle encourages this creditable ambition, arranging for Maria to have lessons with the Smith brothers—the lordly Thomas, reasonable Joshua, and outrageous James. Their eccentric temporary tutor gives the children opportunities to explore their surroundings, and Maria stumbles on a mystery concerning a 17th-century boy. She feels that he is linked with a scrawled message which she discovers on the wall of a stately home. Determination to complete this piece of original research gives Maria the courage to play truant and even to gatecrash the Bodleian. The Oxford setting and historical associations give the book a strong appeal. It has, apparently, sent people to Oxford. Avery thinks it reflects her own romantic yearnings: "As an adolescent I felt about the place as many of my contemporaries felt about Hollywood."

The Elephant War also has an Oxford background. Its heroine, Harriet Jessop, is more timid than Maria but equally convincing. The awesome Smith brothers appear once more. Harriet thinks that they typify the intellectual life of Oxford which seems excitingly attractive to her. She is recruited by a formidable aunt into a campaign to save one of the London Zoo's elephants from being sent to America—to "slavery" in Barnum's Circus. This "cause" draws Harriet into a series of farcical events, and she falls foul of the Smith family who ridicule her campaigning zeal; but unexpectedly James Smith suddenly becomes her infuriating and disruptive ally. (Avery is particularly perceptive when describing the irritation that a bumptious small boy or girl can arouse in a more sensitive older child.) The point is effectively made that enthusiasms can get out of control.

In *The Greatest Gresham* the primly brought up Julia and Henry Gresham are—like Harriet Jessop—deeply aware of their own inadequacies. These are highlighted by their relationship with the next door children. Richard and Kate Holt live in a scruffy and disordered home, but they have an independence that Julia and Henry long to emulate. The Greshams force themselves to perform difficult and embarrassing feats suggested by the Holts; this is supposed to broaden their minds. The story has an intriguingly furtive atmosphere. The children form a secret society, and the Greshams are constantly afraid that their parents will declare the Holts "undesirable" and end the association.

A desire for genteel respectability and social position plays a big part in *A Likely Lad.* It was inspired by the reminiscences of Avery's father-in-law about his Lancashire boyhood. Bookish Willy Overs is the likely lad; his self-made, shopkeeper father intends him to begin work at 13 in an insurance office. Mr. Overs sees this as the start of a successful career for his son and also as a means of establishing the superiority of his branch of the family over that of his patronizing in-laws. Willy's apprehensive but persistent resistance to the scheme eventually persuades his father to allow him to continue his education. The atmosphere of a working-class home at the turn of the century is expressed through the effects of unvarying domestic routines on the children. For instance, on their mother's baking day, Willy and his brother have to suffer banishment from the cosy kitchen/living room to the boredom of an immaculate but icy and toyless parlour.

In the stories, the sense of another time is conveyed externally: there are frequent descriptions of cold, dark rooms and the rituals of lighting fires and candles; of plush table covers, knickerbocker suits, and merino dresses. The psychological tone of Avery's books, however, is modern and lively enough to appeal to a wide range of present-day readers. Everything in the books is seen from the children's point of view. This was certainly not the case in stories which were written for real life Victorian children. The naughtiest of their heroines would never have found herself in the situation of the little girl in *Ellen and the Queen* who has an illicit peep at Queen Victoria's legs!

—Mary Cadogan

AWDRY, W(ilbert) V(ere)

Nationality: British. **Born:** Ampfield, Hampshire, 15 June 1911. **Education:** Dauntsey's, West Lavington, Wiltshire, 1923-29; St.

Peter's College, Oxford, 1929-32, M.A. 1932; Wycliffe Hall, Oxford, 1932-33, diploma in theology 1933. **Family:** Married Margaret Emily Wale in 1938; one son and two daughters. **Career:** Schoolmaster, St. George's School, Jerusalem, 1933-36; ordained Church of England deacon, 1936, and priest, 1937; Curate, Odiham, Winchester, Hampshire, 1936-38, West Lavington, 1938-40, and Kings Norton, Birmingham, 1940-46; Rector, Elsworth with Knapwell, Cambridgeshire, 1946-53; Rural Dean, Bourn, Cambridgeshire, 1950-53; Vicar, Emneth, Norfolk, 1953-65; licensed to officiate in the Diocese of Gloucester. **Died:** 21 March 1997.

Publications for Children

Fiction

The Three Railway Engines, illustrated by C. Reginald Dalby. Leicester, Ward, 1945.
Thomas, The Tank Engine, illustrated by Reginald Payne. Leicester, Ward, 1946; as *Thomas the Tank Engine and Friends,* illustrated with photographs by Kenny McArthur, David Mitton, and Terry Permane, New York, Random House, 1989.
James, The Red Engine, illustrated by C. Reginald Dalby. Leicester, Ward, 1948; New York, Random House, 1991.
Tank Engine Thomas Again, illustrated by C. Reginald Dalby. Leicester, Ward, 1949.
Troublesome Engines, illustrated by C. Reginald Dalby. Leicester, Ward, 1950.
Henry, The Green Engine, illustrated by C. Reginald Dalby. Leicester, Ward, 1951.
Toby, The Tram Engine, illustrated by C. Reginald Dalby. Leicester, Ward, 1952; New York, Random House, 1991.
Gordon, The Big Engine, illustrated by C. Reginald Dalby. Leicester, Ward, 1953.
Edward, The Blue Engine, illustrated by C. Reginald Dalby. Leicester, Ward, 1954.
Four Little Engines, illustrated by C. Reginald Dalby. London, Ward, 1955.
Percy, The Small Engine, illustrated by C. Reginald Dalby. London, Ward, 1956.
The Eight Famous Engines, illustrated by John Kenney. London, Ward, 1957.
Duck and the Diesel Engine, illustrated by John Kenney. London, Ward, 1958.
Belinda the Beetle, illustrated by Ionicus. Leicester, Brockhampton Press, 1958.
The Little Old Engine, illustrated by John Kenney. London, Ward, 1959.
The Twin Engines, illustrated by John Kenney. London, Ward, 1960.
Branch Line Engines, illustrated by John Kenney. London, Ward, 1961.
Belinda Beats the Band, illustrated by John Kenney. Leicester, Brockhampton Press, 1961.
Gallant Old Engine, illustrated by John Kenney. London, Ward, 1962.
Stepney, The Bluebell Engine, illustrated by Gunvor and Peter Edwards. London, Ward, 1963.
Mountain Engines, illustrated by Gunvor and Peter Edwards. London, Ward, 1964.
Very Old Engines, illustrated by Gunvor and Peter Edwards. London, Ward, 1965.
Main Line Engines, illustrated by Gunvor and Peter Edwards. London, Ward, 1966.
Small Railway Engines, illustrated by Gunvor and Peter Edwards. London, Kaye and Ward, 1967.
Enterprising Engines, illustrated by Gunvor and Peter Edwards. London, Kaye and Ward, 1968.
Oliver, The Western Engine, illustrated by Gunvor and Peter Edwards. London, Kaye and Ward, 1969.
Duke, The Lost Engine, illustrated by Gunvor and Peter Edwards. London, Kaye and Ward, 1970.
Tramway Engines, illustrated by Gunvor and Peter Edwards. London, Kaye and Ward, 1972.

Other

Railway Map of the Island of Sodor, illustrated by C. Reginald Dalby. London, Ward, 1958; revised version, illustrated by Peter Edwards, 1971; revised version, illustrated by Clive Spong, 1988.
Surprise Packet, illustrated by Peter Edwards. London, Kaye and Ward, 1972.
The Island of Sodor: Its People, History, and Railways. London, Kaye and Ward, 1987.
Thomas's A.B.C. [*Counting Book*]. London, Heinemann, 2 vols., 1987; as *Thomas's ABC Book,* illustrated with photographs by Kenny McArthur, David Mitton, and Terry Permane, New York, Random House, 1990.

Publications for Adults

Our Child Begins to Pray. Leicester, Ward, 1951.
The Birmingham and Gloucester Railway, with Peter Long. Gloucester, Sutton, 1987.

Editor, *Industrial Archaeology in Gloucestershire.* Gloucestershire Community Council, 1973; revised editions, Gloucestershire Society for Industrial Archaeology, 1975, 1988.
Editor, with Chris Cook, *A Guide to the Steam Railways of Great Britain.* London, Pelham, 1979; revised edition, 1984.

*

W.V. Awdry comments:

My father was a country clergyman very knowledgeable about railways. I was brought up accordingly. Naturally, when my son fell ill at the age of three, I amused him by telling him stories about engines. The first book, *The Three Railway Engines,* resulted.

Its popularity led the publisher to ask for more. As the series grew so did the need for consistency between book and book. A localised background area became essential. Hence the "discovery" of the fictional Island of Sodor between Barrow-in-Furness and the Isle of Man. Sodor was mapped for private use by 1951, and a map was published in 1958 (with much improved versions appearing in 1971 and 1988).

The stories are all based on fact. Granted the fiction that steam engines have personality and can express it, all else is authentic. Each story is based on some "off beat" incident which has happened to some engine, somewhere, some time. Thus all have an authentic railwaylike explanation.

* * *

When W.V. Awdry's *The Three Railway Engines* appeared in 1945, privately owned steam trains still covered Great Britain. Using the popular format of around 50 pages with an illustration opposite each page of text, the book—like its 25 successors—consists of three stories, loosely connected by theme. With the exception of the Fat Controller, the major protagonists in the Railway Series are types of transport, predominantly steam engines. About their colourful flanks and enormous expressive faces, the luckless passengers, forever clearing the tracks or pushing the train, swarm like creatures from Lilliput. It often seems in the early books that these skilfully differentiated characters, Gordon the boastful bully or Edward the querulous newcomer, are pupils in a public school for trains. If the recalcitrant trucks represent youths from the local village to be licked into shape by their natural leaders, then the coaches, for instance Thomas the Tank Engine's Clarabel, are treated more respectfully, like sisters being shown the school.

The stories themselves frequently present little homilies (Awdry was after all a clergyman who once wrote a book on children's prayer) such as "more haste less speed," i.e. don't leave your coaches at the station the way Thomas did. Or "pride comes before a fall": the trains that boast of their hill climbing fail as surely as those who, like Daisy the Diesel Engine, claim a skill in confronting stray animals. Inevitably in a series of this length one encounters repetition; the track round the next bend is ever likely to be blocked by subsidence, and one headstrong train after another is hauled from pond, field, or quarry. Presiding over this endearing world and offering its two rewards—a new coat of paint and the benediction "You are a really useful engine"—is the Fat Director (appropriately after nationalisation, the Fat Controller). His squire-archical power over both engines and passengers seems as limitless as the "blue remembered hills" of C. Reginald Dalby's exquisite illustrations.

In the late 1950s, with steam on the wane, and John Kenney as illustrator, significant changes overtook the Railway Series. Fairly early on Awdry appears to have conceived a fictional home for his creations. As life and railways in England changed so the need may have become more pressing. He settled on the "Island of Sodor." Maps show it artfully filling the Irish Sea between the Isle of Man and the Lancashire coast. On its more limited scale, the author began constructing the details of his imaginary world with the same loving care that Tolkien brought to his. A rail link with the British mainland, mimicking the function of the Bifrost Bridge of Norse mythology, screens out diesel engines instead of frost giants. In *Enterprising Engines,* in which Oliver escapes to Sodor with the aid of friendly signalmen, the diesels left behind in England are characterised as the nameless denizens of a totalitarian railway system. Yet other diesels, or dismissively "spamcans," co-existing uneasily with the Fat Controller's steam trains, appear to fill much the same role as immigrant workers in the Britain of that period. On Sodor we also find a new complementary railway ruled, fittingly enough, by the Thin Controller.

It must be said that though the stories in which these new trains figure do not want for inventiveness—*Very Old Engines* for instance is a full dress historical novel in miniature—they are not wholly successful. Here engines with unappealing, even unpronounceable names such as Rheneas or Skarloey occasionally break into broad Scots dialect. Such impenetrability in the text is unhappily and inadvertently complemented by the more impressionistic pictures of Gunvor and Peter Edwards. Increasingly too Awdry came to use his stories to advertise steam preservation societies like the Tallylyn Railway. Sometimes one suspects even the intended readership to be railway buffs rather than children. Yet undoubtedly in the Railway Series Awdry found the right medium for his creativity. In the Belinda stories talking cars jar with the people and eccentricity oversteps the mark, but the best of the train books, and these are the earliest, put their author almost on a par with Beatrix Potter or A.A. Milne.

Today the series has become a veritable family industry. Stories are available in compendia, annuals, single tale picture books, pop-ups, sequels from Christopher Awdry, and in two simplified versions; one of these last, on boards and illustrated with stills from the television readings, has a charm of its own. No new version however surpasses the originals which to this day provide avid enjoyment for anyone over two. Nor should intending "visitors" to Sodor miss the poker-faced gazeteer of the island put together by Awdry and his brother George.

—John Churcher

AYLESWORTH, Jim

Nationality: American. **Born:** Jacksonville, Florida, 21 February 1943. **Education:** Miami University, Oxford, Ohio, B.A. 1965; Concordia College, River Forest, Illinois, M.A. 1978. **Family:** Married Donna La Puzza; two sons. **Career:** First Grade Teacher, Oak Park, Illinois, 1971-96; writer, from 1980. Professor of Children's Literature, Concordia University, University of Chicago, College of DuPage. **Awards:** Those Who Excel Award, Illinois State Board of Education, 1975; Governor's Master Teacher, 1984; Alumnus of the Year, Concordia University, 1985; Reading Magic Award, *Parenting* Magazine, 1992; Notable Book for Children, American Library Association, 1992, Minnesota Center for the Book Award, 1993, International Reading Association and Children's Book Council Award, 1993, all for *Old Black Fly*; Notable Children's Book, National Council of Teachers of English, 1995, for *My Son John.* **Address:** 55 W. Delaware Place, #407, Chicago, Illinois 60610, U.S.A. **E-mail Address:** oldfly@ayles.com **Website:** www.ayles.com

Publications for Children

Fiction

Hush Up! Illustrated by Glen Rounds. New York, Henry Holt, 1980.

Tonight's the Night, illustrated by John Wallner. Morton Grove, Illinois, Albert Whitman, 1981.

Mary's Mirror, illustrated by Richard Egielski. New York, Holt, 1982.

Siren in the Night, illustrated by Tom Centola. Morton Grove, Illinois, Albert Whitman, 1983.

The Bad Dream, illustrated by Judith Friedman. Morton Grove, Illinois, Albert Whitman, 1985.
Shenandoah, Noah, illustrated by Glen Rounds. New York, Henry Holt, 1985.
Two Terrible Frights, illustrated by Eileen Christelow. New York, Atheneum, 1987.
One Crow: A Counting Rhyme, illustrated by Ruth Young. New York, Lippincott, 1988.
Hanna's Hog, illustrated by Glen Rounds. New York, Atheneum, 1988.
Mother Halverson's New Cat, illustrated by Toni Goffe. New York, Atheneum, 1989.
Mr. McGill Goes to Town, illustrated by Thomas Graham. New York, Henry Holt, 1989.
The Completed Hickory Dickory Doc, illustrated by Eileen Christelow. New York, Atheneum, 1990.
Country Crossing, illustrated by Ted Rand. New York, Atheneum, 1991.
The Folks in the Valley: A Pennsylvania Dutch ABC, illustrated by Stefano Vitale. New York, HarperCollins, 1991.
Old Black Fly, illustrated by Stephen Gammell. New York, Holt, 1992.
The Cat and the Fiddle and More, illustrated by Richard Hull. New York, Atheneum, 1992.
The Good-Night Kiss, illustrated by Walter Krudop. New York, Atheneum, 1993.
My Son John, illustrated by David Frampton. New York, Henry Holt, 1994.
McGraw's Emporium, illustrated by Mavis Smith. New York, Henry Holt, 1995.
Wake Up, Little Children, illustrated by Walter Krudop. New York, Atheneum, 1996.
My Sister's Rusty Bike, illustrated by Richard Hull. New York, Atheneum, 1996.
Teddy Bear Tears, illustrated by Jo Ellen McAllister-Stammen. New York, Atheneum, 1997.'
The Gingerbread Man, illustrated by Barbara McClintock. New York, scholastic, 1998.
Through the Night, illustrated by Pamela Patrick. New York, Atheneum, 1998.

*

Biography: Entry in *Something about the Author,* Vol. 89, Detroit, Gale Research, 1997.

* * *

Jim Aylesworth has been teaching first grade for a long time and he is proud of it. His students should be proud of him as well, for he is a man of good humor and high spirits. And he knows how to tell a rollicking good story, one that is full of fine surprises.

His books for children, in the pre-school to third grade level, speak to everyday joys and discoveries, as well as to everyday trials and tribulations. *Two Terrible Frights* addresses the common childhood dread of the night. A little girl and a little mouse are each told that they may have a bedtime snack if they get it themselves (their mothers have worked all day and are too tired to get it for them). The little girl proceeds from upstairs down to the kitchen; the little mouse proceeds from the basement up to the kitchen. When they meet in the kitchen, one says "Eeek" and the other goes "squeak," and they both retreat from whence they came. The girl's mother and the mouse's mother assure their offspring that the other little creature was probably scared worse than they were. The little girl and the little mouse then go off to bed and dream about eating snacks together one day. The pastel drawings that accompany the text evoke a dreamy atmosphere.

One Crow is a counting rhyme which explores summer and winter on the farm. In the summer one crow sits on a telephone wire; the summer's sun is up and climbing higher. Barnyard animals are introduced, two through nine, and in the end ten children parade through the field. The grass is green, the milkweed is tall, the wild berries glisten. In the winter the same animals and children are shown, but the animals protect themselves from the cold with pigs snuggling in a pile of hay, hens nesting in the old warm coop, sheep huddling in the meadow. Children though play gleefully in the snow, making snowballs and riding sleds. This is a simple book, but one that shows the beauty of the landscape and that provides the fun of learning to count.

Country Crossing is another simple tale with a nighttime setting, but with an explosive feel to it. For the quiet country road, with crickets chirping softly and a lonely owl calling hoo hoo, and a car's old motor puttaput putting along, is rudely invaded by the clanging of the crossing bell, the flashing of the warning lights, and the whistle and the roar of a tremendous freight train that barrels past the crossing and off into the night. When the train disappears, the crossing bell stops ringing, the warning lights stop flashing, and the crossing becomes peaceful as before, with one old car, some crickets, and a lonely owl in his tree. The illustrations in this book are dark and strident, reinforcing the contrast between the big noisy machine and the quiet creatures who normally inhabit the country road.

Old Black Fly, the author reports, is a favorite of his students, who sing the story with him. The story is about a low-down fly who drives a family (Baby, Mama, and Gramma) crazy on a hot summer day. That fly eats the crust of the Apple pie, he bothers the Baby and makes her cry. He coughs on the Cookies with the chocolate bits, and he drives the Dog nearly out of his wits. If that isn't enough, he snoozes on the Quilt on Gramma's bed and rides the red Ribbon on her head. He sniffs the Salami that sister sliced, and runs around her Teacup once or twice. This is an alphabet book, the likes of which hasn't been seen before. And the refrain after every second letter—"Shoo fly! Shoo fly! Shoo"—makes it perfect for group singing. You might wish you were one of Aylesworth's students, just so you could join in this fun. Aylesworth knows children and human nature.

Aylesworth's experience as a teacher led him to writing children's books. Having read hundreds of books to his students over many years, he became interested in being a member of the children's story world and writing books himself. He makes wonderful use of sounds and rhythms, having seen how much children like them in a story, especially one that is being read aloud. In *Hanna's Hog* there is a loud hog call, in *Country Crossing,* a fierce freight train sound. Rhythms are found in *The Completed Hickory Dickory Dock, The Cat in the Fiddle and More,* and *Old Black Fly,* as well as other works.

Aylesworth's sounds and rhythms are echoed and enhanced by the illustrators of his books. In particular Stephen Gammell, Glen Rounds, and Richard Egielski make the author's words reach out to the reader in different yet very lively ways. *Old Black Fly* was an artistic breakthrough for Gammell because in it he is able to let the paint leap and spin from page to page, over fly, baby, dog, and mama. Pink frosting on the birthday cake dribbles to the end of the page, honey slides over and down its pot, an olive oil can spills down the tablecloth on to the floor. The house becomes a gorgeous rainbow of color because of that pesky old fly. This book successfully relates words and pictures to tell a cautionary tale of what could happen to you in the summertime.

—Mary Lystad

B

BABBITT, Natalie (Zane)

Nationality: American. **Born:** Natalie Zane Moore, Dayton, Ohio, 28 July 1932. **Education:** Laurel School for Girls, Cleveland, graduated 1950; Smith College, Northampton, Massachusetts, 1950-54, B.A. in art 1954. **Family:** Married Samuel F. Babbitt in 1954; two sons and one daughter. **Career:** Instructor in writing and illustrating for children, Kirkland College, Clinton, New York, 1969-78. **Awards:** Christopher award, 1976; George G. Stone Center for Children's Books award, 1979; Keene State Children's Literature Festival award, 1993. **Address:** 26 Benefit Street, Providence, Rhode Island 02904, U.S.A.

PUBLICATIONS FOR CHILDREN (ILLUSTRATED BY THE AUTHOR)

Fiction

The Search for Delicious. New York, Farrar Straus, 1969; London, Chatto and Windus, 1975.
Kneeknock Rise. New York, Farrar Straus, 1970.
The Something. New York, Farrar Straus, 1970.
Goody Hall. New York, Farrar Straus, 1971; London, Dent, 1984.
The Devil's Storybook. New York, Farrar Straus, 1974; London, Chatto and Windus, 1976.
Tuck Everlasting. New York, Farrar Straus, 1975; London, Chatto and Windus, 1977.
The Eyes of the Amaryllis. New York, Farrar Straus, 1977; London, Chatto and Windus, 1978.
Herbert Rowbarge. New York, Farrar Straus, 1982; London, Dent, 1984.
The Devil's Other Storybook. New York, Farrar Straus, 1987.
Nellie—A Cat on Her Own. New York, Farrar Straus, 1989.
Bub, or The Very Best Thing. New York, HarperCollins, 1994.

Poetry

Dick Foote and the Shark. New York, Farrar Straus, 1967.
Phoebe's Revolt. New York, Farrar Straus, 1968.

*

Illustrator: *The Forty-Ninth Magician* by Samuel F. Babbitt, 1966; *Small Poems,* 1972, *More Small Poems,* 1976, *Still More Small Poems,* 1978, *Curlicues,* 1980, *Small Poems Again,* 1986, and *All the Small Poems,* 1987, *All the Small Poems and Fourteen More,* 1994, all by Valerie Worth.

Other

Natalie Babbitt, by Michael M. Levy, Boston, Twayne Publishers 1991; "Natalie Babbitt" by Amy Meeker, *Publisher's Weekly,* February 21, 1994.

Media Adaptions: *Tuck Everlasting* (video) Great Plains National Instructional Television Library, 1980; *Kneeknock Rise* (filmstrip) Miller-Brady Productions, 1975.

Natalie Babbitt comments:

I am motivated first by a simple passion for the English language and second by a fascination with the many faces a single reality assumes when viewed through the filter of any given individual's biases, experiences, expectations, and/or desires. Though I am categorized as a writer of fantasy, I have never written about the true fairyland as defined by Tolkien, but rather concern myself with the above mentioned filters which lend every reality an aspect of fantasy. My stories in the main concern human beings and the effects their own fantasies/filters have upon their own realities.

* * *

Natalie Babbitt has made a special place for herself in the world of children's literature. Her stories are highly individual, notable for their humor, which is never condescending, and for their unusual themes. The messages in Babbitt's fiction are not the lessons on personal morality so commonly carried by children's books; the statements made in *Kneeknock Rise, Goody Hall,* and most memorably in *Tuck Everlasting* are philosophic and general, rather than moralistic and particular. They are comments on human ways, needs, and oddities as visible to children as to adults.

One can point to problems. Some instances of Babbitt's humor are almost certainly beyond the ken of her readers, assuming those readers are children and not reviewers. The gentle parodies of Shakespeare, for example—"Rumble, rumble, foil and fumble/Choir adjourn and children mumble," or "Where the sea bucks, there buck I"—are unlikely to mean much to anyone under 12 (or maybe 22). And Babbitt's child characters are sometimes dim in comparison with the adults in the stories: quite often they are not nearly central enough to the action to satisfy a youthful reader. Talk without action is sometimes a drawback; the long prelude to the action of *Goody Hall,* amusing as it is in its scene-setting dialogue, is static and adult. It would play well on a stage, as Shakespeare's comic dialogues play well while they also inform the audience, but whether a child reader will stay with it is another question.

But even when the inaccessible is subtracted from Babbitt's stories, there is much left that is original, funny, and thoughtful. *The Devil's Storybook* is full of lighthearted malice properly ascribed to the devil and his offspring; *Kneeknock Rise* is a kindly look at the pleasures of harmless drama in everyday life; *The Search for Delicious* makes an old point about the relativity of value in a new way.

Babbitt's masterpiece is unquestionably *Tuck Everlasting.* She has chosen for this story a theme no less profound than the meaning and place of death in the universe of living things, yet her handling of this weighty subject is so deft and so gentle that the theme never overwhelms the characters or their poignant, believable tale.

The comparison that comes to mind is with E.B. White's *Charlotte's Web.* Both are fantasies, but barely: just enough to carry forward their themes without becoming so abstract as to lose touch with their young audiences. They are earthbound fantasies, both dealing plainly with life and death, telling stories that are sad and true and funny, all at once. The passage in which Tuck tells Winnie why she must choose mortality over life everlasting is surely one of the most moving in children's literature. He makes it simple, not just because Winnie is 11 years old and could not understand a complex discussion of immortality, but because the matter is to Tuck a simple one: "Life. Moving, growing, changing, never the same two minutes together....Being part of the whole thing, that's the blessing."

Babbitt's work since *Tuck Everlasting* is characteristically varied. *The Eyes of the Amaryllis* adds a touch of fantasy to its basic themes of maturation and acceptance. The quality of writing will hold readers whose tastes run to something more than the average adolescent novel, but the balance between fantasy and realism, and the connection between theme and form is less sure than in *Tuck Everlasting. Herbert Rowbarge* is an off-beat novel which seems to have slipped quietly out of sight since its publication. The reasons are perhaps not hard to guess. Though typically original and subtle, the story asks its readers to remain interested in a protagonist who is an adult for much of the narrative—and none too sympathetic an adult, at that.

The Devil's Other Storybook, on the other hand, easily matches the felicities of the first collection. The stories are brief and amusing, written with an economical wit accessible to almost anyone over the age of eight. Babbitt is not a prolific writer, but she doesn't need to be, for her attention to detail is one of her prose's highest qualities. This meticulous nature is evident in her illustrating as well as her writing.

She began her career in the publishing field as an illustrator. Though she created cover illustrations for her novels she reclaimed her original goal in writing and illustrating picture books. *Bub, or the Very Best Thing* is the story of a king and queen's quest to find the very best of the best in raising their toddler prince. When their search eventually leads to asking the cook's daughter for advice, she suggests asking the prince himself. Though the overly enthusiastic parents do not understand the prince's response of "bub," the readers and other characters know that love is indeed the very best thing.

Babbitt's writing is invariably interesting, with themes readers can identify with: gaining love and acceptance, overcoming fears, and making decisions. Her best work has already placed her firmly in the top rank of contemporary children's writers.

—Anne Scott MacLeod, updated by Lisa A. Wroble

BACON, Martha (Sherman)

Nationality: American. **Born:** Berkeley, California, 2 April 1917. **Education:** Anna Head School, Berkeley; Miss Barry's Foreign School, Florence; Barrington School, Great Barrington, Massachusetts. **Family:** Married 1) Philip Oliver-Smith, three children; 2) R.B. Ballinger in 1963, two stepchildren. **Career:** Editorial assistant, *Atlantic Monthly,* Boston, 1954-56; feature editor, *Vogue,* New York, 1956-57, and *Harper's Bazaar,* New York, 1957-59; Lecturer in Creative Writing, University of Rhode Island, Kingston, 1960-63; Lecturer, later Assistant Professor of English, Rhode Island College, Providence, 1965-81. **Awards:** Borestone Poetry award, 1957. **Died:** 1981.

Publications for Children

Fiction

Sophia Scrooby Preserved, illustrated by Donald Omar White. Boston, Little Brown, 1968; London, Gollancz, 1971.

The Third Road, illustrated by Robin Jacques. Boston, Little Brown, 1971.

In the Company of Clowns: A Commedia, illustrated by Richard Cuffari. Boston, Little Brown, 1973.

Moth Manor: A Gothic Tale, illustrated by Gail Burroughs. Boston, Little Brown, 1978.

Publications for Adults

Novels

A Star Called Wormwood. New York, Random House, 1948; London, Hodder and Stoughton, 1950.

A Masque of Exile. New York, Potter, 1962; London, Heinemann, 1963.

Poetry

Lament for the Chieftains and Other Poems. New York, Coward McCann, 1942.

Things Visible and Invisible. New York, Coward McCann, 1947.

Other

Puritan Promenade (essays). Boston, Houghton Mifflin, 1964.

Translator, *The Child Across the River,* by Giulietta d'Alessandro. New York, McDowell Obolensky, 1958.

*

Manuscript Collection: State University of New York Library, Buffalo.

Martha Bacon commented:

(1978) I began to write for children fairly recently. I found that the ideas which I wished to express were best realized in a story addressed to children. I enjoy writing these books because they allow the fancy to roam freely while the form remains disciplinary and even somewhat restricted. Clarity is essential and I enjoy pursuing it.

* * *

Teacher, poet, and novelist, Martha Bacon used her knowledge of literary craftsmanship to fit diverse writing styles to the small but distinguished and varied contribution she made to literature for children. In her first book, *Sophia Scrooby Preserved,* set in the late 18th century, her heroine is the daughter of an African chieftain; taken as a slave, the child is brought up and educated by the Scrooby family, surpassing in elegance and virtuosity the daughter of the house. While she is captured by pirates, held in bondage by a voodoo queen, and has other high adventures, Sophia preserves the mincing decorum of the period. Even the chapter titles—"As the hart panteth on the mountain so does Pansy pant for the joys of knowledge, and so great is her desire, and so earnest her efforts that success crowns her endeavors and she decks her brows with bays"—are part of Bacon's amusing parody of the florid style of the period; while her plot is clearly concocted pen-in-cheek, it is nevertheless relentlessly vigorous.

The Third Road is a deft time-shaft fantasy in which three lively children from a California household are taken by a unicorn into the formal elegance of a 17th-century Spanish court. While the merger of fantasy and realism is believable, the book lacks the ebullience of its predecessor or the cohesion of its successor, *In the Company of Clowns.* The latter is in the picaresque tradition, an adventure tale set in Italy early in the 18th century, and recreates vividly the casual and flamboyant life of the strolling players who are followed by the protagonist, a 12-year-old orphan who is bored with life as a convent scullery boy. *Moth Manor* is a skillful blend of realism and fantasy, the story of a doll house and its lively family, whose adventures are hidden from the child who tries valiantly to keep her great-aunt from giving the doll house away.

—Zena Sutherland

BACON, R(onald) L(eonard)

Nationality: New Zealander. **Born:** Melbourne, Australia, in 1924. **Family:** Married; three children. **Career:** Has worked as a teacher; principal, Favona Primary School, Auckland. **Address:** Unit 3, 16 Turama Road, Royal Oak, Auckland, New Zealand.

Publications for Children

Fiction

The Boy and the Taniwha, illustrated by Para Matchitt. Auckland and London, Collins, 1966.
Rua and the Sea People, illustrated by Para Matchitt. Auckland and London, Collins, 1968.
Again the Bugles Blow, illustrated by V.J. Livingston. Auckland and London, Collins, 1973.
Hemi Dances, illustrated by Sandra O'Callaghan. Auckland, Waiatarua, 1985.
Hotu-Puku, illustrated by Frank Bates. Auckland, Waiatarua, 1985.
Little Pukeko and the Tiki, illustrated by Frank Bates. Auckland, Waiatarua, 1985.
Maui and Kuri, illustrated by Frank Bates. Auckland, Waiatarua, 1985.
Ruru and the Green Fairies, illustrated by Frank Bates. Auckland, Waiatarua, 1985.
A Legend of Kiwi, illustrated by Steven Dickinson. Auckland, Waiatarua, 1987.
Hemi and the Whale, illustrated by Sharon O'Callaghan. Auckland, Waiatarua, 1988.
The Bone Tree, illustrated by Mark Wilson. Santa Rosa, California, SRA, 1994.

Other

The House of the People (Maori legend), illustrated by Robert F. Jahnke. Auckland, Collins, 1977.
Hatupatu and the Bird Woman (Maori legend), illustrated by Stanley J. Woods. Auckland, Collins, 1979.
The Fish of Our Fathers (Maori legend), illustrated by R.H.G. Jahnke. Auckland, Waiatarua, 1984.
Wind (reader), illustrated by Philippa Stitchbury. Auckland, Ashton, 1984.
Creation Stories, illustrated by R.H.G. Jahnke. Auckland, Shortland, 1984.
Maui Stories, illustrated by Cliff Whiting. Auckland, Shortland, 1984.
Maori Legends: Seven Stories, illustrated by Philippa Stitchbury. Auckland, Shortland, 1984.
The Home of the Winds (Maori legend), illustrated by R.H.G. Jahnke. Auckland, Waiatarua, 1985.
The Bay (reader), illustrated by Sandra Morris. Auckland, Ashton, 1986.
Jessie's Flower (reader), illustrated by Liz Dodson. Auckland, Shortland, 1986.
Codes and Messages. Auckland, Shortland, 1987.
Games and Their Past, illustrated by Ian McNee and Rachel Jones. Auckland, Shortland, 1987.
The Greatest (reader), illustrated by Bryan Pollard and Margaret McGrath. Auckland, Shortland, 1987.
Let's Make Music (reader), illustrated by Deirdre Gardiner. Auckland, Shortland, 1987.
Publishing a Book, photographs by Richard Redgrove. Auckland, Shortland, 1987.
Rainy Day Ideas!, with Carol Hosking, illustrated by Rachel Jones. Auckland, Shortland, 1987.
In My Bed (reader), illustrated by Sandra Morris. Auckland, Shortland, 1988.
In My Room (reader), illustrated by Glenda Jones. Auckland, Shortland, 1988.
Just Me (reader), illustrated by Kelvin Hawley. Auckland, Shortland, 1988.
Off to Work (reader), illustrated by Kelvin Hawley. Auckland, Shortland, 1988.
Our Dog Sam (reader), illustrated by Helen Funnell. Auckland, Shortland, 1988.
Save Our Earth (reader), illustrated by Rodney McRae. Auckland, Shortland, 1988.
The Scarecrow (reader), illustrated by Isabel Lowe. Auckland, Shortland, 1988.
Weaving, illustrated by Heidi Fegan. Auckland, Shortland, 1988.
Grandma's Bicycle (reader), illustrated by Philip Webb. Auckland, Shortland, 1988.

Publications for Adults

Novels

In the Sticks. Auckland, Collins, 1963.
Along the Road. Auckland and London, Collins, 1964.

Other

Auckland: Gateway to New Zealand, photographs by Gregory Riethmaier. Auckland and London, Collins, 1968.
Auckland: Town and Around, photographs by Gregory Riethmaier. Auckland and London, Collins, 1973.

* * *

Writing for R.L. Bacon developed as a by-product of his busy and demanding career as a rural teacher. His first novel, *In the Sticks,* written for an adult audience but of interest to older children, describes the vicissitudes, the heartbreaks, the fun, and the excitement of the teacher working in the backblocks.

His first two picture books for children are both illustrated by the Maori artist Para Matchitt. *The Boy and the Taniwha* describes the life of the little Maori boy Hemi. He lives with his grandmother according to the traditional customs before the coming of the Pakeha. The story tells of Hemi's growth in knowledge and in courage when he finds the taniwha and passes the test of manhood. The text is illustrated magnificently by the lively shapes and colours of Para Matchitt's drawings. Two later picture books continue the theme of Maori life.

Rua and the Sea People tells of another Maori boy, Rua, and his life by the sea. The climax to this tale is the arrival of Captain Cook's ship in 1769, "big, as the meeting house on the marae was big." Rua does not hold as much interest as Hemi, and Para Matchitt has used a great deal of abstraction in his illustrations. These are striking but children do not have for them the warm affection that they have for his earlier illustrations.

In *Again the Bugles Blow* there is a return to the verve of *The Boy and the Taniwha.* This short novel describes one of the great moments in those sad inter-racial conflicts of the mid-19th century, the Land Wars. The main character is another lad named Rua, a contemporary Maori boy who lives in the inner city. By some sort of time shift he finds himself in the Auckland of the early 1860s. Attached to the British military forces during their thrust into the Waikato, Rua sees the tragic waste of war. The climax of the story describes one of the most courageous moments of the Maori warriors. Encircled at Orakau, short of food and water, under bombardment by the Armstrong guns, the defenders fought to the end. Rua had crept into the village or "pa." He observed the call to surrender and the famous reply, "We shall fight on for ever, and ever and ever."

More recently Bacon has made a major contribution to New Zealand writing for children by retelling some of the major stories of Maori mythology in a simple and direct style. *Creation Stories, Maui Stories,* and *Maori Legends: Seven Stories* contain tales that are the heritage of all New Zealanders both Maori and non-Maori, and are a very welcome addition to accessible indigenous material.

The House of the People, The Fish of Our Fathers, and *The Home of the Winds* are a trilogy of books based upon traditional Maori life. They describe the making of a meeting house, the construction of a war canoe, and the building and fortification of a pa on a site that needs to be defended. The books are meticulously researched and finely detailed. The illustrations, especially in the latter two books, beautifully demonstrate the elaborate carving and the dignity of the ritual.

Little Pukeko and the Tiki and *A Legend of Kiwi* are further examples of the excellence the author demonstrates when dealing with material of a traditional nature. *Hemi Dances* brings us to the contemporary world of breakdancing but is skilfully based upon movement in the natural world. Bacon writes a crisp, uncluttered narrative, whether it is of the tragic dilemma of a boy caught between two warring armies or in retelling tales of myth, legend, and folklore. As a sensitive interpreter he has brought spiritual and imaginative nourishment from Maori culture to share with a much wider audience.

—Tom Fitzgibbon

BAGNOLD, Enid (Algerine)

Nationality: British. **Born:** Rochester, Kent, 27 October 1889. **Education:** Prior's Field, Godalming, Surrey, in Marburg, Germany, Lausanne, Switzerland, and at the Villa Leona, Paris; studied painting with Walter Sickert. **Military Service:** Served as a driver with the French Army during World War I. **Family:** Married Sir Roderick Jones in 1920 (died 1962); three sons and one daughter. **Awards:** Arts Theatre prize, 1951; American Academy Award of Merit, 1956. C.B.E. (Commander, Order of the British Empire), 1976. **Died:** 31 March 1981.

Publications for Children

Fiction

Alice and Thomas and Jane, illustrated by the author and Laurian Jones. London, Heinemann, 1930; New York, Knopf, 1931.

National Velvet, illustrated by Laurian Jones. London, Heinemann, and New York, Morrow, 1935.

Play

National Velvet, adaptation of her own novel (produced London, 1946). Published in *Embassy Successes 2,* London, Sampson Low, 1946; published separately, New York, Dramatists Play Service, 1961.

Publications for Adults

Novels

The Happy Foreigner. London, Heinemann, and New York, Century, 1920.

Serena Blandish; or, The Difficulty of Getting Married (as A Lady of Quality). London, Heinemann, 1924; New York, Doran, 1925.

The Squire. London, Heinemann, 1938; as *The Door of Life,* New York, Morrow, 1938.

The Loved and Envied. London, Heinemann, and New York, Doubleday, 1951.

The Girl's Journey: Containing The Happy Foreigner and The Squire. London, Heinemann, and New York, Doubleday, 1954.

Plays

Lottie Dundass (produced Santa Barbara, California, and Wimbledon, 1942; London, 1943). London, Heinemann, 1941; included in *Two Plays,* 1951.

Poor Judas (produced Bradford, 1946; London, 1951). Included in *Two Plays,* 1951.

Two Plays (includes *Lottie Dundass* and *Poor Judas*). London, Heinemann, 1951; as *Theatre: Two Plays,* New York, Doubleday, 1951.

Gertie (produced New York, 1952; as *Little Idiot,* produced London, 1953).

The Chalk Garden (produced New York, 1955; London, 1956). New York, Random House, and London, Heinemann, 1956.

The Last Joke (produced London, 1960). Included in *Four Plays,* 1970.

The Chinese Prime Minister (produced New York, 1964; Cambridge and London, 1965). New York, Random House, and London, French, 1964.
Call Me Jacky (produced Oxford, 1968). Included in *Four Plays,* 1970; revised version, as *A Matter of Gravity* (produced Washington, D.C., 1975; New York, 1976), London, Heinemann, and New York, French 1978.
Four Plays (includes *The Chalk Garden, The Last Joke, The Chinese Prime Minister, Call Me Jacky*). London, Heinemann, 1970; Boston, Little Brown, 1971.

Poetry

The Sailing Ships and Other Poems. London, Heinemann, 1918.
Poems. Andoversford, Gloucestershire, Whittington Press, 1980.

Other

A Diary Without Dates. London, Heinemann, and Boston, Luce, 1918.
Enid Bagnold's Autobiography: From 1889. London, Heinemann, 1969; Boston, Little Brown, 1970.
Letters to Frank Harris and Other Friends, edited by R.P. Lister. Andoversford, Gloucestershire, Whittington Press, 1980.

Translator, *Alexander of Asia,* by Princess Marthe Bibesco. London, Heinemann, 1935.

*

Critical Study: *Enid Bagnold: The Authorized Biography* by Anne Sebba, London, Weidenfeld and Nicolson, 1986; New York, Taplinger, 1987.

* * *

Enid Bagnold was not really a children's writer. She was a playwright of considerable talent, creating forceful characters and plots with real human interest. It is ironic, therefore, that many people know her best for her "children's" story, written many years ago—*National Velvet,* the film of which gave the child Elizabeth Taylor her first starring role. For those who know the story only from the highly inaccurate film I can only urge them to read the book, which deserved far better treatment.

On the surface it is a "pony book." The Sussex butcher's family of five girls and a boy are all horse mad, but they have only the delivery-cart pony between them. The youngest girl, Velvet, a skinny straw-haired child with braces on her teeth, cuts out pictures of horses and daydreams about them. Her chance comes when she wins for a shilling in a raffle a rawboned piebald horse. She rides him in a local gymkhana and he smashes up the jumps except for the wall, over which he sails in great style. Their delivery-lad, an ex-jockey, suggests jokingly that the piebald should enter the Grand National and Velvet takes him seriously. Since the horse will not jump for anyone else, and Velvet can pass for a boy, she trains him herself. She suffers appallingly from nerves, and though they win the race she faints and all is revealed.

It is in the inter-relation of the characters that the author's skill is displayed. The adult reader sees how the different personalities of the sisters are contrasted, the placidity of their outsize mother compared to her eccentric small son who keeps his spit in a bottle, and Velvet herself, horrified by the publicity, insisting she did it not for fame or fortune but for the horse himself, so that he could fulfil his own potential. *National Velvet* can satisfy on many levels.

—Ann G. Hay

BAILEY, Carolyn Sherwin

Nationality: American. **Born:** Hoosick Falls, New York, 25 October 1875. **Education:** Lansingburgh Academy; Teachers College, Columbia University, New York, graduated 1896; Montessori School, Rome; New York School of Social Work. **Family:** Married Eben Clayton Hill in 1936. **Career:** Principal, Jefferson Avenue Kindergarten, Springfield, Massachusetts; taught in New York City public schools; social worker, Warren Goddard House, New York; editor, children's department, *Delineator* magazine, New York; from 1916, editor, *American Childhood* magazine, Springfield, Massachusetts. **Awards:** American Library Association Newbery Medal, 1947. **Died:** 23 December 1961.

PUBLICATIONS FOR CHILDREN

Fiction

Stories for Sunday Telling. Boston, Pilgrim Press, 1916.
Stories for Any Day. Boston, Pilgrim Press, 1917.
Stories for Every Holiday. New York, Abingdon Press, 1918.
Once Upon a Time Animal Stories. Springfield, Massachusetts, Bradley, 1918.
The Outdoor Story Book. Boston, Pilgrim Press, 1918.
Everyday Stories, illustrated by Frederick Knowles. Springfield, Massachusetts, Bradley, 1919.
Hero Stories, illustrated by Frederick Knowles. Springfield, Massachusetts, Bradley, 1919.
The Enchanted Bugle and Other Stories. Dansville, New York, Owen, 1920.
The Torch of Courage and Other Stories. Springfield, Massachusetts, Bradley, 1921.
Flint: The Story of a Trail, illustrated by Charles Lassell. Springfield, Massachusetts, Bradley, 1922.
Reading Time Stories. Chicago, Whitman, 1923.
Surprise Stories. Chicago, Whitman, 1923.
When Grandfather Was a Boy: Stories. Boston, Pilgrim Press, 1923.
Friendly Tales: A Community Story Book. Springfield, Massachusetts, Bradley, 1923.
Lincoln Time Stories. Chicago, Whitman, 1924.
The Wonderful Tree and Other Golden Day Stories, illustrated by Joseph Dash. Chicago, Whitman, 1925.
Little Men and Women Stories. Chicago, Whitman, 1926.
The Wonderful Window and Other Stories, illustrated by Katherine Wireman. Nashville, Cokesbury Press, 1926.
The Wonderful Days, illustrated by C.B. Fall. Chicago, Whitman, 1929.
Read Aloud Stories, illustrated by Hildegard Lupprian. Springfield, Massachusetts, Bradley, 1929.

Li'l' Hannibal. New York, Platt and Munk, 1938.
Country-Stop, illustrated by Grace Paull. New York, Viking Press, 1942; as *Wishing-Well House,* London, Muller, 1950.
Pioneer Art in America, illustrated by Grace Paull. New York, Viking Press, 1944.
The Little Rabbit Who Wanted Red Wings, illustrated by Dorothy Grider. New York, Platt and Munk, 1945.
Miss Hickory, illustrated by Ruth Chrisman Gannett. New York, Viking Press, 1946; London, Hodder and Stoughton, 1977.
Merry Christmas Book, illustrated by Eunice Young Smith. Chicago, Whitman, 1948.
Old Man Rabbit's Dinner Party, illustrated by Robinson. New York, Platt and Munk, 1949; revised edition, 1961.
Enchanted Village (includes play *Land of the Free*), illustrated by Eileen Evans. New York, Viking Press, 1950.
Finnegan II, His Nine Lives, illustrated by Kate Seredy. New York, Viking Press, 1953.
The Little Red Schoolhouse, illustrated by Dorothy Bayley Morse. New York, Viking Press, 1957.
Flickertail, illustrated by Garry Mackenzie. New York, Walck, 1962.

Plays

Plays for the Children's Hour. Springfield, Massachusetts, Bradley, 1931.
This Way to Animal Land, with Ditzy Baker. Akron, Ohio, Saalfield, 1936.

Poetry

Stories and Rhymes for a Child, illustrated by Christine Wright. Springfield, Massachusetts, Bradley, 1909.
Songs of Happiness, music by Mary B. Ehrmann. Springfield, Massachusetts, Bradley, 1912.
A Christmas Party, illustrated by Cyndy Szekeres. New York, Pantheon, 1975.

Other

Mother Goose: Old Rhymes Reproduced in Connection with Their Veracious History, illustrated by Peter Newell. New York, Holt, 1905.
The Jingle Primer: A First Book in Reading Based on Mother Goose Rhymes and Folk Tales, with Clara L. Brown. New York, American Book Company, 1906.
Firelight Stories: Folk Tales Retold, illustrated by Diantha Horne. Springfield, Massachusetts, Bradley, 1907.
Boys' Make-at-Home Things, with Marian Elizabeth Bailey. New York, Stokes, 1912.
Girls' Make-at-Home Things. New York, Stokes, 1912.
The Children's Book of Games and Parties. Chicago, Donohue, 1913.
Every Child's Folk Songs and Games. Springfield, Massachusetts, Bradley, 1914.
Boys and Girls of Colonial Days, illustrated by Uldene Shriver. Chicago, Flanagan, 1917.
The Way of the Gate (reader), with others. New York, Macmillan, 1917.
What to Do for Uncle Sam: A First Book of Citizenship. Chicago, Flanagan, 1918.
Stories of Great Adventures, illustrated by Clara Burd. Springfield, Massachusetts, Bradley, 1919.
Folk Stories and Fables, illustrated by Frederick Nagler. Springfield, Massachusetts, Bradley, 1919.
Broad Stripes and Bright Stars: Stories of American History, illustrated by Power O'Malley. Springfield, Massachusetts, Bradley, 1919.
Wonder Stories: The Best Myths, illustrated by Clara Burd. Springfield, Massachusetts, Bradley, 1920; London, Batsford, 1924.
In- and Out-door Play Games, illustrated by Cobb Shinn. Chicago, Whitman, 1923.
All the Year Play Games, illustrated by Cobb Shinn. Chicago, Whitman, 1924.
Boys and Girls of Pioneer Days. Chicago, Flanagan, 1924.
Stories from an Indian Cave: The Cherokee Cave Builders, illustrated by Joseph Dash. Chicago, Whitman, 1924.
Boys and Girls of Discovery Days, illustrated by Dorothy Dulin. Chicago, Flanagan, 1931.
In Nature's Fairyland. Dansville, New York, Owen, 1927.
Untold History Stories, illustrated by Lillian Titus. Dansville, New York, Owen, 1927.
Forest, Field, and Stream Stories (reader), illustrated by Dorothy Dulin. Chicago, Flanagan, 1928.
Boys and Girls of Today. Chicago, Flanagan, 1928.
Boys and Girls of Modern Days, illustrated by Dorothy Dulin. Chicago, Flanagan, 1929.
Boy Heroes in Making America, illustrated by Lea Norris and Power O'Malley. Chicago, Flanagan, 1931.
Our Friends at the Zoo (reader), with Alice Hanthorn, illustrated by Ruth Hallock. Springfield, Massachusetts, McLoughlin, 1934.
Children of the Handcrafts, illustrated by Grace Paull. New York, Viking Press, 1935.
Tell Me a Birthday Story, illustrated by Margaret Ayer. New York, Stokes, 1935.
Tops and Whistles: True Stories of Early American Toys and Children, illustrated by Grace Paull. New York, Viking Press, 1937.
From Mocassins to Wings: Stories of Our Travel Ways, illustrated by Margaret Ayer. Springfield, Massachusetts, Bradley, 1938.
Garden, Orchard, and Meadow Stories (reader), illustrated by Dorothy Dulin. Chicago, Flanagan, 1939.
Homespun Playdays, illustrated by Grace Paull. New York, Viking Press, 1941.

Editor, with Clara M. Lewis, *For the Children's Hour,* illustrated by C. William Breck. Springfield, Massachusetts, Bradley, 1906.
Editor, *Stories Children Need.* Springfield, Massachusetts, Bradley, 1916.
Editor, *Tell Me Another Story.* Springfield, Massachusetts, Bradley, 1918.
Editor, *The Three Musketeers,* by Alexandre Dumas, illustrated by Harold Brett. Springfield, Massachusetts, Bradley, 1920.
Editor, *Lorna Doone,* by R.D. Blackmore. Springfield, Massachusetts, Bradley, 1921.
Editor, *Merry Tales for Children.* Springfield, Massachusetts, Bradley, 1921.
Editor, *Evangeline,* by Henry Wadsworth Longfellow. Springfield, Massachusetts, Bradley, 1922.
Editor, *In the Animal World.* Springfield, Massachusetts, Bradley, 1924.

Editor, *Stories Children Want,* illustrated by Jack Perkins. Springfield, Massachusetts, Bradley, 1931.
Editor, *Schoolroom Plays and Projects.* Springfield, Massachusetts, Bradley, 1932.

Publications for Adults

Other

Daily Program of Gift and Occupation Work, with Clara M. Lewis. Springfield, Massachusetts, Bradley, 1904.
For the Story-Teller: Story Telling and Stories to Tell. Springfield, Massachusetts, Bradley, 1913.
Montessori Children. New York, Holt, 1915.
Letting in the Gang. Privately printed, 1916.
Everyday Play for Children. Chicago, Donohue, 1916.

Editor, *Sketches along Life's Road,* by Elizabeth Harrison. Boston, Stratford, 1930.
Editor, *The Story-Telling Hour.* New York, Dodd Mead, and London, Harrap, 1934.

* * *

Although the total body of Carolyn Sherwin Bailey's creative work is considerable, those works with the most lasting value are her series on pioneer arts and crafts in America and her *Miss Hickory,* which won the Newbery Medal. Included in the pioneer arts and crafts series are *Children of the Handcrafts, Tops and Whistles, Homespun Playdays,* and *Pioneer Arts in America.* These works are the result of their author's genuine interest in the history and artifacts of a bygone era. *Pioneer Art in America* is representative of the series. Such details in this work as, for example, the weathervane, a wax doll, a silver teapot, a sparking lamp, the jewels of Sandwich, a fiddlin fool, and others are all touched with elements of suspense and drama and a strong flavor of historical accuracy. These stories could have been thinly skeletal and dully factual. Instead they are fully fleshed out, balanced, fluid, and historically appealing, enough so to continue to captivate and hold readers.

Miss Hickory, however, is Bailey's classic work. Although her talent is evident in her early works, close acquaintance with the total body of her writing indicates she experienced a gradual but steady genesis as a creative artist. Like Carlo Collodi, A.A. Milne, L. Frank Baum, E. Nesbit, and others, Bailey used the toy device as literary motif. Her toy doll, Miss Hickory, is by no means a stillborn plaything, for into her Bailey has breathed life that requires no resuscitation from readers. Although Miss Hickory is sometimes as hardheaded as the hickory nut which is, indeed, her head, she is no inert replica of any ordinary toy or real life personage.

Unlike some toys now famous in literature Miss Hickory does not interact, except by implication, with either her creator or with other creatures of the human world. Instead, Miss Hickory's ostensible ties are with animal friends and acquaintances imbued with human characteristics—Crow, Chipmunk, Squirrel, Hen-Pheasant, and Mr. T. Willard-Brown, a barnyard cat. In her relationships with these friends Miss Hickory is spunky, spirited, sharp-tongued, and seemingly inflexible, yet inwardly she is often vulnerable and insecure. She is, nonetheless, never a real loser. Despite numerous near-calamities, with hickory nut for head and applewood twig for body, Miss Hickory proves herself a survivor, even after being deprived of head and brain by Squirrel, for she miraculously becomes a living, blossoming, fruit-bearing branch of an old apple tree. Thus Bailey, in giving Miss Hickory a life after death, has added a new dimension to the use of the toy motif and has given to children and other readers a most satisfying instance of the creative ideal.

—Charity Chang

BAKER, Betty (Lou)

Nationality: American. **Born:** Bloomsburg, Pennsylvania, 20 June 1928. **Education:** In Orange, New Jersey. **Family:** Married Robert George Venturo in 1948 (divorced 1965); one son. **Career:** Dental assistant, owner of gift shop, lecturer. Formerly editor, *Roundup* magazine. **Awards:** Western Heritage award, 1964, 1971; Western Writers of America Spur award, 1968. **Died:** 6 November 1987.

Publications for Children

Fiction

The Sun's Promise, illustrated by Juliette Palmer. New York, Abelard Schuman, 1962; London, Abelard Schuman, 1963.
Little Runner of the Longhouse, illustrated by Arnold Lobel. New York, Harper, and Kingswood, Surrey, World's Work, 1962.
Killer-of-Death, illustrated by John Kaufmann. New York, Harper, 1963.
The Shaman's Last Raid, illustrated by Leonard Shortall. New York, Harper, 1963; as *The Medicine Man's Last Stand,* New York, Scholastic, 1965.
The Treasure of the Padres, illustrated by Leonard Shortall. New York, Harper, 1964.
Walk the World's Rim. New York, Harper, 1965.
The Blood of the Brave. New York, Harper, 1966.
The Dunderhead War. New York, Harper, 1967.
Do Not Annoy the Indians, illustrated by Harold Goodwin. New York, Macmillan, and London, Collier Macmillan, 1968.
The Pig War, illustrated by Robert Lopshire. New York, Harper, 1969; Kingswood, Surrey, World's Work, 1971.
And One Was a Wooden Indian. New York, Macmillan, 1970.
A Stranger and Afraid. New York, Macmillan, and London, Collier Macmillan, 1972.
The Big Push, illustrated by Bonnie Johnson. New York, Coward McCann, 1972.
The Spirit Is Willing. New York, Macmillan, 1974.
Dupper, illustrated by Chuck Eckart. New York, Greenwillow, 1976.
Save Sirrushany! (Also Agotha, Princess Gwyn, and All the Fearsome Beasts), illustrated by Erick Ingraham. New York, Macmillan, 1978.
Partners, illustrated by Emily McCully. New York, Greenwillow, 1978.

All-by-Herself, illustrated by Catherine Stock. New York, Greenwillow, 1980.
Santa Rat, illustrated by Tom Huffman. New York, Greenwillow, 1980.
The Great Desert Race. New York, Macmillan, 1980.
Danby and George, illustrated by Adrianne Lobel. New York, Greenwillow, 1981.
Worthington Botts and the Steam Machine, illustrated by Sal Murdocca. New York, Macmillan, 1981.
Seven Spells to Farewell. New York, Macmillan, 1982.
The Turkey Girl, illustrated by Harold Berson. New York, Macmillan, 1983.
My Sister Says, illustrated by Tricia Taggart. New York, Macmillan, 1984.
The Night Spider Case. New York, Macmillan, 1984.

Other

Arizona. New York, Coward McCann, 1969.
At the Center of the World: Based on Papago and Pima Myths, illustrated by Murray Tinkelman. New York, Macmillan, 1973.
Three Fools and a Horse (Apache folktale), illustrated by Glen Rounds. New York, Macmillan, 1975; Kingswood, Surrey, World's Work, 1977.
Settlers and Strangers: Native Americans of the Desert Southwest and History as They Saw It. New York, Macmillan, 1977.
No Help at All (Mayan legend), illustrated by Emily McCully. New York, Greenwillow, 1978.
Latki and the Lightning Lizard (Indian folktale), illustrated by Donald Carrick. New York, Macmillan, 1979.
Rat Is Dead and Ant Is Sad (Pueblo folktale), illustrated by Mamoru Funai. New York, Harper, 1981.
And Me, Coyote! (Indian folktales), illustrated by Maria Horvath. New York, Macmillan, and London, Macmillan, 1982.

Editor, *Great Ghost Stories of the Old West.* New York, Four Winds Press, 1968.

*

Manuscript Collections: University of California Library, Los Angeles; Kerlan Collection, University of Minnesota, Minneapolis.

* * *

Betty Baker carved a niche for herself as a writer of historical fiction about the southwestern United States and Mexico and of stories dealing with American Indians of the southwest. Her fiction ranges from gentle, humorous tales such as that of a little Iroquois boy who loves maple sugar—this one written using a controlled vocabulary for beginning readers *(Little Runner of the Longhouse)*—to historical fiction for young adolescents. She is at her best with one of these, *Walk the World's Rim,* a tightly plotted, well characterized story of the friendship of a young Indian boy and Esteban, the negro slave who was one of the four survivors of the ill-fated expedition led by Cabeza de Vaca in the 16th century. A companion piece to *Walk the World's Rim* is *A Stranger and Afraid,* the story of a young plains Indian captured by the Pueblo Indians of the southwest, who sees the expedition of Coronado as an opportunity to escape from the Pueblo Indians and to return to his people when he is given to the Spaniards as their guide.

Although Baker's early fiction emphasized the American Indian, she also wrote some interesting historical fiction. In *The Dunderhead War* she pairs an unlikely duo of 17-year-old Quincy Heffendorf from Missouri and his methodical German uncle, Fritz. This fast-paced story of the Mexican War of 1846 tells of the dangers and adventures which befell the ill-trained, undisciplined Missouri Volunteers and Quincy and his uncle, who followed the Volunteers in a wagon train. *The Great Desert Race* is based on an actual automobile race that was run between Los Angeles, California, and Phoenix, Arizona, over questionable or non-existent roads each year from 1908 through 1914. But Baker is at her best with her sensitive and sympathetic novels dealing with the American Indian during the transition period in the southwest when the white man first entered the area. *Killer-of-Death* is the finest of these stories. It is a moving tale of an Apache boy who comes to manhood just as the first white settlers entered Arizona—and what the coming of these strangers meant to the Apache nation.

Demonstrating her considerable versatility, Baker wrote several gently humorous fantasies in the talking beast-sorcerer tradition; *Save Sirrushany!* is the best of these. The author's historical fiction, fantasy, legends, and easy books for younger readers fill a real need for well written literature on a number of themes for children and adolescent readers.

—Margaret F. Maxwell

BAKER, Jeannie

Nationality: British. **Born:** Croydon, England, 2 November 1950. **Education:** Attended Croydon College of Art, 1968-70; Brighton Polytechnic, diploma in graphic design 1972. **Career:** Freelance illustrator, with commissions from *Nova, The Sunday Times,* and Thames Children's Television, 1972-77; full-time writer and illustrator, from 1977. Solo exhibitions of artwork, New York, London, Australia, from 1975; Animated filmmaker and director. **Awards:** Honour book, Australian Picture Book of the Year Award, 1985; Friends of the Earth Earthworm award, 1988; honour book, Australian Picture Book of the Year, 1988; Australian Film Institute Award, for best Australian animated film, 1988; International Board of Books for Young People (IBBY) Honour award, for illustration, 1990; Children's Book Council of Australia Picture Book of the Year, 1992; honour book, Australian Picture Book of the Year award, 1996; notable book, The American Library Association, 1996; Australian Wilderness Society Fiction award, for children's books, 1996. **Address:** c/o Walker Books, 87 Vauxhall Walk, London SE11 5HJ, England; 36 Park Street, Rozelle, Sydney NSW, Australia.

PUBLICATIONS FOR CHILDREN

Fiction (illustrated by the author)

Grandfather. London, Deutsch, 1977.
Grandmother. London, Deutsch, 1978.
Millicent. London, Deutsch, 1980
One Hungry Spider. London, Deutsch, 1982.
Home in the Sky. London, Walker Books, 1983; New York, Greenwillow, 1984.

Where the Forest Meets the Sea. London, Julia MacRae Books, 1987; New York, Greenwillow, 1988.
Window. London, Julia MacRae Books, and New York, Greenwillow, 1991.
The Story of Rosy Dock. New York, Greenwillow and Mark Macleod Books, Random House Australia, 1995.
The Hidden Forest, forthcoming.

*

Media Adaptation: *Where the Forest Meets the Sea* (film based on her book of the same title), 1988; *The Story of Rosy Dock* (film based on her book of the same title), 1995.

Illustrator: *Polar* by Elaine Moss, 1975.

Jeannie Baker comments:

I call my works 'collage constructions'.

The materials I use are mostly natural. Even the greenery is real, although, of course, I have to treat it with chemicals. I bleach it, bathe it in glycerine so that it will feel like it is 'alive', and then spray it finely with oil paint to give a permanent colour.

My work is an illusion in perspective. I try to give as great a feeling of depth to my work as possible, without making it three-dimensional, or a model. Various parts are usually flat at the back, but slightly rounded at the front to give the feeling of solidity and depth I want. Shadows also help me to achieve this.

My work is extremely time consuming; each element is composed of different materials, each posing very different problems.

* * *

Jeannie Baker's collages distinguish her picture books for children. Her artistic training in graphic design took place at the Croydon College of Art; she later graduated from Brighton College of Art with Honors in Art and Design. While at Brighton, Baker first began to work with the medium of collage. After working for a time as a freelance illustrator, Baker emigrated to Tasmania in 1975 and later came to Sydney, where she currently resides.

Her earliest illustrations were done for the book *Polar* (1975), which was written by Elaine Moss. Since that time, Baker has both written as well as illustrated her own work. Her artistry is strongly characterized by a dedication to detail; a preoccupation which she has stated demands much time and tremendous effort. Her work might best be categorized as a type of "art verite," since her emphasis has been upon the re-creation of urban and rural scenes through art. While her technique is visually identifiable as collage, it is collage done with an incredible adherence to natural materials. Wherever possible, Baker uses actual samples and pieces of the objects she portrays in her illustrations, in scale and utilizing realistic perspective. When viewed through the vehicle of a magnifying glass, there is the eerie feeling that the viewer is not just sensing the *essence* of the object portrayed, but can actually almost *touch and feel* the fabrics and textures used in the art. Baker creates models of scenes which are then photographed. Her artwork can stand on its own. Her wordless picture book *Window* (1991) highlights the theme of man's impact upon the environment over time in a quiet, yet powerful manner, evidenced by the urbanization (homes, a McDonald's, cars, etc.) of a quiet, secluded area.

Thematically, she is concerned with relationships between people, and between people and the environment. The books *Grandfather* (1977) and *Grandmother* (1978) offer strong intergenerational themes which center upon the relationships between a young girl and her grandfather in the first book, and the same young girl (wearing identical clothing) and her grandmother, in the second. There is a peace which pervades Baker's work, underscoring the meaningful nature of the relationships, as evidenced in the illustration in *Grandfather* in which the grandfather quietly shares a story with his granddaughter, or in the quiet, yet eminently significant pronouncement of the child at the conclusion of *Grandmother* in which the young girl states "I love my grandmother." These two stories were followed by *Millicent* (1980), a story of a lonely old woman who befriends pigeons in Sydney's Hyde Park, and *One Hungry Spider* (1982).

In 1984, *Home in the Sky,* one of Baker's most enterprising works, was published. Preparation for this book, which is set in New York City, required Baker to spend ten months in New York in order to get a feel of the city and collect materials needed for the art collages. The story skillfully re-creates the New York landscape and the "aura" of the city, both in a positive as well as negative sense, but always with a sensitive touch. It tells the story of Mike, the man who loves pigeons, and the strong relationship he has with his birds. One day, "Light," a white pigeon, flies away. Light has a nasty encounter with some street pigeons, and is later rescued during a ride in a subway train (complete with graffiti and all) by a young boy. The pigeon is taken home by the boy, whose mother informs him that the band on his leg indicates that the pigeon belongs to someone else. Reluctantly, the young boy releases him, and the pigeon safely returns to a grateful Mike. The story contains a beautiful Central Park scene, a "slice of life" so realistic, active yet pastoral, that the reader is encouraged to carefully scrutinize it, savoring its painstaking and marvelous detail.

One of Baker's most successful and ambitious works has been *When the Forest Meets the Sea,* a serene yet stirring portrayal of the story of a young boy taken to an Australian forest by his father, where he imagines himself returned to a point in time when, with the exception of native Aboriginal inhabitants, the place was untouched by man's influence. Muted ghosts of prehistoric creatures are rendered mystically, superimposed upon the eminently "tangible" forest environment. The reader is left with the troubling image of the young boy wondering what the environment will look like as the years pass; thoughts disturbingly portrayed by the imposition of shadowy images of a Coca Cola can, a hotel, a swimming pool and cars as foreshadowing of the future. The final sentence, "But will the forest be here when we come back?" aptly summarizes the concerns of both the boy as well as Jeannie Baker, artist and environmental advocate. As the model for this book, Baker visited and studied the Daintree-Bloomfield region of North Queensland, Australia, setting up camp at Cape Tribulation, where she was able to make excursions as needed into the rain forest. During this time she collected specimens for her impressive collages in the book that were later exhibited at (among other places) Dromkeen, the Institute of Children's Literature in Riddells Creek, Victoria. Baker also directed a ten minute film (same title) based upon the book; it was the 1988 recipient of the Australian Film Institute Award for Best Australian Animated Film. *The Story of Rosy Dock* was also made into an animated film.

Baker's work has been exhibited in New York, London, and throughout Australia. She has won numerous awards and commendations in Australia and the United States, including the Australian Picture Book of the Year Award for *Home in the Sky* (1985), *Where the Forest Meets the Sea* (1988) and *Window* (1992).

—Karen Patricia Smith

BANG, Garrett. See **BANG, Molly.**

BANG, Molly Garrett

Has also written as Garrett Bang. **Nationality:** American. **Born:** Molly Garrett, 29 December 1943, Princeton, New Jersey. **Family:** Married Richard H. Campbell, 1974; one daughter. **Education:** Wellesley College, B.A. 1965; University of Arizona, M.A. 1969; Harvard University, M.A. 1971. **Career:** Author, illustrator, and translator; English teacher, Doshisha University, Kyoto, Japan, 1965-67; interpreter of Japanese, Asahi Shimbun, New York, 1969; reporter, Baltimore Sunpapers, Baltimore, 1970. Illustrator and consultant for UNICEF, Johns Hopkins Center for Medical Research and Training, and Harvard Institute for International Development. **Awards:** ALA Notable Book award, 1977, 1980; Caldecott honor, 1981; Kate Greenaway honor, 1983; Hans Christian Andersen award nomination, 1988; *Boston Globe/Horn Book* award for illustration, 1988. **Address:** 89 Water St., Woods Hole, Massachusetts 02543, U.S.A.

Publications for Children

Fiction (illustrated by the author)

The Grey Lady and the Strawberry Snatcher. New York, Four Winds, 1980.
Ten, Nine, Eight. New York, Greenwillow, 1983.
Delphine. New York, Morrow, 1988.
Yellow Ball. New York, Morrow, 1991.
One Fall Day. New York, Greenwillow, 1994.
Sunshine's Book. New York, Greenwillow, 1994.
Goose. New York, Blue Sky Press, 1996.
Chattanooga Sludge. San Diego, Harcourt Brace, 1996.
Common Ground: The Water, Earth, and Air We Share. New York, Blue Sky Press, 1997.
When I Get Angry. New York, Blue Sky Press, 1998.

Adaptor, *Dawn* (Japanese folktale). New York, Morrow, 1983.
Adaptor, *The Paper Crane* (Chinese folktale). New York, Greenwillow, 1985.
Adaptor and editor, *Tye May and the Magic Brush* (Chinese folktale). New York, Greenwillow, 1981.

Compiler, *The Goblins Giggle, and Other Stories* (folktales from France, China, Japan, Ireland, and Germany). New York, Scribner, 1973.
Editor, *Wiley and the Hairy Man* (adapted from an American folktale by mother, Betsy Bang). New York, Macmillan, 1975.
Editor, *The Buried Moon and Other Stories* (folktales from China, Japan, England, and India). New York, Scribner, 1977.

Translator and compiler, *Men from the Village Deep in the Mountains, and Other Japanese Folk Tales* (as Garrett Bang). New York, Macmillan, 1973.

Other

Picture This: Perception and Composition. Boston, Little, Brown, 1991.

*

Illustrator: *The Old Woman and the Red Pumpkin: A Bengali Folk Tale,* translated and edited by Betsy Bang, Macmillan, 1975; *The Old Woman and the Rice Thief,* translated and edited by B. Bang, Greenwillow, 1977; *Tuntuni, the Tailor Bird,* translated and edited by B. Bang, Greenwillow, 1978; *The Demons of Rajpur,* translated and edited by B. Bang, Greenwillow, 1980; *David's Landing* by Judith Benet Richardson, Woods Hole Historical Collection, 1984; *Red Dragonfly on My Shoulder,* translated by Sylvia Cassedy and Suetake Kunihirs, Harper, 1992.

* * *

A picture book artist who commands an array of media, Molly Bang reveals a unique artistic vision. In *Picture This: Perception and Composition,* Bang articulates that vision in concrete terms. She considers the fundamental elements required of anyone building a picture and identifies the principles of design. She places shapes on the page, manipulates color, size, and shape, then analyzes the resulting emotional responses. The book concludes with a series of exercises with construction paper to experiment with the relationships Bang discovers between a picture's structure and the viewer's feeling.

Picture This proves an insightful key to Bang's work in picture books. Her early illustrations, largely for folk tales retold by Bang or by her mother, Betsy Bang, reflect not only her wide-ranging interest in multicultural folklore, but also the insistent connection between visual images and mood. *The Goblins Giggle and Other Stories* uses a dark background against which sometimes frightening, sometimes endearing goblins in shades of grey and white act out. Bang's seventeen illustrations capture the stories' attitudes and accent the dynamic interplay of art and text to create a unified reading experience. Similarly, in the Bengali folk tales *Tintuni, the Tailor Bird, The Demons of Rajpur, The Old Woman and the Rice,* and *The Old Woman and the Red Pumpkin,* the artist uses palettes limited in color to complement strong lines and culturally stylized illustrations.

In *Wiley and the Hairy Man,* Bang adapts an American folk tale to a "Ready-to-Read" format. She highlights the river setting by using a muddy grey-green set against a white background. The frequent pictures, large typeface, and sparse per-page text ease the beginning reader into confidence with reading skills as they keep him/her fully involved in a rousing tale with dynamic illustrations. Paper cut-out and collage illustrations mark Bang's contribution to Amy L. Cohn's collection of intrinsically American folklore, *From Sea to Shining Sea.* These figures and objects serve a decorative rather than narrative function.

With *The Grey Lady and the Strawberry Snatcher,* named as a Caldecott Honor Book, Molly Bang unites visual and verbal storytelling. This full-color, wordless picture book adopts a folkloric tone. The title "grey lady" is depicted as a grey shape who moves silently through hallways, into grey forests, and finally home. Bang details only her expressive face and the hand that tightly holds the basket of vibrant red strawberries. This soft, harmless character outwits her hunched, pointed pursuer, whose sharp violet hat, pointed purple nose, and bony purple fingers reach out in menacing ways. Touches of strawberry red emanate from the follower's lips, fingertips, and cape, connecting him always with the delicacies he so desires.

Bang maintains her full range of color in *Ten, Nine, Eight,* also a Caldecott Honor Book; however, as she moves to the interior setting of a young child's room, Bang exchanges the earthy colors and many textures of the forest and berry patch for solid blocks of primary colors and backgrounds of soft pastels. With minimum text, she casts a father's bedtime story to his little girl as a countdown from "ten small toes all washed and warm" to a single child snuggled in bed. As in many other works from Molly Bang, the main characters are people of color whose specific ethnicity remains undefined and whose story can be shared by all children.

Dawn earned recognition as a *Boston Globe-Horn Book* Honor Book for its eloquent reshaping in words and pictures of the Japanese legend of the crane wife into a 19th-century American setting. Now an old man, the once poor shipbuilder narrates for his daughter the enigmatic life of her absent mother. Bang rejects standard typefaces and prints the man's words in calligraphy, thus keeping alive the passion and sense of loss from which he speaks. Full color paintings and black-and-white sketches alternate to unravel this powerful tale. Set against borders that foreshadow the story's action, the paintings establish a dynamic tension between color and white, between the texture and flat shapes that underscore the dominant weaving motif. These borders also signify the secrecy essential to the story.

The artist continues to paint in vibrant colors and to tell stories in simple, direct language for the youngest audiences in *Delphine, Yellow Ball,* and *One Fall Day.* Bang's interest in texture appears in *Delphine,* though a sense of speed and movement dominate as a girl rushes to the post office to pick up the surprise present from Gram. Bright, flat greens give way to sweeping strokes of white as her anticipation escalates. All action comes to a halt in a balanced double-page spread showing an unwrapped bicycle and resumes with controlled animation after Delphine masters riding. Bang maintains tight control over movement in *Yellow Ball.* Vibrant crayon pastels against a smooth beige background show many colored blankets and people on a beach. The single yellow ball gains readers' immediate focus when a family, now paper cut-out figures colored in pastels, plays catch and loses the ball to the water. Varying the ball's size from scene to scene, Bang describes its journey across the sea, into the sky, through wind and storms, and finally to a new home in single words or two-word phrases. The simplicity of the words match the simplicity of the object. Objects take the whole stage in the unusual preschool book *One Fall Day.* Bang invokes the voice of a mother talking to her child to narrate the adventures of this group of toys. She combines collage art and sharp color photographs to establish three dimensions and a playful sense of activity.

The Paper Crane may be the most well-known and celebrated work by Molly Bang. It won the *Boston Globe-Horn Book* Award for illustration and stands as a unique contribution to children's literature. Fine paper cut-outs placed in collage relate this story of a mysterious customer's gift to a troubled restaurant owner. Careful composition combines with precise placement of the cutouts at various distances from the level background to establish a three-dimensional quality. Though largely earth tones, the collages take on blocks of color from the clothing that adorns the multicultural customers. Introduction of the origami paper crane reinforces its magical influence, and its stark white color connects it immediately to the white-aproned restaurateur and his similarly dressed young helper. Bang depicts the crane's transformation into a living bird by invoking and then disrupting the three-dimensional space she creates; the crane metamorphoses from a folded paper crane into a bird painted into the picture's background, a space not held by any other figure in the book.

Foreground and background, collage art, clear photography, and manipulation of varied textures join in the illustrations for *Red Dragonfly on My Shoulder,* a collection of haiku. Bang collects recognizable objects to extend the "ease and playfulness" of haiku. She uses rocks and buttons, screws and thread, scissors and cloth, vegetables and discarded crustacean shells, candy and cookies to animate these thirteen short poems about animals. The materials may be familiar, but Bang's original assembly and innovative compositions distinguish this collection.

Any overview of Molly Bang's work quickly shows her artistic vision to be multifaceted. She demonstrates a ranging interest in people, their places and stories. Well-traveled, Bang produces books that benefit from sound research. These elements alone will surely expose readers to cultural diversity. Add to these traits her thoughtful consideration of the compositional elements of a picture, the emotional responses they cause, and a consistent exploration of texture and color, and one sees an individual imagination exploring unique forms of meaningful expression and communication.

—Cathryn M. Mercier

BANNER, Angela

Pseudonym: Angela Mary Maddison. **Nationality:** British. **Born:** Bombay, India, 14 May 1923. **Education:** Ancaster Gate and House, Bexhill, Sussex, 1933-37. **Family:** Married Lionel Parsons in 1941; two children. **Address:** The Ant and Bee Partnership, c/o Grindlays Bank, 13 St. James's Square, London SW1Y 4LF, England.

Publications for Children

Fiction

Ant and Bee: An Alphabetical Story for Tiny Tots, illustrated by Bryan Ward. Leicester, Ward, 1950; New York, Watts, 1963.

More Ant and Bee, illustrated by Bryan Ward. London, Ward, 1956; New York, Watts, 1960.

Mr. Fork and Curly Fork: A Time Story. London, Ward, 1956.

One, Two, Three with Ant and Bee: A Counting Story, illustrated by Bryan Ward. London, Ward, 1958; New York, Watts, 1963.

Around the World with Ant and Bee, illustrated by Bryan Ward. London, Ward, 1958; New York, Watts, 1960.

More and More Ant and Bee: Another Alphabetical Story, illustrated by Bryan Ward. London, Ward, 1961; New York, Watts, 1962.
Ant and Bee and the Rainbow: A Story about Colours, illustrated by Bryan Ward. London, Ward, and New York, Watts, 1962.
Ant and Bee and Kind Dog: An Alphabetical Story, illustrated by Bryan Ward. London, Ward, and New York, Watts, 1963.
Happy Birthday with Ant and Bee, illustrated by Bryan Ward. London, Ward, and New York, Watts, 1964.
Ant and Bee and the ABC, illustrated by Bryan Ward. London, Ward, and New York, Watts, 1966.
Ant and Bee Time, illustrated by the author. London, Kaye and Ward, and New York, Watts, 1969.
Ant and Bee and the Secret, illustrated by the author. London, Kaye and Ward, and New York, Watts, 1970.
Ant and Bee and the Doctor, illustrated by the author. London, Kaye and Ward, and New York, Watts, 1971.
The Ant and Bee Big Buy Bag, illustrated by the author. London, Kaye and Ward, 1971.
Ant and Bee Go Shopping, illustrated by the author. London, Kaye and Ward, and New York, Watts, 1972.
Kind Dog on Monday, illustrated by the author. London, Ant and Bee Partnership, 1972.
Kind Dog Up and Down the Hill, illustrated by the author. London, Ant and Bee Partnership, 1972.
Which Two Will Meet?, illustrated by the author. London, Ant and Bee Partnership, 1972.
Dear Father Christmas, illustrated by the author. London, Ant and Bee Partnership, 1984.

*

Angela Banner comments:

The best reading teacher for a child is another child. My books are made for shared-reading between children. No child is too young to "read" a few words from memory and so contribute to a story telling. Early "memory reading" leads to reading confidence, too often destroyed by educating adults.

* * *

Angela Banner is the author (and sometimes also the illustrator) of the enormously popular series about Ant and Bee. She says she chose an ant and a bee because she used to be afraid of insects and she hoped her children would be different. But, in fact, their insectness is merely incidental. Their smallness is nicely exploited, and Bee does a good deal of flying about, often with Ant on his back. But they are not insects in the way that Mr. Jackson is a toad or Samuel Whiskers a rat. And they are not trying to be. They are zany, one-dimensional characters with enormous appeal for children. They come in small, fat, colourful packets as tempting as a box of Smarties.

The text may be tedious stuff for reading-aloud parents but at least they have the consolation of some bizarre ideas and surrealistic conjunctions and the knowledge that the books are educational as well as entertaining. The books are designed to encourage reading (with key words from a limited vocabulary), counting, telling the time, knowing the colours. The least overtly educational is one of the most successful. *Happy Birthday with Ant and Bee* is supposed to make children aware of the order of the days of the week, but is in fact more of a juvenile guide to the proper conduct of a birthday party. *One, Two, Three with Ant and Bee* can be guaranteed to teach children not only how to count but how to write and read their numbers. As for the reading books, Banner once said she chooses the key words first, "like cooking ingredients." Some of the key words are definitely odd. If you meet a 4-year-old who knows a *yew*-tree and a tea-*urn* when he sees them, you can be sure he has *Ant and Bee* in his house.

The effect of the whole series is to assure a child that books are fun and small, friendly, familiar objects, not glossy beautiful things that need to be treated reverently. The series could be called vulgar, brash, unsubtle, limited, marred by over-emphatic punctuation. But the books combine that mixture of the rational and irrational, the strange and familiar in which children delight. They are lively, funny, inventive, and instructive, and undoubtedly successful.

—Ann Thwaite

BANNERMAN, Helen

Nationality: British (Scottish). **Born:** Helen Brodie Cowan Watson, Edinburgh, Scotland, 25 February 1862; brought up in Madeira. **Education:** At home, and at Miss Olliphant's school; University of St. Andrews, Fife, L.L.A. (external degree) 1887. **Family:** Married William Burney Bannerman in 1889 (died 1924); two daughters and two sons. **Career:** Lived in India from 1889. **Died:** 13 October 1946.

PUBLICATIONS FOR CHILDREN (ORIGINAL EDITIONS PUBLISHED ANONYMOUSLY; ILLUSTRATED BY THE AUTHOR)

Fiction

The Story of Little Black Sambo. London, Grant Richards, 1899; New York, Stokes, 1900.
The Story of Little Black Mingo. London, Nisbet, 1901; New York, Stokes, 1902.
The Story of Little Black Quibba. London, Nisbet, 1902; New York, Stokes, 1903.
Little Degchie-Head: An Awful Warning to Bad Babas. London, Nisbet, 1903; as *The Story of Little Kettle-Head,* New York, Stokes, 1904.
Pat and the Spider: The Biter Bit. London, Nisbet, 1904; New York, Stokes, 1905.
The Story of the Teasing Monkey. London, Nisbet, 1906; New York, Stokes, 1907.
The Story of Little Black Quasha. London, Nisbet, and New York, Stokes, 1908.
The Story of Little Black Bobtail. London, Nisbet, and New York, Stokes, 1909.
The Story of Sambo and the Twins. New York, Stokes, 1936; London, Nisbet, 1937.
The Story of Little White Squibba. London, Chatto and Windus, 1966.

*

Critical Studies: *Little Black Sambo: A Closer Look: A History of...The Story of Little Black Sambo and Its Popularity/Controversy in the United States* by Phyllis J. Yuill, New York, Racism and Sexism Resource Center, 1976; *Sambo Sahib: The Story of Little Black Sambo and Helen Bannerman* by Elizabeth Hay, Edinburgh, Harris, and New York, Barnes and Noble, 1981.

* * *

Helen Bannerman's *The Story of Little Black Sambo* was made up by an Englishwoman living in India in the 1890s to amuse her children. When it was published, embellished by its author's own rather crude coloured illustrations, it was an immediate success and has been continuously in print ever since. It is easy to see why so many generations of children have enjoyed having it read to them—it has even been called "one of the funniest books in existence." The language is simple; there is a picture to look at on almost every other page; and the story-line has the riveting simplicity of a folk-tale. Little Black Sambo, given a fine new Red Coat, Blue Trousers, Purple Shoes, and Green Umbrella, goes out for a walk in the Jungle where he meets four Tigers who, one after another, agree not to eat him in return for one of his pieces of finery. (The Purple Shoes have to be worn as ear-muffs, while the fourth Tiger can only manage to hold the Green Umbrella by tying a knot in his tail.) The Tigers meet and quarrel over which of them is now the grandest. In the end, in a climax which small children find tremendously funny, the Tigers chase each other round a tree so fast that they simply melt away, leaving nothing but a great big pool of melted butter. Sambo's father, Black Jumbo, takes this home with him, and with it his mother, Black Mumbo, makes an enormous feast of pancakes, of which Sambo eats no fewer than "a Hundred and Sixty-nine."

In its various successors there is a similar pattern of repetition-with-variation, culminating in a ludicrous and often innocently bloodthirsty denouement: in *Little Black Mingo* the Mugger swallows the "horrid cross old woman," Black Noggy, complete with a tin of kerosene and a box of matches, with explosive results; in *Little Black Quibba* the Elephant and the Snake engage in a fight in which the Elephant falls over a cliff and ties his trunk together with the Snake into such a tight knot that the Snake (whose rear end is curled round a tree) is pulled out "longer and longer and thinner and thinner" until it breaks "with a Snap! into three pieces."

Since the 1930s in the United States and from 1972 on in Great Britain there has been vociferous unease about the racism implicit in these stories. It is true that if one takes the naming of the characters, together with the garishly coloured clothes they are so proud of, there is evident a certain unwitting condescension towards the black human protagonists which passed unnoticed a century ago but which properly raises qualms in the uneasy multiracial climate of today. In fairness to Bannerman it should be mentioned that much of the American hostility to *Little Black Sambo* related not to her own drawings but to their appallingly offensive vulgarisation by other illustrators in the 50-odd unauthorised versions published in the U.S. (Through the unfortunate action of an intermediary she had lost control of the copyright in 1899 in return for a flat payment of five pounds.) Moreover the caricature style of her own illustrations is applied just as much to the white personae in her now-forgotten volumes as to the black ones in her popular successes. On the whole the fault seems to lie less in Bannerman than in the diseased state of our own culture in which the word Sambo (in the 19th century a proper name) has for several decades now been used only as a term of abuse. It is doubtful whether a normal child in a normal household will take any harm from these books, the more so since the child reader's natural inclination, whatever his colour, is to identify wholeheartedly with the Little Black hero or heroine. Nevertheless the offence they might cause to some readers is real, so that the sensitive teacher will be aware of the need to use tact and caution in introducing them into the classroom.

—Frank Whitehead

BARKER, Cicely Mary

Nationality: British. **Born:** Croydon, Surrey, 28 June 1895. **Education:** At home, and at Croydon School of Art. **Career:** Freelance artist: designed and painted screens and stained glass for St. George's, Waddon, and other churches in Surrey. **Died:** 16 February 1973.

PUBLICATIONS FOR CHILDREN (ILLUSTRATED BY THE AUTHOR)

Fiction

The Lord of the Rushie River. London, Blackie, 1938; New York, Hippocrene, 1977.

Groundsel and Necklaces. London, Blackie, 1946; as *The Fairy's Gift*, Blackie, and New York, Hippocrene, 1977.

Play

When Spring Came In at the Window, music by Olive Linnell. London, Blackie, 1942.

Poetry

Flower Fairies of the Spring. London, Blackie, 1923; New York, Macmillan, 1927.

Flower Fairies of the Summer. London, Blackie, 1925; New York, Macmillan, 1927.

Flower Fairies of the Autumn. London, Blackie, 1926; New York, Macmillan, 1927.

The Book of Flower Fairies. London, Blackie, 1927.

Fairies of the Trees. London, Blackie, 1940; as *Flower Fairies of the Trees,* 1961; New York, Hippocrene, 1976.

Flower Fairies of the Garden. London, Blackie, 1944; New York, Hippocrene, 1976.

Flower Fairies of the Wayside. London, Blackie, 1948; New York, Hippocrene, 1976.

Flower Fairy Picture Book (selection). London, Blackie, 1955.

Flower Fairies of the Winter. London, Blackie, and New York, Bedrick, 1985.

Other

A Flower Fairy Alphabet. London, Blackie, 1934; New York, Hippocrene, 1978.

Lively Stories (readers; *The Little House; Do You Know?; The Click-Clock Man; The Why Girl; Hutch, The Peg Doll*). London, Macmillan, and New York, St. Martin's Press, 5 vols., 1954-55.

Lively Numbers (readers; *The Little Man, The Little Boats, The Lazy Giant*). London, Macmillan, and New York, St. Martin's Press, 3 vols., 1960-62.

Lively Words (readers). London, Macmillan, and New York, St. Martin's Press, 2 vols., 1961-62.

The Sand, The Sea, and the Sun (textbook). Glasgow, Gibson, 1970.

An A.B.C. of Flower Fairies. London, Blackie, 1978; New York, Hippocrene, 1980.

Editor, *Old Rhymes for All Times*. London, Blackie, 1928; New York, Dodge, 1932.

Editor, *Rhymes New and Old*. London, Blackie, 1933; Poughkeepsie, New York, Artists and Writers Guild, 1935; as *A Little Book of Rhymes New and Old*, Blackie, 1937.

Editor, *A Little Book of Old Rhymes*. London, Blackie, 1936; New York, Hippocrene, 1977.

Editor, *The Rhyming Rainbow: Poems*. London, Blackie, and New York, Hippocrene, 1977.

*

Illustrator: *Guardian Angel Birthday Cards*, 1923; *Beautiful Bible Pictures*, 1932; *The Little Picture Hymn Book*, 1933; *He Leadeth Me* by Dorothy O. Barker, 1936; *The Flower Fairies Gardening Year*, 1983.

* * *

For more than two generations the Flower Fairy books by Cicely Mary Barker have enchanted and instructed children. Her meticulous and subtle illustrations are outstanding for their botanical accuracy and detail, but also for the imaginative representation of the essential personification of the plants—the sturdiness of the bugle, the joy of the early crocus, the wistful forget-me-not. She was greatly influenced by the Pre-Raphaelite movement in mood and atmosphere.

It is for the illustrations in her books that she is best remembered, but the verses and text in the stories are worth more than the cursory glance with which they are often dismissed. Her writing could in no way be described as being of great literary merit, and some lines move in a jerky and forced manner. But the individual rhymes contain such a wealth of detail on herbal remedies, plant cultivation, and old folk customs that to read them is to step back 50 years into the provident countryside. Children are exhorted to wait until the conkers fall rather than damage the tree in *Flower Fairies of the Autumn;* Self Heal is acknowledged to be a famous herb of healing in old days in *Flower Fairies of the Wayside*, and in *Fairies of the Trees* there is the instructive verse:

> There are cones on the tall, tall Pine tree,
> With its needles sharp and green;
> Small seeds in the cones are hidden,
> And they ripen there unseen.

The appeal of the verses lies in their simplicity and sincerity—there is nothing coy or vulgar here and they are easy to assimilate by the youngest child, often forming a first and memorable introduction to a knowledge of trees and plants. They have the same ease and brightness as all nursery rhymes, and the same degree of uncomplicated "chattiness."

Barker was deeply religious, and this is apparent in her prose writing, especially *The Lord of the Rushie River*, a moral tale of faith overcoming adversity. A sailor left his little girl in the care of a Dame Dinnage, paying her to look after Susan and his house while he went to sea for one last time. No sooner had his ship sailed than Dame Dinnage showed her true colours and poor Susan was fed on the poorest scraps and watered milk, and her clothes grew ragged while the Dame's old stocking bulged with the money meant for Susan's care. The little girl's only friends were the swans, especially one who seemed to be the Lord of the Rushie River. The swans eventually rescued Susan from her trials and tribulations, her father returned, and even Dame Dinnage returned the money, having had no pleasure in her ill-gotten gains. Susan is saved from being too good to be true by her faith in the swans and her gentle care of the huge birds, and even modern children could find something in this simple and uncomplicated tale. It stops short of sentimentality by the noble portrayal of the birds and also the striking but sympathetic illustrations.

Cicely Mary Barker has a remembered place in 20th-century children's literature, remembered by the countless children who grew up with her drawings and her images printed on the mind's eye, her sensitivity and joy in small things passed on in so unspoilt a manner.

—Fiona Waters

BARNE, Kitty

Nationality: British. **Born:** Marion Catherine Barne, 1883. **Education:** Royal College of Music, London. **Military Service:** Women's Voluntary Service during World War II. **Family:** Married Eric Streatfeild. **Awards:** Library Association Carnegie medal, 1941. **Died:** 1957.

Publications for Children

Fiction

Tomorrow, illustrated by Ethel King-Martyn. London, Hodder and Stoughton, 1912.

The Easter Holidays, illustrated by Joan Kiddell-Monroe. London, Heinemann, 1935; as *Secret of the Sandhills*, New York, Dodd Mead, 1949; London, Nelson, 1955.

Young Adventurers, illustrated by Ruth Gervis. London, Nelson, 1936.

She Shall Have Music, illustrated by Ruth Gervis. London, Dent, 1938; New York, Dodd Mead, 1939.

Family Footlights, illustrated by Ruth Gervis. London, Dent, and New York, Dodd Mead, 1939.

Visitors from London, illustrated by Ruth Gervis. London, Dent, and New York, Dodd Mead, 1940.

May I Keep Dogs?, illustrated by Arnrid Johnston. London, Hamish Hamilton, 1941; New York, Dodd Mead, 1942; as *Bracken My Dog*, London, Dent, 1949.

We'll Meet in England, illustrated by Steven Spurrier. London, Hamish Hamilton, 1942; New York, Dodd Mead, 1943.
Three and a Pigeon, illustrated by Steven Spurrier. London, Hamish Hamilton, and New York, Dodd Mead, 1944.
In the Same Boat, illustrated by Ruth Gervis. London, Dent, and New York, Dodd Mead, 1945.
Musical Honours, illustrated by Ruth Gervis. London, Dent, and New York, Dodd Mead, 1947.
Dusty's Windmill, illustrated by Marcia Lane Foster. London, Dent, 1949; as *The Windmill Mystery,* New York, Dodd Mead, 1950.
Roly's Dogs, illustrated by Alice Molony. London, Dent, 1950; as *Dog Stars,* New York, Dodd Mead, 1951.
Barbie, illustrated by Marcia Lane Foster. London, Dent, 1952; Boston, Little Brown, 1969.
Admiral's Walk, illustrated by Mary Gurnat. London, Dent, 1953.
Rosina Copper, The Mystery Mare, illustrated by Alfons Purtscher. London, Evans, 1954; New York, Dutton, 1956.
Cousin Beatie Learns the Fiddle. Oxford, Blackwell, 1955.
Tann's Boarders, illustrated by Jill Crockford. London, Dent, 1955.
Rosina and Son, illustrated by Marcia Lane Foster. London, Dent, 1956.

Plays

Tomorrow, with D.W. Wheeler. London, Curwen, 1910.
Winds, with D.W. Wheeler, music by Kitty Barne, illustrated by Lucy Barne. London, Curwen, 1912.
Timothy's Garden, verses by D.W. Wheeler, illustrated by Lucy Barne. London, Curwen, 1912.
Celandine's Secret, verses by D.W. Wheeler, illustrated by J.M. Saunders. London, Curwen, 1914.
Peter and the Clock. London, Curwen, 1919.
Susie Pays a Visit. London, Curwen, 1921.
The Amber Gate: A Pageant Play. London, Curwen, 1925.
Philemon and Baucis. London, Gowans and Gray, and Boston, Baker, 1926.
Madge: A Camp-Fire Play. London, Novello, 1928.
Adventurers: A Pageant Play. London, Deane, 1931; Boston, Baker, 1936.
The Grand Party, adaptation of the novel *Holiday House,* by Catherine Sinclair, in *The Theatre Window: Plays for Schools,* edited by W.T. Cunningham. London, Arnold, 1933.
Two More Mimes from Folk Songs: The Wraggle, Taggle Gipsies, O!; Robin-a-Thrush. London, Curwen, 1936.
Two Mimes from Folk Songs: The Frog and the Mouse, The Flowers in the Valley. London, Curwen, 1937.
They Made the Royal Arms. London, Deane, and Boston, Baker, 1937.
Shilling Teas. London, Deane, and Boston, Baker, 1938.
Days of Glory: A Pageant Play. London, Deane, 1946.
The "Local Ass": A Documentary Pageant Play for Girl Guides. London, Girl Guides' Association, 1947.
The Lost Birthday. London, Curwen, n.d.

Other

The Amber Gate, illustrated by Ruth Gervis. London and New York, Nelson, 1933.
Songs and Stories for Acting, illustrated by Ruth Gervis. Glasgow, Brown and Ferguson, 1939.
Listening to the Orchestra. London, Dent, 1941; revised edition, 1946; Indianapolis, Bobbs Merrill, 1946.
Here Come the Girl Guides. London, Girl Guides' Association, 1947.
Elizabeth Fry: A Story Biography. London, Penguin, 1950.
Introducing Handel [Mozart, Schubert], illustrated by Jill Crockford. London, Dent, and New York, Roy, 3 vols., 1955-57.

Publications for Adults

Novels

Mother at Large. London, Chapman and Hall, 1938.
While the Music Lasted. London, Chapman and Hall, 1943.
Enter Two Musicians. London, Chapman and Hall, 1944.
Duet for Sisters. London, Chapman and Hall, 1947.
Vespa. London, Chapman and Hall, 1950.
Music Perhaps. London, Chapman and Hall, 1953.

* * *

Though she produced a good deal of earlier work, mainly plays that are now forgotten, it was not until a few years before World War II that Kitty Barne began to explore a field of children's fiction in which she became something of a pioneer. She would probably have disclaimed a title with quite such aggressive connotations; she was, however, in her quiet way, a very serious and responsible writer. Her junior novels were intended to reflect the real world, in which young characters faced problems and struggled to solve them. She never favoured the child-insulated world in which adults appeared only as fringe characters, tolerated only when the plot demanded their entrance. At a period when most modern stories were frankly escapist, dealing with holiday adventures or improbable juvenile detection, Barne, while not making her books superficially too dissimilar, let in a much-needed draught of fresh air.

The outbreak of war in 1939 gave her inspiration and immediately enlarged opportunities. No one could any longer pretend that young readers could or should be protected from reality. In her Carnegie-winner, *Visitors from London,* she dealt with the impact of London evacuees upon a Sussex village. Later, another Cockney evacuee was a key character in *Three and a Pigeon,* another story of the home front which also involved the black market in farm produce. *In the Same Boat* tells of a Polish girl's escape to Britain and her schooldays there with her new-found English friend. Perhaps most noteworthy of all these novels is *Musical Honours,* in which the father, a returned prisoner-of-war from the Far East, faces all the problems of readjustment, not least the renewal of relationships with his elder children who remember him and with the younger who do not. This was probably one of the earliest children's books in which a parent was depicted as a flesh-and-blood person with faults, not as a love-and-authority symbol.

Both in her thought and in her language, Kitty Barne preferred to stretch her young readers, to overrate rather than underrate their capacity. She was against what she called "patronising simplicity" and "brightness." Children, she declared, did not mind long words or ideas that were a little big for them. She found an exhilaration in writing for them, and this emotion was communicated in the warmth and enthusiasm of her style.

—Geoffrey Trease

BARRIE, (Sir) J(ames) M(atthew)

Nationality: British (Scottish). **Born:** Kirriemuir, Forfarshire (now Angus), Scotland, 9 May 1860. **Education:** Misses Adam School, Kirriemuir; Glasgow Academy, 1868-70; Forfar Academy, 1870-72; Dumfries Academy, 1873-78; University of Edinburgh, 1878-82, M.A. 1882. **Family:** Married the actress Mary Ansell in 1894 (divorced 1909). **Career:** Drama and book critic, Edinburgh *Courant,* 1879-82; leader writer, Nottingham *Journal,* 1883-84. Lived in London after 1885: journalist, contributing to the *St. James's Gazette* and *British Weekly,* 1885-90. President, Society of Authors, 1928-37, and Dramatists' Club, 1934-37. **Awards:** LL.D.: University of St. Andrews, 1898; University of Edinburgh, 1909; D.Litt.: Oxford University, 1926; Cambridge University, 1930. Rector, University of St. Andrews, 1919-22; Chancellor, University of Edinburgh, 1930-37. Created Baronet, 1913; Order of Merit, 1922. **Died:** 19 June 1937.

Publications for Children

Fiction

The Boy Castaways of Black Lake Island. Privately printed, 1901.

The Little White Bird (for adults). London, Hodder and Stoughton, 1902; as *The Little White Bird; or, Adventures in Kensington Gardens,* New York, Scribner, 1902; revised material for children, as *Peter Pan in Kensington Gardens,* illustrated by Arthur Rackham, 1906.

Peter and Wendy, illustrated by F.D. Bedford. London, Hodder and Stoughton, and New York, Scribner, 1911; as *Peter Pan and Wendy,* London, Hodder and Stoughton, 1921.

Plays

Peter Pan; or, The Boy Who Would Not Grow Up (produced London, 1904; Washington, D.C., and New York, 1905; revised version, produced London, 1905). Included in *Plays,* 1928.

When Wendy Grew Up: An Afterthought (produced London, 1908). London, Nelson, 1957; New York, Dutton, 1958.

Publications for Adults

Novels

Better Dead. London, Swan Sonnenschein Lowrey, 1887; Chicago, Rand McNally, 1891.

When a Man's Single: A Tale of Literary Life. London, Hodder and Stoughton, 1888; New York, Lovell, 1892.

The Little Minister. London, Cassell, 3 vols., 1891; New York, Lovell, 1891.

Sentimental Tommy: The Story of His Boyhood. London, Cassell, and New York, Scribner, 1896.

Tommy and Grizel. London, Cassell, and New York, Scribner, 1900.

Farewell Miss Julie Logan: A Wintry Tale. London, Hodder and Stoughton, and New York, Scribner, 1932.

Short Stories

Two of Them. New York, Lovell, 1893.

A Tillyloss Scandal. New York, Lovell, 1893.

Plays

Bandolero, The Bandit (produced Dumfries, 1877).

Caught Napping. Privately printed, 1883.

Richard Savage, with H.B. Marriott Watson (produced London, 1890). Privately printed, 1891.

Ibsen's Ghost; or, Toole Up-to-Date (produced London, 1891). Privately printed, 1939; edited by Penelope Griffin, London, Woolf, 1975.

Walker, London (produced London, 1892). London and New York, French, 1907.

The Professor's Love Story (produced New York, 1892; London, 1894). Included in *Plays,* 1942.

Becky Sharp, adaptation of the novel *Vanity Fair* by W.M. Thackeray (produced London, 1893).

Jane Annie; or, The Good Conduct Prize, with Arthur Conan Doyle, music by Ernest Ford (produced London, 1893). London, Chappell, and New York, Novello Ewer, 1893.

The Little Minister, adaptation of his own novel (produced Washington, D.C., New York, and London, 1897; as *Little Mary,* produced London, 1903). Included in *Plays,* 1942.

A Platonic Friendship (produced London, 1898).

The Wedding Guest (produced London, 1900). London, Fortnightly Review, and New York, Scribner, 1900.

Quality Street (produced London, 1902; New York, 1903). London, Hodder and Stoughton, 1913; New York, Scribner, 1918.

The Admirable Crichton (produced London, 1902; New York, 1903). London, Hodder and Stoughton, 1914; New York, Scribner, 1918.

Pantaloon (produced London, 1905). Included in *Half Hours,* 1914.

Alice Sit-by-the-Fire (produced London and New York, 1905). London, Hodder and Stoughton, and New York, Scribner, 1919.

Josephine (produced London, 1906).

Punch (produced London, 1906).

What Every Woman Knows (produced London, Atlantic City, New Jersey, and New York, 1908). London, Hodder and Stoughton, and New York, Scribner, 1918.

Old Friends (produced London, 1910; New York, 1917). Included in *Plays,* 1928.

A Slice of Life (produced London, 1910; New York, 1912).

The Twelve-Pound Look (produced London, 1910; New York, 1911). Included in *Half Hours,* 1914.

Rosalind (produced London, 1912; New York, 1915). Included in *Half Hours,* 1914.

The Dramatists Get What They Want (produced London, 1912; as *The Censor and the Dramatists,* produced New York, 1913).

The Will (produced London and New York, 1913). Included in *Half Hours,* 1914.

The Adored One: A Legend of the Old Bailey (produced London, 1913; as *The Legend of Leonora,* produced New York, 1914; shortened version, as *Seven Women,* produced London, 1917). *Seven Women* included in *Plays,* 1928.

Half an Hour (produced London and New York, 1913). Included in *Plays,* 1928.

Half Hours (includes *Pantaloon, The Twelve-Pound Look, Rosalind, The Will*). London, Hodder and Stoughton, and New York, Scribner, 1914.
Der Tag (produced London, 1914; as *Der Tag; or, The Tragic Man,* produced New York, 1914). London, Hodder and Stoughton, and New York, Scribner, 1914.
Rosy Rapture, The Pride of the Beauty Chorus, music by H. Darewski and Jerome Kern (produced London, 1915).
The Fatal Typist (produced London, 1915).
The New Word (produced London, 1915; New York, 1917). Included in *Echoes of the War,* 1918.
The Real Thing at Last (produced London, 1916).
Irene Vanbrugh's Pantomime (produced London, 1916).
Shakespeare's Legacy (produced London, 1916). Privately printed, 1916.
A Kiss for Cinderella (produced London and New York, 1916). London, Hodder and Stoughton, and New York, Scribner, 1920.
The Old Lady Shows Her Medals (produced London and New York, 1917). Included in *Echoes of the War,* 1918.
Reconstructing the Crime (produced London, 1917).
Dear Brutus (produced London, 1917; New York, 1918). London, Hodder and Stoughton, and New York, Scribner, 1922.
La Politesse (produced London, 1918).
A Well-Remembered Voice (produced London, 1918). Included in *Echoes of the War,* 1918.
Echoes of the War (includes *The Old Lady Shows Her Medals, The New Word, Barbara's Wedding, A Well-Remembered Voice*). London, Hodder and Stoughton, and New York, Scribner, 1918.
Barbara's Wedding (produced London, 1927; New York, 1931). Included in *Echoes of the War,* 1918.
The Truth about the Russian Dancers (ballet), music by Arnold Bax (produced London, 1920). New York, Dance Perspectives, 1962.
Mary Rose (produced London and New York, 1920). London, Hodder and Stoughton, and New York, Scribner, 1924.
Shall We Join the Ladies? (produced London, 1921; New York, 1925). Included in *Plays,* 1928.
Neil and Tintinnabulum. Privately printed, 1925.
Representative Plays (includes *Quality Street, The Admirable Crichton, What Every Woman Knows, Dear Brutus, The Twelve-Pound Look, The Old Lady Shows Her Medals*), edited by W.L. Phelps. New York, Scribner, 1926.
The Plays of J.M. Barrie (includes *Peter Pan, The Admirable Crichton, Alice Sit-by-the-Fire, What Every Woman Knows, A Kiss for Cinderella, Dear Brutus, Mary Rose, Pantaloon, Half an Hour, Seven Women, Old Friends, Rosalind, The Twelve-Pound Look, The New Word, A Well-Remembered Voice, Barbara's Wedding, The Old Lady Shows Her Medals, Shall We Join the Ladies?*). London, Hodder and Stoughton, 1928; New York, Scribner, 1929; augmented edition, edited by A.E. Wilson (includes *Walker, London; The Professor's Love Story; The Little Minister; The Wedding Guest; The Boy David*), Hodder and Stoughton, 1942.
The Boy David (produced Edinburgh and London, 1936; New York, 1941). London, Davies, and New York, Scribner, 1938.

Screenplays: *The Little Minister,* 1915; *The Real Thing at Last,* 1916; *As You Like It,* with Robert Cullen, 1936.

Poetry

Scotland's Lament: A Poem on the Death of Robert Louis Stevenson. Privately printed, 1895.

Other

The New Amphion. Edinburgh, David Douglas, 1886.
Auld Licht Idylls. London, Hodder and Stoughton, 1888; New York, Cassell, 1891.
A Window in Thrums. London, Hodder and Stoughton, 1889; New York, Waverly, 1891.
An Edinburgh Eleven: Pencil Portraits from College Life. London, Office of the British Weekly, 1889; New York, Lovell, 1892.
My Lady Nicotine. London, Hodder and Stoughton, 1890; New York, Cassell, 1891.
A Holiday in Bed and Other Sketches. New York, New York Publishing Company, 1892.
A Lady's Shoe. New York, Brentano's, 1893.
An Auld Licht Manse and Other Sketches. New York, Knox, 1893.
Allahakbarries C.C. (on cricket). Privately printed, 1893.
Margaret Ogilvy, by Her Son. New York, Scribner, and London, Hodder and Stoughton, 1896.
The Allahakbarrie Book of Broadway Cricket for 1899. Privately printed, 1899.
George Meredith 1909. London, Constable, 1909; as *Neither Dorking nor the Abbey,* Chicago, Browne's Bookstore, 1910.
The Works (Kirriemuir Edition). London, Hodder and Stoughton, 10 vols., 1913.
Charles Frohman: A Tribute. Privately printed, 1915.
Who Was Sarah Findley? by Mark Twain, with a Suggested Solution of the Mystery. Privately printed, 1917.
The Works of J.M. Barrie. New York, Scribner, 10 vols., 1918.
Courage: The Rectorial Address Delivered at St. Andrews University, May 3rd 1922. London, Hodder and Stoughton, and New York, Scribner, 1922.
The Ladies' Shakespeare (lecture). Privately printed, 1925.
The Works (Peter Pan Edition). New York, Scribner, 14 vols., 1929-31.
The Entrancing Life (address). London, Hodder and Stoughton, and New York, Scribner, 1930.
The Greenwood Hat, Being a Memoir of James Anon 1885-1887. Privately printed, 1930; revised edition, London, Davies, and New York, Scribner, 1937.
M'Connachie and J.M.B.: Speeches. London, Davies, 1938; New York, Scribner, 1939.
Letters of J.M. Barrie, edited by Viola Meynell. London, Davies, 1942; New York, Scribner, 1947.
Plays and Stories, edited by Roger Lancelyn Green. London, Dent, 1962.

*

Bibliography: *Sir James M. Barrie: A Bibliography* by B.D. Cutler, New York, Greenberg, 1931.

Manuscript Collections: Beinecke Library, Yale University, New Haven, Connecticut; Lilly Library, Indiana University, Bloomington.

Critical Studies (selection): *J.M. Barrie* by F.J. Harvey Darton, London, Nisbet, 1929; *The Story of J.M.B. (Sir James Barrie)* by Denis Mackail, London, Davies, and New York, Scribner, 1941; *Fifty Years of Peter Pan,* London, Davies, 1954, and *J.M. Barrie,* London, Bodley Head, 1960, New York, Walck, 1961, both by Roger Lancelyn Green; *J.M. Barrie: The Man Behind the Image* by Janet Dunbar, London, Collins, and Boston, Houghton Mifflin,

1970; *Sir James Barrie* by Harry M. Geduld, New York, Twayne, 1971; *J.M. Barrie and the Lost Boys* by Andrew Birkin, London, Constable, and New York, Potter, 1979; *The Case of Peter Pan, or, The Impossibility of Children's Fiction* by Jacqueline Rose, London, Macmillan, 1984; *J.M. Barrie* by Leonée Ormond, Edinburgh, Scottish Academic Press, 1987.

*　　*　　*

It is not always realised that—a few private oddities apart—J.M. Barrie produced only one work for the young. But that one, a major myth of the new century, was written in many forms over many years, before and after the actual stage production. Indeed, it is fair to say that no important work discussed in the present volume can have a more curious history than *Peter Pan*, "that terrible masterpiece," as Peter Davies (see below) once called it. Where for a start is its authentic form to be found? Though that first stage production was in 1904, the play had to wait several years for a definitive printed version. The "story," the full-length definitive narrative (the longest, best, most satisfying of all the versions) did not appear until 1911. Yet clues can be found in Barrie's quite early adult writings.

Certain facts in Barrie's life have so fundamental a part in the making of *Peter Pan* that they should be set out here. He was a small-town Lowlands Scot, one of a weaver's large family. When David, the mother's favourite child, was killed in a skating accident on the eve of his 14th birthday, James, then aged 6 and hitherto of little account, set himself to compensate for the loss. The obsessive relationship that grew between mother and son was to mark the whole of his life, as writer and as man. Another intense relationship began towards the end of the century, when the once penniless young journalist had, quite rapidly, become the rich and celebrated novelist and playwright. This was with Sylvia and Arthur Llewellyn Davies (she was the daughter of George du Maurier) and their several—eventually five—small sons. These boys, devoted childish listeners, were in an immediate sense the kindlers of *Peter Pan*—Jack, Peter, and Michael (as their names confirm) especially.

In print, the magic boy first appeared by name in Barrie's adult novel *The Little White Bird* (1902) a strange first-person narrative about a wealthy bachelor clubman's attachment to a little boy, David. Taking this boy for walks in Kensington Gardens, the narrator tells him of the elusive Peter Pan, who can be found in the Gardens at night, when the gates are closed. A little girl (not motherly Wendy but a sturdy likeable child called Maimie Mannering) bravely stays behind at dusk, though her brother runs away, and she becomes Peter's friend. Four years later these chapters were taken out and reprinted as a separate book called *Peter Pan in Kensington Gardens,* with pictures by Arthur Rackham: its verve and magical atmosphere make it well worth reading today. Told verbally this was the form first known to the Davies boys.

But the roots of the tale go very much further back. In *Margaret Ogilvy* (1896) Barrie recalled how his mother's childhood had ended at 8, when she had to become the family's housekeeper. "The horror of my boyhood was," he noted, "that I knew a time would come when I must also give up games, and how it was to be done, I saw not." More revealing still are his novels *Sentimental Tommy* and *Tommy and Grizel.* Tommy, a clever, feckless dreamer who—disastrously—can't face adult responsibilities, plans a work of fiction:

> a reverie about a little boy who was lost. His parents find him in a wood singing joyfully to himself because he thinks he can now be a boy for ever; and he fears that if they catch him they will compel him to grow into a man, so he runs further from them into the wood and is running still, singing to himself because he is always to be a boy.

But Barrie, unlike Tommy, had a shrewd and positive streak, and the gift of turning fancy into fact. Only a writer of great assurance could have hoped for a theatrical production of *Peter Pan* with its extraordinary cast and sets and flying devices. Beerbohm Tree, who had first offer, thought it hopelessly unworkable, original to excess. But Charles Frohman was more adventurous, and the vastly successful opening productions, on both sides of the Atlantic, were his.

Like most of Barrie's work, *Peter Pan* has been adored and reviled for much the same qualities: what some perhaps call charm, others call sentimental and whimsical. Possibly neither group has taken into account Barrie's outstanding craftsmanship as a playwright, or of his easy gift for gripping a reader's interest on the printed page. The sentimental and whimsical were certainly part of his stock-in-trade, but they were not accidentally used; by the time he wrote *Peter Pan,* the hard glint in the sentimentalist's pale blue eyes becomes increasingly evident. (It is, indeed, a wonderfully *heartless* book—as Barrie was well aware: see the final line of the novel.) A touch of self-satire can possibly be observed even in the obsessional mother-theme. Wendy is given many good lines, in the novel particularly; note her watching the mermaids "combing out their hair in a lazy way that quite irritated her"; note her scornful feelings when Hook has her tied to the mast.

> No words of mine can tell you how Wendy despised those pirates. To the boys there was at least some glamour in the pirate calling, but all that she saw was that the ship had not been scrubbed for years. There was not a porthole on the grimy glass of which you might not have written with your finger "Dirty pig"; and she had already written it several times.

Yet her role holds the seeds of its own defeat. "You need not be sorry for Wendy," writes Barrie. "She was one of the kind that like to grow up. In the end she grew up of her own free will a day quicker than other girls." By ceasing to be a child, she rapidly loses Peter, Ariel of the child-world; she loses in every sense the power to fly. The Wendy portrait, begun with such simple charm (the name was the pet-name of William Ernest Henley's short-lived daughter) has clearly got out of hand, reflecting an unadmitted conflict in Barrie himself.

Peter Pan: landmark or signpost? The first far more than the second; it seems to have stunned imitation at any notable level. Pan-followers ran to coyness rather than wit; and this affects the work's reputation still. True, it did give an impetus to theatre for children; it can also be said that it brought into the open the growing cult of childhood and fairies in writings meant for adults. From Grahame's *The Golden Age* in the 1890s to Milne's *When We Were Very Young* in the 1920s, this cult took in work of de la Mare, Eleanor Farjeon (*Martin Pippin*), Rose Fyleman, Saki, James Stephens (*The Crock of Gold*)—and other prose and verse, now classed as children's reading, which were certainly published for adults in their day. With *Peter Pan* the process works in reverse. Both play and novel were (like *Alice*) specifically meant for the young, but are now (like *Alice*) of increasing interest to adults. *Peter Pan* mirrors its time; it mirrors, though more obliquely, its author's mind. As an instance: Barrie first made his name (and almost wrecked it in his home town) by using his local Scottish background for copy. In *Peter Pan* the Scot is hard to trace. But in fact it is the northern stranger's eye that finds such appeal in the Edwardian middle-class nursery; in the social mystique of Kensington Gardens; in the *mores* of prep school and public school. Is not Hook himself, most enigmatic of pirates, abjuring "bad form" even in death, an old Etonian? James Hook...odd that the author should give him his own name. But nothing is really simple in this work. How to explain the dog-kennel father, say, so many years pre-Thurber?

The position of *Peter Pan* today is a curious one. It is at once known and not known. Like other invented myths (Crusoe, Gulliver) its persons and ideas have currency among many who have neither read nor seen what Barrie wrote. Those who *do* read (or listen) often meet it only through feeble brief retellings (there are, alas, a number of these in print). They are missing much; the full text abounds in richness. *Peter Pan* is the secure child's dream of danger, of wild distances, of freedom from adult rules—but always (as in Sendak's *Where the Wild Things Are*) from a safe home base. It incorporates the traditional boy's adventure yarn which had so much delighted Barrie himself when young; indeed, much of the pirate/redskin material can be seen as a brilliant take-off of the genre. Peter himself is the absolute leader and hero-figure, the animator of action. But the children are not only onlookers; they are *in* the event, as themselves. It incorporates magic; the children actually fly. All these elements are combined on an island which accommodates redskins, pirates, mermaids, wolves with the greatest ease. For the young, the whole thing is a feast which lasts the longer by the skill—the continual sleight-of-hand—with which it is served. A "terrible masterpiece," yes, but the most complex and original of all its author's works, and a mine for Barrie-explorers.

—Naomi Lewis

BARRY, Margaret Stuart

Nationality: British. **Born:** Margaret Stuart Bell, Darlington, County Durham, 7 December 1927. **Education:** At schools in Richmond, Yorkshire, and at teacher training college, Liverpool, diploma 1947. **Family:** Married Pierce Barry in 1957; two daughters and one son. **Career:** Teacher, Lindisfarne Convent Preparatory School, Essex, 1947-49, and Woolten College, 1950-52; art teacher, Huyton, Lancashire; teacher, Alder Hey Children's Hospital, 1957-58. **Agent:** Rosemary Poromley, Juvenilia, Avington, Winchester, Hampshire S021 1DB, England. **Address:** 6 Howard House, Garden Village, Richmond, North Yorkshire, DL10 4UA, England.

Publications for Children

Fiction

Boffy and the Teacher Eater [*Mumford Ghosts*], illustrated by George Adamson. London, Harrap, 2 vols., 1971-74.

Tommy Mac, illustrated by Dinah Dryhurst. London, Longman, 1972.

Woozy, illustrated by John Castle. London, Harrap, 1973.

The Woozies Go to School, illustrated by John Castle. London, Harrap, 1973.

The Woozies on Television, illustrated by John Castle. London, Harrap, 1974.

Tommy Mac Battles On, illustrated by Dinah Dryhurst. London, Kestrel, 1974.

Tommy Mac on Safari, illustrated by Rosemary Evans. London, Kestrel, 1975.

Simon and the Witch, illustrated by Linda Birch. London, Collins, 1976.

Woozy and the Weight Watchers, illustrated by Andrea Smith. London, Harrap, 1977.

The Woozies Go Visiting, illustrated by Andrea Smith. London, Harrap, 1977.

Woozies Hold a Frubarb Week, illustrated by Andrea Smith. London, Harrap, 1977.

The Monster in Woozy Garden, illustrated by Andrea Smith. London, Harrap, 1977.

The Return of the Witch, illustrated by Linda Birch. London, Collins, 1978.

Maggie Gumption [*Flies High*], illustrated by Gunvor Edwards. London, Hutchinson, 2 vols., 1979-81.

The Witch of Monopoly Manor, illustrated by Linda Birch. London, Collins, 1980.

The Witch on Holiday, illustrated by Linda Birch. London, Collins, 1983.

The Witch V.I.P., illustrated by Linda Birch. London, Collins, 1987.

Diz and the Big Fat Burglar, illustrated by Paula Lawford. London, Hamish Hamilton, 1987.

Simon and the Witch in School. London, Collins, 1987.

The Witch and the Holiday Club. London, Collins, 1988.

The Millionaire Witch. London, Collins, 1992.

The Attic Toys

- *Oxfam: The Unloved Bear,* illustrated by Tessa Richardson-Jones. London, Bloomsbury, 1995.
- *Tilly Losh: The Rag Doll,* illustrated by Tessa Richardson-Jones. London, Bloomsbury, 1995.
- *Moggy: The Witch's Cat,* illustrated by Tessa Richardson-Jones. London, Bloomsbury, 1995.
- *Boomer: The Friendly Gorilla,* illustrated by Tessa Richardson-Jones. London, Bloomsbury, 1995.
- *Prissy: The Stuck-up Doll,* illustrated by Tessa Richardson-Jones. London, Bloomsbury, 1997.
- *Mayor Bungle: The Mad Old Dog,* illustrated by Tessa Richardson-Jones. London, Bloomsbury, 1997.

Other

Bill Books (readers), illustrated by Gwen Fulton. London, Collins, 12 vols., 1973.

* * *

Margaret Stuart Barry's reputation as a writer has come to rest upon her *Witch* stories, which have reached a wider reading and viewing public through their television dramatisation at peak children's viewing time.

Her earlier work shows talent and versatility and stands the test of time. Tommy Mac is the imaginative boy who believes that, in his teeming urban community, "there are adventures all around...All you have to do is to *look* for them." The *Woozy* tales are undemanding, but they have a lightness of wit that communicates to children of six to nine. The *Maggie Gumption* collections are delightfully quirky stories about a doll living in the attic of a large house populated by endearing eccentrics such as her rival Pinky Dars and Captain Bombast.

The joke at the center of the hilarious *Witch* books about Simon and his demonic crony is the friendship of a young boy and an apparently harmless old lady. She causes havoc at his school and within his community at the expense, usually, of the beleaguered adults. The fun is wry, ironic, rumbustious, sometimes nihilistic, but never condescending. Readers enjoy the humor that springs from the incongruous: the dear old lady is an anarchist! In her treatment of the teachers, in her behaviour in school, there's an upturning of the natural order of things. An early and brilliant story, *Boffy and the Teacher Eater,* also exploited the essential conservatism of classroom life and routines. Barry is good at depicting the defusion of social pretension. Simon's local do-gooder, Lady Fox-Custard, is ripe for exploitation, as is Maggie Gumption's superior friend Lady Serena Sumptious and the once-grand Ponsonby-Smythe who "could even say 'Ssh' poshly." The new boy who arrives at Tommy Mac's inner-city primary in a Bentley gets off to a bad start too.

Barry's writing proves that she has a fine ear tuned to the linguistic fun of word play, invented names, and jokes. The satisfaction for the reader—especially those called "reluctant"—is in being implicated in narrative which has its roots in the extended jokes that are playground lore. The art extends beyond the comedienne's when Barry draws upon the felt-life of schools and family banter.The confederacy of childhood is also splendidly caught. Simon's schoolmates (including Sally-Who's-on-Book-Four) and Tommy's community, who gather on the bombsite with their sandwiches for the ritual of the gang fight, are ebullient children of the 1980s, multi-cultural in the widest sense, not caricatured or sentimentalised.

—Colin Mills

BASE, Graeme (Rowland)

Nationality: Australian: immigrated to Australia in 1966. **Born:** 6 April 1958, Amersham, England. **Education:** Swinburne Institute of Technology, diploma of art, 1978. **Family:** Married Robyn Anne Paterson, 1981; two sons and one daughter. **Career:** Worked in advertising at design studios, including The Art Producers, Stannard Patten Samuelson, and Paul Pantelis & Partners, 1979-80; keyboard player in band Riki-Tiki-Tavi, with wife, 1980-85; author and illustrator of books for children. **Awards:** Australian Children's Book Award, 1989; Children's Book of Australia Picture Book of the Year, 1989; Young Australian Best Book Award, 1989. **Member:** Australian Society of Book Illustrators. **Address:** c/o Penguin Books Australia Ltd., 487 Maroondah Highway, P.O. Box 257, Ringwood, Victoria 3134, Australia.

Publications for Children

Fiction (illustrated by the author)

My Grandma Lived in Gooligulch. Melbourne, Nelson Australia, 1983.
Animalia. New York, Abrams, 1986.
The Eleventh Hour: A Curious Mystery. London, Viking Kestrel, 1988; New York, Abrams, 1989.
The Sign of the Seahorse. New York, Abrams, 1992.
The Discovery of Dragons. New York, Abrams, 1996.

*

Illustrator: *Adventures with My Best Worst Friend,* Max Dann, Oxford University Press, 1982; *The Island Bike Business* (with Betty Greenhatch), Susan Burke, Oxford University Press, 1982; *Jabberwocky: From "Through the Looking Glass,"* Lewis Carroll, Macmillan, 1985.

Graeme Base comments:

Everyone is influenced by their childhood. The things I write about and illustrate come from a vast range of inputs, some from the earliest impressions of a little child, others from things I saw yesterday and still others from completely out of the blue, though no doubt they owe their arrival to some unconscious stimulus. I have a great love of wildlife, inherited from my parents, which shows through in my subject matter, though always with a view to the humorous, not as a commercial device but as a reflection of my own reasonably happy nature!

My style is tightly controlled and quite linear. I use strong colours largely instinctively having only a mental image of what I hope the picture will look like as a guide. The paintings are done on hot press illustration board with watercolours and transparent inks, using brushes, pencils, technical drawing pens and a scalpel (for scratching). I also use an airbrush for "atmospherics".

The Graphic Design course at Swinburne Institute of Technology in Melbourne, was, when I went through, very much geared for a career in advertising. As a result I worked in a few design studios after I graduated and hated it, but I am certain the training in spatial dynamics, typography and meeting deadlines I received at Swinburne and in the advertising industry was tremendously important in my development as a book illustrator. *Design* is all important—you can spend all the time in the world on technique and detail but if the design is flawed the illustration will never work out satisfactorily.

I aim my books primarily at myself. Although I would have to be a fool to totally disregard the eventual marketplace the most important audience is essentially *me.* When I am happy with a verse or an illustration I let other people see it and hope they will share my enjoyment, and experience the same stimulation of the imagination as I have experienced creating it. I never talk down to kids, believing it far preferable to aim over their heads and risk some subtleties of the text or illustration to go unnoticed rather than to earn their scorn by serving up "kiddie's fare". This makes people think I direct my work mainly at adults, but I don't—I direct it at the child and adult in me and from there to the child and adult in others.

For me the relationship between text and illustration is the very essence of producing a good picture book. Because I write the books I illustrate I have the luxury of being able to refine the text as the illustration ideas emerge. Through the whole life of a project (and it can take several years sometimes) I constantly revise the relationship of the two parts, text and picture, looking for mistakes in continuity, ways of improving what I have come up with to date and unnecessary duplication of information. I started off in the publishing business illustrating other peoples' texts and found it very frustrating mainly because the text was considered sacred and unchangeable, putting ridiculous restrictions on the eventual harmony of text and picture.

When it gets around to finished artwork I work on only one illustration at a time, and on one part of that illustration. After a few weeks most of the board is covered with image and I then go through a process of balancing the whole, bringing all the individual parts together. This is slow work. I live with my pictures in quite an obsessive way during the time it takes to create a book, thinking of hardly anything else, totally involved in the images.

The actual production of a book is a task taken on by several specialized trades—A photographic studio to make 8"X10" transparencies of the artwork; a separator to prepare the images for printing; a paper manufacturer to supply appropriate paper; a printer to print the sheets that make up the book; a binder to collate all the sheets, endpapers, cover and jackets and to stitch the books together; and a publisher to oversee the whole process and distribute the books to the bookshops. In this long chain there are countless opportunities for things to go wrong. I insist on being very involved in all these stages to ensure the quality of the finished book is as high as possible. It would be a great pity to spend months or years on a project and, for the want of a few more weeks of efforts, allow the end result to be of a lesser quality than were possible.

* * *

Graeme Base is one of a newer breed of picture book artists who create books for a more sophisticated audience than is usual with this genre. His illustrations—which are in large part responsible for the appeal of his books—are so complex and intricate that it is not surprising to learn that most of his books take up to three years to produce, which can account for the fact that Base's output is relatively small. Nevertheless, his distinctive style is an important contribution to modern children's literature.

Base's book *Animalia* brought him to worldwide prominence. Taking the well tried formula of an alphabet book, he weaves around it a highly detailed series of prints, while the text uses alliteration to stunning effect: "Diabolical dragons daintily devouring delicious delicacies"; "Wicked warrior wasps wildly waving warlike weapons"; "Lazy lions lounging in the local library." In the pictures there are references to the letter used on that page—the subjects featured on the library shelves include literature and law, and the lions are reading *Lassie Come Home, King Lear,* and a book of limericks. The fonts used reflect the mood of each piece: "Meticulous mice monitoring mysterious mathematical messages" is depicted in computer type, but "Proud peacocks preening perfect plumage" appears in a bold and romantic flowing script. Sometimes the pictures cover a double page spread, at others characters from one scene burst into another on the opposite page. Readers' eyes are constantly dazzled by the images shown, at the same time their minds are intrigued, engaged in detecting as many objects as possible whose names begin with the letter in question. There is also the added interest of trying to locate in each picture the artist himself as a young boy.

It was to be several years before Base's next book appeared. *The Eleventh Hour* is a mystery story in which the reader is given a clue on each page as to the identity of the culprit. The scene of the crime is a birthday party given by Horace the elephant. The number eleven is extremely important for Horace's birthday is on the eleventh day of November, he himself is eleven and he plans to give a feast beginning at eleven o'clock. Unfortunately someone eats the feast, but using the clues, the reader is given the chance to determine who is responsible. The book includes a sealed "top secret" section that can confirm the suspicions of keen-eyed readers. Base's illustrations are again highly intricate, with decorative borders that serve as a link with the theme of each picture. The major problem with the book is the verse which Base uses to tell his story—the rhyme is too often reminiscent of *Rupert* and similar comic strips.

Verse appears again in *The Sign of the Seahorse*—the story is told as a play with eight scenes, a prelude, and an epilogue, all performed in rhyming quatrains. The eventful tale, which includes an epic journey, pollution, extortion, and true love, is enacted on the bottom of the ocean by such sea creatures as crabs, sharks, and trout. Once again the pictures are stunning and full of intricate detail, however, Base's skill is shown at its best in books with little text, as in *Animalia.*

—Keith Barker

BASKIN, Leonard

Nationality: American. **Born:** New Brunswick, New Jersey, 17 August 1922. **Education:** New School for Social Research, A.B. 1949. **Family:** Married 1) Esther Tane, 1946; one son; 2) Lisa Unger, 1967; one son, one daughter. **Military Service:** U.S. Navy, 1943-46. **Career:** Sculptor and graphic artist, since 1949; Professor of Graphics, Smith College, 1953-74. Presenter of one man shows, New York City, 1954, 1956, 1957, 1960-62, 1965-76, and Boston, 1952, 1955, 1959; represented in the permanent collections of Metropolitan Museum of Art, Museum of Modern Art, Library of Congress. National Gallery of Art, Art Institute of Chicago, and Fogg Museum of Harvard University. **Awards:** Tiffany fellow, 1947; Guggenheim fellow, 1953; National Institute of Arts and Letters grant, 1968; first prize in engraving, Sao Paulo Biennial, 1962; American Institute of Graphic Arts, medal, 1965. D.F.A.: New School for Social Research, New York, 1966, and University of Massachusetts, 1968; L.H.D.: Clark University, 1966, and Rutgers University, 1967. **Address:** P.O. Box 413, Leeds, Massachusetts 01053-0413, U.S.A.

PUBLICATIONS FOR CHILDREN (ILLUSTRATED BY THE AUTHOR)

Fiction

Hosie's Alphabet, by Hosea, Tobias, and Lisa Baskin. New York, Viking Press, 1972.

Hosie's Aviary, by Tobias, Lucretia, Hosie, and Lisa Baskin. New York, Viking Press, 1979.

Hosie's Zoo, by Tobias, Lucretia, Hosie, and Lisa Baskin. New York, Viking Press, 1981.

Imps, Demons, Hobgoblins, Witches, Fairies and Elves. New York, Pantheon, 1984.

A Book of Dragons, by Hosie and Leonard Baskin. New York, Knopf, 1985.

Nonfiction

Miniature Natural History. New York, Pantheon Books, 1983.
The Raptors and Other Birds. New York, Pantheon Books, 1985.

Poetry

Season's Songs, by Ted Hughes. Hastings-on-Hudson, New York, Ultramarine Publishers, 1975.
Moon-Whales and Other Moon Poems, by Ted Hughes. Hastings-on-Hudson, New York, Ultramarine Publishers, 1976.
Under the North Star, by Ted Hughes. New York, The Viking Press, 1981.
Did You Say Ghosts?, by Richard Michelson. New York, Simon and Schuster, 1993.
Animals That Ought To Be: Poems About Imaginary Pets, by Richard Michelson. New York, Simon and Schuster, 1996.

PUBLICATIONS FOR ADULTS (ILLUSTRATED BY THE AUTHOR)

Nonfiction

Figures of Dead Men. Amherst, University of Massachusetts, 1968.
Sculpture, Drawings, and Prints. New York, Braziller, 1970.
Leonard Baskin's Natural History. New York, Pantheon, 1983.
A Passover Haggadah, edited by Herbert Bronstein. New York, Grossman Publishers, 1974.

*

Critical Studies: *The Sculpture of Leonard Baskin* by Irma B. Jaffe, New York, Viking Press, 1980.

* * *

Leonard Baskin is the son of a rabbi. At age seven he began Talmudic studies, preparing to become a rabbi himself. His life turned around when he was fourteen and went to a craft demonstration at Macy's department store. He saw a sculptor molding a head, and it was a major event in his life. He watched the sculptor all day and into the evening; when he left he had five pounds of clay with him. The next year he began to study sculpture.

Baskin is one of America's most distinguished artists. He is a sculptor, watercolorist, graphics designer, calligrapher, and engraver. He is internationally renowned as an artist who brought attention to humanism in modern art. He has a mastery of the old techniques of wood engraving and sculpture. And he has a boldness of form and color that bespeaks the Twentieth Century.

In 1962 Baskin founded Gehenna Press in Northampton, Massachusetts, a small publisher of rare books in limited editions. Many of these books are now collector's items. His interest in books extends beyond illustration to all aspects of book design, including the integration of type, paper, illustrations, and bindings to form an object of art. For Baskin book illustration is meaningful when it becomes a partner with the text. His aim is to both comment on the text and elevate it.

Baskin became well known as an illustrator of adult books. He has illustrated books by Conrad Aiken, William Blake, Homer (*The Iliad*), Marianne Moore, Sylvia Plath, and Alfred Tennyson.

It is most fortunate that he then turned his attention to books for children when his three year old son, Hosea, asked him to draw an alphabet. His first attempt, *Hosie's Alphabet,* was a stunning success. It was actually the result of a Baskin family project. His wife Lisa and his children Hosea and Tobias are credited with the text of the book. The pictures far exceed in graphic design and color those of most picture books for children. His amazonian armadillo, bumptious baboon, and carrion crow are incredible in their physical characteristics and in their interpretation of psyche. The demon of this book has a dramatic and devilish face; you can feel its meanness. The gargoyle is eerie and elusive; you can feel its strength. Children enjoy pictures, and with Baskin's pictures they can delight in color and form and small, surprising details. One would be tempted to frame the pictures in this book individually.

Hosie's Aviary shows, in soft pen and watercolor, drawings of hummingbirds in flight, brightly colored finches, and a simple city sparrow. Birds of majesty and plainness are presented, and the wonder and beauty of nature are captured. *Hosie's Zoo* provides more animals to marvel at. And *Miniature Natural History* offers further opportunity to enjoy Baskin's interpretation of the world around.

Baskin also illustrated three children's books by his friend, the poet Ted Hughes. They too show lyrical and beautiful reflections of nature. Most recently Baskin has done paintings for the work of another poet, Richard Michelson. *Animals That Ought to Be* is full of rollicking fantasy, with the text and pictures contributing equally to the entertainment. In this book a young voice states that he loves his dogs and cats, he enjoys chicks and geese and pigs and sheep, but sometimes, when he lies in bed, other creatures fill his head, "Animals you never see. Animals that ought to be." The first such animal is the Nightnoise Gladiator. This animal likes to gobble up his enemy: night noise. Included in such noise are the hissing radiator, the creaking stairs, the squeaking door lock, the rattling refrigerator, and the drip-drip of the bathroom sink. Baskin's interpretation of this creature includes red teeth, red eyes, and a deliciously humped back. Another wonderful animal is the Roombroom. It is he who the young voice calls for when his Mother tells him no more TV until he cleans his room. The Roombroom, as pictured, has whiskers of a whisk broom, nostrils of a dustbuster, backside of a vacuum, and feathers of feather dusters. What great fun for a child to imagine he could have one of his own!

For the child who is genuinely intrigued with Baskin's drawings, one may wish to take out some of his books from the adult section of the library, particularly his *Natural History.* For the child of Jewish faith, *A Passover Haggadah,* with its powerful and beautiful illustrations, will add significantly to his Seder. One may also bring the child to the Museum of Modern Art in New York, the National Gallery of Art in Washington, the Art Institute of Chicago, to view individual Baskin masterpieces. I can think of no gentler or more powerful introduction to fine arts than these children's books illustrated by Leonard Baskin.

—Mary Lystad

BAUM, L(yman) Frank

Pseudonyms: Floyd Akers; Laura Bancroft; John Estes Cooke; Hugh Fitzgerald; Suzanne Metcalf; Schuyler Staunton; Edith Van Dyne. **Nationality:** American. **Born:** Chittenango, New York, 15 May 1856. **Education:** At schools in Syracuse, New York, and Peekskill Military Academy, New York, 1868-69. **Family:** Married Maud Gage in 1882; four sons. **Career:** Reporter, New York *World,* 1873-75; founding editor, *New Era,* Bradford, Pennsylvania, 1876; poultry farmer with B.W. Baum and Son: editor, *Poultry Record,* Syracuse, and columnist ("Poultry Yard"), *New York Farmer and Dairyman,* 1880; actor (as George Brooks) with May Roberts and the Sterling Comedy Company, New York, 1881; owner (as Louis F. Baum), Baum's Opera House, Richburg, New York, 1881-82; toured with his own repertory company, 1882-83; salesman, Baum's Ever-Ready Castorine axle grease, 1883-88; owner, Baum's Bazaar general store, Aberdeen, Dakota Territory, 1888-90; editor, Aberdeen *Saturday Pioneer,* 1890-91; reporter, Chicago *Post,* 1891; buyer, Siegel Cooper and Company, Chicago, 1891; salesman, Pitkin and Brooks crockery firm, Chicago, 1891-97; founder, National Association of Window Trimmers, 1897, and founding editor and publisher, *Show Window* magazine, Chicago, 1897-1902; founding director, Oz Film Manufacturing Company, Los Angeles, 1914-15. **Died:** 6 May 1919.

Publications for Children

Fiction

A New Wonderland, illustrated by Frank Berbeck. New York, Russell, 1900; as *The Surprising Adventures of the Magical Monarch of Mo,* Indianapolis, Bobbs Merrill, 1903.

The Wonderful Wizard of Oz, illustrated by W.W. Denslow. Chicago, Hill, 1900; as *The New Wizard of Oz,* Indianapolis, Bobbs Merrill, 1903; London, Hodder and Stoughton, 1906; edited by Michael Patrick Hearn, New York, Schocken, 1983.

Dot and Tot of Merryland, illustrated by W.W. Denslow. Chicago, Hill, 1901.

The Master Key: An Electrical Fairy Tale, illustrated by Fanny Cory. Indianapolis, Bowen Merrill, 1901; London, Stevens and Brown, 1902.

The Life and Adventures of Santa Claus, illustrated by Mary Cowles Clark. Indianapolis, Bowen Merrill, and London, Stevens and Brown, 1902.

The Enchanted Island of Yew, illustrated by Fanny Cory. Indianapolis, Bobbs Merrill, 1903.

The Marvelous Land of Oz, illustrated by John R. Neill. Chicago, Reilly and Britton, and London, Revell, 1904.

Queen Zixi of Ix, illustrated by Frederick Richardson. New York, Century, 1905; London, Hodder and Stoughton, 1906.

The Woggle-Bug Book, illustrated by Ike Morgan. Chicago, Reilly and Britton, 1905.

John Dough and the Cherub, illustrated by John R. Neill. Chicago, Reilly and Britton, 1906; London, Constable, 1974.

Annabel (as Suzanne Metcalf). Chicago, Reilly and Britton, 1906.

Sam Steele's Adventures on Land and Sea (as Hugh Fitzgerald). Chicago, Reilly and Britton, 1906; as *The Boy Fortune Hunters in Alaska* (as Floyd Akers), 1908.

Twinkle Tales (as Laura Bancroft; *Bandit Jim Crow, Mr. Woodchuck, Prairie-Dog Town, Prince Mud-Turtle, Sugar-Loaf Mountain, Twinkle's Enchantment*), illustrated by Maginel Wright Enright. Chicago, Reilly and Britton, 6 vols., 1906; as *Twinkle and Chubbins,* 1911.

Ozma of Oz, illustrated by John R. Neill. Chicago, Reilly and Britton, 1907; as *Princess Ozma of Oz,* London, Hutchinson, 1942.

Sam Steele's Adventures in Panama (as Hugh Fitzgerald). Chicago, Reilly and Britton, 1907; as *The Boy Fortune Hunters in Panama* (as Floyd Akers), 1908.

Policeman Bluejay (as Laura Bancroft), illustrated by Maginel Wright Enright. Chicago, Reilly and Britton, 1907; as *Babes in Birdland,* 1911.

Dorothy and the Wizard in Oz, illustrated by John R. Neill. Chicago, Reilly and Britton, 1908.

The Boy Fortune Hunters in Egypt [*China, Yucatan, the South Seas*] (as Floyd Akers). Chicago, Reilly and Britton, 4 vols., 1908-11.

The Road to Oz, illustrated by John R. Neill. Chicago, Reilly and Britton, 1909.

The Emerald City of Oz, illustrated by John R. Neill. Chicago, Reilly and Britton, 1910.

The Sea Fairies, illustrated by John R. Neill. Chicago, Reilly and Britton, 1911.

The Daring Twins, illustrated by Pauline Batchelder. Chicago, Reilly and Britton, 1911.

Sky Island, illustrated by John R. Neill. Chicago, Reilly and Britton, 1912.

Phoebe Daring, illustrated by Joseph Pierre Nuyttens. Chicago, Reilly and Britton, 1912.

The Patchwork Girl of Oz, illustrated by John R. Neill. Chicago, Reilly and Britton, 1913.

The Little Wizard Series (*Jack Pumpkinhead and the Sawhorse, Little Dorothy and Toto, Ozma and the Little Wizard, The Cowardly Lion and the Hungry Tiger, The Scarecrow and the Tin Woodman, Tik-Tok and the Nome King*). Chicago, Reilly and Britton, 6 vols., 1913; as *Little Wizard Stories of Oz,* Reilly and Britton, 1914; London, Simpkin, 1939.

Tik-Tok of Oz, illustrated by John R. Neill. Chicago, Reilly and Britton, 1914.

The Scarecrow of Oz, illustrated by John R. Neill. Chicago, Reilly and Britton, 1915.

Rinkitink in Oz, illustrated by John R. Neill. Chicago, Reilly and Britton, 1916.

The Snuggle Tales (*Little Bun Rabbit, Once upon a Time, The Yellow Hen, The Magic Cloak, The Ginger-Bread Man, Jack Pumpkinhead*), illustrated by John R. Neill. Chicago, Reilly and Britton, 6 vols., 1916-17; as *Oz-Man Tales,* 6 vols., 1920.

The Lost Princess of Oz, illustrated by John R. Neill. Chicago, Reilly and Britton, 1917.

The Tin Woodman of Oz, illustrated by John R. Neill. Chicago, Reilly and Britton, 1918.

The Magic of Oz, illustrated by John R. Neill. Chicago, Reilly and Lee, 1919; London, Armada, 1974.

Glinda of Oz, illustrated by John R. Neill. Chicago, Reilly and Lee, 1920.

Jaglon and the Tiger Fairies, illustrated by Dale Ulrey. Chicago, Reilly and Lee, 1953.

A Kidnapped Santa Claus. Indianapolis, Bobbs Merrill, 1961.

The Purple Dragon and Other Fantasies, edited by David L. Greene, illustrated by Tim Kirk. Lakemont, Georgia, Fictioneer, 1976.

Fiction as Edith Van Dyne

Aunt Jane's Nieces [*Abroad, at Millville, at Work, in Society, and Uncle John, on Vacation, on the Ranch, Out West, in the Red Cross*]. Chicago, Reilly and Britton, 10 vols., 1906-15.
The Flying Girl [*and Her Chum*]. Chicago, Reilly and Britton, 2 vols., 1911-12.
Mary Louise [*in the Country, Solves a Mystery, and the Liberty Girls, Adopts a Soldier*]. Chicago, Reilly and Britton, 4 vols., and Reilly and Lee, 1 vol., 1916-19.

Plays

The Wizard of Oz, music by Paul Tietjens, lyrics by Baum, adaptation of the novel by Baum (produced Chicago, 1902; revised version, as *There Is Something New under the Sun,* produced New York, 1903).
The Woggle-Bug, music by Frederic Chapin, adaptation of the novel *The Marvelous Land of Oz* by Baum (produced Chicago, 1905).
The Tik-Tok Man of Oz, music by Louis F. Gottschalk, adaptation of the story *Ozma of Oz* by Baum (produced Los Angeles, 1913).

Poetry

By the Candelabra's Glare, illustrated by W. W. Denslow. Privately printed, 1898.
Father Goose, His Book, illustrated by W. W. Denslow. Chicago, Hill, and London, Werner, 1899.
The Army Alphabet, illustrated by Harry Kennedy. Chicago, Hill, 1900.
The Navy Alphabet, illustrated by Harry Kennedy. Chicago, Hill, 1900.
The Songs of Father Goose, music by Alberta N. Hall, illustrated by W. W. Denslow. Chicago, Hill, 1900.
Father Goose's Year Book: Quaint Quacks and Feathery Shafts for Mature Children, illustrated by Walter Enright. Chicago, Reilly and Britton, 1907.

Other

Mother Goose in Prose, illustrated by Maxfield Parrish. Chicago, Way and Williams, 1897; London, Duckworth, 1899.
American Fairy Tales, illustrated by Ike Morgan and others. Chicago, Hill, 1901; London, Constable, 1978; augmented edition, Indianapolis, Bobbs Merrill, 1908.
L. Frank Baum's Juvenile Speaker (miscellany), illustrated by John R. Neill and others. Chicago, Reilly and Britton, 1910; as *Baum's Own Book for Children,* 1912.
Animal Fairy Tales. Chicago, International Wizard of Oz Club, 1969.

PUBLICATIONS FOR ADULTS

Novels

The Fate of a Crown (as Schuyler Staunton). Chicago, Reilly and Britton, and London, Revell, 1905.
Daughters of Destiny (as Schuyler Staunton). Chicago, Reilly and Britton, 1906.
Tamawaca Folks (as John Estes Cooke). Macatawa, Michigan, Macatawa Press, 1907.
The Last Egyptian (published anonymously). Philadelphia, Stern, and London, Sisley, 1908.

Plays

The Maid of Arran, music and lyrics by Baum, adaptation of the novel *A Princess of Thule* by William Black (also director: produced Syracuse and New York City, 1882).
Matches (produced Richburg, New York, 1882).
Kilmorne; or, O'Connor's Dream (produced Syracuse, 1888).
Stagecraft: The Adventures of a Strictly Moral Man, music by Louis F. Gottschalk (produced Santa Barbara, California, 1914).
The Uplift of Lucifer; or, Raising Hell, music by Louis F. Gottschalk (produced Santa Barbara, California, 1915). Edited by Manuel Weltman, privately printed, 1963.
The Uplifters' Minstrels, music by Byron Gay (produced Del Mar, California, 1916).
The Orpheus Road Company, music by Louis F. Gottschalk (produced Coronado Beach, California, 1917).

Screenplays: *The Fairylogue and Radio-Plays,* 1908; *The Patchwork Girl of Oz,* 1914; *The Magic Cloak of Oz,* 1914; *The Babes in the Wood,* 1914; *The Last Egyptian,* 1914; *The New Wizard of Oz,* 1915.

Poetry

The High-Jinks of L. Frank Baum (songs for Uplifters). Chicago, Wizard Press, 1959.

Other

The Book of the Hamburgs: A Brief Treatise upon the Mating, Rearing, and Management of the Different Varieties of Hamburgs. Hartford, Connecticut, Stoddard, 1886.
The Art of Decorating Dry Goods Windows and Interiors. Chicago, Show Window Publishing Company, 1900.
Our Landlady (*Saturday Pioneer* columns). Mitchell, South Dakota Writers' Project, 1941.

*

Bibliography: In *The Annotated Wizard of Oz* edited by Michael Patrick Hearn, New York, Potter, 1973.

Manuscript Collection: Columbia University, New York.

Critical Studies: *The Wizard of Oz and Who He Was* edited by Russel Nye and Martin Gardner, East Lansing, Michigan State University Press, 1957; *To Please a Child: A Biography of L. Frank Baum, Royal Historian of Oz* by Frank Joslyn Baum and Russell P. MacFall, Chicago, Reilly and Lee, 1961; *Wonderful Wizard, Marvelous Land* by Raylyn Moore, Bowling Green, Ohio, Popular Press, 1974.

* * *

L. Frank Baum has virtually been forced upon scholars and critics by the enduring popularity of *The Wonderful Wizard of Oz.* One result has been the discovery of an unexpected high quality elsewhere in the works of a prolific and uneven writer. And Baum was the kind of writer whose virtues are best appreciated only as one freely admits his shortcomings and his failures. Not that Baum had not had his early partisans. Edward Wagenknecht contributed a study, *Utopia Americana,* by 1929, and James Thurber praised Baum in 1934. But other comments virtually dismissed him as a poor stylist and an unimaginative tale-spinner.

Baum was indeed a poor stylist, but the stilted vocabulary and sentence structure of his early work relaxed considerably by the end of his career. More to the point perhaps is the size of his output. The least of it deserves the neglect it has received. Indeed, it is difficult to believe that the man who wrote the delightful fantasy *Queen Zixi of Ix* also offered the contrived and turgid *Dorothy and the Wizard in Oz.* A further problem has been that Baum wrote series books, and the Oz series kept Oz a vivid and interesting place. But children's series books have traditionally been considered unworthy of any critic's time.

When Baum was good he was very good. And sometimes he was mysteriously good. It is true that in the *Wizard,* the Scarecrow already has the brainpower he seeks from the Wizard, the Tin Woodman already shows the goodness of heart he wants, and the Cowardly Lion is naturally brave. They need only be made aware of their true qualities. And it is clear that Dorothy, after being whirled away from a harsh and lonely existence on the Kansas plains and dropped down into a land of colour and adventure, most wanted (and needed) to find a way home again. But otherwise the effect and meaning of the *Wizard* remain somewhat elusive. If self-reliance is really the message, what about the magic of the slippers? And the simple *accident* of the Wicked Witch's death?

The Marvelous Land of Oz seems more overt and more adult in its intended meaning: it burlesques the suffragette movement. There is some questionable plotting in the book—the six-chapter episode that introduces that memorable pedant, the "highly magnified" and "thoroughly educated" Wogglebug, is otherwise extrinsic and expendable. And in the end, a young girl (Ozma) who had been thought to be a young boy (Tip) is made ruler of Oz—a mysterious conclusion for a satire on feminism. Indeed, the criticism that Oz is a land populated by little men, hollow men, stuffed men, and humbugs ruled over by sweet little girls but where the real power belongs to a strong female figure (Glinda) seems answerable only if one assumes that Baum's tongue was planted firmly and deliberately in his cheek.

The Oz series does include several books in which contrived characters and meandering geography attempt to substitute for plot or even relevant incident. The sprightly *The Patchwork Girl of Oz* rescues the series with interesting characters, broad comedy, and a sustained quest. The stories continued with respectable contributions thereafter, but Baum did have a penchant for repeating himself. *Tik-Tok of Oz* is an amalgam of elements from *The Marvelous Land of Oz* and *Ozma of Oz;* the Frogman of *The Lost Princess of Oz* is another humbug magician.

Thurber pointed out that although Baum rejected "heartache" and "fear" in his "Introduction" to the *Wizard,* we may be thankful that he did not in his tale. Indeed, the Tin Woodman simply chops up some attacking wolves in Chapter XII. And in a true horror, Baum revealed that the Woodman, as an inept forester, gradually became metal because he scarred and chopped away his own limbs. In *The Tin Woodman of Oz* he discovers his own discarded limbs and severed head in his tinsmith's workrooms!

Queen Zixi of Ix is a beautifully paced, more traditional fairy tale of a magic cloak and three wishes which are consistently and sometimes humorously misused. It has been justly called Baum's best book. And *The Life and Adventures of Santa Claus* is an episodic and sustained pagan history of the Christmas figure.Baum's short stories are also uneven but the best of them are equally praiseworthy. Indeed, a collection that included "Jugger-jook" (Baum's Peter Rabbit variant), "A Kidnapped Santa Claus" (partly based on the longer version), "The King Who Changed His Mind," "The Runaway Shadows," "The Yellow Ryl," "A Box of Robbers," and "The Witchcraft of Mary-Marie" might well make a case for Baum as what he once said he hoped to be, an American Hans Christian Andersen. One tale, "Prince Mud-Turtle," is worth dwelling on as a comment on Baum's arbitrary treatment of magic. It is his version of "The Frog Prince," but whereas in the original a tenacious love turns ugliness into beauty, in Baum's story the transformation simply happens. Perhaps we should remind ourselves that magic, even the magic of love, is fine, but self-reliance and a realistic self-knowledge must precede the true gift of love.

A great loss in the Baum canon is represented by *Rinkitink in Oz.* As originally written, it was a beautifully conceived tale of young prince Inga who rescued his imprisoned parents and, symbolically, entered his own manhood. To bring it into the Oz series, Baum had Dorothy take over at the moment of Inga's triumph (another female dea ex machina), utterly (if implicitly) emasculating his hero. If the original manuscript of *Rinkitink* had survived, surely we would have another Baum story to place beside the *Wizard, Queen Zixi, Santa Claus,* and the best of the short tales.

—Martin Williams

BAXTER, Valerie. See **MEYNELL, Laurence.**

BB. See **WATKINS-PITCHFORD, D.J.**

BEACHCROFT, Nina

Nationality: British. **Born:** London, 10 November 1931; daughter of the writer T.O. Beachcroft. **Education:** Wimbledon High School; St. Hilda's College, Oxford, 1950-53, B.A. (honours) in English 1953. **Family:** Married Richard Gardner in 1954; two daughters. **Career:** Sub-editor, *Argosy,* London, 1953-55, and *Radio Times,* London, 1955-57. **Agent:** David Higham Associates Ltd., 5-8 Lower John Street, London W1R 4HA, England.

Publications for Children

Fiction

Well Met by Witchlight. London, Heinemann, 1972; New York, Atheneum, 1973.
Under the Enchanter. London, Heinemann, 1974.
Cold Christmas: A Ghost Story. London, Heinemann, 1974.
A Spell of Sleep. London, Heinemann, 1976.
A Visit to Folly Castle. London, Heinemann, 1977.
A Farthing for the Fair, illustrated by Anthony Colbert. London, Heinemann, 1978.
The Wishing People. London, Heinemann, 1980; New York, Dutton, 1982.
The Genie and Her Bottle. London, Heinemann, 1983.
Beyond World's End. London, Heinemann, 1985.

*

Nina Beachcroft comments:

I have written, on and off, for most of my life. I wrote short stories, of which a few were published, until I worked on a short story magazine, when reading too many soon killed the urge to write them. I wrote two long unpublished (and unpublishable) adult novels, and it was not until my first daughter was about eight that I thought of trying something for children. I wrote three before I eventually got *Well Met by Witchlight* accepted by Heinemann. In trying very hard to please children, I found I was pleasing myself. I enjoy writing fantasy; fairy tales have always appealed to me, as has the best kind of science fiction. It's the imaginative idea behind the story that gets me off the ground; after that, my concern is, I suppose, to work it out in some of its implications and to tell a fast-moving, exciting story, always with its feet in everyday reality even if its head is in the clouds.

* * *

With the exception of *A Farthing for the Fair,* an historical novel written for the Long Ago Children Series, Nina Beachcroft's stories are tales of enchantment that appeal mainly to 8- to 10-year-old children. The underlying pattern is of an unexpected encounter—in a wood, on holiday, in the house next door, through a broken fence—with a mysterious stranger through whom the children are put in danger from some lurking evil. A satisfactory outcome is, of course, assured. In *Well Met by Witchlight* a good witch helps to fill in while Granny is in hospital, comforting the anxious children, assisting them to defeat the evil witch and restoring Granny to health. As the latter returns, the good witch conveniently, but also calmly and reassuringly, retreats into a hibernation which may become death. In *Cold Christmas* the sad little ghost who is seeking to allay the evil that killed her also helps Josephine to make contact with other guests in the chilly Georgian house where her family is spending Christmas. But although in these books the children have a lively individuality, there remains a sense of contrivance, a lack of some inner logic in the intrusion of the supernatural element which prevents satisfactory suspension of disbelief. *Under the Enchanter* suffers less from this problem; it is powerful enough to be convincing, as terrified Laura battles alone to save her brother from the enchanter's fatal spells, her parents being "useless and unnoticing," strangely obtuse and even hostile when she tries to tell them something is seriously wrong with him. In *A Spell of Sleep* it is the relentless, mean-spirited, petty malice reawakened from 800 years ago that causes untold misery and threatens to drive the Turners from their home before the children's persistence finally wins them the appropriate help. Here there is a strong element of reality in the quarrel between neighbours to help carry conviction. *A Visit to Folly Castle* brings a new danger: the attractive, imaginative, and lively Sandra, who longs for a friend and fascinates Emma with all her moods and strange alien powers, nevertheless nearly betrays Emma's young brother to her parents' sinister plots.

After so much fear lurking uneasily behind the normal façade of life, it is almost a relief to turn to *The Wishing People.* For although the wooden figures on Martha's weatherhouse have the gift of granting wishes which, in true folk tradition, rarely turn out as expected, the general tone of this book is happier, more optimistic. Mr. and Mrs. Tom, the wishing people, work together with the children towards an acceptance of their individual imperfections: there is a consequent sense of growth in self-awareness on all sides which includes an understanding that reality can actually be more satisfying than dreams. *The Genie and Her Bottle,* inspired by *The Arabian Nights,* also explores wish granting. It was an enterprising idea to have a female genie for a change, though Leila is no credit to her sex, being a bored, supercilious, spiteful, and capricious Arabian princess, with thoroughly evil intent. But the children to whom she appears are more conventional—a brother and sister who are neglected by their upwardly mobile nouveau riche parents—and in spite of some inventive and comic episodes this is one of the more ordinary and derivative stories. *Beyond World's End,* on the other hand, inspired this time by John Wyndham's *The Kraken Wakes,* uses its material more imaginatively. Both Chris and his friend Jane, who accompanies him in his encounter with the extraterrestrial beings, have an engaging complexity of character and motivation, and their adventures are finely integrated into a story that reflects the ambivalences and untidiness of real life as well as providing an exciting and compelling science fiction story line.

All these stories minister to the child's perception of the unpredictability of the world and his uneasy sense that adults are often unaware of or indifferent to their children's fears, leaving them to struggle unaided—perhaps even actively hindering them in their fight against the unseen evil they sense around them. And in spite of the conventionality of some of the plots there is a lively interest in the variety of detail and situation and in the author's keen depiction of the fluctuations within individual relationships.

—Winifred Whitehead

BEATTY, John and Patricia

Nationality: Americans. **BEATTY, John (Louis): Born:** Portland, Oregon, 24 January 1922. **Education:** Reed College, Portland, B.A. 1943; Stanford University, California, M.A. 1947; University of Washington, Seattle, Ph.D. in history 1953. **Military Service:** United States Army 1943-45: Silver Star, Purple Heart. **Family:** Married Patricia Robbins (i.e., Patricia Beatty) in 1950; one daughter. **Career:** Instructor, Reed College, 1947-49, University of Washington, 1950-52, and University of Delaware, Newark, 1952-53; Assistant Professor, 1953-59, Associate Professor, 1959-75, and Professor of History, 1975, University of California, Riverside. **Awards:** American Philosophical Society grant, 1959. **Died:** 23 March 1975. **BEATTY, Patricia. Pseudonym:** Jean Bartholomew. **Born:** Patricia Robbins, Portland, Oregon, 26 August 1922. **Education:** Reed College, Portland, B.A. in history and English 1944; University of Idaho, Moscow, 1947-50; University of Washington, Seattle, 1951. **Family:** Married 1) John Beatty in 1950 (died 1975), one daughter; 2) Carl G. Uhr in 1977. **Career:** English and history teacher, Coeur d'Alene High School, Idaho, 1947-50; librarian, E.I. du Pont Company, Wilmington, Delaware, 1952-53, and Riverside Public Library, California, 1953-57; Instructor in Creative Writing, University of California, Riverside, 1967-68, and Los Angeles, 1968-69. **Awards:** Western Writers of America award, 1984, 1987; O'Dell award, 1988. **Died:** 9 July 1991.

Publications for Children

Fiction

At the Seven Stars, illustrated by Douglas Gorsline. New York, Macmillan, 1963; London, Chatto and Windus, 1966.
Campion Towers. New York, Macmillan, 1965; London, Chatto and Windus, 1967.
A Donkey for the King, illustrated by Ann Siberell. New York, Macmillan, 1966.
The Royal Dirk, illustrated by Franz Altschuler. New York, Morrow, 1966.
The Queen's Wizard. New York, Macmillan, 1967.
Witch Dog, illustrated by Franz Altschuler. New York, Morrow, 1968.
Pirate Royal. New York, Macmillan, and London, Collier Macmillan, 1969.
King's Knight's Pawn. New York, Morrow, 1971.
Holdfast. New York, Morrow, 1972.
Master Rosalind. New York, Morrow, 1974.
Who Comes to King's Mountain? New York, Morrow, 1975.

Fiction by Patricia Beatty

Indian Canoe-Maker, illustrated by Barbara Beaudreau. Caldwell, Idaho, Caxton Press, 1960.
Bonanza Girl, illustrated by Liz Dauber. New York, Morrow, 1962.
The Nickel-Plated Beauty, illustrated by Liz Dauber. New York, Morrow, 1964.
Squaw Dog, illustrated by Franz Altschuler. New York, Morrow, 1965.
The Queen's Own Grove, illustrated by Liz Dauber. New York, Morrow, 1966.
The Lady from Black Hawk, illustrated by Robert Frankenberg. New York, McGraw Hill, 1967.
Me, California Perkins, illustrated by Liz Dauber. New York, Morrow, 1968.
Blue Stars Watching. New York, Morrow, 1969.
Station Four. Chicago, Science Research Associates, 1969.
Hail Columbia, illustrated by Liz Dauber. New York, Morrow, 1970.
The Sea Pair, illustrated by Franz Altschuler. New York, Morrow, 1970.
A Long Way to Whiskey Creek. New York, Morrow, 1971.
O the Red Rose Tree, illustrated by Liz Dauber. New York, Morrow, 1972.
The Bad Bell of San Salvador. New York, Morrow, 1973.
Red Rock over the River. New York, Morrow, 1973.
How Many Miles to Sundown. New York, Morrow, 1974.
Rufus, Red Rufus, illustrated by Ted Lewin. New York, Morrow, 1975.
By Crumbs, It's Mine! New York, Morrow, 1976.
Something to Shout About. New York, Morrow, 1976.
Billy Bedamned, Long Gone By. New York, Morrow, 1977.
I Want My Sunday, Stranger! New York, Morrow, 1977.
Just Some Weeds from the Wilderness. New York, Morrow, 1978.
Wait for Me, Watch for Me, Eula Bee. New York, Morrow, 1978.
Lacy Makes a Match. New York, Morrow, 1979.
The Staffordshire Terror. New York, Morrow, 1979.
That's One Ornery Orphan. New York, Morrow, 1980.
Lupita Mañana. New York, Morrow, 1981.
Eight Mules from Monterey. New York, Morrow, 1982.
Jonathan Down Under. New York, Morrow, 1982.
Melinda Takes a Hand. New York, Morrow, 1983.
Turn Homeward, Hannalee. New York, Morrow, 1984.
The Coach That Never Came. New York, Morrow, 1985.
Behave Yourself, Bethany Brant. New York, Morrow, 1986.
Charley Skedaddle. New York, Morrow, 1987.
Be Ever Hopeful, Hannalee. New York, Morrow, 1988.
Sarah and Me and the Lady from the Sea. New York, Morrow, 1989.
Eben Tyne, Powdermonkey. New York, Morrow, 1990.
Jayhawker. New York, Morrow, 1991.
Who Comes with Cannons? New York, Morrow, 1992.

Publications for Adults

Novel by Patricia Beatty

The Englishman's Mistress (as Jean Bartholomew). New York, Dell, 1975.

Other by John Beatty

Warwick and Holland, Being the Lives of Robert and Henry Rich. Denver, Alan Swallow, 1965.

Editor, with Oliver A. Johnson, *Heritage of Western Civilization: Select Readings.* Englewood Cliffs, New Jersey, Prentice Hall, 1958.

*

Manuscript Collection: University of California, Riverside.

Patricia Beatty commented:
(1989) For the most part I write of the historical past for young readers—and not only because of a personal, loving interest in history. I sense a growing disinterest among people of the English-speaking world in what has gone on before. This seems particularly true of many university students who say openly, "history began yesterday." I try to make the English and American "pasts" come to life in order to convince the 9 to 14 age group

that people of the past were real people with real personalities and real problems and not text-book, dry-as-a-bone beings, mummified by time and bloodless footnotes.

* * *

John and Patricia Beatty have been two of the more prolific authors of historical fiction for children, collaborating on a series of historical novels set in the British Isles. One hallmark of their work together has been concern for the accuracy of historical detail. Their articles in such journals as *Horn Book* have provided interesting insights on the challenges the authors faced in rendering dialects and period language so that both historic accuracy and clarity are served. Impressive as their careful research and writing are, however, these jointly authored stories are not as interesting as Patricia Beatty's more recent work. The British novels tend to turn complex issues such as the English Civil War and the highland clearances into romantic, swashbuckling affairs. Even the award-winning *The Royal Dirk* lacks the sense of character and place that mark Patricia Beatty's novels with American settings. Alan McCrae's story might have been more powerful if he had stayed in the highlands and faced Lord Cumberland's wrath rather than spend so much of the book with a fencing master in London.

Secondary characters in the Beattys' British novels tend to drift in and out without making a strong impression. Jessie Cameron, the highwayman's wife in *The Royal Dirk,* appears so briefly that the impact of her death on Alan seems exaggerated. In contrast, the characters in Patricia Beatty's American books are more fully developed. When Granny Brant in *Charley Skedaddle* is missing for two days, Charley's search for her and his careful nursing grow from a longterm, well-developed relationship. Other characters, such as Mr. Ponder in *By Crumbs, It's Mine!,* also emerge as integral—and often humorous—parts of Patricia Beatty's stories.

One of the most interesting aspects of Patricia Beatty's recent work is the contrast between her lighter western and first-person novels and her American Civil War books. The lighter works feature liberated young women who face up to the rigors of frontier life and treacherous men. When her father succumbs to "get-rich-quick" disease, Damaris Boyd in *By Crumbs, Its Mine!,* rallies and turns potential tragedy into a money-making venture. In *How Many Miles to Sundown* the heroine treks through the Southwest searching for her absent father. In these and other stories set in the American West Patricia Beatty sets up situations in which young women have a plausible degree of freedom despite the restrictions of their historical era. *Hail Columbia* for instance is one of the first novels for young people that provides a sympathetic portrait of the suffrage movement. For this alone these books would be interesting. It is a delightful bonus that they also display a sense of humor about the conditions that have historically constrained women.

Some of Patricia Beatty's best work are her novels set in the American Civil War. *Charley Skedaddle* is probably the finest of these. Charley is an Irish boy living in New York City. Seeking a way to avenge his brother's death at Gettysburg, and to escape from a prospective brother-in-law he dislikes, Charley joins the Union forces as a drummer boy. At the Battle of the Wilderness, anticipation turns to panic when he sees his friends killed, and shoots his first rebel. Charley "skedaddles"—runs off—and is eventually taken in by an old "witch woman" in the Blue Ridge mountains. Living with Granny Brant, Charley learns the difference between real courage and the bravado that led to his soldiering. The story ends as Charley is forced to escape the retreating Confederates and leave the life he has built for himself in the little mountain community. His promise to return when the war ends closes the story. Beatty does a fine job here of describing the misery of the last years of the Civil War and contrasting it with the hard but satisfying life of the mountain people. While there is some of the same romanticizing of mountain folk here as of highlanders in *The Royal Dirk,* the images of war are more down-to-earth, and Charlie's behavior is more believable.

Following her husband John's death, Patricia Beatty remained a prolific writer of historical fiction—one of the few who can handle so broad a range of periods and styles. Her work is a good introduction to the genre for readers new to historical fiction. She can also be depended upon as a careful author who tries to be true to both the literary and historical qualities of her stories.

—Linda S. Levstik

BECK, Ian

Nationality: British. **Born:** Hove, Sussex, 17 August 1947. **Education:** Brighton College of Art. **Family:** Married Emma Stone, 1977; three children. **Career:** Commercial illustrator doing record covers (including Elton John, *Goodbye Yellow Brick Road,* 1973), greetings cards, calendars, and interior design, 1968-82; clients included Conran Design Group, *Sunday Times* newspaper, *Cosmopolitan* magazine, Trickett and Webb Design Group, Penguin and Puffin books; children's book illustrator, since 1982. Gardening column illustrator, *Saturday Express* magazine. **Address:** c/o Orchard Books, 96 Leonard Street, London EC2A 4RH, England.

PUBLICATIONS FOR CHILDREN: (ILLUSTRATED BY THE AUTHOR)

The Teddy Robber. London, Doubleday, 1989.
Little Miss Muffett. London, Oxford, 1989.
Emily and the Golden Acorn. London, Doubleday, 1992.
Five Little Ducks. London, Orchard Books, 1992.
Orchard ABC. London, Orchard Books, 1994.
Picture Book. London, Deutsch, 1994.
Away in a Manger. London, Orion, 1994.
Oxford Nursery Book. Oxford, Oxford University Press, 1995.
ABC. London, Walker Books, 1995.
Tom and the Island of Dinosaurs. Doubleday, 1995.
Poppy and Pip's Bedtime. London, HarperCollins, 1996.
Poppy and Pip's Walk. London, HarperCollins, 1996.
Home Before Dark. London, Scholastic, 1997.
The Ugly Duckling. London, Orchard Books, 1997.
Lost in the Snow. London, Scholastic, 1998.
The Oxford Nursery Story Book. London, Oxford University Press, 1998.

*

Illustrator: *Round and Round the Garden,* 1983, *Ride a Cock-Horse,* 1986, and *Pudding and Pie,* 1989, all edited by Sarah Williams; *The Lost Domain* (for adults) by Alain-Fournier, 1985; *Short Stories* by Ernest Hemingway, 1986; *Edible Architecture* (for adults), 1986, and *Portable Pleasures* (for adults), 1988, both by M. Coatts; *Pride and Prejudice* by Jane Austen, 1987; *Baby's First Years,* 1989; *Hush-a-bye Baby,* edited by Carolyn Fickling, 1990; *Poems for Christmas,* edited by Jill Bennett, 1992; *Orchard Book of Fairytales,* 1992, and *Sir Billy Bear and Other Friends,* 1996, both by Rose Impey; *Oranges and Lemons* by Karen King, 1994; *Peter and the Wolf* by S. S. Prokoviev, 1994; *The Owl and the Pussycat* by Edward Lear, 1995; *Little Angel* by Geraldine McGaughrean, 1995; *Cork* (for adults) by William Boyd, 1995; *Wit and Wisdom* (for adults), 1995, and *Stories* (for adults), 1997, both by Oscar Wilde; *Noah and the Ark* by Antonia Barber, 1997; *Peter Pan and Wendy* by Rose Impey, 1998.

Ian Beck comments:

I had collected books for children since I was an art student in the 1960s. There was a great revival of interest in illustrators like Arthur Rackham, Edmund Dulac, and Jesse M. King, which itself came out of the Art Nouveau revival. I treated the children's books as collectors items, self-consciously beautiful gift volumes, not the sort of books to survive the rough and tumble of child use. It was not really until the birth of our first child in 1981 that I began to read and use books with a child, and observe the interaction and response that he had to books like *Where the Wild Things Are,* or *Peepo,* or *Each Peach Pear Plum.* Only then did I understand the relation between text and picture, the delight of turning the page to a surprise from, say, a single small picture to a double spread. By coincidence at the same time I was approached by the Oxford University Press, which was at the design concept stage for a book of play rhymes which was to become *Round and Round the Garden.* The designer had seen some of my editorial work for the BBC listings journal *Radio Times,* and thought that my style or approach might be suitable. I was asked to do a test page, and the result was that I was commissioned to illustrate the book.

The book was successful, and a follow up collection was published, and another, and so on, until my editor at Oxford University Press encouraged me to come up with a text for myself to illustrate. This was *Little Miss Muffett,* and it was followed by *The Teddy Robber.* I began a little series of child-centred adventure picture books, very much born out of my own experience of parenting, listening to my children talk and play as they grew, observing their concerns, and excitements. I like the kind of story that involves the child protagonist directly, with the minimum of parental interference. My little heroes and heroines happily fly across the world in hot air balloons, or sail a pirate ship that was a tree in the garden to the edge of the world and back.

The birth of our daughter in 1990 gave me a whole fresh insight, and my *Picture Book* came directly out of my experience of sharing books and life with her. I was brought up by the sea, and now live near the river Thames, and these landscapes frequently appear in my work. My children have contributed immeasurably to my work, not only for themselves but also in allowing me to remember and relive my own childhood.

* * *

Ian Beck spent many years as a commercial illustrator and designer working in interior design and in the record industry, where he painted the cover of one of the best known records of all time, Elton John's *Goodbye Yellow Brick Road.* He took commissions for greetings cards, calendars, packaging and murals. When he broke into the world of children's books, it was as an illustrator of other people's texts, which he still does very skillfully.

Beck's distinctive style is perfectly suited to the nursery, which is why he has been in such demand to illustrate collections of nursery rhymes and party games. His early examples of these—*Round and Round the Garden, Ride a Cock Horse, Pudding and Pie* and *Oranges and Lemons*—brought a freshness to these familiar verses and songs with vibrant illustrations. Although the children in many of these illustrations are often dressed in Edwardian style clothes, and the toys are wooden rocking horses and tin soldiers, putting them very much in a middle-class English tradition of the Nursery, they have a timeless quality that is more universally appealing. The nostalgic imagery suits the subject matter and the books are agreeable to parents and children alike.

Ian Beck's talent for illustration soon led him to write his own texts and produce highly original and discerning picture books. The first of these was *The Teddy Robber,* the story of a little boy whose teddy is stolen one night by a giant. Tom tries desperately to hold on to his teddy, but slips down the giant's leg and hangs on to his boot straps. Inside the castle, Tom discovers that the giant has a whole room full of teddies that he has stolen. However, it appears that the giant is really only looking for his own teddy, which is lost. Tom eventually finds the giant's teddy and helps him return the other lost teddies. This is a deeply satisfying story for very young children. The plot is artfully constructed to include just the right amounts of excitement and fear, fantasy and reality, but with the comfort of a safe ending.

Emily and the Golden Acorn was Beck's second full-length picture book. This is another delicious blend of fantasy and reality in which two children, Emily and Jack, act out their pirate adventures in a huge oak tree in their garden. As a storm is brewing one night Emily makes a wish and the story turns to fantasy. When she wakes the tree has become a real pirate ship and she and Jack set sail for the high seas and adventure. When reality returns in the morning the precious tree has blown down. Luckily, they have brought back a golden acorn from their adventures to plant another tree. Once again, it is a fantasy adventure story that is completely in tune with the imaginations of young children. It gives them the freedom to explore the idea of a great unknown, within the boundaries of a story. Beck uses the device of allowing the children to bring back something from the 'fantasy' part of the story to their 'real' life, which enables child readers/listeners to keep alive the spark of magic that the adventure really happened.

Similarly, in *Tom and the Island of Dinosaurs,* Tom lives with his grandfather in a lighthouse where one day he finds a bottle with a message in it from a girl who is shipwrecked on an island with dinosaurs and an erupting volcano. Tom sets off in a hot-air balloon to rescue Katy and the dinosaurs too before returning to the safety of his grandfather once again. Ian Beck's illustrations for all these books are all encompassing, filling the pages with the details of the stories and drawing the reader into the adventure. Children's imaginations naturally respond to these types of story, where anything is possible and the happy ending is as vital as the drama.

Others of Beck's picture books are gentle tales depicting everyday events in children's lives, as in the Poppy and Pip books, or *Home Before Dark,* the story of a teddy who gets lost and must get himself home before he is needed most. He has also created many books that rely purely on the illustrations, like alphabet and counting books. His *Nursery Book,* for example, is a large format book of pictures of familiar objects or actions—house, flowers, cat, cow, run, jump—one word to each page, with illustrations that combine the by now familiar blend of reality and fantasy.

Ian Beck's style adapts well to other people's texts and he has successfully illustrated classics like *The Owl and the Pussy Cat* and *Peter and the Wolf,* or traditional nursery stories like *The Ugly Duckling.* His soft, muted illustrations for Antonia Barber's fine version of *Noah and the Ark* are wonderfully detailed, adding a new dimension to a familiar story, as in the underwater scene showing the cities beneath the flood waters.

This balance of illustrating the work of others and his own picture books seems to work well for Ian Beck. It allows his talents as an illustrator to flourish and ensures that his own books are of the highest quality in terms of text.

—Fiona Lafferty

BEDARD, Michael

Nationality: Canadian. **Born:** Toronto, 26 June 1949. **Education:** University of Toronto, B.A. 1971. **Family:** Married Martha Bedard; one son, three daughters. **Career:** Worked at St. Michael's College Library for seven years, and as a pressman for a small press for three years; full-time writer. **Awards:** Governor General's Literary Award, 1990, and Canadian Library Association Book of the Year, 1991, both for *Redwork*; Toronto IODE (Imperial Order of the Daughters of the Empire) Children's Book Award, for *The Nightingale,* 1992. **Address:** c/o Bantam Doubleday Dell Books for Young Readers, 1540 Broadway, New York, New York 10036-4094, U.S.A.

Publications for Children

Fiction

A Darker Magic. New York, Atheneum, 1987.
Redwork. Toronto, Lester; New York, Atheneum, 1990.
Painted Devil. Toronto, Lester. 1994.

Picture Books

Woodsedge. Toronto, Gardenshore Press, 1979.
Pipe and Pearls. Toronto, Gardenshore Press, 1980.
The Lightning Bolt, illustrated by Regolo Ricci. Toronto, Oxford University Press, 1989.
Emily (biography), illustrated by Barbara Cooney. Toronto, Lester, and New York, Doubleday, 1992.
The Divide, illustrated by Emily Arnold McCully. Montreal, Tundra Books, 1997.
Glass Town: The Secret World of the Brontë Children, illustrated by Laura Fernandez and Rick Jacobson. Don Mills, Stoddart, 1997.

Contributor, *The Unseen: Scary Stories,* selected by Janet Lunn. Toronto, Lester, 1994.

Reteller, *The Tinder Box,* illustrated by Regolo Ricci. Toronto, Oxford University Press, 1990.
Reteller, *The Nightingale,* illustrated by Regolo Ricci. Toronto, Oxford University Press, 1991.

* * *

Within a relatively short time period, Michael Bedard has established himself as one of Canada's foremost writers of quality juvenile fiction. His works can be divided into two groupings: texts for picture books directed at younger audiences (these would also speak to older readers, however), plus novels for middle school students. Though the picture book texts are very well written, the richness of language, imagery, and theme, as well as the depth of character development found in the longer books for older audiences, causes them to stand out amongst Bedard's output.

A Darker Magic explores the concept of evil's persistent revisitation of the world and mankind's need to be ever vigilant against its seductive aspects. While clearing out student desks, Miss Potts, a teacher for some 40 years, discovers a playbill advertising a children's magic show that is to be performed in the community of Caledon by Professor Mephisto on Saturday, August 8. She recalls the fatal results of such a show 50 years before. Recognizing that the day and date will be the same this year, Miss Potts seeks out the desk's occupant, Emily Endicott, and together they work to see that the darker magic does not achieve its victory. Mephisto is, of course, the diminutive of Mephistopheles, the evil to whom Faustus sold his soul for riches and power. Miss Potts, correctly recognizing that evil is never permanently defeated, exclaims, "He is the Pied Piper, the peddlar of wonder, leading the children into the dark ... All we can do is wait, and watch, and trust that when the night draws near again, there will be someone left who remembers the last time, and is ready for him."

Miss Potts' warning is heeded in *Painted Devil* as Emily Endicott, now a 42-year-old spinster, returns to Caledon, convinced by her dreams that the demonic magician will malevolently reappear on the twenty-eighth anniversary of his last August 8th magic show, again to seek the death of a child. Understanding that the task of vigilance must be passed on to the next generation, Emily enlists the aid of her 14-year-old niece, Alice Higginson, a student assistant at the local public library. Recruited by the new librarian, Mr. Dwyer, to participate in staging a children's Punch and Judy show, Alice is to assume the role of Punch, the character who is ultimately to be dragged off by the painted puppet devil. As the title intimates, while Emily has been appropriately vigilant, she has failed to recognize the darker magic's ability to assume new guises.

Redwork, the novel that appeared between the two darker magic works, revolves around the developing relationship between an old man, Arthur Magnus, and two 15-year-olds, Cass Parry and Maddy Harrington. Magnus, in his nineties, had lost a leg and been gassed during World War I. Cass and his mother Alison rent rooms in Magnus's house while Maddy is one of Cass's co-workers at a local movie theatre. The teens' curiosity about Magnus's nocturnal habits leads to their discovery that Magnus is an alchemist searching for the philosopher's stone, which allegedly possesses the power to cure evil, heal disease, and grant immortality. As the friendship among the three matures, Magnus invites the pair to join him in the final but most dangerous stage of the alchemic work, Redwork. *The Lightning Bolt,* an original fairy tale, initially appeared in a collection of tales Bedard had previously privately printed. In the story, an old woman receives two magic gifts as a reward for a good deed, and then is abused by her husband, who spitefully appropriates one of the objects for his own use.

Having begun to read Emily Dickinson's poetry when he was 17, Bedard acknowledges a fascination with the reclusive poetess. In *Emily,* Bedard breathes life into the character that many may know only through her poetry. While young children who encounter the book's Emily may have no idea who Emily Dickinson was, they can still identify with the emotions and behaviours of the little girl as she joins her mother on a visit to play the piano for their strange neighbour—someone the locals refer to as the "Myth."

Bedard has continued to find inspiration in the lives of famous women writers with *Glass Town: The Secret World of the Brontë Children* and *The Divide.* Bedard's texts for these picture books are fictionalized accounts of the childhoods of the Brontë sisters and Willa Cather, respectively. As with *Emily, Glass Town* and *The Divide* give life to these famous novelists as Bedard introduces them to young audiences and explores their early sources of inspiration. As well, Bedard has retold two of Hans Christian Andersen's classic stories, *The Tinder Box* and *The Nightingale.*

—David H. Jenkinson, updated by Alexandra MacLennan

BEGAY, Shonto

Nationality: Native American. **Born:** Near Shonto, Arizona, 7 February 1954. **Education:** Attended Bureau of Indian Affairs boarding schools at various locations on the Navajo Indian Reservation during his elementary school years; Monument Valley High School, Kayenta, Arizona; Institute of American Indian Arts, Santa Fe, New Mexico, Associate of Fine Arts degree; California College of Arts and Crafts in Oakland, California, B.F.A. 1980. **Family:** Married Cruz; three daughters, one son. **Career:** Herded sheep and drove cattle; National Park Service Ranger, Grand Teton National Park, 1976-81, Navajo National Monument, 1981-86; artist, illustrator, writer, and speaker, since 1981. **Awards:** Reading Rainbow Selection, *The Mud Pony,* 1988; Arizona Author Award, 1993. **Address:** Kayenta, Arizona 86033, U.S.A.

Publications for Children (illustrated by the author)

Ma'ii and Cousin Horned Toad. New York, Scholastic, 1992.

Navajo: Visions and Voices across the Mesa. New York, Scholastic, 1995.

Strawberry Pop and Soda Crackers. Glenview, Illinois, Celebration Press, 1996.

*

Bibliography: "Sacred Places: American Indian Literature from Small Presses" by Kathleen T. Horning, in *Book Links,* July 1992; "Let Our Words Be Heard: Native American Stories Passed from Mouth to Ear to Heart" by Peggy K. Ford, in *Instructor* (New York), Vol. 105, November/December 1995, 47-48.

Illustrator: *The Mud Pony* by Caron Lee Cohen, 1988; *Native People, Native Ways Series,* Vol. 1, *The Native American Book of Knowledge,* 1992, Vol. 2, *The Native American Book of Life,* 1992, Vol. 3, *The Native American Book of Change,* 1992, and Vol. 4, *The Native American Book of Wisdom,* all by White Deer of Autumn; *The Boy Who Dreamed of an Acorn* by Leigh Casler, 1992; *The Magic of Spider Woman* by Lois Duncan, 1996.

* * *

Shonto Begay is a Navajo painter, illustrator, and writer of children's books. His paintings evoke the luminous colors of the Arizona mesa. In his work, he paints and illustrates the world of the *Dinéh,* the Navajo people. His drawings, paintings, and words are infused with the spirit of nature and of Navajo philosophy. Begay's works are part of an effort to balance the "New World" of technology and of those foreign to Navajo tradition with the ancient traditions of his people.

When Begay was five years old, he was sent to a government boarding school, where he was required to go by law. As he tells in his introduction to *Navajo: Voices and Visions Across the Mesa,* at that time, the policy of the U.S. government was to "assimilate" Navajo children, which meant that speaking the Navajo language was forbidden. If children were caught speaking Navajo, their mouths would be washed out with soap. Navajo children at government boarding schools were also required to attend government-sponsored church services. Begay writes: "We were only permitted to go home for two weeks during Christmas, and for the summer. Our parents were forbidden from seeing us in between those times. It was believed that losing our culture would make us become successful." Despite the suffering this policy caused, Begay is not bitter. He draws strength from the values and stories of his tradition, and he seeks to integrate, or at least hold in balance, contemporary American life and the spirituality of Navajo ways.

He has illustrated, with expressive pen and ink drawings, a series of books about Native American people and ways from Beyond Words Publishing, including *The Native American Book of Change* and *The Native American Book of Knowledge,* by White Deer of Autumn (Gabriel Horn). The lyrical drawings in these books affirm the beauty and continuity of Native American culture. They show the relationships between Native American peoples and animals, the spirit world, the traditions of storytelling, and Mother Earth. Noteworthy in these illustrations is Begay's blending of images of the ancestors from before the time of the European invasion and of contemporary American Indian life. For example, his drawings include both Native Americans as they might have appeared before Columbus and young Indians with baseball caps and glasses.

Similarly, in *Navajo: Visions and Voices Across the Mesa* he does not ignore the evidence of the intrusion of alien ways. In a painting "In the Late Light," accompanied by a powerful tribute to Grandmother and her reverence for the earth, a discarded beverage can lies half-buried in the snow in the foreground, close to some shards of traditional pottery, suggesting the destruction of tradition that has been going on for centuries. Nevertheless, the painting is a glowing evocation of the unity of an aged woman with the natural world. It shows a white-haired woman in the glow of evening light, seated on a slope next to a yucca plant, with a dog beside her and goats in the distance. She holds a long staff, and rests her chin on her palm. The sun illuminates the orange-red hillside and patches of snow, while in the shadows and across the valley the snow gleams blue. The rim of the cliffs across the mesa are touched with a thin gold line of sunset. The old woman's posture suggests a patient waiting, harmonious anticipation. The text also emphasizes this union: "The lines in her face were marks of honor, countless winters gazing into the blizzard, many summers in the hot cornfield." Grandmother taught her descendants to revere their grandparents, the young juniper tree and the young piñon tree, by greeting them each morning.

Navajo: Visions and Voices Across the Mesa is a combination of tableaux, a series of poetic reflections and memories paired with paintings by Begay, some recalling moments from his childhood and youth, others evoking scenes of Navajo life. In "Darkness at Noon: Solar Eclipse" he tells of the frightening experience of an eclipse when, as his aunt said, "The sun had died." His father stood on a hill praying, while he and his siblings sat in silence and panic in the hogan, until gradually, beginning with crescents of light on the floor, the sun reappeared. The eclipse taught him to savor the light of the sun, the richness of colors, and the warmth of summer more fully. He now scatters corn pollen every morning before dawn "to thank the sun for its coming gift of light." Another memorable painting, "In My Mother's Kitchen," shows, with tender affection, his mother preparing tortillas at the stove, and is accompanied with a poignant poem that pays tribute to his mother's gentle presence. Other scenes reveal the crowd at the tribal fair, a group of card players at the edge of a healing ceremony, the mystery of a shaman becoming a wolf, a death hogan, abandoned in a canyon, and several glimpses of riders traveling in pick-up trucks.

"Storm Pattern" tells how, as a boy, he urged his mother to weave images he found in magazines into her rugs. She told him she could not, and described to him the gift of a vision she was given as a girl, a vision of storm clouds, which became her pattern. As an adult, he laughs, knowing that the new images he tried to persuade her to weave into her rugs were corporate logos. In a sense, his paintings achieve what he wanted his mother to do: they include corporate logos such as a Grateful Dead trademark (the acknowledgments page has a permission statement for Grateful Dead Merchandising and Harley Davidson, Inc.) and traditional Navajo designs, such as his mother's storm cloud pattern. This duality is characteristic of Begay's work: acknowledging the coexistence of both cultures and, at times, their influence on each other. *Navajo: Visions and Voices Across the Mesa* is his most personal and self-revealing work. It presents a layered series of images of his growth and of his experience of the Navajo community.

Some of Begay's best work has been in collaboration with writers retelling traditional Native American tales. These include Lois Duncan's telling of *The Magic of Spider Woman* and Caron Lee Cohen's version of *The Mud Pony: A Traditional Skidi Pawnee Tale*. Begay dedicates the art for *The Magic of Spider Woman* to "all the guardians of Spider Woman's spirit, the weavers of the Dinéh Nation—especially to my mother, Faye, my Aunt Juanita, and my late grandmother, Bessie Smith." The story tells of how Weaving Woman succumbed to the temptation to pursue her weaving to excess, disobeying her promise to Spider Woman, who taught her how to weave. It is a story about the need for balance in all of life, especially for the artist. Begay's exquisite images show the interconnection between the spirit world and the "Fourth World," which is "on the earth's surface." Begay's palette is resplendent with the purples, blues, and ochres of the Southwest. Duncan writes, "Red clay mesas glowed in the morning sunlight, and valleys sparkled with wildflowers, and deep, green forests blanketed towering mountains," lines which Begay interprets feelingly.

In *The Mud Pony*, another impressive collaboration, a boy is left behind by his people, but Mother Earth turns his mud pony into a living one and he finds his way back to them and becomes an influential leader. With delicate and powerful chalk and watercolor illustrations, Begay illuminates this story. The image of the shadow of the pony over the sleeping chief near the conclusion of the book is particularly powerful.

Ma'ii and Cousin Horned Toad: A Traditional Navajo Story, written and illustrated by Begay, is well told and luminously illustrated. It is a trickster tale about Coyote, Ma'ii, the mischievous one. In this story, Ma'ii is outwitted by the horned toad, and suffers for his greediness. In a note at the end of the story, Begay explains that "whenever we come upon a horned toad, we gently place it over our heart and greet it. '*Ya ateeh shi che*' ('Hello, my grandfather'). We believe it gives strength of heart and mind. We never harm our grandfather." Begay groups this story with the "Coyote out walking stories," which are teaching tales meant to "show proper ways to conduct ourselves." The story has humor, suspense, and the satisfying roundedness belonging to many folk tales. Begay adds a brief glossary with a guide for pronouncing Navajo words.

Drawing on the strength and wisdom of the Navajo tradition, Begay is a contemporary artist interpreting his people's culture both to his people and to American readers generally. He succeeds in conveying reverence for the values of his past without the haze of nostalgia, and in acknowledging the pain of his people's history without being overwhelmed by it. His images and his words convey love of the land and of the people who belong to it.

—J. D. Stahl

BEHN, Harry

Pseudonym: Giles Behn. **Nationality:** American. **Born:** Prescott, Arizona, 24 September 1898. **Education:** Educated at Stanford University, California, 1918; Harvard University, Cambridge, Massachusetts, B.S. 1922. **Family:** Married Alice Lawrence in 1925; one daughter and two sons. **Career:** Scenario writer, Metro-Goldwyn-Mayer, Twentieth Century-Fox, and Universal studios, Hollywood, 1925-35; Professor of Creative Writing, University of Arizona, Tucson, 1938-47. Founding director, Phoenix Little Theatre, 1922-23; Vice President, Tucson Regional Plan, 1940-47; founding editor, *Arizona Quarterly*, Tucson, 1942-47; founder, University of Arizona Press, 1960. **Awards:** George G. Stone Center for Children's Books award, 1965. **Died:** 6 September 1973.

PUBLICATIONS FOR CHILDREN

Fiction

The Painted Cave, illustrated by the author. New York, Harcourt Brace, 1957.

Timmy's Search, illustrated by Barbara Cooney. Greenwich, Connecticut, Seabury Press, 1958.

The Two Uncles of Pablo, illustrated by Mel Silverman. New York, Harcourt Brace, 1959; London, Macmillan, 1960.
Roderick, illustrated by Mel Silverman. New York, Harcourt Brace, 1961.
The Faraway Lurs, illustrated by the author. Cleveland, World, 1963; as *The Distant Lurs,* London, Gollancz, 1965.
Omen of the Birds, illustrated by the author. Cleveland, World, 1964; London, Gollancz, 1965.

Poetry (illustrated by the author)

The Little Hill: Poems and Pictures. New York, Harcourt Brace, 1949.
All Kinds of Time. New York, Harcourt Brace, 1950.
Windy Morning: Poems and Pictures. New York, Harcourt Brace, 1953.
The House Beyond the Meadow. New York, Pantheon, 1955.
The Wizard in the Well: Poems and Pictures. New York, Harcourt Brace, 1956.
The Golden Hive: Poems and Pictures. New York, Harcourt Brace, 1966.
What a Beautiful Noise, illustrated by Harold Berson. New York, World, 1970.
Crickets and Bullfrogs and Whispers of Thunder, edited by Lee Bennett Hopkins. New York, Harcourt Brace, 1984.

Other

Translator, *Cricket Songs* [and *More Cricket Songs*]: *Japanese Haiku.* New York, Harcourt Brace, 2 vols., 1964-71.

Publications for Adults

Plays

Screenplays: *The Big Parade,* 1925; *Proud Flesh,* with Agnes Christine Johnson, 1925; *La Bohème,* with Ray Doyle, 1926; *The Crowd,* with King Vidor and John V.A. Weaver, 1928; *The Racket,* with Del Andrews, 1928; *Frozen River,* 1929; *The Sin Sister,* with Andrew Bennison, 1929; *Hell's Angels,* with Howard Estabrook, 1930.

Poetry

Siesta. Phoenix, Golden Bough Press, 1931.
The Grand Canyon (as Giles Behn). Privately printed, 1935.
Sombra. Copenhagen, Christreu, 1961.

Other

Chrysalis: Concerning Children and Poetry. New York, Harcourt Brace, 1968.

Translator, *The Duino Elegies,* by Rainer Maria Rilke. Mount Vernon, New York, Peter Pauper Press, 1957.
Translator, with Peter Beilenson, *Haiku Harvest.* Mount Vernon, New York, Peter Pauper Press, 1962.

*

Manuscript Collections: Kerlan Collection, University of Minnesota, Minneapolis; University of Oregon Library, Eugene.

* * *

It is a fascinating and far-flung legacy which Harry Behn has left to the child-reader and to those interested in literature for children, characterized, perhaps, by his own words, "Innocence is hardly more than a willingness to wonder." How unusual it is to think of Behn as a man of innocence—born in Arizona when it was still a territory, educated at Harvard, and world-traveled! And yet it is the right phrase, for his willingness to wonder and wander, his enthusiasms and curiosity moved within a changing world which he persisted in viewing, most often, through the eyes of the innocent.

His books, ranging from the child's poetic voice of *Windy Morning* through stories and novels and further poetry as well as translation of haiku, carry a thread of transcendentalism; it is the Indian Earth-Mother, the gods of the Sun People, the god Aplu, the rising of the sun, the "almost imperceptible experience of wonder, removed from knowledge." "When a child," he wrote in *Chrysalis,* "sees his first butterfly and becomes himself a flying flower, such innocence has in it more reality than any however heroic whiz around the planet." So it was that the language of a bug, a chicken, a crow, a storm, rain, or train could spell-bind him into poem or prose-making.

Like Walter de la Mare, he found elves and wizards, fairies and magical beings of whom to write; like Robert Louis Stevenson he became the child speaking in "Swing Song" or "Pirates." Yet his was an American heritage, rooted in world history. *All Kinds of Time* clearly expressed that "Seconds are bugs/minutes are children/hours are people/days are postmen/weeks are Sunday School/months are/north/south/east/west/and in between/seasons are/wild flowers/tame flowers/golden leaves/and snow/years are/Santa Claus/centuries are/George/Washington/and forever is God." This, and the poems within his other books of poetry for children are those of an American child and his particular wonder: "Tell me, tell me everything!/What makes it Winter/And then Spring?" he asks through the child in "Curiosity." Yet, the series of questions of the poem end with his own continuing questions, "Tell me! or don't even grown-ups know?" This search, therefore, led him on; it was not unusual that because of his love for seasons and simplicity he should turn to the translation of Japanese haiku, that he should examine the life of a crow in *Roderick* or Dawn Boy, the Indian, in *The Painted Cave;* that his mother's childhood in Denmark should inspire him to write *The Faraway Lurs* or that his questioning of the correlation between Etruscan and American civilization spun itself out in *Omen of the Birds.*

Poetry, he wrote, "must be presented with careful incompleteness of information." Incompletion thus sustains curiosity; information is not a *raison d'être* for the poet, and "willingness to wonder" is Harry Behn's unique contribution to children's literature.

—Myra Cohn Livingston

BELLOC, (Joseph) Hilaire (Pierre)

Nationality: British (originally French: became British citizen, 1902). **Born:** St. Cloud, near Paris, France, 27 July 1870; brother of the writer Marie Belloc Lowndes. **Education:** Oratory School, Edgbaston, Warwickshire; Balliol College, Oxford (Brackenbury History Scholar), 1892-95, B.A. (honours) in history 1895. **Military Service:** 10th Battery of the 8th Regiment of Artillery of the French Army, 1891. **Family:** Married Elodie Agnes Hogan in 1896 (died 1914); three sons and two daughters. **Career:** Journalist: editor, with A.H. Pollen, *Paternoster Review,* 1890-91; literary editor, London *Morning Post,* 1906-09; editor, with Maurice Baring, *North Street Gazette,* 1910; founder, with G.K. and Cecil Chesterton, and editor, with others, *New Witness,* 1911-12; editor, *G.K.'s Weekly,* 1936-38; columnist ("A Wanderer's Notebook"), *Sunday Times,* 1938-53. Liberal Member of Parliament for South Salford, 1906-10. Head of the English Department, East London College. LL.D.: University of Glasgow, 1902. Knight Commander with Star, Order of St. Gregory the Great, 1934. **Died:** 16 July 1953.

PUBLICATIONS FOR CHILDREN

Poetry

The Bad Child's Book of Beasts: Verses, illustrated by Basil Blackwood. Oxford, Alden Press, and New York, Dutton, 1896.
More Beasts (for Worse Children): Verses, illustrated by Basil Blackwood. London and New York, Arnold, 1897.
A Moral Alphabet, illustrated by Basil Blackwood. London, Arnold, 1899.
Cautionary Tales for Children: Designed for the Admonition of Children Between the Ages of Eight and Fourteen Years: Verses, illustrated by Basil Blackwood. London, Nash, 1907; New York, Knopf, 1922.
New Cautionary Tales: Verses, illustrated by Nicolas Bentley. London, Duckworth, 1930; New York, Harper, 1931.
Cautionary Verses: The Collected Humorous Poems of Hilaire Belloc. London, Duckworth, 1939; New York, Knopf, 1941.
Selected Cautionary Verses. London, Penguin, 1950.

Other

Economics for Helen. Bristol, Arrowsmith, and New York, McBride, 1924; as *Economics for Young People,* London and New York, Putnam, 1925.

PUBLICATIONS FOR ADULTS

Novels

Emmanuel Burden, Merchant.... London, Methuen, and New York, Scribner, 1904.
Mr. Clutterbuck's Election. London, Nash, 1908.
A Change in the Cabinet. London, Methuen, 1909.
Pongo and the Bull. London, Constable, 1910.
The Girondin. London, Nelson, 1911; New York, Doubleday, 1912.
The Green Overcoat. Bristol, Arrowsmith, and New York, McBride, 1912.
The Mercy of Allah. London, Chatto and Windus, and New York, Appleton, 1922.
Mr. Petre. Bristol, Arrowsmith, and New York, McBride, 1925.
The Emerald of Catherine the Great. Bristol, Arrowsmith, and New York, Harper, 1926.
The Haunted House. Bristol, Arrowsmith, 1927; New York, Harper, 1928.
But Soft—We Are Observed! Bristol, Arrowsmith, 1928; as *Shadowed!,* New York, Harper, 1929.
Belinda: A Tale of Affection in Youth and Age. London, Constable, 1928; New York, Harper, 1929.
The Missing Masterpiece. Bristol, Arrowsmith, and New York, Harper, 1929.
The Man Who Made Gold. Bristol, Arrowsmith, 1930; New York, Harper, 1931.
The Postmaster-General. Bristol, Arrowsmith, and Philadelphia, Lippincott, 1932.
The Hedge and the Horse. London, Cassell, 1936.

Short Story

Bona Mors. Horsham, Sussex, Naldrett, 1953.

Play

The Candour of Maturity (produced London, 1912).

Poetry

Verses and Sonnets. London, Ward and Downey, 1896.
The Modern Traveller. London, Arnold, 1898; New York, Knopf, 1923.
Verses. London, Duckworth, 1910; New York, Gomme, 1916.
More Peers. London, Swift, 1911; New York, Knopf, 1924.
Sonnets and Verse. London, Duckworth, 1923; New York, McBride, 1924; revised edition, Duckworth, 1938, 1954; New York, Sheed and Ward, 1939; as *Collected Verse,* London, Penguin, 1958.
(*Poems*). London, Benn, 1925.
The Chanty of the Nona. London, Faber, 1928.
The Praise of Wine: An Heroic Poem. Privately printed, 1931.
Ladies and Gentlemen: For Adults Only and Mature at That. London, Duckworth, 1932.
Songs of the South Country. London, Duckworth, 1951.
The Verse of Hilaire Belloc, edited by W.N. Roughead. London, Nonesuch Press, 1954; as *Complete Verse,* London, Duckworth, 1970.

Other

Danton: A Study. London, Nisbet, and New York, Scribner, 1899.
Lambkin's Remains. Oxford, Simpkin, and New York, Mansfield, 1900.
Paris. London, Arnold, 1900; New York, Scribner, 1907.
Robespierre: A Study. London, Nisbet, and New York, Scribner, 1901.
The Path to Rome. London, George Allen, and New York, Longman, 1902.
The Aftermath; or, Gleanings from a Busy Life, Called upon the Outer Cover, for Purposes of Sale, Caliban's Guide to Letters. London, Duckworth, and New York, Dutton, 1903.
The Great Inquiry (Only Authorised Version) Faithfully Reported. London, Duckworth, 1903.
The Old Road. London, Constable, 1904; Philadelphia, Lippincott, 1911.

Avril, Being Essays on the Poetry of the French Renaissance. London, Duckworth, and New York, Dutton, 1904.
An Open Letter on the Decay of Faith. London, Burns Oates, 1906.
Esto Perpetua: Algerian Studies and Impressions. London, Duckworth, 1906; New York, McBride, 1925.
Sussex, Painted by Wilfrid Ball. London, A. and C. Black, 1906; revised edition, as *The County of Sussex,* London, Cassell, 1936.
Hills and the Sea. London, Methuen, and New York, Scribner, 1906.
The Historic Thames. London, Dent, and New York, Dutton, 1907.
The Eye-Witness (incidents in history). London, Nash, and New York, Kings Treasuries of Literature, 1908.
The Catholic Church and Historical Truth (lecture). Preston, Lancashire, W. Watson, 1908.
On Nothing and Kindred Subjects. London, Methuen, 1908; New York, Dutton, 1909.
An Examination of Socialism. London, Catholic Truth Society, 1908; as *The Alternative,* London, Distributist, 1947.
The Pyrenees. London, Methuen, 1909; New York, Knopf, 1923.
On Everything. London, Methuen, 1909; New York, Dutton, 1910.
Marie Antoinette. London, Methuen, and New York, Doubleday, 1909.
The Church and Socialism. London, Catholic Truth Society, 1910.
The Ferrer Case. London, Catholic Truth Society, 1910.
The International. Philadelphia, Dolphin, 1910.
On Anything. London, Constable, and New York, Dutton, 1910.
On Something. London, Methuen, 1910; New York, Dutton, 1911.
The Party System, with Cecil Chesterton. London, Swift, 1911.
Socialism and the Servile State (debate with J. Ramsay MacDonald). London, South West London Federation of the Independent Labour Party, 1911.
First and Last. London, Methuen, 1911; New York, Dutton, 1912.
The French Revolution. London, Williams and Norgate, and New York, Holt, 1911.
The Battle of Blenheim [Malplaquet, Waterloo, Tourcoing, Crécy, Poitiers]. London, Swift, 5 vols., 1911-12, London, Rees, 1 vol., 1913; *Blenheim* published Philadelphia, Lippincott, 1936; revised edition of *Waterloo,* Rees, 1915; revised edition, as *Six British Battles,* Bristol, Arrowsmith, 1931.
The Four Men: A Farrago. London, Nelson, and Indianapolis, Bobbs Merrill, 1912.
The River of London. London, Foulis, 1912; Boston, Phillip, n.d.
Warfare in England. London, Williams and Norgate, and New York, Holt, 1912.
The Servile State. London, Foulis, 1912; Boston, Phillip, 1913.
This and That and the Other. London, Methuen, and New York, Dodd Mead, 1912.
The Stane Street: A Monograph. London, Constable, and New York, Dutton, 1913.
The Hilaire Belloc Calendar: A Quotation from the Works of Hilaire Belloc for Everyday in the Year. London, Frank Palmer, 1913.
The Book of the Bayeux Tapestry, Presenting the Complete Work in a Series of Colour Facsimiles. London, Chatto and Windus, and New York, Putnam, 1914.
Anti-Catholic History: How It Is Written. London, Catholic Truth Society, 1914.
Three Essays. Portland, Maine, Mosher, 1914.
The History of England from the First Invasion by the Romans to the Accession of King George the Fifth (volume 11 only). New York, Catholic Publications Society of America, and London, Sands, 1915.
A General Sketch of the European War: The First and Second Phase. London, Nelson, 2 vols., 1915-16; as *The Elements of the Great War,* New York, Hearst, 2 vols., 1915-16.
A Picked Company, Being a Selection from the Writings of Hilaire Belloc, edited by E.V. Lucas. London, Methuen, 1915.
High Lights of the French Revolution. New York, Century, 1915.
The Two Maps of Europe and Some Other Aspects of the Great War. London, C. Arthur Pearson, 1915.
Land and Water Map of the War and How to Use It. London, Land and Water, 1915.
At the Sign of the Lion and Other Essays. Portland, Maine, Mosher, 1916.
The Last Days of the French Monarchy. London, Chapman and Hall, 1916.
The Second Year of the War. London, Burrup Mathieson and Sprague, 1916.
The Free Press. London, Allen and Unwin, 1918.
Religion and Civil Liberty. London, Catholic Truth Society, 1918.
The House of Commons and Monarchy. London, Allen and Unwin, 1920; New York, Harcourt Brace, 1922.
The Catholic Church and the Principle of Private Property. London, Catholic Truth Society, 1920.
Europe and the Faith. London, Constable, and New York, Paulist Press, 1920.
Pascal's Provincial Letters. London, Catholic Truth Society, 1921.
Catholic Social Reform Versus Socialism. London, Catholic Truth Society, 1922.
The Jews. London, Constable, 1922; Boston, Houghton Mifflin, 1937.
The Contrast. Bristol, Arrowsmith, 1923; New York, McBride, 1924.
The Road. Manchester, British Reinforced Concrete Engineering Company, and New York, Harper, 1923.
On (essays). London, Methuen, and New York, Doran, 1923.
The Political Effort. London, True Temperance Association, 1924.
The Campaign of 1812 and the Retreat from Moscow. London, Nelson, 1924; as *Napoleon's Campaign of 1812 and the Retreat from Moscow,* New York, Harper, 1926.
The Cruise of the "Nona." London, Constable, and Boston, Houghton Mifflin, 1925.
England and the Faith. London, Catholic Truth Society, 1925.
A History of England. London, Methuen, and New York, Putnam, 4 vols., 1925-31.
Miniatures of French History. London, Nelson, 1925; New York, Harper, 1926.
Hilaire Belloc (essays). London, Harrap, 1926.
The Highway and Its Vehicles, edited by Geoffrey Holme. London, The Studio, 1926.
Short Talks with the Dead and Others. London, Cayme Press, and New York, Harper, 1926.
Mrs. Markham's New History of England, Being an Introduction for Young People to the Current History and Institutions of Our Times. London, Cayme Press, 1926.
A Companion to Mr. Wells's "Outline of History." London, Sheed and Ward, 1926; San Francisco, Ecclesiastical Supply Association, 1927.
Mr. Belloc Still Objects to Mr. Wells's "Outline of History." London, Sheed and Ward, 1926; San Francisco, Ecclesiastical Supply Association, 1927.
The Catholic Church and History. London, Burns Oates, and New York, Macmillan, 1926.

Selected Works. London, Library Press, 9 vols., 1927.
Towns of Destiny. New York, McBride, 1927; as *Many Cities*, London, Constable, 1928.
Oliver Cromwell. London, Benn, 1927.
James the Second. London, Faber, and Philadelphia, Lippincott, 1928.
How the Reformation Happened. London, Cape, and New York, Dodd Mead, 1928.
A Conversation with an Angel and Other Essays. London, Cape, 1928; New York, Harper, 1929.
Joan of Arc. London, Cassell, and Boston, Little Brown, 1929.
Survivals and New Arrivals. London, Sheed and Ward, and New York, Macmillan, 1929.
Richelieu. Philadelphia, Lippincott, 1929; London, Benn, 1930.
Wolsey. London, Cassell, and Philadelphia, Lippincott, 1930.
A Pamphlet, July 27th, 1930. Privately printed, 1930s; as *World Conflict*, London, Catholic Truth Society, 1951.
Cranmer. London, Cassell, 1931; as *Cranmer, Archbishop of Canterbury 1533-1556*, Philadelphia, Lippincott, 1931.
On Translation (lecture). Oxford, Clarendon Press, 1931.
Essays of a Catholic Layman in England. London, Sheed and Ward, 1931; as *Essays of a Catholic*, New York, Macmillan, 1931.
A Conversation with a Cat and Others (essays). London, Cassell, and New York, Harper, 1931.
How We Got the Bible. London, Catholic Truth Society, 1932.
Napoleon. London, Cassell, and Philadelphia, Lippincott, 1932.
The Question and the Answer. New York, Bruce, 1932; London, Longman, 1938.
The Tactics and Strategy of the Great Duke of Marlborough. Bristol, Arrowsmith, 1933.
William the Conqueror. London, Davies, 1933; New York, Appleton, 1934.
Becket. London, Catholic Truth Society, 1933.
Charles the First, King of England. London, Cassell, and Philadelphia, Lippincott, 1933.
Cromwell. London, Cassell, and Philadelphia, Lippincott, 1934.
A Shorter History of England. London, Harrap, and New York, Macmillan, 1934.
Milton. London, Cassell, and Philadelphia, Lippincott, 1935.
Hilaire Belloc (humorous writings), edited by E.V. Knox. London, Methuen, 1935.
An Essay on the Restoration of Property. London, Distribution League, 1936; as *The Restoration of Property*, New York, Sheed and Ward, 1936.
Selected Essays, edited by John Edward Dineen. Philadelphia, Lippincott, 1936.
The Battle Ground (on Syria). London, Cassell, and Philadelphia, Lippincott, 1936.
Characters of the Reformation. London and New York, Sheed and Ward, 1936.
The Crusade: The World's Debate. London, Cassell, 1937; as *The Crusades: The World's Debate*, Milwaukee, Bruce, 1937.
The Crisis of Our Civilization. London, Cassell, 1937; as *The Crisis of Civilization*, New York, Fordham University Press, 1937.
An Essay on the Nature of Contemporary England. London, Constable, and New York, Sheed and Ward, 1937.
The Issue. New York and London, Sheed and Ward, 1937.
The Great Heresies. London and New York, Sheed and Ward, 1938.
Monarchy: A Study of Louis XIV. London, Cassell, 1938; as *Louis XIV*, New York, Harper, 1938.
Stories, Essays, and Poems. London, Dent, 1938.
The Case of Dr. Coulton. London, Sheed and Ward, 1938.
Return to the Baltic. London, Constable, 1938.
Charles II: The Last Rally. New York, Harper, 1939; as *The Last Rally: A Story of Charles II*, London, Cassell, 1940.
The Test Is Poland. London, Weekly Review, 1939.
On Sailing the Sea: A Collection of the Seagoing Writings of Hilaire Belloc, edited by W.N. Roughead. London, Methuen, 1939; Fair Lawn, New Jersey, Essential Books, 1951.
The Catholic and the War. London, Burns Oates, 1940.
On the Place of Gilbert Chesterton in English Letters. London and New York, Sheed and Ward, 1940.
The Silence of the Sea and Other Essays. New York, Sheed and Ward, 1940; London, Cassell, 1941.
Places. New York, Sheed and Ward, 1941; London, Cassell, 1942.
Elizabethan Commentary. London, Cassell, 1942; as *Elizabeth: Creature of Circumstance*, New York, Harper, 1942.
Selected Essays. London, Methuen, 1948.
Hilaire Belloc: An Anthology of His Prose and Verse, edited by W.N. Roughead. London, Hart Davis, and Philadelphia, Lippincott, 1951.
One Thing and Another: A Miscellany from His Uncollected Essays, edited by Patrick Cahill. London, Hollis and Carter, 1955.
Essays, edited by Anthony Forster. London, Methuen, 1955.
Selected Essays, edited by J.B. Morton. London, Penguin, 1958.
Letters from Hilaire Belloc, edited by Robert Speaight. London, Hollis and Carter, and New York, Macmillan, 1958.
Advice. London, Harvill Press, 1960.
Belloc: A Biographical Anthology, edited by Herbert Van Thal and Jane Soames Nickerson. London, Allen and Unwin, and New York, Knopf, 1970.
Hilaire Belloc's Prefaces, Written for Fellow Authors, edited by J.A. De Chantigny. Chicago, Loyola University Press, 1971.

Editor, *Extracts from the Diaries and Letters of Hubert Howard*. Oxford, Hart, 1899.
Editor, *The Footpath Way: An Anthology for Walkers*. London, Sidgwick and Jackson, 1911.
Editor, *Travel Notes on a Holiday Tour in France*, by James Murray Allison. Privately printed, 1931.

Translator, *The Romance of Tristan and Iseult*, by J. Bedier. London, George Allen, 1903; New York, Boni, 1930.
Translator, *The Principles of War*, by Marshal Foch. London, Chapman and Hall, 1918; New York, Holt, 1920.
Translator, *Precepts and Judgments*, by Marshal Foch. London, Chapman and Hall, 1919; New York, Holt, 1920.

*

Bibliography: *The English First Editions of Hilaire Belloc*...by Patrick Cahill, privately printed, 1953.

Critical Studies (selection): *Hilaire Belloc* by Renée Haynes, London, Longman, 1953; *Hilaire Belloc: A Memoir* by J.B. Morton, London, Hollis and Carter, and New York, Sheed and Ward, 1955; *The Young Hilaire Belloc* by Marie Belloc Lowndes, New York, Kenedy, 1956; *The Life of Hilaire Belloc* by Robert Speaight, London, Hollis and Carter, and New York, Farrar Straus, 1957; *Belloc the Man* by Eleanor and Reginald Jebb, Westminster, Maryland, Newman, 1957; *Hilaire Belloc: Edwardian Radical* by

John P. McCarthy, Indianapolis, Liberty Press, 1978; *Hilaire Belloc* by Michael H. Markel, Boston, Twayne, 1982; *Hilaire Belloc* by A.N. Wilson, London, Hamish Hamilton, and New York Atheneum, 1984; *Sailing with Mr. Belloc* by Dermod MacCarthy, London, Collins, 1986.

* * *

There would be no place for Hilaire Belloc in a book of this kind were it not for the gift children have for annexing books designed for their elders. He was no children's writer, although it might be argued that in some important ways he remained an adolescent all his life. His passionate advocacy of improbable, and especially unpopular, theses, his gusto, his dislike of a pedantic adherence to logical processes, all hinted at a certain permanent immaturity at odds with his formidable scholarship.

Young people once liked—and may turn to them again—the "Chester-Belloc" novels, but Belloc's lasting appeal to children rests upon his group of mock cautionary tales in which he made genial fun of a literary convention which was dying, if not dead, in his own childhood. The moral tales in verse written by Elizabeth Turner and others in the early years of the 19th century were serious in intent, concerned with warning the young of the consequences of sin—or even mildly bad behavior. By the end of the century these naive rhymes invited laughter. Belloc adopted the themes, and often the meters, of these archaic poems and, giving them only a slightly different emphasis, made them not merely parody but a genuinely original comic creation. Belloc's *Cautionary Tales* are not an isolated example. Among contemporaries Harry Graham in his *Ruthless Rhymes for Heartless Homes* guyed the same conventions. What gives Belloc's work its rare quality is that he, unlike others playing the same frivolous game, was a real poet. He was one of the outstanding verse technicians of the age with an absolute mastery of his craft, and he was without rival in the brevity and symmetry of his epigrams. The same perfection of craftsmanship that he devoted to "serious" verse he brought to the absurd accounts of Matilda—who cried wolf once too often—and Augustus King, the chewer of string, and Jim, who let go of nurse's hand and was eaten by a lion. Similar qualities are found, perhaps even more characteristically, in the shorter rhymes of *The Bad Child's Book of Beasts* and its sequels.

Belloc's epigrams and sonnets, and the rumbustious verses scattered through the prose works, make regular appearances in anthologies of verse for children, doubtless to the poet's posthumous amusement.

—Marcus Crouch

BEMELMANS, Ludwig

Nationality: American (originally Austrian: emigrated to the United States, 1914; became citizen, 1918). **Born:** Meran, Austria (now Merano, Italy), 27 April 1898. **Education:** At schools in Regensburg and Rothenburg, Bavaria. **Military Service:** United States Army during World War I. **Family:** Married Madeline Freund in 1935; one daughter. **Career:** Worked in hotels and restaurants, 1914-17 and 1919-24; owner, Hapsburg House Restaurant, New York, 1925-35; writer for *New Yorker;* also an artist: exhibitions in galleries in the U.S. and abroad. **Awards:** American Library Association Caldecott medal, 1954. **Died:** 1 October 1962.

Publications for Children (illustrated by the author)

Fiction

Hansi. New York, Viking Press, 1934; London, Lovat Dickson, 1935.
The Golden Basket. New York, Viking Press, 1936.
The Castle Number Nine. New York, Viking Press, 1937.
Quito Express. New York, Viking Press, 1938.
Rosebud. New York, Random House, 1942.
A Tale of Two Glimps. New York, CBS, 1947.
The Happy Place. Boston, Little Brown, 1952.
The High World. New York, Harper, 1954; London, Hamish Hamilton, 1958.
Parsley. New York, Harper, 1955.

Poetry

Madeline. New York, Simon and Schuster, 1939; London, Verschoyle, 1952.
Fifi. New York, Simon and Schuster, 1940.
Sunshine. New York, Simon and Schuster, 1950.
Madeline's Rescue. New York, Viking Press, and London, Verschoyle, 1953.
Madeline's Christmas in Texas. Dallas, Nieman Marcus, 1955.
Madeline and the Bad Hat. New York, Viking Press, 1956; London, Deutsch, 1958.
Madeline and the Gypsies. New York, Viking Press, and London, Deutsch, 1959.
Welcome Home! New York, Harper, 1960; London, Hamish Hamilton, 1961.
Madeline in London. New York, Viking Press, 1961; London, Deutsch, 1962.
Marina. New York, Harper, 1962.
Madeline's Christmas, completed by Madeline and Barbara Bemelmans. New York, Viking Kestrel, and London, Deutsch, 1985.

Publications for Adults

Novels

Now I Lay Me Down to Sleep. New York, Viking Press, 1943; London, Hamish Hamilton, 1944.
The Blue Danube. New York, Viking Press, 1945; London, Hamish Hamilton, 1946.
Dirty Eddie. New York, Viking Press, 1947; London, Hamish Hamilton, 1948.
The Eye of God. New York, Viking Press, 1947; as *The Snow Mountain,* London, Hamish Hamilton, 1950.
The Woman of My Life. New York, Viking Press, and London, Hamish Hamilton, 1957.
Are You Hungry, Are You Cold. Cleveland, World, 1960; London, Mayflower, 1965.
The Street Where the Heart Lies. Cleveland, World, 1963.

Short Stories

I Love You, I Love You, I Love You. New York, Viking Press, 1942; London, Hamish Hamilton, 1943.

Other

My War with the United States. New York, Viking Press, 1937; London, Gollancz, 1938.
Life Class. New York, Viking Press, 1938; London, Lane, 1939.
Small Beer (essays). New York, Viking Press, 1939; London, Lane, 1940.
At Your Service: The Way of Life in a Hotel. Evanston, Illinois, Row Peterson, 1941.
Hotel Splendide. New York, Viking Press, 1941; London, Hamish Hamilton, 1942.
The Donkey Inside. New York, Viking Press, 1941; London, Hamish Hamilton, 1947.
Hotel Bemelmans. New York, Viking Press, 1946; London, Hamish Hamilton, 1956.
The Best of Times: An Account of Europe Revisited. New York, Simon and Schuster, 1948; London, Cresset Press, 1949.
How to Travel Incognito. Boston, Little Brown, 1952.
Father, Dear Father (autobiography). New York, Viking Press, and London, Hamish Hamilton, 1953.
To the One I Love the Best. New York, Viking Press, 1955.
The World of Bemelmans. New York, Viking Press, and London, Hamish Hamilton, 1955.
My Life in Art. New York, Harper, and London, Deutsch, 1958.
How to Have Europe All to Yourself. New York, European Travel Commission, 1960.
Italian Holiday. Boston, Houghton Mifflin, 1961.
On Board Noah's Ark. New York, Viking Press, 1962.
La Bonne Table (writings and drawings), edited by Donald and Eleanor Friede. New York, Simon and Schuster, and London, Deutsch, 1964.
Tell Them It Was Wonderful: Selected Writings, edited by Madeline Bemelmans. New York, Viking, 1985.

Editor, *Holiday in France.* Boston, Houghton Mifflin, 1957; London, Deutsch, 1958.

*

Manuscript Collection: May Massee Collection, Emporia State University, Kansas.

Illustrator: *Noodle* by Munro Leaf, 1937; *Literary Life and the Hell with It* by Whit Burnett, 1939.

* * *

The reputation of Ludwig Bemelmans rests solidly on his five picture books about Madeline, that daring little girl who lived in Paris with 11 other little girls and Miss Clavel in a house "covered with vines." Most of the other Bemelmans books are out of print now—story and picture books that children never adopted as they adopted *Madeline. The High World,* however, is still in circulation, and both *Parsley* and *Hansi* are available on library reference shelves. First a word about these and two others, before we take a closer look at the *Madelines* with their casual, comical couplets, their appealing little girl, and the large bright watercolor settings.

The scenes and people Bemelmans knew as a child growing up in the Austrian Tyrol are reflected in the two illustrated storybooks, *The High World* and *Hansi.* Small escapades and rich local color fill the pages of *Hansi,* while an avalanche and daring rescue based on a real incident bring *The High World* to its climax. Both books keep the reader fully involved and could in themselves have established Bemelmans as an important writer. *Parsley* is a large picture book of the *Madeline* size, filled with beautiful Bemelmans paintings of the forest where the stag named Parsley lived. It evidently failed to equal the *Madeline* books in appeal, perhaps because it verges on sentimentality and an unacceptable anthropomorphism at the end.

Quito Express, illustrated in chalky cinnamon colors, is the satisfying story of little Ecuadorian Pedro, a baby who crawled onto an express train and was carried away for four days, well cared for by a kindly conductor.

It seems a pity that another of the early books, *The Golden Basket,* is no longer available. In this storybook two little girls explore Bruges with their father. And wonder of wonders, they encounter one day 12 uniformed little girls out walking two by two with their Madame Severine. The littlest girl, one Madeleine, skips and hops behind them all saying "Boo-boo-boo!" Which brings us to the famous Madeline of the well-known picture books.

The first book, *Madeline,* was an instant success. Quite apart from the appealing verses and pictures, it offered a heroine to love and a hospital experience (a magnetic topic for young readers). The books that followed were true to the original characterization of the independent little Madeline and continued to blend playful, easy versification with the sweeping pictorial art of the cartoonist-painter. Readers know that foreign cities will be laid out for them to inspect in detail in the Bemelmans illustrations, glowing in color and full of movement—just as the verses move along rapidly and happily through the story. The Bemelmans touch in these books is light and warm, comical and endearing. There is nothing else quite like it. *Madeline's Rescue* brought Bemelmans the Caldecott Medal for "the most distinguished American picture book."

—Claudia Lewis

BENEDICT, Rex (Arthur)

Nationality: American. **Born:** Jet, Oklahoma, 27 June 1920. **Education:** Jet High School, graduated 1938; Northwestern State University, Alva, Oklahoma, B.A. 1949; University of Oklahoma, Norman, 1949-50. **Military Service:** United States Navy Air Corps, 1942-45, 1951-53: lieutenant. **Family:** Married Giusi Maria Usai in 1966. **Career:** Orchestra director, Alva, 1938-41; orchestra manager, San Diego, 1945-46; film dubber, 1953-57, and film translator, 1957-60, Rome; publisher's reader, New York, 1960-65; printer, Corsair Press, New York; reviewer, *New York Times,* 1972-79. **Died:** 21 November 1995.

Publications for Children

Fiction

Good Luck Arizona Man. New York, Pantheon, 1972; London, Hamish Hamilton, 1973.

Goodbye to the Purple Sage: The Last Great Ride of the Sheriff of Medicine Creek. New York, Pantheon, 1973; London, Hamish Hamilton, 1974.
Last Stand at Goodbye Gulch. New York, Pantheon, 1974; London, Hamish Hamilton, 1975.
The Ballad of Cactus Jack. New York, Pantheon, 1975; London, Hamish Hamilton, 1976.
Run for Your Sweet Life, illustrated by David Christiana. New York, Farrar Straus, 1986.

Poetry

In the Green Grass Time. New York, Corsair Press, 1964.

Other

Oh ... Brother Juniper, illustrated by Joan Berg. New York, Pantheon, 1963.

Translator, *One Moonless Night,* by Noële Lavaivre. New York, Braziller, 1964.
Translator, *The Polka Dot Twins,* by Augusto Lunel. New York, Braziller, 1964.

Publications for Adults

Poetry

Moonwash. New York, Corsair Press, 1969.
Nights in the Gardens of Glebe. New York, Corsair Press, 1970.
Epitaph for a Lady. New York, Corsair Press, 1970.
Haloes for Heroes. New York, Corsair Press, 1971.

Translator, *The Prayers of Man,* edited by Alfonso Maria di Nola. New York, McDowell Obolensky, 1961.
Translator, *Amorous Tales from the Decameron.* New York, Fawcett, 1963.
Translator, *Those Cursed Tuscans,* by Curzio Malaparte. Athens, Ohio University Press, 1964.

*

Rex Benedict comments:

(1978) If there is one word that will catch the intent of my efforts in the novel for children, it is the word "mythical." In almost all my novels I have used the Old West as myth. Since facts of the west are so hopelessly lost in myth, I, instead of trying to disentangle them, confuse them even more in the hope of arriving at logic. There is no length to which one cannot go in writing about the west, so long as one is convincing. A professor in Canada is currently dramatizing for television one of the novels under the title *The Magic Lie.* I think, to judge by his title, he is on the right path. The treatment of the west is all a great, beautiful lie, but it is concealed by magic. In short, you don't even notice the prevarication. (I hope.)

* * *

At the beginning of *The Ballad of Cactus Jack* the leader of the once fearsome Pecos Gang finds himself in circumstances befitting mythical geriatrics. Still among the living, he is unwanted—dead or alive. It is a deplorable state, to be sure, for a man whose life has been devoted to spurring otherwise weary minds. He turns to preaching, a corollary trade, both devoted as they are to the proposition that the unaided spirit is often too weak to supply enough excitement to get through a week of ennui. Legendary vigilantes and purveyors of popular religion are both thriving upon a universal need for enthusiasm. However amusing the circumstance, it makes perfectly good sense that a desperado whose antics no longer chill the soul might try the pulpit. Here the hymns become ballads in praise of the backwoods minister, but ballads, as they are inclined to do, dwell on decline and imminent demise. Once again the sad truth will out. Cactus Jack is unwanted, dead or alive. Unwanted perhaps, but not unneeded. He has become a legend that induces a yawn, but the wearied reaction by no means implies that legends are any the less a necessity. It isn't only Cactus Jack who is threatened with premature rigor mortis, but a populace which thrilled to his exploits remains mired in a fatal malnourishment of the spirit.

Fortunately for us, Rex Benedict is able to retread if not resurrect Cactus Jack for those of us who have found his like and the whole landscape of the Wild West a personage and a domain crucial to our existence, but no longer viably transmitted through horse operas or dime novels. Even Benedict acknowledges that he was himself born a century too late to witness the actual phenomenon, and that aside from one writer, Zane Grey, and a single periodical, the spirit of the West was nowhere to be found. Scarce but imperative, the medium must be discovered which will dispense those qualities that the American West has furnished for much of Western civilization. That medium which Benedict supplies seemingly so effortlessly is a satiric blend that demonstrates a studied respect for the subject. Through five books the old western forms are very much at home in a world view that finds it painful to take almost anything seriously. Remarkably, Benedict's characters remain faithful to a world gone by and to the contemporary scene as well, much like Don Quixotes who are loyal to a world seemingly lost, yet who can patiently and efficiently explain its ways to incredulous contemporaries.

In league with the Spanish don, Cactus Jack refuses to acknowledge himself or his world as anachronisms. Adopting the grand old American entrepreneurship of P. T. Barnum, he offers a stupendous, if nonexistent, reward to anyone who might apprehend him. For big bucks lazy imaginations are quickly willing to step lively in forms to which they have become disinterested. They follow the scenario of Cactus Jack who finds it better to be shot in the back by a bounty-hunter than languish in glories past. For all the laughter that follows, *The Ballad of Cactus Jack* along with the rest of Benedict's fiction addresses some serious questions. What happens to a myth which is undead but which still feeds upon the lifeblood of a civilization? How is a legend reintroduced to a lethargic public?

Benedict and his heroes remain wisely attentive to both their own world and the largely incredulous bystanders and readers. It would be unfair and misleading to view his sagas simply as caricature, even if they do cater to a readership that delights in the security of polite ridicule. Not only is there ample savvy in the characters' insights into the human condition, as copiously demonstrated by the mixed-breed narrator of *Good Luck Arizona Man,* but such absurd situations as putting a price on one's own head serve to demonstrate the essential nature of the Western saga rather than flout its conventions.

Benedict depicts the elements comprising the western as games. Actually they are rituals. A game involves a situation where the participants begin as equals and end up unequal, while ritual is the exact opposite. Children's games like Cops and Robbers and Cowboys and Indians should be more properly termed rituals as all are equals in the scenario regardless of which side they stand on, or whether they capture and triumph or are snared and slain. All are equally credited with sustaining an ongoing spectacle. In *Goodbye to the Purple Sage* there is the frequently replayed scenario: "The sheriff had the Pecos Gang within fifty yards of the jail. They was just passin' the Hangin' Tree. That was when the wild shootin' celebration started." The capture never comes, and we are soon to sense that such elusiveness derives neither from the wiliness of the desperadoes nor the ineptitude of the sheriff (though clumsiness and incapacity are everywhere in evidence), but because the event is one of those quintessential rites of life. Even where everyone is a criminal, there inevitably emerges the ceremony in which the participants divide themselves into three groups, the pursuers, the pursued and the onlookers. Goodbye Gulch, the forbidden stretch of land on the other side of the river where degenerates run their own affairs according to their own liking, features one such observance undertaken by a group of ex-marshals, banished to this other side for forsaking the honor of their profession, and an equal number of pure-bred vigilantees. Each day the thugs break out of the jail, are chased by the marshals, are recaptured and returned to the jailhouse. Rest from the invigorating excitement is mutually enjoyed, the gunslingers reposing in their cells, the marshals keeping them company by slumbering on the other side of the bars—all awaiting the next day's break-out jamboree, featuring good fun with real bullets, each of which pierces one of the escapees' black hats.

It seems that there is not only honor among thieves, but a wholesome sense of ritual that unites people of all races and nationalities, all ages, and perhaps just as important, both sexes. Romance is not simply falling in love, but an enactment of aspects of the old Roman novella. The child's game proves to be no mere effort to play grown-up roles, but a crucially necessary rite of interaction. Such universal rituals lie behind the reason for the enduring interest in westerns, and certainly the venture is made all the more satisfying with the playful seriousness and knowing naivety of each of Benedict's sagas. They are always within the Wild West of old, and outside looking in with a chuckle at those absurdities which seem central to the expedition of life.

One of Benedict's subjects dwells not in the American West, but in central Italy. *Oh ... Brother Juniper* features a monk who was a contemporary of St. Francis and St. Clare. Though an ocean and many lifestyles apart from the Wild West figures, Brother Juniper belongs to the same branch of the family of man as the stock characters of Benedict's westerns. Like the sheriff and the Pecos Gang, Brother Juniper takes the guiding principles of his profession with a literalness that is as comic as it is admirable. He gives away the order's silver bells to an impoverished woman, and when harshly rebuked by the general of the order is sorry only that he has been the cause of the hoarseness in his superior's voice. He does not mind being castigated; in fact, he rather likes it. The unassailable simplicity of his faith not only wins for him the admiration of St. Francis, but he is reputed to have driven the devil himself crazy through his unselfconscious display of piety.

The setting and intent of an Umbrian cloister and of a ramshackle sheriff's quarters in Goodbye Glutch could scarcely provide a greater contrast. But the commitment to ritual is as intense in one as in the other. Such rituals are not only a familiar landmark of Benedict's output, but they are probably at the heart of most literary ventures whether real or fictional, or whether intended for adults or for children. Benedict demonstrates that the bald revelation of the rite of life when pushed to its extremes is as delightful as it is serious.

—Leonard R. Mendelsohn

BERENSTAIN, Jan and Stan

BERENSTAIN, Janice. Nationality: American. **Born:** Philadelphia, Pennsylvania, 26 July 1923. **Education:** Attended Philadelphia College of Art, 1941-1945. **BERENSTAIN, Stan. Nationality:** American. **Born:** Philadelphia, Pennsylvania, 29 September 1923. **Education:** Attended Philadelphia College of Art, 1941-42; Pennsylvania Academy of Fine Arts, 1946-1949. **Family:** Married, 13 April 1946; two sons. **Career:** Authors and illustrators; creators of "It's All in the Family," a comic strip published in *McCall's* and *Good Housekeeping.* **Awards:** School Bell Award, National Education Association, 1960; British Book Centre honor book, 1968; Best Book Award, American Institute of Graphic Arts, 1970; University of Chicago Center for Children's Books Best Book Award, 1972, 1974; Philadelphia Library Children's Reading Round Table honor book, 1972, 1973, 1974, 1976, 1980, 1982, 1983, 1984, 1985, 1987, 1988, 1989; Children's Book of the Year, Child Study Association of America, 1977, 1982; Silver Diploma, International Film and Television Festival, Naples, Italy, 1980; Silver Award, International Film and Television Festival, New York City, 1980, 1982, 1987; Young Readers' Award, Michigan Council of Teachers of English, 1981; Drexel Citation, Drexel University, School of Library and Information Science; Children's Classic Award, International Reading Association, 1982, 1983, 1984, 1987; Buckeye Award, Ohio State Library Association, Teachers of English, and International Reading Association, 1982, 1985; Arizona Children's Choice Book Award nomination, and Arizona Young Reader's Award, 1985; Colorado Children's Choice Book Award nomination, 1985; Humanitas Certificate, 1987; Ludington Award, 1989.

Publications for Children

Fiction

The Big Honey Hunt. New York, Beginner Books, 1962.
The Bike Lesson. New York, Beginner Books, 1964.
The Bears' Picnic. New York, Beginner Books, 1966.
The Bear See Scouts. New York, Beginner Books, 1967.
The Bears' Vacation. New York, Beginner Books, 1968.
Inside, Outside, Upside Down. New York, Random House, 1968.
Bears on Wheels. New York, Random House, 1969.
The Bears' Christmas. New York, Beginner Books, 1970.
Old Hat, New Hat. New York, Random House, 1970.
Bears in the Night. New York, Random House, 1971.
The B Book. New York, Random House, 1971.
C Is for Clown. New York, Random House, 1972.

The Bears' Almanac: A Year in Bear Country—Holidays, Seasons, Weather, Actual Facts about Snow, Wind, Rain, Thunder, Lightning, the Sun, the Moon, and Lots More. New York, Random House, 1973.
The Berenstain Bears' Nursery Tales. New York, Random House, 1973.
He Bear, She Bear. New York, Random House, 1974.
The Berenstain Bears' New Baby. New York, Random House, 1974.
The Bears' Nature Guide. New York, Random House, 1975.
The Bear Detectives: The Case of the Missing Pumpkin. New York, Random House, 1975.
The Berenstain Bears' Counting Book. New York, Random House, 1976.
The Berenstain Bears' Science Fair. New York, Random House, 1977.
The Berenstain Bears and the Spooky Old Tree. New York, Random House, 1978.
Papa's Pizza: A Berenstain Bear Sniffy Book. New York, Random House, 1978.
The Berenstain Bears Go to School. New York, Random House, 1978.
The Bears' Activity Book. New York, Random House, 1979.
The Berenstain Bears and the Missing Dinosaur Bone. New York, Random House, 1980.
The Berenstain Bears' Christmas Tree. New York, Random House, 1980.
The Berenstain Bears and the Sitter. New York, Random House, 1981.
The Berenstain Bears Go to the Doctor. New York, Random House, 1981.
The Berenstain Bears' Moving Day. New York, Random House, 1981.
The Berenstain Bears Visit the Dentist. New York, Random House, 1981.
The Berenstain Bears Get in a Fight. New York, Random House, 1982.
The Berenstain Bears Go to Camp. New York, Random House, 1982.
The Berenstain Bears in the Dark. New York, Random House, 1982.
The Berenstain Bears and the Messy Room. New York, Random House, 1983.
The Berenstain Bears and the Truth. New York, Random House, 1983.
The Berenstain Bears and the Wild, Wild Honey, Random House, 1983.
The Berenstain Bears' Soccer Star. New York, Random House, 1983.
The Berenstain Bears Go Fly a Kite. New York, Random House, 1983.
The Berenstain Bears to the Rescue. New York, Random House, 1983.
The Berenstain Bears' Trouble with Money. New York, Random House, 1983.
The Berenstain Bears' Make and Do Book. New York, Random House, 1984.
The Berenstain Bears and the Big Election. New York, Random House, 1984.
The Berenstain Bears and Too Much TV. New York, Random House, 1984.
The Berenstain Bears Shoot the Rapids. New York, Random House, 1984.
The Berenstain Bears and the Neighborly Skunk. New York, Random House, 1984.
The Berenstain Bears and the Dinosaurs. New York, Random House, 1984.
The Berenstain Bears Meet Santa Bear. New York, Random House, 1984.
The Berenstain Bears and Mama's New Job. New York, Random House, 1984.
The Berenstain Bears and Too Much Junk Food. New York, Random House, 1985.
The Berenstain Bears on the Moon. New York, Random House, 1985.
The Berenstain Bears Learn about Strangers. New York, Random House, 1985.
The Berenstain Bears' Toy Time. New York, Random House, 1985.
The Berenstain Bears Forget Their Manners. New York, Random House, 1985.
The Berenstain Bears' Bath Book. New York, Random House, 1985.
The Berenstain Bears Get Stage Fright. New York, Random House, 1986.
The Berenstain Bears: No Girls Allowed. New York, Random House, 1986.
The Berenstain Bears and the Week at Grandma's. New York, Random House, 1986.
The Berenstain Bears and Too Much Birthday. New York, Random House, 1986.
The Berenstain Kids: I Love Colors. New York, Random House, 1987.
The Berenstain Bears Go Out for the Team. New York, Random House, 1987.
Berenstain Bears: Coughing Catfish. New York, Random House, 1987.
The Berenstain Bears Blaze a Trail. New York, Random House, 1987.
The Berenstain Bears on the Job. New York, Random House, 1987.
The Berenstain Bears and the Trouble with Friends. New York, Random House, 1987.
The Berenstain Bears and the Missing Honey. New York, Random House, 1987.
The Berenstain Bears and the Big Road Race. New York, Random House, 1987.
The Berenstain Bears and the Bad Habit. New York, Random House, 1987.
The Berenstain Bears' Trouble at School. New York, Random House, 1987.
After the Dinosaurs. New York, Random House, 1988.
The Berenstain Bears and the Ghost in the Forest. New York, Random House, 1988.
The Berenstain Bears Get the Gimmies. New York, Random House, 1988.
The Berenstain Bears and the Double Dare. New York, Random House, 1988.
The Berenstain Bears and the Bad Dream. New York, Random House, 1988.
The Berenstain Bears Ready, Get Set, Go!. New York, Random House, 1988.
The Berenstain Bears and Too Much Vacation. New York, Random House, 1989.
The Berenstain Bears' Trick or Treat. New York, Random House, 1989.
The Berenstain Bears and the In-Crowd. New York, Random House, 1989.

The Berenstain Bears and the Slumber Party. New York, Random House, 1990.
The Berenstain Bears and the Prize Pumpkin. New York, Random House, 1990.
The Berenstain Bears' Trouble with Pets. New York, Random House, 1990.
The Berenstain Bears Are a Family. New York, Random House, 1991.
The Berenstain Bears at the Super-Duper Market. New York, Random House, 1991.
The Berenstain Bears Say Good Night. New York, Random House, 1991.
The Berenstain Bears' Four Seasons. New York, Random House, 1991.
The Berenstain Bears and the Spooky Fun House. Racine, Wisconsin, Western Publishing Co., 1991.
The Berenstain Bears Don't Pollute (Anymore). New York, Random House, 1991.
The Berenstain Bears and Too Much Pressure. New York, Random House, 1991.
The Berenstain Bears' Big Rummage Sale. Racine, Western Publishing Co., 1991.
The Berenstain Bears Perfect Fishing Spot. Racine, Western Publishing Co., 1991.
The Berenstain Bears and the Trouble With Grownups. New York, Random House, 1992.
The Berenstain Bears and the Broken Piggy Bank. Racine, Western Publishing Co., 1992.
The Berenstain Bears Hug and Make Up. Racine, Western Publishing Co., 1992.
The Berenstain Bears and the Wheelchair Commando. New York, Random House, 1993.
The Berenstain Bears All Year Round. Racine, Western Publishing Co., 1993.
The Berenstain Bears With Nothing to Do. Racine, Western Publishing Co., 1993
The Berenstain Bears and the Bully. New York, Random House, 1993.
The Berenstain Bears Learn About Colors. Racine, Western Publishing Co., 1993.
The Berenstain Bears and the Red-handed Thief. New York, Random House, 1993.
The Berenstain Bears and the Jump Rope Contest. Racine, Western Publishing Co., 1993.
The Berenstain Bears and the Drug Free Zone. New York, Random House, 1993.
The Berenstain Bears and the Spooky Old House. Racine, Western Publishing Co., 1993.
The Berenstain Bears and the Hiccup Cure. Racine, Western Publishing Co., 1993.
The Berenstain Bears and the New Girl in Town. New York, Random House, 1993.
The Berenstain Bears and the Nerdy Nephew. New York, Random House, 1993.
The Berenstain Bears Accept No Substitutes. New York, Random House, 1993.
The Berenstain Bears Family Get-together. Racine, Western Publishing Co., 1993.
The Berenstain Bears and the Baby Chipmunk. Racine, Western Publishing Co., 1993.
The Berenstain Bears' Bedtime Battle. Racine, Western Publishing Co., 1993.
The Berenstain Bears Visit Farmer Ben. Racine, Western Publishing Co., 1993.
The Berenstain Bears Get a Checkup. Racine, Western Publishing Co., 1993.
The Berenstain Bears and the Female Fullback. New York, Random House, 1993.
The Berenstain Bears Gotta Dance! New York, Random House, 1993.
The Berenstain Bears and the Good Deed. Racine, Western Publishing Co., 1993.
The Berenstain Bears and the Wishing Star. Racine, Western Publishing Co., 1993.
The Berenstain Bears and the Dress Code. New York, Random House, 1994.
The Berenstain Bears at Camp Crush. New York, Random House, 1994.
The Berenstain Bears and the Green-eyed Monster. New York, Random House, 1994.
The Berenstain Bears and the School Scandal Sheet. New York, Random House, 1994.
The Berenstain Bears Visit Uncle Tex. Racine, Western Publishing Co., 1994.
The Berenstain Bears' Birthday Boy. Racine, Western Publishing Co., 1994.
The Berenstain Bears and the Giddy Grandma. New York, Random House, 1994.
The Berenstain Bears' New Neighbors. New York, Random House, 1994.
The Berenstain Bears and the Summer Job. Racine, Western Publishing Co., 1994.
The Berenstain Bears and the Galloping Ghost. New York, Random House, 1994.
The Berenstain Bears Lost in a Cave. Racine, Western Publishing Co., 1994.
The Berenstain Bears and the Big Picture. Racine, Western Publishing Co., 1994.
The Berenstain Bears at Big Bear Fair. Racine, Western Publishing Co., 1994.
The Berenstain Bear Scouts in Giant Bat Cave. New York, Scholastic, 1995.
The Berenstain Bears and the Showdown at Chainsaw Gap. New York, Random House, 1995.
The Berenstain Bear Scouts and the Humongous Pumpkin. New York, Scholastic, 1995.
The Berenstain Bears' Media Madness. New York, Random House, 1995.
The Berenstain Bears Count Their Blessings. New York, Random House, 1995.
The Berenstain Bears and Too Much Teasing. New York, Random House, 1995.
The Berenstain Bears in the Freaky Funhouse. New York, Random House, 1995.
The Berenstain Bear Scouts Meet Bigpaw, illustrated by Michael Berenstain. New York, Scholastic, 1995.
The Berenstain Bears Grow-it. New York, Random House, 1996.
The Berenstain Bears' Sampler: The Best of Bear Country. New York, Random House, 1996.
The Berenstain Bears Cook-it. New York, Random House, 1996.
The Berenstain Bears Draw-it. New York, Random House, 1996.
The Berenstain Bears in Big Bear City. New York, Random House, 1996.
The Berenstain Bears in Maniac Mansion. New York, Random House, 1996.

The Berenstain Bears at the Teen Rock Cafe. New York, Random House, 1996.
The Berenstain Bears Fly-it. New York, Random House, 1996.
The Berenstain Bear Scouts and the Sci-Fi Pizza, illustrated by Michael Berenstain. New York, Scholastic, 1996.
The Berenstain Bear Scouts' Ghost Versus Ghost, illustrated by Michael Berenstain. New York, Scholastic, 1996.
Read and Rhyme Bear Country. New York, GT Publications, 1996.
The Berenstain Bears and the Bermuda Triangle. New York, Random House, 1997.
The Berenstain Bears the Whole Year Through: With Earthsaver Tips and Things to Do for Each and Every Month of the Year. New York, Scholastic, 1997.
The Berenstain Bears' Haunted Hayride. New York, Random House, 1997.
The Berenstain Bears at Big Fun Park. New York, Inchworm Press, 1997.
The Berenstain Bears Get the Grouchies. New York, Inchworm Press, 1997.
The Berenstain Bears' Great Scuba Dive. New York, Inchworm Press, 1997.
The Berenstain Bears Go Out to Eat. New York, Inchworm Press, 1997.
The Berenstain Bears Go to the Movies. New York, Inchworm Press, 1997.
The Berenstain Bears Hold Hands at the Big Mall. New York, GT Publications, 1997.
The Berenstain Bears Help Around the House. New York, GT Publications, 1997.
The Berenstains' A Book. New York, Random House, 1997.
The Berenstain Bears and the Blame Game. New York, Random House, 1997.
The Berenstain Bears and the Ghost of the Auto Graveyard. New York, Random House, 1997.
The Berenstain Bears' C Book. New York, Random House, 1997.
The Berenstain Bears' Comic Valentine. New York, Cartwheel Press, 1997.
The Berenstain Bears' Thanksgiving. New York, Scholastic, 1997.
The Berenstain Bears and the Homework Hassle. New York, Random House, 1997.
The Berenstain Bears' Home Sweet Tree. New York, Random House, 1997.
The Berenstain Bears' New Clothes. New York, Random House, 1997.
The Berenstain Bears and Queenie's Crazy Crush. New York, Random House, 1997.
The Berenstain Bear Scouts and the Ice Monster, illustrated by Michael Berenstain. New York, Scholastic, 1997.
The Berenstain Bear Scouts and the Magic Crystal Caper, illustrated by Michael Berenstain. New York, Scholastic, 1997.
The Berenstain Bear Scouts and the Really Big Disaster, illustrated by Michael Berenstain. New York, Scholastic, 1997.
The Berenstain Bear Scouts and the Run-Amuck Robot, illustrated by Michael Berenstain. New York, Scholastic, 1997.
The Berenstain Bear Scouts and the Sinister Smoke Ring, illustrated by Michael Berenstain. New York, Scholastic, 1997.
The Berenstain Bear Scouts and the Giant Bat Cave, illustrated by Michael Berenstain. New York, Scholastic, 1997.
The Berenstain Bears and the Big Date. New York, Random House, 1998.
The Berenstain Bears and the Love Match. New York, Random House, 1998.
The Berenstain Bears Big Bear, Small Bear. New York, Random House, 1998.
The Berenstain Bears by the Sea. New York, Random House, 1998.
The Berenstain Bears' Easter Surprise. New York, Cartwheel Press, 1998.
The Berenstain Bears Get Their Kicks. New York, Random House, 1998.
The Berenstain Bear Scouts and the Terrible Talking Termite, illustrated by Michael Berenstain. New York, Scholastic, 1998.

Television Scripts

The Berenstain Bears' Christmas Tree. National Broadcasting Company, Inc., 1979.
The Berenstain Bears Meet Bigpaw. National Broadcasting Company, Inc., 1980.
The Berenstain Bears' Easter Surprise. National Broadcasting Company, Inc., 1981.
The Berenstain Bears' Comic Valentine. National Broadcasting Company, Inc., 1982.
The Berenstain Bears Play Ball. National Broadcasting Company, Inc., 1983.
The Berenstain Bears' CBS Show. Columbia Broadcasting System, Inc, 1986-87.

Other

Berenstain Bears' around the Clock-Coloring Book. New York, Random House, 1987.
Berenstain Bears' Bear Scout-Coloring Book. New York, Random House, 1987.
Berenstain Bears' Count on Numbers Coloring Book. New York, Random House, 1987.
Berenstain Bears' on the Farm Coloring Book. New York, Random House, 1987.
Berenstain Bears' Safety First-Coloring Book. New York, Random House, 1987.
Berenstain Bears' Storytime Color Book. New York, Random House,1989.

Publications for Adults

Nonfiction (Cartoons)

The Berenstain's Baby Book. New York, Macmillan, 1951.
Sister. New York, Schuman, 1952.
Tax-Wise. New York, Schuman, 1952.
Marital Blitz. New York, Dutton, 1954.
Baby Makes Four. New York, Macmillan, 1956.
Lover Boy. New York, Macmillan, 1958.
It's All in the Family. New York, Dutton, 1958.
Bedside Lover Boy. New York, Dell, 1960.
And Beat Him When He Sneezes. New York, McGraw, 1960.
Call Me Mrs. New York, Macmillan, 1961.
It's Still in the Family. New York, Dutton, 1961.
Office Lover Boy. New York, Dell, 1962.
The Facts of Life for Grown-ups. New York, Dell, 1963.
Flipsville-Squaresville. New York, Dial, 1965.
Mr. Dirty Vs. Mr. Clean. New York, Dell, 1967.
You Could Diet Laughing. New York, Dell, 1969.

Be Good or I'll Belt You. New York, Dell, 1970.
Education Impossible. New York, Dell, 1970.
Never Trust Anyone Over 13. New York, Dell, 1970.
How to Teach Your Children About Sex Without Making a Complete Fool of Yourself. New York, Dutton, 1970.
How to Teach Your Children About God Without Actually Scaring Them Out of Their Wits. New York, Dutton, 1971.
Are Parents for Real? New York, Bantam, 1972.

* * *

Since their marriage in 1946, Stan and Jan Berenstain have devoted their career to writing humorous and, sometimes moralistic, portrayals of family life. In their early years of collaboration, the pair wrote the popular "All in the Family" cartoon series for *McCall's* and *Good Housekeeping,* but in 1962, they began an association with Theodore Geisel, who suggested that they write for the juvenile market. The Berenstain's first attempt, *The Big Honey Hunt,* was highly successful, and when their publisher commissioned subsequent titles the Berenstain Bear dynasty was born.

Initially, the Berenstains focused on "beginner books," texts that were designed to help young children make connections between pictures and words. The backgrounds were kept simple, and the concepts were relatively straightforward. However, by the 1970s, the couple had developed a style of their own which included a greater emphasis on character development and on more sophisticated plot lines. The Berenstain Bear family, which had originally consisted of Papa and Mama Bear and their son, was enlarged to include a female sibling, and the focus of the stories centered around the young bears' anxieties regarding new experiences. These "first time" books, still the most popular in the line, include such topics as the first day of school, the first visit to the dentist's office, and the first time with a babysitter.

Each member of the Berenstain Bear family has his or her own traits and characteristics, and for the most part, the characters are portrayed in predictable ways. Papa Bear is a "traditional" rural type, whose interests lie in woodworking and sports. A relatively simple soul, he is often taken to task by Mama Bear and the children for his bumbling ways. In fact, many critics have argued that the characterization of Papa Bear is somewhat demeaning. Mama Bear, on the other hand, is sensible and domestic. Her interests include quiltmaking and cooking, and hers is the moral voice of the series. For their part, Brother and Sister Bear face the challenges of adolescence with much enthusiasm. As with their parents, their interests fall primarily along traditional gender lines. Brother enjoys sports and science, whereas Sister likes to play with her "Bearbie" doll. Indeed, many of the storylines focus on gender anxiety. In *The Berenstain Bears No Girls Allowed,* for instance, Brother becomes angry and resentful when Sister is able to beat him in sports. Although Mama Bear counsels her daughter that "the important thing is not whether you are a boy or a girl, but the sort of person you are," every effort is made to reestablish Brother's ego.

For the most part, however, the Berenstain Bear series provides its young readers with plot lines that are quite true to life and that are resolved in sensible ways. For instance, in *The Berenstain Bears and the Sitter,* Brother and Sister are afraid that Mrs. Grizzly, their new sitter, will be mean and stodgy. Instead, they find that because she has raised seven cubs of her own, Mrs. Grizzly knows a number of interesting games and stories. Not only are they cured of their fear of being left with a sitter, they also come to appreciate the contributions of their elders. Adding to the learning experience are the humorous and skillful illustrations which are the hallmark of the series.

During the 1980s, the Berenstains added to their repertoire of "First Time Books" by writing intermediate texts (labelled "Big Chapter Books") that focus on such topics as the environment and teenage drug use. These new plot lines are facilitated by the introduction of a number of characters. Professor Actual Factual teaches the Bears about the importance of recycling, and friends such as Queenie McBear and Too-Tall and Lizzy Bruin help Brother and Sister learn lessons about peer pressure. By remaining in touch with current issues facing young readers, the Berenstains have been able to maintain a loyal following. The series has diversified again in the 1990s with the introduction of activity books, television specials, and an interactive web site. In collaboration with their son Michael, the Berenstains have also introduced a mystery series, *The Berenstain Bears Boy Scouts,* designed to appeal to young male readers.

Perhaps the most significant feature of the Berenstain Bears books is the way that the authors use their texts to address parents. Embedded in most of the texts are subtle (and not-so-subtle) parenting tips and guidelines. For example, in *The Berenstain Bears Get the Gimmies,* Papa and Mama Bear are shown to possess radically different parenting styles. While Papa Bear will give in to his children's persistent demands for toys and candy, Mama Bear tries to teach her children to defer gratification. When the parents are unable to reach a compromise, their children become uncontrollable. It is only when the Grandparents visit and suggest a workable strategy that Mama and Papa Bear are able to reestablish order in their household. With their heavily moral tone and their emphasis on the parents' behavioral flaws, such stories as *Get the Gimmies* and *The Berenstain Bears and Too Much Junk Food* (another tale in which the parents must mend their ways) seem geared as much to adults as to children.

By all accounts, the Berenstain Bear series is a publishing phenomenon. Because Stan and Jan Berenstain have kept up with the times, their books continue to delight children and to reassure them regarding many of the difficult rites of passage that they face.

—Gwen A. Tarbox

BERESFORD, Elisabeth

Nationality: British. **Born:** Paris, France. **Education:** St. Mary's Hall, Brighton; St. Catherines, Bramley; Ditchling Dame School, Sussex; Brighton and Hove High School. **Military Service:** Women's Royal Naval Service during World War II; worked as a radio operator. **Family:** Married Max Robertson in 1949; one daughter and one son. **Career:** Since 1948 freelance journalist. Lives in Alderney, Channel Islands. **Agent:** Juvenilia, Avington, Winchester, Hampshire SO21 1DB, England.

Publications for Children

Fiction

The Television Mystery. London, Parrish, 1957.
The Flying Doctor Mystery. London, Parrish, 1958.

Trouble at Tullington Castle. London, Parrish, 1958.
Cocky and the Missing Castle, illustrated by Jennifer Miles. London, Constable, 1959.
Gappy Goes West. London, Parrish, 1959.
The Tullington Film-Makers. London, Parrish, 1960.
Two Gold Dolphins, illustrated by Peggy Fortnum. London, Constable, 1961; Indianapolis, Bobbs Merrill, 1964.
Danger on the Old Pull 'n Push. London, Parrish, 1962.
Strange Hiding Place. London, Parrish, 1962.
Diana in Television. London, Collins, 1963.
The Missing Formula Mystery. London, Parrish, 1963.
The Mulberry Street Team, illustrated by Juliet Pannett. Penshurst, Kent, Friday Press, 1963.
Awkward Magic, illustrated by Judith Valpy. London, Hart Davis, 1964; as *The Magic World,* Indianapolis, Bobbs Merrill, 1965.
The Flying Doctor to the Rescue. London, Parrish, 1964.
Holiday for Slippy, illustrated by Pat Williams. Penshurst, Kent, Friday Press, 1964.
Game, Set, and Match. London, Parrish, 1965.
Knights of the Cardboard Castle, illustrated by C.R. Evans. London, Methuen, 1965.
Travelling Magic, illustrated by Judith Valpy. London, Hart Davis, 1965; as *The Vanishing Garden,* New York, Funk and Wagnalls, 1967.
The Hidden Mill, illustrated by Margery Gill. London, Benn, 1965; New York, Meredith Press, 1967.
Peter Climbs a Tree, illustrated by Margery Gill. London, Benn, 1966.
Fashion Girl. London, Collins, 1967.
The Black Mountain Mystery. London, Parrish, 1967.
Looking for a Friend, illustrated by Margery Gill. London, Benn, 1967.
The Island Bus, illustrated by Robert Hodgson. London, Methuen, 1968.
Sea-Green Magic, illustrated by Ann Tout. London, Hart Davis, 1968.
The Wombles, illustrated by Margaret Gordon. London, Benn, 1968; New York, Meredith Press, 1969.
David Goes Fishing, illustrated by Imre Hofbauer. London, Benn, 1969.
Gordon's Go-Kart, illustrated by Margery Gill. London, Benn, 1970.
Stephen and the Shaggy Dog, illustrated by Robert Hales. London, Methuen, 1970.
Vanishing Magic, illustrated by Ann Tout. London, Hart Davis, 1970.
The Wandering Wombles, illustrated by Oliver Chadwick. London, Benn, 1970.
Dangerous Magic, illustrated by Oliver Chadwick. London, Hart Davis, 1972.
The Invisible Womble and Other Stories, illustrated by Ivor Wood. London, Benn, 1973.
The Secret Railway, illustrated by James Hunt. London, Methuen, 1973.
The Wombles in Danger. London, Benn, 1973.
The Wombles at Work, illustrated by Margaret Gordon. London, Benn, 1973.
Invisible Magic, illustrated by Reg Gray. London, Hart Davis, 1974.
The Wombles Go to the Seaside. London, World Distributors, 1974.
The Wombles Gift Book, illustrated by Margaret Gordon. London, Benn, 1975.
The Snow Womble, illustrated by Margaret Gordon. London, Benn, 1975.
Snuffle to the Rescue, illustrated by Gunvor Edwards. London, Kestrel, 1975.
Tomsk and the Tired Tree, illustrated by Margaret Gordon. London, Benn, 1975.
Wellington and the Blue Balloon, illustrated by Margaret Gordon. London, Benn, 1975.
Orinoco Runs Away, illustrated by Margaret Gordon. London, Benn, 1975.
The Wombles Make a Clean Sweep, illustrated by Ivor Wood. London, Benn, 1975.
The Wombles to the Rescue, illustrated by Margaret Gordon. London, Benn, 1975.
The MacWomble's Pipe Band, illustrated by Margaret Gordon. London, Benn, 1976.
Madame Cholet's Picnic Party, illustrated by Margaret Gordon. London, Benn, 1976.
Bungo Knows Best, illustrated by Margaret Gordon. London, Benn, 1976.
Tobermory's Big Surprise, illustrated by Margaret Gordon. London, Benn, 1976.
The Wombles Go round the World, illustrated by Margaret Gordon. London, Benn, 1976.
The World of the Wombles, illustrated by Edgar Hodges. London, World Distributors, 1976.
Wombling Free, illustrated by Edgar Hodges. London, Benn, 1978.
Toby's Luck, illustrated by Doreen Caldwell. London, Methuen, 1978.
Secret Magic, illustrated by Caroline Sharpe. London, Hart Davis, 1978.
The Happy Ghost, illustrated by Joanna Carey. London, Methuen, 1979.
The Treasure Hunters, illustrated by Joanna Carey. London, Methuen, and New York, Elsevier Nelson, 1980.
Curious Magic, illustrated by Claire Upsdale-Jones. London, Granada, and New York, Elsevier Nelson, 1980.
The Four of Us, illustrated by Trevor Stubley. London, Hutchinson, 1981.
The Animals Nobody Wanted, illustrated by Joanna Carey. London, Methuen, 1982.
The Tovers, illustrated by Geoffrey Beitz. London, Methuen, 1982.
The Adventures of Poon, illustrated by Dinah Shedden. London, Hutchinson, 1984.
The Mysterious Island, illustrated by Joanna Carey. London, Methuen, 1984.
One of the Family, illustrated by Barrie Thorpe. London, Hutchinson, 1985.
The Ghosts of Lupus Street School. London, Methuen, 1986.
Strange Magic, illustrated by Cathy Wood. London, Methuen, 1986.
Emily and the Haunted Castle, illustrated by Kate Rogers. London, Hutchinson, 1987.
Once upon a Time Stories, illustrated by Alice Englander. London, Methuen, 1987.
The Secret Room, illustrated by Michael Bragg. London, Methuen, 1987.
The Armada Adventure. London, Methuen, 1988.
The Island Railway, illustrated by Maggie Harrison. London, Hamish Hamilton, 1988.

Rose. London, Hutchinson, 1989.
Charlie's Ark. London, Methuen, 1989.
The Wooden Gun. London, Hippo, 1989.
The Wandering Wombles. London, Walker, 1990.
Tim the Trumpet. London, Blackie, 1992.
Jamie and the Rola Polar Bear, illustrated by Janet Robertson. London, Blackie, 1993.
Lizzy's War, illustrated by James Mayhew. London, Simon & Schuster. 1993.
Rola Polar Bear and the Heatwave, illustrated by Janet Robertson. London, Blackie, 1994.
The Smallest Whale, illustrated by Susan Field. London, Orchard Books, 1996.
Lizzie's War, Part II, illustrated by James Mayhew. London, Simon and Schuster; as *Lizzy Fights On,* Hove, England, Macdonald Young Books, 1996.
Chris the Climber. N.p., Picadilly Pips, 1997.
Island Treasure. Hove, England, Macdonald Young Books, 1998.

Plays

The Wombles, adaptation of her own stories (produced London, 1974); as screenplay, 1971; as 60 television plays, 1973.

Other

The Wombles Annual 1975-1978. London, World Distributors, 4 vols., 1974-77.
Jack and the Magic Stove (folktale), illustrated by Rita van Bilsen. London, Hutchinson, 1982.

Publications for Adults

Novels

Paradise Island. London, Hale, 1963.
Escape to Happiness. London, Hale, 1964; New York, Nordon, 1980.
Roses round the Door. London, Hale, and New York, Paperback Library, 1965.
Island of Shadows. London, Hale, 1966; New York, Dale, 1980.
Veronica. London, Hale, 1967; New York, Nordon, 1980.
A Tropical Affair. London, Hale, 1967; as *Tropical Affairs,* New York, Dell, 1978.
Saturday's Child. London, Hale, 1968; as *Echoes of Love,* New York, Dell, 1979.
Love Remembered. London, Hale, 1970; New York, Dale, 1978.
Love and the S.S. Beatrice. London, Hale, 1972; as *Thunder of Her Heart,* New York, Dale, 1978.
Pandora. London, Hale, 1974.
The Steadfast Lover. London, Hale, 1980.
The Silver Chain. London, Hale, 1980.
The Restless Heart. New York, Valueback, 1982.
Flight to Happiness. London, Hale, 1983.
A Passionate Adventure. London, Hale, 1983.

Plays

Road to Albutal, with Nick Renton (produced Edinburgh, 1976).
The Best of Friends (produced in the Channel Islands, 1982).

Other

With Peter Spence, *Move On.* London, BBC Publications, 1978.

*

Elisabeth Beresford comments:

The books are roughly in four categories: 1) straight adventure, 2) magic—children with very ordinary backgrounds, to whom quite extraordinary things happen, 3) The Wombles, who, it is hoped, will make children want to fight pollution and to think up ways of "making good use of bad rubbish" (Womble family motto). And will also make readers of all ages laugh!, and 4) romantic thrillers.

* * *

Elisabeth Beresford shares in some degree the dilemma of Conan Doyle. Doyle invented, in a lighter moment, an amateur detective, and Sherlock Holmes hung around his neck like a dead weight. Beresford invented the Wombles. She may not feel as bitterly about her success as Doyle did. There can be no doubt that, in writing these gently humorous tales, she is sharing with readers her own warm affection for these curious creatures. As for the artistic merit of the Wombles, it is difficult to take a cold critical look at a legend. The original stories have been blurred by subsequent translation into other media, and the endearing characters are uncomfortably familiar as toys, puppets, and shambling pop singers. The literary Wombles belong to an ancient tradition, that of the moral tale. In their advocacy of old-fashioned virtues the Wombles are Victorian, but their insistence on conservation strikes a contemporary note. The Wombles have acquired a life independent of the parent stories in which they first appeared; they seem destined for some kind of immortality.

Of course, Beresford was an established writer long before she discovered her first Womble on Wimbledon Common. That she had not won high critical acclaim was due partly to the variety of her work: writers are expected to keep tidily to well-defined paths. A typical example of her stories with a contemporary "realistic" theme is *The Hidden Mill.* In this she takes an actual landscape, one of the decayed rivers of South London, and the derelict buildings on its banks. Three recognisable children from the back streets find that this grubby environment has a rich potential for adventure, dangerous games, and romance, all scaled down to real life. Even the happy ending is based on probability. The same unassuming professionalism underlies a later story, *The Island Railway,* in which a newcomer to the Channel Islands finds common cause with an islander in the revival of a disused railway. The problems and their resolution, the help and opposition of adults, are those of real life. There are no shortcuts, no easy solutions, no extravagant successes. A small book is distinguished by quiet competence.

While writing this kind of story, Beresford was also engaged on more substantial fantasies in the E. Nesbit manner. *Dangerous Magic* is characteristic of these. A great struggle between the forces of good and evil takes place among familiar scenes in London with action mainly in a block of high-rise flats, and a great aerial battle is fought out above the Thames. Like many of the best fantasies it is a tale of high adventure told largely in comic terms. The unicorn which comes to life in a thunderstorm is firmly in the Nesbit tradition in its vanity, its colloquial speech, and its ultimate, if reluctant, heroism.

Among later fantasies *The Ghosts of Lupus Street School* stands out for its closeness to reality. The scene is a London school in the East End which is about to celebrate its centenary by being demolished. A small boy, conspicuously unacademic, is given the holiday task of writing up the school's history. In this he is helped, and sometimes hindered, by Violet, the very solid ghost of one of the original pupils. If there is a degree of didacticism inherent in the theme it is not allowed to come between the reader and his or her enjoyment of a lively and consistent story.

Representative of her post-Wombles work for very young children is the Rola Polar Bear series in which Jamie, a young boy, is extremely nervous and shy until he rescues a friendly polar bear who has wandered onto his street. Jamie's relationship with the Polar Bear is deepened when the two come up with a creative solution to the animal's inability to keep himself cool on warm summer days. Like many of Beresford's characters, Jamie learns to have respect for the natural environment and for himself.

—Marcus Crouch, updated by Gwen A. Tarbox.

BERG, Leila (Rita)

Nationality: British. **Born:** Salford, Lancashire, 12 November 1917. **Education:** Manchester High School; London University. **Family:** Married in 1940; one son and one daughter. **Career:** Children's books editor, Methuen, publishers, London, 1958-60; editor, Salamander Books, Thomas Nelson, publishers, London, 1965; editor, Nippers and Little Nippers series, Macmillan Education Ltd., London, 1968-76. Co-founder, Bookspread (now Leila Berg's Bookspread), 1978. **Awards:** Children's Book Circle Eleanor Farjeon award, 1974. **Address:** Alice's Cottage, Brook Street, Wivenhoe, near Colchester, Essex Colorado 7 9DS, England.

Publications for Children

Fiction

Fourteen What-Do-You-Know Stories, illustrated by Stanley Jackson. London, Epworth Press, 1948; New York, Roy, 1949; as *How John Caught the Sea-Horse and Other Stories* and *The Penguin Who Couldn't Paddle and Other Stories,* London, Penguin, 2 vols., 1966-67.

The Adventures of Chunky, illustrated by George Downs. London, Oxford University Press, 1950.

The Nightingale and Other Stories, illustrated by Garry Mackenzie. London, Oxford University Press, 1951.

The Tired Train and Other Stories, illustrated by Jean Bailey. London, Parrish, 1952.

Little Pete Stories, illustrated by Henrietta Garland. London, Methuen, 1952; revised edition, London, Penguin, 1959.

Trust Chunky, illustrated by Peggy Fortnum. Leicester, Brockhampton Press, 1954.

Fire Engine by Mistake, illustrated by Val Biro. Leicester, Brockhampton Press, 1955.

The Story of the Little Car, illustrated by W.A. Sillince. London, Epworth Press, 1955; as *The Little Car,* London, Methuen, 1972.

Lollipops: Stories and Poems, illustrated by Kathleen Dance. Leicester, Brockhampton Press, 1957.

Andy's Pit Pony, illustrated by Val Biro. Leicester, Brockhampton Press, 1958.

The Hidden Road, illustrated by B. Chapman. London, Hamish Hamilton, 1958.

A Box for Benny, illustrated by Jillian Willett. Leicester, Brockhampton Press, 1958; Indianapolis, Bobbs Merrill, 1961.

Three Men Went to Work, illustrated by Dorothy Clark. London, Methuen, 1960.

The Jolly Farm Book, illustrated by Lindy. London, Collins, 1960.

See How They Work, illustrated by Dorothy Clark. London, Methuen, 1962.

A Newt for Roddy, illustrated by Constance Marshall. London, Nelson, 1965.

My Dog Sunday, illustrated by Dick Hart. London, Hamish Hamilton, 1968.

A Day Out, illustrated by Ferelith Eccles Williams. London, Macmillan, 1968.

Finding a Key, illustrated by Jenny Williams. London, Macmillan, 1968.

Fish and Chips for Supper, illustrated by Richard Rose. London, Macmillan, 1968.

Jimmy's Story, illustrated by Richard Rose. London, Macmillan, 1968.

The Jumble Sale, illustrated by George Craig. London, Macmillan, 1968.

Lesley's Story, illustrated by George Craig. London, Macmillan, 1968.

Julie's Story, illustrated by Richard Rose. London, Macmillan, 1970.

Letters, illustrated by Ferelith Eccles Williams. London, Macmillan, 1970.

The Little Car Has a Day Out, illustrated by Leslie Wood. Leicester, Brockhampton Press, 1970.

Paul's Story, illustrated by Richard Rose. London, Macmillan, 1970.

Robert's Story, illustrated by Richard Rose. London, Macmillan, 1970.

Susan's Story, illustrated by Richard Rose. London, Macmillan, 1970.

Bouncing, illustrated by Margaret Belsky. London, Macmillan, 1971.

Doing the Pools, illustrated by Richard Rose. London, Macmillan, 1972.

The Doctor, illustrated by Val Biro. London, Macmillan, 1972.

Hospital Day, illustrated by Shirley Hughes. London, Macmillan, 1972.

Knitting, illustrated by George Him. London, Macmillan, 1972.

My Brother, illustrated by Linda Birch. London, Macmillan, 1972.

Put the Kettle On!, illustrated by John Dyke. London, Macmillan, 1972.

That Baby, illustrated by Margaret Belsky. London, Macmillan, 1972.

Tracy's Story, illustrated by Richard Rose. London, Macmillan, 1972.

Well, I Never!, illustrated by George Him. London, Macmillan, 1972.

A Band in School, illustrated by John Dyke. London, Macmillan, 1975.

Plenty of Room, illustrated by Joan Beales. London, Macmillan, 1975.
Grandad's Clock, illustrated by Joan Beales. London, Macmillan, 1976.
Snaps (*Presents, The Birthday Races, Waiting for the Dark, Looking for Elephants*), photographs by John Walmsley. London, Macmillan, 4 vols., 1977.
Chatterbooks (*In a House I Know; A Tickle; The Hot, Hot Day; Our Walk*), photographs by John Walmsley. London, Methuen, 4 vols., 1981.
Time for One More (fiction and verse), illustrated by Gerald Rose. London, Methuen, 1986.
Steep Street series (*Rosie and Mister Brown, Loving Jonathan Jones, Call That a Hat!, Having Friends*), illustrated by Lisa Kopper. London, Methuen, 4 vols., 1987.
Dear Billy and Other Stories. London, Viking, 1992.
Mr. Wolf and His Tail. The Knee-high Man. London, BBC Books, 1990.

Other (English language adaptations)

Paint a Black Horse, illustrated by Beatrice Braun-Fock. London, Methuen, 1958.
Bamburu, Boy of Ghana. London, Methuen, 1958.
Noriko-San, Girl of Japan, illustrated by Anna Riwkin-Brick. London, Methuen, 1958.
Little Owl. London, Methuen, 1966.

Other

Folk Tales for Reading and Telling, illustrated by George Him. Leicester, Brockhampton Press, and Cleveland, World, 1966; as *Topsy Turvy Tales,* London, Methuen, 1984.
Small World (*Dogs, Bees, Worms, Blood and Plasters, Ducks, Rainbows, Cars, Vacuum Cleaners*), illustrated by Lisa Kopper. London, Methuen, 8 vols., 1983-85.
Tales for Telling, illustrated by Danuta Laskowska. London, Methuen, 1983.
Christmas, illustrated by Jane Bottomley and John Walmsley. Aylesbury, Buckinghamshire, Ginn, 1985.
Hanukka, illustrated by Jane Bottomley and John Walmsley. Aylesbury, Buckinghamshire, Ginn, 1985.

Editor, *Four Feet and Two, and Some with None: An Anthology of Verse,* illustrated by Shirley Burke and Marvin Bileck. London, Penguin, 1960.
Editor, *Backwards and Forwards: Intertwining Celebration.* Colchester, Quentin Books, 1993.

Translator, with Ruth Baer, *Grown-Ups Don't Understand,* by Irmgard Keun, illustrated by Sylvia Stokeld. London, Parrish, 1955; as *The Bad Example,* New York, Harcourt Brace, 1955.
Translator, with Evelyn Ramsden, *The Singing Town,* by Thorbjørn Egner. London, Methuen, 1959.

PUBLICATIONS FOR ADULTS

Play

Raising Hell (produced Salisbury, 1972; London, 1973).

Other

Risinghill: Death of a Comprehensive School. London, Penguin, 1968.
Neill and Summerhill, photographs by John Walmsley. London, Penguin, 1969.
Children's Rights: Towards the Liberation of the Child, with others, edited by Julian Hall. London, Elek, and New York, Praeger, 1971.
The Train Back: A Search for Parents, with Pat Chapman. London, Allen Lane, 1972.
Look at Kids. London, Penguin, 1972.
Reading and Loving. London, Routledge, 1977.

*

Leila Berg comments:

I simply explore people and situations in a way that I feel is relevant to a child's experience, and that will hold a child through amusement, excitement, or a sense of wonder. This is how one writes for adults too—the only difference is relevance to a *child's* experience.

* * *

Leila Berg is a prolific writer for children and above all a story-teller whose wealth of experience of reading to children is very apparent in her writing. Her style is pruned of unnecessary detail, lively and colloquial, with events surely paced to reach a satisfying conclusion. She writes for the younger age range—stories to listen to or first stories to read for oneself. Her writing has now lost the occasional didacticism of her earlier work. It is based on her own experiences—her Salford Jewish childhood (*A Box for Benny*), her own children, the nursery she ran in her home and so forth. It has also been much shaped both by her desire to show children in literature as they really are—active, argumentative, thinking (e.g., *Little Pete Stories* or the recent *Steep Street* series)—and by her conviction of the need for a literature where the majority of children can read about themselves ("Nippers").

In Berg's supplementary readers for the "Nippers" series (which she also edits), her ideas about children's literature have found their fullest expression. The series has been attacked by teachers who object to the depiction of the realities of working-class life and by others who point to what they see as a stereotyped and patronising view of working people. Berg's books are not to be so lightly dismissed, however. She has an excellent ear, and these books are clear demonstrations of her skill in conveying with verve and wit the speech patterns and vocabulary of those considered until very recently to be "uncultured." Berg also brings to her urban working-class themes the traditional story patterns and repetitions of the teller of tales—in *Fish and Chips for Supper,* for example, we have the lively use of a cumulative tale.

It is not easy to assess Berg's contribution to children's literature. Her major innovations—dialogue true to the cadences of working-class speech and the presentation of positive working-class characters in their own environment—have had a major impact on children's book publishing and extended the range of possibilities open to other writers.

—Rosemary Stones

BERRY, James

Nationality: British (moved to England, 1948). **Born:** Fair Prospect, Jamaica, 1925. **Career:** Overseas telegraphist, Post Office, London, 1951-77. Writer-in-residence, Vauxhall Manor School, London. **Awards:** C. Day Lewis fellowship; Smarties prize, 1987; Signal Poetry Award, for *When I Dance.* **Address:** c/o Hamish Hamilton, 27 Wrights Lane, London W8 5TZ, England.

Publications for Children

Fiction

A Thief in the Village and Other Stories. London, Hamish Hamilton, 1987; New York, Orchard, 1988.
Anancy-Spiderman. London, Walker Books, 1989; as *Spiderman-Anancy,* New York, Holt, 1989.
The Future-telling Lady. Northampton, Hamilton, 1991; as *The Future-telling Lady and Other Stories,* New York, HarperCollins, 1993.
Isn't My Name Magical? London, BBC Books, 1991.
Ajeemah and His Son. New York, HarperCollins, 1994.
Don't Leave an Elephant to Go and Chase a Bird. New York, Simon & Schuster, 1996.
First Palm Trees. New York, Simon & Schuster, 1997.

Poetry

When I Dance. London, Hamish Hamilton, 1988.
Celebration Song, illustrated Louise Brierley. London, Hamish Hamilton, and New York, Simon & Schuster, 1994.
Rough Sketch Beginning, illustrated by Robert Florczak. San Diego, Harcourt Brace, 1996.
Playing a Dazzler. London, Hamish Hamilton, 1996; as *Everywhere Faces Everywhere,* New York, Simon & Schuster, 1997.

Publications for Adults

Short Stories

The Girls and Yanga Marshall. London, Longman, 1987.

Poetry

Fractured Circles. London, New Beacon, 1979.
Cut-Way Feelins, Loving, Lucy's Letters. Stafford, Strange Lime Fruit Stone, 1981.
Chain of Days. Oxford, Oxford University Press, 1985.
Hot Earth, Cold Earth. Newcastle upon Tyne, Bloodaxe, 1995.

Other

Contributor, *Black Poetry,* by Grace Nichols. London, Blackie, 1989.

Editor, *Bluefoot Traveller: An Anthology of West Indian Poets in Britain.* London, Limestone, 1976; revised edition, 1981.
Editor, *Dance to a Different Drum; Brixton Poetry Festival 1983: Poetry from a Community.* London, Brixton Festival, 1983.
Editor, *News for Babylon: The Chatto Book of West Indian-British Poetry.* London, Chatto and Windus, 1984.
Editor, *Classic Poems to Read Aloud.* New York, Kingfisher, 1995.

*

Critical Studies: "An Impulse to Write: An Interview with James Berry" by Brian Merrick, in *Children's Literature in Education* (New York), Vol. 27, No. 4, 1996, 195-208.

* * *

James Berry came late to writing, after settling in Britain, studying English in evening school, and for years being a member of different writing workshops. Interviewed by Brian Merrick in 1996, he described his first serious attempt to compose poetry like this: "I was vacuuming my sitting room and I felt this poem in my head. This voice, you know, with this poem in my Jamaican dialect. I got a pencil and started to write and I was absolutely amazed." From that time he has steadily increased his writing for children and adults, adding a distinct voice to children's literature in Britain and producing short stories and poems of the highest quality.

The stories in the prizewinning *A Thief in the Village* are grounded in the author's memories of growing up in Jamaica, but the vividness and clarity of the child's experiences are recalled with an adult's perceptiveness and moral awareness. Many of the stories deal uncompromisingly with the human poverty, cruelty, and fears that exist in a beautiful natural setting. A spastic boy is set upon by a gang of adolescents who try to kill his pet mongoose. A lad wants a pair of shoes so urgently that he risks severe injury to protect his banana crop and the profit that depends on it. Fanso longs to see the father he has never known, but his hopes of meeting him and his unknown siblings are destroyed by the bitterness that his mother and grandmother feel at having been deserted thirteen years earlier. Small everyday things—a stolen mouth-organ, a pair of shoes, the bicycle that provides one happy ending—take on significance because they embody children's dreams of a better life. "All Other Days Run into Sunday" captures the special associations of a day marked by special activities, better food, and by best clothes for going to church. Berry has told Merrick that he first became interested in the sound of poetry through listening to the Bible read aloud when a small boy, and that he remains "very fond of hymns ... they fill me with a great sense of awe." These Jamaican memories compare fascinatingly with the English experience in his poem "A Different Kind of Sunday." Berry's stories carry conviction both in the re-creation of places and events and in the voices of the characters, like the scruffy child who tempts the church-goer with "Satan life much sweet sweet more than sainty sainty life."

Berry draws directly from folk tradition and the rhythms of speech in his stories of Anancy Spiderman, that cunning, mischievous figure that can change from spider to man and back again. The stories originated in West African culture but were remade when taken by slaves to the West Indies. Berry's Bro Nancy lives comfortably in his own yard with his wife and son, supported by his loyal friend, Bro Dog, and combating his chief antagonist, Bro Tiger. Sometimes he fools others and sometimes he is tricked himself, often because of his greed. Later Anancy stories are told in *First Palm Trees* and *Don't Leave an Elephant to Go and Chase a Bird.*

Berry's later collection, *The Fortune Telling Lady,* also vividly brings alive the Caribbean world, with its dreams and ghosts as well as its colourful surroundings, and some of the stories are based on tales that the author heard as a child in Jamaica. Alongside the gaiety of dancing, singing, and rap rhymes, they tell of children's strong emotions—fear, homesickness, determination, pride—that have a universal appeal. The title story tells how Mother Eesha helps children and their parents by leading them through questions and Name-Stories to understand and solve their problems for themselves. The longest work, "Ajeemah and his Son", tells the historical story of an African slave in a brutal plantation society, and the eventual coming of freedom.

James Berry has done much work in schools, with spells as poet in residence, and has taken a particular interest in awaking a sense of identity and confidence in children from Caribbean backgrounds. He has said that he was alarmed at their "shut in" lack of ambition and resistance to teachers ("I couldn't win them/ They couldn't win me" reflects the school-leaver in "Getting Nowhere"). His story for adults, "The Girls and Yanga Marshall," shows vividly the alienation of Yanga, who wears a rasta hat to school, is in constant trouble with teachers, but understands them with much greater perceptiveness than they comprehend him. Berry has striven to show such youngsters that, like him, they inherit two languages, the Caribbean nation language and Standard English, and he has helped them to see how in responding to experience the tension between language forms can itself be creative. This idea underpins the title story of *A Thief in the Village,* in which an English teacher encourages a girl to write down a story from her own background using Caribbean English.

James Berry's prizewinning collection of poems *When I Dance,* with its directness, vigour, sense of celebration and carnival, gained excellent reviews. Described as "scooped bits of time I've lived in," the poems are written mainly in the first person, but give a vivid sense of the feelings and thoughts of children and adolescents. Like the stories, they reveal a fascination with shifting relationships within families: the younger generation feeling parents stuck in the past, the boy aware of the toughness of his younger sister ("yu nah catch me doin judo with her"), the questioning of chauvinism in "Girls can we educate we dads?" There is a pervasive love of active movement: discos, parties, fast bowling, drum playing. The title poem "When I Dance" celebrates the expansion brought about by music and dance, the way in which "I gather up all my senses ... Telling their poetry in movement / And I celebrate all rhythms." In the later verse of *Celebration Song,* vividly illustrated by Louise Brierley, Berry has transposed the nativity to a Caribbean setting. Mary tells Jesus on his first birthday about how the world celebrated his birth. This picture book takes a refreshingly different look at the traditional Christmas story.

Everywhere faces Everywhere is another collection of poetry for older children, interweaving the imagery and memories of Berry's Jamaican childhood with poems addressing the experience of young Afro-Caribbean people in Britain today. There are more than forty poems in a variety of forms, from rhythmic free verse to dialogues, ballads and haiku, using a range of different voices. Richly human poems are concerned with the nature of teenage relationships, shifting feelings about family and friends, and living in a modern inner city society that is reluctant to embrace diversity. Music, dancing, rapping, carnivals and graffiti artists are juxtaposed with the problems of hunger, racism, isolation and despair. Talking about one of the poems in this volume called "Everywhere faces Everywhere", Berry has said that it draws on experiences of going into multi-cultural schools, with "these faces from all around the globe" that shine "plum-blue to nutmeg-brown, melon-gold to peach pale." Throughout Berry's work runs this concern for breaking down divisions, for widening consciousness: "everybody needs a little bit of everybody," as he writes in the introduction to *When I Dance.* He points out that just as classic English poetry can be read to sound like rap or dub, so black poetry can be presented "straight" in a natural voice. It is with children and with schools that change begins.

—Robert Protherough

BETTINA

Pseudonym for Bettina Ehrlich. **Nationality:** British (originally Austrian: emigrated to Britain, 1938; became citizen, 1947). **Born:** Bettina Bauer, Vienna, Austria, 19 March 1903. **Education:** Kunstgewerbeschule (school of applied arts), Vienna. **Family:** Married the sculptor George Ehrlich in 1930 (died 1966). **Career:** Freelance writer and artist. **Awards:** Paris International Exhibition for Arts and Crafts medal, 1937. **Died:** 10 October 1985.

PUBLICATIONS FOR CHILDREN (ILLUSTRATED BY THE AUTHOR)

Fiction

Poo-Tsee, The Water-Tortoise. London, Chatto and Windus, 1943.
Cocolo. London, Chatto and Windus, 1945; New York, Harper, 1948.
Carmello. London, Chatto and Windus, 1945.
Cocolo Comes to America. New York, Harper, 1949.
Cocolo's Home. New York, Harper, 1950.
Castle in the Sand. New York, Harper, 1951.
A Horse for the Island. New York, Harper, 1952; London, Hamish Hamilton, 1953.
Piccolo. New York, Harper, 1954.
Pantaloni. New York, Harper, 1957; London, Oxford University Press, 1959.
Angelo and Rosaline. London, Collins, 1957.
Trovato. New York, Farrar Straus, 1959; London, Oxford University Press, 1960.
Paolo and Panetto. London, Oxford University Press, 1960; New York, Watts, 1961.
For the Leg of a Chicken. London, Collins, and New York, Watts, 1960.
Francesco and Francesca. London, Oxford University Press, 1962.
Of Uncles and Aunts. London, Oxford University Press, 1963; New York, Norton, 1964.
The Goat Boy. London, Oxford University Press, 1965; New York, Norton, 1966.
Sardines and the Angel. London, Oxford University Press, 1967.
Neretto. London, Oxford University Press, 1969.
A Day in Venice. London, Oxford University Press, 1973.

Other

Show Me Yours: A Little Paintbook. London, Chatto and Windus, 1943.

Dolls. London, Oxford University Press, 1962; New York, Farrar Straus, 1963.

*

Manuscript Collections: Kerlan Collection, University of Minnesota, Minneapolis; University of Oregon Library, Eugene.

Illustrator: *The Swans of Ballycastle* by Walter Hackett, 1954; *The Magic Christmas Tree* by Lee Kingman, 1956; *Piruwayu and the Rainbow* by Gilles Saint-Cérère, 1958; *Favorite Fairy Tales Told in England* by Virginia Haviland, 1959; *The Sorcerer's Apprentice and Other Stories* by John Hosier, 1960; *Tal and the Magic Barruget* by Eva-Lis Wuorio, 1965.

* * *

Bettina is best known for her picture books for five to nine-year-olds. The delicate charm of her watercolours is reminiscent of Ardizzone's and like his, her style is deceptively simple. As a young woman, she said she distrusted her spelling so much that she preferred to tell stories through pictures. Whether or not this is strictly true, her illustrations have the confidence and vigour of someone who habitually communicates visually. Their immediacy and movement carry the story from page to page so that the text can be relaxed and digressive—although nothing is mentioned that is not meticulously illustrated.

Bettina was born in Austria and spent much of her free time in Italy, although she lived in England from the outbreak of the Second World War until her death. The best of her books reflect her memories of pre-war Europe, where nothing more serious than a thunderstorm can trouble the innocent peace of a small community. Her simplicity is, however, not accidental, for she knew how to select the representative detail. The atmosphere she created in her little Italian cafés or Austrian pastures is vivid enough to support her quiet, understated stories. She had the ability—as in a fairy tale—to suspend belief, and, despite her foreign settings, we feel instantly at home. Statues, bronze angels, weathervanes, and the like have a life of their own, just as they would for children. A naiad or a nurse are both equally real.

Her best books have an element of magic. *Sardines and the Angel* tells how, for the price of several ice creams, the gentle Miss Higgins hears the story of Arturo, the little sardine seller. Arturo's family is too poor to afford ice creams, and one day, tempted beyond endurance, he spends some of the money from the sale of his father's fish on a strawberry cone. His father warns him that the bronze angel on the church spire knows about dishonest children, and, sure enough, the next time he gives way to temptation, there is the angel, standing in the café and demanding the largest ice cream cone. Arturo buys it for him, even though he knows he will be punished. Next day, a dreadful storm blows up when he is fishing with his father, but they are both saved when suddenly the angel appears and conjures up a favourable wind. After this, Arturo's parents believe in his strange friendship and they also allow him a weekly ice cream. Magic, moral, and reality are interwoven so well in this story that it is impossible to tell where one ends and the other begins. A similar effect is achieved in *The Goat Boy*, when Toni's goats are saved by a naiad; but this is less successful, largely because Toni himself is too passive in the story.

Bettina's careful attention to the concrete details of everyday life, even in her fantasy, has a child-like assurance, and her books are full of cheerful security, where the occasional cloud only serves to make the sunshine seem brighter.

—Alison Sage

BIANCO, Margery (Winifred) Williams

Also wrote as Margery Williams prior to 1925. **Nationality:** British. **Born:** London, 22 July 1881. **Education:** Privately and at schools in Philadelphia and Sharon Hill, Pennsylvania. **Family:** Married Francisco Bianco; one son and one daughter, the illustrator Pamela Bianco. **Died:** 4 September 1944.

Publications for Children

Fiction

The Velveteen Rabbit; or, How Toys Become Real, illustrated by William Nicholson. London, Heinemann, and New York, Doran, 1922.
The Little Wooden Doll, illustrated by Pamela Bianco. New York, Macmillan, 1925.
Poor Cecco: The Wonderful Story of a Wonderful Wooden Dog Who Was the Jolliest Toy in the House until He Went Out to Explore the World, illustrated by Arthur Rackham. London, Chatto and Windus, and New York, Doran, 1925.
The Apple Tree, illustrated by Boris Artzybasheff. New York, Doran, 1926.
The Adventures of Andy, illustrated by Leon Underwood. New York, Doran, 1927.
The Skin Horse, illustrated by Pamela Bianco. New York, Doran, 1927.
The Candlestick, illustrated by Ludovic Rodo. New York, Doubleday, 1929.
Other People's Houses. New York, Viking Press, 1930.
The House That Grew Smaller, illustrated by Rachel Field. New York, Macmillan, 1931.
A Street of Little Shops, illustrated by Grace Paull. New York, Doubleday, 1932; Kingswood, Surrey, World's Work, 1958.
The Hurdy-Gurdy Man, illustrated by Robert Lawson. New York, Oxford University Press, 1933; London, Oxford University Press, 1937.
The Good Friends, illustrated by Grace Paull. New York, Viking Press, 1934.
Winterbound, illustrated by Kate Seredy. New York, Viking Press, 1936.
Green Grows the Garden, illustrated by Grace Paull. New York, Macmillan, 1936.
Franzi and Gizi, with Gisella Loeffler. New York, Messner, 1941.
Penny and the White Horse, illustrated by Marjory Collinson. New York, Messner, 1942.
Bright Morning, illustrated by Margaret Platt. New York, Viking Press, 1942; London, Collins, 1945.
Forward, Commandos!, illustrated by Rafaello Busoni. New York, Viking Press, 1944; London, Wells Gardner Darton, 1947.

Other

All about Pets, illustrated by Grace Gilkison. New York, Macmillan, 1930.

More about Animals, illustrated by Helen Torrey. New York, Macmillan, 1934.
Tales from a Finnish Tupa, with James Cloyd Bowman, illustrated by Laura Bannon. Chicago, Whitman, 1936; as *Tales from a Finnish Fireside,* London, Chatto and Windus, 1975.
Rufus the Fox: Adapted from the French of Samivel. New York, Harper, 1937.
The Five-and-a-Half Club (reader), with Mabel O'Donnell and Rona Munro, illustrated by Florence and Margaret Hoopes. Evanston, Illinois, Row Peterson, 1942; London, Nisbet, 1956.
Herbert's Zoo and Other Favorite Stories, with others, illustrated by Julian. New York, Simon and Schuster, 1949.
The New Five-and-a-Half Club (reader), with Mabel O'Donnell, illustrated by Margaret Ayer. Evanston, Illinois, Row Peterson, 1951.
Comprehension Cards. London, Nisbet, 24 vols., 1959.

Translator, *The African Saga,* by Blaise Cendrars. New York, Payson and Clarke, 1927.
Translator, *Little Black Stories for Little White Children,* by Blaise Cendrars, illustrated by Pierre Pinsard. New York, Payson and Clarke, 1929.
Translator, with Dagny Mortensen, *Sidsel Longskirt: A Girl of Norway,* by Hans Aanrud, illustrated by Ingri and Edgar Parin d'Aulaire. Philadelphia, Winston, 1935.
Translator, with Dagny Mortensen, *Solve Suntrap: A Boy of Norway,* by Hans Aanrud, illustrated by Ingri and Edgar Parin d'Aulaire. Philadelphia, Winston, 1935.

Publications for Adults

Novels

The Late Returning. London, Heinemann, and New York, Macmillan, 1902.
Spendthrift Summer. London, Heinemann, 1903.
The Price of Youth. London, Duckworth, and New York, Macmillan, 1904.
The Bar. London, Methuen, 1906.
The Thing in the Woods. London, Duckworth, 1913.

Play

Out of the Night: A Mystery Comedy, with Harold Hutchinson. London and New York, French, 1929.

Other

Paris. London, A. and C. Black, and New York, Macmillan, 1910.

Translator, *Four Cents an Acre: The Story of Louisiana under the French,* by Georges Oudard. New York, Brewer and Warren, 1931.

* * *

Some of the greatest books—among them *Alice, The Wind in the Willows,* and *The Hobbit*—have started life as private books. Conceived for the entertainment of individual children, they have only later, and then sometimes after processing, found a wider audience.

Margery Williams Bianco's *Poor Cecco* is of this company. It was made first for the author's daughter Pamela—genius out of genius; at 12 Pamela's drawings inspired Walter de la Mare to create a set of charming "illustrative" verses, and she grew up to be equally distinguished as artist and writer. The Cecco of the title was a battered wooden dog, and the other characters were out of Pamela's toy-cupboard. They live in a necessarily closely knit community, form complicated relationships, and talk their own language. The modern reader who is privileged to look in on this private world is initially puzzled, but not for too long. *Poor Cecco* is one of the classic "toy" stories, deserving a place beside Rachel Field's *Hitty* and Rumer Godden's *Impunity Jane* among the very best of the genre.

Bianco knew, as all who enjoy the company of small children must, that toys are a very serious matter. There is plenty of laughter in *Poor Cecco,* but it is with, not at, the creatures whose destinies are worked out in these pages. The toys feel emotions rather like those of humans, but their actions are governed by certain physical limitations. They are animate but still made of wood, fabric, and stuffing.

They are nicely contrasted with the humans and the animals. There is a particularly convincing portrait of Murrum the cat, who comes nearest in this fundamentally kindly story to being the villain of the piece. The humans play a minor and passive role, apart from the postman who brings home Poor Cecco and his friends from their wanderings, tied together like a parcel and the postage duly paid with Poor Cecco's hard-earned pennies.

Unlike some improvised stories, *Poor Cecco* is tightly constructed. The plot is very compact, even if the entry of a major character—Jensina the Dutch doll—is delayed until well into the book; this is not a flaw so much as a calculated building-up to one of the crises of the narrative. Jensina is a splendid person, strong-minded, resourceful, set against the home-bred dolls with their gossip and petty jealousies. The subtleties of characterisation are expressed always in dialogue rather than in description; each toy has his idiosyncracies of speech and his individual standpoint.

Bianco has always been well served by her illustrators. The first edition of *Poor Cecco* had seven colour-plates in Arthur Rackham's grandest manner, and a recent edition has drawings no less decorative and perhaps more penetrating by Antony Maitland. A lesser book, *The Hurdy-Gurdy Man,* was honoured with masterly designs by Robert Lawson. The book which comes nearest to *Poor Cecco*—*The Velveteen Rabbit*—is one of the very few illustrated by one of the greatest masters of this art, Sir William Nicholson.

The Velveteen Rabbit might be regarded as a trial run for *Poor Cecco.* It too is a story of toys and of the nursery magic which can give them a reality more sharp than that of the ordinary world. But here the writer lacks confidence, and her book is tentative and uncertain, full of the sententiousness into which many writers are prone to slip when the heat of inspiration cools. The moral, instead of being implicit in the narrative, has to be stated and underlined.

Bianco, although not prolific, ranged widely, with translations, educational readers, and a travel book about Paris. For most readers she remains, and rightly, a one-book woman. *Poor Cecco* contains the best of her: the tenderness, the sense of adventure and of fun, the sturdy common sense. As postscript to one of her innumerable letters to Bulka, which fill one memorable chapter, Tubby writes: "I love you more than Christmas and Easter and

Fairyland." These are strong words, but they are rather what the reader feels about this uniquely heart-warming book.

—Marcus Crouch

BIRO, Val

Nationality: British. **Born:** Balint Stephen Biro, Budapest, Hungary, 6 October 1921. **Education:** Cistercian School, Budapest, graduated 1939; Central School of Arts and Crafts, London, 1939-42. **Family:** Married 1) Vivien Woolley in 1945, one daughter; 2) Marie-Louise Ellaway in 1970, two stepchildren. **Career:** Studio manager, Sylvan Press, London, 1944-46; production manager, C. and J. Temple, London, 1946-48; art director, John Lehmann, publishers, London, 1948-53; urban district councillor, 1966-70. Freelance artist and writer. **Awards:** Fellow, Chartered Society of Designers. **Address:** Bridge Cottage, Bosham, West Sussex PO18 8LQ, England.

Publications for Children (illustrated by the author)

Fiction

Bumpy's Holiday. London, Sylvan Press, 1943; New York, Transatlantic Arts, 1945.
Gumdrop: The Adventures of a Vintage Car. Leicester, Brockhampton Press, 1966; Chicago, Follett, 1967.
Gumdrop and the Farmer's Friend. Leicester, Brockhampton Press, 1967; Chicago, Follett, 1968.
Gumdrop on the Rally. Leicester, Brockhampton Press, 1968; Chicago, Follett, 1969.
Gumdrop on the Move. Leicester, Brockhampton Press, 1969; Chicago, Follett, 1970.
Gumdrop Goes to London. Leicester, Brockhampton Press, 1971.
Gumdrop Finds a Friend. Leicester, Brockhampton Press, 1973.
Gumdrop in Double Trouble. Leicester, Brockhampton Press, 1975.
Gumdrop and the Steamroller. London, Hodder and Stoughton, 1976; Chicago, Children's Press, 1977.
Gumdrop Posts a Letter. London, Hodder and Stoughton, 1976; Chicago, Children's Press, 1977; as *Gumdrop and the Birthday Surprise,* Milwaukee, Stevens, 1986.
Gumdrop on the Brighton Run. London, Hodder and Stoughton, 1976.
Gumdrop Has a Birthday. London, Hodder and Stoughton, 1977.
Gumdrop Gets His Wings. London, Hodder and Stoughton, 1979.
Gumdrop Finds a Ghost. London, Hodder and Stoughton, 1980.
Gumdrop and the Secret Switches. London, Hodder and Stoughton, 1981.
Gumdrop Makes a Start. London, Hodder and Stoughton, 1982.
Gumdrop and Horace. London, Hodder and Stoughton, 1982.
Gumdrop Races a Train. London, Hodder and Stoughton, 1982; Milwaukee, Stevens, 1986.
Gumdrop at Sea. London, Hodder and Stoughton, 1983.
Gumdrop at the Zoo. London, Hodder and Stoughton, 1983; Milwaukee, Stevens, 1985.
Gumdrop Gets a Lift. London, Hodder and Stoughton, 1983; Milwaukee, Stevens, 1986.
Gumdrop Goes to School. London, Hodder and Stoughton, 1983; Milwaukee, Stevens, 1986.
Gumdrop in a Hurry. London, Hodder and Stoughton, 1983; as *Gumdrop Beats the Clock,* Milwaukee, Stevens, 1986.
Gumdrop's Magic Journey. London, Hodder and Stoughton, 1984.
Gumdrop Goes Fishing. London, Hodder and Stoughton, 1984.
Gumdrop Has a Tummy Ache. London, Hodder and Stoughton, 1984.
Gumdrop Is the Best Car. London, Hodder and Stoughton, 1984; as *Gumdrop Is the Best,* Milwaukee, Stevens, 1985.
Gumdrop on the Farm. London, Hodder and Stoughton, 1984.
Gumdrop and the Monster. London, Hodder and Stoughton, 1985.
Gumdrop and the Farmyard Caper. Milwaukee, Stevens, 1985.
Gumdrop and the Great Sausage Caper. Milwaukee, Stevens, 1985.
Gumdrop Catches a Cold. Milwaukee, Stevens, 1985.
Gumdrop Floats Away. Milwaukee, Stevens, 1985.
Gumdrop to the Rescue. London, Hodder and Stoughton, 1986.
Gumdrop For Ever! London, Hodder and Stoughton, 1987.
Gumdrop and the Dinosaur. London, Hodder and Stoughton, 1988.
The Bumper Gumdrop Omnibus. London, Hodder and Stoughton, 1989.
Drango Dragon. Loughborough, Leicestershire, Ladybird, 1989.
Gumdrop and the Pirates. London, Hodder and Stoughton, 1989.
Peter Cheater. Aylesbury, Buckinghamshire, Ginn, 1989.
Gumdrop and the Elephant. London, Hodder and Stoughton, 1990.
Look and Find A B C. London, Hippo, 1990.
Miranda's Umbrella. London, Blackie, 1990.
Gumdrop and the Bulldozers. London, Hodder and Stoughton, 1991.
Gumdrop's Merry Christmas. London, Hodder and Stoughton, 1992.
The Monster Pack. London, Longman, 1994.
The Boasting Monsters. London, Longman, 1994.
The Monster Feast. London, Longman, 1994.
Bears Can't Fly. Loughborough, Leicestershire, 1996.
The Monster Birthday. London, Longman, 1997.
Gumdrop and the Martians. London, Hodder Children's Books, 1998.

Language Teaching

New Caribbean Readers, 4 vols. Aylesbury, Ginn, 1995-96.
American Start with English, 8 vols. New York, Oxford University Press, 1996.
The Flying Boot, 50 vols. Walton-on-Thames, Nelson, 1996.
A Bag of Coal, Creepy Castle, Big Snowball, and *Fire in Wild Wood,* by Wess Magee. Oxford, Heinemann, 1996.

Other

The Honest Thief: A Hungarian Folktale. Leicester, Brockhampton Press, 1972; New York, Holiday House, 1973.
Buster Is Lost! (reader). London, Macmillan, 1974.
A Dog and His Bone (reader). London, Macmillan, 1975.
Hungarian Folk-Tales. London, Oxford University Press, 1981; New York, Oxford University Press, 1982.
The Magic Doctor (retelling). London and New York, Oxford University Press, 1982.
Fables from Aesop (retelling). Aylesbury, Buckinghamshire, Ginn, and San Diego, Wright, 18 vols., 1983-88.

The Hobyahs (retelling). Oxford, Oxford University Press, 1985.
The Pied Piper of Hamelin (retelling). Oxford, Oxford University Press, and Morristown, New Jersey, Silver Burdett, 1985.
Tales from Hans Andersen. Aylesbury, Buckinghamshire, Ginn, and San Diego, Wright, 8 vols., 1985-89.
The Donkey That Sneezed (retelling). Oxford and New York, Oxford University Press, 1986.
Jack and the Beanstalk (retelling). Oxford, Oxford University Press, 1989.
Tobias and the Dragon: A Folk Tale from Hungary. London, Blackie, 1989.
The Three Little Pigs (retelling). Oxford, Oxford University Press, 1990.
The Three Billy-Goats Gruff (retelling). Oxford, Oxford University Press, 1993
My Oxford Picture Word Book. Oxford, Oxford University Press, 1994.
Little Treasury of Nursery Rhymes. London, Award Publications, 1995.
Lazy Jack. Oxford, Oxford University Press, 1995.
Jasper's Jungle Journey (poetry). Loughborough, Leicestershire, Ladybird, 1995.
Hansel and Gretel (retelling). Oxford, Oxford University Press, 1997.
Goldilocks and the Three Bears (retelling). Oxford, Oxford University Press, 1998.

Compiler, *Rub-a-dub-dub: Val Biro's 77 Favorite Nursery Rhymes.* London, Blackie, 1991.

*

Illustrator: *The Story of a Carrot* by Kate Barclay, 1944; *No Bombs at All,* 1944, and *Airman's Song Book,* 1945, both by Cyril H.W. Jackson; *Private Gallery* by P. Tabori, 1944; *Worlds Without End* by Denys Val Baker, 1945; *Escape from the Zoo,* 1945, *A Camel from the Desert,* 1947, and *The Penguin Goes Home,* 1951, all by Richard Parker; *Crusading Holiday* by Mary F. Moore, 1946; *England, The Mysterious Island* by P. Treves, 1948; *The Last Days of Pompeii* by Edward Bulwer-Lytton, 1948; *The Story of Joseph and Pharaoh* by Frances Dale, 1950; *Pilgrim's Progress* by John Bunyan, 1951; *Serena Blandish* by Enid Bagnold, 1951; *Zoo for Zanies* by Nicholas Husk, 1952; *The South African Twins,* 1953, and *The Australian Twins,* 1954, both by Daphne Rooke; *The Man Who Made Wine* by J.M. Scott, 1954; *David the Shepherd Boy* by Elizabeth Goudge, 1954; *Fit for a Bishop* by Stephen Bishop, 1955; *Fire Engine by Mistake,* 1955, *Andy's Pit Pony,* 1958, and *The Doctor,* 1972, all by Leila Berg; *The Casket and the Sword* by Norman Dale, 1956; *Tommy the Tugboat,* 1956, *Henry the Helicopter,* 1956, *Tommy Joins the Navy,* 1957, *Henry to the Rescue,* 1959, *Henry the Hero,* 1960, *Tommy's New Engine,* 1961, *Hovering with Henry,* 1961, *Henry in the News,* 1963, *Henry's Busy Winter,* 1964, *Tommy and the Lighthouse,* 1965, *Henry Joins the Police,* 1966, *Tommy and the Oil Rig,* 1967, *Henry and the Astronaut,* 1968, *Tommy and the Spanish Galleon,* 1969, *Henry and the Traction Engine,* 1970, *Tommy and the Yellow Submarine,* 1971, *Henry in the Mountains,* 1972, *Henry in Iceland,* 1973, *Ferryboat Tommy,* 1973, *Tommy in the Caribbean,* 1974, *Henry on Safari,* 1975, *Tommy and the Island,* 1977, and *Lizzie the Lifeboat,* 1985, all by Dora Thatcher; *To Arms for the Queen* by Eric Leyland, 1956; *Kettleby's Zoo* by Margaret Holden, 1957; *Andy and the Mascots,* 1957 [*the Water Crossing,* 1958, *the Sharpshooter,* 1959, *the Display Team,* 1959, *the Secret Papers,* 1961, *the Miniature War,* 1962, *the Royal Review,* 1963, *His Last Parade,* 1968], all by Reginald Taylor; *Hideaway Johnny* by David Scott Daniell, 1959; *The Story of Scotland* by Lawrence Stenhouse, 1961; *The Prisoner of Zenda* by Anthony Hope, 1961; *What a Lark,* 1961, and *Soap-Box Derby,* 1962, both by Rosemary Weir; *Man Makes Towns* by Kenneth Rudge, 1963; *The Ship Stealers,* 1963, and *Big-Head,* 1964, both by Cam Renton; *The Seas of Britain* by Peter Dawlish, 1963; *The Country Year* by Thurlow Craig, 1964; *Arabian Nights,* 1965; *The Wonderful Wizard of Oz,* 1965, and *The Marvelous Land of Oz,* 1967, both by L. Frank Baum; *The Sunday Telegraph Gardening Book* by Fred Whitsey, 1966; *Journal of My Service in India* by J. Corneille, 1966; *The Story of Fanny Burney* by Josephine Kamm, 1966; *The Field Bedside Book,* 1967; *The Ghost of June* by Rupert Croft-Cooke, 1968; *Kangaroo Tennis,* 1968, and *Benjie the Circus Dog,* 1969, both by Donald Bisset; *One Man's Happiness* by Lord Tweedsmuir, 1968; *Sally the Seal,* 1968, *James and Sally Again,* 1970, and *Mr. Bubbus and the Railway Smugglers,* 1976, all by Joan Drake; *Home Is the North* by Walt Morey, 1968; *Discovering Chesham* by Arnold Baines, 1968; *The Untravelled World* by Eric E. Shipton, 1969; *Picture Reference Book of the Georgians* by Boswell Taylor, 1969; *Garden Glory* by Ted Humphris, 1969; *The Terrible Trumpet* by William Wise, 1969; *Soldier Bear* by Geoffrey Morgan, 1970; *The Writ of Green Wax* by Edward Bohan, 1970; *Lovingly,* 1971, *Prayerfully,* 1972, and *Thankfully,* 1975, all by Helen Steiner Rice; *See, Hear and Speak* by Donald Sutherland, 1971; *American Wit and Wisdom* by James Dow, 1971; *The Cook Hostess' Book,* 1971, and *The Sherlock Holmes Cook Book,* 1976, both by Fanny Craddock; *The Good Food Guide,* 1971; *Making Friends with Music* by James Glennon, 1971; *The Jazz Band* by Helen Solomon, 1972; *Country Talk,* 1972, *More Country Talk,* 1973, *New Country Talk,* 1975, *New Country Talk Again,* 1977, *Country Talk Continued,* 1979, and *Latest Country Talk,* 1981, all by J.B.H. Peel; *Mr. Purpose* by Mimi Irving, 1972; *A Reading Book* by Leslie Alexander, 1972; *Tales of the Circus* by Jane MacMichael, 1972; *Victoria in the Wings,* 1972, *The Prince and the Quakeress,* 1976, *Epitaph for Three Women,* 1981, *The Sun in Splendour,* 1982, *The Red Rose of Anjou,* 1982, and other novels by Jean Plaidy; *Play the Best Courses* by Peter Allen, 1973; *Cubs with a Difference,* 1973, *Cubs Away,* 1974, *Cubs on Saturday,* 1976, and *Cubs Ahoy,* 1979, all by Stephen Andrews; *The Dinghy Stories* by Dawn Bowker, 1973; *Garry the Goblin* by Gladys Williams, 1973; *The Reporter* by Michael Pollard, 1973; *The Nose Knows,* 1974, *Dolls in Danger,* 1974, *The Case of the Condemned Cat,* 1975 [*Nervous Newsboy,* 1976, *Invisible Dog,* 1977, *Secret Scribbler,* 1978, *Phantom Frog,* 1979, *Treetop Treasure,* 1980], *The Menaced Midget,* 1975, *The Great Rabbit Robbery,* 1976, and *A Cat Called Amnesia,* 1977, all by E.W. Hildick; *Down the Kitchen Sink* by Beverley Nichols, 1974; *Faster Than Anything* by Peter John Stephens, 1974; *The Robert Carrier Cookery Course,* 1974; *The Sick Cow,* 1974, *George the Fire Engine,* 1976, *Changing of the Guard,* 1978, *The Very, Very Long Dog,* 1978, *The Roundabout Horse,* 1978, *Here Comes Wordman!,* 1979, *King of Beasts,* 1979, *The Big Sneeze,* 1980, *Jungle Silver,* 1981, *The Dial-a-Story Book,* 1981, *The Crawly Crawly Caterpillar,* 1981, *The Tiny Tiny Tadpole,* 1982, *The Scruffy Scruffy Dog,* 1983, *The Tiger Who Couldn't Be Bothered,* 1984, *The Clever Clever Cats,* 1985, *The Silly Silly Ghost,* 1987, *Bobby Brewster's Jigsaw Puzzle,* 1988, and *The Sleeping Policeman,* 1988, all by H.E. Todd; *Brer Rabbit and the Won-*

derful Tar-Baby, 1975 [*Is Trapped,* 1975, *and the Alligator,* 1976, *Saves Brer Terrapin,* 1976], *Buttercup Day,* 1982, *Mike's Monkey,* 1982, *The Runaway Cow,* 1982, *Telltale Tommy,* 1982, *The Magic Mirror,* 1983, *The Forgotten Pets,* 1983, *Dame Topple's Buns,* 1983, and *The Three Wishes,* 1983, all by Enid Blyton; *Food and Drink from Your Garden,* and *The Rough Shoot,* both by Daniel Green, 1975; *Machines on the Farm* by John Denton, 1975; *Jim's Go-Kart* by Jeffrey Bevington, 1975; *The Best Games People Play* by Richard Sharp, 1976; *British Folk Customs* by Christina Hole, 1976; *Colibri Readers* edited by Dorothy Figueroa, 4 vols., 1976-81; *Death to the Strangers!* by Philip Rush, 1977; *Catch the Plane!* by Delia Huddy, 1977; *On Target* by Ken Agar, 1977; *The Devil's Cut* by Clive King, 1978; *The Barley Sugar Ghosts* by Hazel Townson, 1978; *Out of an Egg* by Edward Ramsbottom and Joan Redmayne, 1978; *The Treasure of Dubarry Castle,* 1978, and *The Case of the Silver Lockets,* 1981, both by Lindsay Brown; *Yn Yr Ardd* by Edna Jenkins, 1978; *Sugar and Spice* edited by Giuseppi and Giuseppi, 1978; *Making the Most of It* by Theodora FitzGibbon, 1978; *The Daily Telegraph Cook's Book* by Bon Viveur, 1978; *A Bedside Cookbook* by Sheila Scotter, 1978; *The Sign of the Smiling Lion* by Peter J. Davies, 1979; *A Bucket of Nuts and a Herring Net* by John Jackson, 1979; *Worzel Gummidge* stories, 1979; *New Caribbean Readers* by Hilary Sherlock, 2 vols., 1980-81; *Surprise Bride,* 1980, *The Big Fib,* 1984, and *Haunts and Taunts,* 1993, all by Jean Chapman; *Shopping and Cooking in Europe* by Nicholas Courtney, 1980; *Where Are You Going,* 1980; *100 Bible Stories,* 1980, *100 New Testament Stories,* 1981, and *How Things Began* (3 vols.), 1986, all by Norman J. Bull; *Mr. Wolf and His Tail* by Ronald Deadman, 1981; *Dragon in the Drainpipe,* 1981, *Dragon in the Family,* 1985, and *Wishing Powder,* 1986, all by Maggie Prince; *The Virginian* by Owen Wister, 1981; *Bingo Bones and the Boggart,* 1982, and *Bingo Bones and the Funny Cube,* 1986, both by K.H. Roberts; *The Ivory Elephant's Orchard* by David Gamble, 1983; *The Wind in the Willows* by Kenneth Grahame, 1983; *Pulpit Cricket* by Fergus McKendrick, 1983; *Kokoleoko,* 1983, and *Mrs. Macaroni,* 1985, both by June Tillman; *Jack and the Robbers* by Jill Bennett, 1984; *Gluttony, Pride, and Lust* by Michael Geare and Michael Turner, 1984; *Dilbert* books by Kate Robertson, 4 vols., 1984; *The Brownies in Hospital,* 1984, *Air Day for the Brownies,* 1985, *The Brownies and the Fire,* 1985, *Brownies at the Zoo,* 1986, and *The Brownies and the Flood,* 1987, all by Pamela Sykes; *Computer Studies for You* by Stephen Doyle, 1985; *Time* by Paul Harding, 1985; *Talk It Over* by Sheila Lane, 1985; *Alice in Wonderland* by Lewis Carroll, 1986; *Bread,* 1986, *Mrs. Grindy's Shoes,* 1986, *Up in a Tree,* 1986, and *The Train Ride Story,* 1987, all by Joy Cowley; *Collected Tales from Aesop's Fables* (retelling), 1986, *The Hotchpotch Horse,* 1987, *A Kettle Full of Magic,* 1988, *The Odd Job Man and the Thousand Mile Boots,* 1988, and *Seasons,* 1989, all by Jean Kenward; *The Giant's Footsteps,* 1986, *The Missing Ring,* 1986, *The Mystery Voice,* 1986, and *Strangers in Town,* 1986, all by John Patience; *King Lear,* 1986, *Henry IV Part 1,* 1987, and *Much Ado About Nothing,* 1989, all by Shakespeare; *New Caribbean Readers* by Diane Browne, 1987; *Poor Rabbit,* 1987, *Who Asked the Ants,* 1987, and *Squirrel Is Lonely,* 1990, all by Pat Edwards; *The Jungle Book* adapted by Sheila Lane and Marion Kemp, 1987; *The King's Jokes* by Margaret Mahy, 1987; *New Caribbean Readers* by Pamela Mordecai, 1987; *The Three Billy Goats Gruff* by Diana Perkins, 1987; *Clowns,* and *Races,* both by William Shepherd, 1987; *Crash, Bang, and Wallop* by Linda Allen, 1988; *I Dream,* and *The Wicked Pirates,* both by Jill Eggleton, 1988; *The Crooked Man* and *The Hare and the Tortoise,* both by Helen Arnold, 1989; *Crocodile Tears?: Bedtime Poems for the Very Young* by Penelope Browning, 1990; *Fishing* by Paul Groves, 1990; *Pedro and the Singing Dog* by Jean McKenzie, 1990; *A Visit to Don Otavio: A Traveller's Tale from Mexico* by Sybile Bedford, 1990; *The Christmas Mouse* by Marjory Purves, 1991; *What's up the Coconut Tree?,* 1991, and *Show-off Mouse,* 1993, both by A.H. Benjamin; *When I Was Your Age* by Ken Adams, 1991; *Animal Stories* by Linda Jennings, 1992; *The Dinosaur Egg Mystery* by M. Christina Butler, 1992; *The Dinosaur's Egg* by M. Christina Butler, 1992; *Belinda Beetle* and *Belinda Beats the Band* both by Rev. W. Awdry, 1992; *A Holiday for Mr. Gribble* by Anne Macdonnell, 1993; *Sam and Sue and Lavatory Lou* by Robert Swindells, 1993; *Haunts and Taunts* by Jean Chapman, 1994; *Witches Galore* by Linda Jennings, 1994; *Tall Tale Tom* by Anne Forsyth, 1994; *Grandpa Briny and the Seaweed Garden Centre* by Hilary Sharpe, 1994; *The Landleaguers* by Anthony Trollope, 1995; *Archie the Ugly Dinosaur* by M. Christina Butler, 1996; *The Good Samaritan* by Carol Christian, 1996; *The Father Brown Stories* by G. K. Chesterton, 2 vols., 1997; *The Dinosaur's Dinner* by M. Christina Butler, 1997.

Val Biro comments:

The joy of writing and illustrating the *Gumdrop* books derives partly from the fact that I own the real Gumdrop (a 1926 Austin 12-4) in which I often drive to schools where children can see the "original." As with other vintage car nuts, the old vehicle is my pride and joy, so it is very natural that I should go on writing about it, and feel enthusiastic in doing so. I also get a lot of pleasure in retelling some great stories from fable or folktale, be they from Aesop or from Hungary (my birthplace) in an accessible way for today's children. All the while, I write with a beady eye on the pictorial content, conscious of the luxury of being my own illustrator. Recently I have burst into verse for *Jasper's Jungle Journey,* for very young children. The older I get, the younger my readers become!

(1997)As for illustrating other writers' books, this is my *métier.* The interest in such work lies in the old saying that "books are different": that is, that each book requires something different from the illustrator. In each of the great many books that I have illustrated, I have been transported into a new and different world—be it the wartime R.A.F. in *No Bombs at All,* the fantasy world of *The Wizard of Oz,* or the 1920s magic realism of G. K. Chesterton's Father Brown. In each case I need to adapt not only the mental approach, but often the very style of illustrating itself. And modern technology often adds a new dimension to my work, such as the recent CD-ROM version of *My Oxford Picture Word Book,* where my drawings took on a life of their own!

* * *

Val Biro has made his reputation by picture books for very young children, writing and illustrating them himself. The illustrations are as important as the text, if not more important, for this age group. His chief character is Gumdrop, a vintage car.

"He was a very old car, and his proper name was Austin Clifton Twelve-Four. But everybody called him Gumdrop. His owner, Mr. Oldcastle, was so lonely that he had to go to live with his daughter and sell his car, but he kept the old brass horn." A different incident, portrayed in large dramatic coloured pictures, follows on every page. Burglars steal Gumdrop and crash the car;

various characters, including a gipsy family, secure interesting bits off the vehicle. The rest of the book is taken up with recovering everything, and ends up with a vintage car rally. The last page shows the cross-section of an Austin made in 1926. After that Gumdrop fills many books. He drives round London tangling with crooks, is involved with tractors and cranes, animals and people. A vehicle with real personality, he appeals to the young, who take an interest in cars at a very early age.

"There was a strange sight at the Red Lion one sunny morning in June. The vintage cars had come to start their big rally of the year. Never was there such a collection of fine old cars in the yard. Each had a Rally number fixed to it. Number 1 was an Alvis Duck-Back and Number 2 a Morris Bullnose. The model T Ford was Number 3....And then there was a blue car with a black hood and a brass horn. It was Number 9: an Austin Clifton Heavy Twelve-Four, vintage 1926, driven by Bill McArran. It was Gumdrop." So begins a typical story. This information occupies two pages of large well-spaced print because the vehicles themselves, their owners, and some young spectators, all with expressive faces, fill the entire background.

This particular rally involves a thief, a farmyard, a horse box, a pony club rally, a carnival procession, a crowd of pigs who have to be given a lift, a blazing hayrick, a fire engine, and an angry motor cycle. Gumdrop of course had lost his way, but he was awarded a brass starting handle as a special prize for solving the crime of the stolen prizes. The book ends on a good moral note. "Everyone cheered and all the cars sounded their horns. Gluurk-Gug and Bleep-Blip, Honk-Tonk and Tootle-Toot. Gumdrop was the happiest car in the rally because he had helped a lost little boy, a mayor in a procession, a farmer with ten little pigs...helped put out a fire and found the silver cups."

Gumdrop enjoys his 60th birthday complete with a breakdown adventure and lots of presents, including an old-fashioned AA brass badge presented to him by Lord Montagu at the Beaulieu Historic Motor Show, in *Gumdrop to the Rescue.* Vehicles showing the history of the motor car are drawn and named on the end papers inside the cover. Gumdrop himself is almost human, as in *Gumdrop For Ever!* when the "klaxon stopped bleeping as if it understood, 'though it must have been the wiring unshorting itself." His adventures keep up with the times. In a recent book, *Gumdrop and the Dinosaur,* he travels back in time 65 million years with the help of a computer. The names and lengths of the creatures line the end papers, all with friendly expressive faces which they keep all through the story.

—Margaret Campbell

BISHOP, Claire Huchet

Nationality: French and American. **Born:** Europe; grew up in Brittany. **Education:** Collège Sévigné, Paris; University of London. **Family:** Married Frank Bishop. **Career:** Founding director, L'Heure Joyeuse children's library (the first in France), Paris, 1924-29; worked in the New York Public Library, 1932-36. Contributor to *Commonweal, Saturday Review,* and other periodicals. President, International Council of Christians and Jews, 1975-77, and Jewish-Christian Fellowship of France, 1976-81. **Awards:** Child Study Association of America award, 1953; Nicholas and Hedy International Brotherhood award, 1988. **Died:** 11 March 1993.

PUBLICATIONS FOR CHILDREN

Fiction

The Five Chinese Brothers, illustrated by Kurt Wiese. New York, Coward McCann, 1938; London, Oxford University Press, 1939.
The Kings' Day, illustrated by Doris Spiegel. New York, Coward McCann, 1940.
The Ferryman, illustrated by Kurt Wiese. New York, Coward McCann, 1941; London, Faber, 1943.
The Man Who Lost His Head, illustrated by Robert McCloskey. New York, Viking Press, 1942.
Augustus, illustrated by Grace Paull. New York, Viking Press, 1945.
Pancakes-Paris, illustrated by Georges Schreiber. New York, Viking Press, 1947.
Blue Spring Farm. New York, Viking Press, 1948.
Bernard and His Dogs, illustrated by Maurice Brevannes. Boston, Houghton Mifflin, 1952.
Twenty and Ten, illustrated by William Pène du Bois. New York, Viking Press, 1952; London, Penguin, 1978.
All Alone, illustrated by Feodor Rojankovsky. New York, Viking Press, 1953.
The Big Loop, illustrated by Carles Fontseré. New York, Viking Press, 1955; London, Dent, 1958.
Toto's Triumph, illustrated by Claude Ponsot. New York, Viking Press, 1957; London, Dent, 1959.
A Present from Petros, illustrated by Dimitris Davis. New York, Viking Press, 1961.
Twenty-Two Bears, illustrated by Kurt Wiese. New York, Viking Press, 1964.
The Truffle Pig, illustrated by Kurt Wiese. New York, Coward McCann, 1971.
Georgette, illustrated by Ursula Landshoff. New York, Coward McCann, 1973.

Other

Christopher the Giant (on St. Christopher), illustrated by Berkeley Williams, Jr. Boston, Houghton Mifflin, 1950.
Martin de Porres, Hero, illustrated by Jean Charlot. Boston, Houghton Mifflin, 1954.
French Roundabout. New York, Dodd Mead, 1960; revised edition, 1966.
Lafayette: French-American Hero. Champaign, Illinois, Garrard, 1960.
Yeshu, Called Jesus, illustrated by Don Bolognese. New York, Farrar Straus, 1966; London, Constable, 1967.
Mozart: Music Magician, illustrated by Paul Frame. Champaign, Illinois, Garrard, 1968.
Here Is France. New York, Farrar Straus, 1969.
Johann Sebastian Bach: Music Giant, illustrated by Russell Hoover. Champaign, Illinois, Garrard, 1972.

Editor, *Happy Christmas: Tales for Boys and Girls,* illustrated by Ellen Raskin. New York, Stephen Daye Press, 1956.

PUBLICATIONS FOR ADULTS

Other

French Children's Books for English-Speaking Children: A...Descriptive List... New York, Sheridan Square Press, 1938.

France Alive. New York, McMullen, 1947.
All Things Common. New York, Harper, 1950.
How Catholics Look at Jews: Inquiries into Italian, French and Spanish Teaching Methods. New York, Paulist Press, 1974.

Editor, *Jesus and Israel,* by Jules Isaac, translated by Sally Gran. New York, Holt Rinehart, 1971.

*

Claire Huchet Bishop commented:

(1989) My books for young people range from repeated patterns for the four-year-old up to breathless adventures for the 12- to 13-year old. Writing has always meant for me arduous work and rewarding solace. Poetry was my first dedication which, somehow, evolved into stories for children. Perhaps both kinds of writing have in common a certain aptitude at intense dreamy feeling often typical of people from French Brittany.

* * *

Claire Huchet Bishop brought to American children a taste of Europe—of different people and different customs. In her books one can learn how truffles are found, what it was like to live in war-deprived Paris, how it feels to herd sheep on a mountain by yourself. Yet the author's interest was deeper than mere geographical or historical glimpses. She was discussing important and recurring problems in a child's life.

In *All Alone,* for example, a story designed for older children, a young sheep herder must decide whether to save a new acquaintance from death or abide by a strict village custom of having no dealings with strangers. The peasant lad is faced with a choice between two values—respect for his parents or regard for another human being. It is a serious situation, including fear of punishment, and it is one which could be the experience of any child in some form. Despite his narrow training, the hero chooses the higher law of doing good to his neighbor. Results show the wisdom of his act and encourage a child reader to think for himself.

Pancakes-Paris is still of interest, though it pictures the aftermath of World War II. Its real topic is privation. Butter, milk, oranges, eggs, and cocoa are familiar words to children, but in this story these common foods are very scarce. So the custom of having delectable crêpes before Lent is unknown to the younger children and just a faint memory to the older ones. The disappearance of this tradition is symbolic of a world from which beauty and gracious occasions have been wiped away. It is a bleak scene of mud-colored dripping plaster walls, made so by long periods of no heat, of water and onion as a butter substitute, and of washing without soap. Against this dark picture stands the staunch character of Charles, the oldest child, now man of the family. It is his determination which makes it possible to celebrate the holiday with pancakes as before the war, to bring a shaft of light into the dreary monotony life has become. As in *All Alone* the reader finds a hero who meets difficulties with spirit.

Bishop wrote books for very young children as well as the two just discussed, designed for 8-to-12-year-olds. *The Truffle Pig,* like *Pancakes-Paris,* takes place in France. Using words a child knows well, the author created a story full of country sounds and smells with a lonely boy's love for a pig at its center: "It was tiny with a lovely pink color. It looked very bright. Pierre liked it at once." Pierre elegantly names his pet "Marcel" and the pig signifies his immediate attachment for the boy with loud unmistakable grunts. Pierre's loneliness dissolves. However, pigs usually go to market and Marcel is no exception. In desperation, Pierre runs away with him. "Pierre and Marcel made for the woods. The birds had gone to bed. The smell of earth and plants filled the air. It was very quiet." What a nice description of forest-feeling tucked beside the dark problem! But while in the woods, Marcel displays a talent for finding truffles, and this delicacy delivers the pig from market, Pierre from loneliness, and Pierre's family from poverty.

The Truffle Pig shows the author's versatility. She used simple words and a cadence and format suitable for younger children to portray her vivid scenes and sensations. We do not begrudge the and-they-lived-happily-ever-after ending. Like the other books, it deals with a deep childhood problem—loneliness. Bishop had no hesitation in bringing untrivial subjects to children but the writing is appropriate for the audience.

—Carolyn T. Kingston

BISSET, Donald

Nationality: British. **Born:** London, 30 August 1910. **Education:** Warehousemen, Clerks and Drapers School, Addington, Surrey. **Military Service:** Royal Artillery during World War II; lieutenant. **Family:** Married Nancy Bisset in 1946 (divorced); one son. **Career:** Radio, television, and stage actor. **Died:** 1995.

Publications for Children

Fiction

Anytime Stories, illustrated by the author. London, Faber, 1954.
Sometime Stories, illustrated by the author. London, Faber, 1957.
Next Time Stories, illustrated by the author. London, Methuen, 1959.
This Time Stories, illustrated by the author. London, Methuen, 1961.
Another Time Stories, illustrated by the author. London, Methuen, 1963.
Little Bear's Pony, illustrated by Shirley Hughes. London, Benn, 1966.
Hullo Lucy, illustrated by Gillian Kenny. London, Benn, 1967.
Talks with a Tiger, illustrated by the author. London, Methuen, 1967.
Kangaroo Tennis, illustrated by Val Biro. London, Benn, 1968.
Nothing, illustrated by the author. London, Benn, 1969.
Upside Down Land. Moscow, Progress Publishers, 1969.
Benjie the Circus Dog, illustrated by Val Biro. London, Benn, 1969.
Time and Again Stories, illustrated by the author. London, Methuen, 1970.
Barcha the Tiger, illustrated by Derek Collard. London, Benn, 1971.
Tiger Wants More, illustrated by the author. London, Methuen, 1971.
Yak and the Sea Shell, illustrated by Lorraine Calaora. London, Methuen, 1971.
Yak and the Painted Cave, illustrated by Lorraine Calaora. London, Methuen, 1971.
Yak and the Buried Treasure, illustrated by Lorraine Calaora. London, Methuen, 1972.

Yak and the Ice Cream, illustrated by Lorraine Calaora. London, Methuen, 1972.
Father Tingtang's Journey, illustrated by the author. London, Methuen, 1973.
Jenny Hopalong, illustrated by Derek Collard. London, Benn, 1973.
Yak Goes Home, illustrated by Lorraine Calaora. London, Methuen, 1973.
The Happy Horse, illustrated by David Sharpe. London, Benn, 1974.
The Adventures of Mandy Duck, illustrated by the author. London, Methuen, 1974.
Hazy Mountain, illustrated by Shirley Hughes. London, Kestrel, 1975.
"Oh Dear," Said the Tiger, illustrated by the author. London, Methuen, 1975.
Paws with Shapes, illustrated by Tony Hutchins. Maidenhead, Berkshire, Intercontinental Books, 1976.
Paws with Numbers, with Michael Morris, illustrated by Tony Hutchins. Maidenhead, Berkshire, Intercontinental Books, 1976.
The Lost Birthday, illustrated by the author. Moscow, Progress Publishers, 1976.
The Story of Smokey Horse, illustrated by the author. London, Methuen, 1977.
This Is Ridiculous, illustrated by the author. London, Beaver, 1977.
Journey to the Jungle. London, Beaver, 1977.
The Adventures of Yak, illustrated by the author. London, Methuen, 1978.
What Time Is It When It Isn't?, illustrated by the author. London, Methuen, 1980.
Johnny Here and There, illustrated by the author. London, Methuen, 1981.
The Hedgehog Who Rolled Uphill. London, Methuen, 1982.
The Joyous Adventures of Snakey Boo, illustrated by the author. London, Methuen, 1982.
Sleep Tight, Snakey Boo! London, Methuen, 1985.
Just a Moment! London, Methuen, 1987.
Upside Down Stories. London, Puffin, 1987.
Please Yourself. London, Methuen, 1991.

Plays

Television Series: *Yak,* 1971.

*

Donald Bisset comments:

All my books are modern fairy stories—animistic in concept—and, on the surface, nonsensical, but nevertheless they have meanings.

* * *

Innocence is the essential quality of all Donald Bisset's work—a pure, shining, quite unselfconscious innocence that finds a delighted response in a small child's mind and has an extraordinary *cleansing* effect in an adult's. Of all the writers who protest that they write for only themselves, or the child within them, Bisset is one of the few I would believe. There is genuine simplicity, a total lack of contrivance or artifice or sophisticated humorous hindsight, in his style, plots (if plots there be—perhaps "sequence of events" is more accurate), characters, and dialogue. And yet at the same time there is a kind of artless art in the way he looks at words as if they were as new to him as to a four-year-old and follows them with wide-eyed logic to some daft conclusion; in the way he allows his fantasies to develop by the natural laws of free association; in the way he incorporates the very page itself—the typesetting, his spiky little childlike drawings, the numbering—into the life of the story. The appeal is to the child of around four, five, six, who has learnt just enough of the rules of language, logic, real life, to appreciate seeing them bent, but who still remembers when they were mysterious and unexpected, who is still sufficiently immersed in the world of fairy stories and nursery rhymes to enjoy the comfortable recognition of their patterns, but who has gained enough intellectual distance from them to enjoy playing with and changing those familiar patterns.

The years scarcely changed Bisset. Perhaps the books tend more to be single units, but they still break up into separate chapter-stories, just a few pages long, bedtime reading at its most engaging. Characters zip in and out of different books: Tiger, who grows fat only on words and thrives on a special diet of stories featuring tigers; Komodo the dragon (sometimes papier-mâché) who breathes imaginary fire and dances imaginary polkas, sometimes very old and magical, fuelling a Thames steamboat; and various unnamed but somehow familiar Ducks, Beetles, and Snails. The sun, the moon, icebergs, puddles, clouds, rivers, flowers all have their roles to play, but so do quarrelling railway stations, words like Please and Sorry, complaining of overwork, lost names whose letters become muddled, chapter headings themselves—yet the simple unaffected telling puts paid to hints of whimsy. The sheer effrontery of his little drawings that constantly interrupt the text, and the whole *joie de vivre* that lights up the gentle-hearted world of his imagination charm storyteller and small listener alike.

—Stephanie Nettell

BLACKMAN, Malorie

Nationality: British. **Born:** London, in 1962. **Career:** Has worked as a database manager in positions in Europe and the United States. **Awards:** Feminist Book Fortnight award, 1991, for *Not So Stupid!*; W.H. Smith Mind Boggling Books award, 1994, for *Hacker.* **Address:** c/o Celia MacLachlan, Publicity and Promotions Manager, Children's Books, Transworld Publishers Ltd., 61-63 Uxbridge Road, London W5 5SA, England.

Publications for Children

Fiction

Not So Stupid! Incredible Short Stories. London, Women's Press, 1990.
Blaine, You're a Brat. London, Orchard Books, 1991.
Girl Wonder and the Terrific Twins. London, Gollancz, 1991.
That New Dress. London, Simon and Schuster, 1991.
Girl Wonder's Winter Adventures. London, Gollancz, 1992.
Hacker. London, Doubleday, 1992.
Trust Me. London, Women's Press, 1992.

Operation Gadgetman. London, Doubleday, 1993.
Girl Wonder to the Rescue. London, Gollancz, 1994.
Crazy Crocs, illustrated by Tim Archbold. London, Longman, 1994.
My Friend's a Gris-Quock! London, Scholastic, 1994.
Thief! London, Doubleday, 1995.
Whizziwig, illustrated by Stephen Lee. London, Viking, 1995.
Jack Sweettooth the 73rd. London, Viking, 1995.
Deadly Dare. London, Scholastic, 1995.
Mrs. Spoon's Family, illustrated by Jan McCafferty. London, Andersen Press, 1995.
A.N.T.I.D.O.T.E. London, Doubleday, 1996.
Grandma Gertie's Haunted Handbag, illustrated by David Price. London, Heinemann, 1996.
Computer Ghost. London, Scholastic, 1997.
Pig Heart Boy. London, Doubleday, 1997.
Space Race, illustrated by Colin Mier. London, Corgi Pups, 1997.

"Betsey Biggalow" Series (illustrated by Lis Toft)

Betsey Biggalow Is Here! London, Piccadilly Press, 1992.
Betsey the Detective. London, Piccadilly Press, 1992.
Hurricane Betsey. London, Piccadilly Press, 1993.
Magic Betsey. London, Piccadilly Press, 1994.
Betsey's Birthday Surprise. London, Piccadilly Press, 1997.

Longman Book Project Series, with Wendy Body (illustrated by Kim Harley)

Rachel Versus Bonecrusher the Mighty. London, Longman, 1994.
Rachel and the Difference Thief. London, Longman, 1994.

"Puzzle Planet Adventures" Series (illustrated by Patrice Aggs)

The Mellion Moon Mystery. London, Orchard Books, 1996.
Peril on Planet Pelia. London, Orchard Books, 1996.
The Quasar Quartz Quest. London, Orchard Books, 1996.
The Secret of the Terrible Hand. London, Orchard Books, 1996.

* * *

Malorie Blackman had an auspicious introduction to writing when her first book, *Not So Stupid!,* a collection of astonishing short stories for teenagers featuring strong female characters, was selected for the 1991 Feminist Book Fortnight award in the United Kingdom. Her first novel, *Trust Me,* also for teenagers, is a powerful thriller verging on horror story in which a teenage boy turns into a vampire.

Her *Betsey Biggalow* and *Girl Wonder* books are short stories suitable for reading aloud to five- to six-year-olds, or for beginner readers to tackle alone. The main characters in both series are strong-minded, very lively young black girls who share the conviction that they can do all sorts of things that of course they can't. Betsey Biggalow lives with her family in the Caribbean and is the youngest of three children. She suffers, like all younger siblings, from the frustration that she can't do what her older brother and sister can and is always determined to try to do the same things. Her attempts—riding her big sister's bike and putting on a magic show, for instance—very often end in disaster, but Betsey always manages to come up smiling and invariably turns her disasters into triumphs. Maxine, the Girl Wonder of the titles of that series, is the eldest of three siblings; her two younger brothers are known as the "Terrific Twins." Together the three children get into all sorts of scrapes, usually led by Maxine. For example, her plan for retrieving their ball from the next-door neighbour's garden without being seen resulted in them bringing the whole fence down and ruining her flowers. Like Betsey, though, Maxine bounces back quickly and always looks on the bright side. When her mother had repaired the neighbour's fence, replaced all the damaged flowers, she grounded Maxine and the twins. Maxine complained bitterly and she says of her plan: "But it worked, didn't it? We did get our ball back!"

In the "Puzzle Planet Adventures" Blackman has created series for children who are gaining confidence in reading alone. These are slightly unconventional, as there are puzzles to solve within the story before the main characters can continue with the plot. Each lively adventure is set in space involving disappearing classes, crash landings, vanishing spaceships, and a mystery involving the Terrible Hand. *Space Race,* also for beginner readers, is a simple enough story with a gentle moral about cheating, but children will enjoy it for the idea of living on a Space Station, and owning a spaceship that runs on diamond fuel.

Mrs. Spoon's Family is a deceptively lightweight picture book text with the formidable issue of prejudice at the core. Mrs. Spoon has a cat and a dog that get on well together. The neighbouring cats on one side of the garden and dogs on the other disapprove and indoctrinate each animal into believing they should not be friends. After the cat and dog revert to type the ending is a heartening lesson about true friendship.

Blackman has written several novels aimed at 8- to 12-year-olds which are fast-moving thriller adventures. The first, *Hacker,* won the W.H. Smith Mind Boggling Books award for 1994. It is the story of how Vicky and Gib's father is arrested, accused of stealing over a million pounds from the bank where he works, by computer fraud. Vicky, a computer whiz herself, is determined to prove his innocence, but she must work fast if she is to discover the real thief before she is caught hacking into the bank's computer. Blackman was a systems programmer and database manager before becoming a full-time writer, and she uses this experience to authenticate the plot. It is indeed exciting stuff and has the reader gripped right up to the nail-biting climax.

In *Operation Gadgetman!,* Beatrice, or Beans as her friends call her, lives with her father who is an inventor. When she gets home from school one day to discover her father is not there she immediately smells a rat. She decodes the letter he has left to find he has been kidnapped. The kidnappers want to get their hands on his latest invention—a machine that can override bank cash machines and has the potential to draw out millions of pounds. Beans and her two friends use their spy kits, another of her father's inventions, to find the kidnappers before it's too late.

Thief! deals with Lydia, who is wrongly accused of stealing a school sports cup after she has been set up. Unable to face the consequences, even though she is innocent, she runs away. She then gets caught in a mysterious storm that takes her 37 years into the future. Although a slightly contrived device, it enables the plot to take some curious turns and for Lydia to see herself and her brother as they will be when they grow up. It is, however, a gripping novel that has many surprises with once again a strong female character as the lead.

In *A.N.T.I.D.O.T.E.,* Elliot wishes his mother did something more exciting than being a secretary. This is, it turns out, just a cover for spying, which Eliot discovers when she is wanted by the police for breaking into a pharmaceutical company. He can hardly believe it, but is soon caught up in trying to help clear her name, which puts him in great danger, too. Questions of loyalty are raised, as are the ethics of breaking into somewhere even if the motives are good. It is a fast-moving drama in which children take the major parts, making it compelling reading.

Pig-heart Boy is a thought-provoking book that tackles a highly topical medical and social issue. Cameron is a 13-year-old boy with a heart defect. His only chance of a transplant comes with the offer of some pioneering surgery that could replace his heart with a pig's heart. For him the choice is simple—he has the pig's heart and lives, or he doesn't and he will die before his next birthday. The shock comes when he comes out of hospital and his story becomes headline news. Suddenly his house is under siege with people outraged at the whole idea of his transplant. Blackman manages to get across the many different arguments without being didactic, and keeps the personal experience and responses of the boy and his family at the heart of the issue throughout.

Whatever age group she is writing for, Blackman creates strong, convincing characters, in realistic family situations, with good dialogue and lots of action. An important feature of her books is the deliberately understated way she writes about black people, reflecting the multicultural society to which she belongs. The main characters are very often black, but their nationality and colour are incidental to the stories. This is refreshing to find as so often black characters in children's books are only there as a form of tokenism.

—Fiona Lafferty

BLADES, Ann

Nationality: Canadian. **Born:** Ann Sager in Vancouver, British Columbia, 16 November 1947. **Education:** Crofton House School, Vancouver; University of British Columbia, Vancouver, 1965-70, teaching certificate 1967; British Columbia Institute of Technology, 1972-74, registered nurse's qualification 1974. **Family:** Two sons. **Career:** Elementary school teacher, Peace River North School District, Mile 18, British Columbia, 1967-68, Department of Indian Affairs and Northern Development, Taché, British Columbia, 1969, and Surrey School District, British Columbia, 1969-71; clerk, London, Ontario, 1972; registered nurse, Vancouver General Hospital, 1974-75, and Mt. St. Joseph Hospital, Vancouver, 1975-80. Artist: individual shows: Bau Xi Gallery, Vancouver, 1982, 1983, 1984, 1986, 1987, 1989, 1991, 1997; Bau Xi Gallery, Toronto, 1982, 1983. **Awards:** CACL Book of the Year Award, 1972, and Howard-Gibbon medal, for illustration, 1979; Canada Council Award for illustration, 1979; Elizabeth Mrazik-Cleaver Canadian Picture Book award, 1986. **Address:** 12648 26A Ave., Surrey, British Columbia V4A 2M4, Canada.

PUBLICATIONS FOR CHILDREN (ILLUSTRATED BY THE AUTHOR)

Fiction

Mary of Mile 18. Montreal and Plattsburgh, New York, Tundra, 1971; London, Bodley Head, 1976.

A Boy of Taché. Montreal and Plattsburgh, New York, Tundra, 1973.

The Cottage at Crescent Beach. Toronto, Magook, 1977.

By the Sea: An Alphabet Book. Toronto, Kids Can Press, 1985; Cambridge, Cambridge University Press, 1987.

Seasons Board Books. New York, Lothrop, 1989.

Back to the Cabin. Victoria, Orca, 1996.

*

Illustrator: *Jacques the Woodcutter* by Michael Macklem, 1977; *A Salmon for Simon,* 1978, and *Pettranella,* 1980, both by Betty Waterton; *Six Darn Cows* by Margaret Laurence, 1979; *Anna's Pet* by Margaret Atwood and Joyce Barkhouse, 1980; *A Candle for Christmas* by Jean Speare, 1986; *Ida and the Wool Smugglers* by Sue Ann Alderson, 1987; *The Singing Basket* edited by Kit Pearson, 1990; *A Dog Came, Too* by Ainslie Manson, 1993; *A Ride for Martha,* 1993, and *Pond Seasons,* 1997, by Sue Ann Alderson; contributor, *Mother Goose: A Canadian Sampler,* 1994.

Ann Blades comments:

When I was 19, I went to teach in the two-room school at Mile 18, an isolated farming community in northern British Columbia. In early spring, wanting an activity to help pass the time and impressed by the apparent lack of relevant reading material for children in rural areas, I decided to write and illustrate a book for children. I began to work on *Mary of Mile 18,* using one of my pupils, Mary, and her family as the characters in the book. I finished writing and illustrating *Mary of Mile 18* the following year, while teaching in the two-room school at Taché, an Indian reserve in central British Columbia. The next year I wrote and illustrated *A Boy of Taché,* based on a true episode that occurred while I was teaching there.

Since 1976 I have worked primarily as an illustrator and painter, which I enjoy doing most. In 1982 I began selling paintings through the Bau Xi Gallery in Vancouver and Toronto.

* * *

Requirements for a textbook rarely provoke successful literary endeavours. But the paucity of school material meaningful to children in a schoolhouse tucked away in northern British Columbia became the touchstone of Ann Blades' invention. Her charges in a remote Mennonite community 18 miles off mile 73 of the Alaska Highway would comprehend little of the stoplights, sidewalks, and manicured parks which are veritable landmarks of conventional schoolbooks, but they would have intimate knowledge of the brilliant northern lights, and of isolation, solitude, and an almost overwhelming sense of sameness. And it was these familiar elements that inspired *Mary of Mile 18,* in which the lifestyle of Mary Fehr, bespectacled child within a closely knit family, emerges with simple poignancy. Mary hopes that something different will happen, and she believes the northern lights to be harbingers of promised novelty. Something does happen in the appearance of a pup which is half wolf. But pets are an unaffordable luxury, and the pup cannot be Mary's until he proves capable of contributing to the sustaining pattern of existence. *Mary of Mile 18* suggests that creative pedagogy does indeed border on art.

Blades' second book, *A Boy of Taché,* presents a more elaborate text and a more involved plot. It is also more self-consciously instructive with ecological concerns and observations on northern lifestyles arising from several asides. Za refuses to shoot a pregnant beaver, and it is observed that nowadays there is but an occasional eagle. Two companions pass by a nearby construction camp which is building a railway. But the learning is by no means intrusive. An intriguing theme unites change and continuity. The young Indian boy, Charlie, will now begin to hunt alone, since his beloved grandfather, whose life Charlie has saved, will be forced to retire. But the youthful hero will in fact become a hunter, and his dream of manhood differs little if at all from those of his ancestors.

Blades has written and created two summer vacation books. *The Cottage at Crescent Beach* provides a plausible premise for this total commitment to the graphic arts. In this entrancing little book the picturesque quality of the words dominates any narrative stream. The intrigue of line, colour, and contrast are as apparent in the text as in the drawings. The effect resembles more the presence at a picture gallery than that of sitting at the feet of a raconteur. This is not to say that the writing does not command willing attentiveness, but that the sights and styles of life in summer isolation have an appeal exclusive of any desire to learn what comes next. The lure of the moment makes the potential sameness of the hours into a delighted onslaught of experience of the present. Walks along the railroad track, swinging from trapeze trees, and shadows of maples outside a young girl's bedroom window convey enough suggestions of their own and thus do not require the support of a strong narrative line. To term her art work illustrations is to assume the subordination of pictures to text. Blades' involvement with both art and story suggests that her tales are as graphic as they are plot filled. Neither is servant to the other, as the present tense, that most mysterious of time frames, demands the service of pen and brush. The real plot of *The Cottage at Crescent Beach* is the sustained pleasure in a moment which is continually unfolding, even when arrested.

Back to the Cabin draws on recent vacations Blades and her sons have taken. Unhappy at leaving the attractions of the city, the two boys soon become involved in activities at the lake and, when the vacation is over, they leave reluctantly. Perhaps because she is drawing on more recent experiences, Blades' illustrations lack the evocative quality that those recalling long ago days at Crescent Beach possess. However, the exuberance of the children and their joyful play in sun, rain, and storm are effectively communicated.

Blades' pictures for stories by Betty Waterton and Sue Ann Alderson reveal her ability to reinforce visually character and tone created by the authors' words. A Native boy's feelings of inadequacy and later fulfillment are indicated through his body language and facial expressions in Waterton's *A Salmon for Simon.* As she had for her own stories, Blades depicts the natural landscape in which the boy lives and with which he must come to terms. In Waterton's *Pettranella,* the heroine's sadness at leaving her old world home, her distress at losing the seeds her grandmother had given her, and her joy when they bloom in the spring are amplified by the landscapes, the dingy old world city, the dark woods, and the bright Manitoba spring.

The illustrations for Alderson's *Ida and the Wool Smugglers* and *A Ride for Martha* accurately depict late-19th-century life on a small west coast Canadian Island. The girl's struggles to establish her place in her family and her later understanding of her responsibility to her little sister are communicated through body language and facial expressions and through showing the character in relation to other people and the landscape.

—Leonard R. Mendelsohn, updated by Jon C. Stott

BLAKE, Quentin (Saxby)

Nationality: British. **Born:** 16 December 1932, Sidcup, Kent, England. **Education:** Downing College, Cambridge, M.A. 1956; University of London Institute of Education, P.G.C.E. 1956-57; attended Chelsea School of Art, 1958-59. **Military Service:** Served in the Army Education Corps, 1951-53. **Career:** Illustrator for *Punch,* beginning 1948, and other British magazines, including *Spectator*; also illustrator of children's and educational books. Free-lance illustrator since 1957. Tutor in School of Graphic Design, 1965-78; head of Illustration Department, 1978-86; visiting tutor, 1986-89; senior fellow, 1988; visiting professor since 1989, all for the Royal College of Art, London. Part-time English teacher at French Lycee in London, 1962-65. Work has been exhibited at Workshop Gallery, 1972, 1973, 1974, 1976, at the National Theatre, 1984, at the Royal Academy, 1984, 1986, 1987, and at the London Group, England, 1987. **Awards:** Child Study Association of America's Children's Books of the Year, 1969, 1974, 1985, 1986; International Board on Books for Young People, Hans Christian Andersen honor book for illustration, 1976, 1982, and 1997; *New York Times* Best Illustrated Books of the Year, 1976, 1997; British Library Association Kate Greenaway Medal high commendation, 1980; elected to Royal Designer for Industry, 1980; British Library Association Kate Greenaway Medal, 1981; Federation of Children's Book Groups Children's Book Award, 1981 and 1982; National Book League (England) Kurt Maschler Award runner-up, 1982, 1984, 1985, 1986; Silver Brush (Holland), 1986; officer, Order of the British Empire, 1988; National Book League Kurt Maschler Award 1990; Ragazzi Award, Bologna Book Fair, 1996. **Agent:** Georges Borchardt, Inc., 136 East 57th St., New York, New York 10022; A. P. Watt Ltd., 20 John St., London WC1N 2DR, England. **Address:** Flat 8, 30 Bramham Gardens, London SW5 0HF, England.

PUBLICATIONS FOR CHILDREN

Picture Books (illustrated by the author)

Patrick. London, Cape, 1968; New York, Walck, 1969.
Jack and Nancy. London, Cape, 1969.
Angelo. London, Cape, 1970.
Snuff. Philadelphia, Lippincott, 1973.
Lester at the Seaside. London, Collins Picture Lions, 1975.
With John Yeoman, *The Puffin Book of Improbable Records,* London, Puffin, 1975; as *The Improbable Book of Records,* New York, Atheneum, 1976.
The Adventures of Lester. London, British Broadcasting Corporation, 1978.
Mister Magnolia. Merrimack, 1980.
Quentin Blake's Nursery Rhyme Book. London, Cape, 1983; New York, Harper, 1984.
The Story of the Dancing Frog. London, Cape, 1984; New York, Knopf, 1985.
Mrs. Armitage on Wheels. London, Cape, 1987; New York, Knopf, 1988.
Quentin Blake's ABC. New York, Knopf, 1989.
All Join In. London, Cape, 1990; Boston, Little, Brown, 1991.
Cockatoos. London, Cape, 1992.
Simpkin. London, Cape, 1993.

Clown. London, Cape, 1995.
Mrs. Armitage and the Big Wave. London, Cape, 1997.
Ten Frogs. London, Pavillion, 1997.
The Green Ship. London, Cape, 1998.

Other

Quentin Blake Agenda, 1994.
With John Cassidy, *Drawing for the Artistically Undiscovered.* Klutz Press, 1998.

Compiler, *Custard and Company: Poems by Ogden Nash.* London, Kestrel, 1979; Boston, Little, Brown, 1980.

Editor, *The Quentin Blake Book of Nonsense Verse.* New York, Viking, 1994.
Editor, *The Quentin Blake Book of Nonsense Stories.* New York, Viking, 1996.

Publications for Adults

A Band of Angels (picture book). London, Gordon Fraser, 1969.

*

Media Adaptations: "Patrick" (filmstrip), Weston Woods, 1973; "Snuff" (filmstrip with record or cassette), Weston Woods, 1975; "Great Day for Up!" (filmstrip), Random House.

Illustrator: *The Wonderful Button* by Evan Hunter, 1961; *Good Morning, Miss Dove* by Frances Gray Patton, 1961; *The Boys' Country Book* edited by John Moore, 1961; *Albert the Dragon* by Rosemary Weir, 1961; *Listen and I'll Tell You* by Edward Korel, 1962, Lippincott, 1964; *Punky: Mouse for a Day* by John Moreton, 1962; *My Son-in-Law the Hippopotamus* by Ezo, 1962; *Tales of a Wicked Uncle* by Rupert Croft-Cooke, 1963; *The Gentle Knight* by Richard Schickel, 1964; *The Next-Doors* by Joan Tate, 1964; *Albert the Dragon and the Centaur* by Weir, 1964; *The Further Adventures of Albert the Dragon* by Weir, 1964; *Gardeners' Question Time* by Fred Loads, Alan Gemmell, and Bil Sowerbutts, 1964, second series, 1966; *Riddles, Riddles Everywhere* by Ennis Rees, 1964; *The Oxford Books of Stories for Juniors* edited by James Britton, three volumes, 1964-66; *Pun Fun* by Rees, 1965; *Motoring and the Motorist* by Bill Hartley, 1965; *Aphrodisiacs in Your Garden* by Charles Connell, 1965; *Home Economics* by Barry Ruth, 1966; *Around the World in Eighty Days* by Jules Verne, 1966; *Puzzles for Pleasure and Leisure* by Thomas L. Hirsch, 1966; *Aristide* by Robert Tibber, 1966; *Give a Dog a Good Name* by Marjorie Bilbow and Antony Bilbow, 1967; *Bits and Pieces* by Tate, 1967; *Tiny Tall Tales* by Rees, 1967; *Luke's Garden* by Tate, 1967; *Put on Your Thinking Cap* by Helen J. Fletcher, 1968; *Listen and Read with Peter and Molly* by G. Broughton, 1968; *Your Animal Book* edited by Gordon Fraser, 1969; *Living with Technology* by H. P. Rickman, 1969; *Success with English: The Penguin Course* by Broughton, 1969; *The First Elephant Comes to Ireland* by Nathan Zimelman, 1969; *Mr. Horrox and the Gratch* by James Reeves, 1969; *Gillygaloos and the Gollywhoppers: Tall Tales about Mythical Monsters* by Rees, 1969; *Hogmanay and Tiffany: The Names of Feasts and Fasts* by Gillian Edwards, 1970; *The Birthday Party* by D. Mackay, B. Thompson, and P. Schaub, 1970; *The Good Tiger* by Elizabeth Bowen, 1970; *Puzzles and Quizzles* by Fletcher, 1970; *Kibby's Big Feat* by Thomas Corddry, 1970; *The Witch's Cat* by H. Thomson, 1971; *My Friend Mr. Leakey* by J. B. S. Haldane, 1971; *Play School Play Ideas* by Ruth Craft, 1971; *The Birds* by Aristophanes, translated by Dudley Fitts, 1971; *The Ages of Man: From Sav-age to Sew-age* by Marcus Cunliffe, 1971; *Peter and Molly* by Broughton, 1972; *McBroom's Wonderful One-Acre Farm* by Sid Fleischman, 1972; *Pigeon of Paris* by Natalie Savage Carlson, 1972; *Wizards Are a Nuisance* by Norman Hunter, 1973; *The Armada Lion Book of Young Verse* by Julia Watson, 1973; *The Thingummy-jig* by R. C. Scriven, 1973; *Eating* by F. Knowles and B. Thompson, 1973; *Grimble* by Clement Freud, 1974; *Great Day for Up!* by Dr. Seuss (pseudonym of Theodor Seuss Geisel), 1974; *The Puffin Joke Book* edited by Bronnie Cunningham, 1974; *The Incredible Kidnapping* by Willis Hall, 1975; *Kidnapped at Christmas* by Hall, 1975; *Peter and Molly's Revision Book* by Broughton, 1975; *The Hunting of the Snark* by Lewis Carroll, 1976; *The Bed Book* by Sylvia Plath, 1976; *Horseshoe Harry and the Whale* by Adele De Leeuw, 1976; *Monster Books* by Ellen Blance and Ann Cook, 24 volumes, 1976-1978; *Here Comes McBroom!* by Fleischman, 1976; *The Nonstop Nonsense Book* by Margaret Mahy, 1977; *Of Quarks, Quasars, and Other Quirks: Quizzical Poems for the Supersonic Age* edited by Sara Brewton, John E. Brewton, and John B. Blackburn, 1977; *Willie the Squowse* by Ted Allan, 1977, Hastings House, 1978; *Play School Ideas 2* by Carole Ward, 1977; *Cold Comfort Farm* by Stella Gibbons, 1977; *Funny Business* edited by Cunningham, 1978; *What Difference Does It Make, Danny?* by Helen Young, 1980; *Black Mischief* by Evelyn Waugh, 1981; *McBroom and the Great Race* by Fleischman, 1981; *Cyril Bonhamy v. Madam Big* by Jonathan Gathorne-Hardy, 1981; *Up with Skool!* edited by Tony Lacey, 1981; *Joseph and the Amazing Technicolor Dreamcoat* by Tim Rice and Andrew Lloyd Webber, 1982; *Cyril Bonhamy and the Great Drain Robbery* by Gathorne-Hardy, 1983; *Scoop* by Waugh, 1983; *Animal Farm* by George Orwell, 1984; *How the Camel Got His Hump* by Rudyard Kipling, 1984, Bedrick Books, 1985; *Cyril Bonhamy and Operation Ping* by Gathorne-Hardy, 1984; *A Lamp for the Lambchops* by Jeff Brown, 1985; *The Great Piratical Rumbustification and the Librarian and the Robbers* by Mahy, 1986; *Frankie's Hat* by Jan Mark, 1986; *Can You Get Warts from Touching Toads?: Ask Dr. Pete* by Dr. Pete Rowan, 1986; *Stanley and the Magic Lamp* by Jeff Brown, 1991; *Algernon* by Hilaire Belloc, 1991; *Voyages to the Sun and the Moon* by Cyrano de Bergerac, 1991; *Alphabeasts* by Dick King-Smith, 1992; *The Box of Delights* by John Masefield, 1992; *Cyril Bonhamy and the Great Drain Robbery* by Jonathan Gathorne-Herdy, 1992; *The Midnight Folk* by John Masefield, 1992; *Cautionary Verse* by Helloc, 1993; *The Winter Sleepwalker* by Belloc, 1994; *A Christmas Carol* by Charles Dickens, 1995; *Elephants Have Right of Way* by Sylvia Sherry, 1995; *Meeting Midnight* by Carol Ann Duffy, 1995; *Don Quixote de la Mancha* by Miguel de Cervantes, 1995; *Breakfast with Dolly* by John Hedgecoe, 1995; *The Seven Voyages of Sinbad the Sailor,* 1996.

Illustrator: (All by Joan Aiken) *The Escaped Black Mamba,* 1973; *Tales of Arabel's Raven,* 1974, published as *Arabel's Raven,* 1974; *The Bread Bin,* 1974; *Mortimer's Tie,* 1976; *Mortimer and the Sword Excalibur,* 1979; *The Spiral Stair,* 1979; *Arabel and Mortimer* (includes *Mortimer's Tie, The Spiral Stair,* and *Mortimer and the Sword Excalibur*), 1979; *Mortimer's Portrait on Glass,* 1980; *The Mystery of Mr. Jones's Disappearing Taxi,* 1980;

Mortimer's Cross, 1983; *Mortimer Says Nothing*, 1987; *Mortimer and Arabel*, 1992; *The Winter Sleepwalker and Other Stories*, 1994; *Red Fox*, 1995; *A Handful of Gold*, 1995.

Illustrator: (All by Patrick Campbell) *Come Here Till I Tell You*, 1960; *Constantly in Pursuit*, 1962; *Brewing Up in the Basement*, 1963; *How to Become a Scratch Golfer*, 1963; *The P-P-Penguin Patrick Campbell*, 1965; *Rough Husbandry*, 1965; *A Feast of True Fandangles*, 1979.

Illustrator: (All by Roald Dahl) *The Enormous Crocodile*, 1978; *The Twits*, 1980; *George's Marvellous Medicine*, 1981, published in the United States as *George's Marvelous Medicine*, 1982; *The BFG*, 1982; *Roald Dahl's Revolting Rhymes*, 1982; *The Witches*, 1983; *Dirty Beasts*, 1984; *The Giraffe and the Pelly and Me*, 1985; *Matilda*, 1988; *Rhyme Stew*, 1989; *Esio Trot*, 1990; *The Dahl Diary*, 1991; *Revolting Rhymes and Dirty Beasts*, 1991; *The Vicar of Nibbleswicke*, 1991; *Roald Dahl's Guide to Railway Safety*, 1991; *My Year*, 1993; *The Roald Dahl Quizbook I* and *II* edited by Richard Maher and Sylvia Bond, 1994, 1996; *Roald Dahl's Revolting Recipes* edited by Felicity Dahl and Josie Fison, 1994; *Danny the Chamption of the World*, 1994; *The Magic Finger*, 1995; *Fantastic Mr. Fox*, 1996; *The Roald Dahl Treasury*, 1997.

Illustrator: (All by Nils-Olof Franzen) *Agaton Sax and the Diamond Thieves*, 1965, translated by Evelyn Ramsden, 1967; *Agaton Sax and the Scotland Yard Mystery*, 1969; *Agaton Sax and the Incredible Max Brothers*, 1970; *Agaton Sax and the Criminal Doubles*, 1971; *Agaton Sax and the Colossus of Rhodes*, 1972; *Agaton Sax and the London Computer Plot*, 1973; *Agaton Sax and the League of Silent Exploders*, 1974; *Agaton Sax and the Haunted House*, 1975; *Agaton Sax and the Big Rig*, 1976; *Agaton Sax and Lispington's Grandfather Clock*, 1978.

Illustrator: (All by Russell Hoban) *How Tom Beat Captain Najork and His Hired Sportsmen*, 1974; *A Near Thing for Captain Najork*, 1975; *The Twenty Elephant Restaurant*, 1980; *Ace Dragon Ltd.*, 1980; *The Marzipan Pig*, 1986; *The Rain Door*, 1986; *Monsters*, 1990.

Illustrator: (All by J. P. Martin) *Uncle*, 1964, Coward, 1966; *Uncle Cleans Up*, 1965; *Uncle and His Detective*, 1966; *Uncle and the Treacle Trouble*, 1967; *Uncle and Claudius the Camel*, 1969; *Uncle and the Battle for Badgertown*, 1973.

Illustrator: (All by Michael Rosen) *Mind Your Own Business*, 1974; *Wouldn't You Like to Know?*, 1977; *The Bakerloo Flea*, 1979; *You Can't Catch Me!*, 1981; *Quick, Let's Get Out of Here*, 1984; *Don't Put Mustard in the Custard*, 1986; *Under the Bed*, 1986; *Smelly Jelly Smelly Fish*, 1986; *Spollyolly-diddly-tiddlyitis*, 1987; *Hard-Boiled Legs: The Breakfast Book*, 1987; *Down at the Doctor's: The Sick Book*, 1988; *The Best of Michael Rosen: Poetry for Kids*, 1995; *Don't Put Mustard in the Custard*, 1996; *Tea in the Sugar Bowl*, 1997.

Illustrator: (All by John Yeoman) *A Drink of Water and Other Stories*, 1960; *The Boy Who Sprouted Antlers*, 1961, revised edition, 1977; *The Bear's Winter House*, 1969; *Alphabet Soup*, 1969; *The Bear's Water Picnic*, 1970; *Sixes and Sevens*, 1971; *Mouse Trouble*, 1972; *Beatrice and Vanessa*, 1974; *The Young Performing Horse*, 1977; *The Wild Washerwomen: A New Folktale*, 1979; *Rumbelow's Dance*, 1982; *The Hermit and the Bear*, 1984; *Our Village (Poems)*, 1988; *Old Mother Hubbard's Dog Dresses Up*, 1990; *Old Mother Hubbard's Dog Learns to Play*, 1990; *Old Mother Hubbard's Dog Needs a Doctor*, 1990; *Old Mother Hubbard's Dog Takes up Sport*, 1990; *The Adventures of Old Mother Hubbard's Dog*, 1991; *The World's Laziest Duck and Other Amazing Records*, 1991; *Featherbrains*, 1993; *The Singing Tortoise and Other Animal Folk Tales*, 1993; *The Family Album*, 1993; *The Do-It-Yourself House that Jack Built*, 1994; *Mr. Nodd's Ark*, 1995; *Sinbad the Sailor*, 1996; *The Prince's Gift*, 1997; *Up with Birds*, 1998.

* * *

First, last, and all the time, Quentin Blake is an artist. He thinks in visual terms of line and tone. While he is highly sensitive to the importance of words, their meaning and their music, they are for him a stimulus to design. He has become a writer by default. For most of his professional life there has been no shortage of suitable texts, stories, and poems that echo his own philosophies, reflect his kind of humor, produce in him sympathetic fantasies. Being, as his huge output confirms, a compulsive worker, there are inevitably times when nothing is immediately at hand to fire his creativity; then, he writes his own text. It is still a text that has visual rather than verbal origins. The pictures, whether on paper or still in his mind, lead to the words.

This creative method can be seen in action during his visits to schools and libraries to talk to an audience of young children. Provided with a continuous roll of cartridge paper, he speaks informally and without script, armed only with pen or pencil. His subject matter comes from audience members, who throw out ideas at random, which the artist fields expertly and turns into images on the paper. As a picture-story takes shape in public, Blake seems, and indeed is, working spontaneously in conjuring pictures out of the air. He is drawing upon the vast reserve of pictures stored in his mind, relating them and the words with which he matches them to the ideas offered by his young audience. As a stand-up comedy show, it is magnificent. Sometimes this excellent entertainment may have in it the seeds of a book as yet unwritten.

Eight years passed between the publication of Blake's first illustrated book and that of one to his own texts. Of a total output of more than two hundred illustrated books, few identify him as author. It is a proportion that does not seem to displease him. Unlike some author/artists (Beatrix Potter and Edward Ardizzone, for example, who both thought highly of their skill with words), he makes no special claims for his own stories and rhymes. It does not follow that he lacks a feeling for words. His own stories are told dexterously, with style and economy. Better than most, he knows just where a verbal phrase or description is needed, when a picture will do the job more effectively. As oral storytellers have discovered, he paces his narrative well so that the page turns precisely when sense and image have come together. His words have wit as well as a zany humor.

Reading Blake's books "cold" gives little idea of their potential. They must be performed, whether to a school class or within the family circle. Then it is seen how well they lend themselves to audience participation. The nonsense rhymes in *All Join In* demand this. So, in a less rowdy way, does *Mister Magnolia*, in which a reiterated chorus line, "Mister Magnolia has only one boot," loses none of its poignancy when the audience chants it. Mister Magnolia himself is a typical Blake creation, with his admiral's hat and jacket at odds with the rest of his costume, his sadness and his good humor. Mrs. Armitage, in *Mrs. Armitage on Wheels,* is from the same mould. Mastering her bike, she shows herself to be infinitely resourceful, endlessly patient. Breakspear, her faithful hound who has been provided with his own seat on the vehicle, is a characteristic Blake animal. Breakspear's role is only a supporting one. The frog in *The Story of the Dancing Frog* is a star rising splendidly to his crisis when, trapped in a blazing skyscraper, he dives headlong into a bucket of water.

Blake is no less the creative artist in those books that he shares with an author. Even when the writer has a name as formidable as Roald Dahl, Blake, far from being overawed, can lift the book onto an altogether higher plan by an interpretation that uncovers hidden subtleties in the story. When he is totally at ease with the author, a true cooperation emerges. His work with Joan Aiken in a series of "Mortimer" stories (first made for broadcasting) is of this kind. Aiken's grotesque humor stimulates Blake to diverting excesses of fantasy as raven and child pursue their adventures, verbal and visual caricatures working as one. Blake, too, seems to be singularly in harmony with Russell Hoban in the seriously crazy humor of two "Captain Najork" books. He is closest of all to John Yeoman in a series of picture books spread over many years. Theirs is a two-way collaboration in which author and artist urge one another into higher reaches of absurdity, but always with their feet planted firmly in a recognizable world.

Modern publishing policies have meant that Blake has had relatively limited access to adult books. Most of his work in this field has been with the Folio Society, where he has reacted joyously to quality paper and printing and to the challenge of congenial and demanding texts. Perhaps his most creative work as illustrator is to be found in the Folio *Hunting of the Snark* where, undeterred by the example of definitive illustrations by Henry Holiday and by Mervyn Peake's unforgettable and idiosyncratic designs, he strikes a happy balance between interpretation and decoration in a sequence of simple, provocative, always mysterious images.

Blake's place as an outstanding modern British illustrator has been acknowledged in many ways, not only by his OBE in 1988, but by such marks of popularity as the Post Office adopting his pictures for Dickens' *Christmas Carol* on the 1997 Christmas postage stamps. As Roald Dahl's work is posthumously mined for quiz books and guides to railway safety, Blake seems the inevitable choice for illustrator, his visual interpretations being those most closely identified with Dahl's characters and perspective on the world. The cheerful, self-possessed eccentrics who populate Blake's illustrations give his own flavour to numerous new versions of classics. Blake, who studied English at Cambridge, expresses a sensitivity to language both as author and as illustrator, and his visual reinterpretations of classic texts often reveal new sides to their humour and—sometimes—pathos. The casual and seemingly effortless style of his whimsy matches the deadpan humour of Hilaire Belloc's texts as no other illustrations have done since the original drawings by "B.T.B," while in his monochrome pictures for *Don Quixote* a pensive melancholy underlies the humour.

—Marcus Crouch, updated by Gwyneth Evans

BLEGVAD, Erik

Nationality: Danish. **Born:** Copenhagen, 3 March 1923. **Education:** Copenhagen School of Arts and Crafts, 1941-44. **Military Service:** Royal Danish Air Force, 1945-47. **Family:** Married Lenore Hochman in 1950; two sons. **Career:** Artist and illustrator in Copenhagen, London, and Paris, 1947-1951; illustrator of children's books since 1951. Exhibits include "Fifty Years of Illustration: Erik Blegvad," Duncan of Jordanstone College of Art, Dundee, Scotland, 1991, Grays School of Art, Aberdeen, 1991, and several American Institute of Graphic Arts exhibits. **Awards:** Children's Book Showcase titles, 1975, for *Mushroom Center Disaster,* and 1976, for *The Winter Bear*; *New York Times* Ten Best-Illustrated Books, 1978, for *This Little Pig-A-Wig: And Other Rhymes about Pigs*; *Horn Book* honor list, 1979, for *Self-Portrait: Erik Blegvad.* **Address:** 4 Crescent Mansions, 113 Fulham Rd., London SW3 6RL, England; "Mountain Spring Farm", Wardsboro, Vermont, U.S.A.

PUBLICATIONS FOR CHILDREN (ILLUSTRATED BY THE AUTHOR)

Translator

The Swineherd by Hans Christian Andersen. New York, Harcourt, 1958.

The Emperor's New Clothes by Hans Christian Andersen. New York, Harcourt, 1959.

Hans Christian Andersen: Stories and Fairy Tales by Hans Christian Andersen. London, Heinemann, 1993; as *Twelve Tales,* New York, McElderry, 1994.

Reteller

Burnie's Hill: A Traditional Nursery Rhyme. New York, Atheneum, 1978.

The Three Little Pigs. New York, Atheneum, 1979.

Other

Self-Portrait: Erik Blegvad. Reading, Massachusetts, Addison-Wesley, 1979.

*

Illustrator: *Madame Prunier's Fiskekogebog* by E. Prunier, 1947; *Les Pays Nordiques* by Doré Ogrizek, 1950; *Story of Peace and War* by Thomas Franklin Galt, 1952; *Superstitious: Here's Why!* by Julie F. Batchelor and Claudia de Lys, 1954; *Complete Book of Cheese* by Bob Brown, 1955; *Village Band Mystery,* 1956, and *Flivver,* 1958, by Lee Kingman; *Myrtle Albertina's Secret,* 1956, and *Myrtle Albertina's Song,* 1958, by Lillian Pohlmann; *Greenwillow,* 1956, and *Journey to Christmas,* 1958, by B.J. Chute; *Amazing Vacation* by Dan Wickenden, 1956; *Oddity Land* by Edward Anthony, 1957; *Bed-Knob and Broomstick* by Mary Norton, 1957; *Late Spring* by Jean Fritz, 1957; *The Adventures of Rinaldo* by Isabella Holt, 1959; *The Gammage Cup* by Carol Kendall, 1959; *Having a Friend* by Betty Miles, 1959; *The Little Old Train* by Margaret Otto, 1960; *Jack Mack* by Robert Paul Smith, 1960; *Plenty of Fish* by Millicent Selsam, 1960; *Where's Willie?* by

Seymour Reit, 1961; *The Last of the Wizards* by Ronna Jaffe, 1961; *I'm Hiding,* 1961, *See What I Found,* 1962, *I'm Not Me,* 1963, *Happy Birthday!,* 1964, and *I'm Waiting,* 1966, all by Myra Cohn Livingston; *Mud Pies and Other Recipes* by Marjorie Winslow, 1961; *The Diamond in the Window,* 1962, *The Swing in the Summer House,* 1967, and *The Astonishing Stereoscope,* 1971, all by Jane Langton; *Dusty and the Fiddlers,* 1962, and *Pony in the Schoolhouse,* 1964, by Miska Miles; *Elephi* by Jean Stafford, 1962; *The Ballad of the Pilgrim Cat* by Leonard Wibberley, 1962; *The Pepperidge Farm Cookbook* by Margaret Rudkin, 1963; *The Five Pennies* by Barbara Brenner, 1963; *Elisabeth the Bird Watcher,* 1963, *Elisabeth the Treasure Hunter,* 1964, and *Elisabeth and the Marsh Mystery,* 1966, all by Felice Holman; *A Year Is a Window* by Richard W. Jackson, 1963; *A Time to Recall* by Helen Taylor, 1963; *The Dirty Old Man* by Richard Allingham, 1965; *The Goodbyes of Magnus Marmalade,* 1966, and *Phoebe and the Prince,* 1969, by Doris Orgel; *Beginning to Read Poetry,* edited by Sally Clithero, 1967; *The Cat and the Coffee Drinkers* by Max Steele, 1969; *The Cat from Nowhere* by Monica Stirling, 1969; *Emily's Autumn* by Janice Udry, 1969; *The Conscience Pudding,* 1970, and *The Complete Book of Dragons,* 1972, by E. Nesbit; *Miss Bianca in the Orient,* 1970, *Miss Bianca in the Antarctic,* 1971, and *Miss Bianca and the Bridesmaid,* 1972, all by Margery Sharp; *Bonnie Bess: The Weathervane Horse* by Alvin Tresselt, 1970; *The Tenth Good Thing about Barney* by Judith Viorst, 1971; *The Finches' Fabulous Furnace* by Roger Wolcott Drury, 1971; *The Gift of the Magi* by O. Henry, 1971; *The Wind's Child* by Mark Taylor, 1973; *The Narrow Passage* by Oliver Butterworth, 1973; *Polly's Tiger* by Joan Phipson, 1973; *The Mushroom Center Disaster,* 1974, *Water Pennies and Other Poems,* 1991, and *Hurry, Hurry, Mary Dear,* 1998, by N. M. Bodecker; *The Winter Bear* by Ruth Craft, 1974; *The Dollhouse Caper* by Jean O'Connell, 1975; *The Five in the Forest,* 1974, *The Pleasant Fieldmouse Storybook,* 1977, *The Pleasant Fieldmouse Valentine Trick,* 1977, and *Peter and the Troll Baby,* 1984, all by Jan Wahl; *May I Visit?,* 1976, *Someone New,* 1978, and *I Like to Be Little,* 1990, all by Charlotte Zolotow; *Blueberries Lavender* by Nancy Dingman Watson, 1977; *A Child's Garden of Verses* by Robert Louis Stevenson, 1978; *Yesterday's Snowman* by Gail Mack, 1979; *The Yellow Fairy Book* by Andrew Lang, edited by Brian Alderson, 1980; *Rare Treasures from Grimm: Fifteen Little-Known Tales* compiled and translated by Ralph Manheim, 1981; *Cat Walk* by Mary Stolz, 1983; *Little, Little Sister* by Jane L. Curry, 1990; *With One White Wing: Puzzles in Poems and Pictures,* 1995, and *Riddle Road: Puzzles in Poems and Pictures,* 1999, by Elizabeth Spires.

Illustrator: (All written or edited by Lenore Blegvad) *Mr. Jensen and Cat,* 1965; *One Is for the Sun,* 1968; *The Great Hamster Hunt,* 1969; *Moon-Watch Summer,* 1972; *Mittens for Kittens: And Other Nursery Rhymes about Cats,* 1974; *Hark! Hark! The Dogs Do Bark: And Other Rhymes about Dogs,* 1975; *This Little Pig-a-Wig: And Other Rhymes about Pigs,* 1978; *The Parrot in the Garret: And Other Rhymes about Dwellings,* 1982; *Anna Banana and Me,* 1985; *This Is Me,* 1986; *Rainy Day Kate,* 1988; *A Sound of Leaves,* 1996.

Critical Studies: "A View from the Island: European Picture Books 1967-76" by Brian Alderson, in *Illustrators of Children's Books 1967-1976,* compiled by Lee Kingman, Grace Allen Hogarth, and Harriet Quimby, Boston, Horn Book, 1978; *Self-Portrait: Erik Blegvad* by Erik Blegvad, Reading, Massachusetts, Addison-Wesley, 1979; entry in *Something about the Author,* Vol. 66, Detroit, Gale, 1991; review of *Twelve Tales* by Ann A. Flowers, in *Horn Book,* November-December 1994, 729.

Erik Blegvad comments:

I think the text should be the most important element and the picture should be the complement. I never became a real "gung ho" picture book artist where there are just a few lines of text and this enormous picture in full color. I prefer the other imbalance, where the text is the dominating part and the drawing is just a suggestion of what you're reading. It looks so nice on the page when there is a column of text and then the drawing.

In retrospect it is obvious that I was a very lucky person. A life in aviation was my own choice of career. And as soon as I finished school I was accepted as an apprentice in a famous Danish machine shop, for a four year education, to become a mechanic. World War II, which ruined so many lives, saved, or at least changed mine. I left the factory floor when my employers began working for the Germans in the winter 1940-41 and gained entrance to the municipal art school in Copenhagen. Here my drawing talent, so warmly admired by my family, quickly revealed itself to be quite ordinary. As in my earlier schools I just managed to hang on in the lower echelons of students and graduated in 1944 with the lowest graduation marks possible. It was rumored that the decision to let me graduate was a result of my having been arrested by the Gestapo in the spring of 1944. That summer I was free again and ready to begin a career in Copenhagen as a commercial artist. In that business nobody ever asks about your grades in art school. I worked in two advertising agencies during the last year of the war in Europe. After the liberation of Denmark I served one and a half years in the Danish Air Force. I volunteered for service with the British forces as an interpreter in occupied Germany during the winter and spring of 1946, and, when demobilised I left Copenhagen for Paris. There I stayed in humble circumstances for a couple of years working for "Paris Presse" which published newspapers and the fledgling ladies magazine *Elle.* Working for *Elle* was a watershed for me. I was well paid and had all the work I could handle. In 1950 I married Lenore Hochman from New York. She was an art student at the studios of Andre Lhôte and Fernand Léger and a graduate of Vassar College. In 1951 we left Paris for New York, where I illustrated stories and articles for *Woman's Day* and other magazines. I still illustrate a calendar each year for *Woman's Day.* In 1952 I illustrated the first of many American children's books. *The Story of Peace and War* by Tom Galt, published by Thos y Crowell, in black and white, of course. In 1954 Margaret K. McElderry gave me *Superstitious? Here's Why* by Julie F. Batchelor and Claudia de Lys to illustrate, and the rest is, in a manner of speaking, history. I have a wonderful friendship with Margaret McElderry. Also with some of "my" authors. I'm even married to one of them. I have a wonderful life illustrating. Anyone liking books and eager to draw would be foolish not to become an illustrator.

* * *

As the illustrator of approximately 100 children's books, ranging from novels to retellings of folktales, as well as numerous magazine articles and such features as the *Woman's Day* calendars and the original serial publication of Mary Norton's *The Borrowers,* Erik Blegvad's illustrations are probably more familiar than his name. As his comment indicates, he views his illustrations as secondary to the text. In his autobiographical *Self-Portrait* he comments: "Illustrating a children's book gives me a role which seems natural, accompanist rather than soloist."

Self-Portrait reveals details about Blegvad's life and also shows his development as an artist. The book includes photographs, doodles, envelope designs, the work of other members of his family, and samples of drafts of a title page all combined and unified in strikingly designed pages. Although he has translated and illustrated a few Hans Christian Andersen tales, retold *The Three Little Pigs* (only slightly modifying the classic Joseph Jacobs version), and collaborated with his wife, artist and writer Lenore Blegvad, on collections of nursery rhymes and on her own books, he is one of the few picture book artists who has not written his own texts.

His concentration on images indicates his respect for the texts he has illustrated, which have been consistently high in quality. One of the first books he illustrated was Mary Norton's *Bed-Knob and Broomstick* (1957), followed by Carol Kendall's Newbery honor-winning *The Gammage Cup* in 1959. He began illustrating books written by his wife, Lenore Blegvad, in 1965 with *Mr. Jensen and Cat,* a collaboration that continued into the 1990s, and has included many highly successful books, among them *The Great Hamster Hunt* (1969), *Anna Banana and Me* (1985), and a series of small books of illustrated rhymes beginning with *Mittens for Kittens* (1974) and continuing through *The Parrot in the Garret* (1982).

Lenore Blegvad's *The Great Hamster Hunt* (1969) is illustrated entirely in black and white india-ink drawings with careful attention to detail in the interior and exterior settings, and in the body language and facial expressions of the characters. Nicholas, who longs for a pet, is shown jumping out of his chair with excitement, shoelaces flying, when his friend asks him to take care of his pet hamster while he is on vacation. Harvey, the hamster, looks through the bars of his cage with a melting gaze. Nicholas loves caring for Harvey, and does a good job, until the last night, when Harvey escapes from the cage and disappears. Mother and Father join in the search for the missing Harvey, mother crawling on the floor of Nicholas's room among the clutter of tools, toys, shoes, magazines, and art supplies. Ultimately, Nicholas captures Harvey and all ends happily. The illustrations on nearly every page help develop the story and add attractive spaces between the blocks of text.

The Winter Bear by Ruth Craft, illustrated with ink and water color washes, has continued to be a popular book, although it received little attention at its time of publication in 1974. The book jacket from a distance looks almost photographic, with its web of dark twigs and branches in the foreground, soft brown earth and a pale blue sky behind, and a small brown teddy bear caught upside down in the branches. Brian Alderson, writing in *Illustrators of Children's Books 1967-1976,* praised the conversational rhythms of the text as a "pleasure to read aloud," and found the illustrations "perfectly attuned to it. From the wintery patterning of the board covers, the snow-flecked endpapers, and the scene-setting of the frontispiece, the artist accompanies the reader into the atmosphere of the story. By force of both line and color Erik Blegvad gives visible life to the character at the heart of Ruth Craft's story and the result is a book which, whatever its modest pretensions, is perfectly managed, and hence deeply satisfying."

In *The Doll House Caper* (1975) by Jean S. O'Connell, Blegvad returns to black and white to illustrate a somewhat longer story. He also returns to a fascination with small things and relative sizes that began with *The Borrowers.* Blegvad's pictures manage to convey that the dolls are dolls even when they come alive, and his human characters are never mistaken for dolls. In one vividly realized scene, thick with cross-hatching and a range of light and dark values, the dollhouse family peers out of its dollhouse windows at the enormous faces of human robbers staring in—"All those little fellas are staring at me," said the younger robber, "like real."

Burnie's Hill (1977), a picture-book version of a familiar nursery rhyme, reveals an entirely different style of art—luminescent, atmospheric water colors, with only an occasional use of line. The pictures progress from summer, all in soft greens and blues, to fall, with leaves turning red and orange and a fire throwing sparks into a twilight sky, to the browns, grays, and snow flakes of a winter that becomes white and blue before merging into early spring and back to summer again. In each scene two children, often accompanied by animals, ask the familiar sequence of questions. A later book that uses this same soft style in warmly glowing colors is Charlotte Zolotow's *I Like to Be Little* (1987), with its engaging dialogue between a mother and a little girl who tells what she likes about being little: "I can skip when I'm glad. Grown-ups don't skip when they're glad." The child skips through colorful fallen leaves.

The subdued colors and clean, simple lines of the illustrations in *This Little Pig-A-Wig* (1978) are reminiscent of those of Randolph Caldecott, and lend the book the appearance of a much earlier era. As in the case of Caldecott's own work, the stories are extended through the details in the pictures. One of the poems, "This Little Piggy Went to Market" is a perfect, economical, picture story told through the rhyme and three bands of pictures in black and white, complete on one small page. Blegvad's version of the classic *Three Little Pigs* (1980) is also a small masterpiece with an effectively hairy and wild-looking wolf, who, to the shock of some readers, eats two of the pigs (but not before seasoning and roasting with an apple in the mouth). The wolf himself is eventually eaten by the resourceful third little pig, who accompanies his meal in great style, with wine, a white tablecloth, and candlelight.

Blegvad illustrated two books written by his friend, countryman, and fellow illustrator N. M. Bodecker: *The Mushroom Center Disaster* (1978), which again draws the reader and viewer into a miniature world in detail, and *Water Pennies* (1991), which almost certainly was intended as a tribute to Bodecker, who died in 1988. The pleasant-looking gentleman with a thick mop of hair and bushy mustache who appears throughout the pages of this book of poems about the small creepy-crawlies that inhabit the edges of a pond looks very much like Bodecker.

The illustrations for Andersen's *Twelve Tales* (1994) reveal an attention to detail and an ability to capture the whimsy, pathos, and nuances in the stories without overwhelming them. As Ann Flowers comments in her review in *Horn Book,* "Andersen's opposing qualities of childlike ingenuousness and rueful understanding of human nature are clearly heard. The illustrations, small and neat and delicately detailed, seem to contain the essence of Denmark and Andersen. A perfect collaboration and just right for young readers." Continuing to move in new directions in his fifth decade as an illustrator, his colorful watercolor illustrations for *With One White Wing: Puzzles in Poems and Pictures* by Elizabeth Spires have been praised for providing enough clues to make it possible for young readers to guess the answers to the riddles. Blegvad's long and distinguished career, and the pleasures that his illustrations provide, suggest that the contribution of the artist who plays the role of modest accompanist is, afterall, an important one.

—Linnea Hendrickson

BLOS, Joan W(insor)

Nationality: American. **Born:** New York City, 9 December 1928. **Education:** Vassar College, Poughkeepsie, New York, B.A. 1950; City College of New York, M.A. in psychology 1957. **Family:** Married Peter Blos, Jr., in 1953; one son (deceased) and one daughter. **Career:** Research assistant, Jewish Board of Guardians, New York, 1949-50, and Yale University Child Study Center, New Haven, Connecticut, 1951-53; teacher assistant in psychology, City College of New York, 1950-51; associate editor in the Publications Division, 1959-66, and instructor in the Teacher Education Division, 1960-70, Bank Street College of Education, New York; research assistant and specialist in children's literature, Department of Psychiatry, 1970-72, and lecturer, School of Education, 1972-80, University of Michigan, Ann Arbor. Since 1980 writer and lecturer. Member of the Editorial Board, 1973-77, and U.S. editor, 1976-81, *Children's Literature in Education,* London. **Awards:** American Book award, 1980; American Library Association Newbery Medal, 1980. **Address:** c/o Curtis Brown, Ltd., 10 Astor Place, New York, New York 10003, U.S.A.

Publications for Children

Fiction

Joe Finds a Way, with Betty Miles, illustrated by Lee Ames. Syracuse, Singer, 1967.
"It's Spring," She Said, illustrated by Julie Maas. New York, Knopf, 1968.
Just Think!, with Betty Miles, illustrated by Pat Grant Porter. New York, Knopf, 1971.
A Gathering of Days: A New England Girl's Journal 1830-32. New York, Scribner, 1979.
Martin's Hats, illustrated by Marc Simont. New York, Morrow, 1984.
Brothers of the Heart: A Story of the Old Northwest 1837-38. New York, Scribner, 1985.
Old Henry, illustrated by Stephen Gammell. New York, Morrow, and London, Simon and Schuster, 1987.
The Grampa Days, illustrated by Emily Arnold McCully. New York, Simon and Schuster, 1989.
One Very Best Valentine's Day, illustrated by Emily Arnold McCully. New York, Simon and Schuster, 1989.
The Heroine of the Titanic. New York, Morrow, 1989.
Lottie's Circus, illustrated by Irene Trivas. New York, Morrow, 1989.

Other (readers; illustrated by Dan Dickas)

In the City. New York, Macmillan, 1965.
People Read, with Betty Miles. New York, Macmillan, 1965.

*

Manuscript Collections: Kerlan Collection, University of Minnesota, Minneapolis.

Joan W. Blos comments:

Words, for me, have always been important. It is said that I spoke at an early age, and well before I entered school my father and mother were writing down the "poems" I spoke to them. "First in town it thunders and glitters," begins one surviving example. It rises to the question: "What will you do when the storm is out, and it is beginning to rain?" Observation and question continue to be the basis of what I write.

"Writing begins in caring," I say to the children when asked to speak in schools. By that I mean that writing begins with concern for the world, the events and the people therein. I believe that this world of ours matters and that our small lives count. Writing also means caring about the words which are set down on paper. It's a struggle for me and I wouldn't call it enjoyable. Once I told an interviewer that, although I don't like writing, I *love* having written. That's what keeps me going back—back to the pads and the pens and the pencils, the typewriter, and the wastebaskets (two!) which are under my desk. I think it's important for others to know that writing isn't something you do because you find it easy. Most of the time I'm grateful if I can do it at all. Beyond the caring for words, and one's world, writing has to do with caring for those for whom you write. I suppose that's why I write for children and am happy to hear from them. I like to think of my books, my works, as ways of saying things, to children, for whom I deeply care. However hard I find this work of writing, I would not, do not, want ever to give it up! I hope I get better and better at writing; I know that there is nothing that I would rather do.

* * *

Joan W. Blos's first novel for older children, *A Gathering of Days: A New England Girl's Journal 1830-32,* won numerous awards, among them the Newbery Medal and the American Book award. It is a well-crafted book of historical fiction with a protagonist, Catherine Hall, who is as vividly alive as any of her readers. Catherine's human qualities are revealed early as she wishes "that my hair were curly, as Matty's is, and our mother's." She delights in visiting the Shipmans, their nearest neighbors, but wishes that she could reciprocate with splendid dinners on special occasions (since her mother died years before the journal begins, that is not possible). Here is a real child, loving, usually obedient, but full of fun, too. Having taken great pride in assuming many of her mother's duties, Catherine resents her new stepmother who appears with little warning about halfway through the book, constantly referring to her as "she" or "her" in the journal. On the wedding day, Catherine writes, "On this day, in Boston, they married. I will not call her Mother." Her stepbrother, Daniel, later comes up with a compromise, "Mammann," as Catherine gradually adjusts. In contrast, she dearly loves her friend Cassie, whose death is a terrible blow. Eventually matters sort themselves out as Catherine comes to terms with herself and with those around her. She accepts both Cassie's death and her stepmother; as she prepares to set off on a trip at the end of the journal, she has matured considerably from the girl who first began it.

Since *A Gathering of Days* Blos has created two imaginative picture books and another historical novel. In *Martin's Hats* an array of hats creates the impetus for young Martin's fantasies as he succeeds at one venture after another (cook, fireman, explorer, engineer, etc.). The adventures come to a satisfactory conclusion when he discovers the nightcap waiting for him on his bed. The second picture book, *Old Henry,* is written primarily in rhyming couplets on a timely theme, getting along with others despite differences, as Old Henry refuses to fix up his dilapidated house and rebuffs attempts by neighbors to help him and be friendly. The spirit of compromise eventually results in a potentially happy ending. Stephen Gammell's engaging colored pencil illustrations are a perfect accompaniment.

Blos's recent historical novel, *Brothers of the Heart: A Story of the Old Northwest 1837-38,* has a male protagonist. The tale, set in Michigan, is told through flashback using devices such as letters and journal and diary entries. These fictionalized accounts give the reader a strong sense of verisimilitude; the book rings true, for Blos has also captured the speech cadences and language of the period. Through friendships and relatives several of the characters are linked to Catherine Hall, from *A Gathering of Days,* so that readers can gain a sense of continuity.

The sharp characterization of the first historical fiction novel continues in *Brothers of the Heart* as Shem Perkins, born lame, attempts to make his own way after an unfortunate scene with his upset father. After running away from home, he receives gainful employment and is sent on a dangerous expedition which almost costs him his life but which ensures his maturity and builds his self-confidence, enabling him to return to his family and to the girl he will eventually marry. The reader also learns of another culture as Shem takes in the aged Ottowan Indian, Mary Goodhue, learning from her and tending to her until her death. Through her he discovers his own strengths and makes the realization that he and Mary's long-dead Indian husband were truly brothers of the heart.

The richness of the novel lies in the presentation of the growth of the Michigan region along with the development of characters and insight into the feelings of crippled Shem and the attitudes of others about him. The language, with its rhythms and lilt of earlier times, is remarkably spare, not replete with full-blown descriptions, yet giving the reader a strong sense of place and characterization. Blos has accomplished the fine feat of balancing history with universal human experience, uniting the book's past with the reader's present.

—Marilyn F. Apseloff

BLYTON, Enid (Mary)

Pseudonym: Mary Pollock. **Nationality:** British. **Born:** East Dulwich, London, 11 August 1897. **Education:** St. Christopher's School for Girls, Beckenham, Kent, 1907-15; Froebel Institute, Ipswich High School, 1916-18. **Family:** Married 1) Hugh Pollock in 1924 (divorced 1942), two daughters; 2) Kenneth Darrell Waters in 1943 (died 1967). **Career:** Taught at Bickley Park School, Kent, 1919; nursery governess, Surbiton, Surrey, 1920-24. Columnist, "From My Window," 1923-27, "Letter to Children," 1927-29, and "Children's Page," 1929-45, *Teachers' World,* London; editor, *Sunny Stories* magazine, London, 1926-52, and *Enid Blyton Magazine,* London, 1953-59. Chairman of the Committee, Shaftesbury Society Children's Home, Beaconsfield, Buckinghamshire, 1954-67; Vice-President, Friends of the Cheyne Walk Centre, London, 1960-68. **Died:** 28 November 1968.

Publications for Children

Fiction

The Enid Blyton Book of Fairies, illustrated by Horace J. Knowles. London, Newnes, 1924.
The Zoo Book. London, Newnes, 1924.
The Enid Blyton Book of Bunnies. London, Newnes, 1925.
The Book of Brownies, illustrated by Ernest Aris. London, Newnes, 1926; as *Brownie Tales,* London, Collins, 1964.
Tales Half Told. London, Nelson, 1926.
The Animal Book. London, Newnes, 1927.
Let's Pretend, illustrated by I. Bennington Angrave. London, Nelson, 1928.
Tarrydiddle Town. London, Nelson, 1929.
Cheerio! A Book for Boys and Girls. London, Birn, 1933.
Five [Fifteen, Twenty] Minute Tales. London, Methuen, 3 vols., 1933-40.
Letters from Bobs. Privately printed, 1933.
The Red Pixie Book, illustrated by Kathleen Nixon. London, Newnes, 1934.
Ten Minutes Tales: Twenty-Nine Varied Stories for Children. London, Methuen, 1934.
The Children's Garden. London, Newnes, 1935.
The Green Goblin Book. London, Newnes, 1935; shortened version, as *Feefo, Tuppeny, and Jinks,* London, Staples Press, 1951.
Hedgerow Tales, illustrated by V. Temple. London, Newnes, 1935.
The Famous Jimmy, illustrated by Benjamin Rabier. London, Muller, 1936; New York, Dutton, 1937.
The Yellow Fairy Book. London, Newnes, 1936.
Adventures of the Wishing Chair, illustrated by Hilda McGavin. London, Newnes, 1937.
The Adventures of Binkle and Flip, illustrated by Kathleen Nixon. London, Newnes, 1938.
Billy-Bob Tales, illustrated by May Smith. London, Methuen, 1938.
Mr. Galliano's Circus, illustrated by E.H. Davie. London, Newnes, 1938.
The Secret Island. Oxford, Blackwell, 1938.
Boys' and Girls' Circus Book, illustrated by Hilda McGavin. London, News Chronicle, 1939.
The Enchanted Wood, illustrated by Dorothy M. Wheeler. London, Newnes, 1939.
Hurrah for the Circus! Being Further Adventures of Mr. Galliano and His Famous Circus, illustrated by E.H. Davie. London, Newnes, 1939.
Naughty Amelia Jane! London, Newnes, 1939.
Boys' and Girls' Story Book. London, Newnes, 1940.
The Children of Cherry Tree Farm, illustrated by Harry Rountree. London, Country Life, 1940.
The Little Tree-House, Being the Adventures of Josie, Click, and Bun, illustrated by Dorothy M. Wheeler. London, Newnes, 1940; as *Josie, Click, and Bun and the Little Tree House,* 1951.
Mr. Meddle's Mischief, illustrated by Joyce Mercer and Rosalind M. Turvey. London, Newnes, 1940.
The Naughtiest Girl in the School. London, Newnes, 1940.
The Secret of Spiggy Holes. Oxford, Blackwell, 1940.

Tales of Betsy-May, illustrated by Joan Gale Thomas. London, Methuen, 1940.
The Treasure Hunters, illustrated by E. Wilson and Joyce Davies. London, Newnes, 1940.
The Adventures of Mr. Pink-Whistle. London, Newnes, 1941.
The Adventurous Four. London, Newnes, 1941.
Five O'Clock Tales. London, Methuen, 1941.
The Further Adventures of Josie, Click, and Bun, illustrated by Dorothy M. Wheeler. London, Newnes, 1941.
The Secret Mountain. Oxford, Blackwell, 1941.
The Twins at St. Clare's. London, Methuen, 1941.
The Children of Willow Farm, illustrated by Harry Rountree. London, Country Life, 1942.
Circus Days Again, illustrated by E.H. Davie. London, Newnes, 1942.
Happy Story Book. London, Hodder and Stoughton, 1942.
Enid Blyton's Little Books (*Brer Rabbit, Bed-time Stories, Jolly Tales, Ho-Ho and Too Smart, Tales of the Toys, Happy Stories*), illustrated by Alfred Kerr. London, Evans, 6 vols., 1942.
Five on a Treasure Island. London, Hodder and Stoughton, 1942; New York, Crowell, 1950.
Hello, Mr. Twiddle, illustrated by Hilda McGavin. London, Newnes, 1942.
I'll Tell You a Story, illustrated by Eileen A. Soper. London, Macmillan, 1942.
I'll Tell You Another Story. London, Macmillan, 1942.
John Jolly at Christmas Time [*by the Sea, on the Farm, at the Circus*]. London, Evans, 4 vols., 1942-45.
Mary Mouse and the Doll's House. Leicester, Brockhampton Press, 1942.
The Naughtiest Girl Again. London, Newnes, 1942.
The O'Sullivan Twins. London, Methuen, 1942.
Shadow, The Sheep-Dog. London, Newnes, 1942.
Six O'Clock Tales: Thirty-Three Short Stories for Children, illustrated by Dorothy M. Wheeler. London, Methuen, 1942.
More Adventures on Willow Farm. London, Country Life, 1943.
Bimbo and Topsy, illustrated by Lucy Gee. London, Newnes, 1943.
Dame Slap and Her School, illustrated by Dorothy M. Wheeler. London, Newnes, 1943.
Five Go Adventuring Again. London, Hodder and Stoughton, 1943; New York, Crowell, 1951.
The Magic Faraway Tree, illustrated by Dorothy M. Wheeler. London, Newnes, 1943.
Merry Story Book, illustrated by Eileen A. Soper. London, Hodder and Stoughton, 1943.
More Adventures of Mary Mouse. Leicester, Brockhampton Press, 1943.
The Mystery of the Burnt Cottage, illustrated by J. Abbey. London, Methuen, 1943; Los Angeles, McNaughton, 1946.
The Secret of Killimooin. Oxford, Blackwell, 1943.
Polly Piglet, illustrated by Eileen A. Soper. Leicester, Brockhampton Press, 1943.
Seven O'Clock Tales: Thirty Short Stories for Children. London, Methuen, 1943.
Summer Term at St. Clare's. London, Methuen, 1943.
The Toys Come to Life, illustrated by Eileen A. Soper. Leicester, Brockhampton Press, 1943.
At Appletree Farm. Leicester, Brockhampton Press, 1944.
Billy and Betty at the Seaside. Dundee, Valentine, 1944.
The Boy Next Door, illustrated by Alfred Bestall. London, Newnes, 1944.
The Dog That Went to Fairyland. Leicester, Brockhampton Press, 1944.
Claudine at St. Clare's. London, Methuen, 1944.
Come to the Circus, illustrated by Eileen A. Soper. Leicester, Brockhampton Press, 1944.
Eight O'Clock Tales, illustrated by Dorothy M. Wheeler. London, Methuen, 1944.
Five Run Away Together, illustrated by Eileen A. Soper. London, Hodder and Stoughton, 1944; Chicago, Reilly and Lee, 1960.
The Island of Adventure, illustrated by Stuart Tresilian. London, Macmillan, 1944; as *Mystery Island,* New York, Macmillan, 1945.
Jolly Little Jumbo. Leicester, Brockhampton Press, 1944.
Jolly Story Book, illustrated by Eileen A. Soper. London, Hodder and Stoughton, 1944.
Little Mary Mouse Again. Leicester, Brockhampton Press, 1944.
A Book of Naughty Children: The Mystery of the Disappearing Cat, illustrated by J. Abbey. London, Methuen, 1944; as *The Mystery of the Disappearing Cat,* Los Angeles, McNaughton, 1948.
Rainy Day Stories, illustrated by Nora S. Unwin. London, Evans, 1944.
The Second Form at St. Clare's, illustrated by W. Lindsay Cable. London, Methuen, 1944.
Tales of Toyland, illustrated by Hilda McGavin. London, Newnes, 1944.
The Three Golliwogs. London, Newnes, 1944.
The Blue Story Book, illustrated by Eileen A. Soper. London, Methuen, 1945.
The Brown Family, illustrated by E. and R. Buhler. London, News Chronicle, 1945.
The Caravan Family, illustrated by William Fyffe. London, Lutterworth Press, 1945.
The Conjuring Wizard and Other Stories, illustrated by Eileen A. Soper. London, Macmillan, 1945.
The Family at Red Roofs, illustrated by W. Spence. London, Lutterworth Press, 1945.
Fifth Formers at St. Clare's, illustrated by W. Lindsay Cable. London, Methuen, 1945.
Five Go to Smugglers' Top. London, Hodder and Stoughton, 1945; Chicago, Reilly and Lee, 1960.
Hallo, Little Mary Mouse, illustrated by Olive F. Openshaw. Leicester, Brockhampton Press, 1945.
Hollow Tree House, illustrated by Elizabeth Wall. London, Lutterworth Press, 1945.
The Mystery of the Secret Room. London, Methuen, 1945; Los Angeles, Parkwood Press, 1950.
The Naughtiest Girl Is a Monitor. London, Newnes, 1945.
Round the Clock Stories, illustrated by Nora S. Unwin. London, National Magazine Company, 1945.
The Runaway Kitten, illustrated by Eileen A. Soper. Leicester, Brockhampton Press, 1945.
Sunny Story Book. London, Hodder and Stoughton, 1945.
The Teddy Bear's Party, illustrated by Eileen A. Soper. Leicester, Brockhampton Press, 1945.
The Twins Go to Nursery-Rhyme Land, illustrated by Eileen A. Soper. Leicester, Brockhampton Press, 1945.
Amelia Jane Again. London, Newnes, 1946.
The Bad Little Monkey, illustrated by Eileen A. Soper. Leicester, Brockhampton Press, 1946.
The Castle of Adventure, illustrated by Stuart Tresilian. London, Macmillan, and New York, Macmillan, 1946.

The Children at Happy House, illustrated by Kathleen Gell. Oxford, Blackwell, 1946.
Chimney Corner Stories, illustrated by Pat Harrison. London, National Magazine Company, 1946.
First Term at Malory Towers. London, Methuen, 1946.
Five Go Off in a Caravan, illustrated by Eileen A. Soper. London, Hodder and Stoughton, 1946.
The Folk of the Faraway Tree, illustrated by Dorothy M. Wheeler. London, Newnes, 1946.
Gay Story Book, illustrated by Eileen A. Soper. London, Hodder and Stoughton, 1946.
Josie, Click, and Bun Again, illustrated by Dorothy M. Wheeler. London, Newnes, 1946.
The Little White Duck and Other Stories, illustrated by Eileen A. Soper. London, Macmillan, 1946.
Mary Mouse and Her Family, illustrated by Olive F. Openshaw. Leicester, Brockhampton Press, 1946.
The Mystery of the Spiteful Letters, illustrated by J. Abbey. London, Methuen, 1946.
The Put-em-Rights, illustrated by Elizabeth Wall. London, Lutterworth Press, 1946.
The Red Story Book. London, Methuen, 1946.
The Surprising Caravan, illustrated by Eileen A. Soper. Leicester, Brockhampton Press, 1946.
Tales of Green Hedges, illustrated by Gwen White. London, National Magazine Company, 1946.
The Train That Lost Its Way, illustrated by Eileen A. Soper. Leicester, Brockhampton Press, 1946.
The Adventurous Four Again, illustrated by Jessie Land. London, Newnes, 1947.
At Seaside Cottage, illustrated by Eileen A. Soper. Leicester, Brockhampton Press, 1947.
Five on Kirrin Island Again. London, Hodder and Stoughton, 1947.
The Green Story Book, illustrated by Eileen A. Soper. London, Methuen, 1947.
The Happy House Children Again, illustrated by Kathleen Gell. Oxford, Blackwell, 1947.
Here Comes Mary Mouse Again. Leicester, Brockhampton Press, 1947.
The House at the Corner, illustrated by Elsie Walker. London, Lutterworth Press, 1947.
Little Green Duck and Other Stories. Leicester, Brockhampton Press, 1947.
Lucky Story Book, illustrated by Eileen A. Soper. London, Hodder and Stoughton, 1947.
More about Josie, Click, and Bun, illustrated by Dorothy M. Wheeler. London, Newnes, 1947.
The Mystery of the Missing Necklace. London, Methuen, 1947.
Rambles with Uncle Nat, illustrated by Nora S. Unwin. London, National Magazine Company, 1947.
The "Saucy Jane" Family, illustrated by Kathleen Gell. London, Lutterworth Press, 1947.
A Second Book of Naughty Children: Twenty-Four Short Stories, illustrated by Kathleen Gell. London, Methuen, 1947.
The Second Form at Malory Towers. London, Methuen, 1947.
The Smith Family 1-3 (*At Home, At the Zoo, At the Circus*). Leeds, E.J. Arnold, 3 vols., 1947.
The Valley of Adventure, illustrated by Stuart Tresilian. London, Macmillan, and New York, Macmillan, 1947.
The Very Clever Rabbit. Leicester, Brockhampton Press, 1947.
The Adventures of Pip. London, Sampson Low, 1948.
The Boy with the Loaves and Fishes, illustrated by Elsie Walker. London, Lutterworth Press, 1948; New York, Roy, 1958 (?).
Come to the Circus, illustrated by Joyce M. Johnson (different book from the 1944 title). London, Newnes, 1948.
Bedtime Series. Leicester, Brockhampton Press, 2 vols., 1948.
Five Go Off to Camp. London, Hodder and Stoughton, 1948; as *Five on the Track of a Spook Train,* New York, Atheneum, 1972.
How Do You Do, Mary Mouse. Leicester, Brockhampton Press, 1948.
Just Time for a Story, illustrated by Grace Lodge. London, Macmillan, 1948; New York, St. Martin's Press, 1952.
Let's Have a Story, illustrated by George Bowe. London, Pitkin, 1948.
The Little Girl at Capernaum, illustrated by Elsie Walker. London, Lutterworth Press, 1948; New York, Roy, 1958 (?).
Mister Icy-Cold. Oxford, Blackwell, 1948.
More Adventures of Pip. London, Sampson Low, 1948.
The Mystery of the Hidden House, illustrated by J. Abbey. London, Methuen, 1948.
Nature Tales. London, Johnston, 1948.
Now for a Story, illustrated by Frank Varty. Newcastle-upon-Tyne, Harold Hill, 1948.
The Red-Spotted Handkerchief and Other Stories, illustrated by Kathleen Gell. Leicester, Brockhampton Press, 1948.
The Sea of Adventure, illustrated by Stuart Tresilian. London, Macmillan, and New York, Macmillan, 1948.
The Secret of the Old Mill, illustrated by Eileen A. Soper. Leicester, Brockhampton Press, 1948.
Six Cousins at Mistletoe Farm, illustrated by Peter Beigel. London, Evans, 1948.
Tales after Tea. London, Laurie, 1948.
Tales of the Twins, illustrated by Eileen A. Soper. Leicester, Brockhampton Press, 1948.
They Ran Away Together, illustrated by Jeanne Farrar. Leicester, Brockhampton Press, 1948.
Third Year at Malory Towers, illustrated by Stanley Lloyd. London, Methuen, 1948.
We Want a Story, illustrated by George Bowe. London, Pitkin, 1948.
Bluebell [*Daffodil, Poppy, Buttercup, Snowdrop, Marigold, Foxglove*] *Story Book.* London, Gifford, 7 vols., 1949-55.
Bumpy and His Bus, illustrated by Dorothy M. Wheeler. London, Newnes, 1949.
A Cat in Fairyland and Other Stories. London, Pitkin, 1949.
The Circus Book. London, Latimer House, 1949.
The Dear Old Snow Man. Leicester, Brockhampton Press, 1949.
Don't Be Silly, Mr. Twiddle. London, Newnes, 1949.
The Enchanted Sea and Other Stories. London, Pitkin, 1949.
Good Morning Book, illustrated by Don and Ann Goring. London, National Magazine Company, 1949.
Five Get into Trouble, illustrated by Eileen A. Soper. London, Hodder and Stoughton, 1949; as *Five Caught in a Treacherous Plot,* New York, Atheneum, 1972.
Humpty Dumpty and Belinda. London, Collins, 1949.
Jinky's Joke and Other Stories, illustrated by Kathleen Gell. Leicester, Brockhampton Press, 1949.
Little Noddy Goes to Toyland, illustrated by Harmsen Van Beek. London, Sampson Low, 1949.
Mr. Tumpy and His Caravan, illustrated by Dorothy M. Wheeler. London, Sidgwick and Jackson, 1949; Los Angeles, McNaughton, 1951.

The Mountain of Adventure, illustrated by Stuart Tresilian. London, Macmillan, and New York, Macmillan, 1949.
The Mystery of the Pantomime Cat. London, Methuen, 1949.
Oh, What a Lovely Time. Leicester, Brockhampton Press, 1949.
The Rockingdown Mystery, illustrated by Gilbert Dunlop. London, Collins, 1949.
The Secret Seven, illustrated by George Brook. Leicester, Brockhampton Press, 1949; as *The Secret Seven and the Mystery of the Empty House,* Chicago, Children's Press, 1972.
A Story Party at Green Hedges, illustrated by Grace Lodge. London, Hodder and Stoughton, 1949.
The Strange Umbrella and Other Stories. London, Pitkin, 1949.
Tales after Supper. London, Laurie, 1949.
Those Dreadful Children, illustrated by Grace Lodge. London, Lutterworth Press, 1949.
Tiny Tales. Worcester, Littlebury, 1949.
The Upper Fourth at Malory Towers. London, Methuen, 1949.
Chuff the Chimney Sweep and Other Stories. London, Pitkin, 1950.
The Astonishing Ladder and Other Stories, illustrated by Eileen A. Soper. London, Macmillan, 1950.
Five Fall into Adventure, illustrated by Eileen A. Soper. London, Hodder and Stoughton, 1950; New York, Atheneum, 1972.
Hurrah for Little Noddy, illustrated by Harmsen Van Beek. London, Sampson Low, 1950.
In the Fifth at Malory Towers, illustrated by Stanley Lloyd. London, Methuen, 1950.
The Magic Knitting Needles and Other Stories, illustrated by Eileen A. Soper. London, Macmillan, 1950.
Mister Meddle's Muddles, illustrated by Rosalind M. Turvey and Joyce Mercer. London, Newnes, 1950.
Mr. Pink-Whistle Interferes, illustrated by Dorothy M. Wheeler. London, Newnes, 1950.
The Mystery of the Invisible Thief, illustrated by Treyer Evans. London, Methuen, 1950.
The Pole Star Family, illustrated by Ruth Gervis. London, Lutterworth Press, 1950.
The Rilloby Fair Mystery, illustrated by Gilbert Dunlop. London, Collins, 1950.
Round the Year Stories. London, Coker, 1950.
Rubbalong Tales, illustrated by Norman Meredith. London, Macmillan, 1950.
The Seaside Family, illustrated by Ruth Gervis. London, Lutterworth Press, 1950.
Secret Seven Adventure, illustrated by George Brook. Leicester, Brockhampton Press, 1950; as *The Secret Seven and the Circus Adventure,* Chicago, Children's Press, 1972.
The Ship of Adventure, illustrated by Stuart Tresilian. London, Macmillan, and New York, Macmillan, 1950.
Six Cousins Again, illustrated by Maurice Tulloch. London, Evans, 1950.
Tales about Toys, illustrated by Jeanne Farrar. Leicester, Brockhampton Press, 1950.
The Three Naughty Children and Other Stories, illustrated by Eileen A. Soper. London, Macmillan, 1950.
Tricky the Goblin and Other Stories, illustrated by Eileen A. Soper. London, Macmillan, 1950.
We Do Love Mary Mouse. Leicester, Brockhampton Press, 1950.
Welcome Mary Mouse, illustrated by Olive F. Openshaw. Leicester, Brockhampton Press, 1950.
What an Adventure, illustrated by Eileen A. Soper. Leicester, Brockhampton Press, 1950.
The Wishing Chair Again. London, Newnes, 1950.
The Yellow Story Book, illustrated by Kathleen Gell. London, Methuen, 1950.
Boody the Great Goblin and Other Stories. London, Pitkin, 1951.
The "Queen Elizabeth" Family, illustrated by Ruth Gervis. London, Lutterworth Press, 1951.
Benny and the Princess and Other Stories. London, Pitkin, 1951.
The Big Noddy Book, illustrated by Harmsen Van Beek. London, Sampson Low, 1951 (and later volumes).
The Buttercup Farm Family, illustrated by Ruth Gervis. London, Lutterworth Press, 1951.
Down at the Farm. London, Sampson Low, 1951.
Father Christmas and Belinda. London, Collins, 1951.
Five on a Hike Together, illustrated by Eileen A. Soper. London, Hodder and Stoughton, 1951.
The Flying Goat and Other Stories. London, Pitkin, 1951.
Gay Street Book, illustrated by Grace Lodge. London, Latimer, 1951.
Hello Twins, illustrated by Molly Brett. Leicester, Brockhampton Press, 1951.
Here Comes Noddy Again, illustrated by Harmsen Van Beek. London, Sampson Low, 1951.
Hurrah for Mary Mouse. Leicester, Brockhampton Press, 1951.
Last Term at Malory Towers, illustrated by Stanley Lloyd. London, Methuen, 1951.
Let's Go to the Circus. London, Odhams, 1951.
The Little Spinning House and Other Stories. London, Pitkin, 1951.
The Magic Snow-Bird and Other Stories. London, Pitkin, 1951.
The Mystery of the Vanished Prince, illustrated by Treyer Evans. London, Methuen, 1951.
Noddy and Big Ears Have a Picnic. London, Sampson Low, 1951.
Noddy and His Car, illustrated by Harmsen Van Beek. London, Sampson Low, 1951.
Noddy Has a Shock. London, Sampson Low, 1951.
Noddy Has More Adventures. London, Sampson Low, 1951.
Noddy Goes to the Seaside. London, Sampson Low, 1951.
Noddy Off to Rocking Horse Land. London, Sampson Low, 1951.
Noddy Painting Book. London, Sampson Low, 8 vols., 1951-57.
Noddy's House of Books. London, Sampson Low, 6 vols., 1951.
A Picnic Party with Enid Blyton, illustrated by Grace Lodge. London, Hodder and Stoughton, 1951.
Pippy and the Gnome and Other Stories. London, Pitkin, 1951.
A Prize for Mary Mouse. Leicester, Brockhampton Press, 1951.
The Proud Golliwog, illustrated by Molly Brett. Leicester, Brockhampton Press, 1951.
The Runaway Teddy Bear and Other Stories. London, Pitkin, 1951.
The Six Bad Boys, illustrated by Mary Gernat. London, Lutterworth Press, 1951.
A Tale of Little Noddy. London, Sampson Low, 1951.
"Too-Wise" the Wonderful Wizard and Other Stories. London, Pitkin, 1951.
Up the Faraway Tree, illustrated by Dorothy M. Wheeler. London, Newnes, 1951.
Well Done, Secret Seven, illustrated by George Brook. Leicester, Brockhampton Press, 1951; as *The Secret Seven and the Tree House Adventure,* Chicago, Children's Press, 1972.
Bright Story Book, illustrated by Eileen A. Soper. Leicester, Brockhampton Press, 1952.
The Circus of Adventure, illustrated by Stuart Tresilian. London, Macmillan, 1952; New York, St. Martin's Press, 1953.

Come Along Twins, illustrated by Eileen A. Soper. Leicester, Brockhampton Press, 1952.
Five Have a Wonderful Time, illustrated by Eileen A. Soper. London, Hodder and Stoughton, 1952.
The Mad Teapot, illustrated by Molly Brett. Leicester, Brockhampton Press, 1952.
Mandy, Mops, and Cubby Find a House. London, Sampson Low, 1952.
Mandy, Mops, and Cubby Again. London, Sampson Low, 1952.
Mary Mouse and Her Bicycle, illustrated by Olive F. Openshaw. Leicester, Brockhampton Press, 1952.
Mr. Tumpy Plays a Trick on Saucepan. London, Sampson Low, 1952.
The Mystery of the Strange Bundle, illustrated by Treyer Evans. London, Methuen, 1952.
Noddy and Big Ears. London, Sampson Low, 1952.
Noddy and the Witch's Wand. London, Sampson Low, 1952.
Noddy's Colour Strip Book, illustrated by Harmsen Van Beek. London, Sampson Low, 1952.
Noddy Goes to School. London, Sampson Low, 1952.
Noddy's Ark of Books. London, Sampson Low, 5 vols., 1952.
Noddy's Car Gets a Squeak. London, Sampson Low, 1952.
Noddy's Penny Wheel Car. London, Sampson Low, 1952.
The Queer Mystery, illustrated by Norman Meredith. London, Staples Press, 1952.
The Rubadub Mystery, illustrated by Gilbert Dunlop. London, Collins, 1952.
Secret Seven on the Trail, illustrated by George Brook. Leicester, Brockhampton Press, 1952; as *The Secret Seven and the Railroad Mystery,* Chicago, Children's Press, 1972.
The Very Big Secret, illustrated by Ruth Gervis. London, Lutterworth Press, 1952.
Welcome Josie, Click, and Bun, illustrated by Dorothy M. Wheeler. London, Newnes, 1952.
Well Done, Noddy, illustrated by Harmsen Van Beek. London, Sampson Low, 1952.
Clicky the Clockwork Clown, illustrated by Molly Brett. Leicester, Brockhampton Press, 1953.
Five Go Down to the Sea, illustrated by Eileen A. Soper. London, Hodder and Stoughton, 1953; Chicago, Reilly and Lee, 1961.
Go Ahead Secret Seven, illustrated by Bruno Kay. Leicester, Brockhampton Press, 1953; as *The Secret Seven Get Their Man,* Chicago, Children's Press, 1972.
Gobo and Mr. Fierce. London, Sampson Low, 1953.
Here Come the Twins, illustrated by Eileen A. Soper. Leicester, Brockhampton Press, 1953.
Mandy Makes Cubby a Hat. London, Sampson Low, 1953.
Mary Mouse and the Noah's Ark, illustrated by Olive F. Openshaw. Leicester, Brockhampton Press, 1953.
Mr. Tumpy in the Land of Wishes. London, Sampson Low, 1953.
My Enid Blyton Story Book, illustrated by Willy Schermelé. London, Juvenile Productions, 1953.
The Mystery of Holly Lane, illustrated by Treyer Evans. London, Methuen, 1953.
New Noddy Colour Strip Book. London, Sampson Low, 1953.
Noddy and the Cuckoo's Nest. London, Sampson Low, 1953.
Noddy at the Seaside, illustrated by Harmsen Van Beek. London, Sampson Low, 1953.
Noddy's Cut-Out Model Book. London, Sampson Low, 1953.
Noddy Gets Captured. London, Sampson Low, 1953.
Noddy Is Very Silly. London, Sampson Low, 1953.
Noddy's Garage of Books, illustrated by Harmsen Van Beek. London, Sampson Low, 5 vols., 1953.
The Secret of Moon Castle. Oxford, Blackwell, 1953.
Snowball the Pony, illustrated by Iris Gillespie. London, Lutterworth Press, 1953.
Visitors in the Night, illustrated by Molly Brett. Leicester, Brockhampton Press, 1953.
Well Really Mr. Twiddle!, illustrated by Hilda McGavin. London, Newnes, 1953.
Fun with the Twins, illustrated by Eileen A. Soper. Leicester, Brockhampton Press, 1954.
Enid Blyton's Good Morning Book, illustrated by Willy Schermelé. London, Juvenile Productions, 1954.
Noddy Gets into Trouble. London, Sampson Low, 1954.
What a Surprise!, illustrated by Molly Brett. Leicester, Brockhampton Press, 1954.
The Adventure of the Secret Necklace, illustrated by Isabel Veevers. London, Lutterworth Press, 1954.
The Castle Without a Door and Other Stories. London, Pitkin, 1954.
The Children at Green Meadows, illustrated by Grace Lodge. London, Lutterworth Press, 1954.
Friendly Story Book, illustrated by Eileen A. Soper. Leicester, Brockhampton Press, 1954.
Noddy Goes to the Fair. London, Sampson Low, 1954.
Noddy Giant Painting Book. London, Sampson Low, 1954.
Good Work, Secret Seven!, illustrated by Bruno Kay. Leicester, Brockhampton Press, 1954; as *The Secret Seven and the Case of the Stolen Car,* Chicago, Children's Press, 1972.
Five Go to Mystery Moor. London, Hodder and Stoughton, 1954; Chicago, Reilly and Lee, 1963.
How Funny You Are, Noddy. London, Sampson Low, 1954.
Little Strip Picture Books. London, Sampson Low, 1954 (and other volumes).
The Little Toy Farm and Other Stories. London, Pitkin, 1954.
Mary Mouse to the Rescue. Leicester, Brockhampton Press, 1954.
Merry Mister Meddle, illustrated by Rosalind M. Turvey and Joyce Mercer. London, Newnes, 1954.
More about Amelia Jane, illustrated by Sylvia I. Venus. London, Newnes, 1954.
The Mystery of Tally-Ho Cottage, illustrated by Treyer Evans. London, Methuen, 1954.
Noddy and the Magic Rubber. London, Sampson Low, 1954.
Noddy's Castle of Books, illustrated by Harmsen Van Beek. London, Sampson Low, 5 vols., 1954.
Sooty, illustrated by Pierre Probst. London, Collins, 1955.
Away Goes Sooty, illustrated by Pierre Probst. London, Collins, 1955.
Benjy and the Others, illustrated by Kathleen Gell. London, Latimer, 1955.
Bimbo and Blackie Go Camping, illustrated by Pierre Probst. London, Collins, 1955.
Bobs, illustrated by Pierre Probst. London, Collins, 1955.
Christmas with Scamp and Bimbo, illustrated by Pierre Probst. London, Collins, 1955.
Little Bedtime Books (*The Cloud Kitten, The Doll That Fell Out of the Pram, Silly Sammy, The Surprising Broom, Amanda Going Away, The Balloon Pipe, The Golliwog and the Wireless, The Wizard Who Was Really a Nuisance*). London, Sampson Low, 8 vols., 1955-58.
Neddy the Little Donkey, illustrated by Romain Simon. London, Collins, 1955.

Five Have Plenty of Fun. London, Hodder and Stoughton, 1955.
Gobo in the Land of Dreams. London, Sampson Low, 1955.
The Golliwog Grumbled, illustrated by Molly Brett. Leicester, Brockhampton Press, 1955.
Holiday House, illustrated by Grace Lodge. London, Evans, 1955.
The Laughing Kitten, illustrated by Paul Kaye. London, Harvill Press, and New York, Roy, 1955.
Mandy, Mops, and Cubby and the Whitewash. London, Sampson Low, 1955.
Mary Mouse in Nursery Rhyme Land. Leicester, Brockhampton Press, 1955.
Mischief Again, photographs by Paul Kaye. London, Harvill Press, and New York, Roy, 1955.
Mr. Pink-Whistle's Party, illustrated by Dorothy M. Wheeler. London, Newnes, 1955.
Mr. Tumpy in the Land of Boys and Girls. London, Sampson Low, 1955.
More Chimney Corner Stories, illustrated by Pat Harrison. London, Latimer, 1955.
Noddy in Toyland. London, Sampson Low, 1955.
Noddy Meets Father Christmas. London, Sampson Low, 1955.
Ring o' Bells Mystery. London, Collins, 1955.
The River of Adventure, illustrated by Stuart Tresilian. London, Macmillan, and New York, St. Martin's Press, 1955.
Run-about's Holiday, illustrated by Lilian Chivers. London, Lutterworth Press, 1955.
Secret Seven Win Through, illustrated by Bruno Kay. Leicester, Brockhampton Press, 1955; as *The Secret Seven and the Hidden Cave Adventure,* Chicago, Children's Press, 1972.
Trouble for the Twins, illustrated by Eileen A. Soper. Leicester, Brockhampton Press, 1955.
The Troublesome Three, illustrated by Leo. London, Sampson Low, 1955.
You Funny Little Noddy! London, Sampson Low, 1955.
Be Brave, Little Noddy! London, Sampson Low, 1956.
Bom the Little Toy Drummer, illustrated by R. Paul-Höye. Leicester, Brockhampton Press, 1956.
The Clever Little Donkey, illustrated by Romain Simon. London, Collins, 1956.
Colin the Cow-Boy, illustrated by R. Caillé. London, Collins, 1956.
A Day with Mary Mouse, illustrated by Frederick White. Leicester, Brockhampton Press, 1956.
Animal Tales, illustrated by Romain Simon. London, Collins, 1956.
Noddy Play Day Painting Book. London, Sampson Low, 1956.
Five on a Secret Trail, illustrated by Eileen A. Soper. London, Hodder and Stoughton, 1956.
A Day with Noddy. London, Sampson Low, 1956.
Four in a Family, illustrated by Tom Kerr. London, Lutterworth Press, 1956.
The Mystery of the Missing Man, illustrated by Lilian Buchanan. London, Methuen, 1956.
Noddy and His Friends. London, Sampson Low, 1956.
Noddy and Tessie Bear. London, Sampson Low, 1956.
The Noddy Toy Station Books. London, Sampson Low, 5 vols., 1956.
The Rat-a-Tat Mystery, illustrated by Anyon Cook. London, Collins, 1956.
Scamp at School, illustrated by Pierre Probst. London, Collins, 1956.
Three Cheers Secret Seven, illustrated by Burgess Sharrocks. Leicester, Brockhampton Press, 1956; as *The Secret Seven and the Grim Secret,* Chicago, Children's Press, 1972.
Bom and His Magic Drumstick, illustrated by R. Paul-Höye. Leicester, Brockhampton Press, 1957.
Do Look Out, Noddy! London, Sampson Low, 1957.
Bom Painting Book. London, Dean, 1957.
Five Go to Billycock Hill, illustrated by Eileen A. Soper. London, Hodder and Stoughton, 1957.
Mary Mouse and the Garden Party, illustrated by Frederick White. Leicester, Brockhampton Press, 1957.
Mystery of the Strange Messages, illustrated by Lilian Buchanan. London, Methuen, 1957.
Noddy and the Bumpy Dog. London, Sampson Low, 1957.
Noddy's New Big Book. London, Sampson Low, 1957.
Secret Seven Mystery, illustrated by Burgess Sharrocks. Leicester, Brockhampton Press, 1957; as *The Secret Seven and the Missing Girl Mystery,* Chicago, Children's Press, 1972.
The Birthday Kitten, illustrated by Grace Lodge. London, Lutterworth Press, 1958.
Bom Goes Adventuring, illustrated by R. Paul-Höye. Leicester, Brockhampton Press, 1958.
Bom Goes to Ho Ho Village, illustrated by R. Paul Höye. Leicester, Brockhampton Press, 1958.
Bom Annual, illustrated by R. Paul-Höye and H.W. Felstead. London, Thames, 2 vols., 1958-59.
Clicky Gets into Trouble, illustrated by Molly Brett. Leicester, Brockhampton Press, 1958.
Five Get into a Fix, illustrated by Eileen A. Soper. London, Hodder and Stoughton, 1958.
Mary Mouse Goes to the Fair, illustrated by Frederick White. Leicester, Brockhampton Press, 1958.
Mr. Pink-Whistle's Big Book. London, Evans, 1958.
My Big-Ears Picture Book. London, Sampson Low, 1958.
My Noddy Picture Book. London, Sampson Low, 1958.
Noddy Has an Adventure. London, Sampson Low, 1958.
Puzzle for the Secret Seven, illustrated by Burgess Sharrocks. Leicester, Brockhampton Press, 1958; as *The Secret Seven and the Case of the Music Lover,* Chicago, Children's Press, 1972.
Rumble and Chuff, illustrated by David Walsh. London, Juvenile Productions, 2 vols., 1958.
You're a Good Friend, Noddy! London, Sampson Low, 1958.
The Noddy Shop Book. London, Sampson Low, 5 vols., 1958.
Bom and the Clown, illustrated by R. Paul-Höye. Leicester, Brockhampton Press, 1959.
Bom and the Rainbow, illustrated by R. Paul-Höye. Leicester, Brockhampton Press, 1959.
Hullo Bom and Wuffy Dog, illustrated by R. Paul-Höye. Leicester, Brockhampton Press, 1959.
Mary Mouse Has a Wonderful Idea, illustrated by Frederick White. Leicester, Brockhampton Press, 1959.
Noddy and the Bunkey. London, Sampson Low, 1959.
Noddy Goes to Sea. London, Sampson Low, 1959.
Noddy's Car Picture Book. London, Sampson Low, 1959.
Ragamuffin Mystery. London, Collins, 1959.
Secret Seven Fireworks, illustrated by Burgess Sharrocks. Leicester, Brockhampton Press, 1959; as *The Secret Seven and the Bonfire Mystery,* Chicago, Children's Press, 1972.
Adventure of the Strange Ruby, illustrated by Roger Payne. Leicester, Brockhampton Press, 1960.
Adventure Stories. London, Collins, 1960.
Bom Goes to Magic Town, illustrated by R. Paul-Höye. Leicester, Brockhampton Press, 1960.
Cheer Up, Little Noddy! London, Sampson Low, 1960.

Clicky and Tiptoe, illustrated by Molly Brett. Leicester, Brockhampton Press, 1960.
Five on Finniston Farm, illustrated by Eileen A. Soper. London, Hodder and Stoughton, 1960.
Good Old Secret Seven, illustrated by Burgess Sharrocks. Leicester, Brockhampton Press, 1960; as *The Secret Seven and the Old Fort Adventure,* Chicago, Children's Press, 1972.
Happy Day Stories, illustrated by Marcia Lane Foster. London, Evans, 1960.
Here Comes Bom, illustrated by R. Paul-Höye. Leicester, Brockhampton Press, 1960.
Mary Mouse Goes to Sea, illustrated by Frederick White. Leicester, Brockhampton Press, 1960.
Mystery Stories. London, Collins, 1960.
Noddy Goes to the Fair. London, Sampson Low, 1960.
Noddy's Tall Blue D[Green, Orange, Pink, Red, Yellow] Book. London, Sampson Low, 6 vols., 1960.
Will the Fiddle, illustrated by Grace Lodge. London, Instructive Arts, 1960.
Tales at Bedtime, illustrated by Hilda McGavin. London, Collins, 1961.
Bom at the Seaside, illustrated by R. Paul-Höye. Leicester, Brockhampton Press, 1961.
Bom Goes to the Circus, illustrated by R. Paul-Höye. Leicester, Brockhampton Press, 1961.
Five Go to Demon's Rocks, illustrated by Eileen A. Soper. London, Hodder and Stoughton, 1961.
Happy Holiday, Clicky, illustrated by Molly Brett. Leicester, Brockhampton Press, 1961.
Mary Mouse Goes Out for the Day, illustrated by Frederick White. Leicester, Brockhampton Press, 1961.
Mr. Plod and Little Noddy. London, Sampson Low, 1961.
The Mystery of Banshee Towers, illustrated by Lilian Buchanan. London, Methuen, 1961.
The Mystery That Never Was, illustrated by Gilbert Dunlop. London, Collins, 1961.
Noddy's Toyland Train Picture Book. London, Sampson Low, 1961.
Shock for the Secret Seven, illustrated by Burgess Sharrocks. Leicester, Brockhampton Press, 1961; as *The Secret Seven and the Case of the Dog Lover,* Chicago, Children's Press, 1972.
A Day at School with Noddy. London, Sampson Low, 1962.
Five Have a Mystery to Solve, illustrated by Eileen A. Soper. London, Hodder and Stoughton, 1962.
The Four Cousins, illustrated by Joan Thompson. London, Lutterworth Press, 1962.
Fun with Mary Mouse, illustrated by R. Paul-Höye. Leicester, Brockhampton Press, 1962.
Look Out Secret Seven, illustrated by Burgess Sharrocks. Leicester, Brockhampton Press, 1962; as *The Secret Seven and the Case of the Missing Medals,* Chicago, Children's Press, 1972.
Noddy and the Tootles. London, Sampson Low, 1962.
Stories for Monday [and *Tuesday*]. London, Oliphants, 2 vols., 1962.
The Boy Who Wanted a Dog, illustrated by Sally Michel. London, Lutterworth Press, 1963.
Five Are Together Again, illustrated by Eileen A. Soper. London, Hodder and Stoughton, 1963.
Fun for the Secret Seven, illustrated by Burgess Sharrocks. Leicester, Brockhampton Press, 1963; as *The Secret Seven and the Case of the Old Horse,* Chicago, Children's Press, 1972.
Sunshine Picture Story Book. Manchester, World Distributors, 1964 (and later volumes).
Happy Hours Story Book. London, Dean, 1964.
Mary Mouse and the Little Donkey, illustrated by R. Paul-Höye. Leicester, Brockhampton Press, 1964.
Noddy and the Aeroplane. London, Sampson Low, 1964.
Storybook for Fives to Sevens, illustrated by Dorothy Hall and Grace Shelton. London, Parrish, 1964.
Storytime Book. London, Dean, 1964.
Tell-a-Story Books. Manchester, World Distributors, 1964.
Trouble for the Twins. Leicester, Brockhampton Press, 1964.
The Boy Who Came Back, illustrated by Elsie Walker. London, Lutterworth Press, 1965.
Sunshine Book. London, Dean, 1965.
Treasure Box. London, Sampson Low, 1965.
The Man Who Stopped to Help, illustrated by Elsie Walker. London, Lutterworth Press, 1965.
Noddy and His Friends: A Nursery Picture Book. London, Sampson Low, 1965.
Noddy Treasure Box. London, Sampson Low, 1965.
The Fairy Folk Story Book. London, Collins, 1966.
Fireside Tales. London, Collins, 1966.
John and Mary series (*The Great Big Fish, How John Got His Ducklings, The Dog Who Would Go Digging, The Wheel That Ran Away, The Three Sailors, The Kitten That Disappeared, The Little Brown Bear, Tim Gets a Chance, Granny's Lovely Necklace*), illustrated by Fromont. Leicester, Brockhampton Press, 9 vols., 1966-68.
Pixie Tales. London, Collins, 1966.
Pixieland Story Book. London, Collins, 1966.
Stories for Bedtime. London, Dean, 1966.
Stories for You. London, Dean, 1966.
Holiday Annual [and *Magic, Pixie, Toy*] *Stories.* London, Low Marston, 4 vols., 1967.
Noddy and His Passengers. London, Sampson Low, 1967.
Noddy and the Magic Boots, Noddy's Funny Kite. London, Sampson Low, 1967.
Noddy and the Noah's Ark Adventure Picture Book. London, Sampson Low, 1967.
Noddy in Toyland Picture Book. London, Low Marston, 1967.
Noddy's Aeroplane Picture Book. London, Sampson Low, 1967.
The Playtime Story Book. Manchester, World Distributors, 4 vols., 1967.
Adventures on Willow Farm. London, Collins, 1968.
The Playtime Book. Manchester, World Distributors, 8 vols., 1968.
A Basket of Surprises, illustrated by Caroline Sharpe. London, Knight, 1970.

Fiction as Mary Pollock

Children of Kidillin. London, Newnes, 1940.
Three Boys and a Circus. London, Newnes, 1940.
Mischief at St. Rollo's. London, Newnes, 1943.
The Secret of Cliff Castle. London, Newnes, 1943.
The Adventures of Scamp. London, Newnes, 1943.
Smuggler Ben. London, Laurie, 1943.

Plays

A Book of Little Plays (includes *The Princess and the Swineherd, Sing a Song of Sixpence, Fairy Prisoners, Robin Hood, Peronel's Paint*). London, Nelson, 1926.

The Play's the Thing (includes *The Capture of the Robbers; Rag, Tag, and Bobtail; Rumpelstiltskin; The King's Jester; The Magic Apple; Merry Robin Hood; The King's Pocket Knife; In the Toyshop; The Cuckoo; The Rainbow Flowers; The Wishing-Glove; The Broken Statue*), music by Alec Rowley, illustrated by Alfred Bestall. London, Nelson, 1927; as *Plays for Older Children* and *Plays for Younger Children,* London, Newnes, 2 vols., 1940.
Six Enid Blyton Plays (includes *The Princess and the Enchanter, Robin Hood and the Butcher, The Enchanted Cap, A Visit to Nursery-Rhyme Land, The Squirrel's Secret, The Whistling Brownie*). London, Methuen, 1935.
How the Flowers Grow and Other Musical Plays (includes *The Fairy in the Box, The Magic Ball, The Toys at Night-Time, Who Stole the Crown?, Santa Claus Gets Busy*), music by Cecil Sharman. Exeter, Wheaton, 1939.
Cameo Plays, Book 4 (includes *The Making of a Rainbow, Poor Mr. Twiddle, The Three Wishes, The Donkey's Tail, Santa Claus Comes Down the Chimney, The Wind and the Sun, Brer Rabbit and Mr. Dog, The Little Green Imp*), edited by George H. Holroyd. Leeds, E.J. Arnold, 1939.
The Wishing Bean and Other Plays (includes *The Hole in the Sack, Spreading the News, The Queen's Garden, Sneezing Powder, The Land of Nursery Rhymes*). Oxford, Blackwell, 1939; as *Six Plays for Schools,* 1939.
Noddy in Toyland, music by Philip Green (produced London, 1954). London, Sampson Low, 1956.
Finding the Tickets. London, Evans, 1955.
Mr. Sly-One and Cats. London, Evans, 1955.
Mother's Meeting. London, Evans, 1955.
Who Will Hold the Giant? London, Evans, 1955.
The Famous Five, adaptation of her own stories (produced London, 1955).

Poetry

Child Whispers. London, Saville, 1922.
Real Fairies. London, Saville, 1923.
Songs of Gladness, music by Alec Rowley. London, Saville, 1924.
Silver and Gold, illustrated by Lewis Baumer. London, Nelson, 1925; New York, Nelson, 1928.
The Enid Blyton Poetry Book: Ninety-Six Poems for the Twelve Months of the Year. London, Methuen, 1934.
Noddy Nursery Rhymes. London, Sampson Low, 1956.
Noddy's Own Nursery Rhymes. London, Sampson Low, 1958.

Other

Responsive Singing Games. London, Saville, 1923.
Reading Practice, 1-5, 8-9, 11. London, Nelson, 8 vols., 1925-26.
The Bird Book, illustrated by Roland Green. London, Newnes, 1926.
Aesop's Fables, Retold. London, Nelson, 1928.
Let's Pretend, illustrated by I. Bennington Angrave. London, Nelson, 1928.
Old English Stories, Retold. London, Nelson, 1928.
Pinkity's Pranks and Other Nature Fairy Tales, Retold. London, Nelson, 1928.
Tales of Brer Rabbit, Retold. London, Nelson, 1928.
Nature Lessons. London, Evans, 1929.
The Knights of the Round Table. London, Newnes, 1930.
Tales from the Arabian Nights. London, Newnes, 1930.
Tales of Ancient Greece. London, Newnes, 1930.
Tales of Robin Hood. London, Newnes, 1930.
Let's Read. London, Birn, 1933.
My First Reading Book. London, Birn, 1933.
Stories from World History (*The Adventures of Odysseus, The Story of the Siege of Troy, Tales of the Ancient Greeks and Persians, Tales of the Romans*). London, Evans, 4 vols., 1934.
Round the Year with Enid Blyton: Spring, Summer, Autumn, Winter. London, Evans, 4 vols., 1934.
The Old Thatch series (includes fiction; *The Talking Teapot and Other Tales; Hop, Skip and Jump; The Tale of Mr. Wumble; Brer Rabbit; The Adventures of Bobs; The Little Button-Elves; Animals at Home; Birds at Home; Brer Rabbit and His Friends; The Two Sillies and Other Stories; Round the Year Stories; A Book of Magic; The Watchman with 100 Eyes and Other Greek Tales; Children of Other Lands; A Visit to the Zoo; Tales of Old Thatch; Children of Other Days; King Arthur and His Knights; All about the Circus; Friends of the Countryside*). London, Johnston, 20 vols., 1934-39.
The Children's Garden. London, Newnes, 1935.
Heyo, Brer Rabbit! Tales of Brer Rabbit and His Friends, illustrated by Kathleen Nixon. London, Newnes, 1938.
Birds of Our Gardens, illustrated by Roland Green and Ernest Aris. London, Newnes, 1940.
The News Chronicle Boys' and Girls' Book. London, News Chronicle, 1940.
The Babar Story Book, from stories by Jean de Brunhoff. London, Methuen, 1941; shortened version, as *Tales of Babar,* 1942.
A Calendar for Children. London, Newnes, 1941.
Book of the Year, music by Alec Rowley, illustrated by Eileen A. Soper. London, Evans, 1941 (and later volumes).
Enid Blyton Readers, 1-7, 10-12. London, Macmillan, 10 vols., 1942-50.
The Further Adventures of Brer Rabbit, Being More Tales of Brer Rabbit and His Friends, illustrated by Ernest Aris. London, Newnes, 1942.
The Land of Far-Beyond, based on *Pilgrim's Progress* by John Bunyan. London, Methuen, 1942.
The Children's Life of Christ. London, Methuen, 1943.
The Christmas Book, illustrated by Treyer Evans. London, Macmillan, 1944.
Nature Lover's Book, illustrated by Donia Nachshen and Noel Hopking. London, Evans, 1944.
Tales from the Bible, illustrated by Eileen A. Soper. London, Methuen, 1944.
Nature Readers, 1-30. London, Macmillan, 30 vols., 1945-46.
The First Christmas, illustrated by Paul Henning. London, Methuen, 1945.
The Enid Blyton Holiday Book. London, Sampson Low, 1946 (and 11 later volumes).
Before I Go to Sleep: A Book of Bible Stories and Prayers for Children at Night. London, Latimer, 1947; Boston, Little Brown, 1953.
Enid Blyton's Treasury. London, Evans, 1947.
Jinky Nature Books. Leeds, E.J. Arnold, 4 vols., 1947.
Brer Rabbit and His Friends. London, Coker, 1948.
Brer Rabbit Book, illustrated by Grace Lodge. London, Latimer, 8 vols., 1948-58.
Let's Garden, illustrated by William McLaren. London, Latimer, 1948.

The Enid Blyton Nature Plates, with stories and notes, and reference book. London, Macmillan, 3 vols., 1949.
The Enid Blyton Bible Stories: Old Testament, with Bible pictures and reference book. London, Macmillan, 16 vols., 1949.
My Enid Blyton Bedside Book. London, Barker, 1949 (and 11 later volumes).
A Book of Magic. London, Macmillan, 1949.
My First Enid Blyton Book. London, Latimer, 1952 (and 2 later volumes).
The Enid Blyton Bible Stories: New Testament, with Bible pictures and reference book. London, Macmillan, 16 vols., 1952-53.
Animal Lover's Book. London, Evans, 1952.
Enid Blyton's Omnibus, illustrated by Jessie Land. London, Newnes, 1952.
My First Nature Book, illustrated by Eileen A. Soper. London, Macmillan, 1952 (and 2 later volumes).
Enid Blyton's Christmas Story, illustrated by Fritz Wegner. London, Hamish Hamilton, 1953.
The Story of Our Queen, illustrated by F.Stocks May. London, Muller, 1953.
Little Gift Books, illustrated by Pierre Probst. London, Hackett, 1954 (and later volumes).
Enid Blyton Magazine Annual. London, Evans, 1954 (and 3 later volumes).
The Greatest Book in the World, illustrated by Mabel Peacock. London, British and Foreign Bible Society, 1954.
Bible Stories from the Old [and *New*] *Testament,* illustrated by Grace Lodge. London, Lutterworth Press, 2 vols., 1955.
Favourite Book of Fables, from the Tales of La Fontaine, illustrated by Romain Simon. London, Collins, 1955.
What Shall I Be?, illustrated by Pierre Probst. London, Collins, 1955.
Playing at Home, with Sabine Schweitzer. London, Methuen, 1955.
Let's Have a Party, photographs by Paul Kaye. London, Harvill Press, 1956; New York, Roy, 1957 (?).
A Story Book of Jesus, illustrated by Elsie Walker. London, Macmillan, 1956.
New Testament Picture Books 1-2. London, Macmillan, 2 vols., 1957.
The School Companion, with others. London, New Educational Press, 1958.
A.B.C. with Noddy. London, Sampson Low, 1959.
Old Testament Picture Books. London, Macmillan, 1960.
Noddy's One, Two, Three Book. London, Sampson Low, 1961.
The Big Enid Blyton Book. London, Hamlyn, 1961.
Brer Rabbit Again, illustrated by Grace Lodge. London, Dean, 1963.
Tales of Brave Adventure, Retold. London, Dean, 1963.
Easy Reader. London, Collins, 1965 (and later volumes).
Brer Rabbit's a Rascal, illustrated by Grace Lodge. London, Dean, 1965.
Learn to Count [*Go Shopping, Read about Animals, Tell the Time*] *with Noddy.* London, Sampson Low, 4 vols., 1965.
Tales of Long Ago, Retold. London, Dean, 1965.
Enid Blyton's Bedtime Annual. Manchester, World Distributors, 1966 (and later volumes).
Enid Blyton's Playbook. London, Collins, 1966 (and later volumes).
Gift Book, illustrated by Willy Schermelé. London, Purnell, 1966.
Noddy Toyland ABC Picture Book. London, Sampson Low, 1967.

Editor, *Sunny Stories for Little Folks,* and *Sunny Stories 1937-52.* London, Newnes, 27 vols., 1926-52.
Editor, *Treasure Trove Readers.* Exeter, Wheaton, 4 vols., 1934.
Editor, *Nature Observation Pictures.* London, Warne, 4 vols., 1935.
Editor, *Birds of the Wayside and Woodland,* by Thomas A. Coward. London, Warne, 1936.
Editor, *The Children's Book of Prayers.* London, Muller, 1953.

Publications for Adults

Other

The Story of My Life. London, Pitman, 1952.

Editor, *The Teacher's Treasury.* London, Newnes, 2 vols., 1926.
Editor, *Modern Teaching: Practical Suggestions for Junior and Senior Schools.* London, Newnes, 6 vols., 1928.
Editor, *Modern Teaching in the Infant School.* London, Newnes, 4 vols., 1932.

*

Critical Studies: *Enid Blyton: A Biography* by Barbara Stoney, London, Hodder and Stoughton, 1974; *The Blyton Phenomenon: The Controversy Surrounding the World's Most Successful Children's Writer* by Sheila G. Ray, London, Deutsch, 1982; *The Enid Blyton Story* by Bob Mullan, London, Boxtree, 1987; *A Childhood at Green Hedges* by Imogen Smallwood, London, Methuen, 1989.

* * *

Although her work was first published in a magazine in 1917 and her first book, a 24-page pamphlet of verse, appeared in 1922, the stories which made Enid Blyton a household name with both adults and children did not begin to appear until the late 1930s, first in the weekly magazine *Enid Blyton's Sunny Stories,* and subsequently in book form.

Many adults recall with affection the two short fantasy series which begin respectively with *Adventures of the Wishing Chair* and *The Enchanted Wood.* The origins of both of these may be found in the Norse legends—the wishing chair having overtones of Frey's ship, and the faraway tree of Yggdrasill—but the strange lands which the children visit are far removed from the Norse tradition. They offer plenty of opportunity for slapstick humour and memorable non-human characters, and provide vivid images on which the more imaginative child can weave his own variations.

The Secret Seven and *The Famous Five* have been shown by many reading surveys to be the most widely read series. These provide exciting and undemanding reading material at an age when plenty of reading practice is important. They motivate children to want to read, and there is little which can be offered as an alternative with the same appeal. Blyton never paid any attention to the adult critic of children's literature, who in any case was not much in evidence until long after she was well-established, and she gave the children what she believed they wanted.

There are other series of mystery/adventure stories which are almost as well known and widely read. Blyton's stories in this genre appeal to children at an age when this type of story has the most appeal for them, at a time when links with their peer group are important and membership in a gang is most children's ideal.

The exclusiveness of the Blyton characters may be criticised, but it is an accurate reflection of what children are like at this age. The *Adventure* books are more complex in both plot and characterisation than any of the others, and are therefore bought and praised by librarians and teachers who are selective in their purchase of Blyton books. There are two *Mystery* series: one of them features Fatty, "the master of disguises," and his friends in their attempts to outwit Mr. Goon the policeman in solving mysteries; in the other the central character is the mysterious Barney with his unusual pet. Most memorable of the adventure stories are the five *Secret* books, in which Blyton made use of traditionally British popular literary motifs—the desert island, the kidnapped Ruritanian prince, and the secret Afro-Asian kingdom.

The circus life portrayed in the numerous circus stories was romanticised even for the 1940s, with the horse-drawn caravans and the lack of concern for the realities of compulsory education or regulations about children performing in public; but these stories again provide a setting for unusual characters, exciting adventures, and close contact with animals—early recognised by Blyton as a theme popular with children. Jimmy Brown's success with all kinds of animals in *Mr. Galliano's Circus* is a perfect wish-fulfilment story.

Most boys grow out of Blyton at the age of 10 or 11, but girls may go on reading her longer because of the existence of the school stories. Reading surveys carried out in the 1940s show that the school story was the most popular type of story among girls of 11-14. Blyton's first school stories were those about *The Naughtiest Girl,* set in a progressive, self-governing, coeducational school. Presumably designed so that they would not alienate the boy readers of *Sunny Stories,* in which they appeared as serials, they proved less popular than the later stories about *St. Clare's* and *Malory Towers.* These have worn remarkably well: the girls do not run into troubles of the trivial kind found in comparable stories, which would seem absurd to a schoolgirl of the 1990s, nor did Blyton rely on secret passages, lost heiresses, smugglers, or spies to add interest to the stories. The action arises out of the characters, and the simple psychology, showing why people behave as they do, may well stand the girl reader in good stead in later life; there is also some good slapstick comedy. Although the school story generally has never risen to great literary heights, Blyton's stories are good examples of the genre.

The nearest approach to "social realism" comes in *The Six Bad Boys,* the first edition of which included a preface of praise by Sir Basil Henriques, the well-known juvenile magistrate. This book reflected ideas prevalent in the post-war period; women were being encouraged to stay at home if they had school-age children, and the six boys who eventually come before the juvenile court are shown to have unsatisfactory homes and, particularly, unsatisfactory mothers. Although this may seem oversimplified and out of date in the liberated 1990s, there is still a lot of common sense to be found within the pages of this book.

Although Blyton published over 600 books, some of them (usually those in series) have made much more impact than others. Noddy is the character most frequently criticised by adults, but he probably makes most of his impression on children because of the colourful illustrations and the commercial "spinoffs" rather than because of his adventures.

Blyton has been criticised for her impoverished vocabulary, her undemanding style, her stereotyped characters, her incredible plots, her attitudes towards minority groups, her sexism, and her snobbishness. Although her books do tend to reflect middle-class attitudes of the 1930s and 1940s, these criticisms need to be examined carefully; to Blyton, plot was all important and where necessary she developed strong working-class characters such as Jack, whose skills enable the runaways to survive in *The Secret Island,* and Andy, the fisherman's boy, in *The Adventurous Four.*

The faults of plot, characterisation, and style for which she is criticised by adults contribute largely to her popularity with children. Readers are plunged straight into the plot, are told directly all they need to know and think about the characters, who tend to be all good or all bad, and are not held up by unfamiliar vocabulary or complex sentence structures. Simple and evocative words such as "horrid," "peculiar," and "exciting" tend to be overused. The stories are set in a world which does not exist but is familiar to every reader and the morality is simple and straightforward. Their simplicity makes them appeal to children of all abilities and so long as children are encouraged to move on to other books at the appropriate stage in their development, the reading of Blyton can help them to acquire vital reading skills through practice.

Blyton is perhaps the only children's writer who can be described as a household name. When the Cox Report on the teaching of English to 5 to 11-year-olds was published in 1988, 20 years after her death, the fact that her name was omitted from the list of 200 authors recommended for this age group attracted more media interest than any other feature of the report. The Secretary of State for Education was heard to say that she was a "good" author who didn't need publicity. Each year new editions of her books are published, while old stories and favourite characters appear in new guises. In the early 1980s, some additional titles written by a French author which took the Famous Five to more exotic locations were translated into English and published in paperback. In Germany, the story of Darrell Rivers of Malory Towers was continued, taking her into marriage and motherhood, but so far these have not been introduced to the British market.

Well over 300 Blyton titles were still in print at the end of the 1990s, including editions of the *Famous Five* stories linked to the popular television serialisation and modern adventure games, also based on the *Famous Five* series. Titles such as *The Wrecker's Tower Game* and *The Whispering Island Game* conjure up visions of those elements which helped to make their originator so popular.

Blyton has been the centre of passionate controversy since the 1950s; although the extent of her "banning" by parents, teachers, and librarians has probably been exaggerated, there are signs that in recent years her ability to encourage children to read has been recognised by adults concerned with children's reading. She was, above all, a skilled storyteller and many adults today must owe their pleasure in reading to this quality in her work.

—Sheila G. Ray

BODECKER, N(iels) M(ogens)

Nationality: Danish. **Born:** Copenhagen, Denmark, 13 January 1922; moved to the United States, 1952. **Education:** Technical Society School of Architecture, 1939-41, School of Applied Art, 1941-44, and School of Commerce, 1942-44, all Copenhagen. **Military Service:** Royal Danish Artillery, 1945-47. **Family:** Married Mary Ann Weld in 1952 (marriage dissolved 1959); three sons.

Career: Freelance writer and illustrator. **Awards:** Society of Illustrators award, 1965; Christopher award, 1974, 1977. **Died:** 1 February 1988.

PUBLICATIONS FOR CHILDREN (ILLUSTRATED BY THE AUTHOR)

Fiction

Miss Jaster's Garden. New York, Golden Press, 1971; London, Collins, 1973.

Good Night, Little A.B.C., with Robert Kraus. New York, Springfellow, 1972; London, Cape, 1974.

The Mushroom Center Disaster, illustrated by Erik Blegvad. New York, Atheneum, 1974.

The Lost String Quartet. New York, Atheneum, 1981.

Quimble Wood, illustrated by Branka Starr. New York, Atheneum, 1981.

Poetry

It's Raining Said John Twaining: Danish Nursery Rhymes. New York, Atheneum, and London, Macmillan, 1973.

Let's Marry Said the Cherry and Other Nonsense Poems. New York, Atheneum, 1974; London, Faber, 1977.

Hurry, Hurry, Mary Dear! and Other Nonsense Poems. New York, Atheneum, 1976; London, Dent, 1979.

A Person from Britain Whose Head Was the Shape of a Mitten and Other Limericks. New York, Atheneum, and London, Dent, 1980.

Pigeon Cubes and Other Verse. New York, Atheneum, 1982.

Snowman Sniffles and Other Verse. New York, Atheneum, 1983; London, Faber, 1984.

Carrot Holes and Frisbee Trees, illustrated by Nina Winters. New York, Atheneum, 1983.

PUBLICATIONS FOR ADULTS

Poetry

Digtervandring (Poets Ramble). Copenhagen, Forum, 1943.

Graa Fugle (Grey Birds). Copenhagen, Prior, 1946.

*

Illustrator: *Spillebog for Hus, Hjem, og Kro* (Book of Games for House, Home, and Inn) by Sigfred Pedersen, 1948; *Oh! What a Wonderful Wedding* by Virginia Rowans, 1953; *Half Magic,* 1954, *Knight's Castle,* 1956, *Magic by the Lake,* 1957, *The Time Garden,* 1958, *Magic or Not?,* 1959, *The Well-Wishers,* 1960, and *Seven-Day Magic,* 1962, all by Edward Eager; *The Bulls and the Bees* by Roger Eddy, 1956; *Cousins,* 1956, and *Beaux,* 1958, both by Evan Commager; *Songberd's Grove* by Anne Mainwaring Barrett, 1957; *Cadwallader: A Diversion* by Russell Lynes, 1959; *The S-Man,* by Mark Caine, 1960; *Sylvester, The Mouse with the Musical Ear* by Adelaide Holl, 1961; *David Copperfield* by Charles Dickens, 1962; *The Book of the Dance* by Agnes DeMille, 1963; *The Snake in the Carpool* by Miriam Schlein, 1963; *Lizzie's Twin* by Doris Adelberg, 1964; *Is There a Mouse in the House?* by Josephine Gibson, 1965; *Shoe Full of Shamrock* by Mary Francis Shura, 1965; *Good Night, Little One,* 1972, *Good Night, Richard Rabbit,* 1972, *The Night-Lite Calendar 1974* and *1975,* 1973-74, and *The Night-Lite Storybook,* 1975, all by Robert Kraus; *Mattie Fritts and the Flying Mushroom* by Michael Jennings, 1973; *A Little at a Time* by David A. Adler, 1977.

N.M. Bodecker commented:

(1978) My first collection of Danish verse, written when I was 19, came out in Copenhagen in 1943. Poetry was my first love, illustration came later, and writing for children later still. I changed language and country (though not nationality) at the age of 30, and for the next 20 years made my living as an illustrator, working on my English poetry after hours. When my first English book came out in New York, it may have looked as if an illustrator had suddenly turned writer. Actually the illustrator had been the writer in disguise. A troublesome disguise at times, for illustrating never gave me much pleasure. With *Let's Marry Said the Cherry* I finally picked up the thread I had dropped in Copenhagen 23 years earlier: writing and illustrating my own nonsense. Writing for children took me by surprise, I hadn't planned it, it just happened. The child in me would out.

I'm rather a late bloomer in many ways, and the closer I get to resemble an adult, the easier I find it to give the child in me free range: to sympathize with un-rung bells and boats tugging at their moorings, longing to perform according to their nature: to know that when the longing grows strong enough, the boat sails itself and the bell rings out unaided. Certainly, at night when I'm asleep, the piano in the garden room plays "Oranges and Lemons," or a little Schubert, perhaps.

* * *

Gifted with rare imagination and a wonderful sense of the absurd, N.M. Bodecker wrote both poetry and prose for children. His first English-language work, *Miss Jaster's Garden,* is a gentle tale of a very proper English maiden lady and her good friend Hedgie, and what happens when the flower seeds that Miss Jaster inadvertently drops on Hedgie's back grow and bloom. The simple story of Miss Jaster and her hedgehog friend scarcely prepares the reader for the remarkably imaginative miniature world of *The Mushroom Center Disaster,* a story which in its cozy British warmth and tender feeling for small living things (in this case, insects) is reminiscent of Grahame's *The Wind in the Willows,* but which in its exquisitely careful choice of words and in its poetic rhythm is Bodecker at his best. The story itself, a tale with ecological overtones of what happens when the remains of a picnic lunch are carelessly dropped on a tiny insect village, is slight, but the careful detail with which Bodecker describes the *modus vivendi* of the insects' miniature, and very humanly British, world is captivating.

In contrast to his earlier prose works, Bodecker's later whimsey, *The Lost String Quartet,* details the wacky and wonderful wanderings of the Daffodil String Quartet on their way to a concert in mid-January on the far side of the mountain, which ends with their performance, to considerable applause, of the Spring Quartet in E Minor for string beans, alpen horn, tirelin, and viola constrictor.

Bodecker made his greatest contribution to children's literature, however, with his nonsense verse for children, a growing corpus beginning with *It's Raining Said John Twaining.* This is a translation of Danish nursery rhymes done for Bodecker's three American-born sons; integrated with Bodecker's own illustrations, the poems have a tongue-twisting rhythm and logical illogic which cry to be read aloud. Here we find Miss Jaster reincarnated as Little Miss Price who rode with her mice over the ice, the three guinea pigs who went, like "Pussycat, Pussycat" of the old English nursery rhyme, to see the King, and a host of other zanies in the best nursery-rhyme tradition. The rhythms of traditional skipping rhymes and happily inspired word play animate Bodecker's poetry, which has justly been compared with that of Edward Lear, Ogden Nash, and Lewis Carroll. His further collections enlarged Bodecker's range of subject matter and cast of characters without exhausting his inspired nonsense.

—Margaret F. Maxwell

BOND, (Thomas) Michael

Nationality: British. **Born:** Newbury, Berkshire, 13 January 1926. **Education:** Presentation College, Reading, 1934-40. **Military Service:** Royal Air Force, 1943-44; Middlesex Regiment, British Army, 1944-47. **Family:** Married 1) Brenda Mary Johnson in 1950 (divorced 1981), one daughter and one son; 2) Susan Marfrey Rogers in 1981. **Career:** Cameraman, BBC Television, London, 1947-66. Director, Paddington and Company (Films) Ltd., London. **Agent:** Harvey Unna and Stephen Durbridge Ltd., 24-32 Pottery Lane, London W11 4LZ. **Address:** 22 Maida Avenue, London W2 1SR, England.

Publications for Children

Fiction

A Bear Called Paddington, illustrated by Peggy Fortnum. London, Collins, 1958; Boston, Houghton Mifflin, 1960.
More about Paddington, illustrated by Peggy Fortnum. London, Collins, 1959; Boston, Houghton Mifflin, 1961.
Paddington Helps Out, illustrated by Peggy Fortnum. London, Collins, 1960; Boston, Houghton Mifflin, 1961.
Paddington Abroad, illustrated by Peggy Fortnum. London, Collins, 1961; Boston, Houghton Mifflin, 1972.
Paddington at Large, illustrated by Peggy Fortnum. London, Collins, 1962; Boston, Houghton Mifflin, 1963.
Paddington Marches On, illustrated by Peggy Fortnum. London, Collins, 1964; Boston, Houghton Mifflin, 1965.
Here Comes Thursday, illustrated by Daphne Rowles. London, Harrap, 1966; New York, Lothrop, 1967.
Paddington at Work, illustrated by Peggy Fortnum. London, Collins, 1966; Boston, Houghton Mifflin, 1967.
Paddington Goes to Town, illustrated by Peggy Fortnum. London, Collins, and Boston, Houghton Mifflin, 1968.
Thursday Rides Again, illustrated by Beryl Sanders. London, Harrap, 1968; New York, Lothrop, 1969.
Parsley's Good Deed, illustrated by Esor. London, BBC Publications, 1969.
The Story of Parsley's Tail, illustrated by Esor. London, BBC Publications, 1969.
Thursday Ahoy!, illustrated by Leslie Wood. London, Harrap, 1969; New York, Lothrop, 1970.
Paddington Takes the Air, illustrated by Peggy Fortnum. London, Collins, 1970; Boston, Houghton Mifflin, 1971.
Parsley's Last Stand. London, BBC Publications, 1970.
Parsley's Problem Present. London, BBC Publications, 1970.
Thursday in Paris, illustrated by Leslie Wood. London, Harrap, 1971.
The Tales of Olga da Polga (*Olga Makes a Wish, Olga's New Home, Olga Counts Her Blessings, Olga Makes Her Mark, Olga Takes a Bite, Olga's Second House, Olga Makes a Friend, Olga's Special Day*), illustrated by Hans Helweg. London, Penguin, 1971; New York, Macmillan, 1973.
Parsley the Lion, illustrated by Ivor Wood. London, Collins, 1972.
Parsley Parade, illustrated by Ivor Wood. London, Collins, 1972.
Paddington Bear, illustrated by Fred Banbery. London, Collins, 1972; New York, Random House, 1973; illustrated by John Lobban, New York, HarperCollins, 1992.
Paddington's Garden, illustrated by Fred Banbery. London, Collins, 1972; New York, Random House, 1973; illustrated by John Lobban, New York, HarperCollins, 1993.
The Day the Animals Went on Strike, illustrated by Jim Hodgson. London, Studio Vista, 1972; New York, American Heritage Press, 1973.
Olga Meets Her Match, illustrated by Hans Helweg. London, Longman, 1973; New York, Hastings House, 1975.
Paddington at the Circus, illustrated by Fred Banbery. London, Collins, 1973; New York, Random House, 1974.
Paddington Goes Shopping, illustrated by Fred Banbery. London, Collins, 1973; illustrated by John Lobban, New York, HarperCollins, 1992; as *Paddington's Lucky Day,* New York, Random House, 1974.
Paddington on Top, illustrated by Peggy Fortnum. London, Collins, 1974; Boston, Houghton Mifflin, 1975.
Paddington's Blue Peter Story Book, illustrated by Ivor Wood. London, Collins, 1974; as *Paddington Takes to T.V.,* Boston, Houghton Mifflin, 1974.
Mr. Cram's Magic Bubbles, illustrated by Gioia Fiammenghi. London, Penguin, 1975.
Windmill, illustrated by Tony Cattaneo. London, Studio Vista, 1975.
Paddington at the Seaside, illustrated by Fred Banbery. London, Collins, 1975; New York, Random House, 1978.
Paddington at the Tower, illustrated by Fred Banbery. London, Collins, 1975; New York, Random House, 1978.
Olga Carries On, illustrated by Hans Helweg. London, Kestrel, 1976; New York, Hastings House, 1977.
Paddington at the Station, illustrated by Barry Wilkinson. London, Collins, 1976.
Paddington Takes a Bath, illustrated by Barry Wilkinson. London, Collins, 1976; illustrated by John Lobban, New York, HarperCollins, 1992.
Paddington Goes to the Sales, illustrated by Barry Wilkinson. London, Collins, 1976.
Paddington's New Room, illustrated by Barry Wilkinson. London, Collins, 1976.
Paddington Does It Himself. London, Collins, 1977.
Paddington Hits Out. London, Collins, 1977.
Paddington in the Kitchen. London, Collins, 1977; illustrated by John Lobban, New York, HarperCollins, 1992.
Paddington's Birthday Party. London, Collins, 1977.
Paddington's Picture Book (collection), illustrated by Fred Banbery. London, Collins, 1978.

Paddington Takes the Test, illustrated by Peggy Fortnum. London, Collins, 1979; Boston, Houghton Mifflin, 1980.
J.D. Polson and the Liberty Head Dime, illustrated by Roger Wade Walker. London, Octopus, and New York, Mayflower, 1980.
Paddington in Touch. London, Collins, 1980.
Paddington and Aunt Lucy. London, Collins, 1980.
Paddington Weighs In. London, Collins, 1980.
Paddington at Home. London, Collins, 1980.
Paddington Goes Out. London, Collins, 1980.
J.D. Polson and the Dillogate Affair, illustrated by Roger Wade Walker. London, Hodder and Stoughton, 1981.
Paddington On Screen: A Second Blue Peter Storybook, illustrated by Barry Macey. London, Collins, 1981; Boston, Houghton Mifflin, 1982.
Paddington Has Fun. London, Collins, 1982.
Paddington Works Hard. London, Collins, 1982.
Olga Takes Charge, illustrated by Hans Helweg. London, Kestrel, 1982; New York, Dell, 1983.
J.D. Polson and the Great Unveiling, illustrated by Roger Wade Walker. London, Hodder and Stoughton, 1982.
The Caravan Puppets, illustrated by Vanessa Julian-Ottie. London, Collins, 1983.
Paddington's Storybook, illustrated by Peggy Fortnum. London, Collins, 1983; Boston, Houghton Mifflin, 1984.
Paddington on the River. London, Collins, 1983.
Paddington and the Knickerbocker Rainbow, illustrated by David McKee. London, Collins, 1984; New York, Putnam, 1985.
Paddington at the Zoo, illustrated by David McKee. London, Collins, 1984; New York, Putnam, 1985.
Paddington at the Fair, illustrated by David McKee. London, Collins, 1985; New York, Putnam, 1986.
Paddington's Painting Exhibition. London, Collins, 1985; as *Paddington's Art Exhibition,* New York, Putnam, 1986.
Paddington at the Palace. London, Collins, and New York, Putnam, 1986.
Paddington Minds the House. London, Collins, 1986; as *Paddington Cleans Up,* New York, Putnam, 1986.
Paddington Posts a Letter, with Karen Bond, illustrated by Toni Goffe. London, Hutchinson, 1986; as *Paddington Mails a Letter,* New York, Macmillan, 1986.
Paddington's Clock Book, with Karen Bond, illustrated by Toni Goffe. London, Hutchinson, and New York, Macmillan, 1986.
Paddington at the Airport, with Karen Bond, illustrated by Toni Goffe. London, Hutchinson, and New York, Macmillan, 1986.
On Four Wheels: Paddington's London, with Karen Bond, illustrated by Toni Goffe. London, Hutchinson, 1986; as *Paddington's Wheel Book,* New York, Macmillan, 1986.
Oliver the Greedy Elephant, with Paul Parnes, illustrated by Jim Hodgson. London, Golden Books, 1986.
Paddington and the Marmalade Maze, illustrated by David McKee. London, Collins, 1987.
Paddington's Busy Day, illustrated by David McKee. London, Collins, 1987.
A Mouse Called Thursday. London, Chancellor, 1988.
Paddington's Magical Christmas, illustrated by David McKee. London, Collins, 1988; illustrated by John Lobban, New York, HarperCollins, 1993.
Paddington Meets the Queen, illustrated by John Lobban. London, Carnival, and New York, HarperFestival, 1991.
Paddington Rides On!, illustrated by John Lobban. London, Carnival, and New York, HarperFestival, 1991.
A Day by the Sea, illustrated by Ross Design. London, Young Lions, 1992.
Paddington at the Seashore. New York, HarperCollins, 1992.
Paddington Breaks the Peace. London, Young Lions, 1992.
Something Nasty in the Kitchen. London, Young Lions, 1992.
Paddington's Picnic, illustrated by Nick Ward for Ross Design. London, Young Lions, 1993.
Paddington Does the Decorating. London, Young Lions, 1993.
Paddington's Disappearing Trick. London, Young Lions, 1993.
Paddington's Things I Do, illustrated by John Lobban. New York, HarperCollins, 1994.
Paddington's Things I Feel, illustrated by John Lobban. London, HarperCollins, 1994.
Bears & Forebears: A Life So Far. London, HarperCollins, 1996.
Paddington Bear and the Christmas Surprise, illustrated by R.W. Alley. New York, HarperCollins, 1997.

Plays

The Adventures of a Bear Called Paddington, with Alfred Bradley. London, French, 1974.
Paddington on Stage, with Alfred Bradley, illustrated by Peggy Fortnum. London, Collins, 1974; Boston, Houghton Mifflin, 1977.

Television Series: *The Herbs,* 1970; *The Adventures of Parsley* (puppet films).

Other

Herbs Annual. London, BBC Publications, 2 vols., 1969-70.
The Parsley Annual. London, BBC Publications, 2 vols., 1971-72.
How to Make Flying Things, photographs by Peter Kibble. London, Studio Vista, 1975.
Paddington's Loose-End Book: An ABC of Things to Do, illustrated by Ivor Wood. London, Collins, 1976.
Paddington's Party Book, illustrated by Ivor Wood. London, Collins, 1976.
The Great Big Paddington Book, illustrated by Ivor Wood. London, Collins, 1976; Cleveland, Collins World, 1977.
Fun and Games with Paddington, illustrated by Ivor Wood. London, Collins, 1977; Cleveland, Collins World, 1978.
Paddington's Pop-Up Book, illustrated by Ivor Wood. London, Collins, 1977.
Paddington's Colouring Books (*Paddington Carpenter* [*Conjuror, Cook, Golfer*]). London, Collins, 4 vols., 1977.
Paddington Pastime series (*Paddington's First* [*Word, Counting, Play*] *Book*), illustrated by Barry Wilkinson. London, Collins, 4 vols., 1977.
Paddington's Suitcase (includes *Paddington's Notebook* and *Paddington's Birthday Book*). London, Collins, 1983.
Paddington's First Puzzle Book [and] *Paddington's Second Puzzle Book,* with Karen Bond. New York, Crocodile, 1987.
Paddington's 123. London, Collins, 1990.
Paddington's ABC. London, Collins, 1990; New York, Viking, 1991.
Paddington's Opposites. London, Collins, 1990.
Paddington's Jar of Jokes. London, Carnival, 1992.
Paddington Book and Bear Box (includes plush toy). New York, Viking, 1993.

Editor, *Michael Bond's Book of Bears* [*Mice*]. London, Purnell, 2 vols., 1971-72; New York, Macmillan, 1992.

Translator, with Eve Barwell, *The Motormalgamation,* by H.G. Fischer-Tschop and Barbara von Johnson. London, Studio Vista, 1973.

Publications for Adults

Novels

Monsieur Pamplemousse. London, Hodder and Stoughton, 1984; New York, Beaufort, 1985.
Monsieur Pamplemousse and the Secret Mission. London, Hodder and Stoughton, 1984; New York, Beaufort, 1986.
Monsieur Pamplemousse on the Spot. London, Hodder and Stoughton, and New York, Beaufort, 1986.
Monsieur Pamplemousse Takes the Cure. London, Hodder and Stoughton, 1987; New York, Random House, 1988.
Monsieur Pamplemousse Aloft. London, Hodder and Stoughton, 1989.
Monsieur Pamplemousse Investigates. London, Hodder and Stoughton, 1990.
Monsieur Pamplemousse Rests His Case. London, Headline, and Maine, G.K. Hall, 1991.
Monsieur Pamplemousse on Location. London, Headline, 1992.
Monsieur Pamplemousse Stands Firm. London, Headline, 1992.

Other

The Pleasures of Paris. London, Pavilion, 1987; New York, Potter, 1988.
The Life and Times of Paddington Bear, with Russell Ash. London, Pavilion, 1988.

* * *

It is almost impossible to think of Michael Bond without thinking of Paddington, so identified is he with his creation, one of the outstanding success stories in publishing. This success is due largely to the fact that Paddington is a bear. Teddies and other bears naturally appeal to children as symbolising love and security, and this one is certainly loved. His adventures, as children soon realise, are all certain to go wrong. Thus they have the pleasure of anticipation. Even very young children can become involved. In *Paddington Goes Shopping,* for instance, they can see in a few colourful pictures and brief texts what happens when Paddington is turned loose in a supermarket—he is buried under a load of groceries!

Bond's choice of a bear, although almost accidental, is very skilful. Paddington is not particularly bear-like: he behaves like a child and is generally regarded by the Browns as just another member of the family, albeit very accident-prone. By using a bear in this way, Bond has got the best of both worlds. He interests children who are fascinated by Paddington's propensity for disasters but he also attracts adults to whom the bear epitomises the well-meaning but bumbling adult whose behavior can be so amusing. Perhaps it is too much to say that Bond uses Paddington to illustrate human frailty and failings but undoubtedly he does pin-point many situations familiar to adults. By comparison, Olga da Polga can never match the general appeal of Paddington. She is definitely a guinea pig whose adventures are restricted to her natural surroundings; her relationship with humans is strictly traditional and lacks the supreme touch of fantasy which is the hallmark of the Paddington books where the animal is accepted as "human" throughout all the stories. Nobody looks askance at his going shopping or living as part of the Brown family and it is this dual aspect of Paddington (bear-appeal to children, human personification to adults) that makes Michael Bond's creation so outstanding.

—Margaret Walker

BOND, Ruskin

Nationality: Indian. **Born:** Kasauli, Himachal, 19 May 1934. **Education:** Bishop Cotton School, Simla, 1943-50. **Career:** Freelance writer. **Awards:** Rhys Memorial prize for fiction, 1957; Sahitya Academi award for English writing in India, 1992; nominated for Hans Christian Andersen award for children's literature, 1996 and 1998. **Address:** Ivy Cottage, Landour, Mussoorie, Uttar Pradesh 248179, India.

Publications for Children

Fiction

The Hidden Pool, illustrated by Arup Das. New Delhi, Children's Book Trust, 1966.
Grandfather's Private Zoo, illustrated by Mario Miranda. Bombay, India Book House, 1967.
Panther's Moon, illustrated by Tom Feelings. New York, Random House, 1969.
The Last Tiger. New Delhi, Government of India Publications, 1971.
Angry River, illustrated by Trevor Stubley. London, Hamish Hamilton, 1972.
The Blue Umbrella, illustrated by Trevor Stubley. London, Hamish Hamilton, 1974.
Night of the Leopard, illustrated by Eileen Green. London, Hamish Hamilton, 1979.
Big Business, illustrated by Valerie Littlewood. London, Hamish Hamilton, 1979.
The Cherry Tree, illustrated by Valerie Littlewood. London, Hamish Hamilton, 1980; illustrated by Allan Eitzen, Honesdale, Pennsylvania, Boyds Mills, 1991.
Flames in the Forest, illustrated by Valerie Littlewood. London, MacRae, 1981.
The Adventures of Rusty, illustrated by Imtiaz Dharker. New Delhi, Thomson Press, 1981.
Tigers Forever, illustrated by Valerie Littlewood. London, MacRae, and New York, Watts, 1983.
Earthquake, illustrated by Valerie Littlewood. London, MacRae, 1984.
Getting Granny's Glasses, illustrated by Barbara Walker. London, MacRae, 1985.
Cricket for the Crocodile, illustrated by Barbara Walker. London, MacRae, 1986.
The Adventures of Rama and Sita, illustrated by Valerie Littlewood. London, MacRae, 1987.
The Eyes of the Eagle, illustrated by Valerie Littlewood. London, MacRae, 1987.

Ghost Trouble. London, MacRae, 1989.
Dust on the Mountain. London, MacRae, 1990.
Snake Trouble, illustrated by Mickey Patel. London, MacRae, 1990.
Leopard on the Mountain, illustrated by Duncan Smith. Cambridge, Cambridge University Press, 1997.

Short Stories

The Road to the Bazaar, illustrated by Valerie Littlewood. London, MacRae, 1980.
Panther's Moon and Other Stories, illustrated by Suddhasattwa Basu. New Delhi, Puffin, 1990.
Ruskin Bond Children's Omnibus. New Delhi, Rupa, 1994.
Binya's Blue Umbrella, illustrated by Vera Rosenberg. Honesdale, Pennsylvania, Boyds Mills, 1995.

Poetry

To Live in Magic. New Delhi, Thomson Press, 1983.
Tigers Forever: Poems and Stories. New Delhi, Ratna Sagar, 1996.

Other

Tales Told at Twilight (folktales), illustrated by Madhu Powle. Bombay, India Book House, 1970; as *The Family Ghost and Other Folktales,* New Delhi, Frank Bros., 1996.
World of Trees, illustrated by Siddhartha Banerjee. New Delhi, National Book Trust, 1974.
Who's Who at the Zoo, photographs by Raghu Rai. New Delhi, National Book Trust, 1974.
Once upon a Monsoon Time (autobiography). New Delhi, Orient Longman, 1974.
Man of Destiny: A Biography of Jawaharlal Nehru. New Delhi, Orient, 1976.
A Garland of Memories (essays). New Delhi, Mukul Prakashan, 1982.
Tales and Legends of India, illustrated by Sally Scott. London, MacRae, and New York, Watts, 1982.
An Island of Trees: Nature Stories and Poems, illustrated by Suddhasattwa Basu. Delhi, Ratna Sagar, 1992.

PUBLICATIONS FOR ADULTS

Novels

The Room on the Roof. London, Deutsch, 1956; New York, Coward McCann, 1957.
Love Is a Sad Song. New Delhi, Orient, 1975.
A Flight of Pigeons. Bombay, India Book House, 1980.
The Young Vagrants. Bombay, India Book House, 1981.
Complete Stories and Novels. New Delhi, Viking, 1995.
Strangers in the Nights: Two Novellas. New Delhi, Penguin, 1996.

Short Stories

The Neighbour's Wife and Other Stories. Madras, Higginbothams, 1967.
My First Love and Other Stories. Bombay, Pearl, 1968.
The Man-Eater of Manjari. New Delhi, Sterling, 1974.
A Girl from Copenhagen. New Delhi, India Paperbacks, 1977.
Ghosts of a Hill Station. Bombay, India Book House, 1983.
The Night Train at Deoli. New Delhi, Penguin India, 1988.
Time Stops at Shamli and Other Stories. London, Penguin, 1990.
Our Trees Still Grow in Dehra. New Delhi, Penguin India, 1991.
Delhi Is Not Far: The Best of Ruskin Bond. New Delhi, Penguin India, 1996.

Poetry

It Isn't Time That's Passing: Poems 1970-1971. Calcutta, Writers Workshop, 1972.
Lone Fox Dancing: Lyric Poems. Calcutta, Writers Workshop, 1975.

Other

Strange Men, Strange Places. Bombay, Pearl, 1969.
Beautiful Garhwal. Dehra Dun, English Book Depot, 1988.
Ganga Descends. Dehra Dun, English Book Depot, 1992.
Mussoorie and Landour: Days of Wine and Roses, illustrated by Ganesh Saili. New Delhi, Lustre Press, 1992.
Rain in the Mountains: Notes from the Himalayas. New Delhi, Viking, 1993.
Scenes from a Writer's Life: A Memoir. New Delhi, Penguin India, 1997.

Editor, *Penquin Book of Indian Ghost Stories.* New Delhi, Penquin India, 1993.
Editor, *Penquin Book of Indian Railway Stories.* New Delhi, Penquin India, 1994.
Editor, *Penguin Book of Classical Indian Love Stories & Lyrics.* New Delhi, Penguin India, 1996.

*

Manuscript Collections: Mugar Memorial Library, Boston University.

Ruskin Bond comments:

My early stories, written when I was in my twenties, were about my own childhood in India and some of the people I knew as I grew up. They were written for adults. Then, in my thirties, I began writing for children. By then, I probably had a better perspective on my own childhood and more insight into the lives of other Indian children. Although my father was British, I grew up as an Indian. There has been no division of loyalties; only a double inheritance.

My life, like Scheherazade's, has depended upon my ability to tell stories, and this has been the best and only way in which I have been able to make a living—and also choose the place of my abode, the foothills of the Himalayas. For over 40 years, ever since I was a boy out of school in Simla, I have been a teller of tales—short stories, tall stories, folk stories, true stories, unfinished stories.... I am still a long way from Scheherazade's thousand and one tales, but then, I haven't the executioner's axe poised over me: only the rent to pay and books to buy and sometimes a chicken for myself and the family I share my life with....

The mountains are in my blood. Once you have lived with mountains, there is no escape; you must return, again and again. It was only after I had come to live in the mountains that I began writing for children; for here I was closer to nature, closer to the lives of the children (village or small town) who were growing up on these rugged mountain slopes, where life is never easy. And in stories such as "Dust on the Mountain" and "Leopard on the Mountain," I have made an honest attempt to portray their lives.

* * *

Winner of the 1992 Sahitya Academy award, Ruskin Bond is the most celebrated children's writer in India today. In an autobiographical essay, "What's Your Dream?" published in *A Garland of Memories,* Bond states that his central philosophy has been to first find his dream—a room of his own—and then to pursue it with single-mindedness. He returned from England, where he had gone at the end of the British Raj, to live and work amidst the Himalayan mountains where he was born and raised. In *Rain in the Mountains: Notes from the Himalayas,* a collection of autobiographical notes and essays, Bond writes, "I have been writing in order to sustain the sort of life I like to lead—unhurried, even-paced, sensual, in step with the natural world, most at home with humble people."

The interplay between Bond's personal experiences and their artistic expression in a variety of children's books allows him to weave his literary works into a harmonious pattern. Through well-written, highly entertaining short stories, novels, poems, folktales, and autobiographical essays, Bond gives voice to the things that are important to him: the enchantment of childhood; the belief in the sanctity of nature and wildlife; and the commitment and loyalty in personal relationships.

Through his writings, Bond captures the mood and spirit of a bygone era. His stories for children are set against the gentle and benign environment of a small Himalayan town or village where swiftly-rushing mountain streams, trees, flowers, birds, and animals are part of the characters' lives. The setting is a blend of traditional values and the modern influences of city life; it is a world where rich and poor, rural and urban live side-by-side in harmony. Under this protective atmosphere, the same characters reappear in story after story like old acquaintances. Bond's timeless vision of childhood—which he calls a long summer afternoon of fun and enjoyment—is a re-creation of the romantic view of his own childhood in Jamnagar, where his father was tutor-guardian to the royal children, and in Dehra Dun in the Himalayan foothills, where his grandparents lived. In works like *Once upon a Monsoon Time, The Adventures of Rusty, Big Business,* and *The Road to the Bazaar,* Bond illustrates his vision of childhood as a carefree age of mischief and joy where the only worries are associated with cricket matches, beetle races, and parental anger at bad report cards. In this comfortable and familiar world, there is a sense of security in friendship and the love and guidance of adults.

Living close to nature also instilled in the young Ruskin a reverence for all created beings. *Grandfather's Private Zoo, Who's Who at the Zoo, Our Trees Still Grow in Dehra,* and *To Live in Magic* express his respect for animals and nature. Animals very naturally share the daily lives of his characters. For example, Nakoo the crocodile, in *Cricket for the Crocodile,* resents his sleep being disturbed by the noisy cricket team and his snout being hit by stray balls; and the whimsical antics of the narcissistic python in *Snake Trouble* cause much mirth in an Anglo-Indian household. Even ghosts have their place in this universal harmony. In *Ghost Trouble,* the protagonist acknowledges the rights of a mischievous ghost to move into their house when the peepul tree the ghost lives in is cut down.

Bond has always championed the cause of conservation of wildlife and trees in the Himalayan region. He heightens the reader's consciousness in *An Island of Trees: Nature Stories and Poems* by stressing the importance of trees to animals, plants, and humans. *Tigers Forever* and *Panther's Moon and Other Stories* are his strongest pleas for the preservation of wildlife. In both novels the wild cats turn into man-eaters because of human greed and fear, rapid deforestation and upsetting of the ecosystem, and a violation of the trust placed in humans by nature. *Dust on the Mountain* describes the senseless and indiscriminate exploitation of the Himalayan town of Mussoorie where Bond lives: forests that took hundreds of years to grow are either burned by the fires of careless woodcutters or destroyed to accommodate hotels for the ever-increasing flow of summer tourists; the majestic deodars are felled to make furniture, doors, and beams for houses; and the very mountains are disembowelled in the quarries. In the climactic episode, it is a lone tree that saves the life of Bisnu and the driver when their truck plunges over the winding road while hauling limestone. Sobered and matured by the experience, Bisnu returns to his village to nourish his land for growing things, instead of destroying nature. In Bond's writings, there is sadness in the realization that times are changing in the small, isolated Himalayan towns, but there is also consolation and a sense of permanence in the knowledge that the trees his father had planted in Dehra Dun still exist. Bond is largely responsible for initiating the movement to replant trees on entire mountainsides in Mussoorie.

Just as there was sorrow at the divorce of his parents and death of his adored father, Bond and his characters realize that to live in harmony with nature they must accept both its destructive and nurturing manifestations. His characters attain a mystical understanding of life when they face flood, fire, and earthquake in *Angry River, Flames in the Forest,* and *Earthquake;* while the protagonists of *Night of the Leopard, Panther's Moon,* and *The Eyes of the Eagle* enact the elemental drama of survival against man-eaters and other predators.

At the heart of his writings is the value placed on simplicity and a selfless attitude toward life. Although the stories deal with the pleasures of humble people, their lives are enriched by meaningful experiences and a profound insight into life. Love between brothers and sisters is described in books like *Night of the Leopard;* the mutual dependence between grandparents and grandchildren forms the basis of *The Cherry Tree, Angry River, The Eyes of the Eagle,* and *Getting Granny's Glasses;* and the importance of friendship is the subject of *The Room on the Roof, The Adventures of Rusty,* and *Big Business.* In *The Blue Umbrella,* for example, when young Binya exchanges her leopard's claw pendant for the fancy blue umbrella owned by a city woman, the entire village is envious; in fact, the shopkeeper Ram Bharosa is so jealous that he is willing to hire someone to steal it. When his treachery is exposed, his business is ruined and he ends up a broken man. Binya also realizes that her acquisitiveness had made her insensitive to the feelings of others, and she accepts her share of the responsibility for Ram Bharosa's downfall. She gives the umbrella to him, and this simple gesture leads to his regeneration. These stories touchingly portray the warmth of personal relationships, the passing of traditions from old to young, and the confidence that emanates from children when they are nurtured in a secure and loving environment. Bond's books are also reminiscent of the many friendships that he has maintained over the years and his abiding love for his adopted family, especially his grandchildren. He concludes *Rain in the Mountains* with the thought:

"Most of my life I have given of myself, and in return I have received love in abundance. Life hasn't been a bed of roses. And yet, quite often, I've had roses out of season."

Bond laments the passing away of the simple childhood pleasures he had enjoyed as a boy in Dehra Dun. The safe and joyous world of childhood is shattered when he portrays the loneliness and powerlessness of children as they enter adolescence; they have to face the harsh realities of failure, economic pressures, drunken and abusive adults, and incompatible marriages. In *The Room on the Roof,* which is strongly autobiographical, an Anglo-Indian youth who is without family, friends, or country runs away from his insensitive guardian to find a place for himself in Indian society. The dream of running away in *The Adventures of Rusty* and in "The Great Train Journey" in *The Road to the Bazaar* becomes an essential coping device, as well as a heroic quest that leads to growth and a search for identity. Bond further explores his Anglo-Indian roots in *A Flight of Pigeons,* an historical novel set during the stormy period following the Indian Mutiny of 1857. Bond's ironic vision reveals that the mixed racial heritage of 14-year-old Ruth Labadoor and her mother first makes them victims of the holocaust, and then enables them to survive and communicate with their protectors. As the events move through the three worlds of the Europeans, Hindus, and Muslims, the characters overcome racial, cultural, and political differences to form a common human bond. Although both *The Room on the Roof* and *A Flight of Pigeons* were originally intended for adults, they address the typically adolescent concerns of identity, conflict with adult society, and teenage sexuality with seriousness and candor. Similarly, other works intended for adults such as *Time Stops at Shamli and Other Stories, The Young Vagrants, Love Is a Sad Song, The Night Train at Deoli,* and *An Axe for the Rani* are quite appropriate for young adult reading. These books fill a void in the children's literature of India where adolescent novels, far from exploring the inner person, are limited to mystery and adventure stories and novels of progress.

The several worlds of Bond are further unified by his style and treatment. He is a master storyteller who can take the leisurely setting of the Himalayan hill station, people it with lively characters, and still maintain the tension and drama of the story through a meticulously structured plot. His humorous treatment of the events and characters at once endears them to us, as well as allows the author to distance himself from his personal experiences. Furthermore, recurrent images and metaphors—the shadow of the ancient tree on the house, the bougainvillea branch creeping through the open window, the bazaar as the life-giving principle, and the secret pond in the jungle as the microcosm of the world—which echo through his poetry, autobiographical pieces, and fiction lend depth and continuity to his writings.

—Meena Khorana

BONSALL, Crosby (Newell)

Pseudonym: Crosby Newell. **Nationality:** American. **Born:** Long Island, New York, 2 January 1921. **Education:** American School of Design, New York; New York University School of Architecture. **Family:** Married to George Bonsall. **Career:** Worked in advertising agencies. **Died:** 1995.

PUBLICATIONS FOR CHILDREN

Fiction

Tell Me Some More, illustrated by Fritz Siebel. New York, Harper, 1961; Kingswood, Surrey, World's Work, 1962.

Listen, Listen!, photographs by Ylla. New York, Harper, and London, Hamish Hamilton, 1961.

Who's a Pest?, illustrated by the author. New York, Harper, 1962; Kingswood, Surrey, World's Work, 1963.

Look Who's Talking, photographs by Ylla. New York, Harper, 1962; London, Hamish Hamilton, 1963.

The Case of the Hungry Stranger, illustrated by the author. New York, Harper, 1963; Kingswood, Surrey, World's Work, 1964; New York, HarperCollins, 1992.

What Spot?, illustrated by the author. New York, Harper, and Kingswood, Surrey, World's Work, 1963.

It's Mine, illustrated by the author. New York, Harper, 1964.

I'll Show You Cats, photographs by Ylla. New York, Harper, 1964.

The Case of the Cat's Meow, illustrated by the author. New York, Harper, 1965; Kingswood, Surrey, World's Work, 1966.

The Case of the Dumb Bells, illustrated by the author. New York, Harper, 1966; Kingswood, Surrey, World's Work, 1967.

Here's Jellybean Reilly, photographs by Ylla. New York, Harper, 1966.

Whose Eye Am I?, photographs by Ylla. New York, Harper, 1968.

The Case of the Scaredy Cats, illustrated by the author. New York, Harper, 1971; Kingswood, Surrey, World's Work, 1973.

The Day I Had to Play with My Sister, illustrated by the author. New York, Harper, 1972; Kingswood, Surrey, World's Work, 1974.

Mine's the Best, illustrated by the author. New York, Harper, 1973; Kingswood, Surrey, World's Work, 1974; New York, HarperCollins, 1996.

Piggle, illustrated by the author. New York, Harper, 1973; Kingswood, Surrey, World's Work, 1974.

And I Mean It, Stanley, illustrated by the author. New York, Harper, 1974; Kingswood, Surrey, World's Work, 1975.

Twelve Bells for Santa, illustrated by the author. New York, Harper, 1977; Kingswood, Surrey, World's Work, 1979.

The Goodbye Summer. New York, Greenwillow, 1979.

Who's Afraid of the Dark? New York, Harper, 1980; Kingswood, Surrey, World's Work, 1981.

The Case of the Double Cross. New York, Harper, 1980; Kingswood, Surrey, World's Work, 1981.

The Amazing the Incredible Super Dog. New York, Harper, 1986.

Fiction as Crosby Newell

What Are You Looking At?, with George Bonsall. New York, Treasure Books, 1954.

The Helpful Friends, with George Bonsall. New York, Wonder Books, 1955.

The Surprise Party, illustrated by the author. New York, Wonder Books, 1955.

Captain Kangaroo's Book, illustrated by Evan Jeffrey. New York, Grosset and Dunlap, 1958.

Polar Bear Brothers, photographs by Ylla. New York, Harper, 1960.

Kippy the Koala, photographs by George Leavens. New York, Harper, 1960.

Hurry Up, Slowpoke, illustrated by the author. New York, Grosset and Dunlap, 1961.

Other

Let Papa Sleep (reader), illustrated by Emily Reed. New York, Grosset and Dunlap, 1963.

*

Illustrator: *The Really Truly Treasure Hunt,* 1954, and *The Big Joke,* 1955, both by George Bonsall; *August Explains* by Phil Ressner, 1963; *Go Away, Dog* by Joan L. Nodset, 1963; *Seesaw* by Joan Kahn, 1964; *Great Big Joke and Riddle Book* edited by Oscar Weigler, 1970.

* * *

For 25 years Crosby Bonsall wrote almost exclusively within the *I Can Read* and *Early I Can Read* series of books. While not a school reading scheme, the beginning-to-read-series format is quite different from non-primer, non-series picture story books. Unfortunately authors of such series tend to be overlooked or undervalued. (Imagine if Dr. Seuss had never written anything except *Beginner Books,* or if Arnold Lobel had never written anything except the *Frog and Toad* books, or if Hoban had never written anything except *Frances* stories, and so on.)

Many of Bonsall's books are excellent readers and also impressive picture story books. The *Case* books are amusing stories of a motley assortment of children who investigate mysteries. Readers enjoy thinking through each of the mysteries and anticipating solutions from the clues in the pictures. In *The Case of the Hungry Stranger,* four boys search for the culprit who ate two blueberry pies. When it turns out that Marigold's dog has the guilty blue-stained mouth, Marigold is invited to share the third pie—outside(!) the boys' clubhouse, because a sign on the door says "No Girls Allowed."

Later, in *The Case of the Scaredy Cats,* Marigold and some other girls challenge the boys' pigheadedness with their slogan of "Girls Are As Good As Boys." Pigheadedness being what it is, the boys do not change, but this does not stop them sharing and playing with the girls, or vice versa. Beginning before the recent wave of feminism, some of Bonsall's writing contains gender stereotypes typical of its time. But this is less than might be imagined, and Bonsall has been quick to break down stereotype limitations in her later books.

Even her simplest stories transcend the extremely limited and repetitious vocabulary, letting the pictures and the setting carry almost the whole story. *Mine's the Best,* with its story of rivalry over balloons destroyed in the boastful competition to be "best" and the wholly satisfactory resolution of "Ours was the best," makes sense even without the words. The sense of voice character in boasting challenge and counter-challenge is very clear.

All of Bonsall's books rely on interaction between people, sometimes wordless or onesided, sometimes in full-scale verbal confrontation. *The Day I Had to Play with My Sister* presents a character (possibly a boy, or a girl in jeans) who does all the talking while trying in vain to teach the younger sister how to play hide and seek. *Who's Afraid of the Dark?* shows a young white boy who tells an older black girl that his dog Stella is afraid of the dark. But the accompanying illustrations reveal who really is afraid, and at the end, without words, show how this fear is overcome.

But Bonsall's most significant contribution to children's literature is in the wit and invention of her characters' verbal clashes. *Who's a Pest?* is outstanding, among Bonsall's other good books. Young Homer is plagued by his quadruplet sisters, Lolly, Molly, Polly, and Dolly—a formidable quartet for anyone: confident, self-sufficient, stereotyped girls, they would never want to play with Homer. Or is it that Homer, who disclaims having drawn moustaches on their four baby dolls, is plaguing them? Is Homer a pest? Everyone else seems to think so, even when he is only the victim of verbal circumstances. "What time is it now?" [asks a chipmunk]. "Two to two," said Homer. "Don't toot at me," said the chipmunk. "You're a pest!" This kind of word tangle snares Homer several times, hilariously, elaborately, like an Abbott and Costello vaudeville routine. At this level of readership there is nothing else like it. It is a little like Lewis Carroll for kindergarten!

Bonsall was usually her own illustrator. Her style was not the zany stereotyped grins and exuberance of Steven Kellogg, or the mannered nostalgia of Mercer Mayer, or the artistic streetwise cartoons of Maurice Sendak. Her characters are simple line drawings of robust little kids, a little like Charles Shultz's Charlie Brown mixed with a kewpie doll. They are immediately identifiable and appealing, and match the stories well.

Bonsall wrote one novel for older school-age children. In *The Goodbye Summer* Allie is a natural eccentric, an only child whose father was killed in Vietnam before she was born. Allie explains, "It's no fun having no father and sharing your mother with a bunch of boarders. I am half an orphan!" She also has a remarkable imagination that exaggerates truth beyond recognition. With great humour and narrative invention, Bonsall takes Allie (and her mother) through several domestic adventures, including a Fourth of July parade and a trip to the dump to get rid of the treasured detritus of her entire life. Eventually she realises that, no matter what she does, sooner or later everything says goodbye forever, but that this is balanced by the memories that are left—the lesson that her mother learned when she was widowed. This is a good lesson, very simply, naturally taught, with no didacticism. *The Goodbye Summer* stands comparison with Louis Fitzhugh's *Harriet the Spy,* Mary Rodgers's *Freaky Friday,* or some of Betsy Byars's novels, but with a lighter touch. It deserves to be much better known.

—John Gough

BONTEMPS, Arna(ud Wendell)

Nationality: American. **Born:** Alexandria, Louisiana, 13 October 1902. **Education:** San Fernando Academy, California, 1917-20; Pacific Union College, Angwin, California, A.B. 1923; University of Chicago, M.A. in library science 1943. **Family:** Married Alberta Johnson in 1926; four daughters and two sons. **Career:** Teacher, Harlem Academy, New York, Shiloh Academy, Chicago, and private schools in Huntsville, Alabama, 1924-38; worked for the Illinois Writers' Project of the Works Progress Administration in early 1940s; Professor of English and chief librarian, 1943-66, and writer-in-residence, 1971-73, Fisk University, Nashville; Visiting Professor, University of Illinois, Chicago Circle, 1966-68; Visiting Professor and curator of the James Weldon Johnson Collection at the Beinecke Library, Yale University, New Haven, Connecticut, 1969-71. **Awards:** Pushkin prize, for poetry, 1926, 1927; *Crisis* prize, for poetry, 1927; *Opportunity* prize, for short story, 1932; Rosenwald fellowship, 1938, 1942; Guggenheim fellowship, 1949, 1954; Women's International League for Peace and Freedom Jane Addams award, 1956; Dow award, 1967. L.H.D.: Morgan State College, Baltimore, 1969; honorary degree: Berea College, Kentucky. **Died:** 4 June 1973.

Publications for Children

Fiction

Popo and Fifina, Children of Haiti, with Langston Hughes, illustrated by E. Simms Campbell. New York, Macmillan, 1932.
You Can't Pet a Possum, illustrated by Ilse Bischoff. New York, Morrow, 1934.
Sad-Faced Boy, illustrated by Virginia Lee Burton. Boston, Houghton Mifflin, 1937.
The Fast Sooner Hound, with Jack Conroy, illustrated by Virginia Lee Burton. Boston, Houghton Mifflin, 1942.
Slappy Hooper, The Wonderful Sign Painter, with Jack Conroy, illustrated by Ursula Koering. Boston, Houghton Mifflin, 1946.
Sam Patch, The High, Wide, and Handsome Jumper, with Jack Conroy, illustrated by Paul Brown. Boston, Houghton Mifflin, 1951.
Chariot in the Sky, illustrated by Cyrus Baldridge. Philadelphia, Winston, 1951.
Lonesome Boy, illustrated by Feliks Topolski. Boston, Houghton Mifflin, 1955.
Mr. Kelso's Lion, illustrated by Len Ebert. Philadelphia, Lippincott, 1970.

Other

We Have Tomorrow, photographs by Marian Palfi. Boston, Houghton Mifflin, 1945.
Story of the Negro, illustrated by Raymond Lufkin. New York, Knopf, 1948; revised edition, 1955.
George Washington Carver. Evanston, Illinois, Row Peterson, 1950.
The Story of George Washington Carver, illustrated by Harper Johnson. New York, Grosset and Dunlap, 1954.
Famous Negro Athletes. New York, Dodd Mead, 1954.
Frederick Douglass: Slave, Fighter, Freeman, illustrated by Harper Johnson. New York, Knopf, 1959.
Young Booker: Booker T. Washington's Early Days. New York, Dodd Mead, 1972.

Editor, *Golden Slippers: An Anthology of Negro Poetry for Young Readers,* illustrated by Henrietta Sharon. New York, Harper, 1941.

Publications for Adults

Novels

God Sends Sunday. New York, Harcourt Brace, 1931.
Black Thunder. New York, Macmillan, 1936.
Drums at Dusk. New York, Macmillan, 1939; London, Harrap, 1940.

Short Stories

The Old South: A Summer Tragedy, and Other Stories of the Thirties. New York, Dodd Mead, 1973.

Plays

When the Jack Hollers, with Langston Hughes (produced Cleveland, 1936).
St. Louis Woman, with Countée Cullen, music by Harold Arlen, lyrics by Johnny Mercer, adaptation of the novel *God Sends Sunday* by Bontemps (produced New York, 1946).
Free and Easy (produced Amsterdam, 1949).

Radio Script: *Jubilee,* with Langston Hughes, 1941.

Other plays: *Creole; Careless Love.*

Poetry

Personals. London, Breman, 1964.

Other

They Seek a City: A Study of Negro Migration, with Jack Conroy. New York, Doubleday, 1945; revised edition, as *Anyplace But Here,* New York, Hill and Wang, 1966.
American Missionary Association Archives in Fisk University Library. Nashville, Fisk University, 1947.
100 Years of Negro Freedom. New York, Dodd Mead, 1961.
Free at Last: The Life of Frederick Douglass. New York, Dodd Mead, 1971.
Arna Bontemps-Langston Hughes Letters 1925-1967, edited by Charles H. Nichols. New York, Dodd Mead, 1980.

Editor, *Father of the Blues: An Autobiography,* by W.C. Handy. New York, Macmillan, 1941.
Editor, with Langston Hughes, *The Poetry of the Negro 1746-1949: An Anthology.* New York, Doubleday, 1949; revised edition, as *The Poetry of the Negro 1746-1970,* 1970.
Editor, with Langston Hughes, *The Book of Negro Folklore.* New York, Dodd Mead, 1958.
Editor, *American Negro Poetry.* New York, Hill and Wang, 1963; revised edition, 1974.
Editor, *Hold Fast to Dreams: Poems Old and New.* Chicago, Follett, 1969.
Editor, *Great Slave Narratives.* Boston, Beacon Press, 1969.
Editor, *The Harlem Renaissance Remembered: Essays.* New York, Dodd Mead, 1972.

*

Bibliography: *James Weldon Johnson and Arna Wendell Bontemps: A Reference Guide* by Robert E. Fleming, Boston, Hall, 1978.

Manuscript Collections: Syracuse University Library, New York; Fisk University, Nashville; James Weldon Johnson Collection, Beinecke Library, Yale University, New Haven, Connecticut.

* * *

Arna Bontemps was a prolific, versatile writer whose books were trailblazers for the award-winning works of many of today's black writers—among them Virginia Hamilton, Ashley Bryan, Rosa Guy, Leo and Diane Dillon, and Gwendolyn Brooks. Bontemps's lasting legacy is his writing for children at a time when there were few books written by blacks for black children. His first was *Popo and Fifina,* written with Langston Hughes, whom he met during the Harlem Renaissance in the 1920s. Popo and Fifina, ages eight and ten, are appealing, resourceful children of a Haitian family in a seacoast town. Their father is a fisherman who still finds time to make a red kite, their mother trains them in daily chores, their uncle introduces them to the art of wood designing. The setting is lush and tropical, sunny with mangoes and parrots, vibrant with sudden storms and the midnight music of drums in the forest.

Bontemps turned to Alabama for his next two stories. *You Can't Pet a Possum* is about eight-year-old Shine Boy and his pup Butch who get into trouble but are saved by Aunt Cindy, who finally agrees to let Butch join the family as long as he doesn't act as though he owned the house. "Do, I'm gonna take a stick and run him raggedy," threatens Aunt Cindy in the local vernacular. (Although he used it occasionally in his writing, Bontemps found the Negro dialect mostly offensive and demeaning.) The second story, *Sad-Faced Boy,* is about Slumber and his two brothers who hitchhike to Harlem to visit their uncle. The boys, with harmonica, guitar, and drum, form a successful band, and have adventures in the library and the subway, but come cold weather, thoughts of cotton and ripe persimmons soon send them back to their cabin in Alabama. *Sad-Faced Boy* was the first children's book in which Bontemps touched on the "lonesome boy" theme. He admitted that it was partly autobiographical in origin; as a boy he had looked in vain for lonesome boy stories.

Years later Bontemps explored this theme more fully in the haunting lyrical story *Lonesome Boy.* Bubber is so passionately devoted to his silver trumpet that he blows it loud, fast, and high everywhere he goes. His Grandpa warns him, "It ain't good to go traipsing around with a horn in your hand. You might get into devilment." Bubber grows up still playing his trumpet, all the way down to New Orleans where he plays to his heart's content until the eerie night he learns the meaning of his Grandpa's warning. The mystifying, opaque ending makes the story memorable and tantalizing.

The Fast Sooner Hound, co-written with Jack Conroy, is a lively humorous picture story about a long-legged, lop-eared hound who would "sooner run then eat." He wins a bet for his master by outrunning the Cannon Ball, the fastest train on wheels.

Bontemps's finest achievement is *Story of the Negro,* a book he wished he had had when he was in high school. It is a comprehensive, powerfully written history of the causes and consequences of slavery from the earliest times. The cruelty, suffering, and humiliations are heartbreaking; the struggles, survivals, and triumphs are extraordinary. The book demonstrates that from Aesop to Martin Luther King Jr., slaves and blacks have sought to arouse the conscience of the nation and the world.

—Mary Silva Cosgrave

BOSTON, Lucy (Maria)

Nationality: British. **Born:** Lucy Maria Wood, Southport, Lancashire, 10 December 1892. **Education:** Downs School, Seaford, Sussex; Somerville College, Oxford, 1914; trained in the Voluntary Aid Detachment, St. Thomas's Hospital, London. **Military Service:** Nurse in France during World War I. **Family:** Married in 1917 (marriage dissolved 1935); one son. **Award:** Library Association Carnegie Medal, 1962. **Died:** 25 May 1990.

Publications for Children

Fiction

The Children of Green Knowe, illustrated by Peter Boston. London, Faber, 1954; New York, Harcourt Brace, 1955.

The Chimneys of Green Knowe, illustrated by Peter Boston. London, Faber, 1958; as *Treasure of Green Knowe,* New York, Harcourt Brace, 1958.

The River at Green Knowe, illustrated by Peter Boston. London, Faber, and New York, Harcourt Brace, 1959.

A Stranger at Green Knowe, illustrated by Peter Boston. London, Faber, and New York, Harcourt Brace, 1961.

An Enemy at Green Knowe, illustrated by Peter Boston. London, Faber, and New York, Harcourt Brace, 1964.

The Castle of Yew, illustrated by Margery Gill. London, Bodley Head, and New York, Harcourt Brace, 1965.

The Sea-Egg, illustrated by Peter Boston. London, Faber, and New York, Harcourt Brace, 1967.

The House That Grew, illustrated by Caroline Hemming. London, Faber, 1969.

Nothing Said, illustrated by Peter Boston. London, Faber, and New York, Harcourt Brace, 1971.

The Guardians of the House, illustrated by Peter Boston. London, Bodley Head, 1974; New York, Atheneum, 1975.

The Fossil Snake, illustrated by Peter Boston. London, Bodley Head, 1975; New York, Atheneum, 1976.

The Stones of Green Knowe, illustrated by Peter Boston. London, Bodley Head, and New York, Atheneum, 1976.

Publications for Adults

Novels

Yew Hall. London, Faber, 1954.

Persephone. London, Collins, 1969; as *Strongholds,* New York, Harcourt Brace, 1969.

Play

The Horned Man; or, Whom Will You Send to Fetch Her Away? London, Faber, 1970.

Other

Memory in a House (autobiography). London, Bodley Head, 1973; New York, Macmillan, 1974.

Perverse and Foolish: A Memoir of Childhood and Youth. London, Bodley Head, and New York, Atheneum, 1979.

*

Critical Study: *Lucy Boston* by Jasper Rose, London, Bodley Head, 1965; New York, Walck, 1966.

* * *

Lucy Boston is one of the children's writers who, in the 1950s, began decisively to redirect the course of juvenile fiction. Her earliest books have an unusual delicacy and formality of structure: at a time when predetermined adventure and pony stories were still proliferating, she infused a new seriousness and imaginative honesty into the concept of writing for children.

The underlying theme of the Green Knowe series is continuity, and this is pushed to an extreme in *The Stones of Green Knowe,* when children from various centuries are brought together in a climactic scene. 12th-century Roger is the first boy to live at the Norman stronghold: "All [the] free reaches of the imagination were centred for Roger in the new house that would stand to repel invaders, to receive heroes, to outlast perils, to withstand in its living stone walls the evils of witches and demons." The stories too are centred in the house, and this economical device enables the author to deal effectively with time shifts and episodes of magic and danger. Everything is contained within Green Knowe, which transmits its own validity.

Boston's "ghosts" are rendered in concrete terms, and the interaction between the past and the present (a common aspect of recent fiction) gives an oblique fascination to the straightforward historical events. In context the supernatural has a superrational basis; the convergence of different times in moments of intensity or special insight is an accepted convention. Boston has an unusual sensitivity, nothing to do with whimsy or free-range airy-fairy effects: it is simply expressed in an exquisite clarity of detail (down to the small piece of quilt, "rose-coloured...with minute white sprays") and a judicious use of fantastical motifs. She rarely goes too far: when she does (in several episodes in *The River at Green Knowe,* for instance) she steps back into her stride without fuss.

The River is the weakest of the Green Knowe stories; the children's adventures are balanced awkwardly between the realistic and the dreamlike, and the book lacks a satisfactory conclusion. Of the three children, only Ping, the Chinese boy, reappears later in the series. In *A Stranger at Green Knowe* he befriends an escaped gorilla and helps it to hide in a bamboo thicket: this is the only one of the six books that doesn't contain an element of magic. Instead, a number of complex ideas of freedom and ethics and their violation are presented in symbolical terms. It is entirely fitting that Ping, the displaced boy, should be the hero of this story, not Tolly, great-grandson of the owner of the house.

Tolly is the boy whose special responsiveness gives literal shape to the sequence related by the old lady as she sews her patchwork quilts. The romantic 17th-century children of Green Knowe, Toby, Alexander, and Linnet, with their deer, squirrel, and superb horse Feste, are the most elusive and ethereal of Boston's creations. The historical characters in the second story (*The Chimneys of Green Knowe*) have greater substance: blind Susan and her black companion Jacob are among the most entertaining and resourceful children in fiction. Susan's disability simply makes her "special"; she isn't the least pathetic or repressed. Boston uses the deprivation of one sense to exploit the others: "Everything that touched Susan was something she couldn't see. But far from being afraid she wanted to catch everything in the act of being real. She even put her finger in the candle-flame to see what being burnt was like...."

This is the most perfectly realized of the stories. The narrative works on two levels on a realistic plane, and the historical evocations are highly charged in a way that complements domestic accuracy. It is an excellent blend of adventure and an exercise of the imagination. Its effect, however, is less powerful than that of *An Enemy at Green Knowe* (with its malevolent sorceress actually named Miss Melanie D. Powers). Boston most successfully eliminated all trace of fear from her supernatural confrontations; but in *An Enemy* she acknowledges and examines the concepts of evil and destructiveness. The other stories have a gentle aura of subtlety and precision; this bristles with apprehension and generates a real sense of malignity.

Boston wrote books for younger children: of these, *The Sea-Egg* is the most original and persuasive. The basic motif, the one impossible event that is right in poetic terms, is repeated later with less conviction. The dryad of *Nothing Said,* the regenerated reptile of *The Fossil Snake,* are presented in a context too slight to sustain them. In *The Guardians of the House,* in the episode of the caves, fantasy shades into fallacy. Boston's talent requires scope for extension of the central theme and elaboration of imagery.

Elizabeth Bowen commented on "the insufficiency of so-called real life to the requirements of those who demand to be really alive." The Green Knowe books help to close the gap in one direction: that of belief in a tangible residue of the experience of past generations, the overflow of one consciousness into another, the associative and regenerative power of objects. Taken as a whole, the series is an important contribution to children's literature.

—Patricia Craig

BOWER, Barbara. See **TODD, Barbara Euphan.**

BOYLSTON, Helen Dore

Nationality: American. **Born:** Portsmouth, New Hampshire, 4 April 1895. **Education:** Portsmouth schools; Simmons College, Boston, one year; Massachusetts General Hospital, Boston, qualified nurse 1917. **Military Service:** Anesthesiologist with Harvard Unit at British Army Hospital, France, 1917-18: Captain. **Career:** Head nurse and instructor in Anesthesia, Massachusetts General Hospital, 1918-21; Red Cross nurse, Albania and Poland, 1921-24; nurse, in private practice, New York, 1925-27; head nurse, Norwalk Hospital, Connecticut, in late 1940s. **Died:** 30 September 1984.

Publications for Children

Fiction

Sue Barton, Student Nurse, illustrated by Forrest Orr. Boston, Little Brown, 1936; London, Lane, 1939.

Sue Barton, Senior Nurse, illustrated by Forrest Orr. Boston, Little Brown, 1937; London, Lane, 1940.
Sue Barton, Visiting Nurse, illustrated by Forrest Orr. Boston, Little Brown, 1938; London, Lane, 1941.
Sue Barton, Rural Nurse, illustrated by Forrest Orr. Boston, Little Brown, 1939; London, Lane, 1942.
Sue Barton, Superintendent of Nurses, illustrated by Forrest Orr. Boston, Little Brown, 1940; London, Lane, 1942.
Carol Goes Backstage, illustrated by Frederick Wallace. Boston, Little Brown, 1941; as *Carol Goes on the Stage,* London, Lane, 1943.
Carol Plays Summer Stock, illustrated by Major Felten. Boston, Little Brown, 1942; as *Carol in Repertory,* London, Lane, 1944.
Carol on Broadway, illustrated by Major Felten. Boston, Little Brown, 1944; as *Carol Comes to Broadway,* London, Lane, 1945.
Carol on Tour, illustrated by Major Felten. Boston, Little Brown, 1946; London, Lane, 1948.
Sue Barton, Neighborhood Nurse. Boston, Little Brown, 1949; London, Lane, 1950.
Sue Barton, Staff Nurse. Boston, Little Brown, 1952; London, Lane, 1953.

Jane Cobb Berry was uncredited co-author of *Sue Barton, Student Nurse, Neighborhood Nurse,* and *Staff Nurse,* and of the four Carol books.

Other

Clara Barton: Founder of the American Red Cross, illustrated by Paula Hutchinson. New York, Random House, 1955.

Publications for Adults

Other

"Sister": The War Diary of a Nurse. New York, Washburn, 1927.
Travels with Zenobia: Paris to Albania by Model T Ford, with Rose Wilder Lane, edited by William Holtz. Columbia, University of Missouri Press, 1983.

*

Helen Dore Boylston commented:

(1978) Teenage girls about to decide how they propose to earn a living naturally lean toward the romantic. Nursing and acting have a romantic appeal, but young imaginations conjure up the most wildly inaccurate pictures of life in either profession. I am a nurse myself, and have loved it all my days. But nursing is quite, *quite* different from anything girls imagine. The same is true in regard to the theatre. So, I proposed to give girls as *true* a picture as I was able. The nursing books were easy, naturally. As for the acting profession my neighbor and friend, Eva LeGallienne, is a very famous actress indeed. When I discussed my problem with her, she suggested that I spend an entire autumn and winter backstage in her theatre watching rehearsals, opening nights, and theatre life in general. I did so, and I also brought each completed manuscript to her for her criticisms and suggestions.

* * *

The series books created by the Stratemeyer syndicate were disavowed by educators and librarians, but Helen Dore Boylston offered to the adolescent girl two heroines who were acceptable—Sue Barton and Carol Page. These series were greeted by reviewers as either authoritative vocational stories about the nursing and theatre professions respectively or falsely glamorous. Later, the author was selected by the Landmark Series editor to write a biography of the founder of the American Red Cross, Clara Barton.

In seven volumes, Sue Barton progresses from a student nurse to various professional roles in her career. Plot is the strongest element in Boylston's technique, combining speed and suspense. Romance, mystery, and episodes of typhoid epidemic, hurricane, and pneumonia propel the momentum. Early in her student days, Sue meets Dr. Bill Barry, to whom she becomes married five books and seven years later. A portion of each series book is devoted to reviewing earlier books and previewing the forthcoming book. The fifth book, *Sue Barton, Superintendent of Nurses,* was initially intended to conclude the series, as the couple is finally married and Sue announces a forthcoming child.

Character development is superficial, with changes in circumstances substituted for depth. Sue remains the calm and witty nurse, while Marianna merely changes from waif to sedate wife of an older man. Minor characters such as Tony, the Greek laundryman, and Veazie Ann Cooney, the New Hampshire housekeeper, offer local color through their stereotyped accents. Innumerable people have "twinkling eyes." Humor permeates the books with dialogue such as "superabundance of megalomania arising from excessive local prominence," and situations such as the dachshund sitting on Sue's wedding underwear and then becoming drunk.

Boston, New York City, and New Hampshire are settings drawn from the author's own background. Historical data is limited to the Henry Street Settlement in *Sue Barton, Visiting Nurse.* The authoritative aura created by the author is offset by clichés such as "I'm responsible for the kind of person she becomes," "Doctors should marry nurses," and "There ought always to be a baby in the house." However, there is strong support for the working woman. Sue's father advises, "Show the world what you can do before you settle down" and the nurse postpones marriage for professional experiences.

Although the Sue Barton series is a "period piece" with expressions such as "Zulu gone mad," New York described as "crawling with gangsters and Chinamen and murderers," and nursing procedures from the 1930s, the books remain in print in the United States and in Great Britain, and have been published in other languages.

As with the nurse series, the subject of each of the four Carol Page books is introduced in the title. A girl rises from high school debut to a small part in a New York play to apprenticeship with the summer theater, to Broadway and finally to a tour. Details in background are convincing and ample. As a contemporary reviewer stated, "a career story of this profession must not be rushed." Rightly referred to as a "second string heroine," Carol Page is currently an unknown character, and the books are out of print.

The biography of Clara Barton describes episodes in the nurse's life from age three to more than ninety, and is more substantial and readable than other juvenile biographies about her. The book suffers from superlatives in describing Barton as a faster runner, better pitcher, more politically knowledgeable and in general harder working than her contemporaries.

—Karen Nelson Hoyle

BRADMAN, Tony

Nationality: British. **Born:** London, 22 January 1954. **Education:** Queen's College, M.A. (honors). **Family:** Married to Sally; one son and two daughters. **Career:** Chief sub-editor, *Music Week* magazine, c. 1978; deputy editor, *Parents* magazine (UK edition), 1979-87; writer since 1987. Has worked as a reviewer of specialist children's books, magazines, and national press; visits schools to give book readings. **Agent:** Pat White, Rogers Coleridge & White, 20 Powis Mews, London W11 10N. **Address:** 175 Mackenzie Road, Beckenham, Kent BR3 4SE, England.

Publications for Children

Fiction

The Bad Babies' Counting Book, illustrated by Debbie van der Beek. London, Piccadilly, 1985.
John Lennon, illustrated by Karen Heywood. London, Hamish Hamilton, 1985.
One Nil, illustrated by Gary Wing. London, Viking Kestrel, 1985; new edition, illustrated by Jon Riley, London, Puffin, 1987.
Let's Pretend, illustrated by Susan Hellard. London, Macdonald, 1985.
The Bad Babies' Book of Colors, illustrated by D. van der Beek. London, Piccadilly, 1986.
See You Later, Alligator, illustrated by Colin Hawkins. London, Dial, 1986.
At the Park, illustrated by S. Hellard. London, Macdonald, 1986.
Hide and Seek, illustrated by S. Hellard. London, Macdonald, 1986.
Play Time, illustrated by S. Hellard. London, Macdonald, 1986.
Through My Window, illustrated by Eileen Browne. London, Silver Burdett, 1986.
The Lonely Little Mole (based on a story by Paule Alen), illustrated by Myriam Deru. London, Blackie, 1986.
Night-Time, illustrated by Caroline Holden. London, Methuen, 1986.
Will You Read Me a Story? London, Thorsons, 1986.
Baby's Best Book, illustrated by Lisa Kopper. London, Harper, 1987.
The Baby's Bumper Book, illustrated by L. Kopper. London, Methuen, 1987.
The Bad Babies Book of Months, illustrated by D. van der Beek. London, Piccadilly, 1987.
Smile, Please!, illustrated by Jean Baylis. London, Viking Kestrel, 1987.
I Need a Book! London, Thorsons, 1987.
The Little Cakemaker and the Greedy Magician (based on a story by Alen), illustrated by M. Deru. London, Blackie, 1987.
Look Out, He's Behind You!, illustrated by Margaret Chamberlain. London, Putnam, 1988.
Wait and See, illustrated by E. Browne. London, Oxford University Press, 1988.
Not Like That, Like This!, illustrated by Joanna Burroughes. London, Oxford University Press, 1988.
Bedtime, illustrated by L. Kopper. London, Methuen, 1988.
The Cuddle, illustrated by L. Kopper. London, Methuen, 1988.
Our Cat, illustrated by L. Kopper. London, Methuen, 1988.
Who's Afraid of the Big Bad Wolf?, illustrated by M. Chamberlain. London, Aladdin Books, 1989.
Bub. London, Corgi, 1989.
Gary and the Magic Cat. London, Hodder & Stoughton, 1989, as *The Magic Cat,* 1992.
Tracey's Wish. London, Hamish Hamilton, 1989.
The Sandal: A Story, illustrated by Philippe Dupasquier. London, Viking Kestrel, 1990.
This Little Baby, illustrated by Jenny Williams. London, Putnam, 1990.
Michael, illustrated by Tony Ross. London, Anderson, 1990; New York, Macmillan, 1991.
Let's Go, Ben. London, Dent, 1990.
Gerbil Crazy. London, Viking, 1990.
Miranda the Magnificent. London, Ladybird, 1990.
In a Minute, illustrated by E. Browne. London, Methuen, 1990.
Five Minutes More! London, Collins, 1991.
Morning. London, Collins, 1991.
That's Not a Fish!, illustrated by Susie Jenkins-Pearce. London, Dent, 1991.
Tommy Niner and the Planet of Danger. London, Viking, 1991.
Billy and the Baby, illustrated by Jan Lewis, Barron's, 1992.
It Came from Outer Space, illustrated by Carol Wright. London, Dial, 1992.
Has Anyone Seen Jack?, illustrated by M. Chamberlain. London, Frances Lincoln, 1992.
Frankie Makes a Friend, illustrated by S. Holleyman. London, Andersen, 1992.
My Family, illustrated by Madeleine Baker. London, Collins, 1992.
My Little Baby Brother, illustrated by M. Baker. London, Collins, 1992.
That's Not My Cat!, illustrated by J. Baylis. London, Collins, 1992.
Wally's New Face, illustrated by J. Baylis. London, Collins, 1992.
Winnie's New Broom, illustrated by J. Baylis. London, Collins, 1992.
A Bad Week for the Three Bears, illustrated by J. Williams. London, Random House, 1993.
The Invaders, illustrated by Mark Burgess. London, Blackie, 1993.
Tommy Niner and the Mystery Spaceship, illustrated by Martin Chatterton. London, Viking, 1994.
Night Night, Ben! London, Dent, 1994.
Two Minute Puppy Tales, illustrated by Kim Blundell. London, Ladybird, 1994.
Push Chair Polly, illustrated by A Geoghegan. London, Ladybird, 1996.
What's Wrong With Bertie?, illustrated by P. Stevenson. London, Ladybird, 1996.
Just Us Three, illustrated by Andre Amstutz. London, HarperCollins, 1996.
The Lost Rabbit, illustrated by Susan Winter. London, HarperCollins, 1997.
Magnificent Mummies, illustrated by Martin Chatterton. London, Heinemann, 1997.
Michael, illustrated by Tony Ross. London, Andersen Press, 1997.
The Alien Teacher, illustrated by Peter Kavanagh. London, Corgi Pups, 1997.
Midnight in Memphis, illustrated by Martin Chatterton. London, Heinemann, 1998.
The Frankenstein Teacher, illustrated by Peter Kavanagh. London, Corgi Pups, 1998.

Dilly the Dinosaur Series (illustrated by Susan Hellard):

Dilly the Dinosaur. London, Piccadilly, 1985. New York, Puffin Books, 1986.

Dilly Visits the Dentist. London, Piccadilly, 1986, published as *Dilly Goes to the Dentist.* New York, Viking Kestrel, 1986.
Dilly Tells the Truth. London, Piccadilly, 1986; New York, Viking Kestrel, 1988.
Dilly and the Horror Film. London, Piccadilly, 1987; published as *Dilly and the Horror Movie.* New York, Puffin, 1987.
Dilly's Muddy Day. London, Methuen, 1987.
Dilly and the Tiger. London, Piccadilly, 1988.
Dilly. London, Piccadilly, 1988.
Dilly and the Ghost. London, Piccadilly, 1989.
Dilly Dinosaur, Superstar. London, Piccadilly, 1989.
Dilly Speaks Up. London, Piccadilly, 1990. New York, Viking, 1991.
Dilly Goes on Holiday. London, Piccadilly, 1990.
Dilly the Angel. London, Piccadilly, 1990.
Dilly and His Swamp Lizard. London, Piccadilly, 1991.
Dilly and the Big Kids. London, Piccadilly, 1991.
Dilly's Birthday Party. London, Piccadilly, 1991.
Dilly Goes to School. London, Piccadilly, 1992.
Dilly and the Pirates. London, Piccadilly, 1993.
Dilly—The Worst Day Ever. London, Piccadilly, 1993.
Dilly Goes Swamp Wallowing. London, Mammoth, 1994.
Dilly, Dinosaur Detective. London, Heinemann, 1994.
Dilly's Day In. London, Methuen, 1994.
Dilly's Day Out. London, Methuen, 1994.
Dilly and the Goody Goody. (Blue Banana Series) London, Heinemann, 1996.
Dilly and the Vampire. London, Methuen, 1996.
Dilly and the Cup Final. London, Methuen, 1997.

Daisy Tales (illustrated by Priscilla Lamont):

Daisy and the Babysitter. London, Methuen, 1986.
Daisy and the Crying Baby. London, Methuen, 1986.
Daisy and the Washing Machine. London, Methuen, 1986.
Daisy Goes Swimming. London, Methuen, 1986.
Daisy Feels Ill. London, Methuen, 1988.
Daisy Goes to Playgroup. London, Methuen, 1988.

The Bluebeards Series (illustrated by Rowan Barnes Murphy):

Adventure on Skull Island. London, Piccadilly, 1988; New York, Barron's, 1990.
Mystery at Musket Bay. London, Piccadilly, 1989, New York, Barron's, 1990.
Contest at Cutlass Cove. London, Piccadilly, 1990.
Search for the Saucy Sally. London, Piccadilly, 1990.
Peril at the Pirate School. New York, Barron's, 1990.
Revenge at Ryan's Reef. New York, Barron's, 1991.

Sam, the Girl Detective Series:

Sam, the Girl Detective. London, Yearling, 1989.
Sam, the Girl Detective: The Cash Box Caper. London, Yearling, 1990.
Sam, the Girl Detective: The Case of the Missing Mummy. London, Yearling, 1990.
Sam, the Girl Detective: The Secret of the Seventh Candle. London, Yearling, 1992.
Sam, the Girl Detective: The Great Rock 'n' Roll Ransom. London, Yearling, 1994.

Cambridge Reading Series:

Please, Miss! Cambridge, Cambridge University Press, 1996.
Show and Tell. Cambridge, Cambridge University Press, 1996.
This is the Register. Cambridge, Cambridge University Press, 1996.
Well Done, Sam! Cambridge, Cambridge University Press, 1996.
What's the Time? Cambridge, Cambridge University Press, 1996.
Follow My Leader. Cambridge, Cambridge University Press, 1996.
A Friend for Kate. Cambridge, Cambridge University Press, 1996.
Here Comes Everyone. Cambridge, Cambridge University Press, 1996.
Imran and the Watch. Cambridge, Cambridge University Press, 1996.

Swappers Series (illustrated by Clive Scruton):

Wow! I'm a Whale. London, Bloomsbury, 1996.
Help! I'm a Hamster. London, Bloomsbury, 1996.
Terrific! I'm a Tarnatula. London, Bloomsbury, 1997.

Compiler, *The Magic Kiss,* illustrated by Alan Marks. London, Blackie, 1987.
Compiler, *Animals Like Us,* illustrated by M. Baker. London, Blackie, 1987.
Compiler, *The Mad Family,* illustrated by M. Baker. London, Blackie, 1987.
Compiler, *The Best of Friends.* London, Blackie, 1988.
Compiler, *What a Wonderful Day.* London, Blackie, 1988.
Compiler, *Things That Go.* London, Blackie, 1989.
Compiler, *You're Late, Dad.* London, Methuen, 1989.
Compiler, *That Spells Magic.* London, Penguin, 1989.
Compiler, *The Parents' Book of Bedtime Stories.* London, Viking Kestrel, 1990.
Compiler, *Love Them, Hate Them.* London, Methuen, 1991.
Compiler, *Our Side of the Playground,* illustrated by Kim Palmer. London, Bodley Head, 1991.
Compiler, *Hissing Steam and Whistles Blowing.* London, Puffin, 1991.
Compiler, *Good Sports!,* illustrated by Riley. London, Doubleday, 1992.
Compiler, *A Stack of Story Poems,* illustrated by Tony Blundell. London, Doubleday, 1992.
Compiler, *Amazing Adventure Stories.* London, Doubleday, 1994.
Compiler, *Fantastic Space Stories.* London, Doubleday, 1994.
Compiler, *Dear Mum, Don't Panic,* illustrated by S. Lewis, London, Methuen, 1996.
Compiler, *Incredibly Creepy Stories.* London, Doubleday, 1997.
Compiler, *Football Fever.* London, Doubleday, 1997.
Compiler, *Computer Stories.* London, Doubleday, 1997.
Compiler, *Sensational Cyber Stories.* London, Doubleday, 1997.
Compiler, *Gripping War Stories.* London, Doubleday, 1998.
Compiler, *Off to School,* illustrated by Tony Blundell. London, Macdonald, 1998.

Reteller, *The Ugly Duckling.* London, Methuen, 1990.
Reteller, *The Gingerbread Man.* London, Methuen, 1991.
Reteller, *Goldilocks and the Three Bears.* London, Methuen, 1991.
Reteller, *The Little Red Hen.* London, Methuen, 1991.

Poetry

A Kiss on the Nose, illustrated by Sumiko. London, Heinemann, 1984.

All Together Now!, illustrated by J. Park. London, Viking Kestrel, 1989.

Other

Compiler, *The Essential Father.* London, Unwin, 1985.

Compiler, *So You Want to Have a Baby?* London, Julia MacRae, 1985.

Compiler, *Reading for Enjoyment, 0-6,* 6th edition. London, Baker Book Services, 1989.

* * *

Tony Bradman was a vigorous campaigner for children's books long before he started writing them. As deputy editor of *Parents* magazine, he started the children's book review pages and instigated the *Parents* Best Book for Babies award. He is now a full-time writer and the best word to describe his output is prolific. Having children of his own coupled with his vast experience as a children's book reviewer have greatly contributed to his success, because he certainly has his finger on the pulse of what children like.

His "Dilly the Dinosaur" books are phenomenally popular for the simple reason that Dilly, the world's naughtiest dinosaur, does what every child does, or would like to do. Children are endlessly fascinated by tales of other children naughtier than themselves and Dilly's trademark, the 150-mile-per-hour super scream, is something that children admire and fear at the same time. The stories are about the kinds of situations that will be familiar to any family with young children, from the simply funny, like the time Dilly was chosen to be an angel in the Nativity play, to the more complex, like explaining to a toddler why he has to wait so long for his next birthday. Parents will recognise themselves, too, in, for example, the story about Dilly's parents trying to prepare for a dinner party and looking after a mischievous toddler at the same time. The Dilly stories are perfect for reading aloud to three- to six-year-olds and the clear, large type makes them ideal for beginner readers to tackle alone. The books have translated well to television which has hugely increased their popularity.

Bradman created equally successful and likeable characters in the Bluebeards, a family of pirates who live on the Saucy Sally and sail the high seas hunting for treasure and fighting off other pirates. At a time when parents were keen to avoid giving children toy guns and swords he recognised that children seem to need some sort of fantasy violence—along the lines of the old Cowboys and Indians stories. Consequently these swashbuckling adventures, in which pirates are always threatening to blast other pirates into smithereens, have been very popular amongst children.

His "Tommy Niner" books feature a spaceboy, another character who has the kind of adventures that every boy wants to have. Blasting off into space in his spaceship, the Stardust, with his father and grandfather, on some exciting mission to find missing spaceships, or up against the galaxy's most wanted criminal, Tommy's exploits have even reluctant readers gripped to the end.

The main reason for Bradman's success is that he writes well for children who are just mastering the art of reading alone and fluently. His vocabulary is controlled and his plots are well-paced, which is essential for this age group, who will give up all too quickly if the story does not grip them from the start or the language is too complex. He clearly enjoys language himself and his subjects allow him to play with it, giving him the opportunity to make endless tongue-in-cheek jokes. His series of stories about Sam, the girl detective are one example of where he sends up (or pays tribute to) a genre that the children reading the books may not appreciate at the time. Samantha Marlowe is a girl who likes nothing better than a good mystery to get her teeth into, and her forays into crime detection will have young readers on the edge of their seats.

Many of Bradman's books are published in series' aimed specifically at beginner readers and may consequently appear lightweight. However, his ability to write good believable dialogue, creating realistic relationships between parent and child and between friends make them stand on their own. *One Nil* is an excellent story for young football fanatics and *Invaders* is a fine introduction to science fiction for the eight- to ten-year olds.

Bradman continually comes up with new ideas that fit this series format. His series in which the new teacher in school is an alien, a ghost, or Frankenstein is guaranteed to have children reading to the end. The school setting is always appealing to children beginning to read real books, who enjoy the subversion. He has written stories in the Blue Banana Series, which are excellent for building confidence in children just starting to read, and he includes enough puns and jokes in speech bubbles to keep adults amused as they listen to them being read aloud by a child. Another hugely appealing series for fluent readers is the "Swappers" series, in which a child turns into something else for a while—a whale, a hamster or a tarantula—and is able to do things that would otherwise be impossible. It is an excellent device and one that has great appeal for children imagining life from a different perspective.

Bradman has also built up a highly regarded reputation as a compiler of poems and stories, often an under-rated achievement. Many of these are original in that they include new material from well-known authors and are an excellent way of introducing children to authors within a theme that particularly interests them. His poetry collections, too, are well thought out and span a wide range of material.

Bradman's picture books have good strong storylines, and again his use of language is deliberately controlled with lots of repetition in many cases. They depict scenes at the heart of family life to which children readily respond. In *Not Like That, Like This,* for example, a father gets his head stuck in park railings when he says to his young son "Not like that, like this" and a variety of people stop to tell him how get his head out, all repeating the key phrase, inviting young listeners to join in. In *Frankie Makes a Friend* Bradman clearly has great fun inverting the Frankenstein story. Frankie and his family all look remarkably like creatures from a horror story with green faces and bolts through their necks, but his parents are shocked when he creates a human looking boy from a "Little Professor Kit." *Billy and the Baby* is a refreshing look at the birth of a new baby in a family with one child. As Billy's parents are going through his old baby things in anticipation of the new arrival, Billy keeps taking things for himself. Eventually he reveals he has made a very special box of things to give to his baby sister. It is inspired ideas like these, and his ability to think up new situations for the characters he has created, that will ensure Bradman is an author familiar to most children as they discover books and reading.

—Fiona Lafferty

BRAND, (Mary) Christianna

Pseudonyms: Mary Ann Ashe; Annabel Jones; Mary Roland; China Thompson. **Nationality:** British. **Born:** Mary Christianna Milne, Malaya, 17 December 1907; lived in India as a child. **Education:** Educated at a Franciscan convent, Taunton, Somerset. **Family:** Married Roland S. Lewis in 1939; one adopted daughter. **Career:** Worked as governess, receptionist, dancer, model, salesperson, and secretary. **Died:** 11 March 1988.

Publications for Children

Fiction

Danger Unlimited. New York, Dodd Mead, 1948; as *Welcome to Danger,* London, Foley House Press, 1950.
Nurse Matilda, illustrated by Edward Ardizzone. Leicester, Brockhampton Press, and New York, Dutton, 1964.
Nurse Matilda Goes to Town, illustrated by Edward Ardizzone. Leicester, Brockhampton Press, 1967; New York, Dutton, 1968.
Nurse Matilda Goes to Hospital, illustrated by Edward Ardizzone. London, Hodder and Stoughton, and New York, Dutton, 1974.

Other

Editor, *Naughty Children: An Anthology,* illustrated by Edward Ardizzone. London, Gollancz, 1962; New York, Dutton, 1963.

Publications for Adults

Novels

Death in High Heels. London, Lane, 1941; New York, Scribner, 1954.
Heads You Lose. London, Lane, 1941; New York, Dodd Mead, 1942.
Green for Danger. New York, Dodd Mead, 1944; London, Lane, 1945.
The Crooked Wreath. New York, Dodd Mead, 1946; as *Suddenly at His Residence,* London, Lane, 1947.
The Single Pilgrim (as Mary Roland). London, Sampson Low, and New York, Crowell, 1946.
Death of Jezebel. New York, Dodd Mead, 1948; London, Lane, 1949.
Cat and Mouse. London, Joseph, and New York, Knopf, 1950.
London Particular. London, Joseph, 1952; as *Fog of Doubt,* New York, Scribner, 1953.
Tour de Force. London, Joseph, and New York, Scribner, 1955.
The Three-Cornered Halo. London, Joseph, and New York, Scribner, 1957.
Starrbelow (as China Thompson). London, Hutchinson, and New York, Scribner, 1958.
Court of Foxes. London, Joseph, 1969; Northridge, California, Brooke House, 1977.
The Radiant Dove (as Annabel Jones). London, Joseph, 1974; New York, St. Martin's Press, 1975.
Alas, For Her That Met Me! (as Mary Ann Ashe). London, Star, 1976.
A Ring of Roses (as Mary Ann Ashe). London, Star, 1977.
The Honey Harlot. London, W.H. Allen, 1978.
The Rose in Darkness. London, Joseph, 1979.
The Brides of Aberdar. London, Joseph, 1982; New York, St. Martin's Press, 1983.
Crime on the Coast, and No Flowers by Request, with others. London, Gollancz, 1984.

Short Stories

What Dread Hand? London, Joseph, 1968.
Brand X. London, Joseph, 1974.
Buffet for Unwelcome Guests: The Best Short Stories of Christianna Brand, edited by Francis M. Nevins, Jr., and Martin H. Greenberg. Carbondale, Southern Illinois University Press, 1983.

Plays

Secret People (screenplay), with others, in *Making a Film,* edited by Lindsay Anderson. London, Allen and Unwin, and New York, Macmillan, 1952.

Screenplays: *Death in High Heels,* 1947; *The Mark of Cain,* with W.P. Lipscomb and Francis Cowdry, 1948; *Secret People,* with others, 1952.

Other

Heaven Knows Who. London, Joseph, and New York, Scribner, 1960.

*

Bibliography: "The Works of Christianna Brand" by Otto Penzler, in *Green for Danger,* San Diego, University of California Extension, 1978.

Christianna Brand commented:

(1978) I believe that children, in small families and the permissive age, have too few opportunities to be just mischievously naughty, and that they adore reading about children who *are.* The three "Nurse Matilda" books are about a huge family of children, and each chapter starts with a list of their misdeeds: "Tora was pouring treacle in to the Wellington boots. David was putting glue in the sandwiches," etc., each list ending, "And all the other children were doing simply dreadful things too." This has the children rolling about with laughter and mums write in to thank me for books they can bear to read over and over and over again. The theme is that Nurse Matilda is sent for—she is terribly ugly "with a nose like two potatoes"—and magics them all into goodness again, until they retrogress and she has to be sent for once more. It is an expansion of a story handed down through my family.

The anthology follows the same theme, being extracts from books about naughty children through the ages, from the Bible—where they ran out upon Elijah crying, "Go to, thou baldhead!" and were deservedly eaten up by two large bears—to the present day.

* * *

To the vast majority of English children today, nannies are creatures as mythical as dragons, but like dragons, they have their traditional habits and characteristics enshrined in children's literature. Christianna Brand's Nurse Matilda is a late but notable addition to the small, select band which includes Nana the dog and Mary Poppins.

Nurse Matilda, "the ugliest person you ever saw in your life" with "a nose like two potatoes," descends upon the enormous family of naughty Brown children to teach them the error of their ways. Her method is simple: when they are doing something naughty she bangs her magic stick, and they find themselves unable to stop, so that soon, of course, their naughtiness is no fun at all. As their manners improve she herself grows prettier, until when at last they are reformed characters (temporarily, at least), she leaves. "When my children don't want me, but do need me: then I must stay. When they no longer need me, but they do want me: then I have to go."

This is the pattern of all three books: *Nurse Matilda* is set in the Browns' home, *Nurse Matilda Goes to Town* takes the family to terrible Great-Aunt Adelaide's London house, *Nurse Matilda Goes to Hospital* lands them first in hospital and then by the sea—a seaside which has almost a surrealistic touch of Lewis Carroll about it. Each story contains an ingenious set-piece of naughtiness and culminates in a dream-like chase. These are humorous moral tales set in that Edwardian nursery world which will be most familiar to modern children from the works of E. Nesbit. Part of the appeal of the Brown children's naughtiness, one suspects, lies in the implicit presence of a fairly stern discipline in that nursery world, where you knew where you were and there was no question of you being mentally disturbed rather than plain naughty if you went pouring syrup into your siblings' Wellington boots.

The author tells us that the genesis of the books lies in a story told to the children of her own family, including her cousin Edward Ardizzone, whose illustrations complement the narrative perfectly. In Brand's version these three little *jeux d'esprit* have great style and verve, and perhaps show their oral origin in the success with which they can be read aloud. The story races along in an extravaganza of words, stopping every now and then for a little set-piece, a recital of the various awful things the children are up to, and ending in a chorus of: "And all the other children were doing simply dreadful things too." Very short, very funny, with not a word wasted, the three Nurse Matilda books surely deserve to rank as minor classics of writing for children.

—Anthea Bell

BRANDENBERG, Aliki Liacouras. See **ALIKI.**

BRANFIELD, John (Charles)

Nationality: British. **Born:** Burrow Bridge, Somerset, 19 January 1931. **Education:** Drax Grammar School, Yorkshire, 1943-50; Queens' College, Cambridge, 1950-53, M.A. in English 1956; University of Exeter, Devon, 1970-71, M.Ed. 1972. **Family:** Married Kathleen Peplow in 1955; two daughters and two sons. **Career:** English teacher, 1961-64, head of English department, 1964-75, and sixth form tutor, 1975-81, Camborne Grammar School, later Camborne Comprehensive School, Cornwall. **Awards:** English Speaking Union Page scholarship, 1974; Arts Council award, 1978; Carnegie Medal commendation, 1980. **Agent:** A.P. Watt Ltd., 20 John Street, London WC1N 2DL. **Address:** Mingoose Villa, Mingoose, Mount Hawke, Truro, Cornwall TR4 8BX.

Publications for Children

Fiction

Nancekuke. London, Gollancz, 1972; as *The Poison Factory,* New York, Harper, 1972.
Sugar Mouse. London, Gollancz, 1973; as *Why Me?,* New York, Harper, 1973.
The Scillies Trip. London, Gollancz, 1975.
Castle Minalto; or, the Entertainment of Dr. Trevail. London, Gollancz, 1979.
The Fox in Winter. London, Gollancz, 1980; New York, Atheneum, 1982.
Brown Cow. London, Gollancz, 1983.
Thin Ice. London, Gollancz, 1983.
The Falklands Summer. London, Gollancz, 1987.
The Day I Shot My Dad and Other Stories. London, Gollancz, 1989.
Lanhydrock Days. London, Gollancz, 1991.

Play

Television Play: *The Day I Shot My Dad.* 1976.

Publications for Adults

Novels

A Flag in the Map. London, Eyre and Spottiswoode, 1960.
Look the Other Way. London, Eyre and Spottiswoode, 1963.
In the Country. London, Eyre and Spottiswoode, 1966.

*

Manuscript Collection: Kerlan Collection, University of Minnesota, Minneapolis.

John Branfield comments:

Most of my books are about what I called in the preface to *Nancekuke* "real issues": the right of the individual to protest, the difficulties of a young person learning to cope with a disability, the effects of experimenting with drugs, the problems of old age, and the mutual support that old and young can give to each other. But I am not interested only in "problems," and I hope that I have written without didacticism. I value the traditional functions of the novel, the exploration of character and relationships, the evocation of place—usually Cornwall.

* * *

John Branfield's literary career has been unusual. He began in the 1960s with three adult novels which were received with moderate enthusiasm but have not been kept in print. Then after a six-year gap he produced a successful teenage novel in 1972, rapidly followed by two others in the same purposeful vein. Since 1979 there have been five further novels, including one striking departure from his normal realistic mode, and, most recently, two volumes of short stories. Among his full-length realistic novels, three in particular have stood the test of time well and still have a strong appeal for thoughtful children in the 1990s. All these have pervasive background in the Cornish countryside.

Sugar Mouse, the second to be published, is perhaps the most likely to strike a chord with young teenagers. The 12-year-old heroine is a diabetic and her struggle to come to terms with her condition is described with clinical realism alongside an interesting chain of events featuring ponies, dogs, and boyfriends. Sarah's stubborn folly and her violent quarrels with her family are at times hard to credit, as is her sudden conversion to good sense in the closing pages. Nevertheless, this is both an informative and a very readable story. *Nancekuke* is decidedly more sophisticated, offering some quite complex characters and a selection of social and personal issues for the reader to ponder. Attitudes towards military research and the ramifications of investigative journalism are among the prominent issues, and in each case Branfield strikes a pretty successful balance between making a case and showing that there are pros and cons in most situations. *The Fox in Winter* concentrates largely on a single issue, that of fair treatment for old people, and the author is more concerned to highlight the scandal of callousness than to present a balanced picture. This sort of approach is common enough in adult novels, but one may doubt the wisdom of confronting teenagers with such a harsh indictment when they lack the experience to put it in context. Nevertheless, for those who can cope with sombre theme, and some rather harrowing medical details, this novel has much to commend it, especially the portrayal of Tom Treloar, the indomitable old tyrant who eventually outwits his mercenary relatives.

Of Branfield's five other novels for children, four are concerned with aspects of teenage deviation or self-discovery, and all of these are somewhat marred by overearnestness, together with thin story lines. Probably the most notable is *Thin Ice,* sequel to the rather pedestrian *Brown Cow,* which is primarily concerned with problems of sexual orientation. Here again the author takes on the mantle of crusader for justice and makes few concessions to the needs of immature readers. The remaining novel, *Castle Minalto; or, the Entertainment of Dr. Trevail,* contrasts very sharply with all the rest of Branfield's work. It belongs to the genre of gothic romance, and here Branfield impresses as a most inventive and compulsive storyteller, capable of handling weird situations and larger-than-life characters.

Branfield's two volumes of short stories are interesting in rather different ways. In *Lanhydrock Days* the stories are linked around events in the recent past of a well-known Cornish mansion, with a school visit providing the framework and the child-visitors serving as lively storytellers; the prevailing tone however is serious-minded or even tragic. By contrast, several of the ten separate stories in *The Day I Shot My Dad and Other Stories* are essentially humorous, not to say hilarious. Here Branfield's prime purpose is to expose the follies of adult males in conflict with teenagers, which in the title story and others he brings off with a lightness of touch not often seen in the full-length novels.

—Alasdair K. D. Campbell

BRAZIL, Angela

Nationality: British. **Born:** Preston, Lancashire, 30 November 1869. **Education:** Manchester High School; Ellerslie College, Manchester; Heatherley Studio, London. **Career:** Vice-President, 1920, and President, 1928, Coventry YWCA; Vice-President, Coventry Natural History and Scientific Society. **Died:** 13 March 1947.

Publications for Children

Fiction

A Terrible Tomboy, illustrated by the author and Amy Brazil. London, Gay and Bird, 1904.
The Fortunes of Philippa. London, Blackie, 1906.
The Third Class at Miss Kaye's. London, Blackie, 1908.
The Nicest Girl in the School. London, Blackie, 1909; Boston, Caldwell, 1911.
Bosom Friends: A Seaside Story. London, Nelson, 1910.
The Manor House School, illustrated by F. Moorsom. London, Blackie, 1910; Boston, Caldwell, 1911.
A Fourth Form Friendship. London, Blackie, 1911.
The New Girl at St. Chad's. London, Blackie, 1911.
A Pair of Schoolgirls. London, Blackie, 1912.
The Leader of the Lower School. London, Blackie, 1913.
The Youngest Girl in the Fifth. London, Blackie, 1913.
The Girls of St. Cyprian's. London, Blackie, 1914.
The School by the Sea. London, Blackie, 1914.
The Jolliest Term on Record, illustrated by Balliol Salmon. London, Blackie, 1915.
For the Sake of the School. London, Blackie, 1915.
The Luckiest Girl in the School, illustrated by Balliol Salmon. London, Blackie, and New York, Stokes, 1916.
The Madcap of the School, illustrated by Balliol Salmon. London, Blackie, 1917; New York, Stokes, 1922.
The Slap-Bang Boys. London, Nelson, 1917.
A Patriotic Schoolgirl, illustrated by Balliol Salmon. London, Blackie, 1918.
For the School Colours, illustrated by Balliol Salmon. London, Blackie, 1918.
A Harum-Scarum Schoolgirl, illustrated by John Campbell. London, Blackie, 1919; New York, Stokes, 1920.
The Head Girl at The Gables, illustrated by Balliol Salmon. London, Blackie, 1919; New York, Stokes, 1920.
Two Little Scamps and a Puppy, illustrated by E. Blampied. London, Nelson, 1919.
A Gift from the Sea. London, Nelson, 1920.
A Popular Schoolgirl, illustrated by Balliol Salmon. London, Blackie, 1920; New York, Stokes, 1921.
The Princess of the School, illustrated by Frank Wiles. London, Blackie, 1920; New York, Stokes, 1921; as *A Princess at the School,* London, Armada, 1970.
Loyal to the School, illustrated by Treyer Evans. London, Blackie, 1921.
A Fortunate Term, illustrated by Treyer Evans. London, Blackie, 1921; as *Marjorie's Best Year,* New York, Stokes, 1923.
Monitress Merle, illustrated by Treyer Evans. London, Blackie, 1922.

The School in the South, illustrated by W. Smithson Broadhead. London, Blackie, 1922; as *The Jolliest School of All,* New York, Stokes, 1923.
The Khaki Boys and Other Stories. London, Nelson, 1923.
Schoolgirl Kitty, illustrated by W.E. Wightman. London, Blackie, 1923; New York, Stokes, 1924.
Captain Peggie, illustrated by W.E. Wightman. London, Blackie, and New York, Stokes, 1924.
Joan's Best Chum, illustrated by W.E. Wightman. London, Blackie, 1926; New York, Stokes, 1927.
Queen of the Dormitory and Other Stories, illustrated by P.B. Hickling. London, Cassell, 1926.
Ruth of St. Roman's, illustrated by F. Oldham. London, Blackie, 1927.
At School with Rachel, illustrated by W.E. Wightman. London, Blackie, 1928.
St. Catherine's College, illustrated by Frank Wiles. London, Blackie, 1929.
The Little Green School, illustrated by Frank Wiles. London, Blackie, 1931.
Nesta's New School, illustrated by J. Dewar Mills. London, Blackie, 1932; as *Amanda's New School,* London, Armada, 1970.
Jean's Golden Term. London, Blackie, 1934.
The School at The Turrets. London, Blackie, 1935.
An Exciting Term. London, Blackie, 1936.
Jill's Jolliest School. London, Blackie, 1937.
The School on the Cliff, illustrated by F.E. Hiley. London, Blackie, 1938.
The School on the Moor, illustrated by Henry Coller. London, Blackie, 1939.
The New School at Scawdale, illustrated by M. Mackinlay. London, Blackie, 1940.
Five Jolly Schoolgirls. London, Blackie, 1941.
The Mystery of the Moated Grange. London, Blackie, 1942.
The Secret of the Border Castle, illustrated by Charles Willis. London, Blackie, 1943.
The School in the Forest, illustrated by J. Dewar Mills. London, Blackie, 1944.
Three Terms at Uplands, illustrated by D.L. Mays. London, Blackie, 1945.
The School on the Loch, illustrated by W. Lindsay Cable. London, Blackie, 1946.

Plays

The Mischievous Brownie. Edinburgh, Patterson, 1899.
The Fairy Gifts. Edinburgh, Patterson, 1901.
Four Recitations. Edinburgh, Patterson, 1903.
The Enchanted Fiddle. Edinburgh, Patterson, 1903.
The Wishing Princess. Edinburgh, Patterson, 1904.

Other

My Own Schooldays (autobiography). London, Blackie, 1925.

*

Critical Study: *The Schoolgirl Ethic: The Life and Work of Angela Brazil* by Gillian Freeman, London, Allen Lane, 1976.

* * *

Angela Brazil pioneered the girls' school story in Great Britain and created a genre. Her name is synonymous with "jolly hockey sticks" fiction in spite of many excellent followers. Her first school story, *The Fortunes of Philippa,* was based on her mother's experiences of an English boarding school after early childhood in Rio de Janeiro, and contains a moving, psychologically accurate account of a nervous breakdown occasioned by a persecuting teacher. The book's success brought a commission from Blackie's, who remained her publishers until her death in 1947, although by that time her "works," as she called them, had deteriorated to a formula. The best are those written between 1911 (*The New Girl at St. Chad's* and *A Fourth Form Friendship*) and 1924 (*Captain Peggie*). There was a biography in 1926 (*My Own Schooldays*) which gives a carefully scissored and romanticized account.

Brazil's schooling was academically sound and emotionally disappointing. She longed for secret societies, boarding school, hockey, and amateur dramatics, and created them for her readers. Many girls, inspired by her books, became boarders, and found that real life in no way measured up to Brazil fiction. The books often have perfunctory plots with poor construction. It is the girls, the teaching staffs, and the intense relationships which give them life, and there is no doubt that Brazil really understood adolescent agonies. Passions, jealousies, resentments, and aims were charted with sympathy, as were the problems and responsibilities of headmistresses who appear in a wide range of personalities. Brazil believed in education for its own sake, free from the stress of examinations; loyalty to the family (particularly to mothers—fathers play virtually no part in her books); loyalty to England (*A Patriotic Schoolgirl* and *For the School Colours* are the best examples) and loyalty to *friends.* Aldred and Mabel in *A Fourth Form Friendship* suffer and enjoy the emotional intensity of a heterosexual liaison, and it must be stressed that Brazil was totally innocent of any underlying forces guiding her subconscious. It is interesting to note that in subsequent editions a kiss becomes a handshake, as behaviour patterns changed. In *Loyal to the School* a new principal objected to seeing girls walking about the playground with their arms round each others waists or the display of any affections. She called such behaviour "early Victorian."

Slang is an essential ingredient of the books and made the author unpopular with real headmistresses. Two High Mistresses of St. Paul's Girls' School (Miss Gray and Miss Strudwick) separately condemned her to two generations of pupils. Whether Brazil took the slang from schoolgirls (she claimed she did and rode the commuter train from Coventry to Leamington Spa to take it down from travelling pupils) or the schoolgirls from Brazil, it is difficult to decide. Some of it is incomprehensible—"it's a sneaking rag to prig their bikkies"—and some unlikely—"it's a blossomy idea, O Queen!" What is indisputable is that Brazil drew continuously on her own life, so that her biography can be charted from her work. A visit to a café, a gift of chocolates, hatred of a sister-in-law and adoration of a sick nephew (*A Patriotic Schoolgirl*) are all to be found in the seemingly inflexible format. *Schoolgirl Kitty* is built on personal relationships and events, Carrington is a surname she used as an alias for Brazil, and Lesbia Carrington in *For the School Colours* is based on herself.

—Gillian Freeman

BRENT-DYER, Elinor M.

Pseudonym: Gladys Eleanor May Dyer. **Nationality:** British. **Born:** South Shields, County Durham, 6 April 1894. **Education:** St. Nicholas's school, South Shields and Westoe; City of Leeds Training College, 1915-17; Newcastle Conservatoire of Music. **Career:** Teacher, 1912-15, at Baring Street School and other schools, South Shields, 1917-21, and at Western House School, Fareham, Hampshire, 1922-23; governess in Hereford, 1933-38; founding headmistress, Margaret Roper School, Hereford, 1938-48. **Died:** 20 September 1969.

Publications for Children

Fiction

Gerry Goes to School, illustrated by Gordon Broe. Edinburgh, Chambers, 1922; Philadelphia, Lippincott, 1923.
A Head Girl's Difficulties, illustrated by Nina K. Brisley. Edinburgh, Chambers, 1923.
The Maids of La Rochelle, illustrated by Nina K. Brisley. Edinburgh, Chambers, 1924.
The School at the Chalet, illustrated by Nina K. Brisley. Edinburgh, Chambers, 1925.
Jo of the Chalet School, illustrated by Nina K. Brisley. Edinburgh, Chambers, 1926.
A Thrilling Term at Janeways, illustrated by F.M. Anderson. London, Nelson, 1927.
Seven Scamps Who Are Not All Boys, illustrated by Percy Tarrant. Edinburgh, Chambers, 1927.
The Princess of the Chalet School, illustrated by Nina K. Brisley. Edinburgh, Chambers, 1927.
The Head Girl of the Chalet School, illustrated by Nina K. Brisley. Edinburgh, Chambers, 1928.
Judy the Guide, illustrated by L.A. Govey. London, Nelson, 1928.
The New House Mistress. London, Nelson, 1928.
Heather Leaves School, illustrated by Percy Tarrant. Edinburgh, Chambers, 1929.
The Rivals of the Chalet School, illustrated by Nina K. Brisley. Edinburgh, Chambers, 1929.
Eustacia Goes to the Chalet School. Edinburgh, Chambers, 1930.
The School by the River. London, Burns Oates, 1930.
The Chalet School and Jo, illustrated by Nina K. Brisley. Edinburgh, Chambers, 1931.
The Feud in the Fifth Remove. London, Religious Tract Society, 1931.
Janie of La Rochelle. Edinburgh, Chambers, 1932.
The Little Marie-José. London, Burns Oates, 1932.
The Chalet Girls in Camp. Edinburgh, Chambers, 1932.
The Exploits of the Chalet Girls, illustrated by Nina K. Brisley. Edinburgh, Chambers, 1933.
The Chalet School and the Lintons, illustrated by Nina K. Brisley. Edinburgh, Chambers, 1934.
Carnation of the Upper Fourth. London, Religious Tract Society, 1934.
The New House at the Chalet School. Edinburgh, Chambers, 1935.
Jo Returns to the Chalet School, illustrated by Nina K. Brisley. Edinburgh, Chambers, 1936.
Monica Turns Up Trumps. London, Religious Tract Society, 1936.
Caroline the Second. London, Religious Tract Society, 1937.
The New Chalet School, illustrated by Nina K. Brisley. Edinburgh, Chambers, 1938; as *A United Chalet School,* London, Armada, 1988.
They Both Liked Dogs. London, Religious Tract Society, 1938.
The Chalet School in Exile. Edinburgh, Chambers, 1940.
The Chalet School Goes to It, illustrated by Nina K. Brisley. Edinburgh, Chambers, 1941; as *The Chalet School at War,* London, Armada, 1988.
The Highland Twins at the Chalet School. Edinburgh, Chambers, 1942.
The Little Missus. Edinburgh, Chambers, 1942.
Lavender Laughs in the Chalet School. Edinburgh, Chambers, 1943.
Gay from China at the Chalet School. Edinburgh, Chambers, 1944.
Jo to the Rescue. Edinburgh, Chambers, 1945.
The Lost Staircase. Edinburgh, Chambers, 1946.
Lorna at Wynyards. London, Lutterworth Press, 1947.
Stepsisters for Lorna, illustrated by John Bruce. London, Temple, 1948.
Three Go to the Chalet School. Edinburgh, Chambers, 1949.
Peggy of the Chalet School. Edinburgh, Chambers, 1950.
The Chalet School and the Island. Edinburgh, Chambers, 1950.
Fardingdales. London, Latimer, 1950.
The Chalet School and Rosalie. Edinburgh, Chambers, 1951.
Carola Storms the Chalet School. Edinburgh, Chambers, 1951.
Schoolgirls Abroad (*Verena Visits New Zealand, Bess on Her Own in Canada, A Quintette in Queensland, Sharlie's Kenya Diary*). Edinburgh, Chambers, 4 vols., 1951.
The Chalet School in the Oberland. Edinburgh, Chambers, 1952.
The Wrong Chalet School. Edinburgh, Chambers, 1952.
Shocks for the Chalet School. Edinburgh, Chambers, 1952.
Bride Leads the Chalet School. Edinburgh, Chambers, 1953.
Changes for the Chalet School. Edinburgh, Chambers, 1953.
Janie Steps In. Edinburgh, Chambers, 1953.
The Susannah Adventure. Edinburgh, Chambers, 1953.
Nesta Steps Out. London, Oliphants, 1954.
Kennelmaid Nan. London, Lutterworth Press, 1954.
Joey Goes to the Oberland. Edinburgh, Chambers, 1954.
Chudleigh Hold. Edinburgh, Chambers, 1954.
The Condor Crags Adventure. Edinburgh, Chambers, 1954.
The Chalet School and Barbara. Edinburgh, Chambers, 1954.
Beechy of the Harbour School. London, Oliphants, 1955.
A Chalet Girl from Kenya. Edinburgh, Chambers, 1955.
The Chalet School Does It Again. Edinburgh, Chambers, 1955.
Tom Tackles the Chalet School. Edinburgh, Chambers, 1955.
Top Secret. Edinburgh, Chambers, 1955.
A Problem for the Chalet School. Edinburgh, Chambers, 1956.
Leader in Spite of Herself. London, Oliphants, 1956.
Mary-Lou of the Chalet School. Edinburgh, Chambers, 1956.
A Genius at the Chalet School. Edinburgh, Chambers, 1956; revised edition, London, Collins, 1969.
Excitements at the Chalet School. Edinburgh, Chambers, 1957.
The New Mistress at the Chalet School. Edinburgh, Chambers, 1957.
The Chalet School and Richenda. Edinburgh, Chambers, 1958.
The Coming-of-Age of the Chalet School. Edinburgh, Chambers, 1958.
Theodora and the Chalet School. Edinburgh, Chambers, 1959.
Trials for the Chalet School. Edinburgh, Chambers, 1959.
Joey & Co. in Tirol. Edinburgh, Chambers, 1960.
Ruey Richardson—Chaletian. Edinburgh, Chambers, 1960.

A Leader in the Chalet School. Edinburgh, Chambers, 1961.
The Chalet School Wins the Trick. Edinburgh, Chambers, 1961.
The Feud in the Chalet School. Edinburgh, Chambers, 1962.
A Future Chalet School Girl. Edinburgh, Chambers, 1962.
The School at Skelton Hall. London, Parrish, 1962.
The Chalet School Reunion. Edinburgh, Chambers, 1963.
The Chalet School Triplets. Edinburgh, Chambers, 1963.
Trouble at Skelton Hall. London, Parrish, 1963.
Jane and the Chalet School. Edinburgh, Chambers, 1964.
Redheads at the Chalet School. Edinburgh, Chambers, 1964.
Summer Term at the Chalet School. Edinburgh, Chambers, 1965.
Adrienne and the Chalet School. Edinburgh, Chambers, 1965.
Challenge for the Chalet School. Edinburgh, Chambers, 1966.
Two Sams at the Chalet School. Edinburgh, Chambers, 1967.
Althea Joins the Chalet School. Edinburgh, Chambers, 1969.
Prefects of the Chalet School. Edinburgh, Chambers, 1970.

Other

The Chalet Girls' Cook Book. Edinburgh, Chambers, 1953.

Editor, *The Chalet Book for Girls 1-3.* Edinburgh, Chambers, 3 vols., 1947-49.

PUBLICATIONS FOR ADULTS

Novel

Elizabeth the Gallant. London, Butterworth, 1935.

Plays

My Lady Caprice (produced South Shields, County Durham, 1921).
Polly Danvers, Heiress (produced South Shields, County Durham, 1922).

*

Critical Study: *Behind the Chalet School* by Helen McClelland, Bognor Regis, Sussex, New Horizon, 1981.

* * *

From the early 1920s until her death in 1969 Elinor M. Brent-Dyer wrote almost 100 books for girls. These included historical and adventure stories, but it is for her 58 Chalet School books that this author is remembered. *The School at the Chalet* was published in 1925 and Brent-Dyer's international tri-lingual, non-denominational school in the "Austrian Tirol" soon caught the imagination of readers. It become so popular that a Chalet School Club was formed, attracting a large membership from many parts of the world.

The school, an intriguing amalgam of foreign glamour and British "grit," is founded by Madge Bettany, a young Englishwoman. Although inexperienced, Madge becomes the Chalet School's first headmistress, taking administrative, racial, and language complications in her stride: she is an unconventional principal, sometimes addressing one or other of her pupils as "honey" or "darling."

The school's family atmosphere is accentuated by the presence of Madge's sister, Joey, originally a junior pupil and later Head-Girl. In adult life Joey becomes prolific as a writer of girls' stories and as a breeder (she has eleven children). Despite the variety of pupils who come and go the vitality of the series rests largely on the character of Joey. As this lively and intrepid heroine grows older it is more difficult for the author to make her integral to the stories. However, even in the last book of the series—no. 58, published posthumously in 1970—Joey is still insisting that "if she lived to be a great-grandmother, she would be a Chalet girl to the end."

Initially the Chalet School's appeal owed a great deal to its location. Brent-Dyer ably conveys the charm of the school beside mist-swathed mountains and a lake "alive with dancing shadows." The books are sometimes over-lush. Gentians, marguerites, and alpen roses have a technicolour quality: floweriness spills over into descriptions of the girls in their flame-coloured ties, brown tunics, and shantung blouses. But this is counterbalanced by plenty of action. For instance, *The Princess of the Chalet School* includes—as well as a flowerstrewn masque, a garden party, and a wedding—two kidnapping attempts and an oversize thunderstorm which breaks every window in the valley and sets the school's playing fields on fire. The school buildings are saved from total destruction only by an equally violent hailstorm which opportunely covers everything with five inches of hail in as many minutes. Girls fall into icebound rivers or are stranded on exposed mountain sides: in the first five books alone Joey manages to save the lives of six girls and one dog.

The Chalet School survives after evacuation from the Nazis. It moves first to the Channel Islands, then to Wales and later to the Oberland. Brent-Dyer exploited several of the stock ingredients of girls' fiction including animals, babies, guiding, and country dance. A headmistress for many years, she understood the tastes of girls growing up between the wars, although by the late 1950s her books had become anachronistic.

—Mary Cadogan

BRESLIN, Theresa

Nationality: Scottish/ British. **Born:** Kirkintilloch, Scotland. **Education:** Schools in Kirkintilloch, University of Aston, Birmingham. **Family:** Married; one son and three daughters. **Career:** Youth Services Librarian, East Dunbartonshire District, Scotland. **Awards:** Fidler Award (formerly Kathleen Fidler Award), 1988, and Book Trust's Best of the Decade Award, 1992, for *Simon's Challenge*; Carnegie Gold Medal, 1994, for *Whispers in the Graveyard*; Sheffield Book Award, longer novel category, 1997, for *Death or Glory Boys.* **Address:** 5, Regent Square, Lenzie, Kirkintilloch, Glasgow G66 5AE, Scotland.

PUBLICATIONS FOR CHILDREN

Fiction

Simon's Challenge. Edinburgh, Canongate, 1989.
A Time to Reap. London, Blackie, 1991.
New School Blues. Edinburgh, Canongate, 1992.
Kezzie. London, Methuen, 1993.
Bullies at School. Edinburgh, Canongate, 1994.

Whispers in the Graveyard. London, Methuen, 1994.
Alien Force, illustrated by Bob Harvey. London, Dutton, 1995.
Different Directions. Edinburgh, Canongate, 1995.
A Homecoming for Kezzie. London, Methuen, 1995.
Horrorscopes Sagittarius: Missing. London, Mammoth, 1995.
Death or Glory Boys. London, Methuen, 1996.
Across the Roman Wall. London, A. & C. Black, 1997.
Name Games, illustrated by Kay Widdowson. London, Mammoth, 1997.
Body Parts, illustrated by Janek Matysiak. London, A. & C. Black, 1998.

Short Stories

"Maelstrom," in *Amazing Adventure Stories.* London, Doubleday, 1994.
"You Can Do It," in *Best of Friends.* London, Methuen, 1995.
"Blair, The Boy Who Could Not Be Still," in *Dear Mum, Don't Panic!* London, Methuen, 1995.
"The Gay Goshawk," in *Magic Carpet.* London, Ginn, 1995.
"Act of Love," in *All for Love.* London, Mammoth, 1997.
"The Traveller," in *Just What I Always Wanted.* London, Collins, 1998.

Other

Power Pack: Active Guide to Libraries. London, Library Association, 1995.

*

Theresa Breslin comments:

Rainbows ...

... are inside me, says Solomon, the dyslexic boy in *Whispers in the Graveyard.*

But Solomon's ideas abort, crushed by his lack of skills in literacy. He is unable to write down the thoughts inside his head.

Also, he cannot read ...

Writing *Whispers in the Graveyard* seemed to crystallise my work both as a writer and a librarian. Books are prisms, refracting the light from the minds of others, sending the colours flashing into our own.

And Solomon isn't daft. He knows what he is missing. The stories. He heard someone reading poetry on the radio once ... the words stayed with him for weeks afterwards, searing his mind, thrusting and twisting in his gut.

Children ask me "Is this your book, did you write this?"

Yes I wrote it, and in that sense it is my book. But as soon as it is in print it's yours. The books each one of them; the words, the stories, they belong to the reader.

So that rainbows can arc inside all of us.

* * *

Theresa Breslin's first book won the Kathleen Fidler Award (now the Fidler Award), which was set up to encourage new authors for the eight to twelve age-group. Part of the prize was publication of the winning manuscript and this set Theresa Breslin off on the path to becoming a writer. For this first book, *Simon's Challenge,* she was inspired by her own experience of the local steelworks closing and the consequences of redundancy on children in particular. In the book, Simon's father has been made redundant and has had to go away from home to find work. Simon's deep yearning for a computer has to be put on hold while money is tight. Then he inadvertently witnesses a robbery at his favourite computer shop and is able to help the police to track down the thieves. This is a pretty straightforward adventure, but Theresa Breslin offers pertinent insights into the ways in which parental relationships affect children. The ending is perhaps a little contrived—Simon gets his much-wanted computer as a reward—but it is none the less a satisfying read for the age-group for which it is intended.

Whether she draws on her own experience or on research, Breslin creates real situations and believable characters. The feelings and experiences of children starting secondary school are well portrayed in *New School Blues* in which new girl Mary is fascinated by Jamie, who appears to be a bit of a rebel. The way she befriends him and how they find a mutual interest in archaeology makes a good plot on which to hang the detail of relationships among secondary school children. She is particularly good at writing credible dialogue for this age group; quick and full of humour, it is never patronising.

In another school story, *Bullies at School,* Breslin accurately describes the feelings of a clumsy girl who is teased by her fellow pupils. Her real problem is lack of confidence, but thanks to a supportive teacher, who awakens in her an interest in Celtic literature, she gains a belief in herself that enables her to cope with the bullying. Both these books show accurate observation of children, their conversations and relationships, and manage to convey a real sense of their emotions.

Breslin won the 1994 Carnegie Medal for *Whispers in the Graveyard.* Once again social issues are at the root of the plot, which centres on a dyslexic boy who lives with his alcoholic father. His mother has left home and his teachers have all but given up on him and the only place he can find solace is in a graveyard. In and around this is woven a supernatural story in which a force of evil emerges from the graveyard. The tension is superbly built to a horrifying climax, with such forceful and exciting writing that it is impossible to put down. It is a highly original way of dealing with real issues like dyslexia and its social ramifications, bringing to light as it does adult illiteracy as well.

Alien Force is a science fiction story on the surface. A boy from another planet is sent to investigate an evil force that is steadily growing on Earth. Theresa Breslin combines her ability to tell a good adventure story with her keen perception of children's behaviour. The idea of a higher intelligence that can intervene in other worlds is juxtaposed with warnings that people are gradually destroying planet Earth. All sorts of issues great and small are touched on in a subtle way, from bullying and racism among children to anti-pollution and anti-war propaganda. The ending is a battle of wills between the evil force and the alien and the final twist keeps the reader guessing.

Moving away from the classroom, Theresa Breslin's *Kezzie* and its sequel *Kezzie's Homecoming* are in the historical saga mould. Their historical accuracy makes them equally satisfying for adults and older children. In the first book Kezzie leaves her home in Scotland to search for her younger sister Lucy. The newness of the experience and the apprehension and anxiety Kezzie feels on this enormous journey into the unknown are perceptively captured. Kezzie finds Lucy, who has suffered a traumatic journey herself and together they recover with the kindness shown to them in Canada. At the end of the book war is threatening and Kezzie is convinced that she must return to her grandfather in Scotland.

Kezzie's Homecoming sees Kezzie and Lucy reunited with their beloved grandfather, now living quite a different way of life in a tenement block in Clydebank in Glasgow. Kezzie finds it all strange, but settles down to work in an Italian café and adapts to the way of life. The war brings issues like bigotry and xenophobia to the fore. For example, when the war starts the Italian café is attacked, windows broken, and tables and chairs smashed, because the owners are Italian. Worse is to come in the form of bombings and internment of foreigners and finally, Kezzie and Lucy go to live in the country to relative safety. Both books are emotionally highly charged, the characters completely believable, and the incidents entirely credible, representing something of a tour de force in children's literature.

With the same emotional charge *Death or Glory Boys,* a novel for older children, examines the pros and cons of joining the army, against a background of terrorism. A group of older teenage friends have joined a series of army recruiting evenings to see what the army is all about. The characters discuss the arguments for and against joining. A boy, a pacifist, is against joining, worried that he would lose his sensitivity; one of the girls is keen. Cleverly woven around these conversations is the real plot—a series of terrorist attacks has got the police and army foxed. The story is set in Sheffield and there are definite undertones that the terrorists are IRA. The tension is well created in the scenes of the first bomb and in the final scenes in which the army locates and kills the terrorist, who, in the final twist, turns out to be a girl. The story throws out a lot of thought-provoking ideas and captures particularly well the effects of terrorism on ordinary people.

Theresa Breslin's books deal with "issues" much of the time, but by using credible characters, she manages to treat all sides of a situation sensitively and subtly, leaving the reader to draw his or her own conclusions. Lately, Theresa Breslin's skills have been in demand to write books for a younger age group than in the past. Whether it is in books for beginner or reluctant readers, or in storybooks to read aloud, her writing is of a high quality, her characterisation strong, and her plots interesting.

—Fiona Lafferty

BRETT, Jan (Churchill)

Nationality: American. **Born:** Hingham, Massachusetts, 1 December 1949. **Education:** Attended Colby Junior College (now Colby-Sawyer College), 1968-1969, and Boston Museum of Fine Arts School, 1970. **Family:** Married 1) Daniel Bowler in 1970 (divorced 1979); one daughter; 2) Joseph Hearne in 1980. **Career:** Painter; author and illustrator of children's books. Exhibitions: Master Eagle Gallery, New York City, 1981; Gallery on the Green, Lexington, Massachusetts, 1985; Main Street Gallery, Nantucket, Massachusetts, 1987; Society of Illustration show, New York City, 1991. **Awards:** Parents' Choice award, Parents' Choice Foundation, 1981, and Children's Book Award, University of Nebraska, 1984, for *Fritz and the Beautiful Horses*; *In the Castle of Cats* and *Fritz and the Beautiful Horses* were chosen as "Children's Choices" by the International Reading Association, 1982; Ambassador of Honor Book, English-Speaking Union of the United States, 1983, for *Some Birds Have Funny Names*; Outstanding Science Trade Book for Children, National Science Teachers Association, 1984, for *Some Plants Have Funny Names*; top ten children's books of the year, *Redbook* magazine, 1985, for *Annie and the Wild Animals*; *Booklist* Editor's Choice, 1986, for *The Twelve Days of Christmas,* and 1987, for *Goldilocks and the Three Bears*; first prize, New York Book Show, 1987, for *Mother's Day Mice*; Best of the Year award, *Newsweek,* 1987, for *Goldilocks and the Three Bears*; certificate of merit, Bookbuilders West Book Show, 1987, for *The Enchanted Book*; Pick of the Lists, American Bookseller, and Best Children's Books citation, *New Yorker* magazine, both 1988, both for *The First Dog*; *Parent's* magazine best of the year award, and Parents' Choice award, Parents' Choice Foundation, both 1988, both for *Mother's Day Mice*; Pick of the Lists, American Bookseller, Best Children's Books citation, *New Yorker* magazine, and Booklist best children's book of the 1980s citation, all 1989, all for *The Mitten*; Best Children's Books citation, *New Yorker* magazine, and Pick of the Lists, American Bookseller, both 1990, both for *The Wild Christmas Reindeer*; artist award, New England Booksellers' Association, 1990; Best Children's Books citation, *New Yorker* magazine, and *Newsweek* magazine best of the year award, both 1991, both for *Berlioz the Bear*; Pick of the Lists, American Bookseller, 1991, for *The Owl and the Pussycat* and *Berlioz the Bear*; *Parent's* magazine best of the year award, *School Library Journal* best book of the year citation, Waldenbooks best children's book honor award, and American Library Association notable book citation, all 1991, all for *The Owl and the Pussycat*; Pick of the Lists, American Bookseller, 1992, and Maryland Black-Eyed Susan Picture Book Award, 1994, for *Trouble with Trolls*; Pick of the Lists, American Bookseller, 1993, for *Christmas Trolls*; David McCord Children's Literature Citation, 1993; Pick of the Lists, American Bookseller, Best Children's Books of 1994, *Publisher's Weekly,* Parent's Choice Illustration Award, 1994, and Association of Booksellers for Children Picture Book Award, 1995, all for *Town Mouse Country Mouse*; *New York Times* Books of the Times, 1996, for *Comet's Nine Lives*; Pick of the Lists, American Bookseller, 1997, for *The Hat*; D.H.L.: Fitchburg State College, 1996. **Address:** 132 Pleasant Street, Norwell, Massachusetts 02061, U.S.A. **Website:** http://www.janbrett.com.

Publications for Children (illustrated by the author)

Fritz and the Beautiful Horses. Boston, Houghton Mifflin, 1981.
Annie and the Wild Animals. Boston, Houghton Mifflin, 1985.
Goldilocks and the Three Bears. New York, Dodd, Mead, 1987.
The First Dog. New York, Harcourt Brace Jovanovich, 1988.
Beauty and the Beast. New York, Clarion, 1989.
The Mitten. New York, Putnam's, 1989.
The Wild Christmas Reindeer. New York, Putnam's, 1990.
Berlioz the Bear. New York, Putnam's, 1991.
Trouble With Trolls. New York, Putnam's, 1992.
Christmas Trolls. New York, Putnam's, 1993.
Town Mouse, Country Mouse. New York, Putnam's, 1994.
Armadillo Rodeo. New York, Putnam's, 1995.
Comet's Nine Lives. New York, Putnam's, 1996.
The Hat. New York, Putnam's, 1997.

*

Media Adaptations: *The Great Rescue* (sound recording), Parker Brothers, 1984.

Biography: Entry in *Something About the Author,* Vol. 71, Detroit, Gale, 1992.

Illustrator: *Woodland Crossings* by Stephen Krensky, 1978; *Inside a Sand Castle and Other Secrets* by Mary Louise Cuneo, 1979; *The Secret Clocks: Time Senses of Living Things* by Seymour Simon, 1979; *St. Patrick's Day in the Morning* by Eve Bunting, 1980; *Young Melvin and Bulger* by Mark Taylor, 1981; *In the Castle of the Cats* by Betty Boegehold, 1981; *Some Birds Have Funny Names* by Diana Harding, 1981; *I Can Fly* by Ruth Krauss, 1981; *Prayer: Learning How to Talk to God* by Jeanette L. Groth, 1983; *The Valentine Bears* by Eve Bunting, 1983; *Some Plants Have Funny Names* by Diana Harding Cross, 1983; *The Great Rescue* by Mark Taylor, 1984; *Where Are All the Kittens?* by Jennifer Perryman, 1984; *You Are Special to Jesus* by Annetta Dellinger, 1984; *Old Devil is Waiting: Three Folktales* by Dorothy Van Woerkom, 1985; *The Wizard of Oz: A Story to Color,* 1985; *The Mother's Day Mice* by Eve Bunting, 1986; *The Twelve Days of Christmas,* 1986; *Noelle of the Nutcracker* by Pamela Jane, 1986; *Scary, Scary Halloween* by Eve Bunting, 1986; *The Enchanted Book: A Tale from Krakow* by Janina Porazinska (translated by Bozena Smith), 1987; *Happy Birthday, Dear Duck* by Eve Bunting, 1988; *The Owl and the Pussycat* by Edward Lear, 1991; also illustrator of a calendar for Sunrise Publications.

* * *

Jan Brett had a special love for books and reading since she was a young child: "I remember the special quiet of rainy days when I felt that I could enter the pages of my beautiful picture books," she told *Something About the Author.* "Now I try to recreate that feeling of believing that the imaginary place I'm drawing really exists." Come and enter the richly imaginative world of Jan Brett.

Jan Brett began her career as an illustrator of children's books by others, including Eve Bunting, Ruth Krauss, and Mary Taylor. *Fritz and the Beautiful Horses* was the first book she both wrote and illustrated. Fritz is a pony with a "long, tangled mane, whiskers on his muzzle, and short legs." Unlike the "magnificent jumpers, splendid chargers, and elegant parade horses" for which the old walled city is renowned, Fritz is not beautiful. But he is very gentle and kind, sure-footed and always willing to work. When the old bridge begins to crack, the beautiful horses balk at crossing through the river, and the children get frightened, Fritz comes to their rescue, carefully carrying the children one by one down the steep hill, across the river, and home to safety. And "from that day on, the walled city was known for its beautiful horses and its very dependable pony." The Old World, fairy tale feel that pervades her later work as well as the folkloric design and costume and a wonderful attention to detail are all here in Jan Brett's first, critically-acclaimed picture book.

With her next book, *Annie and the Wild Animals,* Jan Brett adds the fabulous, narrative borders and cumulative storytelling style for which much of her subsequent work has also become known and acclaimed. Something is wrong with Annie's cat Taffy. She has stopped playing. She eats more than usual. She sleeps all day. She curls up in strange places. One day, she completely disappears. (Not to worry, though: the observant reader can watch her travel safely in the woods on the pages' decorative borders.) But Annie worries. She feels lonesome, too, and so places a corn cake on the edge of the wood to attract a new pet. A giant moose is the first to visit. "He's too big to tame," thinks Annie. The next morning, the moose reappears—along with a snarling wildcat: "He's too mean to tame." On succeeding days come a big, growling bear ("too grumpy"), a stag and his family, and a large, gray wolf. But not one of them is soft and friendly like Taffy. Annie runs out of corn meal, so all the wild animals return to the wood. Meanwhile, Taffy has been preparing a wonderful surprise for Annie. As unexpectedly as a warm spring breeze, she proudly returns into the yard. "Taffy," Annie exclaims, "Where have you been?" Taffy turns and looks back the way she has come, out of the wood come three soft and friendly kittens, and Annie will not be lonely any more.

In *The First Dog,* Brett tells an imaginative and cumulative tale about the Paleowolf who might have become the first domesticated animal, finding the inspiration for her border designs in Ice Age cave paintings and artifacts. *The Wild Christmas Reindeer* returns to a Scandinavian Old World setting, as Jan Brett tells the story of Teeka, who must get Santa's reindeer ready to fly on Christmas Eve. She's never worked with the reindeer before, though, and is not sure how to tame them. In her bungling attempts, Teeka learns a valuable lesson about the power of gentleness and patience. (Santa's elves are busily preparing for Christmas, day by day, in the side borders of the triptych-like page spreads.)

In *Berlioz the Bear,* readers watch the borders with eager anticipation as townspeople prepare for their gala town ball and Berlioz and friends encounter one difficulty after another as they struggle to make it to the village square in time for the big event; in *Comet's Nine Lives,* the lighthouse keeper and his cat look out for their new arrival, Comet the cat, if he ever makes it before his nine lives are used up!

The Mitten, based on a Ukranian folktale, is the story of Nicki, who asks his grandmother, Baba, to make him mittens as white as snow. "If you drop one..." Baba warns, "you ll never find it." But Nicki wants snow-white mittens, and finally Baba makes them for him. On his first trip into the woods, he unwittingly drops one, of course, and readers watch the woodland animals, now the center of the page-spreads (with the oblivious Nicki in the side borders) burrow into the mitten, one after another, until it is so big that Nicki has no trouble finding it, once he realizes he's lost it! Brett's most recent book, *The Hat,* is a beautiful variation on this theme, as Lisa hangs her winter clothes on the line, and a stocking blows off and is found by Hedgie the hedgehog. The curious Hedgie pokes his nose into the stocking, but when he pulls it out, the stocking gets stuck on his prickles. "How embarrassing," Hedgie thinks. Naturally, he soon encounters a mother hen, who clucks at him and laughs, "What's that on your head, Hedgie?" "Why, it's my new hat," is his clever reply. "Isn't it beautiful?" Soon, the other farmyard animals see Hedgie's "new hat" and laugh at it, too, but as he tells them how cozy and warm it is, they all come to want one themselves. When, one by one, Lisa's other winter things blow off the line, the animals all get their chance to have a "hat" of their very own.

"My imagination has always run away with me," Jan Brett told *Something About the Author.* "Often I put borders in my books to contain the overflow of thoughts." In her site on the World Wide Web, Jan Brett has found a perfect, multi-faceted outlet for her imaginative energies as she writes and talks about her books and offers a wide variety of book-related activities, from baking Holiday hedgehog cookies to making an iron-on t-shirt from *The Hat* and a sailor's bracelet and making *The Hat* into a play. Welcome to the brave new "cyber world" of Jan Brett!

—Marcia Welsh

BRIDWELL, Norman

Nationality: American. **Born:** Kokomo, Indiana, 15 February 1928. **Education:** John Herron Art Institute, 1945-49; Cooper Union Art School, 1953-54. **Family:** Married Norma Howard, 1958; one son, one daughter. **Career:** Raxon Fabrics, New York City, artist and designer, 1951-53; H.D. Rose Company (film strips), New York City, artist, 1953-56; free-lance commercial artist, 1956-70; writer and Illustrator, from 1962. **Awards:** Lucky Book Club/Four-Leaf Clover Award for Author of the Year, Scholastic, 1971; Children's Choice Award for best picture book, 1987, for *Clifford the Big Red Dog*; Jeremiah Ludington Memorial Award, Educational Paperback Association, 1991. Honorary Degree, Indiana University, 1994. **Address:** Box 869, High Street, Edgartown, Massachusetts 02539, U.S.A.

Publications for Children

Fiction (illustrated by the author)

The Adventures of Clifford the Big Red Dog. New York, Scholastic, 1963.
Zany Zoo. New York, Scholastic, 1963.
Bird in the Hat. New York, Scholastic, 1964.
Clifford Gets a Job. New York, Scholastic, 1965
The Witch Next Door. New York, Scholastic, 1965.
Clifford Takes a Trip. New York, Scholastic, 1966.
Clifford's Halloween. New York, Scholastic, 1966.
A Tiny Family. New York, Scholastic, 1968.
The Country Cat. New York, Scholastic, 1969.
What Do They Do When It Rains? New York, Scholastic, 1969.
Clifford's Tricks. New York, Scholastic, 1969.
How to Care for Your Monster. New York, Scholastic, 1970.
The Witch's Christmas. New York, Scholastic, 1970.
Monster Jokes and Riddles. New York, Scholastic, 1972.
Clifford The Small Red Puppy. New York, Scholastic, 1972
The Witch's Vacation. New York, Scholastic, 1973.
The Dog Frog Book. New York, Xerox Education Publications, 1973.
Merton the Monkey Mouse. New York, Xerox Education Publications, 1973.
Clifford's Riddles. New York, Scholastic, 1974.
Monster Holidays. New York, Scholastic, 1974.
Ghost Charlie. New York, Scholastic, 1975.
Clifford's Good Deeds. New York, Scholastic, 1975.
My Pet the Rock. New York, Xerox Education Publications. 1975.
Boy on the Ceiling. New York, Xerox Education Publications, 1976.
The Witch's Catalog. New York, Scholastic, 1976.
The Big Water Fight. New York, Scholastic, 1977.
Clifford at the Circus. New York, Scholastic, 1977.
Kangaroo Stew. New York, Scholastic, 1979.
The Witch Grows Up. New York, Scholastic, 1979.
Clifford Goes to Hollywood. New York, Scholastic, 1980.
Clifford's ABC. New York, Scholastic, 1984.
Clifford's Sticker Book. New York, Scholastic, 1984.
Clifford's Story Hour. New York, Scholastic, 1984.
Clifford's Family. New York, Scholastic, 1984.
Clifford's Kitten. New York, Scholastic, 1984.
Clifford's Christmas. New York, Scholastic, 1984.
Clifford's Pals. New York, Scholastic, 1985.
Clifford's Neighborhood. New York, Scholastic, 1985.
Clifford and the Grouchy Neighbors. New York, Scholastic, 1985.
Count on Clifford. New York, Scholastic, 1985.
Clifford's Manners. New York, Scholastic, 1987.
Clifford's Birthday Party. New York, Scholastic, 1987
Clifford's Sing Along. New York, Scholastic, 1987
Clifford Wants a Cookie. New York, Scholastic, 1988.
Where Is Clifford? A Lift-a-Flap Book. New York, Scholastic, 1989.
Fun with Clifford Activity Book. New York, Scholastic, 1989.
Clifford's Word Book. New York, Scholastic, 1990.
Clifford's Happy Days: A Pop-up Book. New York, Scholastic, 1990.
Clifford, We Love You. New York, Scholastic, 1991.
Clifford's Animal Sounds. New York, Scholastic, 1991.
Clifford's Bathtime. New York, Scholastic, 1991.
Clifford's Bedtime. New York, Scholastic, 1991.
Clifford's Growth Chart. New York, Scholastic, 1991.
Clifford's Peekaboo. New York, Scholastic, 1991.
Hello, Clifford: A Puppet Book. New York, Scholastic, 1991.
Clifford Counts Bubbles. New York, Scholastic, 1992.
Clifford the Small Red Puppy Follows His Nose. New York, Scholastic, 1992.
Clifford the Firehouse Dog. New York, Scholastic, 1994.
Clifford's Big Book of Stories. New York, Scholastic, 1994
Clifford's Happy Easter. New York, Scholastic, 1994.
Clifford's I Love You. New York, Scholastic, 1994.
Clifford's Springtime. New York, Scholastic, 1994.
Clifford's Thanksgiving. New York, Scholastic, 1994.
Clifford and The Big Storm. New York, Scholastic, 1995.
Clifford's Sports Day. New York, Scholastic, 1996.
Clifford The Big Red Dog Board Book. New York, Scholastic, 1997.
Clifford's First Autumn. New York, Scholastic, 1997.
Clifford's Furry Friends. New York, Scholastic, 1998.
Clifford's First Snow Day. New York, Scholastic, 1998.

*

Biography: Entry in *Something about the Author,* Vol. 68, Detroit, Gale Publishing, 1992.

Illustrator: *How to Care for Your Dog* by Jean Bethell, 1964; *The Real Magnet Book* by Mae Freeman, 1967; *Ickle Bickle Robin* by Edna Mitchell Preston, 1974.

Norman Bridwell comments:

Although the critics find little to like in my books children seem to like them. I am told that many teachers use the *Clifford* books to get children interested in reading. I didn't plan that, but I'm glad it works out that way.

I have been very lucky to have this career. I originally wanted to be an illustrator but had to write my own stories because nobody wanted my art for their books.

* * *

There are certain picture books for the pre-school and beginner reader crowd that are so popular they get their own shelf in the children's section of the public library. The *Spot* books of Eric Hill, the *Curious George* books of H.A. Rey, the *Bear* books of Stan and Jan Berenstain, the *Babar* books by Laurent and Jean de

Brunhoff, the *Arthur* books by Marc Brown, and the *Clifford* books by Norman Bridwell are good examples. They are all series books about animals that show the animals in simple day-to-day situations.

Bridwell has written and illustrated many books about a large dog named Clifford and his proud owner Emily Elizabeth, named after Bridwell's daughter. Bridwell has also written and illustrated several books about a friendly witch, but it is the Clifford books that have brought him his great popularity.

Bridwell's books are rarely praised or even singled out by critics and specialists in children's literature; they are slight in text and simple in illustration. But teachers and librarians have found them to be very useful in getting children interested in reading. Why? They are visually inviting. Clifford is a very large dog, almost as large as an elephant, and he is very red in color, about the red of a fire-engine. He has soulful eyes and floppy ears. You'd be inclined to pet him, and even hug the parts of him you could reach. And Clifford has adventures in his daily life that children can relate to: he celebrates Christmas and Easter, he goes on trips, he tries to do good deeds, and he has manners. Most important, he cares about others.

Clifford came to Emily Elizabeth in a special way. The man down the hall in her apartment house in the city gave her a choice of puppies when his dog had a litter. One puppy in the litter was smaller than the rest, and the man told her not to take that one because he was the runt and would always be small and sick.

But Emily Elizabeth knew at once that this puppy needed her and she chose him above the others. She fed him with her doll's baby bottle. Clifford was so little that he was always getting lost, even in Emily Elizabeth's small apartment. But she looked after him.

Emily Elizabeth did the right thing, of course. Her excellent care of Clifford enabled him to grow, and grow and grow until he was too big for the apartment and had to be sent to live with her uncle in the country. Emily Elizabeth missed Clifford and he missed her. Luckily, she and her parents were able to move to the country, with her father taking a job with her uncle, and Emily Elizabeth reuniting with her dog.

Clifford by now is bigger than a human being, bigger than a car, bigger than Emily Elizabeth's house in the country. Well you can see how delightful it would be to have a dog that big, who had his own very large house in back of Emily Elizabeth's house, and who rides her to school every day on his back. Emily Elizabeth and her friends climb all over Clifford and have good times sliding down his back when he is seated.

There is one problem with Clifford, from Emily's family's point of view: he eats a lot of dog food, which costs a lot of money. But in *Clifford Gets a Job,* he becomes a police dog; he is paid not in money but in dog food. Problem solved. Naturally such a dog might have trouble with the neighbors. In *Clifford and the Grouchy Neighbors,* he indeed does have trouble because he makes so much noise and in an effort to help them, only upsets their grocery cart. Clifford wants to do good, and when he saves the birds in the neighbors' yard from a predatory cat, they are won over and actually thank Clifford for his assistance.

Clifford's Good Deeds describes his efforts at being helpful, and the difficulties he has in doing just the right thing. He tries to help a small paper boy, but throws his newspaper so hard that it goes through the front and back windows of a house. And other mishaps follow. At the end of this book, he manages to rescue two little children out of the third floor of a burning house. Bridwell himself says on one of his dust jackets that he thinks the key to Clifford's charm is that he is not perfect. Clifford always tries to do the right thing, but he makes many mistakes along the way. Children too make mistakes, and they often are misunderstood, so they relate to Clifford's trials and tribulations.

Clifford provides a word book, a counting book, an ABC book, a riddle book, a pop-up book, a puppet book. He even has a book on manners. In *Clifford's Manners,* he says "please" when asking for something, "thank you" when receiving something. Clifford writes thank you notes, shares his toys with friends, puts his toys away when he is finished with them. He is a good sport when he loses. What a role model!

No child is going to read all of these books, but those who read one are likely to enjoy reading others because Clifford becomes a friend, a friend who has funny and familiar adventures, and predictable problems. And he does motivate children to read on. An admirable dog, Clifford. Bridwell's works have been translated into Spanish, Danish, German, Chinese, French, Italian and Greek. The situations depicted and the accompanying drawings are genuine and may be enjoyed by children of many cultures.

—Mary Lystad

BRIGGS, K(atharine) M(ary)

Nationality: British. **Born:** London, 8 November 1898. **Education:** Lansdowne House; Lady Margaret Hall, Oxford, M.A. 1923, Ph.D. 1952. **Military Service:** Women's Auxiliary Air Force, 1941-45. **Career:** Free-lance writer. Headed an amateur theatrical touring company for 15 years. Visiting Professor, University of Pennsylvania, Philadelphia, 1970, and University of California, Berkeley, 1973. President, Folklore Society of London, 1967-70. **Award:** D.Litt.: Oxford University, 1969. **Died:** 15 October 1980.

Publications for Children

Fiction

The Legend of Maiden-Hair. London, Stockwell, 1915.

The Witches' Ride, illustrated by Winifred Briggs. Dunkeld, Perthshire, Capricornus, 1937.

The Prince, The Fox, and the Dragon, illustrated by Winifred Briggs. Dunkeld, Perthshire, Capricornus, 1938.

Hobberdy Dick. London, Eyre and Spottiswoode, 1955; New York, Greenwillow, 1977.

Kate Crackernuts. Oxford, Alden Press, 1963; revised edition, London, Kestrel, and New York, Greenwillow, 1979.

Play

Stories Arranged for Mime (*The Golden Goose; Whuppity Stories; Jesper, Who Herded Hares*). Dunkeld, Perthshire, Capricornus, 3 vols., 1937.

Poetry

Whispers: An Experiment in Lino Cuts, with Elspeth Briggs, illustrated by the authors and Winifred Briggs. Dunkeld, Perthshire, Capricornus, 1940.

The Twelve Days of Christmas, with others, illustrated by Winifred Briggs. Dunkeld, Perthshire, Capricornus, 1952.

Other

Mime for Guides and Brownies. London, Girl Guides Association, 1955.

Abbey Lubbers, Banshees, and Boggarts: A Who's Who of Fairies, illustrated by Yvonne Gilbert. London, Kestrel, and New York, Pantheon, 1979.

Publications for Adults

Novels

The Lisles of Ellingham. Oxford, Alden Press, 1935.

The Castilians. Oxford, Alden Press, 1950.

Plays

The Garrulous Lady. London, Golden Vista Press, 1931.

The Peacemaker (produced Murthly, Perthshire, 1933). Dunkeld, Perthshire, Capricornus, 1938.

The Fugitive. Dunkeld, Perthshire, Capricornus, 1938.

The Lady in the Dark. Dunkeld, Perthshire, Capricornus, 1949.

Other

A History of 75 Years. Privately printed, 1935.

The Personnel of Fairyland: A Short Account of the Fairy People of Great Britain for Those Who Tell Stories to Children. Oxford, Alden Press, 1953; Cambridge, Massachusetts, Bentley, 1954.

Dunkeld and Birman Guide. Oxford, Alden Press, 1956.

The Anatomy of Puck: An Examination of Fairy Beliefs among Shakespeare's Contemporaries and Successors. London, Routledge, 1959; New York, Arno Press, 1977.

Pale Hecate's Team: An Examination of the Beliefs on Witchcraft and Magic among Shakespeare's Contemporaries and His Immediate Successors. London, Routledge, and New York, Humanities Press, 1962.

The Fairies in Tradition and Literature. London, Routledge, 1967; as *The Fairies in English Tradition and Literature,* Chicago, University of Chicago Press, 1967.

A Dictionary of British Folk-tales in the English Language:

Folk Narratives. London, Routledge, 2 vols., 1970; as *Folktales,* Bloomington, Indiana University Press, 2 vols., 1970.

Folk Legends. London, Routledge, and Bloomington, Indiana University Press, 2 vols., 1971.

The Folklore of the Cotswolds. London, Batsford, and Totowa, New Jersey, Rowman and Littlefield, 1974.

A Dictionary of Fairies: Hobgoblins, Brownies, Bogies, and Other Supernatural Creatures. London, Allen Lane, 1976; as *An Encyclopedia of Fairies,* New York, Pantheon, 1976.

A Sampler of British Folk-tales (selection from *A Dictionary of British Folk-tales*). London, Routledge, 1977; as *British Folktales,* New York, Pantheon, 1977.

The Vanishing People: A Study of Traditional Fairy Beliefs. London, Batsford, and New York, Pantheon, 1978.

Nine Lives: Cats in Folklore. London, Routledge, and New York, Pantheon, 1980.

Editor, with Ruth Lyndall Tongue, *Folktales of England.* London, Routledge, and Chicago, University of Chicago Press, 1965.

Editor, *Somerset Folk-lore,* by Ruth Lyndall Tongue. London, Folklore Society, 1965.

Editor, *The Last of the Astrologers: Mr. William Lilly's History of His Life and Times from the Year 1602 to 1681.* London, Folklore Society, 1974.

*

Critical Study: *Katharine Briggs: Story-Teller* by H. Ellis Davidson, Cambridge, Lutterworth Press, 1986.

* * *

This is sadly not the place to try to assess the whole of K.M. Briggs's work, which culminated in the enormous, definitive *A Dictionary of British Folk-tales.* However, it was her long study of folk-tales, and in particular the fairyfolk in all their manifestations, which gave rise to her children's books, and her knowledge and authority are evident in everything she wrote.

Neither *Hobberdy Dick* nor *Kate Crackernuts* are particularly easy books for children. *Hobberdy Dick* is the more accessible of the two—it is younger in tone, with a good deal of fun in it—but it contains the death of a much-loved grandmother, besides demonstrating the period convention that children obey their parents automatically, however harsh the command, and presenting a heroine who must endure slights, insults, and overwork with no real hope of anything better (Anne's fortune does change—but only through the intervention of Dick himself). *Kate Crackernuts* is set in the Scottish Borders and Yorkshire, and most of the speech is in dialect. Besides this, the glamour cast on Katherine, in which she believes her head has been turned into that of a sheep, could be very frightening for some children—and the carnal aspects of diabolism are admitted in the passages to do with witchcraft.

For the persevering, though, both stories are immensely rewarding. Hobberdy Dick is a most endearing hobgoblin, and the reader sympathises enormously with the problems, both practical and spiritual, which he must solve through his characteristic domestic loyalty. Kate Maxwell, one of the two Katherines in *Kate Crackernuts,* is a memorable heroine. Her bravery, determination, and love for her stepsister, which take her twice into the fairy realms on behalf of those weaker than she is (journeys which result in the saving of two lives), are admirable and inspiring. Briggs set her two novels in the 17th century, a time when people believed in witches and fairies as a matter of course. Yet it is a period near enough our own to be reasonably recognisable in its domestic detail: some of the rather old-fashioned themes present in the stories, while absolutely appropriate for the period, also recall the Victorian children's novel.

Briggs started investigating folk-lore in the 1920s and 1930s, as a reaction against the sentimental rubbish offered so frequently to children. As one reads her work, one has the assurance that in all things to do with the fairy kingdoms Briggs's knowledge is impeccable. This gives her books enormous strength: they are triumphant examples of what good modern fairy stories should be. And for those whose appetite is whetted and who want more, books like *Abbey Lubbers, Banshees, and Boggarts* are most satisfying first reference material. One can go on, too, to the many adult works, for K.M. Briggs's fascination with Fairyland communicates itself to readers young and old.

—Felicity Trotman

BRIGGS, Raymond (Redvers)

Nationality: British. **Born:** London, 18 January 1934. **Education:** Rutlish School, Merton, Surrey; Wimbledon School of Art; Slade School of Fine Art, national diploma in design 1953; University of London, diploma in fine art. **Military Service:** British Army, 1953-55. **Family:** Married Jean Taprell Clark in 1963 (died 1973). **Career:** Since 1957 free-lance illustrator and writer; since 1961 part-time lecturer in illustration, Brighton Polytechnic, Sussex. **Awards:** All for illustration: Library Association Kate Greenaway medal, 1967, 1974; Boston *Globe-Horn Book* award, 1979; Victoria and Albert Museum Francis Williams prize, 1982; Children's Rights Workshop other award, 1982; Broadcasting Press Guild award, 1984, for radio play. **Address:** Weston, Underhill Lane, Westmeston, Hassocks, Sussex BN6 8XG, England.

Publications for Children (illustrated by the author)

Fiction

Midnight Adventure. London, Hamish Hamilton, 1961.
The Strange House. London, Hamish Hamilton, 1961.
Sledges to the Rescue. London, Hamish Hamilton, 1963.
Jim and the Beanstalk. London, Hamish Hamilton, and New York, Coward McCann, 1970.
Father Christmas. London, Hamish Hamilton, and New York, Coward McCann, 1973.
Father Christmas Goes on Holiday. London, Hamish Hamilton, 1975.
Fungus the Bogeyman. London, Hamish Hamilton, 1977; New York, Random House, 1979.
The Snowman. London, Hamish Hamilton, and New York, Random House, 1978.
Gentleman Jim. London, Hamish Hamilton, 1980.
The Tin-Pot Foreign General and the Old Iron Woman. London, Hamish Hamilton, and Boston, Little Brown, 1984.
The Snowman (*Building the Snowman, Dressing Up, Walking in the Air, The Party*). London, Hamish Hamilton, and Boston, Little Brown, 4 volumes, 1985.
The Man. London, MacRae, 1992.
Father Christmas Having a Wonderful Time. London, Hamish Hamilton, 1993.
The Bear. London, MacRae, 1994; New York, Random House, 1994.

Play

Gentleman Jim (adaptation of his own story; produced Nottingham, 1985).

Poetry

Ring-a-Ring o' Roses. London, Hamish Hamilton, and New York, Coward McCann, 1962.

Other

The Snowman Pop-up. London, Hamish Hamilton, 1986.
The Snowman Storybook. New York, Random House, 1990.
The Snowman Flap Book. New York, Random, 1991.
The Snowman Tell-the-Time Book. London, Hamish Hamilton, 1991.
The Snowman Clock Book. New York, Random House, 1992.
Snowman: Songbook. Milwaukee, Wisconsin, Hal Leonard, 1993.

Editor, *The White Land: A Picture Book of Traditional Rhymes and Verses.* London, Hamish Hamilton, and New York, Coward McCann, 1963.
Editor, *Fee Fi Fo Fum: A Picture Book of Nursery Rhymes.* London, Hamish Hamilton, and New York, Coward McCann, 1964.
Editor, *The Mother Goose Treasury.* London, Hamish Hamilton, and New York, Coward McCann, 1966.

Publications for Adults

Plays

When the Wind Blows (adaptation of his own book; broadcast on radio, 1983; produced Bristol and London, 1983; Washington, D.C., 1984; adapted for the screen, 1987). London, French, 1983.

Other (illustrated by the author)

When the Wind Blows. London, Hamish Hamilton, and New York, Schocken, 1982.
Unlucky Wally. London, Hamish Hamilton, 1987.
Unlucky Wally Twenty Years On. London, Hamish Hamilton, 1989.

*

Illustrator: *The Wonderful Cornet* by Barbara Ker Wilson, 1958; *Peter and the Piskies* by Ruth Manning-Sanders, 1958; *The Hamish Hamilton Book of Magical Beasts,* 1965, and *Festivals,* 1972, both edited by Manning-Sanders; *Peter's Busy Day* by A. Stephen Tring, 1959; *Look at Castles,* 1960, and *Look at Churches,* 1961, both by Alfred Duggan; *William's Wild Day Out* by Meriol Trevor, 1963; *The Hamish Hamilton Book of Myths and Legends* edited by Jacynth Hope-Simpson, 1964; *Whistling Rufus,* 1964, and *The Hamish Hamilton Book of Giants,* 1968, both edited by William Mayne; *Stevie,* 1965, and *The Elephant and the Bad Baby,* 1969, both by Elfrida Vipont; *The Way over Windle* by Mabel Esther Allan, 1966; *The Flying 19* by James Aldridge, 1966; *The Christmas Book,* 1968, and *The Forbidden Forest,* 1973, both edited by James Reeves; *Nuvolari and the Alfa Romeo,* 1968, and *Jimmy Murphy and the White Dusenberg,* 1968, both by Bruce Carter; *Lindbergh the Lone Flier,* 1968, and *Richthofen the Red Baron,* 1968, both by Nicholas Fisk; *Shackleton's Epic Voyage* by Michael Brown, 1969; *First Up Everest* by Showell Styles, 1969; *The Tale of Three Landlubbers* by Ian Serraillier, 1970; *The Fairy Tale Treasury* by Virginia Haviland, 1972; *All in a Day* by Mitsumasa Anno, 1986.

Critical Studies: "The Film of the Picture Book: Raymond Briggs's 'The Snowman' as Progressive and Regressive Texts" by Geoff Moss, in *Children's Literature in Education* (New York), Vol. 22, No. 3, 1991, 195-204; interview in *Independent,* 24 December 1995.

* * *

The artistic and storytelling style of Raymond Briggs has become so celebrated that it is hard to realise how long it took him to establish his unique mode. After art school and a period working in advertising, he became an illustrator of children's books and was awarded the Kate Greenaway Medal for his illustrations to a bumper nursery rhyme book, *The Mother Goose Treasury,* in 1966. During this time he wrote straightforward adventure stories like *Sledges to the Rescue* in which a group of children with their toboggans help a sick milkman to make his Christmas deliveries. His version of *Jack and the Beanstalk* showed hints of a more anarchic approach—at the top of the beanstalk Jack finds an aging giant who is quite incapable of eating plump little boys and helps him to adapt by getting him fitted out with false teeth, glasses, and a wig.

In order to get away from the constraints of the typical 32-page illustrated children's book, Briggs produced his first wholly individual and highly successful work, *Father Christmas,* in 1973. This used the adaptation of comic-strip format—alternating tiny pictures with full and double page spreads and speech bubbles—that has become associated with Briggs and won him another Kate Greenaway medal. It centres on a resolutely uncheery Santa Claus who complains: "Blooming snow! I hate winter! Work, work, work!" Briggs has recorded that the book was influenced by memories of his father, a milkman with the Cooperative Dairies, having to go out to work early in the morning. It gives a lovingly detailed picture of a vanishing working class life in a terrace house with an old sink and gas stove in the kitchen and an outside lavatory. In the central section, Father Christmas, with his reindeer-powered sledge, flies through to deliver presents to a variety of places. Then he returns home to his pet dog and cat, to enjoy his own solitary turkey and plum pudding. Two years later, and in response to popular demand, Briggs produced *Father Christmas Goes on Holiday,* in which the central character grumpily tries France, Scotland, and Las Vegas (each with some allusive visual jokes) before returning to the piles of accumulated Christmas mail.

Fungus the Bogeyman was the first of a number of books centred on victims or outsiders that produced mixed critical reactions. For children (and some adults) Fungus fascinatingly embodied playground obsessions with snot and pus, forbidden interests and behaviours, so that his very repulsiveness was an attraction. Those who found Fungus unhealthy and regressive were even more critical of what seemed the negative way in which the dim, smelly, spotty protagonist of *Unlucky Wally* was presented. In *Gentleman Jim,* an uneducated attendant in a public lavatory is resentful of the way in which he is oppressed by figures of authority and has Mittyish fantasies that make him wish to be a highwayman. There seems some ambivalence in the way that characters like Fungus, Wally, and Jim are depicted as simultaneously absurd or repellent and yet apparently designed to awake sympathy or compassion.

Briggs's greatest commercial success has been *The Snowman,* a wordless book about a boy's snowman who comes alive in the night, explores the house, and flies with the boy to a northern party with other snowmen. When the boy wakes again in the sunny morning, his friend the snowman has melted away. The book became widely known through a film version shown on British television one Christmas and frequently repeated thereafter. The film, with its evocative music, effectively caught the mixture of happy and sad moods in the book. Perhaps less happily it led the way for other exploitations of the story: a miniature edition, a "build the snowman" book, a clock book, a flap book, a "cuddle cloth" book, a song book, and a story book (rather missing the point that the original's strength lay in the fact that the child reader had to tell the story from the picture cues).

A similar storyline runs through *The Bear.* A girl retires to bed with her teddy, and during the night her room is invaded by a huge white bear. Her excitement at a secret from her parents is modified by the needs of coping with the bear's needs, as he needs to be fed, breaks furniture, and excretes in her room. The borderlines between reality and fantasy are again unclear: in the morning she sees huge footsteps leading away from the house.

In some of Briggs's later work he has moved away from strictly child audiences and has adopted a more ideologically committed stance. Jim Bloggs reappears with his wife Hilda in *Where the Wind Blows,* where the comic strip style is used for deadly serious effect. With black humour it queries the idea of "survival" in a nuclear war, and shows how irrelevant are the memories which the elderly have of earlier wars. Terrifying and sad, the story is made accessible for younger readers by Briggs's concentration on the particular human story of two naive old folk. The book has since been adapted for the stage. In a similar way Briggs used the Falklands war as the basis for a more general critique of the political behaviours that lead to conflict. *The Tin-Pot Foreign General and the Old Iron Woman* begins in nursery tale style, caricaturing the conflicting leaders as they behave with the selfishness and cruelty of naughty quarrelling children. The savage parodying of individuals and attitudes gives way at the ending to a different style and a concern for the sufferings of "real men, made of flesh and blood."

Publication of *The Man,* in 1992, marked a new departure for Briggs, because it grafted a longer and more complex written text on to his familiar mix of comic strip style with larger illustrations of different sizes. Confined almost entirely within the setting of a small bedroom, it tells the story of a boy's shifting relationship with the Man, a tiny hand-sized figure who suddenly appears to him. The boy befriends this figure, looking after him for four days, hiding, feeding, and entertaining him, but on the fifth day he discovers that he has gone, leaving only a semi-literate note. The Man is presented as a Pinterish character who is alternately friendly and aggressive, wheedling and assertive, likable and repellent. The relationship between the two characters is explored in depth through their dialogue and the pictures. The book is also available, well read, on audiotape, but this inevitably misses the complex interrelationship of word and image.

Interviewed for the *Independent,* Briggs remarked: "You can only work out of your own experience. Draw the things you know, write about the things you remember." His great achievement has been to transmute his own experiences of growing up in south London and later of living in East Sussex into vividly realised, unsentimental fantasies with which countless readers can identify. In different ways Briggs has revolutionised the art of telling pictures with stories. He can also claim to have made a significant contribution to the increasing acceptance of strip cartoons as a legitimate art form.

—Robert Protherough

BRIGHT, Robert

Pseudonym: Michael Douglas. **Nationality:** American. **Born:** Sandwich, Massachusetts, 5 August 1902. **Education:** Phillips

Academy, Andover, Massachusetts; Princeton University, New Jersey, B.A. 1923. **Family:** Married Katherine Bailey in 1931; one daughter and one son. **Career:** Reporter, Baltimore *Sun,* 1925-26, and Paris *Times,* 1926-27; assistant to the President, Condé Nast Publications, New York, 1927-28; advertising manager, Revillon Frères, New York, 1928-36; instructor, Massachusetts Department of Education, Boston, 1948-51; lecturer, Emerson College, Boston, 1949; case worker, Department of Welfare, Taos, New Mexico, 1952; music and art critic, Santa Fe *New Mexican,* 1964-65. **Died:** 21 November 1988.

Publications for Children (illustrated by the author)

Fiction

The Travels of Ching. New York, Scott, 1943; London, Collins, 1945.
Georgie. New York, Doubleday, 1944; London, Collins, 1945.
Me and the Bears. New York, Doubleday, 1951.
Hurrah for Freddie!, with Dorothy Brett. New York, Doubleday, 1953.
Miss Pattie. New York, Doubleday, 1954.
I Like Red. New York, Doubleday, 1955; Kingswood, Surrey, World's Work, 1964.
Georgie to the Rescue. New York, Doubleday, 1956; Kingswood, Surrey, World's Work, 1964.
The Friendly Bear. New York, Doubleday, 1957; Kingswood, Surrey, World's Work, 1967.
Georgie's Hallowe'en. New York, Doubleday, 1958; Kingswood, Surrey, World's Work, 1967.
My Red Umbrella. New York, Morrow, 1959.
Which Is Willy? New York, Doubleday, 1962; Kingswood, Surrey, World's Work, 1963.
Georgie and the Robbers. New York, Doubleday, 1963; Kingswood, Surrey, World's Work, 1964.
Georgie and the Magician. New York, Doubleday, 1966; Kingswood, Surrey, World's Work, 1967.
Gregory, The Noisiest and Strongest Boy in Grangers Grove. New York, Doubleday, 1969; Kingswood, Surrey, World's Work, 1970.
Georgie and the Noisy Ghost. New York, Doubleday, 1971; Kingswood, Surrey, World's Work, 1973.
Georgie Goes West. New York, Doubleday, 1973; Kingswood, Surrey, World's Work, 1975.
Georgie's Christmas Carol. New York, Doubleday, 1975; Kingswood, Surrey, World's Work, 1978.
Georgie and the Buried Treasure. New York, Doubleday, 1979; Kingswood, Surrey, World's Work, 1981.
Georgie and the Baby Birds [Ball of Yarn, Little Dog, Runaway Balloon]. New York, Doubleday, 4 vols., 1983.

Poetry

Round, Round World (as Michael Douglas). New York, Golden Press, 1960.
My Hopping Bunny. New York, Doubleday, 1960; Kingswood, Surrey, World's Work, 1967.

Other

Richard Brown and the Dragon. New York, Doubleday, 1952; Kingswood, Surrey, World's Work, 1964.

Publications for Adults

Novels

The Life and Death of Little Jo. New York, Doubleday, 1944; as *Little Jo,* London, Cresset Press, 1946.
The Intruders. New York, Doubleday, 1946; London, Cresset Press, 1948.
The Olivers: The Story of an Artist and His Family. New York, Doubleday, 1947.
The Spirit of the Chase. New York, Scribner, 1956; London, Cresset Press, 1957.

*

Robert Bright commented:

(1978) I intended to make a career as a novelist. But by the time I had published my third novel I realized that while I was gaining critical success I was not getting sufficient return to support a family. I had to be sensible, and so, sensibly, I turned to writing and illustrating picture books for children whose imagination commanded my respect and affection. What I have tried to do in my books is to present fantasy in the way of good stories with interesting characters and lots of humor and fun but with no silliness. So much of fantasy is apt to be silly, but good fantasy is logical and true. It teaches without straining, and above all, it does not abuse the confidence of the reader. I like to think therefore that those who have been brought up and are still being brought up in part with my books may always look back with pleasure at the imaginary worlds to which these stories introduced them.

* * *

The picture books of Robert Bright represent a curious divergence of opinion between the tastes of children and those of certain adult critics of children's literature. Bright's books continue to receive enthusiastic endorsements from young children, but he is seldom referred to in any serious discussion of children's literature, such as those written for teachers or librarians. While a note on his Georgie books is found in the American Library Association *Books for Elementary Schools* and *Children's Catalog,* Bright's work is generally dismissed out of hand by most compilers of selective bibliographies, even those exclusively of picture books.

Although Bright wrote this kind of book with several themes, what literary recognition he received comes almost entirely from his Georgie books. Their qualities help explain their attractiveness to children. These books are pleasant distortions of reality about a wise and brave but altogether gentle little ghost, named Georgie, who resides, unknown to them, with a rather docile and witless old couple. Bright recalled that the idea for Georgie stemmed from his own children badgering him to make up for them a ghost story. While they probably wanted a tale of dread and awe, it was to Bright's ultimate advantage as a publishable writer for the young that he decided against doing a genuine ghost story. Instead he chose a tongue-in-cheek treatment of the supernatural. This is the kind of book which fulfilled his ambition to enter into the child's world so as to invest it with stories that would have delighted him as a child. But one probable reason for lack of critical acclaim lies in his decision to illustrate his own books. While he did a generally good job of melding the pictures with the stories, his drawings are so utterly lacking in artistic merit that they have negatively influenced critics not perceptive to the obvious merits of plots and dialogue.

His illustrations aside, there is little doubt that Bright succeeded in his goal of delighting children. In each of his books about Georgie this smallish apparition heroically undertakes to set to rights some villainous action or unfortunate mishap. For example, in *Georgie and the Robbers* (to this point Georgie "never scared anybody, he was much too shy for that") Bright updated the well-known folk tale, "The Three Musicians." In this case Georgie and his animal playmates do scare away robbers hiding out in a barn and recover their loot. It is obvious here, and in other of his Georgie stories, that Bright took advantage of some of the motifs and traditions of folk literature that children enjoy hearing about. Among these motifs are the small person journeying away from home to a confrontation with a villain, followed by a showdown between good and evil and finally a rescue of the helpless. Bright's characters, as those in folk tales, are habitual in their behavior and unchanging in their motives. They are flat fictional personages whose behavior in stress situations is easily, and therefore happily, predictable by the child reader. Bright also borrowed from traditional literature his manner of talking directly to the reader, his highly melodramatic climaxes, his use of repetition and refrain for the sake of emphasis, and his choice of archaic settings. Other of Bright's books are reflections of the cumulative stories of folk literature. In *My Red Umbrella* and *I Like Red,* simple, repetitive, plotless structures, in which one thing or event in a sequence is much like that which it precedes and follows, Bright demonstrated again his dependence on folk literature.

—Patrick Groff

BRINDLE, Max. See **FLEISCHMAN, (Albert) Sid(ney).**

BRINK, Carol Ryrie

Nationality: American. **Born:** Moscow, Idaho, 28 December 1895. **Education:** Portland Academy, 1912-14; University of Idaho, Moscow, 1914-17; University of California, Berkeley, B.A. 1918. **Family:** Married Raymond Woodard Brink in 1918 (died); one son and one daughter. **Awards:** American Library Association Newbery Medal, 1936; University of Minnesota Kerlan award, 1978. D.Litt.: University of Idaho, 1965. **Died:** 15 August 1981.

Publications for Children

Fiction

Anything Can Happen on the River!, illustrated by W. W. Berger. New York, Macmillan, 1934.

Caddie Woodlawn: A Frontier Story, illustrated by Kate Seredy. New York, Macmillan, 1935; London, Collier Macmillan, 1963.

Mademoiselle Misfortune, illustrated by Kate Seredy. New York, Macmillan, 1936.

Baby Island, illustrated by Helen Sewell. New York, Macmillan, 1937.

All over Town, illustrated by Dorothy Bayley. New York, Macmillan, 1939.

Lad with a Whistle, illustrated by Robert Ball. New York, Macmillan, 1941.

Magical Melons: More Stories about Caddie Woodlawn, illustrated by Marguerite Davis. New York, Macmillan, 1944.

Family Grandstand, illustrated by Jean McDonald Porter. New York, Viking Press, 1952.

The Highly Trained Dogs of Professor Petit, illustrated by Robert Henneberger. New York, Macmillan, 1953.

Family Sabbatical, illustrated by Susan Foster. New York, Viking Press, 1956.

The Pink Motel, illustrated by Sheila Greenwald. New York, Macmillan, 1959; London, Collier Macmillan, 1963.

Andy Buckram's Tin Men, illustrated by W.T. Mars. New York, Viking Press, 1966.

Winter Cottage, illustrated by Fermin Rocker. New York, Macmillan, 1968.

Two Are Better Than One, illustrated by Fermin Rocker. New York, Macmillan, and London, Collier Macmillan, 1968.

The Bad Times of Irma Baumlein, illustrated by Trina Schart Hyman. New York, Macmillan, and London, Collier Macmillan, 1972.

Louly, illustrated by Ingrid Fetz. New York, Macmillan, 1974.

Plays

The Cupboard Was Bare. Franklin, Ohio, Eldridge, 1928.

The Queen of the Dolls. Franklin, Ohio, Eldridge, 1928.

Caddie Woodlawn, adaptation of her own story (produced Minneapolis, 1957). New York, Macmillan, 1954.

Salute Mr. Washington, in *Plays* (Boston), March 1976.

Other

Narcissa Whitman: Pioneer to the Oregon Country, illustrated by Samuel Armstrong. Evanston, Illinois, Row Peterson, 1950.

Lafayette, illustrated by Dorothy Bayley Morse. Evanston, Illinois, Row Peterson, 1953.

Editor, *Best Short Stories for Children.* Evanston, Illinois, Row Peterson, 6 vols., 1936-41.

Publications for Adults as Carol Brink

Novels

Buffalo Coat. New York, Macmillan, 1944; London, Cassell, 1949.

Stopover. New York, Macmillan, 1951.

The Headland. New York, Macmillan, 1955; London, Gollancz, 1956.

Strangers in the Forest. New York, Macmillan, 1959.

Château St. Barnabé. New York, Macmillan, 1963.

Snow in the River. New York, Macmillan, 1964.

The Bellini Look. New York, Bantam, 1976.

Other

Harps in the Wind: The Story of the Singing Hutchinsons. New York, Macmillan, 1947.
The Twin Cities (on Minneapolis—St. Paul). New York, Macmillan, 1961.
Four Girls on a Homestead (reminiscences). Moscow, Idaho, Latah County Museum Society, 1978.

*

Manuscript Collections: Kerlan Collection, University of Minnesota, Minneapolis; University of Idaho Library, Moscow.

* * *

Carol Ryrie Brink's books indicate that she is equally at home in the past and the present. Her strength lies in presenting realistic family relationships and vivid personal portraits, made all the more interesting by her background knowledge of history. *Caddie Woodlawn* was reprinted more than 30 times during its first 30 years. Subtitled "A Frontier Story" it tells of 11-year-old Caddie's life with her family on a farm in Wisconsin. Although set at the time of the Civil War, the war plays no part in the story, for Brink has focused on the tense situation between the Indians and the white settlers. Caddie's long friendship with the Indians and their innate trust in her help to avert a threatened uprising and offer the reader an exciting and believable pioneer story. Brink must have been aware that books such as *Caddie Woodlawn* play an important part in the process of growing up, for in writing about the pioneer family and their way of life she reminds the reader that frontier life required qualities from children unheard of today. They took on real responsibilities as co-workers and shared equally in the family fortunes and failures.

Caddie Woodlawn was followed in 1944 by *Magical Melons* which gives further adventures of Caddie and her brothers but was never as popular as its predecessor. She wrote many other books, one of which, *Baby Island,* put forward the absurd and delightful situation of two girls shipwrecked with a lifeboat full of babies whom they cared for with love and ingenuity on a desert island. In her foreword Brink says she wrote this book for girls who love minding babies and couldn't find enough candidates. It is a delightful and amusing story lost to today's readers through the misfortunes of publishing. *Winter Cottage* tells of a city family feeling the hopelessness of the great depression. They leave the city for a winter in the country where their spirits are raised by the beauties of country living.

Whether writing of past or present, the strength of Brink's books lies in the carefully observed family relationships, which provide the basis for a wider circle as the child develops.

—Ann Bartholomew

BRINSMEAD, Hesba (Fay)

Nationality: Australian. **Born:** Hesba Fay Hungerford, Blue Mountains, New South Wales, 15 March 1922. **Family:** Married Reginald Brinsmead in 1943; two sons. **Education:** Correspondence school; high school in Wahroonga; Avondale College. **Career:** Governess in Tasmania, two years; speech therapy teacher, western Victoria, 1945-48; kindergarten supervisor, Melbourne, two years; amateur actress, Box Hill City Drama Group, Melbourne, 1950-60; since 1960 full-time writer. **Awards:** Australian Children's Book Council Book of the Year award, 1965, 1972. **Address:** Weathertop, Shamara Road, Terranora, New South Wales 2485, Australia.

Publications for Children

Fiction

Pastures of the Blue Crane, illustrated by Annette Macarthur-Onslow. London, Oxford University Press, 1964; New York, Coward McCann, 1966.
Season of the Briar, illustrated by William Papas. London, Oxford University Press, 1965; New York, Coward McCann, 1967.
Beat of the City, illustrated by William Papas. London, Oxford University Press, 1966; New York, Coward McCann, 1968.
A Sapphire for September, illustrated by Victor Ambrus. London, Oxford University Press, 1967.
Isle of the Sea Horse, illustrated by Peter Farmer. London, Oxford University Press, 1969.
Listen to the Wind, illustrated by Robert Micklewright. London, Oxford University Press, 1970.
Longtime Passing. Sydney and London, Angus and Robertson, 1971.
Who Calls from Afar?, illustrated by Ian Ribbons. London, Oxford University Press, 1971.
Echo in the Wilderness, illustrated by Graham Humphreys. London, Oxford University Press, 1972.
The Ballad of Benny Perhaps. Sydney, Cassell, 1977.
The Honey Forest, illustrated by Louise Hogan. Sydney, Hodder and Stoughton, 1978.
Once There Was a Swagman, illustrated by Noela Young. Melbourne and London, Oxford University Press, 1979.
Time for Tarquinia, illustrated by Bruce Riddell. Sydney and London, Hodder and Stoughton, 1981.
Longtime Dreaming. London, Angus and Robertson, 1982.
Christmas at Longtime. Sydney and London, Angus and Robertson, 1983.
The Sand Forest. Sydney, Angus and Robertson, 1985.
Someplace Beautiful, illustrated by Betina Ogden. Sydney, Hodder and Stoughton, 1986.
When You Come to the Ferry. Sydney, Hodder and Stoughton, 1988.
Bianca and Roja, illustrated by Ron Brooks. Chicago, Allen and Unwin, 1993.
The Silver Train to Midnight. Hunter's Hill, New South Wales, Margaret Hamilton Books, 1994.

Other

Under the Silkwood, illustrated by Michael Payne. Sydney, Cassell, 1975.
The Wind Harp. Sydney, Cassell, 1977.
High Dive, and Free Is Lonely, illustrated by Craig Smith. Sydney and London, Hodder and Stoughton, 1979.

PUBLICATIONS FOR ADULTS

I Will Not Say the Day Is Done. Chippendale, New South Wales, Alternative Publishing, 1983.

*

Manuscript Collection: National Library of Australia, Canberra.

Hesba Brinsmead comments:

I have stopped writing, as at age 75 it seemed to me to have been long enough since I began, way back in history. My *Pastures of the Blue Crane* is still being studied in schools, remarkably enough—teachers still visit to gather material for their classes. One reason to stop writing is plain physical. Writing is hard manual work, as well as a thought process, and I'm no longer up to it! But also, I feel that I'm no longer relevant in the writing world. The picture moves on, the scene changes. My "Longtime" books, based on my own childhood, are mainly read by older people, I think, but to most young ones are in a different language from the one they speak. It's best to know when to stop! I so much enjoyed my work as a writer, my life as a writer. I'm so glad I spent any money I earned on travel and seeing all sorts of cultures and people. Now I just read and read. I can thoroughly devote my time to being a reader and appreciate the work that others are doing! My days are always so busy now, I can't imagine how I ever had time to write.

* * *

Hesba Brinsmead's early novels have contemporary settings and modern, outgoing girls for heroines. In contrast, *Longtime Passing,* widely regarded as Brinsmead's best book, is the first of four books that draw on the author's own childhood on a remote farm. Brinsmead's particular talent is in the touch of magic she lends to her portrayal of people and places. Coincidence and chance keep the plots moving along, with the more improbable events tending to mar what are nominally realistic settings. Her joy of life is evident in all her books although in some of the earlier novels, and in *The Sand Forest* and *Someplace Beautiful,* exuberance gives way to sweetness.

Ryl Mereweather, the heroine of the best of Brinsmead's early novels, *Pastures of the Blue Crane,* enjoys opportunities that would have astounded non-conforming literary forebears like *Little Women*'s Jo March. Ryl has wealth and independence but lacks "an island of peace." She finds this security in a run-down farm which was once the family home and which she is forced to share with her churlish (but with a-heart-of-gold) grandfather. The crane of the title is a symbol of continuity, leaving its home each year but returning always to the same place. Ryl is the first of a series of heroines that have become something of a trademark for Brinsmead. She is good-looking, impetuous, flamboyant, and energetic, a contrast to the more somber and studious heroines in other Australian children's fiction of the 1960s and 1970s. The vitality of Brinsmead's characters is a welcome change from the usual emphasis on heroines negotiating "thorny paths," but as other critics have pointed out, there is a cloying sameness about the string of characters with fanciful names that followed Ryl.

Other, more recent, books have contemporary settings. *The Sand Forest* is a return to the brash heroine and adventures of Brinsmead's earlier novels. Shipwrecks and lost treasure and two eccentric uncles make for a compelling, if unlikely, story. Clippie Nancarrow, a daredevil pilot from *Echo in the Wilderness* and *Who Calls from Afar?,* makes a reappearance in *The Sand Forest* to take part in a rescue mission and to provide a romantic interest. *Someplace Beautiful* is a whimsical novel about an attempt by children to save their local bookshop, and in *When You Come to the Ferry* two children and their grandmother have some unexpected adventures.

The "Longtime" series of books best show the author's talent for creating memorable characters and situations both poignant and humourous. Although set in the 1920s, the Longtime books are about pioneering life. The Truelance farm at Longtime, surrounded by forest, is only accessible by bullock team or on horseback. Edwin Truelance is an unlikely farmer, with a theology degree and a passion for music, and his wife Letty was a city girl. Somehow, their apparent unsuitability fits them for a life in a place that had broken others, and they and their five children thrive despite isolation and hardship. The stories are told from the viewpoint of the youngest child, Teddy, who chaffs against the burdens of being "too little." *Longtime Passing* and *Longtime Dreaming* are full-length novels, while *Once There Was a Swagman* and *Christmas at Longtime* are illustrated stories intended for younger children. Somewhat connected to this group of books is a short novel, *The Honey Forest.* All are nostalgic—evoking and celebrating a lifestyle long gone from Australia. In the foreground is the theme of the importance of belonging to a place, and a concern for the environment apparent in Brinsmead's earlier novels.

Also with an historical setting, but far removed from twentieth century Australia, is *Time for Tarquinia* set in ancient Etruria. *Bianca and Roja* is also set in the past, but it is the indefinite anytime of fairy tale, and Brinsmead draws on the well known story of Snow White and Rose Red in this magical and romantic story of sisters living in an ancient forest. The tales in *The Silver Train to Midnight* mark a return to the Longtime tradition (although the characters have different names) of a mildly eccentric family and their extensive network of relations. The haunting title story is Brinsmead at her best with a evocative tale about a child's imagination and how her dreams colour reality.

—Kerry White

BRISLEY, Joyce Lankester

Nationality: British. **Born:** Bexhill, Sussex, 6 January 1896. **Education:** At a day school, Bexhill; Lambeth Art School, London. **Career:** Freelance illustrator. **Died:** 20 September 1978.

PUBLICATIONS FOR CHILDREN (ILLUSTRATED BY THE AUTHOR)

Fiction

Milly-Molly-Mandy Stories. London, Harrap, 1928; New York, McKay, 1976 (?).

More of Milly-Molly-Mandy. London, Harrap, 1929; New York, McKay, 1977.

Further Doings of Milly-Molly-Mandy. London, Harrap, and New York, McKay, 1932.

The Dawn Shops and Other Stories. London, Harrap, and New York, McKay, 1933.
Marigold in Godmother's House. London, Harrap, 1934.
Bunchy. London, Harrap, and New York, McKay, 1937.
The Adventures of Purl and Plain. London, Harrap, 1941.
Milly-Molly-Mandy Again. London, Harrap, 1948; New York, McKay, 1977.
Another Bunchy Book. London, Harrap, 1951.
Milly-Molly-Mandy & Co. London, Harrap, 1955; New York, McKay, 1977.
Milly-Molly-Mandy and Billy Blunt. London, Harrap, 1967; New York, McKay, 1977.
The Joyce Lankester Brisley Book, edited by Frank Waters. London, Harrap, 1981.

Plays

Three Little Milly-Molly-Mandy Plays (includes *Milly-Molly-Mandy Goes Errands [Keeps Shop, Meets Her Great Aunt]*). London, Harrap, 1938.

Poetry

Lambs'-Tails and Suchlike: Verses and Sketches. London, Harrap, and New York, McKay, 1930.

Other

My Bible-Book. London, Harrap, 1940; New York, McKay, 1941.
Children of Bible Days. London, Harrap, 1970.

Editor, *The Wide, Wide World,* by Elizabeth Wetherell. London, University of London Press, 1950.

*

Illustrator: *Adventures of a Little Wooden Horse,* 1938, and *Pretenders' Island,* 1940, both by Ursula Moray Williams.

* * *

Most of Joyce Lankester Brisley's short stories concern the domestic events in the life of a small girl. Milly-Molly-Mandy "had a Father, and a Mother, and a Grandpa, and a Grandma, and an Uncle, and an Aunty; and they all lived together in a nice white cottage with a thatched roof."

In Milly-Molly-Mandy she created a likeable, believable little girl who is every child's better self, a child so cheerful, affectionate, and generous that she could very well seem too good to be true. It was no small achievement to bring this off so well, and to hit off so exactly the things which most please a child: the errands successfully run, the present for mother stitched in secret, the store-room transformed into a new bedroom all to herself, the railway carriage discovered in a field.

Her style is simple and exclamatory, designed for reading aloud, the vocabulary limited. There is little description but her own illustrations give a minimum of character to the various adults who might otherwise appear undifferentiated in their general twinkling benevolence.

Using the same basic setting of village life, in her stories about Bunchy Brisley crossed the boundary into fantasy. In a series of tales following one pattern, a lonely little girl who lives with her grandmother makes playmates for herself out of a pastry girl and cat, the figures on a scrap-work screen, the people in a pack of Happy Families cards and others. In her grandmother's absence these characters come to life and keep her company. These adventures are less convincing than the real doings of Milly-Molly-Mandy, but they have the same underlying warmth and affection for children.

Brisley's work now seems slightly dated and remote. There are an underlying condescension and sentimentality inherent, for example, in referring to a character throughout as "little-friend-Susan." She wrote of a world without war or poverty or illness or anger, a world as warm and as welcoming, as comforting and as kindly as hot tea and toast beside the fire in winter, and if the country setting is romanticised, a land where every cottage is thatched and where mushrooms spring up in high summer, it is within its limitations none the worse for that, a place where everyone might like to have spent their childhood.

—Mary Rayner

BRITTAIN, Bill

Nationality: American. **Born:** William Brittain, Rochester, New York, 16 December 1930. **Education:** Spencerport High School, Spencerport, New York, graduated 1948; Colgate University, Hamilton, New York, 1948-50; Brockport State Teachers College (now State University College), New York, 1950-52, B.S. in education 1952; Hofstra University, Hempstead, New York, 1956-58, M.S. in education 1958. **Family:** Married Virginia Connorton in 1954; one son and one daughter. **Career:** Teacher, LeRoy Central Schools, New York, 1952-54, and in a public school, Lawrence, New York, 1954-60; teacher of English and reading, Lawrence Junior High School, New York, 1960-86. **Address:** 17 Wisteria Drive, Asheville, North Carolina 28804, U.S.A.

PUBLICATIONS FOR CHILDREN

Fiction

All the Money in the World, illustrated by Charles Robinson. New York, Harper & Row, 1979.
Devil's Donkey, illustrated by Andrew Glass. New York, Harper & Row, 1981.
The Wish Giver, illustrated by Andrew Glass. New York, Harper & Row, 1983.
Who Knew There'd Be Ghosts?, illustrated by Michele Chessare. New York, Harper & Row, 1985.
Dr. Dredd's Wagon of Wonders, illustrated by Andrew Glass. New York, Harper & Row, 1987.
The Fantastic Freshman. New York, Harper & Row, 1988.
My Buddy, The King. New York, Harper & Row, 1989.
Professor Porkin's Prodigious Polish, illustrated by Andrew Glass. New York, HarperCollins, 1990.
Wings. New York, HarperCollins, 1991.
The Ghost from Beneath the Sea, illustrated by Michele Chessare. New York, HarperCollins, 1992.

The Mystery of the Several Sevens, illustrated by James Warhola. New York, HarperCollins, 1994.
Shape-Changer. New York, HarperCollins, 1994.
The Wizards and the Monster, illustrated by James Warhola. New York, HarperCollins, 1994.

Publications for Adults

Other

Survival Outdoors. Derby, Connecticut, Monarch, 1977.

*

Manuscript Collection: American Heritage Center, University of Wyoming, Laramie.

Bill Brittain comments:

I'm fascinated by the supernatural, particularly as it applies to wish fulfillment. My books reflect this fascination and deal with witchcraft, demons, haunted houses, and the like. I especially enjoy creating my "Coven Tree" series—*Devil's Donkey, The Wish Giver,* and *Dr. Dredd's Wagon of Wonders*—because the town of Coven Tree is an idealized form of the small village where I grew up.

I don't try to teach lessons in my books. If the yarns send a shiver up some young spines and provide a laugh or two, I feel I've done my job well. I agree with the late Samuel Goldwyn: "If you want to send a message, use Western Union."

* * *

Although Bill Brittain is a prolific writer of mystery stories for adults, he is better known among young readers as the creator of weird and tantalizing characters. Brittain frequently flirts with a concept of evil cloaked in an often deceptively funny facade. *The Coven Tree* stories—several books are set in this town—are moral tales based on the protagonists being driven by a strong wish or goal. In *The Wish Giver,* three characters must each confront the results of their wishes and finally reverse the wish. Brittain's use of an evocative dark character to entice the protagonist into accepting great power reflects the theme revealed in Faust and other Mephistopheles tales. If human nature did not respond, there would be no story. In *Devil's Donkey* Daniel's challenge to beliefs in the power of an old witch leads to his enchantment as a donkey and the final encounter with Mr. Beel, the devil. *Dr. Dredd's Wagon of Wonders* pits evil Dr. Hugo Dredd against Calvin as both take up the challenge to bring rain to a drought-ridden town. In the fourth *Coven Tree* novel, *Professor Popkin's Prodigious Polish,* Luther Gilpin sees a bright future for himself and foolishly buys more than he bargains for in a fancy polish. Dorcas and Hester Gilpin have the wisdom to cope with a saw that polished, takes on a life of its own. Each of the *Coven Tree* stories told by Stew Meat is written in a smooth narrative mode with details that scare but do not terrorize, the language fostering moods of fear and revulsion but always balanced with a bit of humor and outrageousness.

The hilarious and exaggerated tickles the reader in Quenten's adventures in *All the Money in the World* when, after capturing Flan, a leprechaun, and wishing for all the money in the world, he discovers the consequences are a disaster. In *The Fantastic Freshman,* Stanley is driven by one goal, to be a very important person. Given a tiny golden figurine enclosed in a blue glass pyramid and inscribed with the words "We will take good care of you," Stan takes the reader on a series of wildly improbable events, all leading to the attainment of this goal. As in many of his other stories, the protagonist rethinks his goal and learns the heavy price one may have to pay for it.

Wings is a puzzling book, leaving the reader guessing as to its message or purpose. Young Ian Carras is simply not valued in his family; he grows a set of wings, learns to fly and eventually to face his role in his family with the aid of his friend Anita and her mother. Brittain may be exploring adolescent pain, or he may not, but this novel certainly makes the reader think in a variety of directions.

Shape-Changer is a funny science fiction story in which two visitors from Rodinam invade the lives of Frank Dunn and Lauren Kyle. Assuming any form they choose, these aliens are tracking each other; Zymel is a futuristic policeman and Fek is an insane master criminal and who but two earth children can come to the rescue. Brittain provides a youthful cleverness in the antics of Zymel and a clever plot twist in the conclusion that makes this novel work.

In *The Wizards and the Monster,* Simon Toller, Becky Rush and their mentor, Mr. Merlin, meet and travel through time, to test Simon's wish to become a wizard and Becky's to conquer a monster. In the sequel, *The Mystery of the Several Sevens,* they continue their adventures, this time in a mystery set in a fairyland that requires language and mathematical skills. This new series is written for a much younger audience and should attract third and fourth grade readers, particularly girls who will find Becky a strong role model.

Brittain offers the reader a chance both to be scared and to laugh as he draws characters and events that challenge the mind and fix firmly a concept of consequences to action taken. He often uses an unusual or quirky approach to make a wish come true. Polly's temper and bad language are controlled by making her Jug-a-rum like a bull frog whenever she misspeaks. Brittain has a wonderful way of unmasking people so that what appears to be beautiful and enviable is revealed as often ugly and undesirable.

—Jane Anne Hannigan

BROOKE, L(eonard) Leslie

Nationality: British. **Born:** Birkenhead, Cheshire, 24 September 1862. **Education:** Birkenhead School; Birkenhead Art School, 1880-82; St. John's Wood Art School, London, 1882-84; Royal Academy Art School, London (Armitage medal, 1888), 1884-88. **Family:** Married his cousin Sybil Diana Brooke in 1894; two sons. **Career:** Freelance artist and illustrator from 1888. **Died:** 1 May 1940.

Publications for Children (illustrated by the author)

Poetry

Johnny Crow's Garden. London and New York, Warne, 1903.
Johnny Crow's Party. London and New York, Warne, 1907.
Johnny Crow's New Garden. London and New York, Warne, 1935.

*

Critical Study: *Leslie Brooke and Johnny Crow* by Henry Brooke, London, Warne, 1981; New York, Warne, 1982.

Illustrator: *Miriam's Ambition,* 1889, and *The Secret of the Old House,* 1890, both by Evelyn Everett-Green; *Thorndyke Manor* by Mary C. Rowsell, 1889; *The Light Princess and Other Fairy Stories* by George MacDonald, 1890; *Nurse Heatherdale's Story,* 1891, *The Girls and I,* 1892, *Mary,* 1893, *My New Home,* 1894, *The Carved Lions,* 1895, *Sheila's Mystery,* 1895, *The Oriel Window,* 1896, and *Miss Mouse and Her Boys,* 1897, all by Mary Louisa Molesworth; *Marian* by Annie E. Armstrong, 1892; *A Ring of Rubies* by L. T. Meade, 1892; *Bab* by Ismay Thorn, 1892; *Brownies and Rose-leaves,* 1892, and *Moonbeams and Brownies,* 1894, both by Roma White; *Penelope and Others* by Amy Walton, 1892; *A Hit and a Miss* by Eva Knatchbull Hugessen, 1893; *School in Fairyland* by E.H. Strain, 1896; *The Nursery Rhyme Book* edited by Andrew Lang, 1897; *Pippa Passes* by Robert Browning, 1898; *A Spring Song* by T. Nash, 1898; *Singing Time* by Arthur Somervell, 1899; *The Pelican Chorus and Other Verses,* 1899(?), *The Jumblies and Other Nonsense Verses,* 1900, and *Nonsense Songs,* 1900, all by Edward Lear; *Travels round Our Village* by Eleanor G. Hayden, 1901; *Barchester Towers* by Anthony Trollope, 1903; *The Story of the Three Little Pigs,* 1904; *Tom Thumb,* 1904; *Leslie Brooke's Children's Books 1-2,* 2 vols., 1904-05; *The Golden Goose,* 1905; *The Three Bears,* 1905; *The Golden Goose Book,* 1905; *The Book of Gilly* by Emily Lawless, 1906; *The House in the Wood and Other Old Fairy Stories,* 1909; *The Truth about Old King Cole* by George F. Hill, 1910; *The Tailor and the Crow,* 1911; *The Man in the Moon,* 1913; *Oranges and Lemons,* 1913; *A Nursery Rhyme Picture Book 1-2,* 2 vols., 1913-22; *Nursery Rhymes,* 1916; *Rhymes and Lullabies,* 1916; *Songs and Ditties,* 1916; *Tales and Jingles,* 1916; *Little Bo-Peep,* 1922; *This Little Pig Went to Market,* 1922; *Ring o' Roses,* 1922; *Mad Shepherds and Other Human Studies* by Lawrence P. Jacks, 1923; *A Roundabout Turn* by Robert H. Charles, 1930.

* * *

L. Leslie Brooke's stories have been described as "collector's pieces," but they are much more than this: they are perfect examples of the kind of writing which both parent and child can enjoy, each on his own level. The traditional tale—*The Three Little Pigs, The Three Bears, Tom Thumb, The Golden Goose*—are told directly and simply, with the repetition children love, and also with an ear for both the rhythms of English prose and its variety of sentence structure which lend a tough vitality to the stories even after much re-telling. The line drawings and colour illustrations are delightful, well integrated into the story, with a sly sense of humor which points up significant episodes. The morning after the abortive excursion to the turnip field, for instance, there is a picture of the wolf, waking up tardily at four o'clock, a partly eaten turnip still on the chair by his bed, and a picture on the wall of a wolf cooking fried back bacon, while on the next page the little pig is pictured already precariously climbing up the apple tree, his back legs dangling as he clutches the branch desperately with his front trotters. There is much fun for both alert adult and child in these stories and their accompanying illustrations, as also in the cunningly illustrated nursery rhymes of *Ring o'Roses.*

The gem of the collection is the *Johnny Crow* series, in which a dapper Johnny Crow creates a superb garden where he entertains a fascinating variety of farmyard and jungle animals. The pictures are again so detailed, so full of humour and so thoroughly integrated with the text that they enhance and expand the child's understanding particularly in those occasional wickedly satirical episodes which, as in Beatrix Potter's books, make no concessions to the myth that children cannot cope with words of more than two syllables.

Then the Stork
Gave a Philosophic Talk
Till the Hippopotami
Said: "Ask no further 'What am I?'"
While the Elephant
Said something quite irrelevant
In Johnny Crow's Garden.

Here the long words roll off the adult's tongue in a manner very satisfying to the small child, for whom the accompanying illustrations make the joke explicit enough without any laboured explanations from a well-meaning parent or teacher. Most of the rhymes, of course, are much simpler than the ones just quoted; amusing, memorable verse which, together with the wealth of meaning in the drawings above them, makes the storyrite a pleasure for both parent and child, an excellent answer to the complaints of some parents that children's stories bore them stiff.

—Winifred Whitehead

BROOKE, William J.

Nationality: American. **Born:** Washington, D.C., 28 November 1946. **Education:** William and Mary College, B.A. English; University of North Carolina at Chapel Hill, M.A. Drama. **Family:** Married Lynne Greene-Brooke in May 1975. **Career:** Actor and singer specializing in Gilbert and Sullivan operas since high school; also briefly freelanced as a writer for jacket copy and as a ghostwriter. **Awards:** American Library Association Notable Book, 1991, for *A Telling of the Tales.* **Address:** c/o Author Mail, 7th Floor, HarperCollins Publishers, 10 East 53rd St., New York, New York 10022, U.S.A.

Publications for Children

A Telling of the Tales: Five Stories, illustrated by Richard Egielski. New York, HarperCollins, 1990.
Untold Tales. New York, HarperCollins, 1992.
A Brush With Magic; Based on a Traditional Chinese Story, illustrated by Michael Koelsch. New York, HarperCollins, 1993.
Teller of Tales. New York, HarperCollins, 1994.

Publications for Adults

Operantics; Fun and Games for the Opera Buff. Georgetown, Connecticut, Spectacle Lane Press, 1988.

*

William J. Brooke comments:

I am assured by competent authorities that I was once a child, but I have no real memory of how that felt. So I don't feel qualified to write for children. Therefore I try to pick subjects that would appeal to any age and then write to please myself. My editors tell me the results are children's books. I'm not sure whether that says more about their critical abilities or my mental development, but as long as they publish me I don't care.

* * *

William J. Brooke's fiction for children comes under the rubric of "fractured fairy tales," fairy-tale retellings that are retold with new twists in the familiar traditional narrative. Though often humorous, Brooke's reworkings stem from serious questioning of the nature of stories. The unifying thread running through each collection individually and through his body of work as a whole is the act of storytelling itself: what it is, why we do it, and how it affects those who hear the stories we tell.

Brooke takes common fairy tales and twists them sideways, posing a "what if?" question and then following it to its logical conclusion. What if, for example, Sleeping Beauty did not believe that she had been asleep? Or, what if she wanted adventure instead of marriage to a handsome prince? What if Cinderella's unenchanted foot were too big for the enchanted slipper, or what if she realized that a prince who is in love with an illusion would make a very poor husband? "The Waking of the Prince" and "The Fitting of the Slipper," two stories from the first collection, are the delightful outcomes of these questions, stories which belie the traditional fairy-tale happy endings of marriage and staid respectability.

The third story of *A Telling of the Tales,* "The Working of John Henry," gives that story a happier ending, as John Henry, after proving that the quality of a man's soul is what really counts, decides that he could "learn to make noise for a living" and use a steam hammer, since technology and progress are inescapable facts of modern life—and since, after all, he does still need a job. Brooke further draws from American tall-tale mythology in "The Growing of Paul Bunyan," a parable that pleads for environmental awareness as it pits environmental consciousness against conspicuous consumption, personified in two extremes drawn from American tall-tale mythology, Johnny Appleseed and Paul Bunyan.

The last story of the first collection, "The Telling of a Tale," is much more than a simple twist in the traditional version of Jack and the Beanstalk: it enacts Brooke's storytelling philosophy itself. The narrative shifts back and forth between times, narrators, and traditional storyline until the reader, while no longer really sure who is telling the story, nevertheless realizes the truth that "the telling of a tale links you with everyone who has told it before. There are no new tales, only tellers, telling in their own way...." This theme runs throughout the entire set of tales, culminating in the theme of *Teller of Tales* that voices dictate the tales to the teller; these voices are the voices of storytellers everywhere in all times and places.

Even more thought-provoking than the first collection, *Untold Tales* has as its theme the idea of middle-aged regret and the wish that one could relive what's already been done. The first story, "A Prince in the Throat," plays off the popular version of "The Frog Prince," in which a kiss is the agency of disenchantment, while it examines the nature of husband-and-wife relationships and of self-fulfillment. Like Jon Scieszka's *The Frog Prince Continued,* Brooke's retelling picks up many years after the traditional Grimm story, in the midst of a stale marriage; also like Scieszka's story, Brooke's retelling constructs its happy and romantic ending by having the protagonists abandon human life and its dull and oppressive responsibilities altogether. In "A Fate in the Door," Sleeping Beauty's Prince Charming comes knocking on her door twenty-five years later, having been sidetracked, he said, by another princess asleep in a glass coffin and now wanting to go back and fulfill his true destiny.

Brooke's short novel, *A Brush with Magic,* is an expanded version of the Chinese folktale familiar to some readers as Molly Bang's *Tye May and the Magic Brush* (Morrow 1992) or Demi's *Liang and the Magic Paintbrush* (Holt 1988). This novel also explores the nature of art and its purpose in the world, although here the art is visual rather than literary. Liang, the young artist whose pictures come to life seemingly with a will of their own, must learn to accept responsibility for his talent and for his role as an artist.

Brooke did not set out to join the current trend of writing humorous take-offs of fairy tales; in fact, he criticizes this trend by saying that such tales, when produced solely to get a laugh, are the easy way out for an author. Nor does Brooke consider that his stories are particularly children's stories. Instead, they are the result of a personal desire to explore the how and why of the impact that fairy tales have on contemporary audiences, and he readily admits that his retellings are not based on the oral fairy-tale tradition as much as they are on modern popular culture renditions of these tales. Allusions to the Disney versions of "Sleeping Beauty," "Cinderella," and "Snow White" abound in Brooke's retellings of those fairy tales, while "A Prince in the Throat" begins and ends with the popular motif of disenchantment by a kiss rather than the traditional Grimms' ending in which the princess angrily throws the frog against the wall of her bedroom. Modern media was an influence on the creation of the stories in other ways, as well: the first retelling that Brooke wrote, "The Growing of Paul Bunyan," was originally intended to be the basis of a children's musical, and *A Brush with Magic* was originally a screenplay for an animated film.

An actor and singer specializing in light opera, William Brooke has played over thirty roles, has sung with the New York Grand Opera, and has delivered stage performances in Central Park before several thousand people. He and his wife Lynne met on stage and, Brooke says, they have been married "many times over" in various productions. Brooke's training and long experience in the theater are evident in his strong use of dialogue and the fast-moving pace of his plots, as well as in his attention to the immediate effect of the story upon his audience and in the voice in which each story is told.

—Martha P. Hixon

BROOKS, Walter R(ollin)

Nationality: American. **Born:** Rome, New York, 9 January 1886. **Education:** Rochester University, New York, 1904-06; New York Homeopathic Medical College, 1906-08. **Family:** Married 1) Anne Shepard in 1909 (died); 2) Dorothy Collins in 1953. **Career:** Associate editor, *Outlook,* New York, 1923-32; member of the editorial staff, *New Yorker,* 1933, and *Fiction Parade,* New York, 1933-37. **Died:** 17 August 1958.

Publications for Children (illustrated by Kurt Wiese, except as noted)

Fiction

To and Again, illustrated by Adolfo Best-Maugard. New York, Knopf, 1927; as *Freddy Goes to Florida,* 1949; as *Freddy's First Adventure,* London, Lane, 1949.
More To and Again. New York, Knopf, and London, George Allen, 1930; as *Freddy the Explorer,* London, Lane, 1949; as *Freddy Goes to the North Pole,* Knopf, 1951.
Freddy the Detective. New York, Knopf, 1932; London, Lane, 1950.
The Story of Freginald. New York, Knopf, 1936; as *Freddy and Freginald,* London, Lane, 1952.
The Clockwork Twin. New York, Knopf, 1937.
Wiggins for President. New York, Knopf, 1939; as *Freddy the Politician,* 1948.
Freddy's Cousin Weedly. New York, Knopf, 1940.
Freddy and the Ignormus. New York, Knopf, 1941.
Freddy and the Perilous Adventure. New York, Knopf, 1942.
Freddy and the Bean Home News. New York, Knopf, 1943.
Freddy and Mr. Camphor. New York, Knopf, 1944.
Freddy and the Popinjay. New York, Knopf, 1945.
Freddy the Pied Piper. New York, Knopf, 1946.
Freddy the Magician. New York, Knopf, 1947.
Jenny and the King of Smithia, illustrated by Decie Merwin. New York, Grosset and Dunlap, 1947.
Freddy Goes Camping. New York, Knopf, 1948.
Freddy Plays Football. New York, Knopf, 1949.
Freddy the Cowboy. New York, Knopf, 1950.
Freddy Rides Again. New York, Knopf, 1951.
Freddy the Pilot. New York, Knopf, 1952.
Freddy and the Space Ship. New York, Knopf, 1953.
Freddy and the Men from Mars. New York, Knopf, 1954.
Freddy and the Baseball Team from Mars. New York, Knopf, 1955.
Freddy and Simon the Dictator. New York, Knopf, 1956.
Freddy and the Flying Saucer Plans. New York, Knopf, 1957.
Freddy and the Dragon. New York, Knopf, 1958.
Henry's Dog Henry, illustrated by Aldren Watson. New York, Knopf, 1965.
Jimmy Takes Vanishing Lessons, illustrated by Don Bolognese. New York, Knopf, 1965.

Poetry

The Collected Poems of Freddy the Pig. New York, Knopf, 1953.

Publications for Adults

Novel

Ernestine Takes Over. New York, Morrow, 1935; London, Jarrolds, 1937.

Other

New York: An Intimate Guide. New York, Knopf, 1931.

* * *

One of the most difficult juvenile genres to create is that of the anthropomorphic animal. Historically few of these characters have survived more than one generation, and deservedly so. One of the great American exceptions is Walter R. Brooks's Freddy the pig. This talking and thinking pig, jack of all trades and master of none, wore many hats, ranging from detective to magician to politician and beyond. For the child reader, events on Mr. Bean's farm are solely episodic, ranging from the hilarious to the darkly sinister, only slightly familiar to the present world. For the adult, the Bean farm, Freddy, and the other animals are boldly familiar archetypes of daily events and people. A little of all the human traits can be found here through both the human and animal characters. Judging the series by contemporary children's literature standards, the books are beginning to date. The illustrations denote scenes, costumes, and vehicles no longer in use. Brooks's handling of stock character types, the American Indian for example, are now regarded as overtly stereotypical and thus harmful. Valid as these criticisms may be, the series should be considered in its proper scheme. Brooks indisputably raised the anthropomorphic genre to a higher level with Freddy when one stops to consider the 1950s output when the series was beginning. Freddy could not help but lessen library and bookseller's shelves of romantically portrayed doe-eyed kittens and puppies by being a real (human) animal with real feelings, ideas, and faults.

In the 1980s the U.S. publisher Alfred Knopf reissued the Freddy books in the hopes of capturing a new child audience. A failed attempt, it was stopped after eight books because sales did not live up to the publisher's expectations, despite wide reviewer notice and a well-designed publicity effort.

—Jim Roginski

BROWN, Marc (Tolon)

Nationality: American. **Born:** Erie, Pennsylvania, 25 November 1946. **Education:** Cleveland Institute of Art, 1964-69, B.F.A. 1969. **Family:** Married 1) Stephanie Marini in 1968 (divorced 1977), two sons; 2) Laurene Krasny in 1983, one daughter. **Career:** Art director, WICU-TV, Erie, Pennsylvania, 1968-69; Assistant Professor of Art, Garland Junior College, Boston, 1969-76. Artist: numerous individual shows. **Awards:** Children's Choice awards, Children's Book Council and International Reading Association, 1976, for *Arthur's Nose,* 1980, for *Arthur's Eyes,* 1981, for *Arthur's Valentine,* 1982, for *The True Francine, Arthur's Halloween,* and *Arthur Goes to Camp,* and 1983, for *Arthur's April Fool*; *Boston Globe/Horn Book* honor award for illustration, 1985, for *Oh, Kojo! How Could You!*; Notable Children's Trade Book in the Field of Social Studies citations, joint committee of the National Council for Social Studies and the Children's Book Council, 1982, for *The True Francine*; Notable Book citation, *New York Times,* 1986, for *Dinosaurs Divorce: A Guide for Changing Families*; Gold Medal award for best children's software, Bologna, Italy, 1997, for *Arthur's Reading Race.* **Address:** 562 Main Street, Hingham, Massachusetts 02043, U.S.A.

PUBLICATIONS FOR CHILDREN (ILLUSTRATED BY THE AUTHOR)

Fiction

Full House. Boston, Addison Wesley, 1977.
Lenny and Lola. New York, Dutton, 1978.
Moose and Goose. New York, Dutton, 1978.
The Cloud over Clarence. New York, Dutton, 1979.
Pickle Things. New York, Parents' Magazine Press, 1980.
Witches Four. New York, Parents' Magazine Press, 1980; London, Hamish Hamilton, 1981.
The True Francine. Boston, Little Brown, 1981; London, Pepper Press, 1982.
The Silly Tail Book. New York, Parents' Magazine Press, 1983.
The Bionic Bunny Show, with Laurene Krasny Brown. Boston, Little Brown, and London, Collins, 1984.
There's No Place like Home. New York, Parents' Magazine Press, 1984; London, Collins, 1986.
D.W. Flips! Boston, Little Brown, 1987; as *Roll Over D.W.,* London, Piccadilly Press, 1988.
D.W. All Wet. Boston, Little Brown, 1988.
D.W. Rides Again! Boston, Little Brown, 1993.
D.W. Thinks Big. Boston, Joy Street, 1993.
Monster's Lunchbox. Boston, Little Brown, 1994.
Rex and Lilly Playtime, with Laurene Krasny Brown. Boston, Little Brown, 1995.
Rex and Lilly Family Time, with Laurene Krasny Brown. Boston, Little Brown, 1995.
Glasses for D.W. New York, Random House, 1996.
Kiss Hello, Kiss Goodbye. New York, Random House, 1997.
Say the Magic Word. New York, Random House, 1997.

Arthur Adventure Series:

Arthur's Nose. Boston, Little Brown, 1976.
Arthur's Eyes. Boston, Little Brown, 1979; London, Pepper Press, 1981.
Arthur and the True Francine. Boston, Little Brown, 1981.
Arthur's Valentine. Boston, Little Brown, 1980.
Arthur Goes to Camp. Boston, Little Brown, 1982.
Arthur's Halloween. Boston, Little Brown, 1982.
Arthur's April Fool. Boston, Little Brown, and London, Pepper Press, 1983.
Arthur's Thanksgiving. Boston, Little Brown, 1983.
Arthur's Christmas. Boston, Little Brown, 1984; London, Piccadilly Press, 1985.
Arthur's Tooth. Boston, Little Brown, 1985; London, Corgi, 1987.
Arthur's Teacher Trouble. Boston, Little Brown, 1986; London, Piccadilly Press, 1987.
Arthur's Baby. Boston, Little Brown, 1987; London Piccadilly Press, 1988.
Arthur's Birthday. Boston, Little Brown, 1988; London, Piccadilly Press, 1990.
Arthur's Pet Business. Boston, Little Brown, 1990.
Arthur Meets the President. Boston, Little Brown, 1991.
Arthur Babysits. Boston, Joy Street, and London, Little Brown, 1992.
Arthur's Secret Admirer. London, Piccadilly Press, 1992.
Arthur's Family Vacation. Boston, Little Brown, 1993.
Arthur's New Puppy. Boston, Little Brown, 1993.
Arthur's Chicken Pox. Boston, Little Brown, 1994.
Arthur's First Sleepover. Boston, Little Brown, 1994.
Arthur's Television Trouble. Boston, Little Brown, 1995.
Arthur Goes to School. New York, Random House, 1995.
Arthur's Reading Race. New York, Random House, 1996.
Arthur Writes a Story. Boston, Little Brown, 1996.
Arthur's Neighborhood. New York, Random House, 1996.
Arthur's Computer Disaster. Boston, Little Brown, 1997.

Other

One, Two, Three: An Animal Counting Book. Boston, Little Brown, 1976.
Your First Garden Book. Boston, Little Brown, 1981.
Marc Brown's Boat Book. New York, Golden Press, 1982.
Count to Ten. New York, Golden Press, 1982.
Dinosaur, Beware! A Safety Guide, with Stephen Krensky. Boston, Little Brown, 1982; London, Collins, 1983.
Wings on Things. New York, Random House, and London, Collins, 1982.
Perfect Pigs: An Introduction to Manners, with Stephen Krensky. Boston, Little Brown, 1983; London, Collins, 1984.
Spooky Riddles. New York, Random House, 1983; London, Collins, 1984.
What Do You Call a Dumb Bunny? and Other Rabbit Riddles, Games, Jokes, and Cartoons. Boston, Little Brown, and London, MacRae, 1983.
Dinosaurs Divorce: A Guide for Changing Families, with Laurene Krasny Brown. Boston, Little Brown, 1986; London, Collins, 1987; London, Little Brown, 1993.
Visiting the Art Museum, with Laurene Krasny Brown. New York, Dutton, 1986; as *Visiting an Exhibition,* London, Collins, 1986.
Dinosaurs Travel: A Guide for Families on the Go, with Laurene Krasny Brown. Boston, Little Brown, 1988; London, Collins, 1989.
Baby Time: A Grownup's Handbook to Use with Baby, with Laurene Krasny Brown. New York, Knopf, 1989; London, Bodley Head, 1990.
The Family Read-Aloud Christmas Treasury, edited by Alice Low. Boston, Little Brown, 1989.
Toddler Time: A Book to Share with Your Toddler, with Laurene Krasny Brown. Boston, Little Brown, 1990.
Dinosaurs Alive and Well: A Guide to Good Health, with Laurene Krasny Brown. London, Collins, 1991.
Dinosaurs to the Rescue: A Guide to Protecting Our Planet, with Laurene Krasny Brown. Boston, Joy Street, 1992.
When the Dinosaurs Die, with Laurene Krasny Brown. Boston, Little Brown, 1996.

Editor, *Finger Rhymes.* New York, Dutton, 1980.
Editor, *Hand Rhymes.* New York, Dutton, and London, Collins, 1985.
Editor, *Play Rhymes.* New York, Dutton, 1987; London, Collins, 1988.
Editor, *Party Rhymes.* New York, Dutton, 1988; London, Collins, 1989.
Editor, *One, Two, Buckle My Shoe.* New York, Dutton, 1989.
Editor, *Can You Jump Like a Frog?* New York, Dutton, 1989.
Editor, *Teddy Bear, Teddy Bear.* New York, Dutton, and London, Collins, 1989.
Editor, *Two Little Monkeys.* New York, Dutton, and London, Collins, 1989.

Editor, *Scared Silly: A Book for the Brave.* Boston, Little Brown, 1994.

*

Media Adaptations: *Arthur* (daily animated television series) adapted from *Arthur Adventure* characters, Boston, WGBH-TV and PBS, from 1996; *Arthur Adventure* series have also been adapted for CD-ROM by Living Books-Broderbund.

Illustrator: *What Makes the Sun Shine?* by Isaac Asimov, 1971; *The Dragon with a Thousand Wrinkles* by Mary Daem, 1971; *The Iron Lion* by Peter Dickinson, 1972; *I Found Them in the Yellow Pages,* 1973, and *There Goes Feathertop!,* 1979, both by Norma Farber; *The Little Green Thumb Window Garden* by Doug Morse, 1974; *Ride, Ride, Ride* by Marcia Wiesbauer, 1974; *The Four Corners of the Sky* by Ted Clymer, 1975; *Science Games [Puzzles, Tricks, Toys]* by Laurence White, 4 vols., 1975; *Super Sam and the Salad Garden* by Patty Wolcott, 1975; *How the Rabbit Stole the Moon* by Louise Moeri, 1977; *My Doctor Bag Book* by Kathleen Daly, 1977; *Little Owl* by Janwillem van de Wetering, 1978; *Why the Tides Ebb and Flow* by Joan Chase Bowden, 1979; *Rabbit's New Rug* by Judy Delton, 1979; *The Banza* by Diane Wolkstein, 1981; *What's So Funny, Ketu?,* 1981, and *Oh, Kojo! How Could You?,* 1984, both by Verna Aardema; *Swamp Monsters,* 1983, and *Go West, Swamp Monsters!,* 1985, both by Mary Blount Christian; *Little Witch's Big Night,* 1984, *Happy Birthday, Little Witch,* 1985, and *Little Witch Book and Doll Package,* 1988, all by Deborah Hautzig; *Read-Aloud Rhymes for the Very Young* edited by Jack Prelutsky, 1986; *A World Full of Monsters* by John T. McQueen, 1986; *Little Witch's Book of Magic Spells* by Deborah Hautzig, 1993; *Rex and Lilly at Play,* by Laurene Krasny Brown, 1994.

Marc Brown comments:

I had a modest, no frills childhood. I was lucky to be surrounded by a lot of wonderful people. My great-grandmother and grandmother were both storytellers. My grandmother would tell me a beautiful story whenever I wanted one—and she'd give me a back rub at the same time! When I look back at my childhood, I see that my destiny was right in front of me. Arthur reflects the way I was in third grade. My teacher and the principal of my school eventually became characters in my books. And my three sisters became Arthur's little sister, D.W.!

* * *

Learning and growing experiences are serious subjects for Marc Brown, but as his work so ably demonstrates, even serious subjects have their humorous aspects. In a body of work for children that ranges from discussions of gardening and museum visiting to the adventures of an anteater and his friends, Brown abandons neither his sense of purposefulness nor his sense of humor. A trained artist who was profoundly influenced by the interplay of pictures and text in Maurice Sendak's *Where the Wild Things Are,* he is also adept at using illustrations to give added dimension to his written text.

Brown is best known for the "Arthur Adventure" books, a series of picture books about a second-grade (and more recently, third-grade) anteater named Arthur, his friends, and his family. The honors garnered by these books from both children and adults testify to the various levels at which they may be enjoyed. Children easily identify with the likable Arthur; his family and schoolmates, from the obnoxious Francine to his little sister D.W., who wants to know whether she can have Arthur's room after the school bully pulverizes him, are equally recognizable to most elementary school children.

Thematically Brown demonstrates keen sensitivity to the problems and fears of his young audience. In *Arthur's Eyes, Arthur's Nose,* and *Arthur's Tooth,* the hero attempts to find acceptance when he is the only one of his friends to have an obvious physical difference. The stories emphasize self-acceptance as well as acceptance of others. Even more interesting are episodes in which Arthur finds himself in circumstances where there is a large discrepancy between how he knows he is supposed to feel about the situation, and the way he actually does feel. For instance, in *Arthur's Halloween,* Arthur's fears contrast with the excitement and confidence displayed by his friends and even his baby sister, to make the approach of the holiday a dreaded occasion. He is the envy of the class when the teacher selects him to direct the school play in *Arthur's Thanksgiving,* but is privately surprised by the burden of personal responsibility brought by this honor. *Arthur's Baby,* according to his mother and father, is going to be a wonderful addition to their household—but Arthur, like most children, has his doubts. Brown's consistent message, always delivered with sensitivity and humor, is that it is normal to feel apprehensive in these situations, and that they usually turn out well in the end.

The interplay between artwork and narrative in Brown's books makes them useful tools for encouraging children to develop the habit of noticing details as they read. Brown's gimmick of hiding his family's names in the illustrations can be used constructively as a stimulus for picking up other details. For instance, when Arthur worries about being the only first-grader who has not lost a tooth, Brown subtly inserts a picture of a student in a wheelchair, suggesting to the observant reader a more serious aspect of the problem of fitting in, without making a major issue of it. In the same book, Arthur's wild imaginings of what his trip to the dentist will be like are immediately followed by a more realistic but no less horrible depiction of the chaos in the child-filled waiting room; the observant reader will note the subtle irony. Thus Brown's texts and illustrations work together to promote a deeper understanding for the more sophisticated child, and to develop the invaluable skill of attention to detail in any child.

Brown has recently added stories about Arthur's sister D.W. to his repertoire. While generally appealing from a child's level, they do not have the depth of the best of the Arthur books. However, one recent work outside the Arthur series has received accolades from children and adults: *The Bionic Bunny Show,* a collaboration with Brown's wife Laurene. Humor and instruction combine as the reader observes superhero Bionic Bunny (who has appeared in previous texts on Arthur's lunchbox) making an episode of his television show. The show itself proceeds in tandem with a backstage look at how the illusions of superpowers are produced. The book is interesting in its own right, and also useful for stimulating discussions about reality and fantasy with respect to television. In his insistence on attending to the serious concerns of elementary school-age children, as well as to the humor inherent in situations developing from those concerns, Marc Brown continues to create children's books which can be appreciated for their simplicity but enjoyed on more complex levels as well.

—Christine Doyle Stott

BROWN, Marcia

Nationality: American. **Born:** Rochester, New York, 13 July 1918. **Education:** Woodstock College of Painting, New York, summers 1938-39; New York College for Teachers (now State University of New York), Albany, B.A. 1940; New School for Social Research, Art Students' League, and Columbia University, all New York. **Career:** Drama teacher in high school, Cornwall, New York, 1940-43; library assistant, New York Public Library, 1943-48; teacher of puppetry, University of the West Indies, Kingston, Jamaica, 1953. **Awards:** American Library Association Caldecott Medal, 1955, 1962, 1983. **Address:** c/o Scribner's, 866 Third Ave., New York, New York 10022, U.S.A.

PUBLICATIONS FOR CHILDREN (ILLUSTRATED BY THE AUTHOR)

Fiction

The Little Carousel. New York, Scribner, 1946.
Henry, Fisherman: A Story of the Virgin Islands. New York, Scribner, 1949.
Skipper John's Cook. New York, Scribner, 1951.
Felice. New York, Scribner, 1958.
Taramindo! New York, Scribner, 1960.
The Neighbors. New York, Scribner, 1967.
How, Hippo! New York, Scribner, 1969.
The Blue Jackal. New York, Scribner, 1977.

Other

Stone Soup (retelling). New York, Scribner, 1947.
Dick Whittington and His Cat (retelling). New York, Scribner, 1950.
Puss in Boots (retelling). New York, Scribner, 1952.
Cinderella (retelling). New York, Scribner, 1954.
The Flying Carpet (retelling). New York, Scribner, 1956.
Peter Piper's Alphabet. New York, Scribner, 1959.
Once a Mouse (retelling). New York, Scribner, 1961.
Backbone of the King (retelling). New York, Scribner, 1966.
The Bun: A Tale from Russia. New York, Harcourt Brace, 1972.
All Butterflies: An ABC. New York, Scribner, 1974.
Listen to a Shape. New York, Watts, 1979.
Touch Will Tell. New York, Watts, 1979.
Walk with Your Eyes. New York, Watts, 1979.
Shadow (retelling). New York, Scribner, 1982.

PUBLICATIONS FOR ADULTS

Other

Lotus Seeds: Children, Pictures, and Books. New York, Scribner, 1986.

*

Illustrator: *The Trail of Courage* by Virginia Watson, 1948; *The Steadfast Tin Soldier,* 1953, *The Wild Swans,* 1963, and *The Snow Queen,* 1972, all by Hans Christian Andersen; *Anansi* by Philip Sherlock, 1954; *The Three Billy Goats Gruff* by Peter C. Asbjoernsen and J.E. Moe, 1957; *Giselle* by Violette Verdy, 1970; *Of Swans, Sugarplums, and Satin Slippers: Ballet Stories for Children* by Violette Verdy, 1991; *How the Ostrich Got Its Long Neck,* retold by Verna Aardema, 1995.

* * *

Although Marcia Brown is best known as an illustrator, she is also an author and the adapter of many traditional tales for children. Since she illustrates her own work and uses very different media and techniques to complement the essence of each text there is a special unity and sense of wholeness to her books. Brown's first picture book *The Little Carousel* is a realistic story which grew out of a scene she observed from her Greenwich Village apartment during her early years in New York City. Her experience as a storyteller for the New York Public Library also proved useful to her in capturing the sounds and the rhythms of a well-told tale in such works as *Stone Soup, Dick Whittington and His Cat,* and other tales adapted for picture-book audiences.

Brown's books represent different ways of making traditional literature accessible to young children. *Cinderella* retains the airy elegance and magical qualities of the original court drama in words as well as in illustrations. The language of the Indian fable *Once a Mouse* has the simple earthy strength of its character the hermit who "sat thinking about big and little" on both the opening and concluding pages.

Wherever Brown traveled she absorbed both visual and verbal images of the land and its traditions. Not only did her trip to Africa influence *Shadow,* but a visit to the Virgin Islands stimulated the creation of *Henry, Fisherman* and a stay in Hawaii led to her retelling of a Polynesian legend in *Backbone of the King,* her novel-length story of Pakaa and his son Ku.

In addition to her interpretations of folk literature, Brown has also written a number of concept books. *All Butterflies: An ABC* demonstrates her ability to use language sparsely, effectively, and in a way that can still delight children. Two words, in harmony with the illustration, make a statement or raise a question while introducing two letters of the alphabet. Thus: "All Zoo."

Brown has published three concept books illustrated with her own full-color photographs of nature, inviting young readers to observe their work and *Listen to a Shape, Walk with Your Eyes,* and know that *Touch Will Tell.* Poetic language serves as more than captions for the photographs as in "Looking can be/flying/with someone else's wings—/feeling/the beat of the rain/on the face/of a flower—/watching/a spider mending her web, torn by the rain."

—Kay E. Vandergrift

BROWN, Margaret Wise

Pseudonyms: Timothy Hay; Golden MacDonald; Juniper Sage. **Nationality:** American. **Born:** Brooklyn, New York, 23 May 1910. **Education:** Chateau Brilliantmont, Lausanne, Switzerland, 1923-25; Dana Hall, Wellesley, Massachusetts, 1926-28; Hollins College, Virginia, 1928-32, B.A. in English 1932; Columbia University, New York, 1932; Bureau of Educational Experiments (now Bank Street College of Education), New York. **Career:** Assistant to Lucy Sprague Mitchell, Bank Street Publications, New York, mid-1930s; editor, William R. Scott, publishers, New York, 1938-41. **Died:** 13 November 1952.

Publications for Children

Fiction

When the Wind Blew, illustrated by Rosalie Slocum. New York, Harper, 1937.
Bumble Bugs and Elephants, illustrated by Clement Hurd. New York, Scott, 1938.
The Fish with the Deep Sea Smile, illustrated by Roberta Rauch. New York, Dutton, 1938.
The Little Fireman, illustrated by Esphyr Slobodkina. New York, Scott, 1938.
The Streamlined Pig, illustrated by Kurt Wiese. New York, Harper, 1938.
Little Pig's Picnic and Other Stories, illustrated by Walt Disney Studio. Boston, Heath, 1939; London, Collins, 1949.
Noisy Book, illustrated by Leonard Weisgard. New York, Scott, 1939.
Country Noisy Book, illustrated by Leonard Weisgard. New York, Scott, 1940.
Baby Animals, illustrated by Mary Cameron. New York, Random House, 1941.
The Polite Penguin, illustrated by H.A. Rey. New York, Harper, 1941.
The Poodle and the Sheep, illustrated by Leonard Weisgard. New York, Dutton, 1941.
The Seashore Noisy Book, illustrated by Leonard Weisgard. New York, Scott, 1941.
Don't Frighten the Lion!, illustrated by H.A. Rey. New York, Harper, 1942.
Indoor Noisy Book, illustrated by Leonard Weisgard. New York, Harper, 1942.
Night and Day, illustrated by Leonard Weisgard. New York, Harper, 1942.
The Runaway Bunny, illustrated by Clement Hurd. New York, Harper, 1942.
A Child's Good Night Book, illustrated by Jean Charlot. New York, Scott, 1943.
Little Chicken, illustrated by Leonard Weisgard. New York, Harper, 1943.
The Noisy Bird Book, illustrated by Leonard Weisgard and Audubon. New York, Scott, 1943.
SHHhhhh...bang: A Whispering Book, illustrated by Robert de Veyrac. New York, Harper, 1943.
The Big Fur Secret, illustrated by Robert de Veyrac. New York, Harper, 1944.
Black and White, illustrated by Charles Shaw. New York, Harper, 1944.
Horses (as Timothy Hay), illustrated by Dorothy Wagstaff. New York, Harper, 1944.
They All Saw It, photographs by Ylla. New York, Harper, 1944.
Willie's Walk to Grandmama, with Rockbridge Campbell, illustrated by Lucienne Bloch. New York, Scott, 1944.
The House of a Hundred Windows, illustrated by Robert de Veyrac. New York, Harper, 1945.
The Little Fisherman, illustrated by Dahlov Ipcar. New York, Scott, 1945.
Little Fur Family, illustrated by Garth Williams. New York, Harper, 1946.
The Man in the Manhole and the Fix-It Men (as Juniper Sage, with Edith Thacher Hurd), illustrated by Bill Ballantine. New York, Scott, 1946.
The Bad Little Duckhunter, illustrated by Clement Hurd. New York, Scott, 1947.
The Golden Egg Book, illustrated by Leonard Weisgard. New York, Simon and Schuster, 1947.
The First Story, illustrated by Marc Simont. New York, Harper, 1947.
Goodnight, Moon, illustrated by Clement Hurd. New York, Harper, 1947; Kingswood, Surrey, World's Work, 1975; pop-up edition, as *The Goodnight Moon Room,* New York, Harper, and London, Hardy, 1984.
The Sleepy Little Lion, photographs by Ylla. New York, Harper, 1947; London, Harvill Press, 1960.
The Winter Noisy Book, illustrated by Charles Shaw. New York, Harper, 1947.
Five Little Firemen, with Edith Thacher Hurd, illustrated by Tibor Gergely. New York, Simon and Schuster, 1948.
The Golden Sleepy Book, illustrated by Garth Williams. New York, Simon and Schuster, 1948.
The Little Farmer, illustrated by Esphyr Slobodkina. New York, Scott, 1948.
Wonderful Storybook, illustrated by J.P. Miller. New York, Simon and Schuster, 1948.
The Color Kittens, illustrated by Alice and Martin Provensen. New York, Simon and Schuster, 1949; London, Muller, 1951.
The Important Book, illustrated by Leonard Weisgard. New York, Harper, 1949.
The Little Cowboy, illustrated by Esphyr Slobodkina. New York, Scott, 1949.
My World, illustrated by Clement Hurd. New York, Harper, 1949.
A Pussycat's Christmas, illustrated by Helen Stone. New York, Crowell, 1949.
Two Little Miners, with Edith Thacher Hurd, illustrated by Richard Scarry. New York, Simon and Schuster, 1949.
Two Little Trains, illustrated by Jean Charlot. New York, Scott, 1949; Kingswood, Surrey, World's Work, 1960.
O, Said the Squirrel, photographs by Ylla. London, Harvill Press, 1950.
The Dream Book: First Comes the Dream, illustrated by Richard Floethe. New York, Random House, 1950.
The Little Fat Policeman, with Edith Thacher Hurd, illustrated by Alice and Martin Provensen. New York, Simon and Schuster, 1950.
The Peppermint Family, illustrated by Clement Hurd. New York, Harper, and London, Hamish Hamilton, 1950.
The Quiet Noisy Book, illustrated by Leonard Weisgard. New York, Harper, and London, Hamish Hamilton, 1950.
The Wonderful House, illustrated by J. P. Miller. New York, Simon and Schuster, and London, Muller, 1950; revised edition, Simon and Schuster, 1960.
Fox Eyes, illustrated by Jean Charlot. New York, Pantheon, 1951; London, Collins, 1979.
The Summer Noisy Book, illustrated by Leonard Weisgard. New York, Harper, 1951.
The Train to Timbuctoo, illustrated by Art Seiden. New York, Simon and Schuster, 1951; London, Muller, 1952.
Two Little Gardeners, with Edith Thacher Hurd, illustrated by Gertrude Elliott. New York, Simon and Schuster, 1951.

Christmas in the Barn, illustrated by Barbara Cooney. New York, Crowell, 1952.
Dr. Squash, The Doll Doctor, illustrated by J.P. Miller. New York, Simon and Schuster, 1952.
Mister Dog, The Dog Who Belonged to Himself, illustrated by Garth Williams. New York, Simon and Schuster, 1952; London, Muller, 1954.
The Noon Balloon, illustrated by Leonard Weisgard. New York, Harper, 1952.
Seven Little Postmen, with Edith Thacher Hurd, illustrated by Tibor Gergely. New York, Simon and Schuster, 1952.
The Duck, photographs by Ylla. New York, Harper, and London, Harvill Press, 1952.
The Golden Bunny and 17 Other Stories and Poems, illustrated by Leonard Weisgard. New York, Simon and Schuster, 1953.
The Hidden House, illustrated by Aaron Fine. New York, Holt, 1953.
The Sailor Dog, illustrated by Garth Williams. New York, Simon and Schuster, 1953; London, Muller, 1954.
The Friendly Book, illustrated by Garth Williams. New York, Simon and Schuster, 1954.
The Little Fir Tree, illustrated by Barbara Cooney. New York, Crowell, 1954.
Little Indian, illustrated by Richard Scarry. New York, Simon and Schuster, 1954; London, Golden Pleasure Books, 1964.
Wheel on the Chimney, illustrated by Tibor Gergely. Philadelphia, Lippincott, 1954.
Willie's Adventures, illustrated by Crockett Johnson. New York, Scott, 1954.
The Little Brass Band, illustrated by Clement Hurd. New York, Harper, 1955.
Seven Stories about a Cat Named Sneakers, illustrated by Jean Charlot. New York, Scott, 1955; as *Sneakers,* Reading, Massachusetts, Addison Wesley, 1979.
Young Kangaroo, illustrated by Symeon Shimin. New York, Scott, 1955; Kingswood, Surrey, World's Work, 1959.
Big Red Barn, illustrated by Rosella Hartman. New York, Scott, 1956.
David's Little Indian, illustrated by Remy Charlip. New York, Scott, 1956.
Home for a Bunny, illustrated by Garth Williams. New York, Simon and Schuster, 1956; London, Hamlyn, 1961.
Three Little Animals, illustrated by Garth Williams. New York, Harper, 1956.
The Dead Bird, illustrated by Remy Charlip. New York, Scott, 1958.
Four Fur Feet, illustrated by Remy Charlip. New York, Scott, 1961.
On Christmas Eve, illustrated by Beni Montresor. New York, Scott, 1961; London, Collins, 1963.
The Whispering Rabbit, illustrated by Garth Williams and Lilian Obligado. New York, Golden Press, 1965.
The Steamroller, illustrated by Evaline Ness. New York, Walker, 1974.
Once upon a Time in a Pigpen and Three Other Stories, illustrated by Ann Strugnell. Reading, Massachusetts, Addison Wesley, 1980; London, Hutchinson, 1981.
Wonderful Storybook (selection), illustrated by J.P. Miller. Racine, Wisconsin, Western, 1985.

Fiction as Golden MacDonald (illustrated by Leonard Weisgard)

Red Light, Green Light. New York, Doubleday, 1944.
Little Lost Lamb. New York, Doubleday, 1945.
Little Frightened Tiger. New York, Doubleday, 1953.
Whistle for the Train. New York, Doubleday, 1956.

Poetry

Big Dog, Little Dog (as Golden MacDonald), illustrated by Leonard Weisgard. New York, Doubleday, 1943.
The Little Island (as Golden MacDonald), illustrated by Leonard Weisgard. New York, Doubleday, 1946.
Wait till the Moon Is Full, illustrated by Garth Williams. New York, Harper, 1948.
The Dark Wood of the Golden Birds, illustrated by Leonard Weisgard. New York, Harper, 1950.
A Child's Good Morning, illustrated by Jean Charlot. New York, Scott, 1952.
Where Have You Been?, illustrated by Barbara Cooney. New York, Crowell, 1952.
Sleepy ABC, illustrated by Esphyr Slobodkina. New York, Lothrop, 1953.
Nibble Nibble, illustrated by Leonard Weisgard. New York, Scott, 1959.

Other

The Children's Year (adapted from a work by Y. Lacôte), illustrated by Feodor Rojankovsky. New York, Harper, 1937.
The Comical Tragedy or Tragical Comedy of Punch and Judy, illustrated by Leonard Weisgard. New York, Scott, 1940.
The Fables of La Fontaine, illustrated by André Hellé. New York, Harper, 1940.
Brer Rabbit: Stories from Uncle Remus, illustrated by A.B. Frost. New York, Harper, 1941.
Animals, Plants, and Machines (reader), with Lucy Sprague Mitchell, illustrated by Clare Bice. Boston, Heath, 1944.
Farm and City (reader), with Lucy Sprague Mitchell. Boston, Heath, 1944.
Pussy Willow, illustrated by Leonard Weisgard. New York, Simon and Schuster, 1952.
The Diggers, illustrated by Clement Hurd. New York, Harper, and London, Hamish Hamilton, 1961.

*

Manuscript Collections: Westerly Public Library, Rhode Island; Kerlan Collection, University of Minnesota, Minneapolis.

* * *

Author of more than one hundred children's stories, Margaret Wise Brown pioneered by the late 1930s a new approach to writing for children in which a story goes beyond traditional narrative borders to focus directly on important aspects of a young child's world. She saw the latter consisting of such things as: a fascination with the world's colors and sights and smells which were so new to the child's senses; a concern with being lost and being found, good and bad, shy or lonely; and a delight in the recognizably nonsensical. Reflecting these interests, her books aimed at penetrating the child's reality.

The Noisy Books Series early exemplified the author's intent by appealing to the child's growing sensory awareness. In *Noisy Book* a dog named Muffin hears the noises a child would hear and has to guess the identity of one—a device employed in every book.

Muffin listens to indoor sounds in *Indoor Noisy Book,* to rural sounds in *Country Noisy Book,* and to a quiet sound he can't recognize (until with the reader selects from such imaginative possibilities as fog drifting and birds dreaming) in *The Quiet Noisy Book.* The books use words and images in an imaginative and poetic manner to capture the child's attention.

New or familiar sights, the seasons, travel, and the child-feared night are subjects touched upon in stories like *The Noon Balloon, Wheel on the Chimney, Night and Day,* to mention a few. In the first a cat is airlifted over cities and natural topography. In *Wheel on the Chimney* a stork loses his family as they migrate south but rejoins them again in the spring as they return to their chimney nest. A lonely night cat and day cat visit in each other's worlds in *Night and Day,* and the latter stays with his companion after losing his fear of the night world. All three books persuasively accomplish the aim of their author.

A group of Brown's works center on a child's concerns with getting lost, being lonely or alone, and being loved and protected. The title character of *Young Kangaroo* leaves his mother's pouch only narrowly to escape being eaten by dingoes before gratefully returning to his mother's warm security. In *The Runaway Bunny* a rabbit is dissuaded from running away because his mother strongly reaffirms her love. *Little Chicken* deals with a chick who is left alone for the first time and returns home wiser for the experience. On a deeper plane, *The Little Island* tells of a kitten who learns that he, like an isolated island connected to one land under the sea, is a world of his own yet part of the world. These stories perceptively treat the child's innermost concerns.

Offering a valuable spectrum of the author's work is *The Fish with the Deep Sea Smile,* a collection of stories (including "Sneakers, That Rapscallion Cat") and poems demonstrating her sensitivity and skill as a poet as well as writer.

Margaret Wise Brown emerges as a major writer of children's literature. The rich legacy of work she has left us admirably testifies to her success in writing of the child's world.

—Christian H. Moe

BROWN, Pamela (Beatrice)

Nationality: British. **Born:** Colchester, Essex, 31 December 1924. **Education:** Colchester County High School, 1930-39; Brecon County School, 1939-41; Royal Academy of Dramatic Art, London, 1942-43. **Family:** Married Donald Masters in 1949 (died 1962); two daughters. **Career:** Producer, BBC Television, London, 1950-55, Scottish Television, Glasgow, 1956-57, and Granada Television, Manchester and London, 1958-62. **Died:** 26 January 1989.

Publications for Children

Fiction

The Swish of the Curtain, illustrated by Newton Whittaker. London, Nelson, 1941; Philadelphia, Winston, 1943; revised edition, Leicester, Brockhampton Press, 1971; revised edition, Aylesbury, Buckinghamshire, Goodchild, 1984.

Maddy Alone, illustrated by Newton Whittaker. London, Nelson, 1945.

Golden Pavements, illustrated by Newton Whittaker. London, Nelson, 1947.

Blue Door Venture, illustrated by Newton Whittaker. London, Nelson, 1949.

To Be a Ballerina and Other Stories, illustrated by Marcia Lane Foster. London, Nelson, 1950.

Family Playbill, illustrated by Marcia Lane Foster. London, Nelson, 1951; as *Family Troupe,* New York, Harcourt Brace, 1953.

The Television Twins, illustrated by Marcia Lane Foster. London, Nelson, 1952.

Harlequin Corner, illustrated by Marcia Lane Foster. London, Nelson, 1953; New York, Meredith Press, 1969.

The Windmill Family, illustrated by Marcia Lane Foster. London, Nelson, 1954; New York, Crowell, 1955.

Louisa, illustrated by Sax. London, Nelson, 1955; New York, Crowell, 1957.

Maddy Again, illustrated by Drake Brookshaw. London, Nelson, 1956.

The Bridesmaids, illustrated by Peggy Beetles. Leicester, Brockhampton Press, 1956; Philadelphia, McKay, 1957.

Showboat Summer, illustrated by Charles Paine. Leicester, Brockhampton Press, 1957.

Back-stage Portrait, illustrated by Drake Brookshaw. London, Nelson, 1957.

Understudy, illustrated by Drake Brookshaw. London, Nelson, 1958.

First House, illustrated by Drake Brookshaw. London, Nelson, 1959.

As Far as Singapore, illustrated by Peggy Beetles. Leicester, Brockhampton Press, 1959.

The Other Side of the Street, illustrated by Nathan Mayer. Leicester, Brockhampton Press, 1965; Chicago, Follett, 1967.

The Girl Who Ran Away, illustrated by Nathan Mayer. Leicester, Brockhampton Press, 1968.

A Little Universe, illustrated by Faith Jaques. Leicester, Brockhampton Press, 1970.

Summer Is a Festival. Leicester, Brockhampton Press, 1972.

Looking after Libby. Leicester, Brockhampton Press, 1974.

Every Day Is Market Day. London, Hodder and Stoughton, 1977.

The Finishing School. Aylesbury, Buckinghamshire, Goodchild, 1984.

Play

The Children of Camp Fortuna. London, French, 1949.

*

Pamela Brown commented:

(1983) When I started writing I was still a child, and I wrote purely for my own enjoyment. On finding that it amused other children as well I continued to write for their diversion, and have done so ever since.

* * *

Pamela Brown wrote *The Swish of the Curtain* when she was still at school, and it has a freshness and liveliness of plot which surely reflect the youthfulness of the writer. Some of the reasons for its success may include the overriding commitment to acting and to the theatre which permeates much of Brown's work, the creation of a group of completely individual characters with whom readers can identify, and an action-packed and often highly entertaining plot.

For children interested in acting it is easy to see the appeal of a plot that consists of a series of drama-related activities: a drama competition, pantomime, open air production, and even a vividly recounted visit to Stratford-on-Avon. The seven children of the three families (Faynes, Halfords, and Darwins) are united in their theatrical ventures whatever the parental and adult opposition. The reader is fascinated by the diversity of character of the seven children involved, each of whom stands out as a definite individual. Some of the adult characters such as the children's friend the Bishop are affectionately portrayed, but others, particularly the children's arch-enemy Mrs. Potter-Smith, are presented with a degree of ruthlessness which a more mature writer might have diluted. It is a measure of the power and verve of this novel that a revised version was published in 1984. It has been fairly skilfully updated where necessary, although G.C.E. has already been superseded, the coinage was changed in 1971, and little maids belong to another era.

After the merited success of *The Swish of the Curtain,* Brown continued the series with *Maddy Alone, Golden Pavements, Maddy Again,* and *Blue Door Venture.* The Maddy volumes are shorter than the rest of the series, but equally readable. Of the sequels, *Golden Pavements* is perhaps the most successful, and could rank as an excellent example of a career story with its account, now perhaps unfortunately dated, of life at drama school in London, the rigours of touring, the demands of repertory work, and the changing fortunes of the Darwins, Faynes, and Halfords before returning to Fenchester to form their own professional theatre company.

Brown continued over a period of almost 50 years to make a noteworthy contribution to fiction for children. Having trained for the stage herself, she frequently brought this interest to her novels whether the setting is historical or contemporary. *Family Playbill,* set in the Victorian period, is of particular interest with its account, through the eyes of Lexy Mannering, of the fluctuating fortunes of her actor-manager father, other members of the family, and the actors associated with them as they move from one grim town and seedy lodging to another to offer their repertoire to an often unresponsive audience.

Brown's last work was *The Finishing School,* a somewhat misleading title as it is an absorbing story of adjustment to life in Singapore during World War II. This story reflects the fears of the British in Singapore before Japanese occupation, the courage of a teenage girl Rosemary Langford in adapting to restricted prison camp life, and the inherent goodness of individuals faced with great crisis in their lives. The book portrays the contrast between the sheltered, affluent life of Rosemary's family before the Japanese occupation and the rigours of prison camp life. Strengths and weaknesses of character are painfully evident in the crisis situation.

Whatever her theme, Brown's strong points include the ability to tell an absorbing story, the skill to create convincing characters, an aptitude for highlighting the humour of differing situations and predicaments, and a realistic, perceptive, and unromanticised presentation. Brown used a formidable combination of factors to ensure her success over a long period.

—Anne W. Ellis

BROWN, Roy (Frederick)

Nationality: British. **Born:** Vancouver, British Columbia, Canada, 10 December 1921. **Family:** Married Wendy Landman; two sons and two daughters. **Career:** Primary school teacher, 1946-69; deputy head, Helen Allison School for autistic children, 1969-75. **Died:** 14 September 1982.

Publications for Children

Fiction

A Saturday in Pudney, illustrated by James Hunt. London, Abelard Schuman, 1966; New York, Macmillan, 1968.

The House on the Green, illustrated by Trevor Parkin. Edinburgh, Oliver and Boyd, 1967.

Little Brown Mouse, illustrated by Constance Marshall. London, University of London Press, 1967.

The Wonderful Weathercock, illustrated by Ferelith Eccles Williams. London, University of London Press, 1967.

The Viaduct, illustrated by James Hunt. London, Abelard Schuman, 1967; New York, Macmillan, 1968.

The Day of the Pigeons, illustrated by James Hunt. London, Abelard Schuman, and New York, Macmillan, 1968.

The Saturday Man, illustrated by Trevor Ridley. London, BBC Publications, 1969.

The Wapping Warrior, illustrated by James Hunt. London, Chatto and Windus, 1969.

The River, illustrated by James Hunt. London, Abelard Schuman, 1970; as *Escape the River,* New York, Seabury Press, 1972.

The Thunder Pool, illustrated by Gareth Floyd. London, Abelard Schuman, 1971.

The Battle of Saint Street, illustrated by James Hunt. London, Abelard Schuman, and New York, Macmillan, 1971.

Flight of Sparrows. London, Abelard Schuman, 1972; New York, Macmillan, 1973.

Bolt Hole. London, Abelard Schuman, 1973; as *No Through Road,* New York, Seabury Press, 1974.

The White Sparrow. London, Abelard Schuman, 1974; New York, Seabury Press, 1975.

Shep the Second, illustrated by Clifford Bayly. London, Abelard Schuman, 1975.

The Siblings. London, Abelard Schuman, 1975; as *Find Debbie!,* New York, Seabury Press, 1976.

The Million Pound Mouse, illustrated by Joanna Stubbs. London, Abelard Schuman, 1975.

Chubb on the Trail, illustrated by Margaret Belsky. London, Abelard Schuman, 1976.

The Big Test, illustrated by James Hunt. London, Andersen Press, 1976.

The Cage. London, Abelard Schuman, and New York, Seabury Press, 1977.

A Nag Called Wednesday, illustrated by Jeroo Roy. London, Andersen Press, 1977.

Chubb to the Rescue, illustrated by Margaret Belsky. London, Abelard Schuman, 1977.

The Swing of the Gate. London, Andersen Press, and New York, Seabury Press, 1978.

Trojan Rides Again, illustrated by Ivan Hissey. London, Abelard Schuman, 1978.

Undercover Boy, illustrated by Pauline Carr. London, Andersen Press, 1978.
Cover Drive. London, Abelard Schuman, 1979.
Chips and the Crossword Gang, illustrated by Pauline Carr. London, Andersen Press, 1979.
Chubb Catches a Cold, illustrated by Margaret Belsky. London, Abelard Schuman, 1979.
Collision Course. London, Andersen Press, 1980; as *Suicide Course,* New York, Clarion, 1980.
Octopus. London, Andersen Press, 1981.
Chips and the River Rat, illustrated by Victoria Cooper. London, Andersen Press, 1981.
Chips and the Black Moth. London, Andersen Press, 1982.

Plays

Radio Plays: *News Extra!* series, 1973.

Other

A Book of Saints. London, Cassell, 1959.
The Children's Book of Old Testament Stories, illustrated by Hugh T. Marshall. London, Harrap, 1959.
The Children's Pinocchio, illustrated by Sheila Rose. London, Harrap, 1960.
The Children's Heidi, illustrated by Sheila Connelly. London, Harrap, 1963.
Port of Call, illustrated by Jack Trodd. London and New York, Abelard Schuman, 1965.
The Legend of Ulysses, illustrated by Mario Logli and Gabriele Santini. London, Hamlyn, 1965.
The Battle Against Fire, with William Stuart Thomson, illustrated by James Hunt. London, Abelard Schuman, 1966.
Reynard the Fox, illustrated by John Vernon Lord. London and New York, Abelard Schuman, 1969.
Runaway Guy (reader). London, Macmillan, 1980.

* * *

Among major children's writers of the 1970s Roy Brown was one particularly open to his times, in tune with their issues and concerns, and while the readability and human interest of his stories guarantee a wide readership the settings indicate a conscious desire to offer the non-academic urban child a means of identification. The years brought development in technique but not deviation from city backgrounds and characters at risk or disadvantage in modern society.

Brown first came to notice with *A Saturday in Pudney* which had an uncomplicated story line—the tracking down of a lost child and subsequent discovery of thieves—a large cast list of neighbourhood children (including two statutory girls, one West Indian), and a satisfying ending. *The Days of the Pigeons* used the twin search theme again, here the children's pursuit of the lost racing pigeons and the attempts of Mousy Lawson, on the run from an approved school, to contact his father, but this time plot structure and detailing moved forward in complexity. *The River* introduced three characters who recur with variations in later stories: the backward, disturbed child; the ex-Borstal bully; the boy who lets himself be led into crime through threats, promises, or his own inadequacies. We meet them in *Bolt Hole,* where Barry drifts into criminal associations because of the failure of other relationships, and in *Flight of Sparrows. The Siblings* centres on the disappearance of a psychotic 14-year old, but here we have moved up in the social scale to a block of flats, home of a local government official and his very desperate family.

One looks to Brown not for stylistic qualities nor for great originality but for good plots, authenticity of setting, and compassionate engagement with characters. Sympathy is shown to the petty criminal, the old and defenceless, the subnormal, who are seen as the victims of an unfeeling society: the settings with which readers grow familiar are London's river and waste grounds, its derelict houses, warehouses, and building sites. At first classified with Hildick, rather dismissively, as a "cement street" writer, Brown emerged as a key figure in the "relevant" children's fiction fashionable in the 1970s. Yet assessment of his contribution is difficult. The sentiment sometimes moves over into sentimentality: judgments like "Inside the big tough guy there's a wee laddie—maybe even a guid laddie—trying to get out" (*The Day of the Pigeons*) grate; the purple passages (see the last sequence of *The White Sparrow*) embarrass because they are out of key with the prevailing tone; characters are too often explained rather than revealed. The critical question is "If the themes weren't so topical would the literary merits be more suspect?" *The Siblings,* Brown's most powerful book, provides a partial answer. More than compensating for the weaknesses are the mastery of pace, the accessibility and humanity of the stories, and the enlargement of the reader's sympathies.

Later work consisted mainly of tough, fast-moving crime stories, such as *Cover Drive,* still with the characteristic Brown touches—the city settings, the interest in the outsider, the exploration of the father/son relationship—or the series of undemanding mysteries centred around Chips Regan, son of a policeman and, if anything, more astute than his father. Andersen Press, who publish the Chips series, have long been concerned to meet the demand for exciting but simple stories, and it would be churlish not to recognize the appeal of these predictable tales. One cannot, however, regard them as having marked an advance in Brown's development as a writer. Of the later books, the most typical—and most revealing of its author's preoccupation—is *Collision Course,* which charts the slow road to recovery of a disturbed and alienated young man, and the problems of the doctors and social workers who tried to help him.

—Peggy Heeks

BROWNE, Anthony (Edward Tudor)

Nationality: British. **Born:** Sheffield, Yorkshire, 11 September 1946. **Education:** Whitcliffe Mount Grammar School, Cleckheaton, Yorkshire, 1957-63; Leeds College of Art, B.A. (honours) in graphic design 1967. **Family:** Married Jane Franklin in 1980; one son and one daughter. **Career:** Medical artist, Royal Infirmary, University of Manchester, 1968-70; designer, Gordon Fraser Greeting Cards, London, 1971-87. **Awards:** Library Association Kate Greenaway Medal, 1983, 1992; Maschler Award, 1983, 1988; Children's Literature Prize (Germany), 1985; Dutch Silver Pencil, 1989. **Address:** The Chalk Garden, The Length, St.-Nicholas-at-Wade, Birchington, Kent CO7 0PJ, England.

PUBLICATIONS FOR CHILDREN (ILLUSTRATED BY THE AUTHOR)

Fiction

Through the Magic Mirror. London, Hamish Hamilton, and New York, Greenwillow, 1976.
A Walk in the Park. London, Hamish Hamilton, 1977.
Bear Hunt. London, Hamish Hamilton, 1979; New York, Atheneum, 1980.
Look What I've Got! London, MacRae, 1980; New York, Knopf, 1988.
Bear Goes to Town. London, Hamish Hamilton, 1982.
Gorilla. London, MacRae, 1983; New York, Knopf, 1985.
Willy the Wimp. London, MacRae, and New York, Knopf, 1984.
Willy the Champ. London, MacRae, and New York, Knopf, 1985.
Piggybook. London, MacRae, and New York, Knopf, 1986.
The Little Bear Book. London, Hamish Hamilton, 1988; New York, Doubleday, 1989.
I Like Books. London, MacRae, and New York, Knopf, 1989.
A Bear-y Tale. London, Hamish Hamilton, 1989.
The Tunnel. London, MacRae, 1989.
Things I Like. London, MacRae, 1989.
Changes. London, MacRae, 1990.
Willy and Hugh. London, MacRae, 1991.
Zoo. New York, Knopf, 1992.
The Big Baby: A Little Joke. New York, Knopf, and London, MacRae, 1994
King Kong. London, MacRae, 1994; as *Anthony Browne's King Kong,* Atlanta, Turner Publications, 1994.
Willy the Wizard. New York, Knopf, 1995.
Willy the Dreamer. Cambridge, Massachusetts, Candlewick Press, 1998.

Other

Hansel and Gretel (retelling). London, MacRae, 1981; New York, Knopf, 1988.

*

Illustrator: *Knock, Knock! Who's There?* by Sally Grindley, 1985; *The Visitors Who Came to Stay,* 1985, and *Kirsty Knows Best,* 1987, both by Annalena McAfee; *Alice's Adventures in Wonderland* by Lewis Carroll, 1988; *Trail of Stones,* 1990, *The Night Shimmy,* 1992, both by Gwen Strauss; *The Topiary Garden,* by Janni Howker, 1994; *The Daydreamer,* by Ian McEwan, 1994.

Anthony Browne comments:

I have now produced a body of picture books which are unified by style and themes, and which offer a very particular view of the world of my characters. I try to make my books work on different levels—so what seems a very simple story, appreciated on one level—can also stimulate reflection upon the nature of society and its complex values. While my style is often concerned with the materiality of objects and figures, I assemble them then to refute the possibility of material reality—in this way revealing the interior states of the protagonists. I also try to make them funny!

* * *

Whether in picture book or illustrated book, to accompany prose or poetry, as author-illustrator or collaborator, Anthony Browne—for nearly two decades—has given a large audience (of all ages) consistently interesting work that, at every level, contains something to be enjoyed, discovered, and considered.

As one who has made a major contribution to the development of the modern picture book, Browne's own works are unified by style and themes that are entertaining, demanding, and provocative. The settings are generally domestic, and the stories are of survival strategies. His heroes and heroines, whether human or humanized animals, build bridges between social differences, deal with boredom, loneliness, and jealousy, compensate for spiritual neglect, overcome inappropriate dependency, and when possible, care for others. Browne eschews heavy-handed moral messages and radical transformations of circumstance; he shows the way things are and how his protagonists respond. In so doing, Browne offers his readers models of good nature, generosity of spirit, pluck, and, above all, resourcefulness.

Resourcefulness is the constant value that Browne celebrates. In Browne's first picture book, Toby escapes the indifference of his parents with a bold step *Through the Magic Mirror,* which is a metaphor for the frontier between his internal and external worlds. Smudge and Charles are accompanied by a yob and a snob, but win for themselves a brief spell of perfect happiness in *A Walk in the Park. Look What I've Got!* tells the story of two boys, Jeremy and Sam. The former is blinded by his material advantages, while the latter has none; Sam, however, is more than compensated by the power of his imagination to transform the world. Hannah in *Gorilla,* which won for Browne the first of his two Maschler awards, is encircled by goods and toys rather than the comfort of her father's arms, and he dreams up a gorilla to kiss. Browne's three picture books for the very young also affirm the value of resourcefulness. Bear, the eponymous hero, draws himself and his friends out of many dangers and difficulties, but his magic pencil is no wand: It has to be used constructively. The Piggots of *Piggybook* (which challenges sexual stereotyping) and Willy, whether as wimp or champ, have all demonstrated their inner strengths by the time the boardcovers close upon their adventures. Resourcefulness manifests itself through the exercise of the imagination in all of Browne's characters, and the workings of the imagination are depicted rather than described.

Browne's prose style is flat and undecorated, his verbal texts brief, in contrast to his distinctive pictorial style and complex, sometimes puzzling pictures. When the two modes are brought together, the composite text is always capable of a wide range of interpretations. The pictures display the thoughts and conflicting emotions that lie behind the drama of events. These revelations of the inner and imaginative life of his characters greatly extend the perspectives Browne offers his reader/viewers.

The characteristics of his pictorial style are a fondness for surrealistic and fantastic imagery with symbolic functions, and a mode of depiction that, with its intense care to selected details and textures, gives the quality of non-photographic realism. His illustrations are rich with transtextual and intertextual allusions, as well as occasional allusions to famous paintings. Browne often makes free use of the images of the Belgian painter René Magritte and occasionally reworks ideas on which the latter has based easel paintings. Examples may be found in *Through the Magic Mirror, A Walk in the Park, The Visitors Who Came to Stay,* and *Alice's Adventures in Wonderland.* The juxtapositions of ill-assorted objects and fantastic imagery with which Browne creates the surreal states of mind of his characters are a source of visual humor and surprise that keep children searching and turning the picture book pages. Browne's pictures contain a strong element of play, the rule for which is that any given object appearing out of context or odd in scale has a place in the internal logic of the visual narrative.

An enduring and recurring major image is that of a gorilla. It appears as commentator, consort, dream figure, agent of fate, hero, outsider, metaphorical symbol; animal, toy, dressing-up suit; in sleep or daydream, as fact or fantasy. Its first important appearance is in *Look What I've Got:* it became one of the two main characters as well as appearing in other guises; in *Gorilla,* and with the creation of Willy, it is the eponymous hero of a series. Twice Browne has painted unforgettable large-scale close-up images of an ape, both as its empirical self and a demanding symbol. In *Gorilla,* a chimpanzee gazes directly at the beholder in sad resignation, muzzle pressed out against the bars of its cage. In *Zoo,* an outstanding work which moves beyond the domestic sphere to wider social concerns, the image becomes inescapably disturbing in a series of pictures of animals—dignified, demeaned, and defeated. *Zoo* is a satirical account of a family outing that contrasts the conscious and unconscious beastliness of homo sapiens (camouflaged in acrylic stripes and patches) with the tenderly observed plight of the captive animals. The resulting extremes of visual irony raise uncomfortable and topical questions about conservation, as well as showing that humans too can be captives of patterns of thought and behaviour.

In the relationship between word and image, the illustrations have many functions. As well as elaborating, specifying, and amplifying the verbal narrative, Browne's illustrations sometimes exemplify emotional moods at variance with the words. Always, what looks like a collision between the two languages is no perverse accident, but an assertion of the contradictory nature of reality. As in *The Visitors Who Came to Stay,* Browne never hides the truth that social relationships are beset with risks and conflicting feelings, though he manages to make children laugh while conveying that truth.

Browne has contributed picture books to the folk/fairy tale genre, interpreting such texts as expressions of the psychic processes of the unconscious. His radical paintings for *Hansel and Gretel* by the Brothers Grimm accords with a Freudian analysis of the tale. Browne employs a highly symbolic mode which includes sets of recurring images to represent the children's progression and independence, as well as regression and negative feelings about their mother, who is shown with the same facial features as those of the witch. His interest in the genre is also displayed in illustrations for *Trail of Stones,* a poetry anthology by Gwen Strauss. Browne offers both fresh perspectives on characters in well-known tales, as well as a change in his graphic style, in a series of fine drawings, some of which have tones and textures so finely judged and balanced that the effects move close to the subtleties of etchings. Two of the compositions have echoes of Aubrey Beardsley and Gustave Doré and others mark his own originality. Browne's picture book *The Tunnel,* which won the Dutch Silver Pencil, is characteristically capable of sustaining different levels of meaning. On the surface, it is an enjoyable minor variant on *The Snow Queen,* with visual allusions to fairy tales and fairy-tale illustrators. Looking at the pictures, one follows the psychological journey of male and female principles moving toward integration, or the unity of ego and id, or the reconciliation of opposites.

Browne's illustrated books include the major work *Alice's Adventures in Wonderland,* by Lewis Carroll, and *The Topiary Garden,* Janni Howker's short story, in small book format. The Carroll collaboration shows Browne concentrating on the dream-vision of Alice's adventures and using the devices of surrealism to reflect Alice's unconscious. For many children who discover Wonderland by way of Browne, the visual punning and puzzles, the element of play and the strangeness consciously experienced when looking into the pictures may well have more allure than Carroll's text. For Howker's feminist text, Browne compliments her sensuous prose style—that describes so fully the sights and scents and burgeoning feelings of the heroine's world—by limiting his paintings to views of the topiary garden, the Devil's own art, shaped by the will of man to please a man. The style and content is restrained, static, intense, and controlled, thus promoting the theme of male dominance against which the heroine struggles. The overtly comic details that pervade almost all of Browne's illustration are not to be found. It will be interesting to see whether Browne's capacity to interpret serious matters in a more directly serious style will be a developing strand in the future.

—Jane Doonan

BRUCE, Dorita Fairlie

Nationality: British. **Born:** 1885. Lived in London for many years. **Died:** September 1970.

Publications for Children

Fiction

The Senior Prefect, illustrated by Wal Paget. London, Oxford University Press, 1920; as *Dimsie Goes to School,* 1933.

Dimsie Moves Up, illustrated by Wal Paget. London, Oxford University Press, 1921.

Dimsie Moves Up Again, illustrated by Gertrude D. Hammond. London, Oxford University Press, 1922.

Dimsie among the Prefects, illustrated by Gertrude D. Hammond. London, Oxford University Press, 1923.

The Girls of St. Bride's, illustrated by Henry Coller. London, Oxford University Press, 1923.

Dimsie Grows Up, illustrated by Henry Coller. London, Oxford University Press, 1924.

Dimsie, Head-Girl, illustrated by M.S. Reeve. London, Oxford University Press, 1925.

That Boarding School Girl, illustrated by Roy. London, Oxford University Press, 1925.

The New Girl and Nancy. London, Oxford University Press, 1926.

Nancy to the Rescue. London, Oxford University Press, 1927.

Dimsie Goes Back, illustrated by M.S. Reeve. London, Oxford University Press, 1927.

The New House-Captain, illustrated by M.S. Reeve. London, Oxford University Press, 1928.

The King's Curate. London, Murray, 1930.

The Best House in the School, illustrated by M.S. Reeve. London, Oxford University Press, 1930.

The Best Bat in the School. London, Oxford University Press, 1931.
The School on the Moor, illustrated by M.S. Reeve. London, Oxford University Press, 1931.
Captain of Springdale, illustrated by Henry Coller. London, Oxford University Press, 1932.
Mistress-Mariner. London, Murray, 1932.
Nancy at St. Bride's, illustrated by M.D. Johnston. London, Oxford University Press, 1933.
The New House at Springdale, illustrated by M.D. Johnston. London, Oxford University Press, 1934.
Nancy in the Sixth. London, Oxford University Press, 1935.
Dimsie Intervenes, illustrated by M.D. Johnston. London, Oxford University Press, 1937.
Nancy Returns to St. Bride's, illustrated by M.D. Johnston. London, Oxford University Press, 1938.
Prefects at Springdale, illustrated by M.D. Johnston. London, Oxford University Press, 1938.
Captain Anne, illustrated by M.D. Johnston. London, Oxford University Press, 1939.
The School in the Woods, illustrated by G.M. Anson. London, Oxford University Press, 1940.
Dimsie Carries On, illustrated by W. Bryce Hamilton. London, Oxford University Press, 1942.
Toby at Tibbs Cross, illustrated by Margaret Horder. London, Oxford University Press, 1943.
Nancy Calls the Tune, illustrated by Margaret Horder. London, Oxford University Press, 1944.
A Laverock Lilting, illustrated by Margaret Horder. London, Oxford University Press, 1945.
Wild Goose Quest. London, Lutterworth Press, 1945.
The Serendipity Shop, illustrated by Margaret Horder. London, Oxford University Press, 1947.
Triffeny, illustrated by Margaret Horder. London, Oxford University Press, 1950.
The Bees on Drumwhinnie, illustrated by Margaret Horder. London, Oxford University Press, 1952.
The Debatable Mound, illustrated by Patricia M. Lambe. London, Oxford University Press, 1953.
The Bartle Bequest, illustrated by Sylvia Green. London, Oxford University Press, 1955.
Sally Scatterbrain, illustrated by Betty Ladler. London, Blackie, 1956.
Sally Again, illustrated by Betty Ladler. London, Blackie, 1959.
Sally's Summer Term, illustrated by Joan Thompson. London, Blackie, 1961.
Dimsie Takes Charge (stories). Aylesbury, Buckinghamshire, Goodchild, 1985.

* * *

Between the first and second world wars Dorita Fairlie Bruce was an extremely popular writer for girls. Her most memorable books—the Dimsie, Nancy, and Springdale series—have school settings and clearly defined, likeable heroines with whom several generations of schoolgirl readers have identified. Bruce has sometimes been dismissed as merely an imitator of Angela Brazil, the creator of the 20th-century girls' school story. There *are* similarities in the intentional—and unconscious—humour of both authors, but Bruce's plots and characterizations have a subtlety and an uncontrived exuberance that are lacking in many of Brazil's stories.

Bruce's main characters grow up gradually during the course of a series: they progress from being naive but endearing juniors to responsible young adults. The well-ordered life of many girls' private schools is convincingly conveyed through descriptions of regular music practices and walks in crocodile, of girls discarding gymslips for silk dresses on special occasions, or standing around for hours on the boundary, fielding at cricket matches. School is shown as the world in microcosm; there is plenty of challenge—in rivalries between individuals and groups, or in the destructive influence of one girl over another. The author is at her best in describing friendships which are "fervent" but "healthy-minded." Strong aversion to excessively sentimental relationships is the keynote of many of Bruce's books. Prefects encourage sport as a potent corrective, while Dimsie and other juniors form an effective and long-lived "Anti-Soppist League" to put down "mushy" behaviour.

Bruce is less successful at manipulating the relationships in which her heroines become involved as adults. Most of them eventually marry, but schoolgirlish anti-soppism complicates the courting process: "Oh Peter....How can you say anything so horrible?," responds Dimsie when the man who she later marries first declares his love.

The authentic backgrounds of Bruce's stories partly derive from her own experiences as a boarding school pupil. She once wrote of her characters: "I go back to school with them...." Bruce was an officer in the Girls' Guildry and her fiction sometimes exploited this organization's character-building propensities.

She possessed a sense of scene and mood. The cosiness of a study tête-à-tête, for instance, is enhanced by its contrast with a winter gale raging outside over the sodden downs. Bruce was Scottish, and several of her books contain evocative descriptions of her country's lochs, islands, and hills. As well as schoolgirls' adventures she wrote several historical short stories and novels.

Bruce's books tended to dismiss intellectuals and progressives as cranks or useless day-dreamers. Through her straightforward schoolgirls she projected her ideals of practical Christianity (which she occasionally expressed as "helping lame dogs over stiles"), patriotism, and esprit de corps. It is a measure of her skill that she did so without obtrusively moralizing. Many adults today feel that her books constructively influenced their childhood and adolescence.

—Mary Cadogan

BRUCE, Mary Grant

Nationality: Australian. **Born:** Sale, Victoria, in 1878. **Education:** Sale local schools and in Gippsland district, Victoria. **Military Service:** Writer and broadcaster for the Australian Imperial Forces during World War I. **Family:** Married her cousin George E. Bruce in 1914 (died 1949); one son. **Career:** From c.1900 children's page editor (as "Cinderella"), *Leader* magazine of Melbourne *Age;* briefly editor, *Woman's World* and *Woman;* broadcaster. Lived in England and Ireland, 1913-18 and 1927-39, and in England, 1954-58. **Award:** Fellow, Royal Society of Literature. **Died:** 2 July 1958.

Publications for Children

Fiction

A Little Bush Maid, illustrated by J. Macfarlane. Melbourne and London, Ward Lock, 1910.

Mates at Billabong, illustrated by J. Macfarlane. Melbourne and London, Ward Lock, 1911.
Timothy in Bushland, illustrated by J. Macfarlane. Melbourne and London, Ward Lock, 1912.
Glen Eyre, illustrated by J. Macfarlane. Melbourne and London, Ward Lock, 1912.
Norah of Billabong, illustrated by J. Macfarlane. Melbourne and London, Ward Lock, 1913.
Gray's Hollow, illustrated by Patric Dawson. Melbourne and London, Ward Lock, 1914.
From Billabong to London, illustrated by Fred Leist. Melbourne and London, Ward Lock, 1915.
Jim and Wally, illustrated by Bruno Salmon. Melbourne and London, Ward Lock, 1916.
'Possum, illustrated by J. Macfarlane. Melbourne and London, Ward Lock, 1917.
Dick, illustrated by J. Macfarlane. Melbourne and London, Ward Lock, 1918.
Captain Jim, illustrated by J. Macfarlane. Melbourne and London, Ward Lock, 1919.
Dick Lester of Kurrajong, illustrated by J. Macfarlane. Melbourne and London, Ward Lock, 1920.
Rossiter's Farm, illustrated by Esther Paterson. Melbourne, Whitcombe and Tombs, 1920.
Back to Billabong, illustrated by J. Macfarlane. Melbourne and London, Ward Lock, 1921.
The Cousin from Town, illustrated by Esther Paterson. Melbourne, Whitcombe and Tombs, 1922.
The Twins of Emu Plains, illustrated by Dewar Mills. Melbourne and London, Ward Lock, 1923.
Billabong's Daughter, illustrated by J. Macfarlane. Melbourne and London, Ward Lock, 1924.
The Houses of the Eagle, illustrated by Harold Copping. Melbourne and London, Ward Lock, 1925.
Hugh Stanford's Luck. Sydney, Cornstalk, 1925.
The Tower Rooms, illustrated by Dewar Mills. Melbourne and London, Ward Lock, 1926.
Robin, illustrated by Edgar A. Holloway. Sydney, Cornstalk, 1926; London, Angus and Robertson, 1938.
Billabong Adventurers, illustrated by J. Macfarlane. Melbourne and London, Ward Lock, 1927.
Anderson's Jo. Sydney, Cornstalk, 1927.
Golden Fiddles, illustrated by Dewar Mills. Melbourne and London, Ward Lock, 1928.
The Happy Traveller, illustrated by Laurie Taylor. Melbourne and London, Ward Lock, 1929.
Bill of Billabong, illustrated by A.A. Kent. Melbourne and London, Ward Lock, 1931.
Road to Adventure, illustrated by Laurie Taylor. Melbourne and London, Ward Lock, 1932; New York, Minton Balch, 1933.
Billabong's Luck, illustrated by Laurie Taylor. Melbourne and London, Ward Lock, 1933.
"Seahawk," illustrated by J.F. Campbell. Melbourne and London, Ward Lock, 1934.
Wings above Billabong, illustrated by J.F. Campbell. Melbourne and London, Ward Lock, 1935.
Circus Ring, illustrated by J.F. Campbell. Melbourne and London, Ward Lock, 1936; New York, Putnam, 1937.
Billabong Gold, illustrated by J.F. Campbell. Melbourne and London, Ward Lock, 1937.
Told by Peter, illustrated by J.F. Campbell. Melbourne and London, Ward Lock, 1938.
Son of Billabong, illustrated by J.F. Campbell. Melbourne and London, Ward Lock, 1939.
Peter and Co., illustrated by J.F. Campbell. Melbourne and London, Ward Lock, 1940.
Karalta. Sydney and London, Angus and Robertson, 1941.
Billabong Riders. Melbourne and London, Ward Lock, 1942.

Other

The Stone Axe of Burkamukk: Aboriginal Legends Retold, illustrated by J. Macfarlane. Melbourne and London, Ward Lock, 1922.

PUBLICATIONS FOR ADULTS

Other

The Power Within: Four Broadcast Talks. Privately printed, 1941.

*

Critical Studies: *Seven Little Billabongs: The World of Ethel Turner and Mary Grant Bruce* by Brenda Niall, Melbourne, Melbourne University Press, 1979; *Billabong's Author: The Life of Mary Grant Bruce* by Alison Alexander, Sydney, Angus and Robertson, 1979; London, Angus and Robertson, 1980.

* * *

Mary Grant Bruce not only had a devoted following in her own country but many young English readers first learned about the hazards of the Australian bush, its strange bandicoots, wombats, kangaroos, and native bears, its exotic bell-birds and the laughing jackass, and other indigenous creatures, including the mythical Bunyip, through well-thumbed copies of her popular *Timothy in Bushland.* Others were introduced to aboriginal legends through *The Stone Axe of Burkamukk.* Most of her books were first published in England, but in the period between the first and second world wars many an Australian home gathered on its bookshelves, for family reading, a collection of the famous Billabong books, a series which began with *A Little Bush Maid* in 1910.

The Lintons of Billabong were a motherless family who lived on a prosperous station property in the north of Victoria, 17 miles from Cunjee, the nearest town. Billabong is a comfortably secure world in microcosm. Threat is usually external in the form of natural disaster—drought, flood, or bushfire—or of lawless creatures such as vagrant swagmen, cattle duffers, or gold thieves. The world outside only occasionally casts its shadow as when the Linton men are involved in World War I. But Billabong is always there, its wide shady verandahs, its long lagoon in which to swim, its creek for fishing which can dry up or run high, its scrub through which cattle roam, and its open paddocks across which to canter. Against this background Norah Linton, the little bush maid, grows from childhood to womanhood; a fresh open country girl—stalwart yet feminine; resourceful yet lovingly dependent on her menfolk. Her older brother Jim, too, is proudly upright and dependable, and Norah is to marry his boisterous mate, Wally Meadows, who "laughed at life just as he laughed at Death, when it came near to touching him." Only when trouble threatens the Billabong folk does life become serious. This stable family group benignly ruled over by Mr. Linton embraces the homestead servants and the station hands. Brownie, ample, motherly, astutely aware that her cooking will hold the family together in any crisis and "regarded by the station as a species of stout angel in petticoats," and Murty O'Toole, the dry-mouthed Irish stockman, are closest to the family. But the arch-enemies Hogg the gardener and Lee Wing his Chinese help, along with Black Billy the stockboy, are all treated with the same respect as is meted to all visitors and to the many lame-dogs whom the Lintons befriend over the years.

The series reflects the social and economic climate of Australia which weathered both a world war and a depression. Gold is discovered on the property, and to meet expanding needs the Lintons turn to their own air transport in *Wings above Billabong.*

Mary Grant Bruce gives a good deal of explanatory background information, but because she is a first-class storyteller, she is able to regulate the pace of her narrative to her readers' interests. Her characters are made of stern stuff but are not unsentimental, perhaps predictable as well as being reliable. Their conflicts and alarms are always transitory and there is always a happy issue from any kind of adversity. Hence her plots are melodramatic rather than tragic. But her many books epitomised, even if they idealised, a recognisably outback Australian life-style of warm-hearted characters committed to the ideal of "mateship."

—H.M. Saxby

BRUCHAC, Joseph, III

Nationality: American. **Born:** 16 October 1942. **Education:** Cornell University, B.A. 1965; Syracuse University, M.A. 1966; SUNY/Albany, 1970-73; Union Graduate School, Yellow Springs, Ohio, Ph.D. 1975. **Family:** Married Carol Worthen; two sons. **Career:** English teacher and Liaison Officer, Teachers for West Africa, Ghana, 1966-69; English instructor, Skidmore College, 1969-1973; instructor and coordinator for the writing program, Great Meadow Correctional Facility, 1974-1981; faculty member, Hamilton College, 1983, 1985, and 1987; faculty adjunct, SUNY/Albany, 1987, 1988; director, The Greenfield Review Literary Center, and founder and co-editor, The Greenfield Review Press, Greenfield Center, New York, from 1969. Editor, *The Greenfield Review,* 1969-87; board member, 1973-74, 1981-85, national chairman, 1984-85, COSMEP-National Independent Publishers Association; editor, *The Prison Writing Review,* 1976-85; co-editor, *Moccasin Telegraph,* Fairfax, Virginia; poetry editor, *Studies in American Indian Literature,* from 1989; national chair, Returning the Gift Project, 1991-92; acting chair, Native Writers Circle of the Americas, 1992-93; advisory board, Wordcraft Circle of Native American Writers, 1992-93; board member of the National Association for Storytelling, 1992-94; member of editorial boards of *Parabola, Storytelling Magazine, Melus, Obsidian,* Cross Cultural Communications Press, and others. **Awards:** NEA Creative Writing Fellowship (poetry), 1974; CCLM Editors Fellowship, 1980; Rockefeller Humanities Fellowship, 1982; New York State CAPS Poetry Fellowships, 1973, 1982; NEA/PEN Syndicated Fiction Award, 1983; American Book Award, 1984, for *Breaking Silence*; Yaddo Residency Fellowships, 1984, 1985; Cherokee Nation Award (prose), 1986; New York State Council on the Arts Editors Fellowship, 1986; PMA Benjamin Franklin Audio Award, 1992, for *The Boy Who Lived with the Bears*; Hope S. Dean Memorial Award for lifetime contribution to children's books, 1993; PMA Person of the Year Award, 1993; with Gayle Ross, Skipping Stones Book Award, 1995, for *Multicultural Children's Literature*; Knickerbocker Award for Juvenile Literature, New York State Library Association, 1995; Mountains and Plains Booksellers Association Regional Book Award, 1995, for *A Boy Called Slow*; Scientific American Award for Young Readers, 1996; *Boston Globe/Horn Book* Honor Award, 1996, for *The Boy Who Lived with the Bears*; Parents' Choice Award, 1996; American Library Association Notable Children's Books, 1996, for *The Boy Who Lived with the Bears* and *A Boy Called Slow*; Paterson Children's Book Award, 1996, for *Dog People.* **Agent:** Barbara Kautz, P. O. Box 558, Bellport, New York 11713. **Address:** P.O. Box 308, Greenfield Center, New York 12833, U.S.A. **Website:** http://www.greenfieldreview.org.

Publications for Young Adults

Fiction

Turtle Meat and Other Stories. Duluth, Minnesota, Holy Cow! Press, 1992.
Dawn Land. Golden, Colorado, Fulcrum Publishing, 1993.
Long River. Golden, Colorado, Fulcrum Publishing, 1995.
Dog People: Native Dog Stories, illustrated by Murv Jacob. Golden, Colorado, Fulcrum Publishing, 1995.
Children of the Longhouse (with glossary and reading list). New York, Dial Books for Young Readers, 1996.
Eagle Song, illustrated by Dan Andreasen (with glossary and pronunciation guide).New York, Dial Books for Young Readers, 1997.
The Arrow Over the Door, illustrated by James Watling. New York, Dial Books for Young Readers, 1998.
The Waters Between. Hanover, New Hampshire, Hardscrabble Books, 1998.

Folk Stories

Turkey Brother and Other Tales: Iroquois Folk Stories. Freedom, California, The Crossing Press, 1975.
Stone Giants & Flying Heads: Adventure Stories of the Iroquois. Freedom, California, The Crossing Press, 1978.
Iroquois Stories: Heroes and Heroines, Monsters and Magic. Freedom, California, The Crossing Press, 1985.
The Wind Eagle: And Other Abenaki Stories. Greenfield Center, New York, Bowman Books, 1985.
The Faithful Hunter: More Abenaki Stories. Greenfield Center, New York, Bowman Books, 1988.
The Return of the Sun: Native American Tales from the Northeast Woodlands. Freedom, California, The Crossing Press. 1990.
Hoop Snakes, Hide-Behinds and Sidehill Winders. Freedom, California, The Crossing Press, 1991.
Native American Stories (selections from *Keepers of the Earth,* with Michael J. Caduto.) Golden, Colorado, Fulcrum Publishing, 1991.
Native American Animal Stories (selections from *Keepers of the Earth,* with Michael J. Caduto.) Golden, Colorado, Fulcrum Publishing, 1992.

Flying with the Eagle, Racing the Great Bear: Stories from Native North America, illustrated by Murv Jacob. Mahwah, New Jersey, Troll/BridgeWater Books, 1993.

With Gayle Ross, *The Girl Who Married the Moon,* with illustrations by S. S. Burrus. Mahwah, New Jersey, Troll/BridgeWater Books, 1994.

Four Ancestors (songs and poems, with stories retold by Bruchac), illustrated by Cherokee, Ojibway, and San Carlos/Yavapai Apache artists. Mahwah, New Jersey, Troll/BridgeWater Books, 1994.

The Boy Who Lived with the Bears: And Other Iroquois Stories, illustrated by Murv Jacob. New York, Harper Collins Children's Books, 1995.

Native American Plant Stories (selections from *Keepers of the Earth,* with Michael J. Caduto.) Golden, Colorado, Fulcrum Publishing, 1995.

When the Chenoo Howls, illustrated by William Netamuxwe Sauts Bock. New York, Walker and Company, 1998.

Non-Fiction

With Michael J. Caduto, *Keepers of the Earth: Native American Stories and Environmental Activities for Children.* Golden, Colorado, Fulcrum Publishing, 1988.

With Michael J. Caduto, *Keepers of the Animals: Native American Stories and Wildlife Activities for Children.* Golden, Colorado, Fulcrum Publishing, 1990.

The Native American Sweat Lodge, History and Legends. Freedom, California, The Crossing Press, 1993.

With Michael J. Caduto, *Keepers of Life: Discovering Plants through Native American Stories and Earth Activities for Children.* Golden, Colorado, Fulcrum Publishing, 1994.

With Michael J. Caduto, *Keepers of the Night: Native American Stories and Nocturnal Activities for Children.* Golden, Colorado, Fulcrum Publishing, 1994.

Roots of Survival: Native American Storytelling and the Sacred. Golden, Colorado, Fulcrum Publishing, 1996.

Tell Me a Tale: A Book about Storytelling. San Diego, California, Harcourt Brace, 1997.

Lasting Echoes: An Oral History of Native American People. San Diego, Harcourt Brace, 1997.

Bowman's Store: A Journey to Myself (autobiography with photographs). New York, Dial Books for Young Readers, 1998.

Editor, *Native Wisdom.* San Francisco, Harper San Francisco, 1995.

Publications for Children

Folk Stories

The First Strawberries, illustrated by Anna Vojtech. New York, Dial Books for Young Readers, 1993.

The Great Ball Game: A Muskogee Story. New York, Dial Books for Young Readers, 1994.

Gluskabe and the Four Wishes, illustrated by Christine Nyburg Shrader. New York, Dutton/Cobblehill Books, 1995.

With Gayle Ross, *The Story of the Milky Way: A Cherokee Tale,* illustrated by Virginia A. Stroud. New York, Dial Books for Young Readers, 1995.

Between Earth and Sky: Legends of Native American Sacred Places, illustrated by Thomas Locker. San Diego, California, Harcourt Brace, 1996.

The Maple Thanksgiving, illustrated by Anna Vojtech. Glenview, Illinois, Celebration Press, 1996.

With Melissa Jayne Fawcett, *Makiawisug: Gift of the Little People.* Uncasville, Connecticut, Little People, 1997.

Picture Books

With Jonathan London, *Thirteen Moons on Turtle's Back: A Native American Year of Moons* (poetry), illustrated by Thomas Locker. New York, Philomel/Putnam, 1992.

Fox Song, illustrated by Paul Morin. New York, Philomel/Putnam, 1993.

The Earth Under Sky Bear's Feet: Native American Poems of the Land, illustrated by Thomas Locker. New York, Philomel/Putnam, 1995.

The Circle of Thanks (songs and poems), illustrated by Murv Jacob. Mahwah, New Jersey, Troll/BridgeWater Books, 1996.

Many Nations: An Alphabet of Native America, illustrated by Robert Goetzl. Mahwah, New Jersey, Troll/BridgeWater Books, 1997.

Biography

A Boy Called Slow: The True Story of Sitting Bull, illustrated by Rocco Baviera. New York, Philomel/Putnam, 1995.

Publications for Adults

Poetry

Indian Mountain and Other Poems. Ithaca, New York, Ithaca House, 1971.

The Buffalo in the Syracuse Zoo. Greenfield Review Press, 1972.

Great Meadow Poems. Paradise, California, Dustbooks, 1973.

The Manabozho Poems. Marvin, South Dakota, Blue Cloud Quarterly, 1973.

Flow. Austin, Texas, Cold Mountain Press, 1975.

This Earth is a Drum. Austin, Texas, Cold Mountain Press, 1976.

Entering Onondaga. Austin, Texas, Cold Mountain Press, 1978.

There Are No Trees inside the Prison. Brunswick, Maine, Blackberry Press, 1978.

Mu'undu Wi Go. Marvin, South Dakota, Blue Cloud Quarterly, 1978.

The Good Message of Handsome Lake. Greensboro, North Carolina, Unicorn Press, 1979.

Translator's Son. Merrick, New York, Cross Cultural Communications, 1980.

Ancestry. Fort Kent, Maine, Great Raven Press, 1981.

Remembering the Dawn. Marvin, South Dakota, Blue Cloud Quarterly, 1983.

Tracking. Memphis, Tennessee, Ion Books, 1985.

Walking with My Sons. Minneapolis, Minnesota, Landlocked Press, 1985.

Near the Mountains. Fredonia, New York, White Pine Press, 1986.

Langes Gedachtnis/Long Memory. Osnabruck, West Germany, OBEMA, 1988.

Nonfiction

Survival This Way: Interviews with Native American Poets. Tucson, Arizona, University of Arizona Press, 1990.

Roots of Survival: Native American Storytelling and the Sacred. Golden, Colorado, Fulcrum Publishing, 1996.
With Michael J. Caduto, *Native American Gardening: Stories & Recipes for Families.* Golden, Colorado, Fulcrum Publishing, 1996.

Editor

Songs from This Earth on Turtle's Back: Contemporary American Indian Poetry. New York, Greenfield Review Press, 1983.
Breaking Silence: An Anthology of Contemporary Asian American Poets. New York, Greenfield Review Press, 1984.
The Light from Another Country: Poetry from American Prisons. New York, Greenfield Review Press, 1984.
North Country: An Anthology of Contemporary Writing from the Adirondacks and the Upper Hudson Valley. New York, Greenfield Review Press, 1986.
New Voices from the Longhouse: An Anthology of Contemporary Iroquois Writing. New York, Greenfield Review Press, 1988.
Raven Tells Stories: An Anthology of Alaskan Native Writing. New York, Greenfield Review Press, 1991.
Singing of Earth. Berkeley, California, The Nature Company, 1993.
Returning the Gift: Poetry and Prose from the First North American Native Writers' Festival. Tucson, Arizona, University of Arizona Press, 1994.
Aniyunwiya/Real Human Beings: An Anthology of Contemporary Cherokee Prose. New York, Greenfield Review Press, 1995.
Smoke Rising: The Native North American Literary Companion. Detroit, Visible Ink Press, 1995.

*

Media Adaptations: *Abenaki Cultural Heritage, Alnobak: The Dawnland Singers,* and *Iroquois Stories* (recordings), Good Mind Recordings; *The Boy Who Lived with the Bears* (recording), Caedmon/Parabola; *Dawn Land* (recording), Fulcrum; *Gluskabe Stories* (recording), Yellow Moon Press; *Keepers of the Earth, Keepers of the Animals,* and *Keepers of the Plants* (recordings), Fulcrum Publishing.

Critical Studies: *Children's Literature in the Elementary School* by Huck, Hepler, Hickman and Kiefer, Brown and Benchmark Publications, 1997; "Joseph Bruchac III," in *Children's Literature Review,* Vol. 46, Detroit, Gale Research, 1998.

Joseph Bruchac III comments:

One of the reasons I have devoted so much of my own life to the understanding and the respectful telling of traditional Native stories is my strong belief that now, more than ever, these tales have much to teach us—whether we are of Native ancestry or not. We learn about ourselves by understanding others. Our own traditions can be made stronger only when we pay attention to and respect the traditions of people who are different from ourselves. Hearing or reading the stories of the Native peoples of North America will not make any of us Native Americans, but it may help make all of us more human.

* * *

As a master storyteller, poet, author, songwriter, teacher, publisher and editor, Joseph Bruchac is a quiet force behind the recognition and proliferation of Native American writing. Drawing on his own Native American heritage, and parallel with his career as a professional storyteller, his children's and young adult books, both fiction and non-fiction, follow the theme of Indian folk stories and incorporate the fellowship with nature and the strong oral tradition that he inherited from his Abenaki grandfather. Bruchac sees himself as a "tradition bearer." He has worked all his writing life to preserve the myths and legends of the Native peoples of North America. "Stories are the life of a people. They tell of the deepest hopes and fears of a nation," he writes in his introduction to the collection, *The Return of the Sun.*

There are many Indian nations in North America, five hundred recognized tribes in the United States alone, with more than two million members speaking hundreds of different languages. Native American storytellers keep the creation myths, the lesson stories, and the nature myths alive from generation to generation. Some tales are passed down in the telling and remembering, while others have been collected and written down. Bruchac believes that "writing can be a way of making a bridge," between the oral traditions of the remaining Native American storytellers and the young readership of today, though he does not write down folk stories that have never appeared in print.

Native folklore is full of anecdotes, jokes, and wonderful explanations of the ways of the natural world. A wry quality in Indian storytelling is particularly effective in the characterization and dialogue in Bruchac's short forms, both folk stories and fiction. Two collections of Indian tales which represent tribes from different parts of North America, *The Girl Who Married the Moon,* written with Gayle Ross, and *Flying with the Eagle, Racing the Great Bear,* are companion volumes which explore the passage from childhood to adulthood for girls and boys, though each may be read by everyone, adults included. *Turtle Meat and Other Stories,* a collection of fiction and folktales, includes "How the Mink Stole Time," which manages to laugh at one of the awful consequences of the arrival of Europeans in North America, the imposition of European Time on a people once free to make their own time.

Bruchac's first novel for young adults, *Dawn Land,* set in an era long before European contact, focuses on the coming of age of Young Hunter, who is chosen to protect his people from powerful, stone-hearted beings, the Ancient Ones of Indian legend. This adventure story draws on a deep knowledge of nature and the lifeways of an independent and flexible people long established on this continent. Its sequel, *Long River,* continues the story of Young Hunter and, like the earlier novel, weaves Native myth and oral history into the narrative. *The Arrow Over the Door* is historical fiction, set on the eve of the Battle of Saratoga during the Revolutionary War. In alternating narratives a Quaker youth and a young Abenaki Indian relate the story of an actual incident, when an Abenaki scouting party joined a silent Quaker meeting. The forces that pulled Native Americans into white men's wars are explored. Appended author's notes provide short histories of the Abenakis and the Quakers, as well as some historical background to the story.

The series of four *Keepers* books, published between 1988 and 1995 with Michael J. Caduto, integrate Indian tales and scientific, environmental, and craft activities for children. This interdisciplinary approach to teaching about earth and Native American cultures is designed to help children feel a part of their surroundings. *Keepers of the Earth: Native American Stories and Environmental Activities for Children* (1988), *Keepers of the Animals: Native American Stories and Wildlife Activities for Children* (1991), *Keep-*

ers of Life: Discovering Plants through Native American Stories and Earth Activities for Children (1994), and *Keepers of the Night: Native American Stories and Nocturnal Activities for Children* (1995) can be used as teachers' aides or parents' resource books. Reviewer Donna Nurse writes in *Books in Canada* that in this uniquely conceived series of books, Caduto and Bruchac "tie storytelling to its original purpose—the passing along of wisdom from generation to generation."

Though it is possible to divide Bruchac's books for young people roughly into Young Adult and Children's Books, many of them appeal to anyone who has any interest in the natural world, in folklore, in the chance to look at life in a different, more peaceful way. "Stories are wonderful teachers," writes Bruchac in his introduction to *Tell Me a Tale: A Book About Storytelling* (1997), a book that passes on the gift of his heritage to anyone willing to receive it. "Stories helped me overcome my problems and stories taught me many things: that I didn't have to be ashamed when I was afraid, that I could learn to be brave, that there were times for sorrow and times for joy, that things were always going to change, and that some things—like love and courage, hope and faith—were unchanging. I learned through hearing stories that I had my own stories to tell, and that if I told them well, people would want to hear them."

Joseph Bruchac's books for younger readers, illustrated by leading children's illustrators, include *Fox Song,* the story of an Abenaki child whose great-grandmother has just died, but who remembers the gifts of knowledge and understanding she has inherited, including the feeling that she will never be alone in the natural world her great-grandmother has shown her; *Between Earth and Sky,* a collection of poems, illustrated by Thomas Locker, which explores ten sacred places in North America; and *The Earth Under Sky Bear's Feet,* also illustrated by Locker, which includes stories and songs from different Native peoples about the sky and the stars. "Although they speak hundreds of different languages, the Native peoples of North America all share an awareness that the world around them is very much alive," writes Bruchac in his author's note for the latter book. In a companion book, *Thirteen Moons on Turtle's Back: A Native American Year of Moons,* co-written with Jonathan London and once again illustrated by Locker, short tales from thirteen different Native groups explore an alternative calendar based on lunar changes. *The First Strawberries: A Cherokee Story* explains how strawberries helped heal a rift between the first man and the first woman.

Bruchac's work has extended beyond the realm of writing for young people into writing for adults and into acting as a kind of cultural ambassador. When the National Museum of the American Indian was established in the old U.S. Custom House at the tip of Manhattan in New York City in 1994, it was Joseph Bruchac, as a representative of the Native peoples of America, who was invited to write the text for the panels which welcome visitors to the building, and which tell the story of Manhattan's pre-contact past. Writing of The Greenfield Review Press, which he runs with his wife, Carol Bruchac, and one of his sons, he says: "We were a multicultural publisher before the term gained wide currency, although we define 'multicultural' as inclusive of all cultures, not just those neglected in the past." He told interviewer Carl L. Bankston of *The San Francisco Review of Books*: "The awareness and the strengthening of multiculturalism has been one of the best things to happen to literature in this country. We have a much more vital literature today as a result of it."

Bruchac's work as a poet, as well as author and storyteller, has appeared in hundreds of magazines and anthologies. In 1996, he told Kit Alterdice of *Publisher's Weekly* that his career "wasn't really a matter of choice. It was a matter of finding what road I was supposed to be on and then staying on it." His books for young people may be just a bend in the long road of his career. His real accomplishment, one that encompasses everything he has done, is as a translator of the richness of myth, of culture and ideas, from the past into the present and on into the future.

—Angela Wigan

BRYAN, Ashley

Nationality: American. **Born:** New York, New York, 13 July 1923. **Education:** Cooper Union for the Advancement of Science and Art, Columbia University. **Military Service:** U.S. Army, World War II. **Career:** Painter; reteller and illustrator of books for children. Taught painting and drawing, Queen's College, Brooklyn; taught Black American Poetry, Lafayette College, Easton, Pennsylvania; taught children at Brooklyn Museum and The Dalton School, New York City; Professor Emeritus of Art and Visual Studies, Dartmouth, Hanover, New Hampshire. **Awards:** American Library Association Notable Book, 1974, for *Walk Together Children*; Parents Choice Award, 1980, and Coretta Scott King Book Award, 1981 for *Beat the Story-Drum*; American Library Association Notable Book, 1982, for *I'm Going to Sing: Black American Spirituals*; Coretta Scott King Honor Book Citation, 1983, for *I'm Going to Sing: Black American Spirituals,* 1986, for *Lion and the Ostrich Chicks and Other African Folk Tales,* 1988, for *What a Morning: The Christmas Story in Black Spirituals,* 1992, for *All Night, All Day: A Child's First Book of African American Spirituals,* and 1998, for ABC of African American Poetry; Parents' Choice citation, 1992, for *Sing to the Sun*; Silver Medallion, for contributions to children's literature, University of Southern Mississippi, Hattiesburg. **Address:** Hadlock St, Isleford, Maine 04646, U.S.A.

Publications for Children (illustrated by the author)

Folktales, retold by the author

The Ox of the Wonderful Horns and Other African Folktales. New York, Atheneum, 1971.

The Adventures of Aku; or, How it Came about That We Shall Always See Okra the Cat Lying on a Velvet Cushion while Okraman the Dog Sleeps among the Ashes. New York, Atheneum, 1976.

The Dancing Granny. New York, Macmillan, 1977.

Beat the Story-Drum, Pum-Pum. New York, Atheneum, 1980.

The Cat's Purr. New York, Atheneum, 1985.

Lion and the Ostrich Chicks and Other African Folk Tales. New York, Athenaeum, 1986.

Turtle Knows Your Name. New York, Macmillan, 1989.

The Story of Lightning and Thunder. New York, Atheneum, 1993.

Ashley Bryan's ABC of African American Poetry. New York, Atheneum, 1997.

Other

Compiler and illustrator, *Black American Spirituals.* Volume 1: *Walk Together Children,* New York, Atheneum, 1974; Volume 2: *I'm Going to Sing,* New York, Macmillan, 1982.
Compiler and author of introduction, *I Greet the Dawn: Poems,* by Paul Laurence Dunbar. New York, Atheneum, 1978.

Reteller, *Sh-Ko and His Eight Wicked Brothers,* illustrated by Fumio Yoshimura. New York, Macmillan, 1988.

Recordings: *Anansi the Spider in Search of a Fool, The Cat's Purr, The Story of Lightning and Thunder,* Belfast, Maine, Audio Bookshelf, 1994; *The Dancing Granny and Other African Tales,* Caedmon Audio, 1994.

*

Biography: Entry in *Something about the Author,* Volume 72, Detroit, Gale, 1993; *Meet the Author: Ashley Bryan* (video), American School Publishers.

Critical Studies: *Illustrators of Children's Books, 1967-76* by Lee Kingman, Boston, Horn Book, 1978; entry in *Children's Literature Review,* Volume 18, Detroit, Gale, 1993.

Illustrator: *What a Morning; The Christmas Story in Black Spirituals,* selected and edited by John Langstaff, 1987; *All Night, All Day: A Child's First Book of Spirituals,* 1991; *Climbing Jacob's Ladder: Heroes of the Bible in African-American Spirituals,* 1991; *Sing to the Sun,* 1992; *Christmas Gift: An Anthology of Christmas Poems, Songs, and Stories Written by and about African-Americans,* compiled by Chalemae Rollins, 1993; *What a Wonderful World* by George Weiss and Bob Thiele, 1993; *It's Kwanzaa Time* by Linda and Clay Goss, 1995; *The Story of the Three Kingdoms* by Walter Dean Myers, 1995; *The Sun is So Quiet* by Nikki Giovanni, 1996; *The House with No Door: African Riddle Poems* by Brian Swann, 1998; *Carol of the Brown King: Nativity Poems* by Langston Hughes, New York, Atheneum, 1998.

* * *

Ashley Bryan is a teller of tales, a singer of songs, and a painter of the world around. He celebrates lives of Black Americans, Black Africans, and Black West Indians. Bryan grew up within a large family in the Bronx, New York. He discovered early on that the way to survive in his tough neighborhood was through his drawings and paintings; they were the toughest assets he had to offer his community. He attended public schools in New York and then went on to two private colleges in New York: Cooper Union for the Advancement of Science and Art and Columbia University.

Bryan has lived in France and Germany, has traveled extensively throughout Europe and visited Kenya and Uganda. For many years he spent summers on an island off the coast of Maine, where he would paint and exhibit his work. Once he became Professor Emeritus at Dartmouth, he moved to the island year-round, where he paints and creates books full time. He works in oils, outdoors when he is able. He likens his style to that of the early Impressionist painters, but he is less interested in light and more in a sense of rhythm than were these painters.

Bryan first illustrated tales from France and India. When he turned to illustrate African folktales, he was dissatisfied with the way they had been transcribed into English. So he retold them in his own fashion, as well as illustrated them. Bryan used as his source material translations by anthropologists and missionaries who had lived and worked in third world areas. Bryan studied their materials and reworked the stories so they came alive in both the text and accompanying illustrations.

Bryan encourages people to read aloud his tales, so that the meaning as well as the spirit of the stories may be fully appreciated. He has made several audio tapes of stories and poems himself, and his strong, vibrant voice brings them to life. He encourages those who listen to his tapes to clap, dance, shout, and laugh with him. Many of the tapes are now available in the children's section of public libraries.

Bryan's first book of African folk tales, *The Ox of the Wonderful Horns and Other African Folktales,* contains five stories, one of which is about Anansi the Spider. Stories about Anansi are great favorites in West Africa; there are lots of them. In this particular story Anansi decides to fish for profit. There are good fishing waters nearby, and he knows he can grow rich in the fish business. But Anansi does not wish to work at making, setting, and pulling in the traps. No, that is too much trouble for him. So he decides to hire a fool to do the work, and when the fool catches enough fish, Anansi will sell the fish at the market and keep the money for himself. However, things do not go as planned. Anene the crow agrees to help Anansi, but turns the table on him and gets Anansi to make, set, and pull in the traps. Anene then sells the fish and pockets the money. In the end Anansi realizes that when one seeks to make a fool of someone else, one is bound to make a bigger fool of himself. The book ends: "This is my story. Whether it be bitter or whether it be sweet, take some of it elsewhere and let the rest come back to me." The woodcuts in the book are bold and expressive. The colors used—red, orange, and black—are familiar colors in traditional African kente cloth.

More African tales are found in *Lion and the Ostrich Chicks,* which contain stories from the Masai of East Africa, the Bushmen of Angola and southern Africa, and the Hausa of West Africa. In the first story, "Lion and the Ostrich Chicks," a lion captures six small ostrich chicks and says they are his children. Everyone in the forest knows he just wants to eat them, but no one has the courage to stand up to the lion. No one, that is, but the mongoose. The mongoose manages to outsmart the cunning lion, and the chicks are set free to return to their parents. Again, the woodcuts make dramatic use of line and color; the village scenes are alive with activities of people and of animals.

Turtle Knows Your Name is set in the West Indies. It is a charming tale about the love and friendship of a boy and his grandmother. Both of them have very long names. The boy's name is UPSILIMANA TUMPALERADO, and since it is so long, his playmates can never remember it. They simply call him "Long Name." His grandmother tells him though that he should teach his playmates his real name. Now it turns out that his grandmother has an even longer name, MAPASEEDO JACKALINDY EYE PIE TACKARINDY. When the boy finds this out, and they both call each other by their real names, it becomes too much. They decide to call each other simply, "Granny" and "Son." The book ends: "Mmm I love you, Granny!" "Mmmm'mmm I love you, Son!" In this book, the illustrations are done in soft pastels: yellows, greens, blues.

The Story of Lightning and Thunder comes from southern Nigeria. Thunder is a mother sheep and lightning is her son. They live on the west coast of Africa. The villagers are pleased to have them because they are able to call down rain when it is needed. But Son Ram Lightning is young and does not always think before he acts. When he butts people with his horns in order to get close to the King, when he brings rain down when it isn't needed, the villagers complain to their King. The King has to tell Ma Sheep Thunder and Son Ram Lightning that his people no longer feel safe with them living on earth amongst them. When Son Ram Lightning tries to help, he sometimes hurts. So the King banishes them from his kingdom and from the earth; their home must be far away, high up in the sky. In this book the colorful costumes worn by the villagers provide page after page of stunning pictures.

Bryan is also well known for his compilations of Black American spirituals. His interest in spirituals goes back to his own childhood, when families and friends gathered together Sunday afternoons to sing them. Most recently Bryan has produced *Ashley Bryan's ABC of African American Poetry,* another prize-winning volume with compelling illustrations.

—Mary Lystad

BUFFIE, Margaret

Nationality: Canadian. **Born:** Winnipeg, Manitoba, 29 March 1945. **Education:** University of Manitoba, B.A. (Fine Arts) 1967, certificate in education 1976. **Family:** Married James Macfarlane in 1968; one daughter. **Career:** Illustrator, Hudson's Bay Co., Winnipeg, Manitoba, 1968-70; painting instructor, Winnipeg Art Gallery, 1974-75; high school art teacher, River East School Division, Winnipeg, 1976-77; freelance illustrator and painter, 1977-84. Writer since 1984. **Awards:** Canadian Library Association Young Adult Novel Award, 1987-88, for *Who is Frances Rain?*; Governor General's Award honour book; Canadian Library Association best fiction, 1989 and 1992; Ruth Schwartz Children's Book Award nomination, 1989, 1992, 1996; Mr. Christie Book Award nomination, 1992 and 1996; Vicky Metcalfe Award, for Body of Work, 1996; McNally Robinson Book for Young People Award, 1996, for *The Dark Garden.* **Address:** 165 Grandview St., Winnipeg, Manitoba R2G 0L4, Canada.

Publications for Children

Fiction

Who Is Frances Rain?, Toronto, Kids Can Press, 1987; London, Viking, 1989; as *The Haunting of Frances Rain,* New York, Scholastic Inc., 1989.

The Guardian Circle. Toronto, Kids Can Press, 1989; as *The Warnings,* New York, Scholastic, 1991.

My Mother's Ghost. Toronto, Kids Can Press, 1992; as *Someone Else's Ghost,* New York, Scholastic, 1994.

The Dark Garden. Toronto and New York, Kids Can Press, 1995.

*

Media Adaptations: *My Mother's Ghost* (film), Credo Entertainment and Buffalo Gals Pictures, 1996.

Critical Studies: *About Novels* by David W. Booth and Stanley Skinner, Toronto, Globe/Modern Curriculum Press, 1990; *The CANSCAIP Companion: A Biographical Record of Canadian Children's Authors, Illustrators, and Performers,* edited by Barbara Greenwood, Markham, Ontario, Pembroke, 1994; *Meet Canadian Authors and Illustrators,* Richmond Hill, Ontario, Scholastic Canada, 1994; *Writing Stories, Making Pictures,* Toronto, Canadian Children's Book Centre, 1994; *Behind the Story: The Creators of Our Best Children's Books and How They Do It,* edited by Barbara Greenwood, Markham, Ontario, Pembroke, 1995.

* * *

The relationship between the past and the present, particularly in the patterns of family life and family conflict, is a major theme in the novels of Margaret Buffie. While each of the novels centers on a psychic encounter with apparitions of people long dead, these apparitions are not there simply to add a thrill of horror. Rather, they appear for the benefit of the young protagonist; through witnessing the painful events of the past she discovers a resolution of some of her problems with her own family in the present. Buffie's novels are both psychic thrillers and realistic novels about family problems; for the most part, she holds these two elements in a successful balance and knits them together to a conclusion that is absorbing and credible.

The protagonists in Buffie's novels have much in common with each other. All are girls in their mid-teens who are seriously angry with their parents—and with good reason. In three novels, Buffie tells of a girl whose family is on the verge of falling apart, and in a fourth describes a family that has already disintegrated. Badly needing love and security, but too angry, proud, and inexperienced to express her needs effectively, each of these girls finds herself in a situation where her wishes are completely disregarded by adults absorbed in their own difficulties. Helping to bring about the crisis is the family's removal to a less familiar environment: Liz in *Who is Frances Rain?* goes with her family to stay with her grandmother on a lake in northern Manitoba; after her mother leaves home, Rachel in *The Guardian Circle* is sent to live with her father's Aunt Irene in a peculiar old house shared by a lot of peculiar old people; Jessica in *My Mother's Ghost* reluctantly leaves the city to help her father run a guest ranch. In *The Dark Garden* the family does not leave their home, but their routine is disrupted when Thea suffers traumatic amnesia after a bicycle accident. In addition, conflict is created by her parents' planned sabbatical trip to England.

In *Who is Frances Rain?* and *My Mother's Ghost,* some of the adults hope that the move will help to heal rifts within the family. Liz's mother has remarried rather hastily after a painful desertion and divorce, and her three children are full of resentment and bitterness against both mother and stepfather, whose new marriage is already in serious difficulties. Jessica blames her father for the recent death of her young brother and the subsequent withdrawal of her mother into a serious depression. In both these novels, as well as in *The Dark Garden,* the problems of the adults, while presented through the eyes of a hostile teenager, are evoked with sympathy and understanding, and their at least partial resolution at the end of the novel has been prepared for convincingly. In *The Guardian Circle* the background of Rachel's parents' incompatibility is effectively evoked, but in the later parts of the novel the individuality of the characters and their problems are overshadowed by sensationalist psychic scenes involving a poltergeist, ouiji board, and seance. The psychic struggle for Rachel's spirit between her two ghostly uncles—one good and one evil—is somehow less interesting, as well as less plausible, than the earlier realistic accounts of family events which had led her to outbursts of anger and despair.

In *Who is Frances Rain?, My Mother's Ghost,* and *The Dark Garden,* the present-day problems of the protagonist and her family are more successfully interwoven with the ghost story. In the first novel, by putting on a pair of old spectacles she has found on a deserted island, Liz becomes witness to a series of scenes between two women living on the island decades earlier—her gradual discovery of the identity of these women and their link to the crisis in her own family life provides a very satisfying puzzle to solve. Virtually all of the characters in this story prove to be more vulnerable and more lovable than they initially appear. The story reveals, on a number of different levels, the human need for love. This theme recurrs in *The Dark Garden* as Thea works to recover her own memory and resolve the questions of the ghost who invades her life. The conflict that runs through Liz's family history between people who crave to live in the country or the wilderness and people who seek city sophistication is a theme in Buffie's other novels as well. This is most notable in *My Mother's Ghost,* wherein these opposite urges, embodied in the two parents, are shown to have horribly destructive consequences for their children both in Jessica's own family and in the former occupants of the ranch house, where restless spirits re-enact their tragedy.

Buffie's heroines are doughty girls who may make themselves thoroughly unpleasant to other people; they also have a fundamental honesty and the courage to look squarely at situations and not shrink from unpleasant encounters, psychic or otherwise. All four tell their own stories in first-person narratives that generally have an authentic ring of adolescent dialogue and introspection, although occasionally the sense of voice is damaged by an over-elaborate turn of phrase. Each heroine receives significant help from a wise older person and an attractive and almost improbably sympathetic boy of her own age. The romantic interest of these boys is, however, kept subordinate to the family problems the protagonist is learning to understand—and at least partially to resolve, through her disturbing encounters with the ghosts. The early scenes, where the girls first become aware of the eruption of the uncanny into their lives, are vividly created, and Buffie's skill in bringing the ghosts to full life in the climatic confrontations has increased from novel to novel. While she has not achieved the eerie, poetic mastery of such writers in this genre as William Mayne and Margaret Mahy, she tells a compelling story, the chilling, ghostly encounters of which have relevance to everyday life and its problems.

—Gwyneth Evans, updated by Alexandra MacLennan

BULL, Angela (Mary)

Nationality: British. **Born:** Angela Mary Leach, Halifax, Yorkshire, 28 September 1936. **Education:** Badminton School, Bristol, 1948-54; Edinburgh University (Mackenzie prize, 1959), 1955-59, M.A. (honours) in English 1959; St. Hugh's College, Oxford, 1959-61. **Family:** Married Martin Wells Bull in 1962; one son and one daughter. **Career:** English teacher, Casterton School, Kirkby Lonsdale, Westmorland, 1961-62; assistant, Medieval Manuscript Room, Bodleian Library, Oxford, 1962-63. **Awards:** Children's Rights Workshop Other award, 1980. **Agent:** David Higham Associates, 5-8 Lower John Street, Golden Square, London W1R 4HA, England. **Address:** The Vicarage, Gargrave, Skipton, North Yorkshire BD23 3NQ, England.

Publications for Children

Fiction

The Friend with a Secret, illustrated by Lynton Lamb. London, Collins, 1965; New York, Holt Rinehart, 1967.
Wayland's Keep, illustrated by Shirley Hughes. London, Collins, 1966; New York, Holt Rinehart, 1967.
Child of Ebenezer. London, Collins, 1974.
Treasure in the Fog, illustrated by Joanna Worth. London, Collins, 1976.
Griselda. London, Collins, 1977.
The Doll in the Wall, illustrated by Gareth Floyd. London, Collins, 1978.
The Bicycle Parcel, illustrated by Jane Paton. London, Hamish Hamilton, 1980.
The Accidental Twins, illustrated by Jill Bennett. London, Faber, 1982.
A Hat for Emily, illustrated by Sue Dolman. London, Collins, 1986.
The Visitors, illustrated by Valerie Littlewood. London, Hamish Hamilton, 1986.
Green Gloves, illustrated by Thelma Lambert. London, Blackie, 1987.
A Wish at the Baby's Grave. London, Hippo, 1988.
The Jiggery-Pokery Cup, illustrated by Pauline Hazelwood. London, Scholastic, 1990.
Pink Socks and Green Gloves. London, Puffin, 1992.
The Shadows of Owlsnap. London, Dent, 1992; London, Orion Children's Books, 1995.
The Winter Phantoms, London, Dent, 1993; London, Orion Children's Books, 1995.
The Kitchenmaid, illustrated by Tony Morris. London, Ginn, 1994.
Yellow Wellies, illustrated by Marie Louise Comer. London, Blackie, 1994.
Blue Shoes, illustrated by Jacqui Thomas. London, Oxford University Press, 1996.
Purple Buttons, illustrated by Sue Porter. London, Oxford University Press, 1996.
A Patchwork of Ghosts. London, Scholastic Children's Books, 1996.
The Terrible Birthday Present, illustrated by Jacqui Thomas. London, Oxford University Press, 1998.

Other

The Machine Breakers: The Story of the Luddites. London, Collins, 1980.
Anne Frank, illustrated by Stephen Gulbis. London, Hamish Hamilton, 1984.
Florence Nightingale, illustrated by Karen Heywood. London, Hamish Hamilton, 1985.
Marie Curie, illustrated by Edward Mortelmans. London, Hamish Hamilton, 1986.

Elizabeth Fry, illustrated by Edward Mortelmans. London, Hamish Hamilton, 1987.

Publications for Young Adults

Up the Attic Stairs (novel). London, Virago, 1989.

Publications for Adults

With Gillian Avery, *Nineteenth Century Children: Heroes and Heroines in English Children's Stories 1780-1900.* London, Hodder and Stoughton, 1965.
Noel Streatfeild: A Biography. London, Collins, 1984.

*

Angela Bull comments:

Because history sparks my imagination, nearly all my stories have a historical, or partly historical, background. My earliest stories were mainly Victorian. I spent two years researching Victorian children's books, and considerably longer building up a collection of them, so I had plenty of material to draw on. Social conditions were such that Victorian children did not have the independence necessary for active adventures. Their dramas tended to be inward, especially the drama of personal relationships; and this was the theme of most of my early books.

Moving from fiction to biography, I thought it was important to stress the ideas and ideals which motivated my subjects; and so, when I recently turned back to fiction, I found myself continuing to write about people and ideas, particularly in *Up the Attic Stairs,* which traces 80 years of the women's movement, as illustrated in the lives of four generations of provincial girls.

(1998) In the last few years I have been diverted on to ghost stories. Publishers seem to consider this a painless way of presenting history; sugaring the pill, perhaps. Although working out the mechanics of ghostly apparitions can be tiresome, I enjoy the scope for drama and emotion which a supernatural story offers.

* * *

In the last twenty years Angela Bull has diversified her work in a way that could not easily have been foreseen in the 1960s and 1970s. The main body of her fiction writing at the present time comprises five longish, meticulously structured novels with fairly obvious moral or social implications, and seven short but still carefully plotted and purposeful stories for children in the middle age-ranges. She has also produced a number of simple, generously illustrated stories for younger readers. All the full-length stories are set at least partly in Edwardian or Victorian times, while in all three categories the chief protagonists are usually female.

Not much need be said about the stories for younger readers. Most, like *The Accidental Twins* or *Blue Shoes,* are gentle mini-comedies with realistic modem backgrounds, never didactic but reflecting a muted consensus view about social behaviour. *The Kitchenmaid,* written for a history teaching series, gives a vivid picture of life below stairs in a Victorian mansion, and *A Hat for Emily* is also a period piece. In the medium-length category, *A Wish at the Baby's Grave, The Shadows of Owlsnap, The Winter Phantoms,* and *A Patchwork of Ghosts* are time-switch fantasies or ghost stories with a purpose, the purpose being to draw a sharp contrast between the comfortable lives of British middle class children and the hardships or prejudices endured by less fortunate groups in earlier times. The portrayal of pre-Victorian child mill-workers struggling for survival in *The Winter Phantoms* is truly heart-rending, though the time-shift machinery has an awkwardness about it and the modern characters seem rather wooden. The same may be said of *A Patchwork of Ghosts,* where the family of wealthy Edwardians torn apart by selfishness and lethal jealousy are decidedly more convincing than their latter-day descendants.

The other three stories in this medium-length group are quite dissimilar. *Treasure in the Fog* is a Victorian nighttime adventure, not very probable and somewhat marred by an over-prominent moral lesson. *The Visitors* is a domestic episode from one of Queen Victoria's Scottish tours, this time totally convincing, rich in atmosphere and with its morality embedded in the action. *The Doll in the Wall* is a modern holiday adventure in which the author contrives to set up and resolve a genuine mystery involving nine or ten distinct characters and providing some quite digestible food for thought about the hazards of insensitive do-gooding.

Up the Attic Stairs stands apart from the rest of Bull's work as a novel for young adults with no child characters. The author's approach here is quite openly didactic, her aims being to trace the development of feminist movements in Britain in the present century and to encourage readers to think about the variety of relationships now open to women. There is a very large cast of characters; the central contemporary figure, Gabriel, who struggles to reconcile her passion for costume and design with the demands of everyday life, is an interesting creation, but the others seem to exist largely to represent lifestyles. With its non-chronological narrative and constantly changing viewpoints this book certainly calls for a high level of concentration, but those who have the stamina to persist with it may well gain something in the way of social awareness or empathy.

The other full-length novels, all published before 1980, are definitely for children, though they do have quite complicated plots and large casts of characters. The two shortest, *Griselda* and *Wayland's Keep,* should certainly appeal to girls from a wide range of ages who happen to have an interest in tracing their ancestors, since family trees are a major concern in both. *Griselda* is basically a heart-warming story of town and country, with a strong element of fairy-tale romance in the second half, whereas *Wayland's Keep* is more down-to-earth, presenting a sharp contrast between a squabbling modern family and their tragically afflicted Victorian ancestors. Both stories are good examples of their kind, with the moralistic strain rarely obtruding too far, but in my opinion the two remaining novels with their greater range and depth are the most notable of all. *A Friend with a Secret* recreates most convincingly the divisions of society and the pervasive influence of religion in a Victorian seaport; for child-readers there is also an ingenious plot, a succession of dramatic incidents, and a memorable heroine in Olivia Lang, whose family adhere strictly to the Children of Ebenezer sect. *In Child of Ebenezer,* published nine years later, Bull is at her very best. Here there is a political as well as a religious dimension as the Anglo-Irish conflict impinges on the lives of children and adults in three contrasting families. Sombre and even tragic elements are part of the pattern, but in the best Victorian tradition, courage and loyalty have their reward in the end. The richness of this book gives it a claim to classical status, and it should certainly be kept in print.

—Alasdair K.D. Campbell

BULLA, Clyde Robert

Nationality: American. **Born:** King City, Missouri, 9 January 1914. **Education:** Bray school, 1920-26; King City High School, 1926-27. **Career:** Farmer until 1942; linotype operator and columnist, *Tri-County News,* King City, 1942-47. **Awards:** George G. Stone Center for Children's Books award, 1968; Christopher award, 1972. **Agent:** Bill Berger Associates, 444 East 58th Street, New York, New York 10022. **Address:** 1230 Las Flores Drive, Los Angeles, California 90041, U.S.A.

Publications for Children

Fiction

The Donkey Cart, illustrated by Lois Lenski. New York, Crowell, 1946.
Riding the Pony Express, illustrated by Grace Paull. New York, Crowell, 1948.
The Secret Valley, illustrated by Grace Paull. New York, Crowell, 1949.
Surprise for a Cowboy, illustrated by Grace Paull. New York, Crowell, 1950.
A Ranch for Danny, illustrated by Grace Paull. New York, Crowell, 1951.
Johnny Hong of Chinatown, illustrated by Dong Kingman. New York, Crowell, 1952.
Song of St. Francis, illustrated by Valenti Angelo. New York, Crowell, 1952.
Star of Wild Horse Canyon, illustrated by Grace Paull. New York, Crowell, 1953.
Eagle Feather, illustrated by Tom Two Arrows. New York, Crowell, 1953.
Squanto, Friend of the White Men, illustrated by Peter Burchard. New York, Crowell, 1954; as *Squanto, Friend of the Pilgrims,* New York, Crowell, 1969.
Down the Mississippi, illustrated by Peter Burchard. New York, Crowell, 1954.
White Sails to China, illustrated by Robert Henneberger. New York, Crowell, 1955.
The Poppy Seeds, illustrated by Jean Charlot. New York, Crowell, 1955.
John Billington, Friend of Squanto, illustrated by Peter Burchard. New York, Crowell, 1956.
The Sword in the Tree, illustrated by Paul Galdone. New York, Crowell, 1956.
Old Charlie, illustrated by Paul Galdone. New York, Crowell, 1957.
Ghost Town Treasure, illustrated by Don Freeman. New York, Crowell, 1957.
Pirate's Promise, illustrated by Peter Burchard. New York, Crowell, 1958.
The Valentine Cat, illustrated by Leonard Weisgard. New York, Crowell, 1959.
Three-Dollar Mule, illustrated by Paul Lantz. New York, Crowell, 1960.
The Sugar Pear Tree, illustrated by Taro Yashima. New York, Crowell, 1961.
Benito, illustrated by Valenti Angelo. New York, Crowell, 1961.
Viking Adventure, illustrated by Douglas Gorsline. New York, Crowell, 1963.
Indian Hill, illustrated by James Spanfeller. New York, Crowell, 1963.
White Bird, illustrated by Leonard Weisgard. New York, Crowell, 1966; London, Macdonald, 1969.
The Ghost of Windy Hill, illustrated by Don Bolognese. New York, Crowell, 1968.
Mika's Apple Tree: A Story of Finland, illustrated by Des Asmussen. New York, Crowell, 1968.
The Moon Singer, illustrated by Trina Schart Hyman. New York, Crowell, 1969.
New Boy in Dublin: A Story of Ireland, illustrated by Jo Polseno. New York, Crowell, 1969.
Pocahontas and the Strangers, illustrated by Peter Burchard. New York, Crowell, 1971.
Open the Door and See All the People, illustrated by Wendy Watson. New York, Crowell, 1972.
Dexter, illustrated by Glo Coalson. New York, Crowell, 1973.
The Wish at the Top, illustrated by Chris Conover. New York, Crowell, 1974.
Shoeshine Girl, illustrated by Leigh Grant. New York, Crowell, 1975.
Marco Moonlight, illustrated by Julia Noonan. New York, Crowell, 1976.
The Beast of Lor, illustrated by Ruth Sanderson. New York, Crowell, 1977.
Keep Running, Allen!, illustrated by Satomi Ichikawa. New York, Crowell, 1978.
With Michael Syson, *Conquista!,* illustrated by Ronald Himler. New York, Crowell, 1978.
Last Look, illustrated by Emily McCully. New York, Crowell, 1979.
Daniel's Duck, illustrated by Joan Sandin. New York, Harper, 1979.
The Stubborn Old Woman, illustrated by Anne Rockwell. New York, Crowell, 1980.
My Friend the Monster, illustrated by Michele Chessare. New York, Crowell, 1980.
A Lion to Guard Us, illustrated by Michele Chessare. New York, Crowell, 1981.
Almost a Hero, illustrated by Ben Stahl. New York, Dutton, 1981.
Poor Boy, Rich Boy, illustrated by Marcia Sewall. New York, Harper, 1982.
Dandelion Hill, illustrated by Bruce Degen. New York, Dutton, 1982.
Charlie's House, illustrated by Arthur Dorros. New York, Crowell, 1983.
The Cardboard Crown, illustrated by Michele Chessare. New York, Crowell, 1984.
The Chalk Box Kid, illustrated by Thomas B. Allen. New York, Random House, 1987.
Singing Sam, illustrated by Susan Magurn. New York, Random House, 1989.
The Christmas Coat, illustrated by Sylvie Wickstrom. New York, Knopf, 1990.

Other

A Dog Named Penny (reader), illustrated by Kate Seredy. Boston, Ginn, 1955.

Stories of Favorite Operas, illustrated by Robert Galster. New York, Crowell, 1959.
A Tree Is a Plant, illustrated by Lois Lignell. New York, Crowell, 1960; London, A. and C. Black, 1962.
What Makes a Shadow?, illustrated by Adrienne Adams. New York, Crowell, 1962; London, A. and C. Black, 1965.
The Ring and the Fire: Stories from Wagner's Niebelung Operas, illustrated by Clare and John Ross. New York, Crowell, 1962.
St. Valentine's Day, illustrated by Valenti Angelo. New York, Crowell, 1965; as *The Story of Valentine's Day,* illustrated by Susan Estelle Kwas, New York, HarperCollins, 1999.
More Stories of Favorite Operas, illustrated by Joseph Low. New York, Crowell, 1965.
Lincoln's Birthday, illustrated by Ernest Crichlow. New York, Crowell, 1966.
Washington's Birthday, illustrated by Don Bolognese. New York, Crowell, 1967.
Flowerpot Gardens, illustrated by Henry Evans. New York, Crowell, 1967.
Stories of Gilbert and Sullivan Operas, illustrated by James and Ruth McCrea. New York, Crowell, 1968.
Jonah and the Great Fish, illustrated by Helga Aichinger. New York, Crowell, 1970.
Joseph the Dreamer, illustrated by Gordon Laite. New York, Crowell, 1971.
A Grain of Wheat: A Writer Begins. Boston, Godine, 1985.

Translator, *Noah and the Rainbow,* by Max Bollinger, illustrated by Helga Aichinger. New York, Crowell, 1972.

Publications for Adults

Novel

These Bright Young Dreams. Philadelphia, Penn, 1941.

*

Manuscript Collections: Kerlan Collection, University of Minnesota, Minneapolis; University of Oregon Library, Eugene; de Grummond Collection, University of Southern Mississippi, Hattiesburg.

Music: Incidental music for plays—*The Bean-Pickers,* 1952, *A Change of Heart,* 1952, and *Strangers in a Strange Land,* 1952, all by Lois Lenski; songs—*We Are Thy Children,* 1952, *Songs of Mr. Small,* 1954, *Songs of the City,* 1956, *Up to Six,* 1956, *At Our House,* 1959, and *When I Grow Up,* 1960, all by Lois Lenski.

Clyde Robert Bulla comments:

When I was a boy I made up my own stories. Some were high adventure, with buried treasure, perilous journeys, and hair-breadth escapes. Some were quiet, about everyday people like those I knew. Others were about the mysteries of life—things that puzzled and haunted me and left me with a sense of wonder. These are the stories I began to write a long time afterward and the stories I am writing now.

* * *

Clyde Robert Bulla attracts young people to his books by building his plots quickly and believably, using simple language without condescension. He skillfully interweaves the plot with a sense of good and evil, right and wrong. The story of *White Bird* is contingent upon love as known and interpreted by the foundling boy and by the seemingly stern farmer who raises him. Plot develops from their relationship.

In *The Moon Singer* complex ideas are described in simple language. The peasant boy sings because he must, and sings especially well when the moon is full. His need to sing might be a microcosm of the need of any artist, the inner drive to create in spite of, rather than because of, society. There is the gentle yet persuasive suggestion that this is more than just a medieval tale of a boy who felt compelled to sing.

Shoeshine Girl is the story of stubborn and defiant 10-year-old Sarah Ida who must have money in her pocket and goes to work for Al, the shoeshine man. Bulla retains his direct style, and Sarah Ida's growth toward self-acceptance and a concern for other people is believable and sound.

The Stubborn Old Woman evokes the folktale tradition. She refuses to leave her endangered cliff farm or to show any sympathy for the orphan girl who determinedly seeks the old woman's guardianship for herself and her eight siblings. The happy solution to both problems and the cadence of language give texture to the tale.

Charlie in *Charlie's House* runs away from his peasant family, hoping to find a better life in London. He is caught, sold into white slavery, and sent to America as an indentured servant. His first master loses Charlie's bond in a card game with a cousin, a cruel man. Charlie's pluck and determination help him in his new life, even in his attempt to escape. Bulla recreates life in the early 19th century with a clear sense of time and place. Charlie emerges as a credible boy whose life and adventures are well placed and blend well with the background Bulla provides.

Gregory is *The Chalk Box Kid.* When his father loses his job the family must move and Gregory has to share his room with Uncle Max, an unlikable man. He has no place of his own, but finds his escape in an abandoned building where he creates a fanciful chalk garden on the walls, the start of a possible resolution of his problems. At school, where his imagination and artistic ability are recognized and appreciated, Gregory finds that life need not be so grim. The teachers' compassionate interest and the friendliness of the students bolster his spirit. The sensitive picture of a struggling blue-collar family lends credence to the story. Bulla blends fantasy and reality smoothly and effectively, and provides a moving experience for the reader.

Whether Bulla is retelling stories of the opera or the Old Testament, or writing historical fiction or stories that reflect different cultures or inner conflict, there is a satisfying consistency in his treatment of each theme. His more than 60 books reveal integrity and respect for his audience.

—Mae Durham Roger

BURGESS, Thornton Waldo

Nationality: American. **Born:** Sandwich, Massachusetts, 14 January 1874. **Education:** Sandwich High School, graduated 1891; attended business college in Boston, one year. **Family:** Married 1)

Nina E. Osborne in 1905 (died 1906), one son; 2) Fannie P. Johnson in 1911 (died 1950). **Career:** Worked as cashier and bookkeeper in shoe store; office boy, 1895, reporter, 1895-1911, and literary and household editor for Orange Judd weeklies, Phelps Publishing Company, New York; wrote as W.B. Thornton for *Country Life in America,* New York, 1902-03; associate editor, *Good Housekeeping,* New York, 1904-11; story columnist, Associated News, 1912-20, and New York *Herald Tribune* syndicate, 1920-48; founder, and commentator for six years, Burgess Radio Nature League. **Award:** Litt.D.: Northeastern University, Boston, 1938. **Died:** 5 June 1965.

Publications for Children

Fiction

Mother West Wind series:
Old Mother West Wind, illustrated by George Kerr. Boston, Little Brown, 1910; London, Lane, 1937.
Mother West Wind's Children, illustrated by George Kerr. Boston, Little Brown, 1911; London, Lane, 1937.
Mother West Wind's Animal Friends, illustrated by George Kerr. Boston, Little Brown, 1912; London, Lane, 1937.
Mother West Wind's Neighbors, illustrated by George Kerr. Boston, Little Brown, 1913; London, Lane, 1950.
Mother West Wind "Why" Stories, illustrated by Harrison Cady. Boston, Little Brown, 1915; London, Lane, 1950.
Mother West Wind "How" Stories, illustrated by Harrison Cady. Boston, Little Brown, 1916; London, Lane, 1950.
Mother West Wind "When" Stories, illustrated by Harrison Cady. Boston, Little Brown, 1917; London, Lane, 1950.
Mother West Wind "Where" Stories, illustrated by Harrison Cady. Boston, Little Brown, 1918; London, Lane, 1950.
Boy Scouts series:
The Boy Scouts of Woodcraft Camp, illustrated by C.S. Corson. Philadelphia, Penn, 1912.
The Boy Scouts on Swift River, illustrated by C.S. Corson. Philadelphia, Penn, 1913.
The Boy Scouts on Lost Trail, illustrated by C.S. Carson. Philadelphia, Penn, 1914.
The Boy Scouts in a Trapper's Camp, illustrated by F.A. Anderson. Philadelphia, Penn, 1915.
Bedtime Story-Books (illustrated by Harrison Cady):
The Adventures of Reddy Fox. Boston, Little Brown, 1913; London, Lane, 1931.
The Adventures of Johnny Chuck. Boston, Little Brown, 1913; London, Lane, 1938.
The Adventures of Peter Cottontail. Boston, Little Brown, 1914; London, Lane, 1931.
The Adventures of Unc' Billy Possum. Boston, Little Brown, 1914; London, Lane, 1940.
The Adventures of Mr. Mocker. Boston, Little Brown, 1914; London, Lane, 1938.
The Adventures of Jerry Muskrat. Boston, Little Brown, 1914.
The Adventures of Danny Meadow Mouse. Boston, Little Brown, 1915; London, Lane, 1939.
The Adventures of Grandfather Frog. Boston, Little Brown, 1915; London, Lane, 1931.
The Adventures of Chatterer, The Red Squirrel. Boston, Little Brown, 1915; London, Lane, 1931.
The Adventures of Sammy Jay. Boston, Little Brown, 1915; London, Lane, 1932.
The Adventures of Buster Bear. Boston, Little Brown, 1916; London, Lane, 1931.
The Adventures of Old Mr. Toad. Boston, Little Brown, 1916; London, Lane, 1932.
The Adventures of Prickly Porky. Boston, Little Brown, 1916; London, Lane, 1932.
The Adventures of Old Man Coyote. Boston, Little Brown, 1916; London, Lane, 1938.
The Adventures of Paddy the Beaver. Boston, Little Brown, 1917; London, Lane, 1931.
The Adventures of Poor Mrs. Quack. Boston, Little Brown, 1917; London, Lane, 1932.
The Adventures of Bobby Coon. Boston, Little Brown, 1918; London, Lane, 1939.
The Adventures of Jimmy Skunk. Boston, Little Brown, 1918; London, Lane, 1938.
The Adventures of Bob White. Boston, Little Brown, 1919; London, Lane, 1940.
The Adventures of Ol' Mistah Buzzard. Boston, Little Brown, 1919.
Wishing-Stone Stories, illustrated by Harrison Cady. Boston, Little Brown, 1935.
Tommy and the Wishing Stone. New York, Century, 1915.
Tommy's Wishes Come True. Boston, Little Brown, 1921.
Tommy's Change of Heart. Boston, Little Brown, 1921.
The Burgess Big Book of Green Meadow Stories, illustrated by Harrison Cady. Boston, Little Brown, 1932.
Happy Jack. Boston, Little Brown, 1918; London, Lane, 1934.
Mrs. Peter Rabbit. Boston, Little Brown, 1919; London, Lane, 1934.
Bowser the Hound. Boston, Little Brown, 1920; London, Lane, 1934.
Old Granny Fox. Boston, Little Brown, 1920; London, Lane, 1934.
Green Forest series (illustrated by Harrison Cady):
Lightfoot the Deer. Boston, Little Brown, 1921; London, Lane, 1933.
Blacky the Crow. Boston, Little Brown, 1922; London, Lane, 1933.
Whitefoot the Wood Mouse. Boston, Little Brown, 1922; London, Lane, 1933.
Buster Bear's Twins. Boston, Little Brown, 1923; London, Lane, 1933.
Smiling Pool series (illustrated by Harrison Cady):
Billy Mink. Boston, Little Brown, 1924; London, Lane, 1935.
Little Joe Otter. Boston, Little Brown, 1925; London, Lane, 1935.
Jerry Muskrat at Home. Boston, Little Brown, 1926; London, Lane, 1935.
Longlegs the Heron. Boston, Little Brown, 1927; London, Lane, 1935.
Happy Jack Squirrel Helps Unc' Billy, illustrated by Harrison Cady. New York, Eggers, 1924.
Grandfather Frog Gets a Ride, illustrated by Harrison Cady. New York, Eggers, 1924.
A Great Joke on Jimmy Skunk, illustrated by Harrison Cady. New York, Eggers, 1924.
Baby Possum's Queer Voyage, illustrated by Harrison Cady. New York, Eggers, 1924.

The Neatness of Bobby Coon, illustrated by Harrison Cady. New York, Eggers, 1924.
Digger the Badger Decides to Stay, illustrated by Harrison Cady. New York, Eggers, 1924.
Animal Folk, illustrated by Harrison Cady. Akron, Ohio, Saalfield, 1925.
Friendly Animals, illustrated by Harrison Cady. Akron, Ohio, Saalfield, 1925.
Picture Book, illustrated by Harrison Cady. Akron, Ohio, Saalfield, 1925.
The Christmas Reindeer, illustrated by Rhoda Chase. New York, Macmillan, 1926.
Cubby Bear Books (*A Frightened Baby, Farmer Brown's Boy Becomes Curious, What Farmer Brown's Boy Did, Cubby Bear Has a Mind of His Own, An Imp of Mischief, Cubby in Mother Brown's Pantry, A Woe-Begone Little Bear, Cubby Gets a Bath, Milk and Honey, Cubby Finds an Open Door*), illustrated by Nina Jordan. Racine, Wisconsin, Whitman, 10 vols., 1929.
Wee Little Books (*Little Joe Otter's Slide, Betty Bear's Lesson, Unc' Billy Gets Even, Whitefoot's Secret, Jimmy Skunk's Justice, Peter Rabbit's Carrots*). Racine, Wisconsin, Whitman, 6 vols., 1929-33.
Tales from the Storyteller's House, illustrated by Lemuel Palmer. Boston, Little Brown, 1937; London, Lane, 1938.
While the Story-Log Burns, illustrated by Lemuel Palmer. Boston, Little Brown, 1938; London, Lane, 1939.
Animal Stories, illustrated by Harrison Cady. New York, Platt and Munk, 1942; as *The Animal World of Thornton Burgess,* 1961.
  Bobby Coon's Mistake. New York, Platt and Munk, 1940; as *Bobby Coon's Surprise,* 1961.
  The Three Little Bears. New York, Platt and Munk, 1940; as *A Bear Scare,* 1961.
  Peter Rabbit Proves a Friend. New York, Platt and Munk, 1940; as *Peter Rabbit Goes Scouting,* 1961.
  Reddy Fox's Sudden Engagement. New York, Platt and Munk, 1940; as *Reddy Fox Leaves in a Hurry,* 1961.
  Paddy's Surprise Visitor. New York, Platt and Munk, 1940; as *Paddy the Beaver's Visitor,* 1961.
  A Merry Coasting Party. New York, Platt and Munk, 1940; as *Fun at the Queer Trail,* 1961.
  Young Flash, The Deer. New York, Platt and Munk, 1940; as *Flash the Young Deer,* 1961.
  A Robber Meets His Match. New York, Platt and Munk, 1940; as *Robber the Rat Loses Out,* 1961.
Little Color Classics (*Little Pete's* [*Chuck's, Red's*] *Adventure*), illustrated by Harrison Cady. Springfield, Massachusetts, McLoughlin, 3 vols., 1941-42.
Nature Stories (illustrated by Harrison Cady):
  On the Green Meadows. Boston, Little Brown, 1944.
  At the Smiling Pool. Boston, Little Brown, 1945.
  The Crooked Little Path. Boston, Little Brown, 1946.
  The Dear Old Briar-Patch. Boston, Little Brown, 1947.
  Along Laughing Brook. Boston, Little Brown, 1949.
  At Paddy the Beaver's Pond. Boston, Little Brown, 1950.
Baby Animal Stories, illustrated by Phoebe Erickson. New York, Grosset and Dunlap, 1949.
A Thornton Burgess Picture Story Book, illustrated by Nino Carbe. New York, Garden City Publishing, 1950.
The Littlest Christmas Tree, illustrated by Mary and Carl Hauge. New York, Wonder Books, 1954.
Peter Rabbit and Reddy Fox, illustrated by Mary and Carl Hauge. New York, Wonder Books, 1954; as *Peter Cottontail and Reddy Fox,* 1974.
Aunt Sally's Friends in Fur; or, The Woodhouse Night Club, photographs by the author. Boston, Little Brown, 1955.
Stories Around the Year, illustrated by Phoebe Erickson. New York, Grosset and Dunlap, 1955.
Little Peter Cottontail, illustrated by Phoebe Erickson. New York, Wonder Books, 1956.
Bedtime Stories, illustrated by Mary and Carl Hauge. New York, Grosset and Dunlap, 1959; London, Macdonald, 1960.
Nature Stories, illustrated by Adrianna Mazza. New York, Wonder Books, 1959; London, Golden Pleasure Books, 1966.
The Million Little Sunbeams, illustrated by Harrison Cady. Toledo, Ohio, Six Oaks Press, 1963.
The Burgess Book of Nature Lore: Adventures of Tommy, Sue, and Sammy with Their Friends of Meadow, Pool, and Forest, illustrated by Robert Candy. Boston, Little Brown, 1965.

Poetry (illustrated by Harrison Cady)

Animal Paint Book. Akron, Ohio, Saalfield, 1925.
Peter Cottontail's Own Paint Book. Akron, Ohio, Saalfield, 1925.
Animal Pictures. Akron, Ohio, Saalfield, 1925.
Mother Nature's Song and Story Book, music by Rebecca Richards, illustrated by Henry Johnson and Lemuel Palmer. Boston, Worley, 1938.

Other

Natural History series:
  The Burgess Bird Book for Children, illustrated by Louis Agassiz Fuertes. Boston, Little Brown, 1919.
  The Burgess Animal Book for Children, illustrated by Louis Agassiz Fuertes. Boston, Little Brown, 1920.
  The Burgess Flower Book for Children. Boston, Little Brown, 1923.
  The Burgess Seashore Book for Children, illustrated by W.H. Southwick and George Sutton. Boston, Little Brown, 1929.
Wild Flowers We Know [*We Should Know*]. Racine, Wisconsin, Whitman, 2 vols., 1929.
Birds You Should Know, illustrated by Louis Agassiz Fuertes. Boston, Little Brown, 1933.
The Book of Animal Life, with Thora Stowell. Boston, Little Brown, 1937.
The Little Burgess Animal [and *Bird*] *Book for Children,* illustrated by Louis Agassiz Fuertes. Chicago, Rand McNally, 2 vols., 1941.
Nature Almanac, illustrated by Phoebe Erickson. New York, Grosset and Dunlap, 1949.

Publications for Adults

Other

The Bride's Primer, Being a Series of Quaint Parodies on the Ways of Brides..., with others. New York, Phelps, 1905.
Now I Remember: Autobiography of an Amateur Naturalist. Boston, Little Brown, 1960.

*

Bibliography: *Thornton Waldo Burgess: A Descriptive Book Bibliography* by Wayne W. Wright, Sandwich, Massachusetts, Burgess Society, 1979.

Manuscript Collections: Burgess Society, Sandwich, Massachusetts; Sandwich Public Library.

* * *

Thornton Waldo Burgess, one of the most prolific writers of animal stories for children, published over 70 books during his lifetime and over fifteen thousand story columns during his 44 years of daily syndication in American newspapers. His animal stories belong to a genre which includes, at one extreme, stories featuring animals which are actually humans masquerading in feathers or fur, and, at the other, stories presenting the cycles of animal life with strict and often brutal realism. Burgess's animal stories fall somewhere around the middle of this generic continuum. His bestiary is made up of anthropomorphic creatures which reason, converse, and gossip. They do not, however, ride bicycles, snooze in armchairs, or sew the clothes they are always depicted as wearing in the whimsical Harrison Cady illustrations which accompany almost all of Burgess's works. In short, Burgess's animals are hybrids: they operate in a realm at once natural and yet infused with a human moral code. This accommodation between the human and the bestial allowed Burgess to entertain his youthful readers while offering them moral guidance and teaching them nature lore. These three intentions inform nearly all of Burgess's works.

Burgess's career was determined by the success of *Old Mother West Wind* (1910), the first of eight volumes comprising the Mother West Wind series. Each volume offers a collection of short moral fables and explanatory tales which focus on a particular animal's dominant physical traits or behavioral characteristics and conclude with a moral lesson. For example, in the tenth story of *Old Mother West Wind,* "How Sammy Jay Was Found Out," Burgess's narrator presents the vain, lazy Sammy Jay making fun of Johnny Chuck's industrious preparations for winter. When Old Mother West Wind hears that someone has been stealing Happy Jack Squirrel's store of nuts, she convenes all the creatures, blows a stick from Sammy's nut-filled nest, and exposes him as the thief. As a punishment for stealing and as a sign that those who steal can no longer be trusted. Sammy Jay is made to cry "Thief! Thief!" whenever he opens his mouth. The uncomplicated dramatic conflicts of these tales, their unambiguous moral truths, and their genial animal characters account for the prevailing innocence and charm which helped to make the Mother West Wind series among Burgess's most popular works.

In the 20 volumes of the Bedtime Story-Books series, initiated in 1913 with *The Adventures of Reddy Fox* and *The Adventures of Johnny Chuck,* Burgess attempted to render the subject animal of each volume in the round, to delineate its habits, pursuits, and pastimes while refraining from any depiction of natural processes which might be considered unpleasant or pathetic by his child audience. In addition, the formula for the Bedtime Story-Books called for the inclusion of didactic verses and moral asides prompted by life incidents or characteristic habits of the animal depicted. This series, and the Mother West Wind volumes, comprise Burgess's best-known works.

Two other series show Burgess's intention to instruct children in nature lore. The Wishing-Stone series aimed to produce that empathy necessary to convert the child audience into protectors and conservators of wild creatures. Through the agency of the wishing stone, Tommy Brown is transformed into the various animals which he had hitherto menaced. His understanding enlarged through his experiences, Tommy retires his rifle and retrieves his traps, vowing to become a friend to nature's children. In the Bird, Animal, Flower, and Seashore Books for Children, Burgess presented illustrations and information about North American flora and fauna. In each volume, Burgess arranged this encyclopedic information in highly contrived and generally unsuccessful narrative frames involving Peter Rabbit's tuition by various instructors, from Old Mother Nature herself to the sharp-tongued Jenny Wren.

Burgess's works strike many modern readers as formulaic and didactic. His plots lack complexity, and his supra-zoological animal characters are often one-dimensional, embodying a single emblematic characteristic. Because Burgess occasionally descends into racial, sexual, and jingoistic stereotyping, his works often seem dated, though their concern for conservation is certainly current. In spite of their literary flaws, however, Burgess's works continue to be read. The animals which populate Burgess's world are charming, cuddly and gently whimsical; they live and play in a pastoral landscape which reflects the author's longing for a simpler time out of time, an edenic rural past. The world depicted is governed by a clear, unambiguous moral code framed from traditional homespun rural values. The works of Thornton Waldo Burgess thus share the appeal of all popular formulaic literature which reduces life's disturbing complexities into simple and comfortable clarity.

—Lucien L. Agosta

BURMAN, Ben Lucien

Nationality: American. **Born:** Covington, Kentucky, 12 December 1896. **Education:** Harvard University, Cambridge, Massachusetts, A.B. 1920. **Military Service:** United States Army Field Artillery in France during World War I: wounded; Legion of Honor, for journalism, 1947. **Family:** Married Alice Caddy in 1927 (died 1977). **Career:** Reporter, Boston *Herald,* 1920; assistant city editor, Cincinnati *Times Star,* 1921; special writer, New York *Sunday World,* 1922; staff writer, Newspaper Enterprise Association, 1927; war correspondent, in Africa and the Middle East, 1941. **Died:** 12 November 1984.

Publications for Children

Fiction (illustrated by Alice Caddy)

High Water at Catfish Bend. New York, Messner, 1952; with *Seven Stars for Catfish Bend,* London, Kestrel, 1975.

Seven Stars for Catfish Bend. New York, Funk and Wagnalls, 1956; with *High Water at Catfish Bend,* London, Kestrel, 1975.

The Owl Hoots Twice at Catfish Bend. New York, Taplinger, 1961; with *Blow a Wild Bugle for Catfish Bend,* London, Kestrel, 1975.

Blow a Wild Bugle for Catfish Bend. New York, Taplinger, 1967; with *The Owl Hoots Twice at Catfish Bend,* London, Kestrel, 1975.

High Treason at Catfish Bend. New York, Vanguard Press, and London, Kestrel, 1977.
The Strange Invasion of Catfish Bend. New York, Vanguard Press, 1980.
Thunderbolt at Catfish Bend. New York, Wieser and Wieser, 1984.

Publications for Adults

Novels

Mississippi. New York, Cosmopolitan, 1929; as *Then There's Cripple Creek,* London, Lutterworth, 1930.
Steamboat round the Bend. New York, Farrar and Rinehart, 1933; London, Nelson, 1936.
Blow for a Landing. Boston, Houghton Mifflin, 1938; London, Lutterworth Press, 1948.
Rooster Crows by Day. New York, Dutton, 1945; London, Lutterworth Press, 1948.
Everywhere I Roam. New York, Doubleday, 1949; London, Longman, 1957.
The Four Lives of Mundy Tolliver. New York, Messner, 1953; London, Vallentine Mitchell, 1955.
The Street of the Laughing Camel. New York, McGraw Hill, 1959.
The Sign of the Praying Tiger. New York, New American Library, 1966.

Other

Big River to Cross: Mississippi Life Today. New York, Day, 1940.
Miracle on the Congo: Report from the Free French Front. New York, Day, 1942; London, Macmillan, 1943.
Children of Noah: Glimpses of Unknown America. New York, Messner, 1951.
It's a Big Country: America Off the Highways. New York, Reynal, 1956.
It's a Big Continent. New York, McGraw Hill, 1961.
The Generals Wear Cork Hats. New York, Taplinger, 1963; London, Harrap, 1965.
Look Down That Winding River: An Informal Profile of the Mississippi. New York, Taplinger, and Newton Abbot, Devon, David and Charles, 1973.

*

Manuscript Collections: University of Kentucky, Lexington; Tulane University, New Orleans.

* * *

Ben Lucien Burman was born in the river town of Covington, Kentucky, and is most famous for his stories of the rural south, particularly his novels of the Mississippi River. He started writing in childhood, was editor of his high school paper and later had reporting jobs on several major newspapers.

Burman wrote a series of six books for children—and I would certainly recommend them for adults as well—about the talented and wise animals of Catfish Bend. Catfish Bend is located in a swampy area on the banks of the Mississippi River, and the animals who live there include Doc Raccoon, Judge Black (a black watersnake), and the frogs of the Indian Bayou Glee Club. In *High Treason at Catfish Bend* the whole lot of them are taken with the idea that the humans who are moving to Paradise Valley in California may have found paradise. Life is hard enough in Catfish Bend to warrant their making the long trek to the West Coast to find heaven-on-earth. Their difficulties along the way, and their very human ups-and-downs, are reassuring to a child reader. The Catfish Bend crowd, like the characters in Burman's books for older readers, are down and out. And their approach to the high and mighty (mostly human beings living in fancy northern states) is both understandable and sympathetic. Further, these animals know that it is important for survival to help one another, to stick together. "Fighting is the stupidest thing in the world," says the raccoon to some newcomers to the area. He then tells them about the pact the animals at Catfish signed during the big flood, when they'd found out they couldn't stay alive if they kept on quarreling.

Burman, like Mark Twain, is as popular with adult as with adolescent readers. Like Twain, he brings alive the rural poor who have few advantages and limited life experiences. These individuals, animals or human, usually looked down upon as unintelligent and dull, are shown in Burman's tales as amazingly acute, perceptive, and considerably better able to cope than are some of their more sophisticated critics. Their views of nature, of people, and of the world around them, can be excruciatingly insightful and funny. One of Burman's stories for adults, *The Sign of the Praying Tiger,* takes a Kentucky mountaineer out of his rural setting to New Orleans, all the way to Singapore, and finally to the exotic Malaysian island of "Menang," in a great, yarn-spinning adventure.

Beneath Burman's outright foolishness lies a concern and respect for individuals at the bottom, who most often remain unnoticed and unappreciated. Burman makes these individuals, human and animal, come alive and their societies—with their hopes, inconsistencies, and frustrations—come alive as well. He does this in a gentle and humorous manner, and his books provide marvelous entertainment.

—Mary Lystad

BURNETT, Frances (Eliza) Hodgson

Nationality: American (originally British: emigrated with her mother to New Market, Tennessee, 1865, became citizen, 1905. **Born:** Cheetham Hill, Manchester, England, 24 November 1849. **Education:** Various schools in Manchester. **Family:** Married 1) Dr. Swan Moses Burnett in 1873 (divorced 1898), two sons; 2) Stephen Townesend in 1900 (separated 1901; died 1914). **Career:** Lived in Knoxville, 1869-74, Europe, 1875-76, and Washington, D.C., 1877-87; after 1887 traveled frequently between the U.S. and Europe. **Died:** 29 October 1924.

Publications for Children

Fiction

Little Lord Fauntleroy. New York, Scribner, and London, Warne, 1886.

Sara Crewe; or, What Happened at Miss Minchin's. London, Warne, and New York, Scribner, 1888.
Editha's Burglar. Boston, Jordan Marsh, 1888.
Editha's Burglar, and Sara Crewe. London, Warne, 1888.
Little Saint Elizabeth and Other Stories. New York, Scribner, and London, Warne, 1890.
Children I Have Known. London, Osgood McIlvaine, 1892; as *Giovanni and the Other: Children Who Have Made Stories,* New York, Scribner, 1892.
Piccino and Other Child Stories. New York, Scribner, 1894; as *The Captain's Youngest, Piccino, and Other Child Stories,* London, Warne, 1894.
Two Little Pilgrims' Progress: A Story of the City Beautiful. New York, Scribner, and London, Warne, 1895.
A Little Princess, Being the Whole Story of Sara Crewe Now Told for the First Time. New York, Scribner, and London, Warne, 1905.
Racketty-Packetty House. New York, Century, 1906; London, Warne, 1907.
Queen Silver-Bell. New York, Century, 1906; as *The Troubles of Queen Silver-Bell,* London, Warne, 1907.
The Cozy Lion, as Told by Queen Crosspatch. New York, Century, 1907; London, Stacey, 1972.
The Spring Cleaning, as Told by Queen Crosspatch. New York, Century, 1908; London, Stacey, 1973.
The Good Wolf. New York, Moffat, 1908.
Barty Crusoe and His Man Saturday. New York, Moffat, 1909.
The Land of the Blue Flower. New York, Moffat, 1909; London, Putnam, 1912.
The Secret Garden, illustrated by Charles Robinson. New York, Stokes, and London, Heinemann, 1911.
The Lost Prince. New York, Century, and London, Hodder and Stoughton, 1915.
The Way to the House of Santa Claus: A Christmas Story. New York and London, Harper, 1916.
The Little Hunchback Zia. New York, Stokes, and London, Heinemann, 1916.

Plays

The Real Little Lord Fauntleroy, adaptation of her own novel (produced London, Boston, and New York, 1888).
Editha's Burglar, with Stephen Townesend, adaptation of the novel by Burnett (produced Neath, Glamorgan, 1890; as *Nixie,* produced London, 1890).
A Little Princess, adaptation of her novel *Sara Crewe* (as *A Little Unfairy Princess,* produced London, 1902; as *A Little Princess,* produced London and New York, 1903). Published in *Treasury of Plays for Children,* edited by Montrose J. Moses, Boston, Little Brown, 1921.
Racketty-Packetty House, adaptation of her own story (produced New York, 1912).

PUBLICATIONS FOR ADULTS

Novels

That Lass o' Lowrie's. New York, Scribner, and London, Warne, 1877.
Dolly: A Love Story. Philadelphia, Porter and Coates, and London, Routledge, 1877; as *Vagabondia,* New York, Scribner, 1883.
Haworth's. London, Macmillan, and New York, Scribner, 1879.
Louisiana. New York, Scribner, 1880; with *That Lass o' Lowrie's,* London, Macmillan, 1880.
A Fair Barbarian. Boston, Osgood, and London, Warne, 1881.
Through One Administration. Boston, Osgood, 3 vols., 1883; London, Warne, 1883.
A Woman's Will; or, Miss Defarge. London, Warne, 1887; as *Miss Defarge,* with *Brueton's Bayou,* by John Habberton, Philadelphia, Lippincott, 1888.
The Fortunes of Philippa Fairfax. London, Warne, 1888.
The Pretty Sister of José. New York, Scribner, and London, Blackett, 1889.
A Lady of Quality.... New York, Scribner, and London, Warne, 1896.
His Grace of Osmonde.... New York, Scribner, and London, Warne, 1897.
In Connection with the De Willoughby Claim. New York, Scribner, and London, Warne, 1899.
The Making of a Marchioness. New York, Stokes, and London, Smith Elder, 1901.
The Methods of Lady Walderhurst. New York, Stokes, 1901; London, Smith Elder, 1902.
In the Closed Room. London, Hodder and Stoughton, and New York, McClure, 1904.
The Dawn of a To-morrow. New York, Scribner, 1906; London, Warne, 1907.
The Shuttle. New York, Stokes, and London, Heinemann, 1907.
My Robin. New York, Stokes, 1912; London, Putnam, 1913.
T. Tembarom. New York, Century, and London, Hodder and Stoughton, 1913.
The White People. New York, Harper, 1917; London, Heinemann, 1920.
The Head of the House of Coombe. New York, Stokes, and London, Heinemann, 1922.
Robin. New York, Stokes, and London, Heinemann, 1922.

Short Stories

Surly Tim and Other Stories. New York, Scribner, and London, Ward Lock, 1877.
Theo: A Love Story. Philadelphia, Peterson, and London, Ward Lock, 1877.
Pretty Polly Pemberton: A Love Story. Philadelphia, Peterson, 1877; London, Routledge, 1878.
Kathleen: A Love Story. Philadelphia, Peterson, and London, Routledge, 1878.
Miss Crespigny: A Love Story. Philadelphia, Peterson, and London, Routledge, 1878.
Earlier Stories. New York, Scribner, 1878; London, Routledge, 1879.
Earlier Stories, second series. New York, Scribner, 1878; London, Chatto and Windus, 1879.
A Quiet Life, and The Tide on the Moaning Bar. Philadelphia, Peterson, 1878; London, Routledge, 1879.
Our Neighbour Opposite. London, Routledge, 1878.
Jarl's Daughter and Other Stories. Philadelphia, Peterson, 1879.
Natalie and Other Stories. London, Warne, 1879.

Plays

That Lass o' Lowrie's, with Julian Magnus, adaptation of the novel by Burnett (produced New York, 1878).

Esmeralda, with William Gillette (produced Newark, New Jersey, and New York, 1881; as *Young Folks' Ways,* produced London, 1883). New York, French, 1881(?).
Phyllis, adaptation of her novel *The Fortunes of Philippa Fairfax* (produced London, 1889).
The Showman's Daughter, with Stephen Townesend (produced Worcester, 1891; London, 1892).
The First Gentleman of Europe, with Constance Fletcher (produced New York and London, 1897).
A Lady of Quality, with Stephen Townesend, adaptation of the novel by Burnett (produced Detroit and New York, 1897; Cambridge and London, 1899).
The Pretty Sister of José, adaptation of her own novel (produced Syracuse, New York, New York City, and London, 1903).
That Man and I, adaptation of her novel *In Connection with the De Willoughby Claim* (produced London, 1903; New York, 1904).
The Dawn of a Tomorrow, adaptation of her own novel (produced New York, 1909; Liverpool and London, 1910).

Other

The Drury Lane Boys' Club. Washington, D.C., Moon Press, 1892.
The One I Knew the Best of All: A Memory of the Mind of a Child (autobiography). New York, Scribner, and London, Warne, 1893.
In the Garden. New York, Medici Society, 1925.

*

Manuscript Collection: Princeton University Library, New Jersey.

Critical Studies: *Mrs. Ewing, Mrs. Molesworth, and Mrs. Hodgson Burnett* by Marghanita Laski, London, Barker, 1950, New York, Oxford University Press, 1951; *Waiting for the Party: The Life of Frances Hodgson Burnett 1849-1924* by Ann Thwaite, London, Secker and Warburg, and New York, Scribner, 1974; *Frances Hodgson Burnett* by Phyllis Bixler, Boston, Twayne, 1984.

* * *

The bulk of Frances Hodgson Burnett's work for children was written in the 19th century, but her two best books—the final version of *Sara Crewe,* called *A Little Princess,* and *The Secret Garden*—both belong to the 20th. These are the two books which are still read and enjoyed by thousands of children every year, not as period pieces but in exactly the same way as they read contemporary writers. A third book, *Little Lord Fauntleroy,* is also enjoyed; but the critic, anyway, if not the child reader, is more affected in his judgment by the date it was written.

Burnett was well established as a writer for adults when she published *Fauntleroy.* Her early novels were compared with those of George Eliot, and in 1883 an article in the *Century* magazine listed her as one of those with Henry James "who hold the front rank today in general estimation." Her first stories for children were short ones, which appeared in *St. Nicholas.* It was only after the phenomenal success of *Fauntleroy* that she regularly published children's books. The quality of these was variable, and her most impressive work continued to be for adults until the publication of *A Little Princess* in 1905.

The history of this book is curious and is worth going into in some detail. Indeed, a comparison of the three versions of the story gives a rewarding insight into Burnett's working methods and her development as a children's writer. *Sara Crewe* first appeared in 1887. It was a story drawing on some of her experiences as a child at the Miss Hadfields' school in Manchester, but was set in London. Like nearly all Burnett's stories, its theme is the reversal of fortune. In *Fauntleroy* Cedric Erroll had left a small house in New York, wearing clothes made out of his mother's old gown, for the life of the heir to an earldom and an English castle. Sara Crewe had gone to school as an heiress and been reduced, after her bankrupt father's death, to living in an attic as a drudge and an outcast. In both cases, the moral is firmly drawn and cannot be missed by even the most unperceptive child reader: we are what we are, and our outward trappings and possessions have nothing to do with real nobility.

In 1902 Burnett turned the story of *Sara Crewe* into a play. The following year, her editor at Scribner's came up with the suggestion that she write a new, longer version of the book under the play's title, *A Little Princess,* incorporating the new material she had introduced in the play. He wanted the book quickly, the play was still running and sales would be splendid. Fortunately at that point Burnett was committed to two other plays. The book was not rushed and was not finally finished until November 1904.

In the original version, Sara's experiences up until her father's death took no more than four and a half pages. In *A Little Princess* they take ninety. The earlier book is little more than a series of notes for the rich rewards of the full-scale novel. The basic story is an excellent one, and the final version demonstrates with what tremendous skill Burnett was able to make the most of it. The detail is excellent too: Burnett was always good at detail. As she once said, "It is not enough to mention they have tea; you must specify the muffins."

A Little Princess is a great deal more interesting than *Fauntleroy,* partly because Sara is seen not from the adult point of view, but from her own viewpoint. *The Secret Garden* is even more interesting. "It is the most satisfying children's book I know," the critic Marghanita Laski once wrote, and countless people have shared that view. Burnett wrote much of the book in the rose garden of Great Maytham Hall in Rolvenden in Kent. All her life, she said, she had felt "a sort of curious kinship with things which grew," and *The Secret Garden* is, among many other things, an expression of this kinship.

The place is important: the atmosphere of the huge house and garden is romantic and mysterious. The small orphan from India comes to Misselthwaite across the moors. Her arrival is strongly reminiscent of that of Jane Eyre at Thornfield, and there are other points of resemblance between the two books. Burnett did not in fact know Yorkshire well, and her setting owes more to the Brontës than to real life. She stayed with Lord Crewe at Fryston Hall in 1895, but that is her only recorded visit to the area. We don't know where she acquired her knowledge of the Yorkshire dialect Dickon and his family speak so convincingly, but she had always been interested in dialect, ever since the days as a child in Manchester and Salford when one of her greatest pleasures was to sneak out and gossip with the "back street" children.

The setting, as I say, is important, but much more important are the children. The most original thing about the book is that its heroine and one of its heroes are both thoroughly unattractive children. The first sentence makes it compulsive reading: "When Mary Lennox was sent to Misselthwaite Manor to live with her uncle, everybody said she was the most disagreeable-looking child ever seen." And Colin is a hysterical hypochondriac. It is the entirely convincing transformation of these two unhappy children that gives the story its great appeal, even to readers who do not find the natural world particularly attractive.

Other Victorian writers had made deprived children behave quite inappropriately, but Burnett's instinct has since been confirmed by child psychologists. A child denied love does behave as Mary behaved. But *The Secret Garden* is far more than a parable or a demonstration of child behaviour. With Burnett the story always came first, and she was far too good a writer to spoil it with propaganda. Only at the beginning of Chapter 27 does she lapse, with explicit explanations of her symbolism and a bad definition of what the rest of the book conveys so subtly: "to let a sad thought or a bad one get into your mind is as dangerous as letting a scarlet fever germ get into your body." *The Secret Garden* was a book of the new, the 20th century. Far from encouraging the attitudes instilled in Frances as a child ("speak when you're spoken to, come when you're called..."), it suggested children should be self-reliant and have faith in themselves, that they should listen, not to their elders and betters, but to their own hearts and consciences.

The Secret Garden did not make a great impact on its first appearance, but it has never been out of print. It is this book which establishes Mrs. Burnett as undoubtedly one of the most important writers of the century.

—Ann Thwaite

BURNFORD, Sheila (Philip Cochrane)

Nationality: Canadian (originally British (Scottish): emigrated to Canada, 1951). **Born:** Sheila Philip Cochrane Every, Scotland, 11 May 1918. **Education:** St. George's School, Edinburgh; Harrogate College, Yorkshire; studied in Germany. **Family:** Married David Burnford in 1941; three daughters. **Career:** Served in the Royal Naval Hospitals Voluntary Aid Detachment, England, 1939-41; ambulance driver, 1941-42. **Award:** Canadian Library Association Book of the Year Medal, 1963. **Died:** 20 April 1984.

Publications for Children

Fiction

The Incredible Journey, illustrated by Carl Burger. Boston, Little Brown, 1961; revised edition, London, Hodder and Stoughton, 1961.

Mr. Noah and the Second Flood, illustrated by Michael Foreman. Toronto, McClelland and Stewart, London, Gollancz, and New York, Praeger, 1973.

Publications for Adults

Novel

Bel Ria. London, Joseph, 1977; Boston, Little Brown, 1978.

Other

The Fields of Noon (autobiographical essays). Toronto, McClelland and Stewart, Boston, Little Brown, and London, Hodder and Stoughton, 1964.

Without Reserve (on the Indians of Ontario). Toronto, McClelland and Stewart, Boston, Little Brown, and London, Hodder and Stoughton, 1969.

One Woman's Arctic. London, Hodder and Stoughton, 1972; Boston, Little Brown, 1973.

* * *

Of Sheila Burnford's two books for children, *The Incredible Journey* is by far the most popular. In the same genre as Anna Sewell's *Black Beauty,* the story is a sentimental account of the adventures of three pets who survive incredible hardships in an attempt to return to their owners. A young Labrador Retriever, a Siamese cat, and an old Bull Terrier regularly overcome tremendous problems—attack by wild animals, hunger, inclement weather, to name a few—and eventually do succeed in becoming reunited with their owners. Perhaps such an adventure is possible in reality, but it seems implausible that three house pets could so readily adapt to the rigours of wilderness survival in northern Ontario.

The author ascribes just about every human characteristic except speech to her protagonists. In fact, her animals could easily be three children since they think and act much more like people than animals. Allusions are made, for example, to the terrier's "irrepressible air of sly merriment" and his "apologetic grin." The relationship between the three pets seems to be unrealistically altruistic. On one occasion, the cat attacks a bear cub in an effort to save one of the dogs and later gives up his supper in order that the dog might regain his strength. References are made to the Labrador Retriever as the group's "gentle, worried leader." All of the animals, indeed, are invested with commendable traits and human-like emotions. Burnford created a memorable story but not one that is a fair representation of the true nature of animals.

Mr. Noah and the Second Flood is an entirely different type of book. Obviously the vehicle for a strong anti-pollution crusade, this overly long contemporary fable about Noah's descendents is sometimes humorous, sometimes depressing. The theme of man's carelessness in upsetting the ecological balance is very heavily stressed to the detriment of the story. The characters tend to be stereotypes—Mrs. Noah is the epitome of the befuddled, kind-hearted grandmother and Noah is ever the serene patriarch. Most of the humor is derived from observations made by the isolated Noah family on events taking place in the world outside their mountain retreat. The story would probably be more successful in a format less reminiscent of a picture book and cut down to half of its present length.

—Fran Ashdown

BURNINGHAM, John (Mackintosh)

Nationality: British. **Born:** Farnham, Surrey, 27 April 1936. **Education:** Summerhill School, Leiston, Suffolk; Central School of Art, London, 1956-59, diploma. **Family:** Married the illustrator Helen

Oxenbury in 1964; one son and two daughters. **Awards:** Library Association Kate Greenaway medal, 1964, 1971; Boston *Globe-Horn Book* award, 1972; Maschler award, 1984. **Address:** c/o Jonathan Cape Ltd., 32 Bedford Square, London WC1B 3EL, England.

PUBLICATIONS FOR CHILDREN (ILLUSTRATED BY THE AUTHOR)

Fiction

Borka: The Adventures of a Goose with No Feathers. London, Cape, 1963; New York, Random House, 1964.
Trubloff: The Mouse Who Wanted to Play the Balalaika. London, Cape, 1964; New York, Random House, 1965.
ABC, illustrated by the author and Leigh Taylor. London, Cape, 1964; Indianapolis, Bobbs Merrill, 1967.
Humbert, Mister Firkin and the Lord Mayor of London. London, Cape, 1965; Indianapolis, Bobbs Merrill, 1967.
Cannonball Simp. London, Cape, 1966; Indianapolis, Bobbs Merrill, 1967.
Harquin, The Fox Who Went Down to the Valley. London, Cape, 1967; Indianapolis, Bobbs Merrill, 1968.
Seasons. London, Cape, 1969; Indianapolis, Bobbs Merrill, 1971.
Mr. Gumpy's Outing. London, Cape, and New York, Holt Rinehart, 1970.
Mr. Gumpy's Motor Car. London, Cape, 1973; New York, Crowell, 1976.
Come Away from the Water, Shirley. London, Cape, and New York, Crowell, 1977.
Time to Get Out of the Bath, Shirley. London, Cape, and New York, Crowell, 1978.
Would You Rather.... London, Cape, and New York, Crowell, 1978.
The Shopping Basket. London, Cape, and New York, Crowell, 1980.
Avocado Baby. London, Cape, and New York, Crowell, 1982.
Granpa. London, Cape, and New York, Crown, 1984.
Where's Julius? London, Cape, and New York, Crown, 1986.
John Patrick Norman McHennessy: The Boy Who Was Always Late. London, Cape, and New York, Crown, 1987.
Oi! Get Off Our Train. London, Cape, 1989; as *Hey! Get Off Our Train,* New York, Crown, 1990.
Owen John Owen—blwlch-y-gwyntyn hwyr unwaith eto. N.p., Dref Wen, 1990.
H'e! Imigh Leat Den Traein. Dublin, Gill and Macmillan, 1991.
Aldo. London, Cape, 1991; New York, Crown, 1992.
Harvey Slumfenburger's Christmas Present. Cambridge, Massachusetts, Candlewick, 1993.
Courtney. London, Cape, and New York, Crown, 1994.
Cloudland. London, Cape, 1996.

Other

Birdland: Wall Frieze. London, Cape, and New York, Braziller, 1966.
Lionland: Wall Frieze. London, Cape, 1966.
Storyland: Wall Frieze. London, Cape, 1966.
Jungleland: Wall Frieze. London, Cape, 1968.
Wonderland: Wall Frieze. London, Cape, 1968.
Around the World: Two Wall Friezes. London, Cape, 1972.
Around the World in Eighty Days. London, Cape, 1972.
Little Books (readers; *The Baby, The Rabbit, The School, The Snow, The Blanket, The Cupboard, The Dog, The Friend*). London, Cape, 8 vols., 1974-75; New York, Crowell, 8 vols., 1975-76.
Number Play (*Count Up, Read One, Ride Off, Pigs Plus, Just Cats, Five Down*). London, Walker, and New York, Viking Press, 6 vols., 1983.
First Words (*Cluck Baa, Skip Trip, Slam Bang, Sniff Shout, Wobble Pop, Jangle Twang*). London, Walker, 6 vols., 1984; New York, Viking Kestrel, 6 vols., 1984-85.
Play and Learn (*123, Opposites, Colours*). London, Sainsbury-Walker, 3 vols., 1985; as *It's Great to Learn!* (*ABC, 123, Opposites, Colors*), New York, Crown, 4 vols., 1986; as *First Steps: Letters, Numbers, Colors, Opposites,* Cambridge, Massachusetts, Candlewick, 1994; *123* as *John Burningham's Numbers Book,* London, Walker, 1987; *ABC* as *John Burningham's Alphabet Book,* London, Walker, 1987; *Colours* as *John Burningham's Colours Book,* London, Walker, 1987; *Opposites* as *John Burningham's Opposites Book,* London, Walker, 1987; *ABC* as *John Burningham's ABC,* New York, Crown, 1993.
England. London, Cape, 1992.

*

Illustrator: *Chitty-Chitty Bang-Bang* by Ian Fleming, 1964; *The Extraordinary Tug-of-War* by Letta Schatz, 1968; *The Wind in the Willows* by Kenneth Grahame, 1983.

* * *

John Burningham is one of the most outstanding author-illustrators of children's books writing today, creating books that delight both children and their parents and teachers. He manages to appeal to a young child's imagination without appearing condescending, and he creates models of what books for children learning to read should be. Burningham uses vocabulary that is controlled but not restrictive, and his use of repetition of key phrases encourages children to join in and anticipate the sequence of the story as it is read to them, and gives them confidence as they begin to read for themselves. His books abound with humour and their subjects ensure their attraction to children.

Burningham burst onto the children's book scene in 1963 with *Borka: The Adventures of a Goose with No Feathers,* for which he won the Kate Greenaway medal for illustration. It is a gentle story of a goose who never develops feathers and is rejected by the other geese. It ends happily with Borka living in Kew Gardens amongst so many different species of bird that she is no longer out of place.

In the early 1970s Burningham produced a classic among picture books with *Mr. Gumpy's Outing.* The story is a simple one in which Mr. Gumpy goes on a boat trip and is persuaded to take on board some children, a rabbit, a cat, a dog, a pig, a sheep, a chicken, a calf, and a goat. Despite their undertaking to behave and not to antagonize the other passengers, the inevitable happens and they all end up in the water. The tension is well built up and the ending is no less enjoyable for being predictable. The sequel, *Mr. Gumpy's Motor Car,* features the same characters; this time a car ride ends in chaos.

Two books that capture exactly what it is like to be a child are *Come Away from the Water, Shirley* and *Time to Get Out of the Bath, Shirley.* Shirley's exciting make-believe world is shown in stark contrast to her parents' drab everyday world. As her mother nags her about trivial, mundane things, Shirley conjures up fantastic adventures in her imagination. Although the subject is treated humorously the underlying note is a serious one: Shirley's parents are either unable or unwilling to appreciate her fantasies and they are, by implication, the poorer for not doing so. Burningham returns to the same theme in *Where's Julius?,* but on an altogether more cheerful note. Julius can never join his parents for meals because he is always doing something more important. At each meal his reasons for not joining them become more farfetched, but Mr. and Mrs. Troutbeck are able to accept and enjoy Julius's fantasy world and, uncomplaining, take his meals to him on a tray. The illustrations of Mr. Troutbeck scaling the Changa Benang mountains or Mrs. Troutbeck shooting the rapids on the Chico Neeko River, tray held aloft, are marvelous interpretations of the text.

The Shopping Basket and *Avocado Baby* also depict the stuff of children's fantasies. The latter is the story of a sickly baby born into a family of weaklings. After being fed an avocado pear he becomes progressively stronger until he is a "superbaby," carrying the shopping, frightening away burglars, and fighting off bullies in the park. The illustrations of the baby in his blue stretch suit accomplishing these feats of strength make the book a winner. *The Shopping Basket* is, to my mind, one of the best children's books ever conceived. Not only is it a nicely moralistic tale of a rather weedy-looking boy who is able to get the better of his physically stronger assailants by using his intelligence, but it is also a near perfect book for children beginning to read. The vocabulary is controlled, there is plenty of repetition, and new words are introduced within a format that becomes familiar to the child as he reads the story. Steven is sent shopping by his mother and on his way home is accosted by a variety of greedy animals all demanding some of his shopping. He outwits them by challenging them to do something; each animal cannot resist the challenge and falls into the trap. Each time a wordless picture shows the hilarious outcome of the challenge.

John Patrick Norman McHennessy: The Boy Who Was Always Late, is in similar vein. John Patrick is always late for school because of the extraordinary things that happen to him on the way. He manages to get out of some extremely tricky situations in a humorous way, but is always severely punished for his lateness. Although the tables are turned on the stern, unbelieving teacher in the end, the lasting impression is of the unjust punishment John Patrick has to endure.

Granpa stands out as being different in style and tone to Burningham's other books. It depicts the relationship between a small girl and her grandfather in a series of interchanges between the two. The humour here is subtle, unlike the slapstick humour of some books. For example, the little girl says, "When we get to the beach can we stay there forever?" to which her grandfather replies "Yes, but we must go back for our tea at four o'clock." The emphasis is as much on what is left unsaid as what is said, as in the spread that shows them walking away from each other and the words "That was not a nice thing to say to Granpa." The illustrations are a mixture of sepia line drawings and pastel-coloured pictures which balance the text perfectly throughout. The poignant ending with the little girl staring at an empty chair, suggesting Granpa's death, has been too much for many adult reviewers to bear, but children, it seems, cope much better.

Burningham's later books retain this certain wistfulness underlying the humour, for example the implied loneliness of a child largely ignored by its parents. In *Aldo* and *Courtney* he is once again the champion of the child. Aldo, a large imaginary rabbit, is a lonely little girl's only friend. He protects her from bullies at school and reads her stories at night, but the overall feeling is of a sad child deprived of a happy family life. In *Courtney* the children want a dog, but their snobbish parents disapprove of the unwanted mongrel they bring home. Courtney turns out to be an amazing cook, violinist, juggler—you name it Courtney can do it. Then one day he disappears without warning, to which the cynical parents' response is that you can only trust thoroughbreds. Courtney, however, continues to keep an eye on the family from afar.

Harvey Slumfenburger's Christmas Present has a very tired Father Christmas hitching his way to the top of the Roly Poly Mountain to deliver Harvey Slumfenburger's Christmas present because it is the only one he will get. His journey is very funny and the use of language is Burningham at his best in this touching tale.

Oi! Get Off Our Train has a conservation message. A little boy, told to stop playing with his train and go to sleep, dreams he is on the train with his pajama-case dog. Every time they stop a different animal gets on the train. Their initial reaction is to shout "Oi! Get Off Our Train," but each animal is an endangered species and has a good reason why it should be saved. The final page has his mother asking if the elephant, the seal, the crane, the tiger, and the polar bear have anything to do with him—pure understated John Burningham!

In *Cloudland* Burningham develops in an exciting way with a strikingly original idea for the artwork, using photographic images of clouds as the background onto which his characteristic sketchy figures are cut out and overlaid, creating a three-dimensional effect. The story combines, with Burningham's consummate ease, the reality of a child falling off a cliff with the fantasy of being saved by Cloud Children, who make him light and airy by saying some magic words. Albert loses all sense of time and reality with the Cloud Children and thoroughly enjoys himself jumping off clouds, swimming in rain and walking on the path left by an aeroplane. It is not until he sees the lights of the city below that he suddenly remembers his family and wants to go home. Again, in true understated Burningham style, Albert's parents, who were last seen distraught on the mountain, welcome him home, safely tucked up in bed, without questioning where he has been. This ability to leave these mundane details unexplained mirrors the capacity of children to do the same.

—Fiona Lafferty

BURTON, Virginia Lee

Nationality: American. **Born:** Newton Center, Massachusetts, 30 August 1909. **Education:** California School of Fine Arts, San Francisco, 1926-28; Boston Museum School, 1930. **Family:** Married George Demetrios in 1931; two sons. **Career:** Sketcher, Boston *Transcript,* 1928-31. **Award:** American Library Association Caldecott Medal, 1943. **Died:** 15 October 1968.

PUBLICATIONS FOR CHILDREN (ILLUSTRATED BY THE AUTHOR)

Fiction

Choo Choo: The Story of a Little Engine Who Ran Away. Boston, Houghton Mifflin, 1937; London, Faber, 1944.

Mike Mulligan and His Steam Shovel. Boston, Houghton Mifflin, 1939; London, Faber, 1941.
Calico the Wonder Horse; or, The Saga of Stewy Stinker. Boston, Houghton Mifflin, 1941; London, Faber, 1942.
The Little House. Boston, Houghton Mifflin, 1942; London, Faber, 1946.
Katy and the Big Snow. Boston, Houghton Mifflin, 1943; London, Faber, 1947.
Maybelle the Cable Car. Boston, Houghton Mifflin, 1952.

Other

Life Story. Boston, Houghton Mifflin, 1962.

*

Illustrator: *Sad-Faced Boy* by Arna Bontemps, 1937, and *The Fast Sooner Hound* by Bontemps and Jack Conroy, 1942; *Manual of American Mountaineering* edited by Kenneth A. Henderson, 1941; *Don Coyote* by Leigh Park, 1942; *Song of Robin Hood* edited by Anne Malcolmson, 1947; *The Emperor's New Clothes* by Hans Christian Andersen, 1949.

Manuscript Collections: Free Library, Philadelphia; University of Oregon Library, Eugene.

* * *

Writing her books was always the most difficult part, Virginia Lee Burton claimed—a hundred times harder than drawing pictures, of which she never tired. After her few ventures with illustrating stories written by others, she wanted to be in complete control of every aspect of her books, so she wrote them herself. But rather than let an idea develop freely into a story, she approached the text in terms of composing it to fit space on an illustrated page.

Despite this limitation, her texts are effective, especially when read aloud. Continual elimination of extra words plus trial-and-error to assure each word used was the best choice produced simple and strong texts. Burton found a subject she wanted to draw (a machine or a house); then she worked out a story with that subject as heroine by planning a series of drawings to enliven a thin plot thread. The text length was dictated by the number of pages available and the situations for drawings to be spread over them. The actual attention to individual words came last, as she created the text to accompany the pictures. The final step came after the text was set, when she would cut or substitute words so the shape of the type pattern would be an integral part of the page design.

That *Choo Choo* is still a success after more than 50 years says a great deal about the effectiveness of the story despite changing times. The spare but energetic text, full of read-aloud sound effects, catches the exuberant motion in the black-and-white drawings of the runaway steam engine on its dramatic adventure. A child today who has never seen nor heard a steam engine will gain a definite idea of what one was like from hearing *Choo Choo* read, and gain, too, a comforting feeling when the naughty engine is rescued and welcomed back by its crew.

Mike Mulligan and His Steam Shovel is wordier (but only because the story covers a longer span of time) and introduces more characters, and the surprise ending takes verbal as well as visual explanation. Here Burton allows her words to express more than mere accompaniment to the action of the color pictures; she introduces suspense as Mike Mulligan wonders if his long-unemployed, old-fashioned steam-shovel, Mary Anne, really can "dig as much in a day as a hundred men could dig in a week." This suspense becomes the crux of the story as Mary Anne and Mike take on a race against time, digging the cellar for the new town hall in Popperville in just one day. Then a puzzle: how can Mike get Mary Anne out of the cellar? The entire story keeps children's interest and the ingenious ending intrigues them. This is an all-time favorite among American picture books with Mary Anne and Mike Mulligan enshrined in any Hall of Fame of children's book characters.

Burton also used the theme of machine as heroine with a snowplow in *Katy and the Big Snow* and with a cable-car in *Maybelle the Cable Car. Katy* has the appeal inherent in fighting a bad storm, a subject all children can understand. It is told with a strong, direct text. *Maybelle* is complicated, involving technical explanations about San Francisco's cable-cars and the citizens' vote to save them; and even introducing a villain, Big Bill the bus, doesn't make it an entertaining story.

Calico the Wonder Horse has more plot than her other books and the writing is as sharp and vivid as the drawings (some of her most exciting black-and-white work is in this book, which she drew as an antidote to the comics her sons read). It is parody of westerns and tall tales. The style, slap-bang in pace, is just right for this grand mix of funny desperados and frantic action.

A story with a lyric quality which comes partly from the repetition of words that sound well read aloud and partly from the repetition of patterns of the seasons and the years is *The Little House* who "shall never be sold for gold or silver and she will live to see our great-great-grandchildren's great-great-grandchildren living in her." Bestowing feminine genre on her like a ship, Burton also gives the house human qualities—curiosity, sadness, loneliness, fear, and finally happiness when she is rescued from the engulfing city and restored to country life. Children identify with having things happen to them that they cannot prevent and, like the welcoming back of naughty Choo Choo, they find great satisfaction in a happy ending; the little house being lived in and loved once more. They also absorb the complex concepts of times (the sun rising and setting each day; the moon waxing and waning each month; the seasons changing each year) and of change (from country to city to country) through just such a simple and moving story as *The Little House.*

Burton conceived of *Life Story,* "The Story of Life on Our Earth from Its Beginnings Up to Now," as a drama. Her carefully detailed color paintings are framed by the proscenium arch of a stage as an astronomer, a geologist, a paleontologist, a historian, a grandmother, and the author herself stand in the spotlight to show and tell. New scientific discoveries since 1962 may alter theories of creation and evolution and the date man first existed, but *Life Story* will always be brilliant presentation of infinitely complicated material. The text is specifically written to fit each illustration and the reduction of each enormous scientific era or area of study to a few brief sentences sometimes leads to obvious oversimplification. But the brevity is an invitation to a child to discover more. The last section recapitulates *The Little House* and the author's own experience. It also projects and shares emotionally with the reader Burton's deep respect for the designs of nature and the forces of life.

—Lee Kingman

BUTTERWORTH, Nick

Nationality: British. **Born:** Kingsbury, London, 24 May 1946. **Education:** Royal Liberty School, Havering. **Family:** Married Annette in 1975; two children. **Career:** Designer, for printers and design consultancies, including Pentagram; formed own design consultancy with three others, including friend Mick Inkpen, from 1970; began concentrating on illustration, from 1980. Regular presenter on TV-AM; contributor, *Sunday Express* magazine feature called "Upney Junction." **Address:** c/o HarperCollins Publishers, 77-85 Fulham Palace Road, Hammersmith, London W6 8JB, England.

PUBLICATIONS FOR CHILDREN (ILLUSTRATED BY THE AUTHOR)

Fiction

B. B. Blacksheep and Company. London, MacDonald, 1981.
Jack the Carpenter and His Friends. London, Walker, 1986.
Jill the Farmer and Her Friends. London, Walker, 1986.
One Snowy Night. London, HarperCollins, 1989.
My Dad Is Brilliant. London, Walker/Sainsburys 1989.
My Mum Is Fantastic. London, Walker/Sainsburys 1989.
Nursery Rhymes. London, Aurum Books, 1990.
My Grandpa Is Amazing. London, Walker, 1991.
My Granma Is Wonderful. London, Walker, 1991.
After the Storm. London, HarperCollins, 1992.
Amanda's Butterfly. London, HarperCollins, 1992.
Making Faces. London, Walker, 1993.
The Rescue Party. London, HarperCollins, 1993.
The Secret Path. London, HarperCollins, 1994.
The Cross Rabbit. London HarperCollins, 1995.
The Fox's Hiccups. London, HarperCollins, 1995.
A Year in Percy's Park. London, HarperCollins, 1995.
The Badger's Bath. London, HarperCollins, 1996.
The Hedgehog's Balloon. London, HarperCollins, 1996.
Percy Helps Out. London, HarperCollins, 1996.
Tales from Percy's Park London, HarperCollins, 1996.
The Treasure Hunt. London, HarperCollins, 1996.
One Warm Fox. London, HarperCollins, 1997.
The Owl's Lesson. London, HarperCollins, 1997.
Thud! London, HarperCollins, 1997.
All Together Now! London, HarperCollins, 1997.
Four Feathers in Percy's Park. London, HarperCollins, 1998.
Jingle Bells. London, HarperCollins, 1998.

Fiction, with Mick Inkpen

The Lost Sheep, The Precious Pearl, The Two Sons, and *The House on the Rock.* London, Marshall Pickering 1986.
The Nativity Play. London, Hodder and Stoughton, 1986.
I Wonder at the Zoo, I Wonder in the Country, I Wonder in the Garden, and *I Wonder on the Farm.* London, Marshall Pickering, 1987.
Sports Day! London, Hodder and Stoughton, 1988.
The Fox's Tale: Jesus Is Born, The Cat's Tale: Jesus at the Wedding, The Magpie's Tale: Jesus and Zacchaeus, and *The Mouse's Tale: Jesus and the Storm.* London, Marshall Pickering, 1988.
The Ten Silver Coins, The Little Gate, The Good Stranger, and *The Rich Farmer.* London, Marshall Pickering, 1989.
The School Trip. London, Hodder and Stoughton, 1990.
Just Like Jasper. London Hodder and Stoughton, 1990.
Wonderful Earth. London, Hunt and Thorpe, 1990.
Jasper's Beanstalk. London, Hodder and Stoughton, 1993.
Stories Jesus Told. London, Marshall Pickering/HarperCollins, 1996.
Opposites. London, Hodder and Stoughton, 1997.

Board Books

When It's Time for Bed. London, HarperCollins, 1994.
When We Play Together. London, HarperCollins, 1994.
When We Go Shopping. London, HarperCollins, 1994.
When There's Work to Do. London, HarperCollins, 1994.

*

Illustrator: *Jake,* 1995, *Jake Again,* 1996, and *Jake in Trouble,* 1998, all by Annette Butterworth.

Nick Butterworth comments:

When I left school, my dad's counsel was to "find something that you like doing and get somebody else to pay you for doing it."

Happily, I have been able to do exactly that! I consider myself to be very lucky to make my living in the way that I do. I have always loved drawing, ever since I was first able to hold a pencil. I also love stories and storytelling. Children's books provide, for me, the perfect combination.

Having my own children helped me to distinguish between what children actually enjoy and the rather misty-eyed nostalgia for childhood that besets some writing for children.

Reading to Ben and Amanda every night when they were small (and later when not so small!) helped me to re-enter their world. It was hugely enjoyable, great fun and a real privilege. Now they are grown up, I keep in touch with that world (like someone flitting back and forth through the wardrobe to Narnia) by spending what time I can, visiting schools and children's book festivals.

My aim is to produce books that children will love. I want them to remember them when they are grown up. It is very rewarding to get a letter from a child telling me that one of my books is their favourite. I do not set out to teach or even encourage children to read. (In any case that is usually the inevitable byproduct of giving children books that they will want to read.)

I don't like preachiness or moralising in children's books. I want to entertain and stimulate the imagination. But values will come across in any writing and if I have an emphasis that I would be happy to be known for, it is the value of friendship and good old-fashioned kindness.

I strive for excellence in writing and illustration. In picture books the two must both illuminate each other and still contribute something of their won. Design is another factor to which I attach great importance. Too often it is assumed that great pictures will make a great book, but without creative and sensitive layout and appropriate, supportive typography, a book's potential can be all but thrown away.

Conversely, a book with a good story and pictures, which is well presented and inviting to read can become an oft revisited favourite and a friend for life.

To open the cover of such a book is like opening a doorway into a world of imagination where the things that happen have the effect of sending the reader back to the real world with a new sense of possibilities.

* * *

Nick Butterworth is probably best known for the phenomenally successful character that he created in Percy the Park Keeper in his first adventure *One Snowy Night.* This overnight recognition was preceded by much hard work, however, and there will be many who do not know the wealth of material he produced before this outstanding success. His early partnership with Mick Inkpen produced some delightful books, in particular a series retelling Bible stories. They manage to convey quite complex ideas by telling them simply in the format and language of the picture book that young children understand. These are wonderful examples of the humour in language and pictures that both author/illustrators were to continue using in partnership and on their own.

The subjects of Nick Butterworth's books appeal particularly to the younger end of the picture book market, many of them portraying familiar events at home. In his "Baby and Toddler" board books he depicts the under-twos doing everyday things like shopping, playing, and getting ready for bed, all the time stressing the importance of their imaginary relationships with their toys. His illustrations are cartoon-like with crisp, white backgrounds and figures whose irresistible smiling faces are so effectively drawn with so few lines.

His books for younger children often use questions, making a spare text into a discussion point for pre-school children, as in *Jill the Farmer* and *Jack the Carpenter* in which children are invited to talk about people in various occupations and what they use in their work. *The Nativity Play, Sports Day!* and *The School Trip* all use school as the background that children will recognise and adults will enjoy the tongue-in-cheek humour that these stories provoke.

Inevitably, in books for the under-sixes, imagination plays a vital part and many lessons are taught through fantasy. In *Amanda's Butterfly* a little girl out to catch butterflies shelters from the rain in the garden shed and finds a fairy with a broken wing. The story is simple enough, but the pictures of the girl figuring out for herself how to mend the wing are enchanting and manage to suspend our disbelief.

In *Making Faces* Butterworth creates a marvellously interactive book with a mirror at the back to enable children to make the faces suggested in the text. Each double-page spread takes a new subject, asking children to imagine that they are at the fairground, on the beach, or in the jungle, or what it feels like to be a snail, or that they are ill and need medicine, or that they are simply having a boring day. The text then asks the child to make a face to show how they are feeling or to imitate something—"How do you look when you're angry?" or "Can you make an amazed bird face?" Apart from being great fun, it is a book that allows children to explore their feelings and imagine themselves in different situations.

When Nick Butterworth wrote *One Snowy Night* he hit on a perfect structure for a picture book. One snowy night Percy is about to go to bed when he hears a tapping at the door. A very cold squirrel is standing on the doorstep because his bed is full of snow and he can't sleep. Percy invites him in. Another knock, and another, and Percy is soon sharing his bed with two rabbits, a fox, a badger, two ducks, a hedgehog, and a whole family of mice. Then they all hear the noise of something coming up through the floor and run to hide. All the ingredients of a classic picture book are there—repetition making the structure predictable and safe to a point, growing suspense creating a frisson of uncertainty in the middle, and finally a shared joke and a happy ending. Young children instantly relate to the anthropomorphic relationships among the animals and their feelings for each other and for Percy, through which they learn much about their own relationships. Most important, though, are the pictures in which the marvellous expressions on the faces of the animals say it all.

Not surprisingly, Nick Butterworth has gone on to create more adventures for Percy and his animal friends in a series of equally successful stories. In *The Secret Path* Percy's well-laid plans go awry when a helpful squirrel gathers up all the string he has carefully unrolled to find his way out of the maze. The last page opens out with a picture of the maze for readers to help Percy and the animals. *The Rescue Party* shows how Percy and all the animals try to rescue a rabbit who has fallen down an old well—with another surprise ending. *After the Storm* presents Percy with the problem of finding new homes for the animals made homeless when the oak tree in which they lived is blown down in the storm. Once again, a surprise fold-out page adds to the fun.

In addition to these full-length picture books are a series of smaller books—*The Cross Rabbit, The Fox's Hiccups, The Badger's Bath, The Hedgehog's Balloon, The Owl's Lesson,* and *One Warm Fox*—in which a shorter story deals with one animal at a time. The same attention to detail in illustration and character ensure these are both good introductions to Percy for younger children and excellent supplements to the main books for those who know and love him.

There is no doubt that in Percy the Park Keeper Butterworth has created an endearing character that seems to have touched the spot. This first book and its many sequels and offshoots have never been out of print since first publication and seem set to run for a long time to come.

—Fiona Lafferty

BUTTERWORTH, Oliver

Nationality: American. **Born:** Hartford, Connecticut, 23 May 1915. **Education:** Kent School, Connecticut, 1930-33; Dartmouth College, Hanover, New Hampshire, 1933-37, A.B. 1937; Middlebury College, Vermont, M.A. 1947. **Family:** Married Miriam Brooks in 1940; three sons and one daughter. **Career:** Teacher, Kent School, 1937-48, and The Junior School, West Hartford, Connecticut, 1948-49. Since 1949 Instructor in English, Hartford College, Connecticut. **Died:** 17 September 1990.

PUBLICATIONS FOR CHILDREN

Fiction

The Enormous Egg, illustrated by Louis Darling. Boston, Little Brown, 1956; London, Sidgwick and Jackson, 1975.

The Trouble with Jenny's Ear, illustrated by Julian de Miskey. Boston, Little Brown, 1960.

The Narrow Passage, illustrated by Eric Blegvad. Boston, Little Brown, 1973.

The First Blueberry Pig, illustrated by the author. Lubec, Maine, Stone Man Press, 1986.

A Visit to the Big House, illustrated by Vinny Collins. Hartford, Connecticut, Families in Crisis, 1987.

*

Oliver Butterworth comments:

(1989) I feel that my approach to writing for children is related to a deeply rooted American skepticism of social institutions, and a corresponding tendency to believe in the independent *untaught* individual self. Mark Twain has been a strong influence on me, especially in his book *Huckleberry Finn,* and I see my child characters as "innocent" persons who find themselves having to make moral or personal decisions on the basis of their own inner feelings or instincts or convictions, much as Huck Finn has to do. I suppose Mark Twain became a model for me in part because he lived in Hartford, not far from my birthplace, and I felt he was my kind of writer, because he wrote children's books for grownups.

* * *

Some of the world's best-loved stories are "what ifs?" What if the impossible were to happen in everyday, ordinary surroundings, among ordinary folk? What if two young lads, tagging along with an archaeological expedition exploring caves in France, were to struggle through a tiny, narrow passage, impassable to adults, and discover a series of wonderful prehistoric cave paintings, with the artist still in residence? What if they struck up a wordless friendship with him, and realized that his paintings are sacred to the old, old man, and that he will suffer greatly if they are profaned by the eyes of the curious outside world? Will they tell of their discovery, or keep his secret?

Another what if: suppose Jenny, at six years old too young to understand its implications, had incredible powers of mental telepathy. Suppose the child's family was in dire need of money, immediately, and that the child, by appearing in a "whiz kid" contest, could be eligible to win a large prize. Jenny's family are honest folk, but their need is desperate, and the child is willing. What might be the consequences?

Best of all, the "what if" daydream of untold numbers of children brought up on the fantasy of the loveable dinosaur: suppose, one fine day, a common barn-yard hen should lay a truly *enormous* egg? What if that egg, carefully tended over many weeks by a tremulously hopeful young boy, should hatch into a tiny, perfect, charming triceratops? What then if the dear little creature should double his weight daily, threatening to eat the state of New Hampshire, never mind the family, out of house and home? Suppose a publicity-seeking senator declares that feeding the always-hungry triceratops (now lovingly named Uncle Beasley) to be a waste of public funds, demanding that he be stuffed and mounted as a museum exhibit? Surely the boy who has raised him from a pup, so to speak, will hurry to his defence, and just as surely a warm-hearted nation will rise to defend the threatened dinosaur from extinction....

With these three fantasies, Oliver Butterworth has earned a lasting place in the hearts of child readers, and viewers too; for his best-loved creation, *The Enormous Egg,* was filmed for television with great success. Butterworth had a rare ability to recall the substance of childhood dreams of glory; finding treasure; making contact with the unreachable past; controlling the omnipresent adult population, and setting it gently but firmly in its (subordinate) place. His adult figures are a bit dated and stereotyped: Mom never sheds her apron and can't remember difficult words like microphone, and Dad is none too sure of himself outside the farm fence; but Butterworth's lively kids have a lot of fun and adventure, and so do his countless child readers.

—Joan McGrath

C

CANNAN, Joanna (Maxwell)

Nationality: British. **Born:** Oxford, in 1898. **Education:** Wychwood School, Oxford, and in Paris. **Family:** Married H.J. Pullein-Thompson in 1918 (died 1957); three daughters, the writers Diana, Christine, and Josephine Pullein-Thompson, *qq.v.*, and one son, the writer Denis Cannan. **Died:** 22 April 1961.

Publications for Children

Fiction

A Pony for Jean, illustrated by Anne Bullen. London, Lane, 1936; New York, Scribner, 1937.
We Met Our Cousins, illustrated by Anne Bullen. London, Collins, 1937; New York, Dodd Mead, 1938.
Another Pony for Jean, illustrated by Anne Bullen. London, Collins, 1938.
London Pride, illustrated by Anne Bullen. London, Collins, 1939.
More Ponies for Jean, illustrated by Anne Bullen. London, Collins, 1943.
They Bought Her a Pony, illustrated by Rosemary Robertson. London, Collins, 1944.
Hamish: The Story of a Shetland Pony, illustrated by Anne Bullen. London, Penguin, 1944.
Gaze at the Moon, illustrated by Sheila Rose. London, Collins, 1957.

Other

Editor, with M.D. and May W. Cannan, *The Tripled Crown: A Book of English, Scotch and Irish Verse for the Age of Six to Sixteen.* London, Frowde, 1908.

Publications for Adults

Novels

The Misty Valley. London, First Novel Library, 1922; New York, Doran, 1924.
Wild Berry Wine. London, Unwin, and New York, Stokes, 1925.
The Lady of the Heights. London, Unwin, 1926.
Sheila Both-Ways. London, Benn, 1928; New York, Stokes, 1939.
The Simple Pass On. London, Benn, 1929; as *Orphan of Mars,* Indianapolis, Bobbs Merrill, 1930.
No Walls of Jasper. London, Benn, 1930; New York, Doubleday, 1931.
Ithuriel's Hour. London, Hodder and Stoughton, 1931; New York, Doubleday, 1932.
High Table. London, Benn, and New York, Doubleday, 1931.
Snow in Harvest. London, Hodder and Stoughton, 1932.
North Wall. London, Hodder and Stoughton, 1933.
Under Proof. London, Hodder and Stoughton, 1934.
The Hills Sleep On. London, Hodder and Stoughton, 1935.
A Hand to Burn. London, Hodder and Stoughton, 1936.
Frightened Angels. London, Gollancz, and New York, Harper, 1936.
Pray Do Not Venture. London, Gollancz, 1937.
Princes in the Land. London, Gollancz, 1938.
They Rang Up the Police. London, Gollancz, 1939.
Death at The Dog. London, Gollancz, 1940; New York, Reynal, 1941.
Idle Apprentice. London, Gollancz, 1940.
Blind Messenger. London, Gollancz, 1941.
Little I Understood. London, Gollancz, 1948.
The Hour of the Angel; Ithuriel's Hour. London, Pan, 1949.
Murder Included. London, Gollancz, 1950; as *Poisonous Relations,* New York, Morrow, 1950; as *The Taste of Murder,* New York, Dell, 1951.
Body in the Beck. London, Gollancz, 1952; New York, Garland, 1983.
And All I Learned. London, Gollancz, 1952.
Long Shadows. London, Gollancz, 1955.
People to Be Found. London, Gollancz, 1956.
And Be a Villain. London, Gollancz, 1958.
All Is Discovered. London, Gollancz, 1962.

Other

I Wrote a Pony Book. London, Collins, 1950.

* * *

Joanna Cannan was already the author of several satirical adult novels when she wrote her first children's book. *A Pony for Jean* tells the story of Jean Leslie who, exiled from London to the country when her father loses his money "in pepper," acquires a half-starved pony nicknamed The Toastrack, nurses him back to health, learns to ride him, and scoops most of the prizes in the local gymkhana.

A Pony for Jean followed years crowded with other writers' pony biographies or autobiographies, written in the style of *Black Beauty.* Each assumed that horses were morally good, their faults due only to mistreatment; and by 1936 this procession of blameless animals scarred by humanity had become tediously repetitive. Cannan, wanting to write about the ponies she loved and seeking a new angle, shrewdly moved the focus of interest away from the pony to the rider. Nor was Jean just any rider. As the first fanatical pony addict to appear in a book, she left a lasting mark on children's literature.

Early in the story Jean goes to visit her horsy cousins. Goaded by their scorn she mounts a pony, heads for a jump—and recovers consciousness on the drawing room sofa. The fall doesn't matter; the experience of riding has, like a religious conversion, changed Jean's life forever. She staggers off the sofa so that her cousins can show her the despised Toastrack, waiting bony and unkempt in the stable. He turns and gives her "a long soft look," and it is love at first sight.

Cavalier, as the pony is renamed, is everything to Jean: her child, as she nurses him back to health; her teacher, as she learns to ride; her heroic lover, leaping a stile for her at midnight, and winning her glory in the gymkhana. He is a dream pony, yet he is always second in interest. Jean—passionate, resolute, brave, but lighthearted—dominates the book.

A Pony for Jean was an immediate success, and Cannan followed it with other pony stories. *Another Pony for Jean* and *More Ponies for Jean* show the same heroine enlarging her experience and starting her own riding school. *We Met Our Cousins* and *London Pride* also include ponies, but their importance is slighter in these two books based on Cannan's childhood visits to Scotland. *They Bought Her a Pony* proved as archetypal as *A Pony for Jean,* describing how an ignorant rider mismanages her pony until taken in hand by the horse-mad children she has previously despised.

The themes of the girl who adores her pony and the young rider learning from sad experience were well-established by the mid 1940s, taken up, and continued by Cannan's daughters—the Pullein-Thompsons—and many other writers. "Pony books," after Cannan, meant "rider books": stories of heroines struggling with ponies who may at first seem difficult but who, through schooling and cherishing, become winners in the last chapter.

Yet there is an originality and a stylishness in Cannan's books which no other pony book author achieved; and it is perhaps surprising that her work is so little valued. Unfortunately the Cannan personality glimpsed behind the pages seems nowadays uncongenial. Against the realistic, egalitarian, tolerant books of today, Cannan's appear highbrow, intolerant, perversely romantic, and glaringly snobbish.

These traits were the result of her upbringing. She was the descendant of dons and upper-class Scottish soldiers. The Cannans kept aloof from everyday society; in their lonely nursery the children steeped themselves in family tradition and historical romance, constructing stern, heroic dramas imbued with the attitudes that mark all Cannan's books. Courage, courtesy, generosity, and self-control are prized; materialism and indulgence in fantasy or emotionalism are abhorred.

Embodied in fiction, these attitudes make for an unbridgeable gulf between "good" and "bad" characters. Cannan does not, in the usual manner of snobs, prefer the rich to the poor, the thoroughbred to the moorland pony. Instead she directs her readers to empathise with the characters she approves of and scorn those she doesn't. Ideal behaviour is illustrated when Jean saves a horse's life by applying a tourniquet to its injured leg, and then rides away, with no thought of thanks or reward, grateful that her mother taught her "sensible things about arteries, instead of idiotic things about fairies."

Cannan's rigid standards, acceptable once but now outdated, inevitably jar; and that is why her books, for all their originality, passion, wit, and love of animals, are forgotten. If they were ever rediscovered as period pieces, their attractive qualities might be found to counterbalance their unattractive characteristics.

—Angela Bull

CARLE, Eric

Nationality: American. **Born:** Syracuse, New York, 25 June 1929. **Education:** Akademie der Bildenden Künste, Stuttgart, Germany, 1945-50. **Military Service:** United States Army, 1952-54. **Family:** Married 1) Dorothea Wohlenberg in 1954 (divorced 1964), one daughter and one son; 2) Barbara Morrison in 1973. **Career:** Poster designer, United States Information Center, Stuttgart, 1950-52; graphic designer, *New York Times,* 1954-56; art director, L.W. Frohlich and Co., New York, 1956-63; guest instructor, Pratt Institute, Brooklyn, New York, 1964. Freelance writer, illustrator, and designer, from 1963. Individual shows: Frans Hals Museum, Haarlem, Netherlands, 1988; Zeeuwse Bibliotheek, Middelburg, Openbare Bibliotheek, Hengelo, and Bisschoppelijk Museum, Breda, all Netherlands, 1989; Klingspor Museum, Germany, 1989. **Awards:** American Institute of Graphic Arts award, 1970 (twice); Children's Literature prize (Germany), 1970; Nakamori Reader's Prize, Japan, 1975; David McCord Children's Literature citation, Framingham State College and Nobscot Reading Council of the International REading Association, 1995; University of Southern Mississippi Medallion, 1997. **Address:** P.O. Box 485, 38 Main Street, Northampton, Massachusetts 01060, U.S.A.

PUBLICATIONS FOR CHILDREN (ILLUSTRATED BY THE AUTHOR)

Fiction

1, 2, 3, to the Zoo. Cleveland, World, 1968; London, Hamish Hamilton, 1969.

The Very Hungry Caterpillar. Cleveland, World, and London, Hamish Hamilton, 1969.

Pancakes, Pancakes! New York, Knopf, and London, Hamish Hamilton, 1970.

Do You Want to Be My Friend? New York, Crowell, and London, Hamish Hamilton, 1971.

The Rooster Who Set Out to See the World. New York, Watts, and London, Dent, 1972; as *Rooster's Off to See the World,* London, Hodder and Stoughton, 1988.

The Secret Birthday Message. New York, Crowell, and London, Hamish Hamilton, 1972.

Have You Seen My Cat? New York, Watts, and London, Dent, 1973.

I See a Song. New York, Crowell, and London, Hamish Hamilton, 1973.

All About Arthur (an Absolutely Absurd Ape). New York, Watts, 1974; London, Dent, 1975.

My Very First Library. New York, Crowell, 1974.

The Mixed-Up Chameleon. New York, Crowell, and London, Hamish Hamilton, 1975; revised edition, New York, HarperCollins, 1984; London, Hamish Hamilton, 1985.

The Grouchy Ladybug. New York, Crowell, 1977; as *The Bad-Tempered Ladybird,* London, Hamish Hamilton, 1978.

Watch Out! A Giant! New York, Collins World, 1978; London, Hamish Hamilton, 1979.

The Honeybee and the Robber. New York, Philomel, and London, MacRae, 1981.

The Very Busy Spider. New York, Philomel, 1984; London, Hamish Hamilton, 1985.

All Around Us. Natick, Massachusetts, Picture Book Studio, 1986.

Papa, Please Get the Moon for Me. Natick, Massachusetts, Picture Book Studio, 1986; London, Hodder and Stoughton, 1987.

A House for Hermit Crab. Natick, Massachusetts, Picture Book Studio, 1987; London, Hodder and Stoughton, 1988.

The Very Quiet Cricket. New York, Philomel and London, Hamish Hamilton, 1990.

Draw Me a Star. New York, Philomel, 1992; London, Hamish Hamilton, 1993.
Today Is Monday. New York, Philomel, 1993; London, Hamish Hamilton, 1994.
My Apron. New York, Philomel, 1994.
The Very Lonely Firefly. New York, Philomel and London, Hamish Hamilton, 1995.
Little Cloud. New York, Philomel, 1996; London, Hamish Hamilton, 1997.

Other

The Say-with-Me ABC Book. New York, Holt Rinehart, 1967.
The Tiny Seed. New York, Crowell, 1970; as *The Tiny Seed and the Giant Flower,* London, Nelson, 1970.
The Very Long Tail. New York, Crowell, 1972.
The Very Long Train. New York, Crowell, 1972.
Walter the Baker (retelling). New York, Knopf, 1972; revised edition, New York, Simon and Schuster, 1995.
My Very First Book of Colors [*Numbers, Shapes, Words, Food, Growth, Heads and Tails, Homes, Motion, Sounds, Tools, Touch*]. New York, Crowell, 12 vols., 1974-86.
Storybook: Seven Tales by the Brothers Grimm. New York and London, Watts, 1976.
Seven Stories by Hans Christian Andersen. New York and London, Watts, 1978.
Twelve Tales from Aesop. New York, Philomel, 1980.
Catch the Ball! New York, Philomel, and London, Collins, 1982.
Let's Paint a Rainbow. New York, Philomel, and London, Collins, 1982.
What's for Lunch? New York, Philomel, and London, Collins, 1982.
Eric Carle's Animals, Animals. London, Hodder and Stoughton, 1990.
Eric Carle's Dragons, Dragons. New York, Philomel, 1991.
The Art of Eric Carle. New York, Philomel, 1996.
From Head to Toe. New York, HarperCollins, 1997; London, Hamish Hamilton, 1998.
Flora and Tiger. New York, Philomel, 1997.
Catch the Ball! New York, Scholastic Inc., 1998.
Let's Paint a Rainbow. New York, Scholastic Inc., 1998.
What's for Lunch? New York, Scholastic Inc., 1998.

Editor, *Treasury of Classic Stories for Children.* New York, Orchard, and London, Hamish Hamilton, 1988.

*

Illustrator: *The Sun Is a Star,* 1963, and *Gravity at Work and Play,* 1963, both by Sune Engelbrektson; *If You Can Count to Ten,* 1964, *Brown Bear, Brown Bear, What Do You See?,* 1967, and *A Ghost Story,* 1970, all by Bill Martin; *Nature Thoughts,* 1965, and *On Friendship,* 1966, both edited by Louise Bachelder; *Red-Flannel Hash and Shoo-Fly Pie: America's Regional Foods and Festivals* by Lila Perl, 1965; *Aesop's Fables for Modern Readers,* 1965, and *The Whale with a Jail,* 1968, both by Nora Roberts Wainer; *Indoor and Outdoor Grow-It Book* by Samm S. Baker, 1966; *In Search of Meaning: Living Religions of the World* by Carl H. Voss, 1968; *Pandekager til Jens,* 1970, and *Vil du Vaere Min Ven?,* 1971, both by Martin Berg; *Tales of the Nimipoo* by Eleanor B. Heady, 1970; *The Boastful Fisherman* by William Knowlton, 1970; *Feathered Ones and Furry,* 1971, and *Do Bears Have Mothers Too?,* 1973, both by Aileen Fisher; *The Scarecrow Clock* by George Mendoza, 1971; *Why Noah Chose the Dove* by Isaac Bashevis Singer, 1974; *The Hole in the Dike* by Norma B. Green, 1974; *Otter Nonsense* by Norton Juster, 1982; *Chip Has Many Brothers* (renamed as *Thank You, Brother Bear*) by Hans Baumann, 1985; *The Foolish Tortoise* and *The Greedy Python* both by Richard Buckley, 1985; *The Mountain That Loved a Bird* by Alice McLerran, 1985; *All in a Day* by Mitsumasa Anno, 1986; *The Lamb and the Butterfly* by Arnold Sundgaard, 1989; *Polar Bear, Polar Bear, What Do You Hear?* by Bill Martin, 1992.

Eric Carle comments:

I am fascinated by the period in a child's life when he or she, for the first time, leaves home to go to school. What a gulf a child must cross then; from home and security, a world of play and the senses, to a world of reason and abstraction, order and discipline. I should like my books to bridge that great divide. Some of my books have holes, cutouts, flaps to lift, raised, touchable surfaces or computer chips with lights and sound. They are half toy (home) and half book (school). A book that can be touched and felt, a toy that can be read. And, indeed, don't we speak of "grasping" an idea, or of being in "touch" with our feelings!

For me, leaving the warmth of home to go to school was traumatic. It occurs to me that I am still trying to make that difficult first step from home to school easier.

* * *

An author-illustrator must be judged on both arts. Eric Carle is a master craftsman in words and pictures, showing boldness not only in his use of colour but also in the themes he has chosen for his picture books. Although almost all of his books feature an animal or insect, interwoven in the storyline of a humanised creature there is the real natural world, authentically depicted. Added emphasis is given by the use of fable format and humour.

Carle's most famous and probably best-loved book is *The Very Hungry Caterpillar.* Its appeal to young children and adults lies in the multiplicity of attractions within the 16 main pages. The low-key scene-setting text on the white left edge of the first double spread bold colour picture; the contrasting sunny picture on the next page, with the developing storyline, whet the appetite for the eye-catching split pages to follow, through which the caterpillar literally eats his way. Holes in the page indicate his progress through a succession of types of food. The natural aspects of growth, cocoon, and the final glorious double spread butterfly make an impact on the reader after the masterly build up of action, cause and effect, humour, and the possibility for child readers to identify with some of the proxy human similarities.

Therein lies Carle's success, the construction of story and picture providing meat for the eye and the mind while simultaneously carrying the reader forward towards a satisfying end. The same skill can be seen in many of his other books, such as *The Grouchy Ladybug,* where in 40 pages, many of them split, the ladybug meets and retreats from natural and unnatural enemies, involving the reader in recognition of size, shape, and response to her bad temper.

Carle's empathy with the natural world has led him to concentrate most of his books on that theme—he has also written about roosters, spiders, crabs, cats, chameleons, bears, and pythons. In the counting book *1, 2, 3 to the Zoo* each double page has a railway carriage with a growing number of animals in it.

Carle's illustrative style, now well known for the use of collage, is effective and extends the reader's perception. His methods of using the physical page to add knowledge, interest, and imaginative stimulus are also admired. They include split pages in *The Grouchy Ladybug;* different lengths of page and holes in *The Very Hungry Caterpillar;* pages folding and unfolding outwards and upwards in *Papa, Please Get the Moon for Me,* in which Papa climbs up a ladder on the unfolding upwards page to bring home the moon for little Monica; and the die-cut pages with raised surfaces to feel the story in *The Very Busy Spider.* Here the spider, the spider's web, and a fly are in thermo-plastic relief, enabling both visually handicapped and sighted children to read the pictures.

The impact of Carle's dramatic illustrations may cause the adult reader to overlook the carefully designed text, brief though it is in each book. The fable format requires and receives a simple storyline, narrative flow, and both the economical use of words and evocative vocabulary with imaginative stimulus. The build up of atmosphere and tension by repetitive phrases is another feature as is the unforced message or moral inherent in the story and humorously transmitted.

Carle's books though for young children are not childish, but appeal to the child in all of us, to our curiosity, our emotions, to our interest in change, exemplified in *A House for Hermit Crab:* "'Time to move,' said Hermit Crab one day in January. 'I've grown too big for this little shell.'"

Growth is the thread running through Carle's books: growth in knowledge, understanding, concepts, and self-awareness, absorbed painlessly and enjoyably. For underlying all is the author-illustrator's capacity for entertaining through word and picture.

—Margaret R. Marshall

CARLSON, Natalie Savage

Nationality: American. **Born:** Winchester, Virginia, 3 October 1906. **Education:** Attended high school in California. **Family:** Married Daniel Carlson in 1929; two daughters. **Career:** Reporter, Long Beach *Morning Sun,* California, 1926-29. **Award:** Child Study Association of America award, 1966. **Address:** 3220 Highway 19, North Lot 17, Clearwater, Florida 34615, U.S.A.

Publications for Children

Fiction

Alphonse, That Bearded One, illustrated by Nicolas Mordvinoff. New York, Harcourt Brace, 1954.

Wings Against the Wind, illustrated by Mircea Vasiliu. New York, Harper, 1955.

Hortense, The Cow for a Queen, illustrated by Nicolas Mordvinoff. New York, Harcourt Brace, 1957.

The Happy Orpheline, illustrated by Garth Williams. New York, Harcourt Brace, 1957; illustrated by Pearl Falconer, London, Blackie, 1960.

The Family under the Bridge, illustrated by Garth Williams. New York, Harper, 1958; as *Under the Bridge,* London, Blackie, 1969.

A Brother for the Orphelines, illustrated by Garth Williams. New York, Harper, 1959; illustrated by Pear Falconer, London, Blackie, 1961.

Evangeline, Pigeon of Paris, illustrated by Nicolas Mordvinoff. New York, Harcourt Brace, 1960; as *Pigeon of Paris,* illustrated by Quentin Blake, London, Blackie, 1972.

The Tomahawk Family, illustrated by Stephen Cook. New York, Harper, 1960; London, Hamish Hamilton, 1961.

The Song of the Lop-Eared Mule, illustrated by Janina Domanska. New York, Harper, 1961.

Carnival in Paris, illustrated by Fermin Rocker. New York, Harper, 1962; illustrated by Geraldine Spence, London, Blackie, 1964.

A Pet for the Orphelines, illustrated by Fermin Rocker. New York, Harper, 1962; illustrated by Pear Falconer, London, Blackie, 1963.

School Bell in the Valley, illustrated by Gilbert Riswold. New York, Harcourt Brace, 1963.

Jean-Claude's Island, illustrated by Nancy Ekholm Burkert. New York, Harper, 1963; London, Blackie, 1966.

The Orphelines in the Enchanted Castle, illustrated by Adriana Saviozzi. New York, Harper, 1964; illustrated by Pearl Falconer, London, Blackie, 1965.

The Letter on the Tree, illustrated by John Kaufmann. New York, Harper, 1964; London, Blackie, 1967.

The Empty Schoolhouse, illustrated by John Kaufmann. New York, Harper, 1965.

Sailor's Choice, illustrated by George Loh. New York, Harper, 1966.

Chalou, illustrated by George Loh. New York, Harper, 1967; illustrated by Jillian Willett, London, Blackie, 1968.

Luigi of the Streets, illustrated by Emily McCully. New York, Harper, 1967; as *The Family on the Waterfront,* London, Blackie, 1969.

Ann Aurelia and Dorothy, illustrated by Dale Payson. New York, Harper, 1968.

Befana's Gift, illustrated by Robert Quackenbush. New York, Harper, 1969; as *A Grandson for the Asking,* London, Blackie, 1969.

Marchers for the Dream, illustrated by Alvin Smith. New York, Harper, 1969; illustrated by Bernard Blatch, London, Blackie, 1971.

The Half Sisters, illustrated by Thomas di Grazia. New York, Harper, 1970; illustrated by Faith Jaques, London, Blackie, 1972.

Luvvy and the Girls, illustrated by Thomas di Grazia. New York, Harper, 1971.

Marie Louise and Christophe, illustrated by Jose Aruego and Ariane Dewey. New York, Scribner, 1974.

Marie Louise's Heydey, illustrated by Jose Aruego and Ariane Dewey. New York, Scribner, 1975; London, MacRae, 1980.

Runaway Marie Louise, illustrated by Jose Aruego and Ariane Dewey. New York, Scribner, 1977.

Jaky or Dodo?, illustrated by Gail Owens. New York, Scribner, 1978.

Time for the White Egret, illustrated by Charles Robinson. New York, Scribner, 1978.

The Night the Scarecrow Walked, illustrated by Charles Robinson. New York, Scribner, 1979.

A Grandmother for the Orphelines, illustrated by David White. New York, Harper, 1980.

Marie Louise and Christophe at the Carnival, illustrated by Jose Aruego and Ariane Dewey. New York, Scribner, 1981.

Spooky Night, illustrated by Andrew Glass. New York, Lothrop, 1982.
Surprise in the Mountains, illustrated by Elise Primavera. New York, Harper, 1983.
The Ghost in the Lagoon, illustrated by Andrew Glass. New York, Lothrop, 1984.
Spooky and the Ghost Cat, illustrated by Andrew Glass. New York, Lothrop, 1985.
Spooky and the Wizard's Bats, illustrated by Andrew Glass. New York, Lothrop, 1986.
Spooky and the Bad Luck Raven, illustrated by Andrew Glass. New York, Lothrop, 1988.
Spooky and the Witch's Goat, illustrated by Andrew Glass. New York, Lothrop, 1989.

Other

The Talking Cat and Other Stories of French Canada, illustrated by Roger Duvoisin. New York, Harper, 1952.
Sashes Red and Blue, illustrated by Rita Fava. New York, Harper, 1956.
King of Cats and Other Tales (Breton folktales), illustrated by David Frampton. New York, Doubleday, 1980.

*

Manuscript Collections: Kerlan Collection, University of Minnesota, Minneapolis; de Grummond Collection, University of Southern Mississippi, Hattiesburg.

* * *

Natalie Savage Carlson acknowledges that she sought professional training to learn to write. Though this training may account for her well-structured books, her inherent ability is reflected in her graceful style and her amused and amusing observations of human behavior. Her writing has a genial overtone, derived perhaps partly from her childhood in the American South and partly from her French-Canadian roots.

One of her early books, *The Talking Cat and Other Stories of French Canada,* consists of tales told to her mother by a French relative, Michel Meloche. Her version of a well-known French-Canadian folktale about the skunk in the kitchen is a good example of her warm style and gentle humor. Another book in the same temper is *The Song of the Lop-Eared Mule* in which Janina Domanska's illustrations synchronize nicely with the story.

Perhaps her most successful work is *The Family under the Bridge,* a story which developed during an extended stay in Paris. Here, for instance, the tramp, Armand, feeds on the rich odours from a restaurant: "For two hours, Armand sat on the curb enjoying the food smells, because that is the length of time a Frenchman allows himself for lunch in the middle of the day. Then he daintily wiped his whiskered lips with his cuff and rose...."

Another popular book which grew out of her Paris experience is *The Happy Orpheline,* with pictures by Garth Williams. The plot has a clever twist: in an orphanage outside Paris, 20 orphans don't want to be adopted—they are happy where they are!

Beginning with *Marie Louise and Christophe* in 1974, and continuing through *Surprise in the Mountains* and the *Spooky* series, Carlson has devoted her time to writing picture books. In *Spooky and the Ghost Cat* a ghost cat becomes a real one when Spooky outwits a witch. In *Spooky and the Wizard's Bats* he outwits a wizard and in *Spooky and the Bad Luck Raven* he outwits a witch's raven. The illustrations of all these stories by Andrew Glass complement the not-too-scary texts, which inform children that the mysterious elements in life add sparkle to experience.

She attempts always to tell a story which no one else has told, or at least one which she feels she is especially able to tell well. Some wry satire can be detected in *Alphonse, That Bearded One,* in which a trained bear masquerades successfully as a soldier and helps bring peace with the Indians. Less successful are her attempts to adapt her talent to social needs, as in *The Empty Schoolhouse* and *Marchers for the Dream. The Half Sisters* is semi-autobiographical, and an interesting account of how truth is adapted to the fictional form has been written by her daughter, Dr. Julie Carlson McAlpine (*Children's Literature,* 1976). In his work *The Nesbit Tradition* Marcus Crouch praises Carlson highly for her effortless lightness of touch and fine dialogue.

—Francelia Butler

CARTER, Bruce

Pseudonym for Richard Alexander Hough, who has also written as Elizabeth Churchill and Pat Strong. **Nationality:** British. **Born:** Brighton, Sussex, 15 May 1922. **Education:** Frensham Heights School, Farnham, Surrey, 1931-40. **Military Service:** Royal Air Force, 1941-46: fighter pilot. **Family:** Married 1) Helen Charlotte Woodyatt (i.e., Charlotte Hough, *q.v.*), in 1943 (divorced 1980); four daughters; 2) Judy Taylor in 1980. **Career:** General manager and children's books editor, The Bodley Head, London, 1947-55; managing director, Hamish Hamilton Books for Children, London, 1955-70. Chairman, Auxiliary Hospitals Committee, King Edward's Hospital Fund, 1975; Member of the Council, 1970-73 and 1975-84, and Vice-President, 1977-82, Navy Records Society. **Awards:** *Daily Express* Best Book of the Sea award, 1972. **Agent:** Heather Jeeves, 9 Dryden Place, Edinburgh EH9 1RP. **Address:** 31 Meadowbank, Primrose Hill Road, London NW3 1AY, England.

PUBLICATIONS FOR CHILDREN

Fiction

The Perilous Descent into a Strange Lost World, illustrated by Tony Weare. London, Lane, 1952; as *Into a Strange Lost World,* New York, Crowell, 1953.
Speed Six!, illustrated by Tony Weare. London, Lane, 1953; New York, Harper, 1956.
Peril on the Iron Road, illustrated by Charlotte Hough. London, Hamish Hamilton, 1953.
Gunpowder Tunnel, illustrated by Charlotte Hough. London, Hamish Hamilton, 1955.
Target Island, illustrated by Tony Weare. London, Hamish Hamilton, 1956; New York, Harper, 1957; revised edition, Hamish Hamilton, 1967.
Juliet in Publishing (as Elizabeth Churchill). London, Lane, 1956.
Tricycle Tim, illustrated by Prudence Seward. London, Hamish Hamilton, 1957.

The Kidnapping of Kensington, illustrated by C. Walter Hodges. London, Hamish Hamilton, and New York, Harper, 1958; as *The Children Who Stayed Behind,* London, Penguin, 1964.
Four-Wheel Drift. London, Bodley Head, and New York, Harper, 1959; revised edition, London, Heinemann, 1973.
The Night of the Flood, illustrated by Prudence Seward. London, Hamish Hamilton, 1959.
Ballooning Boy, illustrated by Prudence Seward. London, Hamish Hamilton, 1960.
The Motorway Chase, illustrated by Bernard Wragg. London, Hamish Hamilton, 1961.
The Plane Wreckers (as Pat Strong), illustrated by Bernard Wragg. London, Hamish Hamilton, 1961.
Fast Circuit. London, Hamish Hamilton, and New York, Harper, 1962.
The Playground, illustrated by Prudence Seward. London, Hamish Hamilton, 1964.
The Airfield Man. London, Hamish Hamilton, 1965; New York, Coward McCann, 1966.
The Gannet's Nest, illustrated by Constance Marshall. London, Hamish Hamilton, 1966.
B Flight. London, Hamish Hamilton, 1970; as *Flight to Victory* (as Richard Hough), New York, Dutton, 1985.
Upley United, illustrated by Harry Bloom. London, Heinemann, 1972.
The Deadly Freeze. London, Dent, 1976.
Buzzbugs. London, Dent, and New York, Warne, 1977.
Miaow! London, Dent, 1978.
Razor Eyes (as Richard Hough). London, Dent, 1981; New York, Lodestar, 1983.

Other as Richard Hough

The Battle of Midway. New York, Macmillan, and London, Collier Macmillan, 1970.
The Battle of Britain. New York, Macmillan, and London, Collier Macmillan, 1971.
Galápagos: The Enchanted Islands, illustrated by Charlotte Hough. London, Dent, and Reading, Massachusetts, Addison Wesley, 1975.

Other

Motor Racing: A Guide for the Younger Enthusiast, with Michael Frostick. London, Lane, 1955.
The Wright Brothers. London, Newnes, 1955.
Neville Duke. London, Newnes, 1955.
Tim Baker, Motor Mechanic: A Career Book. London, Chatto and Windus, 1957.
Nuvolari and the Alfa Romeo, illustrated by Raymond Briggs. London, Hamish Hamilton, and New York, Coward McCann, 1968.
Jimmy Murphy and the White Dusenberg, illustrated by Raymond Briggs. London, Hamish Hamilton, and New York, Coward McCann, 1968.
The Bike Racers (reader), illustrated by John Crawley. London, Longman, 1974; revised edition, 1979.

Editor, *Great Motor Races.* London, Weidenfeld and Nicolson, 1960; as *Great Auto Races,* New York, Harper, 1961.

Publications for Adults as Richard Hough

Novels

The Fighter. London, Joseph, 1963.
Angels One-Five. London, Cassell, 1978; as *Wings Against the Sky,* New York, Morrow, 1979.
The Fight of the Few. London, Cassell, 1979; New York, Morrow, 1980.
The Fight to the Finish. London, Cassell, 1979; as *Wings of Victory,* New York, Morrow, 1980.
Buller's Guns. London, Weidenfeld and Nicolson, and New York, Morrow, 1981.
Buller's Dreadnought. London, Weidenfeld and Nicolson, and New York, Morrow, 1982.
Buller's Revenge. London, Weidenfeld and Nicolson, and New York, Morrow, 1983.
Buller's Victory. London, Weidenfeld and Nicolson, and New York, Morrow, 1984.
The Raging Sky. London, Macdonald, 1989.

Other

Six Great Railwaymen: Stephenson, Hudson, Denison, Huish, Stephen, Gresley. London, Hamish Hamilton, 1955.
Tourist Trophy: The History of Britain's Greatest Motor Race. London, Hutchinson, 1957.
W.O.: An Autobiography, with Walter Owen Bentley. London, Hutchinson, 1958.
The Fleet That Had to Die. London, Hamish Hamilton, and New York, Viking Press, 1958; abridged edition, London, Chatto and Windus, 1963.
British Grand Prix: A History. London, Hutchinson, 1958.
Admirals in Collision. London, Hamish Hamilton, and New York, Viking Press, 1959.
B.P. Book of the Racing Campbells. London, Stanley Paul, 1960.
The Potemkin Mutiny. London, Hamish Hamilton, 1960; New York, Pantheon, 1961.
Sky Fever, with Geoffrey de Havilland. London, Hamish Hamilton, 1961.
A History of the World's Sports Cars, with Michael Frostick. London, Allen and Unwin, and New York, Harper, 1961.
A History of the World's Classic Cars, with Michael Frostick. London, Allen and Unwin, and New York, Harper, 1963.
The Hunting of Force Z. London, Collins, 1963; as *Death of the Battleship,* New York, Macmillan, 1963.
Dreadnought: A History of the Modern Battleship. New York, Macmillan, 1964; London, Joseph, 1965; revised edition, Cambridge, Stephens, and New York, Macmillan, 1975.
The Battle of Jutland. London, Hamish Hamilton, 1964.
A History of the World's Racing Cars, with Michael Frostick. London, Allen and Unwin, and New York, Harper, 1965.
Rover Memories: An Illustrated Survey of the Rover Car, with Michael Frostick. London, Allen and Unwin, 1966.
A History of the World's Motorcycles, with L.J.K. Setright. London, Allen and Unwin, and New York, Harper, 1966; revised edition, 1973.
The Big Battleship; or, The Curious Career of H.M.S. Agincourt. London, Joseph, 1966; as *The Great Dreadnought: The Strange Story of the H.M.S. Agincourt, The Mightiest Battleship of World War I,* New York, Harper, 1967.

Racing Cars. London, Hamlyn, 1967.
A History of the World's High Performance Cars, with Michael Frostick. London, Allen and Unwin, and New York, Harper, 1967.
Fighting Ships. London, Joseph, and New York, Putnam, 1969.
First Sea Lord: An Authorised Biography of Admiral Lord Fisher. London, Allen and Unwin, 1969; revised edition, London, Severn House, 1977; as *Admiral of the Fleet: The Life of John Fisher,* New York, Macmillan, 1970.
The Pursuit of Admiral von Spee. London, Allen and Unwin, 1969; as *The Long Pursuit,* New York, Harper, 1969.
The Blind Horn's Hate. London, Hutchinson, and New York, Norton, 1971.
Captain Bligh and Mr. Christian: The Men and the Mutiny. London, Hutchinson, 1972; New York, Dutton, 1973; revised edition, London, Cassell, 1979; revised edition as *The Bounty,* London, Corgi, 1984.
Louis and Victoria: The First Mountbattens. London, Hutchinson, 1974; as *The Mountbattens,* New York, Dutton, 1975.
One Boy's War: Per Astra Ad Ardua (autobiography). London, Heinemann, 1975.
The Great Admirals. London, Weidenfeld and Nicolson, 1977; New York, Morrow, 1978.
Man o'War: The Fighting Ship in History. London, Dent, and New York, Scribner, 1979.
The Murder of Captain James Cook. London, Macmillan, 1979; as *The Last Voyage of Captain James Cook,* New York, Morrow, 1979.
Mountbatten, Hero of Our Time. London, Weidenfeld and Nicolson, 1980; as *Mountbatten,* New York, Random House, 1981.
Nelson. London, Park Lane Press, 1980.
The Great War at Sea 1914-1918. London and New York, Oxford University Press, 1983.
Edwina: Countess Mountbatten of Burma. London, Weidenfeld and Nicolson, 1983; New York, Morrow, 1984.
Former Naval Person: Churchill and the Wars at Sea. London, Weidenfeld and Nicolson, 1985; as *The Greatest Crusade: Roosevelt, Churchill, and the Naval War,* New York, Morrow, 1986.
The Ace of Clubs: A History of the Garrick. London, Deutsch, 1986.
The Longest Battle: The War at Sea 1939-45. London, Weidenfeld and Nicolson, and New York, Morrow, 1986.
Born Royal: The Lives and Loves of the Young Windsors (1894-1937). London, Deutsch, and New York, Bantam, 1988.
The Battle of Britain: The Jubilee History, with Denis Richards. London, Hodder and Stoughton, 1989; New York, Norton, 1990.
Other Days Around Me (memoirs). London, Hodder and Stoughton, 1992.
Winston and Clementine: The Triumph of the Churchills. London and New York, Bantam, 1990.
Bless Our Ship: Mountbatten & The Kelly. London, Hodder and Stoughton, 1991.
Edward and Alexandra: Their Private and Public Lives. London, Hodder and Stoughton, 1992; New York, St. Martin's, 1993.
Captain James Cook. London, Hodder and Stoughton, 1994; New York, Norton, 1995.

Editor, *First and Fastest: A Collection of the World's Great Motor Races.* London, Allen and Unwin, 1963; as *First and Fastest: A Collection of Accounts of the World's Greatest Auto Races,* New York, Harper, 1964.
Editor, *The Enzo Ferrari Memoirs: My Terrible Joys,* by Enzo Ferrari, translated by Ivan Scott. London, Hamish Hamilton, 1963.
Editor, *The Motor Car Lover's Companion.* London, Allen and Unwin, and New York, Harper, 1965.
Editor, *Advice to a Grand-daughter: Letters from Queen Victoria to Princess Victoria of Hesse.* London, Heinemann, and New York, Simon and Schuster, 1975.

*

Bruce Carter comments:

My writing for children stems directly from, first, the tastes of my own children, and, second, from my experience as an editor of children's books. (I started the Bodley Head children's list in 1947, the Hamish Hamilton list in 1955, and participated as a consultant editor in the redevelopment of the Heinemann list 1971-76.) Except for one or two educational books, my adventure books, historical novels, science fiction (my first *and* most recent), and motor racing stories reflect my own enthusiasms, which have been widely varied, from flying in the war to canoeing on old canals, from long-distance bicycling to ornithology. If they have had any success, I think it must be because I enormously enjoy writing them, and always turn back to writing them with relief and delight after a long, heavily researched adult work.

* * *

Most of Bruce Carter's stories centre on mechanical transport, and the amount of technical detail increases with the age range of the readers. His adult books are non-fiction on the same themes, suggesting sound knowledge.

His stories, even for the youngest readers, are vigorous and lively, and often have a strong comic line. Tim, in *Tricycle Tim,* is lost, though he hardly realises it, and Jim and Bryony in *The Gannet's Nest,* too young to appreciate the very real danger, are rescued at the vital moment. Boisterous older children fend for themselves in Robinson Crusoe situations in *Target Island* and *The Kidnapping of Kensington.* For teenage readers there are car-racing stories full of thrills and spills where the characters are all adult. *The Perilous Descent into a Strange Lost World* and *The Deadly Freeze* are both science fiction, two lively thrillers where the imaginative use of technology mixed with fantasy blends with politics.

Two historical novels—*Peril on the Iron Road* and *Gunpowder Tunnel*—are carefully researched accounts of tunnel building for an early railway and a pioneer canal. Local opposition is strong in both cases, but trouble in *Gunpowder Tunnel* comes from the rival contractor. Both have plenty of excitement—battles with and among miners and attempts to blow up the tunnels. The young people succeed in foiling the plans of the villains, but in neither book do the characters wholly convince the reader.

The car-racing stories—*Speed Six!, Four-Wheel Drift, Fast Circuit,* and the two imaginative reconstructions of real races, *Jimmy Murphy and the White Dusenberg* and *Nuvolari and the Alfa Romeo*—are good examples of the genre, by an enthusiast for enthusiasts. Team work and brilliant driving succeed against all odds, but heroism also has its place. Unfortunately, with its lower standards, big business is also involved in motor-racing; unscrupulous rivals extend the dimensions of the plot. Yet Carter shows, for instance in *Nuvolari,* that he can write a really gripping fast-moving story in quite simple language by concentrating on the race and the personality of the driver only.

Carter's best books are his air stories—*B Flight, The Airfield Man,* and *Razor Eyes.* Here technicalities are submerged beneath the personalities of the characters—Will, flying fighter planes in the First World War; Simon's father, a failure as the proprietor of the hardware shop who only really lived as a wartime pilot; the deranged farmer. War is never glorified, heroes are heroic not through bravado but through determination, and often the ending is wistful rather than happy.

—Margaret M. Tye

CARTER, Peter

Nationality: British. **Born:** Manchester, Lancashire, 13 August 1929. **Education:** Wadham College, Oxford (mature state scholar, 1958), M.A. 1972. **Family:** Married Gudrun Willege in 1974. **Career:** Apprentice in the building trade, 1942-49; formerly teacher in Birmingham. Freelance writer. **Awards:** *Guardian* award, 1981; *Observer* prize, 1983, 1986; ALA Best Book award, 1986, 1990; Premio Europa di Letteraturo Giovanille; Preis Leseratten. **Address:** c/o Oxford University Press Educational Books, Walton Street, Oxford OX2 6DP, England.

Publications for Children

Fiction

The Black Lamp, illustrated by David Harris. London, Oxford University Press, 1973; Nashville, Nelson, 1975.
The Gates of Paradise, illustrated by Fermin Rocker. London, Oxford University Press, 1974; New York, Oxford University Press, 1979.
Madatan, illustrated by Victor Ambrus. London, Oxford University Press, 1974; New York, Oxford University Press, 1979.
Under Goliath, illustrated by Ian Ribbons. London, Oxford University Press, 1977; New York, Oxford University Press, 1979.
The Sentinels. Oxford and New York, Oxford University Press, 1980.
Children of the Book. Oxford, Oxford University Press, 1982; New York, Oxford University Press, 1987.
Bury the Dead. Oxford, Oxford University Press, 1986; New York, Farrar Straus, 1987.
Captain Teachum's Buried Treasure, with Korky Paul. Oxford, Oxford University Press, 1989.
Borderlands. New York, Farrar Straus, 1990.
Leaving Cheyenne. Oxford, Oxford University Press, 1990.
The Hunted. New York, Farrar Straus, 1994.
Union Blues. Oxford, Oxford University Press, forthcoming.

Play

The Sea Green Man (televised 1984). London, Heinemann, 1986.
The Black Lamp.

Other

Mao. London, Oxford University Press, 1976; New York, Viking Press, 1979.

Translator, *The Snowman Who Went for a Walk,* by Mira Lobe, illustrated by Winifried Opgenoorth. Oxford, Oxford University Press, 1982; New York, Morrow, 1984.
Translator, *Grimms' Fairy Tales,* illustrated by Peter Richardson. Oxford, Oxford University Press, 1982.
Translator, *Valerie and the Good-Night Swing,* by Mira Lobe, illustrated by Winifried Opgenoorth. New York, Oxford University Press, 1983.

*

Peter Carter comments:

The best writers (I don't count myself as one), while deeply rooted in their own communities and cultures, are able to reach out to people everywhere. I remember as a youth being absorbed in William Faulkner's novels, although Mississippi was as alien to me as Mars. This sounds a little odd to my ears since my own work ranges from Iron Age Britain to the Berlin of the Cold War—taking in Mao's China and the Kansas of the Old West, but while drawing on my own experiences I have tried (I put it no higher) to speak to those who, brought up in vastily different circumstances, nonetheless face, as we all do, those implacable certainties of growing up, earning a living in a tough world, getting old, and finally hearing, as the great Ray Charles says, Death, "That old tom-cat scratching at the door, and you got no choice but to let him in."

But "One touch of nature makes the whole world kin," and, without being pious, kin is what we are; and even if we don't actually believe it we had better start acting as if we do or the Four Horseman of the Apocalypse are really going to whoop it up; you might already hear them in the distance; as Jefferson said about slavery, "Like a fire-bell in the night."

* * *

A common theme in Peter Carter's books is the fate of ordinary individuals caught up at times of historical change and enduring life-threatening situations they can neither evade nor control. *The Black Lamp* concerns the impact of both the Napoleonic Wars and the Industrial Revolution on the lives of handloom weavers, whose attempts to protect their way of life by combining under the Luddite banner and breaking the machines culminate in the massacre of Peterloo in 1918. Daniel Cregg, the hero of the story, is orphaned during the massacre, and his young sister is threatened with a lifetime of slavery in the mills. Daniel's fight to save them both is depicted with thoughtful appreciation for the loss of work, rising taxes, and increasing poverty facing the ordinary people of that time.

Carter's next book, *The Gates of Paradise,* is an ambitious and interesting story about William Blake. However, the various aspects of Blake's character—the moody and slightly batty visionary, the lucid poet, and the calm, compassionate man whose clearsighted understanding of the world around him seemed so remarkably penetrating and sane—never quite come together.

More successful is *Madatan,* a complex book set in the eighth century. Madaah's relatively peaceful herdsman's life comes to an abrupt end when he is carried off by fierce raiding Norsemen. The book's main theme is the conflict generated in Madaah through his ensuing encounters with various brutal and bold adventurers—both Norse and English—and with the more peaceful, meditative, yet potentially dangerous men of the new Christian religion with whom he briefly finds refuge. In consequence Madaah becomes both betrayed and betrayer, probing the uneasy mixture of self-interest and idealism in himself and others in this tough and powerful story of revenge and outlawry, but also, finally, of reconciliation.

Under Goliath is set in Belfast in 1969. Two boys, the Protestant Alan Kenton and the Catholic Fergus Riley, strike up an ambivalent, uneasy friendship in spite of the growing hostility between their two communities. There is comedy as well as tension in the story and a close observation of the small details of life as well as the far-reaching effects of action at the barricades. Also pervading *Under Goliath* is a sense of the possibilities of friendship as well as bitterness at the divisive prejudices that have frustrated their ambitions and left them with a sense of tragedy, futility, and waste.

The Sentinels is dedicated to the "memory of the millions of Africans taken into slavery, and the thousands of seamen of the Royal Navy who died to free them." The story follows by turns the fortunes of Lyapo—a Yoruba sold into captivity—the American slaver *Phantom,* and the men on board the Royal Navy's rescuing vessel, the *Sentinel.* The British seamen are by no means as altruistic as the dedication may suggest, and the brutality of life at sea in the 1840s is vividly evoked through the eyes of the "gentleman volunteer," 15-year-old John Spencer.

Children of the Book, an account of the Siege of Vienna by the armies of the Ottoman Empire in 1783, also follows several different groups of characters. The sequence of events powerfully illustrates the horror and futility of war, the petty personal ambitions and cruelties that affect its course, and the ironic parallels and differences of belief which both inspire and betray each side.

Bury the Dead concerns more recent history: the ways in which the Nazi legacy of extermination camps and anti-Semitism and the unspeakable cruelties of the war years live on for the Nordern family in East Germany. They have made valiant attempts to rebuild their lives, to work earnestly and conscientiously for the future, and to forget the past. But all, including the innocent children, find themselves implicated against their will in the plots of their uncle, a former Nazi. Through his activities, readers are reminded of the horrendous consequences of the Nazi ideology still threatening those who at the time tried to avert their eyes from what was happening or to deny complicity in the violence that is inevitable in time of war. Like *Under Goliath,* though for different reasons, this story takes on added resonance as the years pass and attitudes change or harden.

The Nazi theme is taken up again in Carter's more recent book, *The Hunted,* but with a more hopeful and heartening outcome. The author tells us in his preface that in 1943, after the defeat of Italy under Mussolini, the Italian soldiers still stationed in Vichy, France, "immediately and sensibly dashed for the mountain passes to their homeland, taking with them as many refugees as they could. To their eternal honour, more shining than any brutal victories, Italian infantrymen, burdened enough, carried Jewish children over the mountains." *The Hunted* is the compelling account of Salvani and his dogged refusal to abandon the boy, Judah, to his relentless pursuers, and so to the gas chambers of Auschwitz. The scenes of violence and torture are discreetly inserted to make clear the true horror of the time, but they also serve to establish the extent of the courage and humanity shown by this ordinary soldier and those who, for a variety of reasons, risk their lives to help him.

Leaving Cheyenne is a very different story, set in Texas in the "Wild West" of the early 1870s. The 13-year-old narrator, Ben, and his older brother join an outfit driving cattle north to the railroad at Abilene. Ben's story, told in a dryly lucid idiom, establishes him as an innocent youngster who nevertheless quickly learns to survive in the tough Western scene of the time: herding more than a thousand head of cattle over long stretches of plain and across swift-flowing rivers; living from hand to mouth in the rough and tough town of Abilene and the even tougher settlement at Dodge; attempting, vainly, to become a successful "all-American business man"; riding the range after the buffalo, killing and skinning the animals while constantly on the lookout for potential enemies, either Indian or white. Pervading *Leaving Cheyenne* is a sense of the changes taking place—often for the worse—as both the buffalo and the Indians are threatened with extinction by the ruthless hunting of the remaining herds. Amid all this excitement readers are constantly invited to assess for themselves the historical, social, and moral aspects involved in Ben's adventures.

In all his books Carter is clearly on the side of the ordinary man, while attempting always to give a balanced picture of events and to suggest—with few exceptions—that neither good nor evil are the monopoly of any one side or individual.

—Winifred Whitehead

CASSEDY, Sylvia

Nationality: American. **Born:** Brooklyn, New York, 29 January 1930. **Education:** Brooklyn College, 1946-51, B.A. 1951; Johns Hopkins University, Baltimore, 1959-60. **Family:** Married 1) Leslie Verwiebe in 1949 (died 1950); 2) Edward Cassedy in 1952, three daughters and one son. **Career:** Teacher of creative writing to children, Queens College, City University of New York, Flushing, 1973-74, Great Neck Public Library, New York, 1975-79, and Manhasset Public Schools, New York, 1977-84. Instructor in teaching creative writing to children, Nassau County Board of Cooperative Education, New York, 1978-79. **Died:** 6 April 1989.

Publications for Children

Fiction

Little Chameleon, illustrated by Rainey Bennett. Cleveland, World, 1966.

Pierino and the Bell, illustrated by Evaline Ness. New York, Doubleday, 1966.

Marzipan Day on Bridget Lane, illustrated by Margot Tomes. New York, Doubleday, 1967.

Behind the Attic Wall. New York, Crowell, 1983; London, Bodley Head, 1984.

M.E. and Morton. New York, Crowell, and London, Bodley Head, 1987.

Lucie Babbidge's House. New York, Crowell, 1989.

Poetry

Roomrimes, illustrated by Michele Chessare. New York, Crowell, 1987.

Other

In Your Own Words: A Beginner's Guide to Writing. New York, Doubleday, 1979.

Editor, and Translator with Kunihiro Suetake, *Birds, Frogs, and Moonlight,* illustrated by Vo-Dinh. New York, Doubleday, 1967.
Editor, and Translator with Parvathi Thampi, *Moon-Uncle, Moon-Uncle: Rhymes from India,* illustrated by Susanne Suba. New York, Doubleday, 1973.

* * *

Sylvia Cassedy wrote with the inward eye of a child. In her fiction and poetry the boundary between children and adults—a boundary often blurred or absent in literature for this age group—is firmly present. On one side are the acute perceptions, fantasies, and helplessness of being young, on the other the rigidity and misunderstanding of grown ups. In her books the children have a relationship to the physical world that adults have lost. They revel in odd, messy minutiae—smeary pink silver polish, the red strings from cigarette papers, the way a bubble of tar pops on a hot roof—and they haven't yet developed the armour to shield themselves from either the pleasant or unpleasant sensations of their world.

In particular, the author's child characters all possess the transforming power of imagination. This is most obvious in her fantasy *Behind the Attic Wall.* Orphaned Maggie is a child stripped of love and security. Appropriately, she invents a game of domineering the imaginary "Backwoods Girls," who have even less than she. The talking dolls that Maggie later discovers spring naturally out of this needy game; now she can really give, instead of just pretending to. Although the book is a fantasy, the line between how much the dolls are Maggie's own creation and how much they are "real" is very fine—which makes their existence all the more haunting. The result is a remarkably powerful novel about caring and continuity.

In *M.E. and Morton* Mary Ella—or M.E., as she prefers to call herself—also uses fantasy as a solace. In a game similar to the "Backwoods Girls," M.E. pretends that her bottles of paints are orphans. She also deludes herself into believing that she is more popular and loved than she is. Her neighbour Polly has fantasies as well—she imagines that the bugs on her ceiling are dancing or that she can shrink herself to fit into a toy train. Unlike the unhealthy fantasies of M.E., however, Polly's inventions enable her to transfer the dull reality of her poverty-stricken life into joy. M.E.'s childlike adolescent brother Morton is a perfect companion for Polly. His slowness saves him from the guilty confusion of his sister and he can engage with Polly in simple play. Although *M.E. and Morton* is realistic, the use of imagination in both books results in a similar "magic": make-believe comes true through the healing power of love.

The two novels show the strong characterizations that are Cassedy's hallmark. She carefully and gradually shows how Maggie, M.E., Polly, and Morton react in different ways to being victims of adult neglect. Desperately lonely Maggie, posturing M.E., resilient Polly, and stolid Morton—all emerge as unforgettable personalities. While the leisurely pace of her fiction may discourage readers looking for continuous action, each novel builds suspense in delicate layers to reach a surprise ending.

The elements in Cassedy's writing are so consistent that the poems in her newest book *Roomrimes* could have been written by either Maggie or M.E.. Using a variety of poetical forms, an alphabet of interior and exterior rooms and spaces is set forth in fresh and whimsical images, as if observed by a solitary, listening, watching child. Closets are inhabited by whoozits, boys live behind mirrors, and the comments on attics, parlors, and roofs especially are similar to those in her novels.

The author's precise language is another strength in her books. The carefully chosen words that are the foundation of her own and her translated poetry result in impeccable prose as well. Cassedy was a compelling writer whose work showed a unique promise.

—Kit Pearson

CATHERALL, Arthur

Pseudonyms: J. Baltimore; A.R. Channel; Dan Corby; Peter Hallard; Trevor Maine; Linda Peters; Margaret Ruthin. **Nationality:** British. **Born:** Bolton, Lancashire, 6 February 1906. **Military Service:** Royal Air Force, 1940-45: Staff Officer. **Family:** Married Elizabeth Benson in 1936; one daughter and one son. **Died:** 6 January 1980.

Publications for Children

Fiction

Rod o' the Rail. London, Pearson, 1936.
The Rival Tugboats. London, Partridge, 1937.
Adventurers, Ltd. London, A. and C. Black, 1938.
Black Gold. London, Pearson, 1939.
Vanished Whaler, illustrated by S. Drigin. London, Nelson, 1939.
Keepers of the Khyber. London, Nelson, 1940.
Lost with All Hands. London, Nelson, 1940.
Raid on Heligoland. London, Collins, 1940.
The Flying Submarine. London, Collins, 1942.
The River of Burning Sand. London, Collins, 1947.
The Bull Patrol. London, Lutterworth Press, 1949.
Riders of the Black Camel. Bath, Venturebooks, 1949.
Cock o' the Town, illustrated by Kenneth Brookes. London, Boy Scouts Association, 1950.
Wings for a Gull. London and New York, Warne, 1951.
Pirate Sealer. London, Collins, 1953.
Shanghaied! London, Collins, 1954.
Ten Fathoms Deep, illustrated by Geoffrey Whittam. London, Dent, 1954; New York, Criterion, 1968.
Jackals of the Sea, illustrated by Geoffrey Whittam. London, Dent, 1955.
The Scuttlers, illustrated by A. Bruce Cornwell and Drake Brookshaw. London, Nelson, 1955.

Sea Wraith. London, Lutterworth Press, 1955.
Wild Goose Saboteur, illustrated by Kenneth Brookes. London, Dent, 1955.
Forgotten Submarine, illustrated by Geoffrey Whittam. London, Dent, 1956.
Land under the White Robe, illustrated by Geoffrey Whittam. London, Dent, 1956.
Jamboree Challenge, illustrated by Kenneth Brookes. London, Dent, and New York, Roy, 1957.
Java Sea Duel, illustrated by Geoffrey Whittam. London, Dent, 1957.
Jungle Trap, illustrated by Paul Hogarth. London, Dent, 1958; New York, Roy, 1967.
Tenderfoot Trapper, illustrated by Edward Osmond. London, Dent, 1958; New York, Criterion, 1959.
Sea Wolves, illustrated by Geoffrey Whittam. London, Dent, 1959; New York, Roy, 1960.
Dangerous Cargo illustrated by Geoffrey Whittam. London, Dent, 1960; New York, Roy, 1961.
Lapland Outlaw, illustrated by Fred Wood. London, Dent, 1960; New York, Lothrop, 1966.
Blue Veil and Black Gold (as Trevor Maine), illustrated by Richard Kennedy. London, Odhams Press, 1961; New York, Roy, 1965.
China Sea Jigsaw, illustrated by Geoffrey Whittam. London, Dent, 1961; New York, Roy, 1962.
Orphan Otter, illustrated by N. Osten-Sacken. London, Dent, 1962; New York, Harcourt Brace, 1963.
Vagabond Ape, illustrated by N. Osten-Sacken. London, Dent, 1962.
Yugoslav Mystery, illustrated by Stuart Tresilian. London, Dent, 1962; New York, Lothrop, 1964.
Prisoners under the Sea, illustrated by Geoffrey Whittam. London, Dent, 1963.
Lone Seal Pup, illustrated by Edward Osmond. London, Dent, 1964; New York, Dutton, 1965.
The Strange Invader, illustrated by Stuart Tresilian. London, Dent, 1964; as *The Strange Intruder,* New York, Lothrop, 1965.
Tanker Trap, illustrated by Geoffrey Whittam. London, Dent, 1965; New York, Roy, 1966.
Reindeer Rescue (as Linda Peters), illustrated by F.M. Johnson. Leeds, E.J. Arnold, 1966.
Sicilian Mystery, illustrated by Stuart Tresilian. London, Dent, 1966; New York, Lothrop, 1967.
A Zebra Came to Drink, illustrated by Edward Osmond. London, Dent, and New York, Dutton, 1967.
Prisoners in the Snow, illustrated by Victor Ambrus. London, Dent, and New York, Lothrop, 1967.
Death of an Oil Rig, illustrated by Geoffrey Whittam. London, Dent, 1967; New York, Phillips, 1969.
Night of the Black Frost, illustrated by Roger Payne. London, Dent, and New York, Lothrop, 1968.
Camel Caravan, illustrated by Joseph Papin. New York, Seabury Press, 1968; as *Desert Caravan,* London, Macdonald, 1969.
Kidnapped by Accident, illustrated by Victor Ambrus. London, Dent, 1968; New York, Lothrop, 1969.
Island of Forgotten Men, illustrated by Geoffrey Whittam. London, Dent, 1968.
Duel in the High Hills, illustrated by Stanley Smith. London, Dent, 1968; New York, Lothrop, 1969.
Red Sea Rescue, illustrated by Victor Ambrus. London, Dent, 1969; New York, Lothrop, 1970.
Antlers of the King Moose, illustrated by Edward Mortelmans. London, Dent, and New York, Dutton, 1970.
The Big Tusker, illustrated by Douglas Phillips. London, Dent, and New York, Lothrop, 1970.
Keepers of the Cattle, illustrated by Bernard Brett. London, Dent, 1970.
Freedom for a Cheetah, illustrated by Shyam Varma. London, Dent, and New York, Lothrop, 1971.
Barracuda Mystery, illustrated by Gavin Rowe. London, Dent, 1971.
The Unwilling Smuggler, illustrated by Geoffrey Whittam. London, Dent, 1971.
Last Horse on the Sands, illustrated by David Farris. London, Dent, 1972; New York, Lothrop, 1973.
Cave of the "Cormorant." London, Dent, 1973.
A Wolf from the Sky, illustrated by Derek Lucas. London, Dent, 1974.
Stranger on Wreck Buoy Sands. London, Dent, 1975.
Twelve Minutes to Disaster and Other Stories, illustrated by Derek Lucas. London, Dent, 1977.
The Ghost Elephant. London, Abelard Schuman, 1977.
The Last Run and Other Stories. London, Dent, 1977.
No Surrender! and Other Stories. London, Dent, 1979.
The Thirteen Footprints and Other Stories. London, Dent, 1979.
Smuggler in the Bay. London, Dent, 1980.

Fiction as A.R. Channel

Phantom Patrol. London, Collins, 1940.
The Tunnel Busters. London, Collins, 1960.
The Million-Dollar Ice Floe, illustrated by Eric Mudge-Marriott. London, Dobson, 1961.
Operation V.2. London, Collins, 1961.
Arctic Spy, illustrated by Horace Gaffron. London, Collins, 1962.
The Forgotten Patrol. London, Collins, 1962.
The Rogue Elephant, illustrated by D.J. Watkins-Pitchford. London, Dobson, 1962; Philadelphia, Macrae Smith, 1963.
Mission Accomplished. London, Collins, 1964.
Red Ivory, illustrated by D.J. Watkins-Pitchford. London, Dobson, and Philadelphia, Macrae Smith, 1964.
Jungle Rescue, illustrated by D.J. Watkins-Pitchford. London, Dobson, 1967; New York, Phillips, 1968.

Fiction as Margaret Ruthin

Kidnapped in Kandy, illustrated by C. Cane. London, Blackie, 1951.
The Ring of the Prophet. London and New York, Warne, 1953.
White Horse of Hungary. London and New York, Warne, 1954.
Strange Safari. London and New York, Warne, 1955.
The Secret Pagoda. London and New York, Warne, 1960.
Jungle Nurse, illustrated by Hugh Marshall. London, Dobson, and New York, Watts, 1960.
Reindeer Girl, illustrated by Marie Whitby. London, Dobson, 1961; as *Elli of the Northland,* New York, Farrar Straus, 1968.
Lapland Nurse, illustrated by Marie Whitby. London, Dobson, 1962.
Secret of the Shetlands, illustrated by Gwen Gibson. London, Dobson, 1963.
Katrina of the Lonely Isles, illustrated by Gwen Gibson. London, Dobson, 1964; New York, Farrar Straus, 1965.
Kidnapped on Stromboli. London, Dobson, 1966.
Hungarian Rebel. London, Dobson, 1970.

Fiction as Peter Hallard

Coral Reef Castaway, illustrated by Terence Greer. London, Phoenix House, 1958; New York, Criterion, 1960.
Barrier Reef Bandits, illustrated by Hugh Marshall. London, Dobson, and New York, Criterion, 1960.
Guardian of the Reef, illustrated by Hugh Marshall. London, Dobson, 1961.
Boy on a White Giraffe, illustrated by Sheila Bewley. London, Macdonald, and New York, Seabury Press, 1969.
Lost in Lapland, illustrated by Judith Ann Lawrence. London, Macdonald, 1970; as *Puppy Lost in Lapland,* New York, Watts, 1971.
Kalu and the Wild Boar, illustrated by W.T. Mars. New York, Watts, 1973.

Fiction as Dan Corby (U.S. editions as Arthur Catherall)

A Shark on the Saltings. London, Parrish, 1959.
The Little Sealer. London, Parrish, 1960; as *The Arctic Sealer,* New York, Criterion, 1961.
Lost Off the Grand Banks. London, Parrish, 1961; New York, Criterion, 1962.
Man-Eater, illustrated by Richard Lewis. London, Parrish, 1963; New York, Criterion, 1964.
Thunder Dam, illustrated by Omar Davis. London, Parrish, 1964; New York, Criterion, 1965.
Conqueror's Gold. London, Parrish, 1965.

Other

Camp-Fire Stories and How to Tell Them. London, Jenkins, 1935.
The Steam and Steel Omnibus, with George W. Blow, illustrated by Blow. London, Collins, 1950.
The Scout Story Omnibus. London, Collins, 1954.
The Young Baden-Powell, illustrated by William Randell. London, Parrish, 1961; New York, Roy, 1962.
Vanishing Lapland. New York, Watts, 1972.

PUBLICATIONS FOR ADULTS

Novels

Tomorrow's Hunter. London, Jenkins, 1950.
Vibrant Brass. London, Dent, 1954.
Singapore Sari (as J. Baltimore). Leicester, Fiction House, 1958.
No Bouquets for These. London, Tempest Press, 1958.

Play

Step in My Shoes, with David Reade (produced Southport, Lancashire, 1958).

*

Arthur Catherall commented:

(1978) As a young reader I always took for gospel whatever I got from a book. For that reason I have endeavoured throughout my life as a writer to be authentic. As far as possible I have been to the places where I set my stories. I have worked with young people for over 40 years, and I have tried to get the feel of what they look for. You don't find any unnecessary clubbing or shooting in my books. Boys can be little savages without the inspiration of a story to start them off. They look for heroes in a story. I try to give them the right kind of heroes, for boys are great imitators.

* * *

Arthur Catherall, with his many pseudonyms, must have been one of the most prolific of writers for the young, but the truly amazing thing is not so much the output as the consistently authentic standard, the fidelity to fact. The stories are all set in places which Catherall had personal knowledge of, so that although the scenes are immensely varied they are all authentic. And furthermore, he never cheated on plot, he is as clever at extricating his hero from his predicament as he is at devising it.

Catherall served in World War II in various zones of action, including the Pacific; he travelled in all parts of the British Commonwealth, Europe, North America, the Arctic. But his intimate knowledge of a region is no mere backcloth; it also provides the warp and weft of the plot. In other words, plot is intrinsic to place—that of *Red Sea Rescue* could never be adapted for a book about Sicily or Scotland, nor could *Jungle Trap* be adapted to the Arctic or Lancashire. Monsoons, floods, drug-smuggling, working elephants all belong to the India of *The Big Tusker.* Not only did the author know the climate and terrain but also the methods used by local smugglers, the behaviour of elephants, and the way they work with timber. Every detail is thoroughly studied. Catherall's mastery of the cliffhanger consisted in exploiting to the full the hazards intrinsic to the scene and situation by bringing them into the narrative at the exact point where they will maximize the drama and create the greatest surprise.

Let us take a close look at one of his best animal stories, *Freedom for a Cheetah.* First the spellbinding atmosphere of the Indian plains. Dum-dum the cheetah had spent the two years of her life in a stable with only the occasional company of pariah dogs. The air had never been really clean. When her master hunted she was sent dashing across the dusty plains in pursuit of black buck. Now, a youth with a spite against her trainer offers the cheetah her freedom. But freedom held many terrors for Dum-dum and the story follows her adventures with wild dogs, treacherous mud, hunger, tiger, cobra, bees, fire, and finally men. Pursued by a pack of wild dogs, Dum-dum finds that the river mud which had almost fatally trapped her when first she was free now became her ally, for the dogs could not trust themselves to it.

When children are the heroes, their ingenuity and intelligence are stretched to the full to deal with their predicament but always in a way that fits their young experience. In *Prisoners in the Snow* we are in the Austrian mountains. Two children are trapped with their grandfather in their farmhouse after an aeroplane crashing into the mountain causes an avalanche which buries the house in snow. Cows from the damaged cowshed have to be brought into the parlour and hay to feed them brought from the threatened hay loft; the injured pilot who bailed out has to be rescued from the roof—but the roof may collapse and it is a long fall. So they rig up a net, but the idea came quite naturally from the children's experience of a travelling circus. And the children's own excitement is yet another factor adding to the tension and excitement of the reader. It can be explicit in a way not possible in animal stories; but emotion never interferes or takes over.

Catherall in books such as the Bulldog series wrote adventures with men as heroes: Jack Frodsham and Husky Hudson of the salvage tug *Bulldog* in China seas. These resourceful fellows are always up against the same enemy, Karmey, an unscrupulous villain who is constantly balked of his plan to sink them. These are superb yarns, all the more satisfying because it is the same team of heroes being brought time and again to the brink of disaster but turning the tables on the same enemy. *Death of an Oil Rig, Island of Forgotten Men,* and *Ten Fathoms Deep* are a few of these marvellously thrilling novels.

It is a comment on our times that a writer of exciting adventures with real believable heroes was considered a writer for young people. To exploit the same talents in the adult market today he would have to write grisly whodunnits or novels with an anti-hero like Flashman. But this would not be Catherall at all. Throughout his long writing career he always held up to his readers an image of a hero or heroine with courage, kindness, loyalty, and spirit.

—Gwen Marsh

CAUSLEY, Charles (Stanley)

Nationality: British. **Born:** Launceston, Cornwall, 24 August 1917. **Education:** Launceston National School; Horwell Grammar School; Launceston College; Peterborough Training College, 1946-47. **Military Service:** Royal Navy, 1940-46. **Career:** Clerk in builder's office and in electrical supply company, Launceston, 1933-40; teacher in Cornwall, 1947-76. Honorary Visiting Fellow in Poetry, University of Exeter, Devon, 1973-74. Literary editor of BBC radio magazines *Apollo in the West* and *Signature,* 1953-56. Member, Arts Council Poetry (later Literature) Panel, 1962-66; Vice-President, West Country Writers' Association; Vice-President, Poetry Society, London. **Awards:** Society of Authors travelling scholarship, 1954, 1966; fellow, Royal Society of Literature, 1958; Queen's Gold Medal for Poetry, 1967; Cholmondeley award, for verse, 1971; C.B.E. (Commander, Order of the British Empire), 1986; *Signal* Poetry award, 1987; Maschler award, 1987. D. Litt.: University of Exeter, 1977; M.A.: Open University, 1982. **Agent:** David Higham Associates, 5-8 Lower John Street, London W1R 4HA. **Address:** 2 Cyprus Well, Launceston, Cornwall PL15 8BT, England.

Publications for Children

Fiction

The Last King of Cornwall, illustrated by Krystyna Turska. London, Hodder and Stoughton, 1978.

Plays

The Gift of a Lamb, music by Vera Gray, illustrated by Shirley Felts. London, Robson, 1978.

The Ballad of Aucassin and Nicolette, music by Stephen McNeff, illustrated by Yvonne Gilbert (produced London, 1978). London, Kestrel, 1981.

Poetry

Figure of 8: Narrative Poems, illustrated by Peter Whiteman. London, Macmillan, 1969.

Figgie Hobbin: Poems for Children, illustrated by Pat Marriott. London, Macmillan, 1970; New York, Walker, 1973.

The Tail of the Trinosaur, illustrated by Jill Gardiner. Leicester, Brockhampton Press, 1973.

As I Went Down Zig Zag, illustrated by John Astrop. London and New York, Warne, 1974.

Here We Go Round the Round House, illustrated by Stanley Simmonds. Leicester, New Broom Press, 1976.

The Hill of the Fairy Calf, illustrated by Robine Clignett. London, Hodder and Stoughton, 1976.

The Animals' Carol, illustrated by Judith Horwood. London, Macmillan, 1978.

Schondilie, illustrated by Robert Tilling. Leicester, New Broom Press, 1982.

Quack! Said the Billy-Goat, illustrated by Barbara Firth. London, Walker, and New York, Lippincott, 1986.

Early in the Morning: A Collection of New Poems, music by Anthony Castro, illustrated by Michael Foreman. London, Viking Kestrel, 1986; New York, Viking Kestrel, 1987.

Jack the Treacle Eater and Other Poems, illustrated by Charles Keeping. London, Macmillan, 1987.

The Young Man of Cuky: Poems for Children, illustrated by Michael Foreman. London, Macmillan, 1991.

Bring in the Holly: Poems for Children, illustrated by Lisa Kopper. N.p., Frances Lincoln, 1991.

Other

When Dad Felt Bad (reader), illustrated by Richard Rose. London, Macmillan, 1975.

Dick Whittington, illustrated by Antony Maitland. London, Penguin, 1976.

Three Heads Made of Gold (folktale), illustrated by Pat Marriott. London, Robson, 1978.

Editor, *Dawn and Dusk: Poems of Our Time,* illustrated by Gerald Wilkinson. Leicester, Brockhampton Press, 1962; New York, Watts, 1963.

Editor, *Rising Early: Story Poems and Ballads of the 20th Century,* illustrated by Anne Netherwood. Leicester, Brockhampton Press, 1964; as *Modern Ballads and Story Poems,* New York, Watts, 1965.

Editor, *In the Music I Hear: Poems by Children.* Gillingham, Kent, ARC Press, 1970.

Editor, *Oats and Beans and Barley: Poems by Children.* Gillingham, Kent, ARC Press, 1971.

Editor, *The Puffin Book of Magic Verse,* illustrated by Barbara Swiderska. London, Penguin, 1974.

Editor, *The Puffin Book of Salt-Sea Verse,* illustrated by Antony Maitland. London, Kestrel, 1978.

Editor, *The Batsford Book of Stories in Verse for Children,* illustrated by Charles Keeping. London, Batsford, and New York, Hippocrene, 1979.

Editor, *The Sun, Dancing: Christian Verse,* illustrated by Charles Keeping. London, Kestrel, 1982.

Publications for Adults

Short Stories

Hands to Dance. London, Carroll and Nicholson, 1951; augmented edition, as *Hands to Dance, and Skylark,* London Robson, 1979.

Plays

Runaway. London, Curwen, 1936.
The Conquering Hero. London, Curwen, and New York, Schirmer, 1937.
Benedict. London, Muller, 1938.
How Pleasant to Know Mrs. Lear: A Victorian Comedy. London, Muller, 1948.

Poetry

Farewell, Aggie Weston. Aldington, Kent, Hand and Flower Press, 1951.
Survivor's Leave. Aldington, Kent, Hand and Flower Press, 1953.
Union Street. London, Hart Davis, 1957; Boston, Houghton Mifflin, 1958.
The Ballad of Charlotte Dymond. Privately printed, 1958.
Johnny Alleluia. London, Hart Davis, 1961.
Penguin Modern Poets 3, with George Barker and Martin Bell. London, Penguin, 1962.
Ballad of the Bread Man. London, Macmillan, 1968.
Underneath the Water. London, Macmillan, 1968.
Pergamon Poets 10, with Laurie Lee, edited by Evan Owen. Oxford, Pergamon Press, 1970.
Timothy Winters, music by Wallace Southam. London, Turret, 1970.
Six Women. Richmond, Surrey, Keepsake Press, 1974.
Collected Poems 1951-1975. London, Macmillan, and Boston, Godine, 1975.
St. Martha and the Dragon, music by Phyllis Tate. London, Oxford University Press, 1978.
Hymn. North Tawton, Devon, Morrigu Press, 1983.
Secret Destinations. London, Macmillan, 1984.
Kings' Children and Other German Ballads in English Versions. Ashington, Mid-Northumberland Arts Group, 1986.
21 Poems. Shipston-on-Stour, Warwickshire, Celandine Press, 1986.
A Field of Vision. London, Macmillan, 1988.
Secret Destinations: Selected Poems 1976-88. Boston, Godine, 1988.
Poets in Hand, with others, chosen and introduced by Anne Harvey. London, Puffin, 1990.
Collected Poems. London, Macmillan, 1992.

Recordings: *Here Today 1,* Jupiter; *The Poet Speaks 8,* Argo; British Council tapes, 1960, 1966, 1968; *Causley Reads Causley,* Sentinel, 1975; *Pushing the Business On,* Plant Life, 1977; *Secret Destinations,* Sentinel, 1984.

Published Songs: *Shore Leave,* music by Michael Hurd; *Round the Town,* music by Michael Hurd; *Cowboy Song,* music by William Bowie; *The Sheep on Blackening Fields,* music by William Bowie; *Three Masts,* music by William Bowie; *Nursery Rhyme of Innocence and Experience,* music by Betty Rice; *Daystar in Winter,* music by Geoffrey Bush; *Mary, Mary Magdalene,* music by Phyllis Tate; *Jonah,* music by William Mathias.

Other

Editor, *Peninsula: An Anthology of Verse from the West-Country.* London, Macdonald, 1957.
Editor, *An Octave,* by Siegfried Sassoon. London, Arts Council, 1966.
Editor, *Modern Folk Ballads.* London, Studio Vista, 1966.
Editor, *Selected Poems,* by Frances Bellerby. London, Enitharmon Press, 1971.

Translator, *Twenty-five Poems,* by Hamdija Demirovic. Richmond, Surrey, Keepsake Press, 1980.

*

Manuscript Collections: State University of New York, Buffalo; University of Exeter Library, Devon.

Critical Studies: *Causley at 70: Poem and Prose Tribute* edited by Harry Chambers, Calstock, Cornwall, Peterloo, 1987.

Charles Causley comments:
If there is a "best" way to set about writing poems for children, I think it may be by concentrating first on trying to produce a *poem,* and by deciding afterwards on its most appropriate audience. The test of an authentic "children's" poem, surely, is that it should work equally successfully with both the child and the adult. My guiding principle here has always been something I found in W.H. Auden's matchless introduction to his *A Choice of de la Mare's Verse* in which, among many other good things, he wrote "while there are some good poems which are only for adults, because they pre-suppose adult experience in their readers, there are no good poems which are only for children."

* * *

The poet Charles Causley, in his work for both adults and children, is above all things else a rooted man: rooted in his native Cornwall and in the best traditions of English verse. Some poets have one subject matter for adults—adulthood—and an entirely different one for children—childhood—and a manner of writing, including a separate vocabulary, for each. Other poets' work seems to encompass quite naturally the world and preoccupations of children without self-consciously writing down to them—I think in this context not only of Causley but of Eleanor Farjeon. Causley's imagination, steeped as it is in myth, folklore, and the world of the ballad, a world which in its anonymity tends to speak for Everyman, is perpetually moving back and forth, from childhood to adulthood and back again. He is careful not to overestimate the adult taste for a sophisticated poetic veneer, nor to underestimate the extent to which narrative verse, for example, can continue to speak to us now. Such collections for children as *Early in the Morning* and *Jack the Treacle Eater* are steeped in the world of children's nursery rhymes, and the poems in these books, appropriately, have bouncing, infectious rhythms and that haunting and mysterious flavour that one associates with the best kinds of Nonsense: they are a familiar Causley blend of ancient and modern. In *Jack the Treacle Eater* the modern is represented by a poem entitled "I've Never Seen the Milkman" and the ancient by the balladic

"Lady Jane Grey." Both these poems have a clarity, a simplicity, and a freshness that render the notion of whether or not the subject matter is culled from the past or the present quite irrelevant—the fact is that they speak to us now. If anything it is the poem about the milkman, that spectral visitant who leaves evidence of his calls on the doorstep daily but who is never in fact seen by the child, that continues to resonate in the mind long after one has read it:

I wonder if he's thin or fat
Or fair or dark or bald,
Or short or tall, and most of all
I wonder what he's called.

He goes to bed so early
That not an owl has stirred
And rises up again before
The earliest early bird...

Causley returns again and again as a poet to the lore and legends of his native Cornwall, and this strain is represented in these collections by such poems as "At Linkinhorne" (where, it is said by those who should know, the Devil was born) and "The Twelve O'Clock Stone," a haunting poem which recounts how children who suffered from rickets were carried to a certain part of West Penwith to be laid on a logan-stone (a giant boulder with seemingly magical properties which can be rocked by the gentlest of touches) in the expectation of a cure. This particular stone could not be rocked by human hand, but swayed of its own accord at the stroke of midnight. Causley can make the Matter of Britain come alive for children in a way that is unmatched by any other poet of his generation.

—Michael Glover

CHALMERS, Mary (Eileen)

Nationality: American. **Born:** Camden, New Jersey, 16 March 1927. **Education:** Philadelphia College of Art, 1945-48, graduated 1948; Barnes Foundation, Merion, Pennsylvania, 1949-50. **Career:** Commercial artist in the 1950s. **Address:** 4Q Laurel Hill Road, Greenbelt, Maryland 20770, U.S.A.

PUBLICATIONS FOR CHILDREN (ILLUSTRATED BY THE AUTHOR)

Fiction

Come for a Walk with Me. New York, Harper, 1955.
Here Comes the Trolley Car. New York, Harper, 1955.
A Hat for Amy Jean. New York, Harper, 1956.
A Christmas Story. New York, Harper, 1956.
George Appleton. New York, Harper, 1957.
Kevin. New York, Harper, 1957.
Boats Finds a House. New York, Harper, 1958.
Throw a Kiss, Harry. New York, Harper, 1958.
The Cat Who Liked to Pretend. New York, Harper, 1959.
Mr. Cat's Wonderful Surprise. New York, Harper, 1961.
Take a Nap, Harry. New York, Harper, 1964.
Be Good, Harry. New York, Harper, 1967.
Merry Christmas, Harry. New York, Harper, 1977.
Come to the Doctor, Harry. New York, Harper, 1981.
Six Dogs, Twenty-Three Cats, Forty-Five Mice, and One Hundred Sixteen Spiders. New York, Harper, 1986.
The Easter Parade. New York, Harper, 1987; London, Methuen, 1988.

*

Manuscript Collections: Kerlan Collection, University of Minnesota, Minneapolis.

Illustrator: *Every Day Is a World* by Raymond Bechtle, 1957; *I Would Like to Be a Pony and Other Wishes* by Dorothy W. Baruch, 1959; *The Secret Language* by Ursula Nordstrom, 1960; *Big Brother,* 1960, and *The Three Funny Friends,* 1961, both by Charlotte Zolotow; *The Happy Birthday Present* by Joan Heilbroner, 1962; *The House of Thirty Cats* by Mary Calhoun, 1965; *Three to Get Ready* by Betty Boegehold, 1965; *The Crystal Tree* by Jenny D. Lindquist, 1966; *Goodnight Andrew Goodnight Craig* by Marjorie Weinman Sharmat, 1969; *I Write It* by Ruth Krauss, 1970; *When Will It Snow?* by Syd Hoff, 1971; *The Snuggle Bunny* by Nancy Jewell, 1972; *Letitia Rabbit's String Song* by Russell Hoban, 1973; *Crickety Cricket! The Best-Loved Poems of James S. Tippett,* 1973; *When Daisies Pied, and Violets Blue: Songs from Shakespeare,* 1974; *The Day after Christmas* by Alice Bach, 1975; *Oh No, Cat!* by Janice Udry, 1976; *Mule in the Mail* by Stephen Manes, 1978; *Home at Last* by Patricia Lauber, 1980; *Marigold and Grandma on the Town* by Stephanie Calmenson, 1994.

Mary Chalmers comments:

The books of which I am both author and illustrator are all for the very young child—they are "picture books." The books by other authors that I have illustrated range from picture books to stories for young teenagers. There is a different ratio of pictures to words in these books. For instance, Jenny D. Lindquist's *The Crystal Tree* is nearly 300 pages long and has 20 illustrations by me; Russell Hoban's *Letitia Rabbit's String Song* has a picture on every page. I have worked almost entirely with pen and ink, pencil and water color.

* * *

Mary Chalmers is best known for Harry, the beguiling, anthropomorphic cat who has appeared in five tiny books which span 23 years. However, a handful of other small books, which present a childlike point of view, predate and presage Harry. With leisurely language and an artless fusion of fantasy and reality, they describe the simplest of adventures which begin and end in the cozy, nurturing climate of home. Trilby, the cat in *George Appleton,* wakes in human fashion in a fourposter with his head on a pillow but later huddles in classic cat position under the family car; he meets a peaceful, lonely dragon in the woods and they have a "perfectly marvelous time" playing together all day. In *Come for a Walk with Me* Susan invites Will Rabbit to accompany her to Mrs. Horseyfeather's house to borrow molasses; upon arrival they "had had such a lovely walk and they were so happy that they did a little dance." In these narratives there is time for hellos and goodbyes, cups of hot chocolate, and smelling flowers—time for exploration, reflection, communion, and celebration.

Harry demanded a new style. With condensed prose, the elimination of precious words such as "little" and names such as "Harry Hop Toad," and with the whimsy sharpened into wit, the tranquil, domestic happiness is stretched to incorporate conflict and resolution. A more pungent happiness emerges through Harry's first small struggles for autonomy. Familiar parental commands, signalized in titles like *Throw a Kiss, Harry* and *Take a Nap, Harry,* rouse these minor mutinies. Harry throws a kiss to the fireman who rescues him from a rooftop—but only after his mother stops cajoling him to do so and disappears; then he throws an independent, heartfelt kiss. Similarly, he takes a nap, not when his mother, eager to get on with making a cake, rushes him to bed, but later, when a yawn comes after they begin the cake. These are small struggles, but eminently important to a small cat ... and a small child.

Despite their young ages, Harry and Chalmers's other protagonists operate with an appealing aplomb and assiduously overcome obstacles. When a star is needed to complete the tree in *A Christmas Story,* tiny Elizabeth states matter-of-factly, "I'll go get one," and does so, returning with the simple, self-satisfied pronouncement, "There," as the star shines from atop the tree. Harry enters the doctor's office with considerable trepidation in *Come to the Doctor, Harry,* but emerges unimpaired, proudly waving his tail bandage. These attributes are missing in *Merry Christmas, Harry,* Chalmer's least successful Harry book; an uncharacteristically passive role—requesting and receiving a baby kitten from Santa Claus—places Harry in a disappointingly dependent position.

In the early books the illustrations are decorative accessories; in the Harry series they carry the feelings and drama. All but the essentials are eliminated in the sketches and sufficient empty space surrounds Harry so attention is directed to the tiny soft-pencil lines that animate and denote changes in his expressions and actions. When combined judiciously with an understated text that effectively uses silences and pauses, Harry's small powers loom large.

—Nancy C. Hammond

CHANCE, Stephen. See **TURNER, Philip.**

CHANEY, Jill

Nationality: British. **Born:** Radlett, Hertfordshire, 5 June 1932. **Education:** Downs School, Seaford, Sussex, graduated 1947; Waterperry Horticultural School, Oxfordshire, 1948-50, Royal Horticultural Society diploma 1950. **Family:** Married Walter Leeming in 1960; one daughter and one son. **Career:** Gardener, Jewish Board of Guardians, London, 1954-59; director, Chorleywood Bookshop, Hertfordshire, 1971-88. **Address:** Glen Rosa, Colleyland, Chorleywood, Hertfordshire, England.

Publications for Children

Fiction

On Primrose Hill, illustrated by Jane Paton. London, Methuen, 1962.

Half a Candle, illustrated by Carolyn Dinan. London, Dobson, 1968; New York, Crown, 1969.

A Penny for the Guy, illustrated by John Dyke. London, Dobson, 1970.

Mottram Park, illustrated by Carolyn Dinan. London, Dobson, 1971.

Christopher's Dig, illustrated by John Dyke. London, Dobson, 1972.

Taking the Woffle to Pebblecombe-on-Sea, illustrated by Elizabeth Ogan. London, Dobson, 1974.

Return to Mottram Park, illustrated by Carolyn Dinan. London, Dobson, 1974.

Christopher's Find, illustrated by John Dyke. London, Dobson, 1975.

Woffle, R.A., illustrated by Catherine Leeming. London, Dobson, 1976.

The Buttercup Field, illustrated by Elizabeth Ogan. London, Dobson, 1976.

Canary Yellow, illustrated by Carolyn Dinan. London, Dobson, 1977.

Angel Face, illustrated by Carolyn Dinan. London, Dobson, 1979.

Vectis Diary, illustrated by Catherine Leeming. London, Dobson, 1979.

Leaving Mottram Park, illustrated by Carolyn Dinan. Lewes, Sussex, Book Guild, 1989.

Three Weeks in August, illustrated by Catherine Todd. Cross Publishing, 1995.

*

Jill Chaney comments:

Each of my books, even if it is part of a series, is an entity in itself. The books are usually set in an actual place, although these are not always named: I have written one set in East Anglia, several in London, two on the Isle of Wight, one in Oxfordshire. The characters are always entirely fictitious, and what is described is usually a momentous time in the lives of the characters, although to an outsider the incidents might appear unremarkable. It is only now, looking back at the books, that I can discern a pattern common to them all. They seem to be about people trying to get on well with each other, not wanting to quarrel. The books for older children are also about bridging the gap between childish expectations and adult reality. I see this now, but each time I embark on a new book I am only concerned with writing a story about a group of people, many of whom happen to be between the ages of 10 and 20.

* * *

Jill Chaney writes equally successfully for the eight-year-old level and the older adolescent reader. One of her most appealing stories in the former category is *Christopher's Dig,* in which a young boy, after a visit to the Natural History Museum, is fired by enthusiasm to emulate Mary Anning, the 19th-century Dorset girl who dug up a dinosaur. Christopher, who lives in a small London flat, has to borrow a spade from an elderly gardener, but his main problem is finding somewhere to dig. He gets into trouble when he starts excavating the London parks, the Square gardens, and even disused building sites. Eventually he starts work by a sewer outlet on the Thames embankment and finds not a fossilised dinosaur but a box of jewels and gold coins. With the proceeds he takes his family on holiday to the Dorset coast to continue his hunt. The second book, *Christopher's Find,* is equally satisfactory, with the single-minded boy again triumphing over his disbelieving elders. The Woffle stories are for younger readers and make good bedtime tales.

As a writer of teenage fiction, Chaney appeals mainly to girls. *Canary Yellow* is the story of 16-year-old Julia who leaves home because of the incessant squabbling of her parents. She makes friends with a lonely old man living on a canal boat and when he has to go into hospital she moves in to look after his canary. A homeless young couple with small children camping out in a derelict cottage seem to have even greater problems than she has, and she offers to babysit while Dave takes his young wife to the hospital. Eventually the children get put into care and Julia's sympathy for Dave blossoms into love. He takes advantage of this and her initiation is painful. *Vectis Diary* is also the story of a girl on her own for the first time, working in a hotel on the Isle of Wight and writing her diary each night, exploring her feelings as she fumbles her way through the complications of growing up. These are sensitively handled stories and the teenager will not feel "talked-down-to" as she reads them.

—Ann G. Hay

CHANNEL, A.R. See **CATHERALL, Arthur.**

CHARLES, Nicholas. See **KUSKIN, Karla.**

CHAUNCY, Nan(cen Beryl)

Nationality: British. **Born:** Nancen Beryl Masterman, Northwood, Middlesex, 28 May 1900. **Education:** St. Michael's Collegiate School, Hobart, Tasmania. **Family:** Married Antony Chauncy in 1938; one daughter. **Awards:** Australian Children's Book award, 1958, 1959, 1961. **Died:** 1 May 1970.

PUBLICATIONS FOR CHILDREN

Fiction

They Found a Cave, illustrated by Margaret Horder. Melbourne and London, Oxford University Press, 1948; New York, Watts, 1961.

World's End Was Home, illustrated by Shirley Hughes. Melbourne and London, Oxford University Press, 1952; New York, Watts, 1961.

A Fortune for the Brave, illustrated by Margaret Horder. Melbourne and London, Oxford University Press, 1954; New York, Watts, 1961.

Tiger in the Bush, illustrated by Margaret Horder. London, Oxford University Press, 1957; New York, Watts, 1961.

Devil's Hill, illustrated by Geraldine Spence. London, Oxford University Press, 1958; New York, Watts, 1960.

Tangara: "Let Us Set Off Again," illustrated by Brian Wildsmith. London, Oxford University Press, 1960; as *The Secret Friends,* New York, Watts, 1962.

Half a World Away, illustrated by Annette Macarthur-Onslow. London, Oxford University Press, 1962; New York, Watts, 1963.

The "Roaring 40," illustrated by Annette Macarthur-Onslow. London, Oxford University Press, and New York, Watts, 1963.

High and Haunted Island, illustrated by Victor Ambrus. London, Oxford University Press, 1964; New York, Norton, 1965.

The Skewbald Pony, illustrated by David Parry. London, Nelson, 1965.

Panic at the Garage, illustrated by Peter Lloyd. Edinburgh, Oliver and Boyd, 1965.

Mathinna's People, illustrated by Victor Ambrus. London, Oxford University Press, 1967; as *Hunted in Their Own Land,* New York, Seabury Press, 1973.

Lizzie Lights, illustrated by Judith White. London, Oxford University Press, 1968.

The Lighthouse Keeper's Son, illustrated by Victor Ambrus. London, Oxford University Press, 1969.

Other

Beekeeping, illustrated by Jane Walker. Melbourne, Oxford University Press, 1967.

*

Manuscript Collection: State Archives, Hobart, Tasmania.

* * *

Nan Chauncy began writing at a time when Australian children's literature was dominated by melodramatic and romantic post-war fiction. Her early stories for children were in the existing mode except that *They Found a Cave,* although retaining conventional eccentric adult characters and exploiting a strong story line, was about a group of children who emerged as dynamic interacting individuals. They exist in a strong family relationship, and the Tasmanian bush setting is recognisably real. These two characteristics were so refined and strengthened in *Tiger in the Bush* and *Devil's Hill* that both books won the Australian Children's Book of the Year award in successive years and established the author's reputation as a realist. Indeed it can well be claimed that she established the contemporary realistic novel for children in Australia which has now been extended and developed in style and technique, as well as in content, by writers such as Patricia Wrightson and Ivan Southall.

In *Tiger in the Bush, Devil's Hill* and *The "Roaring 40"* Nan Chauncy explores the personal relationships of the Lorenny family. Badge Lorenny, "the little boy, the odd man out, the pest and the hanger-on" whom his older brother Lance and his sister Iggy call a "Bidgee burr" and a "wattle tick" because they can't do anything without his irritating presence, is the stalwart younger son of a strongly drawn family. There is Liddle-ma, a big woman in every way with strong principles and a warm heart, Dad, of few words but inspiring utter confidence in his offspring, the children, and their cousins from "outside." For "the world as Badge Lorenny knew it was just home—home tucked between the rough-wrought mountains of Tasmania like a drop of dew between cabbage leaves." To each of the children "home was home...as soon as you opened the door you saw the great blaze of the fire in the wide black hearth...you saw Dad slowly put down his newspaper—Liddle-ma's comforting smile." Home was a valley sanctuary hewn from the bush and accessible only by flying-fox—"The Wire." Here Badge learns that honesty and loyalty are more important than possessions or popularity, and that retaining his integrity brings a glow "greater than any sunset, uplifting him with joy and pride and a great relief." Through the incident of the lost cow in *Devil's Hill,* which had actually happened to the writer and one of her brothers, Badge's cousin, Sam, the Skite, the blusterer, and the shirker, learns the value of honest toil and the necessity for interdependence as well as independence to weld a family into an enduring unit.

Tangara made a different contribution to Australian children's literature. Perhaps for the first time there was a successful blending of realism with fantasy, and the plight of the aborigines who had been exterminated by white settlers in the early days of the colony of Tasmania was treated with dignity and spirituality. *Tangara* is a journey in time, a psychic rediscovery of the life of the Tasmanian aborigines through the "vision" of Lexie Pavemont whose deep affinity with her great-great-aunt Rita summons the aboriginal girl, Merrina, Rita's friend, from the past to prevent a latter-day tragedy, so that yet another debt is added to the past. The novel moves by implication and imagery to evoke insight into the unspeakable past and ends elegiacally with Merrina keening, "her thin arms reaching up imploringly," "alone and calling to her dead." A more formal lament was to be sung by Chauncy in *Mathinna's People,* a series of tableaux from the day that the young chief Wyrum gazed with awe at the white sails of the *Heemskerck* in 1642 to the death of Towterer, the chief, who went to the Old Ones broken in body and spirit by the contamination of white culture. Ironically the white man, George Robinson, who sought to do good from the highest motives is the one most responsible for a psychological affliction that was far more traumatic than bodily hurt.

Mathinna's People is Chauncy's finest composition. In *The "Roaring 40"* and *High and Haunted Island* she had written evocatively of Tasmania's lonely and threatening South-West coast, and had then created a fictitious island where a colony of Circlists act out the rituals of their religious faith. Even here, where there is a hint of the mysterious, Chauncy's writing is poetically realistic and convincing. Her last two stories, *Lizzie Lights* and *The Lighthouse Keeper's Son,* were less satisfying in that her work had come almost full circle with a return to some early weaknesses of plotting and characterisation.

In spite of a changing society and a greater sophistication in more recent writers, Nan Chauncy, through the Lorenny books and her aboriginal studies in particular, remains among the foremost Australian writers for children.

—H.M. Saxby

CHAUNDLER, Christine

Nationality: British. **Born:** Biggleswade, Bedfordshire, 5 September 1887. **Education:** Queen Anne's School, Caversham, Berkshire; St. Winifred's School, Bangor, Wales. **Career:** Editor, *Little Folks* magazine, London, 1914-17; children's editor, Nisbet, publishers, London, 1919-23; book reviewer, *Quiver* magazine, London, 1923-48; reader, Robert Hale, publishers, London, from 1939. **Died:** December 1972.

Publications for Children

Fiction

The Magic Kiss. London, Cassell, 1916.
Little Squirrel Tickletail, illustrated by Harry Rountree. London, Cassell, 1917; New York, Stokes, 1918.
Ronald's Burglar, illustrated by Helen Stratton. London, Nelson, 1919; New York, Nelson, 1921.
The Reputation of the Upper Fourth. London, Nisbet, 1919.
Pat's Third Term, illustrated by Harold Earnshaw. London, Oxford University Press, 1919.
The Thirteenth Orphan, illustrated by Honor Appleton. London, Nisbet, 1920; New York, Stokes, 1921.
Just Gerry. London, Nisbet, 1920.
The Right St. John's, illustrated by Savile Lumley. London, Oxford University Press, 1920.
The Binky Books (*The Motor Bandits, The Circus Lion*), illustrated by Will Owen. London, Nisbet, 2 vols., 1920.
Snuffles for Short, illustrated by Honor Appleton. London, Nisbet, 1921.
The Fourth Form Detectives. London, Nisbet, 1921.
The Reformation of Dormitory Five. London, Nisbet, 1921.
A Fourth Form Rebel. London, Nisbet, 1922.
Captain Cara. London, Nisbet, 1923.
Jan of the Fourth. London, Nisbet, 1923.
Tomboy Toby. London, Partridge, 1923.
Dickie's Day. London, Nelson, 1924.
Winning Her Colours. London, Nisbet, 1924.
Sally Sticks It Out. London, Partridge, 1924.
Judy the Tramp. London, Nisbet, 1924.
Princess Carroty-Top and Timothy. London, Warne, 1924.
Jill the Outsider, illustrated by Elizabeth Earnshaw. London, Cassell, 1924.
An Unofficial Schoolgirl. London, Nisbet, 1925.
Bunty of the Blackbirds. London, Nisbet, 1925.
The Adopting of Mickie, illustrated by T. Peddie. London, Religious Tract Society, 1925.
A Credit to Her House. London, Ward Lock, 1926.
Twenty-Six Christine Chaundler School Stories for Girls, illustrated by Arthur Twidle. London, Religious Tract Society, 1926.
The Exploits of Evangeline. London, Nisbet, 1926.
Reforming the Fourth. London, Ward Lock, 1927.
The Chivalrous Fifth, illustrated by Anne Rochester. London, Nelson, 1927.
Philippa's Family. London, Nisbet, 1927.
Meggy Makes Her Mark. London, Nisbet, 1928.
The Games Captain. London, Ward Lock, 1928.
Friends in the Fourth. London, Ward Lock, 1929.

The Technical Fifth. London, Ward Lock, 1930.
A Disgrace to the Fourth, illustrated by M.D. Swales. London, Nelson, 1930.
The New Girl in Four A. London, Nisbet, 1930.
The Madcap in the School. London, Nelson, 1930.
Two in Form Four. London, Cassell, 1931.
The Junior Prefect. London, Ward Lock, 1931.
The Story-Book School. London, Oxford University Press, 1931.
Jill of the Guides. London, Nisbet, 1932.
Five B and Evangeline. London, Newnes, 1932.
The Feud with the Sixth. London, Nisbet, 1932.
Cinderella Ann. London, Ward Lock, 1932.
The Amateur Patrol. London, Nisbet, 1933.
The Lonely Garden, and Ronald's Burglar. London, Nelson, 1934.
Tales of Nicky-Nob. London, Chambers, 4 vols., 1937.
The Children's Story Hour, illustrated by Alfred E. Kerr. London, Evans, 1938.
The Odd Ones, illustrated by Harry Rountree. London, Country Life, 1941.
Winkie Wee and the Silver Sixpence. London, Museum Press, 1947.
Winkie-Wee's Spring Cleaning. London, Museum Press, 1947.
Prize for Gardening, illustrated by L.M. Dufty. London, Nelson, 1948.
More Stories for the Children's Hour, illustrated by Cyril Foster. London, Hale, 1949.

Play

A Child Is Born: A Nativity Play. London, Evans, 1949.

Poetry

Curious Creatures, illustrated by Fred Robinson. London, The Naturist, 1944.
The Golden Years: Some Verses for Nurseries. London, Hale, 1950.

Other

My Book of Beautiful Legends, with Eric Wood, illustrated by A.C. Michael. London, Cassell, and New York, Funk, 1916.
My Book of Stories from the Poets, illustrated by A.C. Michael. London, Cassell, 1919; New York, Funk, 1920.
Arthur and His Knights, illustrated by Mackenzie. London, Nisbet, 1920; as *Legends and Tales of King Arthur,* New York, Stokes, 1920.
The Children's Christmas Book. London, Mowbray, 1949.
The Blue [Brown, Red] Book of Saints' Stories, Retold. London, Mowbray, 3 vols., 1952.
A Year-Book of Legends [Fairy Tales, the Stars, Customs, Saints, Folk-lore, Nursery Tales], illustrated by Tom Godfrey. London, Mowbray, 7 vols., 1954-63; *A Year-Book of Customs* published New York, Morehouse Gorham, 1957.
The End of the Rainbow (reader), illustrated by Hilda Boswell. Edinburgh, McDougall, 1958.
Through the Christian Year. London, Mowbray, 1960.
Great Saints Library: Simply-Written Lives for Christian Reading (St. Bridget, St. Christopher, St. Elizabeth and St. Teresa, St. Francis of Assisi, St. George and St. Alban, St. Hilda of Whitby, St. Hugh of Lincoln, St. Joan of Arc, St. Margaret of Scotland, St. Martin of Tours, St. Nicholas, St. Vincent de Paul), illustrated by Jennifer Miles. London, Mowbray, 12 vols., 1961.
Everyman's Book of Legends. London, Mowbray, 1963.
Everyman's Book of Ancient Customs. London, Mowbray, 1968.
Every Man's Book of Superstitions, illustrated by Margaret Francis. London, Mowbray, and New York, Philosophical Library, 1970.

Publications for Adults

Other

The Children's Author: A Writer's Guide to the Juvenile Market. London, Pitman, 1934.

* * *

Christine Chaundler was a colourful writer who, for several decades, contributed stories on school, Girl Guide, and fairy themes to many children's magazines and annuals, as well as producing full-length books. She was an editor of *Little Folks* from 1914 to 1917, and some of her most memorable works (*Meggy Makes Her Mark, Jill of the Guides,* etc.) were first published in that periodical. Her fairy poems and stories for younger children were refreshingly unsentimental. She was best known during the 1920s and 1930s, however, for her school stories. These were variations on classic themes of the genre established by Angela Brazil and developed by Dorita Fairlie Bruce. But Chaundler failed to achieve a comparable degree of recognition—possibly because her charactizations were less acute, and because she never extended the adventures of any of her heroines beyond a single novel into a series.

She managed to inject a strong sense of realism into her books, even when exploiting vivid and dramatic situations. One of the most distinctive elements of her writing was the capacity to deal with the girl who finds herself suddenly against the tide of popular standards and opinion. She first used this theme persuasively in *Pat's Third Term* with a junior who refused to make the expected gestures of homage to the generally idolized Head Girl; she developed and refined it in *Jill the Outsider* and *A Disgrace to the Fourth,* and, with considerable wit and style, in *The Chivalrous Fifth.* This was an attack on the type of snobbery that was so often associated with traditional, elitist boarding-schools: a new girl, Jane, is tolerated rather than accepted because she has told her form-mates that her mother keeps a second-hand shop, but this turns out to be a Bond Street antique gallery, and Jane's mother is a Viscountess!

Chaundler wrote numerous stories that catered for the enormous enthusiasm that surrounded the early days of the Girl Guide Movement. Here again, however, she was careful to steer clear of high-flown sentiment; her Girl Guides were not always the epitomes of efficiency and preparedness that they were in stories by many other Guiding writers. In *Bunty of the Blackbirds,* for example, one girl is shown as unable to light a campfire without setting the common alight, ripping her skirt from hem to waist, and burning a hole in her knickers. Similar uninflated realism was the keynote of her excellent 1919 series of *Little Folks* short stories, "How We Won the War," in which the over-ambitious patriotic efforts of a family of children repeatedly and entertainingly misfire.

Christine Chaundler continued to produce inventive fiction well into the 1930s. Later, in the 1950s and 1960s, she concentrated on writing a series of informative, religious non-fiction books, and "re-tellings" for younger children.

—Mary Cadogan

CHEETHAM, Ann. See **PILLING, Ann.**

CHIPPERFIELD, Joseph E(ugene)

Pseudonym: John Eland Craig. **Nationality:** British. **Born:** St. Austell, Cornwall, 20 April 1912. **Education:** Educated privately. **Family:** Married Mary Anne Tully in 1936. **Career:** Editor, Author's Literary Service, London, 1930-34; editor and script-writer for documentary films, 1934-40. **Died:** 3 January 1976.

PUBLICATIONS FOR CHILDREN

Fiction

Two Dartmoor Interludes. London, Boswell Press, 1935.
An Irish Mountain Tragedy. London, Boswell Press, 1936.
Three Stories (includes *Two Dartmoor Interludes, An Irish Mountain Tragedy, The Ghosts from Baylough*). London, Boswell Press, 1936.
This Earth—My Home: A Tale of Irish Troubles. Dublin, Padraic O'Follain, 1937.
Storm of Dancerwood, illustrated by C. Gifford Ambler. London, Hutchinson, 1948; New York, Longman, 1949; revised edition, Hutchinson, 1967.
Greatheart, The Salvation Hunter: The Epic of a Shepherd Dog, illustrated by C. Gifford Ambler. London, Hutchinson, 1950; New York, Roy, 1953.
Beyond the Timberland Trail, illustrated by Raymond Shepard. London, Hutchinson, 1951; New York, Longman, 1953.
Windruff of Tor Links, illustrated by Helen Torrey. New York, Longman, 1951; London, Hutchinson, 1954.
Grey Chieftain, illustrated by C. Gifford Ambler. London, Hutchinson, 1952; New York, Roy, 1954.
The Dog of Castle Crag (as John Eland Craig), illustrated by Leslie Atkinson. London, Nelson, 1952.
Silver Star, Stallion of the Echoing Mountain, illustrated by C. Gifford Ambler. London, Hutchinson, 1953; New York, Roy, 1955.
Greeka, Eagle of the Hebrides, illustrated by C. Gifford Ambler. London, Hutchinson, 1953; New York, Longman, 1954; revised edition, Hutchinson, 1962.
Rooloo, Stag of the Dark Water, illustrated by C. Gifford Ambler. London, Hutchinson, 1955; New York, Roy, 1962; revised edition, Hutchinson, 1962, Roy, 1963.
Dark Fury, Stallion of Lost River Valley, illustrated by C. Gifford Ambler. London, Hutchinson, 1956; New York, Roy, 1957.
Wolf of Badenoch: Dog of the Grampian Hills, illustrated by C. Gifford Ambler. London, Hutchinson, 1958; New York, Longman, 1959.
Ghost Horse: Stallion of the Oregon Trail, illustrated by C. Gifford Ambler. London, Hutchinson, 1959; New York, Roy, 1962.
Grasson, Golden Eagle of the North, illustrated by C. Gifford Ambler. London, Hutchinson, 1960.
Petrus, Dog of the Hill Country, illustrated by Stuart Tresilian. London, Heinemann, and New York, Longman, 1960.
Seokoo of the Black Wind, illustrated by C. Gifford Ambler. London, Hutchinson, 1961; New York, McKay, 1962.
The Grey Dog from Galtymore, illustrated by Stuart Tresilian. London, Heinemann, 1961; New York, McKay, 1962.
Sabre of Storm Valley, illustrated by C. Gifford Ambler. London, Hutchinson, 1962; New York, Roy, 1965.
A Dog Against Darkness, illustrated by F.R. Exell. London, Heinemann, 1963; as *A Dog to Trust: The Saga of a Seeing-Eye Dog,* New York, McKay, 1964.
Checoba, Stallion of the Comanche, illustrated by C. Gifford Ambler. London, Hutchinson, 1964; New York, Roy, 1966.
Boru, Dog of the O'Malley, illustrated by C. Gifford Ambler. London, Hutchinson, 1965; New York, McKay, 1966.
The Two Fugitives, illustrated by John Lathey. London, Heinemann, 1966.
Lone Stands the Glen, illustrated by Barry Driscoll. London, Hutchinson, 1966.
The Watcher on the Hills. London, Heinemann, 1968.
Rex of Larkbarrow, illustrated by Robert Hales. London, Hutchinson, 1969.
Storm Island, illustrated by Gareth Floyd. London, Hutchinson, 1970.
Banner, The Pacing White Stallion, illustrated by Robert Hales. London, Hutchinson, 1972.
Lobo, Wolf of the Wind River Range, illustrated by Robert Hales. London, Hutchinson, 1974.
Hunter of Harter Fell, illustrated by Victor Ambrus. London, Hutchinson, 1976.

Other

The Story of a Great Ship: The Birth and Death of the Steamship Titanic, illustrated by Charles King. London, Hutchinson, 1957; New York, Roy, 1959.

* * *

Joseph E. Chipperfield's *Storm of Dancerwood* has been revised and reprinted and is probably his best book. It tells of an alsatian dog and a blind vixen who have a curious, gentle relationship which ends in her death. The dog becomes gradually attached to a man who succeeds in winning his confidence. So develops that extraordinary empathy between human and animal that this author understood so well. Children understand this too because so many of them have just such close ties with their pets.

Often Chipperfield's dogs, or horses, are wild, intractable, or misunderstood, which adds spice to the stories. He has been said to "revive nostalgically the dramatic quality of Jack London," and this is a fair comparison. He had the same gift for interpreting animals' reactions without becoming too anthropomorphic. Only in *A Dog Against Darkness* does one have doubts about the subtlety of the thoughts that run through Arno's brain as he is being trained to be a guide dog for the blind. But this book has its own peculiar fascination, for readers of any age, because of the descriptions of this very special training.

The horse stories are violent and vivid and greatly enriched by the background of pioneering days in America. *Banner* is a tale of men obsessively determined to capture a horse that has become a legend. Banner is the last of the wild white stallions driven up the Colorado Rockies into a country being ravaged by men and their new railroads. He finally escapes his most persistent and crazy pursuer, leaving man and horse to the vultures. But there is no doubt left in the reader's mind that the frontiers of the west are pushing on and destroying the old ways of life.

Many of Chipperfield's books have remained in print, and *Ghost Horse* is available also in paperback. Children love animal stories. You will not find Chipperfield books learnedly analysed in manuals on children's literature, or hear them seriously discussed at conferences, but neither will you find them sitting unread on library shelves.

—Cecilia Gordon

CHORPENNING, Charlotte (Lee Barrows)

Nationality: American. **Born:** 3 January 1872. **Education:** Iowa Agricultural College, Ames; Cornell University, Ithaca, New York, 1892-94, B.L. 1894; Harvard University, Cambridge, Massachusetts (John Craig prize, 1915), 1913-15. **Family:** Married John C. Chorpenning. **Career:** Teacher, Wolf Hall school, Denver, 1901-04; English teacher, Winona Normal School, Minnesota, 1904-13, and 1915 to early 1920s; dramatic director, Recreation Training School, Hull House, Chicago; member of the Speech Department, Northwestern University, Evanston, Illinois; head of the Children's Theatre, Goodman Theatre, Art Institute of Chicago, 1931-52; worked with the U.S.O. during World War II. Co-founder, Children's World Theatre, late 1940s. **Died:** January 1955.

Publications for Children

Plays

The Emperor's New Clothes, adaptation of the story by Hans Christian Andersen (produced New York, 1935). New York, French, 1932.

Rhodopis, The First Cinderella. Chicago, Coach House Press, 1934.

Jack and the Beanstalk (produced New York, 1937). Anchorage, Kentucky, Children's Theatre Press, 1935.

The Indian Captive (produced Chicago, 1936). Anchorage, Kentucky, Children's Theatre Press, 1937.

Tom Sawyer's Treasure Hunt, adaptation of the story *Tom Sawyer* by Mark Twain. New York, French, 1937.

Hans Brinker and the Silver Skates, adaptation of the story by Mary Mapes Dodge. Anchorage, Kentucky, Children's Theatre Press, 1938.

Little Black Sambo and the Tigers, adaptation of the story by Helen Bannerman (produced New Orleans, 1939). New York, Dramatists Play Service, 1938; as *Rama and the Tigers,* Chicago, Coach House Press, 1954.

The Prince and the Pauper, adaptation of the story by Mark Twain. New York, Dramatists Play Service, 1938.

Radio Rescue (produced London, 1958). New York, Dramatists Play Service, 1938.

The Return of Rip Van Winkle, adaptation of the story "Rip Van Winkle" by Washington Irving. New York, Dramatists Play Service, 1938; as *Rip Van Winkle,* Chicago, Coach House Press, 1954.

Cinderella, adaptation of the story by Charles Perrault. Anchorage, Kentucky, Children's Theatre Press, 1940.

Abe Lincoln—New Salem Days (produced Chicago, 1941). Chicago, Coach House Press, 1954.

Rumpelstiltskin (produced New York, 1947). Anchorage, Kentucky, Children's Theatre Press, 1944.

The Secret Weapon. Washington, D.C., National Education Association, 1944.

Alice in Wonderland, adaptation of the story by Lewis Carroll. Chicago, Dramatic Publishing Company, 1946.

The Adventures of Tom Sawyer, adaptation of the story by Mark Twain. Chicago, Dramatic Publishing Company, 1946.

Many Moons, adaptation of the story by James Thurber (produced New York, 1947). Chicago, Dramatic Publishing Company, 1946.

The Elves and the Shoemaker, with Nora Tully (produced Chicago, 1946). Anchorage, Kentucky, Children's Theatre Press, 1946.

Little Red Riding Hood; or, Grandmother Slyboots (produced New York, 1947). Anchorage, Kentucky, Children's Theatre Press, 1947.

The Sleeping Beauty. Anchorage, Kentucky, Children's Theatre Press, 1947.

Little Lee Bobo, Chinatown Detective, with R.H. Lee. Anchorage, Kentucky, Children's Theatre Press, 1948.

The Three Bears. Anchorage, Kentucky, Children's Theatre Press, 1949.

King Midas and the Golden Touch. Anchorage, Kentucky, Children's Theatre Press, 1950.

Flibbertygibbet (His Last Chance), with Nora Tully MacAlvay. Anchorage, Kentucky, Children's Theatre Press, 1952.

Robinson Crusoe, adaptation of the novel by Daniel Defoe. Anchorage, Kentucky, Children's Theatre Press, 1952.

The Magic Horn: A Story of Roland and Charlemagne, with Anne Nicholson. Chicago, Coach House Press, 1954.

Lincoln's Secret Messenger—Boy Detective to a President. Chicago, Coach House Press, 1955.

Hansel and Gretel, adaptation of the story by the Grimm Brothers. Chicago, Coach House Press, 1956.

Three Adventure Plays (includes *The Adventures of Tom Sawyer, Radio Rescue, The Magic Horn).* Chicago, Coach House Press, 1972.

Publications for Adults

Other

Twenty One Years with Children's Theatre. Anchorage, Kentucky, Children's Theatre Press, 1954.

* * *

Charlotte Chorpenning is acknowledged as the first lady of children's theatre in the United States; both as playwright and producer, her influence has been immeasurable. Her plays are chiefly adaptations of fairy tales and children's literary classics but include dramatizations of history and legend. The dramas demonstrate the principles she preached about writing plays for children in *Twenty One Years with Children's Theatre,* such as the need for conventionally constructed plots allowing physical action, central characters with whom the child could identify, moral values, and colorful settings.

Adaptations of well-known fairy tales such as *Jack and the Beanstalk* and *Rumpelstiltskin* constitute the largest body of the Chorpenning canon. The hero of *Jack and the Beanstalk* aids his mother and neighbors by outwitting a cruel giant after climbing a magic beanstalk into the sky and returning with riches courageously won. Despite the characters' one-dimensionality, the fanciful plot provides imaginative action and theatricality that make this early play continually popular. The characters in *Rumpelstiltskin* assume more dimension in a tale of a miller's daughter who wins a prince by spinning straw into gold through the proffered magical services of an evil dwarf who demands a cruel bargain from which she only narrowly escapes. Also representative is a charming dramatization of Thurber's *Many Moons,* in which a spoiled princess maturely accepts that she does not possess the only moon. Evident in all three plays is a well-structured plot projecting appealing characters, fanciful settings, and a traditional moral.

Children's literary classics are another Chorpenning source. One example is *The Return of Rip Van Winkle,* whose title character is sensitively portrayed with his frailties and warmheartedness. Rip's adventures in fleeing from an exasperated wife, meeting Henry Hudson's crew, and waking up after a 20 year sleep are both affecting and stageworthy. In *Hans Brinker and the Silver Skates,* to give another example, the young hero's courageous efforts save his family's sanity and security, and enable his sister to win a skating match on the Holland canals. Characteristic of these audience-appealing adaptations is the presence of familiar scenes from the original stories and a theatrically efficacious *pièce bien faite* plot pattern.

Three plays exemplify Chorpenning dramas trotting out the material of history and legend. A pioneer girl actually captured and adopted by the Seneca Indians is the protagonist of *The Indian Captive* who is forbidden by a loving but possessive Chief to reveal herself to her mother come in search of her, but is finally returned to her own people. The drama credibly depicts Indian life and theatrically interprets historical incident. Young Abe is convincingly recreated amid Lincoln lore in *Abe Lincoln—New Salem Days* as a debt-ridden Illinois storekeeper. Also successfully portrayed, President Lincoln is saved by a boy from a Copperhead kidnapping plot in *Lincoln's Secret Messenger.* These stageworthy dramas hold particular appeal for young adults.

The plotting and production requirements of many of Chorpenning's plays seem out of fashion today. Yet that her plays continue to be performed attests to their durability and to their author's craftsmanship and merited reputation.

—Christian H. Moe

CHURCH, Richard (Thomas)

Nationality: British. **Born:** London, 26 March 1893. **Education:** Dulwich Hamlet School, London, 1905-08. **Family:** Married 1) Caroline Parfett in 1915; 2) Catherina Schimmer in 1930 (died 1965); 3) Dorothy Beale in 1967; three daughters and one son. **Career:** Civil servant, London, 1909-33; editor, J.M. Dent, publishers, London, 1933-51. Co-founder, the *Criterion,* London, 1921; regular contributor to the *Spectator* and *New Statesman,* London; for 40 years contributor of a monthly essay to the "Home Forum Page" of the *Christian Science Monitor,* Boston. Director, English Festival of Spoken Poetry, until it merged with the Arts Council Poetry Panel. President, PEN, 1958-59, and the English Association, 1964-65. **Awards:** Femina Vie Heureuse prize, 1938; *Sunday Times* Gold Medal, 1955; Foyle Poetry prize, 1957. Fellow, 1950, and Vice-President, 1968, Royal Society of Literature; Fellow, Royal Society of Art, 1970. C.B.E. (Commander, Order of the British Empire), 1957. **Died:** 4 March 1972.

Publications for Children

Fiction

A Squirrel Called Rufus, illustrated by John Skeaping. London, Dent, 1941; Philadelphia, Winston, 1946.
The Cave, illustrated by Clarke Hutton. London, Dent, 1950; as *Five Boys in a Cave,* New York, Day, 1951; revised edition, Dent, 1953.
Dog Toby: A Frontier Tale, illustrated by Laurence Irving. London, Hutchinson, 1953; New York, Day, 1958.
Down River, illustrated by Laurence Irving. New York, Day, 1957; London, Heinemann, 1958.
The Bells of Rye. London, Heinemann, 1960; New York, Day, 1961.
The White Doe, illustrated by John Ward. London, Heinemann, 1968; New York, Day, 1969.
The French Lieutenant: A Ghost Story. London, Heinemann, 1971; New York, Day, 1972.

Publications for Adults

Novels

Oliver's Daughter: A Tale. London, Dent, 1930.
High Summer. London, Dent, 1931; New York, Smith, 1932.
The Prodigal Father. London, Dent, and New York, Day, 1933.
The Apple of Concord. London, Dent, 1935.
The Porch. London, Dent, 1937.
The Stronghold. London, Dent, 1939.
The Room Within. London, Dent, 1940.
The Sampler. London, Dent, 1942.
The Nightingale. London, Hutchinson, 1952.
The Dangerous Years. London, Heinemann, 1956; New York, Dutton, 1958.
The Crab-Apple Tree. London, Heinemann, 1959.
Prince Albert. London, Heinemann, 1963.
Little Miss Moffatt: A Confession. London, Heinemann, 1969.

Play

The Prodigal: A Play in Verse (produced Canterbury, 1953). London, Staples Press, 1953.

Poetry

The Flood of Life and Other Poems. London, Fifield, 1917.
Hurricane and Other Poems. London, Selwyn and Blount, 1919.
Philip and Other Poems. Oxford, Blackwell, 1923.

The Portrait of the Abbot: A Story in Verse. London, Benn, 1926; New York, Dial Press, 1927.
The Dream and Other Poems. London, Benn, 1927.
Mood Without Measure. London, Faber and Gwyer, 1927.
Theme with Variations. London, Benn, 1928.
The Glance Backward: New Poems. London, Dent, 1930.
News from the Mountain. London, Dent, 1932.
Twelve Noon. London, Dent, 1936.
The Solitary Man and Other Poems. London, Dent, 1941.
Twentieth-Century Psalter. London, Dent, 1943.
The Lamp. London, Dent, 1946.
Collected Poems. London, Dent, 1948; New York, AMS Press, 1976.
Selected Lyrical Poems. London, Staples Press, 1951.
The Inheritors: Poems 1948-1955. London, Heinemann, 1957.
(*Poems*). London, Hulton, 1959.
North of Rome. London, Hutchinson, 1960.
The Burning Bush: Poems 1958-1966. London, Heinemann, 1967.
25 Lyrical Poems. London, Heinemann, 1967.

Other

Mary Shelley. London, Howe, and New York, Viking Press, 1928.
An Essay in Estimation of Dorothy Richardson's "Pilgrimage." London, Dent-Cresset Press, 1938.
Calling for a Spade. London, Dent, 1939.
Eight for Immortality. London, Dent, 1941; Freeport, New York, Books for Libraries Press, 1969.
Plato's Mistake. London, Routledge, 1941.
British Authors: A Twentieth Century Gallery. London, Longman, 1943; revised edition, 1948; Freeport, New York, Books for Libraries Press, 1969.
Green Tide. London, Country Life, 1945.
Richard Jefferies Centenary 1848-1948: Memorial Lecture. Swindon, Council of the Borough of Swindon, 1948.
Kent. London, Hale, 1948.
A Window on a Hill. London, Hale, 1951.
The Growth of the English Novel. London, Methuen, 1951; New York, Barnes and Noble, 1961.
A Portrait of Canterbury. London, Hutchinson, 1953; revised edition, 1968.
Over the Bridge: An Essay in Autobiography. London, Heinemann, 1955; as *Over the Bridge: An Autobiography,* New York, Dutton, 1956.
The Royal Parks of London. London, Ministry of Works, 1956.
Small Moments. London, Hutchinson, 1957; New York, Dutton, 1958.
The Golden Sovereign: A Conclusion to "Over the Bridge." London, Heinemann, and New York, Dutton, 1957.
A Country Window: A Round of Essays. London, Heinemann, 1958.
Calm October: Essays. London, Heinemann, 1961.
The Voyage Home (autobiography). London, Heinemann, 1964; New York, Day, 1966.
A Stroll Before Dark: Essays. London, Heinemann, 1965.
A Look at Tradition. London, Oxford University Press, 1965.
London: Flower of Cities All. London, Heinemann, and New York, Day, 1966.
Speaking Aloud. London, Heinemann, 1968.
A Harvest of Mushrooms and Other Sporadic Essays. London, Heinemann, 1970.
The Wonder of Words. London, Hutchinson, 1970.
London in Colour. London, Batsford, and New York, Norton, 1971.
Kent's Contribution. Bath, Adams and Dart, 1972.

Editor, *Poems and Prose,* by Swinburne. London, Dent, and New York, Dutton, 1940.
Editor, with M.M. Bozman, *Poems of Our Time 1900-1942.* London, Dent, 1945.
Editor, *John Keats: An Introduction and a Selection.* London, Phoenix House, 1948.
Editor, *Poems,* by Shelley. London, Folio Society, 1949.
Editor, *Poems for Speaking.* London, Dent, 1950.
Editor, *A Selection of Poems,* by Spenser. London, Grey Walls Press, 1954.
Editor, *Out of the Dark: New Poems,* by Phoebe Hesketh. London, Heinemann, 1954.
Editor, *The Spoken Word: A Selection from Twenty-Five Years of "The Listener."* London, Collins, 1955; revised edition, 1960.
Editor, *The Little Kingdom: A Kentish Collection.* London, Hutchinson, 1964.
Editor, *Essays by Divers Hands.* London, Oxford University Press, 1965.

*

Manuscript Collection: University of Texas, Austin.

* * *

Unlike many authors Richard Church is not easy to categorize; he belongs to no obvious group or movement, apparently owes nothing to older writers, and was content every so often to publish a skilful, polished, craftsmanlike story, capable of catching the attention on more than one level, that of the younger reader who might possibly remain unaware of a deeper significance, and that of the adult who is not afraid to dip into what ostensibly is a story for children and find there a satisfying and perceptive commentary on the human condition. *Dog Toby* is such a story, a moving and poignant tale which takes place on both sides of a barbed wire frontier. Three children and their two dogs, innocently oblivious of the significance of the wire, ignore the division it represents, and reach a close understanding with ordinary people on the other side. A simple allegory but none the less effective.

Similarly, *A Squirrel Called Rufus* is the story of an old-established family of red squirrels, secure in the heart of a forest, who are confronted by a deadly and ruthless enemy, a horde of grey squirrels invading their home, threatening to usurp their rights and freedoms. After a great battle, the climax of the struggle, the invaders are hurled back, to leave the red squirrels triumphant. Once again to all intents and purposes this is nothing more than an unpretentious if exciting and dramatic adventure story, but then we notice the date of publication—1941, and so presumably written when England itself stood in the same perilous situation.

The world of nature also provides the backcloth to *The White Doe,* about Tom Winter's concern for a white doe and her fawn he befriends in the forest where his father is woodman. At the same time Tom is troubled in his mind by the effect of his parting with his close friend Billy Lander, the Squire's son away for the first time at boarding school. And then another complicating factor enters his life, the arrival of snobbish Harold Sims into the locality, with whom Tom immediately crosses swords, and whose determination to hunt the deer occasions the life-and-death climax. In this instance the angry thread of human relationships, entangled even further by Tom's friendship with Harold's sister, is thrown into sharp contrast with the orderly passing of the seasons in the forest and on the shore.

The Cave relates the exploration by a group of five boys who call themselves the Tomahawk Club of a limestone cave one of them stumbles across. Again Church focuses attention on human relationships: when danger comes the dominating Alan Hobbs fails to measure up to it and another of the group, George Reynolds, assumes authority and responsibility, and displays the qualities of leadership. Compared to this compelling series of character studies, *Down River,* the further adventures of the Tomahawk Club, is slightly pedestrian. But no author can sustain such a high level of excellence indefinitely, not even Richard Church.

—Alan Edwin Day

CIARDI, John (Anthony)

Nationality: American. **Born:** Boston, Massachusetts, 24 June 1916. **Education:** Bates College, Lewiston, Maine, 1934-36; Tufts College, Medford, Massachusetts, B.A. (magna cum laude) 1938 (Phi Beta Kappa); University of Michigan, Ann Arbor (Hopwood award, 1939), A.M. 1939. **Military Service:** United States Army Air Corps, 1942-45: Air Medal, Oak Leaf Cluster. **Family:** Married Myra Judith Hostetter in 1946; one daughter and two sons. **Career:** Instructor, University of Kansas City, Missouri, 1940-42 and 1945-46; Briggs Copeland Instructor in English, 1946-48, and Assistant Professor, 1948-53, Harvard University, Cambridge, Massachusetts; Lecturer, 1953-54, Associate Professor, 1954-56, and Professor of English, 1956-61, Rutgers University, New Brunswick, New Jersey; Lecturer, 1947-73, and Director, 1956-72, Bread Loaf Writers Conference, Vermont. Editor, Twayne Publishers, New York, 1949; lecturer, Salzburg Seminar in American Studies, 1951; poetry editor, 1956-73, and contributing editor, 1973-80, *Saturday Review,* New York; host, *Accent* program, CBS-TV, 1961-62; contributing editor, *World Magazine,* New York, 1972-73. Director, 1955-57, and President, 1958-59, National College English Association. **Awards:** Bread Loaf Writers Conference fellowship, 1940; Oscar Blumenthal prize, 1943, Eunice Tietjens Memorial prize, 1944, Levinson prize, 1946, and Harriet Monroe Memorial prize, 1955 (*Poetry,* Chicago); New England Poetry Club Golden Rose, 1948; American Academy in Rome fellowship, 1956; National Council of Teachers of English award, for poetry, 1982. D. Litt.: Tufts College, 1960; Ohio Wesleyan University, Delaware, 1971; Washington University, St. Louis, 1971; Hum.D.: Wayne State University, Detroit, 1963; LL.D.: Ursinus College, Collegeville, Pennsylvania, 1964; D.L.H.: Kalamazoo College, Michigan, 1964; Bates College, 1970; Honorary Doctorate: Kean College, Union, New Jersey, 1977. **Member:** American Academy, and American Academy of Arts and Sciences. **Died:** 30 March 1986.

Publications for Children

Fiction

The Wish-Tree, illustrated by Louis Glanzman. New York, Crowell Collier, 1962.

Poetry

The Reason for the Pelican, illustrated by Madeleine Gekiere. Philadelphia, Lippincott, 1959.
Scrappy the Pup, illustrated by Jane Miller. Philadelphia, Lippincott, 1960.
I Met a Man, illustrated by Robert Osborn. Boston, Houghton Mifflin, 1961.
The Man Who Sang the Sillies, illustrated by Edward Gorey. Philadelphia, Lippincott, 1961.
You Read to Me, I'll Read to You, illustrated by Edward Gorey. Philadelphia, Lippincott, 1962.
John J. Plenty and the Fiddler Dan: A New Fable of the Grasshopper and the Ant, illustrated by Madeleine Gekiere. Philadelphia, Lippincott, 1963.
You Know Who, illustrated by Edward Gorey. Philadelphia, Lippincott, 1964.
The King Who Saved Himself from Being Saved, illustrated by Edward Gorey. Philadelphia, Lippincott, 1965.
The Monster Den; or, Look What Happened at My House—and to It, illustrated by Edward Gorey. Philadelphia, Lippincott, 1966.
Someone Could Win a Polar Bear, illustrated by Edward Gorey. Philadelphia, Lippincott, 1970.
Fast and Slow: Poems for Advanced Children and Beginning Parents, illustrated by Becky Gaver. Boston, Houghton Mifflin, 1975.
Doodle Soup, illustrated by Merle Nacht. Boston, Houghton Mifflin, 1985.
The Hopeful Trout and Other Limericks, illustrated by Susan Meddaugh. Boston, Houghton Mifflin, 1989.

Publications for Adults

Poetry

Homeward to America. New York, Holt, 1940.
Other Skies. Boston, Little Brown, 1947.
Live Another Day. New York, Twayne, 1949.
From Time to Time. New York, Twayne, 1951.
As If: Poems New and Selected. New Brunswick, New Jersey, Rutgers University Press, 1955.
I Marry You: A Sheaf of Love Poems. New Brunswick, New Jersey, Rutgers University Press, 1958.
39 Poems. New Brunswick, New Jersey, Rutgers University Press, 1959.
In the Stoneworks. New Brunswick, New Jersey, Rutgers University Press, 1961.
In Fact. New Brunswick, New Jersey, Rutgers University Press, 1962.
Person to Person. New Brunswick, New Jersey, Rutgers University Press, 1964.
This Strangest Everything. New Brunswick, New Jersey, Rutgers University Press, 1966.
An Alphabestiary: Twenty-Six Poems. Philadelphia, Lippincott, 1967.
A Genesis: 15 Poems. New York, Touchstone, 1967.
The Achievement of John Ciardi: A Comprehensive Selection of His Poems with a Critical Introduction, edited by Miller Williams. Chicago, Scott Foresman, 1969.

Lives of X. New Brunswick, New Jersey, Rutgers University Press, 1971.
The Little That Is All. New Brunswick, New Jersey, Rutgers University Press, 1974.
Limericks: Too Gross, with Isaac Asimov. New York, Norton, 1978.
For Instance. New York, Norton, 1979.
A Grossery of Limericks, with Isaac Asimov. New York, Norton, 1981.
Selected Poems. Fayetteville, University of Arkansas Press, 1984.
The Birds of Pompeii. Fayetteville, University of Arkansas Press, 1985.
Ciardi, Measure of the Man, edited by Vince Clemente. Fayetteville, University of Arkansas Press, 1987.

Recordings: *As If,* Folkways; *John Ciardi,* Everett Edwards, 1972.

Other

Dialogue with an Audience. Philadelphia, Lippincott, 1963.
Dante Alighieri: Three Lectures, with J.C. Mathews and Francis Fergusson. Washington, D.C., Library of Congress, 1965.
On Poetry and the Poetic Process, with Joseph B. Roberts, Jr. Troy, Alabama, Troy State University Press, 1972.
Manner of Speaking (*Saturday Review* columns). New Brunswick, New Jersey, Rutgers University Press, 1972.
A Browser's Dictionary and Native's Guide to the Unknown American Language. New York, Harper, 1980; *A Second Browser's Dictionary,* New York, Harper, 1983.
Plain English in a Complex Society, with Laurence Urdang and Frederick Dickerson. Bloomington, Indiana University Poynter Center, 1980.
Good Words to You: An All-New Dictionary and Native's Guide to the Unknown American Language. New York, Harper, 1987.
Saipan: The War Diary of John Ciardi. Fayetteville, University of Arkansas Press, 1988.

Editor, *Mid-Century American Poets.* New York, Twayne, 1950.
Editor, *How Does a Poem Mean?* Boston, Houghton Mifflin, 1960; revised edition, with Miller Williams, 1975.
Editor, with James M. Reid and Laurence Perrine, *Poetry: A Closer Look.* New York, Harcourt Brace, 1963.

Translator, *The Divine Comedy,* by Dante. New York, Norton, 1977.
Translator, *The Inferno,* by Dante. New Brunswick, New Jersey, Rutgers University Press, 1954.
Translator, *The Purgatorio,* by Dante. New York, New American Library, 1961.
Translator, *The Paradiso,* by Dante. New York, New American Library, 1970.

*

Bibliography: *John Ciardi: A Bibliography* by William White, Detroit, Wayne State University Press, 1959.

Manuscript Collections: Wayne State University, Detroit; Library of Congress, Washington, D.C.; Lockwood Library, State University of New York, Buffalo.

Critical Study: *John Ciardi* by Edward Francis Krickel, Boston, Twayne, 1980.

John Ciardi commented:

(1978) I gather that there is a professionalism about writing for children. The professionals I have met seem to have rules, some of which make me uneasy. I began writing children's poems first as a game with my nephews, then with my own children. I do not know how to do it by rule, only by ear. I know I am happy when I reach children. I want the contact to be *fun.* A few years ago the National Council of Teachers of English surveyed American school children and had them vote for their 25 favorite poems. The poem they put at the top of the list was my "Mummy Slept Late and Daddy Fixed Breakfast." No citation has ever given me more pleasure, especially as evidence that my amateur sense of it has been right, that I am reaching children where it is fun.

* * *

It is one thing to write nonsense verse for children, as many do, with outrageously silly situations, concocted creatures, and humorous story lines as well as attention to contemporary concerns—but quite another matter when a poet, in command of his craft, puts his mind and heart to it. John Ciardi, whose background was that of a scholar, critic, and adult poet, was such a craftsman who kept in touch with the matters that delight the young and, through numerous books, presented them with a wealth of observations, creatures, and situations deriving their strength from pattern and rhyme that ring clear and true to the ear and often invite active participation and much laughter.

Ciardi's imagination was in tune with the young who enjoy the absurdity of ridiculous names; he, in a sense, updated Edward Lear for the contemporary child with his "Brobinyak" who lives in the "Forest of Foffenzee/In the land of the Pshah of Psham," where one might also meet "Radio Eeels" or the "Banjo Tern" or the "Scrawny Shank," or the "Saginsack" whose "Radio Horns/And Aerials for ears" could "be listening to you." Again, in the story of "The Army Horse and the Army Jeep" there are echoes of the inanimate table and chair of Lear. Yet Ciardi was not imitating; he was his own man, unlike others writing for children who seize nonsense and preposterous names and situations and who do not, in craft or in use of symbol, measure up to Lear.

Ciardi's interest in animals, the shark, python, whale, crow, ape, boa constrictor, and others, permeates his books in an imaginative series of short-story poems. Nature is also given emphasis in "How to Tell the Top of a Hill" or "The River Is a Piece of Sky." Ecological concerns crop up in "And They Lived Happily Ever After for a While," all of which focus on the same wonder and imaginative speculation as in "The Reason for the Pelican" or "Fast and Slow" where the "fast young crow" does not know "...Where to go."

The occasional cuteness of "Mummy Slept Late and Daddy Fixed Breakfast" or "Prattle," although these poems are popular, seems to me to show Ciardi at less than his best. The strength and haunting quality of "There once was an Owl perched on a shed./Fifty years later the Owl was dead./Some say mice are in the corn./Some say kittens are being born" prove his ability to soar beyond mere childishness.

In whatever form he chose to write, his control was always admirable; his couplets, tercets, quatrains, limericks attest to his carefully constructed meter and rhyme; his technique went happily beyond what he himself called "spillage of raw emotion." Ciardi wrote to entertain in a rhythm to which the young respond, and if occasional morals creep in now and again, they are done with a sophistication and humor that are so carefully worked into the poem that they cannot be faulted.

—Myra Cohn Livingston

CLARE, Helen. See **CLARKE, Pauline.**

CLARK, Ann Nolan

Nationality: American. **Born:** Las Vegas, New Mexico, 5 December 1896. **Education:** New Mexico Highlands University, Las Vegas, graduated 1919. **Family:** Married Thomas Patrick Clark in 1919 (died); one son (deceased). **Career:** Schoolteacher near Las Vegas, 1917 and 1919; worked in Tacoma, Washington, 1918; assistant English teacher, Highlands University; educational supervisor, Bureau of Indian Affairs, 1920-62; trained teachers in Latin America, 1945-50; education consultant, Institute of Latin-American Affairs, 1946-62. United States delegate to UNESCO Conference, Brazil. **Awards:** American Library Association Newbery Medal, 1953; United States Bureau of Indian Affairs Distinguished Service award, 1962; Catholic Library Association Regina Medal, 1963. **Died:** 13 December 1995.

PUBLICATIONS FOR CHILDREN

Fiction

Buffalo Caller: The Story of a Young Sioux Boy of the Early 1700s, Before the Coming of the Horse, illustrated by Marian Hulsizer. Evanston, Illinois, Row Peterson, 1942.
Young Hunter of Picuris, illustrated by Velino Herrara. Chilocco, Oklahoma, Bureau of Indian Affairs, 1943.
Little Navajo Bluebird, illustrated by Paul Lantz. New York, Viking Press, 1943.
Magic Money, illustrated by Leo Politi. New York, Viking Press, 1950.
Secret of the Andes, illustrated by Jean Charlot. New York, Viking Press, 1952; London, Penguin, 1976.
Looking-for-Something: The Story of a Stray Burro of Ecuador, illustrated by Leo Politi. New York, Viking Press, 1952.
Blue Canyon Horse, illustrated by Allan Houser. New York, Viking Press, 1954.
Santiago, illustrated by Lynd Ward. New York, Viking Press, 1955.
A Santo for Pasqualita, illustrated by Mary Villarejo. New York, Viking Press, 1959.
World Song, illustrated by Kurt Wiese. New York, Viking Press, 1960.
Paco's Miracle, illustrated by Agnes Tait. New York, Farrar Straus, 1962.
Tia Maria's Garden, illustrated by Ezra Jack Keats. New York, Viking Press, 1963.
Medicine Man's Daughter, illustrated by Don Bolognese. New York, Farrar Straus, 1963.
This for That, illustrated by Don Freeman. San Carlos, California, Golden Gate Books, 1965.
Summer Is for Growing, illustrated by Agnes Tait. New York, Farrar Straus, 1968.
Hoofprint on the Wind, illustrated by Robert Andrew Parker. New York, Viking Press, 1972.
Year Walk. New York, Viking Press, 1975.
All This Wild Land. New York, Viking Press, 1976.
To Stand Against the Wind. New York, Viking Press, 1978.

Poetry

In My Mother's House, illustrated by Velino Herrara. New York, Viking Press, 1941.
Third Monkey, illustrated by Don Freeman. New York, Viking Press, 1956.
Bear Cub, illustrated by Charles Fracé. New York, Viking Press, 1965.

Other

Who Wants to Be a Prairie Dog? (reader), illustrated by Van Tishnahjinnie. Phoenix, Office of Indian Affairs, 1940.
Little Herder in Spring [*Autumn, Winter, Summer*] (readers), illustrated by Hoke Denetsosie. Phoenix, Office of Indian Affairs, 4 vols., 1940-42.
Little Boy with Three Names: Stories of Taos Pueblo (reader), illustrated by Tonita Lujan. Chilocco, Oklahoma, Office of Indian Affairs, 1940.
The Pine Ridge Porcupine (reader), illustrated by Andrew Standing Soldier. Lawrence, Kansas, Office of Indian Affairs, 1941.
A Child's Story of New Mexico, with Frances Carey. Lincoln, Nebraska, University Publishing, 1941.
There Still Are Buffalo (reader), illustrated by Andrew Standing Soldier. Lawrence, Kansas, Office of Indian Affairs, 1942.
About the Slim Butte Raccoon (reader), illustrated by Andrew Standing Soldier. Lawrence, Kansas, Office of Indian Affairs, 1942.
About the Grass Mountain Mouse (reader), illustrated by Andrew Standing Soldier. Lawrence, Kansas, Office of Indian Affairs, 1942.
About the Hen of Wahpeton (reader), illustrated by Andrew Standing Soldier. Lawrence, Kansas, Office of Indian Affairs, 1943.
Bringer of the Mystery Dog (reader), illustrated by Oscar Howe. Lawrence, Kansas, Office of Indian Affairs, 1943.
Brave Against the Enemy: A Story of Three Generations—of the Day Before Yesterday, of Yesterday, and of Tomorrow (reader), illustrated by Helen Post. Lawrence, Kansas, Office of Indian Affairs, 1944.
Sun Journey: A Story of the Zuñi Pueblo (reader), illustrated by Percy T. Sandy. Chilocco, Oklahoma, Office of Indian Affairs, 1945.
Singing Sioux Cowboy Reader, illustrated by Andrew Standing Soldier. Lawrence, Kansas, United States Indian Service, 1947.
Linda Rita (reader). Washington, D.C., Government Printing Office, 1948.
Los Patos Son Diferentes (reader). Washington, D.C., Government Printing Office, 1948.
El Buey Que Quería Vivir en la Casa (reader). Washington, D.C. Government Printing Office, 1948.

Juan el Poblano (reader). Washington, D.C., Government Printing Office, 1949.

El Cerdito Que Fué al Mercado (reader). Washington, D.C., Government Printing Office, 1949.

El Maestro Rural en la Comunidad, with Manuel Arce and Miguel Gordillo. Guatemala, Ministerio de Educacibon Publica, 1955.

The Little Indian Pottery Maker, illustrated by Don Perceval. Los Angeles, Melmont, 1955.

Third Monkey, illustrated by Don Freeman. New York, Viking Press, 1956.

The Little Indian Basket Maker, illustrated by Harrison Begay. Los Angeles, Melmont, 1957.

The Desert People, illustrated by Allan Houser. New York, Viking Press, 1962.

Father Kino: Priest to the Pimas, illustrated by H. Lawrence Hoffman. New York, Farrar Straus, and London, Burns Oates, 1963.

Brother Andre of Montreal, illustrated by Harold Lang. New York, Vision Books, and London, Burns Oates, 1967.

Arizona Is for Young People, with Glenna Craw. Lincoln, Nebraska, University Publishing, 1968.

Along Sandy Trails, illustrated by Alfred A. Cohn. New York, Viking Press, 1969.

Circle of Seasons, illustrated by W.T. Mars. New York, Farrar Straus, 1970.

In the Land of Small Dragon: A Vietnamese Folktale, with Dang Manh Kha, illustrated by Tony Chen. New York, Viking Press, 1979.

Publications for Adults

Other

Journey to the People. New York, Viking Press, 1969.

These Were the Valiant: A Collection of New Mexico Profiles. Albuquerque, Horn, 1969.

*

Manuscript Collections: Kerlan Collection, University of Minnesota, Minneapolis; de Grummond Collection, University of Southern Mississippi, Hattiesburg; University of Oregon Library, Eugene.

Ann Nolan Clark comments:

When I entered the Bureau of Indian Affairs (B.I.A.) in the 1920s, I quickly realized that there were no textbooks which Indian children could relate to—vocabulary, background, and values in the books then available were foreign to them and could not be understood. I wrote what was then called "Third Grade Geography" which I thought would help to build concepts of people in relation to places and modes of living. Each child bound (in Indian calico) his own book and illustrated it. Someone from the B.I.A. Washington office showed a copy to May Massee at Viking Press, and the book was published as *In My Mother's House.* This led the B.I.A. to encourage me to write Indian readers for Indian children. These were illustrated by Indian students and published at Indian schools where printing was being taught. I did a series of Pueblo, Navajo, Sioux, and Papago stories, but World War II cut off our appropriation for printing. After that I continued to work for the B.I.A., and tried to write a book every year.

* * *

In My Mother's House is one of the most unusual books ever written for children in the United States. Ann Nolan Clark wrote it so that her small class of third graders in the tiny Tewa Indian village of Tesuque, New Mexico, would have a book that they could read and understand about the everyday life of their people.

It is no wonder the five Indian children took the book to their hearts. It is a book filled with their ways, their world, their words; and said in a way that they would say it. Yes, the book must be *said.* If one just looks at the words it could easily be mistaken for any other primer for early readers, but when the words are given sound, the Indian child's deep feeling for nature and love of family are poetically revealed.

Ordinarily teaching children and writing for them doesn't mix well, but then Clark is no ordinary woman. Like that of Sylvia Ashton-Warner, the remarkable teacher-writer who worked among the Maori children of New Zealand, Clark's writing is extraordinary because her approach to teaching was extraordinary. For instance, she found in the written work of older Indian children the quiet beauty of straightforward "Talk" that comes naturally to a person raised in the oral tradition. Here, in "Sleep," is but one of those she shares in *Journey to the People:*

The sun goes down
and night falls.
Then I close my eyes
and go to sleep
in my bed under the trees.

These served as her models when she turned to writing books for their younger brothers and sisters, who could not as yet read or write, but whose minds and hearts she knew and understood, books like *Blue Canyon Horse* and *The Desert People* (a companion piece to *In My Mother's House*). It begins:

I am a boy
of the Desert People.

White men call me Indian
White men call me Papago
but the wild animals
call me Brother
because they know me
and love me.

Simple beauty remains the most succinct and apt description of Clark's books, even when one considers those that are addressed to more sophisticated readers. The plots of books like *Secret of the Andes* and *Santiago* revolve around the difficulties faced by young Indians in meeting the demands of two conflicting cultures. These works appeal most to those readers who appreciate the special delights of atmosphere and mood that are captured only by a writer who not only knows the cultures of the Indians of the Americas but who also has a reverential understanding for the people and their ways, all gained through a lifetime of living with them.

As she says: "children need children's books that have been written with honesty, accuracy, and reality. They need books that develop deeper understandings and broader acceptances, that enrich imagination. Their need is my challenge." Ann Nolan Clark has met that challenge.

—James E. Higgins

CLARK, Catherine Anthony

Nationality: British. **Born:** Catherine Anthony Smith, London, 5 May 1892; emigrated to Canada, 1914. **Education:** Convent of Jesus and Mary, Ipswich, Suffolk. **Family:** Married Leonard Clark in 1919; one son and one daughter. **Career:** Columnist, *Prospector,* Nelson, British Columbia. **Awards:** Canadian Library Association Book of the Year medal, 1952. **Died:** 24 February 1977.

Publications for Children

Fiction

The Golden Pine Cone, illustrated by Clare Bice. Toronto, Macmillan, 1950.
The Sun Horse, illustrated by Clare Bice. Toronto, Macmillan, 1951.
The One-Winged Dragon, illustrated by Clare Bice. Toronto, Macmillan, 1955.
The Silver Man, illustrated by Clare Bice. Toronto, Macmillan, 1958; London, Macmillan, 1959.
The Diamond Feather; or, The Door in the Mountain: A Magic Tale for Children, illustrated by Clare Bice. Toronto and London, Macmillan, 1962.
The Man with the Yellow Eyes, illustrated by Gordon Raynor. Toronto, Macmillan, and New York, St. Martin's Press, 1963; London, Macmillan, 1964.
The Hunter and the Medicine Man, illustrated by Clare Bice. Toronto, Macmillan, 1966.

* * *

As the author of six books of fantasy Catherine Anthony Clark was an important contributor to a field of writing sparsely represented in Canadian children's literature. Her books are set in British Columbia and the magic adventures they recount take place in wilderness areas and the foothills of the Rocky Mountains where the spirits of the land and the people who have inhabited it are alive. They draw strongly on the legendary figures and the beliefs of the Indians of the Pacific Northwest, and indeed native peoples play an important role in all the stories. Clark has created folk spirits of the countryside, the Lake Snake, the Head Canada Goose, which add humour and imaginative vigour. On the periphery of the enchanted lands are prospectors and settlers. It is often through these characters, for whom the boundaries of reality have become blurred, that the spirits are introduced.

The protagonists are children, generally a boy and girl. At odds with their lives, they are drawn to fantastic adventures in which they undertake a quest. In following it they come to a better understanding of themselves and the problems with which they must contend. While this forms the unifying theme of the plots, the author's purpose is more closely involved in portraying the land and its inheritance. Her strength as a descriptive writer is a major factor in her success. There is a marked similarity between the stories. *The Golden Pine Cone* relates the magic adventures of two children who find a golden pine cone belonging to the ruler of the lands, lakes, and the forests and must withstand those who seek the power it holds. In *The Sun Horse* a boy and girl search for her father who has been lured by a golden stallion into the idyllic valley of forgetfulness. The Chinese and Indian strains in British Columbia's past are brought together in *The One-Winged Dragon,* the story of an old Chinese farmer who keeps a dragon in his well and the children who, with the dragon's help, return his daughter to him. The life of native peoples of the Pacific Northwest is well reflected in their adventures. The book is more well constructed than the earlier fantasies, its characterization is fuller and more sympathetic. *The Silver Man* tells of a troubled boy who, in his dazed contemplation of a rock crystal, experiences an adventure in which he restores a lost young chieftain to his tribe. Clark's last two novels are weakened by a plethora of incident and plot. In *The Diamond Feather* an orphaned brother and sister go through the door in a mountain to the Valley at the Edge of Time in search of the children of a bitter old prospector. *The Hunter and the Medicine Man* tells of two children who explore a haunted mountain and become involved in an evil medicine man's attempt to usurp the position of a tribe's rightful chief.

The books are limited in their imaginative scope. There is often little distinction between the real world and the fantastic. Although the children are believable, their dialogue natural and colloquial, the conduct clearly expected of them is very exacting. Written with ease and inventiveness the stories are, however, entertaining reading.

Clark also produced a book of historical fiction for early readers, *The Man with the Yellow Eyes.* Set near Nelson, British Columbia, at the turn of the century it tells of a boy's race against an unscrupulous prospector to stake his father's claim to land containing rich deposits of silver. The handling of the plot is banal but the descriptions of the foothills and the practical ways of the hardworking settlers are here, as in the other books, noteworthy.

—Ruth Osler

CLARK, David. See **HARDCASTLE, Michael.**

CLARK, Emma Chichester

Nationality: British. **Born:** London, England, 15 October 1955. **Education:** Chelsea School of Art, B.A. (with Honours) 1978; Royal College of Art, M.A. 1983. **Family:** Married Lucas van Praag. **Career:** Illustrator and author of children's books, from 1983. Visiting lecturer at Middlesex Polytechnic and City and Guilds School of Art, 1984-86. **Awards:** Mother Goose Award, 1988. **Address:** c/o Laura Cecil, 17 Alwyne Villas, London N 1, England.

Publications for Children (illustrated by the author)

Catch That Hat! London, Bodley Head, 1988; New York, Little, Brown, 1990.
Myrtle, Tertle, and Gertle. London, Bodley Head, 1989.

The Story of Horrible Hilda and Henry. New York, Little, Brown, 1988.
The Bouncing Dinosaur. London, Methuen, and New York, Farrar, Straus & Giroux, 1990.
I Never Saw a Purple Cow and Other Nonsense Rhymes. London, Walker, 1990; New York, Little, Brown, 1991.
Tea with Aunt Augusta. London, Methuen, 1991; as *Lunch with Aunt Augusta,* New York, Dial, 1992.
Miss Bilberry's New House. London, Methuen, 1993; as *Across the Blue Mountains,* San Diego, Harcourt Brace, 1993.
With others, *Tom's Pirate Ship and Other Stories.* Oxford, Heinemann, 1996.
Little Miss Muffet Counts to Ten. London, Andersen, 1997; as *Little Miss Muffet's Count-Along Surprise,* New York, Doubleday, 1997.
With others, *Mostly Animal Poetry.* Oxford, Heinemann, 1997.
More! London, Andersen, 1998.

*

Illustrator: *Listen to This,* 1987, *Stuff and Nonsense,* 1989, *Boo! Stories to Make You Jump,* 1990, *A Thousand Yards of Sea,* 1993, *Mesoscopic Quantum Physics,* 1995, all compiled by Laura Cecil; *Cissy Lavender* by Primrose Lockwood, 1989; *Wild Robert* by Diana Wynne Jones, 1989; *Good Night, Stella* by Kate McMullan, 1990; *James and the Giant Peach* by Roald Dahl, 1990; *Ragged Robin: Poetry from A to Z* by James Reeves, 1990; *Rock-a-Bye Baby* by Jane Romer, 1990; *Beware of the Aunts!* by Pat Thomson, 1991; *Delilah and the Dogspell* by Jenny Nimmo, 1991; *The Queen's Goat* by Margaret Mahy, 1991; *The Haunting of Pip Parker* by Anne Fine, 1992; *The Orchard Book of Greek Myths,* 1992, and *The Orchard Book of Greek Gods and Goddesses,* 1997, by Geraldine McCaughrean; *Tertius and Pliny* by Ben Frankel, 1992; *The Way of the Cat* by D. J. Enright, 1992; *The Minstrel and the Dragon Pup* by Rosemary Sutcliff, 1993; *Time and the Clockmice* by Peter Dickinson, 1993; *The Frog Princess* retold by Laura Cecil, 1994; *I Have a Song to Sing, O!: An Introduction to the Songs of Gilbert and Sullivan* selected and edited by John Langstaff, 1994; *Ruth and the Blue Horse* by Charles Ashton, 1994; *Too Tired* by Ann Turnbull, 1994; *Piper* by Laura Cecil, 1995; *Something Rich & Strange: A Treasury of Shakespeare's Verse* compiled by Gina Pollinger, 1995; *Dimanche Diller at Sea* by Henrietta Branford, 1996; *Little Red Riding Hood* edited by Sam McBratney, 1996; *Mrs. Vole the Vet* by Allan Ahlberg, 1996; *Preposterous Pets* edited by Laura Cecil, 1996; *Sinan* by Emma Allcock, 1996; *Thumbelina* by Jane Falloon, 1996; *Glove Puppet Man* by John Yeoman, 1997; *Little Book of Shakespeare* edited by Gina Pollinger, 1997; *Mehmet the Conqueror* by Laura Mare, 1997; *Adventures of Robin Hood & Marian* by Adrian Mitchell, 1998; *Noah and the Space Ark* by Laura Cecil, 1998.

* * *

Emma Chichester Clark's career as an illustrator began auspiciously, when her pictures for Laura Cecil's *Listen to This* won her the prestigious Mother Goose Award in 1988 for the best newcomer to children's illustration. Since then, she has established herself as one of England's leading children's illustrators, with nearly 50 books published in her first decade of work. Clark has developed into an artist with words as well as pictures, producing a number of fine picture books to her own texts. A gentle humour and an enjoyment of quirky individualism in both the human and the animal worlds mark both her interpretations of traditional stories and poems, and her invention of new fables. She uses colour with subtlety and skill, and is able to suggest character and emotions without a hint of sentimentality. Although she has illustrated some books for older children, including an edition of *James and the Giant Peach,* her principal work has been as a creator of picture books, and as an illustrator of poetry and anthologies.

Many of Clark's illustrations have an old-fashioned quality: her figures inhabit a world of gardens, leisure time, and large, floppy-brimmed hats. This pastoral world is, however, never smug or over-sweet. In her own stories, conflicts and danger colour the adventures, although a certain lightness of tone and a humorous edge keep them from being overly alarming. The darkest of Clark's picture book illustrations are those for *Piper,* by her frequent collaborator Laura Cecil; this story of a dog rescued from a cruel owner is presented in somber shades unlike her usual palette of bright or soft pastels. Even here, however, the slightly tongue-in-cheek melodrama of colour and gesture reveal such evident villainy in the wicked owner and such good-hearted innocence in Piper the dog that a happy resolution seems inevitable. The distancing of the pictured world by the old-fashioned air of the characters, their homes, and their dress allows for a somewhat ironic distancing of the reader from what is going on: the reader can enjoy Cissy Lavender, Miss Bilberry, and Gertle without being entirely caught up in their own view of things.

Clark presents comical and even absurd situations with delicate humour, avoiding ridicule or obvious satire. Her characters often seem bemused by their own experiences, but they are always allowed to retain their dignity and their illusions, even as the reader is invited to see through them. In *Miss Bilberry's New House,* for example, after Miss Bilberry has become discontented with her home, packed up her household, and trundled her possessions and animal companions on an arduous journey through forests and "across the blue mountains," she finds another house which she decides will suit them well. The reader recognizes immediately from the pictures that Miss Bilberry has travelled in a circle back to her old home—but the text and Miss Bilberry herself prefer to ignore this possibility. The fable makes its point, humorously and without didacticism, and no one is diminished or embarrassed.

Clark's affinities as an illustrator and as an author of picture books are with her great English predecessors Beatrix Potter and Edward Ardizzone. Like them, she is a fantasist and a fabulist, whose skilful use of line and watercolour is delicate and understated. Her stories are reassuring, but have an underlying toughness. They often feature characters who, like Peter Rabbit or Ardizzone's Tim, journey away from home into danger but return safely at the end. Animal siblings, such as the charming ring-tailed lemurs of *Tea at Aunt Augusta's* or the donkeys of *Myrtle, Yertle and Gertle,* are used to tell humorous fables reflecting on human behaviour. In them, the reader is led to identify with the haplessly absent-minded or greedy youngest child, who nonetheless triumphs in the end. Their mishaps have an element of absurdity: Jemima, the little lemur, eats too much at tea and falls through the trees, while Gertle daydreams and misses the departure of her cruise ship. Like Potter, Clark often presents her animals in human dress, and in Frankl's *Tertius and Pliny* her characters are animated toys. Clark's settings are less precise and more geographically varied than Potter's lovingly-detailed Lake District scenes, but often share their characteristically English palette of soft watercolour blues, yellows, greens, and lavenders. Like

Ardizzone's, Clark's human heroes are small but resolute individualists whose own choices, rather than external demands, determine the course of their adventures.

Two characteristic details serve almost as a trademark in Clark's illustrations. In her earlier books, particularly, she draws the eyes of her characters in a distinctive way, as circles with pupil dots, which is both child-like and curiously expressive. Many of her books also feature characters wearing broad-brimmed hats, which both fit with the loosely Edwardian settings and become personalized features in themselves, suggesting sometimes the self-concealment of villainy (as in *Piper*) but most often a kind of pleasure in dress and a casually civilized outdoor comfort. These two attributes help to make her illustrations quickly recognizable. A more fundamental quality of her artistry is her ability to convey a sense of movement: the rhythmic quality and expressive gestures of her characters animate her illustrations for song books and poetry collections, and add to the energy of her picture books—as in the pictures of the lemurs leaping through the trees in *Tea at Aunt Augusta's.* While her illustrations often suggest the serenity and charm of a timeless world, her work has a vitality and a multicultural perspective which also make it highly contemporary.

—Gwyneth Evans

CLARK, Leonard

Nationality: British. **Born:** St. Peter Port, Guernsey, 1 August 1905. **Education:** Monmouth School, 1917-22; Normal College, Bangor, Caernarvonshire, 1928-30, Cert. Ed. 1930. **Military Service:** Home Guard, Devon Regiment, 1940-43. **Family:** Married Jane Callow in 1954; one son and one daughter. **Career:** Teacher in Gloucestershire, 1922-28, and London, 1930-36; Assistant Inspector, 1936-45, and Inspector of Schools, 1945-70, Board of Education, later Ministry of Education, in Devon, Yorkshire, and London; from 1970 editor, Longmans Poetry Library series; consultant editor, Chatto and Windus Poetry Books for the Young, London, and Thornhill Press, Gloucester. **Awards:** Children's Literature Association award, for criticism, 1979. Liveryman of Haberdashers' Company, 1965; Freeman of City of London, 1965. Honorary Associate, London Academy of Music and Dramatic Art, 1969. Fellow, Royal Society of Literature, 1953. Knight of the Order of St. Sylvester, 1970. O.B.E. (Officer, Order of the British Empire), 1966. **Member:** Arts Council Literature panel, 1965-69, and Westminster Diocesan Schools Commission, 1970-76. **Died:** 10 September 1981.

Publications for Children

Fiction

Robert Andrew Tells a Story [and Tiffy, by the Sea, and the Holy Family, and the Red Indian Chief, and Skippy, in the Country], illustrated by James Scargill. Leeds, E.J. Arnold, 7 vols., 1965-66.

Mr. Pettigrew's Harvest Festival, illustrated by Toffee Sanders. Gloucester, Thornhill Press, 1974.

Mr. Pettigrew's Train, illustrated by Toffee Sanders. Gloucester, Thornhill Press, 1975.

Mr. Pettigrew and the Bell-ringers, illustrated by Toffee Sanders. Gloucester, Thornhill Press, 1976.

Poetry

Daybreak: A First Book of Poems, illustrated by Selma Nankivell. London, Hart Davis, 1963.

The Year Round: A Second Book of Poems, illustrated by Edward Ardizzone. London, Hart Davis, 1966.

Fields and Territories. London, Turret, 1967.

Good Company, illustrated by Jennie Corbett. London, Dobson, 1968.

Near and Far, illustrated by Kozo Kakimoto and others. London, Hamlyn, 1968.

Here and There, illustrated by Kuniro Fukazawa. London, Hamlyn, 1969.

Secret as Toads. London, Chatto and Windus, 1972.

Singing in the Streets: Poems for Christmas. London, Dobson, 1972.

The Broad Atlantic. London, Dobson, 1974.

Four Seasons, illustrated by Jennie Corbett. London, Dobson, 1975.

Collected Poems and Verses for Children. London, Dobson, 1975.

The Tale of Prince Igor, illustrated by Charles Keeping. London, Dobson, 1979.

Stranger Than Unicorns, illustrated by Jennie Corbett. London, Dobson, 1979.

The Singing Time: Poems and Verses for Children, illustrated by Doreen Caldwell. London, Hodder and Stoughton, 1980.

The Corn Growing, illustrated by Lisa Kopper. London, Hodder and Stoughton, 1982.

Other

When They Were Children, illustrated by William Randell. London, Parrish, and New York, Roy, 1964.

St. Felix and the Spider. London, Catholic Truth Society, 1974.

St. Patrick. London, Catholic Truth Society, 1974.

St. Anthony of Egypt. London, Catholic Truth Society, 1974.

St. Dorothea and the Flowers of Paradise. London, Catholic Truth Society, 1974.

Tales from the Panchatantra, illustrated by Jeroo Roy. London, Evans, 1979.

Editor, *The Magic Kingdom: An Anthology of Verse for Seniors.* London, Mathews and Marrot, 1937.

Editor, *The Open Door: An Anthology of Verse for Juniors.* London, Mathews and Marrot, 1937.

Editor, *Quiet as Moss: Thirty Six Poems,* by Andrew Young. London, Hart Davis, 1959.

Editor, *Drums and Trumpets: Poetry for the Youngest,* illustrated by Heather Copley. London, Bodley Head, 1962.

Editor, *Common Ground: An Anthology for the Young,* illustrated by M.E. Eldridge. London, Faber, 1964.

Editor, *Selected Poems by John Clare 1793-1864.* Leeds, E.J. Arnold, 1964.

Editor, *All Things New: An Anthology,* illustrated by Ann Tout. London, Constable, 1965.

Editor, *The Poetry of Nature.* London, Hart Davis, 1965.

Editor, *Following the Sun: Poems by Children,* illustrated by Tony Dyson. London, Odhams Press, 1967.

Editor, *Burning as Light: Thirty Seven Poems,* by Andrew Young, illustrated by Joan Hassall. London, Hart Davis, 1967.
Editor, *Flutes and Cymbals: Poetry for the Young,* illustrated by Shirley Hughes. London, Bodley Head, 1968; New York, Crowell, 1969.
Editor, *Sound of Battle,* illustrated by Ewart Oakeshott. Oxford, Pergamon Press, 1969.
Editor, *Poems by Children.* London, Studio Vista, 1970.
Editor, *All Along, Down Along: A Book of Stories in Verse,* illustrated by Pauline Baynes. London, Longman, 1971.
Editor, *Fire of Spring: Prose and Poetry from IAPS Schools.* Tunbridge Wells, Kent, Fenrose, 1974.
Editor, *The Way the Wind Blows: A Book of Verse,* illustrated by Lisa Kopper. London, Evans, 1979.

Publications for Adults

Poetry

Poems. London, Fortune Press, 1940.
Passage to the Pole and Other Poems. London, Fortune Press, 1944.
Rhandanim. Leeds, Salamander Press, 1945.
The Mirror and Other Poems. London, Wingate, 1948.
XII Poems. Birmingham, City of Birmingham School of Printing, 1948.
English Morning and Other Poems. London, Hutchinson, 1953.
Selected Poems 1940-1957. London, Hutchinson, 1958.
Walking with Trees. London, Enitharmon Press, 1970.
Every Voice. Guildford, Surrey, Words Press, 1971.
The Hearing Heart. London, Enitharmon Press, 1974.
Winter to Winter and Other Poems. London, Dobson, 1977.
Silence of the Morning. London, Enitharmon Press, 1977.
Twelve Poems from St. Bartholomew's. Privately printed, 1978.
As I Looked Over Jordan: Sixteen Poems. Kinnesswood, Kinross, Lomond Press, 1984.

Other

Alfred Williams: His Life and Work. Oxford, Blackwell, 1945; New York, Kelley, 1969.
Ideas in Poetry. Birmingham, City of Birmingham School of Printing, 1947.
Sark Discovered: The Prospect of an Island, Being a Literary and Pictorial Record of the Island of Sark. London, Dent, 1956; revised edition, London, Dobson, 1971, 1979.
Walter de la Mare: A Checklist. Cambridge, University Press, 1956.
Walter de la Mare. London, Bodley Head, 1960; New York, Walck, 1961.
Green Wood: A Gloucestershire Childhood. London, Parrish, 1962.
Andrew Young. London, Longman, 1964.
A Fool in the Forest (autobiography). London, Dobson, 1965.
Prospect of Highgate and Hampstead. London, Highgate Press, 1967.
Grateful Caliban (autobiography). London, Dobson, 1968.
A Tribute to Walter de la Mare, with Edmund Blunden. London, Enitharmon Press, 1974.
Three Poets, Two Children, with Vernon Scannell and Dannie Abse, edited by Desmond Badham-Thornhill. Gloucester, Thornhill Press, 1975.
The Inspector Remembers: A Diary of One of Her Majesty's Inspectors of Schools 1936-1970. London, Dobson, 1976.
Writing for the Public. Gloucester, Thornhill Press, 1976.
The Story of Rahere. Privately printed, 1978.
An Intimate Landscape. London, Nottingham Court Press, 1981.

Editor, *The Kingdom of the Mind: Essays and Addresses 1903-1937 of Albert Mansbridge.* London, Dent, 1944.
Editor, *Andrew Young: Prospect of a Poet: Essays and Tributes by Fourteen Writers.* London, Hart Davis, 1957.
Editor, *The Collected Poems of Andrew Young.* London, Hart Davis, 1960.
Editor, (*Poems*), by Robert Graves and D.H. Lawrence. London, Longman, 1967.
Editor, with others, *The Complete Poems of Walter de la Mare.* London, Faber, 1969; New York, Knopf, 1970.
Editor, *Poems of Ivor Gurney 1890-1937.* London, Chatto and Windus, 1973.
Editor, *Complete Poems of Andrew Young.* London, Secker and Warburg, 1974.
Editor, *Great and Familiar: The Heritage of English Poetry.* Tunbridge Wells, Kent, Fenrose, 1974.
Editor, *They Looked at Gloucestershire: An Anthology of Poetry and Prose.* London, Dobson, 1980.

Translator, with Iris Allam, *The Zemganno Brothers,* by E.L.A. Goncourt. London, Redman, 1957.

*

Leonard Clark commented:
(1978) It is natural that, as the father of two children, a former teacher, and one of Her Majesty's Inspectors of Schools for many years, I should write prose and poetry for the young. In addition, as editor of many anthologies of poetry for the young, I have seen the need for providing for them, in attractive form, collections of poetry by other poets. In essence, my poetry for the young does not differ greatly from any other poetry I write, for I have always believed that a good poem for children must be a good poem for everybody else. This poetry, which has largely concerned itself with nature, and with the thoughts and feelings of children as they grow up and inherit the world, is successful, perhaps, because I believe I am the child for whom the poems have been written. Although I owe a great deal to Walter de la Mare's advice and guidance, my voice is my own. It is a very English voice which tries to speak of things eternal, without any condescension, sentimentality, or undue nostalgia. It faces up to life as life is lived imaginatively, with always an eye on the visionary and mystical.

* * *

Despite his popular Mr. Pettigrew stories, Leonard Clark was best known for poetry. Teaching experience enabled him to speak directly to children. "You are the child for whom the poem is written," Kathleen Raine told him. He was also the only Inspector of Schools since Matthew Arnold to publish a substantial body of verse. After de la Mare, only he and James Reeves produced their collected children's poems. His influence on educational literary policy has been considerable, and he originated the Arts Council's "Writers in Schools" project. He edited many anthologies, some of poems by children themselves. All his books are very carefully designed. In *Following the Sun* the chapter headings from Traherne make a continuous and developing accompaniment to the poems themselves. In *All Things New,* seasonal changes, the Six Days and varied manifestations of Creation, the illustrations, link the verse to a subtle whole. His own poem "Earthworm" is shaped like a worm, the rhythms of "Snow" approximate that of the fall of snow itself. Clark was particularly sympathetic to the 5-12 age group but always "a poem for children must be a good poem." He never hesitated to include a difficult work, confident that even a small response is ample justification. Too much easy reading rots the imagination; a poem, wrote T.S. Eliot, can communicate before it is understood.

Clark's range was wide: the undeservedly obscure, neglected, and forgotten may flank some famous name, testifying not to the insignificance but unimportance of fashion. Throughout, originality of theme is rated less than originality of perception. He was quick to notice the child who sees the ocean as an angry cat but who may yet allow people to lie on its wet back: and the teenager who sadly, memorably, wonders whether her own indifference has killed a baby. His concern with tradition placed poems and individual words against total history, the changing values and perspectives. "Sleep" is shown treated by John Fletcher, Wordsworth, Tennyson, Edward Thomas, Auden. This concern informed his choices among contemporaries. When an Inspector, he set himself to remedy their neglect in schools. His *The Poetry of Nature,* starting with Chaucer and Lydgate, ends with Wain, Thwaite, Kirkup, Ted Hughes. A teacher, he realised that little can be taught, much implied. He seldom wrote a "children's poem," but first wrote, then decided the audience. His own verse included lyrics, narratives of travel and adventure, and, above all, nature poetry in the tradition of Clare, Christina Rossetti, Frost, and Edward Thomas, with affinities to de la Mare and Andrew Young, on both of whom he was an authority. It is not the slack pastoral of nymphs and shepherds, but of observation, precise, sharp, at times ironic. Edith Sitwell once called him "a practical mystic." He saw not Man and Nature but Man with Nature. There are also echoes of Blake and Samuel Palmer. His most consistent influence was the English countryside, its centuries of order, work—he enjoyed *things* in action—conflict, and evolution, landscapes of peace made strong despite inescapable present pollutions and past cruelties. Quiet Somerset contains sad, once-bloody Sedgemoor. With little violence but much intensity his is a poetry of special places, private dreams, secret sounds, the precious autonomy of field and wood, the gaps within silence of an abandoned house. Conflict is suggested, not between Science and Nature, but irresponsible bits of Science exploiting or ruining a Nature which, if left wholly to itself, would likewise distort and overwhelm. Clark spoke to those for whom trees are more than timber, hedges more than barriers. Birds are simultaneously remote and personal: they are pattern and colour, carrion and myth, pet and victim.

He recorded the permutations of the child's day, the complex gradations of light and emotion, overlappings of morning, afternoon, and evening, of play and dream. He largely ignored current events but not history: was grieved and angered by the murder both of the Inca Atahualpa and of J.F. Kennedy. He knew that for certain minds a cave painting or Spanish ingot can be more contemporary than a transistor. Many poems, ostensibly simple, can ultimately reveal the unexpected. In his long writing life—he began publishing at 18—he kept an evenness of texture which may have prevented many obvious anthology pieces. This at least leaves much to be discovered. That he always wanted to delight gently rather than bruise and crudely shock may have robbed him of some critical esteem but undeniably won him a very wide readership.

—Peter Vansittart

CLARK, Mavis Thorpe

Has also written as M.R. Clark and Mavis Latham. **Nationality:** Australian. **Born:** Melbourne, Victoria, in 1912. **Education:** Methodist Ladies College, Melbourne. **Family:** Married Harold Latham (died); two daughters. **Career:** Member of Committee of Management, Australian Society of Authors, 15 years. President, International PEN, Melbourne (two terms); Member of Committee, National Book Council, seven years; named Member of the General Division of the Order of Australia (AM), 1996. **Awards:** Australian Children's Book Council commendation, 1957, 1968, and Book of the Year award, 1967; ALA Notable Book commendation, 1969. **Address:** 1/22 Rochester Road, Canterbury, Victoria 3126, Australia.

Publications for Children

Fiction

Hatherly's First Fifteen (as M.R. Clark), illustrated by F.E. Wiley. Sydney, Whitcombe and Tombs, and London, Oxford University Press, 1930.
Dark Pool Island. Melbourne, Oxford University Press, 1949.
The Twins from Timber Creek. Melbourne, Oxford University Press, 1949.
Home Again at Timber Creek. Melbourne, Oxford University Press, 1950.
Missing Gold. London, Hutchinson, 1951.
Jingaroo. Melbourne, Oxford University Press, 1951.
The Brown Land Was Green, illustrated by Harry Hudson. Melbourne and London, Heinemann, 1956; as *Kammoora,* London, Octopus, 1990.
Gully of Gold, illustrated by Anne Graham. Melbourne and London, Heinemann, 1958.
Pony from Tarella, illustrated by Jean M. Rowe. Melbourne and London, Heinemann, 1959.
They Came South, illustrated by Joy Murray. Melbourne and London, Heinemann, 1963.
The Min-Min, illustrated by Genevieve Melrose. Melbourne, Lansdowne Press, 1966; London, Angus and Robertson, 1967; New York, Macmillan, 1969.
Blue above the Trees, illustrated by Genevieve Melrose. Melbourne, Lansdowne Press, 1967; London, Angus and Robertson, 1968; New York, Meredith Press, 1969.
Spark of Opal, illustrated by Genevieve Melrose. Melbourne, Lansdowne Press, 1968; London, Methuen, 1971; New York, Macmillan, 1973.
Nowhere to Hide, illustrated by Genevieve Melrose. Melbourne, Lansdowne Press, 1969.
Iron Mountain, illustrated by Ronald Brooks. Melbourne, Lansdowne Press, 1970; New York, Macmillan, 1971; London, Methuen, 1972.
New Golden Mountain. Melbourne, Lansdowne Press, 1973; as *If the Earth Falls In,* New York, Seabury Press, 1975.
Wildfire. Sydney, Hodder and Stoughton, and Leicester, Brockhampton Press, 1973; New York, Macmillan, 1974.
The Sky Is Free. Sydney, Hodder and Stoughton, 1974; Leicester, Brockhampton Press, and New York, Macmillan, 1976.
The Hundred Islands, illustrated by Astra Lacis. Sydney and London, Hodder and Stoughton, 1976; New York, Macmillan, 1977

The Lilly-Pilly, illustrated by Prue Chammen. Adelaide, Rigby, 1979.
A Stranger Came to the Mine, illustrated by Jane Walker. Richmond, Victoria, Hutchinson, 1980.
Solomon's Child. Richmond, Victoria, and London, Hutchinson, 1981.
Soft Shoe, illustrated by Iiba Wentenberg. Melbourne, Martin Educational, 1988.

Radio Plays

The Brown Land Was Green, 1961.
Gully of Gold, 1962.
They Came South, 1965.
The Boy from Cummeroogunga, 1981.
Jingaroo, 1981.

Other

Fishing (as Mavis Latham), illustrated by Joy Murray. Melbourne, Oxford University Press, 1963.
The Pack-Tracker, illustrated by Shirley Turner. Melbourne, London, and New York, Oxford University Press, 1968.
The Opal Miner, illustrated by Barbara Taylor. Melbourne, Oxford University Press, 1969.
Iron Ore Mining, illustrated by Jocelyn Bell. Melbourne, Oxford University Press, 1971.
Spanish Queen (reader), illustrated by Joan Saint. Sydney and London, Hodder and Stoughton, 1977.
The Boy from Cumeroogunga: The Story of Sir Douglas Nicholls, Aboriginal Leader. Sydney, Hodder and Stoughton, 1979.
Joey (reader), illustrated by Joanna McKeown. Mount Gravatt, Queensland, Mount Gravatt College of Advanced Education, 1980.
Boo to a Goose (reader), illustrated by Bruce Riddell. Mount Gravatt, Queensland, Mount Gravatt College of Advanced Education, 1981.
The Thief Who Came Quietly. Mount Gravatt, Queensland, Mount Gravatt College of Advanced Education, 1982.
Young and Brave. Sydney, Hodder and Stoughton, 1984.

PUBLICATIONS FOR ADULTS

Other

John Batman (as Mavis Latham). Melbourne, Oxford University Press, 1962.
Pastor Doug: The Story of an Aboriginal Leader. Melbourne, Lansdowne Press, 1965; London, Newnes, 1966; revised edition, as *Pastor Doug: The Story of Sir Douglas Nicholls, Aboriginal Leader,* Lansdowne Press, 1972.
Strolling Players. Melbourne, Lansdowne Press, 1972.
No Mean Destiny: The Story of the War Widows' Guild of Australia 1945-1985. Melbourne, Hyland House, 1986.

*

Manuscript Collection: National Library of Australia, Canberra.

Critical Study: In *Innocence and Experience: Essays on Contemporary Australian Children's Writers,* Thomas Nelson, 1982.

Mavis Thorpe Clark comments:

Individual writers concentrate their work effort, usually, on a particular category of literature. Among the many forms, he or she may be a novelist, an historian, an essayist, a playwright, a biographer, a poet, a writer for children. The genre, I believe, "chooses" its exponents. I began to write in my early school years, about children, for children. These first steps revealed my path. As a result my main body of work has been for young people, though I have written biographies and factual books for adults.

As a writer for today's youth, I am writing for the most important generation ever born. Today's young ones will be the caretakers of the world's uncertain future, and responsible for its preservation, even survival. It is a sobering thought, but an honour and a privilege to be "chosen" to work in this field of literature.

Writing, however, has given me as a person much more than a vocation. It has led me through many physical journeys, of many miles, to certain discoveries about life. Not sudden or quick discoveries, but rather a distillation of ideas. It all began with that first journey—into South Australia's remote Northwest—which produced *The Min-Min.* This book, with it's outback setting and characters, won the Children's Book Council of Australia Book of the Year award in 1967, and has not been out of print since.

That first journey from city to outback was followed by many such journeys, especially into those desert miles of spinifex, saltpan, and sky, where scarcely a mulga tree breaks the line of Earth's rim. And there is nothing, indeed, to separate or distract from a pervasive sense of oneness with this land.

Now, writing my autobiography, comes the discovery of how consistent was the journey-track that led me, not only to those places that yielded so much of my writing material—prompting a young student to describe me as "the author who writes about Australia"—but also a satisfying awareness, as the indigenous people of this land, the Aborigines, have always been aware.

* * *

Mavis Thorpe Clark is a prolific and well-organized writer; her teenage novels are set in different parts of Australia, and she first investigates these backgrounds very thoroughly before she begins to write. In *Blue above the Trees* and *The Brown Land Was Green,* two early novels, she relates the experiences of two (fictional) pioneer families. In these two stories, plot and characterization can be more readily separated than in her later novels, when her skill in characterization increases to the point where events and characters interact upon each other. Her plots, however, are always strong, with events and their outcome a vital force in each story. *Nowhere to Hide,* another earlier work, is interesting as being one of the few novels for young readers which has a background of Australia during the Second World War.

The Min-Min (Australian Children's Book of the Year, 1967) is undoubtedly Clark's most outstanding work; in telling the story of an outback railway settler's family, living cut off from civilization, she displays a degree of conviction and compassion which she has not quite achieved since, perhaps because in *The Min-Min* she was content to pursue one outstanding theme. In several of her other novels, by contrast, she tends to introduce a number of parallel or sub-themes, diffusing the reader's interest between characters of almost equal importance. *The Sky Is Free* and *The Hun-*

dred Islands are each concerned with topical and social questions, which tend now and then to dominate characterization and plot. In *The Sky Is Free,* the young hero runs away from a comfortable suburban home to the opal fields; on the way he teams up with a boy who is also on the run, from an institutional home. While this novel has many admirable qualities, including well-assimilated information about the opal fields, the plot is perhaps too neatly contrived. Conservation, especially that of the fauna of the Bass Strait islands, is the theme of *The Hundred Islands,* which contains fascinating first-hand observation of the mutton-bird, in particular; but in this novel, too, the author tends to subject characterization to the theme, and manipulate the plot a little too firmly.

Solomon's Child, again a purposeful novel, is concerned with present-day social issues. It tells how the teenage daughter of separated parents comes to terms with the decision of which parent will have custody, and describes the anti-social behaviour induced in her by her emotional conflict.

—Barbara Ker Wilson

CLARKE, Gus

Nationality: British. **Born:** Suffolk, 1948. **Education:** Studied at Edinburgh and Kingston Schools of Art, DipAD in graphic design 1971. **Family:** married, Carole; two sons. **Career:** Held various jobs designing for print and packaging exhibitions, television and video productions for five years before forming partnership with former Art school friend to do much the same sort of work. **Awards:** Runner-up for Mother Goose Award, 1990; Prix Versele, 1992, for *Bilou et Titou* (french translation of *Eddie and Teddy*). **Address:** c/o Andersen Press, 20 Vauxhall Bridge Road, London SW1V 2SA, England; 194 Southampton Way, London SE5 7EU, England.

Publications for Children: (illustrated by the author)

Eddie and Teddy. London, Andersen Press, 1990.
Along Came Eric. London, Andersen Press, 1991.
How Many Days to My Birthday? London, Andersen Press, 1992.
E I E I O. London, Andersen Press, 1992.
Betty's Not Well Today. London, Andersen Press, 1993.
Ten Green Monsters. London, Andersen Press, 1993.
Helping Hector. London, Andersen Press, 1994.
Pat, the Dog. London, Andersen Press, 1994.
Too Many Teddies. London, Andersen Press, 1995.
Cheeky Monkey. London, Andersen Press, 1995.
Michael's Monsters. London, Andersen Press, 1996.
Scratch 'n' Sniff. London, Andersen Press, 1996.
Nothing But Trouble. London, Andersen Press, 1997.
Lucy's Bedtime Book. London, Andersen Press, 1998; as *Goodnight Lucy,* New York, Simon and Schuster, 1998.

*

Illustrator: *Anthony and the Aardvark* by Lesley Sloss, 1990; *Big Brave Brother Ben* by Kara May, 1991; *Juggling with Jeremy* by Chris d'Lacey, 1996.

Gus Clarke comments:

Like a lot of other people at Art School I thought illustrating children's books seemed like a nice way to earn a living.

Then I left Art School, got a job or two and suddenly it was eighteen years later. I still hadn't illustrated a children's book but by now I'd read a lot of them, having two sons aged six and three. I'd taken some time off work following an illness and was thinking about the next eighteen years.

Children's books seemed even more appealing now and I certainly knew a lot more about children than I did all those years ago.

However, since I hadn't done a great deal of drawing in that time it seemed unlikely that I would be asked to illustrate anybody's books. The only thing to do was to write one myself. With a little bit of help from my boys, three months later I sent photos of the finished artwork for *Eddie and Teddy* to four London publishers and held my breath.

Andersen Press, a name we'd seen on a lot of our favorite books, phoned first: Would I mind redrawing a few of the pictures where I had put the boy and his bear in what were very "English" school uniforms—it might adversely affect international sales. Well, what could I say?

I've done a few others since then. And I hope to do one or two more, with a little bit of help from my, now rather big, boys.

* * *

Gus Clarke has that wonderful ability in a picture-book writer to amuse the adult reader as much as the child listener. His books appeal widely to the under-fives, many of them featuring situations that will be familiar in families—sibling rivalry, having to wait for a birthday, fear of the unknown, and so on. What makes these books refreshingly different is the way that Clarke injects humour and irony into his pictures to make the whole greater than the sum of its parts. His books can be used with older children, too, who appreciate the irony in the pictures once they have grown beyond the particular stage with which the story deals.

In *Along Came Eric* a little boy called Nigel is happily enjoying the undivided attention of his parents when "along came Eric," a new little brother. Everyone makes such a fuss of Eric that Nigel feels that nobody likes him any more. "Sometimes Nigel wasn't sure that Nigel liked Eric at all." However, as Eric grows up the two become good friends, and Nigel is just thinking "Life's not so bad," when along comes Alice! The text is controlled and spare, with the pictures filling in all the things that have been left unsaid. The expressions on the faces of the characters—even the cat—speak volumes.

A similar approach works well in *How Many Days to My Birthday?* Three-year-old Danny has to wait for what seems like a very long time until his next birthday. His long-suffering mother patiently explains and they make a chart to cross off the days, but still he finds it hard to understand. Finally his birthday arrives. A marvellously frenzied series of pictures illustrate his birthday party, and suddenly it's all over. A happy mother and son survey the havoc wreaked. "'Well,' said Mum. 'Was it worth waiting for?'" Danny answers in true child-like style "'Yes... But, Mum ... How many days till Christmas?'" Once again, the very funny pictures of Danny's exasperated mother stoically enduring the endless questioning elicit a wry smile from adult readers.

Michael's Monsters tackles a common fear amongst children that there are monsters or other frightening things lurking in dark corners. Michael won't go to the bathroom unless there is someone standing at the bottom of the stairs looking out for monsters. When Dad goes with him and shows Michael that there is a simple explanation for everything he sees as a monster. But then Dad gets a surprise!

Humour keeps children going back to Clarke's books, even though they know the ending. Two books in which the punch line is all-important are *Betty's Not Well Today* and *Nothing But Trouble.* All through *Betty's Not Well Today* Betty is referred to as not being well enough to go to school and the pictures show a little girl and her doll lying in bed thinking about what they are missing. When the doctor arrives to see Betty, the final page shows that she is the doll, not the girl! In *Nothing But Trouble* Maisie's day starts badly and gets worse and each page shows another problem, which range from her mother pouring cereal on her head, to opening her lunch to find the baby's bottle. She looks forward to the next day being better. It certainly looks as if it is going to be—until the last page, when she goes off to school with her dress tucked into her pants. The jokes in these books are so enjoyable that children delight in knowing the ending and waiting for it.

Gus Clarke's tremendous sense of humour translates well to novelty books. *Ten Green Monsters* uses the song "Ten Green Bottles" as its base, with flaps to lift to see the monsters falling off the wall one at a time. *Helping Hector* has flaps to lift and wheels to turn to help Hector the Mouse get to the Beach. *Cheeky Monkey* comes with lots of press-out tabs with pictures of things that can be fitted into slots to involve the reader in the story by helping Cheeky Monkey to confuse everything. Similarly, in *Lucy's Bedtime* the child reader is actively encouraged to change the scene by moving items from slots in one page to the next, thus changing the scene and "animating" the story.

In *Scratch 'n' Sniff* Clarke develops a longer story in a book that marks a transitional stage between picture books and those for beginner readers. Sniff the dog is searching everywhere to find out where a particularly exciting smell is coming from. Scratch the cat sends him off outside in pursuit, while in the background we see Scratch's feline friends sneaking into the house. Sniff searches for the smell all day, asking all his friends if they can smell it. The descriptions of what he thinks it is are wonderful and the encounters with other dogs highly amusing. Just before he returns, Scratch ushers out all the cats, with the promise to see them again tomorrow. In a marvellously covert ending the reader discovers just what the smell was as Scratch puts some drops of powerful smelling compound on Sniff's nose!

The key elements of Clarke's books are his capacity to pick up a familiar incident and turn it into an amusing and entertaining story with deceptively simple illustrations and a wry sense of humour, perfectly integrating text and pictures.

—Fiona Lafferty

CLARKE, Pauline

Has also written as Helen Clare. **Nationality:** British. **Born:** Born in Kirkby-in-Ashfield, Nottinghamshire, 19 May 1921. **Education:** Somerville College, Oxford, B.A. (honours) in English 1943. **Family:** Married the historian Peter Hunter Blair in 1969 (died 1982). **Career:** Writer; contributor of essays and reviews to periodicals, including *Times Literary Supplement, Eastern Daily Press* (Norwich), and *Junior Bookshelf.* **Awards:** Library Association Carnegie medal, 1963; Lewis Carroll Shelf award, 1963; Deutshe Jugendbuch Preis (Germany), 1968. **Agent:** Curtis Brown, 162-168 Regent Street, London W1R 5TB. **Address:** Church Farm House, Bottisham, Cambridgeshire CB5 9BA, England.

Publications for Children

Fiction

The Pekinese Princess, illustrated by Cecil Leslie. London, Cape, 1948.

The Great Can, illustrated by Cecil Leslie. London, Faber, 1952.

The White Elephant, illustrated by Richard Kennedy. London, Faber, 1952; New York, Abelard Schuman, 1957.

Smith's Hoard, illustrated by Cecil Leslie. London, Faber, 1955; as *Hidden Gold,* New York, Abelard Schuman, 1957; as *The Golden Collar,* Faber, 1967.

Sandy the Sailor, illustrated by Cecil Leslie. London, Hamish Hamilton, 1956.

The Boy with the Erpingham Hood, illustrated by Cecil Leslie. London, Faber, 1956.

James the Policeman [and the Robbers, and the Smugglers, and the Black Van], illustrated by Cecil Leslie. London, Hamish Hamilton, 4 vols., 1957-63.

Torolv the Fatherless, illustrated by Cecil Leslie. London, Faber, 1959.

The Lord of the Castle, illustrated by Cecil Leslie. London, Hamish Hamilton, 1960.

The Robin Hooders, illustrated by Cecil Leslie. London, Faber, 1960.

Keep the Pot Boiling, illustrated by Cecil Leslie. London, Faber, 1961.

The Twelve and the Genii, illustrated by Cecil Leslie. London, Faber, 1962; as *The Return of the Twelves,* New York, Coward McCann, 1964.

The Bonfire Party, illustrated by Cecil Leslie. London, Hamish Hamilton, 1966.

The Two Faces of Silenus. London, Faber, and New York, Coward McCann, 1972.

Fiction as Helen Clare (illustrated by Cecil Leslie)

Five Dolls in a House. London, Lane, 1953; Englewood Cliffs, New Jersey, Prentice Hall, 1965.

Merlin's Magic. London, Lane, 1953.

Bel the Giant and Other Stories, illustrated by Peggy Fortnum. London, Lane, 1956; as *The Cat and the Fiddle, and Other Stories,* Englewood Cliffs, New Jersey, Prentice Hall, 1968.

Five Dolls and the Monkey. London, Lane, 1956; Englewood Cliffs, New Jersey, Prentice Hall, 1967.

Five Dolls in the Snow. London, Bodley Head, 1957; Englewood Cliffs, New Jersey, Prentice Hall, 1967.

Five Dolls and Their Friends. London, Bodley Head, 1959; Englewood Cliffs, New Jersey, Prentice Hall, 1968.

Seven White Pebbles, illustrated by Cynthia Abbott. London, Bodley Head, 1960.

Five Dolls and the Duke. London, Bodley Head, 1963; Englewood Cliffs, New Jersey, Prentice Hall, 1968.

Picture Books

Crowds of Creatures, illustrated by Cecil Leslie. London, Faber, 1964.

Poetry

Silver Bells and Cockle Shells, illustrated by Sally Ducksbury. London and New York, Abelard Schuman, 1962.

PUBLICATIONS FOR ADULTS

Editor (as Pauline Hunter Blair), with Michael Lapidge, *Anglo-Saxon Northumbria,* by Peter Hunter Blair. London, Variorum, 1984.

* * *

The greatest single achievement of Pauline Clarke is undoubtedly her original fantasy *The Twelve and the Genii.* Once the concept is accepted that the toy soldiers given to Branwell Brontë when he was eight might be rediscovered and brought to life by another young boy in the present, the rest follows with compelling and inevitable logic. The Twelve are sharply individualised characters but always retain their soldierly nature, and the saga of their final journey, helped by children, is full of fascinating detail. Her other stories can be grouped for convenience into historical novels, contemporary adventures, and first readers. Among the historical stories, *Torolv the Fatherless* is a striking example of her skill in combining a feeling of period with a strong narrative and the ability to create character. The conflict between Torolv's loyalty to his Saxon foster family and to the Viking raider to whom he owed his first allegiance is shown with compassion. Life in medieval Norwich is vividly described in *The Boy with the Erpingham Hood* and the everyday detail is combined with the excitement and heartbreak of action at Agincourt and Harfleur.

Her contemporary stories such as *Keep the Pot Boiling,* a collection of nostalgic episodes about a family trying to make money, *The White Elephant,* a fast-moving but unlikely thriller about jewel thieves in London, and *Smith's Hoard,* in which children fight to save some Iceni treasures from the scrap merchant, are mostly well-written and full of vitality with authentic backgrounds and straightforward narrative style. *The Two Faces of Silenus* is a fantasy for older readers—a difficult undertaking—in which she captures the transition between childhood and adult emotions. Clarke has a special ability in writing for the very young which sparkles from her James stories, *Sandy the Sailor,* and *The Bonfire Party,* for instance. She uses simple vocabulary and repetition to create interesting stories in which her knowledge of children and her ability to capture them on paper are ably demonstrated. However remote the historical setting or bizarre the fantasy, her books are enriched and given plausibility by the description of everyday events and characters: the children in *The Twelve,* the detail of London in *The White Elephant,* the skills and rivalries in *Torolv* and the factual research in *Erpingham Hood.* Above all, she has that most essential talent for writers for children: the ability to tell a story.

—Valerie Brinkley-Willsher

CLEARY, Beverly

Nationality: American. **Born:** Beverly Bunn, McMinnville, Oregon, 12 April 1916. **Education:** University of California, Berkeley, B.A. 1938; University of Washington, Seattle, B.A. in librarianship 1939. **Family:** Married Clarence Cleary in 1940; twin daughter and son. **Career:** Children's librarian, Yakima Public Library, Washington, 1939-40; post librarian, United States Army Hospital, Oakland, California, 1942-45. Lives in Carmel, California. **Awards:** American Library Association Laura Ingalls Wilder award, 1975; Catholic Library Association Regina medal, 1980; American Book award, for paperback, 1981; University of Southern Mississippi award, 1982; George G. Stone Center for Children's Books award, 1983; Society of Children's Writers Golden Kite award, 1983; Christopher award, 1984; American Library Association Newbery medal, 1984; Doctor of Humane Letters, Cornell College. **Address:** c/o William Morrow Inc., 1350 Avenue of the Americas, New York, New York 10019, U.S.A.

PUBLICATIONS FOR CHILDREN

Fiction

Henry Huggins, illustrated by Louis Darling. New York, Morrow, 1950.

Ellen Tebbits, illustrated by Louis Darling. New York, Morrow, 1951.

Henry and Beezus, illustrated by Louis Darling. New York, Morrow, 1952; London, Hamish Hamilton, 1982.

Otis Spofford, illustrated by Louis Darling. New York, Morrow, 1953.

Henry and Ribsy, illustrated by Louis Darling. New York, Morrow, 1954; London, Hamish Hamilton, 1979.

Beezus and Ramona, illustrated by Louis Darling. New York, Morrow, 1955; London, Hamish Hamilton, 1978.

Fifteen, illustrated by Beth and Joe Krush. New York, Morrow, 1956; London, Penguin, 1962.

Henry and the Paper Route, illustrated by Louis Darling. New York, Morrow, 1957.

The Luckiest Girl. New York, Morrow, 1958.

Jean and Johnny, illustrated by Beth and Joe Krush. New York, Morrow, 1959.

Leave It to Beaver (fictionalization of tv series). New York, Berkley, 1960.

The Real Hole, illustrated by Mary Stevens. New York, Morrow, 1960; London, Collins, 1962; reillustrated by DyAnne DiSalvo-Ryan, New York, Morrow, 1986.

Two Dog Biscuits, illustrated by Mary Stevens. New York, Morrow, 1961; London, Collins, 1963; reillustrated by DyAnne DiSalvo-Ryan, New York, Morrow, 1986.

Emily's Runaway Imagination, illustrated by Beth and Joe Krush. New York, Morrow, 1961.

Henry and the Clubhouse, illustrated by Louis Darling. New York, Morrow, 1962; London, Hamish Hamilton, 1981.

Sister of the Bride, illustrated by Beth and Joe Krush. New York, Morrow, 1963.

Ribsy, illustrated by Louis Darling. New York, Morrow, 1964.

The Mouse and the Motorcycle, illustrated by Louis Darling. New York, Morrow, 1965; London, Hamish Hamilton, 1974.

Mitch and Amy, illustrated by George Porter. New York, Morrow, 1967.
Ramona the Pest, illustrated by Louis Darling. New York, Morrow, 1968; London, Hamish Hamilton, 1974.
Runaway Ralph, illustrated by Louis Darling. New York, Morrow, 1970; London, Hamish Hamilton, 1974.
Socks, illustrated by Beatrice Darwin. New York, Morrow, 1973.
Ramona the Brave, illustrated by Alan Tiegreen. New York, Morrow, and London, Hamish Hamilton, 1975.
Ramona and Her Father, illustrated by Alan Tiegreen. New York, Morrow, 1977; London, Hamish Hamilton, 1978.
Ramona and Her Mother, illustrated by Alan Tiegreen. New York, Morrow, and London, Hamish Hamilton, 1979.
Ramona Quimby, Age 8, illustrated by Alan Tiegreen. New York, Morrow, and London, Hamish Hamilton, 1981.
Ralph S. Mouse, illustrated by Paul O. Zelinsky. New York, Morrow, and London, Hamish Hamilton, 1982.
Dear Mr. Henshaw, illustrated by Paul O. Zelinsky. New York, Morrow, and London, MacRae, 1983.
Lucky Chuck, illustrated by J. Winslow Higginbottom. New York, Morrow, and London, MacRae, 1984.
Ramona Forever, illustrated by Alan Tiegreen. New York, Morrow, and London, MacRae, 1984.
Janet's Thingamajigs, illustrated by DyAnne DiSalvo-Ryan. New York, Morrow, 1987.
The Growing-Up Feet, illustrated by DyAnne DiSalvo-Ryan. New York, Morrow, 1987.
Here Come the Twins. London, Hamilton, 1989.
The Twins Again. London, Hamilton, 1989.
Muggie Maggie. New York, Morrow, 1990.
Strider. New York, Morrow, 1991.
Petey's Bedtime Story, illustrated by David Small. New York, Morrow, 1993.

Play

The Sausage at the End of the Nose. New York, Children's Book Council, 1974.

Poetry

The Hullabaloo ABC, illustrated by Earl Thollander. Berkeley, California, Parnassus Press, 1960.

Other

The Ramona Quimby Diary, illustrated by Alan Tiegreen. New York, Morrow, 1984.
The Beezus and Ramona Diary, illustrated by Alan Tiegreen. New York, Morrow, 1986.
A Girl from Yamhill: A Memoir. New York, Morrow, 1988.
My Own Two Feet: A Memoir. New York, Morrow, 1995.

*

Beverly Cleary comments:

As a child I had difficulty learning to read. The discovery, when I was about eight years old, that I could actually read, and read with pleasure, was one of the most exciting moments of my life. From that moment on, as I read through the shelves of the library, I searched for, but was unable to find, the books I wanted to read most of all: books about the sort of children who lived in my neighborhood, books that would make me laugh. The stories I write are the stories I wanted to read as a child, and the experience I hope to share with children is the discovery that reading is one of the pleasures of life and not just something one must do in school.

* * *

For over forty years, since the appearance of *Henry Huggins,* Beverly Cleary has been a children's book writer of remarkable success and critical importance. Her global popularity with four generations of reading children is rivalled only by the critical acclaim her books have garnered. The appeal of Cleary's work can be attributed to her extraordinary talent in creating memorable young characters whose exuberant spirit and zest for life attract young and old readers alike.

Perhaps the most significant statement one can make about Cleary's children's books is that they are read, over and over again, aloud and alone; they are shared by adults and children, and passed from child to child. Her creation of picture books, young adult novels, books about animals, fantasy, and realism attest to her versatility as an author. Reading, the library, and the power of literature are recurring elements in her novels. Humor and clarity characterize her writing style no matter what the genre. Marked by plot-intensive episodes usually recounted in chapter format, her stories revolve around the antics and adventures of engaging characters. Primary attributes of Cleary's characters remain their highly creative play, their dominant ties to neighborhood friends, and a strong sense of community. Still, these characters struggle, not with heavy-handed issues which threaten to consume their naive lives, but with emotions and concerns familiar to young and intermediate readers. Their universal experiences range from Henry Huggins's challenge to demonstrate his ability to manage a paper route, to the often physical and emotionally trying sibling rivalry between Beezus and Ramona Quimby, to the psychological impact of divorce on young Leigh Botts.

Cleary's four picture books stand as the least successful of her work. *The Real Hole* and *The Growing-Up Feet* focus on twins Jimmy and Janet as they investigate the world around them. Told in static, at times forced rhyme, *The Hullabaloo ABC* features nameless twins exploring a farm in the morning. *Lucky Chuck* represents a change both for Cleary and in the expectations of a picture book: uncharacteristically the book focuses on a teenaged boy who must suffer the consequences of his carefree recklessness while riding a motorcycle. The illustrations detail Chuck's motorcycle, its parts, and his loving attention to its maintenance.

Motorcycles also figure prominently in three books about Ralph S. Mouse. *The Mouse and the Motorcycle, Runaway Ralph,* and *Ralph S. Mouse* exemplify Cleary's most successful ventures into fantasy as they trace a mouse's first communication with a human, his acquisition of a motorcycle, his ensuing journey into the dangers away from his family, and his satisfying return home. The worlds of fantasy and realism co-exist; their interaction is governed by clearly prescribed rules which are strictly observed. The combination results in a tantalizing tale of an adventurous mouse.

Without question Beverly Cleary's best known and most loved characters reside on or near Klickitat Street in Portland, Oregon, the bustling neighborhood of Henry Huggins, Ellen Tebbits, Otis Spofford, and the unforgettable Beezus and Ramona Quimby. Above all, these children are normal; they genuinely care for their parents and friends and their love is fully returned. They act as real children act. Sometimes they misunderstand or are misunderstood. Readers closely identify with the older children feeling pestered by their younger friends as they simultaneously recognize the younger child's attraction to the stimulating games enjoyed by older counterparts. While some aspects of the wholesome lifestyle Cleary depicts now appear dated, her sensitive, penetrating awareness of individual children and their needs endures. She must be commended for writing about real children faced with difficult circumstances without becoming fixated on the issues themselves. Published in 1953, *Otis Spofford* depicts one of the first latchkey, single-parent children in children's literature. Yet the story is about Otis, his pleasures and pains, his friends, and his feelings; it is not about his stereotyped problems.

The earlier books shift focus from character to character, developing a community of individual children with unique attributes and interests. With a greater number of books focusing on Henry and his dog Ribsy, Beezus, and Ramona, readers form strong alliances with these three special characters. Of them, Ramona emerges most fully. She makes her first appearance in *Henry Huggins* and immediately threatens to steal the spotlight from well-meaning, reliable Henry. Ramona's spunk, her impermeable but often ambivalent bond to Beezus, and her unsurpassed creativity intrigue and entertain readers. Cleary never cheapens her characters; she never sacrifices Ramona's integrity or intelligence for a laugh. Through Ramona, Cleary touches young readers on an emotional level which engages and challenges, but does not overwhelm. Her ability to sustain their attention over time, from book to book, remains an accomplishment beyond evaluation.

Cleary's novels for young adults, especially adolescent girls, do not possess the timeless qualities of the Ramona and Henry books. *Fifteen, Jean and Johnny,* and *The Luckiest Girl* do not speak to contemporary young adults. Partly thanks to spirited Ramona, 15-year-old girls no longer define themselves solely by their boyfriends or lack of boyfriends. Their future aspirations extend beyond wife and mother to include careers in a range of professions. Despite such limitations these novels are historically interesting as they recall social practices and attitudes less prevalent in contemporary times. Similarly, *Muggie Maggie,* which depicts a girl whose comfort in writing on a personal computer interferes with her willingness to learn cursive penmanship, stems from contemporary concerns. Its relevance to young readers may not outlive the ever-changing technology.

In *Dear Mr. Henshaw,* Cleary definitively enters the 1980s. The story opens as Leigh M. Botts writes to his favorite author in fulfillment of a school assignment. The letters gradually move into revealing diary entries as Leigh gains confidence in himself and demonstrates greater writing skill. With tenacity characteristic of Ramona, Leigh struggles with his parents' divorce, his working mother's absence, his father's emotional absence, and adjustment to a new school and town. The atypical shape of the narrative successfully breaks from Cleary's usual form as she stakes out new territory as a writer. Unlike earlier books, *Dear Mr. Henshaw* turns not on dramatic episodes but on Leigh's introspection.

Leigh Botts won over critics and Cleary garnered the Newbery Award for crafting *Dear Mr. Henshaw.* Readers who quickly identified with Leigh can follow his growth in *Strider.* Once again, Cleary uses the journal format to showcase Leigh's deliberations on life, friends, and family. He narrates his movement into adolescence as he acquires a new friend, a first girlfriend, and a special dog, Strider. Cleary highlights specific events to track Leigh's changing perspective on his parents' divorce and to trace his evolving emotional maturity.

If *Dear Mr. Henshaw* and *Strider* reveal Leigh Botts in personal dialogue with himself, *A Girl from Yamhill* represents Cleary's self-contemplation. This candid autobiography traces the author from her early childhood through young adolescence. Cleary deftly portrays herself as an animated, curious, and often misunderstood little girl, a kindred spirit of Ramona. The book reveals the author's ongoing struggle to resolve troublesome issues about her possessive mother and their less-than-perfect relationship. Voracious readers and avid Cleary fans will recognize here familiar sights, sounds, names, and happenings which have been disclosed in stories. As in all her work, Cleary moves readers with humorous but controlled prose emanating from genuine emotion and familiar experience.

—Cathryn M. Mercier

CLEWES, Dorothy (Mary)

Nationality: British. **Born:** Dorothy Mary Parkin, Nottingham, 6 July 1907. **Education:** Privately in Nottingham; University of Nottingham. **Family:** Married Winston David Armstrong Clewes in 1932 (died 1957). **Career:** Secretary and physician's dispenser, Nottingham, 1924-32. **Agent:** Curtis Brown, 162-168 Regent Street, London WIR 5TB. **Address:** Soleig, Kings Ride, Alfriston, Sussex BN26 5XP, England.

Publications for Children

Fiction

The Rivals of Maidenhurst. London, Nelson, 1925.

The Cottage [*Stream, Treasure, Fair*] *in the Wild Wood,* illustrated by Irene Hawkins. London, Faber, 4 vols. 1945-49.

The Wild Wood (includes *The Cottage in the Wild Wood* and *The Stream in the Wild Wood*), illustrated by Irene Hawkins. New York, Coward McCann, 1948.

Henry Hare's Boxing Match, illustrated by Patricia W. Turner. London, Chatto and Windus, and New York, Coward McCann, 1950.

Henry Hare's Earthquake, illustrated by Patricia W. Turner. London, Chatto and Windus, 1950; New York, Coward McCann, 1951.

Henry Hare, Painter and Decorator, illustrated by Patricia W. Turner. London, Chatto and Windus, 1951.

Henry Hare and the Kidnapping of Selina Squirrel, illustrated by Patricia W. Turner. London, Chatto and Windus, 1951.

The Adventure of the Scarlet Daffodil, illustrated by R.G. Campbell. London, Chatto and Windus, 1952; as *The Mystery of the Scarlet Daffodil,* New York, Coward McCann, 1953.

The Mystery of the Blue Admiral, illustrated by J. Marianne Moll. New York, Coward McCann, 1954; London, Collins, 1955.

The Secret, illustrated by Peggy Beetles. London, Hamish Hamilton, and New York, Coward McCann, 1956.

The Runaway, illustrated by Peggy Beetles. London, Hamish Hamilton, and New York, Coward McCann, 1957.

Adventure on Rainbow Island, illustrated by Shirley Hughes. London, Collins, 1957; as *Mystery on Rainbow Island,* New York, Coward McCann, 1957.

The Jade Green Cadillac, illustrated by Shirley Hughes. London, Collins, 1958; as *The Mystery of the Jade-Green Cadillac,* New York, Coward McCann, 1958.
The Happiest Day, illustrated by Peggy Beetles. London, Hamish Hamilton, 1958; New York, Coward McCann, 1959.
The Old Pony, illustrated by Peggy Beetles. London, Hamish Hamilton, 1959; New York, Coward McCann, 1960.
Hide and Seek, illustrated by Peggy Beetles. London, Hamish Hamilton, 1959; New York, Coward McCann, 1960.
The Lost Tower Treasure, illustrated by Shirley Hughes. London, Collins, 1960; as *The Mystery of the Lost Tower Treasure,* New York, Coward McCann, 1960.
The Hidden Key, illustrated by Peggy Beetles. London, Hamish Hamilton, 1960; New York, Coward McCann, 1961.
The Singing Strings, illustrated by Shirley Hughes. London, Collins, 1961; as *Mystery of the Singing Strings,* New York, Coward McCann, 1961.
All the Fun of the Fair, illustrated by Juliette Palmer. London, Hamish Hamilton, 1961; New York, Coward McCann, 1962.
Wilberforce and the Slaves, illustrated by Peter Edwards. London, Hutchinson, 1961.
Skyraker and the Iron Imp, illustrated by Peter Edwards. London, Hutchinson, 1962.
The Purple Mountain, illustrated by Robert Broomfield. London, Collins, 1962; as *The Golden Eagle,* New York, Coward McCann, 1962.
The Birthday, illustrated by Juliette Palmer. London, Hamish Hamilton, 1962; New York, Coward McCann, 1963.
The Branch Line, illustrated by Juliette Palmer. London, Hamish Hamilton, and New York, Coward McCann, 1963.
Operation Smuggle, illustrated by Shirley Hughes. London, Collins, 1964; as *The Mystery of the Midnight Smugglers,* New York, Coward McCann, 1964.
Boys and Girls Come Out to Play, illustrated by Jane Paton. London, Hamish Hamilton, 1964.
The Holiday, illustrated by Janet Duchesne. London, Hamish Hamilton, and New York, Coward McCann, 1964.
Guide Dog, illustrated by Peter Burchard. London, Hamish Hamilton, and New York, Coward McCann, 1965; as *Dog for the Dark,* London, White Lion, 1974.
Red Ranger and the Combine Harvester, illustrated by Peter Edwards. London, Hutchinson, 1966.
Roller Skates, Skooter and Bike, illustrated by Constance Marshall. London, Hamish Hamilton, and New York, Coward McCann, 1966.
A Boy like Walt. London, Collins, and New York, Coward McCann, 1967.
A Bit of Magic, illustrated by Robert Hales. London, Hamish Hamilton, 1967.
A Girl like Cathy. London, Collins, 1968.
Adopted Daughter. New York, Coward McCann, 1968.
Upsidedown [Special Branch, Fire-Brigade] Willie, illustrated by Edward Ardizzone. London, Hamish Hamilton, 3 vols., 1968-70.
Peter and the Jumbie, illustrated by Robert Hales. London, Hamish Hamilton, 1969.
Library Lady, illustrated by Robert Hales. London, Chatto Boyd and Oliver, 1970; as *The Library,* New York, Coward McCann, 1971.
Two Bad Boys, illustrated by Lynette Hemmant. London, Hamish Hamilton, 1971.
The End of Summer. New York, Coward McCann, 1971.
Storm over Innish. London, Heinemann, 1972; Nashville, Nelson, 1973.
A Skein of Geese, illustrated by Janet Duchesne. London, Chatto Boyd and Oliver, 1972.
Ginny's Boy. London, Heinemann, 1973.
Hooray for Me, illustrated by Michael Jackson. London, Heinemann, 1973.
Wanted—A Grand, illustrated by Robert Micklewright. London, Chatto and Windus, 1974.
Missing from Home. London, Heinemann, 1975; New York, Harcourt Brace, 1978.
Nothing to Declare. London, Heinemann, 1976.
The Testing Year. London, Heinemann, 1977.
The Adventures of Willie. London, MacRae, 1991.

Other

The Brown Burrows Books, illustrated by Patricia W. Turner. London, Chatto and Windus, 4 vols., 1950-51.
Guide Dogs for the Blind. London, Hamish Hamilton, 1966.

Editor, *The Secret of the Sea: An Anthology of Underwater Exploration and Adventure,* illustrated by Jeroo Roy. London, Heinemann, 1973.

Publications for Adults

Novels

She Married a Doctor. London, Jenkins, 1943; as *Stormy Hearts,* New York, Arcadia House, 1944.
Shepherd's Hill. London, Sampson Low, 1945.
To Man Alone. London, Jenkins, and New York, Arcadia House, 1945.
A Stranger in the Valley. London, Harrap, 1948.
The Blossom on the Bough. London, Harrap, 1949.
Summer Cloud. London, Harrap, 1951.
Merry-Go-Round. London, Hodder and Stoughton, 1954.
I Came to a Wood. London, Hale, 1956.

* * *

Dorothy Clewes writes for a variety of ages. Her work for younger children, the stories of preschool Willie, or Penny and her friends, are undemanding tales in everyday settings, with children who get up to amusing little naughtiness. In another series the Hadley children, who seem to enjoy eternal summer holidays, spend them in detecting crimes; it is important to score off the adult world. The trouble with these stories is that the characters are not sufficiently well drawn or interesting enough to get the reader "hooked" on the series, and anyone finding them safe, comfortable reading would quickly find his palate cloying. It is a case of "read one, you've read them all."

Her books for teenagers are rather more successful, apart from the ever present premise that problem teenagers will be helped by reading about fictional characters with the same problems. That sort of child does not read that sort of book. *Nothing to Declare* tells of Dave, not very bright at school, who takes on a cross-channel driving job. He quickly realises that it involves smuggling, and starts to worry not just about getting caught but about the moral aspects of his actions. He has to choose between the easy money and his conscience, complicated by the fact that other people do not seem to think it is wrong. *Ginny's Boy* is a story of young love, though Ginny tries to blind herself to the fact that her boyfriend is irresponsible and selfish, and that the love is mostly on her side. *Storm over Innish* is her most successful book. Her heroine Letty, a highly imaginative girl who escapes into a secret world of writing, loses her brother in a boating accident. A few years later a boy of the same age is washed up unconscious on the same beach, suffering from amnesia. Letty looks after him and tries to help him recover his identity, fearing all the while that when he does so she will lose him. It is not quite a love story but very nearly so, a tentative reaching-out into uncharted waters.

In some ways it is difficult to make a satisfying meal out of Clewes's books. Perhaps it is because she tries so hard to help us to identify and emphathise with the protagonists that other figures in her stories, particularly the adults, become stereotypes; children prefer adults to be real and recognisable.

—Ann G. Hay

CLIFFORD, Martin. See **RICHARDS, Frank.**

CLIFTON, (Thelma) Lucille

Nationality: American. **Born:** Thelma Lucille Sayles, Depew, New York, 27 June 1936. **Education:** Howard University, Washington, D.C., 1953-55; Fredonia State Teachers College, New York, 1955. **Family:** Married Fred J. Clifton in 1958; four daughters and two sons. **Career:** Claims clerk, New York State Division of Employment, Buffalo, 1958-60; literature assistant, U.S. Office of Education, Washington, D.C., 1969-71. Visiting writer, Columbia University School of the Arts; poet-in-residence, Coppin State College, Baltimore, 1972-76; visiting writer, George Washington University, Washington, D.C., 1982-83. **Awards:** YM-YWHA Poetry Center Discovery award, 1969; National Endowment for the Arts grant, 1970, 1972; Juniper prize, 1980; American Library Association Coretta Scott King award, 1984; Pulitzer Prize Nominations for Poetry, 1980, 1988; Lannan Literary Award for Poetry, 1996; honorary degrees from the University of Maryland and Towson State University, 1996. **Agent:** Marilyn Marlow, Curtis Brown, 10 Astor Place, New York, New York 10003, U.S.A.

Publications for Children

Fiction

All Us Come Cross the Water, illustrated by John Steptoe. New York, Holt Rinehart, 1973.

Don't You Remember?, illustrated by Evaline Ness. New York, Dutton, 1973.

The Boy Who Didn't Believe in Spring, illustrated by Brinton Turkle. New York, Dutton, 1973.

The Times They Used to Be, illustrated by Susan Jeschke. New York, Holt Rinehart, 1974.

My Brother Fine with Me, illustrated by Moneta Barnett. New York, Holt Rinehart, 1975.

Three Wishes, illustrated by Stephanie Douglas. New York, Viking Press, 1976.

Amifika, illustrated by Thomas di Grazia. New York, Dutton, 1977.

The Lucky Stone, illustrated by Dale Payson. New York, Delacorte Press, 1979.

My Friend Jacob, illustrated by Thomas di Grazia. New York, Dutton, 1980.

Sonora Beautiful, illustrated by Michael Garland. New York, Dutton, 1981.

Ten Oxherding Pictures, illustrated by Lisa Bulawsky. Santa Cruz, California, Moving Parts Press, 1988.

Poetry

Some of the Days of Everett Anderson, illustrated by Evaline Ness. New York, Holt Rinehart, 1970.

Everett Anderson's Christmas Coming, illustrated by Evaline Ness. New York, Holt Rinehart, 1971.

Good, Says Jerome, illustrated by Stephanie Douglas. New York, Dutton, 1973.

Everett Anderson's Year, illustrated by Ann Grifalconi. New York, Holt Rinehart, 1974.

Everett Anderson's Friend, illustrated by Ann Grifalconi. New York, Holt Rinehart, 1976.

Everett Anderson's 1—2—3, illustrated by Ann Grifalconi. New York, Holt Rinehart, 1977.

Everett Anderson's Nine Month Long, illustrated by Ann Grifalconi. New York, Holt Rinehart, 1978.

Everett Anderson's Goodbye, illustrated by Ann Grifalconi. New York, Holt Rinehart, 1983.

Dear Creator: A Week of Poems for Young People and Their Teachers, illustrated by Gail Gordon Carter. New York, Doubleday, 1997.

Other

The Black BC's, illustrated by Don Miller. New York, Dutton, 1970.

Publications for Adults

Novel

Generations of Americans: A Memoir. New York, Random House, 1976.

Poetry

Good Times. New York, Random House, 1969.

Good News about the Earth. New York, Random House, 1972.

An Ordinary Woman. New York, Random House, 1974.

Two-Headed Woman. Amherst, University of Massachusetts Press, 1980.
Good Woman: Poems and a Memoir, 1969-1980. Rochester, New York, BOA Editions, 1987.
Next: New Poems. Rochester, New York, BOA Editions, 1987.
Quilting: Poems 1987-1990. Rochester, New York, BOA Editions, 1991.
The Book of Light. Port Townsend, Washington, Copper Canyon Press, 1993.
The Terrible Stories: Poems. Rochester, New York, BOA Editions, 1996.

* * *

In her picture books, poetry, and prose for young readers, Lucille Clifton emphasizes the importance of trust, compassion, and friendship in the formation of a fulfilling life. In the popular *Everett Anderson* series, Mrs. Anderson encourages her son to "walk tall in the world," and Everett attempts to follow her advice, even when the pain of his father's death compels him to question the meaning of life itself. In *Everett Anderson's Goodbye,* Everett's grief is expressed masterfully in Clifton's free-flowing poetic style: "Everett Anderson tries to sleep/but it is too hard and/the hurt is too deep./Everett Anderson likes his food/but how can a dinner/do any good?/Everett Anderson just sits staring/wondering what's the use of caring." Everett's eventual recovery and his acceptance of a new stepfather and baby sister encourage young readers that they too can accept changes in their lives.

In *Amifika,* Clifton portrays in the anxieties of a young boy who misinterprets his mother's off-hand comment that she plans to get rid of a number of things from the house that have accumulated while her husband was away serving in the military. Assuming that his mother is referring to him, Amifika thinks, "I be what Mama get rid of. Like she said, [daddy] can't miss what he don't remember. I be the thing they get rid of." In these poignant lines, Clifton underscores Amifika's vulnerability and provides a compelling insight into the fear of abandonment felt by many young children.

Clifton's work also contains a powerful examination of African-American heritage and culture. In *The Black BCs,* the letters of the alphabet are used to introduce discussions, in prose and poetry, of the contributions of African-American men and women to American history, literature, and politics. In *The Times They Used to Be,* a mother tells her children about the conditions for African-Americans back in 1948, and in *The Lucky Stone,* a great-grandmother weaves four stories around a little black stone that brought luck to its owners, from slave times up into the present.

For intermediate readers, Clifton focuses on peer interaction. In *Three Wishes,* young Zenobia learns that a fight with a best friend can actually lead both parties to reexamine the importance of friendship and acceptance. In *My Friend Jacob,* Clifton depicts a highly-valued friendship between an eight year-old African-American boy named Sam and his neighbor Jacob, a seventeen year-old white boy who is mildly retarded, but who can be helped to learn. In fact, Sam learns the importance of self-esteem by teaching Jacob vital survival skills. In *Sonora Beautiful,* another illustrated book, Clifton provides the reader with an intriguing glimpse into the life of a white teenage girl who is struggling to establish her sense of self within a highly individualistic family.

In all her books for young people, Lucille Clifton presents events and then allows her young readers to draw conclusions for themselves. Often, a protagonist's change of heart is depicted through the illustrations or through abrupt changes of scene. Thus, while much of Clifton's work contains important cultural messages, she allows her readers to grow and to mature at their own pace along with her characters.

—Claudia Lewis, updated by Gwen A. Tarbox.

CLIMO, Shirley

Nationality: American. **Born:** Shirley Beistle in Cleveland, Ohio, 25 November 1928. **Education:** Attended DePauw University, 1946-49. **Family:** Married George F. Climo, 17 June 1950; one son and two daughters. **Career:** Scriptwriter for weekly juvenile series "Fairytale Theatre," Cleveland, 1949-53; free-lance writer since 1976. President of Morning Forum of Los Altos, 1971-73. **Agent:** Kendra Marcus, *Bookstop,* 67 Meadow View Road, Orinda, California 94563, U.S.A. **Address:** 24821 Prospect Ave., Los Altos, California 94022, U.S.A.

Publications for Children

Fiction

The Cobweb Christmas, illustrated by Joe Lasker. New York, Crowell, 1982.
Gopher, Tanker, and the Admiral, illustrated by Eileen McKeating. New York, Crowell, 1984.
Someone Saw a Spider, illustrated Dirk Zimmer. New York, Crowell, 1985.
A Month of Seven Days. New York, Crowell, 1987.
King of the Birds, illustrated by Ruth Heller. New York, Harper, 1988.
T. J.'s Ghost. New York, Crowell, 1988.
The Egyptian Cinderella, illustrated by R. Heller. New York, Crowell, 1989.
The Korean Cinderella, illustrated by R. Heller. New York, HarperCollins, 1993.
The Little Red Ant and the Great Big Crumb: A Mexican Fable, illustrated by Francisco X. Mora. New York, Clarion, 1995.
The Irish Cinderlad, illustrated by Loretta Krupinski. New York, HarperCollins, 1996.

Other

Piskies, Spriggans, and Other Magical Beings: Tales from the Droll-Teller, Retold by Shirley Climo, illustrated by Joyce Audy dos Santos. New York, Crowell, 1981.
City! New York. New York, Macmillan, 1990.
City! San Francisco. New York, Macmillan, 1990.
City! Washington, D.C. New York, Macmillan, 1991.
The Match between the Winds, illustrated by Roni Shepherd. New York, Macmillan, 1991.
Stolen Thunder: A Norse Myth, illustrated by Alexander Koshkin. New York, Clarion, 1994.
Atalanta's Race: A Greek Myth, illustrated by Alexander Koshkin. New York, Clarion, 1995.

Why Monkeys Live in Trees. Forthcoming.

Compiler and reteller, *A Treasury of Princesses: Princess Tales from around the World,* illustrated by Ruth Sanderson. New York, HarperCollins, 1996.

Compiler and reteller, *A Treasury of Mermaids: Mermaid Tales from around the World,* illustrated by Jean and Mou-sien Teng. New York, HarperCollins, 1997.

Compiler and reteller, *Magic and Mischief: Tales from Cornwall* (from stories by Robert Hunt and William Bottrell). New York, Clarion, 1998.

Publications for Adults

Contributor, *Writing and Selling Fillers, Light Verse, and Short Humor.* New York, Writer, Inc., 1982.

* * *

Shirley Climo's best work mixes fact and fancy; she is extraordinarily skilled at using an already-existing frame as the basis of a story and embellishing it with details that make it come to life for the reader. In two collections of folk tales, *Piskies, Spriggans, and Other Magical Beings: Tales from the Droll-Teller* and *Someone Saw a Spider,* and in several one-tale picture books, Climo re-tells old stories from many cultures, expertly capturing the cultural background of each of the tales. *Piskies* re-creates long-ago Cornwall, not only through the use of the accurate dialect she employs, but also by means of an accomplished storyteller's flair for language. The Spriggans, for example, "jump about on tabletop like hoptoads," and the sea king is "so old he appeared to be carved of driftwood." Climo's spider stories come from all over the world, but the details of each—the sunbeams that "fall straight as bamboo poles" in the Japanese tale, or Zachary Dee from the Ozarks who was "so quick he could bag a weasel in the chicken house without even waking the hens"—indicate careful research and language selection that perfectly matches each tale to its particular source. Additionally, Climo often appends factual details that augment her stories, such as explanations of, and folk superstitions about, the fantastic creatures that are the subjects of the *Piskies* tales. In some cases, the facts about real creatures such as the spiders are even more interesting—that a fever-reducing drug was once made from spider webs, for instance.

Some critics have averred that Climo's collections of tales suit the adult storyteller better than the child reader. It is true, for example, that only the most arachnophilic reader would devour her entire collection of spider stories at once; nevertheless, well-written collections of tales are valuable resources for dipping into from time to time and need not be read en masse. In any case, Climo's picture-books recounting single tales, especially the Cinderella variations, exhibit the same care in re-telling as do her larger collections, and most of these also contain interesting factual material on the tales' sources. *King of the Birds* falls short in this regard, for although the tale itself is well-told, Climo's note regarding the origins of her particular version of the story is rather vague. *The Little Red Ant and the Great Big Crumb* also seems to draw on so many variants that the tale itself lacks the precision usually associated with the "fable" it purports to be. Readers may find its use of Spanish words and characters (with an appended glossary) enjoyable, but the text becomes a bit cumbersome as it attempts to blend fable with cumulative tale and to develop individual characters as well.

Shirley Climo's "city" books, which delineate the history and present state of San Francisco, Washington, and New York, demonstrate the same flair for taking a set story structure—in this case, the history of certain American cities—and skillfully blending in nuggets of fascinating information, as she does when working with folk tales. For instance, her recounting of the history of the Capitol building and the governmental functions that take place within it includes the story of how the term "lobbyist" originated, as well as the information that young people who work as congressional pages must get up early enough in the morning to attend high school classes *before* they go to work for Congress. Climo is adept at including just enough tidbits to enliven the factual narrative and to make the prospect of a visit to any of these cities sound most inviting.

Climo's ventures into standard fiction, however, are markedly less effectual than her work that uses history or folk tale as a structure. She brings historical accuracy to the Civil War novel *A Month of Seven Days,* but many aspects of young Zoe's character and the issues the novel addresses seem unfinished. *Gopher, Tanker, and the Admiral* has the feel of a story from the 1950s, even though it was published in 1984. The attempts at humor in this novel, such as a pickle that somehow leaps out of Gopher's sandwich and into his sister's glass of milk, or his attempt to scavenge in a surly neighbor's garbage, fall flat. Repeated references to the fact that the new mail carrier is female come across as dated and sexist. The requisite reference to modern life—the fact that Gopher's parents are separated—occurs, but is only marginally explored, much less resolved. Climo seems to need the structure provided by tradition or history to do her best writing; her considerable talents are more successfully utilized in rendering old stories with lively and engaging language, than they are in creating new ones.

—Christine Doyle

CLYMER, Eleanor

Pseudonyms: Janet Bell; Elizabeth Kinsey. **Nationality:** American. **Born:** Eleanor Lowenton, New York City, 7 January 1906. **Education:** Barnard College, New York, 1923-25; University of Wisconsin, Madison, B.A. 1927; New York University; Bank Street College of Education, New York. **Family:** Married Kinsey Clymer in 1933; one son. **Career:** Teacher in camps and nursery schools. Worked for Dodd Mead, publishers, 1928-32. **Awards:** Child Study Association of America award, 1975. **Address:** 3118 Elm, The Quadrangle, 3300 Darby Road, Haverford, Pennsylvania 19041, U.S.A.

Publications for Children

Fiction

A Yard for John, illustrated by Mildred Boyle. New York, McBride, 1943.

Here Comes Pete, illustrated by Mildred Boyle. New York, McBride, 1944.

The Grocery Mouse, illustrated by Jeanne Bendick. New York, McBride, 1945.
Little Bear Island, illustrated by Ursula Koering. New York, McBride, 1945.
Sunday in the Park (as Janet Bell), illustrated by Aline Appel. New York, McBride, 1946.
Monday-Tuesday-Wednesday Book (as Janet Bell), illustrated by Mary Stevens. New York, McBride, 1946.
The Country Kittens, illustrated by Jeanne Bendick. New York, McBride, 1947.
The Trolley Car Family, illustrated by Ursula Koering. New York, McKay, 1947.
The Latch Key Club, illustrated by Corinne Dillon. New York, McKay, 1949.
Treasure at First Base, illustrated by Jean MacDonald Porter. New York, Dodd Mead, 1950.
Tommy's Wonderful Airplane, illustrated by Kurt Wiese. New York, Dodd Mead, 1951.
Thirty-Three Bunn Street, illustrated by Jane Miller. New York, Dodd Mead, 1952.
Chester, illustrated by Ezra Jack Keats. New York, Dodd Mead, 1954.
Not Too Small after All, illustrated by Tom O'Sullivan. New York, Watts, 1955.
Sociable Toby, illustrated by Ingrid Fetz. New York, Watts, 1956.
Mr. Piper's Bus, illustrated by Kurt Wiese. New York, Dodd Mead, 1961.
Benjamin in the Woods. New York, Wonder Books, 1962.
Now That You Are Seven, illustrated by Ingrid Fetz. New York, Association Press, 1963.
Harry, The Wild West Horse, illustrated by Leonard Shortall. New York, Atheneum, 1963; London, Hamish Hamilton, 1964.
The Tiny Little House, illustrated by Ingrid Fetz. New York, Atheneum, 1964.
Chipmunk in the Forest, illustrated by Ingrid Fetz. New York, Atheneum, 1965.
The Adventure of Walter, illustrated by Ingrid Fetz. New York, Atheneum, 1965.
My Brother Stevie. New York, Holt Rinehart, 1967.
The Big Pile of Dirt, illustrated by Robert Shore. New York, Holt Rinehart, 1968.
Horatio, illustrated by Robert Quackenbush. New York, Atheneum, 1968.
Belinda's New Spring Hat, illustrated by Gioia Fiammenghi. New York, Watts, 1969.
We Lived in the Almont, illustrated by David Stone. New York, Dutton, 1970.
The House on the Mountain, illustrated by Leo Carty. New York, Dutton, 1971.
The Spider, The Cave, and the Pottery Bowl, illustrated by Ingrid Fetz. New York, Atheneum, 1971.
Me and the Eggman, illustrated by David Stone. New York, Dutton, 1972.
How I Went Shopping and What I Got, illustrated by Trina Schart Hyman. New York, Holt Rinehart, 1972.
Santiago's Silver Mine, illustrated by Ingrid Fetz. New York, Atheneum, 1973.
Luke Was There, illustrated by Diane de Groat. New York, Holt Rinehart, 1973.
Leave Horatio Alone, illustrated by Robert Quackenbush. New York, Atheneum, 1974.
Take Tarts as Tarts Is Passing, illustrated by Roy Doty. New York, Dutton, 1974.
Engine Number Seven, illustrated by Robert Quackenbush. New York, Holt Rinehart, 1975.
Hamburgers—And Ice Cream for Dessert, illustrated by Roy Doty. New York, Dutton, 1975.
Horatio's Birthday, illustrated by Robert Quackenbush. New York, Atheneum, 1976.
Horatio Goes to the Country, illustrated by Robert Quackenbush. New York, Atheneum, 1978.
The Get-Away Car. New York, Dutton 1978.
Horatio Solves a Mystery, illustrated by Robert Quackenbush. New York, Atheneum, 1980.
A Search for Two Bad Mice, illustrated by Margery Gill. New York, Atheneum, 1980.
My Mother Is the Smartest Woman in the World, illustrated by Nancy Kincade. New York, Atheneum, 1982.
The Horse in the Attic, illustrated by Ted Lewin. Scarsdale, New York, Bradbury Press, 1983.

Fiction as Elizabeth Kinsey

Teddy, illustrated by Jeanne Bendick. New York, McBride, 1945.
Patch, illustrated by James Davis. New York, McBride, 1946.
Sea View Secret, illustrated by Mary Stevens. New York, Watts, 1952.
Donny and Company, illustrated by Mary Stevens. New York, Watts, 1953.
This Cat Came to Stay!, illustrated by Don Sibley. New York, Watts, 1955.

Other

Make Way for Water, illustrated by J.C. Wonsetler. New York, Messner, 1953.
Modern American Career Women, with Lillian Erlich. New York, Dodd Mead, 1959.
The Case of the Missing Link, illustrated by Robert Macguire. New York, Basic Books, 1962; revised edition, 1968.
Search for a Living Fossil: The Story of the Coelacanth, illustrated by Joan Berg. New York, Holt Rinehart, 1963; London, Lutterworth Press, 1965.
Communities at Work. Boston, Heath, 1964; revised edition, 1969.
Wheels, illustrated by Charles Goslin. New York, Holt Rinehart, 1965.
The Second Greatest Invention: Search for the First Farmers, illustrated by Lili Réthi. New York, Holt Rinehart, 1969.

PUBLICATIONS FOR ADULTS

Other

Management in the Home, with Lillian Gilbreth. New York, Dodd Mead, 1954.

*

Manuscript Collections: Kerlan Collection, University of Minnesota, Minneapolis; de Grummond Collection, University of Southern Mississippi, Hattiesburg.

Eleanor Clymer comments:

I began writing for children under the guidance of Lucy Sprague Mitchell, who is not so well remembered now, but in the 1930s revolutionized children's literature with her "Here and Now" realistic approach. My first books were based on the everyday familiar world of my young son and his friends. As they grew older I wrote stories about their interests: baseball, airplanes, exploring, photography, pets. I also wrote about the history of science, an earlier interest of mine. In the 1950s and 1960s, however, the world was changing. My child was grown up, but there were other children to write for. I wanted to say something about the emotions and problems of children dealing with a sometimes hostile world. In *My Brother Stevie* I tried to tell what a child of the "inner city" might have said in talking about her own life. I tried to write simply enough not to put off older children who might not be facile readers but who had already had difficult life experience. I had moved from the city to a small country village, but that was the first of a number of books about the city I had known well. After traveling in the Southwest and Mexico I became interested in the life of present-day Native Americans and wrote *The Spider, The Cave and the Pottery Bowl* and *Santiago's Silver Mine.* More recently I have been writing about life in a small town. *My Mother Is the Smartest Woman in the World* is about small-town politics and how much women are needed to participate in them. *The Get-Away Car* is based partly on the village where I live. *The Horse in the Attic* is a mystery story but its central theme is that of a loving family.

It has been a long road. I have several more books which I hope to write in the time remaining.

* * *

Eleanor Clymer has written 50 books for children, enough surely to earn her the label of a prolific writer. But there are other writers who turn out books regularly; the difference is that Clymer is an *excellent* as well as a prolific writer of children's books. She exhibits the same fine literary quality in a non-fiction book such as *Search for a Living Fossil: The Story of the Coelacanth* as she does in her renowned works of fiction such as *My Brother Stevie, The House on the Mountain,* and *Luke Was There.*

Clymer writes both for the picture book crowd, young readers, and older readers from age 10 up. While *My Brother Stevie* and *Luke Was There* may be catalogued for an audience of 9 to 11, adults will be as deeply moved as children by these books. Both books throw doubt on the claim that only ethnic writers can know the ethnic experience, for one of these stories is from the viewpoint of a young black girl, the other from that of a young black boy. And in both tales, the reader intensely identifies with the characters. Clymer doesn't let the environment and life style of the protagonists occupy the foreground. She is unsparing in her depiction of the problems facing the children, of the less-than-ideal treatment they receive both from their situations and from the people surrounding them. In her books, the facts of reality must be accepted; what is important to the reader is how the children cope with them. In the coping, they reveal to us some important truths about ourselves. Clymer never *tells* us; the characters and their actions *show* us. When we see Stevie's negative responses to his grandmother's punishing attitudes, and his loving response to his understanding teacher, we learn something about helping human needs. In *Luke Was There* we live in the skin of an institutionalized child and feel in our bones his despair and anger as adults betray his trust again and again. After experiencing these books (and *The House on the Mountain*), we can never again view ghetto children as before; we have walked in their shoes. These three books alone place Clymer in the foremost rank of children's writers.

Clymer's style is deceptively simple; but it is the simplicity that results from the painstaking paring away of superfluous or extraneous words and thoughts. Her characters' speech seems to be their natural speech; in actuality, it is Clymer's skill in subtly deleting all but the important prose yet retaining the flavor and rhythm of natural speech that allows us to understand the needs and personalities of the characters. For instance, these two lines from *The House on the Mountain:* "I tell Gloria, 'Why don't you watch the kids?' She says, 'Why don't you leave me alone?'" Here we glimpse the concern of the 10-year-old "I" who is relating the story, and his teenage sister's indifference—in just seventeen words!

Clymer's books about Horatio the cat, for younger children, are much more amusing and lighter in theme. Parents who are inveigled into reading them aloud will chuckle in recognition of the "characteristic cat" that is Horace. Only an appreciative watcher of cats could so unerringly portray Horace in all his set ways! Clymer must have as much fun in creating these adventures as children will in listening to them.

—Betty Boegehold

COATSWORTH, Elizabeth (Jane)

Nationality: American. **Born:** Buffalo, New York, 31 May 1893. **Education:** Park Street School, 1899-1907; Los Robles School, Pasadena, California, 1907-09; Buffalo Seminary, 1909-11; Vassar College, Poughkeepsie, New York, B.A. 1915 (Phi Beta Kappa); Columbia University, New York, M.A. 1916; Radcliffe College, Cambridge, Massachusetts. **Family:** Married the writer Henry Beston in 1929 (died 1968); two daughters. **Awards:** American Library Association Newbery medal, 1931; New England Poetry Club Golden Rose, 1967; University of Minnesota Kerlan award, 1975. Litt.D.: University of Maine, Orono, 1955; L.H.D.: New England College, Henniker, New Hampshire, 1958. **Died:** 2 September 1986.

Publications for Children

Fiction

The Cat and the Captain, illustrated by Gertrude Kaye. New York, Macmillan, 1927.

Toutou in Bondage, illustrated by Thomas Handforth. New York, Macmillan, 1929.

The Boy with the Parrot, illustrated by Wilfred Bronson. New York, Macmillan, 1930.

The Cat Who Went to Heaven, illustrated by Lynd Ward. New York, Macmillan, 1930; London, Dent, 1949.

Knock at the Door, illustrated by F.D. Bedford. New York, Macmillan, 1931.

Cricket and the Emperor's Son, illustrated by Weda Yap. New York, Macmillan, 1932; revised edition, Kingswood, Surrey, World's Work, 1962.

Away Goes Sally, illustrated by Helen Sewell. New York, Macmillan, 1934; London, Woodfield, 1955.

The Golden Horseshoe, illustrated by Robert Lawson. New York, Macmillan, 1935; revised edition, as *Tamar's Wager,* London, Blackie, 1971.

Sword of the Wilderness, illustrated by Harve Stein. New York, Macmillan, 1936; London, Blackie, 1972.

Alice-All-by-Herself, illustrated by Marguerite de Angeli. New York, Macmillan, 1937; London, Harrap, 1938.

Dancing Tom, illustrated by Grace Paull. New York, Macmillan, 1938; London, Combridge, 1939.

Five Bushel Farm, illustrated by Helen Sewell. New York, Macmillan, 1939; London, Woodfield, 1958.

The Littlest House, illustrated by Marguerite Davis. New York, Macmillan, 1940; Kingswood, Surrey, World's Work, 1958.

The Fair American, illustrated by Helen Sewell. New York, Macmillan, 1940; London, Blackie, 1970.

A Toast to the King, illustrated by Forrest Orr. New York, Coward McCann, 1940; London, Dent, 1941.

Tonio and the Stranger, illustrated by Wilfred Bronson. New York, Grosset and Dunlap, 1941.

You Shall Have a Carriage, illustrated by Henry Pitz. New York, Macmillan, 1941.

Forgotten Island, illustrated by Grace Paull. New York, Grosset and Dunlap, 1942.

Houseboat Summer, illustrated by Marguerite Davis. New York, Macmillan, 1942.

The White Horse, illustrated by Helen Sewell. New York, Macmillan, 1942; as *The White Horse of Morocco,* London, Blackie, 1973.

Thief Island, illustrated by John Wonsetler. New York, Macmillan, 1943; Kingswood, Surrey, World's Work, 1960.

Twelve Months Make a Year, illustrated by Marguerite Davis. New York, Macmillan, 1943.

The Big Green Umbrella, illustrated by Helen Sewell. New York, Grosset and Dunlap, 1944.

Trudy and the Tree House, illustrated by Marguerite Davis. New York, Macmillan, 1944.

The Kitten Stand, illustrated by Kathleen Keeler. New York, Grosset and Dunlap, 1945.

The Wonderful Day, illustrated by Helen Sewell. New York, Macmillan, 1946; London, Blackie, 1973.

Plum Daffy Adventure, illustrated by Marguerite Davis. New York, Macmillan, 1947; Kingswood, Surrey, World's Work, 1965.

Up Hill and Down: Stories, illustrated by James Davis. New York, Knopf, 1947.

The House of the Swan, illustrated by Kathleen Voute. New York, Macmillan, 1948; Kingswood, Surrey, World's Work, 1959.

The Little Haymakers, illustrated by Grace Paull. New York, Macmillan, 1949.

The Captain's Daughter, illustrated by Ralph Ray. New York, Macmillan, 1950; London, Collier Macmillan, 1963.

American Adventures 1620-1945, illustrated by Robert Frankenburg. New York, Macmillan, 1968.

- *First Adventure,* illustrated by Ralph Ray. New York, Macmillan, 1950.
- *The Wishing Pear,* illustrated by Ralph Ray. New York, Macmillan, 1951.
- *Boston Bells,* illustrated by Manning Lee. New York, Macmillan, 1952.
- *Aunt Flora,* illustrated by Manning Lee. New York, Macmillan, 1953.
- *Old Whirlwind: A Story of Davy Crockett,* illustrated by Manning Lee. New York, Macmillan, 1953.
- *The Sod House,* illustrated by Manning Lee. New York, Macmillan, 1954.
- *Cherry Ann and the Dragon Horse,* illustrated by Manning Lee. New York, Macmillan, 1955.

Door to the North, illustrated by Frederick Chapman. Philadelphia, Winston, 1950; Kingswood, Surrey, World's Work, 1960.

Dollar for Luck, illustrated by George and Doris Hauman. New York, Macmillan, 1951; as *The Sailing Hatrack,* London, Blackie, 1972.

The Last Fort, illustrated by Edward Shenton. Philadelphia, Winston, 1952; London, Hamish Hamilton, 1953.

Cat Stories, illustrated by Feodor Rojankovsky. New York, Simon and Schuster, 1953; London, Publicity Products, 1955.

Dog Stories, illustrated by Feodor Rojankovsky. New York, Simon and Schuster, 1953; London, Publicity Products, 1954.

Horse Stories, with Kate Barnes, illustrated by Feodor Rojankovsky. New York, Simon and Schuster, 1954.

Hide and Seek, illustrated by Genevieve Vaughan-Jackson. New York, Pantheon, 1956.

The Peddler's Cart, illustrated by Zhenya Gay. New York, Macmillan, 1956; as *The Pedlar's Cart,* London, Blackie, 1971.

The Dog from Nowhere, illustrated by Don Sibley. Evanston, Illinois, Row Peterson, 1958.

Down Tumbledown Mountain, illustrated by Aldren Watson. Evanston, Illinois, Row Peterson, 1958.

The Cave, illustrated by Allan Houser. New York, Viking Press, 1958; as *Cave of Ghosts,* London, Hamish Hamilton, 1971.

You Say You Saw a Camel!, illustrated by Brinton Turkle. Evanston, Illinois, Row Peterson, 1958.

Pika and the Roses, illustrated by Kurt Wiese. New York, Pantheon, 1959.

Desert Dan, illustrated by Harper Johnson. New York, Viking Press, 1960; London, Harrap, 1963.

Lonely Maria, illustrated by Evaline Ness. New York, Pantheon, 1960; London, Hamish Hamilton, 1967.

The Noble Doll, illustrated by Leo Politi. New York, Viking Press, 1961.

Ronnie and the Chief's Son, illustrated by Stefan Martin. New York and London, Macmillan, 1962.

Jock's Island, illustrated by Lilian Obligado. New York, Viking Press, 1963; London, Angus and Robertson, 1965.

Jon the Unlucky, illustrated by Esta Nesbitt. New York, Holt Rinehart, 1964; Chalfont St. Giles, Buckinghamshire, Sadler, 1968.

The Secret, illustrated by Don Bolognese. New York, Macmillan, 1965; Kingswood, Surrey, World's Work, 1967.

The Hand of Apollo, illustrated by Robin Jacques. New York, Viking Press, 1965; Kingswood, Surrey, World's Work, 1967.

The Place, illustrated by Marjorie Auerbach. New York, Holt Rinehart, 1966.

The Fox Friend, illustrated by John Hamberger. New York, Macmillan, 1966.

Chimney Farm Bedtime Stories, with Henry Beston, illustrated by Maurice Day. New York, Holt Rinehart, 1966.

Bess and the Sphinx (includes verse), illustrated by Bernice Loewenstein. New York, Macmillan, 1967; London, Blackie, 1974.

Troll Weather, illustrated by Ursula Arndt. New York, Macmillan, 1967; Kingswood, Surrey, World's Work, 1968.
The Ox-Team, illustrated by Peter Warner. London, Hamish Hamilton, 1967.
Bob Bodden and the Good Ship "Rover," illustrated by Ted Schroeder. Champaign, Illinois, Garrard, 1968; London, Watts, 1972.
The Lucky Ones: Five Journeys Toward a Home, illustrated by Janet Doyle. New York, Macmillan, 1968.
Lighthouse Island, illustrated by Symeon Shimin. New York, Norton, 1968.
George and Red, illustrated by Paul Giovanopoulos. New York, Macmillan, 1969.
They Walk in the Night, illustrated by Stefan Martin. New York, Norton, 1969.
Indian Mound Farm, illustrated by Fermin Rocker. New York, Macmillan, and London, Collier Macmillan, 1969.
Grandmother Cat and the Hermit, illustrated by Irving Boker. New York, Macmillan, 1970.
Bob Bodden and the Seagoing Farm, illustrated by Frank Aloise. Champaign, Illinois, Garrard, 1970; London, Watts, 1972.
The Snow Parlor and Other Bedtime Stories, illustrated by Charles Robinson. New York, Grosset and Dunlap, 1971.
Under the Green Willow, illustrated by Janina Domanska. New York, Macmillan, 1971.
Good Night, illustrated by Jose Aruego. New York, Macmillan, 1972.
The Wanderers, illustrated by Trina Schart Hyman. New York, Four Winds Press, 1972.
Daisy, illustrated by Judith Gwyn Brown. New York, Macmillan, 1973.
Pure Magic, illustrated by Ingrid Fetz. New York, Macmillan, 1973; as *The Were-fox,* New York, Collier, 1975; as *The Fox Boy,* London, Blackie, 1975.
All-of-a-Sudden Susan, illustrated by Richard Cuffari. New York, Macmillan, 1974.
Marra's World, illustrated by Krystyna Turska. New York, Greenwillow, 1975.

Poetry

Night and the Cat, illustrated by Foujita. New York, Macmillan, 1950.
Mouse Chorus, illustrated by Genevieve Vaughan-Jackson. New York, Pantheon, 1955.
The Peaceable Kingdom and Other Poems, illustrated by Fritz Eichenberg. New York, Pantheon, 1958.
The Children Come Running, illustrated by Roger Duvoisin. New York, Golden Press, 1960.
The Sparrow Bush: Rhymes, illustrated by Stefan Martin. New York, Norton, 1966.
Down Half the World, illustrated by Zena Bernstein. New York, Macmillan, 1968.

Other

Runaway Home (reader), illustrated by Gustaf Tenggren. Evanston, Illinois, Row Peterson, 1942.
The Princess and the Lion, illustrated by Evaline Ness. New York, Pantheon, 1963.
Daniel Webster's Horses, illustrated by Cary. Champaign, Illinois, Garrard, 1971.

Editor, *Tales of the Gauchos,* by W.H. Hudson, illustrated by Henry Pitz. New York, Knopf, 1946.
Editor, *Indian Encounters: An Anthology of Stories and Poems,* illustrated by Frederick Chapman. New York, Macmillan, 1960.

PUBLICATIONS FOR ADULTS

Novels

Here I Stay. New York, Coward McCann, 1938; London, Harrap, 1939.
The Trunk. New York, Macmillan, 1941.
The Enchanted. New York, Pantheon, 1951; London, Dent, 1952.
Silky: An Incredible Tale. New York, Pantheon, and London, Gollancz, 1953.
Mountain Bride: An Incredible Tale. New York, Pantheon, 1954.
The White Room. New York, Pantheon, 1958; London, Dent, 1959.

Poetry

Fox Footprints. New York, Knopf, 1923.
Atlas and Beyond. New York, Harper, 1924.
Compass Rose. New York, Coward McCann, 1929.
Country Poems. New York, Macmillan, 1942.
Summer Green. New York, Macmillan, 1948.
The Creaking Stair. New York, Coward McCann, 1949.
Poems. New York, Macmillan, 1957.

Other

The Sun's Diary: A Book of Days for Any Year. New York, Macmillan, 1929.
Country Neighborhood. New York, Macmillan, 1944.
Maine Ways. New York, Macmillan, 1947.
South Shore Town. New York, Macmillan, 1948.
Maine Memories. Brattleboro, Vermont, Stephen Greene Press, 1968.
Personal Geography: Almost an Autobiography. Brattleboro, Vermont, Stephen Greene Press, 1976; London, Prior, 1979.

Editor, *Especially Maine: The Natural World of Henry Beston from Cape Cod to the St. Lawrence.* Brattleboro, Vermont, Stephen Greene Press, 1970.

*

Manuscript Collections: Kerlan Collection, University of Minnesota, Minneapolis; Bowdoin College Library, Brunswick, Maine.

* * *

Elizabeth Coatsworth wrote about "things which touch my imagination." Her imagination was as boundless as her pen was prolific. The author of some 90 books for children, Coatsworth wrote on such diverse subjects as Viking-raided Ireland (*The Wanderers*), the ancient inhabitants of the fjords and mountains in Norway (*Troll Weather*), and a city boy's summer in *Lighthouse Island.* Her vision encompassed lonely children and their search for independence, magic dolls, refugees, forests where animals can turn into people, and, above all, nature.

Although she travelled widely, the bulk of her work concerns America in all its phases. History books aside, she wrote of the desert, the plains, the mountains, Indians, pioneers, immigrants. But it is from Maine that her finest books have come, and in Maine that she found for decades the resources to create one lapidary tale after another.

Although born in 1893, the author continued to understand the perceptions of the young throughout her long writing career. One of her most successful themes is that of the lonely and different child learning to cope in an adverse world. *Lonely Maria* and *Grandmother Cat and the Hermit* both deal with this idea, as does *Marra's World* which combines the theme with Coatsworth's favorite setting—an island off the Maine Coast. With the subtle use of magic and fantasy it conveys the mood of a legend. Marra is regarded as hopeless by her teacher and schoolmates and even by her father and grandmother: "Everything about her life bewildered her." But when it comes to nature, Marra excels. She knows everything about the island. Gradually, with the help of a friend, she accepts herself as different, and the enchantment begins. Marra's mother is Nerea, a seal who was human for a time and who returned to the sea. Here, and in *The Enchanted,* Coatsworth touches on the ancient mythic theme where one being is able to work extraordinary changes for love of another.

Coatsworth reached her apogee in her nature writing, notably "The Incredible Tales" tetralogy about New England originally written for adults. As critic Edmund Fuller observes: "As with all Miss Coatsworth's work, *Silky* is a poet's book, mystic, delicate, lovely. With these 'Incredible Tales' she has created a rich, fresh medium that is at once original and yet the revival of a tradition neglected or distorted in this material age." *The Enchanted,* the best of the four, begins: "There is in northern Maine a township or, as they say here, a 'plantation,' called the Enchanted. It lies in the heart of the forest country and is seldom entered except by lumbermen bound for some winter logging camp from which they return with curious stories." A young man, David Ross, decides to try farming and buys a place right next to the Enchanted. His neighbors are a warm, closely knit family named Perdry, and he falls in love with one of the daughters and marries her. For their honeymoon they camp in the forest: "The stream seemed to sing its continual braided song especially for them, and the big pine sheltered them as though it liked them. They sat for many hours between its curving roots, their backs to its wide trunk, looking out at the water flowing by, always new water, and new ripples of light, yet always essentially the same stream catching the sunlight in the same net of motion." The magic in this tale and in Coatsworth's others is not arbitrary. It is all planned, provided for. Her special gift was the weaving together of a local story and her own vivid characters. The events that conclude *The Enchanted,* the metamorphosis of the Perdrys, are at once anticipated and surprising.

It was Coatsworth's intention to instruct through her stories, but she was never pedantic. The works do not come together with quite the ease of a folk tale that has been repeated from generation to generation, but are a combination of good New England common sense and modern legend. In *All-of-a-Sudden Susan,* building a feeling of danger, Coatsworth writes: "Everything was uneasy, except people, who are always the last to notice what's happening around them." A weakened dam bursts in a storm and Susan is carried away on the flood with her magic doll, Emelida, who talks to her. Susan sees uprooted houses, bloated animals, even a dead woman. "You can't keep people from dying," Emelida comforts her. "They do it all the time and we may be doing it, too, for all we know. But meantime, enjoy yourself."

The Sod House follows immigrants from their arrival in Boston to the settling of a community in Kansas. The New England Emigrant Aid Society helps the Traubels buy land on the Osage River. They are not welcome as northerners at a time when North and South are angling for control of the territory. Political reasons are carefully explained. The Indians the Traubels meet are portrayed solemnly and informatively (Coatsworth was always interested in their way of life), and Ilse, the child in the story, is allowed to fulfill her possibilities, as are most of Coatsworth's fictive children.

The Lucky Ones, a collection of five stories about the homeless and the stateless from different parts of the world—Tibet, Algeria, Rwanda, Hungary, and Hong Kong—explains why they are refugees, and describes the adversity they meet in trying to adjust to another way of life. Each story is preceded by a poem, and while in some cases the political background is not given enough detail, the children in the stories, and the children who read them, are treated with the respect that marks all Coatsworth's work.

Using her considerable creativeness and knowledge, her love of the natural world and her regard for children, Coatsworth was responsible for consistently fine literature for readers whose imaginations are as young and fresh as her own was.

—Angela Wigan

COCKETT, Mary

Nationality: British. **Born:** 1915 in Yorkshire. **Education:** Bedford College, University of London; Institute of Education, London. **Family:** Married to Reginald Cockett; one son and one daughter. **Career:** Editor, National Institute of Industrial Psychology, 1943-48, and International Congress of Mental Health, 1948-49. **Address:** 24 Benville Avenue, Bristol BS9 2RX, England.

Publications for Children

Fiction

Jonathan on the Farm, illustrated by Joan and Dick Robinson. London, Harrap, 1954.

Jonathan and Felicity, illustrated by Joan and Dick Robinson. London, Harrap, 1955.

Fourteen Stories about Jonathan, illustrated by Sheila Connelly. London, Harrap, 1956.

More about Jonathan, illustrated by Dick Robinson. London, Harrap, 1957.

Jan the Market Boy, illustrated by Peggy Beetles. Leicester, Brockhampton Press, 1957.

Bouncing Ball, illustrated by Peggy Beetles. London, Hamish Hamilton, 1958.

Jasper Club, illustrated by Mary Shillabeer. London, Heinemann, 1959.

When Felicity Was Small, illustrated by Dick Robinson. London, Harrap, 1959.

Rolling On, illustrated by Shirley Hughes. London, Methuen, 1960.

Seven Days with Jan, illustrated by Peggy Beetles. Leicester, Brockhampton Press, 1960.

Mary Ann Goes to Hospital, illustrated by Shirley Hughes. London, Methuen, 1961.

Out with Felicity and Jonathan, illustrated by Dick Robinson. London, Harrap, 1962.

Cottage by the Lock, illustrated by Shirley Hughes. London, Methuen, 1962.

Benny's Bazaar, illustrated by Jennifer Cook. Edinburgh, Oliver and Boyd, 1964.

Acrobat Hamster, illustrated by Lynette Hemmant. London, Hamish Hamilton, 1965.

The Birthday Ride, illustrated by W.F. Phillipps. Edinburgh, Oliver and Boyd, 1965.

Sunflower Giant, illustrated by Lynette Hemmant. London, Hamish Hamilton, 1966.

There for the Picking, illustrated by Maureen Eckersley. Edinburgh, Oliver and Boyd, 1966.

Ash Dry, Ash Green, illustrated by Diana Stanley. Edinburgh, Oliver and Boyd, 1966; New York, Criterion, 1968.

Strange Valley, illustrated by Mary Dinsdale. Edinburgh, Oliver and Boyd, 1967.

Twelve Gold Chairs, illustrated by Margery Gill. Edinburgh, Oliver and Boyd, 1967.

Something Big, illustrated by Robert Hales. Edinburgh, Oliver and Boyd, 1968.

The Wild Place, illustrated by Margery Gill. Edinburgh, Oliver and Boyd, 1968.

Rosanna the Goat, illustrated by Reginald Gray. London, Chatto Boyd and Oliver, 1969; Indianapolis, Bobbs Merrill, 1970.

Pelican Park, illustrated by Frank Francis. London, Harrap, and New York, Warne, 1969.

Another Home, Another Country, illustrated by Sandra Archibald. London, Chatto Boyd and Oliver, 1969.

Farthing Bundles, illustrated by Jane Paton. London, Chatto Boyd and Oliver, 1970.

The Joppy Stories (*Joppy Crawling, and Joppy on His Feet; Joppy Steps Out, and Caught on a Tree Stump; Joppy in a Bucket, and The Moving Cat*), illustrated by Mary Cossey. London, Chatto and Windus, 3 vols., 1972.

Boat Girl, illustrated by Gareth Floyd. London, Chatto and Windus, 1972.

As Big as the Ark, illustrated by Barry Wilkinson. London, Methuen, 1974.

Look at the Little One, illustrated by Margaret Palmer. London, Hodder and Stoughton, 1974; Chicago, Children's Press, 1976.

Snake in the Camp, illustrated by Joan Beales. Leicester, Brockhampton Press, 1975; Chicago, Children's Press, 1976.

Tower Raven, illustrated by Sally Launder. London, Abelard Schuman, 1975.

Backyard Bird Hospital, illustrated by Gareth Floyd. London, Hodder and Stoughton, 1976.

The Balloon That Brought Luck, illustrated by Mary Dinsdale. London, Kaye and Ward, 1978.

The Drowning Valley, illustrated by Trevor Stubley. London, Hodder and Stoughton, 1978.

Monster in the River, illustrated by Mary Dinsdale. Exeter, Devon, Wheaton, 1979.

Pig at the Market, illustrated by David Anstey. Exeter, Devon, Wheaton, 1979.

Ladybird at the Zoo, illustrated by Caroline Sharpe. Exeter, Devon, Wheaton, 1979.

The Birthday, illustrated by Doreen Caldwell. London, Hodder and Stoughton, 1979.

The Christmas Tree, illustrated by Carol Walklin. London, Collins, 1979.

Enough Is Enough, illustrated by Nancy Petley-Jones. London, Hodder and Stoughton, 1980.

Shadow at Applegarth, illustrated by Gavin Rowe. London, Hodder and Stoughton, 1981.

Witch of Candlewick, illustrated by Janet Duchesne. London, Kaye and Ward, 1981.

Hoo-Ming's Discovery, illustrated by Valerie Littlewood. London, Hamish Hamilton, 1982.

The Cat and the Castle, illustrated by Doreen Caldwell. London, Hodder and Stoughton, 1982.

The School Donkey, illustrated by Valerie Littlewood. London, Hamish Hamilton, 1982.

Strange Hill, illustrated by Mark Peppé. London, Hodder and Stoughton, 1984.

Tracker, illustrated by Maria Majewska. London, Hamish Hamilton, 1984.

Better Than a Party, illustrated by Karen Heywood. London, Hamish Hamilton, 1985.

Zoo Ticket, illustrated by Doreen Caldwell. London, Hodder and Stoughton, 1985.

Rescue at the Zoo, illustrated by Colin Threadgall. London, Hamish Hamilton, 1986.

The Day of the Squirrels, illustrated by Doreen Caldwell. London, Hodder and Stoughton, 1987.

Kate of Candlewick, illustrated by Janet Duchesne. London, Hodder and Stoughton, 1987.

The Little Leaf and the Loose Tooth, with Rosalie Eisenstein. London, Macmillan, 1987.

The Paper Boy and Other Stories. London, Macmillan, 1987.

Bridesmaids, illustrated by Annabel Spenceley. London, Hodder and Stoughton, 1988.

Mystery on the Farm, illustrated by Janet Duchesne. London, Hamish Hamilton, 1988.

Bickering Bridesmaids. London, Hodder and Stoughton, 1991.

Other

Roads and Travelling, illustrated by Trevor Stubley. Oxford, Blackwell, 1964.

Bridges, illustrated by Diana Stanley. Edinburgh, Oliver and Boyd, 1965.

Tufty (reader), illustrated by George Adamson. London, Macmillan, 1968.

Frankie's Country Day (reader), illustrated by Mary Dinsdale. London, Macmillan, 1968.

The Lost Money (reader), illustrated by Mary Dinsdale. London, Macmillan, 1968.

The Wedding Tea (reader), illustrated by Mary Dinsdale. London, Macmillan, 1970.

Magic and Gold: Tales from Northern Europe, illustrated by Peter Kesteven. Oxford and New York, Pergamon Press, 1970.

Towns, illustrated by W.G.D. Hill. Oxford, Blackwell, 1971.

The Marvellous Stick (reader), illustrated by Mary Dinsdale. London, Macmillan, 1972.

Bells in Our Lives, illustrated by Janet Duchesne. Newton Abbot, Devon, David and Charles, 1973.

Treasure, illustrated by Desmond Knight. London, Dent, 1973.
The Rainbow Walk (reader), illustrated by Prudence Seward. London, Burke, 1973.
An Armful of Sparrows (reader), illustrated by George Adamson. London, Macmillan, 1973.
Dolls and Puppets. Newton Abbot, Devon, David and Charles, 1974.
Walls, illustrated by W.G.D. Hill. Oxford, Blackwell, 1974.
He Cannot Really Read (reader), illustrated by Prudence Seward. London, Oxford University Press, 1975.
The Story of Cars, illustrated by Ralph Hodgson. Oxford, Blackwell, 1976.
The Magician (reader), illustrated by Richard Rose. London, Oxford University Press, 1976.
Fly High, Magpie (reader), illustrated by Jeroo Roy. London, Macmillan, 1977.
Missing (reader), illustrated by Peter Edwards. London, Oxford University Press, 1978.
For Children on Wheels, with A.M.L. Miller, illustrated by Edward Carr. London, Royal Automobile Club, 1979.
The Bell (reader), illustrated by Pat Nessling. London, Macmillan, 1980.
Money to Spend (reader), illustrated by Chris Masters. London, Macmillan, 1980.
At the Tower (reader). London, Macmillan, 1984; Cleveland, Modern Curriculum Press, 1985.
Crab Apples (reader). London, Macmillan, 1984; Cleveland, Modern Curriculum Press, 1985.
Paper Boys (reader). London, Macmillan, 1985.
A Place of His Own (reader). London, Macmillan, 1987.
Winning All the Way (reader). London, Macmillan, 1987.

* * *

Mary Cockett is one of those figures familiar in all fields of literary endeavour, the conscientious professional more noted for reliability than outstanding talent. Her output is considerable, numbering some 70 books as well as stories for radio and television. Over three decades she has worked for several publishers, producing fiction for many different age groups, information books, and supplementary readers. However, she is best known for series books intended for 5-to-9-year-olds. Recent titles such as *The Day of the Squirrels* or *Tracker* show her ability to write satisfying stories within the length and language restraints of series requirements. While her books have attracted little critical attention, they are of the kind likely to form the bulk of the average child's reading, and as such deserve closer assessment.

Reading a whole batch at a time makes one aware that there has been neither significant development nor a falling off over the years, but rather the maintenance of a dependable standard. The peak of recognition probably came in 1961 when *Rolling On,* a predictable but warmhearted tale of one summer Dan spends with his grandfather, was one of the three British titles considered for the Hans Christian Andersen Award. One can find in it, as in some of the other non-series titles such as *Shadow at Applegarth,* a greater freedom in the writing and a sense of personal engagement. Mary Cockett's work in general shows a recognition of contemporary issues and interests, for example in the world of *Hoo-Ming's Discovery* or *Kate of Candlewick* with its bridges between old age and childhood, but she never allows the story to be lost in didacticism.

Most stories are set in the present and treat everyday happenings, relying for success on traditional factors: a clear, simple plot, sympathetic characters, and perception of children's interests, the whole imbued with a belief in kindness, courage, and perseverance. The shortage of accessible stories for children at the post-picture book stage is often deplored, and Cockett has made a substantial contribution to this area, managing to achieve credible characters and a fresh style within the series format. The ability to compose a spare text resonant with meaning and close to children's interests is seen in some of the picture books, for instance *Monster in the River,* the tall tale which turns out to be true, and similar features characterise the supplementary readers such as *The Rainbow Walk,* diminishing current arguments which polarise "real books" and "readers."

—Peggy Heeks

COERR, Eleanor (Beatrice)

Has also written as Eleanor Page. **Pseudonym:** Eleanor B. Hicks. **Born:** Eleanor Page, 29 May 1922, Kamsack, Saskatchewan, Canada. **Education:** Attended University of Saskatchewan; graduated from Kadel Airbrush School, Chicago, 1945; American University, B.A. 1969; University of Maryland, M.L.S. 1971. **Family:** Married Wymberley De Renne Coerr in 1965. **Career:** Reporter and editor, *Edmonton Journal,* Edmonton, Alberta, 1944-49; editorial post, *Advertiser-Journal,* Montgomery, Alabama, 1953-58; editorial post, *Manila Times,* Manila, Republic of the Philippines, 1958-60; editor, U.S. Information Service, Taipei, Taiwan, 1960-62; contributing editor, Voice of America Special English Division, Washington, D.C., 1963-65; librarian, Davis Memorial Library, Bethesda, Maryland, 1971-72. Lecturer at Chapman and Monterey Peninsula colleges. Visiting author to schools, organizations, and reading councils in the United States and other countries. **Awards:** West Australia Book Award, 1982; OMAR Award, 1982; National Teachers Assocation/CBC Outstanding Science Trade Book for Children, 1976; National Council on the Social Studies/CBC Notable Children's Trade Book in the Field of Social Studies, 1986. **Address:** Putnam Publishing Group, 200 Madison Ave., New York, New York 10016, U.S.A.

Publications for Children

Fiction

Snoopy (as Eleanor Page), self-illustrated. Institute of Applied Art, 1945.
Circus Day in Japan (as Eleanor B. Hicks), self-illustrated. Tuttle, 1954.
The Mystery of the Golden Cat, self-illustrated. Tuttle, 1968.
Twenty-five Dragons, illustrated by Joann Daley. Chicago, Follet, 1971.
Biography of a Giant Panda, illustrated by Kazue Mizumura. New York, Putnam, 1974.
Biography of a Kangaroo, illustrated by Linda Powell. New York, Putnam, 1976.
The Mixed-up Mystery Smell, illustrated by Tomie de Paola. New York, Putnam, 1976.

Biography of Jane Goodall, illustrated by Kees de Kiefte. New York, Putnam, 1976.
Sadako and the Thousand Paper Cranes, illustrated by Ronald Himler. New York, Putnam, 1977.
Waza Wins at Windy Gulch, illustrated by Janet McCaffery. New York, Putnam, 1977.
Gigi: A Baby Whale Borrowed for Science and Returned to the Sea, with William E. Evans. New York, Putnam, 1980.
The Big Balloon Race, illustrated by Carolyn Croll. New York, Harper, 1981.
The Bell Ringer and the Pirates, illustrated by Joan Sandin. New York, Harper, 1983.
The Josefina Story Quilt, illustrated by Bruce Degen. New York, Harper, 1986.
Lady with a Torch: How the Statue of Liberty Was Born, illustrated by Oscar de Mejo. New York, Harper, 1986.
Chang's Paper Pony, illustrated by Deborah K. Ray. New York, Harper, 1989.
Mieko and the Fifth Treasure. New York, Putnam, 1993
Buffalo Bill and the Pony Express. New York, Harper, 1995.

* * *

Eleanor Coerr has written both fiction and nonfiction for children. *Sadako and the Thousand Paper Cranes* is her best-known and most outstanding contribution. Sadako Sasaki died from leukemia at twelve years old as a result of the radiation in Hiroshima. It is the strength of this young woman as she fights to survive that Coerr writes about, and it is the folding of the paper cranes that has captured the hearts of young people all over the world. Sadako only folded 644 cranes before she died, but her classmates finished for her. Sadako, illustrated by Ed Young and based on the video narrated by Liv Ullmann, is a retelling of the same story in a picture book format. There is a statue of Sadako in Hiroshima Peace Park and children from all over the world fold and send paper cranes each year for Peace Day, August 6. Surely this is a tribute to the power of this story in the lives of young people. Coerr writes of Sadako, "If you tell people that 200,000 died as a result of the bombing of Hiroshima, it doesn't have as much impact as the story of one little girl."

Biography of Jane Goodall is a revealing portrayal of patience and determination presenting the early years of Goodall's childhood through her first years in Africa working on chimpanzee behavior. Coerr's *Biography of a Giant Panda,* the story of Mela, the young panda, gives the reader a sense of the actual day-to-day existence of this animal in China. Coerr has the knack of compelling the reader to turn the page and learn more about the animal and the environment. She demonstrates this in the *Biography of a Kangaroo,* a study of the red kangaroo of the Australian outback. The story is of young Max, his early journeys in his mother's pouch, through his young joey years, into adulthood, learning how to survive and finally realizing that man is his greatest enemy.

Coerr has made an enormous contribution with her "I Can Read" books, particularly, *Chang's Paper Pony, The Bell Ringer and the Pirates,* and *The Josefina Story Quilt.* The books are more complex than many beginning readers. In each story, Coerr weaves elements of history into the lives of her characters. She is sensitive to the Chinese immigration to the United States during the period of the Gold Rush as well as the building of the railroad. Yet Chang's dream of owning his own pony is a focal point for the reader. Coerr is up-front in presenting prejudice while imbuing her characters with a sense of values and honesty. Young Pio wants to ring the great bells at the mission and he is determined to save the people from the danger of the pirates. Like many of her books the story is based on the true stories of mission days in California. General Bouchard and his pirates did raid the mission, and the importance of the bells in mission life is the central theme of the story. Josefina is a remembered hen who had a part in the westward journey. Faith uses a quilt as a means of showing her love and tracing their history of the journey to California.

Mieko and the Fifth Treasure stresses the importance of a very ancient Japanese art form, calligraphy, in the life of a young child. Mieko's hand was injured at Nagasaki, and this story tells of her struggle to gain back sufficient courage and strength of will to reach the level of artistic performance that she had in the past. Her grandfather and Yoshi, among others, contribute to her change and achievement, and an unhappy child becomes a joy to herself and others.

Coerr is a writer who cares about sharing stories from a variety of cultures and providing the insights to grasp some of the unjust and horrendous things our world has allowed. Her books raise questions in the minds of readers and even more they raise feelings and emotions that help children grow.

—Jane Anne Hannigan

COHEN, Barbara

Nationality: American. **Born:** Barbara Kauder, Asbury Park, New Jersey, 15 March 1932. **Education:** Barnard College, New York, 1950-54, B.A. 1954; Rutgers University, New Brunswick, New Jersey, 1954-55, M.A. 1957. **Family:** Married Gene Cohen in 1954; three daughters. **Career:** English teacher in New Jersey public high schools, Tenafly, 1955-57, Somerville, 1958-60, and Hillsborough, 1970-78. **Awards:** Association of Jewish Libraries Best Book award and Sydney Taylor award, 1982; National Jewish Book award, 1983 (twice). **Died:** 1992.

Publications for Children

Fiction

The Carp in the Bathtub, illustrated by Joan Halpern. New York, Lothrop, 1972.
Thank You, Jackie Robinson, illustrated by Richard Cuffari. New York, Lothrop, 1974.
Bitter Herbs and Honey. New York, Lothrop, 1976.
Where's Florrie?, illustrated by Joan Halpern. New York, Lothrop, 1976.
Benny. New York, Lothrop, 1977.
R, My Name Is Rosie. New York, Lothrop, 1978.
The Innkeeper's Daughter. New York, Lothrop, 1979.
Fat Jack. New York, Atheneum, 1980.
I Am Joseph, illustrated by Charles Mikolaycak. New York, Lothrop, 1980.
Unicorns in the Rain. New York, Atheneum, 1980.
Queen for a Day. New York, Lothrop, 1981.

Gooseberries to Oranges, illustrated by Beverly Brodsky. New York, Lothrop, 1982.
King of the Seventh Grade. New York, Lothrop, 1982.
Seven Daughters and Seven Sons, with Bahija Lovejoy. New York, Atheneum, 1982.
Lovers' Games. New York, Atheneum, 1983.
Molly's Pilgrim, illustrated by Michael Deraney. New York, Lothrop, 1983.
Here Come the Purim Players!, illustrated by Beverly Brodsky. New York, Lothrop, 1984.
Roses, illustrated by John Steptoe. New York, Lothrop, 1984.
Coasting. New York, Lothrop, 1985.
The Secret Grove, illustrated by Michael Deraney. New York, Union of American Hebrew Congregations, 1985.
The Christmas Revolution, illustrated by Diane de Groat. New York, Lothrop, 1987.
First Fast. New York, Union of American Hebrew Congregations, 1987.
Headless Roommate. New York, Bantam, 1987.
People Like Us. New York, Bantam, 1987.
The Orphan Game, illustrated by Diane de Groat. New York, Lothrop, 1988.
Tell Us Your Secret. New York, Bantam, 1989.
The Long Way Home, illustrated by Diane de Groat. New York, Lothrop, 1990.
The Chocolate Wolf, illustrated by Troy Howell. New York, Philomel, 1993.
David: A Biography, illustrated by Charles Mikolaycak. New York, Clarion, 1993.
Two Hundred Thirteen Valentines, illustrated by Wil Clay. New York, Holt, 1993.
Make a Wish, Molly, illustrated by Jan Naimo Jones. New York, Doubleday, 1994.

Other (retellings)

The Binding of Isaac, illustrated by Charles Mikolaycak. New York, Lothrop, 1978.
Lovely Vassilisa, illustrated by Anatoly Ivanov. New York, Atheneum, 1980.
Yussel's Prayer, illustrated by Michael Deraney. New York, Lothrop, 1981.
The Demon Who Would Not Die, illustrated by Anatoly Ivanov. New York, Atheneum, 1982.
Even Higher, illustrated by Anatoly Ivanov. New York, Lothrop, 1987.
The Donkey's Story: A Bible Story, illustrated by Susan Jeanne Cohen. New York, Lothrop, 1988.
Canterbury Tales, illustrated by Trina Schart Hyman. New York, Lothrop, 1988.

*

Manuscript Collection: Rutgers University Library, New Brunswick, New Jersey.

Barbara Cohen commented:

(1989) I've loved stories for as long as I can remember—nursery tales my mother told me, family anecdotes recounted by relatives around countless holiday dinner tables, books of all kinds that I consumed voraciously on my own. I decided as soon as they taught me to form letters that writing stories was a good thing to do, and I still think so. I write children's stories because inside my own head I'm stuck at 12 years old. That's OK. It's worked out.

* * *

Barbara Cohen was best known as a writer of stories reflecting her Jewish heritage, but she was far more than just a Jewish writer. She was a master storyteller who dealt with universal themes, drawing on her own childhood experiences and those of friends and family members to create stories that reveal commonalties among people from different times, places, and cultural and religious backgrounds. Although the family is of paramount importance, most of Cohen's protagonists are struggling to maintain their unique identities and to fit into a larger world outside the family.

Cohen was especially strong writing for 6-9-year-olds who want to read alone but are not ready for a full-length novel. *The Carp in the Bathtub* centers around the preparation of gefilte fish for Passover, but all youngsters can identify with Leah and Harry Katz who refuse to eat the carp their mother has kept in the bathtub. *First Fast,* also about the Katz family in Brooklyn, tells of young Harry's bet with an older boy that he can fast on Yom Kippur although he is too young to be required to do so. Harry keeps the fast even when he catches Bernie, the older boy, eating a big hotdog with mustard. With this simple story, Cohen explains the celebration of the Jewish Day of Atonement. *Molly's Pilgrim* is about a young Russian immigrant who, after much anguish as an outsider, eventually helps her third-grade class appreciate what it means to be a pilgrim. Cohen made a cameo appearance as a school crossing guard in the film version of this story which won an Academy Award in 1986. In a related story, *Make a Wish, Molly,* Molly learns about the customs of birthday celebrations in America. Molly is invited to Emma's birthday party and is anxious to taste a fancy cake like one she saw in a bakery window. Unfortunately, the party takes place during Passover when Molly can't eat the beautifully decorated cake. Her new friends don't understand, and Molly leaves the party in tears because she is different. On Molly's birthday, Emma and the other girls show up at Molly's home to wish her a happy birthday and celebrate with a candle on a plate of rugelach, proving that not all parties need fancy invitations and frosted cakes. *The Secret Grove,* based on a true story, tells of a Jewish boy and an Arab boy who meet in an orange grove between their lands, share an orange, and plant the seeds. Years later, after many wars between their nations, the Jewish boy, now a former soldier, returns to the grove and wonders about the fate of his Arab friend.

Several of her stories, such as *I Am Joseph* and *The Binding of Isaac,* are retellings and elaborations of Old Testament stories. Balaam is the focus of her *Donkey's Story,* taken from the Bible but told with humor that demonstrates that any of us can rise to the occasion. Even Higher is her adaptation of an old Yiddish tale about the doubter, which is delicate in its simplicity. Cohen collaborated with illustrator Anatoly Ivanov on retellings of Russian folktales including *The Demon Who Would Not Die.* Ivan Tsarevich exhibits such kindness to all the animals he encounters that they, in turn, repay him by helping him find the one token that will kill the evil demon who had captured his wife. Lovely Vassilisa, the Russian Cinderella, earns the respect of Baba Yaga, the witch, in a lively telling of one of the many Baba Yaga stories.

King of the Seventh Grade moves to a more contemporary time to share Vic Abram's resentment of Hebrew School and his Bar Mitzvah, which he feels separate him from his non-Jewish friends. In *213 Valentines,* Wade Thompson reluctantly leaves his friends to go to a gifted and talented class in a new school. As a new student from a poorer district and one of only a few African-Americans, Wade feels out of place with "the snobs" in the fourth grade. *Valentine's Day* is a big deal in this school and, believing that no one will send him a valentine, Wade buys 213 valentines and sends most of them to himself. He doesn't fool his classmates, but he does make them laugh when he reads the signatures of Ronald Reagan, Bill Cosby, Michael Jackson, Nelson Mandela and Oprah Winfrey. Of course, he also got valentines from many classmates in this easy chapter book for new readers.

Each of these stories, set in different times, deals with the problem of a young person whose religious and cultural heritage sets him/her apart from schoolmates and friends. Cohen's voice as a storyteller brought what might appear to be foreign or strange to today's young people and made it familiar and worthy of thoughtful consideration. Although Cohen died in 1992, she left behind several manuscripts to be published in late 1994 and in 1995.

—Kay E. Vandergrift

COLE, Babette

Nationality: British. **Born:** Jersey, Channel Islands, 10 September 1949. **Education:** Canterbury College of Art, B.A. (honors) 1974. **Career:** Author and illustrator of childrens books, since 1973; has worked as an animator for television and an illustrator of greeting cards. **Awards:** Children's Book of the Year, Child Study Association of America, 1980, for *Nungu and the Hippopotamus*; New York Public Library's Best Children's Book citation, 1983, for *The Wind in the Willows Pop-Up Book*; Kate Greenaway Medal Commendation, Library Association, 1986, both for *Princess Smartypants*; Annabell Fargeon Award, Library Association, 1986, for *Princess Smartypants,* and 1987, for *Prince Cinders*; Kate Greenaway Medal, 1987, for *Prince Cinders*; Kurt Mascher Award, Book Trust, 1996, for *Drop Dead.* **Address:** c/o Hamish Hamilton, 27 Wrights Lane, London W8 5TZ, England; Ivy Cottage, Wingmore Lane, Wingmore, Elham, North Canterbury, Kent CT4 6LS, England.

PUBLICATIONS FOR CHILDREN (ILLUSTRATED BY THE AUTHOR)

Fiction

Basil Brush of the Yard. London, Purnell, 1977.
Promise Solves the Problem. London, Kaye and Ward, 1977.
Nungu and the Crocodile. London, Purnell, 1978; New York, McGraw Hill, 1979.
Nungu and the Hippopotamus. London, Macdonald, 1978.
Nungu and the Elephant. London, Macdonald, and New York, McGraw Hill, 1980.
Promise and the Monster. London, Granada, 1981.
Beware of the Vet. London, Hamish Hamilton, 1982.
Don't Go Out Tonight. London, Hamish Hamilton, 1982.
The Trouble with Mum. Kingswood, Surrey, Kaye and Ward, 1983; as *The Trouble with Mom,* New York, Coward McCann, 1984.
The Hairy Book. London, Cape, 1984; New York, Random House, 1985.
The Slimy Book. London, Cape, 1985; New York, Random House, 1986.
The Trouble with Dad. London, Heinemann, 1985; New York, Putnam, 1986.
Princess Smartypants. London, Hamish Hamilton, 1986; New York, Putnam, 1987.
Prince Cinders. London, Hamish Hamilton, 1987; New York, Putnam, 1988.
The Smelly Book. London, Cape, 1987; New York, Simon and Schuster, 1988.
The Trouble with Gran. London, Heinemann, and New York, Putnam, 1987.
The Trouble with Grandad. London, Heinemann, 1988.
King Change-a-Lot. London, Hamish Hamilton, 1988; New York, Putnam, 1989.
Three Cheers for Errol. London, Heinemann, 1988; New York, Putnam, 1989.
Cupid. London, Hamilton, 1989; New York, Putnam, 1990.
The Silly Book. London, Cape, 1989; New York, Doubleday, 1990.
Babette Cole's Beastly Birthday Book, with Ron Van der Meer. London, Heinemann, 1990; New York, Doubleday, 1991.
Hurrah for Ethelyn! Boston, Massachusetts, Little, Brown, and London, Heinemann, 1991.
Tarzanna. London, Hamish Hamilton, 1991; New York, Putnam, 1992.
Supermoo! New York, Putnam, and London, BBC Books, 1992.
The Trouble with Uncle. Boston, Little, Brown, and London, Heinemann, 1992.
Mommy Laid an Egg!; or, Where Do Babies Come From?. New York, Chronicle Books, 1993; as *Mummy Laid an Egg!; or Where Do Babies Come From?,* London, Cape, 1993.
Winni Allfours. Mahwah, New Jersey, BridgeWater Books, and London, Hamish Hamilton, 1993.
Dr. Dog. New York, Knopf, and London, Cape, 1994.
Babette Cole's Cats. New York, Warner Books, and London, Heinemann, 1995.
Babette Cole's Dogs. New York, Warner Books, and London, Heinemann, 1995.
Babette Cole's Fish. New York, Warner Books, and London, Heinemann, 1995.
Babette Cole's Ponies. New York, Warner Books, and London, Heinemann, 1995.
The Bad Good Manners Book. London, Hamish Hamilton, 1995; New York, Dial, 1996.
Drop Dead. London, Cape, 1996; New York, Knopf, 1997.
Brother. London, Heinemann, 1997.
Dad. London, Heinemann, 1997.
Mother. London, Heinemann, 1997.
Sister. London, Heinemann, 1997.
Two of Everything. London, Cape, 1997.

*

Illustrator: *Your Dog* by Joan Tate, 1975; *Daisy* by Jenny Butterworth, 1976; *The Unicorn Drum* by Annabel Farjeon, 1976; *Mice and Mendelson* by Joan Aiken, 1978; *A Flying Bird* and *The Marrow Boat,* 1978, both by Oliver Postgate; *Count Bakwerdz* *on the Carpet,* 1979, and *Sneeze and Be Slain,* 1980, both by Norman Hunter; *Grasshopper and the Unwise Owl* [*Pickle Factory, Poisoned River*], all by Jim Slater, 3 volumes, 1979-82; *The Last Vampire,* 1982, *The Inflatable Shop,* 1984, *The Vampire's Holiday,* 1992, all by Willis Hall; *The Wind in the Willows* by Kenneth Grahame, 1983; *Hocus Pocus* edited by Lesley Young, 1983.

* * *

Text and illustration are inseparable in Babette Cole's picture books, which all demonstrate her uniquely quirky sense of humour. Zany is the word that most succinctly describes her output and it is this unpredictability that makes the humour almost anarchic in places and ensures her appeal to children. The characters she writes about are larger than life and her cartoon-like illustrations capture their grotesqueness. Her imagination almost runs away with her at times as she creates ever more bizarre situations. In *Beware of the Vet,* the vet Mr. MacPlaster mistakes cow hormone accelerator tablets for aspirin and grows horns and a tail. In *Winni Allfours,* Winni's vegetarian parents refuse to buy her a horse, but as a result of eating too many vegetables, she finally turns into one and wins the Grand National.

In *The Trouble with Mum,* Cole exaggerates every schoolchild's fear that his or her mother is different. Here the mother is a witch, complete with witch's hat, and brings her child to school on a broomstick. The embarrassment caused by this mother will make any normal child's fears pale into insignificance. This book was followed by four more in similar vein. *The Trouble with Dad* features a father whose boring job makes him seek excitement by making robots that never quite work as one might expect them to. The granddad in *The Trouble with Grandad* grows giant vegetables that unfortunately produce giant caterpillars that cause chaos, and *The Trouble with Gran* is that she's an alien! This gran livens up the OAP's outing and ends up having to transport everyone home in the bus shelter, but not before taking them on a quick visit to her planet. The uncle in *The Trouble with Uncle* is a larger than life pirate, who does more than mess around with boats. The humour in all these books is wonderfully underplayed in the text and hilariously depicted in the pictures.

Cole delights in turning language and situations upside down. She inverts the traditional role of the fairy-tale princess in *Princess Smartypants,* in which the princess wears dungarees and wants to remain unmarried. All her suitors fail the classic ordeals she sets them until Prince Swashbuckle comes along. He successfully feeds her revolting pets, rides pillion on her motorbike, outlasts her at the roller-disco, and finally wins a kiss from the princess, which turns him into a toad. This ensures the princess's future as a single woman as no other suitors want to risk winning her hand. In *Prince Cinders* she turns the Cinderella story on its head with her tale of the prince who is "small, spotty, scruffy and skinny" and who is persecuted by his three big hairy brothers. He finally wins the hand of Princess Lovelypenny (no thanks to the dirty fairy, however) by being able to fit into, not a glass slipper, but some tight blue jeans. Cole has great fun with the Superman/Batman genre in *Supermoo,* in which a cow with super powers and her sidekick Calf Crypton are determined to keep the country clean and green. She combats the Bots who are polluting the air with their foul gases and saves Miss Pimple's swimming class from a treacle slick.

Cole is expert at portraying the revolting or disgusting—the things that young children revel in reading about—and does so most effectively and amusingly in her trio *The Hairy Book, The Slimy Book,* and *The Smelly Book.* Each of these has children squealing with delight as the rhyming texts list the ever more revolting subjects. The humour is extended in the illustrations, which are equally disgusting and feature grotesque noses, monsters, and the like. However, despite the distasteful nature of the subject matter, none of these books is in any way offensive.

Although her books are not serious in design they can have an underlying moral. In *Three Cheers for Errol,* for example, Errol the rat is bad at sums, spelling, science, and art. He is, however, good at sport and is chosen to represent his school in the Interschool Ratathalon. In other words, you don't have to be academically clever to succeed.

Cole's humour has a lightness of touch that makes the whole simply fun. *Dr. Dog,* for example, takes a humorous look at the serious subject of health and hygiene. The Gumboyle's family dog is a doctor, who explains to the family the effects of cigarette smoking and how head lice and worms are transmitted. Informative and fun at the same time, the climax, illustrating what happens when Grandad's gases build up inside him, is not for the fainthearted. The same must be said of *Mummy Laid an Egg!* which attracted a lot of controversy when first published. Ostensibly an introduction to sex education, it shows two parents giving some very far-fetched explanations for how babies are born. The children are better informed and do a series of hilarious drawings to show mum and dad what really happens, leaving a rather red-faced mum and dad in the end.

Following on from the facts of life came "the facts of death" in *Drop Dead* in which two children ask their grandparents why they are such "bald old wrinklies." They tell how they started life as bald wrinkly babies, then went to school and college, and gave up the idea of being scientists to become film stars. They have indeed lived life to the full and point out that "one day we'll just drop down dead like everyone else."

Two of Everything tackles the difficult subject of divorce in similar matter-of-fact style and with outrageous humour. Two children ask the vicar if he will un-marry their warring parents. They agree and the un-wedding is a huge success and they depart on separate un-honeymoons. The shrewd children order two of everything, now that their parents will be living apart. Hilarious illustrations show how years of being unhappy have changed the parents physical features from being quite good looking to being ugly. Any underlying seriousness in these last two books is introduced subtly by way of the humour.

Humour can often attract those who are less keen to read. Cole's brand of infectious humour can show such children that reading can be as much fun as watching television, for example. For this reason alone her books are to be enthusiastically recommended.

—Fiona Lafferty

COLUM, Padraic

Nationality: Irish. **Born:** Longford, 8 December 1881. **Education:** Glasthule National School, Sandycove, County Dublin. **Family:** Married the writer Mary Catherine Gunning Maguire in 1912 (died 1957). **Career:** Clerk, Irish Railway Clearing House, Dublin, 1898-1904; member of the National Theatre Society and associated with the founding of the Abbey Theatre, Dublin; founder, with others, 1911, and editor, 1912-13, *Irish Review,* Dublin; moved to the United States, 1914, and lived in Pittsburgh, Connecticut, and New York; lived in France, 1930-33; lecturer, Columbia University, New York, from 1939. President, James Joyce Society, New York, and Poetry Society of America, 1938-39. **Awards:** Academy of American Poets fellowship, 1952; Irish Academy of Letters Gregory medal, 1953; Catholic Library Association Regina medal, 1961; Georgetown University medal, 1964. Litt.D: Columbia University, New York, 1958; Trinity College, Dublin, 1958. **Member:** Irish Academy of Letters, and American Academy. **Died:** 11 January 1972.

Publications for Children

Fiction

A Boy in Eirinn, illustrated by Jack B. Yeats. New York, Dutton, 1913; London, Dent, 1915.
The Boy Apprenticed to an Enchanter, illustrated by Dugald Stuart Walker. New York, Macmillan, 1920.
The Peep-Show Man, illustrated by Lois Lenski. New York, Macmillan, 1924; London, Macmillan, 1932.
The White Sparrow, illustrated by Joseph Low. New York, Macmillan, 1933; as *Sparrow Alone,* London, Blackie, 1975.
Where the Winds Never Blew and the Cocks Never Crew, illustrated by Richard Bennett. New York, Macmillan, 1940.

Play

The Destruction of the Hostel (produced Dublin, 1910).

Other

The King of Ireland's Son, illustrated by Willy Pogány. New York, Macmillan, 1916; London, Harrap, 1920.
The Boy Who Knew What the Birds Said, illustrated by Dugald Stuart Walker. New York, Macmillan, 1918.
The Adventures of Odysseus and the Tale of Troy, illustrated by Willy Pogány. New York, Macmillan, 1918; London, Harrap, 1920; as *The Children's Homer,* Macmillan, 1946.
The Girl Who Sat by the Ashes, illustrated by Dugald Stuart Walker. New York, Macmillan, 1919; London, Collier Macmillan, 1968.
The Children of Odin: A Book of Northern Myths, illustrated by Willy Pogány. New York, Macmillan, 1920; London, Harrap, 1922.
The Golden Fleece and the Heroes Who Lived Before Achilles, illustrated by Willy Pogány. New York, Macmillan, 1921.
The Children Who Followed the Piper, illustrated by Dugald Stuart Walker. New York, Macmillan, 1922.
The Six Who Were Left in a Shoe, illustrated by Dugald Stuart Walker. Chicago, Volland, 1923; London, Brentano, 1924.
Tales and Legends of Hawaii: At the Gateways of the Day, and *The Bright Islands,* illustrated by Juliette May Fraser. New Haven, Connecticut, Yale University Press, 2 vols., 1924-25; as *Legends of Hawaii,* Yale University Press, and London, Oxford University Press, 1937.
The Island of the Mighty, Being the Hero Stories of Celtic Britain Retold from the Mabinogion, illustrated by Wilfred Jones. New York, Macmillan, 1924.
The Voyagers, Being Legends and Romances of Atlantic Discovery, illustrated by Wilfred Jones. New York, Macmillan, 1925.
The Forge in the Forest, illustrated by Boris Artzybasheff. New York, Macmillan, 1925.
The Fountain of Youth: Stories to Be Told, illustrated by Jay Van Everen. New York, Macmillan, 1927.
Orpheus: Myths of the World, illustrated by Boris Artzybasheff. New York, Macmillan, 1930; as *Myths of the Old World,* New York, Universal Library, n.d.
The Big Tree of Bunlahy: Stories of My Own Countryside, illustrated by Jack B. Yeats. New York, Macmillan, 1933; London, Macmillan, 1934.
The Frenzied Prince, Being Heroic Stories of Ancient Ireland, illustrated by Willy Pogány. Philadelphia, McKay, 1943.
The Stone of Victory and Other Tales, illustrated by Judith Gwyn Brown. New York, McGraw Hill, 1966.

Editor, *Gulliver's Travels,* by Swift, illustrated by Willy Pogány. New York, Macmillan, 1917; London, Harrap, 1919.
Editor, *The Arabian Nights, Tales of Wonder and Magnificence,* illustrated by Lynd Ward. New York, Macmillan, 1953.

Publications for Adults

Novels

Castle Conquer. New York, Macmillan, 1923.
The Flying Swans. New York, Crown, 1957.

Short Stories

Three Men: A Tale. London, Mathews and Marrot, 1930.
Selected Short Stories of Padraic Colum, edited by Sanford Sternlicht. Syracuse, New York, Syracuse University Press, 1985.

Plays

The Children of Lir, and *Brian Boru* in *Irish Independent* (Dublin), 1902.
The Kingdom of the Young (produced 1902). Published in *United Irishman* (Dublin), 1903.
The Foleys, and *Eoghan's Wife,* in *United Irishman* (Dublin), 1903.
The Saxon Shillin' (produced Dublin, 1903). Published in *Lost Plays of the Irish Renaissance,* edited by Robert Hogan and James Kilroy, Dixon, California, Proscenium Press, 1970.
The Fiddler's House (as *Broken Soil,* produced Dublin, 1903; London, 1904; revised version, as *The Fiddler's House,* produced Dublin, 1907; New York, 1941). Dublin, Maunsel, 1907; in *Three Plays,* 1916.
The Land (produced Dublin and London, 1905). Dublin, Abbey Theatre, 1905; in *The Three Plays,* 1916.
The Miracle of the Corn: A Miracle Play (produced Dublin, 1908; London, 1911). Included in *Studies,* 1907; in *Dramatic Legends and Other Poems,* 1922.
Thomas Muskerry (produced Dublin and London, 1910). Dublin, Maunsel, 1910; in *Three Plays,* 1916.
The Desert. Dublin, Devereux, 1912; as *Mogu the Wanderer; or, The Desert: A Fantastic Comedy,* Boston, Little Brown, 1917; as *Mogu of the Desert* (produced Dublin, 1931).

The Betrayal (produced Manchester, 1913; Pittsburgh, 1914). Published in *One-Act Plays of To-Day 4,* edited by J.W. Marriott, London, Harrap, 1928; in *Selected Plays,* 1986.
Three Plays: The Fiddler's House, The Land, Thomas Muskerry. Boston, Little Brown, 1916; Dublin and London, Maunsel, 1917; revised edition, New York, Macmillan, 1925.
The Grasshopper, with F.E. Washburn-Freund, adaptation of a play by Count Keyserling (produced New York, 1917).
Balloon (produced Ogunquit, Maine). New York, Macmillan, 1929.
The Show-Booth, adaptation of a play by Alexander Blok (produced Dublin, 1948).
Moytura: A Play for Dancers. Dublin, Dolmen Press, 1963.
The Challengers: Monasterboice, Glendalough, Cloughoughter (produced Dublin, 1966). *Monasterboice* and *Glendalough* included in *Selected Plays,* 1986.
The Road round Ireland, with Basil Burwell, adaptation of works by Colum (produced Norwalk, Connecticut, 1967; as *Carricknabauna,* produced New York, 1967).
Selected Plays of Padraic Colum (includes *The Land, The Betrayal, Glendalough, Monasterboice*), edited by Sanford Sternlicht. Syracuse, New York, Syracuse University Press, 1986.

Poetry

Heather Ale. Privately printed, 1907.
Wild Earth. Dublin, Maunsel, 1907; revised edition, as *Wild Earth and Other Poems,* Maunsel, and New York, Holt, 1916.
Dramatic Legends and Other Poems. New York, Macmillan, 1922.
The Way of the Cross: Devotions on the Progress of Our Lord Jesus Christ from the Judgment Hall to Calvary. Chicago, Seymour, 1926.
Creatures. New York, Macmillan, 1927.
Old Pastures. New York, Macmillan, 1930.
Poems. New York, Macmillan, and London, Macmillan, 1932; revised edition, as *The Collected Poems of Padraic Colum,* New York, Devin Adair, 1953.
The Story of Lowry Maen. New York, Macmillan, 1937.
Flower Pieces: New Poems. Dublin, Orwell Press, 1938.
The Jackdaw. Dublin, Gayfield Press, 1939.
The Vegetable Kingdom. Bloomington, Indiana University Press, 1954.
Ten Poems. Dublin, Dolmen Press, 1957.
Garland Sunday. Dublin, Dolmen Press, 1958.
Irish Elegies. Dublin, Dolmen Press, 1958; revised edition, 1961, 1966; London, Oxford University Press, 1963.
The Poet's Circuits: Collected Poems of Ireland. London, Oxford University Press, 1960.
Images of Departure. Dublin, Dolmen Press, 1969.

Other

Studies (miscellany). Dublin, Maunsel, 1907.
My Irish Year. London, Mills and Boon, and New York, Pott, 1912.
The Irish Rebellion of 1916 and Its Martyrs: Erin's Tragic Easter, with others, edited by Maurice Joy. New York, Devin Adair, 1916.
The Road round Ireland. New York, Macmillan, 1926.
Cross-Roads in Ireland. New York, Macmillan, 1930.
Ella Young: An Appreciation. London and New York, Longman, 1931.
A Half-Day's Ride: or, Estates in Corsica. New York, Macmillan, 1932.
The Legend of Saint Columba. New York, Macmillan, 1935; London, Sheed and Ward, 1936.
Our Friend James Joyce, with Mary Colum. New York, Doubleday, 1958; London, Gollancz, 1959.
Arthur Griffith. Dublin, Browne and Nolan, 1959; as *Ourselves Alone! The Story of Arthur Griffith and the Origin of the Irish Free State,* New York, Crown, 1959.
Story Telling Old and New. New York, Macmillan, 1961.

Editor, *Oliver Goldsmith.* London, Herbert and Daniel, and Chicago, Browne, 1913.
Editor, *Broad-Sheet Ballads, Being a Collection of Irish Popular Songs.* Dublin and London, Maunsel, 1913; Baltimore, Remington, 1914.
Editor, with Edward J. O'Brien, *Poems of the Irish Revolutionary Brotherhood.* Boston, Small Maynard, 1916; revised edition, 1916.
Editor, *Anthology of Irish Verse.* New York, Boni and Liveright, 1922; revised edition, New York, Liveright, 1948.
Editor, *A Treasury of Irish Folklore: The Stories, Traditions, Legends, Humor, Wisdom, Ballads, and Songs of the Irish People.* New York, Crown, 1954; revised edition, 1962, 1967.
Editor, with Margaret Freeman Cabell, *Between Friends: Letters of James Branch Cabell and Others.* New York, Harcourt Brace, 1962.
Editor, *The Poems of Samuel Ferguson.* Dublin, Figgis, 1963.
Editor, *Roofs of Gold: Poems to Read Aloud.* New York, Macmillan, and London, Collier Macmillan, 1964.

*

Manuscript Collection: Berg Collection, New York Public Library.

Critical Study: *Padraic Colum: A Biographical-Critical Introduction* by Zack R. Bowen, Carbondale, Southern Illinois University Press, 1970.

Theatrical Activities:
Actor: **Plays**—Buinne in *Deirdre* by AE, Dublin, 1902; Pupil in *The Hour-Glass* by W.B. Yeats, Dublin, 1903; A Cripple in *The King's Threshold* by W.B. Yeats, Dublin, 1903.

* * *

Padraic Colum's fictional work for the young ranges from the retelling of traditional tales, like his Cinderella story *The Girl Who Sat by the Ashes* to the partially autobiographical novel *A Boy in Eirinn.* Working in collaboration with many different artists his picture books vary greatly in their length and complexity. The bulk of his output lies in the period 1914 to 1939, and much of it is now unavailable to the general British public.

It is in *A Boy in Eirinn* that Colum's version of the Ancient Mariner first appears. Carrying the tiny closed theatre on his back like a hunch, the peep-show man with his fund of stories and concealed pictures both anticipates Ray Bradbury's Illustrated

Man in having been terrified by his own exhibits, and more directly represents the author himself, accompanied by his Muse. This equivocal figure is developed further in the three short stories titled *The Peep-Show Man;* while, by the simple expedient of never revealing its contents, the portable theatre projects itself to the reader as a Pandora's Box of unconscious images, its owner narrates to a young boy, outside whose house he has paused, the first two tales, which concern noble young men brought low by fickle women. But of greater significance in the totality of Colum's work is the third tale. The peep-show man here switches roles to become an off-stage character, who has given the same lonely boy a caged white blackbird. The bird, which must be free to sing on Easter morning, is released in spiritual exchange for the return of the boy's missing father. In its employment of bird symbolism, in its portrayal by analogy of a specially gifted child, and in its moving scene of paternal reunion, this episode draws together three of the author's most abiding motifs. The latter two, very Joycean in their sympathies (Colum and Joyce were long-standing friends), certainly have their origin in the three years Colum spent in the care of an uncle, while Colum senior ineffectually sought his fortune in America. Such figures as the peep-show man, the entertainer in *The White Sparrow,* and the evil guardian magician in *The Boy Apprenticed to an Enchanter* may therefore be partially regarded as ambivalent father surrogates. Even such a mundane story as *The Six Who Were Left in a Shoe* is elevated by the keenly conveyed desolation of the deserted animals. And at the end of *Where the Winds Never Blew and the Cocks Never Crew* the characters pass away across the edge of the world, as one figuratively would when leaving Ireland for America.

Through the fictional persona of Finn O'Donnell these crucial years are explored most candidly in *A Boy in Eirinn.* This *bildungsroman,* illustrated by Jack B. Yeats in his naturalistic phase, is both a summing up of the author's Irish childhood and an introduction to the mother country for Irish-American boys. The dissolute elder Colum is here transformed as Finn's father into a political prisoner of the British. Like his author, the child hero is farmed out to an uncle and grandfather. Cleverly interleaved with a calendar of country customs and the adventures of Finn and his friend Tim (another boy without a father) on a set-piece visit to the Dublin of horse trams and gaslight are mythical stories like the Children of Ler and patriotic lessons in Irish history. Although one would not particularly expect a child to read it today, *A Boy in Eirinn,* with its whitewashed houses and long dusty roads full of tinkers and show people, has not lost its period charm. While that book, with among others its caged goldfinch and tame jackdaw, abounds in birds, and birds figure prominently as the guardian angel starlings of *The Girl Who Sat by the Ashes* and in *The Boy Who Knew What the Birds Said,* it is with *The White Sparrow* that they crowd out the landscape and reach their apogee. Here the famous flock of starlings in the Luxembourg Gardens are ingeniously equated with western city dwellers who have sold their souls for industry and gossip. In their midst and identifying himself with more melodious and solitary species is the White Sparrow. Spurned by his fellows, conscious of his difference from the herd, the hero in temperament and some of his adventures is really another incarnation of the fair-haired Finn. This 60-page book is Colum's most enduring creation in the genre.

—John Churcher

CONLON-McKENNA, Marita

Nationality: Irish. **Born:** Dublin, Ireland, 5 November 1956. **Education:** St. Nicholas Montessori College, diploma 1983. **Family:** Married James David McKenna, 26 August 1977; three daughters and one son. **Career:** Writer. **Awards:** Reading Association of Ireland Award, International Reading Association award, and Irish Arts Council Bursary award, all 1991; Bisto Book of the Year shortlist, 1990-91, and 1995-96; Bisto Book of the Year, 1991-92, and 1992-93; Irish Children's Book Trust award, 1992, for historical fiction, and Book of the Year award, 1993; Osterreichischen Kinder und jugendbuchpreis 1993; Grand Prix Europeen du Roman pour Enfants (France), runner-up, 1994. **Address:** Homewood, 50 Stillorgan Grove, Blackrock, County Dublin, Ireland.

Publications for Children

Fiction

My First Holy Communion. Dublin, Veritas, 1990.
Under the Hawthorn Tree: Children of the Famine. New York, Holiday House, and London, Viking, 1990.
Wildflower Girl. New York, Holiday House, and London, Viking, 1992.
The Blue Horse. Dublin, O'Brien Press, 1993.
Little Star, illustrated by Christopher Coady. New York, Little, Brown, and London, ABC, 1993.
The Very Last Unicorn, illustrated by C. Coady. New York, Little, Brown, and London, ABC, 1994.
No Goodbye. Dublin, O'Brien Press, 1994.
Safe Harbour. Dublin, O'Brien Press, 1995.
Fields of Home, illustrated by Donald Teskey. Dublin, O'Brien, and New York, Holiday House, 1996.

Publications for Young Adults

"The Old Dog" (short story), in *First Times,* edited by Robert Dunbar. Dublin, Poolbeg, 1997.

*

Media Adaptations: "Under the Hawthorn Tree" (radio serialization of her novel), RTE; "Under the Hawthorn Tree" (film), Young Film-makers Ireland, 1997.

Manuscript Collections: National Library of Ireland, Dublin.

Marita Conlon-McKenna comments:

Growing up in Ireland in the 1950s and 1960s all I ever dreamed of, or wanted, was to be a writer, but most important, a *children's* writer. Someone who could write the type of books that I loved to read. I wrote to lots of children's authors hoping to find out the key; unfortunately, I never heard back from any of them. Ireland and the world of children's literature in those days seemed to be very far apart. Nowadays my stories and words cross borders and boundaries, continents and oceans. I am so lucky to be part of the wondrous world of children's books.

(1997) Creating characters is what I do best. Breathing life into them, they become flesh and bone, heat and spirit, almost as real as my own four children. The story is the world they live in. My heroes and heroines are not the the dragon-slaying type, for truth to tell they fight battles too big for most heroes. My readers, from the first chapters, are forced to enter the arena of the words. Time and again they tell me, "I felt I was in the story." I thank them for joining me there.

* * *

Writing in *Children's Books in Ireland,* Marita Conlon-McKenna comments: "It all started when I heard a story on the radio about an unmarked children's grave which had been found under a hawthorn tree. 'There must,' I thought to myself, 'be a story there!' At more or less the same time I had been doing some research into the Famine—I'm always doing research into something!—consulting lots of scholarly texts without quite realising that I would soon be using some of this information in a book for children."

Conlon-Kenna's novels have one uniting theme, that of the courage, fortitude, and abiding hope of her young protagonists. All the plots and places are very different and from different worlds yet there is a similarity of spirit between Eily of *Under the Hawthorn Tree,* Peggy of *Wildflower Girl,* Katie of *The Blue Horse,* and Sophie of *Safe Harbour.*

Conlon-McKenna writes convincingly and with gentle wit and humanity of families dispossessed either by the ravages of famine in Ireland or the discrimination of modern society. But despite the strangeness of their situation, each family is real, ordinary in a most extraordinary way. Conlon-McKenna's plots are skilfully and deftly unfolded with a pace that keeps the reader turning the pages and with an emotional core that leaves an ache that lingers long after the book is closed. The author writes with deftness and simplicity, very often giving us in one sentence a distillation of emotion, reaction, and response as in: "Peggy pinned a smile across her face."

Under the Hawthorn Tree, Conlon-McKenna's first novel, has an unlikely setting, the single greatest disaster in Irish history, the Great Potato Famine of 1845. When Bridget, the baby of the O'Driscoll family, dies in a village ravaged by famine she is buried under the hawthorn tree. While her distracted mother goes in search of her husband, the children, Eily, Michael, and Peggy, are left to fare for themselves. The story is the story of their flight and journey across Ireland fleeing the dreaded workhouse in search of their mother's maiden aunts Lena and Nano who figured so large in their bedtime stories. For Eily—the eldest, the "little mother"—it is the end of a childhood as she assumes responsibility for her brother and sister and fights to quell her own panic and fear in the need to provide encouragement—but not without resentment. "Eily knew exactly how she felt and wished that she was still a small child and could scream and shout and let all her feelings out." However, when confronting death and starvation, she sums up all her strengths and rallies the family. "Up you lazy lumps," she scolded. "Back indoors. There's work to be done." Many of the adults they encounter on the way show scant sympathy for the children—the priest who passes the exhausted children on his horse and traps a handkerchief to his face, or the soldier whose cries of "come on you brats move away"—which brings tears and blushes to sensitive Eily. Not all the adults are unsympathetic and many of Conlon-McKenna's novels have a wise woman with special gifts or powers. It is old Kate in *Under the Hawthorn Tree* who has a gift for healing and whose little cottage is filled with jars of lotions and herbs and indeed whose parting advice to Eily is "let nature be your friend." In *The Blue Horse* it is Nan Maguire, the old travelling woman who is a famed fortune teller and "who has the gift," who advises Katie "follow your instincts, trust to them and they'll see you right." At moments of great poignancy or tension, the author frequently allows us a wry smile. "I don't exactly know where to start," he mumbled. "The beginning, it's usually the best place," smiled Nano."

Wildflower Girl takes up the fortunes of Peggy, youngest of the O'Driscolls in *Under the Hawthorn Tree.* Seven years have passed and the children are on the brink of adulthood: Eily about to marry a young farmer; Michael finding his hearts desire working as a stable boy; Peggy, spirited, impulsive, and warm hearted, sets out on her own to seek her fortune in the new world and learned to battle against seasickness and homesickness and to seek happiness in the enjoyment of her beloved wildflowers and the small events of her working day. The forty days boat journey travelling steerage is harrowing reading as travellers are buffeted by the elements and their spirits battered by exploitative ship owners. The pages are filled with smells and sounds that all add to the sense of claustrophobia.

Responding to the demands of her many fans Conlon-McKenna completes the trilogy begun with *Under the Hawthorn Tree* and *Wildflower Girl* with *Fields of Home.* It is twelve years since Eily, Michael, and Peggy set off on their journey to find their grandmother. Each lives their own separate lives and each confronts loneliness, danger, and insecurity. In her most complex narrative structure to date we meet up with the trio as they make their way in the adult world. Eily, married with children, is eking out a living in their small rented cottage; Michael works as a stable-boy for Lord Buckland, one of the landed gentry, whilst Peggy continues as house maid in Boston. The chapters weave back and forth across the Atlantic as we once again witness the resilience and ingenuity of the three protagonists. Eventually Michael, now out of work because the stately home was burned to the ground, returns to live with Eily and becomes both catalyst and saviour in their lives. *Fields of Home* ends appropriately with Peggy married and on her way West with a wagon trail on yet another journey, "this .. one [a] journey she really wanted to make."

A more uncertain future awaits the protagonists of *The Blue Horse,* set in contemporary urban Ireland. It charts the ups and downs of a travelling family who are tempted to "settle" after their caravan is burnt to the ground. Again, Katie is the eldest and wavers between her longing for fun and childhood games and the demands placed on her in helping her mother and younger brother and sister to adjust to the settled lifestyle. This is not a comfortable book, confronting as it does the cruelties and prejudices of society to those who seem not to conform. One of the most telling episodes is when Katie attempts to have her mop of red hair cut at a hairdressers and suffers total humiliation as she faces excuses by one, outright refusal by another, and shouts by yet another that they didn't want the likes of her. Finally her friend Sally comes to the rescue and cuts it for her. Katie looks at her reflection, deciding that she looks older and maybe even wiser.

Once again Conlon-McKenna roots her narrative firmly in twentieth-century urban Ireland with all its social ills in *No Goodbye.* Few parents understand the heavy burden of guilt that children automatically assume, believing themselves responsible when things go wrong. In this story of marital breakdown each of the children is given a voice as chapters alternate, allowing the reader to share their bewilderment and grief at their mother's sudden departure.

With few words in her picture books, Conlon-McKenna continues to touch children's emotional responses. The author conveys sorrow, sadness, joy, and love with a focus both simple and direct. Poetic, lyrical, memorable, and fantastic are the words that spring to mind in assessing the prose in *Little Star* and *The Last Unicorn.* In the range of work produced since her first published book, Conlon-McKenna has shown herself to be a consummate storyteller who never cheats her readers and who treats them as equals capable of complex and contradictory emotions.

—Pat Donlon

COONEY, Barbara

Nationality: American. **Born:** 6 August 1917, Brooklyn, New York. **Education:** Smith College, B.A. 1938; also attended Art Students League, 1940. **Military Service:** Women's Army Corps, World War II, 1942-43; became second lieutenant. **Family:** Married Guy Murchie in 1944 (divorced 1947), one daughter; married Charles Talbot Porter in 1949, one daughter and one son. **Career:** Free-lance author and illustrator since 1938. **Awards:** American Library Association Caldecott Medal, 1959 and 1980; *New York Times* Notable Books of the Year, 1974, 1975, 1979; University of Southern Mississippi Silver Medallion, 1975, for Outstanding Contributions in the Field of Children's Books; medal from Smith College for body of work, 1976; *New York Times* Best Illustrated Books of the Year, 1979; National Council for Social Studies/Children's Book Council, Notable Children's Trade Book in the Field of Social Studies, 1982 and 1986; Association of American Publishers, American Book Award for Hardcover Picture Book, 1983; *New York Times* Best Book of the Year, 1983; Fitchburg State College, Ph.D. 1988; *Boston Globe-Horn Book* Picture Book Honor, 1989; Keene State College Children's Literature Festival Award, 1989. McCord Children's Literature Citation, 1990; Lupine Award, 1990, for *Hattie and the Wild Waves;* Kerlan Award, 1992, for body of work; honorary doctorates from the University of Maine at Machais, Westbrook College, and Bowdoin College, 1994, 1995, and 1996 respectively; proclaimed an official state treasure of Maine, 1996.

Publications for Children

Fiction (illustrated by the author)

The King of Wreck Island. New York, Farrar & Rinehart, 1941.
The Kellyhorns. New York, Farrar & Rinehart, 1942.
Captain Pottle's House. New York, Farrar, 1943.
The Little Juggler: Adapted from an Old French Legend. New York, Hastings House, 1961, new edition, 1982.
Christmas. New York, Crowell, 1967.
A Garland of Games and Other Diversions: An Alphabet Book. New York, Holt, 1969.
Miss Rumphius. New York, Viking, 1982.
Island Boy. New York, Viking, 1988.
Hattie and the Wild Waves. New York, Viking, 1990.

Adapter, *Chanticleer and the Fox* by Geoffrey Chaucer. New York, Crowell, 1958.
Adapter, *The Courtship, Merry Marriage, and Feast of Cock Robin and Jenny Wren: To Which Is Added the Doleful Death of Cock Robin.* New York, Scribner, 1965.
Adapter, *Snow White and Rose Red* by Jacob Grimm and Wilhelm Grimm. New York, Delacorte, 1966.

Editor, *A Little Prayer.* New York, Hastings House, 1967.

Reteller, *Little Brother and Little Sister* by J. Grimm. New York, Doubleday, 1982.

Publications for Adults

Other

Twenty-Five Years A-Graying: The Portrait of a College Graduate, a Pictorial Study of the Class of 1938 at Smith College, Northampton, Massachusetts, Based on Statistics Gathered in 1963 for the Occasion of Its 25th Reunion, Boston, Little, Brown, 1963.

*

Illustrator: Carl Malmberg, *Ake and His World,* Farrar & Rinehart, 1940; Frances M. Frost, *Uncle Snowball,* Farrar & Rinehart, 1940; Oskar Seidlin and Senta Rypins, *Green Wagons,* Houghton, 1943; Anne Molloy, *Shooting Star Farm,* Houghton, 1946; Phyllis Crawford, *The Blot: Little City Cat,* Holt, 1946; Nancy Hartwell, *Shoestring Theater,* Holt, 1947; L. L. Bein, *Just Plain Maggie,* Harcourt, 1948; Lee Kingman, *The Rocky Summer,* Houghton, 1948; Ruth C. Seeger, *American Folk Songs for Children in Home, School and Nursery School: A Book for Children, Parents and Teachers,* Doubleday, 1948; Child Study Association of America, *Read Me Another Story,* Crowell, 1949; Rutherford Montgomery, *Kildee House,* Doubleday, 1949; L. Kingman, *The Best Christmas,* Doubleday, 1949, reprinted, Peter Smith, 1985; Phyllis Krasilovsky, *The Man Who Didn't Wash His Dishes,* Doubleday, 1950; R. C. Seeger, *Animal Folk Songs for Children: Traditional American Songs,* Doubleday, 1950; Nellie M. Leonard, *Graymouse Family,* Crowell, 1950; Child Study Association of America, *Read Me More Stories,* Crowell, 1951; R. Montgomery, *Hill Ranch,* Doubleday, 1951; Elisabeth C. Lansing, *The Pony That Ran Away,* Crowell, 1951; L. Kingman, *Quarry Adventure,* Doubleday, 1951, published in England as *Lauri's Surprising Summer,* Constable, 1957; E. C. Lansing, *The Pony That Kept a Secret,* Crowell, 1952; Mary M. Aldrich, *Too Many Pets,* Macmillan, 1952; M. W. Brown, *Where Have You Been?,* Crowell, 1952, reprinted, Scholastic Book Services, 1966; Barbara Reynolds, *Pepper,* Scribner, 1952; Miriam E. Mason, *Yours with Love, Kate,* Houghton, 1952; Margaret W. Brown, *Christmas in the Barn,* Crowell, 1952; Catherine Marshall, *Let's Keep Christmas,* Whittlesey House, 1953; R. C. Seeger, *American Folk Songs for Christmas,* Doubleday, 1953; N. M. Leonard, *Grandfather Whiskers, M. D.: A Graymouse Story,* Crowell, 1953; L. Kingman, *Peter's Long Walk,* Doubleday, 1953; E. C. Lansing, *A Pony Worth His Salt,* Crowell, 1953; Jane Quigg, *Fun for Freddie,* Oxford University Press, 1953; Margaret Sidney, *The Five Little Peppers,* Doubleday, 1954.

M. W. Brown, *The Little Fir Tree,* Crowell, 1954, reissued, 1985; Margaret G. Otto, *Pumpkin, Ginger, and Spice,* Holt, 1954; Helen Kay (pseudonym of Helen C. Goldfrank), *Snow Birthday,* Farrar, Straus, 1955; Louisa May Alcott, *Little Women; or, Meg, Jo, Beth, and Amy,* Crowell, 1955; Louise A. Kent, *The Brookline Trunk,* Houghton, 1955; Catherine S. McEwen, *Away We Go! One-Hundred Poems for the Very Young,* Crowell, 1956; Catherine Marshall, *Friends with God: Stories and Prayers of the Marshall Family,* Whittlesey House, 1956; H. Kay, *City Springtime,* Hastings House, 1957; Neil Anderson (pseudonym of Jerrold Beim), *Freckle Face,* Crowell, 1957; Henrietta Buckmaster, *Lucy and Loki,* Scribner, 1958; Harry Behn, *Timmy's Search,* Seabury, 1958; M. G. Otto, *Little Brown Horse,* Knopf, 1959; Elizabeth G. Speare, *Seasonal Verses Gathered by Elizabeth George Speare from the Connecticut Almanack for the Year of the Christian Era, 1773,* American Library Association, 1959; *Le Hibou et la Poussiquette* (French adaptation of *The Owl and the Pussycat* by Edward Lear), translated by Francis Steegmuller, Little, Brown, 1961; Walter de la Mare, *Peacock Pie: A Book of Rhymes,* Knopf, 1961; Noah Webster, *The American Speller: An Adaptation of Noah Webster's Blue-Backed Speller,* Crowell, 1961; M. G. Otto, *Three Little Dachshunds,* Holt, 1963; Sarah O. Jewett, *A White Heron: A Story of Maine,* Crowell, 1963; Virginia Haviland, *Favorite Fairy Tales Told in Spain,* Little, Brown, 1963; *Papillot, Clignot, et Dodo* (French adaptation of *Wynken, Blynken, and Nod* by Eugene Field), translated by F. Steegmuller and Norbert Guterman, Farrar, Straus, 1964; Hugh Latham, translator, *Mother Goose in French,* Crowell, 1964; A. Molloy, *Shaun and the Boat: An Irish Story,* Hastings House, 1965; Jane Goodsell, *Katie's Magic Glasses,* Houghton, 1965; Samuel Morse, *All in a Suitcase,* Little, Brown, 1966; Aldous Huxley, *Crowns of Pearblossom,* Random House, 1967; Alastair Reid and Anthony Kerrigan, *Mother Goose in Spanish,* Crowell, 1968; Edward Lear, *The Owl and the Pussy-Cat,* Little, Brown, 1969; Natalia M. Belting, *Christmas Folk,* Holt, 1969; E. Field, *Wynken, Blynken and Nod,* Hastings House, 1970.

William Wise, *The Lazy Young Duke of Dundee,* Rand McNally, 1970; Homer, *Dionysus and the Pirates: Homeric Hymn Number 7,* translated and adapted by Penelope Proddow, Doubleday, 1970; Felix Salten (pseudonym of Siegmund Salzman), *Bambi: A Life in the Woods,* Simon & Schuster, 1970; *Book of Princesses,* Scholastic Book Services, 1971; Homer, *Hermes, Lord of Robbers: Homeric Hymn Number Four,* translated and adapted by P. Proddow, Doubleday, 1971; Homer, *Demeter and Persephone: Homeric Hymn Number Two,* translated and adapted by P. Proddow, Doubleday, 1972; John Becker, *Seven Little Rabbits,* Walker, 1972; May Garelick, *Down to the Beach,* Four Winds, 1973; Robyn Supraner, *Would You Rather Be a Tiger?,* Houghton, 1973; Dorothy Joan Harris, *The House Mouse,* Warne, 1973; Edna Mitchell Preston, *Squawk to the Moon, Little Goose* Viking, 1974; Zora L. Olsen, *Herman the Great,* Scholastic Book Services, 1974; E. L. Horwitz, *When the Sky Is Like Lace,* Lippincott, 1975; Jean P. Colby, *Lexington and Concord, 1775: What Really Happened,* Hastings House, 1975; E. M. Preston, *The Sad Story of the Little Bluebird and the Hungry Cat,* Four Winds, 1975; Marjorie W. Sharmat, *Burton and Dudley,* Holiday House, 1975; M. J. Craig, *The Donkey Prince,* Doubleday, 1977; Aileen Fisher, *Plant Magic,* Bowmar, 1977; Ellin Greene, compiler, *Midsummer Magic: A Garland of Stories, Charms, and Recipes,* Lothrop, 1977; Donald Hall, *Ox-Cart Man,* Viking, 1979; Delmore Schwartz, *I Am Cherry Alive, the Little Girl Sang,* Harper, 1979; Norma Farber, *How the Hibernators Came to Bethlehem,* Walker, 1980; Wendy Kesselman, *Emma,* Doubleday, 1980; Margot C. Griego and others, selectors and translators, *Tortillitas para Mama and Other Nursery Rhymes: Spanish and English,* Holt, 1982; John Bierhorst, translator, *Spirit Child: A Story of the Nativity,* Morrow, 1984; Rumer Godden, *The Story of Holly and Ivy,* Viking, 1985; Toni de Gerez, reteller, *Louhi, Witch of North Farm,* Viking, 1986; Sergei Prokofiev, *Peter and the Wolf Pop-Up Book,* Viking, 1986; Elinor L. Horwitz, *When the Sky Is Like Lace,* Lippincott, 1987; Gloria M. Houston, *The Year of the Perfect Christmas Tree: An Appalachian Tale,* Dial, 1988. Alice McLerran, *Roxaboxen,* Lothrop, 1991; Michael Bedard, *Emily,* Doubleday, 1992; Jane Yolen, *Letting Swift River Go,* Little, Brown, 1992; Ruth Sawyer, *The Remarkable Christmas of the Cobbler's Sons,* Viking, 1994; Opal Whitley, *Only Opal: The Diary of a Young Girl,* selected and adapted by Jane Boulton, Philomel, 1994.

Media Adaptations: *Chanticleer and the Fox* was adapted as a sound filmstrip by Weston Woods, 1959; *Wynken, Blynken and Nod* was adapted as a sound filmstrip by Weston Woods, 1967; *Owl and the Pussycat* was adapted as a sound filmstrip, 1967; *The Man Who Didn't Wash His Dishes* was adapted as a sound filmstrip by Weston Woods, 1973; *Squawk to the Moon, Little Goose* was adapted as a sound filmstrip by Viking, 1975; *Miss Rumphius* was adapted as a filmstrip with cassette by Live Oak Media, 1984; *Ox-Cart Man* was adapted as a filmstrip with cassette by Random House and as a videocassette by Live Oak Media; *How the Hibernators Came to Bethlehem* was adapted as a filmstrip with cassette by Random House; *American Folksongs for Children* was adapted as a cassette.

* * *

Barbara Cooney is one of the most prolific and most versatile author/illustrators in the children's book field. By the time she won her first Caldecott Award for *Chanticleer and the Fox,* an adaptation of "The Nun's Priest's Tale" from Chaucer's *Canterbury Tales,* she had already created approximately fifty books. The bold, yet simple, black-and-white scratchboard illustrations with red, blue, green, and gold capture the haughty pride of Chanticleer the rooster. In her Caldecott acceptance speech, Cooney spoke of her characteristic use of detail, pointing out that the magpie in the pollarded willow was an evil omen and that all of the many plants pictured are authentic to Chaucer's England. Twenty-one years after her first Caldecott winner, Cooney won again, this time for her illustrations for Donald Hall's *Ox-Cart Man.* Her paintings for this tale of the cycle of the seasons in the life of a New England family in the 1830s are based on the early American tradition of painting on wood.

In recent years, Cooney has continued to illustrate others' work while also creating her own perfectly balanced picture story books. These latter works seem more personal, more sensitive, and more demanding of readers than earlier books. Her preferred technique for illustrations now seems to be painting with acrylics on fabric, usually silk, coated with gesso and mounted on illustration board, adding special effects with pastels and colored pencils.

Island Boy was inspired by an 1899 record of life in Maine. This is the story of Matthais who grows up on the island and, although he left to make his fortune, returns there to raise his own family. Before his death, he passes on to his grandson, Young Matthais, both his love of the island and the skills to survive there.

Hattie and the Wild Waves seems to include scenes both from Cooney's mother's life and from her own in this story of a young girl who became an artist. Miss Rumphius, narrated by the grandniece of the character, may not contain as many specific details of Cooney's life in Brooklyn, Long Island, and Maine; but it certainly appears to reflect her love of nature, of travel, and of the sea as well as her desire to leave something of beauty behind as her life's legacy. All three of these stories express the continuity of caring and concern from one generation to another and the sense of permanence of a place that is home to all of them.

Two of the best-known and most loved creators of children's books combined their talents to produce *Letting the Swift River Go,* based on the actual creation of the Quabbin Reservoir in Massachusetts. Cooney's exquisite watercolors accented with pastels and colored pencils perfectly capture the spirit of Jane Yolen's telling of the flooding of small towns to provide water for the city of Boston. Sally Jane, who was a child when this happened, returns to the reservoir years later with her father who points from the rowboat to places that used to be. As Sally Jane remembers what is gone, she also remembers her mother's voice telling her, when she used to catch fireflies, "You have to let them go." Cooney's evocative pictures remind us that we can both hold on to the memory of the past and let it go to appreciate what has replaced it.

Michael Bedard's story based on the life of Emily Dickinson is told from the point of view of a young girl who lives across the street. Cooney's paintings in *Emily* capture the gentleness and the warmth of the characters and the essence of another time and a quieter way of life. She visited the poet's home in Amherst to make sketches to insure the accuracy of her illustrations. One does not have to be familiar with Dickinson or her work to enjoy the details of homes and flowers and costumes, but poetry lovers will especially appreciate this loving tribute to one who pondered and preserved life's mysteries.

Only Opal: The Diary of a Young Girl is a tribute to a young woman who lived a very different type of life from that of Emily Dickinson. Opal Whitely was a real child, born around the turn of the century, who kept a diary when she was five and six years old. An orphan, she traveled from one Oregon lumber camp to another with her adopted parents. She reports that "The mama where I live says I am a nuisance," but she works hard at all her many chores. Opal loves trees, flowers, and all the animals; and she names them all with names of great artists, painters and poets and musicians, from a book her angel parents left her. Opal's love of language and of nature, akin to that of Cooney herself, makes this perfect subject for her art. The delicacy of detail and the quiet, pensive mood are characteristic of many of Cooney's illustrations. So too is her sensitivity to young children and to the elderly, especially those who are slightly different and more attuned to the natural world.

—Kay E. Vandergrift

COOPER, Lettice (Ulpha)

Nationality: British. **Born:** Eccles, Lancashire, 3 September 1897. **Education:** St. Cuthbert's School, Southbourne; Lady Margaret Hall, Oxford, 1916-18, B.A. **Career:** Editorial assistant and drama critic, *Time and Tide,* London, 1939-40; public relations officer, Ministry of Food, London, 1940-45. President, Robert Louis Stevenson Club, 1958-74; Vice-Chairman, 1975-78, and President, 1979-81, English PEN Club. **Awards:** Arts Council bursary, 1968, 1979; Eric Gregory travelling scholarship, 1977; O.B.E. (Officer, Order of the British Empire), 1980. **Died:** 1994.

Publications for Children

Fiction

Blackberry's Kitten, illustrated by Mary Shillabeer. Leicester, Brockhampton Press, 1961; New York, Vanguard Press, 1963.
The Bear Who Was Too Big, illustrated by Nicholas Fisk. London, Parrish, 1963; Chicago, Follett, 1966.
Bob-a-Job, illustrated by Mary Dinsdale. Leicester, Brockhampton Press, 1963.
Contadino, illustrated by Antony Maitland. London, Cape, 1964.
The Twig of Cypress, illustrated by W.F. Phillipps. London, Deutsch, 1965; New York, Washburn, 1966.
We Shall Have Snow. Leicester, Brockhampton Press, 1966.
Robert the Spy Hunter. London, Kaye and Ward, 1973.
Parkin, illustrated by Rosie Evans. London, Harrap, 1977.

Other

Great Men of Yorkshire (West Riding). London, Lane, 1955.
The Young Florence Nightingale, illustrated by Denise Brown. London, Parrish, 1960; New York, Roy, 1961.
The Young Victoria, illustrated by Denise Brown. London, Parrish, 1961; New York, Roy, 1962.
James Watt, illustrated by W.F. Phillipps. London, A. and C. Black, 1963.
Garibaldi, illustrated by Ronald Ferns. London, Methuen, 1964; New York, Roy, 1966.
The Young Edgar Allan Poe, illustrated by William Randell. London, Parrish, 1964; New York, Roy, 1965.
The Fugitive King, illustrated by Denise Brown. London, Parrish, 1965.
A Hand upon the Time: A Life of Charles Dickens. New York, Pantheon, 1968; London, Gollancz, 1971.
Robert Louis Stevenson. London, Burns and Oates, 1969.
Gunpowder: Treason and Plot, illustrated by Elisabeth Grant. London, Abelard Schuman, 1970.

Publications for Adults

Novels

The Lighted Room. London, Hodder and Stoughton, 1925.
The Old Fox. London, Hodder and Stoughton, 1927.
Good Venture. London, Hodder and Stoughton, 1928.
Likewise the Lyon. London, Hodder and Stoughton, 1928.
The Ship of Truth. London, Hodder and Stoughton, and Boston, Little Brown, 1930.
Private Enterprise. London, Hodder and Stoughton, 1931.
Hark to Rover! London, Hodder and Stoughton, 1933.
We Have Come to a Country. London, Gollancz, 1935.
The New House. London, Gollancz, and New York, Macmillan, 1936.

National Provincial. London, Gollancz, and New York, Macmillan, 1938.
Black Bethlehem. London, Gollancz, and New York, Macmillan, 1947.
Fenny. London, Gollancz, 1953.
Three Lives. London, Gollancz, 1957.
A Certain Compass. London, Gollancz, 1960.
The Double Heart. London, Gollancz, 1962.
Late in the Afternoon. London, Gollancz, 1971.
Tea on Sunday. London, Gollancz, 1973.
Snow and Roses. London, Gollancz, 1976.
Desirable Residence. London, Gollancz, 1980.
Unusual Behaviour. London, Gollancz, 1986.

Other

Robert Louis Stevenson. London, Home and Van Thal, 1947; Denver, Alan Swallow, 1948.
Yorkshire: West Riding. London, Hale, 1950.
George Eliot. London, Longman, 1951; revised edition, 1960, 1964.

*

Manuscript Collections: Eccles Public Library, Lancashire.

Lettice Cooper comments:
I want to write books that children will *enjoy,* and I hope the books will stimulate their imaginations. I should like to write them so that they give children an example of good English.

* * *

Lettice Cooper is known to adults both as a novelist and for her scholarly but readable biography of Dickens, *A Hand upon the Time,* but she also wrote delightful books for the very young and some intended for the newly independent reader. The child who is just beginning to master this new skill and can cope with a limited vocabulary will have great fun with the adventures of Robert the spy hunter, and will identify joyfully with the heroic Robert as he survives exciting perils like a mini-James Bond. Young children love stories where the small and underprivileged score over the large and powerful, and this is one of the book's great charms.

Blackberry's Kitten and *Parkin* are further tales for this age group. They read aloud well and provide a good vehicle for shared appreciation as books for bedtime. *Bob-a-Job* is the story of a couple of attractive but incompetent small boys attempting to do their good deeds for Scout Week; the humour here will appeal to young readers as the situations are familiar and the escapades only slightly over-the-top. The improbably plausible is the style of comedy that nine-to-eleven-year-olds relish. *We Shall Have Snow* is in a more serious vein, telling how a lonely little girl left with relatives comes to terms with her difficulties.

Cooper's work for older children is set in the Italian countryside which is described in loving detail. She knows Tuscany and its people well, and in *Contadino* we see the region through the eyes of a young American boy coming to live with his Italian grandparents, exploring the totally new way of life and beliefs. There is some plot excitement to spice the descriptive writing when young Nicolo is instrumental in persuading the local landlord against the eviction of his grandfather from the family home. *The Twig of Cypress* takes us back to the 19th century, and we follow the story of a youngster who supports Garibaldi and his freedom fighters in an exciting adventure story.

Apart from the last-mentioned story her books could be said to sacrifice plot to description and character delineation. We learn a lot about appearances, scenery, motives and feelings, but the why seems more important than the what. Perhaps this is oversimplification, but the stories have a candyfloss quality, a frothy delicacy that is so evanescent that as soon as you put the book down you wonder whether you really enjoyed it after all. With the tales for the little ones this does not really matter.

—Ann G. Hay

CORBETT, (Winfield) Scott

Nationality: American. **Born:** Kansas City, Missouri, 27 July 1913. **Education:** Kansas City Junior College, 1930-32; University of Missouri, Columbia, bachelor of journalism 1934. **Military Service:** Correspondent, United States Army 42nd (Rainbow) Infantry Division, 1943-46. **Family:** Married Elizabeth Grosvenor Pierce in 1940; one daughter. **Career:** Part-time teacher, Moses Brown School, Providence, 1957-65. **Award:** Mystery Writers of America Edgar Allan Poe award, 1963. **Agent:** Curtis Brown, 10 Astor Place, New York, New York 10003. **Address:** 149 Benefit Street, Providence, Rhode Island 02903, U.S.A.

Publications for Children

Fiction

Susie Sneakers, illustrated by Leonard Shortall. New York, Crowell, 1956.
Midshipman Cruise. Boston, Little Brown, 1957.
Tree House Island, illustrated by Gordon Hansen. Boston, Little Brown, and London, Dent, 1959.
Dead Man's Light, illustrated by Leonard Shortall. Boston, Little Brown, 1960.
The Lemonade [Mailbox, Disappearing Dog, Limerick, Baseball, Turnabout, Hairy Horror, Hateful Plateful, Home Run, Hockey, Black Mask, Hangman's Ghost] Trick, illustrated by Paul Galdone. Boston, Little Brown, 12 vols., 1960-77.
Cutlass Island, illustrated by Leonard Shortall. Boston, Little Brown, 1962; London, Dent, 1964.
Danger Point: The Wreck of the "Birkenhead." Boston, Little Brown, 1962.
One by Sea, illustrated by Victor Mays. Boston, Little Brown, 1965.
The Cave above Delphi, illustrated by Gioia Fiammenghi. New York, Holt Rinehart, 1965.
Pippa Passes, illustrated by Judith Gwyn Brown. New York, Holt Rinehart, 1966.
The Case of the Gone Goose, illustrated by Paul Frame. Boston, Little Brown, 1966.
Diamonds Are Trouble. New York, Holt Rinehart, 1967; revised edition as *The Trouble with Diamonds,* New York, Dutton, 1985.

Cop's Kid, illustrated by Jo Polseno. Boston, Little Brown, 1968.
Ever Ride a Dinosaur?, illustrated by Mircea Vasiliu. New York, Holt Rinehart, 1969.
The Case of the Fugitive Firebug, illustrated by Paul Frame. Boston, Little Brown, 1969.
Diamonds Are More Trouble. New York, Holt Rinehart, 1969.
Steady, Freddie, illustrated by Lawrence Beall Smith. New York, Dutton, 1970.
The Baseball Bargain, illustrated by Wallace Tripp. Boston, Little Brown, 1970.
The Mystery Man, illustrated by Nathan Goldstein. Boston, Little Brown, 1970.
The Case of the Ticklish Tooth, illustrated by Paul Frame. Boston, Little Brown, 1971.
The Big Joke Game, illustrated by Mircea Vasiliu. New York, Dutton, 1972.
The Red Room Riddle, illustrated by Geff Gerlach. Boston, Little Brown, 1972.
Dead Before Docking, illustrated by Paul Frame. Boston, Little Brown, 1972.
Run for the Money, illustrated by Bert Dodson. Boston, Little Brown, 1973.
Dr. Merlin's Magic Shop, illustrated by Joe Mathieu. Boston, Little Brown, 1973.
Take a Number. New York, Dutton, 1974.
Here Lies the Body, illustrated by Geff Gerlach. Boston, Little Brown, 1974.
The Case of the Silver Skull, illustrated by Paul Frame. Boston, Little Brown, 1974.
The Great Custard Pie Panic, illustrated by Joe Mathieu. Boston, Little Brown, 1974.
The Boy with Will Power, illustrated by Ed Parker. Boston, Little Brown, 1975.
The Case of the Burgled Blessing Box, illustrated by Paul Frame. Boston, Little Brown, 1975.
The Boy Who Walked on Air, illustrated by Ed Parker. Boston, Little Brown, 1975.
The Great McGoniggle's Gray Ghost, illustrated by Bill Ogden. Boston, Little Brown, 1975.
The Great McGoniggle's Key Play, illustrated by Bill Ogden. Boston, Little Brown, 1976.
The Hockey Girls. New York, Dutton, 1976.
Captain Butcher's Body, illustrated by Geff Gerlach. Boston, Little Brown, 1976.
The Great McGoniggle Rides Shotgun, illustrated by Bill Ogden. Boston, Little Brown, 1977.
The Foolish Dinosaur Fiasco, illustrated by Jon McIntosh. Boston, Little Brown, 1978.
The Discontented Ghost. New York, Dutton, 1978.
The Donkey Planet, illustrated by Troy Howell. New York, Dutton, 1979.
The Mysterious Zetabet, illustrated by Jon McIntosh. Boston, Little Brown, 1979.
The Great McGoniggle Switches Pitches, illustrated by Bill Ogden. Boston, Little Brown, 1980.
The Deadly Hoax. New York, Dutton, 1981.
Grave Doubts. Boston, Little Brown, 1982.
Down with Wimps!, illustrated by Larry Ross. New York, Dutton, 1984.
Witch Hunt. Boston, Little Brown, 1985.

Other

What Makes a Car Go?, illustrated by Len Darwin. Boston, Little Brown, 1963; London, Muller, 1968.
What Makes TV Work?, illustrated by Len Darwin. Boston, Little Brown, 1965; London, Muller, 1968.
What Makes a Light Go On?, illustrated by Len Darwin. Boston, Little Brown, 1966; London, Muller, 1968.
What Makes a Plane Fly?, illustrated by Len Darwin. Boston, Little Brown, 1967.
Rhode Island. New York, Coward McCann, 1969.
What Makes a Boat Float?, illustrated by Victor Mays. Boston, Little Brown, 1970.
What about the Wankel Engine?, illustrated by Jerome Kühl. New York, Four Winds Press, 1974.
Bridges, illustrated by Richard Rosenblum. New York, Four Winds Press, 1978.
Jokes to Read in the Dark, illustrated by Annie Gusman. New York, Dutton, 1980.
Home Computers: A Simple and Informative Guide. Boston, Little Brown, 1980.
Jokes to Tell Your Worst Enemy, illustrated by Annie Gusman. New York, Dutton, 1984.

PUBLICATIONS FOR ADULTS

Other

The Reluctant Landlord. New York, Crowell, 1950.
Sauce for the Gander. New York, Crowell, 1951.
We Chose Cape Cod. New York, Crowell, 1953.
Cape Cod's Way: An Informal History. New York, Crowell, 1955.
The Sea Fox: The Adventures of Cape Cod's Most Colorful Rum-runner, with Manuel Zora. New York, Crowell, 1956; London, Hale, 1957.

*

Manuscript Collections: de Grummond Collection, University of Southern Mississippi, Hattiesburg; Kerlan Collection, University of Minnesota, Minneapolis.

Scott Corbett comments:

I am a storyteller devoted to the proposition that suspense and humor are a worthwhile combination. My books, especially the Trick books, have been widely used in schools to trap reluctant readers and get them started on books. My most successful efforts of late have been ghost stories of a slightly more modern flavor than those Victorian chillers which today are not only period pieces but, all too often, semi-colon pieces. The What Makes It Work books were successful in explaining difficult subjects to beginning readers—mainly because I started with no knowledge of the subjects myself and thus did not make the expert's mistake of assuming too much basic understanding on the part of his readers. *What Makes a Car Go?* was published in an Arabic edition, not for children but as a workable introduction to the internal combustion engine for adult Arabs. Perhaps this was a mistake—I may have let something slip about the importance of all that oil. An interest in computer led me to write about them—and now I write all my books on my computer, while my typewriter gathers dust.

* * *

A strange old lady gave Kerby Maxwell a magic chemistry set. Think what different comic authors might do with this beginning. What Scott Corbett did was to have Kerby and his friend Fenton concoct a lemonade that made whoever drank it *good.* There are humorous consequences for Kerby's relationships with his surprised parents, the bully next door, and for the school play. *The Lemonade Trick* turned out to be the first of the successful series of "trick books" for which Corbett is best known.

In these and many of his other stories, Corbett blends a little magic and plot with a lot of boyish humor. *Ever Ride a Dinosaur?* begins "I don't know how you feel about garbage. Personally, I agree with the fellow who said 'I can take it out, or leave it alone.' The only trouble was at my cousin Charlie's house, I seemed to do the taking out, and he did the leaving alone." As this opening suggests, Corbett establishes an amiable relationship with the reader and gets on with his story. His themes are basic ones for the pre-adolescent boy. Corbett treats these themes in such a way as to keep them fun but non-threatening. "As usual," he writes in *The Limerick Trick* "when [Kerby] secretly worked with his chemistry set, he felt a bit guilty. What would his parents think if they knew?" In the work of Sendak, du Bois, or Dahl the explosive potential of this chemistry set would become apparent. In Corbett's stories the chemicals are used in a pro-social way. The lemonade trick makes one good, the hockey trick must be used to maintain a fair balance between the rival Panthers and Wildcats, etc.

Corbett has applied his skills to a non-fiction series, ranging from *What Makes a Car Go?* and *What Makes a Boat Float?* to a book on home computers. He has also written easy-to-read adventures, ghost stories, mysteries, and science fiction. In the quarter of a century from 1960 to 1985 he published an average of two to three books a year. In some of his stories the main characters are older than Kerby Maxwell. For example, two 16-year-olds, Wally and Les, are sleuths in the fairly complex mysteries *Grave Doubts* and *Witch Hunt.* Two young male scientists are the heroes of *The Donkey Planet,* but to disguise them for a secret mission their boss turns the pair into a 14-year-old boy with horns on his head and a donkey. The donkey has to resist the advances of female donkeys while the boy outwits the villain. When the boss commends them after their return to Earth, they tell him that "any ass could do it."

The chemistry of Corbett's appeal shows consistencies over time. He is a skilled craftsman but not a perfectionist. Though his humor and invention lack the brilliance of authors who are more daring and more invested in their creativity, he is a friendly and enjoyable author for pre-adolescent boys.

—Ravenna Helson

CORBETT, W(illiam) J(esse)

Nationality: British. **Born:** Birmingham, Warwickshire, 21 February 1938. **Education:** Billesley Secondary School, Birmingham, 1942-53. **Military Service:** Physical training instructor in the British Army. **Career:** Has worked as a merchant seaman, baker's assistant, furniture removal man, slaughterman, and builder. **Award:** Whitbread award, 1983. **Address:** 6 Selborne Grove, Billesley, Birmingham, England.

Publications for Children

Fiction

The Song of Pentecost, illustrated by Martin Ursell. London, Methuen, 1982; New York, Dutton, 1984.
Pentecost and the Chosen One, illustrated by Martin Ursell. London, Methuen, 1984; New York, Delacorte Press, 1987.
The End of the Tale and Other Stories, illustrated by Tony Ross. London, Methuen, 1985.
Pentecost of Lickey Top, illustrated by Martin Ursell. London, Methuen, 1987.
The Bear Who Stood on His Head, illustrated by Martin Ursell. London, Methuen, 1988.
Dear Grumble. London, Methuen, 1989.
Toby's Iceberg. London, Methuen, 1990.
Little Elephant. London, Methuen, 1991.
Duck Soup Farm. London, Methuen, 1992.
The Granson Boy, illustrated by Tony Ross. London, Methuen, 1993.
The End of the Tale. London, Mammoth, 1994.
Hamish Climbing Father's Mountain, illustrated by Susan Hellard. London, Hodder, 1995.
The Dragon's Egg and Other Stories, illustrated by Wayne Anderson. London, Hodder, 1996.

*

Media Adaptations: *The Song of Pentecost* has been adapted for the stage.

W.J. Corbett comments:

Although my books are classed as children's, I like to think that they can be enjoyed by a wide age group. My publications to date have all had animal characters with human parallels.

I never write down to children. I believe that they can grasp situations very quickly, and can enjoy sadness as well as humour in a book. I try to keep the ending under wraps as long as possible, allowing the reader's own imagination full play.

* * *

W.J. Corbett's first book *The Song of Pentecost* was a deserved winner of the Whitbread award. It is a splendid saga story, telling of the journey of a group of assorted animals across a dangerous country to a new home in the Lickey Hills. An ingenuous snake is cheated of his inheritance, a beautiful pond, and is helped by harvest mice, led by their hereditary chief Pentecost. They agree to help the snake regain his home in return for a place to live, since their own dwellings have become hazardous through slum clearance plans. The characters are lively, the wit is adult, and we follow with keen interest their adventures, stirred up by a frog who is a pathological liar, an untrustworthy fox, and a strange seven-legged bug who is a born troublemaker.

The sequels, *Pentecost and the Chosen One* and *Pentecost of Lickey Top,* continue the adventure of Pentecost, his family, and the various animals living in the Lickey Hills. These books are less successful, however; most of the new characters are far less attractive, and the adult reader at least is aware of disturbing overtones.

Corbett's first novel for younger children, *The Bear Who Stood On His Head,* relates four tales (one for each season of the year) of a family of bears who live in the Rocky Mountains, bears who, like his Pentecost characters, are as much human as animal. Ben Bear, clumsy and disobedient though eminently lovable, continually causes trouble for his brother and sister. But *he* avoids every unpleasantness because everyone, from the bees to the lightning to the fierce wolves, loves him. In *Dear Grumble,* Corbett features human characters for the first time, albeit in a fantasy about children getting dragons for pets. While the storylines of both books are appropriate for their intended audience, the difficulty of Corbett's prose often strikes an overly sophisticated note.

Corbett returned to the animal world with *Toby's Iceberg,* the story of the grandson of Moby Dick, who sets off on a quest to deliver an iceberg to the equator for his cousins to lick when they are thirsty. Along the way, he is joined by a series of intriguing, and often humourous, companions. The journey undertaken by *Little Elephant,* whose mother is killed by ivory poachers, is more serious, and more frightening, but contains both funny and touching moments. Although the plot of *Hamish Climbing Father's Mountain*—a child (or, in this case, a goat) conquering his fear in order to rescue his sweetheart—sounds hackneyed, in Corbett's hands it comes off as a wonderfully witty read.

In much of his recent work, Corbett returns to his original audience—middle grade readers. And although the novels often include animals, humans are typically their main characters. In *Duck Soup Farm,* Daisy, Chris, and Dave decide to start a pet-sitting business. Their initial adventures (with an elderly neighbor's annoying parrot and a tarantula) are lightheartedly amusing, but a later job involving a mysterious horse leads to intrigue. *The Grandson Boy,* though filled with fast-paced action and farcical situations, is noteworthy for the strength of its characterizations—Jenny, a tough country girl; Aunt Rose, the witch whom Jenny "adopts,"; Aunt Rose's Grandson Boy, Tim, sent to Aunt Rose's while his parents sort through their divorce; and Nutty, captain of a gang who helps Tim adjust to country life. The tales in *The Dragon's Egg and Other Stories* are related by Sniffy, a magical dragon who passes his cold onto George and who then must entertain the boy while he recovers from his illness.

As is the case with many authors who achieve accolades early in their careers, Corbett's later novels have had difficulty living up to the standard set by his first. Much of his post-Pentecost work has met with the same reaction of disappointment as did his Pentecost sequels, particularly those titles for younger readers published immediately after the Pentecost tales. But Corbett certainly has his admirers. While some reviewers and critics find fault with the adult tone of Corbett's humour, others deem it brilliantly witty. Some feel that the "literary" quality of his writing—its detailed descriptions, its strong characterizations, its telling turns of phrase—is far too sophisticated for its intended audience; others rejoice in its very sophistication. Corbett's claim that he "never writes down to children" is certainly behind these two divergent attitudes toward his work.

—Ann G. Hay, updated by Jackie C. Horne

CORBY, Dan. See **CATHERALL, Arthur.**

CORLETT, William

Nationality: British. **Born:** Darlington, County Durham, 8 October 1938. **Education:** St. Olave's School, Ripon, Yorkshire; Fettes College, Edinburgh; Royal Academy of Dramatic Art, London, 1956-58, diploma. **Career:** Repertory and television actor in London and the provinces. **Award:** Pye award, for television play, 1978. **Address:** Churchfields, Hope Mansell, near Ross-on-Wye, Herefordshire HR9 5TA, England.

Publications for Children

Fiction

The Gate of Eden. London, Hamish Hamilton, 1974; Scarsdale, New York, Bradbury Press, 1975.
The Land Beyond. London, Hamish Hamilton, 1975; Scarsdale, New York, Bradbury Press, 1976.
Return to the Gate. London, Hamish Hamilton, 1975; Scarsdale, New York, Bradbury Press, 1977.
The Dark Side of the Moon. London, Hamish Hamilton, 1976; Scarsdale, New York, Bradbury Press, 1977.
Barriers. London, Hamish Hamilton, 1981.
Bloxworth Blue. London, MacRae, 1984; New York, Harper, 1985.
The Secret Line. London, Walker, 1988.
With Carla Lane, *Mrs. Boswell's Slice of Bread.* London, BBC Books, 1989.
The Steps Up the Chimney. London, Bodley Head, 1990.
The Door in the Tree. London, Bodley Head, 1991.
The Tunnel Behind the Waterfall. London, Bodley Head, 1991.
The Bridge in the Clouds. London, Bodley Head, 1993.
The Gondolier's Cat. London, Hodder and Stoughton, 1993.
The Summer of the Haunting. London, Bodley Head, 1993.
Now and Then. London, Abacus, 1996.
Two Gentlemen Sharing. London, Little Brown 1997.

Plays

Orlando the Marmalade Cat Buys a Cottage, adaptation of the story by Kathleen Hale (produced London, 1975).
Orlando's Camping Holiday, adaptation of the story by Kathleen Hale (produced London, 1976).

Television Plays: *Barriers* series, 1980; *The Machine-Gunners,* from the story by Robert Westall, 1983; *The Watchouse,* from the story by Robert Westall, 1988; *Torch,* 1992; *Moonacre,* 1994.

Poetry

The Ideal Tale, illustrated by Maria Lancaster. Salisbury, Compton Russell, 1975.

The Once and Forever Christmas, with John Moore. Tisbury, Wiltshire, Compton Russell, 1975.

Other

Questions series (*The Question of Religion, The Christ Story, The Hindu Sound, The Judaic Law, The Buddha Way, The Islamic Space*), with John Moore. London, Hamish Hamilton, 6 vols., 1978-79; as *Their Questions,* Scarsdale, New York, Bradbury Press, 6 vols., 1980.

Publications for Adults

Plays

The Gentle Avalanche (produced Farnham, Surrey, 1962; London, 1963). London, French, 1964.
Another Round (produced Farnham, Surrey, 1962). London, French, 1963.
Return Ticket (produced Farnham, Surrey, 1962; London, 1965). London, English Theatre Guild, 1966.
The Scallop Shell (produced Farnham, Surrey, 1963).
Flight of a Lone Sparrow (produced Farnham, Surrey, 1965).
The Scourging of Matthew Barrow (produced Leicester, 1966).
Tinker's Curse (produced Nottingham, 1968). Published in *Plays of the Year 34,* London, Elek, 1968; New York, Ungar, 1969.
We Never Went to Cheddar Gorge (televised 1968; produced Perth, 1969).
The Illusionist (produced Perth, 1969).
National Trust (produced Perth, 1970).
The Deliverance of Fanny Blaydon (produced Perth, 1971).

Television Plays: *Dead Set at Dream Boy,* 1965; *We Never Went to Cheddar Gorge,* 1968; *The Story Teller,* 1969; *A Memory of Two Loves,* 1972; *Conversations in the Dark,* 1972; *Mr. Oddy,* from story by Hugh Walpole, 1975; *The Orsini Emeralds,* from story by G.B. Stern, 1975; *Emmerdale Farm* series, 1975-77; *Philip,* 1979; *Going Back,* 1979; *Kids,* 1979; *The Red Signal,* from a work by Agatha Christie, 1982; *Dearly Beloved,* 1984; *The Christmas Tree,* from novel by Jennifer Johnston, 1986; *Dreams Lost, Dreams Found,* from work by Pamela Wallace, 1987.

* * *

William Corlett works at the boundary between teenage and adult fiction. His first novel, *The Gate of Eden,* appeared before publishers began using labels such as "Young Adult" to categorise novels that seem suitable for mid to late adolescence. Classification at this level is often difficult. Corlett's writing does not fit easily in such a slot, despite the usual presence of young adult characters. They are not late adolescents preoccupied by their own world, but people in a larger world of children and adults. Corlett's novels are serious and "adult" in a way that defies attempts to categorise possible readership.

The Gate of Eden is, apparently, a simple story about a teenage schoolboy who makes friends with an eccentric retired bachelor school teacher. This is the boy's first step beyond the confines of home and school. By the end of the book the boy has found his first girlfriend and rejects the old man in favour of the young woman. But there is much more. The character of the vulnerable old man is presented as vividly as that of the boy, the unnamed first-person narrator, who tells the story—recalling, quoting from letters, and commenting on his own memories and failings—long after the events. The balance of interest between youth and old age is equal and the point of view is strictly adult, tinged with bittersweet nostalgia and regret, poetically told.

Taken on its own *The Gate of Eden,* with its symbolic title, poetic writing, vigorous dialogue, compelling characterisation, and penetrating insight, compares very well with other outstanding books about complex relationships between teenagers and old people, such as John Branfield's *The Fox in Winter* and Penelope Lively's *The House in Norham Gardens,* where ideas about the start of adult life are balanced by thoughts of old age and death. But Corlett's first novel is actually the beginning of a trilogy.

The Land Beyond takes the unnamed young man through the aftermath of a three-year relationship with a different girl. Although the end of an affair can be of interest to teenagers, all the characters are adult. The narrative progresses through several different styles and levels: stream of consciousness, notebook, diary, TV screenplay, meditation, memory, a time-slip narrative as the man explores the temples at Delphi, and metaphysical speculation about life. There is a rebirth of the individual, framed within a confrontation or mutual haunting between the young man and the young Greek who was the model for the famous statue of the charioteer of Delphi. This use of time fantasy and living mythology links the book with the recently popular children's genre of a modern story haunted by the presence of ancient mythology. However the experimental nature of the writing demands far more than is usual with children's books.

Return to the Gate presents the unnamed narrator as an old man, surviving alone in an era of political collapse and economic scarcity. The old man meets a young woman. They establish a tentative relationship and help each other try to cope with the violence of the authoritarian society they live in. This subtly reworks the structure of relationships in *The Gate of Eden.* Although the book can be described as a kind of political science fiction, its characters are concerned to find some purpose in being alive, some way to make sense of life, and to know who they are and what they value. Corlett's vision is religious, broadly and humanely, rather than political.

After the trilogy, Corlett has worked on a more compressed scale. *The Dark Side of the Moon* interweaves three stories: an innocent(?) school boy is kidnapped as a philosophical protest against confining social values; a policeman tries to investigate the kidnapping; and an astronaut breaks down on the first trip behind the moon. Each story reflects on the other, and each raises serious questions about the meaning of life, madness, identity, good and evil, and social decay—questions which cannot reasonably be answered but deserve to be considered. The boy and the policeman are well realised, but the moon story does not integrate convincingly, despite its metaphorical significance. Much of the book's poetic speculative questioning resembles Corlett's non-fictional *Questions* series on religions. It is a brave experiment, deserving comparison with John Fowles's *The Collector* and William Golding's *Free Fall.*

Bloxworth Blue (named after a species of rare butterfly), much less experimental in prose style, explores many of Corlett's usual themes through five related strands of story. There is a medieval legend of two imps and Lincoln Cathedral, memories of the very elderly uncle, marital crisis of the mother, first sexual encounter of the daughter, and adventures of the son as he explores the cathedral, relives the legend, and discovers his uncle's bitter secret. Guilt, death, love, betrayal, murder, pain, lust, youth, old age, time, and God: a strong mixture—but "children's," "Young Adult," or adult? At times there is more telling than showing, but counterbalanced by insight and honesty, strong dialogue, complex emotion, and a range of interesting characters.

Corlett may not be to everyone's taste, but his individual voice, intelligence, and undeniable skill are always challenging and he deserves serious attention.

—John Gough

COWLEY, (Cassia) Joy

Nationality: New Zealander. **Born:** 7 August 1936. **Education:** Girls' High School, Palmerston North, Wellington. **Family:** Married Malcolm Mason (died 1985); two daughters and two sons (from a previous marriage); remarried, 1989. **Career:** Pharmacist's apprentice, 1953-56. **Awards:** New Zealand Buckland Literary Award, 1970; New Zealand Literary Achievement Award, 1980; AIM Children's Book Award (picture book) 1982, 1996, (fiction) 1992; New Zealand Children's Book of the Year award, 1983, 1993; Russell Clark Award, 1985; New Zealand Commemoration Medal, 1990; Order of the British Empire (for services to Children's Literature), 1992; Margaret Mahy Lecture Award, 1993. **Address:** c/o Shortland Publications, P.O. Box 56-133, Auckland 3, New Zealand; Fish Bay, Kenepuru, RD2, Picton 7372, New Zealand.

Publications for Children

Fiction

The Duck in the Gun, illustrated by Edward Sorel. New York, Doubleday, 1969.
The Silent One, illustrated by Hermann Greissle. New York, Knopf, 1981; London, Methuen, 1982.
The Terrible Taniwha of Timberditch, illustrated by Rodney McRae. Auckland, Oxford University Press, 1982.
Two of a Kind: Stories, with Mona Williams, illustrated by Jane Amos. Upper Hutt, Blackberry Press, 1984.
Salmagundi, illustrated by Philip Webb. Auckland and Oxford, Oxford University Press, 1985.
Captain Felonius, illustrated by Elizabeth Fuller. Auckland, Shortland, 1986.
The Lucky Feather, illustrated by Philip Webb. Auckland, Shortland, 1986.
My Tiger (stories), illustrated by Jan van der Voo. Auckland, Shortland, 1986.
Pawprints in the Butter: A Collection of Cats, illustrated by New Zealand Children. Wellington, Mallinson Rendel, 1991.
Bow Down, Shadrach, illustrated by Robyn Belton. Auckland, Hodder & Stoughton, 1991; Bothell, Washington, Wright Group, 1996.
Happy Birthday, Mrs. Felonius, illustrated by Trevor Pye. Norwood, Australia, Omnibus, 1992.
The Day of the Rain, illustrated by Bob Kerr. Wellington, Mallinson Rendel, 1993.
Little Unicorn Library: The Park Street Playground, Robotwalk, illustrated by Jan Van der Voo. Beecroft, New South Wales, Custom Book Company, 1993.
The Screaming Mean Machine, illustrated by David Cox. Auckland and New York: Scholastic, 1993.
Beep and the Telephone, illustrated by Rob De Tombe. Wellington, Telecom New Zealand, 1994.
Beyond the River. Auckland, Scholastic, 1994.
The Day of the Snow, illustrated by Bob Kerr. Wellington, Mallison Rendel, 1994.
Gladly Here I Come. Auckland, Viking, 1994; Bothell, Washington, Wright Group, 1996.
Song of the River, illustrated by Elizabeth Fuller. Auckland, Scholastic, and Bothell, Washington, Wright Group, 1994.
The Cheese Trap, illustrated by Linda McClelland. Auckland, Scholastic, 1995.
Babysitter Bother, Chicken Dinners, and *Croack-a-roo-roo-roo* ("The Happy Hens Series"), illustrated by Yvonne Sutherland. Auckland, Scholastic, 1995.
The Day of the Wind, illustrated by Trevor Pye. Wellington, Mallison Rendel, 1995.
The Mouse Bride, illustrated by David Christiana. Auckland and New York, Scholastic, 1995.
Brave Mama Puss, Papa Puss to the Rescue, Mabel and the Marvellous Meow, and *Oscar in Danger* ("Puss Quartet"). Auckland, Reed, 1995-96.
The Sea Daughter, illustrated by Manu Smith. Auckland, Scholastic, 1995.
Tulevai and the Sea, illustrated by Manu Smith. Auckland, Scholastic, 1995.
Gracias the Thanksgiving Turkey, illustrated by Joe Cepeda. New York, Scholastic, 1996.
Nicketty-Nacketty-Noo-Noo-Noo, illustrated by Tracey Moroney. Auckland, Scholastic, 1996.
Snake and Lizard. Bothell, Washington, Wright Group, 1996.
Elephant Rhymes, illustrated by Brent Putze. Auckland, Scholastic, 1997.
The Great Bamboozle, illustrated by Philip Webb. Auckland, Scholastic, 1997.
A Haunting Tale, illustrated by Philip Webb. Auckland, Scholastic, 1997.
The Hitchhikers: Stories from Joy Cowley. New York, Scholastic, 1997.
Singing Down the Rain, illustrated by Jan Spivey Gilchrist. New York, HarperCollins, 1997.
Ticket to the Sky Dance. Auckland, Viking, 1997.
The Bump, illustrated by Linda McClelland. Auckland, Scholastic, 1997.
Agapanthus Hum and the Eyeglasses, illustrated by Jennifer Plecas. New York, Philomel, 1998.

Nonfiction

Write On!: Joy Cowley's Guide for Young Authors, illustrated by Trevor Pye. Auckland, Scholastic, 1994; published as *A Guide For Young Authors,* illustrated by Mits Katayama, Bothell, Washington, Wright Group, 1995.
Joy Cowley Answers Kids' Questions. Auckland, Scholastic, 1995.

Readers

Fish in the Trough, A New Friend, Johnny's Guitar, The Fire-Fighters, The Meeting House, Wendy Makes a Poi, all illustrated by Nancy Parker. 6 vols., Wellington, Kea Press, 1968; as *The Tu[illegible] and Sis Books,* 6 vols., Wellington, Price Milburn, 1977.
With June Melser, "Story Chest Read-Together Books": *Mrs. Wishy-Washy, Smarty Pants, The Big Toe, Boo-Hoo, Grandpa Grandpa*

Hairy Bear, The Hungry Giant, In a Dark Dark Wood, Lazy Mary, Obadiah!, One Cold Wet Night, Poor Old Polly, Sing a Song, Three Little Ducks, Woosh!, Yes Ma'am, The Red Rose, To Town, Dan the Flying Man, The Farm Concert, The Jigaree, Meanies, The Monster's Party, and *Who Will Be My Mother?,* illustrated by Elizabeth Fuller, Murray Grimsdale, Philip Webb, Martin Bailey, Andrew Reid, David Cowe, Deirdre Gardiner, Jenny Cochrane, Christine Ross, Jo Davies, Gary Hebley, Rosemary Turner, Annie Dickeson, Isabel Lowe, and Rita Parkinson. 24 vols., Auckland, Shortland, 1980-83; 24 vols., Leeds, Arnold Wheaton, 1982-83; Bothell, Washington, Wright Group, 1988-90.

With June Melser, "Story Chest Books": *The Birthday Cake, The Dragon, A Terrible Fright, A Barrel of Gold, Clever Mr. Brown, Hungry Monster, Jack-in-the-Box, The Kick-a-Lot Shoes, The Pirates, Wet Grass, Where Is My Spider?, Yum and Yuk, Captain Bumble, Countdown, A Day in Town, The Big Tease, Cat on the Roof, The Ghost and the Sausage, Grandma's Stick, Hatupatu and the Birdwoman, Little Brother's Haircut, The Sunflower That Went FLOP, Tell-Tale,* and *Sun Smile,* illustrated by Philip Webb, Martin Bailey, David Cowe, Deirdre Gardiner, Glenda Jones, Murray Grimsdale, Annie Dickeson, Robyn Kahukiwa, Helen Humphries, Sherryl Jordan, Isabel Lowe, and Christine Ross. 24 vols., Auckland, Shortland, 1981-82; 24 vols., Leeds, Arnold Wheaton, 1982; Bothell, Washington, Wright Group, 1989-94.

With June Melser, "Story Chest Ready-Set-Go Books": *The Bee, The Chocolate Cake, Come with Me, Copy-Cat, Flying, I Want an Ice Cream, Little Pig, Lost, My Home, Plop!, Round and Round, Splosh, To New York, Who Lives Here?, Where Are They Going?, Who's Going to Lick the Bowl?, Horace, The Night Train, The Pumpkin, Rum-Tum-Tum, Sleeping Out, Too Big for Me, What a Mess!,* and *Look for Me,* illustrated by Christine Ross, Robyn Belton, Deirdre Gardiner, Murray Grimsdale, Jenni Webb, Philip Webb, Isabel Lowe, David Cowe, Martin Bailey, Annie Dickeson, Robyn Kahukiwa, Lynette Vondruska, and Rodney McRae. 24 vols., Auckland, Shortland, 1981-82; 24 vols., Leeds, Arnold Wheaton, 1982; Bothell, Washington, Wright Group, 1990.

With June Melser and Margaret Mahy, "Story Chest Books": *Cooking Pot, Fast and Funny, Roly-Poly, Sing to the Moon, Tiddalik,* illustrated by Deirdre Gardiner, Lynette Vondruska, Jo Davies, Isabel Lowe, Annie Dickeson, Philip Webb, and others. 5 vols., Auckland, Shortland, and Leeds, Arnold Wheaton, 1982.

"Story Box Books": *The Pie Thief, The Tale of the Cook, The Trader from Currumbin, The War of the Winds,* and *Poor Old Robot,* illustrated by Robyn Belton, David Cowe, and Jan van der Voo. First volume, Leeds, Arnold Wheaton, 1982; 5 vols., Auckland, Shortland, 1982-85.

"Story Chest Ready-to-Read Books": *Number One, The Biggest Cake in the World, Fasi Sings; Fasi's Fish, Greedy Cat, Our Teacher Miss Pool, Rain Rain, Words, I'm the King of the Mountain, Rosie at the Zoo, The Wild Wet Wellington Wind, Did You Say Five?, The Smile,* and *Where Is Miss Pool?,* illustrated by Jill McDonald, Diane Perham, Murray Grimsdale, Robyn Belton, Nina Price, Lesley Moyes, Dick Frizzell, Christine Ross, Clare Bowes, and Penny Newman. 13 vols., Wellington, Department of Education School Publications Branch, 1982-87.

With June Melser, "Story Chest Get Ready Books": *The Bicycle, The Big Hill, Feet, The Ghost, Go Go Go, Houses, If You Meet a Dragon, In the Mirror, A Monster Sandwich, Mouse, Night-Time, On a Chair, Painting, The Party, The Storm,* and *The Tree-House,* illustrated by Debbie Britten, Rita Parkinson, Sandra Morris, Robyn Belton, Rodney McRae, Elizabeth Fuller, Deirdre Gardiner, Glenda Jones, Sherryl Jordan, Isabel Lowe, Annie Dickeson, Jo Davies, and Rachel Waddy. 16 vols., Leeds, Arnold Wheaton, 1983; Bothell, Washington, Wright Group, 1990.

The Fierce Little Woman and the Wicked Pirate, illustrated by Jo Davies. Auckland, Shortland, 1984.

Old Tuatara, illustrated by Clare Bowes. Wellington, Department of Education School Publications Branch, 1983; as *Old Lizard,* Melbourne, Nelson, 1985.

"Jellybeans Books": *Don't Wake the Baby, The Kangaroo from Woolloomooloo, Lavender the Library Cat, Let's Get a Pet, The Little Brown House, The Magician's Lunch, Morning Dance, The Most Scary Ghost, Mouse Monster, The Plants of My Aunt, Ten Loopy Caterpillars, The Terrible Armadillo, The Train That Ran Away, The Yukadoos, Monster, The Amazing Popple Seed, The Bull and the Matador, Cow Up a Tree, The Difficult Day, The Gumby Shop, A Handy Dragon, The Horrible Thing with Hairy Feet, Mr. Beep, Boggity-Bog, Do-Whacky-Do, The Shoe Grabber, A Silly Old Story, A Walk with Grandpa, The Wonder-Whizz, The Wild Woolly Child, I Saw A Dinosaur, The Hat Sale, Papa's Spaghetti, The Springtime Rock And Roll, Talk, Talk, Talk,* and *Woolly, Woolly,* illustrated by Elizabeth Fuller, Philip Webb, Rodney McRae, Jo Davies, Murray Grimsdale, Sherryl Jordan, David Cowe, Mary Davy, Rita Parkinson, Jan van der Voo, Kelvin Hawley, Martin Bailey, Ian McNee, Marie Low, and Deborah Fletcher. First 23 vols. published Leeds, Arnold Wheaton, 1986-87; 36 vols., Auckland, Shortland, 1985-89.

Birth of the Terrible. Auckland, Shortland, 1986.

The King's Pudding, illustrated by Martin Bailey. Auckland, Shortland, 1986.

Turnips for Dinner, illustrated by Jan van der Voo. Auckland, Shortland, 1986; Leeds, Arnold Wheaton, 1987.

Mrs. Grindy's Shoes, illustrated by Val Biro. Auckland, Shortland, and Leeds, Arnold Wheaton, 1986.

"Sunshine Books": *Yuk Soup, Baby Gets Dressed, Big and Little, Buzzing Flies, Dinner!, Down to Town, A Hug Is Warm, Huggles' Breakfast, Huggles Can Juggle, Huggles Goes Away, I Am a Bookworm, I Can Fly, I Can Jump, I Love My Family, Ice Cream, Little Brother, The Long Long Tail, Major Jump, My Home, My Puppy, Our Granny, Our Street, The Race, Scat! Said the Cat, Shark in a Sack, Shoo!, Snap!, Uncle Buncle's House, Up in a Tree, What Is a Huggles?, When Itchy Witchy Sneezes, Along Comes Jake, Bread, Come for a Swim, The Cooking Pot, Dad's Headache, Don't You Laugh at Me!, The Giant's Boy, Good for You, Goodbye Lucy, I'm Bigger Than You!, Let's Have a Swim!, Little Car, The Monkey Bridge, Mr. Grump, Mr. Whisper, My Boat, My Sloppy Tiger, Noise, Nowhere and Nothing, Old Grizzly, One Thousand Currant Buns, The Poor Sore Paw, Ratty-Tatty, Red Socks and Yellow Socks, The Seed, Spider Spider, The Terrible Tiger, The Tiny Woman's Coat, Wake Up, Mum!, What Would You Like?, Where Are You Going Aja Rose?, The Wind Blows Strong, 31111002798708, Boggywooga, The Dippy Dinner Drippers, In the Middle of the Night, Mrs Muddle Mud-Puddle, The Person from Planet X, Bogle's Card, Jim's Trumpet, A Magician's House, Mr Fixit, Rubbish, Sloppy Tiger and the Party, Sloppy Tiger Bedtime,* and *When the Cookernup Store Burned Down,* illustrated by Rodney McRae, Robyn Belton, Miranda Witford, Rita Parkinson, Judith Cowley, Isabel Lowe, Philip Webb, Sandy

Nightingale, Jill Allpress, Madeline Beasley, Jan van der Voo, Susan Moxley, Annie Dickeson, Korky Paul, Val Biro, Wendy Hodder, Lynn Breeze, Terry Burton, Nick Price, Martin Bailey, Eric Kincaid, Peter Stevenson, Astrid Matijasevic, Jeff Fowler, Michelle Stuart, John Francis, Rosemary Murphy, Vicki Smillie-McItoull, Robert Roennfeldt, Deirdre Gardiner, Mary Davy, John Bennett, Terry Burton, and Mark Sofilas. 77 vols., Auckland, Heinemann, 1986-89; Bothell, Washington, Wright Group, 1986-90.

"Windmill Books": *Growing, The Little Red Hen, My Little Brother, Splish Splash!, Where Can We Put an Elephant?, Where's the Egg Cup, Lucy's Sore Knee,* and *My Wonderful Chair,* illustrated by Miranda Witford, Wendy Hodder, Judith Trevelyan, Dawn Johnston, Dick Frizzell, Jan van der Voo, and Trevor Pye. 8 vols., Auckland, Heinemann, 1986-88.

The Train Ride Story, illustrated by Val Biro. Auckland, Shortland, and Leeds, Arnold Wheaton, 1987.

Giant on the Bus, illustrated by Ian McNee. Auckland, Shortland, 1987.

Seventy Kilometers from Ice Cream, photographs by Winton Cleal. Wellington, Department of Education School Publications Branch, 1987.

"Cocky's Circle Little Books": *Timothy Flynn, Tom's Trousers,* and *When The Moon Was Blue,* illustrated by Jenni Webb, Lise Knowles, Kelvin Hawley. Artarmon, New South Wales, Advertiser Magazines, 1988-89.

"Interaction Books": *Far Out* and *The White Horse,* illustrated by James Cowley and Fraser Williamson. Auckland, Shortland, 1988.

"Ready to Read Books": *Greedy Cat* and *Greedy Cat Is Hungry,* illustrated by Robyn Belton. Wellington, School Publications, Department of Education, 1988.

My Bad Mood, illustrated by Ruth Kiel. Wellington, Highgate/Price Milburn, 1989.

"Cocky's Circle Little Books": *The Things I Like, Cow Up a Tree, Do-Whacky-Do, Monster, Across the Nullarbor, The Gonna Bird, The Yellow Tractor,* and *The Wild Woolly Child,* illustrated by Philip Webb, Rita Parkinson, and Martin Bailey. North Sydney, New South Wales, Murdoch Books, 1990-95.

"Literacy Links": *The Cabbage Princess, Yellow Overalls, Baba Yaga: A Traditional Russian Tale,* and *A Froggy Tale,* illustrated by Trevor Pye, Robyn Belton, Sam Thiewes, and Clive Taylor. Auckland, Shortland, 1990, 1996.

"Ready to Read Books": *Rosie at the Zoo, Uncle Tim's Sleep, Woolly Sally, Hoiho's Chicks, Pukelo Morning, The Shag Goes Fishing, The Water Boatman, The New Cat, Robber Cat, Bedtime Cat, What Does Greedy Cat Like?,* and *Off Goes the Hose!,* illustrated by Judith Kunzle, Sharon Murdoch, Dean Schneider, Nic Bishop, Allan Hope, Tim Galloway, Robyn Belton, Jennifer Lautusi, Penny Newman, and Christine Ross. Wellington, Learning Media, 1991-97.

Stolen Food: A Maori Legend, illustrated by Murray Grimsdale. Wellington, Learning Media, 1993.

"The Story Basket series": *Who Spilled The Beans?, Wishy-Washy Day, Ballyhoo!, Cats, Cats, Cats, Greedy Cat's Breakfast, Kitzikuba, The Meanies Came to School, Mr. Beakman's Deli, The Pirate Feast,* and *Water! Water!,* illustrated by Diana Magnuson, Elizabeth Fuller, Sandra Shields, David Lund, Laura Lydecker, Lidia Taranovic, and Jean Pidgeon. Bothell, Washington, Wright Group, 1993-95.

Ten Happy Elephants, illustrated by Philip Webb. British Virgin Islands, Wendy Pye, 1995.

"Country Kids series": *The Boomy Buzzer, Crabs, Egg Stuff, The Island, Leaves, Playhouse, Rabbit Hunt,* and *Running Away,* illustrated by Jenny Scown. Auckland, Heinemann Primary, 1996.

From Sky to Sea, illustrated by Nic Bishop. Wellington, Learning Media, 1996.

"Get-Ready Books": *The Boogie-Woogie Man: A Play, Brenda's Birthday, The Bridge, Chick's Walk, Dan Gets Dressed, The Escalator, Fishing, The Gifts, The "Gotcha" Box, Green Grass, Halloween, Happy Birthday, Frog: A Play, How to Make a Hot Dog, Ice Cream Stick, Jump, Jump, Kangaroo, Look Out, Dan!, Microscope, Mouse Train, Mrs. Wishy-Washy's Tub, My Picture, The Nest, New Pants, Rat's Funny Story, Salad, Shoo, Fly!, Snowman, Sunflower Seeds, The Surprise, Swing, Tick-Tock, Waiting,* and *What Can Jigarees Do?,* illustrated by Robyn Belton, Jennifer Lautusi, Wade Shotter, Annie Hayward, Christine Ross, Sandra Cammell, Tony Stoddard, Philip Webb, Jan Van der Voo, George Baxter, Chris Norfolk, Brent Putze, Kathryn Pond, Ian McNee, Elizabeth Fuller, Andrew Coffey, Bryan Pollard, Murray Grimsdale, Damon Keen, Martin Bailey, Fred Ooms, Richard Hoit, Sarah Irvine, Lise Knowles, Margaret Power, Annette Hislop, and Glenda Jones. Auckland, Shortland Publications, 1997.

"Ready-Set-Go Books": *Barn Dance, The Bears' Picnic, The Best Children in the World, Blueberry Muffins: A Two-Part Chant, Chicken for Dinner, The Clown in the Well, Dr. Boondoggle, Ducks, Ebenezer and the Sneeze, The Fantastic Cake, Fire and Water, The Giggle Box, Gulp!, How Many Hot Dogs?, How to Make Can Stilts, The Hungry Giant's Lunch, I Love Chickens: A Play, The Lift, Little Hearts, Little Meanie's Lunch: A Play, My Brown Cow, My Mum and Dad, Pet Shop, Roberto's Smile, Roy G. Biv, Skating, Teeth, Tittle-Tattle Goose, Umbrella, Valentine's Day, Where is Skunk?,* and *Who Can See the Camel?*) illustrated by Brent Chambers, Gavin Bishop, Marjorie Scott, Jo Davies, Christine Ross, Christine Hansen, Kelvin Hawley, Helen Humphries, Philip Webb, Tim Tripp, Rodney McRae, Rita Parkinson, Jenni Webb, Anthony Sang, Chris Norfolk, Fraser Williamson, Sandra Cammell, Brian Pollard, Marjorie Scott, John Hurford, Mary Davy, Mike Spoor, Martin Bailey, Boris Pokos, and Kyle Graeme. Auckland, Shortland Publications, 1997.

Publications for Adults

Novels

Nest in a Falling Tree. New York, Doubleday, and London, Secker and Warburg, 1967.

Man of Straw. New York, Doubleday, 1970; London, Secker and Warburg, 1971.

Of Men and Angels. New York, Doubleday, 1972; London, Hodder and Stoughton, 1973.

The Mandrake Root. New York, Doubleday, 1975; London, Hodder and Stoughton, 1976.

The Growing Season. New York, Doubleday, 1978; London, Hodder and Stoughton, 1979.

Short Stories

Heart Attack and Other Stories. Auckland, Hodder and Stoughton 1985; London, Hodder and Stoughton, 1986.

The Complete Short Stories. Auckland, Harper Collins, 1997.

Other

Aotearoa Psalms: Prayers of a New People, illustrated by Terry Coles. Wellington, Catholic Supplies, 1989.
Whole Learning: Whole Child. Bothell, Washington, Wright Group, 1994.
Psalms Down-Under, illustrated by Terry Coles. Wellington, Catholic Supplies, 1996.
Everything 'Round Us Is Praise: Extraordinary Prayers for Ordinary Days, photographs by Terry Coles. Notre Dame, Indiana, Ave Maria Press, 1997.

Editor, with Thelma France, *Women Writers of New Zealand 1932-1982.* Wellington, Colonial, 1982.

*

Media Adaptations: *Carry Me Back* (film based on a short story), 1982; *The Night Digger* (film adaptations of *Nest in a Falling Tree*); *The Silent One* (film); *Captain Castor* (sound recording), Department of Education, Audio Production Unit, 1988; *Uncle Joe* (sound recording), Audio Production Unit, Dept. of Education, 1988; *The Yukadoos; Ten Loopy Caterpillars; The Kangaroo from Woolloomooloo* (video recording), Shortland Publications, 1988; *The Biggest Cake in the World* (sound recording), Learning Media, 1989, *Did You Say Fire?* (sound recording), Learning Media, 1989; *Greedy Cat is Hungry* (sound recording), Learning Media, 1989; *The Lost Tune* (sound recording), Learning Media, 1989; *Nana's Spectacles* (sound recording), Learning Media, 1989; *Old Tuatara* (sound recording), Learning Media, 1990; *The Wild Wet Wellington Wind* (sound recording), Learning Media, 1991; *Our Teacher, Miss Pool ; Where is Miss Pool?* (sound recording), Learning Media, 1991; *Flowers* (sound recording), Learning Media, 1991; *The Sea Of Peace Stories* (sound recording), Radio New Zealand, Replay Radio, c. 1992-1993; *Uncle Timi's Sleep* (sound recording), Learning Media, 1996.

Joy Cowley comments:

Who says you live only once? As often as you pick up a book and enter it, you live another life. Books enlarge our experience of ourselves, others, and the worked in a way that can never be measured. We grow through reading. And we are hugely disadvantaged if we can't read.

As a child, I was a slow learner. Because my early reading experiences were dull and difficult, I was nearly a failed reader. At nine, I discovered real stories and from then on, my life changed. Reading was not about dull words, lists, and boring exercises. Reading was about excitement and adventure!

My new love of reading flowed into writing. By the time I was twenty-two I was having short stories published in magazines. But in the following years, while I was writing adult stories and novels, I was aware they my own children were expected to learn to read from the same kind of dull and difficult school texts that I had been given. I was aware that children were being taught to read and to hate reading at the same time, because the experience was not enjoyable.

For the last 30 years I have lived with a commitment that borders on obsession, to give children easy and exciting stories in well-illustrated and well-produced books that will make learning to read a pleasure instead of a boring chore. My philosophy of learning has not been borrowed from any of the academic reading stances—e.g. Basal/Phonics/Whole Language—but from the needs of the child. Thirty years of working with teachers and students in classrooms in many countries have helped me understand stages of child development and ability, child interest and innovation. All the stories I write are tested in classrooms by teachers and students and if they do not work, they are trashed. A story must work on several levels: it must be a real story, with a beginning, middle, and ending. It must entertain. It must relate to the child's world rather than to some adult concept of what the world should be. It must include skills and strategies that the teacher can use to teach word and letter sounds and language structure at the appropriate level. It must be open to the child's innovation, to be a springboard or model for the child's own creative story.

We know that we never learn information in a vacuum. All learning takes place in an emotional context. When the first reading experiences are pleasurable, 50 years later, that pleasure will still be felt every time we pass a bookshop or library.

* * *

With nearly five hundred books to her credit, Joy Cowley has proven herself one of the most prolific, as well as one of the most popular, writers for children working in New Zealand today. And with her work translated into Japanese, Swedish, Maori, Samoan, and even Tokelauan and Rarotongan, her readership has grown far beyond her original English-speaking audience.

Cowley had her first stories (for adults) published in the New Zealand *Listener* in the 1960s. Since then she has published five novels for adults and a book of collected short stories. This body of writing is significant and valuable. But her most important contributions to literature have come in her works for children. Not only has she had her work published in the public arena, but she has also made a tremendous contribution the educational field, with a wealth of series directed specifically to schools.

Cowley has said that "Reading should be 'magic.' Humour is valuable (children can't be tense when they are laughing) and also rhyme, rhythm, alliteration, etc. The two crimes in early reading are giving children books which are dull, and books which are difficult." The author follows her own advice exactly in the scores of stories she has written for children.

The Duck in the Gun first appeared in an American edition in 1969 and did not receive the attention it deserved until the 1984 New Zealand publication illustrated by Robyn Belton. The superb pictures underline the comic irony of a story in which the foolishness of war is gently derided.

In a picture book designed for older children, *Salmagundi,* the tone is sharper and the satire more direct. Even after the rival arms manufacturers, Dr. Foster and Major Brassblow, have replaced their factories with trees, gardens, and playgrounds their wickedness lives on.

The Terrible Taniwha of Timberditch goodhumouredly dramatises Josephine's search for the mysterious Maori monster, and her discovery of the mythical creatures of other countries such as trolls, gorgons, and the Loch Ness monster.

Pirates are the protagonists of *The Lucky Feather* and *The Fierce Little Woman and the Wicked Pirate.* In the first, Captain Castor discovers after a nasty accident that he needs no talisman but only his own independent judgement to keep himself out of trouble. The delightfully fierce little woman who lives in a cottage on the end of a jetty knits socks for sailors and plays her bagpipes to the seagulls. When the pirate finds humility, and she finds love, they live happily ever after.

Short stories in a volume shared with Mona Williams entitled *Two of a Kind* and the novel *The Silent One* demonstrate Cowley's deep, compassionate, and realistic knowledge of human values and behavior. *The Silent One* deserves the critical acclaim it has received. Set on a tropical island in the South Pacific, the story describes the ordeal of the deaf child Jonasi. Ostracised by the people of the village because of their superstition, he has only the love of his stepmother, and of the chief and his son. He spends most of his time fishing in the lagoon where he discovers and makes friends with the mysterious white turtle, who is the spirit of age-old wisdom and of light and grace. The story is mythic in quality, in style poetic, and simple and direct in the telling.

The bulk of Cowley's work during the 1980s and 1990s has focused on readers for educational publishers. But she continues to keep her hand in the trade book field, proving equally adept at writing for children of all ages. Her picture books include four titles in the "Happy Hens" series, gently humorous tales based on the characters created by Yvonne Sutherland. *The Screaming Mean Machine* tells of a young girl finally big enough to ride the scariest roller coaster who isn't sure she's brave enough to climb aboard. Cowley's three "Day" books (*The Day of the Rain, The Day of the Snow,* and *The Day of the Wind*) feature the fantastic adventures of the students in Miss Mcmillan's class. Laughter abounds in *The Cheese Trap,* the story of two mice determined to get some tasty cheese and the old grey cat who devises a cunning plan to catch them, as well as in *The Puss Quartet,* four tales about a family of felines plagued by catnappers, robot rats, and alley cat gangs. *Nicketty-Nacketty-Noo-Noo-Noo* relates the adventures of an ogre called Gobbler Magoo who lives in a swamp and captures a maker of good tasty stew.

Cowley's more serious side comes into play in her folktales. *The Sea Daughter* is a retelling of the story of Hinemoana, daughter of the sea, who falls in love with Kahu the fisherman. To stay with him she must promise never to speak of who she is, or the curse of the sea will fall upon her. Tulevai's mother proves her love is stronger than the sea and the wind and rescues her son from their clutches in *Tulevai and the Sea. The Mouse Bride,* frustrated by her own weakness, is determined to marry the strongest husband in the world; her quest to find him proves her stronger than she thinks.

Among her picture books with contemporary settings are *Gracias, The Thanksgiving Turkey,* the story of a bird given to New York City-dweller Miguel by his father to fatten for the holiday table. Problems result when Miguel becomes attached to the endearing turkey. In *Singing Down the Rain,* a drought has made the town's adults, usually friendly and kind, all "scritchy with each other." Arguments ensue until a mysterious woman in a pickup arrives, claiming to specialize in rainsong.

Cowley has also followed up on the success of her early novel, *The Silent One,* with infrequent, but well received, works for older readers, books filled with suspense and adventure. *Bow Down, Shadrach,* winner of the New Zealand Children's Book of the Year award, tells of a young girl who must rescue her horse, Shadrach, after discovering that the "Rest Home for Aged Equestrian Friends" where she has placed her aged Clydesdale is not what its owners portrayed it to be. Its sequel, *Glady Here I Come,* features Shadrach's daughter, Gladly, and the problems she and her owner encounter when an underprivileged boy named Eden comes to stay with their family. And in *Ticket to the Sky Dance,* Shog and his twin sister Jancie are street kids signed up by an international modelling agency. The twins can't believe their luck, but soon become suspicious of what is happening in the agency's building. The short story format is also one Cowley has mastered, as can be seen in *The Hitchhikers,* a book of horror stories featuring young adult protagonists.

Though nonfiction has not played a major role in her work, Cowley has penned several titles in which she shares her knowledge of the craft of writing with her ever curious audience. *Write On! Joy Cowley's Guide for Young Authors* is a guide to the main aspects of story writing, including punctuation and grammar, structure, getting ideas, editing, and final presentation. And in *Questions Kids Ask Joy Cowley,* the author describes her life and work by answering some of the many questions that children have asked her during her long career.

Cowley comes to her writing from a background of varied experiences. As a writer she is gifted and committed. Her imagination, her depth of understanding, her sense of fun, and her exhilaration give her books lasting qualities.

—Tom Fitzgibbon, updated by Jackie C. Horne

CRESSWELL, Helen

Nationality: British. **Born:** Nottinghamshire, 11 July 1934. **Education:** Nottingham Girls' High School; King's College, University of London, B.A. (honours) in English 1955. **Family:** Married Brian Rowe in 1962; two daughters. **Career:** Worked as a literary assistant, fashion buyer, and teacher. **Awards:** Gold Rose Chicago Award, 1988, for *The Haunted School*; BAFTA nomination, 1991, for the *Five Children and It* series, and 1996, for *The Demon Headmaster.* **Agent:** A.M. Heath, 79 St. Martin's Lane, London WC2N 4AA, England. **Address:** Old Church Farm, Eakring, Newark, Nottinghamshire NG22 0DA, England.

Publications for Children

Fiction

Sonya-by-the-Shore, illustrated by Robin Jane Wells. London, Dent, 1960.

Jumbo Spencer, illustrated by Clixby Watson. Leicester, Brockhampton Press, 1963; Philadelphia, Lippincott, 1966.

The White Sea Horse, illustrated by Robin Jacques. Edinburgh, Oliver and Boyd, 1964; Philadelphia, Lippincott, 1965; reissued 1997 as *The Little Sea Horse,* illustrated by Jason Cockcroft, London, Hodder, 1995, New York, HarperCollins, 1997 (also issued by HarperCollins as *The Little Sea Pony,* 1997).

Jumbo Back to Nature, illustrated by Leslie Wood. Leicester, Brockhampton Press, 1965.

Pietro and the Mule, illustrated by Maureen Eckersley. Edinburgh, Oliver and Boyd, and Indianapolis, Bobbs Merrill, 1965.

Jumbo Afloat, illustrated by Leslie Wood. Leicester, Brockhampton Press, 1966.

Where the Wind Blows, illustrated by Peggy Fortnum. London, Faber, 1966; New York, Funk and Wagnalls, 1968.

The Piemakers, illustrated by V.H. Drummond. London, Faber 1967; Philadelphia, Lippincott, 1968.

A Day on Big O, illustrated by Shirley Hughes. London, Benn, 1967; Chicago, Follett, 1968.
A Tide for the Captain, illustrated by Robin Jacques. Edinburgh, Oliver and Boyd, 1967.
The Signposters, illustrated by Gareth Floyd. London, Faber, 1968.
Jumbo and the Big Dig, illustrated by Leslie Wood. Leicester, Brockhampton Press, 1968.
The Barge Children, illustrated by Lynette Hemmant. London, Hodder and Stoughton, 1968.
The Sea Piper, illustrated by Robin Jacques. Edinburgh, Oliver and Boyd, 1968.
The Night-Watchmen, illustrated by Gareth Floyd. London, Faber, and New York, Macmillan, 1969.
A Gift from Winklesea, illustrated by Janina Ede. Leicester, Brockhampton Press, 1969.
A Game of Catch, illustrated by Gareth Floyd. London, Chatto Boyd and Oliver, 1969; New York, Macmillan, 1977.
A House for Jones, illustrated by Margaret Gordon. London, Benn, 1969.
The Outlanders, illustrated by Doreen Roberts. London, Faber, 1970.
Rainbow Pavement, illustrated by Shirley Hughes. London, Benn, 1970.
The Wilkses, illustrated by Gareth Floyd. London, BBC Publications, 1970; as *Time Out,* Cambridge, Lutterworth Press, 1987.
The Bird Fancier, illustrated by Renate Meyer. London, Benn, 1971.
Up the Pier, illustrated by Gareth Floyd. London, Faber, 1971; New York, Macmillan, 1972.
The Weather Cat, illustrated by Margery Gill. London, Benn, 1971.
The Beachcombers, illustrated by Errol Le Cain. London, Faber, and New York, Macmillan, 1972.
Bluebirds over Pit Row, illustrated by Richard Kennedy. London, Benn, 1972.
Jane's Policeman, illustrated by Margery Gill. London, Benn, 1972.
The Long Day, illustrated by Margery Gill. London, Benn, 1972.
Roof Fall! illustrated by Richard Kennedy. London, Benn, 1972.
Short Back and Sides, illustrated by Richard Kennedy. London, Benn, 1972.
The Beetle Hunt, illustrated by Anne Knight. London, Longman, 1973.
The Bongleweed, illustrated by Ann Strugnell. London, Faber, 1973; New York, Macmillan, 1974.
The Bower Birds, illustrated by Margery Gill. London, Benn, 1973.
Lizzie Dripping, illustrated by Jenny Thorne. London, BBC Publications, 1973.
Lizzie Dripping by the Sea, illustrated by Faith Jaques. London, BBC Publications, 1974.
Lizzie Dripping and the Little Angel, illustrated by Faith Jaques. London, BBC Publications, 1974.
Lizzie Dripping Again, illustrated by Faith Jaques. London, BBC Publications, 1974.
Two Hoots [*Go to Sea, in the Snow, and the Big Bad Bird, and the King, Play Hide-and-Seek*], illustrated by Martine Blanc. London, Benn, 6 vols., 1974-77; New York, Crown, 6 vols., 1978.
More Lizzie Dripping, illustrated by Faith Jaques. London, BBC Publications, 1974.
Butterfly Chase, illustrated by Margery Gill. London, Kestrel, 1975.
The Winter of the Birds. London, Faber, 1975; New York, Macmillan, 1976.
Donkey Days, illustrated by Shirley Hughes. London, Benn, 1977.
Awful Jack, illustrated by Joanna Stubbs. London, Hodder and Stoughton, 1977.
The Flyaway Kite, illustrated by Bridget Clarke. London, Kestrel, 1979.
My Aunt Polly by the Sea, illustrated by Margaret Gordon. Exeter, Wheaton, 1980.
Dear Shrink. London, Faber, and New York, Macmillan, 1982.
The Secret World of Polly Flint, illustrated by Shirley Felts. London, Faber, 1982; New York, Macmillan, 1984.
Ellie and the Hagwitch, illustrated by Jonathan Heap. London, Hardy, 1984.
Petticoat Smuggler, illustrated by Shirley Bellwood. London, Macmillan, 1985.
Greedy Alice, illustrated by Martin Honeysett. London, Deutsch, 1986.
Whodunnit? illustrated by Caroline Browne. London, Cape, 1986.
Dragon Ride, illustrated by Liz Roberts. London, Kestrel, 1987.
Moondial. London, Faber, and New York, Macmillan, 1987.
Trouble, illustrated by Margaret Chamberlain. London, Gollancz, 1987; New York, Dutton, 1988.
Rosie and the Boredom Eater. London, Heinemann, 1989.
Hokey Pokey Did It! Loughborough, Ladybird, 1989.
Whatever Happened in Winklesea? London, Lutterworth, 1989.
Almost Goodbye Guzzler. London, Black, 1990.
Time Out. New York, Macmillan, 1990.
Meet Posy Bates. London, Bodley Head, and New York, Macmillan, 1990.
Posy Bates Again! London, Bodley Head, and New York, Macmillan, 1991.
Posy Bates and the Bag Lady. London, Bodley Head, and New York, Macmillan, 1993.
The Watchers: A Mystery at Alton Towers. London, Viking, 1993; New York, Macmillan, 1994.
Polly Thumb. Hemel Hempstead, Simon and Schuster, 1994.
Giant! Cambridge, Cambridge University Press, 1994.
Birdspell, illustrated by Aafke Brouwer, London, Puffin, 1993; New York, Macmillan, 1994.
Stonestruck. London, Viking Penguin, 1995.
Mystery at Winklesea, illustrated by Susan Winter. London, Hodder and Stoughton, 1995.
Mister Maggs, illustrated by Jamie Smith. London, Picadilly, 1996.
Bag of Bones. London, Hodder and Stoughton, 1997.
Sophie and the Sea Wolf. London, Hodder and Stoughton, 1997.
The Little Grey Donkey. London, Hodder and Stoughton, 1998.

The Bagthorpe Saga (illustrated by Jill Bennett)

Ordinary Jack. London, Faber, and New York, Macmillan, 1977.
Absolute Zero. London, Faber, and New York, Macmillan, 1978.
Bagthorpes Unlimited. London, Faber, and New York, Macmillan, 1978.
Bagthorpes v. the World. London, Faber, and New York, Macmillan, 1979.
Bagthorpes Abroad. London, Faber, and New York, Macmillan, 1984.
Bagthorpes Haunted. London, Faber, and New York, Macmillan, 1985.
Bagthorpes Liberated. London, Faber, and New York, Macmillan, 1989.
Bagthorpes Triangle. London, Faber, 1992.
Bagthorpes Besieged. London, Hodder and Stoughton, 1995.

Plays

Lizzie Dripping and the Witch (produced London, 1977).

Television Plays: *Lizzie Dripping* (from her own stories), BBC, 1973, 1975; *Dick Whittington,* BBC, 1974; *Jumbo Spencer* (from her own story), BBC, 1976; *The Day Posy Bates Made History* (from her own story), 1977; *The Haunted School* series, Revcom/Australian Broadcasting, 1986; The *Secret World of Polly Flint* series (from her own story), ITV, 1987; *Moondial* (from her own story), 1988; *Five Children and It* series, 1991; *The Return of the Psammead* series (released on videocassette as *Return of the Sand Fairy),* BBC, 1993; *The Watchers* series, 1995; *The Demon Headmaster,* 1995; *The Famous Five* (seven episodes), 1996-97; *The Demon Headmaster 2,* 1996; *The Phoenix and the Carpet,* 1997; *The Demon Headmaster 3,* 1998.

Other (readers)

Rug Is a Bear, illustrated by Susanna Gretz. London, Benn, 1968.
Rug Plays Tricks, illustrated by Susanna Gretz. London, Benn, 1968.
Rug Plays Ball, illustrated by Susanna Gretz. London, Benn, 1969.
Rug and a Picnic, illustrated by Susanna Gretz. London, Benn, 1969.
John's First Fish, illustrated by Prudence Seward. London, Macmillan, 1970.
At the Stroke of Midnight: Traditional Fairy Tales Retold, illustrated by Carolyn Dinan. London, Collins, 1971.
The Weather Cat, illustrated by Margery Gill. London, Benn, 1971.
The Key, illustrated by Richard Kennedy. London, Benn, 1973.
Cheap Day Return, illustrated by Richard Kennedy. London, Benn, 1974.
Shady Deal, illustrated by Richard Kennedy. London, Benn, 1974.
The Trap, illustrated by Richard Kennedy. London, Benn, 1974.
Nearly Goodbye, illustrated by Tony Morris. London, Macmillan, 1980.
Penny for the Guy, illustrated by Nicole Goodwin. London, Macmillan, 1980.
The Story of Grace Darling, illustrated by Paul Wright. London, Viking, 1988.

Editor, *Puffin Book of Funny Stories.* New York, Viking, 1992.
Editor, *Best Stories for Six Year Olds.* London, Hodder, 1995.
Editor, *Mystery Stories.* London, Kingfisher, 1996.

Reteller, *Classic Fairy Tales.* New York, Golden Books, 1993.
Reteller, *Collins Treasury of Fairy Tales.* London, Collins, 1997.
Reteller, *The Phoenix and the Carpet.* London, Puffin, 1997.

Publications for Adults

For Bethlehem Read Little Thraves (television play), 1977.

*

Helen Cresswell comments:

Whatever I have to say that is of any value whatever, is contained in my work itself. If I could say what I have to say in any other form, then I would do so. And in any case, I do not usually know what I *do* think until I have said it.

* * *

Although Helen Cresswell began her career as a writer of delicate poetic fantasies, her reputation was made of stronger stuff. Her major books have something fantastic, if not always fantasy, in them. *The Piemakers,* her first outstanding success, includes no magical elements; the fantasy comes from telling a story larger than life. *The Signposters* was from a similar mould. With *The Night-Watchmen* in 1969 her work changed direction. The scene was still an enlarged version of the ordinary world, but the supernatural crept in, and it has stayed with her ever since. From *The Outlanders* to *The Winter of the Birds* her stories have occupied the frontier country between a world of commonplace niceness and nastiness and the terrors and wonders that lurk just out of sight. Part of the strength of the novels lies in their implications; she rarely brings the reader face to face with magic.

In her Lizzie Dripping stories, originally designed for television, Cresswell leaves it to the reader to decide whether the supernatural exists. Lizzie is a very ordinary girl in an ordinary family. Does she really have adventures with a witch? Television is a medium that by its nature cannot deal effectively with implications. The viewer has to see the witch as Lizzie does. In the more subtle written version options are left open. That gloriously colourful and embarrassing witch may be real, or she may exist only in Lizzie Dripping's inventive head.

Attractive as they are, the Lizzie Dripping stories are a byproduct of the major novels. So too are the Jumbo Spencer stories, and the disciplined brief texts that Cresswell has written for reluctant older readers, these latter are perhaps the finest examples of a creative artist accepting restrictions on vocabulary, syntax, and subject matter. It is as a writer of humorous and poetic fantasies that Cresswell is best known and is likely to be best remembered.

The Piemakers is the real foundation stone of her work. This is a story of the Roller family, hereditary piemakers of Danby Dale in Yorkshire. A recurrent theme in all Cresswell's books is that of craftsmanship, of work done with skill and pride. The Rollers, like the Signposters and the entertainers in *Up the Pier* and even the scavengers and beachcombers, like to do a job well. Even Gravella Roller, who hates the family trade and wants to go on the stage, recognizes her father's supreme artistry. Faced with the newly baked royal pie "faintly golden, smooth and yet promising a rough, satisfying crustiness, and decorated with the Royal Coat of Arms, a slightly deeper gold, perfect as if it had been carved from stone by the chisel of a master," Gravella breathes: "Oh, it's beautiful!" and her mother dabs her eyes with "the pinafore that wasn't there."

The Piemakers is a funny book, but it takes the fun quite seriously. It is a comedy of incongruity, achieved by blowing a commonplace situation up to gigantic proportions. Baking a pie is not funny. Baking a pie for two thousand eaters *is,* the more so because the logistics of the operations are worked out in detail Cresswell sets her very tall story neatly in a pseudo-historical context, producing archival evidence. Archaeological too; in an exquisite epilogue she takes sceptical readers back to Danby Dale to look at the duck pond on the village green. Yes, it *is* the pie-dish.

Funny as the book is, real life is sometimes funnier. Having spun *The Piemakers* out of her imagination, Cresswell discovered that the piemakers of Danby Dale had really existed. Documentary evidence was to be had, and earnest historical researchers sought her acquaintance and cooperation.

In *The Signposters* Helen Cresswell pursued a similar theme, but with a little less gusto. Again the emphasis is on craftsmanship, but the crafts are many and the effect diffuse. This is a story of the open road, and the best of it is the atmosphere and the pervasive happiness.

She is at her best in drawing eccentrics, and this is perhaps a small criticism of her work. Every fantasy needs a touchstone of reality. In *The Night-Watchmen* the story turns on a very normal little boy who lacks the sharp individuality of, for example, Alice. Consequently, instead of providing a bridge between the real and the fantastic worlds, Henry tends to be an obstacle to one's acceptance of the fantasy. The same is true, in a lesser degree, of the small lodger in *The Beachcombers.*

This apart, *The Night-Watchmen* is an absorbing novel as well as a key to Cresswell's later work. The central idea is marvellous in its originality and simplicity. Josh and Caleb are tramps who have devised the perfect protection against being moved on by the police. A hole in the ground, a Danger Men at Work sign, and tramps become night-watchmen, part of the scenery and not worth a second glance. A whole comic novel could be grown from this seed, and this writer could have brought it off splendidly with such richly humorous characters as Josh and Caleb. But Cresswell had already written two purely funny books, and she was pushing outwards the frontiers of her craft. So the night-watchmen are threatened by Greeneyes, a half-explained and less than half-seen terror of the night. Henry helps to frustrate the Greeneyes and Josh and Caleb catch the night train to There. The story is masterly in its rise to a climax and a swift resolution, but some readers are left with the vague feeling that they have been cheated.

The Winter of the Birds is the latest of her stories in the category of poetic and grotesque fantasy. It is perhaps her cleverest book, but it is not necessarily for that reason more original and important than the earlier work. There are signs that with greater maturity she is becoming more serious, or more sober. There is not much sheer fun in *The Winter of the Birds.* Edward Flack, who has dedicated his life to the achievement of heroism, is a nice invention but he barely raises a smile. Patrick Finn, who *is* a hero, is one of Cresswell's larger-than-life people; he is very noisy but hardly very amusing. The best touches of Cresswell humour come from the terrible MacKays, enormously antisocial small boys.

The power and seriousness of much of *The Winter of the Birds* may have led some admirers to think that Cresswell was turning away from humour. They were reassured by the Bagthorpe books. In one of those abrupt changes of direction in which she delights, she turned to uproarious situation comedy. The Bagthorpes are a family of geniuses, all, that is, except Jack, who is ordinary. They are also lacking in the ordinary faculties of commonsense and self-preservation, and their brilliance leads them into ever more hilarious dilemmas. Take, for example, the great competition phase. The family decide to make capital out of their preternatural intelligence by entering for every available competition. To this end Father removes all the labels from the food tins in the larder. Thereafter every meal in the Bagthorpe household becomes a matter of high adventure as each member of the family in turn takes pot-luck among the anonymous cans. Fostered by a television series the Bagthorpes have become something of a cult, good for sales but not so good for creativity. Indeed there was a sad failure of imagination in the last two books of the series, when the author strove hard to inject some of the old humour into contrived situations and tired characters.

Before this Cresswell had made another of her abrupt changes of direction. In *Dear Shrink* she entered an area so far unfamiliar to her, that of the sociological novel. The sensitive, cultured, and reasonably affluent Saxon children find themselves, through an unforeseen change in their parents' plans, at the mercy of the Social Services Department. They are put into "care," first with a foster mother of positively Dickensian horror, then in a children's home. In his distress Oliver Saxon, who tells the story, takes to confiding his inmost thoughts to Carl Jung, whom he addresses in his journal as "Dear Shrink." The writer strains probability, both in the basic situation and in some of the details, but she paints a memorable picture of a modern human problem, the more effective because it comes through the words of an articulate small boy.

The most successful of her later work has come from a renewed interest in the possibilities offered by television drama. *Moondial* was written simultaneously for television and as a novel, and it proved outstandingly excellent in both forms. In the reality of Belton House, a recent acquisition of the National Trust, Cresswell tapped a powerful source of imaginative energy. Her purely fictional story of a young girl who solves her own personal problem by taking to herself the troubles of long-dead children in the great house carries particular conviction because it is so closely related to the topography of a real house and its landscape. *Moondial* is the most moving, as it is the most personal, of her writings to date. It may prove to be a turning point in her development. It certainly confirms that she is among the most unpredictable as well as the most exciting of the writers of her generation.

The Watchers, too, is based on an actual location, though one far removed from the classical restraint of Belton. The scene is Alton Towers, an incongruous mixture of picturesque landscape and fun park in the English Midlands. Orphans and other deprived children, resident in an unlovely home, come here as a welcome treat in their drab lives, and two of them make an unauthorized return trip that they propose to extend indefinitely. Dangers lurk among the wooded glades and the stomach-churning rides, from a cruel dropout who plans to use the runaways for his own criminal purposes, to less tangible creatures out of Alton's past. Cresswell's blend of past and present, reality and magic, works a little less well in this context, but her social conscience is as strongly in evidence as ever.

Involvement with television drama continued with a highly successful adaptation of E. Nesbit's *Five Children and It,* which combined close fidelity to the original with imaginative exploitation of the magic of TV. Inevitably there was a demand for a sequel, and in default of a satisfactory story—Nesbit's own *Story of the Amulet* was judged unsuitable—Cresswell wrote her own in which she captured the period atmosphere and the characteristic rhythms of Nesbit's style. *The Return of the Psammead* proved rather better on screen than in print, but the book still gave much pleasure to a large audience.

In recent years Cresswell has done more editing, for all ages as usual, ranging from six-year-olds (*Best Stories for Six Year Olds*) to middle-grade readers (*The Puffin Book of Funny Stories* and *Classic Fairy Tales*) and above (*Mystery Stories*). All show her characteristic taste and good organization. Notably, the anthology of fairy tales presents traditional versions, not the revisionist stories that have been so popular with critics and educators. The mystery volume, making a parallel statement, includes mainly classic authors such as Conan Doyle and Christie rather than contemporary writers for children. Although her production of original stories seems to have slowed somewhat, it still serves young readers from the smallest (*Mister Maggs)* to the teenaged (*Stonestruck).* Unfortunately, although Cresswell's mystery and fairy-tale anthologies have been published on both sides of the Atlantic, her recent fiction is not available in the United States (where the Bagthorpes, however, remain continuously in print).

With a huge output ranging from Easy Readers for beginners to demanding novels for teenagers, Cresswell's humor, understanding, and resourcefulness continue to impress. The big prizes still elude her. Adult judges seem reluctant to admit that so prolific and varied a talent is to be taken seriously. Her best book, I suspect, has yet to be written.

—Marcus Crouch, updated by Caroline C. Hunt

CREWS, Donald

Nationality: American. **Born:** 30 August 1938, Newark, New Jersey. **Education:** Graduated from Cooper Union for the Advancement of Science and Art, 1959. **Military Service:** U.S. Army, 1962-64. **Family:** Married Ann Jonas (see her entry in this volume) in 1963; two daughters. **Career:** Illustrator and author; free-lance artist, photographer, and designer. Assistant art director, *Dance* (magazine), New York City, 1959-60; staff designer, Will Burton Studios, New York City, 1961-62. **Awards:** One of American Institute of Graphic Arts Fifty Books of the Year, 1968; Children's Book Council Children's Book Showcase selection, 1974; American Library Association Notable Book, 1978 and 1980; American Institute of Graphic Arts Book Show selection, 1979; Caldecott Honor Book, 1979 and 1981; one of ten *New York Times* Best Illustrated Books, 1986. **Address:** c/o Greenwillow Books, 1350 Avenue of the Americas, New York, New York 10019, U.S.A.

Publications for Children

Picture Books (illustrated by the author)

We Read: A to Z. New York, Harper, 1967.
Ten Black Dots. New York, Scribner, 1968; revised edition, New York, Greenwillow, 1986.
Freight Train. New York, Greenwillow, 1978.
Truck. New York, Greenwillow, 1980.
Light. New York, Greenwillow, 1981.
Harbor. New York, Greenwillow, 1982.
Carousel. New York, Greenwillow, 1982.
Parade. New York, Greenwillow, 1982.
School Bus. New York, Greenwillow, 1984.
Bicycle Race. New York, Greenwillow, 1985.
Flying. New York, Greenwillow, 1986.
Bigmama's. New York, Greenwillow, 1991.
Shortcut. New York, Greenwillow, 1992.
Sail Away, New York, Greenwillow, 1995.
Night at the Fair, New York, Greenwillow, 1998.

*

Illustrator: Harry Milgrom, *ABC Science Experiments,* Crowell, 1970; J. Richard Dennis, *Fractions Are Parts of Things,* Crowell, 1971; H. Milgrom, *ABC of Ecology,* Macmillan, 1972; Franklyn M. Branley, *Eclipse: Darkness in Daytime,* Crowell, 1973, revised edition, HarperCollins, 1988; Robert Kalan, *Rain,* Greenwillow, 1978; R. Kalan, *Blue Sea,* Greenwillow, 1979; Dorothy de Wit, editor, *The Talking Stone: An Anthology of Native American Tales and Legends,* Greenwillow, 1979; Paul Giganti, Jr., *How Many Snails?: A Counting Book,* Greenwillow, 1988; P. Giganti, Jr., *Each Orange Had 8 Slices,* Greenwillow, 1991; Patricia Lillie, *When this Box Is Full,* Greenwillow, 1993; George Shannon, *Tomorrow's Alphabet,* Greenwillow, 1995; Miriam Schlein, *More than One,* Greenwillow, 1996.

Media Adaptations: *Freight Train* (sound filmscript), Educational Enrichment Material, 1980; *Truck* (sound filmscript), Live Oak Media, 1981.

Manuscript Collections: Kerlan Collection, University of Minnesota.

* * *

Donald Crews's books about transportation are favorites with young readers. Using simple language, mostly color, and action words, *Freight Train* roars through the pages moving right through the book into children's memories. Uncluttered lines with mood designed through blurring motion makes this an exciting read. *Truck* traces the journey of a truck carrying tricycles by keeping the reader's eye focused on the bright red-labeled truck as it moves from city to country to city again. The stylized images, the various angles, and the movement of partial illustrations from one page to another is strong and powerful. Young people will read traffic signs and search to find their red truck on the maze of roadways.

The Bicycle Race is exciting and fast-paced, with 12 numbered racers in various bright colors. From the very start of the race, number nine is delayed because of mechanical trouble. The reader is asked to keep track of who is winning as the racers speed along the raceway. This counting book has the basic numbers from one to 12, but the order of the numbers changes to correspond to the order of the bicycles in the race. The surprise ending adds to the excitement in the reading. *Parade* is a joyous romp through the day of a parade with people watching and colors everywhere as the band struts and the flags move forward. One even sees bicycles from bygone days and antique automobiles. Even Crews's ending is realistic; after the parade is over, the sanitation truck moves in to clean the street.

The night is not as dark as the reader might think in the exploration of *Light* in both city and country. Crews encourages the reader to think about all kinds of light in windows of homes in the county as well as in city buildings. He draws attention to head lights and taillights and to flashing lights and the beauty of glimmering lights on a bridge.

Bigmama's is a fun-filled reminiscence of the author's summer visits to his grandparents with his own mama, his brother, and his two sisters. Observant young people will notice that the trai car they travel on has a sign designating "colored." On their arrival in Florida from New Jersey, the children check to see that all is the same as previous summers. Family sharing and lazy summer days are effectively conveyed in the warm colors of the illustrations.

In *Shortcut,* Crews combines his fascination with trains with a memory from his childhood. Here a group of children take a shortcut along the railroad tracks as a train ominously approaches. The close-up movement of the train roaring past and the fear it evokes is heightened by the blurred images.

Crews also illustrates the work of others. His images for Patricia Lillie's *When This Box Is Full* are very different from most of his other work. For this book photographs are used not for reference but for the actual images screened onto the page through a laser process.

Bold illustrations with simple texts, an ability to see things from a child's perspective, and the development of the sensitive eye of the reader are characteristic of Donald Crews's work. He says in the video about himself that "I take photographs ... more than I sketch things. If I need some information, I just as soon photograph it ... and use that for inspiration." Both his simple object or transportation books and his more fully plotted family stories are themselves inspirations for young readers.

—Kay E. Vandergrift

CROCKETT, Samuel Rutherford

Nationality: British. **Born:** Little Duchrae, Balmaghie, Kirkcudbrightshire, 24 September 1860. **Education:** Laurieston Free Church School, 1865-67; Cowper's Free Church School, Castle Douglas, Kirkcudbrightshire, 1867-76; Edinburgh University, 1876-79; Heidelberg University; New College, Edinburgh, 1882-86. **Family:** Married Ruth Mary Milner in 1887; two sons and two daughters. **Career:** Travelling tutor in Germany, Sicily, and Italy, 1879-82. Entered the Free Church of Scotland and ordained minister, 1886: minister, Penicuik, Midlothian, 1886-95 (resigned). Editor, *Worker's Monthly,* London, 1890-91. **Died:** 21 April 1914.

Publications for Children

Fiction

Sweetheart Travellers: A Child's Book for Children, for Women, and for Men, illustrated by Gordon Browne and W.H.C. Groome. London, Wells Gardner Darton, and New York, Stokes, 1895.

The Surprising Adventures of Sir Toady Lion with Those of General Napoleon Smith: An Improving History for Old Boys, Young Boys, Good Boys, Bad Boys, Little Boys, Cowboys, and Tom-Boys, illustrated by Gordon Browne. London, Wells Gardner Darton, and New York, Stokes, 1897.

Sir Toady Crusoe, illustrated by Gordon Browne. London, Wells Gardner Darton, and New York, Stokes, 1905.

Sweethearts at Home: Assisted by Sweetheart Herself, and with Additions and Corrections by Hugh John, Sir Toady Lion, Maid Margaret, and Miss Elizabeth Fortinbras, illustrated by C.E. Brock. London and New York, Hodder and Stoughton, 1912.

Other

Editor, *Red Cap Tales Told from Ivanhoe* [*The Fortunes of Nigel, Quentin Durward, Guy Mannering, Rob Roy, The Antiquary, Waverley, The Pirate,* and *A Legend of Montrose*], by Walter Scott. London, A. and C. Black, and New York, Macmillan, 8 vols., 1904-10.

Publications for Adults

Novels

The Play-Actress. London, Unwin, and New York, Putnam, 1894.

The Lilac Sunbonnet. London, Unwin, and New York, Appleton, 1894.

Mad Sir Uchtred of the Hills. London, Unwin, and New York, Macmillan, 1894.

The Raiders, Being Some Passages in the Life of John Faa, Lord and Earl of Little Egypt. London, Unwin, and New York, Macmillan, 1894.

The Men of the Moss Hags. London, Isbister, and New York, Macmillan, 1895.

A Galloway Herd. New York, Fenno, 1895.

The Grey Man. London, Unwin, and New York, Harper, 1896.

Cleg Kelly, Arab of the City. London, Smith Elder, and New York, Appleton, 1896.

Lochinvar. London, Methuen, 1897; New York, Harper, 1898.

The Standard Bearer. London, Methuen, and New York, Appleton, 1898.

The Red Axe. London, Smith Elder, 1898; New York, Harper, 1899.

The Silver Skull. New York, Stokes, 1898; London, Smith Elder, 1901.

The Black Douglas. London, Smith Elder, and New York, Doubleday, 1899.

Kit Kennedy, Country Boy. London, Clarke, and New York, Harper, 1899.

Ione March. London, Hodder and Stoughton, and New York, Dodd Mead, 1899.

Joan of the Sword Hand. London, Ward Lock, and New York, Dodd Mead, 1900.

Little Anna Mark. London, Smith Elder, 1900; as *The Isle of the Winds: An Adventurous Romance,* New York, Doubleday, 1900.

Cinderella. London, Clarke, and New York, Dodd Mead, 1901.

The Firebrand. London, Macmillan, and New York, McClure, 1901.

The Dark o' the Moon, Being Certain Further Histories of Folk Called "Raiders." London, Macmillan, and New York, Harper, 1902.

The Banner of Blue. New York, McClure, 1902; London, Hodder and Stoughton, 1903.

Flower o'-the-Corn. London, Clarke, 1902; New York, McClure, 1903.

The Adventurer in Spain. London, Isbister, and New York, Stokes, 1903.

The Loves of Miss Anne. London, Clarke, and New York, Dodd Mead, 1904.

Strong Mac. London, Ward Lock, and New York, Dodd Mead, 1904.

Raiderland: All about Grey Galloway. London, Hodder and Stoughton, and New York, Dodd Mead, 1904.

Maid Margaret of Galloway. London, Hodder and Stoughton, 1905; as *May Margaret: Called "The Fair Maid of Galloway,"* New York, Dodd Mead, 1905.
The Cherry Ribband. London, Hodder and Stoughton, and New York, Barnes, 1905.
Kid McGhie: A Nugget of Dim Gold. London, Clarke, 1906.
Fishers of Men. New York, Appleton, 1906.
The White Plumes of Navarre: A Romance of the Wars of Religion. London, Religious Tract Society, 1906; as *The White Plume,* New York, Dodd Mead, 1906.
Me and Myn. London, Unwin, 1907.
Vida; or, The Iron Lord of Kirktown. London, Clarke, 1907; as *The Iron Lord,* New York, Empire Book Company, 1907.
Little Esson. London, Ward Lock, 1907.
Deep Moat Grange. London, Hodder and Stoughton, and New York, Appleton, 1908.
Princess Penniless. London, Hodder and Stoughton, 1908.
The Bloom o' the Heather. London, Nash, 1908.
The Men of the Mountain. London, Religious Tract Society, and New York, Harper, 1909.
Rose of the Wilderness. London, Hodder and Stoughton, 1909.
The Seven Wise Men. London, Religious Tract Society, 1909.
Love's Young Dream. New York, Macmillan, 1910.
The Dew of Their Youth. London, Hodder and Stoughton, 1910.
The Smugglers. London, Hodder and Stoughton, 1911.
The Lady of the Hundred Dresses. London, Nash, 1911.
Love in Pernicketty Town. London and New York, Hodder and Stoughton, 1911.
Patsy. New York, Macmillan, 1912.
Anne of the Barricades. London and New York, Hodder and Stoughton, 1912.
The Moss Troopers. London and New York, Hodder and Stoughton, 1912.
Sandy's Love Affair. London, Hutchinson, 1913; as *Sandy,* New York, Macmillan, 1914.
A Tatter of Scarlet. London, Hodder and Stoughton, 1913.
Silver Sand. London, Hodder and Stoughton, and Chicago, Revell, 1914.
Hal o' the Ironsides. London, Hodder and Stoughton, and New York, Revell, 1915.
The Azure Hand. London and New York, Hodder and Stoughton, 1917.
The White Pope, Called "The Light Out of the East." Liverpool, Books Ltd., 1920; as *The Light Out of the East,* New York, Doran, 1920.
Rogues' Island. London, Faber, 1926.

Short Stories

The Stickit Minister and Some Common Men. London, Unwin, 1893; New York, Macmillan, n.d.
Bog-Myrtle and Peat: Tales, Chiefly of Galloway. London, Bliss Sands, and New York, Appleton, 1895.
Lad's Love: Tales. London, Bliss Sands, and New York, Appleton, 1897.
The Stickit Minister's Wooing and Other Galloway Stories. London, Hodder and Stoughton, and New York, Doubleday, 1900.
Love Idylls. London, Murray, and New York, Dodd Mead, 1901.
Young Nick and Old Nick: Yarns for the Year's End. London, Stanley Paul, 1910.

Poetry

Dulce Cor, Being the Poems of Ford Berêton. London, Kegan Paul, 1886.

Other

My Two Edinburghs: Searchlights Through the Mists of Thirty Years. London, Cedar Press, 1909.

* * *

Sir Toady Lion, otherwise Arthur George Picton Smith—the *nom de guerre* derives from his early attempts to twist his tongue round the name of his favorite character in history, Richard *Coeur de Lion*—is the younger brother of Hugh John Smith who assumes the imperial title of General Napoleon Smith at the age of twelve before leading his army in a campaign against the town "Smoutchies" who are holding a pet lamb hostage in the Black Sheds, the slaughterhouse yard, and who are trespassing in the grounds of The House of Windy Standard, Sir Toady's home in the Scottish border country. The army musters in its ranks their literary sister Priscilla, Sammy and Cissy Carter from the neighbouring estate of Oaklands, and two stable boys, Mike O'Donelly and Peter Greg. And it is Sir Toady himself who stealthily rescues the lamb for all the military ardour, staffwork, and planning of the commander-in-chief after the first set encounter with the enemy had decidedly ended in the Smoutchies' favour.

Nevertheless Samuel Rutherford Crockett's *The Surprising Adventures of Sir Toady Lion with Those of General Napoleon Smith* really belongs to the elder brother as he emerges from a series of adventures with honour unblemished and his sense of duty undiminished in true romantic fashion whereas Sir Toady demands a fair measure of patience and toleration in the reader. He appears as a more sympathetic and engaging character in *Sir Toady Crusoe* when befriending an Australian boy searching for his sister, but even here his precocious cunning is in no way alleviated by the mawkish sentimentality constantly surrounding him. In many respects this is a pity because Crockett writes with a fresh and affectionate nostalgia in the earlier volume which is largely based on his own childhood upbringing. Of *Sweetheart Travellers* and *Sweethearts at Home,* described by the author as "vagrom chronicles," little need be said; their excessively sentimental approach has earned for them a truly deserved and lasting oblivion.

—Alan Edwin Day

CROMPTON, Richmal

Nationality: British. **Born:** Richmal Crompton Lamburn in Bury, Lancashire, 15 November 1890. **Education:** St. Elphin's Clergy Daughters' School, Warrington, Lancashire, later Darley Dale, Derbyshire; Royal Holloway College, University of London 1911-14 (Driver scholar, 1914), B.A. (honours) in classics 1914. **Career:** Teacher, St. Elphin's, 1915-17; classics mistress, Bromley High School for Girls, Kent, 1917-24. Crippled by poliomyelitis in 1923. **Military Service:** Volunteer in the Auxiliary Fire Service, Bromley, during World War II. **Died:** 11 January 1969.

PUBLICATIONS FOR CHILDREN

Fiction (William books illustrated by Thomas Henry through 1962)

Just—William. London, Newnes, 1922.
More William. London, Newnes, 1922.
William Again. London, Newnes, 1923.
William the Fourth. London, Newnes, 1924.
Still William. London, Newnes, 1925.
William the Conqueror. London, Newnes, 1926.
William the Outlaw. London, Newnes, 1927.
William in Trouble. London, Newnes, 1927.
William the Good. London, Newnes, 1928.
William. London, Newnes, 1929.
William the Bad. London, Newnes, 1930.
William's Happy Days. London, Newnes, 1930.
William's Crowded Hours. London, Newnes, 1931.
William the Pirate. London, Newnes, 1932.
William the Rebel. London, Newnes, 1933.
William the Gangster. London, Newnes, 1934.
William the Detective. London, Newnes, 1935.
Sweet William. London, Newnes, 1936.
William the Showman. London, Newnes, 1937.
William the Dictator. London, Newnes, 1938.
William and A.R.P. London, Newnes, 1939; as *William's Bad Resolution,* 1956.
Just William: The Story of the Film. London, Newnes, 1939.
William and the Evacuees. London, Newnes, 1940; as *William the Film Star,* 1956.
William Does His Bit. London, Newnes, 1941.
William Carries On. London, Newnes, 1942.
William and the Brains Trust. London, Newnes, 1945; abridged edition, as *William the Hero,* London, Collins, 1972.
Just William's Luck. London, Newnes, 1948.
Jimmy. London, Newnes, 1949.
William the Bold. London, Newnes, 1950.
Jimmy Again, illustrated by Lunt Roberts. London, Newnes, 1951.
William and the Tramp. London, Newnes, 1952.
William and the Moon Rocket. London, Newnes, 1954.
William and the Space Animal. London, Newnes, 1956.
William's Television Show. London, Newnes, 1958.
William the Explorer. London, Newnes, 1960.
William's Treasure Trove. London, Newnes, 1962.
William and the Witch, illustrated by Thomas Henry and Henry Ford. London, Newnes, 1964.
Jimmy the Third, illustrated by Lunt Roberts. London, Armada, 1965.
William and the Monster, illustrated by Peter Archer and Thomas Henry. London, Armada, 1965.
William the Ancient Briton, illustrated by Peter Archer and Thomas Henry. London, Armada, 1965.
William the Cannibal, illustrated by Peter Archer and Thomas Henry. London, Armada, 1965.
William the Globetrotter, illustrated by Peter Archer and Thomas Henry. London, Armada, 1965.
William and the Pop Singers, illustrated by Henry Ford. London, Newnes, 1965.
William and the Masked Ranger, illustrated by Henry Ford. London, Newnes, 1966.
William the Superman, illustrated by Henry Ford. London, Newnes, 1968.
William the Lawless, illustrated by Henry Ford. London, Newnes, 1970.

Play

William and the Artist's Model. London, J. Garnet Miller, 1956.

PUBLICATIONS FOR ADULTS

Novels

The Innermost Room. London, Melrose, 1923.
The Hidden Light. London, Hodder and Stoughton, 1924.
Anne Morrison. London, Jarrolds, 1925.
The Wildings. London, Hodder and Stoughton, 1925.
David Wilding. London, Hodder and Stoughton, 1926.
The House. London, Hodder and Stoughton, 1926; as *Dread Dwelling,* New York, Boni and Liveright, 1926.
Millicent Dorrington. London, Hodder and Stoughton, 1927.
Leadon Hill. London, Hodder and Stoughton, 1927.
Enter—Patricia. London, Newnes, 1927.
The Thorn Bush. London, Hodder and Stoughton, 1928.
Roofs Off! London, Hodder and Stoughton, 1928.
The Four Graces. London, Hodder and Stoughton, 1929.
Abbot's End. London, Hodder and Stoughton, 1929.
Blue Flames. London, Hodder and Stoughton, 1930.
Naomi Godstone. London, Hodder and Stoughton, 1930.
Portrait of a Family. London, Macmillan, 1932.
The Odyssey of Euphemia Tracy. London, Macmillan, 1932.
Marriage of Hermione. London, Macmillan, 1932.
The Holiday. London, Macmillan, 1933.
Chedsy Place. London, Macmillan, 1934.
The Old Man's Birthday. London, Macmillan, 1934; Boston, Little Brown, 1935.
Quartet. London, Macmillan, 1935.
Caroline. London, Macmillan, 1936.
There Are Four Seasons. London, Macmillan, 1937
Journeying Wave. London, Macmillan, 1938.
Merlin Bay. London, Macmillan, 1939.
Steffan Green. London, Macmillan, 1940.
Narcissa. London, Macmillan, 1941.
Mrs. Frensham Describes a Circle. London, Macmillan, 1942.
Weatherley Parade. London, Macmillan, 1944.
Westover. London, Hutchinson, 1946.
The Ridleys. London, Hutchinson, 1947.
Family Roundabout. London, Hutchinson, 1948.
Frost at Morning. London, Hutchinson, 1950.
Linden Rise. London, Hutchinson, 1952.
The Gypsy's Baby. London, Hutchinson, 1954.
Four in Exile. London, Hutchinson, 1955.
Matty and Dearingroydes. London, Hutchinson, 1956.
Blind Man's Buff. London, Hutchinson, 1957.
Wiseman's Folly. London, Hutchinson, 1959.
The Inheritor. London, Hutchinson, 1960.

Short Stories

Kathleen and I, and, of Course, Veronica. London, Hodder and Stoughton, 1926.
A Monstrous Regiment. London, Hutchinson, 1927.

Mist and Other Stories. London, Hutchinson, 1928.
The Middle Things. London, Hutchinson, 1928.
Felicity Stands By. London, Newnes, 1928.
Sugar and Spice and Other Stories. London, Ward Lock, 1929.
Ladies First. London, Hutchinson, 1929.
The Silver Birch and Other Stories. London, Hutchinson, 1931.
The First Morning. London, Hutchinson, 1936.

*

Bibliography: *William: A Bibliography* by W.O.G. Lofts and Derek J. Adley, privately printed, 1980.

Critical Studies: *Richmal Crompton: The Woman Behind William* by Mary Cadogan, London, Allen and Unwin, 1986; *Just Richmal: The Life Work of Richmal Crompton* by Kay Williams, Guildford, Surrey, Genesis, 1986.

* * *

Richmal Crompton never achieved distinction as a writer of adult novels, but ironically her success as a children's author rests almost entirely on her William stories which were originally created for mature readers. William Brown first appeared in the February 1919 issue of *Home Magazine* in a story called "Rice Mould," which was later included in the book *More William* (1922). Nearly all the William books (the exception is the full length *Just William's Luck*) comprise a series of separate episodes; this pattern was established because up to the publication of *William and the Evacuees* in 1940 each chapter was a reprint of a short story that had first been published in the *Home* or *Happy* magazines.

The books work on several levels and interest readers of differing ages and tastes. If the irony and subtlety of the early episodes were over the heads of juvenile readers, they were still bound to respond to the absurd situations in which William finds himself and to the facetious tone which Crompton uses to describe these. The stories lost something of their satirical edge when, after 1940, Crompton began to write them specifically for children, but they remained inventive and anarchic.

In the early 1920s William, the anti-hero, emerged as something new in children's fiction, a welcome departure from the impeccably honourable boys and girls who had for so long been leading characters in juvenile books. William is not particularly truthful; he carries untidiness and dirtiness almost to the point of fetishism; he is intellectually lazy, acquisitive, and belligerent. But in the stories these traits are appealing rather than repulsive. William's boisterous proclivities seem natural and require no justification (though he is always complaining that grown-ups misunderstand his good intentions). He is the ultimate unbookish, adventurous, outdoor child. Crompton, whose main ambition was to produce serious adult novels, had without realizing it made the character that she called her "pot-boiler" into an archetype, and today the name of William Brown—like Cinderella or Billy Bunter—has symbolic meaning even for people who have never read the stories.

The William books are almost parodies of Crompton's adult family sagas. The genre is drawing-room comedy, with William as the ingenuous initiator of social chaos and embarrassment for his elders. His family belongs to the cook-gardener-and-house-maid-employing class, and by placing William in a genteel environment Crompton makes his rugged non-conformity and rebelliousness more effective than if he came from a working-class home.

Although Crompton had been a supporter of the campaign for women's suffrage, there is little evidence of feminism in the books. The "Outlaws" (William and his friends Ginger, Henry, and Douglas) firmly despise women and girls. Of course, the females in William's world tend to be stereotypes. Mrs. Brown is the typical wife who always concurs with her husband's opinions by absently reiterating "Yes dear," as she constantly darns the socks of her menfolk. (In one book she is described as darning on five separate occasions.) William's sister Ethel is a bright but useless young thing (she never works except in times of National Emergency when she becomes a fetching V.A.D.), a flirt whose red-gold hair and eyelash-fluttering techniques eventually take their toll of every male in the village. Violet Elizabeth Bott, the rather vulgar sauce-magnate's daughter, is the only interesting girl character in the stories, and William frequently meets his match in this six-year-old bundle of frills, fluffiness, and precocious obstinacy who gets her own way so often by threatening to "thcream and thcream" till she's "thick." Of course Crompton is not usually concerned with complex presentation of character, either male or female; she simply exploits stereotypes, like the outraged clergyman, the batty artist, the ageing spinster apostle of higher thought, to trigger off a series of preposterous situations—which nevertheless in the William context are somehow believable.

The character of William was partly inspired by events in the lives of Crompton's own family. She drew on memories of the childhood of her brother and, later, that of her nephew. Her stories featuring Jimmy were less addictive and ran only to three books. Several years younger than the 11-year-old William, Jimmy engaged in less memorable adventures that were described in lively but very short and simple stories.

It appears that Crompton made one or two unsuccessful attempts to create a female character who would have something of William's irrepressible nature. However, Veronica, in *Kathleen and I, and, of Course, Veronica* (1926), is a little girl whose amusing antics are merely cute, and the determinedly bouncy heroines of *Enter—Patricia* (1927) and *Felicity Stands By* (1928) are young adults rather than juveniles.

—Mary Cadogan

CRUICKSHANK, Margrit

Nationality: British. **Born:** Scotland. **Education:** Graduated from Aberdeen University. **Career:** Works in a children's bookshop, Dun Laoghaire; reviewer of children's literature, the *Irish Times*. Writer since 1990. **Awards:** Readers' Association of Ireland Special Merit Award, 1993; Bisto Book of the Year shortlist, 1992-93, and special commendation, 1995-96.

PUBLICATIONS FOR CHILDREN

Fiction

S.K.U.N.K. and the Ozone Conspiracy. Dublin, Poolbeg, 1990.
S.K.U.N.K. and the Splitting Earth. Dublin, Poolbeg, 1991.
Circling the Triangle. Dublin, Poolbeg, 1991.
A Monster Called Charlie. Dublin, Poolbeg, 1992.

S.K.U.N.K. and the Nuclear Waste Plot. Dublin, Poolbeg, 1992.
S.K.U.N.K. and the Freak Flood Fiasco. Dublin, Poolbeg, 1994.
Down by the Pond. London, Frances Lincoln, 1995.
Anna's Six Wishes. Dublin, Poolbeg, 1995.
Liza's Lamb. Dublin, Poolbeg, 1995.
S.K.U.N.K. and the Bride of Dracula. Dublin, Poolbeg, 1996.
The Door. Dublin, Poolbeg, 1996.

Other

Contributor, *Goodbye and Hello* (stories). London, Viking, 1992.
Contributor, *Chiller* (short stories). Dublin, Poolbeg, 1995.
Contributor, *First Times* (short stories). Dublin, Poolbeg, 1997.

*

Margrit Cruickshank comments:

I was one of the lucky children—I had a parent who told us stories. My father read books to us: *Winnie the Pooh, The Jungle Book* and *Heidi* stick in my mind. (As we had only the German version of *Heidi,* a present from my Swiss grandparents, he had to work out each chapter in advance—a real labour of love.) But he also told us stories, mainly autobiographical ones, especially on walks—and he was a great walker. It was a lesson on how to get recalcitrant children the last mile home which I then put into practise when I had children of my own. From telling stories to writing them down was an obvious step—and eventually I tried sending them off to a publisher. The age of my protagonists rose as my children grew older, even though I was no longer writing primarily for them. And now I have started to write picture stories for the very young. Latent granny-urges? Perhaps.

* * *

Margrit Cruickshank's first book, *S.K.U.N.K. and the Ozone Conspiracy,* introduces us to the lively adventure-prone Aisling—to all intents living a normal life between school, hockey, and home—that is until she becomes embroiled with her bedridden eccentric godfather Seamus. *S.K.U.N.K. and the Ozone Conspiracy* is the first in the series followed by *S.K.U.N.K. and the Splitting Earth, S.K.U.N.K. and the Nuclear Waste Plot, S.K.U.N.K. and the Freak Flood Fiasco,* and *S.K.U.N.K. and the Bride of Dracula.* All the plots are centred on environmental issues and the very bad baddies in the terrorist organisation S.K.U.N.K. They are, in the words of Seamus, "as nasty a bunch of central European gentleman as you are ever likely to meet. You could say the letters stand for Skulduggery, Killing, Unscrupulousness, Nastiness and Corruption." You could indeed. These are fast moving light-hearted adventure stories strong on plot and place. The one truly flesh-and-blood person is Ashling, who is something of a Walter Mitty figure constantly seeing her life unfold in high drama before her eyes as headlines in *The Irish Times.* There are occasional insightful glimpses of Aisling's social background. Aisling's father was described as "the street organiser for the Neighbourhood Watch Scheme. Kevin and Aisling had tried to convince him that, with Mrs. Hegarty living opposite and looking out her windows all day long, it was quite unnecessary on their street...."

Cruickshank's Stephen, the central character of her young adult novel, *Circling the Triangle,* is from a middle-class family and with some musical talent who finds himself on a roller coaster of misdemeanour and misadventure, a catalogue of woes and misunderstandings leading to worse and worse behaviour: total drunkenness, defacing walls, stealing, lying, mitching school, and totally alienating his bewildered family. Why then do we not hate this young monster? Because Cruickshank has caught the deep down panic and confusion which keeps him on his collision course with everyone around him and because the story is presented as autobiography we cannot help siding with him. The triangle of the title is that eternal love triangle—A loves B who loves C; the circling is Stephen's confusion and searching for direction and for a centre in his life. This circling is also the search for an ending where the author provides us with three alternative possible endings: the final triangle of the book. It is a perfect resolution to something that is never finally resolved. The shadow between longing for what might have been, the memory of how it was, and present reality is the dilemma presented finally to the reader. The book ends with the phrase, "Only it wasn't quite like that either."

Circling the Triangle is adolescent life in urban Ireland as it is and as it has never before been shown, written with honesty that is sometimes brutal and depicting a society where the adolescents have no copyright on vulnerability or confusion.

The Door is also written for young adults and centres around Hugh's Transition Year in a Dublin school. Unlike Stephen in *Circling the Triangle* Hugh is an instantly likeable, normal young man, bumbling and awkward, but sincere in his efforts to become friend and boyfriend to Rachel, an avid feminist and campaigner on a myriad of issues. The door of the title is both real and symbolic and becomes the *leitmotif* of the work. It is the title of the school newspaper which Hugh and his friends are editing—a title inspired by a poem by Miroslav Holub which urges us to "Go out and open the door" and concludes that "at least/there'll be/a draught." For the group it is a door opening to the adult world as they seek to confront sexual harassment and censorship. It has a physical reality too—Rachel's front door slams against Hugh leading him to some wild conjectures as to the underlying cause of her moodiness. Cruickshank is an expert at form and structure, hanging the novel on an end-of-year essay assignment and heading each chapter with quotations which comment on, or counterpoint the events of the chapter, sometimes ironically, always appropriately.

Liza's Lamb, Anna's Six Wishes and *Down by the Pond* are all for younger children, with a range of themes from the hospitalisation of a young boy, a magic wishes story with a difference, and a boisterous farmyard chase. *Liza's Lamb* tells how Shane, six-years-old and suddenly in hospital far from his farm and animals, copes with the fear and strangeness of his new environment. His helplessness against the tyranny of hospital procedures is handled in a straightforward, completely honest manner. It is all there: the tedium of the waiting room, the futility of the cheerfully-posed questions—"'I think we'd better do some tests. Is that all right, Shane? Just blood tests and an X-ray.' It wasn't all right. 'I want to go home,' Shane said.' ...people wouldn't leave him alone. There were more thermometers, more blood pressure bandages, more poking and pushing him about"—not to mention the indignities of bedpans and bed baths. This is not just a "going to hospital" story, but the story of a developing friendship between two children from different backgrounds thrown together by a common bond of their illness. Many of Cruickshank's books have an underlying awareness of green issues and nature in general which are demonstrated in an amusing fashion in *Anna's Six Wishes* as Anna's fairy godmother appears to her in a series of highly-unusual guises, all of them liable to attack from Anna—a spider, mouse, bluebottle, slug, wasp and woodlouse. Anna learns not only not to judge on appearance but to think twice before making a wish. The book ends with one page blank but for a question posed to the reader: "If you had a fairy godmother, what would YOU wish for?"

Down by the Pond is a multi-layered picture book. The straightforward, bouncy rhyme has us follow the trail of the red fox with the black-tipped tail down by the pond, watched by jersey cow, pink pig, clucking hens, and collie dog, until the least likely heroine emerges in the shape of a little grey kitten. As the chase ends and each of the animals claims credit for the predator's watery Waterloo in the pond, the little grey kitten winks at us and "went back to sleep in the sun by and by." It is a book which invites noisy participation by even the youngest child.

—Pat Donlon

CUMMINGS, Pat (Marie)

Nationality: American. **Born:** 9 November 1950, Chicago, Illinois. **Education:** Attended Spelman College, Atlanta, Georgia, 1970-71, and Atlanta School of Art, 1971-72; Pratt Institute, Brooklyn, New York, B.F.A. 1974. **Family:** Married Chuku Lee in 1975. **Career:** Freelance author and illustrator since 1974; adjunct professor of illustration, Parsons School of Design. **Awards:** National Council on the Social Studies/Children's Book Council Notable Children's Trade Book in the Field of Social Studies, 1982; American Library Association Coretta Scott King Honorable Mention, 1983 and 1987; Coretta Scott King Award, 1984; Black Women in Publishing Illustration Award, 1988. **Member:** Society of Children's Book Writers, Graphic Artists Guild, Author's Guild, Writer's Guild of America, East. **Address:** c/o HarperCollins, 10 E. 53rd St., New York, New York 10022, U.S.A.

Publications for Children

Fiction (illustrated by the author)

Jimmy Lee Did It. New York, Lothrop, 1985.
C.L.O.U.D.S. New York, Lothrop, 1986.
Clean Your Room, Harvey Moon! New York, Bradbury, 1991.
Petey Moroni's Camp Runamok Diary. New York, Bradbury, 1992.
Carousel. New York, Bradbury, 1994.
Dear Mabel! Glenview, Illinois, Celebration Press, 1996.
The Blue Lake. New York, HarperCollins, 1997.
My Aunt Came Back. New York, HarperCollins, 1998.

Other

Editor and compiler, *Talking with Artists.* New York, Bradbury, 1991.
Editor and compiler, *Talking with Artists 2.* New York, Simon and Schuster, 1995.

*

Illustrator: *Good News* by Eloise Greenfield, 1977; *Beyond Dreamtime: The Life and Lore of the Aboriginal Australian* by Trudie MacDougall, 1978; *The Secret of the Royal Mounds* by Cynthia Jameson, 1980; *Just Us Women* by Jeanette Caines, 1982; *My Mama Needs Me* (Reading Rainbow book) by Mildred Pitts Walter, 1983; *Fred's First Day* by Cathy Warren, 1984; *Chilly Stomach* by Jeanette Caines, 1986;*Springtime Bears* (also known as *Playing with Mama*) by Cathy Warren, 1986; *I Need a Lunch Box* by Jeanette Caines, 1988; *Storm in the Night* by Mary Stolz, 1988; *Willie's Not the Hugging Kind,* by Joyce Durham Barrett, 1989; *Two and Too Much* by Mildred Pitts Walter, 1990; *Go Fish* by Mary Stolz, 1991; *"C" Is for City* by Nikki Grimes, 1994; *Barry and Bennie* by Angela Shelf Medearis, 1996; *Pickin' Peas* retold by Margaret Read MacDonald, 1998;

* * *

Pat Cummings has made an impact upon the genre of multicultural picture story books for children by creating, through her stories and illustrations, characters and story lines depicting family values, positive relationships, and elements of fantasy and humor. Working primarily with mixed medium of colored pencil, watercolor, and gouache, Cummings captures the attention of children by placing colorful surprises within her illustrations and creating story lines that offer young readers elements of both fanciful imagination and realistic conflict resolution. Cummings successfully allows her young audience to experience glimpses of her happy, active childhood.

Having grown up in a military family, Cummings, together with her parents and three siblings, moved frequently. While she was always was the "new kid" on the block, the security and support of her family provided both a consistency and a source for thematic material for her stories and illustrations. Early exposure to fairy tales, fantasy literature as well as the diversified cultures of the Asian and European cities in which she has lived, allows Cummings to freely utilize, with versatility, fanciful and imaginative themes within her stories and illustrations. Cummings utilizes biographical elements within her stories; often, images of her family members are found in the pages or on the covers of her books. Young Artie, in *Jimmy Lee Did It,* is mischievous. He conveniently blames the imaginary character "Jimmy Lee" for all the mysterious happenings about the house. For this publication, Cummings recalls the many playful pranks her younger brother performed as a child. The illustrations within this volume provide the reader and viewer with surprises not evident within the text of the story. Illustrations bleeding off the page suggest an action had occurred; a picture on the wall suddenly changes perspective once "Jimmy Lee" appears taking some treats from a table, and finally, shadows hinting that Artie, is indeed, the guilty character. Depicting the warm supportive family unit, young Alex, in *Carousel,* is very disappointed that her father did not arrive from his business trip in time for her birthday. Although Alex opens the gift he left for her, a toy carousel, she is unable to contain her hurt and is sent to her room because of rude behavior. While in her room, Alex falls asleep and dreams that the animals in the carousel come to life. As they begin to run outside, each animal encourages Alex to join them amidst the dark of the night and the bright stars. After a time of play, Alex and the animals return to her room. Feeling her fingers around the zebra's mane, Alex awakes to a new morning. Embracing Alex, her father apologizes for the delay in his return for her party. Observing the faces of the characters, the viewer experiences the emotions and spontaneity Cummings captures within the illustrations. The brilliant colors utilized for the animals of the carousel are contrasted with the warmer hues chosen for the moments when the reader or viewer is not to be distracted by fancifulness, but is to concentrate on Cummings' theme for the moment: resolving difficult situations within relationships. Biographical, imaginative, and humorous elements appear collectively in other works that Cummings has written and illustrated. The poetic text in *Clean Your Room Harvey Moon!* reveals the method Harvey selects to clean his room. As in Cummings' other works, the illustrations contain several elements of surprise and humor, not always evident in the text. Based on a true tale told by a friend, Cummings created *Petey Moroni's Camp Runamok Diary,* a daily account of the mysterious happenings of a cleptomaniac raccoon. Choosing her husband as model for the character Chuku, an artist in *C.L.O.U.D.S.,* Cummings reveals her attraction for aerial views and designs in the sky while telling a creative and imaginative tale. Winning the 1992 Boston Globe-Horn Book award for her non-fiction, *Talking with Artists,* Cummings successfully shares with her young audiences the process involved in the creation of the picture story book.

When collaborating with other writers, Cummings' illustrations portray a more serious realistic tone. Utilizing her sister and niece as models for illustration in *Just Us Women,* Cummings captures the close relationship between aunt and niece as they spend quality time traveling together. Preferring to illustrate stories containing relationships and family values, Cummings offers the young viewer an opportunity to experience the story through the faces and expressions she illustrates. Jason's expressions of anticipation in *My Mama Needs Me* as he patiently waits for his new born sister to awaken from her nap, and Willie's look of relief, in *Willie's Not the Hugging Kind* as he discovers that it is acceptable for a boy to be hugged, are examples of Cummings' artistic technique of demonstrating realistic emotions through facial expressions. Other picture books illustrated by Cummings portraying children's emotional responses within a supportive family environment include *Good News, Fred's First Day, Chilly Stomach, Storm in the Night, I Need a Lunchbox, Two and Too Much,* and *Go Fish.*

In a recent interview, Cummings expressed her commitment to the creation of picture story books that offer young readers positive solutions to every day challenges. Her plans for the future include an exploration of the folklore genre and volume two of *Talking with Artists.*

—Linda J. Zoppa

CUNLIFFE, John (Arthur)

Nationality: British. **Born:** Colne, Lancashire, 16 June 1933. **Education:** The Grammar School, Colne, 1944-50; Leeds School of Librarianship, 1954-55; A.L.A. 1955; Northwest London Polytechnic School of Librarianship, 1956-57; F.L.A. 1957; Charlotte Mason College of Education, Ambleside, Westmorland, 1973-75, Cert. Ed. 1975. **Family:** Married Sylvia May Thompson in 1960; one son. **Career:** Branch librarian, Earby, Yorkshire, 1951-54; mobile librarian, Wooler, Northumberland, 1955-56; deputy information officer, Decca Radar Research Laboratories, Tolworth, Surrey, 1957-58; senior assistant librarian, Hendon, London, 1958; manager, rare books department, Foyle's booksellers, London, 1958-59; regional children's librarian, Bletchley, Buckinghamshire, 1959-62; librarian in charge of work with young people, Reading, Berkshire, 1962-64, and Brighton, 1967-73; librarian, British Council, Belgrade, Yugoslavia, 1964-66; education librarian, Newcastle-upon-Tyne, 1966-67; teacher, Castle Park School, Kendal, Cumbria, 1975-79; teacher-organiser, Manchester Education Committee, 1979-80. Full-time writer, from 1985.

Publications for Children

Fiction

Farmer Barnes Buys a Pig, illustrated by Carol Barker. London, Deutsch, 1964; New York, Lion Press, 1968.
Farmer Barnes and Bluebell, illustrated by Carol Barker. London, Deutsch, 1966.
Farmer Barnes at the County Show, illustrated by Jill McDonald. London, Deutsch, 1969; as *Farmer Barnes at the County Fair,* New York, Lion Press, 1969.
The Adventures of Lord Pip, illustrated by Robert Hales. London, Deutsch, 1970.
The Giant Who Stole the World, illustrated by Faith Jaques. London, Deutsch, 1971.
Farmer Barnes and the Goats, illustrated by Jill McDonald. London, Deutsch, 1971.
Riddles and Rhymes and Rigamaroles, illustrated by Alexy Pendle. London, Deutsch, 1971.
The Giant Who Swallowed the Wind, illustrated by Faith Jaques. London, Deutsch, 1972.
Farmer Barnes Goes Fishing, illustrated by Jill McDonald. London, Deutsch, 1972.
Giant Kippernose and Other Stories, illustrated by Fritz Wegner. London, Deutsch, 1972.
The King's Birthday Cake, illustrated by Faith Jaques. London, Deutsch, 1973.
The Great Dragon Competition and Other Stories, illustrated by Alexy Pendle. London, Deutsch, 1973.
The Farmer, The Rooks, and the Cherry Tree, illustrated by Prudence Seward. London, Deutsch, 1974.
Small Monkey Tales, illustrated by Gerry Downes. London, Deutsch, 1974.
Farmer Barnes and the Snow Picnic, illustrated by Joan Hickson. London, Deutsch, 1974.
Giant Brog and the Motorway, illustrated by Alex Pendle. London, Deutsch, 1976.
Farmer Barnes Fells a Tree, illustrated by Joan Hickson. London, Deutsch, 1977.
Farmer Barnes and the Harvest Doll, illustrated by Joan Hickson. London, Deutsch, 1977.
Mr. Gosling and the Runaway Chair, illustrated by William Stobbs. London, Deutsch, 1978.
Farmer Barnes' Guy Fawkes Day, illustrated by Joan Hickson. London, Deutsch, 1978.
Mr. Gosling and the Great Art Robbery, illustrated by William Stobbs. London, Deutsch, 1979.
Sara's Giant and the Upside-Down House, illustrated by Hilary Abrahams. London, Deutsch, 1980.
Our Sam: The Daftest Dog in the World, illustrated by Maurice Wilson. London, Deutsch, 1980.
Postman Pat and the Mystery Thief [*Takes a Message, Goes Sledging, to the Rescue*], illustrated by Celia Berridge. London, Deutsch, 4 vols., 1981-86.

Postman Pat's Treasure Hunt [*Secret, Rainy Day, Difficult Day, Foggy Day, Tractor Express, Thirsty Day, Letters on Ice, Breezy Day*], illustrated by Celia Berridge. London, Deutsch, 9 vols., 1981-85.
Postman Pat Easy Readers (*Postman Pat's Wet Day* [*Messy Day, Safari, Day in Bed, Washing Day, Sore Tooth, Christmas Tree*], *Postman Pat Plays for Greendale* [*and the Christmas Puddings, and the Greendale Ghost, Makes a Splash, and the Dinosaur Bone, and the Spring Cleaning Day, and the Pet Show, and the Bees*]), illustrated by Joan Hickson. London, Deutsch, 14 vols., 1986-89.
Postman Pat Beginners (*Postman Pat's 123 Story* [*ABC Story, Three Wishes*] *Postman Pat Gets Fat*), illustrated by Joan Hickson. London, Deutsch, 4 vols., 1986-90.
Postman Pat's Summer Storybook [*Winter Storybook*], illustrated by Celia Berridge. London, Deutsch, 2 vols., 1987.
Postman Pat's Parcel of Fun, illustrated by Stuart Trotter. London, Deutsch, 1987.
My Postman Pat Storytime Book. London, Treasure, 1987.
Fog Lane School and the Great Racing Car Disaster, illustrated by Andrew Tiffen. London, Deutsch, 1988.
Postman Pat and the Letter-Puzzle. London, Hippo, 1988.
Postman Pat Gets a Pet. London, Hippo, 1988.
Postman Pat Goes Sailing. London, Hippo, 1988.
The Minister's Cat, illustrated by David Parkins. London, Deutsch, 1989.
Postman Pat Goes to Town. London, Hippo, 1989.
Postman Pat's Cat-Up-a-Tree Party. London, Hippo, 1989.
Postman Pat's Greendale Storybook. London, Hippo, 1989.
Postman Pat's Zodiac Storybook, illustrated by Celia Berridge. London, Deutsch, 1989.
Readaloud Stories, with Elizabeth Lindsay and Joan Stimson. London, Hippo, 1990.
Ted Glen's New Year Promises, illustrated by Ray Mutimer. London, Hippo, 1990.
Granny Dryden's Runaway Pig, illustrated by Ray Mutimer. London, Hippo, 1991.
Julian and the Vacuum Cleaner. London, Deutsch, 1991.
My Favourite Postman Pat Stories. London, Treasure, 1991.
Pat and the Puzzle Parcels, illustrated by Ray Mutimer. London, Hippo, 1991.
Postman Pat and the Toy Soldiers. London, Deutsch, 1991.
Postman Pat's Sleepy Days. London, Hippo, 1991.
Dare You Go? London, Deutsch, 1992.
Miss Hubbard's New Hat. London, Hippo, 1992.
Postman Pat Takes the Bus. London, Deutsch, 1992.
Postman Pat Wins a Prize. London, Hippo, 1992.
Postman Pat's Wild Cat Chase. London, Deutsch, 1992.
Rosie & Jim. London, Deutsch, 1992.
Rosie & Jim and the Man in the Wind. London, Deutsch, 1992.

Plays

Postman Pat's Adventures (produced Wimbledon, 1987).

Television Plays: *Postman Pat* series, from 1981.

Poetry

Standing on a Strawberry and Other Poems, illustrated by David Parkins. London, Deutsch, 1987.

Other

Fun and Games with Postman Pat: An Activity Book, with Ivor Wood, illustrated by Joan Hickson. London, Deutsch, 1983.
Play Logo. London, Deutsch, 1984.
The Postman Pat Fun Book, illustrated by Celia Berridge. London, Deutsch, 1987.
Postman Pat and the Toy Soldiers Sticker Fun Book, with Susannah Bradley, illustrated by Ray Mutimer. London, Hippo, 1991.

* * *

John Cunliffe is a well-established storyteller who has written a number of charming picture book stories and some original fairy tales. His earliest picture books, about Farmer Barnes, are simple, appealing stories, written at a slow measured pace, about a somewhat harassed farmer and his family. They are rather long for reading aloud, but the language is simple enough for children of about seven with a reasonable reading ability. Unfortunately, these pleasant stories lack visual uniformity as a series by having three illustrators, Jill McDonald, Joan Hickson, and Carol Barker.

Cunliffe has been a storyteller to groups of children of different ages for a number of years, and has used this experience very effectively in his various collections of original tales. The giant stories are to my mind the most pleasing. "Giant Kippernose" is a very amusing story about a kindly giant who gets very lonely because the people in the village always run away from him. It is only one day when everyone has a streaming cold that the truth is revealed: he stinks! He turns the cheese green, the milk sour, the butter rancid (children revel in such details!). When Giant Kippernose turns over a new leaf and starts having a bath, washing his hair and beard and socks, the villagers are happy to talk to him again. These are all nicely written tales, in the folk tradition, although often with a distinctly modern flavour. *The Great Dragon Competition and Other Stories* is in a similar vein, with some nicely controlled stories, again suitable for reading aloud.

Undoubtedly Cunliffe's most well-received venture has been his stories about Postman Pat and his black and white cat and the residents of a slightly sleepy small valley called Greendale. Part of a television series as well as published books, the stories have had wide exposure and proved immensely popular with preschool aged children. They are competently written, using lively language, short sentences, and simple dialogue. They draw upon a stock of characters peopling Greendale, and present an innocent, fanciful view of small-town life where Pat is given cups of tea and cake on his rounds, collects stamps from the letters he delivers, and bats and bowls the town's cricket team to victory (celebrated with nothing stronger than rhubarb wine). While seeming to look to the past, the stories have amusing touches of the 1980s and 1990s—in *Postman Pat's Day in Bed,* for instance, Pat's replacement while he is ill is a young woman with wonderful spiky green and pink hair.

—Judith Elkin

CUNNINGHAM, Julia (Woolfolk)

Nationality: American. **Born:** Spokane, Washington, 4 Octobe[r] 1916. **Education:** St. Anne's School, Charlottesville, Virgini[a] graduated 1933. **Career:** Clerk, Guaranty Trust Company, New York, 1937-40; co-ordinating editor, G. Schirmer music publishers, New York, 1940-44; associate editor, Dell Publishing Company, New York, 1944-47; secretary, Air Reduction Company, New York, 1947-49; assistant to the advertising manager, Sherman Clay and Company, San Francisco, 1950-51; free-lance writer, France, 1952; salesperson, Metropolitan Museum of Art, New York, 1953-56; bookseller and children's book buyer, Tecolote Book Shop, Santa Barbara, California, 1960-76. **Awards:** *Book World* Children's Spring Festival award, 1962; Southern Council for Children and Young People award, 1966; *New York Times* Outstanding Book of the Year, 1970; Lewis Carroll Shelf award, 1972; Christopher award, 1977; *Boston Globe* honor book, 1981. **Agent:** Bill Berger Associates, 444 East 58th Street, New York, New York 10022. **Address:** 122-A West Valerio Street, Santa Barbara, California 93101, U.S.A.

Publications for Children

Fiction

The Vision of François the Fox, illustrated by Nicholas Angelo. Boston, Houghton Mifflin, 1960.
Dear Rat, illustrated by Walter Lorraine. Boston, Houghton Mifflin, 1961.
Macaroon, illustrated by Evaline Ness. New York, Pantheon, 1962; London, Harrap, 1963.
Candle Tales, illustrated by Evaline Ness. New York, Pantheon, 1964.
Dorp Dead, illustrated by James Spanfeller. New York, Pantheon, 1965; London, Heinemann, 1967.
Viollet, illustrated by Alan Cober. New York, Pantheon, 1966.
Onion Journey, illustrated by Lydia Cooley. New York, Pantheon, 1967.
Burnish Me Bright, illustrated by Don Freeman. New York, Pantheon, 1970; London, Heinemann, 1971.
Wings of the Morning, photographs by Katy Peake. San Carlos, California, Golden Gate Books, 1971.
Far in the Day, illustrated by Don Freeman. New York, Pantheon, 1972.
The Treasure Is the Rose, illustrated by Judy Graese. New York, Pantheon, 1973.
Maybe, A Mole, illustrated by Cyndy Szekeres. New York, Pantheon, 1974.
Come to the Edge. New York, Pantheon, 1977.
Tuppenny. New York, Dutton, 1978.
A Mouse Called Junction, illustrated by Michael Hague. New York, Pantheon, 1980.
Flight of the Sparrow. New York, Pantheon, 1980.
The Silent Voice. New York, Dutton, 1981.
Wolf Roland. New York, Pantheon, 1983.
Oaf, illustrated by Peter Sis. New York, Knopf, 1986.

*

Manuscript Collections: Kerlan Collection, University of Minnesota, Minneapolis; University of Oregon Library, Eugene.

* * *

Since the publication of her first children's book in 1960, Julia Cunningham's works for children have been praised for their originality and for their carefully crafted, highly concentrated, indeed poetic, prose. Cunningham has written such appealing animal fables as *Maybe, A Mole, Macaroon,* and *The Vision of François the Fox* and quasi-gothic stories in the manner of *The Treasure Is the Rose* and *Tuppenny.* In several spare, fable-like stories which feature lost children in search of home, identity, love, and self-worth, Cunningham has brought her work to a high level of excellence.

Among Cunningham's most memorable creations are her anthropomorphic animal characters. Most often in her animal fables Cunningham reveals the power of love to bring forth the highest and the best self. In *The Vision of François the Fox* François begins his adventures as a pleasure-loving and urbane trickster. But when he enters a cathedral, he is awed by the stained-glass vision of a saint. Thenceforth, he surrenders his life of pleasure and aesthetic enjoyment, devoting himself to self-sacrifice. In reversing her readers' expectations about fox behavior, Cunningham suggests that we may break out of conventional molds which limit our possibilities. In *Macaroon* Cunningham depicts a spoiled raccoon who loves only his own pleasure until he finds a little girl, Erika, who truly needs him. This charming animal story reveals Cunningham's gifts for writing descriptions of the natural world and for creating character. *Maybe, A Mole* features a lovable mole who is nevertheless an outsider because he loves the light. Maybe's capacity for loyalty and friendship transforms the worldly fox, who realizes that Maybe is "someone to be trusted, to be company, to be loved." This delightful story provides fine examples of Cunningham's talent for writing droll dialogue. In *A Mouse Called Junction* Cunningham presents an over-protected child mouse who lives in perfect security in a large family. Character motives remain ambiguous in this animal story; the tale strains to realize allegorical significance which remains obscure.

Cunningham's animal characters please the reader with their memorable and vividly depicted personalities, their amusing dialogue, and their capacity for friendship. At times, however, readers may feel that the allegory in the animal fables is strained, that the design upon the reader is perhaps too palpable. At their best, then, Cunningham's stories please with wry humor and vivid characterization; at their worst, they are excessively didactic.

One of Cunningham's most popular children's books is *Dear Rat* which features Andrew the Rat. Cunningham clearly enjoys blending the conventions of detective fiction with the romance of fairy tale in this tale of Andrew the detective from Hampton, Wyoming, who encounters and successfully defeats a tough gangster, Groge, and his muscled goons, Snatch and Flicker. When Andrew arrives in France, he finds that these three gangsters are involved in stealing jewels from the Lady's crown in Chartres Cathedral. Outwardly tough but inwardly honest and tender, Andrew makes friends with Richet, a sensitive and cultivated bird. Through his tenacious powers of ratiocination, Andrew succeeds in returning the jewels to Chartres Cathedral and in winning the hand of the delicately lovely princess rat, Angelique.

Several of Cunningham's works for children reveal strongly gothic elements. In *Viollet* a lovely thrush is a gifted singer who can perform only when she is alone, despite the encouragement of her friends, Warwick the fox and Oxford the hound. An innocent and kind-hearted Count, owner of a vineyard, is keenly in tune with nature and hears the lovely song of the thrush. The setting of this tale with its ruined castle and its lush ripening grapes is powerfully depicted. Tressac, the villainous foreman, is duly thwarted by Viollet, Warwick, and Oxford when he tries to murder the Count and to seize the estate by means of a forged will. Another gothic tale, *The Treasure Is the Rose,* is set in the medieval world of 1100. This tale combines the terrors of the gothic with the charms of medieval romance: love again redeems spiritual and emotional paralysis. In *Tuppenny* Cunningham creates the powerful story of Tuppenny, a lovely and mysterious young girl who enters the lives of three families, each of which hides unspeakable dark secrets from the past. Tuppenny, who strongly suggests that she is a supernatural agent, quite literally rids the town of a horrifying nightmare. *Tuppenny* makes use of more sophisticated gothic dimensions; it conveys a remarkable sense of moral and psychological horror.

One of Cunningham's most significant achievements is her use of what critics have called the "Romantic child." This child is characterized by innocence, affinity with the imagination and with nature. In many of her most compelling children's books Cunningham places this homeless, outcast child in a hostile, sometimes insane, world. This child character not only endures and prevails but brings blessedness and reconciliation to all who are able to receive these gifts.

Certainly Cunningham's most famous and controversial book of this kind is *Dorp Dead.* In this troubling, intensely allegorical work, the first-person narrator, Gilly Ground, hides his intelligence and sensitive nature in the gray, prison-like atmosphere of an orphanage. Driven to distraction by this existence, Gilly runs away for a day to his haven, an ancient crumbling tower "in the center of a tall stand of pines." Gilly regards this isolated pastoral tower as his home, his kingdom; it is the shelter for his dreaming and imagining. On the day when Gilly has fled, Mrs. Heister, the director, has placed him in the foster home of Master Kobalt, an eccentric carpenter who makes ladders. At the tower, Gilly meets a hunter whose gun carries no bullets. The Hunter explains to Gilly that he "hunts to see." Once he finds himself caught up in Master Kobalt's rigid routine, he barely remembers the hunter. At first Gilly is attracted to Kobalt's regimented ways, for Gilly enjoys the benefits of good food, warm clothing, and a comfortable house for the first time in his life. Gradually, however, he learns that Kobalt is not a caring parent, but a mad tyrant, who plans to enslave Gilly in a cage, just as he has enslaved his dog Mash. Gilly narrowly escapes death at Kobalt's hands. As he escapes from his prison with Kobalt (what the Hunter has called Gilly's "bewitchment"), Gilly is encouraged by the vision of a star, by the chorusing of birds in the garden, and by his love for Mash. In this powerful story Cunningham suggests that the Hunter represents the questing, imagining human spirit which perceives its oneness with the universe yet dares to be itself. Kobalt, a fixed element with destructive connotations, seems to represent the regimentation and life-denying aspects of the technological world which values only the practical. Happily Gilly chooses the Hunter's way even at the risk of his life, leaving an unequivocal message to Kobalt, "Dorp Dead." Gilly has not mastered his spelling problems, but he has made the right and the human choice.

In *Flight of the Sparrow* Cunningham reveals a young, homeless girl's attempts to survive on her own in the streets of Paris. "Little Cigarette" is adopted by the boy, Mago, who provides for several homeless children. Eventually Little Cigarette finds herself caught between her loyalty for Mago and her own ideals and values. Cunningham explores a similar theme in the novel *Come to the Edge.*

In her three books about Auguste, the gifted deaf-mute mime artist, Cunningham reveals her creative talent at its best. Her feeling for art and the imagination, her belief that beauty and innocence can survive and even change the worst cruelty and evil, her conviction that human love can exert a powerful moral and spiritual force all find expression in these highly poetic and beautifully crafted books—*Burnish Me Bright, Far in the Day,* and *The Silent Voice.*

In sum, Cunningham has created a distinctive place for herself in 20th-century American children's literature. Her stories present a powerful vision of human possibility and only occasionally strain for allegorical significance or lapse into melodramatic sentimentality. She affirms that innocence, love, human art, and the imagination can prevail in the face of moral blindness, human cruelty, and ignorance.

—Anita Moss

CURRY, Jane Louise

Nationality: American. **Born:** East Liverpool, Ohio, 24 September 1932. **Education:** Pennsylvania State University, State College, 1950-51; Indiana State College (now Indiana University of Pennsylvania), 1951-54, B.S. in education 1954; University of California, Los Angeles, 1957-59; Stanford University, California (teaching assistant), 1959-61, 1964-65, 1967-68, M.A. 1962, Ph.D. 1969; Royal Holloway College, University of London (Fulbright fellow), 1961-62; University College, University of London (Leverhulme fellow), 1965-66. **Career:** Art instructor, East Liverpool, 1955, and Los Angeles city schools, 1955-59; shop assistant, Vroman's Bookstore, Pasadena, California, 1963; acting instructor, 1967-68, and lecturer, 1984, 1987, Stanford University. **Address:** c/o Margaret K. McElderry Books, Simon & Schuster Children's Publishing Division, 1230 Avenue of the Americas, New York, New York 10020.

Publications for Children

Fiction

Beneath the Hill, illustrated by Imero Gobbato. New York, Harcourt Brace, 1967; London, Dobson, 1968.

The Sleepers, illustrated by Gareth Floyd. New York, Harcourt Brace, 1968; London, Dobson, 1969.

The Change-Child, illustrated by Gareth Floyd. New York, Harcourt Brace, 1969; London, Dobson, 1970.

The Daybreakers, illustrated by Charles Robinson. New York, Harcourt Brace, and London, Longman, 1970.

Mindy's Mysterious Miniature, illustrated by Charles Robinson. New York, Harcourt Brace, 1970; as *The Housenapper,* London, Longman, 1971.

Over the Sea's Edge, illustrated by Charles Robinson. New York, Harcourt Brace, and London, Longman, 1971.

The Ice Ghosts Mystery. New York, Atheneum, 1972; London Longman, 1973.

The Lost Farm, illustrated by Charles Robinson. New York, Atheneum, and London, Longman, 1974.

Parsley Sage, Rosemary and Time, illustrated by Charles Robinson. New York, Atheneum, 1975.
The Watchers. New York, Atheneum, 1975; London, Kestrel, 1976.
The Magical Cupboard, illustrated by Charles Robinson. New York, Atheneum, 1976.
Poor Tom's Ghost, illustrated by Janet Archer. New York, Atheneum, and London, Kestrel, 1977.
The Birdstones. New York, Atheneum, 1977; London, Kestrel, 1978.
The Bassumtyte Treasure. New York, Atheneum, and London, Kestrel, 1978.
Ghost Lane. New York, Atheneum, 1979.
The Wolves of Aam. New York, Atheneum, 1981.
Shadow Dancers. New York, Atheneum, 1983.
The Great Flood Mystery. New York, Atheneum, and London, Hippo, 1985.
The Lotus Cup. New York, Atheneum, 1986.
Me, Myself and I. New York, McElderry, 1987.
The Big Smith Snatch. New York, Macmillan, 1989.
Little, Little Sister. New York, Macmillan, 1989.
What the Dickens! New York, Macmillan, 1991.
The Christmas Knight, illustrated by DyAnne DiSalvo-Ryan. New York, McElderry, 1993.
The Great Smith House Hustle. New York, McElderry, 1993.
Robin Hood and His Merry Men. New York, McElderry, 1994.
Robin Hood in the Greenwood. New York, McElderry, 1996.
Moon Window. New York, McElderry, 1996.
Dark Shade. New York, McElderry, 1998.
The Far Side of the Sea, forthcoming.

Other

Down from the Lonely Mountain: California Indian Tales, illustrated by Enrico Arno. New York, Harcourt Brace, 1965; illustrated by the author, London, Dobson, 1968.
Back in the Beforetime: Tales of the Californian Indians, illustrated by James Watts. New York, McElderry, 1987.
Turtle Island: Tales of the Algonquian Peoples, forthcoming.

*

Manuscript Collections: Kerlan Collection, University of Minnesota, Minneapolis.

Jane Louise Curry comments:

After I began work on *The Far Side of the Sea,* I was reminded once again that the books which have given me the most pleasure have been those for which I had to work hardest and learn most. Some stories—the comical adventures—were great fun to tell, and others may have been more suspenseful or exciting, but the titles that leap to mind first when children ask "Which book is your favorite," are *Over the Sea's Edge, Poor Tom's Ghost, The Wolves of Aam* and, *Dark Shade.* I suspect now that *The Far Side of the Sea* may join them. It is set in eighteenth-century Scotland and Virginia, but though I had visited both places, I knew their histories only in a general fashion. I am learning.

I usually happen upon my stories quite unexpectedly. I think, or read, or hear of an odd idea, a surprising event, a place: that in the nineteenth century many people believed that the Mandan Indians were descended from ancient adventurers who sailed from Wales with a Prince Madoc (*Over the Sea's Edge*); or that a house might hold within it a ghost of its long-ago self (*Poor Tom's Ghost*); or that the Indians of the Northeast believed that long ago giants and little people lived in the Great Forest (*The Wolves of Aam*); or that being lost in that Great Forest, parts of which the early settlers called "The Shades of Death," must have been truly terrifying (*Dark Shade*). With *The Far Side of the Sea,* while looking for records of ancestors in Virginia, I happened upon a paragraph about shiploads of stolen Scottish children sold as bond slaves.

Soon, like a magnet collecting iron fillings, a story idea settles in at the back of my mind and begins to collect not characters, but their odd quirks; not scenery, but a great tree here or a stone stair there. Then suddenly I hear something—you might call it a whisper from the bottom of a deep well—that tells me, "Madoc did (not "could have," but a flat, irrational "*did*") sail to America"; or "That odd, castellated house you saw in Isleworth *does* have the ghost of its seventeenth-century self inside it"; or "During the last Ice Age there *were* giants and little people in eastern North American"; or "One of the Highlander soldiers Colonel Bouquet of the British Army reported as getting lost during the expedition that cut a road through the Great Forest in 1758 *stayed* lost for days, and is found by a girl who lives near that same spot in the twentieth century."

Each time this heart-of-the-story feels more like a discovery than an invention. I ask myself, "All right—but *how*? Who was Prince Madoc? When did he live? What was life like there, and then? Who were his family? Why would he have sailed away from Wales in the first place? In what sort of ship? What would he have found if he *did* land in Mobile Bay in Alabama, as some claim? And how did native Americans there live eight hundred or more years ago? Often young readers will say, "You can just make all that up, can't you?" But I can't. I need to *find out*, and the finding-out is more than half the fun. "Detective work," I tell them. But for me it is more complex than a game of or exercise in detection. As I do my research I am both explorer and maker, and I begin to feel as if I am uncovering what happened to my characters rather than inventing it. I learn the names of each of Madoc's (no, Madauc's) half-brothers; I recite the poems the real Llywarch wrote; I learn the actual method by which his followers and workers would have built an ocean-going ship, and I follow on maps the routes upon which caution and the ocean currents would have taken them. I learn that there were *cities* in America long before Columbus came. I discover that the rivers there yielded freshwater pearls by the basketful. And much more. When I began to write, my characters of course did what I planned for them, but their world became so solid, so real to me that, more than once, it seemed as if one had put out a hand to brush me aside—and gone on to do something quite unexpected. And that *is* exciting.

* * *

Since publication of her first book in 1965, Jane Louise Curry has produced works of fantasy and modern fiction, each imbued with the sense of a past that may be gone but certainly is not dead or forgotten. In works like *The Lotus Cup* and *The Great Flood Mystery* the protagonists, intrigued by mysteries and artifacts from the past, seek to learn more; in the course of solving the mystery they realize that history is not barren but made up of the stories of lively, interesting people whose lives still touch their own. Most of Curry's many fantasies concern time and time travel. They are rich with a sense that time past and time present are not separate; the present and the past resonate, each affecting the other, as children of the 20th century help those in earlier times and are themselves helped in return. This resonance is strongest in *Poor Tom's Ghost,* a time fantasy set as much in the England of Elizabeth I as in that of Elizabeth II, as a young boy seeks to alter the destiny of an Elizabethan actor who haunts the boy's father in the 20th century.

Central among Curry's works are her Abáloc novels, eight loosely connected works of high fantasy set on the North American continent. *The Wolves of Aam* and *Shadow Dancers* postulate that magical beings lived here in prehistoric times; *The Watchers, The Birdstones, The Daybreakers, Over the Sea's Edge, The Change-Child,* and *Beneath the Hill* chronicle the remains of that magic in historical times. These works are as much about time and its passage as they are about the struggle between good and evil, as lands and peoples replace earlier lands and peoples. Before the Ice Age, eastern North America is inhabited by the magical Silvrin, who move on and leave the land to the Aldar, an equally magical people. During the Ice Age the region, populated by giants and men and the nomadic Tiddi, is called Astarlind. By the 4th century, when the Aldar have traveled to a land beyond the world, what remains has been replaced by Ebhélic. Ebhélic becomes Abáloc long before the 12th century; by the 20th century, even Abáloc has been forgotten, though Apple Lock, West Virginia, has grown up in the area. Each age forgets what has gone before—the shy, long-established families of 20th-century Twilly's Green, West Virginia, have no knowledge of the Aldar from whom they are descended, and the 12th-century Abalockians cannot read the ancient book of history preserved from 4th-century Ebhélic. But the magic has lived on in the land: each period feels the touch of evil powers imprisoned beneath the mountains in the first age of Astarlind; and in the 20th century an ancient ammarn tree remains from the powerful groves that protected the land long before the 4th century. Time is a real presence in those novels. Represented as an endless ring surrounding a tree, it appears several places in the novels: the gentle Abalockians see it as the ring of eternity cradling the fruitfulness of life, while the savage people of Cibotlán see it as the ring of death binding the life inside.

Ultimately the past, in almost all Curry's novels, is something we ignore at our peril. Destroying the writings of earlier ages, the people of Ebhélic are defenseless against those who use knowledge to hold them in thrall; the evil forces held beneath the mountains almost destroy the descendants of their keepers, who are ignorant of earlier events. In *Poor Tom's Ghost,* Roger Nicholas, happy when his family finally settles in the house his father has inherited, finds that its history may destroy the security he has built. In several works—including Curry's modern fiction—the protagonists find in the past a sort of saving grace. In *The Daybreakers* artifacts of Abáloc when sold will bolster the Apple Lock school system's sagging budget and help reopen the schools. In *The Lotus Cup* Corry Tipson finds the key to her future in her family's past: reconstructing a porcelain-making process, she discovers both her true talents and confidence in herself.

Curry's work is graceful and evocative, her characters lively, especially in *The Lotus Cup* and *Poor Tom's Ghost.* Her attempt to create for North America a mythical past is especially interesting for the reader of fantasy. Reading the Abáloc novels in order of publication is like watching an archaeological dig: having "discovered" the artifacts of Astarlind in *Beneath the Hill,* Curry seems to have dug deeper and deeper into her mythical past with each successive book, and part of the reader's pleasure is in fitting together the history of the land.

—Pat Pflieger

D

DALE, Penny

Nationality: British. **Born:** London 1954. **Education:** Bristol Polytechnic Faculty of Art and Design, Foundation Course, 1971-2; Exeter College of Art and Design, B.A. (honours) in Fine Art 1977. **Family:** Married Bryan Dale in 1978; one daughter. **Career:** Member of Natural Theatre company, Bath, 1972-73; costume designer and maker, Northcott Theatre, Exeter, 1977-78; graphic design, Northumbrian Energy Workshop, 1979-80; print maker and watercolour artist, 1981-84; writer and illustrator of children's books, from 1985. **Awards:** Commended for Kate Greenaway Medal, 1988; Best Books for Babies Award, 1990. **Address:** c/o Walker Books, 87 Vauxhall Walk, London SE11 5HJ, England.

Publications for Children (illustrated by the author)

Fiction

Bet You Can't. London, Walker Books, 1987.
Ten in the Bed. London, Walker Books, 1988.
Wake Up, Mr. B! London, Walker Books, 1988.
The Elephant Tree. London, Walker Books, 1991.
All about Alice. London, Walker Books, 1992.
Play with Alice and Laura. London, Walker Books, 1993.
Ten Out of Bed. London, Walker Books, 1993.
Daisy Rabbit's Tree House. London, Walker Books, 1995.
Big Brother, Little Brother. London, Walker Books, 1997.
Ten Play Hide and Seek. London, Walker Books 1998.

*

Illustrator: *Unknown* by Philippa Hunt, 1986; *The Stopwatch* by David Lloyd, 1986; *Once There Were Giants,* 1989, *Rosie's Babies,* 1990, and *When the Teddy Bears Came,* 1994, all by Martin Waddell; *The Mushroom Hunt* by Simon Frazer, 1994.

Penny Dale comments:

I discovered I wanted to write and illustrate books for children after doing quite a lot of other things/activities although all of them were related to art and theatre in some way. It was when my daughter started to enjoy being read to that I began to look more carefully at the books we read and thought I would like to do that!

I realised I had always liked the combination of words and pictures. Back at school I remembered how I had continued to draw pictures alongside essays or pieces of writing, e.g. in history or geography that were more elaborate than the teachers really wanted or expected. When I was about 14 and studying medieval castles in Britain, the teacher asked for a simple plan of the castle to go beside our writing—I made a kind of lift the flap plan in my exercise book so you could reveal all the levels or floors in the castle. I drew dungeons and kitchens on the lower levels, grand halls with a banqueting table higher up and bedrooms with four posters. I drew the food on the table, people in the beds, and cannons on the roof. My teacher was rather stunned. I think he liked it, but by that age I suspect he would have preferred more writing and less drawing.

I realised later on when I looked back to school days that what I was doing was writing *and* illustrating. Even though I studied fine art, mostly sculpture, at college, and worked in the theatre quite extensively, the seeds of what I do nowadays were obviously starting to grow a long time ago.

I often work with words and pictures simultaneously. I tend to work on large sheets of paper, putting words and very basic sketches together to see if they work, sometimes writing much of it like a screen play or film storyboard. Words themselves are necessarily simple for young readers. Pictures add to the emotional and atmospheric depth of the book—standing in for detailed descriptive passages and scene setting, adding to the depth of characterisation with facial expressions, gestures, and body language.

The most exciting part of writing with words and pictures for me is the magic that happens when the two feel as if they are communicating a mysterious third world that lies in the space between them, a place for the audience to inhabit and add to with their own imaginations.

*   *   *

Penny Dale's work is characterised by realism in both text and pictures. Her illustrations have a photographic quality and the text is often accurate reporting of children's activities and speech. Her storylines are the familiar everyday events that make up family life with the under-fives, much of it focusing on the very real imaginary relationships children have with their toys. Her children are carefree individuals, unhindered by adult restraints, completely absorbed in their adventures.

Her first book, *Bet You Can't,* features two small children trying very hard to tidy up while being thwarted in an amusing way throughout. The text is minimal—just the short, repetitive speech of the children—making it easy to understand for the very youngest. The humour is in the pictures that show what is really happening.

Ten in the Bed shows a child in a big bed with nine soft toys playing along to the nursery song "There were ten in the bed and the little one said, 'Roll over.'" Each time they roll over one of the toys falls out of bed, until at last: "There was one in the bed and the little one said, 'I'm cold! I miss you!'" The pictures show the toys getting up to mischief and finally all bounding back to bed and going to sleep. In *Ten Out of Bed,* the same child and toys start off playing wild imaginary games and one by one the toys fall asleep, until only the child is left awake. In *Ten Play Hide and Seek* the toys are back for a bedtime game of hide-and-seek, which finishes when they cannot find Mouse. Eventually he pops up from under the bedclothes and all ends happily once more with them tucked up in bed and asleep. These three books successfully combine realism in the accuracy of the pictures and imaginative fantasy in the actions of the child and the toys.

The Elephant Tree is in a similar vein, with two children playing in the garden with their toys. Gradually reality changes to make-believe as they go in search of a tree for elephant to climb. They come across a "bird tree," a "monkey tree," a "tiger tree," and finally a wood full of "bear trees." The text is minimal, but the pictures lead children masterfully through this adventure. Each shows echoes of the last picture and, in the distance, a foretaste of the next page. These may not even be noticed by children at first, but they provide a wonderful sense of continuity as the adventure ends up back in the garden with a mound of snow made into an elephant tree with twigs.

Daisy Rabbit's Tree House is a variation on the theme, but the same toys now have lives and families of their own. Daisy Rabbit learns not to feel homesick when she stays the night at her friends' houses. This familiar anxiety of young children is thoughtfully explored through the toys, enabling children to recognise and deal with their own fears from a safe distance.

Wake Up, Mr. B! is an example of Penny Dale's skill at filling out a minimal text with the irony and humour in the pictures. An early-rising Rosie has little success in rousing her brother or her parents, so she wakes Mr. B, a huge dog, with whom she plays some delightful games before they both fall asleep again under the kitchen table. Beautifully observed domestic detail make this accessible to very young children.

All about Alice is an amiable and realistic portrait of family life with young children. Alice and her big sister, Laura, are getting dressed. "Here are some of Alice's clothes. What do you think she put on?" The pictures show shiny shoes, green trousers, a party dress, dungarees, and more. The next page shows her putting on a strange combination of clothes, until Dad comes and helps her dress properly. The text continues in this vein, following Alice's day having breakfast, taking Laura to school with her mother, playing at home, collecting Laura and so on. Each page invites the reader to guess what Alice will do on the next page. All these questions make this an excellent book to share with preschool children to develop language and explore the idea of making choices.

Big Brother, Little Brother portrays another affectionate sibling relationship that is familiar to many families. When the little brother cries only his big brother knows what is wrong and what to do to cheer him up—and he's always right. But when little brother wants his big brother's truck there is a contretemps. When big brother cries this time, little brother knows why. Once again the text is simple, and the pictures wonderfully evocative of the warmth of the relationship.

Penny Dale has illustrated books by other writers, most successfully with Martin Waddell, perhaps because the themes are similar to her own: the relationships between very young children and their siblings and parents. For example, *Rosie's Babies* and *When the Teddy Bears Came* deal with children's feelings about a new baby in the family. *Once There Were Giants* looks at how a child grows from being a baby to having a baby of her own. Her style fits beautifully with Waddell's gentle lilting prose, perfectly portraying these domestic situations.

—Fiona Lafferty

DALGLIESH, Alice

Nationality: American (emigrated to the United States, 1902; naturalized citizen). **Born:** Trinidad, West Indies, 7 October 1893. **Education:** Pratt Institute, Brooklyn, New York, diploma in kindergarten teaching; Teachers College, Columbia University, New York, A.B. in English and education, M.A. **Career:** Teacher of kindergarten and elementary education for 17 years; teacher at Horace Mann School, New York; editor, Books for Young Readers, Charles Scribner's Sons, New York, 1934-60. Contributing editor, *Saturday Review,* New York, 1960-66. **Died:** 11 June 1979.

Publications for Children

Fiction

West Indian Play Days, illustrated by Margaret Evans Price. Chicago, Rand McNally, 1926.

The Little Wooden Farmer, and The Story of the Jungle Pool, illustrated by Theodora Baumeister. New York, Macmillan, 1930; revised edition, 1968; London, Hamish Hamilton, 1969.

The Blue Teapot: Sandy Cove Stories, illustrated by Hildegard Woodward. New York, Macmillan, 1931.

The Choosing Book, illustrated by Eloise Burns Wilkin. New York, Macmillan, 1932.

Relief's Rocker, illustrated by Hildegard Woodward. New York, Macmillan, 1932.

Roundabout, illustrated by Hildegard Woodward. New York, Macmillan, 1934.

Sailor Sam, illustrated by the author. New York, Scribner, 1935.

The Smiths and Rusty, illustrated by Berta and Elmer Hader. New York and London, Scribner, 1936.

Wings for the Smiths, illustrated by Berta and Elmer Hader. New York and London, Scribner, 1937.

The Young Aunts, illustrated by Charlotte Becker. New York and London, Scribner, 1939.

The Hollyberrys, illustrated by Pru Herric. New York and London, Scribner, 1939.

Wooden Shoes in America, illustrated by Lois Maloy. New York, Scribner, 1940.

A Book for Jennifer: A Story of London Children in the Eighteenth Century and of Mr. Newbery's Juvenile Library, illustrated by Katherine Milhous. New York, Scribner, 1940.

Three from Greenways, illustrated by Gertrude Howe. New York, Scribner, and London, Hodder and Stoughton, 1941.

Gulliver Joins the Army, illustrated by Ellen Segner. New York, Scribner, 1942.

The Little Angel, illustrated by Katherine Milhous. New York, Scribner, 1943.

The Silver Pencil, illustrated by Katherine Milhous. New York, Scribner, 1944.

Along Janet's Road, illustrated by Katherine Milhous. New York, Scribner, 1946.

Reuben and His Red Wheelbarrow, illustrated by Ilse Bischoff. New York, Grosset and Dunlap, 1946.

The Davenports Are at Dinner, illustrated by Flavia Gág. New York, Scribner, 1948.

The Davenports and Cherry Pie, illustrated by Flavia Gág. New York, Scribner, 1949.

The Bears on Hemlock Mountain, illustrated by Helen Sewell. New York, Scribner, 1952; London, Epworth Press, 1965.

The Courage of Sarah Noble, illustrated by Leonard Weisgard. New York, Scribner, 1954; London, Hamish Hamilton, 1970.

Adam and the Golden Cock, illustrated by Leonard Weisgard. New York, Scribner, 1959.

Other

A Happy School Year (reader), illustrated by Mary Spoor Brand. Chicago, Rand McNally, 1924.
Peregrin and the Goldfish, illustrated by Tom Seidmann-Freud. New York, Macmillan, 1929.
First Experiences with Literature (textbook). New York, Scribner, 1932.
America Travels: The Story of a Hundred Years of Travel in America, illustrated by Hildegard Woodward. New York, Macmillan, 1933; revised edition, 1961.
Long Live the King! A Story Book of English Kings and Queens, illustrated by Lois Maloy. New York, Scribner, 1937.
America Begins: The Story of the Finding of the New World, illustrated by Lois Maloy. New York, Scribner, 1938; revised edition, 1959.
America Builds Homes: The Story of the First Colonies, illustrated by Lois Maloy. New York, Scribner, 1938.
Wings Around South America, illustrated by Katherine Milhous. New York, Scribner, 1941.
The True Story of Fala, with Margaret Suckley. New York, Scribner, 1942.
They Live in South America, illustrated by Katherine Milhous and Frances Lichten. New York, Scribner, 1942.
The Thanksgiving Story, illustrated by Helen Sewell. New York, Scribner, 1954.
The Columbus Story, illustrated by Leo Politi. New York, Scribner, 1955.
The Fourth of July Story, illustrated by Marie Nonnast. New York, Scribner, 1956.
Ride the Wind (on Charles Lindbergh), illustrated by Georges Schreibner. New York, Scribner, 1956.

Editor, *Christmas: A Book of Stories New and Old,* illustrated by Hildegard Woodward. New York, Scribner, 1934; as *A Christmas Holiday Book,* London, Dent, 1934.
Editor, *Once on a Time* (folktales), illustrated by Katherine Milhous. New York, Scribner, 1938.
Editor, with Françoise, *The Gay Mother Goose,* illustrated by Françoise. New York, Scribner, 1938.
Editor, *The Will James Cowboy Book.* New York, Scribner, 1938.
Editor, *Happily Ever After: Fairy Tales,* illustrated by Katherine Milhous. New York, Scribner, 1939.
Editor, *St. George and the Dragon,* by Richard Johnson, illustrated by Lois Maloy. New York, Scribner, 1941.
Editor, *The Enchanted Book,* illustrated by Concetta Cacciola. New York, Scribner, 1947.

Publications for Adults

Other

Selected Books for Young Children, with *Selected Pictures for Young Children,* by Rita Scherman. New York, Educational Playthings, 1934.
The Horace Mann Kindergarten for Five-Year-Old Children, with Charlotte Garrison and Emma Sheehy. New York, Columbia University Teachers College, 1937.

Editor, with Annis Duff, *Aids to Choosing Books for Your Children.* New York, Children's Book Council, 1957.

* * *

Alice Dalgliesh's rich background as a British and American subject, as a kindergarten and elementary school teacher, and as a children's book editor are all reflected in her many different types of children's books, with their wide variety of locale, period, and subject matter. Perhaps Dalgliesh's information books are her most popular ones; many have gone through various editions, and, in the case of *America Travels,* the second edition is revised and enlarged. This work is characteristic of Dalgliesh's competent treatment of information and history. The style is casual, with a strong emphasis on dialogue, factual exposition, and indirect characterization. This particular work contains eight "traveling tales," as diverse as the story about a young pioneer child who travels alone by stage coach, and a story about "two boys and the first automobile that came to town." The intent of the author is to give a young reading audience a taste of a broad range of accurate subject matter related to travel.

This attention to accuracy, detail, and diversity is also characteristic of *The Thanksgiving Story, The Fourth of July Story,* and *Christmas: A Book of Stories New and Old.* The exactness of detail and perspective in the information books is reflected in Dalgliesh's juvenile historical novels, such as *Adam and the Golden Cock,* based on a true story that occurred around Newton, Connecticut, in 1781, and *The Courage of Sarah Noble,* also a true story, about an eight-year-old child who travels through the wilderness into Indian country to cook for her father while he builds a new home. Sarah's perceptions about the Indian community and the "humanness" of its members are of real value to the child who grows up with a demeaning and stereotyped impression of American Indians superimposed on him from all sides.

Alice Dalgliesh's characters and stories are all given life and moment because of the author's attention to image, detail, and believability. For this reason, two of Dalgliesh's picture books for young children have remained perennial favorites. *The Little Wooden Farmer,* in a 1968 edition with fine illustrations by Anita Lobel, is a repetition book emphasizing the progressive steps one takes to produce a well-appointed farm. Because of the dialogue, repetition, and progression, the book reads well aloud. Dalgliesh apparently realized this when she first published the story in 1930 as one "to read and play." The dramatic quality of Dalgliesh's picture books is seen best in *The Bears on Hemlock Mountain.* This is a tense, suspenseful, and characteristically imaginative tale that lends itself both to reading aloud and acting out. Behind all of Dalgliesh's work is a strong sense of the child audience for which it is written, and a delight in language, detail, situation, and action.

—Rachel Fordyce

DALLAS, Ruth

Pseudonym for Ruth Mumford. **Nationality:** New Zealander. **Born:** Invercargill, 29 September 1919. **Education:** Southland Technical College, Invercargill. **Awards:** New Zealand Literary Fund achievement award, 1963; University of Otago Robert Burns fellowship, 1968; New Zealand Book award, for poetry, 1977; Buckland award, for poetry, 1977. Litt.D.: University of Otago, Dunedin, 1978. **Address:** 448 Leith Street, Dunedin, New Zealand.

Publications for Children

Fiction

The Children in the Bush, illustrated by Peter Campbell. London, Methuen, 1969.
Ragamuffin Scarecrow, illustrated by Els Noordhof. Dunedin, University of Otago Bibliography Room, 1969.
A Dog Called Wig, illustrated by Edward Mortelmans. London, Methuen, 1970.
The Wild Boy in the Bush, illustrated by Peter Campbell. London, Methuen, 1971.
The Big Flood in the Bush, illustrated by Peter Campbell. London, Methuen, 1972; New York, Scholastic, 1974.
The House on the Cliffs, illustrated by Gavin Rowe. London, Methuen, 1975.
Shining Rivers, illustrated by Gareth Floyd. London, Methuen, 1979.
Holiday Time in the Bush, illustrated by Gary Hebley. London, Methuen, 1983.

Other

Sawmilling Yesterday, illustrated by Juliet Peter. Wellington, Department of Education, 1958.
Curved Horizon: An Autobiography. Dunedin, University of Otago Press, 1991.

Publications for Adults

Poetry

Country Road and Other Poems 1947-1952. Christchurch, Caxton Press, 1953.
The Turning Wheel. Christchurch, Caxton Press, 1961.
Experiment in Form. Dunedin, University of Otago Bibliography Room, 1964.
Day Book: Poems of a Year. Christchurch, Caxton Press, 1966.
Shadow Show. Christchurch, Caxton Press, 1968.
Song for a Guitar and Other Songs, edited by Charles Brasch. Dunedin, University of Otago Press, 1976.
Walking on the Snow. Christchurch, Caxton Press, 1976.
Steps of the Sun. Christchurch, Caxton Press, 1979.
Collected Poems. Dunedin, University of Otago Press, 1987.

*

Manuscript Collections: Hocken Library, University of Otago, Dunedin, New Zealand.

Ruth Dallas comments:

In New Zealand when I was a child, the books I read came from England and were to a certain extent foreign, in that I had never seen the environment I was reading about: big cities, attached houses, upstairs bedrooms, nurseries, nannies, fathers who were abroad, English villages, gamekeepers, and all historical material, including very old houses—in short, the common paraphernalia of children's fiction as I first encountered it. Even the elderly people in my family had grown up in a setting that was quite different from the "old country." Between the oral New Zealand tales I heard and storybook stories from overseas, there was a gap that disturbed me for a long time. I began to write stories about New Zealand children for the school journals in 1958. My first children's novel was published in London in 1969 and was based on tales I had heard in my own family. I had noticed that children were growing up who did not know that much of their green farmland was once covered with the forest that is now found in reserves and that not only old pioneers had lived in the bush but children, too. I plan to continue writing New Zealand stories, both historical and contemporary, as well as poetry.

* * *

Ruth Dallas is best known in her own country as a poet who particularly evokes the landscape of southern South Island. Both her prose and poetry for children have been made available to numerous young New Zealanders through the School Journals, enlightened publications put out by the Department of Education for reading in schools.

The connection with educational purpose may in part contribute to the slightly didactic nature of her earlier works. *The Children in the Bush, The Wild Boy in the Bush,* and *The Big Flood in the Bush* all rather self-consciously teach about the life of the early settlers but are made vivid by the liveliness of their characterization. All three books feature a family of four 19th-century children whose vigour, enthusiasm, and propensity for getting into not unlikely scrapes in the absences of their widowed mother, the Settlement's nurse, are reminiscent of E. Nesbit's. Ruth Dallas has the rare gift of conveying a "child's eye view," and these books are recounted by the youngest—8-year-old Jean. The angle of the narrative is convincingly hers, whether she describes laughing and talking after bedtime so that "Mrs. Bain came into the room in her petticoat" or the frequent crises with their cow, who rejoiced in the inspired name of "Hokey-Pokey."

The numerous animal stories, plays, and poems published in the "Journals" reached fruition in *A Dog Called Wig,* which must be one of the most unusual of all animal stories. Here a boy, who initially has to plead with his parents to keep the stray dog which has appeared in the garden, subsequently feels betrayed and disillusioned by the animal's attachment to his father. Only after the dog is badly injured and the boy involved in an exciting adventure with escaped Borstal inmates, is the relationship restored.

These books are all in an "easy to read" format which, while most suitable to the less confident reader, are stylistically cramping. In *The House on the Cliffs,* however, Dallas has profited by a longer book for an older reader. In this evocative story the images of shells, wind, rocks, and solitary sea-birds, which occur so frequently in her poems, become symbols of the delicate balance between loneliness and independence in the relationship between eccentric old Biddy Bristow and two present-day schoolgirls. This story has the different levels of meaning so characteristic of both good poetry and good children's literature, and in Biddy's single-minded beach searchings for "a bell to ring when the wind blows" we learn something of the nature of creative seeking.

Friendship between old and young is again central in *Shining Rivers,* set in the Otago goldfields of the 1860s, in which a young immigrant boy leaves a safe bakery job to go to "the diggings," lured by prospects of speedy wealth. His disenchantment with the rough scene there is tempered by the guidance and generosity of an old miner, and this carefully researched novel presents a thoughtful and convincing picture of the past.

—Betty Gilderdale

DALTON, Annie

Nationality: British. **Born:** Dorset, England, 1948. **Awards:** Nottinghamshire Book Award, 1991; Carnegie Medal commendation, 1991.

Publications for Children

Fiction

Out of the Ordinary. London, Methuen, 1988.
Night Maze. London, Methuen, 1989.
The Witch Rose. London, Methuen, 1990.
The Afterdark Princess. London, Methuen, 1990.
The Alpha Box. London, Methuen, 1991.
Demon-Spawn. London, Blackie, 1991.
The Real Tilly Beany. London, Methuen, 1991.
Swan Sister. London, Methuen, 1992.
Naming the Dark. London, Methuen, 1992.
Tilly Beany and the Best Friend Machine. London, Methuen, 1993.
Ugly Mug. London, Hamish Hamilton, 1994.

Other

Contributor, *Love Them, Hate Them: Stories of Brothers and Sisters,* edited by Tony Bradman. London, Methuen, 1991.

* * *

Annie Dalton has set her personal trademark on the genre of children's and teenage fantasy with, so far, four novels for young adults and four for children, plus three more realistic stories for under-11s. The children's fantasy genre, regarded by connoisseurs as the highest achievement in children's literature, has the drawback of a literary and allusive style, so that reluctant readers may find its assumptions intimidating, whether the book is a classic by Kipling or Nesbit, a modern classic by Alan Garner, or a secondary-world fantasy by Tolkien or Le Guin. While still crafting literary fantasies, Dalton has made an explicit and consistent effort to involve disadvantaged readers in her books.

All the leading characters in her young adult books are either orphans, from single-parent families, or do not live with their parents. They are usually short of money and awkward with the opposite sex. Her books are optimistic: supernatural encounters go some way to solve her characters' problems, in the tradition of Nesbit and Diana Wynne Jones. As in a number of Nesbit's books, the setting is usually the run-down part of town, with families in ordinary or decrepit housing. As her heroes and heroines begin to experience supernatural events, they ridicule themselves and use modern slang to deprecate the magic opening up around them. Then Dalton builds to her climaxes where phrases like "rainbow dazzle," "dim blue incandescence," and "burning golden whirlpool" evoke the intense spirituality of transforming magic.

In *Out of the Ordinary,* a restless teenage girl scribbles a note offering her services in any quest going; soon she is entrusted with a changeling from another world and must guard him from an evil wizard. When the wizard snatches the boy, she goes into the magic dimension to rescue him. In *Night Maze,* the one exception to the rule that her characters live in dilapidated housing, two orphans find themselves in an ancient house, adopted into a family that lives under a 400-year-old curse. They must lift the curse by undergoing the ordeal of the Night Maze.

In *The Alpha Box,* Asha finds a box in a junk shop. It proves to be Pandora's Box itself, and she has been selected by the Great Goddess to save the world from pollution and space aliens (thus the story is a mixture of sci-fi and fantasy). Asha attracts the interests of Joss, a youth who has acquired what might be Orpheus's lyre from the junk shop, a lyre transformed into a modern guitar.

In *Naming the Dark,* the teenage hero discovers that he is descended from the long-lost rulers of Atlantis, and is destined to follow the "ancient golden road" and find and mend a magic sword: the Grail legend lies behind this fantasy. Both the latter novels also feature the theme of the war between men and women, and how individuals may tackle and improve the situation.

The Witch Rose, The Afterdark Princess, and *Swan Sister* are poetical fantasies for 8- to 13-year-olds. In the first, a mother and daughter live alone, waiting for the father to realise he needs them, and for the mother to overcome her resentment against his love of magic; in the second, a teenage schoolgirl comes to babysit, and takes her charges into a world of quests and monsters; and in the third, a baby girl is kidnapped by wild swans as revenge for humans polluting their environment. These charming little books introduce children to the concepts of high and fairy-tale fantasy within a relatively short and welcoming text, with *Swan Sister,* echoing Hans Andersen, the longest of the three.

The Real Tilly Beany and *Tilly Beany and the Best Friend Machine* are not fantasies, but depict the daily life of a young girl with a highly coloured inner life. Matilda, "Tilly," at only five years old has the gift of improvising herself a fresh costume and personality right down to the makeup, and giving herself wholeheartedly to her play. Her family and friends try to accept her transformation into a witch, mermaid, and teddy bear, but when she can't snap out of her Cindertilly impersonation, her parents realise she needs a special kind of drama teacher.

Tilly Beany and the Best Friend Machine shows Tilly in search of a new "best friend" when everyone else in her school class has paired off. She copes with losing her former best friend, gets an idea from her teenage sister about computer dating, and builds a crazy machine out of an old mangle—but her wish comes true in the end. These stories are perfect to read aloud or alone for children in the transition from picture books to children's novels.

In a relatively short time Annie Dalton has attracted a crowd of teenage and adult admirers to hail this latest entrant to the roster of living children's poetic fantasists such as Garner, Wynne Jones, Farmer, and Yolen.

—Jessica Yates

DALY, Niki

Nationality: South African. **Born:** Nicholas Daly, Cape Town, 13 June 1946. **Education:** Cape Technikon, diploma (in art and design) 1970. **Family:** Married Judith Mary Kenny in 1973; two sons. **Career:** Singer and songwriter, C.B.S. Record Company, London, 1970-72; junior art director, Advertising Agency, London, 1973-75; free-lance illustrator, London, from 1975, and author, from 1978; graphics teacher, East Ham College of Technology, London, 1976-79; head of graphic design, Stellenbosch University, 1983-89; head of Songololo Books division, David Philip Publishers, 1989-92. **Awards:** British Arts Council and Provincial Booksellers Award for Illustration, 1978; *Horn Book* Honor List, 1987; Parents' Choice Foundation Parents' Choice Book Award for Literature, 1988; Katrien Harries Award (South Africa) for illustration, 1988; IBBY Honours Award, for illustration, 1995, for *All the Magic in the World*; one of the ten best illustrated books to be publihsed in the U.S.A., *New York Times Literary Supplement,* 1995, for *Why the Sun and Moon Live in the Sky,* and 1996, for *One Round Moon and a Star for Me*; Anne Izard Story Teller's Choice Award, Westchester, New York, Library System, 1996, for *Why the Sun and Moon Live in the Sky.* Member: Association of Illustrators (London). **Agent:** Laura Cecil, 17 Alwyne Villas, London N1 2HG, England. **Address:** 36 Strubens Road, Cape Town, South Africa. E-mail Address: inkman@iafrica.com.

PUBLICATIONS FOR CHILDREN

Fiction (illustrated by the author)

The Little Girl Who Lived Down the Road. London, Collins, 1978.
Vim the Rag Mouse. London, Gollancz, and New York, McElderry, 1979.
Joseph's Other Red Sock. London, Gollancz, and New York, McElderry, 1982.
Leo's Christmas Surprise. London, Gollancz, 1983.
Not So Fast, Songololo. London, Gollancz, 1985, New York, Atheneum, 1986.
The Walker Storytime series
- *Ben's Gingerbread Man.* London, Walker Books, and New York, Viking, 1985.
- *Teddy's Ear.* London, Walker Books, 1985.
- *Monsters Are Like That.* London, Walker Books, 1985.
- *Just Like Archie.* London, Walker Books, 1986.
- *Look at Me!* London, Walker Books, 1986.
- *Thank You Henrietta.* London, Walker Books, 1986.

With Ingrid Mennen, *Ashraf of Africa,* illustrated by Nikolaas Maritz. Cape Town, Songololo Books, 1991; as *Somewhere in Africa,* New York, Dutton, and London, Bodley Head, 1992.
Mama, Papa and Baby Joe. London, Viking Kestrel, and New York, Viking, 1991.
Mary Malloy and the Baby Who Wouldn't Sleep. Racine, Wisconsin, Western, 1991; as *Mary Malloy, the Crescent Moon and the Baby Who Couldn't Sleep,* London, Heinemann, 1993.
Papa Lucky's Shadow. New York, Margaret K. McElderry, 1991, London, The Bodley Head, 1993.
With Wendy Hartmann, *All the Magic in the World,* New York, Dutton, and London, Bodley Head, 1993.
Why the Sun and Moon Live in the Sky. New York, Lothrop, 1994.
With Ingrid Mennen, *One Round Moon and a Star for Me.* New York, Orchard Books, and London, Bodley Head, 1994.
My Dad: Story and Pictures. New York, Margaret K. McElderry, 1995.
With Nola Turkington, *The Dancer.* Cape Town, Human and Rousseau, 1996
With Wendy Hartmann, *The Dinosaurs are Back and it's All Your Fault Edward.* New York, Margaret McElderry, and London, Bodley Head, 1996.
Zan Angelo. New York, Farrar, Straus & Giroux, and London, Frances Lincoln, 1998.

*

Illustrator: Kathleen Hersom, *Maybe It's a Tiger,* Macmillan (London), 1981; Christopher Gregorowski, *Fly Eagle Fly,* Tafelberg Publishers (Cape Town), 1982; Louis Baum, *I Want To See the Moon,* Bodley Head, 1984, Overlook Press, 1989; Ruth Craft, *The Day of the Rainbow,* Viking Kestrel, 1989; Reviva Shermbrucker, *Charlie's House,* London, Walker Books, 1992; Cari Best, *Red Light, Green Light, Mama and Me,* New York, Orchard Books, 1995.

Media Adaptations: With Weston Woods, video presentation of *Not So Fast, Songololo,* 1990.

* * *

Although he has lived and worked in Britain, Niki Daly is South African and currently lives in that country. He uses his experience of different races and continents to very great effect. What binds all Niki Daly's work together, whether he is artist, artist-author, or co-author, is his deep affection for children, as well as his acknowledgement of and respect for their imaginative powers.

His books for very young children show a keen awareness of a small child's life and surroundings. These are portrayed with a simplicity and tenderness that speaks very directly to the reader. *Teddy's Ear,* one of a series of six small books, tells how Teddy's ear comes off, and is sewn on again. At the end, the picture alone shows how Tim holds Teddy: by the ear. For slightly older readers, we find the same qualities in *Red Light, Green Light, Mama and Me,* where Daly's artwork depicts the day Lizzie spends with Mama working in the library. A world away from the American setting of this story, *One Round Moon and a Star for Me* takes us to rural Lesotho in southern Africa. Mama has a new baby, and friends and relatives bring gifts. "I'm the baby's father", Papa says—but is swift to reassure the unnamed narrator that he's the narrator's father too. The small fears of childhood are as real, and as sympathetically dealt with, in a hut on the African plains as in the hurly-burly of an American city. *Not So Fast, Songololo* is a delightful story about Shepherd and Gogo, his Granny, going into town to buy some new shoes. Both Shepherd and Gogo are slow in their movements, though Shepherd looks after Gogo when it comes to traffic and crossing the road. The affection between the pair is evident—including Granny's nickname for Shepherd, Songololo.

Many of Daly's books show a rich vein of humour. Joseph's frantic hunt for his missing sock, in *Joseph's Other Red Sock,* produces a wonderful monster in the cupboard! The crowded mess that is Joseph's bedroom will be familiar to every reader. Children will particularly appreciate the last page, in which Joseph, having defeated the cupboard monster, goes off with two red socks ... and one blue shoe. *Mama, Papa, and Baby Joe* is the story of a shopping trip; written in simple verse, it demands to be read aloud. This time the pictures are much more cartoonish—full of bustling activity that repays careful exploration. There are, for example, more animals, aliens, and legendary characters around than is usual in the shops! That tramp with a bowler hat, cane, and big boots standing in a doorway looks very familiar. And Baby Joe finds plenty to play with—one has more than a fleeting sympathy with his parents' repeated cries of "DON'T DO THAT!" and "YOU CAN'T HAVE THAT!" *The Dinosaurs Are Back and It's All Your Fault Edward* is a riotous fantasy in which a small boy tries to convince his brother Edward that the rock under his bed is about to hatch into a dinosaur, with hideous consequences. He ends up terrifying himself, having to ask Edward (who has in the meantime fallen asleep) for help. There is a lavatorial turn to some of the fun that may shock prudish adults, but which will delight small boys.

Daly's third, and perhaps most important, group of books are those in which he makes social comments. Books that come into this category can all be read and enjoyed for the surface level of stories and pictures. However, on another level, Daly is making serious statements about the world that many children live in. This can be as simple as *Somewhere in Africa* which tells us that many African children live in cities, and know lions and crocodiles only through pictures in books. *All the Magic in the World* is about poor black children playing, but however poor they are they have the ability to imagine. Little Lena who is clumsy, stumbling on stairs and falling out of trees, triggers the discovery by getting old Joseph to show her the oddments he keeps in a tin. Her disabilities are only there for those that can see—and her imagination is as good as anyone's. *In Maybe It's a Tiger,* Daly uses slum children from a variety of ethnic backgounds. From the poverty of a street of crumbling terraced houses and grafitti-covered walls, the children pretend Granny's tabby cat is a tiger, and Beverley's puppy is a bear. When little Joseph, foiled in his attempt to add an ostrich, a crocodile, and an octopus to the menagerie, produces by a magnificent leap of imagination the best animal of all, the shabby front steps become a place of brilliant colour and life. The contrast between the arid surroundings and the text, which tells of the power and luxuriance of children's imagination, could not be greater.

Charlie Mogotsi, in *Charlie's House,* imagines as he builds a house out of mud and sticks and paper that this is a smart dwelling for him and his family. The detailed pictures reflect the intensity of his dream—and show the hideous reality of his actual life in a leaky corrugated iron shelter in a South African township. This one of Daly's most powerful and moving statements about social conditions, for those who wish to extract it from the loving depiction of a little boy playing.

Perhaps the most devastating of all Daly's work in this area is *My Dad,* a quiet, painful picture book about a child whose father is an alcoholic. It is a courageous look at a child's disillusionment with an adult who nearly destroys the thing he loves best. At the end there is a gleam of hope, but Daly and his co-author are honest about the difficulties to be faced.

Why the Sun and Moon Live in the Sky is a Nigerian story, but the artwork, in ink and wash, is full of Renaissance images. It represents a change of direction for Niki Daly, and it will be most interesting to see where he goes next and how he will continue to use his gifts of humour, observation, and empathy.

—Felicity Trotman

DANIELL, David Scott

Pseudonym for Albert Scott Daniell. **Other Pseudonyms:** Richard Bowood; John Lewesdon. **Nationality:** British. **Born:** London, 1 July 1906. **Education:** Bedford Modern School. **Military Service:** Royal Engineers, Eighth Army, in Sicily and Italy, 1941-46: captain; mentioned in dispatches. **Family:** Married Elizabeth Mary Thirlby in 1939; one son. **Career:** Worked for the Commonwealth Trust, Gold Coast, 1929-30. **Died:** 29 August 1965.

Publications for Children

Fiction

Mission for Oliver, illustrated by William Stobbs. London, Cape, 1953.
Polly and Oliver, illustrated by William Stobbs. London, Cape, 1954.
The Dragon and the Rose, illustrated by Sheila Stratton. London, Cape, 1955; New York, Abelard Schuman, 1957.
Hunt Royal, illustrated by William Stobbs. London, Cape, 1958.
Hideaway Johnny, illustrated by Val Biro. Leicester, Brockhampton Press, 1959.
The Boy They Made King, illustrated by William Stobbs. London, Cape, 1959; New York, Duell, 1960.
Polly and Oliver at Sea, illustrated by William Stobbs. London, Cape, 1960.
The Rajah's Treasure, illustrated by William Stobbs. New York, Duell, 1960.
Sandro's Battle, illustrated by Colin Spencer. London, Cape, and New York, Duell, 1962.
By Jiminy, illustrated by D.G. Valentine. Leicester, Brockhampton Press, 1962.
Saved by Jiminy, illustrated by D.G. Valentine. Leicester, Brockhampton Press, 1963.
Polly and Oliver Besieged, illustrated by William Stobbs. London, Cape, 1963.
By Jiminy Ahoy, illustrated by D.G. Valentine. Leicester, Brockhampton Press, 1963.
By Jiminy in the Jungle, illustrated by D.G. Valentine. Leicester, Brockhampton Press, 1964.
Polly and Oliver Pursued, illustrated by William Stobbs. London, Cape, 1964.
Horsey and Co. and the Bank Robbers (as Richard Bowood), illustrated by A. Oxenham. London, Golden Pleasure Books, 1965.
By Jiminy in the Highlands, illustrated by D.G. Valentine. Leicester, Brockhampton Press, 1966.
Red Gaskell's Gold (as Richard Bowood), illustrated by Peter Kesteven. London, Macmillan, and New York, St. Martin's Press, 1966.

Plays

Children's Theatre Plays (includes *Hide-and-Seek; The Queen and Mr. Shakespeare; The King's Messenger; Stand and Deliver; The Adventure; The Jester, The Queen, and the Hen*). London, Harrap, 1948.

More Children's Theatre Plays (includes *Hereward the Wake, The Gascon Ring, The Stowaway, The Silver Snuff Box*), illustrated by Elizabeth Thirlby. London, Harrap, 1951.

Costume Plays for Schools (includes *Hunt Royal, The Ring of Gold, Roses for the Queen, Tyger's Hart, Treasure Hunt*). London, Harrap, 1955.

Faith of Our Fathers: The Story of Christianity in Britain (includes *A.D. 150-878: Go Preach in Heathen Britain, 1100-1382: The Glory of the Medieval Church, 1537-1620: The Years of Conflict, 1662-1960: Freely to Worship*), with G.W.H. Lampe. London, University of London Press, 4 vols., 1961.

Letters for the Prince, in *Junior One-Act Plays of To-Day, Fourth Series,* edited by Harold Gardiner. London, Harrap, 1963.

Other

Flight One to Six: Australia, Canada, United States of America, India, Africa, and *The Holy Land,* illustrated by Jack Matthew. Loughborough, Leicestershire, Wills and Hepworth, 6 vols., 1958-62.

The Golden Pomegranate, illustrated by George Adamson. London, University of London Press, 1960.

Ladybird Book of London (as John Lewesdon). Loughborough, Leicestershire, Wills and Hepworth, 1961.

Battles and Battlefields, illustrated by William Stobbs. London, Batsford, 1961.

Discovering the Bible, with G.W.H. Lampe, illustrated by Graham Oakley. London, University of London Press, 1961; Nashville, Abingdon Press, 1966.

Explorers and Exploration, illustrated by William Stobbs. London, Batsford, 1962.

Discovering the Army, illustrated by Crispin Fisher. London, University of London Press, 1965.

Sea Fights. London, Batsford, 1966.

Your Body, illustrated by Robert Ayton. Loughborough, Leicestershire, Wills and Hepworth, 1967.

Other as Richard Bowood

The Story of Flight [*Railways, Ships, Houses and Homes, Clothes and Costume, Our Churches and Cathedrals*], illustrated by Robert Ayton. Loughborough, Leicestershire, Wills and Hepworth, 6 vols., 1960-64.

Great Inventions, illustrated by Robert Ayton. Loughborough, Leicestershire, Wills and Hepworth, 1961.

The Weather, with F.E. Newing, illustrated by J.H. Wingfield. Loughborough, Leicestershire, Wills and Hepworth, 1962.

Magnets, Bulbs and Batteries, with F.E. Newing, illustrated by J.H. Wingfield. Loughborough, Leicestershire, Wills and Hepworth, 1962.

Lights, Mirrors and Lenses, with F.E. Newing, illustrated by J.H. Wingfield. Loughborough, Leicestershire, Wills and Hepworth, 1962.

Levers, Pulleys and Engines, with F.E. Newing, illustrated by J.H. Wingfield. Loughborough, Leicestershire, Wills and Hepworth, 1963.

Air, Wind and Flight, with F.E. Newing, illustrated by J.H. Wingfield. Loughborough, Leicestershire, Wills and Hepworth, 1963.

Naples Ahead, illustrated by David Knight. London, Macmillan, and New York, St. Martin's Press, 1964.

Soldiers. London, Hamlyn, 1965.

Animals [and *Birds*] *and How They Live,* with F.E. Newing, illustrated by Ronald Lampitt. Loughborough, Leicestershire, Wills and Hepworth, 2 vols., 1965-66.

Plants and How They Grow, with F.E. Newing, illustrated by Ronald Lampitt. Loughborough, Leicestershire, Wills and Hepworth, 1965.

Our Land in the Making: Earliest Times to the Norman Conquest and *Norman Conquest to Present Day,* illustrated by Ronald Lampitt. Loughborough, Leicestershire, Wills and Hepworth, 2 vols., 1966.

Underwater Exploration, illustrated by B. Knight. Loughborough, Leicestershire, Wills and Hepworth, 1967.

PUBLICATIONS FOR ADULTS

Novels

Young English. London, Cape, 1931.

Morning's at Seven. London, Cape, 1940.

The Time of the Singing. London, Cape, 1941.

Nicholas Wilde. London, Cape, 1948.

Fifty Pounds for a Dead Parson. London, Cape, 1960.

Other

Cap of Honour: The Story of the Gloucestershire Regiment (the 28th/61st Foot) 1694-1950. London, Harrap, 1951.

Royal Hampshire Regiment 1918-1950, vol. 3. Aldershot, Hampshire, Gale and Polden, 1955.

History of the East Surrey Regiment 1920-1952, vol. 4. London, Benn, 1957.

4th Hussar: The Story of the 4th Queen's Own Hussars 1685-1958. Aldershot, Hampshire, Gale and Polden, 1959.

World War 1 and *2: An Illustrated History.* London, Benn, 2 vols., 1965-66.

* * *

David Scott Daniell was a full-time professional writer with many interests. Whatever he wrote is distinctive for the enthusiasm he brought to his subject and for the desire to share that enthusiasm with his readers. As a storyteller he tends to stand outside the action, so that the effect is as if we were watching a film or a play. Indeed his first published work for children was a collection of some of the costume plays he had written for Bertha Waddell's theatre, and from these and his work for radio come his ability to handle dialogue and his penchant for dramatic happenings and swift change of fortune.

The five Polly and Oliver stories, two of which were originally written as radio plays, are in effect costume dramas in narrative form. Oliver is a drummer boy in the 111th Regiment of Foot at the time of the Napoleonic Wars. His long-suffering sergeant is also his uncle, whose daughter Polly accompanies the regiment everywhere and Oliver most places. The adventures of the pair of them take place on land and sea in Sicily, Spain, and India, and involve soldiers and bandits, spies and subterfuges, chases and captures, misunderstandings and mistaken identities. They are fun to read and are also full of authentic military and nautical detail.

Another series of adventure stories is that woven round the lively and resourceful By Jiminy, a modern Neapolitan shoeshine boy, and his English friends, the twins Tom and Sukie, children of an archaeologist. Though basically these are straightforward and easily assimilable variations on the theme of children versus crooks, there are sufficient characterisation, genuine humour, and accurate archaeological background to lift them above many other stories of this kind.

Of the individual historical novels, *The Boy They Made King* successfully illuminates the story of Lambert Simnel. The character of Lambert himself is especially well drawn, and his transition from shoe-maker's son to royal imposter and back again to ordinary boy is completely convincing. *Hunt Royal,* about the flight of Charles II, is along more conventional lines, but Daniell is a good enough writer to make Charles a character in his own right and to take advantage of opportunities for dramatic irony. A particularly good scene is that in which three boys staying in the house in which Charles is hiding are interrogated by Cromwell's officers.

In *Sandro's Battle* a boy, living with his composer father and a beloved donkey in a castle in Italy during World War II, is involved with soldiers on both sides when the area becomes a no-man's land between the two armies and the castle a strategic position. The dialogue sparkles and the fun is fast, but the underlying message is serious—war destroys innocent bystanders and causes them to lose their homes and possessions; it also makes ordinary and friendly people range themselves against each other to kill.

—Antony Kamm

DARKE, Marjorie (Sheila)

Nationality: British. **Born:** Birmingham, Warwickshire, 25 January 1929. **Education:** Worcester Grammar School for Girls, 1938-46; Leicester College of Art and Technology, 1946-50; Central School of Art, London, 1950. **Family:** Married in 1952; two sons and one daughter. **Career:** Textile designer, John Lewis Partnership, London, 1951-54. Lives in Somerset. **Awards:** *Guardian* Award commendation, 1975, and runner-up, 1977. **Agent:** Rogers Coleridge and White, 20 Powis Mews, London W11 1JN, England.

Publications for Children

Fiction

Ride the Iron Horse, illustrated by Michael Jackson. London, Longman, 1973.
The Star Trap, illustrated by Michael Jackson. London, Longman, 1974.
Mike's Bike, illustrated by Jim Russell. London, Kestrel, 1974.
A Question of Courage, illustrated by Janet Archer. London, Kestrel, and New York, Crowell, 1975.
What Can I Do?, illustrated by Barry Wilkinson. London, Kestrel, 1975.
The Big Brass Band, illustrated by Charles Front. London, Kestrel, 1976.
Kipper's Turn, illustrated by Mary Dinsdale. London, Blackie, 1976.
My Uncle Charlie, illustrated by Jannat Houston. London, Kestrel, 1977.
The First of Midnight, illustrated by Anthony Morris. London, Kestrel, 1977; New York, Seabury Press, 1978.
A Long Way to Go. London, Kestrel, 1978.
Kipper Skips, illustrated by Thelma Lambert. London, Blackie, 1979.
Carnival Day, illustrated by Nita Sowter. London, Kestrel, 1979.
Comeback. London, Kestrel, 1981.
Tom Post's Private Eye. London, Macmillan, 1983.
Messages: A Collection of Shivery Tales. London, Viking Kestrel, 1984.
Imp, illustrated by Margaret Chamberlain. London, Heinemann, 1985.
The Rainbow Sandwich, illustrated by Joanna Worth. London, Methuen, 1989.
Night Windows, illustrated by Annabel Spenceley. London, Macmillan, 1990.
A Rose from Blighty. London, Collins, 1990.
Emma's Monster, illustrated by Shelagh McNicholas. London, Walker, 1992.
Just Bear and Friends, illustrated by Duncan Smith. London, Walker, 1996.

*

Media Adaptations: *My Uncle Charlie* (cartoon), BBC-TV, 1982; *Carnival Day,* BBC-TV, 1982; *The First of Midnight,* BBC Radio, 1985; *Emma's Monster,* Channel 4 TV, 1985, *Toothache,* Channel 4 TV, 1988; *A Question of Courage* (dramatization), Oxford University Press, 1990; *A Question of Courage,* BBC Radio, 1992.

Marjorie Darke comments:

Unlike many writers I came to the craft late. Although I have always been an avid reader, the idea of writing stories did not occur until greater leisure—when my children went to school—made me aware of an ever-growing need to do something more creative and demanding than housework. Writing specifically for children was not a conscious choice. In my opinion too much emphasis is placed on the dividing line between stories for children and those for adults. I write for myself, the characters and storyline often beginning with a chance conversation, a few words overheard in the street, something read in a book or seen on television. Once born, the people in my imagination have a curious knack of assuming a life of their own, their actions often veering away from paths I have planned for them. I find it difficult to pin-point the reasons why I have often chosen historical backgrounds for my books. They may stem from a lifelong love of hearing tales told by my mother and grandmother of "when I was a girl." Certainly it had nothing to do with school history which I found dry and boring except for the rare times we studied the lives of ordinary people. People, in fact, are my main concern—whether in past or present-day settings—trying to make them live and be as real as I possibly can.

Short stories were a later development in my writing career, as were stories written specially for very young children. Both need a refreshingly different approach, I find, although the writing of novels remains my first love. But whatever the length of the story, because children are clear-sighted and perceptive, endeavouring to entertain them continues to be a great challenge and an ever-growing pleasure.

* * *

Marjorie Darke has largely confined herself to writing historical novels for older children, concentrating on late 18th-, 19th-, and early 20th-century British history. In many of her stories she demonstrates a very sympathetic understanding of how ordinary working people cope in difficult and often rapidly changing circumstances. In this way she has tackled a number of "problem" areas, including the effects in urban and rural areas of the Industrial Revolution, the brutalising effects of the slave trade, and the growing consciousness of women through the Suffragette movement. The background historical detail is carefully researched and has an authentic feel to it, the settings and stories are realistic, and the characters drawn with a conviction that gives credence to the story and a real "feel" for that particular period of history.

With her first novel, *Ride the Iron Horse,* Marjorie Darke began a run of powerful historical novels in which she showed that stories with socio-economic themes can be just as dramatic as those with a military background. *Ride the Iron Horse* is set in 18th-century Britain, in the pioneering days of the new railway system. The hero, John, a village lad, has a talent for engineering, but is restricted by his poverty and illiteracy. The villagers riot against the railway navvies who lay the railway track. John will have a real career, however, thanks to Frances, the squire's daughter, who secretly teaches him to read. The sequel, *The Star Trap,* describes how Frances runs away to become an actress and is eventually engaged to John.

Darke's interest in women's oppression comes to full bloom in her most popular work, *A Question of Courage,* a novel about the Suffragettes which has been dramatized for stage performance. Emily Palmer, a poor seamstress, is recruited by wealthy upper-class Louise to commit acts of sabotage, first in Birmingham and then in London, where they are arrested, go on hunger strike, and are force-fed.

Darke then turned to another form of oppression: racism, combined with injustice to women. Jess, an orphaned girl who is sold as a servant, falls in love with and shelters Midnight, an escaped slave. Midnight becomes a boxer, seeing this as a way of saving money for his passage home to Africa, but Jess feels that she cannot go with him and bears their child in England. In two more novels Darke told the story of Midnight's descendants.

A Long Way to Go is about the twins Luke and Bella, who are living in London during World War I. At a time when native dark-skinned Britons were rare, Luke and Bella suffer racial taunts because of their different-colored skin. Luke decides that conscription is unjust and becomes a conscientious objector, or "oonchie." He is arrested and sent to the front in France. Bella works in a munitions factory where she meets Emily Palmer—both get sacked for demanding pay equal with male workers.

Gail Knight in *Comeback,* a young adult novel set in the 1980s, also suffers racial name-calling, but at least she has friends among the black British community, as well as white friends. Abandoned by a mother who dared not tell her family she was pregnant, she grows up in council homes. Ambitious to develop her gymnastic talents to Olympic level, she must not only discipline her body, but also her suspicious mind, distrustful of others because of previous experiences. Meetings with Emily, now an elderly widow, provide clues to her family tree, but what matters most to her is her own talent and determination.

Darke did not publish her Midnight Quintet in chronological order; a more recent title takes up Emily's adventures during World War I. *A Rose from Blighty* describes Emily's growing romance with Louise's brother Peter—in defiance of social class barriers—and Louise's consequent jealousy. The book also tells of the girls' estrangement after Peter's death in action. In France they meet again, nursing wounded soldiers. Fast-paced, authentic, passionate, not shirking the gruesome details, it is vintage Darke, demonstrating her genius in bringing her characters to life and taking up the story of Emily and Louise years after *A Question of Courage* was published.

Darke has also written a number of books for younger, early readers, the most successful being *My Uncle Charlie* and *Carnival Day.* Two stories for slightly older children which provide a useful early introduction to historical novels are *Kipper's Turn* and *Kipper Skips,* both set in Birmingham in the 1880s. Young Kipper works for a jeweller earning enough money to pay for his board and lodging. By law he should be at school, but if he cannot work, he cannot pay his way and will be sent to the workhouse. Kipper's dilemma and desperate attempts to remain honest while needing to survive are well portrayed. *Night Windows,* a time fantasy, offers an unusual perspective on the Industrial Revolution. Some schoolchildren studying the period find that by drawing pictures of 18th-century people they have visions at night of a crisis that took place on their own street, when wreckers burned mill machinery.

Darke has continued to write for the younger reader in two books of linked stories about imaginative play and the role of a special companion, the first book about a girl, Emma, and the second about a boy, Pip. Emma's "monster" supposedly lives under her bed, and her understanding Dad takes the monster very seriously; however, Monster goes too far when he falls into a paint tin when Dad is decorating Emma's bedroom. Bear, in *Just Bear and Friends,* is a real toy, given to Pip when he was born, and now rather dilapidated and at risk from Pip's boisterous friends. Pip has to move on to the next stage in life—his eight birthday—and give, or at least lend, his bear to his friend's little sister.

—Judith Elkin, updated by Jessica Yates

DAUGHERTY, James (Henry)

Nationality: American. **Born:** Asheville, North Carolina, 1 June 1889. **Education:** Corcoran School of Art, Washington, D.C.; Pennsylvania Academy of Fine Arts, Philadelphia; London School of Art. **Military Service:** Worked as a ship camouflager during World War I. **Family:** Married Sonia Medvedeva in 1913; one son. **Career:** Artist and illustrator: murals in Cleveland, and in Weston, Fairfield, and Stamford, Connecticut; retrospective exhibition, New York, 1971. **Awards:** American Library Association Newbery medal, 1940. **Died:** 12 February 1974.

PUBLICATIONS FOR CHILDREN (ILLUSTRATED BY THE AUTHOR)

Fiction

Andy and the Lion. New York, Viking Press, 1938.
The Picnic. New York, Viking Press, 1958.

Poetry

The Wild, Wild West. Philadelphia, McKay, 1948.
West of Boston. New York, Viking Press, 1956.

Other

Daniel Boone. New York, Viking Press, 1939.
Poor Richard. New York, Viking Press, 1941.
Abraham Lincoln. New York, Viking Press, 1943.
The Landing of the Pilgrims. New York, Random House, 1950.
Of Courage Undaunted: Across the Continent with Lewis and Clark. New York, Viking Press, 1951.
Trappers and Traders of the Far West. New York, Random House, 1952.
Marcus and Narcissa Whitman, Pioneers of Oregon. New York, Viking Press, 1953.
The Magna Charta. New York, Random House, 1956.
William Blake. New York, Viking Press, 1960.

Editor, *The Kingdom and the Power and the Glory: Stories of Faith and Marvel.* New York, Knopf, 1929.
Editor, *Their Weight in Wildcats: Tales of the Frontier.* Boston, Houghton Mifflin, 1936.
Editor, *In the Beginning, Being the First Chapter of Genesis from the King James Version.* New York and London, Oxford University Press, 1941.
Editor, *Walt Whitman's America* (selections). Cleveland, World, 1964.
Editor, *Henry David Thoreau, A Man of Our Time.* New York, Viking Press, 1967.
Editor, *The Sound of Trumpets: Selections from Ralph Waldo Emerson.* New York, Viking Press, 1971.

PUBLICATIONS FOR ADULTS

Other

An Outline of Government in Connecticut, edited by Philip E. Curtiss. Hartford, Connecticut, House Committee on Public Information, 1944.

*

Bibliography: "James Henry Daugherty: A Bibliography" by Edward and Elaine Kemp, in *Imprint: Oregon* (Eugene), Fall 1975.

Manuscript Collections: University of Oregon Library, Eugene; May Massee Collection, Emporia State University, Kansas.

Illustrator: *Tad Sheldon, Boy Scout* by John Fleming Wilson, 1913; *King Penguin* by Richard Henry Horne, 1925; *The Lost Gospel* by Arthur Cheney Train, 1925; *The Plucky Allens* by Clara Pierson, 1925; *The Adventures of Johnny T. Bear* by Margaret McElroy, 1926; *Daniel Boone, Wilderness Scout* by Stewart Edward White, 1926; *The Mountain of Jade* by Violet Irwin and Vilhjalmur Stefansson, 1926; *Drake's Quest* by Cameron Rogers, 1927; *Kris and Kristina* by Marie Bruce, 1927; *The Splendid Spur* edited by Arthur Quiller-Couch, 1927; *The Story of Bread,* 1927, *The Story of Milk,* 1927, and *The Story of Textiles,* 1928, all by Elizabeth Watson; *Abe Lincoln Grows Up* 1928, and *Early Moon,* 1930, both by Carl Sandburg; *The Blacksmith and the Blackbirds* by Edith Rickert, 1928; *The Conquest of Montezuma's Empire* by Andrew Lang, 1928; *Hugh Gwyeth* by Beulah Dix, 1928; *Irene of Tundra Towers,* 1928, and *Judy of the Whale Gates,* 1930, both by Elizabeth Burrows; *Knickerbocker's History of New York,* 1928, and *The Bold Dragoon,* 1930, both by Washington Irving; *The Stream of History* by Geoffrey Parsons, 1928; *Tuftoo, The Clown* by Howard Garis, 1928; *The White Company* by Arthur Conan Doyle, 1928; *Wulnoth, The Wanderer* by Herbert Inman, 1928; *Courageous Companions* by Charles J. Finger, 1929; *Three Comedies* by William Shakespeare, 1929; *Uncle Tom's Cabin* by Harriet Beecher Stowe, 1929; *The Adventures of Johnny Appleseed* by Henry Chapin, 1930; *John Brown's Body* by Stephen Vincent Benét, 1930; *The Oregon Trail* by Francis Parkman, 1931; *The Adventures of Tom Sawyer* by Mark Twain, 1932; *Mashinka's Secret,* 1932, *All Things New,* 1936, *Vanka's Donkey,* 1940, *Wings of Glory,* 1940, *The Way of an Eagle,* 1941, *Ten Brave Men,* 1951, *Ten Brave Women,* 1953, and *Thomas Jefferson,* 1963, all by Sonia Medvedeva Daugherty; *The Memoirs of Benvenuto Cellini,* 1932; *The Railroad to Freedom,* by Hildegarde Swift, 1932; *The Sign of the Buffalo Skull* by Peter O. Lamb, 1932; *Windows on Henry Street* by Lillian D. Wald, 1934; *Girls of Glen Hazard,* 1937, and *Clue of the Faded Dress,* 1938, both by Maristan Chapman; *Green Gravel* by Dora Aydelotte, 1937; *Over the Blue Wall* by Etta Lane Matthews, 1937; *Call of the Mountain* by Cornelia Meigs, 1940; *Morgan's Fourth Son* by Margaret Isabel Ross, 1940; *Almanac for Americans* by Willis Thornton, 1941, 1954; *Barnaby Rudge* by Charles Dickens, 1941; *A Treasury of Best-Loved Hymns* edited by Daniel Poling, 1942; *Yankee Thunder,* 1944, *John Henry and the Double-Jointed Steam Drill,* 1945, *Joe Magarac and His U.S.A. Citizen Papers,* 1948, and *Heroes in American Folklore,* 1962, all by Irwin Shapiro; *Lincoln's Gettysburg Address,* 1947; *American Folklore and Its Old-World Backgrounds* by Carl Lamsen Carmer, 1949; *American Life in Literature* edited by Jay Hubbell, 1949; *The Authentic Revolution* by Erwin Canham, 1950; *Better Known as Johnny Appleseed* by Mabel Leigh Hunt, 1950; *Comanche* by David Appel, 1951; *A Long Way to Frisco* by Alfred Powers, 1951; *The Loudest Noise in the World,* 1954, and *Gillespie and the Guards,* 1956, both by Benjamin Elkin; *The Rainbow Book of American History* by Earl Schenck Miers, 1955, 1968; *The Last of the Mohicans* by James Fenimore Cooper, 1957; *Wisher,* 1960, and *Robert Goddard,* 1964, both by Charles Michael Daugherty; *A Promise to Our Country* by James Francis Calvert, 1961; *The Three Musketeers* by Alexandre Dumas, 1962.

* * *

Only an occasional page, such as James Daugherty's salute as illustrator to Father Knickerbocker in *Knickerbocker's History of New York,* foretells the remarkable command of English, the talent for melodic lines, exhibited privately in the journals young Daugherty kept while traveling as an art student of 16 in England. That one page, along with bold, witty illustrations of typical Daugherty women and men with keen eyes, thrust jaws, and angular bodies, presaged Daugherty the writer.

Daugherty was nearly fifty when he became established as a writer, and perhaps because this talent had been dammed up for so many years, it seemed to pour forth rapidly after Daugherty completed his first book as author and illustrator, *Andy and the Lion.* The illustrations in *Andy* stand independently of the text, and, indeed, Daugherty had submitted them to his editor at Viking without words. However, with the addition of a simple, charming narration, he secured a balance between words and illustrations.

His second book, the first in which his talents as a writer are fully displayed, was *Daniel Boone.* Daugherty's appreciation, understanding, and admiration of this typically American figure are constantly evident. The prose, illustrations, and subject are a successful blend, and introduce the qualities which appear in nearly every book written by this artist, a major exponent of the Synchromist art school in the 1910s.

Daugherty's love of country, of American life and customs, the expanding frontier in American history, and of heroes, both legendary and historic, became the source for many books. Like the poet Walt Whitman, he celebrated many national events and people, but unlike Whitman, he did not sing of himself nor did he accept all American history at face value. He combined a serious regard for human values, when writing of Thoreau, Emerson, or Lincoln, with a somewhat sceptical view of the possible motivation of some American patriots. His sincere admiration for the Pilgrims (*The Landing of the Pilgrims*), the exploration of the American west (*Of Courage Undaunted: Across the Continent with Lewis and Clark*), and the hardy pioneer (*Marcus and Narcissa Whitman, Pioneers of Oregon*) is exemplified by his warm descriptions in prose and illustration. While he proclaimed in resonant prose or poetry, or both in combination, the deeds of his forebears, Daugherty was a good critic, with a turn of phrase or malicious facial expression shared with the reader; *West of Boston, The Wild, Wild West,* and *Their Weight in Wildcats* are good examples. Concern for fellow man, for the honest, self-reliant individual is expressed as Daugherty writes of Lincoln or introduces the transcendental philosophy of Emerson and Thoreau. Daugherty accepts the philosophy, which appears as an underlying theme in his work, while warning his reader that meditation cannot demand inward commitment: Thoreau and Emerson have obligations to their society. The matter is cause for comment in *West of Boston.*

Daugherty's place as a writer is assured. Although his subjects are American by birth or nature, their appeal is universal. Daugherty's mastery of language and humor, his appeal to the senses, his celebration of life, understanding of mankind, and his love of all things fill each book. As a writer and illustrator with a good editorial sense, he knew how to combine, balance, and strengthen the art of writing and of illustration.

—Edward Kemp

d'AULAIRE, Edgar and Ingri Parin

d'AULAIRE, Edgar Parin: Nationality: American (originally German: emigrated to the United States, 1929, became citizen, 1939.) **Born:** Munich, Germany, 30 September 1898. **Education:** Institute of Technology, 1917-19, and School of Applied Arts, 1919-22, Munich; studied art with Hans Hofmann, Munich, 1922-24, and with Andre Lhote and Pola Gauguin, Paris, 1925-29. **Family:** Married Ingri Maartenson (i.e., Ingri d'Aulaire) in 1925 (died 1980); two children. **Career:** Artist: book illustrator, 1922-26; painted frescoes, Norway, 1926-27; graphic work exhibited in United States, Italy, Norway, Czechoslovakia, France. **Died:** 1 May 1986. **d'AULAIRE, Ingri (Maartenson) Parin: Nationality:** American (originally Norwegian: emigrated to the United States, 1929, became citizen, 1940). **Born:** Kongsberg, Norway, 27 December 1904. **Education:** Kongsberg Junior College, 1918-23; Institute of Arts and Crafts, Oslo, 1923-24; studied art with Hans Hofmann, Munich, 1924-25, and with Andre Lhote and Pola Gauguin, Paris, 1925-29. **Career:** Portrait artist. **Died:** 24 October 1980. **Awards:** American Library Association Caldecott medal, 1940; Catholic Library Association Regina medal, 1970.

Publications for Children (illustrated by the authors)

Fiction

The Magic Rug. New York, Doubleday, 1931.
Ola. New York, Doubleday, 1932.
Ola and Blakken and Line, Sine, Trine. New York, Doubleday, 1933; revised edition, as *The Terrible Troll-Bird,* 1976.
Children of the Northlights. New York, Viking Press, 1935; London, Woodfield, 1960.
Animals Everywhere. New York, Doubleday, 1940; revised edition, 1954.
Don't Count Your Chicks. New York, Doubleday, 1943.
Wings for Per. New York, Doubleday, 1944.
Too Big. New York, Doubleday, 1945.
Nils. New York, Doubleday, 1948.
Foxie. New York, Doubleday, 1949; revised edition, as *Foxie, The Singing Dog,* 1969.
The Two Cars. New York, Doubleday, 1955.
The Magic Meadow. New York, Doubleday, 1958.

Other

The Conquest of the Atlantic. New York, Viking Press, 1933.
George Washington. New York, Doubleday, 1936.
Abraham Lincoln. New York, Doubleday, 1939; Birmingham, Combridge, 1957; revised edition, New York, Doubleday, 1957.
Leif the Lucky. New York, Doubleday, 1941.
Pocahontas. New York, Doubleday, 1946.
Benjamin Franklin. New York, Doubleday, 1950.
Buffalo Bill. New York, Doubleday, 1952.
Columbus. New York, Doubleday, 1955.
Book of Greek Myths. New York, Doubleday, 1962.
Norse Gods and Giants. New York, Doubleday, 1967.
Trolls (Norwegian folktales). New York, Doubleday, 1972.

Translator, *East of the Sun and West of the Moon: Twenty-One Norwegian Folktales,* by Peter Christen Asbjørnsen. New York, Viking Press, 1938; revised edition, 1966.

*

Manuscript Collections: Dartmouth College, Hanover, New Hampshire; University of Oregon Library, Eugene; Kerlan Collection, University of Minnesota, Minneapolis; de Grummond Collection, University of Southern Mississippi, Hattiesburg.

Illustrator (Edgar Parin d'Aulaire): 17 books in Germany, 1922-26; *Rama, The Hero of India* by Dhan Gopal Mukerji, 1930; *Blood* by Hanns J. Ewers, 1930; *Needle in a Haystack* by John Mattheson, 1930; *Coming of the Dragon Ships* by Florence McClurg Everson, 1931; *Kari* by Gabriel Scott, 1931; *Gao of the Ivory Coast* by Katherine Seabrook, 1931; *Children of the Soil* by

Nora Burglon, 1932; with Ingri Parin d'Aulaire: *The Lord's Prayer,* 1934; *Sidsel Longskirt,* 1935, and *Solve Suntrap,* 1936, both by Hans Aanrud, translated by Margery Williams Bianco and Dagay Mortenson; *The Star Spangled Banner* by Francis Scott Key, 1942; *Johnny Blossom* by Dikken Zwilgmeyer, 1948.

Edgar and Ingri Parin d'Aulaire commented:

(1978) For almost 50 years we have been working together on picture books, and still like it as much as when we first began. But when a book is finished we return to our individual paintings—which are still as different as when we first met. We have created a third personality for our books—it is not Edgar, it is not Ingri—it is a mixture of us both. We have no intention of ever becoming a monster with one head and four hands.

* * *

Working as a couple Edgar and Ingri Parin d'Aulaire created over 20 picture books for children from their extensive research and travel. They become "one unity with two heads, four hands, and one handwriting when working." Producing books with Norwegian and American backgrounds predominantly, they steeped themselves in the subject and locale for about a year prior to executing each one.

The most authoritative books are the seven with Norwegian settings. *Ola* incorporates Norwegian folklore motifs, customs, and local color in the realistic story about a contemporary child. The sequel, *Ola and Blakken and Line, Sine, Trine,* is more fanciful (and was reworked for a new edition called *The Terrible Troll-Bird*). Laplanders are followed through a year of seasonal activities in *Children of the Northlights. Norse Gods and Giants* treats mythology, and folklore is the source of *East of the Sun and West of the Moon* and *Trolls.* Three books link Norway and the United States. *Leif the Lucky* is a biography of the man who discovered Vineland on the American shores, and *The Conquest of the Atlantic* describes voyages from the Vikings to Balboa. The countries are not specifically identified in *Wings for Per,* which juxtaposes traditional law and justice with tyranny and occupation. In *Nils* a school boy is called a sissy when he wears hand-knit stockings to school, but this second generation Norwegian-American eventually achieves acceptance and respect among his classmates. Edgar was generally credited for the dramatic quality in the texts, Ingri for the humor.

As immigrants to the United States, the d'Aulaires selected national heroes and patriotic subjects. *George Washington, Abraham Lincoln, Pocahontas, Benjamin Franklin, Buffalo Bill,* and *Columbus* were published in a span of 19 years. These biographies are propelled by the chronological action and seem stiff when compared to *Ola* and the more imaginative books. The d'Aulaires came to American themes "as children," offering a fresh approach to the national anthem, *The Star Spangled Banner.* Even *The Lord's Prayer* was interpreted from the viewpoint of an American child, which annoyed Bertha E. Mahony and Marguerite M. Mitchell, who felt that children's imagination should provide the images. *Don't Count Your Chicks,* though based on the Danish Hans Christian Andersen work, has an early American interpretation.

The d'Aulaires used research and travel to ensure the accuracy of their books. Their first book, *The Magic Rug,* was written in the style of a travelogue in response to a Norwegian child's request for information about their winter stay in Kairawan in Tunisia. To write *The Conquest of the Atlantic,* they studied in the New York Public Library and University of Norway in Oslo, and viewed ship models and costumes in the Musée de la Marine in the Louvre in Paris. They established a base in Geneva, and become acquainted with Swiss history, literature, and art before beginning *The Magic Meadow.* The authors once remarked that a thousand pages of research may be compressed into each picture book, and that they may rework a manuscript ten or twenty times before being satisfied. In an interview with Art Buchwald (*Herald Tribune,* 30 October 1956), Ingri d'Aulaire said: "We found out many wicked stories about Mr. Franklin and we were tempted to use them, but we were afraid because it would spoil the market for the children's books. The mothers and grandmothers would say 'no.'" As well as accumulating notes, the couple visited the locales they wrote about: while working on *Buffalo Bill,* they spent six weeks camping out on the midwest plains; they walked over George Washington's Virginia, and pitched tents along the Lincoln trail.

Unlike the biographies, which have little dialogue, the imaginative books have lively conversation. *Foxie* is based in part on Anton Chekhov's *Kashtanka,* about a performing theatrical dog. While Kashtanka's master is a poor carpenter and her fellow performers are a cat, a gander, and a pig, Foxie's master is a boy and her coperformers a cat and a rooster. Ingri's humor is apparent in *The Two Cars,* one of which remarks, "My paint is hardly dry behind my fenders," while the other states, "I am one hundred thousand miles old." A statement in this book, published midway in their career, is indicative of the manner in which the couple worked—"you won the race but not the praise." Striving for perfection, they produced both quantity and quality.

—Karen Nelson Hoyle

DAVIES, Andrew (Wynford)

Nationality: British. **Born:** Cardiff, Glamorgan, 20 September 1936. **Education:** Whitchurch Grammar School, Glamorgan; University College, London, B.A. in English 1957. **Family:** Married Diana Huntley in 1960; one son and one daughter. **Career:** Teacher, St. Clement Danes Grammar School, 1958-61, and Woodberry Down School, 1961-63, both London; lecturer, Coventry College of Education and University of Warwick, Coventry, 1963-87. **Awards:** *Guardian* award, 1979; Boston *Globe-Horn Book* award, 1980; Broadcasting Press Guild award, 1981, for television play; Pye award, 1982, for television play; Royal Television Society award, 1987, for television series; Bafta award, 1991, 1993; Writers Guild award, 1991, 1992; Silver Nymph award (Monte Carlo), 1993, for television show. **Agent:** Harvey Unna and Stephen Durbridge Ltd., 24-32 Pottery Lane, London W11 4LZ. **Address:** 21 Station Road, Kenilworth, Warwickshire CV8 1JJ, England.

Publications for Children

Fiction

The Fantastic Feats of Doctor Boox, illustrated by Tony Escott. London, Collins, 1972; Scarsdale, New York, Bradbury Press, 1973.

Conrad's War. London, Blackie, 1978; New York, Crown, 1980.
Marmalade and Rufus, illustrated by John Laing. London, Abelard Schuman, 1979; New York, Crown, 1983; as *Marmalade Atkins' Dreadful Deeds,* London, Abelard Schuman, 1982.
Marmalade Atkins in Space, illustrated by John Laing. London, Abelard Schuman, 1982.
Educating Marmalade, illustrated by John Laing. London, Abelard Schuman, 1983.
Badger Girl. London, BBC Publications, 1984.
Danger: Marmalade at Work, illustrated by John Laing. London, Abelard Schuman, 1984.
Marmalade Hits the Big Time, illustrated by John Laing. London, Blackie, 1984.
Alfonso Bonzo, illustrated by Tony Ross. London, Methuen, 1986.
Poonam's Pets, with Diana Davies, illustrated by Paul Dowling. New York, Viking, 1990.
Boot Street Band, with Steve Attridge. London, BBC Publications, 1993.
Raj in Charge, with Diana Davies. London, Hamish Hamilton, 1995.
Marmalade on the Ball. London, Hamish Hamilton, 1995.

Plays

Marmalade Atkins in Space (televised 1981). London, Abelard Schuman-Methuen, 1982.

Radio Play: *Hey Jude,* 1982.

Television Plays: *The Legend of King Arthur,* 1979; *Marmalade Atkins in Space,* 1981; *Educating Marmalade,* 1982; *Danger: Marmalade at Work,* 1984.

Other

The Legend of King Arthur, illustrated by Peter Archer. London, Armada, 1979.

Publications for Adults

Novels

A Very Peculiar Practice (novelization of television series). London, Methuen, 1986.
A Very Peculiar Practice: The New Frontier (novelization of television series). London, Methuen, 1988.
Getting Hurt. London, Methuen, 1989.
Dirty Faxes and Other Stories. London, Minerva, 1990.
B. Monkey. London, Lime Tree, 1992.

Plays

Can Anyone Smell Gas? (produced Richmond, Surrey, 1972).
The Shortsighted Bear (broadcast 1972; produced Coventry, 1979).
Filthy Fryer and the Woman of Mature Years (produced Richmond, Surrey, 1974).
Linda Polan: Can You Smell Gas?, What Are Little Girls Made Of? (produced Leicester, 1975).
Rohan and Julie (produced London, 1975).
Randy Robinson's Unsuitable Relationship (produced London, 1976).
Teacher's Gone Mad (produced Richmond, Surrey, 1977).
Going Bust (produced Coventry, 1977). London, French, 1982.
Fearless Frank (televised 1978; revised version, music by Dave Brown, produced London, 1979; New York, 1980).
Brainstorming with the Boys (produced Richmond, Surrey, 1978).
Battery (produced Coventry, 1979).
Diary of a Desperate Woman (produced Coventry, 1979).
Rose (produced London, 1980; New York, 1981). London, French, 1980; New York, French, 1981.
Thermal Underwear. London, French, 1987.
Prin (produced London, 1989; Broadway, 1990). London, French, 1989.

Radio Plays: *The Hospitalisation of Samuel Pellett,* 1964; *Getting the Smell of It,* 1967; *A Day in Bed,* 1967; *Curse on Them, Astonish Me!,* 1970; *Steph and the Man of Some Distinction,* 1971; *The Innocent Eye,* 1971; *The Shortsighted Bear,* 1972; *Steph and the Simple Life,* 1972; *Steph and the Zero Structured Life Style,* 1976; *Accentuate the Positive,* 1980; *Campus Blues,* 1984.

Television Plays: *Who's Going to Take Me On?,* 1967; *Is That Your Body, Boy?,* 1970; *The Christmas Present,* 1970; *No Good Unless It Hurts,* 1973; *The Water Maiden,* 1974; *Grace,* 1975; *The Imp of the Perverse,* 1975; *The Signalman,* 1976; *A Martyr to the System,* 1976; *Eleanor Marx,* 1977; *Happy in War,* 1977; *The Velvet Glove,* 1977; *Fearless Frank,* 1978; *Renoir My Father,* 1978; *To Serve Them All My Days,* from the novel by R.F. Delderfield, 1980; *Bavarian Night,* 1981; *Heartattack Hotel,* 1983; *Diana,* from the novel by R.F. Delderfield, 1984; *Pythons on the Mountain,* 1985; *A Very Peculiar Practice* series, 1986, 1988; *Inappropriate Behaviour,* 1987; *Lucky Sunil,* 1988; *Baby, I Love You,* 1988; *Mother Love,* 1988; *House of Cards,* 1989; *A Very Polish Practice,* 1990; *Filipina Dream Girls,* 1991; *To Play the King,* 1992; *The Old Devils,* 1993; *Anglo Saxon Attitudes,* 1993; *Harnessing Peacocks,* 1993; *Middlemarch,* 1994; *A Few Short Journeys of the Heart,* 1994; *Game On,* 1994.

* * *

It was the smooth veneer of genteel unreality over much of what has been written for children that irritated Andrew Davies into making his own robust scratch marks. Children's emotional relationships, particularly with their families, their private opinions, and, most of all, their sense of humour, were all rougher and tougher than it seemed to him were reflected in the sensitive well-meaning works that they were being offered. And in *Conrad's War* Davies did create a true original.

Davies' *Conrad's War* is a skillfully constructed little book, written in a direct, simple style (deceptively so, for beneath the simplicity and slapstick are some provocative and subtle ideas for ten-to-twelve-year old children to tackle), and it knits together realism and Monty Python-type fantasy, farce, and genuine emotions, into a neat seamless unit. It tells of how a small boy's consuming passion for war—for war toys, games, comics, defiant heroism, all the clichés of war, in fact—is distinctly cooled by finding himself (and his dog, his Airfix Lancaster, and his fat, absent-minded Dad) in a series of grotesque time leaks into World War II, episodes that begin as hilarious parodies of Conrad's fantasies but alarmingly become more and more realistic. The attitude of Conrad to his father, suggested (but never explained) in all its tangled reality of simmering rage, frustration, affectionate contempt, dependence, and love, is both very funny and instantly recognisable. I can think of no other like it in British fiction for children.

Conrad's War is a hugely successful joke, but a joke with a real punch to its punch line, and it is the—admittedly deliberate—lack of weight behind the punch that keeps the bad girl Marmalade Atkins stories on the levels of jolly farce. Some of the happiest effects are familiar from *Conrad's War:* there is the same teasing warping of dreams by real life; the same energetic dialogue, effortlessly heard in the reader's head—no accident that Davies, the adult dramatist, introduced Marmalade so successfully to children's television. There are some memorably daft characters who are marvelously alive in their own right—Rufus, the tough old chauvinist donkey, who aids and abets Marmalade in her wicked ways, and Sister Conception, she of the moustache and the great hairy hands and the baseball bat, who tries to teach Marmalade at the Convent of the Blessed Limit. But there are also more predictable caricatures, painted with a very broad brush indeed and jokey capital letters. And indeed, the welcome energy and gutsy bounce of Davies's writing owe much to the spirit of traditional comics. After a gap of more than a decade the incorrigible pair return in *Marmalade Atkins on the Ball,* with Marmalade and Rufus revitalizing the English football team, winning an international cricket test match, and, *pièce de résistance,* Rufus giving an ice-dancing display.

The intermediary *Alfonso Bonzo,* though powered by the same high spirits, echoes the tensions and sense of shadows lurking behind the fun of *Conrad's War:* a young boy finds more than he bargained for (literally—with an enchantingly mysterious doorstep salesman) when magical wish-fulfillment transports him into what's happening on the TV screen. Although Davies had meantime become an admired and prolific dramatist and television writer, he touched base again among children's books with *Poonam's Pets,* an endearingly surreal picture-book text for the very young, co-written with his wife Diana. When an infant school class is asked to bring in their pets, unassuming and silent little Poonam proves to be an all-powerful lion tamer, a story as notable for the prominence given to the ethnic-minority children in the class (who are never commented on) as for its tongue-in-cheek imagination. In a sequel, *Raj in Charge,* a teacher decides to put an exceedingly naughty infant in charge of good behaviour, a weighty responsibility that sucks him into a Sendak-like fantasy. Though gentle in comparison with his novels, the sense of romping *joie de vivre* is unmistakable.

It is a relief that he has not abandoned writing for children, for, at his best, Davies pans the comic rough stuff through a mesh of dramatic skill and an understanding of young minds to produce gems glinting with sharp edges.

—Stephanie Nettell

DAWLISH, Peter

Pseudonym for James Lennox Kerr. Also wrote as Lennox Kerr. **Nationality:** British. **Born:** Paisley, Renfrewshire, 1 July 1899. **Education:** North School, Paisley. **Military Service:** Royal Naval Volunteer Reserve, 1915-19 and 1942-46: mentioned in despatches. **Family:** Married Elizabeth Lamorna Birch in 1932; one son. **Career:** Gold prospector; member of the British Mercantile Marine, 1919-29, 1939-42. **Died:** 11 March 1963.

Publications for Children

Fiction

The Blackspit Smugglers (as Lennox Kerr), illustrated by Rowland Hilder. London, Nelson, 1935.
The Eye of the Earth (as James Lennox Kerr), illustrated by F.P. Paterson. London, Nelson, 1936.
Peg-Leg and the Fur Pirates, illustrated by Norman Hepple. London, Oxford University Press, 1939.
Captain Peg-Leg's War, illustrated by J.D. Evans. London, Oxford University Press, 1939.
Peg-Leg and the Invaders, illustrated by Jack Matthew. London, Oxford University Press, 1940.
Peg-Leg Sweeps the Sea, illustrated by Leonard Boden. London, Oxford University Press, 1940.
Dauntless Finds Her Crew, illustrated by P.A. Jobson. London, Oxford University Press, 1947; as *Dauntless Finds a Crew,* Wendover, Buckinghamshire, Goodchild, 1984.
The First Tripper, illustrated by P.A. Jobson. London, Oxford University Press, 1947.
Dauntless Sails Again, illustrated by P.A. Jobson. London, Oxford University Press, 1948; as *Dauntless and the Smugglers,* Wendover, Buckinghamshire, Goodchild, 1984.
Dauntless and the Mary Baines, illustrated by P.A. Jobson. London, Oxford University Press, 1949; as *Dauntless and the Wreck of the Mary Baines,* Wendover, Buckinghamshire, Goodchild, 1985.
North Sea Adventure, illustrated by P.A. Jobson. London, Oxford University Press, 1949.
Dauntless Takes Recruits, illustrated by P.A. Jobson. London, Oxford University Press, 1950; as *Dauntless and the Poplar Pirates,* Wendover, Buckinghamshire, Goodchild, 1985.
MacClellan's Lake, illustrated by Roy Sharp. London, Oxford University Press, 1951.
Aztec Gold, illustrated by P.A. Jobson. London, Oxford University Press, 1951.
Dauntless Sails In, illustrated by P.A. Jobson. London, Oxford University Press, 1952.
The Bagodia Episode, illustrated by P.A. Jobson. London, Oxford University Press, 1953.
Dauntless in Danger, illustrated by P.A. Jobson. London, Oxford University Press, 1954.
Way for a Soldier. London, Oxford University Press, 1955.
He Went with Drake, illustrated by P.A. Jobson. London, Harrap, 1955.
Sailors All. Oxford, Blackwell, 1958.
The Race for Gowrie Bay, illustrated by Christopher Brooker. London, Oxford University Press, 1959.
Dauntless Goes Home, illustrated by P.A. Jobson. London, Oxford University Press, 1960.
The Boy Jacko, illustrated by William Stobbs. London, Oxford University Press, 1962; New York, Watts, 1963.

Other

Young Drake of Devon. London, Oxford University Press, 1954.
Martin Frobisher, illustrated by William Stobbs. London, Oxford University Press, 1956.
Johnno the Deep-Sea Diver: The Life Story of Diver John Johnstone as Told to Peter Dawlish. London, Harrap, and New York, Watts, 1960.
The Royal Navy, illustrated by Victor Ambrus. London, Oxford University Press, 1963.
The Seas of Britain, illustrated by Val Biro. London, Benn, 1963.
The Merchant Navy, illustrated by Victor Ambrus. London, Oxford University Press, 1966.

Editor (as James Lennox Kerr), *On—and Under—the Ocean Wave: A Book of Modern Sea Stories.* London, Nelson, 1933.

Publications for Adults as James Lennox Kerr

Novels

Old Ship. London, Constable, 1930; New York, Macmillan, 1931.
Glenshiels. London, Lane, 1932.
Ice: A Tale of Effort. London, Lane, 1933.
Woman of Glenshiels. London, Collins, 1935.
The Fool and the Tractor. London, Collins, 1936.

Other

Backdoor Guest. London, Constable, and Indianapolis, Bobbs Merrill, 1930.
The Young Steamship Officer. London, Nelson, 1933.
Cruising in Scotland: The Log of the Migrant, Describing How a 35 Pound Cruiser Gave Pleasure to a Distinguished Artist and His Family. London, Collins, 1938.
The Eager Years: An Autobiography. London, Collins, 1949.
The Great Storm, Being the Authentic Story of the Loss at Sea of the "Princess Victoria" and Other Vessels Early in 1953. London, Harrap, 1954.
The R.N.V.R.: A Record of Achievement, with Wilfred Granville. London, Harrap, 1957.
Wilfred Grenfell: His Life and Work. London, Harrap, and New York, Dodd Mead, 1959.
The Unfortunate Ship: The Story of H.M. Troopship Birkenhead. London, Harrap, 1960.
Harbour Spotter. London, Newman Neame, 1962.
The Yachtsman's Log and Astronomical Position Line Formula. Privately printed, 1963.

Editor, *A Modern Sinbad: An Autobiography,* by Aylward Edward Dingle. London, Harrap, 1948.
Editor, with David James, *Wavy Navy by Some Who Served.* London, Harrap, 1950.
Editor, *Touching the Adventures of Merchantmen in the Second World War.* London, Harrap, 1953.

* * *

Peter Dawlish's books for boys, along with many others of the 1930-60 period, are now regrettably considered outdated and outmoded. Contemporary trends and standards have retreated from his stern and exacting regard for duty and service. Sociological cries protesting against the slightest taint of "elitism" wherever it can be discerned, or imagined where it cannot, contrast painfully with his disciplined, salt-crusted yarns. His books are in fact as dated as the wireless, Saturday morning cinemas, or stop-me-and-buy-one cyclists. Not surprisingly, most of them are long out of print.

His first fictional hero was the formidable figure of Captain Peg-Leg, a nautical equivalent to Biggles, admirably suited to the mood of wartime Britain. Unlike Biggles, however, Captain Peg-Leg was pensioned off at the end of hostilities in 1945. So Dawlish embarked upon series of books about the voyages of a 45-foot schooner, *Dauntless,* which when first encountered was apparently destined for the breaker's yard. Reconditioned and recommissioned by a group of school boys under the command of a former naval captain, *Dauntless* eventually put to sea. Dawlish's own extensive marine experience and know-how were evident on every page, and no boy with salt in his veins could resist the authentic tang of the sea. Landlubbers might find themselves in difficulties wading through oceans of seafaring terminology but they too could wallow in these exhilarating and intoxicating sea stories.

Subsequently Dawlish took to historical adventures set in Tudor and Stuart times. *Aztec Gold* narrates the fortunes of an expedition mounted by a Devon farmer to rescue his brother, reported to be held captive on an isolated Aztec island stronghold. *He Went with Drake* is a return to the Henty tradition of enlisting a young hero in the company of a great captain, while *The Boy Jacko* tells of a voyage to Virginia in response to a summons from a rich uncle, hindered by villainy and skulduggery at every turn, which a London street urchin is instrumental in thwarting.

In the not-so-distant past sea stories were a recognizable and respected genre of both adult and junior fiction. Why they should have almost totally disappeared from publishers' lists is not altogether clear, unless it is because many of them, especially those written for children, were set in times of war or in historical periods when the prevailing national mood and temper was one of expansion, a concept now regarded as neither practical nor creditable. Possibly the English Tourist Board's Maritime England promotion might encourage enterprising publishers to reprint titles from their backlists. Should this prove feasible Peter Dawlish's books must surely be among the first to re-emerge from the shadows. Their refreshing, open-air, good-natured comradeship has a lot to offer present day readers.

—Alan Edwin Day

DAY LEWIS, C(ecil)

Pseudonym: Nicholas Blake. **Nationality:** British. **Born:** Ballintubbert, Queen's County (now County Laois), Ireland, 27 April 1904; brought to England in 1905. **Education:** Wilkie's Preparatory School, London, 1912-17; Sherborne School, Dorset, 1917-23; Wadham College, Oxford, 1923-27, B.A. 1927, M.A. **Military Service:** Editor in the Ministry of Information, London, 1941-46. **Family:** Married 1) Mary King in 1928 (divorced 1951), two sons; also one other son; 2) Jill Balcon in 1951, one daughter and one son. **Career:** Assistant master, Summer Fields School, Oxford, 1927-28; master, Larchfield School, Helensburgh,

Dunbartonshire, 1928-30, and Cheltenham Junior School, Gloucestershire, 1930-35; reader, John Lehmann Ltd., publishers, London, 1946; reader from 1946, and Director from 1954, Chatto and Windus, publishers, London. Professor of Poetry, Oxford University, 1951-56; Norton Professor of Poetry, Harvard University, Cambridge, Massachusetts, 1964-65. Clark Lecturer, 1946, and Sidgwick Lecturer, 1956, Cambridge University; Warton Lecturer, British Academy, London, 1951; Byron Lecturer, University of Nottingham, 1952; Chancellor Dunning Lecturer, Queen's University, Kingston, Ontario, 1954; Compton Lecturer, University of Hull, Yorkshire, 1968. Member, Arts Council of Great Britain, 1962-67: Chairman of the Poetry, later Literature, Panel. **Awards:** Honorary Fellow, Wadham College, 1968. D.Litt.: University of Exeter, 1965; University of Hull, 1970; Litt.D.: Trinity College, Dublin, 1968. Fellow, 1944, Vice-President, 1959, and Companion of Literature, 1965, Royal Society of Literature; Honorary Member, American Academy, 1966; Member, Irish Academy of Letters, 1968. C.B.E. (Commander, Order of the British Empire), 1950. Poet Laureate, 1968. **Died:** 22 May 1972.

Publications for Children

Fiction

Dick Willoughby. Oxford, Blackwell, 1933; New York, Random House, 1938.
The Otterbury Incident, illustrated by Edward Ardizzone. London, Putnam, 1948; New York, Viking Press, 1949.

Other

Poetry for You: A Book for Boys and Girls on the Enjoyment of Poetry. Oxford, Blackwell, 1944; New York, Oxford University Press, 1947.

Editor, *The Echoing Green: An Anthology of Verse.* Oxford, Blackwell, 3 vols., 1937.
Editor, *The Midnight Skaters: Poems for Young Readers,* by Edmund Blunden, illustrated by David Gentleman. London, Bodley Head, 1968.

Publications for Adults

Novels

The Friendly Tree. London, Cape, 1936; New York, Harper, 1937.
Starting Point. London, Cape, 1937; New York, Harper, 1938.
Child of Misfortune. London, Cape, 1939.

Novels as Nicholas Blake

A Question of Proof. London, Collins, and New York, Harper, 1935.
Thou Shell of Death. London, Collins, 1936; as *Shell of Death,* New York, Harper, 1936.
There's Trouble Brewing. London, Collins, and New York, Harper, 1937.
The Beast Must Die. London, Collins, and New York, Harper, 1938.
The Smiler with the Knife. London, Collins, and New York, Harper, 1939.
Malice in Wonderland. London, Collins, 1940; as *The Summer Camp Mystery,* New York, Harper, 1940; as *Malice with Murder,* New York, Pyramid, 1964.
The Case of the Abominable Snowman. London, Collins, 1941; as *The Corpse in the Snowman,* New York, Harper, 1941.
Minute for Murder. London, Collins, 1947; New York, Harper, 1948.
Head of a Traveller. London, Collins, and New York, Harper, 1949.
The Dreadful Hollow. London, Collins, and New York, Harper, 1953.
The Whisper in the Gloom. London, Collins, and New York, Harper, 1954; as *Catch and Kill,* New York, Bestseller, 1955.
A Tangled Web. London, Collins, and New York, Harper, 1956; as *Death and Daisy Bland,* New York, Dell, 1960.
End of Chapter. London, Collins, and New York, Harper, 1957.
A Penknife in My Heart. London, Collins, 1958; New York, Harper, 1959.
The Widow's Cruise. London, Collins, and New York, Harper, 1959.
The Worm of Death. London, Collins, and New York, Harper, 1961.
The Deadly Joker. London, Collins, 1963.
The Sad Variety. London, Collins, and New York, Harper, 1964.
The Morning after Death. London, Collins, and New York, Harper, 1966.
The Private Wound. London, Collins, and New York, Harper, 1968.

Plays

Screenplays (documentaries): *The Colliers,* 1939; *The Green Girdle,* 1940.

Radio Play: *Calling James Braithwaite,* 1940.

Poetry

Beechen Vigil and Other Poems. London, Fortune Press, 1925.
Country Comets. London, Hopkinson, 1928.
Transitional Poem. London, Hogarth Press, 1929.
From Feathers to Iron. London, Hogarth Press, 1931.
The Magnetic Mountain. London, Hogarth Press, 1933.
Collected Poems 1929-1933. London, Hogarth Press, 1935; with *A Hope for Poetry,* New York, Random House, 1935.
A Time to Dance and Other Poems. London, Hogarth Press, 1935.
Noah and the Waters. London, Hogarth Press, 1936.
A Time to Dance, Noah and the Waters, and Other Poems, with an Essay, Revolution in Writing. New York, Random House, 1936.
Overtures to Death and Other Poems. London, Cape, 1938.
Poems in Wartime. London, Cape, 1940.
Selected Poems. London, Hogarth Press, 1940.
Word over All. London, Cape, 1943; New York, Transatlantic, 1944.
(*Poems*). London, Eyre and Spottiswoode, 1943.
Short Is the Time: Poems 1936-1943 (includes *Overtures to Death* and *Word over All*). New York, Oxford University Press, 1945.
Poems 1943-1947. London, Cape, and New York, Oxford University Press, 1948.

Collected Poems 1929-1936. London, Hogarth Press, 1949.
Selected Poems. London, Penguin, 1951; revised edition, 1957, 1969, 1974.
An Italian Visit. London, Cape, and New York, Harper, 1953.
Collected Poems. London, Cape-Hogarth Press, 1954.
Christmas Eve. London, Faber, 1954.
The Newborn: D.M.B., 29th April, 1957. London, Favil Press of Kensington, 1957.
Pegasus and Other Poems. London, Cape, 1957; New York, Harper, 1958.
The Gate and Other Poems. London, Cape, 1962.
Requiem for the Living. New York, Harper, 1964.
On Not Saying Everything. Privately printed, 1964.
A Marriage Song for Albert and Barbara. Privately printed, 1965.
The Room and Other Poems. London, Cape, 1965.
C. Day Lewis: Selections from His Poetry, edited by Patric Dickinson. London, Chatto and Windus, 1967.
Selected Poems. New York, Harper, 1967.
The Abbey That Refused to Die: A Poem. County Mayo, Ireland, Ballintubber Abbey, 1967.
The Whispering Roots. London, Cape, 1970; as *The Whispering Roots and Other Poems,* New York, Harper, 1970.
Going My Way. London, Poem-of-the-Month Club, 1970.
Poems of C. Day Lewis 1925-1972, edited by Ian Parsons. London, Cape-Hogarth Press, 1977.
Posthumous Poems. Andoversford, Gloucestershire, Whittington Press, 1979.

Recording: *Poems,* Argo, 1974.

Other

A Hope for Poetry. Oxford, Blackwell, 1934; with *Collected Poems,* New York, Random House, 1935.
Revolution in Writing. London, Hogarth Press, 1935; New York, Random House, 1936.
Imagination and Thinking, with L. Susan Stebbing. London, British Institute of Adult Education, 1936.
We're Not Going to Do Nothing: A Reply to Mr. Aldous Huxley's Pamphlet "What Are You Going to Do about It?" London, Left Review, 1936.
The Poetic Image. London, Cape, and New York, Oxford University Press, 1947.
Enjoying Poetry: A Reader's Guide. London, National Book League, 1947.
The Colloquial Element in English Poetry. Newcastle-upon-Tyne, Literary and Philosophical Society, 1947.
The Poet's Task. Oxford, Clarendon Press, 1951.
The Grand Manner. Nottingham, University of Nottingham, 1952.
The Lyrical Poetry of Thomas Hardy. London, Oxford University Press, 1953.
Notable Images of Virtue: Emily Brontë, George Meredith, W.B. Yeats. Toronto, Ryerson Press, 1954.
The Poet's Way of Knowledge. Cambridge, University Press, 1957.
The Buried Day (autobiography). London, Chatto and Windus, and New York, Harper, 1960.
The Lyric Impulse. Cambridge, Massachusetts, Harvard University Press, and London, Chatto and Windus, 1965.
Thomas Hardy, with R.A. Scott-James. London, Longman, 1965.
A Need for Poetry? Hull, University of Hull, 1968.
On Translating Poetry: A Lecture. Abingdon-on-Thames, Berkshire, Abbey Press, 1970.

Editor, with W.H. Auden, *Oxford Poetry 1927.* Oxford, Blackwell, 1927.
Editor, with John Lehmann and T.A. Jackson, *A Writer in Arms,* by Ralph Fox. London, Lawrence and Wishart, 1937.
Editor, *The Mind in Chains: Socialism and the Cultural Revolution.* London, Muller, 1937.
Editor, with Charles Fenby, *Anatomy of Oxford: An Anthology.* London, Cape, 1938.
Editor, with L.A.G. Strong, *A New Anthology of Modern Verse 1920-1940.* London, Methuen, 1941.
Editor, with others, *Orion 2-3.* London, Nicholson and Watson, 2 vols., 1945-46.
Editor, *The Golden Treasury of the Best Songs and Lyrical Poems in the English Language,* by Francis Turner Palgrave. London, Collins, 1954.
Editor, with John Lehmann, *The Chatto Book of Modern Poetry 1915-1955.* London, Chatto and Windus, 1956.
Editor, with Kathleen Nott and Thomas Blackburn, *New Poems 1957.* London, Joseph, 1957.
Editor, *A Book of English Lyrics.* London, Chatto and Windus, 1961; as *English Lyric Poems 1500-1900,* New York, Appleton Century Crofts, 1961.
Editor, *The Collected Poems of Wilfred Owen.* London, Chatto and Windus, 1963; New York, New Directions, 1964.
Editor, *The Poems of Robert Browning.* Cambridge, Limited Editions Club, 1969; New York, Heritage Press, 1971.
Editor, *A Choice of Keats's Verse.* London, Faber, 1971.
Editor, *Crabbe.* London, Penguin, 1973.
Editor, *A Lasting Joy: An Anthology.* London, Allen and Unwin, 1973.

Translator, *The Georgics of Virgil.* London, Cape, 1940; New York, Oxford University Press, 1947.
Translator, *The Graveyard by the Sea,* by Paul Valéry. London, Secker and Warburg, 1947.
Translator, *The Aeneid of Virgil.* London, Hogarth Press, and New York, Oxford University Press, 1952.
Translator, *The Eclogues of Virgil.* London, Cape, 1963; with *The Georgics,* New York, Doubleday, 1964.
Translator, with Mátyás Sárközi, *The Tomtit in the Rain: Traditional Hungarian Rhymes,* by Erzsi Gazdas. London, Chatto and Windus, 1971.

*

Bibliography: *C. Day Lewis, The Poet Laureate: A Bibliography* by Geoffrey Handley-Taylor and Timothy d'Arch Smith, London and Chicago, St. James Press, 1968.

Manuscript Collections: New York Public Library; State University of New York, Buffalo; British Library, London; University of Liverpool.

Critical Studies: *C. Day Lewis* by Clifford Dyment, London, Longman, 1955, revised edition, 1963; *C. Day Lewis* by Joseph N. Riddel, New York, Twayne, 1971; *C. Day-Lewis: An English Literary Life* by Sean Day-Lewis, London, Weidenfeld and Nicolson, 1980.

Theatrical Activities:
Actor: **Radio**—Tom Moore in *Blame Not the Bard,* 1942.

* * *

C. Day Lewis is best known as a children's writer for *The Otterbury Incident.* It has been "one of those books that work" to grateful teachers and librarians in the United Kingdom for some 40 years.

His heroes attend a day school in post-war England, a departure from the timeless cloisters of boarding schools which were still a feature of boys' comics of the period. Their exploits are described by George, himself a participant in the kids-catch-crooks adventure—a device which allows confidential asides to his reader and a mock-heroic style as the boys go into action with the discipline of a commando unit. His idiom is firmly middle-class and, inevitably, of its time: chaps in the company shut up "j. quick" when their leader tells them off; a couple of spivs are "a pair of blisters" or "fearful outsiders." There are unselfconscious references to a search proving as difficult as looking for "a nigger in a dark cellar" and to a pawnbroker "jewing" the boys, and a carefree objectivity about "females."

The abiding success of the book lies in the fact that it reworks, in a particularly lively way, a situation of unfailing appeal to children. A group of kids, unaided, outwit a trio of grown-ups; and since the grown-ups are criminals, the children earn the gratitude and admiration of adult society, embodied in a police inspector and their headmaster.

The basic formula was well-tried even in 1948. Day Lewis's story is distinguished by the rapid and entertaining ride he offers over a steeplechase of a plot. Each hurdle requires ingenious negotiation: inventive and comic fund-raising to pay for a broken window; bizarre detection by the local newsagent, E. Sidebotham, who suffers periodic delusions that he is Sherlock Holmes; and a satisfying denouement as the boys' practised military strategies are brought into play against a criminal with a cut-throat razor he means to use.

Characters are simply sketched, but for many children the stereotypes may provide readier access to the narrative than subtler portraits. Day Lewis had already demonstrated his control of an exciting plot peopled by boldly drawn figures in *Dick Willoughby,* where he charted the progress of a young Elizabethan. Secret tunnels, sword-play on the Spanish Main, an evil Catholic kinsman, and a dash of innocent romance spice the mixture. The dialogue is entangled in what Geoffrey Trease calls "tushery": "Marry, come up, thou tun of a booby, that hairy comet of thine, that hollybush thou grow'st to keep thy neck warm for the rope med frighten Spaniards but not a Dorset maiden," cries a serving maid to a bluff retainer "in high glee."

Even in *Dick Willoughby,* however, there are many of the qualities which mark *The Otterbury Incident*: the clarity of the issues at stake, the pace of the action, and a pervading high spiritedness.

—Geoff Fox

de ANGELI, Marguerite

Nationality: American. **Born:** Marguerite Lofft, Lapeer, Michigan, 14 March 1889. **Education:** Schools in Lapeer and Philadelphia. **Family:** Married John de Angeli in 1910 (died 1969); four sons and one daughter. **Career:** Professional singer, 1904-21. **Awards:** American Library Association Newbery medal, 1950; Catholic Library Association Regina medal, 1968. Marguerite de Angeli Library, Lapeer, Michigan, named in 1981. **Died:** 16 June 1987.

Publications for Children (illustrated by the author)

Fiction

Ted and Nina Go to the Grocery Store. New York, Doubleday, 1935.
Ted and Nina Have a Happy Rainy Day. New York, Doubleday, 1936.
Henner's Lydia. New York, Doubleday, 1936; Kingswood, Surrey, World's Work, 1965.
Petite Suzanne. New York, Doubleday, 1937.
Copper-Toed Boots. New York, Doubleday, 1938; Kingswood, Surrey, World's Work, 1965.
Skippack School. New York, Doubleday, 1939; Kingswood, Surrey, World's Work, 1964.
A Summer Day with Ted and Nina. New York, Doubleday, 1940.
Thee, Hannah! New York, Doubleday, 1940; Kingswood, Surrey, World's Work, 1962.
Elin's Amerika. New York, Doubleday, 1941; Kingswood, Surrey, World's Work, 1964.
Up the Hill. New York, Doubleday, 1942.
Yonie Wondernose. New York, Doubleday, 1944.
Turkey for Christmas. Philadelphia, Westminster Press, 1944.
Bright April. New York, Doubleday, 1946.
Jared's Island. New York, Doubleday, 1947.
The Door in the Wall. New York, Doubleday, 1949; Kingswood, Surrey, World's Work, 1959.
Just Like David. New York, Doubleday, 1951.
Black Fox of Lorne. New York, Doubleday, 1956; Kingswood, Surrey, World's Work, 1959.
Fiddlestrings. New York, Doubleday, 1974.
The Lion in the Box. New York, Doubleday, 1975.
Whistle for the Crossing. New York, Doubleday, 1977.
Friendship and Other Poems. New York, Doubleday, 1981.

Other

A Pocket Full of Posies: A Merry Mother Goose. New York, Doubleday, 1961.
The Goose Girl. New York, Doubleday, 1964.

Editor, *Book of Nursery and Mother Goose Rhymes.* New York, Doubleday, 1954.
Editor, *The Old Testament.* New York, Doubleday, 1960.
Editor, *Book of Favorite Hymns.* New York, Doubleday, 1963.

Publications for Adults

Other

Libraries and Reading: Their Importance in the Lives of Famous Americans, with others, edited by Donald H. Hunt. Philadelphia, Drexel Press, 1964.

Butter at the Old Price: The Autobiography of Marguerite de Angeli. New York, Doubleday, 1971.

*

Manuscript Collection: Free Library, Philadelphia.

Illustrator: *The New Moon,* 1924, and *The Covered Bridge,* 1936, both by Cornelia Meigs; *Meggy MacIntosh* by Elizabeth Janet Gray, 1930; *A Candle in the Mist* by Florence Crannell Means, 1931; *The Christmas Nightingale* by Eric Kelly, 1932; *Joan Wanted a Kitty* by Jane Brown Gemmill, 1937; *Alice-All-by-Herself* by Elizabeth Coatsworth, 1937; *Red Sky over Rome* by Anne D. Kyle, 1938; *The Princess and the Gypsy* by Jean Rosmer, 1938; *Prayers and Graces for Little Children* edited by Quail Hawkins, 1941; *They Loved to Laugh* by Kathryn Worth, 1942; *In and Out: Verses* by Tom Robinson, 1943; *The Empty Barn,* 1966, and *The Door in the Wall: A Play,* 1968, both by Arthur C. de Angeli.

* * *

Most famous of all Marguerite de Angeli's long list of titles is *The Door in the Wall,* which won for her the Newbery Medal. Set in the England of Edward III, it is a beautifully realized piece of historical fiction: the young hero's brave acceptance of his handicap and his determination to fight on against all but insuperable hardship have an inspiring message for youngsters of any era. The writer conveys with jewel-like clarity both the differences and the similarities of that distant time and this: green, wild England with its glorious, comfortless castles and noisome narrow streets, and the inhabitants in so many ways like their counterparts of today. Robin is a boy of the 13th century, but he speaks very clearly to the 20th-century reader.

De Angeli had a gift for making the exotic, peculiar, or particular seem universal and unthreatening to young readers, who are often xenophobic in their rejection of the unfamiliar. She wrote with equal sympathy and understanding of families of varied ethnic backgrounds and creeds; and just as her illustrations bring their outward appearances vividly to life, her gentle, simple stories make their daily lives and the small concerns of their children those of all loving families everywhere. If at first glance her works seem concerned with contrasting cultures, in fact her study was that of the universality of happy childhood.

She reserved the larger dramatic themes, such as war and revenge, for her few tales of the remote past; young Robin of *The Door in the Wall* is the saviour of his besieged castle in the mist; in *Black Fox of Lorne* Jan and Brus, twin Viking lads of the 10th century, avenge their father's death by treachery; but these ambitious novels for older children are atypical. De Angeli was best known and loved for her shorter stories of ordinary, day-to-day childhood concerns; of the boy who longs above all things for a pair of copper-toed boots; the working lad whose stern but loving father must be made to see that there is a place for artists as well as for miners; little Hannah who painfully discovers for herself the meaning of her drab Quaker bonnet and learns to wear it with pride; and all her other believable, loveable children.

Many of her stories and their illustrations are based upon de Angeli's own family and its folklore, and have both the strength and weakness of family tradition revealed to the outsider. There is a suggestion of the "separateness" enveloping any close-knit family, however large-hearted its members, and a natural tendency to overrate family stories and catch-phrases that have meaning only to the inner circle of intimates. But more than offsetting the effect of partiality is the depth of love, trust, and understanding that informs de Angeli's writings with the glow of happiness remembered and preserved.

—Joan McGrath

de GRAFT-HANSON, J(ohn) O(rleans)

Nationality: Ghanaian. **Born:** Sunyani, 7 October 1932. **Education:** Mfantsipim School, Cape Coast, 1947-50; University College of Gold Coast (now Ghana), 1951-56, B.A. (honours) in classics 1956; Cambridge University, England, 1957-61, B.A. 1959, M.Litt. in classics 1961. **Family:** Married; 10 children. **Career:** Lecturer, 1960-65, Senior Lecturer, 1965-74, and Associate Professor of Classics, 1974-82, University of Ghana, Legon; Associate Professor of Classics, Fourah Bay College, University of Sierra Leone, Freetown, 1982-86. Professor of Classics, University of Cape Coast, from 1987. Dean, Faculty of Arts, University of Ghana, Legon, 1970-76; member of the Board of Directors, Graphic Corporation, 1971-72, and Museums and Monuments, 1973-74; visiting lecturer, University of British Columbia, Vancouver, 1976-77; President, Council of the Children's Literature Foundation (Ghana), 1978-82; vice-chairman, Ghana Book Development Board, 1980-82. **Awards:** Ghana Library award, 1975; Ghana Book Development award, 1979; Fellow, Ghana Academy of Arts and Sciences, 1979; International Board of Books for Young People (IBBY) Honours list, 1994; Valco Fund Literary Prize, 1995. **Address:** c/o Department of Classics, University of Cape Coast, Cape Coast, Ghana.

Publications for Children

Fiction

The Secret of Opokuwa, illustrated by John Kedjani. Accra, Ghana, Anowuo, 1967.

The Little Sasabonsam. Tema, Ghana Publishing Corporation, 1972.

Papa Ewusi and the Magic Marble. Tema, Ghana Publishing Corporation, 1973.

Papa and the Animals. Tema, Ghana Publishing Corporation, 1973.

The Fetish Hide-Out. Tema, Ghana Publishing Corporation, 1975.

The People from the Sea. Tema, Ghana Publishing Corporation, 1988.

The Singing Tortoise. Tema, Ghana Publishing Corporation, 1989.

The Little Rain Cloud. Accra, Sedco Publishing, 1989.

Antobam's Dream. Accra, Quick Service Books, 1993.

The Golden Oware Counters. Tema, Ghana Publishing Corporation, 1993.

Black Baby Jesus. Accra, Quick Service Books, 1995.
The Harmattan Man. Accra, Quick Service Books, 1995.
Who Has Stolen the Sky? Accra, Quick Service Books, 1995.
Mpotse—Mpotse—Eguamba—Na—Feow. Accra, Quick Service Books, 1995.
Amanfi's Gold. Accra, Ghana Universities, 1996.
Dukudukuduku. Accra, Black Mask, 1997.
The Pear That Would Not Drop. Accra, Sedco Publishing, 1997.

Other

Ancient Greek Stories About Africa, illustrated by Fred Odametey. Accra, Adwinsa Publications, 1982.
Children's Literature—The Ghanaian Experience (J.B. Danquah Memorial Lectures, series 24). Accra, Ghana Academy of Arts and Sciences, 1991.

*

J. O. de Graft-Hanson comments:
In my children's books I aim at utilizing our rich heritage of traditional stories, mainly folktales and legends, for original creative writing for our children—to stimulate their curiosity and imagination, to thrill them with a sense of adventure and discovery, and also to give them a feeling for literature.

The traditional stories are not simply retold; rather they serve as sources of inspiration from which my own stories take off or, where appropriate, as content material around which they are woven. For example, from our folktales comes *The Little Sasabonsam:* a child hears a story about the Sasabonsam, a forest demon of our Ananse tales, just before bedtime, and he sets out to find a little one, his adventures taking the form of a dream that is almost nightmarish. But in *Papa and the Animals* a substantial portion is taken up by a number of animals who come to console a child weeping for the loss of his marbles by narrating, each in turn, their own stories of how they too lost some precious possession. Their stories are essentially from well-known Akan folktales of the "why or how so?" kind, but are made more dramatic by being told by the animals themselves.

On the other hand *The Secret of Opokuwa* has its germ in the alleged historical attempt to get possession of the famous sacred Golden Stool of Ashanti by a British Governor of the Gold Coast (now Ghana). Similarly *The Fetish Hide-Out* is woven around the legend of the destruction of what was once the most famous oracular shrine of the Fanti states; while in *The People from the Sea* a group of children in search of information for a history lesson get involved in tracking down the perpetrators of a burglary and helping to effect their capture.

In all my books I try as much as possible to make the language simple and direct, bearing in mind that my target readership is children between the ages of 8 and 14.

* * *

J.O. de Graft-Hanson believes that folklore provides important source material for Ghanaian children's literature. In all of his fiction he places contemporary children in contact with persons or places that are important in Fante or Akan folklore or tells folk tales in the context of the story. His fiction, like the folklore upon which it is based, includes implicit and sometimes explicit morals.

Papa Ewusi is the young, highly imaginative boy hero of a series of stories that make extensive use of folk tales and well-known characters in Ghanaian folklore such as Sasabonsam and dwarves. In *The Little Sasabonsam* Papa Ewusi becomes very curious about the fierce, gigantic, hairy, scaly Sasabonsam about which his grandfather told him. In his dreams he enters the forest, talks with birds and animals, plays and sings with dwarves, and meets and befriends a baby Sasabonsam. However, the father Sasabonsam is not friendly and chases and breathes fire on Papa when he wakes up. In *Papa Ewusi and the Magic Marble* Papa obtains a magic marble from dwarves in their forest home. When the marble is lost (actually stolen by another boy) the dwarves help Papa find it. They also help Papa with his household chores and provide his grandparents with food. However, Papa's good fortune is short-lived, for he really loses the magic marble in a well.

In the final story in the series, *Papa and the Animals,* Papa becomes bored and cries. When a mouse laughs at him, Papa tells the mouse a story, and the mouse reciprocates. The same events occur with a pig, monitor lizard, and vulture. As a result Papa hears four explanatory tales including how vulture became bald and how monitor lizard lost his hearing. De Graft-Hanson includes few details about the folkloric characters that appear in the Papa Ewusi series, for they are familiar to the Ghanaian children for whom he writes.

De Graft-Hanson's historical adventure stories are based on oral traditions about real historical events or on legends about the distant past. *The People from the Sea* takes place at the time of the Cape Coast earthquake of 1939. The hero hears the legend of Asebu told by his uncle and learns that it has contemporary relevance in the robbery of a store, which he helps to solve. *The Secret of Opokuwa* is based on a well-known event in Ghanaian history, the "theft" of the Ashanti golden stool by British colonial officials. In the context of the story, part of a yam festival is performed and children tell ananse stories to entertain themselves. The three child heroes and heroines actually save the state stool by substituting a newly made facsimile. The same three children are the main characters in *The Fetish Hide-Out* which is based on a legend about the Fante shrine of Nananompow. This story also includes rituals associated with "traditional" rulers. The children save Nana Otei's pet lamb, and in the process find a fetish hide-out where "bad" medicine is made. The hide-out is eventually destroyed after one of the children who was being held captive there is rescued, and the "good" medicine of the chief priest prevails, bringing rain to end a drought.

In de Graft-Hanson's stories the past lives in the present. His written stories continue an old African storytelling tradition in which each storyteller creates well-known stories anew for a contemporary audience.

—Nancy J. Schmidt

de HAMEL, Joan (Littledale)

Nationality: British (emigrated to New Zealand, 1955). **Born:** Joan Littledale Pollock, London, 31 March 1924. **Education:** Queen's Gate School, London, 1932-40; Ecole S. Georges (Switzerland) at Onslow Hall, Shrewsbury, 1940-42; Lady Margaret Hall, Oxford, 1942-44, B.A. (honours) in modern languages 1944, M.A. 1949. **Family:** Married Francis de Hamel in 1948; five sons. **Career:** Assistant mistress, St. Nicholas School, Hemel

Hempstead, Hertfordshire, 1944-45; head of languages, Francis Holland School, London, 1945-48; Lecturer in French, Teachers College, Dunedin, 1967-79. **Awards:** New Zealand Library Association Esther Glen award, 1979; Reed Memorial award, 1985. **Agent:** Ray Richards, 3/43 Aberdeen Road, Castor Bay, Auckland; or, A.P. Watt Ltd., 20 John Street, London WC1N 2DL, England. **Address:** 25 Howard Street, Macandrew Bay, Dunedin, New Zealand.

Publications for Children

Fiction

X Marks the Spot, illustrated by the author. Guildford, Surrey, Lutterworth Press, 1973.
Take the Long Path, illustrated by Gareth Floyd. Guildford, Surrey, Lutterworth Press, 1978.
Hemi's Pet, illustrated by Christine Ross. Auckland, Reed Methuen, and London, Angus and Robertson, 1985; Boston, Houghton Mifflin, 1987.
The Third Eye. Auckland, Viking Kestrel, 1987.
Hideaway. London, Puffin, 1992.
Hemi and the Shortie Pyjamas, illustrated by Lyn Kriegler. Auckland, Puffin, 1996.

*

Joan de Hamel comments:

X Marks the Spot is an adventure story about three children surviving under difficult circumstances after a helicopter crash in the New Zealand bush. There is a strong slant towards natural history and survival techniques—in addition to the mystery of "X." *Take the Long Path* is set on Otago Peninsula. David lives on an isolated farm and follows the fortunes of the local yellow-eyed penguins. He meets an old Maori and finds his own life is mysteriously bound up with the history of the Maoris on the peninsula and paralleled by the lives of the penguins he protects. *Hemi's Pet* is a picture story book. If a pet is something alive that you love and look after, why not enter your little sister in the school pet show? In *Hemi and the Shortie Pyjamas,* Hemi devises a way to visit Rata, who is in the hospital. *The Third Eye* is a story of intrigue for the older age group. The secret work of a scientist on the rare tuatara, the prophecies of the Maori ancestors, and the plans of a property developer involve the three children from *X Marks the Spot* (now four years older) during a working holiday in the mountains near Takaka, New Zealand. Hideaway is also a mystery/adventure story, set in Dunedin on a Peninsula Angora goat farm, where Becky, aged 11, is staying with her uncle and aunt and cousin Chloe.

* * *

Joan de Hamel is an English immigrant to New Zealand whose great strength is her freshness of vision in interpreting the local scene. Her novels show an awareness of such New Zealand issues as the conservation of rare species and the human problems inherent in a multiracial society. Above all, however, they demonstrate her exuberant response to the New Zealand landscape, which assumes as great an importance to her canvases as her convincingly portrayed human relationships.

X Marks the Spot is a celebration of the remote southwestern forests of the South Island in which a family of children have to survive after a plane crash. Against all the beauty of the clear atmosphere and the exhilaration of the high peaks are set the discomfort of sandflies and the real dangers of rushing rivers. When their backpacks are swept away and they are left with only a gun and matches, these city-bred children realize that they will have to kill a deer to avoid starvation, and their ensuing agony of mind is memorably portrayed. The subplot is the discovery of South American poachers out to capture the rare kakapo parrot.

The landscape alters in *Take the Long Path* to the bare sheep country of southeastern Otago, which is flanked by lupin-clad sand dunes and the treacherously beautiful Pacific. A deserved winner of the Esther Glenn medal, the book is much more copmplex than *X Marks the Spot,* deftly interweaving three themes. The main one is that of the relationship between the hero, David, and his parents, but it has strong Maori and animal story components. David, who loves his rather disorganised mother, while he fears his forbidding, sheep-farming father, turns for consolation to the penguins that nest in the sand dunes, adopting one family of them in particular as his own. It is there that he meets an old Maori man, who tells David that he is there on "family business" to look for an ancient whalebone club that had belonged to one of his ancestors. David finds the club and discovers that he has been talking to the ghost of his own grandfather, who had "taken the long path" from the spirit world. David then realizes that he himself is half-Maori and that the man he has thought of as his father is in fact his stepfather. He is able to come to terms with the situation when he sees it parallels the plight of his penguin family, whose father has been killed but whose rather feckless mother—like his own—needs a mate to protect her. David, too, has taken the long path to self-knowledge in a book that portrays, on an individual level, the conflict between the differing attitudes of Maoris and Europeans.

In *The Third Eye,* the children of *X Marks the Spot,* now in their late teens, become involved in a conservation issue when they discover that rare lizards—tuataras—are being smuggled out of the country by an American woman scientist. She suspects that their pineal, third eye may hold the secret of their survival on barren rocks—information that might be relevant to humans after a nuclear war. The novel unobtrusively raises the whole question of whether bad means are justified by laudable ends. Another underlying issue is whether remote areas should be developed if doing so would create local employment. There are never easy answers, but within the framework of well-written, highly readable adventure stories, Joan de Hamel offers food for thought on current issues.

She does, however, present an unusual solution to a problem in her only picture book. In the engagingly related *Hemi's Pet,* a seven-year-old Maori boy has no animal to show at the school pet show, until he realizes that his little sister fits all the criteria for a "pet," for which he wins first prize for originality.

In her novel, *Hideaway,* de Hamel moves away from the larger themes of conservation, instead highlighting the adventure on an Otago goat farm where Becky is staying with an aunt and uncle. Becky gradually realizes that her cousin Chloe is involved with the delinquent element in Dunedin and is deceiving her parents. However, Becky herself becomes involved in a deception when she discovers a young Russian who has jumped ship and whom she feeds and shelters in a disused hut. A goat farmer herself, de Hamel paints a convincing picture of the farm and ensures that a little hand-reared kid has an important part in the jigsaw plot, which sees all the elements slot neatly into place in the last chapter.

—Betty Gilderdale

DE JONG, Meindert

Nationality: American (brought to the United States at age eight). **Born:** Wierum, Netherlands, 4 March 1906. **Education:** Calvin College, Grand Rapids, Michigan, A.B. 1928; University of Chicago. **Military Service:** United States Army Air Corps during World War II: historian of the Chinese-American Wing, 14th Air Force. **Family:** Married 1) Hattie Overeinter in 1932; 2) Beatrice DeClaire McElwee in 1962 (died 1969), five stepchildren. **Career:** College teacher, then farmer, in Iowa, 1928-38; worked with the Federal Writers Project, Grand Rapids, Michigan. Lived in Mexico, 1962-67. **Awards:** American Library Association Newbery medal, 1955; Child Study Committee award, 1957; Hans Christian Andersen International medal, 1962; National Book award, 1969; Catholic Library Association Regina medal, 1972. **Died:** 16 July 1991.

Publications for Children

Fiction

The Big Goose and the Little White Duck, illustrated by Edna Potter. New York, Harper, 1938; London, Heinemann, 1939.
Dirk's Dog Bello, illustrated by Kurt Wiese. New York, Harper, 1939; London, Lutterworth Press, 1960.
Wheels over the Bridge, illustrated by Aldren Watson. New York, Harper, 1941.
Bells of the Harbor, illustrated by Kurt Wiese. New York, Harper, 1941.
The Cat That Walked a Week, illustrated by Tessie Robinson. New York, Harper, 1943; London, Lutterworth Press, 1965.
The Little Stray Dog, illustrated by Edward Shenton. New York, Harper, 1943.
Billy and the Unhappy Bull, illustrated by Marc Simont. New York, Harper, 1946; London, Lutterworth Press, 1966.
Good Luck Duck, illustrated by Marc Simont. New York, Harper, and London, Hamish Hamilton, 1950.
Tower by the Sea, illustrated by Barbara Comfort. New York, Harper, and London, Hamish Hamilton, 1950.
Smoke above the Lane, illustrated by Girard Goodenow. New York, Harper, 1951.
Shadrach, illustrated by Maurice Sendak. New York, Harper, 1953; London, Lutterworth Press, 1957.
Hurry Home, Candy, illustrated by Maurice Sendak. New York, Harper, 1953; London, Lutterworth Press, 1962.
The Wheel on the School, illustrated by Maurice Sendak. New York, Harper, 1954; London, Lutterworth Press, 1956.
The Little Cow and the Turtle, illustrated by Maurice Sendak. New York, Harper, 1955; London, Lutterworth Press, 1961.
The House of Sixty Fathers, illustrated by Maurice Sendak. New York, Harper, 1956; London, Lutterworth Press, 1958.
Along Came a Dog, illustrated by Maurice Sendak. New York, Harper, 1958; London, Lutterworth Press, 1959.
The Last Little Cat, illustrated by Jim McMullen. New York, Harper, 1961; London, Lutterworth Press, 1962.
The Singing Hill, illustrated by Maurice Sendak. New York, Harper, 1962; London, Lutterworth Press, 1963.
Nobody Plays with a Cabbage, illustrated by Tom Allen. New York, Harper, 1962; London, Lutterworth Press, 1963.
Far Out the Long Canal, illustrated by Nancy Grossman. New York, Harper, 1964; London, Lutterworth Press, 1965.
Puppy Summer, illustrated by Anita Lobel. New York, Harper, and London, Lutterworth Press, 1966.
Journey from Peppermint Street, illustrated by Emily McCully. New York, Harper, 1968; London, Lutterworth Press, 1969.
A Horse Came Running, illustrated by Paul Sagsoorian. New York, Macmillan, and London, Lutterworth Press, 1970.
The Easter Cat, illustrated by Lillian Hoban. New York, Macmillan, 1971; Guildford, Surrey, Lutterworth Press, 1972.
The Almost All-White Rabbity Cat, illustrated by H.B. Vestal. New York, Macmillan, and Guildford, Surrey, Lutterworth Press, 1972.

Other

Bible Days, illustrated by Kreigh Collins. Grand Rapids, Michigan, Fideler, 1949.
The Mighty Ones: Great Men and Women of Early Bible Days, illustrated by Harvey Schmidt. New York, Harper, 1959; London, Lutterworth Press, 1960.

*

Manuscript Collections: Kerlan Collection, University of Minnesota, Minneapolis; Park Library, Central Michigan University, Mount Pleasant.

* * *

Great writers have a quality far more important than facility with words, more than observation and a graphic portrayal of what is observed. It is a quality that might be called compassionate perception. Certain writers of children's literature have this characteristic. Children are often loving by nature, perceptive, sensitive, and they respond to an author who is spiritually akin to them.

Meindert De Jong, whose books spanned many years and assorted ages, was such a writer. That De Jong liked animals can be quickly seen from his titles: *Puppy Summer, The Last Little Cat, The Cat That Walked a Week, A Horse Came Running, Good Luck Duck.* But titles do not reveal his wonderful ability to describe sensitively but without sentimentality the shimmering love which sometimes springs up between a child and a pet.

The Easter Cat is the story of Millicent, a little girl who adored cats but was prevented from having one of her own by her Mother's allergy. Gradually the reader learns that Millicent is the only small person in a world of adults. Her desire for a kitten is really her need for a being smaller than herself who depends upon her love and care. How universal a situation from a child's eye level! In solving the problem, De Jong uses carefully selected diction. Note this description of a clock at night—"The white dial of the big clock was a murky nothing sending out its heavy tick-tocks"—or the description of an emotional reaction—"Your heart sort of gets like cheap ice cream when it melts—all watery and mushy." The vocabulary of *The Easter Cat* is familiar to little children—ice cream and tick-tocks and mush—yet De Jong's artistry is obvious. Adults may forget the pain of being always too small or too weak, but a child recognizes the feeling readily and finds in Millicent a heroine who learns to cope and conquer.

In *The Wheel on the School,* written for older children, De Jong begins his story in a sleepy Dutch school with a little girl's composition about storks. Storks may not be familiar to the average child, but school rooms and compositions are and so he slips easily into the barren seaside community of Shora whose children desire the return of the great birds to nest upon their roofs as they did in the past. Now the roofs of Shora are all sharp, too slippery for nesting, but the children intend to entice the storks by placing a wheel on the school house roof. This simple plot becomes complicated because the children must overcome hostility from adults, violent storms, and finally a close brush with death to rescue two bedraggled storm-weakened birds. *The Wheel on the School* is an absorbing adventure story but it has a larger meaning. It is a monumental struggle which touches a whole community. A fisherman learns that his mind and his courage can supplement the use of legs; the children find that physical strength is second to spiritual tenuousness; the whole village encounters elemental forces of wind and tide but the common project causes a deep emotional stirring which finally washes away petty feelings and unifies Shora's people. It is a lovely story and one which shows a child that he need not be unimportant just because he is not an adult.

Shadrach is a classic and as such is confined to no age group. *Shadrach* is about the finding of identity, the nucleus of being which a child must discover so that his own uniqueness may stand forth. Grandfather has promised Davie a rabbit—not just any rabbit—a black rabbit. Perceiving its specificity even before it is a reality, Davie names his rabbit carefully—a wonderful name with Biblical undertones—Shadrach. Like Millicent in *The Easter Cat,* this child needs a smaller being to care for, and his affection for his rabbit is very deep. When the rabbit is lost, the family suggests a replacement (as families do) but Davie becomes ill at the thought. He understands the animal's uniqueness. There can be no casual substitution. This child is "all-children." Will no one *see?* At last the busy adults pause and try to comprehend what a small voice is saying. At last they listen. *Shadrach* is a definition of love—perceptive, sensitive love because it rests on the ability to understand and accept each individual as special. Meindert De Jong's books are important contributions to literature, examining problems of childhood with depth and beauty.

—Carolyn T. Kingston

de la MARE, Walter

Pseudonym: Walter Ramal. **Nationality:** British. **Born:** Charlton, Kent, 25 April 1873. **Education:** St. Paul's Cathedral Choristers' School, London (founder, *Choristers Journal,* 1889). **Family:** Married Constance Elfrida Ingpen in 1899 (died 1943); two sons and two daughters. **Career:** Clerk, Anglo-American Oil Company, London, 1890-1908. Reviewer for the *Times, Westminster Gazette, Bookman,* and other journals, London. **Awards:** Royal Society of Literature Polignac prize, 1911; James Tait Black Memorial prize, for fiction, 1922; Library Association Carnegie medal, 1948; Foyle Poetry prize, 1954. D.Litt.: Oxford, Cambridge, Bristol, and London universities; LL.D.: University of St. Andrews. Honorary Fellow, Keble College, Oxford. Granted Civil List pension, 1908; Companion of Honour, 1948; Order of Merit, 1953. **Died:** 22 June 1956.

Publications for Children

Fiction

The Three Mulla-Mulgars, illustrated by Dorothy P. Lathrop. London, Duckworth, 1910; New York, Knopf, 1919; as *The Three Royal Monkeys; or, The Three Mulla-Mulgars,* London, Faber, 1935.

Story and Rhyme: A Selection from the Writings of Walter de la Mare, Chosen by the Author. London, Dent, and New York, Dutton, 1921.

Broomsticks and Other Tales, illustrated by Bold. London, Constable, and New York, Knopf, 1925.

Miss Jemima, illustrated by Alec Buckels. Oxford, Blackwell, 1925; Poughkeepsie, New York, Artists and Writers Guild, 1935.

Old Joe, illustrated by C. T. Nightingale. Oxford, Blackwell, 1927.

The Dutch Cheese and the Lovely Myfanwy, illustrated by Dorothy P. Lathrop. New York, Knopf, 1931.

The Lord Fish and Other Tales, illustrated by Rex Whistler. London, Faber, 1933.

The Old Lion and Other Stories, illustrated by Irene Hawkins. London, Faber, 1942.

Mr. Bumps and His Monkey, illustrated by Dorothy P. Lathrop. Philadelphia, Winston, 1942.

The Magic Jacket and Other Stories, illustrated by Irene Hawkins. London, Faber, 1943.

The Scarecrow and Other Stories, illustrated by Irene Hawkins. London, Faber, 1945.

The Dutch Cheese and Other Stories, illustrated by Irene Hawkins. London, Faber, 1946.

Collected Stories for Children, illustrated by Irene Hawkins. London, Faber, 1947.

A Penny a Day, illustrated by Paul Kennedy. New York, Knopf, 1960.

Play

Crossings: A Fairy Play, music by C. Armstrong Gibbs, illustrated by Randolph Schwabe (produced Hove, Sussex, 1919; London, 1925). London, Beaumont Press, 1921; New York, Knopf, 1923.

Poetry

Songs of Childhood (as Walter Ramal). London, Longman, 1902 New York, Garland, 1976; revised edition, as Walter de la Mare Longman, 1916, 1923.

A Child's Day: A Book of Rhymes, illustrated by Carine and Wi Cadby. London, Constable, 1912; New York, Holt, 1923.

Peacock Pie: A Book of Rhymes. London, Constable, 1913; Ne York, Holt, 1917.

Down-Adown-Derry: A Book of Fairy Poems, illustrated by Do othy P. Lathrop. London, Constable, and New York, Holt, 192

Stuff and Nonsense and So On, illustrated by Bold. London, Constable, and New York, Holt, 1927; revised edition, London, Faber, 1946.
Poems for Children. London, Constable, and New York, Holt, 1930.
This Year, Next Year, illustrated by Harold Jones. London, Faber, and New York, Holt, 1937.
Bells and Grass: A Book of Rhymes, illustrated by Rowland Emett. London, Faber, 1941; New York, Viking Press, 1942.
Collected Rhymes and Verses, illustrated by Berthold Wolpe. London, Faber, 1944.
Rhymes and Verses: Collected Poems for Children, illustrated by Elinore Blaisdell. New York, Holt, 1947.
Poems, edited by Eleanor Graham, illustrated by Margery Gill. London, Penguin, 1962.
The Voice, edited and illustrated by Catherine Brighton. London, Faber, 1986; New York, Delacorte Press, 1987.

Other

Told Again: Traditional Tales, illustrated by A.H. Watson. Oxford, Blackwell, 1927; as *Told Again: Old Tales Told Again,* New York, Knopf, 1927; as *Tales Told Again,* London, Faber, and Knopf, 1959.
Stories from the Bible, illustrated by Theodore Nadejen. London, Faber, and New York, Cosmopolitan, 1929.
Letters from Mr. Walter de la Mare to Form Three. Privately printed, 1936.
Animal Stories, Chosen, Arranged, and in Some Part Re-Written. London, Faber, 1939; New York, Scribner, 1940.
Selected Stories and Verses, edited by Eleanor Graham. London, Penguin, 1952.
Molly Whuppie, illustrated by Errol Le Cain. London, Faber, and New York, Farrar Straus, 1983.

Editor, *Come Hither: A Collection of Rhymes and Poems for the Young of all Ages,* illustrated by Alec Buckels. London, Constable, and New York, Knopf, 1923; revised edition, 1928.
Editor, with Thomas Quayle, *Readings: Traditional Tales Told by the Author,* illustrated by A.H. Watson and C. T. Nightingale. Oxford, Blackwell, 6 vols., 1925-28; New York, Knopf, 1 vol., 1927.
Editor, *Tom Tiddler's Ground: A Book of Poetry for the Junior and Middle Schools.* London, Collins, 3 vols., 1932; New York, Knopf, 1 vol., 1962.
Editor, *Old Rhymes and New, Chosen for Use in Schools.* London, Constable, 2 vols., 1932.

Publications for Adults

Novels

Henry Brocken: His Travels and Adventures in the Rich, Strange, Scarce-Imaginable Regions of Romance. London, Murray, 1904; New York, Knopf, 1924.
The Return. London, Arnold, 1910; New York, Putnam, 1911; revised edition, London, Collins, and New York, Knopf, 1922; London, Faber, 1945.
Memoirs of a Midget. London, Collins, 1921; New York, Knopf, 1922.

Short Stories

Lispet, Lispett, and Vaine. London, Bookman's Journal, 1923.
The Riddle and Other Stories. London, Selwyn and Blount, 1923; as *The Riddle and Other Tales,* New York, Knopf, 1923.
Ding Dong Bell. London, Selwyn and Blount, and New York, Knopf, 1924.
Two Tales: The Green-Room, The Connoisseur. London, Bookman's Journal, 1925.
The Connoisseur and Other Stories. London, Collins, and New York, Knopf, 1926.
At First Sight. New York, Crosby Gaige, 1928.
On the Edge: Short Stories. London, Faber, 1930; New York, Knopf, 1931.
Seven Short Stories. London, Faber, 1931.
A Froward Child. London, Faber, 1934.
The Nap and Other Stories. London, Nelson, 1936.
The Wind Blows Over. London, Faber, and New York, Macmillan, 1936.
The Picnic and Other Stories. London, Faber, 1941.
Best Stories of Walter de la Mare. London, Faber, 1942.
The Collected Tales of Walter de la Mare, edited by Edward Wagenknecht. New York, Knopf, 1950.
A Beginning and Other Stories. London, Faber, 1955.
Ghost Stories. London, Folio Society, 1956.
Some Stories. London, Faber, 1962.
Eight Tales. Sauk City, Wisconsin, Arkham House, 1971.

Poetry

Poems. London, Murray, 1906.
The Listeners and Other Poems. London, Constable, 1912; New York, Holt, 1916.
The Old Men. London, Flying Fame, 1913.
The Sunken Garden and Other Poems. London, Beaumont Press, 1917.
Motley and Other Poems. London, Constable, and New York, Holt, 1918.
Flora, drawings by Pamela Bianco. London, Heinemann, and Philadelphia, Lippincott, 1919.
Poems 1901 to 1918. London, Constable, 2 vols., 1920; as *Collected Poems 1901 to 1918,* New York, Holt, 2 vols., 1920.
The Veil and Other Poems. London, Constable, 1921; New York, Holt, 1922.
Thus Her Tale: A Poem. Edinburgh, Porpoise Press, 1923.
A Ballad of Christmas. London, Selwyn and Blount, 1924.
The Hostage. London, Selwyn and Blount, 1925.
St. Andrews, with Rudyard Kipling. London, A. and C. Black, 1926.
(*Poems*). London, Benn, 1926.
Alone. London, Faber, 1927.
Selected Poems. New York, Holt, 1927.
The Captive and Other Poems. New York, Bowling Green Press, 1928.
Self to Self. London, Faber, 1928.
A Snowdrop. London, Faber, 1929.
News. London, Faber, 1930.
To Lucy. London, Faber, 1931.
The Sunken Garden and Other Verses. Birmingham, Birmingham School of Printing, 1931.
Two Poems. Privately printed, 1931.

The Fleeting and Other Poems. London, Constable, and New York, Knopf, 1933.
Poems 1919 to 1934. London, Constable, 1935; New York, Holt, 1936.
Poems. London, Corvinus Press, 1937.
Memory and Other Poems. London, Constable, and New York, Holt, 1938.
Two Poems, with Arthur Rogers. Privately printed, 1938.
Haunted: A Poem. London, Linden Press, 1939.
Collected Poems. New York, Holt, 1941; London, Faber, 1942.
Time Passes and Other Poems, edited by Anne Ridler. London, Faber, 1942.
The Burning-Glass and Other Poems, Including The Traveller. New York, Viking Press, 1945.
The Burning-Glass and Other Poems. London, Faber, 1945.
The Traveller. London, Faber, 1946.
Two Poems: Pride, The Truth of Things. London, Dropmore Press, 1946.
Inward Companion. London, Faber, 1950.
Winged Chariot. London, Faber, 1951.
Winged Chariot and Other Poems. New York, Viking Press, 1951.
O Lovely England and Other Poems. London, Faber, 1953.
The Winnowing Dream. London, Faber, 1954.
Selected Poems, edited by R.N. Green-Armytage. London, Faber, 1954.
The Morrow. Privately printed, 1955.
(*Poems*), edited by John Hadfield. London, Vista Books, 1962.
A Choice of de la Mare's Verse, edited by W.H. Auden. London, Faber, 1963.
Envoi. Privately printed, 1965.
The Complete Poems of Walter de la Mare, edited by Leonard Clark and others. London, Faber, 1969; New York, Knopf, 1970.
The Collected Poems of Walter de la Mare. London, Faber, 1979.

Other

M.E. Coleridge: An Appreciation. London, The Guardian, 1907.
Rupert Brooke and the Intellectual Imagination (lecture). London, Sidgwick and Jackson, and New York, Harcourt Brace, 1919.
Some Thoughts on Reading (lecture). Bembridge, Isle of Wight, Yellowsands Press, 1923.
Some Women Novelists of the 'Seventies. London, Cambridge University Press, 1929.
The Printing of Poetry (lecture). London, Cambridge University Press, 1931.
The Early Novels of Wilkie Collins. London, Cambridge University Press, 1932.
Lewis Carroll. London, Faber, 1932.
Early One Morning in the Spring: Chapters on Children and on Childhood as It Is Revealed in Particular in Early Memories and in Early Writings. London, Faber, and New York, Macmillan, 1935.
Poetry in Prose (lecture). London, Oxford University Press, 1936; New York, Oxford University Press, 1937.
Arthur Thompson: A Memoir. Privately printed, 1938.
An Introduction to Everyman. London, Dent, 1938.
Stories, Essays, and Poems, edited by M.M. Bozman. London, Dent, 1938.
Pleasures and Speculations. London, Faber, 1940; Freeport, New York, Books for Libraries Press, 1969.
Private View (essays). London, Faber, 1953; Westport, Connecticut, Hyperion, 1979.
Walter de la Mare: A Selection from His Writings, edited by Kenneth Hopkins. London, Faber, 1956.

Editor, *Desert Islands and Robinson Crusoe.* London, Faber and New York, Fountains Press, 1930; revised edition, Faber 1932.
Editor, *Poems,* by Christina Rossetti. Newtown, Wales, Gregynog Press, 1930.
Editor, *The Eighteen-Eighties: Essays by Fellows of the Royal Society of Literature.* London, Cambridge University Press 1930.
Editor, *Behold, This Dreamer! Of Reverie, Night, Sleep, Dream Love-Dreams, Nightmare, Death, The Unconscious, The Imagination, Divination, The Artist, and Kindred Subjects.* London Faber, and New York, Knopf, 1939.
Editor, *Love.* London, Faber, 1943; New York, Morrow, 1946.

*

Bibliography: In *L'Oeuvre de Walter de la Mare: Une Aventure Spirituelle* by Luce Bonnerot, Paris, Didier, 1969.

Manuscript Collections: Syracuse University, New York; Temple University, Philadelphia; University of Chicago; King's College Cambridge.

Critical Studies (selection): *Walter de la Mare: A Critical Study* by Forrest Reid, London, Faber, and New York, Holt 1929; *Walter de la Mare: An Exploration* by John Atkins, London, Temple, 1947; *Walter de la Mare* by Kenneth Hopkins London, Longman, 1953; *Tea with Walter de la Mare* by Russell Brain, London, Faber, 1957; *Walter de la Mare* by Leonard Clark, London, Bodley Head, 1960, New York, Walck, 1961 *Walter de la Mare* by Doris Ross McCrosson, New York Twayne, 1966.

* * *

Walter de la Mare, though one of the most gifted and original writers of the 20th century, is currently one of the most neglected. His poetry, much admired on its first appearance, has steadily lost ground and is now regarded as incontrovertibly minor. The preference for traditional forms and refusal to tackle contemporary social problems or to indulge in the direct expression of personal feeling have condemned it. His prose never received due appreciation, the dated settings, sexual reticence, and determined rejection of contemporary life mitigating against success; yet, like Kipling, de la Mare was arguably at his best in the short story. He wrote a great deal specifically for children, and this has been more consistently admired since here his supposed deficiencies might be felt to be advantages. It is more rewarding, however, to treat his work for adults and children as a whole, in which the child's apprehension of the world represents a central and passionate mode of experience. De la Mare held strong and slightly odd convictions about childhood, associating it with intuition and a natural physical grace that was subsequently lost; like dreams it afforded fresher, more intense visions whose ultimate source might lie beyond, as well as within the individual. A profoundly platonic thinker, de la Mare felt that children lived closer to pri mal truths, being as yet unshadowed by the miseries and burdens of adult life. He resisted the temptation to idealise, and several stories (e.g., "In the Forest") reveal the callousness, even cruelty of the young; but despite their prevailing self-absorption, children seemed to him powerfully, if only too briefly, in contact with underlying spiritual truths.

De la Mare's most sustained work for children is *The Three Mulla-Mulgars*—later reprinted as *The Three Royal Monkeys*—and written to amuse his own. It is a powerfully original creation, a complete and consistent secondary world, with its own powers for good and evil, invented cultures, hierarchies, even language. This world is inhabited primarily by the various races of monkeys ("Mulgars"), among whom man is only another sub-species (or "Oomgar-Mulgar"). The highest in rank are the "Mulla-Mulgars" or royal monkeys such as the book's heroes, the brothers Thumb, Thimble, and Nod. Their quest for the paradisal land of Tishnar, their destined home, provides the main narrative thread. Although most of the book's denizens are familiar enough—zebras, jackals, eagles—everything that appears is endowed with a new significance, being changed "into something rich and strange." The tropical forest is altered beyond recognition by heavy falls of snow, the panther Immanâla becomes the very principle of evil itself, the zebras are "the Little Horses of Tishnar." The youngest brother, Nod, has the standard folkloric virtues of luck, pluck, and determination to carry him through his various adventures—his digressive stay with the shipwrecked sailor Andy Battle, the near loss of his talismanic Wonderstone to the enchantingly beautiful Water Midden, and the final underground journey to the very borders of Tishnar. De la Mare continually echoes traditional folk tales and as continually transforms them.

Like Tolkien's hobbits, the brothers are at once human in their ways of thinking and responding, and yet distinctively alien in their habits and instincts; their mother has taught them that, as royal monkeys, they must never walk on all fours, taste blood, nor, unless in danger and despair, climb trees or grow a tail. De la Mare seems to have been intrigued by the human potentiality within the simian. A later story, "The Old Lion," relates the experiences of a uniquely intelligent monkey, Jasper, his friendship with the first mate of "The Old Lion," and his later exploitation as a music-hall turn. Human greed and cruelty are sharply contrasted to Jasper's trust and innocence, and his role within the story resembles that of the child observer in the world of adults, a device de la Mare used particularly effectively. This is one of 17 stories selected from *Broomsticks* and *The Lord Fish* to form *Collected Stories for Children.* In subject matter these are surprisingly heterogeneous. Most make use of magic or folklore motifs in one way or another, but some openly inhabit a fairytale world ("Dick and the Beanstalk," "A Penny a Day," "The Three Sleeping Boys of Warwickshire"), others approach it obliquely ("Lucy," "Alice's Godmother," "Miss Jemima," "The Scarecrow"), while others barely glance at it ("Maria-Fly," "Visitors"). All are illuminated by an instinctive grasp of the child's imaginative life and an intense apprehension of unknown modes of being which make them deeply rewarding for adult readers. It is, however, rare to find a child who has read them with real pleasure because their subtle, understated, and indirect approach creates delays and difficulties avoided in the more obviously exciting adventures of the travellers to Tishnar.

If de la Mare's short stories for children inadvertently erect barriers, his children's verse has an irresistible rhythmic force and immediacy. With the exception of Blake and Carroll, no poet has more effectively recaptured the direct appeal of the nursery-rhyme, at its most hypnotic when at its most incantatory:

> *Applecumjocaby,* blindfold eye!
> How many rooks come sailing by;
> Caw—caw in the deep blue sky?
> Eeka, Neeka, Leeka, Lee—
> Here's a lock without a key...
> Do diddle di do
> Poor Jim Jay
> Got stuck fast
> In Yesterday.

Like his short stories, de la Mare's verse for children ranges over a wide variety of subjects, combining an extraordinary degree of technical virtuosity with a characteristic complexity. The moods comprehended include terror, enchantment, laughter and tears, while time passing, evil, unhappiness, and cruelty are as often present as the pleasures and energies of nature. These are poems that should be part of every child's reading experience.

In addition to these achievements, de la Mare edited *Come Hither* and *Tom Tiddler's Ground,* delightful anthologies of children's verse, as well as retelling fairy stories (*Told Again*), and Bible stories, and collecting *Animal Stories,* many of which were of his own invention.

—Julia Briggs

DEMI

Nationality: American. **Born:** Charlotte Dumaresq Hunt, in Cambridge, Massachusetts, 2 September 1942. **Education:** Instituto Allende, Guanajuate, Mexico; Rhode Island School of Design, 1960; Immaculate Heart College, Los Angeles, California, B.A. 1962; Fulbright Scholarship to India, 1962-1963; University of Baroda, M.S. 1965; graduate study at China Institute. **Family:** Married John Rawlins Hitz (an artist and writer) in 1965 (marriage ended), one son; married Taesi Jesse Huang. **Career:** Artist and writer; invited speaker at children's events, libraries, colleges, and universities. **Awards:** Fulbright Fellow, 1962; various art awards from California State Fair, California Arts and Science Fair, Los Angeles County Museum, and Los Angeles Outdoor Art Festival; Notable Book, American Library Association, 1980; Pick of the Lists, American Bookseller Association, 1990.

PUBLICATIONS FOR CHILDREN (ILLUSTRATED BY THE AUTHOR)

Fiction

The Leaky Umbrella. New York, Prentice-Hall, 1980.
The Elephant Book. New York, Random House, 1981.
Follow the Line. New York, Henry Holt, 1981.
Where's Willie Worm? New York, Random House, 1981.
Peek-A-Boo. New York, Random House, 1982.
Watch Harry Grow! New York, Random House, 1984.
So Soft Kitty. New York, Putnam, 1986.
Fleecy Lamb. New York, Putnam, 1987.

Fluffy Bunny. New York, Putnam, 1987.
Fuzzy Wuzzy Puppy. New York, Putnam, 1987.
Cuddly Chick. New York, Putnam, 1988.
Downy Duckling. New York, Putnam, 1988.
Jolly Koala Bear. New York, Putnam, 1989.
Roly Poly Panda. New York, Putnam, 1989.
Demi's Christmas Surprise. New York, Putnam, 1990.
Little Bitty Bunny. New York, Putnam, 1992.
Little Chick Chick. New York, Putnam, 1992.
Little Baby Lamb. New York, Putnam, 1993.
Little Lucky Ducky. New York, Putnam, 1993.
Su Tung Po. New York, St. Martins Press, 1996.

Folklore

Liang and the Magic Paintbrush. New York, Henry Holt, 1980.
Cinderella on Wheels. New York, Henry Holt, 1982.
Dragon Kites & Dragonflies: A Collection of Chinese Nursery Rhymes. New York, Harcourt, 1986.
Chen Ping and His Magic Axe. New York, Dodd, 1987.
The Hallowed Horse: A Folktale from India. New York, Putnam, 1987.
A Chinese Zoo: Fables and Proverbs. New York, Harcourt, 1988.
Demi's Reflective Fables. New York, Grosset, 1988.
The Empty Pot. New York, Henry Holt, 1990.
The Magic Boat. New York, Henry Holt, 1990.
Bamboo Hats and a Rice Cake. New York, Crown Books for Young Readers, 1993.
Demi's Secret Garden. New York, Henry Holt, 1993.
Demi's Dragons & Fantastic Creatures. New York, Henry Holt, 1993.
The Firebird. New York, Henry Holt, 1994.
Santa's Furry Friends. New York, Henry Holt, 1994.
The Magic Goldfish. New York, Henry Holt, 1995.
The Stonecutter. New York, Crown Books for Young Readers, 1995. *The Dragon's Tale & Other Animal Fables of the Chinese Zodiac.* New York, Henry Holt, 1996.
Buddha Stories. New York, Henry Holt, 1997.
One Grain of Rice: A Mathematical Folktale. New York, Scholastic, 1997.
The Greatest Treasure. New York, Scholastic, 1998.
Donkey and the Rock. New York, Henry Holt, 1999.

Nonfiction

The Book of Moving Pictures. New York, Knopf, 1979.
Under the Shade of the Mulberry Tree. New York, Prentice Hall, 1979.
Where Is It? Garden City, New York, Doubleday, 1979.
Light Another Candle: The Story and Meaning of Hanukkah. Boston, Houghton Mifflin, 1981.
Demi's Find the Animals A B C. New York, Grosset, 1985.
Demi's Count the Animals 1 2 3. New York, Grosset, 1986.
Demi's Opposites. New York, Grosset, 1987.
Find Demi's Dinosaurs: An Animal Game Book. New York, Putnam, 1989.
Find Demi's Baby Animals. New York, Putnam, 1990.
Kung-Hsi Fa-Ts'Ai!: Happy New Year Kung-Hsi. New York, Crown Publishing, 1998.

Biography

The Adventures of Marco Polo. New York, Henry Holt, 1981.
Chingis Khan. New York, Henry Holt, 1991.
Buddha. New York, Henry Holt, 1996.
Grass Sandals. New York, Simon & Schuster, 1997.
Dalai Lama. New York, Henry Holt, 1998.

Poetry

In the Eyes of the Cat: Japanese Poetry for All Seasons. New York, Henry Holt, 1994.

*

Critical Studies: Entry in *Something about the Author,* Vol. 66, Detroit, Gale Research, 1991, 128-130; entry in *Sixth Book of Junior Authors and Illustrator,* New York, H.W. Wilson, 1996, 77-79.

Illustrator: *The Surangini Tales* by Partap Sharma, 1973; *The Classic of Tea* by Lu Yu, translation by Francis Ross Carpenter, 1974; *Feelings* by Smith and Wardhough, 1975; *The Tom Glazer Guitar Book* by Tom Glazer, 1976; *The Old China Trade: Americans in Canton, 1784-1843* by Francis Ross Carpenter, 1976; *The Shape of Water* by Augusta Goldin, 1979; *Bong Nam and the Pheasants* by Yushin Yoo, 1979; *Dragon Night and Other Lullabies* by Jane Yolen, 1980; *Light Another Candle: The Story and Meaning of Hankkah* 1981, and *Make Noise, Make Merry: The Story and Meaning of Purim* 1983, both by Miriam Chaikin; *Eucalyptus Wings* by J. Alison James, 1995.

* * *

Demi grew up in a household where artistic expression was natural and encouraged. Both immediate and extended family were artists in the fields of painting, theater, and architecture. Christened at birth Charlotte Dumaresq Hunt, her mother was herself a painter and made certain that her young daughter experienced various types of artistic media. This continued as Demi entered Immaculate Heart College in Los Angeles, a college renowned for its eclectic approach to art, inclusive of many styles, media, and techniques. Here she was greatly influenced by the unconventional artist Sister Corita, a controversial figure within the Church. After receiving a degree from Immaculate Heart College, Demi continued her education at various institutions in diverse areas—Rhode Island, U.S.A., Mexico, Brazil, India (as a Fulbright scholar), and China. Her artistic inclinations have led her to express herself in many different forms. She works in mediums of serigraph, water-color, mobile, collage, and textile design. Besides being a prolific author of children's books, she also has painted murals, the church dome of St. Peter's and Paul's Church in Wilmington, California, paintings and silkscreen prints which have been exhibited in galleries, and art for private homes.

Despite these diverse experiences and artistic interests, Demi has a recognizable style as a children's book illustrator. Her freedom of expression gained in childhood and her ability to reproduce styles and details from the various artistic contexts in which she studied abroad has resulted in bold colorful drawings that appeal to young readers. For example, the clarity of *Demi's Count the Animals 1 2 3* has been praised for clearly presenting words digits, and illustrations of animals. However, influencing this counting book, as well as other literature, is Demi's use of numerous repeated items within one illustration. Witnessing repetitious religious drawings in India during Hindu and Buddhist worship, Demi has employed this to add to the complexity and exuberance of her art style. *Demi's Opposites* is another example of clarity in explaining a basic concept, but it works while offering complex attention-grasping illustrations full of detail, color, and repetition of line, form, and figures. The interactive nature of this book uses elements of art to fine-tune children's skills of discrimination and observation.

Readers are immediately aware of the Chinese influence in Demi's children's books. Three sources of this influence are her travels and studies in China, a book by Wang Kai called the *Mustard Seed Garden Manual of Painting,* written in 1679, and the stories shared by her husband Taesi Jesse Huang. Demi has stated that "Life is magic. Everything alive is magic. To capture life on paper is magic. To capture life on paper was the aim of Chinese painters. That is my aim too."

Many of Demi's stories for children are folktales. *Liang and the Magic Paintbrush* is an earlier work that evidences the Chinese influence as well as a simply retold story with a moral. In most of these folktales, such as *The Empty Pot,* sophisticated language and universal understandings make the book one for readers of all ages. In addition to carefully chosen language, Demi's attention to detail, bright colors, and unusual borders and placement of text on each page help to tell the story. This is the story of a young boy who admits to being the only child in the emperor's kingdom who cannot grow a beautiful flower from the seed given him by the emperor. He is rewarded with the kingdom for his honesty as the king had given each child a cooked seed, so obviously they could not have grown the many flowers they brought before the emperor. *The Magic Goldfish,* a Russian tale, contains poetic narrative in telling a story about greed. Again, the reader sees evidence of the repetitious, numerous drawings characteristic of Demi's work. Each section of text is encircled with repetitive drawings of some person, animal, or symbol representing that particular incident in the story. On each opposing page, the illustration is encircled with a wide bold gold band. The reader's attention is drawn with equal attention to both text and illustration, as the two weave a story of a poor fisherman who is granted wishes by a magic goldfish for sparing the goldfish's life. His greedy wife is never satisfied with what the fisherman asks from the fish and in the end, she is left as poor as in the beginning.

Demi has also distinguished herself in yet another genre. Biographical accounts of historical figures are found in texts with quite advanced text in terms of language and concepts. *Chingis Khan* describes with much detail the emergence of the Mongul leader who, at the time of his death, had conquered and ruled the largest empire ever created by one man. With great attention to the historical and legendary aspects of Khan's story, Demi describes his early lessons of survival, his ability to unite feuding Mongol tribes, and his perseverance as he conquered China and Persia. Again the color gold permeates the illustrations and heightens the powerful aspects of Khan's rise to power. *Buddha* describes the emergence of Siddhartha, one of the Buddhas who came to earth as royalty. This retelling of the ancient story has bordered rectangular drawings that frequently spread across two pages. Again, detail, bright colors, fine lines, and repeated figures distinguish Demi's work. Within this story of Siddhartha's search for life's truths are two parables that he used to teach his ideas. Both books are for readers of all ages, as the combination of text and illustrations cast new perspectives on both of these historical figures.

Demi shares with young readers the power of story through her art. The freedom of expression that was encouraged in her childhood supports her creations that grasp the attention of young readers through lively design and color. The tales she creates and retells celebrate her ability to capture the magic of life on paper.

—Janelle B. Mathis

dePAOLA, Tomie

Nationality: American. **Born:** Thomas Anthony dePaola, Meriden, Connecticut, 15 September 1934. **Education:** Pratt Institute, Brooklyn, New York, B.F.A. 1956; California College of Arts and Crafts, Oakland, M.F.A. 1969; Lone Mountain College, San Francisco, doctoral equivalency 1970. **Career:** Since 1956 freelance artist and designer: paintings and murals for churches and monasteries in New England; set designer for night clubs and theatres; several individual shows since 1961, and numerous group shows. Instructor, 1962-63, and Assistant Professor of Art, 1963-66, College of the Sacred Heart, Newton, Massachusetts; Assistant Professor of Art, San Francisco College for Women (now Lone Mountain College), 1967-70; Instructor in Art, Chamberlayne Junior College, Boston, 1972-73; Associate Professor, designer, and technical director in the Speech and Theater departments, Colby College, New London, New Hampshire, 1973-76; Associate Professor of Art, 1976-78, and artist-in-residence, 1978-79, New England College, Henniker, New Hampshire. **Awards:** Boston Art Directors' Club award, 1968; Franklin Typographers award, 1969; American Library Association Caldecott Honor, 1975; Japan's Nakamori Prize, 1978; University of Minnesota Kerian award, 1981; *Boston Globe/Horn Book* Honor Award, 1982; Society of Children's Book Writers Golden Kite award for illustration, 1982, 1983; Catholic Library Association Regina medal, 1983; David McCord Children's Literature Citation, 1986; U.S. nominee, IBBY Hans Christian Andersen Award, 1990; Smithson Medal, 1990; Helen Keating Ott Award, 1993; University of Mississippi Medallion, 1995; Keene State College Children's Literature Festival Award, 1998. **Address:** c/o Putnam's Sons, 200 Madison Avenue, New York, New York 10022, U.S.A.

PUBLICATIONS FOR CHILDREN (ILLUSTRATED BY THE AUTHOR)

Fiction

The Wonderful Dragon of Timlin. Indianapolis, Bobbs Merrill, 1966.
Fight the Night. Philadelphia, Lippincott, 1968.
Joe and the Snow. New York, Hawthorn, 1968.
Parker Pig, Esquire. New York, Hawthorn, 1969.
The Journey of the Kiss. New York, Hawthorn, 1970.
The Monsters' Ball. New York, Hawthorn, 1970.
Nana Upstairs and Nana Downstairs. New York, Putnam, 1973; London, Methuen, 1983; revised edition, New York, Putnam, 1998.

Andy (That's My Name). Englewood Cliffs, New Jersey, Prentice Hall, 1973.
The Unicorn and the Moon. Lexington, Massachusetts, Ginn, 1973.
Charlie Needs a Cloak. Englewood Cliffs, New Jersey, Prentice Hall, 1974; London, Collins, 1975.
Watch Out for the Chicken Feet in Your Soup. Englewood Cliffs, New Jersey, Prentice Hall, 1974.
Michael Bird-Boy. Englewood Cliffs, New Jersey, Prentice Hall, 1975.
When Everyone Was Fast Asleep. New York, Holiday House, 1976.
Four Stories for Four Seasons. Englewood Cliffs, New Jersey, Prentice Hall, 1977.
Helga's Dowry: A Troll Love Story. New York, Harcourt Brace, 1977.
Bill and Pete. New York, Putnam, 1977; Oxford, Oxford University Press, 1982.
Pancakes for Breakfast. New York, Harcourt Brace, 1978.
Oliver Button Is a Sissy. New York, Harcourt Brace, 1979; London, Methuen, 1981.
Big Anthony and the Magic Ring. New York, Harcourt Brace, 1979.
Flicks. New York, Harcourt Brace, 1979.
Songs of the Fog Maiden. New York, Holiday House, 1979.
The Knight and the Dragon. New York, Putnam, and London, Methuen, 1980.
The Hunter and the Animals. New York, Holiday House, 1981; London, Andersen Press, 1982.
Now One Foot, Now the Other. New York, Putnam, 1981; London, Methuen, 1982.
The Friendly Beasts: An Old English Christmas Carol. New York, Putnam, 1981; London, Methuen, 1984.
Marianna May and Nursey. New York, Holiday House, 1983.
Sing, Pierrot, Sing (wordless book). New York, Harcourt Brace, and London, Methuen, 1983.
Merry Christmas, Strega Nona. San Diego, Harcourt Brace, 1986; London, Methuen, 1987.
Bill and Pete Go Down the Nile. New York, Putnam, and Oxford, Oxford University Press, 1987.
An Early American Christmas. New York, Holiday House, 1987.
Baby's First Christmas. New York, Putnam, 1988.
The Art Lesson. New York, Putnam, 1989.
Haircuts for the Woolseys. New York, Putnam, 1989.
Too Many Hopkins. New York, Putnam, 1989.
Little Grunt and the Big Egg: A Prehistoric Fairy Tale. New York, Holiday House, 1990.
Tomie dePaola's Book of Bible Stories. New York, Putnam/Zondervan, 1990.
Bonjour Mr. Satie. New York, Putnam, 1991.
My First Passover. New York, Putnam, 1991.
My First Halloween. New York, Putnam, 1991.
Tony's Bread. London, ABC, 1990.
My First Thanksgiving. New York, Putnam, 1992.
The Legend of the Poinsettia. Putnam, 1994.
The Country Angels' Christmas. Putnam, 1995.
Mary, the Mother of Jesus. New York, Holiday House, 1995.
The Baby Sister. New York, Putnam, 1996.
Strega Nona: Her Story. New York, Putnam, 1996.
The Bubble Factory. New York, Grosset & Dunlap, 1996.
Get Dressed Santa. New York, Grosset & Dunlap, 1996.
The Days of the Blackbird. New York, Putnam, 1997.
Bill and Pete to the Rescue. New York, Putnam, 1998.
Big Anthony: His Story. New York, Putnam, 1998.
26 Fairmount Avenue. New York, Putnam, 1999.

Play

A Rainbow Christmas (puppet play; also director and designer: produced Cambridge, Massachusetts, 1971).

Poetry

Book of Poems. New York, Putnam, 1988; London, Methuen, 1989.

Other

The Wind and the Sun (tale from Aesop). Lexington, Massachusetts, Ginn, 1972.
The Cloud [Quicksand, Popcorn, Kids' Cat, Family Christmas Tree] Book. New York, Holiday House, 5 vols., 1975-80.
Strega Nona: An Old Tale. Englewood Cliffs, New Jersey, Prentice Hall, 1975; as *The Magic Pasta Pot,* London, Hutchinson, 1979.
Things to Make and Do for Valentine's Day. New York, Watts, 1976.
The Clown of God: An Old Story. New York, Harcourt Brace, 1978; London, Methuen, 1979.
Criss-Cross, Applesauce, photographs by B.A. King. New York, Addison House, 1979.
The Lady of Guadalupe. New York, Holiday House, 1980.
The Prince of the Dolomites: An Old Italian Tale. New York, Harcourt Brace, 1980; London, Methuen, 1981.
The Legend of Old Befana: An Italian Christmas Story. New York, Harcourt Brace, 1980.
Fin M'Coul: The Giant of Knockmany Hill. New York, Holiday House, and London, Andersen Press, 1981.
The Comic Adventures of Old Mother Hubbard and Her Dog. New York, Harcourt Brace, and London, Methuen, 1981.
Giorgio's Village. New York, Putnam, and London, Methuen, 1982.
Francis, The Poor Man of Assisi. New York, Holiday House, 1982.
Strega Nona's Magic Lessons. New York, Harcourt Brace, 1982; London, Methuen, 1983.
Bible Story Cut-Outs (*Noah and the Ark, David and Goliath*). Minneapolis, Winston Press, 2 vols., 1983-84.
The Legend of the Bluebonnet: An Old Tale of Texas. New York, Putnam, and London, Methuen, 1983.
The Story of the Three Wise Kings. New York, Putnam, and London, Methuen, 1983.
The Mysterious Giant of Barletta. New York, Harcourt Brace, 1984; London, Andersen Press, 1985.
Queen Esther. New York, Harper, 1986.
The Miracles of Jesus. New York, Holiday House, 1987.
The Parables of Jesus. New York, Holiday House, 1987.
Bob and Bobby. London, Puffin, 1988.
The Legend of the Indian Paintbrush. New York, Putnam, 1988.
The Legend of the Persian Carpet. New York, Putnam, 1993.
Strega Nona Meets Her Match. New York, Putnam, 1993.
Tom. New York, Putnam, 1993.
Christopher: The Holy Giant. New York, Holiday House, 1994.
Patrick: Patron Saint of Ireland. New York, Holiday House, 1994.

Editor, *Mother Goose.* New York, Putnam, and London, Methuen, 1985.
Editor, *Favorite Nursery Tales.* New York, Putnam, and London Methuen, 1986.
Editor, *Book of Christmas Carols.* New York, Putnam, and London, Methuen, 1987.

*

Manuscript Collections: Kerlan Collection, University of Minnesota, Minneapolis.

Illustrator: *Sound,* 1965, and *Wheels,* 1965, both by Lisa Miller; *The Tiger and the Rabbit and Other Tales* by Pura Belpré, 1965; *Tricky Peik and Other Picture Tales* edited by Jeanne B. Hardendorff, 1967; *Finders Keepers, Losers Weepers* by Joan M. Lexau, 1967; *Sound Science,* 1968, and *Light and Sight,* 1969, both by Melvin L. Alexenberg; *The Cabinet of the President of the United States* by James A. Eichner, 1968; *Poetry for Chuckles and Grins* edited by Leland Blair Jacobs, 1968; *Take This Hammer,* 1969, *Who Needs Holes?,* 1970, *Pick It Up,* 1971, *Hold Everything,* 1973, and *Look in the Mirror,* 1973, all by Samuel and Beryl Epstein; *The Rocking-Chair Ghost* by Mary C. Jane, 1969; *Hercules, The Gentle Giant* by Nina Schneider, 1969; *The Morning Glory* by Robert Bly, 1969; *How to Be a Puppeteer* by Eleanor Boylan, 1970; *Rutherford T. Finds 21 B* by Barbara Rinkoff, 1970; *The Folklore of Love and Courtship* and *The Folklore of Weddings and Marriage* both edited by Duncan Emrich, 1970; *Hot as an Ice Cube* by Philip Balestrino, 1971; *John Fisher's Magic Book* by John Fisher, 1971; *Monsters of the Middle Ages* by William Wise, 1971; *Authorized Autumn Charts of the Upper Red Canoe River Country* by Peter Zachary Cohen, 1972; *What Is Fear* by Jean Rosenbaum and Lutie McAuliffe, 1972; *Mario's Mystery Machine* by Sibyl Hancock, 1972; *The Franklin Watts Concise Guide to Baby-Sitting* by Rubie Saunders, 1972; *Let's Find Out about Communications* by Valerie Pitt, 1973; *Danny and His Thumb* by Kathryn F. Ernst, 1973; *David's Windows* by Alice Low, 1974; *The Star-Spangled Banana* edited by Charles Keller and Richard Baker, 1974; *Let's Find Out about Houses* by Martha and Charles Shapp, 1975; *Old Man Whickutt's Donkey* by Mary Calhoun, 1975; *This Is the Ambulance Leaving the Zoo,* 1975, and *Six Impossible Things Before Breakfast,* 1977, both by Norma Farber; *The Tyrannosaurus Game,* 1976, *Santa's Crash-Bang Christmas,* 1978, and *Fat Magic,* 1978, all by Steven Kroll; *If He's My Brother* by Barbara Williams, 1976; *Good Morning to You, Valentine,* 1976, *Beat the Drum, Independence Day Has Come,* 1977, and *Easter Buds Are Springing,* 1979, all edited by Lee Bennett Hopkins; *I Love You, Mouse* by John Graham, 1976; *The Whatchamacallit Book* by Bernice Kohn Hunt, 1976; *The Mixed-Up Mystery Smell* by Eleanor Coerr, 1976; *Let's Find Out about Summer* by Martha Shapp, 1976; *Can't You Make Them Behave, King George?,* 1977, *The Good Giants and the Bad Pukwudgies,* 1982, and *Shh! We're Writing the Constitution,* 1987, all by Jean Fritz; *Once upon a Dinkelsbühl,* 1977, and *The Little Friar Who Flew,* 1980, both by Patricia Lee Gauch; *The Ghost with the Halloween Hiccups,* 1977, *Funnyman's First Case,* 1981, and *Funnyman and Penny Dodo,* 1984, all by Stephen Mooser; *Simple Pictures Are Best,* 1977, and *The Mountains of Quilt,* 1987, both by Nancy Willard; *Odd Jobs,* 1977, *Four Scary Stories,* 1978, *Odd Jobs and Friends,* 1982, *The Vanishing Pumpkin,* 1983, *The Quilt Story,* 1985, and *Pages of Music,* 1988, all by Tony Johnston; *The Badger and the Magic Fan: A Japanese Folktale* adapted by Tony Johnston, 1990; *The Surprise Party,* 1977, *The Spooky Halloween Party,* 1981, and *Party Time for Nicky,* 1983, all by Annabelle Prager; *Solomon Grundy, Born on Oneday* by Malcolm E. Weiss, 1977; *The Giants' Farm,* 1977, *The Giants Go Camping,* 1979, and *Hark! A Christmas Sampler,* 1991, all by Jane Yolen; *The Christmas Pageant* (text from Bible), 1978; *Oh, Such Foolishness!* edited by William Cole, 1978; *Jamie's Tiger* by Jan Wahl, 1978; *Marc the Magnificent* by Sue Alexander, 1978; *Ghost Poems* edited by Daisy Wallace, 1979; *The Cat on the Dovrefell* translated by George Webbe Dasent, 1979; *My Daddy's Mustache* by Naomi Panush Salus, 1979; *The Triumphs of Fuzzy Fogtop* by Anne K. Rose, 1979; *The Night Before Christmas* by Clement C. Moore, 1980; *The Walking Coat* by Pauline Watson, 1980; *The Wuggie Norple Story* by Daniel Pinkwater, 1980; *Moon, Stars, Frogs, and Friends* by Patricia MacLachlan, 1980; *Edward, Benjamin, and Butter* by Malcolm Hall, 1981; *Robin Goodfellow and the Giant Dwarf* by Michael Jennings, 1981; *The Friendly Beasts: An Old English Christmas Carol,* 1981; *Nicholas Bentley Stoningpot III* by Ann McGovern, 1982; *Tattie's River Journey* by Shirley Rousseau Murphy, 1983; *The Carsick Zebra and Other Animal Riddles* by David A. Adler, 1983; *The Mother Goose Frieze,* 1984; *Mother Goose Story Streamers,* 4 vols., 1984; *Mary Had a Little Lamb* by Sarah Josepha Hale, 1984; *The First Christmas,* 1984; *Country Farm,* 1984; *Miracle on 34th Street* by Valentine Davies, 1984; *Teeny Tiny* retold by Jill Bennett, 1986; *For Every Child a Star* by Thomas Yeomans, 1986; *The Kitten Kids,* 4 vols., 1986; *Maggie and the Monster* by Elizabeth Winthrop, 1987; *What the Mailman Brought* by Carolyn Craven, 1987; *Who's a Friend of the Water-Spurting Whale?* by Sanna Anderson Baker, 1987; *Petook* by Caryll Houselander, 1988; *Cookie's Week,* 1988, and *Caspar's Week,* 1989, both by Cindy Ward; *The Story of Rabbit and Coyote* by Tony Johnston, 1994; *I Love You Sun, I Love You Moon* by Karen Pandell, 1994; *Alice Nizzy Nazzy: The Witch of Santa Fe* by Tony Johnston, 1995; *The Eagle and the Rainbow,* retold by Antonio Hernandez Madrigal, 1997; *Benny's Big Bubble* by Jane O'Connor, 1997; *Mice Squeak, We Speak* by Arnold Shapiro, 1997; *Erandi's Braids* by Antonio Hernandez Madrigal, 1999.

* * *

Tomie dePaola's creative brush and pen have fashioned more than 200 informational books, imaginative stories, realistic picture books, and folktales, bringing him recognition as a creative writer and illustrator and as a favorite choice of children. Though dePaola has been criticized for being too prolific, a close inspection finds versatility and a distinct style to be the significant hallmarks of his work.

Humor, often an innate part of dePaola books, surfaces even in his concept books, a genre where amusement is too rarely found. *The Quicksand Book,* while giving concise and factual details about Jungle Girl and her particular dilemma in the sinking mud, also tells a funny story. *The Popcorn Book* and *The Kids' Cat Book* are patterned in that same tradition.

DePaola's imaginative stories, including the early *Helga's Dowry* and the more recent *Little Grunt and the Big Egg: A Prehistoric Fairy Tale,* also provide a showcase for the author-artist's nimble wit. While simple but clever wordplay is evident in *Haircuts for the Woolseys* (about a family of sheep who get "haircuts" too early in the spring), *Bonjour, Mr. Satie* expresses a more sophisticated humor; both reflect dePaola's continuing delight in making children laugh.

A serious side to the author-artist's nature also exists. Such religious titles as *The Clown of God: An Old Story*; *Francis, The Poor Man of Assisi*; *The Miracles of Jesus*; and *Jingle* are sensitive but not sentimental, thoughtful but not didactic. Some of his folktales also sound a somber note. *The Legend of the Bluebonnet: An Old Tale of Texas* and *The Legend of the Indian Paint-*

brush, both native American tales, deal with sacrifice and personal courage. *Bluebonnet,* in which a young girl throws her doll into the fire to help bring rain to her starving people, is particularly compelling.

This serious strain can also be found in his realistic stories, which tend to be autobiographical. One of his most popular has been *Nana Upstairs and Nana Downstairs,* which he re-illustrated in full color in 1998, heightening the emotions and making it more appealing to end-of-the-century readers. *Now One Foot, Now the Other,* which deals with aging and death, is also based on childhood relationships with his own grandparents. *Oliver Button Is a Sissy* and *The Art Lesson* address such issues as name calling and student-teacher confrontations, with threads of humor imaginatively woven into the plots; in *Tom,* his Irish grandfather inadvertently gets him in trouble at school, and in *The Baby Sister* Tommy waits impatiently for the birth of his baby sister. Children's authors rarely reveal such personal details; that he does so, and without any self-aggrandizement, it is to dePaola's credit.

Folktales, which have generated some of the most critical attention accorded dePaola, provide a generous stage for his wide-ranging talents. He has retold and illustrated folktales from both the Italian and Irish sides of his heritage and has also incorporated his own New England background into his Americana works. His illustrations for *The Night Before Christmas* (by Clement C. Moore), *Mary Had a Little Lamb* (by Sarah Josepha Hale), and *An Early American Christmas* evoke his interest in antique quilts, old houses, and 19th-century objects. Concern with authenticity can be seen in the source notes provided, and, in the latter book, his careful choice of words and dialogue results in a tale that rings true.

Strega Nona: An Old Tale, an original work often mistaken for a folktale, brought early recognition with a Caldecott Honor award in 1976. Since then several other Strega Nona tales, including *Big Anthony and the Magic Ring* and *Strega Nona: Her Story,* have amused children with their fun-loving plots and spry artwork. This prolific artist counts five major anthologies to his credit. In addition to the popular *Mother Goose,* he selected and illustrated collections of Christmas carols, bible stories, nursery tales, and poems. Large diverse collections, they are all generously and lavishly illustrated with appealing artwork that extends the written words. Perusal of these books shows the selections have been made carefully and thoughtfully, with the attention span and interest of readers and the appeal of the chosen tales and poems in mind.

In an effort to encourage new talent and make children aware of lesser-known folktales, dePaola and Putnam created a special line called Whitebird Books in 1989, for which the author served as creative director. DePaola wrote and illustrated some of the titles, illustrated others, and served as creative mentor to others; the line, however, folded five years later as the books became lost in the flood of folktales coming on the market in the mid 1990s. In 1999, dePaola began a new writing venture, creating chapter books for older children. The first, *26 Fairmount Avenue,* sounds themes of individuality amid relationships in a story that is amusing and appealing to his audience.

Whether original story, autobiographical vignette, folktale, informational book, or anthology, the books dePaola creates are child-centered and inviting. Through all, the child dePaola once was shines brightly, captivating readers and enriching the field of children's books.

—Barbara Elleman

de REGNIERS, Beatrice Schenk

Pseudonym: Tamara Kitt. **Nationality:** American. **Born:** Beatrice Schenk Freedman, Lafayette, Indiana, 16 August 1914. **Education:** University of Illinois, Urbana, 1931-33; University of Chicago, Ph. B. 1935, and graduate student, 1936-37; University of Toulouse, 1935; the Sorbonne, Paris, 1935-36; Winnetka Graduate Teachers College, Illinois, M.Ed. 1941. **Family:** Married Francis de Regniers in 1953. **Career:** Member of the Eloise Moore Dance Group, Chicago, 1942-43; copywriter, Scott Foresman, publishers, Chicago, 1943-44; welfare officer, UNRRA, Egypt, 1944-46; copywriter, American Book Company, New York, 1948-49; director of educational materials, American Heart Association, New York, 1949-61; editor, Lucky Book Club, Scholastic Book Services, New York, 1961-81.

Publications for Children

Fiction

The Giant Story, illustrated by Maurice Sendak. New York, Harper, 1953.

A Little House of Your Own, illustrated by Irene Haas. New York, Harcourt Brace, 1954; London, Collins, 1957.

A Child's Book of Dreams, illustrated by Bill Sokol. New York, Harcourt Brace, 1957.

The Snow Party, illustrated by Reiner Zimnik. New York, Pantheon, 1959; London, Faber, 1961; new edition, illustrated by Bernice Myers, New York, Lothrop, 1990.

What Happens Next: Adventures of a Hero, illustrated by Remo. New York, Macmillan, 1959.

Who Likes the Sun?, illustrated by Leona Pierce. New York, Harcourt Brace, 1961; London, Collins, 1962.

The Little Book, illustrated by the author. New York, Walck, 1961; as *Going for a Walk,* New York, Harper, 1982; new edition, illustrated by Robert Knox, HarperCollins, 1993.

The Little Girl and Her Mother, illustrated by Esther Gilman. New York, Vanguard Press, 1963.

How Joe the Bear and Sam the Mouse Got Together, illustrated by Brinton Turkle. New York, Parents' Magazine Press, 1965; new edition, illustrated by Bernice Myers, New York, Lothrop, 1990.

Penny, illustrated by Marvin Bileck. New York, Viking Press, 1966; new edition, illustrated by Betsy Lewin, New York, Lothrop, 1987.

The Giant Book, illustrated by William Lahey Cummings. New York, Atheneum, 1966.

The Day Everybody Cried, illustrated by Nonny Hogrogian. New York, Viking Press, 1967.

The Boy, The Rat, and the Butterfly, illustrated by Haig and Regina Shekerjian. New York, Atheneum, 1971.

Laura's Story, illustrated by Jack Kent. New York, Atheneum, 1979.

Waiting for Mama. New York, Clarion, 1984.

Fiction as Tamara Kitt

The Adventures of Silly Billy, illustrated by Jill Elgar. New York, Grosset and Dunlap, 1961; London, Muller, 1966.

The Secret Cat, illustrated by William Russell. New York, Grosset and Dunlap, 1961.
Billy Brown Makes Something Grand, illustrated by Rosalind Welcher. New York, Grosset and Dunlap, 1961; London, Muller, 1970.
Billy Brown the Baby Sitter, illustrated by Rosalind Welcher. New York, Grosset and Dunlap, 1962; London, Muller, 1970.
The Surprising Pets of Billy Brown, illustrated by Rosalind Welcher. New York, Grosset and Dunlap, 1962.
The Boy Who Fooled the Giant, illustrated by William Russell. New York, Grosset and Dunlap, 1963; London, Muller, 1968.
The Boy, The Cat, and the Magic Fiddle, illustrated by William Russell. New York, Grosset and Dunlap, 1964.
A Special Birthday Party for Someone Very Special, illustrated by Brinton Turkle. New York, Norton, 1966.
Sam and the Impossible Thing, illustrated by Brinton Turkle. New York, Norton, 1967.
Jake, illustrated by Brinton Turkle. New York and London, Abelard Schuman, 1969.

Plays

Picture Book Theater: The Mysterious Stranger, and The Magic Spell, illustrated by William Lahey Cummings. New York, Clarion, 1982.
Everyone Is Good for Something (musical play for all ages; first produced Louisville, Kentucky, 1986), based on her book of the same title; script and lyrics by the author; music by Victoria Bond. New York, French, 1990.

Poetry

What Can You Do with a Shoe?, illustrated by Maurice Sendak. New York, Harper, 1955.
Was It a Good Trade?, illustrated by Irene Haas. New York, Harper, 1956; London, Collins, 1957.
Something Special, illustrated by Irene Haas. New York, Harcourt Brace, 1958; London, Collins, 1959.
Cats Cats Cats Cats Cats, illustrated by Bill Sokol. New York, Pantheon, 1958.
May I Bring a Friend?, illustrated by Beni Montresor. New York, Atheneum, 1964; London, Collins, 1966.
Circus, photographs by Al Giese. New York, Viking Press, 1966.
Willy O'Dwyer Jumped in the Fire: Variations on a Folk Rhyme, illustrated by Beni Montresor. New York, Atheneum, 1968; London, Collins, 1970.
Catch a Little Fox: Variations on a Folk Rhyme, illustrated by Brinton Turkle. New York, Seabury Press, 1970; London, Hamish Hamilton, 1971.
It Does Not Say Meow and Other Animal Riddle Rhymes, illustrated by Paul Galdone. New York, Seabury Press, 1972; Kingswood, Surrey, World's Work, 1973.
Red Riding Hood, Retold in Verse..., illustrated by Edward Gorey. New York, Atheneum, 1972; London, Collins, 1973.
A Bunch of Poems and Verses, illustrated by Mary Jane Dunton. New York, Seabury Press, 1977.
Jack and the Beanstalk Retold in Verse, illustrated by Anne Wilsdorf. New York, Atheneum, 1985.
So Many Cats!, illustrated by Ellen Weiss. New York, Clarion, 1985.
This Big Cat, and Other Cats I've Known, illustrated by Alan Daniel. New York, Crown, 1985.
A Week in the Life of Best Friends and Other Poems of Friendship, illustrated by Nancy Doyle. New York, Atheneum, 1986.
Jack the Giant-Killer Retold in Verse, illustrated by Anne Wilsdorf. New York, Atheneum, 1987.
The Way I Feel...Sometimes, illustrated by Susan Meddaugh. New York, Clarion, 1988.

Other

The Shadow Book, photographs by Isabel Gordon. New York, Harcourt Brace, 1960.
The Abraham Lincoln Joke Book, illustrated by William Lahey Cummings. New York, Random House, 1965.
David and Goliath, illustrated by Richard Powers. New York, Viking Press, 1965.
The Enchanted Forest: From a Story by La Comtesse de Ségur, illustrated by Gustave Doré and others. New York, Atheneum, 1974.
Little Sister and the Month Brothers (Slav folktale), illustrated by Margot Tomes. New York, Seabury Press, and London, Hamish Hamilton, 1976.
Everyone Is Good for Something (based on folktale motifs), illustrated by Margot Tomes. New York, Clarion, 1980.

Editor, with Eva Moore and Mary M. White, *Poems Children Will Sit Still For: A Selection for Primary Grades.* New York, Citation Press, 1969; revised edition, as *Sing a Song of Popcorn: Every Child's Book of Poems,* illustrated by several Caldecott award-winning illustrators, New York, Scholastic, 1988.

* * *

"Sometimes you just want everyone to leave you alone. No children. No grownups. Then it is a good thing to have a little house. A false face is a little house for your face."

Those lines from Beatrice Schenk de Regniers's *A Little House of Your Own* are marked by the deceptively simple style that characterizes her writing. On closer examination, one becomes aware of the pleasing rhythm, the precise choice of words, the genuinely childlike point-of-view, and the *speakability* of the lines. These are qualities that distinguish most of the more than 30 books for young children that de Regniers has written and published since 1953.

While unified in style, her output can be separated into several distinct categories. First there are the concept books, of which *A Little House of Your Own* is a notable example. Others in this group would include the poetic *Who Likes the Sun?, The Shadow Book* with its lovely blend of photographs and text, and *The Little Girl and Her Mother,* which gently describes what each can, and cannot, do and ends with the little girl growing up and becoming a mother herself.

Another category to which de Regniers has made some important contributions is that of the retold folk tale. In *Everyone Is Good for Something, Little Sister and the Month Brothers,* and *Red Riding Hood* she employs her gift for simple directness to achieve texts that young children can read by themselves, while at the same time maintaining an unobtrusive elegance—no mean accomplishment. And her original story *The Snow Party* adheres to many of the classic folk tale patterns as it recounts what happened when a bunch of snowbound people—and animals—turned what might have been a disaster into a frolic. *The Snow Party* is one of de Regniers's most unbridled, and most zestful, books.

The largest section in her body of work is comprised of picture book variations on folk rhymes, and original texts with the same lilting, musical quality. *What Can You Do with a Shoe?* is one of the most amusing and imaginative examples, and *Was It a Good Trade?, Catch a Little Fox,* and *It Does Not Say Meow* have their share of sparkling moments too. *Willy O'Dwyer Jumped in the Fire* seems too frail as a text, however, perhaps because Beni Montresor's pictures for it are so dark and heavy. Earlier, Montresor won the Caldecott Medal with another of de Regniers's texts in the folk rhyme genre, *May I Bring a Friend?* While this sustains a pleasingly gentle tone as it tells of all the animals that accompany a little boy on his visits to the King and Queen, it lacks some of the energy that infuses de Regniers's other songlike picture books.

In the 1980s de Regniers concentrated her energies on collections of original poems for children, most notably *A Week in the Life of Best Friends and Other Poems of Friendship* and *The Way I Feel...Sometimes.* The latter is a refreshingly honest exploration of the strong emotions, ranging from anger to jealousy to joy, that all children experience at one time or another. Her lasting affection for cats and their ways reveals itself in another collection of this period, *This Big Cat, and Other Cats I've Known,* and in her counting story told in verse, *So Many Cats!*

Occupying a special place in de Regniers's *oeuvre* are the exceptions, books that fit into no particular category as they experiment with new forms and themes. *The Day Everybody Cried* explores feelings of sadness and happiness but stays on too abstract a level to make its point successfully. *Penny,* a modern reworking of the Thumbelina theme, is a fascinating attempt to create a miniature novel. And *The Boy, The Rat, and the Butterfly* attempts even more—a parable of life, death, and rebirth expressed through the relationship of the three title characters, all of whom are named Peter. "Now they are going down the road," the book ends. "The boy, the rat, and the butterflies. They don't seem to be going very far. And wherever they are going, they are not getting there very fast. And it doesn't matter, really."

There it is again—the deceptive simplicity that stamps so many of Beatrice de Regniers's books for children.

—James Cross Giblin

de ROO, Anne (Louise)

Nationality: New Zealander. **Born:** 1931, in Gore. **Education:** New Plymouth Girls' High School; University of Canterbury, Christchurch, 1949-52, B.A. 1952. **Career:** Library assistant, Dunedin Public Library, 1956; assistant librarian, Dunedin Teachers' College, 1957-59; governess and part-time gardener, Church Preen, Shropshire, England, 1962-68; part-time secretary, Barkway, Hertfordshire, England, 1969-73; part-time medical typist, Palmerston North, New Zealand, 1974-78. Since 1978 full-time writer. **Awards:** ICI bursary, 1981. **Died:** 1997.

PUBLICATIONS FOR CHILDREN

Fiction

The Gold Dog. London, Hart Davis, 1969.
Moa Valley. London, Hart Davis, 1969.
Boy and the Sea Beast, illustrated by Judith Anson. London, Hart Davis, 1971; New York, Scholastic, 1974.
Cinnamon and Nutmeg. London, Macmillan, 1972; Nashville, Nelson, 1974.
Mick's Country Cousins. London, Macmillan, 1974.
Scrub Fire. London, Heinemann, 1977; New York, Atheneum, 1980.
Traveller. London, Heinemann, 1979.
Because of Rosie. London, Heinemann, 1980.
Jacky Nobody. Auckland, Methuen, 1983; London, Methuen, 1984.
The Bats' Nest. Auckland and London, Hodder and Stoughton, 1986.
Friend Troll, Friend Taniwha, illustrated by R.H.G. Jahnke. Auckland and London, Hodder and Stoughton, 1986.
Mouse Talk. Palmerston North, Church Mouse Press, 1989.
The Good Cat. Palmerston North, Church Mouse Press, 1990.
Hepzibah Mouse's ABC. Palmerston North, Church Mouse Press, 1991.
Sergeant Sal. Auckland, Random Century, 1991.
Hepzibah's Book of Famous Mice. Palmerston North, Church Mouse Press, 1993.
Henry, Does God Eat Pumpkins?: A Mouse Journey Through the Church Year. Palmerston North, Church Mouse Press, 1995.
Henry, from a Church Mousehole. Palmerston North, Church Mouse Press, 1996.

Plays

The Dragon Master, music by John Schwabe (produced Palmerston North, 1978).
The Silver Blunderbuss, music by John Schwabe (produced Palmerston North, 1984).

PUBLICATIONS FOR ADULTS

Fiction

Hope Our Daughter. Palmerston North, Church Mouse Press, 1990.
Becoming Fully Human. Palmerston North, Church Mouse Press, 1991.
And We Beheld His Glory. Palmerston North, Church Mouse Press, 1994.
Christ Be My Courage. Palmerston North, Church Mouse Press, 1997.

*

Anne de Roo comments:

As a child in New Zealand I had only books that told of strange faraway places where Christmas came in midwinter and children gathered bluebells in the woods in May. Books in fact that had nothing to do with the world I saw about me. Tales of strange distant places are fine and exciting and I like to think I provide them for English and American children—New Zealand is a new wild place in which exciting things can still happen. But much more important to me are the New Zealand children who as well as strange stories of Christmas by the fireside instead of in the summer sunshine have a right to stories that belong to the world they see about them and to parts of their country they have not yet explored for themselves.

* * *

Anne de Roo's first book reveals a style which is unpretentious and sparing. *The Gold Dog* is a good, lively "yarn," skilfully constructed with vigorous scenes of outdoor adventure as children, following their own hunches, perform feats of courage. Set in a very authentic and distinctive part of New Zealand, the mountainous district of Central Otago, scene of the gold discoveries of Gabriel Read in 1861, the book describes a search for lost treasure. The most interesting part of the story concerns the reverberations of the area's romantic past when the old digger, Seb, wins the love and respect of the little community of Marston on the Oxburn.

Moa Valley is also set in the mountains in the southern part of the South Island of New Zealand. The book describes courage in the face of hardship when young people become lost in unexplored territory. An older man is again the focus of the story: Mr. Peacock dreams he will find a living moa, a giant flightless bird, long thought extinct.

Boy and the Sea Beast marks a stage when a new dimension enters her work. Up to this point, it is clear that de Roo is technically very effective but while the quality of suspense is strong, the solution to the action comes too easily and character is subordinated to the need for a happy ending. This is much less so in *Boy and the Sea Beast* which is about a child's friendship with a dolphin. The book is inspired by the charming stories of two famous dolphins, Pelorous Jack and Opo, who have been friends to man in New Zealand. Despite the very indifferent illustrations which in no way convey with accuracy the Maori or his environment, Boy-at-Last Rangi and his family who live in the far North of the North Island of New Zealand are spontaneous and vital people. The delightful dolphin, Thunder, is saved by Boy from exploitation but must finally leave for the free and wild life with his own kind.

This theme is extended and deepened in *Cinnamon and Nutmeg* and *Mick's Country Cousins,* two closely related stories of the lush rolling dairy lands of the North Island province of Taranaki in which characters matter far more than the adventures which follow from their predicaments. In the second novel, Mick has no father and, as a consequence, becomes unmanageable. Sent to wholesome surroundings in the country, he feels the tension between his old values and the newer ones on the farm. Significantly, it is the love of animals which has a large part in the development of a feeling for those around him.

Traveller and *Because of Rosie* show the author's mastery of the writing of the historical novel for children. *Traveller* is the effortlessly told story of the highly intelligent sheep dog which the legendary Mackenzie used in the South Island High Country of the 1850s. *Because of Rosie* describes a very different scene—that of the North Island bush of the Manawatu Plain in 1872. Though the theme is a well-used one—an orphaned family surviving amid the hardships of pioneering days in the bush—the author brings to it a sense of fresh vigour.

Scrub Fire is based on the well-worn theme of children lost in the bush. However, the author handles her material with a light touch even including humour within a tense drama of survival in the rugged North Island bush. Surehanded as ever in her characterisation, she does not fudge the near-fatal consequences of such a plight as the children struggle to conquer their fears and overcome their mistakes.

De Roo returned to history in the award-winning *Jacky Nobody* and its sequel *The Bats' Nest.* When the chief Hone Heke refers to Jacky as a relative he begins to realise he is not a *pakeha* boy who is kept and educated by a missionary as one of his own family. He is Maori, the son of an English sailor and a highborn Maori mother. Despite the pain of parting Jacky finally joins the Maori warriors and recognises them as his own people. The reader sees through the eyes of Jacky the frustrations that the Maori had with the Treaty of Waitangi, the cutting of the flag pole at Kororareka, defeat of the Redcoats at Ohaeawai, and the Maori defeat on a Sunday at Ruapekapeka. Frustrated by and disillusioned with the Treaty of Waitangi, Hone Heke takes what he considers to be peaceful means of protest. In the course of misunderstandings between Maori and European, violence erupts and many innocent people suffer. These carefully researched novels bring the past vividly back and show us how relevant such events are to the state of society in New Zealand today.

Friend Troll, Friend Taniwha demonstrates de Roo's versatility, for here she succeeds with fantasy firmly based on New Zealand soil. She brings together the Scandanavian giant and the Maori sea beast who enlist the support of the dolphins and the cheeky keas. Children will love the humour.

De Roo moved a long distance from her early novels of adventure to works that delve deeply into the most important elements of life—love and laughter, loyalty and courage, peace and forgiveness.

—Tom Fitzgibbon

DESAI, Anita

Nationality: Indian. **Born:** Anita Mazumbar, Mussoorie, 24 June 1937. **Education:** Queen Mary's Higher Secondary School, New Delhi; Miranda House, Delhi University, B.A. (honours) in English literaure 1957. **Family:** Married Ashvin Desai in 1958; two sons and two daughters. **Career:** Professor of creative writing, Smith College, 1987, and Mount Holyoke College, 1988-1993; since 1993, professor of writing, Massachusetts Institute of Technology. Fellow, Royal Society of Literature, American Academy of Arts and Letters; Helen Cam Fellow of Girton College, University of Cambridge, 1986; Ashby Fellow of Clare Hall, University of Cambridge, 1989. **Awards:** Royal Society of Literature Winifred Holtby prize, for adult fiction, 1978; Sahitya Academy award, 1979; *Guardian* award, 1982; Hadassah award (U.S.A.), 1989; Padma Sri award (India), 1990; Neil Gunn International Fellowship (Scotland), 1994. **Agent:** Rogers, Coleridge, & White, Ltd., 20 Powis Mews, London W11 1JN, England.

PUBLICATIONS FOR CHILDREN

Fiction

The Peacock Garden. Bombay, India Book House, 1974; London, Heinemann, 1979.
Cat on a Houseboat. Bombay, Orient Longman, 1976.
The Village by the Sea. London, Heinemann, 1982.

Publications for Adults

Novels

Cry, The Peacock. Calcutta, Rupa, n.d.; London, Owen, 1963.
Voices in the City. London, Owen, 1965.
Bye-Bye, Blackbird. New Delhi, Hind, and Thompson, Connecticut, InterCulture, 1971.
Where Shall We Go This Summer? New Delhi, Vikas, 1975.
Fire on the Mountain. New Delhi, Allied, London, Heinemann, and New York, Harper, 1977.
Clear Light of Day. New Delhi, Allied, London, Heinemann, and New York, Harper, 1980.
The Village by the Sea: An Indian Family Story. London, Heinemann, 1982.
In Custody. London, Heinemann, 1984; New York, Harper, 1985.
Baumgartner's Bombay. London, Heinemann, 1988.
Journey to Ithaca. London, Heinemann, 1995.

Short Stories

Games at Twilight and Other Stories. New Delhi, Allied, and London, Heinemann, 1978; New York, Harper, 1980.

*

Critical Studies: *Indian Writing in English* by Paul Verghese, Bombay, Asia Publishing House, 1970; *Anita Desai: A Study of Her Fiction* by Meena Belliappa, Calcutta, Writers Workshop, 1971; *The Twice-Born Fiction* by Meenakshi Mukherjee, New Delhi, Arnold-Heinemann, 1972; *Indian Writing in English* by Srinivas Iyyengar, Bombay, Asia Publishing House, 1972; *The Novels of Mrs. Anita Desai* by B.R. Rao, New Delhi, Kalyani, 1977; *Anita Desai the Novelist* by Madhusudan Prasad, Allahabad, New Horizon, 1981; *Perspectives on Anita Desai,* edited by Ramesh K. Srivastava, Ghaziabad, Vimal, 1984.

Anita Desai comments:

As soon as I was taught the alphabet, I started to write. I would come home from school and sit down on a wicker stool at a low green table and spend the long, silent afternoons writing. No experience or sensation seemed quite complete till I had found words for it and written it down: it became a habit and a way of life. I would write little stories, stitch them together, illustrate them and give them to my family who thought of me as "the writer in the family." Later I had small pieces published in a children's magazine. When I was in college, I had short stories and reviews published in journals. I wrote my first novel between the age of 21 and 23. It has been a long lifetime of which at least half has been made up of words, books and writing. Life is chaotic but when I write I can impose order and meaning and sense and, I hope, clarity.

* * *

One of India's most respected authors of books for adults, Anita Desai is acquiring an increasingly strong international reputation as a children's writer as well—a reputation deriving primarily from two books, *The Peacock Garden* and *The Village by the Sea: An Indian Family Story*. Because her adult novels decry the rootlessness, materialism, and spiritual schizophrenia of modern society, Desai is sometimes believed to oppose all traditional constructs, including marriage and the family, and to champion an institutionless society. But her children's novels are strong ammunition against this reading of any of her works: they assert that the family can be a safe harbor on the sea of change—and that of all social entities, the family is most effective in nurturing individuals through tragedy and crisis or in facilitating growth and reformation.

The Peacock Garden is a short novel that can be read and enjoyed by third graders, but that speaks effectively to much older readers as well. Told from the perspective of a young Muslim girl whose family escapes the 1947 Zuni race riots in Punjab, its focus is on the enclosed garden of a mosque where, thanks to the generosity of an old Hindu man, the family finds refuge. There, the family effectively endures additional tragedy, gathering strength and unity. The conclusion of the novel suggests that a promising new life awaits the family as they prepare to return to the outside world.

Older readers will perceive, however, that underlying ironies mute the book's optimism. While the garden is most certainly a symbol of peace, security, and the continuity of life, it is also the very clear embodiment of an artificial and transitory existence. Once they leave its walls, the family is not guaranteed survival, let alone happiness. And unless they are wary, the relationships carefully cultivated during their time in the garden will wither and die.

The Village by the Sea is the story of two children who are forced into adulthood early. Their mother is chronically ill (and is eventually hospitalized); their unemployed father spends increasingly long periods of time away from the family, drinking. Finally, when it becomes clear the family will self-destruct unless something is done, the twelve-year-old boy strikes out for Bombay to earn money to bring back to his family. In his absence (and largely in the absence of both parents), the boy's thirteen-year-old sister remolds the family, increasing its self-sufficiency and unity.

Less structured and less focused in characterization or theme than *The Peacock Garden, The Village by the Sea* is nevertheless a richer and more engaging novel despite its flaws. And some of its flaws are serious: the casual structure of the novel and its multiple plot lines cause many readers to become impatient and bored. Some of the book's "problems" are much more real, much more convincing than its "solutions." When Hari wishes that his reprobate father were dead, for example, the reader believes him. But when the father is suddenly transformed as a consequence of his wife's being hospitalized, the skeptical reader wants a more thorough explanation of the change. Finally, the book's chapters are divided between its dual protagonists, Lila and her brother Hari. This could be seen as a strength, potentially increasing the novel's appeal to both female and male readers. In actuality, however, the reader is distanced from both Lila and Hari, knowing neither intimately.

Still, the novel provides an engaging and enlightening view of Indian life earlier in this century. Its portraits of Bombay city life and of the grinding poverty of the countryside are vivid and heartwrenching. And its cultural implications are profound, albeit unsettling. Most crucially, the novel skillfully portrays the "no-win choices" with which the Third World has been confronted during the past sixty or seventy years—the poverty of the status quo on one hand and the headlong plunge into industrialization (whereby traditions, values, and the environment itself are discarded) on the other. Sensitive students will be rewarded for the time they spend with Desai: they will come away from her novels knowing they have been taught.

—Keith Lawrence

de TREVIÑO, Elizabeth Borton

Nationality: American. **Born:** Bakersfield, California, 2 September 1904. **Education:** Stanford University, California, B.A. (Phi Beta Kappa) 1925; Boston Conservatory of Music. **Family:** Married Luis Treviño Gomez in 1935; two sons (one deceased). **Career:** Reporter, *Jamaica Plain Journal,* Boston, 1927-28; apprentice in production and advertising, Ginn and Company, publishers, Boston, 1928-31; interviewer, Boston *Herald American,* 1930-34; publicist, Mexico City Tourist Department, Mexican National Railways, and Mexican National Symphony, 1942-52; violinist, Vivaldi Orchestra, Mexico City, 1962-67. **Awards:** American Library Association Newbery medal, 1966. **Agent:** Mrs. Ray Pierre Corsini, 12 Beekman Place, New York, New York 10022, U.S.A. **Address:** Apartado Postal 827, Cuernavaca, Morelos, Mexico.

Publications for Children

Fiction

Pollyanna in Hollywood, illustrated by H. Weston Taylor. Boston, Page, 1931.
Our Little Aztec Cousin of Long Ago, Being the Story of Coyotl and How He Won Honor under His Kings, illustrated by Harold Cue. Boston, Page, 1934.
Pollyanna's Castle in Mexico, illustrated by Harold Cue. Boston, Page, 1934.
Our Little Ethiopian Cousin: Children of the Queen of Sheba. Boston, Page, 1935.
Pollyanna's Door to Happiness, illustrated by Harold Cue. Boston, Page, 1936.
Pollyanna's Golden Horseshoe, illustrated by Griswold Tyng. Boston, Page, 1939.
About Bellamy, illustrated by Jessie Robinson. New York, Harper, 1940.
Pollyanna and the Secret Mission, illustrated by Harold Cue. Boston, Page, 1951.
A Carpet of Flowers, illustrated by Alan Crane. New York, Crowell, 1955; Kingswood, Surrey, World's Work, 1956.
Nacar, the White Deer, illustrated by Enrico Arno. New York, Farrar Straus, 1963; Kingswood, Surrey, World's Work, 1964.
I, Juan de Pareja. New York, Farrar Straus, 1965; London Gollancz, 1966.
Casilda of the Rising Moon: A Tale of Magic and of Faith, of Knights and a Saint in Medieval Spain. New York, Farrar Straus, 1967; London, Gollancz, 1968.
Turi's Poppa. New York, Farrar Straus, 1968; as *Turi's Papa,* London, Gollancz, 1969.
Beyond the Gates of Hercules: A Tale of the Lost Atlantis. New York, Farrar Straus, and London, Gollancz, 1971.
El Guëro. New York, Farrar Straus, 1989.
Leona, a Love Story. Farrar Straus, 1994.

Other

Here Is Mexico. New York, Farrar Straus, 1970.

Publications for Adults

Novels

Even As You Love. New York, Crowell, 1957.
The Greek of Toledo: A Romantic Narrative about El Greco. New York, Crowell, 1959.
The Fourth Gift. New York, Doubleday, 1966.
The House on Bitterness Street. New York, Doubleday, 1970.
The Music Within. New York, Doubleday, 1973.
The Heart Possessed: A Love Story. New York, Doubleday, 1978.
Among the Innocent. New York, Doubleday, 1981.

Other

My Heart Lies South: The Story of My Mexican Marriage. New York, Crowell, 1953.
Where the Heart Is (memoirs). New York, Doubleday, 1962.
Juarez, Man of Law. New York, Farrar Straus, 1974.
The Hearthstone of My Heart (memoirs). New York, Doubleday, 1977.

*

Manuscript Collections: Boston University Library.

Critical Studies: *Mexico in the Work of Elizabeth Borton de Treviño* by Patricia Vickers, unpublished dissertation, Christian College, Lubbock, Texas, 1976.

Elizabeth Borton de Treviño comments:

All my books enclose a little kernel of truth ... something that really happened. *Nacar, the White Deer* enlarges upon a note in the history of the Manila galleon, the Spanish vessel that plied between the Orient and Acapulco, New Spain (now Mexico). According to the note, at one time the great ship carried across the Pacific a beautiful albino deer, which was reshipped from Veracruz to Spain as a gift for the king. *I, Juan de Pareja* retells the story of the lifelong friendship and regard of the famous Spanish painter Velasquez and his Negro slave, Juan; Juan taught himself to paint, in secret, and later Velasquez freed him and made him his assistant. *Casilda of the Rising Moon: A Tale of Magic and of Faith, of Knights and a Saint in Medieval Spain* recounts the story of a young Moorish princess of Spain in the 11th century who became a Christian convert and a saint. *Turi's Poppa* is the tale of a small boy and his father who walked halfway across Europe so that the father could take up a position as a violin-maker in Cremona, Italy. *Here Is Mexico* explores historical and contemporary Mexico, revealing a potpourri of truths and legends which combine to give this country its unique flavor.

At the same time, each of my stories tries to show some phase of love, that powerful emotion "which makes the world go round." *Nacar, the White Deer* portrays the love between a child and a gentle wild creature, the deer. *I, Juan de Pareja* shows the strong affection and esteem that can exist between persons of different races. *Casilda of the Rising Moon* is a study of the way in which the love of God may express itself in compassion for all living things. *Turi's Poppa* tells of the love between a boy and his father, and *Here Is Mexico* is an account of my beloved adopted country.

* * *

"All my life," writes Elizabeth Borton de Treviño, "I have been fascinated by imaginative speculation," and each of her stories is such a speculation, triggered by some legend or historical incident.

Of her books, *I, Juan de Pareja* has had most acclaim. It is based on Velasquez's paintings, and on the known facts of his life, but the hero is Juanico, his slave, who tells the story. It is an unusual and memorable book, concerned with the problems and frustrations of slavery, and the parallel constraints imposed on artistic freedom by the requirements of court convention. Tolerance, understanding, and love of art and truth are its moral values, as exemplified by Velasquez himself, whose words, "Art should be Truth, and Truth, unadorned, unsentimentalised, is Beauty," lie at the centre of the book.

This attitude is explicit also in *Beyond the Gates of Hercules,* a tale of the lost Atlantis which becomes, finally, a modern moral fable. The Atlanteans are deeply religious, and committed to the civilised peaceful way of life, though one might question here their uncritical acceptance of voluntary human sacrifice to the angry Sea God. The story elaborates the idyllic life of Atlantis in a Golden Age of mutual understanding and cooperation, though its happiness is soon shot through with trouble and anxiety as events move inexorably forward. For Baka, lacking the intuitive thought-reading of his people, becomes a scientist, and eventually, to compensate for his increasing alienation from his family, an aggressive power seeker. He turns his master's potentially good invention to evil use, becomes a military dictator, and Atlantis is destroyed. Its fate is clearly a warning to the Atomic Age, but the diagnosis of its ills is too superficial and simplistic. The book has charm, all the same.

Turi's Poppa, though set in post-war Europe, with echoes of its confusions and distresses, is less fraught with warnings. Turi is half gypsy. After his mother's death he and his father, a penniless violin maker, walk to Italy where work is waiting. Turi's gypsy lore and cunning, though of great help on the journey and in encounters with border guards, are also a source of trouble and distress: the conflicting attitudes and values of father and son are recounted with engaging simplicity, though with some of the lapses into sentimentality which so mar *Casilda of the Rising Moon.* This latter book tells the story of a frail, suffering Moorish princess, whose faith transforms her into an incredibly enduring and miracle working saint. But the writing is strained and overinsistent, and the story remains a fervidly romantic idealisation which contrasts unfavourably with the calmer achievements of the other books. *Nacar, the White Deer* is a more appealing story, with its loving and detailed account of pastoral life in 17th-century Mexico, exciting encounters with snakes and brigands, a voyage to Spain, and a climax in which the hitherto dumb hero makes an impassioned plea for the life of his deer, now threatened with a sacrificial role in a glorious royal hunt. This story, too, is concerned with extolling and defending the gentler things of life against violence and greed—a theme that runs through all these stories and, in spite of the sentimentality which sometimes creeps in, remains refreshing and appealing to the sensitive, thoughtful young reader.

El Guëro is a more personal story, a tribute to the memory of de Treviño's husband's grandfather, Judge Cayetano Treviño, and more particularly of his father, the eponymous hero and narrator of the story. It begins in the Mexico of the late 1870s, a time of violence and chaos within the country, when the lawful president had been deposed by a military coup. El Guëro's father, the judge, remained steadfastly loyal to the legally elected government, and with exemplary courage singlehandedly declared his opposition both to the usurping president, and, later, to the venal military commander in the remote region to which he and his family had been exiled. The young El Guëro's own contribution to events is an equally courageous attempt to seek help for his wrongfully imprisoned father, undertaking alone a hazardous journey through hostile territory, with no certainty of success at the end. The central theme is a familiar one: courage, steadfastness, and truth are virtues to hold on to whatever the consequences—and they can indeed win out, even against unprecedented odds. The story is quietly told, with no exaggerated heroics, though the stubborn uprightness of the judge comes across clearly as he faces endless dangers without flinching. There is throughout the story a great deal of fascinating detail, not only of the countryside during the hazardous initial journey to Ensenada, but also of the family's efforts to survive when they are ruthlessly abandoned on a remote and desolate shore, and as they later try to establish a home, a court and law and order in the almost nonexistent town of Ensenada. But perhaps the book's greatest appeal is that this is a true story, told with loving respect for these heroes of the past, whose belief in justice overrode all considerations of personal safety or gain.

—Winifred Whitehead

DODD, Lynley (Stuart)

Nationality: New Zealander. **Born:** Lynley Stuart Weeks, Rotorua, 5 July 1941. **Education:** Tauranga College, 1954-57; Elam School of Fine Arts, Auckland University, 1959-61, diploma in fine arts 1962; Auckland Teachers College, 1962. **Family:** Married Anthony R.F. Dodd in 1965; one son and one daughter. **Career:** Art mistress, Queen Margaret College, Wellington, 1963-68; freelance illustrator, 1968-83. **Awards:** New Zealand Library Association Esther Glen award, 1975; Choysa bursary, 1978; New Zealand Book award, for illustration, 1981; New Zealand Picture Book of the Year award, 1984, 1986, 1988; New Zealand Commemoration medal, 1990; AIM Picture Book of the Year Award, 1992. **Address:** Edward Avenue, R.D.3, Tauranga, New Zealand.

PUBLICATIONS FOR CHILDREN

Fiction (illustrated by the author)

Titimus Trim. Auckland, Hodder and Stoughton, and London, Hamish Hamilton, 1979.

The Apple Tree. Wellington, Mallinson Rendel, 1982; Milwaukee, Stevens, 1985.

The Smallest Turtle. Wellington, Mallinson Rendel, and Barnstaple, Devon, Spindlewood, 1982; Milwaukee, Stevens, 1985.

Hairy Maclary from Donaldson's Dairy. Wellington, Mallinson Rendel, and Barnstaple, Devon, Spindlewood, 1983; Milwaukee, Stevens, 1985.

Hairy Maclary's Bone. Wellington, Mallinson Rendel, and Barnstaple, Devon, Spindlewood, 1984; Milwaukee, Stevens, 1985.

Hairy Maclary, Scattercat. Wellington, Mallinson Rendel, and Barnstaple, Devon, Spindlewood, 1985; Milwaukee, Stevens, 1987.
Wake Up, Bear. Wellington, Mallinson Rendel, and Barnstaple, Devon, Spindlewood, 1986; Milwaukee, Stevens, 1988.
Hairy Maclary's Caterwaul Caper. Wellington, Mallinson Rendel, and Barnstaple, Devon, Spindlewood, 1987.
A Dragon in a Wagon. Wellington, Mallinson Rendel, and Barnstaple, Devon, Spindlewood, 1988.
Hairy Maclary's Rumpus at the Vet. Wellington, Mallinson Rendel, and Barnstaple, Devon, Spindlewood, 1989.
Slinky Malinki. Wellington, Mallinson Rendel, and Barnstaple, Devon, Spindlewood, 1990; Milwaukee, Stevens, 1991.
Find Me a Tiger. Wellington, Mallinson Rendel, and Barnstaple, Devon, Spindlewood, 1991; Milwaukee, Stevens, 1992.
Hairy Maclary's Showbusiness. Wellington, Mallinson Rendel, and Barnstaple, Devon, Spindlewood, 1991; Milwaukee, Stevens, 1992.
The Minister's Cat ABC. Wellington, Mallinson Rendel, and Barnstaple, Devon, Spindlewood, 1992; Milwaukee, Stevens, 1994.
Slinky Malinki, Open the Door. Wellington, Mallinson Rendel, and Barnstaple, Devon, Spindlewood, 1993; Milwaukee, Stevens, 1994.
Schnitzel von Krumm's Basketwork. Wellington, Mallinson Rendel, and Barnstaple, Devon, Spindlewood, 1994.
Hairy Maclary, Sit. Milwaukee, Stevens, 1998.
Schnitzel von Krumm Forget-Me-Not. Milwaukee, Stevens, 1998.

Other

The Nickle Nackle Tree. London, Hamish Hamilton, 1976; New York, Macmillan, 1978; Wellington, Mallinson Rendel, 1985.

*

Illustrator: *My Cat Likes to Hide in Boxes* by Eve Sutton, 1973; *Pussyfooting* by Jillian Squire, 1978; *I'm a Tree* by James K. Baxter, 1979; *Druscilla* by Clarice England, 1980; *Kindness* and *Barnyard Song* (traditional rhymes), 1981; *Pop Pop Pop* (adaptation of traditional rhyme), and *One Big Dinosaur,* both by Beverley Randell, 1981; *The Pesky Paua* by Robin Cunningham and Fran Hunia, 1983.

Lynley Dodd comments:

I came to writing late. It was through my illustrating work for *My Cat Likes to Hide in Boxes* that I became hooked on picture books; the heady excitement of a first publication, plus the fact that my own two children were active "consumers" at that stage, meant that ideas began germinating and with the confidence of ignorance I decided to give writing a try. The result, after much sweated labour, was *The Nickle Nackle Tree.* Since then I have written and illustrated my own books.

The big advantage of being author and illustrator lies in being able to plan the whole book from scratch. There is no conflict over interpretation and from the first rough rhythms and images in the head through to final result, words and pictures can evolve together in mood, balance, style, and sympathy.

I don't set out with earnest messages in mind. I like to have fun with words and characters and I aim to amuse and entertain—if a little learning creeps in occasionally, that's fine. I keep an eye and ear open for the whimsical; my "ideas" book is full of things earmarked for possible future use, from improbable names on a Royal Banquet guest list to a sketch of my mother's cat wearing an upturned supermarket bag.

Children often ask, "Will you write 'chapter ' books?" That would probably mean giving up "writing the pictures," as a two-year-old friend once put it. I think I'll stick with picture books.

* * *

If the mantle of Beatrix Potter has descended on any one contemporary picture book author it must surely be upon Lynley Dodd. Both writers have created unforgettable animal characters, and both achieve equal excellence in text and pictures with a total cohesion between the two. But there the similarities end. Dodd's books are not pale imitations of Potter's; their individuality and vigour are totally original.

Undoubtedly Dodd's success rests largely upon the sequence of stories which begins with *Hairy Maclary from Donaldson's Dairy* and which hopefully is not yet ended. Within these books she has created a range of canine and feline protagonists who inhabit the world of the small, shaggy, terrier-like Hairy Maclary. His friends include the mastiff "Hercules Morse as big as a horse," dalmation "Bottomley Potts covered in spots," old English sheepdog "Muffin Maclay like a bundle of hay," the greyhound-like "Bitzer Maloney all skinny and bony," and the dachshund "Schnitzel von Krumm with the very low tum." In the first book they are all routed by the "toughest tom in town," the formidable Scarface Claw, who also defeats Hairy Maclary in *Hairy Maclary Scattercat,* but the dogs gain something of a revenge in *Hairy Maclary's Caterwaul Caper* when Scarface Claw is stuck up a tree. It is then the dogs' turn to get stuck at various obstacle points when they are trying to divest Hairy Maclary of his bone in *Hairy Maclary's Bone.* Hairy Maclary also features more recently at the vet's, where he again meets old acquaintances, and even gets himself into a cat show in *Hairy Maclary's Show Business.*

Of his canine companions, so far only Schnitzel von Krumm has had a book to himself; in *Schnitzel von Krumm's Basketwork* he does not at all welcome a new basket in place of his old one. Among the featured cats, the lithe black Slinky Malinky has deserved his own books. In the first title he leads a secret life of crime, stealing by night, while in *Slinky Malinky Open the Door* he discovers how to open all the doors and create mayhem when he and a parrot are left alone in the house. The series has deserved its enormous success for the vivacity and humour of both the cumulative texts and the pictures, in which an animal's-eye view of vanishing tails, pavements, plants, walls, and feet is depicted.

Although Dodd's animals have marked personalities, she is never tempted into anthropomorphism. Her characters stay within the limitations of their species. Her earlier books, *The Apple Tree* and *The Smallest Turtle,* are virtually non-fiction; in the former a possum steals apples, while in the latter a young turtle, newly hatched from his egg, has to make his way to the sea. In the later *Wake up Bear* a succession of animals are unable to waken Bear from his hibernation—until a passing bee reminds him of honey and succeeds where everyone else has failed. In *Find Me A Tiger*—artistically one of the most ambitious of Dodd's books—a number of animals are so cleverly camouflaged that the child has to look hard to find them. In *The Minister's Cat ABC* Dodd takes the old alphabet game, "The Parson's Cat," and adapts it as an opportunity to show splendidly observed cats in a variety of moods and circumstances.

In one of her few forays into fantasy, *A Dragon in a Wagon,* a small girl, Susie Fogg, daydreams that her dog Sam becomes something more exciting, like a "dragon in a wagon" or "a gnu with 'flu." She herself plays an active part in these Walter Mitty-like departures from reality, but is delighted when she falls over to find the real Sam with his "friendly doggy face" ready to comfort her.

There has been a steady development in Dodd as an artist. Her pictures in Eve Sutton's *My Cat Likes to Hide in Boxes,* and her own *The Nickle Nackle Tree* and *Titimus Trim* (the story of an old man who muddles his routine), display a strong decorative element, with much flat use of primary colour. Her later stories, although still exhibiting a marked ability in drawing and design, rely more upon her own visual experiences to produce greater subtlety of atmosphere and colour, with a correspondingly stronger sense of space and realism.

From *The Nickle Nackle Tree* (a splendidly alliterative counting book) onwards, she has always shown a command of the sound and rhythms of language. These are excellent books to read aloud to children. The names, rhymes, repetition, refrains, and cumulative effects all invite participation, and the total unity of text and pictures ensures an economical, disciplined, and artistic entity.

—Betty Gilderdale

DORRIT, Susan. See **SCHLEIN, Miriam.**

DOUGLAS, Michael. See **BRIGHT, Robert.**

DOWNIE, Mary Alice (Dawe)

Nationality: Canadian (originally American: moved to Canada, 1940). **Born:** Mary Alice Dawe Hunter, Alton, Illinois, 12 February 1934. **Education:** St. Clement's School, Toronto; Trinity College, University of Toronto, 1951-55, B.A. (honours) in English 1955. **Family:** Married John Downie in 1959; three daughters. **Career:** Stenographer, Maclean-Hunter, Toronto, 1955; reporter, *Marketing* magazine, Toronto, 1955-56; editorial assistant, *Canadian Medical Association Journal,* Toronto, 1956-57; librarian, later publicity manager, Oxford University Press, Toronto, 1958-59; book review editor, Kingston *Whig-Standard,* Ontario, 1973-78. Founding editor, Kids Canada series, Kids Can Press, Toronto, and Northern Lights series, Peter Martin Associates, Toronto. **Awards:** Ontario Arts Council award, 1970, 1975, 1981, 1987, 1989, 1990; Canada Council bursary, 1971, 1981, 1987; Ontario Heritage Foundation grant, 1988; Multicultural Directorate grant, 1990. **Address:** 190 Union Street, Kingston, Ontario K7L 2P6, Canada.

Publications for Children

Fiction

Honor Bound, with John Downie, illustrated by Joan Huffman. Toronto, Oxford University Press, and New York, Walck, 1971; revised edition, Kingston, Ontario, Quarry Press, 1981.
Scared Sarah, illustrated by Laszlo Gal. Toronto, Nelson, 1974.
Dragon on Parade, illustrated by Mary Lynn Baker. Toronto, Peter Martin Associates, 1974.
The King's Loon, illustrated by Ron Berg. Toronto, Kids Can Press, 1979.
The Last Ship, illustrated by Lissa Calvert. Toronto, Peter Martin Associates, 1980.
A Proper Acadian, with George Rawlyk, illustrated by Ron Berg. Toronto, Kids Can Press, 1981.
Jenny Greenteeth, illustrated by Ann Powell. Toronto, Rhino, 1981; revised edition, Toronto, Kids Can Press, 1984.
Alison's Ghosts, with John Downie. Toronto, Nelson, 1984; Independence, Ohio, Schoolhouse Press, 1986.
The Cat Park, illustrated by Kathryn Naylor. Kingston, Ontario, Quarry Press, 1993.

Other

The Magical Adventures of Pierre (French-Canadian fairy tale), illustrated by Yüksel Hassan. Toronto, Nelson, 1974.
The Witch of the North: Folk Tales of French Canada, illustrated by Elizabeth Cleaver. Ottawa, Oberon Press, 1975.
Seeds and Weeds: A Book of Country Crafts, with Jillian Hulme Gilliland. Toronto, North Winds Press, 1981.
The Wicked Fairy-Wife: A French-Canadian Folktale, illustrated by Kim Price. Toronto, Kids Can Press, 1983.
Stones and Cones: Country Crafts for Kids, with Jillian Hulme Gilliland. Toronto, Scholastic, 1984.
How the Devil Got His Cat (French-Canadian folktale), illustrated by Jillian Hulme Gilliland. Kingston, Ontario, Quarry Press, 1988.
The Buffalo Boy and the Weaver Girl (Chinese folktale), with Mann Hwa Huang-Hsu, illustrated by Jillian Hulme Gillilano. Kingston, Ontario, Quarry Press, 1991.
Cathal the Giant Killer and the Dun Shaggy Filly (Scottish folktale), illustrated by Jillian Hulme Gillilano. Kingston, Ontario, Quarry Press, 1991.

Editor, with Barbara Robertson, *The Wind Has Wings: Poems from Canada,* illustrated by Elizabeth Cleaver. Toronto, Oxford University Press, and New York, Walck, 1968; London, Oxford University Press, 1969.
Editor, with Mary Hamilton, *And Some Brought Flowers: Plants in a New World,* illustrated by E.J. Revell. Toronto, University of Toronto Press, 1980.
Editor, with Barbara Robertson, *The New Wind Has Wings: Poems from Canada,* illustrated by Elizabeth Cleaver. Toronto and London, Oxford University Press, 1984; New York, Oxford University Press, 1985.
Editor, with Elizabeth Greene and M.-A. Thompson, *The Window of Dreams: New Canadian Writing for Children.* Toronto, Methuen, 1986.
Editor, with Barbara Robertson, *The Well-Filled Cupboard: Everyday Pleasures of Home and Garden.* Toronto, Lester and Orpen Dennys, 1987.

Editor, with Barbara Robertson, *Doctor Dwarf and Other Poems for Children* by A.M. Klein. Kingston, Ontario, Quarry Press, 1990.

Editor, with M.-A. Thompson, *Written in Stone: A Kingston Reader.* Kingston, Ontario, Quarry Press, 1993.

*

Mary Alice Downie comments:

My books are for children, and my themes are usually drawn from the Canadian past. It's a short past when you consider the country but stretches out when the heritage of the immigrant is included.

The books have resulted from a mixture of writing, translating, retelling, and rediscovery of little-known materials. My aim is to entertain and occasionally inform young Canadians. My hope is that the stories and poems will appeal beyond the borders of the country and the age of childhood.

* * *

Mary Alice Downie's junior fiction breathes life into distant periods of Canadian history. Her youthful Canadians of long ago are irresistible creations: believably of their period, yet as lively and full of fun as their distant descendants who people the playgrounds of today.

Her most ambitious historical fiction to date, written in collaboration with her husband, is *Honor Bound,* set in 1784. This suspenseful story depicts the terrifying times that brought an important segment of the Canadian population—the United Empire Loyalists—to strengthen a struggling new nation.

The Averys of Philadelphia are Loyalists, faithful to England's King George III. The War of Independence is now over, but the persecution of the defeated goes on unabated. Unwilling "Americans" who doggedly remain faithful to the King to whom they had sworn allegiance are being persecuted in the name of freedom. Many, like the Averys, left homes and possessions to make their hazardous way to Canada; and in those days, going to Canada meant going to the wilderness.

Unused as they are to rough backwoods ways, the Averys make Cataraqui (now Kingston) a haven and a home. The heaviest burden the family has to bear is that of separation from Honor, the 17-year-old eldest daughter of the family, who had been visiting an aunt in upstate New York when the Yankee vigilantes struck, and of whom they have since had no word. If only Honor can be found, these proud new Canadians will be very content in their "uncivilized" home.

A Proper Acadian, for younger readers, simplifies a complex tragedy into dimensions within the grasp of children. 12-year-old Timothy is an orphaned Bostonian of the 1750s, sent to live with his dead mother's sister to keep him out of the trouble for which he shows too much aptitude. Thus it happens that he is living with his Acadian kinsfolk in Minas when in 1775 the dread order for the deportation of all Acadians is carried out.

Timothy elects to accompany his aunt's family into exile rather than return to his home in Boston. The lives of the puritanical Bostonians and the warm-hearted, happy-go-lucky Acadians are nicely contrasted, and it is easy to understand Timothy's choice. The story is vividly told from the perspective of a young lad torn between loyalties to his New England birthplace and to his beloved adoptive family.

In *The King's Loon* the thankless foundling Andre learns through the ungrateful behavior of the captive loon he releases to freedom exactly how hurtful his own carelessness has been to his adoptive parent, Tante Louet. The appealing story is imbedded in a mini-history lesson of the expedition of Count Frontenac, the haughty new Governor of New France, to make himself known to the Iroquois and impress them with his power.

The Last Ship, too, is a tiny, well-sugared lesson in Canadian history. The departure of the last supply ship of the year from New France before winter ends all navigation has always signalled a time of deep gloom to the exiles in this bleak place now cut off for long, empty months from all they hold dear. Yet somehow this year, *real* life goes on just as before, for suddenly Quebec, not the France of Louis XIV, is where Madeleine's life, and the lives of her family and friends, are really lived. Quebec is no longer exile, but home.

Contemporary in setting, yet evoking the past, *Alison's Ghosts* is the mildly otherwordly story of a youngster troubled by the possession of an Indian artifact, the bowl of an ancient medicine pipe. She becomes convinced that it is necessary for her to locate the missing stem, and to restore the pipe intact to the questing spirit of a Micmac shaman. In her search for the spirit pipe, Alison uncovers the story of its haunted history.

Her interest in history probably influenced Downie's adapted versions of two French-Canadian folktales, the slightly chilling *The Wicked Fairy-Wife,* and the more cheerful *How the Devil Got His Cat,* in which a clever Mother Superior plays a sly trick upon the mysterious stranger who has tried to trick *her* by volunteering to build the bridge the convent needs, if he may claim for his own the first thing to cross that bridge when it is completed.

For much younger readers, *Dragon on Parade* is a small-town summer idyll of three little girls who want to be the hit of the Bayfield Lions Club Carnival by creating a stunning dragon costume out of cardboard boxes, drapery, paint, and sequins, in every child's dress-up dream come true.

Downie is a writer who understands children, and has a rare talent for speaking directly to them by focussing upon that carefully selected aspect of her subject most surely calculated to appeal to the hearts of young readers.

—Joan McGrath

DRUMMOND, V(iolet) H(ilda)

Nationality: British. **Born:** London, 30 July 1911. **Education:** The Links, Eastbourne, Sussex; St. Martin's School of Art, London. **Family:** Married Anthony Swetenham in 1948; one son by previous marriage. **Career:** Chairman, V.H. Drummond Productions since 1960. **Awards:** Library Association Kate Greenaway medal, for illustration, 1957.

PUBLICATIONS FOR CHILDREN (ILLUSTRATED BY THE AUTHOR)

Fiction

Phewtus the Squirrel. London, Oxford University Press, 1939; revised edition, London, Constable, 1966; New York, Lothrop, 1987.

Mrs. Easter's Parasol. London, Faber, 1944.
Miss Anna Truly. London, Faber, 1945; Boston, Houghton Mifflin, 1949.
Lady Talavera. London, Faber, 1946.
Tidgie's Innings. London, Faber, 1947.
The Charming Taxi-cab. London, Faber, 1947.
The Mountain That Laughed. London, Grey Walls Press, 1947.
The Flying Postman. London, Penguin, 1948; Boston, Houghton Mifflin, 1949.
Mr. Finch's Pet Shop. London, Faber, 1953; New York, Oxford University Press, 1954.
Mrs. Easter and the Storks. London, Faber, 1957; New York, A.S. Barnes, 1960.
Little Laura's Cat. London, Faber, 1960.
Little Laura on the River. London, Faber, 1960.
Little Laura and the Thief. London, Nelson, 1963.
Little Laura and Her Best Friend. London, Nelson, 1963.
Little Laura and the Lonely Ostrich. London, Nelson, 1963.
Miss Anna Truly and the Christmas Lights. London, Longman, 1968.
Mrs. Easter and the "Golden Bounder." London, Faber, 1970.
Mrs. Easter's Christmas Flight. London, Faber, 1972.

Plays

Television Series: *Little Laura,* 1963.

Other

I'll Never Be Asked Again. London, Debrett's, 1979.

*

Illustrator: *The Twelfth* by J.K. Stanford, 1944; *Here and There a Lusty Trout* by Thomas A. Powell, 1947; *Verse and Worse* by Arnold Silcock, 1947; *The Shaggy Dog Story* by Eric Partridge, 1948; *Carbonel* by Barbara Sleigh, 1955; *The Wild Little House* by Eilís Dillon, 1955; *Esprit de Corps* by Lawrence Durrell, 1957; *The Piemakers* by Helen Cresswell, 1967.

V.H. Drummond comments:

I wrote my first children's book for my son aged four; the idea for my next book, *Mrs. Easter's Parasol,* came to me while walking with him in Kensington Gardens. In 1963 I drew the pictures and wrote the stories for the *Little Laura* series on BBC "Children's Hour," and my last three children's books were written for my three grandchildren.

* * *

V.H. Drummond won the Kate Greenaway medal in 1957, but her talent as an imaginative and original writer of stories for young children is at least as great as her talent as an illustrator. Her characters—Little Laura and her beloved Nannie, Laura's best friend, Billie Guftie, his Aunt Mrs. Easter, and even Miss Anna Truly (though she hates washing-up)—inhabit a world which has so little connection with reality that surely no one could call it dated or class-ridden. Certainly, Drummond has a decided preference for things that are not new-fangled and automatic, useful as the escalator is in disposing of Vilewort the Villain. And Laura may cry "What larking fun!" This is hardly the expression of a contemporary child, but one with as much appeal for such children as her ride on the swan's back and her unselfconscious converse with the King.

Drummond's characters are all tremendously spirited. The King reacts to the story of Mrs. Easter and the storks with "What courage! What a tale of romance!" We can only say the same. One of Drummond's favourite words is elegant. The King's tea table is, of course, elegant. So is the main lodge in *Lady Talavera.* More surprisingly, so is the ice cream in *The Flying Postman.* And Drummond's style and language are never less than elegant: "So they descended from the roof and made their way towards the harbour, followed by the grieving bird."

The Flying Postman is the best of all these delightful books. Shorter than most, with bolder yet softer artwork, the story tells of Mr. Musgrove, who delivered letters by helicopter and foolishly crashed into the church when entertaining the children with his aerobatics. The Postal Authorities dismiss him and Mr. Musgrove is forced to make a living by selling pink ice cream. Fortunately one day the Post Master General has an accident outside Mr. Musgrove's house and, in return for his kindness and the reviving elegant ice cream, reinstates him in his job—a logical, unbureaucratic procedure any child would applaud.

—Ann Thwaite

du BOIS, William Pène

Nationality: American. **Born:** Nutley, New Jersey, 9 May 1916. **Education:** Miss Barstow's School, New York; Lycée Hoche, Versailles, 1924-28; Lycée de Nice, 1928-29; Morristown School, New Jersey, 1930-34. **Military Service:** United States Army, 1941-45: correspondent, *Yank* magazine. **Family:** Married 1) Jane Bouché in 1943; 2) Willa Kim in 1955. **Career:** Art editor and designer, *Paris Review.* **Awards:** American Library Association Newbery medal, 1948. **Died:** 5 February 1993.

PUBLICATIONS FOR CHILDREN (ILLUSTRATED BY THE AUTHOR)

Fiction

Elisabeth, The Cow Ghost. New York, Nelson, 1936; London, Museum Press, 1944.
Giant Otto. New York, Viking Press, 1936; London, Harrap, 1937; revised edition, as *Otto in Africa,* New York, Viking Press, 1961, Leicester, Brockhampton Press, 1962.
Otto at Sea. New York, Viking Press, 1936; London, Harrap, 1937.
The Three Policemen; or, Young Bottsford of Farbe Island. New York, Viking Press, 1938.
The Great Geppy. New York, Viking Press, 1940; London, Hale, 1942
The Flying Locomotive. New York, Viking Press, 1941; London Museum Press, 1946.
The Twenty-One Balloons. New York, Viking Press, 1947; London, Hale, 1950.
Peter Graves. New York, Viking Press, 1950; Kingswood, Surrey World's Work, 1974.
Bear Party. New York, Viking Press, 1951; Kingswood, Surrey World's Work, 1975.

Squirrel Hotel. New York, Viking Press, 1952.
The Giant. New York, Viking Press, 1954.
Lion. New York, Viking Press, 1956.
Otto in Texas. New York, Viking Press, 1959; Leicester, Brockhampton Press, 1961.
The Alligator Case. New York, Harper, 1965.
Lazy Tommy Pumpkinhead. New York, Harper, 1966.
The Horse in the Camel Suit. New York, Harper, 1967.
Pretty Pretty Peggy Moffitt. New York, Harper, 1968.
Porko Von Popbutton. New York, Harper, 1969.
Call Me Bandicoot. New York, Harper, 1970.
Otto and the Magic Potatoes. New York, Viking Press, 1970.
Bear Circus. New York, Viking Press, 1971; Kingswood, Surrey, World's Work, 1975.
Mother Goose for Christmas. New York, Viking Press, 1973.
The Forbidden Forest. New York, Harper, and London, Chatto and Windus, 1978.
Gentleman Bear. New York, Farrar Straus, 1985.

Other

The Hare and the Tortoise, and The Tortoise and the Hare/La Liebre y la Tortuga, & la Tortuga y la Liebre (bilingual edition), with Lee Po. New York, Doubleday, 1972.

*

Manuscript Collection: May Massee Collection, Emporia State University, Kansas.

Illustrator: *S.O.S. Geneva* by Richard Plant and Oskar Seidlin, 1939; *Harriet* by Charles McKinley, Jr., 1946; *The Witch of Scrapfaggot Green* by Patricia Gordon, 1948; *The Mousewife* by Rumer Godden, 1951; *The Young Visiters* by Daisy Ashford, 1951; *Moon Ahead* by Leslie Greener, 1951; *Twenty and Ten* by Claire Huchet Bishop, 1952; *My Brother Bird* by Evelyn Ames, 1954; *The Rabbit's Umbrella* by George Plimpton, 1955; *In France* by Marguerite Clement, 1956; *Jexium Island* by Madeleine Grattan, 1957; *Castles and Dragons* edited by the Child Study Association, 1958; *Fierce John* by Edward Fenton, 1959; *Billy the Barber* by Dorothy Kunhardt, 1961; *The Owl and the Pussycat* by Edward Lear, 1962; *The Light Princess* by George MacDonald, 1962; *The Three Little Pigs,* 1962; *Dr. Ox's Experiment* by Jules Verne, 1963; *The Poison Belt* by Arthur Conan Doyle, 1964; *A Certain Small Shepherd* by Rebecca Caudill, 1965; *The Magic Finger* by Roald Dahl, 1966; *The Tiger in the Teapot* by Betty Yurdin, 1968; *Digging for China: A Poem* by Richard Wilbur, 1970; *The Topsy-Turvy Emperor of China* by Isaac Bashevis Singer, 1971; *Seal Pool* by Peter Matthiessen, 1972; *William's Doll,* 1972, *My Grandson Lew,* 1974, *The Unfriendly Book,* 1975, and *It's Not Fair,* 1976, all by Charlotte Zolotow; *Where's Gomer?* by Norma Farber, 1974; *Moving Day* by Tobi Tobias, 1976; *The Runaway Flying Horse* by Paul J. Bonzon, 1976; *We Came A-Marching—One, Two, Three* by Mildred Hobzek, 1978; *The Sick Day* by Patricia MacLachlan, 1979; *The Planet of Lost Things,* 1982, and *The Night Book,* 1985, both by Mark Strand; *Anna Witch* by Madeleine Edmondson, 1982; *Bear in Mind,* edited by Bobbye S. Goldstein, 1989; *Just My Size* by May Garelick, 1990.

* * *

If the prolific writings of William Pène du Bois suggest any common theme, it would have to be the celebration of eccentricity. His Newbery Medal winner, *The Twenty-One Balloons,* begins with a retired arithmetic teacher being retrieved from the Atlantic Ocean where he clung for dear life to the workings of twenty-one deflated balloons. But instead of pursuing the reason why, the author focused instead upon outrageously idiosyncratic Professor Sherman as he rebuffs entreaties of benefactors and dignitaries—even the President of the United States—rather than relate his experiences prior to addressing the Western American Explorer's Club. His accidental landing on the island of Krakatoa had brought him into contact with people whose proclivities were if anything more peculiar than his own. The gentleman who originally discovered Sherman unconscious and naked upon the beach, waits in a stolid, butler-like stance to provide the survivor with spats, a detachable collar, and a starched white dickey in order to commence a brief expedition through tropical brush and into the society of Krakatoa.

Although the virtues of loyalty and perseverence are implicitly applauded throughout du Bois's writings, overbearing commitment to excess commands the essential spotlight. In separate studies of the seven deadly sins (four of these theological fictions for children have appeared so far) he paraded impish delight in excess with one central character demonstrating comic ingenuity in perpetuating an obvious psychological imbalance. There is no denunciation of vice. Porko von Popbutton's swelled belly and voracious gastronomic compulsion cast him ultimately as unlikely hero as victorious goalie against an arch rival school. Ermine Bandicoot, the youthful miser, is as well a charming teller of tales who eschews cigarettes because they are too costly. He does, however, collect the butts with the intention of reprocessing valuable tobacco. His comic lust for gain provokes the ingenious venture of using the Statue of Liberty as an advertising pedestal and he later uses a football field to roll the world's largest cigarette. *Peter Graves* features two eccentrics, Peter the fearless, who urges his school gang across the bay via sharply peaking and declining bridge cables, and Houghton F. Furlong, whose horrible house and preposterous inventions scare off even the authorities. Furlong's latest concoction defies the inventor and his youthful accomplice in the search for a possible use. Five small books concern Otto, a Bunyanesque otterhound who can snuggle up to the Sphinx, fan a windmill with his tail, and casually bury 171 Arab warriors in the sand. *The Alligator Case* and its sequel, *The Horse in the Camel Suit,* concern a young boy's preoccupation with being a detective. His over zealous imagination is matched by equally peculiar villains, one of whom knocks bullet peas into the air with pork chop mallets, each time adroitly retrieving the vegetables in his open mouth. The comedy of humours continues throughout the du Bois opus.

After a seven-year absence, du Bois returned to writing with the most preposterous theme of them all—himself. Any devotee of du Bois, and there are many of them, might suspect that his own life would provide a stream of fictional excesses quite exceeding any of the idiosyncratic figures in the du Bois canon. To assure that the tale not be constrained by an undue focus upon the author, the major personage in *Gentleman Bear* is not Sir Billy Browne-Browne, but a teddybear named Bayard. After all, the achievements of flesh and blood are all too tame a preoccupation when compared with activating the personality of a stuffed creature. That's why few writers would want to confine themselves with uncovering the mundane realities of the man on the street. In the life of the fictional du Bois, only the dates, some of the names, and the superabundance of absurdities sustain a connection with the author. Certainly the real Billy Browne-Browne is so truly and grandly ridiculous in his whims and accomplishments that he would be a hard act to follow. True allegiance, after all, is spiritual not biological. The book provides a steady stream of studied excessiveness, and the most ludicrous revelation of all is that the compounding of excessive improbables turns out to be so calmly rational. The sustained laughter notwithstanding, *Gentleman Bear* makes one wonder if the true absurdities do not reside in the literal reading of one's own pursuits and achievements. Most readers are likely to be convinced, as are all the characters in the book, that we all need the attendance of a stuffed bear, at least through the seemingly important junctures of what we are apt to call life.

—Leonard R. Mendelsohn

DUGGAN, Maurice (Noel)

Nationality: New Zealander. **Born:** Auckland, 25 November 1922. **Education:** University of Auckland. **Family:** Married Barbara Platts in 1945; one child. **Career:** Worked in advertising from 1961: with J. English Wright (Advertising) Ltd. Auckland, 1965-72. **Awards:** Hubert Church Prose award, 1957; New Zealand Library Association Esther Glen award, 1959; Katherine Mansfield Memorial award, for short story, 1959; University of Otago Robert Burns fellowship, 1960; New Zealand Literary Fund scholarship, 1966; Buckland award, 1969. **Died:** 11 December 1974.

Publications for Children

Fiction

Falter Tom and the Water Boy, illustrated by Kenneth Rowell. Auckland, Blackwood and Janet Paul, 1957; London, Faber, and New York, Criterion, 1958.

The Fabulous McFanes and Other Children's Stories, illustrated by Richard Kennedy. Whatamongo Bay, Cape Catley, 1974.

Publications for Adults

Short Stories

Immanuel's Land. Auckland, Pilgrim Press, 1956.

New Authors: Short Story I, with others. London, Hutchinson, 1961.

Summer in the Gravel Pit. Auckland, Blackwood and Janet Paul, and London, Gollancz, 1965.

O'Leary's Orchard and Other Stories. Christchurch, Caxton Press, 1970.

Collected Stories, edited by C.K. Stead. Auckland, Auckland University Press-Oxford University Press, 1981.

* * *

Maurice Duggan's claim to distinction as a children's author stems undoubtedly from his award-winning novel *Falter Tom and the Water Boy.* A collection of three short stories, *The Fabulous McFanes,* reveals a capacity for energetic storytelling and considerable insight into the concerns of childhood; but to *Falter Tom* must go the ultimate tribute. It remains, without doubt, the most distinguished work to have emerged so far from the pen of a New Zealand author for children.

The story is a fantasy, told in simple, almost faultless prose, the whole a mere 64 pages long. Falter Tom, an old, tale-spinning sailor whose nickname derives from a stiff leg which imparts "a peculiar style to his walk" is enticed into the underwater world by the water boy, an ageless child of the sea, a mixture of wisdom and innocence, gravity and gaiety. Duggan's sea-world is a timeless one, a setting in which the old man's age is irrelevant, his lameness unhampering. It is simultaneously a real world, inhabited by live fish, furnished with ghostly wrecks of ancient and modern ships, embellished here and there with lost treasure and spilled cargo. Duggan invents a minimum of artificial detail; even the Sea Kings, who must be consulted, ultimately, as to Falter Tom's destiny, are heard but not seen, their awesome voices intoning the conditions in unison. The boy himself is at once all-child and all-spirit, humanity and immortality.

It would be possible to theorize that Duggan, a man of robust, outdoor temperament to whom the loss of a leg was a major tragedy, and who before his early death suffered in turn a series of debilitating illnesses, saw in Falter Tom's story the enactment of his own wish fulfilment—deliverance from a world in which pain and despair must often have threatened to extinguish the wit and humour that were his by nature. Certainly, the underwater world as Falter Tom, escorted by the boy, experiences it, seems to contain all of eternity. There, the old become young, the halt and the lame are made whole.

But to the child reader, preoccupied quite properly with his own enjoyment of the story, such speculation is irrelevant. The pace and shape of the tale, the humanity of the characters, the green reality of the underwater world, and the mounting of the tension are all. Falter Tom's agony of choice (to remain forever, or to leave and resume mortal life) elevates his story to the level of high drama. His decision is an affirmation of life, his story heroic.

—Dorothy Butler

DUNCAN, Jane

Pseudonym for Elizabeth Jane Cameron. **Other Pseudonym:** Janet Sandison. **Nationality:** British (Scottish). **Born:** Dunbartonshire, Scotland, 10 March 1910. **Education:** Lenzie Academy, Dumbarton; University of Glasgow, M.A. 1930. **Military Service:** Served in the photographic intelligence division of the Women's Auxiliary Air Force, 1939-45: flight officer. **Career** Worked in various jobs, mainly secretarial, 1931-39; worked in the Bahamas, 1945-58. **Died:** 20 October 1976.

Publications for Children

Fiction

Camerons on the Train, illustrated by Victor Ambrus. London, Macmillan, 1963.

Camerons on the Hills, illustrated by Victor Ambrus. London, Macmillan, 1963.
Camerons at the Castle, illustrated by Victor Ambrus. London, Macmillan, 1964; New York, St. Martin's Press, 1965.
Camerons Calling, illustrated by Victor Ambrus. London, Macmillan, and New York, St. Martin's Press, 1966.
Camerons Ahoy!, illustrated by Victor Ambrus. London, Macmillan, and New York, St. Martin's Press, 1968.
Herself and Janet Reachfar, illustrated by Mairi Hedderwick. London, Macmillan, 1975; as *Brave Janet Reachfar,* New York, Seabury Press, 1975.
Janet Reachfar and the Kelpie, illustrated by Mairi Hedderwick. London, Macmillan, and New York, Seabury Press, 1976.
Janet Reachfar and the Chickabird, illustrated by Mairi Hedderwick. London, Macmillan, and New York, Seabury Press, 1978.

Publications for Adults

Novels

My Friends the Miss Boyds. London, Macmillan, and New York, St. Martin's Press, 1959.
My Friend Muriel. London, Macmillan, 1959; New York, St. Martin's Press, 1960.
My Friend Monica. London, Macmillan, and New York, St. Martin's Press, 1960.
My Friend Annie. London, Macmillan, and New York, St. Martin's Press, 1961.
My Friend Sandy. London, Macmillan, 1961; New York, St. Martin's Press, 1962.
My Friend Martha's Aunt. London, Macmillan, and New York, St. Martin's Press, 1962.
My Friend Flora. London, Macmillan, 1962; New York, St. Martin's Press, 1963.
My Friend Madame Zora. London, Macmillan, and New York, St. Martin's Press, 1963.
My Friend Rose. London, Macmillan, and New York, St. Martin's Press, 1964.
My Friend Cousin Emmie. London, Macmillan, 1964; New York, St. Martin's Press, 1965.
My Friends the Mrs. Millers. London, Macmillan, and New York, St. Martin's Press, 1965.
My Friends from Cairnton. London, Macmillan, and New York, St. Martin's Press, 1966.
My Friend My Father. London, Macmillan, 1966; New York, St. Martin's Press, 1967.
My Friends the MacLeans. London, Macmillan, and New York, St. Martin's Press, 1967.
My Friends the Hungry Generation. London, Macmillan, and New York, St. Martin's Press, 1968.
My Friend the Swallow. London, Macmillan, and New York, St. Martin's Press, 1970.
My Friend Sashie. London, Macmillan, and New York, St. Martin's Press, 1972.
My Friends the Misses Kindness. London, Macmillan, and New York, St. Martin's Press, 1974.
My Friends George and Tom. London, Macmillan, and New York, St. Martin's Press, 1976.

Novels as Janet Sandison

An Apology for the Life of Jean Robertson:
Jean in the Morning. London, Macmillan, and New York, St. Martin's Press, 1969.
Jean at Noon. London, Macmillan, 1971; New York, St. Martin's Press, 1972.
Jean in the Twilight; or, The Mists of Autumn. London, Macmillan, 1972; New York, St. Martin's Press, 1973.
Jean Towards Another Day; or, Can Spring Be Far Away? London, Macmillan, and New York, St. Martin's Press, 1975.

Other

Letter from Reachfar (memoir). London, Macmillan, 1975; New York, St. Martin's Press, 1976.

* * *

Jane Duncan's chief contribution to children's literature is a series of five books written about the Cameron family. These imaginary children are based on the author's own nieces and nephews—one sister (the eldest), two brothers a little younger, and a much smaller brother, Iain. Iain—or Nink as he is known to his relatives and friends—is retarded, and the loving relationship between Nink and the rest of the family may well prove most helpful to many readers in a similar situation.

The Cameron children are accustomed to spending their summer holidays with an aunt in Scotland; although they themselves live north of the Border, Aunt Liz lives much further north. Each time they visit her, fresh excitements occur. They become very attached to a Scottish stately home called "Castle Vannich," which in one story is being turned into a hotel to make ends meet, but whatever is happening there becomes part of the tale. As one might expect, there are legends concerning Castle Vannich, notably one around the disappearance of the White Hart of Vannich, and it is little Nink who accidentally solves this mystery.

The characters of the children are cleverly drawn, and the Scottish countryside adds a great deal to the background of the stories. The author weaves a blend of history into each narrative. For example, it may be a professor friend of Aunt Liz who is an expert on Viking ships, so imagine the delight when it seems likely that the remains of a Viking ship may lie buried nearby. It may be the discovery of the stone of Strathdonan, but whatever it is, Jane Duncan's family stories have this additional quality which gives them a certain appeal for historically minded young readers.

It must be borne in mind, however, that these family stories were written in the 1960s and reflect a style of family holiday which, sadly enough, is less common today. Nowadays, individual members of a family tend to go their separate ways. This in no way detracts from the sound values inherent in the Cameron series, and their very difference may well provide an added attraction to some readers.

In 1975 Duncan wrote the first of three picture books which have the same setting—Black Isle in Ross-shire—as her popular novels for adult readers. In *Herself and Janet Reachfar* Janet is the little granddaughter living on the farm, and Herself is, of course, Janet's grandmother. Granny is a wonderful combination of stern attitude and overwhelming warmth. One day there is a sudden snowstorm, and against orders Janet goes with her sheepdog Fly to rescue the sheep marooned on East Hill. Not only does she save the sheep, but finds the first lamb of the spring as well! This is a picture book for younger readers, but ideally it should be read to them, as the author has made no concessions in the text to lack of reading ability.

—Berna C. Clark

DUNCAN, Norman (McLean)

Nationality: Canadian. **Born:** Brantford, Ontario, 2 July 1871. **Education:** University of Toronto, 1891-95. **Career:** Journalist, Auburn *Bulletin,* New York, 1895-97, and New York *Evening Post,* 1897-1900; Newfoundland and Labrador correspondent, *McClure's* magazine, New York, 1900-04; Professor of Rhetoric, Washington and Jefferson College, Washington, Pennsylvania, 1901-06; Middle and Far East correspondent, *Harper's* magazine, New York, 1907, 1912-13; Professor of English, University of Kansas, Lawrence, 1909-11. **Died:** 18 October 1916.

PUBLICATIONS FOR CHILDREN

Fiction

The Adventures of Billy Topsail. New York, Revell, and London, Hodder and Stoughton, 1906.
Billy Topsail and Company. New York, Revell, 1910.
Billy Topsail, M.D.: A Tale of Adventure with Doctor Luke of the Labrador. New York, Revell, 1916; London, Hodder and Stoughton, 1917.

PUBLICATIONS FOR ADULTS

Novels

The Way of the Sea. New York, McClure, 1903; London, Hodder and Stoughton, 1904.
Doctor Luke of the Labrador. New York, Revell, and London, Hodder and Stoughton, 1904.
The Mother. New York, McClure, and London, Hodder and Stoughton, 1905.
The Cruise of the Shining Light. Toronto, Oxford University Press, and New York, Harper, 1907.
Every Man for Himself. New York, Harper, 1908.
The Suitable Child. New York, Revell, 1909.
The Measure of a Man: A Tale of the Big Woods. New York, Revell, 1911; London, Hodder and Stoughton, 1912.
The Best of a Bad Job: A Hearty Tale of the Sea. Toronto, Oxford University Press, and New York, Revell, 1912.
Finding His Soul. New York, Harper, 1913.
The Bird-Store Man: An Old-Fashioned Story. New York, Revell, 1914.
Christmas Eve at Swamp's End. New York, Revell, 1915.
Battles Royal Down North. New York, Revell, 1918.
Harbour Tales Down North. New York, Revell, 1918.

Short Stories

The Soul of the Street: Correlated Stories of the New York Syrian Quarter. New York, McClure, 1900.

Other

Dr. Grenfell's Parish: The Deep Sea Fisherman. Toronto and New York, Revell, and London, Hodder and Stoughton, 1905.
Higgins: A Man's Christian. New York, Harper, 1909.
Going Down from Jerusalem: The Narrative of a Sentimental Traveller, illustrated by Lawren S. Harris. New York, Harper, 1909.
Australian Byways: The Narrative of a Sentimental Traveller, illustrated by George Harding. New York, Harper, 1915.

* * *

Norman Duncan wrote more than twenty books, most of which can be categorized as popular fiction for adults. However, a number of these adult books, such as *The Cruise of the Shining Light,* were read by adolescents as well as by adults. Although the characters in Duncan's books for adults are drawn from subjects as diverse as New York prostitution and the fishermen of Labrador and Newfoundland, it is generally agreed that he is as his best when writing stories of the sea. His technique is to employ a mixture of sentimentality and sharply focused realism, and his emphasis is usually on action and the documentary presentation of a particular region rather than on an in-depth exploration of character.

The popular Billy Topsail novels, which Duncan wrote specifically for young readers, are episodic adventure stories set on the Newfoundland and Labrador coast. The early years of the boy protagonist Billy Topsail are the focus of *The Adventures of Billy Topsail;* the sequel, *Billy Topsail and Company* covers some of the same time-span, but focuses on a merchant-trading venture of Billy's adolescent years; *Billy Topsail, M.D.* again reworks some of the earlier material, but it focusses on Billy's later teen years, during which time he assists Duncan's famous Dr. Luke and decides to become a doctor himself. (The fictional Dr. Luke, based partly on the real Dr. Wilfred T. Grenfell, is the protagonist of *Doctor Luke of the Labrador,* one of Duncan's well-known works for adults.)

Despite some repetition, the novels are exciting to read, and they give the reader a sense of what it was like to grow up on the rugged, sparsely populated Canadian coast around the turn of the century. Billy Topsail is a lively, red-blooded little boy whose curiosity and sense of adventure often take him into danger on either land or sea, but his pluck, common sense, and courage always save him. One memorable portion of the first book, for instance, describes Billy and a friend's encounter with a giant squid who plays dead until the curious boys bring their boat near him; then his ubiquitous tentacles appear from all angles, behind and under their punt, and the terrified boys fight for their lives. Another scene which appears in many variations in the Topsail series is that in which Billy (or someone else, like Dr. Luke) takes a shortcut across the cove on floating ice pans in order to save a life or to do a good deed. These perilous trips, so dangerous because the boys (or men) either may slip off the ice and drown, or fall through "rotten" ice and suffocate, or float out to sea and freeze, serve to underline Duncan's admiration for the hardiness and bravery of these people of Newfoundland and Labrador. *Billy Topsail, M.D.,* for example, includes an extraordinarily effective long episode in which Billy is rushing a little lame boy across th ice in the huge bay on the fateful night that the spring ice breaks up and begins drifting out to sea. The two boys are left helplessly marooned on an ice pan with the starving, vicious, part-wolf sled dogs who try to attack and eat the weakening boys.

Duncan stresses bravery, loyalty, kindness, humour, manners, friendliness, and helpfulness to others, especially weaker people. Although he often lapses into didacticism and sentimental idealization of character, Duncan reveals remarkable narrative and descriptive powers in the Billy Topsail series.

—Mary Rubio

DURACK, (Dame) Mary

Nationality: Australian. **Born:** Adelaide, South Australia, 20 February 1913. **Education:** Loreto Convent, Perth. **Family:** Married Horace Clive Miller in 1938 (died 1980); four daughters (two deceased) and two sons. **Career:** Columnist (as "Virgilia"), Western Australian Newspapers, Perth, 1937-38; worked for Australian Broadcasting Corporation. President, Western Australian Branch, Fellowship of Australian Writers, Swanbourne, 1958-63; from 1983 Emeritus Fellow, Literature Board of Australia. **Awards:** Commonwealth Literary Fund grant, 1973, 1977; Australian Research Committee grant, 1980, 1984; Australian Society of Women Writers Alice award, 1982; Australian Council fellowship, 1983. D.Litt.: University of Western Australia, Nedlands, 1978. O.B.E. (Officer, Order of the British Empire), 1966; D.B.E. (Dame Commander, Order of the British Empire), 1978; AC (Order of Australia), 1989. **Agent:** Curtis Brown (Australia) Pty. Ltd., 86 William Street, Paddington, New South Wales 2021. **Address:** 12 Bellevue Avenue, Nedlands, Western Australia 6009, Australia.

Publications for Children

Fiction

The Way of the Whirlwind, illustrated by Elizabeth Durack. Sydney, Consolidated Press, 1941; London, Angus and Robertson, 1956; revised edition, Angus and Robertson, 1979.

Plays

The Ship of Dreams (produced Fremantle, Western Australia, 1968).
The Way of the Whirlwind, adaptation of her own story (produced Broome, Western Australia, 1970).

Poetry

Little Poems of Sunshine by an Australian Child. Perth, Sampson, 1923.
Piccaninnies, illustrated by Elizabeth Durack. Sydney, Offset Printing, 1940.
The Magic Trumpet, illustrated by Elizabeth Durack. Melbourne, London, and New York, Cassell, 1946.
Kookanoo and Kangaroo, illustrated by Elizabeth Durack. Adelaide, Rigby, 1963; London, Angus and Robertson, 1964; Minneapolis, Lerner, 1966.
Red Jack, illustrated by Michael Wilkin. Melbourne, Macmillan, 1987; London, Macmillan, 1988.

Other

All-About: The Story of a Black Community on Argyle Station, Kimberley, illustrated by Elizabeth Durack. Sydney, The Bulletin, 1935.
Chunuma, illustrated by Elizabeth Durack. Sydney, The Bulletin, 1936.
Son of Djaro, illustrated by Elizabeth Durack. Sydney, The Bulletin, 1938.
To Ride a Fine Horse, illustrated by Elizabeth Durack. Melbourne and London, Macmillan, and New York, St. Martin's Press, 1963.
The Courteous Savage: Yagan of Swan River, illustrated by Elizabeth Durack. Melbourne and London, Nelson, 1964; as *Yagan of the Bibbulmun,* Melbourne, Nelson, 1976.
An Australian Settler, illustrated by David Parry. Melbourne and London, Oxford University Press, 1964; as *A Pastoral Emigrant,* Melbourne, London, and New York, Oxford University Press, 1965.
Tjakamarra: Boy Between Two Worlds. Perth, Vanguard, 1977.

Publications for Adults

Novel

Keep Him My Country. Sydney, Angus and Robertson, and London, Constable, 1955.

Plays

Dalgerie, music by James Penberthy (produced Perth, 1966).
Swan River Saga (produced Perth, 1971). Perth, Service Printing, 1975.

Radio Play: *The Dallying Llama,* 1959.

Other

With Florence Rutter, *Child Artists of the Australian Bush.* London, Harrap, 1950.
Kings in Grass Castles. London, Constable, 1959; reprinted with new introduction, 1979.
The Rock and the Sand. London, Constable, 1969.
To Be Heirs Forever (biography of Eliza Shaw). London, Constable, 1976.
The Aborigines in Australian Literature. Perth, Western Australian Institute of Technology, 1978.
With B. Mulholland, *A Legacy of Love.* Perth, Artlook, 1981.
Sons in the Saddle. London, Constable, 1983.
With others, *The Land Beyond Time.* Sydney, Lansdowne Press, 1984.
With others, *The Stockman.* Sydney, Lansdowne Press, 1984.

Editor, *The Fifth Sparrow,* by M.L. Skinner. Sydney, Sydney University Press, 1972.
Editor, *The End of Dreaming,* by Ingrid A. Drysdale. Adelaide, Rigby, 1974; London, Hale, 1975.

*

In *Reflections—Profile of 150 Women Who Helped Make Western Australia,* Perth, Carroll's, 1978; in *Australia's Writers* by Graeme Kinross-Smith, Sydney, Thomas Nelson, 1980.

* * *

Mary Durack and her sister Elizabeth, whose illustrations form an integral part of all her books, have a unique position in Australian children's literature. As the grandchildren of one of Australia's most picturesque pioneers who drove his flocks and herds thousands of miles through unexplored country in one of the greatest pioneering feats of the 19th century, their name was already known when the *Bulletin* in Sydney published their first book in 1935. This and two subsequent books depicted life on Argyle Station in remote northwestern Australia, telling of the day-to-day events of the aborigines living on the station. Though the books often told of the doings of aboriginal children, they are not necessarily books *for* children. Several years later, in 1941, they produced a real fairy story, *The Way of the Whirlwind.* In the old fairy tale tradition it told of two children who set out on a quest, their adventures, and the ultimate success of their search. But in this story the children were aborigines, whose baby brother had been stolen by a whirlwind. Their search involved them with such creatures, of the spirit or animal world, that imaginary aboriginal children could possibly have encountered. The young children, for whom the book was written, could identify with the aboriginal hero and heroine, and the story was skilfully told, the suspense being maintained throughout. This was at the time the most successful attempt to create a fantasy based on aboriginal life. Though it did not purport to interpret aboriginal mythology, the device lent a new dimension to the conventional fairy story, and it enabled Australian children to relate to the aboriginal children they had probably never seen, and the country and creatures who formed their environment. This story has not the richness or conviction of imaginative power to move the reader as do the great works of the imagination, but its liveliness and originality still appeal to young children. It advanced children's stories in Australia through the author's unselfconscious acceptance of aboriginal characters and a primitive setting, which was then an innovation.

The Magic Trumpet, a lyrical fantasy in verse, was imaginatively illustrated throughout with some of her sister's most successful drawings printed both in colour and in sepia. *The Courteous Savage* is a sympathetic account of the tragic relations between the early white settlers in Western Australia and the aboriginal inhabitants. Mary Durack has interpreted aboriginal life in many books for Australian children with understanding and imagination.

—Marcie Muir

DUVOISIN, Roger (Antoine)

Nationality: American (emigrated to the United States, 1927, naturalized citizen, 1938). **Born:** Geneva, Switzerland, 28 August 1904. **Education:** Ecole Professionelle, Geneva, 1915-17; Ecole des Arts Decoratifs, Geneva, 1917-23, teaching diploma. **Family:** Married Louise Fatio, *q.v.,* in 1925; two sons. **Career:** Stage designer, Geneva Opera, 1922-24; manager of a ceramics firm, Ferney-Voltaire, France, 1924-25; textile designer, in Lyon and Paris, 1927, and for Mallinson Silk Company, New York, 1927-32; Visiting Professor, Parsons School of Art, New York, 1942-50. Freelance illustrator, 1932-60. Group shows: Art Alliance Gallery, Philadelphia, 1946; Museum of Modern Art, New York, 1946; Durand Rue Gallery, New York, 1949; Philadelphia Museum School of Art, 1953; "Graphic Art in the U.S.A.," European tour, 1963; Bratislava Biennale; Rutgers University Museum of Art, 1973. **Awards:** American Library Association Caldecott medal, for illustration, 1948; Society of Illustrators award, 1961; University of Southern Mississippi award, 1971; New York Academy of Science award, for nonfiction, 1975; University of Minnesota Kerlan award, 1976. Honorary Doctorate: Kean College, Union, New Jersey, 1978. **Died:** 30 June 1980.

PUBLICATIONS FOR CHILDREN (ILLUSTRATED BY THE AUTHOR)

Fiction

A Little Boy Was Drawing. New York, Scribner, 1932.

Donkey-Donkey: The Troubles of a Silly Little Donkey. Racine, Wisconsin, Whitman, 1933; London, Chatto Boyd and Oliver, 1969.

All Aboard! New York, Grosset and Dunlap, 1935.

The Christmas Cake in Search of Its Owner. New York, American Artists Group, 1941.

The Christmas Whale. New York, Knopf, 1945.

Chanticleer. New York, Grosset and Dunlap, 1947.

Petunia. New York, Knopf, 1950; London, Lane, 1958.

Petunia and the Song. New York, Knopf, 1951.

A for the Ark. New York, Lothrop, 1952; London, Bodley Head, 1961.

Petunia's Christmas. New York, Knopf, 1952; London, Bodley Head, 1960.

Petunia Takes a Trip. New York, Knopf, 1953; London, Bodley Head, 1959.

Easter Treat. New York, Knopf, 1954.

One Thousand Christmas Beards, See Smith Toy Shop, Eat at Joe's. New York, Knopf, 1955; Kingswood, Surrey, World's Work, 1975.

Two Lonely Ducks: A Counting Book. New York, Knopf, 1955; London, Bodley Head, 1966.

The House of Four Seasons. New York, Lothrop, 1956; Leicester, Brockhampton Press, 1960.

Petunia, Beware! New York, Knopf, 1958; London, Bodley Head, 1962.

Day and Night. New York, Knopf, 1960.

The Happy Hunter. New York, Lothrop, 1961; Edinburgh, Oliver and Boyd, 1962.

Veronica. New York, Knopf, 1961; London, Bodley Head, 1962.

Our Veronica Goes to Petunia's Farm. New York, Knopf, 1962; as *Veronica Goes to Petunia's Farm,* London, Bodley Head, 1963.

Lonely Veronica. New York, Knopf, 1963; London, Bodley Head, 1964.

Spring Snow. New York, Knopf, 1963; Kingswood, Surrey, World's Work, 1966.

Veronica's Smile. New York, Knopf, 1964; London, Bodley Head, 1965.

Petunia, I Love You. New York, Knopf, 1965; London, Bodley Head, 1966.
The Missing Milkman. New York, Knopf, 1967; Kingswood, Surrey, World's Work, 1968.
What Is Right for Tulip. New York, Knopf, 1969.
Veronica and the Birthday Present. New York, Knopf, 1971; London, Bodley Head, 1972.
The Crocodile in the Tree. London, Bodley Head, 1972; New York, Knopf, 1973.
Jasmine. New York, Knopf, 1973; London, Bodley Head, 1974.
Petunia's Treasure. New York, Knopf, 1975; London, Bodley Head, 1977.
Periwinkle. New York, Knopf, 1976.
Crocus. New York, Knopf, and London, Bodley Head, 1977.
Snowy and Woody. New York, Knopf, 1979.
The Importance of Crocus. London, Bodley Head, 1980; New York, Knopf, 1981.
Petunia the Silly Goose Stories: Five Read-Aloud Classics. New York, Knopf, 1987.

Other

And There Was America. New York, Knopf, 1938.
The Three Sneezes and Other Swiss Tales. New York, Knopf, 1941; London, Muller, 1943; as *Fairy Tales from Switzerland,* Muller, 1958.
They Put Out to Sea: The Story of the Map. New York, Knopf, 1943; London, University of London Press, 1947.
The Four Corners of the World. New York, Knopf, 1948.
The Miller, His Son, and Their Donkey. New York, McGraw Hill, 1962; London, Bodley Head, 1963.
See What I Am. New York, Lothrop, 1974; Kingswood, Surrey, World's Work, 1977.

*

Bibliography: *A Roger Duvoisin Bibliography* by Irvin Kerlan, Charlottesville, Bibliographic Society of the University of Virginia, 1958.

Manuscript Collections: Kerlan Collection, University of Minnesota, Minneapolis; University of Oregon Library, Eugene; Rutgers University Library, New Brunswick, New Jersey; de Grummond Collection, University of Southern Mississippi, Hattiesburg.

Illustrator: *Mother Goose* edited by William Rose Benét, 1936; *The Pied Piper of Hamelin* by Robert Browning, 1936; *Riema, Little Brown Girl of Java,* 1937, *Soomoon, Boy of Bali,* 1938, and *Jo-Yo's Idea,* 1939, all by Kathleen Morrow Elliot; *The Feast of Lamps* by Charlet Root, 1938; *Tales of the Pampas* by W.H. Hudson, 1939; *Rhamon, A Boy of Kashmir* by Heluiz Washburne, 1939; *Language Arts for Modern Youth,* 1939; *The Dog Cantbark* by Marjorie Fischer, 1940; *Petits Contes Vrais* by Mary Riley and Andre Humbert, 1940; *Military French,* n.d.; *At Our House* by John G. McCullough, 1943; *A Child's Garden of Verses,* 1944, and *Travels with a Donkey,* 1957, both by Robert Louis Stevenson; *Fair, Fantastic Paris* by Harold Ettlinger, 1944; *Jumpy the Kangaroo* by Janet Howard, 1944; *The Christmas Book of Legends and Stories,* by Elva Smith and Alice Hazeltine, 1944; *Virgin with Butterflies* by Tom Powers, 1945; *The Happy Time* by Robert Fontaine, 1945; *Bhimsa the Dancing Bear* by Christine Weston, 1945; *"I Won't," Said the King* by Mildred Jordan, 1945; *The Life and Adventures of Robinson Crusoe* by Daniel Defoe, 1946; *The Successful Secretary* by Margaret Pratt, 1946; *At Daddy's Office* by Robert Jay Misch, 1946; *Daddies: What They Do All Day,* 1946, and *The Sitter Who Didn't Sit,* 1949, both by Helen Walker Puner; *Moustachio* by Douglas Rigby, 1947; *White Snow, Bright Snow,* 1947, *Johnny Maple-Leaf,* 1948, *Sun Up,* 1949, *Follow the Wind,* 1950, *Hi, Mr. Robin!,* 1950, *Autumn Harvest,* 1951, *Follow the Road,* 1953, *I Saw the Sea Come In,* 1954, *Wake Up, Farm!,* 1955, *Wake Up, City!,* 1957, *The Frog in the Well,* 1958, *Timothy Robbins Climbs the Mountain,* 1960, *Under the Trees and Through the Grass,* 1962, *Hide and Seek Fog,* 1965, *The World in the Candy Egg,* 1967, *It's Time Now!,* 1969, *The Beaver Pond,* 1970, and *What Did You Leave Behind?,* 1978, all by Alvin Tresselt; *The Steam Shovel That Wouldn't Eat Dirt* by George Walters, 1948; *Christmas Pony,* 1948, and *Winkie's World,* 1958, both by William Hall; *The Little Whistler* by Frances Frost, 1949; *The Man Who Could Grow Hair* by William Attwood, 1949; *Dozens of Cousins* by Mabel Watts, 1950; *Vavache, The Cow Who Painted Pictures* by Frederic Attwood, 1950; *Love and Dishes* by Niccolo de Quattrociocchi, 1950; *The Christmas Forest,* 1950, *Anna the Horse,* 1951, *The Happy Lion,* 1954, *The Happy Lion in Africa,* 1955, *The Happy Lion Roars,* 1957, *A Doll for Marie,* 1957, *The Three Happy Lions,* 1959, *The Happy Lion's Quest,* 1961, *Red Bantam,* 1963, *The Happy Lion and the Bear,* 1964, *The Happy Lion's Vacation,* 1967, *The Happy Lion's Treasure,* 1971, *Hector Penguin,* 1973, *The Happy Lion's Rabbits,* 1974, *Marc and Pixie and the Walls in Mrs. Jones's Garden,* 1975, *Hector and Christina,* 1977, and *The Happy Lioness,* 1980, all by Louise Fatio; *The Camel Who Took a Walk,* 1951, and *Tigers Don't Bite,* 1956, both by Jack Tworkov; *Farm Wanted* by Helen Hilles, 1951; *Gian-Carlo Menotti's Amahl and the Night Visitors,* 1952; *The Talking Cat and Other Stories of French Canada* by Natalie Savage Carlson, 1952; *Busby and Co.* by Herbert Coggins, 1952; *Chef's Holiday* by Idwal Jones, 1952; *Tell Me, Little Boy* by Doris Van Liew Foster, 1953; *The Night Before Christmas* by Clement C. Moore, 1954; *Sophocles the Hyena* by James Moran, 1954; *Flash of Washington Square* by Margaret Pratt, 1954; *Little Red Nose* by Miriam Schlein, 1955; *One Step, Two...,* 1955, *Not a Little Monkey,* 1957, *In My Garden,* 1960, and *The Poodle Who Barked at People,* 1964, all by Charlotte Zolotow; *Ride with the Sun* edited by Harold Courlander, 1955; *Trillium Hill* by E.L. Marsh, 1955; *Christmas on the Mayflower* by Wilma Pitchford Hays, 1956; *Bennie, The Bear Who Grew Too Fast* by Beatrice and Ferrin Frasher, 1956; *The Sweet Pattotie Doll,* 1957, *Wobble the Witch Cat,* 1958, *Houn' Dog,* 1959, *The Nine Lives of Homer C. Cat,* 1961, and *The Hungry Leprechaun,* 1962, all by Mary Calhoun; *Does Poppy Live Here?* by Arthur Gregor, 1957; *Wait Till Sunday* by Susan Dorritt, 1957; *The Little Church on the Big Rock* by Hazel Allen, 1958; *Favorite Fairy Tales Told in France* edited by Virginia Haviland, 1959; *A Fish Is Not a Pet* by May Natalie Tabak, 1959; *The Pointed Brush* by Patricia Miles Martin, 1959; *The Three-Cornered Hat* by Pedro Antonio de Alarcón, 1959; *Please Pass the Grass* by Leone Adelson, 1960; *The Children Come Running* by Elizabeth Coatsworth, 1960; *Angelique,* 1960, and *Mr. and Mrs. Button's Wonderful Watchdogs,* 1978, both by Janice; *The Wishing Well in the Woods,* 1961, and *The April Umbrella,* 1963, both by Priscilla and Otto Friedrich; *Lisette,* 1962, *The Rain Puddle,* 1965, and *The Remarkable Egg,* 1968, all by Adelaide Holl; *The Lamb and the Child,* 1963, and *Days of Sunshine, Days* *of Rain,* 1965, both by Dean Frye; *Teddy* by Grete Janus Hertz, 1964; *Around the Corner* by Jean B. Showalter, 1966; *Nubber Bear* by William Lipkind, 1966; *Poems from France* edited by William Jay Smith, 1967; *The Old Bullfrog,* 1968, and *The Web in the Grass,* 1972, both by Berniece Freschet; *Earth and Sky* by Mona Dayton, 1969; *The Owl Book* edited by Richard Shaw, 1970; *Which Is the Best Place?* translated by Mirra Ginsburg, 1976; *What Ever Happened to the Baxter Place?* by Pat Ross, 1976; *Heinz Hobnail and the Great Shoe Hunt* by Anne Duvoisin, 1976.

Roger Duvoisin commented:

(1978) The childhood impressions that are still alive in Louise Fatio and me help us to understand children and to communicate with them. I love the lively curiosity children show toward their surroundings; I love their questions, and the free way they have of expressing their reactions in their conversation, in their drawings and paintings, and even in their poems and letters. Adults often lose this refreshing freedom and curiosity as they form set, conventional opinions about their world. That is why it is so interesting to converse with children, to learn from them as well as to teach them.

It is good to observe that children are now more and more encouraged to express themselves, to create, and that they are taken more seriously. Because of this, making books for children is a more captivating form of art for the writer and illustrator.

* * *

Whether illustrating his own stories or those by others (including his wife, Louise Fatio), Roger Duvoisin's pictures became part of the whole. It's almost impossible to separate his visuals from the texts because Duvoisin's innate and professionally developed gifts insured that his illustrations complement the tales. And this sense of design served him as well in the construction of a narrative; he was an artist with words as well as with his brush. Most critics would agree, however, that the reason for the author-illustrator's lasting appeal is that readers knew he cared, about them and his subjects.

Specifically he was appreciated for his delicious sense of humor, the playfulness which infuses a Duvoisin production even on a serious theme. Everyone loves to laugh at Petunia, the silly goose who convinces herself and the other farm animals that she knows everything because she owns a book. After a succession of convulsive mishaps based on Petunia's pretensions as an expert, she learns: "I can't carry wisdom under my wing...I must learn to read." Another of Duvoisin's charming characters is the cow Jasmine, who argues the case for individuality. Finding a fancy hat, she wears it and sticks to her principles even when the chapeau makes her the laughing-stock of the barnyard.

Jasmine, Petunia, and their companions are well known to millions of children as are Duvoisin's other animal stars—cats, dogs, and more exotic fauna like the hippo and the giraffe. *A for the Ark*—one of the catchiest alphabet books for beginners to cut their literary teeth—brings a whole menagerie to joyous life. And sometimes his plots involve humans as well. In *The House of Four Seasons* Suzy and Billy are helping their parents paint their house, a task which gives Duvoisin the chance to present a nifty lesson in how to create various colors and, not incidentally, to tell a suspenseful story. *The Missing Milkman* invigorates the maxim concerning all work and no play and vice versa. Here we follow the adventures of a dairy worker who runs away to spend a bucolic holiday until idleness palls and duty calls.

In all the original and witty books Roger Duvoisin conjured up for 50 years, he taught implicitly while he entertained. That characteristic is no small part of his appeal.

—Jean F. Mercier

E

EAGER, Edward (McMaken)

Nationality: American. **Born:** Toledo, Ohio, in 1911. **Education:** Harvard University, Cambridge, Massachusetts. **Family:** Married Jane Eberly in 1938; one son. **Died:** 23 October 1964.

Publications for Children

Fiction

Mouse Manor, illustrated by Beryl Bailey-Jones. New York, Farrar Straus, 1952.
Half Magic, illustrated by N.M. Bodecker. New York, Harcourt Brace, and London, Macmillan, 1954.
Playing Possum, illustrated by Paul Galdone. New York, Putnam, 1955.
Knight's Castle, illustrated by N.M. Bodecker. New York, Harcourt Brace, and London, Macmillan, 1956.
Magic by the Lake, illustrated by N.M. Bodecker. New York, Harcourt Brace, and London, Macmillan, 1957.
The Time Garden, illustrated by N.M. Bodecker. New York, Harcourt Brace, 1958; London, Macmillan, 1959.
Magic or Not?, illustrated by N.M. Bodecker. New York, Harcourt Brace, and London, Macmillan, 1959.
The Well-Wishers, illustrated by N.M. Bodecker. New York, Harcourt Brace, 1960; London, Macmillan, 1961.
Seven-Day Magic, illustrated by N.M. Bodecker. New York, Harcourt Brace, 1962; London, Macmillan, 1963.

Poetry

Red Head, illustrated by Louis Slobodkin. Boston, Houghton Mifflin, 1951.

Publications for Adults

Plays

Pudding Full of Plums (produced Cambridge, Massachusetts).
Dream with Music (lyrics only), book by Sidney Sheldon, Dorothy Kilgallen, and Ben Roberts, music by Clay Warnick (produced New York, 1944).
The Liar, with Alfred Drake, music by John Mundy, lyrics by Eager, adaptation of a play by Goldoni (produced New York, 1950).
The Gambler, with Alfred Drake, adaptation of a play by Ugo Betti (produced New York, 1952).
The Adventures of Marco Polo: A Musical Fantasy (lyrics only), book by William Friedberg and Neil Simon, music by Clay Warnick and Mel Pahl (televised, 1956). New York, French, 1959.
Call It Virtue, adaptation of a play by Luigi Pirandello (produced New York, 1963).
Gentlemen, Be Seated, with Jerome Moross, music by Moross, lyrics by Eager (produced New York, 1963).
Rugantino (lyrics only), book by Alfred Drake, music by Armando Trovaioli, adaptation of a play by Pietro Garinei, Sandro Giovanini, Festa Campanile, and Franciosa (produced New York, 1964).
The Happy Hypocrite, music by James Bredt, adaptation of the story by Max Beerbohm (produced New York, 1968).

Television Plays: *The Marriage of Figaro,* from the libretto by Lorenzo da Ponte, music by Mozart, 1954; *The Adventures of Marco Polo* (lyrics only), 1956.

Musical Adaptations: *Orpheus in the Underworld,* music by Jacques Offenbach, National Broadcasting Company (NBC-TV), 1954; *The Marriage of Figaro,* music by Mozart, NBC-TV, 1954.

* * *

Seldom has a major author been imitated so blatantly and in many ways so successfully as E. Nesbit by Edward Eager. In *Half Magic* and its sequels, Eager's indebtedness is gracefully acknowledged; Nesbit is his group of children's favorite author, and they want the sort of real magic that came into her characters' ordinary lives to enter theirs. This magic has rules that enable you to direct it, or, if they are not respected, cause the magic to thwart you.

This basic paradigm Eager takes from Nesbit, along with the family of four or five clever but believable children. The coin of *Half Magic* recalls Nesbit's amulet, *Knight's Castle* the Magic City, the Natterjack of *The Time Garden* is her Psammead, etc. The adventures are like hers and the humor is like hers, perhaps even more abundant. Sometimes there is also a scene, setting, or mood from Baum, Boston, or Carroll. Eager loved books and was a natural at entering the literary worlds of others with appreciation and zest.

Eager's experience of "magic" was almost certainly less deep than Nesbit's. Perhaps he resembled Mr. Smith in *Half Magic,* who says: "The trouble with life is that not enough impossible things happen for us to believe in, don't you agree?" In some of his best books, *Magic or Not?* and *The Well-Wishers,* Eager uses the device of tantalizing uncertainty about the reality of the magic. Nowhere in Eager's books is there the powerful force field of inner psychic happenings that Nesbit can create.

As a fantasist, Eager is looser and less compelling than his model. On the other hand, he is more interested in his characters as people in real relationships. Compare Mr. Smith in *Half Magic* with "the gentleman upstairs" in *The Story of the Amulet.* Eager is at his best when he uses his affection and perceptiveness to delineate his characters and integrate his story at the level of real life. In other books, such as *Seven-Day Magic,* he remains witty and inventive but seems to be repeating his own adaptations.

—Ravenna Helson

EDMONDS, Walter D(umaux)

Nationality: American. **Born:** Boonville, New York, 15 July 1903. **Education:** Cutler School, New York, 1914-16; St. Paul's School, Concord, New Hampshire, 1916-19; Choate School, Wallingford, Connecticut, 1919-21; Harvard University, Cambridge, Massachusetts (staff member, from 1922, secretary, 1924-25, and president, 1925-26, *Harvard Advocate*), 1921-26, A.B. 1926; Utica College, 1993. **Family:** Married 1) Eleanor Livingston Stetson in 1930 (died 1956), one son and two daughters; 2) Katharine Howe Baker-Carr in 1956 (deceased). **Career:** Member of the Board of Overseers, Harvard College, 1945-50; director, 1955-72, and president and publisher, 1957-66, *Harvard Alumni Bulletin.* **Awards:** Harvard University Phi Beta Kappa (honorary); American Library Association Newbery Medal, 1942; National Book award, 1976; Christopher award, 1976. Litt.D.: Union College, Schenectady, New York, 1936; Rutgers University, New Brunswick, New Jersey, 1940; Colgate University, Hamilton, New York, 1947; Harvard University, 1952, Syracuse University Press John Ben Snow Prize, 1995. **Member:** American Academy of Arts and Sciences. **Agent:** Harold Ober Associates, 425 Madison Avenue, New York, New York 10017. **Address:** 27 River Street, Concord, Massachusetts 01742, U.S.A.

Publications for Children

Fiction

The Matchlock Gun, illustrated by Paul Lantz. New York, Dodd Mead, 1941.
Tom Whipple, illustrated by Paul Lantz. New York, Dodd Mead, 1942.
Two Logs Crossing: John Haskell's Story, illustrated by Tibor Gergely. New York, Dodd Mead, 1943.
Wilderness Clearing, illustrated by John de Martelly. New York, Dodd Mead, 1944.
Cadmus Henry, illustrated by Manning Lee. New York, Dodd Mead, 1949.
Mr. Benedict's Lion, illustrated by Doris Lee. New York, Dodd Mead, 1950.
Corporal Bess, illustrated by Manning Lee. New York, Dodd Mead, 1952.
Hound Dog Moses and the Promised Land, illustrated by William Gropper. New York, Dodd Mead, 1954.
Uncle Ben's Whale, illustrated by William Gropper. New York, Dodd Mead, 1955.
They Had a Horse, illustrated by Douglas Gorsline. New York, Dodd Mead, 1962.
Time to Go House, illustrated by Joan Berg Victor. Boston, Little Brown, 1969.
Seven American Stories, illustrated by William Sauts Bock. Boston, Little Brown, 1970.
Wolf Hunt, illustrated by William Sauts Bock. Boston, Little Brown, 1970.
Beaver Valley, illustrated by Leslie Morrill. Boston, Little Brown, 1971.
The Story of Richard Storm, illustrated by William Sauts Bock. Boston, Little Brown, 1974.
Bert Breen's Barn. Boston, Little Brown, 1975.
The Night Raider and Other Stories. Boston, Little Brown, 1980.

Publications for Adults

Novels

Rome Haul. Boston, Little Brown, and London, Sampson Low, 1929.
The Big Barn. Boston, Little Brown, 1930; London, Sampson Low, 1931.
Erie Water. Boston, Little Brown, 1933; London, Hurst and Blackett, 1934.
Drums along the Mohawk. Boston, Little Brown, and London, Jarrolds, 1936.
Chad Hanna. Boston, Little Brown, and London, Collins, 1940.
Young Ames. Boston, Little Brown, and London, Collins, 1942.
In the Hands of the Senecas. Boston, Little Brown, and London, Collins, 1947; as *The Captive Woman,* New York, Bantam, 1962.
The Wedding Journey. Boston, Little Brown, 1947.
The Boyds of Black River. New York, Dodd Mead, and London, Collins, 1953.
The South African Quirt. Boston, Little Brown, 1985.

Short Stories

Mostly Canallers: Collected Stories. Boston, Little Brown, 1934.

Other

Moses. Privately printed, 1939.
The First Hundred Years, 1848-1948: 1848, Oneida Community; 1880, Oneida Community Limited; 1935, Oneida Ltd. Oneida, New York, Oneida Ltd., 1948; revised edition, 1958.
They Fought with What They Had: The Story of the Army Air Forces in the Southwest Pacific 1941-1942. Boston, Little Brown, 1951.
The Erie Canal: The Story of the Digging of Clinton's Ditch. Utica, New York, Munson Williams Proctor Institute, 1960.
The Musket and the Cross: The Struggle of France and England for North America. Boston, Little Brown, 1968.
Tales My Father Never Told. Syracuse, Syracuse University Press, 1995.

*

Critical Studies: *Walter D. Edmonds, Storyteller* by Lionel D. Wyld, Syracuse, New York, Syracuse University Press, 1982.

Walter D. Edmonds comments:

I am no good at this sort of thing, but perhaps my remarks accepting the National Book award for *Bert Breen's Barn* may be apropos.

"It's a fine thing to be given a National Book award, and I am deeply grateful—though I'm not sure my book deserves recognition as a book for children. I'm not sure there really is such a book, anyway. The great children's classics belong equally to adults. Though I have no classics to my name, all but three of my children's books' appeared originally in adult magazines or were written for adult readers. The three I started out deliberately to write for children seem to me not much more so than the others—which may, I see, be a commentary on my writing. So I think categories do not mean a great deal. The story is the important thing.

"In *Bert Breen's Barn* I set out to make a story about an occurrence that happened on our place and neighborhood in upstate

New York when I was a very small boy, just learning to tie my own shoes. As a matter of fact it was an old man on whom I modelled the character of Birdy Morris who showed me how to tie the laces so they never came undone, until you wanted them to. I did not write the story for children but for my own pleasure, finding myself, in the process, overwhelmed with remembrances of how things were just after the turn of the century and by the qualities of life we were brought up to think valuable.

"So to be given a National Book award near the end of fifty years of writing means a great deal more than I can put into words. Especially as I never have been much of a hand to win a prize. Except in marriage."

* * *

Although Walter D. Edmonds has been known as a fine writer of adult books, his work for children has been equally well received. His first, *The Matchlock Gun,* won the Newbery Medal; a later novel, and his best so far, *Bert Breen's Barn,* won the 1976 National Book Award.

Edmonds now lives in Concord, Massachusetts, but it is the Boonville area of New York in the Mohawk Valley, the place he returns to each summer, that he uses for the settings for most of his books. Through his skill as a writer, he recreates the past there, thoroughly immersing the reader in various periods with his clear prose. In *The Matchlock Gun,* set in the 18th century, savage Indians on the warpath attacking innocent people may now seem one-sided from the perspective of the 1980's because social attitudes have changed a great deal in the last 40 years. Time has a way of giving a different view, but the book remains effective.

Bert Breen's Barn, set around Boonville at the beginning of the 20th century, is quality writing for young adults. The simple but eloquent prose, laced with country imagery ("like a raccoon peering sideways through the slats of a chicken coop") and vernacular, first catches the reader and then absorbs him completely in the narrative. The pace is steady, but suspense builds as the characters become more sharply defined and the plot unfolds. Although there is a search for buried treasure, this is no run-of-the-mill mystery story and hunt, but a well-crafted book that improves with each rereading. With its strong emphasis on characterization, the novel should appeal to readers for generations to come.

All of Edmonds's books contain strong characterizations that have much in common: many of the protagonists have an indomitable, unquenchable spirit that keeps them going even in the face of adversity, and that determination, combined with a strong moral fiber, creates a sure knowledge in the reader that the character will succeed. Edward, in *The Matchlock Gun,* kills the Indians and saves his mother and sister; Tom, in *Bert Breen's Barn,* gains his family a fine reputation (they had been considered shiftless) through his hard work and honesty; in two shorter works, *Two Logs Crossing* and *They Had a Horse,* each protagonist's determination brings success out of failure. The successes are hard-won, often preceded by tears and discouragement, but these weaknesses make the characters more convincing. In *They Had a Horse* the final scene where Jacob's tears mingle with his wife's remains with the reader long after the tale has been finished. In most of the books, too, the protagonists are willing to heed the advice of others.

Edmonds has said that, except for three books, he has not intentionally written for children. His latest book perhaps demonstrates that best, for *The Night Raider and Other Stories* contains four tales for older readers or adults. Set in the Boonville area, each is very different from the others, even the humorous ones: "Perfection of Orchard View" includes great comic correspondence between a gentleman farmer and his hired hand about a prize pig, and "Charlie Phister's Famous Bee Shot" demonstrates how gullible people can be. The other two tales are much more somber, especially "Raging Canal," which reveals the brutality that many boy canallers had to face. "The Night Raider" gradually discloses a mystery: something is killing the guinea hens. When the raiding owl is discovered and caught, but not killed, the result is a moving one.

In all of his books, for children or for adults, Edmonds displays his skill with words. He has an ear carefully tuned to each situation, and he plays with the language accordingly. He can be detailed in his description when it serves his purpose, or spare, and simple; his humor can be tongue-in-cheek or satirical; and he ably uses dialogue to reveal character as well as to further the action. His books stand up well to rereading, the ultimate test of any writer.

—Marilyn F. Apseloff

EDMUND, Sean. See **PRINGLE, Laurence P(atrick).**

EDWARDS, Dorothy

Nationality: British. **Born:** Dorothy Brown, Teddington, Middlesex, 6 November 1914. **Education:** Schools in Teddington and Sunbury. **Family:** Married Francis P. Edwards in 1942; one daughter and one son. **Career:** Secretary for Odeon cinemas; freelance editor for many years, and producer of *Listen with Mother* series, 1969-70, BBC, London; lecturer and broadcaster. **Awards:** Children's Rights Workshop Other award, 1975, 1981. **Died:** 9 August 1982.

Publications for Children

Fiction

My Naughty Little Sister: Stories from "Listen with Mother," illustrated by Henrietta Garland. London, Methuen, 1952.

My Naughty Little Sister and Some Others, illustrated by Caroline Guthrie. London, Methuen, 1957.

My Naughty Little Sister's Friends, illustrated by Una J. Place. London, Methuen, 1962.

When My Naughty Little Sister Was Good, illustrated by Shirley Hughes. London, Methuen, 1968.

Tales of Joe and Timothy, illustrated by Reintje Venema. London, Methuen, 1969.

All about My Naughty Little Sister, illustrated by Shirley Hughes. London, Methuen, 1969.

Listen, Listen!, illustrated by Elizabeth Davies. London, BBC Publications, 1970.
More Naughty Little Sister Stories, illustrated by Shirley Hughes. London, Methuen, 1970.
Peter Nick-Nock and the Cuckoo Clock, illustrated by Alexy Pendle. London, Transworld, 1971.
Roger's Trains, illustrated by Alexy Pendle. London, Transworld, 1971.
Joe and Timothy Together, illustrated by Reintje Venema. London, Methuen, 1971.
Janie's Cooking Day, illustrated by Elizabeth Davies. London, Transworld, 1973.
Sam's Woolly Hat, illustrated by Elizabeth Davies. London, Transworld, 1973.
My Naughty Little Sister and Bad Harry, illustrated by Shirley Hughes. London, Methuen, 1974.
The Magician Who Kept a Pub and Other Stories, illustrated by Jill Bennett. London, Kestrel, 1975.
A Wet Monday, illustrated by Jenny Williams. London, Methuen, 1975; New York, Morrow, 1976.
Dad's New Car, illustrated by John Dyke. London, Methuen, 1976.
My Naughty Little Sister Goes Fishing, illustrated by Shirley Hughes. London, Methuen, 1976.
My Naughty Little Sister and Bad Harry's Rabbit, illustrated by Shirley Hughes. London, Methuen, 1977; Englewood Cliffs, New Jersey, Prentice Hall, 1981.
My Naughty Little Sister at the Fair, illustrated by Shirley Hughes. London, Methuen, 1979.
Here's Sam, illustrated by David Higham. London, Methuen, 1979.
A Strong and Willing Girl, illustrated by Robert Micklewright. London, Methuen, 1980.
Crash!!, illustrated by Lynne Cousins. London, Hippo, 1980.
The Witches and the Grinnygog. London, Faber, 1981.
My Naughty Little Sister and *My Naughty Little Sister's Friends* (collections), illustrated by Shirley Hughes. London, Methuen, 2 vols., 1982.
The Old Man Who Sneezed: Read Aloud Stories, illustrated by Thelma Lambert. London, Methuen, 1983.
Mark the Drummer-Boy. London, Methuen, 1983.
Emmie and the Purple Paint, illustrated by Priscilla Lamont. London, Methuen, 1984.
Robert Goes to Fetch a Sister, illustrated by Carolyn Dinan. London, Methuen, 1986.
King Dicky Bird and the Bossy Princess. London, Methuen, 1987.

Plays

Radio Plays: *The Girl Who Wanted to Eat Boys,* 1974; *The Old Woman Who Lived in a Real Glass Vinegar Bottle,* 1976; *Listen with Mother* series.

Television Scripts: *Playschool* series.

Poetry

Listen and Play Rhymes 1-2, illustrated by Prudence Seward. London, Methuen, 2 vols., 1973.

Other

Look, Look, A Cookery Book, illustrated by Prudence Seward. London, Methuen, 1973.
Look, Look, My Garden Book, illustrated by Prudence Seward. London, Methuen, 1973.
A Look, See and Touch Book, illustrated by Peter Edwards. London, Methuen, 1976.
A Walk Your Fingers Story, illustrated by Peter Edwards. London, Methuen, 1976.
My Naughty Little Sister's Birthday Book, illustrated by Shirley Hughes. London, Methuen, 1982.

Editor, *"Listen with Mother" Stories,* illustrated by Caroline Sharpe. London, BBC Publications, 1972.
Editor, *The Read-to-Me Story Book,* illustrated by Lynnette Hemmant. London, Methuen, 1974.
Editor, *The Read-to-Me-Another Story Book,* illustrated by Jenny Williams. London, Methuen, 1976.
Editor, *Once, Twice, Thrice upon a Time,* illustrated by Juliette Palmer. Guildford, Surrey, Lutterworth Press, 1976.
Editor, *Once, Twice, Thrice and Then Again,* illustrated by Juliette Palmer. Guildford, Surrey, Lutterworth Press, 1976.
Editor, *Ghosts and Shadows,* illustrated by Jane Walmsley. Guildford, Surrey, Lutterworth Press, 1980.
Editor, *Mists and Magic,* illustrated by Jill Bennett. Guildford, Lutterworth Press, 1983.

* * *

Children delight in tales of bad behaviour in their peers and who could sound more promising than "My Naughty Little Sister" and her boon companion Bad Harry. The enormous following and affection for the Naughty Little Sister stories, Dorothy Edwards's chief success, stem from several masterly devices. The first must be the use of the first person throughout. There is the obvious connotation of once upon a time when Mummy (or Granny or whoever is reading the story) was young and all the implications of the story unfolding with the added bonus of the closeness of the relationship. There is the marvellous mixture of envy, respect, and disapproval evinced by the older sister—somehow above such bad behaviour and yet longing to be young and carefree again. The stories are just the right length for reading aloud, and there is enough action and development to satisfy both reader and listener. The style is conversational (very suited to the late lamented *Listen with Mother* which first broadcast many of the stories), and the stories of simple everyday adventures. Above all else there are the warmth and security of the family. Whatever awful thing My Naughty Little Sister does, all ends well, on the "and they all lived happily ever after" note.

Joe and Timothy, and Sam, are less successful creations, lacking the character and indomitable will of the Naughty Little Sister, but well worth closer attention is *A Strong and Willing Girl,* winner of the Other Award. The girl in question was Edwards's own Auntie Nan, and the book portrays in fascinating detail what it was like to be in service in Victorian times. Again the style is conversational, confiding, but richly humorous and full of life. The picture painted is realistic without being melodramatic or sentimental, and the book eminently readable.

All Edwards's books are full of domestic detail, and herein lies much of their appeal—the familiar and the recognizable, bound together in day-to-day adventures.

—Fiona Waters

EDWARDS, Monica (le Doux)

Nationality: British. **Born:** Belper, Derbyshire, 8 November 1912. **Education:** Wakefield High School; Thornes House School, Wakefield; St. Brandon's School for the Daughters of the Clergy, Bristol. **Family:** Married William Edwards in 1933; one son and one daughter. **Agent:** Curtis Brown Ltd., 162-168 Regent Street, London W1R 5TB, England. **Address:** Cowdray Cross, Thursley, Godalming, Surrey, England.

Publications for Children

Fiction

Wish for a Pony, illustrated by Anne Bullen. London, Collins, 1947.
No Mistaking Corker, illustrated by Anne Bullen. London, Collins, 1947.
The Summer of the Great Secret, illustrated by Anne Bullen. London, Collins, 1948.
The Midnight Horse, illustrated by Anne Bullen. London, Collins, 1949; New York, Vanguard Press, 1950.
The White Riders, illustrated by Geoffrey Whittam. London, Collins, 1950.
Black Hunting Whip, illustrated by Geoffrey Whittam. London, Collins, 1950.
Punchbowl Midnight, illustrated by Charles Tunnicliffe. London, Collins, 1951.
Cargo of Horses, illustrated by Geoffrey Whittam. London, Collins, 1951.
Spirit of Punchbowl Farm, illustrated by Joan Wanklyn. London, Collins, 1952.
Hidden in a Dream, illustrated by Geoffrey Whittam. London, Collins, 1952.
The Wanderer, illustrated by Joan Wanklyn. London, Collins, 1953.
Storm Ahead, illustrated by Geoffrey Whittam. London, Collins, 1953.
No Entry, illustrated by Geoffrey Whittam. London, Collins, 1954.
Punchbowl Harvest, illustrated by Joan Wanklyn. London, Collins, 1954.
The Nightbird, illustrated by Geoffrey Whittam. London, Collins, 1955.
Frenchman's Secret, illustrated by Geoffrey Whittam. London, Collins, 1956.
Strangers to the Marsh, illustrated by Geoffrey Whittam. London, Collins, 1957.
Operation Seabird, illustrated by Geoffrey Whittam. London, Collins, 1957.
The Cownappers, illustrated by Geoffrey Whittam. London, Collins, 1958.
Killer Dog, illustrated by Sheila Rose. London, Collins, 1959.
No Going Back, illustrated by Geoffrey Whittam. London, Collins, 1960.
The Outsider, illustrated by Geoffrey Whittam. London, Collins, 1961.
The Hoodwinkers, illustrated by Geoffrey Whittam. London, Collins, 1962.
Dolphin Summer, illustrated by Geoffrey Whittam. London, Collins, 1963; New York, Hawthorn, 1971.
Fire in the Punchbowl, illustrated by Geoffrey Whittam. London, Collins, 1965.
The Wild One, illustrated by Geoffrey Whittam. London, Collins, 1967.
Under the Rose, illustrated by Richard Kennedy. London, Collins, 1968.
A Wind Is Blowing. London, Collins, 1969.

Plays

Joan Goes Farming. London, Lane, 1954.
Rennie Goes Riding. London, Lane, 1956.
The Dawn Killer (screenplay). 1958.

Publications for Adults

The Unsought Farm. London, Joseph, 1954.
The Cats of Punchbowl Farm. London, Joseph, and New York, Doubleday, 1964.
The Badgers of Punchbowl Farm. London, Joseph, 1966.
The Valley and the Farm. London, Joseph, 1971.
Badger Valley. London, Joseph, 1976.

*

Monica Edwards comments:
My books for children are all based on fact. They form two series: one ("Romney Marsh") was inspired by my own youth in a Sussex fishing village, the other ("Punchbowl Farm") by my children's life on a Surrey farm. Both places are real, and the events can be followed on Ordnance Survey maps for the areas.

* * *

From a seemingly inauspicious start in the late 1940s, with the publication of *Wish for a Pony* and *No Mistaking Corker,* Monica Edwards developed two very real and memorable series in the "Romney Marsh" and "Punchbowl" books. In spite of the heavy emphasis on the pony-lovers in the first two books, there was even then a noticeable depth of character in the children, usually missing from the horse-show-and-rosette story which was published in such great numbers in the late 1940s and 1950s. Edwards takes each character and builds identity within a setting she knows and, obviously, loves.

Tamzin, Rissa, Roger, and Meryon love the Romney Marsh, with its sheep and wide sky and distant sea, and their adventures in and around it often arise out of the plight of one aspect of their way of life: the fishing in *The Nightbird,* or sheep farming in *The White Riders* and *No Entry.* The author is not afraid of blood and fighting as in *Cargo of Horses,* or of the emotional problems of growing up, in *No Going Back* and *A Wind Is Blowing.*

The Thorntons of Punchbowl Farm move from Hampshire into Surrey after the caravan holiday described in the first person by Lindsey in *No Mistaking Corker.* These are much more family stories, with Andrea, Dion, Lindsey, and Peter leading normal, bickering, loving family lives in the setting of the wild Devil's Punchbowl and the derelict farm they own beside it. Most of the adventures in this series arise out of normal farming crises, like the animals poisoned by yew in *Spirit of Punchbowl Farm,* or the escaping animals in *The Wanderer.* Andrea is followed through her adolescent years, Lindsey remains staunch in her defence of wild creatures and the old ways, and Dion's ever-present determination to farm the wild acres is seen to reach fruition by the last in the series—*The Wild One.* Peter alone plays no major part in any of the stories, except to preserve normality by being the imitating younger brother whose mice have always got out or who needs looking after. Touches of time travel and fantasy (in *Black Hunting Whip* and *Spirit of Punchbowl Farm*) add to the exceptional quality of these realistic tales of farm life.

As Edwards herself shows from the beginning of her writing a touch of the qualities of Arthur Ransome, whose titles are often mentioned in her text, so is she now being seen to influence the writings of younger authors. Much of her style of writing is apparent in the books by Tasmanian author Anne Farrell, who quotes Edwards titles as Edwards quoted Ransome. Such developments are proof of the author's quality: that her writing ability is admirable, and that her stories are memorable.

—Mary Nettlefold

EHLERT, Lois (Jane)

Nationality: American. **Born:** Beaver Dam, Wisconsin, 9 November 1934. **Education:** Graduated from Layton School of Art, Milwaukee, Wisconsin, B.F.A. 1957; University of Wisconsin, graduate study 1959. **Family:** Married John Reiss, 1967 (separated 1977). **Career:** Writer and illustrator; teacher, Layton School of Art Junior School; layout and production assistant, John Higgs Studio, Milwaukee, Wisconsin; freelance illustrator and designer, from 1962; designer of toys and games for children, a series of basic art books, banners for libraries and public spaces, posters and brochures, and sets for the Moppet Players, a children's theater. Exhibits include Creativity on Paper Show, New York, 1964, Society of Illustrators shows, 1971, 1989, and 1990, and International Children's Book Exhibit, Bologna, Italy, 1979. **Awards:** Best Children's Book citation, New York Public Library, 1987, for *Growing Vegetable Soup*; Pick of the Lists citation, American Booksellers, 1988, and New York Public Library Best Children's Book citation, Outstanding Science Trade Books for Children by the National Science Teachers Association, and John Burroughs list of nature books for young readers, all 1989, all for *Planting a Rainbow*; Pick of the Lists citation, American Booksellers, Book-of-the-Month Club Selection, and *Parenting* magazine's Reading Magic award, all 1989, all for *Eating the Alphabet*; Pick of the Lists citation, American Booksellers, 1989, and Caldecott Honor Book, American Library Association, 1990, for *Color Zoo*; Notable Children's Books, American Library Association, Book-of-the-Month Club Citation, and *Boston Globe/Horn Book* Honor award, 1990, Parent's choice award, 1991, both for *Chicka Chicka Boom Boom*; National Science Teachers Association award, 1990, and Silver Award, Dimensional Illustrators Awards Show, 1991, both for *Color Farm*; *Parenting* magazine Best Books citation, 1990, for *Color Farm* and *Fish Eyes*; *New York Times* Ten Best Illustrated Books, Parent's Choice Honor for Story Books, Certificate of Merit, Graphics Arts Awards, both 1990, and Children's Choices, IRA-CBC, 1993, all for *Fish Eyes*; *Redbook*'s Ten Best Picture Books, 1990, *Boston Globe/Horn Book* Nonfiction Honor Award, 1992, Outstanding Science Trade Book, National Science Teachers Association, 1993, all for *Feathers for Lunch*; Certificate of Excellence, *Parenting* magazine, 1991, Outstanding Science Trade Book, National Science Teachers Association, 1991, Elizabeth Burr Award of the Wisconsin Library Association, 1992, *Boston Globe/Horn Book* Nonfiction Honor Book, 1992, and California children's Media Award for Nonfiction, 1992, all for *Red Leaf, Yellow Leaf*; Gold Award, Dimensional Illustrators Awards Show, 1991, for *Color Zoo*; First Place, New York Book Show, for Juvenile Trade Specialty, and *Parenting* magazine's Reading Magic Awards, the year's ten best books, both 1992, both for *Circus*; New York Public Library Best Children's Books, ALA Notable Book, *Booklist* Editors' Choice, all 1992, and *Horn Book*'s Fanfare list, 1993, all for *Moon Rope*; Best Book Children's Books, Printing Industry of America, 1994, for *Nuts to You!*; Gold Seal Award, Oppenheim Portfolio, 1996, for *Eating the Alphabet*; New York Book Show Award, 1996, *Snowballs*; Best Books of 1997, *Book Links, Parenting* Magazine Reading Magic Award, and *Booklist* Editors' Choice, 1997, for *Hands*; D.H.L.: University of Wisconsin, Milwaukee, 1994. **Address:** c/o Children's Books, Harcourt Brace and Company, 525 B Street, Suite 1900, San Diego, California 92101, U.S.A.

PUBLICATIONS FOR CHILDREN (ILLUSTRATED BY THE AUTHOR)

I Like Orange. New York, Franklin, 1961.
Making Music Your Own. Silver-Burdett, 1962.
Animals to See 1 2 3. Racine, Wisconsin, Western Publishing, 1963.
Limericks by Lear. Cleveland, Ohio, world, 1965.
What Is that Sound? New York, Atheneum, 1967.
Mathematical Games for 1 or 2. New York, Crowell, 1971.
Milwaukee Children's Zoo. E.F. Schmidt, 1972.
The Great Flower Pie. New York, Bradbury, 1972.
Sing a Song of Sound. Scroll Press, 1973.
What Do You Think I Saw? New York, Pantheon, 1975.
The Visit. New York, Knopf, 1976.
Number Families. Crowell Publishing, 1978.
Beginning to Learn about Shapes. Raintree, 1979.
Growing Vegetable Soup. San Diego, Harcourt, 1987.
Planting a Rainbow. San Diego, Harcourt, 1988.
Color Zoo. New York, HarperCollins, 1989.
Eating the Alphabet: Fruits and Vegetables from A to Z. San Diego, Harcourt, 1989.
Rat-Tat-Tat, Thump, Thump. New York, HarperCollins, 1989.
Chicka Chicka Boom Boom. New York, Simon and Schuster, 1989.
Color Farm. New York, HarperCollins, 1990.
Feathers for Lunch. San Diego, Harcourt, 1990.
Fish Eyes: A Book You Can Count On. San Diego, Harcourt, 1990.
Red Leaf, Yellow Leaf. San Diego, Harcourt, 1991.
Circus. New York, HarperCollins, 1992.
Moon Rope: A Peruvian Folktale/ Un lazo a la luna: una layenda peruana (translated into Spanish by Amy Prince). San Diego, Harcourt, 1992.
Nuts to You! San Diego, Harcourt, 1993.
Mole's Hill: A Woodland Tale. San Diego, Harcourt, 1994.
Crocodile Smile. New York, HarperCollins, 1994.
Snowballs. San Diego, Harcourt, 1995.
Under My Nose. Katonah, New York, Richard C. Owen, 1996.
Cuckoo: A Mexican Folktale/Cucú: Un cuento folklórico mexicano (translated into Spanish by Gloria de Aragón Andújar). San Diego, Harcourt, 1997.

Hands. San Diego, Harcourt, 1997.
Top Cat. San Diego, Harcourt, 1998.

*

Manuscript Collection: Kerlan Collection, University of Minnesota.

Illustrator: *I Like Orange* by Patricia M. Zens, 1961; *Limericks* by Edward Lear, 1965; *What Is That Sound!* by Mary L. O'Neill, 1966; *Mathematical Games for One or Two* by Mannis Charosh, 1972; *Great Flower Pie* by Andrea Di Noto, 1973; *Sing a Song of Sound* by Vicki Silvers, 1973; *What Do You Think I Saw?: A Nonsense Number Book* by Nina Sazer, 1976; *The Visit* by Diane Wolkstein, 1977; *Number Families* by Jane J. Srivastava, 1979; *Shapes* by Richard Allington, 1979; *Chicka Chicka Boom Boom* by Bill Martin, Jr. and John Archambault, 1989; *Thump, Thump, Rat-a-tat-tat* by Gene Baer, 1989; *Words* by Bill Martin and John Archambault, 1993; *Crocodile Smile* by Sarah Weeks, 1994; *A Pair of Socks* by Stuart J. Murphy, 1996; *Angel Hide and Seek* by Ann Turner, 1998.

Critical Studies: "The Artist at Work: Card Tables and Collage" by Anita Silvey, in *Horn Book,* November-December 1991, 695-704; "Lois Ehlert," in *Talking with Artists* by Pat Cummings, New York, Bradbury, 1991, 36-41; "Alive with Color: An Interview with Lois Ehlert" by Connie Goddard, in *Publisher's Weekly,* 12 February 1992, 18-19; entry in *Something about the Author,* Vol. 69, Detroit, Gale, 1992; "Lois Ehlert" in *Children's Book Illustration and Design,* edited by Julie Cummins, New York, Library of Applied Design, 1992, 50-52; entry in *Children's Literature Review,* Vol. 28, Detroit, Gale, 1992; *Color World: A Video Visit* (video), Orlando, Florida, Harcourt, 1994; "Lois Ehlert" by Maeve Visser Knoth, in *Children's Books and Their Creators,* edited by Anita Silvey, Boston, Houghton Mifflin, 1995, 220-22.

* * *

Lois Ehlert's background as a graphic artist and designer is evident in her innovative, colorful, and visually stunning books. These are books that immediately capture the attention with their boldness while they also reward deeper looking and repeated readings. In each of them, Ehlert's attention to detail and her involvement in the total design of the books is evident. In some ways her books are like puzzles, both for Ehlert herself as she becomes totally involved in the complexities of their creation, and for the reader who uncovers additional details, connections, patterns, and delights as time goes by.

Ehlert was not satisfied with her earliest attempts at creating books in the 1960s. The technology available for printing could not do justice to her colors. "The printed book was so awful that I didn't want a child to have it," she told Anita Silvey in her 1992 *Horn Book* interview. At that time she wasn't given permission to go to the printer to approve colors on a press run for a book the way she was allowed to do with her graphic arts projects. But as years passed and there was more emphasis on graphics in picture books, and friends and colleagues spurred her on, she decided the time was right to try again. A course in book-making at the University of Wisconsin encouraged her to explore and experiment, resulting in the book that eventually became *Color Zoo* (1989). "That was the start of what I consider almost a second career in the children's book field—a twenty-five-year overnight success story!" she told Silvey.

For the most part *Growing Vegetable Soup* (1987), the first book Ehlert wrote and illustrated in her second career, was greeted with enthusiasm by critics and reviewers. "The boldest, brassiest garden book to hit the market, and what a delight," wrote Barbara Peklo Serling in *School Library Journal.* But others criticized the colors as "painfully vivid" and decried the book's "minimal information" and failure to depict the vegetables and garden tools in a more true-to-life manner. "A plausible notion for a book, shouted down by garish illustrations," wrote a reviewer for *Kirkus Reviews.* Despite the reservations of these reviewers, the book has remained in print and is available in several editions.

Although Ehlert's use of bold shapes and colors and her experiments with positive and negative space and figure/ground may be startling in the world of children's books, her style is reminiscent of the cut paper designs of Matisse, as well as of works by such pop and op art artists as Frank Stella and Robert Indiana; for example, Stella's "Protractor" painting, and the famous Indiana "Love" design that became a best-selling postage stamp. Ehlert has also drawn on folk traditions, including "ancient Peruvian textiles, jewelry, ceramic vessels, sculpture, and architectural detail" in the bilingual *Moon Rope* (1992); the ribbon applique, and beadwork designs of Woodland Indians in *Mole's Hill* (1994); and Mexican "cut-paper fiesta banners, tin work, textiles, metal *milagros,* clay, 'tree of life' candelabra, and wooden toys and sculptures" for her retelling of the Mayan *Cuckoo* (1997). All of these influences are carefully detailed in notes in the books themselves.

The art in *Growing Vegetable Soup, Circus, Moon Rope,* and *Cuckoo* consists of colored paper layered upon vividly colored or black backgrounds, sometimes resulting in a sense of vibration between adjacent colors. In other books, such as *Red Leaf, Yellow Leaf* and *Snowballs,* Ehlert constructs her collages out of actual objects, ribbons, seeds, bottle caps, string, twigs, and pieces of clothing, as well as varieties of layered paper. In *Snowballs* Ehlert actually provides a photographed page of the "good stuff" or found objects she used to decorate her snow family, thus inspiring children and teachers to make their own collections of objects to use in their designs. Reader participation is strongly encouraged in most of Ehlert's books. An easy-to-make soup recipe is included in *Growing Vegetable Soup,* a recipe for popcorn balls in *Snowballs,* and directions for selecting and planting a tree in *Red Leaf, Yellow Leaf.* Collage itself is a technique that lends itself to children's creations.

Beginning with *Color Zoo* Ehlert also experimented with die-cut pages. In this book and in the companion *Color Farm* Ehlert has ingeniously used cut-out windows in various geometric shapes to create her animals, providing a stunning demonstration of the relationships between shapes, the possibilities in their combinations, and the way various colors and shapes transform each other when used in combination. The text is minimal, consisting only of an introductory paragraph, which, in true Ehlert fashion, invites participation: "Look at beaks and snouts with me./Make some more for us to see," and of labels for the animals, such as "Rooster," and of the names of the shapes such as hexagon, octagon, oval, heart, and square.

Hands (1997) moves closer to the realm of the toy book. A tribute to Ehlert's parents, both of whom liked to make things and who encouraged their daughter's artistic aspirations, the book sounds much like the project Ehlert describes to Connie Goddard in a 1992 interview in *Publisher's Weekly.* An assignment "to create a portrait of someone without using photographs" resulted in "a book of sorts" called *My Father Always Worked with His Hands.*

"Using a series of mementos, like pigskin work gloves for the book's cover, helped her understand what makes a book; that it is, among other things, a 'gathering of leaves. Learning how I could express something taught me a different way to communicate.'" *Hands,* as a mass-produced book, does not, of course, have pigskin work gloves for a cover, but it does have a photograph of work gloves bound along their knit cuffs with a carpenter's folding ruler and two screws.

Because the book works on so many levels, it is much more than a gimmick. There are several die-cut pages, including the image of a tin box with "screwdrivers" written in red pencil on masking tape on top, and inside, along with the half-title page of the book, one finds a collection of small screwdrivers. As the story continues, there are more tools, pencils, rulers, paint-spattered fabrics, quilts, lace, a pin-cushion, scissors, a tissue-paper pattern piece pinned to fabric, and a pot-holder that is the same one that is identified in *Talking with Artists* as one that Ehlert made at age eight. Best of all is the ending: "I want to be an artist. Then I'll join hands with my mom and dad. I love to make things with my hands. Do you?" These last two pages and the back cover consist of a sequence of three hands: one small hand covered with paint as though it has been finger painting, one medium-sized hand covered in a green cloth glove decorated with tiny hearts, and finally, for the back cover, the large hand of the father in its fuzzy yellow work glove. "This is really my autobiography," Ehlert said in an interview on Bookwire's internet site.

There is a sense of adventure, fun, and experimentation in all of Ehlert's books that inspires and encourages readers to try their own artistic experiments. Yet, her books are infused with an artistry and design, and a careful attention to detail that makes them much more complex than they at first appear.

—Linnea Hendrickson

EHRLICH, Bettina. See **BETTINA.**

EKWENSI, Cyprian (Odiatu Duaka)

Nationality: Nigerian. **Born:** Minna, Niger State, 26 September 1921. **Education:** Government School, Jos, 1931-36; Government College, Ibadan, 1936-41; Higher College, Yaba, 1941-43; School of Forestry, Ibadan, 1942-45; Achimota College, Gold Coast, 1943; School of Pharmacy, Yaba, 1947-49; Chelsea School of Pharmacy, University of London, 1951-56; University of Iowa, Iowa City, 1974. **Family:** Married Eunice Anyiwo; five children. **Career:** Teacher, Igbobi College, Yaba, 1947-49; lecturer, School of Pharmacy, Lagos, 1949-51; pharmacist superintendent, Nigerian Medical Services, 1956-57; head of features, Nigerian Broadcasting Corporation, 1957-61; director, Federal Information Services, 1961-67; director-general, Broadcasting Corporation of Biafra, during Nigerian civil war, 1967-70; proprietor, East Niger Chemists and East Niger Trading Company, from 1970; chairman, East Central State Library Board, 1972-75; managing director, Star Printing and Publishing Company, 1975-79; consultant, *Weekly Trumpet* and *Daily News,* both Anambra State, and *Weekly Eagle,* Imo State, 1980-81; commissioner for information, Anambra State, 1983. Member of the Board of Governors, Federal Radio Corporation, Lagos, 1985; chairman, Anambra State Hospitals Board, 1986-88. **Award:** Dag Hammarskjöld International award, 1968. **Agent:** David Bolt Associates, 12 Heath Drive, Send, Surrey GU23 7EP, England. **Address:** 12 Hillview, P.O. Box 317, Enugu, Anambra State, Nigeria.

Publications for Children

Fiction

When Love Whispers. Onitsha, Nigeria, Tabansi Bookshop, 1947.
The Leopard's Claw. London, Longman, 1950.
The Drummer Boy. London, Cambridge University Press, 1960.
The Passport of Malam Ilia. London, Cambridge University Press, 1960.
Yaba Roundabout Murder. Lagos, Tortoise, 1962.
The Rainmaker and Other Stories. Lagos, African Universities Press, 1965.
Trouble in Form Six, illustrated by Prue Theobalds. London, Cambridge University Press, 1966.
Juju Rock, illustrated by Bruce Onabrakpeya. Lagos, African Universities Press, 1966.
Coal Camp Boy. Lagos, Longman, 1973.
Samankwe in the Strange Forest. Ikeja, Longman Nigeria, 1973.
The Rainbow-Tinted Scarf and Other Stories, illustrated by Gay Galsworthy. London, Evans, 1975.
Samankwe and the Highway Robbers. London, Evans, 1975.
Motherless Baby. Enugu, Fourth Dimension, 1980.
Gone to Mecca. Ibadan, Heinemann, 1991.
Masquerade Time. London, Heinemann, 1991.

Other

Ikolo the Wrestler and Other Ibo Tales. London, Nelson, 1947.
An African Night's Entertainment: A Tale of Vengeance, illustrated by Bruce Onabrakpeya. Lagos, African Universities Press, and London, Deutsch, 1962.
The Great Elephant-Bird (folktale), illustrated by Rosemary Tonks and John Cottrell. London, Nelson, 1965.
The Boa Suitor, illustrated by John Cottrell. London, Nelson, 1966.

Publications for Adults

Novels

People of the City. London, Dakers, 1954; revised edition, London, Heinemann, 1963; New York, Fawcett, 1969.
Jagua Nana. London, Hutchinson, 1961; New York, Fawcett, 1969.
Burning Grass: A Story of the Fulani of Northern Nigeria. London, Heinemann, 1962.
Beautiful Feathers. London, Hutchinson, 1963.
Iska. London, Hutchinson, 1966.
Survive the Peace. London, Heinemann, 1976.

Divided We Stand. Enugu, Fourth Dimension, 1980.
Jagua Nana's Daughter. Ibadan, Spectrum, 1986.
For a Roll of Parchment. Ibadan, Heinemann, 1987.

Short Stories

Lokotown and Other Stories. London, Heinemann, 1966.
Restless City and Christmas Gold with Other Stories. London, Heinemann, 1975.

Other

Editor, *Festac Anthology of Nigerian New Writing.* Lagos, Federal Ministry of Information, 1977.

*

Critical Study: *Cyprian Ekwensi* by Ernest Emenyona, London, Evans, 1974.

* * *

Cyprian Ekwensi is an acknowledged pioneer in writing Nigerian youth literature. He is nearly unique among African writers in publishing stories for children as early as the 1940s, in *West African Review* and T. Cullen Young's *African New Writing,* before children's literature was emphasized, and in continuing to write for children after becoming an internationally known novelist. The reissue of his stories in collections and new editions attests to his popularity among young readers.

Ekwensi's writing for children is thoroughly grounded in the realities of contemporary life in the three main geographical regions of Nigeria. Folk tales, including *An African Night's Entertainment,* and adventure stories, such as *Juju Rock* and *The Passport of Malam Ilia,* are set in northern Nigeria among the Hausa and Fulani people. Most of the stories in *The Rainbow-Tinted Scarf* take place in western Nigeria among the Yoruba people, while *Coal Camp Boy* and the new series about Samankwe are set in eastern Nigeria among the Igbo people. *The Drummer Boy* and many of the stories in *The Rainmaker* have urban settings. Ekwensi is truly a national writer, yet his work is not so localized as to prevent its being enjoyed by children outside Nigeria.

Ekwensi's folklore, like his fiction, is told in contemporary Nigerian idiom. The folk tales reflect some of the diversity of Nigerian folklore by including tales told by several ethnic groups, tales with human as well as animal characters, and long tales like the one in *An African Night's Entertainment.* Versions of widespread themes in West African folklore, such as a woman who marries an animal, melting girl, a king who refuses to let his beautiful daughter marry, and tortoise trickster tales are found in his collections, along with local themes. Numerous stylistic features of oral narratives such as epigrammatic naming, proverbs, songs, choral responses, and extensive dialogue are used, though considerably simplified for children. Ekwensi has chosen to retell folk tales with implicit or explicit morals, reflecting the strong didactic emphasis in all his writing for children.

Ekwensi's fiction includes the same elements he enjoyed reading as a youth: truth, poetic justice, heroism, romance, folkloric mystery, and adventure. His stories, most of which are about the adventures of boys and men, reflect real experiences, such as going to school in the colonial and post-colonial eras, poverty in urban areas, and the aftermath of the Nigerian Civil War, as well as fictional experiences prominent in the mass media, such as capturing thieves and searching for lost treasure.

Adventure is a focus of all Ekwensi's fiction, regardless of its setting. The adventure may be sheer fun, as when school boys play pranks in *Trouble in Form Six,* but more often it involves apprehending wrong-doers. The blind hero of *The Drummer Boy* unknowingly becomes involved with thieves who purport to be his friends, while the hero of *Coal Camp Boy*, who resettles near Enugu after the Nigerian Civil War, discovers looters who are reselling property stolen from war victims. In *Juju Rock* a search for a man lost in a boat crash leads to the discovery of a gold mine whose riches are being concealed by a group of men who use secret society rituals to frighten away potential discoverers of their wealth. In his various adventures, Samankwe encounters highway robbers, kidnappers, money doublers, and illicit palm-wine makers. The adventures often include fighting and violence, but those who do wrong always are punished and the heroes receive praise for their bravery and attempts to uphold justice.

—Nancy J. Schmidt

ELLIN, E(lizabeth) M(uriel)

Nationality: New Zealander. **Born:** Waiuku, 22 March 1905. **Education:** Secondary school in Auckland. **Agent:** Minerva Bookshop Ltd., C.P.O. Box 2597, 13 Commerce Street, Auckland 1, New Zealand.

Publications for Children

Fiction

The Children of Clearwater Bay, illustrated by Garth Tapper. Auckland, Minerva, and London, Macmillan, 1969.
The Greenstone Axe, illustrated by Elizabeth Sutherland. Albany, New Zealand, Stockton House, 1975.

* * *

E.M. Ellin's two published novels have, in high degree, what educationists call "readability." Both books show children coping with situations which are dangerous in a very real sense; both, by the use of a deceptively simple prose style, a swift evocation of setting and character, and sure handling of energetic narrative, ensure reader attention to the last page.

The Children of Clearwater Bay is a tale of endurance, of desperate measures taken to ensure survival in the face of catastrophe. The Cameron children, six of them ranging in age from 14 to two-year-old twins, are real children: quarrelsome, joyful, and, in the face of danger, sensibly dismayed. This dismay emphasises their subsequent resourcefulness; in common with their counterparts in *The Greenstone Axe* (the three Archer children) they demonstrate a proper balance of anxiety evoked by consciousness of their own immaturity, and determination to do the best in the circumstances.

This capacity for bringing the characters alive and bestowing credibility on the action is the hallmark of Ellin's writing. One senses in her prose—particularly in the dialogue—a memory for the preoccupations of childhood, an effortless recapturing of childish reaction to circumstance, as well as a retention of that particular quality of zest and resilience which belongs, alone, to the healthy child.

Ellin's childhood, spent on a farm in the far north of New Zealand, obviously equipped her with a strong sense of place. This she transmits smoothly to her books, which are both set in this area. The isolation of pioneer life, the necessity for children to behave responsibly and independently, while yet retaining the ebullience of childhood, the ever-present influence of the bush and the sea, all emerge strongly.

The historical details in Ellin's stories are accurately researched and presented without comment. There are friendly Maoris and hostile Maoris; the author sees as her concern the recounting of the children's adventures against an authentic background rather than the espousal of any cause. In this—and in her predilection for banishing parents so that the action centres around her children, unencumbered and unassisted—she reflects a tradition earlier than her own in children's writing though several other modern authors (notably Southall in his earlier work) favoured this device.

If one is to believe (with Geoffrey Trease) that "whatever the other valuable elements in a story, the single indispensable one is entertainment," one must acknowledge Ellin's achievement. Her characters interact vigorously against a background which exists. The result is entertainment of a high order.

—Dorothy Butler

ELY, George Herbert. See **STRANG, Herbert.**

EMECHETA, (Florence Onye) Buchi

Nationality: British. **Born:** Lagos, Nigeria, 21 July 1944. **Education:** Methodist Girls' High School, Lagos; University of London, B.Sc. (honours) in sociology 1972. **Family:** Married Sylvester Onwordi in 1960 (separated 1969); two sons and three daughters. **Career:** Librarian, 1960-64; library officer, British Museum, London, 1965-69; youth worker and resident student, Race, 1974-76; community worker, Camden Council, London, 1976-78; visiting lecturer at universities in the United States, 1979; Senior Research Fellow and Visiting Professor of English, University of Calabar, Nigeria, 1980-81; Lecturer, Yale University, New Haven, Connecticut, 1982; Lecturer, University of London, since 1982. Proprietor, Ogwugwu Afo Publishing Company, London; member of the Home Secretary's Advisory Council on Race, since 1979. **Address:** 7 Briston Grove, London N8 9EX, England.

Publications for Children

Fiction

The Bride Price. London, Allison and Busby, and New York, Braziller, 1976.
Titch the Cat, illustrated by Thomas Joseph. London, Allison and Busby, 1979.
Nowhere to Play, illustrated by Peter Archer. London, Allison and Busby, 1980.
The Moonlight Bride. Oxford, Oxford University Press, 1980.
The Wrestling Match. Oxford, Oxford University Press, 1980; New York, Braziller, 1983.
Naira Power. London, Macmillan, 1982.

Publications for Adults

Novels

Adah's Story. London, Allison and Busby, 1983.
In the Ditch. London, Barrie and Jenkins, 1972.
Second-Class Citizen. London, Allison and Busby, 1974; New York, Braziller, 1975.
The Slave Girl. London, Allison and Busby, and New York, Braziller, 1977.
The Joys of Motherhood. London, Allison and Busby, and New York, Braziller, 1979.
Destination Biafra. London, Allison and Busby, 1982.
Double Yoke. London, Ogwugwu Afo, 1982; New York, Braziller, 1983.
The Rape of Shavi. London, Ogwugwu Afo, 1983; New York, Braziller, 1985.
A Kind of Marriage. London, Macmillan, 1986.
Head above Water. London: Ogwugwu Afo, 1986.
Gwendolen. London, Collins, 1989; as *The Family,* New York, Braziller, 1990.
Kehinde. Oxford and Portsmouth, New Hampshire, Heinemann, 1994.

Plays

Television Plays: *A Kind of Marriage,* 1976; *The Ju Ju Landlord,* 1976.

Other

Our Own Freedom, photographs by Maggie Murray. London, Sheba, 1981.
Head above Water (autobiography). London, Ogwugwu Afo, 1986.
"Feminism with a Small 'f'!," in *Criticism and Ideology: Second African Writers' Conference, Stockholm 1986,* edited by Kirsten Holst Petersen, Stockholm, Scandinavian Institute for African Studies, 1988.

*

Biography: *Buchi Emecheta* (videocassette), Cicero, Illinois, Roland, 1988; *The Joys of Motherhood: A Conversation with Buchi Emecheta* (videocassette), Fairleigh Dickinson University, Ballantine, 1992; "Buchi Emecheta" by Kirsten Holst Petersen, in *Dictionary of Literary Biography,* Vol. 117, *Caribbean and Black African Writers, First Series,* Detroit, Gale, 1992.

Critical Studies: "Women and Migration in Four Emecheta Novels" by Consuela Fernetta Bennet, unpublished dissertation, University of the West Indies, 1988; "The African Female Experience in Selected Novels of Buchi Emecheta" by Constance Joy

Magnus, unpublished dissertation, University of the West Indies, 1989; "What They Told Buchi Emecheta: Oral Subjectivity and the Joys of Otherhood" by Cynthia Ward, in *PMLA,* Vol. 105, 1990, 83-97; *Reading Buchi Emecheta: Cross-cultural Conversations,* edited by Katherine Fishburn, Westport, Greenwood, 1994; "'He Neo-Tarzan, She Jane?': Buchi Emecheta's *The Rape of Shavi*" by Judie Newman, in *College Literature,* Vol. 22, No. 1, 1995, 161-170; *Emerging Perspectives on Buchi Emecheta,* edited by Marie Umeh, Trenton, New Jersey, Africa World, Press, 1996; "Buchi Emecheta's *The Bride Price* and *The Slave Girl*: A Schizoanalytic Perspective" by Rose Ure Mezu, in *ARIEL,* Vol. 28, No. 1, 1997, 131-47.

* * *

Buchi Emecheta is one of Africa's best-known women writers, whose books for adults, for teenagers, and for children all concern the values inherent in African culture at home and overseas. Emecheta currently lives in London, and many of her works focus on the experience of Nigerian characters in Britain. Whether set in Britain or in Nigeria, however, all question the effects of caste and of gender discrimination upon the individual and her society.

Though not written specifically for young readers, Emecheta's two autobiographical novels, *In the Ditch* and *Second Class Citizen,* have long appealed to young women for their scathing portrayal of Adah's (Emecheta's) experiences; denied schooling because she was "only a girl," she eventually achieved an excellent education but was at the mercy of a husband who treated her as property and even burned her novel. Through these experiences, compounded by a series of children, Adah's spirit is unquenchable. For young adults, these novels make a good introduction to *The Bride Price* (which is, significantly, the novel burned by the husband in *Second Class Citizen*). In this novel, set in Nigeria, it is clear that young womanhood (in fact, womanhood in general) has been poorly served by African male writers. The narrator does not say anything positive about traditional ways of life discussed in the novel. Emecheta sees the custom of Bride Price as the barbaric reduction of marriage to wife-buying, and the custom of "Osu," or outcast, as barbaric and inhuman. In spite of the fact that Chike's father is one of the wealthiest and most educated people in Ibuza Community, he and his family are regarded as slaves since one of his ancestors had been sold into slavery. As far as Emecheta is concerned, these are customs humans should mercilessly fight against, but she refrains from direct criticism. For all its protest, *The Bride Price* is non-didactic. (Nevertheless, this and several other Emecheta novels have been attacked by male African writers for their negative portrayal of Nigerian customs.)

Emecheta switches from a focus on tradition to an examination of contemporary issues in *Naira Power,* a more didactic work. The novel explores the decadence and corruption which excessive love of money can unleash on a society. The plot unfolds mainly through flashback spanning colonial days through the present and is narrated by Amina to Bintu as they sit in a car during a strong tropical rainstorm. The major didactic element in *Naira Power* concerns limitation of Nigerian currency (the naira) and the general limitation of the power of money; as Bintu tells Amina, "I am glad to hear that there are instances in which naira can't ferry one through." In the novel young Ramonu's robbery career ends in disgrace: he is burnt to death when the community who knows him mistakes him for an actual robber. Ramonu's moral degeneration begins after his expulsion from home by his father. Lacking parental guidance, he drifts into a bad group of business associates. Unlike Amina's father, who is quite concerned with the welfare and progress of his children and the company they keep, Ramonu's father does not seem to worry about his son's associates and how he makes his money. Instead, he glories in enjoying his son's ill-gotten money. Emecheta uses Ramonu's father's relationship with his son and Amina's father's relationship with his children to stress the need for parental guidance of children. *Naira Power* also addresses the issue of overpopulation, a serious problem which has the potential to ruin Nigeria. Part of the novel is set in contemporary Lagos, and the congestion of the city and the physical squalor are reflected in the moral decadence of many of the characters. Most of the problems in the novel arise either from a lack of moral integrity or an ignoble lust for money.

The Bride Price and *Naira Power* occupy the borderline between an adult and a young adult readership and have been enjoyed by both. Emecheta's real juvenile titles are less serious than these two; in fact, some scholars regard her series of four consecutive books for young readers as an interlude between two phases of her career. A young adult book with a Nigerian setting, *The Wrestling Match* portrays a sixteen-year-old orphan boy's efforts to win a wrestling match in order to be taken seriously by his aunt and uncle. *The Moonlight Bride* centers on an accidentally overheard wedding plan; though its material overlaps with that of *The Bride Price,* its mood is less somber. In her two picture books for younger children, *Titch the Cat* and *Nowhere to Play,* the setting is unmistakably English. The families shown in both books are of Nigerian origin but English upbringing. Because of the younger audience of these books, Emecheta's characteristic savage analysis of injustice is missing; though realistic, the books are not pessimistic.

—Osayimwense Osa, updated by Caroline C. Hunt

ENRIGHT, Elizabeth (Wright)

Nationality: American. **Born:** Oak Park, Illinois, 17 September 1909. **Education:** Edgewood School, Greenwich, Connecticut; Art Students' League, New York, 1927-28; in Paris, 1928; Parsons School of Design, New York. **Family:** Married Robert Marty Gillham in 1930; three sons. **Career:** Teacher of creative writing, Barnard College, New York, 1960-62. **Awards:** American Library Association Newbery Medal, 1939. LL.D.: Nasson College, Springvale, Maine, 1966. **Died:** 8 June 1968.

PUBLICATIONS FOR CHILDREN (ILLUSTRATED BY THE AUTHOR)

Fiction

Kintu: A Congo Adventure. New York, Farrar and Rinehart, 1935.

Thimble Summer. New York, Farrar and Rinehart, 1938; London, Heinemann, 1939.

The Sea Is All Around. New York, Farrar and Rinehart, 1940; London, Heinemann, 1959.

The Saturdays. New York, Farrar and Rinehart, 1941; London, Heinemann, 1955.
The Four-Story Mistake. New York, Farrar and Rinehart, 1942; London, Heinemann, 1955.
Then There Were Five. New York, Farrar and Rinehart, 1944; London, Heinemann, 1956.
The Melendy Family (includes *The Saturdays, The Four-Story Mistake, Then There Were Five*). New York, Farrar and Rinehart, 1947.
A Christmas Tree for Lydia. New York, Rinehart, 1951.
Spiderweb for Two: A Melendy Maze. New York, Rinehart, 1951; London, Heinemann, 1956.
Gone-Away Lake, illustrated by Beth and Joe Krush. New York, Harcourt Brace, and London, Heinemann, 1957.
Return to Gone-Away, illustrated by Beth and Joe Krush. New York, Harcourt Brace, 1961; London, Heinemann, 1962.
Tatsinda, illustrated by Irene Haas. New York, Harcourt Brace, 1963; London, Heinemann, 1964.
Zeee, illustrated by Irene Haas. New York, Harcourt Brace, 1965; London, Heinemann, 1966.

Publications for Adults

Short Stories

Borrowed Summer and Other Stories. New York, Rinehart, 1946; as *The Maple Tree and Other Stories,* London, Heinemann, 1947.
The Moment Before the Rain. New York, Harcourt Brace, and London, Heinemann, 1955.
The Riddle of the Fly and Other Stories. New York, Harcourt Brace, 1959; London, Heinemann, 1960.
Doublefields: Memories and Stories. New York, Harcourt Brace, 1966; London, Heinemann, 1967.

*

Illustrator: *Kees,* 1930, *Amnon, A Lad of Palestine,* 1931, and *Kees and Kleintje,* 1934, all by Marian King; *The Crystal Locket* by Nellie M. Rowe, 1935.

* * *

Elizabeth Enright's keen perception of childhood and her remarkable gifts as a writer place her books among the select few that are timeless and enduring. In *The Sea Is All Around* one of her characters says, "I like people to look at things wholeheartedly...learning and absorbing them so that their memories are full of accurate impressions." Her books are full of "accurate impressions"; they ring true. The children in her books, too, have this ability to look, learn, and absorb wholeheartedly. They are interesting and full of life.

The heroine of *Thimble Summer* is 10-year-old Garnet Linden. Her Wisconsin summer starts out to be dull and hopeless; her family's farm is in serious trouble because of drought, and it is the time of the Great Depression. Soon after she finds a silver thimble in a dried up river bed, the rains come and a lovely summer of adventure begins. The book is full of the feel of a midwest farm and the dry little towns nearby, and the mood of America in the 1930's. A child of the depression, an orphan named Eric whose life has been lonely wandering, accidentally finds his way to the Linden family and is cared for and eventually adopted by them. There is a tree-house adventure, a wonderful chapter about being locked in the town library after closing time, a rebellious trip to a distant city. The summer, and the book, come to an end on a note of joy when Garnet's own personal pig whom she has raised from babyhood wins the blue ribbon at the county fair.

The Sea Is All Around is full of the mood of a storm-swept wintery island thirty miles out in the Atlantic. Once a busy port and home for prosperous whaling captains, the island is rich in tradition, scenery, and characters as well. Mab Kendall is an orphan who comes from Iowa to live with an aunt on Pokenick Island. This book is unforgettable for its description of loneliness and the awakening of contentment in a child. There are many lovely old people: "They carry with them memories of a long life starred with adventures." Her warm descriptions are delightful—she makes us see and feel storms and cold, snow and spring, the presence of the sea, northern lights, dune plants, swamp flowers and mosses, always called by their right names and more vivid as a result.

In the Melendy books the children are satisfying characters, particularly now when television gives ready-made dreams and makes watchers of us. All Enright children do things that children dream of doing. In *The Saturdays* they contrive ways of making New York City their private source of joy. *The Four-Story Mistake* takes Mona, Rush, Randy, and Oliver Melendy out of the city and into an old house in the country, full of secrets and mysteries. The grounds are "thirty acres of land that hold a sample of everything delightful short of an active volcano and an ocean that one could want on his own territory: brook, woods, stable, hollow tree and summer house."

Then There Were Five continues Melendy life in the country. World War II plays a part in this book, with Father in Washington and the children involved in at-home war efforts. The Melendy children have many talents and use them in fascinating ways. They also love to talk, and say things the way one wishes one could, and they are funny. A new Melendy comes on the scene, Mark, a young boy with no home, who adds much to the family and the book. *Spiderweb for Two* finds the older children away and Randy and Oliver home alone. For a little while their lives are empty. Then the mail brings the first of a series of clues in the form of cryptic poems, which, when deciphered, lead the children to strange hiding places and many adventures.

Gone-Away Lake and *Return to Gone-Away* are about two realistically drawn families who live in the country. Witty, original old people give a sense of history with stories of the past. Animals abound, and secrets and clubs, danger and daring, and always nature, authentic and fascinating, accessible and an accessory to what happens.

Tatsinda is a "once-upon-a-time" fairy tale, traditional in feeling. But Enright's knowing characterizations and lovely language make it special and fresh. *Zeee* is a funny down-to-earth fairy tale about a "bad" fairy, the size of a bee, who lives in the present and has personality problems. Zeee eventually finds a home and a friend and makes peace with herself and the cruel world which looms around her.

These are all beautiful books, to become deeply involved in, to absorb easily and happily and to remember always.

—Irene Haas

ESTES, Eleanor (Ruth)

Nationality: American. **Born:** Eleanor Ruth Rosenfeld, West Haven, Connecticut, 9 May 1906. **Education:** Union Grammar School, West Haven; West Haven High School, graduated 1923; Pratt Institute Library School, New York (Hewins scholar), 1931-32. **Family:** Married Rice Estes in 1932; one daughter. **Career:** Children's librarian, Free Public Library, New Haven, Connecticut, 1924-31, and branches of the New York Public Library, 1932-40. **Awards:** American Library Association Newbery Medal, 1952; Pratt Institute Alumni Medal, 1968. **Died:** 15 July 1988.

Publications for Children

Fiction

The Moffats, illustrated by Louis Slobodkin. New York, Harcourt Brace, 1941; London, Bodley Head, 1959.
The Middle Moffat, illustrated by Louis Slobodkin. New York, Harcourt Brace, 1942; London, Bodley Head, 1960.
Rufus M., illustrated by Louis Slobodkin. New York, Harcourt Brace, 1943; London, Bodley Head, 1960.
The Sun and the Wind and Mr. Todd, illustrated by Louis Slobodkin. New York, Harcourt Brace, 1943.
The Hundred Dresses, illustrated by Louis Slobodkin. New York, Harcourt Brace, 1944.
The Sleeping Giant and Other Stories, illustrated by the author. New York, Harcourt Brace, 1948.
Ginger Pye, illustrated by the author. New York, Harcourt Brace, 1951; London, Bodley Head, 1961.
A Little Oven, illustrated by the author. New York, Harcourt Brace, 1955.
Pinky Pye, illustrated by Edward Ardizzone. New York, Harcourt Brace, 1958; London, Constable, 1959.
The Witch Family, illustrated by Edward Ardizzone. New York, Harcourt Brace, 1960; London, Constable, 1962.
The Alley, illustrated by Edward Ardizzone. New York, Harcourt Brace, 1964.
Miranda the Great, illustrated by Edward Ardizzone. New York, Harcourt Brace, 1967.
The Tunnel of Hugsy Goode, illustrated by Edward Ardizzone. New York, Harcourt Brace, 1971.
The Coat-Hanger Christmas Tree, illustrated by Susanne Suba. New York, Atheneum, 1973; London, Oxford University Press, 1976.
The Lost Umbrella of Kim Chu, illustrated by Jacqueline Ayer. New York, Atheneum, 1978; London, Oxford University Press, 1980.
The Moffat Museum. New York, Harcourt Brace, 1983.
The Curious Adventures of Jimmy McGee, illustrated by John O'Brien. San Diego, Harcourt Brace, 1987.

Play

The Lollipop Princess: A Play for Paper Dolls, illustrated by the author. New York, Harcourt Brace, 1967.

Publications for Adults

Novel

The Echoing Green. New York, Macmillan, 1947.

*

Manuscript Collection: Kerlan Collection, University of Minnesota, Minneapolis.

Eleanor Estes commented:

(1983) I have no aim other than to entertain, and to do this in the most complete and artistic way that I can.

* * *

Eleanor Estes's most exceptional feat, in her long and much-lauded career as an author of books for children, was her ability to distill the very essence of childhood. Estes's prose, simple and direct, and written with a rare authenticity of voice, never for an instant betrays her adult perceptions and perspectives. Estes wrote as a child writing for children, not as an adult writing for children, capturing with keen insight and sharp observation the vibrancy and vitality of that which is "long ago and far away" for many adults, but everyday reality for the child.

Perhaps Estes's best-known and best-loved creation is the Moffat family of Cranbury, Connecticut. *The Moffats* centers around bashful Joey, inspired Jane, irrepressible Rufus, and big sister Sylvie. Estes paints a portrait of each child as special and individual, and simultaneously gives them a firm grounding as part of a cohesive family unit. A string-of-pearls format characterizes the book—episodic in nature, each chapter focuses on a single event or incident, rather than having a formal plot structure. This lack of plot movement does not detract from the strength of the book, however. Estes's finesse at powerfully evoking the sights and sounds and the pleasures and pains of childhood is unwavering. The ebullient and energetic adventures of the indomitable Moffat family spill across every page of the Moffat book and its successors, *The Middle Moffat, Rufus M.,* and finally, *The Moffat Museum,* written 42 years after the first Moffat story.

Ginger Pye, the 1952 Newbery Medal winner, and *Pinky Pye* are also set in Cranbury. Warm family stories, they are written with the same realistic humor and understanding of the child psyche that plays such an integral role in the Moffat books. Pets are important in the lives of the Pye children—in *Ginger Pye* Jerry and Rachel, with the special tenacity of children, spend months searching for their new puppy Ginger after she disappears on Thanksgiving Day. *Pinky Pye* combines fantasy and reality in the account of an extraordinary black kitten who, after being adopted by the family, learns to type on Mr. Pye's typewriter.

Connie Ives and her best friend Billy Maloon spring to life in *The Alley,* a mystery story set in Brooklyn, New York. When Connie's house is burglarized Connie and Billy turn detective, determined to solve the crime. Shot through with charm and originality, *The Alley* is all "cops and robbers," and distinguished by a stronger plot design than the Moffat and Pye stories.

The Hundred Dresses, like *The Alley,* is more solidly plotted than much of Estes's work, and also has a more serious theme than a great deal of her writing. Told with Estes's trademark sensitivity to and understanding of child character, it stands as a tribute to the invincibility of the human spirit. Wanda Petronski wears the same faded blue dress to school every day, but tells her classmates she has one hundred dresses at home. After becoming the subject of incessant teasing and prejudiced remarks, Wanda drops out of school and her family moves away. In an emotional, cathartic ending, Wanda's disconsolate and guilt-ridden persecutors are taught an enduring lesson in compassion and forgiveness.

With *The Witch Family* Estes again ventures into the realm of fantasy. By drawing pictures, best friends Amy and Clarissa create and manipulate Old Witch, head witch of all the witches, Little Witch Girl, Weeny Witch, and Malachi, the spelling bee. Filled with wit, wordplay, and plenty of "hurly-burlies," the book is a salute to the transforming power of a child's imagination. A less successful fantasy than *The Witch Family, The Curious Adventures of Jimmy McGee* reintroduces the reader to Amy and Clarissa, but the hero of the story is Jimmy McGee, a plumber who wears a stovepipe hat and a bombazine suit. The melding of fantasy and reality is not accomplished seamlessly, and Jimmy McGee and his antics are not as engrossing as are those of the witch family.

The reader does become involved in *The Lost Umbrella of Kim Chu,* however. Estes impeccably captures the ethnic flavor of New York, in particular Manhattan's Chinatown, in the early years of the 20th century. At the library, Kim Chu forgets her father's unique umbrella, which contains a scroll hidden in a secret compartment in the handle. Her grandmother sends Kim Chu on a quest in search of the umbrella, and she becomes involved in a chase on an elevated train and the Staten Island ferry before it is retrieved. At times the story seems manipulated to suit the author's intentions, but the direct prose style and sure eye for telling detail is distinctive of all of Estes's writing.

Estes was a celebrant of childhood. She moved in the kingdom of the young as if her passport for that country had never expired—indeed, in her mind it had not. Her books are immediate and have kept their appeal despite spanning four generations of readers. They have the kind of staying power springing from the authenticity of recreated experience that begins, and ends, in the joy that is so characteristic of childhood.

—Carolyn Shute

ETS, Marie Hall

Nationality: American. **Born:** North Greenfield, Wisconsin, 16 December 1893. **Education:** Lawrence College, Appleton, Wisconsin, 1915-16; New York School of Fine and Applied Art, 1916-17; University of Chicago, Ph.B. 1924, and graduate work; Art Institute, Chicago; Columbia University, New York. **Family:** Married 1) Milton T. Rodig in 1917 (died 1918); 2) Harold N. Ets in 1929 (died 1943). **Career:** Artist for San Francisco and Los Angeles decorating firms, 1917-18; social worker, Department of the Navy, 1918; part-time volunteer resident, Chicago Commons Settlement House, 1919-29; child health worker for the American Red Cross in Pilsen, Czechoslovakia, 1921-22; agent, United States Coal Commission in West Virginia and Illinois, 1923. Individual show (drawings): Columbia University Teachers College, New York, 1963. **Awards:** American Library Association Caldecott Medal, 1960; University of Minnesota Kerlan award, 1975. **Died:** 1984.

Publications for Children (illustrated by the author)

Fiction

Mister Penny. New York, Viking Press, 1935; London, Woodfield, 1957.

In the Forest. New York, Viking Press, 1944; London, Faber, 1955.

My Dog Rinty, with Ellen Tarry, illustrated by Alexander and Alexandra Alland. New York, Viking Press, 1946.

Oley, The Sea Monster. New York, Viking Press, 1947.

Little Old Automobile. New York, Viking Press, 1948.

Mr. T.W. Anthony Woo: The Story of a Cat and a Dog and a Mouse. New York, Viking Press, 1951.

Another Day. New York, Viking Press, 1953; London, Faber, 1956.

Play with Me. New York, Viking Press, 1955; London, Penguin, 1976.

Mister Penny's Race Horse. New York, Viking Press, 1956; London, Woodfield, 1958.

Cow's Party. New York, Viking Press, 1958; London, Faber, 1959.

Nine Days to Christmas, with Aurora Labastida. New York, Viking Press, 1959.

Mister Penny's Circus. New York, Viking Press, 1961.

Gilberto and the Wind. New York, Viking Press, 1963.

Automobiles for Mice. New York, Viking Press, 1964.

Just Me. New York, Viking Press, 1965; London, Angus and Robertson, 1966.

Bad Boy, Good Boy. New York, Crowell, 1967.

Talking Without Words: I Can, Can You? New York, Viking Press, 1968.

Elephant in a Well. New York, Viking Press, 1972.

Jay Bird. New York, Viking Press, 1974.

Poetry

Beasts and Nonsense. New York, Viking Press, 1952.

Other

The Story of a Baby. New York, Viking Press, 1939.

Publications for Adults

Other

Rosa: The Life of an Italian Immigrant. Minneapolis, University of Minnesota Press, 1970.

*

Manuscript Collection: Kerlan Collection, University of Minnesota, Minneapolis.

Marie Hall Ets comments:

I lived in a family with several children who loved to hear stories and have me draw for them. I found it to be as enjoyable for me as for my nieces and nephew, so have tried to entertain children with my stories and pictures ever since.

* * *

The best work of Marie Hall Ets is deceptively simple. Most picture books that speak directly to the young child of nursery school age stand the risk of not at first impressing the adult who selects it. Very often it is only after the adult witnesses the secret appeal that such books hold for children that he returns to examine and appreciate the subtle craftsmanship of the author-illustrator.

A book like *In the Forest* or *Play with Me* is so simple in construction and syntax that one may be tempted to say that it wouldn't be very hard to write a book like that—when in fact these are the most difficult books of all to write. The distance in years and experience between the writer and the young child is so great that only a special few, like Ets, have been successful in creating picture books that the child intuitively recognizes as having been written expressly for him.

In these books Ets daringly selects a first person telling. In order for her to do this she not only must feel comfortable with the mental furniture of the young child's mind, but she must also be sure to select a content and a style with which the child is both familiar and comfortable. She skillfully blends fancifulness with matter-of-factness: both are integral ingredients of a child's imaginative play. Repetition, artfully employed, gives the effect of the muted chant that a child often creates when he plays alone:

> I had a new horn and a paper hat
> And I went for a walk in the forest.
> A big wild lion was taking a nap.
> But he woke up when he heard my horn.
> "Where are you going?" he said to me.
> "May I go too, if I comb my hair?"
> So he combed his hair and he came too
> When I went for a walk in the forest.

Her longer stories, like *Mister Penny* and *Mr. T.W. Anthony Woo,* are reminiscent of the earlier stories of Hugh Lofting. Like Doctor Dolittle in fiction (and Doctor Schweitzer in life), Mr. Penny and the cobbler of Shooshko are superb adult models for children. They show a great love and reverence for all God's creatures, and they demonstrate great patience towards them, no matter how mischievous they may be. These books are alive with silly names and slapstick humor that make children laugh out loud, but beneath all the fun, and devoid of moralistic pronouncement, are such notions as: "People always hate the things they are afraid of" and "How nice it is to have peace."

The works of Ets are perfect for sharing: there is much to savor for both child and adult.

—James E. Higgins

EUPHAN. See **TODD, Barbara Euphan.**

EVANS, Hubert (Reginald)

Nationality: Canadian. **Born:** Vankleek Hill, Ontario, 9 May 1892. **Education:** Galt Collegiate, Ontario, graduated 1909. **Military Service:** Kootenay Battalion, Rocky Mountain Rangers, in France and Flanders, 1915-19. **Family:** Married Anna Winter in 1920 (died 1960); three children. **Career:** Newspaper reporter, Toronto and British Columbia, 1910-14; worked for commercial fisheries and on salmon conservation as a fisheries officer; lived in Indian villages, Northern British Columbia, 1946-53. **Died:** 17 June 1986.

Publications for Children

Fiction

Forest Friends: Stories of Animals, Fish and Birds West of the Rockies. Philadelphia, Judson Press, 1926.
Derry, Airedale of the Frontier. New York, Dodd Mead, 1928.
Derry's Partner, illustrated by Frank E. Schoonover. New York, Dodd Mead, 1929.
Derry of Totem Creek, illustrated by H.E.M. Sellen. New York, Dodd Mead, 1930.
The Silent Call. New York, Dodd Mead, 1930.
Mountain Dog. Philadelphia, Westminster Press, 1956; as *Son of the Salmon People,* Madeira Park, British Columbia, Harbour, 1981.

Other

North to the Unknown: The Achievement and Adventures of David Thompson, illustrated by Ruth Collins. Toronto, McClelland and Stewart, and New York, Dodd Mead, 1949.

Publications for Adults

Novels

The New Front Line. Toronto, Macmillan, 1927.
Mist on the River. Toronto, Copp Clark, 1954.
O Time in Your Flight. Madeira Park, British Columbia, Harbour, 1979.

Poetry

Whittlings. Madeira Park, British Columbia, Harbour, 1976.
Endinas. Madeira Park, British Columbia, Harbour, 1978.
Mostly Coast People. Madeira Park, British Columbia, Harbour, n.d.

* * *

Hubert Evans's writings are concerned for the most part with the Skeena River area of British Columbia, an area whose facets he knew very well from his life there working first in the commercial fisheries and later as a fisheries officer. This background is evident in his writing for adults, which reflects his knowledge of life in the province, particularly the life of the Indians.

In his children's books Evans drew on much of his own experience of close contact with the outdoors for his material. His two collections of animal stories, *Forest Friends* and *The Silent Call,* are told in a familiar, anecdotal style. Their chief interest is their reflection of the natural world Evans appeared to know very well. His fictionalized biography of David Thompson (1770-1857), *North to the Unknown,* written for teenagers, is marred by his lack of familiarity with the historical period about which he wrote.

Perhaps his most successful writing is to be seen in his novels about Derry, an Airedale terrier, which appeared in Grosset's *Famous Dog Stories* series, and *Mountain Dog.* In these, Evans writes animal biographies against a background of carefully described and obviously well-loved settings in British Columbia. His love of nature and his desire for its conservation are evident throughout these books. Like most attempts at rendering intelligible the thoughts and activities of animals, these books could be accused of, at times, sentimentalizing and anthropomorphizing dogs. While Evans can at times be accused of both practices, the stories, with their well-observed detail and their exciting and imaginative plots, sustain interest very well. As a writer of nature stories, and particularly of dog stories, Evans was quite successful, and much of his work bears favourable comparison with that of the two most prominent Canadian writers of the genre, Ernest Thompson Seton and Charles G.D. Roberts.

—Janet E. Baker

EYRE, Elizabeth. See **STOREY, Margaret.**

F

FARJEON, Eleanor

Pseudonyms: Tomfool; Chimaera. **Nationality:** British. **Born:** London, 13 February 1881; daughter of the novelist Benjamin Leopold Farjeon; sister of the writers Herbert and Joseph Jefferson Farjeon and the composer Harry Farjeon. **Education:** Educated privately. **Career:** Regular contributor to *Punch,* London, 1914-17; wrote verse (as Tomfool) for the London *Daily Herald,* 1917-30; staff member and verse contributor (as Chimaera), *Time and Tide,* London, in the 1920s. **Awards:** Hans Christian Andersen International Medal, 1956; Library Association Carnegie Medal, 1956; Catholic Library Association Regina Medal, 1959. **Died:** 5 June 1965.

PUBLICATIONS FOR CHILDREN

Fiction

Martin Pippin in the Apple-Orchard, illustrated by C.E. Brock. London, Collins, 1921; New York, Stokes, 1922.
Tom Cobble, illustrated by M. Dobson. Oxford, Blackwell, 1925.
Nuts and May: A Medley for Children, illustrated by Rosalind Thornycroft. London, Collins, 1926.
Italian Peepshow and Other Tales, illustrated by Rosalind Thornycroft. New York, Stokes, 1926; as *Italian Peepshow and Other Stories,* Oxford, Blackwell, 1934; revised edition as *Italian Peepshow,* London, Oxford University Press, 1960.
The Wonderful Knight, illustrated by Doris Pailthorpe. Oxford, Blackwell, 1927.
The King's Barn; or, Joan's Tale. London, Collins, 1927.
The Mill of Dreams; or, Jennifer's Tale. London, Collins, 1927.
Young Gerard; or, Joyce's Tale. London, Collins, 1927.
A Bad Day for Martha, illustrated by Eugenie Richards. Oxford, Blackwell, 1928.
Kaleidoscope. London, Collins, 1928; New York, Stokes, 1929.
The Perfect Zoo. London, Harrap, and Philadelphia, McKay, 1929.
The King's Daughter Cries for the Moon, illustrated by May Smith. Oxford, Blackwell, 1929.
The Tale of Tom Tiddler, illustrated by Norman Tealby. London, Collins, 1929; New York, Stokes, 1930.
Westwoods, illustrated by May Smith. Oxford, Blackwell, 1930; Poughkeepsie, New York, Artists and Writers Guild, 1935.
The Old Nurse's Stocking Basket, illustrated by E. Herbert Whydale. London, University of London Press, and New York, Stokes, 1931.
Perkin the Pedlar, illustrated by Clare Leighton. London, Faber, 1932.
Katy Kruse at the Seaside; or, The Deserted Islanders. London, Harrap, and Philadelphia, McKay, 1932.
Ameliaranne's Prize Packet, illustrated by S.B. Pearse. London, Harrap, 1933; as *Ameliaranne and the Magic Ring,* Philadelphia, McKay, 1933.
Pannychis, illustrated by Clare Leighton. Shaftesbury, Dorset, High House Press, 1933.
Ameliaranne's Washing Day, illustrated by S.B. Pearse. London, Harrap, and Philadelphia, McKay, 1934.
Jim at the Corner and Other Stories, illustrated by Irene Mountfort. Oxford, Blackwell, 1934; as *The Old Sailor's Yarn Box,* New York, Stokes, 1934.
The Clumber Pup, illustrated by Irene Mountfort. Oxford, Blackwell, 1934.
And I Dance Mine Own Child, illustrated by Irene Mountfort. Oxford, Blackwell, 1935.
Jim and the Pirates, illustrated by Roger Naish. Oxford, Blackwell, 1936.
Martin Pippin in the Daisy-Field, illustrated by Isobel and John Morton-Sale. London, Joseph, 1937; New York, Stokes, 1938.
One Foot in Fairyland: Sixteen Tales, illustrated by Robert Lawson. London, Joseph, and New York, Stokes, 1938.
The Silver Curlew, from her own play, illustrated by Ernest H. Shepard. London, Oxford University Press, 1953; New York, Viking Press, 1954.
The Little Book-Room, illustrated by Edward Ardizzone. London, Oxford University Press, 1955; New York, Oxford University Press, 1956.
The Glass Slipper, from the play by Eleanor and Herbert Farjeon, illustrated by Ernest H. Shepard. London, Oxford University Press, 1955; New York, Viking Press, 1956.
Mr. Garden, illustrated by Jane Paton. London, Hamish Hamilton, and New York, Walck, 1966.

Plays

Grannie Gray: Children's Plays and Games with Music and Without, illustrated by Joan Jefferson Farjeon. London, Dent, 1939.
The Glass Slipper, with Herbert Farjeon, music by Clifton Parker, illustrated by Hugh Stevenson (produced London, 1944). London, Wingate, 1946.
The Silver Curlew: A Fairy Tale, music by Clifton Parker (produced London, 1949). London, French, 1953.

Poetry

Nursery Rhymes [and *More Nursery Rhymes*] *of London Town,* illustrated by Macdonald Gill. London, Duckworth, 2 vols., 1916-17; with music by the author, London, Oxford University Press, 4 vols., 1919-26.
All the Way to Alfriston, illustrated by Robin Guthrie. London, Morland Press, 1918.
Singing Games for Children, illustrated by J. Littlejohns. London, Dent, and New York, Dutton, 1919.
A First [and *Second*] *Chap-Book of Rounds,* music by Harry Farjeon, illustrated by John Garside. London, Dent, and New York, Dutton, 2 vols., 1919.
Tunes of a Penny Piper, illustrated by John Aveten. London, Selwyn and Blount, 1922.
Songs for Music and Lyrical Poems, illustrated by John Aveten. London, Selwyn and Blount, 1922.
All the Year Round. London, Collins, 1923; as *Around the Seasons,* London, Hamish Hamilton, and New York, Walck, 1969.
The Country Child's Alphabet, illustrated by William Michael Rothenstein. London, Poetry Bookshop, 1924.

The Town Child's Alphabet, illustrated by David Jones. London, Poetry Bookshop, 1924.
Songs from "Punch" for Children, music by the author. London, Saville, 1925.
Young Folk and Old. Shaftesbury, Dorset, High House Press, 1925.
Joan's Door, illustrated by Will Townsend. London, Collins, 1926; New York, Stokes, 1927.
Singing Games from Arcady, music by the author. Oxford, Blackwell, 1926.
Come, Christmas, illustrated by Molly McArthur. London, Collins, 1927; New York, Stokes, 1928.
An Alphabet of Magic, illustrated by Margaret Tarrant. London, Medici Society, 1928.
Poems for Children. Philadelphia, Lippincott, 1931.
Kings and Queens, with Herbert Farjeon, illustrated by Rosalind Thornycroft. London, Gollancz, and New York, Dutton, 1932; revised edition, London, Dent, 1953; Philadelphia, Lippincott, 1955.
Heroes and Heroines, with Herbert Farjeon, illustrated by Rosalind Thornycroft. London, Gollancz, and New York, Dutton, 1933.
Over the Garden Wall, illustrated by Gwendolen Raverat. London, Faber, and New York, Stokes, 1933.
Sing for Your Supper, illustrated by Isobel and John Morton-Sale. London, Joseph, and New York, Stokes, 1938.
Songs of Kings and Queens, with Herbert Farjeon, music by Eleanor Farjeon. London, Arnold, 1938.
A Sussex Alphabet, illustrated by Sheila M. Thompson. Bognor Regis, Sussex, Pear Tree Press, 1939.
Cherrystones, illustrated by Isobel and John Morton-Sale. London, Joseph, 1942; Philadelphia, Lippincott, 1944.
A Prayer for Little Things, illustrated by Elizabeth Orton Jones. Boston, Houghton Mifflin, 1945.
The Mulberry Bush, illustrated by Isobel and John Morton-Sale. London, Joseph, 1945.
The Starry Floor, illustrated by Isobel and John Morton-Sale. London, Joseph, 1949.
Mrs. Malone, illustrated by David Knight. London, Joseph, 1950; New York, Walck, 1962.
Silver-Sand and Snow. London, Joseph, 1951.
The Children's Bells: A Selection of Poems, illustrated by Peggy Fortnum. London, Oxford University Press, 1957; New York, Walck, 1960.
A Puffin Quartet of Poets, with others, edited by Eleanor Graham, illustrated by Diana Bloomfield. London, Penguin, 1958.
Then There Were Three, Being Cherrystones, The Mulberry Bush, The Starry Floor, illustrated by Isobel and John Morton-Sale. London, Joseph, 1958; Philadelphia, Lippincott, 1965.
Morning Has Broken, illustrated by Gordon Stowell. Oxford, Mowbray, 1981.
Invitation to a Mouse and Other Poems, edited by Annabel Farjeon, illustrated by Antony Maitland. London, Pelham, 1981.
Something I Remember, edited by Anne Harvey, illustrated by Alan Marks. London, Blackie, 1987.

Other

Mighty Men: Achilles to Julius Caesar, Beowulf to Harold, illustrated by Hugh Chesterman. Oxford, Blackwell, 2 vols., 1924-25; New York, Appleton, 2 vols., 1925.
Tales from Chaucer: The Canterbury Tales Done into Prose, illustrated by W. Russell Flint. London, Medici Society, and New York, Cape and Smith, 1930.
Ten Saints, illustrated by Helen Sewell. New York, Oxford University Press, 1936; London, Oxford University Press, 1953.
Lector Readings (reader), illustrated by Ruth Westcott. London, Nelson, 1936.
The Wonders of Herodotus, illustrated by Edmund Nelson. London, Nelson, 1937.
Paladins in Spain..., illustrated by Katharine Tozer. London, Nelson, 1937.
The New Book of Days, illustrated by Philip Gough and Meredith W. Hawes. London, Oxford University Press, 1941; New York, Walck, 1961.
Eleanor Farjeon's Book: Stories, Verses, Plays, edited by Eleanor Graham, illustrated by Edward Ardizzone. London, Penguin, 1960.

Editor, with William Mayne, *The Hamish Hamilton Book of Kings,* illustrated by Victor Ambrus. London, Hamish Hamilton, 1964; as *A Cavalcade of Kings,* New York, Walck, 1965.
Editor, with William Mayne, *The Hamish Hamilton Book of Queens,* illustrated by Victor Ambrus. London, Hamish Hamilton, 1965; as *A Cavalcade of Queens,* New York, Walck, 1965.
Editor, *The Green Roads: Poems for Young Readers,* by Edward Thomas, illustrated by Bernard Brett. London, Bodley Head, and New York, Holt Rinehart, 1965.

Publications for Adults

Novels

The Soul of Kol Nikon. London, Collins, and New York, Stokes, 1923.
Ladybrook. London, Collins, and New York, Stokes, 1931.
The Fair of St. James: A Fantasia. London, Faber, and New York, Stokes, 1932.
The Humming Bird. London, Joseph, 1936; New York, Stokes, 1937.
Miss Granby's Secret. London, Joseph, 1940; as *Miss Granby's Secret; or, The Bastard of Pinsk,* New York, Simon and Schuster, 1941.
Brave Old Woman. London, Joseph, 1941.
The Fair Venetian. London, Joseph, 1943.
Golden Coney. London, Joseph, 1943.
Ariadne and the Bull. London, Joseph, 1945.
Love Affair. London, Joseph, 1947; New York, Macmillan, 1949.
The Two Bouquets, from the play by Eleanor and Herbert Farjeon. London, Joseph, 1948.

Short Stories

Gypsy and Ginger. London, Dent, and New York, Dutton, 1920.
Faithful Jenny Dove and Other Tales. London, Collins, 1925; revised edition, as *Faithful Jenny Dove and Other Illusions,* London, Joseph, 1963.

Plays

Floretta (opera), music by Harry Farjeon (produced London, 1899). London, Henderson and Spalding, 1899.
The Registry Office (opera), music by Harry Farjeon (produced London, 1900). London, Henderson and Spalding, 1900.

A Gentleman of the Road (operetta), music by Harry Farjeon (produced London, 1902). London, Boosey and Hawkes, 1903.
St. John's Eve, music by Alexander C. Mackenzie (produced Liverpool, 1924).
The Two Bouquets: A Victorian Comedy with Music, with Herbert Farjeon, music by the authors (produced London, 1936). London, Gollancz, 1936.
An Elephant in Arcady, with Herbert Farjeon, music by Ernest Irving (produced London, 1938).
A Room at the Inn: A Christmas Masque, with Herbert Farjeon, music by Harry Farjeon (broadcast, 1938). Privately printed, 1956.
Aucassin and Nicolette, with Herbert Farjeon, music by Clifton Parker. London, Chappell, 1952.

Radio Play: *A Room at the Inn: A Christmas Masque,* with Herbert Farjeon, 1938.

Poetry

Pan-Worship and Other Poems. London, Elkin Mathews, 1908.
Dream-Songs for the Beloved. London, Orpheus Press, 1911.
Sonnets and Poems. Oxford, Blackwell, 1918.
Tomfooleries (as Tomfool). London, Daily Herald, 1920.
Moonshine (as Tomfool). London, Labour Publishing-Allen and Unwin, 1921.
The ABC of the B.B.C. London, Collins, 1928.
Snowfall. London, Favil Press, 1928.
A Collection of Poems. London, Collins, 1929.
First and Second Love: Sonnets. London, Joseph, 1947.

Other

Arthur Rackham: The Wizard at Home. New York, Century, 1914.
Trees. London, Batsford, 1914.
A Nursery in the Nineties (autobiography). London, Gollancz, 1935; as *Portrait of a Family,* New York, Stokes, 1936.
Magic Casements (essays). London, Allen and Unwin, 1941.
Dark World of Animals. London, Sylvan Press, 1945.
Elizabeth Myers. Aylesford, Kent, St. Albert's Press, 1957.
Edward Thomas, The Last Four Years: The Memoirs of Eleanor Farjeon, Book One. London, Oxford University Press, 1958.

Translator, with Herbert Farjeon, *The Fan,* in *Four Comedies,* by Carlo Goldoni, edited by Clifford Bax. London, Cecil Palmer, 1922.

*

Critical Studies: *Eleanor Farjeon* by Eileen Colwell, London, Bodley Head, and New York, Walck, 1961; *The Eleanor Farjeon Book: A Tribute to Her Life and Work 1881-1965,* London, Hamish Hamilton, 1966, as *A Book for Eleanor Farjeon,* New York, Walck, 1966; *Eleanor: Portrait of a Farjeon,* London, Gollancz, 1966, and *In Search of Elsie Piddock,* London, Favil Press, 1967, both by Denys Blakelock; *Morning Has Broken: A Biography of Eleanor Farjeon* by Annabel Farjeon, London, MacRae, and New York, Watts, 1986.

* * *

Eleanor Farjeon's writing was so much part of her own bubbling, enthusiastic personality that it is impossible not to see her as one of her own characters. She is, without doubt, the motherly, generous animal-lover Mrs. Malone "Whose heart was so big/It had room for us all...." And she is the Nurse in *The Old Nurse's Stocking Basket.* Old Nurse has been around a long while and nursed such charges as King Neptune, the Brothers Grimm, the Spanish Infanta "who had to be best at everything," and tiny Lipp the Lapp "who was so small his mother couldn't find him." She tells wise and witty stories to her present family.

Farjeon enjoyed this device of circling stories around a central character, and it also works well in *Jim at the Corner,* in which Sailor Jim spins yarns for the boy Derry. She first used it in *Martin Pippin in the Apple-Orchard,* a romantic pastoral originally intended for adults. It caught the imaginations of young girls in the 1920s, though its whimsical charm has dated. The sequel, *Martin Pippin in the Daisy-Field,* is a sturdier book for a younger age group, where the batch of tales told by the minstrel are also Sussex-based, and well plotted and sustained. One story, "Elsie Piddock Skips in Her Sleep," stands out, and was the writer's own favorite.

In later life Farjeon wrote that it was her absorption in imaginative play that led to "that flow of ease that makes writing a delight." She was also fortunate in her unorthodox father's dislike of formal education and encouragement to read freely in his well-stocked library. "That little bookroom," she wrote, "opened magic casements for me through which I looked out on other worlds and times than those I lived in." *The Little Book-Room* was an apt title for the 1955 collection she made from her own stories. It is her finest work, and a worthy winner of the Andersen and Carnegie medals. The range is wide, the stories are amusing and unsentimental; fantasy combines with sharp observation, lit by unexpected twists and turns. Reading these 27 stories one learns of her own experience and values. Trust, friendship, and justice are more important than rank or material possessions. She is never far away from her own childhood, and the wisest of her adult characters know the importance of "a life kept always young." The humour is rich and firm, but she never glosses over death, old age, or disappointment. It is a collection of quality, of depth, of ageless appeal, to return to over and over again.

Among the stories *And I Dance Mine Own Child* is unusual. The two main characters, Griselda and her Great Grandmother, separated by a span of 100 years, have reversed roles. The old lady enjoys sorting beads, playing with Bella the doll, and stealing currants. Her eyes grow bright and greedy for sweets to take with the medicine Grissie doses her with. Grissie is capable, wise to Gramma's ways, adept at tucking her up and telling her stories. They are descendants of the poet, Thomas Dekker, and own an ancient book of his; Bella sits by it—"it props her up beautiful"—but it turns out to be so valuable that Gramma need not go to the Almshouse and Grissie can go on singing her the song Dekker wrote for that other, long ago Griselda: "Hush ... hush ... hush.... And I dance mine own child."

Farjeon was the friend of many poets, among them D.H. Lawrence, Robert Frost, and Edward Thomas, and in her youth she too "dreamed of being a real poet, but half way through my life the dream died and whatever figments of it remained went into writing songs and verses for children." The best of her poetry matches the best of her prose, but at times she allowed her delight in words, rhyme, and rhythm to dance along into slight, rather tripping verse. She never quite caught the chilling edge, the sense of menace, of her friend Walter de la Mare; but her work offers amazing variety and craftsmanship. The two stand together as the most important English children's poets of the 20th century. She drew on a vast store of knowledge, and wrote of town and country, good and bad children, old folk, magic and the sea, school and home. She liked to weave poems around the alphabet letters, or a theme like the zodiac or party games. Her poems on kittens, on a special golden cat, on the cats that "Sleep anywhere,/ Any table, any chair..." are very popular. She practiced no formal religion until she became a Catholic in old age, but "Morning Is Broken" is sung as a hymn, she wrote much on saints, and no-one captures the holiness, as well as the festivity, of Christmas as she did. *Nursery Rhymes of London Town,* includes inventive and quirky play on London place names: "King's Cross! What shall we do?/Leave him alone for a minute or two"; "Wormwood scrubs the City streets,/Wormwood scrubs St. Paul's." Herbert Farjeon's collaboration with his sister was a happy one; his more caustic humour combined well with her light-hearted touch. Their masterpiece, *Kings and Queens,* offers a tongue in cheek glimpse at the monarchy, with such observations as:

> Bluff King Hal was full of beans,
> He married half a dozen Queens,
> For three called Kate they cried the banns
> And one called Jane, and a couple of Anne's....

They also collaborated on a play, *The Glass Slipper,* and later she wrote one on her own, *The Silver Curlew.* Both are highly professional theatre pieces, with attractive characters and sparkling dialogue, and are far less dated than one would expect.

Farjeon's final piece of writing, the perceptive introduction to a selection of Edward Thomas's poems for young readers, was completed the day before her 84th birthday. This closed a career that is recognised annually when the Children's Book Circle give the Eleanor Farjeon award in her memory. In the 1930s she told would-be children's writers: "Don't write down to children...don't try to be on their level...don't think there is a special tone they will respond to. Don't be afraid of words and things you think they can't yet grasp...." It was advice she always followed herself.

—Anne Harvey

FARR, Diana. See **PULLEIN-THOMPSON, Diana.**

FARROW, G(eorge) E(dward)

Nationality: British. **Born:** Ipswich, Suffolk, 17 March 1862. **Education:** United States and London. **Died:** 1920(?).

Publications for Children

Fiction

The Wallypug of Why, illustrated by Harry and Dorothy Furniss. London, Hutchinson, 1895; New York, Dodd Mead, 1896.
The King's Gardens: An Allegory, illustrated by A.L. Bowley. London, Hutchinson, 1896.
The Missing Prince, illustrated by Harry and Dorothy Furniss. London, Hutchinson, 1896; New York, Dodd Mead, 1897.
The Wallypug in London, illustrated by Alan Wright. London, Methuen, 1897.
Adventures in Wallypug-Land, illustrated by Alan Wright. London, Methuen, 1898; New York, Burt, 1900.
The Little Panjandrum's Dodo, illustrated by Alan Wright. London, Skeffington, and New York, Stokes, 1899; as *Dick, Marjorie, and Fidge: The Adventures of Three Little People,* New York, Burt, 1901.
The Mandarin's Kite, illustrated by Alan Wright. London, Skeffington, 1900.
Baker Minor and the Dragon, illustrated by Alan Wright. London, Pearson, 1901.
The New Panjandrum, illustrated by Alan Wright. London, Pearson, 1901; New York, Dutton, 1902.
In Search of the Wallypug, illustrated by Alan Wright. London, Pearson, 1902.
All About the Wallypug. London, Tuck, 1903.
Professor Philanderpan. London, Pearson, 1903.
The Cinematograph Train and Other Stories, illustrated by Alan Wright. London, Johnson, 1904.
Pixie Pickles: The Adventures of Pixene and Pixette in Their Woodland Haunts, illustrated by Harry B. Neilson. London, Skeffington, 1904; New York, Warne, 1906.
The Wallypug Birthday Book, illustrated by Alan Wright. London, Routledge, 1904.
The Wallypug in Fog-land, illustrated by Alan Wright. London, Pearson, and Philadelphia, Lippincott, 1904.
The Mysterious "Mr. Punch." London, S.P.C.K., 1905.
The Wallypug Book, illustrated by Harry Furniss. London, Treherne, 1905.
The Wallypug in the Moon; or, His Badjesty, illustrated by Alan Wright. London, Pearson, and Philadelphia, Lippincott, 1905.
Ruff and Ready: The Fairy Guide, with May Byron, illustrated by John Hassall. London, Cooke, 1905.
Ten Little Jappy Chaps, illustrated by John Hassall. London, Treherne, 1905.
The Adventures of Ji, illustrated by G.C. Tresidder. London, Partridge, 1906.
The Escape of the Mullingong: A Zoological Nightmare, illustrated by Gordon Browne. London, Blackie, 1906.
The Adventures of a Dodo, illustrated by Willy Pogány. London, Unwin, 1907; New York, Wessels, 1908; as *A Mysterious Voyage,* London, Partridge, 1910.
Zoo Babies, illustrated by Cecil Aldin. London, Hodder and Stoughton, 1907; New York, Stokes, 1908.
The Dwindleberry Zoo, illustrated by Gordon Browne. London, Blackie, 1908.
Don't Tell, illustrated by John Hassall. New York, Stokes, n.d.
The Mysterious Shin Shira. London, Hodder and Stoughton, 1913.

Poetry

An A.B.C. of Every-Day People, illustrated by John Hassall. London, Blackie, 1902.
Absurd Ditties, illustrated by John Hassall. London, Routledge, and New York, Dutton, 1903.
Wallypug Tales. London, Tuck, 1903.
Round the World A.B.C., illustrated by John Hassall. London, Nister, and New York, Dutton, 1904.

PUBLICATIONS FOR ADULTS

Other

Lovely Man, Being the Views of Mistress A. Crosspatch. London, Skeffington, 1904.
Food of the Dogs and What Became of It: A Travesty, with Ample Apologies to Mr. H.G. Wells. London, Johnson, 1904.

Editor, *Essays in Bacon: An Autograph Book.* London, Treherne, 1906.

* * *

G.E. Farrow was perhaps the best, and certainly the most prolific, of the many Victorian and Edwardian Lewis Carroll imitators, who felt they too had an aptitude for paradox, puns, and versifying, and that a dream setting was a convenient excuse for a loose and inconsequential plot. It is startling now to observe how closely they followed their model: *The Wallypug of Why,* Farrow's first and most popular book, begins, like *Alice in Wonderland,* with its heroine (who greatly resembles Alice) waking in a dreamland filled with strange and combative creatures against whom she struggles to assert herself. But the Wallypug himself is genuinely original, a nervous little nonentity who in theory rules the land of Why but in practice is ruled by his subjects whom he addresses as "Your Majesty." Harry Furniss's drawings of this pathetic little being with his crown tipped over one eye were so apt that they were followed by subsequent illustrators of Wallypug sequels. There were many of these. The Wallypug and his entourage are brought to London in *The Wallypug in London* to see the sights of Queen Victoria's Diamond Jubilee; sent to Fog-land in 1904, and to the Moon in 1905, adventures which lack the spontaneity and sprightliness of the first book.

The Little Panjandrum's Dodo, his best book, is better constructed than any of these, and much his most original writing. Three children float away on a high tide to a land ruled by the Little Panjandrum who sends them, under pain of "subtransexdistrication," to find his Dodo. The Dodo himself is an endearing character for all his vanity, touchiness, and consequential airs. "It's lovely being extinct. Have you ever tried it?....It's most convenient, if anyone calls whom you don't wish to see, just tell the servant to say that you're extinct, and there is an end of the matter." The Dodo's final arrival in London, his attempt to take a job as a "typewriter," and his disappearance are depicted with a light humour that Farrow never achieved anywhere else, and certainly not in the two subsequent stories of the Dodo's adventures.

—Gillian Avery

FATCHEN, Max

Nationality: Australian. **Born:** Adelaide, South Australia, 3 August 1920. **Education:** Angle Vale Primary School; Gawler High School. **Military Service:** Royal Australian Air Force, 1940-45. **Family:** Married Jean Wohlers in 1942; two sons and one daughter. **Career:** Journalist, Adelaide *News* and *Sunday Mail,* 1946-55; journalist, 1955-84, literary editor, 1971-81, and special writer, 1981-84, Adelaide *Advertiser.* **Awards:** A.M. (Member, Order of Australia), 1980; Walkey award, 1996, for outstanding journalism; Primary English Teaching Association of Australia award, 1996, for excellence in writing poetry for children. **Agent:** John Johnson Ltd., 45-47 Clerkenwell Green, London ECIR 0HT, England. **Address:** 15 Jane Street, Smithfield, South Australia 5114, Australia.

PUBLICATIONS FOR CHILDREN

Fiction

The River Kings, illustrated by Clyde Pearson. Sidney, Hicks Smith, and London, Methuen, 1966; New York, St. Martin's Press, 1968.
Conquest of the River, illustrated by Clyde Pearson. Sydney, Hicks Smith, and London, Methuen, 1970.
The Spirit Wind, illustrated by Trevor Stubley. Sydney, Hicks Smith, and London, Methuen, 1973.
Chase Through the Night, illustrated by Graham Humphreys. Sydney and London, Methuen, 1977.
The Time Wave, illustrated by Edward Mortelmans. Sydney and London, Methuen, 1978.
Closer to the Stars. Sydney and London, Methuen, 1981.
Had Yer Jabs? Sydney, Methuen, 1987.

Poetry

Songs for My Dog and Other People, illustrated by Michael Atchison. London, Kestrel, 1980.
Wry Rhymes for Troublesome Times, illustrated by Michael Atchison. London, Kestrel, 1983.
A Paddock of Poems, illustrated by Kerry Argent. Adelaide, Omnibus, 1987.
A Pocketful of Rhymes, illustrated by Kerry Argent. Adelaide, Omnibus, 1989.
The Country Mail Is Coming: Poems from Down Under, illustrated by Catharine O'Neill. Boston, Joy Street Books, 1990.
With Colin Thiele, *Tea for Three.* Melbourne, Moondrake, 1994.
Peculiar Rhymes and Lunatic Lines. London, Orchard Books, 1995.

Other (in verse)

Drivers and Trains, illustrated by Iris Millington. Melbourne, Longman, 1963.
Keepers and Lighthouses, illustrated by Iris Millington. Melbourne, Longman, 1963.
The Plumber, illustrated by Iris Millington. Melbourne, Longman, 1963.
The Electrician, illustrated by Iris Millington. Melbourne, Longman, 1963.

The Transport Driver, illustrated by Iris Millington. Melbourne, Longman, 1965.
The Carpenter, illustrated by Iris Millington. Melbourne, Longman, 1965.
Mostly Max. Adelaide, Wakefield Press, 1995.

PUBLICATIONS FOR ADULTS

Poetry

Peculia Australia: Verses. Privately printed, 1965.

Other

Just Fancy, Mr. Fatchen! A Collection of Verse, Prose and Fate's Cruel Blows. Adelaide, Rigby, 1967.
Forever Fatchen. Adelaide, Advertiser, 1983.

*

Manuscript Collections: South Australia State Library, Adelaide.

Max Fatchen comments:
My work as a journalist has taken me along Australia's river systems, particularly the Murray. I have covered its floods, talked to its oldtimers, ridden on some of the last of its riverboats and thus gathered material for my two books on the Murray—*The River Kings* and *Conquest of the River.* I have also seen the Mississippi, and it was a visit there in 1963 that helped to trigger my interest in writing books myself. My assignments have also taken me to sea aboard lighthouse ships and landing servicing crews by boat and helicopter on lonely islands of the southern Australian coast. I have also been at sea with trawlermen, naval surveyors, and lobster fishermen. I know particularly the windy coastline of South Australia where the last squareriggers came to load grain for their race around the Horn. I have also roamed over Australia's outback, particularly in the area under the Gulf of Carpentaria and across the lonely rivers and coastline of Arnhem Land in the Northern Territory. Here again I have found material for my books. The sea and the land are not just background but characters in my books because I feel they are alive, have a personality of their own and react on the people I write about. So I describe weather, the moods of landscape and climate, the fact that in the loneliness of the outback, particularly at night, the land can be felt like a presence padding around in the darkness outside. I feel that children like a strong storyline, action, character, good dialogue, and no humbug. I find them honest, attentive, and perceptive once their interest is captured. A book is a voyage, and I don't want them just to be passengers but members of the crew.

* * *

The sea, rivers, and sailing craft, combined with his deep feeling for his native South Australia, lie at the heart of Max Fatchen's writing for young readers. His first two novels (for younger teenagers) formed a slightly tentative approach into the area of children's literature. *The River Kings* and *Conquest of the River,* set in South Australia's pioneering days when riverboats used to trade and cruise along the Murray River, both follow the fortunes of teenaged Shane, who runs away from an unhappy home and becomes a member of a riverboat crew. Both stories are well constructed, though perhaps a little too tightly organized, and they are filled with dramatic and humorous incident and deft characterization of typical riverboat people—a tough but kindly Cap'n, a Chinese cook, Scottish engineer, and so forth. They are also soundly based on riverboat knowledge and research. The choice of incidents and their outcome tend to be predictable, but, given the riverboat setting, this is to some extent inevitable—fire, flood, bunyips, and races between one riverboat and another are obvious ingredients of stories set on the Murray—and Fatchen was one of the first to choose this setting for junior fiction. Well in the background lurks the author's almost mystic and certainly poetic feeling for the great river. Here is a sound professional journalist producing exciting and very readable fiction, with just a hint of more significant power behind him. His narrative style is exceptionally clear-cut, free of any excess verbiage.

The publication of *The Spirit Wind* marked an important new departure for Fatchen. This is a much deeper and more ambitious work, in which the strain of poetry and mysticism emerges strongly, linked to Aboriginal lore through the character of Nunganee, an outcast from his tribe because he once "sang" a man's death. This book is set, once again, in the last century; the central character is 15-year-old Jarl Hansen, deckhand aboard the *Hootzen,* a squarerigger out of Norway bound for Australia, and ruled by a sadistic Mate. Jarl encounters Nunganee when he jumps ship in South Australia; their destinies, as well as that of the Mate and of the *Hootzen* herself, become entwined and are eventually fulfilled during a night of fierce storm when the mysterious Spirit Wind is unleashed. In this work Fatchen shows new powers and has launched his writing beyond the shallower seas of predictable incident and nicely observed characterization.

—Barbara Ker Wilson

FATIO, Louise

Nationality: American (emigrated to the United States in 1925; naturalized citizen, 1938). **Born:** Lausanne, Switzerland, 18 August 1904. **Education:** Boarding school, Basel, Switzerland; Collège des Jeunes Filles, Geneva. **Family:** Married Roger Duvoisin, *q.v.,* in 1925 (died 1980); two sons.

PUBLICATIONS FOR CHILDREN (ILLUSTRATED BY ROGER DUVOISIN)

Fiction

The Christmas Forest. New York, Aladdin, 1950.
Anna the Horse. New York, Aladdin, 1951.
The Happy Lion. New York, McGraw Hill, 1954; London, Lane 1955.
The Happy Lion in Africa. New York, McGraw Hill, 1955; London, Bodley Head, 1963.
The Happy Lion Roars. New York, McGraw Hill, 1957; London, Bodley Head, 1959.
A Doll for Marie. New York, McGraw Hill, 1957.
The Three Happy Lions. New York, McGraw Hill, 1959; London, Bodley Head, 1960.

The Happy Lion's Quest. New York, McGraw Hill, 1961; London, Bodley Head, 1962.
Red Bantam. New York, McGraw Hill, and London, Bodley Head, 1963.
The Happy Lion and the Bear. New York, McGraw Hill, 1964; London, Bodley Head, 1965.
The Happy Lion's Vacation. New York, McGraw Hill, 1967; as *The Happy Lion's Holiday,* London, Bodley Head, 1968.
The Happy Lion's Treasure. New York, McGraw Hill, and London, Bodley Head, 1971.
Hector Penguin. New York, McGraw Hill, and London, Bodley Head, 1973.
The Happy Lion's Rabbits. New York, McGraw Hill, 1974; London, Bodley Head, 1975.
Marc and Pixie and the Walls in Mrs. Jones's Garden. New York, McGraw Hill, 1975; London, Hodder and Stoughton, 1977.
Hector and Christina. New York, McGraw Hill, 1977; London, Bodley Head, 1978.
The Happy Lioness. New York, McGraw Hill, 1980.

*

Manuscript Collection: Kerlan Collection, University of Minnesota, Minneapolis.

Louise Fatio comments:

(1978) As in the case of most of those who translate their thoughts and beliefs into books, my books are an extension of my life. Or, I should say, our lives, my husband's and mine, for we have similar backgrounds, share the same tastes, and collaborate on many of our books.

Our love of people, of nature, our respect for animals—all often expressed in my books—date from our childhoods. We spent many summer vacations on farms or in villages, my husband in a Savoy village or a fishing village on the Mediterranean, I in a French-Swiss village. The need for a full country life not too far from a civilized city led us to settle in New Jersey (then a farming land which deserved its name of garden state) when we came to America. It is in this country atmosphere that we composed most of our books and brought up our children.

* * *

Louise Fatio is best known for her Happy Lion picture books, a series with general unifying qualities, perhaps the most significant the characterization of the genial lion and the quiet themes of friendship and acceptance.

The Happy Lion lives in the zoo, but, thanks to his friendship with François, the zookeeper's son, is able to wander out of the zoo whenever it suits him. Uncharacteristically gentle and thoroughly kind, the Happy Lion shows great concern for others—visitors as well as fellow zoo-dwellers. He is pensive, restless, lonely, helpful; when he is free, he occasionally frightens townspeople, but not by his fierceness.

In addition to the memorable character of the Happy Lion, the themes of the books are important. To love and be loved is a treasure. We need someone like ourselves, as the Happy Lion discovers when he finds a mate in *The Happy Lion Roars.* Where we live is home, not where we come from, the Happy Lion discovers in *The Happy Lion in Africa.* He challenges rules and finds that sometimes new rules are needed, and in another story he discovers that befriending others makes one happy. Aggressive behavior is rewarded with aggression, kind behavior with kindness, as in *Red Bantam.* Hector in *Hector Penguin* finds it important to be what he is not to conform.

These direct, straightforward stories with little imagery or stylistic complexity, illustrated by Roger Duvoisin, have warmth and acceptance in their tone: they are important as comfortable affirmations of love and loyalty.

—Rebecca J. Lukens

FENTON, Edward

Nationality: American. **Born:** New York City, 7 July 1917. **Education:** Amherst College, Massachusetts. **Military Service:** American Field Service and the British 8th Army in North Africa during World War II. **Family:** Married Sophia Harvati in 1963. **Career:** Staff member in the print department, Metropolitan Museum of Art, New York, 1950-55. **Awards:** Mystery Writers of America Edgar Allan Poe award, 1962; Batchelder award, for translation, 1970, 1974, 1980. **Died:** 24 December 1995.

Publications for Children

Fiction

Us and the Duchess, illustrated by Reisie Lonette. New York, Doubleday, 1947.
Aleko's Island, illustrated by Dimitris Davis. New York, Doubleday, 1948; London, Oxford University Press, 1953.
Hidden Trapezes, illustrated by Reisie Lonette. New York, Doubleday, 1950.
Nine Lives; or, The Celebrated Cat of Beacon Hill, illustrated by Paul Galdone. New York, Pantheon, 1951.
The Golden Doors, illustrated by Gioia Fiammenghi. New York, Doubleday, 1957; as *Mystery in Florence,* London, Constable, 1959.
Once upon a Saturday, illustrated by Rita Fava. New York, Doubleday, 1958.
Fierce John, illustrated by William Pène du Bois. New York, Doubleday, 1959.
The Nine Questions, illustrated by C. Walter Hodges. New York, Doubleday, 1959; Kingswood, Surrey, World's Work, 1962.
The Phantom of Walkaway Hill, illustrated by Jo Ann Stover. New York, Doubleday, 1961.
An Island for a Pelican, illustrated by Dimitris Davis. New York, Doubleday, and Kingswood, Surrey, World's Work, 1963.
The Riddle of the Red Whale. New York, Doubleday, 1966.
The Big Yellow Balloon, illustrated by Ib Ohlsson. New York, Doubleday, 1967.
A Matter of Miracles. New York, Holt Rinehart, 1967.
Penny Candy, illustrated by Edward Gorey. New York, Holt Rinehart, 1970.
Duffy's Rocks. New York, Dutton, and London, Hamish Hamilton, 1974.
The Refugee Summer. New York, Delacorte Press, 1982; London, MacRae, 1983.

The Morning of the Gods. New York, Delacorte Press, and London, MacRae, 1987.

Other

Translator, *Wildcat under Glass,* by Alki Zei. New York, Holt Rinehart, 1968; London, Gollancz, 1969.
Translator, *Petros' War,* by Alki Zei. New York, Dutton, and London, Gollancz, 1972.
Translator, *The Sound of the Dragon's Feet,* by Alki Zei. New York, Dutton, 1979.

Publications for Adults

Novels

The Double Darkness. New York, Doubleday, 1947; London, Cresset Press, 1948.
Anne of the Thousand Days (novelization of screenplay). New York, New American Library, 1970.

Poetry

Soldiers and Strangers. New York, Macmillan, 1945.

Other

Translator, *Greek Shop Signs,* by George Vakirtzis and others. Athens, Papastratos, 1974.

*

Manuscript Collections: de Grummond Collection, University of Southern Mississippi, Hattiesburg.

* * *

Through a writing career stretching over a period of 40 years, Edward Fenton has written books in a wide range of styles for young readers. His many novels have been published in numerous languages, and it is this cosmopolitan appeal that is unusual in a children's writer. Although American born, Fenton now considers himself a Greek by adoption, while retaining his sense of *kosmos* in his themes. *The Morning of the Gods,* his latest work, is set in a Greece repressed by the rule of the Colonels, a repressive military junta. Fenton identifies in exact detail the Greece of the mind's eye: "There was hardly anything to see: a small square with a couple of stunted palm trees in the middle of it and some yellowish houses clutching the dry rocks; the sea behind them; and then, the vast sky." Location clarified, the reader is not allowed to lose this shared vision of the colour and beauty of the land, a daily life of encounters and experience, where myth and poetry are still vital elements. This is Carla's first visit home. Her, and Fenton's, native New York is a world removed from her mother's birthplace. However, she soon comes to empathise with the people—their warmth, heritage, and loathing of the Colonels. "Colonels, generals, they all come, and eventually they all go away again. We are the ones who remain." Carla soon finds a practical way to share this mutual abhorrence of the military rule, and contribute a step, albeit a small one, on the return to the fields of Asphodel.

Fenton's time living in both Greece and Italy has naturally been a major influence on his writing, giving him a breadth of experience that allows his books to transcend the restrictive themes of much modern writing for young readers. *Aleko's Island, An Island for a Pelican, The Golden Doors,* as well as *The Morning of the Gods,* are all triumphant testiments to his travels. The atmospheric and descriptive writing has a stamp of authority that surpasses the vividest of imaginations or depth of research. Naturally because of his strong American roots much of Fenton's work is based on his early experiences growing up in and around New York City. One of these, *The Phantom of Walkaway Hill,* first gained him public recognition through its selection as winner of the prestigious Edgar Allen Poe award in 1962. Others to recommend from this period include *Once upon a Saturday,* based upon his own adolescence, *Fierce John,* and *The Riddle of the Red Whale.* An extension of the American experience theme is attempted successfully in *Duffy's Rocks.* Although Fenton was New York born and bred, he manages to convey the Depression years in industrial Pittsburgh in an inspired piece of imagined-experience writing.

Penny Candy, a magical picture book, shows Fenton's skills in yet further areas of the writer's art. Widow Shinn has a candy store. But, is she really a witch? Who's going to hang around long enough to put her to the test? Those tempted to sneak in and try the candy tend to find they turn a strange colour—a bit of a give-away.

Carla's mother had told her that "You will see it all for yourself when I take you there." With Fenton that promise is never made, but the result is certainly achieved. Fenton's settings, whether they are in New York or Greece, or indeed wherever, fill the mind's imaginings. To say that he is a word photographer in sympathy with his locations undervalues the writer. To visit, to experience, to inhabit even, does not mean at all that you can capture the essence for the delight of the reader. Fenton has that gift, not just for the physical appearances of terrain, but for the capturing of the soul, the spirit, the sense of any place he portrays.

—Bill Boyle

FIDLER, Kathleen (Annie)

Nationality: British. **Born:** Coalville, Leicestershire, 10 August 1899. **Education:** Girls' High School, Wigan, Lancashire, 1911-18; St. Mary's College, Bangor, North Wales, 1918-20, Teacher's Certificate 1920. **Family:** Married J.H. Goldie in 1930 (died); one son and one daughter. **Career:** Headmistress, Scot Lane Evening Institute, 1924-30, and St. Paul's Girls' School, Wigan, 1925-30; script writer, Authors' Panel for Schools Broadcasting in Scotland, 1938-62. **Award:** Moscow Film Festival award, 1967. **Died:** 1980.

Publications for Children

Fiction

The Borrowed Garden. London, Lutterworth Press, 1944.
St. Jonathan's in the Country: A Sequel to "The Borrowed Garden," illustrated by Charles Koolman. London, Lutterworth Press, 1945; revised edition, 1952.

Fingal's Ghost. London, John Crowther, 1945.
The Brydons at Smugglers' Creek, illustrated by H. Tilden Reeves. London, Lutterworth Press, 1946.
The White Cockade Passes. London, Lutterworth Press, 1947.
The Mysterious Mr. Simister. London, Lutterworth Press, 1947.
More Adventures of the Brydons, illustrated by Victor Bertoglio. London, Lutterworth Press, 1947; revised edition, London, Hodder and Stoughton, 1971.
The Brydons Go Camping, illustrated by A.H. Watson. London, Lutterworth Press, 1948.
Mr. Simister Appears Again, illustrated by Margaret Horder. London, Lutterworth Press, 1948.
Mr. Simister Is Unlucky, illustrated by Margaret Horder. London, Lutterworth Press, 1949.
The Brydons Do Battle, illustrated by A.H. Watson. London, Lutterworth Press, 1949.
The Brydons in Summer, illustrated by A.H. Watson. London, Lutterworth Press, 1949.
Guest Castle. London, Lutterworth Press, 1949.
I Rode with the Covenanters, illustrated by E. Boyce Uden. London, Lutterworth Press, 1950.
The Brydons Look for Trouble, illustrated by T.R. Freeman. London, Lutterworth Press, 1950.
The Brydons in a Pickle, illustrated by T.R. Freeman. London, Lutterworth Press, 1950.
Surprises for the Brydons, illustrated by T.R. Freeman. London, Lutterworth Press, 1950.
The White-Starred Hare and Other Stories, illustrated by A.H. Watson. London, Lutterworth Press, 1951.
The Brydons Get Things Going, illustrated by T.R. Freeman. London, Lutterworth Press, 1951; revised edition, Hodder and Stoughton, 1971.
The Brydons Hunt for Treasure, illustrated by T.R. Freeman. London, Lutterworth Press, 1951.
The Brydons Catch Queer Fish, illustrated by T.R. Freeman. London, Lutterworth Press, 1952.
The Brydons Stick at Nothing, illustrated by T.R. Freeman. London, Lutterworth Press, 1952.
Fedora the Donkey, illustrated by Iris Gillespie. London, Lutterworth Press, 1952.
The Stallion from the Sea, illustrated by G.S. Ronald. London, Lutterworth Press, 1953.
The Brydons Abroad, illustrated by T.R. Freeman. London, Lutterworth Press, 1953.
The Deans Move In, illustrated by Reg Forster. London, Lutterworth Press, 1953.
Pete, Pam and Jim, the Investigators, illustrated by Lunt Roberts. London, Lutterworth Press, 1954.
The Deans Solve a Mystery, illustrated by Reg Forster. London, Lutterworth Press, 1954.
The Deans Follow a Clue, illustrated by Reg Forster. London, Lutterworth Press, 1954.
The Bank House Twins, illustrated by Frank Bellamy. London, Lutterworth Press, 1955.
The Droving Lad, illustrated by Geoffrey Whittam. London, Lutterworth Press, 1955.
The Deans Defy Danger, illustrated by Reg Forster. London, Lutterworth Press, 1955.
The Brydons on the Broads, illustrated by T.R. Freeman. London, Lutterworth Press, 1955; revised edition, London, Hodder and Stoughton, 1971.
Challenge to the Brydons, illustrated by T.R. Freeman. London, Lutterworth Press, 1956.
Mr. Punch's Cap, illustrated by Shirley Hughes. London, Lutterworth Press, 1956.
The Deans Dive for Treasure, illustrated by Reg Forster. London, Lutterworth Press, 1956.
The Deans to the Rescue, illustrated by Reg Forster. London, Lutterworth Press, 1957.
The McGills at Mystery Farm, with Jack Gillespie, illustrated by Leo Davy. London, Lutterworth Press, 1958.
Lanterns over the Lune, illustrated by David Walsh. London, Lutterworth Press, 1958.
The Deans' Lighthouse Adventure, illustrated by Reg Forster. London, Lutterworth Press, 1959.
More Adventures of the McGills, with Jack Gillespie, illustrated by Hodgson. London, Lutterworth Press, 1959.
The Deans and Mr. Popple, illustrated by Reg Forster. London, Lutterworth Press, 1960.
The Brydons at Blackpool, illustrated by T.R. Freeman. London, Lutterworth Press, 1960.
Escape in Darkness, illustrated by Geoffrey Whittam. London, Lutterworth Press, 1961.
The Deans' Dutch Adventure, illustrated by Reg Forster. London, Lutterworth Press, 1962.
The Brydons Go Canoeing, illustrated by T.R. Freeman. London, Lutterworth Press, 1963.
The Little Ship Dog, illustrated by Antony Maitland. London, Lutterworth Press, 1963.
The Desperate Journey, illustrated by Michael Charlton. London, Lutterworth Press, 1964.
Flash the Sheep Dog, illustrated by Antony Maitland. London, Lutterworth Press, 1965.
Police Dog, illustrated by Sheila Rose. London, Lutterworth Press, 1966.
The Boy with the Bronze Axe, illustrated by Edward Mortelmans. Edinburgh, Oliver and Boyd, 1968.
Haki the Shetland Pony, illustrated by Victor Ambrus. London, Lutterworth Press, 1968; Chicago, Rand McNally, 1970.
Treasure of Ebba, illustrated by Trevor Ridley. London, Lutterworth Press, 1968.
Mountain Rescue Dog, illustrated by Mary Russon. London, Lutterworth Press, 1969.
School at Sea, illustrated by David Grice. London, Epworth Press, 1970.
The Gold of Fast Castle, illustrated by Trevor Ridley. London, Lutterworth Press, 1970.
The Thames in Story. London, Epworth Press, 1971.
Turk, The Border Collie, illustrated by Mary Dinsdale. Guildford, Surrey, Lutterworth Press, 1975.
The Railway Runaways, illustrated by Terry Gabbey. London, Blackie, 1977.
The Lost Cave. London, Blackie, 1978.
Seal Story, illustrated by Douglas Phillips. Guildford, Surrey, Lutterworth Press, 1979.
Pablos and the Bull. London, Blackie, 1979.
The Ghosts of Sandeel Bay, illustrated by Annabel Large. London, Blackie, 1981.

Plays

Screenplay: *Flash the Sheepdog,* 1968.

Radio Plays: *Children's Hour* series.

Television Play: *Haki the Shetland Pony,* from her own story, 1970.

Other

Stories from Scottish Heritage, with Lennox Milne. Edinburgh, Chambers, 3 vols., 1951.
Tales of the North Country, illustrated by Jack Matthew. London, Lutterworth Press, 1952.
To the White North: The Story of Sir John Franklin, illustrated by F. Furnivall. London, Lutterworth Press, 1952.
Tales of London, illustrated by Douglas Relf. London, Lutterworth Press, 1953.
Tales of the Midlands, illustrated by Douglas Relf. London, Lutterworth Press, 1954.
The Man Who Gave Away Millions: The Story of Andrew Carnegie, illustrated by Hodgson. London, Lutterworth Press, 1955; New York, Roy, 1956.
Tales of Scotland, illustrated by Douglas Relf. London, Lutterworth Press, 1956.
Look to the West: Tales of Liverpool, illustrated by Henry Toothill. London, Lutterworth Press, 1957.
Tales of the Islands, illustrated by Douglas Relf. London, Lutterworth Press, 1959.
Tales of Pirates and Castaways, illustrated by Charles Keeping. London, Lutterworth Press, 1960.
Tales of the West Country, illustrated by Charles Keeping. London, Lutterworth Press, 1961.
True Tales of Treasure, illustrated by W.F. Phillipps. London, Lutterworth Press, 1962.
Tales of the South Country, illustrated by W.F. Phillipps. London, Lutterworth Press, 1962.
True Tales of Escapes, illustrated by W.F. Phillipps. London, Lutterworth Press, 1965.
New Lamps for Old (reader), illustrated by John Dugan. Edinburgh, Oliver and Boyd, 1965.
Adventure Underground (reader), illustrated by Forth Studios. Edinburgh, Oliver and Boyd, 1966.
Forest Fire (reader), illustrated by Laszlo Acs. Edinburgh, Oliver and Boyd, 1966.
True Tales of Mystery, illustrated by Bonar Dunlop. London, Lutterworth Press, 1967.
True Tales of Castles, illustrated by Imre Hofbauer. London, Lutterworth Press, 1969.
Flodden Field, September 9, 1513, illustrated by F.R. Exell. London, Lutterworth Press, 1971.
Diggers of Lost Treasure. London, Epworth Press, 1972.
Stories of Old Inns. London, Epworth Press, 1973.
The '45 and Culloden, July 1745 to April 1746, illustrated by F.R. Exell. Guildford, Surrey, Lutterworth Press, 1973.
Pirate and Admiral: The Story of John Paul Jones, illustrated by Bernard Brett. Guildford, Surrey, Lutterworth Press, 1974.
Wrecks, Wreckers and Rescuers, with Ian Morrison, illustrated by Morrison. Guildford, Surrey, Lutterworth Press, 1977.

*

Kathleen Fidler commented:

(1978) My writing first began for my own children's interest and amusement. The "Brydon Family" books, written first as broadcasts, later as books, reflected my own happy and simple family life. As my children grew, my writing expanded into historical, biographical, and archaeological fields, representing my and their varied interests. I now write to interest my grandchildren. Broadcasting has been a large part of my writing, and this sharpened the focus of books and dialogue. I also give talks to children in schools and libraries, and this keeps me actively in touch with children.

* * *

To remark that Kathleen Fidler earned an enviable reputation for good stories well told is not to damn with faint praise but to place her firmly in the mainstream of professional children's writers who year in, year out continue to publish well constructed books that satisfy an ever widening circle of readers. During her long writing career, spanning four decades, she confirmed her craftsmanlike ability to come to grips with most types of children's fiction. With undiminished skill she fashioned good, honest plots, moving at a brisk pace, in two family series, the Brydons and the Deans; holiday adventures, usually set in remote and isolated countryside; imaginative historical fiction; and in her extremely popular animal stories. Authors who turn to this last category, especially those favouring dog tales, sometimes find it difficult to avoid that mawkish sentimentality so easily aroused in doggie people, young or old. Aware of the danger, she was careful to write only about working dogs mostly in a harsh environment: *Police Dog; Mountain Rescue Dog,* an authentic account of training in the Scottish Highlands; and *The Little Ship Dog,* who guards a valuable cargo voyaging up the Grand Union Canal. *Turk, The Border Collie* relates what might have happened to the dog actually given the starring role in the filming of her earlier book, *Flash the Sheep Dog,* whose inconsolable grief caused him to slip away from his farm when his master died. At the end Turk returns, a rare move away from reality, but in this case her readers would expect no less.

Fidler's amateur knowledge of archaeology was sometimes enlisted to good effect, nowhere more so than in *The Boy with the Bronze Axe,* inspired by a visit to the Stone Age settlement of Skara Brae, in the Orkneys. The events following the arrival of a strange boy from over the sea, equipped with a bronze axe, and the impact this advance in technology had on a backward and pastoral community, are unveiled with a deceptively light and easy touch. Her enthusiasm for archaeology is also evident in *Treasure of Ebba,* the holiday adventures of a group of four, two families of brother and sister, a typical Fidler cast, who reappear in *The Gold of Fast Castle.* Purists might object to adding the glamorous concept of treasure: the realist author would reply that treasure is indispensable if life is to be breathed into archaeology for children.

This sense of realism is the hallmark of Fidler's contribution to children's literature. Essentially she portrays ordinary people caught up in slightly extraordinary circumstances, in exciting but not unduly perilous adventures, usually arising out of everyday matter-of-fact occurrences. The unlikely attains credibility by contrast with its mundane surroundings. This is not an easy balance to achieve, or to maintain: Fidler achieved it, and maintained it.

—Alan Edwin Da

FIELD, Rachel (Lyman)

Nationality: American. **Born:** New York City, 19 September 1894. **Education:** Springfield High School, Massachusetts; Radcliffe College, Cambridge, Massachusetts, 1914-18. **Family:** Married Arthur Siegfried Pederson in 1935; one adopted daughter. **Career:** Member of the editorial department, Famous Players-Lasky film company, Hollywood, 1918-23. **Awards:** Drama League of America prize, 1918; American Library Association Newbery Medal, 1930. **Died:** 15 March 1942.

Publications for Children

Fiction

Eliza and the Elves, illustrated by Elizabeth MacKinstry. New York, Macmillan, 1926.
The Magic Pawnshop: A New Year's Eve Fantasy, illustrated by Elizabeth MacKinstry. New York, Dutton, 1927; London, Dent, 1928.
Little Dog Toby, illustrated by the author. New York, Macmillan, 1928.
Polly Patchwork, illustrated by the author. New York, Doubleday, 1928.
Hitty, Her First Hundred Years, illustrated by Dorothy P. Lathrop. New York, Macmillan, 1929; as *Hitty: The Life and Adventures of a Wooden Doll,* London, Routledge, 1932.
Pocket-Handkerchief Park, illustrated by the author. New York, Doubleday, 1929.
Calico Bush, illustrated by Allen Lewis. New York, Macmillan, 1931; London, Collier Macmillan, 1966.
The Yellow Shop, illustrated by the author. New York, Doubleday, 1931.
The Bird Began to Sing, illustrated by Ilse Bischoff. New York, Morrow, 1932.
Hepatica Hawkes, illustrated by Allen Lewis. New York, Macmillan, 1932.
Just Across the Street, illustrated by the author. New York, Macmillan, 1933.
Susanna B. and William C., illustrated by the author. New York, Morrow, 1934.
The Rachel Field Story Book (includes *The Yellow Shop, Pocket-Handkerchief Park, Polly Patchwork*), illustrated by Adrienne Adams. New York, Doubleday, 1958; Kingswood, Surrey, World's Work, 1960.

Plays

Everygirl, in *St. Nicholas* (New York), October 1913.
Three Pills in a Bottle (produced Cambridge, Massachusetts, 1917; New York, 1923). Included in *Six Plays,* 1924.
Rise Up, Jennie Smith (produced Cambridge, Massachusetts, 1918). New York, French, 1918.
Time Will Tell (produced Cambridge, Massachusetts, 1920).
The Fifteenth Candle. New York, French, 1921.
Six Plays (includes *Cinderella Married, Three Pills in a Bottle, Columbine in Business, The Patchwork Quilt, Wisdom Teeth, Theories and Thumbs*). New York, Scribner, 1924; *The Patchwork Quilt* published in *One-Act Plays of Today,* edited by J.W. Marriott, London, Gollancz, 1928.
The Cross-Stitch Heart and Other Plays (includes *Greasy Luck, The Nine Days' Queen, The Londonderry Air, At the Junction, Bargains in Cathay*). New York, Scribner, 1927.
Patchwork Plays (includes *Polly Patchwork; Little Square-Toes; Miss Ant, Miss Grasshopper, and Mr. Cricket; Chimney Sweeps' Holiday; The Sentimental Scarecrow*), illustrated by the author. New York, Doubleday, 1930.
First Class Matter. New York, French, 1936.
The Bad Penny. New York, French, 1938.

Poetry (illustrated by the author)

The Pointed People: Verses and Silhouettes. New Haven, Connecticut, Yale University Press, and London, Oxford University Press, 1924.
An Alphabet for Boys and Girls. New York, Doubleday, and London, Heinemann, 1926.
Taxis and Toadstools: Verses and Decorations. New York, Doubleday, and London, Heinemann, 1926.
A Little Book of Days. New York, Doubleday, and London, Heinemann, 1927.
Christmas Time. New York, Macmillan, 1941.
Poems. New York, Macmillan, 1957.
Poems for Children, illustrated by Lynette Hemmant. Kingswood, Surrey, World's Work, 1978.

Other

Fortune's Caravan, from translation by Marion Saunders of a work by Lily Jean-Javal, illustrated by Maggie Salcedo. New York, Morrow, 1933; London, Oxford University Press, 1935.
All Through the Night, illustrated by the author. New York, Macmillan, 1940; London, Collins, 1954.
Prayer for a Child, illustrated by Elizabeth Orton Jones. New York, Macmillan, 1944.

Editor, *The White Cat and Other Old French Fairy Tales,* by Marie Catherine d'Aulnoy, illustrated by Elizabeth MacKinstry. New York, Macmillan, 1928.
Editor, *American Folk and Fairy Tales,* illustrated by Margaret Freeman. New York, Scribner, 1929.
Editor, *People from Dickens: A Presentation of Leading Characters from the Books of Charles Dickens,* illustrated by Thomas Fogarty. New York, Scribner, 1935.

Publications for Adults

Novels

Time Out of Mind. New York, Macmillan, 1935; London, Macmillan, 1937.
To See Ourselves, with Arthur Pederson. New York, Macmillan, 1937; London, Collins, 1939.
All This and Heaven Too. New York, Macmillan, 1938; London, Collins, 1939.
And Now Tomorrow. New York, Macmillan, 1942; London, Collins, 1943.

Short Story

Christmas in London. Privately printed, 1946.

Poetry

Points East: Narratives of New England. New York, Brewer and Warren, 1930.
A Circus Garland. Washington, D.C., Winter Wheat Press, 1930.
Branches Green. New York, Macmillan, 1934.
Fear Is the Thorn. New York, Macmillan, 1936.

Other

God's Pocket: The Story of Captain Samuel Hadlock, Junior, of the Cranberry Isles, Maine. New York, Macmillan, 1934; London, Macmillan, 1937.
Ave Maria: An Interpretation from Walt Disney's "Fantasia" Inspired by the Music of Franz Schubert. New York, Random House, 1940.

*

Illustrator: *Punch and Robinetta* by Ethel May Gate, 1923; *Come, Christmas* by Eleanor Farjeon, 1928; *The House That Grew Smaller* by Margery Williams Bianco, 1931.

* * *

Rachel Field's reputation as a children's book author today rests almost solely on her book *Hitty, Her First Hundred Years* which won the Newbery Medal in 1930. The book is a picaresque, first-person narrative of the memoirs of the doll Mehitabel's first hundred years. The strong personality of the doll binds the narration together, although individual scenes and a wide variety of characters are given considerable dimension. The setting ranges from New England to India and eventually back again, with realistic scenes devoted to plantation life, whale sightings, the singing of Jenny Lind, and sitting for a daguerreotypist intermixed. The book is enhanced by illustrations by Dorothy P. Lathrop who frequently illustrated for Field. For a discussion of Field's work habits and how *Hitty* came into being, one should consult Louise Bechtel's *Books in Search of Children.*

Field was also an illustrator of books for children and adults, but she is best known for her literary canon which includes fantasy, historical fiction, non-fiction, poetry, and plays, as well as a selected edition of Mme. d'Aulnoy's fairy tales and a slightly saccharine *Prayer for a Child.* One aspect of her work that is largely ignored today, but merits attention, is her playwriting for children. Her best known works in this genre are five diverse plays anthologized in a volume entitled *Patchwork Plays.* These plays are good in that they are all playable, making few highly technical demands on child players but considerable demands on the child audience's imagination. Each of the plays is packed with action and believability. Perhaps a distance of fifty years precludes immediacy and dramatic impact on a modern audience of a play about a sentimental scarecrow, but Field would capture a modern audience with her play *Little Square-Toes.* This short work is about a young girl who is captured by Indians during King Philip's war and who is reluctant to return to "civilization" when given the chance. It is marked by highly realistic dialogue, swift action, and a strong, developmental plot. Field's best-known book of poetry for children is *Taxis and Toadstools,* a town-and-country anthology on subjects as diverse as the conjunction of the two subjects in the title would suggest. The best poems read naturally with flowing enjambment; the weakest scan methodically and almost monotonously, though the latter are much in the minority.

—Rachel Fordyce

FIENBERG, Anna

Nationality: Australian. **Born:** United Kingdom 1956; moved with her family to Australia in 1959. **Career:** New South Wales *School Magazine,* 1980–1990 (editor 1988–1990); national book club consultant. **Awards:** Children's Book Council of Australia Book of the Year, younger readers, 1992; Alan Marshall Prize for Children's Literature, Victorian Premier's Literary awards, 1993. **Address:** c/o Allen & Unwin Pty Ltd, 9 Atchison Street, St Leonards, New South Wales 2065, Australia.

PUBLICATIONS FOR CHILDREN

Fiction

Billy Bear and the Wild Winter, illustrated by Astra Lacis. North Ryde, New South Wales, Angus & Robertson, 1988.
The Champion [*Con the Whiz Kid, Marisa's Party, My Goldie, Stefano's Nonna, A Teddy for Louise, Please, Teresa Trouble, Tien Tells Minh*], illustrated by Felicity Meyer. Sydney, Traffic Authority of New South Wales, 1988.
Wiggy and Boa, illustrated by Ann James. Melbourne, Dent, 1988; Boston, Houghton Mifflin, 1990; as *Pirate Trouble for Wiggy and Boa,* St. Leonards, New South Wales, Allen & Unwin, 1996.
The 9 Lives of Balthazar, illustrated by Donna Gynell. Ferntree Gully, Victoria, Houghton Mifflin, 1989.
The Magnificent Nose, and Other Marvels, illustrated by Kim Gamble. St. Leonards, New South Wales, Allen & Unwin, 1991; Oxford, Oxford University Press, 1992.
Ariel, Zed and the Secret of Life, illustrated by Kim Gamble. St. Leonards, New South Wales, Allen & Unwin, 1992.
The Hottest Boy Who Ever Lived, illustrated by Kim Gamble. St. Leonards, New South Wales, Allen & Unwin, 1993; Morton Grove, Illinois, Whitman, 1995.
Madeline the Mermaid and Other Fishy Tales, illustrated by Ann James. St. Leonards, New South Wales, Allen & Unwin, 1995.
Power to Burn. St. Leonards, New South Wales, Allen & Unwin, 1995.
With Barbara Fienberg, *Tashi,* illustrated by Kim Gamble. St. Leonards, New South Wales, Allen & Unwin, 1995.
With Barbara Fienberg, *Tashi and the Giants,* illustrated by Kim Gamble. St. Leonards, New South Wales, Allen & Unwin, 1995
Dead Sailors Don't Bite, illustrated by Ann James. St. Leonards New South Wales, Allen & Unwin, 1996.
With Barbara Fienberg, *Tashi and the Ghosts,* illustrated by Kin Gamble. St. Leonards, New South Wales, Allen & Unwin, 1997
The Doll's Secret. Melbourne, Australia Post, 1997.
With Barbara Fienberg, *Tashi and the Genie,* illustrated by Kin Gamble. St. Leonards, New South Wales, Allen & Unwin, 1997
Reteller, *Snugglepot and Cuddlepie* [*Snugglepot and Cuddlepie at Se Snugglepot and Cuddlepie Meet Little Obelia, Cuddlepie Goes t the Dentist, Snugglepot and Cuddlepie and the Banksia Me Snugglepot and Cuddlepie Go Home*], illustrated by Vicky Kitano Pymble, New South Wales, Harper Collins Publishers, 1997.

Minton Goes Flying [*Minton Goes Sailing*], illustrated by Kim Gamble. St. Leonards, New South Wales, Allen & Unwin, 1998.
With Barbara Fienberg, *Tashi and the Baba Yaga,* illustrated by Kim Gamble. St. Leonards, New South Wales, Allen & Unwin, 1998.

Other

Eddie. Milton, Queensland, Jacaranda Wiley, 1988.

* * *

Anna Fienberg's novels, short stories and picture books for younger readers feature resourceful children who develop their special talents in worlds where almost anything is possible. Some characters have difficulties overcoming prejudices against difference, but are often helped by friends who appreciate their special qualities. Friendship between girls and boys is characteristic as is humour, from the slapstick of the novel *Wiggy and Boa* and its sequel *Pirate Trouble for Wiggy and Boa,* to the amusing word play in the picture book *The Hottest Boy Who Ever Lived.* The naming of characters points to the light-hearted allegorical nature of much of Fienberg's writing. In *The Magnificent Nose,* Andy Umm is a seemingly timid boy, Wendelin B. Wordforce an author, and Valentina Lookwell is a portrait painter, while "Ariel" and "Zed" reflect that novel's concern with words, writing, and the creation of character.

Despite the variety of settings and characters in Fienberg's novels, all feature protagonists who seek improvement in their lives and find that, with some effort (and magic), things can change. In *Wiggy and Boa,* Wiggy (Ludwig van Weezelman) and Boa (Boadicea Bolderack) are from very different but equally unsatisfactory households and depend on each other for some relief from their misery. Wiggy's house is poorly run; his music-obsessed parents are quite uninterested in housework or cooking, while Boa's grandfather, Admiral Bolderack, selfishly insists on a shipshape household. When Boa mistakenly calls up a band of wicked pirates, this apparent disaster has some unexpected benefits. Nevertheless, the pirates can't be entirely tamed and despite a newfound dedication to toothpaste and other domestic matters, in *Dead Sailors Don't Bite* they kidnap the children's teacher who has confiscated their marbles leaving Wiggy and Boa to find a solution. The Island in *Ariel, Zed and the Secret of Life* is where writers send their rebellious characters. Friends Ariel and Zed go there too, for a holiday, and come back wiser, happier with themselves, and armed with the knowledge that they can make choices about their own life and attitudes. Billy in *Billy Bear and the Wild Winter* doesn't hibernate in winter, unlike his friends and relations, and so he plans to wake everyone up with music. The successful *Tashi* series of short illustrated novels features the small but heroic Tashi, an alter ego for young Jack, who recounts Tashi's extraordinary stories of cleverness and courage to his admiring parents.

The Magnificent Nose is five magical tales about children with unusual talents—such as carpentry skills, a sensitive nose, special sight, and language abilities—each character linked by a golden spider, Aristan, who encourages them in their endeavours. The final and sixth tale sees them all meeting on a plane flying to Kathmandu to meet Lindylou, the clever carpenter, and "the children had such a wonderful time, they stayed for dinner and then for a year". Outstanding production, together with Kim Gamble's illustration, helped *The Magnificent Nose* to be recognised with the Children's Book Council of Australia Book of the Year award for Younger Readers in 1992. Similarly, *Madeline the Mermaid and Other Fishy Tales,* four tales about a mermaid and her "merdog" and "mercat" who all live in a conch shell on the ocean floor, is enhanced by illustrator Ann James' fine detail. In these "Fishy Tales", Madeline makes friends with a Kraken who is scared of the dark, is saved from the boring pufferfish by Horatio the jellyfish, reunites a pirate with his lost love and deals cleverly with two troublesome sea witches. Gamble and James, to date, have been the chief illustrators of Fienberg's work, the former, in particular with the *Tashi* books, creating a signature appearance for their books.

Harold, in the picture book, *The 9 Lives of Balthazar,* is another talented child. He wants to be a scientist, just like his mum, and he takes heed of her advice to test everything out for himself. But when he uses Balthazar the alley cat to discover whether cats really do have nine lives, he learns there is more to knowledge than experiments. The major idea in *The Hottest Boy Who Ever Lived* is the well-worn theme of an outsider being accepted by others, but the situation and characters are bizarre and inventive. Hector is such a hot boy that a sigh from him can shrivel grass. His loneliness is eased when, due to an accident, he meets Gilda the Adventurer who, coming from chilly parts, appreciates his warmth. Unfortunately, the other Vikings reject him as a freak—but Hector proves himself useful in their cold world. There is considerable play on the idiomatic use of temperature terms to describe character: "The truth is, I am too hot to handle." Kim Gamble's illustrations equal the text for inventiveness and gentle humour. Hector's companion, Minton, a salamander, features in an illustrated adventure series of his own.

Power to Burn, a novel for adolescent readers, is a significant change in readership for Fienberg but nevertheless retains elements of magic and difference so central to her other writing. Even the notion of a burningly hot person as in *The Hottest Boy Who Ever Lived* is repeated although here linked to anger and power. This is an extraordinary story set in Italy about a father's battle to control the magic abilities that are inherited by his children from his wife's family. His wife seems to accept restraint, but not their daughter, Lucrezia, who, kept from the love of her life, leaves home with revenge in her heart. Major themes are the persecution of witches, fear of difference and unease about women's abilities. Another departure for Fienberg is a series of re-told stories based on May Gibbs' famous gumnut baby characters. Intended to introduce younger children to the works of an Australian icon there is some debate as to the worth of the exercise as the originals are still so highly regarded.

—Kerry White

FINE, Anne

Nationality: British. **Born:** Leicester, 7 December 1947. **Education:** Northampton High School for Girls, 1958-65; University of Warwick, Coventry, 1965-68, B.A. (honours) in history and politics 1968. **Family:** Married Kit Fine in 1968; two daughters. **Career:** Teacher, Cardinal Wiseman Secondary School, Coventry, 1968-69, and Saughton Prison, Edinburgh, 1971-72; information officer, Oxfam, Oxford, 1969-71. **Awards:** Scottish Arts Council award, 1986; Carnegie medal, 1989, 1992; Smarties Award, 1990; Guardian Children's Fiction Award, 1990; British Book Awards Children's Author of the Year, 1990, 1993; Whitbread Children's Novel Award, 1993, 1997; Nasen Special Educational Needs Book Award, 1996; British nomination for the Hans Christian Andersen Award, 1998.

Publications for Children

Fiction

The Summer-House Loon. London, Methuen, 1978; New York, Crowell, 1979.
The Other, Darker Ned. London, Methuen, 1979.
The Stone Menagerie. London, Methuen, 1980.
Round Behind the Ice-House. London, Methuen, 1981.
The Granny Project. London, Methuen, and New York, Farrar Straus, 1983.
Scaredy-Cat, illustrated by Vanessa Julian-Ottie. London, Heinemann, 1985.
Anneli the Art Hater. London, Methuen, 1986.
Madame Doubtfire. London, Hamish Hamilton, 1987; as *Alias Madame Doubtfire,* Boston, Little Brown, 1988.
Crummy Mummy and Me, illustrated by David Higham. London, Deutsch, 1988.
A Pack of Liars. London, Hamish Hamilton, 1988.
Goggle-Eyes. London, Hamish Hamilton, 1989.
The Country Pancake, illustrated by Philippe Dupasquier. London, Methuen, 1989.
Bill's New Frock, illustrated by Philippe Dupasquier. London, Methuen, 1989.
Goggle Eyes. London, Hamish Hamilton, 1989; as *My War with Goggle Eyes,* Boston, Little Brown, 1989.
Stranger Danger?, illustrated by Jean Baylis. London, Hamish Hamilton, 1989.
Bill's New Frock, illustrated by Philippe Dupasquier. London, Methuen, 1989.
A Sudden Puff of Glittering Smoke, illustrated by Adriano Gon. London, Piccadilly, 1989.
Only A Show, illustrated by Valerie Littlewood. London, Hamish Hamilton, 1990.
A Sudden Swirl of Icy Wind, illustrated by David Higham. London, Piccadilly, 1990.
A Sudden Glow of Gold. London, Piccadilly, 1991.
The Worst Child I Ever Had, illustrated by Clara Vulliamy. London, Hamish Hamilton, 1991.
The Book of the Banshee. London, Hamish Hamilton, 1991; New York, Scholastic, 1994.
Designing a Pram. London, Heinemann, 1991.
The Angel of Nitshill Road, illustrated by K. Aldous. London, Methuen, 1992.
Poor Monty, illustrated by Clara Vulliamy. New York, Clarion, 1991; London, Methuen, 1992.
The Same Old Story Every Year. London, Hamish Hamilton, 1992.
Flour Babies. Boston, Little Brown, 1992; as *Flour Babies and the Boys of Room 8,* 1992.
The Chicken Gave It To Me, illustrated by Cynthia Fisher. London, Hamish Hamilton, 1992; Boston, Joy Street, 1993; as *The True Story of Harrowing Farm,* 1993.
The Haunting of Pip Parker. London, Walker, 1992.
The Genie Trilogy (includes *A Sudden Puff of Glittering Smoke, A Sudden Swirl of Icy Wind,* and *A Sudden Glow of Gold*). London, Mammoth, 1992.
The Diary of a Killer Cat, illustrated by Steve Cox. London, Hamish Hamilton, 1994.
Press Play, illustrated by Terry McKenna. London, Piccadilly Press, 1994.
Step by Wicked Step. London, Hamish Hamilton, 1995.
The Tulip Touch. London, Hamish Hamilton, 1996.
Countdown. London, Heinemann, 1996.
Jennifer's Diary, illustrated by Kate Aldous. London, Hamish Hamilton, 1996.
How to Write Really Badly, illustrated by Philippe Dupasquier. London, Methuen, 1996.
Care of Henry, illustrated by Paul Howard. London, Walker, 1996.
Ruggles. London, Mammoth, 1998.
Charm School. London, Transworld, 1999.
Loudmouth Louis. London, Hamish Hamilton, forthcoming.

Plays

The Granny Project, adaptation of her own story. London, Collins, 1986.
Bill's New Frock. London, Longman Educational, 1992.
Angel of Nitshill Road. London, Ginn, 1993,
Stranger Danger? London, Ginn, 1994,
Celebrity Chicken (adaptation of *The Chicken Gave It To Me*). London, Longman Educational, 1995.
Goggle Eyes. London, Heinemann Educational, 1995.
The Book of the Banshee. London, Collins Educational, 1995.
Flour Babies. London, Collins Educational, 1996.
The Country Pancake. London, Ginn, 1997.

Publications for Adults

Novels

The Killjoy. London, Bantam, 1986; New York, Mysterious Press, 1987.
Taking the Devil's Advice. London, Viking, 1990.
In Cold Domain, London, Viking, 1994.
Telling Liddy. London, Transworld, 1998.

Play

Radio Play: *The Captain's Court Case,* 1987.

Other

Facing Three Ways: Woodfield Lecture VXI. Woodfield, 1993.
The Family Tree: The Ronald M. Hubbs and Margaret S. Hubb Lectures. No. 3, St. Paul, Minnesota, University of St. Thomas, 1995.

*

Anne Fine comments:

I find I write mostly about that period during which the stabi ity of childhood, when almost all decisions are made by others, giving way to a wider world. A sense of the need for a sort of personal elbow-room is developing, and people outside the family seem to be showing other ways to go. Growing through to full autonomy is, for anyone, a long and doggy business; for some, more sabotaged than others by their nature or upbringing, it can seem impossible. I try to show that the battle through the chaos and confusions is worthwhile and can, at times, be seen as very funny.

* * *

Anne Fine's outstanding quality is humour: she has a good eye for a comic situation and commands a trenchantly witty style. Her first books are 20th-century comedies of manners, offering stylish entertainment to older children with a certain amount of sophistication. Academic passions, running high over early Sardinian trade routes in *The Summer-House Loon,* make a change from the earnest subjects chosen by many contemporary writers for this age group. Ione Muffet, the book's heroine, has to disentangle the romantic affairs of her father's secretary and a promising young academic, besides dealing with her father himself, a blind historian who is a pleasing variation on the perennial theme of the eccentric professor. The same characters return with further complications in the book's sequel, *The Other, Darker Ned,* in which Ione, her social conscience aroused, organizes a fete in aid of Oxfam—and finds new emotions emerging in her.

In her third book, *The Stone Menagerie,* Fine again takes as her central situation one in which a young couple impinge upon the life of a child with family problems, in this case the boy Ally. Riley and the captivating Flora—vegetarian, wholefoods enthusiast and basket weaver—are an attractive pair, and the spirit of comedy hovers over the book. *Round Behind the Ice-House* is a more overtly serious novel: a study of the difficulties of growing up, complicated by the relationship of two of the central figures, twins who were previously very close.

Subsequently, Anne Fine has both deepened and widened her range, always turning her gift for comedy to excellent account. Social problems of widespread relevance in an age where the conventional nuclear family is less and less of the norm emerge as subjects in her novels for older children; they include divorce in *Madame Doubtfire* and its aftermath in *Goggle-Eyes,* where the child narrator Kitty eventually comes to terms with her mother's initially-much-resented new partner. Similarly, Simon Martin in *Flour Babies,* landed with the class project of caring for a six-pound bag of flour as if it were a baby, not only comes to feel fiercely protective of his imaginary infant but also to make allowances for the father who walked out of his life, and to appreciate his mother's efforts in bringing him up alone. *The Granny Project* hinges on the problem of old age, and *A Pack of Liars,* beneath the entertaining surface sparkle that is the hallmark of Fine's style, conducts a serious debate on the nature and consequences of veracity.

Ingenious plot construction is another feature of Fine's work; even when the basic premise of *Madame Doubtfire* may seem a little farfetched, the sheer comic verve of her writing brings it off. There is much perceptive warmth in the description of her young protagonists' relationships with their parents, siblings, friends, and teachers—particularly in her two outstanding novels for older children, *Goggle-Eyes* and *Flour Babies,* both of them lessons in adaptation and both winners of the Carnegie Medal.

The same characteristics are carried over to her books for younger children: *Only a Show* and *The Worst Child I Ever Had* (for children who have just mastered reading skills); *Bill's New Frock, Anneli the Art Hater, The Country Pancake* and *"The Chicken Gave it To Me".* In the last-named title Fine departs from her usual realistic backgrounds to present, within a framework narrative of two children talking, a fantasy ostensibly written by a chicken transported to another planet, where little green men farm human beings for the pot: an ecologically angled fable successfully making its point through humour.

Fantasy also appears in Anne Fine's trilogy of short stories for younger children: *A Sudden Puff of Glittering Smoke, A Sudden Swirl of Icy Wind* and *A Sudden Glow of Gold,* in which genies appear to three different children offering to grant wishes. In the proper tradition of such tales, they illustrate the vanity of human wishes—unless made for someone else's benefit—and there is also a touch of magic, reminiscent of Walter de la Mare, about them.

Anne Fine has a notable ability to write wittily for all age groups, making valid moral points while leaving the reader on the child protagonist's side, and never writing down or condescending. *Goggle-Eyes,* dramatized as a serial shown on British television in adult prime viewing-time, and *Madame Doubtfire,* made into a highly successful film, show that a genuinely funny book can easily transcend barriers of age-group and genre.

In the award-winning *Bill's New Frock,* Bill Simpson wakes up and finds that he is a girl. The story follows his day at school during which he discovers what it is like to be treated as a member of the opposite sex. This is a book full of comedy which provokes much discussion among young people about gender roles and behaviour. The school setting is also central to *How to Write Really Badly.* Chester Howard, a new arrival at Walbottle Manor (Mixed) primary school, persuades his classmate Joe Gardener "the writer from Hell" to "trade on his strengths" and produce a school project describing "how to write really badly." In the process both boys learn something about their true talents. This novel, which shows how intelligence and skill can manifest themselves in myriad ways, won an award for a book which portrays positively a child with special educational needs.

In *The Angel of Nitshill Road,* a new girl arrives at a primary school. During the few weeks that she attends Nitshill Road, the class bully is routed and his erstwhile victims gain new confidence in themselves. However, Celeste does not perform her miracles by any magical means, but by making the bully, his victims, and their teacher face up to what is happening. Whether Celeste is heaven sent or not is for readers to decide. However, by believing in her, some of her classmates come to believe in themselves.

In a short, well-constructed novel, teacher Mr. Oakway needs to write the end of term reports and asks his class to *Design a Pram.* They divide themselves into two groups and the way in which they approach the task from somewhat differing perspectives is the central theme. This brief novel shows Anne Fine's insight into, as Margaret Meek has described it, the "shared understandings of the cultural codes of the classroom, its rituals and interactions."

In Anne Fine's more recent novels for older children, the family is the focal point at least as much as the school. In *The Book of the Banshee* Will Flowers describes the battles between his parents and his sister Estelle as she asserts her own personality on reaching adolescence. While he is writing his account of "war in the family" (the title the book has been given in its Spanish translation), Will is reading a book written by a young soldier about life in the trenches in the first world war and he makes frequent comparisons.

Anne Fine also uses the discovery of another's writings as a spur to storytelling in *Step by Wicked Step,* a novel with a number of narrators, each one taking over from the last. The framework for this book is a school trip where the accommodation is in an old house. After the gothic opening set in a thunderstorm, the finding of a diary written by a former occupant serves as the trigger for the five children thrown together to discover what they have in common. Each of the five tell their own, highly individual stories of life with step-parents, revealing much domestic detail of family life in the modern world.

The Tulip Touch takes Anne Fine into new territory. Gone is the wry humour, although the sharp detailed observation of human behaviour remains. From the perspective of Natalie, whose family run a large country hotel, she explores how a child can become manipulative and eventually commit cruel and criminal acts. The book charts the friendship of Natalie and Tulip, a child from an unloving and abusive family. Like the relationship between the two girls, the narrative is both chilling and compulsive. The games that Tulip initiates become more and more dangerous until eventually Natalie realises that she must break free. Readers are left to draw their own conclusions as to the reasons for Tulip's behaviour. Anne Fine demonstrates that there are no clear or easy answers. Tulip's home background is shadowy and unsatisfactory, but other adults in her life as well as her parents are unable or unwilling to help her in ways which might have set her on a different path in life. Only Natalie at the conclusion of this thought-provoking novel feels both pity for Tulip and guilt at her own role in her former friend's downfall. Although Anne Fine has rarely provided a conventional happy ending in her fiction for older children, never before has she left matters quite so open-ended or treated such a chilling theme.

Anne Fine continues to be popular with children and highly regarded by critics. Her books appear on all the major award shortlists in Britain, and her work has been translated into more than twenty languages. In 1998 she was the British nomination for the Hans Christian Andersen Award.

—Anthea Bell, updated by Ann Lazim

FINKEL, George (Irvine)

Nationality: British. **Born:** South Shields, County Durham, 13 May 1909. **Education:** At public primary schools; Bede Collegiate School, Sunderland, County Durham, 1919-26. **Military Service:** Royal Auxiliary Air Force, 1930-34; sub-lieutenant, Royal Naval Volunteer Reserve, 1939-45; lieutenant Commander, Royal Navy, 1945-50; technical training officer, Australian Fleet Air Arm, Nowra, New South Wales, during the Korean War; engineer officer, Naval Air Base, Nowra, 1952-58. **Family:** Married Lena Almond in 1930; three sons and one daughter. **Career:** Cadet chemical engineer, 1927-34; aviator, Imperial Airways, England, Europe, and Africa, 1934-39; professional officer and later teaching hospitals planning officer, University of New South Wales, Kensington, 1958-69. **Died:** March 1975.

PUBLICATIONS FOR CHILDREN

Fiction

The Mystery of Secret Beach. Sydney, Angus and Robertson, 1962; London, Angus and Robertson, 1963.
Ship in Hiding. Sydney, Angus and Robertson, 1963.
Cloudmaker. Sydney and London, Angus and Robertson, and New York, Roy, 1965.
The Singing Sands. Sydney and London, Angus and Robertson, 1966.
The Long Pilgrimage, illustrated by George Tetlow. Sydney and London, Angus and Robertson, 1967; New York, Viking Press, 1969.
Twilight Province, illustrated by George Tetlow. Sydney and London, Angus and Robertson, 1967; as *Watch Fires to the North,* New York, Viking Press, 1967.
The "Loyall Virginian." Sydney and London, Angus and Robertson, 1968; as *The Loyal Virginian,* New York, Viking Press, 1968.
Journey to Jorsala. Sydney and London, Angus and Robertson, 1969.
The Peace Seekers. Sydney and London, Angus and Robertson, 1970.
The Stranded Duck, illustrated by Andrew Parnell. Sydney, Angus and Robertson, 1973.
Operation Aladdin, illustrated by Walter Stackpool. Sydney and London, Hodder and Stoughton, 1976.

Other

Navigator and Explorer: James Cook, illustrated by Amnon Sadubin. Sydney, Wentworth Press, 1969.
James Cook, Royal Navy, illustrated by Amnon Sadubin. Sydney and London, Angus and Robertson, 1970.
Community Services: Power, Transport. Melbourne, Nelson, 2 vols., 1970.
Laws: Making and Keeping Them. Melbourne, Nelson, 1970.
Migrants of Legend [Who Changed the World, Who Had No Choice, Who Made Britain]. Melbourne, Nelson, 4 vols., 1970.
Producing Food: Cereals, Fish, Fruit, Meat. Melbourne, Nelson, 4 vols., 1970.
William Light. Sydney, Angus and Robertson, 1972.
Matthew Flinders, Explorer and Scientist, illustrated by Victor Hatcher. Sydney and London, Collins, 1973.
New South Wales 1788-1900. Melbourne, Nelson, 1974.
Victoria 1834-1900. Melbourne, Nelson, 1974.
The Dutchman Bold: The Story of Abel Tasman. Sydney and London, Angus and Robertson, 1975.
Governor Lachlan Macquarie. Melbourne, Nelson, 1975.
South Australia 1836-1900. Melbourne, Nelson, 1975.
Queensland 1824-1900. Melbourne, Nelson, 1975.
Antarctica: The Heroic Age. Sydney and London, Collins, 1976.
Tasmania 1803-1900. Melbourne, Nelson, 1976.
Western Australia 1829-1900. Melbourne, Nelson, 1976.

* * *

George Finkel began his literary career by writing a few well structured adventure stories for boys. He then became absorbed in a much deeper vein of creative fiction, and produced a numb of originally researched historical novels, as well as fictional biographies. In both novels and biographies he often presents ingenious theories and fresh viewpoints on the significance of certain events or character motivation. Thus, in *Twilight Province* he presents his view of the Arthur legend; *The "Loyall Virginian"* explores an unusual aspect of the secession of the North American colonies from Britain; *The Peace Seekers* attempts an explanation of the infiltration of a North American Indian tribe by men of Celtic stock. Attention to detail and exact explanation of, for example, mechanical parts is a recognizable facet of his writing, reflecting his own inquiring mind. The careful plotting of his novels tends to occupy first place in the scheme of work; characterization is not the dominant aspect. George Finkel's fictional biographies, especially *James Cook, Royal Navy* (he felt a particular empathy in relation to Cook for they belonged to the same part of England, and Finkel's own seagoing experience was considerable) and *William Light*—the gallant, artistic ex-Army officer who became first Surveyor General for South Australia—are clear-cut and strike a happy balance between fiction and fact. They are neither romanticized nor are they bereft of the attribute of story.

Latterly, Finkel turned to a new form of fiction: short, compelling novels set in the present day whose main appeal is to boys in the 10-14 age group. In *The Stranded Duck* and *Operation Aladdin* he related two stories concerning salvage operations carried out by a family of cousins and their grandfather. But for the author's untimely death, these stories might well have developed into a continuing series. They are tightly structured, told with economy of narrative, and show a considerably deeper degree of characterization than do his longer novels.

—Barbara Ker Wilson

FINLAY, Winifred (Lindsay Crawford)

Nationality: British. **Born:** Newcastle-upon-Tyne, Northumberland, 27 April 1910. **Education:** High School for Girls, Whitley Bay, Northumberland; King's College, University of Newcastle, 1928-33, M.A. (honours) in English. **Family:** Married Evan Finlay in 1935; one daughter. **Career:** Schoolmistress and college lecturer, Newcastle-upon-Tyne, 1933-35, Stratford-on-Avon, 1941-44, Leeds, 1944-48, and Northampton, 1948-50. Regular contributor, *Child Education*, London. **Award:** Mystery Writers of America Edgar Allan Poe award, 1970. **Died:** 1989.

Publications for Children

Fiction

The Witch of Redesdale. London, Harrap, 1951.
Peril in Lakeland. London, Harrap, 1953.
Peril in the Pennines. London, Harrap, 1953.
Cotswold Holiday, illustrated by Shirley Macgregor. London, Harrap, 1954.
The Lost Silver of Langdon. London, Harrap, 1955.
Storm over Cheviot. London, Harrap, 1955.
Judith in Hanover. London, Harrap, 1955.
Canal Holiday. London, Harrap, 1957.
The Cruise of the "Susan." London, Harrap, 1958.
The Castle and the Cave, illustrated by John S. Goodall. London, Harrap, 1960.
The Lost Emeralds of Black Howes. London, Harrap, 1961.
Alison in Provence, illustrated by John S. Goodall. London, Harrap, 1963.
Mystery in the Middle Marches. London, Harrap, 1964.
Castle for Four. London, Harrap, 1966.
Adventure in Prague. London, Harrap, 1967.
Danger at Black Dyke. London, Harrap, and New York, Phillips, 1968.
The Cry of the Peacock. London, Harrap, 1969.
Summer of the Golden Stag. London, Harrap, 1969.
Singing Stones. London, Harrap, 1970.
Beadbonny Ash. London, Harrap, 1973; Nashville, Nelson, 1975.

Plays

Radio Plays: *Children's Hour* series, 1947-63, including *The Clues of the Sickle Moon*, 1961, *Mystery in the Middle Marches*, 1962, *Castle for Four*, 1963.

Other

Folk Tales from the North, illustrated by Victor Ambrus. London, Kaye and Ward, 1968; New York, Watts, 1969.
Folk Tales from Moor and Mountain, illustrated by Victor Ambrus. London, Kaye and Ward, 1969; New York, Roy, 1970.
Cap o' Rushes and Other Folk Tales, illustrated by Victor Ambrus. London, Kaye and Ward, and Eau Claire, Wisconsin, Hale, 1974.
Tattercoats and Other Folk Tales, illustrated by Shirley Hughes. London, Kaye and Ward, 1976; New York, Harvey House, 1977.
Ghosts, Ghouls, and Spectres: English Ghost Stories, with Gillian Hancock, illustrated by Gavin Rowe. London, Kaye and Ward, 1976.
Spies and Secret Agents, with Gillian Hancock, illustrated by Gavin Rowe. London, Kaye and Ward, 1977.
Treasure Hunters, with Gillian Hancock, illustrated by Edward Mortelmans. London, Kaye and Ward, 1978.
Tales from the Hebrides and Highlands, illustrated by Bernadette Watts. London, Kaye and Ward, 1978.
Clever and Courageous Dogs, with Gillian Hancock, illustrated by Gavin Rowe. London, Kaye and Ward, 1978.
Famous Flights of Airships and Balloons, with Gillian Hancock, illustrated by David Armitage. London, Kaye and Ward, 1979.
Tales from the Borders, illustrated by Victor Ambrus. London, Kaye and Ward, 1979.
Tales of Sorcery and Witchcraft, illustrated by Laszlo Acs. London, Kaye and Ward, 1980.
Tales of Fantasy and Fear, illustrated by Victor Ambrus. London, Kaye and Ward, 1981.
Fight for Life, illustrated by Gavin Rowe. London, Kaye and Ward, 1981.
Secret Rooms and Hiding Places, illustrated by Gavin Rowe. London, Kaye and Ward, 1982.
Vampires, Werewolves and Phantoms of the Night: Demonic Tales from Different Lands, illustrated by Kate Mellor. London, Methuen, 1983.

*

Winifred Finlay comments:

I have written stories ever since I can remember. I first wrote professionally for my own daughter during the war when there was a shortage of suitable books. My stories and plays are set in real places which I know well: Britain, France, Germany, Czechoslovakia. I have tried to show that, because of the action in which they were involved, my principal characters have developed in their understanding of themselves and other people.

As a Northumbrian with Scottish parents, I have often drawn on areas I knew when young: the Roman Wall, the Border Country, and the Scottish Highlands and Islands. For my later work I have collected fascinating folk and ghost tales, ballads and legends. I was taught to have a healthy respect for the English language, and I have always tried to maintain sound literary standards as I feel very strongly that only the best is good enough for children.

* * *

Winifred Finlay had a prolific career as a writer of children's books and radio plays. Most of her novels followed the same pattern: some children on holiday are involved in a mystery which they eventually solve, finding after dramatic and often dangerous events that the mystery itself was not as spectacular as they had thought. The anti-climactic conclusion keeps her stories realistic and sensible, and the hordes of international crooks and caves stuffed with treasure remain firmly in the children's imaginations.

She narrates not only a story, but also the emotional journey taken by one or more children who have to come to terms with a difficult relationship or one of the problems of growing up. From her observation and experience Finlay best describes the adolescent girl, and though her heroines are from the same mould, the different situations they face bring plenty of variety to the basic theme of a girl growing up, finding out how to relate to her mother and to boyfriends, finding a suitable career and perhaps going against her parents wishes.

Several of her books, like *Summer of the Golden Stag* and *Adventure in Prague,* deal with a teenage girl alone, abroad. As she copes with foreigners, plus the inevitable mystery, she learns about her own personality and needs. Whether abroad or at home, the mystery element is usually associated with a genuine historical background. Finlay is especially sympathetic to the scenery and antiquities of North Britain—the lakes, the Roman Wall, ancient stones, etc., which are described in detail, while she also ridicules childish fantasies, e.g., of Druids: "Stonehenge and mistletoe and long white beards."

In 1970 Finlay deserted the typical adventure story for full-blooded fantasy of the Alan Garner kind, where supernatural creatures from the past come alive now. *Singing Stones* and *Beadbonny Ash* are magical adventures in Scotland's Celtic past. They resemble the earlier books in their well-drawn family relationships and historical detail, but they abandon the cynical attitude to mystery for a genuine commitment to the power of the supernatural and the war between Good and Evil.

Singing Stones is about the discovery of the ancient carved coronation stone of Scotland; *Beadbonny Ash* about a girl's rediscovery of her love for her mother, through a journey in time to the days when the Old Gods were replaced by Christ. The girl's mother is identified with the great Celtic goddess, Ugly Hag and Beautiful Lady in one, just as in real life her daughter loves and hates her.

She later wrote several collections of folk-tales from oral and literary sources. Her retellings are not mere paraphrases, but expansions of the old tales with detail and humour. Several collections of ghost and spy stories extended her work, but *Beadbonny Ash* is her masterpiece.

—Jessica Yates

FISHER, Aileen (Lucia)

Nationality: American. **Born:** Iron River, Michigan, 9 September 1906. **Education:** University of Chicago, 1923-25; University of Missouri, Columbia, Bachelor of Journalism 1927. **Career:** Director, Women's National Journalistic Register, Chicago, 1929-32; research assistant, Labor Bureau of the Middle West, Chicago, 1931-32. **Awards:** Western Writers of America award, for nonfiction, 1967; National Council of Teachers of English award, for poetry, 1978. **Address:** 505 College Avenue, Boulder, Colorado 80302, U.S.A.

Publications for Children

Fiction

Over the Hills to Nugget, illustrated by Sandra James. New York, Aladdin, 1949.

Trapped by the Mountain Storm, illustrated by J. Fred Collins. New York, Aladdin, 1950.

Homestead of the Free: The Kansas Story. New York, Aladdin, 1953.

Timber! Logging in Michigan, illustrated by Pers Crowell. New York, Aladdin, 1955.

Off to the Gold Fields, illustrated by R.M. Powers. New York, Nelson, 1955; as *Secret in the Barrel,* New York, Scholastic, 1965.

Cherokee Strip: The Race for Land, illustrated by Walt Reed. New York, Aladdin, 1956.

A Lantern in the Window, illustrated by Harper Johnson. New York, Nelson, 1957.

Skip, illustrated by Genevieve Vaughan-Jackson. New York, Nelson, 1958.

Fisherman of Galilee, illustrated by John De Pol. New York, Nelson, 1959.

Summer of Little Rain, illustrated by Gloria Stevens. New York, Nelson, 1961.

My Cousin Abe, illustrated by Leonard Vosburgh. New York, Crowell, 1962.

Arbor Day, illustrated by Nonny Hogrogian. New York, Crowell, 1965

Human Rights Day, with Olive Rabe, illustrated by Lisl Weil. New York, Crowell, 1966.

Plays

The Squanderbug's Christmas Carol. Washington, D.C., United States Treasury Department, 1943.

The Squanderbug's Mother Goose. Washington, D.C., United States Treasury Department, 1944.

A Tree to Trim: A Christmas Play. Evanston, Illinois, Row Peterson, 1945.
What Happened to Toyland. Evanston, Illinois, Row Peterson, 1945.
Nine Cheers for Christmas: A Christmas Pageant. Evanston, Illinois, Row Peterson, 1945.
Before and After: A Play about the Community School Lunch Program. Washington, D.C., War Food Administration, 1945.
All Set for Christmas. Evanston, Illinois, Row Peterson, 1946.
Here Comes Christmas! A Varied Collection of Christmas-Program Materials for Elementary Schools. Evanston, Illinois, Row Peterson, 1947.
Witches, Beware: A Hallowe'en Play. New York, Play Club, 1948.
Set the Stage for Christmas: A Collection of Pantomimes, Skits, Recitations, Readings, Plays and Pageants. Evanston, Illinois, Row Peterson, 1948.
Christmas in Ninety-Nine Words (lyrics only), music by Rebecca Welty Dunn. Evanston, Illinois, Row Peterson, 1949.
Angel in the Looking-Glass, in *Plays,* Boston, 1950.
The Big Book of Christmas: A Collection of Plays, Songs, Readings, Recitations, Pantomimes, Skits, and Suggestions for Things to Make and Do for Christmas. Evanston, Illinois, Row Peterson, 1951.
Health and Safety Plays and Programs. Boston, Plays Inc., 1953.
Holiday Programs for Boys and Girls. Boston, Plays Inc., 1953; revised edition, 1980.
United Nations Plays and Programs, with Olive Rabe. Boston, Plays Inc., 1954.
Patriotic Plays and Programs, with Olive Rabe. Boston, Plays Inc., 1956.
Christmas Plays and Programs. Boston, Plays Inc., 1960.
Plays about Our Nation's Songs. Boston, Plays Inc., 1962.
The King's Toothache, and *One-Ring Circus,* in *Thirty Plays for Classroom Reading,* edited by Donald D. Durrell. Boston, Plays Inc., 1965.
Time for Mom, and *Young Abe Lincoln,* in *Fifty Plays for Holidays,* edited by Sylvia E. Kamerman. Boston, Plays Inc., 1969.
Bicentennial Plays and Programs. Boston, Plays Inc., 1975.
Year-Round Programs for Young Players. Boston, Plays Inc., 1985.

Poetry

The Coffee-Pot Face, illustrated by the author. New York, McBride, 1933.
Inside a Little House, illustrated by the author. New York, McBride, 1938.
That's Why, illustrated by the author. New York, Nelson, 1946.
Up the Windy Hill: A Book of Merry Verse with Silhouettes, illustrated by the author. New York, Abelard Press, 1953; London, Abelard Schuman, 1958.
Runny Days, Sunny Days: Merry Verses, illustrated by the author. New York and London, Abelard Schuman, 1958.
Going Barefoot, illustrated by Adrienne Adams. New York, Crowell, 1960.
Where Does Everyone Go?, illustrated by Adrienne Adams. New York, Crowell, 1961.
I Wonder How, I Wonder Why, illustrated by Carol Barker. New York and London, Abelard Schuman, 1962.
Like Nothing at All, illustrated by Leonard Weisgard. New York, Crowell, 1962.
I Like Weather, illustrated by Janina Domanska. New York, Crowell, 1963.
Cricket in a Thicket, illustrated by Feodor Rojankovsky. New York, Scribner, 1963.
Listen, Rabbit, illustrated by Symeon Shimin. New York, Crowell, 1964.
In the Middle of the Night, illustrated by Adrienne Adams. New York, Crowell, 1965.
In the Woods, In the Meadow, In the Sky, illustrated by Margot Tomes. New York, Scribner, 1965; Kingswood, Surrey, World's Work, 1967.
Best Little House, illustrated by Arnold Spilka. New York, Crowell, 1966.
Skip Around the Year, illustrated by Gioia Fiammenghi. New York, Crowell, 1967.
My Mother and I, illustrated by Kazue Mizumura. New York, Crowell, 1967.
Up, Up the Mountain, illustrated by Gilbert Riswold. New York, Crowell, 1968.
We Went Looking, illustrated by Marie Angel. New York, Crowell, 1968.
Clean as a Whistle, illustrated by Ben Shecter. New York, Crowell, 1969.
In One Door and Out the Other: A Book of Poems, illustrated by Lillian Hoban. New York, Crowell, 1969.
Sing, Little Mouse, illustrated by Symeon Shimin. New York, Crowell, 1969.
But Ostriches..., illustrated by Peter Parnall. New York, Crowell, 1970.
Feathered Ones and Furry, illustrated by Eric Carle. New York, Crowell, 1971.
Do Bears Have Mothers Too?, illustrated by Eric Carle. New York, Crowell, 1973.
My Cat Has Eyes of Sapphire Blue, illustrated by Marie Angel. New York, Crowell, 1973.
Once We Went on a Picnic, illustrated by Tony Chen. New York, Crowell, 1975.
I Stood upon a Mountain, illustrated by Blair Lent. New York, Crowell, 1979.
Anybody Home?, illustrated by Susan Bonners. New York, Crowell, 1980.
Out in the Dark and Daylight, illustrated by Gail Owens. New York, Harper, 1980.
Rabbits, Rabbits, illustrated by Gail Niemann. New York, Harper, 1983.
In Summer, with Jane Belk Moncure, illustrated by Marie-Claude Monchaux. Elgin, Illinois, Children's World, 1985.
When It Comes to Bugs, illustrated by Chris and Bruce Degen. New York, Harper, 1986.
The House of a Mouse, illustrated by Joan Sandin. New York, Harper, 1988.
Always Wondering. New York, HarperCollins, 1991.

Other

Guess Again! (riddles). New York, McBride, 1941.
All on a Mountain Day, illustrated by Gardell Christensen. New York, Nelson, 1956.
We Dickinsons: The Life of Emily Dickinson as Seen Through the Eyes of Her Brother Austin, with Olive Rabe, illustrated by Ellen Raskin. New York, Atheneum, 1965.
Valley of the Smallest: The Life Story of a Shrew, illustrated by Jean Zallinger. New York, Crowell, 1966.

We Alcotts: The Life of Louisa May Alcott as Seen Through the Eyes of "Marmee"..., illustrated by Ellen Raskin. New York, Atheneum, 1968.
Easter, illustrated by Ati Forberg. New York, Crowell, 1968.
Jeanne d'Arc, illustrated by Ati Forberg. New York, Crowell, 1970.
The Ways of Animals (in verse) (*Animal Houses,* illustrated by Jan Wills; *Animal Jackets,* illustrated by Muriel Wood; *Filling the Bill,* illustrated by Betty Fraser; *No Accounting for Taste,* illustrated by Gloria Gaulke; *Now That Days Are Colder,* illustrated by Gordon Laite; *Sleepy Heads,* illustrated by Phero Thomas; *"You Don't Look Like Your Mother," Said the Robin to the Fawn,* illustrated by Ati Forberg; *Tail Twisters,* illustrated by Albert John Pucci; *Going Places,* illustrated by Midge Quenell; *Animal Disguises,* illustrated by Tim and Greg Hildebrandt). Glendale, California, Bowmar, 10 Vols., 1973-74.
The Ways of Plants (in verse) (*Plant Magic,* illustrated by Barbara Cooney; *Mysteries in the Garden,* illustrated by Ati Forberg; *Swords and Daggers,* illustrated by James Higa; *And a Sunflower Grew,* illustrated by Trina Schart Hyman; *Petals Yellow and Petals Red,* illustrated by Albert John Pucci; *Now That Spring Is Here,* illustrated by Symeon Shimin; *As the Leaves Fall Down,* illustrated by Barbara Smith; *Prize Performances,* illustrated by Margot Tomes; *A Tree with a Thousand Uses,* illustrated by James Endicott; *Seeds on the Go,* illustrated by Hans Zander). Glendale, California, Bowmar, 10 Vols., 1977.

*

Manuscript Collections: Kerlan Collection, University of Minnesota, Minneapolis.

Aileen Fisher comments:

I enjoy writing for children. I especially enjoy writing verse. It gives me such a good chance for remembering how things looked and felt and *were* when I was a child.

* * *

Aileen Fisher draws upon observation and research to produce children's literature in various genres. She has written poetry, prose in the form of nature stories, and biographies, nonfiction, and plays.

Poetry has been her most significant contribution; as one *New York Times* reviewer wrote, "She lights the commonplace moment with wonder." While in college, she published her first collection, *The Coffee-Pot Face.* Subjects which she would treat for a lifetime were here—nature, such as a ladybug and icicles, objects such as a chair, childhood conditions such as a tummy-ache, and seasons. Well-known illustrators were selected to interpret her one-poem picture books, such as *In the Middle of the Night* and *Once We Went on a Picnic.* Inspired by her verse, Adrienne Adams, Marie Angel, and Symeon Shimin earned honors for their work. While praising *Going Barefoot* for its "rare synthesis of information and imagination," a reviewer considered it too long for one sitting with a small child.

Fisher's rhymed verses may be short (*Sing, Little Mouse*), or sustained as a story (*My Mother and I* and *Where Does Everyone Go?*). Many of them open with a query (*Anybody Home?*), or musing (*In the Middle of the Night*), and expand to include observations on many animals. Fisher uses a light and lilting tone and often injects humor, as in the description of a skunk who investigates animal homes. Her special experiences with northern climes make the anticipation of "the wonderful month of the Barefoot Moon" convincing.

Close observation of nature and research on the Upper Peninsula in Michigan are the basis of *Timber! Logging in Michigan.* Colorado mountains are the setting for a number of books, such as *Trapped by the Mountain Storm* and *Valley of the Smallest: The Life Story of a Shrew.* The shrew was an unusual selection of an animal for a full-length narrative, but the author introduces other animals to show the natural interrelationships, and the author acknowledged a British zoologist who had published a book on the behaviour of a shrew. Virginia Haviland wrote in the *Horn Book* (December 1966): "A sharp observer, with a poet's imagination, the author records what she has seen near her mountain home. Her account is both more vivid and more suspenseful than most nature books...."

Her biographies have fared less well under the scrutiny of reviewers. By having Simon Peter, the brother of Emily Dickinson, and the mother of the March girls tell the stories of *Fisherman of Galilee, We Dickinsons,* and *We Alcotts,* she ensures a fresh approach. But despite direct quotations from primary sources, the books pale when compared to the Biblical narrative and authors' autobiographical writing. *Jeanne d'Arc,* according to the reviewer Barbara Wersba in the *New York Times Review* (24 May 1970), lacks passion, and "remains less of the journey of a saint than a biography of a very nice girl." Fisher's other non-fiction publications are the result of the same research, observation, and literary style. The collections of plays have the usefulness of being free of royalty fees for the performers, but, perhaps for the same reason, are unimpressive.

—Karen Nelson Hoyle

FISHER, Dorothy Canfield

Pseudonym: Stanley Cranshaw. **Nationality:** American. **Born:** Dorothea Frances Canfield, Lawrence, Kansas, 17 February 1879. **Education:** Ohio State University, Columbus, Ph.B. 1899; the Sorbonne, Paris; Columbia University, New York, Ph.D. in romance languages 1905. **Family:** Married John Redwood Fisher in 1907; one daughter and one son. **Career:** Secretary, Horace Mann School, New York, 1902-05; relief worker in France, 1916-19. Member of the Vermont Board of Education, 1921-23. **Awards:** Delta Kappa Gamma Society Educator's award, 1946; Women's National Book Association Skinner award, 1951; Sarah Josepha Hale Special award, 1958. D.Litt.: Middlebury College, Vermont, 1921; Dartmouth College, Hanover, New Hampshire, 1922; University of Vermont, Burlington, 1922; Columbia University, 1929; Northwestern University, Evanston, Illinois, 1931; Rockford College, Illinois, 1934; Ohio State University, 1935; Williams College, Williamstown, Massachusetts, 1935; Swarthmore College, Pennsylvania, 1935; University of Nebraska, Lincoln, 1936; Mount Holyoke College, South Hadley, Massachusetts, 1936; Marlboro College, Vermont, 1951; Smith College, Northampton, Massachusetts, 1954. **Died:** 9 November 1958.

Publications for Children

Fiction

Understood Betsy, illustrated by Ada C. Williamson. New York, Holt, 1917; London, Constable, 1922; as *Betsy,* London, Bodley Head, 1962; revised edition, New York, Holt Rinehart, 1972.
Made-to-Order Stories, illustrated by Dorothy P. Lathrop. New York, Harcourt Brace, 1925; London, Cape, 1926.
Tell Me a Story: A Book of Stories to Tell to Children, illustrated by Tibor Gergely. Lincoln, Nebraska, University Publishing Company, 1940; London, Mitre Press, n.d.
Nothing Ever Happens and How It Does, with Sarah N. Cleghorn, illustrated by Esther Boston Bristol. Boston, Beacon Press, 1940.
Something Old, Something New: Stories of People Who Are America, illustrated by Mary D. Shipman. Chicago, Scott Foresman, 1949.

Plays

A Family Talk about War. New York, Children's Crusade for Children, 1940.
Liberty and Union, with Sarah N. Cleghorn. New York, Book of the Month Club, 1940.

Other

What Shall We Do Now? Five Hundred Games and Pastimes; A Book of Suggestions for Children's Games and Employments, with others. New York, Stokes, 1907.
On a Rainy Day, with Sarah Fisher Scott. New York, A.S. Barnes, 1938.
In the City and on the Farm (reader), with Eunice Crabtree and Lu Verne Walker, illustrated by Terry Townsend. Lincoln, Nebraska, University Publishing Company, 1940; London, Mitre Press, n.d.
My First Book: A Reading Readiness Book, with Eunice Crabtree and Lu Verne Walker. Lincoln, Nebraska, University Publishing Company, 1940.
Runaway Toys (reader), with Eunice Crabtree and Lu Verne Walker, illustrated by Terry Townsend. Lincoln, Nebraska, University Publishing Company, 1940.
To School and Home Again (reader), with Eunice Crabtree and Lu Verne Walker, illustrated by Terry Townsend. Lincoln, Nebraska, University Publishing Company, 1940; London, Mitre Press, n.d.
More about the City and the Farm (reader), with Eunice Crabtree and Lu Verne Walker, illustrated by Terry Townsend. Lincoln, Nebraska, University Publishing Company, 1941.
Under the Roof (reader), with Eunice Crabtree and Lu Verne Walker, illustrated by Terry Townsend. Lincoln, Nebraska, University Publishing Company, 1941; London, Mitre Press, n.d.
Under the Sun (reader), with Eunice Crabtree and Lu Verne Walker, illustrated by Terry Townsend. Lincoln, Nebraska, University Publishing Company, 1941; London, Mitre Press, n.d.
Highroads and Byroads (reader), with Eunice Crabtree and Lu Verne Walker, illustrated by Mary Royt and George Buctel. Lincoln, Nebraska, University Publishing Company, 1948; London, Mitre Press, n.d.
Next Door (reader), with Eunice Crabtree and Lu Verne Walker. Lincoln, Nebraska, University Publishing Company, 1949.
Paul Revere and the Minute Men, illustrated by Norman Price. New York, Random House, 1950.
Our Independence and the Constitution, illustrated by Robert Doremus. New York, Random House, 1950.
A Fair World for All: The Meaning of the Declaration of Human Rights, illustrated by Jeanne Bendick. New York, McGraw Hill, 1952.
And Long Remember: Some Great Americans Who Have Helped Me, illustrated by Ezra Jack Keats. New York, McGraw Hill, 1959.

Publications for Adults

Novels

Gunhild: A Norwegian-American Episode. New York, Holt, 1907.
The Squirrel-Cage. New York, Holt, and London, Constable, 1912.
The Bent Twig. New York, Holt, 1915, and London, Constable, 1916.
The Brimming Cup. New York, Harcourt Brace, and London, Cape, 1921.
Rough-Hewn. New York, Harcourt Brace, 1922; London, Cape, 1923.
Raw Material. New York, Harcourt Brace, 1923.
The Home-Maker. New York, Harcourt Brace, and London, Cape, 1924.
Her Son's Wife. New York, Harcourt Brace, and London, Cape, 1926.
The Deepening Stream. New York, Harcourt Brace, and London, Cape, 1930.
Bonfire. New York, Harcourt Brace, and London, Cape, 1933.
Seasoned Timber. New York, Harcourt Brace, and London, Cape, 1939.

Short Stories

Hillsboro People, verse by Sarah N. Cleghorn. New York, Holt, 1915; London, Cape, 1923.
The Real Motive. New York, Holt, and London, Constable, 1916.
Home Fires in France. New York, Holt, 1918; London, Constable, 1919.
Basque People. New York, Harcourt Brace, and London, Cape, 1931.
Fables for Parents. New York, Harcourt Brace, 1937; London, Cape, 1938.
Four-Square. New York, Harcourt Brace, 1949.
A Harvest of Stories, from a Half Century of Writing. New York, Harcourt Brace, 1956.

Other

Emile Angier, Playwright-Moralist-Poet: A Study. Columbus, Ohio State University, 1899.
Corneille and Racine in England: A Study of the English Translations of the Two Corneilles and Racine, with Especial Reference to Their Presentation on the English Stage. New York, Columbia University Press, and London, Macmillan, 1904.
Elementary Composition, with George R. Carpenter. New York and London, Macmillan, 1906.

A Montessori Mother. New York, Holt, 1912; London, Constable, 1913; as *Montessori for Parents,* Cambridge, Massachusetts, Bentley, 1965.
The Montessori Manual, in Which Dr. Montessori's Teachings and Educational Occupations Are Arranged in Practical Exercises or Lessons.... Chicago, Richardson, 1913; London, Kegan Paul, 1914.
Mothers and Children. New York, Holt, 1914; London, Constable, 1915.
A Peep into the Educational Future. Buffalo, New York, Park School, 1915.
Self-Reliance: A...Discussion of Teaching Self-Reliance...to Modern Children. Indianapolis, Bobbs Merrill, 1916; London, Constable, 1917.
Fellow Captains!, with Sarah N. Cleghorn. New York, Holt, 1916.
The Day of Glory. New York, Holt, 1919.
What Grandmother Did Not Know. Boston, Pilgrim Press, 1922.
The French School at Middlebury. Middlebury, Vermont, Middlebury College, 1923.
Why Stop Learning? New York, Harcourt Brace, 1927.
Learn or Perish (lecture). New York, Liveright, and London, Oxford University Press, 1930.
Vermont Summer Homes. Montpelier, Vermont Bureau of Publicity, 1932.
Moral Pushing and Pulling (lecture). Townsend, Vermont, Leland and Gray Seminary, 1933.
Tourists Accommodated: Some Scenes from Present Day Summer Life in Vermont. New York, Harcourt Brace, 1934.
Wells College Phi Beta Kappa Address. Aurora, New York, Wells College, 1936.
Another Night for America. New York, Harrison, 1942.
Our Young Folks. New York, Harcourt Brace, 1943.
American Portraits. New York, Holt, 1946.
Book Clubs (lecture). New York, New York Public Library, 1947.
Vermont Traditions: The Biography of an Outlook on Life. Boston, Little Brown, 1953.
Memories of My Home Town. Privately printed, 1956; as *Memories of Arlington, Vermont.* New York, Duell, 1957.

Editor, with Sidonie Matsner Grunberg, *Our Children: A Handbook for Parents.* New York, Viking Press, 1932.

Translator, *Life of Christ,* by Giovanni Papini. New York, Harcourt Brace, 1923.
Translator, *Work: What It Has Meant to Men Through the Ages,* by Adriano Tilgher. New York, Harcourt Brace, and London, Harrap, 1931.

*

Critical Studies: *Pebble in a Pool: The Widening Circles of Dorothy Canfield Fisher's Life* by Elizabeth Yates, New York, Dutton, 1958, as *The Lady from Vermont,* Brattleboro, Vermont, Stephen Greene Press, 1971; *Dorothy Canfield Fisher: A Biography* by Ida H. Washington, Shelburne, Vermont, New England Press, 1981.

* * *

Dorothy Canfield Fisher used her own background as a basis for her written work. Her unusual ability to create realistic tales was based on her own experiences as a girl and young woman. She was a professor's daughter, born in Kansas of strong New England heritage. The atmosphere of learning and the familiarity with her family history shaped her character. She had a privileged position from which to view her surroundings. Yet her Vermont values, strengthened and broadened by education and travel, helped mold an individual sensitive to the needs and aspirations of human beings.

Understood Betsy certainly reflects all of her powers of observation as well as her biases and interests. In this book a young girl, raised by two aunts in a midwestern city, must spend time with distant relatives in Vermont. Two prim, affluent, city-dwelling aunts have provided for their niece, but they have turned her into a dependent, nervous, and neurotic being. It is not a pleasant view of urban life. The Vermonters who take Betsy in are deftly characterized. Uncle Harry is a taciturn yet warm-hearted man the likes of whom are disappearing from New England. Cousin Ann and Aunt Abigail are the very embodiment of the stern, upright, resourceful, yet loving Yankee. In this new atmosphere, Betsy learns to adjust, adapt, and grow in self-reliance and warm personal relationships. One is impressed with the characters and background in the story: they are psychologically and historically accurate. The theme of learning to overcome problems and adjust has been accomplished without becoming overbearing or maudlin.

Made-to-Order Stories is more unusual. These stories originated in tales made up for Fisher's ten-year-old son who disliked trite and usual plots. All of the stories are based on diverse objects. For example, a ship's anchor, a library, a woodchuck, a spider, a bed, a doorknob and usually a little boy are woven into an exciting and unusual tale. Only when one reads through the innumerable stories can one fathom the incredible well of creativity from which she drew.

Fisher's stories have entertained children for generations. Her writing, of course, reflects the rural attitudes and values of her era as well as her respect for children and their intelligence. Her characters are always real and the author never talks down to her readers. Teachers and parents who want accurate American historical and cultural material in children's literature will want to see her work on every library shelf. It is interesting to note that *Understood Betsy,* with a setting that may be unfamiliar to a late-20th-century urban child, is most unusual. This book about a girl growing up in the early 20th century stresses Betsy's human rather than her feminine identity. The author's creativity, humor, insight, and observation have been used to construct tales which have held and will continue to hold the attention of children aged 8 to 12.

—Dorothy D. Siles

FISHER, Leonard Everett

Nationality: American **Born:** Bronx, New York, 24 June 1924. **Education:** Attended Art Students League, 1941, and Brooklyn College 1941-42; Yale University, B.F.A. 1949, M.F.A. 1950. **Family:** Married Margery M. Meskin (a school librarian), 1952; three children. **Military Service:** United States Army Corps of Engineers, 1942-46; became technical sergeant; participated in topographic mapping of five major campaigns in European and Pacific areas. **Career:** Painter, illustrator, author, and educator; exhibited works at museums, libraries, galleries, and universities throughout the United States. Graduate teaching fellow, Yale Ar

School, 1949-50; Whitney School of Art, New Haven, Connecticut, dean, 1951-53; faculty member, 1966-78, academic dean, 1978-82, dean emeritus, from 1982, and visiting professor, 1982-87, Paier College of Art. Visiting professor, artist, or consultant at various universities and colleges, including Case Western Reserve University, Silvermine Guild School of the Arts, Hartford University School of Art, Fairfield University, and University of California; lecturer and speaker at art institutes, academic seminars, education workshops, and children's book programs nationwide. Designer of United States postage stamps for the United States Postal Service, 1972-77; design consultant, Postal Agent, Staffa and Bernera Islands, Scotland, 1979-82. **Awards:** William Wirt Winchester traveling fellowship, Yale University, 1949; Joseph Pulitzer scholarship in art, Columbia University and the National Academy of Design, 1950; Carle J. Blenner Prize for painting, New Haven Paint and Clay Club, 1965; premio grafico, Fiera di Bologna, 5th Fiera Internazionale del Libro per l'Infanzia e la Gioventu, Italy, 1968, for *The Schoolmasters;* Leonard Everett Fisher Day, Fairview Park, Ohio, opening National Children's Book Week, November 12, 1978; New York Library Association/School Library Media Section Award for Outstanding Contributions in the Fields of Art and Literature, 1979; Medallion of the University of Southern Mississippi for Distinguished Contributions to Children's Literature, 1979; Christopher Medal for illustration, 1981 for *All Times, All Peoples*; National Jewish Book Award for Children's Literature, and Association of Jewish Libraries Award for Children's Literature, both 1981, both for *A Russian Farewell*; *Parenting*'s Reading Magic Award, Time-Life, 1988, for *Monticello*; Children's Book Guild/*Washington Post* Nonfiction Award, 1989; nominee, Orbis Pictus Award for Outstanding Nonfiction for Children, National Council Teachers of English, 1989, for *The White House*; Parents' Choice Award, 1989, for *The Seven Days of Creation*; Regina Medal, Catholic Library Association, 1991, for "lifetime distinguished contributions to children's literature"; Kerlan Award, University of Minnesota, 1991, for "singular attainments in the creation of children's literature"; Arbuthnot Honor Lecturer, Association of Library Services to Children of the American Library Association, 1995. **Address:** 7 Twin Bridge Acres Road, Westport, Connecticut 06880, U.S.A. **E-mail Address:** LeonardoE1@aol.com.

PUBLICATIONS FOR CHILDREN (ILLUSTRATED BY THE AUTHOR)

Fiction

A Head Full of Hats. New York, Dial, 1962.
Storm at the Jetty. New York, Viking, 1980.
The Seven Days of Creation. New York, Holiday House, 1981.
Star Signs. New York, Holiday House, 1983.
The Olympians: Great Gods and Goddesses of Ancient Greece. New York, Holiday House, 1984.
Theseus and the Minotaur. New York, Holiday House, 1988.
Jason and the Golden Fleece. New York, Holiday House, 1990.
The ABC Exhibit. New York, Macmillan, 1991.
Cyclops. New York, Holiday House, 1991.
Sailboat Lost. New York, Macmillan, 1991.
Kinderdike. New York, Macmillan, 1994.
William Tell. New York, Farrar, Straus & Giroux, 1996.

Nonfiction

Pumpers, Boilers, Hooks, and Ladders. New York, Dial, 1961.
Pushers, Spads, Jennies and Jets. New York, Dial, 1961.
Leonard Everett Fisher's Liberty Book. New York, Doubleday, 1976.
Alphabet Art: Thirteen ABC's from Around the World. New York, Four Winds, 1979.
Number Art: Thirteen 1,2,3's from Around the World. New York, Four Winds, 1982.
Boxes! Boxes! New York, Viking, 1984.
Symbol Art: Thirteen Squares, Circles and Triangles from Around the World. New York, Four Winds, 1984.
The Great Wall of China. New York, Macmillan, 1986.
Calendar Art: Thirteen Days, Weeks, Months and Years from Around the World. New York, Four Winds, 1987.
The Tower of London. New York, Macmillan, 1987.
Look Around: A Book About Shapes. New York, Viking, 1987.
Pyramid of the Sun, Pyramid of the Moon. New York, Macmillan, 1988.
The Wailing Wall. New York, Macmillan, 1989.
Prince Henry the Navigator. New York, Macmillan, 1990.
Galileo. New York, Macmillan, 1992.
Gutenberg. New York, Macmillan, 1993.
Stars and Stripes. New York, Holiday House, 1993.
David and Goliath. New York, Holiday House, 1993.
Marie Curie. New York, Macmillan, 1994.
Moses. New York, Holiday House, 1995.
Gandhi. New York, Simon & Schuster/Atheneum, 1995.
Anasazi. New York, Simon & Schuster/Atheneum, 1997.
The Gods and Goddesses of Ancient Egypt. New York, Holiday House, 1997.
Alexander Graham Bell. New York, Atheneum, 1998.

PUBLICATIONS FOR YOUNG ADULTS (ILLUSTRATED BY THE AUTHOR)

Fiction

The Death of Evening Star: The Diary of a Young New England Whaler. New York, Doubleday, 1972.
The Warlock of Westfall. New York, Doubleday, 1974.
Across the Sea from Galway. New York, Four Winds, 1975.
Sweeney's Ghost. New York, Doubleday, 1975.
Letters from Italy. New York, Four Winds, 1977.
Noonan. New York, Doubleday, 1981.
A Russian Farewell. New York, Four Winds, 1980.
The Jetty Chronicles. New York, Marshall Cavendish, 1997.

Nonfiction

The "Colonial Americans" Series, New York, Watts, 1964-1976; Boston, Godine, 1986-1990; New York, Cavendish, 1996-1997. Includes *The Architects, Blacksmiths, Cabinetmakers, Doctors, Glassmakers, Hatters, Homemakers, Limners, Papermakers, Peddlers, Potters, Printers, Schoolmasters, Shipbuilders, Shoemakers, Silversmiths, Tanners, Weavers, Wigmakers.*
Two If by Sea. New York, Random House, 1970.
Picture Book of Revolutionary War Heroes. New York, Stockpole, 1970.

The Art Experience: Oil Painting 15-19th Centuries. New York, Franklin Watts, 1973.

The "Nineteenth-Century America" Series, New York, Holiday House. Includes *The Factories,* 1979; *The Railroads,* 1979; *The Hospitals,* 1980; *The Sports,* 1980; *The Newspapers,* 1981; *The Unions,* 1982; *The Schools,* 1983.
The Statue of Liberty. New York, Holiday House, 1985.
Ellis Island. New York, Holiday House, 1986.
The Alamo. New York, Holiday House, 1987.
Monticello. New York, Holiday House, 1988.
The White House. New York, Holiday House, 1989.
The Oregon Trail. New York, Holiday House, 1990.
Tracks Across America: The Story of the American Railroad, 1825-1900. New York, Holiday House, 1992.
Niagara Falls: Nature's Wonder. New York, Holiday House, 1996.

Publications for Adults

Masterpieces of American Painting. New York, Bison/Exeter, 1985.
Remington and Russell. New York, W. H. Smith, 1986.

*

Media Adaptations: *The Golden Frog, The Burning Mountain, A Jungle Jumble, Monsieur Jolicouer's Umbrella, Ride the Cold Wind,* and *Lora Lorita* (filmstrips), Random House.

Manuscript Collections: Leonard Everett Fisher Archive, University of Connecticut, Storrs; Kerlan Collection, University of Minnesota, Minneapolis; de Grummond Collection, University of Southern Mississippi, Hattiesburg; University of Oregon Library, Eugene; Postal History Collection, Smithsonian Institution, Washington, D.C.

Biography: Entry in *Something about the Author Autobiography Series,* Vol. 1, Detroit, Gale, 1986.

Critical Studies: *American Artist,* September 1966, 42-47, 67-70; *Six Artists Paint a Still Life* by Charles M. Daugherty, North Light, 1977; *Magic and Other Realism,* edited by Howard Munce, New York, Holiday House, 1979; *Dictionary of Literary Biography,* Vol. 61, *American Writers for Children since 1960: Poets, Illustrators and Nonfiction Authors,* Detroit, Gale, 1987; *Children's Literature Review,* Vol. 18, Detroit, Gale, 1989; *The Voice of the Narrator* edited by Charlotte F. Otten and Gary D. Schmidt, New York, Greenwood Press, 1989; *Major Authors and Illustrators for Children and Young Adults* edited by Laurie Collier and Joyce Nakamura, Detroit, Gale, 1993; *The Maze, the Minotaur, the Matador* by Camille Hayward, Chicago, Book Links, 1993; *Leonard Everett Fisher: A Life in Art,* Storrs, The University of Connecticut, 1998; *Leonard Everett Fisher,* Frostburg, Maryland, Companion, 1998.

Illustrator: *The Exploits of Xenophon* by Geoffrey Household, 1955; *Carrier Boy* by Florence Walton Taylor, 1956; *To Unknown Lands* by Manley Wade Wellman, 1956; *My Eskimos: A Priest in the Arctic* by Roger P. Buliard, 1956; *The First Book of the American Revolution* by Richard B. Morris, 1956; *The First Book of New England* by L. D. Rich, 1957; *America, America, America* by Kenneth S. Giniger, 1957; *The First Book of American History* by Henry Steele Commager, 1957; *Mike Fink* by James C. Bowman, 1957; *The Splendor of Persia* by Robert Payne, 1957; *The First Book of the Constitution* by Morris, 1958; *America's Own Mark Twain* by Jeanette Eaton, 1958; *The Arabs* by Harry B. Ellis, 1958; *Energy and Power* by Robert Irving, 1958; *Digging into Yesterday* by Estelle Friedman, 1958; *Dynamite and Peace* by E. B. Meyer, 1958; *Kateri Tekakwitha* by E. M. Brown, 1958; *Here Come the Clowns* by C. Edell, 1958; *The World of Jo Davidson* by L. H. Kuhn, 1958; *David's Campaign Buttons* by Catherine Wooley, 1959; *Paul Bunyan* by M. Dolbier, 1959; *Boy Joe Goes to Sea* by E. L. Boyd, 1959; *America is Born* by Gerald W. Johnson, 1959; *The First Book of Indian Wars* by Morris, 1959; *Westward, Westward, Westward,* edited by Elizabeth Abell, 1959; *This Is the Desert* by Philip H. Ault, 1959; *Sound and Ultrasonics* by Irving, 1959; *America Moves Forward* by Johnson, 1960; *America Grows Up* by Johnson, 1960; *Electromagnetic Waves* by Irving, 1960; *Declaration of Independence,* 1960; *Military History of Civil War Naval Actions* by Trevor N. Dupuy, 1960; *Military History of Civil War Land Battles* by Dupuy, 1960; *The Man Without a Country* by Edward E. Hale, 1960; *Ride the Cold Wind* by Anico Surnay, 1960; *Indy and Mrs. Lincoln* by Natalia Belting, 1960; *Verity Mullens and the Indians* by Belting, 1960; *The First Book of the War of 1812* by Morris, 1961; *Vasco Nunez De Balboa* by Emma G. Sterne, 1961; *The Queen's Most Honorable Pirate* by James P. Wood, 1961; *A Horse Named Justin Morgan* by Harold W. Felton, 1962; *Great Archaeologists* by Charles M. Daugherty, 1962; *But Not Our Daddy* by Margery M. Fisher, 1962; *Modern Discoveries in Archaeology* by Robert C. Suggs, 1962; *Golden Child* by Paul Engle, 1962; *Man of the Monitor* by Jean L. Latham, 1962; *The Supreme Court* by Johnson, 1962; *Sergeant O'Keefe and His Mule* by Felton, 1962; *The Presidency* by Johnson, 1962; *Before Adam* by Jack London, 1962; *Pilgrim Courage* by Eric Smith and Robert Meredith, 1962; *Message of Garcia* by E. Hubbard, 1962; *Getting to Know the U.S.A.* by Charles Ferguson, 1963; *Golden Frog* by A. Surany, 1963; *The Congress* by Johnson, 1963; *One and One* by M. Fisher, 1963; *The Weigher of Souls* by Andre Maurois, 1963; *Star Rover* by London, 1963; *Patriotism, Patriotism, Patriotism,* edited by Helen Hoke, 1963; *Gettysburg Address,* 1963; *Communism: An American View* by Johnson, 1964; *Coming of the Pilgrims* by Smith and Meredith, 1964; *Our Presidents* by Richard Armour, 1964; *Riding with Coronado* by Meredith and Smith, 1964; *Alexander the Great, Scientist-King* by Robert C. Suggs, 1964; *John F. Kennedy's Inaugural Address,* 1964; *Archaeology of San Francisco* by Suggs, 1965; *Archimedes* by Martin Gardner, 1965; *The Story of Aida* by Florence Stevenson, 1965; *The First Book of the White House* by Lois P. Jones, 1965; *Casey at the Bat* by Ernest L. Thayer, 1965; *Rebel Sea Raider* by John Foster, 1965; *The Burning Mountain* by Surany, 1965; *Let's Find Out About John Fitzgerald Kennedy* by Martha and Charles Shapp, 1965; *Archaeology of New York* by Suggs, 1966; *The Story of the Thirteen Colonies* by Clifford L. Alderman, 1966; *Guadalcanal General* by Foster, 1966; *Forgotten by Time* by Robert Silverberg, 1966; *The Cabinet* by Johnson, 1966; *The Legend of Sleepy Hollow* by Washington Irving, 1966; *Kati and Kormos* by Surany, 1966; *A Jungle Jumble* by Surany, 1966; *Quest of Columbus* by Meredith and Smith, 1966; *Journey with Jonah* by Madeleine L'Engle, 1967; *The Story of Science in America* by L. Sprague and Catherine C. De Camp, 1967; *Great Stone Face and Two Other Stories* by Nathaniel Hawthorne, 1967;

Franklin D. Roosevelt by Johnson, 1967; *The Devil's Disciple* by G. B. Shaw, 1967; *Covered Bridge* by Surany, 1967; *Monsieur Policoeur's Umbrella* by Surany, 1967; *Rip Van Winkle* by Irving, 1967; *The First Book of the Founding of the Republic* by Morris, 1968; *Malachy's Gold* by Surany, 1968; *The Luck of Roaring Camp* by Bret Harte, 1968; *Napoleon's Marshall* by J. Foster, 1968; *The British Empire* by Gerald W. Foster, 1969; *Exploring the Great River* by Meredith and Smith, 1969; *Lora Lorita* by Surany, 1969; *Why the Earth Quakes* by Julian May, 1969; *The Year of the Whale* by Victor B. Scheffer, 1969; *The Year of the Seal* by Scheffer, 1970; *American Popular Music* by Berenice R. Morris, 1970; *Little Calf* by Scheffer, 1970; *The Land Beneath the Sea* by May, 1971; *The Night Country* by Loren Eisely, 1971; *The Wicked City* by Isaac B. Singer, 1972; *Juan Diego and the Lady* by Jan Wahl, 1973; *The Journey of the Gray Whales* by Gladys Conklin, 1974; *Some Dreams are Nightmares* by James E. Gunn, 1974; *The Joy of Crafts* by Blue Mountain Crafts Council, 1975; *The White Falcon* by E. Thompson, 1976; *All Times, All Peoples: A World History of Slavery* by Milton Meltzer, 1980; *A Circle of Seasons* by Myra Cohn Livingston, 1982; *Our Presidents* by Richard Armour, 1983; *Sky Songs* by Livingston, 1984; *Celebrations* by Livingston, 1985; *Sea Songs* by Livingston, 1986; *Earth Songs* by Livingston, 1986; *Space Songs* by Livingston, 1988; *Up in the Air* by Livingston, 1989; *Little Frog's Song* by Alice Schertle, 1992; *If You Ever Meet a Whale* by Livingston, 1992; *The Spotted Pony: A Collection of Hanukkah Stories,* edited by Eric A. Kimmel, 1992.

Illustrator of Textbooks and Learning Materials: *Our Reading Heritage,* 6 Vols., New York, Holt, 1956-1958; *Good English Through Practice* by Marjorie Wescott Barrows, New York, Holt, 1956; *The Reading Laboratories,* edited by Don Parker, 8 Vols., Chicago, Science Research Associates, 1957-1962; *Reading Skills* by M. W. Barrows and E. N. Woods, New York, Holt, 1958; *The Literature Sampler,* edited by Dolores Betler, 2 Vols., New York, Learning Materials, Inc. 1962, 1964; *How Things Change,* New York, Field Enterprise, 1964.

Illustrator of Filmstrips: *Murders in the Rue Morgue* by Edgar Allan Poe, *Dr. Jekyll and Mr. Hyde* by Robert Louis Stevenson, 1978, *The Judge's House* by Bram Stoker, 1978, *Snow* (from *The Phantom Coach*) by A. B. Edwards, 1978, and *The Tell Tale Heart* by Poe, 1980, all Encyclopaedia Britannica.

Leonard Everett Fisher comments:

There is in my temperament a love of form, shape, line, and their arrangements as seen rhythmically, with or without color, under a light. Everything I look at or imagine is translated in these terms and stored in my memory bank. These are the elements to which I as an artist respond. These, the cells that structure an artistic soul, are the unmeasurable passage to my artistic nirvana. While form, rhythm, color, and light—words, too—serve my artistic passion, the immediate focus of my work in books for young readers is on who we are, where we originated, and what we have done for and to each other. I am not interested in having children see mirror images of themselves. I want my books to be avenues of knowledge, grace, and civility, literarily and artistically expressed. I try to convey to young readers both the worthiness of their survival in a hostile world and the humanizing aspects of art beyond the illustrative match of picture and word. It matters little whether that is expressed in nonfiction or fiction. In the process, I hope to widen a youngster's knowledge base and to communicate purpose, pictorially and verbally, as dramatically as I can to make it stick in one's memory. Also, what I illustrate and write for young readers has much to do with the pleasures of discovering and retaining information. My artistic compulsion, welded as it is to varied interests, and having been transposed—in large part—to the book, has resulted, more or less, in the communication of my internal visions of the observable world, past and present, the dynamics of which I try to graphically and verbally express. I work mightily in language and pictures to deliver from the depths of my soul an indelible sense of the human experience. Whether nonfiction or fiction, I work to satisfy myself. But I like to think that I work to make a difference. Thus it shall always be with me. (Excerpted with the author's permission from a lecture delivered at the University of Wisconsin, Milwaukee, 5 May 1995.)

* * *

Leonard Everett Fisher is an amazingly versatile and prolific producer of high quality, factually accurate books for young readers. During the thirty-six years from 1961-1997 he has written 75 self-illustrated children's books, has done the illustrations for approximately 122 books by other authors, and in addition, has written textbooks and other learning materials as well as producing audio visual materials and filmstrips.

His books are both fiction and nonfiction. A large number are concerned with American and world history. His "Nineteenth Century America" series describes various aspects of American society, including the growth of the nation's railroads, the development of factories, favorite sports, and the development of schools during this century. Both text and illustration are accurate reflections of the period. They are also often witty and amusing. His desire to connect the reader with the institutions of the past are obvious.

"The Colonial Americans" series contains a total of nineteen books illustrated in detailed black and white drawings. The books describe Colonial crafts, trades, and professions. They all follow the format of beginning with a brief history of the craft or profession followed by a description of the actual techniques used by Colonial craftsmen. According to O. Mell Busbin, writing in the *Dictionary of Literary Biography,* the series has been widely used in classrooms throughout the United States, especially in the arts and social sciences. More than a half-million copies of the series have been sold.

Fisher's interest in writing about immigrants is illustrated in a number of books. *Across the Sea from Galway* tells of a group of Irish immigrants who flee famine and oppression in Ireland only to be shipwrecked off the coast of Massachusetts. *Letters from Italy* recounts the experiences of several generations of an Italian-American family, beginning with the grandfather who fought with Garibaldi for Italian independence and ending with a grandson who dies in World War II fighting Mussolini. *A Russian Farewell* traces a Jewish-Ukranian family from their sufferings under the Czarist government to the time they decide to leave for America. *Ellis Island* describes the entry point for many immigrants to a new life in the United States.

Several books have their inspiration in Fisher's childhood on the seashore. The family home at Sea Gate in Brooklyn is situated on the jetty of land where the Atlantic Ocean meets the waters of Gravesend Bay. This family home has a breath taking view of passing ships, storms at sea, and the local lighthouse. *Storm at the Jetty* is a descriptive story of how a lovely August afternoon changes into a violent frightening thunderstorm at sea. *The Death of Evening Star* tells the story of a nineteenth-century whaling ship and the many dangers of its final voyage.

Fisher has also done a number of books about places of importance in American and world history, including books on *The Statue of Liberty, Monticello, The White House, The Alamo,* and *The Wailing Wall.* His most recent such book is *Niagara Falls: Nature's Wonder* (1996). This book, intended for readers grades seven through nine, focuses on Niagara Falls as a cultural and historical institution rather than as a natural phenomenon. Beginning with the European discovery of the Falls in 1678, the book traces the Falls' emergence in the last two centuries as an attraction for sightseers and daredevils. The black-and-white illustrations include nineteenth century paintings and engravings as well as photographs. This is a factual book which middle school readers will read with the same interest they usually reserve for sports stories and adventure novels.

Biographies are also important in Fisher's work. Among his more recent biographies are *Prince Henry the Navigator* (1990), *Galileo* (1992), *Gutenberg* (1993), *Gandhi* (1995), and *William Tell* (1996). These biographies follow a similar format, consisting of 32 pages of text, numerous original illustrations and reproductions, and occasional timelines and maps. Each of the books offers a unique or original perspective on these important figures: the Gutenberg biography features a fascinating reproduction of a page from a 1455 Gutenberg Bible; the Gandhi biography focusses on Gandhi's role as a champion of Indian rights in South Africa rather than on the struggle for Indian independence; and the William Tell book contains acrylic paintings with unusual color combinations—red against berry, for example—and deep shadows, all of which work together to create a dramatic effect. In each case Fisher offers interesting ways to engage the reader in the subject.

Fisher's art work and writing are blended best in his books about mythology. Among these are *The Olympians: Great Gods and Goddesses of Ancient Greece* (1984), *Theseus and the Minotaur* (1988), *Jason and the Golden Fleece* (1990), *Cyclops* (1991), and *David and Goliath* (1993). The latter, a picture book for readers age five through eight, has many thickly painted images set against a desert background. This is a concise telling which will lead children to other Bible stories, or to Fisher's own books of myths.

Anasazi (1997) is a 32-page picture book for grades four through six. It tells the story of the Anasazi, or "ancient ones," who lived in the Four Corners area of Utah, Colorado, New Mexico, and Arizona. A compressed text with dramatic solid and sepia-toned art combine to tell of the homes, agriculture, and art work of this ancient people. It is a good introduction to the lives of these Native Americans.

—Reba Pinney

FITCH, Sheree

Nationality: Canadian. **Born:** Moncton, New Brunswick, 3 December 1956. **Education:** St. Thomas University, Frederickton, New Brunswick, B.A.; Acadia University, Wolfeville, Nova Scotia, M.A. **Family:** Married Gilles Plante; one son, one daughter. **Career:** Writer. **Awards:** Mr. Christie's Book Award, 1993, for *There Were Monkeys in My Kitchen!* **Address:** Chocolate Lake, Halifax, Nova Scotia B3N, Canada.

Publications for Children

Poetry

Toes in My Nose and Other Poems. Toronto, Doubleday, 1987.
Sleeping Dragons All Around. Toronto, Doubleday, 1989.
Merry-Go-Day. Toronto, Doubleday, 1991.
There Were Monkeys in My Kitchen! Toronto, Doubleday, 1992.
I Am Small. Toronto, Doubleday, 1994.
Mabel Murple. Toronto, Doubleday, 1995.
If You Could Wear My Sneakers: A Book About Children's Rights. Toronto, Doubleday, 1997.

Other

In This House Are Many Women. Halifax, Goose Lane, 1994.

* * *

The topic of Sheree Fitch's master's thesis, "The Oral Tradition in Children's Poetry," reveals not only her academic interest but also the focus of her own poetry. The poems in her seve volumes of children's books are designed to be read aloud, as th Nova Scotia poet has done in dozens of performances acros Canada. Experimenting with a variety of voices, rhyme and rhythr patterns, and several sound devices, Fitch has created what sh has often called "utterature," which presents real and imagine events as perceived and experienced by children.

Fitch's first book, *Toes in My Nose,* based on rhymes she cre ated for her own children, presents, from the point of view of young child, both the ordinary and the fantastic. On the one hanc the speaker may describe a naughty action, such as putting rock in a brother's socks, or a happy memory, such as visiting a favor ite grandparent. On the other, the accounts may be of a boy wh exploded after eating too much popcorn, or of an orangutan wh is a household pet. Most of the poems have short lines contain ing four to six syllables; the longest is 39 lines. This brevity, alon with the strong rhythms, pronounced rhymes, and frequent us of onomatopoeia, emphasizes the comic treatment of most of th topics. The quiet tones of "I Wonder About Thunder" and "I Ca Fly" capture the reflective moments of childhood.

Sleeping Dragons All Around, There Are Monkeys in M Kitchen, and *Merry-Go-Day* are book-length narrative poems tha reveal Fitch's skill in capturing the child's love of both real an imaginary characters and situations. In the first two, the speake is confronted with a potentially chaotic situation: a midnight tri to the refrigerator must be made without disturbing the dragon who sleep about the house; a child, home alone, must find a wa to rid the house of hordes of invading monkeys. In each book Fitch skillfully portrays the reactions of the narrator and the ec centric dragons and monkeys. In *Merry-Go-Day,* the varied inci dents and emotions of a day at the exhibition are sensitivel evoked by the changing rhythms and tones of individual section of the poem.

I Am Small and *Mabel Murple* are each made up of a number o poems that, taken as a group, define the personalities of two ver different children. The unnamed speaker in the former is a sma child sensitively responding to different aspects of her life. Un like Fitch's earlier books, this one does not make extensive use o rhyme, onomatopoeia, or pronounced rhythms. Fitch create longer, more gently flowing free verse and precise visual image to reveal the child's growing awareness of her physical, emotional, and imaginary worlds. *Mabel Murple* is an make-believe character from a purple planet. Her comic habits and actions, presented in rhymed, strongly accented lines, include wild, reckless skiing, skateboarding, and motorcycle riding. In many ways she represents an escape from ordinary life for the narrator, who describes the character with amazement and admiration.

The fact that most of the poems in *If You Could Wear My Sneakers* are considerably longer than those in the earlier collections suggests that they are intended for older children. The fourteen poems deal with items in the United Nations Declaration of the Rights of Children by portraying interactions between individuals and those outside of their own families. Themes include the value of the self and of other people and the importance of respecting differences and recognizing similarities. By making the characters animals from around the world, and using alliteration and tongue-twisting phrases, Fitch gives a light and humorous but still serious tone to the messages.

Whether writing about such occurrences as a visit to a grandmother's house or the exhibition, imaginary adventures with dragons or monkeys, the thoughts of a small child, or the interactions of groups of animals, Fitch exhibits her ability to create a wide range of tones through the skilful use of rhyme, meter, alliteration, and onomatopoeia. Sheree Fitch's command of what she has called the "lipslipperiness" of language and her understanding of younger children's many views about the dimensions of their lives have made her an important Canadian children's poet of the 1990s.

—Jon C. Stott

FITZGERALD, John D(ennis)

Nationality: American. **Born:** Utah, in 1906. **Career:** Worked as a journalist and musician. **Died:** 21 May 1988.

Publications for Children

Fiction (Great Brain series illustrated by Mercer Mayer)

The Great Brain. New York, Dial Press, 1967; London, Dent, 1969.
More Adventures of the Great Brain. New York, Dial Press, 1969; London, Dent, 1972.
Me and My Little Brain. New York, Dial Press, 1971; London, Dent, 1974.
The Great Brain at the Academy. New York, Dial Press, 1972.
The Great Brain Reforms. New York, Dial Press, 1973.
Brave Buffalo Fighter (Waditaka Tatanka Kisisohitka), illustrated by John Livesay. Independence, Missouri, Independence Press, 1973.
Private Eye. Nashville, Nelson, 1974.
The Return of the Great Brain. New York, Dial Press, 1974.
The Great Brain Does It Again. New York, Dial Press, 1975; London, Dent, 1976.

Publications for Adults

Novels

Papa Married a Mormon. Englewood Cliffs, New Jersey, Prentice Hall, 1955; London, W.H. Allen, 1956.
Mamma's Boarding House. Englewood Cliffs, New Jersey, Prentice Hall, and London, W.H. Allen, 1958.
Uncle Will and the Fitzgerald Curse. Indianapolis, Bobbs Merrill, 1961; London, W. H. Allen, 1962.

Other

The Professional Story Writer and His Art, with Robert C. Meredith. New York, Crowell, 1963.
Structuring Your Novel: From Basic Idea to Finished Manuscript, with Robert C. Meredith. New York, Barnes and Noble, 1972.

*

Manuscript Collections: Kerlan Collection, University of Minnesota, Minneapolis.

* * *

The Great Brain series, for which John D. Fitzgerald is best known, focuses on the lives—part fictional, part real—of the Fitzgerald family in southern Utah between 1896 and 1899. The main characters are John D. and Tom D. Fitzgerald, aged seven and 10 respectively at the beginning of the series. John is the narrator, but it is his brother Tom's activities as the Great Brain which provide most of the interest and plot action.

The genesis of the series lies in the real John D. Fitzgerald's origins and childhood, detailed in his early biographical novel *Papa Married a Mormon.* Indeed, much of the second half of *Papa* recounts various real-life exploits of the Great Brain and family. In tone, style, phraseology, and ethics these tales are very similar to those in the subsequent works of fiction, but there are also some important differences: for example, Fitzgerald's real-life sister, Katie, and his Uncle Will and Aunt Queenie (a former saloon owner and dance-hall girl), though very prominent in the family history, have no place in the children's novels; even more striking, the real Tom, unlike his brothers, became a Mormon, attended a Mormon, not a Catholic, academy, and eventually (surprise!) went to the Orient as a Mormon missionary.

However, it is the children's books which are the most important works, and they show Fitzgerald's creativity transcending autobiography and reaching into the realms of the tall tale and the American myth. Typically, in the fiction, Tom, stimulated by a particular situation to use his Great Brain, develops an ingenious scheme or idea and recruits J.D. as his assistant (frequently to J.D.'s at least partial disadvantage). Sometimes Tom will tackle a community problem (the Alkali Flats Stock Swindle, the Adenville Bank Robbery). Sometimes he'll provide a service (the education of Britches Dotty, the Americanizing of a Greek immigrant boy). Sometimes he'll con his companions into accepting what amount to sure bets on his part (the Magnetic Stick Swindle, the Tin Can Swindle). And, almost always, he is on watch for the opportunity to make a profit from the situation via rewards, pay for services rendered, kickbacks, and outright con-artist cheating.

J.D. describes the problem as Tom's Great Brain plus his money-loving heart, but the reality is a bit more subtle than this. As events prove time and again, the problem is not really Tom's Great Brain but, instead, the conflict within his heart between, on the one hand, the money-loving impulse (self-interest and perhaps, in a larger metaphor, the capitalist element in American society) and, on the other hand, the ethical sense, compassion for one's fellow man, the kind of cooperative neighbourliness which did much to build American society. This conflict is the key to Tom's character. His dilemma is not brain versus heart but rather the uses to which the heart, motivated two conflicting ways, puts the powers of his brain. Thus, in many instances, Tom's sheer conniving impulse, his pride, and his desire to make a profit bring his brain into play with these goals alone in mind. Yet in other instances his brain is harnessed not primarily by the need for profit but instead by compassion: two good instances are his rehabilitation (with fee refunded) of one-legged Andy Anderson and his organization of a funeral for Old Butch, a mongrel loved by the dogless children. Then of course there are the various times both impulses work together to benefit both society and Tom himself; for example, solving various robberies and finding two boys lost in a labyrinthine cave. This is as it should be in American society, and indeed the books in many ways are quintessentially American: the profit motive and the ethic of helpfulness mutually reinforcing one another, all held together under the aegis of the democratic ideal, best exemplified in the story of the starving Paiute Indians in the seventh book. Here, conviction of the rightness of the American ideal leads Tom to write to the President when he feels that ideal is being violated. And, by exercising this very basic American concept of free speech to call for redress of grievances he in fact achieves just that, a redress of Indian grievances and a cleansing of a slightly corrupt system. Right triumphs here, and it is because of Tom's ethical values, his intelligence (his Great Brain), and his self-confident willingness to act.

The books are all of a kind, with little to separate one from its fellows. Though somewhat episodic, they yet retain one or more narrative threads integrating each book and connecting the series as a whole. As individual works, probably the most satisfactory overall are *The Great Brain* and *More Adventures of the Great Brain,* while *Me and My Little Brain*—though still a good read—is the least humorous and therefore least satisfactory.

The strengths of the series are its portrayal of close-knit family and community life in the late 19th-century American west, its ecumenical aspects, its very American value system, and its humour—deriving partly from the American tradition of the tall tale and partly from a form of dramatic irony: the contrast between J.D.'s over-naive attitude in the stories and the reader's larger perspective. In addition, Fitzgerald treats childhood with respect, as an arena of life where good and evil are present and where real choices must be made as part of the growing-up process, but also an arena where courage, intelligence, and ethical action, in the end, prevail.

—John Robert Sorfleet

FITZHUGH, Louise

Nationality: American. **Born:** Memphis, Tennessee, 5 October 1928. **Education:** Hutchison School, Memphis; Southwestern College, Memphis; Florida Seminary College, Lakeland; New York University School of Education; Bard College, Annandale-on-Hudson, New York; Art Students' League, New York; Cooper Union, New York. **Awards:** Children's Rights Workshop Other award, 1976. **Died:** 19 November 1974.

Publications for Children (illustrated by the author)

Fiction

Harriet the Spy. New York, Harper, 1964; London, Gollancz, 1974.
The Long Secret. New York, Harper, 1965; London, Gollancz, 1975.
Bang, Bang, You're Dead, with Sandra Scoppettone. New York, Harper, 1969.
Nobody's Family Is Going to Change. New York, Farrar Straus, 1974; London, Gollancz, 1976.
I Am Five. New York, Delacorte Press, 1978.
Sport. New York, Delacorte Press, 1979.
I Am Three, illustrated by Susanna Natti. New York, Delacorte Press, 1982.
I Am Four, illustrated by Susan Bonners. New York, Delacorte Press, 1982.
I Know Everything about John and He Knows Everything about Me, illustrated by Lillian Hoban. New York, Doubleday, 1993.

*

Illustrator: *Suzuki Beane* by Sandra Scoppettone, 1961.

* * *

During her brief career as a children's writer Louise Fitzhugh was perhaps most well known for creating memorable and psychologically realistic characterizations of upper-middle-class urban children. Zena Sutherland called *Harriet the Spy* a "milestone" in children's literature because of the power with which Fitzhugh reveals the emotional anguish of the contemporary American child. Other critics agree that the book's artistry makes it a masterpiece. At her best, certainly, Fitzhugh created a moving vision of lonely intelligent urban children caught in the complexities of modern life and fragmented families, thrown painfully upon their own emotional resources.

In *Harriet the Spy* Fitzhugh delineates the character of a highly intelligent and imaginative child living in an affluent home. Though imaginative and resourceful, Harriet is nevertheless lonely; to assuage her insecurities, she leads an obsessively regimented existence: she writes compulsively in her "spy" notebook; she eats only tomato sandwiches at precisely the same time each day; she insists upon cake and milk on the dot each day after school. Fitzhugh makes it clear almost at once that Harriet is misusing her talent for writing by spying on others and by writing unkind remarks about her friends. Yet Harriet has no one to offer real guidance to her.

Harriet's father is a highly pressured television executive, who is too exhausted at the end of the day to do anything but sip martinis and slump in front of the television. Her mother is preoccupied with social activities and asks Harriet only the most inane questions about school life. Harriet's teachers are apparently oblivious to her obvious talent for writing and her imagination they give her an appallingly unimaginative role in the school Thanksgiving play, that of an onion. Only Harriet's nurse, "Ole Golly," understands anything about the inner life of this vibrant, intelligent child. Yet Ole Golly is herself not entirely emotionally whole. In response to Harriet's incessant questions, her voracious need to know everything, Ole Golly can only quote in pedantic fashion from her enormous store of reading—everything from Dostoevsky to Emerson. Sometimes Ole Golly's continual quoting irritates Harriet, who wishes that she "would just shut up."

Yet the nurse is Harriet's lifeline. When Ole Golly marries Mr. Waldenstein, Harriet's emotional problems began to mount. When her friends discover her notebook and the unkind remarks she has written about them, they give her the silent treatment, and the notebook is taken away from her. When the notebook is removed, Harriet no longer possesses the smallest stay against confusion. She rapidly declines into an emotional breakdown. Finally, psychotherapy, a letter from Ole Golly reminding Harriet that the purpose of writing is "to put love in the world, not to use against your friends," and a job on the school paper help to make Harriet whole again.

In some respects Harriet's character reminds the reader of such conventional naughty, imaginative, high-spirited children as Twain's Tom Sawyer. Such children seem to realize their imaginative and creative potentiality most fully apart from the intrusion of adults. Yet such a vision of childhood assumes a safe and secure home and community. Harriet's isolation from adults conveys a sense of painful alienation, not joyous anarchy. *Harriet the Spy,* despite its delightful characterizations and humorous dialogue, shocks the reader with its insight into the dreadful freedom of contemporary children.

The Long Secret is ostensibly a sequel to *Harriet the Spy* but actually centers upon the character of shy, wealthy Beth Ellen Hansen. Beth Ellen and Harriet both spend their summers in Water Mill, New York. Two events bring Beth Ellen's smoldering emotional problems to a crisis. First, Harriet is determined to track down the notewriter who has been leaving shocking notes around town (a grocery store clerk receives the message "Jesus hates you"). At the same time Beth Ellen discovers that her wealthy, vain, and spoiled mother, Zeebey, and her equally shallow husband, Wallace, are coming to visit her for the first time since she was a small child. As a counterpoint to the inane and trivial socializing of the idle rich, Fitzhugh creates an unlikely family of religious fanatics from Mississippi. Mama Jenkins, the mother of this family, is making her fortune manufacturing toe medicine from watermelons. Fitzhugh is clearly interested in Mama Jenkins's capacity to blend her religious doctrine with her greed for money. The purpose of this family in the fabric of the novel remains ambiguous, although it does lead Harriet to ask her father some hard religious questions. In the denouement of *The Long Secret* Beth Ellen finally expresses her repressed anger towards her narcissistic mother and experiences emotional liberation, and Harriet figures out that Beth Ellen has written the notes, clearly as an outlet for her anger.

One of Fitzhugh's most disturbing novels (and in the minds of some readers, her best) is *Nobody's Family Is Going to Change.* In this novel Fitzhugh focuses upon 11-year old, overweight Emma Sheridan, the daughter of an ambitious middle-class black lawyer. Emma desperately wishes to become a lawyer and to win her father's approval. Her little brother, Willis, is a gifted dancer. Mrs. Sheridan exists in the shadow of her husband, a domineering patriarch, who dislikes Emma for her intelligence and her ambitions to be a lawyer. Likewise he harshly refuses to accept Willie's identity as a dancer. Emma tries many tactics to win her father's love; at one point she even joins the Children's Army to fight for children's rights. All of her attempts signally fail. In a riveting and shocking illumination, Emma recognizes the bitter fact that her father hates her, "that fathers and mothers don't change. It's up to us to change....We have to stop trying to make them love us." Emma's painful insight perhaps strains credibility; yet the novel attests to Fitzhugh's tough-minded vision of the family. A family, she suggests unequivocally, may be a trap and a tomb, where children are doomed to shrink and to die rather than to grow. Despite the novel's dark implications, Emma's final word is triumphant and assertive. If the father cannot accept who she is, what her talents are, "That," she says emphatically, "is your problem."

Sport, published posthumously in 1979, centers upon Harriet's friend, Simon Rocque ("sport"). Despite its rather improbable plot, this novel features another memorable portrait of a tough child who survives because of his own resourcefulness and because of the support of his father and friends. The relationship between Sport and his father is moving and tender; Sport's growing love and acceptance of his new step-mother, Kate, is also convincingly presented.

Fitzhugh's picture book, *Bang, Bang, You're Dead,* was a controversial book prominently associated with the so-called "New Realism" in children's literature. Published in the Vietnam War era, the book conveyed a vehement message against the folly of war and violence. Part of the controversy over the book occurred because of its graphic language (including such expressions as "pukeface") and its graphic depiction of violence. In this book, the message overshadows everything else; the characters are barely developed.

Flannery O'Connor has written that to reach a morally blind audience, the writer must exaggerate and distort. Fitzhugh's works resonate with social consciousness and with just indignation against human selfishness, greed, and ignorance. She sometimes creates grotesque characterizations, apparently in an attempt to shock her readers into an awareness that middle-class, affluent children may be lost in the wilderness, the emotional and moral chaos of contemporary urban life. Fitzhugh's mastery in writing witty dialogue, her gift for creating memorable characters, and her moral honesty in relentlessly depicting psychologically realistic portraits of contemporary American children have earned for her a lasting place in children's literature.

—Anita Moss

FLACK, Marjorie

Nationality: American. **Born:** Greenport, Long Island, New York, 23 October 1897. **Education:** Art Students' League, New York, 1918-20. **Family:** Married 1) the artist Karl Larsson in 1919 (divorced 1940), one daughter; 2) the poet William Rose Benét in 1941 (died 1950). **Career:** Art teacher, Bronxville, New York. **Died:** 29 August 1958.

Publications for Children

Fiction (illustrated by the author)

Taktuk, An Arctic Boy, with Helen Lomen. New York, Doubleday, 1928; London, Lane, 1956.

All Around the Town. New York, Doubleday, 1929.
Angus and the Ducks. New York, Doubleday, 1930; London, Lane, 1933.
Angus and the Cat. New York, Doubleday, 1931; London, Lane, 1933.
Angus Lost. New York, Doubleday, 1932; London, Lane, 1933.
Ask Mr. Bear. New York, Macmillan, 1932.
The Story about Ping, illustrated by Kurt Wiese. New York, Viking Press, 1933; London, Lane, 1935.
Wag-Tail Bess. New York, Doubleday, 1933; as *Angus and Wag-Tail Bess,* London, Lane, 1935.
Tim Tadpole and the Great Bullfrog. New York, Doubleday, 1934.
Humphrey: One Hundred Years Along the Wayside with a Box Turtle. New York, Doubleday, 1934.
Christopher. New York, Scribner, 1935.
Topsy. New York, Doubleday, 1935; as *Angus and Topsy,* London, Lane, 1935.
Up in the Air, illustrated by Karl Larsson. New York, Macmillan, 1935.
Wait for William. Boston, Houghton Mifflin, 1935.
What to Do about Molly, illustrated by the author and Karl Larsson. Boston, Houghton Mifflin, 1936; London, Lane, 1938.
Willy Nilly. New York, Macmillan, 1936; London, Lane, 1939.
Lucky Little Lena. New York, Macmillan, 1937.
The Restless Robin. Boston, Houghton Mifflin, 1937.
Walter, The Lazy Mouse. New York, Doubleday, 1937; Edinburgh, Chambers, 1964.
William and His Kitten. Boston, Houghton Mifflin, 1938; London, Lane, 1939.
Pedro, with Karl Larsson, illustrated by Larsson. New York, Macmillan, 1940.
The New Pet. New York, Doubleday, 1943; London, Lane, 1956.
I See a Kitty, illustrated by Hilma Larsson. New York, Doubleday, 1943.
The Boats on the River, illustrated by Jay Hyde Barnum. New York, Viking Press, 1946.
Happy Birthday Letter, illustrated by Jay Hyde Barnum. Boston, Houghton Mifflin, 1947.

Poetry

Adolphus; or, The Adopted Dolphin and the Pirate's Daughter, with William Rose Benét. Boston, Houghton Mifflin, 1941.
Away Goes Jonathan Wheeler, illustrated by Hilma Larsson. New York, Doubleday, 1944.

Other

Neighbors on the Hill, with Mabel O'Donnell, illustrated by Florence and Margaret Hoopes. Evanston, Illinois, Row Peterson, 1943.

*

Manuscript Collections: University of Oregon Library, Eugene.

Illustrator: *Knights, Goats, and Battleships* by Terry Strickland Colt, 1930; *Scamper, The Bunny Who Went to the White House,* 1934, and *Scamper's Christmas,* 1934, both by Anne Roosevelt Dall; *Here, There, and Everywhere,* 1936, and *All Together,* 1952, both by Dorothy Aldis; *The Country Bunny and the Little Gold Shoes* by DuBose Heyward, 1939; *A Black Velvet Story* by Dee Smith, 1940; *Olaf, Lofoten Fisherman* by Fru Constance Schram, 1940.

* * *

Marjorie Flack's picture books are good for reading aloud to small children. Angus is a Scottie dog who chases ducks, strongly objects to sharing his home with a cat, gets lost, and helps to overcome the excessive timidity of Bess the airedale and to solve the problems of the spaniel Topsy. Each simple story is illustrated with clear realistic line drawings and told with a good eye for the detail of a lively young dog's life. The young child will enjoy Angus's experiences as they are also his own: the "Things Which Come Apart" though clearly they shouldn't; the fascination of things on the other side of the hedge; the terrors of being lost; and the jealousy when a rival appears in the household. There is a comforting progression in the books, too; the alarums and excursions with the ducks in the first book are followed by later episodes in which the same ducks are routed by an older and more confident Angus. These stories are for under-fives; *The Story about Ping* is a favorite with five to six-year-olds. Ping is a duckling who lives on a Chinese boat on the Yangtze River. He runs away to escape punishment, but after a frightening day alone on the river returns thankfully to the safety of his wise-eyed boat, along with his father, mother, and all his other relations. This is a varied and entertaining story, with a touch of fantasy and the exotic, illustrated with bright, quaint, and intriguing pictures by Kurt Wiese.

Walter, The Lazy Mouse is a longer story for five to seven-year-olds. Walter is so lazy that he is perpetually out of phase with both home and school. Eventually, when his family forget his existence altogether and move house without him he finds refuge with a family of bullfrogs who are even more happy-go-lucky than himself. Rather perversely, he is so anxious to establish himself in their singularly unretentive memories that he becomes punctual, active, and hardworking, labouring at a more-than-usually thankless task of perpetually teaching these frogs what they don't need to know and will inevitably forget. The illogicality of this teacher's nightmare, however, will not be apparent or important to the child reader, for whom the amusing detail of Walter's efforts at swimming and furniture-making and his wholly delightful first encounter with the chorus of frogs will make this a memorable tale.

Taktuk, An Arctic Boy, written in collaboration with Helen Lomen, is a very different kind of book. It gives an informative picture of the life of a ten-year-old Eskimo boy, but though the detail is good and the story simply told, the tone is a little condescending, and amid the welter of information and the rather wooden prose the Eskimo family never comes alive. It is a useful rather than an enthralling book.

—Winifred Whitehead

FLEISCHMAN, (Albert) Sid(ney)

Pseudonyms: Max Brindle, Carl March. **Nationality:** American. **Born:** Brooklyn, New York, 16 March 1920. **Education:** San Diego State College, B.A. 1949. **Military Service:** United States

Naval Reserve, 1941-45. **Family:** Married Betty Taylor in 1942; two daughters and one son, Paul Fleischman, *q.v.* **Career:** Magician in vaudeville and night clubs, 1938-41; reporter, San Diego *Daily Journal,* 1949-50; associate editor, *Point* magazine, San Diego, 1950-51. **Awards:** Western Writers of America Spur award, 1964; George G. Stone Center for Children's Books award, 1972; Society of Children's Book Writers Golden Kite award, 1974; Boston *Globe-Horn Book* award, 1979; American Library Association Newbery Medal, 1987. **Address:** 305 Tenth Street, Santa Monica, California 90402, U.S.A.

Publications for Children

Fiction

Mr. Mysterious and Company. Boston, Little Brown, 1962; London, Hutchinson, 1963; pictures by Eric von Schmidt. New York, Greenwillow Books, 1997.
By the Great Horn Spoon!, illustrated by Eric von Schmidt. Boston, Little Brown, 1963; London, Hamish Hamilton, 1965; as *Bullwhip Griffin,* New York, Avon, 1967.
The Ghost in the Noonday Sun, illustrated by Warren Chappell. Boston, Little Brown, 1965; London, Hamish Hamilton, 1966.
McBroom Tells the Truth, illustrated by Kurt Werth. New York, Norton, 1966.
Chancy and the Grand Rascal, illustrated by Eric von Schmidt. Boston, Little Brown, 1966; London, Hamish Hamilton, 1967.
McBroom and the Big Wind, illustrated by Kurt Werth. New York, Norton, 1967.
McBroom's Ear, illustrated by Kurt Werth. New York, Norton, 1969.
Longbeard the Wizard, illustrated by Charles Bragg. Boston, Little Brown, 1970.
Jingo Django, illustrated by Eric von Schmidt. Boston, Little Brown, and London, Hamish Hamilton, 1971.
McBroom's Ghost, illustrated by Robert Frankenberg. New York, Grosset and Dunlap, 1971.
The Wooden Cat Man, illustrated by Jay Yang. Boston, Little Brown, 1972.
McBroom's Zoo, illustrated by Kurth Werth. New York, Grosset and Dunlap, 1972.
McBroom's Wonderful One-Acre Farm (includes *McBroom Tells the Truth, McBroom and the Big Wind, McBroom's Ghost*), illustrated by Quentin Blake. London, Chatto and Windus, 1972.
McBroom the Rainmaker, illustrated by Kurt Werth. New York, Grosset and Dunlap, 1973.
The Ghost on Saturday Night, illustrated by Eric von Schmidt. Boston, Little Brown, 1974; London, Heinemann, 1975; pictures by Laura Cornell, New York, Greenwillow Books, 1997.
McBroom Tells a Lie, illustrated by Walter Lorraine. Boston, Little Brown, 1976.
Here Comes McBroom (includes *McBroom Tells a Lie, McBroom the Rainmaker, McBroom's Zoo*), illustrated by Quentin Blake. London, Chatto and Windus, 1976.
Me and the Man on the Moon-Eyed Horse, illustrated by Eric von Schmidt. Boston, Little Brown, 1977; as *The Man on the Moon-Eyed Horse,* London, Gollancz, 1980.
Kate's Secret Riddle Book, illustrated by Barbara Bottner. New York and London, Watts, 1977.
McBroom and the Beanstalk, illustrated by Walter Lorraine. Boston, Little Brown, 1978.
Jim Bridger's Alarm Clock and Other Tall Tales, illustrated by Eric von Schmidt. New York, Dutton, 1978.
Humbug Mountain, illustrated by Eric von Schmidt. Boston, Little Brown, 1978; London, Gollancz, 1980.
The Hey Hey Man, illustrated by Nadine Bernard Westcott. Boston, Little Brown, 1979.
McBroom and the Great Race, illustrated by Walter Lorraine. Boston, Little Brown, 1980; London, Chatto and Windus, 1981.
The Case of the Cackling Ghost, illustrated by Anthony Rao. New York, Random House, 1981.
The Case of the Flying Clock, illustrated by William Harmuth. New York, Random House, 1981.
The Case of Princess Tomorrow, illustrated by Bill Morrison. New York, Random House, 1981.
The Case of the Secret Message, illustrated by William Harmuth. New York, Random House, 1981.
The Case of the 264-Pound Burglar, illustrated by Bill Morrison. New York, Random House, 1982.
The Bloodhound Gang's Secret Code Book, illustrated by Bill Morrison. New York, Random House, 1983.
McBroom's Almanac, illustrated by Walter Lorraine. Boston, Little Brown, 1984.
The Whipping Boy, illustrated by Peter Sis. New York, Greenwillow, 1986; London, Methuen, 1988.
The Scarebird, illustrated by Peter Sis. New York, Greenwillow, 1988.
The Ghost in the Noonday Sun, illustrated by Peter Sis. New York, Greenwillow, 1989.
The Midnight Horse. New York, Greenwillow, 1990; London, Methuen, 1991.
Jim Ugly, illustrated by Joseph A. Smith. New York, Greenwillow, 1992; London, Hamilton, 1993.
The 13th Floor: A Ghost Story, illustrations by Peter Sis. New York, Greenwillow Books, 1995.
Bandit's Moon, illustrations by Joseph A. Smith. New York, Greenwillow Books, 1998.

Other

Mr. Mysterious's Secrets of Magic, illustrated by Eric von Schmidt. Boston, Little Brown, 1975; as *Secrets of Magic,* London, Chatto and Windus, 1976.
The Abracadabra Kid: A Writer's Life (autobiography). New York, Greenwillow Books, 1996.

Publications for Adults

Novels

The Straw Donkey Case. New York, Phoenix Press, 1948.
Murder's No Accident. New York, Phoenix Press, 1949.
Shanghai Flame. New York, Fawcett, 1951; London, Fawcett, 1957.
Look Behind You, Lady. New York, Fawcett, 1952; London, Muller, 1953; as *Chinese Crimson,* London, Jenkins, 1962.
Danger in Paradise. New York, Fawcett, 1953; London, Muller, 1954.
Counterspy Express. New York, Ace, 1954.

Malay Woman. New York, Fawcett, 1954; London, Fawcett, 1955; as *Malaya Manhunt,* London, Jenkins, 1965.
Blood Alley. New York, Fawcett, 1955; London, Fawcett, 1956.
Yellowleg. New York, Fawcett, and London, Muller, 1960.
The Venetian Blonde. New York, Fawcett, 1963; London, Muller, 1964.

Plays

Screenplays: *Blood Alley,* 1955; *Good-bye My Lady,* 1956; *Lafayette Escadrille,* with William A. Wellman, 1958; *The Deadly Companions, Yellowleg,* both 1961; *Scalawag,* 1972; *The Whipping Boy* (as Max Brindle), 1994.

Other

Between Cocktails. N.p., Abbott Magic Company, 1939.
Magic Made Easy (as Carl March). N.p., Croydon, 1953.
Crosscurrents of Criticism, with others, edited by Paul Heins. Boston, Horn Book, 1977.
The Charlatan's Handbook. L and L Publishing, 1993.

*

Manuscript Collection: Kerlan Collection, University of Minnesota, Minneapolis.

Sid Fleischman comments:
While my books rarely draw upon direct personal experience, I catch ghostly glimpses of my presence on almost every page. The stories inevitably reveal my interests and enthusiasms—my taste for the comic in life, my love of adventure, the seductions (for me) of the 19th-century American frontier, and my enchantment with the folk speech of that period. Language is a wondrous toy and I have great literary fun with it.

Since I don't plot my stories in advance, the experience of writing a book is, for me, very much the same as reading a book. I rarely know what is going to happen next and have to sit at the typewriter to find out. My starting point is almost always a background, such as the California Gold Rush in *By the Great Horn Spoon!* or the age of piracy in *The Ghost in the Noonday Sun.* On other occasions I begin with an idea for a character: the magician in *Mr. Mysterious and Company,* for example, or a Midwest teller of tall tales as in the McBroom stories.

* * *

The tall tale is a special branch of folklore. It has its own language, its own pacing, its own outrageous logic. But it is also tied to a specific place: rural America. Coming out of the European Munchausen tradition, the tall tale found a permanent home on the American frontier where it was frontier in spirit, style, and tone. The tall tale can still be found in its oral form in the rural Southern and Western United States. In its literary form it can be found, occasionally, in children's books.

Sid Fleischman comes neither from the South or West, nor from the country at all. He is a product of the urban East. Yet he has made the particular voice of the tall tale so much his own that, if any one author can be said to be master of the genre, it is he. His oddball characters include Chancy, so skinny he has to stand twice to cast a shadow; McBroom, who owns the richest one-acre farm in the world; Jingo Hawks, the biggest liar in Mrs. Duggart's Beneficent Orphan Home (and proud of it); the irrepressible Hey-Hey Man; and hosts of others.

Fleischman's wit and style are deceptive. His flagrant humor disguises the fact that he is a careful craftsman who chooses each scene with infinite care and sets it down with a straight face. He may be pulling your leg, but he does it with a poker face. His slang-oriented style, with its tall-tale helpings of grandiloquence, hyperbole, and exaggeration, are the result of impeccable research. He fills looseleaf notebooks with data on names, phrases, places, all culled from period novels, newspapers, and other primary sources. For Fleischman, the tall tale is both a literary dialect and a literary folklore. He takes it seriously.

Fleischman's many novels combine adventure with history, humor with serious statement. But the stories themselves are told at such a breakneck pace that the reader is given little time to consider how finely drawn the strange characters are, or how definitively rendered are the villains. Instead it seems, at first reading, that story is all. Nowhere does this craftsmanship, this use of language, this swiftness of pace show more clearly than in *Chancy and the Grand Rascal.* One part quest story, two parts braggadocio, it concerns the travels of young Chancy Dundee and his uncle—the Grand Rascal—by foot, by raft, by train, by steamboat, and by willpower through the U.S.A. as they look for the scattered remnants of their family. There are tall tales within tall tales, whoppers told offhandedly by Chancy, his Uncle Will, his sister Indiana, and others. And by the time the book is through, the reader has laughed a lot, learned a great deal about frontier life, and added some marvelous new/old words to his vocabulary—words such as *yawhawin', pineries, mudshoes, jayhawkers,* and *beeves.*

Fleischman writes for television and has done riddle books, young mysteries, and adult Westerns, but it is in the tall tale that he throws a shadow—singular and irresistible.

In 1986 Fleischman published *The Whipping Boy,* a novel more historically based, and less flamboyant, than some of his tall tales. But his command of story is still strong, the characters still engaging. The book won the Newbery Medal, a tribute not just to that one volume, but to Fleischman's highly original contributions to the literature of childhood.

In 1996, Fleischman released his autobiography, *The Abracadabra Kid: A Writer's Life,* to widespread critical acclaim. Though it is the story of a grown man—a man 76 years old, in fact—Fleischman writes as ever to a youthful audience. Given its title, it is not surprising that his narrative, broken into 43 short chapters, should play heavily on the author's ability with magic. He tells of card tricks and early magic shows, but he also describes his experiences in the Navy during World War II. Along the way, Fleischman gives valuable insights for young writers, coupled with useful knowledge he gained as a screenwriter on John Wayne's movies. One insight comes from director William "Wild Bill" Wellman, who optioned Fleischman's *Blood Alley:* "[he] insisted that every scene end with a strong curtain line.... I carried this over as an effective writing habit into my novels. Unless my imagination dries up, my chapters inevitably end with the dramatic flourish of a curtain line." For all his teaching, though, Fleischman is not above seeing himself in a humorous light, as he shows with various mordant comments culled from fan mail and excerpted as chapter epigraphs—e.g., "I read *The Ghost in the Noonday Sun.* Don't quit your day job."

—Jane Yolen, updated by Judson Knight

FLORA, James (Royer)

Nationality: American. **Born:** Bellefontaine, Ohio, 25 January 1914. **Education:** Urbana College, Ohio, 1931-33; Art Academy of Cincinnati, 1934-39. **Family:** Married Jane Sinnickson in 1941; five children. **Career:** Co-founding publisher, Little Man Press, Cincinnati, 1939-42; art director and sales promotion manager, Columbia Recording Corporation, New York and Bridgeport, Connecticut, 1942-50; consultant art director and board member, Benwill Publishing Corporation, Boston, 1957-62; art director and board member, Computer Design Publishing Company, 1962-80. Freelance magazine illustrator, 1952-80. **Address:** St. James Place, Bell Island, Rowayton, Connecticut 06853, U.S.A.

PUBLICATIONS FOR CHILDREN (ILLUSTRATED BY THE AUTHOR)

Fiction

The Fabulous Firework Family. New York, Harcourt Brace, 1955; revised edition, with new illustrations by the author, New York, Atheneum, 1994.
The Day the Cow Sneezed. New York, Harcourt Brace, 1957.
Charlie Yup and His Snip-Snap Boys. New York, Harcourt Brace, 1959.
Leopold, The See-Through Crumbpicker. New York, Harcourt Brace, 1961.
Kangaroo for Christmas. New York, Harcourt Brace, 1962.
My Friend Charlie. New York, Harcourt Brace, 1964.
Grandpa's Farm: Four Tall Tales. New York, Harcourt Brace, 1965.
Sherwood Walks Home. New York, Harcourt Brace, 1966.
Fishing with Dad. New York, Harcourt Brace, 1967.
The Joking Man. New York, Harcourt Brace, 1968.
Little Hatchy Hen. New York, Harcourt Brace, 1969.
Pishtosh, Bullwash, and Wimple. New York, Atheneum, 1972.
Stewed Goose. New York, Atheneum, 1973.
The Great Green Turkey Creek Monster. New York, Atheneum, 1976.
Grandpa's Ghost Stories. New York, Atheneum, 1978.
Wanda and the Bumbly Wizard. New York, Atheneum, 1980.
Grandpa's Witched-Up Christmas. New York, Atheneum, 1982.

Plays

Animated Film Screenplays: *The Fabulous Firework Family,* 1959; *Leopold, The See-Through Crumbpicker,* 1972.

PUBLICATIONS FOR ADULTS

New Orleans Wood Engravings in Portfolio. Cincinnati, Little Man Press, n.d.

*

Manuscript Collections: Kerlan Collection, University of Minnesota, Minneapolis.

Illustrator: *3 Fragments and a Story* by William Saroyan, 1939; *Murderpie,* 1939, *I'll Never Be the Same,* 1939, and *Gup,* 1942, all by Robert Lowry; *The Talking Dog and the Barking Man* by Elizabeth Seeman, 1960; *101 Words and How They Began,* 1979, and *101 More Words and How They Began,* 1980, both by Arthur Steckler.

James Flora comments:

Aside from my own personal pleasure in writing and illustrating for children my only aim is entertainment. I always try to write a bang-up good story that will intrigue a child and demonstrate how much fun reading can be. The process of learning to read is so protracted, difficult, and boring in our schools that many children find it distasteful and never learn at all.

I keep my work light and rollicking and my reward is the letters I get from children telling me how much they *enjoy reading* my books. To impart the joy of reading is the single thread that runs through all my stories.

* * *

Hyperbole, humor, action, and invention are hallmarks of James Flora's cumulative and tall tales and fanciful adventures. Elaborating on what might happen if a seed company sent the wrong order, a hen could hatch anything, or the North Pole was stolen, he lets his imagination run rampant. In *The Day the Cow Sneezed* the sneeze exposes a mouse, which eludes a cat, who claws a goat, and on and on until breathtaking rides involving a policeman's motorcycle, a steam roller, a Ferris wheel, and a truck loaded with fireworks, they roll—shooting rockets and all—onto a boat; whereupon the fireworks are extinguished and Fletcher, the boy protagonist, is summarily punished for allowing the cow to get chilled and wet. In *The Great Green Turkey Creek Monster* a Hooligan vine, which grows so fast "you had to run to keep ahead of it," rampages through Turkey Creek, its multitudinous tendrils invading town buildings. Causing chaos, confusion, and eventually consternation, it opens fireplugs to take a shower, pushes the garbage truck into the movie theater (patrons rush out exclaiming, "Hoo boy! What a stinky picture") and forces the school principal into the girl's room, eliciting the shocked pronouncement, "*and he isn't a girl.*" Fun, funny, fast-paced, and exuberant, these stories show events and objects appearing out of control.

Flora loses control, however, in stories which ignore logic while building nonsense. In *Stewed Goose,* which smacks of animated cartoons, the action is frenetic rather than funny as a bear contrives endlessly to catch a goose that he could in reality snare with one swat of his paw. Similarly, in *The Joking Man,* the final revelation that the two boy protagonists are, in fact, the mysterious joking man, undermines the plot when there is no accounting for their ability to perform the impossible pranks. These books, like *Pishtosh, Bullwash, and Wimple* and *My Friend Charlie,* have little plot or characterization to sustain them; they rise and fall on the invention and silliness concocted upon each page.

The most successful narratives such as *Little Hatchy Hen, Grandpa's Farm,* and *Grandpa's Ghost Stories,* with their emphasis on superlatives, invincibility, growth, and invention, are in the mode of traditional American folklore and benefit from its structure. Their conversational storytelling tone and direct authorial appeals, like "Did you ever hear...?" and "You don't believe...?," draw readers into the tall tales about the hen who is kidnapped by the world's champion chicken thief, and the farm where cornstalks grow so fast Grandpa can't chop them down because he can "never chop twice in the same place." The "too terrible to tell" ghost stories ghoulishly reek of "shrouds that smell like a toad's underwear," and promote "goosebumps in between ... goosebumps."

At his best Flora communes with the roguish, playful qualities in children. His aim is to entertain; his method is boisterous, zany action and clever invention. His flat, stylized cartoon drawings animate and extend the hilarity even onto the title pages.

—Nancy C. Hammond

FOON, Dennis

Nationality: American/Canadian (dual). **Born:** Detroit, Michigan, 18 November 1951. **Education:** University of Michigan, Ann Arbor (Hopwood award, 1972), 1969-73, B.A. (honors) in religious studies and creative writing 1973; University of British Columbia, Vancouver, 1973-75, M.F.A. in playwriting 1975. **Family:** Married Jane Howard Baker in 1975 (divorced); two daughters. **Career:** Instructor in playwriting, University of British Columbia Centre for Continuing Education, 1974-79. Co-founder and artistic director, Green Thumb Theatre for Young People, Vancouver, 1975-88. Playwright-in-residence, Young People's Theatre, Toronto, 1983-84. Consultant, Sesame Street Canada, 1988-92; Canadian Vice-President, International Association of Theatres for Children and Youth, 1979-82. **Awards:** *Writers Digest* award, 1973; Canadian Broadcasting Corporation award, 1985; British Theatre award, 1986; Jesse award (directing), 1984, 1985, 1986, 1987; Chalmers award, 1987; International Arts for Young Audiences award, for outstanding contribution to theater for young audiences, 1989; Scott Newman award, 1990. **Agent:** Peter Zednik, Green Thumb Theatre, 1885 Venables, Vancouver, British Columbia V5L 2H6. **Address:** 647 East 12th Avenue, Vancouver, British Columbia V5T 2H7, Canada.

Publications for Children

Fiction

The Short Tree and the Bird That Could Not Sing, illustrated by John Bianchi. Vancouver, Douglas and McIntyre, 1986.

Plays

The Last Days of Paul Bunyan (puppet play; produced Vancouver, 1977). With *The Windigo,* Toronto, Playwrights, 1978.
Heracles (produced Vancouver, 1978). Vancouver, Talonbooks, 1978.
Raft Baby (produced Vancouver, 1978).
The Windigo (produced Vancouver, 1979; London, 1980). With *The Last Days of Paul Bunyan,* Toronto, Playwrights, 1978.
The Hunchback of Notre Dame, adaptation of a novel by Victor Hugo (produced Vancouver, 1981). Toronto, Playwrights, 1983.
New Canadian Kid (produced Vancouver, 1981; London, 1985). Vancouver, Pulp Press, 1982.
Trummi Kaput, adaptation of the play by Volker Ludwig (produced Vancouver, 1982; New York, 1983). Published in *Canadian Theatre Review* (Toronto), Spring 1983.
Feeling Yes, Feeling No (produced Vancouver, 1982).
Skin (produced Vancouver, 1984; revised version, also director: produced Toronto, 1986). With *Liars,* Toronto, Playwrights, 1988.
Invisible Kids (also director: produced London, 1985).
Liars (produced Vancouver, 1986). With *Skin,* Toronto, Playwrights, 1988.
Bedtimes and Bullies, adaptation of a play by Volker Ludwig (also director: produced Toronto, 1987).
Mirror Game (also director: produced Quebec City, 1988). Winnipeg, Blizzard, 1992.
War (produced Vancouver, 1994).
The Short Tree and the Bird That Could Not Sing (produced Vancouver, 1994).
Seesaw (produced Vancouver, 1994), Winnipeg, Blizzard, 1993.
Sunspots (produced Vancouver, 1995).

Other

Am I the Only One? A Young People's Book about Sex Abuse, with Brenda Knight. Vancouver, Douglas and McIntyre, 1985.

Publications for Adults

Plays

Hotsy Totsy, with others (produced Vancouver, 1978).
Children's Eyes (produced Vancouver, 1983).
Afternoon Tea (produced Vancouver, 1986).
Differences (screenplay, 1986).
Boogeymen (television play, in *Lies from Lotusland* series, 1987).
Wheels (television play, in *Lies from Lotusland* series, 1987).
Zaydok (produced Vancouver, 1987; New York, 1988).
Little Criminals (television play, Canadian Broadcasting Corporation, 1996).

*

Theatrical Activities:
Director: **Plays**—Many of his own plays, and *Portrait of an Adult as a Young Kid* by John Carroll, Vancouver, 1980; *Schoolyard Games* by John Lazarus, Vancouver, 1981; *The Bittersweet Kid* by Peggy Thompson, Vancouver, 1982, and subsequent tours; *One Thousand Cranes* by Colin Thomas, Vancouver, 1983, and Pacific tour, 1985; *Not So Dumb* by John Lazarus, Vancouver, 1984, and Canadian tour, 1985; *Herot,* Adelaide, Australia, 1985; *Secrets of an Usherette* by Gordon Armstrong, Vancouver, 1986; *Nightlight* by John Lazarus, Vancouver, 1986; *One in a Million* by David Holman, Vancouver, 1987; *No Worries* by David Holman, Toronto, 1989; *Dancing in the Garden ... Like Momma* by Elizabeth Dancoes, Vancouver, 1990; *Amigo's Blue Guitar* by Joan MacLeod, Toronto, 1990; *Naomi's Road* by Joy Kogawa, adapted by Paula Wing, Toronto, 1992.

Dennis Foon comments:
When I was growing up in Detroit I used to spend my summers in Algonquin Park, Ontario. The tranquility of those lakes and forests always served as an antidote to the rising racial tension I was experiencing in my home town. Some years later when I was invited to pursue my M.F.A. at the University of British

Columbia I jumped at the chance. I hated Detroit, hated the fact that things had become so polarized, so far gone that I couldn't see an end to the social problems. Canada had always represented a kind of Mecca to me. I had always sworn I'd get here somehow.

When I finished my degree and we started Green Thumb Theatre, I had little idea in the beginning what theatre for young people could be. But very soon it became clear to me that theatre could be a way to communicate ideas, a way to work toward change.

By comparison with the violence and chaos in Detroit, Vancouver is a very calm and sensible place. But it is clear that the seeds of many of the same problems that I experienced in Detroit are pervasive in Canada. To me they are like St. Exupery's baobab seeds: if we ignore them, they will destroy us.

I believe in the possibility for change and that it is up to each of us to make it happen, both inside and outside. My plays and other writings are a vote for the future.

* * *

The written products of Dennis Foon, playwright and director of theatre for children and young adults, have been both consistent and changing over the last decade. His plays, which generally contain few characters and require little elaborate staging, are available to small companies and can reach wide audiences. Foon's subject matter has undergone transformation: many of his early plays are plot- or character-oriented, but more recently they have focused on contemporary social issues.

Among the "story" plays is *The Last Days of Paul Bunyan,* a puppet play in which Paul, tall tale hero, is told "The thing you cannot fight has come." While seeking this thing Paul overcomes other challenges but, unable to defeat the reality that "the big trees are gone" and his days as a lumberjack are over, Paul and his blue ox Babe go to the Land of Tall Tales.

An Ojibwa Indian belief regarding a spirit, the Windigo, which drives starving hunters mad and leads them into cannibalism, is the basis for *The Windigo.* Red Bird, a shaman, wants Sweet Grass to be his wife. When she chooses Half Sky instead, Red Bird places a curse on him. During a harsh winter, the pregnant Red Bird risks murder by a starving Half Sky unless he defeats the Windigo.

Raft Baby is a dramatized version of an event that ostensibly happened in British Columbia in the late 19th century. As a white man and his Blackfoot wife are dying they place their infant daughter on a raft which they float down the Peace River. By chance the woman's brother rescues the child but, not recognizing her parentage, gives her to a couple to raise. Some two decades later, the brother recovers his brother-in-law's diary, realizes the child's identity, and searches for his niece, discovering her on her wedding day.

The Hunchback of Notre Dame provides the essential storyline around the relationships of Esmerelda, Frollo, Quasimodo, Phoebus, and Gringoire. *Heracles,* which commences following the death of the mythical Greek hero of enormous strength, reviews the events leading up to Heracles's death caused by his donning the poisoned shirt given him by his wife. *Bedtimes and Bullies* examines children's fears and the quality of communication between parents and children.

Probably the most recognized of Foon's plays treating social issues is *New Canadian Kid,* which reflects the immigrant experience, especially its impact on children. Audiences can participate in what a new Canadian might experience because Nick, the boy from Homeland, speaks English while the Canadian characters speak "gibberish." Anxious about lost friends and learning a new language, Nick is reassured by his mother that "It won't even take a week." Nick interacts principally with Mug and Mench. Focusing on Nick's differences, Mug mocks Nick's smelly food and inability to speak "English." Mench, a girl, supports Nick and becomes his first Canadian friend.

Mirror Game portrays the destructive cycle of child and spouse abuse. Luke, physically abused by his father, becomes an abuser of his girlfriend Sara. She in turn allows the mistreatment because she observes her mother's submission to her live-in boyfriend's battering. Foon shows that appearances are not reality. Luke and Sara, "the beautiful people" on the outside, are tormented by inner blemishes; Bob and Maggie, the seemingly "normal kids" with exterior imperfections of zits and excess weight, have been emotionally abused by parents and carry into relationships the effects of diminished self-respect. By the play's end all but Luke have apparently broken the cycle.

As five preteens play in *Invisible Kids,* listeners learn that Georgie's parents are saving money to bring her older sister from Jamaica. Achieving the needed amount, the family discovers their daughter must wait two further years for her papers. The children conclude the delay is because "we're the wrong colour" since European applicants are delayed but months while Asians, South Americans, and Africans wait years. Deciding they are neither powerless nor invisible, the children create a petition demanding equality of treatment and send one copy to the prime minister and another to a television network since politicians "won't listen to us. We're just kids."

Skin and *Liars* are published together. *Skin* deals with racial prejudice, especially its expression within schools. A Canadian-born girl of West Indian parents hears a teacher categorizing her as lazy and capable of no higher aspirations than vocational school. Fearing rejection of her heritage, Bombay-born Phiroza describes herself as Persian to a boy she likes. Tuan, a Vietnamese boatperson, is physically harassed in the halls and loses his part-time job because of being Asian. In *Liars* a pair of 16-year-olds, Jace, a headbanger, and Lenny, a preppy girl, share a problem—parental alcoholism. Jace's father is a physically abusive drunk while Lenny's mother is the protected, hidden alcoholic. Initially Jace and Lenny provide mutual emotional support, but Jace eventually escapes into drugs.

In addition to his plays Foon has co-edited a book and authored a picture book. With Brenda Knight, Foon created *Am I the Only One? A Young People's Book about Sex Abuse.* Some two dozen boys and girls, in prose, poetry, and art, powerfully share their experiences of being abused by parents, relatives, babysitters, and neighbors. As the title implies, the contents attempt to reassure abused readers they are not alone in having experienced sexual abuse, and the text offers suggestions for obtaining help. The theme of friendship, which recurs in many of Foon's plays, appears in *The Short Tree and the Bird That Could Not Sing.* Being short, the tree could not see the world's goings-on. A bird with an atrocious voice begins roosting in the tree's branches and becomes the tree's eyes to the wider world. Their friendship grows until autumn migration when the tree is convinced he will lose his friend forever, but spring brings the bird back. While the text carries the storyline, John Bianchi's illustrations reinforce the book's emotions.

Perhaps it is the fate of playwrights to have their names forgotten because, while audiences see plays and may remember their titles, they do not carry away a script bearing the playwright's name. Foon's plays have won awards and been performed internationally, but in Canada his name might first be connected to one of his books rather than to his principal literary vehicle, plays.

—David H. Jenkinson

FOREMAN, Michael

Nationality: British. **Born:** Pakefield, Suffolk, 21 March 1938. **Education:** Notley Road Secondary Modern School, Lowestoft, Suffolk; Lowestoft School of Art, National Diploma in Design 1958; Royal College of Art, London (Silver Medal, 1963), A.R.C.A. (honours) 1963. **Family:** Married 1) Janet Charters in 1959 (divorced 1966), one son; 2) Louise Phillips in 1980, two sons. **Career:** Lecturer, St. Martin's School of Art, London, 1963-65, London School of Printing, 1967, Royal College of Art, 1968-70, and Central School of Art, London, 1971-72. Art director, *Playboy,* Chicago, 1965, and *King,* London, 1966. Since 1960 art director, *Ambit,* London. Individual show: Royal Festival Hall, London, 1985. **Awards:** Schweppes travelling scholarship, 1961-63; Festival International du Livre Silver Eagle award (Nice), 1972; Victoria and Albert Museum Francis Williams prize, 1972, 1977; Graphics prize (Bologna), 1982; Maschler award, 1982; Library Association Kate Greenaway Medal, 1983, 1990; Federation of Children's Books Group award, 1984; *Signal* Poetry award, 1987; Smarties prize, 1993, 1997. **Agent:** Eilleen McMahon, P.O. Box 1062, Bayonne, New Jersey 07002, U.S.A. **Address:** 5 Church Gate, London, S.W.6, England.

Publications for Children (illustrated by the author)

Fiction

The Perfect Present. London, Hamish Hamilton, and New York, Coward McCann, 1967.
The Two Giants. Leicester, Brockhampton Press, and New York, Pantheon, 1967.
The Great Sleigh Robbery. London, Hamish Hamilton, 1968; New York, Pantheon, 1969.
Horatio. London, Hamish Hamilton, 1970; as *The Travels of Horatio,* New York, Pantheon, 1970.
Moose. London, Hamish Hamilton, 1971; New York, Pantheon, 1972.
Dinosaurs and All That Rubbish. London, Hamish Hamilton, 1972; New York, Crowell, 1973.
War and Peas. London, Hamish Hamilton, and New York, Crowell, 1974.
All the King's Horses. London, Hamish Hamilton, 1976; Scarsdale, New York, Bradbury Press, 1977.
Panda's Puzzle, and His Voyage of Discovery. London, Hamish Hamilton, 1977; Scarsdale, New York, Bradbury Press, 1978.
Winter's Tales, illustrated by Freire White. London, Benn, and New York, Doubleday, 1979.
Trick a Tracker. London, Gollancz, and New York, Philomel, 1981.
Panda and the Odd Lion. London, Hamish Hamilton, 1981.
Land of Dreams. London, Andersen Press, and New York, Holt Rinehart, 1982.
Cat and Canary. London, Andersen Press, 1984; New York, Dial Press, 1985.
Panda and the Bunyips. London, Hamish Hamilton, 1984; New York, Schocken, 1987.
Private Zoo. London, Methuen, 1985.
Panda and the Bushfire. London, Hamish Hamilton, and Englewood Cliffs, New Jersey, Prentice Hall, 1986.
Ben's Box (pop-up). London, Hodder and Stoughton, 1986.
Ben's Baby. London, Andersen Press, 1987; New York, Harper, 1988.
The Angel and the Wild Animal. London, Andersen Press, 1988; New York, Atheneum, 1989.
War Boy. London, Pavilion, 1989.
Michael Foreman's World of Fairy Tales. London, Pavilion, 1990.
One World. London, Andersen Press, 1990.
Michael Foreman. N.P., Beetles, 1990.
Michael Foreman's Mother Goose. London, Walker, 1991.
The Boy Who Sailed with Columbus, with Richard Seaver. London, Pavilion, and New York, Arcade, 1991.
Jack's Fantastic Voyage. London, Andersen Press, and San Diego, Harcourt Brace, 1992.
Grandfather's Pencil and the Room of Stories. London, Andersen Press, 1993; San Diego, Harcourt Brace, 1994.
War Game. London, Pavilion, 1993.
Dad! I Can't Sleep. London, Andersen Press, 1994.
After the War Was Over. London, Pavilion Books, 1995; New York, Arcade, 1996.
Surprise! Surprise! London, Andersen Press, 1995; San Diego, Harcourt Brace, 1995.
Seal Surfer. London, Andersen Press, 1996; San Diego, Harcourt Brace, 1997.
The Little Reindeer. London, Andersen Press, 1996; New York, Dial, 1997.
Look! Look! London, Andersen Press, 1997.
Angel and the Box of Time. London, Andersen Press, 1997.
Jack's Big Race. London, Andersen Press, 1998.

*

Illustrator: *The General* by Janet Charters, 1961; *Making Music* by Gwen Clemens, 1966; *I'm for You and You're for Me* by Mabel Watts, 1967; *Let's Fight and Other Russian Fables* by Sergei Vladimirovich Mikhalkov, 1968; *Adam's Balm* by William Ivan Martin, 1970; *The Birthday Unicorn,* 1970, and *Alexander in the Land of Mog,* 1973, both by Janet Elliott; *The Living Arts of Nigeria* edited by William Fagg, 1971; *Fischer v. Spassky* by C.O. Alexander, 1972; *The Living Treasures of Japan* by Barbara Adachi, 1973; *Mr. Noah and the Second Flood* by Sheila Burnford, 1973; *Rainbow Rider* by Jane Yolen, 1974; *Private Zoo* by Georgess McHargue, 1975; *Teeny-Tiny and the Witch Woman* by Barbara K. Walker, 1975; *The Stone Book,* 1976, *Tom Fobble's Day,* 1977, *Granny Reardun,* 1977, *The Aimer Gate,* 1978, and *Fairy Tales of Gold,* 4 vols., 1979, all by Alan Garner; *The Push-cart War* by Jean Merrill, 1976; *Hans Christian Andersen: His Classic Fairy Tales* translated by Erik Haugaard, 1976; *Monkey and the Three Wizards* translated by Peter Harris, 1976; *Borrowed Feathers and Other Fables* retold by Bryna Stevens, 1978; *The Selfish Giant,* 1978, and *The Nightingale and the Rose,* 1981, both by Oscar Wilde; *The Brothers Grimm: Popular Folk Tales* translated by Brian Alderson, 1978; *Mickey's Kitchen Contest* by Kurt Baumann, 1978; *Seven in One Blow,* 1978; *How to Catch a Ghost* by Noodles, 1979; *The Faithful Bull* by Ernest Hemingway, 1980; *The Tiger Who Lost His Stripes* by Anthony Paul, 1980; *City of Gold* by Peter Dickinson, 1980; *The Pig Plantagenet* by Allen Andrews, 1980; *After Many a Summer* by Aldous Huxley, 1980; *Over the Bridge* edited by John Loveday, 1981; *Fairy Tales,* 1981, *The Saga of Eric the Viking,* 1983, *Nicobobinus,* 1985, and *The Curse of the Vampire's Socks and Other Doggerel,* 1988, *Terry Jones' Fantastic Stories,* 1993, *A Fish of the World,* 1994, *The Beast with a Thousand Teeth,* 1994, all by Terry Jones; *The Magic Mouse and the Millionaire,* 1982, *The Brontosaurus Birthday Cake,* 1983, and *Brontosaurus Superstar!,* 1985, all by Robert McCrum; *Sleeping Beauty and Other Favourite Fairy Tales* retold by Angela Carter, 1982; *Long Neck and Thunder Foot* by Helen Piers, 1982; *The Crab That Played with the Sea,* 1982, *The Jungle Book,* 1987, and *Just So Stories,* 1987, all by Rudyard Kipling; *A Christmas Carol* by Charles Dickens, 1983; *Poems for 7-Year-Olds and Under* edited by Helen Nicoll, 1983; *Poems for 9-Year-Olds and Under* [*10-Year-Olds and Over*] edited by Kit Wright, 2 vols., 1984; *A Cat and Mouse Love Story,* 1984, *Spider the Horrible Cat,* 1992, *There's a Bear in the Bath!,* 1994, all by Nanette Newman; *A Child's Garden of Verses* by Robert Louis Stevenson, 1985; *Charlie and the Chocolate Factory,* 1985, *The Complete Adventures of Charlie and Mr. Willy Wonka,* 1990, *Charlie and the Great Glass Elevator,* 1993, all by Roald Dahl; *Shakespeare Stories* by Leon Garfield, 1985; *Seasons of Splendour: Tales, Myths and Legends of India* by Madhur Jaffrey, 1985; *I'll Take You to Mrs. Cole* by Nigel Gray, 1985; *Letters from Hollywood* by Michael Moorcock, 1986; *The Magic Ointment and Other Cornish Legends* by Eric Quayle, 1986; *Tales for the Telling: Irish Folk and Fairy Stories* by Edna O'Brien, 1986; *Fun* by Jan Mark, 1987; *Classics of the Macabre* by Daphne du Maurier, 1987; *The Night Before Christmas* by Clement C. Moore, 1988; *Early In the Morning,* 1988, *Young Man of Cury and Other Poems,* 1993, both by Charles Causley, 1988; *Peter Pan and Wendy* by J.M. Barrie, 1988; *Worms Wiggle* by David Pelham, 1989; *The Sand Horse* by Ann Turnbull, 1989; *Edmond Went Far Away* by Martin Bax, 1989; *Land of the Long White Cloud* by Kiri Te Kanawa, 1989; *Once Upon a Planet* by Christina Martinez, 1989; *The Shining Princess and Other Japanese Legends* edited by Eric Quayle, 1989; *Busy! Busy! Busy!* by Jonathan Shipton, 1991; *Over In the Meadow: A Pop-Up Counting Rhyme* by Stacie Strong, 1992; *The Echoing Green* by Mary Rayner, 1992; *The Arabian Nights* translated by Brian Alderson, 1992; *Funnybunch* by Kit Wright, 1993; *Arthur: High King of Britain,* 1994, *Robin of Sherwood,* 1996, *Farm Boy,* 1997, and *Joan of Arc of Domrémy,* 1998, all by Michael Morpurgo, 1998; *The Long Weekend* by Troon Harrison, 1994; *Wyvern Spring,* 1993, *Wyvern Summer* and *Wyvern Fall,* both 1994, all by Toby Forward; *Sarah and the Sandhorse* by Andrew Baynes, 1994; *Shakespeare Stories II* by Leon Garfield, 1994; *Peter's Place* by Sally Grindley, 1995; *The Little Prince* by Antoine de Saint-Exupéry, 1995; *The Songs My Paddle Sings* by James Riordan, 1996; *Beyond the Rainbow Warrior* edited by Michael Morpurgo, 1996; *The Little Ships* by Louise Borden, 1997; *The Knight and the Squire* by Terry Jones, 1997.

* * *

Michael Foreman is one of the outstanding creators of children's picture books working today, and is also a prolific and versatile illustrator of other writers' books. He combines a distinctive style of flowing watercolour with a genius for conveying atmosphere, and the visual richness of his work is always a feast for the eye.

As a writer, Foreman is in turn serious, whimsical, and poetic. He displayed almost from the start the ability to wrap up a political point or social theme in an engaging story with considerable appeal to children. *Horatio,* which featured a hippopotamus who is dissatisfied with squelching in mud and who longs for "fields of corn and marigolds," made a point both about the world and man's nature, while *Moose* took a more political theme: the gentle Moose, caught in the middle of a flaming row between Bear and Eagle, builds himself a shelter that the other animals come to share. Cartoon-like elements indicate Bear (in his yellow dictator's uniform) and Eagle are the superpowers. At the same time there are plays on words to relish ("Very amoosing ... I'll shout at you if you don't vamoose, Moose").

War and Peas (a play, of course, on the word "peace") contrasted, very graphically, overconsumption with poverty as the enormously fat king of a country groaning with food refuses to help his starving neighbor, King Lion. The effects of pollution were demonstrated in *Dinosaurs and All That Rubbish,* but the dinosaurs who come to clear the planet are jolly creatures full of fun. These early works have certainly stood the test of time, since several of them have been reissued 15 years and more after first publication.

All the King's Horses was one of the first fairy tales to be stood on its conventional head: the princess, far from the "milk-white, golden-haired, pink little number princesses are supposed to be," throws her prospective husbands at wrestling and gallops away. Princesses in picture books have not looked back since. *Panda's Puzzle* depicted one of the first "searches for identity" in picture books, and is rated as a modern classic. Panda travels the world to find out whether he is a white bear with black bits or a black bear with white bits, and, faced with conflicting advice, finally discovers it does not matter.

In the 1980s Foreman explored some more whimsical and poetic themes. *Cat and Canary* was a fantasy set against the glimmering skyline of New York as Cat is blown about at the end of a kite high above the streets—giving the opportunity for some dazzling perspectives. *Jack's Fantastic Voyage,* which took its inspiration from the Cornish background that Foreman knows very well, features some of his most masterly artwork: dramatic seascapes as Jack and his grandfather sail through the storm-tossed night. A sequel, *Jack's Big Race,* was published in 1998. *Grandfather's Pencil and the Room of Stories* was another imaginative foray investing the ordinary with poetic power.

Foreman has also handled domestic themes, and several child-centered picture books were inspired by his young sons. In *Ben's Baby* a small boy looks forward to the birth of a baby brother in a warm and realistic story, while *The Angel and the Wild Animal* features a small boy in his many moods, with a spare text ("Sometimes we have an Angel in our house. Most times at night, and mostly asleep..."). *Dad! I Can't Sleep* is an amusing bedtime story with a twist, as Little Panda summons up a whole menagerie to keep him company when he can't sleep. Little Panda also features in *Surprise! Surprise!* and *Look! Look!,* which together form a sort of trilogy; the last title makes a wry comment on computer games: Little Panda, enthralled by his Cops and Robbers game, is oblivious to the fact that a real robbery is taking place nearby, and does not even notice the cops in hot pursuit passing through his room.

Several of Foreman's books in the 1990s have had a nonfiction slant. *One World* was one of the first picture books with an ecological theme. Although a didactic note creeps in, the whole is suffused with the beauty of the natural world at risk from pollution. *The Boy Who Sailed with Columbus,* which came out for the 500-year anniversary of Christopher Columbus's discovery of the New World, tells the story from the point of view of the cabin boy.

Three books have been concerned with war. *War Boy* was an account of Foreman's own childhood in a Suffolk coastal village during the Second World War. Although barrage balloons and air raids are vividly represented, his child's eye-view of events is understated: "I woke up when the bomb came through the roof." And everyday life continued, with childhood games among the sandbags and tank traps.

If *War Boy* is evocative and informative, *War Game* is even more poignant, dedicated to Foreman's uncles who died in France during the First World War. It conveys superbly the discomforts and dangers for men in the trenches living "like bedraggled moles in a world of mud." It has its lighter moments when both sides venture across No Man's Land on Christmas Day to sing carols and play football, but it ends on a sombre note, with bloodstains on the snow. This book, which won the 1993 Smarties prize, is one of Foreman's most impressive achievements. The final part of the war trilogy, *After the War Was Over,* carries on the story from *War Boy* with the same immediacy and humorous detail.

Foreman's more recent titles include *The Little Reindeer,* an engaging Christmas story with great child appeal which duly won the 6-8 category of the Smarties prize in 1997, and *Angel and the Box of Time,* an imaginative story in which a small girl, on the road with her showman grandfather and his performing goat, dreams of the past . She sees the scenes that her greatgrandfather, and his father before him, would have taken part in, set against widely different backgrounds.

A significant title is *Seal Surfer,* set in Cornwall over several seasons as a boy and his grandfather come to watch the seals on the rocks. The boy gets to know one seal pup in particular, and eventually they surf together side by side. As always with Foreman, the lyrical illustrations are matched with an eloquent text. What is remarkable is that the boy is disabled, but it is necessary to look closely at the illustrations to see his crutches, as the fact is never mentioned in the text. The story was widely praised for this refreshing lack of patronising assumptions about disability.

—Jennifer Taylor

FOREST, Antonia

Nationality: British. **Born:** London. **Awards:** Commendation from British Library Association, 1961, for *Peter's Room.* **Address:** c/o Faber and Faber Ltd., 3 Queen Square, London WC1N 2AU, England.

PUBLICATIONS FOR CHILDREN

Fiction

Autumn Term, illustrated by Marjorie Owens. London, Faber, 1948.
The Marlows and the Traitor, illustrated by Doritie Kettlewell. London, Faber, 1953.
Falconer's Lure: The Story of a Summer Holiday, illustrated by Tasha Kallin. London, Faber, 1957.
End of Term. London, Faber, 1959.
Peter's Room. London, Faber, 1961.
The Thursday Kidnapping. London, Faber, 1963; New York, Coward McCann, 1965.
The Thuggery Affair. London, Faber, 1965.
The Ready-Made Family. London, Faber, 1967.
The Player's Boy. London, Faber, 1970.
The Players and the Rebels. London, Faber, 1971.
The Cricket Term. London, Faber, 1974.
The Attic Term. London, Faber, 1976.
Run Away Home. London, Faber, 1982.

* * *

Although four of Antonia Forest's books are primarily school stories, the rest of her series about the Marlow family is set mainly outside school in holiday periods. In all these stories the upper middle-class background is evident, particularly in the stories set at home, which have casual references to servants, hunting, parties, and private chapels, more akin to children's books of the 1930s than to the 1980s.

The most original and outstanding plot in the series is that of *Peter's Room,* a brilliant blend of reality and fantasy woven around the intense fascination of the Brontë kingdoms of Gondal and Angria for the young Marlows. The interest in these imaginary kingdoms is aroused when one of the sisters, Ginty, has to produce an essay on some aspect of the Brontës' life or work. The Marlows create their own kingdom of Angora and become utterly absorbed in it for an entire Christmas holiday. This highly successful book well deserved the commendation it received from the Library Association in 1961.

In 1982 *Run Away Home* was a welcome addition to the Marlow saga. Set in a Christmas holiday period, it introduces an original approach to the ever popular running-away theme with the gripping sailing incident which reaches a peak of suspense. This book will delight devotees of the Marlow family with its totally consistent evolution of the characters of the sisters Rowena, Ann, Nicola, and Lawrie. It also continues the tradition of eloquent dialogue for which Forest is noted.

However, Forest is likely to be remembered primarily for her school stories in which she follows accepted formulae, but gives the Marlows a rare form of immortality with school years spanning a period of nearly 30 years, and also introduces ingenious variations. The twins' hopes of academic triumph are doomed to failure. Running away is an ignominious experience for Nick who is immediately sent back to school by her elder brother, and has not even been missed in her absence. Starts of term are highlighted by the incident of the pulling of the communication cord in the train or a bolt across the fields to catch an escaped merlin. Dramatics perhaps occupy an undue proportion of certain plots, but this is acceptable to the wariest reader because of Forest's enthusiastic details.

It is not Forest's skilful handling of the school story plot that ensures her success, but her positive flair for characterisation, her presentation of violent clashes of personality, her understanding of the fluctuations of schoolgirl friendships, and her insight into sisterly relationships.

Antonia Forest's able handling of plot and character, combined with sound literary style, enable her to present the traditional school story in a new and lasting dimension, unlikely to have many if any successful imitators.

—Anne W. Ellis

FOULDS, E.V. See **VIPONT, Elfrida.**

FOX, Mem

Nationality: Australian. **Born:** Merrion Frances Partridge in Melbourne, 5 March 1946. **Education:** Rose Bruford Drama School, London, diploma, 1968; Flinders University of South Australia, B.A. 1978; South Australian College of Advanced Education, B. Ed. 1979, graduate diploma 1981. **Family:** Married Malcolm Fox; one daughter. **Career:** Teacher of English, Zimbabwe and Ruwanda, 1968-69; drama teacher, Cabra Dominican School, Adelaide, South Australia, 1970; English tutor, South Australian Institute of Technology, 1971-72; lecturer, 1973-86, senior lecturer, 1987-1994, associate professor, since 1994, Flinders University of South Australia. **Awards:** Literary Award for best children's book of 1984 from the Premier of New South Wales; Australian Children's Book Council Highly Commended Picture Book of the Year Award, 1984; Child Study Association of America children's books of the year, 1985; American Library Association Notable Book, 1985; *New York Times* Notable Book, 1986; Dromkeen Medal for Outstanding Contribution to Children's Literature in Australia, 1990; Advance Australia Award for Distinguished Services to Literature, 1991; Chancellor's Award, Flinders University, 1994; Alice Award, Fellowship of Australian Woman Writers, 1994; honorary doctorate, University of Wollongong, 1996. **Agent:** Caroline Lurie, 2A Armstrong St., Middle Park 3206, Australia. **Website:** www.va.com.au\memfox.

Publications for Children

Fiction

Possum Magic, illustrated by Julie Vivas. Adelaide, Omnibus, 1983; Nashville, Abingdon, 1987.
Wilfrid Gordon McDonald Partridge, illustrated by Julie Vivas. Adelaide, Omnibus, 1984; New York, Kane Miller, 1985.
A Cat Called Kite, illustrated by K. Hawley. Auckland, Ashton Scholastic, 1985.
Hattie and the Fox, illustrated by Patricia Mullins. Auckland, Ashton Scholastic, 1986; New York, Bradbury, 1987.
Sail Away, illustrated by Pamela Lofts. Auckland, Ashton Scholastic, 1986.
Arabella: The Smallest Girl in the World, illustrated by Vicky Kitanov. Auckland, Ashton Scholastic, 1986; New York, Scholastic, Inc., 1987.
Just Like That, illustrated by Kilmeny Niland. Sydney, Hodder & Stoughton, 1986.
Zoo Looking, illustrated by Rodney McRae. Melbourne, Martin Educational, 1987.
Koala Lou, illustrated by Pamela Lofts. Drakeford, 1987; New York, Harcourt Brace Jovanovich, 1989.
A Bedtime Story, illustrated by Sisca Verwoert. Melbourne, Martin Educational, 1987.
The Straight Line Wonder, illustrated by Meredith Thomas. Melbourne, Martin Educational, 1987.
Night Noises, illustrated by Terry Denton. Adelaide, Omnibus, 1988; New York, Harcourt Brace Jovanovich, 1989.
Guess What? illustrated by Vivienne Goodman. Adelaide, Omnibus, 1988; New York, Harcourt Brace Jovanovich, 1988.
Feathers and Fools, illustrated by Lorraine Ellis. Mount Waverly, Victoria, Ashwood House, 1988.
Sophie, illustrated by Craig Smith. Drakeford, 1988; New York, Harcourt, 1994.
With Love, at Christmas, illustrated by Gary Lippincott. Nashville, Abingdon, 1988.
Shoes from Grandpa, illustrated by Patricia Mullins. Auckland, Ashton Scholastic, 1989; New York, Orchard Books, 1990.
Time for Bed, illustrated by Jane Dyer. Auckland, Ashton Scholastic, and New York, Harcourt, 1993.
Tough Boris, illustrated by Kathryn Brown. New York, Harcourt, 1994.
Great Scott!, illustrated by Terry Denton. San Diego, Harcourt Brace Jovanovich, 1996.
Wombat Divine, illustrated by Kerry Argent. San Diego, Harcourt Brace Jovanovich, 1996.
Whoever You Are, illustrated by Leslie Staub. San Diego, Harcourt Brace Jovanovich, 1997.
The Straight Line Wonder, illustrated by Marc Rosenthal. Greenvale, New York, Mondo, 1997.
Boo to a Goose, illustrated by David Miller. New York, Dial, 1998.

Publications for Adults

Other

Mem's the Word (autobiography). Melbourne, Books, 1990; New York, Harcourt Brace Jovanovich, 1992.
How to Teach Drama to Infants Without Really Crying. Auckland, Ashton Scholastic, 1984; as *Teaching Drama to Young Children,* illustrated by Bob Graeme, New York, Heinemann, 1987.
"Dear Mem Fox, I've Read All Your Books Even the Pathetic Ones." New York, Harcourt Brace Jovanovich, 1992.
Articles of Faith. New York, Harcourt, 1993.
With L. Wilkinson, *English Essentials: The Wouldn't-Be-Without-It Handbook on Writing Well.* Melbourne, Macmillan, 1993.
Radical Reflections: Passionate Opinions on Teaching, Living, and Learning. New York, Harcourt, 1993.

Also contributor of essays to anthologies and periodicals, including *The New Advocate, Language Arts,* and *Reading Teacher.*

*

Media Adaptations: *Wilfrid Gordon McDonald Partridge* (filmstrip/audio cassette; narrated by the author), Weston Woods Studios, 1988; *Mem Fox Reads* (two audio tapes by Mem Fox narrating her own stories), Harcourt Brace Jovanovich, 1993.

Critical Studies: "Mem Fox: Magic Writer" by Jill Brislan, in *Orana* (Australia), Vol. 24, No. 2, May 1988, 95-102.

* * *

Mem Fox, one of Australia's most popular children's writers, has created the texts for a number of internationally popular picture books that feature Australian settings, rhyme, and rhythm, as well as close, caring relationships between children and adults. A professional storyteller and teacher of drama and language arts who has also written textbooks and essays for teachers and educators, Fox has a love of language and wordplay which is reflected in the simple, poetic tales she relates.

Fox's best-selling *Possum Magic,* typical of much of her work, is full of repetition and alliteration and highlights Australian culture. An elderly possum, Grandma Pos, one of Fox's many positive adults, searches all over Australia, from Adelaide to Hobart, to find the right food to undo the Bush Magic she has used to make young Hush invisible. As Fox herself has noted, the book is an archetypal quest story in which a child secretly hopes that an adult can make right something that has gone wrong. Part of the appeal of the book is Fox's use of various Australian dishes, such as "lamington" (a sponge cake) and "vegemite" (a yeast spread), which she endows with magical qualities.

Like *Possum Magic,* several of Fox's other picture books also focus on elderly characters who eventually learn how to communicate with children. In *Night Noises,* the protagonist, 99 year-old Lily Laceby, lives in an old cottage in the hills with her fat old dog, Butch Aggie. While Lily dozes, dreaming about the past, her family and friends gather for a surprise party. At the end of the book, she reveals to her great-great-grandchild, Emily, that inside, she too is only four-and-a half. That Lily and Emily have similar feelings, despite the differences in their ages, helps young readers empathize with those who are older.

An elderly woman, Mrs. Cavallaro, is also the protagonist of the somewhat controversial *With Love, at Christmas,* in which she gives away her family's Christmas presents to the poor, only to have them reappear when she dies after seeing the Christ Child in a trunk. In a similar vein, the title character of *Wilfrid Gordon McDonald Partridge* is a small boy who befriends his neighbors, the inhabitants of a home for the elderly—especially Miss Nancy Alison Delacourt, who has lost her memory. When Wilfrid Gordon shares various objects that are important to him, some of her memories return.

Koala Lou, one of Fox's most effective stories, focuses on a child and her mother. Koala Lou, a baby koala, is used to having her mother say that she loves her. As she grows older, however, her mother is increasingly busy and does not openly express her love every day. Koala Lou trains for the Bush Olympics to win back her mother's love, only to learn that she has never lost it, and that it is not conditional on her achievements.

Several of Fox's stories reflect a storyteller's interest in folk genres, especially cumulative tales and nursery rhymes. *Hattie and the Fox* is, in structure, reminiscent of "The Little Red Hen." Repeatedly interrupted by negative comments from a variety of barnyard animals, Hattie the black hen tries to warn them about an approaching fox. *Shoes from Grandpa* is a cumulative rhyme, much like "The House that Jack Built," in which young Jesse's many relatives each plan to give her an article of clothing to go with the shoes from her grandfather, only to learn that she'd really much prefer a pair of jeans. *Feathers and Fools* is a more developed tale which has been described as an anti-nuclear war fable in which peacocks and swans stockpile weapons in case they need to fight each other.

Both *Guess What?* and *Time for Bed* are simple, predictable stories especially appropriate for beginning readers or young children. *Guess What?* focuses on Daisy O'Grady who, in a series of questions and answers, is revealed to be a witch. Most of the questions posed are answered by "Guess!", followed by "Yes!", although at the end Fox breaks the pattern to reveal that Daisy is not a mean witch. *Time for Bed* is a collection of couplets in which a variety of animal creatures tell their offspring that it is "time for bed." In tone and feeling, it resembles Margaret Wise Brown's *Goodnight Moon* (1947), which also treats the ritual of going to sleep. All of Fox's picture books have a simplicity, musical quality, and emotional core that speak to young children and, it seems likely, will ensure their popularity for some time to come.

—Joel D. Chaston

FREEMAN, Barbara C(onstance)

Nationality: British. **Born:** Ealing, Middlesex, 29 November 1906. **Education:** Tiffin Girls' School, Kingston-upon-Thames, Surrey; Kingston School of Art. **Career:** Painter, Green and Abbott, wallpaperers, London, 1926-27; then freelance illustrator and writer. Individual show of art at the Heritage Centre, Kingston-upon-Thames Museum, 1989. **Address:** 62 Hook Road, Surbiton, Surrey KT6 5BH, England.

Publications for Children (illustrated by the author)

Fiction

Timi. London, Faber, 1961; New York, Grosset and Dunlap, 1970.
Two-Thumb Thomas. London, Faber, 1961.
A Book by Georgina. London, Faber, 1962; New York, Norton, 1968.
Broom-Adelaide. London, Faber, 1963; Boston, Little Brown, 1965.
The Name on the Glass. London, Faber, 1964; New York, Norton, 1966.
Lucinda. London, Faber, 1965; New York, Norton, 1967.
Tobias. London, Faber, 1967.
The Forgotten Theatre. London, Faber, 1967.
The Other Face. London, Macmillan, 1975; New York, Dutton, 1976.
A Haunting Air. London, Macmillan, 1976; New York, Dutton, 1977.
A Pocket of Silence. London, Macmillan, 1977; New York, Dutton, 1978.
The Summer Travellers. London, Macmillan, 1978.
Snow in the Maze. London, Macmillan, 1979.
Clemency in the Moonlight. London, Macmillan, 1981.

*

Manuscript Collection: de Grummond Collection, University of Southern Mississippi, Hattiesburg.

Illustrator: *Stories from Hans Andersen,* 1949; *Stories from Grimm,* 1949; *Jan and His Clogs,* 1951, *Jan Klaassen Cures the*

King, 1952, *Puppet Plays for Children,* 1953, and *Never Run from the Lion and Another Story,* 1958, all by Antonia Ridge; *The Magic Candles* by Mary Steward, 1954; *The Sleeping Beauty and Other Tales* by Charles Perrault, 1954; *Granny's Wonderful Chair* by Frances Browne, 1955; pictures for *The Children's Encyclopedia.*

Barbara C. Freeman comments:

I write, I suppose, chiefly because I enjoy writing and I like living in two worlds: the one I was born into and the other (which becomes entirely real) which I write about. I'm deeply interested in the way ordinary people lived in the past and the way in which the past thrusts into the present. I believe that most writers find that their characters develop lives of their own and sometimes take charge of both conversations and plots. This, for me, is pure delight, and I allow my people all the freedom that is possible.

At art school I was trained to observe details of every kind, and it is a habit that one never grows out of. Details, especially those of the past, fascinate me.

* * *

"Don't you understand? *I must* take charge of my own life. If I don't, I don't know what will happen to me." Rose, the heroine of *Snow in the Maze,* sums up the underlying theme of all of Barbara C. Freeman's work, whether fantasy, like the early novels *Timi* and *Two-Thumb Thomas,* or historical, like *The Name on the Glass* or *The Summer Travellers,* or ghost stories, like *Snow in the Maze* and *Clemency in the Moonlight.* The heroines (or hero, in *Two-Thumb Thomas*) tend to be rather lonely people for whom it is an effort to resist outside pressures and be decisive. It is cheerful to know that they can and do succeed. In the case of the ghost stories, success comes through contact with the past, where an older unhappiness to be righted gives the heroine an absorbing interest—and the necessary impetus to help herself.

Freeman's handling of these ghostly episodes is masterly. They are never frightening, but the sense of a place and of the people who inhabited that place are conveyed so strongly that the reader is taken quite naturally into the "other" part of the plot. Indeed, in one book, *Snow in the Maze,* Freeman has depicted a most interesting combination of place (Briarcourt House) and a ghost who isn't—the rather splendid, definitely flesh-and-body young caretaker turns out to be the original 18th-century owner, trapped in time. It is particularly satisfying to find that he can mend a bike. The most memorable character of all is undoubtedly Linette, the school cat, in *Two-Thumb Thomas.* Thomas himself is rather a timid boy (hardly surprising in one raised in the school stationery cupboard), but Linette, who looks after him, is a great personality, full of resource and warmth.

All the novels show the author's love of gardens, of art, and of many crafts, some now almost forgotten. Lacemaking, the cutting of silhouettes, and fanmaking, for example, contribute substantially to the plots of those books in which they appear, while the reader takes in, almost without realizing, some interesting details of how these things were done. Her love of such things is also evident in the author's pictures, which decorate every book.

Barbara C. Freeman is a gentle writer, with a particular appeal to girls. She makes no great demands on her readers, but does provide good entertainment. Anyone wanting easy, fluent, romantic stories would do well to consider her work.

—Felicity Trotman

FREEMAN, Bill

Nationality: Canadian. **Born:** William Bradford Freeman, London, Ontario, 21 October 1938. **Education:** Acadia University, Wolfville, Nova Scotia, B.A. in philosophy 1964; McMaster University, Hamilton, Ontario, M.A. 1970, Ph.D. in sociology 1979. **Family:** Married Marsha Hewitt (divorced); two sons and two daughters. **Career:** Probation officer, Hamilton, Ontario, 1964-69; community organizer, Hamilton Welfare Rights, 1970; Lecturer, McMaster University, 1971-73; teacher, Vanier College, Montreal, 1977-86; financial consultant, 3rd Street Funding, Toronto since 1988. **Awards:** Canada Council prize, 1976; Vicky Metcalf award, 1984. **Address:** 16 Third Street, Ward's Island, Toronto, Ontario M5J 2B2, Canada.

Publications for Children

Fiction

Shantymen of Cache Lake. Toronto, Lorimer, 1975.
The Last Voyage of the Scotian. Toronto, Lorimer, 1976.
Cedric and the North End Kids, photographs by Lutz Lille. Toronto, Lorimer, 1978.
First Spring on the Grand Banks. Toronto, Lorimer, 1978.
Trouble at Lachine Mill. Toronto, Lorimer, 1983.
Harbour Thieves. Toronto, Lorimer, 1984.
Danger on the Tracks. Toronto, Lorimer, 1987.

Play

Ghosts of the Madawaska (produced Ottawa, 1985).

Publications for Adults

Play

Glorydays (produced Hamilton, Ontario, 1988).

Other

1005: Political Life of a Local Union. Toronto, Lorimer, 1982.

Editor, with Marsha Hewitt, *Their Town: The Mafia, The Media, and the Party Machine.* Toronto, Lorimer, 1979.

*

Bill Freeman comments:

I am perhaps best known for my series of books that have come to be called "Adventures in Canadian History." These books are an attempt to portray the life of ordinary Canadians in the 1870s. Each book, in a different setting, is an adventure story that is engaging and fast moving. The Bains children, heroes of the stories, are not "superkids" but they have learned to struggle against odds for their survival.

* * *

Adventures in Canadian History, the series title of Bill Freeman's novels for children, reflects one of his purposes in writing for younger Canadian readers: a desire to introduce them to the excitement of their country's past. A more important, underlying purpose is revealed in his statement that "economic factors shaped ordinary people's lives." The difficulties faced by members of the working class and the pressures placed on them by the controllers of society are revealed in each story.

The central characters in the series are John and Meg Bains, young teenagers, and later Jamie, their little brother. In *Shantymen of Cache Lake,* set in the Ottawa Valley in the 1870s, the two older siblings seek work at a lumber camp to aid their impoverished and widowed mother. In addition to the dangers of logging and the harshness of the elements, they must confront a selfish and evil foreman and overcome the skepticism of their co-workers. In the later books they work on a schooner carrying immigrants to the New World, on a Newfoundland fishing boat, in a Quebec textile mill, and on the newly built railroad in southern Ontario. Each adventure tests their courage and their resolve to provide financial aid to their mother; and in each the children learn about the dignity of the common laborers and about the economic forces and personal selfishness threatening these people.

For the novels Freeman has done extensive historical research and incorporated his findings smoothly into the narratives. As Meg, John, and Jamie enter a new job they experience difficulties which give Freeman the opportunity to explain techniques and, equally important, the dangers that all the workers must face. Included are diagrams and rare historical photographs enabling readers to visualize clearly the different occupations.

While his contention that a rich few controlled the lives of the impoverished laborers is quite likely true, his presentation of this theme is awkward. Foremen become stereotypical villains, while owners are incredibly ignorant of the hardships endured by those who make their wealth possible. Although each new book introduces a new area of Canada, the plot structures and character types become predictably similar. Having clearly and vividly presented his thesis in the first book, Freeman does little more than expound it in the rest of the series. Moreover, the characters of the children seem to develop very little: John is somewhat timid, Meg combines assertiveness and motherly concern, and Jamie reveals his talent for getting into scrapes.

In spite of these limitations, Freeman's historical novels have earned a significant place in Canadian children's literature, exploring as they do aspects of Canadian history frequently ignored by writers: the difficult lives of ordinary people struggling to make their lives worthwhile while laboring in occupations generally little known by younger readers of today.

—Jon C. Stott

FREEMAN, Don

Nationality: American. **Born:** San Diego, California, 11 August 1908. **Education:** Principia High School, St. Louis; San Diego School of Fine Arts; Art Students' League, New York. **Military Service:** United States Army Infantry, Rainbow Division, for two years. **Family:** Married Lydia Cooley in 1931; one son. **Career:** Trumpeter in jazz band; drama artist, *New York Times,* 1934-52. Individual show: Margo Feiden Galleries, New York, 1975. **Died:** 1 February 1978.

PUBLICATIONS FOR CHILDREN (ILLUSTRATED BY THE AUTHOR)

Fiction

Chuggy and the Blue Caboose, with Lydia Freeman. New York, Viking Press, 1951.
Pet of the Met, with Lydia Freeman. New York, Viking Press, 1953.
Beady Bear. New York, Viking Press, 1954; London, Penguin, 1977.
Mop Top. New York, Viking Press, 1955.
Fly High, Fly Low. New York, Viking Press, 1957.
The Night the Lights Went Out. New York, Viking Press, 1958.
Norman the Doorman. New York, Viking Press, 1959; Leicester, Brockhampton Press, 1972.
Space Witch. New York, Viking Press, 1959.
Cyrano the Crow. New York, Viking Press, 1960.
Come Again, Pelican. New York, Viking Press, 1961.
Botts, The Naughty Otter. San Carlos, California, Golden Gate Books, 1963.
Ski Pup. New York, Viking Press, 1963.
Dandelion. New York, Viking Press, 1964; Kingswood, Surrey, World's Work, 1965.
The Turtle and the Dove. New York, Viking Press, 1964; Kingswood, Surrey, World's Work, 1965.
A Rainbow of My Own. New York, Viking Press, 1966; Kingswood, Surrey, World's Work, 1967.
The Guard Mouse. New York, Viking Press, 1967; Kingswood, Surrey, World's Work, 1970.
Corduroy. New York, Viking Press, 1968; London, Penguin, 1976.
Quiet! There's a Canary in the Library. San Carlos, California, Golden Gate Books, 1969.
Tilly Witch. New York, Viking Press, 1969.
Forever Laughter. San Carlos, California, Golden Gate Books, 1970.
Hattie the Backstage Bat. New York, Viking Press, 1970.
Penguins of All People! New York, Viking Press, 1971.
Inspector Peckit. New York, Viking Press, 1972; Kingswood, Surrey, World's Work, 1973.
Flash the Dash. Chicago, Children's Press, 1973.
The Seal and the Slick. New York, Viking Press, 1974; as *The Sea Lion and the Slick,* Kingswood, Surrey, World's Work, 1976.
The Paper Party. New York, Viking Press, 1974; Kingswood, Surrey, World's Work, 1977.
Will's Quill. New York, Viking Press, 1975.
Bearymore. New York, Viking Press, 1976.
The Chalk Box Story. Philadelphia, Lippincott, 1976.
A Pocket for Corduroy. New York, Viking Press, and London, Penguin, 1978.
Corduroy's Toys [*Party Day*], illustrated by Lisa McCue. New York, Viking Kestrel, 2 vols., 1985.

Plays

Screenplays (short films): *Lollipop Opera,* 1970; *Storymaker,* 1972.

Television Play: *The Baker* (*Sesame Street* series), 1971.

Other

Add-a-Line Alphabet. San Carlos, California, Golden Gate Books, 1968.

PUBLICATIONS FOR ADULTS

Other

It Shouldn't Happen. New York, Harcourt Brace, 1945.
Come One, Come All!, (autobiography). New York, Rinehart, 1949.

*

Manuscript Collections: May Massee Collection, Emporia State University, Kansas.

Bibliography: *The Prints of Don Freeman: A Catalogue Raisonné* by Edith McCulloch, Charlottesville, University Press of Virginia, 1987.

Illustrator: *My Name Is Aram,* 1940, and *The Human Comedy,* 1943, both by William Saroyan; *Diedrich Knickerbocker's History of New York* by Washington Irving, 1940; *The White Deer* by James Thurber, 1945; *Once Around the Sun* by Brooks Atkinson, 1951; *Sauce for the Gander* by Scott Corbett, 1951; *Mike's House* by Julia Sauer, 1954; *Third Monkey,* 1956, and *This for That,* 1965, both by Ann Nolan Clark; *The Uninvited Donkey* by Anne H. White, 1957; *Ghost Town Treasure* by Clyde Robert Bulla, 1957; *Angelenos, Then and Now,* 1966; *Best Friends,* 1967, and *Best of Luck,* 1969, both by Myra Brown; *Voltaire's Micromegas* by Elizabeth Hall, 1967; *California Indian Days* by Helen Bauer, revised edition 1968; *Seven in a Bed* by Ruth Sonneborn, 1968; *Joey's Cat* by Robert Burch, 1969; *Burnish Me Bright,* 1970, and *Far in the Day,* 1972, both by Julia W. Cunningham; *Edward and the Night Horses* by Jacklyn Matthews, 1971; *The Wild Cats of Rome* by Elizabeth Cooper, 1972; *The Christmas Strangers,* 1976, and *The April Foolers,* 1978, both by Marjorie Thayer; *Monster Night at Grandma's House* by Richard Peck, 1977; *Dinosaur, My Darling* by Edith Thacher Hurd, 1978; *The Day Is Waiting* by Linda Z. Knab, 1980; *Uncle Sam Presents* by Tony Buttitta and Barry B. Witham, 1982.

* * *

Don Freeman's picture books sing out with a playfulness that strikes the child's imagination. He sees his themes and subjects with an artist's eye from which comes a flow of pictures followed by a stream of words.

Pet of the Met, one of his first books (written in collaboration with his wife, Lydia), set a high standard for his work. He blends his intimate knowledge of the Opera House and Mozart's *The Magic Flute* with mouse and cat antics. Mr. Petrini, the page turner at the opera house, and a *Magic Flute* enthusiast, deftly confronts a mouse's traditional enemy, Mefisto, the cat. There is a jauntiness of writing that gives the book a lasting spirit.

Norman the Doorman is a master at collecting mousetraps set for him in the museum where he is the doorman and guide to his relatives, including Maestro Petrini and family. He hears of a sculpture competition, enters his sculpture *Trapeese,* and wins first prize. This is a caper to be enjoyed for what it is, with an implicit commentary on the meaning of art exhibits to be detected by the more sophisticated reader. *The Guard Mouse* continues the fanciful escapades of the Petrini family. Their cousin, Clyde, a Grenadier guard at Buckingham Palace, welcomes the Petrinis. The children, Do, Re, Mi, tired after their long trip from New York, are left behind as Clyde takes the parents on a tour of London, a light-hearted romp that indicates more than a chance acquaintance with the city. In each of these books an element of surprise adds marked interest to the story. Freeman is an effective storyteller, interweaving information that can arouse the undiscovered interests of the young child.

Freeman's imagination reaches out into unlikely areas. Peary B. Penguin, in *Penguins of All People!,* is urgently requested to attend a special meeting of the United Nations, to share with the members the secret of how penguins live together so peacefully. Might the U.N. members learn from him? In *Will's Quill* Willoughby, a country goose, is rescued by Young Will, and, to show his gratefulness for Will's kindness, tells the story with overtones of archaic language about a country goose who helped William Shakespeare in the writing of his plays.

Freeman also created books that capture spontaneously, without ulterior motive, the imaginative world to which the young child responds. *Mop Top* is the story of a little boy who will not have his hair cut until he is mistaken for a mop. In *Dandelion* a lion receives an invitation to a tea-and-taffy party from Jennifer Giraffe, and sets about with meticulous preparation to look his best. The results are preposterous, sustained by Freeman's clear vision and obvious zest for the development of this situation. Children can identify with the implicit, gentle wisdom. In *Corduroy* a shopworn bear yearns for a home in which his sense of belonging can be satisfied. Lisa sees Corduroy, the bear, and empties her piggy bank to buy him. He must belong to her. Freeman develops the not-uncommon theme of a stuffed animal and a child with understanding and compassion.

Freeman's visual sense gave strength to his picture books even when his text did not reach the same height. At his best, he offers rich visual experiences with sparkle and harmony in his writing.

—Mae Durham Roger

FRENCH, Fiona (Mary)

Nationality: British. **Born:** Bath, Somerset, 27 June 1944. **Education:** Devon; at Croydon College of Art, Surrey, 1961-66, National Diploma in Design for painting and lithography 1966. **Career:** Children's art therapy teacher, Long Grove Psychiatric Hospital, Epsom, Surrey, 1967-69; design teacher, Wimbledon School of Art, 1970-71, and Leicester and Brighton polytechnics, 1973-74. Assistant to the painter Bridget Riley, 1967-72. Since 1974 freelance illustrator. **Award:** Library Association Kate Greenaway Medal, 1987. **Agent:** Pat White, Rogers Coleridge and White, 20 Powis Mews, London W11 1JN. **Address:** 48 Hungate Street, Aylsham, Norfolk NR11 6AA, England.

Publications for Children (illustrated by the author)

Fiction

Jack of Hearts. London, Oxford University Press, and New York, Harcourt Brace, 1970.
Huni. London, Oxford University Press, 1971.
The Blue Bird. London, Oxford University Press, and New York, Walck, 1972.
King Tree. London, Oxford University Press, and New York, Walck, 1973.
City of Gold. London, Oxford University Press, and New York, Walck, 1974.
Aio the Rainmaker. London, Oxford University Press, 1975; New York, Oxford University Press, 1978.
Matteo. London, Oxford University Press, 1976; New York, Oxford University Press, 1978.
Hunt the Thimble. London and New York, Oxford University Press, 1978.
The Princess and the Musician. London, Evans, 1981.
Future Story. Oxford, Oxford University Press, 1983; New York, Bedrick, 1984.
Maid of the Wood. Oxford, Oxford University Press, 1985.
Snow White in New York. Oxford, Oxford University Press, 1986; New York, Oxford University Press, 1987.
The Song of the Nightingale. London, Blackie, 1986.
The Magic Vase. Oxford, Oxford University Press, 1991.
Anancy and Mr. Dry-Bone. London, Frances Lincoln, and New York, Little Brown, 1991.
King of Another Country. New York, Oxford University Press, 1992.
Little Inchkin. New York, Dial, 1994.
Nikos the Fisherman. New York, Oxford University Press, 1996.
Lord of the Animals. London, Frances Lincoln, and Brookfield, Connecticut, Millbrook Press, 1997.

Other

John Barleycorn (retelling). London, Abelard Schuman, 1982.
Cinderella (retelling). Oxford, Oxford University Press, 1987; New York, Oxford University Press, 1988.
Rise, Shine! London, Methuen, and as *Rise & Shine,* New York, Little Brown, 1989.

Publications for Adults

Short Stories

Un-Fairy Tales. Privately printed, 1966.

*

Illustrator: *Book of Magical Birds* by Margaret Mayo, 1977; *Fabulous Beasts* by Richard Blythe, 1977; *The Star Child* by Oscar Wilde, abridged by Jennifer Westwood, 1979; *The Necklace of Princess Fiorimonde* by Mary de Morgan, 1980; *Clowns and Clowning* by Carol Crowther, 1980; *Hidden Animals* by Josephine Karavasil, 1982; *Fat Cat,* 1984, and *Going to Squintum's,* 1985, both by Jennifer Westwood; *Pepi and the Secret Names* by Jill Paton Walsh, 1994; *The Dragon Takes a Wife* by Walter Dean Myers, 1994.

* * *

By steeping herself in the culture or period content of her picture books, Fiona French produces not only authentic detail but an almost tangible atmosphere, a feat perceiveable in her gloriously rich illustrative style and in the entirely suitable economy and relevance of the texts.

All her books are full of the powerful elemental themes found in myth and fairy tale. Envy, greed, and power appear in the first book, *Jack of Hearts,* based on the playing card Kings of Hearts, Diamonds, Clubs, and Spades, represented as happy, rich, warlike, and evil respectively and the 18th birthday feast of Jack of Hearts. Research shows in the description of the feast, including "wild boar and peacock and paradise sauce and herring pie and hedgehog, gingerbread, sea-holly candy and rich red wine." Elemental emotions appear also in *King Tree,* in a Louis XIV Garden of Versailles setting, where Orange Tree organises nominations for king, and the oak, laurel, pomegranate, olive, and vine vie with each other in election promises; but the ladies choose Orange Tree as King. Pride and the fight between good and evil appear in *City of Gold,* a medieval, Biblical style tale of John and Thomas, brothers journeying on the roads easy and hard, thwarting the Devil in a series of encounters. *The Blue Bird* reveals the evil Enchantress when the Chinese girl Blue Jade seeks a cure for her pet bird's loss of voice, a revelation spectacularly accomplished in transition from Wedgwood blue illustration to a burst of colour when the Enchantress is demolished and her victims freed. *Matteo,* too, follows the practical jokers through apparent success to just retribution.

Survival and proving oneself to the gods are the themes of *Huni* and *Aio the Rainmaker.* Huni, possible successor to Pharaoh, meets some of the gods from Egyptian mythology—Ra, the cat, the serpent, Osiris—survives ordeals to prove health and strength, and is deemed fit to be the new Pharaoh. In *Aio* African tribal art and legend are interwoven to form an African "experience" of a parched land, of Aio's powers to call on the Ancestors for rain to relieve the thirsty animals, graphically described in text and pictures.

These simple but strong emotions lend themselves to a textual treatment in which French retains the essence of the concept in short yet strongly phrased sentences with the narrative flow and the underlying moral message of the oral tradition. The striking use of colour is a feature of her powerful illustrative style: playing cards based on a real design, medieval stained glass windows in *City of Gold,* Egyptian art in *Huni,* Chinese style in *The Blue Bird,* French mannered style in *King Tree,* African art in *Aio,* and Florentine style in *Matteo.* Sombre shades to stunning colours match the events in *The Song of the Nightingale* which, with St. Francis, brings peace and new life to war-torn Assisi. *Maid of the Wood,* a wooden doll into whom life is breathed with unexpected results, carries on the bold colour and simple text story.

Two departures from traditional themes are first, the extraordinary *Future Story* in which the influence of space photography and high tech form the basis of life and relationships in future times and places—a strong and beautiful space age theme. The second example also has strength of line and colour. *Snow White in New York,* which won a Greenaway award, is a retelling with a 1920s setting and jazz musicians instead of the seven dwarfs. The illustrations are in perfect harmony with the 1920s-style humorous text.

After transposing that fairy tale into the 20th century French reverted to traditional treatment with *Cinderella,* giving prominence to the characters rather than the scenery, with sumptuous detailed costume and brief text set on multicoloured wash backgrounds.

French's picture books are not, in theme and style, for the young child, but for those over eight, for young people, and for adults who see the masterly relationships between the verbal and visual concept of each book.

—Margaret R. Marshall

FRIEL, Maeve

Nationality: Irish. **Born:** Derry, Northern Ireland, 10 December 1950. **Education:** Thornhill College, Derry, 1960-68; University College Dublin, 1968-1972, B.A. in Sociology and Social Research. **Family:** Married Paul Kennedy in 1970; two children. **Career:** Social research assistant, University College Dublin, 1972-73; teacher, British School, Genoa, Italy, 1973-75; assistant lecturer, Londonderry College of Technology, Northern Ireland, 1975-76; administrative assistant, Jordanian Embassy, London 1976-78, and Britannia Summer Schools, Genoa, Italy, 1978-79; writer. **Awards:** Hennessy Literary Award for Emerging Writer, 1990; Bisto Book of the Year short list, 1992-93, 1994-95; Reading Association of Ireland short list, 1995, 1997; Bisto Merit Award, 1996-97. **Address:** 10 Maretimo Villas, Blackrock, County Dublin, Ireland.

Publications for Children

The Deerstone. Dublin, Poolbeg, 1992.
Distant Voices. Dublin, Poolbeg, 1994.
The Lantern Moon. Dublin, Poolbeg, 1996.

Publications for Young Adults

Charlie's Story. Dublin, Poolbeg, 1993; Atlanta, Peachtree, 1997.

Other

Here Lies: A Guide to Irish Graves. Dublin, Poolbeg, 1997.

*

Critical Studies: Unpublished interview with Maeve Friel by Pat Donlon, 1998.

Maeve Friel comments:

The principal reason why I write is that I was brought up in a family of book-readers and library-goers and inherited an addiction to the printed word, although I did not submit anything for publication until I was in my late thirties when I started writing short stories for adults.

Three of my children's novels have an historical setting. I have always had a strong interest in social history and the social forces that shape the lives of ordinary people. Children of course do not figure much in history books but I relish the challenge of recreating an historical period by researching sources as diverse as medieval manuscripts, census returns, newspapers, letters, advertisements, parliamentary reports, photographs, even gravestones. Childhood was rarely a very happy experience—children died young and not just from plagues, famines and wars but because they were often abused, exploited, enslaved, or ignored, but contemporary children have no problem in identifying with children from the past because the essential experience of childhood has not changed. Using an historical setting also allows one to touch upon issues in the lives of contemporary children. The inner emotional life of the child is as complicated as any adult's so one can employ as wide-ranging an emotional palette as when one is writing for adults. Anger, fear, jealousy, loneliness are as much a part of the child's life as are happiness, wonder, excitement and love.

Charlie's Story, the only one of my novels to date that has a contemporary setting, was born not with a location in mind at all but because I wanted to engage on a deeper level with strong emotion, with the pain of growing up, and with the blindness and deafness of many adults, parents and teachers, to what is going on in their children's lives. It is quite a harrowing read at times. It is sometimes described by people as about bullying, but I did not set out to write that sort of "issue-led" book. I write principally because I like to tell stories.

* * *

In *Charlie's Story* Maeve Friel gives us an intense and unforgettable story of one girl's loneliness and sense of isolation. Abandoned by her mother as a baby, Charlie is the victim of bullying at her school. The story, told in the first person narrative, unfolds with sickening inevitability as we watch helplessly and with horror her loss of self-esteem and her inexorable move towards self-immolation. Her recovery and determination to shed her victim status is a little too sudden, too successful to ring true. Nevertheless, such is Charlie's impact that the reader entrapped by the deep emotions of the story would demand nothing less than her salvation and redemption.

Historical fiction is Friel's true metier and amongst the growing numbers of Irish writers excelling in this genre she holds a special place because of her acute sense of time and place. In two of her novels, Friel has used the time-slip narrative device with great deftness and style. In *The Deerstone* the setting is the ruined monastic city of Glendalough in county Wicklow, the present-day haunt of tourists and school outings. The story is inspired by an ancient legend about two newborn children fed by a deer and centers on a lonely modern child who escapes from his school friends to explore Glendalough on his own. Encountering the deerstone he unlocks its magic powers and finds himself back in 12th century. There he meets Luke, the son of King Dermot MacMurrough, now fostered out to the monks of the abbey. Both are lonely, separated from their parents, and each is indistinguishable from the other, twins separated by time. It is a well-paced, exciting story which uses to great effect the unfamiliarity of each with the trappings and contraptions of the other's life.

"Only you will know where to find me. Ellie opened her eyes. A tall boy-man was standing at her bedroom window, his slim face and golden hair caught in a pall of ghostly green moonlight." From these compelling first lines we are thrust deep into the mystery that haunts Ellie's dreams in *Distant Voices.* Powerful and gripping, it is a story of obsession. The Viking Harald haunts Ellie's dreams, drawing her back into his world, his search for his own sod of death. The violence of the Viking raids is set against the every day violence of Ellie's home town

Derry. "I like to give my books a strong sense of place," Friel told Pat Donlon in an interview, "and my third book, *Distant Voices,* is set in Derry, the town where I grew up. It came about through reading a reference in the Annals of Ulster to a short-lived settlement of Vikings on Lough Foyle in the 9th century." The period of the Viking invasions of Ireland was a very violent time, but Ellie, the modern protagonist of the novel, has also grown up in a violent society of random killings and towns reduced to rubble, so she can empathize with the Viking Harald. She is called upon to literally unearth his story and the past by discovering his uncorrupted bog body.

A strong sense of place also informs *The Lantern Moon,* which is set in Ludlow, England, where Friel was living at the time of writing. The idea for the book came from Friel's discovery that the economy of this handsome historical town was built upon the vicious exploitation of young children in the glove-making business. "While researching conditions in the town in the early nineteenth century," Friel told Donlon, "I read contemporary accounts of children as young as nine being transported to Australia and of an exiled prince under house arrest in the town, and I was shown an early prototype of a collapsible silk top hat. I had a book!" *The Lantern Moon* has resonances of Dickens and Kingsley, peopled as it is with the poor and the exploited of nineteenth-century England. William and Annie Spears, brother and sister, endure the fate of their class. Overworked, misunderstood, and hounded for crimes they never committed, they are eventually deported to Australia, all the time hoping against hope to be reunited with their convict father. The children are comforted on their nightmare voyage by the discovery of letters from their father, whose one solace in exile was to suppose that his wife and family might just be looking at the same moon, a moon "like a huge white lantern." When the family is finally reunited—on the last page of the book—Friel wisely leaves us to conjecture the unwritten story that happens after the final sentence: "And as her brother flew into the man's open arms, Annie knew she was finally surfacing from a nightmare that had gone on far too long. She hurried towards her father, with warm rain-drops coursing down her face. The moon hung overhead like a lantern behind a veil of rain."

—Pat Donlon

FRITZ, Jean

Pseudonyms: Ann Scott. **Nationality:** American. **Born:** Hankow, China, 16 November 1915; lived in China until 1928. **Education:** Wheaton College, Norton, Massachusetts, 1933-37, A.B. 1937; Columbia University Teachers College, New York, 1938-39. **Family:** Married Michael G. Fritz in 1941; one son and one daughter. **Career:** Author of historical biographies and novels for young people. Associate editor, Wheaton *News,* 1933-37; research assistant, Silver Burdett, publishers, New York, 1937-41; researcher, Boy Scouts of America, New York, 1941; reviewer, San Francisco *Chronicle,* and Tacoma *Ledger-News-Tribune,* Washington, and free-lance writer, Macmillan and Prang publishers, 1940s-early 1950s; children's librarian, Dobbs Ferry Library, New York, 1955-57; founder and teacher, Jean Fritz Writers' Workshops, Katonah, New York, 1962-70; teacher, Board of Cooperative Educational Service, Westchester County, New York, 1971-73; faculty member, Appalachian State University, Boone, North Carolina, summers 1981-83. Book reviewer, *San Francisco Chronicle,* 1941-43, and *New York Times,* since 1970, and *Washington Post*; lecturer. **Awards:** Named *New York Times* outstanding book of the year, 1973, for *And Then What Happened, Paul Revere?,* 1974, for *Why Don't You Get a Horse, Sam Adams?,* 1975, for *Where Was Patrick Henry on the 29th of May?,* 1976, for *What's the Big Idea, Ben Franklin?,* 1981, for *Traitor: The Case of Benedict Arnold,* and 1982, for *Homesick: My Own Story*; named *Boston Globe-Horn Book* honor book, 1974, for *And Then What Happened, Paul Revere?,* 1976, for *Will You Sign Here, John Hancock?,* and 1980, for *Stonewall*; named outstanding Pennsylvania author, Pennsylvania School Library Association, 1978; Honor award for Nonfiction, Children's Book Guild, 1979, for the "body of her creative writing"; American Book award nomination, 1980, for *Where Do You Think You're Going, Christopher Columbus?,* and 1981, for *Traitor: The Case of Benedict Arnold*; Child Study award and Christopher award, both 1982, Newbery Honor Book award, American Book award, and named *Boston Globe-Horn Book* honor book, all 1983, all for *Homesick: My Own Story*; *Boston Globe-Horn Book* Nonfiction award, 1984, and Knickerbocker award for Juvenile Literature, 1992, both for *The Double Life of Pocahontas*; Regina award, 1985; Laura Ingalls Wilder award, 1986; Orbis Pictus award, National Council of English Teachers, 1989, and Boston Globe/Horn Book award, 1990, both for *The Great Little Madison*; LL.D.: Washington and Jefferson College, 1982; Wheaton College, 1987; **Address:** 50 Bellewood Ave., Dobbs Ferry, New York 10522, U.S.A.

Publications for Children

Fiction

Bunny Hopwell's First Spring, illustrated by Rachel Dixon. New York, Wonder Books, 1954.

Help Mr. Willy Nilly, illustrated by Jean Tamburine. New York, Treasure Books, 1954.

Fish Head, illustrated by Marc Simont. New York, Coward McCann, 1954; London, Faber, 1956.

121 Pudding Street, illustrated by Sofia. New York, Coward McCann, 1955.

Hurrah for Jonathan!, illustrated by Violet La Mont. Racine, Wisconsin, Whitman, 1955.

The Late Spring, illustrated by Erik Blegvad. New York, Coward McCann, 1957.

The Cabin Faced West, illustrated by Feodor Rojankovsky. New York, Coward McCann, 1958.

Champion Dog, Prince Tom, with Tom Clute, illustrated by Ernest Hart. New York, Coward McCann, 1958.

How to Read a Rabbit, illustrated by Leonard Shortall. New York, Coward McCann, 1959.

Brady, illustrated by Lynd Ward. New York, Coward McCann, 1960; London, Gollancz, 1966.

December Is for Christmas (as Ann Scott), illustrated by Alcy Kendrick. New York, Wonder Books, 1961.

Tap, Tap, Lion—One, Two, Three, illustrated by Leonard Shortall. New York, Coward McCann, 1962.

I, Adam, illustrated by Peter Burchard. New York, Coward McCann, 1963; London, Gollancz, 1965.

Magic to Burn, illustrated by Beth and Joe Krush. New York, Coward McCann, 1964.
Early Thunder, illustrated by Lynd Ward. New York, Coward McCann, 1967; London, Gollancz, 1969.
George Washington's Breakfast, illustrated by Paul Galdone. New York, Coward McCann, 1969.
The Secret Diary of Jeb and Abigail: Growing Up in America 1776-1783, illustrated by Kenneth Bald and Neil Boyle. Pleasantville, New York, Reader's Digest, 1976.

Other

Growing Up, illustrated by Elizabeth Webbe. Chicago, Rand McNally, 1956.
The Animals of Dr. Schweitzer, illustrated by Douglas Howland. New York, Coward McCann, 1958; Edinburgh, Oliver and Boyd, 1962.
San Francisco, illustrated by Emil Weiss. Chicago, Rand McNally, 1962.
Surprise Party (reader), illustrated by George Wiggins. New York, Initial Teaching Alphabet Publications, 1965.
The Train (reader), illustrated by Jean Simpson. New York, Grosset and Dunlap, 1965.
And Then What Happened, Paul Revere?, illustrated by Margot Tomes. New York, Coward McCann, 1973.
Why Don't You Get a Horse, Sam Adams?, illustrated by Trina Schart Hyman. New York, Coward McCann, 1974.
Where Was Patrick Henry on the 29th of May?, illustrated by Margot Tomes. New York, Coward McCann, 1975.
Who's That Stepping on Plymouth Rock?, illustrated by J.B. Handelsman. New York, Coward McCann, 1975.
Will You Sign Here, John Hancock?, illustrated by Trina Schart Hyman. New York, Coward McCann, 1976.
What's the Big Idea, Ben Franklin?, illustrated by Margot Tomes. New York, Coward McCann, 1976.
Can't You Make Them Behave, King George?, illustrated by Tomie de Paola. New York, Coward McCann, 1977.
Brendan the Navigator, illustrated by Enrico Arno. New York, Coward McCann, 1979.
Stonewall, illustrated by Stephen Gammell. New York, Putnam, 1979.
Back to Early Cape Cod. Washington, D.C., National Park Service, 1979.
Where Do You Think You're Going, Christopher Columbus?, illustrated by Margot Tomes. New York, Putnam, 1980.
The Man Who Loved Books (on St. Columba), illustrated by Trina Schart Hyman. New York, Putnam, 1981.
Traitor: The Case of Benedict Arnold, illustrated by John André. New York, Putnam, 1981.
The Good Giants and the Bad Pukwudgies (folktale), illustrated by Tomie de Paola. New York, Putnam, 1982.
Homesick: My Own Story, illustrated by Margot Tomes. New York, Putnam, 1982.
The Double Life of Pocahontas, illustrated by Ed Young. New York, Putnam, 1983.
China Homecoming, photographs by Michael Fritz. New York, Putnam, 1985.
Make Way for Sam Houston, illustrated by Elise Primavera. New York, Putnam, 1986.
Shh! We're Writing the Constitution, illustrated by Tomie de Paola. New York, Putnam, 1987.
China's Long March: 6000 Miles of Danger, illustrated by Yang Zhr Cheng. New York, Putnam, 1988.
The Great Little Madison. New York, Putnam, 1989.
Bully for You, Teddy Roosevelt! New York, Putnam, 1991.
George Washington's Mother, illustrated by DyAnne DiSalvo-Ryan. New York, Putnam, 1992.
The World in 1492, with Katherine Paterson, Frederick and Patricia McKissack, Margaret Mahy, and Jamake Highwater, illustrated by Stefano Vitale. New York, Holt, 1992.
The Great Adventure of Christopher Columbus, illustrated by Tomie dePaola. New York, Putnam, 1992.
Around the World in a Hundred Years: Henry the Navigator—Magellan, illustrated by Anthony B. Venti. New York, Putnam, 1993.
Just a Few Words, Mr. Lincoln: The Story of the Gettysburg Address, illustrated by Charles Robinson. New York, Putnam, 1993.
Surprising Myself, photographs by Andrea F. Pfleger. Katonah, New York, Richard C. Owen, 1993.
Harriet Beecher Stowe and the Beecher Preachers. New York, Putnam, 1994.
You Want Women to Vote, Lizzie Stanton? illustrated by DyAnne DiSalvo-Ryan, New York, Putnam, 1995.

PUBLICATIONS FOR ADULTS

Other

Cast for a Revolution: Some American Friends and Enemies 1728-1814. Boston, Houghton Mifflin, 1972.

*

Manuscript Collections: Kerlan Collection, University of Minnesota, Minneapolis; Children's Literature Collection at the University of Oregon Library, Eugene; University of Southern Mississippi.

Critical Studies: *Jean Fritz: A Critical Biography* by Elizabeth Hostetler, unpublished dissertation, University of Toledo, 1981; entry in *Dictionary of Literary Biography,* Vol. 52: *American Writers for Children since 1960: Fiction,* Detroit, Gale, 1986; essay in *Something About the Author Autobiography Series,* Vol. 2, Detroit, Gale, 1986; entry in *Children's Literature Review,* Detroit, Gale, Vol. 2, 1976, Vol. 14, 1988.

Jean Fritz comments:
Although I experiment in various kinds of writing, my curiosity, I suppose, drives me most often to the past where there are more people, more stories, more truths, more secrets than I can ever hope to exhaust. I like having more than one century at my disposal. And I seem to need to put my roots down deeper and deeper into my own country.

* * *

Early in the 1970s, Jean Fritz began to write the short, beguiling biographies which promise to make her as famous literarily as her subjects are historically. For readers aged 7 through 11 years, the books bear such jaunty titles as, *And Then What Happened, Paul Revere?, Will You Sign Here, John Hancock?,* and *Where Do*

You Think You're Going, Christopher Columbus? Her zesty account of Plymouth Rock, for instance, proves that the author can infuse even a stone with personality.

The little histories have been applauded by critics and read eagerly—not just by children but by adults who are amused by Fritz's lighthearted approach to weighty subjects. But the author is in no way guilty of debunking heroes. On the contrary, she is one of the few writers who convince us, by stressing their humanity, that the American Founding Fathers were even more remarkable than we had realized.

These books are the logical culmination of Fritz's background and interests. During the 1950s, she began to invent characters to people stories rooted in actuality. (Even her fantasies, like the adventurous *Magic to Burn,* center around British/American relations.) *The Cabin Faced West* is an affectionate *roman à clef* about her own great-great-grandmother, Ann Hamilton. When Ann was a child, her father moved his family from their staid home in Gettysburg, across the Allegheny Mountains into trackless western Pennsylvania. The little girl's initial loneliness and growing love for her new home in the wilds are the backbone of an appealing novel, and readers can't help feeling Ann's joyous excitement when George Washington stops on his travels to dine with her family in the rough cabin on Hamilton Hill in 1784.

It isn't surprising that a gifted woman author can capture and convey the days of a girl child seeking cheer in bleak, strange surroundings. But Fritz does equally well by her boy heroes. During the 1960s, she created several historical novels featuring young men, teenagers whose involvement in chaotic events make history vital and interesting to modern readers. In *Early Thunder,* Daniel West battles split loyalties during the tense days of 1765, when his town of Salem endures conflicts between Whigs and Tories that presage the coming Revolutionary War. In *I, Adam,* the suspenseful adventures of Adam Crane convince him that coming of age in 1850 doesn't equal attaining manhood, that part of his destiny is to work for the shaping of the young nation. Brady Minton of *Brady* is a kid who learns the hard way not to tell everything he knows. His father is helping slaves to escape, just before the outbreak of the Civil War, a secret Mr. Minton can't trust his son to keep until Brady comes through a crisis and proves he has grown reliable.

With *Harriet Beecher Stowe and the Beecher Preachers* and *You Want Women to Vote, Lizzie Stanton?,* Fritz was back on familiar ground, portraying pivotal figures in American history. The former earned her favorable reviews because it presented the nineteenth-century writer and activist in a more accessible manner than many of the young people's biographies of Stowe already on the market. Likewise the portrayal of voting-rights crusader Stanton is a powerful one, showing the private struggles that marked her career from its beginning to her heroic final speech in 1892: "In the end, she said, everybody, men and women, were alone. They were responsible for themselves; no one could represent them."

The hallmarks of all Fritz's books are their literary quality, authenticity, empathy with her characters, and respect for her young readers—the latter quality clearly visible in writing that bears no hint of condescension. And her natural, unforced sense of humor doesn't hurt either.

—Jean F. Mercier

FUJIKAWA, Gyo

Nationality: American. **Born:** Berkeley, California, 3 November 1908. **Education:** Attended Chouinard Art Institute. **Career:** Free-lance commercial illustrator and author/illustrator of books for children. Instructor in color and design, Chouinard Art Institute, 1933-39; promotion department artist, Walt Disney Studios, Anaheim, California, 1939-41; designer of movie advertisements, Fox Film Co., New York City, 1942; art director, William Douglas McAdams (pharmaceutical advertising agency), New York City, 1943-51. Work includes U.S. postage stamps commemorating Lady Bird Johnson's beautification program, Eskimo Pies advertisements, Beechnut baby foods advertisements, the centennial of golden anniversary of the International Peace Garden, illustrations in *Family Circle, Ladies' Home Journal,* and *McCalls,* and cover illustrations for *Saturday Evening Post.* **Address:** 325 East 57th St., Apt. 5B, New York, New York 10022, U.S.A.

Publications for Children

Picture Books (illustrated by the author)

Babies. New York, Grosset, 1963.
Baby Animals. New York, Grosset, 1963.
A to Z Picture Book. New York, Grosset, 1974.
Let's Eat. New York, Grosset, 1975.
Let's Play. New York, Grosset, 1975.
Puppies, Pussycats, and Other Friends. New York, Grosset, 1975.
Sleepy Time. New York, Grosset, 1975.
Gyo Fujikawa's Oh, What a Busy Day! New York, Grosset, 1976.
Babies of the Wild. New York, Grosset, 1977.
Betty Bear's Birthday. New York, Grosset, 1977.
Can You Count? New York, Grosset, 1977.
Our Best Friends. New York, Grosset, 1977.
Millie's Secret. New York, Grosset, 1978.
Let's Grow A Garden. New York, Grosset, 1978.
My Favorite Thing. New York, Grosset, 1978.
Surprise! Surprise! New York, Grosset, 1978.
Come Follow Me...to the Secret World of Elves and Fairies and Gnomes and Trolls. New York, Grosset, 1979.
Jenny Learns A Lesson. New York, Grosset, 1980.
Welcome Is a Wonderful Word. New York, Grosset, 1980.
Come Out and Play. New York, Grosset, 1981.
Dreamland. New York, Grosset, 1981.
Fairyland. New York, Grosset, 1981.
Faraway Friends. New York, Grosset, 1981.
The Flyaway Kite. New York, Grosset, 1981.
Good Morning! New York, Grosset, 1981.
Here I Am. New York, Grosset, 1981.
Jenny and Jupie. New York, Grosset, 1981.
The Magic Show. New York, Grosset, 1981.
Make-Believe. New York, Grosset, 1981.
My Animal Friends. New York, Grosset, 1981.
One, Two, Three, A Counting Book. New York, Grosset, 1981.
Shags Has a Dream. New York, Grosset, 1981.
Mother Goose. New York, Grosset, 1981.
A Tiny Word Book. New York, Grosset, 1981.
Year In, Year Out. New York, Grosset, 1981.
Jenny and Jupie to the Rescue. New York, Grosset, 1982.

Fraidy Cat. New York, Grosset, 1982.
Me Too! New York, Grosset, 1982.
Sam's All-Wrong Day. New York, Grosset, 1982.
Shags Finds a Kitten. New York, Grosset, 1983.
That's Not Fair. New York, Grosset, 1983.
Are You My Friend Today? New York, Random House, 1988.
Sunny Books: Four Favorite Tales. J. B. Communications, 1989.
Ten Little Babies. New York, Random House, 1989.
See What I Can Be! New York, Putnam, 1990.
Good Night, Sleep Tight, Shh. New York, Random House, 1990.

*

Illustrator: Robert Louis Stevenson, *A Child's Garden of Verses,* Grosset, 1957; Clement C. Moore, *The Night Before Christmas,* Grosset, 1961; *Mother Goose,* Grosset, 1968; *A Child's Book of Poems,* Grosset, 1969; Eve Morel, editor, *Fairy Tales and Fables,* Grosset, 1970; *Poems for Children,* Platt, 1980; *Baby Mother Goose,* Random House, 1989; Bobbi Katz, *Poems for Small Friends,* Random House, 1989; *Gyo Fujikawa's A Child's Book of Poems,* Grosset, 1989.

* * *

One of the grandnames of American children's book illustration, Gyo Fujikawa has produced some four dozen works, many of them modestly-priced, jacketless board books for the leading U.S. mass-market publishers. Though her output may appear modest when compared to other popular illustrators' lists of publications, few of her books ever go out of print, and her audience—because of the size of mass-market printings and reprintings—is incalculably large. Fujikawa's illustrations are characterized by pleasingly soft colors and clear, unambiguous images—small children and animals, familiar household objects, etc. Her work is imbued as well with a genuine sweetness and a timeless appeal that seems to both comfort children and speak to adults' nostalgic recollections of the fleeting joys of childhood.

Fujikawa came to children's book illustration relatively late in a successful career—in the mid-1950s—and turned then to greeting cards as well. Because she began her working life as a commercial artist (becoming an art director for a succession of advertising agencies on both the East and West coasts), and counts her early apprenticeship at the Walt Disney Studios in Hollywood as "a most memorable and profound experience," we know that behind her simple and seemingly artless children's book drawings of cuddly animals and appealing small fry of all races and colors lies a hard-won sophistication about how best to reach—and satisfy—a wide audience.

Typically, her pictures have a minimum of background detail and a superfluity of near-irresistible children and animals exuding good cheer at center stage on her uncluttered pages. In *Sam's All-Wrong Day,* a bear cub devours all of the small hero's laboriously-picked berries, but we don't for a moment doubt a happy outcome.

Among the artist's most popular works are *Babies* and *Baby Animals,* and, later, more elaborate versions of the same themes: *Let's Play, Let's Eat, Sleepy Time* and *Babes of the Wild.* These books are straightforward catalogs of endearing examples of the title subject matter, accompanied by minimal texts (i.e. "Babies are very little...soft, warm and cuddly").

Fujikawa has also illustrated her own selections of nursery rhymes from *Mother Goose* and done a popular *A to Z Picture Book* and *One, Two, Three: A Counting Book,* work that can be fairly described as the meat-and-potatoes staples of children's books. Clement Moore's *The Night Before Christmas,* Robert Louis Stevenson's *A Child's Garden of Verses,* and various fairy tales and fables can also be found in sunny Fujikawa illustrated editions. The artist's work always reflects a careful reading of traditional texts. When mention is made of particular objects or events, she unfailingly includes them, knowing that children are likely to seek them out.

If the darker side of childhood, or life itself, never clouds her happy pictures, she has rarely overstepped the border into the saccharine or sententious. Her 80-page compendium of childhood activities, *Oh, What A Busy Day!* was chosen for exhibition in the American Institute of Graphic Arts' annual book show, and the artist has richly merited the affectionate regard of a wide audience of children and former children.

—Selma G. Lanes

FULLER, Roy (Broadbent)

Nationality: British. **Born:** Failsworth, Lancashire, 11 February 1912. **Education:** Blackpool High School, Lancashire; qualified as a solicitor, 1934. **Military Service:** Royal Navy, 1941-46; Lieutenant, Royal Naval Volunteer Reserve. **Family:** Married Kathleen Smith in 1936; one son, the writer John Fuller. **Career:** Staff member of various legal firms, 1934-38; assistant solicitor, 1938-58, solicitor, 1958-69, and director, 1969-88, Woolwich Equitable Building Society, London. Chairman of the Legal Advisory Panel, 1958-69, and Vice-President, 1969-87, Building Societies Association. Professor of Poetry, Oxford University, 1968-73. Chairman, Poetry Book Society, London, 1960-68; a Governor, BBC, 1972-79; member, Arts Council of Great Britain, and Chairman of the Literature Panel, 1976-77; member, Library Advisory Council, 1977-79. **Awards:** Fellow, Royal Society of Literature, 1958; Arts Council Poetry award, 1959; Duff Cooper Memorial prize, for poetry, 1968; Queen's Gold Medal for Poetry, 1970; C.B.E. (Commander, Order of the British Empire), 1970; Cholmondeley award, for poetry, 1980. M.A.: Oxford University; D.Litt.: University of Kent, Canterbury, 1986. **Died:** 27 September 1991.

Publications for Children

Fiction

Savage Gold, illustrated by Robert Medley. London, Lehmann, 1946.
With My Little Eye, illustrated by Alan Lindsay. London, Lehmann, 1948; New York, Macmillan, 1957.
Catspaw, illustrated by David Gollins. London, Alan Ross, 1966.
The Other Planet and Three Other Fables, illustrated by Paul Peter Piech. Richmond, Surrey, Keepsake Press, 1979.

Poetry

Seen Grandpa Lately?, illustrated by Joan Hickson. London, Deutsch, 1972.

Poor Roy, illustrated by Nicolas Bentley. London, Deutsch, 1977.
More about Tompkins and Other Light Verse. Edinburgh, Tragara Press, 1981.
Upright, Downfall, with Barbara Giles and Adrian Rumble. Oxford and New York, Oxford University Press, 1983.
The World Through the Window: Collected Poems for Children, illustrated by Nick Duffy. London, Blackie, 1989.

Publications for Adults

Novels

The Second Curtain. London, Verschoyle, 1953; New York, Macmillan, 1956.
Fantasy and Fugue. London, Verschoyle, 1954; New York, Macmillan, 1956; as *Murder in Mind,* Chicago, Academy, 1986.
Image of a Society. London, Deutsch, 1956; New York, Macmillan, 1957.
The Ruined Boys. London, Deutsch, 1959; as *That Distant Afternoon,* New York, Macmillan, 1959.
The Father's Comedy. London, Deutsch, 1961.
The Perfect Fool. London, Deutsch, 1963.
My Child, My Sister. London, Deutsch, 1965.
The Carnal Island. London, Deutsch, 1970.
Omnibus (includes *With My Little Eye, The Second Curtain,* and *Fantasy and Fugue*). Manchester, Carcanet, 1988.

Poetry

Poems. London, Fortune Press, 1940.
The Middle of a War. London, Hogarth Press, 1942.
A Lost Season. London, Hogarth Press, 1944.
Epitaphs and Occasions. London, Lehmann, 1949.
Counterparts. London, Vershoyle, 1954.
Brutus's Orchard. London, Deutsch, 1957; New York, Macmillan, 1958.
Collected Poems 1936-1961. London, Deutsch, 1962.
Buff. London, Deutsch, 1965.
New Poems. London, Deutsch, 1968.
Pergamon Poets 1, with R.S. Thomas, edited by Evan Owen. Oxford, Pergamon Press, 1968.
Off Course. London, Turret, 1969.
Penguin Modern Poets 18, with A. Alvarez and Anthony Thwaite. London, Penguin, 1970.
To an Unknown Reader. London, Poem-of-the-Month Club, 1970.
Song Cycle from a Record Sleeve. Oxford, Sycamore Press, 1972.
Tiny Tears. London, Deutsch, 1973.
An Old War. Edinburgh, Tragara Press, 1974.
Waiting for the Barbarians: A Poem. Richmond, Surrey, Keepsake Press, 1974.
From the Joke Shop. London, Deutsch, 1975.
The Joke Shop Annexe. Edinburgh, Tragara Press, 1975.
An Ill-Governed Coast. Sunderland, Ceolfrith Press, 1976.
Re-treads. Edinburgh, Tragara Press, 1979.
The Reign of Sparrows. London, London Magazine Editions, 1980.
The Individual and His Times: A Selection of the Poetry of Roy Fuller, edited by V.J. Lee. London, Athlone Press, 1982.
House and Shop. Edinburgh, Tragara Press, 1982.
As from the Thirties. Edinburgh, Tragara Press, 1983.
Mianserin Sonnets. Edinburgh, Tragara Press, 1984.
New and Collected Poems 1934-1984. London, Secker and Warburg, 1985.
Subsequent to Summer. Edinburgh, Salamander Press, 1985.
Outside the Canon. Edinburgh, Tragara Press, 1986.
Consolations. London, Secker and Warburg, 1987.
Available for Dreams. London, Collins, 1989.

Other

Owls and Artificers: Oxford Lectures on Poetry. London, Deutsch, and New York, Library Press, 1971.
Professors and Gods: Last Oxford Lectures on Poetry. London, Deutsch, 1973; New York, St. Martin's Press, 1974.
Souvenirs (memoirs). London, London Magazine Editions, 1980.
Vamp Till Ready: Further Memoirs. London, London Magazine Editions, 1982.
Home and Dry: Memoirs 3. London, London Magazine Editions, 1984.
Twelfth Night: A Personal View. Edinburgh, Tragara Press, 1985.
The Strange and the Good:
Home and Dry. London, Collins, 1989.
Souvenirs. London, Collins, 1989.
Vamp Till Ready. London, Collins, 1989.
Stares. London, Sinclair-Stevenson, 1990.
Spanner and Pen: Post-War Memoirs. London, Sinclair-Stevenson, 1991.

Editor, *Byron for Today.* London, Porcupine Press, 1948.
Editor, with Clifford Dyment and Montagu Slater, *New Poems 1952.* London, Joseph, 1952.
Editor, *The Building Societies Acts 1874-1960: Great Britain and Northern Ireland,* 5th edition. London, Franey, 1961.
Editor, *Supplement of New Poetry.* London, Poetry Book Society, 1964.
Editor, *Fellow Mortals: An Anthology of Animal Verse.* Plymouth, Macdonald and Evans, 1981.
Editor, with John Lehmann, *The Penguin New Writing 1940-1950: An Anthology.* London, Penguin, 1985.

*

Manuscript Collections: Brotherton Collection, Leeds University; State University of New York, Buffalo; British Library, London.

Bibliography: *Roy E. Fuller: A Bibliography* by Steven E. Smith, Brookfield, Vermont, Ashgate, 1996.

Critical Studies: *Roy Fuller* by Allan E. Austin, Boston, Twayne, 1979; *Dictionary of Literary Biography,* Vol. 15, *British Novelists, 1930-1959,* Detroit, Gale, 1983; *Roy Fuller: A Tribute,* edited by A.T. Tolley, Ottawa, Carleton University Press, 1993; *Roy Fuller, Writer and Society* by Neil Powell, Manchester, Carcanet, 1995.

Roy Fuller comments:
Though writing for children has always given me a certain sense of freedom, I have never thought of my children's books as "written down" to an audience. Indeed, possibly I have erred the other way; *With My Little Eye* was published in the United States as an adult crime novel! The separation in time between the two groups of children's books is to be accounted for by the fact that I was

stimulated to write them first by my son's childhood, then my grandchildren's. I spoke about (*inter alia*) my own writings for children and their relation to my other work in a Sidney Robbins Memorial Fund lecture in 1975 (printed in *Children's Literature in Education,* Spring 1976) called "The Influence of Children on Books."

* * *

Savage Gold, written for Roy Fuller's son, is the story of two lads who find themselves caught up in a clash of interests between rival mining corporations in East Africa. It is well told, its setting is an attractive one, the action comes at a fast and exciting pace, but in the end Fuller's literariness leaves doubts as to whether his talents are really suitable for the writing of junior fiction. These misgivings are reinforced by *With My Little Eye,* a boy's detective novel which examines the effects of a court-room murder on the mind of an exceptionally intellectual and literate adolescent, Frederick French, only son of a County Court judge, and which follows his peripatetic efforts to hunt down the killer.

French bears an undoubted resemblance to Michael Innes's erudite sleuth John Appleby—he finds his first clue in Sir Walter Scott's *The Black Dwarf*—and in general *With My Little Eye* contains the same bizarre mixture of intellectual cerebration and outlandish adventures that characterize the early Innes detective novels. But in all seriousness we can only conclude that Fuller sadly misdirected his inventiveness; even in 1948 the market for this type of story, aimed at that almost indefinable range of reader between 12 and 17, could not have been very large, and although the book attracted much praise from the critics, it is difficult to believe it held much interest for that age group. Take this passage, for example, which comes from a discussion between father and son:

> Well, on the highest level I think that the hunt for a murderer—fictional or in real life—satisfied a moral longing. It is all part of a revolution of our time. We—my generation—have no general and dogmatic views about right and wrong. And yet we want good to be rewarded and evil punished. Murder is a happening which usually is quite unarguably evil even from our disillusioned viewpoint. And so in that little limited sphere we have a disproportionate interest. On a lower level, of course, the pursuit of a murderer has the interest of a puzzle. But if you go on to ask me why men are fascinated by puzzles, I am afraid I cannot answer you.

Few teenage readers, either then or now, will surely continue for very long to read even a detective novel if it stops the action to moralize in this fashion, especially when the son, whose speech it is, and who also tells the story in the first person, is demonstrably in today's terms an unashamed, unrepentent elitist in his language and attitude.

Catspaw belongs to the verges of science fiction: Victoria, a little girl, wanders into a country inhabited solely by dogs who somewhat improbably are living in constant fear of Pussia the land of the cats. A clever parable about the cold war, the whole ghastly twilight world of espionage, intelligence, and security is mirrored there in fantasy, but again the message is wasted on the wrong audience.

—Alan Edwin Day

FYLEMAN, Rose

Nationality: British. **Born:** Rose Amy Feilmann in Basford, Nottinghamshire, 6 March 1877. **Education:** University College, Nottingham; Royal College of Music, London, diploma; studied singing in Germany and Paris. **Career:** Singer: first public performance, Queen's Hall, London, 1903. Teacher and lecturer; regular contributor to *Punch,* London; founding editor, *Merry-Go-Round* children's magazine, Oxford 1923-24. **Died:** 1 August 1957.

Publications for Children

Fiction

The Rainbow Cat and Other Stories, illustrated by Thelma Cudlipp Grosvenor. London, Methuen, 1922; New York, Doran, 1923.
Forty Good-Night Tales, illustrated by Thelma Cudlipp Grosvenor. London, Methuen, 1923; New York, Doran, 1924.
The Adventure Club, illustrated by A.H. Watson. London, Methuen, 1925; New York, Doran, 1926.
Letty: A Study of a Child, illustrated by Lisl Hummel. London, Methuen, 1926; New York, Doran, 1927.
Forty Good-Morning Tales. London, Methuen, 1926; New York, Doran, 1929.
Twenty Tea-Time Tales. London, Methuen, 1929; as *Tea Time Tales,* New York, Doubleday, 1930.
The Dolls' House, illustrated by Margaret Tempest. London, Methuen, 1930; New York, Doubleday, 1931.
The Katy Kruse Play Book, illustrated by Katy Kruse. London, Harrap, and Philadelphia, McKay, 1930.
The Strange Adventures of Captain Marwhopple, illustrated by Gertrude Lindsay. London, Methuen, 1931; New York, Doubleday, 1932.
The Easter Hare and Other Stories, illustrated by Decie Merwin. London, Methuen, 1932.
Jeremy Quince, Lord Mayor of London, illustrated by Cecil Leslie. London, Cape, 1933.
The Princess Dances, illustrated by Cecil Leslie. London, Dent, 1933.
Timothy's Conjuror. London, Methuen, 1942.
The Timothy Boy Trust, illustrated by Marjorie Wratten. London, Methuen, 1944.
Hob and Bob: A Tale of Two Goblins, illustrated by Charles Stewart. London, Hollis and Carter, 1944.
Adventures with Benghazi, illustrated by Peggy Fortnum. London, Eyre and Spottiswoode, 1946.
The Smith Family 4-6 (*At the Seaside, In the Country, In Town*). Leeds, E.J. Arnold, 3 vols., 1947.
Nursery Stories. London, Evans, 1949.
Lucy the Lamb. London, Eyre and Spottiswoode, 1951.
Neddy the Donkey. London, Eyre and Spottiswoode, 1951.
The Sparrow and the Goat. London, Eyre and Spottiswoode, 1951.
The Starling and the Fox. London, Eyre and Spottiswoode, 1951.
White Flower, illustrated by M.E. Stewart. Leeds, E.J. Arnold, 1953.

Plays

Eight Little Plays for Children (includes *Darby and Joan, The Fairy Riddle, Noughts and Crosses, The Weather Clerk, The Fairy and the Doll, Cabbages and Kings, In Arcady, Father Christmas*). London, Methuen, 1924; New York, Doran, 1925.

Seven Little Plays for Children (includes *The Princess and the Pirate; The Butcher, The Baker, The Candlestickmaker; The Mermaid; Peter Coffin; The Arm-Chair; Mother Goose's Party; The Coming of Father Christmas*). London, Methuen, 1928.

Happy Families: A Comic Opera, music by Thomas F. Dunhill (produced Guildford, Surrey, 1933). London, Methuen, 1933.

Nine New Plays for Children (includes *The Whisker; The Moon; Cinderella "At Home"; The Sampler; Three Naughty Imps; Surprise, The Imp; The Test; Sleeping Beauty; Father Christmas Comes to Supper*), illustrated by Eleanor L. Halsey. London and New York, Nelson, 1934.

Six Longer Plays for Children (includes *Snow-White, Porridge, Pork-Pie Night, The Bear, The Gus-Plug, The Angry Brownies*), illustrated by Eleanor L. Halsey. London, Nelson, 1936.

The Magic Pencil and Other Plays from My Tales (includes *The Carpet of Truth, Captain Marwhopple, The Rhyming Prince, The Chestnut Man, The Three Princesses, Troodle, A Legend of St. Nicholas*). London, Methuen, 1938.

The Spanish Cloak. London, Methuen, 1939.

Red-Riding-Hood, music by Will Grant. London, Oxford University Press, 1949.

Poetry

The Sunny Book, illustrated by Millicent Sowerby. London, Oxford University Press, 1918.

Fairies and Chimneys. London, Methuen, 1918; New York, Doran, 1920.

The Fairy Green. London, Methuen, 1919; New York, Doran, 1923.

The Fairy Flute. London, Methuen, 1921; New York, Doran, 1923.

A Small Cruse, illustrated by Katy Kruse. London, Methuen, 1923.

The Rose Fyleman Fairy Book. London, Methuen, and New York, Doran, 1923.

Fairies and Friends. London, Methuen, 1925; New York, Doran, 1926.

The Rose Fyleman Calendar, illustrated by Lisl Hummell. London, Methuen, 1927.

Joy Street Poems, with others. Oxford, Blackwell, 1927.

A Princess Comes to Our Town, illustrated by Gertrude Lindsay. London, Methuen, 1927; New York, Doubleday, 1928.

Old-Fashioned Girls and Other Poems, illustrated by Ethel Everett. London, Methuen, 1928.

A Garland of Rose's: Collected Poems of Rose Fyleman, illustrated by René Bull. London, Methuen, 1928.

Gay Go Up, illustrated by Decie Merwin. London, Methuen, 1929; New York, Doubleday, 1930.

Fifty-One New Nursery Rhymes, illustrated by Dorothy Burroughes. London, Methuen, 1931; New York, Doubleday, 1932.

The Blue Rhyme Book, music by Thomas F. Dunhill, illustrated by M. Bantock. London, Boosey-Methuen, 1933.

Runabout Rhymes, illustrated by Margaret Tempest. London, Methuen, 1941.

Number Rhymes. Leeds, E.J. Arnold, 1946.

Rhyme Book for Adam. London, Methuen, 1949.

Other

A Little Christmas Book, illustrated by Lisl Hummel. London, Methuen, 1926; New York, Doran, 1927.

The Katy Kruse Dolly Book, illustrated by Katy Kruse. London, Harrap, and New York, Doran, 1927; *The Second Katy Kruse Dolly Book,* Harrap, 1930.

Hey! Ding-a-Ding. London, University of London Press, 1931.

The Rose Fyleman Birthday Book, illustrated by Muriel Dawson and Margaret Tarrant. London, Medici Society, 1932.

Bears, illustrated by Stuart Tresilian. London and New York, Nelson, 1935.

Monkeys. London and New York, Nelson, 1936.

Billy Monkey: A True Tale of a Capuchin, with E.M.D. Wilson, illustrated by Cecil Leslie. London, Nelson, 1936; New York, Nelson, 1937.

A Book of Saints: Joan of Arc to St. Nicholas, illustrated by Gertrude Mittelman. London, Methuen, 1939.

Folk-Tales from Many Lands. London, Methuen, 1939.

Daphne and Dick (*An Uncle from Canada, Round and About, Adventures*), illustrated by Jeannetta Vise. London, Macdonald, 3 vols., 1952.

Editor, *Round the Mulberry Bush, Being a Book of Stories and Verse for Children.* London, Partridge, and New York, Dodd Mead, 1928.

Editor, *Sugar and Spice: A Collection of Nursery Rhymes, New and Old,* illustrated by Janet Laura Scott. Racine, Wisconsin, Whitman, 1935.

Editor, *Here We Come A'Piping* (verse), illustrated by Irene Mountfort. Oxford, Blackwell, 4 vols., 1936-37; New York, Stokes, 1 vol., 1937.

Editor, *A'Piping Again* (verse), illustrated by Irene Mountfort. Oxford, Blackwell, 1936; New York, Stokes, 1938.

Editor, *Bells Ringing: An Anthology of Verse for Young Children,* illustrated by Irene Mountfort. Oxford, Blackwell, 1938; New York, Stokes, 1939.

Editor, *Pipe and Drum: An Anthology of Verse for Young Children,* illustrated by Irene Mountfort. Oxford, Blackwell, 1939; New York, Stokes, 1940.

Editor, *Let's Play.* London, Grout, 1943.

Editor, *Punch and Judy,* illustrated by Paul Henning. London, Methuen, 1944.

Editor, *Over the Tree Tops: Nursery Rhymes from Many Lands.* Oxford, Blackwell, 1949.

Translator, *Bibi,* by Karin Michaelis, illustrated by Hedvig Collin. London, Allen and Unwin, 1933.

Translator, *Bibi Goes Travelling,* by Karin Michaelis, illustrated by Hedvig Collin. London, Allen and Unwin, 1934.

Translator, *Widdy-Widdy-Wurkey: Nursery Rhymes from Many Lands,* illustrated by Valerie Carrick. Oxford, Blackwell, 1934; as *Picture Rhymes from Foreign Lands,* New York, Stokes, 1935; as *Nursery Rhymes from Many Lands,* New York, Dover, 1971.

Translator, *Green Island,* by Karin Michaelis, illustrated by Hedvig Collin. London, Allen and Unwin, 1936.

Translator, *Père Castor's Wild Animal Books* (*Bourru, The Brown Bear; Frou, The Hare; Mischief, The Squirrel; Plouf, The Wild Duck; Scaf, The Seal; Quipic, The Hedgehog; Martin, The Kingfisher; Cuckoo*), by Lida, illustrated by Rojan. London, Allen and Unwin, 8 vols., 1937-42.

Translator, *Fireflies,* by Jan Karafiat, illustrated by Emil Weiss. London, Allen and Unwin, 1942.

Translator, *Tuck, The Story of a Snow Hare,* by Alfred Flueckiger, illustrated by Grace Huxtable. London, Lane, 1949.

Translator, *Simone and the Lilywhites,* by Marie-Louise Ventteclaye. London, Museum Press, 1949.
Translator, *The Adventures of Tommy, The Cat Who Went to Sea,* by Lillian Miozzi, illustrated by Charlotte Hough. London, Lane, 1950.
Translator, *Peter and His Friend Toby,* by Lily Martini, illustrated by Wolfgang Felten. London, Lane, 1955.

Publications for Adults

Play

After All. London, Methuen, 1939.

Other

Translator, *Songs.* London, Curwen, 1927.

* * *

Rose Fyleman is one of the people responsible for the modern tiny fairy, as distinct from the Elizabethan kind like Puck, who were full-sized, often grotesque, and capable of metamorphosis. Her first poem, "There are fairies at the bottom of my garden," established for all time the tiny flower-fairies, dainty, gossamer-winged, and glamorous, wearing crowns and gaily-coloured dresses. Yet they live in surroundings familiar to her young readers, as in the poem called "The Fairy House," where a little girl discovers a tiny house with

> Teeny weeny carpets
> On shiny polished floors
> Teeny weeny handles
> On little painted doors

and the rest of its furnishings to match. Fairies are at the same time wonderful and understandable.

As a teacher she knew what appealed to little children. Some of the earlier work she produced was adapted from French and German folk tales and poems, and other work, though original, has a continental flavour, such as the tale called "The Broom," where the poor crossing-sweeper gets a witch's broom by mistake and becomes rich by hiring it out for journeys, until a scientist rents it to go to the moon and meets its rightful owner.

A skilled musician, she turned many of her poems into songs and indeed composed a children's opera. Though the present taste for magic in fiction tends to be darker and more sinister, there is still a place for Fyleman to give small children their first taste of the supernatural world.

—Ann G. Hay

FYSON, J(enny) G(race)

Nationality: British. **Born:** Jenny Grace Harrison, Bromley, Kent, 3 October 1904. **Education:** St. Swithens School, Winchester, 1918-21. **Family:** Married Christopher Fyson in 1940 (died 1945); one son. **Career:** Painter, 1921-37, and weaver. **Address:** c/o Oxford University Press, Walton Street, Oxford OX2 6DP, England.

Publications for Children

Fiction

The Three Brothers of Ur, illustrated by Victor Ambrus. London, Oxford University Press, 1964; New York, Coward McCann, 1967.
The Journey of the Eldest Son, illustrated by Victor Ambrus. London, Oxford University Press, 1965; New York, Coward McCann, 1967.
Friend Fire and the Dark Wings, illustrated by Annabel Large. Oxford, Oxford University Press, 1983.

Play

Radio Play: *Saul and David,* 1952.

*

J.G. Fyson comments:

In my first two published books I have tried to fill in the background of the time of Abraham from archaeological discoveries. The pitfall that one meets in trying to write religious books for children is the snare of becoming a religious propagandist: of manufacturing facts and twisting behaviour to fit a theory. I have tried all the time to let the facts speak for themselves and to make my characters complete human beings, then found they inevitably led me to conclusions unthought of.

In *The Journey of the Eldest Son* it became clear that there was no way of freeing man from the load of guilt that his imagination has cooked up except by the intervention of the New Testament. As when a man recovers from a neurosis he sees God and is cured. The "dark wings" of the third book are primeval fears which still affect our judgment.

* * *

Which is the more difficult historical novel to write, one of a period which is fully documented, or one where the documentation is so thin as to be virtually invisible? J.G. Fyson chose the latter and made it seem an easy matter to recreate a 4000-year-old scene. The setting of her two linked novels is Ur of the Chaldees. Here is a sophisticated society, a city-state which has achieved a highly developed form of government, fine crafts, and a system of trade. Outside the city walls lies the wilderness where savages threaten the trade routes. The wealth of Teresh the Stern and the welfare of his family depend on the courage of those who will dare the dangers and trade in distant parts.

The Three Brothers of Ur is largely a family story. Haran the youngest son is a harum-scarum, "that king of all the jackdaws of Ur," as Mushinti the Beautiful puts it neatly. His flair for mischief is the motive-force of much of the story. The malice of Maychor, the middle son, also plays a part. Shamashazir is above mischief and malice. As the elder son he is head of the house when Teresh is away; moreover, he needs to have his father's agreement to travel on the next trade journey. But father will give no permission without a favourable sign from the Teraphim, the household god. Haran manages to break the Teraphim, but Shamashazir receives messages from someone greater than a clay image, a voice coming out of the White Mountains.

In *The Journey of the Eldest Son* Shamashazir takes the trail over the mountains and is able to test both his courage and endurance and the relative power of the gods of the tribes he meets. He also meets the Lord of All the Earth and realizes the source of the voice which he had heard from the mountains.

The advent of monotheism seems an unlikely theme on which to base two stories for children. In Fyson's hands adventure and character and philosophy become one. Many readers who delight in the fun and the excitement remain unaware that in another book Shamashazir is called Abraham, and that they are reading the story of a great turning-point in history. It is not important. No reader can be unaware that on his adventurous journey Shamashazir discovers a great truth, even if the nature of that truth remains hidden for a time. These are not the only children's books whose true meaning is understood only in adult life.

A gap of nearly 20 years separates the Ur stories from Fyson's next book. In that time she gave much thought to the mystery of man's origins and to the biology and philosophy of evolution (expressing these thoughts most precisely in a long as-yet-unpublished poem). For her next book she went back to the emergence of homo sapiens, the "Wise-Animal" who is the central figure of *Friend Fire and the Dark Wings.* The small cave boy Lari carelessly breaks the tip of his father's precious hunting spear. While making a new one he inadvertently discovers the secret of fire and so transforms the lives of his family and changes the course of prehistory. It is a great theme. Instead of treating it with due solemnity Fyson develops it in human terms, dwelling on the impact of a major invention on a few primitive people. She avoids the common weakness of most stories about early man—hindsight. Lari and his family are inarticulate, almost without benefit of language, and the reader sees their situation through their eyes. The book is as honest as it is sensitive. The warmth that pervades it comes as much from love as from fire.

—Marcus Crouch

G

GÁG, Wanda (Hazel)

Nationality: American. **Born:** New Ulm, Minnesota, 11 March 1893. **Education:** New Ulm High School, graduated 1912; St. Paul Art School, 1913-14; Minneapolis Art School, 1914-17; Art Students' League, New York, 1917-18. **Family:** Married Earle Marshall Humphreys in 1931. **Career:** Schoolteacher, 1912-13; commercial artist, 1918-23. Individual shows: New York Public Library, 1923; Weyhe Gallery, New York, 1926, 1930, 1940 (retrospective); group shows: Museum of Modern Art, New York, 1939; Metropolitan Museum, New York, 1943. **Award:** University of Minnesota Kerlan award, 1977. **Died:** 27 June 1946.

PUBLICATIONS FOR CHILDREN (ILLUSTRATED BY THE AUTHOR)

Fiction

Millions of Cats. New York, Coward McCann, 1928; London, Faber, 1929.
The Funny Thing. New York, Coward McCann, 1929; London, Faber, 1962.
Snippy and Snappy. New York, Coward McCann, 1931; London, Faber, 1932.
The ABC Bunny. New York, Coward McCann, 1933; London, Faber, 1962.
Storybook. New York, Coward McCann, 1940.
Nothing at All. New York, Coward McCann, 1941; London, Faber, 1942.

Other

Gone Is Gone; or, The Story of a Man Who Wanted to Do Housework. New York, Coward McCann, 1935; London, Faber, 1936.
Tales from Grimm. New York, Coward McCann, 1936; London, Faber, 1937.
Snow White and the Seven Dwarfs. New York, Coward McCann, and London, Faber, 1938.
Three Gay Tales from Grimm. New York, Coward McCann, 1943; London, Heinemann, 1946.
More Tales from Grimm. New York, Coward McCann, 1947; London, Faber, 1962.

PUBLICATIONS FOR ADULTS

Other

Growing Pains: Diaries and Drawings for the Years 1908-1917. New York, Coward McCann, 1940.

*

Manuscript Collections: Kerlan Collection, University of Minnesota, Minneapolis; New York Public Library; Free Library, Philadelphia; Minneapolis Institute of Art.

Critical Studies: *Wanda Gág: The Story of an Artist* by Alma Scott, Minneapolis, University of Minnesota Press, 1949; *50 Years of Wanda Gág's Millions of Cats 1928-1978* by Michael Patrick Hearn, New York, Coward McCann, 1978.

Illustrator: *The Day of Doom* by Michael Wigglesworth, 1929.

* * *

Wanda Gág's undertakings supply an enchanting course in aesthetics for the young, as well as a display of what is good in children's fiction. *Nothing at All* articulates through simple narrative the process by which an airy notion achieves apprehensible form. An invisible puppy, whose existence is suggested by nothing more than a dog house and a name which defines his condition, emerges through desire, design, and poetry to acquire outline, colour, and form, and finally to become a bona fide pet. Cohesion and limitless possibility are key concepts for comprehending the achievement of Gág's classic, *Millions of Cats.* Primitive woodcuts mingle with a hand-lettered narrative, and serve as a means to expand narration, instead of lapsing into illustration's habitual role of incidental ornamentation. All things cohere, as a simple peasant longing soon becomes over-abundant fulfillment. Straightforward prose erupts into unforgettable lyric outbursts as the author delves into the mundane and emerges with the marvellous. The cottage environs, serene, secure, and clean, yet require a cat to love. Absolute contentment is but a wish away, a dream whose reality is induced by nothing more than a jaunt over hills, through villages to a nearby place where fancy yields surcharged plenty. The avalanche of lovely felines laps up ponds and eats the grass lands bare until the too-much becomes resolved into one straggly kitten. This homely residue, through care and love, rises in time to become the embodiment of beauty.

In *The ABC Bunny* individual images resist every static tendency and break forth into activity. Instead of the usual abcederia where each letter has its calligraphic moment and then is seen no more, here A's apple becomes C's crash which propels B's bunny into D's dash towards E's everywhere. Interlacing objects with activity, the sounds, basic segments of language, lead onward to boundless possibility. Infinite growth rather than happy end is likewise the final scene in the tale *The Funny Thing,* where a fanciful diet of jum jills causes a ceaseless succession of segments to append themselves to the tail of an already improbable creature who defies a name and must be termed an *aminal* since he fits no genus at all.

Gág's attitude toward characters, as well as author and audience, appears to be fascinated involvement. Even the plot seems susceptible to enchantment. Her 52 fairy tales, translations from the brothers Grimm, are tempered to sustain the magic of the story-telling experience recalled from her own childhood. Where literal renderings will serve, so much the better. Where phrasing, episodes, and endings must be altered, the sensibility of the narrator becomes, as it did with the ancient bards, the ultimate arbiter. However much her tamperings might dismay the folklorist, her heart is with her auditors. The lyric sound leads to a mood of distilled wonderment. The tale is no mere narrative sequence. Above all, it is an atmosphere.

—Leonard R. Mendelsohn

GAGE, Wilson. See **STEELE, Mary Q.**

GAL, Laszlo

Nationality: Canadian. **Born:** Budapest, Hungary, 18 February 1933. **Education:** Academy of Dramatic Arts, Budapest, 1951-52; Superior School of Pedagogy, Budapest, diploma 1955. **Family:** Married Armida Romano Gagarella in 1962; two daughters. **Career:** Teacher, freelance artist, graphic designer, illustrator, author. **Awards:** Canadian Library Association Book of the Year for Children Award, 1971, for *Cartier Discovers the St. Lawrence*; Imperial Order of Daughters of the Empire Best Children's Book of the Year, 1978, for *My Name is Not Odessa Yarker, The Shirt of the Happy Man,* and *Why the Man in the Moon Is Happy*; Amelia Frances Howard-Gibbon Illustrator's Medal from the Canadian Library Association, Imperial Order of Daughters of the Empire Best Children's Book of the Year, and the Canada Council Children's Literature Prize for illustration, all 1980, all for *The Twelve Dancing Princesses*; Canada Council Children's Literature Prize for illustration, 1984, for *Hans Christian Andersen's "The Little Mermaid."* **Address:** c/o Key Porter Books, 70 The Esplanade, Toronto, Ontario M5E 1R2, Canada.

Publications for Children

Fiction (illustrated by the author)

Prince Ivan and the Firebird. Toronto, McClelland and Stewart, 1991.
East of the Sun and West of the Moon. Toronto, McClelland and Stewart, 1993.
Merlin's Castle. Toronto, Stoddart, 1995.
With Raffaella Gal, *The Parrot.* Toronto, Groundwood, 1997.

*

Illustrator: *Chanson de Roland,* 1966, *El Cid: Soldier and Hero,* 1968 (as *La Gesta del Cid,* 1969), *I Nibelunghi* (as *Siegfried: The Mighty Warrior,* 1968), *Orlando Paladino de Francia,* 1968, and *Aeneide,* 1969, all by Maria Luisa Gefaell de Vivanco; *Fiable de Andersen* by Hans Christian Andersen, 1967; *Cartier Discovers the St. Lawrence* by William Toye; *Raven, Creator of the World,* 1970, and *Why the Man in the Moon is Happy and Other Eskimo Tales of Creation,* 1977, by Ronald Melzack; *The Moon Painters and Other Estonian Folk Tales* by Selve Maas, 1971; *How the Chipmunk Got Its Stripes* by Nancy Cleaver, 1973; *Scared Sarah* by Mary Alice Downie, 1974; *My Name Is Not Odessa Yarker* by Marian Engel, 1977; *The Shirt of the Happy Man* by Mariella Bertelli, 1977; *Sword of Egypt* by Bert Williams, 1977; *The Twelve Dancing Princesses: A Fairy Story* by Janet Lunn, 1979; *Christobel: A Story for Young People* by Catherine Ahearn, 1982; *Hans Christian Andersen's "The Little Mermaid",* 1983, and *The Goodman of Ballengiech,* 1991, by Margaret Maloney; *Canadian Fairy Tales* by Eva Martin, 1984 (as *Tales of the Far North,* 1987); *The Willow Maiden* by Meghan Collins, 1985; *The Enchanted Tapestry: A Chinese Folktale* by Robert D. San Souci, 1987; *Iduna and the Magic Apples,* 1988, and *The Spirit of the Blue Light,* 1990, by Marianna Mayer; *A Flask of Sea Water* by P. K. Page, 1989; *Sea Witches* by Joanne Robertson, 1991; *The Moon and the Oyster* by Donia Blumenfeld Clenman, 1992; *Pome and Peel* by Amy Erlich, 1993; *Tiktala* by Margaret Shaw-MacKinnon, 1996. **For Adults:** *Forgotten Pathways of the Trent* by Leslie Frost, 1973; *Comparative Mythology* by Marion Ralston, 1974; *Hamlet* and *A Midsummer Night's Dream* by William Shakespeare, 1988; *Folklore of Canada: Tall Tales, Songs, Stories, Rhymes, Jokes from Every Corner of Canada* by Edith Fowke, 1990; *Dracula* by Bram Stoker, retold by Tim Wynne-Jones, 1997.

* * *

Laszlo Gal is one of Canada's foremost illustrators of adaptations of traditional tales. In his own stories and in those written by others, Gal carefully researches the historical and cultural backgrounds and creates a series of tableau-like pictures that embody frozen moments of narrative action. A one-time theatre student, he composes his illustrations like stage sets containing appropriate period costumes, objects, and architectural styles, lighting suitable to tone and mood, and characters positioned not only to reflect action but also to complete the design of the picture.

In *Cartier Discovers the St. Lawrence,* a condensation of a history by William Toye, Gal's full-color illustrations, which depict small figures against a rugged landscape, contrast the plain dress of the Native peoples with the clothing of the French, and portray the winter suffering of the Europeans. The watercolor-and-tempura paintings for Janet Lunn's adaptation of *The Twelve Dancing Princesses,* a Grimm Brothers' folktale, are in the style of the High Renaissance. Separated from the text, the doublespreads are visual islands that readers are invited to contemplate before continuing the narrative. However, in *The Little Mermaid,* Margaret Maloney's retelling of the Hans Christian Andersen classic, Gal uses a variety of shapes and sizes for the pictures, relating them to the text and making them part of the rhythm of the story.

Gal's range of styles is apparent in illustrations for several adaptations of traditional stories from many different cultures. Meghan Collins' *The Willow Maiden,* a Celtic tale about a young man in an enchanted forest, features vaguely medieval costumes and uses the illumination from the full moon to create a backlit effect that enhances the elements of the mysterious and supernatural. *The Goodman of Ballengiech,* Maloney's version of a realistic legend from 16th-century Scotland, contrasts realistically depicted dwellings and costumes of peasants and royalty in the story of a friendship between a king and a yeoman. The style of Oriental landscape painting and tapestry art are used in *The Enchanted Tapestry,* a Chinese folktale adapted by Robert de San Souci.

Gal's recent illustrations for original stories of other writers reveal his ability to adapt his techniques to the moods and tones of the narratives. In the paintings for P. K. Page's literary fairytale *A Flask of Sea Water,* in which a goatherd wins the love of a prin cess, the star-bedecked arches above each illustration, along with the turbans and robes of the characters, complement the Arabian Nights style of the story. In *Tiktala,* in which a modern Eskimo girl discovers her vocation as a traditional carver, the illustrations of the heroine's brief transformation into a seal are dominated by a variety of green and blue tones that evoke both the wintery sea and ice and the spiritual powers the girl encounters.

Gal has also written and illustrated three books that are based on traditional narratives and themes. His adaptation of the Norse folktale *East of the Sun and West of the Moon* is shorter than the original, particularly in the account of the heroine's long and arduous quest to recover her lost lover. He also removes specific Christian references and emphasizes family unity by having the girl's parents and siblings join her and the prince after the marriage. The illustrations, which accurately present Scandinavian architecture and scenery, amplify the quest for a safe, happy home. Humble dwellings are contrasted to castles, with the castle to which the couple finally move being the most secure, beautiful, and brightly lit of the three castles depicted.

In *Merlin's Castle,* a brother and sister and their pet lizard magically enter into a book created by their artist father, encounter the legendary Merlin, and take part in defeating an evil dragon. The story, which celebrates the power of the literary imagination, is illustrated with doublespreads that depict the main events and, through the use of luminescent shades and hues, evokes the magical quality of these. *The Parrot,* a loose adaptation of an Italian folktale, co-written and illustrated with his daughter Raffaella, also celebrates the power of the literary imagination. As long as the hero (who has been transformed into a parrot) can tell a story without interruption the young woman he loves will be safe from an evil king. Objects from 16th-century Italy give the illustrations a period flavor. The use of black and white drawings to depict the girl as she listens to the story create an impression of detachment and passivity, as though she is dependant on the males, good and evil, in her life.

In the books Gal has illustrated, the pictures are not essential for the communication of the narrative. The texts could stand and, in some cases, have stood alone. The illustrations amplify, rather than expand on the words, giving visual representations of historical and cultural settings with which readers may be unfamiliar, and they visually reenforce the emotions and moods of the stories. Laszlo Gal's success in this method of illustration has not only earned him a reputation as one of Canada's top children's book artists, but also a place as an important painter in the classic tradition of illustration that includes Howard Pyle, Walter Crane, and N. C. Wyeth.

—Jon C. Stott

GANNETT, Ruth Stiles

Nationality: American. **Born:** New York City, 12 August 1923. **Education:** City and Country School; George School, Pennsylvania; Vassar College, Poughkeepsie, New York, B.A. 1944. **Family:** Married Peter Kahn in 1947; seven children. **Career:** Medical technician, Boston City Hospital; radar research technician, Massachusetts Institute of Technology, Cambridge; staff member, Children's Book Council, New York. **Address:** 8315 Rte. 227, Trumansburg, New York 14886, U.S.A.

Publications for Children

Fiction

My Father's Dragon, illustrated by Ruth Chrisman Gannett. New York, Random House, 1948; London, Macmillan, 1957.
The Wonderful House-Boat-Train, illustrated by Fritz Eichenberg. New York, Random House, 1949.
Elmer and the Dragon, illustrated by Ruth Chrisman Gannett. New York, Random House, 1950.
The Dragons of Blueland, illustrated by Ruth Chrisman Gannett. New York, Random House, 1951.
Katie and the Sad Noise, illustrated by Ellie Simmons. New York, Random House, 1961.
My Father's Dragon, Elmer and the Dragon, and The Dragons of Blueland. New York, Random House, 1997.

*

Manuscript Collections: May Massee Collection, Emporia State University, Kansas; Kerlan Collection, University of Minnesota, Minneapolis.

Ruth Stiles Gannett comments:
I wrote the first "Dragon" story to amuse myself while between jobs, with no thought of publication, in 1946. I am astonished and grateful that it has remained popular all the years since.

* * *

In her trilogy (*My Father's Dragon, Elmer and the Dragon, The Dragons of Blueland*), Ruth Stiles Gannett sets her pace with verve and freshness, with a childlike matter-of-factness, and an inherent logic. Her use of the fantastic reflects a sensibility for the imagination of young children. So skillfully does she develop Elmer Elevator that the incredible becomes credible without strain. In *My Father's Dragon* her understanding of what little boys are like, especially Elmer, is apparent. The reader accepts, without question, Elmer's decision to make the journey to Wild Island to free the baby dragon. Unafraid of words, Gannett selects exactly the right ones for her tale. Clearly American in spirit, her language takes on universality.

Elmer and the Dragon continues naturally Elmer's high adventure. The humor and the nonsense are typical of the imaginative world of any child. She offers details that indicate an intuitive understanding of a child's curiosity. Whether it is food or history or even the contents of a treasure chest, everything is described with relish.

The Dragons of Blueland brings to an end Elmer's adventures as he sets out with Boris, the baby dragon, to rescue Boris's family entrapped in a cave. Although the humor and excitement are not so well sustained as in the two earlier books, this is a finale for a saga that reflects completely the child's world. One is reminded of the world of Christopher Robin. There is the same kind of naturalness, believability, and whimsy.

The author's mother, Ruth Chrisman Gannett, illustrated the books. Her work interprets the text perfectly; they complement the text so that there is not only reading but visual pleasure.

The Wonderful House-Boat-Train, the story of the search by Pops Pops, the retired railroad engineer, and his four grandchildren for a home, is more deliberate and lacks the quality that is associated with a natural, creative flow. *Katie and the Sad Noise* appears to be a book for the beginning reader. Katie hears strange noises and tells her parents of them. Their concern leads to a consultation with Katie's teachers. One situation follows another, building up a sense of mystery. The resolution is neatly presented, and ends with a Christmas surprise, but the complexity of plot tends to throw off course the simplicity of text.

Gannett will be remembered for her singular approach to creativity. Children, hearing or reading the Elmer Elevator books, can say, "Of course!" The cultivated adult will recognize the touch of the real storyteller who has accomplished what she has set out to do—to tell her tales with grace, childlike humor, and literary style.

—Mae Durham Roger

GARD, Joyce

Pseudonym for Joyce Reeves. **Nationality:** British. **Born:** London, 13 January 1911; sister of James Reeves, *q.v.* **Education:** Wycombe Abbey School, Buckinghamshire, 1924-29; Lady Margaret Hall, Oxford (honours), B.A. in English 1933. **Career:** Assistant, Foreign Rights Department, Curtis Brown Ltd., London, 1934-35; teacher, Varndean School for Girls, Brighton, 1935-37; lived in Paris, 1937-39; temporary administrative assistant, Ministry of Economic Warfare, London, 1939-45; civil servant, Frankfurt and Hamburg, 1945-47; apprentice, Winchcombe Pottery, Gloucestershire, 1947-48; studio potter, London and Newhaven, Sussex, 1948-56; part-time private secretary and research assistant to Sir Roland Penrose, London, 1956-72. Translator and contributor, *XX Siècle* art review, Paris, 1939-70. **Address:** 1 Eliza Cottages, Charing, Ashford, Kent TN27 0JG, England.

Publications for Children

Fiction

Woorroo, illustrated by Ronald Benham. London, Gollancz, 1961.
The Dragon of the Hill. London, Gollancz, 1963.
Talargain, The Seal's Whelp. London, Gollancz, 1964; New York, Holt Rinehart, 1965.
Smudge of the Fells. London, Gollancz, 1965; New York, Holt Rinehart, 1966.
The Snow Firing. London, Gollancz, 1967; New York, Holt Rinehart, 1968.
The Mermaid's Daughter. London, Gollancz, and New York, Holt Rinehart, 1969.
Handysides Shall Not Fall, illustrated by Carolyn Dinan. London, Kaye and Ward, 1975.
The Hagwaste Donkeys, illustrated by Gareth Floyd. London, Pelham, 1976.

Other

Translator, *Journey to the Centre of the Earth,* by Jules Verne, illustrated by Dick Hart. London, Hutchinson, 1961.

Publications for Adults

Other

Translator (as Joyce Reeves), *Marc Chagall: Drawings and Water Colors for the Ballet,* by Jacques Lassaigne. Paris, XX Siècle, and New York, Tudor, 1969.

*

Joyce Gard comments:

(1978) The only way I can write for children is to write for myself as a child—to become a child again, the person I was and still essentially am.

My books are not easy to introduce or categorize briefly. However, I think the basic essentials of any children's fiction, which I have tried to provide, are: 1) a good story, 2) good writing, 3) credible, interesting people, not too complex, 4) a sound setting—an individual and distinctive *place,* and 5) something *extra.*

This "extra" could be an unusual insight into a particular way of life, for instance, or a special magic or mystery. In my first children's books I attempted to recapture the ecstasy of pure physical sensation which only children, I believe, can experience unmixed: either imagined—flying like a bird in *Woorroo*—or real—ocean-swimming in *Talargain,* here enhanced by communion with the seals.

I explored other childhood dreams and obsessions, such as finding buried treasure, confronting dragons, entering into the lives of beautiful people of the past—*The Dragon of the Hill* and *Talargain.* Then I turned to practical lives I would have liked to live—a sheep farmer in the Lake District in *Smudge of the Fells*—or had myself lived—a studio potter in *The Snow Firing.* There is as much technical know-how in these two books as I could squeeze in without, I hope, giving up the first requisite of a good story.

The Mermaid's Daughter is for an older age-group; it is the story of a girl growing up in the Scilly Isles in Roman times and her adventures as she strives to reconcile her two roles—that of the chosen mortal embodiment of the Sea Goddess of the islands and of a flesh-and-blood human being and her relationships with family and lovers, friends and enemies.

I don't believe in an explicit "message"; in my experience this causes an automatic switch-off of interest in a healthy child. I believe strongly, however, that worthwhile fiction is a power for good and feeds the imagination—in the same way that Shelley claimed for poetry.

(1983) I am not writing for children any more. That vein ran out after I went to the Orkneys and Shetlands some years ago looking for a children's book and became so severely infected with the archaeological virus that the resulting book was unpublishable even after two rewritings. For a long time now I have been researching and am now writing a book which no serious archaeologist would dare to undertake, as it consists of an attempt to reconstruct a lost period of our history for which the evidence is all too scanty. However, the editor of *Current Archaeology,* Andrew Selkirk, has been good enough to publish a few short pieces of mine in a similar speculative vein, of course taking no responsibility.

* * *

Joyce Gard writes for children prepared to savour a book rather than romp through it for the sake of the story. Her novels are strongly rooted in place—the English Lakes, Gloucestershire, th

Scillies—often luminously evoked. In each the author explores one of her many interests, which include pottery, sheep-farming, and archaeology, and these are the real focus of the story. Though they may begin with exciting action, such as the memorable horror and beauty of the dragon's flight, successive events move more slowly and are sometimes impeded by a straight recapitulation of events that the reader has not shared. The characters also are usually subordinate to the theme or plot, perfectly satisfactory for their purpose but not explored in any great depth and not much changed or developed by the things that happen to them. Gard's best gift is that of sensory perception. *Woorroo* shares the wild joy and freedom of winged flight, *Talargain* the physical sensation, the delight and fear, of swimming with the seals, and the boy's relationship with them. In *The Snow Firing* one can feel the smooth wet clay and the warmly sensuous beauty of the finished pots.

The stories intended for younger readers will appeal only to a limited audience of rather sheltered children. But in the present spate of books for the mass there may still be a need for a few for minority groups.

It is in the novels dealing with the past that the writer shows her real quality. *The Dragon of the Hill, Talargain,* and *The Mermaid's Daughter* are all wholly or partly set in the period of Roman Britain. The life and manners of the time are handled convincingly and lightly; the reader can share in them without feeling burdened by conscientious social history. Gard is particularly interested in ancient cults and can identify herself imaginatively with the religious feeling of other times and countries. Woorroo's aboriginal magic, as he chants and paints in the dawn at the edge of the lake, is one of the most memorable moments in the novel. *The Mermaid's Daughter,* by far her most ambitious and successful book, attempts to recreate the cult of the Great Mother, the Sea Goddess, as it may once have existed in the Scilly Islands. The heroine, Astria, is the secret representative of the goddess among her people. The story moves between the islands and the Roman fortress at Caerleon, both vividly evoked. It develops slowly despite times of excitement, of romantic love and tragedy, but it immerses the reader completely in its own world. Individual episodes remain most vividly in the mind—the ritual marriage in the dark cave by the sea, Astria dancing on the bright spring grass beyond Caerleon, watched by the wild, shy hill people, the meeting with St. Alban in the Roman garrison. But above all one is haunted by the images of sea and sky and flowers, a sense of grace and light. This is a book of unusual quality.

—Margaret Greaves

GAUCH, Patricia Lee

Nationality: American. **Born:** Patricia Lee, Detroit, Michigan, 3 January 1934. **Education:** Miami University, Oxford, Ohio, A.B. 1956; Manhattanville College, Purchase, New York, M.A.T. 1969; Drew University, Ph.D. 1988. **Family:** Married Ronald Raymond Gauch, 1955; one son, two daughters. **Career:** Writer and editor. Reporter, Louisville *Courier-Journal,* 1957-59; writer, Coward-McCann and Geoghegan/Putnam, New York, from 1969; teacher, Gill-St. Berhards School, Gladstone, New Jersey, 1972-83; part-time professor, Drew University, Madison, New Jersey, Rutgers University, New Brunswick, New Jersey, Manhattanville College, Purchase, New York; vice president and editorial director, Philomel Books, New York, from 1985. **Awards:** Cited in *Writers of Children's Books of the Year,* New Jersey Institute of Technology, 1971, for *Christina Katerina and the Box,* 1972, for *A Secret House,* 1973, for *Grandpa and Me* and *Aaron and the Green Mountain Boys,* and 1983, for *Night Talks*; Notable Children's Trade Book in the Field of Social Studies, National Council for the Social Studies/Children's Book Council, 1975, for *This Time, Tempe Wick?* **Agent:** Dorothy Marinko, McIntosh and Otis, Inc., 18 East 41st St., New York, New York, 10014. **Address:** 21 Curry Lane, Hyde Park, New York 12538, U.S.A.

PUBLICATIONS FOR CHILDREN

Fiction

My Old Tree, illustrated by Doris Burn. New York, Coward, McCann, 1970.

A Secret House, illustrated by Margot Tomes. New York, Coward, McCann, 1970.

Christina Katerina and the Box, illustrated by Doris Burn. New York, Coward, McCann, 1971.

Aaron and the Green Mountain Boys, illustrated by Margot Tomes. New York, Coward, McCann, 1972.

Grandpa and Me, illustrated by Symeon Shimin. New York, Coward, McCann, 1972.

Christina Katerina and the First Annual Grand Ballet, illustrated by Doris Burn. New York, Coward, McCann, 1973.

This Time, Tempe Wick?, illustrated by Margot Tomes. New York, Coward, McCann, 1974.

Thunder at Gettysburg, illustrated by Stephen Gammell. New York, Coward, McCann, 1975.

The Impossible Major Rogers, illustrated by Robert Andrew Parker. New York, Putnam, 1977.

Once Upon a Dinkelsbuhl, illustrated by Tomie de Paola. New York, Putnam, 1977.

On to Widecombe Fair, illustrated by Trina Schart Hyman. New York, Putnam, 1978.

The Little Friar Who Flew, illustrated by Tomie de Paola. New York, Putnam, 1980.

Christina Katerina and the Time She Quit the Family, illustrated by Elise Primavera. New York, Putnam, 1987.

Dance, Tanya, illustrated by Satomi Ichikawa. New York, Philomel, 1989.

Christina Katerina and the Great Bear Train, illustrated by Elise Primavera. New York, Putnam, 1990.

Bravo, Tanya, illustrated by Satomi Ichikawa. New York, Philomel, 1992.

Uncle Magic, illustrated by Deborah Kogan Ray. New York, Holiday House, 1992.

Noah, illustrated by Jonathan Green. New York, Philomel, 1994.

Tanya and Emily in a Dance for Two, illustrated by Satomi Ichikawa. New York, Philomel, 1994.

Christina Katerina and Fats Watson and the Great Neighborhood War, illustrated by Stacey Schuett. New York, Putnam, 1997.

Tanya and the Magic Wardrobe, illustrated by Satomi Ichikawa. New York, Philomel, 1997.

Publications for Young Adults

Fiction

The Green of Me. New York, Putnam, 1978.
Fridays. New York, Putnam, 1979.
Kate Alone. New York, Putnam, 1980.
Morelli's Game. New York, Putnam, 1981.
Night Talks. New York, Putnam, 1983.
The Year the Summer Died. New York, Putnam, 1985.

*

Biography: Entry in *Something about the Author,* Vol. 80, Detroit, Gale, 1995.

Patricia Lee Gauch comments:

For me, my love of children's literature started when I read *Ping* by Marjorie Flock. Not only did I have the tale of the little duck who had an adventure on the Yangtze River, but I realize now, I wandered out into the world myself looking for adventure. Writing for young people has given me the opportunity to inner and outer worlds, past and present. Even now I look so fondly on my forays into the 18th and 19th century while researching and writing *This Time Tempe Wick?* and *Thunder at Gettysburg.* In writing my novels, I explored the inner worlds of adolescents, frequently applying the "what-if" to relationships and pivotal moments in a young person's life. I suppose that is a mark of even what appears to be my simplest books: this look at the human spirit. How it moves and survives in the face of a world laden with obstacles. Back to Ping. He misses the call of the boatmaster (his head is under water), so he can't get home that night to his cozy boat. Can he survive? Tanya the littlest dancer, isn't the best in class, doesn't hear the teacher's call as the other young people do; will she survive? Of course, because like Ping she discovers her own world, goes her own way. Literature is the music of the soul. I will go on singing as long as I hear the music.

* * *

Patricia Lee Gauch is an excellent writer and editor of children's books. Her own writing covers three genres: picture books for the very young, historical fiction for the middle reader, and novels for the young adult.

Popular among her picture books are those about two young girls: Christina Katerina and Tanya. Christina Katerina is a spirited, independent young lady. In *Christina Katerina and the Box* she and her friend Fats Watson have great fun playing in a huge refrigerator box. In *Christina Katerina and the Time She Quit the Family* she quits the family so that she can do whatever she pleases, without her brother and her parents to bother her. In *Christina Katerina and the Great Bear Train,* she runs away from home to avoid the arrival of a new sibling. Gauch likes to draw on the experiences of real people for her stories. Her own daughter, Christine, was the model for the Christina stories.

The books about Tanya were written for the illustrator-writer Satomi Ichikawa, who is a devotee of the ballet, like little Tanya. In the first book of the series, *Dance Tanya,* Tanya is enamored of the dance. When her older sister Elise practices her positions—first, second, fourth, fifth—so does Tanya. When Elise does the perfect plié, so does Tanya. When Elise goes to her lessons, Tanya is allowed to come along to watch, but not to dance. Tanya does get to attend Elise's dance recital in the spring, and when she comes home, with no one looking, Tanya dances too, just the way Elise did. The next Christmas Tanya receives a shiny case, a pair of leotards, and ballet slippers. Now she is big enough to take dancing lessons.

The watercolor illustrations by Satomi Ichikawa are soft-hued and lyrical. Tanya's arabesques and jetés dance all over the pages. In the companion book, *Bravo, Tanya,* Tanya is now in dancing class. But dancing with others, to Miss Bessinger's clapping (one, two, three, four), Tanya is no longer able to hear the music she once heard when she danced alone. In class, she trips, she falls, she twirls into another dancer. One day though, while dancing in the meadow, she discovers music anew and is able to dance in class as well as by herself. The quiet watercolors, the joyous portrait of a young girl twirling to her heart's content, complete a satisfying book.

In a note to *Aaron and the Green Mountain Boys,* Gauch explains that in 1776, in Bennington, Vermont, there was a real boy named Aaron Robinson, the tavern keeper's grandson. Legend has it that he chopped the wood so that his mother and other village women could bake bread to feed the patriot army. The bread the villagers made and their fires enable the Green Mountain Boys to get to the battle scene with full stomachs and dry rifles just at the right time. Gauch tells Aaron's story, the story of a nine-year-old who wants to be part of the excitement of fighting the British Redcoats. But every time he offers his services, he is told to help bake the bread for the real soldiers. That seems too tame for a boy who can shoot a blackbird at 100 paces! The rumble of cannons, the shots of guns, and the quiet work of villagers who support their troops, are shown with honesty and pride.

Temperance Wick is another young heroine from Revolutionary times. Legend has it that she lived near Morristown, New Jersey, and was known for her strength and courage. In *This Time, Tempe Wick?,* Tempe artfully prevents Revolutionary soldiers from stealing her horse. This Revolution-era story describes the fact that a large war is made up of many small wars, sometimes among people who are fighting against the same side: soldiers against soldiers, soldiers against the farmers they are supposed to protect, farmers against soldiers that are fighting for them. In this story a group of tired, cold, unpaid soldiers from Pennsylvania turn against their captains and the farmers who feed them. Gauch shows in this story that war is not simple, a straight contest between good and evil. She shows as well that humans are not simple, all strong or all weak.

Gauch's novels for young adults also are impressive in their complex characterizations. She is sensitive to the way relationships between young people get formed and friendships develop. She is aware of the joys and the hurts that are a part of growing up. In *Morelli's Game* the English teacher at Lockewood Academy, a private high school in Pennsylvania, sends two groups of students on a journey through the Pennsylvania hills on to Washington, D.C. The boys are allowed only five dollars spending money. The journey brings out raw emotions and raw language. The boys slowly realize that some of their own precious individuality has to be sacrificed to a group effort if they are to survive a sometimes exhilarating, other times terrifying adventure. And they learn about people who do not attend private schools.

Gauch also cuts into the psyches of teen-age girls in books such as *Fridays* and *Kate Alone.* She brings alive family function and dysfunction, peer group pressure and companionship. Gauch is skillful in addressing the fears and challenges and joys of young adulthood.

—Mary Lysta

GAY, Marie-Louise

Nationality: Canadian. **Born:** Québec City, 17 June 1952. **Education:** Institute of Graphic Arts, Montreal, 1970-71; Montreal Museum of Fine Arts School, 1973; Academy of Art College, San Francisco, 1977-79. **Family:** Married David Homel; two sons. **Career:** Children's clothing designer; art director; set designer; editorial illustrator; graphic designer; lecturer in illustration; author/ illustrator; playwright. Contributor of illustrations to periodicals including *Perspectives, Mother Jones,* and *Psychology Today.* **Awards:** Canada Council Children's Literature Prize, 1984, for *Lizzy's Lion*; Canada Council Children's Literature Prize, 1984, for *Drole d'école*; The Amelia Frances Howard-Gibbon Illustrator's Award, 1987, for *Moonbeam on a Cat's Ear*; The Amelia Frances Howard-Gibbon Award, 1988, and the Governor General's Literary Award, 1988, both for *Rainy Day Magic*; Mr. Christie's Book Award, 1997, for *The Fabulous Song.* **Address:** c/o Groundwood Books, 585 Bloor Street West, Toronto, Ontario M6G 1K5, Canada.

Publications for Children

Fiction (illustrated by the author)

De zéro a minuit. Montreal, La Courte Echelle, 1981.
La soeur de Robert. Montreal, La Courte Echelle, 1983.
Drole d'école. Québec, Ovale, 1984.
The Garden. Toronto, James Lorimer, 1985.
Moonbeam on a Cat's Ear. Don Mills, Ontario, Stoddart, 1986; as *Voyage Au Clair de Lune.* Saint-Lambert, Québec, Héritage, 1986.
Rainy Day Magic. Don Mills, Ontario, Stoddart, 1987; as *Magie d'un jour de pluie.* Saint-Lambert, Québec, Héritage, 1986.
Angel and the Polar Bear. Don Mills, Ontario, Stoddart, 1988; as *Angèle et l'ours polaire,* Saint-Lambert, Québec, Héritage, 1988.
Fat Charlie's Circus. Don Mills, Ontario, Stoddart, 1989; as *Le Cirque de Charlie Chou,* translated by Christiane Duchesne, Saint-Lambert, Québec, Héritage, 1989.
Willy Nilly. Don Mills, Ontario, Stoddart, 1990; as *Bonne fête Willy,* translated by Christiane Duchesne. Saint-Lambert, Québec, 1990.
Mademoiselle Moon. Don Mills, Ontario, Stoddart, 1992.
Rabbit Blue. Don Mills, Ontario, Stoddart, 1993; as *Lapin bleu,* Saint-Lambert, Québec, Héritage, 1993.
Midnight Mimi. Don Mills, Ontario, Stoddart, 1994; as *Mimi-la-Nuit* Saint-Lambert, Québec, Héritage, 1994.
The Three Little Pigs. Toronto, Groundwood Books, 1994.
Rumpelstiltskin. Toronto, Groundwood Books, 1997.

Other

Author and set, costume, and puppet designer, *Bonne fête Willy* (children's puppet play; first produced National Arts Center Atelier, Montreal, Montreal, November 26, 1989).
Author and set, costume, and puppet designer, *Qui a peur de Loulou?* (children's puppet play; first produced in 1994).

*

Illustrator: *Hou Ilva,* 1976, *Hébert Luée,* 1980, and *Dou Ilvien,* 1981, all by Bertrand Gauthier; *Hands On: A Media Resource Book for Teachers* by Anne Taylor, National Film Board of Canada, 1977; *Lizzy's Lion* by Dennis Lee, 1985; *That's Enough, Maddie,* 1991, *Maddie in Goal,* 1992, *Maddie Wants Music,* 1993, *Maddie Goes to Paris,* 1994, and *Maddie in Danger,* 1995, all by Louise Leblanc, translated by Sarah Cummins; *The Last Piece of Sky* by Tim Wynne-Jones, 1993; *When Vegetables Go Bad!,* 1994, and *The Fabulous Song,* 1996, by Don Gillmor.

Marie-Louise Gay comments:

When I hear people (adults, of course) saying that today, children are much more interested in computers, electronic games, videos, and television, than reading books ... when these same people say that books well disappear altogether in a few decades ... *I do not believe it for one minute.* There will always be books. There will always be children ready to devour books; to dive happily into a story, an adventure, a mystery; there will always be bookworms.

I know, I was one, and I will continue writing for them.

* * *

Marie-Louise Gay, winner of several English and French Canadian illustrators' awards, celebrates children's love of energetic, often chaotic play, and the exuberance of their adventures in imaginative worlds they create or enter. Her cartoon-like pictures—generally pen-and-ink sketches with bright water color washes—capture the energy and enthusiasm of her characters as they confront, with joy and, often, courage, the real and make-believe elements of their lives.

Gay had established a reputation as an important illustrator in Québec before her work for Dennis Lee's poem *Lizzy's Lion,* the story of a girl whose pet lion devours a burglar, brought her to national attention. The smug grin of the tousle-headed heroine, who controls her pet by tugging on its tail, the clutter of her bedroom, and the changing expressions on the robber's face complement and expand on the humorous exaggeration of Lee's verse.

In several books she has written and illustrated, Gay explores children's relationships to real, make-believe, and magical worlds. Her short rhymed poem for *Moonbeam on a Cat's Ear* gives only an outline of events. A small boy and his sister sneak outside on a moonlight night, then lasso and ride the moon. At the conclusion, the narrator asks if this were a dream or an actual experience. The pictures suggest an answer and fill out meaning and characterization. The cat and mouse who had been sleeping on the bed now rest on the curve of the moon. As the children stand at the door, bolts of lightning cutting across the wallpaper and an outside landscape with no familiar objects suggest that the children are moving into an alternative world. Whether or not their experiences are real, their emotions are, and their different facial expressions and body language reveal their varying responses to the events.

The two children in *Rainy Day Magic* also experience a sense of release as an exasperated parent sends them to play in the basement and they enter into a strange world they find there. The closing lines also raise questions about the nature of their experience. Although details from their house appear in the other world, one of the characters returns with a starfish not found in the house. The joyous chaos of the children's actions is fully embodied in the illustrations: they careen through the house, upsetting objects, and leaving toys all around, and they find even more exciting activities for the release of their energies in the magical realm into which they enter.

In *Angel and the Polar Bear* and *Willy Nilly,* fantastic events take place in this world: Angel must cope with a series of disasters in her apartment, including the arrival of a polar bear; Willy must find a way to undue the mistakes caused by his misuse of a magic kit he discovers. In the former, white borders surrounding part of each doublespread represent the world of Angel's apartment. However, these borders cannot contain the fantastic events, which burst beyond them. Angel's daring and cleverness are paralleled by a tiny little kitten who, though not mentioned in the words, is seen performing brave actions. The foolish pride of Willy Nilly is indicated by his largeness in the pictures; his humbling when he seeks help to remedy his mistakes is indicated by his smallness in relation to the magician he visits. In each picture, the facial expressions of a rabbit and turtle, also not mentioned in the text, reveal their attitudes towards the boy's foolish behavior.

Recently Gay has illustrated two very different works: Don Gillmor's realistic story, *The Fabulous Song,* and the Brothers Grimm's *Rumpelstiltskin.* In the former, a humorous narrative about a boy's learning the true nature of his musical talents, the initially unhappy hero is the smallest in the illustrations. After he has triumphantly conducted his family orchestra, he sits proudly in the center of the page, eating ice cream with the spoon he had used as a baton. Torn zig-zag pieces of musical scores that had crossed the page when he is unhappy are replaced by wavy, rainbow-colored ribbons containing musical notes. The story of a woman's struggle for freedom from the domination of three men in her life, *Rumpelstiltskin* is the most somber work Gay has illustrated. Early in the narrative the king's horse and then his shadow loom over the young woman. Rumpelstiltskin strides confidently into her prison cell. However, as the girl gains power, she assumes a more dominant position in the illustrations. Gay's cartoon-like figures are intended to lighten the horror of the story, but seem somewhat out of key with its underlying mood.

In her books, Gay humorously and insightfully presents children confidently confronting and seeking to control their worlds. These are splashed with a variety of color, each presented in varying degrees of brilliance to reflect her characters' changing moods. The simple texts and humorous, almost child-like illustrations successfully present the child's love of wildness and play, of chaos and control. Gay is one of Canada's foremost interpreters of young children's perceptions of important real and imaginary elements of their lives.

—Jon C. Stott

GEE, Maurice (Gough)

Nationality: New Zealander. **Born:** Whakatane, 22 August 1931. **Education:** Avondale College, Auckland, 1945-49; University of Auckland, 1950-53, M.A. (honours) in English 1953; Auckland Teachers College, 1954. **Family:** Married Margaretha Garden in 1970; one son (from previous marriage) and two daughters. **Career:** Schoolteacher, 1955-57; held various jobs, 1958-66; assistant librarian, Alexander Turnbull Library, Wellington, 1967-69; city librarian, Napier Public Library, 1970-72; deputy librarian, Teachers Colleges Library, Auckland, 1974-76. Since 1976 full-time writer. **Awards:** New Zealand Literary Fund scholarship, 1962, 1976, and Award of Achievement, 1967, 1973; University of Otago Robert Burns fellowship, 1964; Hubert Church Prose award, 1973; New Zealand Book award, 1976, 1979, 1982, 1991; James Tait Black Memorial prize, 1979; Sir James Wattie award, 1979, 1993; New Zealand Children's Book of the Year award, 1984, 1995; New Zealand Library Association Esther Glen award, 1986, 1995; D.Litt.: Victoria University, Wellington, 1987. **Agent:** Richards Literary Agency, P.O. Box 31240, Milford, Auckland 9. **Address:** 41 Chelmsford St., Wellington, New Zealand.

Publications for Children

Fiction

Under the Mountain. Wellington, London, and New York, Oxford University Press, 1979.
The World Around the Corner, illustrated by Gary Hebley. Wellington, Oxford University Press, 1980; Oxford and New York, Oxford University Press, 1981.
The Halfmen of O. Auckland and Oxford, Oxford University Press, 1982; New York, Oxford University Press, 1983.
The Priests of Ferris. Auckland and Oxford, Oxford University Press, 1984; New York, Oxford University Press, 1985.
Motherstone. Auckland and Oxford, Oxford University Press, 1985.
The Fire-Raiser. Auckland, Oxford University Press, 1986; Boston, Houghton Mifflin, 1992.
The Champion. Auckland, Puffin, 1989; New York, Simon and Schuster, 1993.
The Fat Man. Auckland, Penguin, 1994; New York, Simon and Schuster, 1997.

Television Series: *The Fire-Raiser,* from his own story, 1986; *The Champion,* from his own story, 1989.

Publications for Adults

Novels

The Big Season. London, Hutchinson, 1962.
A Special Flower. London, Hutchinson, 1965.
In My Father's Den. London, Faber, 1972.
Games of Choice. London, Faber, 1976.
Plumb. London, Faber, 1978.
Meg. London, Faber, 1981; New York, St. Martin's Press, 1982.
Sole Survivor. London, Faber, and New York, St. Martin's Press 1983.
Prowlers. London, Faber, 1987.
The Burning Boy. London, Faber, and New York, Viking, 1990.
Going West. London, Faber, 1993.
Crime Story. Auckland, Penguin, 1994; London, Faber, 1995.
Loving Ways. Auckland, Penguin, 1996; London, Faber, 1997.

Short Stories

A Glorious Morning, Comrade. Auckland, Auckland University Press-Oxford University Press, 1975.
Collected Stories. Auckland and London, Penguin, 1986; New York, Penguin, 1987.

Other

Nelson Central School: A History. Nelson, Nelson Central School Centennial Committee, 1978.
Mortimer's Patch (television plays). 1980.

*

Critical Studies: *Introducing Maurice Gee* by David Hill, Auckland, Longman Paul, 1981; *Maurice Gee* by Bill Manhire, Auckland and Oxford, Oxford University Press, 1986.

* * *

Maurice Gee, in his vision of the traditional fantasy struggle between good and evil, sees evil as the abuse of power, with pollution and devastation as a result. *Under the Mountain* portrays huge, worm-like creatures lurking under Auckland's volcanic cones. When activated by metamorphosing alien slugs, they will destroy Earth. *The World Around the Corner* describes a band of goblin-like Grimbles, championed by a dragon cloud of poisonous gas. *The Halfmen of O, The Priests of Ferris,* and *Motherstone* as a trilogy examine at length the corruption of absolute power—political, religious, royal, and military. In turn, the satanic Otis Claw, the Paingiver, rules with his Deathguards in his spreading hell of a city; the High Priest and his police-priests use cruelty and killing in their religious rites to keep order ("There is no other way to run the State"); mad Osro is determined to be king, and mad Widd is determined to fight him, even though they each have the ultimate weapon to destroy all.

Against these evil characters are the child-protagonists. Helped by Nature, their special gifts, each other, and sympathetic, sometimes symbolically drawn adults, all discover the necessary strength to meet each challenge. The red-haired twins Rachel and Theo develop telepathic powers and control of magic stones to make the volcanoes erupt just in time. Caroline saves the magic glasses from the Grimbles and returns them, revitalised by the sun, to the elvish Moon-girl who can then win the yearly fight against the dragon. Nicholas supports his cousin Susan Ferris on her long journeys in her quest for the magic charms. With help she succeeds in destroying each set of oppressive rulers and, as a final solution, wipes out all memory so that life on O returns to the Neanderthal stage.

But this struggle demands sacrifice. Gee's "colouring" shows that in the overthrow of evil, because of human imperfections, innocent people must suffer, for which we "do right to grieve." Since "Good must be won daily in the battle that never ends," some repetition in the trilogy is inevitable, but each story ends successfully. And Gee underlines the duality of his vision by pairing and paralleling characters, creatures (notably cats, domestic and wild), magic stones, and images.

The storylines are carried by an assurance of tone and dialogue. Danger builds effectively to its climax. Humour, a shorter length, and a lighter touch make Gee's polished second title suitable for younger readers. Humour also relieves the grimness of the trilogy, mainly through greedy, shifty, garrulous Jimmy Jaspers: "Cling ... I'm gunner ram yer skinny legs down yer throat." Jimmy is indeed a "Mixie ... in Balance ... probably more bad than good, that is the way with men." But he chooses to repent (an important theme in Gee's adult writing) and to fight against evil. Besides Jimmy Jaspers, the trilogy embraces an imaginative cast of helpful and hindering creatures.

Like other fantasy writers, Gee brings credibility to his stories through detail. He moves his settings from explicit Auckland to unnamed Nelson (where he is supported by nine full-page pencil drawings), to his Otherworld of O which is entered through a drug-induced, time-space flip. He appeals to the senses—the pervading stink of the slugs, the constantly recurring screams in O. To clarify his details, however, he leans on similes which are sometimes unnecessary, even distracting. For example, when in O the living hill dies, the awesome quality is diminished through comparison with house-timbers, herds, trucks, and battleships. Some pages lack editorial polish as well.

For his television-linked historical novel, *The Fire-Raiser,* Gee turns to the realistic world of his adult fiction. He sets the action in Jessop, a small town based on Nelson but reflecting any small New Zealand town during World War I. In a penetratingly taut opening chapter, on the night of 23 March 1915 the fire-raiser strikes again. The four children know who the fire-raiser is before the adults do. Unlike children in Blyton formula stories, these children tell the police, which doesn't reduce tension and does increase credibility.

Standing out as characters are the eccentric, tyrannical, Dickensian Mrs. Marwick and her unbalanced, middle-aged son Edgar. Refreshingly, teacher Clippy Hedges is one who likes children, has a sense of humour, and is cheerful though aware of "meanness, cruelty and pain," and colonial snobbery in the community. Patriotic fervour turns ugly in war-fanned mob hysteria that explodes in an attack on the gentle German piano teacher. The dramatic rhythms and quick scene cuts of television techniques influence the shaping of this novel, but it is handled with power and skill. As it encompasses human strengths, weaknesses, and social comment, it adds considerably to Gee's compelling, thought-provoking contribution to children's literature in New Zealand.

—Diane Hebley

GIBBONS, Gail (Gretchen)

Nationality: American. **Born:** Oak Park, Illinois, 1 August 1944. **Education:** University of Illinois, B.F.A. 1967. **Family:** Married 1) Glenn Gibbons in 1966 (died 1972); 2) Kent Ancliffe, 1976; two stepchildren. **Career:** Artist, WCIA-Television, Champaign, Illinois, 1967-1969; promotions and animation artist, WMAQ-TV, Chicago, 1969; staff artist, Bob Hower Agency, Chicago, 1969-70; staff artist, WNBC-Television, House of Animation, New York, New York, 1970-76; freelance writer and illustrator of children's books, since 1975; free-lance artist, United Press International, New York City, since 1977. **Awards:** New York City Art Director Club award, 1979; American Institute of Graphic Arts award, 1979; National Science Teachers Association/Children's Book Council Award, 1980 and 1982; certificate of appreciation for *The Post Office Book: Mail and How it Moves* from U. S. Postmaster General, 1982; American Library Association Notable Book award, 1983, 1985; National Council of Social Studies Notable Children's Trade Book in the Field of Social Studies, 1983, 1987, 1989, 1990, and 1992; National Science Teachers Association's Outstanding Science Trade Books for Children, 1983, 1987, 1991, 1996, 1998; Washington Post Childen's Book Guild Award, 1987; International Reading Association Children's Choice Award, 1989,

1995; American Bookseller Pick of the Lists, 1992. **Address:** Goose Green, Corinth, Vermont 05039, U.S.A.

PUBLICATIONS FOR CHILDREN (ILLUSTRATED BY THE AUTHOR)

Nonfiction

Things to Make and Do for Halloween. New York, F. Watts, 1976.
Things to Make and Do for Columbus Day. New York, F. Watts, 1977.
Things to Make and Do for Your Birthday. New York, F. Watts, 1978.
Clocks and How They Go. New York, Crowell, 1979.
Lock and Keys. New York, Crowell, 1980.
The Too-Great Bread Bake Book. New York, Warne, 1980.
Trucks. New York, HarperCollins, 1981.
Christmas Time. New York, Holiday House, 1982.
The Post Office Book: Mail and How it Moves. New York, HarperCollins, 1982.
Tool Book. New York, Holiday House, 1982.
Boat Book. New York, Holiday House, 1983.
New Road! New York, HarperCollins, 1983.
Sun Up, Sun Down. San Diego, Harcourt Brace, 1983.
Thanksgiving Day. New York, Holiday House, 1983.
Department Store. New York, Crowell, 1984.
Fire! Fire! New York, HarperCollins, 1984.
Halloween. New York, Holiday House, 1984.
The Seasons of Arnold's Apple Tree. New York, Harcourt Brace, 1984.
Tunnels. New York, Holiday House, 1984.
Check it Out: The Book About Libraries. New York, Harcourt Brace, 1985.
Fill It Up! New York, HarperCollins, 1985.
The Milk Makers. New York, Simon & Schuster, 1985.
Playgrounds. New York, Holiday House, 1985.
Flying. New York, Holiday House, 1986.
From Path to Highway: The Story of the Boston Post Road. New York, HarperCollins, 1986.
Happy Birthday! New York, Holiday House, 1986.
Up Goes the Skyscraper! New York, Simon & Schuster, 1986.
Valentine's Day. New York, Holiday House, 1986.
Deadline!: From News to Newspaper. New York, HarperCollins, 1987.
Dinosaurs. New York, Holiday House, 1987.
Trains. New York, Holiday House, 1987.
Weather Forecasting. New York, Simon & Schuster, 1987.
Zoo. New York, HarperCollins, 1987.
Farming. New York, Holiday House, 1988.
Prehistoric Animals. New York, Holiday House, 1988.
Sunken Treasure. New York, HarperCollins, 1988.
Catch the Wind!: All about Kites. Boston, Little Brown, 1989.
Easter. New York, Holiday House, 1989.
Marge's Diner. San Diego, HarperCollins, 1989.
Monarch Butterfly. New York, Holiday House, 1989.
Beacons of Light: Lighthouses. New York, Morrow, 1990.
How a House Is Built. New York, Holiday House, 1990.
Weather Words and What They Mean. New York, Holiday House, 1990.
From Seed to Plant. New York, Holiday House, 1991.
The Puffins Are Back! New York, HarperCollins, 1991.
Whales. New York, Holiday House, 1991.
The Great St. Lawrence Seaway. New York, Morrow, 1992.
Recycle!: A Handbook for Kids. Boston, Little Brown, 1992.
Sharks. New York, Holiday House, 1992.
Stargazers. New York, Holiday House, 1992.
Caves & Caverns. New York, Harcourt Brace, 1993.
Frogs. New York, Holiday House, 1993.
Pirates: Robbers of the High Seas. Boston, Little Brown, 1993.
The Planets. New York, Holiday House, 1993.
Puff—Flash—Bang!: A Book about Signals. New York, Morrow, 1993.
Spiders. New York, Holiday House, 1993.
Christmas on an Island. New York, Morrow, 1994.
Country Fair. Boston, Little Brown, 1994.
Emergency! New York, Holiday House, 1994.
Nature's Green Umbrella: Tropical Rain Forests. New York, Morrow, 1994.
St. Patrick's Day. New York, Holiday House, 1994.
Wolves. New York, Holiday House, 1994.
Bicycle Book. New York, Holiday House, 1995.
Catch the Wind!: All About Kites. Boston, Little Brown, 1995.
Knights in Shining Armor. Boston, Little Brown, 1995.
Planet Earth/Inside Out. New York, Morrow, 1995.
The Reasons for Seasons. New York, Holiday House, 1995.
Saint Patrick's Day. New York, Holiday House, 1995.
Sea Turtles. New York, Holiday House, 1995.
Wolves. New York, Holiday House, 1995.
Cats. New York, Holiday House, 1996.
Deserts. New York, Holiday House, 1996.
Dogs. New York, Holiday House, 1996.
Music Maker. New York, Simon & Schuster, 1996.
The Reasons for Seasons. New York, Holiday House, 1996.
Click!: A Book about Cameras & Taking Pictures. Boston, Little Brown, 1997.
Gulls ... Gulls ... Gulls.... New York, Holiday House, 1997.
The Honey Makers. New York, Morrow, 1997.
The Moon Book. New York, Holiday House, 1997.
Paper, Paper Everywhere. San Diego, Harcourt Brace, 1997.
Marshes & Swamps. New York, Holiday House, 1998.
Soaring With the Wind: The Bald Eagle. New York, Morrow, 1998.
Yippee-Yay!: A Book About Cowboys & Cowgirls. Boston, Little Brown, 1998.
Dragons. New York, Morrow, forthcoming.
How You Were Born. New York, Simon & Schuster, forthcoming.
Santa Claus. New York, Morrow, forthcoming.

Fiction

Willie and His Wheel Wagon. New York, Prentice Hall, 1975.
Salvador and Mister Sam: A Guide to Parakeet Care. New York, Prentice Hall, 1976.
The Missing Maple Syrup Sap Mystery; or, How Maple Syrup is Made. New York, Frederick Warne, 1979.
The Magnificent Morris Mouse Clubhouse. New York, F. Watts 1981.

*

Illustrator: *Rounds about Rounds* by Jane Yolen, 1977; *Goo Junk* by Judith Enderle, 1979; *Hot & Cold,* 1979, *My Balloor* 1979, *Pete, the Wet Pet,* 1979, *The Mouse at the Show,* 1980, a by Catherine Chase; *Cars and How They Go* by Joanna Cole, 1983; *Baby in the Box* by Frank Asch, 1989.

Critical Studies: *Children's Literature Review,* Vol. 8, Detroit, Gale Research, 1985, 88-99; entry in *Something about the Author,* Vol. 72, Detroit, Gale Research, 1993, 76-80.

* * *

As a child, Gail Gibbons had an insatiable curiosity about the world around her, and frequently approached adults with many "why" questions. At the same time, she began her interest in creating books when at the age of four she created her first wordless picture book—four pages attached with yarn. Realizing her artistic potential through her early love of drawing and painting, her family encouraged her endeavors which eventually led to her receiving a degree from the University of Illinois in graphic design. Her talents were immediately put to work in a position with a CBS affiliate in Chicago. When she moved to New York City she worked on a children's show entitled "Take a Giant Step," a forerunner to PBS's successful program "The Electric Company." It was here that Gibbons was encouraged to return to her love of writing, prompted by children on the show who asked if she had ever written a children's book.

Gibbon's artistic beginnings were not the only aspect of her childhood to be nurtured and fulfilled as time passed. Her curiosity became more intent as she not only continued asking questions but began researching and travelling to find answers, then sharing these answers with children of all ages. A diversity of topics characterizes Gibbons informational books as she explores both the natural world and those aspects designed by man. Lighthouses, rainforests, spiders, skyscrapers, cowboys, puffins, dinosaurs, the post office, and photography are the subjects of but a few of her many inquiries. Her explorations within books of the "inner workings" of places, things, animals, and events are noted for their accuracy. Her love of the outdoor natural world is quite evident, as is the fun that she has in exploring the world around her. Gibbon's topics include both those that require travel to research and those that reflect the immediate world around her, such as whales, puffins, lighthouses, and *Christmas on an Island,* all describing her part-time home on an island off the coast of Maine.

While Gibbons' earlier books used fiction as a vehicle to provide information to readers, such as in her first book, *Willy and His Wagon Wheel,* or *The Missing Maple Syrup Sap Mystery,* informational nonfiction emerged as the genre most suited for the complexity of topics and her precise illustrative style. Brightly colored illustrations, often with labels, diagrams, and charts, add technical information and provide entertaining and understandable explanations of what could be difficult topics for young readers. These explanations, though, are never condescending. Both art and text support the new insights by providing numerous examples of an animal or object of focus, different perspectives on a topic, understanding of its historical significance or environmental importance, and detailed behind-the-scenes happenings, as in *Zoo* or *Department Store.* The judges of the prestigious *Washington Post* Children's Book Guild Award said in 1987 that "The enormous breadth of subjects that Gail Gibbons has brought to life is astonishing.... Her books are free-flowing fountains of information." Since then she has extended both the breadth of topics and the depth of perspectives while retaining readability for young readers.

The comprehensiveness of Gibbons's creations is evident in such titles as *Yippee-Yay!: A Book about Cowboys and Cowgirls.* This book provides historical perspectives on cowboys and cowgirls, as well as information on clothing, equipment, lifestyle, and the daily language that describes this way of life. The round-up and trail drive are described in detail with information on branding, the most famous cow trails, strategies and particular jobs during the drive, and potential dangers. In a more contemporary light, rodeos and modern ranching are described. A concluding annotation profiling famous cowboys and cowgirls and a glossary of interesting facts extend thinking on this topic.

Gulls ... Gulls ... Gulls... and *The Bald Eagle* describe the significance of each species of bird to our environment and exemplify Gibbons' attention to the details of nature. Fascinating facts about nesting, hatching, hunting, communication, and lifestyle are found in each book as she seeks to distinguish each species. *The Bald Eagle* additionally addresses the significance of this bird as the emblem of the United States and its danger of extinction. *The Honey Makers,* which has been described as "humming with information, energy, and charm," as the two preceding books, shares amazing facts about the life of these natural inhabitants. She identifies three types of bees and their importance to ecology as well as for the honey they produce.

Marshes and Swamps gives insights into these wetlands which store water and provide homes for many endangered life forms. The different roles each of these wetlands play are comprehensively portrayed, while additional facts conclude the book. Gibbons provides lots of information to invite inquiry about a topic which is not often sufficiently considered in geography studies in school.

Whether the topic is kites or recycling or knights in shining armor, Gail Gibbons clearly and comprehensively introduces and explains topics that not only answer questions, but are the source for further inquiry and personal investigation for young readers. For adult readers, likewise, each book is a source of learning with the subtle, though unintended, reminder that much of what is enjoyed in life is taken for granted. Gibbons has provided grand explanations through text and art of very basic concepts and systems for all ages. She is, as one critic described her, a "master of picture-book nonfiction."

—Janelle B. Mathis

GIBBS, (Cecilia) May

Nationality: Australian. **Born:** Surrey, England, 1877; emigrated to Australia, 1881. **Education:** Church of England Girls' School, Perth, Cope and Nichol School, Chelsea Polytechnic, and Henry Blackburn School of Black and White Art, London. **Family:** Married B.J. Ossoli Kelly in 1913. **Career:** M.B.E. (Member, Order of the British Empire). **Died:** 27 November 1969.

PUBLICATIONS FOR CHILDREN (ILLUSTRATED BY THE AUTHOR)

Fiction

About Us. London, Nister, and New York, Dutton, 1912.
Gum Blossom Babies. Sydney, Angus and Robertson, 1916.

Gumnut Babies. Sydney, Angus and Robertson, 1916.
Boronia Babies. Sydney, Angus and Robertson, 1917.
Flannel Flowers and Other Bush Babies. Sydney, Angus and Robertson, 1917.
Wattle Babies. Sydney, Angus and Robertson, 1918.
Snugglepot and Cuddlepie: Their Adventures Wonderful. Sydney, Angus and Robertson, 1918.
Little Ragged Blossom, and More about Snugglepot and Cuddlepie. Sydney, Angus and Robertson, 1920.
Little Obelia, and Further Adventures of Ragged Blossom, Snugglepot and Cuddlepie. Sydney, Angus and Robertson, 1921.
Nuttybub and Nittersing. Melbourne, Osboldstone, 1923.
Chucklebud and Wunkydoo. Melbourne, Osboldstone, 1924; as *Two Little Gumnuts,* Sydney, Cornstalk, 1929.
Scotty in Gumnut Land. Sydney, Angus and Robertson, 1941; London, Angus and Robertson, 1956.
Mr. and Mrs. Bear and Friends. Sydney, Angus and Robertson, 1943; London, Angus and Robertson, 1957.
Prince Dande Lion: A Garden Whim-Wham. Sydney, Ure Smith, 1953; London, Angus and Robertson, 1954.
The May Gibbs Collection: Gumnut Classics, edited by Maureen Walsh. Sydney, Angus and Robertson, 1985.

Poetry

Bib and Bub: Their Adventures. Sydney, Cornstalk, 2 vols., 1925.
The Further Adventures of Bib and Bub. Sydney, Cornstalk, 1927.
More Funny Stories about Old Friends Bib and Bub. Sydney, Cornstalk, 1928.
Bib and Bub in Gumnut Town. Waterloo, New South Wales, Halstead, 1929.
Bib and Bub Painting Book: New Stories. Sydney, Penfold, n.d.
Gumnuts. Sydney, Angus and Robertson, 1940.

Other

Alphabet Frieze. Sydney, Angus and Robertson, 1984.

*

Manuscript Collections: Mitchell Library, Sydney.

Critical Studies: *May Gibbs and Her Fantasy World* (exhibition catalogue) by Robert Holden, Sydney, Royal Botanic Gardens, 1985; *The May Gibbs Collection: Mother of the Gumnuts, Her Life and Work* by Maureen Walsh, Sydney, Angus and Robertson, 1985.

Illustrator: *Barons and Kings (1215-1485)* by Estelle Ross, 1912; *Scribbling Sue and Other Stories* by Amy Eleanor Mack, 1913; *Gem of the Flat* by Constance Mackness, 1914; *A Little Bush Poppy* by Edith Graham, 1915.

* * *

May Gibbs gave Australian children a sense of identity with their own land. She told them amusing stories about the wild creatures of the "bush," and of appealing "buds" and "blossoms"—imaginary figures evoked from the unique Australian flora. Like Beatrix Potter, she was a talented artist before she turned to writing. Having dwelt in her childhood amid the enchantingly beautiful West Australian bushland, she spent most of her life recreating its charm for children. She was an excellent draftswoman, and meticulous in her attention to detail. After producing calendars, post-cards, and the like during World War I, she wrote and illustrated some exquisite little booklets, beginning with *Gum Blossom Babies* in 1916. Their success encouraged her to create her best-known book, *Snugglepot and Cuddlepie,* which became a favourite, especially when it was later combined with two subsequent books to form *The Complete Adventures of Snugglepot and Cuddlepie.*

She also began to produce a comic strip, with the two main characters, Bib and Bub, closely resembling the gum-nuts in her stories. Each strip told a simple story in doggerel, but they were loved by children, and appeared weekly in Australian newspapers from 1925 for over 40 years, so that most Australians of different generations shared one childhood experience. Her humour and invention were always entertaining, though the strips in later years were sometimes reprinted. She was not fortunate in the production of her books, though the first editions of the earlier ones were well-produced with a generous number of illustrations. Later production was of a crude quality on poor paper with blurred or faint illustrations. Some of her stories were rewritten and illustrations redrawn with the addition of garish colour. However, recent years have seen more sensitive reproductions of her work in response to widely attended exhibitions of her original drawings. A beautifully produced two-volume set, comprising a compendium volume of her main books together with a biography illustrated with many hitherto unpublished drawings and watercolours was published in 1985. This reflects her wider recognition as one of Australia's finest authors and illustrators for children. The charm, gentleness, and fun of her stories and illustrations and their originality is appreciated as never before. A nationwide campaign is at present afoot to preserve her Sydney harbourside home, "Nutcote," as part of the nation's heritage.

—Marcie Muir

GILBERT, Manu. See **WEST, Joyce (Tarlton).**

GILMAN, Phoebe

Nationality: Canadian/American. **Born:** New York, 4 April 1940. **Education:** Hunter College, New York, and Art Students League, New York, 1957-59; Bezalel Academy, Jerusalem, 1968. **Family:** Married 1) Mani Deligtisch (divorced); 2) Brian Bender, two daughters, one son. **Career:** Freelance artist, writer, and illustrator, from 1968; fine arts instructor, Ontario College of Arts, 1975-1990. **Awards:** Vicky Metcalfe Award, 1993, for her body of work; Ruth Schwartz Children's Book Award and Sydney Taylor Award, 1993, for *Something From Nothing.* **Address:** c/o Scholastic Canada Ltd., 123 Newkirk Rd., Richmond Hill, Ontario L4C 3G5, Canada.

Publications for Children (illustrated by the author)

The Balloon Tree. Richmond Hill, Scholastic Canada, 1984; as *L'arbre aux balloons,* Richmond Hill, Scholastic-TAB, 1985.
Jillian Jiggs. Richmond Hill, Scholastic Canada, 1985; as *Lili Tire-bouchon,* Richmond Hill, Scholastic-TAB, 1985.
Little Blue Ben. Richmond Hill, Scholastic Canada, 1986.
The Wonderful Pigs of Jillian Jiggs. Richmond Hill, Scholastic Canada, 1988; as *Les beau cochons de Lili Tire-bouchon,* translated by Christiane Duchesne, Richmond Hill, Scholastic-TAB, 1988.
Grandma and the Pirates. Richmond Hill, Scholastic Canada, 1990; as *Grand-mere et les pirates,* translated by Christiane Duchesne, Toronto, Scholastic, 1990.
Something from Nothing. Richmond Hill, Scholastic Canada, 1992; as *Un merveilleux petit rien!,* translated by Marie-Andree Clermont, Richmond Hill, Scholastic Canada, 1992.
Jillian Jiggs to the Rescue. Richmond Hill, Scholastic Canada, 1994.
The Gypsy Princess. Richmond Hill, Scholastic Canada, 1995; as *La princesse gitane,* translated by Christiane Duchesne, Richmond Hill, Scholastic Canada, 1995.
Pirate Pearl. Richmond Hill, Scholastic Canada, 1998.

*

Phoebe Gilman comments:

I've come to accept that stories develop a life and a will of their own. Even a story like *Something from Nothing,* which I adapted from an old Jewish folktale, *The Tailor,* changed as the characters created themselves in my hands. I had meant to parallel the original tale, but as soon as I decided to turn the tailor into a Grandpa, *he* wanted to make everything for his grandson.

My book *Jillian Jiggs,* was originally going to be a simple riff on the Mother Goose rhyme, *Gregory Griggs,* who wore twenty-seven different wigs. I thought he would turn everything in the house into a wig and I sketched him wearing a mop as a wig. Well, *he* looked more like a *she* in the sketch, which set me thinking ... maybe I'll make him a girl. the only three syllable girl's name I could come up with was Gillian. Gillian Griggs didn't have the right bounce so I dropped the 'r' in Griggs and it became Giggs. Gillian Giggs was born! She took over immediately ... didn't want to be restricted to just wigs and didn't want her name spelled with G's.

I think that's what I like the most about my chosen profession ... its un-predictableness. I never know who's going to pop up next when I set pen to paper, or to be more precise, fingers to computer keyboard. One thing I do know though. I am in complete agreement with a seven year old boy name Adam who once sent me a letter saying, "When I grow up I want to be an illustrator because I like making people happy." Me too, Adam. Me too.

* * *

As a child, Phoebe Gilman demanded that the illustrations in the books she read be accurate in relation to the written texts, creative in expanding the stories' meanings, and challenging to viewers, inviting them to interact with pictures to create further meanings. Many years later, as she began writing and illustrating her own books, Gilman made the same demands on herself—and met them. Words and pictures interrelate to present narratives about imaginative creative characters and their interactions.

Gilman's first two books, *The Balloon Tree* and *Little Blue Ben,* introduce the themes of creativity and freedom. In the former, a princess devises a clever scheme to escape from her evil, power-hungry uncle; in the latter, two brothers work out a plan to escape from their mother's constant diet of eggs. Princess Leora remembers her father's telling her that, in case of trouble, she should release a balloon into the sky to call for help. Finding a balloon and releasing it requires courage and creativity, as well as cooperation with others. Although the details of the pictures suggest some meanings not found in the words, human figures are so small that facial expressions that could reveal character and emotion are difficult to see. Little Blue Ben, a tiny man who lives with his brother, Blue Cat, suggests a game of hide-and-seek with the loser eating the other's eggs. Gilman effectively employs doublespreads to reflect the enjoyment the two experience as they leave the confining house. Gilman's invitation to readers to spot the hiding Ben prefigures her implicit invitation to notice significant details in her later, more complex works.

Grandma and the Pirates parodies conventional adventure stories as an old woman and girl create an ingenious, daring plan for escaping their captors. Gilman uses facial expressions to generate much of the book's humor: the pirates, who try to look fierce, appear foolish; the heroines assume increasingly more resolute and sly expressions. The different materials forming the borders of the pictures reinforce the action. For example, knotted ropes surround the illustration in which the grandmother is captured, while fish traps border the scene in which the girl and woman are confined on the ship.

Jillian Jiggs and its two sequels celebrate a modern child's love of exuberant, almost wild play. With her friends, the heroine creates toys and other objects from materials around her house, makes constant messes, and annoys her mother. As Jillian's creative enthusiasm grows, more small objects appear in the pictures and spill beyond the borders of each illustration.

In *Something from Nothing* and *The Gypsy Princess,* Gilman uses her art most fully to expand on themes, conflicts, and characterization. Drawing on an eastern European Jewish folktale, Gilman, in the former book, presents the relationship between Joseph and his grandfather, who makes the boy a baby blanket and then, as the child grows and the cloth wears out, creates increasingly smaller articles from it. When the cloth is finally gone, the boy uses his memories of it to create a story for his family and classmates—something from nothing. The written narrative celebrates the ingenuity of the old man and his grandson. The illustrations celebrate community and interrelationship: among members of the family, between the family and the larger community, and within a family of mice who live beneath the floorboards on scraps, including cloth, that come from the human family above them. Each doublespread depicts the three groups, their separate activities, and the relationships among them.

The Gypsy Princess is a variation on a well-known story pattern: a young person, dissatisfied with life at home, moves to a new, desired place only to discover that it is not what she expects, and returns home wiser and more content. Cinnamon, in spite of her grandmother's warnings, leaves her gypsy community and beloved pet bear to live in the palace. However, after being ignored and slighted by the princess, she escapes from her new home and returns to the forest. Just before entering the camp, she looks at her reflection in a pond, declares "I am who I am," and plunges into the water, where she washes away all traces of palace life.

Each doublespread for *The Gypsy Princess* contains three closely related illustrations: on the left, a small framed picture above the written text and, surrounding it, a full-paged picture; on the right, a full-paged picture framed with a formal border. Early in the story, the girl's dream of dancing with a prince appears in the small picture; surrounding the text are images from tales told by her grandmother; on the facing picture, the grandmother, girl, and pet bear are grouped together as if in a portrait. However, when the girl is at the palace, the bear stands alone in the wood, she is being fitted for a fancy but confining dress, and, in the facing picture, she sits alone and sad in the formal palace garden.

Phoebe Gilman's works contain fairly conventional plots, themes, and conflicts—the triumph of the underdog over oppressors, the escape from confinement to freedom, the joy of play, and the contrast between reality and what is imagined. Gilman's originality comes from the new twists she gives to familiar patterns. Balloons become magical objects; a tiny man and a cat are brothers who resist a hen's food; a girl's bedroom and backyard are the locales for wondrous activity; a grandmother who cooks noodle-pudding outwits ferocious buccaneers; and a lonely girl's best friend is not another girl but a dancing bear. Through her illustrations, Gilman infuses her plots with exuberance, joy, and a sense of freedom, inviting her audiences to interact creatively with text and pictures so that they may experience the stories more fully.

—Jon C. Stott

GIOVANNI, Nikki (Yolande Cornelia Giovanni)

Nationality: American. **Born:** Nashville, Tennessee, 7 June 1943. **Education:** Fisk University, Nashville, Tennessee, 1960-61, 1964-67, B.A. (honors) in history, 1967; University of Pennsylvania Social Work School, Philadelphia; Columbia University School of the Arts, New York. **Family:** One son. **Career:** Poet, writer, lecturer. Assistant Professor of Black Studies, Queens College of the City University of New York, Flushing, 1968; Associate Professor of English, Rutgers University, Livingston College, New Brunswick, New Jersey, 1968-72; visiting Professor of English at Ohio State University, 1984; Professor of Creative Writing at Mount St. Joseph on the Ohio, 1985; Professor, Virginia Polytechnic Institute and State University, 1987—; Director, Warm Hearth Writer's Workshop, 1988—. Editorial Consultant, *Encore* magazine and *Encore American and Worldwide News,* Albuquerque, New Mexico; founder of publishing firm, Niktom Ltd., 1970; co-chair of Literary Arts Festival for State of Tennessee Homecoming, 1986; author of columns "One Woman's Voice," for Anderson-Moberg Syndicate of the *New York Times,* and "The Root of the Matter," in *Encore American and Worldwide News.* **Awards:** Ford Foundation grant, 1967; National Endowment for the Arts grant, 1968; Harlem Cultural Council grant, 1969; named one of ten most admired black women by the *Amsterdam News,* 1969; *Mademoiselle* award for outstanding achievement, 1971; Omega Psi Phi Fraternity award for outstanding contribution to arts and letters, 1971; Meritorious Plaque for Service, Cook County Jail, 1971; Prince Matchabelli Sun Shower award, 1971; life membership and scroll, National Council of Negro Women, 1972; National Association of Radio and Television Announcers award for best spoken word album, for *Truth Is on Its Way,* 1972; Woman of the Year Youth Leadership award, *Ladies' Home Journal,* 1972; National Book award nomination for *Gemini,* 1973; American Library Association commendation for *My House,* 1973; Cincinnati Chapter YWCA Woman of the Year, 1983; elected to Ohio Women's Hall of Fame, 1985; named Outstanding Woman of Tennessee, 1985; Post-Corbett Award, 1986; Ohioana Book Award, 1988; Woman of the Year, NAACP (Lynchburg chapter), 1989; Jeanine Rae Award for the Advancement of Women's Culture, 1995; Langston Hughes Award, 1996; awarded keys to numerous cities, including Lincoln Heights, Ohio, Dallas, Texas, and Gary, Indiana, all 1972, New York City, 1975, Buffalo, New York, and Cincinnati, Ohio, both 1979, Savannah, Georgia, and Clarksdale, Mississippi, both 1981, Miami, Florida, 1982, New Orleans, Louisiana, Monroe, Louisiana, Fort Lauderdale, Florida, and Los Angeles, California, all 1984; Honorary Doctorates: Wilberforce University, 1972, University of Maryland, Princess Anne Campus, 1974, Ripon University, 1974, Smith College, 1975, and Mount St. Joseph on the Ohio, 1983, Fisk University, 1988, Indiana University, 1991, Otterbein College, 1992, Widener University, 1993, Albright College, 1995, Cabrini College, 1995, and Allegheny College, 1997. **Address:** Department of English, Virginia Polytechnic Institute and State University, P.O. Box 0112, Blacksburg, Virginia 24063-0112, U.S.A.

Publications for Children

Poetry

Spin a Soft Black Song: Poems for Children, illustrated by Charles Bible. New York, Hill & Wang, 1971; reprinted with illustrations by George Martin, Westport, Connecticut, Lawrence Hill, 1985; revised edition, New York, Farrar, Straus, 1987.

Ego-Tripping and Other Poems for Young People, illustrated by George Ford. Westport, Connecticut, Lawrence Hill, 1973.

Vacation Time: Poems for Children, illustrated by Marisabina Russo. New York, Morrow, 1980.

Knoxville, Tennessee, illustrated by Larry Johnson. New York, Scholastic, 1994.

The Genie in the Jar, illustrated by Chris Raschka. New York, Holt, 1996.

The Sun is So Quiet, illustrated by Ashley Bryan. New York, Holt, 1996.

Publications for Young Adults

Poetry

Black Feeling, Black Talk. Detroit, Broadside Press, 1968.

Black Judgement. Detroit, Broadside Press, 1968.

Black Feeling, Black Talk/Black Judgement. New York, Morrow, 197[illegible]

Poem of Angela Yvonne Davis. New York, Afro Arts, 1970.

Re:Creation. Detroit, Broadside Press, 1970.

My House, with foreword by Ida Lewis. New York, Morrow, 197[illegible]

The Women and the Men. New York, Morrow, 1975.

Cotton Candy on a Rainy Day, with introduction by Pau[illegible] Giddings. New York, Morrow, 1978.

Those Who Ride the Night Winds. New York, Morrow, 1983.
Sacred Cows ... and Other Edibles. New York, Morrow, 1988.
The Selected Poems of Nikki Giovanni. New York, Morrow, 1996.
Love Poems. New York, Morrow, 1997.

Other

Racism 101. New York, Holt, 1994.

Editor, *Grandmothers: Poems, Reminiscences, and Short Stories about the Keepers of Our Traditions.* New York, Holt, 1994.
Editor, *Shimmy, Shimmy, Shimmy Like My Sister Kate: Looking at the Harlem Renaissance through Poems.* New York, Henry Holt, 1996.

Recordings: *Truth Is on Its Way,* Right-On Records, 1971; *Like A Ripple on a Pond,* Niktom, 1973; *The Way I Feel,* Atlantic Records, 1974; *Legacies: The Poetry of Nikki Giovanni,* Folkways Records, 1976; *The Reason I Like Chocolate,* Folkways Records, 1976; *Cotton Candy on a Rainy Day,* Folkways Records, 1978.

PUBLICATIONS FOR ADULTS

Nonfiction

Gemini: An Extended Autobiographical Statement on My First Twenty-five Years of Being a Black Poet. Indianapolis, Bobbs-Merrill, 1971.
A Dialogue: James Baldwin and Nikki Giovanni, with James Baldwin. Philadelphia, Lippincott, 1973; London, Joseph, 1975.
A Poetic Equation: Conversations Between Nikki Giovanni and Margaret Walker, with Margaret Walker. Washington, D.C., Howard University Press, 1974.

Other

Author of foreword, *The Abandoned Baobob: The Autobiography of a Woman,* Chicago, Chicago Review Press, 1991.

Editor, *Night Comes Softly: An Anthology of Black Female Voices.* Newark, New Jersey, Medic Press, 1970.
Editor, *Appalachian Elders: A Warm Hearth Sampler.* Blacksburg, Virginia, Pocahontas Press, 1991.

*

Media Adaptations: *Spirit to Spirit: The Poetry of Nikki Giovanni* (television film, featuring the poet reading from her published works), Public Broadcasting Corporation, 1986.

Manuscript Collections: Mugar Memorial Library, Boston University, Massachusetts.

Biographies: Entry in *Authors in the News,* Volume 1, Detroit, Gale, 1976; *Dictionary of Literary Biography,* Detroit, Gale, Volume 5: *American Poets since World War II,* 1980, Volume 41: *Afro-American Poets since 1955,* 1985.

Critical Studies: *Dynamite Voices I: Black Poets of the 1960s* by Don L. Lee, Broadside Press, 1971; *Modern Black Poets: A Collection of Critical Essays* edited by Donald B. Gibson, Prentice-Hall, 1973; *Understanding the New Black Poetry: Black Speech and Black Music as Poetic References* by Stephen Henderson, Morrow, 1973; entry in *Contemporary Literary Criticism,* Detroit, Gale, Volume 2, 1974, Volume 4, 1975, Volume 19, 1981, Volume 64, 1991; *Beautiful, Also, Are the Souls of My Black Sisters: A History of the Black Woman in America* by Jeanne Noble, Prentice-Hall, 1978; *Black Women Writers at Work* by Claudia Tate, Crossroad Publishing, 1983; entry in *Children's Literature Review,* Volume 6, Detroit, Gale, 1984; *Black Women Writers, 1950-1980: A Critical Evaluation* edited by Mari Evans, Doubleday, 1984; *Black Literature Criticism,* Detroit, Gale, 1992; *Nikki Giovanni* by Virginia Fowler, Boston, Twayne, 1992; *Conversations with Nikki Giovanni* by Virginia Fowler, Jackson, University Press of Mississippi, 1992.

* * *

Nikki Giovanni, known as one of the angry poets of the black revolution of the 1960s, also wrote three volumes of sensitive and passionate poetry for young people, and individual poems from her poetry books are often anthologized in other collections. The first edition of *Spin a Soft Black Song,* published in 1971, appears to be, in format and style of illustration, for younger children than the 1985 revised edition. The voices and points of view of African-American youngsters, however, remain with all their poignancy, joy, pain, boisterousness, and quiet reflection. Although the majority of the poems are about home, family, and everyday life; there is a political undertone that cries out for young African-Americans to "dance to our own song / we must spin to our own word / we must spin a soft Black song."

Most of the poems in *Ego-Tripping and Other Poems for Young People* were published earlier and selected for their relevance for young people. The title poem is a celebration of the mythic powers of black women and has often been compared to male counterparts such as Langston Hughes's "The Negro Speaks of Rivers" or Walt Whitman's "Song of Myself." The overall voice of the poems in this collection is bold and proud, angry and revolutionary, as was much of the poet's early work. *Vacation Time,* on the other hand, is a much more relaxed and joyous collection which portrays the world of children as full of wonder and delight. Although the immediacy of her poetry and the references to contemporary people and events date some of her early work, a sense of African-American history and of universal human concerns remains for today's readers. Both as a radical social reformer and as a celebrant of the everyday life of African-American youth, Giovanni uses vernacular language to speak directly to young people of all races. Her message to them from "poem for black boys (with special love to james)," written in 1967, is as true today as it was then. "And you will understand all too soon / That you, my children of battle, are your heroes / You must invent your own games and teach us old / ones how to play."

Grand Mothers: Poems, Reminiscences, and Short Stories About the Keepers of Our Tradition begins with Giovanni's memories of her own grandmother and ends with her mother's essay about her grandmother, representing four generations of Watson/Giovanni women. This continuity of caring women within a family is a thread that runs through Giovanni's own writing, so this edited collection is a natural extension of her work.

"Knoxville, Tennessee," one of the poems from *Black Feeling, Black Talk, Black Judgment,* was made into an enchanting picture book, a celebration of summer at home in the mountains with a grandmother and a very loving family. It celebrates together, eating freshly picked vegetables from the garden, enjoying the warmth of the season and the companionship of those who care about you.

—Kay E. Vandergrift, updated by Mary Lystad

GLEESON, Libby

Nationality: Australian. **Born:** Young, New South Wales, September 19, 1950. **Education:** University of Sydney, Sydney, Australia, B.A., 1973. **Family:** Married Euen Tovey; three children. **Career:** Held a number of instructorships at various secondary schools and universities, 1974-1986. Employed as a consultant for teachers of English as a Second Language, 1986-1990. **Awards:** Angus & Robertson Award for Writers For Young Readers, 1984; South Australia's Premier's Award, 1985; Guardian Newspaper's Award for Children, 1988; Children's Literature Peace Prize, 1991; International Board on Books for Young People, 1992; Children's Book Council of Australia Picture Book of the Year honor, 1993; Children's Book Council of Australia Children's Book of the Year award, 1997. **Address:** 11 Oxford Street, Petersham, NSW 2049, Australia.

Publications for Children

Fiction

Eleanor, Elizabeth. Ringwood, Victoria, Penguin, 1984.
I Am Susannah. Ringwood, Victoria, Penguin, 1986.
One Sunday. Pymble, New South Wales, HarperCollins, 1988.
Dodger. Ringwood, Victoria, Penguin, 1990.
Big Dog. Lisarow, New South Wales, Ashton Scholastic, 1991.
Uncle David. Lisarow, New South Wales, Ashton Scholastic, 1992.
Mum Goes to Work. Lisarow, New South Wales, Ashton Scholastic, 1992.
Where's Mum? Lisarow, New South Wales, Ashton Scholastic, 1992.
Hurry Up! illustrated by Mitch Vane. Santa Rosa, CA: SRA School Group, 1992.
Sleep Time. Lisarow, New South Wales, Ashton Scholastic, 1993.
Love Me, Love Me Not (short stories), Lisarow, New South Wales, Ashton Scholastic, 1993.
Sleeptime, Gosford, New South Wales, Ashton Scholastic, 1993.
Walking to School, illustrated by Linda McClelland. Santa Rosa, California, SRA School Group, 1994.
Skating on Sand, illustrated by Ann James. Ringwood, Victoria, Viking, 1994.
The Princess and the Perfect Dish, illustrated by Armin Greder. Sydney, Scholastic, 1995.
Hannah Plus One, illustrated by Anne James. Ringwood, Victoria, Puffin, 1996.
Queen of the Universe, illustrated by David Cox. Norwood, New South Wales, Omnibus Books, 1997.

*

Bibliography: "Typical Turbulence: Writing and Raising a Family" by Karen Jameyson, in *The Horn Book,* March/April 1997, 225-227.

* * *

The contribution of Libby Gleeson to Australian children's literature has been manifold: through picture books, short stories, and fiction for both children and young adults. The common thread in all her writing is an astute and penetrating understanding of family relationships and peer group interaction. Although many of her characters could well fit the category of the boy or girl "next door," Gleeson is socially aware without ever becoming strident. Her females—and these predominate—are invariably independent thinkers and "doers." Few writers equal her ability to record the overt behaviour of contemporary young people even as she slides beneath the skin to expose what they are really thinking and feeling—or to make such revelation the stuff of story. In doing so, Gleeson's prose is always straightforward, unadorned, and never showy, yet is never impoverished. She uses teenage idiom and the vernacular with sufficient restraint to make her dialogue ring true; and her colloquialisms are carefully controlled.

Gleeson's picture book texts make for entertaining yet involving storytime reading for parent and child. In *Sleep Time,* a small child's resistance to sleep—"'But it's not dark,' says the girl"—takes the form of mental play, almost day-dreaming. She counts the stars on her ceiling, begs her toys to sleep for her; until she squeezes her teddy tightly and together they fall asleep. *Mum Goes to Work* and *Where's Mum?* have been carefully planned so that text and illustration work together. *Mum Goes to Work* presents a variety of women from diverse cultures and classes involved in their daily work while their children are engaged in creative play related to those occupations. *Where's Mum?* features lateral thinking made into creative play, a game, a challenge, in that when Mum fails to turn up on time it could just be that "she was walking home when she saw Humpty Dumpty have a great fall". And the game continues until Mum arrives with a gaggle of nursery and storybook characters in tow.

In each story, Gleeson, draws out the humour, drama, and full meaning of everyday incidents, and uses the mundane as a door to the imagination. Gleeson is also interested in portraying young children who develop coping devices to deal with changes in their environment. In *Hannah Plus One,* seven year-old Hannah, the youngest child in her family, learns to work through her fear of sharing her mother with a newborn baby. In *Big Dog* (released in the United States as *The Great Big Scary Dog*), a young boy and his sister are afraid to walk past a barking dog that lives next door to their house. Everyone has an opinion on how the children can stop the dog from barking: "Dad says to ignore it. Mom says to look the dog in the eye and keep on walking. [The parents' friend Cindy] says to walk on the other side of the road." However, the children decide to confront their fears directly by dressing up in their friend Diep's New Year's dragon costume to scare the dog themselves. To their surprise, the dog is not only unafraid of their dragon costume, he rolls over on his back and allows the children to pet him. In this way, Gleeson encourages her young readers to create unique, forthright solutions to their problems.

In addition to portraying the inner world of young children Gleeson also does battle with societal forces that she feels ar harmful to teenagers' self-esteem. As Karen Jameyson notes in a *Horn Book* article, Gleeson is particularly worried "about what can happen to girls in a society so filled with the slim super-model imagery of girls' magazines." In *The Princess and the Perfect Dish,* Gleeson addresses this issue by creating a princess who loves to eat, is proud of her body image, and still manages to live happily ever after.

For her intermediate readers, Libby Gleeson emphasizes the inner worlds of her characters; it is this quality that made both *Eleanor, Elizabeth* and *I Am Susannah* honour books in the Australian awards for 1985 and 1988. Both books explore the themes of friendship lost, disruptions to the even tenor of life, the influence of the past upon the present, and the continuity of human experience. Both focus upon strong but sensitive girls working to establish their identity. The first has a rural setting and revolves around a family group; the second has an inner-city setting and revolves around a single mother and her daughter. Both open up the inner life and depths of the protagonist through direct narration, dialogue, and a judicious use of thought stream. Eleanor's discovery of her grandmother's diary helps her come to terms with her new environment and provides her with the means of establishing her self-esteem. Susie's relationship with the mysterious Blue Lady, who now lives in the house once occupied by her best friend, helps Susie come to terms with her parents' separation and her own uncertainties.

Gleeson's young adult novel, *Dodger,* is more experimental—almost post-modernist. It opens with a first-person sensory exploration: "Cool dark place. Cement floor. Under the washtubs. Loud voices..." Passages of mental monologue follow and then a more conventional narrative broken up by letters, reports, notices, jottings, memory flashes and stream-of-consciousness. Here the protagonist is a teenage boy, an outsider grieving for his dead mother and absentee father. Mick's pain and vulnerability are sensed by a sympathetic teacher, and his rehabilitation begins when Penny involves him in a production of the musical *Oliver.* A deeper psychological stream flows through the book: the nature of obsession and guilt and what causes teachers to become sadistic bullies. More subtle is the careful peeling away of the masks young people wear to conceal their uncertainties. This is the process at work in Gleeson's short stories, especially those collected in *Love Me, Love Me Not.* Here the shifting nature of teenage relationships is made overt in nine interconnected stories set in a Sydney high school. As in all her work, Gleeson provides space for the reader to ponder, to make connections, and to grow a little in self-understanding.

—Maurice Saxby, updated by Gwen A. Tarbox.

GLEITZMAN, Morris

Nationality: British. **Born:** Sleaford, Lincolnshire, 1953; emigrated with family to Australia in 1969. **Education:** Attended school in London; Canberra College of Advanced Education, degree in Professional Writing. **Family:** Married; two children. **Career:** Screenwriter, journalist. **Awards:** Children's Book Council of Australia Honour Book Award, 1992. **Address:** c/o Macmillan, 25 Eccleston Place, London SW1W 9NF, England.

Publications for Children

The Other Facts of Life. Australia, McPhee Gribble, 1985; London, Puffin, 1994.
Second Childhood. Australia, Penguin, 1990; London, Puffin, 1995.
Two Weeks with the Queen. London, Pan, 1990.
Misery Guts. London, Blackie, 1991.
Worry Warts. London, Blackie, 1992.
Blabber Mouth. London, Macmillan, 1994.
Puppy Fat. London, Macmillan, 1995.
Sticky Beak. London, Macmillan, 1995.
Belly Flop. Australia, Macmillan, 1996; London, Macmillan, 1996.
Water Wings. Australia, Macmillan, 1996; London, Macmillan 1997.
With Paul Jennings, *Wicked.* London, Puffin, 1998.

Other

Two Weeks with the Queen, edited by Mary Morris. London, Pan, 1994.

* * *

Although Morris Gleitzman was born and brought up in England, his writing style and subject matter are very far from English. He takes on difficult subjects and confronts them head on, with inexhaustible humour. Despite his sometimes side-splitting humour he manages to deal with raw emotion without getting mawkish, or being insincere.

His first book, *The Other Facts of Life,* starts with the mother of a teenage boy worrying that they need to tell him about "the facts of life." Actually, he is worried about the starving millions in the world and how he and his family can possibly go on being well fed without doing anything. The book focuses on the intense and very real feelings that many adolescents have about being helpless in the context of so much world suffering. Seeing the whole from the perspective of the parents and how their son's behaviour is merely embarrassing to them gives another dimension to the situation. The fact that his father is a butcher, and his sister anorexic, only adds to the farcical possibilities. The family relationships are well observed and the different perspectives realistically portrayed.

The interaction between parents/adults and children is at the centre of all Gleitzman's books. He conveys the sense that parents and children seem to be opposing forces, while at the same time acknowledging that each wants to do their best for the other. Many of his child characters seem to take on roles that the adults should be fulfilling. They are trying to sort out their parents' problems, for example, but they do so from a childlike perspective. When the children get the slightly wrong end of the stick and then take matters into their own hands is when Gleitzman's humour is so strong.

The book that made Gleitzman's name in Britain was *Two Weeks with the Queen,* in which he tackles the portentous issues of cancer, AIDS, and ultimately death. A young boy's brother is dying of cancer and he is sent to stay with relatives in London. While there he decides that he will ask the Queen if one of her doctors could help his brother. In a hospital he meets a man whose partner is dying of AIDS and learns a little about how people come to terms with death. These are huge and immensely difficult subjects to encounter, particularly in children's books, but Gleitzman handles them in a touching and sensitive way. It is difficult to imagine how a book dealing with such issues could be so funny, but it is. The humour is derived from the way the boy so naively tries to go about getting help. The genuine trust and belief that the Queen of England's doctor will be able to do things ordinary people's doctors are unable to do evokes a deep emotional response in the reader.

In his next two books Gleitzman's natural aptitude for telling a slick story with a highly inventive plot shines through. *Misery Guts* is the first book in which Keith attempts to control his parents' lives. Keith is a child with a passion for painting things bright colours, but his idea to paint their fish-and-chip shop Tropical Mango does not cheer up his mum and dad, who remain permanently miserable. Keith decides they need to emigrate to Australia, but it takes a near disaster to make them do it. Underneath a series of hilarious and rather far-fetched episodes are serious issues of what actually makes people happy.

The saga continues in *Worry Warts.* Now in what should be paradise in Australia, Keith's parents are no happier. When he overhears them discussing splitting up he decides that lack of money is the root of their problem and sets off to make a fortune in the opal fields. Needless to say things go woefully wrong and his parents split up anyway. Gleitzman's characters are not afraid of raw emotion and Keith lets his show when he is trapped underground in a mining accident. Finally, having had time to think about the meaning of life, Keith accepts his parents' decision to return to England and live apart.

Puppy Fat is the third book about Keith. Now back in England, he continues to worry about his parents' chances of happiness on their own. Who is going to want to go out with anyone with a saggy tummy, wobbly bottom, and dodgy legs? He tries advertising them and when that doesn't work he resorts to painting again, hoping that a mural of what they could look like if they tried will motivate them to get into shape. Aunty Bev, the beautician, and his old friend Tracy arriving from Australia are his last hope. Amongst the humour are perceptive insights into the way that children are affected by their parents' problems.

Far from having run out of "big issues," in *Blabber Mouth* Gleitzman takes as his main character a girl who is mute and whose mother has died. Rowena Batt finds her father hugely embarrassing, especially when he sings. Her relationship with him is honestly portrayed, their mutual diffidence perfectly described. She needs to find a way of telling him not wear loud shirts and sing without hurting his feelings. Her embarrassment is complete when he asks her teacher for a date. *Blabber Mouth* is fundamentally about the difficulty people have communicating with the people they love the most, surely a universal problem.

The sequel, *Sticky Beak,* sees Rowena's father happily married to her teacher, who is expecting a baby. Rowena is as headstrong as ever, it seems, and her effort to reform a deranged cockatoo, convinced that all he needs is a little love and understanding, leads to disaster. She hasn't bargained for his extreme behaviour and outbursts of bad language, and things hit rock bottom when he destroys the new nursery. Once again the outrageous humour and sometimes rude language make this a hilarious book.

Belly Flop says much about people and the way they treat each other. The main character, Mitch Webber, is in trouble—he's being chased by two of the toughest kids in town. His grandmother has told him he has a guardian angel, so he decides to call him up to ask him to get him out of this hopeless situation. The novel is written in a series of hilarious one-way conversations with this guardian angel, Doug. The town is in the middle of the worst drought ever and Mitch's Dad is the much-hated Bank Liaison Officer, whose job it is to report on families who can't pay back their loans. Mitch decides to become a champion diver to help his family gain back the respect of the townsfolk and places all his trust in Doug as he steps onto the board. This novel is so fast moving that it hardly draws breath, but its sentiments are warm-hearted and its execution extremely amusing.

In *Water Wings* Gleitzman tackles death once more. Pearl is overjoyed when she discovers her mother's new boyfriend's mother: she now has a grandmother, of sorts. She prepares for a grey-haired old lady coming to stay, getting her a rocking chair and fluffy slippers. So it is quite a shock when she turns up looking like an ex-wrestler and chain smoking! She is in fact Mitch Webber's grandmother from *Belly Flop,* who turns out to be dying of cancer. This is one of Gleitzman's wisest books, exploring as it does the contemplation of euthanasia. True to form, however, although it is an intensely funny book in parts, it is overwhelmingly moving, without being nauseatingly sentimental. Gleitzman once again demonstrates his ability to get the perfect balance.

—Fiona Lafferty

GOBLE, Paul

Nationality: British/American. **Born:** Haslemere, Surrey, England, 27 September 1933. **Education:** Central School of Arts and Crafts, London, England, Central School of Arts and Crafts Diploma (with distinction) and National Design Diploma 1959. **Family:** Married 1) Dorothy Lee in 1960 (divorced 1978), one son and one daughter; 2) Janet A. Tiller in 1978, one son. **Military Service:** First Battalion the King's Shropshire Light Infantry, Great Britain. **Career:** Freelance industrial designer, 1960-68; senior lecturer at Ravensbourne College of Art and Design, London, England, 1968-77; author and illustrator, from 1969. Fellow, Royal Society of Arts (FRSA) and Society of Industrial Artists and Designers (FSIAD). **Awards:** Horn Book Honor List, 1969, for *Red Hawk's Account of Custer's Last Battle*; American Library Association Notable Book award, 1970, for *Red Hawk's Account of Custer's Last Battle,* 1977, for *The Sound of Flutes,* 1979, for *The Girl Who Loved Wild Horses,* and 1985, for *Buffalo Woman*; Art Books for Children Award, 1974, for *The Friendly Wolf,* and, 1979, for *The Girl Who Loved Wild Horses*; Caldecott Medal, 1979, for *The Girl Who Loved Wild Horses*; Aesop Award, 1992, for *Love Flute.* **Address:** Oak Tree Canyon, Black Hawk, South Dakota 57718, U.S.A.

Publications for Children (illustrated by the author)

With Dorothy Goble, *Red Hawk's Account of Custer's Last Battle.* New York, Pantheon, 1969.

With Dorothy Goble, *Brave Eagle's Account of the Fetterman Fight 21 December 1866.* New York, Macmillan, 1972; in England as *The Hundred in the Hands: Brave Eagle's Account of the Fetterman Fight, 21 December 1866.*

With Dorothy Goble, *Lone Bull's Horse Raid.* New York, Macmillan, 1973.

With Dorothy Goble, *The Friendly Wolf.* Scarsdale, New York, Bradbury, 1974; revised by Paul Goble as *Dream Wolf,* New York, Bradbury, 1990.

The Girl Who Loved Wild Horses. Scarsdale, New York, Bradbury, 1978.

The Gift of the Sacred Dog. Scarsdale, New York, Bradbury, 1980.

Star Boy. Scarsdale, New York, Bradbury, 1980.

Buffalo Woman. Scarsdale, New York, Bradbury, 1984.
The Great Race of the Birds and Animals. New York, Bradbury, 1985.
Death of the Iron Horse. New York, Bradbury, 1987.
Her Seven Brothers. New York, Bradbury, 1988.
Iktomi and the Boulder: A Plains Indian Story. New York, Orchard Books, 1988.
Beyond the Ridge. New York, Bradbury, 1989.
Iktomi and the Berries: A Plains Indian Story. New York, Orchard Books, 1989.
Iktomi and the Ducks: A Plains Indian Story. New York, Orchard Books, 1990.
I Sing for the Animals. New York, Bradbury, 1991.
Iktomi and the Buffalo Skull: A Plains Indian Story. New York, Orchard Books, 1991.
Crow Chief. New York, Orchard Books, 1992.
Love Flute. New York, Bradbury, 1992.
The Lost Children. New York, Bradbury, 1993.
Adopted by the Eagles. New York, Bradbury, 1994.
Iktomi and the Buzzard. New York, Orchard Books, 1994.
Remaking the Earth: A Creation Story from the Great Plains of North America. New York, Orchard Books, 1996.
The Return of the Buffaloes. Washington, National Geographic Society, 1996.
The Legend of the White Buffalo Woman. Washington, National Geographic Society, 1998.
Iktomi and the Coyote. New York, Orchard Books, 1998.

*

Media Adaptations: *Red Hawk's Account of Custer's Last Battle* (recording; read by Arthur S. Junaluska), Caedmon Records, 1972.

Illustrator: *The Sound of Flutes and Other Indian Legends,* edited by Richard Erdoes, 1976.

* * *

The texts of Paul Goble's picturebooks are relatively short and his illustrations expand on and deepen the pictures. Whether he is adapting Native myths and trickster tales from the northern plains, retelling historical events, or telling original stories based on traditional myths, he creates pictures that not only accurately depict settings, dwellings, clothing, and objects, but also embody Native symbolism necessary for the full expression of each narrative's thematic significance.

The Lakota (Sioux) phrase "mitakuye oyasin," or "we are all related," expresses a major belief of the Plains peoples and is embodied in many of Goble's books. In *Buffalo Woman,* a Lakota myth, and *The Girl Who Loved Wild Horses,* an original story, the relationship is literal; marriages between human beings and animals who were essential to Plains culture cement the bond of respect between the two species. In *Dream Wolf,* another original story, and *Adopted by the Eagles,* a Lakota myth, kindly animals help human beings. The myths *Her Seven Brothers* and *The Lost Children* expand the relationships to the stars, who were once human beings. The former concludes: "It is good to learn that they once lived here on earth.... We are never alone at night." The stories about the Lakota trickster Iktomi are humorous narratives about an individual who has no sense of relationship to other people or the rest of the creation. He is alone in his adventures, striving to fulfill his greed and ego through tricks and manipulations.

Goble's carefully researched, exquisitely executed illustrations, both singly and grouped together, precisely communicate factual, historical, social, and spiritual elements of the narratives. In *Red Hawk's Account of Custer's Last Battle, Brave Eagle's Account of the Fetterman Fight,* and *Lone Bull's Horse Raid*—all works of fictionalized history—Goble adapted ledger-book art, a style developed in the 1870s by Native American men who, imprisoned by the army, used the ledger paper given them to depict scenes from their past. In these mythical stories he adapts elements of vision painting, in which waving lines indicate the presence of supernatural forces. The radiating sun-circle design, a symbol of unity and spiritual power, is also used frequently. Interestingly, these symbols are not found in the Iktomi stories, an indication of the fact that the trickster acknowledges no power beyond himself.

The pictures from the Caldecott Medal-winning *The Girl Who Loved Wild Horses* (about a character who "understood horses in a special way") reveals Goble's narrative art at its best. According to the author, the book expresses "the Native American rapport with nature." The radiating arcs of semi-circles on the half-title page are behind the girl, who is mounted on a horse. At the conclusion, the girl, transformed into a horse, stands with her mate, the line of her mane that now forms a part of the arc of the circle a symbol of her new union. Within the story, a series of illustrations depict her moving away from camp toward the herd of wild horses. In the background, thunderclouds and forks of lighting indicate the spiritual powers operating in her life.

Goble gives his Iktomi stories a late 20th-century setting, an indication that the tales continue to be told by contemporary Native peoples. Under the traditional regalia that looks so foolish on him, the trickster wears a T-shirt, gym shorts, and sneakers. The author's statement that "Tales about Iktomi remind us ... that chaotic behavior is never far below the surface" is reflected in the paintings. Frequently the character is pictured as off-balance or upside down; at times only part of his body is depicted, as he is being pulled off the page because of his foolish deeds.

Although recently some Native and non-Native readers have criticized Goble, a white man, for presuming to retell the stories of another culture, the largest number of readers have praised his work. Limiting his books to the northern Plains peoples, members of a culture he has long studied and for which he reveals great respect, he has introduced his audiences to an important element of the traditional past. Using illustrations that are physically and symbolically accurate, he has produced narratives that embody the many elements of traditional Plains life and reveal their importance for all readers.

—Jon C. Stott

GODDEN, (Margaret) Rumer

Nationality: British. **Born:** Sussex, 10 December 1907. **Education:** Privately and at Moira House, Eastbourne, Sussex. **Family:** Married 1) Laurence Sinclair Foster in 1934 (died), two daughters; 2) James Lesley Haynes Dixon in 1949 (died 1973). **Career:** Director of a children's ballet school, Calcutta, in the 1930s. **Awards:** Spring Book Festival award, 1951, for *Candy Floss,* and 1961, for *Miss Happiness and Miss Flower;* commended for Carnegie Medal by the British Library Association, 1957, for *The*

Fairy Doll, and 1962, for *Miss Happiness and Miss Flower;* International Board on Books for Young People Honor List, 1958, for *The Fairy Doll;* America's Children's Books of the Year, Child Study Association, 1969, for *Operation Sippacik,* 1972, for *The Diddakoi* and *The Old Woman Who Lived in a Vinegar Bottle,* and 1975, for *Mr. McFadden's Hallowe'en;* Whitbread award, 1972, for *The Diddakoi;* Parents Choice award, 1984, for *Thursday's Children;* Notable Children's Trade Book in the Field of Social Studies, National Council for Social Studies and the Children's Book Council, for *The Story of Holly and Ivy,* 1986; Silver Pen award for Children's Book of the Year (Holland), for *The Diddakoi;* Order of the British Empire, 1993. **Agent:** Curtis Brown London, Haymarket House, 28/29 Haymarket, SW1Y 4SP, England; or, 10 Astor Place, New York, New York 10003, U.S.A. **Address:** Ardnacloich, Moniaive, Thornhill, Dumfries and Galloway DG3 4HZ, Scotland.

Publications for Children

Fiction

The Dolls' House, illustrated by Dana Saintsbury. London, Joseph, 1947; New York, Viking Press, 1948; as *Tottie,* London, Penguin, 1983.

The Mousewife, illustrated by William Rene du Bois. London, Macmillan, and New York, Viking Press, 1951.

Four Dolls, illustrated by Pauline Baynes. London, Macmillan, 1983; New York, Greenwillow, 1984.

- *Impunity Jane: The Story of a Pocket Doll,* illustrated by Adrienne Adams. New York, Viking Press, 1954; London, Macmillan, 1955.
- *The Fairy Doll,* illustrated by Adrienne Adams. London, Macmillan, and New York, Viking Press, 1956.
- *The Story of Holly and Ivy,* illustrated by Adrienne Adams. London, Macmillan, and New York, Viking Press, 1958.
- *Candy Floss,* illustrated by Adrienne Adams. London, Macmillan, and New York, Viking Press, 1960.

Mouse House, illustrated by Adrienne Adams. New York, Viking Press, 1957; London, Macmillan, 1958.

Miss Happiness and Miss Flower, illustrated by Jean Primrose. London, Macmillan, and New York, Viking Press, 1961.

Little Plum, illustrated by Jean Primrose. London, Macmillan, and New York, Viking Press, 1963.

Home Is the Sailor, illustrated by Jean Primrose. London, Macmillan, and New York, Viking Press, 1964.

The Kitchen Madonna, illustrated by Carol Barker. London, Macmillan, and New York, Viking Press, 1967.

Operation Sippacik, illustrated by James Bryan. London, Macmillan, and New York, Viking Press, 1969.

The Old Woman Who Lived in a Vinegar Bottle, illustrated by Mairi Hedderwick. London, Macmillan, and New York, Viking Press, 1972.

The Diddakoi, illustrated by Creina Glegg. London, Macmillan, and New York, Viking Press, 1972.

Mr. McFadden's Hallowe'en, illustrated by Ann Strugnell. London, Macmillan, and New York, Viking Press, 1975.

The Rocking Horse Secret, illustrated by Juliet Stanwell Smith. London, Macmillan, 1977; New York, Viking Press, 1978.

A Kindle of Kittens, illustrated by Lynne Byrnes. London, Macmillan, 1978; New York, Viking Press, 1979.

The Dragon of Og, illustrated by Pauline Baynes. London, Macmillan, and New York, Viking Press, 1981.

The Valiant Chatti-Maker, illustrated by Jeroo Roy. London, Macmillan, and New York, Viking Press, 1983.

Thursday's Children, London, Pan Macmillan, 1984.

Fu-Dog, illustrated by Valerie Littlewood. London, MacRae, 1989.

Listen to the Nightingale. London, Pan Macmillan, 1992.

Great Grandfather's House, illustrated by Valerie Littlewood. London, MacRae, 1992; New York, Greenwillow, 1993.

Premlata and the Festival of Lights, illustrated by Ian Andrew. London, Macmillan, and New York, Greenwillow Books, 1996.

Poetry

In Noah's Ark. London, Joseph, and New York, Viking Press, 1949.

St. Jerome and the Lion, illustrated by Jean Primrose. London, Macmillan, and New York, Viking Press, 1961.

Other

Editor, *Round the Day, Round the Year, The World Around: Poetry Programmes for Classroom or Library.* London, Macmillan, 6 Vols., 1966-67.

Editor, *A Letter to the World: Poems for Young Readers,* by Emily Dickinson, illustrated by Prudence Seward. London, Bodley Head, 1968; New York, Macmillan, 1969.

Publications for Adults

Novels

Chinese Puzzle. London, Davies, 1936.

The Lady and the Unicorn. London, Davies, 1937.

Black Narcissus. London, Davies, and Boston, Little Brown, 1939.

Gypsy, Gypsy. London, Davies, and Boston, Little Brown, 1940.

Breakfast with the Nikolides. London, Davies, and Boston, Little Brown, 1942.

A Fugue in Time. London, Joseph, 1945; as *Take Three Tenses: A Fugue in Time,* Boston, Little Brown, 1945.

The River. London, Joseph, and Boston, Little Brown, 1946.

A Candle for St. Jude. London, Joseph, and New York, Viking Press, 1948.

A Breath of Air. London, Joseph, 1950; New York, Viking Press, 1951.

Kingfishers Catch Fire. London, Macmillan, and New York, Viking Press, 1953.

An Episode of Sparrows. New York, Viking Press, 1955; London, Macmillan, 1956.

The Greengage Summer. London, Macmillan, and New York, Viking Press, 1958.

China Court: The Hours of a Country House. London, Macmillan, and New York, Viking Press, 1961.

The Battle of the Villa Fiorita. London, Macmillan, and New York, Viking Press, 1963.

In This House of Brede. London, Macmillan, and New York, Viking Press, 1969.

The Peacock Spring. London, Macmillan, 1975; New York, Viking Press, 1976.

Five for Sorrow, Ten for Joy. London, Macmillan, and New York, Viking Press, 1979.

The Dark Horse. London, Macmillan, 1981; New York, Viking Press, 1982.
Coromandel Sea Change. London, Macmillan, and New York, Morrow, 1991.

Short Stories

Mooltiki and Other Stories and Poems of India. London, Macmillan, and New York, Viking Press, 1957.
Swans and Turtles: Stories. London, Macmillan, 1968; as *Gone: A Thread of Stories,* New York, Viking Press, 1968.
Mercy, Pity, Peace, and Love. with J. Godden. New York, Morrow, 1989.
Indian Dust. with J. Godden. London, Macmillan, 1989.
Cromartie V. the God Shiva Acting through the Government of India. London, Macmillan, and New York, Morrow, 1997.

Plays

Screenplays: *The River,* with Jean Renoir, 1951; *Innocent Sinners,* with Neil Patterson, 1958.

Other

Rungli-Rungliot (*Thus Far and No Further*). London, Davies, 1943; as *Rungli-Rungliot Means in Paharia, Thus Far and No Further,* Boston, Little Brown, 1946; as *Thus Far and No Further,* London, Macmillan, 1961.
Bengal Journey: A Story of the Part Played by Women in the Province 1939-1945. London, Longman, 1945.
Hans Christian Andersen: A Great Life in Brief. London, Hutchinson, and New York, Knopf, 1955.
Two under the Indian Sun (autobiography), with Jon Godden. London, Macmillan, and New York, Knopf, 1966.
The Tale of the Tales: The Beatrix Potter Ballet. London, Warne, 1971.
Shiva's Pigeons: An Experience of India, with Jon Godden. London, Chatto and Windus, and New York, Viking Press, 1972.
The Butterfly Lions: The Story of the Pekingese in History, Legend, and Art. London, Macmillan, 1977; New York, Viking Press, 1978.
Gulbadan: Portrait of a Rose Princess at the Mughal Court. London, Macmillan, 1980; New York, Viking Press, 1981.
A Time to Dance, No Time to Weep (autobiography). London, Macmillan, and New York, Morrow, 1987.
A House with Four Rooms (autobiography). London, Macmillan, and New York, Morrow, 1989.

Editor, *Mrs. Manders' Cookbook,* by Olga Manders. London, Macmillan, and New York, Viking Press, 1968.
Editor, *The Raphael Bible.* London, Macmillan, and New York, Viking Press, 1970.

Translator, *Prayers from the Ark* (verse), by Carmen de Gasztold. New York, Viking Press, 1962, reprinted with illustrations by Barry Moser, 1992; London, Macmillan, 1963.
Translator, *The Creatures' Choir* (verse), by Carmen de Gasztold. New York, Viking Press, 1965; as *The Beasts' Choir,* London, Macmillan, 1967.

*

Manuscript Collections: Mugar Memorial Library, Boston University.

Critical Studies: *Rumer Godden* by Hassell A. Simpson, New York, Twayne, 1973.

Rumer Godden comments:

I am supposed to be a novelist but between each novel I try to write a children's book. "Why?" and I can almost always see a glimmer of misconception in the people's eyes. Because you need to write something easy: says that glimmer. Whereas the answer is the exact opposite. "Because of the discipline."

"Discipline?"

"Yes, It is far more difficult to write a children's book than, say a novel. With a novel the writer can do anything she likes but for children? There must be very little description. They find it boring as they do soliloquies, so dear to a novelist's heart. If there is anything essential for your plot it must be given to a child to say or better to an animal because children don't really listen to grown-ups. Flashbacks, too, are intensely muddling to a small child.

In my book, *The Story of Holly and Ivy,* I had to give the whole sad history of the little orphan child Ivy, who had no father or mother or grandmother in just a few lines. How? Well I wrote: *Sometimes in Ivy there was an empty feeling and the emptiness ached; it ached so much that she had to say something quickly in case she cried and, I don't care. I don't care at all, said Ivy.*

These are just some of the snags in writing for children."

* * *

In her over forty years of writing for both adults and children, Rumer Godden has revealed a fascination with the private worlds of childhood, and empathy with the loneliness and insecurity of the child who doesn't "fit in." Her early books about the miniature worlds of dolls and mice brilliantly evoke the childlike capacity to animate and humanize, while the recognition in those stories of the reality of cruelty and evil is developed in a more strictly realistic context, along with adventure and humor, in such later novels as *The Diddakoi* and *Mr. McFadden's Hallowe'en.* While the improbably convenient gifts and rescues with which Godden tends to end her stories are better suited to the fantasies than to realistic fiction, in both these genres, as well as in her adaptations of folk tales, Godden is a gripping story-teller, with a vivid sense of the drama inherent in even the smallest of details and situations.

Finding a home—be it a doll house, a mouse house, or a human home for an orphan child—is the major concern for most of Godden's characters. The mother cat in *A Kindle of Kittens* searches among the human inhabitants of her village to find the right home for each of her four kittens, and her thoughtful match-making benefits the humans as much as the kittens. Just any home is not enough: Godden's characters seek homes that will confirm and strengthen their own individual identities, and what suits Candy Floss would not at all please Mr. Plantagenet of *The Dolls' House.* Godden delights in detailing the miniature charms of the dolls' houses in *The Dolls' House, Mouse House, Miss Happiness and Miss Flower,* and *Home is the Sailor.* Some of her doll characters, however, prefer less-settled accommodations: intrepid Impunity Jane has a great time riding around in boys' pockets and tied to balloons, while Candy Floss much prefers the rough and adventurous life she leads with an itinerant fair-stall operator to the luxury offered her by spoiled Clementina, who selfishly steals her from him.

The dolls Candy Floss, Impunity Jane, Curly in *Home is the Sailor* and Tottie in *The Dolls' House* all suffer, as many children do, when they are forced to leave their homes and the people they love; their homesickness is as powerfully conveyed as the longing of other characters to have a home and someone to belong to. The homesickness of a refugee woman, their housekeeper, moves Gregory in *The Kitchen Madonna* to make for her an elaborately decorated icon like the one she remembered from childhood. Godden's detailed description of his construction of the picture, like the children's creation of an authentically Japanese house for Miss Happiness and Miss Flower, reveals her understanding of how the sense of beauty and belonging are enhanced in children through these small-scale acts of creativity. Making a home in miniature seems an important way of finding one's place in the larger world as well.

Through child-substitutes such as doll or mouse, as well as real child characters like stubborn, clumsy Selina in *Mr. McFadden's Halloween* or outcast Kizzy the Diddakoi, Godden arouses the reader's sympathy with small, disregarded, and sometimes actively persecuted children. The determined and resilient spirit of dolls like Tottie and Impunity Jane carries them through adventures that are harrowing to them but more than half-comical when seen from a human perspective; when Selina and Kizzy, however, are cruelly bullied by other school-children, their sufferings are painfully real. Godden makes us cheer for the courage and persistence of these "difficult" children, although the happily-ever-after resolutions she eventually provides may be less than wholly convincing. Godden's subjects of old-fashioned dolls, village life, and children raised in genteel nurseries might seem quaint, but the emotions—of jealousy, loneliness, anger, longing, fear, and sibling rivalry—that are at the heart of all her stories are timeless, and powerfully conveyed. Friendship and family feeling are central values in all of the stories, and various doll, mouse, and child characters provide memorable examples of loyalty, honesty, tolerance, and true concern for their friends. Perhaps because Godden is not afraid to include some really nasty, malevolent behavior in her stories, the figures who rise above it and defeat it are credible and interesting.

Godden's writing style is precise and elegantly spare, sometimes suggestive of that of Beatrix Potter, whom she admired and impersonated in an amusing set of fictitious letters to a publisher wanting to "simplify" her books. Apart from two collections of poetry and several adaptations of folk tales, Godden's work for children is chiefly short novels appealing to readers from ages eight to 11. In some of her earlier stories the roles of the sexes are very conventionally defined, albeit in a slightly satirical tone and from the point of view of limited characters—dolls locked into a certain age and role forever. Godden's adult fiction is notable for its evocation of young girls awakening to sexual feeling and discovering the complexities of social boundaries; several novels, including *The Greengage Summer* and *The Peacock Spring,* have been reissued as young adult titles, thus extending the range of Godden's work for young people from the fantasy play-world of younger children to the physical and emotional crises of later adolescence. Across this range, her insight into the inner life of the imagination, and her conviction of the possibilities for and value of generous actions in one's everyday life, make her a writer of depth and significance.

—Gwyneth Evans

GODFREY, Martyn

Nationality: Canadian. **Born:** Birmingham, England, 17 April 1949; moved with family to Canada, 1957; naturalized citizen. **Family:** Married Carolyn Boswell in 1973 (divorced 1985); two children. **Education:** University of Toronto, B.A. Honours 1973; B.Ed. 1974. **Career:** Elementary school teacher, Kitchener-Waterloo, Ontario, 1974-77, Mississauga, Ontario, 1977-80, and Assumption, Alberta, 1980-82; junior high school teacher, Edson, Alberta, 1983-85; children's writer, since 1985. **Awards:** Vicky Metcalf Short Story Award, 1985; award for best children's book from the University of Lethbridge, 1987; co-winner, Geoffrey Bilson Award for Historical Fiction, 1989; Manitoba Young Reader's Choice Award, 1993. **Agent:** Joanne Kellock, 11017-80 Avenue, Edmonton, Alberta T6G OR2, Canada.

Publications for Children

Fiction

The Vandarian Incident. Richmond Hill, Scholastic-TAB, 1981; as *The Day the Sky Exploded,* Richmond Hill, Scholastic Canada, 1991.

Here She Is, Ms Teeny-Wonderful. Richmond Hill, Scholastic Canada, 1984.

Plan B Is Total Panic. Toronto, J. Lorimer, 1986.

It Isn't Easy Being Ms Teeny-Wonderful. Richmond Hill, Scholastic Canada, 1987.

Baseball Crazy. Toronto, J. Lorimer, 1987.

It Seemed Like a Good Idea at the Time. Edmonton, Tree Frog Press, 1987.

Send in Ms Teeny-Wonderful. Richmond Hill, Scholastic Canada, 1988.

Why Just Me? Toronto, McClelland & Stewart, 1989.

Can You Teach Me to Pick My Nose? New York, Avon Books, 1990.

I Spent My Summer Vacation Kidnapped into Space. New York, Scholastic, 1990.

Monsters in the School. Richmond Hill, Scholastic Canada, 1991.

With Frank O'Keeffe, *There's A Cow in My Swimming Pool.* Richmond Hill, Scholastic Canada, 1991.

Wally Stutzgummer, Super Bad Dude. Richmond Hill, Scholastic Canada, 1992.

The Great Science Fair Disaster. Richmond Hill, Scholastic, 1992; New York, Scholastic, 1992.

Meet You in the Sewer. Richmond Hill, Scholastic-Canada, 1993.

Please Remove Your Elbow From My Ear. New York, Avon, 1993.

Just Call Me Boom Boom. Richmond Hill, Scholastic Canada 1994.

Do You Want Fries with That? Toronto, Scholastic Canada, 1996.

Adventures in Pirate Cove #1: The Mystery of Hole's Castle. New York, Avon Books, 1996.

Adventures in Pirate Cove #2: The Hunt for Buried Treasure. New York, Avon Books, 1996.

Adventures in Pirate Cove #3: The Desperate Escape. New York Avon Books, 1997.

Welcome to the Club. Richmond Hill, Scholastic Canada, 1998.

PUBLICATIONS FOR YOUNG ADULTS

Fiction

Alien Wargames. Richmond Hill, Scholastic Canada, 1984.
The Beast. Don Mills, Collier Macmillan Canada, 1984.
Spin Out. Don Mills, Collier Macmillan Canada, 1984.
Ice Hawk. Don Mills, Collier Macmillan Canada, 1985.
Fire! Fire! Don Mills, Collier Macmillan Canada, 1985.
The Last War. Don Mills, Collier Macmillan, 1986; New York, Collier Books, 1989.
Wild Night. Don Mills, Collier Macmillan Canada, 1987.
More Than Weird. Don Mills, Collier Macmillan Canada, 1987.
Rebel Yell. Don Mills, Collier Macmillan Canada, 1987.
Mystery in the Frozen Lands. Toronto, J. Lorimer, 1988.
Break Out. Toronto, Collier Macmillan Canada, 1988.
In the Time of the Monsters. Don Mills, Collier Macmillan Canada, 1989.
Don't Worry About Me, I'm Just Crazy. Toronto, Stoddart, 1992.
Mall Rats. Edmonton, OZ New Media/Duval, 1994.
The Things. Edmonton, OZ New Media/Duval, 1994.

Other

Is It Okay If This Monster Stays for Lunch?, illustrated by Susan Wilkinson (picture book). Toronto, Oxford University Press, 1992.

*

Bibliography: *Canadian Books for Children: A Guide to Authors and Illustrators* by Jon C. Stott and Raymond E. Jones, Toronto, Harcourt Brace Jovanovich, 1988.

Martyn Godfrey comments:

When I was young, I had an awful time with Language Arts. In fact, I had to repeat the third grade because I couldn't spell or write a sentence. But I do remember enjoying writing from the seventh grade on.

I started writing for young people the day one of my sixth grade students, Thomas, was searching for a space adventure novel to read in the school library. When Thomas came up empty-handed, he said, "You know, Mr. Godfrey, every week I write a story for you. Why don't you write a story for me this week? Why don't you write me a space story?"

So I did. the story got longer and longer. Over a hundred pages. I sent it to Scholastic Canada and they published it as *The Vandarian Incident.* (I changed the title a few years later. Now it's called *The Day the Sky Exploded.*)

I taught for eleven years before quitting to become a fulltime writer thirteen years ago. But I still get to talk to students. Every year I'm invited to speak at over 50 schools a year. I've visited schools in every Canadian province and many U.S. states.

I try to write two novels a years on my Mac. I write a story three times on the computer before printing a paper copy. Then I read it out loud to a wall in my house. I want to hear what it sounds like if your teacher is reading it to you. Then I take copies to a school in my neighborhood and ask the teachers to read it to their students and tell me what they liked, and more importantly, what they didn't like. Then I rewrite it another six or seven times.

The most asked question I hear is, "Where do you get your ideas?"

The answer is, "From real life."

Some of it comes from my teaching experience. If you read *Why Just Me?,* you'll read about a boy who gets a raisin caught up his nose one lunchtime. It's true; it happened in my class. In *Can You Teach Me to Pick My Nose?,* there's a chapter about a boy who gets his head stuck in his desk. It happened in my classroom. Honest.

Sometimes my friends give me ideas. Frank O'Keeffe, my buddy and fellow writer, lives on a farm. A lot of funny events in *There's a Cow in My Pool* are true tales from Frank's farm.

Sometimes it's people I meet on my travels. My *Adventures in Pirate Cove* series is based on a conversation I had with a twelve-year-old Nova Scotia girl in the dining room of her grandmother's Bed and Breakfast Inn. she gave me the ideas for all those wacky characters.

I get my ideas from the newspaper. *Don't Worry about Me, I'm Just Crazy* began when I read the story of an incredible rescue on the brink of Niagara Falls.

I must also give credit to my son, Marcus and my daughter, Selby. A lot of the action in *Do You Want Fries with That?* happened on our vacation to Disney World several years ago.

And, lastly, the things I do often appear in my novels. Check out chapter seven of *Meet You in the Sewer.* The stuff that happens to J. B. and Erin at the bottom of the wave pool actually happened to me.

The second most asked question I hear is, "How cam I become a good writer?"

Easy. Read. The best training for a writer is to read. I don't know a single published writer who doesn't like to read.

On a more personal note, my hobbies are collecting comic books, growing older, and playing oldtimers softball. I like watching movies, *The Simpsons* and The Learning Channel. I'm a big Blue Jays fan ever since writing a book about them (*Baseball Crazy*) and because I live in Edmonton, I cheer for the hockey Oilers.

I hope you enjoy my books and if we haven't met each other face to face yet, I hope we get a chance to do that real soon.

* * *

In *Canadian Books for Children,* Jon C. Stott and Raymond E. Jones quote Martyn Godfrey's description of two kinds of books: "First, there are the stories that kids devour. Then there are the ones that get the gold crests...." Godfrey calls the medal winners "super books," but he notes that in libraries "their covers don't fall off because kids don't take them home." Godfrey therefore produces the first kind, books that children seek because they know that they will enjoy reading them. His success is indisputable: he is one of Canada's best-selling children's authors, and libraries across the country contain tattered and torn copies of his fiction.

Godfrey pursues a wide audience, but he began with the aim of satisfying a single reader. As the jacket notes on his books state, he wrote his first novel, *The Vandarian Incident* (reissued as *The Day the Sky Exploded*), in response to a student's challenge. Godfrey followed this conventional space adventure about battles against reptilian aliens with a more original and serious book. *Alien War Games* dramatizes the conflict between humans from Earth and the population of a planet they colonize. By forcing readers to sympathize with the indigenous hunting culture, whom the settlers mislead and abuse, this novel criticizes imperialism and racial prejudice. Periodically, Godfrey returns to science fiction, but such books are not among his best. *I Spent My Summer Vacation Kidnapped into Space,* for example, is an uninspired "space opera" in which two adolescents are kidnapped by aliens, sold as slaves who fight slime worms in a circus, and then sent to rescue a princess. Its combination of bizarre aliens, ludicrous heroics, and light banter prevents it from succeeding as a genuine adventure, but it is not funny enough to be a spoof. Other books, such as *The Last War,* about the grim aftermath of an atomic war, and *The Things,* about adolescents fighting monsters created by an experimental laboratory, focus on action at the expense of character development.

These last two titles, though, are among Godfrey's contributions to publishers' series designed for reluctant readers. Written in the first-person to establish character identification, such novels have an unchallenging vocabulary. Their short chapters present fast-paced action and conclude with cliff-hangers. In *Wild Night,* for example, a boy working in a convenience store improbably contends in a single night with a robbery, an attempted suicide, a birth, and a nearly fatal accident. Other high interest titles explore such issues as the moral conflict of a hockey player ordered to injure an opposing superstar (*Ice Hawk*) and the violent lives of troubled teens hanging around a large mall (*Mall Rats*).

Godfrey has been most successful in attracting readers with stories about pre-teen life. Like those for reluctant readers, these novels use first-person narration to invite identification with the central character. They hook readers with relatively dramatic openings, and they maintain interest with slapstick situations. Extensive dialogue, often studded with jokes to make it entertaining, develops both conflicts and personalities. The eccentricities of the characters also create humor, but the central characters exhibit the common anxieties and insecurities of youth. Although the plots contain absurd events, they illustrate serious issues involving parent-child relationships (many of the parents are recently divorced) and friendships, especially with the opposite sex. The themes emphasize understanding and acceptance of others.

Godfrey's most popular comic novel is *Here She Is, Ms Teeny-Wonderful,* in which Carol Weatherspoon, whose talent is jumping her bicycle over garbage cans, enters a preteen beauty contest. When the obnoxious Campbell twins try to sabotage Carol's chances, they initiate a series of ludicrous retaliations. Its unified action, fast pace, frequent reversals of expectation, and colorful characters make this novel a satisfying comedy in the tradition of Gordon Korman's "Bruno and Boots" books. As is often the case, however, the sequels are disappointing: they mix excessive amounts of slapstick comedy with implausible physical heroism, and eccentric characters with artificial concerns about maturation. The same lack of control weakens *The Great Science Fair Disaster,* which uses slapstick chaos to resolve the central conflict between the narrator and her parents, but forgets to resolve the subplot about an underachieving student. In contrast, *Please Remove Your Elbow From My Ear* successfully resolves several conflicts. The motif of mistaken perceptions unites its comic episodes, in which Stormy Sprague, a social misfit, stops a gang from extracting protection money from students and then helps other social outcasts to win a floor hockey tournament. In much the same way, *Can You Teach Me to Pick My Nose?* focuses on the comic dilemma of Jordy Shepherd, who is trapped into entering a half-pipe contest even though his over-protective mother has never let him try skateboarding. The climactic contest teaches his mother to give him some freedom and Jordy to have faith in himself.

Similar changes in perceptions and relationships are central in some of Godfrey's other books. In *Why just Me?,* Shannon MacKenzie dreads approaching puberty, but she learns to welcome it, showing appropriate psychological maturity by supporting a friend even after they quarrel, by forming a closer relationship with her divorced mother, and by trying to share her new boyfriend's interest in hockey. Shannon's assumption that her father's hair restorer is a medication for preventing insanity weakens plausibility, but the novel otherwise succeeds. The same mixture of serious and comic perceptions appears in *Don't Worry About Me, I'm Just Crazy.* Roob Fowler ludicrously daydreams about being stranded with Rachel Parsons and entertains misguided hopes of solving his problems at school by moving in with his divorced father. The novel ends with the cliché of Roob saving a friend's life, but it shows Roob developing more mature visions of both Rachel and his drunken father. *Do You Want Fries with That?* also concludes with a rescue, but it focuses on the misperceptions of an adult. Brittany Prentice's divorced father is smotheringly over-protective until she saves a boy from drowning. The underlying theme is serious—that parents must alter their behavior as their children grow—but it barely escapes trivialization because it depends on a father who is only a caricature and a change of heart occasioned by a melodramatic contrivance.

Many of Godfrey's books exhibit the flaws of commercial fiction: contrived plots, one-dimensional characters, and weak themes. Nevertheless, Godfrey amuses child readers with jokes, slapstick episodes, engaging characters, and plots involving issues important to adolescents. Such novels don't win gold crests, but they may convince many children that reading is truly pleasurable.

—Raymond E. Jones

GORDON, Gaelyn

Nationality: New Zealander. **Born:** Hawela, New Zealand, 26 November 1939. **Education:** University of New Zealand, B.A. 1961; also attended Canterbury University and Christchurch Teachers College. **Family:** Married Peter Gordon, 16 May 1964; one son and one daughter. **Career:** Taught English and drama in secondary schools; worked in the theatre as an actor and director. **Awards:** Frank Sargeson Fellow; Cheysa Bursary; QE11 Literary Grant. **Member:** Children's Book Founder; New Zealand Book Council, PEN, New Zealand Writers Guild. **Died:** 1997.

Publications for Children

Fiction

Stonelight. Auckland, Reed Heinemann, 1988.
Tales from Another Now. Auckland, Reed Heinemann, 1989.
Above Suspicion. Auckland, Random Century, 1990.
Several Things Are Alive and Well and Living in Alfred Brown's Head. Auckland, HarperCollins, 1990.
Mindfire. Auckland, HarperCollins, 1991.
Prudence M. Muggeridge, Damp Rat. Auckland, HarperCollins, 1991.
Duckat. Auckland, Scholastic, 1992.

Fuss Finds Out. Auckland, HarperCollins, 1993.
Skateboarders. Auckland, Scholastic, 1993.
Take Me to Your Leaders. Auckland, HarperCollins, 1993.
Tripswitch. Auckland, HarperCollins, 1993.
Why Some Things Happen in Our Town. Auckland, HarperCollins, 1993.
David and the Monster. Auckland, HarperCollins, 1994.
Fuss the Farm Dog. Auckland, HarperCollins, 1994.
Fuss the Collector. Auckland, HarperCollins, 1994
Walter and the Too-Big Dog. Auckland, HarperCollins, 1994.
Robert's Robot. Auckland, HarperCollins, 1994.
Fuss and Friend. Auckland, HarperCollins, 1995.
River Song. Auckland, HarperCollins, 1995.
The Other Worlds of Andrew Griffin. Auckland, HarperCollins, 1995.
Magginty. Auckland, HarperCollins, 1996.

* * *

Gaelyn Gordon's earlier work was remarkable for being the first European writing to assimilate and interpret Maori folklore. However, more recently she has moved to quirky and often satirical commentary on contemporary society.

Her first novel, *Stonelight,* saw a rather uneasy partnership between Angela, a Maori "street kid," and Thomas, a European boarding school boy. Both possessed unusual gifts, Thomas could communicate with trees and Angela could breathe under water. Together, helped by the red-headed fairy people of Maori folklore, they set out on a quest to discover why their land is in turmoil and earthquakes are intensifying.

The same protagonists appear in Gordon's *Mindfire,* in which a teenage boy is bewitched by a daughter of the sun. This time it is the weather that is out of balance and Angela and Thomas are called upon to help restore it. There are three years between the publication of Gordon's first novel and her second novel, but *Mindfire* shows a considerable development in Gordon's skill as an author in the portrayal of atmosphere and of convincing relationships.

With *Several Things Are Alive and Well and Living in Alfred Brown's Head,* however, she turns to science fiction. Alfred Brown's head is suddenly taken over by Opie, an intergalactic researcher from a more advanced civilization. She regards our own civilization as primitive, because in her world all menial tasks are performed by mind control. But she herself becomes obsessed by the different tastes and textures of food on earth. It is a light-hearted and amusing story, but its sequel, *Take Me to Your Leaders,* has more satirical bite. This time Opie is researching systems of government on earth and Gordon takes the opportunity to articulate some trenchant reflections on Parliamentary proceedings as well as holding up to ridicule a gullible public's toleration of the "hype" of the Lottery game "Blotto."

Her healthy sense of the absurd is again evident in *Prudence M. Muggeridge, Damp Rat,* in which 15-year-old Prudence is kept a virtual prisoner by her grandmother, head of a financial empire. Prudence is told that she will not be adult until she is forty and is kept in a nursery routine, although given a rigorous intellectual training. But when she learns the truth she escapes and arrives in a modern city, lacking colloquial speech or contemporary knowledge until she is befriended by some "street kids." They all then rob a bank and use Prudence's knowledge of finance to manipulate the stock exchange with the proceeds. As a consequence of this they become exceedingly rich and ruin the grandmother. It is all highly improbable fun. Prudence combines the skills of a Houdini with a Machiavellian brain and the persistence of a long distance runner, while the street kids are loyal and angelic friends. But underlying the crisp prose is a deft management of plot and satirical comment on an adult world where minor crime is heavily punished but where money laundering and stock market manipulation are richly rewarded.

There is a return to the "wicked guardian" theme in *Tripswitch,* where three contemporary schoolgirl cousins, all tragically orphaned, live with their wicked aunt, who is a witch. By drugging the girls and plaiting their hair together she hopes to gain power over them and their inheritances, until her plans are foiled by a latter-day, if unlikely, Prince Charming, and by the girls' realization that they are not lacking in power if they use their mental resources.

Once again it is a preposterous story, made credible by the compelling narrative and humour but which continues to explore Gordon's interest in the manipulation and nature of mental processes. Even in a picture book for young children *Duckat,* things are not what they seem, when a duck suffers an identity crisis which must be resolved.

Her latest books all implicitly ask the reader to view the world with fresh eyes. Even in the "Fuss" books for reluctant readers the little dog Fuss experiences an alien environment when she is moved from city to country.

In *River Song,* the last in the "Stonelight" trilogy, a Maori river monster transforms itself into a young man who views the late 20th century with astonished eyes. This is a novel for young adults but in her books for younger children, *David and the Monster from Outer Space* and *Magginty,* promptings from alien creatures get children into trouble, although with ultimately happy outcomes.

Andy Griffin, in *The Other Worlds of Andrew Griffin,* learns to ask important questions when he is transported into other worlds through the medium of a magic ring. Once again Gordon's use of fantasy highlights philosophical concepts, but this is balanced by a shrewd depiction of the thrust and parry of everyday life in Andy's large family.

In the ten years since her first published novel Gordon has revealed herself to be a new and original voice in New Zealand literature for children. Although she frequently uses well-known traditional themes, her whimsical interpretations invest them with a humour and liveliness which challenge readers to reexamine old assumptions. Her untimely death has deprived New Zealand of one of its most versatile and innovative writers.

—Betty Gilderdale

GORDON, John (William)

Nationality: British. **Born:** Jarrow, County Durham, 19 November 1925. **Education:** Wisbech Grammar School, Cambridgeshire. **Military Service:** Royal Navy, 1943-47. **Family:** Married Sylvia Ellen Young in 1954; one son and one daughter. **Career:** Reporter, 1947-49, and sub-editor, 1949-51, *Isle of Ely and Wisbech Advertiser;* chief reporter and sub-editor, *Bury Free Press,* Bury St. Edmunds, Suffolk, 1951-58; sub-editor, *Western Evening Herald,* Plymouth, 1958-62; sub-editor and columnist, *Eastern Evening*

News, Norwich, 1962-73; sub-editor, *Eastern Daily Press,* Norwich, 1973-85. **Address:** 99 George Borrow Road, Norwich, Norfolk NR4 7HU, England.

PUBLICATIONS FOR CHILDREN

Fiction

The Giant under the Snow. London, Hutchinson, 1968; New York, Harper, 1970.
The House on the Brink. London, Hutchinson, 1970; New York, Harper, 1971.
The Ghost on the Hill. London, Kestrel, 1976; New York, Viking Press, 1977.
The Waterfall Box. London, Kestrel, 1978.
The Spitfire Grave and Other Stories. London, Kestrel, 1979.
The Edge of the World. London, Hardy, and New York, Atheneum, 1983.
Catch Your Death, illustrated by Jeremy Ford. London, Hardy, 1984.
The Quelling Eye. London, Bodley Head, 1986.
The Grasshopper. London, Bodley Head, 1987.
Ride the Wind. London, Bodley Head, 1989.
Blood Brothers. London, Signpost, 1989.
Secret Corridor. London, Blackie, 1990.
The Burning Baby and Other Ghosts. London, Walker, 1992; New York, Candlewick, 1993.
Gilray's Ghost. London, Walker, 1995.

Other

Ordinary Seaman (memoir). London, Walker, 1992.

*

John Gordon comments:

There's no better place than the Fens of East Anglia for stirring the imagination—a land so flat and open must have secrets, and it has—so the stories I write come from there or thereabouts. I like the land and I like the people, and I often write about the supernatural because it is always there, beyond the edge of things. One of the pleasures of storytelling is turning things upside down, so at various times I have turned the Fens into a red desert (*The Edge of the World*), had people flying from the top of Norwich Cathedral spire (*The Giant under the Snow*), or had a malign corpse rise from the mud of the River Nene in Wisbech and threaten a woman who lives in a house at the riverside (*The House on the Brink*). But stories are nothing without people, and people are almost nothing without other people, so my stories, no matter how chilling, are love stories, especially, odd as it may seem, in *Gilray's Ghost* and the forthcoming *The Flesh Eater.* Snow and Christmas come together, as they should, in another forthcoming book, *The Starveling Boy.*

* * *

After completing war service in the Royal Navy (vividly recounted in his autobiographical *Ordinary Seaman*) and while working as a journalist, John Gordon wrote his first children's book in the 1960s. When *The Giant under the Snow* appeared in 1968, a new and powerful voice in fantasy was identified: a writer ranking with Alan Garner. Between them, Garner and Gordon extended the range of fantasy into urgent realism. The "other world" was here and now: today's children could stumble into it at any time.

The Giant under the Snow rehearsed several themes Gordon develops in later works. The worlds his child characters, Jonk and the rest, inhabit is contemporary East Anglia, England, where Gordon lives: an eerie place of lonely landscapes and wide skies where the supernatural never seems far away. In solid, present day Norwich the children find themselves in an ancient, magic world where witches live, the deeply troubling and imaginatively-created Leathermen invade, and the children gain the power to fly. There is a tremendous climax when the prehistoric giant under the snow rises as evil forces have an even older revenge taken on them. The book formed a stunning debut for a writing career which flourishes and constantly surprises.

This was undoubtedly a children's book: his second, *The House on the Brink,* was written for young adults. This subtle psychological thriller contains finely-realised sexual tension, another feature to become a regular theme. The house is real: Peckover House in Wisbech, by the River Nene. As the relationship between Dick Dodds and Helen Johnson develops, they are involved in the haunting of rich Mrs. Knowles from the house. A black shape "like a man, all tied up, no arms, no legs" is coming up from the river, dreadful, threatening, into the house. Is it just a log, or a cursed, prehistoric body? Is Mrs. Knowles merely neurotic? Is "the tall, grey, gentle man" Miller her tormentor or saviour? This is a riddling, difficult, memorable book close to the status of classic.

Adolescent sexual awakening and the terror in everyday things are also present in *The Ghost on the Hill,* another story with the ambiguous reality of the East Anglian landscape at its heart. This meticulously written book moves, like the others, from quiet beginnings to a towering climax, epitomizing Gordon's exact powers of construction in building up a long, complex narrative. This power also shows in the free-ranging fantasy *The Edge of the World* and the disturbingly powerful *The Quelling Eye.* Here the imaginative leap into human flight so effectively rendered in *The Giant under the Snow* is taken a step further. Can Peregrine Falconer, possessor of the quelling eye, really fly? Can he actually become a hawk? Chuck and Tessa are meshed in a supernatural mystery. *The Grasshopper* also develops intricately the themes of earlier works. Here is the whole society of an East Anglian Fen town: the growing relationship between a boy and girl, Harry and Charlotte; tension caused by different social levels—Harry is middle-class, Charlotte poor with a jail-bird father; a fearless leap into the imaginative—instinctive Charlotte can ride the grasshopper; self-conscious Harry cannot.

However, like most novelists who are masters of construction, Gordon is equally at home in the short story. *The Spitfire Grave and Other Stories, Catch Your Death,* and *The Burning Baby and Other Ghosts* contain narratives which, in their uncompromising spareness, are disturbing, even shocking. In *The Burning Baby,* Bernard Friend has murdered 16-year old Barbara Pargeter on hearing she was pregnant. He burns the body in a Fireworks Night bonfire—but the baby is born in the fire and seeks Bernard out to consume him. Rupert and the narrator go skating on the fens. Is there a body under the ice? Rupert's uncle was drowned: his ghost rises from the ice to take a terrible revenge. Sophie won't stay with Martin all night in the hall where Clive died years before. Martin loses his key and is locked in with a malevolent ghost. No one knew Miss Jervis once had a daughter or that she murdered her granddaughter and fed her to the eels. Nor did Miss Jervis know what would come one night out of water.

These stories push to the very edge the power of imagination to work in real, tangible settings. They form a definite stage in Gordon's development as a writer of serious, compelling fantasy.

—Dennis Hamley

GOREY, Edward (St. John)

Has also written as Eduard Blutig, Mrs. Regera Dowdy, Raddory Gewe, Om, Edward Pig, E.D. Ward, Ogdred Weary, Dogear Wryde, Garrod Weedy, Aedwyrd Gore. **Nationality:** American. **Born:** Chicago, Illinois, 22 February 1925. **Education:** Harvard University, Cambridge, Massachusetts, A.B. in French Literature; attended Art Institute of Chicago, Chicago, Illinois. **Military Service:** United States Army, 1943-46. **Career:** Writer, illustrator, and designer; worked at a variety of jobs, including bookstore clerk, in Boston, Massachusetts, 1950-53; staff artist and book jacket designer, Doubleday & Co., New York City, 1953-60; founder, Fantod Press, 1962; illustrations exhibited in museums and galleries, including Graham Gallery, New York City, and Yale University Library, New Haven, Connecticut, both 1974; designer of record jacket for recording of his stories produced by Watt 4, 1976; set designer for productions of *Les Ballets Trocadero de Monte Carlo,* 1977, and of sets and costumes for stage productions of *Dracula* and *Gorey's Stories,* both 1978; designer of shower curtain for Metropolitan Opera catalogue; contributor of cartoons to periodicals, including the *New York Times, Sports Illustrated, Evergreen,* and *Esquire.* **Awards:** *New York Times* Best Illustrated Book of the Year award, 1966, for *The Monster Dens; or, Look What Happened at My House and to It,* 1969, for *The Dong with the Luminous Nose,* and 1971, for *The Shrinking of Treehorn*; American Institute of Graphic Arts Fifty Books Exhibit and Children's Book Show, and American Library Association Notable Book citation, both 1971, and Bologna Children's Book Fair best graphics for children award, 1977, all for *The Shrinking of Treehorn*; Children's Book Showcase selection, 1972, for *Lions and Lobsters and Foxes and Frogs: Fables from Aesop, The Shrinking of Treehorn,* and *Sam and Emma,* and 1973, for *Red Riding Hood: Retold in Verse for Boys and Girls to Read Themselves*; Brooklyn Museum Art Books for Children citation, 1974, for *Red Riding Hood*; Antoinette Perry ("Tony") Award, best costume and set design for a Broadway play, 1978, for *Dracula*; Parents Choice award for illustration, 1982, for *The Dwindling Party.* **Address:** Box 146, Yarmouthport, Massachusetts 02675, U.S.A.

Publications for Children

Fiction (illustrated by the author)

The Doubtful Guest. Garden City, New York, Doubleday, 1958.
The Bug Book. New York, Looking Glass Library, 1959.
The Hapless Child. New York, Ivan Obolensky, 1961.
The Wuggly Ump. Philadelphia, Pennsylvania, J.B. Lippincott, 1963.
[The Nursery Frieze]. New York, The Fantod Press, 1964.
The Gilded Bat. New York, Simon & Schuster, 1967.
As Mrs. Regera Dowdy, *The Pious Infant.* New York, The Fantod Press, 1966.
With Peter F. Neumeyer, *Donald and the....* New York, Young Scott Books, 1969.
With Peter F. Neumeyer, *Donald Has a Difficulty.* New York, The Fantod Press, 1970.
With Peter F. Neumeyer, *Why We Have Day and Night.* New York, Young Scott Books, 1970.
The Lavender Leotard; or, Going a Lot to the New York City Ballet. New York, Gotham Book Mart, 1973.
The Eclectic Abecedarium. Boston, Massachusetts, Anne & David Bromer, 1983.

Fiction (illustrated by others)

With Victoria Chess, *Fletcher and Zenobia,* illustrated by Chess. New York, Meredith Press, 1967.
With Victoria Chess, *Fletcher and Zenobia Save the Circus,* illustrated by Chess. New York, Dodd, Mead, 1971.

Publications for Adults (illustrated by the author)

The Unstrung Harp. New York, Duell, Sloan & Pearce/Little, Brown, 1953.
The Listing Attic. New York, Duell, Sloan & Pearce/Little, Brown, 1954.
The Object Lesson. Garden City, New York, Doubleday, 1957.
The Fatal Lozenge: An Alphabet. New York, Ivan Obolensky, 1960.
Under pseudonym Ogdred Weary, *The Curious Sofa.* New York, Ivan Obolensky, 1961.
The Gorey Alphabet. London, Constable, 1961.
Under pseudonym Ogdred Weary, *The Beastly Baby.* New York, The Fantod Press, 1962.
The Willowdale Handcar or The Return of the Black Doll. Indianapolis, Indiana, Bobbs Merrill, 1962.
The Gashlycrumb Tinies or After the Outing. New York, Simon & Schuster, 1963.
The Insect God. New York, Simon & Schuster, 1963.
The Vinegar Works/Three Volumes of Moral Instruction. New York, Simon & Schuster, 1963.
The West Wing. New York, Simon & Schuster, 1963.
The Sinking Spell. New York, Ivan Obolensky, 1964.
The Remembered Visit: A Story Taken From Life. New York, Simon & Schuster, 1965.
Under pseudonym Mrs. Regera Dowdy, *The Evil Garden: Eduard Blutig's Der Böse Garten in a Translation by Mrs. Regera Dowdy with the Original Pictures of O. Müde.* New York, The Fantod Press, 1966.
The Inanimate Tragedy. New York, The Fantod Press, 1966.
Under pseudonym Mrs. Regera Dowdy, *The Pious Infant.* New York, The Fantod Press, 1966.
3 Books from the Fantod Press: The Evil Garden, The Inanimate Tragedy, and The Pious Infant. New York, The Fantod Press, 1966.
The Utter Zoo. New York, Meredith Press, 1967.
The Blue Aspic. New York, Meredith Press, 1968.

Secrets: Volume One, The Other Statue. New York, Simon & Schuster, 1968.
The Epiplectic Bicycle. New York, Dodd, Mead, 1969.
The Iron Tonic: or A Winter Afternoon in Lonely Valley. New York, Albondocani Press, 1969.
The Chinese Obelisks: Fourth Alphabet. New York, The Fantod Press, 1970.
The Osbick Bird. New York, The Fantod Press, 1970.
The Sopping Thursday. New York, Gotham Book Mart and Gallery, 1970.
Three Books from the Fantod Press: The Chinese Obelisks, Donald Has a Difficulty, and The Osbick Bird. New York, The Fantod Press, 1970.
The Deranged Cousins or, Whatever. New York, The Fantod Press, 1971.
The Disrespectful Summons. New York, The Fantod Press, 1971.
Under pseudonym Raddory Gewe, *The Eleventh Episode.* New York, The Fantod Press, 1971.
Under pseudonym Edward Pig, *[The Untitled Book].* New York, The Fantod Press, 1971.
Three Books from the Fantod Press: The Deranged Cousins, The Eleventh Episode, and [The Untitled Book]. New York, The Fantod Press, 1971.
The Abandoned Sock. New York, The Fantod Press, 1972.
Amphigorey. New York, G.P. Putnam's, 1972.
The Awdrey-Goré Legacy. New York, Dodd, Mead, 1972.
Leaves from a Mislaid Album. New York, Gotham Book Mart, 1972.
Categorey: Fifty Drawings. New York, Gotham Book Mart, 1973.
Fantod IV: Three Books from the Fantod Press: The Abandoned Sock, The Disrespectful Summons, and The Lost Lions. New York, The Fantod Press, 1973.
A Limerick. Dennis, Massachusetts, Salt-Works Press, 1973.
The Lost Lions. New York, The Fantod Press, 1973.
The Listing Attic and The Unstrung Harp. London, Abelard, 1974.
Amphigorey, Too. New York, G.P. Putnam's, 1975.
The Glorious Nosebleed, Fifth Alphabet. New York, Dodd, Mead, 1975.
L'Heure Bleu. New York, The Fantod Press, 1975.
Les Passementeries Horribles. New York, Albondocani Press, 1976.
Dogear Wryde Postcards: Scènes de Ballet Series (designed for the New York City Ballet). N.p., 1976.
The Loathsome Couple. New York, Dodd, Mead, 1977.
Dogear Wryde Postcards: Alms for Oblivion Series. N.p., 1978.
The Green Beads. New York, Albondocani Press, 1978.
The Broken Spoke. New York, Dodd, Mead, 1979.
Dogear Wryde Postcards: Interpretive Series. N.p., 1979.
Dracula: A Toy Theater. New York, Scribner's, 1979.
Gorey Posters. New York, Harry N. Abrams, 1979.
Dancing Cats and Neglected Murderesses. New York, Workman, 1980.
Dogear Wryde Postcards: Neglected Murderesses Series. N.p., 1980.
F.M.R.A. New York, Andrew Alpern, 1980.
Les Urnes Utiles. Cambridge, Massachusetts, Halty-Ferguson, 1980.
Le Mélange Funeste. New York, Gotham Book Mart, 1981.
The Dwindling Party. New York, Fandom House, 1982.
The Water Flowers. New York, Congdon & Weed, 1982.
Amphigorey Also. New York, Congdon & Weed, 1983.
E.D. Ward: A Mercurial Bear. New York, Gotham Book Mart, 1983.
The Prune People. New York, Albondocani Press, 1983.
The Tunneÿl Calamity. New York, G.P. Putnam's, 1984.
Les Echanges Malandreux. Worcester, Massachusetts, Metacom Press, 1985.
The Prune People II. New York, Albondocani Press, 1985.
The Improvable Landscape. New York, Albondocani Press, 1986.
The Raging Tide; or, The Black Doll's Imbroglio. New York, Beaufort Book Publishers, 1987.
Dogear Wryde Postcards: Menaced Objects Series. N.p., 1989.
Dogear Wryde Postcards: Tragédies Topiares Series. N.p., 1989.
The Dripping Faucet/Fourteen Hundred & Fifty Eight Tiny, Tedious, & Terrible Tales. Worcester, Massachusetts, Metacom Press, 1989.
The Helpless Doorknob/A Shuffled Story. N.p., 1989.
Q.R.V. Boston, Massachusetts, Anne and David Bromer, 1989.
Dogear Wryde Postcards: Whatever Next? Series. N.p., 1990.
The Fraught Settee. Cape Cod, Massachusetts, The Fantod Press, 1990.
Under pseudonym Eduard Blutig, *The Stupid Joke: Translation by Mrs. Regera Dowdy with original pictures by O. Müde.* Cape Cod, Massachusetts, The Fantod Press, 1990.
Under pseudonym Eduard Blutig, *The Tuning Fork. Translation by Mrs. Regera Dowdy with original pictures by O. Müde.* Cape Cod, Massachusetts, The Fantod Press, 1990.
La Ballade Troublante. Cape, Cod, Massachusetts, The Fantod Press, 1991.
The Betrayed Confidence/Seven Series of Dogear Wryde Postcards. Orleans, Massachusetts, Parnassus Imprints, 1992.
Two Novels: The Grand Passion [and] The Doleful Domesticity. Cape Cod, Massachusetts, The Fantod Press, 1992.
Under pseudonym Dogear Wryde, *The Floating Elephant,* and under pseudonym Ogdred Weary, *The Dancing Rock* (2 volumes bound back to back). N.p., 1993.
Under pseudonym Garrod Weedy, *The Pointless Book: or, Nature & Art.* Cape Cod, Massachusetts, The Fantod Press, 1993.
Under pseudonym Aedwyrd Goré, *Figbash Acrobate.* N.p., 1994.
The Retrieved Locket. Cape Cod, Massachusetts, The Fantod Press, 1994.
The Fantod Pack. New York, Gotham Book Mart, 1995.
The Unknown Vegetable. Cape Cod, Massachusetts, The Fantod Press, 1995.

Plays

More Gorey Stories (entertainment with music; produced Barnstable, Massachusetts, 1981).
Lost Showlaces (entertainment with music; produced Woods Hole, Massachusetts, 1985).
Tinned Lettuce; or, The New Musical (entertainment with music by David Aldrich; produced by Tisch School of the Arts Undergraduate Theatre, New York University, New York City, 1985).
Useful Urns (entertainment with music; produced Provincetown, Massachusetts, 1990).
Stuffed Elephants (entertainment with music; produced Woods Hole, Massachusetts, 1990).
Flapping Ankles (entertainment with music; produced Provincetown, Massachusetts, 1991).

Amphigorey: The Musical (music by Peter Golub; produced at American Music Theater Festival, Philadelphia, Pennsylvania, 1992).

Other

The Black Doll: A Silent Film (film script). New York, Gotham Book Mart, 1973.

*

Media Adaptations: *Gorey Stories* (adaptation for the stage by Stephen Currens of several of Gorey's Tales, including *The Loathsome Couple, The Deranged Cousins,* and *The Blue Aspic*; produced Broadway, 1978, Los Angeles, 1992); *The Vinegar Works* (adaptation for stage; produced London, 1989); *Gorey by Grimes* (sound recording), Caedmon Records, 1980; selections from Gorey's work recorded with jazz accompaniment, Watt 4, 1976.

Critical Studies: Review of *The Vinegar Works,* in *Newsweek,* 26 August 1963; *American Picturebooks From Noah's Ark to the Beast Within* by Barbara Bader, New York, Macmillan, 1976; *Something About the Author,* Vol. 70, Detroit, Gale, 1993; *The World of Edward Gorey* by Clifford Ross and Karen Wilkin, New York, Harry N. Abrams, 1996; review of *The World of Edward Gorey* by Richard B. Woodward, in *Village Voice* (New York), 15 October 1996, 45-46; review of *The World of Edward Gorey,* in *People,* 23 December 1996, 34; review of *The World of Edward Gorey* by Michael Dirda, in *Smithsonian* (Washington, D.C.), June 1997, 150-53.

Illustrator: *Case Record from a Sonnetorium* by Merrill Moore, 1951; *Men and Gods* by Rex Warner, 1959; *The Man Who Sang the Sillies* by John Ciardi, 1961; *Quake, Quake, Quake: A Leaden Treasury of English Verse* by Paul Dehn, 1961; *You Read to Me, I'll Read to You* by John Ciardi, 1962; *You Know Who* by John Ciardi, 1964; *Die Offene Tur* by Saki, 1964; *Die Orgie—eine Idylle* by Walter De La Mare, 1965; *The King Who Saved Himself From Being Saved* by John Ciardi, 1965; *Alvin Steadfast on Vernacular Island* by Frank Jacobs, 1965; *Monster Festival* edited by Eric Potter, 1965; *Christmas Bower* by Polly Redford, 1966; *Cultural Slog* by Felicia Lamport, 1966; *The Monster Den or Look What Happened at My House—and To It* by John Ciardi, 1966; *Brer Rabbit and His Tricks* by Ennis Rees, 1967; *Die neununddreissig Stufen* by John Buchan, 1967; *Son of the Martini Cookbook* by Jane Trahey, 1967; *Cobweb Castle* by Jan Wahl, 1968; *Hauntings: Tales of the Supernatural* edited by Henry Mazzeo, 1968; *He Was There from the Day We Moved In* by Rhoda Levin, 1968; *More of Brer Rabbit's Tricks* by Ennis Rees, 1968; *The Very Fine Clock* by Muriel Spark, 1968; *The Jumblies* by Edward Lear, 1968; *At the Top of My Voice and Other Poems* by Felice Holman, 1969; *The Dong with the Luminous Nose* by Edward Lear, 1969; *Merry, Rose, and Christmas-Tree June* by Doris Orgel, 1969; *Penny Candy* by Edward Fenton, 1970; *Someone Could Win a Polar Bear* by John Ciardi, 1970; *Lions and Lobsters and Foxes and Frogs: Fables from Aesop* by Ennis Rees, 1971; *Miss Clafooty and the Demon* by Jacob David Townsend, 1971; *Sam and Emma* by Donald Nelsen, 1971; *The Shrinking of Treehorn* by Florence Parry Heide, 1971; *Red Riding Hood: Retold in Verse for Boys and Girls to Read Themselves* retold by Beatrice Schenk de Regniers, 1972; *The House with a Clock in Its Walls* by John Bellairs, 1973; *Jack the Giant Killer,* 1973; *Rumpelstiltskin by the Grimm Brothers,* retold by Edith Tarcov, 1973; *The Enchanted Forest* by Beatrice Schenk de Regniers, 1974; *Instant Lives* by Howard Moss, 1974; *The Rats of Rutland Grange* by Edmund Wilson, 1974; *Rotkaeppchen: Ein Maearchen der Brueder Grimm* by Jacob Grimm, 1974; *All Strange Away* by Samuel Beckett, 1976; *Nuns: Poems* by Terence Winch, 1976; *Treehorn's Treasure* by Florence Parry Heide, 1981; *Light Metres* by Felicia Lamport, 1982; *Old Possum's Book of Practical Cats* by T.S. Eliot, 1982; *Saki's Stories* by Saki, 1982; *The Adventures of Treehorn* by Florence Parry Heide, 1983; *The Curse of the Blue Figurine* by John Bellairs, 1983; *The Mummy, the Will, and the Crypt* by John Bellairs, 1983; *The Dark Secret of Weatherend* by John Bellairs, 1984; *Treehorn's Wish* by Florence Parry Heide, 1984; *Freshwater, a Comedy* by Virginia Woolf, 1985; *The Revenge of the Wizard's Ghost* by John Bellairs, 1985; *The Eyes of the Killer Robot* by John Bellairs, 1986; with Joe Servello, *High Jinx* by Donald Westlake, 1987; *Beginning to End* by Samuel Beckett, 1988; *The Twelve Terrors of Christmas* by John Updike, 1993; title sequence animation for Public Broadcasting Service (PBS) television series *Mystery.*

* * *

Teachers and children's librarians have become well acquainted with the work of Edward Gorey, largely through his illustrations for John Bellairs' spooky mysteries for middle readers, for Florence Parry Heide's *Treehorn* picture books for younger readers, and for Edward Lear's nonsense verse.

But are Edward Gorey's own books actually for children? Indeed, Gorey's books fall into the standard categories of children's literature. Hand-lettered picture books all (illustrated with Gorey's own unique pen-and-ink drawings), they include alphabet books, such as *The Gashlycrumb Tinies, The Fatal Lozenge, The Chinese Obelisks,* and *Figbash Acrobate.* But "A is for AMY who fell down the stairs" and "B is for BASIL assaulted by bears" (both from *The Gashlycrumb Tinies*) and "The Baby, lying meek and quiet/Upon the customary rug,/Has dreams about rampage and riot/And will grow up to be a thug" (from *The Fatal Lozenge*) are hardly the stuff of the typical toddler's alphabet book. Children are the main characters of many of his books, but even the titles—*The Hapless Child, The Beastly Baby,* and *The Pious Infant* (who dies, at age four, after going out in a hailstorm to give his breadpudding to an unfortunate widow)—give one pause. There are animal stories: *The Doubtful Guest* (a huge black bird "of peculiar appearance" who comes to visit unexpectedly and stays seventeen years, "with no intention of going away"), *The Bug Book* (the tale of some charming—and uncharacteristically colorful—red and blue and yellow bugs who combine their forces to squash a mean and menacing black bug), *The Nursery Frieze* (in which a large, boar-like creature utters edifying words like "archipelago," "cardamom," and "obloquy"), *The Wuggly Ump* (a dinosaurian monster who eats "umbrellas, gunny sacks,/Brass doorknobs, mud, and carpet tacks," and finally the three child-protagonists of the story) and *The Salt Herring.* And there are limericks, like those in *The Listing Attic*: "A headstrong young woman in Ealing/Threw her two weeks' old child at the ceiling;/When quizzed why she did,/She replied, 'To be rid/Of a strange, overpowering feeling.'" Absurdist texts, sinister situations, child-eating monsters and child-throwing parents, strange-sounding words (some of the limericks are all in French)—just the sort of thing to shock, thrill, and amuse many a child.

"I suppose I know a few tots who would like my books.... I would have loved them as a child," Gorey told a reviewer for *Newsweek.* Above all, though, Gorey's settings, situations, and characters—from Charlotte Sophia, the hapless child, to the evil man who carries her off and sells her to a "drunken brute"—exhibit a particular nonchalance that raises them above sheer meanness and tragedy. "I remember somebody once telling me that there is a phrase in the Beatitudes, in the French version, that literally translated means 'Blessed are the nonchalant.' Well, the kinds of things I'm attracted to are nonchalant," Gorey explained to Clifford Ross in *The World of Edward Gorey.*

Edward Gorey is a great balletophile, and, until the death of George Balanchine in 1980, attended (attired, like many of the male characters in his books, in a fur coat, sneakers, and a long knitted scarf) nearly every performance of the New York City Ballet. In *The Gilded Bat,* five year-old Maudie Splaytoes grows up to become a prima ballerina renowned for her portrayal of a golden bat in a ballet created just for her, "La Chauve-Souris Doree." In *The Lavender Leotard,* Gorey's wryly unabashed tribute to his favorite ballet company, "the author introduces two small distant, ageless, and wholly imaginary relatives to fifty seasons of the New York City Ballet."

Gorey began publishing his books at the urging of the owners of the Gotham Book Mart, which published many of the small editions that have become highly sought-after collectors' items, and ultimately he formed his own publishing company, The Fantod Press ("fantod," a delightfully Gorey word, is a Victorian term for "a fit of irritability and tension"). Soon, major publishers were publishing omnibus collections of his work, like the series *Amphigorey, Amphigorey Too,* and *Amphigorey Also,* and he was asked to design the set for a Broadway production of *Dracula,* for which he won a prestigious "Tony" award. Most recently, he has become widely known to television viewers as the designer of the memorable title sequences for the Public Broadcasting Service's *Mystery* series. And he has even rated his own celebrity tribute in *People* magazine: "Gorey in his glory is a sight to behold/For young and old."

—Marcia Welsh

GOUDGE, Elizabeth (de Beauchamp)

Nationality: British. **Born:** Wells, Somerset, 24 April 1900. **Education:** Grassendale School, Southbourne, Hampshire; Reading University School of Art. **Career:** Taught design and applied art, Ely and Oxford, 1922-32. **Awards:** Library Association Carnegie Medal, 1947. Fellow, Royal Society of Literature, 1945. **Died:** 1 April 1984.

Publications for Children

Fiction

The Fairies' Baby and Other Stories. Amersham, Buckinghamshire, and London, Morland-Foyle, 1920.

Sister of the Angels: A Christmas Story, illustrated by C. Walter Hodges. London, Duckworth, and New York, Coward McCann, 1939.

Smoky-House, illustrated by C. Walter Hodges. London, Duckworth, and New York, Coward McCann, 1940.

The Well of the Star. New York, Coward McCann, 1941.

Henrietta's House, illustrated by Lorna R. Steele. London, University of London Press-Hodder and Stoughton, 1942; as *The Blue Hills,* New York, Coward McCann, 1942.

The Little White Horse, illustrated by C. Walter Hodges. London, University of London Press, 1946; New York, Coward McCann, 1947.

Make-Believe, illustrated by C. Walter Hodges. London, Duckworth, 1949; Boston, Bentley, 1953.

The Valley of Song, illustrated by Steven Spurrier. London, University of London Press, 1951; New York, Coward McCann, 1952.

Linnets and Valerians, illustrated by Ian Ribbons. Leicester, Brockhampton Press, and New York, Coward McCann, 1964.

I Saw Three Ships, illustrated by Richard Kennedy. Leicester, Brockhampton Press, and New York, Coward McCann, 1969.

Other

God So Loved the World: A Life of Christ. London, Hodder and Stoughton, and New York, Coward McCann, 1951.

Publications for Adults

Novels

Island Magic. London, Duckworth, and New York, Coward McCann, 1934.

The Middle Window. London, Duckworth, 1935; New York, Coward McCann, 1939.

A City of Bells. London, Duckworth, and New York, Coward McCann, 1936.

Towers in the Mist. London, Duckworth, and New York, Coward McCann, 1938.

The Bird in the Tree. London, Duckworth, and New York, Coward McCann, 1940.

The Castle on the Hill. London, Duckworth, and New York, Coward McCann, 1941.

Green Dolphin Country. London, Hodder and Stoughton, 1944; as *Green Dolphin Street,* New York, Coward McCann, 1944.

The Herb of Grace. London, Hodder and Stoughton, 1948; as *Pilgrim's Inn,* New York, Coward McCann, 1948.

Gentian Hill. London, Hodder and Stoughton, and New York, Coward McCann, 1949.

The Heart of the Family. London, Hodder and Stoughton, and New York, Coward McCann, 1953.

The Rosemary Tree. London, Hodder and Stoughton, and New York, Coward McCann, 1956.

The White Witch. London, Hodder and Stoughton, and New York, Coward McCann, 1958.

The Dean's Watch. London, Hodder and Stoughton, and New York, Coward McCann, 1960.

The Scent of Water. London, Hodder and Stoughton, and New York, Coward McCann, 1963.

The Child from the Sea. London, Hodder and Stoughton, and New York, Coward McCann, 1970.

Short Stories

A Pedlar's Pack and Other Stories. London, Duckworth, and New York, Coward McCann, 1937.
The Golden Skylark and Other Stories. London, Duckworth, and New York, Coward McCann, 1941.
The Ikon on the Wall and Other Stories. London, Duckworth, 1943.
The Reward of Faith and Other Stories. London, Duckworth, 1950; New York, Coward McCann, 1951.
White Wings: Collected Short Stories. London, Duckworth, 1952.
The Lost Angel. London, Hodder and Stoughton, and New York, Coward McCann, 1971.

Plays

The Brontës of Haworth (produced London, 1932). Included in *Three Plays,* 1939.
Joy Will Come Back (produced London, 1937).
Suomi (produced London, 1938). Included in *Three Plays,* 1939.
Three Plays: Suomi, The Brontës of Haworth, and Fanny Burney. London, Duckworth, 1939.
Fanny Burney (produced Oldham, Lancashire, 1949). Included in *Three Plays,* 1939.

Poetry

Songs and Verses. London, Duckworth, 1947; New York, Coward McCann, 1948.

Other

The Elizabeth Goudge Reader, edited by Rose Dobbs. New York, Coward McCann, 1946; as *At the Sign of the Dolphin: An Elizabeth Goudge Anthology,* London, Hodder and Stoughton, 1947.
Saint Francis of Assisi. London, Duckworth, 1959; as *My God and My All: The Life of St. Francis of Assisi,* New York, Coward McCann, 1959.
The Chapel of the Blessed Virgin Mary, Buckler's Hard, Beaulieu. Privately printed, 1966.
A Christmas Book (anthology). London, Hodder and Stoughton, and New York, Coward McCann, 1967.
The Ten Gifts (anthology), edited by Mary Baldwin. London, Hodder and Stoughton, and New York, Coward McCann, 1969.
The Joy of the Snow: An Autobiography. London, Hodder and Stoughton, and New York, Coward McCann, 1974.
Pattern of People: An Elizabeth Goudge Anthology, edited by Muriel Grainger. London, Hodder and Stoughton, 1978; New York, Coward McCann, 1979.

Editor, *A Book of Comfort: An Anthology.* London, Joseph, and New York, Coward McCann, 1964.
Editor, *A Diary of Prayer.* London, Hodder and Stoughton, and New York, Coward McCann, 1966.
Editor, *A Book of Peace: An Anthology.* London, Joseph, 1967; New York, Coward McCann, 1968.
Editor, *A Book of Faith.* London, Hodder and Stoughton, and New York, Coward McCann, 1976.

*

Elizabeth Goudge commented:

(1978) I have always loved writing for children; I have enjoyed writing my children's books even more than writing my novels. Of all my books the two I care for most are *The Little White Horse* and *The Valley of Song.* And I have enjoyed the children themselves, both receiving their letters and being visited by them. They have been one of the greatest joys of my life.

* * *

Elizabeth Goudge was in many ways a writer born out of her time, and always liable to be judged old-fashioned. Young readers, however, are themselves strongly inclined to have old-fashioned tastes, so that the best of her works, like the best of Victorian work, are unlikely to lose their appeal. The openly religious, sometimes Anglican, element which runs through all her writing may perhaps seem increasingly strange if the habit of church-going continues to decline, but her highly evocative powers of description, her gift for creating memorable characters, and her ability to work through an intricately woven plot and bring it to a satisfactory conclusion, are virtues which will surely survive. Among her other qualities one may note Goudge's habit of surrounding her child characters with interesting adults, often advanced in years, and her flair for giving personality to animals, especially dogs and horses.

At their best Goudge's stories are strongly rooted in everyday reality, with magic and fantasy used only to enliven; similarly, her much-criticised lapses into sentimentality and sickly-sweetness are quite rare in the two or three books on which her reputation depends. Little need be said here about *Smoky-House* and *The Valley of Song.* The former is an odd mixture of smuggling adventure, fairy-story, and cosy moralizing, while the latter, though palpably sincere, is too much concerned with the author's personal vision of heaven, and not enough with the child's normal interests. Two other books are interesting but uneven. *Sister of the Angels* is very sentimental, though redeemed by flashes of humour and a fine portrayal of an artist's dedication; and the collection called *Make-Believe* contains one story—"The Forester's Ride"—which one might recommend for any high-spirited ten-year-old, but otherwise it seems more suitable for nostalgic adults than for children.

Most of Goudge's children's books came in the earlier part of her writing career. One exception, *Linnets and Valerians,* also happens to be in her very best vein, with a plot of nicely judged complexity and a sparkling cast of heroes, villains, and eccentrics. Ezra Oake, the one-legged sailor-servant, is certainly among her finest creations. Possibly, however, her two previous great successes, *The Little White Horse* and *Henrietta's House,* deserve higher praise by virtue of their originality. *Henrietta's House* must be almost unique in giving pride of place to a group of elderly clergymen, and the combination in this book of rollicking entertainment with a deep religious purpose is a notable achievement. *The Little White Horse* is lengthy, complicated, and concerned with emotions such as sexual passion, pride, jealousy, and loneliness; yet the principal characters and incidents are exceptionally captivating, and an atmosphere of joyous enchantment persists throughout. Goudge's reputation could stand on this book alone.

—Alasdair K.D. Campbell

GRAHAM, Bob

Nationality: Australian. **Born:** Robert Graham, Sydney, New South Wales, 20 October 1942. **Education:** Julian Ashton Art School, Sydney, 1964-68. **Family:** Married Carolyn Smith in 1968; one daughter and one son. **Career:** Artist, New South Wales Government printers, Sydney, 1973-75; resource designer, Department of Technical Education, Sydney, 1975-82; illustrator, Five Mile Press, Melbourne, 1982-85. **Awards:** Australian Children's Book Council Picture Book of the Year award, 1988, 1990 (Honour book), 1991, 1993; Children's Peace Literature Award, Psychologists for the Prevention of War, Australian Psychological Society, 1993; UNICEF Bologna Illustrator of the Year, 1994. **Address:** "Greystones," Vale St., Henstridge BA8 O5Q, Somerset, United Kingdom.

PUBLICATIONS FOR CHILDREN (ILLUSTRATED BY THE AUTHOR)

Fiction

Pete and Roland. Sydney and London, Collins, 1981; New York, Viking, 1984.
Here Comes John. Adelaide, Omnibus, 1983; London, Hamish Hamilton, 1985; Boston, Little Brown, 1988.
Here Comes Theo. Adelaide, Omnibus, 1983; London, Hamish Hamilton, 1985; Boston, Little Brown, 1988.
Pearl's Place. Melbourne, Lothian, 1983; London, Blackie, 1983; New York, Bedrick, 1985.
Libby, Oscar and Me. Melbourne, Lothian, 1984; London, Blackie, and New York, Bedrick, 1985.
Bath Time for John. Adelaide, Omnibus, 1985; London, Hamish Hamilton, 1985; Boston, Little Brown, 1988.
First There Was Frances. Melbourne, Lothian, 1985; London, Blackie, 1985; New York, Bradbury Press, 1986.
Where Is Sarah? Adelaide, Omnibus, 1985; London, Hamish Hamilton, 1985; Boston, Little Brown, 1988.
The Wild. Melbourne, Lothian, 1986; London, Blackie, and New York, Bedrick, 1987.
The Adventures of Charlotte and Henry. Paris, Centurion, 1987; London and New York, Viking Kestrel, 1987.
Crusher Is Coming! Melbourne, Lothian, 1987; London, Collins, 1987; New York, Viking Kestrel, 1988.
The Red Woollen Blanket. London, Walker, 1987; Boston, Little Brown, 1988.
Has Anyone Here Seen William? London, Walker, 1988; Boston, Little Brown, 1989.
Sitting Ducks and The Duck's Revenge. Fitzroy, Victoria, The Five Mile Press, 1988.
Bringing Home the New Baby [*Getting to Know the New Baby, Visiting the New Baby, Waiting for the New Baby*]. London, Walker, 1989.
Grandad's Magic. London, Walker, 1989; Boston, Little Brown, 1989.
Greetings from Sandy Beach. Melbourne, Lothian, 1990; London, Blackie, 1990; New York, Kane/Miller, 1992.
Rose Meets Mr. Wintergarten. London, Walker, 1992; Cambridge, Massachusetts, Candlewick, 1992.
Brand New Baby. London, Walker, 1992.
Spirit of Hope. Port Melbourne, Victoria, Lothian, 1993; Greenvale, New York, Mondo, 1996.
Zoltan the Magnificent. Port Melbourne, Victoria, Lothian, 1994.
Queenie the Bantam. London, Walker, 1997; as *Queenie, One of the Family,* Cambridge, Massachusetts, Candlewick, 1997.

Other (readers)

I Can series (*Actions 1, Actions 2, Babies, Bikes, Colour, Families, Helping, In the Water, My Senses, Pets, School, Shopping*). Fitzroy, Victoria, Five Mile Press, 12 vols., 1984; as *Reading Is Fun* series, London, Blackie, 12 vols., 1986.
Science Early Learners series (*Heat, Moving, Push, Senses, Sound, Water*). Fitzroy, Victoria, Five Mile Press, and London, Blackie (*Push* as *Wheels*), 6 vols., 1986; as *It's Much Too Hot!, Look Out for Rosy!, Pig's Wild Cart Ride, Rupert's Big Splash,* Balwyn, Victoria, Five Mile Press, 1991.
Busy Day Board Books (*Helping, Playing, Sleeping, Waking*). Fitzroy, Victoria, Five Mile Press, 4 vols., 1988.

*

Illustrator: *The Useful Book,* 1979 (and other editions); *Round and Round* and *Special Times* by Diane Snowball and Faye Bolton, 1980; *A Boggle of Bunyips* edited by Edel Wignall, 1981; *Jenny's Baby Brother* by Peter Smith, 1981; *Sing Together,* 1982; *Time to Sing!,* 1982; *A First Australian Poetry Book* compiled by June Factor, 1983; *Second Ever Book of Things to Make and Do* by Roland Harvey, 1983; *Scratch, Scratch, Scratch* by Heather Fidge, 1984; *The Kids' Letter Writing Book,* 1985; *Microwave Cooking for Kids,* 1984, and *The Second Microwave Cooking for Kids,* 1985, both by Judith Ryles; *How Does Your Garden Grow?* by Kevin Heinze, 1985; *It's Fun to Be Two* by Mijo Beccaria, 1985; *More Free Stuff for Kids,* 1985; *Ford Family Car Fun Book* edited by Anne Bower Ingram and Peggy O'Donnell, 1986; *Camping: Let's Do It Together,* and *Making a Picture Book,* both by Anne Bower Ingram, 1987; *Songs from There's a Bear in There,* 1987; *Sounds and Music* by Stella Turner, 1990; *Babies: Unsentimental Anthology* by Iona Opie, 1990; *Poems for the Very Young* edited by Michael Rosen, 1993; *This is Our House* by Michael Rosen, 1996; *Full House* by Nigel Gray, 1998.

Bob Graham comments:

Our little terrier Buffy is not as young as he used to be. Age may have wearied him, but he still has an essential charisma (and a stringy knotted coat that has a magnetic attraction to small sticks and burrs, and blends him perfectly with his surroundings.)

Occasionally we become separated on a walk, and with increasing alarm I double back on my tracks, look under bushes, and scan the horizon. And he's usually in the last place that I look.

Right at my feet.

So it is with my stories. I somehow find them in small, seemingly insignificant things that are part of my everyday life.

Sometimes I patiently scrape away to reveal some event, or sometimes I can suddenly find a story, like turning over a rock with my boot ... and there it is.

Either way, it always surprises me.

Ultimately, when my story is written and the pictures are done I like it to have the feeling and the authenticity of opening someone's Family Photo Album and peering inside.

Then I can call it "finished."

* * *

Bob Graham's picture books always feature young children and their toys and pets in family situations. His stories are most often about something very important to the major child character. A continuing theme in the author's works is the affection children have for animals. In *Pete and Roland* a brief but warm relationship grows between a little blue budgerigar and a young boy, while *The Wild* concerns a child whose pets choose between domesticity and the lure of the bush surrounding his home. The restrictions of flat dwelling compared to what Graham obviously considers a "proper home" are contrasted in *Pearl's Place*, and *The Red Woollen Blanket* traces the life and times of a much loved security blanket. In *Crusher is Coming!* a young boy worries that his home life may show him up as less tough than he would like to appear to the school football star, and *Has Anyone Here Seen William?* depicts the extraordinary curiosity of a newly mobile toddler. With a skill reminiscent of other highly regarded author-illustrators, including Shirley Hughes and John Burningham, Graham presents childhood concerns with dignity and humour. His portrayal of very young children has been particularly successful, and no doubt part of his popularity and success is due to the pleasure both child readers and their parents find in Graham's depiction of familiar home situations.

In the author's best books, the economical text and cartoon-like illustrations appear spontaneous and uncontrived. The illustrations are ink with colour wash, and Graham uses a variety of quarter-, half-, full- and double-page illustrations, constantly altering perspective to enlarge on the text. In *Pearl's Place*, the block of flats where Arthur lives unhappily with his mother leans threateningly over diminutive figures while at Pearl's house Arthur and Jessica can easily climb on the roof. Similarly in *The Wild,* human figures fill the foreground in domestic scenes, but outside towering eucalypti make them seem vulnerable. *Crusher is Coming!* is an example of the ironic relationship Graham sets up between his somewhat understated text and his illustrations. Peter has invited the local tough boy, Crusher, to tea. Desperate to appear tough himself, he hides away his teddies and plans "boyish" activities, but Crusher is beguiled by Peter's young sister Claire and enjoys a tea-party with the toddler and a family of stuffed toys. The dialogue gives us Peter's perception of Crusher, contradicting the illustrations (for example, a large red-haired boy feeding a toy duck from a teacup) and providing a multi-layered text usually associated with more obviously sophisticated writing. This technique has been used with considerable success by Graham in a number of illustrated readers. One of the best is *Here Comes Theo,* where a deliberate echo of old school readers—"Here comes Theo. Look at him go"—is undercut, both by less conventional text—"Down she goes, and gets the licking treatment"—and by the funny illustrations of a manic dog knocking over his child friends with his overenthusiastic greetings.

Distinctive features of all Graham's books are humour and optimism, the latter characteristic particularly evident in his depiction of relationships. In six recent titles, love and understanding are central themes, with the suggestion in *Spirit of Hope* that love is humankind's last hope. *Grandad's Magic* is a bittersweet tale of the decline of one's powers in old age and emphasises the strong links between the old and very young. In *Greetings from Sandy Beach,* a girl and her family share a camping site, at first reluctantly, with motorcycle riders, The Disciples of Death, and a busload of school children. "Don't go near them," says Dad, but there is a warmer relationship by the end of the weekend. Young Rose Summers brings old Mr. Wintergarten from cranky isolation into a world of colour and companionship in *Rose Meets Mr. Wintergarten. Spirit of Hope* is Graham's strongest statement so far about the importance of friendship and love, especially family love, in times of trouble. The Fairweathers live in a house dwarfed by huge relics of industry and threatened with demolition, but together they find a (temporary) solution. This book has disturbed a number of adult commentators, perhaps because of its suggestion of the fragility of the human situation or even because of the industrial setting, but it is a continuation of many of the author's concerns, including a tendency towards allegory that was first apparent in *Rose Meets Mr. Wintergarten.* Similarly *This is Our House* by Michael Rosen is a modern fable. George won't share the cardboard cubbyhouse with anyone—not with girls, or small people, or twins, or people with glasses—but when he goes to the toilet everyone jumps in, telling George the house isn't for people with red hair like him! In his illustrations (which must be "read" from the end papers through to the back cover) Graham goes beyond this authentic play time incident to make a telling comment about the necessity of getting along with others when urban situations involve close living.

Relationships are central to *Zoltan the Magnificent.* Dad works such long hours that his son Jack rarely sees him, a used tea-bag on the sink the only sign of Dad's presence in the house. Fortunately a holiday reveals a creative side of Dad that is new and delightful to Jack. The text in *Zoltan the Magnificent* is uncharacteristically stilted, with a hint of finger-wagging, although the illustrations are rich with incident and humour. In *Queenie the Bantam* Graham returns to his (apparently) easy rhythms with a story about birth, change and the tides of family life. Queenie is a red bantam hen rescued from a pond by Caitlin's dad. She makes herself "very much at home," but after some time has passed is returned to her proper home, a farm a short distance away. But Queenie steadfastly returns each morning to lay an egg which is carefully collected from the dog's basket by little Caitlin. However when routine is disturbed by the arrival of a new baby the accumulated eggs are hatched by Bruno the dog! Progressing in a series of mini-climaxes, one expects Queenie's tale to be over when she is rescued from the dam, and later returned to the farm, but the story changes direction much as Caitlin's family changes as she grows. The author appears to have had fun creating the twists in the narrative with the text inviting the reader to share in the possibilities of story. The last scene depicts Caitlin and the new baby leaning against Bruno with one of Queenie's chicks perched on the dog's head, possibilities for "another story" as the text notes.

Recognition of Graham's talent in the form of literary awards was slow in coming, but he has now won the Australian Children's Book Council Picture Book of the Year award three times (in 1988, 1991 and 1993), an acknowledgement that he is Australia's premier author-illustrator of books for young children. Now living in England and still contributing a serial comic strip to a French children's magazine (as he has done for many years) Graham is Australia's most internationally well-known picture book creator. In 1996 an illustration from *Greetings from Sandy Beach* was reproduced as an Australia Post stamp, one of a set of four postage stamps (the others were illustrations from books by Pamela Allen, Ron Brooks and Graeme Base) to mark the fiftieth anniversary of the Australian Children's Book Council awards.

—Kerry White

GRAHAM, Eleanor

Nationality: British. **Born:** Walthamstow, Essex, 9 January 1896. **Education:** Chingford High School, Essex, 1902-09; North London Collegiate School for Girls, 1910-14; London School of Medicine, 1914-16. **Career:** Bumpus' children's book room, London, 1926-30; children's book editor, William Heinemann, Ltd., publishers, London, 1930-33, and Methuen Ltd., publishers, London, 1933-36; librarian, private children's lending library, 1936-37; children's book editor and founder of the Puffin series, Penguin Books Ltd., London, 1939-61. Children's book reviewer, *Sunday Times* and the *Bookman,* both London, 1930s. **Award:** Children's Book Circle Eleanor Farjeon award, 1973. **Died:** 8 March 1984.

Publications for Children

Fiction

The Night Adventures of Alexis, illustrated by Winifred Langlands. London, Faber, 1925.
Six in a Family, illustrated by Alfred Sindall. London, Nelson, 1935.
The Children Who Lived in a Barn, illustrated by J.T. Evans. London, Routledge, 1938; revised edition, London, Penguin, 1955.
Head o' Mey, illustrated by Arnold Bond. London, Benn, 1947.

Other

High Days and Holidays: Stories, Legends and Customs of Red-Letter Days and Holidays, illustrated by Priscilla M. Ellingford. London, Benn, 1932; as *Happy Holidays: Stories, Legends and Customs of Red-Letter Days and Holidays,* New York, Dutton, 1933.
Change for Sixpence. London, University of London Press, 1937.
When the Fun Begins. London, University of London Press, 1937.
Adventure in Natal: A Book for Boys of Early Hunting Adventures in Natal, with George Gordon Campbell. London, Pitman, 1938.
The Making of a Queen: Victoria at Kensington Palace. London, Cape, 1940.
The Story of "The Wind in the Willows": How It Came to Be Written. London, Methuen, 1950.
True Dog Stories, with Lillian Gask. London, Harrap, 1950.
The Story of Charles Dickens, illustrated by Norman Meredith. London, Methuen, 1952; New York, Abelard Schuman, 1954.
The Story of Jesus, illustrated by Brian Wildsmith. London, Penguin, 1959.
J.M. Barrie's Peter Pan: The Story of the Play, illustrated by Edward Ardizzone. Leicester, Brockhampton Press, and New York, Scribner, 1962.

Editor, *Welcome Christmas! Legends, Carols, Stories, Riddles,* illustrated by Priscilla M. Ellingford. London, Benn, 1931; New York, Dutton, 1932.
Editor, *Tents in Mongolia: A Youth Edition,* by Henning Haslund-Christensen. London, Kegan Paul, 1935.
Editor, *More Travels and Adventures in Mongolia: A Youth Edition of "Men and Gods in Mongolia,"* by Henning Haslund-Christensen. London, Kegan Paul, 1936.
Editor, *Selected Stories and Verses,* by Walter de la Mare. London, Penguin, 1952.
Editor, *A Puffin Book of Verse,* illustrated by Claudia Freedman. London, Penguin, 1953.
Editor, *A Puffin Quartet of Poets,* illustrated by Diana Bloomfield. London, Penguin, 1958.
Editor, *Eleanor Farjeon's Book: Stories, Verses, Plays,* illustrated by Edward Ardizzone. London, Penguin, 1960.
Editor, *Poems,* by Walter de le Mare, illustrated by Margery Gill. London, Penguin, 1962.
Editor, *Secret Laughter* (anthology). London, Penguin, 1964.
Editor, *A Thread of Gold: An Anthology of Poetry,* illustrated by Margery Gill. London, Bodley Head, 1964; Freeport, New York, Books for Libraries Press, 1969.
Editor, *The Music of the Feast: Poems for Young Readers,* by Robert Herrick, illustrated by Lynton Lamb. London, Bodley Head, 1969.

Publications for Adults

Other

Kenneth Grahame. London, Bodley Head, and New York, Walck, 1963.

* * *

Eleanor Graham's most notable contribution to children's fiction is *The Children Who Lived in a Barn.* It merits serious consideration, as the plot offers a complete contrast to the highly successful holiday adventure plot initiated by Arthur Ransome and imitated by M.E. Atkinson, Aubrey de Selincourt, M. Pardoe, and many other writers. Graham accepts the convention of disposing of parents by means of an air crash, but this does not ensure a carefree, parentless existence. Instead, it highlights the stark realities which face a group of children left temporarily without parents. It does not prove possible to dispense with adults, and an incredibly large number of adults, pleasant and unpleasant, interfere helpfully and unhelpfully with the children's affairs. In the best tradition of Arthur Ransome, Graham extols the virtues of self-reliance. She perhaps differs from him in her relentless emphasis on the unromanticized mechanics of everyday life. It is inevitable that some of these details are now obsolete, e.g., the wash day procedure. Perhaps the greatest weakness of the plot is the return of the parents, but these are minor criticisms of an original story.

Unlike numerous forgotten writers of the period whose characterization was so nominal as to be nonexistent, Graham succeeds with the Dunnett children in creating five individual and consistent personalities. She gives convincing details of their relationships with each other, of their quarrels, and of the problems which arise in the absence of parents. She also succeeds in giving a valid account of family solidarity in a time of crisis. The strains imposed on the eldest girl, Susan, who is only 13 years old, are particularly well handled.

By the post-World War II period a family in a similar situation would normally be caught in the safety net of the social services, although John Rowe Townsend offered an alternative in *Gumble's Yard* (1961). The young reader of today might feel that the family situation of *The Children Who Lived in a Barn* has little resemblance to any situation known to him, but he might also admire the Dunnetts' success in coming to terms with a crisis, and he might even envy them a degree of freedom unlikely today. This book was a deliberate antidote to the often far-fetched holiday adventure stories of the 1930s, and Graham might be said to have had a definite didactic purpose in writing it. It is easy to understand that with her wide experience in the field of children's publishing, she must have felt deep concern over the proliferation of second-rate material for children, particularly in the 1920s. Her serious endeavours in the fields of publishing and editing led to an improvement in the quality of children's books in the 1930s, and ensures her a lasting place in the history of children's literature.

—Anne W. Ellis

GRAHAM, Harry (Jocelyn Clive)

Pseudonyms: Coldstreamer; Col. D. Streamer. **Nationality:** British. **Born:** London, 23 December 1874. **Education:** Eton College; Royal Military College, Sandhurst, Surrey. **Military Service:** Coldstream Guards, 1895: Aide-de-Camp to the Earl of Minto, Governor-General of Canada, 1898; served in South Africa, 1901-02; rejoined Coldstream Guards, 1914: Captain. **Family:** Married Dorothy Fraser in 1910; one daughter. **Career:** Journalist. Trustee, British Museum. **Died:** 30 October 1936.

Publications for Children

Fiction

Happy Families: A Story for the Young of All Ages. London, Cape, 1934.

Poetry

Ruthless Rhymes for Heartless Homes (as Col. D. Streamer), illustrated by G.H. London, Arnold, 1899; New York, Russell, 1901.
A Song-Garden for Children: A Collection of Children's Songs (adaptations of French and German songs), with Rosa Newmarch, music by Norman O'Neill. London, Arnold, and New York, Longman, 1906.
More Ruthless Rhymes for Heartless Homes, illustrated by Ridgewell. London, Arnold, and New York, Putnam, 1930.
When Grandmamma Fell Off the Boat: The Best of Harry Graham. London, Methuen, 1986.

Publications for Adults

Novels

Lord Bellinger. London, Arnold, and New York, Duffield, 1911.
Biffin and His Circle. London, Mills and Boon, 1919.
The Last of the Biffins. London, Methuen, 1925.
The Biffin Papers. London, Lane, 1933.
The Private Life of Gregory Gorm. London, Davies, 1936.

Plays

Little Miss Nobody. London, Hopwood and Crew, 1901.
The "Mind the Gates" Girl, with others (produced London, 1912).
The Cinema Star. London, Chappell, 1914.
State Secrets (produced London, 1914). London, French, 1924.
Tina, with Paul A. Rubens (produced London, 1915).
Sybil, music by Victor Jacobi, adaptation of a play by Max Brody and Ferenc Martos (produced Baltimore and New York, 1916; Manchester, 1920; London, 1921). London, Chappell, 1915.
The Maid of the Mountains (lyrics only, with others), book by Frederick Lonsdale, music by Harold Fraser-Simson (produced Manchester, 1916; London, 1917; New York, 1918).
A Southern Maid, with D.C. Calthorp, music by Harold Fraser-Simson (produced Manchester, 1917; London, 1920). London, Ascherberg, 1920.
A Little Dutch Girl, with Seymour Hicks, music by E. Kalman (produced London, 1920). London, Chappell, 1920.
The Lady of the Rose (lyrics only), book by Frederick Lonsdale, music by Jean Gilbert, adaptation of a work by Rudolf Schanzer and Ernest Welisch (produced Manchester, 1921; London, 1922). London, Ascherberg Hopwood, 1922; as *The Lady in Ermine* (produced New York, 1922).
Our Nell (lyrics only), book by Louis N. Parker and Reginald Arkell, music by Harold Fraser-Simson and Ivor Novello (produced New York, 1922; London, 1924).
Whirled into Happiness, music by Robert Stolz, adaptation of a work by Robert Bodanzky and Bruno Hardt-Warden (produced London, 1922).
Toni, with Douglas Furber, music by Hugo Hirsch (produced Hanley, Staffordshire, 1923; London, 1924).
Madame Pompadour, with Frederick Lonsdale, music by Leo Fall, adaptation of an Austrian play (produced London, 1923). London, Ascherberg Hopwood and Crew, 1924.
Head over Heels (lyrics only, with Adrian Ross), book by Seymour Hicks, music by Harold Fraser-Simson (produced London, 1923).
The Buried Cable; or, Dirty Work at the Cross-Roads (produced London, 1924). London, French, 1924.
Orange Blossom, adaptation of a French play (produced London, 1924).
Katja the Dancer, with Frederick Lonsdale, music by Jean Gilbert, lyrics by Graham, adaptation of a work by L. Jacobsohn and R. Osterreicher (produced Bradford, 1924; London, 1925; as *Katya,* produced New York, 1926).
The Grand Duchess, adaptation of a play by Alfred Savoir (produced London, 1925).
Clo-Clo, with Douglas Furber, music by Franz Lehár (produced Liverpool and London, 1925).
Betty in Mayfair (lyrics only), book by J. Hastings Turner, music by Harold Fraser-Simson, adaptation of the book *The Lilies of the Field* by Turner (produced London, 1925). London, French, 1929.
Cleopatra (lyrics only), book by J. Hastings Turner, music by Oscar Straus (produced London, 1925).
Sky High, with Harold Atteridge, music by Robert Stolz and others (produced New York, 1925).
Riquette (lyrics only), book by Gertrude E. Jennings, music by Oscar Straus, adaptation of a play by Rudolf Schanzer and Ernest Welisch (produced Detroit and Glasgow, 1925).

Merely Molly (lyrics only), book by J. Hastings Turner, music by Herman Finck and Joseph Meyer (produced London, 1926).
The Blue Mazurka (lyrics only), book by Monckton Hoffe, music by Franz Lehár, adaptation of a play by Leo Stein and Bella Jenbach (produced London, 1927).
By Candle Light, adaptation of a play by Siegfried Geyer (produced Southsea, Hampshire, and London, 1928). London, French, 1930.
Lady Mary (lyrics only), book by Frederick Lonsdale and J. Hastings Turner, music by Albert Sirmay (produced London, 1928).
Our Peg (lyrics only), book by Edward Knoblock, adaptation of the play *Masks and Faces* by Tom Taylor and Charles Reade. London, French, 1929.
Hunter's Moon, adaptation of a play by Sophus Michaelis (produced London, 1929).
There's No Fool Like an Old Fool (produced London, 1929).
The Good Companions (lyrics only, with Frank Eyton), book by J.B. Priestley and Edward Knoblock, music by Richard Addinsell, adaptation of the novel by Priestley (produced London and New York, 1931). London and New York, French, 1935.
White Horse Inn, music by Ralph Benatzky and Robert Stolz, adaptation of a play by Blumenthal and Kadelburg (produced London, 1931; New York, 1936).
The Land of Smiles, music by Franz Lehár, adaptation of a play by Ludwig Herzer and Fritz Lohner (produced London, 1931; as *Yours Is My Heart,* produced New York, 1946).
Lady-in-Waiting, adaptation of a play by Ottillo Orbok and Jacques Natanson (produced London, 1931).
Viktoria and Her Hussar, music by Paul Abraham, adaptation of a work by Alfred Grunwald and Fritz Lohner (produced London, 1931). London, Fox, 1945.
Casanova, music by Johann Strauss, adaptation of a play by Hans Muller (produced London, 1932).
Doctor's Orders, adaptation of a play by Louis Verneuil (produced London, 1933).
Roulette, adaptation of a play by Laszlo Fodor (produced London, 1935).
Rise and Shine, with Desmond Carter, music by Robert Stolz, adaptation of a work by Arnold and Gilbert (produced London, 1936).

Poetry

Ballads of the Boer War (as Coldstreamer). London, Richards, 1902.
Fiscal Ballads. London, Arnold, 1905.
More Misrepresentative Men. New York, Fox Duffield, 1905.
Verse and Worse. London, Arnold, 1905.
Misrepresentative Women and Other Verses. London, Arnold, and New York, Duffield, 1906.
Familiar Faces. London, Arnold, and New York, Duffield, 1907.
Deportmental Ditties and Other Verses. London, Mills and Boon, and New York, Duffield, 1909.
Canned Classics and Other Verses. London, Mills and Boon, 1911.
The Motley Muse: Rhymes for the Times. London, Arnold, and New York, Longman, 1913.
Rhymes for Riper Years. London, Mills and Boon, 1916.
The World We Laugh In: More Deportmental Ditties. London, Methuen, 1924.
Strained Relations. London, Methuen, 1926.
The World's Workers. London, Methuen, 1928.
Adam's Apples. London, Methuen, 1930.
The King's Horses (and the King's Men) (song), with Noel Gay. New York, Feist, 1930.

Poetry as Col. D. Streamer

Baby's Baedeker: An International Guide-Book. New York, Russell, 1902.
Perverted Proverbs. New York, Russell, 1903.
Misrepresentative Men. New York, Fox Duffield, 1904; London, Gay and Bird, 1905; augmented edition, London, Gay and Hancock, 1910.

Other

A Group of Scottish Women. London, Methuen, and New York, Duffield, 1908.
The Bolster Book: A Book for the Bedside. London, Mills and Boon, and New York, Duffield, 1910.
The Mother of Parliaments. London, Methuen, 1910; Boston, Little Brown, 1911.
The Perfect Gentleman: A Guide to Social Aspirants. London, Arnold, and New York, Duffield, 1912.
Splendid Failures. London, Arnold, and New York, Longman, 1913.
The Complete Sportsman. London, Arnold, 1914.
(*Selections*). London, Methuen, 1934.

* * *

For nearly 40 years Captain Harry Graham was an indefatigable composer of miscellaneous light verse, but the only products of his skilful pen that remain current are his *Ruthless Rhymes.* The rhymed preface to the first (1899) volume suggested that these were addressed "To children of maturer years / (From seventeen to ninety-nine)"; and urged "fond parents" to keep the volume far from the reach of children "of tender age (from two to eight)." Perhaps this advice should not be taken too seriously; but it does seem that the rhymes were meant originally for the adult sense of humour, and were only later appropriated by the young, presumably for the sake of their cheerful sadism. Typically a "ruthless rhyme" describes with relish some domestic calamity, preferably a violent death, and rounds off the account with some nonchalantly inadequate reflection:

When Grandmamma fell off the boat
And couldn't swim (and wouldn't float)
Matilda just stood by and smiled.
I almost could have slapped the child.

The victim may equally well be a juvenile as an adult, however, as in "Tender-heartedness":

Billy, in one of his nice new sashes,
Fell in the fire and was burnt to ashes.
Now, although the room grows chilly,
I haven't the heart to poke poor Billy.

In *More Ruthless Rhymes* the catastrophes are even more enterprisingly varied, and the rhyming is as deft and the phrasing as neatly witty as ever. W. H. Auden and John Garrett in *The Poet's Tongue* (1935) seem to have been the first to introduce

Harry Graham into a poetry anthology intended for the young, but since then their example has been followed by a number of other editors. It would seem that, even in the bloodthirsty world of today, the engaging subtlety of Graham's wit maintains its appeal, even in competition with his cruder imitators.

Graham's prose fiction includes one volume, *Happy Families,* which he described as "A Story for the Young of All Ages." In this, three impeccably upper-class children, Alice and Martin and Timothy, in the guise of their detective agency, "Almartim's Limited," pursue in the park a suspicious character who turns out to be a duke and an old friend of their explorer-father. Taken off for the summer to the duke's delightful country estate they meet adventures which are genuinely dangerous as well as funny, and which lead to the capture of two burglars and a villainous "fence." The story appeals on two levels—to children as straightforward and amusing adventure, and to adults by its more sophisticated touches of characterisation and wit. It must be admitted that it has dated a good deal, however, partly at least because of its excessively elevated social setting in what one reviewer called "the governessed classes."

—Frank Whitehead

GRAHAME, Kenneth

Nationality: British. **Born:** Edinburgh, 8 March 1859. **Education:** St. Edward's School, Oxford, 1868-75. **Family:** Married Elspeth Thomson in 1899; one son. **Career:** Grahame Currie and Spens, parliamentary agent's office, London, 1875-79. From 1879 gentleman-clerk, and secretary, 1898-1907, Bank of England, London. Secretary of the New Shakespere Society, London, 1877-91. **Died:** 6 July 1932.

Publications for Children

Fiction

The Golden Age. London, Lane, and Chicago, Stone and Kimball, 1895.
Dream Days. London and New York, Lane, 1898; revised edition, 1899.
The Wind in the Willows, illustrated by Graham Robertson. London, Methuen, and New York, Scribner, 1908.
First Whisper of "The Wind in the Willows," edited by Elspeth Grahame. London, Methuen, 1944; Philadelphia, Lippincott, 1945.

Other

My Dearest Mouse: "The Wind in the Willows" Letters. London, Pavilion, 1988.

Editor, *Lullaby-Land: Songs of Childhood,* by Eugene Field, illustrated by John Lawrence. New York, Scribner, 1897; London, Lane, 1898.
Editor, *The Cambridge Book of Poetry for Children.* London, Cambridge University Press, 2 vols., and New York, Putnam, 1916.

Publications for Adults

Short Stories

The Headswoman. London and New York, Lane, 1898.

Other

Pagan Papers. London, Elkin Mathews and Lane, 1893; Chicago, Stone and Kimball, 1894.
Fun o' the Fair. London, Dent, 1929.
The Kenneth Grahame Day Book, edited by Margery Coleman. London, Methuen, 1937.
Paths to the River Bank: The Origins of "The Wind in the Willows," edited by Peter Haining. London, Souvenir Press, 1983.

*

Critical Studies: *Kenneth Grahame: Life, Letters, and Unpublished Work* by Patrick R. Chalmers, London, Methuen, 1933; *Kenneth Grahame 1859-1932: A Study of His Life, Work, and Times,* London, Murray, 1959, as *Kenneth Grahame: A Biography,* Cleveland, World, 1959, abridged as *Beyond the Wild Wood: The World of Kenneth Grahame,* Exeter, Devon, Webb and Bower, 1982, and New York, Facts on File, 1983, by Peter Green; *Kenneth Grahame* by Eleanor Graham, London, Bodley Head, and New York, Walck, 1963.

* * *

It was *The Golden Age,* presently followed by *Dream Days,* that "made" Kenneth Grahame's name. Indeed, so great was the success of these books, both in Britain and America, that *The Wind in the Willows* at first disappointed readers. Several publishers (including those who held the earlier books) had in fact turned down the manuscript. Publishing history is full of these wry mischances. Yet all three books have more in common than may at first appear. All have a seminal place in later fiction. And all derive so much from the accidents of their author's life that some relevant facts should first be set out here.

Grahame's childhood was one of uprooting and loss. He was born in Edinburgh in 1859, the third of four children; in his first few years the family lived in the Western Highlands, near Loch Fyne. This pleasant time was ended by the mother's death when Kenneth was five. The children were despatched to their maternal grandmother at Cookham Dene in Berkshire—a loved place that relives in Grahame's books—but three years later they were moved again. Meanwhile the advocate father, destroyed by the loss of his wife, resigned his post (as Sheriff-Substitute of Argyllshire), drifted to France, and died, an alcoholic, at Le Havre. The fates of the four young Grahames (presently three, for the oldest, Willie, died at 16) lay with unimaginative southern relatives; they inflicted their worst blow on Kenneth by refusing to let him go on to Oxford, though his record at school should have made this a natural step. Such luxuries were thought unsuitable, and a place was found for him in the Bank of England. He had a conformist streak, and rose in time to one of the Bank's three top positions. But the sense of deprivation remained. His other half-life, of intense dream-fantasy, was to channel itself, by various chances, into the books we know.

Grahame's first printed writings were lightweight period essays, ephemeral stuff, though fashionable at the time. But William Ernest Henley, editor of the *National Observer,* noticed one that was different: "The Olympians"; he urged Grahame to write more in this kind. Grahame did; and *The Golden Age* and *Dream Days* were the result. They are, in simplest terms, made up of events in the daily lives of five orphaned children, living in a country house with unloved relatives. Allies are mostly found among the servants, or the odd bachelor solitaries—an artist, maybe a doctor. But the adult and child worlds are distinct. The children live, with marvellous vividness, in the imagination, acting out each book they read, entering, as it were, each picture. (See "Its Walls Were As of Jasper.") One may note that when Edward the oldest goes away to school, the narrator stays behind, still in childhood. In life, Kenneth went off too. Wild Wood? Wide World? Not for Rat; not for Grahame, either.

Grahame was not by temperament an original, yet here he was an original indeed. Nobody yet had so fully pursued this sharp child's view of child and adult, seen with a child's exactness, set down with an adult's skill. The books would affect not only children's fiction (notably the Nesbit-style family story), but the whole child-cult for adults in the new century. Not widely read today, they yet will always be a brilliant find for perceptive readers.

The Wind in the Willows (whose influence can be seen in animal fantasies from Uttley to Adams), began as a series of episodes told to Grahame's 4-year-old son Alistair. Without this waiting listener the book as we know it would probably never have been written. The animal cast, which at first so much perplexed Grahame's adult readers, came naturally enough in a nursery narrative. Are they not creatures of fable and fairy tale? What else, after all? The child-theme of *The Golden Age* and *Dream Days* was, for Grahame, played out; all five children at the end of the tale were already moving towards the Olympian world. Yet animal comrades, neither old nor young, free both from childhood's rules and adult burdens (like undergraduates) exactly fitted the need. As it happens, Grahame had already given thought (expressed in his Introduction to Aesop and elsewhere) to the unjust human roles imposed on animals in didactic fables. Even so, like most major works of children's fiction, *The Wind in the Willows* is not so much a book for the young as a book for Grahame himself about himself, for the streak of childhood that stayed in him undissolved: an autobiography of the mind. Some episodes can be seen as wholly personal: "Wayfarers All," in which Rat is held by friends from the lure of bohemian wanderings, and is offered the consolation of turning the whole affair into poetry, is notably of this kind.

But the first reviews suggest the general perplexity. "For ourselves," the *Times* critic wrote, "we lay *The Wind in the Willows* reverently aside, and again, for the hundredth time, take up *The Golden Age.*" "Grown-up readers," this writer adds, "will find it monstrous and elusive." For *Punch* it was "a sort of irresponsible holiday story in which the chief characters are woodland animals, who are represented as enjoying most of the advantages of civilisation." Arnold Bennett took a bolder view. "The author may call his chief characters the Rat, the Mole, the Toad—they are human beings, and are meant to be nothing but human beings....The book is an urbane exercise in irony at the expense of the English human character and mankind. It is entirely successful."

Yet Grahame was not by intent an adult ironist. As narrative, the book is truly in key with a young child's mind, not least in the merging of outward fact with the inward fact of fantasy. Motor and train exist with mediaeval dungeon. The very size of the creatures varies easily with the scene. "The Toad was train-size; the train was Toad-size"—thus Grahame answered a query on this point. As a result, no pictures, even Shepard's, even Rackham's, are wholly satisfactory, though both are fine on the scenery. It might be worth pointing out that much that is characteristic in *The Wind in the Willows* is foreshadowed in the two earlier books—the camaraderie, the food and feasts, the secret haunts, the obsession with ships (or boats) and water, the long days of summer, the pantheism, the woods under winter snow—and the literary ambiences. But in those earlier books the Wide World is always near. In *The Wind in the Willows* the carefree days are held. It is a book which (in Peter Green's apt comment) stops the clock. Its potent English pastoral dream—reflected too in so much Georgian poetry—remains unchanged. The earliest readers in 1908 and thereafter must have thought this permanence true of Edwardian life itself. History was soon to give the book a further asset—nostalgia, and nostalgia is one of the few commodities that do not decline with time.

And so, *The Wind in the Willows* has been for most of the century a prime best-seller and an unmistakeable landmark in child-literature. Few educated people grow up without meeting its characters, its phrases ("messing about in boats," for instance), its evocative woods and waters. Children mainly prefer the preposterous deeds of Toad (a character almost certainly evolved for the small-boy Alistair); adults more often remember Rat and Mole, in the early chapters especially. A newcomer may quite reasonably wonder what keeps the book in living currency. The style is far from simple; it abounds with absorbed quotations, parody, and pastiche. Its values are not only "middle-class" but almost feudal. Not a girl or woman can be seen except when about some needed chore. But the central fusion of fact and fantasy still drives through these feelings.

—Naomi Lewis

GRAMATKY, Hardie

Nationality: American. **Born:** Dallas, Texas, 12 April 1907. **Education:** Stanford University, California, 1926-28; Chouinard Art School, Los Angeles, 1928-30. **Military Service:** Training film supervisor in the United States Air Force, 1942-45. **Family:** Married Dorothea Cooke in 1932; one daughter. **Career:** Head animator, Walt Disney Productions, Hollywood, 1930-36; artist and reporter, *Fortune* magazine, New York, 1937-39, and other magazines. Commissioned Air Force war artist, Vietnam, 1966. Secretary of the American Watercolor Society, 1946-48. **Award:** American Watercolor Society High Winds Medal, 1979. **Died:** 29 April 1979.

Publications for Children (illustrated by the author)

Fiction

Little Toot. New York, Putnam, 1939; London, Dent, 1946.

Hercules: The Story of an Old-Fashioned Fire Engine. New York, Putnam, 1940; Kingswood, Surrey, World's Work, 1960.

Loopy. New York, Putnam, 1941; London, Dent, 1947.
Creeper's Jeep. New York, Putnam, 1948; Kingswood, Surrey, World's Work, 1960.
Sparky: The Story of a Little Trolley Car. New York, Putnam, 1952; Kingswood, Surrey, World's Work, 1959.
Homer and the Circus Train. New York, Putnam, 1957; Kingswood, Surrey, World's Work, 1960.
Bolivar. New York, Putnam, 1961; Kingswood, Surrey, World's Work, 1962.
Nikos and the Sea God. New York, Putnam, 1963; Kingswood, Surrey, World's Work, 1964.
Little Toot on the Thames. New York, Putnam, 1964; Kingswood, Surrey, World's Work, 1965.
Little Toot on the Grand Canal. New York, Putnam, 1968; Kingswood, Surrey, World's Work, 1969.
Happy's Christmas. New York, Putnam, 1970; Kingswood, Surrey, World's Work, 1971.
Little Toot on the Mississippi. New York, Putnam, 1973; Kingswood, Surrey, World's Work, 1974.
Little Toot Through the Golden Gate. New York, Putnam, 1975; Kingswood, Surrey, World's Work, 1977.
Little Toot and the Loch Ness Monster, completed by Dorothea Gramatky and Linda Gramatky. New York, Putnam, 1989.

*

Manuscript Collections: University of Oregon Library, Eugene; Kerlan Collection, University of Minnesota, Minneapolis; de Grummond Collection, University of Southern Mississippi, Hattiesburg.

Illustrator: *The Treasure Hunter* by Isabel Boyd Proudfit, 1939; *Skwee-Gee* by Darwin and Hildegarde Teilhat, 1940.

Hardie Gramatky commented:

(1978) I like to feel that my work is designed to reach out to children of the younger age group (ages 5 to 8) as a challenge to their potential imaginations. Through an exciting visual approach (paintings that I do in full color) I relate picture to story in a way that makes children love and enjoy the power of words.

Research for my books is actually done right on the spot, as it were. The background of the story is authentic, which every child seems to appreciate. Through picture and story the reader travels to far-off worlds that he may never have an opportunity to see.

This is a creative venture—working with young minds. From the amount of mail I receive I feel certain the experiment has worked.

* * *

Mention *Sparky: The Story of a Little Trolley Car* to anyone, child or adult, and you'll probably get a puzzled look. Say *Little Toot* and the response will be, in all likelihood, a smile and an instant nod of recognition. The trolley car is demonstrably first cousin to the famous tugboat in character and plot. But Hardie Gramatky, author-illustrator of both books and of several others, grew rich and famous with the story of the perky tug while his other works are comparatively unknown. *Little Toot* is now years old, and, along with its sequels, is as much in demand as ever.

Gramatky's style is attractive; his stories are carefully constructed, simply written but never condescending. He builds on locales familiar to him, on characters children can empathize with. A prime example is *Nikos and the Sea God,* about a modern Greek boy who becomes involved with the formidable Poseidon. The text is enlivened by Gramatky's use of Greek words, readily understood in context. The author also created *Homer and the Circus Train, Creeper's Jeep,* and other satisfying entertainments.

His popularity and assurance of lasting renown, however, rest on the cornerstone of his career, *Little Toot,* and its successors. What makes some books classics and others, which seem equally appealing, also-rans, is a question which all authors (and publishers) would love to have the answer to. Most critics and readers agree that the doughty tugboat grabs and keeps its large audience, generation after generation, because of Toot's innate qualities. Always faced with overwhelming odds, sneered at because of his lack of size and strength, Little Toot is nevertheless the soul of pluck, comparable to the fellow who loses battles but wins the war. Boys and girls who are also small exult in his victories. Children respond to a well-told, suspenseful story which keeps them turning the pages to find out what happens next. But, most of all, they like the assurance they get from discovering that, like their hero, they count too—little though they be. A fringe benefit of the Little Toot books (which parents and educators value) is that they give readers information about life in various parts of America, England, and Italy. Still, the magnet of the stories is Gramatky's skillful adaptation of a theme at least as old as that familiar since Biblical time, the triumph of David over Goliath.

—Jean F. Mercier

GRAY, Nicholas Stuart

Nationality: British. **Born:** Scotland, 23 October 1922. **Education:** Privately. **Career:** Actor and stage director. **Award:** Scottish Arts Council award, 1979. **Died:** 17 March 1981.

Publications for Children

Fiction

Over the Hills to Fabylon, illustrated by the author. London, Oxford University Press, 1954; New York, Hawthorn, 1970.
Down in the Cellar, illustrated by Edward Ardizzone. London, Dobson, 1961.
The Seventh Swan: An Adventure Story, illustrated by Joan Jefferson Farjeon. London, Dobson, 1962.
The Stone Cage, illustrated by the author. London, Dobson, 1963.
Grimbold's Other World, illustrated by Charles Keeping. London, Faber, 1963; New York, Meredith Press, 1968.
The Apple-Stone, illustrated by William Stobbs. London, Dobson, 1965; New York, Meredith Press, 1969.
Mainly in Moonlight, illustrated by Charles Keeping. London, Faber, 1965; New York, Meredith Press, 1967.
The Boys, illustrated by Robin Adler. London, Dobson, 1968.
The Further Adventures of Puss in Boots, illustrated by W.M. Hatch. London, Faber, 1971.
The Edge of Evening, illustrated by Charles Stewart. London, Faber, 1976.

The Wardens of the Weir, illustrated by Carolyn Dinan. London, Dobson, 1978.
A Wind from Nowhere. London, Faber, 1978.
The Garland of Filigree, illustrated by W.M. Hatch. London, Dobson, 1979.

Plays

The Haunted (produced London, 1948).
Beauty and the Beast, illustrated by Joan Jefferson Farjeon (produced London, 1950). London, Oxford University Press, 1951.
The Tinder-Box, adaptation of a story by Hans Christian Andersen, illustrated by Joan Jefferson Farjeon. London, Oxford University Press, 1951.
The Princess and the Swineherd, illustrated by Joan Jefferson Farjeon (produced London, 1952). London, Oxford University Press, 1952.
Rapunzel (puppet play; produced London, 1953).
The Hunters and the Henwife, illustrated by Joan Jefferson Farjeon. London, Oxford University Press, 1954.
The Marvellous Story of Puss in Boots, music by Ronnie Hill, illustrated by Joan Jefferson Farjeon (also director: produced London, 1954). London, Oxford University Press, 1955.
The Imperial Nightingale, adaptation of a story by Hans Christian Andersen, illustrated by Joan Jefferson Farjeon (also director: produced London, 1956). London, Oxford University Press, 1957.
New Clothes for the Emperor, adaptation of a story by Hans Christian Andersen, illustrated by Joan Jefferson Farjeon (produced London, 1957). London, Oxford University Press, 1957.
The Other Cinderella, with Due Acknowledgements to All the Earlier Versions, illustrated by Joan Jefferson Farjeon (produced London, 1982). London, Oxford University Press, 1958.
The Seventh Swan, illustrated by Joan Jefferson Farjeon. London, Dobson, 1962.
The Wrong Side of the Moon, based on the story by the Grimm brothers and his own story *The Stone Cage* (produced Edinburgh, 1966; London, 1968).
Lights Up (produced London, 1967).
New Lamps for Old, illustrated by Joan Jefferson Farjeon (also director: produced Guildford, Surrey, 1968). London, Dobson, 1968.
Gawain and the Green Knight, illustrated by Victor Ambrus. London, Dobson, 1969.

Publications for Adults

Novel

Killer's Cookbook. London, Dobson, 1976.

*

Illustrator: *James and Macarthur* by Jenny Laird, 1951.

Theatrical Activities:
Director: **Plays**—*Beauty and the Beast,* London, 1953; *The Marvellous Story of Puss in Boots,* London, 1954; *The Imperial Nightingale,* London, 1956; *New Clothes for the Emperor,* London, 1963; *The Wrong Side of the Moon,* tour, 1967; *New Lamps for Old,* Guildford, Surrey, 1968; *The Shepherd's Play,* Gloucestershire, 1975.

Actor: **Plays**—Francis in *The Haunted,* London, 1948; understudied The Beast in *Beauty and the Beast,* London, 1951; Prince Etienne in *The Princess and the Swineherd,* London, 1952; Puss in *The Marvellous Story of Puss in Boots,* London and tours; Second Suspicious Character, London, 1956, and later Four Winds in *The Imperial Nightingale;* Piers in *New Clothes for the Emperor,* London, 1957; Tomlyn in *The Wrong Side of the Moon,* Edinburgh, 1966, London, 1968; Slave of the Lamp in *New Lamps for Old,* Guildford, Surrey, 1968; Iago in *Othello* by Shakespeare, Malvern, Worcestershire, 1969.

* * *

Nicholas Stuart Gray's writing sprang first from his work in the theatre. His plays, ostensibly for children, often a development of familiar fairy tales, have the range and subtlety to attract an adult audience as well. Beneath the sparkle and the gaiety there are profounder themes—the beauty and the kindness and the terror of Death in *The Imperial Nightingale,* the inward shadows of self-distrust and the loneliness of being different in *Gawain and the Green Knight.* However familiar the story, the events are always unexpected. This is the kind of material, sensitive and intelligent, that children most need.

Some of the stories appear both as plays and novels. One of the most satisfying is *The Stone Cage,* the story of Rapunzel told by Tomlyn, the witch's cat and half-unwilling, half-fascinated familiar. A daring, impudent, and devious cat, with a wry sense of humour, he believes himself to hate everyone and trust no one. His fellow-familiar, Marshall, the ancient raven, is terrified of magic. Between them they save Rapunzel, but are punished by exile to the terrible far side of the moon. Yet when Mother Gotel is caught by her own black magic, Marshall and Tomlyn elect to stay with her in her desolation until she has learned to grow a human heart again. Under Tomlyn's racy, throw-away, ironic account of things runs always the current of deeper feeling, the tragedy and triumphs of human experience. Through the witch herself, vicious, treacherous, and cruel as she is, we become increasingly aware of pity for self-inflicted misery as much as for the griefs of those who love.

The novels with original plots, such as *Down in the Cellar, The Apple-Stone,* and *The Garland of Filigree* (with its tiny, engaging, and quite irresponsible dragon), give scope for the author's hilarious inventiveness, but are never merely funny. They are peopled by redoubtable but completely credible children, whose encounters with magic are interwoven with their normal lives, and who slowly learn the heavy responsibilities of its power. Their adventures—exciting, absurd, sad, or horrific—always enlarge their understanding and sympathy.

The books of short stories, *Mainly in Moonlight, The Edge of Evening,* and *A Wind from Nowhere,* exhibit the full range and versatility of Gray's writing. They have the wildly unpredictable humour, the sudden darknesses and shadows, the poise between the worlds of night and day, of magic and reality, that show their author's Highland origin. Their demons and hippogriffs, knights and mermaids, sad little witches and perplexed humans are funny, touching, and fascinating. So are the animals—dogs, cats, horses, goats—beautifully drawn by a writer who loves and respects them. Some of the stories haunt the heart for a long time afterwards—

the tragedy of stupidity and misunderstanding in "The Star Beast" and its curiously inverted reflection in "The Blot on the Landscape" (both "space" stories of a very unusual kind), the nostalgic sadness of "The Golden Beasts" or "The Stranger." Beneath them all is his deep caring for people and the haunting sense that we dwell in a lost paradise.

The last story of *A Wind from Nowhere,* "Once Upon a Time There Was a Chance," is on this theme, and is developed into the most unusual of all his novels, *The Wardens of the Weir.* The Avatar of the short story, by whose error our world went awry, is given his second chance, with the help of a small group of children, an old carthorse, a dog, and two cats, to redeem his mistake, to save the lost things of this earth and give them a new beginning. Here too ordinary life with its comedy and heartbreak still goes on, but the "magic" is powerful and moving. It leaves the reader convinced, as the author is, of the infinite value of all living creatures.

Laughter, magic, courage, and caring are the stuff of all Gray's work. His book have the rare gift of enlarging the spirit.

—Margaret Greaves

GREAVES, Margaret

Nationality: British. **Born:** Birmingham, Warwickshire, 13 June 1914. **Education:** Alice Ottley School, Worcester, 1927-33; St. Hugh's College, Oxford (scholar), 1933-38, B.A. (honours) in English 1936, B. Litt. 1938, M.A. 1944. **Military Service:** British Women's Land Army, 1941-43. **Career:** High school English teacher, Lincoln, 1938-40, Priory School, Shrewsbury, 1940-41; English teacher, Pate's Grammar School, Cheltenham, 1943-46; lecturer, 1946-60, and principal lecturer and head of the English department, 1960-70, St. Mary's College, Cheltenham. **Died:** 28 June 1995.

Publications for Children

Fiction

Gallimaufry series (*The Snowman of Biddle, The Rainbow Sun, King Solomon and the Hoopoes, The Great Bell of Peking*), illustrated by Jill McDonald. London, Methuen, 4 vols., 1971; Glendale, California, Bowmar, 4 vols., 1975.
The Dagger and the Bird, illustrated by Jill McDonald. London, Methuen, 1971; New York, Harper, 1975.
The Grandmother Stone. London, Methuen, 1972; as *Stone of Terror,* London, Target, and New York, Harper, 1974.
Little Jacko and the Wolf People, illustrated by Jill McDonald. London, Methuen, 1973.
The Gryphon Quest. London, Methuen, 1974.
Curfew. London, Methuen, 1975.
The Night of the Goat, illustrated by Trevor Ridley. London, Abelard Schuman, 1976.
Nothing Ever Happens on Sundays, illustrated by Gareth Floyd. London, BBC Publications, 1976.
The Abbotsbury Ring, illustrated by Laszlo Acs. London, Methuen, 1979.
A Net to Catch the Wind, illustrated by Stephen Gammell. New York, Harper, 1979.
Cat's Magic, illustrated by Joanna Carey. London, Methuen, 1980; New York, Harper, 1981.
Charlie, Emma, and Alberic, illustrated by Eileen Browne. London, Methuen, 1980.
The Snake Whistle, illustrated by Gareth Floyd. London, BBC Publications, 1980.
Charlie, Emma, and the Dragon Family, illustrated by Eileen Browne. London, Methuen, 1982.
Charlie, Emma, and the School Dragon, illustrated by Eileen Browne. London, Methuen, 1984.
The Monster of Roundwater, illustrated by Michael Bragg. London, Methuen, 1984.
Little Bear and the Papagini Circus, illustrated by Francesca Crespi. London, Methuen, and New York, Dial Press, 1986.
Charlie, Emma, and Dragons to the Rescue, illustrated by Eileen Browne. London, Methuen, 1986.
Hetty Pegler, Half-Witch, illustrated by Derek Crowe. London, Methuen, 1987.
Charlie, Emma, and the Juggling Dragon. London, Methuen, 1989.
Mouse Mischief, illustrated by Jane Pinkney. London, M. Malin/ Deutsch, 1989.
Henry's Wild Morning, illustrated by Teresa O'Brien. London, Dent, 1990; New York, Dial, 1991.
Juniper's Journey. London, Methuen, 1990.
Magic from the Ground. London, Dent, 1990.
The Lucky Coin, illustrated by Liz Underhill. New York, Stewart, Tabori and Chang, 1990.
Amanda and the Star Child, illustrated by Diane Catchpole. London, Dent, 1991.
The Lost Ones, illustrated by Honey de Lacey. London, Dent, 1991.
Charlie, Emma, and the Runaway Dragon. London, Methuen, 1991.
Rosie's Lion. London, Dent, 1992.
The Naming, illustrated by Pauline Baynes. London, Dent, 1992; San Diego, Harcourt Brace, 1993.
The Star Horse, illustrated by Jan Nesbitt. London, Dent, 1992.
Littlemouse Alone. London, Scholastic, 1992.
Sarah's Lion, illustrated by Honey de Lacey. Hauppauge, New York, Barron's Educational Series, 1992.
Ice Journey, illustrated by A.C. Darke. London, Dent, 1993.
Henry in the Dark. London, Dent, 1993.
The Serpent Shell, illustrated by Jane Nesbitt. Hauppauge, New York, Barron's Educational Series, 1993.

Play

A Star for My Son (television play). 1980.

Poetry

Nicky's Knitting Granny and the Cat, illustrated by Alice Englander. London, Methuen, 1985.
The Mice of Nibbling Village, illustrated by Jane Pinkney. London, M. Malin, and New York, Dutton, 1986.

Other

English for Juniors series (*Your Turn Next, One World and Another, Gallery, Two at Number Twenty, What Am I?*), illustrated by Jill McDonald. London, Methuen, 5 vols., 1966-72; as *Gallery Wonders,* Glendale, California, Bowmar, 1975.

A Little Box of Witches (retellings; *The Witch Cat, Kate Crackernuts, The Witch's Servant, Mother Cuspen*), illustrated by Francesca Crespi. London, Methuen, and New York, Dial Press, 4 vols., 1985.

Fairy Tale series (retellings; *The Princess and the Pea, Lucky Hans, The Musicians of Bremen, Red Riding Hood*), illustrated by Annegart Fuchschuber, Michèle Lemieux, Renate Mörtl-Rangnick, and Eva Scherbarth. London, Methuen, 4 vols., 1985.

Once There Were No Pandas: A Chinese Legend, illustrated by Beverley Gooding. London, Methuen, and New York, Dutton, 1985.

A Little Box of Ballet Stories (retellings; *Petrushka, Firebird, Coppelia*), illustrated by Francesca Crespi. London, Methuen, and New York, Dial Press, 3 vols., 1986.

Goldilocks and the Three Bears (retelling), illustrated by Maria Claret. London, Methuen, 1987.

The Magic Flute: The Story of Mozart's Opera, illustrated by Francesca Crespi. London, Methuen, and New York, Greenwillow, 1989.

Tattercoats (retelling), illustrated by Margaret Chamberlain. London, F. Lincoln, and New York, Crown, 1990.

Stories from the Ballet, illustrated by L. Kopper. London, F. Lincoln, 1993.

Editor, *Scrap-Box: Poems for Grown-Ups to Share with Children,* illustrated by Jill McDonald. London, Methuen, 1969.

Publications for Adults

The Blazon of Honour: A Study in Renaissance Magnanimity. London, Methuen, and New York, Barnes and Noble, 1964.

Regency Patron: Sir George Beaumont. London, Methuen, 1966.

*

Margaret Greaves comments:

I have never outgrown the children's books that I loved. As I have grown older I have only added to the range and depth of my imaginative reading. So, when I write for children, I write also for myself. Because I have lived nearly always in the country I think I have a particular caring for natural things, a feeling for the past, and a predisposition towards folklore and magic. But above all I care about people; and whether my stories are those of "real life" or "fantasy" (what is the distinction?—they are only different ways of presenting such glimmers of truth as one is privileged to see), the core of my interest is in human relationships.

* * *

In *Little Jacko and the Wolf People* Margaret Greaves presents a "western." There are dangers and courage, friendship and cooperation, ritual magic and celebration, wolves and desperadoes—an exciting package in a story told with swift economy and but a few hundred words for the very young. At the other end of the range, in *Curfew,* she explores a profound ethical problem. Set in the early 19th century, the story concerns a boy on the run from justice whose gullibility has led him into a state where false witness can be held against him. His struggles to survive involve him in petty thefts and deceit, and eventually lead him to become entangled with smuggling and murder. As the boy-hero searches for honest values in a world both perfidious and generous he finds that the law and justice are not in themselves sufficient guides to conduct. Only in probing a deeper moral understanding, he learns, will resolution be found for the dilemmas he must face. The adolescent reader who is used to having his stories neatly tied up at the end with evil overcome and triumphant virtue rewarded will find this novel's refusal to offer cut and dried answers salutary and stimulating.

If Greaves has the courage to leave her heroes (and readers!) in uncertainty and nagging doubt it is because, enriched in self-knowledge, they emerge from adventure equipped to face a more complex world. Neither the heroes and heroines of *The Dagger and the Bird,* nor of *The Grandmother Stone* are assured of living happily ever after. In the former their long-lost brother has yet to adjust to the family, to fit into the warmth and harsh reality of the smithy after the insubstantial and wish-fulfilling faerie world. Like his brother and sister before him, he will have to learn to choose wisely between truth and show.

Greaves conjures up a world of faerie magic in *The Dagger and the Bird,* and also in *The Gryphon Quest,* through a richness of language drawing concrete images, a world both tangibly present and shiftingly insubstantial, whereas the magic of books as various as the lighthearted Charlie and Emma series, *The Monster of Roundwater,* and the romping *Cat's Magic,* on the one hand, and the more profound *The Snake Whistle* and *The Abbotsbury Ring,* on the other, manifests itself in commonplace and thoroughly modern settings. Indeed, in Abbotsbury, it seems that magic is after all nothing special, it can be stumbled on: it is love that, though freely offered, must also be earned, as Magnus finds in *The Snake Whistle* where he has to struggle to reject the corrupting facility of undeserved magical powers. Recently Greaves has produced a number of delightfully illustrated picture stories and tales for the youngest readers where enchantment remains prosaic. In *Magic from the Ground* it is to be found in the wild plants of the gardens and hedgerows of Somerset, but carrying a stern moral health warning. Knowledge of the use of magic, no less than any other power, is a heavy responsibility and, as the readers of *The Lost Ones* learn, is a healing gift only when mixed with love.

In *The Grandmother Stone,* a novel likely to attract an older readership, the power of magic and its association with credulity and popular superstition are measured against courage and independence of mind. Greaves handles the themes of witchcraft, iconolatry, and bigotry in a story set in Stark about the time of the English civil wars. Her heroes survive in displaying a clear-sighted faith in the worth of people. They emerge, not to blaring trumpets and popular acclaim, but to a sense of personal maturity. Still isolated, they are, if sadder, wiser in self-knowledge and with fewer illusions about others. A remarkable feature of this novel, too, is its handling of dawning sexuality. Awakening physical awareness is evoked with sensitivity and totally without prurience.

Few children's writers have commanded the range, assurance, and depth of Margaret Greaves.

—Myles McDowell

GREEN, Roger (Gilbert) Lancelyn

Nationality: British. **Born:** Norwich, Norfolk, 2 November 1918. **Education:** Dane Court, Pyrford, Surrey; Liverpool College; Merton College, Oxford, 1937-42, B.A. 1940, B.Litt. and M.A. 1944. **Family:** Married June Burdett in 1948; two sons and one daughter. **Career:** Actor, Oxford and London, 1942-45; antiquarian bookseller, Oxford, 1943; deputy librarian, Merton College, Oxford, 1945-50; William Noble Research Fellow in English, 1950-52, and member of Council, 1964-70, University of Liverpool. Editor, *Kipling Journal,* London, 1957-79. Andrew Lang Lecturer, St. Andrews University, Scotland, 1968. Played Pirate Noodler in the play *Peter Pan* by J.M. Barrie, London and tour, 1942-43. **Awards:** Mythopoeic Society award, 1975; Scout Association Chief Scout's Medal, 1976; Mystery Writers of America Edgar Allan Poe award, for nonfiction, 1984. D.Litt.: University of Liverpool, 1981. **Died:** 8 October 1987.

Publications for Children

Fiction

The Wonderful Stranger: A Holiday Romance, illustrated by John Baynes. London, Methuen, 1950.

The Luck of the Lynns, illustrated by Sheila Macgregor. London, Methuen, 1952.

The Secret of Rusticoker, illustrated by Sheila Macgregor. London, Methuen, 1953.

The Theft of the Golden Cat, illustrated by Edward McGrath. London, Methuen, 1955.

Mystery at Mycenae: An Adventure Story of Ancient Greece, illustrated by Margery Gill. London, Bodley Head, 1957; New York, A.S. Barnes, 1959.

The Land Beyond the North, illustrated by Douglas Hall. London, Bodley Head, 1958; New York, Walck, 1959.

The Land of the Lord High Tiger, illustrated by John S. Goodall. London, Bell, 1958.

The Luck of Troy, illustrated by Margery Gill. London, Bodley Head, 1961.

Other

The Sleeping Beauty and Other Tales, illustrated by Rene Cloke. Leicester, Ward, 1947.

Beauty and the Beast, and Other Tales, illustrated by Rene Cloke. Leicester, Ward, 1948.

The Story of Lewis Carroll. London, Methuen, 1949; New York, H. Schuman, 1950.

King Arthur and His Knights of the Round Table, illustrated by Lotte Reiniger. London, Penguin, 1953.

The Adventures of Robin Hood, illustrated by Arthur Hall. London, Penguin, 1956.

Old Greek Fairy Tales, illustrated by Ernest H. Shepard. London, Bell, 1958; New York, Roy, 1969.

Tales of the Greek Heroes, illustrated by Betty Middleton-Sandford. London, Penguin, 1958.

The Tale of Troy: Retold from the Ancient Authors, illustrated by Betty Middleton-Sandford. London, Penguin, 1958.

Heroes of Greece and Troy (includes *Tales of the Greek Heroes* and *The Tale of Troy*), illustrated by Heather Copley and Christopher Chamberlain. London, Bodley Head, 1960; New York, Walck, 1961; revised edition, Bodley Head, 1973.

The Saga of Asgard: Retold from the Old Norse Poems and Tales, illustrated by Brian Wildsmith. London, Penguin, 1960; as *Myths of the Norsemen,* London, Bodley Head, 1962.

The True Book about Ancient Greece, illustrated by N.G. Wilson. London, Muller, 1960.

Ancient Greece, illustrated by Carol Barker. London, Weidenfeld and Nicolson, 1962; New York, Day, 1969.

Once, Long Ago: Folk and Fairy Tales of the World, illustrated by Vojtêch Kubasta. London, Golden Pleasure Books, 1962; as *Once upon a Time: Folk and Fairy Tales of the World,* New York, Golden Press, 1962; as *My Book of Favourite Fairy Tales,* London, Hamlyn, 1969.

Authors and Places: A Literary Pilgrimage, illustrated by John Bowers. London, Batsford, 1963; New York, Putnam, 1964.

Ancient Egypt, illustrated by Elizabeth Hammond. London, Weidenfeld and Nicolson, 1963; New York, Day, 1964.

Tales of the Greeks and Trojans, illustrated by Janet and Anne Grahame-Johnstone. London, Purnell, 1964.

Tales from Shakespeare (*The Comedies* and *Tragedies and Romances*), illustrated by Richard Beer. London, Gollancz, 2 vols., 1964-65; New York, Atheneum, 1965.

Tales the Muses Told: Ancient Greek Myths, illustrated by Shirley Hughes. London, Bodley Head, and New York, Walck, 1965.

A Book of Myths, illustrated by Joan Kiddell-Monroe. London, Dent, and New York, Dutton, 1965.

Myths from Many Lands, illustrated by Janet and Anne Grahame-Johnstone. London, Purnell, 1965.

Folk Tales of the World, illustrated by Janet and Anne Grahame-Johnstone. London, Purnell, and Boston, Ginn, 1966.

Sir Lancelot of the Lake, illustrated by Janet and Anne Grahame-Johnstone. London, Purnell, 1966.

Stories of Ancient Greece, illustrated by Doreen Roberts. London, Hamlyn, 1967.

Tales of Ancient Egypt, illustrated by Heather Copley. London, Bodley Head, 1967; New York, Walck, 1968.

Jason and the Golden Fleece, illustrated by Janet and Anne Grahame-Johnstone. London, Purnell, 1968.

The Tale of Ancient Israel, illustrated by Charles Keeping. London, Dent, and New York, Dutton, 1969.

The Tale of Thebes, illustrated by Jael Jordan. London and New York, Cambridge University Press, 1977.

Editor, *Modern Fairy Stories,* illustrated by Ernest H. Shepard. London, Dent, and New York, Dutton, 1955.

Editor, *The Book of Nonsense,* illustrated by Charles Folkard. London, Dent, and New York, Dutton, 1956.

Editor, *Fairy Stories,* by Mary Louisa Molesworth. London, Harvill Press, 1957.

Editor, *Tales of Make-Believe,* illustrated by Harry Toothill. London, Dent, and New York, Dutton, 1960.

Editor, *The Book of Verse for Children,* illustrated by Mary Shillabeer. London, Dent, 1962.

Editor, *Ten Tales of Detection.* London, Dent, and New York, Dutton, 1967.

Editor, *Stories and Poems,* by Rudyard Kipling. London, Dent, 1970.

Editor, *Thirteen Uncanny Tales,* illustrated by Ray Ogden. London, Dent, and New York, Dutton, 1970.

Editor, *The Hamish Hamilton Book of Dragons,* illustrated by Krystyna Turska. London, Hamish Hamilton, 1970; as *A Cavalcade of Dragons,* New York, Walck, 1970.
Editor, *Alice's Adventures in Wonderland, and Through the Looking-Glass and What Alice Found There,* by Lewis Carroll, illustrated by John Tenniel. London and New York, Oxford University Press, 1971.
Editor, *Tales of Terror and Fantasy: Ten Stories from "Tales of Mystery and Imagination,"* by Edgar Allan Poe, illustrated by Arthur Rackham. London, Dent, 1971.
Editor, *Ten Tales of Adventure,* illustrated by Philip Gough. London, Dent, 1972.
Editor, *The Hamish Hamilton Book of Magicians,* illustrated by Victor Ambrus. London, Hamish Hamilton, 1973; as *A Cavalcade of Magicians,* New York, Walck, 1973; as *A Book of Magicians,* London, Penguin, 1977.
Editor, *Strange Adventures in Time,* illustrated by George Adamson. London, Dent, and New York, Dutton, 1974.
Editor, *The Hamish Hamilton Book of Other Worlds,* illustrated by Victor Ambrus. London, Hamish Hamilton, 1976; as *The Beaver Book of Other Worlds,* London, Beaver, 1978.

Publications for Adults

Novel

From the World's End: A Fantasy. Leicester, Ward, 1948; New York, Ballantine, 1971.

Poetry

The Lost July and Other Poems. London, Fortune Press, 1945.
The Singing Rose and Other Poems. Leicester, Ward, 1947.

Other

Tellers of Tales. Leicester, Ward, 1946; revised edition, 1953; revised edition, London, Ward, and New York, Watts, 1965; revised edition, London, Kaye and Ward, 1969.
Andrew Lang: A Critical Biography with a Short Title Bibliography. Leicester, Ward, 1946.
Poulton-Lancelyn: The Story of an Ancestral Home. Oxford, Oxonian Press, 1948.
A.E.W. Mason: The Adventures of a Story Teller. London, Parrish, 1952.
Fifty Years of Peter Pan. London, Davies, 1954.
Into Other Worlds: Space-Flight in Fiction from Lucian to Lewis. London, Abelard Schuman, 1957; New York, Arno Press, 1975.
Lewis Carroll. London, Bodley Head, 1960; New York, Walck, 1962.
J.M. Barrie. London, Bodley Head, 1960; New York, Walck, 1961.
Mrs. Molesworth. London, Bodley Head, 1961; New York, Walck, 1964.
Andrew Lang. London, Bodley Head, and New York, Walck, 1962.
The Lewis Carroll Handbook, Being a New Version of a Handbook of the Literature of the Rev. C.L. Dodgson. London, Oxford University Press, 1962; revised edition, London, Dawson, and New York, Barnes and Noble, 1970.
C.S. Lewis. London, Bodley Head, and New York, Walck, 1963; revised edition, in *Three Bodley Head Monographs,* Bodley Head, 1969.
Kipling and the Children. London, Elek, 1965.
C.S. Lewis: A Biography, with Walter Hooper. London, Collins, and New York, Harcourt Brace, 1974.
"Holmes, This Is Amazing": Essays in Unorthodox Research. Privately printed, 1975.

Editor, *The Diaries of Lewis Carroll.* London, Cassell, 2 vols., 1953; New York, Oxford University Press, 1954.
Editor, *A Century of Humorous Verse 1850-1950.* London, Dent, and New York, Dutton, 1959.
Editor, *The Readers' Guide to Rudyard Kipling's Work.* Canterbury, Gibbs, 1961.
Editor, *Plays and Stories,* by J.M. Barrie. London, Dent, and New York, Dutton, 1962.
Editor, *The Works of Lewis Carroll,* illustrated by John Tenniel. London, Hamlyn, 1965.
Editor, *Kipling: The Critical Heritage.* London, Routledge, and New York, Barnes and Noble, 1971.
Editor, with Morton Cohen, *The Letters of Lewis Carroll.* London, Macmillan, 2 vols., 1979.
Editor, *The Selected Letters of Lewis Carroll.* New York, Pantheon, 1982.

Translator, *The Searching Satyrs,* by Sophocles. Leicester, Ward, 1946.
Translator, *Two Satyr Plays: Euripides' Cyclops and Sophocles' Ichneutai.* London, Penguin, 1957.

*

Roger Lancelyn Green commented:

(1978) My intention with my first four works of fiction was to write exciting adventure stories set against a background of the way of life on a country estate in the 1920s and 1930s—a way of life that had almost passed away even as I wrote. But the setting was too "out of date" and not yet sufficiently "period" to satisfy the critics. None of the four reached a second edition—and two more (the set) remain unpublished.

Meanwhile, however, I had begun retelling myths, legends, and fairy tales—with great success. And I set myself to give young readers as many of the great stories of the ancient world as I could—mainly of ancient Greece but also Egypt, the Middle East, Scandinavia, and our own national legends. That many of these have been reprinted almost annually show that I have at least made good a "felt want" now that Latin and Greek are so little taught.

Deep study of Greek legends and my great love for Greece and its literature led me to attempt to use Greek legends as the basis of fictional narratives—"historical romances" in which the history was that of the world of Homer: *Mystery at Mycenae,* a detective story with Odysseus as the detective; *The Land Beyond the North,* an adventure story of the Argonauts' return from Calchis with the Golden Fleece; and, the most successful, *The Luck of Troy,* a spy story told from the point of view of a Greek boy in Troy during the siege and fall.

The Land of the Lord High Tiger was a departure in the direction of the Carroll-Nesbit tradition written round my old "stuffed animals" and the stories I told them as a child. This is my own favourite (*The Luck of Troy* is my best)—but again the sequel remains unpublished.

* * *

Although Roger Lancelyn Green's main contribution to children's literature is his distinguished work as a compiler, editor, and reteller of tales, there are in his impressively long list of titles some eight books, all, with the exception of *The Luck of Troy* (1961), published in the 1950s (and all except the last out of print), that are works of fiction in a stricter sense. It is a pity that Green should have neglected this form of writing for so long, for in the three "classical" novels for older readers, *Mystery at Mycenae, The Land Beyond the North,* and *The Luck of Troy,* there is evidence of a developing skill in creating intelligent and imaginative novels.

The Land of the Lord High Tiger, a whimsical tale for younger children, is a hotchpotch fantasy which Roger and Priscilla enter through a picture of a tiger on the bedroom wall. They become a prince and princess, encountering more or less predictable pieces of pantomime machinery such as three wishes, lost slippers, giants, wizards, a robber captain memorably named Habbakuk Hak, magic carpets (eaten by Tiger Moths!), and last-minute rescues. Odd oaths ("Screwtape and Slogarithma") and tortured puns ("only school-girls and tidal-waves have serge on them") have a period charm, while the villains are too funny to be frightening.

Green is much more at home in ancient Greece, where his inventive flair combines well with his deep knowledge and love of classical myth, legend, and literature. *Mystery at Mycenae,* the story of Helen of Troy's earlier abduction as a young girl, told in the style of a detective novel, is perhaps marred by excessive schoolmasterly explanation and lines of dialogue such as "It's all a beastly muddle," and "I hawk at higher game, ha-ha," while halfway through the gaff is blown on the mystery. But the blend of classical authenticity with imaginative speculation is vindicated in the sequel, *The Luck of Troy,* which is, as it were, the inside story of the last year of the great siege as experienced by the 12-year-old Nicostratus, Helen's son by Menelaus, who had been taken as a baby to Troy by Paris along with his mother. The complexities of the narrative are skilfully and imaginatively handled in clear, unfussy prose, while questions of loyalty, courage, and civilised conduct are explored through the boy's awakening consciousness of the conflict between his Greek origin and his Trojan upbringing. With the decline of the classics in schools, this novel, together with *The Land Beyond the North,* which is an audacious but not too implausible story linking Jason's journey to the Hyperboreans with Daedalus and the building of Stonehenge, is an imaginative as well as an effective way for a young reader to become acquainted with classical antiquity.

—Graham Hammond

GREENE, Bette

Nationality: American. **Born:** Bette Evensky, Memphis, Tennessee, 28 June 1934. **Education:** University of Alabama, University, 1952; Memphis State University, 1953-54; Columbia University, New York, 1955. **Family:** Married Donald Sumner Greene in 1959; one daughter and one son. **Career:** Reporter, Memphis *Commercial Appeal,* 1950-52, and United Press, Memphis bureau, 1953-54; information officer, American Red Cross, Memphis, 1958-59, and Boston State Psychiatric Hospital, 1959-61. **Awards:** Society of Children's Writers Golden Kite award, 1973. **Address:** 338 Clinton Road, Brookline, Massachusetts 02146, U.S.A.

PUBLICATIONS FOR CHILDREN

Fiction

Summer of My German Soldier. New York, Dial Press, 1973; London, Hamish Hamilton, 1974.
Philip Hall Likes Me. I Reckon Maybe, illustrated by Charles Lilly. New York, Dial Press, 1974; London, Hamish Hamilton, 1976.
Morning Is a Long Time Coming. New York, Dial Press, and London, Hamish Hamilton, 1978.
Get On Out of Here, Philip Hall. New York, Dial Press, 1981; London, Hamish Hamilton, 1982.
Them That Glitter and Them That Don't. New York, Knopf, 1983.
I've Already Forgotten Your Name, Philip Hall! New York, Knopf, 1983.
The Drowning of Stephen Jones. New York, Bantam, 1991.

*

Manuscript Collection: Kerlan Collection, University of Minnesota, Minneapolis.

Bette Greene comments:

I grew up in a small town in the Arkansas Delta (the very eye of the Bible Belt) during the war bond and pin-up picture days of World War II. My friends considered me the luckiest girl in town because, while sugar was being rationed, my parents owned a country store full of gum and candy. But, on the contrary, I considered myself the unluckiest, unhappiest girl in town because my religion (Jewish) was alien to my community, my friends and especially myself. I used to sneak into the tents of itinerant Protestant preachers the way a teenager today might sneak into an X-rated movie. And as the evangelist spoke with easy familiarity of the fires of Hell, I could feel its heat. So I "caught" religion as simply as others caught colds.

And it is from these roots—of childhood sights, smells, and memories—that I write.

* * *

Bette Greene's young-adult novels address the problems of particular individuals who, because they are "different," are alienated from the societies in which they live. To make matters worse, they are badly treated by their own parents, from whom they must break away in order to achieve independence.

Greene's best-known work, *Summer of My German Soldier,* has freshness of approach and an intensity of focus and feeling. Twelve-year-old Patty Bergen is alienated from family and community, and the irony is that, as a Jew in a conservative WASP town, her only friends are also outsiders—a black housemaid and a German soldier who has escaped from a nearby prisoner-of-war camp and whom she harbours. The portrayal of Patty's self-centred mother and bitter, brutal, tyrannical father is a particularly savage one. Conversely, the young German soldier, the epitome of everything admirable, is perhaps too idealised, embodying Patty's romantic view of another world and better people.

In a sequel, *Morning Is a Long Time Coming,* Patty, now 18, escapes from her hateful parents and her stifling Arkansas hometown. In Paris she meets and lives with a young Frenchman. The book's climax involves an attempt to make contact with the mother of the German soldier. This is a clumsy, pathetic venture, but it frees Patty from her obsession with him.

Carol Anne Delaney, a lonely 18-year-old daughter of uncaring parents, seeks a new life as a country singer in Nashville, "all aglitter in a gown sequins and feathers" in *Them That Glitter and Them That Don't.* Like Patty Bergen, she survives social isolation in her small Arkansas town and emerges strengthened in character. In *The Drowning of Stephen Jones,* the title character is harassed and then murdered by bigoted local Bible-belt teenagers because he is gay. In researching this outspoken and controversial novel, which is based on an actual event, Greene interviewed hundreds of victims of gay-bashing (and their homophobic tormentors) but, as she has said, "It isn't at all necessary to be homosexual to be marked as one of America's designated victims." Stephen Jones, Carol Anne Delaney, and Patty Bergen are all designated victims of societies in which they are different.

A remarkable contrast to the emotional intensity and seriousness of these books can be found in Greene's "Philip Hall" stories for younger readers. These are bright, sunny books consisting of episodes from the green and pleasant childhood days of 11-year-old Beth Lambert, a vivacious, happy, and intelligent high achiever. The unifying theme in each book is Beth's affection for her friend and rival, classmate Philip Hall. These are relaxed, "fun" books, written with economy, drive, and directness, with especially polished and convincing dialogue.

—Walter McVitty

GREENE, Constance C(larke)

Nationality: American. **Born:** New York City, 27 October 1924. **Education:** Marymount Academy, New York, graduated 1942; Skidmore College, Saratoga Springs, New York, 1942-44. **Family:** Married Philip M. Greene in 1946; two sons and three daughters. **Agent:** Marilyn Marlow, Curtis Brown, 10 Astor Place, New York, New York 10003. **Address:** 21 North Main Street, East Hampton, New York 11937, U.S.A.

PUBLICATIONS FOR CHILDREN

Fiction

A Girl Called Al, illustrated by Byron Barton. New York, Viking Press, 1969.
Leo the Lioness. New York, Viking Press, 1970.
The Good-Luck Bogie Hat. New York, Viking Press, 1971.
The Unmaking of Rabbit. New York, Viking Press, 1972.
Isabelle the Itch, illustrated by Emily McCully. New York, Viking Press, 1973.
The Ears of Louis, illustrated by Nola Langner. New York, Viking Press, 1974.
I Know You, Al, illustrated by Byron Barton. New York, Viking Press, 1975; London, Kestrel, 1977.
Beat the Turtle Drum, illustrated by Donna Diamond. New York, Viking Press, 1976.
Getting Nowhere. New York, Viking Press, 1977.
I and Sproggy, illustrated by Emily McCully. New York, Viking Press, 1978.
Your Old Pal, Al. New York, Viking Press, 1979.
Dotty's Suitcase. New York, Viking Press, 1980.
Double-Dare O'Toole. New York, Viking Press, 1981.
Al(exandra) the Great. New York, Viking Press, 1982.
Ask Anybody. New York, Viking Press, 1983.
Isabelle Shows Her Stuff. New York, Viking Kestrel, 1984.
Star Shine. New York, Viking Kestrel, 1985.
Just Plain Al. New York, Viking Kestrel, 1986.
The Love Letters of J. Timothy Owen. New York, Harper, 1986.
Monday I Love You. New York, Harper, 1988.
Isabelle and Little Orphan Frannie. New York, Viking Kestrel, 1988.
Al's Blind Date. New York, Viking Kestrel, 1989.
Nora: Maybe a Ghost Story. New York, Harcourt Brace, 1993.
Odds on Oliver, illustrated by S.D. Schindler. New York, Viking Press, 1993.

Short Stories

Funny You Should Ask. New York, Delacorte, 1992.
Within Reach. Harper/Collins, 1993.
Don't Give Up the Ghost. Delacorte, 1993.

PUBLICATIONS FOR ADULTS

Novel

Other Plans. New York, St. Martin's Press, 1985.

*

Constance C. Greene comments:

One of the funnest (I know this isn't a word but sometimes a writer makes up words to fill a bill) things about writing for children is creating a character who is a composite of a lot of things and people. Oneself, one's children, children met in passing, and made up people. Mr. Richards from my first book *A Girl Called Al* was such a character. The assistant super in the apartment building Al and her friend, the book's narrator, live in, Mr. Richards is a fine, funny, kind and helpful man. He has a unique way of polishing his kitchen floor which kids like.

"A good laugh is good for the soul," Mr. Richards says. It's true. It's also good for the disposition, and for a general outlook on life. Laughter lightens the heart and I do think kids need heart lightening. They did almost 30 years ago when *Al* was written and they need it even more today. Childhood seems to have been shortened some, innocence is often damaged, bruised, maybe forever. I have thought long and hard what I could do about this and came to the conclusion that the only thing I can do is to make children laugh. So I try.

And sometimes, if I'm lucky, a child says to me, or writes, "Your books seem real," they say. "They make me laugh. There are things in it that are just like me."

And that is my reward. No small thing.

* * *

Warmth, vitality, and wit, three distinguishing marks in Constance C. Greene's novels, are particularly evident in her characterizations. Her ability to draw believable characters, identifiable to the boy or girl next door, is Greene's strength and accounts for her high popularity with young readers. These distinctive creations successfully carry her stories, and though the plots are usually slim and episodic, they are accomplished with finesse.

With a sharply observant eye, Greene firmly roots her young protagonists in reality and rounds them out with individualized, sometimes quirky personalities who spout casual, glib, and often amusing dialogue. The result is a range of lively characters such as Ben (*The Good-Luck Bogie Hat*), who sees himself as a second Humphrey Bogart and Timothy (*The Love Letters of J. Timothy Owen*), who cribs from published love letters to woo his lady love. Two others that immediately come to mind are Al, who brightly debuted in Greene's first book (*A Girl Called Al*) and who has continued to shine through four others, and Isabelle from *Isabelle the Itch,* a feisty character who is probably most remembered for the daily fights she arranges with her friend and opponent Herbie. Supporting characters are not slighted either as evidenced by Herbie, who delights in making neck boils from wads of chewing gum and Al's long suffering but ever-supportive friend, the nameless narrator of the Al books.

Perhaps the most interesting of Greene's inventions, however, are the elderly, somewhat eccentric friends who bolster the protagonists' confidence, provide emotional refuge, and occasionally disperse tidbits of wisdom. One need only remember Mrs. Beebe (*The Ears of Louis*) who cheats at poker; Mr. Richards (*A Girl Called Al*), who polishes his kitchen floor with cloths tied to his shoes; the sympathetic teacher (*Monday I Love You*) who bolsters Gracie's confidence when she is tormented about her looks, and Mrs. Stern (*Isabelle the Itch*), who continually paints her house and who, in a later book, announces that she might marry again—completely unsettling Isabelle.

The underlying theme in Greene's work is self-adjustment. Sometimes the problem may loom large in the beholder's eye but is nevertheless just a growing-up pain, such as Al's fears of attending her father's wedding or Timothy's lovesick adoration of unreachable Sophie. Other times Greene probes at a more serious level: Gracie's embarrassment about her size 38D breasts, Frannie's inability to read, or Al's awakened consciousness to homeless people. Regardless, the resolution is brought about slowly through the character's own realization of the problem and his or her ability to cope with it. All of Isabelle's coaching to help Guy be less of a goody-goody, for example, is for naught until he tackles the job himself.

Following a number of lighter, episodic books, Greene's first foray into more heavily plotted novels came in 1976 with *Beat the Turtle Drum.* In this story she explores the adjustment of a young girl to her sister's death and in doing so shows an ability to deepen character portrayals to create a more complex novel. While still using a series of episodes to propel the action, the author moves each situation inevitably forward—toward Joss's death—with the characters, though griefstricken, able to handle the tragedy. *Dotty's Suitcase* was Greene's second attempt; here she uses a 1930s Depression setting with a sustained plotline running through the story. It is one of her best books and serves as a milestone in the author's career.

Greene's successful and well-loved characters (Isabelle and Al) continue to appear, and their awareness of social issues, such as the homeless and illiterate, bring a texture to the books that shows growth in the writer and her characters and is meaningful for readers as well. Greene continues to grow and though she hasn't yet reached her potential, her delivery of believable characters ensures an ongoing popularity. Readers gravitate toward the strong personalities, the flow of frankness, and the strains of humor that Greene so smoothly and effectively provides.

—Barbara Elleman

GREENFIELD, Eloise

Nationality: American. **Born:** Eloise Little, Parmele, North Carolina, 17 May 1929. **Education:** Miner Teachers College, Washington, D.C., 1946-49. **Family:** Married Robert J. Greenfield in 1950; one son and one daughter. **Career:** Clerk-typist, 1949-56, and supervisory patent assistant, 1956-60, U.S. Patent Office, Washington, D.C.; staff member, Unemployment Compensation Board, Washington, D.C., 1963-64; secretary, case control technician, and administrative assistant, Washington, D.C., 1964-68; director of adult fiction, 1971-73, and of children's literature, 1973-74, District of Columbia Black Writers Workshop; writer-in-residence, District of Columbia Commission on the Arts, 1973, 1985-86. **Awards:** National Council for the Social Studies Woodson award, 1974; Women's International League for Peace and Freedom Jane Addams award, 1976; American Library Association Coretta Scott King award, 1978; Award from Black Sisterhood for Action, 1983; Washington D. C. Mayor's Art Award for Literature, 1983; National Council of Teachers of English Award for Excellence in Poetry for Children, 1997. **Agent:** Maria Brown Associates, 412 West 154th Street, New York, New York 10034, U.S.A.

Publications for Children

Fiction

Bubbles. Washington, D.C., Drum and Spear Press, 1972; as *Good News,* New York, Coward McCann, 1977.

Sister, illustrated by Moneta Barnett. New York, Crowell, 1974.

She Come Bringing Me That Little Baby Girl, illustrated by John Steptoe. Philadelphia, Lippincott, 1974.

Me and Nessie, illustrated by Moneta Barnett. New York, Crowell, 1975.

First Pink Light, illustrated by Moneta Barnett. New York, Crowell, 1976.

Africa Dream, illustrated by Carole Byard. New York, Day, 1977.

Talk about a Family, illustrated by James Calvin. Philadelphia, Lippincott, 1978.

I Can Do It by Myself, with Lessie Jones Little, illustrated by Carole Byard. New York, Crowell, 1978.

Grandmama's Joy, illustrated by Carole Byard. New York, Collins, 1980.

Darlene. New York, Methuen, 1980.

Grandpa's Face, illustrated by Floyd Cooper. New York, Philomel, 1988.

Lisa's Daddy and Daughter Day, illustrated by Jan Spivey Gilchrist. New York, Sundance, 1991.

Big Friend, Little Friend, illustrated by Jan Spivey Gilchrist. New York, Sundance, 1991.

Aaron and Gayla's Alphabet Book, illustrated by Jan Spivey Gilchrist. New York, Black Butterfly Children's Books, 1993.

Aaron and Gayla's Counting Book, illustrated by Jan Spivey Gilchrist. New York, Black Butterfly Children's Books, 1993.
William and the Good Old Days, illustrated by Jan Spivey Gilchrist. New York, HarperCollins, 1993.
Sweet Baby Coming, illustrated by Jan Spivey Gilchrist. New York, HarperCollins, 1994.
Koya Delaney and the Good Girl Blues. New York, Scholastic, 1995.
On My Horse, illustrated by Jan Spivey Gilchrist. New York, HarperFestival, 1995.

Board Books

Daddy and I, illustrated by Jan Spivey Gilchrist. New York, Black Butterfly Children's Books, 1991.
I Make Music, illustrated by Jan Spivey Gilchrist. New York, Black Butterfly Children's Books, 1991.
My Doll Keisha, illustrated by Jan Spivey Gilchrist. New York, Black Butterfly Children's Books, 1991.
Kia Tanisha, illustrated by Jan Spivey Gilchrist. New York, HarperFestival, 1997.
Kia Tanisha Drives Her Car, illustrated by Jan Spivey Gilchrist. New York, HarperFestival, 1997.

Poetry

Honey, I Love and Other Love Poems, illustrated by Diane and Leo Dillon. New York, Crowell, 1978.
Daydreamers, illustrated by Tom Feelings. New York, Dial Press, 1981.
Nathaniel Talking, illustrated by Jan Spivey Gilchrist. New York, Writers and Readers, 1988.
Under the Honey Tree, illustrated by Amos Ferguson. New York, Harper, 1988.
For the Love of the Game: Michael Jordan and Me, illustrated by Jan Spivey Gilchrist. New York, HarperCollins, 1997.

Other

Rosa Parks, illustrated by Eric Marlow. New York, Crowell, 1973.
Paul Robeson, illustrated by George Ford. New York, Crowell, 1975.
Mary McLeod Bethune, illustrated by Jerry Pinkney. New York, Crowell, 1977.
Childtimes: A Three-Generation Memoir, with Lessie Jones Little, illustrated by Jerry Pinkney. New York, Crowell, 1979.
Alesia, with Alesia Revis, illustrated by George Ford, photographs by Sandra Turner Bond. New York, Putnam, 1981.

*

Media Adaptations: *Honey, I Love* (recording), Honey Productions, 1982.

Critical Studies: "Something to Shout About" by Eloise Greenfield, in *Horn Book,* December 1975; "Writing for Children—a Joy and a Responsibility" by Eloise Greenfield, in *Interracial Books for Children Bulletin,* Vol. 10, No. 3, 1979, 3-4; entry in *Something About the Author,* Vol. 19, Detroit, Gale Research, 1980; entry in *Children's Literature Review,* Detroit, Gale Research, Vol. 4, 1982, Vol. 38, 1996; *Children's Books and Their Creators* by Anita Silvey, Boston, Houghton Mifflin, 1995; "Profile: Eloise Greenfield" by Rudine Sims, in *Language Arts,* Vol. 74, No. 8, 1997, 630-634.

* * *

The late 1960s and early 1970s saw the introduction of many black writers to mainstream children's publishing. Eloise Greenfield was one of them, and her works, all of which portray aspects of the black American experience, collectively carry a positive message to both the black and the white youngsters who read them. Greenfield wrote in *Horn Book*: "I want to encourage children to develop positive attitudes toward themselves and their abilities, to love themselves. I want to present to children alternative methods for coping with the negative aspects of their lives and to inspire them to seek new ways of solving problems." These desires are clearly reflected in her work, which includes picture books, several biographies of important black heroes, poetry, two short novels, and a family memoir.

A strong sense of family is apparent in all Greenfield's fiction. No matter what the story level, there is much love. In *First Pink Light,* a picture book, young Tyree wants to stay up to greet his father who will be arriving at dawn. In *Talk about a Family,* a brief novel, a girl named Genny begins to adjust to her parent's separation by coming to realize that they still love her and she surely loves them. *Childtimes,* a memoir for older children, contains narratives by Greenfield, her mother, and her grandmother, all of whom recall childhoods shaped by differing eras but nurtured by warm family relationships.

Greenfield's wish to inspire and accent the positive is easily seen throughout her work. *Darlene* and *Alesia* are particularly strong examples. Both are about disabled black youngsters, one of them real, the other fictional. Both books encourage the view that the disabled are not unable. The fact that Alesia, a 17-year-old who is struggling to walk again after a severely disabling accident, is a real person will have particular meaning to handicapped minority youngsters in need of a role model.

Her wish to provide black youngsters positive role models and inform them of their past is also carried through in her simple biographies, which present the figures of Mary McLeod Bethune, Rosa Parks, and Paul Robeson. These were, in a sense, groundbreaking books, for they presented strong black men and women little written about in a format easily accessible for younger readers. They were a significant contribution toward easing the dearth of black history material available for young readers.

The artistic success of Greenfield's work varies. Her weakness is a didacticism which flaws some of her more pointedly bibliotherapeutic works such as *Bubbles,* about a boy learning to read, or *Darlene,* whose protagonist manages to have fun despite being confined to a wheelchair. Her best writing involves the warm evocation of tender childhood moods and emotions. *First Pink Ligh* and *She Come Bringing Me That Little Baby Girl* exemplify thi in picture books. The poems of *Honey, I Love* are lyrical and emotionally appealing. For example it's impossible not to be caugh up in the snapping, evocative rhythms of "Way Down in the Music": "I get way down in the music / Down inside the music / I le it wake me / take me / Spin me around and make me / Uh-ge down." *Talk about a Family* and *Sister,* two brief novels, are wel knit stories that achieve their purposes, though the messages i *Sister* are sometimes too strongly stated. Greenfield's most ambitious and mature work is *Childtimes,* her three-generational memoir. Its intimacy, pride, and reverence are compelling. It's a mo ing story that embodies all of its author's aims in a manner that qualifies as both art and living history.

Greenfield's desire to share her love of words with those who are new to the world is evident in her recently published board books for toddlers. Using rhythmic and poetic language, she portrays African-American children engaged in daily routines, finding pride in themselves and delight in their relationships with others. She also reveals children coping with the frustrations of being small. In *Kia Tanisha* she paints a charming portrait of an active little girl who just *loves* to run but is disheartened by her very practical family's admonitions about running inside the house. Eventually, her parents take her outside to run in the yard. As poetry, these works do not possess the rich resonance of earlier works such as *Honey, I Love.* However, their appeal to children who are just beginning to manipulate language is undeniable. These beautifully illustrated board books also fill a void because there are few books which feature African-American characters for the youngest reader.

In addition to the pleasure of writing for children, Greenfield has a keen sense of responsibility about her work. She observed in *Interracial Books for Children Bulletin* that books should "make children aware of their strength and leave them with a sense of hope and direction." This conviction is evident in her poem, *For the Love of the Game: Michael Jordan and Me.* This picture book is an invocation for children to rise to challenges in their young lives, to soar like basketball superstar Michael Jordan. In the first half of the poem, Greenfield celebrates Jordan's fabled ability to defy gravity as he takes to the air to slam dunk a basketball: "...he forgets to obey / the Law of Gravity / jumps not up and down / but up and up / and up, then *stops* / stands right there / on a little piece of air." The second half of the poem focuses upon an eleven year old African-American boy and girl who muse about their future. They recognize the obstacles, dread the dangers, and recoil from onslaughts of negativity: "But I hear the voices / of naysayers / You can't, too hard / you can't." However, the children also hear the encouragement of those who love them, "*If you fall / you will rise again* / I breathe their words / I feel the strength / of my spirit." This poem is a departure for Greenfield since it is not grounded in daily life but focused on dreams and ambitions.

Clearly this work achieves a purpose about which Greenfield feels strongly—inspiring children to believe in themselves. The message dominates the poem and the language fluctuates between being graceful and being stilted.

Eloise Greenfield frequently states her conviction that a need exists for more African-American literature for children in which they can see a reflection of themselves, their lives and their history. She has expressed her desire to be a part of building that body of literature. There is no doubt that she has succeeded.

—Denise Murcko Wilms, updated by Frank Corbett, Jr.

GREENWOOD, Ted

Nationality: Australian. **Born:** Edward Alister Greenwood, Melbourne, Victoria, 4 December 1930. **Education:** Balwyn Primary School, 1936-41; Mont Albert Central School, 1942-43; Melbourne Boys' High School, 1944; Camberwell High School, 1945-47; Melbourne Teachers' College, 1949-50, teaching diploma; Royal Melbourne Institute of Technology, 1954-59, Diploma of Art 1959. **Family:** Married Florence Lorraine Peart in 1954; three daughters and one son. **Career:** Primary teacher, Melbourne, 1948-56; lecturer in art education, Melbourne Teachers' College, 1956-60, and Toorak Teachers' College, Melbourne, 1960-68. Deputy chairman, Australia Arts Council Community Arts Board, 1978-83. **Awards:** Australian Children's Book Council Picture Book of the Year award, 1969; Churchill fellowship, 1972; Australian Literary fellowship, 1975; Visual Art Board award, 1976. **Address:** 50 Hilton Road, Ferny Creek, Victoria 3786, Australia.

Publications for Children

Fiction (illustrated by the author)

Obstreperous. Sydney and London, Angus and Robertson, 1970.
Aelfred. Sydney, Angus and Robertson, 1970; London, Angus and Robertson, 1971.
V.I.P.: Very Important Plant. Sydney and London, Angus and Robertson, 1971.
Joseph and Lulu and the Prindiville House Pigeons. Sydney and London, Angus and Robertson, 1972.
Terry's Brrrmmm GT. Sydney, Angus and Robertson, 1974; London, Angus and Robertson, 1976.
The Pochetto Coat, illustrated by Ron Brooks. Richmond, Victoria, Hutchinson, 1978; London, Hutchinson, 1980.
A Day in the Life of Curious Eddie. London, Angus and Robertson, 1979.
Ginnie. London, Kestrel, 1979.
The Boy Who Saw God, illustrated by Genevieve Rees. Richmond, Victoria, Hutchinson, 1980; London, Penguin, 1983.
Everlasting Circle. Richmond, Victoria, Hutchinson, 1981; London, Hutchinson, 1982.
Flora's Treasures. London, Hutchinson, 1982.
Marley and Friends. Richmond, Victoria, Hutchinson, 1983; London, Hutchinson, 1984.
Ship Rock. Richmond, Victoria, and London, Hutchinson, 1985.
Windows. McPhee Gribble/Penguin Books Australia, 1989.
Uncle Theo is a Number Nine. McPhee Gribble/Penguin Books Australia, 1990.
Spooner or Later. with Paul Jennings, illustrated by Terry Denton. London, Viking, 1993.
The Ventriloquist. McPhee Gribble/Penguin Books Australia, 1994.
With Paul Jennings, *Duck for Cover,* illustrated by Terry Denton. Melbourne and London, Viking, 1994.
What Do We Do with Dawson?, illustrated by Terry Denton. Puffin, 1996.
With Paul Jennings, *Freeze a Crowd,* illustrated by Terry Denton. Ringwood, Victoria, Viking, 1996.
After Dusk, illustrated by Ann James. Ringwood, Victoria, Puffin, 1997.

Other

Warts and All: A Book of Body Talk, with Shane Fennessy, illustrated by Elizabeth Honey. Richmond, Victoria, and London, Hutchinson, 1984.
I Don't Want to Know, with Shane Fennessy. Hawthorn, Victoria, Hutchinson, 1986.

*

Illustrator: *Sly Old Wardrobe,* 1968, and *The Glass Room,* 1970, both by Ivan Southall; *Children Everywhere,* 1970.

Ted Greenwood comments:

Whether working in the picture-book or longer prose forms, I remain interested in the episodic, the cyclical, the open-ended, rather than the rounded, defined experience.

* * *

Ted Greenwood became a picture-book artist by accident rather than intent. He happened to be painting a portrait of the children's author Ivan Southall, who had just been asked by his publisher to supply a picture-book text. He suggested that Greenwood be invited to illustrate it. ("I don't think he knew any other artist!" Greenwood says.) The result was *Sly Old Wardrobe.* Although it was Greenwood's first attempt at book illustration, it won the 1969 Australian Picture Book of the Year award and set him off on a new career which has seen him develop from being an illustrator to becoming a serious author in his own right.

His books are, like the man himself, original and unconventional. He works from principle rather than precedent, being more concerned with philosophies and ideas than trends and formulas. His picture books don't even look like those of other illustrators. He sometimes distorts the shape of the type-matter itself, to match the sense of the text, e.g. in *Joseph and Lulu and the Prindiville House Pigeons* it is sometimes elongated to match the high-rise city buildings, and in *Terry's Brrrmmm GT* it goes "downhill" to match the descent of the fragile billy cart in the "soap-box derby." His drawings are sometimes fractured or incomplete, leading off the page in order to make the reader anticipate what might be on the following page, as in *V.I.P.: Very Important Plant.*

His previous career as a schoolteacher perhaps explains the didacticism in his work, which, even in the picture books, sets out to challenge children by presenting them with abstract ideas, sometimes obscurely portrayed, so that the reader is forced to ask questions, being cajoled into making necessary connections, into sharing with the author-illustrator the experience of "creating" the book's idea and message with every reading.

Greenwood is fascinated by the continuity of natural life, especially its cyclic nature, and has produced a number of interesting picture books exploring this idea. In *V.I.P.,* for instance, his text deliberately avoids capital letters, even at the start, suggesting that things (in this case, plants) do not suddenly *begin,* appearing from nowhere. Nor, in the case of Australian eucalyptus, with their capacity for self-renewal after devastating bushfires, is there an abrupt end. There is always hope—shown here by the sprouting of a leaf bud on an apparently dead tree: life goes on in its inevitable way. Even an ancient rock, as in *Ship Rock,* is being constantly eroded, forever changing and adding life and sustenance to its environment. The cycle is most explicitly presented in *Everlasting Circle,* which presents children with the wonder of the migratory flight of the shearwater (mutton-bird) in its awesome circuit of the vast Pacific basin, repeated endlessly, year after year.

Greenwood's early novels have a poignancy about them. *The Pochetto Coat* is a sort of wistful dialogue between an aging and jaded circus clown and a little girl, while the hero of *The Boy Who Saw God,* struggling to come to terms with a spiteful stepfather and an obsession with the Bible, imagines he has been commanded by God to sacrifice a real live sheep. Like the picture books, these novels challenge the reader, with their multiple layers of meaning, some too obscure for the average child to grasp, but always with a deep, underlying humanity in exploring the need for friendship, trust, and acceptance in our lives.

Greenwood's simplest and most enjoyable books are *Ginnie* and *Marley and Friends,* which consist of episodic, child-centered stories based on the author's observations of, and responses to, the behavior of his youngest daughter. These stories are written with warmth and humour, the natural grace of the language making them excellent for reading aloud to young children.

More recently he has combined with a doctor friend, Shane Fennessy, to produce some non-fiction books designed to give children honest, value-free information about things that concern them. For instance, *Warts and All: A Book of Body Talk,* written in straightforward and sensibly uncensored language, discusses such things as smelly feet, bed-wetting, nose-bleeding, masturbation, and even farting!

In all his work, Greenwood shows a deep concern and respect for children, and a desire to give them the best of his careful craftsmanship, as both a writer and illustrator.

—Walter McVitty

GRICE, Frederick

Nationality: British. **Born:** Durham, 21 June 1910. **Education:** Johnston School, Durham, 1922-28; King's College, University of London (Brewer prize), 1928-31, B.A. (honours) in English; Hatfield College, Durham University, 1931-32, teaching diploma. **Military Service:** Royal Air Force, 1941-46: Flight Lieutenant. **Family:** Married Gwendoline Simpson in 1939; two daughters. **Career:** Assistant master, A.J. Dawson School, County Durham, 1934-40; Head of the English Department, Worcester College of Further Education, 1946-72. **Award:** Children's Rights Workshop Other award, 1977. **Died:** 8 February 1983.

PUBLICATIONS FOR CHILDREN

Fiction

Aidan and the Strollers, illustrated by William Stobbs. London, Cape, 1960; as *Aidan and the Strolling Players,* New York, Duell, 1961.

The Bonny Pit Laddie, illustrated by Brian Wildsmith. London, Oxford University Press, 1960; as *Out of the Mines: The Story of a Pit Boy,* New York, Watts, 1961.

The Moving Finger, illustrated by Joan Kiddell-Monroe. London, Oxford University Press, 1962; as *The Secret of the Libyan Caves,* New York, Watts, 1963.

A Severnside Story, illustrated by William Papas. London, Oxford University Press, 1964.

The Luckless Apple, illustrated by Ian Ribbons. London, Oxford University Press, 1966.

The Oak and the Ash, illustrated by Trevor Ridley. London, Oxford University Press, 1968.

The Courage of Andy Robson, illustrated by Victor Ambrus. London, Oxford University Press, 1969.

The Black Hand Gang, illustrated by Doreen Roberts. London, Oxford University Press, 1971.

Young Tom Sawbones, illustrated by Ian Ribbons. London, Oxford University Press, 1972.
Nine Days' Wonder, illustrated by Paul Ritchie. London, Oxford University Press, 1976.
Johnny-Head-in-Air. London, Oxford University Press, 1978.
Water Breaks Its Neck. Oxford, Oxford University Press, 1986.

Other

Folk Tales of the North Country Drawn from Northumberland and Durham. London, Nelson, 1944.
Folk Tales of the West Midlands, illustrated by N.J.P. Turnbull. London, Nelson, 1952.
Folk Tales of Lancashire, illustrated by N.J.P. Turnbull. London, Nelson, 1953.
Rebels and Fugitives, illustrated by William Stobbs. London, Batsford, 1963; New York, Norton, 1964.
A Northumberland Missionary, illustrated by Ralph Lavers. London, Oxford University Press, 1963.
Jimmy Lane and His Boat (reader), illustrated by Eileen Green. London, Oxford University Press, 1963; New York, Watts, 1968.
The Rescue, and The Poisoned Dog (reader), illustrated by Gwyneth Cole. London, Oxford University Press, 1963; New York, Watts, 1968.
Bill Thompson's Pigeon (reader), illustrated by Maureen Warren. London, Oxford University Press, 1963; New York, Watts, 1968.
The Lifeboat Haul (reader), illustrated by John Lawrence. London, Oxford University Press, 1965.
Dildrum, King of the Cats, and Other English Folk Stories, illustrated by Julia Ball. London, Oxford University Press, 1967; New York, Watts, 1968.
Tales and Beliefs (reader), illustrated by Gunvor Edwards. London, Nelson, 1974.

PUBLICATIONS FOR ADULTS

Poetry

Night Poem and Other Pieces. Tunbridge Wells, Kent, Peter Russell, 1955.
The Faithful City. Privately printed, 1960.

Other

Francis Kilvert: Priest and Diarist. Hereford, Kilvert Society, 1975.
Francis Kilvert and His World. London, Caliban, 1982.

Editor, *A Kilvert Symposium.* Hereford, Kilvert Society, 1975.

*

Manuscript Collections: de Grummond Collection, University of Southern Mississippi, Hattiesburg.

Frederick Grice commented:

(1978) I was born in the North of England, within hearing distance of the bells of Durham Cathedral. My father worked in a small colliery a few miles out of Durham. I think I had the best of three worlds—the world of the pit village with its stories of strikes, evictions, lock-outs, and accidents; the world of the beautiful mediaeval city of Durham where I went to school; and the world of the austerely beautiful countryside that encircled the colliery village.

The first book I wrote was a simple collection of North Country legends and folk tales. I was interested in them because they seemed to embody the spirit of the land and the people that were to be the main theme of my writing—*The Bonny Pit Laddie, The Oak and the Ash, The Courage of Andy Robson, Nine Days' Wonder,* etc. The variety of my interests, and in particular my interest in literature (for the greater part of my working life I have been a college tutor) has prompted me to investigate other themes such as the fortunes of strolling players in the late 18th and early 19th centuries, the lives of railway navvies, etc., but I write best and most authentically about the North, and these are the stories to which children most eagerly respond.

* * *

At a time when working-class children's stories were rare, *The Bonny Pit Laddie,* set in Frederick Grice's native Durham, came as a welcome phenomenon, its subject matter handled with deep feeling and skilful craftsmanship. True, it did not depict the contemporary scene. Set back more than half a century, it had the nostalgia that is apt to creep into this author's fiction. Thus, *A Severnside Story* has jukeboxes and leather-jacketed motor-cyclists to denote the 1960s, but one feels that the boy-hero, and certainly the author, would have been more at home in the Worcester of Elgar's youth. That is really the atmosphere which is so sensitively and poetically evoked. Grice stuck to the locations he knew. Even in *The Moving Finger* he is utilising his North African service in World War II, but understandably this book has less intimate, affectionate feeling, and is more of a conventionally contrived adventure story. *Johnny-Head-in-Air,* by contrast, after a Saharan prologue, goes back to the Hurricane pilot's boyhood holiday in the quiet English countryside and the origins of his obsession with flying.

Grice's strengths and weaknesses are very clearly exemplified in *Aidan and the Strollers,* a delightful tale of travelling actors of 1825. Characters and atmosphere are splendidly handled—indeed, there is a prodigality of almost Dickensian characters passing all too briefly across the everchanging scene. Plot construction and the maintenance of tension are less successful. Time lapses of several weeks are cursorily bridged in a paragraph or two, leaving the reader with unanswered questions. The author has tried to pour a heady quart into a pint-pot, yet shortage of space does not deter him from introducing long Shakespearean quotations and charming but not altogether necessary descriptions of rural sights and sounds.

If Grice excelled in male characterization, he seemed curiously uninterested in depicting the other sex. The absence of women in the Saharan adventure is understandable, but in a theatrical story one would have expected the actresses to make their presence felt. Aidan and his friend Jeremy might appear to a modern child unbelievably blind to the girls they must have met. Possibly the author, already 50 when this book appeared, was following the tradition of his own childhood reading, when there were books for boys and books for girls, as rigidly separated as school cloakrooms.

In his posthumous book, *Water Breaks Its Neck,* Grice used as setting the Radnorshire hills to which he had been increasingly drawn by the enthusiasm for Kilvert which became a dominant interest in his final years. It is a simple but eventful story, narrated by a shepherd boy in 1872, and shows no sign of any failing in his sensitivity or vigour.

Grice was a literary storyteller of style and integrity. For the "gentle" reader—the more bookish, imaginative child—his work offers great satisfaction.

—Geoffrey Trease

GRIFFITH, Helen V(irginia)

Nationality: American. **Born:** Wilmington, Delaware, 31 October 1934. **Education:** Henry C. Conrad High School, Woodcrest, Delaware, graduated 1952. **Career:** Secretary/treasurer, S.G. Williams and Brothers, Wilmington, from 1976. **Awards:** Children's Choice Citation from International Reading Association/Children's Book Council, 1981; Best Books Citation from the School Library Journal, 1982. **Address:** 410 Country Club Drive, Wilmington, Delaware 19803, U.S.A.

Publications for Children

Fiction

Mine Will, Said John, illustrated by Muriel Batherman. New York, Greenwillow, 1980; reissued by Greenwillow, 1992, illustrated by Joseph A. Smith.
Alex and the Cat, illustrated by Joseph Low. New York, Greenwillow, 1982.
Alex Remembers, illustrated by Donald Carrick. New York, Greenwillow, 1983.
More Alex and the Cat, illustrated by Donald Carrick. New York, Greenwillow, 1983.
Foxy. New York, Greenwillow, 1984; London, MacRae, 1985.
Nata, illustrated by Nancy Tafuri. New York, Greenwillow, 1985; London, MacRae, 1986.
Georgia Music, illustrated by James Stevenson. New York, Greenwillow, 1986.
Grandaddy's Place, illustrated by James Stevenson. New York, Greenwillow, 1987.
Journal of a Teenage Genius. New York, Greenwillow, 1987.
Baby Bears Get Dressed. New York: Derrydale, 1988.
Emily and the Enchanted Frog, illustrated by Susan Condie Lamb. New York, Greenwillow, 1989.
Caitlin's Holiday, illustrated by Susan Condie Lamb. New York, Greenwillow, 1990.
Plunk's Dreams, illustrated by Susan Condie Lamb. New York, Greenwillow, 1990.
Grandaddy and Janetta, illustrated by James Stevenson. New York, Greenwillow, 1993.
Doll Trouble, illustrated by Susan Condie Lamb. New York, Greenwillow, 1993.
Dream Meadow, illustrated by Nancy Barnet. New York, Greenwillow, 1994.
Granddaddy's Stars, illustrated by James Stevenson. New York, Greenwillow, 1995.
Alex and the Cat, illustrated by Sonia Lamut. New York, Greenwillow, 1997.
Dinosaur Habitat, illustrated by Sonja Lamut. New York, Greenwillow, 1998.

*

Helen V. Griffith comments:

The memory of a story can last a lifetime. I try to make the memory a pleasant one.

* * *

Helen V. Griffith emerged on the children's book scene in a way reminiscent of her prose: quiet, poetic, and subtly powerful. She continues to attain success in a variety of forms (picture books, short chapter books, read-alone stories, and books for intermediate readers). A gentle humor and ardent respect for human integrity and frailty permeate all her works. Already accomplished, Griffith continues to be an exciting and engaging writer.

Mine Will, Said John, Griffith's first picture book, recounts John's insistent search for the perfect pet. The author effectively portrays John's emotions, from slight irritation to genuine joy, with few, simple words. Readers delight as the chorus "Mine does, said John" ends each episode with a new animal and finally crescendos in John's triumphant "Mine will" as he hugs his yearned-for puppy. Griffith's story takes on added charm in the understanding parent-child relationship; John and his parents share not only a mutual love but also mutual respect.

The picture book *Dream Meadow* explores the life-long friendship between an old lady and her old dog. In their "waking dreams" the woman and dog alike revisit their younger days, days when Jenny and Frisky ran after butterflies in sunshine-drenched meadows. Griffith uses the dreams as a metaphoric pull toward death: though tempted to live in her dream meadow, the unsurpassably loyal dog waits for her owner to enter that world first. Aptly quiet and somber, this picture book reveals the blessing of an enduring friendship.

Griffith's funny stories of Alex the dog and his unlikely feline buddy appear in four books to date. As Alex grows from a puppy, his friendship with the cat deepens, and their adventures extend beyond the safe boundaries of their young owner's backyard. The cat delivers his advice in an utterly feline deadpan and quietly supports and educates child-like Alex. Griffith captures these anthropomorphic characters and their amusing antics in lively dialogue constructed from limited vocabulary.

Foxy, a novel for intermediate readers, again reveals Griffith's concern with connections, be they between animals, humans, or animals and humans. Preadolescent Jeff feels uncomfortable camping for the first time with his parents in the Florida Keys. One night he mistakenly identifies a ragged, abandoned, starving dog as a fox. When he learns his error, he also recognizes both his bond to this outcast animal and his ability to nurture it. Griffith tenderly explores Jeff's loneliness and desire to belong as she simultaneously focusses on his friend's ambivalence toward Jeff. The chapters, which alternate point of view between three primary characters, highlight unique personal struggles. Unfortunately the novel's popularity could suffer from its introspective qualities and the gentleness uncharacteristic of boys' books.

Griffith shifts into outright comedy in the hilarious fantasy *Journal of a Teenage Genius.* Zack's plight as a misunderstood scientist is engagingly related through his self-conscious diary entries. The consistency of the novel's construction allows readers insight into Zack's home life, love life, career ambitions, and self-assessments. His straightforward accounting and genuineness provide laughs, even guffaws, at the expense of the unassuming young scientist.

Caitlin's Holiday also reflects Griffith's sense of humor, but in this case, the slant is decidely satiric. Caitlin, the likable young protagonist, is so taken with a beautiful doll she sees in a thrift shop that she secretly substitutes her own doll for the new one and sneaks out of the shop unnoticed. Caitin's punishment for this act occurs on several levels. Predictibly, once her mother finds out, Caitlin is encouraged to return the doll. However, because the store owner has already sold Caitlin's original doll, Caitlin is allowed to keep her "stolen" toy. On a less conventional level, Caitlin is punished by the doll herself. After only a few moments in Caitlin's possession, Holiday comes to life and turns out to be a spoiled, self-centered, clothes conscious pest. When Caitlin is unable to afford new clothes for Holiday and asks her to wear ones that she has on hand, the doll tosses her blond hair and screams, "'I wouldn't be caught dead in these things.'" All Holiday wants to do is try on make up, listen to music, and get a tan. Caitlin learns an important lesson before eventually taming her unruly doll; namely, beauty does not guarantee a kind disposition. In a highly economical manner, Griffith manages to criticize idealized images of feminine beauty and to weave a humorous morality tale well-suited for the pre-teen reader.

In three companion picture books featuring a curious young protagonist Janetta and her grandfather, Griffith's gift of style, melodious flair with words, and talent in telling a compelling story about characters who are also sensitive, whole human beings. Although published secondly, *Grandaddy's Place* introduces Janetta and her mother as they visit Grandaddy on his Georgia farm. The book's shining success emanates from Janetta's and her grandfather's integrity of character. A city girl, Janetta needs time, patience, and the strength of will to peacefully co-exist with noisy farm animals and outdoor creatures. Grandaddy's life experience instilled in him the gentility and kindness to embrace his granddaughter with both humor and seriousness.

Grandaddy and Janetta opens a year later, when Janetta travels alone from Baltimore to visit her grandfather in Georgia. Brief chapters and James Stevenson's delicate, lush watercolor illustrations mark the girl's continuing journey into a rich, loving relationship with the farm, its animals, and her reliable, earthy, and delightful grandaddy.

Georgia Music emphasizes the vital connection between generations. Physical frailty prevents Grandaddy from maintaining his Georgia farm, and brings him reluctantly to live with his daughter and granddaughter in Baltimore. His depression deepens as the days pass. After many futile attempts, his granddaughter finally reaches and frees him by sharing the very music he taught her to love. Griffith's decision not to name the characters, ambiguously referred to as "the girl" and "grandaddy," strikes a resonant chord. This book stands as Griffith's crowning achievement. Her characters convey the complexity and interdependency of human relationships. Her elegant prose reminiscently evokes Georgia as a time and place. Her words poetically capture the quiet essence of togetherness as she conducts the communal night chorus of birds singing, insects chirping, and humans breathing.

—Cathryn M. Mercier, updated by Gwen A. Tarbox.

GRIFFITHS, G(ordon) D(ouglas)

Nationality: British. **Born:** Wallasey, Cheshire, 19 July 1910. **Education:** Wallasey Grammar School, 1920-27; St. Luke's College, Exeter, 1957-58. **Military Service:** Reconnaissance Corps, and acting sergeant, Intelligence Corps, British Army, 1943-46. **Family:** Married Edith Grace Chalmers Lane in 1948. **Career:** Farmer prior to 1943; French, Latin, and Greek teacher, Devon preparatory schools and Exeter Cathedral School, 1959-60; publishers' reader. **Died:** July 1973.

Publications for Children

Fiction

Mattie: The Story of a Hedgehog, illustrated by Elsie Wrigley. Kingswood, Surrey, World's Work, 1967; New York, Delacorte Press, 1977.

Silver Blue: A Story of the Ponies That Run Free on Dartmoor, illustrated by Elsie Wrigley. Kingswood, Surrey, World's Work, 1970.

Abandoned. Kingswood, Surrey, World's Work, 1973; Chicago, Follett, 1974.

Publications for Adults

Other

History of Teignmouth, with E.G.C. Griffiths. Teignmouth, Devon, Brunswick Press, 1965.

* * *

Judged by quantity only, the output of G.D. Griffiths might seem slight: no more than three books, whose economy of writing makes each rather less in length than the average novel. But these three books place their author in the highest rank of their special genre, the animal narrative. (See also Roberts, Williamson, and others.) It is a scrupulous genre, needing both informed observation and the ability to record its findings. It does *not* include the (often bestselling) humorous records of an author's adventures as vet or zoo-keeper. Animals are rarely themes for comedy, especially those caught up in the human world. A central feature of the form—and Griffiths illustrates this particularly well—is that, while neither sentimental nor anthropomorphic, it rouses a sympathetic understanding through the explicit presentation of its facts.

All of Griffiths's books are set in the Dartmoor region of Devon, one of the last surviving "wild" areas in southern England. Each focusses on a particular animal, living in a natural habitat yet affected both for good and ill by human contact. The subject of *Mattie* is a hedgehog, one of a family born in an old neglected garden near the moor. Outside a textbook there can be few more exact accounts of the creature's looks, behaviour, cycle of life from birth to old age and death. Griffiths, though, is not writing a textbook but a work lit by creative imagination; its impact stays. Characteristically, he shows how inescapably his creature is linked with the larger world around, not only that of insects, plants, other woodland fauna, but of the human kind. One nameless human kicks and kills; another tries to mend the harm, puts out milk, or a grass-filled flowerpot for shelter. *Mattie* is a memorable little book, a classic of its kind.

Silver Blue is far more ambitious in plan, but also—no doubt for this reason—the least "popular" work of the three. As if in contrast to the minuscule scale of the hedgehog story, this ranges widely over the moor, and over the years of the 19th century—a time when a certain wild strain of Dartmoor pony appeared and vanished. Thus, the tale follows a line of creatures, not one individual member. Yet it has all the essential Griffiths qualities—the knowledge, the sense of place, the austere and moving distinction. A beautiful book, it deserves to be better known.

Abandoned, arguably the peak work of the three, has the particularity of *Mattie* and the wider range of *Silver Blue.* Here, the focus returns to the individual creature—in this case, a cat. At 12 weeks old it is thrown out of a car on to a lonely Dartmoor road, and, after further human rejections, learns to accept the life of the moor. The deep snows of winter, the drought of summer, a heath fire (started by campers), floods when the swollen river overflows, illegal gintraps, a fox hunt—all these the cat survives, though not without scars. Humans betray but humans are also rescuers. A watchman at the claypits tends her after the fire; an old "lifer" at the prison finds her half dead and frozen in the stables, and shelters her through the winter; an elderly couple very gradually win her confidence at the end. In all the books, but especially in *Abandoned,* the sense of the moorland seasons is Brontëan in its beauty and its vividness. At the same time, the reader is always kept aware—if only by an illuminating line or two—of the human lives that touch the creature's anxious world: now, say, a difficult husband back from sea; now a prison warder sharing his charges' isolation. This grasp of the total scene, animal, human, elemental, makes *Abandoned* more than a genre example; it is a small but distinguished novel in its own right.

—Naomi Lewis

GRIFFITHS, Helen

Pseudonym: Helen Santos. **Nationality:** British and Spanish. **Born:** London, 8 May 1939. **Education:** Balham and Tooting College of Commerce, London (Matthew Arnold Memorial prize), 1953-55. **Family:** Married Pedro Santos de la Cal in 1959 (died 1973); three daughters. **Career:** Cowgirl, Bedfordshire, 1956; secretary, Blackstock Engineering, Cockfosters, Hertfordshire, 1957-58; office worker, Selfridge's, 1959, and Oliver and Boyd, publishers, 1959-60, both London; teacher of English as a foreign language, Madrid, 1973-76. **Address:** 42 Newbridge Road, Bath, Avon, England.

PUBLICATIONS FOR CHILDREN

Fiction

Horse in the Clouds, illustrated by Edward Osmond. London, Hutchinson, 1957; New York, Holt Rinehart, 1958.

Wild and Free, illustrated by Edward Osmond. London, Hutchinson, 1958.

Moonlight, illustrated by Edward Osmond. London, Hutchinson, 1959.

Africano. London, Hutchinson, 1961.

The Wild Heart, illustrated by Victor Ambrus. London, Hutchinson, 1963; New York, Doubleday, 1964.

The Greyhound, illustrated by Victor Ambrus. London, Hutchinson, 1964; New York, Doubleday, 1966.

The Wild Horse of Santander, illustrated by Victor Ambrus. London, Hutchinson, 1966; New York, Doubleday, 1967.

León, illustrated by Victor Ambrus. London, Hutchinson, 1967; New York, Doubleday, 1968.

Stallion of the Sands, illustrated by Victor Ambrus. London, Hutchinson, 1968; New York, Lothrop, 1970.

Moshie Cat: The True Adventures of a Majorcan Kitten, illustrated by Shirley Hughes. London, Hutchinson, 1969; New York, Holiday House, 1970.

Patch, illustrated by Maurice Wilson. London, Hutchinson, 1970.

Federico, illustrated by Shirley Hughes. London, Hutchinson, 1971.

Russian Blue, illustrated by Victor Ambrus. London, Hutchinson, and New York, Holiday House, 1973.

Just a Dog, illustrated by Victor Ambrus. London, Hutchinson, 1974; New York, Holiday House, 1975.

Witch Fear, illustrated by Victor Ambrus. London, Hutchinson, 1975; as *The Mysterious Appearance of Agnes,* New York, Holiday House, 1975.

Pablo, illustrated by Victor Ambrus. London, Hutchinson, 1977; as *Running Wild,* New York, Holiday House, 1977.

The Kershaw Dogs, illustrated by Douglas Hall. London, Hutchinson, 1978; as *Grip: A Dog Story,* New York, Holiday House, 1978.

The Last Summer: Spain 1936, illustrated by Victor Ambrus. London, Hutchinson, and New York, Holiday House, 1979.

Blackface Stallion, illustrated by Victor Ambrus. London, Hutchinson, and New York, Holiday House, 1980.

Love Forever. London, Macmillan, 1981.

Dancing Horses. London, Hutchinson, 1981; New York, Holiday House, 1982.

Hari's Pigeon. London, Hutchinson, 1982.

Rafa's Dog. London, Hutchinson, and New York, Holiday House 1983.

The Dog at the Window. London, Hutchinson, and New York, Holiday House, 1984.

Caleb's Lamb (as Helen Santos). London, Scripture Union 1984.

If Only (as Helen Santos). London, Scripture Union, 1987.

Other

Jesus as Told by Mark: A Simple Retelling of the Gospel of Mark, illustrated by Jenny Kisler. London, Scripture Union 1983.

Publications for Adults

Novel

The Dark Swallows. London, Hutchinson, 1966; New York, Knopf, 1967.

*

Helen Griffiths comments:

I had my first book published at an early age, and my first few titles are obviously immature. Their purpose, I think, was sheer self-entertainment together with encouragement from my publishers to continue.

The main theme behind all my work, which I have endeavoured to express from the beginning, is to show animals free from the sentimental light in which they are so often portrayed in fiction. I have not tried to write sad books, as I have been accused of doing. I have tried and continue trying to portray a section of life as I see and feel it to be.

Many of my later books have a Spanish background, and in these I have tried to portray the country and the people as they really are, not as foreigners so often imagine them to be. I have also attempted to express how Spaniards feel towards animals, not cruel but indifferent, an attitude often misunderstood outside the country. I would like to think that these books may help people to know a little more about Spain.

* * *

Helen Griffiths's first published book was written when she was a schoolgirl of 15 or 16. Though she has gained in depth and range in her many subsequent novels, her strong descriptive manner and her central kindling theme (the lot of animals—those especially linked with man—in a predatory human world) remain the same. In almost every book it is some rare child, briefly sharing the genius of the animal, who makes a link between creature and humankind. Though knowledgeable enough about her horses, dogs, and cats, she is probably more of a novelist than a naturalist writer and because of the key role given to children in her stories, she is aptly ranked as a children's novelist.

Her first few stories were about horses in the South American plains—free wild creatures, mostly doomed to be caught and "broken" or slaughtered for their skins. The note of violence and cruelty that must attend such themes may not have lessened their popularity with the young. But she occasionally shows a greater subtlety. Perhaps the two best of her horse novels are *The Wild Heart* and *The Wild Horse of Santander* (note the recurring adjective). The first of these tells of a mare born wild on the pampas; left motherless at four months and surviving only by theft, she grows up a natural loner, even among her kind. But she is coveted by traders and others for her supreme racing speed. At the end of a terrible hunt she finds strange sanctuary—in a church. A foundling boy, brought up by the village priest, has to solve the problem of how to give her both liberty and life. The second novel tells of an 8-year-old blind Spanish boy, languid and over-cosseted, who is "given" a new-born foal, born to a half-wild mare after an escapade. A deep alliance grows between the two young creatures, and presently, without either bit or bridle, the horse (which no one else is able to touch) will race along day after day with the blind boy on his back. (What most disturbs the adults is that the horse and not the human is master of the two.) This perfect trust is cracked when the boy leaves for an operation to restore his sight.

In more recent novels she has written of dogs and cats—chiefly in the Spanish setting that she herself knows well. They are, inevitably, grim and poignant stories, though most have consoling endings. *León* is one of the most complex and important of these books—a classic of dog fiction. A clever Spanish village boy, Hilario, has the chance of going to medical school, but has to leave his beloved mongrel sheep-dog with relatives. Caught in the Civil War, and badly wounded, he does not return for several years, while León—chained, starved, beaten, abused, abandoned—tastes the fate of most of his kind in a Latin country. It is the chance of Hilario's medical skill that at last reunites the two. In other novels, based on personal fact, a nameless human (in fact, the author herself) has an operative part in the tale, and ensures a happier end. *Just a Dog,* a vivid account of the life of mongrel strays in Madrid, is of this kind; *Moshie Cat* is another. Two characteristic tales—*The Greyhound* and *Russian Blue*—have a London setting.

Of all her books, *Witch Fear* seems most to diverge from the pattern of the rest, yet basically it is still of the Griffiths kind. This interesting tale describes the situation of what we might now call an autistic child in a superstitious European village several centuries ago—a condition in this case caused by shock: the frightful death of her mother, a herbal healer, as a witch. Unable to communicate in expected human fashion, this girl is in much the same unhappy position as an animal in the rough peasant setting—indeed, her only natural alliance is with a rescued cat. Though (since this is fiction) truth comes out and the girl is saved from death, the basic Griffiths point is sharply made.

If the note of her novels is often sombre, this is because of their truth to human behaviour, too often where the normal is the mindless, mean, and gross. Yet (with equal truth), the animals are always shown as uncorrupt, and this increases the poignancy of their lot. Sad to say—whether through a paucity of ideas or total surrender to the mores of her adopted home—she has devoted her recent book *Dancing Horses* to lauding the miserable business of bullfighting.

—Naomi Lewis

GRIMES, Nikki

Has also written as Naomi McMillan. **Nationality:** American. **Born:** Harlem, New York, 20 October 1950. **Education:** Rutgers University, B.A. in English 1974. **Family:** One daughter (deceased). **Career:** Talent coordinator, Blackafrica Promotions, Inc., New York City, 1970-71; instructor in writing and applied sociolinguistics, Rutgers University, New Brunswick, New Jersey, 1972-74; documentary photographer, Harlem Teams for Self-Help, 1975-76; scriptwriter and producer, The Kid Show, WBAI-FM Radio, New York City, 1977-78; scriptwriter and producer, Riksradio, Sweden, 1979-80; proofreader and translator, AB Exportsprak Translators, Sweden, 1980-84; freelance writer and editor, 1984-88; writer and editor, Walt Disney Company, 1988-90; freelance writer, from 1990. Lecturer at colleges, universities, and workshops, including Pratt Institute, City University of New York, Studio Museum of Harlem, University of Massachusetts,

New York University; consultant to Swedish Educational Radio and New York's Cultural Council Foundation. **Awards:** Ford Foundation grant for research in Tanzania, 1974-75; Best Books of the Year selection, Child Study Association, and Children's Book of the Year Award, Bank Street College, both for *Growin'*; Coretta Scott Kimg award; Books for Free Children citation, *Ms.* magazine, Children's Book citation, Library of Congress, Best Books of the Year, *Philadelphia Inquirer,* Best Books of the Season, *Saturday Review,* all 1978, and Notable Books citation, American Library Association (ALA), 1978-79, all for *Something on My Mind*; Benjamin Franklin Picture Book Award, 1994, for *From a Child's Heart*; Honor Book, Coretta Scott King Award, and ALA Notable Books citation, all for *Meet Danitra Brown: 100 Titles for Reading and Sharing*; New York Public Library Best Books selection, for *Meet Danitra Brown* and *C is for City*; ALA Notable Books citation, 1997, for *Come Sunday.* **Address:** 903 N. 71st Street, Seattle, Washington 98103, U.S.A.

Publications for Children

Fiction

Growin', illustrated by Charles Lilly. New York, Dial, 1977.
Oh, Bother! Someone's Baby-Sitting!, illustrated by Sue DiCicco. Racine, Wisconsin, Western Publishing, 1991.
Oh, Bother! Someone's Fighting!, illustrated by Darrell Baker. Racine, Wisconsin. Western Publishing, 1991.
Minnie's New Friend, illustrated by Peter Emslie and Darren Hunt. Racine, Wisconsin, Western Publishing, 1992.
Baby's Bedtime, illustrated by Sylvia Walker. Racine, Wisconsin, Western Publishing Golden Board Book, 1995.
C is for City, illustrated by Pat Cummings. New York, Lothrop, 1995.
Wild, Wild Hair, illustrated by George Ford. New York, Scholastic, 1996.
At the Break of Day, illustrated by Paul Morin. Grand Rapids, Michigan, Eerdmans, forthcoming.

Poetry

Something on My Mind, illustrated by Tom Feelings. New York, Dial, 1978.
From a Child's Heart, illustrated by Brenda Joysmith. East Orange, New Jersey, Just Us Books, 1993.
Meet Danitra Brown, illustrated by Floyd Cooper. New York, Lothrop, 1994.
Come Sunday, illustrated by Michael Bryant. Grand Rapids, Michigan, Eerdmans. 1996.
It's Raining Laughter, Photographs by Myles Pinkney. New York, Dial, 1997.
Danitra Brown Leaves Town, illustrated by Floyd Cooper. New York, Lothrop, forthcoming.
Is It Far to Zanzibar?, illustrated by Michael Bryant. New York, Lothrop, forthcoming.

Other

Adapter, *Walt Disney's Pinocchio,* illustrated by Phil Ortiz and Diana Wakeman. Racine, Wisconsin, Western Publishing, 1992.
Reteller, *Cinderella,* illustrated by Don Williams and Jim Story. Racine, Wisconsin, Western Publishing, 1993.

Author of several books based on Walt Disney characters, including *Mickey Mouse Tales* and *The Little Mermaid,* Philadelphia, Pennsylvania, Running Press; *The Viking's Eye* and *Sky Island,* both in the "Mickey Mouse Adventures" Series; *My Favorite Book* and *The Great Castle Contest,* in the "Minnie 'n' Me" Series; *Fast Friends, Eeyore's Tail Tale,* and *Rabbit Marks the Spot,* in the "Winnie the Pooh Twin" series; *Her Chance to Dream,* in the "Tale Spin" series; and *Fake Me to Your Leader* and *Catteries Not Included,* in the "Rescue Rangers" series.

Fiction, under pseudonym Naomi McMillan

Wish You Were Here, illustrated by Vaccaro Associates. New York, Disney Press, 1991.
Baby's Colors, illustrated by Keaf Holliday. Racine, Wisconsin. Western Publishing Golden Board Book, 1995.
Busy Baby, illustrated by Anna Rich. Racine, Wisconsin, Western Publishing Golden Board Book, 1996.

Other, under pseudonym Naomi McMillan

Reteller, *Cinderella.* New York, McClanahan Book Co., 1995.
Reteller, *Jack and the Beanstalk.* New York, McClanahan Book Co., 1995.

Publications for Young Adults

A Dime a Dozen (poetry). New York, Dial, 1998.
Jazmin's Notebook (novel). New York, Dial, 1998.
Malcolm X: A Force for Change. New York, Fawcett Columbine, 1992.
Talkin' 'Bout Bess: The Story of Aviator Bessie Coleman. New York, Orchard, forthcoming.

Publications for Adults

Poems By Nikki Grimes. New York, CB Broadside Publications, 1970.
Portrait of Mary (historical fiction). New York, Harcourt, 1994.

*

Biography: Entry in *Something about the Author,* Vol. 93, Detroit, Gale, 1997, 73-76.

Critical Studies: Entry in *Children's Literature Review,* Vol. 42 Detroit, Gale, 1997.

Nikki Grimes comments:

The written word has always held a special fascination for me. It seemed uncanny that words, spread across a page just so, had the power to transport me to another time or place. But they could. I spent many hours ensconced in the local library reading—no, devouring—book after book after book. Books were my soul's delight. Even so, in one sense, the stories I read betrayed me. Too few featured African Americans. Fewer still spoke to, or acknow edged the existence of, the particular problems I faced as a black foster child from a dysfunctional and badly broken home. I couldn't articulate it then, but I sensed a need for validation which the books I read did not supply. *When I grow up,* I thought, *I'll write books about children who look and feeel like me.*

* * *

Nikki Grimes has written for very young children, middle readers, young adults, and adults. She is a versatile and insightful observer of human nature, writing prose that is precise, poetry that is lyrical.

For the very young she has written board books on familiar themes. Her poetry for children is some of the most joyous on the children's library bookshelf. In *Meet Danitra Brown* Zuri Jackson introduces her best friend, Danitra Brown, because she is the most splendiferous girl in town. Danitra Brown only wears purple, because her Mom has told her stories about queens in Timbuktu, who all wore purple. Danitra thinks that she might very well be a princess. Who's to say? Just in case, she dresses in purple every day. Bright pictures show Danitra in purple socks and jeans and sneakers; she wears purple ribbons in her hair. Danitra Brown and Zuri Jackson jump rope, stage plays, and ride bikes together. Danitra takes her feet right off the pedals, throws her arms to the sky, while her friend yells out, "Fly, Danitra! Fly!" And Danitra does fly through the pictures. Though some people call her "Coke-bottle Brown "(her bifocals are big and thick and round) and though she doesn't have money for the ice cream man, she says she's going to win the Nobel Prize. Zuri says that she can tell by looking in her eyes, that Danitra means it. And Danitra shows Zuri some of her writing rhymes and stories. The dignity and strength of both girls come through in text and illustrations.

Another artful picture book is Grimes's *Come Sunday.* The poems in this book describe LaTasha's celebration of Sunday at the Paradise Baptist Church. It shows the religious ritual and response through the eyes of a young child. For Latasha it is a day of wonderful sounds: the pipe organ, the tambourine, the drum, the choir, and the strong voice of the preacher. LaTasha sings along with the congregation. It is also a day of wonderful color, as she studies ladies' hats with feathers, bows, flowers, ribbons; there are hats of peach, plum red, and pale pink. Her mother tells her that people should dress up for the Lord. It is a day of wonderful ceremony: Baptism, Sunday School, the offering. LaTasha prays at the altar with one eye open; her head is bowed, but she is hoping to catch a miracle as it takes place. And then there is the church supper which comes after the service; LaTasha is ready for the good food even before the service ends. The joyous illustrations add to the sense of togetherness and peace which a day of worship brings to the child.

Grimes has also written novels for the middle reader and for young adults. *Growin'* is the story of an African-American fifth grader named Yolanda who must adjust to her father's death, subsequent move to a new neighborhood and a new school, continued disagreements with her mother as she keeps on growin'.

Malcolm X is one of Grimes' heroes. In *Malcolm X: A Force for Change,* she provides a sympathetic but honest record of his life. The poverty and petty crime of his early childhood, the conversion to Black Muslin religion while he was in jail, the continuous search for truth and justice of his young adulthood; all are eloquently presented. Grimes is particularly adept at showing the concerns among and frictions between Black leaders of the 1950s and 1960s as they struggled to effect social change, to bring respect and opportunities for all Americans. Grimes portrays Malcolm X as a symbol of hope for the dropout, the drug addict, the bigot, black and white. He demonstrated through his own life that it is possible to change. Persons can change, groups can change, as they define goals and work towards them.

Grimes' books are for all people. They speak to the joys and challenges of life, as people grow, explore, dream.

—Mary Lystad

GRUELLE, Johnny

Nationality: American. **Born:** John Barton Gruelle, Arcalo, Illinois, 25 December 1880. **Education:** At schools in Indianapolis. **Family:** Married Myrtle Swann in 1900; one daughter and two sons. **Career:** Cartoonist and illustrator for Indianapolis *Star* and Cleveland *Press* from mid-1890s; wrote Sunday comic strip Mr. Twee Deedle for New York *Herald,* 1910-16, and Brutus page for New York *Herald Tribune,* 1929-38. **Died:** 9 January 1938.

PUBLICATIONS FOR CHILDREN (ILLUSTRATED BY THE AUTHOR)

Fiction

Mr. Twee Deedle. New York, Cupples and Leon, 1913.
Mr. Twee Deedle's Further Adventures. New York, Cupples and Leon, 1914.
The Travels of Timmy Toodles. Garden City, New York, Martin, 1916.
My Very Own Fairy Stories. Chicago, Volland, 1917; as *My Very Own Fairy Book,* London, Brentano's, 1923.
The Funny Little Book. Chicago, Donohue, 1917.
Raggedy Ann Stories. Chicago, Volland, 1918; London, Brentano's, 1923.
Little Sunny Stories. Joliet, Illinois, Volland, 1919.
Friendly Fairies. Chicago, Volland, 1919; London, Brentano's, 1923.
Raggedy Andy Stories: Introducing the Little Rag Brother of Raggedy Ann. Chicago, Volland, 1920; London, Collins, 1978.
The Little Brown Bear. Chicago, Volland, 1920.
Orphant Annie Story Book. Indianapolis, Bobbs Merrill, 1921.
Eddie Elephant. Chicago, Volland, 1921.
Johnny Mouse and the Wishing Stick. Indianapolis, Bobbs Merrill, 1922.
The Magical Land of Noom. Chicago, Volland, 1922.
Raggedy Ann and Andy and the Camel with the Wrinkled Knees. Chicago, Donohue, 1924; as *The Camel with the Wrinkled Knees,* Springfield, Massachusetts, McLoughlin, 1941; London, Hutchinson, 1942.
Raggedy Ann's Wishing Pebble. Joliet, Illinois, Volland, 1925.
Raggedy Ann's Alphabet Book. Joliet, Illinois, Volland, 1925.
The Paper Dragon: A Raggedy Ann Adventure. Joliet, Illinois, Volland, 1926.
Beloved Belindy. Chicago, Donohue, 1926.
Wooden Willie. Joliet, Illinois, Volland, 1927.
Raggedy Ann's Magical Wishes. Joliet, Illinois, Volland, 1928.

Raggedy Andy's Number Book. Chicago, Volland, n.d.
Marcella Stories. Chicago, Volland, 1929.
The Cheery Scarecrow. Chicago, Donohue, 1929.
Golden Book. Chicago, Donohue, 1929.
A Mother Goose Parade. Chicago, Donohue, 1929.
Raggedy Ann in the Deep Deep Woods. Joliet, Illinois, Volland, 1930.
Raggedy Ann's Sunny Songs, music by Will Woodin. Chicago, Volland, 1930.
Raggedy Ann in Cookie Land. New York, n.i., 1931.
Raggedy Ann's Lucky Pennies. Joliet, Illinois, Volland, 1932.
Raggedy Ann and the Left-Handed Safety Pin. Racine, Wisconsin, Whitman, 1935.
Raggedy Ann in the Golden Meadow. Racine, Wisconsin, Whitman, 1935.
Raggedy Ann's Joyful Songs, music by Charles Miller. New York, Miller Music, 1937.
Raggedy Ann in the Magic Book, illustrated by Worth Gruelle. New York, Gruelle, 1939.
Raggedy Ann and the Golden Butterfly. New York, Gruelle, 1940.
Raggedy Ann and the Hoppy Toad. Springfield, Massachusetts, McLoughlin, 1940.
Raggedy Ann and the Laughing Brook. Springfield, Massachusetts, McLoughlin, 1940; London, Hutchinson, 1942.
Raggedy Ann Helps Grandpa Hoppergrass. Springfield, Massachusetts, McLoughlin, 1940; London, Hutchinson, 1942.
Raggedy Ann in the Garden. Springfield, Massachusetts, McLoughlin, 1940.
Raggedy Andy Goes Sailing. Springfield, Massachusetts, McLoughlin, 1941; London, Hutchinson, 1942.
Raggedy Ann and Andy and the Nice Fat Policeman, illustrated by Worth Gruelle. New York, Gruelle, 1942.
Raggedy Ann and Betsy Bonnet String. New York, Gruelle, 1943.
Raggedy Ann and Andy, illustrated by Julian Wehr. Akron, Ohio, Saalfield, 1944.
Raggedy Ann in the Snow White Castle, illustrated by Justin Gruelle. New York, Gruelle, 1946.
Raggedy Ann and the Slippery Slide, illustrated by Ethel Hays. Akron, Ohio, Saalfield, 1947.
Raggedy Ann at the End of the Rainbow, illustrated by Ethel Hays. Akron, Ohio, Saalfield, 1947.
Raggedy Ann's Adventure, illustrated by Ethel Hays. Akron, Ohio, Saalfield, 1947.
Raggedy Ann's Mystery, illustrated by Ethel Hays. Akron, Ohio, Saalfield, 1947.
Raggedy Ann's Fairy Stories. Chicago, Donohue, n.d.
Raggedy Ann's Marcella. Chicago, Donohue, n.d.
Stories about Raggedy Ann to Read Aloud, illustrated by Rachel Taft Dixon. London, Spring Books, 1960.
Raggedy Ann and the Golden Ring, illustrated by Worth Gruelle. Indianapolis, Bobbs Merrill, 1961.
Raggedy Ann and the Happy Meadow, illustrated by Worth Gruelle. Indianapolis, Bobbs Merrill, 1961.
Raggedy Ann and the Hobby Horse, illustrated by Worth Gruelle. Indianapolis, Bobbs Merrill, 1961; London, Collins, 1978 (?).
Raggedy Ann and the Wonderful Witch, illustrated by Worth Gruelle. Indianapolis, Bobbs Merrill, 1961.
Raggedy Ann and Andy and the Kindly Ragman, illustrated by John Hopper. Indianapolis, Bobbs Merrill, 1975.
Raggedy Ann and Andy and the Witchie Kissabye, illustrated by John Hopper. Indianapolis, Bobbs Merrill, 1975.
More Raggedy Ann and Andy Stories, edited by Martin Williams, illustrated by the author and Worth and Justin Gruelle. Indianapolis, Bobbs Merrill, 1977.

*

Illustrator: *Grimm's Fairy Tales* translated by Margaret Hunt, 1914; *Rhymes for Kindly Children* by Fairmont Snyder, 1916; *All about Hansel and Gretel,* 1917; *All about Mother Goose,* 1918; *The All about Story Book,* 1929; *The Bam Bam Clock* by J.P. McEvoy, 1936; *Rhymes for Kindly Children* by Ethel Fairmont, 1937; *The Old-Fashioned Raggedy Ann and Andy ABC Book* by Robert Kraus, 1981.

* * *

Like a number of other American writers for children—L. Frank Baum and Thornton Waldo Burgess, for example—Johnny Gruelle was a highly prolific early 20th-century writer. He was also the reputed author of much material turned out in his name long after his death. One result has been that Gruelle, like the others, has only just begun to receive critical and scholarly attention. His major creation was the fictional rag doll, Raggedy Ann, who, with the other dolls and toy animals from Marcella's nursery, had a secret life of her own when the "real for sure people," in Gruelle's child-like phrase, were asleep or away from the house.

Their around-the-house adventures filled the first volume in the Raggedy Ann series, *Raggedy Ann Stories,* and eventually three others, *Raggedy Andy Stories, Beloved Belindy,* and *Marcella Stories.* They are the sort of tales that delight small children. Raggedy Ann, carelessly left outdoors, is washed down a drainpipe and eventually rescued. She is dripped on by a careless house-painter and has to be given a new face and knitting-yarn hair. However, an episode like "The Taffy Pull" in the *Raggedy Andy* collection has a suspense that all ages can appreciate: the dolls stage an evening invasion of the kitchen, make candy, make a mess, and manage to clean up, escape to the nursery and exactly resume their former positions before the family returns from an outing.

In the best stories, however, the dolls enter Johnny Gruelle's very personal (but very 20th-century American) version of fairyland, the "deep, deep woods" behind Marcella's house, "full of elves, and fairies, and everything." Beginning with *Raggedy Ann and Andy and the Camel with the Wrinkled Knees* and *Raggedy Ann's Wishing Pebble* they have charming, book-length adventures which feature amiable creatures like the Snarlyboodle and the Snoopwiggy, more traditional figures like witches and goblins (some of them helpful and none of them very cruel), eccentric kings, handsome princes and beautiful princesses, and magic spells which can be broken with the answer to such riddles as, "Why does a snicker-snapper snap snickers from snuckers?"—altogether an adventurous place where simple "kindliness," in Gruelle's word, usually wins out in the end.

In the best of these longer tales—and *Wooden Willie* and, above all, *The Paper Dragon* should be added to the list—Gruelle reveals unique qualities, for the stories move at the charming pace of a group of children playing an improvisational adventure game among themselves. Gruelle's style, moreover, is whimsically child like in its playful vocabulary and its invented proper names, and its tumbling cadences. Adopting the narrative manner and the styl of children in telling his stories for children—that is Johnny Gruelle's unique contribution to their literature.

—Martin Williams

H

HADER, Berta and Elmer

Nationality: Americans. **Berta—Born:** Berta Hoerner, San Pedro, Coahuila, Mexico, in 1891. **Education:** University of Washington, Seattle, 1909-12; California School of Design, San Francisco, 1915-18. **Family:** Married Elmer Hader in 1919; one son. **Career:** Staff artist, San Francisco *Bulletin,* 1916-18. **Died:** 6 February 1976. **Elmer (Stanley)—Born:** Pajaro, California, 7 September 1889. **Education:** California School of Design, San Francisco, 1907-10; Julian Academy, Paris, 1912-14. **Military Service:** Army Camouflage Corps during World War I. **Career:** Worked as apprentice silversmith, surveyor's assistant, and locomotive fireman, 1906-10; vaudeville actor. **Died:** 7 September 1973. **Award:** American Library Association Caldecott Medal, 1949.

PUBLICATIONS FOR CHILDREN (ILLUSTRATED BY THE AUTHORS)

Fiction

Two Funny Clowns. New York, Coward McCann, 1929.
Lions and Tigers and Elephants Too, Being an Account of Polly Patchin's Trip to the Zoo. London and New York, Longman, 1930.
Under the Pig-Nut Tree. New York, Knopf, and London, Allen and Unwin, 2 vols., 1930-31.
The Farmer in the Dell. New York, Macmillan, 1931.
Tooky, The Story of a Seal Who Joined the Circus. New York and London, Longman, 1931.
Chuck-a-Luck and His Reindeer. Boston, Houghton Mifflin, 1933.
Spunky. New York, Macmillan, 1933.
Whiffy McMann. New York and London, Oxford University Press, 1933.
Midget and Bridget. New York, Macmillan, 1934.
Jamaica Johnny. New York, Macmillan, 1935.
Billy Butter. New York, Macmillan, 1936.
Tommy Thatcher Goes to Sea. New York, Macmillan, 1937.
Cricket, The Story of a Little Circus Pony. New York, Macmillan, 1938; Birmingham, Combridge, 1939.
Cock-a-Doodle Doo: The Story of a Little Red Rooster. New York, Macmillan, 1939.
The Cat and the Kitten. New York, Macmillan, 1940.
Little Town. New York, Macmillan, 1941.
The Story of Pancho and the Bull with the Crooked Tail. New York, Macmillan, 1942; London, Hale, 1946.
The Mighty Hunter. New York, Macmillan, 1943; London, Hale, 1947.
Rainbow's End. New York, Macmillan, 1945.
The Skyrocket. New York, Macmillan, 1946.
Big City. New York, Macmillan, 1947.
The Big Snow. New York, Macmillan, 1948.
Little Appaloosa. New York, Macmillan, 1949.
Squirrely of Willow Hill. New York, Macmillan, 1950.
Lost in the Zoo. New York, Macmillan, 1951.
Little White Foot. New York, Macmillan, 1952.
Wish on the Moon. New York, Macmillan, 1954.
Home on the Range: Jeremiah Jones and His Friend Little Bear in the Far West. New York and London, Macmillan, 1955.
The Runaways. New York, Macmillan, 1956.
Ding Dong Bell, Pussy's in the Well. New York, Macmillan, 1957.
Little Chip of Willow Hill. New York, Macmillan, 1958.
Reindeer Trail. New York, Macmillan, 1959.
Mister Billy's Gun. New York, Macmillan, and London, Macmillan, 1960.
Quack Quack. New York, Macmillan, 1961.
Little Antelope: An Indian for a Day. New York, Macmillan, 1962.
Snow in the City. New York, Macmillan, and London, Collier Macmillan, 1963.
Two Is Company, Three's a Crowd. New York, Macmillan, and London, Collier Macmillan, 1965.

Poetry

What'll You Do When You Grow Up??? New York and London, Longman, 1929.

Other

The Picture Book of Travel. New York, Macmillan, 1928.
Picture Book of Mother Goose. New York, Coward McCann, 1930.
Picture Book of the States. New York, Harper, 1932.
Stop, Look, Listen. New York, Longman, 1936.
Green and Gold: The Story of the Banana. New York, Macmillan, 1936.
The Inside Story of the Hader Books. New York, Macmillan, 1937.
The Little Stone House: A Story of Building a House in the Country. New York, Macmillan, 1944.
The Friendly Phoebe. New York, Macmillan, 1953.

*

Bibliography: By Edward Kemp, in *Imprint: Oregon* (Eugene), Spring-Fall 1977.

Manuscript Collections: University of Oregon Library, Eugene; May Massee Collection, Emporia State University, Kansas.

Illustrators: *The Ugly Duckling,* 1927; *Chicken Little,* 1927; *Wee Willie Winkie,* 1927; *Hansel and Gretel,* 1927; *Donald in Numberland* by Jean Murdoch Peedie, 1927; *The Little Red Hen,* 1928; *The Old Woman and the Crooked Sixpence,* 1928; *The Story of the Three Bears,* 1928; *The Wonderful Locomotive* by Cornelia Meigs, 1928; *The Story of Mr. Punch* by Octave Feuillet, 1929; *A Monkey Tale,* 1929, *Little Elephant,* 1930, *Baby Bear,* 1930, *Lion Cub,* 1931, *Humpy,* 1937, and *Stripey,* 1939, all by Hamilton Williamson; *Timothy and the Blue Cart* by Elinor Whitney, 1930; *Big Fellow at Work,* by Dorothy Baruch, 1930; *Sonny Elephant* by Madge Bigham, 1930; *A Good Little Dog,* 1930, *Bingo Is My Name,* 1931, and *Here, Bingo!,* 1932, all by Anne Stoddard; *The Play-Book of Words* by Prescott Lecky, 1933; *Jimmy the Groceryman* by Jane Miller, 1934; *Everyday Fun,* 1935, and *Who Knows,* 1937, both by Julia Hahn; *The Smiths and Rusty,* 1936, and *Wings for the Smiths,* 1937, both by Alice Dalgliesh; *A Visit* *from St. Nicholas* by Clement C. Moore, 1937; *Marcos, A Mountain Boy of Mexico* by Melicent Lee, 1937; *The Farmer* by Henry B. Lent, 1937; *Banana Tree House* by Phillis Garrard, 1938; *Timothy Has Ideas* by Miriam E. Mason, 1943; *Mr. Peck's Pets* by Louise Hunting Seaman, 1947. Elmer Hader only: *Charm* by Mary Margaret McBride and Alexander Williams, 1927, and *How Dear to My Heart* by McBride, 1940; *Adventures of Theodore Roosevelt* by Edwin Emerson, 1928; *The Story of Water Supply,* 1929, and *The Story of Health,* 1931, both by Hope Holway; *The Story of Markets* by Ruth Orton Camp, 1929; *The Garden of the Lost Key* by Forrestine Hooker, 1929; *Down Ryton Water* by Eva Gaggin, 1941; *The Isle of Que* by Elsie Singmaster, 1948.

* * *

Berta and Elmer Hader, a husband and wife team, wrote and illustrated children's books from the 1920s through the 1960s. The upgrading of children's literature during the nearly five decades that the Haders were associated with children's books can be seen in their works. While some of their earlier works may be considered of dubious quality, their later books possess good literary style and careful coordination of pictures and text. There is variety in their books, though most of them are stories about animals. At a time when children's picture books contained anthropomorphic animals that were overly "cute," the Haders carefully created animals in all their animal dignity.

A common setting of books by the Haders is Willow Farm, which is sure to be the rural area where they lived in the little house they built themselves. The story of the building of this house is told in their picture book *The Little Stone House.* Willow Farm is the setting of *Squirrely of Willow Hill,* a story about Mr. and Mrs. McGinty who care for a squirrel, tame him and spoil him; but when spring comes, set him free in a park. Mr. and Mrs. McGinty and Willow Farm are revisited in *Little White Foot,* about the peaceful coexistence of a mouse family and a human family which results in the belling of the family cat to protect the lives of the mice.

The care and understanding of animal ways shown in both *Squirrely of Willow Farm* and *Little White Foot* are shown over and over again in the Haders' books. *Quack Quack* is a mallard duck aided for a time by people, but allowed to return to the wilds again. The skunk and the fawn, kept for a while by the retired carpenter in *Rainbow's End,* both return to their lives in the forest. A similar event occurs in *Cock-a-Doodle Doo* when Little Red, a baby chick hatched with ducks, finds his way back to the barnyard to live with his own kind.

The best known of the Haders' works is *The Big Snow,* which received the Caldecott Medal in 1949. It is a book that shows the careful detail that typifies many of their works. *The Big Snow* is an animal book. People appear in the illustrations only twice, and are important only because of their relationship with the animals. The story has three parts. The animals prepare for winter, there is a snowstorm, and animals and people cope with the results of the heavy snow. The many details of the book deserve attention. Bright blue endpapers show many designed snowflakes. On the page preceding the title page a wild goose, the late fall symbol, is shown flying into the book. The frontis-piece is a full color picture of a snow scene, a promise of the major intent of the book. Central to this picture are the many animals in it: deer, raccoons, skunks, squirrels, rabbits, a cardinal, and a blue jay. The title page itself is almost stark, reminiscent of a quiet heavy snowfall; it is decorated only with seven snowflakes. The back of the title page shows a man and a woman surrounded by snow, a small self portrait of the Haders, which is a trademark of a Hader book.

On the first page of the story, the geese return. These heralds of winter appear across the top of each page throughout the first half of the book guiding the reader's eye through the pages. The final appearance of the geese is a full-color page that is shared with no other animal. The geese at the top of each page have been witness to the preparation made for winter by a variety of animals. With their disappearance midway in the book, winter takes over. Snow starts to fall and the reader is witness to the simple drama of a tremendous snowfall.

The story tells of the effect of the snowfall, the shoveling out, and of an old couple who share food with animals whose survival is threatened by the heavy snow. The story ends on Ground Hog Day when the ground hog predicts six more weeks of winter in this uncomplicated and satisfying paragraph: "The ground hog was right. It was a long cold winter for the birds and the animals on the hill, but the little old man and the little old woman put out food for them until the warm spring came. And that was the end of the BIG SNOW."

In *Rainbow's End* the reader sees a reflection of the main character as he examines the injured birds the children bring him to be cared for: "Toby always felt sad for these feathered creatures that made his day happier with their pretty ways and their sweet songs." So it seems this genuine appreciation for the companionship of animal life permeates Berta and Elmer Hader's books. This care is expressed through the stories—animals characterize only themselves, behave according to their instincts, and are allowed to remain happily in natural surroundings with their own kind—and is displayed even more clearly in the illustrations, beautiful representations of animals in careful proportion showing each animal as it really is. Surely this is one of the Haders' greatest contributions to children's books.

—Mary J. Lickteig

HAGON, Priscilla. See **ALLAN, Mabel Esther.**

HAIG-BROWN, Roderick (Langmere)

Nationality: Canadian (originally English: emigrated to Canada 1926). **Born:** Lancing, Sussex, England, 21 February 1908. **Edu**cation:** Charterhouse, Godalming, Surrey. **Military Service:** Ca nadian Army, 1939-45: major. **Family:** Married Ann Elmore i 1934; one son and three daughters. **Career:** Worked as a logge trapper, fisherman, and guide, Washington, U.S.A., 1926, and Bri ish Columbia, 1927-29; provincial magistrate and judge, Campbe River Children's and Family Court, British Columbia, 1942-7 Frequent broadcaster and moderator of television programs. Cha cellor, University of Victoria, British Columbia, 1970-73. **Award** Canadian Library Association Book of the Year Medal, 194

1964; Governor-General's citation, 1948; Crandell Conservation Trophy, 1955; Vicky Metcalf award, 1966. LL.D.: University of British Columbia, Vancouver, 1952. **Died:** 9 October 1976.

PUBLICATIONS FOR CHILDREN

Fiction

Silver: The Life of an Atlantic Salmon, illustrated by J.P. Moreton. London, A. and C. Black, 1931.
Ki-yu: A Story of Panthers, illustrated by Kurt Wiese. Boston, Houghton Mifflin, 1934; as *Panther,* London, Cape, 1934.
Starbuck Valley Winter, illustrated by Charles De Feo. New York, Morrow, 1943; London, Collins, 1944.
Saltwater Summer. Toronto, Collins, and New York, Morrow, 1948; London, Collins, 1949.
Mounted Police Patrol. London, Collins, and New York, Morrow, 1954.
Fur and Gold, illustrated by Paul Duff. Toronto, Longman, 1962.
The Whale People, illustrated by Mary Weiler. London, Collins, 1962; New York, Morrow, 1963.
Alison's Fishing Birds, illustrated by Jim Rimmer. Vancouver, Colophon, 1980.

Other

Captain of the Discovery: The Story of Captain George Vancouver, illustrated by Robert Banks. Toronto and London, Macmillan, 1956.
The Farthest Shores, illustrated by Frank Newfeld. Toronto, Longman, 1960.

PUBLICATIONS FOR ADULTS

Novels

Pool and Rapid: The Story of a River, illustrated by C.F. Tunnicliffe. Toronto, McClelland and Stewart, and London, A. and C. Black, 1932.
Timber: A Novel of Pacific Coast Loggers. New York, Morrow, 1942; as *The Tall Trees Fall,* London, Collins, 1943.
On the Highest Hill. Toronto, Collins, and New York, Morrow, 1949; London, Collins, 1950.

Short Stories

Woods and River Tales, edited by Valerie Haig-Brown. Toronto, McClelland and Stewart, 1980.

Other

The Western Angler: An Account of Pacific Salmon and Western Trout in British Columbia. New York, Derrydale Press, 1939.
Return to the River: A Story of the Chinook Run. New York, Morrow, 1941; London, Collins, 1942.
A River Never Sleeps. Toronto, Collins, and New York, Morrow, 1946; London, Collins, 1948.
Measure of the Year. Toronto, Collins, and New York, Morrow, 1950.
Fisherman's Spring. Toronto, Collins, and New York, Morrow, 1951.
Spring Congregation Address 1952: Power and People. Vancouver, University of British Columbia, 1952.
Fisherman's Winter. New York, Morrow, 1954.
Divine Discontent: An Address to the Annual Assembly of Victoria College. Victoria, British Columbia, Victoria Daily Times, 1954.
The Case for the Preservation of Strathcona Park. Victoria, British Columbia, Daily Colonist, 1955.
Fabulous Fishing in Latin America.... New York, Pan American World Airways, 1956.
The Face of Canada, with others. Toronto, Clarke Irwin, 1959; London, Harrap, 1960.
Fisherman's Summer. Toronto, Collins, and New York, Morrow, 1959.
The Living Land: An Account of the Natural Resources of British Columbia. Toronto, Macmillan, and New York, Morrow, 1961.
The Pacific Northwest, with Stewart Holbrook and Nard Jones, edited by Anthony Netboy. New York, Doubleday, 1963.
A Primer of Fly Fishing. Toronto, Collins, and New York, Morrow, 1964.
Fisherman's Fall. Toronto, Collins, and New York, Morrow, 1964.
Canada's Pacific Salmon, revised edition. Ottawa, Queen's Printer, 1967.
The Canadians 1867-1967. Toronto, Macmillan, 1967.
The Salmon. Ottawa, Queen's Printer, 1974.
Bright Waters, Bright Fish: An Examination of Angling in Canada. Vancouver, Douglas and McIntyre, and Portland, Oregon, Timber Press, 1980.
The Master and His Fish, edited by Valerie Haig-Brown. Toronto, McClelland and Stewart, and Seattle, University of Washington Press, 1981.
Writings and Reflections: From the World of Roderick Haig-Brown, edited by Valerie Haig-Brown. Toronto, McClelland and Stewart, and Seattle, University of Washington Press, 1982.

*

Manuscript Collections: University of British Columbia Library, Vancouver.

Theatrical Activities:
Actor: **Films**—*Out of the North,* 1952; *Rural Magistrate.*

* * *

Before the "boom period" of the last two decades, Roderick Haig-Brown was an undisputed giant of Canadian children's literature. The two-time winner of the Canadian Library Association Medal had distinguished himself as a writer of animal stories, boys' adventures, history, biography, and a bildungsroman of pre-contact Native life. His works combined well-established genres, especially the animal and adventure story, with his deep knowledge and appreciation of the Canadian landscape and his respect for what he called "quiet heroes." His work as logger, fisherman, trapper, and guide sharpened his knowledge of nature and deepened his understanding of human nature; his lifelong love of nature provided inspiration and guides for his writing.

Four works illustrate his achievements in the different genres. *Ki-yu: A Story of Panthers* draws on detailed study of panthers; but, in the manner of the realistic animal story, he elevates his presentation of details to the level of symbol. Ki-yu, the most noble animal of the area, engages in heroic confrontation with the most dedicated hunter, one who respects and understands his prey. *Captain of the Discovery* combines historical facts with sensitive understanding of the challenges and responsibilities of leadership to present the life of George Vancouver, the 18th-century explorer who showed respect for his own men as well as the lands and people he encountered.

Starbuck Valley Winter describes the coming of age of teenager Don Morgan, who spends a winter trapping to earn money for a new fishing boat. While Haig-Brown draws on ideas of manly virtue found in boys' adventure novels, his presentations of Don's inner life and of his struggles and achievements in the rugged West Coast landscape are convincing and authentic, drawn as they are on the author's own experience and knowledge. *The Whale People* is also an initiation novel, this time about a Nootka Indian teenager who assumes the role of chief after the death of his father. As in his other books, Haig-Brown's research is impeccable. More significant, he succeeds in recreating the inner life of someone of another culture and time, capturing the hero's response to his physical, social, and, perhaps most important, spiritual environments.

Although some critics consider Haig-Brown's writing old-fashioned, using 19th- and early 20th- century forms and focussing mainly on heroic male figures, his books are important treatments of a significant aspect of the Canadian experience: the human encounter with the grandeur and danger of the natural environment.

—Jon C. Stott

HALDANE, J(ohn) B(urdon) S(anderson)

Nationality: Indian (originally British: moved to India, 1957, became citizen, 1961). **Born:** Oxford, England, 5 November 1892; son of the scientist John Scott Haldane; brother of Naomi Mitchison, *q.v.* **Education:** Lynam's School, Oxford; Eton College, 1905-11; New College, Oxford, 1911-14, B.A. 1914, M.A. **Military Service:** Black Watch in France, Iraq, and India, 1914-19: Captain. **Family:** Married 1) Charlotte Franken in 1926 (divorced 1945), one stepson; 2) Helen Spurway in 1945. **Career:** Fellow of New College, 1919-22; Reader in Biochemistry, Cambridge University, 1923-33; geneticist, John Innes Horticultural Research Institution, London, 1927-36; Fullerian Professor of Physiology, Royal Institution, London, 1930-32; Professor of Genetics, 1933-36, and Weldon Professor of Biometry, 1936-57, University College, London; Research Professor, Indian Statistical Institute, Calcutta, 1957-61; worked for Council of Scientific and Industrial Research, Calcutta, 1961-62; Head of Genetics and Biometry, Government of Orissa, Bhubaneswar, 1962-64. President, Genetical Society, 1932-36; science correspondent, 1937-50, and chairman of the Editorial Board, 1940-50, *Daily Worker,* London (joined Communist Party, 1942; resigned, 1950). **Awards:** Royal Society Darwin Medal, 1952; Royal Anthropological Institute Huxley Medal, 1956; Linnean Society Darwin-Wallace Medal, 1958; National Academy of Sciences Kimber Medal, 1961; Accademia dei Lincei Feltrinelli prize, 1961. D.Sc.: University of Groningen, 1946; Oxford University, 1961; Honorary Doctorate: University of Paris, 1949; LL.D.: University of Edinburgh, 1956. Honorary Fellow, New College, 1961. Corresponding member, Société de Biologie, 1928; Fellow, Royal Society, 1932; Chevalier, Legion of Honour, 1937; honorary member, Moscow Academy of Sciences, 1942; corresponding member, Deutsche Akademie der Wissenschaften, 1950, National Institute of Sciences of India, 1953, and Royal Danish Academy of Sciences, 1956. **Died:** 1 December 1964.

Publications for Children

Fiction

My Friend Mr. Leakey, illustrated by Leonard Rosoman. London, Cresset Press, 1937; New York, Harper, 1938.

Publications for Adults

Novel

The Man with Two Memories. London, Merlin Press, 1976.

Other

Daedalus; or, Science and the Future: A Paper Read to the Heretics, Cambridge, on February 4th, 1923. London, Kegan Paul Trench Trubner, 1923; New York, Dutton, 1924.
Callinicus: A Defence of Chemical Warfare. London, Kegan Paul Trench Trubner, and New York, Dutton, 1925.
Animal Biology, with Julian Huxley. Oxford, Clarendon Press, 1927.
The Last Judgment: A Scientist's Vision of the Future of Man. New York and London, Harper, 1927.
Possible Worlds and Other Essays. London, Chatto and Windus, 1927; as *Possible Worlds and Other Papers,* New York, Harper, 1928.
Science and Ethics (lecture). London, C.A. Watts, 1928.
Enzymes. London, Longman, 1930; Cambridge, Massachusetts Institute of Technology Press, 1965.
Materialism (miscellany). London, Hodder and Stoughton, 1932.
The Causes of Evolution. London, Longman, and New York, Harper, 1932.
The Inequality of Man and Other Essays. London, Chatto and Windus, 1932; as *Science and Human Life,* New York, Harper, 1933.
Biology in Everyday Life, with John Randal Baker. London, Allen and Unwin, 1933.
Fact and Faith. London, C.A. Watts, 1934.
Human Biology and Politics. London, British Science Guild, 1934.
Science and the Supernatural: A Correspondence Between Harold Lunn and J.B.S. Haldane. London, Eyre and Spottiswoode, and New York, Sheed and Ward, 1935.
The Outlook of Science, edited by William Empson. London, Routledge, 1935.
Science and Well-Being, edited by William Empson. London, Routledge, 1935.
The Chemistry of the Individual (lecture). London, Oxford University Press, 1938.
The Marxist Philosophy. London, Birkbeck College, 1938.

A.R.P. [Air Raid Precautions]. London, Gollancz, 1938.
Heredity and Politics. London, Allen and Unwin, and New York, Norton, 1938.
How to Be Safe from Air Raids. London, Gollancz, 1938.
The Marxist Philosophy and the Sciences. London, Allen and Unwin, 1938; New York, Random House, 1939.
Science and Everyday Life. London, Lawrence and Wishart, 1939; New York, Macmillan, 1940.
Science and You. London, Fore Publications, 1939.
Keeping Cool and Other Essays. London, Chatto and Windus, 1940; as *Adventures of a Biologist,* New York, Harper, 1940.
Science in Peace and War. London, Lawrence and Wishart, 1940.
New Paths in Genetics. London, Allen and Unwin, 1941; New York, Harper, 1942.
Dialectical Materialism and Modern Science. London, Labour Monthly, 1942.
Why Professional Workers Should Be Communists. London, Communist Party, 1945.
A Banned Broadcast and Other Essays. London, Chatto and Windus, 1946.
Science Advances. London, Allen and Unwin, and New York, Macmillan, 1947.
What Is Life? New York, Boni and Gaer, 1947; London, Lindsay Drummond, 1949.
Is Evolution a Myth? A Debate Between Douglas Dewar, C. Merson Davies and J.B.S. Haldane. London, Paternoster Press, 1949.
Everything Has a History (essays). London, Allen and Unwin, 1951.
The Biochemistry of Genetics. London, Allen and Unwin, and New York, Macmillan, 1954.
The Argument from Animals to Men: An Examination of Its Validity for Anthropology (lecture). London, Royal Anthropological Institute, 1956.
Karl Pearson 1857-1957 (address). London, Biometrika Trustees, 1958.
The Unity and Diversity of Life (lecture). Delhi, Government of India Publications Division, 1958.
Science and Indian Culture. Calcutta, New Age Publishers, 1965.
Science and Life: Essays of a Rationalist. London, Pemberton-Barrie and Rockliff, 1968.
On Being the Right Size and Other Essays. Oxford, Oxford University Press, 1985.

Editor, *You and Heredity,* by Amram Scheinfeld and Morton D. Schweitzer. London, Chatto and Windus, 1939.

*

Critical Studies: *J.B.S.: The Life and Work of J.B.S. Haldane* by Ronald W. Clark, London, Hodder and Stoughton, 1968, New York, Coward McCann, 1969; *Haldane: The Life and Work of J.B.S. Haldane with Special Reference to India* by Krishna R. Dronamraju, Aberdeen, Aberdeen University Press, 1985.

* * *

It was a mathematician who wrote *Alice in Wonderland* a century ago. It was one of the greatest polymaths of our own time who wrote another of the best books for children ever published, *My Friend Mr. Leakey,* but who, unlike Lewis Carroll, left it at that. Perhaps in Carroll work and play were more sharply divided. All the zest and delight in the strangeness of the universe that illuminated J.B.S. Haldane's scientific research, all "the power to connect things in his mind in unexpected ways" noted in Sir Peter Medawar's preface to *J.B.S.* are at their height in this volume. The paperback edition is especially valuable for a preliminary paragraph in which the author's voice speaks as directly as it does in the narrative. "Professor Haldane has been used for experiments ever since he was three.... Some of the things that happened to him are nearly as queer as the things that happen in this book. He thinks ... science can be more exciting than magic ... the nearest things he has to a dragon in his house are two she-newts, Flosshilda and Berenice.... He is bald, weighs about 15 stone, and is fond of swimming." Children were still writing to him about the book in 1962, when he told one that "a green lizard 4 feet long" had trespassed into his Indian bathroom.

There are three minor stories in the volume: one about a man who gives rats biscuits containing powdered iron filings and then draws them by a powerful magnet into a pit, one about an anaconda fitted with status-symbolic golden teeth by his millionaire owner, and one about the naiad Miss Wandle with a magic shop in Wandsworth. All have startling freshness and ingenuity, but in the actual Mr. Leakey adventures invention tumbles over itself in glory. He is a real magician, a member of the International Congress of Sorcerers on the Brocken, and has his meals grilled by a small dragon (who wears asbestos boots when out of the fire) and served by an octopus. Strawberries are fetched from New Zealand by a jinn whose incautious colleagues get stomach ache from radio waves, find the lower air crowded with aeroplanes, and are pelted with shooting stars by angels if they fly too high. When Mr. Leakey gives a party he temporarily transforms his guests into human-sized versions of whatever they choose (a whimsical film star turned butterfly finds herself with goggly eyes and a proboscis). He travels on a magic carpet which "hovers stiffly" a foot above floors covered with books. He makes the author practise being invisible, which produces a (physiologically justified) "nasty giddy feeling." And so on. Nothing could be more characteristic of the man who wrote in his last years "the world is not only queerer than anyone has imagined but queerer than anyone *can* imagine."

—Renée Haynes

HALE, Kathleen

Nationality: British. **Born:** Broughton, Biggar, Lanarkshire, 24 May 1898. **Education:** Manchester High School for Girls; Manchester School of Art; University College, Reading (scholar), 1916-18; Central School of Art, London; East Anglian School of Painting and Drawing. **Family:** Married Douglas McClean in 1926 (died 1967); two sons. **Career:** Artist: paintings exhibited at New English Arts Club, London Group, Grosvenor Galleries, Vermont Gallery, Warwick Public Library Gallery, Gallery Edward Harvane, New Grafton Gallery, Parkin Gallery; metal groups and pictures exhibited at Lefevre Galleries, Leicester Galleries, and Oxford Arts Centre; mural for Festival of Britain Schools Section, London, 1951; Orlando Ballet for Festival Gardens, London, 1951. Fellow, Society of Industrial Artists and Designers. O.B.E. (Officer, Order of the British Empire), 1976. **Address:** Tod House, Forest Hill, Oxford, England.

Publications for Children (illustrated by the author)

Fiction

Orlando, The Marmalade Cat: A Camping Holiday. London, Country Life, and New York, Scribner, 1938.
Orlando's Evening Out. London, Penguin, 1941.
Orlando's Home Life. London, Penguin, 1942.
Orlando, The Marmalade Cat, Buys a Farm. London, Country Life, 1942.
Henrietta, The Faithful Hen. London and New York, Transatlantic Arts, 1943.
Orlando, The Marmalade Cat: His Silver Wedding. London, Country Life, 1944.
Orlando, The Marmalade Cat, Becomes a Doctor. London, Country Life, 1944.
Orlando's Invisible Pyjamas. London, Transatlantic Arts, 1947.
Orlando, The Marmalade Cat: A Trip Abroad. London, Country Life, 1949.
Orlando, The Marmalade Cat, Keeps a Dog. New York, Country Life, 1949.
Orlando, The Judge. London, Murray, 1950.
Orlando's Country Life: A Peep-Show Book. London, Chatto and Windus, 1950.
Puss-in-Boots: A Peep-Show Book. London, Chatto and Windus, 1951.
Orlando, The Marmalade Cat: A Seaside Holiday. London, Country Life, 1952.
Manda. London, Murray, 1952; New York, Coward McCann, 1953.
Orlando's Zoo. London, Murray, 1954.
Orlando, The Marmalade Cat: The Frisky Housewife. London, Country Life, 1956.
Orlando's Magic Carpet. London, Murray, 1958.
Orlando, The Marmalade Cat, Buys a Cottage. London, Country Life, 1963.
Orlando and the Three Graces. London, Murray, 1965.
Orlando, The Marmalade Cat, Goes to the Moon. London, Murray, 1968.
Orlando, The Marmalade Cat, and the Water Cats. London, Cape, 1972.
Henrietta's Magic Egg. London, Allen and Unwin, 1973.

Publications for Adults

Other

A Slender Reputation (autobiography). London, Warne, 1994.

*

Illustrator: *I Don't Mix Much with Fairies,* 1928, and *Plain Jane,* 1929, both by Mary R. Harrower; *Basil Seal Rides Again* by Evelyn Waugh, 1963.

Kathleen Hale comments:

I began writing my books for my own children. Then I wrote for children who were deprived of family love—especially those evacuated during the last war, torn from their parents and sent to sometimes unsympathetic homes. I've tried to keep the parent relationship, with love and understanding, alive for children who are denied it. I also wrote the books for *my own* rather cold childhood, thereby living out a warmth that was lacking when I was a child.

* * *

Kathleen Hale's numerous picture books about Orlando the Marmalade Cat provide an excellent example of the kind of book which is enjoyed most when it is read aloud to a child of the right age, and at the same time pored over with the fascinated alertness that brings to light new things to notice in the illustrations with every re-reading. For Orlando's adventures have come in books of varied shapes and sizes (including some very large ones); but invariably the text and the pictures have been carefully integrated so that the story-line carried by the words is echoed and often embellished by the richly inventive lithographs. As an instance of what the pictures can add to the words one might mention *Orlando's Evening Out,* where the "cots" in which the kittens are fast asleep are shown to be Master's slippers, while Master himself, with Orlando on one knee and Orlando's wife Grace on the other, is no more than a bald head hidden behind the *Daily Mews.* This story involves a visit to the circus in the course of which Orlando involuntarily becomes a star performer, and the orchestra ends up by playing "He's a Jolly Good Feline...." It will be seen that Kathleen Hale's verbal humour relies a good deal upon puns; sometimes these are not particularly good ones, but the word-play can at times be wittily original—Tinkle's coinage "Hot Wartle" must surely have passed into the accepted lingo of not a few families.

The humour hinges also on a complex interweaving of the humanised feline world of Orlando and his family and a richly eccentric human world. One of the very best of the stories is *Orlando's Invisible Pyjamas.* This starts with Orlando slipping out one snowy evening to take a dead mouse to the nightwatchman who is guarding a hole in the road (the kitten Tinkle sees him and says: "Hello Farver, you've grown a Mousetache!"); unfortunately Mr. Pusey, the nightwatchman, does not really appreciate Orlando's gift when it is deposited in his frying-pan alongside his sausages, and in the ensuing flurry Orlando's hind quarters are drenched with paraffin. The following day Tinkle finds an embarrassed Orlando hiding in the snowy pampas grass, "quite bald from the waist to the tip of his tail." His family smuggles him home camouflaged by a "Modesty Awning," and while the kittens and Mr. Pusey do their best to entertain him as he lies in bed, Grace knits him a pair of pyjamas which look just like real fur. Trouble comes only when he meets a dog and all his fur stands on end except his pyjamas—an incident entertainingly reinforced by the illustration. The later stories have tended to become increasingly fantastical and highly elaborated, but the series as a whole offers a wealth of enjoyment—ideal, one would say, for the intelligent six-year-old, but capable of being appreciated on some level at almost any age from four to eight.

—Frank Whitehead

HANSEN, Joyce

Nationality: American. **Born:** New York City, 18 October 1942. **Education:** Pace University, New York, B.A. in English 1972; New York University, M.A. in English Education 1978. **Family:** Married to Matthew Nelson. **Career:** English teacher, New York from 1973; Mentor, Empire State College, Brooklyn, New York, from 1987.

Publications for Children

Fiction

The Gift-Giver. Boston, Houghton Mifflin, 1980.
Home Boy. Boston, Houghton Mifflin, 1982.
Which Way Freedom? New York, Walker, 1986.
Yellowbird and Me. Boston, Houghton Mifflin, 1986.
Out from This Place. New York, Walker, 1988.
The Captive. New York, Scholastic, 1994.
I Thought My Soul Would Rise and Fly: The Diary of Patsy, a Freed Girl. New York, Scholastic, 1997.
Women of Hope: African Americans Who Made a Difference, foreword by Moe Foner. New York, Scholastic Press, 1998.

Publications for Adults

Other

Between Two Fires: Black Soldiers in the Civil War. New York, Franklin Watts, 1993.
With Gary McGowan, *Breaking Ground, Breaking Silence: The Story of New York's African Burial Ground.* New York, Henry Holt, 1997.

* * *

Joyce Hansen has a gift for interweaving socio-political themes with problems of personality. In her novels about family vulnerability in American inner cities, she draws upon autobiographical material and her knowledge of West Indian immigrants in New York. *The Gift-Giver* and its sequel *Yellowbird and Me* are about youngsters in the Bronx; *Home Boy* alternates between a Caribbean setting and a chaotic urban environment. Hansen's two fictionalized treatments of the Civil War, *Which Way Freedom?* and *Out from This Place,* reflect the scholarly advances of revisionist historians.

Family dispersion is emphasized in the inner city stories—a diffusion of parents and children resulting from problems of poverty, substandard housing, and job insecurity. Ghetto schools come under particular scrutiny, although Hansen does not target the school as a unique social failure. She places the shortcomings of the school within the larger context of urban disintegration. This thematic content makes her stories issue-oriented in the sense that they are life-oriented; they do not gloss over the impact of public policies on the daily struggles of the urban poor.

Hansen is a creative storyteller who builds her cosmopolitan settings in ways that shed light on character motivation. She lets Doris, a ten year old, narrate *The Gift-Giver.* This strategy allows the author to reveal indirectly the child's resentment toward overprotective parents. Doris supplies clues that explain parental anxieties and the other personal and environmental conditions that disrupt family life. The novel's structure is episodic, but the author's unmistakable tie with her characters produces its own dramatic power.

Hansen counterbalances characterizations of Doris and her friend Amir. Major themes come into focus primarily through the actions of Amir, while a strong sense of verisimilitude is felt through her child narrator. Amir is a somewhat mysterious figure and serves as a symbol of Hansen's positive values: the importance of family, belief in self, a determination to progress and act responsibly. On the other hand Doris represents the immaturities of a normal ten year old. By placing her in the narrator role, Hansen keeps her astute observations of childhood in the foreground, and lets her idealism emerge symbolically and unobtrusively.

Home Boy juxtaposes Caribbean and New York settings and their impact upon a father-son relationship. The author uses a different technique in this narrative: fast cinematic intercuts from one time frame to another. This fracturing of time parallels the alienation of the central characters as their long-held American Dream is rapidly extinguished.

Early chapters set up the basic dimensions of the family's hardships in New York. A deeper character development occurs when Hansen backtracks to St. Cruz Island—to the boyish antics of young Marcus and his friends, the peace-making efforts of a grandmother, the foolishness of a well-meaning but thoroughly de-Africanized teacher. Details of setting are sometimes used to highlight frustration, as when Marcus and his father Rudy meet and a painful awkwardness engulfs them: "Rudy gulped down his beer and they let the television absorb their discomfort."

The two historical novels, *Which Way Freedom?* and *Out from This Place,* are organized around a group of epigraphs drawn from historical studies and documents. These quotations often foretell what the slave protagonists, Obidiah and Easter, will encounter as they experience the American Civil War. For example, a Northern general's actual statement to his Southern captives hints at the Northern betrayal of blacks that the fictional slaves will ultimately face: "Not only will we [the Union Army] abstain from all interferences with your slaves, but we will, with an iron hand, crush any attempt at insurrection on their part."

Besides using this documentary method of linking history and the inventions of fiction, Hansen constructs a plot that exposes the workings of the plantation system. She draws a convincing picture of how slaves had limited access to information and had to improvise accordingly. She reveals the necessity of ever-evolving and supportive slave networks.

Whether Hansen aims to evoke the life and times of a 20th-century Northern city or a 19th-century Southern plantation, she has such a firm grasp of regional and historical detail that she builds characterization spontaneously from that base. This combination of background knowledge and novelistic technique accounts for her success in reconstructing the realities of black experience.

—Donnarae MacCann

HARDCASTLE, Michael

Pseudonym: David Clark. **Nationality:** British. **Born:** Huddersfield, Yorkshire, 6 February 1933. **Education:** At schools in Huddersfield. **Military Service:** Royal Army Educational Corps, 1951-56. **Career:** Newspaper reporter, 1956-59; literary editor, Bristol *Evening Post,* 1959-65; chief feature writer, Liverpool *Daily Post,* 1965-67. Since 1967 freelance writer. **Award:** M.B.E. (Member, Order of the British Empire), 1988. **Address:** 17 Molescroft Park, Beverley, North Humberside HU17 7EB, England.

PUBLICATIONS FOR CHILDREN

Fiction

Soccer Is Also a Game. London, Heinemann, 1966; as *Soccer Comes First,* London, Dragon, 1971.
Redcap. London, Collins, 1967.
Shoot on Sight. London, Heinemann, 1967.
Aim for the Flag. London, Heinemann, 1967; Chicago, Follett, 1969.
The Chasing Game. London, Heinemann, 1968; revised edition, Southport, Lancashire, Hardcastle, 1976.
Goal, illustrated by James Hunt. London, Heinemann, 1969.
Dive to Danger, illustrated by Richard Kennedy. London, Benn, 1969.
Shilling a Mile, illustrated by Richard Kennedy. London, Benn, 1969; as *Walk for Us,* n.d.
Stop That Car!, illustrated by Richard Kennedy. London, Benn, 1970.
Reds and Blues, illustrated by Richard Kennedy. London, Benn, 1970.
The Hidden Enemy. London, Epworth Press, 1970; revised edition, as *Hidden Enemy,* Southport, Lancashire, Hardcastle, 1976.
Strike!, illustrated by Richard Kennedy. London, Benn, 1970.
Smashing!, illustrated by Richard Kennedy. London, Benn, 1970.
Don't Tell Me What to Do. London, Heinemann, 1970.
Come and Get Me, illustrated by Richard Kennedy. London, Benn, 1971.
Live in the Sky, illustrated by Richard Kennedy. London, Benn, 1971.
Shelter, illustrated by Richard Kennedy. London, Benn, 1971.
A Load of Trouble, illustrated by Richard Kennedy. London, Benn, 1971.
Blood Money, illustrated by Richard Kennedy. London, Benn, 1971.
It Wasn't Me, illustrated by Richard Kennedy. London, Benn, 1971.
In the Net, illustrated by Trevor Stubley. London, Methuen, 1971.
Playing Ball. London, Heinemann, 1972.
Goals in the Air. London, Heinemann, 1972.
Island Magic. London, Heinemann, 1973.
United!, illustrated by Trevor Stubley. London, Methuen, 1973.
Away from Home, illustrated by Trevor Stubley. London, Methuen, 1974.
Free Kick, illustrated by Trevor Stubley. London, Methuen, 1974.
The Demon Bowler. London, Heinemann, 1974.
The Big One. London, Nelson, 1974.
The Chase. London, Nelson, 1974.
On the Run. London, Nelson, 1974.
Heading for Goal. London, Nelson, 1974.
Contact series (*Last Across, The Match, Dead of Night, Road Race, A Hard Man, Catch, Day in the Country, The Long Drop*), illustrated by Gareth Floyd. London, Collins, 8 vols., 1974.
Flare Up. London, Nelson, 1975.
Get Lost. London, Nelson, 1975.
Money for Sale, illustrated by Fermin Rocker. London, Heinemann, 1975.
Life Underground, illustrated by Roger Harris. London, Heinemann, 1975.
Mark Fox series (*The First Goal, Breakaway, On the Ball, Shooting Star, Goal in Europe, Kick Off, Attack!*). London, Armada, 7 vols., 1976-82.
Where the Action Is. London, Heinemann, 1976.
The Saturday Horse, illustrated by Trevor Stubley. London, Methuen, 1977.
First Contact series (*Go and Find Him, River of Danger, The Great Bed Race, Night Raid*), illustrated by Maureen and Gordon Gray. London, Collins, 4 vols., 1977.
Strong Arm, illustrated by Gareth Floyd. London, Benn, 1977.
Fire on the Sea, illustrated by Gareth Floyd. London, Benn, 1977.
Holiday House, illustrated by Gareth Floyd. London, Benn, 1977.
Crash Car, illustrated by Gareth Floyd. London, Benn, 1977.
Soccer Special, illustrated by Paul Wright. London, Methuen, 1978.
Top of the League. London, Heinemann, 1979.
The Reporters (*Top Soccer, Top Fishing, Top Speed*). London, Harrap, 3 vols., 1979-81.
The Switch Horse, illustrated by Paul Wright. London, Methuen, 1980.
Go for Goal, illustrated by Ron Sandford. London, Benn, 1980.
Racing Bike, illustrated by Ron Sandford. London, Benn, 1980.
Snakerun, illustrated by Ron Sandford. London, Benn, 1980.
Hot Wheels, illustrated by Ron Sandford. London, Benn, 1980.
Behind the Goal. London, Pelham, 1980.
Half a Team, illustrated by Trevor Stubley. London, Methuen, 1980.
The Gigantic Hit. London, Pelham, 1982.
Roar to Victory, illustrated by Patrice Aitken. London, Methuen, 1982.
Fast from the Gate, illustrated by Patrice Aitken. London, Methuen, 1983.
Caught Out, illustrated by Trevor Parkin. London, Methuen, 1983.
Hooked! London, Longman, 1984.
The Team That Wouldn't Give In, illustrated by Trevor Parkin. London, Methuen, 1984.
Double Holiday, illustrated by Shirley Bellwood. London, Blackie, 1985.
Winning Rider. London, Methuen, 1985.
Tiger of the Track. London, Methuen, 1985.
The Shooters. London, Methuen, 1986.
James and the TV Star. London, Blackie, 1986.
No Defence. London, Deutsch, 1986.
One Kick. London, Faber, 1986.
Snookered! London, Blackie, 1987.
Mascot. London, Methuen, 1987.
Quake. London, Faber, 1988.
The Rival Games. London, Methuen, 1988.
The Magic Party, illustrated by Vanessa Julian-Ottie. London, Blackie, 1988.
Kickback. London, Faber, 1989.
The Green Machine. London, Methuen, 1989.
Penalty. London, Dent, 1990.
Walking the Goldfish. London, Heinemann, 1990.
Joanna's Goal. London, Blackie, 1990.
Lucky Break. London, Blackie, 1990.
Mark England's Cap, illustrated by Margaret de Souza. London, Heinemann, 1990.
Advantage Miss Jackson. London, Methuen, 1991.
James and the House of Fun. London, Blackie, 1991.
Second Chance. London, Faber, 1991.
The Away Team. London, Methuen, 1992.
Own Goal. London, Faber, 1992.
Dog Bites Goalie (short stories). London, Methuen, 1993.

One Good Horse. London, Dent, 1993.
Racing to Win. London, Mammoth, 1993
Soccer Star. London, Heinemann, 1993.
Shooting Boots. London, Ginn, 1993.
You Won't Catch Me. London, Methuen, 1994.
Soccer Captain. London, Orion, 1994.
Netball Shooters. London, Mammoth, 1995.
Please Come Home. London, Faber, 1995.
Winning Goal. London, Methuen, 1995.
Carole's Camel. London, Heinemann, 1995.
Puzzle. London, Orion, 1995.
The Fastest Bowler in the World. London, Faber, 1996.
Matthew's Goals, illustrated by Bob Moulder. London, A. C. Black, 1997.

Fiction as David Clark (illustrated by Richard Kennedy)

Goalie. London, Benn, 1972.
Splash. London, Benn, 1972.
Run. London, Benn, 1973.
Top Spin. London, Benn, 1973.
Grab. London, Benn, 1974.
Winner. London, Benn, 1975.
Volley. London, Benn, 1975.
Roll Up. London, Benn, 1975.

* * *

Sporting fiction for young readers is still in its formative stages, and has not yet reached the point where individual writers may be acclaimed as masters of the genre. But Michael Hardcastle's football novels clearly demonstrate that he must be seriously regarded as a writer of children's fiction and not simply as a successful author of football stories. First with his Scorton Rovers novels following the fortunes of a Football League team winning promotion to the first Division, then in his Bank Vale United series about the local rivalries of a Sunday Junior League, and in the Mark Fox sequence, one football-daft lad's progress from school football to the twin towers of Wembley, he displays an uncanny understanding of what passes through the young footballer's mind and a true awareness of what really goes on in football on and off the field.

The First Goal introduces Mark, the youngest member of his school team, for whom "the next match in which he played was always the most important of his life." In *Breakaway* his career appears to falter, he is suspended from his school team, and then gets sent off the field in a youth league match. The news that he has been selected for the County Youth XI for a representative match in London (which forms the central narrative of *On the Ball*) sets him back on course. Mark Fox is no stereotyped Roy of the Rovers hero; he is flesh and blood, no stranger to despair when the world seems against him.

In the Net, the first of the Bank Vale United series, presents an agonizing dilemma often confronting keen and enthusiastic soccer players, the shadow of the School Rugby XV looming over their Saturday afternoons. In *United!* the team goes through a bad patch and recruits a star forward who proves to be a troublemaker. Two of the regular stalwarts of the side have a hard time keeping the side together. *Away from Home,* in fact, concerns only three of the team invited to join an arduous Town Boys' three matches in five days tour. Each member of the party comes under scrutiny in turn, his character subjected to a deeper inspection than is usually the case in other books of the series where two or three players at the most can feature at all prominently.

If the rewards of sports fiction are tempting, the pitfalls awaiting authors who venture into this specialized field can be daunting. One false line of dialogue, one error in either description or situation, and the vital effect of the total reality is irretrievably lost. Hardcastle triumphantly surmounts these difficulties. Capturing the hard slog young footballers put into their training, their anxieties about fitness, team rivalries and jealousies, the iniquities of referees, the seemingly callous attitude of coaches and sportsmasters to potentially serious injuries, and the exhaustion of the dressing room, his stories are authentic and convincing to the last detail.

—Alan Edwin Day

HARDING, Lee (John)

Nationality: Australian. **Born:** Colac, Victoria, 17 February 1937. **Education:** Australian primary schools. **Family:** Married 1) Carla Bleeker in 1960 (divorced 1974), two sons and one daughter; 2) Irene Anne Pagram in 1982, one daughter. **Career:** Freelance photographer, 1953-70. **Awards:** Ditmar award, 1970, 1972; Alan Marshall award, 1978; Australian Children's Book of the Year award, 1980. **Agent:** Virginia Kidd, 538 East Hartford Street, Milford, Pennsylvania 18337, U.S.A.

PUBLICATIONS FOR CHILDREN

Fiction

The Fallen Spaceman, illustrated by Lee Walsh. Melbourne, Cassell, 1973; London, Cassell, 1975; revised edition, New York, Harper, 1980.
The Children of Atlantis, illustrated by Irene Pagram. Melbourne, Cassell, 1976.
The Frozen Sky, illustrated by Kristine Ammitzball. Melbourne, Cassell, 1976.
Return to Tomorrow, illustrated by Irene Pagram. Melbourne, Cassell, 1976.
The Weeping Sky, Melbourne, Cassell, 1977.
Displaced Person, Melbourne, Hyland House, 1979; as *Misplaced Persons,* New York, Harper, 1979.
The Web of Time, Melbourne, Cassell, 1979.
Waiting for the End of the World, Melbourne, Hyland House, 1983.

PUBLICATIONS FOR ADULTS

Novels

A World of Shadows. London, Hale, 1975.
Future Sanctuary. Toronto, Laser, 1976.

Plays

Radio Plays: *Journey into Time* serial, 1978; *The Legend of New Earth* serial, 1979.

Other

Chained, photographs by John Bergland. Melbourne, Ron Smith, 1972.

Editor, *Beyond Tomorrow: An Anthology of Modern Science Fiction.* Melbourne, Wren, 1976; abridged edition, London, New English Library, 1977.
Editor, *The Altered I: An Encounter with Science Fiction.* Melbourne, Norstrilia Press, 1976; revised edition, New York, Berkley, 1978.
Editor, *Rooms of Paradise.* Melbourne, Quartet, 1978; New York, St. Martin's Press, 1979.

* * *

In all his novels for young people, Lee Harding has used the notion of worlds existing very much like our own and only differing in a few vital points as the basis of his plots. These differences tend to highlight aspects of human behaviour rather than, as in many other science-fiction stories, concentrating on technological curiosities. All the novels feature a hero, usually orphaned, who has to face a testing time. Most often the struggle is with his own character more than with external terrors. There is a recurring motif of future possibilities in Harding's novels, an appropriate theme for adolescent readers. Tied to this, and also appropriate for a writer of science fiction, is the idea that the future is not fixed but consists of infinite outcomes.

Harding brought a refreshing liveliness to the area of books for reluctant readers with his first four titles: *The Fallen Spaceman, The Children of Atlantis, The Frozen Sky,* and *Return to Tomorrow.* His first major novel for children, *The Weeping Sky,* takes up many of the themes evident in the readers. The setting is mediaeval Europe, but in the Crusades the enemy is from the North, the pope sits in Athens, and the people worship the "One True God" who had sent his only son to die on a wheel. Set against the power of the church are the Scientists, a group who have to work in secret for fear of persecution. Both groups regard the phenomenon of The Wall, a glass-like sheet seeming to hang in the air and weep, with awe. Beyond The Wall an apprentice Scientist finds another world, even more violent and repellent than the one he knows. *The Weeping Sky* is a tightly written and exciting novel which due to some unfortunate editing has not been available to as wide an audience as it might otherwise have attracted. In *The Web of Time* human ideas about time rather than concepts of the supernatural are examined in a fast-paced adventure story. This is the one novel that features technical wizardry, in this instance a time machine, but the machine is a mere backdrop to a further look at the idea of the co-existence of many worlds, in this case separated by time. Indeed the power of the mind is shown to be more effective than the machine in crossing the boundaries of time.

In Harding's best-known novel, *Displaced Person,* the hero Graeme comes to the conclusion that our world is manipulated by outside forces who adjust space and time as part of some great experiment. Graeme starts to feel out of touch with his everyday world, people look right through him, colour begins to ebb, and he finds himself alone in a grey world. Initially Graeme thinks his mind must be disturbed, but finally he concludes that he is actually displaced from his usual world, and finding two companions in the grey world confirms this view. However, for the reader the questions are left more open. Is Graeme's experience perhaps a manifestation of alienation? Or perhaps the story is suggesting other worlds are within us and can be experienced with an adjustment to our perception. The puzzles about reality are part of the book's fascination. *Waiting for the End of the World* has a more conventional fictional setting in a nasty future when the population is kept under control with drugs, and those outside the cities roam the land in lawless gangs. As in his other novels Harding creates a suspenseful and exciting narrative, and again the theme of possibilities is central. In this novel the notion of another world, in this case a ghostly hoard from ancient European times, seems incongruous in an Australian setting, despite the European origins of the "dreamers." More valid and important to the ideas in the novel is the resolve of a group of three young people to strike out in a new direction with the hope of somehow changing the direction of their bloody world.

Harding uses the resources of science fiction to explore human failings, but despite Graeme's theories about outside control in *Displaced Person,* this author's compelling stories suggest a hopeful view of human resilience.

—Kerry White

HARRIS, Aurand

Nationality: American. **Born:** Jamesport, Missouri, 4 July 1915. **Education:** Jamesport public schools, 1920-32; University of Kansas City, 1932-36, A.B. 1936; Northwestern University, Evanston, Illinois, 1937-39, M.A. 1939; Columbia University, New York (John Golden prize, 1945), 1945-47. **Career:** Auditorium teacher, Gary public schools, Indiana, 1939-41; Head of the Drama Department, William Woods College, Fulton, Missouri, 1942-45; drama teacher, Grace Church School, New York, 1946-77; drama teacher, Columbia University Teachers College, New York, summers 1958-63; playwright-in-residence, University of Florida, Tallahassee, 1972; drama teacher, Western Connecticut State College, Danbury, summer 1976; playwright-in-residence, University of Texas, Austin, 1976-84, University of Kansas, Lawrence, 1979, Young Audiences, Cleveland, autumns 1981-84, California State University, Northridge, 1982, Nebraska Theatre Caravan, Omaha, 1982, Indiana University-Purdue University, Indianapolis, 1985 and 1988, American School of Madrid, Spain, 1986, and New York University, New York, 1988. Associated with summer theatre in Cape May, New Jersey, 1946, Bennington, Vermont, 1947, Peaks Island, Maine, 1948, and Harwich, Massachusetts, 1963-82. **Awards:** American Theatre Association Chorpenning Cup 1967, 1986; National Endowment for the Arts grant, 1976. Fellow, American Theatre Association, 1985; Ohio Theatre Alliance Award for Outstanding Achievement in Theatre; Indiana Governor's highest honor; Alumni Achievement Award, University of Missouri, 1985; Alumni Merit Award, Northwestern University, 1987; Best Children's Published Play, AATE 1992-93; winner of 15 playwriting awards. **Address:** c/o Anchorage Press, Box 8067, New Orleans, Louisiana 70182, U.S.A.

Publications for Children

Plays

Pinocchio and the Fire-Eater (produced Gary, Indiana, 1940). New York, McGraw Hill, 1967.
Once upon a Clothesline (produced Fulton, Missouri, 1944). Boston, Baker, 1945.
The Doughnut Hole. New York, French, 1947.
The Moon Makes Three. New York, French, 1947.
Seven League Boots (produced Cleveland, 1947). Boston, Baker, 1948.
Circus Days (produced Seattle, 1948). New York, French, 1949; revised version, as *Circus in the Wind,* 1960.
Pinocchio and the Indians (produced Seattle, 1949). New York, French, 1949.
Simple Simon; or, Simon Big-Ears (produced Washington, D.C., 1952; Slough, Buckinghamshire, 1964). Anchorage, Kentucky, Children's Theatre Press, 1953.
Buffalo Bill (produced Seattle, 1953). Anchorage, Kentucky, Children's Theatre Press, 1954.
We Were Young That Year. New York, French, 1954.
The Plain Princess, adaptation of the book by Phyllis McGinley (produced Kalamazoo, Michigan, 1954). Anchorage, Kentucky, Children's Theatre Press, 1955.
The Flying Prince (produced Washington, D.C., 1965). New York, French, 1958; revised version (produced Fort Wayne, Indiana, 1984), New Orleans, Anchorage Press, 1985.
Junket (No Dogs Allowed), adaptation of the story by Anne H. White (produced Louisville, Kentucky, 1959). Anchorage, Kentucky, Children's Theatre Press, 1959.
The Brave Little Tailor (produced Charleston, West Virginia, 1960; London, 1966). Anchorage, Kentucky, Children's Theatre Press, 1961.
Pocahontas (produced Birmingham, Alabama, 1961). Anchorage, Kentucky, Children's Theatre Press, 1961.
Androcles and the Lion (produced New York, 1964; Sheffield, 1968). Anchorage, Kentucky, Children's Theatre Press, 1964.
Rags to Riches, adaptation of stories by Horatio Alger, music by Eva Franklin, lyrics by Harris and Franklin (produced Harwich, Massachusetts, 1965; Teddington, Middlesex, 1970). Anchorage, Kentucky, Anchorage Press, 1966.
A Doctor in Spite of Himself, adaptation of a play by Molière (produced New York, 1966). Anchorage, Kentucky, Anchorage Press, 1968.
The Comical Tragedy or Tragical Comedy of Punch and Judy, music by Glenn Mack (produced Atlanta, 1969). Anchorage, Kentucky, Anchorage Press, 1970.
Just So Stories, adaptation of the stories by Rudyard Kipling (produced Tallahassee, Florida, 1971). Anchorage, Kentucky, Anchorage Press, 1971.
Ming Lee and the Magic Tree. New York, French, 1971.
Steal Away Home, adaptation of work by Jane Kristof (produced Louisville, Kentucky, 1972). Anchorage, Kentucky, Anchorage Press, 1972.
Peck's Bad Boy, adaptation of the novel by George Wilbur Peck (produced Harwich, Massachusetts, 1973). Anchorage, Kentucky, Anchorage Press, 1974.
Robin Goodfellow (produced Harwich, Massachusetts, 1974). Anchorage, Kentucky, Anchorage Press, 1977.
Yankee Doodle (produced Austin, Texas, 1975). Anchorage, Kentucky, Anchorage Press, 1975.
Star Spangled Salute (produced Harwich, Massachusetts, 1975). Anchorage, Kentucky, Anchorage Press, 1975.
Six Plays for Children (includes *Androcles and the Lion, Rags to Riches, Punch and Judy, Steal Away Home, Peck's Bad Boy, Yankee Doodle*), edited by Coleman A. Jennings. Austin, University of Texas Press, 1977.
A Toby Show (produced Austin, Texas, 1978). New Orleans, Anchorage Press, 1978.
The Arkansaw Bear (produced Austin, Texas, 1980). New Orleans, Anchorage Press, 1980.
Treasure Island, adaptation of the novel by Robert Louis Stevenson (produced Northridge, California, 1982). New Orleans, Anchorage Press, 1983.
The Magician's Nephew, adaptation of the novel by C.S. Lewis (produced Austin, Texas, 1983). Chicago, Dramatic Publishing, 1984.
Ride a Blue Horse (produced Indianapolis, 1985). New Orleans, Anchorage Press, 1986.
Huck Finn's Story (produced Akron, Ohio, 1987). New Orleans, Anchorage Press, 1988.
Monkey Magic (produced Honolulu, Hawaii, 1989). New Orleans, Anchorage Press, 1990.
The Pinballs (produced Northwestern University, 1992). New Orleans, Anchorage Press, 1992.
Peter Rabbit and Me (produced New York University, 1992). New Orleans, Anchorage Press, 1994.
The Prince and the Pauper, dramatization of the novel by Mark Twain (produced Nashville, Tennessee, 1993). New Orleans, Anchorage Press, 1994.
Young Black Beauty, dramatization of the novel by Anne Sewell (produced Louisville, Kentucky, 1995). New Orleans, Anchorage Press 1996.

Other

Editor, with Coleman A. Jennings, *Plays Children Love: A Treasury of Contemporary and Classic Plays for Children 1-2,* illustrated by Susan Swan and Lee Duran. New York, Doubleday, vol. 1, 1981; New York, St. Martin's Press, vol. 2, 1988.

Publications for Adults

Plays

Ladies of the Mop. Evanston, Illinois, Row Peterson, 1945.
Madam Ada. New York, French, 1948.
And Never Been Kissed, adaptation of the novel by Sylvia Dee. New York, French, 1950.

*

Manuscript Collections: Arizona State University, Tempe, Arizona.

Critical Studies: *The Dramatic Contributions of Aurand Harris to Children's Theatre in the United States* by Coleman A. Jennings, unpublished dissertation, New York University, 1974 (includes bibliography); *The Theatre of Aurand Harris: His Plays, His Life.* Edited by Lowell Swortzell, New Orleans, Anchorage Press, 1995.

Theatrical Activities:
Director: **Play**—*Rags to Riches,* Shanghai, 1987 (first foreigner officially invited to direct a children's play in the People's Republic of China).

Aurand Harris comments:

I write for children because they and I like the same thing in theatre—a good story, interesting characters, excitement, fantasy, beauty, and fun. My plays are usually based on history, legend, myth, or children's classics, and are conceived and executed in a variety of styles ranging from *commedia dell'arte* to melodrama to poetic fantasy. Best of all, there is an increasing and receptive audience that lets you know when it is enjoying itself.

* * *

Aurand Harris, author of some 38 published plays for children, is America's most-produced children's theatre playwright. His plays, constantly produced since the late 1940s, have enormously enriched the literature of American children's theatre.

During the 10-year period from 1946 to 1955, Harris experimented with a variety of plays. He had been writing not only for audiences of children, but for teenagers and adults as well. Writing for children, however, provided Harris with opportunities which were unfettered by the naturalistic limitations usually expected by adult audiences. Because children are imaginative and willing to accept any theatrical form if it is honestly presented, he found great satisfaction in writing for them and since 1955 has written only for children and youth.

To write successful plays for children's theatre, an author must understand the youthful audience with the same thoroughness that he knows the techniques of playwriting. An audience comprised of children of various ages, representing many stages of maturity with widely differing interests and abilities to concentrate, presents an extra dimension of challenge to the playwright. Children are sensitive, perceptive, and quick to react overtly and honestly to whatever they see and hear. Harris's sensitivity to child audiences, his desire to create plays of high quality which adults perform for youth, and his thoroughly practical knowledge of all aspects of theatre have made him the respected professional playwright he is today.

Harris's children's plays are usually derived from fairy tales and legends, history, and other published writing. Harris has written some original plots, but creating new stories has obviously been of secondary interest to him. Of even greater importance is the way he has learned to shape the content. As his craftsmanship has steadily increased throughout his career, so has the range of maturity in the audience for whom he writes. In his late plays he has broadened his approach to include older youth, though he continues to command the attention of the younger audience members.

In writing each of his plays, Harris has recreated a dramatic form from the adult theatre with adjustments that make it suitable for a child audience. His selection of form, such as of *commedia dell'arte,* late-19th-century melodrama, comedy with sober overtones, dramatic chronicle, lighthearted farce, or musical revue is determined by the presence of intrinsic qualities which appeal to children.

Because the six elements of dramatic form, theme, plot, character, dialogue, song, and spectacle are so closely interdependent in Harris's plays, the works exhibit a vital theatricality to which young audiences respond. Each of his plays, unified and satisfactorily resolved, has a unique quality of its own. The most outstanding examples of this unified and unique playwriting are *Androcles and the Lion* and *The Arkansaw Bear.*

—Coleman A. Jennings

HARRIS, Geraldine (Rachel)

Nationality: British. **Born:** 17 October 1951. **Education:** King's College, Cambridge, 1973-77, B.A. (honours) 1977, M.A. 1980; Wadham College, Oxford, 1977-84, D.Phil. in Egyptology 1985. **Family:** Married Richard G.E. Pinch in 1978. **Career:** Lecturer in Egyptology; writer. **Address:** c/o British Museum Press, 46 Bloomsbury Street, London WC1B 3QQ, England.

Publications for Children

Fiction

White Cranes Castle, illustrated by Lisa Jensen. London, Macmillan, 1979.

"Seven Citadels" series

Prince of the Godborn. London, Macmillan, and New York, Greenwillow, 1982.
The Children of the Wind. London, Macmillan, and New York, Greenwillow, 1982.
The Dead Kingdom. London, Macmillan, and New York, Greenwillow, 1983.
The Seventh Gate. London, Macmillan, and New York, Greenwillow, 1983.

Other

Gods and Pharaohs from Egyptian Mythology, illustrated by John Sibbick and David O'Connor. London, Lowe, 1982; New York, Schocken, 1983.
The Junior Atlas of Ancient Egypt. London, Lionheart, 1989.
Ancient Egypt: Cultural Atlas for Young People. Oxford and New York, Facts on File, 1990.
Isis and Osiris. London, British Museum Press, 1996.
Who was Cleopatra, illustrated by Peter Dennis. Brighton, Macdonald, 1997.

Publications for Adults (as Geraldine Pinch)

New Kingdom Votive Offerings to Hathor. Oxford, Griffith Institute, 1989.
Magic in Ancient Egypt. London, British Museum, 1994.

*

Geraldine Harris comments:

All my work draws inspiration from myth and legend. *White Cranes Castle* is based on Japanese myths, legends, and folklore but has an historical setting. The four books that make up the "Seven Citadels" quartet are set in an invented world but they have a classic quest theme and are influenced by the myths of many cultures.

* * *

At first sight there may seem little to connect an academic Egyptologist with a fantasy for younger teenage readers set i mediaeval Japan, and a major and very complex four-volume fantasy epic that appeals to adults as well as to older teenagers. However on closer examination several important connections emerge, all crucial when considering the work of Geraldine Harris.

Both works of fiction are set in highly ordered, hierarchical societies that are in decline. In both, religion permeates the lives of all the participants. It is the failure to remember and observe divine commands that has brought about the decay of nation and inhabitant. In *White Cranes Castle* Akari finds his contemporaries abandoning the old ways in favour of new, more exciting ideas. Kerish-lo-Taan, hero of the "Seven Citadels" series, is a member of the ruling house of Galkis, descended from the god Zeldin—but most of the rest of the Imperial house have chosen to ignore their divine origin and the responsibilities that brings, in pursuit of personal gain and the lust for power. It is knowledge of the old ways, and a willingness to adhere to divine commands, that bring about the spiritual growth enabling both heroes to succeed in their respective tasks—though this is accompanied by personal sacrifice of a high order.

White Cranes Castle tells how the unconsidered cousin, Akari, is able to rouse and converse with the eight-headed dragon, which has had to rise from its lake bed to bring the rain the country so badly needs. Within the confines of a short book there is already in *White Cranes Castle* evidence of the author's love of colour, and of her vivid imaginative powers. The theme of redemption, of great importance when considering Geraldine Harris's work, is also clearly present.

In the much longer "Seven Citadels" Harris's powers blossom: it is no mean feat to sustain the imaginative force required to invent and people the world of Zindar and to engage the reader in Kerish-lo-Taan's quest for the legendary saviour of Galkis. The saviour is imprisoned; it will take seven keys to unlock him. The keys are held by seven sorcerers—remarkably individual creations—each of whom must first be found and then persuaded to give up a key. Surrendering a key means surrendering immortality. One of the redemptions to be found in this tale is that found in facing the limitations of humanity and accepting death. Immortality has emphasized the flaws and imperfections present in the characters of the sorcerers when they were mortal. The damage they have done to themselves and the people they rule cannot be put right while they exist in the sterile rigidity of immortality.

The sorcerers allow Harris much scope for imagination, especially Shubeyash, who, like his kingdom, is dead: a terrifying, trapped, immortal ghost. But it is in the creation of the hideous, cynical, acid-tongued Gidjabolgo, Kerish's companion for so much of the journey, that she has devised one of the most unusual and unexpectedly attractive characters in children's fantasy.

Harris studied many folklores before turning to postgraduate work in Egyptology, but it is from that comparatively little-known and exceptionally rich corpus of myth and legend that one may begin to pick up some of the threads she weaves so well. In *Gods and Pharaohs from Egyptian Mythology* one finds a strongly hierarchical society which did eventually decline, and in which the power and presence of the gods pervaded the whole of mortal life. Concern about death, and interest in life after death, is also a major preoccupation in Ancient Egypt. The story of the unconsidered mouse helping the mighty lion is Egyptian (though better known in its Greek form) and the boats that take souls to the Underworld in Ancient Egypt have a memorably terrifying parallel in "Seven Citadels." Hubris is of course punishable in most religions.

Isis and Osiris is an interesting combination of fiction and nonfiction. It is written for younger readers, and tells how Khonouphis the priest teaches the twin sisters Taous and Thaues stories of the deities Isis and Osiris so they may play the parts of the twin goddesses Isis and Nephthys at the funeral of the Apis Bull. Woven into the priest's tales are details of the girls' problems with their mother and greedy half-brother. Harris uses a simple direct style that includes dialogue and reads like fiction, but the characters and incidents are taken from Ancient Egyptian history. Photographs of paintings, drawings, and artefacts illustrate the story, and are accompanied by lengthy captions giving substantial details about the illustration, and relating it to the story itself. It is a fascinating device, but leaves the reader feeling slightly uneasy, partly because it is an unusual style, and partly because writing history as fiction in this way inevitably imposes restrictions on the author's natural style.

The themes of love, death, and redemption that feature so largely in Harris's work make a refreshing change from the good-versus-evil, or light-against-dark themes of many other fantasies. Her overall narrative drive and sheer imaginative power bring zest, resonance, and a strong individual flavour to her work.

—Felicity Trotman

HARRIS, Mary K(athleen)

Nationality: British. **Born:** Harrow, Middlesex, 22 September 1905. **Education:** Harrow County School for Girls, 1915-22. **Died:** 1966.

Publications for Children

Fiction

Gretel at St. Bride's, illustrated by Drake Brookshaw. London, Nelson, 1941.

The Wolf, illustrated by Kathleen Cooper. London, Sheed and Ward, 1946; revised edition, New York, Sheed and Ward, 1955.

The Niche over the Door. London, Sheed and Ward, 1948.

Henrietta at St. Hilary's. London, Staples Press, 1953.

Thomas, illustrated by Cliff Roberts. New York, Sheed and Ward, 1956.

A Safe Lodging, illustrated by Don Bolognese. New York, Sheed and Ward, 1957.

Emily and the Headmistress. London, Faber, 1958.

Seraphina, illustrated by Sheila Rose. London, Faber, 1960.

Penny's Way, illustrated by Sheila Rose. London, Faber, 1963.

The Bus Girls, illustrated by Eileen Green. London, Faber, and New York, Norton, 1965.

Jessica on Her Own, illustrated by Alison Prince. London, Faber, 1968.

Other

Elizabeth, illustrated by R.M. Sax. New York, Sheed and Ward, 1961.

Helena, illustrated by Michael Hampshire. New York, Sheed and Ward, 1964.

Publications for Adults

Novels

Fear at My Heart. London and New York, Sheed and Ward, 1951.
My Darling from the Lion's Mouth. London, Chatto and Windus, 1956; as *I Am Julie,* New York, Crowell, 1956.
Lucia Wilmot. London, Chatto and Windus, 1959.

* * *

Mary K. Harris had no illusions about childhood. Looking back on her own schooldays (she went to her secondary school in 1915), she recalled that "I found myself amongst a group of children who were consistently horrid to each other," but she realized later "that these hateful school children were only hateful in a mass, that, in their own secret, solitary selves they were as aghast at each other as I was." There's no doubt that, like many less intelligent people, she remained all her life obsessed by her schooldays, but she turned her obsession to splendid account and gave us some of the best school stories we have. Her writing career began slowly and her early work was mainly for Guide magazines and for Sheed and Ward, the Catholic publishers—she was a convert.

Her Faber books, to their advantage, have no special axes to grind but it is interesting to note that her early Catholic story, *The Wolf,* shows her talent much more clearly than her conventional early school stories, *Gretel at St. Bride's* and *Henrietta of St. Hilary's.* Gretel, however, is not a stock heroine. The solitary quality of childhood is seen in her in extreme form. The year is 1941 and she is a refugee from Nazi Germany whereas "all the girls at St. Bride's ever worried about was Saturday sweets and getting into the hockey eleven."

Harris's progression from the boarding schools of these early books and *Emily and the Headmistress,* via the grammar-school boarding hostel of *Seraphina* to the boarder-less grammar schools of *Penny's Way* and *The Bus Girls,* and eventually to the Secondary Modern of *Jessica on Her Own,* seems almost uncannily deliberate, as if Harris with each book was simply attempting to get nearer and nearer to a wider number of potential readers. In fact, her social situations are a lot more complex than this would suggest. Jessica, the first of her heroines to go to a Secondary Modern, is the daughter of a Cambridge graduate mother, a very different type from the mothers in the two previous books. After her not completely successful attempt at the Ruffles (cousins, perhaps, of Eve Garnett's Ruggles) in *Emily and the Headmistress,* Harris never seemed to put a foot wrong in her social nuances. But it is imaginative conviction that counts, of course, not social awareness. Harris's books are never manufactured to support a thesis, but she certainly wrote with purpose. She aimed to make ordinary life interesting and meaningful. She felt it important to help children to understand themselves and each other, to make them realize, as she herself had not realized until much later, that other children are also vulnerable.

Emily and the Headmistress rather stands alone. The typical Harris heroine is 12 or 13; Emily is only eight. But it was in this book that the author first achieved her individuality. It was followed by *Seraphina,* her only novel told in the first person, a marvellously imagined story, rich in detail, strong in plot. Harris had showed there could be a school story which did not suffer from conservatism, xenophobia, snobbery, the underrating of learning (the list is Orwell's).

Nothing Harris wrote was solemn; everything was entertaining. In her books she explored with amused understanding the different pressures on adolescent girls as they come to terms with life, with the conflicting demands of home and school, and the difficulties and rewards of friendship. She had an ability to create not just one or two characters in each book but a whole form, even the feeling of a whole school, of individuals. In her last book, *Jessica on Her Own,* she moved out of the pure school story. School and home were equally important.

—Ann Thwaite

HARRIS, Rosemary (Jeanne)

Nationality: British. **Born:** London, 20 February 1923. **Education:** Thorneloe School, Weymouth; St. Martin's, Central, and Chelsea schools of art, London; Department of Technology, Courtauld Institute, London, 1950. **Military Service:** Red Cross Nursing Auxiliary, Westminster Division, London, 1941-45. **Career:** Picture restorer, 1949; reader, Metro-Goldwyn-Mayer, 1951-52; children's book reviewer, the *Times,* London, 1970-73. **Awards:** Library Association Carnegie Medal, 1969; Arts Council grant, 1971. **Agent:** A.P. Watt Ltd., 20 John Street, London WC1N 2DR, England.

Publications for Children

Fiction

The Moon in the Cloud. London, Faber, 1968; New York, Macmillan, 1969.
The Shadow on the Sun. London, Faber, and New York, Macmillan, 1970.
The Seal-Singing. London, Faber, and New York, Macmillan, 1971.
The Bright and Morning Star. London, Faber, and New York, Macmillan, 1972.
The King's White Elephant, illustrated by Errol Le Cain. London, Faber, 1973.
The Flying Ship, illustrated by Errol Le Cain. London, Faber, 1975.
The Little Dog of Fo, illustrated by Errol Le Cain. London, Faber, 1976.
I Want to Be a Fish, illustrated by Jill Bennett. London, Kestrel, 1977.
A Quest for Orion. London, Faber, 1978.
Green Finger House, illustrated by Juan Wijngaard. London, Eel Pie, 1979.
Tower of the Stars. London, Faber, 1980.
The Enchanted Horse, illustrated by Pauline Baynes. London, Kestrel, 1981.
Janni's Stork, illustrated by Juan Wijngaard. London, Blackie, and New York, Harper, 1982.
Zed. London, Faber, 1982.
Summers of the Wild Rose. London, Faber, and Boston, Faber, 1987.
Colm of the Islands, illustrated by Pauline Baynes. London, Walker, 1989.

Ticket to Freedom. London, Faber, 1991.
The Wildcat Strike. London, Hamish Hamilton, 1995.

Plays

Television Plays: *Peronik,* 1976; *The Unknown Enchantment,* 1982.

Other

The Child in the Bamboo Grove (legend), illustrated by Errol Le Cain. London, Faber, 1971; New York, Phillips, 1972.
The Lotus and the Grail: Legends from East to West, illustrated by Errol Le Cain. London, Faber, 1974; abridged edition, as *Sea Magic and Other Stories of Enchantment,* New York, Macmillan, 1974.
Beauty and the Beast, illustrated by Errol Le Cain. London, Faber, 1979; New York, Doubleday, 1980.
Heidi (retelling), illustrated by Tomi Ungerer. London, Benn, 1983.

Editor, *Love and the Merry-Go-Round,* illustrated by Pauline Baynes. London, Hamish Hamilton, 1988.

PUBLICATIONS FOR ADULTS

Novels

The Summer-House. London, Hamish Hamilton, 1956.
Voyage to Cythera. London, Bodley Head, 1958.
Venus with Sparrows. London, Faber, 1961.
All My Enemies. London, Faber, 1967; New York, Simon and Schuster, 1973.
The Nice Girl's Story. London, Faber, 1968; as *Nor Evil Dreams,* New York, Simon and Schuster, 1974.
A Wicked Pack of Cards. London, Faber, 1969; New York, Walker, 1970.
The Double Snare. London, Faber, 1974; New York, Simon and Schuster, 1975.
Three Candles for the Dark. London, Faber, 1976.
The Haunting of Joey M'basa. London, Hamish Hamilton, 1996.

*

Rosemary Harris comments:

I came to writing almost by chance—not that I hadn't scribbled a lot when I was a child, but there was no fixed intention of becoming a writer. After the restrictions of war work, my career seemed set in painting and picture-restoring, until a series of accidental happenings sent me home, where I filled in time writing an adult novel, which was accepted by Hamish Hamilton. Later on, once established as a Faber author, at the request of their children's book editor, I wrote my first children's book and Carnegie winner *The Moon in the Cloud.* A lot of writers do seem to take indirect paths to their career; so if I were giving advice to any young would-be author, I'd suggest they tried other things first, and get a lot of different experiences—and travel; and certainly acquire computer skills in this day and age.

* * *

Rosemary Harris makes nonsense of any distinction between adult and children's fiction. She writes only for her peers of any age.

Her Egyptian trilogy (1969-72) begins lightheartedly, though it never shirks the realities of human evil. *The Moon in the Cloud* tells how Reuben, the musician and animal tamer, sets out for Kemi to obtain a pair of lions for Noah's ark, and so to earn a passage for himself and his wife Thamar. He suffers dangers and distress, becomes chief musician to the young Pharaoh, Merenkere, and eventually achieves his mission in surprising ways, helped by his formidable cat, Cefalu. The two succeeding books, though witty and engaging as ever, grow increasingly somber in theme. *The Shadow on the Sun* is the story of Merenkere's emerging greatness and of his love for Meri-Mekhmet. It is Reuben who rescues her when she is abducted by the evil Prince of Punt. *The Bright and Morning Star* probes the grief of Reuben and Thamar for their sick autistic son and that of Merenkere for his weak and treacherous heir. Still, the book is a celebration of human greatness and generosity, and the pace never flags, with the excitement generated as much by language as by action. Its vivid images and rhythms, brilliant and sometimes sinister, echo the sunlight and darkness of the characters, the contrasts of the empty desert, the sophisticated yet barbaric beauty of Kemi, and the stifling horror of the voodoo-haunted jungles of Punt. The animals are as delightfully individual as the human characters, yet always retain their own animal nature. Their comments are often the vehicle of the story's delicate and sharp-edged irony.

In *The Seal-Singing* the author moves into the contemporary world, but her Scottish island is tainted by ancient witchcraft. She shows a sympathetic understanding of adolescents in her study of the young cousins, with their loves and jealousies and uncertainties, and a fascinating knowledge of the seals themselves. Rock and wind and sea are unforgettably present. The story is tense and exciting, though lightly handled.

Harris also writes for younger children. *The Child in the Bamboo Grove* and *The Little Dog of Fo* are charming Chinese tales, and *The Enchanted Horse* transfers an English folktale to an Indian setting. *Janni's Stork* tells of a witty Dutch housewife and the boy she befriends.

In *A Quest for Orion* and *Tower of the Stars,* Harris evokes a somber vision of a world crumbling into ruin and slavery beneath a savage totalitarian regime. Tiny, isolated groups of young people resist and struggle to survive. The impression is wholly bleak; and the mixture of magic symbols, science fiction, and "alternative time" theories is not completely convincing. But the characters and their personal relationships are powerfully evoked.

In two of her books from the 1980s, she again breaks new ground. *Zed* is the tense and moving story of an eight-year-old boy taken hostage in a terrorist attack. He recalls it eight years later, so that throughout the book the child's grief and disillusionment are set against the maturity and concern for others which he achieves through the experience. *Summers of the Wild Rose* is a compassionate story of first love between an English girl and a half-Jewish boy under the growing shadow of Nazi power—a tragic journey from innocence to experience. As in all her books, a faith in essential goodness balances her unflinching portrayal of the darkness that threatens it. These are compelling stories through which the reader can grow in understanding, and widen his or her experience.

—Margaret Greaves

HATHORN, Libby

Nationality: Australian. **Born:** Elizabeth Helen Krahe, 26 September 1943, Newcastle, New South Wales. **Education:** Attended Sydney Girl's High School, 1956-60; Sydney Technical College, 1960-61, and Balmain Teacher College (now University of Technology, Sydney), 1962-63. **Family:** Married John Hathorn in 1968; one daughter and one son. **Career:** Teacher and librarian in schools in Sydney, 1965-81, deputy principal, 1977; consultant and senior education officer for government adult education programs, 1981-86. Since 1987 full-time writer. Occasional lecturer in English and children's literature, Sydney University, since 1982; writer in residence, University of Technology, Sydney, 1990, Woollahra Library, 1992; and Edith Cowan University, 1992. Speaker for student, teacher, and parent groups. **Awards:** Children's Book Council of Australia, highly commended, 1982; Children's Book of the Year shortlist, 1986, 1990; honour award, 1987, 1988; honour book of the year, older readers, 1990; notable book, 1991 (2 books), 1992, 1993, 1996, 1997; New South Wales Premier's Literary Awards shortlist, 1986; Literature Board of the Australia Council fellowships, 1987, 1988, 1993, 1994-97; Society of Women Writers commendation, for body of work, 1990; named to American Library Association Best Book for Young Adults list, 1991; New South Wales Children's Week award for literature, 1992; Kate Greenaway award, United Kingdom, 1995, for text for picture storybook; Parent's Choice award, United States, 1995; Australian Violence Prevention Certificate award, 1995. **Agent:** Laura Blake Peterson, Curtis Brown, 10 Astor Place, New York, New York 10003, U.S.A. **Address:** 32 Lang Road, Centennial Park, Sydney, New South Wales 2021, Australia. **Website:** http://www.libbyhathorn.com.

Publications for Children

Fiction

Stephen's Tree, illustrated by Sandra Laroche. London, Methuen, 1979.
Lachlan's Walk, illustrated by S. Laroche. Port Melbourne, Heinemann, 1980.
The Tram to Bondi Beach, illustrated by Julie Vivas. North Blackburn, Victoria, Collins, 1981.
Paolo's Secret, illustrated by Lorraine Hannay. Port Melbourne, Heinemann, 1985.
All About Anna. Port Melbourne, Heinemann, 1986.
Looking Out for Sampson. Rydalmere, New South Wales, Hodder and Stoughton, 1987.
Freya's Fantastic Surprise, illustrated by Sharon Thompson. Lisarow, New South Wales, Ashton Scholastic, 1988.
The Extraordinary Magics of Emma McDade, illustrated by Maya. Rydalmere, New South Wales, Hodder and Stoughton, 1989.
Stuntumble Monday, illustrated by Melissa Web. North Blackburn, Victoria, Collins Dove, 1989.
The Garden of the World, illustrated by Tricia Oktober. Margaret Hamilton Books, 1989.
Thunderwith. Port Melbourne, Heinemann, 1989.
Jezza Says, illustrated by Donna Rawlins. Pymble, New South Wales, Angus and Robertson, 1990.
So Who Needs Lotto? illustrated by Simon Kneebone. Ringwood, Victoria, Penguin, 1990.
Love Me Tender. Rydalmere, New South Wales, Hodder and Stoughton, 1992.
The Lenski Kids and Dracula. Ringwood, Victoria, Penguin, 1992.
Valley Under the Rock. Port Melbourne, Heinemann, 1993.
Way Home, illustrated by Greg Rogers. Random House, 1993.
Feral Kid. Rydalmere, New South Wales, Hodder and Stoughton, 1994.
Grandma's Shoes, illustrated by Elivia Salvadier. New York, Little, Brown, 1994.
The Wonder Thing, illustrated by Peter Gouldthorpe. Ringwood, Victoria, Penguin, 1995.
What a Star. Pymble, New South Wales, HarperCollins, 1994.
The Climb. Ringwood, Victoria, Penguin, 1996.
Chrysalis. Port Melbourne, Reed, 1997.
Rift. Rydalmere, New South Wales, Hodder Headline, 1998.

Poetry

Talks with My Skateboard. Australian Broadcasting Corporation, 1991.

Other

Help for Young Writers. Thomas Nelson, 1991.
Good to Read (textbook). Thomas Nelson, 1991.
Who? (stories). Port Melbourne, Heinemann, 1992.

Editor, *The Blue Dress* (stories). Port Melbourne, Heinemann, 1991.

Publications for Adults

Other

Half-Time: Perspectives on Mid-life, with G. Bates. Fontana Collins, 1987.
Better Strangers (stories). Millenium Books, 1989.
Damascus, a Rooming House (libretto; performed Sydney, 1990).
The Maroubra Cycle: A Journey Around Childhood (performance poetry). Sydney, University of Technology, 1990.
The Blue Dress Suite (music theatre piece; produced Melbourne, 1991).
Grandma's Shoes, composed by Grahame Koehne, (libretto; performed Australian Opera Workshop).

*

Theatrical Activities:
Director: **Musical Theatre**—*The Blue Dress Suite,* 1991.

Libby Hathorn comments:

As a child I loved poetry with a passion—poems my parents recited which were often Australian bush ballads, but also poetry of the English Romantics—and then the poems I discovered on the bookshelves of libraries and bookshops. During my adolescence, whilst British poets remained a strong influence, (with the discovery of the likes of Dylan Thomas or WB Yeats), I began reading older Australian poets such as Shaw Neilson and David Campbell; as well as contemporaries like Judith Wright and Les

Murray. And then translations began arriving in the bookshops and I discovered the joys of poets such as Garcia Lorca and Rainer Maria Rilke. Poetry is still a journey for me with the work of poets like Pablo Neruda and Wallace Stevens being wonderful discoveries for me in adulthood.

Poetry has informed my writing and in particular the picture storybook whose text qualities are much like a 'good' poem-succinct, spare and surprising. I think children are often natural poets with the freedom to 'play' with words and phrases that we adults can sometimes lose, and their writing of poetry should be encouraged. And I think that young people also deserve to hear the best that language has to offer through poetry, even though it may mean some 'work' on their part as the reader/ thinker.

I'm pleased that my picture storybook *Sky Sash So Blue* presented itself to me as a narrative poem, because to me it is all the more powerful, for the 'singing' quality of the text. But picture storybooks are not the only place for poetry in my writing. In nearly every novel I write, I quote poetry. There is generally a character who loves poetry or knows somebody—mother, grandfather, friend who does! It might be just a passing reference but it's there because I feel our lives should not lack poetry. It's best when poetry seems part of the landscape and not something separate to our lives because of course it so powerfully and poignantly reflects our lives—so it is a natural addition to my prose writing.

Quite often a story will present itself as a poem. For example, my novel *Thunderwith* which is currently being made a telemovie by Hallmark Hall of Fame, began as a four line poem about thunder—and from that poem and the stormy night on which it presented, came a whole novel.

When I'm troubled I can find solace in poetry. When I'm happy I can often find still more joy in poetry. When I'm lonely I can find comfort in thoughts exquisitely expressed. And when I'm puzzled Ican sometimes find a meaning, in entering the mind and world of some other human being who is trying to make sense and music of it all!

So you can see that poetry is a much a passion for me now as it was when I was child asking my dad or mum to say the one about nightingale, or the drover, or the billabong, or the highwayman, just one more time!

* * *

A strong sense of place pervades all of Libby Hathorn's writing, whether it occurs in the succinct text of a picture book, poem, or short story, in her exploration of the inner world of play that flows like a current underneath the exuberance of children in junior school, or through her insight into the tumultuous lives of troubled teenagers. It is perhaps most evident in the poems that make up her *Maroubra Cycle* (Maroubra is one of Sydney's eastern seaside suburbs, where Hathorn spent her childhood), but there is also a compelling immediacy to the settings of Coogee Beach in *Love Me Tender* and the inner-city streets and lanes in such novels as *Feral Kid.* In *Thunderwith* and Valley Under the Rock, Hathorn lovingly endows with life the rain forests and valleys of New South Wales. She also recreates with precision and tenderness the sensory perceptions that make childhood a time for the storing up of potent memories.

Hathorn began her writing career with three realistic picture books set in suburban Sydney. She was fortunate to have Sandra Laroche and then Julie Vivas as illustrators; *The Tram to Bondi Beach* is a landmark picture book in which the artwork extends the text by giving added substance to the mental and emotional life of the young protagonist. The same dynamic interaction of text and illustration is present in Hathorn's most recent picture book. *Way Home* is the dramatic monologue of a "street kid" whose odyssey and fierce affection for a stray cat are given added energy and urgency through the highly-charged night scenes depicted by artist Gregory Rogers.

After her successful first picture books, Hathorn introduced a new note into the junior novel in Australia. Both Jessica and Paolo in *Paolo's Secret* are isolated, lonely and suffering; Jessica because her best friend has moved away, Paolo because he is culturally and temperamentally an outsider. A shared secret draws the two into a warm and mutually supportive relationship. In subsequent junior novels Hathorn has created a gallery of sometimes abrasive extroverts. The charismatic but incorrigible and hard-to-live-with Anna in *All About Anna,* dubbed a *singular child* by her father, and the irrepressible over-the-top Emma who can command thunderstorms in *The Extraordinary Magics of Emma McDade* are representative of Hathorn's forceful females, who are able to mask inner anxiety with a boldly aggressive front. Cheryl in *Looking Out for Sampson* is a supercilious but insecure mischief maker; in *So, Who Needs Lotto?* Denise the show-off and bully reveals her inner self when she makes friends with Cosmo, a nervous, reticent classmate. Through his hare-brained schemes for raising money the bombastic hero of *Jezza Says* discovers that it is possible to make dreams come true, but not necessarily in a materialistic way. The Lenski kids of *The Lenski Kids and Dracula* are "the wildest, meanest, screamiest kids you ever saw" and it takes a weird baby-sitter to cut them down to size.

Hathorn's hilarious, fast-paced, riotous tales for junior readers have an underlying seriousness that is given closer focus in the short stories represented in various anthologies and in her own volume, *Who?* There is loss, loneliness, and misunderstanding, but also the promise of ultimate reconciliation and healing, too, in her later novels. In *Feral Kid* it is a runaway from a foster home involved in the mugging of a kindly old lady, also suffering from an inner emptiness, who has the soft underbelly that presages the promise of redemption.

In her novels for adolescents, *Thunderwith, Love Me Tender,* and *Valley Under the Rock,* Hathorn's young people face their fears, inadequacies and suffering, and move toward maturity. Lara's mother in *Thunderwith* dies, but Lara learns to cope with her own emotive response to life, as well as an unsympathetic step-mother, her new family, her not-so-strong father, and the local bully, partly through the sympathetic understanding and wisdom of an Aboriginal storyteller. Alan in *Love Me Tender,* a child of rock and roll, also suffers the pain of separation from his mother, but it is his ultimate faith in the healing power of love that helps him along the path to maturity. Zoe in *Valley Under the Rock,* too, is taut with resentment and feels shut out of her mother's life and that of her brother. She has become *l'etranger.* But, again, love brings revelation and a degree of understanding. In her novels for teenagers, especially, Hathorn exposes, with compassion, sensitivity, and poetry the universal and ongoing struggle of humanity to heal hurts, establish meaningful relationships, and to learn to accept one's self—and, ultimately—those who have wronged us.

—Maurice Saxby

HAUGAARD, Erik (Christian)

Nationality: Danish. **Born:** Copenhagen, 13 April 1923. **Education:** Black Mountain College, North Carolina, 1941-42; New School for Social Research, New York, 1945-47. **Military Service:** Royal Canadian Air Force, 1942-45: flight sergeant; King Christian X Medal (Denmark). **Family:** Married 1) Myrna Seld in 1949 (died 1981), two children; 2) Masako Taira in 1986 (died 1996). **Career:** Worked as farm laborer in Fyn, Denmark, 1938-40, and shepherd in Wyoming. Whittall Lecturer, Library of Congress, Washington, D.C., 1973. **Awards:** Boston *Globe-Horn Book* award, 1967; Women's League for Peace and Freedom Jane Addams award, 1968; Danish Cultural Minister's award, 1970; Chapelbrook Foundation award, 1970; Japan Foundation fellowship, 1981; Children's Literature Association Phoenix award, 1988. **Address:** Toad Hall, The Quay, Ballydehob, County Cork, Ireland.

PUBLICATIONS FOR CHILDREN

Fiction

Hakon of Rogen's Saga, illustrated by Leo and Diane Dillon. Boston, Houghton Mifflin, 1963; as *Hakon's Saga,* London, Faber, 1964.
A Slave's Tale, illustrated by Leo and Diane Dillon. Boston, Houghton Mifflin, 1965; London, Gollancz, 1966.
Orphans of the Wind, illustrated by Milton Johnson. Boston, Houghton Mifflin, 1966; London, Gollancz, 1967.
The Little Fishes, illustrated by Milton Johnson. Boston, Houghton Mifflin, 1967; London, Gollancz, 1968.
The Rider and His Horse, illustrated by Leo and Diane Dillon. Boston, Houghton Mifflin, 1968; London, Gollancz, 1969.
The Untold Tale, illustrated by Leo and Diane Dillon. Boston, Houghton Mifflin, 1971.
A Messenger for Parliament. Boston, Houghton Mifflin, 1976.
Cromwell's Boy. Boston, Houghton Mifflin, 1978.
Chase Me, Catch Nobody! Boston, Houghton Mifflin, 1980; London, Granada, 1982.
Leif the Unlucky. Boston, Houghton Mifflin, 1982.
A Boy's Will, illustrated by Troy Howell. Boston, Houghton Mifflin, 1983.
The Samurai's Tale. Boston, Houghton Mifflin, 1984.
Prince Boghole, illustrated by Julie Downing. New York, Macmillan, 1987.
Princess Horrid. New York, Macmillan, 1989.
The Boy and the Samurai. Boston, Houghton Mifflin, 1991.
The Story of Yuriwaka. Boulder, Colorado, Rinehart, Roberts, 1991.
The Death of Mr. Angel. Boulder, Colorado, Rinehart, Roberts, 1992.
Under the Black Flag. Boulder, Colorado, Rinehart, Roberts, 1993.
The Revenge of the Forty-seven Samurai. Boston, Houghton Mifflin, 1994.

Other

Translator, *The Complete Fairy Tales and Stories of Hans Andersen.* New York, Doubleday, and London, Gollancz, 1974; shortened version, as *Hans Christian Andersen: His Classic Fairy Tales,* illustrated by Michael Foreman, London, Gollancz, 1976; New York, Doubleday, 1978.

PUBLICATIONS FOR ADULTS

Play

The Heroes (produced Antioch, Ohio, 1958).

Poetry

25 Poems. Tappernöje, Denmark, Squire Press, 1957.

Other

Portrait of a Poet: Hans Christian Andersen and His Fairy Tales (lecture). Washington, D.C., Library of Congress, 1973.

*

Critical Studies: *Something About the Author, Autobiography Series, Vol. 12.* Detroit, Gale Research, 1991.

Manuscript Collections: Kerlan Collection, University of Minnesota, Minneapolis; de Grummond Collection, University of Southern Mississippi, Hattiesburg.

Erik Haugaard comments:
I conceive of my fellow men as individuals: lonely figures trying to understand the dilemma they are born into. To live, to survive, is to me an heroic task but not necessarily a tragic one; victory is possible, at least on an individual level. The possibility of love and friendship exists; it is not a matter of chance but of choice. I cannot conceive of literature without this faith; the choiceless man going to his doom is but a silent brute, and he would not have left behind him the literature, art, and music of which we have a right to be justly proud.

* * *

Erik Haugaard, a master craftsman who writes of half a dozen countries and as many time periods, has had a varied career. Now in his fourth decade of writing for young readers, Haugaard continues to experiment with new formats and subject matter. Despite its variety, his work is readily identifiable, not only for its consistently high quality but for certain common themes. In almost every Haugaard novel, a boy comes of age at a time of turmoil and stress. Usually, he is uprooted from his own home and seeks (and often finds) a father figure or mentor who helps him to cope with nightmarish conditions: war, ethnic strife, loss of family, often hunger, and always danger. Settings and time periods include first-century Jerusalem, sixteenth and seventeenth century Japan, seventeenth century England, colonial America, and twentieth century Denmark and Italy. Haugaard's research is impeccable, always including periods spent in the country he is researching.

Haugaard began in the 1950s as a writer for adults, with a published volume of poetry and several plays, followed by his first attempt at a novel: a story of medieval Scandinavia, which he called *The Last Heathen.* Though Houghton Mifflin declined *The Last Heathen,* the children's books editor suggested that Haugaard refashion the story for the juvenile market; the result was *Hakon of Rogen's Saga,* a spare narrative about an orphaned boy on a bleak island off the Norwegian coast. Set at the end of the Viking period, this is not a translation of an actual saga but an original work, as is the sequel, *A Slave's Tale,* with a rare (for Haugaard) female protagonist. Though born a slave, Helga eventually marries Hakon after a journey of hardship and self-discovery that parallel's Hakon's experiences. The sea is almost a character in both books, as it is also in another Haugaard work of the mid-1960s, *Orphans of the Wind* (with a partially American setting). Two of Haugaard's best known books, both from the late 1960s, skirt the edges of despair. *The Little Fishes,* first of his books to be set in the twentieth century, presents the sordid and dangerous lives of a group of homeless Italian children during World War II. There is nothing grand or heroic about Haugaard's version of the war, in which survival at any cost is the constant issue. (Thirteen years later, *Chase Me, Catch Nobody* returns to the subject of World War II but offers a more hopeful view of human nature through a rather simplistic, adventure-oriented plot.) The second of these dark books, *The Rider and His Horse,* was not very successful at the time of its publication but received belated recognition two decades later. In this tale of first-century Judea, ending with the fall of the Masada, villains abound among the Romans, Samaritans, and even the politically divided Jews.

Haugaard returned to European historical settings in the 1970s. *The Untold Tale,* set in his native Denmark during the seventeenth century, marks the lowest point of the author's descent into pessimism; the protagonist not only undergoes the same horrors as Haugaard's other displaced children but does not even survive—in part, because he fails to find a father figure who can protect him. During the next few years, Haugaard was translating Hans Christian Andersen's tales, which appeared in several different versions and on which he lectured at the Library of Congress. He then resumed his seventeenth century European stories with *A Messenger for Parliament,* tracing the career of a boy whose mother dies and whose boastful, irrational father joins Cromwell's army. After weeks with a band of similarly displaced boys, Oliver Cutter becomes a protegee of his namesake, Oliver Cromwell; in a sequel, *Cromwell's Boy,* he undertakes a spying mission. Though human weakness and treachery are plentiful in this war too, the anarchy seems more temporary. Oliver, now settled in America, tells these stories from the point of view of an old man, lending an air of hope and stability not found in some of the earlier books.

Always willing to explore new ground, Haugaard did extensive background research in Japan for *The Samurai's Tale.* Once again, a young boy made homeless by circumstance learns to survive. In this case, the boy is taken into the household of a Japanese nobleman and eventually becomes a samurai himself. In this book, Haugaard achieves a balance between the uncertain world of seventeenth century Japan, with its rival war lords, and the stability of the noble household. He continued mining this vein with *The Boy and the Samurai,* a sixteenth century tale, and the short *Story of Yurikawa,* a rendering of a folk tale. At least one additional Japanese book is forthcoming.

Since 1990, Haugaard has explored new forms and new themes as well as developing his Japanese series. Two of his recent books are for much younger readers and one is for young adults; all three have settings he has not previously used. *Prince Boghole,* a picture book, tells a charming story of three princes who compete for the hand of an Irish princess; *Princess Horrid* describes what happens in a magic country when an ill-behaved princess turns into a kitten. *The Death of Mr. Angel,* Haugaard's only book with a contemporary American setting, examines the dilemma of a lonely teenager in a small town full of narrow-minded adults and virtually mindless peers. The story has not received the attention it deserves, partly because it has been confused with more sensational treatments of death and violence involving teacher figures. All three of these works show a new side of Haugaard's art: the use of external circumstances that, while not dangerous or harrowing as in the earlier books, nevertheless threaten the protagonist's chance to lead a normal life and develop individual values. Haugaard has also added to his list of thought-provoking adventures with *Under the Black Flag,* detailing the friendship between a plantation owner's son and a slave when both sail the Caribbean with Blackbeard.

—Caroline C. Hunt

HAWES, Charles Boardman

Nationality: American. **Born:** Clifton Springs, New York, 24 January 1889. **Education:** Schools in Bangor, Maine; Bowdoin College, Brunswick, Maine, graduated 1911; Harvard University, Cambridge, Massachusetts (Longfellow fellow), 1911-12. **Family:** Married Dorothea Cable in 1916; two sons. **Career:** Taught at Harrisburg Academy, Pennsylvania, one year; staff member, *Youth's Companion,* Boston; associate editor, *Open Road,* Dayton, Ohio. **Awards:** American Library Association Newbery Medal, 1924. **Died:** 15 July 1923.

Publications for Children

Fiction

The Mutineers. Boston, Atlantic Monthly Press, 1920; London, Heinemann, 1923.

The Great Quest, illustrated by George Varian. Boston, Atlantic Monthly Press, 1921; London, Heinemann, 1922.

The Dark Frigate. Boston, Atlantic Monthly Press, 1923; London, Heinemann, 1924.

Publications for Adults

Other

Whaling, completed by Dorothea Hawes. New York, Doubleday, and London, Heinemann, 1924.

Gloucester, By Land and Sea: The Story of a New England Seacoast Town. Boston, Little Brown, 1928.

* * *

Charles Boardman Hawes's untimely death at 35 cut short a career that might have rivaled Robert Louis Stevenson's had it run its course. With the exception of two novels, *The Dark Frigate* and *The Mutineers,* Hawes's work is long out of print. Derivative and flawed as these two books are, they both reveal what an inspired storyteller Hawes at his best could be.

Except for the fact that *The Dark Frigate* and *The Mutineers* are set in different centuries, they could both be the same book.

The lawful masters of the ship are murdered and the vessel taken over by pirates. But once the villains gain the upper hand, their luck deserts them. No longer can they do anything right. Eventually the heroes outwit them and regain the ship, leaving the evildoers to a richly deserved fate. If that sounds familiar it is because we have read that tale before: Stevenson's *Treasure Island.*

Hawes never was able to escape the shadow of that great book. His prose and narrative skill often approach the master's, but he is unable to sustain the performance over an entire novel. *The Mutineers* is the more successful of the two works, and one of the most gripping adventures ever written about the China clipper trade. *The Dark Frigate* is much more uneven. It begins too late, continues too long, and seems awash in an impossibly archaic dialect that owes far too much to Kingsley's *Westward, Ho!* Yet even this leaking, lumbering galleon of a book has its moments. Tom Jordan's takeover of *The Rose of Devon,* the murder of Captain Candle, and the fight with the Porcupine ketch are episodes of high adventure that can stand with the best.

The basic flaw of both *The Dark Frigate* and *The Mutineers* is their lack of a villain of the stature of Long John Silver. It is Silver, so charming, so menacing, who makes *Treasure Island* pulse with excitement. By contrast, Hawes's villains—Jordan, Falk, and Kipping—are weaklings and petty crooks. Hawes is much more successful with his minor characters. In the Fagin-like Jacob of *The Dark Frigate* we apparently have an anomaly: a Jewish pirate! The black cook of *The Mutineers* is shrewd and courageous, an original and admirable figure in spite of his minstrel show dialect. But even his roots may lie in a similar character in Kipling's *Captains Courageous.*

At the time of his death Charles Boardman Hawes was a second-rate writer trying to make up with detail what he lacked in originality. Nevertheless his work showed promise of great things to come. Had he been allowed to live longer, had he been less bookish, had he actually sailed before the mast himself like Jack London and Herman Melville, he might stand today as one of the great writers of the sea. As it is, he is not very far behind them.

—Eric A. Kimmel

HAYES, John F(rancis)

Nationality: Canadian. **Born:** Dryden, Ontario, 5 August 1904. **Education:** University of Toronto evening classes, 1930-45. **Family:** Married Helen Eileen Casselman in 1927; two sons and one daughter. **Career:** Writer, MacLean-Hunter Publishing Company, 1925-27, Consolidated Press, 1927-29, and Saturday Night Press, 1928, all Toronto; sales promotion writer, General Motors of Canada, Oshawa, Ontario, 1929-30; head of the Creative Department, 1930-34, and assistant sales manager, 1935, Brigdens Ltd., Toronto; sales promotion manager, Moffats Ltd., Weston, Ontario, 1937-40; executive assistant, 1940-45, sales manager, 1945-47, vice-president and general manager, 1947-50, vice-president and general manager of the Montreal Branch, 1950-56, and director and member of the Executive Committee, Southam Press Ltd., Toronto; managing director, Southam Printing Company, Toronto, 1956-60. Director, Toronto Graphic Arts Association. **Awards:** Governor-General's award, 1952, 1954; Quebec Government Scientific and Literary award, 1955; Canadian Library Association Book of the Year medal, 1959; Vicky Metcalf award, 1964. **Died:** November 1980.

Publications for Children (illustrated by Fred J. Finley)

Fiction

Buckskin Colonist. Toronto, Copp Clark, 1947; Oxford, Blackwell, 1948.
Treason at York. Toronto, Copp Clark, 1949.
A Land Divided. Toronto, Copp Clark, 1951; Philadelphia, Westminster Press, 1954.
Rebels Ride at Night. Toronto, Copp Clark, 1953.
Bugles in the Hills. Toronto, Copp Clark, 1955; Oxford, Blackwell, and New York, Messner, 1956.
The Dangerous Cove: A Story of Early Days in Newfoundland. Toronto, Copp Clark, 1957; New York, Messner, 1960.
Quest in the Cariboo. Toronto, Copp Clark, 1960.
Flaming Prairie: A Story of the Northwest Rebellion of 1885. Toronto, Copp Clark, 1965.
The Steel Ribbon. Toronto, Copp Clark, 1967.
The Nation Builders. Toronto, Copp Clark, 1968.
On Loyalist Trails: A Story about the United Empire Loyalists, illustrated by J. Merle Smith. Toronto, Copp Clark, 1971.

Publications for Adults

Other

The Renovation Business. Toronto, Crane, 1962.
Switzerland. Toronto, Air Canada, 1962.
The Challenge of Change: 50 Years 1912-1962. Toronto, Downtown Church Workers Association, 1962.
Into a Nation. Toronto, Canadian Council of Churches, 1966.
Wilderness Mission: The Story of Sainte-Marie-among-the-Hurons. Toronto, Ryerson Press, 1969.

* * *

The historical novels of John F. Hayes provide a near panorama, in fiction, of pre-20th-century Canadian history. The earliest setting is Newfoundland in 1676; the latest, the Prairies in 1885. Hayes dealt with most regions of Canada (the Maritimes, Ontario, the Prairies, British Columbia), omitting only the far north and, significantly, Quebec. And he tackled all major conflicts—again with one important exception involving Quebec: the Battle of the Plains of Abraham which resulted in the final fall of New France to the British. Why Hayes assiduously avoided Quebec subjects seems to be due to a reluctance to confront English-French antagonisms within Canada. Accordingly, another potentially divisive topic—the removal of the Acadians (*A Land Divided*)—is treated so as to defuse the historical situation of the long-lasting hostilities felt by the actual participants. Thus the expulsion is smoothed over with pro-British justifications; thus the cruelty of the eviction is minimized; and thus the Acadian co-hero, Pierre—though his family is expelled—even joins the English Navy. The reality was starker, and passions ran deeper, than Hayes allowed. Accordingly, though the novel certainly contains moments of excitement and various authentic details of the period, it nevertheless violates the spirit of the time.

Hayes's other historical novels treat the settlement of Newfoundland (*The Dangerous Cove*), the Loyalist emigration to Canada (*On Loyalist Trails*), the War of 1812 (*Treason at York*), the Selkirk settlers (*Buckskin Colonist*), the Mackenzie Rebellion (*Rebels Ride at Night*), the British Columbia gold rush (*Quest in the Cariboo*), the early days of the Mounties (*Bugles in the Hills*), the building of the Canadian Pacific Railway (*The Steel Ribbon*), and the Riel Rebellion (*Flaming Prairie*). In these books he was generally true to the reality of the times he treats, and the historical facts, though accurate and reasonably detailed, are usually not intrusions into the story but rather enrichments of it. The historical events are quite exciting in themselves, and this contributes to the total excitement and interest that the novels create.

Hayes's fiction typically locates a teen-age male hero plus a close friend in an exciting historical time or place. Soon the boys, for reasons often connected with their fathers, find themselves at the focal point between good and evil groups and, acting, prevent calamities from happening—or at least attenuate them. The main hero generally has a close relationship with his father, and the father's praise of his son's manly achievements is frequent. In various books (*The Dangerous Cove, A Land Divided*) the hero is even allowed the wish-fulfilment situation of rescuing his father from dangerous enemies. Further, where the hero's father is dead (*Rebels Ride at Night*), a substitute father soon steps forth to become the beneficiary of good deeds and the source of praise that boys desire. The father's (or substitute's) occupation is often important, incidentally, for the boy frequently follows in his footsteps. Action so satisfactory of boyhood dreams and male role expectations is one of the prominent elements in the books and one of the reasons that boys like them.

The defects in Hayes's fiction are sporadic, occurring to different degrees in different books, but fatal to none. These include the improbabilities of plot, repetitious action, weak concluding paragraphs, and dialogue which is acceptable but not inspired. His strength, besides historical authenticity, was the ability to create, notwithstanding defects, tales of excitement with which a boy can easily identify because they meet his psychological needs for adventure, manly behaviour, success, and parental praise.

—John Robert Sorfleet

HAYWOOD, Carolyn

Nationality: American. **Born:** Philadelphia, Pennsylvania, 3 January 1898. **Education:** High School for Girls and Normal School, both Philadelphia; Pennsylvania Academy of Fine Arts (Cresson traveling scholar), 1923-25. **Career:** Teacher, Friends Central School, Philadelphia; assistant in the studio of Violet Oakley; portrait painter and mural artist. **Died:** 11 January 1990.

PUBLICATIONS FOR CHILDREN (ILLUSTRATED BY THE AUTHOR)

Fiction

When I Grow Up. Racine, Wisconsin, Whitman, 1931.
"B" Is for Betsy. New York, Harcourt Brace, 1939.
Two and Two Are Four. New York, Harcourt Brace, 1940.
Betsy and Billy. New York, Harcourt Brace, 1941.
Primrose Day. New York, Harcourt Brace, 1942.
Back to School with Betsy. New York, Harcourt Brace, 1943.
Here's a Penny. New York, Harcourt Brace, 1944.
Betsy and the Boys. New York, Harcourt Brace, 1945.
Penny and Peter. New York, Harcourt Brace, 1946.
Little Eddie. New York, Morrow, 1947.
Penny Goes to Camp. New York, Morrow, 1948.
Eddie and the Fire Engine. New York, Morrow, 1949.
Betsy's Little Star. New York, Morrow, 1950.
Eddie and Gardenia. New York, Morrow, 1951.
The Mixed-Up Twins. New York, Morrow, 1952.
Eddie's Pay Dirt. New York, Morrow, 1953.
Betsy and the Circus. New York, Morrow, 1954.
Eddie and His Big Deals. New York, Morrow, 1955.
Betsy's Busy Summer. New York, Morrow, 1956.
Eddie Makes Music. New York, Morrow, 1957.
Betsy's Winterhouse. New York, Morrow, 1958.
Eddie and Louella. New York, Morrow, 1959.
Annie Pat and Eddie. New York, Morrow, 1960.
Snowbound with Betsy. New York, Morrow, 1962.
Here Comes the Bus! New York, Morrow, 1963.
Eddie's Green Thumb. New York, Morrow, 1964.
Robert Rows the River. New York, Morrow, 1965.
Eddie the Dog Holder. New York, Morrow, 1966.
Betsy and Mr. Kilpatrick. New York, Morrow, 1967.
Ever-Ready Eddie. New York, Morrow, 1968.
Taffy and Melissa Molasses. New York, Morrow, 1969.
Eddie's Happenings. New York, Morrow, 1971.
A Christmas Fantasy, illustrated by Glenys and Victor Ambrus. New York, Morrow, 1972; Leicester, Brockhampton Press, 1973.
Away Went the Balloons. New York, Morrow, 1973.
"C" Is for Cupcake. New York, Morrow, 1974.
Eddie's Valuable Property. New York, Morrow, 1975.
A Valentine Fantasy, illustrated by Glenys and Victor Ambrus. New York, Morrow, 1976.
Betsy's Play School, illustrated by James Griffin. New York, Morrow, 1977.
Eddie's Menagerie, illustrated by Ingrid Fetz. New York, Morrow, 1978.
The King's Monster, illustrated by Victor Ambrus. New York, Morrow, 1980.
Halloween Treats, illustrated by Victoria de Larrea. New York, Morrow, 1981.
Santa Claus Forever!, illustrated by Glenys and Victor Ambrus. New York, Morrow, 1983; Oxford, Oxford University Press, 1986.
Happy Birthday from Carolyn Haywood, illustrated by Wendy Watson. New York, Morrow, 1984.
Summer Fun, illustrated by Julie Durrell. New York, Morrow, 1986.
How the Reindeer Saved Santa, illustrated by Victor Ambrus. New York, Morrow, 1986; Oxford, Oxford University Press, 1987.
Merry Christmas from Eddie. New York, Morrow, 1986.
Hello, Star, illustrated by Julie Durrell. New York, Morrow, 1987.

Other

Editor, *Make a Joyful Noise! Bible Verses for Children.* Philadelphia, Westminster Press, 1984.

*

Manuscript Collections: Free Library, Philadelphia; Kerlan Collection, University of Minnesota, Minneapolis; de Grummond Collection, University of Southern Mississippi, Hattiesburg.

Carolyn Haywood commented:

(1989) I write for children because I feel that they need to know what is going on in their world and they can best understand it through stories about their world.

* * *

Carolyn Haywood was a prolific writer of very popular books that appeal to children in the 7 to 10 age group. Since her first junior novel appeared many years ago, her recognition as one of the premier writers of mildly exciting adventure stories involving the typical concerns of normal, middle-class children has steadily grown.

The reasons for Haywood's immense success are numerous. One of these surely must be the attractive plots of her stories, centered on the day-by-day experiences of ordinary yet extremely vigorous, active, and dominant children. Haywood created imaginative yet wholesome situations for these children to live through, often with problems to solve. These problem conditions, of little actual consequence except for the great deal of activity they allow her characters to perform, are typical of those found in children's lives. These are predicaments which the child reader easily recognizes as ones that could actually happen to him. They are situations spun through narrative plots much like those found in the typical social novel, that is, a telling out of ever-widening social arrangements rather than the depiction of well-developed representations of personality. As well, they use an episodic, short-story form of organization. The chapters of Haywood's books are so lightly threaded, one to the other, that each of them can be read almost by itself.

The main characters of Haywood's tales are idealized, unsophisticated, even stereotyped children. They are flat or "mythical" people who enter and leave the episodes in her stories with much of the same set of qualities. These fictional children, who seldom if ever pause to question their responses to the forces set against them, are nonetheless highly endearing to young readers. Furthermore, Haywood made sure these readers understand fully the motives of her fictionalized subjects by describing them in direct and steadfast fashion. By this means her readers are left with little or nothing to infer about their personalities or motivations. This may seem defective writing, but it is a style that young children have repeatedly shown they prefer over an indirect or subtle development of character in books. It obviously was soon apparent to Haywood that these characters were so believable to her readers that she could successfully write a series on some of them. Thus Betsy and Eddie emerged as main attractions in several of Haywood's different stories.

—Patrick Groff

HEDDERWICK, Mairi

Nationality: British. **Born:** Gourock, Renfrewshire, Scotland, 2 May 1939. **Education:** St. Columba's Girls School, Kilmacolm, Renfrewshire, until 1957; Edinburgh College of Art, 1957-61; Jordanhill College of Education, Glasgow, 1961-62. **Family:** Divorced; one son and one daughter; three grandchildren. **Career:** Writer, illustrator, and teacher. **Address:** Greenbanks, Roberton, by Hawick, Scottish Borders TD9 7ND, Scotland.

Publications for Children (illustrated by the author)

Fiction

Peedie Peebles' Summer or Winter Book. London, Bodley Head, 1989; as *P.D. Peebles' Summer or Winter Book.* Boston, Little Brown, 1989.
The Spell Singer and Other Stories. London, Blackie, 1989.
Peedie Peebles' Colour Book. London, Bodley Head, 1994.

Reteller, *The Tale of Carpenter MacPheigh: a Scottish Folk Tale.* London, Blackie, 1994.

"Katie Morag" Series

Katie Morag Delivers the Mail. London, Bodley Head, 1984; Boston, Little Brown, 1988.
Katie Morag and the Two Grandmothers. London, Bodley Head, and Boston, Little Brown, 1985.
Katie Morag and the Tiresome Ted. London, Bodley Head, and Boston, Little Brown, 1986.
Katie Morag and the Big Boy Cousins. London, Bodley Head, and Boston, Little Brown, 1987.
Katie Morag and the New Pier. London, Bodley Head, 1993.
Katie Morag and the Wedding. London, Bodley Head, 1995.
The Big Katie Morag Storybook. London, Bodley Head, 1996.
Katie Morag and the Grand Concert. London, Bodley Head, 1997.

"Robbie" Series

Dreamy Robbie! Harlow, Oliver & Boyd, 1993.
Robbie's First Day at School. Harlow, Oliver & Boyd, 1993.
Robbie's Trousers. Harlow, Oliver & Boyd, 1993.
Robbie and Granpa. Harlow, Oliver & Boyd, 1994.
Robbie's Birthday. Harlow, Oliver and Boyd, 1994.
Robbie's Next Day at School by Margaret Burnell, Sallie Harkness and Helen MacLullich. Harlow, Oliver & Boyd, 1994.
Oh, Robbie! by Margaret Burnell, Sallie Harkness and Helen MacLullich. Harlow, Oliver & Boyd, 1994.

Publications for Adults

Other

Views of Scotland. Gartocharn, Dunbarton, Famedram, 1981.
An Eye on the Hebrides. Edinburgh, Canongate, 1989.
Highland Journey: A Sketching Tour of Scotland Retracing the Footsteps of Victorian Artist John T. Reid. Edinburgh, Canongate, 1992.

*

Illustrator: *The Old Woman Who Lived in a Vinegar Bottle* by Rumer Godden, 1972; *Herself and Janet Reachfar,* 1975, *Jane*

Reachfar and the Kelpie, 1976, and *Janet Reachfar and Chickabird,* 1978, all by Jane Duncan; *The Gift of the Tarns* by E.R. Taylor, 1977; *A Cat Called Rover; A Dog Called Smith* by Wendy Body, 1981; *Hamish and the Wee Witch,* 1986, *Hamish and the Fairy Bairn,* 1989, and *Meet Maggie McMuddle,* 1989, all by Moira Miller; *Our Best Stories* edited by Anne Wood and Ann Pilling, 1986; *The Haggis* by Alexander Maclean, 1987; *Venus Peter Saves the Whale* by Christopher Rush, 1992; *Hands off Our School!* by Joan Lingard, 1992.

Mairi Hedderwick comments:

All my work comes from the hotch potch jumble of events and feelings that float around in my memory box. I am a totally subjective writer/illustrator/communicator. (I prefer the last description—must be the African Missionary Grandfather in me).

I can only write, draw, and talk about what I have experienced. The Katie Morag books are a pure nostalgia rerun of the young family-rearing island years in the Inner Hebrides of Scotland. Katie Morag is the late third child, my family long since grown up. Her bedroom is full of the toys and detritus that were my own children's. She wears my daughter's clothes. Grannie Island cooks on my Rayburn stove. Katie Morag's good moods and bad moods are all mine. As a mature(?) woman, I threw my old teddy bear into the sea—twice....

I have recently moved to the Scottish Borders after a life time association with the island that is the source material for much of my work especially Katie Morag. But life is too short to stay in the one place forever. It is time for me to now explore mainland, and beyond, mountains and forests in contrast to shell sand strands and seascape horizons. I would like to travel more and write adult books. I am presently writing up the story of the voyage of *Anassa.* Summer of '97 I and a friend lived for six weeks on this small and very low tech but beautiful little yacht, taking her down the Caledonian Canal through Scotland's finest mountain scenery and once at sea on the West Coast explored the many fiords that indent the coastline. I learned that it is very difficult to do watercolours on a moving boat!

Summer of '98 I am off to Central Africa to follow in my missionary parents footsteps. I hope a book will come of that too.

But wherever I go or whatever I do Katie Morag will always be calling me back to the island. all the many children I visit in schools and libraries will see to that!

* * *

Mairi Hedderwick depicts Scottish island life with affection and understanding, mercifully devoid of the sentimentality that often afflicts similar books. She herself was an island dweller in the 1960s when she became a classic "drop-out" from civilisation running a small printing press with her family on the island of Coll in the Hebrides. She looks back to this time with nostalgia but no regrets, using her experiences as a background for her highly successful picture books. *Katie Morag Delivers the Mail* was welcomed not only as a first-rate picture book for young children but for the arrival of a Scots artist and writer—a rare being. Katie Morag is a resourceful small girl living in the post office on the island of Struay, based on life on Coll. The success of the illustrations lies in the minute detail so beloved by children—the animals wreaking unseen havoc, the clutter of goods on the shelves of the shops, and the bustling, everyday life of the community.

Grannie Island plays a central role in all the Katie Morag books. She is usually depicted in dungarees, often with her head deep in the innards of a tractor. Hedderwick was surprised when the book was chosen as an example of a nonsexist picture book. With no crusading in mind, she had simply portrayed a woman doing everyday 'male' tasks, a common occurrence in rural communities. To date there are eight Katie Morag books with a ninth in production. Each book concerns the feelings of young children such as sibling rivalry in *Katie Morag and the Tiresome Ted,* in which Katie Morag vents her feelings over the arrival of a new baby by tossing her beloved teddy to the waves. A particular favourite at its creator's storytelling sessions, as the highlight is the production from a box of her own battered teddy which suffered a similar fate!

Hedderwick has two picture books for younger children. *Peedie Peebles' Summer or Winter Book* is a small "Lift the Flap" book which follows the routine of a toddler in both summer and winter, and in which the child can watch the antics of Peedie Peebles blissfully unaware of the disturbance to his long-suffering parents. The lavish details of the illustrations and the pleasure of investigating underneath the flaps make this a particularly enjoyable book for sharing. *Peedie Peebles' Colour Book* has large colourful pictures depicting Peedie Peebles "assisting" his parent's efforts at decorating the house which allows full reign to the creativity of the illustrator with lively detail which allows the young reader to identify the myriad colours used.

There are two books for adults which capture Hedderwick's deep love of Scotland. *An Eye on the Hebrides* charts her six month continuous journey with sketch pad and watercolours to many Scottish islands and *Highland Journey: A Sketching Tour of Scotland.* The latter is particularly fascinating as she followed in the footsteps of Victorian artist John T. Reid. Travelling alone, mostly on foot but occasionally hitching lifts on boats and local transport, she traced Reid's journey from Leith to Lewis. Her beautiful water colours sit alongside Reid's black and white engravings of 1876 and her pithy comments note the many changes which have taken place since his day.

—Valerie Bierman

HEIDE, Florence Parry

Pseudonyms: Alex B. Allen; Jamie McDonald. **Nationality:** American. **Born:** Pittsburgh, Pennsylvania, 27 February 1919. **Education:** Ellis School, Pittsburgh, graduated 1935; Wilson College, Chambersburg, Pennsylvania; University of California, Los Angeles, B.A. 1939. **Family:** Married Donald C. Heide in 1943; three sons and twin daughters. **Career:** Worked for RKO, and in public relations and advertising, New York; former public relations director, Pittsburgh Playhouse. **Awards:** Children's Book of the Year award, Child Study Association of America, 1970, for *Sound of Sunshine, Sound of Rain,* 1972, for *My Castle*; American Library Association (ALA) Notable Book, 1971, for *The Shrinking of Treehorn,* 1978, for *Banana Twist,* 1981, for *Treehorn's Treasure,* 1982, for *Time's Up!,* and 1990, for *The Day of Ahmed's Secret*; Children's Book Showcase, 1972, for *The Shrinking of Treehorn*; First Prize, Council for Wisconsin Writers, 1976, for *Growing Anyway Up,* 1982, for *Treehorn's Treasure,* 1982, for

Treehorn's Wish, and 1990, for *The Day of Ahmed's Secret*; Golden Kite Honor Book, 1976, for *Growing Anyway Up*; Golden Archer Award, Wisconsin Public Schools, 1976; Jugenbuchpreis (Best Children's Book in Germany), 1977, for *The Shrinking of Treehorn*; Children's Reading Round Table award, 1984; Omar's Book award, 1986, for *Banana Blitz*; Best Books of 1990 selection, *School Library Journal,* ALA Booklist Editor's Choices selection, Notable Children's Trade Book in the Field of Social Studies, Notable Trade Book in the Language Arts, listed on The Children's Book Council's 1990 selection of Children's Trade Books in cultural diversity, all 1990, all for *The Day of Ahmed's Secret*; Notable Wisconsin Author, 1991; Outstanding Children's Book award, New Hampshire Writers and Publishers Project, 1992, Notable Children's Trade Book in the Field of Social Studies, 1992, Editors' Choice 1992, *Booklist,* Best Books of 1992 list, *Parent's* magazine, *Hungry Mind Review* Children's Book of Distinction, 1993, and Rhode Island Children's Book award master list, 1993, all for *Sami and the Time of Troubles*; Major Achievement award, 1996. Litt.D.: Carthage College, Kenosha, Wisconsin, 1979. **Agent:** Marilyn Marlow, Curtis Brown, 10 Astor Place, New York, New York 10003. **Address:** 7700 Third Avenue, Kenosha, Wisconsin 53143-6003, U.S.A.

Publications for Children

Fiction

Benjamin Budge and Barnaby Ball, illustrated by Sally Mathews. New York, Four Winds Press, 1967.
Maximilian, with Sylvia W. Van Clief, illustrated by Ed Renfro. New York, Funk and Wagnalls, 1967.
The Day It Snowed in Summer, with Sylvia W. Van Clief, illustrated by Kenneth Longtemps. New York, Funk and Wagnalls, 1968.
How Big Am I?, with Sylvia W. Van Clief, illustrated by George Suyeoka. Chicago, Follett, 1968.
It Never Is Dark, with Sylvia W. Van Clief, illustrated by Don Almquist. Chicago, Follett, 1968.
Sebastian, with Sylvia W. Van Clief, illustrated by Betty Fraser. New York, Funk and Wagnalls, 1968.
That's What Friends Are For, with Sylvia W. Van Clief, illustrated by Brinton Turkle. New York, Four Winds Press, 1968.
Hannibal (as Jamie McDonald), with Anne and Walter Thiess, illustrated by Anne and Walter Thiess. New York, Funk and Wagnalls, 1968.
Maximilian Becomes Famous, illustrated by Ed Renfro. New York, Funk and Wagnalls, 1969.
The New Neighbor, with Sylvia W. Van Clief, illustrated by Jerry Warshaw. Chicago, Follett, 1970.
Alphabet Zoop, illustrated by Sally Mathews. New York, McCall, 1970.
Giants Are Very Brave People, illustrated by Charles Robinson. New York, Parents' Magazine Press, 1970.
The Little One, illustrated by Kenneth Longtemps. New York, Lion Press, 1970.
Sound of Sunshine, Sound of Rain, illustrated by Kenneth Longtemps. New York, Parents' Magazine Press, 1970.
Look! Look! A Story Book, illustrated by Carol Nicklaus. New York, McCall, 1971.
The Key, illustrated by Ati Forberg. New York, Atheneum, 1971.
The Shrinking of Treehorn, illustrated by Edward Gorey. New York, Holiday House, 1971; London, Kestrel, 1975.
Some Things Are Scary, illustrated by Robert Osborne. New York, Scholastic, 1971.
Who Needs Me?, illustrated by Sally Mathews. Minneapolis, Augsburg, 1971.
My Castle, illustrated by Symeon Shimin. New York, McGraw Hill, 1972.
The Mystery of the Missing Suitcase, with Sylvia W. Van Clief, illustrated by Seymour Fleishman. Chicago, Whitman, 1972.
The Mystery of the Silver Tag, with Sylvia W. Van Clief, illustrated by Seymour Fleishman. Chicago, Whitman, 1972.
The Hidden Box Mystery, with Sylvia W. Van Clief, illustrated by Seymour Fleishman. Chicago, Whitman, 1973.
Mystery at MacAdoo Zoo, with Sylvia W. Van Clief, illustrated by Seymour Fleishman. Chicago, Whitman, 1973.
Mystery of the Whispering Voice, with Sylvia W. Van Clief, illustrated by Seymour Fleishman. Chicago, Whitman, 1974.
Mystery of the Melting Snowman, with Roxanne Heide, illustrated by Seymour Fleishman. Chicago, Whitman, 1974.
Mystery of the Vanishing Visitor, with Roxanne Heide, illustrated by Seymour Fleishman. Chicago, Whitman, 1975.
Mystery of the Bewitched Bookmobile, with Roxanne Heide, illustrated by Seymour Fleishman. Chicago, Whitman, 1975.
When the Sad One Comes to Stay. Philadelphia, Lippincott, 1975.
Growing Anyway Up. Philadelphia, Lippincott, 1976.
Mystery of the Lonely Lantern, with Roxanne Heide, illustrated by Seymour Fleishman. Chicago, Whitman, 1976.
Mystery at Keyhole Carnival, with Roxanne Heide, illustrated by Seymour Fleishman. Chicago, Whitman, 1977.
Brillstone Break-In, with Roxanne Heide. Chicago, Whitman, 1977.
Mystery of the Midnight Message, with Roxanne Heide, illustrated by Seymour Fleishman. Chicago, Whitman, 1977.
Fables You Shouldn't Pay Any Attention To, with Sylvia W. Van Clief, illustrated by Victoria Chess. Philadelphia, Lippincott, 1978.
Banana Twist. New York, Holiday House, 1978.
Secret Dreamer, Secret Dreams. Philadelphia, Lippincott, 1978.
Fear at Brillstone, with Roxanne Heide. Chicago, Whitman, 1978.
Mystery at Southport Cinema, with Roxanne Heide, illustrated by Seymour Fleishman. Chicago, Whitman, 1978.
Face at the Brillstone Window, with Roxanne Heide. Chicago, Whitman, 1979.
Mystery of the Mummy's Mask, with Roxanne Heide, illustrated by Seymour Fleishman. Chicago, Whitman, 1979.
Body in the Brillstone Garage, with Roxanne Heide. Chicago, Whitman, 1980.
Mystery of the Forgotten Island, with Roxanne Heide, illustrated by Seymour Fleishman. Chicago, Whitman, 1980.
A Monster Is Coming! A Monster Is Coming!, with Roxanne Heide, illustrated by Rachi Farrow. New York, Watts, 1980.
Black Magic at Brillstone, with Roxanne Heide, illustrated by Joe Krush. Chicago, Whitman, 1981.
Treehorn's Treasure, illustrated by Edward Gorey. New York, Holiday House, 1981; London, Kestrel, 1983.
Time's Up!, illustrated by Marylin Hafner. New York, Holiday House, 1982.
The Problem with Pulcifer, illustrated by Judith Glasser. New York, Lippincott, 1982.
The Wendy Puzzle. New York, Holiday House, 1982.

Time Bomb at Brillstone, with Roxanne Heide, illustrated by Joe Krush. Chicago, Whitman, 1982.
Banana Blitz. New York, Holiday House, 1983.
Mystery on Danger Road, with Roxanne Heide, illustrated by Seymour Fleishman. Chicago, Whitman, 1983.
Treehorn's Wish, illustrated by Edward Gorey. New York, Holiday House, 1984; Oxford, Oxford University Press, 1986.
Time Flies!, illustrated by Marylin Hafner. New York, Holiday House, 1984.
Tales for the Perfect Child, illustrated by Victoria Chess. New York, Lothrop, 1985; London, Piccadilly Press, 1986.
The Day of Ahmed's Secret, with Judith Heide Gilliland, illustrated by Ted Lewin. New York, Lothrop, 1990; London, Gollancz, 1991.
Sami and the Time of Troubles, with Judith Heide Gilliland, illustrated by Ted Lewin. Boston, Clarion, 1992.
The Bigness Contest, illustrated by Victoria Chess. Boston, Joy Street Books, 1993.
Timothy Twinge, with Roxanne Heide Pierce, illustrated by Barbara Lehman. New York, Lothrop, 1993.
It's about Time, with Roxanne Heide Pierce and Judith Heide Gilliland. Boston, Clarion, 1998.
Tio Armando, with Roxanne Heide Pierce, illustrated by Ann Grifalconi. New York, Lothrop, 1998.
The House of Wisdom, with Judith Heide Gilliland. New York, DK Publishing, 1999.

Fiction (as Alex B. Allen, with Sylvia W. Van Clief)

Basketball Toss Up, illustrated by Kevin Royt. Chicago, Whitman, 1972.
No Place for Baseball, illustrated by Kevin Royt. Chicago, Whitman, 1973.
Danger on Broken Arrow Trail, illustrated by Michael Norman. Chicago, Whitman, 1974.
Fifth Down, illustrated by Dan Siculan. Chicago, Whitman, 1974.
The Tennis Menace, with David Heide, illustrated by Timothy Jones. Chicago, Whitman, 1975.

Poetry (songs)

Songs to Sing about Things You Think About, music by Sylvia W. Van Clief, illustrated by Rosalie Schmidt. New York, Day, 1971.
Christmas Bells and Snowflakes, music by Sylvia W. Van Clief. New York, Southern Music, 1971.
Holidays! Holidays!, music by Sylvia W. Van Clief. New York, Southern Music, 1971.
Grim and Ghastly Goings On, illustrated by Victoria Chess. New York, Lothrop, 1992.
Oh, Grow Up!, with Roxanne Heide Pierce, New York, Orchard, 1996.

Other

Lost! (textbook), with Roxanne Heide. New York, Holt Rinehart, 1973.
I See America Smiling (textbook), with Roxanne Heide. New York, Holt Rinehart, 1973.
No Roads for the Wind (textbook), with David Fisher Parry. New York, Macmillan, 1974.
Who Can? (reader), with Sylvia W. Van Clief. New York, Macmillan, 1974.
Lost and Found (reader), with Sylvia W. Van Clief. New York, Macmillan, 1974.
Hats and Bears (reader), with Sylvia W. Van Clief. New York, Macmillan, 1974.
Tell about Someone You Love (textbook), with Roxanne Heide. New York, Macmillan, 1974.
God and Me, illustrated by Ted Smith. St. Louis, Concordia, 1975.
You and Me, illustrated by Ted Smith. St. Louis, Concordia, 1975.
Changes, illustrated by Kathy Counts. St. Louis, Concordia, 1978.
I Love Every-People, with Roxanne Heide, illustrated by John Sandford. St. Louis, Concordia, 1978.
Who Taught Me? Was It You, God?, illustrated by Terry Whittle. St. Louis, Concordia, 1978.
By the Time You Count to Ten, illustrated by Pam Erickson. St. Louis, Concordia, 1979.

*

Florence Parry Heide comments:

A late bloomer, I started to write only when my five children had started school. Since I'd never written before, I wasn't sure then (and am not sure yet) what I want most of all to write or what I am best at writing, so I keep trying a great variety: picture books, poetry, juvenile novels, mysteries; funny books, sad books—I love them all. There are so many ideas waiting out there, so many unwritten stories, so many characters yet to be invented, so many many words to spin. What an adventure!

* * *

Florence Parry Heide has drawn most sustained notice as author of the Treehorn books, drolleries enhanced by the witty drawings of Edward Gorey. As much for adults as children are her three spoofs on perfect and obnoxious children. Hilarity reigns in the two books about Jonah, as well as the two about Noah. Worthy of note are three stories for young adolescents in which Heide deftly fleshes out the character of the troubled, female protagonists. For reluctant readers Heide offers the action of 20 mysteries, each solved in 128 pages by the children of The Spotlight Detective Club or two teenagers of Brillstone Apartments. For young children Heide has authored two dozen fair-to-middling picture books including some for Lutheran publishing houses and some textbook readers. In two decades Heide has written about 75 books. Until her death Sylvia Van Clief was second author for nearly one-third of the titles. Then Heide's twin daughter Roxanne became collaborator for 15 of the mysteries and five other titles.

Diminutive in an adult-dominated setting, the deadly serious Treehorn believes he is becoming even smaller in *The Shrinking of Treehorn.* The various, unruffled responses of mother (as long as you don't do it at the table), father, friend, teacher (we don't shrink in this class), and principal to the shrinking of Treehorn endow the story with clichés that are cleverly twisted and generate the reader's empathy for his neglected feelings. The writing is scrupulously controlled; Heide adroitly unfolds the perplexing and preposterous circumstances with restraint and sobriety, and allows Treehorn himself to put an end to his unusual condition. The delectable, bridled humor is taken up in the pen and ink drawings.

In *Treehorn's Treasure* he is possessed of an even more fertile imagination, largely fed by a craving for comic books and the fantastic products of their ads, which money can buy. Father urges Treehorn to save his dollar allowance because "money doesn't grow on trees." Treehorn puts the dollar in an envelope already addressed to Instant Magic and tucks it in a tree. Before long he observes the leaves are changing to dollar bills, thus furnishing him the wherewithal to make his purchases. The reader readily accepts the fantasy while the unbelieving adults of Treehorn's universe consistently react obliquely. The engaging interplay of illustration and text augment meaning and refine the portrayal of the unique boy. Gorey's trenchant black-on-white drawings place lovable Treehorn on the latticework of an angular environment, except for the occasional balloons that convey the little fellow's wild imaginings.

One does not reveal the wish made before blowing out the candles on a birthday cake lest the wish not come true. In *Treehorn's Wish* the wish of the final page of text is not shared with the reader but a wry story is built around the three wishes granted to Treehorn by a genie of golden earrings and long robe who appears out of a puff of smoke from the jug Treehorn has found in the yard. Although at the beginning of the day Treehorn hopes his parents may lavish him with presents to make up for the past meager years, by breakfast he has reason to believe his father and mother are more concerned about matters other than his birthday. Treehorn's first wish assures he will have a birthday cake and the second, candles. Neglect and admonishments of the day are countered by Treehorn's effusive thoughts about ways to use his third wish. Gorey's sophisticated line drawings perfectly complement the bittersweet account of stoical Treehorn's unusual birthday. The final illustration, at once conclusive and provocative, shows Treehorn alone at the kitchen table blowing the candles of his cake; two empty chairs attend him.

The format of Heide's spoofs might suggest the books are for beginning readers but the titles should be read as warning labels. These tales are for the worldly wise of all ages, those ready for a dose of irreverence. *The Problem with Pulcifer* introduces a child who will not watch television. Parents and school personnel worry about the boy who prefers to read books and refuses to succumb to television addiction as everybody else in the book has. Seven short pieces in *Fables You Shouldn't Pay Any Attention To* and in *Tales for the Perfect Child* treat the flip side of moral sketches. Greedy Gretchen (the gluttonous fish in *Fables*), after displaying her disgusting eating habits at lunch, is satiated and doesn't go for the worm on the hook while the other fish, who have eaten daintily and are still hungry, meet their doom. *Tales* might have been subtitled Techniques to Get Your Own Way. Arthur prefers his comfortable old clothes but acquiesces to his mother's command to get dressed up for the visit to Aunt Eunice. Arthur dutifully puts on his finest clothes and then goes to the kitchen to pour himself a large glass of grape juice. The three books might not be appreciated by the perfect parents who try so hard but anyone ready to chuckle at some sprightly commentary on proper behavior will be amused by the tongue-in-cheek humor.

Jonah in *Banana Twist* applies for admission to a boarding school that promises a television set and refrigerator in every dorm room. Upon arrival in *Banana Blitz* Jonah finds his roommate to be none other than the antagonist of the earlier book, Goober. Zany antics and slapstick humor give one meaning to the common word of the titles, although bananas play their part in each book. Surely both Jonah and Goober are one-of-a-kind boys, even though one-dimensional. Similar in tone are the books about Noah, *Time's Up!* and *Time Flies!.* The son of an efficiency fanatic shares, in first person, his viewpoints about adjusting to a new neighborhood and a baby sister. The writing style is breezy; coincidence and misunderstanding advance the plots and bring about satisfying endings.

Keenly sensitive characterization and tight prose distinguish Heide's first-person narratives for emerging adolescents. The point of view, like an autobiographical monologue, is consistently of the girl protagonist, who introduces the audience to other characters in the dimensions she sees fit but also freely reveals to the reader her innermost feelings. The author provides a vivid and profound character study.

Sara (*When the Sad One Comes to Stay*) is ultimately confronted with the choice between her calculating, success-bent mother and the shabby, elderly neighborhood character who proffers warmth and friendship, recalling in Sara's mind the halcyon days before she was snatched from her easygoing father. Crazy Maisie, who staves off loneliness (the sad one) with aberrant behavior, loses out to mother, an inevitable denouement, realistic but vexing.

In *Growing Anyway Up* Florence shuns facing up to relationships with adults and classmates. Convinced that her thoughts and feelings are kept secret by not letting anyone look into her eyes, Florence veils herself behind peculiar ocular rituals and other distancing mannerisms. Exuberant Aunt Nina helps her become more forbearing of her taciturn mother and the lump who will be her stepfather.

Severely disturbed Caroline of *Secret Dreamer, Secret Dreams* cannot speak to anyone, not even her patient and loving father. Her delight in her dog gives promise of recovery but in the last sentence Caroline laments, "Brumm barks helplessly, his voice unintelligible as my own, his message and mine forever undelivered."

Heide skillfully handles the egocentric adolescent's testing and tasting of life, evolving alliances with parents and other adults, who usually represent contending values. The transitory solutions of early teen years, neither tidy nor assuredly optimistic, are used to fashion bothersome and provocative endings. Heide's particular strength lies in her delineation of character.

—Selma K. Richardson

HENRY, Marguerite

Nationality: American. **Born:** Marguerite Breithaupt, Milwaukee, Wisconsin, 13 April 1902. **Education:** Riverside High School, Milwaukee; Milwaukee State Teachers College, two years. **Family:** Married to Sidney Crocker Henry. **Awards:** American Library Association Newbery medal, 1949; Western Heritage award, 1967; University of Minnesota Kerlan award, 1975. **Died:** 26 November 1997.

Publications for Children

Fiction

Auno and Tauno: A Story of Finland, illustrated by Gladys Blackwood. Chicago, Whitman, 1940.

Dilly Dally Sally, illustrated by Gladys Blackwood. Akron, Ohio, Saalfield, 1940.

Geraldine Belinda, illustrated by Gladys Blackwood. New York, Platt and Munk, 1942.

Their First Igloo on Baffin Island, with Barbara True, illustrated by Gladys Blackwood. Chicago, Whitman, 1943; London, Gifford, 1945.

A Boy and a Dog, illustrated by Diana Thorne and Ottilie Foy. Chicago, Wilcox and Follett, 1944.
Justin Morgan Had a Horse (stories), illustrated by Wesley Dennis. Chicago, Wilcox and Follett, 1945; revised edition, Chicago, Rand McNally, 1954.
The Little Fellow, illustrated by Diana Thorne. Philadelphia, Winston, 1945; revised edition, Chicago, Rand McNally, 1975.
Misty of Chincoteague, illustrated by Wesley Dennis. Chicago, Rand McNally, 1947; London, Collins, 1961.
Always Reddy, illustrated by Wesley Dennis. New York, McGraw Hill, 1947.
King of the Wind, illustrated by Wesley Dennis. Chicago, Rand McNally, 1948; London, Constable, 1957.
Little-or-Nothing from Nottingham, illustrated by Wesley Dennis. New York, McGraw Hill, 1949.
Sea Star: Orphan of Chincoteague, illustrated by Wesley Dennis. Chicago, Rand McNally, 1949; London, Collins, 1968.
Born to Trot, illustrated by Wesley Dennis. Chicago, Rand McNally, 1950; excerpts, as *One Man's Horse,* 1977.
Brighty of the Grand Canyon, illustrated by Wesley Dennis. Chicago, Rand McNally, 1953; London, Collins, 1970.
Cinnabar, The One O'Clock Fox, illustrated by Wesley Dennis. Chicago, Rand McNally, 1956.
Misty, The Wonder Pony, illustrated by Clare McKinley. Chicago, Rand McNally, 1956.
Black Gold, illustrated by Wesley Dennis. Chicago, Rand McNally, 1957.
Muley-Ears, Nobody's Dog, illustrated by Wesley Dennis. Chicago, Rand McNally, 1959.
Gaudenzia, Pride of the Palio, illustrated by Lynd Ward. Chicago, Rand McNally, 1960; London, Collins, 1971; as *The Wildest Horse Race in the World,* Rand McNally, 1976; as *Palio: The Wildest Horse Race in the World,* London, Fontana, 1976.
Five O'Clock Charlie, illustrated by Wesley Dennis. Chicago, Rand McNally, 1962; London, Collins, 1963.
Stormy, Misty's Foal, illustrated by Wesley Dennis. Chicago, Rand McNally, 1963; London, Collins, 1965.
White Stallion of Lipizza, illustrated by Wesley Dennis. Chicago, Rand McNally, 1964; London, Blackie, 1976.
Mustang, Wild Spirit of the West, illustrated by Robert Lougheed. Chicago, Rand McNally, 1966; London, Collins, 1968.
San Domingo, The Medicine Hat Stallion, illustrated by Robert Lougheed. Chicago, Rand McNally, 1972; London, Collins, 1975; as *Peter Lundy and the Medicine Hat Stallion,* Rand McNally, 1977.
Stories from Around the World. Chicago, Rand McNally, 1974.
Misty Treasury (omnibus). Chicago, Rand McNally, 1982.
Misty's Twilight, illustrated by Karen G. Pre. New York, Macmillan, 1992.
Marguerite Henry's Horseshoe Library: Stormy, Misty's Foal; Sea Star, Orphan of Chincoteague; Misty of Chincoteague. New York, Macmillan, 1992.
Brown Sunshine of Sawdust Valley, illustrated by Bonnie Shields. New York, Simon and Schuster, 1996.

Other

Alaska [Argentina, Brazil, Canada, Chile, Mexico, Panama, West Indies, Australia, The Bahamas, Bermuda, British Honduras, Dominican Republic, Hawaii, New Zealand, and *Virgin Islands] in Story and Pictures,* illustrated by Kurt Wiese. Chicago, Whitman, 16 vols., 1941-46.
Birds at Home, illustrated by Jacob Bates Abbott. Chicago, Donohue, 1942; revised edition, Northbrook, Illinois, Hubbard Press, 1972.
Robert Fulton, Boy Craftsman, illustrated by Lawrence Dresser. Indianapolis, Bobbs Merrill, 1945.
Benjamin West and His Cat Grimalkin, illustrated by Wesley Dennis. Indianapolis, Bobbs Merrill, 1947.
Album of Horses, illustrated by Wesley Dennis. Chicago, Rand McNally, 1951; shortened version, as *Portfolio of Horses,* 1952; as *Portfolio of Horse Paintings,* 1964.
Wagging Tails: An Album of Dogs, illustrated by Wesley Dennis. Chicago, Rand McNally, 1955; as *Album of Dogs,* 1970.
All about Horses, illustrated by Wesley Dennis. New York, Random House, 1962; London, W.H. Allen, 1963; revised edition, Chicago, Rand McNally, 1967.
Dear Readers and Riders. Chicago, Rand McNally, 1969.
A Pictorial Life of Misty, illustrated by Wesley Dennis. Chicago, Rand McNally, 1976.
Dear Marguerite Henry. Chicago, Rand McNally, 1978.
The Illustrated Marguerite Henry, illustrated by Wesley Dennis, Robert Lougheed, Lynd Ward, and Rich Rudich. Chicago, Rand McNally, 1980.
Our First Pony. Chicago, Rand McNally, 1984.
Marguerite Henry's Album of Horses: A Pop-up Book, illustrated by Ezra N. Tucker. New York, Aladdin, 1993.

*

Manuscript Collections: Kerlan Collection, University of Minnesota, Minneapolis.

* * *

Mention horse stories to any young reader of the genre and the name Marguerite Henry is sure to enter the conversation. These readers are usually so passionate in their love for horses that they place few demands upon the literary quality of a book so long as it is about their favorite animal. Yet even among these readers, Henry's works are recognized as above and apart from the usual fare of animal adventure stories.

The quality that separates her from most writers of animal stories is her historical perspective. Her works are best appreciated if they are thought of and judged as historical romance, whether it be a fictional biography like *Benjamin West and His Cat Grimalkin,* or a fictional exploration of the events which historically trace the emergence of a particular breed of horse, as in *Justin Morgan Had a Horse* or *King of the Wind.*

It is partly because children do not come to her books thinking of them as historical works that they are so especially appealing. Teachers, and far too many writers, often ignore the needs of children, forgetting that if they are to be attracted to the study of history their interests must be aroused and their sympathies enlisted; and also forgetting that children want action, drama, adventure, and heroes. All of these can be found by children in the historical animal romances of Henry.

The use of the word "romance" here should not be interpreted as meaning trite and improbable, but rather to identify the romantic tradition for young readers sired so brilliantly by Stevenson. Although Will James's *Smoky* was based on the first-hand experience of a cowboy while Henry's stories are the result of painstaking research, both writers are in the same tradition. As writers of horse stories they demonstrate, first of all, a thorough knowledge of the breed depicted. The animals are objectively reported, and yet 0they are portrayed in such a way that their "character" is known and felt by humans, both within and outside the stories. The human characters, too, since most of them are actual people, are neither one-dimensional nor stereotyped.

However, it is the magical appeal of history—the merging of fact with imagination with legend—that gives the Henry books their trademark. Her stories are either implicitly or explicitly marked with prologues and epilogues, so that the web of history, the connection of things distant in time, place, person, and circumstance, reaches the consciousness of the young reader. The distant past touches the more recent past of the story time, which in turn touches the present and reaches out to the future of the reader's time.

The last paragraph of the epilogue in *Brighty* is a characteristic ending of a Henry book: "Especially on moonlit nights a shaggy little form can be seen flirting along the ledges, a thin swirl of dust rising behind him. Some say it is nothing but moonbeams caught up in a cloud. But the older guides swear it is trail dust out of the past, kicked up by Brighty himself, the roving spirit of the Grand Canyon—forever wild, forever free."

—James E. Higgins

HEWARD, Constance

Nationality: British. **Born:** 1884. **Died:** 1968.

Publications for Children

Fiction

Ameliaranne and the Green Umbrella, illustrated by S.B. Pearse. London, Harrap, and Philadelphia, Jacobs, 1920.
Cheery Tales [and *More Cheery Tales*] *for Little People.* London, S.P.C.K., 2 vols., 1920; New York, Macmillan, 2 vols., 1921.
The Twins and Tabiffa, illustrated by S.B. Pearse. London, Harrap, and Philadelphia, Jacobs, 1923.
Sunshiny Stories. London, Sheldon Press, 1924.
Grandpa and the Tiger, illustrated by Lilian Govey. London, Harrap, and Philadelphia, Jacobs, 1924.
The Story Book, edited by Isa M. Jackson. London, Collins, 1924.
Chappie and the Others, illustrated by Savile Lumley. London, Warne, 1926.
A Handful of Happiness, illustrated by Patience Arnold. London, Sheldon Press, 1926.
Kitty's Tea Party. London, Sheldon Press, 1926.
Mr. Pickles and the Party, illustrated by Anne Anderson. London, Warne, 1926.
Fairy Circle series (*Fairy* [*Gnome, Laughter, Story, Nonsense, Magic*] *Circle*). London, Collins, 6 vols., 1927.
Faithful Teddy. London, Sheldon Press, 1927.
The Fortune Finders. Leeds, E.J. Arnold, 1928.
An Eventful Holiday. Leeds, E.J. Arnold, 1928.
Ameliaranne Keeps Shop, illustrated by S.B. Pearse. London, Harrap, and Philadelphia, McKay, 1928.
A Tale of Two Mysteries. Leeds, E.J. Arnold, 1928.
Ameliaranne, Cinema Star, illustrated by S.B. Pearse. London, Harrap, 1929.
Ameliaranne and the Monkey, illustrated by S.B. Pearse. Philadelphia, McKay, 1929.
Rolf's First Earnings and Other Stories, illustrated by G. Robinson. London, Sheldon Press, 1929.
Tommy's Little Grains of Sand and Other Stories. London, Sheldon Press, 1930.
Benjy Comes. London, Wells Gardner, 1931.
Grandpa Nog and the Nimblies, illustrated by Muriel Gill. London, Harrap, and Philadelphia, McKay, 1937.
Billety Bill and the Big Brown Bear, illustrated by Muriel Gill. London, Harrap, and Philadelphia, McKay, 1937.
Ameliaranne at the Farm, illustrated by S.B. Pearse. London, Harrap, and Philadelphia, McKay, 1937.
Ameliaranne Gives a Christmas Party, illustrated by S.B. Pearse. London, Harrap, and Philadelphia, McKay, 1938.
Ameliaranne Camps Out, illustrated by S.B. Pearse. London, Harrap, and Philadelphia, McKay, 1939.
Ameliaranne Keeps School, illustrated by S.B. Pearse. London, Harrap, and Philadelphia, McKay, 1940.
Ameliaranne Goes Touring, illustrated by S.B. Pearse. London, Harrap, and New York, McKay, 1941.
Chappie, illustrated by M.K. Mountain. London, Warne, 1945.
Dick in Command. Leeds, E.J. Arnold, 1950.
Bobby Budge from Nowhere. Leeds, E.J. Arnold, 1950.
Midnight, Our Pony, illustrated by C. Instrell. Leeds, E.J. Arnold, 1953.
Adventures [and *Further Adventures*] *of Christabel Jane and Chirpy,* illustrated by S.B. Pearse. London, Harrap, 2 vols., 1955.
Jonathan's Children, illustrated by Jane Paton. London, Harrap, 1963.
The House on the Edge of the Moor, illustrated by Edward Mortelmans. London, Harrap, 1968.

* * *

Constance Heward is best known for creating Ameliaranne, a helpful little girl related in spirit to Pollyanna, whose most striking features are her competence and her curl rags "which she wore from Friday night to Sunday morning."

Heward's career was a long one. The first picture book, *Ameliaranne and the Green Umbrella,* was published in 1920. It is also the simplest and best, introducing the heroine and her five little brothers and sisters, as well as their mother, Mrs. Stiggins, "who was poor and took in washing." Ameliaranne goes to the Squire's tea party while the rest of the family stay at home with a cold. Anxious that they should not miss out on all the good things, Ameliaranne hides her own tea cakes in her green umbrella, planning to smuggle them home. Miss Josephine, the Squire's strict sister, discovers the hoard; but all ends happily because the Squire soon realises Ameliaranne's unselfishness and he sends her home with cakes for everyone.

Although her last Ameliaranne book appeared in 1941, Heward continued to write for children until 1968, turning her hand to full-length adventure stories. These seem of less interest than her earlier books. Ameliaranne, in fact, took on a life apart from her creator. 12 additional Ameliaranne books were written by an assortment of authors. Continuity was preserved by using the same artist, S.B. Pearse, whose chubby, cheerful children, with their slightly vacant expressions, so brilliantly encapsulated the warm and cosy world of Ameliaranne.

In the hands of Eleanor Farjeon, Ameliaranne appears at her best—resourceful, engaging, and good natured, living in a safe and comfortable land next door to fantasy, where magic does not exactly exist, but where, all the same, the poor but pretty school mistress can have a beautiful new dress for the ball. At worst, the Ameliaranne imitators have merely copied the Heward style, emphasising what is static and priggish about the character. It is noticeable that Heward's own Ameliaranne becomes more wooden over the years. The spirited little girl who battles with Miss Josephine in *Green Umbrella* has become a collection of virtues by the final books.

Yet it is not difficult to see why she has always had readers. Heward was an extremely good storyteller, and she never allowed the action to flag. There is no bewildering uncertainty in her books; the world she creates is entirely under control and Ameliaranne is never at a loss. At best, this creates a sense of freshness and optimism. What is more, Ameliaranne's solutions to the various problems she encounters are simple, yet delightfully enterprising. She immediately recognises the thief who is pretending to be the shopkeeper's sailor son—because he does not roll from side to side as sailors do; and she hides the coins from the till for safety in a jar of pickled onions; the notes she wraps in her hair as curl papers.

Heward's books are easy to read. Her descriptions are well-worn but they are graphic, concrete, and so confidently used that they all contribute to the sense of friendly familiarity in her writing. Every child is apple-cheeked and no eye seems without a twinkle. The characters are stereotypes; but this makes them instantly recognisable. "Oh, no! I wouldn't take it upon myself to be so bold," cries Mrs. Stiggins, and she continues to say the same thing at intervals throughout 20 books. On the other hand, Heward was undoubtedly writing for the undemanding 1920s. By today's tastes she is rather slavish in her support of a society where the rich man kept to his castle and the poor man stayed at his gate. Ameliaranne does not let us forget that she is the daughter of a washerwoman. "To think we've been hobnobbing with the gentry!" she cries in *Ameliaranne Camps Out.* You must know your place—and there is no room for complexity of thought or character. In *Grandpa and the Tiger,* a very curious early story, a tiger, whose only crime is that he has escaped and wandered into the hero's garden, is summarily shot and made into a rug.

Ameliaranne can appear almost banal in her simplicity; but she conveys an implicit assurance, and somewhere there is a world of security and order, where no disaster is so complete that common sense will not eventually triumph, to be rewarded by high tea and pink-iced cakes with cherries on top.

—Alison Sage

HEWETT, Anita

Pseudonym: Anne Wellington. **Nationality:** British. **Born:** Wellington, Somerset, 23 May 1918. **Education:** University of Exeter, 1936-39, teaching diploma, National Froebel Foundation, 1939. **Military Service:** Women's Royal Air Force, 1940-45. **Family:** Married Richard Duke in 1966. **Career:** Primary school teacher, 1945-52; Principal, Shirley Hall School, Kingston Hill, Surrey, 1952-61; producer, Schools Broadcasting Department, BBC, London, 1962-70. **Died:** 13 March 1989.

PUBLICATIONS FOR CHILDREN

Fiction

Elephant Big and Elephant Little, and Other Stories, illustrated by Charlotte Hough. London, Lane, 1955; New York, A.S. Barnes, 1960.

The Little Yellow Jungle Frogs and Other Stories, illustrated by Charlotte Hough. London, Lane, 1956; New York, A.S. Barnes, 1960.

Honey Mouse and Other Stories, illustrated by Margery Gill. London, Lane, 1957.

Think, Mr. Platypus, illustrated by Anne Marie Jauss. New York, Sterling, 1958.

Koala Bear's Walkabout, illustrated by Anne Marie Jauss. New York, Sterling, 1959.

The Laughing Bird, illustrated by Anne Marie Jauss. New York, Sterling, 1959.

A Hat for Rhinoceros and Other Stories, illustrated by Margery Gill. London, Bodley Head, 1959; New York, A.S. Barnes, 1960.

Piccolo, illustrated by Dick Hart. London, Bodley Head, 1960; New York, A.S. Barnes, 1961.

The Tale of the Turnip, illustrated by Margery Gill. London, Bodley Head, and New York, McGraw Hill, 1961.

The Little White Hen, illustrated by William Stobbs. London, Bodley Head, 1962; New York, McGraw Hill, 1963.

Piccolo and Maria, illustrated by Dick Hart. London, Bodley Head, 1962.

The Elworthy Children, illustrated by Margery Gill. London, Bodley Head, 1963.

Dragon from the North, illustrated by Gioia Fiammenghi. London, McGraw Hill, 1965.

The Pebble Nest illustrated by Jennie Corbett. London, University of London Press, 1965.

The Bull Beneath the Walnut Tree and Other Stories, illustrated by Geraldine Spence. London, Bodley Head, 1966; New York, McGraw Hill, 1967.

Mrs. Mopple's Washing Line, illustrated by Robert Broomfield. London, Bodley Head, and New York, McGraw Hill, 1966.

Fire Engine Speedy, illustrated by Edward McLachlan. London, University of London Press, 1966.

Mr. Faksimily and the Tiger, illustrated by Robert Broomfield. London, Bodley Head, 1967; Chicago, Follett, 1969.

Animal Story Book, illustrated by Margery Gill and Charlotte Hough. London, Bodley Head, 1972.

Mr. Bingle's Apple Pie (as Anne Wellington), illustrated by Nita Sowter. London, Abelard Schuman, 1978.

Grandfather Gregory (as Anne Wellington), illustrated by Nita Sowter. London, Abelard Schuman, 1980.

Other (readers)

Clip the Crab's Adventure. Leeds, E.J. Arnold, 1950.

The Seven Proud Sisters and Other Stories, illustrated by M. Jarman. London, Ginn, 1952.

The Crocodile That Couldn't Swim, illustrated by C. Instrell. Leeds, E.J. Arnold, 1953.
Slink the Shadow. Leeds, E.J. Arnold, 1953.

* * *

Anita Hewett's background as a teacher is evident in her work. She wrote for the children she enjoyed teaching—the little ones, the eights and under. At one stage in her career she worked as a Schools Radio producer. Most of her stories are suitably short, to be read or told at one sitting. They almost always point a moral, unobtrusively and often humorously, but the educational content is there. They make ideal standbys for the classroom bookshelf.

The majority are animal fables in the Just-So tradition but lighter and tighter in texture. In the omnibus *Animal Story Book,* the stories are grouped geographically in four sections covering Africa, Australia, South America, and South-East Asia. They are informative as well as entertaining about wildlife. Most of them use the well-tried techniques of repetition and cumulative construction and, at times, these technical devices are in danger of becoming mechanical. But the style is always elegant and the pay-offs refreshingly unpredictable. In "The Leopard That Lost a Spot," for instance, Monkey teases Leopard by painting out one of his spots. When the rain washes it back, to the bewildered creature's relief, Monkey laughs and laughs till he falls out of his tree. "He did not fall on the soft leaves. Nor did he fall in the long grass. He fell where he deserved to fall—in the pot of yellow paint."

Hewett's picture books benefit from the contribution of distinguished artists. But the texts deserve the pictures. *Mr. Faksimily and the Tiger* is particularly successful—a charming, original tale about an intrepid photographer who goes into the jungle to snap Terrible Tiger. All he has for protection is his umbrella—but he uses it to good effect. Again, the end comes as a surprise and gives the story an unusual, satisfying twist.

Her two novels about Piccolo, an Italian urchin, and his donkey are different in kind. These are realistic stories—the first effortless, the second somewhat contrived. But both give an English child real insight into an unfamiliar lifestyle and, again, there is educational value in the way Piccolo matures through his experiences. *The Elworthy Children,* another realistic story, also stands out from the main body of her work. With affectionate humour, Hewett describes the small adventures of a typical middle-class family. Five-year-old Polly and her older sister are the main characters and there is no doubt by the end of the book that the author understood the workings of a small child's mind.

—Joy Whitby

HIGHTOWER, Florence

Nationality: American. **Born:** Boston, Massachusetts, 9 June 1916. **Education:** Vassar College, Poughkeepsie, New York, A.B. 1937. **Family:** Married James R. Hightower in 1940; four children. **Career:** Lived in China, 1940-41, 1946-47. **Died:** 6 March 1981.

Publications for Children

Fiction

Mrs. Wappinger's Secret, illustrated by Beth and Joe Krush. Boston, Houghton Mifflin, 1956; London, Lane, 1957.
The Ghost of Follonsbee's Folly, illustrated by Ati Forberg. Boston, Houghton Mifflin, 1958.
Dark Horse of Woodfield, illustrated by Joshua Tolford. Boston, Houghton Mifflin, 1962; London, Macdonald, 1964.
Fayerweather Forecast, illustrated by Joshua Tolford. Boston, Houghton Mifflin, 1967; London, Macdonald, 1968.
The Secret of the Crazy Quilt, illustrated by Beth and Joe Krush. Boston, Houghton Mifflin, 1972.
Dreamwold Castle. Boston, Houghton Mifflin, 1978.

*

Manuscript Collections: University of Wisconsin Library, Madison.

Florence Hightower commented:

(1978) I write novels in which I hope intelligent, reading children will find the same sustaining pleasure which intelligent, reading adults find in novels written for them. My novels deal with children in their relations with each other, their families, and their communities. My characters, like those in adult novels, are beset by problems and conflicts. Sometimes they can and do cope. Sometimes they can't or won't. Although I rely on a mechanical plot to bring my characters together in dramatic situations, I consider the unfolding of the plot of secondary importance to the unfolding of characters in their various relationships. The effectiveness of a novel, however, depends not on the intention of the author, but on the way he uses words. A story, well told, seems to grow and blossom as naturally and beautifully as a plant. A clumsily told story, though its intentions be of the best, never comes to life. It has been suggested to me by school teachers that I write stories using only words that are on lists which children of various ages are required in school to recognize. If I did this, my stories would be born dead. In writing each sentence, I use the best words I can think of and deploy them as skilfully as I know how. I always wish that my vocabulary were larger and my skill greater. Educators and other propagandists often expect writers for children to connive with them by sneaking doses of instruction, guidance, or uplift into their books. For a novelist, especially a children's novelist, to do this strikes me as stupid and degrading. He destroys the artistic integrity of his own work, lessens its impact, and perverts his true purpose in writing—which is to reveal insights into the human condition in such a stirring, appealing, and moving way that he fires the imagination of his reader and inspires him to sharpen his own insights, challenges him to increase his knowledge, and persuades him to enlarge his sympathies by reading more novels, that he may grow up into a cultivated, discerning, novel-reading adult.

* * *

Perhaps it is because much of her writing reflected the activities of her own children and of the Maine island where they spent their vacations that Florence Hightower's stories have such lively and believable characters and such convincing settings. In her first book, *Mrs. Wappinger's Secret,* the action centers on an eccentric old woman who enlists the help of a young neighbor to help her find some treasure she believes is buried on her property, but the appeal lies not only in the plot but also in the insight into the likeable if often exasperating characters, especially in the depiction of Charlie's summer-weary father.

All of the Hightower books abound in humor, and in *Dark Horse of Woodfield* the author incorporates this through her distinctive characters yet manages to give a convincing picture of the Depression Era. In this story, as in others, there is a smooth blending of elements, of main plot and minor plots. The old, once-splendid house, Woodfield, is the setting for a warm family story, a horse story, and a love story, all nicely merged, and told with credible suspense. In *The Ghost of Follonsbee's Folly,* another vigorous family story, much of the appeal lies in the compatible union of odd and everyday events. Again, in *Fayerweather Forecast* the ebullient Fayerweather clan tolerates affectionately each member's idiosyncracies—and even uses them to advantage, as in the episode in which mother is working for a new school and employs the talents of her histrionic young daughter, who obligingly quavers a pitiful tale about how dreadfully antiquated the old school is. And yet, for all its buoyant humor, the story explores a mysterious murder. *The Secret of the Crazy Quilt* is a fast-paced, intricate story of rum-runners of the Prohibition Era, but the wit and humor of her style balance the grimness of the events, which are told in retrospect by two of the characters; here Hightower again proved adroit in weaving plot threads into a seamless whole.

—Zena Sutherland

HIGHWATER, Jamake

Tribal name: Piitai Sahkomaapii [Eagle Son]. **Other Pseudonym:** J Marks. **Nationality:** American (Blackfeet Indian). **Career:** Worked with San Francisco Contemporary Theatre, 1955-67; editor, Fodor Travel Guides, New York, 1970-75; Lecturer, New York University School of Continuing Education, 1980-85; Assistant Professor, Columbia University School of the Arts, 1983-86, and Graduate School of Architecture, since 1984; Guest Professor, University of Texas Health Science Center, Houston, 1985. Contributing editor, *Stereo Review,* New York, 1972-79; classical music editor, *SoHo Weekly News,* New York, 1975-79; columnist or contributor, *Indian Trader,* Billings, Montana, 1977-80, *New York Arts Journal,* 1978-84, *Native Arts/West,* Santa Fe, 1980-81, *Lone Star Review,* Dallas, 1981-83, *Christian Science Monitor,* Boston, and *Commonweal.* Host, *Indian America* program, WNET-TV, New York, 1982. Founding President, American Indian Community House, New York, 1976-78. Consultant, 1975-80, and member of the Literature Panel, New York State Council on the Arts, from 1981; founding board member, Indian Arts Foundation, Albuquerque, from 1980. Member of the Executive Board, PEN American Center, 1983-85, and Children's Literature Board, PEN, 1985-88. Founding President, Native Land Foundation, from 1984; general director, Native Arts festival, from 1986. **Awards:** Women's International League for Peace and Freedom Jane Addams award, for non-fiction, 1979; Anisfield-Wolf award, 1980. D.F.A.: Minneapolis College of Art and Design, 1986. **Address:** Native Land Foundation, 1201 Larrabee Street, Suite 202, Los Angeles, California 90069, U.S.A.

Publications for Children

Fiction

Anpao: An American Indian Odyssey, illustrated by Fritz Scholder. Philadelphia, Lippincott, 1977.
The Sun, He Dies: The End of the Aztec World. New York, Lippincott, 1980.
Ghost Horse Cycle:
Legend Days. New York, Harper, 1984.
The Ceremony of Innocence. New York, Harper, 1985.
I Wear the Morning Star. New York, Harper, 1986.
Dark Legend. New York, Grove, 1994.
Eyes of Darkness. New York, Lothrop, 1985.
Rama, a Legend, illustrated by Kelli Glancey. New York, Holt, 1994.
A Myth of Our Own: Adventures in World Religions. New York, Holt, 1996.

Poetry

Moonsong Lullaby, photographs by Marcia Keegan. New York, Lothrop, 1981.

Other

Many Smokes. Many Moons: A Chronology of American Indian History Through Indian Art. Philadelphia, Lippincott, 1978.
Anpao (recording). Folkways, n.d.

Publications for Adults

Novel

Journey to the Sky. New York, Crowell, 1978.

Other

Rock and Other Four Letter Words: Music by the Electric Generation (as J Marks). New York, Bantam, 1968.
Mick Jagger: The Singer Not the Song (as J Marks). New York, Curtis, 1973.
Fodor's Indian America: A Cultural and Travel Guide. New York, McKay, 1975; London, Hodder and Stoughton, 1976.
Song from the Earth: American Indian Painting. Boston, New York Graphic Society, 1976.
Ritual of the Wind: North American Indian Ceremonies, Music and Dances. New York, Viking Press, 1977; revised edition, New York, Van der Marck, 1984.
Dance: Rituals of Experience. New York, A and W, 1978.
Masterpieces of American Indian Painting. Santa Fe, Bell Editions, 2 Vols., 1979-83.
The Sweet Grass Lives On: 50 Contemporary North American Indian Artists. New York, Crowell, 1980.
The Primal Mind: Vision and Reality in Indian America. New York, Harper, 1981.
Arts of the Indian Americas: Leaves from the Sacred Tree. New York, Harper, 1983.
Native Land: Sagas of the Indian Americas. Boston, Little Brown, 1986; *Native Land* (television series and narrator), 1984, 1986.

Shadow Show: An Autobiographical Insinuation. New York, Van der Marck, 1986.
Myth and Sexuality. New York, New American Library, 1990.
Kill Hole. Grove, 1992.
The Language of Vision: Twenty-two Meditations on Myth and Metaphor in the Arts. New York, Grove, 1994.
Songs for the Seasons (poems), illustrated by Sandra Speidel. New York, Lothrop, 1994.
The Mythology of Transgression: Homosexuality as Metaphor. New York, Oxford University Press, 1997.

Contributor, *The World of 1492: "The Americas."* Holt, 1992.

Editor, *Words in the Blood: Contemporary Indian Writers of North and South America.* New York, New American Library, 1984.

*

Manuscript Collections: Native Land Foundation, New York.

Jamake Highwater comments:

I am an author who is Indian (not an Indian author), and as such I have spent my life attempting to transliterate into languages other than my own (Blackfeet) the essences of my cultural precepts which are fundamentally different from the conceptualizations of the dominant society. Happily my work seems to have significance both for Native Americans and non-Indians alike—which makes me believe that I have succeeded in producing a series of metaphors which bridge that great distance between peoples—a distance which consists not of space but of culture. I am equally trained in the culture of my own Indian people (the Blood Band of the Blackfeet Nation) and of the Western world; and it is this duplexity which gives me a strong motivation—since I discover in Western arts a ritual essence not unlike the mentality which is Indian. I have therefore used art to produce histories alternative to the Western chronicles which are, finally, but one way of looking at the past and one way of evaluating the events of the present.

* * *

Jamake Highwater is the author of several books, fiction and non-fiction, on Native American culture. *Anpao,* his best-known juvenile work, is a Native American *Alice in Wonderland.* Like Alice, it fits no category but its own. In *Anpao* characters suddenly appear, divide, change shape, vanish, and reappear like the Cheshire Cat. *Anpao* can be a bewildering book for it too rejects the logical, sequential patterns underlying the western concept of history. Where Carroll follows the byways of anti-logic and disorder down the rabbithole into Wonderland, Highwater takes his hero Anpao across a pre-Columbian landscape of the mind.

Anpao begins with a hero cut off from his past, from his people, from his beloved, and in the symbolic figure of his twin brother Oapna, from himself. Anpao's love for Ko-ko-mik-e-is, his search for his father, the Sun, and all his adventures become quests to restore what has been lost. Anpao's journey encompasses all planes. He moves through space and time, above the earth and below. There is no distinction between the physical world and the realm of dreams. Internal and external are one. Whatever can be imagined becomes real. Like a Zen koan, *Anpao* strives to break up the definitions by means of which the Western mind attempts to impose itself on the natural world.

In *Legend Days* and *The Ceremony of Innocence* Highwater takes the primal figure of Anpao and makes him a woman. Amana descends from the realm of myth into history. Rescued from the owls by the foxes, she becomes Memory, incorporating within herself the old songs and stories, the mythic soul of the Native American peoples. She is male and female, mother and warrior, hunter and nurturer, witness to the physical and spiritual extinction of the Plains tribes in the 19th century. Amana's own family disintegrates under the pressures from outside: poverty, intermarriage, alcoholism, false ideals, rejection of the old ways. No one wants to hear the old songs; no one believes the old stories. Sitko, Amana's grandson, is the only hope for the future. Sitko will listen.

Sitko is Highwater. Both these books and those to come in this series can be considered efforts to define his personal history. In the figures of Jemima and Jaime, Highwater compassionately depicts how easily dreams go awry when people forget their roots. He also directs barbs at hypocritical Indians. Amana's being denied land on the Blackfoot reservation because there is no record of her on the tribal register is an ironic reflection of Highwater's own recent legal difficulties.

Many authors describe the details of the Native American's culture. Highwater is one of the few to open a window into his soul.

—Eric A. Kimmel

HILDICK, E(dmund) W(allace)

Nationality: British. **Born:** Bradford, Yorkshire, 29 December 1925. **Education:** Wheelwright Grammar School, Dewsbury, Yorkshire, 1937-41; City of Leeds Training College, Yorkshire, 1948-50, teachers certificate. **Military Service:** Royal Air Force, 1946-48. **Family:** Married Doris Clayton in 1950. **Career:** Junior assistant, Dewsbury Public Library, 1941-42; clerk, truck repair depot, Leeds, 1942-43; laboratory assistant, Admiralty Signals Establishment, Haslemere, Surrey, and Sowerby Bridge, Yorkshire, 1943-46; teacher, Dewsbury Secondary Modern School, 1950-54. Since 1954 self-employed writer. Visiting critic and associate editor, *Kenyon Review,* Kenyon College, Gambier, Ohio, 1966-67. **Awards:** Tom-Gallon Trust award, for short story, 1957; Mystery Writers of America Edgar Allan Poe award, 1979. **Address:** c/o Coutts and Company Ltd., 440 The Strand, London WC2R 0QS, England.

Publications for Children

Fiction

Jim Starling, illustrated by Roger Payne. London, Chatto and Windus, 1958.
Jim Starling and the Agency, illustrated by Roger Payne. London, Chatto and Windus, 1958.
Jim Starling and the Colonel, illustrated by Roger Payne. London, Heinemann, 1960; New York, Doubleday, 1968.
Jim Starling's Holiday, illustrated by Roger Payne. London, Heinemann, 1960.
The Boy at the Window, illustrated by Ionicus. London, Chatto and Windus, 1960.

Jim Starling Takes Over, illustrated by Roger Payne. London, Blond, 1963; revised edition, London, New English Library, 1971.
Jim Starling and the Spotted Dog, illustrated by Roger Payne. London, Blond, 1963.
Jim Starling Goes to Town, illustrated by Roger Payne. London, Blond, 1963.
Meet Lemon Kelly, illustrated by Margery Gill. London, Cape, 1963; as *Lemon Kelly,* New York, Doubleday, 1968.
Birdy Jones. London, Faber, 1963; Harrisburg, Pennsylvania, Stackpole, 1969.
Mapper Mundy's Treasure Hunt, illustrated by John Cooper. London, Blond, 1963.
Lemon Kelly Digs Deep, illustrated by Margery Gill. London, Cape, 1964.
Louie's Lot. London, Faber, 1965; New York, David White, 1968.
The Questers, illustrated by Richard Rose. Leicester, Brockhampton Press, 1966; New York, Hawthorn, 1970.
Calling Questers Four, illustrated by Richard Rose. Leicester, Brockhampton Press, 1967.
The Questers and the Whispering Spy, illustrated by Richard Rose. Leicester, Brockhampton Press, 1967.
Lucky Les: The Adventures of a Cat of Five Tales, illustrated by Peter Barrett. London, Blond, 1967; revised edition, Leicester, Brockhampton Press, 1974.
Lemon Kelly and the Home-Made Boy, illustrated by Iris Schweitzer. London, Dobson, 1968.
Louie's S.O.S., illustrated by Iris Schweitzer. London, Pan, 1968; New York, Doubleday, 1970.
Birdy and the Group, illustrated by Richard Rose. London, Pan, 1968; Harrisburg, Pennsylvania, Stackpole, 1969.
Here Comes Parren, illustrated by Michael Heath. London, Macmillan, 1968; New York, World, 1972.
Back with Parren, illustrated by Michael Heath. London, Macmillan, 1968.
Birdy Swings North, illustrated by Richard Rose. London, Pan, 1969; Harrisburg, Pennsylvania, Stackpole, 1971.
Manhattan Is Missing illustrated by Jan Palmer. New York, Doubleday, 1969; London, Stacey, 1972.
Top Boy at Twisters Creek, illustrated by Oscar Liebman. New York, David White, 1969.
Birdy in Amsterdam, illustrated by Richard Rose. London, Pan, 1970; Harrisburg, Pennsylvania, Stackpole, 1971.
Ten Thousand Golden Cockerels, illustrated by Richard Rose. London, Evans, 1970.
The Dragon That Lived under Manhattan, illustrated by Harold Berson. New York, Crown, 1970.
The Secret Winners, illustrated by Gustave Nebel. New York, Crown, 1970.
The Secret Spenders, illustrated by Gustave Nebel. New York, Crown, 1971.
The Prisoners of Gridling Gap: A Report, With Expert Comments from Doctor Ranulf Quitch, illustrated by Paul Sagsoorian. New York, Doubleday, 1971; London, Stacey, 1973.
My Kid Sister, illustrated by Iris Schweitzer. New York, World, 1971; Leicester, Brockhampton Press, 1973.
The Doughnut Dropout, illustrated by Kiyo Komoda. New York, Doubleday, 1972.
Kids Commune, illustrated by Oscar Liebman. New York, David White, 1973.
The Active-Enzyme Lemon-Freshened Junior High School Witch, illustrated by Iris Schweitzer. New York, Doubleday, 1973.
The Nose Knows, illustrated by Unada Gliewe. New York, Grosset and Dunlap, 1973; London, Hodder and Stoughton, 1974.
Birdy Jones and the New York Heads. New York, Doubleday, 1974.
Dolls in Danger, illustrated by Val Biro. London, Hodder and Stoughton, 1974; as *Deadline for McGurk,* New York, Macmillan, 1975.
Louie's Snowstorm, illustrated by Iris Schweitzer. New York, Doubleday, 1974; London, Deutsch, 1975.
The Menaced Midget, illustrated by Val Biro. Leicester, Brockhampton Press, 1975.
The Case of the Condemned Cat, illustrated by Val Biro. London, Hodder and Stoughton, and New York, Macmillan, 1975.
Time Explorers Inc., illustrated by Nancy Ohanian. New York, Doubleday, 1976.
A Cat Called Amnesia, illustrated by Val Biro. New York, David White, 1976; London, Deutsch, 1977.
The Case of the Nervous Newsboy, illustrated by Val Biro. London, Hodder and Stoughton, and New York, Macmillan, 1976.
The Great Rabbit Robbery, illustrated by Val Biro. London, Hodder and Stoughton, 1976; as *The Great Rabbit Rip-Off,* New York, Macmillan, 1977.
The Top-Flight Fully-Automated Junior High School Girl Detective, illustrated by Iris Schweitzer. New York, Doubleday, 1977; as *The Top-Flight Fully-Automated Girl Detective,* London, Deutsch, 1979.
The Case of the Invisible Dog, illustrated by Lisl Weil. New York, Macmillan, and London, Hodder and Stoughton, 1977.
Louie's Ransom. New York, Knopf, 1978; London, Deutsch, 1979.
The Case of the Secret Scribbler, illustrated by Lisl Weil. New York, Macmillan, and London, Hodder and Stoughton, 1978.
The Case of the Phantom Frog, illustrated by Lisl Weil. New York, Macmillan, and London, Hodder and Stoughton, 1979.
The Case of the Treetop Treasure, illustrated by Lisl Weil. New York, Macmillan, and London, Hodder and Stoughton, 1980.
The Case of the Snowbound Spy, illustrated by Lisl Weil. New York, Macmillan, 1980.
The Case of the Bashful Bank Robber, illustrated by Lisl Weil. New York, Macmillan, 1981.
The Case of the Four Flying Fingers, illustrated by Lisl Weil. New York, Macmillan, 1981.
McGurk Gets Good and Mad, illustrated by Lisl Weil. New York, Macmillan, 1982.
The Case of the Felon's Fiddle, illustrated by Lisl Weil. New York, Macmillan, 1982.
The Case of the Slingshot Sniper, illustrated by Lisl Weil. New York, Macmillan, 1983.
The Ghost Squad Breaks Through. New York, Dutton, 1984.
The Ghost Squad Flies Concorde. New York, Dutton, 1985.
The Ghost Squad and the Halloween Conspiracy. New York, Dutton, 1985.
The Case of the Vanishing Ventriloquist, illustrated by Kathy Parkinson. New York, Macmillan, 1985.
The Ghost Squad and the Ghoul of Grünberg. New York, Dutton, 1986.
The Case of the Muttering Mummy, illustrated by Blanche Sims. New York, Macmillan, 1986.
The Ghost Squad and the Prowling Hermits. New York, Dutton, 1987.
The Case of the Wandering Weathervanes, illustrated by Denise Brunkus. New York, Macmillan, 1988.
The Ghost Squad and the Menace of the Malevs. New York, Dutton, 1988.

The Memory Tap. London, Macmillan, 1989.
The Case of the Purloined Parrot. New York, Macmillan, 1990.
The Case of the Dragon in Distress. New York, Macmillan, 1991.
The Case of the Weeping Witch. New York, Macmillan, 1992.
My Famous Father. London, Macmillan, 1990.
The Case of the Desperate Drummer. New York, Macmillan, 1993.
The Case of the Fantastic Footprints. New York, Macmillan, 1994.
Hester Bidgood: Investigatrix of Evill Deedes. New York, Macmillan, 1994.
The Case of the Absent Author (editor). New York, Macmillan, 1995.
The Case of the Wiggling Wig. New York, Simon & Schuster, 1996.
The Purloined Corn Popper: A Felicity Snell Mystery. New York, Marshall Cavendish, 1997.
The Serial Sneak Thief: A Felicity Snell Mystery. New York, Marshall Cavendish, 1997.

Other

A Close Look at Newspapers [Magazines and Comics, Television and Sound Broadcasting, Advertising]. London, Faber, 4 vols., 1966-69.
Cokerheaton (storypack), illustrated by Roger Payne. London, Evans, 1971.
Rushbrook (storypack). London, Evans, 1971.

Publications for Adults as Wallace Hildick

Novels

Bed and Work. London, Faber, 1962.
A Town on the Never. London, Faber, 1963.
Lunch with Ashurbanipal. London, Faber, 1965.
Monte Carlo or Bust! (novelization of screenplay; as E.W. Hildick). London, Sphere, 1969; as *Those Daring Young Men in Their Jaunty Jalopies,* New York, Berkley, 1969.
Bracknell's Law. New York, Harper, 1975; London, Hamish Hamilton, 1976.
The Weirdown Experiment. New York, Harper, and London, Hamish Hamilton, 1976.
Vandals. London, Hamish Hamilton, 1977.
The Loop. London, Hamish Hamilton, 1977.

Other

Word for Word: A Study of Authors' Alterations, with Exercises. London, Faber, 1965; abridged edition, as *Word for Word: The Rewriting of Fiction,* New York, Norton, 1966.
Writing with Care: 200 Problems in the Use of English. London, Weidenfeld and Nicolson, and New York, David White, 1967.
Thirteen Types of Narrative. London, Macmillan, 1968; New York, Potter, 1970.
Children and Fiction: A Critical Study in Depth of the Artistic and Psychological Factors Involved in Writing Fiction for and about Children. London, Evans, 1970; New York, World, 1971; revised edition, Evans, 1974.
Storypacks: A New Concept in English Teaching (as E.W. Hildick). London, Evans, 1971.
Only the Best: Six Qualities of Excellence. New York, Potter, 1973.

*

E.W. Hildick comments:

In my fiction for children I have always been compelled to give an accurate reflection of the contemporary background as I know it. That is why the first half-dozen or so books are set in the industrial working-class North of England, where I was brought up and worked and taught until the mid-1950s. Then comes a batch (*Meet Lemon Kelly,* the Questers books, and others) influenced by 7 years spent in the New Town of Stevenage, near London. After that come the stories with American settings (New York City, as in *Manhattan Is Missing,* Ohio, and various Long Island and Connecticut suburbs). Such a strong emphasis on the contemporary always courts the danger of ephemerality—and to avoid this there must be some kind of preservative; some acid or salt. Fortunately, my adolescent bent as the Clown of the Class—so much the despair of my teachers at the time—seems to have stood me in good stead as a writer, with the humour, the slapstick, the occasional wit acting so effectively as a preservative that many of my early books are still in print. About my adult fiction in relation to the children's books, I've been interested to note, when compiling the list, that there are often overlapping themes and settings. Thus *Meet Lemon Kelly* was written around the same time as *A Town on the Never* (both New Town books); *Lemon Kelly Digs Deep* (a children's archeological quest) links with *Lunch with Ashurbanipal* (British Museum background); while *Bracknell's Law* and *Vandals* give rather sombre accounts of the vicissitudes of British families living in the U.S., in contrast to the lighter shades of my Anglo-U.S. children's books.

* * *

E.W. Hildick has firm views about children and fiction and his considerable output is aimed at putting his theory into practice. In order to broaden the social background of children's books he concentrates on working-class, or classless, characters and his pioneering has paved the way for others. His intentions sometimes dominate the story but generally he has created lively, humorous plots, a style which is deceptively fluent, although deliberately constructed for less able readers, and characterisation which is sound, if not always deep.

The books about Jim Starling and The Questers demonstrate a new approach to the school story in which school is shown as an integral part of the boys' lives, not a separate way of life as in many pre-war stories. The Cement Street Secondary Modern and its teachers will be familiar to many readers, and the boys he writes about are recognisably those he hopes will read the books. In *The Questers* he avoids the sentimentality inherent in the theme by the pace and ingenuity of the plots in which the boys attempt to involve their bed-ridden friend in their activities. Aimed similarly at nine-to-12-year-olds, the series about Lemon Kelly is action-packed with a minimum of narrative and shows the imagination and humour typical of his work. The exuberance of Hildick's writing is especially noticeable in the stories about Louie, a highly professional milkman with a trained band of schoolboy helpers who overcome every hazard including rival milk companies, snowstorms, and muggers to see that the milk gets through. The farcical situations are anchored in reality by the down-to-earth Louie, and the short, staccato sentences, particularly in *Louie's Lot,* stimulate an awareness of words, their meanings and shape. Two further groups of stories are those about Birdy Jones and McGurk, for slightly older and younger readers respectively. Keen observation of the contemporary world helps to make Birdy and his manager credible, but the concept is farfetched and more obviously contrived to appeal to the non-reading teenager. The McGurk books are an attempt to construct a conventional detective mystery in a simple style around a trivial incident such as whether the cat was guilty of catching and eating the bird.

Some of Hildick's more recent titles show the influence of the time he has spent in America. In particular, the Ghost Squad books have transatlantic settings, dialogue, and style. *The Ghost Squad Breaks Through* is an original idea: the first of a series of adventure stories centred around a gang of youngsters, four of whom are ghosts. They continue to communicate with their two living friends by means of a word processor, and Hildick creates the logic of the ghost world and its interplay with the living with great ingenuity. The plots are fast-moving and eventful and although there are flashes of humor there is also menace and real danger for the squad. Like much of his earlier output, the Ghost Squad books have no great literary quality but they are professionally crafted and well designed for the non-literary reader. It would be churlish not to be grateful for Hildick's many books which offer action, humour, some believable characters, and lively dialogue, and which are dedicated to the idea that reading is fun.

—Valerie Brinkley-Willsher

HILL, David

Nationality: New Zealander. **Born:** Napier, New Zealand, in 1942. **Education:** Napier Boys' High School; Victoria University, Wellington, M.A. 1964. **Family:** Married; two children. **Career:** High school teacher, Tanaki College, Takapuna Grammar School, and schools in England, 1965 to 1982; full-time writer since 1982. **Awards:** Northland Youth Theatre Award, 1986, for *Ours But To Do*; *Times Educational Supplement* Award, and Sheffield Children's Book Award Merit Prize, both 1995, and Silver Feather Award (Germany), all for *See Ya Simon*. **Address:** 21, Timandra Street, New Plymouth, New Zealand. **E-mail Address:** dhill@tpsun.taranki.ac.nz.

Publications for Children

The Games of Nanny Miro. Tauranga, Moana Press, 1990.
See Ya Simon. Wellington, Mallinson Rendel, 1992.
Kick Back. Auckland, Ashton Scholastic, 1995.
The Winning Touch. Auckland, Ashton Scholastic, 1995.
Take It Easy. Wellington, Mallinson Rendel, 1995.
Help Yourself. Auckland, Wendy Pye, 1995.
Old Bones. Auckland, Wendy Pye, 1995.
Hats Off! Auckland, Wendy Pye, 1995.
Seconds Best. Auckland, Ashton Scholastic, 1996.
Cold Comfort. Wellington, Mallinson Rendel, 1996.
Fat, Four-eyed and Useless. Auckland, Scholastic, 1997.
Treasure Deep. Wellington, Mallinson Rendel, 1997.
Good Move. Sydney, Addison Wesley Longman, 1997.
Ganging Up. Sydney, Addison Wesley Longman, 1997.
Give It Hoops. Auckland, Scholastic, 1998.
Boots 'n All. Auckland, Scholastic, 1998.
Comes Naturally. Wellington, Mallinson Rendel, 1998.

Publications for Young Adults

Plays

The Big Drip. Auckland, Longman Paul, 1983.
Down Broad Street. Auckland, Longman Paul, 1985.
Get in the Act. Auckland, Heinemann, 1985.
Ours But to Do. Auckland, Longman Paul, 1986.
Been There. Auckland, Longman Paul, 1990.
A Time to Laugh. Auckland, Longman Paul, 1990.
Branches. Auckland, Longman Paul, 1993.
A Day at a Time. Auckland, New House, 1994.
Takes Two. Auckland, Heinemann, 1996.
Be All Right. Auckland, New House, 1998.

Publications for Adults

The Seventies Connection. Dunedin, John McIndoe, 1980.
Moaville Magic. Auckland, Hodder & Stoughton, 1985.
Taranaki. Auckland, Hodder & Stoughton, 1987.
The Boy. Auckland, Benton Ross, 1988.
More from Moaville. Auckland, Hodder & Stoughton, 1988.
The Year in Moaville. Wellington, Inprint, 1991.

*

David Hill comments:

I have very little imagination. People never believe me when I say this but it's true. I can't invent worlds or stories or people. Everything I do starts from something that's happened to me or to someone I know. As I start to make notes about it, I usually find that other ideas start arriving. I believe the best way to get yourself started is to sit down with paper in front of you, and start writing on it. I'll do four or five drafts in longhand, then transfer it to the word-processor and edit, edit, edit on that. Most of my editing seems to involve cutting things out; it's amazing how much flab there is in early drafts.

I like writing about fears and embarrassments. I reckon that these are common ground which we all recognise and I believe that writing anything which gives you that "I know that" response is likely to be effective. I like writing for children and teenagers because they're such a truthful audience. They recognise padding and boring bits very quickly, and they keep you on your toes. I also find that writing for young readers challenges the author to keep *the story paramount.* Adults can be satisfied with significant themes, felicities of style, social sharpness and fashion, but children expect—gasp—a good plot! This is a real and recurring challenge.

* * *

David Hill's work is characterised by humour and compassion. He does not hesitate to tackle large problems, but they are seen within the total context of a community. Most of his novels are written for teenagers. They fall into the categories either of school stories, which include sport, or of survival in a hostile outdoor environment.

His first book for children, however, which attracted wide acclaim, did not fall neatly into either genre. *See Ya Simon* chronicles the friendship between two boys, Nathan and Simon. In most respects they are typical teenagers, but one important difference separates them: Simon has muscular dystrophy and is in a wheelchair. His cheerful acceptance of his condition and his sense of humour contrast with Nathan's increasing awareness that his friend's condition is deteriorating and that he will soon die. Hill never avoids the real philosophic problems of pain and death, but far from becoming maudlin the narrative is lightened by highly amusing incidents and is sustained by lively dialogue.

Hill's experiences as a secondary school teacher permeate his books. His depictions of both staff and students are balanced; these are real people enduring the daily round with a shrewd sense of humour and with enough common sense to know when to worry and when to accept the situation. In *Kick Back* Chris Atkinson is a keen practitioner of kick boxing. He is also very interested in Stacey Jones and is delighted when she joins the class. He is, however, puzzled by her reluctance to be touched. Only towards the end of the novel does it become evident that Stacey had been the victim of sexual abuse. Once again a "problem" situation is invested with good humour. Chris is an exceptionally well-balanced young man and his relationship with Stacey will help her to overcome the trauma she has suffered.

In a lighter vein, *Curtain Up* follows developments during rehearsals for a drama production at school. The central character, Nick, suffers from rollercoaster emotions as he first focuses his attentions on the prettiest girl in the cast then, undaunted by lack of success, switches to the most sympathetic. All the time he fails to recognize the real friendship of his stage "wife." It is an affectionate, funny novel in which the embarrassments, daydreams, and conflicting loyalties of the teenage male are astutely captured.

The picture given of school play productions is highly authentic as, step by step, a group of anmaesic wooden students is alternately cajoled and bullied into a convincing cast of actors. This state of affairs is brought about by the excellence of the drama teacher, aptly named Ms. Bright, and another excellent teacher of English, Mr. Richards, features in *Fat, Four-Fyed and Useless.* Here Ben Hambleton wears glasses, is overweight, hates sport, and feels useless. But his life improves considerably when Mr. Richards starts a lunchtime writers group. Through sharing their work the six members of the group gradually develop friendships as well as writing ability. The process also leads to understanding a mystery surrounding one of the group members, who had lost two brothers in a boating accident. The school milieu is totally authentic, there is very little unusual here, but Hill transforms the ordinary into the memorable as he deftly portrays Ben's progress from naiveté to a greater realization of human complexities.

The Winning Touch and *Seconds Best* both focus on sport, the former on a group of pupils who lack the necessary brawn to form a rugby team but do very well at touch-rugby. *Seconds Best* features cricket where once again a second rate team is encouraged by an enterprising teacher, who also has to contend with a very difficult former "street-kid".

Hill's survival stories are darker than his school-based novels. *Take It Easy* takes place against the background of remote and inhospitable terrain. Rob Kennedy is the only experienced tramper amongst an inexperienced group of teenagers exploring the New Zealand bush. But when the adult leader of the group dies from a heart attack Rob has to take charge. He knows the rules of tramping but his advice is ignored and he cannot prevent the group from plunging into life-threatening danger. The taut narrative is compelling reading but underlying the action is Rob's concern for his father, who has been withdrawn since the death of his wife. One of the happy outcomes of what narrowly misses becoming a tragedy is that his father is jolted into realising that Rob too, has been bereaved and needs attention.

In *Cold Comfort* another young man, Craig Dawson, is a reasonably experienced climber travelling by helicopter to join a mountaineering expedition headed by his uncle. But as a result of an argument between the arrogant young pilot and a female passenger the helicopter crashes on a mountain side. The inherent drama is intensified by the interplay of totally incompatible characters as they face cold, hunger, and whiteout conditions with inadequate equipment and no radio. Once again, as in *Take It Easy,* the experienced voice is not listened to and as a result the pilot dies.

The "survival" novels are bleak, lacking the humour that is so much a feature in the other books, but these characters are in life-and-death situations. They are also isolated, with no supportive network of family or school in such remote situations. In the school stories characters may have problems but they are not left to suffer alone.

Throughout all the books, however, there is an exploration of friendship, emerging in the survival stories, more established in novels set in school. In his latest book, *Treasure Deep,* for younger readers, a long-standing friendship between a white New Zealand boy and a young Maori is threatened when differences between race and background emerge after their discovery of valuable Maori artifacts.

Apart from his willingness to tackle very real problems with a lightness of touch Hill's outstanding quality is the excellence of his writing. He is a master of the crisp, lively sentence and achieves the rare distinction of portraying teenage speech convincingly but without recourse to swearing or to slang.

—Betty Gilderdale

HILL, Lorna

Nationality: British. **Born:** Lorna Leatham, Durham, 21 February 1902. **Education:** Durham High School for Girls; LeManoir, Lausanne; University of Durham, B.A. 1926. **Family:** Married V.R. Hill in 1928; one daughter. **Died:** 1991.

PUBLICATIONS FOR CHILDREN

Fiction

Marjorie & Co., illustrated by Gilbert Dunlop. London, Art and Educational, 1948.

Stolen Holiday, illustrated by Gilbert Dunlop. London, Art and Educational, 1948.

Border Peel, illustrated by Esmé Verity. London, Art and Educational, 1950.

A Dream of Sadler's Wells, illustrated by Eve Guthrie. London, Evans, 1950; New York, Holt, 1955.

Veronica at the Wells, illustrated by Eve Guthrie. London, Evans, 1951; as *Veronica at Sadler's Wells,* New York, Holt, 1955.

They Called Her Patience, illustrated by Gilbert Dunlop. London, Burke, 1951.
Masquerade at the Wells, illustrated by Eve Guthrie. London, Evans, 1952; as *Masquerade at the Ballet,* New York, Holt, 1957.
It Was All Through Patience, illustrated by Gilbert Dunlop. London, Burke, 1952.
No Castanets at the Wells, illustrated by Eve Guthrie. London, Evans, 1953; as *Castanets for Caroline,* New York, Holt, 1956.
Jane Leaves the Wells, illustrated by Eve Guthrie. London, Evans, 1953.
Castle in Northumbria, illustrated by Gilbert Dunlop. London, Burke, 1953.
Ella at the Wells, illustrated by Eve Guthrie. London, Evans, 1954.
Dancing Peel, illustrated by Esmé Verity. London, Nelson, 1954.
So Guy Came Too, illustrated by Joanna Curzon. London, Burke, 1954.
Return to the Wells, illustrated by Eve Guthrie. London, Evans, 1955.
Dancer's Luck, illustrated by Esmé Verity. London, Nelson, 1955.
The Five Shilling Holiday, illustrated by Joanna Curzon. London, Burke, 1955.
Rosanna Joins the Wells, illustrated by Eve Guthrie. London, Evans, 1956.
The Little Dancer, illustrated by Esmé Verity. London, Nelson, 1956; New York, Nelson, 1957.
Principal Role, illustrated by Esmé Verity. London, Evans, 1957.
Swan Feather, illustrated by Esmé Verity. London, Evans, 1958.
Dancer in the Wings, illustrated by Esmé Verity. London, Nelson, 1958.
Dress-Rehearsal, illustrated by Esmé Verity. London, Evans, 1959.
Back-Stage, illustrated by Esmé Verity. London, Evans, 1960.
Dancer in Danger, illustrated by Esmé Verity. London, Nelson, 1960.
The Vicarage Children, illustrated by Marcia Lane Foster. London, Evans, 1961.
Vicki in Venice, illustrated by Esmé Verity. London, Evans, 1962.
Dancer on Holiday, illustrated by Esmé Verity. London, Nelson, 1962.
No Medals for Guy, illustrated by Gilbert Dunlop. London, Nelson, 1962.
More About Mandy, illustrated by Ann Kent Robinson. London, Evans, 1963.
The Secret, illustrated by Esmé Verity. London, Evans, 1964.
The Vicarage Children in Skye, illustrated by Elizabeth Grant. London, Evans, 1966.

Other

La Sylphide: The Life of Marie Taglioni. London, Evans, 1967.

Publications for Adults

Novels

The Other Miss Perkin. London, Hale, 1978.
The Scent of Rosemary. London, Hale, 1978; New York, Pinnacle, 1980.

*

Lorna Hill comments:

My "pony" books, set in Northumberland where I lived for most of my life, were written for my daughter Vicki when she was small. Vicki became a dancer and trained at the Sadler's Wells Ballet School (now the Royal Ballet School), and this was how I obtained the background for my ballet books.

* * *

Lorna Hill's *A Dream of Sadler's Wells* set a pattern which she was to follow consistently through the 1950s and early 1960s. It is a wish-fulfilment story about Veronica Weston, a child dancer, recently orphaned, who is sent to live with some rich, snobbish relations in Northumberland. Here, besides riding and enjoying a romantic friendship with a boy musician, she secretly practices her dancing, until, in the end, she auditions for Sadler's Wells Ballet School and is accepted as a student. *A Dream of Sadler's Wells* was the first of a long series of interlocking "Wells" novels, following Veronica's entirely predictable progress through the ballet school to starring roles at Covent Garden and marriage with the young musician, while at the same time widening out to include the dancing careers of other talented orphans, or daughters of Northumbrian county families.

In the early books Hill attempts to show something of the genuinely hard life of a ballet student—"groans, sighs and panting breath filled the studio"—but reality soon drowns in syrupy romance. Hill may assert that "a ballet school is full of heartache," but the heartache is of a most novelettish kind. Her heroines struggle with malicious guardians who refuse them dancing lessons, or jealous rivals who plot against them, but never with the technical demands of their art. They are clearly born to be ballerinas, with their strong, slender feet and huge dark eyes; and they acquire their perfect "line" as much by instinct as from their lessons. The only conflict they experience is between their careers and marriage to some devoted suitor, but a satisfactory, fairy-tale ending is invariably reached.

These books' popularity came from the glamour they offered, a decorous glamour which suited the unsophisticated teenagers of the 1950s, who could overlook the stereotyped, class-ridden characterization and repetitive plots. Hill presents a day-dream world of famous, beautiful, aristocratic people—occasionally contrasted with the vulgar lower classes—who inhabit Scottish castles and Northumbrian stately homes, who hunt and go to balls, wear Dior models, dance at Royal Gala performances before the Queen, receive proposals from Ruritanian monarchs, and subside into happy-ever-after marriages while still emotionally, if not actually, teenagers.

Among all the candy-floss romance, one book, *The Vicarage Children,* stands out. This is a realistic, everyday chronicle of a clergy family without wealth or talent, who find plenty to enjoy in spite of the limitations of life in their small Northumberland village. With her feet on the ground for once, Hill depicted genuine family situations, and showed that she could draw ordinary characters with warmth and humour.

—Angela Bull

HOBAN, Russell (Conwell)

Nationality: American. **Born:** Lansdale, Pennsylvania, 4 February 1925. **Education:** Lansdale High School; Philadelphia Museum School of Industrial Art, 1941-43. **Military Service:** Served in the United States Army Infantry, 1943-45: Bronze Star. **Family:** Married 1) Lillian Aberman (i.e., the illustrator Lillian Hoban) in 1944 (divorced 1975), one son and three daughters; 2) Gundula Ahl in 1975, three sons. **Career:** Magazine and advertising agency artist and illustrator; story board artist, Fletcher Smith Film Studio, New York, 1951; television art director, Batten Barton Durstine and Osborn, 1951-56, and J. Walter Thompson, 1956, both in New York; freelance illustrator, 1956-65; advertising copywriter, Doyle Dane Bernbach, New York, 1965-67. Since 1967 full-time writer. **Awards:** Christopher award, 1972; Whitbread award, 1974; Ditmar award (Australia), 1982; John W. Campbell Memorial award, 1982. **Agent:** David Higham Associates Ltd., 5-8 Lower John Street, London W1R 4HA, England. **Address:** Fulham, London, England.

PUBLICATIONS FOR CHILDREN

Fiction

Bedtime for Frances, illustrated by Garth Williams. New York, Harper, 1960; London, Faber, 1963.
Herman the Loser, illustrated by Lillian Hoban. New York, Harper, 1961; Kingswood, Surrey, World's Work, 1972.
The Song in My Drum, illustrated by Lillian Hoban. New York, Harper, 1962.
London Men and English Men, illustrated by Lillian Hoban. New York, Harper, 1962.
Some Snow Said Hello, illustrated by Lillian Hoban. New York, Harper, 1963.
The Sorely Trying Day, illustrated by Lillian Hoban. New York, Harper, 1964; Kingswood, Surrey, World's Work, 1965.
A Baby Sister for Frances, illustrated by Lillian Hoban. New York, Harper, 1964; London, Faber, 1965.
Bread and Jam for Frances, illustrated by Lillian Hoban. New York, Harper, 1964; London, Faber, 1966.
Nothing to Do, illustrated by Lillian Hoban. New York, Harper, 1964.
Tom and the Two Handles, illustrated by Lillian Hoban. New York, Harper, 1965; Kingswood, Surrey, World's Work, 1969.
The Story of Hester Mouse Who Became a Writer, illustrated by Lillian Hoban. New York, Norton, 1965; Kingswood, Surrey, World's Work, 1969.
What Happened When Jack and Daisy Tried to Fool the Tooth Fairies. New York, Four Winds Press, 1965.
Henry and the Monstrous Din, illustrated by Lillian Hoban. New York, Harper, 1966; Kingswood, Surrey, World's Work, 1967.
The Little Brute Family, illustrated by Lillian Hoban. New York, Macmillan, 1966.
Save My Place, with Lillian Hoban, illustrated by Lillian Hoban. New York, Norton, 1967.
Charlie the Tramp, illustrated by Lillian Hoban. New York, Four Winds Press, 1967.
The Mouse and His Child, illustrated by Lillian Hoban. New York, Harper, 1967; London, Faber, 1969.
A Birthday for Frances, illustrated by Lillian Hoban. New York, Harper, 1968; London, Faber, 1970.
The Stone Doll of Sister Brute, illustrated by Lillian Hoban. New York, Macmillan, and London, Collier Macmillan, 1968.
Harvey's Hideout, illustrated by Lillian Hoban. New York, Parents' Magazine Press, 1969; London, Cape, 1973.
Best Friends for Frances, illustrated by Lillian Hoban. New York, Harper, 1969; London, Faber, 1971.
The Mole Family's Christmas, illustrated by Lillian Hoban. New York, Parents' Magazine Press, 1969; London, Cape, 1973.
Ugly Bird, illustrated by Lillian Hoban. New York, Macmillan, 1969.
A Bargain for Frances, illustrated by Lillian Hoban. New York, Harper, 1970; Kingswood, Surrey, World's Work, 1971.
Emmet Otter's Jug-Band Christmas, illustrated by Lillian Hoban. New York, Parents' Magazine Press, and Kingswood, Surrey, World's Work, 1971.
The Sea-Thing Child, illustrated by Brom Hoban. New York, Harper, and London, Gollancz, 1972.
Letitia Rabbit's String Song, illustrated by Mary Chalmers. New York, Coward McCann, 1973.
How Tom Beat Captain Najork and His Hired Sportsmen, illustrated by Quentin Blake. New York, Atheneum, and London, Cape, 1974.
Ten What? A Mystery Counting Book, illustrated by Sylvie Selig. London, Cape, 1974; New York, Scribner, 1975.
Dinner at Alberta's, illustrated by James Marshall. New York, Crowell, 1975; London, Cape, 1977.
Crocodile and Pierrot, with Sylvie Selig, illustrated by Selig. London, Cape, 1975; New York, Scribner, 1977.
A Near Thing for Captain Najork, illustrated by Quentin Blake. London, Cape, 1975; New York, Atheneum, 1976.
Arthur's New Power, illustrated by Byron Barton. New York, Crowell, 1978; London, Gollancz, 1980.
The Twenty-Elephant Restaurant, illustrated by Emily McCully. New York, Atheneum, 1978; London, Cape, 1980.
The Dancing Tigers, illustrated by David Gentleman. London, Cape, 1979.
La Corona and the Tin Frog, illustrated by Nicola Bayley. London, Cape, 1979.
Flat Cat, illustrated by Clive Scruton. London, Methuen, and New York, Philomel, 1980.
Ace Dragon Ltd., illustrated by Quentin Blake. London, Cape, 1980.
The Serpent Tower, illustrated by David Scott. London, Methuen, 1981.
The Great Fruit Gum Robbery, illustrated by Colin McNaughton. London, Methuen, 1981; as *The Great Gumdrop Robbery,* New York, Philomel, 1982.
They Came from Aargh!, illustrated by Colin McNaughton. London, Methuen, and New York, Philomel, 1981.
The Battle of Zormla, illustrated by Colin McNaughton. London, Methuen, and New York, Philomel, 1982.
The Flight of Bembel Rudzuk, illustrated by Colin McNaughton. London, Methuen, and New York, Philomel, 1982.
Ponders (*Jim Frog, Big John Turkle, Charlie Meadows, Lavinia Bat*), illustrated by Martin Baynton. London, Walker, and New York, Holt Rinehart, 4 vols., 1983-84.
The Rain Door, illustrated by Quentin Blake. London, Gollancz, 1986; New York, Crowell, 1987.

The Marzipan Pig. London, Cape, 1986; New York, Farrar Straus, 1987.
Monsters, illustrated by Quentin Blake. New York, Scholastic, 1989.
Jim Hedgehog and the Lonesome Tower, illustrated by Betsy Lewin. New York, Clarion, 1990.
Jim Hedgehog's Supernatural Christmas, illustrated by Betsy Lewin. New York, Clarion, 1992.
M.O.L.E.: Much Overworked Little Earthmover. London, Jonathan Cape, 1993.
The Court of the Winged Serpent, illustrated by Patrick Benson. London, Trafalgar Square, 1995.
The Trokeville Way. New York, Knopf, 1996; London, Random House, 1997.

Poetry

Goodnight, illustrated by Lillian Hoban. New York, Norton, 1966; Kingswood, Surrey, World's Work, 1969.
The Pedaling Man and Other Poems, illustrated by Lillian Hoban. New York, Norton, 1968; Kingswood, Surrey, World's Work, 1969.
Egg Thoughts and Other Frances Songs, illustrated by Lillian Hoban. New York, Harper, 1972; London, Faber, 1973.

Nonfiction

What Does It Do and How Does It Work? Power Shovel, Dump Truck, and Other Heavy Machines. New York, Harper, 1959.
The Atomic Submarine: A Practice Combat Patrol under the Sea. New York, Harper, 1960.

Publications for Adults

Novels

The Lion of Boaz-Jachin and Jachin-Boaz. London, Cape, and New York, Stein and Day, 1973.
Kleinzeit. London, Cape, and New York, Viking Press, 1974.
Turtle Diary. London, Cape, 1975; New York, Random House, 1976.
Riddley Walker. London, Cape, and New York, Summit, 1980.
Pilgermann. London, Cape, and New York, Summit, 1983.
The Medusa Frequency. London, Cape, and New York, Atlantic Monthly Press, 1987.
Fremder. London, Cape, 1996.

Plays

Come and Find Me (television play). 1980.
The Carrier Frequency, with Impact Theatre Co-operative (produced London, 1984).
Riddley Walker, adaptation of his own novel (produced Manchester, 1986).

*

Critical Studies: "Thoughts on a Shirtless Cyclist, Robin Hood, Johann Sebastian Bach, and One or Two Other Things," in *Children's Literature in Education,* no. 4, 1971, 5-23; "An Interview With Russell Hoban" by Edward Myers, in *Literary Review,* 1983, 5-16; "Always a Dance Going on in the Stone: An Interview With Russell Hoban," by Rhonda M. Bunbury, in *Children's Literature in Education,* Vol. 17, No. 3, 1986, 138-149; *Through the Narrow Gate: The Mythological Consciousness of Russell Hoban* by Christine Wilkie, Fairleigh, Fairleigh Dickinson University Press, 1989; "Wilde Pommegranates: The Ghost of a Room and the Soul of a Story," in *Children's Literature in Education* vol. 28, no. 1, 1997, 19-29.

* * *

The virtues of Russell Hoban's picture books surely owe something to his early years as a television art director, copywriter, and freelance illustrator. There are an elegance and wit about them, combined with the fairly unerring selection of apt illustrations (often by Lillian Hoban) which, one suspects, are the product of a talent and industry normally summed up by the word professionalism. And though these books, because of their repetitive sentence-structures and simplified vocabularies, are sometimes included in Reading Schemes, it is important to realise that many of them are more than that implies.

The best known is probably the series about Frances the Badger, who, with her father and mother, baby sister, and best friend Thelma, goes through the kinds of experiences that children between the ages of 4 and 7 enjoy reading about. The books are anthropomorphic, with the badgers wearing clothes, and talking and behaving like humans generally. But what is so captivating about them is the combination of witty observations and shrewd common sense. When Frances begins to feel that her mother is busier than usual because of the new baby, she decides to run away:

> "Well," said Frances, "things are not very good here anymore. No clothes to wear. No raisins for the oatmeal. I think maybe I'll run away."
> "Finish your breakfast," said Mother. "It is about time for the school bus."
> "What time will dinner be tonight?" said Frances.
> "Half past six," said Mother.
> "Then I shall have plenty of time to run away after dinner," said Frances, and she kissed her mother goodbye and went to school.

The pattern of these stories is reassuringly familiar and almost cosy at times, with the liberal middle-class badger parents exercising just the right degree of permissive control in dealing with Frances's problems, which are usually resolved happily. But occasionally the parents' patience wears thin, and Frances has to learn that some things have to be accepted for the way they are.

The combination of wit and elegance with something rather more formidable is also presented a shade less delicately in some of the other picture books, such as *The Stone Doll of Sister Brute,* for example. In *How Tom Beat Captain Najork and His Hired Sportsmen* (illustrated by Quentin Blake) Tom has a hilarious time outwitting his aunt Miss Fidget Wonkham-Strong and her efforts to subdue him. The very qualities of fooling around, which his aunt tries so hard to crush, prove just the thing to defeat Captain Najork at the games of Womble, Muck, and Sneedball, and so a deeply serious defence of natural joy is seen to underpin this whole delightful fantasy.

Similar use of fantasy, though of an increasingly sombre kind, dominates the longer stories which have begun to appear since *The Mouse and His Child* in the mid-1960s. Increasingly recognised as a modern children's classic, or a modern classic which uses the form of children's fiction, this picaresque story describes the adventures of a clockwork-toy mouse and his son after they have been rescued from a dustbin by a passing tramp. Their wanderings through a modern urban civilisation bring them close to disaster and failure many times. They meet a variety of toys and animals, including a prophetic Frog, an aristocratic toy Elephant and a philosophical Muskrat; they constantly need rewinding, and flounder for a time in a muddy lake. Above all, they are pursued by Manny Rat, a ruthless and ingenious predator, who can be viciously cruel, for example, to a broken down toy-donkey:

> "You're not well," said Manny Rat. "I can see that easily. What you need is a long rest." He picked up a heavy rock, lifted it high, and brought it down on the donkey's back, splitting him open like a walnut. "Put his works in the spare-parts can," said Manny Rat to Ralphie.

Increasingly, as this powerful, comic, and disturbing narrative develops, however, we become aware that the pilgrimage of the mouse and his child is centred upon three very human needs, the desire for a territory or home of their own, like the one they knew in the toyshop, their desire to become self-winding and independent, and finally their desire to know what is beyond "The Last Visible Dog" they see mentioned everywhere, and which comes to represent Infinity. Again the ending is deceptively ambiguous, for though the mouse and his child do find the apparent security of a renovated Dolls' House and are surrounded by their friends, they also learn that there is nothing "beyond the Last Visible Dog but us," and that no one is ever completely self-winding—"That's what friends are for." Even more ominously for some readers, however, is the fact that Manny Rat himself remains at large, if apparently reformed.

The violence and witty allusiveness found in *The Mouse and His Child,* including a theatre which parodies Beckett's work, for example, is not something which all children find palatable, and one suspects that, though its reputation will continue to grow, it will appeal to children of at least 12 and upwards. *The Sea-Thing Child* may be found even more oblique by young readers, for it has none of the narrative energy of *The Mouse and His Child,* dealing, as it does, with an animal washed up on the sea-shore and his conversations mainly with a fiddler-crab and an albatross. Even so, its themes, the need for absolute honesty with oneself and being true to one's own nature, in this case trying to make a bow for a violin if you are a fiddler-crab and going back to sea if you are a sea-bird, are absolutely central to Hoban's work. There is nothing "beyond the Last Visible Dog but us."

Equally the adult novels will probably prove too demanding for all but the most alert adolescent readers, though there are elements of wit and fantasy in them, especially *Kleinzeit* and *Turtle Diary,* which many will enjoy. Since the late 1970s, in fact, and the emergence of Hoban as a serious adult novelist, particularly with the publication of *Riddley Walker,* an amazing picture of the future relayed to us by an illiterate 12-year-old, it is tempting to suggest that Hoban has put most of his energy into his adult books. *Pilgermann,* ostensibly a historical novel set in the Middle East in the 11th century, and *The Medusa Frequency,* a contemporary novel about a writer of comic serials, engage with themes that will daunt all but the brightest teenager.

Among his children's books since 1975, *Arthur's New Power* and *Dinner at Alberta's* are very like a continuation of the Badger series, with stories about a crocodile family, while *The Twenty-Elephant Restaurant* is no more than a cheerful anecdote. *La Corona and the Tin Frog* and *The Marzipan Pig* contain some typically Hobanesque features, but, though a new vein of gentle domestic humour appears in *The Great Fruit Gum Robbery* and *They Came from Aargh!, A Near Thing for Captain Najork* and *The Rain Door* by contrast seem more laboured. *Ponders,* a set of linked stories about the creatures who live near a pond, including a bat, a frog, and a heron, evokes an amusing, gentle world, with a hint of melancholy that will fascinate some children, but may lack sufficient grip for others.

Jim Hedgehog adds a Gothic layer to the animal-suburbia tales of Frances and Albert, reminiscent of James Marshall's suburban fables of pigs, snakes, and tortoises. Jim is a heavy metal fan who listens to groups such as Giant Squid and Crashing Boars. Mr. Strange, a sly stoat, sells Jim a cassette called "Lonesome Tower," by Itsa Thing. Jim's mother teaches him to read and write music, explaining the treble clef lines and spaces as Eating Green Bananas Doesn't Fatten, and Fat Alligators Cautiously Eat Grapefruit. But Jim prefers his own mnemonics! He finds Itsa (a lonely tower-walking girl-thing) and her lost song. When Itsa plays for Jim's School Summer Festival "windows shattered for miles around." Pretty heavy! Jim lives in the latter days (or daze) of the twentieth century, leaving Frances's cosy world far behind.

The Trokeville Way, Hoban's first novel actually published for Young Adults is a fantasy world-slip full of word play. Thirteen-year-old Nick, knocked on the head by the school bully, finds himself entering the mysterious world of the jigsaw puzzle he is persuaded to buy from Moe Nagic, a street musician who may be a magician. The puzzle is a painting with a dark wood, a bridge, a damsel in distress, and the bully. Nick must travel through the landscape of the puzzle to reach Trokeville, and solve his own dreaming and rebuild his life, attempting to make sense of the strange events, the characters he meets, and the Carrolian twists of language, where "troke" is a dream tongue-slip for "stroke."

Hoban is a remarkable writer, and whatever he publishes is bound to be of interest, but perhaps only *The Dancing Tigers* comes near the quality of his earlier children's stories, an apparently modest picture book, but witty, powerful, and mythic, like an idiosyncratic mixture of Blake and Woody Allen.

—Dennis Butts

HOBERMAN, Mary Ann

Nationality: American. **Born:** Mary Ann Freedman, Stamford, Connecticut, 12 August 1930. **Education:** Smith College, A.B (magna cum laude) 1951; Yale University, M.A. 1985. **Family** Married Norman Hoberman, 1951; two daughters, two sons. **Ca-reer:** Writer, poet, speaker, consultant, and artist-in-the-schools from 1955; founder and member of The Pocket People (children' theater group), 1968-75; adjunct professor, Fairfield University Fairfield, Connecticut, 1980-83; program coordinator, C.G. Jun Center, New York City, 1981. **Awards:** Book Week Poem awar from Children's Book, Council, 1976; American Book Award, 198 for *A House Is a House for Me*; *The Looking Book* and *A Hous*

Is a House for Me were both selections of the Junior Literary Guild. **Agent:** Gina Maccoby Literary Agency, P. O. Box 60, Chappaqua, New York 10514-0060, U.S.A. **Address:** 98 Hunting Ridge Road, Greenwich, Connecticut 06831, U.S.A.

Publications for Children

Poetry

All My Shoes Come in Two's, illustrated by Norman Hoberman. Boston, Little, Brown, 1957.
How Do I Go?, illustrated by Norman Hoberman. Boston, Little, Brown, 1958.
Hello and Good-by, illustrated by Norman Hoberman. Boston, Little, Brown, 1959.
What Jim Knew, illustrated by Norman Hoberman. Boston, Little, Brown, 1963.
Not Enough Beds for the Babies, illustrated by Helen Spyer. Boston, Little, Brown, 1965.
A Little Book of Little Beasts, illustrated by Peter Parnall. New York, Simon and Schuster, 1973.
The Looking Book, illustrated by Jerry Joyner. New York, Viking, 1973.
The Raucous Auk, illustrated by Joseph Low. New York, Viking, 1973.
Nuts to You and Nuts to Me, illustrated by Ronni Solbert. New York, Knopf, 1974.
I Like Old Clothes, illustrated by Jacqueline Chwast. New York, Knopf, 1976.
Bugs, illustrated by Victoria Chess. New York, Viking, 1976.
A House Is a House for Me, illustrated by Betty Fraser. New York, Viking, 1978.
Yellow Butter, Purple Jelly, Red Jam, Black Bread: Poems, illustrated by Chaya Burstein. New York, Viking, 1981.
The Cozy Book, illustrated by Tony Chen. New York, Viking, 1982; illustrated by Betty Fraser, San Diego, Browndeer Press, 1995.
Mr. and Mrs. Muddle, illustrated by Catharine O'Neill. New York, Little, Brown, 1988.
A Fine Fat Pig, and Other Animal Poems, illustrated by Malcah Zeldis. New York, HarperCollins, 1991.
Fathers, Mothers, Sisters, Brothers: A Collection of Family Poems, illustrated by Marilyn Hafner. Boston, Little, Brown, 1991.
One of Each, illustrated by Marjorie Priceman. Boston, Little, Brown, 1997.
The Seven Silly Eaters, illustrated by Marla Frazee. San Diego, Harcourt Brace, 1997.
The Llama Who Had No Pajama, illustrated by Betty Fraser. San Diego, Harcourt Brace, 1998.
Miss Mary Mack: A Hand-Clapping Rhyme, illustrated by Nadine Bernard Westcott. Boston, Little, Brown, 1998.
The Strange Tale of the Marvelous Mouse Man, illustrated by Laura Forman. San Diego, Harcourt Brace, 1999.

Other

Editor, *My Song is Beautiful: Poems and Pictures in Many Voices.* Boston, Little, Brown, 1994.

*

Biographies: Entry in *Something about the Author,* Vol. 72, Detroit, Gale, 1993, 112-114; *Something about the Author, Autobiography Series,* Vol. 18, Detroit, Gale, 1994, 113-131.

Critical Study: Entry in *Children's Literature Review,* Vol. 22, Detroit, Gale, 1991.

Mary Ann Hoberman comments:

I have always loved to write, to make up poems and songs and stories, and can hardly remember a time when I did not want to be a writer. When my children were born, I turned naturally to composing songs and poems and stories for *them*; and in this way my lifelong vocation as a writer for children originated. But while my four young children were the catalyst for this writing, they did not always furnish its content. Most of my poems, especially those written early in my career, draw upon my own well-remembered childhood for their subject matter. I imagine that most children's writers share this capacity to recall in vivid detail the sights and sounds and smells and feelings of their first years in the world. Indeed, this store of experience has been referred to as "a writer's capital," the hoard that *all* writers draw on to achieve their vision.

However, there is another motivation for my writing that is undoubtedly its primary inspiration; and that is language itself. Before I could read, before I could write, I loved words. Their sounds, their rhythms, their rhymes. And as I grew older, their shades of meaning, their spelling, their etymologies, the whole mysterious riddle of our marvelous language, began to enchant me and enchants me still. To configure some of these words into verses that lure young reader/listeners into a love of language is my abiding pleasure.

* * *

Mary Ann Hoberman is a poet who likes to write poetry, who can hardly wait to finish one poem so she can start on another. She especially likes to write for children, because she enjoys rhythm and rhyme as they do. For Hoberman, an odd fact or the sound of a name catches her ear, or rhythm catches her feet, and she can't get rid of it. So she writes her poem to be free of it; then she is able to turn her attention to another poem.

Her first four books were illustrated by her husband. *All My Shoes Comes in Twos* ruminates about various kinds of footwear; *How Do I Go?* is about various means of transportation. The poems are engaging and the simple illustrations make a satisfying presentation for the very young.

Hoberman's books are usually about ordinary topics—animals or people or daily events—but the topics are not approached in ordinary ways. In *A Little Book of Little Beasts* rhymes describe the habitats of frogs, snakes, mice, ants, turtles, and other small animals. The child learns something while being amused. In *The Raucous Auk: A Menagerie of Poems,* there are poems about lions, tigers, and bears. But there are also poems about the bandicoot (who is fond of fruit), the auk (the raucous auk must squawk to talk), the ocelot (a clever cat, who knows a lot of this and that). Hoberman offers poems in this volume about animal habitats (Alaska has the grizzly bear, but bats and rats live everywhere) and about relationships between animals (slow down for a minute or two, and consider the apes, for they are all related to you). The monochromatic drawings wriggle across the pages, adding more humor.

A House Is a House for You uses the noun "house" generically. There are houses for animals of all sorts: houses for rabbits are hutches, and a house for a mule is a shed. Whereas a castle is a house for a duchess, a bedbug lies himself down in a bed. There are houses for machines. A garage is that for a car, a hanger's a house for a plane, a dock is a house for a ship, and a terminal is a house for a train. And there are splendid houses for small children: tree houses, refrigerator cartons, umbrellas on the ground, dining room tables covered with a long white cloth, tents made from a sheet.

The author points to houses for food: barrels for pickles, bottles for jam, pots for potatoes, a sandwich for ham. A book is a house for a story, a rose is a house for a smell, and a head is a house for a secret that you will never tell. Hoberman's own imagination entices the reader/listener to use his imagination, to add more houses for more things. The illustrations in this book are good fun: busy and bright, with small surprises here and there.

Mr. and Mrs. Muddle takes up the art of compromise, which is an art of importance to child as well as adult. Mr. and Mrs. Muddle are a horse couple who disagree over purchasing a car for transportation. Mr. Muddle is of the opinion that cars are too loud and too fast. Mrs. Muddle likes the sound of cars and likes their speed. Since they cannot agree on a car, they settle on a canoe and paddle along together. Paddling together, they cooperate, and thus they come closer together. They haven't really solved the transportation issue, but maybe they will one day.

In *A Fine Fat Pig* the usual collaboration between author and illustrator was reversed: the paintings by Malcah Zeldis were done first, and the poems written to accompany the pictures. Pictures and poetry are well matched here; they are spirited and witty. The big smiling zebra is accompanied by the question: Is it black striped with white, or white striped with black, striped from the front, or striped from the back? A happy blue pig in his pen wallows in mud and muck. The accompanying poem comments: "What lucky fun/What funny luck." The folk art in this book is truly superb. Zeldis's folk paintings are in the permanent collections of many museums around the world, including the Musee d'Art Naif de l'Ile-de-France, the Museum of American Folk Art, and the Smithsonian Institution. The paintings are bold in design, simple in detail, and glorious in color. They might encourage a trip to a local museum to see other examples of folk art from this and from other countries.

Fathers, Mothers, Sisters, Brothers: A Collection of Family Poems offer poems about families, families of varying composition and families of varying parts of the world. The author starts off with the poem, "What is a family?" And she answers in this way: "Either a lot or a few is a family;/But whether there's ten or there's two in your family,/All of your family plus you is a family." This reassuring thought enables her to bring up families with only one child, families with adoptive children, families with half-sisters and half-brothers, families with absent fathers. In "My Father," a young boy misses his father, who does not live with him but has another family. The boy is happy when his father comes to visit, and misses him when he leaves again.

Part of the real fun of this book is the approach, not to family structure, but to family function. "Pick Up Your Room," is a poem about what many mothers say to many children. In this poem the daughter explains that the room is too heavy to pick up. "Relatives" is a poem about people who pinch your cheek and make a fuss, and say you've got the family's hazel eyes and will probably reach your father's size. "Eat It—It's Good for You," shows how ridiculous is the assertion that something which tastes so bad is so good for you. The last poem, "Our Family Comes from Round the World," shows in words and pictures people of different races and interests enjoying themselves in a green, park-like setting. The two-page spread is descriptive and not preachy, funny and not weighty.

Hoberman is fortunate in having illustrators of her works who pick up on her delight with life and who are as interested as she is in its quirky aspects. Her verses will cause giggles as they are read to the preschool child and by the primary grader. Young children will relate to Hoberman's rhythms and to the fine illustrations of her raucous auk, fat pig, and head that houses a secret. These works may even encourage the reader to try a rhyme, a picture of his own, or to read another book of poetry.

—Mary Lystad

HODGES, C(yril) Walter

Nationality: British. **Born:** Beckenham, Kent, 18 March 1909. **Education:** Dulwich College, London, 1922-25; Goldsmiths' College School of Art, London, 1925-28. **Military Service:** British Army, 1940-46. **Family:** Married Greta Becker in 1936; two sons. **Career:** Since 1929 stage and exhibition designer, mural painter, and freelance book, magazine, and advertisement illustrator. Designer of productions, Mermaid Theatre, 1951-52, 1964, and St. George's Theatre, 1976, London; Art director, Encyclopaedia Britannica Films, Chicago, 1959-61; Judith E. Wilson Lecturer, Cambridge University, 1974; Adjunct Professor of Theatre, Wayne State University, Detroit, 1980-83; visiting scholar, University of Maryland, College Park, 1983. Since 1979 design consultant and adviser for Globe Theatre Reconstruction Project; has designed exhibitions for Lloyds and the U.K. Provident Institution, and murals for the Chartered Insurance Institute, 1934, and the U.K. Provident Institution, 1957. Collections: Elizabethan theatre reconstructions and designs, Folger Shakespeare Library, Washington, D.C.; Shakespeare Centre & Birthplace Trust, Stratford-upon-Avon, England. **Awards:** Library Association Kate Greenaway Medal, for illustration, 1965. D. Litt.: University of Sussex, Brighton, 1979. **Address:** 36 Southover High Street, Lewes, East Sussex BN7 1HX, England.

Publications for Children (illustrated by the author)

Fiction

Columbus Sails. London, Bell, and New York, Coward McCann 1939.

The Flying House: A Story of High Adventure. London, Benn, 1947 as *Sky High: The Story of a House That Flew,* New York, Cow ard McCann, 1947.

The Namesake. London, Bell, and New York, Coward McCanr 1964.

The Marsh King. London, Bell, and New York, Coward McCanr 1967.

The Overland Launch. London, Bell, 1969; New York, Cowar McCann, 1970.

Playhouse Tales. London, Bell, and New York, Coward McCann, 1974.
Plain Lane Christmas. London, Dent, and New York, Coward McCann, 1978.

Other

Shakespeare and the Players. London, Bell, and New York, Coward McCann, 1948.
Shakespeare's Theatre. London, Oxford University Press, and New York, Coward McCann, 1964.
The Norman Conquest. London, Oxford University Press, and New York, Coward McCann, 1966.
Magna Carta. London, Oxford University Press, and New York, Coward McCann, 1966.
The Spanish Armada. London, Oxford University Press, 1967; New York, Coward McCann, 1968.
The English Civil War. London, Oxford University Press, 1972; as *The Puritan Revolution,* New York, Coward McCann, 1972.
The Emperor's Elephant. London, Oxford University Press, 1975.
The Battlement Garden: Britain from the Wars of the Roses to the Age of Shakespeare. London, Deutsch, 1979; New York, Clarion, 1980.

PUBLICATIONS FOR ADULTS

Other

The Globe Restored: A Study of the Elizabethan Theatre. London, Benn, 1953; revised edition, London, Oxford University Press, and New York, Coward McCann, 1968.
The Globe Playhouse 1599-1613: A Conjectural Drawing. London, Benn, and New York, Coward McCann, 1959.
Shakespeare's Second Globe: The Missing Monument. London, Oxford University Press, 1973.

Editor, with Samuel Schoenbaum and Leonard Leone, *The Third Globe: Symposium for the Reconstruction of the Globe Playhouse.* Detroit, Wayne State University Press, 1981.

*

Illustrator: *King Richard's Land,* 1933, and *Mr. Sheridan's Umbrella,* 1935, both by L.A.G. Strong; *Treasures of English Verse* edited by Herbert Strang, 1934; *The Happy Mariners* by Gerald W. Bullet, 1935; *Plays in Verse and Mime* by Rosalind Vallance, 1935; *Know Ye Not Agincourt* by Leslie Barringer, 1936; *The Squirrel's Granary* by William Beach Thomas, 1936; *My Garden by the Sea* by Robert A. Foster-Melliar, 1936; *The Schoolboy King* by Mark Dallow, 1937; *Trixie* (*Stories of the Circus*) by Bob Barton and G. Ernest Thomas, 1937; *New Tales from Shakespeare,* 1938, *More New Tales from Shakespeare,* 1939, *New Tales from Malory,* 1939, and *New Tales of Troy,* 1940, all by G.B. Harrison; *A Book of Famous Pirates* by A.M. Smyth, 1940; *The Watchers* by A.E.W. Mason, 1940; *Mutiny in the Caribbean* by G.W. Keeton, 1940; *They Wanted Adventure* by Kenneth Macfarlane, 1940; *Sister of the Angels,* 1940, *Smoky-House,* 1940, *The Little White Horse,* 1946, and *Make Believe,* 1949, all by Elizabeth Goudge; *The Ship Aground,* 1940, and *Painted Ports,* 1948, both by C. Fox Smith; *They Raced for Treasure,* 1946, *Flight to Adventure,* 1947, *There's No Escape,* 1950, *Mountain Rescue,* 1955, and *The Silver Sword,* 1956, all by Ian Serraillier; *Adventures of Button and Mac* by Ursula Hourihane, 1946; *The Story of the Treasure Seekers,* 1947, *The New Treasure Seekers,* 1947, and *The Would-Be-Goods,* 1947, all by E. Nesbit; *The Swiss Family Robinson* by Johann David and Johann Rudolf Wyss, 1949; *Cocos Gold* by Ralph Hammond, 1950; *The Chronicles of Robin Hood,* 1950, *The Queen Elizabeth Story,* 1951, *The Armourer's House,* 1951, *Brother Dusty-Feet,* 1952, *The Eagle of the Ninth,* 1954, and *The Shield Ring,* 1956, all by Rosemary Sutcliff; *Redcap Runs Away* by Rhoda Power, 1952; *The Crown of Violet,* 1952, and *Bows Against the Barons,* revised edition, 1966, both by Geoffrey Trease; *Sea-Dogs and the Pilgrim Fathers* edited by John Hampdon, 1953; *Queen Elizabeth and the Spanish Armada* by Frances Winwar, 1954; *A Swarm in May,* 1955, *Chorister's Cake,* 1956, and *Cathedral Wednesday,* 1960, all by William Mayne; *Will Shakespeare and the Globe Theatre* by Anne Terry White, 1955; *The King's Snare* by Helen Lobdell, 1955; *The Adventures of Huckleberry Finn* and *The Adventures of Tom Sawyer,* both by Mark Twain, 1955; *Cold Hazard* by Richard Armstrong, 1956; *Ransom for a Knight* by Barbara Leonie Picard, 1956; *The Three Musketeers* by Dumas, 1957; *Once-upon-a-Time Storybook* by Rose Dobbs, 1958; *The Flight and Adventures of Charles II* by Charles Norman, 1958; *The Kidnapping of Kensington* by Bruce Carter, 1958; *The Golden Stile* by Gwen Walker, 1958; *Castles and Kings* by Henry Treece, 1959; *Red Indian Folk and Fairy Tales* by Ruth Manning-Sanders, 1960; *The Siege and Fall of Troy* by Robert Graves, 1962; *Three Against London* by Rachel Varble, 1962; *Growing Up in the Thirteenth Century,* 1962, *The Story of the Crusades,* 1963, and *Growing Up with the Norman Conquest,* 1965, all by Alfred Duggan; *The Shoe Shop Bears,* 1963, and *Hannibal and the Bears,* 1965, both by Margaret J. Baker; *The Lion in the Gateway* by Mary Renault, 1964; *The Richleighs of Tantamount* by Barbara Willard, 1966; *The Complete Pelican Shakespeare* edited by Alfred Harbage, 1969; *The Nine Questions* by Edward Fenton, 1969; *The Rime of the Ancient Mariner* by Samuel Taylor Coleridge, 1971; *The Pied Piper of Hamelin* by Robert Browning, 1971; *The Sea-Beggar's Son* by F.N. Monjo, 1974; *Here Come the Clowns* by Lowell Swortzell, 1978; *The New Cambridge Shakespeare,* 29 vols., 1984—; *The Boar's Head Playhouse,* 1986, and *Shakespeare's Playhouses,* 1987, both by Herbert Berry.

C. Walter Hodges comments:

It is a truth more or less universally acknowledged by those concerned with literature for children, that children ought not to be written down to. But is the opposite also true, that they ought not to be *written up from?* Surely not. Those who are nowadays called Children's Writers (and their illustrators) are adults, engaged as adults in highly-skilled creative, imaginative work; and children in their own imaginations are as near adult as need be for an intelligent readership. Many of the books that most attracted me and my friends when I was young were not specifically written as "children's books"—as for example the works of Stevenson or Kipling; therefore today, when I write for children, I do not go out of my way to make my books only suitable for them at their younger age. I like to make them also suitable for me at mine. Besides, I am quite sure that children of any age ought not to be given children's books that are not suitable for adults to read.

*   *   *

C. Walter Hodges's particular talent is for the making of novels out of historical events, always those which have a momentum and a grandeur of their own. He is a quiet author, using no tricks of technique, and obtruding his own personality scarcely at all. This method gives an extraordinary verisimilitude to his stories; the author's cunning and skill become invisible, and one is apparently reading "what really happened."

In *Columbus Sails,* Hodges's first full-length book, the story is told from three different viewpoints; that of a monk who knows about the difficulties that Columbus surmounted to get his expedition financed, that of a sailor who can relate the events of the voyage, and that of an Indian in Spain, who knows how it all ended. The diffusion of the narrative voice, and the fact that each narrator tells not really his own story—the narrators are barely characterised—but that of the voyage, establishes Hodges's predominant tone.

Alfred Daneleg, through whose eyes the early years of King Alfred are told in *The Namesake,* is a more rounded character, yet still functions largely as a clear-eyed narrator of the course of history. But the change from *Columbus Sails* is very great. In Alfred, Hodges found a subject that set his imagination alight. The battles and shifts of fortune of those grim times, the iron hearts and wolf's hunger of the Danes, and the brave, thoughtful, capable, and loving young man who rescued England have inspired the writer, and shine for the reader. A moral as well as a physical struggle was waged by Alfred; and that gives a depth and subtlety to the story. *The Namesake* is a fine historical novel and probably Hodges's best book.

The Marsh King, a sequel to *The Namesake,* completes the tale of Alfred's early wars. The opening page tells us that the story has been garnered from two eye-witnesses, but much more is in the book than these two could probably have known, and once again we are looking at very transparent narrators. In effect this is straight narration, lacking the central consciousness of Alfred Daneleg in *The Namesake.* This is a fast moving, adventurous story, a tale of battles and treachery, but a certain resonance is missing, and it is not quite the equal of the earlier book.

In *The Overland Launch* Hodges found a more modern subject. This is the true, though incredible, story of the determination of a lifeboat coxswain to get his boat in the sea and launched on a rescue mission, even though it meant hauling it up and over a hill with the most notorious ascent and descent in the West Country, in the teeth of a terrible storm. The successful achievement of this impossible task gives Hodges an epic and thrilling subject. He catches very well the temper of West Country men, and the burr of their voices. A memorable book.

Playhouse Tales is a set of short stories all about actors and playwrights of Shakespeare's time, on which Hodges is an expert. Entirely at home in this period, not now very fashionable for historical writers, Hodges is in a relaxed and humorous mood. We do not need his careful notes to tell us that many of the incidents are authentic; sunny, intricate and ornate, these tales feel right for the Elizabethan atmosphere.

Hodges is an admirable craftsman; his self-effacing manners as an author should not lead one to undervalue his skill.

—Jill Paton Walsh

HODGES, M(argaret) M(oore)

Nationality: American. **Born:** Sarah Margaret Moore in Indianapolis, Indiana, 26 July 1911. **Education:** Attended public schools in Indianapolis, Indiana; Tudor Hall, Indianapolis, Indiana, 1924-28; Vassar College, Poughkeepsie, New York, A.B. in English 1932 (with honors); Carnegie Institute of Technology, Pittsburgh, Pennsylvania (now Carnegie Mellon University), M.L.S. 1958. **Family:** Married Fletcher Hodges, Jr.; three sons. **Career:** Special assistant and children's librarian, Carnegie Library of Pittsburgh, Pittsburgh, Pennsylvania, 1953-64; story specialist in compensatory education department, Pittsburgh, Pennsylvania public schools, 1964-68; lecturer 19964-68, assistant professor, 1968-72, associate professor, 1972-75, professor, 1975-77, and professor emeritus, from 1977, University of Pittsburgh Graduate School of Library and Information Sciences, Pittsburgh. Storyteller for "Tell Me a Story", WQED-TV, Pittsburgh, 1965-76. **Awards:** Carnegie Staff Scholarship, 1956-58; Caldecott Honor Award, 1964, *New York Times* ten best picture books of the year award, 1964, and Silver Medal Bienal (Brazil), 1965, all for *The Wave*; *Lady Queen Anne* was selected as the best book for young adults by an Indiana author, 1970; outstanding juvenile book selection by the *New York Times,* 1971, for *The Making of Joshua Cobb*; John G. Bowman Memorial grant for research abroad, 1974; Outstanding Pennsylvania Children's Author Award, Pennsylvania Librarians Association, 1977; Daughter of Mark Twain Award, 1980; *New York Times* Best Illustrated Children's Book Award, 1984, Carolyn W. Field Award for best children's book by a Pennsylvania author, *Horn Book* Honor Book Award and Caldecott Award, all 1985, all for *St. George and the Dragon*; "Margaret Hodges Day" Citation, University of Pittsburgh School of Library and Information Science, 1985; Keystone State Reading Award, 1985; Margaret Hodges scholarship established, 1989; American Library Association Best Books for Young Adults citation, 1989, for *Making a Difference: The Story of an American Family*; Notable Children's Trade Book citation, National Council for Social Studies and Children's Book Council, 1989, for *The Arrow and the Lamp: The Story of Psyche*; Parents' Choice Honor for Story Books, and Children's Book Council Award, both 1990, both for *Buried Moon*; American Library Association Notable Books List, 1991, for *St. Jerome and the Lion*; Park Tudor Distinguished Alumna Award, 1992. **Address:** University of Pittsburgh, Room 600, Library and Information Science Building, Bellefield Ave., Pittsburgh, Pennsylvania 15260, U.S.A.

PUBLICATIONS FOR CHILDREN

Fiction

One Little Drum, Chicago, Follett, 1958.
What's for Lunch, Charlie?. New York, Dial, 1961.
A Club against Keats, illustrated by Rick Schreiter. New York Dial, 1962.
The Secret in the Woods illustrated by Judith Brown. New York Dial, 1963.
The Wave, illustrated by Blair Lent. Boston, Houghton, 1964.
The Hatching of Joshua Cobb. New York, Farrar, Straus, 1967.
Sing Out, Charley!, illustrated by Velma Ilsley. New York, Farrar and Straus, 1968.

The Making of Joshua Cobb. New York, Farrar, Straus, 1971.
The Gorgon's Head: A Myth from the Isles of Greece, illustrated by Charles Mikolaycak. Boston, Little, Brown, 1972.
The Fire Bringer: A Paiute Indian Legend, illustrated by Peter Parnall. Boston, Little, Brown, 1972.
Persephone and the Springtime: A Greek Myth, illustrated by Arvis Stewart. Boston, Little, Brown, 1973.
The Other World: Myths of the Celts, illustrated by Eros Keith. New York, Farrar, Straus, 1973.
The Freewheeling of Joshua Cobb. New York, Farrar, Straus, 1974.
Baldur and the Mistletoe: A Myth of the Vikings, illustrated by Gerry Hoover. Boston, Little, Brown, 1974.
The Little Humpbacked Horse: A Russian Tale, illustrated by Chris Conover. New York, Farrar, Straus, 1980.
The Avenger. New York, Scribner, 1982.
If You Had a Horse: Steeds of Myth and Legend, illustrated by D. Benjamin Van Steenburg. New York, Scribner, 1984; London, Hippo, 1987.
Saint George and the Dragon: A Golden Legend, illustrated by Trina Schart Hyman. Boston, Massachusetts, Little, Brown, 1984.
The Arrow and the Lamp: The Story of Psyche, illustrated by Donna Diamond. Boston, Little, Brown, 1989.
The Voice of the Great Bell, illustrated by Ed Young. Boston, Little, Brown, 1989.
Buried Moon, illustrated by Jamichail Henterly. Boston, Little, Brown, 1990.
The Kitchen Knight, illustrated by Trina Schart Hyman. New York, Holiday House, 1990.
Hauntings: Ghosts and Ghouls from around the World, illustrated by David Wenzel. Boston, Little, Brown, 1991.
St. Jerome and the Lion, illustrated by Barry Moser. New York, Orchard Books, 1991.
Brother Francis and the Friendly Beasts, illustrated by Ted Lewin. New York, Scribner, 1991.
The Golden Deer, illustrated by Daniel Sans Souci. New York, Charles Scribner's Sons, 1992.
Don Quixote and Sancho Panza, illustrated by Stephen Marchesi. New York, Scribner's, 1992.
Saint Patrick and the Peddler, illustrated by Paul Brett Johnson. New York, Orchard Books, 1993.
The Hero of Bremen, illustrated by Charles Mikolaycak. New York, Holiday House, 1993.
Of Swords and Sorcerers: The Adventures of King Arthur and His Knights, illustrated by David Frampton. New York, Scribner, 1993.
Hidden in Sand, illustrated by Paul Birling. New York, Scribner, 1994.
Gulliver in Lilliput, illustrated by Kim Bulcken Root. New York: Holiday House, 1995.
Comus, illustrated by Trina Schart Hyman. New York, Holiday House, 1996.
Molly Limbo, illustrated by Elizabeth Miles. New York, Atheneum, 1996.
The True Tale of Johnny Appleseed, illustrated by Kimberly Bulcken Root. New York, Holiday House, 1997.
Saint Christopher, illustrated by Richard Watson. Grand Rapids, Michigan, W.B. Erdman's, 1997.
Up the Chimney, illustrated by Amanda Harvey. New York, Holiday House, 1998.
Joan of Arc: The Lily Maid, illustrated by Robert Rayevsky. New York, Holiday House, 1999.
Moses, illustrated by Mike Wimmer. San Diego, Harcourt Brace, 1999.

Biography

Lady Queen Anne: A Biography of Queen Anne of England. New York, Farrar, Straus & Giroux, 1969.
Hopkins of the Mayflower: Portrait of a Dissenter. New York, Farrar, Straus, 1972.
Knight Prisoner: The Tale of Sir Thomas Malory and His King. New York, Farrar and Straus, 1989.
Making a Difference: The Story of an American Family. New York, Scribner, 1989.

Editor

The Young Traveler in Australia, by Kathleen Monypenny. New York, Dutton, 1954.
The Young Traveler in New Zealand, by H. M. Harrop. New York, Dutton, 1954.
The Young Traveler in the West Indies, by Lucille Iremonger. New York, Dutton, 1955.
The Young Traveler in Greece, by Geoffrey Trease. New York, Dutton, 1956.
Stories to Tell to Children, with others. Pittsburgh, Carnegie Library of Pittsburgh, 1960.
Tell It Again: Great Tales from around the World, illustrated by Joan Berg. New York, Dial, 1963.
Constellation: A Shakespeare Anthology. New York, Farrar, Straus, 1968.
Elva S. Smith's The History of Children's Literature: A Syllabus with Selected Bibliographies, with Susan Steinfirst. Chicago, American Library Association, 1980; London, Eurospan, 1980.

*

Critical Studies: *Children's Books and their Creators,* edited by Anita Silvey, Boston, Houghton Mifflin, 1995, 315-316; entry in *Something about the Author,* edited by Diane Telgen, Detroit, Gale Research, Inc., 1994, 88-94; entry in *Something about the Author Autobiography Series,* edited by Joyce Nakamura, Detroit, Gale Research, Inc., 1990, 183-201.

* * *

The life and career of Margaret Hodges is characterized by her affinity for storytelling and her belief in the importance of story in children's lives. In a speech given at the University of Pittsburgh in April, 1992, Hodges expressed her ardent conviction that children need to be exposed to the finest of their literary heritage. She pointed out that fine literature is a way to speak to children's hearts and quoted James Stephens from *Crock of Gold* that "the head does not hear anything until the heart has listened and what the heart hears today, the head will understand tomorrow." Hodges' opinion about the importance of story is most evident in her retellings of folklore.

Hodges' professional life began when she was asked to volunteer as a storyteller at the Carnegie Library of Pittsburgh. She adapted and told Arthurian legends to children in the library and thus began a remarkable career of telling and writing stories that would speak to the hearts of children. Hodges' work falls in three categories: realistic fiction, biography, and folklore. Of the three, Hodges is best known and has garnered the most awards for her retellings of folktales. The earliest of her retellings was an adaptation of a Japanese folktale, *The Wave,* originally collected by Lafcadio Hearn. This folktale is the dramatic account of an old man's wisdom and the sacrifice he makes to save his people. An editor's note observes that Hodges' retelling of this tale was honed by the response of many children who listened to her tell it. The voice of the storyteller is evident in this and many of Hodges' retellings. This book won the Caldecott Honor award in 1965.

One of the most renowned of Hodges' adaptations of folklore is *St. George and the Dragon.* This classic adventure tale is based upon Spenser's legend, *The Fairie Queen,* but Hodges' adaptation eschews the legend's subplots to focus upon the efforts of the Red Cross Knight to rid the Princess Una of the horrific dragon that has terrorized her people. Trina Schart Hyman's lavish illustrations earned this book a Caldecott award in 1985. Hyman and Hodges collaborated again in *The Kitchen Knight,* the story of Sir Gareth of Orkney, a nephew of King Arthur who poses as a stranger and asks to be given an adventure through which he may prove his valor and worthiness to be a knight in the king's service. In both of these retellings, Hodges recreates the age of chivalry where unblemished heroes pit their own goodness against the forces of evil. Both heroes follow the mythic pattern of the hero who leaves home, faces trials and returns, victorious, only to take up the challenge again. Both tales are a significant part of Anglo-Saxon literary heritage and in each, Hodges employs the cadence of the storyteller, creating vivid images that are enhanced by Hyman's illustrations.

In addition to these illustrated versions of classic English tales, Hodges has also compiled collections of folklore from the British Isles. *The Other World: Myths of the Celts* is a collection of powerful tales from Ireland, Scotland, and Wales that reveals the mysticism of the ancient Celts in classic tales of gods, fairies and heroic men and women. Again, the voice of the storyteller is clear in these stories. As is her custom, Hodges scrupulously identifies the sources of her tales, indicating the oldest and most significant sources she consulted for her retellings.

Hodges strives to bring stories of many lands to young readers. She carefully researches the tales she adapts or retells but her travels to other countries were occasionally the springboard for her stories. For example, travels to Greece inspired her retellings of *The Gorgon's Head* and the well known myth, *Persephone and the Springtime,* as well as the novel, *The Avenger,* which features the Olympic Games and the Battle of Marathon. Her research is evident in the Russian tale, *The Little Humpbacked Horse,* a story of foolish Ivan whose goodness and simplicity earns him the assistance of the humpbacked horse that no one else values. Together, Ivan and the horse overcome his brothers' jealousy and greed and meet and exceed all the tasks the Tsar sets before them. Hodges' retelling is lively, retaining the linguistic flavor of traditional folklore, incorporating such phrases as, "Morning brings more wisdom than the evening".

Hodges' inclination to provide a retelling that retains the flavor and language of the original is evident in most of her folktales. She alters the text only when she deems it necessary to make the story more accessible to the modern reader. The additions she makes are so subtle that they seem like a part of the original tale but they serve as polish for the literary gems she brings to her readers. For example, in *The Buried Moon,* Hodges relates an English tale of how the kindly moon is captured and buried in a black pool by the evil creatures who dwell in the dark corners of the bogs in the English countryside. The beautiful moon is found and released by the folk who live near the bog and depend on her light to protect them from the haunts of the night. Hodges' retelling is faithful to the original, using such terms as "squishy mools" and referring to the light from "will o' the wisps." However, she adds that since that long ago time, the moon shines more brightly over the bog than anywhere else as a sign of her gratitude to those good folk who rescued her when she was buried and left for dead. This graceful addition to an ancient tale provides a connection for the modern reader and gives the story the flavor of a pourquoi tale.

An exception to Hodges' assiduous adherence to original renditions is her story, *St. Patrick and the Peddler.* For this retelling, Hodges drew upon several variants of the folk tale in which a poor, humble villager receives a message in a dream that he must travel to a city to receive an important message, or a treasure. When he arrives at the distant city, he is scoffingly told by a city resident that such dreams are sheer nonsense since the resident himself had had a similar dream about treasure being buried under a poor man's hearth in his village. The villager then returns to his home and finds the treasure buried under his own hearth. In her version of the story, Hodges used a village in Ireland as the setting; the poor man is a peddler who gives away his wares when people suffering from the potato famine cannot pay him and St. Patrick himself is the message bearer in the dream.

Hodges' research and travel enhanced more than her retellings of folklore. They also served as the foundation for the biographies she has written. Although Hodges professed that as a student she had an aversion to history, she discovered, as a writer, that compelling stories existed in the lives of historically significant, but lesser known, figures from the past. She conducted painstakingly thorough research to create the biography of Queen Anne and was pleasantly surprised by how much she enjoyed the work. Critics applauded her efforts; *Lady Queen Anne: A Biography of Queen Anne of England* was named best book for Young Adults by an Indiana author. In *Lady Queen Anne,* as in subsequent biographical studies, readers find the hallmarks of strong biography. Hodges creates well rounded, flesh-and-blood characters who are convincing products of their era. Hodges also reveals the influence these individuals had on history. The settings created in these biographies impart a flavor of the period, describing clothing, housing and the manner of life. Her attention to detail is meticulous and inclusion of primary sources is noteworthy. However, the presentation of a compelling story and the presentation of information are often competing forces in biography and, at times, Hodges' scholarship takes the upper hand. Readers who are less motivated by the subject or who demand fast-paced action may lose interest in these books.

Hodges is not concerned solely with the stories of the past. She has also written several realistic fiction books. Much of her realistic fiction is based upon family experiences, her remembrance of her own childhood experiences and those of her sons and their friends. The plots of these stories revolve around daily life and explore such themes as gaining independence and insight into relationships with friends and acquaintances. *The Freewheeling of Joshua Cobb* relates the summer adventures and understanding that await a preteenage boy as he travels with a former camp counselor, a friend and an eccentric newcomer on a bicycle camping trip. Joshua Cobb is the subject of several of Hodges' realistic fiction books and through his adventures, the reader witnesses the coming of age of a preadolescent. These books are solidly written and relate stories which have significance for contemporary readers but are less likely to speak to children's hearts in quite the same way as the folklore for which the consummate storyteller, Margaret Hodges, is best known.

—Anne Drolett Creany

HOFF, Syd(ney)

Nationality: American. **Born:** New York City, 4 September 1912. **Education:** New York public schools; National Academy of Design. **Family:** Married Dora Berman in 1937; two daughters. **Career:** Daily cartoonist ("Laugh It Off"), King Features Syndicate, 1957-71. **Agent:** Scott Meredith Literary Agency, 845 Third Avenue, New York, New York 10022, U.S.A. **Address:** Lives in Miami Beach, Florida.

PUBLICATIONS FOR CHILDREN (ILLUSTRATED BY THE AUTHOR)

Fiction

Muscles and Brains. New York, Dial Press, 1940.
Eight Little Artists. New York, Abelard Schuman, 1954.
Patty's Pet. New York, Abelard Schuman, 1955.
Danny and the Dinosaur. New York, Harper, 1958; Kingswood, Surrey, World's Work, 1969.
Sammy, The Seal. New York, Harper, 1959; Kingswood, Surrey, World's Work, 1960.
Julius. New York, Harper, 1959; Kingswood, Surrey, World's Work, 1960.
Ogluk, The Eskimo. New York, Holt Rinehart, 1960.
Where's Prancer? New York, Harper, 1960.
Oliver. New York, Harper, 1960; Kingswood, Surrey, World's Work, 1961.
Who Will Be My Friends? New York, Harper, 1960; Kingswood, Surrey, World's Work, 1964.
Little Chief. New York, Harper, 1961; Kingswood, Surrey, World's Work, 1962.
Albert the Albatross. New York, Harper, 1961; Kingswood, Surrey, World's Work, 1962.
Chester. New York, Harper, 1961; Kingswood, Surrey, World's Work, 1969.
Stanley. New York, Harper, 1962; Kingswood, Surrey, World's Work, 1963.
Grizzwold. New York, Harper, 1963; Kingswood, Surrey, World's Work, 1964.
Lengthy. New York, Putnam, 1964; Kingswood, Surrey, World's Work, 1965.
Mrs. Switch. New York, Putnam, 1967.
Irving and Me. New York, Harper, 1967.
Wanda's Wand. Norwalk, Connecticut, Gibson, 1968.
The Witch, The Cat, and the Baseball Bat. New York, Grosset and Dunlap, 1968.
Slithers. New York, Putnam, 1968.
Baseball Mouse. New York, Putnam, 1969.
Jeffrey at Camp. New York, Putnam, 1969.
Mahatma. New York, Putnam, 1969.
Roberto and the Bull. New York, McGraw Hill, 1969; Kingswood, Surrey, World's Work, 1971.
Herschel the Hero. New York, Putnam, 1969; Kingswood, Surrey, World's Work, 1971.
The Horse in Harry's Room. New York, Harper, 1970; Kingswood, Surrey, World's Work, 1971.
The Litter Knight. New York, McGraw Hill, 1970.
Palace Bug. New York, Putnam, 1970.
Siegfried, Dog of the Alps. New York, Grosset and Dunlap, 1970.
Wilfred the Lion. New York, Putnam, 1970.
The Mule Who Struck It Rich. Boston, Little Brown, 1971.
Thunderhoof. New York, Harper, 1971; Kingswood, Surrey, World's Work, 1972.
When Will It Snow?, illustrated by Mary Chalmers. New York, Harper, 1971.
Ida the Bareback Rider. New York, Putnam, 1972.
My Aunt Rosie. New York, Harper, 1972.
Pedro and the Bananas. New York, Putnam, 1972.
A Walk Past Ellen's House. New York, McGraw Hill, 1973; Kingswood, Surrey, World's Work, 1980.
Amy's Dinosaur. New York, Windmill, 1974.
Kip Van Wrinkle. New York, Putnam, 1974.
Katy's Kitty. New York, Windmill, 1975.
Pete's Pup. New York, Windmill, 1975.
Barkley. New York, Harper, 1975; Kingswood, Surrey, World's Work, 1976.
The Littlest Leaguer. New York, Windmill, 1976.
Walpole. New York, Harper, 1977; Kingswood, Surrey, World's Work, 1978.
Henrietta Lays Some Eggs. Champaign, Illinois, Garrard, 1977.
Henrietta, The Early Bird. Champaign, Illinois, Garrard, 1978.
Henrietta, Circus Star. Champaign, Illinois, Garrard, 1978.
Henrietta Goes to the Fair. Champaign, Illinois, Garrard, 1979.
Slugger Sal's Slump. New York, Windmill, 1979.
Santa's Moose. New York, Harper, 1979.
Nutty Noodles. New York, Scholastic, 1979.
Scarface Al and His Uncle Sam. New York, Coward McCann, 1980.
Henrietta's Halloween. Champaign, Illinois, Garrard, 1980.
Merry Christmas, Henrietta. Champaign, Illinois, Garrard, 1980.
Henrietta's Fourth of July. Champaign, Illinois, Garrard, 1981.
Soft Skull Sam. New York, Harcourt Brace, 1981.
Happy Birthday, Henrietta! Champaign, Illinois, Garrard, 1983.
Barney's Horse. New York, Harper, 1987.
Mrs. Brice's Mice. New York, Harper, 1988.
Bernard on His Own. New York, Clarion, 1993.
Captain Cat. New York, HarperCollins, 1993.
Duncan, the Dancing Duck. New York, Clarion, 1994.
The Lighthouse Children. New York, HarperCollins, 1994.
Arturo's Baton. New York, Clarion Books, 1995.
Happy Birthday, Danny and the Dinosaur!. New York, HarperCollins, 1995.
Danny and the Dinosaur Go to Camp. New York, HarperCollins, 1996.

Plays

Giants and Other Plays for Kids (includes *Lion in the Zoo, Children on the Moon, The Family, Wild Flowers*). New York, Putnam, 1973.

Television Plays: *Tales of Hoff* series, 1947.

Other

Syd Hoff's Joke Book. New York, Putnam, 1972.
Jokes to Enjoy, Draw, and Tell. New York, Putnam, 1974; as *Sid Hoff Shows You How to Draw Cartoons,* New York, Scholastic, 1979.
Dinosaur Do's and Don't's. New York, Windmill, 1975.
Gentleman Jim and the Great John L. New York, Coward McCann, 1977; Kingswood, Surrey, World's Work, 1979.
Sid Hoff's Best Jokes Ever. New York, Putnam, 1978.
Boss Tweed and the Man Who Drew Him (on Thomas Nast). New York, Coward McCann, 1978.
Mighty Babe Ruth. New York, Scholastic, 1980.
How to Draw Dinosaurs. New York, Windmill, 1981.
The Man Who Loved Animals (on Henry Bergh). New York, Coward McCann, 1982.
The Young Cartoonist: The ABC's of Cartooning. New York, Farrar Straus, and Windlesham, Surrey, Springwood, 1983.
Syd Hoff's Animal Jokes. New York, Lippincott, 1985.
Drawing with Letters and Numbers. New York, Scholastic, 1993.

Publications for Adults

Other

Military Secrets. New York, Hillair, 1943.
Feeling No Pain: An Album of Cartoons. New York, Dial Press, 1944.
Mom, I'm Home! (cartoons). New York, Dutton, 1945.
Oops! Wrong Party (cartoons). New York, Dutton, 1951.
It's Fun Learning Cartooning. New York, Stravon, 1952.
Oops! Wrong Stateroom! (cartoons). New York, Washburn, 1953.
Out of Gas! (cartoons). New York, Washburn, 1954.
Okay—You Can Look Now! (cartoons). New York, Duell, 1955.
The Better Hoff (cartoons). New York, Holt Rinehart, 1961.
Upstream, Downstream, and Out of My Mind. Indianapolis, Bobbs Merrill, 1961.
Twixt the Cup and the Lipton. Indianapolis, Bobbs Merrill, 1962.
So This Is Matrimony (cartoons). New York, Pocket Books, 1962.
Hunting, Anyone? (cartoons). Indianapolis, Bobbs Merrill, 1963.
From Bed to Nurse; or, What a Way to Die (cartoons). New York, Dell, 1963.
Learning to Cartoon. New York, Stravon, 1966.
The Art of Cartooning. New York, Stravon, 1973.
Editorial and Political Cartooning: From Earliest Times to the Present.... New York, Stravon, 1976.

*

Manuscript Collections: Kerlan Collection, University of Minnesota, Minneapolis; University of California, Los Angeles; de Grummond Collection, University of Southern Mississippi, Hattiesburg; Syracuse University, New York; Library of Congress, Washington, D.C.

Illustrator: *Parm Me* by Alex Kober, 1945; *Hello Muddah, Hello Fadduh!,* 1964, and *I Can't Dance!,* 1964, both by Allan Sherman; *I Should Have Stayed in Bed!,* 1965, *The Homework Caper,* 1966, and *The Rooftop Mystery,* 1968, all by Joan M. Lexau; *A Chanukah Fable for Christmas* by Jerome Coopersmith, 1969; *Henri Goes to the Mardi Gras* by Mildred Wright, 1971; *Donald and the Fish That Walked* by Edward R. Ricciuti, 1974; *The Snake That Couldn't Slither* by Peggy Bradbury, 1976; *The Boy Who Could Find Anything,* 1978, and *Bigfoot Makes a Movie,* 1979, both by Joan Lowery Nixon; *Arthur Gets What He Spills* by Louise Armstrong, 1979; *Play Ball with Roger the Dodger* by Al Campanis, 1980; *Don't Be My Valentine* by Joan M. Lexau, 1985; *I Saw You in the Bathtub* edited by Alvin Schwartz, 1989.

* * *

At his best, Syd Hoff creates likable human and animal characters whose simple, often humorous exploits provide the beginning reader with an engaging stimulus to read the easily managed texts. The plots themselves are generally straightforward, dealing positively with concepts familiar to and easily grasped by early elementary audiences. Very often, an animal character will leave its normal environment to explore the larger world, returning home safely after a series of adventures (*Lengthy, Barkley, Slithers,* and *Danny and the Dinosaur,* for instance). During these escapades, humor is created by adult figures who respond to the animal as if it were human and usually in the way, and by children who welcome it as a delightful new playmate, offering acceptance when adults do not.

Another typical Hoff plot involves unlikely heroes in either human or animal form, such as Bernard in *Baseball Mouse,* who helps a human baseball team emerge victorious, and Harold in *The Littlest Leaguer,* who manages a home run after a whole season of bench-sitting. A closely related theme is that of people who are "different" but eventually come to be appreciated, such as Stanley, a caveman who prefers painting to hunting, and the good witch Mrs. Switch. Even when reworking these basic themes with different characters but barely altered plots, Hoff generally manages the telling with such bright good humor that children continue to respond with delighted enthusiasm.

However, from an adult perspective, some of Hoff's work is marred by lapses that are not easily overlooked. There are some characters in the beginning readers who are not particularly likable, and whose exploits are not especially funny. Jeffrey Spink, who spends virtually his entire session of summer camp either eating or sleeping, is one of these; Bernard (*Baseball Mouse*), who ultimately saves the day by cheating for his team, is another. These occasional problems become more obvious in the full-length *Irving and Me,* in which the main character treats his only friend with puzzling insensitivity, and continually badgers his parents to buy him a dog. Artie's own remorse for his behavior is intended to make it more palatable and even humorous, but the humor falls flat, largely because he is an unappealing character. In fact, the only character in the novel who is at all endearing is the reformed town bully; the others are too realistic to be caricatures, but drawn too broadly to be acceptable on a realistic level. The humor that usually works in the shorter tales, partly because it is never examined too deeply, wears much too thin in this longer work.

More serious flaws are Hoff's reinforcement of ethnic prejudices and sexual stereotypes in this novel, and in some of the shorter works as well. *Little Chief,* for instance, is blatantly stereotypical in its portrayal of the main character; sexual stereotypes abound in "The Family," one of the plays in *Giants and Other Plays for Kids.* The treatment of characters does not seem to be deliberately unkind; nevertheless, Hoff's attitudes seem rather antiquated and insensitive.

Hoff's more recent work does not indicate much positive development as a children's writer. In *Barney's Horse* he abandons his standard formula of animals and children to pair an animal and an adult, but neither character is particularly interesting, and even its basic plot is unconvincing. Despite the flaws that become apparent in a close examination of Hoff's work, however, the humor and simplicity which combine in his most deserving stories will probably keep works such as *Danny and the Dinosaur, Amy's Dinosaur,* and *The Horse in Harry's Room* among the perennial favorites of children just beginning to read.

—Christine Doyle Francis

HOFFMAN, Mary M(argaret)

Has also written as Mary Lassiter. **Nationality:** British. **Born:** Eastleigh, Hampshire, 20 April 1945. **Education:** Attended school in Dulwich; Cambridge University, M. A. English literature 1971; University College, London, post-graduate study in linguistics. **Family:** Married Stephen Barber, 1972; three daughters. **Career:** Lecturer, Open University, London, 1975-80; full-time writer (including journalist and book reviewer), from 1980. **Agent:** Rogers, Coleridge and White, 20 Powis Mews, London W11 1JN, England. **Address:** 28 Crouch Hall Road, London N8 8HJ, England. **E-mail Address:** marushka@worldash.deman.co.uk.

Publications for Children

Fiction

White Magic. London, Rex Collings, 1975.
With Chris Callery, *Buttercup Busker's Rainy Day.* London, Heinemann, 1982.
With Willis Hall, *The Return of the Antelope.* London, Heinemann, 1985.
Beware Princess! London, Heinemann, 1986.
The Second-hand Ghost. London MMB/Deutsch, 1986.
King of the Castle. London, Hamish Hamilton, 1986.
A Fine Picnic. London, Macdonald, 1986.
Animal Hide and Seek. London, Macdonald, 1986.
The Perfect Pet. London, Macdonald, 1986.
Clothes for Sale. London, Macdonald, 1986.
Nancy No-Size. London, Methuen, 1987.
Specially Sarah. London, Methuen, 1987.
My Grandma Has Black Hair. London, Methuen, 1988.
Dracula's Daughter. London, Heinemann, 1988.
All About Lucy. London, Methuen, 1989.
Min's First Jump. London, Hamish Hamilton, 1989.
Mermaid and Chips. London, Heinemann, 1989.
Dog Powder. London, Heinemann, 1989.
Catwalk. London, Methuen, 1989.
Just Jack. London, Methuen, 1990.
Leon's Lucky Lunchbreak. London, Dent, 1991.
The Babies' Hotel. London, Dent, 1991.
Amazing Grace. London, Frances Lincoln, 1991.
Max in the Jungle. London, Hamish Hamilton, 1991.
The Ghost Menagerie. London, Orchard Books, 1992.
The Four-Legged Ghosts. London, Orchard Books, 1993.
Henry's Baby. London, Dorling Kindersley, 1993.
Cyril MC. London, Viking, 1993.
Bump in the Night. London, Collins, 1993.
Grace and Family. London, Frances Lincoln, 1995; as *Boundless Grace,* New York, Dial, 1995.
Song of the Earth. London, Orion, 1995.
Trace in Space. London, Hodder, 1995.
A Vanishing Tail. London, Orchard Books, 1996.
Quantum Squeak. London, Orchard Books, 1996.
Special Powers. London, Hodder, 1997.
An Angel Just Like Me. London, Frances Lincoln, 1997.
Comet. London, Orchard Books, 1997.
Sun Moon and Stars. London, Orion, 1998.
A Twist in the Tail. London, Frances Lincoln, 1998.
Virtual Friend. Barrington Stoke, 1998.
Clever Katya. London, Barefoot Books. 1998.
Three Wise Women. London, Frances Lincoln, 1999.
Women of Camelot. London, Frances Lincoln, 2000.

Nonfiction

Tiger. London, Belitha/Windward, 1983.
Monkey. London, Belitha/Windward, 1983.
Elephant. London, Belitha/Windward, 1983.
Panda. London, Belitha/Windward, 1983.
Lion. London, Belitha/Methuen, 1985.
Zebra. London, Belitha/Methuen, 1985.
Hippo. London, Belitha/Methuen, 1985.
Gorilla. London, Belitha/Methuen, 1985.
Whales and Sharks. London, Brimax Books, 1986.
With Trevor Weston, *Dangerous Animals.* London, Brimax Books, 1986.
Wild Cat. London, Belitha/Methuen, 1986.
Giraffe. London, Belitha/Methuen, 1986.
Snake. London, Belitha/Methuen, 1986.
Bear. London, Belitha/Methuen, 1986.
Wild Dog. London, Belitha/Methuen, 1987.
Seal. London, Belitha/Methuen, 1987.
Antelope. London, Belitha/Methuen, 1987.
Bird of Prey. London, Belitha/Methuen, 1987.
Amazing Mammals Kit. London, Dorling Kindersley Educational, 1993.

Other

A First Bible Storybook. London, Dorling Kindersley, 1997.

Editor, *Ip, Dip, Sky Blue.* London, Collins, 1990.
Editor, *Stacks of Stories.* London, Hodder, 1997.

Publications for Adults

Reading, Writing and Relevance. London, Hodder & Stoughton, 1976.
As Mary Lassiter, *Our Names, Our Selves.* London, Heinemann, 1983.

*

Mary Hoffman comments:

You can find out more about me on two websites: www.okukbooks.com and www.name.co.uk. I have been writing for children for more than twenty-five years and have no plans to stop. I don't see myself ever retiring, because I have so many ideas for new books that I think it will take the rest of my life to get them all written.

One of the best things about writing for children is the letters you get. Only last week I had a letter from an Asian girl in Glasgow who liked *Special Pavers,* one from a child in a local secondary school, who had read a short story of mine "Children" (about dares that got out of hand) *26* times and two packets of letters, one from a school I had visited in Ilford and one from an elementary school in Wichita, Kansas, with whom I'd had a telephone conference call interview a few weeks before.

It takes time to answer all these but it does make me feel my work is worthwhile when I find out that something I have written has made a difference to people I've never met.

Re-telling myths, legends fairytales and fables now takes up about a third of my time. I am working on two collections this summer (1998) one of myths and legends for Dorling Kindersley and one of stories about brother and sisters for Barefoot Books.

One of the things that makes my working life so untidy as that I have books in every stage of their life from having the first idea to answering letters about books which may have been published years ago. So all the stages in between: drafting, talking to publishers and my agent, getting a contract, deciding on an illustrator, editing, working at rough drawings and storyboards, commenting on final artwork, reading or writing blurbs and press releases, checking sources, checking proofs, reading reviews, agreeing to subsidiary rights, talking to children in schools and libraries—all these thing happen on each book. I have now written around 70 books, not all published yet, and you can see that the actual *writing* bit takes up quite a small proportion of my time. It's only when a deadline is looming that I sit down and just write every day till it's done.

I have several ideas and potential books in mind all the time. As time goes by and I write more of them, others move up the queue and they get done eventually too. Meanwhile other ideas are suggested to me by publishers, so they have to be slotted in too. Also I want to try my hand at adult novels. Every night, before I fall asleep, I think about my stories and write a bit more of one of them in my head. Or I develop a character a bit more, get to know more about her or him.

That means that, when I start to write, I already know a lot about what I want the character and the story to be like. Then, of course, as I write, more ideas come along and flush the story out. That is one of the parts of my job which is the most fun, feeling the story come alive.

I often feel that stories have an independent existence, they are in some sense there already and I just have to find them. I don't know what they are like beforehand, but I recognise them as I start to write; it is like uncovering something. The sculptor Michelangelo talked about his work in the same way. He believed that the figures he made were inside the blocks of marble he worked on; his job was to release them from their stone prisons. That's how I feel too.

Releasing my stories into the world is what I most want to do and I am incredibly lucky that this is what I am allowed to do as my daily job. I get paid for making things up. What could possibly be better?

* * *

Mary Hoffman was steeped in books from an early age, writing her own plays, which her friends performed at primary school, and reading anything that came to hand. When she decided to become a full-time writer she channelled much of her energy into fighting the cause of children's books and libraries in newspaper articles and campaigns.

Her first book, *White Magic,* a novel about a boy and a girl living in Italy who find a unicorn and have to look after it, was published after being recommended to the publisher by Richard Adams (of *Watership Down* fame). Hoffman then wrote a number of non-fiction texts for a series of books about animals before breaking into junior fiction. Many of these shorter books have been published in series like Banana Books, Toppers, Superchamps, and Cartwheels, for beginner and early readers. For example, *Beware Princess!, Dracula's Daughter,* and *Mermaid and Chips* were published in Heinemann's Banana Books series; *King of the Castle, Max in the Jungle* and *Min's First Jump* were published in Hamish Hamilton's Cartwheels series; and *Dog Powder* in Heinemann's Superchamps series. All these books are well written, have interesting plots, tongue-in-cheek ideas, and believable, feisty characters. Although these series are never classified as "great literature" they have a vital place in encouraging children to practise their reading skills, and their importance should not be underestimated.

In similar vein, though longer, are her Magic Mouse stories in the Orchard Super Crunchies series for fluent readers. These stories feature animal ghosts, who are the perfect pets for children who are allergic to animals, or whose parents do not want them. Cedric the mouse, who conjures up ghosts of pets and can make himself and the children invisible, is an appealing character and the idea provides endless scope for amusing situations, as the three titles testify: *The Four-Legged Ghosts, A Vanishing Tail,* and *Quantum Squeak.*

Mary Hoffman also has a talent for writing picture books with strong storylines and real substance. It is no easy option to reduce an idea down to a minimal text. In *My Grandma Has Black Hair* she reflects contemporary society, challenging the stereotype of the old grey-haired grandmother, sitting knitting in her rocking chair. It is a good idea and provides an amusing story. Family relationships and peer pressure are well portrayed in the picture book *Henry's Baby.* Henry desperately wants to be one of the in-crowd, but cannot think of anything that is cool enough to make him popular. When he invites his friends to play he does not want his style cramped by a baby brother and organises for the baby to go to a friend's house. Fate intervenes and the baby has to stay, proving to be even more popular than skateboards and the latest music. The gang just can't wait to come to play with his baby brother again. It is a nice recognition of the pride that Henry really feels for his baby brother, but is too embarrassed to admi to his friends.

Although Mary Hoffman had written over 40 books when she wrote *Amazing Grace* in 1991, it was this picture book that catapulted her into the limelight. In this she hit on something that touched so many people—the stereotypes of sex and colour, and particularly the limitations that are placed on people because of them. Her heroine Grace is always acting out her favourite stories so naturally wants the star part in the school play of *Peter Pan.* As well as being a girl, Grace is black, both reasons why her classmates think she could not be Peter Pan. Grace auditions, gets th part, and plays it brilliantly, proving "You can be anything yo want, if you put your mind to it." It is neither sentimental n didactic, but sensitively and intelligently written, and incidentally beautifully illustrated by Caroline Binch. It literally took off, particularly in the United States, selling over a quarter of a million copies. In the sequel *Grace and Family,* Mary Hoffman follows the same characters back to their native country of the Gambia, and explores the difficult feelings that are aroused when families are kept apart by divorce. Grace's father was not in the first book and the sequel shows him living in Africa. Once again, Mary Hoffman is honest in her portrayal of this situation and the book is a touching and powerful portrait of a family who, though divided, feel deeply about each other.

An Angel Just Like Me is an equally thought-provoking story that takes a new look at the way society portrays Christmas. As a black family decorates a Christmas tree they discover their angel is broken. Tyler, the young boy, wonders why angels are always girls and always pink-skinned. He sets out to find a black angel, just like him. His friend Carl, whose holiday job is being Father Christmas in a store, has the answer and carves him a very special black boy angel. Like the Grace books, this story is not moralistic. None the less, it makes the point that questioning the status quo from time to time is no bad thing.

More recently Mary Hoffman has taken up the longer novel again with two books for readers of 10 and over. They champion the female protagonist, with spirited girl heroines who are in control of their own destiny. The first, *Trace in Space,* is a fairly straightforward detective adventure set in space, in which Trace is an interstellar police cadet who seems to get all the worst cases. Humour abounds in the plot and dialogue.

The protagonist of *Special Powers,* Emily Grey, is an ordinary sort of girl with a passion for fantasy novels. She spends a lot of her time in the library, alternating between falling in love with the librarian and creating her own fantasy world. When new girl Archie Powers turns up Emily's life immediately becomes more exciting. The Powers family is definitely alternative and absolutely fascinating to Emily. They are from another dimension and their special powers are put to great use when they get caught up in trying to save the local library from closure. Mary Hoffman manages to expertly intertwine fantasy and reality to create an exciting and credible story.

In addition to a wide range of picture books, fiction and nonfiction, Mary Hoffman has built a reputation as an accomplished reteller of traditional stories. She has sensitively rewritten collections of Bible stories, myths and legends, and animal stories from around the world. She has also recently edited a collection of short stories by top children's authors, *Stacks of Stories,* which have the importance of libraries as their common theme, carrying on very much as she started.

—Fiona Lafferty

HOGARTH, Grace (Weston)

Pseudonyms: Amelia Gay; Allen Weston. Has also written as Grace Allen. **Nationality:** American. **Born:** Grace Weston Allen, Newton, Massachusetts, 5 November 1905. **Education:** Newton High School, 1919-23; University of California, Berkeley, 1923-24; Vassar College, Poughkeepsie, New York, 1924-27, B.A. 1927; Massachusetts School of Art, 1927-28; Yale University School of Fine Arts, New Haven, Connecticut, 1928-29; Columbia University, New York, 1935-36. **Family:** Married 1) William David Hogarth in 1936 (died 1965), two children; 2) Philip L. Sayles in 1971 (divorced 1977). **Career:** Staff artist, then children's books editor, Oxford University Press, New York and London, 1929-38, Chatto and Windus, London, 1938-39, and Houghton Mifflin, Boston, 1940-43; British representative for Houghton Mifflin, 1943-47, and other publishers, 1947-56, London; children's book editor, 1956-63, managing director, 1963-66, and chairman and managing director, 1966-72, Constable, later Longman Young Books, London. Editor, Lifetime Library, 1968-70. Governor, North London and Camden Schools for Girls, 1963-71; member of the Executive Committee, Association of Governing Bodies of Girls' Public Day School Trust, 1969-71. **Died:** 1996.

PUBLICATIONS FOR CHILDREN

Fiction

Lucy's League (as Amelia Gay), illustrated by Nora S. Unwin. London, Hodder and Stoughton, 1950; as Grace Hogarth, New York, Harcourt Brace, 1951.

John's Journey (as Amelia Gay), illustrated by Nora S. Unwin. London, Hodder and Stoughton, 1952; as Grace Hogarth, New York, Harcourt Brace, 1952.

The Funny Guy, illustrated by Fritz Wegner. London, Hamish Hamilton, and New York, Harcourt Brace, 1955.

As a May Morning. New York, Harcourt Brace, and London, Hamish Hamilton, 1958.

A Sister for Helen, illustrated by Pat Marriott. London, Deutsch, 1976.

Other

Australia: The Island Continent, illustrated by Howard W. Willard. Boston, Houghton Mifflin, 1943.

PUBLICATIONS FOR ADULTS

Novels

This to Be Love (as Grace Allen). London, Cape, 1949.

The End of Summer. London, Cape, 1951.

Children of This World. London, Cape, 1953.

Murders for Sale (as Allen Weston, with Andre Norton). London, Hammond, 1954; as *Sneeze on Sunday,* New York, Tor, 1992.

Other

Editor, with Caroline Hogarth, *American Cooking for English Kitchens.* London, Hamish Hamilton, 1957.

Editor, with Lee Kingman and Harriet Quimby, *Illustrators of Children's Books 1967-1976.* Boston, Horn Book, 1978.

*

Manuscript Collection: Vassar College Library, Poughkeepsie, New York.

Illustrator: *A Bible ABC,* 1943.

Grace Hogarth comments:

For nearly all of my working life I was an editor of children's books rather than a writer of them. I think it is always a temptation for editors to write because they are so constantly exposed to writing, but I confess that I found publishing books for children far easier than writing them.

My first job, after university and two years of art school, was as Staff Artist in the Oxford University Press in New York just before the depression. I survived this by illustrating and editing some of the books on the children's list and by designing jackets, laying out ads, etc. Although I am not an artist of much ability, I found this experience and training of the greatest help to me when I became a publisher of books for children.

My most successful children's books were *The Funny Guy* and *As a May Morning,* and I wrote both of them when my own children were the appropriate ages for them. There is nothing like a young audience for honest criticism and assistance!

* * *

Grace Hogarth made a dual contribution to the field of children's books, both as an editor and an author. Her first job was as children's editor at the Oxford University Press in New York and then as children's editor for a number of publishing houses in Britain. In 1957 she started the children's list at Constable and discovered many distinguished authors and artists who are at the peak of their careers today. Although there have been talented editors in both Britain and the United States, Hogarth was unique in her experience in the field of children's books on both sides of the Atlantic. She was of immense value in introducing important children's writers from one country to another. There had long been a tendency to feel that children must not be subjected to books which are "too foreign," and Hogarth tried hard to change this attitude. In an article she wrote for the *Horn Book* in 1965 she says, "Editors on both sides of the Atlantic are apt to say 'American children would never understand this' or 'Whatever will English children make of these peculiar clothes?' What we tend to overlook is the obvious truth that children everywhere are keenly interested in, and ready to learn about, other children, and the odder the better."

Perhaps because she started her career as an art student her interest in book illustration has always been as keen as her insistence on quality in writing. She illustrated her own editions of *A Bible ABC* for the youngest readers.

The Funny Guy, perhaps the most popular of her children's books, takes place in America in 1900 and tells of the year when Helen Hamilton's mother goes into hospital and Helen acquires the nickname of "the funny guy" from her classmates at school. Through a subscription to *St. Nicholas* magazine Helen learns that writing is fun and can bring new friends. This book was followed by *As a May Morning,* a novel for older children which explored the pleasures and pains of leaving childhood for an alien adult world. Hogarth's writing is very much concerned with human relations and the importance of coming to terms with one another.

—Ann Bartholomew

HOLLAND, Isabelle

Pseudonym: Francesca Hunt. **Nationality:** American. **Born:** Basel, Switzerland, 16 June 1920. **Education:** Private schools in England; University of Liverpool, 1938-40; Tulane University, New Orleans, B.A. in English 1942. **Career:** Publicity director, Crown Publishers, New York, 1956-60, and Lippincott, publishers, Philadelphia, 1960-66; assistant to the publisher, *Harper's* magazine, New York, 1967-68; publicity director, Putnam's Sons, publishers, New York, 1968-69. **Awards:** Church and Synagogue Library Association Ott award, 1983 (twice). **Agent:** Elaine Markson Literary Agency, 44 Greenwich Avenue, New York, New York, 10011, U.S.A. **Address:** 49 E. 73rd Street, Apt. 8A, New York, New York 10021, U.S.A.

Publications for Children

Fiction

Amanda's Choice. Philadelphia, Lippincott, 1970.

The Man Without a Face. Philadelphia, Lippincott, 1972 (made into film, 1993).

The Mystery of Castle Renaldi (as Francesca Hunt). Middletown, Connecticut, Xerox, 1972.

Heads You Win, Tails I Lose. Philadelphia, Lippincott, 1973.

Journey for Three, illustrated by Charles Robinson. Middletown, Connecticut, Xerox, 1974; London, Macdonald and Jane's, 1978.

Of Love and Death and Other Journeys. Philadelphia, Lippincott, 1975; as *Ask No Questions,* London, Macdonald and Jane's, 1978.

Alan and the Animal Kingdom. Philadelphia, Lippincott, 1977; London, Macdonald and Jane's, 1979.

Hitchhike. Philadelphia, Lippincott, 1977.

Dinah and the Green Fat Kingdom. Philadelphia, Lippincott, 1978.

Now Is Not Too Late. New York, Lothrop, 1980.

Summer of My First Love. New York, Fawcett, 1981; London, Severn House, 1987.

A Horse Named Peaceable. New York, Lothrop, 1982.

Abbie's God Book, illustrated by James McLaughlin. Philadelphia, Westminster Press, 1982.

Perdita. Boston, Little Brown, 1983; London, Severn House, 1987.

God, Mrs. Muskrat, and Aunt Dot, illustrated by Beth and Joe Krush. Philadelphia, Westminster Press, 1983.

After the First Love. New York, Fawcett, 1983; London, Severn House, 1988.

The Empty House. New York, Lippincott, 1983; London, Severn House, 1985.

Kevin's Hat, illustrated by Leonard B. Lubin. New York, Lothrop, 1984.

Green Andrew Green, illustrated by Pat Steiner. Philadelphia, Westminster Press, 1984.

The Island. Boston, Little Brown, 1985; London, Severn House, 1986.

Jenny Kiss'd Me. New York, Fawcett, 1985; London, Severn House, 1986.

Henry and Grudge. New York, Walker, 1986.

Love and the Genetic Factor. New York, Fawcett, 1987.

The Christmas Cat, illustrated by Kathy Mitchell. New York, Golden, 1987.

Toby the Splendid. New York, Walker, 1987.
Thief. New York, Fawcett, 1989.
The Easter Donkey. New York, Golden, 1989.
The Journey Home. New York, Scholastic, 1990.
The Unfrightened Dark. Boston, Little Brown, 1990.
The House in the Woods. Boston, Little Brown, 1991.
Behind the Lines. New York, Scholastic, 1994.
The Promised Land. New York, Scholastic, 1996.

Publications for Adults

Novels

Cecily. Philadelphia, Lippincott, 1967; London, Severn House, 1985.
Kilgaren. New York, Weybright and Talley, 1974; London, Collins, 1975.
Trelawny. New York, Weybright and Talley, 1974; as *Trelawny's Fell,* London, Collins, 1976.
Moncrieff. New York, Weybright and Talley, 1975; as *The Standish Place,* London, Collins, 1976.
Darcourt. New York, Weybright and Talley, 1976; London, Collins, 1977.
Grenelle. New York, Rawson, 1976; London, Collins, 1978.
The deMaury Papers. New York, Rawson, 1977; London, Collins, 1978.
Tower Abbey. New York, Rawson, 1978; London, Collins, 1979.
The Marchington Inheritance. New York, Rawson, 1979; London, Collins, 1980.
Counterpoint. New York, Rawson, 1980; London, Collins, 1981.
The Lost Madonna. New York, Rawson, 1981; London, Collins, 1982.
A Death at St. Anselm's. New York, Doubleday, 1984; London, Severn House, 1985.
Flight of the Archangel. New York, Doubleday, 1985; London, Severn House, 1986.
A Lover Scorned. New York, Doubleday, 1986; London, Severn House, 1987.
Bump in the Night. New York, Doubleday, 1988; London, Severn House, 1989 (made into television movie, 1991).
A Fatal Advent. New York, Fawcett, 1989.
The Long Search. Thorndike, Maine, Thorndike, 1990.
Love and Inheritance. Thorndike, Maine, Thorndike, 1991.
Family Trust. HAL/Dutton, 1994.

*

Manuscript Collections: Kerlan Collection, University of Minnesota, Minneapolis; de Grummond Collection, University of Southern Mississippi, Hattiesburg.

Isabelle Holland comments:

The Greek philosopher Heraclitus said "character is destiny." Some well-known contemporary writer—possibly the late Elizabeth Bowen—said "character is plot." In my books I write about what interests me most: the development of character, its growth of understanding of self, and its relationship to others. To me this is the basis of all stories, and I look upon myself primarily as a story teller.

* * *

After a productive career in publishing, Isabelle Holland began writing for children in the late 1960s. Her first novel, *Cecily,* originally published for adults, appeared in 1967 and was praised for its lucid prose and convincing characterizations. It concerns the experiences of an unhappy 13-year-old girl in an English boarding school whose brilliant and beautiful teacher rejects her. Because the novel revealed exceptional insight into the young girl's psyche, Holland was asked to write for children, and *Amanda's Choice* was published in 1970. Since that time, Holland has written many fine books for children. She often treats controversial subjects—death, homosexuality, rape, the dangers of hitchhiking—but she avoids treating these topics with a didactic tone. Rather she skillfully embeds social, psychological, and moral messages within believable dramatic situations.

A great many of Holland's protagonists are lonely, isolated children or young adults. Often these characters are struggling to survive in a painful family situation. In *Amanda's Choice* the central character is the daughter of a loving father and his selfish second wife. Amanda herself belongs to a tradition of obnoxious, misunderstood children in children's literature. When her conflicts become unbearable, she runs away and seeks her friend Manuel in New York City. Without family, friends, or resources, Amanda at last begins to accept her father's love. In *Dinah and the Green Fat Kingdom* Holland portrays a 12-year-old plagued with weight problems. She experiences intense conflicts with her slim attractive mother and her gifted older brother. Dinah finds relief in a secret woodland bower, where she spins humorous fantasies about a clever nation of fat people. Eventually Dinah learns to manage her weight problem and also effects a reconciliation with her mother. Because of Holland's deft uses of detail, the novel is much more than a tract about how to solve the problems of juvenile obesity.

Several of Holland's books treat controversial topics with tact and psychological insight. *Hitchhike* depicts the dangers of hitchhiking. Angry at her father, Pat Mallory hitches rides first with a middle-aged man and later with four young men. In the second instance, she barely escapes gang rape. Although the book is well written, it is Holland's most didactic work. She handles taboo subjects much more skillfully in *The Man Without a Face* and *Perdita.* Charles Norstadt isolates himself in resentment from his older sister Gloria and his attractive unstable mother and finds comfort, like Salinger's Holden Caulfield, in his younger sister Meg and a tomcat. When he learns that Gloria will return home in the fall, Charles is desperate to enter boarding school and enlists the tutoring services of Justin McLeod, "the man without a face," a teacher who had been disfigured in an accident involving a student and alcohol. By the end of the summer, Charles has faced some disillusionments about his dead war hero father, grieved about the tomcat's sudden death, and experienced a homosexual encounter with Justin. Charles does gain some maturity and insight but not without immense pain.

At the time of its publication *The Man Without a Face* was highly controversial. Many parents objected to Holland's sympathetic treatment of the homosexual teacher. Holland presents Justin as a compassionate, caring, if flawed human being, not a monstrous child abuser.

With similar psychological perception and sympathy, Holland depicts the emotional struggles of a young girl, Perdita, who is found unconscious in a dry well after having been raped and beaten.

Though she must summon all of her courage, Perdita manages to find the strength to heal.

Many critics claim that Holland's novel, *Of Love and Death and Other Journeys* is her masterpiece. In this realistic work the 15-year-old Meg has lived a fascinatingly unconventional life in Europe with her mother and latest stepfather. Her life changes painfully with her mother's surgery for cancer and her father's arrival. Meg must come to terms with losing her mother and also adapt to an entirely new way of life. In this fine novel Holland portrays death and grief compassionately but unsentimentally and displays remarkable skill in revealing the nuances of family conflict. Plot, setting, theme, and character are admirably integrated, and Holland creates believable dialogue among her witty, sophisticated characters.

In a difficult world Holland's characters are amazingly resourceful. They find unexpected ways to survive. Some characters turn to animals for comfort, as do Dinah in *The Green Fat Kingdom,* Alan in *Alan and the Animal Kingdom,* and Jessamy in *A Horse Named Peaceable.* Others find a stay against loneliness in creating imaginary friends. In *God, Mrs. Muskrat, and Aunt Dot* Rebecca Smith, an 11-year-old orphan, is lonely, imaginative, and verbal. She turns to her imaginary friend, Mrs. Muskrat, a kindly earthmother who freely gives her cookies, comfort, and love. Eventually Rebecca must reconcile her real and imaginary worlds. In *Abbie's God Book* a young character survives emotionally through expressing her religious beliefs.

Holland justly deserves her reputation as an accomplished novelist for children and young adults. She expresses in lucid prose the complexities of relationships, insists upon the need for young adults to accept responsibility for their lives, as well as the consequences of their actions, and celebrates the power of the human spirit to heal itself and to survive the most painful circumstances.

—Anita Moss

HOLLING, Holling C(lancy)

Nationality: American. **Born:** Holling Corners, Michigan, 2 August 1900. **Education:** Leslie High School, Michigan, graduated 1917; Art Institute of Chicago, graduated 1923. **Family:** Married Lucille Webster in 1925. **Career:** Member of the Zoology Department, Chicago Museum of Natural History, 1923-26; taught on the New York University World Cruise, 1926-27. After 1927 freelance designer, advertising artist, and book illustrator. **Died:** 7 September 1973.

PUBLICATIONS FOR CHILDREN

Fiction (illustrated by the author)

Little Big-Bye-and-Bye. Chicago, Volland, 1926.

Choo-Me-Choo, illustrated by Lucille Holling. Minneapolis, Buzza, 1928.

Rum-Tum-Tummy, The Elephant Who Ate. Akron, Ohio, Saalfield, 1928.

Claws of the Thunderbird: A Tale of Three Lost Indians. Chicago, Volland, 1928.

Rocky Billy: The Story of the Bounding Career of a Rocky Mountain Goat. New York, Macmillan, 1928.

The Twins Who Flew round the World. New York, Platt and Munk, 1931.

Little Buffalo Boy, illustrated by Holling C. and Lucille Holling. New York, Garden City Publishing Company, 1939.

Paddle-to-the-Sea. Boston, Houghton Mifflin, 1941; London, Collins, 1945.

Tree in the Trail. Boston, Houghton Mifflin, 1942; London, Collins, 1948.

Seabird, illustrated by Holling C. and Lucille Holling. Boston, Houghton Mifflin, 1948; London, Collins, 1960.

Minn of the Mississippi. Boston, Houghton Mifflin, 1951.

Pagoo, illustrated by Holling C. and Lucille Holling. Boston, Houghton Mifflin, 1957.

Other

New Mexico Made Easy, with Words of Modern Syllables. Chicago, Clancy, 1923.

The Book of Indians, illustrated by Holling C. and Lucille Holling. New York, Platt and Munk, 1935; London, Cassell, 1938.

The Book of Cowboys, illustrated by Holling C. and Lucille Holling. New York, Platt and Munk, 1936; London, Cassell, 1938.

PUBLICATIONS FOR ADULTS

Poetry

Sun and Smoke: Verse and Woodcuts of New Mexico. Privately printed, 1923.

*

Manuscript Collections: University of Oregon Library, Eugene.

Illustrator: *Blot, The Little City Cat* by Phyllis Crawford, 1930; *The Road in Storyland* edited by Watty Piper, 1932, and *Children of Other Lands* by Piper, 1943.

* * *

A writer with the consummate gift of storytelling and the ability to teach through sharing remarkable bits and pieces of information, Holling C. Holling moved from his companion collections *The Book of Indians* and *The Book of Cowboys* of the 1930s to a group of singular books which offer blendings of rare elements. He offered in these books "a unique vision of the country, each focusing first on the wild life Mr. Holling knew so well, but spreading wide into the works of men and the sweep of history."

The first of these geo-historical-fiction volumes, *Paddle-to-the-Sea,* is a tremendously original and arresting story with a mixture of imagination and a wealth of information employing techniques pioneered and perfected by Holling and his artist wife. The story follows the adventures of Paddle, carved into a miniature canoe by an Indian boy. Paddle comes to travel from "the hills above Lake Superior" across the Great Lakes, and eventually to France encountering suspenseful situations of many kinds. The values of this story for today's readers are described fully in a penetrating analysis, "The Teaching of Paddle-to-the-Sea," by Terry Borten in *Learning* (January, 1977). He comments on the energy, simplicity, understanding, and appeal in the story, and the allowance Holling makes for the feelings of children. "What we teachers need is Holling's insight into the relationship between narrative action and factual information."

Holling's consuming interest in nature combined with history is further developed in *Tree in the Trail* which traced the beginnings (1610) of a cottonwood tree in the Great Plains to the ox yoke which "traveled with a tune" to the Santa Fe Trail. To Indians this lonely giant represented a peace-medicine tree; to other travelers a landmark until 1834 when lightning and wind struck it down. Blending anthropology and zoology with geography and history, the prose captures the excitement of both the historical setting, the old Southwest—together with the realia linked with its emergence. The authenticity stems from the author's personal saddle-horse contact with thousands of miles of plains, deserts, and mountains; he was able to transfer to the reader the sights, knowledge, and awe he absorbed.

In *Seabird* Holling told the intriguing story of an ivory gull carved by a young lad onto a whaling ship. Traveling on the family's vessels over four generations, this marvelous gull witnessed the enormous changes sailors and their ships experienced as they moved around the seas of the world into modern times. In *Minn of the Mississippi* a mud turtle travels from the head-waters of the great waterway along its colorful shores to the Gulf, bringing alive the people, their work, and evidences of early exploration. *Pagoo* is an experimental narrative about a hermit crab, drawn into a whirlwind of action described in vivid detail. He eventually returns to the "endless rocking rhythms of the sea." In each of these books Holling makes himself felt through his vibrant text and imagery.

—Clara O. Jackson

HOOKS, William H.

Nationality: American. **Born:** Whiteville, North Carolina, 14 November 1921. **Education:** University of North Carolina at Chapel Hill, B.A. 1948, M.A. 1950. **Military Service:** United States Army Medical Corps, 1942-1946. **Career:** High school history and social studies teacher, Chapel Hill, North Carolina, 1949; history and dance instructor, Hampton Institute, Hampton, Virginia, 1950; choreographer at opera workshop, Brooklyn College of the City University of New York, Brooklyn, New York, 1955-64; owned dance studio, New York, New York, 1965-70; publications division staff member, 1970-72, and chairperson of division, 1972-91, Bank Street College, New York City; managing editor, "Bank Street Readers"; vice-president, Ballet Concepts, Inc.; educational consultant, American Broadcasting Company, Columbia Broadcasting Company, and National Broadcasting Company; reviewer, *Dance Digest*; script writer, *Captain Kangaroo* television program. **Address:** 718 E. Franklin St., Chapel Hill, North Carolina 27514, U.S.A.

Publications for Children

The Seventeen Gerbils of Class 4A. New York, Coward, 1976.
Maria's Cave. New York, Coward, 1977.
Doug Meets the Nutcracker. New York, F. Warne, 1977.
The Mystery on Bleecker Street. New York, Knopf, Inc., 1980.
Mean Jake and the Devils. New York, Dial, 1981.
The Mystery on Liberty Street. New York, Knopf, 1982.
Three Rounds With Rabbit. New York, Lothrop, 1984.
With Seymour V. Reit and Betty D. Boegehold, *When Small Is Tall, and Other Read-Together Tales.* New York, Random House, 1985.
With Betty D. Boegehold and Joanne Openheim, *Read-a-Rebus: Tales and Rhymes in Words and Pictures.* New York, Random House, 1986.
Moss Gown. Boston, Houghton Mifflin Company, 1987.
The Legend of the White Doe. New York, Simon & Schuster, 1988.
Pioneer Cat. New York, Random House, 1988.
With Barbara Brenner, *Lion and Lamb.* New York, Bantam, 1989.
Mr. Bubble Gum. New York, Bantam, 1989.
The Three Little Pigs and the Fox. New York, Macmillan, 1989.
The Ballad of Belle Dorcas. New York, Knopf, 1990.
Mr. Monster. New York, Bantam, 1990.
A Dozen Dizzy Dogs. New York, Bantam, 1990.
The Gruff Brothers. New York, Bantam, 1990.
With Barbara Brenner, *Lion & Lamb Step Out.* New York, Bantam Doubleday, 1990.
Lo-Jack & Pirates. New York, Bantam Doubleday, 1991.
Where's Lulu? New York, Bantam, 1991.
With Barbara Brenner, *Ups and Downs With Lion and Lamb.* New York, Bantam, 1991.
Mr. Baseball. New York, Bantam, 1991.
With Betty Beogehold, *The Rainbow Ribbon: A Bank Street Book About Values.* New York, Viking, 1991.
Peach Boy. New York, Bantam Doubleday Dell, 1992.
With Barbara Brenner and Joanne Oppenheim, *How Do You Make a Bubble?* New York, Bantam, 1992.
Monster from the Sea. New York, Bantam, 1992.
Little Poss & Horrible Hound. New York, Gareth Stevens, 1992.
Rough, Tough, and Rowdy: A Bank Street Book About Values. New York, Viking, 1992.
The Monster From the Sea. New York, Bantam, 1992.
Feed Me!: An Aesop Fable. New York, Gareth Stevens, 1992
The Mighty Santa Fe. New York, Simon & Schuster, 1993.
Mr. Dinosaur. New York, Bantam Doubleday Dell, 1994.
The Rainbow Ribbon. New York, Puffin, 1994.
Snowbear Whittington: An Appalachian Beauty & the Beast. New York, Macmillan, 1994.
The Girl Who Could Fly. New York, Macmillan, 1995.
Freedom's Fruit. New York, Knopf, 1996.
Mr. Garbage. New York, Bantam, 1996.
The Mystery of Missing Tooth. New York, Bantam Doubleday Dell, 1997.
Mr. Big Brother. New York, Bantam, 1998.
The Legend of the Christmas Rose. New York, HarperCollins, 1999.

Other

Co-author, *Barron's Book of Fun and Learning: Preschool Learning Activities.* New York, Barron's, 1987.
With Barbara Brenner and Joanne Openheim, *No Way, Slippery Slick! A Child's First Book About Drugs.* New York, HarperCollins, 1991.

Publications for Young Adults

Crossing the Line. New York, Knopf, 1978.
Circle of Fire. New York, Simon & Schuster, 1982.
A Flight of Dazzle Angels. New York, Macmillan, 1988.

Other

With Ellen Galinsky, *The New Extended Family: Day Care That Works.* Boston, Houghton, 1977.

*

Critical Studies: Review of *Circle of Fire* by Nancy Sheridan, in *Horn Book,* October 1982, 517; review of *Freedom's Fruit* by Maeve Visser Knoth, in *Horn Book,* May-June 1996, 325; entry in *Sixth Book of Junior Authors and Illustrators,* New York, H.W. Wilson, 1996, 133-134; entry in *Something about the Author,* Vol. 94, Detroit, Gale Research, 1998, 105-109.

William H. Hooks comments:

Much of my work, especially the novels, draws heavily on my personal and family background. I am also deeply interested, and have done much research, into the folk literature of North Carolina in particular, and the South in general. I have spent much time in Appalachia where I collected a storehouse of tales from the oral tradition. I was fortunate in growing up with a family of storytellers in the eastern, coastal section of North Carolina where a rich heritage of Elizabethan and African folklore share equal billing.

* * *

William H. Hooks is recognized both in the fields of education and dance, for his career combines a love of fine arts and an ability to share them with others through choreography, media presentation, and writing. The roots of his significant contribution to children's literature is found in his own beginnings in rural eastern North Carolina where he grew up with storytellers in his family and strong youthful impressions of the historical era and setting of the coastal Tidewater country. Although his appearance as an author of children's books would not take place until later in his life, his earlier career was an intricate combination of teaching, dance, and creating learning contexts for both children and adults. When after age 50 he began his career as an author of children's books, he drew upon both his professional and personal experiences to create highly regarded works within the genres of historical and realistic fiction, folklore, and fantasy.

A significant element of Hooks' work is his preservation of authentic descriptions of the rural South as they were found in the lore of local storytellers. The language, characters, and wisdom of these folktales are described from a storyteller's perspective. *Mean Jake and the Devils* is framed around a grandmother telling her grandson stories about mean Jake. The grandmother was created from Hooks' recollections of his own grandmother and an aunt who told him stories of the region. The humorous portrayal of the devil and his two children trying to outwit mean Jake is typical of this body of folklore but represents just one of the personalities given to this supernatural creature. Later works that retell and capture the context of this southern folklore include "conjure" stories such as *The Ballad of Belle Dorcas* and *Freedom's Fruit.* In both stories a conjurer is called upon to perform magic to save loved ones from the tragedies of slavery. Belle Dorcas is a free person, being the white plantation owner's daughter by his black mistress. When she falls in love with a young slave, the conjurer is called upon to find a way to save him from being sold. He is turned into a tree which is later cut to make the roof of a smoke house. Belle, however, has been given the power to turn him back into himself at night and they spend a life of night meetings. The story ends with her death and the mysterious appearance of two cedar tress where the smokehouse stood. *Freedom's Fruit* also has the theme of the innocent outwitting the greedy master who is going to sell his slaves. The mother of a young girl casts a spell on a grapevine, which in turn causes those who eat of the fruit to turn old and weak. The conjure woman's daughter and her boyfriend eat the fruit and because they become old, they are not worth much. The old woman can then afford to buy their freedom and all ends well the following spring when they return to their normal youthful state. Maeve Visser Knoth notes in a *Horn Book* review that William Hooks "weaves a poetic story about the ability of the oppressed to outwit those with power."

The social and geographical context of the 1930s directly influenced two of his novels for young readers. *Crossing the Line* and *Circle of Fire* both are stories of racial prejudice and the hatred that it invokes within a community. In the former, a young boy named Harrison befriends an elderly African-American woman. Captivated by her stories, he discovers they have a common relative, her nephew. His murder and the woman's disappearance create a story of bigotry seen through the innocence perspective of adolescence. *Circle of Fire* again focuses on Harrison and his African-American friends as they are confronted with activities of the Ku Klux Klan and their planned attacks on gypsies who are camping in their community. Nancy Sheridan of *Horn Book* characterizes this novel as "filled with vivid characters and mounting tension.... a powerful lingering tale of shattered innocence and changing relationships."

His earlier historical fiction includes *Maria's Cave* and *A Flight of Dazzle Angels. Maria's Cave* is about young Maria Sautuola, who discovers stone age paintings in Spain. The anthropological and historical community fails to acknowledge the value of her findings at first but Maria is persistent throughout her life in assuring the paintings receive their just recognition. *A Flight of Dazzle Angels,* Hooks's third book for young adolescents focuses on the romance between two young people in the summer of 1908.

William Hooks has also provided readers with stories reflective of fairy tales. *Moss Gown* is often thought to be a Southern Cinderella tale as it tells the story of a good-hearted daughter who is ill-treated. Candace is the outcast daughter whose father is more pleased with her two sisters. Hooks has combined the Southern tale often known as "Rush Cape" with recognizable story elements from King Lear. *Snowbear Whittington: An Appalachian Beauty and the Beast* is another addition to that unique sub-genre of fairy tale variants. *Three Little Pigs and the Fox* also recount this familiar tale in an Appalachian setting.

Other of Hooks's stories also reflect his prior professional experiences that focused on children. His first book, *The Seventee[n] Gerbils of Class 4A,* describes from a child's perspective the perplexing problem of caring for 17 gerbils and dividing them among four children. The simplistic, yet insightful approach to the mat[h] dilemma highlights the realistic character portrayal in this earl[y] reader chapter book.

The Mighty Santa Fe and *The Girl Who Could Fly* are both examples of Hooks's ability to write about that which delights a child's sense of fantasy. *The Mighty Santa Fe* tells of a young boy and his grandmother who embark on a magical Christmas Eve train ride. The thrill of such a fantastical ride is warmed by the shared experience between the two. *The Girl Who Could Fly* is a delightfully humorous story about the magical gifts of Tomasina Jones that make her ideal for the boys baseball team.

William Hooks writes text that is rich in descriptive language, characterization developed through dialogue, and setting. The elements of his writing not only support his plot, but capture both an historical era and geographical culture to be enjoyed and understood by readers. His contribution to the field exceeds that of providing authentic and entertaining stories to preserving a bit of the heritage of the South as he experienced it as a boy.

—Janelle B. Mathis

HOPE-SIMPSON, Jacynth

Pseudonym: Helen Dudley. **Nationality:** British. **Born:** Jacynth Cureton, Birmingham, Warwickshire, 10 November 1930. **Education:** King Edward VI High School, Birmingham; University of Lausanne, 1949; St. Hugh's College, Oxford, Dip. Ed. 1953, M.A. 1956. **Family:** Married Dermot Hope-Simpson in 1955; one daughter. **Career:** English teacher, Bournemouth School for Girls, 1953-54, and Croham Hurst School, Croydon, 1954-57; examiner, Oxford and Cambridge General Certificate of Education, 1957-58. Chairman, West Country Writers' Association, 1980-82. **Address:** Franchise Cottage, Newtown, Milborne Port, Sherborne, Dorset DT9 5BJ, England.

Publications for Children

Fiction

Anne, Young Swimmer. London, Constable, 1960.
The Stranger in the Train, illustrated by Prudence Seward. London, Hamish Hamilton, 1960.
The Great Fire, illustrated by Pat Marriott. London, Hamish Hamilton, 1961; New York, Dutton, 1962.
Young Netball Player. London, Constable, 1961.
Danger on the Line, illustrated by Janet Duchesne. London, Hamish Hamilton, 1962.
The Man Who Came Back. London, Hamish Hamilton, 1962.
The Ice Fair, illustrated by Pat Marriott. London, Hamish Hamilton, 1963.
The Ninepenny, illustrated by Janet Duchesne. London, Hamish Hamilton, 1964.
The Witches' Cave, illustrated by Janet Duchesne. London, Hamish Hamilton, 1964.
The Edge of the World, illustrated by Peter Warner. London, Hamish Hamilton, 1965; New York, Coward McCann, 1966.
The High Toby, illustrated by Lynette Hemmant. London, Hamish Hamilton, 1966.
Escape to the Castle, illustrated by Mary Russon. London, Hamish Hamilton, 1967.
The Unknown Island. London, Hamish Hamilton, 1968; New York, Coward McCann, 1969.
The Gunner's Boy. London, Heinemann, 1973.
Save Tarranmoor! London, Heinemann, 1974.
The Hijacked Hovercraft, illustrated by Jeroo Roy. London, Heinemann, 1975.
Black Madonna. London, Heinemann, 1976; Nashville, Nelson, 1977.
Vote for Victoria, illustrated by Jael Jordan. London, Heinemann, 1976.

Other

Basic Certificate English: A Revision Course in the Grammar and Structure of the English Language, with Answers. London, Hamish Hamilton, 1966.
They Sailed from Plymouth. London, Hamish Hamilton, 1970.
Elizabeth I. London, Hamish Hamilton, 1971.
Who Knows? Twelve Unsolved Mysteries. London, Heinemann, 1974; Nashville, Nelson, 1976.
Always on the Move, illustrated by Jolyne Knox. London, Heinemann, 1975.
The Making of the Machine Age. London, Heinemann, 1978.

Editor, *The Hamish Hamilton Book of Myths and Legends,* illustrated by Raymond Briggs. London, Hamish Hamilton, 1964; as *The Curse of the Dragon's Gold: European Myths and Legends,* New York, Doubleday, 1969.
Editor, *The Hamish Hamilton Book of Witches,* illustrated by Krystyna Turska. London, Hamish Hamilton, 1966; as *A Cavalcade of Witches,* New York, Walck, 1967; as *Covens and Cauldrons,* London, Beaver, 1977.
Editor, *Tales in School: An Anthology of Boarding-School Life,* illustrated by John Lawrence. London, Hamish Hamilton, 1971.

Publications for Adults

Novels

The Bishop of Kenelminster. London, Putnam, 1961.
The Bishop's Picture. London, Putnam, 1962.
The Unravish'd Bride. London, Putnam, 1963.
The Hooded Falcon (as Helen Dudley). London, Futura, 1979.
Island of Perfumes. London, Hale, 1985.
Cottage Dreams. London, Hale, 1985.

*

Jacynth Hope-Simpson comments:

I should like to feel that I write for a wide range of children, with enough incident and pace to attract the reluctant reader and with (one hopes) enough depth of content to appeal to more "bookish" readers. One of my basic beliefs is that while one may need to simplify both language and one's material in writing for children, one must never write down to them, I believe accuracy to be of the utmost importance, especially as so many ideas are formed at a surprisingly early age. On an imaginative level, I am particularly interested in places and the interaction between place and personality.

* * *

The earliest traditions of storytelling for children were strongly moral and didactic in their intention; children were taken seriously because their instruction was a serious matter. Increasingly since the 1950s, this emphasis has changed to an attempt to evoke the nature of childhood itself as being of prime significance.

Jacynth Hope-Simpson's position is more consistent with the older tradition. She takes her subject matter from a wide range of incident and location, and its seriousness is represented more by a talent for realism, but this is of a kind that grows from mundane and continuous contact with children. In *Danger on the Line,* for example, the small crisis is prompted by Antony's discovery that Clare, the small daughter of the master in charge of the outdoor model steam railway, was upset because "A large piece of sharp black gravel was stuck in her left nostril." In the same way in the more ambitious *Escape to the Castle,* Vaclav's adventure begins on a hot night in his Prague attic when he becomes unendurably aware of being shut out from a larger life, an unwilling prisoner (not helped by his younger brother's preoccupation with squeezing his insect bites). He locates this larger life in the Castle where his delight in Mozart's music is challenged by a meeting with the composer weighed down by problems of his own. This theme possibly needs fuller treatment to realise its complexity; but the neat ordering of surprise—where stock stories involve improbable escapes from realistic castles, this escape is from cramping domesticity in search of an ideal in a castle—is characteristic of the author's unobtrusive originality. This originality is given fuller scope in *The Gunner's Boy.* Mark and Peter are the sons of a Dartmoor parson sent to stay with an aunt in Plymouth while their mother impatiently awaits the tardy arrival of the latest child in competition with the family cat which is similarly disadvantaged. Mark is bookish and Peter, the younger boy, is mad to go to sea. Peter runs away to join a Spanish expedition but hurts his leg on the way down to the harbour, and Mark, going to bring him back, is taken in his place and becomes the reluctant, and sensitive, narrator of the story. This, again, provides more than conventional battle scenes on *The Revenge* and hardships at sea, for Mark is taken on board the *San Pablo* after the battle and sees the humane side of the despised and hated Spaniards.

The characteristic qualities of these stories include: respect for the child reader which entails such authentic details as, in the London of *The Great Fire,* "The shop signs swung over their heads; a striped pole for the barber, a knee boot for the bootmaker"; a precise sense of place whether 17th-century London, the Prague of Mozart, or Drake's Plymouth and contemporary Finistère; and pre-eminently a strong sense of dramatic realism so that child adventures, of the past and of today, are consistently related to an encircling and clearly defined adult world.

—Kenneth J. Sterck

HOUGH, (Helen) Charlotte

Nationality: British. **Born:** Helen Charlotte Woodyatt, Brockenhurst, Hampshire, 24 May 1924. **Education:** Frensham Heights School, Farnham, Surrey. **Military Service:** Women's Royal Naval Service. **Family:** Married Richard Hough (i.e., Bruce Carter, *q.v.*) in 1943 (divorced 1980); four daughters; married Dr. Louis Ackroyd in 1997. **Agent:** Curtis Brown, 162-168 Regent Street, London WIR 5TB. **Address:** 1-A Ivor Street, London NW1 9PL, England.

Publications for Children (illustrated by the author)

Fiction

Jim Tiger. London, Faber, 1956; Indianapolis, Bobbs Merrill, 1958.
Morton's Pony. London, Faber, 1957.
The Home-Makers. London, Hamish Hamilton, 1957.
The Hampshire Pig. London, Hamish Hamilton, 1958.
The Story of Mr. Pinks. London, Faber, 1958.
The Animal Game. London, Faber, 1959.
The Trackers. London, Hamish Hamilton, 1960.
Algernon. London, Faber, 1961; New York, A.S. Barnes, 1962.
Anna and Minnie. London, Faber, 1962.
Three Little Funny Ones. London, Hamish Hamilton, 1962.
The Owl in the Barn. London, Faber, 1964.
More Funny Ones. London, Faber, 1965.
Red Biddy and Other Stories. London, Faber, 1966; New York, Coward McCann, 1967.
Sir Frog and Other Stories. London, Faber, 1968.
Educating Flora and Other Stories. London, Faber, 1968.
Abdul the Awful (includes *Sir Frog and Other Stories* and *Educating Flora and Other Stories*). New York, McCall, 1970.
Queer Customer. London, Heinemann, 1972.
Wonky Donkey. London, Heinemann, 1975.
Bad Cat. London, Heinemann, 1975.
Pink Pig. London, Heinemann, 1975.
Charlotte Hough's Holiday Book. London, Heinemann, 1975; as *The Holiday Story Book,* London, Beaver, 1976.
The Mixture as Before. London, Heinemann, 1976.

Poetry

A Bad Child's Book of Moral Verse. London, Faber, and New York, Walck, 1970.

Other

My Aunt's Alphabet, with Billy and Me (reader). London, Hamish Hamilton, 1969.
Verse and Various (miscellany). London, Dent, 1979.

Publications for Adults

Novel

The Bassington Murder. London, Elek, and New York, St. Martin's Press, 1980.

*

Illustrator: *The House on the Moor,* 1948, *The Thirteenth Adventure,* 1949, *Steeple Folly,* 1950, *Castaway Camp,* 1951, and *The Barnstormers,* 1953, all by M.E. Atkinson; *The Adventures of Tommy* by Lillian Miozzi, 1950; *I Carried the Horn,* 195[illegible] *Goodbye to Hounds,* 1952, and *Riders from Afar,* 1954, all [illegible]

Christine Pullein-Thompson; *Land of Ponies* by Marjorie M. Oliver, 1951; *Barry's Exciting Year,* 1951, *Barry Gets His Wish,* 1952, and *Barry's Great Day,* 1954, all by A. Stephen Tring; *Two of Us* by Janet Branford, 1952; *Mystery at Winton's Park,* 1952, and *Hotel Doorway,* 1953, both by Lorna Lewis; *The Wonderful Farm* by Marcel Aymé, 1952; *Smoky Joe,* 1952, *Smoky Joe in Trouble,* 1953, and *Smoky Joe Goes to School,* 1956, all by Laurence Meynell; *Prince among Ponies* by Josephine Pullein-Thompson, 1952; *Five Proud Riders* by Ann Stafford, 1953; *The Sheepdog Adventure* by Ethelind Fearon, 1953; *The Enchanted Horse* by April Jaffé, 1953; *Peril on the Iron Road,* 1953, and *Gunpowder Tunnel,* 1955, both by Bruce Carter; *Black Beauty* by Anna Sewell, 1954; *Elephant Big and Elephant Little,* 1955, *The Little Yellow Jungle Frogs,* 1956, and *Animal Story Book,* 1972, all by Anita Hewett; *The Boy with the Green Thumb* by Barbara Euphan Todd, 1956; *The Flying Jacket* edited by Betty Willsher, 1964; *Time for a Story* edited by Eileen Colwell, 1967; *Galápagos* by Richard Hough, 1975; *What Katy Did* by Susan Coolidge.

* * *

Charlotte Hough is a writer of marked individuality and versatility, qualities not easily combined. She writes in both prose and verse, and for a wide age-span, ranging from the very small children to whom *Wonky Donkey* is meant to be read aloud, to the eleven-year-olds who want junior novels such as *Queer Customer.* Further—though this is not the place to attempt an assessment of her talents as an illustrator—it must be remarked that in some of her books, notably *Wonky Donkey,* her pictures are so integrated with her text that the latter (often no more than a single sentence or a single word per page) cannot be criticised in isolation.

Within the purely verbal context, however, it can be said that all her work, for whatever age, exhibits certain consistent features. There is always a great sense of fun, and infectious enthusiasm for words, a delight in juggling with them. This dexterity is naturally most marked in her use of rhyme and assonance. *A Bad Child's Book of Moral Verse* is not unworthy to stand on the shelf beside the Belloc volumes of an earlier day. But this same verbal dexterity is also a feature of her prose, which shows much of the same neatness and economy. Exuberance without waste of words is the paradox she contrives to achieve, so that the reader is whirled along.

These high spirits and robust good humour cannot obscure the fact that Hough is in the great moralist tradition of English children's literature. Whether writing of children or adults or of animals to whom human frailties are transferred—the conceited guinea-pig, Mr. Pinks, the maladroit Jim Tiger, or Morton's pony, the elderly and sagacious pony as reliable and protective as a grown-up—she makes her points with a light touch, so that the very weaknesses of her characters render them the more lovable.

Probably it is her shorter pieces—her animal stories and fairy tales making fresh use of old material, giant and goblin, mermaid and princess—that represent her most original contribution. At the same time, a junior novel such as *Queer Customer,* with its central theme of a boy's natural but unnecessary dread of an operation, must not be underrated. It displays another, more realistic side to her work, and her sympathetic depiction of the characters is full of insight and humanity.

—Geoffrey Trease

HOUGH, Richard. See **CARTER, Bruce.**

HOWE, James

Nationality: American. **Born:** Oneida, New York, 2 August 1946. **Education:** Boston University, 1964-68, B.F.A 1968; Hunter College, New York, M.A. 1977. **Family:** Married 1) Deborah Smith in 1969 (died 1978); 2) Betsy Imershein in 1981, one daughter. **Career:** Freelance actor and director, 1971-75; literary agent, Lucy Kroll Agency, New York, 1976-81. Lives in Hastings-on-Hudson, New York. **Agent:** Amy Berkower, Writers House Inc., 21 West 26th Street, New York, New York 10010, U.S.A.

Publications for Children

Fiction

Bunnicula: A Rabbit Tale of Mystery, with Deborah Howe, illustrated by Alan Daniel. New York, Atheneum, 1979; London, Hodder and Stoughton, 1984.

Teddy Bear's Scrapbook, with Deborah Howe, illustrated by David S. Rose. New York, Atheneum, 1980.

Annie Joins the Circus, illustrated by Leonard Shortall. New York, Random House, 1982.

Howliday Inn, illustrated by Lynn Munsinger. New York, Atheneum, 1982; London, Dragon, 1987.

The Case of the Missing Mother, illustrated by William Cleaver. New York, Random House, 1983.

The Celery Stalks at Midnight, illustrated by Leslie Morrill. New York, Atheneum, 1983; London, Hodder and Stoughton, 1986.

A Night without Stars. New York, Atheneum, 1983.

The Day the Teacher Went Bananas, illustrated by Lillian Hoban. New York, Dutton, 1984; London, Viking Kestrel, 1985.

How the Ewoks Saved the Trees, illustrated by Walter Helez. New York, Random House, 1984.

Morgan's Zoo, illustrated by Leslie Morrill. New York, Atheneum, 1984.

Mister Tinker in Oz, illustrated by David S. Rose. New York, Random House, 1985.

What Eric Knew. New York, Atheneum, 1985.

Eat Your Poison, Dear. New York, Atheneum, 1986.

A Love Note for Baby Piggy. New York, Marvel, 1986.

Stage Fright. New York, Atheneum, 1986.

There's a Monster under My Bed, illustrated by David S. Rose. New York, Atheneum, 1986.

I Wish I Were a Butterfly, illustrated by Ed Young. New York, Harcourt Brace, 1987.

Nighty-Nightmare, illustrated by Leslie Morrill. New York, Atheneum, 1987.

The Fright before Christmas, illustrated by Leslie Morrill. New York, Morrow, 1988.

Scared Silly, illustrated by Leslie Morrill. New York, Morrow, 1989.

Dew Drop Dead. New York, Atheneum, 1990.

Hot Fudge, illustrated by Leslie Morril. New York, Morrow, 1990.
Pinky and Rex, illustrated by Melissa Sweet. New York, Atheneum, 1990.
Pinky and Rex Get Married, illustrated by Melissa Sweet. New York, Atheneum, 1990.
Creepy-Crawly Birthday, illustrated by Leslie Morrill. New York, Morrow, 1991.
Adaptor, *Dances with Wolves: A Story for Children* (adapted from the screenplay by Michael Blake). New York, Newmarket Press, 1991.
Pinky and Rex and the Spelling Bee, illustrated by Melissa Sweet. New York, Atheneum, 1991.
Pinky and Rex and the Mean Old Witch, illustrated by Melissa Sweet. New York, Atheneum, 1991.
Pinky and Rex Go to Camp, illustrated by Melissa Sweet. New York, Atheneum, 1992.
Return to Howliday Inn, illustrated by Alan Daniel. New York, Atheneum, 1992.
The Bunnicula Fun Book. New York, Morrow, 1993.
Pinky and Rex and the New Baby, illustrated by Melissa Sweet. New York, Atheneum, 1993.
Rabbit-Cadabra!, illustrated by Alan Daniel. New York, Morrow, 1993.
Bunnicula Escapes!, a Pop-up Adventure, illustrated by Alan and Lea Daniel; paper engineering by Vicki Teague-Cooper. New York, Tupelo Books, 1994.
There's a Dragon in My Sleeping Bag, illustrated by David S. Rose. New York, Atheneum, 1994.
The New Nick Kramer, or My Life as a Baby-sitter. New York, Hyperion Books for Children, 1995.
Pinky and Rex and the Double-dad Weekend, illustrated by Melissa Sweet. New York, Atheneum; Toronto, Maxwell Macmillan Canada; New York, Maxwell Macmillan International, 1995.
Pinky and Rex and the Bully, illustrated by Melissa Sweet.
New York, Atheneum Books for Young Readers, 1996.
Horace and Morris But Mostly Dolores, illustrated by Ana Lopez Escriva. New York, Atheneum Books for Young Readers, 1997.
Pinky and Rex and the New Neighbors, illustrated by Melissa Sweet. New York, Atheneum Books for Young Readers, 1997.
The Watcher. New York, Atheneum Books for Young Readers, 1997.
Pinky and Rex and the Perfect Pumpkin, illustrated by Melissa Sweet. New York, Atheneum Books for Young Readers, 1998.
Pinky and Rex and the School Play, illustrated by Melissa Sweet. New York, Atheneum Books for Young Readers, 1998.

Other

The Hospital Book, photographs by Mal Warshaw. New York, Crown, 1981.
The Muppet Guide to Magnificent Manners, illustrated by Peter Elwell. New York, Random House, 1984.
When You Go to Kindergarten, photographs by Betsy Imershein. New York, Knopf, 1986; revised and updated edition, New York, Morrow Junior Books, 1994.
Babes in Toyland (retelling), illustrated by Allen Atkinson. New York, Harcourt Brace, 1986.
Carol Burnett: The Sound of Laughter. New York, Viking, 1987.
The Secret Garden (retelling), illustrated by Thomas B. Allen. New York, Random House, 1987.
My Life as a Babysitter (television play). The Disney Channel, 1990.
Playing with Words, photographs by Michael Craine. Katonah, New York, R.C. Owen, 1994.

*

James Howe comments:

As a writer for children, I have many responsibilities—the responsibility to give the reader well-crafted language that is appropriate for the story at hand, to use language that respects the reader's intelligence while stretching his or her appreciation of what language can do, to articulate what the child cannot, to give positive values in a world where values have been demeaned, to make demands on the reader's mind and spirit, to entertain, and to make the reader laugh. Humor is the most precious gift I can give to my reader, a reminder that the world is not such a terribly serious place. There is more than video games and drugs and nuclear threats; there is laughter—and there is hope. In the end, however, my primary responsibility as a writer is to the hidden child in the reader and in myself, and to the belief that—though we are years apart—when I open my mouth to speak, the child will understand. Because in that hidden part of ourselves, we are one.

* * *

James Howe has an outrageous funny bone that makes the reader laugh out loud while reading the adventures of Harold, Chester, Howie, Bunnicula, and the Monroe family. It is the delicious humor permeating Howe's stories that often enables the reader to accept the various plots and storylines. In *Playing With Words,* his photo-autobiography, Howe writes "I don't know what I'll write next. But whatever it is, I hope I'll be surprised."

His first story, written with his wife, is *Bunnicula: A Rabbit Tale of Mystery.* The story is told by Harold, the Monroe family dog, and details the peculiar events after the arrival of a tiny rabbit found in a local movie theater during a showing of *Dracula* and named Bunnicula. Chester, the observant and clever cat, is convinced of Bunnicula's nefarious antecedents and thus begins a romp through a series of hilarious adventures trying to prove Chester correct. Although the other animals in the story talk, Bunnicula does not speak. Howe sets up a series of situations which inevitably cause all kinds of complications. Howe has Chester reading books and doing reference work in his search for the truth about Bunnicula while Harold is a carefree dog who loves chocolate cupcakes with cream centers. By a series of inferences we come to the conclusion that Chester could be right, especially when the veggies turn white and fang-like teeth of Bunnicula are notices. At the same time we love Bunnicula who seems so misunderstood and our love is conveyed through Harold who becomes his protector. Chateau Bow-Wow is the setting of *Howliday Inn* where Chester and Harold are boarded while their family is on vacation. Unusual things happen at the Chateau, and Chester convinces Harold that they must solve this terrifying mystery and even possible murder. The importance of Howard and Heather, the two dachshunds, is overlooked by all, including the criminal harrison. All is solved by Chester and the Monroes gain a new member of their family. In *Return to Howliday Inn,* the adventurous animals are on the prowl as they meet a new eerie voice, warnings of impeding doom, and cries from a ghostly pile of bones. Hamlet, the Great Dane, and the yuppie dogs, Linda and Bob, all contribute to the caricature nature of this story with endless puns and clever references. In *The Celery Stalks at Midnight* Howe has created a madcap chase of Bunnicula, who Chester is convinced will turn the neighborhood gardens into a vast field of zombie vegetables. *Night-Nightmare* is the story of an overnight camping trip which includes the story of how Bunnicula came to be a vampire—according to Chester. *Rabbit-Cadabra!* is a magical adventure when Howie and Harold track Bunnicula to the amazing Karlovsky's hat. Garlic-pizza is Chester's solution to a plague of vampire rabbits he envisions.

Howe created another series with Pinky and Rex who are the protagonists of chapter book stories for those readers emerging from picture books and I Can Read stories. *Pinky and Rex and the Spelling Bee* uses two things quite familiar to young children: the desire to win a spelling bee when you know that you're good and a peeing accident as an embarrassment. What Howe adds, however, is a careful expression of friendship between Pinky and Rex that rises above either plot item. In *Pinky and Rex Go to Camp,* all of the fears about camp are merged in Pinky being afraid of camp and Rex determined that her fear will only be true if Pinky doesn't join her at Camp Wackatootchee. *Pinky and Rex and the New Baby* explores both the addition of a sibling as well as adoption when Rex's family decide to adopt a baby boy. But it is the soccer ball gift that helps resolve this story.

Stage Fright is a *Sebastian Barth* mystery, another series that Howe has created for an older group of children. In this story drawn from Howe's theater background, Sebastian really wants to work with the famous actress Michaele Caraway but someone else has other ideas. David and Corrie join forces with him to solve another mystery. *Eat Your Poison, Dear* engages the reader with an answer to the question about food in the cafeteria, that is, what if it were poisoned? This sets Sebastian Barth off on the chase and the mystery is begun. *Dew Drop Dead* is much more of a serious story in which death and homelessness play a part in the mystery.

Howe's books are clever, often spoofs, and filled with contemporary references that entertain. It is the sheer fun of following the suspicions of Chester while feeling comforted in Harold's calmness and developing a real concern for Bunnicula that captures a child reader. Howe creates characters because he sees a story in his mind and obviously asks himself the age-old question "What if...?" That he answers this in a variety of stories in exciting and sound adventures with always a heavy dose of humor is the measure of his success; all of this because he "loved playing with words."

—Jane Anne Hannigan

HOWES, Edith (Annie)

Nationality: New Zealander. **Born:** London, England, c. 1874. **Education:** Schools in Kaiapoi and Christchurch. **Career:** Teacher, Wellington Girls' College; infant mistress, Gore Public School. **Member:** Royal Society of New Zealand. **Died:** July 1954.

PUBLICATIONS FOR CHILDREN

Fiction

The Sun's Babies, illustrated by Frank Watkins. London, Cassell, 1910.
Fairy Rings, illustrated by Frank Watkins. London, Cassell, 1911.
Rainbow Children, illustrated by Alice B. Woodward. London, Cassell, 1912.
Where Bell-Birds Chime. Christchurch, Whitcombe and Tombs, 1912.
The Cradle Ship, illustrated by Florence Mary Anderson. London, Cassell, 1916.
Wonderwings and Other Fairy Stories, illustrated by Alice Polson. Auckland, Whitcombe and Tombs, 1918.
Little Make-Believe, illustrated by Alice Polson. Auckland, Whitcombe and Tombs, 1919.
The Singing Fish, illustrated by Florence Mary Anderson. London, Cassell, 1921.
Snowdrop. Auckland, Whitcombe and Tombs, 1923.
The Dream Girl's Garden. London, Ward Lock, 1923.
The Enchanted Road, illustrated by Janet Smalley. New York, Morrow, 1927.
Silver Island, illustrated by Kathleen Coales. Auckland, Whitcombe and Tombs, and London, Oxford University Press, 1928.
Sandals of Pearl, illustrated by Audrey Chalmers. New York, Morrow, 1928; London, Dent, 1929.
The Golden Forest, illustrated by M. Lee Thompson. London, Dent, 1933.
Mrs. Kind Bush, illustrated by Anne Anderson. London, Cassell, 1933.
Riverside Family, illustrated by McGregor Williams. Auckland, Collins, 1944.

Other

Maoriland Fairy Tales. London, Ward Lock, 1913.
Whitcombe's Story Books (*The Rainbow, The Poppy Seed, More Tales of Maori Magic, Drums of the Sea, The Lovely Lady and Other Stories, Lizzie Limpet and Other Stories, Willie Wagtail and Other Tales, Safe Going, Out of the Night, Young Pioneers*). Auckland, Whitcombe and Tombs, 10 vols., 1923-34; *Drums of the Sea* published London, Burns Oates, 1939.
The Long Bright Land: Fairy Tales from Southern Seas, illustrated by Dorothy P. Lathrop. Boston, Little Brown, 1929.
The Great Experiment, illustrated by William Smith. London, Dent, 1932.

PUBLICATIONS FOR ADULTS

Other

Stewart Island. Christchurch, Whitcombe and Tombs, 1913.
Marlborough Sounds: The Waters of Restfulness. Auckland, Whitcombe and Tombs, 1919.
Tales Out of School. Auckland, Whitcombe and Tombs, 1919.
The World So Full. London, Cassell, 1922.

* * *

Edith Howes was a school teacher whose major interest was nature study, and a great many of her stories have the strongly didactic intention of informing children about New Zealand's bush, beach, and marine life.

Writing within the fashion of the period she delivered her messages through the medium of fantasy, and every variety of gossamer-winged fairy flits through the pages of her books. The most famous was *The Cradle Ship,* which ran into numerous editions and was translated into French, Italian, and Danish. Daringly advanced for the period it aimed to teach children "the facts of life" when twins who wanted to know where the new baby had come from were taken by their mother onto the Cradle Ship. On their voyage they saw every variety of animal with its young, beginning with insects and fish who abandoned their eggs, progressing to the more caring birds, marsupials, and mammals, until they finally understood that human babies "grow beneath their Mother's heart."

Edith Howes believed firmly in the power of knowledge and deplored the prevailing secrecy in sexual matters. In an adventure story for older readers, *The Golden Forest,* she left the reader in no doubt that a young man had died from venereal disease: "he wasted his youth, he depleted his vitality...there must be growth and maturity before the giving of cells." The speaker is the boy's father who concluded, "You are fortified, strengthened, cleansed by knowledge."

When liberated from the sentimental "Flower Fairy" syndrome, Howes wrote directly and well, as in the first really indigenous New Zealand adventure story, *Silver Island,* which has the Swiss Family Robinson theme of a family of children marooned on an off-shore island. *Riverside Family* gives a good picture of a country family of the period, and *Young Pioneers* is a well-researched story about early settlers. These are the books which still appeal; her fairy stories can only be regarded as interesting period pieces.

—Betty Gilderdale

HUDSON, Jan

Nationality: Canadian. **Born:** Janis Wiedrick in Calgary, Alberta, 27 April 1954. **Education:** University of Calgary, B.A. 1978; University of Alberta, L.L.B. 1984. **Family:** Married Ernie Emil Hudson in 1977 (divorced); one stepdaughter. **Career:** Legal editor and writer; legal researcher, administrative assistant, and editor for Attorney General of British Columbia. **Awards:** Canada Council Children's Literature Prize, and Canadian Library Association Book of the Year for Children, both 1984, both for *Sweetgrass*; Parents' Choice Award, and Notable Book and Best Book for Young Adults Citation, American Library Association, both 1989, both for *Dawn Rider*; R. Ross Annett Award, Writers Guild of Alberta, 1991. **Died:** Edmonton, Alberta, 22 April 1990.

Publications for Children

Fiction

Sweetgrass. Edmonton, Tree Frog Press, 1984; New York, Philomel Books, 1989.

Dawn Rider. Toronto, HarperCollins, 1990; New York, Philomel Books 1990.

*

Critical Studies: "Portraits: Jan Hudson" by Dave Jenkinson, in *Emergency Librarian,* Vol. 12, September-October 1984, 46-47; "The Plains Truth: Indians and Metis in Recent Fiction" by Raymond E. Jones, in *Children's Literature Association Quarterly,* Vol. 12, Spring 1987, 36-39; "Jan Hudson," in *Canadian Books for Children: A Guide to Authors and Illustrators,* by Jon C. Stott and Raymond E. Jones, Toronto, Harcourt Brace Jovanovich Canada, 1988, 78-80.

* * *

Jan Hudson had only a brief career, dying of respiratory failure shortly before the publication of her second novel. Nevertheless, she earned a significant place among Canadian writers for children. Combining an anthropologist's detailed knowledge of Plains Indian culture and a contemporary feminist's concern for the treatment of females in a patriarchal society, Hudson produced well-researched and entertaining historical fiction.

Because her first novel, *Sweetgrass,* won Canada's two most prestigious awards for children's writing, Hudson became a celebrity. She was not, however, a true overnight success. As Jon C. Stott and Raymond E. Jones note in *Canadian Books for Children,* Hudson frequently described herself as "a rewriter, not a writer"; she thus produced seventeen drafts of her novel over a five-year period. As she learned more about her craft and her own attitudes to her subject, the book underwent a conceptual change. When she began it, Hudson has said, she intended to write an adventure portraying native life in nineteenth-century Alberta. Believing that she could get the book published only if the adventures appealed to boys, she made the central character a male. Eventually, Hudson listened to her own inner voice and changed the main character to a girl. In doing so, she transformed a formulaic adventure into a novel that is both a moving study of social codes and a tense survival story.

Set in 1837, *Sweetgrass* focuses on the coming of age of the title character, a fifteen-year-old Blackfoot girl. The central conflict is between Sweetgrass and her father, Shaggy Bull, who represents patriarchal values. Sweetgrass loves and longs to marry a young warrior named Eagle Sun. Her desires are of little account, however, because her culture teaches that "Wanting is not right for a young woman." In fact, Sweetgrass lives in a bad time for Blackfoot females. Blackfoot men, eager for the horses, guns, and manufactured goods offered by white traders, have abandoned the tradition of monogamy because they need extra wives to tan the great number of hides required for trade. Sweetgrass thus fears that, like her impoverished friend Pretty Girl, she will be forced into a polygamous marriage in which she will be little more than a slave.

The first-person narrative clearly portrays Sweetgrass as bitter that she lacks power and freedom merely because she is a female. Sweetgrass thus repeatedly expresses envy of her little brother who has choices, who gets more respect than she does, and who seldom receives the criticism that is her daily lot. Nevertheless to prove to her father that she is mature and worthy of choosing her own husband, she behaves in the fashion expected of Blackfoot girls and does not complain. When her father burdens her with tasks designed to show that marriage is not romantic, she silently endures the drudgery. The only support that she receives comes from her grandmother, a warrior woman who represents the independent females of the past. When Sweetgrass shows bravery during an Assiniboin attack on their camp, grandmother proclaims that Sweetgrass will also become a warrior woman.

The second part of the novel is a survival story in which physical suffering tests the maturity and develops the inner power of Sweetgrass. Sweetgrass begins to show her abilities after her father leaves the starving family's isolated winter camp to seek game. When smallpox strikes, Sweetgrass takes charge because the only remaining adult, her Almost-Mother, is paralyzed with grief over the death of her baby. Resisting the urge to desert her sick family, Sweetgrass employs all of her once-hated female skills to nurse them and feed them. Finally, unable to find food, she shows her inner strength and resourcefulness by accepting that she must violate the taboo against eating fish if she is to save the family. Sweetgrass thus demonstrates that a woman need not be a warrior to be a hero. When her father finally returns and realizes all that she has done, he rewards her, granting her the right to marry the man she loves.

Sweetgrass is a vivid presentation of Blackfoot life. What makes it gripping, however, is its psychological focus. Modern without being anachronistic, this novel evokes the tensions that a female experiences when society unfairly restricts her. It shows the strength females need to cope with imposed social inferiority, and it celebrates the heroic selflessness they demonstrate in spite of it. In fact, this tough-minded novel makes only one concession to the conventions of popular romance: Sweetgrass alone avoids having her face scarred by smallpox.

Dawn Rider is also about a Blackfoot female coming of age within a restrictive society, but it is set in the early eighteenth-century, when the Blackfoot people first acquired horses. The central character, Kit Fox, is a sixteen-year-old who believes that she is nothing special to anyone because she is both a middle child and a girl. Kit Fox does feel special, however, to the fiercely wild horse her tribe has just acquired because it lets her touch him. Although she has had a sacred dream about riding a horse, her tribe's elders believe that riding horses is for males and therefore refuse to let her near the horse again. Eventually, Kit Fox proves that she is special. When her camp suffers a surprise attack, she does the only thing that will save her people: she rides the horse to summon help. In addition to proving that she is special, Kit Fox matures psychologically, recognizing that she loves and wants to marry a young man whom she had thought to be merely a friend.

Kit Fox's struggle to achieve psychological maturity and social acceptance occurs against the background of the domestic lives of three generations of her family and a full range of tribal activities: a buffalo hunt, a celebratory dance, a war party, a young man's ritual display of bravery, and a marriage ceremony. These scenes exude historical authenticity, but most of them are set pieces displaying native customs; they are not essential to communicating the anxieties and developing maturation of Kit Fox. Consequently, *Dawn Rider* lacks a tight social and psychological focus.

Jan Hudson did not have the chance to develop into a major talent, but she deserves respect for writing *Sweetgrass.* This gripping novel portrays accurately, intelligently, and sensitivity a group too often ignored in historical literature: native women.

—Raymond E. Jones

HUGHES, Shirley

Nationality: British. **Born:** Hoylake, Lancashire, 16 July 1929. **Education:** West Kirby High School for Girls; Liverpool Art School; Ruskin School of Art, Oxford. **Family:** Married John Vulliamy in 1952; two sons and one daughter. **Career:** Freelance illustrator and writer. Member of the Management Committee, Society of Authors, 1983-86. Since 1985 member of the Registrar's Advisory Committee for Public Lending Right; member, The Council of the Society of Authors; chair, Children's Writers Group of the Society of Authors, 1994-96. **Awards:** Children's Rights Workshop Other award, 1976; Library Association Kate Greenaway Medal, 1977; Eleanor Farjeon award, 1984; honorary fellow, Library Association (United Kingdom), 1997. **Address:** c/o Bodley Head, Random House, 20 Vauxhall Bridge Road, London SW1V 2SA, England.

Publications for Children (illustrated by the author)

Fiction

Lucy and Tom's Day. London, Gollancz, and New York, Scott, 1960.

The Trouble with Jack. London, Bodley Head, 1970.

Lucy and Tom Go to School. London, Gollancz, 1973.

Sally's Secret. London, Bodley Head, 1973.

Helpers. London, Bodley Head, 1975; as *George the Babysitter,* Englewood Cliffs, New Jersey, Prentice Hall, 1977.

Lucy and Tom at the Seaside. London, Gollancz, 1976.

Dogger. London, Bodley Head, and New York, Mulberry, 1977; as *David and Dog,* Englewood Cliffs, New Jersey, Prentice Hall, 1978.

It's Too Frightening for Me! London, Hodder and Stoughton, 1977; as *Haunted House,* Englewood Cliffs, New Jersey, Prentice Hall, 1978.

Moving Molly. London, Bodley Head, 1978; Englewood Cliffs, New Jersey, Prentice Hall, 1979.

Up and Up. London, Bodley Head, and Englewood Cliffs, New Jersey, Prentice Hall, 1979.

Here Comes Charlie Moon. London, Bodley Head, 1980; New York, Lothrop, 1986.

Lucy and Tom's Christmas. London, Gollancz, 1981; New York, Viking Kestrel, 1986.

Alfie Gets in First. London, Bodley Head, 1981; New York, Lothrop, 1982.

Alfie's Feet. London, Bodley Head, and New York, Lothrop, 1982.

Alfie Gives a Hand. London, Bodley Head, and New York, Lothrop, 1983.

An Evening at Alfie's. London, Bodley Head, and New York, Lothrop, 1984.

Charlie Moon and the Big Bonanza Bust-up. London, Bodley Head, 1982.

Lucy and Tom's ABC. London, Gollancz, 1984; New York, Viking Kestrel, 1986.

Chips and Jessie. London, Bodley Head, 1985; New York, Lothrop, 1986.

Nursery Collection (*Bathwater's Hot, When We Went to the Park, Noisy, All Shapes and Sizes, Colours, Two Shoes New Shoes*). London, Walker, and New York, Lothrop, 6 vols., 1985-86.

Another Helping of Chips. London, Bodley Head, 1986; New York, Lothrop, 1987.
Lucy and Tom's 123. London, Gollancz, and New York, Viking Kestrel, 1987.
The Big Alfie and Annie Rose Storybook. London, Bodley Head, 1988; New York, Lothrop, 1989.
Angel Mae: A Tale of Trotter Street. London, Walker, 1989; New York, Morrow, 1992.
The Big Concrete Lorry: A Tale of Trotter Street. London, Walker, 1989.
The Snow Lady: A Tale of Trotter Street. London, Walker, 1990.
Wheels: A Tale of Trotter Street. London, Walker, 1991.
The Big Alfie Out of Doors Storybook. London, Bodley Head, and New York, Lothrop, Lee & Shepard, 1992.
The Alfie Collection. New York, Morrow, 1993.
Stories by Firelight. London, Bodley Head, and New York, Lothrop, Lee & Shepard, 1993.
Bouncing. London, Walker, and Cambridge, Massachusetts, Candlewick Press, 1993.
Giving. London, Walker, and Cambridge, Massachusetts, Candlewick Press, 1993.
Hiding. London, Walker, and Cambridge, Massachusetts, Candlewick Press, 1994.
Chatting. London, Walker, and Cambridge, Massachusetts, Candlewick, 1994.
Enchantment in the Garden. London, Bodley Head, and New York, Lothrop, Lee & Shepard, 1996.
Playing (selected from *Giving, Hiding, Chatting, and Bouncing*). London, Walker, and Cambridge, Massachusetts, Candlewick, 1997.
Alfie and the Birthday Surprise. London, Bodley Head, and New York, Lothrop, 1997.
The Lion and the Unicorn, London and New York, Dorling Kindersley, 1998.

Poetry

Out and About. London, Walker, and New York, Lothrop, 1988.
Rhymes for Annie Rose. London, Bodley Head, and New York, Lothrop, 1995.

Other

Editor, *Over the Moon: A Book of Sayings.* London, Faber, 1980.

*

Critical Studies: "Hughes in Flight" by Aidan Chambers, in *Horn Book* (Boston), Vol. 56 , 1980, 211-15; "Drawn towards Children" by Susan Thomas, in *Times Educational Supplement,* 27 May 1994, A3.

Illustrator: *World's End Was Home* by Nan Chauncy, 1952; *Follow the Footprints,* 1953, *The World Upside Down,* 1954, and *The Toffee Join,* 1968, all by William Mayne; *Little Women* by Louisa May Alcott, 1953; *All Through the Night* by Rachel Field, 1954; *The Bell Family,* 1954, *New Town,* 1960, and *The Painted Garden* revised edition, 1961, all by Noel Streatfeild; *The Journey of Johnny Rew* by Anne Mainwaring Barrett, 1954; *Mr. Punch's Cap* by Kathleen Fidler, 1956; *The Man of the House* by Allan Campbell McLean, 1956; *William and the Lorry,* 1956, and *The Merry-Go-Round,* 1963, both by Diana Ross; *Guns in the Wild,* 1956, *Katy at Home,* 1957, and *Katy at School,* 1959, all by Ian Serraillier; *Lost Lorrenden,* 1956, *Fiona on the Fourteenth Floor,* 1964, *The Sign of the Unicorn,* 1968, *The Wood Street Group,* 1970, *The Wood Street Secret,* 1970, *The Wood Street Rivals,* 1971, *The Wood Street Helpers,* 1973, and *Away from Wood Street,* 1976, all by Mabel Esther Allan; *Adventure on Rainbow Island,* 1957, *The Jade Green Cadillac,* 1958, *The Lost Tower Treasure,* 1960, *The Singing Strings,* 1961, and *Operation Smuggle,* 1964, all by Dorothy Clewes; *The Boy and the Donkey* by Diana Pullein-Thompson, 1958; *Rolling On,* 1960, *Mary Ann Goes to Hospital,* 1961, and *Cottage by the Lock,* 1962, all by Mary Cockett; *Flowering Spring* by Elfrida Vipont, 1960; *The Curious Adventures of Tabby* by E.H. Lang, 1959; *Fell Farm Campers* by Marjorie Lloyd, 1960; *The Bronze Chrysanthemum* by Sheena Porter, 1960; *Fairy Tales,* 1961, and *More Fairy Tales,* 1970, both by Hans Christian Andersen; *Plain Jane,* 1961, *Place Mill,* 1962, and *A Stone in a Pool,* 1964, all by Barbara Softly; *Willy Is My Brother* by Peggy Parish, 1963; *Tales of Tigg's Farm,* 1963, *Meet Mary Kate,* 1963, *A Dream of Dragons,* 1965, *Satchkin Patchkin,* 1966, *Mary Kate and the Jumble Bear* [*School Bus*], 2 vols., 1967-70, *Mrs. Pinny and the Blowing Day* [*Sudden Snow, Salty Sea Day*], 3 vols., 1968-72, and *Mother Farthing's Luck,* 1971, all by Helen Morgan; *The Shinty Boys,* 1963, and *The New Tenants,* 1968, both by Margaret MacPherson; *Tim Rabbit's Dozen,* 1964, and *From Spring to Spring,* 1978, both by Alison Uttley; *Stories for Seven-Year-Olds* [*Six-Year-Olds, Five-Year-Olds, Under-Fives, Nine-Year-Olds*] and *More Stories for Seven-Year-Olds,* all edited by Sara and Stephen Corrin, 6 vols., 1964-79; *Roller Skates,* 1964, and *Lucinda's Year of Jubilo,* 1965, both by Ruth Sawyer; *The Cat and Mrs. Cary* by Doris Gates, 1964; *Stories from Grimm,* 1964; *Tales the Muses Told* by Roger Lancelyn Green, 1965; *The Twelve Dancing Princesses,* 1965; *Kate and the Family Tree,* 1965, *The Smallest Doll,* 1966, and *The Smallest Bridesmaid,* 1966, all by Margaret Storey; *The Faber Book of Nursery Stories* edited by Barbara Ireson, 1966; *The Witch's Daughter,* 1966, and *Squib,* 1971, both by Nina Bawden; *Little Bear's Pony,* 1966, and *Hazy Mountain,* 1975, both by Donald Bisset; *Wayland's Keep* by Angela Bull, 1966; *Porterhouse Major* by Margaret J. Baker, 1967; *Home and Away* by Ann Thwaite, 1967; *A Day on Big O,* 1968, *Rainbow Pavement,* 1970, and *Donkey Days,* 1977, all by Helen Cresswell; *My Naughty Little Sister* series by Dorothy Edwards, 10 vols., 1968-91; *A Crown for a Queen,* 1968, *The Toymaker's Daughter,* 1968, *Malkin's Mountain* revised edition, 1970, *The Three Toymakers* revised edition, 1970, and *Bogwoppit,* 1978, all by Ursula Moray Williams; *Flutes and Cymbals* edited by Leonard Clark, 1968; *The Bicycle Wheel,* 1969, *The Ruth Ainsworth Book,* 1970, *The Phantom Fisherboy,* 1974, *The Phantom Roundabout,* 1977, and *The Pirate Ship and Other Stories,* 1980, all by Ruth Ainsworth; *Moshie Cat,* 1969, and *Federico,* 1971, both by Helen Griffiths; *Voices in the* Fog, by Elizabeth Cheatham Walton, 1969; *Goldie* by Irma Chelton, 1969; Cinderella by Charles Perrault, 1970; *Eight Days to Christmas,* 1970, and *Ginger,* 1972, both by Geraldine Kaye; *The Lost Angel* by Elizabeth Goudge, 1971; *The Smell of Privet* by Barbara Sleigh, 1971; *Burnish Me Bright* by Julia W. Cunningham, 1971; *The Little Broomstick* by Mary Stewart, 1971; *Dancing Day* by Robina Willson, 1971; *Robbie's Mob,* by Jo Rice, 1971; *The*

Thirteen Days of Christmas by Jenny Overton, 1972; *A House in the Square* by Joan G. Robinson, 1972; *The First [Second, Third] Margaret Mahy Story Book,* 3 vols., 1972-75; *Hospital Day* by Leila Berg, 1972; *Mother's Help* by Susan Dickinson, 1972; *The Hollywell Family* by Margaret Kornitzer, 1973; *The Gauntlet Fair* by Alison Farthing, 1974; *Jacko and Other Stories* by Jean Sutcliffe, 1974; *Miss Hendy's House* by Joan Drake, 1974; *Peter Pan and Wendy* retold by May Byron, 1976; *The Snake Crook* by Ruth Tomalin, 1976; *Tattercoats and Other Folk* Tales, edited by Winifred Finlay, 1976; *Make Hay While the Sun Shines* edited by Alison Abel, 1977; *A Throne for Sesame* by Helen Young, 1977; *Trouble with Dragons* by Oliver Selfridge, 1978; *The Snailman* by Brenda Sivers, 1978; *Pottle Pig* by Nancy Northcote, 1978; *Witchdust* by Mary Welfare, 1980; *A Cat's Tale* by Rikki Cate, 1982; *Five to Eight* by Dorothy Butler, 1985; *The Secret Garden* by Frances Hodgson Burnett, 1988; *The Boy Who Bounced and Other Magic* Tales, 1986, *The Horrible Story and Others,* 1987, *Chocolate Porridge and Other Stories,* 1989, and *The Girl with the Green Ear: Stories About Magic in Nature,* 1992, all by Margaret Mahy; *The Baby Pack* by Penelope Leach, 1990; *Rainbow Tales* by Alison Utley, 1991; *The Railway Children* by E. Nesbit, 1994.

Shirley Hughes comments:

I was born and brought up in a quiet, well-behaved suburb of Liverpool. When in childhood our lives were rudely interrupted by World War II we went to school carrying gas masks, saved up mountains of silver paper, and learned to knit mufflers for the troops (mine were rather long, as I never quite got the hang of casting off). Wartime, when it's not frightening, is intolerably dull. We combatted boredom by reading, writing, and illustrating stories and getting up plays. Later we became hopelessly stage and movie struck. On the whole, an ideal upbringing for someone fascinated by visual narrative.

After art school I freelanced as an illustrator and learned that a story for a young child is not words with pictures added at a later stage to make the thing more attractive but must evolve as a unified whole from the outset, like making a film. I use sketchbooks all the time. You develop an eye for a telling gesture, for the way people, especially children, group themselves when absorbed in a game or conversation, for emotion revealed in hands and feet as well as faces. You develop a memory bank of observations, them you go home and make it all up.

A successful picture book gets read aloud over and over again, often in nightly succession. However short the text you aim to make it flow like a poem but with much of the characterisation, the background, and humour there to be discovered in the pictures. A delightful dialogue emerges, with the child making all sorts of contributions. It is one of the great shared pleasures of early childhood, and one of the most satisfying and demanding of audiences which any author could aspire to address.

* * *

Over the years of Shirley Hughes's remarkable creativity and output, children's visual literacy has grown in competence and complexity. Television, advertising, and picture books have contributed to this process, especially in the early stages of reading. From words and images, late twentieth-century children now pick up narrative cues very quickly.

Shirley Hughes's response to this is *Stories by Firelight,* a book of great subtlety, three years in the making, which entices readers into new literary experiences. She describes it as "a combination of prose, verses and paintings to celebrate the winter season." The pages glow with early sunsets and firelight looped with deep shadows for half-seen images and lurking magic. The three main stories are reading adventures for those who have outgrown their earlier picture books. The first story has at its heart the Gaelic folk tale of the selkie or seal-wife who, tricked into living on land, bears children, but at last returns to the sea. This is embedded in another narrative, of a schoolgirl who is convalescing in the house of an artist who paints seascapes and tells her about the selkie. The device works by means of shifts in page design and the colours and tones of the two tellings. This rich intricacy makes the way it works quite clear to the reader and, at the same time, is a double magic, because the whole is about imagination—inner seeing as well as outer looking.

The second tale, "A Midwinter Night's Dream" has no words; the reader's self-telling has to do it all. A small boy wanders in his dream in a nether world full of passages and caves filled with small fantastic creatures, clear in all their unlikely detail to the reader, but, as the artist says, "just outside the firelight", like other half-perceptions in reading that children enjoy but can't begin to explain. Here are traces of other literary and artistic inheritances, details from the artist's sketchbooks of places where inspiration mingled with current awareness of the fragility of ancient treasures the young might never see, like the angel in the town hall of Siena, in a world threatened by different kinds of vandalism. The intrepid night wanderer isn't afraid of gargoyles, gryphons, the inhabitants of old stories, a threatening bird with a light bulb in its beak. He finds himself in the whale's mouth (Jonah and Kipling for bookish adults), before he returns to bed, through time and space again designed as shifts of tone and colour in the background of the action. In the third story, William and his grandfather are dismantling the Christmas tree to burn it in the garden. William is plagued by guilt at having opened a special box in his grandfather's room without telling him. When his grandfather tips the contents of the box on to the last of the bonfire William confesses what he has done and learns an unexpected lesson. His grandfather watches the fire burn low. The gaps in the text are for growing readers, as are the feelings, reflected in the firelight. In between the stories are poems which echo their originals in Hardy and Milton, another intertext of rhythm, sound and meanings. This is an important book, which could have been four different books. But the totality is both traditional, in the best sense of "retelling," and at the same time it is a post-modern production, the work of a mature artist whose intellectual grasp of the kinds of text contemporary children read is matched by her imagination and skill.

One can see how Shirley Hughes has children's reading and understanding development at heart by looking at the differences between the books for babies and pre-school readers and those that children are likely to read for themselves. These differences are apparent throughout her long and distinguished career, and indeed the success of some of her picture books in translation shows their universality. Recent books for the very young include *Giving, Bouncing, Chatting,* and *Hiding.* The activities described in these books are especially interesting. As they learn language, children name not only things but also events attached to the things words describe, although the context and details are different. Thus hiding behind curtains is the same as, but different from, hiding one's feelings. Giving goes with a present, a tea party, a cross look. What psycholinguists take pages to explain, Shirley Hughes clearly shows as action in context, so that the reader puts the two together and separates out the differences.

This kind of book cohesion develops readerly imagination. Shirley Hughes's books are interwoven with each other in that the world of children is recognizably the same in each. Alfie and Annie Rose, for example, grow as their readers do. In *The Big Alfie Out of Doors Story Book,* Alfie has new experiences, such as sleeping in a tent and waking up to be the only person about, and learning to tolerate the loss of something precious. The listening or early reader begins to feel different layers of meaning. *Rhymes for Annie Rose* focuses more on Annie, who was a follower in earlier Alfie stories. In *Alfie and the Birthday Surprise,* a more serious theme emerges as Alfie and his family try to help their neighbor, Bob McNally, recover from the loss of his beloved cat, Smoky. Hughes takes this story from an unusual angle as it is the adult neighbor who grieves while the children are more detached and analytical (though sympathetic). Her subtly colored illustrations convey emotion without the slightest touch of sentimentality.

The children in the series of books called *Tales of Trotter Street* are different although, in London, the shift in the landscape is not a great distance. They are a multicultural group, streetwise, with working mothers. The stable features of their lives are neighborliness, social and peer pressure, shared anxieties about child-minding, bikes, and babies. What, in the text, seems to be descriptive writing underlined by the pictures is in fact the complexity of everyday living in cities: the amazing, cramped, *things-ness* of it all in *The Big Concrete Lorry*; the mixed preoccupations of a young schoolchild in *Angel Mae*; passionate peer-group longings in *Wheels*; and the unease of being less than kind in *The Snow Lady.* Each book is a totality of seeing, thinking, and feeling.

Two recent books for middle-grade readers have been somewhat less successful. *Enchantment in the Garden,* a fantasy set in Italy during the 1920s, concerns a solitary young girl who brings a statue to life. Reviewers felt that the characteristic Hughes style was too overpowering for the fantasy mode and criticized the slow pace of the narrative. *The Lion and the Unicorn,* offered by the new DK Ink fiction line, also strikes out into territory Hughes has not tried before. In this World War II story, a Jewish boy from London must cope with the physical and psychological stresses of being evacuated to the countryside. The subject of child evacuees has been explored so well and so often before, notably by Nina Bawden in *Carrie's War* and Michelle Magorian in *Good Night, Mr. Tom,* that Hughes's competent book does not stand out above the rest as do her picture books for the very young.

All our concerns about children learning to read are upheld and helped by the work of Shirley Hughes. Right at the beginning of their encounters with the literary, children discover what reading can be like. Later, when children take books in hand for themselves, they confidently inhabit the worlds of the characters who have become familiar. When they take the bigger step of discovering just how many complex, intriguing, and beautiful forms of imaginative reading there are, they will expect adventures and surprises. Two generations of readers, at least, have reason to be grateful to Shirley Hughes for all of these experiences. The recent success of her books translated into Welsh, French, Spanish, and Chinese attest to her enduring qualities.

—Margaret Meek, updated by Caroline C. Hunt

HULL, Katharine, and WHITLOCK, Pamela

Nationality: British. **HULL, Katharine: Born:** London, 18 July 1921. **Education:** St. Mary's Convent, Ascot, Berkshire; Lady Margaret Hall, Oxford. **Military Service:** Women's Royal Air Force, 1941-45: Flight Officer. **Family:** Married Paul Buxton in 1950 (divorced 1970); two sons and one daughter. **Died:** November 1977. **WHITLOCK, Pamela (Frances): Born:** Penang, Malaysia, 21 March 1920. **Education:** St. Mary's Convent, Ascot, Berkshire, 1934-39. **Military Service:** Women's Royal Air Force, 1941-45. **Family:** Married John Bell in 1954; five daughters. **Career:** Publicity assistant, Jonathan Cape, publishers, London, 1939-40; children's books editor, Collins, publishers, London, 1946-52, and founding editor, *Collins Magazine,* 1947-52; children's books editor, Oxford University Press, in the 1950s. **Died:** 3 June 1982.

Publications for Children

Fiction (illustrated by Pamela Whitlock)

The Far-Distant Oxus. London, Cape, 1937; New York, Macmillan, 1938.
Escape to Persia. London, Cape, 1938; New York, Macmillan, 1939.
Oxus in Summer. London, Cape, 1939; New York, Macmillan, 1940.
Crowns. London, Cape, 1947.

Other by Pamela Whitlock

Editor, *All Day Long: An Anthology of Poetry for Children,* illustrated by Joan Hassall. London, Oxford University Press, 1954.
Editor, *The Open Book: A Collection of Stories, Essays, Poems, Songs and Music,* illustrated by Marcia Lane Foster. London, Collins, and New York, Kenedy, 1956.

* * *

The initial claim to fame of Katharine Hull and Pamela Whitlock arose from the fact that they were teenagers when their first book was written. That *The Far-Distant Oxus* is still read with enjoyment over 50 years later indicates that it had more than curiosity value. It is basically a holiday adventure story with all the elements loved by young readers: ponies, camping, and an absence of interfering adults. Readers identify with the exploits of the six children on Exmoor because they imagine they would enjoy this sort of self-directed holiday. It is full of incident, ranging from the trivial to the epic, but the difficulties they encounter are not ignored. The journey by raft down the "Oxus" to the sea, for instance is undertaken with never a thought of how they will get back against the current.

Although there are obvious parallels with writers like Arthur Ransome and M.E. Atkinson, there is nothing imitative about *The Far-Distant Oxus* and its sequels. The authors had a direct, clear style, and the dialogue and continuous action, pared of unnecessary description, carry the reader through the now unfashionable length of the stories. There is, however, a certain amateurish qual ity in the writing. The characterisation is less detailed and deep than it might be and the children have a tendency to make speeches rather than to talk.

This is not true of the more mature *Crowns,* a later book not in the Oxus sequence. This is also wish-fulfilment of a kind in which four cousins invent a private kingdom where they can order things to suit their own natures: romantic, organising, impulsive, or solitary and contemplative. Through their imaginings they discover more about what they want in life and what they are. Their "real" lives—comfortable, middle-class, and monied—are sharply observed and their secret world vividly imagined.

—Valerie Brinkley-Willsher

HUNT, Francesca. See **HOLLAND, Isabelle.**

HUNT, Mabel Leigh

Nationality: American. **Born:** Coatesville, Indiana, 1 November 1892. **Education:** DePauw University, Greencastle, Indiana, 1910-12; Western Reserve University Library School, Cleveland, 1923-24. **Career:** Children's and branch librarian, Indianapolis, 1926-38. **Died:** 3 September 1971.

Publications for Children

Fiction

Lucinda, A Little Girl of 1860, illustrated by Cameron Wright. New York, Stokes, 1934.
The Boy Who Had No Birthday, illustrated by Cameron Wright. New York, Stokes, 1935.
Little Girl with Seven Names, illustrated by Grace Paull. New York, Stokes, 1936.
Susan, Beware!, illustrated by Mildred Boyle. New York, Stokes, 1937.
Benjie's Hat, illustrated by Grace Paull. New York, Stokes, 1938.
Little Grey Gown, illustrated by Ilse Bischoff. New York, Stokes, 1939.
Michel's Island, illustrated by Kate Seredy. New York, Stokes, 1940.
John of Pudding Lane, illustrated by Clotilde Funk. New York, Stokes, 1941.
Billy Button's Butter'd Biscuit, illustrated by Katherine Milhous. New York, Stokes, 1941; London, Standard Art Book Company, 1943.
Corn-Belt Billy, illustrated by Kurt Wiese. New York, Grosset and Dunlap, 1942.
Peter Piper's Pickled Peppers, illustrated by Katherine Milhous. New York, Stokes, 1942; London, Standard Art Book Company, 1943.
The Peddler's Clock, illustrated by Elizabeth Orton Jones. New York, Grosset and Dunlap, 1943.
Young Man of the House, illustrated by Louis Slobodkin. Philadelphia, Lippincott, 1944.
Sibby Botherbox, illustrated by Marjory Collison. Philadelphia, Lippincott, 1945.
Such a Kind World, illustrated by Edna Potter. New York, Grosset and Dunlap, 1947.
The Double Birthday Present, illustrated by Elinore Blaisdell. Philadelphia, Lippincott, 1947.
Matilda's Buttons, illustrated by Elinore Blaisdell. Philadelphia, Lippincott, 1948.
The Wonderful Baker, illustrated by Grace Paull. Philadelphia, Lippincott, 1950.
The 69th Grandchild, illustrated by Elinore Blaisdell. Philadelphia, Lippincott, 1951.
Ladycake Farm, illustrated by Clotilde Funk. Philadelphia, Lippincott, 1952.
Singing among Strangers, illustrated by Irene Gibian. Philadelphia, Lippincott, 1954.
Miss Jellytot's Visit, illustrated by Velma Ilsley. Philadelphia, Lippincott, 1955.
Stars for Cristy, illustrated by Velma Ilsley. Philadelphia, Lippincott, 1956; London, Blackie, 1958.
Cristy at Skippinghills, illustrated by Velma Ilsley. Philadelphia, Lippincott, 1958; London, Blackie, 1960.
Cupola House, illustrated by Nora S. Unwin. Philadelphia, Lippincott, 1961.
Johnny-Up and Johnny-Down, illustrated by Harold Berson. Philadelphia, Lippincott, 1962.
Beggar's Daughter. Philadelphia, Lippincott, 1963.

Other

"Have You Seen Tom Thumb?" (biography of Charles Sherwood Stratton), illustrated by Fritz Eichenberg. New York, Stokes, 1942.
Better Known as Johnny Appleseed, illustrated by James Daugherty. Philadelphia, Lippincott, 1950.
Tomorrow Will Be Bright (reader), illustrated by Tommy Shoemaker. Boston, Ginn, 1958.

*

Manuscript Collections: Kerlan Collection, University of Minnesota, Minneapolis.

* * *

An author whose books appeal chiefly to pre-teenage girls, Mabel Leigh Hunt drew on her Quaker upbringing for several of her stories. *Lucinda,* her first book, the story of an Indiana Quaker child during the Civil War, has been praised for its well-chiseled prose and for the author's power to evoke the feeling of the Indiana countryside. A second book about a Quaker child, *Little Girl with Seven Names* has retained its popularity, dealing as it does with a perennial childhood problem, the child who is teased in school because she is different. In Melissa-Louisa-Amanda-Miranda-Cynthia-Jane-Farlow's case, it is not her Quaker upbringing which brings her ridicule from her schoolmates, but her excessively long name. The ingenious way in which Melissa Louisa manages to rid herself of a couple of her forenames is the main thrust of the slim plot of this warm little book.

Miss Jellytot's Visit is the story of Kate O'Dea, who, after her mother has had a visitor, decides that she, too, wishes to be treated as a guest, and who, as Miss Jellytot, comes for a six-day "visit" to the O'Dea family. One of the first books to deal in a realistic, sympathetic way with a mother-child relationship, this gently humorous story still appeals to girls in the early grades.

Ladycake Farm, although it has been kept in print, has not fared as well as some of her other books at the hands of contemporary critics. One of the first books to attempt a realistic and sympathetic portrayal of blacks, it deals with a black family which buys a farm in a previously all-white area. Hard work and determination lead to the family's acceptance by their neighbors at the end of the story, but the father's advice to his children to smile in the face of insults has been felt by many reviewers to be degrading. In comparison with most current fiction for children about blacks, *Ladycake Farm* now seems dated; few children will read it with pleasure.

Hunt's juvenile biographies are characterized by meticulous research and a feeling for the kind of interesting detail which serves to make the period come alive for a young reader. Still in print, her *Better Known as Johnny Appleseed,* the life of the legendary John Chapman, was a Newbery Honor Book in 1951. Also well and accurately written is *"Have You Seen Tom Thumb?,"* a biography of the midget Charles Sherwood Stratton.

—Margaret F. Maxwell

HUNT, Peter (Leonard)

Nationality: British. **Born:** Rugby, Warwickshire, 2 September 1945 **Education:** University College of Wales, Aberystwyth, 1963-67, B.A. in English 1966, M.A. 1969; University of Wales, Cardiff, Ph.D. 1981. **Family:** Married Sarah Wilkinson in 1981; four daughters. **Career:** Lecturer in English, University of Wales Institute of Science and Technology, Cardiff, 1968-87. Senior Lecturer in English 1988-95, Reader in English 1995-96, Professor of English from 1996, University of Wales, Cardiff. Visiting Professor, University of Michigan, Arm Arbor, 1977; Visiting Lecturer, Massachusetts Institute of Technology, Cambridge, 1982. Principal Associate, John Kirkman Communication Consultancy, from 1983; Adjunct Professor, San Diego State University, 1990; Visiting Fellow, University of Wollongong, 1991. Fellow, Institute of Scientific and Technical Communicators. Member, International Research Society of Children's Literature. **Awards:** Society for Technical Communication (U.S.A.) award, 1987; Distinguished Scholarship Award, International Research Society for the Fantastic in the Arts, 1996. **Address:** West Sundial Cottage, Downend, Horsley, Stroud, Gloucestershire GL6 OPF, England. **E-mail Address:** HuntP@cardiff.ac.uk.

Publications for Children

Fiction

The Maps of Time. London, MacRae, 1983.
A Step Off the Path. London, MacRae, 1985.
Backtrack. London, MacRae, 1986; London, Walker 1992.
Sue and the Honey Machine. illustrated by Duncan Smith. London, MacRae, 1989.
Fay Cow and the Missing Milk. illustrated by Duncan Smith. London, MacRae, 1989; as *Fay Cow and the Honey Machine,* London, Walker, 1992; reissued in one volume, London, Walker, 1992.
Going Up. London, MacRae, 1989; London, Walker, 1991.

Publications for Adults

Children's Book Research in Britain. Cardiff, University of Wales, 1977; revised edition, with Beth Humphries and Sarah Wilkinson, Cardiff, University of Wales, 1982.
Critic into Author: Woodfield Lecture XIII. Huddersfield, Woodfield and Stanley, 1990.
Arthur Ransome. Boston, Twayne, 1991; revised as *Approaching Arthur Ransome,* London, Cape, 1992.
Criticism, Theory and Children's Literature. Oxford and Cambridge, Massachusetts, Blackwell, 1991.
An Introduction to Children's Literature. Oxford and New York, Oxford University Press, 1994.
The Wind in the Willows: A Fragmented Arcadia. New York, Twayne, 1994.

Editor, *Further Approaches to Research in Children's Literature.* Cardiff, University of Wales, 1982.
Editor, *Bevis* by Richard Jefferies. Oxford and New York, Oxford University Press, 1989.
Editor, *Children's Literature: The Development of Criticism.* London and New York, Routledge, 1990.
Editor, *Literature for Children: Contemporary Criticism.* London and New York, Routledge, 1992.
Editor, *Children's Literature: An Illustrated History.* London and New York, Oxford University Press, 1995.
Editor, *The Routledge International Companion Encyclopedia of Children's Literature.* London and New York, Routledge, 1996.

*

Peter Hunt comments:

As a professional academic, and critic of children's books, I feel that children should be treated with the greatest respect: and so, my first three novels are consciously experimental—trying to push back the possibilities of narrative and of style. As such, they are a "difficult" read, but that perhaps is one way to challenge the sophistication of other media. My newer books try to reach a wider audience by making style and structure less complex, while refusing to compromise on viewpoint and content. I hope that my commitment to narrative theory and the intelligence of developing readers comes out in the books. My publications for adults have been designed to both further the academic study of children's literature and to make it—and ideas about it—accessible to the widest possible audience. Although I have had to concentrate recently on books *about* children's literature, I am continuing to tell stories to, and to write experimental books for children.

* * *

The transition from critic to writer is so tricky that it is no[t] surprising so few have attempted it. One who has successfull[y] transfered from being a writer on children's books to a writer o[f] them is Peter Hunt. Well known for his series of essays on aspects of children's literature which appeared before his first novel was published, Hunt must be one of the few writers for young people to possess a Ph.D. in children's literature. His intellectually vigorous articles have been a regular feature of the journal *Signal*. Hunt's attitude towards children's books is illuminated by his three novels for young people and reinforces his belief that children's books benefit from experimentation.

The Maps of Time uses themes of fantasy, combines them with reality, and also comments on the art of telling stories. Four teenagers are on a camping holiday with Simon, a curate, and the younger, introverted Sam. Sam is a fascinating character whose personality emerges slowly in the slight glimpses the reader is given and whose full depth is hardly realised by the others in the party. His powers, recognised by the mysterious Harald, centre around a series of maps and a pencil Sam has bought in a second-hand bookshop in Hay on Wye. As the story emerges it is discovered that Sam can restore a part of the country to the last century by drawing around the map in pencil. This part of the narrative covers the main body of the book until a particularly climatic event occurs. Hunt then provides the reader with four different versions of subsequent events, one each from two of the teenagers which shows that the love affair that appears to have developed between them is in fact one-sided, one told at last through Sam's eyes, and one that could possibly have been the truth. The final chapter brings these threads together only to end on a note of uncertainty. *The Maps of Time* is a skillfully constructed piece of writing, with subtle characterisation often developing through oblique glimpses of personality and some felicities of style; Sam, for instance, is introduced to the reader as "hot and sweating and four years behind the others."

A Step off the Path is also experimental but in this case the attempt to be consistently clever seems to have overridden other considerations. A group of characters who might have stepped out of an Iris Murdoch novel (with names to match) is thrown together in a commune on the England-Wales border. While the four elder children—Seb, Perdy, Tim, and Anna—spend a camping weekend helping the last descendants of King Arthur's court escape over the border, fighting treachery both within and outside their ranks, Jo, Seb's sister, stays at home telling a remarkably similar story to the twins,Matt and Jassy. However, where does the reality start and the fiction end, the author asks, to the accompaniment of a series of quotations from the likes of D.H. Lawrence and Cyril Connolly and apposite comments from the novel's characters. Although the book contains some pleasing features (the Arthurian tribe is uncompromisingly realistic, Merlin being a particularly powerful creation), it fails mainly because it is too explicit and wordy. Hunt's first book benefitted as much by what was implied rather than stated: with some judicious pruning *A Step off the Path* might have achieved the same powerful effect.

Nevertheless there is nothing too clever about *Backtrack,* Hunt's next novel. An almost straightforward exposition of detection, it loses none of its effect by being more simple. Rill and Jack, thrown together by accident, develop a fascinating love-hate relationship as they unravel another accident which happened 70 years previously and in which, by chance, both of their great uncles were involved. The plots they discover change so quickly that again it is difficult to distinguish between fact and fiction, a feature emphasised by the apparently contemporary references to the accident scattered through the book which equally could be genuine or fabricated. *Backtrack* gets to the same point as *A Step off the Path*; however, it also successfully says what it wants to say and encompasses the quirky relationship between the two main protagonists.

Going up, is even simpler in its plot. It tells a not unusual story of two young people, Tom and Sue, and their exploits in their first year at university. Here they encounter hopeless romantics, drinking companions and neurotics who make up a typical student body. Their year is told with wit and humour and inevitably they end the year together. Hunt's main concessions to the cleverness he has shown in previous books are seen mainly in the quotes which begin chapter headings and in the glittering conversation demonstrated by many of the characters.

Hunt's writings have not often achieved easy popularity with either critics or children. There are some who would maintain that for this reason he would be wise not to pursue any experimentation. However, Hunt in his critic mode would be the first to say that children's tastes cannot be so easily assessed. There is a significant number of young people, not necessarily the most sophisticated or proficient readers, who would find these books both rewarding and beneficial.

—Keith Barker

HUNTER, Bernice Thurman

Nationality: Canadian. **Born:** 3 November 1922, Toronto, Ontario. **Education:** Runnymede Collegiate Institute, commercial diploma 1939. **Family:** Married Lloyd George Hunter 16 November 1942; two daughters. **Career:** Bookkeeper and machine operator, Eaton Co. Ltd., Toronto, 1942-70; general office clerk, 1970-75; writer. Volunteer worker for Canadian Cancer Society. **Awards:** Imperial Order of Daughters of the Empire (of Canada) award, 1981; IODE award, 1981; Vicky Metcalf award, 1990; Toronto Historical Commendation, 1994; City of Scarborough Bicentennial award, 1996. **Member:** Writers Union of Canada, Canadian Society of Children's Authors, Illustrators and Performers. **Address:** 3333 Finch Ave. E, Scarborough, Ontario M1S 2P4, Canada.

Publications for Children

Fiction

That Scatterbrain Booky. Richmond Hill, Ontario, Scholastic, 1981.
With Love from Booky. Richmond Hill, Ontario, Scholastic, 1983.
A Place for Margaret. Richmond Hill, Ontario, Scholastic, 1984.
As Ever, Booky. Richmond Hill, Ontario, Scholastic, 1985.
Margaret in the Middle. Richmond Hill, Ontario, Scholastic, 1986.
Lamplighter. Richmond Hill, Ontario, Scholastic, 1987.
Margaret on Her Way. Richmond Hill, Ontario, Scholastic, 1988.
The Railroader. Richmond Hill, Ontario, Scholastic, 1990.
The Firefighter. Richmond Hill, Ontario, Scholastic, 1991.
Hawk and Stretch. Richmond Hill, Ontario, Scholastic, 1994.
Amy's Promise. Richmond Hill, Ontario, Scholastic, 1996.

*

Bernice Thurman Hunter comments:

Those of my young readers who know me as "Booky" (Boo-key) will already know that most of my stories are based on real life and real people and that they are often set in the past.

For instance, "Booky" is based on my own childhood during The Great Depression. And *Lamplighter* is my father's story, set in the late 1800s. In the "Margaret" trilogy you find out what life was like for a friend of mine during the 1920s. And the adventures in *The Railroader* and *The Firefighter* take place in 40s and 50s.

The question I am most often asked by young people is: "How do you remember what happened so long ago? That stuff is history!" (Imagine my amazement when I discovered that my life is now considered history!)

Well, there are many ways to recapture the past besides remembering. One way that really worked for me was to ask someone, even older than me, to share their memories. That's how I came to write *Amy's Promise* (and the sequel to *Amy's Promise* which is in the works).

I was always fascinated with my cousin Amy's story, and I was grateful to her when she gave me permission to write it.

Amy is twelve years old when her story begins, but she was only six when she made an important promise to her dying mother. And that is the theme of the story: how Amy copes with that promise.

Somebody said: "Long term memory is the gift of old age." I think I've got it!

* * *

One of Canada's foremost writers of juvenile fiction employing historical settings, Bernice Thurman Hunter attracts middle school audiences through her consistent ability to create likeable, but ordinary, central juvenile characters whom she places in loving, supporting environments and surrounds with interesting, historically accurate details. In addition to providing readers with glimpses of everyday life during other time periods, Hunter's writings allow young readers to recognize that, while the fictional historical individuals encounter happenings unique to the era in which they live, the characters' emotional experiences parallel their own. Hunter's 10 books to date fall into two principal groupings: a pair of trilogies featuring female central characters, and four titles each utilizing a male protagonist.

The "Booky" trio, *That Scatterbrain Booky, With Love From Booky,* and *As Ever, Booky,* is essentially fictionalized autobiography. The books' contents consist of chronologically linked episodes drawn from Bernice's life during the Depression years as she grew up in Toronto, Ontario, the middle child of five in a financially poor but emotionally rich family. Beginning in September, 1932, when Beatrice "Booky" Thompson is 10, the series concludes seven years later with the outbreak of World War II. Pronounced "Boo-key," Booky is the actual nickname given Bernice by her mother. The chapters of the episodic plot, which record the large and small happenings within the family, can often stand alone as separate reads. The inclusion of pages reproduced from the Eaton's Catalog, excerpts from period newspapers, and numerous photos from the Thurman family albums enhances the 1930s atmosphere in these titles.

Hunter's second trilogy, the fictional "Margaret" books, includes *A Place for Margaret, Margaret in the Middle* and *Margaret on Her Way*. In the summer of 1925, 11-year-old Margaret Emerson, who has contracted tuberculosis, is sent to recover on the farm of her childless aunt and uncle. Though Margaret's illness is cured by September, her journey home is delayed, first when family members are quarantined and then when Margaret's mother gives birth to her tenth child. By the time Margaret can return to Toronto, the strong emotional bond that has formed among the threesome causes Aunt Marg and Uncle Herb to ask to have Margaret permanently, a request Margaret's child-rich parents grant. Margaret's relationship with the farm's Clydesdale horse leads to her decision to become a veterinarian, then a most unusual career choice for a female. While the three books' episodic plots record a range of everyday occurrences in Margaret's life, the central thread uniting the works is Margaret's gradual progress toward attaining her vocational choice in that day's more sexist society. The trilogy concludes with Margaret's 1932 high school graduation, which sees her "on her way" to veterinary college.

The titles of Hunter's next three books, *Lamplighter, The Railroader* and *The Firefighter,* suggest a vocational thrust to the books' plots. Of all of Hunter's books, *Lamplighter* uses the earliest time setting, 1888, and the youngest central character, Willie Adams, 6 3/4, who lives in a log house in northern Ontario. During a visit to Toronto with his mother, Willie encounters a lamplighter igniting the streets' gas lamps, an event which provides Willie with an answer to an uncle's persistent question: "What are you going to be when you grow up?" Since the book covers but a year in Willie's life, he makes little progress toward his goal, but readers do get to share fully in the life of an extended pioneer family as its members engage in such activities as preparing for Christmas, enduring a five-day blizzard, or burying one of their number.

While *The Railroader* and *The Firefighter* are acceptable reads, they are the least successful of Hunter's books, possibly because, in attempting to tell a complete story, Hunter moves away from her episodic, anecdotal style. Both books feature young boys who, while aspiring to a career, become heroes. In 1947, "Skip" Skinner, 12, hopes to work for the railroad some day, perhaps as an engineer. By befriending Charlie, the watchman who controls the crossing gates, Skip learns how to signal trains with a lantern, and, when Charlie has a heart attack, he uses this knowledge to prevent an accident. In 1955, recently orphaned Terry Dawson, 11, lives with his two spinster aunts in Toronto. Spending time hanging around the local fire hall, Terry becomes interested in firefighting. While he struggles with his grief, however, Terry's behaviour deteriorates, and his repeated presence at fires causes him to become an arson suspect—but Terry clears his name by spotting the firebug and alerting the authorities.

With *Hawk and Stretch,* Hunter returns both to the family and the style of the "Booky" books. Using the time period 1943-4 and Booky's younger brother Billy, aka Stretch, now 11, as the central character, Hunter exposes readers to the Second World War's effects on families. As well, the book considers the issue of friendship as Billy encounters Daniel "Hawk" Thunder, the new kid in school, and finds himself being forced to choose between an old and a new chum. Interestingly, by repeating a Thompson family ghost story, Hunter ties *Hawk and Stretch* and *Lamplighter* together.

—David H. Jenkinson

HUNTER, Norman (George Lorimer)

Nationality: British. **Born:** Sydenham, Kent, 23 November 1899. **Education:** Beckenham County School, Kent. **Military Service:** London Irish Rifles, and at Headquarters, 9th Division, 1918-19. **Family:** Married Sylvia Mary Rangel in 1923; one son and two daughters. **Career:** Chief copywriter, S.H. Benson Ltd., London, 1938-49, P.N. Barrett Company, Johannesburg, 1949-58, and Central Advertising Ltd., Johannesburg, 1958-70. Also a conjurer: performed at Maskelyne's Theatre of Magic, St. George's Hall, London, and at the Little Theatre, London; Associate of the Inner Magic Circle. **Awards:** Silver Cross of St. George, 1993. **Died:** 23 February 1995.

Publications for Children

Fiction

The Bad Barons of Crashbania, illustrated by Eve Garnett. Oxford, Blackwell, 1932.
The Incredible Adventures of Professor Branestawm, illustrated by W. Heath Robinson. London, Lane, 1933.
Professor Branestawm's Treasure Hunt and Other Incredible Adventures, illustrated by James Arnold. London, Lane, 1937.
Larky Legends, illustrated by James Arnold. London, Lane, 1938; abridged edition, as *The Dribblesome Teapots and Other Incredible Stories,* London, Bodley Head, 1969.
Stories of Professor Branestawm, illustrated by W. Heath Robinson. Leeds, E.J. Arnold, 1939.
Jingle Tales. London, Warne, 1941.
The Peculiar Triumph of Professor Branestawm, illustrated by George Adamson. London, Bodley Head, 1970.
The Home-Made Dragon and Other Incredible Stories, illustrated by Fritz Wegner. London, Bodley Head, 1971.
Professor Branestawm Up the Pole, illustrated by George Adamson. London, Bodley Head, 1972.
The Frantic Phantom and Other Incredible Stories, illustrated by Geraldine Spence. London, Bodley Head, 1973.
Wizards Are a Nuisance, illustrated by Quentin Blake. London, BBC Publications, 1973.
Professor Branestawm's Great Revolution, illustrated by David Hughes. London, Bodley Head, 1974.
Dust-Up at the Royal Disco, illustrated by Fritz Wegner. London, Bodley Head, 1975.
Professor Branestawm 'round the Bend, illustrated by Derek Cousins. London, Bodley Head, 1977.
Count Bakwerdz on the Carpet, illustrated by Babette Cole. London, Bodley Head, 1979.
Professor Branestawm's Perilous Pudding, illustrated by Derek Cousins. London, Bodley Head, 1979.
Sneeze and Be Slain and Other Incredible Stories, illustrated by Babette Cole. London, Bodley Head, 1980.
The Best of Branestawm. London, Bodley Head, 1980.
Professor Branestawm and the Wild Letters, illustrated by Gerald Rose. London, Bodley Head, 1981.
Professor Branestawm's Pocket Motor Car, illustrated by Gerald Rose. London, Bodley Head, 1981.
Professor Branestawm's Building Bust-Up, illustrated by Gerald Rose. London, Bodley Head, 1982.
Professor Branestawm's Mouse War, illustrated by Gerald Rose. London, Bodley Head, 1982.
Professor Branestawm's Crunchy Crockery, illustrated by Gerald Rose. London, Bodley Head, 1983.
Professor Branestawm's Hair-Raising Idea, illustrated by Gerald Rose. London, Bodley Head, 1983.

Other

Puffin Book of Magic, illustrated by Jill McDonald. London, Penguin, 1968; as *Norman Hunter's Book of Magic,* London, Bodley Head, 1974; as *The Wizard Book of Magic,* New York, Sterling, 1978.
Professor Branestawm's Dictionary, illustrated by Derek Cousins. London, Bodley Head, 1973.
Professor Branestawm's Compendium of Conundrums, Riddles, Puzzles, Brain-Twisters, and Dotty Descriptions, illustrated by Derek Cousins. London, Bodley Head, 1975.
Professor Branestawm's Do-It-Yourself Handbook, illustrated by Jill McDonald. London, Bodley Head, 1976.
Vanishing Ladies and Other Magic, illustrated by Jill McDonald. London, Bodley Head, 1978.

Publications for Adults

Other

Simplified Conjuring for All: A Collection of New Tricks Needing No Special Skill or Apparatus, With Suitable Patter. London, Pearson, 1923.
Advertising Through the Press: A Guide to Press Publicity. London, Pitman, 1925.
New and Easy Magic: A Further Series of Novel Magical Experiments Needing No Special Skill or Apparatus for Their Performance, With Suitable Patter. London, Pearson, 1925.
Hey Presto: A Book of Effects for Conjurers, illustrated by Sid Lorraine. London, Bagshawe, 1931.
New Conjuring Without Skill. London, Lane, 1935.
Successful Conjuring for Amateurs, edited by F.J. Camm. London, Pearson, 1951; as *Successful Magic for Amateurs,* New York, Arco, 1952; revised edition, as *Successful Conjuring,* Arco, 1964.

*

Critical Studies: "Professor Branestawm's Magic Theatre," in *Lights,* January 1991; "The Incredible Stories of Norman Hunter" by Richard Dalby, in *Book Collector,* November 1993, 72-80.

Norman Hunter comments:

I write two kinds of children's books—well, three kinds if you include my books on magic and how-to-do-it. I began by writing stories about funny kings and queens in which I took plots from traditional fairy tales and bent them out of shape a bit. These stories have now developed into a series of adventures of the King and Queen of Incrediblania. The other books deal with the adventures of Professor Branestawm, a highly learned gentleman who spends so much time knowing about extraordinary things he has no time to think of ordinary ones. He invents machines which eventually turn on him and has the kind of adventures an absent-minded professor might well have, only a great deal more so. The magic overflows into the stories to some extent because I frequently visit libraries, schools, book exhibitions, and bookshops and do a little magic show in which some of the magic is tied up with Professor Branestawm and his inventions. I am sometimes asked what age children my books appeal to. I think the Incrediblania stories are appreciated by children from about seven or perhaps younger, while the Professor Branestawm stories are for slightly older ones, say from nine, but a lot depends on the children. As the books are funny I also have a number of adult readers and I find mums and dads are quite happy to read my stories to their children and sometimes sneak the books away from the children to read themselves, which I like very much.

* * *

Sheer high spirits and exuberant good humour are the hallmarks of Norman Hunter's popular comic stories. *The Incredible Adventures of Professor Branestawm* and its sequel, *Professor Branestawm's Treasure Hunt,* were first published in the 1930s and have retained their comic appeal for children ever since. Taking the stock figure of the eccentric, absentminded Professor, Hunter made an engagingly dotty and unworldly character of him, gave his two faithful companions—Colonel Dedshott of the Catapult Cavaliers, none too bright but a loyal friend, and the much-tried housekeeper Mrs. Flittersnoop, always on the point of going off to stay with sister Aggie until the latest trouble is over—and involved them in a series of crazy misadventures arising from the Professor's weird machines, which never, of course, perform in exactly the way intended.

Some of these earlier stories, though they are enjoyed by children as much as ever, show their age now, with their emphasis, for instance, on radio broadcasting and mention of the long defunct Children's Hour. But Hunter has kept his hero up with the times, and since his own retirement and return to England from South Africa has published further Professor Branestawm collections, where the Professor shows himself quite at home with television, supermarkets, and so on (even if he falls foul of the Way Ahead and Right Outside Group of Advanced Artists by agreeing with Mrs. Flittersnoop that her little nephew could do better. The irate Artists take their revenge on the Professor's painting machine, "loosening screws and inserting plastic spanners of very bad design into the works"). Perhaps the humour of these later collections is slightly too sophisticated, compared to that of their predecessors, to suit the taste of the modern child, but the appeal still lies in the delightfully farcical situations and the author's command of comic language, with many incidental touches such as the alarm clock which "sounded more like Robin Hood's wedding in technicolour than an alarm clock." This is a very English type of humour, including the timeless setting of the little town of Great Pagwell with its municipal bureaucracy.

Hunter's other stories have been comic fairy tales. This is a difficult genre to tackle; the dangers of coyness and whimsy lie in wait, but Hunter avoids them, again by the genial verve of his language; who could resist the King of Incrediblania's comment that he sees "a most second-hand-looking person" coming down the street, or the remark that "horses are deliberately unsuitable on battleships." These stories are well served by the pleasingly ornate illustrations of Fritz Wegner, as was Professor Branestawm first by Heath Robinson and later by George Adamson.

—Anthea Bell

HURD, (John) Thacher

Nationality: American. **Born:** Burlington, Vermont, 6 March 1949. **Education:** University of California, Berkeley, 1967-68; California College of Arts and Crafts, B.F.A. 1972. **Family:** Married Olivia Scott, 12 June 1976; two sons. **Career:** Writer and illustrator of children's books; apprentice printer, Grabhorn-Hoyem Press (now Arion Press), 1967, 1969; self-employed builder, designer, and cabinetmaker, 1972-78; teacher of writing and illustrating children's books, California College of Arts and Crafts and Dominican College, 1981-86; co-owner with wife, Olivia Hurd, of Peaceable Kingdom Press, since 1983; lecturer and guest speaker at seminars, conferences, and schools. Exhibits include group show at California College of Arts and Crafts, 1972, one-man show in Monkton, Vermont, 1973, and group show at Roberson Museum, Binghamton, New York, 1997. **Awards:** *Boston Globe/Horn Book* award for illustration,1985, for *Mama Don't Allow*; *Reading Rainbow* selections, both 1984, for *Mystery on the Docks* and *Mama Don't Allow*; *Instructor* magazine's Year's Best Books for Children, 1996, for *Art Dog.* **Address:** 188 Tamalpais Road, Berkeley, California 94708. **Agent:** Marilyn Marlow, Curtis Brown Ltd., 10 Astor Place, New York, New York 10003, U.S.A.

PUBLICATIONS FOR CHILDREN (ALSO ILLUSTRATED BY EXCEPT AS NOTED)

The Old Chair. New York, Greenwillow, 1978.
The Quiet Evening. New York, Greenwillow, 1978.
Hobo Dog. New York, Scholastic, 1980.
Axle the Freeway Cat. New York, Harper, 1981.
Mystery on the Docks. New York, Harper, 1983.
Hobo Dog's Christmas Tree. New York, Scholastic, 1983.
Mama Don't Allow. New York, Harper, 1984.
Hobo Dog in the Ghost Town. New York, Scholastic, 1985.
Pea Patch Jig. New York, Crown, 1986.
A Night in the Swamp (pop-up book). New York, Harper, 1987.
Blackberry Ramble. New York, Crown, 1989.
Little Mouse's Big Valentine. New York, HarperCollins, 1990.
Tomato Soup. New York, Crown, 1991.
Little Mouse's Birthday Cake. New York, HarperCollins, 1992.
Art Dog. New York, HarperCollins, 1996.
Zoom City (board book). New York, HarperCollins, 1998.
Santa Mouse and the Ratdeer. New York, HarperCollins, 1998.

Other

With mother, Edith Hurd, *Little Dog Dreaming,* illustrated by father, Clement Hurd. New York Harper, 1965.
With John Cassidy, *Watercolor for the Artistically Undiscovered.* Palo Alto, Klutz Press, 1992.

*

Media Adaptations: *Mystery on the Docks* and *Mama Don't Allow* were adapted for television and broadcast on *Reading Rainbow,* Public Broadcasting Service, 1984; *Mama Don't Allow* was adapted for television and broadcast on *CBS Storybreak,* Columbia Broadcasting System, 1986, for videocassette, Random House, 1988, and as a children's opera, *Muskrat Lullaby,* performed by the Los Angeles City Opera Company, 6 October 1989.

Critical Studies: *Something about the Author,* Detroit, Gale, Vol. 45, 1986, Vol. 94, 1997; "Thacher Hurd: A Talent in His Own Right" by Diane Roback, in *Publisher's Weekly* 231, 23 January 1987, 33-37; review of *Blackberry Ramble* by Mary Lou Budd, in *School Library Journal,* November 1989, 84; *Contemporary Authors: New Revision Series,* Vol. 36, Detroit, Gale, 1992; review of *Tomato Soup* by Trev Jones, in *School Library Journal,* June 1992, 95; review of *Art Dog* by Virginia Golodetz, in *School Library Journal,* February 1996, 84-85; "One Picture Is Worth a Thousand Web Sites" by J.D. Biersdorfer, in *New York Times Book Review,* 19 May 1996, 28.

Illustrator: *Mattie and the Chicken Thief* by Ida Luttrell, 1988; *Wheel Away!* by Dayle Ann Dodds, 1989; *Dinosaur Chase* by Carolyn Otto, 1991; *Fritzi Fox Flew in from Florida* by Leah Komaiko, 1995.

Thacher Hurd comments:

I think that I like to write the books that I would have liked to have read when I was a child—books with strong characters and a sense of mystery. Children often identify so completely with the characters they read about in books that they live through these characters and see themselves as the characters. So I feel that the main character in a picture book should be strong and full of energy with a spirit of adventure and a sense of his own power to solve whatever comes his way.

* * *

As the son of the renowned picture book creators Edith Thacher Hurd and Clement Hurd, young Thacher felt that his parents led charmed lives. He hung around his father's cluttered, cozy studio and watched him work on books. "I think I got this feeling for what it was like to lead that life ... so completely free—he did exactly what he wanted every day. There was this wonderful aura of creativity around him that seemed very magical," Thacher told Diane Roback in a *Publisher's Weekly* interview in 1987. He grew up aware of the kinds of books his parents did and the kinds of books Margaret Wise Brown did. "My mother always made me very aware of rhythm. She always read to me at night; she has a very rhythmical voice, and is very aware of the inner pace of a book. She and my father always had this idea that a picture book is a little dance between the words and the pictures," Hurd told Roback. It is evident that he learned his lessons well, for his own best books are a "dance between the words and the pictures," full of rhythm, with perfect pacing and strong forward movement.

One of his earliest books, *A Quiet Evening* (1978), reflects perhaps overly much the influence of his parents and Margaret Wise Brown. Although it is a nice enough bedtime book, it lacks the mystery and tension of *Goodnight Moon,* and of Hurd's later books. With *Hobo Dog* (1980) and *Axle the Freeway Cat* (1981), the reader begins to hear Hurd's own distinctive voice, and detect themes that would become recurrent in his work. Both Hobo and Axle are loners who live on the fringes of society, picaresque heroes who elicit admiration and smiles, not pity. They persevere as they travel along their individual paths, and eventually find rewards, acceptance, and friendship.

The opening words of *Axle* beg to be read aloud: "Under the freeway overpass,/behind the guardrail,/down by a muddy drainage ditch,/lived Axle, the Freeway Cat." Axle's home is "an abandoned car with four flat tires and an engine that couldn't be fixed," while Hobo lives in a little "shack by the side of the tracks" when he isn't riding the rails. But, Axle has made his car "cozy" with all the comforts of home. His job is to collect litter along the freeway, where no one pays him any attention. He finds a shiny new harmonica among the litter, and enjoys playing it every evening, although no one hears his music. Then one day there is a tremendous traffic jam caused by a little female cat whose car has quit. Axle comes to the rescue, and the rest is history. After spinning around on the freeways for awhile, "over the underpass,/under the overpass," they end up at Axle's car where after supper as the sun goes down they play "a duet for harmonica and auto horn/ down by the muddy ditch/under the freeway overpass."

Mystery on the Docks (1983) builds on conventions of mystery stories, waterfront movies, comics, and cartoons to create a highly original, action-packed picture book. In characteristic Hurd fashion, the hero is unlikely: an opera-loving short-order cook mouse who sings as he works. A poster of Eduardo Bombasto, the famous singer, and various other opera posters adorn the walls of his diner. On a starless night, with a cold and clammy fog creeping in, two suspicious-looking, nasty rats slink into the diner. As luck would have it, these are the rats who have kidnapped Eduardo, and it is Ralph who helps free him. Eduardo is able to use his phenomenal voice to sing from the crow's nest "Halllpp!" to the tune of the Toreador Song. The bad rats are captured in a rush—"Whap!," "Bam!," "Kapow!,"—and the good guys enjoy a concert, a party, and a toast to Ralph, the hero. The design of the book is lively, with variations in the placement and style of the text, and size and placement of the pictures.

Mama Don't Allow (1984) is even more free-flowing, colorful, and rhythmical than *Mystery on the Docks.* Again, the heroes are outcasts of sorts, members of the Swamp Band whose music is not appreciated by anyone but "the sharp-toothed, long-tailed, yellow-eyed alligators" who like their music "really loud." Inspired by the traditional jazz song, "Mama Don't Allow," the book follows the pattern of *Where the Wild Things Are* with naughty outcasts, dangerous alligators, the taming of the hero, and the return home. When the alligators decide to eat the band members, the band tricks them with an offer of "one more song before dinner," and then cleverly chooses "A Lullaby of Swampland," which puts all the alligators to sleep. The band tiptoes home "playing that lullaby as quiet as could be" so even Mama finally says, "Oh, how nice..."

From the mid 1980s to the mid 1990s, Hurd's books moved in slightly different directions. *Pea Patch Jig* in 1986 marked the first of three stories about Baby Mouse and her family who live, mostly unobserved by humans, in Farmer Clem's garden, an imaginative and emotional reconstruction of Hurd's childhood home in Vermont. The books consist of lively adventures and close calls caused by humans and other large animals and the irrepressible Baby's naughtiness. *Pea Patch Jig* was well received, although the sequels, *Blackberry* and *Tomato Soup* garnered a mixed response. Mary Lou Budd, writing in *School Library Journal,* praised *Blackberry Ramble*'s "vibrant watercolor illustrations done in an exuberant cartoon style" and found that they "far surpass a mediocre slapstick story." But Trev Jones, reviewing *Tomato Soup* for *School Library Journal,* felt this "*Soup* is missing some seasoning and some logic, too." Judging by the wear on library copies of these books, however, they appear to be as loved by children as the others. There were also some other mouse books during these years: *Little Mouse's Big Valentine* and *Little Mouse's Birthday Cake,* both of them warm, whimsical stories of lone mice who find they have friends after all. During these years Hurd also illustrated several books by other writers.

In 1996, Hurd returned to the imaginative, free-wheeling energy of *Mystery on the Docks* and *Mama Don't Allow* with *Art Dog.* Another loner, Arthur Dog, is a guard at the Dogopolis Museum of Art, with its paintings by Vincent Van Dog, Pablo Poodle, Leonardo Dog Vinci, and Henri Muttisse. He leads a quiet life, but on nights when the moon is full, werewolf-like, his eyes grow bright and his fur glistens, and he takes to the streets with his mask, beret, paints, and paint-brush. When thieves break into the museum and steal the Mona Woofa, Art is jailed by mistake but escapes by painting himself a ladder and a window and leaping, Batman-like, into the air. Art Dog then paints himself a brushmobile worthy of Richard Scarry, in which he zooms off in pursuit of the crooks. In what reviewer Virginia Golodetz in *School Library Journal* describes as "perhaps the brightest double-page spread ever painted—an open pastiche on Matisse—he is shown subduing the crooks with paints and slashing brush."

Hurd has said that he was influenced not only by the work of his parents and Margaret Wise Brown, but also by Maurice Sendak's *Where the Wild Things Are,* by Don Freeman's *Pet of the Met,* by Taro Yashima's *Crow Boy,* and by the work of William Steig. All of these influence and others can be seen in his work, yet Hurd's work is distinctly his own. As he said in *Something About the Author,* "I believe that children's books should be for children, and not for the coffee tables of educators and librarians. I remember I loved to read as a child, and I think I try to write ... something that could draw me into another world: an alive, vibrant world of energy and wild and bursting color."

—Linnea Hendrickson

HURWITZ, Johanna

Nationality: American. **Born:** Johanna Frank, New York City, 9 October 1937. **Education:** Queens College, Flushing, New York, 1955-58, B.A. in English 1958; Columbia University, New York, 1958-59, M.L.S. 1959. **Family:** Married Uri Levi Hurwitz in 1962; one daughter and one son. **Career:** Children's librarian, New York Public Library, 1959-64; Lecturer in Children's Literature, Queens College, 1965-68; librarian, Calhoun School, 1968-75, and New Hyde Park school district, 1975-77, both New York; children's librarian, Great Neck Public Library, New York, 1978-92. Visiting storyteller, New York Public Library, 1964-67; teacher of writer's workshops in children's literature, Hofstra University, Hempstead, New York, 1981, 1986, and University of Vermont, 1995. **Award:** Swedish Institute grant, 1988. **Address:** 10 Spruce Place, Great Neck, New York 11021, U.S.A.

PUBLICATIONS FOR CHILDREN

Fiction

Busybody Nora, illustrated by Susan Jeschke. New York, Morrow, 1976.

Nora and Mrs. Mind-Your-Own-Business, illustrated by Susan Jeschke. New York, Morrow, 1977.

The Law of Gravity, illustrated by Ingrid Fetz. New York, Morrow, 1978.

Much Ado about Aldo, illustrated by John Wallner. New York, Morrow, 1978.

Aldo Applesauce, illustrated by John Wallner. New York, Morrow, 1979.

New Neighbors for Nora, illustrated by Susan Jeschke. New York, Morrow, 1979.

Once I Was a Plum Tree, illustrated by Ingrid Fetz. New York, Morrow, 1980.

Superduper Teddy, illustrated by Susan Jeschke. New York, Morrow, 1980.

Aldo Ice Cream, illustrated by John Wallner. New York, Morrow, 1981.

Baseball Fever, illustrated by Ray Cruz. New York, Morrow, 1981.

The Rabbi's Girls, illustrated by Pamela Johnson. New York, Morrow, 1982.

Tough-Luck Karen, illustrated by Diane deGroat. New York, Morrow, 1982.

Rip-Roaring Russell, illustrated by Lillian Hoban. New York, Morrow, 1983.

DeDe Takes Charge!, illustrated by Diane deGroat. New York, Morrow, 1984.

The Hot and Cold Summer, illustrated by Gail Owens. New York, Morrow, 1984.

The Adventures of Ali Baba Bernstein, illustrated by Gain Owens. New York, Morrow, 1985.

Russell Rides Again, illustrated by Lillian Hoban. New York, Morrow, 1985.

Hurricane Elaine, illustrated by Diane deGroat. New York, Morrow, 1986.

Yellow Blue Jay, illustrated by Donald Carrick. New York, Morrow, 1986.

Class Clown, illustrated by Sheila Hamanaka. New York, Morrow, 1987.

Russell Sprouts, illustrated by Lillian Hoban. New York, Morrow, 1987.

The Cold and Hot Winter, illustrated by Carolyn Ewing. New York, Morrow, 1988.

Teacher's Pet, illustrated by Sheila Hamanaka. New York, Morrow, 1988.

Hurray for Ali Baba Bernstein, illustrated by Gail Owens. New York, Morrow, 1989.

Russell and Elisa, illustrated by Lillian Hoban. New York, Morrow, 1989.

Aldo Peanut Butter, illustrated by Diane deGroat. New York, Morrow, 1990.

Class President, illustrated by Sheila Hamanaka. New York, Morrow, 1990.

"E" Is for Elisa, illustrated by Lillian Hoban. New York, Morrow, 1991.

School's Out, illustrated by Sheila Hamanaka. New York, Morrow, 1991.

Ali Baba Bernstein: Lost and Found, illustrated by Karen Milone. New York, Morrow, 1992.

Roz and Ozzie, illustrated by Eileen McKeating. New York, Morrow, 1992.

Make Room for Elisa, illustrated by Lillian Hoban. New York, Morrow, 1993.

New Shoes for Silvia, illustrated by Jerry Pinkney. New York, Morrow, 1993.

The Up and Down Spring, illustrated by Gail Owens. New York, Morrow, 1993.
School Spirit, illustrated by Karen Dugan. New York, Morrow, 1994.
A Word to the Wise, illustrated by Robert Rayefsky. New York, Morrow, 1994.
A *Llama in the Family,* illustrated by Mark Graham. New York, Morrow, 1994.
Elisa in the Middle, illustrated by Lillian Hoban. New York, Morrow, 1995.
Ozzie on His Own, illustrated by Eileen McKeating. New York, Morrow, 1995.
Even Stephen, illustrated by Michael Dooling. New York, Morrow, 1996.
The Down and Up Fall, illustrated by Gail Owens. New York, Morrow, 1996.
Spring Break, illustrated by Karen Dugan. New York, Morrow, 1997.
A Llama in the Library. Forthcoming.
Jericho Journey. Forthcoming.
Ever Clever Elisa. Forthcoming.
Starting School. Forthcoming.
The One and Only Lucas Cott. Forthcoming.

Other

Anne Frank: Life in Hiding, illustrated by Vera Rosenberry. Philadelphia, Jewish Publication Society, 1988.
Astrid Lindgren: Storyteller to the World, illustrated by Michael Dooling. New York, Viking, 1989.
Leonard Bernstein, A Passion for Music, illustrated by Sonia Lisker. Philadelphia, Jewish Publication Society, 1993.
Helen Keller. New York, Random House, 1997.

Editor, *Birthday Surprises: Ten Great Stories to Unwrap.* New York, Morrow, 1995.

*

Manuscript Collections: Kerlan Collection, University of Minnesota, Minneapolis.

Johanna Hurwitz comments:

More than anything else, I hope children gain pleasure from my books. I do not write with deep messages or hidden meanings. If upon completion of my book, the reader is eager to read another (by me or by someone else too), then I know I have been successful.

* * *

After a career as a children's librarian that began nearly forty years ago, Johanna Hurwitz knows what children like to read; her considerable writing talent and gentle but accurate sense of humor have enabled her to translate this knowledge into a series of successful short novels for elementary school children. In the typical Hurwitz novel, the protagonist is a likable young child facing common difficulties of childhood: making friends in a new school, getting along with siblings at home, and trying to find a place to fit in, both at home and in school. The children are always resourceful and amusing, but never ridiculous; their major problem is usually resolved by book's end.

A Hurwitz novel is like a finely-focused close-up photograph; the main character is well-defined, but other characters remain mostly in the background, furthering the plot as it relates to the central figure. This is not to say that Hurwitz can only describe childhood from a single point of view; it is often the case that characters who make cameo appearances in one story come into full focus as central figures in later works. Occasionally even incidents that have been described in one novel are encountered from another point of view in another book, such as the class play about French history which turns up in both *Tough-Luck Karen* and *DeDe Takes Charge!* Hurwitz is adept at depicting the world according to fourth-grader Aldo Sossi, but works equally well from the perspectives of his middle sister Karen, older sister Elaine, and his best friend DeDe. The Michaels family, first introduced through the exploits of their oldest son, "rip-roaring Russell," gained added dimension for readers when Russell's younger sister Elisa became the focus of her own stories; Elisa in turn became a "middle child" with the addition of baby brother Marshall in 1985. The technique of concentrating on one personality at a time allows Hurwitz to develop in-depth character portrayals without burdening her novels with a complexity beyond the grasp of her intended audience.

Hurwitz's novels for early elementary school, those about Nora, her brother Teddy, and their friend Russell, make excellent beginning chapter books for reading aloud. Each chapter is self-contained while furthering a more general plot, which provides for the closure sought by children around the first-grade level. Humorous twists and gentle irony abound as Hurwitz explores common experiences such as the first day of kindergarten, experimentation with crude language, and children's birthday parties. Often the adults as well as the children are apt to learn a few things, as when Russell gives his parents a report card evaluating their child-rearing skills. Hurwitz is often at her best in novels involving upper-elementary to junior high children. Three especially fine novels featuring two nine-year-olds and a girl of 13 demonstrate that Hurwitz is able to deal powerfully and poignantly with some of the more complex problems of growth and self-discovery, without abandoning her trademark humor.

In *Baseball Fever* Ezra Kaufman attempts to reconcile his own interests with his father's diametrically opposed expectations. Karen Sossi, the heroine of *Tough-Luck Karen,* is a 13-year-old whose normal adolescent difficulties are complicated by her position as a middle child between two academically superior siblings. Cricket Kaufman faces a bewildering shift in self-image when for the first time in her life she is not the undisputed top student in her class (*Teacher's Pet*). In all three novels the protagonists demonstrate identifiable growth between the opening and the conclusion. Their problems are serious, but the Hurwitz touch, from gentle irony to all-out hilarity, makes getting to the solutions a joy as well as a challenge. If *Even Stephen* is a true indicator, however, thirteen may be the upper limit at which Hurwitz operates effectively from the child's perspective. This novel, which concerns fourteen-year-old Sunny and her seventeen-year-old brother, is funniest in situations which befit younger characters better, and has Sunny speaking in a distinctly non-fourteen voice, wondering, for example, why a boyfriend is "so hard for me to attain." Further, while Sunny's boy troubles and sibling troubles ring reasonably true, Hurwitz's inclusion of the tragedy of a gym teacher dying of a massive heart attack, and its aftermath, seems unmanageable in a 100-page novel.

In fact, the only Hurwitz novels that do not work well are those in which the protagonists encounter difficulties that are more extraordinary than universal. While humor carries the day and makes her recent "Llama" tales engaging if less convincing than some of her earlier work, she errs in treating circumstances such as the death of a parent (*The Rabbi's Girls*) and divorce (*DeDe Takes Charge!*) with much the same serio-comic attitude she employs when Aldo has difficulty making friends in his new school. There are undeniably lighter moments in the most dreadful circumstances; however, glossing over the intense pain in these novels makes their happy resolutions finally unconvincing.

An unfortunate aspect of Hurwitz's work is the occasional lapse into ethnic stereotypes. In two of her best works she makes the poorest student in the class a Hispanic in one case, and an oriental refugee in the other. These negative references are especially puzzling since she so rarely alludes to ethnicity at all, other than in *The Rabbi's Girls,* in which the Levin family encounters the pain of discrimination. While serious in themselves, these misjudgments are not frequent in Hurwitz's work, and could easily be edited out of future editions of the novels. Most of the time Hurwitz provides her young readers with believable heroes and heroines facing the common but important crises of childhood, and treats them to much laughter on the way to convincing, attainable solutions of their problems.

—Christine Doyle

HUTCHINS, Hazel

Nationality: Canadian. **Born:** Calgary, Alberta, 9 August 1952. **Education:** University of Calgary , 1970-72. **Family:** Married Ted Hutchins in 1973; two sons, one daughter. **Career:** Store clerk, office clerk, waitress, author. **Awards:** White Ravens Selection of the International Youth Library, 1987, for *Leanna Builds a Genie Trap*; Reading Magic Award, 1988, for *The Three and Many Wishes of Jason Reid*; R. Ross Annett Award for Children's Literature, Writers' Guild of Alberta, 1992, for *A Cat of Artimus Pride*; Storytelling World Award, 1996, for *Tess.* **Address:** Annick Press, 15 Patricia Ave., Willowdale, Ontario M2M 1H9, Canada. **E-mail Address:** wjhutchi@banff.net. **Website:** http://www.inkspot.com/author/hutchins/

Publications for Children:

The Three and Many Wishes of Jason Reid. Willowdale, Ontario, Annick Press, 1983.
Anastasia Morning Star and the Crystal Butterfly. Willowdale, Annick Press, 1983; as *Anastasia Filipendule et la papillon de verre,* Willowdale, 1984; as *Anastasia Morningstar,* New York, Viking, 1990.
Leanna Builds a Genie Trap. Willowdale, Annick Press, 1984; as *Marie-Eve et le piege a genies,* Willowdale, Annick Press, 1989.
Ben's Snow Song: A Winter Picnic. Willowdale, Annick Press, 1987.
Casey Webber the Great. Willowdale, Annick Press, 1988.
Norman's Snowball. Willowdale, Annick Press, 1989.
Nicholas at the Library. Willowdale, Annick Press, 1990.
Katie's Babbling Brother. Willowdale, Annick Press, 1991.
A Cat of Artimus Pride. Willowdale, Annick Press, 1991; as *Un Chat nomme Cortez,* Willowdale, Annick Press, 1994.
And You Can Be the Cat. Willowdale, Annick Press, 1992.
The Catfish Palace. Willowdale, Annick Press, 1992.
The Best of Arlie Zack. Willowdale, Annick Press, 1993.
Within a Painted Past. Willowdale, Annick Press, 1994.
Believing Sophie. Martin Grove, Illinois, A. Whitman, 1995.
Tess. Toronto, Annick Press, 1996.
Yancy and Bear. Toronto, Annick Press, 1996.
The Prince of Tarn. Toronto, Annick Press, 1997.
Shoot for the Moon, Robyn. Halifax, Nova Scotia, Formac, 1997.
It's Raining, Yancy and Bear. Toronto, Annick Press, 1998.

*

Hazel Hutchins comments:

OK—I admit it. I love to write. I *have* to write. I'm addicted to the strange habit of putting words, ideas, people, places and happenings onto that blank, white landscape known as paper.

If I don't spend some time writing each day I feel as if something is missing. If I have to go a week or more, I begin to snap and growl and snarl.

And writing comes easy to me. Well, the unconscious kind of writing comes easy. Do you know what I mean by the unconscious kind? It's the kind that just flows out of your brain onto the paper without much effort. That's where most of my stories start—with ideas just flowing onto paper.

But it's not where my stories end.

After that first wonderful flow of ideas, inevitably, the story begins to go rapidly down hill. Does that happen to you? Do your great ideas slowly begin to falter and fail and finally fade away? Mine try to do just that, but I've found a couple of ways to breath life back into them.

One way is brainstorming and culling. I think of all the things that could happen in my story—and then I throw out 90 percent of them. I keep only the very best, only the most unique and intriguing happenings for my story. Only the best is what I want to write. Only the best is what the reader wants to read.

Next, I try to come up with a great ending. If I've got a great ending in the back of my mind, I'll *just have* to write a great story to lead up to it!

And finally, I sit down and write some of the best parts. I don't write the boring parts that lead up to them, I just jump right in and write the good parts. Later, if I need to, I'll fill in the gaps that lead up to them. Later, if I need to, I'll change some of the events themselves to fit in with the story as it evolves. But often, when I'm finished some of the good parts, I discover that many of them can be linked together with very little extra explanation and that gives wonderful energy to the story and keeps it moving at a swift pace.

And is that the end of it? Far from it. Now begins the part I both hate and love. I rewrite and rewrite and rewrite.

I hate it because it's just plain hard work to go over and over a story until every paragraph, every sentence, every word is smooth and clear and says exactly what I want it to say, exactly the way it needs to be said.

I love it because when the words do finally, magically, fit together as perfectly as I can possibly make them, the story takes an enormous leap and becomes alive and even larger than life there on the page before me.

It isn't easy. It isn't always fun.
But it's always worth it.
May all your stories be a discovery. May all your words speak with eloquence.
And may the Muse be kind.

* * *

At the beginning of a Hazel Hutchins' novel, magical powers suddenly enter into the lives of ordinary children. For example, the opening sentence of *Anastasia Morningstar and the Crystal Butterfly* states: "On a bright morning in May, the lady at the corner grocery story turned Derek Henshaw into a frog." At the end of each novel, the magic has left their lives; however, because of its influence, the central characters have come to a better understanding of themselves and the people around them. For a boy granted a seemingly endless supply of wishes, another who finds a jacket that makes him invisible, or a girl who can enter the paintings hanging in her aunt's guest room, the magic is a catalyst for the inner changes of their lives.

In *The Three and Many Wishes of Jason Reid,* a being from another universe must, in order to return to his own world, grant the hero three wishes. An inept baseball player, Jason first wishes for a magic fielder's glove and then discovers how to extend the wishes indefinitely. He learns not only to wish worthily but also to accept responsibility for the consequences of his wishes. The title hero of *Anastasia Morningstar,* who has the ability to transform people into other creatures, helps Sarah to transform her lack of confidence into self-worth. *Casey Weber, the Great* examines the effect of a magical jacket on the character of a boy who wishes to appear on a popular talent show. He learns that inner imagination and thoughtfulness are more important than marvelous powers.

When a century old, talking cat who enters a girl's life in *A Cat of Artemis Pride* tells Claire about the nobility of its original owner, she is able to enter the Heritage Days Parade with a real sense of pride in both her city's past and her own float. The magical objects in *The Best of Arlie Zack* help a boy who hangs around with bad kids to develop inner strength and a healthier relationship with and attitude to his father, who had left the family years earlier. The central characters in *Within a Painted Past* and *The Prince of Tarn* leave this world and, in helping the people they encounter, they learn to help themselves. In the former, Allison, entering the pioneer world of western Canada depicted in a group of paintings, initially feels inadequate around people her own age; but as she comes to the aid of a brother and sister from the past, her confidence grows. In the latter, Fred meets a character from a story written by his now deceased mother and helps the prince to regain his kingdom. Both learn the truth of the mother's belief that "You've got to write your own story."

In the short texts for several picture books, Hutchins presents psychologically true, although sometimes literally fantastic, experiences of younger children. *Ben's Snow Song, Norman's Snowball,* and *The Catfish Palace* are realistic stories based on incidents in her own children's lives. *Katie's Babbling Brother,* in which a sometimes annoying little boy is made tiny with magic powder, and *Nicholas at the Library,* in which a boy helps a little monkey find the book from which he has become separated, deal with sibling rivalry and parent-child conflicts respectively.

Hutchins's stories are both light and serious, humorous and profound. The magic in them relates to fantasies, such as unlimited wishes or invisibility, in which most children have indulged. However, it does not overwhelm the stories; it is an intriguing and entertaining plot device that enhance the events, but more important, provides a means of examining the personalities of the people it touches. The heroes, boys and girls around the ages of eleven or twelve (younger in the picture books), face problems not uncommon to children of their ages: insecurity, sense of peer group inadequacy, the difficulties of single parent families. With the exception of *The Best of Arlie Zack,* parents play minor roles. The significant adults, often the possessors or granters of magical powers, are frequently like the god-parents or enchanted characters of folk tales who provide the children with opportunities to help themselves. Unlike folktales, however, the central characters do not face their struggles alone. They usually befriend another person their own age, usually of the opposite sex, who becomes a trusted companion. Their relationships are not romances, but deep friendships.

Hutchins treats her characters with seriousness and respect. They participate in adventures that are convincing to readers both as stories and as explorations of conflicts with which the readers can quickly identify.

—Jon C. Stott

HUTCHINS, Pat

Nationality: British. **Born:** Pat Goundry, Catterick Camp, Yorkshire, 18 June 1942. **Education:** Darlington School of Art, County Durham, 1958-60, intermediate certificate; Leeds College of Art, 1960-62, national diploma in illustration. **Family:** Married Laurence Hutchins in 1966; two children. **Career:** Assistant art director, J. Walter Thompson advertising agency, London, 1963-66. **Award:** Library Association Kate Greenaway Medal, 1975. **Address:** 75 Flask Walk, London NW3 1ET, England.

PUBLICATIONS FOR CHILDREN (ILLUSTRATED BY THE AUTHOR)

Fiction

Rosie's Walk. New York, Macmillan, and London, Bodley Head, 1968.
Tom and Sam. New York, Macmillan, 1968; London, Bodley Head, 1969.
The Surprise Party. New York, Macmillan, 1969; London, Bodley Head, 1970.
Clocks and More Clocks. New York, Macmillan, and London, Bodley Head, 1970.
Changes, Changes. New York, Macmillan, and London, Bodley Head, 1971.
Titch. New York, Macmillan, 1971; London, Bodley Head, 1972.
Good Night, Owl. New York, Macmillan, 1972; London, Bodley Head, 1973.
The Silver Christmas Tree. New York, Macmillan, and London, Bodley Head, 1974.
The House That Sailed Away, illustrated by Laurence Hutchins. New York, Greenwillow, 1975; London, Bodley Head, 1976.

Follow That Bus!, illustrated by Laurence Hutchins. New York, Greenwillow, and London, Bodley Head, 1977.
Happy Birthday, Sam. New York, Greenwillow, and London, Bodley Head, 1978.
The Best Train Set Ever. New York, Greenwillow, 1978; London, Bodley Head, 1979.
One-Eyed Jake. New York, Greenwillow, and London, Bodley Head, 1979.
The Mona Lisa Mystery, illustrated by Laurence Hutchins. New York, Greenwillow, and London, Bodley Head, 1981.
One Hunter. New York, Greenwillow, and London, Bodley Head, 1982.
You'll Soon Grow into Them, Titch. New York, Greenwillow, and London, Bodley Head, 1983.
The Curse of the Egyptian Mummy, illustrated by Laurence Hutchins. New York, Greenwillow, and London, Bodley Head, 1983.
King Henry's Palace. New York, Greenwillow, and London, Bodley Head, 1983.
The Very Worst Monster. New York, Greenwillow, and London, Bodley Head, 1985.
The Doorbell Rang. New York, Greenwillow, and London, Bodley Head, 1986.
Where's the Baby? New York, Greenwillow, and London, Bodley Head, 1986.
Rats! New York, Greenwillow, and London, Bodley Head, 1989.
Which Witch Is Which? New York, Greenwillow, 1989; London, MacRae, 1990.
What Game Shall We Play? New York, Greenwillow, and London, MacRae, 1990.
Tidy Titch. New York, Greenwillow, and London, MacRae, 1991.
Silly Billy! New York, Greenwillow, and London, MacRae, 1992.
My Best Friend. New York, Greenwillow, and London, MacRae, 1993.
Three-Star Billy. New York, Greenwillow, and London, MacRae, 1994.
Little Pink Pig. New York, Greenwillow, and London, MacRae, 1994.
Titch and Daisy. New York, Greenwillow, and London, Bodley Head, 1996.
Shrinking Mouse. New York, Greenwillow, and London, Bodley Head, 1997.

Poetry

The Wind Blew. New York, Macmillan, and London, Bodley Head, 1974.
Don't Forget the Bacon! New York, Greenwillow, and London, Bodley Head, 1976.
The Tale of Thomas Mead. New York, Greenwillow, and London, Bodley Head, 1980.

* * *

If Pat Hutchins had only produced one book—*Rosie's Walk*—she would nevertheless have earned her place in *Twentieth-Century Children's Writers.* Yet *Rosie's Walk* has a text of a mere 36 words. It is a picture book, of course, and its art work (which shows Rosie the hen going for a walk "across the yard, around the pond...past the mill...under the beehives" and getting home in time for dinner) is strong and attractive. But it is neither the 36 words on their own nor the art work on its own that would entitle Hutchins to her entry: it is the brilliant interplay of the two, the assured use of dramatic irony. For young children listening to the story of Rosie, walking, will never hear a mention of the fox who, they can see from the pictures, is one step behind her, always tripped up (whether accidentally or intentionally is Hutchins's secret) by the strutting hen.

A close second to *Rosie's Walk* is *Good Night, Owl,* where, again, the text plays a large part in the book's success. Owl tries to sleep—but all day long the birds and animals in his tree wake him up, each with its own cry; but when at nightfall the tree quietens down at last, then it is owl's turn to screech. In *Titch* Hutchins uses her talent with combined word and picture to show dramatically how the youngest member of a family—only allowed the smallest and most boring of options by his elder brother and sister—has to be content with a mere seed when it comes to gardening. But he plants the seed—which grows and grows....

In a sequel, *You'll Soon Grow into Them, Titch,* careful picture watchers will pick up clues pointing to the arrival of a new baby in the family, someone to whom Titch, hitherto the youngest, can assign *his* cast-off clothes. Recently Hutchins has experimented with a Monster family, in *The Very Worst Monster* and *Where's the Baby?*. The Monsters may be green-nosed, long-eared, and clawed but, especially Grandma who sings the praises of the Baby no matter what misdemeanours he has been up to, they are immensely human and lovable.

This author-artist, whose every picture book is a magnet for young listeners and readers, has also created three extraordinary picture books that enticingly explore the importance of learning to read (*The Tale of Thomas Mead* "who never, ever learned to read") and basic mathematics: *1 Hunter* is a witty counting book, and in *The Doorbell Rang* Ma's 12 cookies, made for Victoria and Sam, have to be shared by an ever-increasing number of children as the doorbell rings...and rings.

Hutchins is an excellent storyteller. As an artist she naturally first turned to the picture book as her medium. But, gloriously alive to family lore and to children's fantasies, she has since written four attractive stories for under nines, each illustrated by her husband, Laurence Hutchins. *The House That Sailed Away* is the most complete and best planned of these: readers willingly adop[t] the dotty Hutchins family who sail away inside their house in a flood and find themselves on a desert island—with pirates, and treasure, and Grandma! The school stories, *Follow That Bus!, The Mona Lisa Mystery,* and *The Curse of the Egyptian Mummy* are funny, too, but more complex and, because less personal, lacking just that touch of sharp idiosyncrasy that is the hall-mark of a true Hutchins.

—Elaine Mos[s]

HYMAN, Trina Schart

Nationality: American. **Born:** Philadelphia, Pennsylvania, 8 April 1939. **Education:** Philadelphia Museum College of Art, 1956-59; Boston Museum School of the Arts, 1959-60; Konstfackskola (Swedish State Art School), Stockholm, 1960-61. **Family:** Married Harris Hyman in 1959 (divorced 1968); one daughter. **Career:** Artist and illustrator. Art director, *Cricket* Magazine

1972-79; greeting card artist, *Pawprints* and *Recycled Paper Products.* **Awards:** *Boston Globe/Horn Book* honor award for illustration, 1968, for *All in Free but Janey,* 1973, for *King Stork,* 1978, for *On to Widecombe Fair*; *Bookworld* Spring Book Festival Award, 1969, for *A Walk Out of the World,* and 1971, for *A Room Made of Windows*; American Institute of Graphic Arts Children's Books selection, 1970, for *The Pumpkin Giant*; *New York Times* Outstanding Books of the Year, 1971, for *A Room Made of Windows*; Canadian Library Association award, 1973, for *The Marrow of the World*; Children's Book Showcase of the Children's Book Council, 1975, for *Greedy Mariani,* and 1976, for *Magic in the Mist*; *Boston Globe/Horn Book* honor award for nonfiction, 1976, for *Will You Sign Here, John Hancock?*; Jewish Welfare Board National Jewish Book Award, 1982, for *The Night Journey*; Golden Kite Award for Illustration and Parents' Choice Award for Illustration, 1983, and Caldecott honor book, 1984, for *Little Red Riding Hood*; *New York Times* Best Illustrated Books, 1984, and Caldecott Medal, 1985, for *Saint George and the Dragon*; Dorothy Canfield Fisher Award, 1987, for *Castle in the Attic*; Golden Kite Picture-Illustration honor, 1988, for *Canterbury Tales*; Caldecott honor, 1990, for *Hershel and the Hanukkah Goblins*; Children's Literature Festival Award, Keene State College, New Hampshire, 1991; Golden Kite Picture-Illustration honor, *New York Times* Best Illustrated Books, Parents Choice Storybook Award, 1992, and *Boston Globe-Horn Book* Award for Illustration, 1993, for *The Fortune Tellers*; Drexel Citation, School of Library and Information Science of Drexel University and the Free Library of Philadelphia, for body of work, 1993; *Booklist*'s Top of the List, 1997, for *Bearskin.* **Address:** Brick Hill Rd., Lyme, New Hampshire 03768, U.S.A.

PUBLICATIONS FOR CHILDREN (ILLUSTRATED BY THE AUTHOR)

How Six Found Christmas. Boston, Little, Brown, 1969.
A Little Alphabet. Boston, Little, Brown, 1980; revised, New York, Morrow, 1993.
Self-Portrait: Trina Schart Hyman. Reading, Massachusetts, Addison-Wesley, 1981.
The Enchanted Forest (movable book). New York, Putnam, 1984.

Reteller, *The Sleeping Beauty.* Boston, Little, Brown, 1977.
Reteller, *Little Red Riding Hood.* New York, Holiday House, 1983.

*

Media Adaptations: *Dragon Stew* (filmstrip and record), BFA Educational Media, 1975; *Tight Times* was filmed as a *Reading Rainbow* special, PBS-TV, 1983; *Little Red Riding Hood* (filmstrip with cassette), Listening Library, 1984.

Manuscript Collections: Kerlan Collection, University of Minnesota, Minneapolis; Baker Library, Dartmouth College; de Grummond Collection, University of Southern Mississippi Library, Hattiesburg; University of Connecticut Special Collections, Storrs, Connecticut.

Critical Studies: "The 'Ubiquitous' Trina Schart Hyman" by Michael Patrick Hearn, in *American Artist,* May 1979, 36-43, 96-97; *Self-Portrait: Trina Schart Hyman,* Reading, Massachusetts, Addison-Wesley, 1981; "How Picture Books Work" by Perry Nodelman, in *Festschrift: A Ten Year Retrospective,* edited by Perry Nodelman and Jilly May, Lafayette, Indiana, 1983, 20-25; "Profile: Trina Schart Hyman" by David E. White, in *Language Arts,* September 1983, 782-92; "Who Does Snow White Look At?" by Hugh Crago, in *Signal,* September 1984, 129-45; "Caldecott Medal Acceptance" by Trina Schart Hyman, in *Horn Book,* July/August 1985, 410-21; "Illustration as Interpretation: Trina Schart Hyman's Folk Tales" by Jill P. May, in *Children's Literature Association Quarterly,* Fall 1985, 127-131; *Something about the Author,* Detroit, Gale, Vol. 46, 1986, Vol. 95, 1997; "Trina Schart Hyman" by Hugh Crago, in *Dictionary of Literary Biography,* Vol. 61, *American Writers for Children since 1960,* Detroit, Gale, 1987, 108-115; "Once-Upon-a-Time Artist in the Land of Now: An Interview with Trina Schart Hyman" by Wendy Saul, in *The New Advocate,* No. 1, 1988, 8-17; "Trina Schart Hyman," in *Children's Book Illustration and Design* edited by Julie Cummins, New York, Library of Applied Design, 1991, 78-80; "'Cut It Down, and You Will Find Something at the Roots'" by Trina Schart Hyman, in *The Reception of Grimms' Fairy Tales: Responses, Reactions, Revisions,* edited by Donald Haase, Detroit, Wayne State University Press, 1993, 293-300; "Zen and the Art of Children's Book Illustration" by Trina Schart Hyman, in *The Zena Sutherland Lectures,* edited by Betsy Hearne and Marilyn Kaye, New York, Clarion, 1993, 186-205; "*The Fortune-tellers*" (*Boston Globe/Horn Book Award* acceptance speech) by Trina Schart Hyman, in *Horn Book,* January/February 1994, 48-49; "Trina Schart Hyman" by Christine C. Behr, in *Children's Books and Their Creators,* edited by Anita Silvey, Boston, Houghton Mifflin, 1995, 337-39; "Creating a Picture Book: Trina Schart Hyman," in *The Potential of Picturebooks* by Barbara Kiefer, Upper Saddle, New Jersey, Prentice-Hall, 1995; "The Art of Trina Schart Hyman in *Comus* and *The Golem*" by Dilys Evans, in *Book Links,* March 1997, 27-29.

Illustrator: *Toffe och den lilla bilen* (*Toffe and the Little Car*) by Hertha Von Gebhardt, 1961; *Riddles, Riddles, from A to Z* by Carl Memling, 1963; *Bow Wow! Meow!* by Melanie Bellah, 1963; *Curl Up Small* by Sandol S. Warburg, 1964; *Children of the Salmon* by Eileen O'Faolain, 1965; *All Kinds of Signs,* 1965; *Joy to the World: Christmas Legends* by Ruth Sawyer, 1966; *The Magic Maker,* 1966, and *The Half-Time Gypsy,* 1968, by Joyce Varney; *Favorite Fairy Tales Told in Czechoslovakia* retold by Virginia Haviland, 1966; *Billy Finds Out* and *Billy Celebrates* by Edna B. Trickey, 1966; *Five Trials of the Pansy Bed* by Jacob D. Townsend, 1967; *Stuck with Luck,* 1967, *All in Free but Janey,* 1968, and *Break a Magic Circle,* 1971, by Elizabeth Johnson; *Moon Eyes* by Josephine Poole, 1967; *Cinnamon Seed* by John T. Moore, 1967; *Little Red Flower,* 1968, and *The Vi-Daylin Book of Minnie the Mump,* 1970, by Paul Tripp; *Epaminondas* by Eve Merriam, 1968; *Wreath of Carols* edited by Betty M. Owen and Mary MacEwen, 1968; *Dragon Stew* by Tom McGowen, 1969; *The Cabin on the Fjord* by Susan Meyers, 1969; *The Coming of Pout* by Peter Hunter Blair, 1969; *The Moon Singer* by Clyde R. Bulla, 1969; *A Walk Out of the World,* 1969, and *The Marrow of the World,* 1972, by Ruth Nichols; *Benjamin the True* by Claudia Paley, 1969; *Greta the Strong* by Donald J. Sobol, 1970; *Let's Steal the Moon: Jewish Tales, Ancient and Recent* retold by Blanche Luria Serwer, 1970; *The Walking Stones* by Mollie Hunter, 1970; *Sir Machinery* by Tom McGowen, 1970; *The Shy Little Girl,* 1970, and *The Popular Girls Club,* 1972, by Phyllis Krasilovsky; *The Pumpkin Giant,* 1970, and *Princess Rosetta and the Popcorn Man,*

1971, retold by Ellin Greene, 1970; *The Ghost Next Door* by Wylly Folk St. John, 1971; *The Bigger They Come* and *Take it or Leave It* by Osmond Molarsky, 1971; *The Bread Book* by Carolyn Meyer, 1971; *A Room Made of Windows* by Eleanor Cameron, 1971; *How I Went Shopping and What I Got* by Eleanor Clymer, 1972; *Sarah and Katie* by Dori White, 1972; *The Fairy Tale Life of Hans Christian Andersen* by Eva Moore, 1972; *Magic Heart* by Jan Wahl, 1972; *Who Says So?* by Paul Hendrich, 1972; *Listen Children, Listen,* 1972, *Christmas Poems,* 1984, and *Cat Poems,* 1987, by Myra Cohn Livingston; *The Bad Times of Irma Baumlein,* 1972, and *Caddie Woodlawn* (revised edition), 1973, by Carol Ryrie Brink; *King Stork,* 1973, and *Bearskin,* 1997, by Howard Pyle; *The Ugly Duckling and Two Other Stories* by Hans Christian Andersen, edited by Lilian Moore, 1973; *Joanna Runs Away* by Phyllis LaFarge, 1973; *Clever Cooks: A Concoction of Stories, Recipes and Riddles* compiled by Ellin Greene, 1973; *The Wanderers* by Elizabeth Coatsworth, 1973; *The Everything Book* by Eleanor G. Vance, 1974; *Two Queens of Heaven: Aphrodite and Demeter* by Doris Gates, 1974; *Greedy Mariani and Other Folktales of the Antilles* edited by Dorothy S. Carter, 1974; *Figgie Hobbin* (poetry) by Charles Causley, 1974; *You've Come a Long Way, Sybil McIntosh: A Book of Manners and Grooming for Girls* by Charlotte Herman, 1974; *Snow White* by J. and W. Grimm, translated by Paul Heins, 1974; *Why Don't You Get a Horse, Sam Adams?,* 1974, *Will You Sign Here, John Hancock?,* 1976, and *The Man Who Loved Books,* 1981, by Jean Fritz; *The Quitting Deal,* 1975, and *Wishing,* 1977, by Tobi Tobias; *Magic in the Mist,* Margaret Kimmel, 1975; *The Watchers* by Jane Curry, 1975; *Star Mother's Youngest Child* by Louise Moeri, 1975; *Witch Poems,* 1976, and *Fairy Poems,* 1980, edited by Daisy Wallace; *Among the Dolls* by William Sleator, 1976; *Meet Guguze,* by Spiridon Vangheli, 1977; *Six Impossible Things Before Breakfast,* 1977, and *How Does it Feel to Be Old?,* 1979, by Norma Farber; *South Star,* 1977, and *Home,* 1979, by Betsy Hearne; *On to Widecombe Fair* by Patricia Gauch, 1978; *The Mechanical Doll* by Pamela Stearns, 1979; *Tight Times* by Barbara Hazen, 1979; *Peter Pan* by J. M. Barrie, 1980; *Ranger Rick's Holiday Book* edited by Elizabeth G. Jones, 1980; *The Night Journey* by Kathryn Lasky, 1981; *Rapunzel* by J. and W. Grimm, retold by Barbara Rogasky, 1982; *For Reading Out Loud! A Guide to Sharing Books with Children* by Margaret Mary Kimmel and Elizabeth Segel, 1983; *Big Sixteen* by Mary Calhoun, 1983; *Ronia the Robber's Daughter* by Astrid Lindgren, 1983; *A Christmas Carol* by Charles Dickens, 1983; with Hilary Knight and others, *The Cat Walked through the Casserole and Other Poems for Children* by Pamela Espeland and Marilyn Waniek, 1984; *Saint George and the Dragon: A Golden Legend Adapted from Edmund Spenser's Faerie Queen* by Margaret Hodges, 1984; *The Castle in the Attic* by Elizabeth Winthrop, 1985; *A Child's Christmas in Wales* by Dylan Thomas, 1985; *The Water of Life* by J. and W. Grimm, retold by Barbara Rogasky, 1986; *A Hidden Magic* by Vivian Vande Velde, 1986; *A Connecticut Yankee in King Arthur's Court* by Mark Twain, 1988; *Canterbury Tales* by Geoffrey Chaucer, adapted by Barbara Cohen, 1988; with Marcia Brown and others, *Sing a Song of Popcorn* compiled by Beatrice Schenk de Regniers, 1988; *Swan Lake* retold by Margot Fonteyn, 1989; *Hershel and the Hanukkah Goblins,* 1989, and *The Adventures of Hershel of Ostropol,* 1995, by Eric C. Kimmel; *The Kitchen Knight: A Tale of King Arthur* by Margaret Hodges, 1990; *Winter Poems* compiled and edited by Barbara Rogasky, 1991; *The Fortune-tellers* by Lloyd Alexander, 1992; *Ghost Eye* by Marion Dane Bauer, 1992; *Iron John* retold by Eric C. Kimmel, 1994; *The Golem* retold by Barbara Rogasky, 1996; *Comus* adapted by Margaret C. Hodges, 1996; *Five Hair-Raising Tales* by Angela Shelf Medearis, 1996; *The Serpent Slayer and Other Stories of Strong Women* retold by Katrin Tchana, forthcoming; *A Child's Calendar* by John Updike, forthcoming.

Trina Schart Hyman comments:

I illustrate books because I love stories almost as much as I love to draw. A story creates a whole world of its own. Making the pictures to illustrate the story gives me a chance to enter that world and help bring it to life, adding some special stories of my own through pictures. Drawing, for me, is a way of trying to understand the world—both the story world and the real world. It is also a way of saying what I think and feel about things. It is a kind of love letter.

* * *

Trina Schart Hyman is one of America's most prolific, best-known, and best-loved illustrators. She has illustrated over 130 children's books, ranging from poetry, to nonfiction, to story collections, to novels, to retellings of classic stories. She was also the first art director and a long-time contributor to *Cricket,* the children's literary magazine. She is probably best-known, however, for her highly original and sometimes controversial illustrations of folk and fairy tales. Preferring illustrating to writing, Hyman has written only a few of the many texts she has illustrated. Among them are *How Six Found Christmas,* a small, whimsical tale she wrote and illustrated for her daughter; her autobiography, *Self-Portrait: Trina Schart Hyman*; and her retellings of *Sleeping Beauty* and *Little Red Riding Hood.*

As Hyman makes clear in her autobiography and other writings, fairy tales—especially those of the Grimms, and in particular *Little Red Riding Hood*—were central to her childhood. In "'Cut it Down and You Will Find Something at the Roots,'" Hyman wrote of Little Red Riding Hood, "I so strongly identified with that less-than-clever trusting little twit of a heroine, and was so fascinated by her encounter with the wolf and her adventures in the forest and at Grandmother's house, that I became literally enchanted by the tale. I was so obsessed with it that the fine and wavering line between story and real life became invisible to me." Hyman's mother sewed her a little red velvet cape which she wore "every day for almost a year." She also constantly drew pictures of herself in the red cape, of grandmother's house, of the wolf, and of the forest "with an angel or two thrown in for good measure." Even when she was grown up, fairy tales continued to speak to her.

Hyman's first full-color picture book, *Snow White and the Seven Dwarfs* (1974), marked a turning point in her career. "I had recently gone through one of those life experiences that involve coincidences, jealousies, a lot of fierce emotions, treacheries, rebirths—all the emotional underpinnings of 'Snow White.' I put it all into that book," Hyman wrote in '"Cut It Down." The highly emotional illustrations have attracted both praise and criticism from reviewers and critics. Perry Nodelman wrote that the emphasis on emotion opposes "the spirit of fairy tales" and causes the viewer to align with "the one person in the story who gives in to her emotions—the Queen." Hugh Crago, on the other hand, writing in the *Dictionary of Literary Biography,* considered *Snow White* Hyman's masterpiece and "perhaps the finest *Snow White* of the century." He praised Hyman's refusal "to retreat from feelings into decoration: her Witch-Queen is both stately and passionately jealous; her minor characters (the King, the serving women, the Hunter) come vividly alive as individuals; her Prince is a real man, not a handsome dummy.... [T]he longing, devotion, hatred, suspicion, and fear that are explicit in the Grimm tale are given full rein as never before." Crago concluded that "the artist presents *Snow White* as a statement about human closeness and human loneliness," a theme "presumably central to Trina Schart Hyman's own life." Jill May, taking still another approach, saw in Hyman's illustrations "the struggle between superstition and Christianity." The old queen's "obsession for youth and beauty, for life in this sphere, have driven her to insanity. Her rage against youth and death has caused her destruction." May pointed out that the final illustration of the mirror contains faces of the young and old and future children, and at the bottom "outstretched hands in the sacrificial position reminiscent of Christ's suffering on the cross. Combined, the images point to the salvation of the innocent and the rebirth of the virtuous."

The portrait of the young Snow White was based on Hyman's eleven-year-old daughter Katrin, the Prince on writer and storyteller Jane Yolen's husband, and the Queen on artist Nancie Swanberg, with whom Hyman had lived for seven years. Among the dwarves are Hyman herself, her own father, Katrin's father, Paul Heins (translator of the text), and Konrad Lorenz, whom she had never met but whose work she had admired. Her neighbor, Hugh, who also appeared in *Little Red Riding Hood,* became the Huntsman.

Hyman followed her *Snow White* with the less personal and emotional *Sleeping Beauty* (1977). In some ways this is a more beautifully constructed book, with its text integrated with the illustrations through frames of arches, trees, and vines. Hyman wrote in "'Cut It Down," that the *Sleeping Beauty* was "intentionally more lighthearted, romantic, and softer" than *Snow White.* The model for Briar Rose was her daughter's best friend, Annie, fifteen years old. When the book was going to press Annie was killed in a car accident. "I still cannot let myself think too much about that coincidence or examine too closely the parallels between the fairy tale and real life. It was five years before I could think about illustrating another Grimms' tale."

Among the books Hyman illustrated in those five years was one of her favorites, Norma Farber's *How Does It Feel to Be Old?* (1979), a book very different in tone and feeling from the fairy tales, but equally rich in human warmth. During this time she also illustrated Barrie's *Peter Pan* (1980) with eloquent line drawings and warm color plates.

Rapunzel appeared in 1982, followed by *Little Red Riding Hood* in 1983, for which Hyman was awarded a Caldecott honor medal, and *St. George and the Dragon,* retold by Margaret Hodges, in 1984, for which she received the coveted Caldecott Medal. The illustrations for these books were influenced by Hyman's discovery of the use of borders in the folklore illustrations of Russian illustrator Ivan Bilbin. While some critics have felt the borders in *Rapunzel* and *Little Red Riding Hood* are too cluttered, confining, and distracting, others feel that in these books she at last reached a mature and successful style. *Little Red Riding Hood* is set in the New Hampshire forests of a century ago, on familiar woodland paths, and in Hyman's own kitchen. Fabric patterns from remembered clothing from her childhood appear in the border designs. It is easy to believe that the little girl Hyman portrays is the four-year-old Trina, and the wolf the paradoxical wolf of her childhood memories and dreams, who manages to be both attractive and frightening.

St. George and the Dragon, a retelling from Spenser's *Faerie Queene,* marked Hyman's first collaboration with Margaret Hodges, and a high point in her career. The book is cleaner in design than Hyman's previous picture books, with beautifully executed window-like borders, framing both the pictures and the text. While the illustration borders are undecorated, allowing the viewer to look through them into the scenes portrayed, as though looking through a window, those bordering the text contain designs and extensions of the story much like those in medieval illuminated manuscripts. Even into this allegorical tale Hyman manages to inject the personal. In her award acceptance speech she vividly recalls the process of envisioning the dragon, which she actually saw one morning rising over the hill in a neighbor's field, and also reveals that the scene on the back of the book jacket shows Margaret and Fletcher Hodges coming up the path, toward Trina at her drawing table.

In the years since *St. George and the Dragon* Hyman has continued to explore new techniques. Known for her flowing lines drawn first in pencil, then darkened with India ink and colored over in acrylics, Hyman has also used crayon and oil paints to create her illustrations. In *The Water of Life* (1986) she combines the page lay-outs of *Little Red Riding Hood* with the less-cluttered style of *St. George. Canterbury Tales* (1988), an illustrated book, contains striking, vividly-colored portraits and scenes, surrounded by intricate borders traced in gold, reminiscent of the elaborate page decorations of William Morris. *Hershel and the Hanukkah Goblins* (1989), which earned Hyman a second Caldecott honor medal, uses a style similar to that of her *Snow White,* with white blocks of text set into a dark background. *The Fortune Tellers* (1992), a folktale by Lloyd Alexander, which Hyman decided to set in Cameroon, uses less line and no borders, but retains the tradition of modeling the characters on friends and family. In this case the hero of the tale is her son-in-law, Eugene Tchana, while daughter Katrin can be seen as the Peace Corps worker "hanging around on the outskirts of things." In *Iron John* (1994), a male Cinderella story, Hyman abandons both her trademark borders and her use of line, using oil paints for the first time to create a much softer look, that still has the unmistakable look of a Hyman illustration. *Bearskin* (1997), from Howard Pyle's *Wonderbook,* incorporates a multicultural cast of characters in a fairy tale setting, including a Hyman trademark stunningly beautiful princess and a manly hunk of a hero.

Hyman's illustrations typically combine beauty, romanticism, and fantasy with warm, real, human, down-to-earth characters, but most of all, and perhaps rarest of all, her books communicate an investment of herself in her work and a dedication that has continued unabated throughout a long career, regardless of the changing tides of critical opinion.

—Linnea Hendrickson

I-J

ISADORA, Rachel

Nationality: American. **Born:** New York City, New York, c. 1953. **Education:** American School of Ballet. **Family:** Married 1) Robert Maiorano in 1977 (divorced 1982); 2) James Turner; one daughter, one son. **Career:** Dancer, Boston Ballet Company, Boston, Massachusetts; author and illustrator of children's books. **Awards:** Children's Book of the Year awards, Child Study Association, 1976, for *Max,* 1985, for *I Hear and See,* and 1986, for *Flossie and the Fox* and *Cutlass in the Snow*; Children's Choice award, International Reading Association and Children's Book Council, 1976, Children's Book Showcase award, Children's Book Council, 1977, American Library Association (ALA) Notable Book citation, and Reading Rainbow selection, all for *Max*; Junior Literary Guild citation, for *Willaby*; ALA Notable Book citation, 1979, for *Seeing Is Believing*; *Boston Globe/Horn Book* Honor Book for Illustration, 1979, Best Book for Spring award, *School Library Journal,* 1979, and Caldecott Honor Book, ALA, 1980, all for *Ben's Trumpet*; *A Little Interlude* was included in American Institute of Graphic Arts Book Show, 1981; Best Book award, School Library Journal, and ALA Notable Book citation, both 1982, both for *The White Stallion*; Children's Book award, New York Public Library, 1983, for *City Seen from A to Z*; Outstanding Science Trade Book citation, National Council for Social Studies and Children's Books Council, 1985, for *I Touch*; *Horn Book* Honor List citation, 1987, for *Flossie and the Fox*; ALA Notable Book citation, for *At the Crossroads.* **Address:** c/o William Morrow and Co., 1350 Avenue of the Americas, New York, New York 10019, U.S.A.

PUBLICATIONS FOR CHILDREN (ILLUSTRATED BY THE AUTHOR)

Fiction

Max. New York, Macmillan, 1976.
The Potter's Kitchen. New York, Greenwillow, 1977.
Willaby. New York, Macmillan, 1977.
Ben's Trumpet. New York, Greenwillow, 1979.
My Ballet Class. New York, Greenwillow, 1980.
No, Agatha! New York, Greenwillow, 1980.
Jesse and Abe. New York, Greenwillow, 1981.
City Seen from A to Z. New York, Greenwillow, 1983.
Opening Night. New York, Greenwillow, 1984.
I Hear. New York, Greenwillow, 1985.
I See. New York, Greenwillow, 1985.
I Touch. New York, Greenwillow, 1985.
The Pirates of Bedford Street. New York, Greenwillow, 1988.
Babies. New York, Greenwillow, 1990.
Friends. New York, Greenwillow, 1990.
At the Crossroads. New York, Greenwillow, 1991.
Over the Green Hills. New York, Greenwillow, 1992.
Lili at the Ballet. New York, Putnam, 1993.
Lili On Stage. New York, Putnam, 1995.
My Ballet Diary. New York, Putnam, 1995.
Newsboy. New York, Greenwillow, 1995.
A South African Night. New York, Greenwillow, 1998.

Adaptations and Retellings

The Nutcracker. New York, Macmillan, 1981.
The Little Match Girl (based on "The Little Match Girl" by Hans Christian Anderson). New York, Putnam, 1987.
The Princess and the Frog (based on "The Frog King and Iron Heinrich" by Wilhelm and Jacob Grimm). New York, Greenwillow, 1989.
Swan Lake: A Ballet Story (based on the ballet *Swan Lake* by Peter Ilich Tchaikovsky). New York, Putnam, 1989.
Firebird (based on *The Firebird* by Igor Stravinsky). New York, Putnam, 1994.
The Steadfast Tin Soldier (based on "The Steadfast Tin Soldier" by Hans Christian Anderson). New York, Putnam, 1996.

Biography

Young Mozart. New York, Viking, 1997.
Isadora Dances. New York, Greenwillow, 1998.

*

Media Adaptations: *Ben's Trumpet* (videocassette and filmstrip with audiocassette).

Illustrator: *Backstage,* 1978, *Francisco,* 1978, and *A Little Interlude,* 1980, all by Robert Maiorano; *Seeing Is Believing,* 1979, *The White Stallion,* 1982, and *Cutlass in the Snow,* 1986, all by Elizabeth Schub; *Flossie and the Fox* by Patricia C. McKissack, 1986; *Golden Bear* by Ruth Young, 1990; *Prayers, Praises, and Thanksgivings* edited by Sandol Stoddard, 1992; *Grandfather's Lovesong,* by Reve Lindberg, 1993.

* * *

Rachel Isadora writes and illustrates books for children of all ages. In books like *Babies* and *Friends* for her youngest readers, she offers darling toddlers depicted in round lines and bright colors playing and hugging and waving goodbye. Books for her older readers offer a strong contrast in style and storyline. From the dramatically evocative black and white drawings in the Newbery honor book *Ben's Trumpet* to the colorful dynamics of *Firebird* and the soft pencil drawings in books like *Max, Willaby,* and *My Ballet Class,* Isadora's impressive artistic range effectively matches style to text.

Isadora's first career as a dancer with the Boston Ballet Company ended after she suffered an injury to her foot. She had danced since she was a toddler and had drawn almost as long, though unlike the years of training for ballet, her drawing was self-taught. After she could no longer dance professionally she turned to her art and had immediate success with *Max,* her first book about a boy headed to his baseball game who tags along with his sister to her ballet lesson. After he dances with the other children and then hits a home run at his ball game, he decides that ballet will make him a better ball player. In *Max* and subsequent books, art, music, and ballet figure strongly as Isadora draws from her dance experience to tell stories about the ballet, dancers, and creative children.

Although most of her work is original fiction, she also does pictorial adaptations of ballets, biographies, and retellings of classic stories. Children of diverse races and nationalities in action—dancing, drawing, playing baseball, making music—people her work. Like Max, who warms up for his baseball games by going to dancing class, children in Isadora's books dare to be different, though in the relatively ideal worlds Isadora invents for creative children, conflicts are gentle and resolved without undue stress.

In *Willaby* and *The Pirates of Bedford Street,* children who like to draw face mild crises when, as does Willaby, they draw when they should do other things or, like Joey, they draw on surfaces they should not. Though the stories are similar, the illustrations are very different. In *Willaby* the pencil-drawn illustrations show scenes at school and home in black and white, except for Willaby and her drawings, which are given a light pink-red wash to emphasize how this creative child tunes out school and the world to draw. When other children skip rope or play with balls, Willaby draws on the playground pavement; when other children copy a get-well poem for their teacher, Willaby draws a fire truck. When time runs out, she must turn in her fire truck unsigned as her get-well car to the teacher. This causes her crisis: she likes her teacher and is afraid the teacher will be hurt if she doesn't see a card with Willaby's name on it. The crisis ends when the teacher thanks Willaby for the get-well drawing, and Willaby is happy again. Lively watercolor illustrations show Joey as he draws his way through his neighborhood; Isadora pictures the ships and pirates he sees in his imagination on the outside edges of the page while showing Joey at work on his own pictures. Joey's crisis comes when the landlady orders him to scrub his pirate-movie inspired chalk drawings off the sidewalk, front door, and steps. With his father's help, Joey does as the landlady has asked. Then the landlady defuses the crisis by giving Joey crayons and a drawing pad so "when you draw you can keep your pictures." One element these and other of Isadora's books share is the representation of various races being friends, sharing the classroom, the neighborhood, the stage, the world. Willaby, for instance, is African-American; Joey is white. But, as in all of Isadora's books, race is never mentioned; children just are what they are.

Several of Isadora's books center on the ballet, or in the case of *Isadora Dances,* her biography of Isadora Duncan, on dancing other than ballet. *My Ballet Class* offers soft pencil drawings with occasional soft pink and blue washes as Isadora pictures young dancers getting ready for dance class and then demonstrating the various steps they practice. As is typical of her work, she captures beautifully the children's postures and movement, a skill honed by observation during her years of ballet training and performance. *Opening Night* moves from class to actual performance as Heather prepares to make her stage debut. The slightly impressionistic, softly colored illustrations, each captured in a brown line frame, show Heather moving through the excitement of arriving at the theater, greeting other dancers, getting made up, dressing in her costume, and, finally, dancing on stage. Another performance story is told in *Lili on Stage.* Here the unframed watercolors again prettily sketch the pre-performance dancers and stage crew before, during, and after the ballet. Like Heather, Lili also has a "favorite ballerina," an adult to whom she takes a gift and from whom the girl receives kind encouragement. Isadora shifts from fictional girls to a real one in *Isadora Dances,* a remarkably effective introduction through anecdote and watercolor illustration to Isadora Duncan, the woman whose flowing, natural approach to dance changed the world of dance. The author-illustrator captures turn of the century style in clothing and attitudes. The controversy surrounding Duncan's approach to dance is suggested through sepia tones and darker colors in scenes like the one picturing the performance where, shocked as they were by Duncan's "filmy" costume, "forty women instantly got up and left in a huff."

Other non-fiction work includes retellings and adaptations of traditional tales and ballets. Two of these are *The Steadfast Tin Soldier* and *Firebird.* Both are rendered in dramatic, romantic watercolor illustrations which capture the tensions and emotions of the stories. Inspired by George Balanchine's interpretation of Igor Stravinsky's *The Firebird* ballet, *Firebird* plays intense reds, greens, and blues against light colors to set the tone and mood while swirling lines capture the movement of the dance. Moody browns, blacks, and blues capture the sweet sadness of Hans Christian Andersen's tale of love between the Steadfast Tin Soldier and the lovely paper ballerina. All of Isadora's retellings and adaptations remain true to the spirit of the original work, but her versions capture the essential qualities of narrative and conflict on a level with which young readers can readily connect.

Some of her most recent work draws from her experiences of traveling in South Africa. *At the Crossroads, Over the Green Hills,* and *A South African Night* offer views into the way children live in another culture. All three books are done in Isadora's impressionistic watercolor, though each allows a distinctly different view of South Africa. *A South African Night* offers a simple, soothing view: wild animals go about their business at night while the people of the city sleep. Tawny renditions of the big cats are especially appealing in this book. *Over the Green Hills* traces the journey a boy, his mother, and baby sister make on foot to visit the grandmother. This gentle family story invites Isadora's young readers to appreciate a way of life very different than their own. *At the Crossroads* pictures children of a segregated South African township who are excited that their fathers are coming home after ten months of working in the distant mines. The shanty town looks bleak: browns and grays capture the bare land and corrugated tin shacks, the one water tap that serves the entire neighborhood, and the general clutter of old tires, buckets, and wires. But though Isadora realistically depicts the squalor of such living conditions as one effect of apartheid, her emphasis is on the children's spirit and creativity as they create guitars, drums, and rhythm instruments so they can celebrate with song and dance the return of the fathers. Their joy affects the entire community, as does their disappointment when the evening arrival time comes and goes without the anticipated reunion. Determined, the children wait at the crossroads all night and are rewarded with the dawn arrival of their fathers. Then the celebration begins again as the united families "march home together."

The 1980 Newbery honor book *Ben's Trumpet* remains the best known expression of Isadora's artistic range. The powerful black-and-white drawings masterfully capture in art deco style the rhythmic energy of the 1920s Jazz Age. Jagged lines, energetic diagonals, and sweeping curves capture the boy's tension as well as the rhythm of the music he so longs to be a part of. Ben wants more than anything to play the trumpet like the musician he hears nightly from the jazz club across the street from his apartment, and the art so effectively depicts the power of the music that readers readily understand the attraction it holds for Ben. But this boy lives in the ghetto, and scenes depicting his family in their apartment make clear that they cannot afford the instrument he longs for. Finally, the trumpet player he idolizes responds by giving him a trumpet and lessons. Typical of the creative child in Isadora's books, the boy's obsession is rewarded.

One of the most appealing elements in Rachel Isadora's work is that no matter what the storyline or the style of illustration the child and the child's interests are taken seriously. Her story lines and characters invite children into the world of music and art and dance. There young readers see characters who look very much like themselves, no matter what race or nationality, enjoying their talents and creativity as they practice, perform, or simply celebrate the joys of life.

—Linda Benson

ISH-KISHOR, Sulamith

Nationality: American. **Born:** London, England, in 1896. **Education:** Hunter College, New York. **Awards:** Jewish Book Council of America Charles and Bertie Schwartz award, 1964, 1972; Association of Jewish Libraries Sydney Taylor award, 1969. **Died:** 23 June 1977.

Publications for Children

Fiction

The Heaven on the Sea and Other Stories, illustrated by Penina Ish-Kishor. New York, Bloch, 1924.
Little Potato and Other Stories, illustrated by J. Russack. New York, Board of Education, 1937.
How the Weatherman Came, illustrated by Rebecca Andrews. New York, Board of Education, 1938.
The Palace of Eagles and Other Stories, illustrated by Alice Horodisch. New York, Shoulson Press, 1948.
The Stranger Within the Gates and Other Stories, illustrated by Alice Horodisch. New York, Shoulson Press, 1948.
A Boy of Old Prague, illustrated by Ben Shahn. New York, Pantheon, 1963; London, Chatto and Windus, 1966.
Our Eddie. New York, Pantheon, 1969.
Drusilla: A Novel of the Emperor Hadrian, illustrated by Thomas Morley. New York, Pantheon, 1970.
The Master of Miracle: A New Novel of the Golem, illustrated by Arnold Lobel. New York, Harper, 1971.

Other

The Bible Story. New York, United Synagogue of America, 1921.
The Children's Story of the Bible. New York, Educational Stationery House, 1930.
Children's History of Israel from the Creation to the Present Time. New York, Jordan, 3 vols., 1930-33.
Jews to Remember, illustrated by Kyra Markham. New York, Hebrew Publishing Company, 1941.
American Promise: A History of Jews in the New World, illustrated by Grace Hick. New York, Behrman House, 1947.
Friday Night Stories, 1, 2, and 4. New York, Women's League of the United Synagogue of America, 3 vols., 1949.
The Carpet of Solomon: A Hebrew Legend, illustrated by Uri Shulevitz. New York, Pantheon, 1966.
Pathways Through the Jewish Holidays, edited by Benjamin Efron. New York, Ktav, 1967.

Publications for Adults

Other

Magnificent Hadrian: A Biography. New York, Minton Balch, and London, Gollancz, 1935.
Everyman's History of the Jews. New York, Fell, 1948.
How Theodor Herzl Created the Jewish National Fund. New York, Jewish National Fund, 1960.
Blessed Is the Daughter, with Meyer Waxman and Jacob Sloan. New York, Shengold, 1960.

* * *

Sulamith Ish-Kishor's writing reveals substantial and sure knowledge of her subject matter. Her contribution lies especially in two novels and a legend.

Her book *A Boy of Old Prague* represents a difficult feat. Tomás, a Christian boy, is bound to a Jewish family. He takes with him insidious, evil tales he has heard about the Jews. As he experiences life in the Ghetto, and a pogrom, he is drawn to Jews and develops compassion and understanding. The plight of the Jews in the 16th century is so skillfully related that the reader gains insight into the injustices dealt to them throughout history. Without pyrotechnics, the author lets her story unfold, and it is her understatement that gives the novel a quiet but gripping power. Ish-Kishor not only interprets the past but also illuminates the present, a true mark of excellence.

Our Eddie offers another facet of Jewish life. The story of the Raphel family, first in England and then in New York, centers on Eddie and on the rest of the family. There is keen perception of Eddie as a human being, and as the son of a man who cannot bring himself to a realization of what society apart from his own vision is like. This is a tapestry of a particular kind of Jewish life, full of emotion, conflict, and contrast. The author's reminiscences are deeply moving, agonizing at times, with a masterful blending of story and style.

Ish-Kishor retells a brief but important Hebrew legend in *The Carpet of Solomon.* Her love for the tale is evident as she describes Solomon's dream in which he goes to the end of the Earth by means of a magic carpet. His humbling experiences draw him closer to the wisdom for which he is known. The author creates an appropriate atmosphere and sets a dreamlike mood. The underlying message is delivered with no sermonizing.

Her knowledge of Jewish history, mores, and legends is enhanced by an intensity of style appropriate for each book. She had the touch of the craftsman coupled with an artistic use of language.

—Mae Durham Roger

IWAMATSU, Jun Atsushi. See **YASHIMA, Taro.**

JACKSON, Jesse

Nationality: American. **Born:** Columbus, Ohio, 1 January 1908. **Education:** Attended Ohio State University, Columbus, 1927-29. **Family:** Married Ann Newman in 1938; one daughter. **Career:** Worked in boys' camps and with private youth agencies, and as a juvenile probation officer; worked for the Bureau of Economic Research. From 1974 lecturer, Appalachian State University, Boone, North Carolina. **Awards:** MacDowell Colony fellowship; National Council for the Social Studies Woodson award, 1975. D. Litt.: Appalachian State University, 1982. **Died:** 14 April 1983.

PUBLICATIONS FOR CHILDREN

Fiction

Call Me Charley, illustrated by Doris Spiegel. New York, Harper, 1945.
Anchor Man, illustrated by Doris Spiegel. New York, Harper, 1947.
Room for Randy, illustrated by Frank Nicholas. New York, Friendship Press, 1957.
Charley Starts from Scratch. New York, Harper, 1958.
Tessie, illustrated by Harold James. New York, Harper, 1968.
The Sickest Don't Always Die the Quickest. New York, Doubleday, 1971.
The Fourteenth Cadillac. New York, Doubleday, 1972.

Other

Black in America: A Fight for Freedom, with Elaine Landau. New York, Messner, 1973.
Make a Joyful Noise unto the Lord! The Life of Mahalia Jackson, Queen of Gospel Singers. New York, Crowell, 1974.

* * *

Jesse Jackson wrote of ordinary people and ordinary events with extraordinary skill. He wrote of communication breakdowns at the family breakfast table, of high heel shoes that are too tight to be comfortable but also too new to discard, of Halloween night dances with masks and musicians, of nurturing hope, and of recurrent despair. Jackson's fictional people are not heroes and heroines, they are everyday mothers, fathers, sisters, brothers, nurses, doctors, printers, librarians, domestics—persons to be found in all communities. His novels of teenagers depict the struggles of young blacks for dignity and for excellence among their own people and among their white contemporaries. Portraits of whites as well as of blacks show individuals in turmoil, with not entirely dissimilar goals and dreams, frustrations, and fears.

Call Me Charley, Jackson's first novel, is a forthright story of a young black who has come to a white neighborhood and finds himself unwelcome on the block and in the school. It is only with time and effort that he wins some respect and friendship and is able to participate in group activities. The book ends with Charley still making adjustments; there are no easy solutions.

Tessie is the story of a Harlem girl who wins a scholarship to a Fifth Avenue private school. It is hard for Tessie, her father, her mother, her brother, her old Harlem friends, and her new school friends to relate to her changed roles. Tessie learns that she cannot please all the people in her life all of the time, and that she has to please herself as well as others. The ending of this book shows the beginning of Tessie's adjustment to life in two worlds; but it is only a beginning and the future remains uncertain. This story also rings true.

Jackson was one of the most successful of black American writers focusing on the interrelationships, feelings, and values of persons of several cultures, several religious groups, and several classes. His stories are fast moving, and his characters come alive to express a multi-ethnic society, with both difficulties and rewards for those striving for equity within it.

—Mary Lystad

JAMES, Will(iam Roderick)

Pseudonym for Joseph Ernest Nephtali Dufault. **Nationality:** Canadian. **Born:** St. Nazaire de Acton, Quebec, 6 June 1892. **Education:** Catholic primary school, Montreal; California School of Fine Arts, San Francisco, 1919; Yale University School of Fine Art, New Haven, Connecticut, 1921. **Military Service:** United States Army, 1918-19. **Family:** Married Alice Conradt in 1920 (separated 1935). **Career:** Cowhand, rodeo rider, and stunt man for Thomas Ince Studio, Hollywood. Served a prison sentence for cattle rustling, 1915. **Awards:** American Library Association Newbery Medal, 1927. **Died:** 3 September 1942.

PUBLICATIONS FOR CHILDREN (ILLUSTRATED BY THE AUTHOR)

Fiction

Smoky the Cowhorse. New York, Scribner, 1926.
Sand. New York, Scribner, 1929.
Sun Up: Tales of the Cow Camps. New York, Scribner, 1931.
Big Enough. New York, Scribner, 1931.
Uncle Bill: A Tale of Two Kinds of Cowboy. New York, Scribner, 1932.
In the Saddle with Uncle Bill. New York, Scribner, 1935.
Young Cowboy. New York, Scribner, 1935.
Scorpion, A Good Bad Horse. New York, Scribner, 1936.
Look-See with Uncle Bill. New York, Scribner, 1938.
The Dark Horse. New York, Scribner, 1939.
My First Horse. New York, Scribner, 1940.
Horses I've Known. New York, Scribner, 1940.

Other

Cowboys North and South. New York, Scribner, 1924.
Drifting Cowboy. New York, Scribner, 1925.
Lone Cowboy: My Life Story. New York, Scribner, 1930.
Cowboy in the Making. New York, Scribner, 1937.
The Will James Cowboy Book, edited by Alice Dalgliesh. New York, Scribner, 1938.

Publications for Adults

Novels

The Three Mustangeers. New York, Scribner, 1933.
Home Ranch. New York, Scribner, 1935.
Flint Spears, Cowboy Rodeo Contestant. New York, Scribner, 1938.
The American Cowboy. New York, Scribner, 1942.

Short Stories

Book of Cowboy Stories. New York, Scribner, 1951; London, Phoenix House, 1952.

Other

Cow Country. New York and London, Scribner, 1927.
All in a Day's Riding. New York and London, Scribner, 1933.
Will James: The Spirit of the Cowboy (exhibition catalogue), edited by J.M. Neil. Lincoln, Nebraska, Nicolaysen Art Museum, 1985.

*

Critical Studies: *Will James, The Gilt Edged Cowboy* by Anthony A. Amaral, Los Angeles, Westernlore Press, 1967, revised edition, as *Will James: The Last Cowboy Legend,* Reno, University of Nevada Press, 1980; *Will James: The Life and Work of a Lone Cowboy* by William Gardner Bell, Flagstaff, Arizona, Northland Press, 1987.

Illustrator: *Wild Animal Homesteads* by Enos A. Mills, 1923; *Tombstone: An Iliad of the Southwest* by Walter Noble Burns, 1933.

* * *

The stories written by Will James, a cowboy himself, concern cowboys and horses, all that relates to the lives of cowboys and horses. *Smoky the Cowhorse* is James at his best. At one time controversial for its colloquial quality, James's style is the spoken language of the range-rider, or seems to be; its grammatical structures are convincingly those of idiomatic language. Despite the credible dialect of poorly educated cowhands, the stories are filled with fine stylistic elements. With visual imagery, James describes the cow country and its rugged terrain, the range and its prairie vastness. When James writes of horses, his language is equally vivid, for he recreates the squeak of saddle leather, the shaking of a corral as a pony hits the earth, the stirring of dust that looks like a "young cloud." The action of the horses, as they writhe, bucking and struggling, or plunge, gallop, or buck, is convincingly vivid. Since the publication of *Smoky* in 1926, attitudes toward treatment of animals have changed, of course. *Young Cowboy,* for example, seems brutal though accurate in its description of steer roping. Publication dates, however, alert the reader to the fact that the life and work of the cowboy, too, have changed. The stories, despite the expected limitations of subject matter, come alive when they describe the actions of the cow ponies.

Characterization is most convincing when James writes of horses, the "crethures" he loves so well. One horse is different from another, despite the similar natures of their lives. Perhaps James assumes more knowledge of the horse's thinking than a realistic story should, but James is not overwhelmingly sentimental. He confines himself largely to telling what Smoky, his most famous horse character, sees, rather than revealing Smoky's emotions. This reserve is necessary, helpful in making the horses convincing characters. Although James's stories do not have clear themes beyond the unifying idea that a cowboy's life is filled with hard work he loves, they explicitly detail pieces and parts of equipment as well as techniques for working with horses.

When James's stories focus on the cowboy rather than on the horse as central character, as in *Flint Spears* and *Uncle Bill,* for example, they lose some of their vitality. In recreating the routine, the training, the activities of cowboy life, James seems to make a typical cowboy of every character, rather than making a cowboy a believable human being.

James, his own illustrator, shows great skill in depicting horses in all attitudes and poses; his realistic pictures are alive with motion, and his horses seem alive with muscular vitality.

—Rebecca J. Lukens

JARRELL, Randall

Nationality: American. **Born:** Nashville, Tennessee, 6 May 1914. **Education:** Attended schools in California and Tennessee; Vanderbilt University, Nashville (editor, *Masquerader*), B.S. in psychology 1936 (Phi Beta Kappa), M.A. in English 1939. **Military Service:** Served as a celestial navigation tower operator in the United States Army Air Corps, 1942-46. **Family:** Married 1) Mackie Langham in 1940 (divorced); 2) Mary Eloise von Schrader in 1952, two stepdaughters. **Career:** Instructor in English, Kenyon College, Gambier, Ohio, 1937-39, University of Texas, Austin, 1939-42, and Sarah Lawrence College, Bronxville, New York, 1946-47; associate professor, 1947-58, and professor of English, 1958-65, Woman's College of the University of North Carolina (later University of North Carolina at Greensboro). Lecturer, Salzburg Seminar in American Civilization, 1948; visiting fellow in Creative Writing, Princeton University, New Jersey, 1951-52; fellow, Indiana School of Letters, Bloomington, Summer 1952; visiting professor of English, University of Illinois, Urbana, 1953; Elliston Lecturer, University of Cincinnati, Ohio, 1958. Acting literary editor, the *Nation,* New York, 1946-47; poetry critic, *Partisan Review,* New Brunswick, New Jersey, 1949-53, and *Yale Review,* New Haven, Connecticut, 1955-57; member of the Editorial Board, *American Scholar,* Washington, D.C., 1957-65. Consultant in poetry, Library of Congress, Washington, D.C., 1956-58. **Awards:** *Southern Review* prize, 1936; Jeannette Sewell Davis prize, 1943, Levinson prize, 1948, and Oscar Blumenthal prize, 1951 (*Poetry,* Chicago); John Peale Bishop Memorial prize (*Sewanee Review*), 1946; Guggenheim fellowship, 1946; American Academy grant, 1951; National Book award, 1961; University of North Carolina Gardner award, 1962; American Association of University Women award, 1964; Ingram Merrill award, 1965. D.H.L.: Bard College, Annandale-on-Hudson, New York, 1962. Member, American Academy, 1961; Chancellor, Academy of American Poets, 1965. **Died:** 14 October 1965.

Publications for Children

Fiction

The Gingerbread Rabbit, illustrated by Garth Williams. New York, Macmillan, and London, Collier Macmillan, 1964.
The Bat-Poet, illustrated by Maurice Sendak. New York, Macmillan, 1964; London, Kestrel, 1977.
The Animal Family, illustrated by Maurice Sendak. New York, Pantheon, 1965; London, Hart Davis, 1967.
Fly by Night, illustrated by Maurice Sendak. New York, Farrar Straus, 1976; London, Bodley Head, 1977.

Poetry

A Bat Is Born, illustrated by John Schoenherr. New York, Doubleday, 1978.

Other

The Rabbit Catcher and Other Fairy Tales of Ludwig Bechstein. New York, Macmillan, and London, Macmillan, 1962.
The Golden Bird and Other Fairy Tales by the Brothers Grimm. New York, Macmillan, and London, Macmillan 1962.
Snow-White and the Seven Dwarfs: A Tale from the Brothers Grimm, illustrated by Nancy Ekholm Burkert. New York, Farrar Straus, 1972; London, Kestrel, 1974.
The Juniper Tree and Other Tales from Grimm, with Lore Segal, illustrated by Maurice Sendak. New York, Farrar Straus, 1973; London, Bodley Head, 1974.
The Fisherman and His Wife, illustrated by Margot Zemach. New York, Farrar Straus, 1980.

Publications for Adults

Novel

Pictures from an Institution: A Comedy. New York, Knopf, and London, Faber, 1954.

Play

The Three Sisters, adaptation of a play by Chekhov (produced New York, 1964; London, 1965). New York, Macmillan, 1969.

Poetry

Five Young American Poets, with others. New York, New Directions, 1940.
Blood for a Stranger. New York, Harcourt Brace, 1942.
Little Friend, Little Friend. New York, Dial Press, 1945.
Losses. New York, Harcourt Brace, 1948.
The Seven-League Crutches. New York, Harcourt Brace, 1951.
Selected Poems. New York, Knopf, 1955; London, Faber, 1956.
Uncollected Poems. Privately printed, 1958.
The Woman at the Washington Zoo: Poems and Translations. New York, Atheneum, 1960.
Selected Poems. New York, Atheneum, 1964.
The Lost World: New Poems. New York, Macmillan, 1965; London, Eyre and Spottiswoode, 1966.
The Complete Poems. New York, Farrar Straus, 1969; London, Faber, 1971.
The Achievement of Randall Jarrell: A Comprehensive Selection of His Poems with a Critical Introduction, edited by Frederick J. Hoffman. Chicago, Scott Foresman, 1970.
Jerome: The Biography of a Poem. New York, Grossman, 1971.

Other

Poetry and the Age. New York, Knopf, 1953; London, Faber, 1955.
Poets, Critics, and Readers (address). Charlottesville, University Press of Virginia, 1959.
A Sad Heart at the Supermarket: Essays and Fables. New York, Atheneum, 1962; London, Eyre and Spottiswoode, 1965.
The Third Book of Criticism. New York, Farrar Straus, 1969; London, Faber, 1975.
Kipling, Auden & Co.: Essays and Reviews 1935-1964. New York, Farrar Straus, 1980; Manchester, Carcanet, 1981.
About Popular Culture. Winston-Salem, North Carolina, Palaemon Press, 1981.
Randall Jarrell's Letters: An Autobiographical and Literary Selection, edited by Mary Jarrell. Boston, Houghton Mifflin, 1985; London, Faber, 1986.

Editor, *The Anchor Book of Stories.* New York, Doubleday, 1958.
Editor, *The Best Short Stories of Rudyard Kipling.* New York, Hanover House, 1961; as *In the Vernacular: The English in India* and *The English in England,* New York, Doubleday, 2 vols., 1963.
Editor, *Six Russian Short Novels.* New York, Doubleday, 1963.

Translator, with Moses Hadas, *The Ghetto and the Jews of Rome,* by Ferdinand Gregorovius. New York, Schocken, 1948.
Translator, *Goethe's Faust, Part One.* New York, Farrar Straus, 1976; London, Faber, 1978.

*

Bibliographies: "Randall Jarrell: A Bibliography of Criticism 1941-1981" by Jeffrey Meyers, in *Bulletin of Bibliography* (Boston), December 1982; *Randall Jarrell: A Descriptive Bibliography 1929-1983* by Stuart Wright, Charlottesville, University Press of Virginia, 1986.

Manuscript Collections: Walter Clinton Jackson Library, University of North Carolina, Chapel Hill; Berg Collection, New York Public Library.

Critical Studies: *Randall Jarrell 1914-1965* edited by Robert Lowell, Peter Taylor, and Robert Penn Warren, New York, Farrar Straus, 1967; *Randall Jarrell* by Karl Shapiro, Washington, D.C., Library of Congress, 1967; *The Poetry of Randall Jarrell* by Suzanne Ferguson, Baton Rouge, Louisiana State University Press, 1971, and *Critical Essays on Randall Jarrell* edited by Ferguson, Boston, Hall, 1983; *Randall Jarrell* by M.L. Rosenthal, Minneapolis, University of Minnesota Press, 1972; *Randall Jarrell* by Bernetta Quinn, Boston, Twayne, 1981; *Worlds and Lives: The Poetry of Randall Jarrell* by Charlotte H. Beck, New York, Associated Faculty Press, 1983; *Randall Jarrell's Children's Books,* La Jolla, California, Green Tiger Press, 1984, and *The Children's Books of Randall Jarrell,* Athens, University of Georgia Press, 1988, both by Jerry Griswold; "Randall Jarrell Issue" of *South Carolina Review* (Clemson), Fall 1984.

* * *

"The trouble isn't making poems," Randall Jarrell's little bat-poet bitterly says, "the trouble's finding somebody that will listen to them." Such an assertion, made by one of America's leading contemporary poets, gives rise to a series of speculations about Jarrell and his unique contribution to children's literature. For whereas reviewers hailed *The Animal Family,* the story of a lonely hunter who finds a mermaid, a bear, a lynx, and a boy who live together in understanding, it becomes apparent that joy and a happy ending are what make most readers comfortable.

In his first book, *The Gingerbread Rabbit,* Jarrell also devises a happily-ever-after. But here he was only wetting his feet. Elements of "The Gingerbread Boy" permeate this story for the very young; there is but one verse in the book, the call of the vegetable man hawking turnip-greens (published in another form as an adult poem) and yet one can find all the embryonic themes which were used in his subsequent books—innocence, loneliness, the search for a home and fulfillment, fear, love, and forebodings of death.

These themes recur on a more poetic level in *The Animal Family, The Bat-Poet,* and *Fly by Night,* and these books, one suspects, will stir and elicit a response now and in future years by the most sensitive adults and children. For the reaction of many reviewers and critics, among these (most amazingly!) other poets, often makes it painfully clear that the entire point of what Jarrell has so beautifully done is completely misunderstood. These critics fail to recognize that they are the pompous, egotistical mockingbirds of *The Bat-Poet* who listen only to their own songs and voices, who do not hear the little bat crying out in loneliness, with a need to be heard, loved, protected, and accepted for his individual contribution. The hunter and mermaid of *The Animal Family* and David of *Fly by Night* represent, among others, those with this same loneliness and search. The knowledge that they are different from others, that growth is painful and love hard-won takes a different turn in all three books; each character has his mentor, his own personality, and whether in human or animal form the fall from innocence is dealt with on various meaningful levels.

Jarrell drew from the animal world a symbolic level that deserves careful study. Is the owl of fear and possible death in *The Bat-Poet* any relation to the owl of security and mother-love of *Fly by Night?* The symbols are many, and Jarrell explored them through beautiful prose and magnificent poetry. It is quite possible, one feels, that the lack of formal poetry in *The Animal Family* makes it a less formidable, more comfortable story for some readers.

As in his adult poetry, Jarrell was laying bare his own emotions in his work for children, and never more so than in *The Bat-Poet* which is, to me, the most eloquent story ever written about the sensitivity and life of a poet, about pompous critics, or, indeed, what the making of poems is all about.

—Myra Cohn Livingston

JELLICOE, (Patricia) Ann

Nationality: British. **Born:** Middlesbrough, Yorkshire, 15 July 1927. **Education:** Polam Hall, Darlington, County Durham; Queen Margaret's, Castle Howard, Yorkshire; Central School of Speech and Drama, London (Elsie Fogarty prize, 1947), 1944-47. **Family:** Married 1) C.E. Knight-Clarke in 1950 (marriage dissolved 1961); 2) Roger Mayne in 1962, one son and one daughter. **Career:** Actress, stage manager, and director, in London and the provinces, 1947-51; founding director, Cockpit Theatre Club, London, 1952-54; lecturer and director, Central School of Speech and Drama, 1954-56; literary manager, Royal Court Theatre, London, 1973-75; founding director, 1979-85, and president, 1986, Colway Theatre Trust. O.B.E. (Officer, Order of the British Empire), 1984. **Address:** c/o Cassarotto Ramsay Ltd., National House, 60-66 Wardour St., London W1V 3HP, England.

Publications for Children

Plays

You'll Never Guess (also director: produced London, 1973). Included in *3 Jelliplays,* 1975.
Two Jelliplays: Clever Elsie, Smiling John, Silent Peter, and A Good Thing or a Bad Thing (also director: produced London, 1974). Included in *3 Jelliplays,* 1975.
3 Jelliplays. London, Faber, 1975.

Publications for Adults

Plays

Rosmersholm, adaptation of the play by Ibsen (also director: produced London, 1952; revised version produced London, 1959). San Francisco, Chandler, 1960.
The Sport of My Mad Mother (also co-director: produced London, 1958). Published in *The Observer Plays,* London, Faber, 1958; revised version, London, Faber, 1964; with *The Knack,* New York, Dell, 1964.
The Lady from the Sea, adaptation of a play by Ibsen (produced London, 1961).
The Knack (produced Cambridge, 1961; also co-director: London, 1962; Boston, 1963; New York, 1964). London, Encore, and New York, French, 1962.
The Seagull, with Adriadne Nicolaeff, adaptation of a play by Chekhov (produced London, 1964).
Der Freischütz, translation of the libretto by Friedrich Kind, music by Weber (produced London, 1964).
Shelley; or, The Idealist (also director: produced London, 1965). London, Faber, and New York, Grove Press, 1966.
The Rising Generation (produced London, 1967). Published in *Playbill 2,* edited by Alan Durband, London, Hutchinson, 1969.
The Giveaway (produced Edinburgh, 1968; London, 1969). London, Faber, 1970.
Flora and the Bandits (also director: produced Dartington, Devon, 1976).
The Reckoning (also director: produced Lyme Regis, Dorset, 1978).
The Bargain (also director: produced Exeter, 1979).
The Tide (also director: produced Axminster, Devon, 1980).
The Western Women, music by Nick Brace, adaptation of a story by Fay Weldon (also co-director: produced Lyme Regis, Dorset, 1984).

Other

Some Unconscious Influences in the Theatre. London and New York, Cambridge University Press, 1967.
Devon: A Shell Guide, with Roger Mayne. London, Faber, 1975.
Community Plays: How to Put Them On. London, Methuen, 1987.

Theatrical Activities:
Director: **Plays**—*The Confederacy* by Vanbrugh, London, 1952; *The Frogs* by Aristophanes, London, 1952; *Miss Julie* by Strindberg, London, 1952; *Rosmersholm* by Ibsen, London, 1952; *Saint's Day* by John Whiting, London, 1953; *The Comedy of Errors,* London, 1953; *Olympia* by Ferenc Molnar, London, 1953; *The Sport of My Mad Mother* (co-director, with George Devine), London, 1958; *For Children* by Keith Johnstone, London, 1958; *The Knack* (co-director, with Keith Johnstone), London, 1962; *Skyvers* by Barry Reckord, London, 1963; *Shelley,* London, 1965; *You'll Never Guess,* London, 1973; *Two Jelliplays,* London, 1974; *A Worthy Guest* by Paul Bailey, London, 1974; *Six of the Best,* London, 1974; *Flora and the Bandits,* Dartington, Devon, 1976; *The Reckoning,* Lyme Regis, Dorset, 1978; *The Bargain,* Exeter, 1979; *The Tide,* Axminster, Devon, 1980; *The Poor Man's Friend* by Howard Barker, Bridport, Dorset, 1981; *The Garden* by Charles Wood, Sherborne, Dorset, 1982; *The Western Women* (co-director, with Chris Fog and Sally-Ann Lomax), Lyme Regis, Dorset, 1984; *Entertaining Strangers* by David Edgar, Dorchester, Dorset, 1985.

* * *

Ann Jellicoe's first play for children was *You'll Never Guess,* a superb version of the Rumpelstiltskin story. This was followed by *Clever Elsie, Smiling John, Silent Peter,* and *A Good Thing or a Bad Thing.* These two plays demonstrate many of the aspects of the style which has made her adult plays so successful. In both plays a spare, realistic dialogue is used, and there is a sense of rhythm in the text which is particularly characteristic of her writing and requires careful attention in production. There is in neither play a hint of her using a special style for children, no fear of the whimsical patronising stuff children's plays are so often made of. She understands what will make children laugh or simply engage their attention.

In *Clever Elsie* she takes a traditional tale as the basis for her play. In fact several age old ideas are there, besides the tale of Elsie's overactive imagination projecting a series of future disasters, all of them based on misunderstandings. It is a play of ideas, and works well with the full age range under 11 years, but it especially appeals to infants who are quite capable of grasping the fact that the characters' simplicity and lack of logic lead them up the wrong path. The young audience is placed in a position of greater knowledge, but knowledge gained by the children using their own powers of logic, and this adds to their delight.

In *A Good Thing or a Bad Thing* the overall story or plot is of more importance—again a story using traditional elements. There is a queen, a princess in need of rescue, and a monster to threaten both her and the audience. Her rescuer, however, is not the traditional prince but a mere gardener's boy, whom we see living in very ordinary circumstances with his mother. The monster is quite imaginary—it is never seen, only heard—but in production there is not a child in the audience who fails to see it, claws and all, marching across the stage and dangerously near the front row! The tale is again a simple one but the conflicts presented are extremely powerful. The play is in fact essentially about power—the power of the mother, the ruler, the unknown and feared—which is why it evokes such a strong response from children.

This play differs from *Clever Elsie* in structure, in that Jellicoe leaves more room for direct contact with the audience and suggests areas where ad-libbing and consultation with the children is vital to the play. *Clever Elsie* has a much more contained, constructed feel to it, so that if played with *A Good Thing or a Bad Thing* the two nicely complement each other in style and make up an excellent programme.

Jellicoe, who has herself both acted and directed, leaves room in both plays for the actor and director to complete the production. Neither play requires elaborate settings or effects and can be played not only in theatres but on tour in schools very easily, the only vital technical requirements being a reasonable sound system.

—Joan Mills

JOHNS, W(illiam) E(arl)

Pseudonyms: William Earle; Jon Early. **Nationality:** British. **Born:** Bengeo, Hertfordshire, 5 February 1893. **Education:** Attended school in Bengeo; Hertford Grammar School, 1905-07; articled to a Hertford surveyor, 1907-12. **Family:** Married Maude Hunt in 1914 (died 1961), one son; lived with Doris May Leigh from 1924. **Career:** Sanitary inspector, Swaffham, Norfolk, 1912-13. Served in the Norfolk Yeomanry, 1913-15, and in the Machine Gun Corps, in Egypt and Salonika, 1916-17; transferred to the Royal Flying Corps (later Royal Air Force), 1917, and served until 1927: shot down and captured in France, 1918; Flight Officer, 1920-27; lecturer, Air Defence Cadet Corps, later Air Training Corps, and writer for the Ministry of Defence, London, 1939-45. Aviation illustrator from 1927; founding editor, *Popular Flying,* 1932-39, and *Flying,* 1938-39, both London; columnist ("The Passing Show"), *My Garden* magazine, London, 1937-44, and for *Modern Boy, Pearson's, Boys' Own Paper,* and *Girls' Own Paper.* **Died:** 21 June 1968.

Publications for Children

Fiction (Biggles series from 1945, and Worrals and Gimlet series all illustrated by Leslie Stead)

The Camels Are Coming. London, John Hamilton, 1932; as *Biggles, Pioneer Air Fighter,* London, Armada, 1982.
The Cruise of the Condor: A Biggles Story. London, John Hamilton, 1933.
Biggles of the Camel Squadron. London, John Hamilton, 1934.
Biggles Flies Again. London, John Hamilton, 1934.
Biggles Learns to Fly. London, Boys' Friend Library, 1935.
Biggles Flies East, illustrated by Howard Leigh and Alfred Sindall London, Oxford University Press, 1935.
Biggles Hits the Trail, illustrated by Howard Leigh and Alfrec Sindall. London, Oxford University Press, 1935.
Biggles in France. London, Boys' Friend Library, 1935.
The Black Peril: A Biggles Story. London, John Hamilton, 1935 as *Biggles Flies East* (not same as 1935 book), London, Boy' Friend Library, 1938.
Biggles in Africa, illustrated by Howard Leigh and Alfred Sindal London, Oxford University Press, 1936.
Biggles & Co., illustrated by Howard Leigh and Alfred Sindal London, Oxford University Press, 1936.

Biggles—Air Commodore, illustrated by Howard Leigh and Alfred Sindall. London, Oxford University Press, 1937.
Biggles Flies West, illustrated by Howard Leigh and Alfred Sindall. London, Oxford University Press, 1937.
Biggles Flies South, illustrated by Howard Leigh and Jack Nicolle. London, Oxford University Press, 1938.
Biggles Goes to War, illustrated by Howard Leigh and Martin Tyas. London, Oxford University Press, 1938.
Champion of the Main, illustrated by H. Gooderman. London, Oxford University Press, 1938.
Biggles Flies North, illustrated by Howard Leigh and Will Narraway. London, Oxford University Press, 1939.
Biggles in Spain, illustrated by Howard Leigh and J. Abbey. London, Oxford University Press, 1939.
The Rescue Flight: A Biggles Story, illustrated by Howard Leigh and Alfred Sindall. London, Oxford University Press, 1939.
Biggles in the Baltic, illustrated by Howard Leigh and Alfred Sindall. London, Oxford University Press, 1940.
Biggles in the South Seas, illustrated by Norman Howard. London, Oxford University Press, 1940.
Biggles—Secret Agent, illustrated by Howard Leigh and Alfred Sindall. London, Oxford University Press, 1940.
Worrals of the W.A.A.F. London, Lutterworth Press, 1941.
Spitfire Parade: Stories of Biggles in War-Time, illustrated by Ratcliffe Wilson. London, Oxford University Press, 1941.
Biggles Sees It Through, illustrated by Howard Leigh and Alfred Sindall. London, Oxford University Press, 1941.
Biggles Defies the Swastika, illustrated by Howard Leigh and Alfred Sindall. London, Oxford University Press, 1941.
Biggles in the Jungle, illustrated by Terence Cuneo. London, Oxford University Press, 1942.
Sinister Service, illustrated by Stuart Tresilian. London, Oxford University Press, 1942.
Biggles Sweeps the Desert, illustrated by Leslie Stead. London, Hodder and Stoughton, 1942.
Worrals Flies Again. London, Hodder and Stoughton, 1942.
Worrals Carries On. London, Lutterworth Press, 1942.
Worrals on the War-Path. London, Hodder and Stoughton, 1943.
Biggles—Charter Pilot, illustrated by Mendoza. London, Oxford University Press, 1943.
Biggles "Fails to Return", illustrated by Leslie Stead. London, Hodder and Stoughton, 1943.
Biggles in Borneo, illustrated by Stuart Tresilian. London, Oxford University Press, 1943.
King of the Commandos, illustrated by Leslie Stead. London, University of London Press, 1943.
Gimlet Goes Again. London, University of London Press, 1944.
Worrals Goes East. London, Hodder and Stoughton, 1944.
Biggles in the Orient. London, Hodder and Stoughton, 1945.
Worrals of the Islands: A Story of the War in the Pacific. London, Hodder and Stoughton, 1945.
Biggles Delivers the Goods. London, Hodder and Stoughton, 1946.
Gimlet Comes Home. London, University of London Press, 1946.
Sergeant Bigglesworth C.I.D. London, Hodder and Stoughton, 1947.
Comrades in Arms. London, Hodder and Stoughton, 1947.
Gimlet Mops Up. Leicester, Brockhampton Press, 1947.
Worrals in the Wilds. London, Hodder and Stoughton, 1947.
Biggles Hunts Big Game. London, Hodder and Stoughton, 1948.
Biggles' Second Case. London, Hodder and Stoughton, 1948.
Gimlet's Oriental Quest. Leicester, Brockhampton Press, 1948.
The Rustlers of Rattlesnake Valley. London, Nelson, 1948.
Worrals Down Under. London, Lutterworth Press, 1948.
Biggles Breaks the Silence. London, Hodder and Stoughton, 1949; as *Biggles in the Antarctic,* London, Armada, 1970.
Biggles Takes a Holiday. London, Hodder and Stoughton, 1949.
Gimlet Lends a Hand. Leicester, Brockhampton Press, 1949.
Worrals Goes Afoot. London, Lutterworth Press, 1949.
Worrals in the Wastelands. London, Lutterworth Press, 1949.
Worrals Investigates. London, Lutterworth Press, 1950.
Biggles Gets His Men. London, Hodder and Stoughton, 1950.
Gimlet Bores In. Leicester, Brockhampton Press, 1950.
Another Job for Biggles. London, Hodder and Stoughton, 1951.
Biggles Goes to School. London, Hodder and Stoughton, 1951.
Biggles Works It Out. London, Hodder and Stoughton, 1951.
Gimlet Off the Map. Leicester, Brockhampton Press, 1951.
Biggles—Air Detective. London, Latimer, 1952.
Biggles Follows On. London, Hodder and Stoughton, 1952.
Biggles Takes the Case. London, Hodder and Stoughton, 1952.
Gimlet Gets the Answer. Leicester, Brockhampton Press, 1952.
Biggles and the Black Raider. London, Hodder and Stoughton, 1953.
Biggles in the Blue. Leicester, Brockhampton Press, 1953.
Biggles in the Gobi. London, Hodder and Stoughton, 1953.
Biggles of the Special Air Police. London, Thames Publishing Company, 1953.
Biggles and the Pirate Treasure, and Other Biggles Adventures. Leicester, Brockhampton Press, 1954.
Biggles Cuts It Fine. London, Hodder and Stoughton, 1954.
Biggles, Foreign Legionnaire. London, Hodder and Stoughton, 1954.
Biggles, Pioneer Airfighter. London, Thames Publishing Company, 1954.
Gimlet Takes a Job. Leicester, Brockhampton Press, 1954.
Kings of Space, illustrated by Leslie Stead. London, Hodder and Stoughton, 1954.
Adventure Bound, illustrated by Douglas Relf. London, Nelson, 1955.
Biggles' Chinese Puzzle and Other Biggles Adventures. Leicester, Brockhampton Press, 1955.
Biggles in Australia. London, Hodder and Stoughton, 1955.
Return to Mars, illustrated by Leslie Stead. London, Hodder and Stoughton, 1955.
Biggles of 266. London, Thames Publishing Company, 1956.
Biggles Takes Charge. Leicester, Brockhampton Press, 1956.
No Rest for Biggles. London, Hodder and Stoughton, 1956.
Now to the Stars, illustrated by Leslie Stead. London, Hodder and Stoughton, 1956.
Biggles Makes Ends Meet. London, Hodder and Stoughton, 1957.
Adventure Unlimited, illustrated by Douglas Relf. London, Nelson, 1957.
Biggles of the Interpol. Leicester, Brockhampton Press, 1957.
Biggles on the Home Front. London, Hodder and Stoughton, 1957.
To Outer Space, illustrated by Leslie Stead. London, Hodder and Stoughton, 1957.
Biggles Buries a Hatchet. Leicester, Brockhampton Press, 1958.
Biggles on Mystery Island. London, Hodder and Stoughton, 1958.
Biggles Presses On. Leicester, Brockhampton Press, 1958.
The Edge of Beyond, illustrated by Leslie Stead. London, Hodder and Stoughton, 1958.
Biggles at World's End. Leicester, Brockhampton Press, 1959.

Biggles' Combined Operation. London, Hodder and Stoughton, 1959.
Biggles in Mexico. Leicester, Brockhampton Press, 1959.
The Death Rays of Ardilla, illustrated by Leslie Stead. London, Hodder and Stoughton, 1959.
Adventures of the Junior Detection Club. London, Parrish, 1960.
Biggles and the Leopards of Zinn. Leicester, Brockhampton Press, 1960.
Biggles Goes Home. London, Hodder and Stoughton, 1960.
To Worlds Unknown, illustrated by Leslie Stead. London, Hodder and Stoughton, 1960.
Where the Golden Eagle Soars, illustrated by Colin Gibson. London, Hodder and Stoughton, 1960.
The Quest for the Perfect Planet, illustrated by Leslie Stead. London, Hodder and Stoughton, 1961.
Biggles and the Missing Millionaire. Leicester, Brockhampton Press, 1961.
Biggles and the Poor Rich Boy. Leicester, Brockhampton Press, 1961.
Biggles Forms a Syndicate. London, Hodder and Stoughton, 1961.
Biggles Goes Alone. London, Hodder and Stoughton, 1962.
Biggles Sets a Trap. London, Hodder and Stoughton, 1962.
Orchids for Biggles. Leicester, Brockhampton Press, 1962.
Worlds of Wonder: More Adventures in Space, illustrated by Leslie Stead. London, Hodder and Stoughton, 1962.
Biggles and the Plane That Disappeared. London, Hodder and Stoughton, 1963.
Biggles Flies to Work. London, Dean, 1963.
Biggles' Special Case. Leicester, Brockhampton Press, 1963.
Biggles Takes a Hand. London, Hodder and Stoughton, 1963.
Biggles Takes It Rough. Leicester, Brockhampton Press, 1963.
The Man Who Vanished into Space. London, Hodder and Stoughton, 1963.
Biggles and the Black Mask. London, Hodder and Stoughton, 1964.
Biggles and the Lost Sovereigns. Leicester, Brockhampton Press, 1964; as *Biggles and the Lost Treasure,* London, Knight, 1978.
Biggles Investigates and Other Stories of the Air Police. Leicester, Brockhampton Press, 1965.
Biggles and the Blue Moon. Leicester, Brockhampton Press, 1965.
Biggles and the Plot That Failed. Leicester, Brockhampton Press, 1965.
Biggles Looks Back. London, Hodder and Stoughton, 1965.
Biggles Scores a Bull. London, Hodder and Stoughton, 1965.
Biggles in the Terai. Leicester, Brockhampton Press, 1966.
Biggles and the Gun Runners. Leicester, Brockhampton Press, 1966.
Biggles and the Penitent Thief. Leicester, Brockhampton Press, 1967.
Biggles Sorts It Out. Leicester, Brockhampton Press, 1967.
Biggles and the Dark Intruder. London, Knight, 1967.
Biggles in the Underworld. Leicester, Brockhampton Press, 1968.
The Boy Biggles. London, Dean, 1968.
Biggles and the Deep Blue Sea. Leicester, Brockhampton Press, 1968.
Biggles and the Little Green God. Leicester, Brockhampton Press, 1969.
Biggles and the Noble Lord. Leicester, Brockhampton Press, 1969.
Biggles Sees Too Much. Leicester, Brockhampton Press, 1970.
Biggles of the Royal Flying Corps (selection), edited by Piers Williams. Maidenhead, Berkshire, Purnell, 1978.

Other

Fighting Planes and Aces, illustrated by Howard Leigh. London, John Hamilton, 1932.
The Modern Boy's Book of Pirates. London, Amalgamated Press, 1939.
The Biggles Book of Heroes. London, Parrish, 1959.
The Biggles Book of Treasure Hunting, illustrated by William Randell. London, Parrish, 1962.

Editor, *The Modern Boy's Book of Aircraft.* London, Amalgamated Press, 1931.

PUBLICATIONS FOR ADULTS

Novels

Mossyface (as William Earle). London, Mellifont Press, 1932.
The Spy Flyers. London, John Hamilton, 1933.
Sky High. London, Newnes, 1936; revised edition, London, Latimer, 1951.
Steeley Flies Again. London, Newnes, 1936; revised edition, London, Latimer, 1951.
Blue Blood Runs Red (as Jon Early). London, Newnes, 1936.
Murder by Air. London, Newnes, 1937; revised edition, London, Latimer, 1951.
The Murder at Castle Deeping. London, John Hamilton, 1938; revised edition, London, Latimer, 1951.
Desert Night: A Romance. London, John Hamilton, 1938.
Wings of Romance: A Steeley Adventure. London, Newnes, 1939; revised edition, London, Latimer, 1951.
The Unknown Quantity. London, John Hamilton, 1940.
No Motive for Murder. London, Hodder and Stoughton, 1958; New York, Washburn, 1959.
The Man Who Lost His Way. London, Macdonald, 1960.

Short Stories

The Raid. London, John Hamilton, 1935.
Doctor Vane Answers the Call. London, Latimer, 1950.
Short Sorties. London, Latimer, 1953.
Sky Fever and Other Stories. London, Latimer, 1953.

Plays

Radio Plays (with G.R. Ranier): *The Machine That Disappeared,* 1942; *The Charming Mrs. Nayther,* 1942.

Other

The Pictorial Flying Course, with Harry M. Schofield, illustrated by Johns. London, John Hamilton, 1932.
The Air V.C.'s. London, John Hamilton, 1935.
Some Milestones of Aviation. London, John Hamilton, 1935.
The Passing Show: A Garden Diary by an Amateur Gardener. London, My Garden, 1937.
No Surrender, with R.A. Kelly. London, Harrap, 1969.

Editor, *Wings: A Book of Flying Adventures.* London, John Hamilton, 1931.
Editor, *Thrilling Flights.* London, John Hamilton, 1935.

*

Critical Studies: *Biggles: The Authorised Biography* by John Pearson, London, Sidgwick and Jackson, 1979; *By Jove, Biggles: The Life of Captain W.E. Johns* by Peter Berresford Ellis and Piers Williams, London, W.H. Allen, 1981.

Illustrator: *Desert Wings* by Covington Clarke, 1931.

* * *

The emergence of flying stories in the closing years of the 19th century can be seen not only as an extension of the traditional adventure story, but as a response to the actual developments in aviation at that time. Early writers in the genre owed rather more to fantasy and invention than scientific knowledge, but by the time of World War I, writers such as P.F.Westerman began to produce more realistic stories.

W.E. Johns built upon this tradition. Unlike Westerman, Johns had actually seen a good deal of active service. Originally a soldier who had experienced trench warfare in Gallipoli, he transferred to the Royal Flying Corps in 1917, and was a member of the 55th Squadron involved in bombing raids on Germany. Shot down in 1918, he finished the war in a prison camp, but remained in the R.A.F. until 1927, obtaining further flying experience in India and Iraq.

In 1932 he published in the magazine *Popular Flying* "The White Fokker," his first story about Biggles, the pilot who would become his most enduring creation. "Biggles" is the nickname of James Bigglesworth, at this time a teenager but already a Flight Commander on active service in France during World War I. Members of Biggles's squadron are regularly being ambushed and killed by a German Fokker B. VII, but, though Biggles eventually manages to trap and to shoot down the German pilot, what Johns emphasises is not just the skill and courage of his hero, but the cruelty of war, including its psychological damage.

In these early stories, Biggles is no stereotyped hero but a patriotic, skilful, highly-strung young man, who several times comes close to tears, even hysteria, when comrades are lost. In the magazine stories, collected in such books as *The Camels Are Coming* and *Biggles of the Camel Squadron,* Johns successfully conveys how many flyers felt and behaved, with their mixture of idealism and apparent flippancy, in the days when the average life expectancy of a new pilot was sometimes estimated to be about three weeks.

The problem for Johns was where to go once he had exhausted his early war experiences. *The Cruise of the Condor* pointed the way, in a tale about the post-war adventures of Biggles and two of his wartime comrades, the Hon. Algernon Lacey and flight-sergeant Smyth, on a treasure-hunt in the wilds of Brazil. Later books show Johns adopting equally conventional plots, and with the addition to Biggles's team of 15-year-old Ginger Hebblethwaite, the stories tend to focus upon the group's attempts to solve mysteries. The narrative line becomes increasingly formulaic, as the group separate for their investigations, and one part of the group always has to rescue the other from its difficulties. Thus in *Biggles—Air Commodore,* for example, the characters set out to find out why merchant ships are being sunk in the Indian Ocean, but when the group separate to begin their search, Ginger and Algy crash in the jungle, and have to be rescued by Biggles, and later when Biggles and Ginger are lost on an island Algy has to return the compliment. Thus a device initially used to create suspense soon became predictable and monotonous.

The outbreak of World War II enabled Johns to describe Biggles resuming active service in such books as *Biggles Defies the Swastika* and *Biggles in the Orient.* (He also wrote 11 books about a heroine Squadron Officer Joan Worralson, "Worrals" of the Women's Auxiliary Air Force, as well as a series about an army hero, "Gimlet" King of the Commandos.) After the war, Johns continued to narrate Biggles's career, usually as an officer in the Air Police, in such books as *Sergeant Bigglesworth C.I.D.* and *Biggles Works It Out.* From 1954 he also began to publish a series of science-fiction stories, beginning with *Kings of Space,* the first of 10 books about the adventures of Professor Brane and the crew of his spaceship.

Despite the science fiction, and the stories about Worrals and Gimlet, however, it is the books—102 all told—about Biggles upon which Johns's reputation rests. In 1964 the first UNESCO Statistical Year Book reported that so many books about him had been published worldwide that Biggles was the most popular juvenile hero in the world. Yet these books are the subject of considerable controversy. Although Johns hoped that his flying-story adventures would teach his juvenile readers such virtues as courage, sportsmanship "according to the British idea," teamwork, and loyalty to the Empire, many critics have pointed to the presence of racism implicit in any defence of imperialism, and to the simple, stereotyped view of foreigners present in Johns's works.

As the plots in the later stories became more formulaic and predictable, and the language became increasingly littered with clichés, and as the character of Biggles himself became more tight-lipped and imperturbable, so Johns's attitude seems to have shifted from a differentiation between good and bad Germans in the early war stories to a derogatory treatment of most non-Europeans in the later books. In this respect Johns is partly the product of his time, of course, and it is pleasing to learn that in his last unfinished tale Biggles's successor was to have been an Indian. For these reasons, however, the major interest of most of Johns's books today is likely to be of a cultural or historical kind, but readers and commentators do him a disservice when they ignore the early stories.

—Dennis Butts

JOHNSON, Angela

Nationality: American. **Born:** 18 June 1961, Tuskegee, Alabama. **Education:** Attended Kent State University. **Career:** Child development worker, Volunteers in Service to America (VISTA), Ravenna, Ohio, 1981-82; freelance writer of children's books, from 1989. **Awards:** *School Library Journal* Best Books of the Year, 1989; Ezra Jack Keats Award, 1990; Coretta Scott King honor book, 1990; Coretta Scott King Award, 1994. **Member:** Authors Guild, Authors League of America. **Address:** Orchard Books, 95 Madison Avenue, New York, New York 10016, U.S.A.

PUBLICATIONS FOR CHILDREN

Fiction

Tell Me a Story, Mama, illustrated by David Soman. New York, Orchard Books, 1989.

Do Like Kyla, illustrated by James Ransome. New York, Orchard Books, 1990.

When I Am Old with You, illustrated by David Soman. New York, Orchard Books, 1990.
One of Three, illustrated by David Soman. New York, Orchard Books, 1991.
The Leaving Morning, illustrated by David Soman. New York, Orchard Books, 1992.
The Girl Who Wore Snakes. New York, Orchard Books, 1993.
Julius the Pig. New York, Orchard Books, 1993.
Toning the Sweep. New York, Orchard Books, 1993.
Joshua by the Sea, illustrated by Rhonda Mitchell. New York, Orchard Books, 1994.
Joshua's Night Whispers, illustrated by Rhonda Mitchell. New York, Orchard Books, 1994.
Mama Bird, Baby Birds, illustrated by Rhonda Mitchell. New York, Orchard Books, 1994.
Rain Feet, illustrated by Rhonda Mitchell. New York, Orchard Books, 1994.
Shoes Like Miss Alice's, illustrated by Ken Page. New York, Orchard Books, 1995.
Humming Whispers. New York, Orchard Books, 1995.
The Aunt in Our House, illustrated by David Soman. New York, Orchard Books, 1996.
The Rolling Store, illustrated by Peter Catalanotto. New York, Orchard Books, 1997.
Daddy Calls Me Man, illustrated by Rhonda Mitchell. New York, Orchard Books, 1997.
Gone from Home: Short Takes. New York, DK Publishing, 1998.
Songs of Faith. New York, Orchard Books, 1998.

* * *

Angela Johnson is a master at representing human nature in various guises at different levels. Her work ranges from simple board books to picture books to novels for young adults. The picture book *When I Am Old with You* was designated a 1990 Coretta Scott King Honor Book, and the novel *Toning the Sweep* received the 1994 Coretta Scott King Award.

Toning the Sweep is an ambitious work that succeeds in weaving the strands of a coming-of-age novel into the tapestry of the civil rights movement. The drama centers upon a life cut short by racism, as well as the impact of this event upon the lives of family members in various generations. Also, the young reader sees a community unite for survival and for the mutual support its members can offer one another. The title refers to the ritual of hitting with a hammer a metal sweep (a type of plow) in order to ring a dead person's soul to heaven. This ritual is reminiscent of a West African ritual in which the community comes together and shrieks at the moment of a person's death to strengthen his or her passage through death's door. It must be recognized that death was not viewed as an end, but as a continuation of life; death was seen as a transitional passage between one form of life and another. Also, souls not "announced" were destined to wander about restlessly. Fourteen-year-old Emmie and her mother unite in the long overdue action of toning the sweep for Emmie's grandfather, who was killed by the Ku Klux Klan in 1964. He had decided to spend 30 years worth of patient savings on a car, and had thereby become an unwitting participant in the civil rights drama; his life became a symbol of what happened to Blacks who dared step outside the propertyless position assigned to them.

Johnson connects the participants in this fictional community with rich symbolism. Ola, Emmie's grandmother, is dying of cancer. The trip to the California desert to help her settle her things before moving to Cleveland is a celebration of her life and a tying up of the loose ends frayed by Charles's death in 1964. Johnson cleverly uses the desert plant world to suggest the tenacity of African Americans in pursuing their freedom. The oft-maligned kudzu plant, for example, becomes a symbol of survival and strength when transported by Ola to the desert. This green vine was "something that no one could stop," something growing uncontainably with just a little water and sunshine. Similarly, the Joshua tree, which represents support for the different characters with its long, outstretched branches, is a referent to the Joshua of the Old Testament who was born into slavery but was guided out of Egypt and rose to become a beloved leader of his people.

Johnson's poetic artistry gives her a way with words that negotiates smoothly the rugged terrain of the subtle and the obvious. The 1964 Buick convertible that transported Ola and her child out of the horror of the Alabama lynching is a metaphor for freedom, and it is in this vehicle that Emmie picks up the freedom symbol on her own. In the car she can move about in a world all-to-often unkind to the daughters of a slave heritage. Johnson reveals to us a world where the promise of a better quality of life blooms under the protective embrace of an extended family, formed not just by kinfolk but by "other-mothers" and a community determined to free its children.

Johnson's second novel, *Humming Whispers,* explores fear within loving family relationships. Sophy wonders if she will become schizophrenic like her older sister, Nikki (Nicole). Johnson reveals Sophy's fear as she turns fourteen, the age that Nikki was when the whispers began. Orphaned ten years earlier by a car crash, the sisters live with their aunt Shirley who tries to cope and loves them unconditionally. Within the context of a loving family relationship, Johnson describes Sophy's attempts to cope with her fear.

In her books for a younger audience, Johnson develops a supportive and extended family network around her characters. *Do Like Kyla, One of Three,* and *The Leaving Morning* present the typical challenges of most children in Western societies (e.g., sibling rivalry, birth order challenges, and family relocations). *The Aunt in Our House* focuses on how a woman comes to live with her brother's family and how they try to make her happy, to help her over the sadness of losing her home. Although she and her brother are white and her sister-in-law is black, race is only shown through illustrations, not mentioned. Johnson presents children/families of color leading normal, everyday lives, having normal growing-up experiences, and rising to the occasion with the help of family members and friends. This is a realistic portrayal of African Americans and adds a much needed dimension to children's literature.

Johnson's particular skill in illustrating loving relationships is evidenced in *Daddy Calls Me Man.* The book contains four simple verses written by a boy inspired by four of his father's paintings. The focus is on young Noah's relationship with his loving family. In the final verse Noah's parents show their appreciation for his unselfishness towards his younger sister. The title of the book captures the pride of father and son.

In *Tell Me A Story, Mama,* as well as in *When I Am Old with You,* Johnson experiments with generational stories that depart from a linear time frame. This is also true in *The Rolling Store* where two young friends, one black and one white, prepare their own mini-version of the rolling store like the one in Granddaddy's song about his childhood memories in an almost carless countryside

Here past meets present joyously and lovingly as the song comes to an end and Granddaddy joins the children and their "store". Johnson captures the depth of tenderness enjoyed by children and the breadth of instruction supplied by affectionate elders.

Her picture book talents are especially visible in *The Girl Who Wore Snakes* and *Julius the Pig,* where the unfamiliar is made familiar and the familiar becomes charmingly unfamiliar. In the former she indirectly alludes to a parallel between snakes, which elicit an aversion in some people, and African Americans, who are sometimes reacted to in a similar way. But Johnson subverts that irrational bias by transforming the snake into a thing of beauty—an ornament to be admired and worn proudly. In *Julius the Pig* Johnson has created a spoof of childhood with an outrageously naughty pig. The work teaches the fine art of kindness while illustrating the delights of nonsense humor.

Even in the board books for very young children, Johnson carefully develops a world of poetry for her listeners. In sum, there is a high consistency in Angela Johnson's books—in the poetic quality of writing and in the narrational inventiveness that leave readers hoping for more to come.

—Contributor Lucille H. Gregory,
updated by Marilyn F. Apseloff

JOHNSON, Crockett

Pseudonym for David Johnson Leisk. **Nationality:** American. **Born:** New York City, 20 October 1906. **Education:** Attended Cooper Union, New York, 1924; New York University, 1925. **Family:** Married Ruth Krauss, *q.v.,* in 1940. **Career:** Drew weekly panel "Little Man with the Eyes" for *Collier's,* 1938-41, and the syndicated comic strip "Barnaby," 1941-62, and panel "Barkis," 1955. **Died:** 11 July 1975.

Publications for Children (illustrated by the author)

Fiction

Who's Upside Down? New York, Scott, 1952; as *Upside Down,* Chicago, Whitman, 1969.
Harold and the Purple Crayon. New York, Harper, 1955; London, Constable, 1957.
Is This You?, with Ruth Krauss. New York, Scott, 1955; London, Pitman, 1966.
Harold's Fairy Tale: Further Adventures with the Purple Crayon. New York, Harper, 1956.
Harold's Trip to the Sky. New York, Harper, 1957.
Terrible, Terrifying Toby. New York, Harper, 1957.
Time for Spring. New York, Harper, 1957.
The Blue Ribbon Puppies. New York, Harper, 1958.
Harold at the North Pole: A Christmas Journey with the Purple Crayon. New York, Harper, 1958.
Merry Go Round. New York, Harper, 1958.
Ellen's Lion: Twelve Stories. New York, Harper, 1959; Kingswood, Surrey, World's Work, 1964.
The Frowning Prince. New York, Harper, 1959.
Harold's Circus. New York, Harper, 1959.
Will Spring Be Early or Will Spring Be Late? New York, Crowell, 1960.
A Picture for Harold's Room: A Purple Crayon Adventure. New York, Harper, 1960; Kingswood, Surrey, World's Work, 1963.
Harold's ABC. New York, Harper, 1963.
The Lion's Own Story: Eight New Stories about Ellen's Lion. New York, Harper, 1963; Kingswood, Surrey, World's Work, 1964.
We Wonder What Will Walter Be When He Grows Up? New York, Holt Rinehart, 1964; Kingswood, Surrey, World's Work, 1966.
Castles in the Sand, illustrated by Betty Fraser. New York, Holt Rinehart, 1965; Kingswood, Surrey, World's Work, 1967.
Gordy and the Pirate, and the Circus Ringmaster, and the Knight, and the Major League Manager, and the Western Marshal, and the Astronaut, and a Remarkable Achievement. New York, Putnam, 1965.
The Emperor's Gifts. New York, Holt Rinehart, 1965; Kingswood, Surrey, World's Work, 1966.

Publications for Adults

Other

Barnaby. New York, Holt, 1943.
Barnaby and Mr. O'Malley. New York, Holt, 1944.
Barkis: Some Precise and Some Speculative Interpretations of the Meaning of a Dog's Bark at Certain Times and in Certain (Illustrated) Circumstances. New York, Simon and Schuster, 1956.

*

Illustrator: *The Carrot Seed,* 1945, *How to Make an Earthquake,* 1954, and *The Happy Egg,* 1967, all by Ruth Krauss; *Story of Money* by Constance Foster, 1950; *Willie's Adventures* by Margaret Wise Brown, 1954; *Mickey's Magnet* by Franklin and Branley, 1956; *The Little Fish That Got Away* by Bernardine Cook, 1957.

* * *

Crockett Johnson was the creator of *Barnaby,* a comic strip forever cherished in the memories of those who knew it. Mr. O'Malley, Barnaby's inefficient fairy godfather, is the key figure. Square and squat and hatted, Mr. O'Malley has inadequate wings, a cigar for a wand, and a lifetime membership in the Little Men's Chowder and Marching Society. He is badly miscast as a fairy godfather, and Barnaby spends most of his time extracting himself from the messes Mr. O'Malley gets both of them into.

Johnson wrote a number of children's books as well. These are blessed with the same clear drawings and pervasive humor as the *Barnaby* strip, though the humor is less adult. Johnson managed the delicate feat of writing whimsically for children without falling into sentimentality. *Harold and the Purple Crayon,* perhaps his most successful book for children, is a virtuoso performance. The simple, convincing pictures illustrate a gently humorous text about a little boy creating his own adventurous excursion into the world with his purple crayon. The firm purple line grows from page to page, making a moon, a road, an ocean, a picnic, and animals to eat the leftovers, a city full of windows (but not the right window), until Harold, always calm and in command, draws his own window, his own bed and his own covers to pull up, and so ends his expedition. *A Picture for Harold's Room,* an "I Can Read Book," is a little flatter, perhaps because of the restricted vocabulary; *Harold's ABC* may be slightly too intricate for its audience.

Ellen's Lion and *The Lion's Own Story* demonstrate Johnson's ability to keep a nice balance between imagination and reality. The two books are collections of very brief stories consisting of dialogues between Ellen (perhaps 5 years old) and her stuffed lion. Ellen leads an extremely busy and adventurous life being a knight, a mountain climber, a doctor, and planning to be a "lady fireman." She is sometimes aided, but reluctantly, by her lion, who never for a moment forgets that he is stuffed, has button eyes and no powers of locomotion. He is the realist, she the Walter Mitty; together they make two amusing books, very Crockett Johnson.

Another Walter Mitty character is Gordy, of *Gordy and the Pirate,* who encounters on the way home from school a pirate and several other romantic figures, all of whom invite him to the most tempting adventures. But Gordy remembers each time, just in time, that this is the day he promised to go straight home from school. And so, eventually, he does: "And, for Gordy, that was indeed a remarkable achievement." Unfortunately, the gentle irony of the story may well go over the heads of its intended readers.

And that, indeed, may be the principal problem with some of Johnson's stories. It is not that he was given to winking over the heads of children at the adults who might be reading the stories aloud. It is just that the perspective necessary to catch the joke may be a little beyond the child for whom the story is meant. Johnson always perceived the humor of the human ego, though kindly. Just as Mr. O'Malley's inflated self-esteem is the basis for much of the fun in *Barnaby,* so some of the humor in the two *Ellen* books and the main joke of *We Wonder What Will Walter Be When He Grows Up?* depends upon a recognition of egocentricity. But small children, who are themselves egocentric, may not see it. And some of the word play in *Walter*—the characterization of the mole as the "deepest thinker," the giraffe as the "highest thinker" and so forth—seems to rest upon an acquaintance with certain clichés which little children may not have.

—Anne Scott MacLeod

JONAS, Ann

Nationality: American. **Born:** 28 January 1932, Flushing, New York. **Education:** Cooper Union for the Advancement of Science and Art, New York City, art certificate 1959. **Family:** Married Donald Crews (see his entry) in 1963; two daughters. **Career:** Designer, Rudolph de Harak, Inc. (design company), New York City, 1959-62; designer, Advertis, Inc., Frankfurt, Germany, 1962-63; designer, Donald & Ann Crews (design company), New York City, from 1964. Author and illustrator of children's books, from 1981. **Awards:** *New York Times* Best Illustrated Books of the Year, 1983; *Booklist* Children's Editors' Choice books, 1983; Nebraska Library Association Golden Sower Book Award, 1985; *School Library Journal* Best Books, 1984 and 1985; Child Study Association of America's Children's Books of the Year, 1985; *Boston Globe-Horn Book* Award honor book, 1986; *New York Times* Best Books of the Year, 1989.

PUBLICATIONS FOR CHILDREN

Picture Books (illustrated by the author)

When You Were a Baby. New York, Greenwillow, 1982.
Two Bear Cubs. New York, Greenwillow, 1982.
Round Trip. New York, Greenwillow, 1983.
Holes and Peeks. New York, Greenwillow, 1984.
The Quilt. New York, Greenwillow, 1984.
The Trek. New York, Greenwillow, 1985.
Now We Can Go. New York, Greenwillow, 1986.
Where Can It Be? New York, Greenwillow, 1986.
Reflections. New York, Greenwillow, 1987.
Color Dance. New York, Greenwillow, 1989.
Aardvarks, Disembark! New York, Greenwillow, 1990.
The Thirteenth Clue. New York, Greenwillow, 1992.
Splash! New York, Greenwillow, 1995.
Watch William Walk. New York, Greenwillow, 1997.

* * *

Each picture book by Ann Jonas is an adventure in design—clever, creative, interactive, and fun. From the simple *When You Were a Baby* to the surrealistic *The Quilt,* each book invites the reader to participate in the adventure. Because she is a graphic artist first and a storyteller second, her books depend far more upon illustration than text. On each page, a few well-chosen words suffice; these complement the illustrations and draw the reader into the experience of the book. Readers are asked to find hidden animals, open cupboards on the page, recognize objects by seeing only parts of them, experience the reversal of figure and ground. Deceptively simple, Jonas's illustrations are actually sophisticated approaches to visual perception which engage adults as well as children.

Jonas's first book, *When You Were A Baby,* begins with a view of the top of a crib with a baby's legs and feet in the air and the declaration in large, clear letters: "When you were a baby, you couldn't do very much." On the last page a pair of toddler feet stand upright in shoes and socks, above the words "But now you can!" The illustrations throughout, as bold and uncluttered as the message, reinforce the toddler's sense of accomplishment. Each double-page spread reveals one more task the toddler now finds easy: piling blocks, drinking from a glass, sitting a doll in a chair, taking a toy dog for a walk.

Warmth and joy continue in *Two Bear Cubs* as the cubs, fleeing a skunk, lose sight of their mother. They eagerly explore their world, discover honey and angry bees, and try to fish, while the text repeats innocently, "But where's their mother?" The cubs may not know, but the reader sees the mama bear slightly camouflaged in the flat, green and brown background, safely near as her cubs learn independence. Preschoolers can triumphantly point out the hidden bear, pleased to see what the cubs have missed. In *The Trek,* a child old enough to walk to school alone imagines jungle animals along her path. Slightly camouflaged like the mother bear they are quite visible to the discerning eye. *The Thirteenth Clue* for children who can read, also requires some detecting—readers must decipher upside-down, reversed, hidden, and scrambled messages.

Several books, including *Holes and Peeks* and *Now We Can Go* portray typical toddler situations with sensitivity, humor, and accuracy. Both employ eye-catching, large, bright illustrations as child narrates a simple text. In *Where Can It Be?* a toddler searches for something lost. The reader helps by turning half or three-quarter pages to open closets and cupboards or to look under a bedspread or table. Each opened page reveals Jonas's eye for detail; the refrigerator, for example, is filled with pickles, milk, maple syrup, leftovers—and much more. After a treasure hunt throughout the house—each room is individually wallpapered and furnished—the child is happily reunited with the missing blanket.

Jonas's best known book is unquestionably *Round Trip.* With deftly drawn black and white silhouettes, Jonas takes readers on a trip that begins at home in early morning and ends at night. Passing farm, mountains, wood, and city, readers travel through starkly dramatic scenes until sunset, when it is "time to turn around"—and readers turn the book over to reverse figure and ground on the return trip. Shifting perspective, readers look up at buildings they had looked down on earlier. We see marshy inlets turn into fireworks in a night sky and discover whitecaps in the ocean turning into birds flying overhead. The temptation to turn the book over to compare scenes is irresistible. *Reflections* recreates a child's day at the seashore, using a similar reversible picture technique, but in color. The pictures are pretty, appealing, and equally deft, though not as dramatic as those in *Round Trip.*

The Quilt, more surrealistic and psychologically complex than anything else by Jonas, portrays a child's dream/nightmare adventure as the richly-colored squares on her handmade quilt turn into a town. Observant readers will recognize patterns from individual squares in each dream sequence. In contrast, *Color Dance* is almost too realistic. To illustrate the color wheel, Jonas creates what she calls a "fantasy" of dancers twirling colored scarves. Visually attractive, *Color Dance* is clearly designed to teach. Similarly, *Aardvarks, Disembark!* retells the Noah story in order to introduce all the animals whose names Noah did not know. Presented alphabetically, to scale and in perspective on each page, some animals are familiar (condor, yak, wallaby) while others are either obscure, endangered, or extinct (zeren, aardwolf, quagga, dodo); a glossary identifies which animals fit into each category.

In *Splash!* and *Watch William Walk,* Jonas continues to teach. *Splash!* whimsically encourages counting. As various animals and the child narrator get into and out of a pond, the repeated question "How many are in my pond?" wiggles along the bottom, on the left side of each brightly colored double-page spread. *Watch William Walk* addresses language rather than math, as Jonas plays with alliteration, using the letter W. Aerial-view illustrations of a boy, a girl, a dog, and a duck, all leaving footprints in the sand, accompany the sometimes silly but always correct sentences: "William won't walk with Wilma when Wilma walks Wanda." "Wanda whiffs wetlands." Readers may well be inspired to make up their own tongue-twisters. Interactive as ever, Ann Jonas continues to provide delightful surprises in her imaginatively conceived, artistically sophisticated books.

—Lois Rauch Gibson

JORDAN, Sherryl

Nationality: New Zealander. **Born:** Sherryl Brogden, 8 June 1949, Hawera, New Zealand. **Family:** Married Lee Jordan in 1970; one daughter. **Education:** Attended Tauranga Girls' College, 1962-64; two years of nursing training, 1967-68. **Career:** Illustrator, 1980-85; full-time writer since 1988. Part-time work as a teacher's aide in primary schools, working with profoundly deaf children, 1979-87. Writer-in-residence, University of Iowa, 1993. **Awards:** Winner, national illustrating competition, 1980; Choysa Bursary, 1988; AIM Story Book of the Year Award, New Zealand, 1991, for *Rocco*; Runner-up, AIM Story book of the year award, and short-listed for the New Zealand Library Association Esther Glen Award, 1992, for *The Juniper Game*; short-listed for the New Zealand Library Association Esther Glen Award, and AIM Junior Story Book of the Year Award, 1992, for *The Wednesday Wizard*; short-listed for the AIM Story Book of the Year Award, 1993, for *Denzil's Dilemma*; selected by American Bookseller magazine as a "Pick of the List", 1993, and American Library Association Best Book for Young Adults, 1994, American Library Association Recommended Book for the Reluctant Young Adult Reader, 1994, Children's Book of the Year by Bank Street School of Education, 1994, and short-listed for the New Zealand AIM Book Of the Year Awards, 1994, listed in Whitcoull's New Zealand Top 100 books, 1997, for *Winter of Fire*; short-listed for the New Zealand AIM Book of the Year Awards, short-listed for the New Zealand Library Association Esther Glen Award, and American Library Association Best Book for Young Adults, all 1995, all for *Tanith (Wolf-Woman)*; short-listed for the New Zealand Post Children's Book Awards (formerly the New Zealand AIM Awards), Secret Sacrament, 1997. **Member:** Children's Literature Association (committee member), Bay of Plenty branch. **Agent:** Renee Cho, of McIntosh and Otis, Inc., 310 Madison Avenue, New York, New York 10017, U.S.A. **Address:** 165 Kings Avenue, Matua, Tauranga, New Zealand.

Publications for Children

Fiction

The Firewind and the Song, illustrated by the author. Tokyo, Kagyusha Publishers, 1984.

Matthew's Monsters, illustrated by Dierdre Gardiner. Auckland, Ashton Scholastic, 1986.

No Problem Pomperoy, illustrated by Jan van der Voo. Century Hutchinson, 1988.

Kittens (school reader). Shortlands, 1989.

The Wobbly Tooth. Shortlands, 1989.

Babysitter Bear, illustrated by Trevor Pye. Century Hutchinson, 1990.

Rocco, Auckland, Ashton Scholastic, and London, Scholastic. 1990; as *A Time of Darkness,* New York, Scholastic, 1990.

The Juniper Game. Auckland, Ashton Scholastic, and London and New York, Scholastic, 1991.

The Wednesday Wizard. Auckland, Ashton Scholastic, London and New York, Scholastic, 1991.

Denzil's Dilemma (sequel to *The Wednesday Wizard*). Auckland, Ashton Scholastic, and New York, Scholastic, 1992.

Winter of Fire. Auckland, Ashton Scholastic, London and New York, Scholastic, 1993.

Other Side of Midnight, illustrated by Brian Pollard. Auckland, Ashton Scholastic, 1993.

Tanith. Melbourne, Omnibus, 1994; as *Wolf-woman,* Boston, Houghton Mifflin, 1994.

Sign of the Lion. Auckland, Penguin, 1995.

Secret Sacrament. Auckland, Penguin, 1996.
Denzil's Great Bear Robbery. Wellington, Mallinson Rendel, 1997.

*

Illustrator: (All by Joy Cowley) *Mouse,* Shortland Publications, 1983; *Tell-tale,* Shortland Publications, 1983; *The Silent One,* Whitcoulls, 1984; *Mouse Monster,* Shortland Publications, 1985.

Sherryl Jordan comments:

My first book was created when I was four years old. I had been given a notebook of blue paper, and made it into a picture book story about a mermaid. During my childhood I wrote many stories, including several full-length novels which my teachers at school sent to publishers. Those early works were never published, but they established in me a love for writing that has never faded. The path to publication was long and arduous.

In my adult years I learned the writing craft by attending seminars and listening to other writers; through criticism and rewriting; and through determination and perseverance. During my long apprenticeship, I wrote 27 picture books for children, and 12 novels. Of the picture books, three were published. Not one of the novels was published. In 1988 I began work on the 13th novel, having decided that this was going to be the making or breaking of my literary career: if this book was rejected, I would give up writing. The book was for young adults, and was called *Rocco.* (Published as *A Time of Darkness* in the USA.) It was the turning-point in my career.

Now I am a full-time writer of novels for young adults. I have in the past written several picture books for younger children, but because my writing hours are now limited (due to Occupational Overuse Syndrome), I write only novels, which give me the greater joy. I visit schools regularly to discuss books and writing. I have held several workshops on creative writing, working with adults and with children. I have also spoken at seminars and conferences on my work and life as a writer. In 1993 I won a writing fellowship in the USA, and took part in the International Writing Program at the University of Iowa. During this fellowship I spoke at many high schools in Iowa, since my books were in libraries, and also spoke at seminars in Chicago, and at the University of Wilmington, North Carolina. In 1996 I was guest speaker at a Science Fiction Conference in Copenhagen, Denmark, and twice have been invited to speak at conferences in Melbourne, Australia.

I have one daughter, Kym, of 22 years, who is artistic and who writes wonderful poems; and a husband, Lee, without whose unfailing help and encouragement I would not be a writer. We celebrate our lives in Tauranga, New Zealand, where we enjoy sailing and time by the ocean. I also treasure music, time with friends, and solitude to write. And I enjoy the company of my cat, Jethro, who loves my beautiful studio as much as I do, and who only occasionally walks across my computer keyboard and creates chaos.

All my young adults novels have been gifts. I don't think them up. They hit me over the head when I least expect them; overwhelm me with impressions, sights, and sounds of their new worlds; enchant me with their characters; and dare me to write them. Before I begin writing I have the entire novel in my head like a movie, the first sentence and the last, and everything in between. I believe that every book is whole and complete long before I am given that first inspiration; I have only to tune into it, recognise it, and record it as faithfully as I can. Some books are inspired by a character who suddenly, dramatically, comes into my vision and my heart. Others are inspired by a memory, a subtle but deep truth taught to me by life. They all are expressions of my own spiritual journey through this life—of my dreams, my battles, my fears and triumphs.

One of my favourite quotes is from Keats: "I am certain of nothing but the holiness of the heart's affections and the truth of the imagination." It is this truth of the imagination that is the foundation, I believe, of good fantasy. Fantasy as its own validity. Betty Gilderdale, New Zealand writer and authority on children's books, said: "Fantasy should never be thought of as escapism. Good fantasy explores possibilities. It is the training ground for lateral thinkers, inventors, and philosophers of the future."

In my books I explore the boundless spaces between fact and fantasy, the real and the truth we imagine. I don't write a book unless I believe in it. I don't allow my characters to experience anything that is not valid, worth-while, and honest to the core. I make my characters admirable because I believe young people need heroes who are excellent. I write about truths that life has taught me, because it is only deep conviction within the writer that gives power to words. All my young adult novels contain that seed of truth, though it may be wrapped up in fantasy. I hope my books open doors. I hope they are not answers, but questions. I hope they inspire young people to discover the truth of the imagination, and to explore for themselves the limitless worlds within and beyond their own minds.

* * *

After some pleasing but unremarkable picture books, Sherryl Jordan emerged as a new and original voice in New Zealand's literature for older readers with the publication of *Rocco.* In this thought-provoking novel she not only explores the fascinating possibilities opened up by physics on the nature of time, synchronicity, and parallel worlds, but also takes the reader with Rocco, a contemporary teenager, on his journey towards self-discovery.

The novel opens with his recurring nightmare of being attacked by a wolf, but one day when he wakes up he finds himself no longer in our world but in the stark landscape of Anshur. He is befriended by a tribe of cave dwellers whom he initially judges to be primitive because of their lack of technology, but gradually he realizes that their honesty and kindness, as well as their seasonal rituals, may have more inherent value than the superficial sophistication of his own contemporary world. He is puzzled by the strong feeling of affinity he has with the wise old woman of the tribe, Ayoshe, and suspects that she knows more about him than he is prepared to divulge.

Ironically, just as he becomes reconciled to staying in Anshur, Rocco is involuntarily returned home, and it is a tribute to Jordan's vivid depiction of Anshur that this seems almost anticlimactic. It is, however, a necessary postscript for understanding what has happened. Rocco had thought Anshur was in the past. He now learns that it is in the future. He remembers Ayoshe's words, "I stand on this path and all other paths exist at the same time—all that separates us from them is a tiny action, a word, a human hope."

In this powerful story Jordan avoids didacticism through the quality of her imaginative insights but there is no escaping the overall message that the individual is important, that choices are available and that even apparently insignificant actions matter in the scheme of things.

By placing her characters somewhere between two worlds Jordan invites her readers, as well as her protagonists, to question both sets of values. Have we "progressed" in the sense of getting better? Is the past necessarily worse than the present? What can we learn from it?

Rocco had inherited a gift of dreaming "true" and of telepathy from his father, and in *The Juniper Game* Jordan enlarges upon the latter. Juniper is a lively, intelligent, contemporary girl, who is fascinated both by the medieval world and by the possibilities of telepathy. She persuades a classmate, Dylan, to help her with an experiment because he has the artistic ability she needs. She then proceeds to visit different locations and "send" him mind pictures of where she is, to see whether he can pick up the images and draw them. After considerable success she decides to send him a picture of 15th-century Tewkesbury and Dylan receives it as well as the other actual locations. Gradually they both find themselves in medieval Tewkesbury and they become increasingly involved with a young woman who is accused of witchcraft and subsequently burnt at the stake.

Central to the book is an exploration of the nature of time. "Maybe there's just an eternal Now where all Time occurs simultaneously," Juniper says.

But the metaphysical concerns, although integral to the novel, are balanced by the convincing picture given of Juniper's and Dylan's separate home lives and by the development of their relationship from what began as a scientific cooperation to deeper friendship and dawning romance.

The portrayal of a strong female character continues in *A Winter of Fire* which takes place in a cold world after some cataclysm has permanently hidden the sun. The only way that the people can keep warm is by mining coal for fuel and this is done by the Quelled, or untouchable, supervised by the advantaged Chosen. But Elsha of the Quelled, refuses to be subservient to the Chosen and determines to improve the lot of her people. Her indomitable spirit and strong sense of mission help her to hold to her ideals through much adversity and enable her ultimately to achieve her goal. It is a memorable novel in which rich visual images glow against the somber background of a darkened world.

In her latest book, *Tanith,* human communities are compared to those of the wolves when Tanith, a girl living in the distant past, was reared by wolves until she was three years old and was then discovered by a local tribe. She was brought to the chieftain's house and became a companion to his wife. But when she died Tanith became increasingly uneasy. She had never been fully accepted by the superstitious tribe and gradually she starts returning to the wolves where she experiences the acceptance and affection she lacks in the tribe. In the end she has to choose whether to go back to the village or stay with the wolves and it is the brutality of tribal warfare which dictates her choice.

In four recent books for younger readers Jordan returns to the recorded historical past. In the first of a light-hearted trilogy, *The Wednesday Wizard,* a medieval sorcerer's apprentice discovers a spell which will project him through time and he finds himself in contemporary New Zealand, while in *Denzil's Dilemma* friend he has made there comes to visit him in his world. *Denzil's Great Bear Robbery* sees Denzil in trouble for having saved a dancing bear from cruelty. The uproar his action creates prompts him to return to the 20th century, with the bear. His reception in contemporary suburbia is less than enthusiastic, but results in some highly entertaining mayhem.

The same period, but in more sober mood, features in the picture book *The Other Side of Midnight* in which a medieval girl, orphaned by the plague, goes in search of her brother and finds some of her prejudices about other people to be surprisingly inaccurate.

Secret Sacrament is perhaps her most ambitious novel to date. Once again it is set in an imaginary world, Navora, where 14-year-old Gabriel refuses to follow in his merchant father's footsteps. Instead, he becomes a Healer in the Citadel. There his outstanding gifts bring him to the attention of the Empress. But her favours involve him in political intrigues, his life is threatened and he flees to the dispossessed Shinali people. He falls in love with one of them, fights for their rights, suffers imprisonment and ultimately sacrifices himself for them.

Jordan writes with a passionate integrity. Navora is intensely, almost sensuously, realised. We see its landscapes, we feel its textures. Underpinning the carefully plotted structure is an exploration of the effects of power, both on those who wield it and on those who suffer it.

But primarily this powerful novel traces the development of Gabriel from naive idealism to a mature understanding of life's complexities. With him we are taken through the whole gamut of emotions, from the joys of love to the horror of a Shinali leader's crucifixion.

Jordan's great strength as a writer lies in being able to combine considerable storytelling ability with themes which stimulate readers into examining wider issues than their own day-to-day concerns. She is not didactic. Her readers are not told what to believe, but they are encouraged to think for themselves and to acknowledge that there may be alternatives to our present way of life.

—Betty Gilderdale

JOYCE, William

Nationality: American. **Born:** 11 December 1957. **Education:** Attended Southern Methodist University, Dallas, Texas. **Family:** Married Elizabeth; one daughter and one son. **Career:** Screenwriter, author, and illustrator; contributor of illustrations to periodicals; board member, Stoner Art Center, Shreveport, Louisiana, 1987-89. **Awards:** Best Book Award, *School Library Journal,* 1985, for *George Shrinks*; Christopher Award (best illustration), for Humphrey's Bear, 1987; *New York Times* Best Illustrated Award, 1989, for *Nicholas Cricket*; Silver Medal, Society of Illustrators, 1992, for *Bently & Egg.* **Address:** 3302 Centenary Boulevard, Shreveport, Louisiana 71104, U.S.A.

Publications for Children (illustrated by the author)

Fiction

George Shrinks. New York, Harper & Row, 1985.
Dinosaur Bob and His Adventures with the Family Lazardo. New York, Harper & Row, 1988.
A Day with Wilbur Robinson. New York, Harper & Row, 1990.
Bently & Egg. New York, HarperCollins, 1992.

Santa Calls. New York, HarperCollins, 1993.
The Leaf Men and the Brave Good Bugs. New York, HarperCollins, 1996.
Buddy. New York, HarperCollins, 1997.

*

Critical Studies: "Can I Go Over to Wilbur's?" by David Leavitt, in *New York Times Book Review,* 11 November 1990, 29; "Make Room for Bently" by Malcolm Jones, Jr., in *Newsweek,* 16 March 1992, 72; entry in *Something About the Author,* Detroit, Gale, Vol. 72, 1993; "Leaf It to Joyce" by Ken Tucker, in *Entertainment Weekly,* 29 November 1996, 83; "William in Wonderland" by Susan Hawthorne Nash and Carolanne Griffith Roberts, in *Southern Living,* December 1996, 102-104; "Where the Mind Wanders: Childhood Fantasies" by Rosemary Chance and Erlene Bishop Killeen, in *Emergency Librarian* (Seattle), September/October 1997, 58.

Illustrator: *Tammy and the Gigantic Fish* by Catherine and James Gray, 1983; as Bill Joyce, *My First Book of Nursery Tales: Five Mother Goose Stories* by Marianna Mayer, 1983; *Waiting-for-Spring Stories* by Bethany Roberts, 1984; *Shoes* by Elizabeth Winthrop, 1986; *Humphrey's Bear* by Jan Wahl, 1987; *Nicholas Cricket* by Joyce Maxner, 1989; *Some of the Adventures of Rhode Island Red* by Stephen Manes, 1990.

* * *

As a boy, "I was garrulous, mischievous, always scheming and drawing," William Joyce told Susan Hawthorne Nash and Carolanne Griffith Roberts for *Southern Living* magazine. In fact, Nash and Roberts write, the grown Joyce's mind still "lives in the lyrical land of the fantastic." Let us enter the mischievously fantastic, lyrical wonderland of William Joyce.

Joyce's first picture book for children, *George Shrinks,* is a small book about a small boy who shrinks in his sleep to become even smaller! When George awakens, he finds a note from his parents, who are out. "Dear George," it says. "When you wake up, please make your bed, brush your teeth, and take a bath. Then clean up your room and go get your little brother. Eat a good breakfast, and don't forget to wash the dishes.... Take out the garbage, and play quietly. Make sure you water the plants and feed the fish. Then check the mail and get some fresh air. Try to stay out of trouble." An ordinary list of ordinary activities, but fulfilling them is not so ordinary for the now-tiny George, who must climb on to his mountainous pillow to make his bed and sit on the faucet of the bathroom sink to brush his teeth with a huge, unwieldy toothbrush. Indeed, being very small brings on one extraordinary adventure after another—and it is not so easy to stay out of trouble! Taking a bath is like embarking on an ocean voyage (watch out for the enormous rubber duck!), taking out the garbage requires equipping himself as a mahout and riding an elephant (his baby brother is enlisted) to which a wagon loaded with the overflowing garbage bag is hitched, and watering the plants is an exciting trip through the jungle. But when Mom and Dad return, all is well and back to normal.

Dinosaur Bob and His Adventures with the Family Lazardo is another incredible adventure story. While on safari with his family in Africa, Scotty Lazardo finds a dinosaur. "Can we keep him?" plead his sisters, Zelda and Velma. "I don't see why not," replies Dr. Lazardo. "He looks kind of like my uncle Bob," Mrs. Lazardo comments. When Scotty calls the dinosaur "Bob" and the dinosaur responds with a smile and a wag of his giant tail, the family names him Bob, and the fun begins! Even Joyce's acknowledgements—to Nick and Nora Charles and to "Mr. Kong, eighth wonder of the world" as well as to his own young nephew—set the book's tone of slapstick and wonder.

Spending a day at your best friend's house may seem pretty ordinary, even dull, but when your friend is Wilbur Robinson and there are twin uncles Dmitri and Spike (who greet you from the large flower urns outside the front door), Aunt Billie (who plays with a life-sized train set), Cousin Pete (who walks the "cats" that happen to be tigers), Uncle Gaston (who sits comfortably in the family cannon, then blasts himself across the room), Grandfather (who, along with "Mr. Ellington and Mr. Armstrong," is training frogs to play jazz), and more—all of whom you encounter as you and Wilbur search for Grandfather's false teeth—then your day won't be at all ordinary and, like the narrator of *A Day at Wilbur Robinson's,* you'll think that Wilbur Robinson's house is "the greatest place to visit."

With its gentle pastel tones, *Bently & Egg*—the story of a shy young frog who agrees to watch over a duck's new egg while she visits her sister—is a visual departure from the bold brightness of Joyce's earlier books. But, as Malcolm Jones, Jr., points out in his review of the book for *Newsweek,* "for all its sweetness, Bently is every bit as zestful as its predecessors. Commandeering a hot-air balloon, sailing a toy boat, crashing a garden party, Bently is never at a loss. Jubilantly resourceful, he has a swell time being a hero."

Santa Claus is every child's hero, of course, and when a mysterious box stamped "S.C." arrives at Art Atchinson Aimesworth's house in Abilene, Texas, Art is thrilled to discover that it's from Santa Claus himself. "Open the box. Assemble the contents. Come NORTH. Yours, S.C." reads the note that sets *Santa Calls* in motion. "Gee whiz," sighs Art's sister Esther in awe. "Santa calls." Art and his best friend, Spaulding Littlefeets (a young Comanche brave) set about opening the box. "It appears to be a flying machine," Spaulding observes. "To fly north in," says Art. "To see Santa," says Spaulding. "But why?," Art wonders. Esther smiles but says nothing. The boys assemble the contraption and prepare to fly north. Esther cannot come: "You're too little to come," Art tells her. She threatens to tell if they don't let her go, then begins to cry when Art reminds her sternly that "an Aimesworth never tells." He relents, and they're off to the icy unknown! Santa's land is truly a land of wonders, but it is not without its dangers—like the terrible Dark Elves who kidnap Esther. Art bravely saves her (with candy, the elves' weakness, Santa tells him). The three children then join Santa and Mrs. Claus for the Clauses' annual Christmas voyage. "What's our first stop, Mrs. Claus?" "Abilene, Texas." In no time, the children are home in bed. "Did you enjoy your ride, Mr. Aimesworth?" "Very much," says Art. "But why did you call for us?" Santa doesn't answer right away, but as Art drifts asleep, he hears Santa say softly, "Good night, my fine brave children. Merry Christmas dreams, and remember, some secrets are best left unsolved." Little Esther knows the answer, though: she had written to Santa earlier that year: "Dear Santa, You can send me toys if you like, but what I really wish for is for my brother Art to be my friend. Yours, Esther Aimesworth." And Santa has left her with his personal response: "Dear Esther, Such a rare and wonderful request could not be refused. I'm glad our little adventure did the trick. SC." Only Esther knows the secret—

which the reader can discover too by opening the handwritten letters attached to the last two pages of this wondrous Christmas story.

Joyce has told a reviewer for *Entertainment Weekly* that he is intent on giving children "work that makes them take a leap of imagination." His *The Leaf Men and the Brave Good Bugs*—the story of a team of bald, muscular green men who battle the evil Spider Queen and provide comfort to an old woman—is another wildly imaginative celebration of goodness and bravery. *Buddy,* Joyce's latest book, is based on the true story of Gertrude Lintz, a New York socialite who raises a gorilla she has named Buddy but must reluctantly part with when he gets a hint of his true heritage and becomes unmanageable. The quiet sepia tones of Joyce's illustrations beautifully mirror the sweet nostalgia of this story.

In their comments on Joyce for their essay "Where the Mind Wanders: Childhood Fantasies," Rosemary Chance and Erlene Bishop Killeen note that "fantasy worlds ... always appeal to children" and, further, that "the combination of Joyce's sentimentality and quirky humor ... appeal to a wide age range." But perhaps Malcolm Jones, Jr., sums up the appeal of Joyce's books best: "Droll and unfailingly good-natured, they are as much about childhood as they are for children. Once you enter Joyce's world, you'll never want to leave."

—Marcia Welsh

JUDAH, Aaron

Nationality: British. **Born:** Bombay, India, 19 October 1923. **Education:** Attended Anglo-Indian schools, graduated 1941. **Family:** Married in 1977; one son. **Career:** Bridge boy on a Cunard ship, 1943-44; draughtsman in a munitions factory, London, 1945. Qualified as a physiotherapist, 1949, and practicing physiotherapist in London, Norway, Israel, India, Australia, France, and Spain, 1949-72; part-time physiotherapist, and freelance writer, from 1972. **Address:** 6 Lower Denmark Road, Ashford, Kent TN23 7SU, England.

Publications for Children

Fiction

Tommy with the Hole in His Shoe, illustrated by Sheila Hawkins. London, Faber, 1957.
Tales of Teddy Bear, illustrated by Sheila Hawkins. London, Faber, 1958.
The Adventures of Henrietta Hen, illustrated by Sheila Hawkins. London, Faber, 1958.
Miss Hare and Mr. Tortoise, illustrated by Sheila Hawkins. London, Faber, 1959.
The Pot of Gold and Two Other Tales, illustrated by Mervyn Peake. London, Faber, 1959; New York, A.S. Barnes, 1960.
God and Mr. Sourpuss, illustrated by Richard Kennedy. London, Faber, 1959; New York, A.S. Barnes, 1960.
Basil Chimpy Isn't Bright, illustrated by Sheila Hawkins. London, Faber, 1959.
Henrietta in the Snow, illustrated by Sheila Hawkins. London, Faber, 1960.
Basil Chimpy's Comic Light, illustrated by Sheila Hawkins. London, Faber, 1960.
Anna Anaconda: The Swallowing Wonder, illustrated by John Howson. London, Faber, 1960.
Henrietta in Love, illustrated by Sheila Hawkins. London, Faber, 1961.
The Proud Duck, illustrated by the author. London, Faber, 1961.
The Elf's New House, illustrated by Sheila Hawkins. London, Faber, 1962.
Ex-King Max Forever!, illustrated by the author. London, Faber, 1963.
The Careless Cuckoos, illustrated by Sheila Hawkins. London, Faber, 1963.
The Fabulous Haircut, illustrated by the author. London, Faber, 1964.
On the Feast of Stephen, illustrated by Sheila Hawkins. London, Faber, 1965.

Publications for Adults

Novels

Clown of Bombay. London, Faber, 1963; New York, Dial Press, 1968.
Clown on Fire. London, Macdonald, 1965; New York, Dial Press, 1967.
Cobweb Pennant. London, Dent, 1968.
Lillian's Dam. London, Dent, 1970.

* * *

Aaron Judah peoples his stories with childlike humans of all ages and with animals. The animals inhabit both the real world of nature, where the chase and sudden death are part of the order of things, and also the anthropomorphic world in which they represent the vices and virtues. Foxes are cunning, camels haughty and selfish, monkeys irresponsible, while owls are learned, hedgehogs kindly, and pandas old and wise. Nothing very unusual in all this, of course, the very stuff of the best nursery stories in the tradition of Beatrix Potter and Alison Uttley. Again, like many a good storyteller before him, Judah tells a tale to point a moral without falling into moralising attitudes.

The nursery story is an over-constrained genre: all the more remarkable that this writer should have brought a freshness to it. His language is necessarily simple, direct, used with economy (though he'll stretch the young reader where precision demands it); his images are concrete, his tone often lyrical without being coy or whimsical. There are drama, often heavily charged with emotion, rich humour, and inventive characterisation. No one who has met Mr. Makeshift Monkey in *Tommy with the Hole in His Shoe* or Anna Anaconda is likely easily to forget them.

The tone is central to the success of these tales. The words leap from the page demanding to be read aloud. He *shares* the experience of the stories with the young reader or listener. His voice is that of an enthralled observer excitedly and intimately drawing attention to the wonder he sees around him. Nor is he above admitting ignorance when the wonder runs beyond his grasp. We never know what fearsome presence caused the desperate

Henrietta to scurry to the hollow oak (*The Adventures of Henrietta Hen*). We cannot tell, and Judah doesn't attempt to explain, what it was that God did to change Mr. Sourpuss, but we delight in that gentleman's joy at his new-found happiness.

Miss Hare and Mr. Tortoise brings together all that is best in this writer's work. Desperate fear, tenderness, humour, lyricism, harsh reality, and the celebration of wonder are all artfully balanced in this exquisite love story, and what must surely be the gentlest, most reassuring low-key ending of any bedtime story ever written.

—Myles McDowell

JUKES, Mavis

Nationality: American. **Born:** 3 May 1947, Nyack, New York. **Education:** Attended University of Colorado, Boulder, 1965-67; University of California, Berkeley, B.A. 1969, Elementary Teaching Certificate 1970; Golden Gate University, J.D. 1978. **Family:** Married Robert H. Hudson in 1976; two daughters and two stepsons. **Career:** Teacher, Longfellow Elementary School, Berkeley, California, 1970-73, art specialist, 1973-75; admitted to the Bar of California, 1979; fulltime writer, from 1979. **Awards:** Bank Street College of Education Irma Simonton Black Award for Excellence in Children's Literature, 1983; Parents' Choice Foundation Parents' Choice Award, 1983; *School Library Journal* Best Books of the Year, 1983 and 1984; Bay Area Book Reviewers Association Award for Children's Literature, 1985; *Horn Book* Honor List, 1985; Newbery Honor book, 1985. **Member:** California Bar Association.

Publications for Children

Fiction

No One Is Going to Nashville, illustrated by Lloyd Bloom. New York, Knopf, 1983.
Like Jake and Me, illustrated by Lloyd Bloom. New York, Knopf, 1984.
Blackberries in the Dark, illustrated by Thomas B. Allen. New York, Knopf, 1985.
Lights around the Palm, illustrated by Stacey Schuett. New York, Knopf, 1987.
Getting Even. New York, Knopf, 1988.
Wild Iris Bloom. New York, Knopf, 1991.
I'll See You in My Dreams. New York, Knopf, 1992.
Human Interaction with Mrs. Gladys B. Furley, R.N.: Expecting the Unexpected. New York, Delacorte, 1996.
Losers Weepers, illustrated by Mike Reed. New York, Random House, 1997.

Non-Fiction

It's a Girl Thing: How to Stay Healthy, Safe, and In Charge, illustrated by Debbie Tilley. New York, Knopf, 1996.
It's a Girl Thing: Dating. New York, Random Library, 1998.
It's a Girl Thing: Your First Period. New York, Knopf, 1998.

Film: *Mavis Jukes: A Conversation with the Author.* Disney Educational Productions, 1989.

Film Script: *Who Owns the Sun,* with Patricia McKissack (adapted from Who Owns the Sun by Stacey Chbosky). Disney Educational Productions, 1990.

*

Media Adaptations: *Blackberries in the Dark* and *Like Jake and Me* (films), Disney Educational Productions; *Like Jake and Me* (videotape and filmstrip), Random House, 1984.

* * *

In her first book for children, *No One Is Going to Nashville,* Mavis Jukes shows the form, theme, and style that continue to characterize her work. This slim volume exceeds readers' expectations of the typical picture book. Text outweighs art; the pictures decorate the text rather than interpret it; however, the book is not long, or intricate, enough to be considered a chapter book or a novel. Instead, Jukes begins to define her specific audience of newly independent readers. These readers, like the story's main character, Sonia, focus on a primary narrative element, trace it via a strong character with whom they can identify, and respond to building psychological and emotional complexity. Sonia becomes singularly interested in owning the lost dog with the "weirdears" (sic). Jukes uses eloquent, simply phrased dialogue between Sonia, her father Robert, and her stepmother Annette to develop the three characters. Details about precise physical setting recede as Sonia's care for the dog escalates despite her father's refusal to adopt it. Readers' empathy with Sonia wins affirmation as Annette shares her recollection of a childhood pet dog and the two comfort each other. When Annette claims the dog for Sonia, despite Robert's weak protestations, Sonia and readers alike feel satisfied by the power of love to fortify and nurture.

Like Jake and Me introduces another young child, Alex, and his small family. Like Sonia, who visits her father on weekends only, Alex comes to forge a new bond with his stepparent. Alex clearly struggles to feel that he belongs with his mother, Virginia, now pregnant with twins, and Jake, a cowboy who is so different than Alex's natural father. Alex looks for ways to be helpful to Jake, who appears to be aloof and wholly self-sufficient. Jukes creates an affinity between Jake and Alex in a scene at once humorous and evocative. As Jake watches Virginia out a window, Alex closely watches a pregnant wolf spider crawl into Jake's clothing. Jukes takes readers into her confidence as the parallel conversation shared by Jake and Alex builds in intensity and humor. The child and man overcome their mutual confusion as Jake frantically undresses in search of the feared spider. The energetic pitch of the scene crescendos in an emotionally gratifying conclusion for Jake, Alex, and the reader.

Lights Around the Palm introduces seven-and-a-half-year-old Emma. Like Sonia, Emma not only identifies with, but also communicates with animals. While her parents indulge this tendency her brother can barely tolerate it. In this illustrated book, Jukes once again gives the reader greater information than she does her characters; as a result, young readers comfortably identify with the main character because they know the story will turn out favorably. Here, Jukes plays on words and animal sounds to dispel Bob's doubt that she can indeed teach the horse, pig, dog, sheep owl, and chicken to speak. Emma's parents remain in the story's background; instead, Emma's relationship with her brother takes on new direction.

Two of Jukes's other books, *Blackberries in the Dark* and *I'll See You in My Dreams,* keep the spotlight within the family circle, but shifts it slightly. In Blackberries in the Dark, Austin visits his grandmother on her farm the summer after his grandfather's death. Jukes subtly reveals Austin's profound sadness at his grandfather's absence as Austin seeks out the familiar items and activities they shared. The story achieves unique psychological resonance as his grandmother redefines her relationship with Austin. Together, they carry on family traditions and discover their own grounds for a caring future. A nameless child travels across the country to be with her uncle in the hospital in *I'll See You in My Dreams.* Jukes introduces the child's mother as an integral emotional support in this journey. The girl imagines the ideal good-bye to her dying uncle. She envisions herself as a skywriter, signing her good-byes to her pilot uncle across the darkening skies. In so expanding the domestic circle, Jukes creates another young character grounded in her family and empowered by her imagination.

Jukes writes two novels for intermediate readers. The companion books *Getting Even* and *Wild Iris Bloom* introduce the prepubescent friends Maggie Hunter and Iris Bloom. Like her predecessors in Jukes's fiction, Maggie lives with her mother and visits her father and soon-to-be stepmother on occasion. This family structure causes Maggie almost as much concern as Maggie's relationship with her father and as Iris Bloom causes Maggie's mother. Iris relies on a single adult; although she has two parents in both books, they travel away from home and leave Iris in the care of the housekeeper, Mrs. Fuller. While Getting Even focuses largely on Maggie's troubles at school and Wild Iris Bloom looks at Iris's wildly independent streak, Jukes realizes with veracity the middle-school setting in all its worries, fads, and obsessions. The author describes a believable bully, children misunderstood by adults, and the confidence, antics, and sustenance of childhood friendships. Maggie and Iris survive—and somehow even triumph—with integrity and honesty.

Jukes' books for older readers focus on the pressures that young girls face as they enter puberty. Although her *It's a Girl Thing* series is classified as non-fiction, the books include more than a recital of facts regarding the basics of sex education and peer relationships; Jukes illustrates these topics with examples taken from her own adolescence, including a revealing glimpse into what, in retrospect, she recognizes to be her own battle with issues of self-esteem.

Human Interaction with Mrs. Gladys B. Furley, R.N.: Expecting the Unexpected is a fictional counterpart to the *It's a Girl Thing* books. River, the twelve year-old heroine, uses the information she has learned in Mrs. Furley's sex education classes to determine whether or not her moody older sister is pregnant. On the way to uncovering the truth that it is her mother who is expecting a baby, River also learns to take pride in herself as a student and to become more comfortable with her own body. Peppered with phrases designed to capture her young readers' interest (the popular girls at River's elementary school are referred to as "jerky trendoid celebrity wannabes," for instance), the novel demystifies the process of "human interaction" and is an able successor to Judy Blume's *Are You There God? It's Me, Margaret.*

In all of her writing for children and young adults, Jukes uses language in direct and poetic ways to describe fully the realistic worlds of today's children. Her command of dialogue complements masterful character development. Above all, Jukes proves herself a writer of insightful wisdom about the psychological and emotional realities of young people.

—Cathryn M. Mercier, updated by Gwen A. Tarbox.

K

KAHL, Virginia (Caroline)

Nationality: American. **Born:** Milwaukee, Wisconsin, 18 February 1919. **Education:** Milwaukee-Downer College, 1936-40, B.A. 1940; University of Wisconsin, Madison, 1956-57, Master of Library Science 1957. **Career:** Library assistant, Milwaukee Public Library, 1942-48; librarian, Berlin, and command librarian, Salzburg, United States Army, 1948-55; librarian, Madison public schools, Wisconsin, 1958-61; library director, Menomonee Falls Public Library, Wisconsin, 1961-68. Since 1970 librarian, Alexandria Library, Virginia. Member of the faculty, George Washington University Continuing Education for Women Center, Washington, D.C., 1970-80.

PUBLICATIONS FOR CHILDREN (ILLUSTRATED BY THE AUTHOR)

Fiction

Away Went Wolfgang! New York, Scribner, 1954.
Maxie. New York, Scribner, 1956.
Droopsi. New York, Scribner, 1958.
Here Is Henri!, with Edith Vacheron. New York, Scribner, 1959.
More about Henri!, with Edith Vacheron. New York, Scribner, 1961.
Giants, Indeed! New York, Scribner, 1974.
Whose Cat Is That? New York, Scribner, 1979.

Poetry

The Duchess Bakes a Cake. New York, Scribner, 1955; London, Collins, 1977.
Plum Pudding for Christmas. New York, Scribner, 1956.
The Habits of Rabbits. New York, Scribner, 1957.
The Perfect Pancake. New York, Scribner, 1960.
The Baron's Booty. New York, Scribner, 1963.
How Do You Hide a Monster? New York, Scribner, 1971.
Gunhilde's Christmas Booke. New York, Scribner, 1972.
Gunhilde and the Hallowe'en Spell. New York, Scribner, 1975.
How Many Dragons Are Behind the Door? New York, Scribner, 1977.

*

Virginia Kahl comments:

My books will appeal, I hope, to those children who enjoy a simple fantasy and possess a sense of the ridiculous; they carry no message. I am old-fashioned enough to believe that picture books are to be enjoyed by young readers. I leave to others the job of introducing them to the seamy side of life. Early childhood, when books are introduced, should be a time of joy and gaiety. I want children to enjoy my stories, laugh at the pictures, and think back indulgently on my bumbling characters. Probably the single experience that has most influenced my writing was my sojourn in Austria. I was overwhelmed by the scenery and loved the people; and the city of Salzburg is always in the back of my mind when I write my books. As for my pictures, my first editor, Alice Dalgliesh, remarked that she had seldom seen such simple illustrations. Fortunately, they seem appropriate to the text.

* * *

Virginia Kahl is a humorist of the slapstick school. Her "Duchess" books are founded on exuberant exaggeration, the multiplication of some small incident until a mad chaos engulfs the dukedom. A hint of these madcap happenings comes with a mere mention of the Duchess's over-large family: "Madeleine, Gwendolyn, Jane and Clothilde,/ Willibald, Genevieve, Maud and Mathilde..."—thirteen daughters altogether. This group is soon entangled in the Duchess's innocent-looking ventures, which somehow run riot while the Duke looks on helplessly.

Kahl's success as an entertainer is best seen in *The Duchess Bakes a Cake*—a fantasy which combines rowdy humour with serene rationality. When an over-supply of yeast sends a cake dough rising to heaven with the cook trapped on top, the crisis is resolved when the youngest Duchess child gets hungry. Then everyone simply eats enough of the dough to bring the Duchess down.

> "How lovely!" the Duchess said, "Come, let us sup."
> "I'll start eating down; you start eating up."

The winning combination in this book is apparently the clarity with which silliness and logic have been joined; the personality of the high-born, scatter-brained Duchess; the easily chanted refrain ("All I wanted to make/was a lovely light luscious delectable cake"); the unlabored rhyme and evenly accented rhythm of the verse (which help emphasize the narrative content rather than the form); and the unfamiliar words for small children to savor: pummel, catapult, minstrel, etc.

In *The Baron's Booty* and *The Habits of Rabbits* the plot lines are more familiar: kidnappers overwhelmed by the purely child-like behavior of children they've abducted, rabbits producing an over-population of ridiculous proportions. Yet these are ideal vehicles for the Duchess character and for employing a popular motif of folktales—the central role of the youngest family member.

Another memorable creation is a milk-cart dog (in *Away Went Wolfgang!*) who is so seized by the work ethic that he dashes over the cobblestone streets and spills the milk before it can be delivered. Working out his problem entails a surprise incident which turns the milk into another saleable product: butter. But Wolfgang's characterization—the portrayal of devotion and excess energy in a young dog—outshines other features in this tale.

Such high creativity has not been maintained in works like *Gunhilde's Christmas Booke* or *Maxie.* The former presents a predictable series of episodes in which Christmas customs are explained to non-Christians. The rhymed text provides a lighthearted dimension, but the narrative lacks liveliness as well as the usual Christmas ingredients: reverence or wonder. In the latter book the dachshund, Maxie, is allowed to be an explicit moralizer, and is consequently much less attractive than Wolfgang.

Kahl is a writer whose best works for preschool and kindergarten children should not be permitted to lapse into obscurity. The inspired imagination and good craftsmanship in the early books are not often surpassed; and although runaway cake batter is a motif in folk literature, the treatment applied by Kahl is entirely unprecedented. Her work as a whole offers readers a wealth of fresh images and personalities.

—Donnarae MacCann

KARIUKI, Elijah

Nationality: Kenyan. **Born:** 28 August 1956. **Education:** University of Nairobi, B.Sc. (honors) in agricultural engineering, 1980; University of Reading, United Kingdom, masters in food process engineering, 1985; United States International University, Africa (USIU-A), masters in business administration, 1994. **Family:** Married Salome Wanjiru, 1981; four children. **Career:** Currently senior engineer, Firestone (East Africa), Nairobi. **Address:** c/o Longman Kenya Ltd., P.O. Box 18033, Nairobi, Kenya.

Publications for Children

Fiction

The Sun's Daughter. Nairobi, East African Publishing House, 1976.
Ziki, My Monkey Boy. Nairobi, Longman, 1979.
A Car Named Safari. Nairobi, Longman, 1981.
The Engine Puzzle. Nairobi, Longman, 1981.
The Fire Puzzle. Nairobi, Longman, 1981.
The Irrigation Puzzle. Nairobi, Longman, 1981.
The Underground Water Puzzle. Nairobi, Longman, 1981.
This Country Is My Country. Nairobi, Longman, 1981.

*

Elijah Kariuki comments:

Most of my writing was done while a student at the University. I intend to pick up the pieces again soon. I believe that we who have had the privilege of knowing some science and technology owe our people, especially the children, something. We should make it available to them in a language they can understand, so as to reduce the many puzzles that surround them. This will help them understand the world around them; this will give them a better chance to survive in the liberalized world. I believe African children should be given the chance to know in good time, so that they can choose their lives. My mission is to teach them technological puzzles and good morals. I want to teach them that it is possible to be anything. I want to introduce them to these things before they get scared away by the sheer monstrosity of the puzzles. Once they understand the whys, I believe they will be able to stand up and be self-reliant like the rest of the world.

* * *

Elijah Kariuki writes fiction based on folklore and contemporary life for Kenyan school children. His books have been published in series of supplementary school readers, and as a result his stories are didactic; but they also include events and adventures of interest to primary and secondary school children.

The Sun's Daughter is based on a common theme in East African folklore of a handsome young man, Magasi, who refuses to marry any local woman, including the chief's daughter, because he wants to marry the most beautiful woman of all, the sun's daughter Kasai. While travelling in search of Kasai he is captured by an ogre, who tricks him into choosing between marrying the ogre's cannibal daughter or death. Magasi chooses death, but is able to escape before he is killed. Eventually he finds Kasai and upon first meeting they know they are meant for each other, but Magasi must kill the ogre before they can marry. After the couple is married, their kingdoms are united under Magasi's rule, and there is peace and happiness for many years.

A Car Named Safari is about the repair of a 1949 car which the hero dreams of entering in the East African Safari auto race. Like Kariuki's stories in the Puzzlecrackers Series, this one includes adventure, technical knowledge, and cooperation in the achievement of a common goal. The 13-year-old hero and his friends are assisted by his cousin, an auto mechanic, in repairing the car. Although the car is too old to enter in the East African Safari, they plan to drive it to the site of the race. Because of a flat tire and engine trouble en route, they arrive in time to see only the last car, which crashes. They become heroes by taking the injured drivers to the hospital and a newspaper article is written about their car. The interest of the story is heightened by clearly delineated characters who include the hero's bossy younger brother, his proud and unfriendly "friend" Paul, and his feeble grandfather who cares only about his goats.

The stories in the Puzzlecrackers Series are about science, technology, and the importance of hard work. They are more explicitly didactic than *A Car Named Safari* in including diagrams that illustrate science principles discussed in the stories. As in Kariuki's other books, there also are black and white drawings of action from the stories. *The Engine Puzzle* is about car repair, in this case an old pickup truck. The child heroes learn about the history of the steam engine, and how the engine, battery, and other car parts work. They find learning all the information difficult, but are able to repair the truck and are rewarded by being able to ride in it.

The three boys who founded the Babanyeta Science Club are the core characters in all the stories in the Puzzlecrackers Series. In *The Fire Puzzle* they learn to make a biogas digester. Although they have difficulty believing that good will come of all the cow dung they collect, they successfully build and demonstrate a biogas digester and decide to build a gas factory to aid their community. Their success is a result of careful planning and hard work, as is the success of the heroes and heroines of the other stories in the series. In *The Irrigation Puzzle* a girl is admitted to the science club after overcoming sex prejudice because she is very good a science. The children join with informed adults in the Harambee spirit to acquire knowledge, plan the project, prepare the field and build irrigation structures with community involvement. There is much excitement during the construction and a celebration whe the irrigation system works. In *The Underground Water Puzzl* the children build a borehole in a village that has no water supply. They must learn about water underground and receive help fro an engineer to achieve their goal.

Ziki, My Monkey Boy is about a boy's pet monkey as well community development. Although the boy characters are not fon of monkeys because they steal maize that the boys must guar and sometimes harm children, the hero rescues a monkey with broken leg and cares for him with assistance from a veterinaria

Ziki, the monkey, learns to fetch cattle, harvest maize, scare animals from the farm, and shake hands. Thanks to him there is a record maize harvest, but Ziki runs off to the forest where he belongs. Although he becomes a maize thief, he never steals maize from the hero's farm. The cultural background of this story includes many facets of contemporary rural Kenyan life including seeing a film on deforestation, planting trees for a national project, doing chores at home and school, and making toys from wood.

Some of the same children appear as characters in *This Country Is My Country* as in *A Car Named Safari.* In this story the hero's grandfather tells about the Maasai in the good old days, and a "strange bachelor" tells stories about his experiences in World War II. The boy heroes engage in childhood rivalry, raise rabbits, care for a wounded crown bird, and assist with a community project to build a hospital. As in Kariuki's other fiction, the action is constructed around facets of contemporary life with which Kenyan children are familiar.

Kariuki is nearly unique among African children's writers in selecting science as a focus for fiction. He writes stories about a wide range of topics that both promote nationalism and entertain.

—Nancy J. Schmidt

KAYE, Geraldine

Nationality: British. **Born:** Geraldine Hughesdon, Watford, Hertfordshire, 14 January 1925. **Education:** Felixstowe College, Suffolk, 1934-39; Watford Grammar School, 1939-42; London School of Economics, 1946-49, B.Sc. (honours) in economics 1949. **Military Service:** Women's Royal Naval Service, 1943-46. **Family:** Married Barrington Kaye in 1948 (divorced 1975); two daughters and one son. **Career:** Scriptwriter, Malayan Film Unit, Malaya, 1951-52; teacher, Methodist Girls School, Paya Lebar, Singapore, 1952-54, and Mitford Colmer School, London, 1962-64. **Awards:** Children's Rights Workshop Other award, 1985. **Agent:** A.M. Heath and Co. Ltd., 79 St. Martin's Lane, London WC2N 4AA. **Address:** 39 High Kingsdown, Bristol, Avon BS2 8EW, England.

PUBLICATIONS FOR CHILDREN

Fiction

The Boy Who Wanted to Go Fishing, illustrated by Peggy Fortnum. London, Methuen, 1960; as *Kassim Goes Fishing,* 1969.

Kwasi and the Parrot and Other Stories. London, Oxford University Press, 1961.

Kwasi Goes to Town, illustrated by Valerie Herbst. London and New York, Abelard Schuman, 1962.

Kofi and the Eagle, illustrated by Sheila Hawkins. London, Methuen, 1963.

Chik and the Bottle House, illustrated by Peggy Fortnum. London, Nelson, 1965.

The Raffle Pony, illustrated by Gareth Floyd. Leicester, Brockhampton Press, 1966.

Oh, Essie!, illustrated by Rosemary Honeybourne. London, Benn, 1966.

The Blue Rabbit, illustrated by Clyde Pearson. Leicester, Brockhampton Press, 1967.

Kassim and the Sea Monkey, illustrated by Gay Galsworthy. London, Longman, 1967.

Koto and the Lagoon, illustrated by Joanna Stubbs. London, Deutsch, 1967; New York, Funk and Wagnalls, 1969.

The Tail of the Siamese Cat, illustrated by Ferelith Eccles Williams. London and New York, Nelson, 1967.

The Sea Monkey, illustrated by Gay Galsworthy. London, Longman, and Cleveland, World, 1968.

Tawno, Gypsy Boy, illustrated by Gareth Floyd. Leicester, Brockhampton Press, 1968.

Runaway Boy, illustrated by Michal Morse. London, Heinemann, 1971.

Nowhere to Stop, illustrated by Gareth Floyd. Leicester, Brockhampton Press, 1972.

Marie Alone. London, Heinemann, 1973.

The Rotten Old Car, illustrated by Leslie Wood. Leicester, Brockhampton Press, 1973; Chicago, Children's Press, 1976.

Tim and the Red Indian Headdress, illustrated by Carolyn Dinan. Leicester, Brockhampton Press, 1973; Chicago, Children's Press, 1976.

The Yellow Pom-Pom Hat, illustrated by Margaret Palmer. Leicester, Brockhampton Press, 1974; Chicago, Children's Press, 1976.

Goodbye, Ruby Red, illustrated by Robin Lawrie. Leicester, Brockhampton Press, 1974; Chicago, Children's Press, 1976.

Joanna All Alone, illustrated by Mary Dinsdale. Newton Abbot, Devon, David and Charles, 1974; Nashville, Nelson, 1975.

A Nail, A Stick, and a Lid, illustrated by Linda Birch. Leicester, Brockhampton Press, 1975; Chicago, Children's Press, 1976.

Billy-Boy, illustrated by Gareth Floyd. London, Hodder and Stoughton, 1975.

Children of the Turnpike, illustrated by Gareth Floyd. London, Hodder and Stoughton, 1976.

A Different Sort of Christmas, illustrated by Doreen Caldwell. London, Kaye and Ward, 1976.

Where Is Fred?, illustrated by Mike Cole. London, Knight, 1976; Chicago, Children's Press, 1977.

Penny Black. London, Heinemann, 1976.

Joey's Room. London, Macmillan, 1978.

King of the Knock-Down Gingers, illustrated by Glenys Ambrus. London, Hodder and Stoughton, 1979.

The Beautiful Take-Away Palace, illustrated by Glenys Ambrus. London, Kaye and Ward, 1980.

The Day after Yesterday, illustrated by Glenys Ambrus. London, Deutsch, 1981.

The Plum Tree Party, illustrated by Gabrielle Stoddart. London, Hodder and Stoughton, 1981.

Frangipani Summer. London, Macmillan, 1983.

The Sky-Blue Dragon, illustrated by Glenys Ambrus. London, Hodder and Stoughton, 1983.

The Donkey Strike, illustrated by Glenys Ambrus. London, Hodder and Stoughton, 1984.

Comfort Herself, illustrated by Jennifer Northway. London, Deutsch, 1984.

The Biggest Bonfire in the World, illustrated by Glenys Ambrus. London, Hodder and Stoughton, 1985.

The Call of the Wild Wood, illustrated by Abigail Pizer. London, Hodder and Stoughton, 1986.

The School Pool Gang, illustrated by Glenys Ambrus. London, Hodder and Stoughton, 1986.

A Breath of Fresh Air. London, Deutsch, 1987.
The Rabbit Minders, illustrated by Glenys Ambrus. London, Hodder and Stoughton, 1987.
Great Comfort. London, Deutsch, 1988.
The Donkey Christmas. London, Hodder and Stoughton, 1988.
Summer in Small Street, illustrated by Joanna Carey. London, Methuen, 1989.
The Babysitting Gang. London, Hodder and Stoughton, 1990.
A Dog Called Dog. London, Hodder and Stoughton, 1990.
Winter in Small Street. London, Methuen, 1990.
Someone Else's Baby. London, Deutsch, 1990; New York, Hyperion, 1992.
The Stone Boy. London, Heinemann, 1991.
A Piece of Cake. London, Deutsch, 1991.
Snowgirl. London, Heinemann, 1991.
Birthdays in Small Street, illustrated by L. Toft. London, Methuen, 1993.
Hands Off My Sister. London, Scholastic (Hippo), 1993.
Kelso's Carnival. London, Heinemann, 1994.
The Dragon Upstairs. London, Scholastic, 1997.
My Second Best Friend. London, Scholastic, 1998.

Other (readers)

Tales for Malayan Children. Singapore, Donald Moore, 1956.
The Creek Near Kwarme's Village and Other Stories, illustrated by Lorna Paull. London, Oxford University Press, 1961.
Kwaku and the Bush Baby. London, Oxford University Press, 1961.
Kwaku Goes Shopping. London, Oxford University Press, 1961.
Susie and Sophie and Other Stories, illustrated by Gene Adams. London, Oxford University Press, 1961.
Nii-Ofrang and His Garden and Other Stories, illustrated by Lorna Paull. London, Oxford University Press, 1962.
Kwabena and the Leopard, illustrated by Elizabeth Vaughan. London, Oxford University Press, 1964.
Yaa Goes South, illustrated by Elizabeth Vaughan. London, Oxford University Press, 1967.
Bonfire Night, illustrated by George Adamson. London, Macmillan, 1968.
Eight Days to Christmas, illustrated by Shirley Hughes. London, Macmillan, 1970.
In the Park, illustrated by Lynette Hemmant. London, Macmillan, 1970.
The Rainbow Shirt, illustrated by Lynette Hemmant. London, Macmillan, 1970.
Red Shoes. London, Oxford University Press, 1971.
Nowhere to Go. London, Oxford University Press, 1971.
The Tin Soldier. London, Oxford University Press, 1971.
Donkey Boy, illustrated by Prudence Seward. London, Oxford University Press, 1972.
Ginger, illustrated by Shirley Hughes. London, Macmillan, 1972.
The Children of the Brown Family, illustrated by Gavin Rowe. London, Oxford University Press, 1973.
A Mad Skipping Cat. London, Macmillan, 1974.
Scrap's Club. London, Macmillan, 1974.
To Catch a Thief, illustrated by Trevor Stubley. London, Oxford University Press, 1975.
Adventure [and *Another Adventure*] *in London,* illustrated by Mary Dinsdale. London, Oxford University Press, 2 vols., 1975-78.
Christmas Is a Baby, illustrated by Richard Butler. London, Macmillan, 1975.
Pegs and Flowers, illustrated by Richard Butler. London, Macmillan, 1975.
In Portobello Road, illustrated by Mary Dinsdale. London, Oxford University Press, 1976.
In the New Forest, illustrated by Trevor Stubley. London, Oxford University Press, 1976.
Week Out. London, Longman, 1978.
A Life of Her Own, illustrated by Anne Knight. London, Oxford University Press, 1978.
The Birthday Ball, illustrated by Lesley Smith. London, Macmillan, 1982.

*

Geraldine Kaye comments:

I write for the whole child age range but I have tended to write for older children and teenagers as my own children have grown up. I write quite a lot about children in different cultures and environments and I am especially interested in the child who is culturally an outsider: the Gypsy child or the child of mixed parentage. It also seems to me to be important to try to give recognition to the fact that we live in a very fluid, rapidly changing society in which there is no longer clear consensus on many issues of social behaviour. In recent years I have become more interested in history and think we need to know what went before to understand what is now. Young people are not keen on historical fiction now, but they appreciate a "time-slip" story with perhaps a magical element.

* * *

It is no accident that makes Geraldine Kaye in demand at creative writing courses. Participants encounter no mystique, no sense of the weighty English literary tradition, no talk of inspiration and the Muse. Instead, they meet an unpretentious professional who makes no large claims for her work, someone ever willing to exercise her craft in a commissioned series title, yet no mere cipher but a writer of skill, individuality, and conviction.

The early stories, such as *The Boy Who Wanted to Go Fishing* and *Kofi and the Eagle,* make use of Kaye's knowledge of Malaya and Africa. Within the simple form of Methuen's Read Aloud series they contain a richness characteristic of the author. The background details are authentic, the plot lines clear and uncluttered, the observation precise, with a quiet wisdom imbuing the whole. Many later stories spring from Kaye's long interest in gypsies and the disadvantaged. *Runaway Boy,* for example, takes the adjustment of Danny Baker, on escape from an approved school, to life in the open and eventual adoption by a gypsy family, while *Billy-Boy* and *Nowhere to Stop* both explore the gap between gypsies and the communities in which they settle. More recent work shows a concern for children adapting to new countries and new cultures, as in *The Day after Yesterday,* a moving story of a Chinese girl coming to terms with both life in England and a tragedy in her past, or *The Beautiful Take-Away Palace.*

Kaye's professionalism manifests itself in the range of her publications: a year's output might include a brief supplementary reader, a novel for teenagers with reading difficulties, and a full length book. Inevitably quality does vary, but the results are always competent and readable—and usually much more. *Nowhere to Stop* is typical of Kaye's gifts: the social concern informs but never unbalances the story; the characters live on outside the page the style is accessible, the plot skilfully paced, and we are treated to warmth without sentimentality.

A Breath of Fresh Air, which recreates the horror of the slave trade, and *Comfort Herself,* the story of a girl's struggle to find her own path when torn between relations in England and Ghana, both demonstrate Kaye's ability to center a story in a precise location with specific tensions and yet give its theme a universal quality. Kaye may not be likely to reach the ranks of Carnegie Medal winners but she is read, understood, and enjoyed by a wide audience, and leaves those readers with a sense of sympathies extended.

—Peggy Heeks

KEATS, Ezra Jack

Nationality: American. **Born:** Brooklyn, New York, 11 March 1916. **Education:** Thomas Jefferson High School, Brooklyn. **Military Service:** United States Army Air Corps during World War II. **Career:** Muralist for the Works Progress Administration in the 1930s, then freelance commercial artist; taught in the School of Visual Arts, New York, 1947-48, and Workshop School, New York, 1955-57. **Awards:** American Library Association Caldecott Medal, 1963; Boston *Globe-Horn Book* award, for illustration, 1970; University of Southern Mississippi award, 1980. **Died:** 6 May 1983.

PUBLICATIONS FOR CHILDREN (ILLUSTRATED BY THE AUTHOR)

Fiction

My Dog Is Lost, with Pat Cherr. New York, Crowell, 1960.
The Snowy Day. New York, Viking Press, 1962; London, Bodley Head, 1967.
Whistle for Willie. New York, Viking Press, 1964; London, Bodley Head, 1966.
Jennie's Hat. New York, Harper, 1966.
Peter's Chair. New York, Harper, 1967; London, Bodley Head, 1968.
A Letter to Amy. New York, Harper, 1968; London, Bodley Head, 1969.
Goggles! New York, Macmillan, 1969; London, Bodley Head, 1970.
Hi, Cat! New York, Macmillan, 1970; London, Bodley Head, 1971.
Apt. 3. New York, Macmillan, 1971; London, Hamish Hamilton, 1972.
Pet Show! New York, Macmillan, and London, Hamish Hamilton, 1972.
Psst! Doggie—. New York, Watts, 1973.
Skates! New York, Watts, 1973.
Dreams. New York, Macmillan, and London, Hamish Hamilton, 1974.
Kitten for a Day. New York, Watts, 1974.
Louie. New York, Greenwillow, 1975; London, Hamish Hamilton, 1976.
The Trip. New York, Greenwillow, and London, Hamish Hamilton, 1978.
Maggie and the Pirate. New York, Four Winds Press, 1979.
Louie's Search. New York, Four Winds Press, and London, MacRae, 1980.
Regards to the Man in the Moon. New York, Four Winds Press, 1981; London, Macmillan, 1985.
Clementina's Cactus. New York, Viking Press, 1982; London, Methuen, 1983.

Other

John Henry: An American Legend. New York, Pantheon, 1965.

Editor, *Over in the Meadow* (verse). New York, Four Winds Press, 1971; London, Hamish Hamilton, 1973.

PUBLICATIONS FOR ADULTS

Other

Editor, *God Is in the Mountain* (quotations). New York, Holt Rinehart, 1966.
Editor, *Night* (quotations), photographs by Beverly Hall. New York, Atheneum, 1969.

*

Manuscript Collections: Gutman Library, Harvard University, Cambridge, Massachusetts; de Grummond Collection, University of Southern Mississippi, Hattiesburg.

Theatrical Activities:
Designer: **Play**—*The Trip,* music and lyrics by Stephen Schwartz, New York, 1983.

Illustrator: *Jubilant for Sure,* 1954, and *Sure Thing for Shep,* 1956, both by Elizabeth Lansing, 1956; *Chester* by Eleanor Clymer, 1954; *Wonder Tales of Dogs and Cats* by Florence Carpenter, 1955; *Mystery on the Isle of Skye* by Phyllis A. Whitney, 1955; *A Change of Climate,* 1956, and *The Tournament of the Lions,* 1960, both by Jay Williams, and *Danny Dunn and the Anti-Gravity Paint,* 1956, *Danny Dunn on a Desert Island,* 1957, *Danny Dunn and the Homework Machine,* 1958, and *Danny Dunn and the Weather Machine,* 1959, all by Williams and Raymond Abrashkin; *Three Young Kings* by George Albee, 1956; *Wee Joseph* by William MacKellar, 1957; *The Indians Knew* by Tillie S. Pine, 1957, and *The Pilgrims Knew,* 1957, *The Chinese Knew,* 1958, *The Eskimos Knew,* 1962, and *The Egyptians Knew,* 1964, all by Pine and Joseph Levine; *And Long Remember* by Dorothy Canfield Fisher, 1959; *Grasses* by Irmengarde Eberle, 1960; *Nihal of Ceylon* by Eleanor A. Murphey, 1960; *Desmond's First Case* by Herbert Best, 1961; *In the Night* by Paul Showers, 1961; *The Rice Bowl Pet* by Patricia Miles Martin, 1962; *What Good Is a Tale?* by Solveig P. Russell, 1962; *The Peterkin Papers* by Lucretia P. Hale, 1963; *Tia Maria's Garden* by Ann Nolan Clark, 1963; *The Flying Cow* by Ruth Collins, 1963; *Zoo, Where Are You?* by Ann McGovern, 1964; *Speedy Digs Downside Up* by Maxine Kumin, 1964; *In a Spring Garden* edited by Richard Lewis, 1965; *The Naughty Boy: A Poem* by John Keats, 1965; *How to Be a Nature Detective* by Millicent Selsam, 1966; *The Little Drummer Boy* by Katherine Kennicott Davis, Henry Onorati, and Harry Simeone, 1968; *In the Park* by Esther Hautzig, 1968; *Two Tickets to Free-*

dom by Florence B. Freedman, 1971; *The King's Fountain* by Lloyd Alexander, 1971; *Penny Tunes and Princesses* by Myron Levoy, 1972.

Ezra Jack Keats commented:

(1978) My purpose in creating books for children is to share my experiences with them, ranging from the real world and feeling to fantasy. I hope children, whoever they may be, will discover that they are important, resourceful, and that they can have hope and self-esteem.

* * *

In his early books *The Snowy Day* and *Whistle for Willie* Ezra Jack Keats came forward with his own unmistakable style of illustration and text: the cut-out and gouache collage that gaily and vividly simplifies and stylises urban landscapes while the precise, almost scannable text, a separate statement for each page, concentrates the incidents of the stories—each a learning situation for under-fives—into easily memorable details.

All Keats's books combine the child's excitement at discovering new abilities and attitudes—like whistling (in *Whistle for Willie*), coping with ambivalent emotions (*Peter's Chair*), outwitting tougher and older kids (*Goggles*), or helping (a blind man in *Apt. 3*)—with a strong sense of the grim urban reality in which their little heroes Peter, Archie, Sam, and Louie grow up. Yet the New York street with its litter, its grimy building fronts, and graffiti-covered walls which always serves as a backdrop has the rich and lively atmosphere of home just as much as the interior of Peter, Sam, and Ben's apartment block where every inmate is known to the boys. Keats does not gloss over the stark urban reality. He presents it as the emotionally secure child would experience it, full of solid objects like traffic lights, trees, walls, and pavements to draw on and play around on. This environment is as tangible in the illustrations—which little fingers find irresistibly redrawable, particularly in *The Snowy Day* with its footprints, stickmarks, and "angels" made in the snow, its piling snow mountains and sparkling snow crystals—as in the text which laconically sets out the simple facts of inner and outer landscape in description and dialogue. Small things matter: found objects like sticks, cardboard boxes, pieces of chalk, goggles, cats, landmarks like look-out pipe and traffic light, the patient attention of grown-ups, friendship, planned and unplanned get-togethers like birthday parties (*A Letter to Amy*) and pet shows (*Pet Show*), or improvised street entertainment (*Hi, Cat!, The Trip*).

The world of these little books is at once open to discovery and quite secure, as exemplified in the wordless *Clementina's Cactus,* where Clementina's curiosity and delight in a flowering cactus are held just enough in check by her father to keep her from being hurt by its prickles. It is a world peopled with children, grown-ups, and animals which are ultimately friendly, though they may be scary at first. There the child becomes gently and gradually socialised, yet not without experiencing the normal, ambivalent feelings of pride at achieving and envy at others being better at something, of love for parents and friends and jealousy (for a newly arrived baby sister, for instance), of fear when bullied and triumph when successful through using wit, persistence, or courage. It revolves around the simple games of small children alone or in groups, and because it uses hardly any props except animals, it is universal, classless, and timeless.

There is some development and change in Keats's style from the first books to later work, particularly in the illustrations which have shifted the emphasis from witty cut-out collage to highly impressionistic shadow-play. Also, Keats increasingly tackles emotions on top of the sense-and-action experience of young children, for instance, in the Louie stories *The Trip* and *Louie's Search* where a lonely, uprooted, and fatherless boy overcomes his sense of isolation. He does this in the first with the help of an imaginative game of make-believe, a fantasy trip back to his old neighborhood friends, which gives him the strength to go out into the streets of his new neighborhood, dressed up, because it is Halloween, but confident that he will make new friends there. In the second he goes out into a strange and hostile world like the fairytale hero, not only in search of adventure, but also in search of a father, and he is again successful. But this time he has to pass a difficult test of courage first, because the man he eventually finds is fearsome and suspicious and has to be won round by a proof of Louie's man-to-man honesty. More than other Keats heroes Louie sets an example of how courage and imagination combine in the difficult task of growing up.

—Gertrud Mander

KEEPING, Charles (William James)

Nationality: British. **Born:** London, 22 September 1924. **Education:** Frank Bryant School for Boys, Kennington, London; Regent Street Polytechnic School of Art, London, 1946-52, National Diploma in art and design. **Military Service:** Royal Navy, 1942-46: telegraphist. **Family:** Married Renate Meyer in 1952; three sons and one daughter. **Career:** Printing trade apprentice, 1938; worked as an engineer and rent collector; Visiting Lecturer in Lithography, Regent Street Polytechnic School of Art, 1956-63; Visiting Lecturer in Lithography, Croydon College of Art and Design, Surrey, 1962-78; Visiting Lecturer in Printmaking, Camberwell School of Arts and Crafts, London, from 1979. Artist and book designer and illustrator. Member, Society of Industrial Artists. **Awards:** (for illustration) Library Association Kate Greenaway Medal, 1968, 1982; Victoria and Albert Museum Francis Williams Memorial prize, 1972, 1977; Bratislava Biennale Golden Apple award, 1975; Maschler award, 1987; W.H. Smith award, 1988. **Died:** 16 May 1988.

PUBLICATIONS FOR CHILDREN (ILLUSTRATED BY THE AUTHOR)

Fiction

Black Dolly. Leicester, Brockhampton Press, 1966; as *Molly o' the Moors,* Cleveland, World, 1966.

Shaun and the Cart-Horse. London, Oxford University Press, and New York, Watts, 1966.

Charley, Charlotte, and the Golden Canary. London, Oxford University Press, and New York, Watts, 1967.

Alfie and the Ferry Boat. London, Oxford University Press, 1968; as *Alfie Finds the Other Side of the World,* New York, Watts, 1968.

Joseph's Yard. London, Oxford University Press, and New York Watts, 1969.

Through the Window. London, Oxford University Press, and New York, Watts, 1970.
The Garden Shed. London, Oxford University Press, 1971.
The Spider's Web. London, Oxford University Press, 1972.
The Nanny Goat and the Fierce Dog. London, Abelard Schuman, 1973; New York, Phillips, 1974.
Richard. London, Oxford University Press, 1973.
The Railway Passage. London, Oxford University Press, 1974.
Wasteground Circus. London, Oxford University Press, 1975.
Inter-City. London, Oxford University Press, 1977.
Miss Emily and the Bird of Make-Believe. London, Hutchinson, 1978.
Willie's Fire-Engine. Oxford and New York, Oxford University Press, 1980.
Sammy Streetsinger. Oxford, Oxford University Press, 1984; New York, Oxford University Press, 1987.

Plays

Television Plays: *Joseph's Yard,* and *Through the Window,* both from his own stories, 1970.

Other

River. London, Oxford University Press, 1978.

Editor, *Tinker Tailor: Folk Songs.* Leicester, Brockhampton Press, 1968; Cleveland, World, 1969.
Editor, *Cockney Ding Dong.* London, Kestrel, 1975.
Editor, *Book of Classic Ghost Stories.* London, Blackie, 1986; New York, Bedrick, 1987.
Editor, *Classic Tales of the Macabre.* London, Blackie, and New York, Bedrick, 1987.

*

Illustrator: *Man Must Measure* by Ted Kavanagh, 1955; *Heute und Morgen 2* and *3* by Martha Freudenberger and Magda Kelber, 1956-57; *The Silver Branch,* 1957, *Warrior Scarlet,* 1958, *The Lantern Bearers,* 1959, *Knight's Fee,* 1960, *Dawn Wind,* 1961, *Beowulf,* 1961, *Heroes and History,* 1965, *The Mark of the Horse Lord,* 1965, *Dragon Slayer,* 1966, *The Capricorn Bracelet,* 1973, and *Blood Feud,* 1977, all by Rosemary Sutcliff; *Bridges,* 1958, *Roads,* 1959, *Canals,* 1961, *Ships,* 1962, *Railways,* 1964, *Wells,* 1965, *Dams,* 1966, and *Harbours and Docks,* 1967, all by John Stewart Murphy; *Merrily on High* by Guthrie Foote, 1959; *Riverbend Bricky,* 1960, and *Bricky and the Hobo,* 1964, both by Ira Nesdale; *Tales of Pirates and Castaways,* 1960, and *Tales of the West Country,* 1961, both by Kathleen Fidler; *The Queen of Trent* by Mitchell Dawson, 1961; *King Solomon's Mines* by Rider Haggard, 1961; *The Golden Age,* 1962, and *Dream Days,* 1962, both by Kenneth Grahame; *Lost John* by Barbara Leonie Picard, 1962; *Tipiti the Robin* by René Guillot, 1962; *The Shadow-Line, and Within the Tides* by Joseph Conrad, 1962; *Three Trumpets* by Ruth Chandler, 1962; *Harriet and the Cherry Pie* by Clare Compton, 1963; *The Latchkey Children* by Eric Allen, 1963; *Knights of the Golden Table,* 1963, and *The Treasure of Siegfried,* 1964, both by E.M. Almedingen; *Patrick Kentigern Keenan,* 1963, *The Kelpie's Pearls,* 1964, and *Thomas and the Warlock,* 1967, all by Mollie Hunter; *The Castle and the Harp* by Philip Rush, 1963; *Grimbold's Other World,* 1963, *Mainly in Moonlight,* 1965, *The Apple-Stone,* 1969, and *Over the Hills to Fabylon,* 1970, all by Nicholas Stuart Gray; *The Horned Helmet,* 1963, *The Children's Crusade,* 1964, *The Last of the Vikings,* 1964, *Splintered Sword,* 1965, *Swords from the North,* 1967, *The Dream-Time,* 1967, and *The Invaders,* 1972, all by Henry Treece; *The Moonstone* by Wilkie Collins, 1963; *They Told Mr. Hakluyt* edited by Frank Knight, 1964; *Whitsun Warpath* by Elizabeth Grove, 1964; *The Story of Egypt* by Jacoba Sporry, 1964; *Jenny,* 1964, *The Next-Doors,* 1964, and *Mrs. Jenny,* 1966, all by Joan Tate; *Wuthering Heights* by Emily Brontë, 1964; *The King's Contest,* 1964, *The Sky-Eater,* 1966, and *Poko and the Golden Demon,* 1968, all by James Holding; *The Rain Boat* by Lace Kendall, 1965; *Elidor* by Alan Garner, 1965; *Damien the Leper's Friend* by John Reginald Milsome, 1965; *Your English* by Denys Thompson and R.J. Harris, 1965; *King Horn,* 1965, and *The Wildman,* 1976, both by Kevin Crossley-Holland, and *Beowulf* translated by Crossley-Holland, 1982; *Bent Is the Bow,* 1965, and *The Red Towers of Granada,* 1966, both by Geoffrey Trease; *The Life of Our Lord* by Henry Daniel-Rops, 1965; *An Owl for His Birthday,* 1966, *The Haunted Mine,* 1968, *A Boy and His Bike,* 1976, and *The Story of Tod,* all by Richard Potts; *All Quiet on the Western Front* by Erich Maria Remarque, 1966; *Island of the Great Yellow Ox,* 1966, and *The Flight of the Doves,* 1968, both by Walter Macken; *Komantcia* by Harold Keith, 1966; *Celtic Folk and Fairy Tales* by Eric and N.I.S. Protter, 1967; *With Books on Her Head* by Edna Walker Chandler, 1967; *Champion of Charlemagne* by Marie Butts, 1967; *Bach* by Frederic Westcott, 1967; *The Cold Flame* by James Reeves, 1967, and *An Anthology of Free Verse* edited by Reeves, 1968; *The Christmas Story,* 1968; *The Mixture as Before,* 1968, and *Of Human Bondage,* both by W. Somerset Maugham; *After Many a Summer,* 1969, and *Time Must Have a Stop,* 1969, both by Aldous Huxley; *The Tale of Ancient Israel* by Roger Lancelyn Green, 1969; *The Castle of Otranto* by Horace Walpole, 1969; *Mr. Britling Sees It Through* by H.G. Wells, 1969; *Knights, Beasts and Wonders* by Margaret J. Miller, 1969; *The Heroes* by Charles Kingsley, 1970; *The God Beneath the Sea,* 1970, and *The Golden Shadow,* 1973, both by Leon Garfield and Edward Blishen, and *The Wedding Ghost* by Leon Garfield, 1985; *The Angry Valley* by Nigel Grimshaw, 1970; *Early Encounters* by John Watts, 1970; *Five Fables from France,* 1970, and *The Strange Feathery Beast,* 1973, both by Lee Cooper; *Ruined City,* 1970, and *On the Beach,* 1970, both by Nevil Shute; *The Poet's Tales* edited by William Cole, 1971; *The Idiot* by Feodor Dostoevsky, 1971; *Enjoy Reading!* by R.E. Rogerson, 1971; *The Valley of the Frost Giants* by Mary Francis Shura, 1971; *Wizards and Wampum* by Roger Squire, 1972; *The Twelve Labors of Hercules* by Robert Newman, 1972; *Flood Warning* by Paul Berna, 1972; *Weland, Smith of the Gods* by Ursula Synge, 1972; *I'll Tell You a Tale* by Ian Serraillier, 1973; *The Ghost Stories of M.R. James,* 1973; *Weirdies,* 1973, *Monsters, Monsters, Monsters,* 1974, and *Spectres, Spooks, and Shuddery Shades,* 1977, all by Helen Hoke; *When Darkness Comes* by Robert Swindells, 1973; *The Birds and Other Stories* by Lewis Jones, 1973; *The Magic Horns,* 1974, and *The Mermaid's Revenge and Other Stories,* 1979, both by Forbes Stuart; *The Little Book of Sylvanus* by David Kossoff, 1975; *Tower Blocks* by Marian Lines, 1975; *Terry on the Fence,* 1975, *A Kind of Wild Justice,* 1978, and *Break in the Sun,* 1980, all by Bernard Ashley; *About the Sleeping Beauty* by P.L. Travers, 1975; *Les Misérables* by Victor Hugo, 1976; *The Robbers* by Nina Bawden, 1979; *The Tale of Prince Igor* retold by Leonard Clark, 1979; *The Batsford Book of Stories in Verse for Children,* 1979, and *The Sun, Dancing,* 1982, both edited by Charles Causley, and *Jack the Treacle Eater and Other*

Poems by Charles Causley, 1987;*Breakback Alley* by Tony Drake, 1979; *Gods and Men* by John Bailey and others, 1981; *The Highwayman* by Alfred Noyes, 1981; *The Posthumous Papers of the Pickwick Club,* 1981, *Great Expectations,* 1981, *Our Mutual Friend,* 1982, *The Mystery of Edwin Drood,* 1982, *David Copperfield,* 1983, and *Hard Times,* 1983, all by Charles Dickens; *The Beginning of the Armadilloes,* 1982, and *Rikki-Tikki-Tavi and Other Animal Stories,* 1984, both by Rudyard Kipling; *Stumpy, Dr. Jekyll and Mr. Hyde, The Wrecker, New Arabian Nights,* and *More New Arabian Nights* all by Robert Louis Stevenson; *The Lady of Shalott,* 1986; *The Tale of Sir Gawain* retold by Neil Philip, 1987; *Black Beauty* by Anna Sewell, 1988; *Dracula* by Bram Stoker, 1988; *Frankenstein* by Mary Shelley, 1988.

Charles Keeping commented:

(1978) I suppose many of my picture books for children have grown out of something observed or overheard during my numerous long walks around London. A few relate directly to experiences from my own childhood. *The Spider's Web,* for example, came from early thoughts recalled from childhood, whereas *The Railway Passage* grew out of a conversation with a comparative stranger in a pub.

I like a picture book to be more than just entertaining or a collection of pretty pictures. It should present a variety of ideal and interesting situations to stimulate thought, but I *don't* like moral solutions.

* * *

Always a masterly illustrator of other people's words, Charles Keeping, like many of today's finest children's book artists, moved over to writing and illustrating his own books. While he was not in any way a born writer, although capable of the occasional telling phrase, it is certainly true that he was at his best as an artist when working to his own inspiration. Moreover he learned the trick of making his text a foil for the pictures and pared his words increasingly so as to convey more and more of his information visually, a technique used to great effect in *Richard,* the story of a day in the life of a London police horse, where no detail of stabling or grooming is omitted yet the text is reduced to hardly more than captions. In this way Keeping kept his flat, prosaic sentences simple for young readers and relied on his pictures to provide the imaginative stimulus they need.

Keeping's style changed much over the years but his world remained the same, the streets and yards of London's east end and the banks of London's river which he knew deeply, almost instinctively, and portrayed with a detailed and observant sympathy that makes his books a chronicle for adults as well as a pleasure for children. The bold swathes of colour he used in his cockney fairy tale *Charley, Charlotte, and the Golden Canary,* which won him the Kate Greenaway Medal, and the watery brilliance of *Alfie and the Ferry Boat*—in which a small boy crosses the Thames and discovers "the other side of the world"—gave way to a subtler use of line, but his work, although more delicate, lost nothing of its strength. It became, if anything, more formidable.

There was always a sombre element in Keeping's imagination, but in later years he could become truly frightening, using strange angles and foreshortenings to suggest the transformations that the mind can work on the physical world. The chicken, seen through the fence in *The Spider's Web,* is a crimson, glaring basilisk one moment, a harmless fowl the next. Perhaps his most savage work was in the tormented black, white, and sepia illustrations to Alfred Noyes's poem *The Highwayman,* the most curious, Keeping's own modern fable, *Sammy Streetsinger,* in which a not entirely successful story is redeemed by the manic intensity of his pictures. Fortunately Keeping's perception of things innocent or benevolent was equally acute and the last word may, after all, belong to the gentle melancholy that pervades his 1987 illustrations to *Black Beauty.*

How far, in his later work, Keeping can be called a creator of children's books may be questioned. He can be violent, gloomy, and difficult. He was undoubtedly one of the outstanding figures of his time.

—Anne Carter

KEIR, Christine. See **PULLEIN-THOMPSON, Christine.**

KELLOGG, Steven

Nationality: American. **Born:** Norwalk, Connecticut, 26 October 1941. **Education:** Rhode Island School of Design, Providence, B.F.A. 1963; American University, Washington, D.C. **Family:** Married Helen Hill in 1967; four stepdaughters and two stepsons. **Career:** Instructor in etching, American University, 1966. **Awards:** Silver Paintbrush award (Netherlands), 1974; David McCord Citation, 1987; Regina Medal, 1989; New England Booksellers Award, 1996; Jo Osborn Medal, 1997. **Address:** c/o Dial Books for Young Readers, 2 Park Avenue, New York, New York 10016, U.S.A.

PUBLICATIONS FOR CHILDREN (ILLUSTRATED BY THE AUTHOR)

Fiction

The Wicked Kings of Bloon. Englewood Cliffs, New Jersey, Prentice Hall, 1970.

Can I Keep Him? New York, Dial Press, 1971.

The Mystery Beast of Ostergeest. New York, Dial Press, 1971; London, Warne, 1977.

The Orchard Cat. New York, Dial Press, 1972.

Won't Somebody Play with Me? New York, Dial Press, 1972; London, Warne, 1977.

The Island of the Skog. New York, Dial Press, 1973; London, Warne, 1977.

The Mystery of the Missing Red Mitten. New York, Dial Press, 1974; London, Bodley Head, 1980.

Much Bigger Than Martin. New York, Dial Press, 1976; London, Warne, 1977.

The Mysterious Tadpole. New York, Dial Press, 1977; London, Warne, 1979.

The Mystery of the Magic Green Ball. New York, Dial Press, 1978 London, Bodley Head, 1980.

Pinkerton, Behave! New York, Dial Press, 1979; London, Warne, 1981.
The Mystery of the Flying Orange Pumpkin. New York, Dial Press, 1980.
A Rose for Pinkerton. New York, Dial Press, 1981; London, Warne, 1982.
The Mystery of the Stolen Blue Paint. New York, Dial Press, 1982.
Tallyho, Pinkerton! New York, Dial Press, 1982; London, Hutchinson, 1983.
Ralph's Secret Weapon. New York, Dial Press, and London, Hutchinson, 1983.
Best Friends. New York, Dial Press, 1986; London, Hutchinson, 1988.
Aster Aardvark's Alphabet Adventures. New York, Morrow, 1987.
Prehistoric Pinkerton. New York, Dial Press, 1987.
The Christmas Witch. New York, Dial Press, 1992.

Other (retellings)

There Was an Old Woman. New York, Parents' Magazine Press, 1974; London, Warne, 1978.
Paul Bunyan. New York, Morrow, 1984.
Chicken Little. New York, Morrow, 1985; London, Hutchinson, 1987.
Pecos Bill. New York, Morrow, 1986.
Johnny Appleseed. New York, Morrow, 1988.
Jack and the Beanstalk. New York, Morrow, 1991.
Mike Fink. New York, Morrow, 1992.
Yankee Doodle. New York, Simon & Schuster, 1995.
Sally Ann Thunder Ann Whirlwind Crockett. New York, Morrow, 1995.
I Was Born about 10,000 Years Ago. New York, Morrow, 1996.
The Three Little Pigs. New York, Morrow, 1997.

*

Illustrator: *Gwot! Horrible Funny Hairticklers* by George Mendoza, 1967; *Martha Matilda O'Toole* by James Copp, 1969; *Brave Johnny O'Hare* by Eleanor B. Heady, 1969; *The Rotten Book* by Mary Rodgers, 1969; *Matilda Who Told Lies and Was Burned to Death,* 1970, and *The Yak, The Python, The Frog,* 1975, both by Hilaire Belloc; *Mrs. Purdy's Children* by Ruth Loomis, 1970; *Granny and the Desperadoes* by Peggy Parish, 1970; *Mister Rogers' Songbook* by Fred Rogers, 1970; *Can't You Pretend?* by Miriam Young, 1970; *Here Comes Tagalong* by Anne Mallett, 1971; *Crabapple Night,* 1971, and *The Very Peculiar Tunnel,* 1972, both by Jan Wahl; *The Castles of the Two Brothers* by Aileen Friedman, 1972; *Abby* by Jeanette Franklin Caines, 1973; *Come Here, Cat* by Joan L. Nodset, 1973; *You Ought to See Herbert's House* by Doris Herold Lund, 1973; *Kisses and Fishes* by Liesel Moak Skorpen, 1974; *How the Witch Got Alf* by Cora Annett, 1975; *The Smartest Bear and His Brother Oliver,* 1975, *The Most Delicious Camping Trip Ever,* 1976, *Grouchy Uncle Otto,* 1977, and *Millicent the Magnificent,* 1978, all by Alice Bach; *The Great Christmas Kidnaping Caper* by Jean van Leeuwen, 1975; *The Boy Who Was Followed Home* by Margaret Mahy, 1975; *Yankee Doodle* by Edward Bangs, 1976; *Awful Alexander* by Judith Chaote, 1976; *Gustav the Gourmet Giant* by Lou Anne Bigge Gaeddert, 1976; *Barney Bipple's Magic Dandelions* by Carol Chapman, 1977; *Appelard and Liverwurst,* 1978, and *Liverwurst Is Missing,* 1981, both by Mercer Mayer; *The Pickle Plan* by Marilyn Singer, 1978; *Jill the Pill* by Julia Castiglia, 1979; *There's an Elephant in the Garage* by Douglas Davis, 1979; *Molly Moves Out* by Susan Pearson, 1979; *Once, Said Darlene* by William Sleator, 1979; *Uproar on Hollercat Hill* by Jean Marzollo, 1980; *The Day Jimmy's Boa Ate the Wash,* 1980, and *Jimmy's Boa Bounces Back,* 1984, both by Trinka Noble; *A Change of Plans* by Alan Benjamin, 1982; *The Ten-Alarm Camp-Out* by Cathy Warren, 1983; *A: My Name Is Alice* by Jane Bayer, 1984; *How Much Is a Million?* by David M. Schwartz, 1985; *Iva Dunnit and the Big Wind* by Carol Purdy, 1985; *Leo, Zack, and Emmie Together Again,* and *Tom, Zack, and Emmie in Winter,* both by Amy Ehrlich, 1987; *If You Made a Million* by David M. Schwartz, 1989; *Is Your Mama a Llama?* by Deborah Guarino, 1989; *Jimmy's Boa and the Big Splash Birthday Bash* by Trinka Noble, 1989; *The Day the Goose Got Loose* by Reeve Lindbergh, 1990; *Engelbert the Elephant* by Tom Paxton, 1990; *Parents in the Pigpen, Pigs in the Tub* by Amy Ehrlich, 1992; *The Great Quillow* by James Thurber, 1993; *The Wizard Next Door* by Peter Glassman, 1993; *Adventures of Huckleberry Finn* by Mark Twain, 1994; *The Rattlebang Picnic* by Margaret Mahy, 1994; *Frogs Jump* by Alan Brooks, 1996; *Library Lil* by Suzanne Williams, 1997.

* * *

Steven Kellogg's great Dane Pinkerton provides the most descriptive image of his work: a happy, sprawling romp. Kellogg's picture books can be roughly divided into those stories he writes himself and those he only illustrates. Unlike illustrators such as Maurice Sendak and Arnold Lobel, who have distinctive prose as well as illustrative styles, Kellogg's writing is so nondescript as to make it difficult to distinguish his own stories from those of others without first checking the title pages. There is, however, a distinctive "Kellogg-style" story. This usually features a simple episode getting rapidly out of hand, providing Kellogg with an opportunity to exhibit his talent for depicting crowds of hysterically happy humans and animals knocking into each other.

Kellogg is an enormously prolific illustrator. Few artists achieving his commercial success would bother illustrating the work of unknown and generally undistinguished writers. But Kellogg's need to keep working apparently outstrips his own ability to create new material. This might pose a problem for Sendak, but Kellogg's textual requirements are simple enough that any number of writers can keep him supplied.

Kellogg's style works. It can be successfully and endlessly applied to a variety of subjects ranging from the alphabet (*A: My Name Is Alice*) to American folklore (*Paul Bunyan*) to numerical concepts (*How Much Is a Million?*) as well as to any number of picture books (*Can I Keep Him?, The Day Jimmy's Boa Ate the Wash, The Island of the Skog*). Unlike Chris Van Allsburg or Paul O. Zelinsky, Kellogg is not one to experiment with new forms. He has found his niche.

Recent criticism of Kellogg has been savage. A review of *Johnny Appleseed* described his work as "blowsy...undisciplined..." While accurate in one sense, it must also be noted that it is precisely these overblown qualities that are the basis for Kellogg's appeal. Kellogg does manifest a compulsive need to fill up every inch of blank space. Unlike Peter Spier, Nancy Ekholm Burkert, and Maurice Sendak, artists who also incorporate a great deal of intricate detail in their illustrations, Kellogg's figures and objects jostle and collide. They seem charged with nervous energy, never sitting still. Everything on the page appears to be in frantic motion with no place for the eye to rest. This works well with light, slightly zany material such as *Chicken Little* and *A: My Name Is Alice,* or where unrestrained excess is the book's whole point (*Paul Bunyan, How Much Is a Million?*). It fails in *Johnny Appleseed,* where the theme of the gentle man living in harmony with his surroundings finds itself at odds with the frenetic illustrations.

Kellogg may not be one of the 20th century's great artists, but he deserves recognition as a genial, unpretentious illustrator whose distinctive manic style works effectively when matched with the right material.

—Eric A. Kimmel

KELLY, Eric (Philbrook)

Nationality: American. **Born:** Amesbury, Massachusetts, 16 March 1884. **Education:** Dartmouth College, Hanover, New Hampshire, A.B. 1906, M.A. 1929. **Family:** Married Katherine Collins Merrill in 1924. **Career:** Staff member, Westfield *Times,* Massachusetts, 1906, Springfield *Union,* Massachusetts, 1906-11, *Hunterton Gazette,* High Bridge, New Jersey, 1912, Boston *Herald,* 1914-18, and Boston *Transcript,* summers 1922-24; Instructor in English, 1921-29, Professor of Journalism, 1929-54, and Emeritus Professor, 1954-60, Dartmouth College. Lecturer (Kosciuszko Foundation scholar), University of Krakow, Poland, 1925-26; member of mission to Mexico, Office of Foreign Relief and Rehabilitation Operations, 1943. Vice-President, Paderewski Commission; trustee, Kosciuszko Foundation. **Awards:** American Library Association Newbery Medal, 1929; Kosciuszko Foundation Gold Medal, 1956. Chevalier, 1934, and Commander, 1945, Order Polonia Restituta. **Died:** 3 January 1960.

Publications for Children

Fiction

The Trumpeter of Krakow, illustrated by Angela Pruszynska. New York, Macmillan, 1928; London, Chatto and Windus, 1968.

The Blacksmith of Vilno, illustrated by Angela Pruszynska. New York, Macmillan, 1930.

The Golden Star of Halich, illustrated by Angela Pruszynska. New York, Macmillan, 1931.

The Christmas Nightingale, illustrated by Marguerite de Angeli. New York, Macmillan, 1932.

Three Sides of Agiochook, illustrated by Le Roy Appleton. New York, Macmillan, 1935.

Treasure Mountain, illustrated by Raymond Lufkin. New York, Macmillan, 1937.

At the Sign of the Golden Compass, illustrated by Raymond Lufkin. New York, Macmillan, and Birmingham, Combridge, 1938.

In Clean Hay. Privately printed, 1940.

On the Staked Plain, illustrated by Harve Stein. New York, Macmillan, 1940.

From Star to Star, illustrated by Manning Lee. Philadelphia, Lippincott, 1944.

The Hand in the Picture, illustrated by Irena Lorentowicz. Philadelphia, Lippincott, 1947.

The Amazing Journey of David Ingram. Philadelphia, Lippincott, 1948.

Other

A Girl Who Would Be Queen: The Story and Diary of the Young Countess Krasinska, with Clara Hoffmanowa, illustrated by Vera Bock. Chicago, McClurg, 1939.

Polish Legends and Tales. New York, Polish Publication Society of America, 1971.

Publications for Adults

Other

The Hope of All the Poles in the World. Chicago, Polish Roman Catholic Union Archives and Museum, 1941.

The Land of the Polish People. New York, Stokes, 1943; revised edition, Philadelphia, Lippincott, 1952.

* * *

The larger body of Eric Kelly's creative writing results from his deep love and respect for a land, Poland, and a people not his own except by adoption. Although generally regarded as literature for younger readers, Kelly's fiction has been widely enjoyed by the reading public at large. Characterized by an unerring blend of good story-telling and Poland's colorful history, his fiction has brought to readers an appreciation for the cultural and intellectual history of Poland and the aspirations and ideals of a valiant and honorable people.

Kelly's intense appreciation for medieval art and architecture, his love of natural beauty, and his eye for detail found expression in a variety of Polish tales and legends. In his "By Order of the Queen," which first appeared in 1924 in *St. Nicholas,* Kelly describes Krakow as a city of gold—"yellow in dawn, gray in dusk, blue in the midday, but gold, gold, gold in the sweet hour of sunset." He is equally at ease with characterization. In "By Order of the Queen," for example, the buyers and sellers in the market place are seen in jocular, conversational mood; yet as though setting a stage and chiseling a special character for the engrossing and suspenseful story to follow, Kelly introduces early a woman flitting "from bargain-stall to bargain-stall, glancing within as if searching for someone." She is not an old woman, he says, "but there is that about her which tells of age in other terms than years." "By Order of the Queen" and other Eric Kelly stories which appeared in *St. Nicholas* in the mid-1920s are but earlier harbingers of his highly acclaimed trilogy—*The Trumpeter of Krakow, The Blacksmith of Vino,* and *The Golden Star of Halich.*

The best known and most representative of the trilogy is *The Trumpeter of Krakow* which won the Newbery Medal. The general setting of this unusual historical romance is the city of Krakow; the specific setting, the parish church of St. Mary the Virgin. This church with its gothic architecture, the royal castle on Wawel Hill, the old and renowned Krakow University, and city streets at nighttime provide a proper backdrop for a dramatic, swift-moving, action-packed story. The politics of Krakow's constant threat from invading Tartars or greedy Russian tsars during the 15th century provide warp and woof to Kelly's exciting literary canvas, while a rich historical tradition is continued in the hourly trumpeting of the Polish *Heynal* from a tower in St. Mary's. The young trumpeter Joseph Charnetski and his family, the wise and revered Professor Jan Kanty, alchemists, hypnotists, thieves, and ruffians provide suspenseful action in a drama told in rich, poetic prose. *The Trumpeter of Krakow* is analogous in some respects to Victor Hugo's *Notre-Dame de Paris*; assuredly it places Kelly among the most capable American creators of juvenile fiction of his own period or any other.

—Charity Chang

KEMP, Gene

Nationality: British. **Born:** Gene Rushton, Wigginton, Staffordshire, 27 December 1926. **Education:** Wigginton Church Primary School; Tamworth Girls' High School, Staffordshire; University of Exeter, Devon (exhibitioner), 1945-48, B.A. (honours) in English 1948. **Family:** Married 1) Norman Pattison in 1949 (divorced 1958), one daughter; 2) Allan Kemp in 1958, one daughter and one son. **Career:** Teacher, St. Sidwell's Combined Primary School, Exeter, 1963-79, and Rolle College, Exmouth, Devon, 1974-75. Since 1979 freelance writer. **Awards:** Children's Rights Workshop Other award, 1977; Library Association Carnegie Medal, 1978. M.A.: University of Exeter, 1984. **Agent:** Gerald Pollinger, Laurence Pollinger Ltd., 18 Maddox Street, London W1R 0EU, England. **Address:** 6 West Avenue, Exeter, Devon EX4 4SD, England.

PUBLICATIONS FOR CHILDREN (BOOKS THROUGH 1981 ILLUSTRATED BY CAROLYN DINAN)

Fiction

The Prime of Tamworth Pig. London, Faber, 1972.
Tamworth Pig Saves the Trees. London, Faber, 1973.
Tamworth Pig and the Litter. London, Faber, 1975.
Christmas with Tamworth Pig. London, Faber, 1977.
The Turbulent Term of Tyke Tiler. London, Faber, 1977.
Gowie Corby Plays Chicken (not illustrated). London, Faber, 1979.
Dog Days and Cat Naps (short stories). London, Faber, 1980.
The Clock Tower Ghost. London, Faber, 1981.
No Place Like. London, Faber, 1983.
Charlie Lewis Plays for Time, illustrated by Vanessa Julian-Ottie. London, Faber, 1984.
The Well, illustrated by Chantal Fouracre. London, Faber, 1984.
Jason Bodger and the Priory Ghost. London, Faber, 1985.
Mr. Magus Is Waiting for You, illustrated by Alan Baker. London, Faber, 1986.
Juniper: A Mystery, illustrated by Chloe Cheese. London, Faber, 1986.
Tamworth Pig Stories, illustrated by Carolyn Dinan. London, Faber, 1987.
Crocodile Dog, illustrated by Elizabeth Manson-Bahr. London, Heinemann, 1987.
I Can't Stand Losing. London, Faber, 1987.
Room with No Windows. London, Faber, 1989.
Just Ferret. London, Faber, 1990.
Matty's Midnight Monster, illustrated by Diann Timms. London, Faber, 1991.
The Mink War, illustrated by Andrew Davidson. London, Faber, 1992.
Tamworth Pig Rides Again! London, Faber, 1992.
Wanting a Little Black Gerbil, with Chantal Fouracre. London, Heinemann, 1992.
Roundabout (short stories). London, Faber, 1993.
The Wacky World of Wesley Baker, illustrated Chris Fisher. London, Puffin, 1994.
Zowey Corby's Story. London, Faber, 1995.
A Dog's Journey, illustrated by Alan Howard. London, HarperCollins, 1996.
The Tyke Tiler Terrible Joke Book. London, Faber, 1997.
Zowey Corby and the Black Cat Tunnel. London, Puffin, 1997.

Other

Rebel Rebel (anthology). London, Faber, 1997.

Editor, *Ducks and Dragons: Poems for Children,* illustrated by Carolyn Dinan. London, Faber, 1980.
Editor, *Puffin Book of Ghosts and Ghouls,* illustrated by N. Harris. London, Puffin, 1992.

*

Gene Kemp comments:

I write stories for children hoping they will enjoy them and have a laugh. It's great to create a world and make the characters do what you want them to do—except in many cases they do what *they* want to do!

* * *

The broad appeal of Gene Kemp's stories is indicated by the fact that *The Turbulent Term of Tyke Tiler* was not only awarded the Library Association's Carnegie Medal but was also joint winner of the Other Award for 1977. This truly innovative book gives new dimensions to the day-school story, and an authoritative boost to feminism. More convincingly than any other juvenile book it demolishes many accepted ideas about aspirational and experiential differences between boys and girls. The realization of this is all the more significant to the reader because it only becomes apparent after the tantalizing twist in the story's tail (when the 11-year-old "hero" turns out to be a heroine). The book is also a comically touching account of the friendship between bright-as-a-button Tyke and a dim but engaging boy. The exactly appropriate first person narrative is punctuated by consciously dire playground rhymes and jokes which sharpen its pacy succinctness.

Gowie Corby Plays Chicken, another book with a primary school setting, also deals with a rebellious leading character and an unusual friendship. It never quite rises to Tyke Tiler's literally shattering-rooftop heights, although it has similar style and exhilaration. The lively mood is sustained in Kemp's recent full-length story, *The Clock Tower Ghost.* Once again her main characters are not obviously those with whom readers might easily identify; spiteful, greedy, nine-year-old Amanda is simply awful, and the gloomy ghost that she discovers in her new home is hardly endearing. This is, in a sense, another book about an ill-assorted pair of friends. The bond that is reluctantly forged between girl and ghost brings about not only some anarchically entertaining situations but also the reform of Amanda, and, for the spirit, a long awaited release from his hundred years of haunting.

The Tamworth stories are more magical and innocent, though Thomas, the human hero who shares the honours with the socially crusading pig, is occasionally obstreperous. These tales for younger children combine domestic cosiness and questing outdoor themes, and strike echoes of Milne's Pooh stories. (There is even an inverted reference to these in the naming of the anti-hero Christopher Robin Baggs.) Thomas pursues his adventures in the company of a poetry-spouting rabbit and a mathematically inclined hedgehog—his two floppy toys who, like Pooh, and Piglet, are fully alive in the context of small-boy and animal rapport. Tamworth Pig, of course, is not only really alive but larger than life; his personality, like the ardour of his conservationist campaigns, is comically convincing.

Animals are also enlivening elements in *Dog Days and Cat Naps.* In this collection of short stories Kemp's crispness of style and feeling for the vivid rumbustiousness of primary school cultures are used to good effect. Events and relationships are acutely observed, and each story produces a strong measure of excitement and genuine surprise.

Kemp has produced two thought-provoking but incisively funny books for teenagers, *No Place Like* and *I Can't Stand Losing.* The first of these features a "no nukes" family which, noisy and voluble, hardly lives up to the "peace house" notice adorning its front door. Pete, the leading character who enters the new world of sixth form college life, finds himself in various rites of passage situations. In *I Can't Stand Losing* the serious issues addressed again include that of the nuclear threat. A family of "no-hopers" who draw strength from their toughly idealistic mum have to pull themselves up by their own bootstraps when she packs her case and declares she is off to Greenham Common. Whether Chernobyl, and the spread of AIDS, will ultimately change society is left as an open question.

Juniper is an outstanding addition to Kemp's stories for eight- to 12-year-olds. It is both a mystery and an adventure, and the unlikely heroine Juniper retains her resilience despite disadvantage: "...I only have half an arm and my father is a criminal. And my mother is...a bit loopy." Like *The Turbulent Term of Tyke Tiler, Juniper* focuses on a friendship between a girl and a boy (in this case from different races), but despite flashes of Kemp's characteristically spicy humour, it has a moving and haunting quality.

—Mary Cadogan

KENNEDY, (Jerome) Richard

Nationality: American. **Born:** Jefferson City, Missouri, 23 December 1932. **Education:** Portland State University, Oregon, 1954-58, B.S. (honours) 1958; Oregon State University, Corvallis, 1964-65. **Military Service:** United States Air Force, 1951-54: Staff Sergeant. **Family:** Married Lillian Nance in 1960 (divorced 1974); two sons. **Career:** Janitor (retired), Oregon State University Marine Science Center, Newport, Oregon. Has also worked as a publicist, fireman, deckhand, cab driver, postal worker, elementary school teacher, woodcutter, carpenter, fisherman, and in the used book trade. **Awards:** (International) Pied Piper Literature prize, 1988 for *Amy's Eyes.* **Address:** 415 West Olive, Newport, Oregon 97365, U.S.A.

Publications for Children

Fiction

The Parrot and the Thief, illustrated by Marcia Sewall. Boston, Little Brown, 1974.
The Contests at Cowlick, illustrated by Marc Simont. Boston, Little Brown, 1975.
The Blue Stone, illustrated by Ronald Himler. New York, Holiday House, 1976.
Come Again in the Spring, illustrated by Marcia Sewall. New York, Harper, 1976.
The Porcelain Man, illustrated by Marcia Sewall. Boston, Little Brown, 1976; London, Hamish Hamilton, 1977.
Oliver Hyde's Dishcloth Concert, illustrated by Robert Andrew Parker. Boston, Little Brown, 1977.
The Dark Princess, illustrated by Donna Diamond. New York, Holiday House, 1978.
The Rise and Fall of Ben Gizzard, illustrated by Marcia Sewall. Boston, Little Brown, 1978.
The Leprechaun's Story, illustrated by Marcia Sewall. New York, Dutton, 1979.
The Lost Kingdom of Karnica, illustrated by Uri Shulevitz. San Francisco, Sierra Club, 1979.
The Mouse God, illustrated by Stephen Harvard. Boston, Little Brown, 1979.
Inside My Feet: The Story of a Giant, illustrated by Ronald Himler. New York, Harper, 1979.
Crazy in Love, illustrated by Marcia Sewall. New York, Dutton, 1980.
Song of the Horse, illustrated by Marcia Sewall. New York, Dutton, 1981.
The Boxcar at the Center of the Universe, illustrated by Jeff Kronen. New York, Harper, 1982.
Amy's Eyes, illustrated by Richard Egielski. New York, Harper, 1985; London, MacRae, 1986.
Collected Stories, illustrated by Marcia Sewall. New York, Harper, 1987.

Poetry

Delta Baby and Two Sea Songs, illustrated by Lydia Dabcovich and Charles Mikolaycak. Reading, Massachusetts, Addison Wesley, 1979.
Little Love Song, illustrated by Petra Mathers. New York, Knopf, 1992.

Has also written musical plays *The Snow Queen* and *What a Woman Wants,* with music by Mark Lambert.

* * *

Richard Kennedy's success as a storyteller lies in his fertile imagination, his ability to structure a narrative economically, his philosophical turn of mind, and his lucid, sometimes comical, style. He experiments with different fictional modes—a practice that perhaps contributes to the spontaneity that distinguishes his work.

The Blue Stone is an original fairy tale based upon a riddle; *The Porcelain Man* is a simple magical tale reminiscent of a German *märchen; The Mouse God* is a whimsical satire in the tradition of

Hans Andersen; *The Dark Princess* is a mystical romance after the manner of Laurence Housman fantasies; *Crazy in Love* is a folksy parable, with rich symbolic overtones; *Song of the Horse* is a lyrical celebration of animal-child relationships; *The Boxcar at the Center of the Universe* is an initiation novel that experiments with framing devices and extravagant imagery; *Amy's Eyes* is a doll fantasy, with layer upon layer of implicit commentary about identity formation, obsessive conduct, and the kind of bitterness that hardens into malice.

On rare occasions Kennedy's fanciful plots are too cumbersome to be credible. This flaw impairs *Inside My Feet* and, to a lesser degree, the initiation novel. In all his other works of fiction, form and content are well integrated, the thematic materials are often profound, and the story lines are ingenious.

The Blue Stone illustrates Kennedy's ability to blend the simple and the sublime. The plot is too complicated to paraphrase, and yet it all boils down to a naive "nature" myth. In the end the reader sees how angels are made from bits of sky that fall to earth and are swallowed by swallows. Before this discovery is made, however, there are dozens of twists in the story: men swallow the sky stone and become ducks, women who swallow it are changed to hens, and poems turn pigs into bread loaves. To avoid narrative chaos, the author structures the story in tight relationship to a riddle.

Jack and Bertie are an archetypal peasant couple with a lively sense of wonder and a gift for unpretentious poetic speech. Jack finds the blue stone while he is "splashering about" in the creek and Bertie swallows it while the soup is "starting to agitate." An astrologer, Zork, is one of several intriguing villains: "He had a long stork-like way about him, also a sharp nose and a scraggly little head that popped up through his red cape as if he had squeezed his head small by bearing down too hard on tiny schemes."

Kennedy's overall narrative style is as casual as the dialogue between the characters. This adds unity while also enabling the author to highlight such fragments of poetic description as the lines about "dark and careful cats" crouching in wonder.

Thematic benchmarks help the reader keep track of the complicated rules of magic, as when warnings in the riddle make it easy for a child to follow the moral thread. The art of writing such a complex parable is the art of evoking a clear-cut ethical system, while simultaneously suggesting that there is a reservoir of unstated meaning below the surface. In *The Blue Stone* naive comments carry a wealth of implication: "The working of heaven," says Bertie, "is enough to tire a person out completely."

Kennedy's powers as a lyrical and philosophical writer reach a new height in *Amy's Eyes*. And because he needs an intricate plot in order to share his world view, he makes considerable demands on his readers—demands upon their power of concentration, suspension of disbelief, and acceptance of human enigmas. At the same time the whole fanciful journey is easy. Such plot lines as loving a doll into life and grappling with gold-crazed pirates are already conventional in children's literature. Moreover, Kennedy makes use of simple patterns: inversions (when dolls become people, and people become dolls); superimpositions (when a magnanimous character assumes traits of the most ruthless); contrasts, as when "The Golden Man" (Amy's beloved father) confronts "Goldnose" (a fiendish pirate). And always there is Kennedy the phrase maker, as in this depiction of unrequited love: "...Miss Quince glared at her plate and stabbed at every one of her peas individually, and chewed each to extinction with terrible method."

In *Delta Baby and Two Sea Songs*, Kennedy ventures into mock-scary nonsense poems. "Delta Baby" has all the intrigue of a Gothic romance—an infant marked for assassination is handed from one rescuer to another until finally the child is left with only the forces of nature as unlikely saviors. Kennedy's concern about a power-abusing world is indirectly stated. *Little Love Song* is a set of verses in which the author plays with the idea of a miniature existence: a home inside a peanut shell, a bath in a drop of milk, love letters delivered in pea pod envelopes. The charm is in the detail as well as in seeing a mismatched couple (a human and a Thumbelina) find happiness.

Kennedy's poems as well as his fiction cannot be defined as tales exclusively for the young. *Amy's Eyes* demonstrates this best for it is Kennedy's most multi-leveled work, warranting the accolade bestowed by another eminent fantasy writer, Lloyd Alexander: "[It] sets a new high standard for all of us concerned with quality in literature...."

—Donnarae MacCann

KENNEDY, X. J.

Pseudonym for Joseph Charles Kennedy. **Nationality:** American. **Born:** Dover, New Jersey, 21 August 1929. **Education:** Seton Hall College, South Orange, New Jersey, B.Sc. 1950; Columbia University, New York, M.A. 1951; Sorbonne, Paris, Cert. Litt. 1956. **Military Service:** United States Navy, 1951-55. **Family:** Married Dorothy Mintzlaff in 1962; one daughter and four sons. **Career:** Teaching Fellow, 1956-60, and Instructor, 1960-62, University of Michigan, Ann Arbor; lecturer, University of North Carolina, Greensboro, 1962-63; Assistant Professor, 1963-67, Associate Professor, 1967-73, and Professor of English, 1973-79, Tufts University, Medford, Massachusetts. Visiting Lecturer, Wellesley College, Massachusetts, 1964, and University of California, Irvine, 1966-67; Bruern Fellow in American Civilization, University of Leeds, 1974-75. Poetry editor, *Paris Review*, Paris and New York, 1962-64; editor, with Dorothy M. Kennedy, *Counter/Measures* magazine, 1972-74. **Awards:** (for poetry) Hopwood award, 1959; Bread Loaf Writers Conference fellowship, 1960; Lamont Poetry Selection award, 1961; Bess Hokin prize (*Poetry*, Chicago), 1961; National Endowment for the Arts grant, 1967; Shelley Memorial award, 1970; Guggenheim fellowship, 1973; Golden Rose, New England Poetry Club, 1974; *Los Angeles Times* book award, 1985. L.H.D.: Lawrence University, Appleton, Wisconsin, 1988; Michael Braude award, American Academy and Institute of Arts and Letters, 1989. **Agent:** Curtis Brown, 10 Astor Place, New York, New York 10003. **Address:** 4 Fern Way, Bedford, Massachusetts 01730, U.S.A.

PUBLICATIONS FOR CHILDREN

Fiction

The Owlstone Crown, illustrated by Michele Chessare. New York, Atheneum, 1983.

The Eagle as Wide as the World. New York, McElderry, 1997.

Poetry

One Winter Night in August and Other Nonsense Jingles, illustrated by David McPhail. New York, Atheneum, 1975.
The Phantom Ice Cream Man: More Nonsense Jingles, illustrated by David McPhail. New York, Atheneum, 1979.
Did Adam Name the Vinegarroon?, illustrated by Heidi Johanna Selig. Boston, Godine, 1982.
The Forgetful Wishing-Well, illustrated by Monica Incisa. New York, Atheneum, 1985.
Brats, illustrated by James Watts. New York, Atheneum, 1986.
Fresh Brats, illustrated by James Watts. New York, McElderry, 1990.
The Kite that Braved Old Orchard Beach: Year-Round Poems for Young People, illustrated by Marian Young. New York, McElderry, 1991.
Ghastlies, Goops, and Pincushions: Nonsense Verse, illustrated by Ron Barrett. New York, McElderry, 1989.
The Beasts of Bethlehem, illustrated by Michael McCurdy. New York, McElderry, 1992.
Drat These Brats!, illustrated by James Watts. New York, McElderry, 1993.
Uncle Switch, illustrated by John O'Brien. New York, McElderry, 1997.

Other

Editor, with Dorothy M. Kennedy, *Knock at a Star: A Child's Introduction to Poetry,* illustrated by Karen Ann Weinhaus. Boston, Little Brown, 1982.
Editor, with Dorothy M. Kennedy, *Talking Like the Rain: A First Book of Poems,* illustrated by Jane Dyer. New York, Little Brown, 1992.

Publications for Adults

Poetry

Nude Descending a Staircase: Poems, Song, A Ballad. New York, Doubleday, 1961; Pittsburgh, Carnegie Mellon University Press, 1994.
Growing into Love. New York, Doubleday, 1969.
Bulsh. Providence, Rhode Island, Burning Deck, 1970.
Breaking and Entering. London, Oxford University Press, 1972.
Emily Dickinson in Southern California. Boston, Godine, 1974.
Celebrations after the Death of John Brennan. Lincoln, Massachusetts, Penmaen Press, 1974.
Three Tenors, One Vehicle: A Book of Songs, with James E. Camp and Keith Waldrop. Columbia, Missouri, Open Places, 1975.
French Leave: Translations. Florence, Kentucky, Robert L. Barth, 1983.
Hangover Mass. Cincinnati, Bits Press, 1984.
Cross Ties: Selected Poems. Athens, University of Georgia Press, 1985.
Dark Horses. Baltimore, Maryland, Johns Hopkins University Press, 1992.

Other

An Introduction to Poetry (textbook). Boston, Little Brown, 1966; revised edition, 1971, 1974, 1978, 1982, 1986, 1990; with Dana Gioia, 1994, New York, Longman, 1998.
An Introduction to Fiction. Boston, Little Brown, 1976; revised edition, 1979, 1983, 1987, New York, HarperCollins, 1991, 1995.
Literature: An Introduction to Fiction, Poetry, and Drama. Boston, Little Brown, 1976; revised edition, 1979, 1983, 1987, 1991; with Dana Gioia, New York, HarperCollins, 1994.
The Bedford Reader, with Dorothy M. Kennedy. Boston, Bedford, 1982; revised edition, New York, St. Martin's Press, 1985, 1988; and with Jane Aaron, 1991, 1994, 1997.
The Bedford Guide for College Writers (textbook), with Dorothy M. Kennedy. New York, St. Martin's Press, 1987; revised edition, 1990; and with Sylvia Halliday, 1993.

Editor, with James E. Camp, *Mark Twain's Frontier.* New York, Holt Rinehart, 1963.
Editor, with Keith Waldrop and James E. Camp, *Pegasus Descending: A Book of the Best Bad Verse.* New York, Macmillan, and London, Collier Macmillan, 1971.
Editor, *Messages: A Thematic Anthology of Poetry.* Boston, Little Brown, 1973.
Editor, *Tygers of Wrath: Poems of Hate, Anger, and Invective.* Athens, University of Georgia Press, 1981.

*

X. J. Kennedy comments:

From the titles of my books for children you might get the impression that nonsense is all I care about. Oh, I care about nonsense fervently, but in poetry for kids, more than nonsense is possible. At least a part of each verse collection I've done deals with the world that children know. Two books, *The Forgetful Wishing-Well* and *The Kite that Braved Old Orchard Beach,* are more or less realistic throughout.

At the risk of becoming tricky to pigeonhole (it might be easier to label me "poet" only), I've also written two novels for eight-to-twelve-year-olds, *The Owlstone Crown* and a sequel, *The Eagle as Wide as the World.* These stories mingle realism and fantasy, though the fantasy predominates. They tell the adventures of a couple of twins, a boy and a girl, with the girl usually the leader, despite her being legally blind. In coping with monstrous villainry, they enjoy the help of Lew Ladybug, an insect detective, a Kodiak brown bear named Fardels, and a fortune-telling snail. These books began as yarns that I told aloud to our own kids to pass the time during a vacation blighted by rain. That many other kids have liked the stories has been one of the chief satisfactions of my life.

* * *

One of the worlds of X. J. Kennedy lies just next door in a neighborhood where mothers keep pet pigs, play slide trombones, and bake inedible pies while fathers conjure up a good whirl for their entire families in a concrete mixer. Through their houses pass an assortment of odd aunts, uncles, and grandparents, as well as a monstrous mouse who crashes a birthday party. It is a heady place where the Tooth Fairy, fabric shrinkers, "a birthday cake so full of eggs/It cackles, clucks and scratches," are part of everyday living, where salami subs, gumball machines, staplers, and cough drops enjoy a life of their own. It is, most importantly, a world where children may exercise their own imaginations to create still more fun. "My mother's big green gravy boat/Once thought he was a navy boat./I poured him over my mashed potatoes/And out swam seven swift torpedoes./Torpedoes whizzed and whirred, and—WHAM!/One bumped smack into my hunk of ham..."

Kennedy's imagination overflows with absurdities. Spaghetti, he writes, makes very unusual shoelaces. In winter one can prepare "Snowflake Souffle" by stirring it with "two hind legs," baking it in an igloo and slicing it with a "rusty ice-skate." The Thrift-Rite Supermart provides enough frozen delicacies to whip up an "Instant Storm." A coat made of cocoa skin makes one feel "All warm and scummy."

His "far out family" includes a great-great-Grandma who sleeps in a treehouse, an Aunt Jill who insists that dill stalks will afford "sour puss" pickles "a few good tickles," and Cousin Carrée who serves—both literally and figuratively—"a good square meal" including ground round shaped into bricks with hamburger buns squeezed into squares. His "...uncle, General Doug MacDougal,/ Sleeps nights inside a huge blue bugle" while "All four of my uncle Erics/Tear their hair and throw hysterics." In *Brats* Kennedy conjures up scores of annoying youngsters who are either victims or perpetrators of further hilarity. "At the laundromat Liz Meyer/ Flung her brothers in the dryer./Round and round they've whizzed for years,/Not yet dry behind the ears."

In addition to zany family situations which include household pets, there are "Unheard-Of Birds and Couldn't-Be Beasts" as well as attic ghosts and a variety of "Cheerful Spirits." Dinosaurs fascinate Kennedy, as do creatures of the sea. In addition to a limerick about a nervous sea captain from Cheesequake, there is a rousing story poem about Mackeral Mack and Halibut Hal. Kennedy's lines sing: "With walloping tails, the whales off Wales/ Whack waves to wicked whitecaps..." In this, as in all of his work, Kennedy outshines mere versifiers with a superb use of rhyme, meter, onomatopoeia, alliteration, and delightful wordplay. "The cows that browse in pastures/Seem not at all surprised/That as they moo they mow the lawn/And their milk comes pasture-ized." Digested by a giant snail, Uncle Artemus McPhail remarks that he "finds this whole thing hardly moving." In his animal alphabet, *Did Adam Name the Vinegarroon?,* he writes of a tyrannosaur: "Yet tyrants, under Time's slow hand,/Must one day bow their necks./Now in museums—bones wired—stand/Tyrannosaurus wrecks." Kennedy's work is rich in simile and metaphor; "...bats drowse in houses' eaves/Like tents collapsed for storage," a mole "tunnels underneath your lawn/To shoulder up a wrinkle," and an iguana "demonstrates the signs/Of somewhat hasty wrapping."

While a good portion of Kennedy's early verse for children in *One Winter Night in August* and *The Phantom Ice Cream Man* appear as strictly nonsensical, there is, as in all excellent nonsense, a toehold on reality, a recognition of the human condition. Mothers may not buy "six paper swimming pools" or "backscratchers for a pig" but they do enjoy bargain sales. Mighty Mump cereal may not contain "sugar, corncobs, and dye" but televised, it is "made up to look/simply ethereal." In a recent book of poetry, *The Forgetful Wishing-Well,* lies Kennedy's other world of reality where sticky ice cream cones, forbidden TV watching, excuses to stay up late, reactions to ugly deer statues, and even a child's poignant sense of loss are explored. "I take my plastic rocket ship/ To bed, now that I'm older./My wooly bear is packed away—/ Why do the nights feel colder?" Humor remains keen, as in conversations between a crocus and artichoke, a truck and taxi. A schoolbus, window screen, fog, snow, and old stone mill are personified. But nonsense has been routed. One can see in "Roofscape" a skyscraper shadowing "A low-kneeling church," watch pigeons, traffic snarls and the world as it is. An unforgettable use of onomatopoeia occurs in "Rain into River" where "Rain into river/falling/tingles/one/at/a/time/the trout's/tin shingles." Kennedy's title poem, "To a Forgetful Wishing-Well," sets the tone. "All summer long, your round stone eardrum held/Wishes I whispered down you. None came true./Didn't they make one ripple in your mind?/I even wished a silver pail for you."

Kennedy is at home in both worlds; to each he is making a significant contribution.

—Myra Cohn Livingston

KENNEMORE, Tim

Nationality: British. **Born:** London, 2 February 1957. **Address:** c/o Faber and Faber, 3 Queen Square, London WC1N 3AU, England.

Publications for Children

Fiction

The Middle of the Sandwich. London, Faber, 1981.
The Fortunate Few. London, Faber, 1981; New York, Coward McCann, 1982.
Wall of Words. London, Faber, 1982.
Here Tomorrow, Gone Today (short stories). London, Faber, 1983.
Changing Times. London, Faber, 1984.
Alice's Birthday Pig, illustrated by Alex de Wolf. London, Hamish Hamilton, 1995.
Alice's World Record, illustrated by Alex de Wolf. London, Hamish Hamilton, 1996.

* * *

With only a handful of books to her credit, Tim Kennemore is making her mark on children's fiction. Her first full-length story, *The Middle of the Sandwich,* appeared in 1981, and underlined the fact that there was a resurgence of interest in the school story, even though the new wave in this genre represented a departure from the traditional boarding school sagas of the 1920s and 1930s. *The Middle of the Sandwich* has a day school setting and is concerned with disorientation at the upper junior level. It is a measure of Kennemore's skill that she brings a sense of freshness and discovery to this well-trodden scheme. As in all her books she is an acutely aware, detached observer, who harnesses both comedy and drama to good effect.

Helen, the heroine, has to spend a term at a village primary school; this term is sandwiched between her more permanent education at a private preparatory school and a London comprehensive, and at first everything and everyone seem hostile. There is some extremely perceptive use of the confines of school to heighten emotions and relationships, and the obedient, well-behaved Helen learns how to cope with her new situation by drawing on unexpected inner resources.

Helen turns out to be the most conformist of Kennemore's heroines. Her next, the 14-year-old Jodie Bell in *The Fortunate Few,* starts off with far more assertion and talent. She is a gymnast, whose adventures are set in a world of the future (which nevertheless is related closely to our own) in which gymnastics seems to have taken over from football as the most popular spectator sport. Although Jodie is believable as a character, the book is a merciless send-up of professional exploitation; journalists and publicity men are treated as trenchantly as are officials in sports promotion and big business circles. This book's sparkling satirical edge makes it appropriate for adult audiences as well as for children, and it seems that Kennemore's stories, which show a consistently developing maturity, are likely to appeal to a wide range of readers as they can be appreciated at various levels. *Wall of Words,* for example, is at one level a satisfying family saga; at another it represents black humour as biting as that of *The Fortunate Few* (her leading child characters have a morbid passion for embalming, spontaneous explosion, and other unsocial activities).

Here Tomorrow, Gone Today demonstrates her flair for the short story. Four of the tales in this collection have school settings; three are more concerned with family relationships. They encompass every shade of Kennemore's humour from mild irony to gulping satire. Her ability to convey naturalistic adolescent dialogue (bad jokes and all!) comes across robustly in these episodes which have as their theme the debunking of pompous adults and precocious teenagers. There are threads of feminism too, which are the more telling for being stumbled upon by the reader rather than rammed home. In "The Black Sheep," for example, the M.P. parent so bitterly resented by the weedy, depressive Russell turns out to be his mother and not his father: her agent, prime minister, and rival candidate are also firmly feminine.

There is nothing particularly new about Kennemore's plots and themes, but her treatment of these is always satisfyingly inventive.

—Mary Cadogan

KERR, (Anne) Judith

Nationality: British (originally German: naturalized citizen, 1947). **Born:** Berlin, Germany, 14 June 1923; daughter of the writer Alfred Kerr. **Education:** Schools in Germany, Switzerland, France, and England; Central School of Art, London (scholar), 1945. **Family:** Married the writer Nigel Kneale in 1954; one daughter and one son. **Career:** Secretary, Red Cross, London, 1941-45; teacher and textile designer, 1946-53; reader, script editor, and script writer, BBC-TV, London, 1953-58. Lives in London. **Address:** c/o HarperCollins Publishers, 77-85 Fulham Palace Rd., London W6 8JB, England.

Publications for Children (illustrated by the author)

Fiction

The Tiger Who Came to Tea. London, Collins, and New York, Coward McCann, 1968.
Mog the Forgetful Cat. London, Collins, 1970; New York, Parents' Magazine Press, 1972.
When Hitler Stole Pink Rabbit. London, Collins, 1971; New York, Coward McCann, 1972.
When Willy Went to the Wedding. London, Collins, 1972; New York, Parents' Magazine Press, 1973.
The Other Way Round (not illustrated). London, Collins, and New York, Coward McCann, 1975.
Mog's Christmas. London, Collins, and Cleveland, World, 1976.
A Small Person Far Away. London, Collins, 1978; New York, Coward McCann, 1979.
Mog and the Baby. London, Collins, 1980.
Mog in the Dark. London, Collins, 1983; New York, Larousse, 1984.
Mog and Me. London, Collins, 1984.
Mog's Family of Cats. London, Collins, 1985.
Mog's Amazing Birthday Caper. London, Collins, 1986.
Mog and Bunny. London, Collins, 1988; New York, Knopf, 1989.
Mog and Barnaby. London, Collins, 1991.
How Mrs. Monkey Missed the Ark. London, Collins, 1992.
The Adventures of Mog. London, Collins, 1993.
Mog on Fox Night. London, HarperCollins, 1993.
Mog in The Garden, London, HarperCollins, 1994.
Mog's Kittens, London, HarperCollins, 1994.

*

Judith Kerr comments:

The picture books were for my children—in fact, a lot of the ideas came from my children in the first place, and also from my husband. They were the sort of ideas which amused us all. Mog is our cat. The novels also were written for my children, but deal with my own childhood as a refugee from Hitler, first in Switzerland and France, later in England during the war. It was so different from the way they grew up that I wanted them to know about it, and I wanted also to explain that it wasn't nearly as horrific as it sounded. Perhaps most of all it was a way of remembering my own parents, now long dead.

* * *

Judith Kerr's twin talents as writer and illustrator have been in quantitative balance in her popular picture books about Mog the cat, which were aimed, successfully, at the under-fives. With these she proved herself a thoroughly competent, professional, imaginative children's author—one among many. Real distinction, however, she achieved with her two autobiographical stories for young readers over ten which chart her exceptionally eventful childhood and adolescence as the daughter of a famous German Jewish writer and refugee from Nazi Germany.

Together, *When Hitler Stole Pink Rabbit* and *The Other Way Round* tell Anna's (alias Judith's) 12-year odyssey that takes her to three countries (Switzerland, France, England) and makes her trilingual. It is a lively, detached, and objective narrative, helped by a distance of 30 years between event and writing down, a precise memory, a warm sense of humour, and profound insight into the growing self-awareness and world perception of child and teenager. Both books derive most of their interest from the interaction of outside political events with inside subjective experience of child and teenager, the first story the more poignantly so because little Anna is as yet incapable of grasping the momentous historical changes which force her universally respected father to leave his native country and end his brilliant career, thus changing their lives from wealthy middle-class to destitute stateless. Yet Kerr demonstrates convincingly how all that matters for the child is family togetherness and emotional security, while lack of money or settled home is of secondary importance. Both in Switzerland and France little Anna bravely takes everything in her stride: drastically reduced living conditions, changing playmates and teachers, lack of toys and money, even adjusting to a new language and being cut by Nazi Germans on holiday in their temporary Swiss home. Only a brief separation from her parents proves traumatic, because the warm understanding in a secure family is her be-all and end-all, natural squabbling and disappointments notwithstanding. Anna thus has as happy a childhood as any child growing up in much more sheltered circumstances.

The 18-year old Anna in *The Other Way Round,* however, is learning independence the hard way because of the conditions the war and her enemy-alien status put her into, and because she feels for her aging parents in their appallingly reduced existence. They live in a cheap London hotel full of Central European refugees, her father a German-language writer without work and her mother doing menial jobs—the tragedy of exile! Yet Anna succeeds and overcomes by asserting the importance of her own life (secretary during the day, art student in the evening) in spite of her deep concern for her parents. She experiences first love and loss of love, first success and failure, the reward and monotony of work, the stirrings of creativity. Set against the richly detailed backcloth of the war, the Blitz and the Battle of Britain, rationing, air raids, buzz bombs and finally victory, Kerr's story of Anna's successful transition from lost schoolgirl to self-possessed art student is a chronicle of an epoch as much as of the grim refugee life Anna and her family have to live while waiting for the war to end. Together, the two books give the young reader a bit of important contemporary history, as seen and experienced by somebody who went through it vulnerable, yet open-eyed. There is no better way for the young reader to be brought up both against recent history and the psychological implications such turbulent times had for those growing up in them.

—Gertrud Mander

KHALSA, Dayal Kaur

Nationality: American; immigrated to Canada in 1970. **Born:** Marcia Schoenfeld in Queens, New York, 17 April 1943; changed name in mid-1970s. **Education:** City College of New York, B.A. in English 1963. **Career:** Writer, artist, and yoga teacher. **Awards:** Choice Book from Canadian Children's Book Centre, 1984, 1988; *New York Times* Notable Children's Book, 1986; New York Public Library Best Children's Book, 1986; Canada Council Children's Literature Prize honorable mention for illustration, 1987; Ontario Arts Council Ruth Schwartz Award finalist, 1987; Amelia Frances Howard-Gibbon Award finalist, 1987; American Library Association Notable Book, 1986, 1987, and 1988; American Institute of Graphic Arts Show Winner's List, 1987; American Booksellers Association/Children's Book Council Children's Bestseller List, 1988; Canadian Children's Book Centre Choice Book, 1988-89; New York Public Library Best Children's Book, 1988; Governor General's Literary Award for Children's Illustration finalist, 1988; *Booklist* Most Outstanding Picture Books of the Year, 1988. **Died:** 17 July 1989.

Publications for Children

Fiction (illustrated by the author)

Baabee Books, Series I, four volumes. Westmount, Quebec, Tundra, 1983.

Baabee Books, Series II, four volumes. Westmount, Quebec, Tundra, 1983.

Baabee Books, Series III (includes *Bon Voyage Baabee, Happy Birthday Baabee, Merry Christmas Baabee,* and *Welcome Twins*). Westmount, Quebec, Tundra, 1984.

Tales of a Gambling Grandma. Westmount, Quebec, Tundra, and New York, Potter, 1986; as *Tales of a Gambling Grannie,* London, MacDonald, 1988.

I Want a Dog. Westmount, Quebec, Tundra, and New York, Potter, 1987.

Sleepers. Westmount, Quebec, Tundra, and New York, Potter, 1988.

My Family Vacation. Westmount, Quebec, Tundra, and New York, Potter, 1988.

How Pizza Came to Our Town. Westmount, Quebec, Tundra, 1989; as *How Pizza Came to Queens,* New York, Potter, 1989.

Julian. Westmount, Quebec, Tundra, and New York, Potter, 1989.

Cowboy Dreams. Westmount, Quebec, Tundra, and New York, Potter, 1990.

Snow Cat. Westmount, Quebec, Tundra, and New York, Potter, 1992.

*

Critical Studies: "Dayal Kaur Khalsa (1943-1989): A Publisher's Tribute" by May Cutler, in *CM: Canadian Materials for Schools and Libraries* (Ottawa), Vol. 16, No. 6, November 1989, 228-229; "Dayal Kaur Khalsa" by Terri L. Lyons, in *Canadian Children's Literature* (Guelph), Vol. 59, 1990, 70-74.

* * *

During her brief career as an author-illustrator, Dayal Kaur Khalsa produced picture books that bring to life the world of her childhood with clarity, affection, and humor. Her works effectively offer the child's perspective about details that adults dismiss as mundane, recalling the sights, sounds, tastes, and smells that form the texture of childhood. Khalsa's earliest works consist of three related series, each composed of four board books. These Baabee titles were designed for the very young child. The first books fold out accordion-style, but later titles are bound conventionally. The small format, bright colors, and uncluttered images encourage young children to explore the baabees' world. The brown, blue, yellow, and pink infants get dressed, play with toys, bathe, go for stroller rides, and participate in other simple activities. The books also depict familiar objects such as pets and toys.

These early works pale against Khalsa's full-scale picture books, beginning with *Tales of a Gambling Grandma.* Although Khalsa spent most of her adult life in Canada and created all her picture books there, the subject matter for most of her stories comes straight from her childhood in Queens, New York. The frame for her first story is provided by an adult narrator recalling her grandmother, but the reminiscences are clearly those of a young child. Who wouldn't remember a grandmother who escaped from the Russian Cossacks in a hay cart and warns her granddaughter to keep borscht in the refrigerator in case they appear in Queens? Grandma takes her on excursions to Coney Island, a vaudeville show, a Chinese restaurant. But most of the time they spend "quietly under the willow tree, just the two of us." There Grandma tells how she learned to play poker to earn extra money early in her marriage. Her gambling prowess continues in the Sunshine Ladies Card Club, on her yearly California excursion to play poker with her son's friends, and in dining room card games when she wins the narrator's allowance. Clearly the child's world revolves around Grandma, whose death leaves a void. Two illustrations of Grandma's room capture that loss poignantly. In the first, the girl, who has a cold, sits on the bed under a sheet tent. She counts pennies while Grandma sits in a chair beside her polishing the coins. In the second, the bed is neatly made, the chair empty. The girl is in the closet, seeking comfort by hugging Grandma's dresses with their familiar touch and smell.

Although the girl narrator is unnamed, in Khalsa's next book, *I Want a Dog,* she is identified as May. Her attempts to convince her parents to buy her a dog reveal May's creativity and determination. After leading dogs home with salami and buying a puppy for her mother's birthday fail, May makes a surrogate dog from a roller skate. She walks the skate faithfully in all kinds of weather and soon has neighborhood children pulling skates on leashes. Khalsa brilliantly depicts May's obsession through such touches as giving all her classmates dogs' heads while she daydreams in school. In *Sleepers,* an unnamed May insists that she never sleeps. Brief rhymes identify members of her family, other people, and animals who sleep. All the while she sinks more deeply under the covers.

My Family Vacation returns to the larger and longer format. May and her family drive to Florida for a winter vacation. Uncertain that she wants to leave snow, May quickly develops enthusiasm for the journey despite her older brother's jokes about her continual collecting of souvenirs like motel soap and paper placemats. Khalsa depicts scenes such as a used car lot, miniature golf course, roadside tourist attractions, and motels with bright colors and unerring attention to detail, celebrating the kitsch that captivates May.

May's enthusiasm for life helps her find adventure as home as well as on the road. In *How Pizza Came to Queens,* Mrs. Pellegrino arrives from Italy to stay with the family of May's best friends. Her unhappiness is apparent, but her inability to speak English prevents her from explaining. May and her friends try to cheer Mrs. Pellegrino, but her sadness seems connected to a mysterious word: pizza. Library research helps May and her friends discover the ingredients Mrs. Pellegrino needs to bring delicious smells and wonderful tastes to their neighborhood.

May's final appearance comes in *Cowboy Dreams,* published posthumously. Using first-person narration, the book describes a girl's longing for a horse. She enters a raffle and plans to convert the garage to a stable but has to settle for movie Westerns and a blanket saddle on the basement banister. As usual, her imagination proves a great resource, and the final pages depict May in vast Western landscapes. The accompanying text comes from cowboy songs, including ballads of farewell whose poignancy deepens with the realization that Khalsa faced imminent death from cancer while she completed her work. May's first appearance in *Tales of a Gambling Grandma* includes her wearing Western garb, which she sports in later books as well. Kaur amplifies this recurring motif in her final rendition of May.

Two other books feature different protagonists. *Julian* is told by a woman with two cats who needs a barking dog to chase groundhogs from her garden. Julian, a large yellow dog, proves to be a "real good chaser," whose enthusiasm sometimes gets him into predicaments. The story is based on Khalsa's adulthood. *The Snow Cat,* published several years after Khalsa's death, uses painting rediscovered by artist Brian Grison. The illustrations are more stylized and less detailed that in her other long picture books. Young Elsie, who lives alone in a cottage the edge of the wood, prays for a cat for companionship during the long winter. God sends a huge snow cat, and all is well until Elsie ignores God's command to leave the cat outdoors. The melted cat does not disappear entirely, instead forming a cat-shaped lake that provides Elsie with year-round enjoyment.

Reviewers and critics have noted the details in Khalsa's books that reward careful and repeated readings. She places famous paintings on walls of her interiors or subtly alters them for her own illustrations, such as her transformation of Georges Seurat's "Sunday Afternoon on the Island of La Grande Jatte" into a crowd of dog walkers. She incorporates humorous touches such as placing titles of her own books, some yet unpublished, on library shelves. Even the title page illustrations can extend the story as in *Tales of a Gambling Grandma,* which depicts the hay cart crossing the Atlantic. The endpapers of later books incorporate related motifs, such as wheels and slices of pizza floating through the sky. These techniques help establish the predominant sense of joy and wonder in life that infuses Khalsa's work, giving stories set in a particular time and place an emotional richness that will keep the titles fresh for new generations.

—Kathy Piehl

KIMENYE, Barbara

Nationality: Ugandan. **Born:** East Africa. **Career:** Private secretary to the government of the Kabaka of Buganda; staff member, *Uganda Nation,* Kampala. Since 1974 social worker in London. **Address:** c/o Nelson, Nelson House, Mayfield Road, Walton-on-Thames, Surrey KT12 5PL, England.

Publications for Children

Fiction

The Smugglers, illustrated by Roger Payne. London, Nelson, 1966.

Moses, illustrated by Rena Fennessy. Nairobi, Oxford University Press, 1967.

Moses and Mildred, illustrated by Rena Fennessy. Nairobi, Oxford University Press, 1967.

Moses and the Kidnappers, illustrated by Rena Fennessy. Nairobi, Oxford University Press, 1968.

Moses in Trouble, illustrated by Rena Fennessy. Nairobi, Oxford University Press, 1968.

The Winged Adventure, illustrated by Terry Hirst. Nairobi, Oxford University Press, 1969.

Moses in a Muddle, illustrated by Rena Fennessy. Nairobi, Oxford University Press, 1970.

Moses and the Ghost, illustrated by Rena Fennessy. Nairobi, Oxford University Press, 1971.
Paulo's Strange Adventure, illustrated by Olga J. Heuser. Nairobi, Oxford University Press, 1971.
Moses on the Move, illustrated by Mara Onditi. Nairobi, Oxford University Press, 1972.
Sarah and the Boy. Nairobi, Oxford University Press, 1973.
Martha the Millipede, illustrated by Mara Onditi. Nairobi, Oxford University Press, 1973.
Moses and the Penpal, illustrated by Mara Onditi. Nairobi, Oxford University Press, 1973.
Moses the Camper, illustrated by Mara Onditi. Nairobi, Oxford University Press, 1973.
The Runaways, illustrated by Mara Onditi. Nairobi, Oxford University Press, 1973.
Moses in a Mess, illustrated by George Mogaka. Nairobi, Heinemann Kenya, 1991.
The Mating Game. London, Macmillan, 1992.
The Money Game. Oxford, Heinemann, 1992
Kayo's House. London, Macmillan, 1995.
Moses and the Movie. London, Macmillan, 1996.

Publications for Adults

Novels

The Gemstone Affair. London, Nelson, 1978.
The Scoop. London, Nelson, 1978.

Short Stories

Kalasanda. Nairobi and London, Oxford University Press, 1965.
Kalasanda Revisited. Nairobi and London, Oxford University Press, 1966.

* * *

Barbara Kimenye has written a fantasy *Martha the Millipede* in which a discontented millipede learns the hard way that millipedes do not wear shoes. However, most of her books are boys' and girls' adventure books, the most successful being the delightful Moses series in which she has done for African children what Richmal Crompton did for English children through her famous William books. Like William, Moses is an engaging schoolboy whose well-intentioned actions regularly land him and his gang in trouble with the authorities. But, unlike William, Moses's activities are confined to his boarding school, which bears the pretentious name Mukibi's Educational Institute for the Sons of African Gentlemen, but which is really a shabby, money-making institution for throw-outs from reputable schools.

Kimenye makes a distinction between high-spirited boys like Moses and bad boys such as the bully Magara, and Wakweya, the crook masquerading as a schoolboy. In between is "Itchy Fingers" who "when approached nicely" would always return an article to the owner although he might "absent-mindedly pick it up later in the day." With her humorous style Kimenye manages to keep everything in proportion. The boys' escapades are narrated with indulgent amusement, most of them being simply unfortunate, not wicked. One such escapade is the collapse of the dormitory thatched roof over the heads of the Headmaster and his deputy while Moses is trying to retrieve his pet snake from the roof. On another occasion, the cooks go on strike and stingy Mukibi puts the boys on kitchen duty. Their efforts to provide the school with decent meals in spite of the almost empty store lands Moses in a prickly pineapple patch, and he also gets tossed by a cow during an illegal milking session at night. For his pains he is punished by the authorities.

The adventures of Moses and his friends are most exciting and sound so probable that the reader is drawn into the stories. This is why the books have been so successful. Kimenye's other adventure books are not as successful, especially those about girls, such as *Sarah and the Boy* and *The Winged Adventure. Paulo's Strange Adventure* is full of improbable action while *The Runaways* makes copious use of slang. *The Smugglers* reads like the script of a stereotypical Western film or television thriller. Kimenye is at her best when she writes stories with an authentic African background about real people whose trials and tribulations she portrays with human understanding.

—Mabel D. Segun

KINGMAN, (Mary) Lee

Nationality: American. **Born:** Reading, Massachusetts, 6 October 1919. **Education:** Colby-Sawyer College, New London, New Hampshire, A.A. 1938; Smith College, Northampton, Massachusetts, B.A. 1940. **Family:** Married Robert H. Natti in 1945; one daughter and one son. **Career:** Worked for Boston Manufacturers Mutual Fire Insurance Company, 1940-42; assistant, 1943-44, and juvenile editor, 1944-46, Houghton Mifflin, publishers, Boston; member, Folly Cove Designers, Gloucester, Massachusetts, 1946-71. Book editor, poster and calendar designer, council member, 1964-70, and 1970-90, director, *Horn Book,* Boston. **Address:** 105 High Street, Gloucester, Massachusetts 01930-1165, U.S.A.

Publications for Children

Fiction

Pierre Pidgeon, illustrated by Arnold E. Bare. Boston, Houghton Mifflin, 1943.
Ilenka, illustrated by Arnold E. Bare. Boston, Houghton Mifflin, 1945.
The Rocky Summer, illustrated by Barbara Cooney. Boston, Houghton Mifflin, 1948.
The Best Christmas, illustrated by Barbara Cooney. New York, Doubleday, 1949; London, Constable, 1958.
Philippe's Hill, illustrated by Hildegard Woodward. New York, Doubleday, 1950.
The Quarry Adventure, illustrated by Barbara Cooney. New York, Doubleday, 1951; as *Lauri's Surprising Summer,* London, Constable, 1957.
Kathy and the Mysterious Statue, illustrated by Jean MacDonald Porter. New York, Doubleday, 1953.
Peter's Long Walk, illustrated by Barbara Cooney. New York, Doubleday, 1953.

Mikko's Fortune, illustrated by Arnold E. Bare. New York, Farrar Straus, 1955.
The Magic Christmas Tree, illustrated by Bettina. New York, Farrar Straus, 1956; London, Oxford University Press, 1957.
The Village Band Mystery, illustrated by Erik Blegvad. New York, Doubleday, 1956.
Flivver, The Heroic Horse, illustrated by Erik Blegvad. New York, Doubleday, 1958.
Ginny's First Secret, illustrated by Hazel Hoecker. Newton, Massachusetts, Phillips, 1958.
House of the Blue Horse. New York, Doubleday, 1960.
The Saturday Gang, illustrated by Burt Silverman. New York, Doubleday, 1961.
Peter's Pony, illustrated by Fen Lasell. New York, Doubleday, 1963.
Sheep Ahoy!, illustrated by Lisl Weil. Boston, Houghton Mifflin, 1963.
Private Eyes: Adventures with the Saturday Gang, illustrated by Burt Silverman. New York, Doubleday, 1964.
The Year of the Raccoon. Boston, Houghton Mifflin, 1966.
The Secret Journey of the Silver Reindeer, illustrated by Lynd Ward. New York, Doubleday, 1968; Kingswood, Surrey, World's Work, 1970.
The Peter Pan Bag. Boston, Houghton Mifflin, 1970.
Georgina and the Dragon, illustrated by Leonard Shortall. Boston, Houghton Mifflin, 1972.
The Meeting Post: A Story of Lapland, illustrated by Des Asmussen. New York, Crowell, 1972; London, MacRae, 1985.
Escape from the Evil Prophecy, illustrated by Richard Cuffari. Boston, Houghton Mifflin, 1973.
Break a Leg, Betsy Maybe! Boston, Houghton Mifflin, 1976.
Head over Wheels. Boston, Houghton Mifflin, 1978; London, Hamish Hamilton, 1979.
The Refiner's Fire. Boston, Houghton Mifflin, 1981.
The Luck of the "Miss L." Boston, Houghton Mifflin, 1986.
Catch the Baby!, illustrated by Susanna Natti. New York, Viking, 1990.

Publications for Adults

Other

Editor, *Newbery and Caldecott Medal Books 1956-1965.* Boston, Horn Book, 1965.
Editor, *Newbery and Caldecott Medal Award Winners and Honor Books 1922-1968.* Boston, Horn Book, 1968.
Editor, with Joanna Foster and Ruth Giles Lontoft, *Illustrators of Children's Books 1957-1966.* Boston, Horn Book, 1968.
Editor, *Newbery and Caldecott Medal Books 1966-1975.* Boston, Horn Book, 1975.
Editor, *The Illustrator's Notebook.* Boston, Horn Book, 1978.
Editor, with Grace Hogarth and Harriet Quimby, *Illustrators of Children's Books 1967-1976* Boston, Horn Book, 1978.
Editor, *Newbery and Caldecott Medal Books 1976-1985.* Boston, Horn Book, 1986.

*

Manuscript Collections: Kerlan Collection, University of Minnesota, Minneapolis; de Grummond Collection, University of Southern Mississippi, Hattiesburg.

Lee Kingman comments:

In looking back over 43 years of writing for children and young adults, and over 28 published books, I find them for the most part to have been inspired by the ages and interests of my two children and their friends as they grew up. The subjects range from kindergarten concerns (*Peter's Long Walk*) to young adult relationships (*The Peter Pan Bag*) and family relationships (*The Refiner's Fire*); the styles range from legend-like (*The Secret Journey of the Silver Reindeer*) through humorous (*Georgina and the Dragon*) to realistic (*The Year of the Raccoon* and, more recently, *Head over Wheels,* which I wrote after my son became a quadriplegic in a car accident and I found there was a dearth of fiction dealing with how traumas affect not only the victim but family and friends). Some are mysteries; some have Icelandic, Lapp, and Finnish-American backgrounds, inspired by my husband's Finnish heritage. I have always wanted to explore new subjects, learn new things, and have tried, in writing about them, to be sensitive to the style best suited to the kind and length of the material, the potential age ranges of readers, and the subjects themselves.

My daughter, Susanna Natti, has become a recognized illustrator of children's books and Viking Penguin published our first collaboration of story and pictures, *Catch the Baby!,* in 1990. Also, I am particulary pleased that quite a few of my books have been published in other languages, including Finnish, Swedish, Polish, German, French, and Japanese.

* * *

Lee Kingman has claimed an uncharted territory, Lapland, for her own in children's literature. *The Meeting Post* replaces the northern aura of mystery with an informed and friendly familiarity. Readers of *The Secret Journey of the Silver Reindeer* may well be intrigued to further study of this distant land, traditional home of nomads now imprisoned by the arbitrary boundaries of a nationalism foreign to them. Distant in time as well as in locale, *Escape from the Evil Prophecy* is an adventure of the 11th century, an era of unrest in Iceland. Christianity struggles with paganism, and democratic ideals with anarchy and blood-feud. Her hero and heroine personify the generosity of youth, and the difficulties of commitment to social change in the face of established custom.

Closer to home, *The Peter Pan Bag* owes its success with adolescents to Kingman's empathy with their painful *rites de passage* in a culture that makes a difficult time still more difficult by leaving its boundaries undefined. Runaway Wendy, 17 years old, longs for freedom. A Boston hippie-haven proves intoxicatingly attractive, but offers no solution to her identity problem. Though some of the actualities of life in a hippie pad have been glossed over, Kingman understands youngsters insistent upon recognition of their status as adults while they live, like Peter Pan, in Never-Never Land. *Georgina and the Dragon* stars 10-year-old Georgie, whose name evidences disappointment at the birth of a fifth daughter to a sonless father. In this slight, cheerful, mildly feminist story, dauntless Georgie demonstrates just what girls can do. In the critically acclaimed *The Year of the Raccoon* Joey, an ordinary, normal 15-year-old, is sandwiched between two brilliant brothers, under the shadow of a successful, unconsciously domineering father, who expects great things of all his family. Joey's love for Bertie, his only-partly-tame raccoon, precipitates crisis in a family that has maintained a precarious balance on the edge of catastrophe. *Head over Wheels* might have been a tragedy in other hands. Terry and Kerry are identical twins. No one can tell them apart—until Terry is crippled in a car accident. Now a quadriplegic, he must chart a new course for a life to be spent in a wheelchair, with the support of his family and especially of his twin. This is a most perceptive, often painfully moving story. Sara hardly knows her father, but suddenly must go to live with him—in a barn, no less! Understanding grows between them, as she learns to appreciate his talent and warmth, while discounting his excesses of temperament, in *The Refiner's Fire.*

Alec wins a loathed Cabbage Patch doll in a raffle, instead of the rowboat he longs for, and he feels that his luck is all of one kind: BAD. Then fate takes a hand, when an elderly neighbour who has rescued the prize rowboat from an ignominious fate as a petunia planter decides to let Alec do her rowing for her, and even to enter the coveted craft in the year-end races, in *The Luck of the "Miss L,"* a slight but pleasant summer entertainment.

Though Kingman's picture books and plays for juniors do not rank with her work for more mature readers, and her writings are sometimes slight and uneven, her peaks are very, very high.

—Joan McGrath

KING-SMITH, Dick

Nationality: British. **Born:** Bitton, Gloucestershire, 27 March 1922. **Education:** Marlborough College, Wiltshire, 1936-40; University of Bristol, B.Ed. 1975. **Military Service:** Grenadier Guards, 1941-46: lieutenant; mentioned in despatches. **Family:** Married Myrle England in 1943; two daughters and one son. **Career:** Farmer in Gloucestershire, 1947-67; teacher, Farmborough Primary School, Bath, 1975-82; since 1982 freelance writer. **Awards:** *Guardian* award, 1984. **Agent:** A.P. Watt Ltd., 20 John Street, London WC1N 2DR. **Address:** Diamond's Cottage, Queen Charlton, near Keynsham, Avon BS18 2SJ, England.

PUBLICATIONS FOR CHILDREN

Fiction

The Fox Busters, illustrated by Jon Miller. London, Gollancz, 1978; New York, Delacorte Press, 1988.
Daggie Dogfoot, illustrated by Mary Rayner. London, Gollancz, 1980; as *Pigs Might Fly,* New York, Viking Press, 1982.
The Mouse Butcher, illustrated by Wendy Smith. London, Gollancz, 1981; New York, Viking Press, 1982.
Magnus Powermouse, illustrated by Mary Rayner. London, Gollancz, 1982; New York, Harper, 1984.
The Queen's Nose, illustrated by Jill Bennett. London, Gollancz, 1983; New York, Harper, 1985.
The Sheep-Pig, illustrated by Mary Rayner. London, Gollancz, 1983; as *Babe, The Gallant Pig,* New York, Crown, 1985.
Harry's Mad, illustrated by Jill Bennett. London, Gollancz, 1984; New York, Crown, 1987.
Lightning Fred, illustrated by Michael Bragg. London, Heinemann, 1985.
Saddlebottom, illustrated by Alice Englander. London, Gollancz, 1985.
H. Prince, illustrated by Martin Honeysett. London, Walker, 1986.
E.S.P., illustrated by Peter Wingham. London, Deutsch, 1986.
Farmer Bungle Forgets, illustrated by Martin Honeysett. London, Walker, 1986; New York, Atheneum, 1987.
Noah's Brother, illustrated by Ian Newsham. London, Gollancz, 1986.
Dumpling, illustrated by Jo Davies. London, Hamish Hamilton, 1986.
Yob, illustrated by Abigail Pizer. London, Heinemann, 1986.
Tumbleweed, illustrated by Ian Newsham. London, Gollancz, 1987.
The Hodgeheg, illustrated by Linda Birch. London, Hamish Hamilton, 1987.
Cuckoobush Farm, illustrated by Kazuko. London, Orchard, 1987; New York, Greenwillow, 1988.
Friends and Brothers, illustrated by Susan Hellard. London, Heinemann, 1987.
Martin's Mice, illustrated by Jez Alborough. London, Gollancz, 1988; New York, Crown, 1989.
George Speaks, illustrated by Judy Brown. London, Viking Kestrel, 1988.
The Greatest! London, Heinemann, 1988.
The Jenius, illustrated by Peter Firmin. London, Gollancz, 1988.
Emily's Legs, illustrated by Katinka Kew. London, Macdonald, 1988.
Dodo Comes to Tumbledown Farm, illustrated by John Sharp. London, Heinemann, 1988.
The Toby Man, illustrated by Ian Newsham. London, Gollancz, 1989.
Alice and Flower and Foxianna. London, Heinemann, 1989.
Beware of the Bull! London, Heinemann, 1989.
Henry Pond the Poet, illustrated by Larry Wilkes. London, Hodder and Stoughton, 1989.
Dodos Are Forever, illustrated by David Parkins. London, Viking Kestrel, 1989.
Sophie's Snail. New York, Delacorte, 1989.
The Trouble with Edward. London, Hodder & Stoughton, 1989.
Ace: The Very Important Pig. New York, Crown, 1990.
Alphabeasts, illustrated by Quentin Blake. New York, Macmillan, 1990.
The Jolly Witch. London, Simon & Schuster, 1990.
Paddy's Pot of Gold. London, Viking Kestrel, 1990.
The Water Horse. London, Viking Kestrel, 1990.
The Whistling Piglet. London, Walker, 1990.
Caruso's Cool Cats. London, BBC/Longman, 1991.
The Cuckoo Child, illustrated by Leslie Bowman. New York, Hyperion, 1991.
Find the White Horse. London, Viking, 1991.
Horace and Maurice. London, Doubleday, 1991.
Lightning Strikes Twice. London, Mammoth, 1991.
Sophie's Tom. London, Walker, 1991.
The Animal Parade: A Collection of Stories and Poems, illustrated by Jocelyn Wild. New York, Tambourine Books, 1992.
Blessu and Dumpling. London, Puffin, 1992.
Farm Tales. London, Little Mammoth, 1992.
The Finger Eater. London, Walker, 1992.
The Ghost at Codlin Castle. London, Viking, 1992.
The Guard Dog. Young Corgi, 1992.
Jungle Jingles. London, Picture Corgi, 1992.
Pretty Polly, illustrated by Marshall Peck. New York, Crown, 1992.
The Topsy-turvy Storybook, illustrated by John Eastwood. London, Victor Gollancz, 1992.
Triffic Pig Book. London, Gollancz, 1992.

All Pigs Are Beautiful, illustrated by Anita Jeram. Cambridge, Massachusetts, Candlewick Press, 1993.
The Clockwork Mouse, London, Penguin, 1993.
Dragon Boy, illustrated by J. Wild. London, Viking, 1993.
Horse Pie. London, Doubleday, 1993.
The Merrythought, illustrated by Mike Reid. London, Puffin, 1993.
The Invisible Dog, illustrated by Roger Roth. New York, Crown, 1993.
Lady Daisy, illustrated by Jan Naimo Jones. New York, Delacorte, 1993.
A Narrow Squeak and Other Animal Stories, illustrated by A. Harvey. London, Viking, 1993.
Sophie Hits Six, illustrated by David Parkins. Cambridge, Massachusetts, Candlewick Press, 1993.
Uncle Bumpo. London, AndrÈ Deutsch Children's, 1993.
Bobby the Bad, illustrated by Julie Anderson. London, AndrÈ Deutsch Children's, 1994.
Connie and Rollo, illustrated by Judy Brown. London, Doubleday, 1994.
The Excitement of Being Ernest, illustrated by Nigel McMullen. London, Simon and Schuster, 1994.
Happy Mouseday. London, Doubleday, 1994.
Harriet's Hare, illustrated by Valerie Littlewood. London, Doubleday, 1994.
I Love Guinea-pigs. London, Walker, 1994.
Mr. Potter's Pet, illustrated by Hilda Offen, London, Viking, 1994.
The Schoolmouse, illustrated by Phil Garner. London, Viking, 1994.
Sophie in the Saddle, illustrated by David Parkins. Cambridge, Massachusetts, Candlewick Press, 1994.
Sophie Is Seven. London, Walker, 1994.
The Swoose, illustrated by Marie Corner. New York, Hyperion, 1994.
King Max the Last: A Second Hodgeheg Story, illustrated by Linda Birch. London, Hamish Hamilton, 1995.
All Because of Jackson, illustrated by John Eastwood. London, Doubleday, 1995.
Sophie's Adventures, illustrated by David Parkins. London, Walker, 1995.
Sophie's Lucky, illustrated by David Parkins. London, Walker, 1995.
The Terrible Trins, illustrated by Diz Wallis. London, Viking, 1995.
Warlock Watson, London, Hippo, 1995.
Clever Duck, illustrated by Mike Terry. London, Viking, 1996.
Godhanger, illustrated by Andrew Davidson. London, Doubleday, 1996.
Hogsel and Gruntel, illustrated by Liz Graham-Yooll. London, Gollancz, 1996.
Mrs. Jollipop, illustrated by Frank Rodgers. Hemel Hempstead, Macdonald Young, 1996.
Smasher, illustrated by Michael Terry. London, Viking, 1996.
Treasure Trove, illustrated by Paul Howard. London, Viking, 1996.
Omnibombulator, illustrated by Jim and Peter Kavanagh. London, Young Corgi, 1996.
Animal Stories, illustrated by Mike Terry. London, Puffin, 1997.
Puppy Love, illustrated by Anita Jeram. London, Walker, 1997.
The Spotty Pig, illustrated by Mary Wormell. London, Gollancz, 1997.
The Stray, illustrated by Frank Rodgers. London, Viking, 1997.
What Sadie Saw, illustrated by Julie Anderson. London, Scholastic, 1997.
How Green Was My Mouse, illustrated by Robert Bartelt. London, Viking, 1998.

Other

Pets for Keeps, illustrated by Alan Saunders. London, Penguin, 1986.
Town Watch, illustrated by Catherine Bradbury. London, Penguin, 1987.
Country Watch: Animals to Look Out for in the Countryside, illustrated by Catherine Bradbury. London, Penguin, 1987.
Water Watch, illustrated by Catherine Bradbury. London, Penguin, 1988.
Dick King-Smith's Animal Friends: Thirty-one True Life Stories, illustrated by Anita Jeram. London, Walker, 1996.
Dirty Gertie Macintosh (poetry), illustrated by Ros Asquith. London, Doubleday, 1996.

*

Media Adaptation: *Babe* (the film storybook, adapted by Ron Fontes and Justine Korman, from a screenplay by George Miller and Chris Noonan), based on the novel *The Sheep-Pig* by Dick King-Smith. London, Puffin, 1995.

Dick King-Smith comments:

I came late to writing, after a good long time farming. Later I taught young children (and have 10 grandchildren of my own), and it is their potential enjoyment of a story that makes writing one, for me, so enjoyable.

* * *

Some adults may still dislike Dick King-Smith's jovial anthropomorphism, but most—and all children—were beguiled from the start by his engagingly stylish view of animal family life. His main quality, however, is an ability to tell a jolly good adventure story and to stack danger and adversity and terrible odds against an unlikely hero. Add humour and affection and the result has been a stream of skilful and deserved bestsellers.

Such a combination demands a tricky balance that he had not yet perfected in his first novel, *The Fox Busters.* The joke, not the plot or the characters, dominates the book, and the humour borders on the facetious, over-allusive for readers too young to catch all the underlying references and verbal high jinks. But *Daggie Dogfoot* and *The Mouse Butcher* are both very satisfying: a single hero, whom we grow to love, fights desperately against a terrifying enemy, while the style, dialogue, and characterisation remain light and playful. Daggie is a piglet whose deformed feet, instead of leading him to the slaughterhouse, enable him to become a mighty swimmer and saviour of the farm; the rough-and-ready tomcat Butcher wins the heart of the lovely Persian in the manor and defeats the outcast villain. *The Mouse Butcher,* however, is more self-consciously humanised—the community of cats mirrors the snobberies and prejudices of human society a little laboriously.

With *The Sheep-Pig* he succeeds in balancing in one story the strongest qualities of all the others, and it is clearly right to award it that often overworked encomium, "a modern classic." A piglet, won at a local fair by a sheep farmer, realises that the only sensible way to handle sheep is to speak politely to them, and not only saves the farmer's flock (and his own bacon) from rustlers but goes on to astound the whole world by winning the Sheep-

Dog Trials on television. It is deftly constructed, the animal and human characters are marvelously defined in dialogue, the suspense remains strong and quite unbullied by the joke, and the style is so clean and economic that our hero wins through to a frenzy of cheers without a hint of soppiness. King-Smith's affection for the animal qualities of his characters, springing from the genuine knowledge of an ex-farmer, brings a needed warmth to the jokes and excitement—a warmth typified in the mother-baby relationship (or its equivalent) that recurs throughout his work.

A late starter but prodigiously productive, he has proved remarkably consistent, though his plots are now sometimes thinner. To his regular animal novels he added a range of stories for beginner readers (*The Hodgeheg* is particularly charming, with a nicely judged black edge to its humour), picture-book texts (such as *Farmer Bungle Forgets*), collections of short stories like *The Ghost at Codlin Castle*—some, while invariably entertaining, allow his whimsical, almost fey, aspects too free a rein—and natural history information books, and branched out into novels with human protagonists. But even these predominantly remain fantasies, from the early *The Queen's Nose,* where Harmony learns the best way to handle the wishes bestowed on her by a magic 50p piece, or the slapstick thriller starring a superintelligent parrot, *Harry's Mad,* to *Lady Daisy,* in which King-Smith attacks macho taboos by allowing a nine-year-old boy to love, and talk to, a Victorian doll. *The Merrythought* (a chicken wishbone) actually grants wishes, that familiar King-Smith dream theme, and was conceived as a gentle offering for the family of his own son whose young wife died leaving five children—their fictional counterparts have the initials of their real names.

Other fantasies straddle these two worlds of humans and animals: *Dragon Boy* invents a stirringly adventurous childhood for the Little John of legend, with humour, tenderness, and a typical acceptance of the life-and-death quality of animal life, while *Harriet's Hare* takes the talking animal idea to the verge of science fantasy. (It also has a bright and competent little farm-bred heroine—a specialty of King-Smith's.) He is more tentative about tackling stories of human character, and it is interesting to see how this very moral writer accepts the challenge of an outright liar and cheat in *Uncle Bumpo.*

But splendid though all these are, they miss something of that special élan of his animal stories, which must come from deep within King-Smith's own feelings. It cannot be coincidence that of his more recent work it was *Find the White Horse,* a suspenseful and touching variation on the "Incredible Journey" notion, that won him an award chosen by young readers themselves. It is with such tales as these that his reputation remains, carving a benchmark against which animal novels will now always be judged.

—Stephanie Nettell

KINSEY, Elizabeth. See **CLYMER, Eleanor.**

KIPLING, (Joseph) Rudyard

Nationality: British (of English parents; moved to England, 1872). **Born:** Bombay, India, 30 December 1865. **Education:** United Services College, Devon, 1878-82. **Family:** Married Caroline Starr Balestier in 1892; two daughters and one son. **Career:** Assistant editor, *Civil and Military Gazette,* Lahore, 1882-87; assistant editor and overseas correspondent, *Pioneer,* Allahabad, 1887-89; full-time writer from 1889; lived in London, 1889-92, and Brattleboro, Vermont, 1892-96, then returned to England; settled in Burwash, Sussex, 1902. Rector, University of St. Andrews, 1922-25. **Awards:** Nobel Prize for Literature, 1907; Royal Society of Literature Gold medal, 1926. LL.D.: McGill University, Montreal, 1907; D. Litt.: University of Durham, 1907; Oxford University, 1907; Cambridge University, 1907; University of Edinburgh, 1920; the Sorbonne, Paris, 1921; University of Strasbourg, 1921; D. Phil.: University of Athens, 1924. Honorary Fellow, Magdalene College, Cambridge, 1932. Associate member, Académie des Sciences Morales et Politiques, 1933. Refused the Poet Laureateship, 1895, and the Order of Merit. **Died:** 18 January 1936.

Publications for Children

Fiction

The Jungle Book, illustrated by J. Lockwood Kipling and others. London, Macmillan, and New York, Century, 1894.

The Second Jungle Book, illustrated by J. Lockwood Kipling. London, Macmillan, and New York, Century, 1895; revised edition, Macmillan, 1895.

"Captains Courageous": A Story of the Grand Banks, illustrated by I.W. Taber. London, Macmillan, and New York, Century, 1897.

Stalky & Co. London, Macmillan, and New York, Doubleday, 1899; revised edition, as *The Complete Stalky & Co.,* Macmillan, 1929, Doubleday, 1930.

Kim, illustrated by J. Lockwood Kipling. New York, Doubleday, and London, Macmillan, 1901.

Just So Stories for Little Children, illustrated by the author. London, Macmillan, and New York, Doubleday, 1902.

Puck of Pook's Hill, illustrated by H.R. Millar. London, Macmillan, and New York, Doubleday, 1906.

Kipling Stories and Poems Every Child Should Know, edited by Mary E. Burt and W.T. Chapin, illustrated by Charles Livingston Bull and others. New York, Doubleday, 1909.

Rewards and Fairies, illustrated by Frank Craig. London, Macmillan, and New York, Doubleday, 1910.

Land and Sea Tales for Scouts and Guides. London, Macmillan, and New York, Doubleday, 1923.

Ham and the Porcupine. New York, Doubleday, 1935.

Publications for Adults

Novel

The Light That Failed. New York, United States Book Company, 1890; London, Macmillan, 1891.

Short Stories

Plain Tales from the Hills. Calcutta, Thacker Spink, 1888; New York, Lovell, and London, Macmillan, 1890.
Soldiers Three: A Collection of Stories. Allahabad, Wheeler, 1888; London, Sampson Low, 1890.
The Story of the Gadsbys: A Tale Without a Plot. Allahabad, Wheeler, 1888; London, Sampson Low, and New York, Lovell, 1890.
In Black and White. Allahabad, Wheeler, 1888; London, Sampson Low, 1890; with *Soldiers Three,* New York, Lovell, 1890.
Under the Deodars. Allahabad, Wheeler, 1888; revised edition, London, Sampson Low, 1890.
The Phantom 'Rickshaw and Other Tales. Allahabad, Wheeler, 1888; revised edition, London, Sampson Low, 1890.
Wee Willie Winkie and Other Child Stories. Allahabad, Wheeler, 1888; revised edition, London, Sampson Low, and Chicago, Rand McNally, 1890.
Soldiers Three, and Under the Deodars. New York, Lovell, 1890.
The Phantom 'Rickshaw, and Wee Willie Winkie. New York, Lovell, 1890.
The Courting of Dinah Shadd and Other Stories. New York, Harper, and London, Macmillan, 1890.
Indian Tales. New York, United States Book Company, 1890.
Mine Own People. New York, United States Book Company, 1891.
Life's Handicap, Being Stories from Mine Own People. New York and London, Macmillan, 1891.
The Naulahka: A Story of West and East, with Wolcott Balestier. London, Heinemann, and New York, Macmillan, 1892.
Many Inventions. London, Macmillan, and New York, Appleton, 1893.
Soldier Tales. London, Macmillan, 1896; as *Soldier Stories,* New York, Macmillan, 1896.
The Day's Work. New York, Doubleday, and London, Macmillan, 1898.
The Kipling Reader. London, Macmillan, 1900; revised edition, 1901; as *Selected Stories,* 1925.
Traffics and Discoveries. London, Macmillan, and New York, Doubleday, 1904.
Abaft the Funnel. New York, Dodge, 1909.
Actions and Reactions. London, Macmillan, and New York, Doubleday, 1909.
A Diversity of Creatures. London, Macmillan, and New York, Doubleday, 1917.
Selected Stories, edited by William Lyon Phelps. New York, Doubleday, 1921.
Land and Sea Tales. London, Macmillan, and New York, Doubleday, 1923.
Debits and Credits. London, Macmillan, and New York, Doubleday, 1926.
Selected Stories. London, Macmillan, 1929.
Thy Servant a Dog, Told by Boots. London, Macmillan, and New York, Doubleday, 1930; revised edition, as *Thy Servant a Dog and Other Dog Stories,* Macmillan, 1938.
Humorous Tales. London, Macmillan, and New York, Doubleday, 1931.
Animal Stories. London, Macmillan, 1932; New York, Doubleday, 1938.
Limits and Renewals. London, Macmillan, and New York, Doubleday, 1932.
All the Mowgli Stories. London, Macmillan, 1933; New York, Doubleday, 1936.
Collected Dog Stories. London, Macmillan, and New York, Doubleday, 1934.
More Selected Stories. London, Macmillan, 1940.
Twenty-One Tales. London, Reprint Society, 1946.
Ten Stories. London, Pan, 1947.
A Choice of Kipling's Prose, edited by W. Somerset Maugham. London, Macmillan, 1952; as *Maugham's Choice of Kipling's Best: Sixteen Stories,* New York, Doubleday, 1953.
A Treasury of Short Stories. New York, Bantam, 1957.
(*Short Stories*), edited by Edward Parone. New York, Dell, 1960.
Kipling Stories: Twenty-Eight Exciting Tales. New York, Platt and Munk, 1960.
The Best Short Stories, edited by Randall Jarrell. New York, Hanover House, 1961; as *In the Vernacular: The English in India* and *The English in England,* New York, Doubleday, 2 vols., 1963.
Famous Tales of India, edited by B.W. Shir-Cliff. New York, Ballantine, 1962.
Phantoms and Fantasies: 20 Tales. New York, Doubleday, 1965.
Short Stories, edited by Andrew Rutherford. London, Penguin, 1971.
Twenty-One Tales, edited by Tim Wilkinson. London, Folio Society, 1972.
Tales of East and West, edited by Bernard Bergonzi. Avon, Connecticut, Limited Editions Club, 1973.
Kipling's Kingdom: Twenty-Five of Rudyard Kipling's Best Indian Stories, Known and Unknown, edited by Charles Allen. London, Joseph, 1987.

Play

The Harbour Watch (produced London, 1913; revised version, as *Gow's Watch,* produced London, 1924).

Poetry

Schoolboy Lyrics. Privately printed, 1881.
Echoes (published anonymously), with Alice Kipling. Privately printed, 1884.
Departmental Ditties and Other Verses. Lahore, Civil and Military Gazette Press, 1886; revised edition, London, Thacker Spink, 1890.
Departmental Ditties, Barrack-Room Ballads, and Other Verse. New York, United States Book Company, 1890.
Barrack-Room Ballads and Other Verses. London, Methuen, 1892; as *Ballads and Barrack-Room Ballads,* New York, Macmillan, 1892.
The Seven Seas. New York, Appleton, and London, Methuen, 1896.
Recessional. Privately printed, 1897.
An Almanac of Twelve Sports, illustrated by William Nicholson. London Heinemann, and New York, Russell, 1898.
Poems, edited by Wallace Rice. Chicago, Star, 1899.
Recessional and Other Poems. Privately printed, 1899.
The Absent-Minded Beggar. Privately printed, 1899.
With Number Three, Surgical and Medical, and New Poems. Santiago, Chile, Hume, 1900.
Occasional Poems. Boston, Bartlett, 1900.
The Five Nations. London, Methuen, and New York, Doubleday, 1903.
The Muse among the Motors. New York, Doubleday, 1904.

Collected Verse. New York, Doubleday, 1907; London, Hodder and Stoughton, 1912.

A History of England (verse only), with C.R.L. Fletcher. London, Oxford University Press-Hodder and Stoughton, and New York, Doubleday, 1911; revised edition, 1930.

Songs from Books. New York, Doubleday, 1912; London, Macmillan, 1913.

Twenty Poems. London, Methuen, 1918.

The Years Between. London, Methuen, and New York, Doubleday, 1919.

Verse: Inclusive Edition 1885-1918. London, Hodder and Stoughton, 3 vols., and New York, Doubleday, 1 vol., 1919; revised edition, 1921, 1927, 1933.

A Kipling Anthology: Verse. London, Methuen, and New York, Doubleday, 1922.

Songs for Youth, from Collected Verse. London, Hodder and Stoughton, 1924; New York, Doubleday, 1925.

A Choice of Songs. London, Methuen, 1925.

Sea and Sussex. London, Macmillan, and New York, Doubleday, 1926.

St. Andrews, with Walter de la Mare. London, A. and C. Black, 1926.

Songs of the Sea. London, Macmillan, and New York, Doubleday, 1927.

Poems 1886-1929. London, Macmillan, 3 vols., 1929; New York, Doubleday, 3 vols., 1930.

Selected Poems. London, Methuen, 1931.

East of Suez, Being a Selection of Eastern Verses. London, Macmillan, 1931.

Sixty Poems. London, Hodder and Stoughton, 1939.

Verse: Definitive Edition. London, Hodder and Stoughton, and New York, Doubleday, 1940.

So Shall Ye Reap: Poems for These Days. London, Hodder and Stoughton, 1941.

A Choice of Kipling's Verse, edited by T.S. Eliot. London, Faber, 1941; New York, Scribner, 1943.

Sixty Poems. London, Hodder and Stoughton, 1957.

A Kipling Anthology, edited by W.G. Bebbington. London, Methuen, 1964.

The Complete Barrack-Room Ballads, edited by Charles Carrington. London, Methuen, 1973.

Kipling's English History: Poems, edited by Marghanita Laski. London, BBC Publications, 1974.

Kipling: A Selection, edited by James Cochrane. London, Penguin, 1977.

Early Verse by Rudyard Kipling 1879-1889: Unpublished, Uncollected, and Rarely Collected Poems, edited by Andrew Rutherford. Oxford, Clarendon Press, and New York, Oxford University Press, 1986.

Other

Quartette, with others. Lahore, Civil and Military Gazette Press, 1885.

The City of Dreadful Night and Other Sketches. Allahabad, Wheeler, 1890.

The City of Dreadful Night and Other Places. Allahabad, Wheeler, and London, Sampson Low, 1891.

The Smith Administration. Allahabad, Wheeler, 1891.

Letters of Marque. Allahabad, Wheeler, 1891; selections published London, Sampson Low, 1891.

American Notes, with *The Bottle Imp,* by Robert Louis Stevenson. New York, Ivers, 1891.

Out of India: Things I Saw, and Failed to See, in Certain Days and Nights at Jeypore and Elsewhere. New York, Dillingham, 1895.

The Kipling Birthday Book, edited by Joseph Finn. London, Macmillan, 1896; New York, Doubleday, 1899.

A Fleet in Being: Notes of Two Trips with the Channel Squadron. London and New York, Macmillan, 1898.

From to Sea to Sea: Letters of Travel. New York, Doubleday, 2 vols., 1899; as *From Sea to Sea and Other Sketches,* London, Macmillan, 2 vols., 1900.

Works (Swastika Edition). New York, Doubleday, Appleton, and Century, 15 vols., 1899.

Letters to the Family (Notes on a Recent Trip to Canada). Toronto, Macmillan, 1908.

The Kipling Reader (not same as 1900 collection of short stories). New York, Appleton, 1912.

The New Army (6 pamphlets). New York, Doubleday, 1914; as *The New Army in Training,* London, Macmillan, 1 vol., 1915.

France at War. London, Macmillan, and New York, Doubleday, 1915.

The Fringes of the Fleet. London, Macmillan, and New York, Doubleday, 1915.

Tales of "The Trade." Privately printed, 1916.

Sea Warfare. London, Macmillan, and New York, Doubleday, 1916.

The War in the Mountains. New York, Doubleday, 1917.

To Fighting Americans (speeches). Privately printed, 1918.

The Eyes of Asia. New York, Doubleday, 1918.

The Graves of the Fallen. London, Imperial War Graves Commission, 1919.

Letters of Travel (1892-1913). London, Macmillan, and New York, Doubleday, 1920.

A Kipling Anthology: Prose. London, Macmillan, and New York, Doubleday, 1922.

Works (Mandalay Edition). New York, Doubleday, 26 vols., 1925-26.

A Book of Words: Selections from Speeches and Addresses Delivered Between 1906 and 1927. London, Macmillan, and New York, Doubleday, 1928.

The One Vol. Kipling. New York, Doubleday, 1928.

Souvenirs of France. London, Macmillan, 1933.

A Kipling Pageant. New York, Doubleday, 1935.

Something of Myself for My Friends Known and Unknown. London, Macmillan, and New York, Doubleday, 1937.

Complete Works (Sussex Edition). London, Macmillan, 35 vols., 1937-39; as *Collected Works* (Burwash Edition), New York, Doubleday, 28 vols., 1941 (includes revised versions of some previously published works).

A Kipling Treasury: Stories and Poems. London, Macmillan, 1940.

Kipling: A Selection of His Stories and Poems, edited by John Beecroft. New York, Doubleday, 2 vols., 1956.

The Kipling Sampler, edited by Alexander Greendale. New York, Fawcett, 1962.

Letters from Japan, edited by Donald Richie and Yoshimori Harashima. Tokyo, Kenkyusha, 1962.

Pearls from Kipling, edited by C. Donald Plomer. New Britain, Connecticut, Elihu Burritt Library, 1963.

Rudyard Kipling to Rider Haggard: The Record of a Friendship, edited by Morton Cohen. London, Hutchinson, 1965; Rutherford, New Jersey, Fairleigh Dickinson University Press, 1968.

The Best of Kipling. New York, Doubleday, 1968.

Stories and Poems, edited by Roger Lancelyn Green. London, Dent, 1970.

Kipling's Horace, edited by Charles Carrington. London, Methuen, 1978.

American Notes: Rudyard Kipling's West, edited by Arrell M. Gibson. Norman, University of Oklahoma Press, 1981.

The Portable Kipling, edited by Irving Howe. New York, Viking Press, 1982.

O Beloved Kids: Rudyard Kipling's Letters to His Children, edited by Elliot L. Gilbert. London, Weidenfeld and Nicolson, 1983; New York, Harcourt Brace, 1984.

Kipling's India: Uncollected Sketches 1884-1888, edited by Thomas Pinney. London, Macmillan, and New York, Schocken, 1986.

The Illustrated Kipling, edited by Neil Philip. London, Collins, 1987.

A Choice of Kipling's Prose, edited by Craig Raine. London, Faber, 1987.

Kipling's Japan, edited by Hugh Cortazzi and George Webb. London, Athlone Press, 1988.

Editor, *The Irish Guards in the Great War.* London, Macmillan, and New York, Doubleday, 2 vols., 1923.

*

Bibliographies: *Rudyard Kipling: A Bibliographical Catalogue* by James McG. Stewart, edited by A. W. Keats, Toronto, Dalhousie University-University of Toronto Press, 1959, London, Oxford University Press, 1960; "Kipling: An Annotated Bibliography of Writings about Him" by H.E. Gerber and E. Lauterbach, in *English Fiction in Transition 3* (Tempe, Arizona), 1960, and *8,* 1965.

Manuscript Collections: Cornell University Library, Ithaca, New York; Library of Congress, Washington, D.C.; Houghton Library, Harvard University, Cambridge, Massachusetts; Pierpont Morgan Library, New York.

Critical Studies: *Rudyard Kipling: His Life and Work* by Charles Carrington, London, Macmillan, 1955, revised edition, 1978, as *The Life of Rudyard Kipling,* New York, Doubleday, 1955; *Rudyard Kipling* by Rosemary Sutcliff, London, Bodley Head, 1960, New York, Walck, 1961; *The Readers' Guide to Rudyard Kipling's Work,* Canterbury, Gibbs, 1961, and *Kipling The Critical Heritage,* London, Routledge, and New York, Barnes and Noble, 1971, both edited by Roger Lancelyn Green, and *Kipling and the Children* by Green, London, Elek, 1965; *Kipling's Mind and Art* edited by Andrew Rutherford, Edinburgh, Oliver and Boyd, and Stanford, California, Stanford University Press, 1964; *Rudyard Kipling* by J.I.M. Stewart, London, Gollancz, and New York, Dodd Mead, 1966; *Rudyard Kipling: Realist and Fabulist* by Bonamy Dobrée, London and New York, Oxford University Press, 1967; *Kipling and His World* by Kingsley Amis, London, Thames and Hudson, 1975, New York, Scribner, 1976; *The Strange Ride of Rudyard Kipling: His Life and Works* by Angus Wilson, London, Secker and Warburg, 1977, New York, Viking Press, 1978; *Rudyard Kipling* by Lord Birkenhead, London, Weidenfeld and Nicolson, 1978; *Rudyard Kipling* by James Harrison, Boston, Twayne, 1982; *Rudyard Kipling and the Fiction of Adolescence* by Robert F. Moss, New York, St. Martin's Press, and London, Macmillan, 1982; *Kipling: Interviews and Recollections* edited by Harold Orel, London, Macmillan, 2 vols., 1983, New York, Barnes and Noble, 2 vols., 1984; *A Kipling Companion* by Norman Page, London, Macmillan, 1984; *Kipling and Orientalism* by B.J. Moore-Gilbert, London, Croom Helm, 1986; *Kipling's Hidden Narratives* by Sandra Kemp, Oxford, Blackwell, 1988; *Rudyard Kipling* by Martin Seymour-Smith, London, Macdonald, 1989.

* * *

Looking back over his work a few months before he died, Rudyard Kipling wrote: "Since the tales had to be read by children, before people realised that they were meant for grown-ups,...I worked the material in three or four overlaid tints and textures, which might or might not reveal themselves according to the shifting light of sex, youth, and experience." He wrote this specifically of his last children's book, *Rewards and Fairies,* but it applies to some extent to all his children's books—and this makes it particularly difficult to write of him as a "children's author."

Kipling's approach to the writing of fiction was by way of meticulous fact, originally that of the first-class journalistic reporter (a position which he held for seven years in India—before returning to London at the age of 23, to find himself famous within a few months). In the experimental stage towards the end of his time in India, when his first and some of his most famous stories were written, he was learning to put himself in the place of the various types about whom he was writing, to think their thoughts and to speak their language. It was a period in literary history when writing in dialect was a growing fashion, particularly prevalent in America, and Kipling with his amazingly retentive memory was able to become an expert in many dialects—Cockney, Yorkshire, and Irish for his *Soldiers Three,* native Indians for *In Black and White,* the general conversation of higher-class "Anglo-Indians" at Simla in many of the *Plain Tales*—and it was inevitable for one who loved children as he did from an early age, that he should attempt their forms of speech and thought in the four stories of the original *Wee Willie Winkie* volume at the end of 1888, before he left India.

The next stories which Kipling wrote with children as their intended first readers became *The Jungle Book* and *The Second Jungle Book*—several of which made their first appearance in the American children's magazine *St. Nicholas.* Of these stories the eight concerning Mowgli—the Indian boy who was brought up by the wolves and became the Master of the Jungle, until he returned to his own kind in the end—became immediately among the best loved stories with young readers and a children's classic by the end of the century. "His stories are not animal stories in the realistic sense; they are wonderful, beautiful fairy tales," wrote Ernest Thompson Seton, the great Canadian naturalist and writer of the life-stories of real animals. Many games of "make-believe" in fact and fiction took Mowgli for their hero and his jungle for their new Fairyland, and not twenty years after the publication of *The Jungle Books,* Baden-Powell made such make-believe still more real for small boys all over the world by basing his Wolf-cubs—the junior Boy Scouts—on them.

As was natural for a writer of Kipling's vivid imagination, as soon as he had children of his own he began to invent stories to tell to them. Many of these were never written down, but one series became the established favourite, a series of incantatory tales that had to be told again and again, always in the same words always "just-so." The first three appeared in *St. Nicholas* at the end of 1897. There was then a gap until mid-1900. Josephine, "the daughter that was all to him," who appears as Taffimai, died in 1899 at the age of six; but after a break Kipling was able to write down the rest of the tales he had made for her, and probably added a few more—and *Just So Stories* was published in 1902. This, the most unusual of Kipling's books, is probably the most timeless and the most enduring of his tales for children. It should be read aloud to obtain its best effect, but is enjoyed in different ways at almost any age.

Between writing the first and last of the Just So stories, Kipling published three other books which appeal strongly to boy readers as well as, and perhaps in different ways from, the adults for whom they were intended. The least well known, "*Captains Courageous,*" is a full-length sea-story set among the old fishing-fleets on the Grand Banks in the North Atlantic. The theme is one of Kipling's favorites, that of the "young cub" being "licked into shape"—as of Mowgli learning to become Master of the Jungle before returning to put his particular accomplishments at the service of his own kind. In this case Harvey Cheyne, the spoilt son of an American millionaire, falls overboard from a luxury liner and is picked up by a fishing boat and made to "work his keep" for several months before returning to his family, having by then indeed "suffered a sea-change."

The next book aims at the same goal, but in a highly debatable manner: "There came to me the idea of beginning some tracts or parables for the young," wrote Kipling. "These, for reasons honestly beyond my control, turned themselves into a series of tales called *Stalky & Co.*" This book has probably met with more contradictory criticism than any of his other works. To the adult reader it can be enjoyed again and again as one of the greatest works of humour in the language—or it can be detested and condemned as "an unpleasant book about unpleasant boys at an unpleasant school." With boys themselves, however, it has always been a favorite, is not likely to have led them into any new forms of mischief, and is certainly now too much of a "period piece" to seem anything but a hilarious collection of yarns about a type of academy almost as obsolete as a Dame School.

Kipling's other book about a boy hero is *Kim,* which is now being classed among the great British novels—by Indian and Pakistani critics and scholars as well as British and American. It is as much, or no more, a boy's book as *Huckleberry Finn* and is enjoyed or not at various ages as variously as Mark Twain's classic. Once again it follows the development of a small boy with exceptional chances and at first no sense of duty or obligation as he develops mentally and spiritually to fill the place in the world for which he is uniquely fitted. But in the process Kim, the little Irish orphan brought up more or less as a native Indian, passes through a series of absorbing adventures set against the most vivid and authentic literary picture we have of India as Kipling saw and knew it nearly a century ago.

None of these last three books was meant specifically for young readers: but after *Just So Stories,* written for "the vanished Josephine," Kipling realised that he had two other children fast growing up and just as desirous of tales, even if of a different kind. The family had by now settled in an early 17th-century manor house in a secluded corner of Sussex; this, and a performance of scenes from *A Midsummer Night's Dream* which the two put on for their parents, brought forth *Puck of Pook's Hill.* These tales, and those in the sequel, *Rewards and Fairies,* cover English history, largely as it impinged on their own neighbourhood, from the end of the Roman Occupation to the days of the Napoleonic Wars, and many of them have been acclaimed as among the best historical stories ever written. The historian G.M. Trevelyan, for example, wrote in 1953: "As a piece of historical imagination I know nothing in the world better than the story in *Puck* called 'The Joyous Venture'... I can see no fault in it, and many a merit." And next to this he set "Simple Simon" and "The Tree of Justice" in *Rewards and Fairies.*

As the stories were written for Kipling's own children, who appear in them as Dan and Una, it is only right that the second volume is more difficult than the first, to match their advance in age and understanding. And they were the last books that Kipling wrote for children. "Dan" was killed in the First World War, and, though "Una" married, she had no children—so we can but regret that Kipling wrote no "Tales of a Grandfather," while giving thanks for those stories already written: some of the greatest and most enduring of their kind in whatever compartment of literature we choose to set them.

As Patrick Chalmers wrote: he was one of those who "give their heart's best only when they give to a child."

—Roger Lancelyn Green

KITT, Tamara. See **de REGNIERS, Beatrice Schenk.**

KJELGAARD, Jim

Nationality: American. **Born:** James Arthur Kjelgaard, New York City, 6 December 1910. **Education:** Syracuse University, New York, two years. **Family:** Married Edna Dresen in 1939; one daughter. **Awards:** Western Writers of America Spur award, 1958. **Died:** 12 July 1959.

Publications for Children

Fiction

Forest Patrol, illustrated by Tony Palazzo. New York, Holiday House, 1941; London, Sampson Low, 1948.

Rebel Siege, illustrated by Charles Wilson. New York, Holiday House, 1943.

Big Red, illustrated by Bob Kuhn. New York, Holiday House, 1945; London, Carousel, 1980.

Buckskin Brigade, illustrated by Ralph Ray, Jr. New York, Holiday House, 1947.

Snow Dog, illustrated by Jacob Landau. New York, Holiday House, 1948.

Kalak of the Ice, illustrated by Bob Kuhn. New York, Holiday House, 1949.

A Nose for Trouble, illustrated by Collett. New York, Holiday House, 1949.

Wild Trek, illustrated by Faye. New York, Holiday House, 1950; London, Collins, 1964.

Chip, The Dam-Builder, illustrated by Ralph Ray, Jr. New York, Holiday House, 1950.
Irish Red, Son of Big Red, illustrated by Ames. New York, Holiday House, 1951; London, Collins, 1958.
Fire-Hunter, illustrated by Ralph Ray, Jr. New York, Holiday House, 1951.
Trailing Trouble. New York, Holiday House, 1952.
Outlaw Red, Son of Big Red, illustrated by Ames. New York, Holiday House, 1953.
The Spell of White Sturgeon, illustrated by Stephen Voorhies. New York, Dodd Mead, 1953.
Haunt Fox, illustrated by Glen Rounds. New York, Holiday House, 1954.
Cracker Barrel Trouble Shooter, illustrated by Albert Orbaan. New York, Dodd Mead, 1954.
Lion Hound, illustrated by Jacob Landau. New York, Holiday House, 1955; London, Collins, 1957.
The Lost Wagon, illustrated by Albert Orbann. New York, Dodd Mead, 1955.
Desert Dog, illustrated by Sam Savitt. New York, Holiday House, 1956.
Trading Jeff and His Dog. New York, Dodd Mead, 1956.
Wolf Brother, illustrated by Charles Wilson. New York, Holiday House, 1957; London, Collins, 1963.
Wildlife Cameraman, illustrated by Sam Savitt. New York, Holiday House, 1957.
Double Challenge, illustrated by Chris Kenyon. New York, Dodd Mead, 1957.
Swamp Cat, illustrated by Edward Shenton. New York, Dodd Mead, 1957.
We Were There at the Oklahoma Land Run, illustrated by Chris Kenyon. New York, Grosset and Dunlap, 1957.
Rescue Dog of High Pass, illustrated by Edward Shenton. New York, Dodd Mead, 1958.
The Black Fawn, illustrated by Erk. New York, Dodd Mead, 1958.
The Land Is Bright. New York, Dodd Mead, 1958.
Hound Dog and Other Yarns, illustrated by Paul Brown. New York, Dodd Mead, 1958.
Stormy, illustrated by Louis Darling. New York, Holiday House, 1959; London, Collins, 1964.
Hi Jolly, illustrated by Kendall Rossi. New York, Dodd Mead, 1959.
Boomerang Hunter, illustrated by W.T. Mars. New York, Holiday House, 1960.
Ulysses and His Woodland Zoo, illustrated by Kendall Rossi. New York, Dodd Mead, 1960.
The Duck-Footed Hound, illustrated by Marc Simont. New York, Crowell, 1960.
My Father's Collie. New York, Dodd Mead, 1961.
Tigre, illustrated by Everett Raymond Kinstler. New York, Dodd Mead, 1961.
Hidden Trail, illustrated by Louis Darling. New York, Holiday House, 1962.
Fawn in the Forest and Other Wild Animal Stories, illustrated by Sam Savitt. New York, Dodd Mead, 1962.
Two Dogs and a Horse, illustrated by Sam Savitt. New York, Dodd Mead, 1964.
Furious Moose of the Wilderness, illustrated by Mort Künstler. New York, Dodd Mead, 1965.
Dave and His Dog Mulligan, illustrated by Sam Savitt. New York, Dodd Mead, 1966.
Coyote Song, illustrated by Robert MacLean. New York, Dodd Mead, 1969.

Other

The Explorations of Père Marquette, illustrated by Stephen Voorhies. New York, Random House, 1951.
Coming of the Mormons, illustrated by Stephen Voorhies. New York, Random House, 1953.
The Story of Geronimo, illustrated by Charles Wilson. New York, Grosset and Dunlap, 1958.

Editor, *The Wild Horse Roundup: A Collection of Stories by Members of the Western Writers of America,* illustrated by Paul Brown. New York, Dodd Mead, 1957.
Editor, *Hound Dogs and Others: A Collection of Stories by Members of the Western Writers of America,* illustrated by Paul Brown. New York, Dodd Mead, 1958.

*

Manuscript Collections: Kerlan Collection, University of Minnesota, Minneapolis.

* * *

An engaging animal, a colorful person, and a distinctive habitat are the three ingredients Jim Kjelgaard incorporated into most of his many books for young people. Using a writing mode as simple as his own life-style, he based his books on his own experiences, travels, and investigation.

His most notable books are the series about the Irish setter, his favorite dog. Different temperaments are characterized in *Big Red, Irish Red, Son of Big Red,* and *Outlaw Red, Son of Big Red.* He himself hunted with Irish setters, but he had interest in other dogs, too. His impressive list of dog books includes such breeds as the greyhound in *Desert Dog,* the husky in *Snow Dog* and *Wild Trek,* the wildfowl retriever in *Stormy,* and the collie in *Double Challenge.* Intrigued with the St. Bernard, he found it necessary to inform himself using Alfred Richard Sennett's book *Across the Great St. Bernard* to take notes about a place he was unable to visit. He extended his scope to other creatures of the wild such as *Kalak of the Ice, The Black Fawn, Chip,* and *Haunt Fox* about a polar bear, a deer, a beaver, and his own favorite animal respectively. In a letter to Dr. Irvin Kerlan to whom the last book is dedicated, the author wrote, "When I was a youngster, away back in 1929, it was impossible to get any sort of job. I went into the hills with two fox hounds, and before the winter was over I had 13. Naturally I didn't make any money, but I doubt if I've since had half as much fun!...I like red foxes, I think, better than any other animal."

In most of his books there is a human being in addition to an animal. His debut, *Forest Patrol,* describes a boy yearning to become a forest ranger. The main character in *Swamp Cat* and *Stormy* is a boy, in *Snow Dog* it is a trapper. In *The Story of Geronimo* he interpreted both the Apache Indian renegade and his adversaries. *Rebel Siege* portrayed the struggle of loyalties of a group in the Carolinas in 1780, written and published in the context of World War II.

The wilderness, either contemporary or historical, is the setting for most of Kjelgaard's books. As a child he was drawn to the woods where he observed animal life in natural habitat. During his first year after high school he and a friend spent an entire winter season in the Pennsylvania forest hunting and fishing. *Buckskin Brigade,* one of the author's favorite books, portrays pioneer life on the frontier. "Story hunts have led me from the Atlantic to the Pacific and from the Arctic Circle to Mexico City," he wrote on the jacket of *Coyote Song.* "Stories, like gold, are where you find them—3,000 miles from home or on the doorstep." While living in Wisconsin he wrote *The Spell of White Sturgeon* and *The Explorations of Père Marquette,* both with local settings. Historical fiction, such as *The Lost Wagon* about the Oregon Trail and *Fire-Hunter* suggesting the life of a prehistoric man, were the result of research and an educated imagination.

Kjelgaard was well-known to bibliographers seeking books for the reluctant reader and for occupational counseling. He specialized in telling a good story with simplicity, and encouraged fellow-authors to provide better reading for youth. In a letter to Dr. Kerlan he mused, "As for me, I'm 43 and a very plain sort of person. By that I mean if I had a choice between attending a party at the Stork Club or going bass fishing, I'd go fishing." Reviewers praised him for his fine plots and action. Reviewing for the *Horn Book* (August 1962), Margaret Warren Brown stated, "Much more mysterious than the mystery in *Hidden Trail* (the disappearance of an elk herd) is the author's ability to fashion an absorbing story out of such unlikely materials as a youthful photographer, a Conservation Department, an Airedale, and the migration pattern of elks."

The author's brother, John, provided the model for the forest ranger in the books. A game warden's responsibilities are outlined in *Trailing Trouble* and *A Nose for Trouble,* the wildlife cameraman is portrayed in a book with that title, and a naturalist whose plane is forced to land in the remote Canadian wilderness is described in *Wild Trek.* An avid reader can follow Kjelgaard's books and life chronologically, observing that the camera is substituted for a gun in his later works.

—Karen Nelson Hoyle

KNIGHT, Eric (Mowbray)

Pseudonym: Richard Hallas. **Nationality:** British (moved to the United States, 1912). **Born:** Menston, Yorkshire, 10 April 1897. **Education:** Bewerly School, Yorkshire; Boston Museum of Fine Arts; New York Academy of Design. **Military Service:** Princess Patricia's Canadian Light Infantry during World War I; United States Army during World War II: major; Legion of Merit. **Family:** Married 1) Dorothy Noyes Hall in 1917, three daughters; 2) Jere Knight in 1932. **Career:** Journalist: staff member of several Connecticut newspapers, Bronx *Home News,* and Philadelphia *Sun* and *Public Ledger,* until 1934; film writer in Hollywood. **Died:** Killed in action, 15 January 1943.

Publications for Children

Fiction

Lassie Come-Home, illustrated by Marguerite Kirmse. Philadelphia, Winston, 1940; London, Cassell, 1942.

Publications for Adults

Novels

Invitation to Life. New York, Greenberg, 1934; London, Cassell, 1936.
Song on Your Bugles. London, Boriswood, 1936; New York, Harper, 1937.
The Flying Yorkshireman: Novellas, with others. New York, Harper, 1938.
You Play the Black and the Red Comes Up. London, Cassell, 1938; as Richard Hallas, New York, McBride, 1938.
Now Pray We for Our Country. London, Cassell, 1940; as *The Happy Land,* New York, Harper, 1940; as *This Is the Land,* Leeds, Morley Baker, 1969.
This above All. London, Cassell, and New York, Harper, 1941.
Sam Small Flies Again. New York, Harper, 1942; London, Cassell, 1943; as *Sam Small, The Flying Yorkshireman,* London, Spearman, 1958.

Other

They Don't Want Swamps and Jungles (radio talk). Ottawa, Director of Public Information, 1942.
World of Plenty, with Paul Rotha. London, Nicholson and Watson, 1945.
The Dedicated Life of Rainer Maria Rilke. Shorne, Kent, Ridgeway House, 1949; New York, Haskell House, 1974.
Portrait of a Flying Yorkshireman: Letters from Eric Knight in the United States to Paul Rotha in England, edited by Rotha. London, Chapman and Hall, 1952.

* * *

Eric Knight is one of a number of ambitious authors, starting perhaps with R.D. Blackmore, who contributed quite substantially to various branches of literature but by the verdict of posterity are known largely as writers for children. Within a space of ten years Knight published seven volumes, mainly full-length adult novels, including one that was widely hailed at the time in Britain and America for its originality and boldness, and which is still not entirely forgotten. *This above All* is concerned with problems of conscience and conflict of loyalties under the pressures of war; though written with obvious sincerity, it would probably be too earnest and at times too morbid for most tastes nowadays. Knight's several Yorkshire comedies featuring the amazing Sam Small might be better candidates for revival, but without any doubt his reputation will rest essentially on the merits of *Lassie Come-Home.*

Lassie was published in 1940, but a version of it had previously appeared as a magazine story, and in the last 50 years it has constantly been translated, adapted for the media, and, in the United States, re-issued with new illustrations and varying degrees of simplification. The 1940 version, running to 240 pages and with drawings by the distinguished animal illustrator Marguerite Kirmse, has the best claims to be treated as the standard text. Reviewers appear to have regarded it as an adult novel, and there are certainly a number of passages, especially those dealing with memories of World War I or the process of law in a Scottish court-room, which would be unlikely to interest young children. However, the central story is very simple; the dog-heroine, though by no means humanized, is by far the most interesting character;

and the author is most careful to give vice and virtue their due reward in each chapter. The likelihood is that Knight originally designed the story largely as a pot-boiler which would have the widest possible appeal to people of all ages who enjoy a good read and have no objection to a fairly liberal infusion of sentiment.

Nowadays *Lassie* is usually recommended for children of eight or nine upwards, and I would certainly expect most young readers to enjoy the story, perhaps also to take something of value from it. The author's surely genuine love of dogs and his sense of outrage at the sufferings of the unemployed are likely to make a strong impression on many, while his craftsmanship is generally good enough to avoid the worst pitfalls of didacticism. There is nothing better in the book than the contrasting of humanity and brutality in the chapters featuring Rowlie Palmer, the travelling potter.

All in all, *Lassie* has quite an honourable place in the long line of dog-centred stories accessible to children, a line stretching from *The Dog Crusoe* (Ballantyne) and *Owd Bob* (Ollivant) to *Old Yeller* (Gipson) and *A Dog So Small* (Pearce).

—Alasdair K.D. Campbell

KNOWLES, Mabel Winifred. See **WYNNE, May.**

KONIGSBURG, E(laine) L(obl)

Nationality: American. **Born:** New York City, 10 February 1930. **Education:** Farrell High School, Pennsylvania; Carnegie Institute of Technology (now Carnegie-Mellon University), Pittsburgh, B.S. 1952; University of Pittsburgh, 1952-54. **Family:** Married David Konigsburg in 1952; two sons and one daughter. **Career:** Writer. Bookkeeper, Shenango Valley Provision Company, Sharon, Pennsylvania, 1947-48; science teacher, Bartram School, Jacksonville, Florida, 1954-55, 1960-62. Worked as manager of a dormitory laundry, playground instructor, waitress and library page while in college; research assistant in tissue culture lab and organic chemistry while in graduate school at the University of Pittsburgh. **Awards:** Honor book in *Book Week* Children's Spring Book Festival, 1967, and Newbery Honor Book, 1968, for *Jennifer, Hecate, Macbeth, William McKinley, and Me, Elizabeth;* Newbery Medal, 1968, and William Allen White award, 1970, both for *From the Mixed-Up Files of Mrs. Basil E. Frankweiler;* Carnegie-Mellon Merit award, 1971; American Library Association notable children's book and National Book award nomination, both 1974, both for *A Proud Taste for Scarlet and Miniver;* American Library Association best book for young adults, for *The Second Mrs. Giaconda,* and *Father's Arcane Daughter;* American Library Association notable children's book and American Book award nomination, 1980, both for *Throwing Shadows; Jennifer, Hecate, Macbeth, William McKinley, and Me, Elizabeth, About the B'nai Bagels, A Proud Taste for Scarlet and Miniver,* and *Journey to an 800 Number* were all chosen Children's Books of the Year by the Child Study Association of America. **Address:** c/o Atheneum, 1230 Avenue of the Americas, New York, New York 10020, U.S.A.

Publications for Children (illustrated by the author)

Fiction

Jennifer, Hecate, Macbeth, William McKinley, and Me, Elizabeth. New York, Atheneum, 1967; as *Jennifer, Hecate, Macbeth and Me,* London, Macmillan, 1968.
From the Mixed-Up Files of Mrs. Basil E. Frankweiler. New York, Atheneum, 1967; London, Macmillan, 1969.
About the B'nai Bagels. New York, Atheneum, 1969.
(George). New York, Atheneum, 1970; as *Benjamin Dickinson Carr and His (George),* London, Penguin, 1974.
Altogether, One at a Time, illustrated by Gail E. Haley and others. New York, Atheneum, 1971.
A Proud Taste for Scarlet and Miniver. New York, Atheneum, 1973; London, Macmillan, 1974.
The Dragon in the Ghetto Caper. New York, Atheneum, 1974; London, Macmillan, 1979.
The Second Mrs. Giaconda. New York, Atheneum, 1975; London, Macmillan, 1976.
Father's Arcane Daughter. New York, Atheneum, 1976; London, Macmillan, 1977.
Throwing Shadows (stories). New York, Atheneum, 1979.
Journey to an 800 Number. New York, Atheneum, 1982; as *Journey by First Class Camel,* London, Hamish Hamilton, 1983.
Up from Jericho Tel. New York, Atheneum, 1986.
Samuel Todd's Book of Great Colors. London, Macmillan, 1990.
Samuel Todd's Book of Great Inventions. New York, Atheneum, 1991.
Amy Elizabeth Explores Bloomingdale's. New York, Atheneum, 1992.
T-Backs, T-Shirts, COAT, and Suit. New York, Atheneum, 1993.
The View from Saturday, New York, Atheneum, 1996.

Play

The Second Mrs. Giaconda, adaptation of her own novel (produced Jacksonville, Florida, 1976).

Other

A Children's Book Author Speaks to Grown-Ups, New York, Ath eneum, 1995.

*

Media Adaptations: *From the Mixed-Up Files of Mrs. Basil E Frankweiler* (record; cassette), Miller-Brody/Random Hous 1969; *From the Mixed-Up Files of Mrs. Basil E. Frankweiler* (mo tion picture) starring Ingrid Bergman, Cinema 5, 1973, release under new title *The Hideaways,* Bing Crosby Productions, 197 *Jennifer and Me* (television movie; based on *Jennifer, Hecat Macbeth, William McKinley, and Me, Elizabeth*), NBC-TV, 197

The Second Mrs. Giaconda (play), first produced in Jacksonville, Florida, 1976. *Jennifer, Hecate, Macbeth, William McKinley, and Me, Elizabeth* (cassette), Listening Library, 1986; *Caroline?* (based on *Father's Arcane Daughter*), Hallmark Hall of Fame Presentation, 1990.

Manuscript Collections: University of Pittsburgh, Pennsylvania.

Biographies: Entry in *Third Book of Junior Authors,* New York, H.W. Wilson, 1972; essay in *Authors and Illustrators of Children's Books: Writings on Their Lives and Works,* New York, Bowker, 1972; entry in *Dictionary of Literary Biography,* Volume 52, Detroit, Gale, 1986; *E. L. Konigsburg* by Dorrel Thomas Hanks, Jr., New York, Twayne, 1992; essay in *Speaking for Ourselves, Too* compiled and edited by Donald R. Gallo, National Council of Teachers of English, 1993.

Critical Studies: Entry in *Children's Literature Review,* Volume 1, Detroit, Gale, 1976; *Your Arcane Novelist: E. L. Konigsberg* by David Rees, Horn Book, 1978.

* * *

E.L. Konigsburg is a patchy, unpredictable, and fascinating writer. Her contribution to children's literature can be conservatively assessed as superior, and since she is amazingly inventive and prolific, it is happily permissible to assume that there will be more very good things to come.

She is probably best known for her Newbery Medal winner of 1968, *From the Mixed-Up Files of Mrs. Basil E. Frankweiler,* an inspired piece of wish fulfillment. What youngster with spunk and imagination hasn't dreamed of having the freedom of a great museum: liberty to roam at will, *touching everything;* to sleep in the antique fourposters, bathe in the reflecting pool, and, best of all, collect the good-luck coins from the fountain? Claudia and Jamie Kincaid do all this and more. Their well-ordered plan for running away from home and setting up light housekeeping in New York's Metropolitan Museum of Art is neatly successful; and they return safely home in their own good time: a most satisfying adventure. One would almost hesitate to recommend such an accurate and enticing escape manual to young readers for fear of inspiring emulation, if the story did not so clearly reveal the discomfort and inconvenience of camping out in the world of ancient art as well as its satisfactions. Claudia and Jamie make a success of it, but they are a convincingly special pair of people.

So are the heroines of *Jennifer, Hecate....* Jennifer is a self-proclaimed grade-school witch who enlists the narrator, little Elizabeth, as her apprentice. The half-pretence private world of the two little girls is amusing and touching, and their characters are beautifully contrasted. The developing friendship of two lonely city children is drawn with strokes of feathery delicacy. Jennifer is black, and Elizabeth white, but the irrelevance of this detail makes its point more convincingly than any amount of pious sermonizing could do.

About the B'nai Bagels is less touching and amusing than her earlier books. 12-year-old Mark is aghast when his mother becomes manager of his Little League baseball team, but the family members become closer and learn a lot about each other in a season of shared sportsmanship and problem solving. Then comes *(George).* The title is a thumbnail description of young Ben's personality; it is split in a most companionable way. His invisible other self George lives within Ben's body (in parenthesis, as it were). Ben sees for George, and George remembers and interprets for Ben. They need each other. Though most of the adults who have dealings with Ben see him as neurotic, he gives the impression of doing very well indeed, at least as long as he has George. *Altogether, One at a Time* is a collection of four short stories, all having to do with compromise and the need for coming to terms with reality. From these pithy little pieces it is quite a leap to *A Proud Taste for Scarlet and Miniver,* a not too successful historic fantasy based on the life and times of Queen Eleanor of Aquitaine. The historic facts are accurate, but the flavour is wrong. Unmistakably, this is a cast of 20th-century masqueraders in medieval garb.

From the 12th century Konigsburg moves back to the present for *The Dragon in the Ghetto Caper* in which a youngster from a closed, privileged community makes contact with the realities of life outside his small protected world. His first ventures take him into a black ghetto where he becomes involved with the local numbers runner. Andrew J. Chronister is too knowing and cynical for a sheltered child; this story seems to have been written with one eye on the adult reader. *The Second Mrs. Giaconda* is a story of Leonardo da Vinci, as seen by his young servant, the disrespectful, impish Salai, a true historic personage. Through this brilliant work of historic imagination, Leonardo, the Duke and Duchess of Milan, and the rapscallion Salai become vividly real and alive.

Back again to the present: Caroline Carmichael was kidnapped 17 years ago. Suddenly a woman appears, claiming to be the missing heiress. Her arrival upon the scene dramatically changes the lives of Heidi and Winston, two children who must learn to accept a stranger as their long-lost half-sister, but a surprise ending reveals the fact that it is not after all Caroline (*Father's Arcane Daughter*). Another collection, *Throwing Shadows,* introduces several boy heroes who discover what it is that makes each of them special and unique; and each one of them is a character given strength and vitality in the compass of a few pages. In *Journey to an 800 Number* stuffy young Bo has been raised as a complete snob by his social-climbing mother. When, however, he is despatched to spend the period of her second honeymoon with his father, an itinerant camel-keeper who works the convention circuit selling rides, Bo meets some extremely fascinating characters, and learns a few startling facts about himself, some pleasing, some not, in a very amusing and sometimes moving story of a uniquely American way of life.

In *Up from Jericho Tel* Konigsburg evokes the shade of the late theatrical great Tallulah Bankhead, as compelling a personality in death as ever on stage, to send two children, Jeanmarie Troxell and Malcolm Soo, on a posthumous detective mission. They are required to bring peace to her restless spirit by discovering which of her friends betrayed her trust by stealing her treasure, the Regina Stone.

Konigsburg is fitfully brilliant. When she is good, she is extraordinarily so; when she is a wee bit off form, she is still better than most. Her next work will be as much of a surprise package as her first: but the name Konigsburg on the title page will ensure that it will be well worth reading.

—Joan McGrath

KORMAN, Gordon (Richard)

Nationality: Canadian. **Born:** Montreal, Quebec, 23 October 1963. **Education:** New York University, B.F.A. 1985. **Family:** Married Michelle Iserson in 1996. **Career:** Writer since 1975. **Awards:** Canadian Authors' Association Air Canada Award, "Most Promising Writer under Thirty-five," 1981; International Year of the Youth Committee of the Ontario Government, Ontario Youth Award, for contributions to children's literature, 1985; Markham Civic Award for the Arts, 1987; American Library Association Editors' Choice, 1988; ALA Best Book List, 1987, 1988, 1991; Junior Library Guild selection, 1992. **Member:** Writers Union of Canada; Canadian Society of Children's Authors, Illustrators, and Performers (CANSCAIP); Canadian Authors' Association; Society of Children's Book Writers. **Agent:** Curtis Brown Ltd., 10 Astor Place, New York, New York 10003, U.S.A. **Address:** 20 Dersingham Cres., Thornhill, Ontario L3T 4E7, Canada.

Publications for Children

Fiction

This Can't Be Happening at Macdonald Hall!, illustrated by Affie Mohammed. Richmond Hill, Ontario, Scholastic Canada, 1977.

Go Jump in the Pool!, illustrated by Lea Daniel. Richmond Hill, Ontario, Scholastic Canada, 1979.

Beware the Fish!, illustrated by Lea Daniel. Richmond Hill, Ontario, Scholastic Canada, 1980.

Who Is Bugs Potter? Richmond Hill, Ontario, Scholastic Canada, 1980.

I Want to Go Home! Richmond Hill, Ontario, Scholastic Canada, 1981.

Our Man Weston. Richmond Hill, Ontario, Scholastic Canada, 1982.

The War with Mr. Wizzle. Richmond Hill, Ontario, Scholastic Canada, 1982.

Bugs Potter: Live at Nickaninny. Richmond Hill, Ontario, Scholastic Canada, 1983.

No Coins, Please. Richmond Hill, Ontario, Scholastic Canada, 1984.

Don't Care High. Richmond Hill, Ontario, Scholastic Canada, 1985.

Son of Interflux. Richmond Hill, Ontario, Scholastic Canada, 1986.

A Semester in the Life of a Garbage Bag. Richmond Hill, Ontario, Scholastic Canada, 1987.

The Zucchini Warriors. Richmond Hill, Ontario, Scholastic Canada, 1988.

Radio Fifth Grade. Richmond Hill, Ontario, Scholastic Canada, 1989.

Losing Joe's Place. Richmond Hill, Ontario, Scholastic Canada, 1990.

Macdonald Hall Goes Hollywood. Richmond Hill, Ontario, Scholastic Canada, 1991.

The D- Poems of Jeremy Bloom, with Bernice Korman. Richmond Hill, Ontario, Scholastic Canada, 1992.

The Twinkie Squad. Richmond Hill, Ontario, Scholastic Canada, 1992.

The Toilet Paper Tigers. Richmond Hill, Ontario, Scholastic Canada, 1993.

Why Did the Underwear Cross the Road? Richmond Hill, Ontario, Scholastic Canada, 1994.

Something Fishy at MacDonald Hall. Richmond Hill, Ontario, Scholastic Canada, 1995.

The Last Place Sports Poems of Jeremy Bloom, with Bernice Korman. Richmond Hill, Ontario, Scholastic Canada, 1996.

The Chicken Doesn't Skate. Richmond Hill, Ontario, Scholastic Canada, 1996.

Liar, Liar, Pants on Fire. Richmond Hill, Ontario, Scholastic Canada, 1997.

Monday Night Football Club Series

Quarterback Exchange: I Was John Elway. New York, Hyperion Books, 1997.

Running Back Conversion: I Was Barry Sanders. New York, Hyperion Books, 1997.

Superbowl Switch: I Was Dan Marino. New York, Hyperion Books, 1997.

Heavy Artillery: I Was Junior Seau. New York, Hyperion Books, 1998.

Ultimate Scoring Machine: I Was Jerry Rice. New York, Hyperion Books, 1998.

Gordon Korman comments:

I got started writing in seventh grade, in answer to an English assignment. Our teacher said he was tired of the same old "creative" writing essays. He wanted us to work on the same story for a whole term. So he asked for an outline the first week, and a chapter a week after that. I really got into it, got carried away, and wrote a little over 100 pages of a story that eventually became my first book, *This Can't be Happening at Macdonald Hall.*

People started saying things like, "Hey, this is as good as all that published stuff." So, not knowing how impossible it is to get a first effort published, especially when you're 12, I had my Mom type it. Then we packaged it up, and sent it to Scholastic. And the rest, as they say, is history. I've been writing ever since.

* * *

When a seventh-grade English project led to a 13-year-old's publishing a novel, *This Can't Be Happening at Macdonald Hall!,* likely many people thought the event was just a one-time thing. However, two decades and some 30 books later, humorist Gordon Korman has certainly proven he was no flash-in-the-pan author. Regardless of the segment of the juvenile population for which he is writing, Korman always populates his books with a zany, likeable cast of young and adult characters who are in familiar, but somehow wacky, settings. Korman's output can be divided into two clusters, with the larger grouping principally appealing to middle schoolers. The remaining titles, *Don't Care High, A Semester in the Life of a Garbage Bag, Son of Interflux,* and *Losing Joe's Place* would more likely be enjoyed by older adolescents though they will still be consumed by loyal, younger Korman fans in need of another humour fix.

This Can't Be Happening at Macdonald Hall! introduced readers to a setting and two principal characters to which Korman has returned a half dozen times. Macdonald Hall, an all-boys boarding school, numbers among its 700 students Bruno Walton and "Boots" Melvin O'Neal. Best friends and roommates, the pair exhibit contrasting personalities with Bruno, the leader, always dragging the reluctant, cautious Boots into prankish schemes that invariably lead to their awaiting punishment in the office of Headmaster William Sturgeon, a.k.a "The Fish." Because the Headmaster decides the pair must be separated, the opening book's humour flows naturally from the pair's schemes to cause The Fish to reunite them.

A characteristic of the Bruno and Boots books is that each new title, while presenting additional characters, also reveals fresh aspects of individuals encountered in earlier books. For example, *This Can't Be Happening at Macdonald Hall!* introduced Bruno's new roommate, Elmer Drimsdale, the school's oddball science genius, and also Boot's new bunkmate, the rich, snobbish and full-time hypochondriac George Wexford-Smyth III. In *Go Jump in the Pool,* it is Wexford-Smyth's stock market expertise that successfully multiplies the monies the boys have raised to build a swimming pool. When declining enrolment imperils Macdonald Hall's financial viability in *Beware the Fish!,* only by using one of Drimsdale's inventions is the desired end achieved.

Each Bruno and Boots book acknowledged the across-the-road presence of Miss Scrimmage's Finishing School for Young Ladies, but it was not until *The War With Mr. Wizzle* that the girls assumed any major plot function. Having to cope with unwanted new teachers, the students from the two schools unite in common cause—to rid themselves of both teachers! Miss Scrimmage's girls also play a significant role in *The Zucchini Warriors* as Macdonald Hall's football team attempts to achieve a winning season so that an alumnus will donate a recreational hall. Lacking a talented quarterback, the team secretly recruits Cathy Burton, who masquerades as Elmer Drimsdale. In the most recent Bruno and Boots instalment, *Macdonald Hall Goes Hollywood,* the school's use for a movie setting causes Bruno to become determined to land an extra's role while Miss Scrimmage's 300 girls hound the movie's teen heart-throb star.

In addition to Bruno and Boots, Korman has created some other memorable characters. Readers meet a high school band drummer who accidentally becomes a rock star in *Who is Bugs Potter?,* and then encounter him again in *Bugs Potter Live at Nickaninny* as the young drummer is trapped for two weeks with his parents in a remote northern wilderness. *I Want to Go Home!* features Rudy Miller, a reluctant summer camper who drives his counsellors crazy by continually trying to escape. *Our Man Weston,* a humorous spy mystery, involves twin brothers who are working at a summer resort located next to a military base. Artie Geller, an 11-year-old con artist in *No Coins, Please,* turns a New York to Los Angeles camp-and-tour trip into his own scamming opportunity. *Radio Fifth Grade* finds three students operating their own Saturday FM radio show and exploiting a phone-in trivia contest to complete their homework assignments. *The Twinkie Squad* is the pejorative nickname given to a school's after-school "Special Discussion Group" composed of the school's losers. With his usual witty blend of satire and slapstick, Korman converts this group of social pariahs into the school's most sought-after club. Supposed losers also feature in *The Toilet Paper Tigers,* in which nine Texas Little League draft rejects are moulded into a winning team by the dictatorial granddaughter of their inept coach. Korman co-authored *The D- Poems of Jeremy Bloom* with his mother. Looking for an easy class, sixth grader Jeremy misreads the course offerings and selects "Pottery," only to discover that he has chosen 'Poetry" and now must write poems. During each grading period, Jeremy somehow offends his teacher, and he attributes his D-minus grade to this series of faux pas.

Korman introduced a new series, the Monday Night Football Club books, in 1997 with the publication of *Quarterback Exchange: I Was John Elway, Running Back Conversion: I Was Barry Sanders,* and *Superbowl Switch: I Was Dan Marino.* In these books, members of the Monday Night football club (a group of grade five students) take turns donning a magic football jersey which allows them to trade places with real NFL players. In addition to the adolescent boys' fantasies that Korman spins, this series includes contributions from the players featured, as well as biographical information about them.

—David H. Jenkinson, updated by Alexandra MacLennan

KRASILOVSKY, Phyllis

Nationality: American. **Born:** Phyllis Manning, Brooklyn, New York, 28 August 1926. **Education:** Brooklyn College, evenings 1944-47; Cornell University, Ithaca, New York, 1949-50. **Family:** Married William Krasilovsky in 1948; three daughters and one son. **Career:** Teacher of children's literature, Marymount College, Tarrytown, New York, 1969-70; creative writing teacher, Katonah Library, New York, 1970-72.

Publications for Children

Fiction

The Man Who Didn't Wash His Dishes, illustrated by Barbara Cooney. New York, Doubleday, 1950; Kingswood, Surrey, World's Work, 1962.

The Very Little Girl, illustrated by Ninon MacKnight. New York, Doubleday, 1953; Kingswood, Surrey, World's Work, 1959.

The Cow Who Fell in the Canal, illustrated by Peter Spier. New York, Doubleday, 1957; Kingswood, Surrey, World's Work, 1958.

Scaredy Cat, illustrated by Ninon MacKnight. New York, Macmillan, 1959; Kingswood, Surrey, World's Work, 1961.

Benny's Flag, illustrated by W.T. Mars. Cleveland, World, 1960; Kingswood, Surrey, World's Work, 1961.

The Very Little Boy, illustrated by Ninon MacKnight. New York, Doubleday, 1962; Kingswood, Surrey, World's Work, 1963.

Susan Sometimes, illustrated by Abbi Giventer. New York, Macmillan, and London, Macmillan, 1962.

The Girl Who Was a Cowboy, illustrated by Cyndy Szekeres. New York, Doubleday, and Kingswood, Surrey, World's Work, 1965.

Peter's Wooden Shoe. New York, Tambourine Press, 1966.

The Very Tall Little Girl, illustrated by Olivia Cole. New York, Doubleday, 1969; Kingswood, Surrey, World's Work, 1970.

The Shy Little Girl, illustrated by Trina Schart Hyman. Boston, Houghton Mifflin, 1970; Kingswood, Surrey, World's Work, 1971.

The Popular Girls Club, illustrated by Trina Schart Hyman. New York, Simon and Schuster, 1972; Kingswood, Surrey, World's Work, 1974.

L.C. Is the Greatest. Nashville, Nelson, 1975.

The Man Who Tried to Save Time, illustrated by Marcia Sewall. New York, Doubleday, 1979.

The Man Who Entered a Contest, illustrated by Yuri Salzman. New York, Doubleday, 1980.
The First Tulips in Holland, illustrated by S.D. Schindler. New York, Doubleday, 1982.
The Man Who Cooked for Himself, illustrated by Mamoru Funai. New York, Parents' Magazine Press, 1982.
The Happy Times Storybook, illustrated by Ruth Sanderson. New York, Golden Books, 1987.
The Christmas Tree that Grew, illustrated by Kathy Wilburn. Racine, Wisconsin, Western Publishing, 1987.
The Man Who Was Too Lazy to Fix Things. New York, Tambourine Press, 1992.
The Woman Who Saved Things, pictures by John Emil Cymerman. New York, Tambourine Press, 1993.

*

Phyllis Krasilovsky comments:

I wrote my first book, *The Man Who Didn't Wash His Dishes,* for a four-year-old boy who was dying of cancer. I wrote it as a letter and was told by his mother that he had to hear it "seven times a day." Considering that he was in pain most of the time, I realized I had something there. I have always enjoyed writing books for children, and telling stories to children (I do a lot of speaking and lecturing), but I was not really proud of being a children's book writer until I had to research the field for a course I was invited to give on the history of children's literature at Marymount College. At that time I became overwhelmed with the glory and the scope as well as the value of it, and ever since have been most proud and have felt most like an artist because of the children's books. It is heartwarming to realize that one can open the door to the world of reading by a good story!

* * *

Phyllis Krasilovsky has so mastered the art of providing adventure in small rooms that it would in her case be a deservedly flattering observation to assert that she does indeed create tempests in teapots. In a manner at once picturesque and direct, she snatches excitement out of the ordinary: the growth of flowers; the baking of cakes; the munching of grass—all carry within them expansive delights which she shares with readers and listeners, for it is apparent that she intends to be listened to as well as read.

A tulip bulb (*The First Tulips in Holland*) becomes an improvised history, a romance, a social upheaval, and a character study, all in a matter of 20 pages of text, none of which exceeds a few dozen words. A leisurely intensity compacted within her style enables a great deal to happen without any feeling of being hurried along. The flowers that characterize the Dutch landscape have their roots in Persia and possess a Turkish name. One little seed an everywhere. Why not? The entrancing quality of the tulip has crossed every boundary. In celebration of their universal appeal, Krasilovsky invents the daughter of the mythical first importer of the bulbs drawing crowds to her window, engrossed as they are by the progress of the plants. A once drab landscape flowers with excitement and eventually blossoms forever, or so it seems.

Ordinary-looking seeds can produce dramatic changes. Jack of beanstalk fame exchanged his cow for a few of them, and he ascended the heavens, and after several epic ventures retired a wealthy man. Krasilovsky not only has her seeds, but also a cow (*The Cow Who Fell in the Canal*) who dreams of the world beyond the windmill and the attractive compact cheese farm for which she is the principal producer. From a benign world filled with kindly people (such as populate all of Krasilovsky's books) emerges a restlessness which could be explosive, though never destructive. The dissatisfactions of her characters, and the revolutions they produce, seldom prove unsettling, at least not in the long run. The minds of all her creations show themselves quite capable of assimilating novelty, of learning from their mistakes, and of living, if necessary, in renovated landscapes. Accidents are applauded, as it appears that the whole universe responds happily to the adventure.

The worst that transpires is a series of comic blunders, rectified without any noticeable penalty. One bachelor decides to become super-efficient in order to save time, but the effected changes, which include sleeping in his clothes, have intolerable consequences. He resumes his earlier life-style wiser and happier. Another man who never washes his dishes (but who still insists on using only clean utensils) drinks from vases and the soap dish, amusing postures to say the least. He runs out of space and out of dishes. The conclusion, simple enough, is that it's easier to clean each dish immediately after use. The lessons are always apparent, and probably learned without aid of the narrative. But the muscular prose which turns attention to each of the words, and the continual movement make for a pleasurable experience regardless of the predictability. The experience is worth repeating for the pleasure alone. As Auden says, "Pleasure is by no means an infallible guide, but it is the least fallible."

Krasilovsky exploits some simple but efficient techniques in a successful search for variety. Using her trip to the Netherlands as a basis for at least two books, she allows a super-stuffed bovine (her job, which she fulfills with zeal, is to eat incessantly) to command the perspective. In *The Cow Who Fell in the Canal* it is Hendrika's desire to see the world beyond her own charming environs that converts her accidental plunge into the canal into an excursion by barge to the city. Here the spectator becomes the spectacle. Crowds gather to gaze on a cow who focusses her sights upon ships, draw bridges, and cobblestones. Pulled ashore, she sniffs bicycles as well as flowers, pleasuring particularly in munching the trimming of a green-ribboned straw hat. But the succession of accidents restores everything to a degree of normalcy. Having seen the world beyond, Hendrika is quite content to return to full-time eating, particularly since she now wears the straw hat. This domestic remnant of the strange places has become the stuff which makes the daily chewing of forage an ideal occupation. She may reflect and dream with a leisure filled with productive industry. And she sports the heady remnant of her trip to the city.

The formula is simple enough. The ordinary provokes a longing for something different. This desire for change in turn results in a happy return to the original condition. But the cycle is no mere retracing of the inevitable. A circle is not necessarily circular to those who traipse along the circumference. To reach the starting point means the completion of a journey, enlarged by experience and the imagination.

—Leonard R. Mendelsohn

KRAUS, Joanna Halpert

Nationality: American. **Born:** Portland, Maine, 7 December 1937. **Education:** Sarah Lawrence College, Bronxville, New York, 1955-59, B.A. 1959; Westfield College, University of London, 1957-58; University of California, Los Angeles, 1961-63, M.A. 1963; Columbia University, New York, 1967-72, Ed.D. 1972. **Family:** Married Ted M. Kraus in 1966; one son. **Career:** Associate director, Baltimore Children's Theatre, 1960-61; drama director, Strathmere School of the Arts, North Gower, Ontario, summers 1961-63; director of drama, New Rochelle Academy, New York, 1962-63; chairwoman, Children's Theatre Showcase, New York, 1963-65; assistant director, Clark Center for Performing Arts, New York, 1963-65; drama teacher, YM-YWHA, New York, 1965-70; Instructor, New York City Community College, 1966-69, Columbia University Teachers College, 1970-71, and State University of New York, Purchase, 1970-72; Lecturer, 1972-73, and Assistant Professor, 1973-79, New York State University College at New Paltz. Associate Professor, 1979-85, coordinator of Arts for Children, 1981-90, Professor of Theatre, 1985-95, graduate coordinator of Arts for Children, 1991-95, State University of New York at Brockport; instructor, Gate Gifted and Talented Enrichment, California, from 1997. Contributor to periodicals including *Times Herald Record, Children's Theatre Review, Critical Digest,* and California East Bay's *The Sunday Times.* **Member:** American Alliance for Theatre and Education, Children's Theatre Association of America (recording secretary, 1982-84), Dramatists Guild, International Association of Theatre for Young People. **Awards:** American Theatre Association Chorpenning Cup, for achievement in playwriting, 1971; Creative Artists Public Service fellowship in playwriting, 1976-77; first prize, Indiana University-Purdue University at Indianapolis (IUPUI) National Playwriting Competition, for *Remember My Name,* 1989; Lifetime Achievement award, New York State Theatre Education Association, 1995; Distinguished Play Award, American Alliance for Theatre and Education, 1996, for *Angel in the Night.* **Agent:** c/o Susan Schulman, 454 W. 44th St., New York, New York 10036, U.S.A.

Publications for Children

Fiction

Seven Sound and Motion Stories. Charlottesville, Virginia, New Plays, 1971; revised edition, as *Sound and Motion Stories,* 1980.
Tall Boy's Journey, illustrated by Karen Ritz. Minneapolis, Carolrhoda Books, 1992.

Plays

The Ice Wolf (produced New York, 1964). Charlottesville, Virginia, New Plays, 1967.
Mean to Be Free (produced New York, 1968). Charlottesville, Virginia, New Plays, 1968; in *Plays Plus* series, London, Collins Educational, 1990.
Vasalisa (produced Davidson, North Carolina, 1972). Charlottesville, Virginia, New Plays, 1973.
Circus Home (produced Seattle, 1977). Charlottesville, Virginia, New Plays, 1979.
The Dragon Hammer (produced Charlottesville, Virginia, 1977). Included in *The Dragon Hammer, and The Tale of Oniroku,* 1978.
The Dragon Hammer, and The Tale of Oniroku: Two Plays from the Far East, illustrated by Marisabina Russo. Charlottesville, Virginia, New Plays, 1978.
Why Am I Invisible—Especially at Lunch? (Snapshots of Women in Academe), with others (produced Rochester, New York, 1982).
The Last Baron of Arizona (produced Tempe, Arizona, 1984). Tempe, Arizona, Pyracantha Press, 1985.
Kimchi Kid (produced New Brunswick, New Jersey, 1986). Charlottesville, Virginia, New Plays, 1988.
The Shaggy Dog Murder Trial (produced Rochester, New York, 1986). New Orleans, Anchorage Press, 1988.
Remember My Name: A Story of Survival in Wartime France (produced IUPUI, Indianapolis; Jerusalem Group Theatre, New York). New York, Samuel French, 1989.
Angel in the Night (produced Evanston, Illinois, 1991). Woodstock, Illinois, Dramatic Publishing Company, 1995.
Ms. Courageous: Women of Science (produced Brockport, New York, 1995). Charlottesville, Virginia, New Plays, 1997.
Sunday Gold (produced Raleigh, North Carolina). Woodstock, Illinois, Dramatic Publishing Company, 1998.

Publications for Adults

Plays

Tenure Track (Snapshots of Women in Academe), with Greer Woodward (produced Megan Terry's Magic Theatre) Studio City, California, Players Press, 1993.

Other

The Great American Train Ride: Using Creative Dramatics for a Multi-Disciplinary Classroom Project. Charlottesville, Virginia, New Plays, 1975.
"Dramatizing History," in *Children and Drama,* 2nd edition, edited by Nellie McCaslin, New York, Longman, 1980.

Editor, with Vicki Lewin, *In My Mind/In Your Mind: Rochester Kids Write.* Brockport, State University of New York College at Brockport, 1982.

*

Theatrical Activities:
Director: **Plays**—*The Indian Captive,* New Paltz, New York, 1973; *A Christmas Carol,* Brockport, New York, 1979; *Tom Sawyer,* Brockport, 1980; *A Wrinkle in Time,* 1981; *The Shaggy Dog Murder Trial,* 1986; *Step on a Crack,* 1993; *Ms. Courageous,* 1995.

Joanna Halpert Kraus comments:

I believe that the real purpose of theatre for young people is to illuminate in an exciting way the concerns of children today, to bring greater understanding of both the commonplace and the extraordinary, and to illustrate the concept of alternative choices which exist in everyone's life.

A play, a story, a poem are all personal statements, wrung out of conviction, wrought with care.

I have always worked with concepts and themes that attracted me at the start, such as themes of prejudice, quests for freedom, and the courage of women. Children's literature and theatre for young audience should touch the spirit, ignite the imagination, and engage the intellect.

* * *

Joanna Halpert Kraus has made a considerable name for herself in the fields of children's theatre and creative dramatics, both as an educator and as a playwright. Her best known play, *The Ice Wolf,* is a lyric, provocative, and haunting story of an Eskimo village controlled, mind and body, by shamans and superstitions. A fair-haired child, Anatou, is born to parents who reject her because of village taboos, and the play is essentially a well-honed, undogmatic plea for sanity, humanity, mercy, justice, and compassion. The flow of language and action is at times exquisite, and the play, unlike many contemporary plays for children, has value, in Horatian terms, to educate and entertain both children and adults. This critical evaluation is true of all Kraus's works, especially a play entitled *Mean to Be Free* which is a re-telling of the story of Harriet Tubman and the Underground Railway. The play is accurate and well-researched, but the intensity of the drama goes beyond facts. Early in the play the following speech summarizes the intensity of action, feeling, and dialogue that underlie the entire play:

> But this freedom train is goin' a long way. And the road ain't easy. You've got to sleep by day, walk by night. And never let folks know you're about. Watch me. You'll learn to hide as well as I can. You gotta walk so quiet that there's not even a sound of your bare feet on the earth. When you sleep, you gotta be so quiet that there's not a sound of breathing. Not a cough or a sneeze. Once this train starts, ain't no turning back.

Another of Kraus's works is *Vasalisa,* a technically involved three-act play based on the Russian legend of the evil witch Baba Yaga and the title character, a fur merchant's adventurous daughter in seventeenth-century Russia. Vasalisa, by dint of her virtue, manages to thwart the witch's guile without the action veering toward the dogmatic. Framed by an interesting use of prologue and epilogue involving a Russian troubadour-acting company, the play is rich with music, song, dance, and spectacle. Evident in Kraus's plays is an abundance of action, visual effects, and spirited dialogue. These factors are also particularly apparent in the anthology *Seven Sound and Motion Stories,* which includes "The Winner," based on an Aesop fable; "Chaunteecleer," a retelling of a chaucerian tale based on an African myth about a spider; three contemporary stories; a science fiction tale entitled "The Tale of Oniroku." Each of these tales is tight, detailed, and self-contained.

Again employing characteristic humanitarian themes urging the need for mercy and compassion, Kraus in several works since 1989 has turned to contemporary experiences of World War II and the travail facing Korean orphans. *Remember My Name* is a prize-winning drama about a young girl's survival in wartime France and the courage of those who protect her from the Nazis. The heroine, who matures from a sheltered child to a firm-minded adolescent fighting for her country and her life, is the center of a riveting, well-told story inspired by historical accounts. Also set in wartime Europe, the two-act drama *Angel in the Night* is based on the true story of Polish-Catholic teenage girl who at risk of her life saves the lives of four Jewish persons during two years of the Nazi occupation of Poland by hiding them on her farm (without her parents' approval). Despite imprisonment and beatings by the Nazis, she refuses to betray them. The central character's story of courage and compassion ably demonstrates the concept that one person can make a difference. Also the author of a book for children, Kraus chronicles the emotional and cultural problems of a Korean orphan boy who travels to the home of adoptive parents in the United States in *Tall Boy's Journey* presents a perceptive and well-detailed portrait of the international adoption experience.

Turning to an adult audience in her co-authored play *Tenure Track,* Kraus offers in fourteen scenes with insight and wit a lively look at the hectic and sometimes rewarding lives of women and their male colleagues in modern day universities. It is an effective, stageworthy work. However, Kraus's well-merited reputation rests on her ability as a writer who speaks directly and masterfully to young people.

—Rachel Fordyce, updated by Christian Moe

KRAUS, Robert

Pseudonyms: E.S. Silly; I.M. Tubby. **Nationality:** American. **Born:** Milwaukee, Wisconsin, 21 June 1925. **Education:** Attended Layton Art School, Milwaukee, 1942; Art Students' League, New York, 1945. **Family:** Married Pamela Wong in 1946; two sons. **Career:** Cartoonist and illustrator; work published in *Saturday Evening Post, Esquire,* and *New Yorker.* Founding President and publisher, Windmill Books, 1966-83; from 1972, founding President, Springfellow Books, New York. **Address:** c/o Viking Children's Books, Penguin Books, U.S.A., 375 Hudson St., New York, New York 10014, U.S.A.

Publications for Children

Fiction

Junior, The Spoiled Cat, illustrated by the author. New York and London, Oxford University Press, 1955.

All the Mice Came, illustrated by the author. New York, Harper, 1955.

Ladybug, Ladybug!, illustrated by the author. New York, Harper 1957.

I, Mouse, illustrated by the author. New York, Harper, 1958.

Mouse at Sea, illustrated by the author. New York, Harper, 1959

The Littlest Rabbit, illustrated by the author. New York, Harper 1961.

The Trouble with Spider, illustrated by the author. New York Harper, 1962.

Miranda's Beautiful Dream, illustrated by the author. New York Harper, 1964.

Penguin's Pal, illustrated by the author. New York, Harper, 196[illegible]

The Bunny's Nutshell Library (*The Silver Dandelion, Juniper, Th First Robin, Springfellow's Parade*), illustrated by the autho New York, Harper, 4 vols., 1965.

Amanda Remembers, illustrated by the author. New York, Harper, 1965.
My Son, The Mouse, illustrated by the author. New York, Harper, 1966.
The Little Giant, illustrated by the author. New York, Harper, 1967.
Unidentified Flying Elephant, illustrated by Whitney Darrow. New York, Windmill, 1968.
The Children Who Got Married, illustrated by Edna Eicke. New York, Windmill, 1969.
Hello, Hippopotamus, illustrated by the author. New York, Windmill, 1969.
Rumple Nose-Dimple and the Three Horrible Snaps, illustrated by Mischa Richter. New York, Windmill, 1969.
The Christmas Cookie Sprinkle Snitcher, illustrated by Virgil Partch. New York, Windmill, 1969.
How Spider Saved Christmas, illustrated by the author. New York, Windmill, 1970.
Daddy Long Ears, illustrated by the author. New York, Windmill, 1970.
Whose Mouse Are You?, illustrated by Jose Aruego. New York, Macmillan, 1970; London, Hamish Hamilton, 1971.
Bunya the Witch, illustrated by Mischa Richter. New York, Windmill, 1971.
The Tail Who Wagged the Dog, illustrated by the author. New York, Windmill, 1971.
Ludwig, The Dog Who Snored Symphonies, illustrated by Virgil Partch. New York, Windmill, 1971.
Pip Squeak, Mouse in Shining Armor, illustrated by Richard Oldden. New York, Windmill, 1971.
Lillian, Morgan, and Teddy, illustrated by Edna Eicke. New York, Windmill, 1971.
Leo the Late Bloomer, illustrated by Jose Aruego. New York, Windmill, 1971; London, Hamish Hamilton, 1972.
The Tree That Stayed Up until Next Christmas, illustrated by Edna Eicke. New York, Windmill, 1972.
Good Night, Little A.B.C., with N.M. Bodecker, illustrated by Bodecker. New York, Springfellow, 1972; London, Cape, 1974.
Good Night, Richard Rabbit, illustrated by N.M. Bodecker. New York, Springfellow, 1972; London, Cape, 1974.
Milton the Early Riser, illustrated by Jose Aruego and Ariane Dewey. New York, Windmill, 1972; London, Hamish Hamilton, 1974.
Big Brother. New York, Parents' Magazine Press, 1973.
How Spider Saved Halloween. New York, Parents' Magazine Press, 1973.
Pip Squeaks Through, illustrated by Richard Oldden. New York, Springfellow, 1973.
Poor Mister Splinterfitz!, illustrated by Robert Byrd. New York, Springfellow, 1973.
Herman the Helper, illustrated by Jose Aruego and Ariane Dewey. New York, Windmill, 1974; London, Kestrel, 1977.
Rebecca Hatpin, illustrated by Robert Byrd. New York, Windmill, 1974.
Owliver, illustrated by Jose Aruego and Ariane Dewey. New York, Windmill, 1974; London, Kestrel, 1976.
Pinchpenny Mouse, illustrated by Robert Byrd. New York, Windmill, 1974; London, Andersen Press, 1976.
The Night-Lite Story Book, illustrated by N.M. Bodecker. New York, Windmill, 1975.
I'm a Monkey, illustrated by Hilary Knight. New York, Windmill, 1975.
Three Friends, illustrated by Jose Aruego and Ariane Dewey. New York, Windmill, 1975; London, Kestrel, 1978.
The Gondolier of Venice, illustrated by Robert Byrd. New York, Windmill, 1976; London, Andersen Press, 1977.
Kittens for Nothing, illustrated by Diane Paterson. New York, Windmill, 1976.
Boris Bad Enough, illustrated by Jose Aruego and Ariane Dewey. New York, Windmill, 1976; London, Hardy, 1983.
The Good Mousekeeper, illustrated by Hilary Knight. New York, Windmill, 1977.
Noel the Coward, illustrated by Jose Aruego and Ariane Dewey. New York, Windmill, 1977.
Springfellow, illustrated by Sam Savitt. New York, Windmill, 1978.
The Detectives of London, with Bruce Kraus, illustrated by Robert Byrd. New York, Windmill, 1978; London, Andersen Press, 1979.
Another Mouse to Feed, illustrated by Jose Aruego and Ariane Dewey. New York, Windmill, 1980.
Mouse Work, illustrated by Jose Aruego and Ariane Dewey. New York, Windmill, 1980.
Animal Families. New York, Windmill, 1980.
Mert the Blurt, illustrated by Jose Aruego and Ariane Dewey. New York, Windmill, 1980.
Puppet Pal Books (*Herman the Helper Lends a Hand, Leo the Late Bloomer Bakes a Cake, Milton the Early Riser Takes a Trip, Owliver the Actor Takes a Bow*), illustrated by Jose Aruego and Ariane Dewey. New York, Windmill, 4 vols., 1981; London, Methuen, 4 vols., 1982.
The King's Trousers, illustrated by Fred Gwynne. New York, Windmill, 1981.
How Spider Saved Turkey, illustrated by the author. New York, Windmill, 1981.
Tubby Books (as I.M. Tubby; *I'm a Little Tugboat* [*Fish, Baby, House, Airplane, Choo-Choo*]), illustrated by the author. New York, Windmill, 6 vols., 1981-82.
Leo the Late Bloomer Takes a Bath, illustrated by Jose Aruego and Ariane Dewey. New York, Windmill, 1981.
Herman the Helper Cleans Up, illustrated by Jose Aruego and Ariane Dewey. New York, Windmill, 1981.
Squeaky Books (as E.S. Silly; *Squeaky, Squeaky's One Man Band*), illustrated by the author. New York, Windmill, 2 vols., 1982.
Springfellow's Parade. New York, Windmill, 1982.
Pudgy Car Board Books (*Bumpy the Car, Tony the Tow Truck, Freddy the Fire Engine*). New York, Grosset and Dunlap, 1985.
Mrs. Elmo of Elephant House, illustrated by the author. New York, Delacorte Press, 1986.
How Spider Saved Valentine's Day, illustrated by the author. New York, Scholastic, 1986.
Where Are You Going, Little Mouse?, illustrated by Jose Aruego and Ariane Dewey. New York, Greenwillow, and London, MacRae, 1986.
Come Out and Play, Little Mouse, illustrated by Jose Aruego and Ariane Dewey. New York, Greenwillow, and London, MacRae, 1987.
Babytown Board Books (*The Babytown Express, Meet the Babies, A Sunny Day in Babytown, Welcome to Babytown*), illustrated by the author. New York, Simon and Schuster, 4 vols., 1987.
Happy Plumpy Board Books (*Happy Farm* and *Happy City*). New York, Simon and Schuster, 2 vols., 1987.
The Hoodwinking of Mrs. Elmo, illustrated by the author. New York Delacorte Press, 1987.

Spider's First Day at School, illustrated by the author. New York, Scholastic, 1987.
How Spider Saved Easter, illustrated by the author. New York, Hastings House, 1988.
Spider's Hometown, illustrated by the author. New York, Scholastic, 1988.
Mummy Dearest Creepy Hollow Whooooooodunnit Series (*Creepy Hollow Ghostly Glowing Haunted House, Mummy Knows Best, Mummy Vanishes, Private Eyes Don't Blink, The Phantom of Creepy Hollow,* illustrated by the author. New York, Warner, 5 vols., 1988.
Screamy Mimi, illustrated by Hilary Knight. New York, Simon and Schuster, 1988.
Along Came Duck, illustrated by D. Hockerman and B. Masheris. New York, Scott, Foresman, 1989.
Buggy Bear Cleans Up. Englewood Cliffs, New Jersey, Silver Press, 1989.
Ella the Bad Speller. Englewood Cliffs, New Jersey, Silver Press, 1989.
Phil the Ventriloquist, illustrated by the author. New York, Greenwillow, 1989.
Good Morning, Miss Gator. Englewood Cliffs, New Jersey, Silver Press, 1989.
Here Comes Tardy Toad. Englewood Cliffs, New Jersey, Silver Press, 1989.
How Spider Saved Santa Bug. New York, Scholastic, 1989.
How Spider Saved the Baseball Game. New York, Scholastic, 1989.
Miss Gator's School House. Englewood Cliffs, New Jersey, Messner, 1989.
Spider's Draw-a-Long Book. New York, Scholastic, 1989.
The Big Birthday Mix Up. New York, Warner, 1990.
The Boogie Woogie Bears Go Back to Nature. New York, Warner, 1990.
The Boogie Woogie Bears' Picnic. New York, Warner, 1990.
Daddy Long Ears' Halloween. Englewood Cliffs, New Jersey, Simon & Schuster, 1990.
Klunky Monkey, New Kid in Class. New York, Bantam, 1990.
The Mixed Up Mice Clean House. New York, Warner, 1990.
Musical Max, illustrated by Jose Aruego and Ariane Dewey. Englewood Cliffs, New Jersey, Simon & Schuster, 1990.
Spider's Baby-Sitting Job. New York, Scholastic, 1990.
Squirmy's Big Secret. Englewood Cliffs, New Jersey, Silver Press, 1990.
How Spider Saved the Flea Circus. New York, Scholastic, 1991.
How Spider Stopped Litterbugs. New York, Scholastic, 1991.
Dr. Mouse, Bungle Jungle Doctor. Racine, Wisconsin, Western, 1992.
The Adventures of Wise Old Owl. Mahwah, New Jersey, Troll Associates, 1993.
All My Chickens. Racine, Wisconsin, Western, 1993.
Dance, Spider, Dance! New York, Golden Books, 1993.
Jack O'Lantern's Scary Halloween. Racine, Wisconsin, Western, 1993.
Wise Old Owl's Canoe Trip Adventure. Mahwah, New Jersey, Troll Associates, 1993.
Wise Old Owl's Halloween Adventure. Mahwah, New Jersey, Troll Associates, 1993.
Wise Old Owl's Christmas Adventure. Mahwah, New Jersey, Troll Associates, 1994.
Fables Aesop Never Wrote (But Robert Kraus Did). New York, Viking, 1994.
Strudwick: A Sheep in Wolf's Clothing. New York, Viking, 1995.
Big Squeek, Little Squeek, illustrated by Kevin O'Malley. New York, Orchard Books, 1996.
Near Myths: Dug Up and Dusted Off. New York, Viking, 1996.
Little Louie the Baby Bloomer, illustrated by Jose Aruego and Ariane Dewey. New York, HarperCollins, 1998.

Poetry

Shaggy Fur Face, illustrated by Virgil Partch. New York, Windmill, 1971.
Good Night, Little One, illustrated by N.M. Bodecker. New York, Springfellow, 1972; London, Cape, 1974.
The Old-Fashioned Raggedy Ann and Andy ABC Book, edited by Pam Kraus, illustrated by Johnny Gruelle. New York, Windmill, 1981.

Other

Animal Etiquette, illustrated by Whitney Darrow. New York, Windmill, 1969.
Don't Talk to Strange Bears, illustrated by Edward Koren. New York, Windmill, 1969.
The Rabbit Brothers. New York, Anti-Defamation League of B'nai B'rith, 1969.
Vip's Mistake Book, illustrated by Virgil Partch. New York, Windmill, 1970.
Night-Lite Calendar 1976, 1979, 1980, illustrated by Hilary Knight. New York, Dutton, 3 vols., 1976-79.
Mickey Mouse Calendar 1977, 1980, illustrated by Walt Disney Studios. New York, Dutton, 2 vols., 1976-79.
See the Moon, illustrated by the author. New York, Windmill, 1980.
Box of Brownies (*The Brownies' ABC's* [*Joke Book, Song and Dance Book*], *You Can Count on Brownies*), with Pam Kraus, illustrated by Palmer Cox. New York, Windmill, 4 vols., 1980; London, Hamish Hamilton, 4 vols., 1981.
See the Christmas Lights, illustrated by Pam Kraus. New York, Windmill, 1981.

Editor, *Nanook of the North,* by Robert J. Flaherty. New York, Windmill, 1971.
Editor, *Reggie Jackson's Scrapbook.* New York, Windmill, 1978.

*

Manuscript Collections: Syracuse University, New York.

Illustrator: *Red Fox and the Hungry Tiger* by Paul Anderson 1962; *Rabbit and Skunk and the Big Fight,* 1964, *Rabbit and Skunk and the Spooks,* 1967, and *Rabbit and Skunk and the Scary Rock,* 1970, all by Carla Stevens; *Animail* by Cleveland Amory, 1976.

Robert Kraus comments:

I am fortunate that parents and children like my books and enjoy my sense of humor. I resumed illustrating my own stories in 1983 when I gave up publishing Windmill Books. I now illustrate all of my own books since I was trained as an artist and enjoy writing/drawing. It is the only way for me to fully express my stories. I have many more books planned for author/illustrator Robert Kraus. God bless him!

* * *

There is a consistency about Robert Kraus's storybooks that is comforting. Picking up one of his new offerings is always like greeting an old friend.

Although there's a sprinkling of other furry beings and a human or two, mice populate most of his works, joining his rabbits, frogs, teddy bears, and most recently (and his professed favorites) spiders. Kraus has picked the more helpless creatures—those vulnerable and dependent on the kindness of others for their existence—with which children can so readily identify. And they always triumph in the most delightful and unexpected way. Unexpected—that's a key to a Kraus book. Just when you're sure you know the ending, he applies a mild surprise that can both reassure a child and knock a few pegs from beneath a blasé grown-up.

In *Another Mouse to Feed,* Mr. and Mrs. Mouse figure 30 children are quite enough. She's taken on an extra job as a rollerskating instructor and he's holding down three jobs, and they're always too tired to enjoy the children they have. Then Mouse Thirty One appears on their doorstep. The children rally and take on small after-school jobs and help around the house. In fact, the Mouse family gets so comfortable that Mr. and Mrs. Mouse are able to pursue only those careers they really want and enjoy the family, too. In an ever so gentle way we see that family cooperation gives everyone a little time to relax and enjoy life and each other. In *The Good Mousekeeper* it's a cat who loves mice, but as foster children, not as meals. She cares for them lovingly and teaches her neighbor, Mrs. Tabby, not to "covet her neighbor's mice." Kraus demonstrates the beauty of foster love. In *Where Are You Going, Little Mouse?* a mouse runs away from home in search of a "better" family, only to discover (while hacking through the jungle and crossing the desert by camel) that he misses his own family. Of course in the end they are reunited, with a new appreciation of love.

One of my favorites is not a mouse, though, but a technicolor creature, *Mert the Blurt,* who blurts out family business to the neighbors: Aunt Martha goes skinny dipping; Aunt Patti wears contact lenses. His family worries just what will become of Mert. But in that typical Kraus twist, Mert becomes a successful television newscaster, making his family so proud of him. Along the same lines, *Owliver* is continually pretending day and night, performing in the mode of Sir Laurence Olivier. His mother encourages his talent with acting lessons and praise. His father, preferring his son take up medicine or the law, gives his son appropriate toys. But Kraus has the last laugh on all of us with aspirations for our offspring when the young owl grows up to become a fireman.

Kraus's messages are abundantly clear in his "human tales," too. In *The King's Trousers* he pokes fun at our feelings about the powerful. Bud the royal window-washer spreads the news that the king puts his trousers on one leg at a time—just like the rest of them. His subjects were furious that the king was no better than they. The king switches to royal robes and the disgruntled subjects, satisfied that he's different from them, serve him loyally, from then on.

Whether he writes about people or animals, Kraus makes us see ourselves a little more clearly.

—Mary Blount Christian

KRAUSS, Ruth (Ida)

Nationality: American. **Born:** Baltimore, Maryland, 25 July 1911. **Education:** Public elementary schools; at Peabody Institute of Music, Baltimore; New School for Social Research, New York; Maryland Institute of Art, Baltimore; Parsons School of Art, New York, graduate. **Family:** Married David Johnson Leisk (i.e., Crockett Johnson *q.v.*) in 1940 (died 1975). **Died:** 10 July 1993.

Publications for Children

Fiction

A Good Man and His Good Wife, illustrated by Ad Reinhardt. New York, Harper, 1944; revised edition, 1962.

The Carrot Seed, illustrated by Crockett Johnson. New York, Harper, 1945.

The Great Duffy, illustrated by Richter. New York, Harper, 1946.

The Growing Story, illustrated by Phyllis Rowand. New York, Harper, 1947.

Bears, illustrated by Phyllis Rowand. New York, Harper, 1948.

The Happy Day, illustrated by Marc Simont. New York, Harper, 1949.

The Big World and the Little House, illustrated by Marc Simont. New York, Schuman, 1949.

The Backward Day, illustrated by Marc Simont. New York, Harper, and London, Hamish Hamilton, 1950.

The Bundle Book, illustrated by Helen Stone. New York, Harper, 1951.

A Hole Is to Dig: A First Book of First Definitions, illustrated by Maurice Sendak. New York, Harper, 1952; London, Hamish Hamilton, 1963.

A Very Special House, illustrated by Maurice Sendak. New York, Harper, 1953.

I'll Be You and You Be Me, illustrated by Maurice Sendak. New York, Harper, 1954.

How to Make an Earthquake, illustrated by Crockett Johnson. New York, Harper, 1954.

Charlotte and the White Horse, illustrated by Maurice Sendak. New York, Harper, 1955; London, Bodley Head, 1977.

Is This You?, with Crockett Johnson, illustrated by Johnson. New York, Scott, 1955; London, Pitman, 1966.

I Want to Paint My Bathroom Blue, illustrated by Maurice Sendak. New York, Harper, 1956.

The Birthday Party, illustrated by Maurice Sendak. New York, Harper, 1957.

Monkey Day, illustrated by Phyllis Rowand. New York, Harper, 1957.

Somebody Else's Nut Tree and Other Tales from Children, illustrated by Maurice Sendak. New York, Harper, 1958.

A Moon or a Button, illustrated by Remy Charlip. New York, Harper, 1959.

Open House for Butterflies, illustrated by Maurice Sendak. New York, Harper, and London, Hamish Hamilton, 1960.

"Mama, I Wish I Was Snow" "Child, You'd Be Very Cold," illustrated by Ellen Raskin. New York, Atheneum, 1962.

Eye Nose Fingers Toes, illustrated by Elizabeth Schneider. New York, Harper, 1964.

The Little King, The Little Queen, The Little Monster, and Other Stories You Can Make Up Yourself, illustrated by the author. New York, Scholastic, 1966.

This Thumbprint: Words and Thumbprints, illustrated by the author. New York, Harper, 1967.

The Happy Egg, illustrated by Crockett Johnson. New York, Scholastic, 1967.

Little Boat Lighter Than a Cork, illustrated by Esther Gilman. Westport, Connecticut, and New York, Magic Circle Press-Walker, 1976.

Minestrone: A Ruth Krauss Selection, illustrated by the author. New York, Greenwillow, 1981.

Big and Little, illustrated by Mary Szilagyi. New York, Scholastic, 1987.

Poetry

I Can Fly, illustrated by Mary Blair. New York, Simon and Schuster, 1950.

A Bouquet of Littles, illustrated by Jane Flora. New York, Harper, 1963.

What a Fine Day for..., music by Al Carmines, illustrated by Remy Charlip. New York, Parents' Magazine Press, 1967.

I Write It, illustrated by Mary Chalmers. New York, Harper, 1970.

Everything under a Mushroom, illustrated by Margot Tomes. New York, Four Winds Press, 1974.

Somebody Spilled the Sky, illustrated by Eleanor Hazard. New York, Greenwillow, 1979.

Publications for Adults

Poem-Plays

The Cantilever Rainbow. New York, Pantheon, 1965.

There's a Little Ambiguity Over There among the Bluebells and Other Theatre Poems. New York, Something Else Press, 1968.

If Only. Eugene, Oregon, Toad Press, 1969.

Under Twenty. Eugene, Oregon, Toad Press, 1970.

Love and the Invention of Punctuation. Lenox, Massachusetts, Bookstore Press, 1973.

This Breast Gothic. Lenox, Massachusetts, Bookstore Press, 1973.

If I Were Freedom (produced Annandale-on-Hudson, New York, 1976).

Re-examination of Freedom (produced Boston, 1976). West Branch, Iowa, Toothpaste Press, 1981.

Under 13. Lenox, Massachusetts, Bookstore Press, 1976.

When I Walk I Change the Earth. Providence, Rhode Island, Burning Deck, 1978.

Small Black Lambs Wandering in the Red Poppies (produced New York, 1982).

Ambiguity 2nd (produced Boston, 1985).

Productions include *A Beautiful Day, There's a Little Ambiguity Over There among the Bluebells, Re-Examination of Freedom, Newsletter, The Cantilever Rainbow, In a Bull's Eye, Pineapple Play, Quartet, A Show, A Play—It's a Girl!, Onward, Duet* (or *Yellow Umbrella*), *Drunk Boat, If Only, This Breast,* many with music by Al Carmines, Bill Dixon, and Don Heckman, produced in New York, New Haven, Boston, and other places, since 1964.

*

Manuscript Collection: Dupont School, Wilmington, Delaware.

* * *

After a long silence, Ruth Krauss was heard from again in 1976 when she published a new picture book. *Little Boat Lighter Than a Cork* is almost as tiny as its title, a walnut-shell craft in which a baby sails on a fantasy voyage. The simple, unpunctuated text is a lyrical lullaby and would be greeted as exceptional had it come from anyone else. But since *Little Boat* is by Krauss, it must be noted that it isn't a patch on the marvels of innovation she is capable of. In only one instance of the new text does she dart into an aside reminiscent of her classics. That's when the infant passenger says to the boat, "I will rock you for the small streams and big rivers and for dolphins..." and interrupts the litany with "...for a red apple popping out of the water or is it the sun."

Her faithful following who have found Krauss's books virtual magnets since the appearance of her first in 1944 must miss the mirthful surprises she had previously offered. Millions of readers treasure their well-worn copies of *A Hole Is to Dig: A First Book of First Definitions.* People lined up in book stores to invest in the fun that book offered during the 1950s. Kids (and the kids still alive in adults) felt the pleasant shock of recognition when they met Krauss, an author who knew what they did: of course a hole is to dig; eyebrows are to go over eyes, a face is so you can make faces, a package is to look inside, etc. Another of her welcome earlier productions was *The Carrot Seed,* still enthusiastically read and listened to in a musical adaptation on a recording. The hero is a boy who is the ultimate in passive resistance and inflexible faith. Everyone tells the lad that the carrot seed he plants won't come up. He answers not a word. He bides his time. He pulls the weeds which spring up around his plant and he waters it. For a long time, nothing happens. "And then, one day, a carrot came up. Just as the little boy knew it would."

With *I'll Be You and You Be Me, Somebody Else's Nut Tree and Other Tales,* and her other satisfying stories, Krauss conveys the viewpoint of a child, the awesome imagination of a little one who knows that anything is possible. One of her most pixieish books is *The Little King, The Little Queen, The Little Monster, and Other Stories You Can Make Up Yourself* in which the same things happen to three characters who are each granted a wish by a good fairy. The repetition of plot and sameness of language here are veritable meat for the readers' fantasy feasts. The dessert is the author's wind-up, a hint to her audience that they write their own tales, and her additional suggestions: "The Little Elephant," "The Little Egg," "The Little?"

Krauss has earned lasting fame with the creation of timeless works, clearly understood and valued by everyone who speaks the *lingua franca* of childhood.

—Jean F. Mercier

KURELEK, William

Nationality: Canadian. **Born:** 3 March 1927, Whitford, Alberta. **Family:** Married Jean Andrews in 1962; two daughters and two sons. **Education:** University of Manitoba, B.A. 1949. **Career**

Picture framer in Toronto, Ontario, 1959-71; artist in Toronto, 1960-77. Work exhibited in more than fifty one-man and group exhibitions in galleries throughout Canada, Great Britain, and the United States, including the Isaacs Gallery, Toronto, 1960, 1962-64, 1966, 1968, 1970, 1972-74, 1976, 1978, and 1980, J. B. Speed Art Museum, Louisville, KY, 1962, Banfer Gallery, New York, 1963, Montreal Museum of Fine Arts, 1963, Rochester Memorial Art Gallery, New York, 1963, National Gallery of Canada, Ottawa, 1963, 1965, and 1968, Commonwealth Gallery, London, England, 1963, Edmonton Art Gallery, 1965 and 1970, Winnipeg Art Gallery, 1965, Yellowstone Art Center, Montana, 1967, Cornell University, 1971, Burnaby Art Gallery, British Columbia, 1973, and Canada House Gallery, London, 1978; paintings are also represented in various permanent collections, including Museum of Modern Art, New York, and National Gallery of Canada. **Member:** Royal Canadian Academy of Art. **Awards:** Canada Council senior arts grant, 1969; *New York Times* Best Illustrated Children's Book Award, 1973 and 1974; *Horn Book* Honor Book for Illustration, 1974; Canadian Association of Children's Librarians Illustrators Award; Doctor of Law, University of Windsor, 1976; Christian Culture Award, 1977; Order of Canada, 1977. **Died:** November 1977.

PUBLICATIONS FOR CHILDREN

Fiction

A Prairie Boy's Winter. New York, Houghton, 1973.
Lumberjack. New York, Houghton, 1974.
A Prairie Boy's Summer. New York, Houghton, 1975.
A Northern Nativity: Christmas Dreams of a Prairie Boy. Montreal, Tundra, 1976.

PUBLICATIONS FOR ADULTS

Other

O Toronto. New Press, 1973.
Some One with Me (autobiography). Ithaca, New York, Center for Improvement of Undergraduate Education, Cornell University, 1973; revised edition, Toronto, McClelland & Stewart, 1980.
The Passion of Christ According to St. Matthew. Niagara Falls Art Gallery and Museum, 1975.
Kurelek Country. New York, Houghton, 1975, published as *Kurelek's Canada,* Scarborough, Ontario, Pagurian Press, 1975.
Fields. Plattsburgh, New York, Tundra, 1975.
Jewish Life in Canada, with Abraham Arnold. Hurtig, 1976.
The Last of the Arctic, Scarborough, Ontario, Pagurian Press, 1976.
The Ukrainian Pioneer, Niagara, 1980.

*

Biographies: The following three films have been made of the artist's life and work: *Kurelek,* documentary film, National Film Board of Canada, 1967; *Pacem in Terris,* film of his drawings and paintings, 1971; and *The Maze,* psychological film study of his struggle with depression, Cornell University, 1971.

Illustrator: *Look Who's Coming,* by Mary Paximadas, Press, 1976, *Who Has Seen the Wind,* by W. O. Mitchell, 1976, and *Fox Mykyta,* by Ivan Franko, 1978.

* * *

One of Canada's most respected painters, William Kurelek, quickly established himself as an important Canadian children's author of the 1970s. Three of his books—*A Prairie Boy's Winter, A Prairie Boy's Summer* (both winners of the Canadian Children's Book-of-the-Year award), and *Lumberjack*—are visual and verbal autobiographical reminiscences. *A Northern Nativity* portrays Kurelek's interpretation of how Christ would be received if He were born in modern Canada.

The dedications of *A Prairie Boy's Winter* and *A Praire Boy's Summer* reflect the dual aspects of Kurelek's work. The former bears the inscription: "For everyone who ever spent a winter on the prairies—and for all the others who wonder what it was like." The dedication to the latter book is more complex: "With love for my sister, Nancy, who more than anyone else shared with me the surprise and wonder of prairie seasons as a child—who has added to that surprise and wonder a sense of awe and love for the Creator of those wonders. Many call it the living whole—ultimate cause—nature. We two call it: God." Each of his books is both a realistic portrayal and a religious celebration.

The two prairie books contain twenty chapters, each with a full page painting of a typical activity accompanied by three or four paragraphs discussing it. The theme of *A Praire Boy's Winter* is the relationship between the people and the cold, often dangerous land. Working and playing together, living with rather than in opposition to the land, the people thrive. The book opens with the autumn departure of the crows and concludes with their spring return. In between are such activities as the first snowfall, the making of the skating rink, skiing behind the hayrack, and skating on the bog ditch. The hero is the artist as a young boy, generally an outsider in relation to other children. *A Prairie Boy's Summer* follows the life of young William from his school activities in early June, through the summer, to his September return to school. He is happiest enjoying the prairie landscape alone and engaging in unstructured activities. In the illustrations for both books, one has a sense of the prairie horizon, the distant line with seemingly endless landscape in front of it. Against and in this landscape, children enjoy their daily and seasonal activities. However, while the illustrations focus on the children's work and play, they also reflect the artist's sense of a divine presence infusing the landscape.

Lumberjack describes a summer Kurelek spent as a young man logging in northern Ontario. The pictures capture the beauty of the life in old-time lumber camps, but also portray William as a loner, determined to stick out his time in the bush and acquire greater self-confidence. Interestingly, more of the pictures in this volume deal with people interacting, perhaps is a reflection of William's character growth from the shy, awkward lonely boy he was in the earlier books.

A Northern Nativity, considered by some critics to be Kurelek's finest children's book, presents a hypothesis: what would have happened had Christ been born in twentieth-century Canada. The artist's sense of the Canadian landscape is evident in the depiction of twenty scenes from across Canada as the settings of this hypothetical birth. In each, the bleakness of the landscape mirrors the loneliness of the Holy Family and provides a contrast to the warmth of their love for each other.

Although some critics argue that his are not really children's books, but nostalgic adult looks back at childhood, most consider Kurelek's presentations, in words and pictures, of work and play in a harsh and demanding landscape, his portrayal of the lonely William, and his sense of religious awe to be very suitable for readers in upper elementary grades and to be among the finest Canadian books of their type.

—Jon C. Stott

KUSHNER, Donn

Nationality: Canadian/American. **Born:** Lake Charles, Louisiana, 29 March 1927. **Education:** Harvard University, B.Sc. 1948; McGill University, M.Sc. 1950, Ph.D. 1952. **Family:** Married Eva Milada Dubska in 1949; three children. **Career:** Research Scientist, 1954-65; professor, University of Ottawa, 1965-89, and University of Toronto, from 1989; author. **Awards:** Canadian Library Association Book of the Year Award, 1981, for *The Violin-Maker's Gift*; IODE (Canadian Chapter) Award, 1987, for *A Book Dragon*; Canadian Society of Microbiologists Award, 1992. **Address:** 63 Albany Avenue, Toronto, Ontario, M5R 3C2, Canada. **E-mail Address:** donn.kushner@utoronto.ca.

Publications for Children

Fiction

The Violin-Maker's Gift. Toronto, Macmillan, 1980; New York, Farar Straus & Giroux, 1982.
Uncle Jacob's Ghost Story. Toronto, Macmillan, 1984; New York, Holt Rhinehart and Winston, 1986.
A Book Dragon. Toronto, Macmillan, 1987; New York, Henry Holt, 1988.
The House of Good Spirits. Toronto, Lester and Orpen Dennys, 1990.
The Dinosaur Duster. Toronto, Lester Publishing, 1992.
A Thief Among Statues. Toronto, Annick Press, 1993.
The Night Voyagers. Toronto, Lester Publishing, 1995.

Publications for Adults

Fiction

The Witnesses and Other Stories. Ottawa, Borealis Press, 1980.

Nonfiction

Editor and contributor, *Microbial Life in Extreme Environments.* Academic Press, 1978.

*

Donn Kushner comments:

I have been interested in stories as such since childhood. A story seems to me to have a life of its own and telling a story expresses a part of life. As a writer I want to tell original stories that have come to me from my own experience and imagination.

"What age group do you write for?" This is almost a standard question when others learn that I write "children's books". I even used the question as the title of a talk to a literary congress. I confess that usually I write to please myself, to tell the stories in ways that appeal to me. I try to use humor, and also irony and complexity. As a keen amateur chamber music performer (violin and viola) I have long appreciated counterpoint, the setting of one theme against another. This often appears in my own tales, in which another story is told below the surface of the actual events. I believe that children do appreciate a well-told story, and that they will benefit, as children or adults, from themes which are not stated so openly.

However, I have learned the hard way not to insert complexity for its own sake, nor to pepper my text with literary or historical allusions, unless I provide appropriate information for my young readers (and even their parents, most of whom are young enough to be my children.) This is not "writing down" to the audience but simply following the rule that I have learned as a professor: teach, don't overawe your listeners.

Most of my stories involve elements of the supernatural, but I try to keep them well anchored in the everyday life of their surroundings. My dragon, Nonesuch, did live for centuries of real historical time, through many events that actually happened: the War of the Roses, the Plague and Great Fire of London, the Holocaust. Uncle Jacob and his ghosts did exist in turn of the century Russia and New York City. A story about Martians, that seems likely to be published within a year, is based on the kind of creatures that, conceivably, might exist on the real Mars—even though many of their names are taken from old cowboy movies.

I still have some stories to tell, and am happy to find yet others making their appearance. Currently I'm working on the tale of Aunt Nan, who made a deal with "Mr. Mervyn", a demonic salesman, for a special "oubliette", a very deep hole to contain all her unwanted junk. Later, the oubliette is used as a dump site by a large chemical corporation, with some unexpected results. I'm also redoing my own version of the Bremen Town Musicians, and one or two other tales. A few years ago an editor asked why I didn't "bite the bullet" and write a book for adults. One is perking around in my mind.

* * *

A talking bird that foretells the future, a shrinking dragon, statues that speak, malignant Mayan deities, and a wide variety of ghosts—these are the types of beings encountered by the central characters in Donn Kushner's novels. As they respond to these fabulous presences, the often ordinary heroes develop courage and wisdom, becoming exceptional individuals as they confront and defeat the selfishness, materialism, and evil that threaten their lives and the lives of the people around them.

The noun in the title of Kushner's first novel, *The Violin-Maker's Gift,* refers not only to the hero's special talent, but also to the fact that it is a reward given him for his good actions. An ordinary craftsman who rescues a talking bird which he presents to his friend, Gaspard l'Innocent must steal it back to save the marvelous creature from its now greedy owner. Kushner introduces two themes found in his stories: the importance of artistic expression and the need to protect works of art from grasping materialists. He also portrays the testing of the central character, who proves his ability to act courageously for himself and others.

Uncle Jacob's Ghost Story also examines the importance of artistic expression and introduces the theme of diaspora, the exile of people from their homelands. Ghosts who provide links and continuity between past and present and who help the central character understand his responsibilities also appear for the first time in Kushner's fiction. Jacob, a man who seeks natural, rational explanations for all events, has his empiricism shaken when he encounters the ghosts of friends from his Polish village walking on a New York Street. The story of Jacob's difficult life in New York and his relationship with the ghosts is set within a framework: Paul, a young boy, hears the story from his grandfather, Jacob's brother, and realizes that "Some day, only I will know it [the story], and it must be told." Paul learns the importance of narrative as a means of keeping the past alive, of preserving old traditions and values.

Over several centuries, Nonesuch, the title hero of *A Book Dragon,* has shrunk until he is no bigger than a large insect, a size convenient to him in his self-appointed role as guardian of illuminated manuscripts and rare books. At the novel's climax, he bravely protects a small bookstore in the eastern United States from greedy land developers. As in *The Violin-Maker's Gift,* materialistic, artistically insensitive individuals are satirized, and those who protect works of art and who preserve the wisdom and beauty of the past are heroic. In *A Thief Among Statues,* Brian Newgate, a London orphans living in an Ontario town early in the twentieth century, also plays a central role in preserving works of art. Guided by the ghost of a woodcarver, the boy recovers lost and dispersed statues of a Nativity scene and brings them to the church in which they belong.

In *The House of Good Spirits* and *The Night Voyagers* Kushner drops the relatively light-hearted tone of his earlier fantasies as he presents stories of slavery, civil war, and political repression. In each of these books, the young heroes must confront powerful, deep-rooted forces of evil that have operated in all eras. In the former novel, Amos, who has joined his parents on an exchange trip from Nigeria to eastern Ontario, learns that the town in which they live had been a destination for escaped slaves. A talented sketcher, Amos is able to use one of his drawings to travel magically into the worlds of 19th-century American slavery and contemporary war-torn Africa. In both worlds, he discovers the great evil of those who hold power, and he courageously fights for freedom. Like Paul in *Uncle Joseph's Ghost Story,* he accepts his duty to help complete and conserve stories from the past.

In presenting the life of Manuel in *The Night Voyagers,* Kushner examines political repression in Central America and the lives of those who have fled north across the United States to Canada. Manuel escapes with his family after the death of his father, presumably a victim of the political power structure. The boy, who had not spoken since his father's death (his silence being a symbol of the voicelessness of the political victims of his country), regains his voice as he cries out to save his drowning brother. The family is chased by the Lords of the Dead, figures from Mayan mythology, and their contemporary world agents, military police and evil civilians, but is guided by the ghosts of his father and those of a boy and girl who had also died in their country's struggles. Although the family finds a safe home in Canada, the hero realizes that the evil embodied in his enemies cannot be completely be defeated and that he must main constant vigilance.

Kushner's narratives present worlds in which the ordinary and the fabulous, physical realities and magical, supernatural forces interact. Often because of the powers of art, the characters come in contact with the fabulous world, and, by responding with resolution, courage, and responsibility, they are able to achieve more fulfilled lives. None of the worlds Kushner depicts is perfect: greedy dragons, land developers, gods of evil, and repressive political organizations present formidable adversaries. Each character must bring his own story to a successful resolution, help others to complete theirs, and remember and preserve the moral values found in these stories. Although his fantasies about contemporary political conflicts are occasionally over-complex in plot structure and somewhat over-emphatic in their condemnation of modern, political manifestations of evil, Kushner's narratives and the magical, supernatural elements in them are portrayed with a delicacy and power that have made him a significant Canadian fantasist.

—Jon C. Stott

KUSKIN, Karla

Pseudonym: Nicholas Charles. **Nationality:** American. **Born:** Karla Seidman, New York City, 17 July 1932. **Education:** Elizabeth Irwin High School; Antioch College, Yellow Springs, Ohio, 1950-53; Yale University, New Haven, Connecticut, 1953-55, B.F.A. 1955. **Family:** Married Charles Kuskin in 1955 (divorced 1986); one son and one daughter; married William L. Bell 1989. **Awards:** AIGA awards, 1956, 1958, 1976; National Council of Teachers of English award, for verse, 1979; New York Academy of Sciences award, 1980; Parenting-Reading Magic award for *Soap Soup,* 1992; Parents' Choice Humor Book award for *A Great Miracle Happened There,* 1993; John S. Burroughs Science award for *City Dog,* 1994. **Address:** 96 Joralemon Street, Brooklyn, New York 11201, U.S.A.

Publications for Children (illustrated by the author)

Fiction

Just Like Everyone Else. New York, Harper, 1959.
Which Horse Is William? New York, Harper, 1959.
The Walk the Mouse Girls Took. New York and London, Harper, 1967.
Watson, The Smartest Dog in the U.S.A. New York, Harper, 1968.
What Did You Bring Me? New York, Harper, 1973.
A Space Story, illustrated by Marc Simont. New York, Harper, 1978.
The Philharmonic Gets Dressed, illustrated by Marc Simont. New York, Harper, 1982.
The Dallas Titans Get Ready for Bed, illustrated by Marc Simont. New York, Harper, 1986.
Jerusalem, Shining Still, illustrated by David Frampton. New York, Harper, 1987.
A Great Miracle Happened There: A Chanukah Story, illustrated by Robert Andrew Parker. New York, HarperCollins, 1993.
Paul, pictures by Milton Avery. New York, HarperCollins, 1994.

Poetry

Roar and More. New York, Harper, 1956.
James and the Rain. New York, Harper, 1957; London, Lutterworth Press, 1960.

In the Middle of the Trees. New York, Harper, 1958.
The Animals and the Ark. New York, Harper, 1958; London, Lutterworth Press, 1961.
Square as a House. New York, Harper, 1960.
The Bear Who Saw the Spring. New York, Harper, 1961.
All Sizes of Noises. New York, Harper, 1962.
How Do You Get from Here to There? (as Nicholas Charles). New York, Macmillan, and London, Macmillan, 1962.
Alexander Soames: His Poems. New York, Harper, 1962.
ABCDEFGHIJKLMNOPQRSTUVWXYZ. New York, Harper, 1963.
The Rose on My Cake. New York and London, Harper, 1964.
Sand and Snow. New York, Harper, 1965.
Jane Anne June Spoon and Her Very Adventurous Trip to the Moon (as Nicholas Charles). New York, Norton, 1966.
In the Flaky Frosty Morning. New York, Harper, 1969.
Any Me I Want to Be. New York and London, Harper, 1972.
Near the Window Tree: Poems and Notes. New York, Harper, 1975.
A Boy Had a Mother Who Bought Him a Hat. Boston, Houghton Mifflin, 1976.
Herbert Hated Being Small. Boston, Houghton Mifflin, 1979.
Dogs and Dragons, Trees and Dreams. New York, Harper, 1980.
Night Again. Boston, Little Brown, 1981.
Something Sleeping in the Hall. New York, Harper, 1985.
Soap Soup. New York, HarperCollins, 1992.
Patchwork Island, illustrated by Petra Mathers. New York, HarperCollins, 1994.
City Dog. New York, Clarion, 1994.
City Noises, illustrated by Renee Flower. New York, HarperCollins, 1994.
The Upstairs Cat. New York, Clarion, 1997.
The Sky Is Always in the Sky. New York, HarperCollins, 1998.

Other

Thoughts, Pictures, and Words, photographs by Nicholas Kuskin, Katonah, NY, R. C. Owen, 1995.

PUBLICATIONS FOR ADULTS

What Do You Mean by Design? (screenplay), 1973.
An Electric Talking Picture (screenplay), 1973.

*

Illustrator: *Xingu* by Violette and John Viertel, 1959; *Who Woke the Sun?* by M.S. Seidman, 1960; *Sing for Joy* by Norman and Margaret Mealy, 1961; *The Dog That Lost His Family* by Jean Lee Latham and Bee Lewi, 1961; *Oh Ye Jigs and Juleps,* 1962, and *Credos and Quips,* 1964, both by Virginia Hudson; *Harrison Loved His Umbrella,* by Rhoda Levine, 1964; *Boris the Lopsided Bear* by Gladys Schmitt, 1966; *Look at Me* by Marguerita Rudolph, 1967; *Big Enough* by Sherry Kafka, 1970; *What Shall We Do, and Allee Galloo!* edited by Marie Winn and Allan Miller, 1970; *The Monkey and the Crocodile* by Ellen Babbit, 1984; *Stone Soup* by Marcia Brown, 1984; *The Monster Who Grew Small* by Joan Grant, 1984.

Narrator: *Poetry Explained* (film strip), 1980.

Karla Kuskin comments:

Roar and More is the first book that I wrote and illustrated for children. I was a graphic arts student at Yale University when I designed and printed it on a small motor-driven press. Since then I have written and illustrated, or just written, or just illustrated, over 50 books. Some of them are for very young children, non-readers. For the most part I write out of my imagination. Sometimes I begin with something real, the idea of musicians getting dressed (*The Philharmonic Gets Dressed*) or football players after the game (*The Dallas Titans Get Ready for Bed*), and then I let my imagination take over. I love the sounds and rhythms of language, so I also write a lot of verse and poetry. I read a lot of it too. Readers are writers. Or are writers readers? Both, I think.

* * *

Since Karla Kuskin's first book, a participative poetry book entitled *Roar and More,* this talented author-illustrator has worked imaginatively and successfully with a number of literary genres, always for younger children. These have included an alphabet book (*ABCDEFGHIJKLMNOPQRSTUVWXYZ*), a fanciful animal tale (*Watson, The Smartest Dog in the U.S.A.*), a concept book (*Square as a House*), and a cumulative rhyming tale (*James and the Rain*), much in the tradition of Marjorie Flack. However, it is with her short verse that Kuskin has made her most memorable contribution to literature for children. Beginning with *In the Middle of the Trees,* we find an outpouring of short poems which are universally childlike in their concepts, yet refined in their artlessly simple language. Certain to appeal to a young child's own experience is

I'm very good at climbing
I nearly climbed a tree
But just as I was almost up
I sort of skinned my knee.

The sly humor of "Sweet Delilah," a cat so perfect that

From miles around the people came
To watch her winning ways
And they had nought to say but good
And nought to give but praise

amuses adult readers, while children laugh at the way Delilah routs a pack of hungry wolves with her "barking loud harroo"—her one flaw.

A further book of short poems, *The Rose on My Cake,* tells of winter clothing, birthday parties, and days when nothing goes right. It also includes the delightfully nonsensical "Hughbert and the Glue" and a hauntingly lyrical poem, "Once," which tells of a mouse that was once a queen:

The world turns.
The sun burns.
The moon goes down to dawn....

Kuskin's unusually imaginative and deftly humorous gift for projecting herself into various objects, natural and mechanical, is demonstrated in this same volume with her "If I Were a..." in which she ruminates on the feelings of a bird, a fish, a larkspur, and sandwich. She carries this idea into a later book, *Any Me I Want to Be,* a riddle book in which each of a number of objects, from trees to parrots to mittens to a computer, describes itself. The child is encouraged to imagine what it would be like to be a tiny ant, a complacent parrot, or a rooted tree, and then to go further in expressing his "If I Were..." ideas in verse of his own.

In *Thoughts, Pictures, and Words,* from the "Meet the Author" series, Kuskin uses both prose and poetry to connect with her young readers. The book contains not only her autobiography, told in brief format—as well as pictures from her own childhood and adulthood—but also descriptions of her writing methods, which can be highly valuable to aspiring authors.

Kuskin's most successful poems are those which capture the essence of childish experience; her ability to think herself into a child's skin, she says, is due to the fact that she draws for her inspiration on memories of her own childhood. That she has been able to distill these memories into simple yet lighthearted verses, which at their best are exquisite in their evocation of her small themes, is Kuskin's lasting talent.

—Margaret F. Maxwell, updated by Judson Knight

KUSUGAK, Michael (Arvaarluk)

Nationality: Canadian. **Born:** Repulse Bay, Northwest Territories, 27 April 1948. **Education:** Attended schools in Rankin Inlet, Yellowknife, Churchill, and Saskatoon. **Family:** Married; four sons. **Career:** Worked in various government positions for fifteen years; also worked as director of community programs for Arctic College. Full-time writer. **Awards:** Ruth Schwartz Award, best picture book, 1994. **Address:** Box 61, Rankin Inlet, Northwest Territories X0C 0G0, Canada.

Publications for Children

Fiction

A Promise Is a Promise, with Robert Munsch, illustrated by V. Krykorka. Willowdale, Ontario, Annick Press, 1988.

Baseball Bats for Christmas, illustrated by Vladyana Krykorka. Willowdale, Ontario, Annick Press, 1990.

Hide and Sneak, illustrated by V. Krykorka. Willowdale, Ontario, Annick Press, 1992.

Northern Lights: The Soccer Trails, illustrated by V. Krykorka. Willowdale, Ontario, Annick Press, 1993.

Other

My Arctic 1,2,3, illustrated by V. Krykorka. Toronto, Annick Press, 1996.

* * *

The difficult position of the Native author is exemplified in the life and writing of Canadian Eskimo (Inuit) storyteller Michael Kusugak. During his first seven years, Kusugak and his family lived a traditional nomadic, hunting life, and he spoke no English. Later he completed his high school education in the South and earned a degree in English literature at the University of Saskatchewan. Since 1988, he has published four books that have become very popular among Canadian Inuit and non-Inuit children. Having heard traditional tales told by his grandmother and studied written literature, Kusugak set about to create stories that would combine elements of the old and modern worlds, would appeal to his own people as well as to larger audiences and would catch the attention of children who were primarily interested in television and video games.

Each of Kusugak's stories is about a modern Eskimo child. One is based on his own experiences in the mid-1950s; the others are about contemporary girls. Three of them include traditional spiritual beliefs or encounters with supernatural beings who were characters in the old tales and myths. *Baseball Bats for Christmas* describes the mystification felt by Inuit children of four decades ago when a bush pilot leaves six evergreen trees at their remote village just before Christmas. The children decide that he intended them to use the trunks of the trees to fashion bats so that they could play baseball on the ice. *Northern Lights: The Soccer Trails* is about the continued belief that the northern lights indicate the movement of the spirits of dead people playing soccer in the heavens. When Kataujaq sees the shifting lights one winter evening, her grandmother explains that the spirit of the girl's recently dead mother is playing above and that she need not feel lonely. Her people's traditional beliefs sustain her.

A Promise Is a Promise and *Hide and Sneak* are about Allashua, a girl who escapes two supernatural beings who had always been threats to little children. In the former, she breaks her promise not to go near the thawing springtime sea ice and is captured by a qallupilluit, a creature she does not believe in because she has not seen it on television. To get away, she selfishly promises to bring her brother to the creatures and is only saved through her mother's cleverness. The story is a modern example of a traditional Eskimo cautionary tale, designed indirectly to teach proper behavior. It also is about a girl who must learn that there are more realities than those found on television programs from another culture.

In *Hide and Sneak,* an older Allashua escapes on her own from an Ijiraq, an impish being who captures children who have become lost when they wander out onto the tundra. Again she ignores her mother's warnings, preferring the messages of television; but when she becomes the Ijiraq's victim, she uses an old Inuit custom of ridiculing another person to shame him into proper behavior. Readers from southern Canada recognize in Allashua a familiar story character: the lost little girl who uses her cleverness to save herself. Eskimo children see in her a girl who saves herself by remembering and responding to ancient cultural beliefs. These two books thus represent Kusugak's way of bridging the two worlds and the two types of stories that both he and his readers are familiar with.

In *My Arctic 1, 2, 3,* Kusugak uses the familiar counting book genre to present his unfamiliar northern world to non-Eskimo readers and to teach them about the relationships among animals and between them and traditional and modern Eskimoes. Although he and his family no longer hunt these animals, they observe them and still feel the respect and admiration that traditional people felt.

—Jon C. Stott

KYLE, Elisabeth

Pseudonyms: Agnes Mary Robertson Dunlop; Jan Ralston. **Nationality:** British (Scottish). **Born:** Ayr, Scotland. **Education:** Privately. **Died:** 23 February 1982.

Publications for Children

Fiction

Visitors from England, illustrated by A. Mason Trotter. London, Davies, 1941.
Vanishing Island, illustrated by A. Mason Trotter. London, Davies, 1942; as *Disappearing Island,* Boston, Houghton Mifflin, 1944.
Behind the Waterfall, illustrated by A. Mason Trotter. London, Davies, 1943.
The Seven Sapphires, illustrated by Nora Lavrin. London, Davies, 1944; New York, Nelson, 1957.
Holly Hotel, illustrated by Nora Lavrin. London, Davies, 1945; Boston, Houghton Mifflin, 1947.
Lost Karin, illustrated by Nora Lavrin. London, Davies, 1947; Boston, Houghton Mifflin, 1948.
The Mirrors of Castle Doone, illustrated by Nora Lavrin. London, Davies, 1947; Boston, Houghton Mifflin, 1949.
West Wind, illustrated by Francis Gower. London, Davies, 1948; Boston, Houghton Mifflin, 1950.
The House on the Hill, illustrated by Francis Gower. London, Davies, 1949.
Mystery of the Good Adventure (as Jan Ralston), illustrated by A. Mason Trotter. New York, Dodd Mead, 1950.
The Provost's Jewel, illustrated by Joy Colesworthy. London, Davies, 1950; Boston, Houghton Mifflin, 1951.
The Lintowers, illustrated by Joy Colesworthy. London, Davies, 1951.
The Captain's House, illustrated by Joy Colesworthy. London, Davies, 1952; Boston, Houghton Mifflin, 1953.
The Reiver's Road, illustrated by A.H. Watson. London, Nelson, 1953; as *On Lennox Moor,* New York, Nelson, 1954.
The House of the Pelican, illustrated by Peggy Fortnum. London and New York, Nelson, 1954.
Caroline House, illustrated by Robert Hodgson. London, Nelson, 1955; as *Carolina House,* New York, Nelson, 1955.
Run to Earth, illustrated by Mary Shillabeer. London, Nelson, 1957.
The Money Cat, illustrated by Cecil Leslie. London, Hamish Hamilton, 1958.
Eagle's Nest, illustrated by Juliette Palmer. London and New York, Nelson, 1961.
The Stilt Walkers. London, Heinemann, 1972.
Through the Wall, illustrated by Philip Moon. London, Heinemann, 1973.
The Yellow Coach, illustrated by Alexy Pendle. London, Heinemann, 1976.
The Key of the Castle, illustrated by Joanna Troughton. London, Heinemann, 1976.

Other

Queen of Scots: The Story of Mary Stuart, illustrated by Robert Hodgson. London, Nelson, 1957.
Maid of Orleans: The Story of Joan of Arc, illustrated by Robert Hodgson. London, Nelson, 1957.
Girl with a Lantern, illustrated by Douglas Relf. London, Evans, 1961; as *The Story of Grizel,* New York, Nelson, 1961.
Girl with an Easel, illustrated by Charles Mozley. London, Evans, 1962; as *Portrait of Lisette,* New York, Nelson, 1963.
Girl with a Pen: Charlotte Brontë, illustrated by Charles Mozley. London, Evans, 1963; New York, Holt Rinehart, 1964.
Girl with a Song: The Story of Jenny Lind, illustrated by Charles Mozley. London, Evans, 1964; as *The Swedish Nightingale,* New York, Holt Rinehart, 1965.
Victoria: The Story of a Great Queen, illustrated by Annette Macarthur-Onslow. London, Nelson, 1964.
Girl with a Destiny: The Story of Mary of Orange, illustrated by Charles Mozley. London, Evans, 1965; as *Princess of Orange,* New York, Holt Rinehart, 1966.
The Boy Who Asked for More: The Early Life of Charles Dickens. London, Evans, 1966; as *Great Ambitions,* New York, Holt Rinehart, 1968.
Duet: The Story of Clara and Robert Schumann. London, Evans, and New York, Holt Rinehart, 1968.
Song of the Waterfall: The Story of Edvard and Nina Grieg. London, Evans, and New York, Holt Rinehart, 1970.

Publications for Adults

Novels

The Begonia Bed. London, Constable, and Indianapolis, Bobbs Merrill, 1934.
Orangefield. London, Constable, and Indianapolis, Bobbs Merrill, 1938.
Broken Glass. London, Davies, 1940.
The White Lady. London, Davies, 1941.
But We Are Exiles. London, Davies, 1942.
The Pleasure Dome. London, Davies, 1943.
The Skaters' Waltz. London, Davies, 1944.
Carp Country. London, Davies, 1946.
Mally Lee. London, Davies, and New York, Doubleday, 1947.
A Man of Talent. London, Davies, 1950; as *A Little Fire,* New York, Appleton, 1950.
The Tontine Belle. London, Davies, 1951.
Conor Sands. London, Davies, 1952.
The Regent's Candlesticks. London, Davies, 1954.
The Other Miss Evans. London, Davies, 1958.
Return to the Alcazar. London, Davies, 1962.
Love Is for the Living. London, Davies, 1966; New York, Holt Rinehart, 1967.
High Season. London, Davies, 1968.
Queen's Evidence. London, Davies, 1969.
Mirror Dance. London, Davies, 1970; New York, Holt Rinehart, 1971.
The Scent of Danger. London, Davies, 1971; New York, Holt Rinehart, 1972.
The Silver Pineapple. London, Davies, 1972.
The Heron Tree. London, Davies, 1973.
Free as Air. London, Davies, 1974.
Down the Water. London, Davies, 1975.
All the Nice Girls. London, Davies, 1976.
The Burning Hill. London, Davies, 1977.

The Stark Inheritance. London, Davies, 1978.
A Summer Scandal. London, Davies, 1979.
The Deed Box. London, Hale, 1981.
Bridge of the Blind Man. London, Hale, 1983.

Play

The Singing Wood, with Alec Robertson (produced Glasgow, 1957).

Other

The Mirrors of Versailles. London, Constable, 1939.
Forgotten as a Dream. London, Davies, 1953.
A Stillness in the Air. London, Davies, 1956.
Oh Say, Can You See? London, Davies, 1959.

*

Manuscript Collections: National Library of Scotland, Edinburgh.

* * *

Elisabeth Kyle's many titles made no dramatic contribution to children's literature but provided interesting and exciting stories for young readers for 35 years. Her love of Scotland was a consistent feature, giving authentic atmosphere to such titles as *Caroline House, Run to Earth,* and *The House of the Pelican,* the last a mystery conveying the contrasting moods of Edinburgh. *Caroline House* is a sentimental story and now very dated in terms of clothes, customs, and attitudes, but the underlying theme concerning Caroline's ancestors, Tobacco Lords of Glasgow, is absorbing. Like *Run to Earth,* it is a tale of the miscarriage of justice, and in both books a reliance on coincidence and convenience is evident in the plot. Family relationships are well drawn in Kyle's stories and, despite some stereotyped characters, this is clearly demonstrated in *Eagle's Nest* where a mystery about a 10-year-old burglary is skilfully combined with a background of forestry and the breeding of a rare eagle.

Among more recent books, *The Stilt Walkers* is set in London during the Great Exhibition of 1951. Kyle's feeling for history enabled her to recreate the atmosphere in spite of a rather melodramatic plot and some superimposed historical detail, and she created suspense and tension in an essentially ephemeral tale. In *The Key of the Castle* she returned to Scotland for the story of a page boy who wants to rescue Mary Queen of Scots from Lochleven. She wrote comfortably for 8-to-10-year-olds.

The other main group of her writing consists of fictionalised biographies. She treated her subjects with sympathy, and the story presentation may catch the interest of young readers despite the dangers of over-glamourisation. The historical subjects seem more successful than the musical ones; in particular the romantic story of Grizel Hume intertwines with that of Mary of Orange. In *Girl with a Destiny* Mary's story is told up to her accession to the English throne with William in 1688, while *Girl with a Lantern* tells of Grizel Hume's early life in Scotland, her exile with her father to Holland, and their eventual return with William and Mary. In *Girl with a Pen* the author took some liberties with the chronology, but the details of the Brontës' family life and of Charlotte's early difficulties are accurately researched. The style is old-fashioned and not always subtle but it is an imaginative and interesting reconstruction for young readers. Kyle was an accomplished writer, and her early books were valuable in their time, but many of her novels are now dated and it is to be hoped that publishers will resist the temptation to reprint them unrevised.

—Valerie Brinkley-Willsher

L

LAMPLUGH, Lois

Nationality: British. **Born:** Barnstaple, Devon, 9 June 1921. **Education:** Privately educated; Open University, B.A. (honours) 1980. **Military Service:** Auxiliary Territorial Service, 1939-43. **Family:** Married Lawrence Carlile Davis in 1955; one daughter and one son. **Career:** Member of the editorial staff, Jonathan Cape Ltd., publishers, London, 1947-57. **Agent:** A.P. Watt Ltd., 20 John Street, London WC1N 2DL. **Address:** Springside, Bydown, Swimbridge, Devon EX32 0QB, England.

Publications for Children

Fiction

The Pigeongram Puzzle, illustrated by William Stobbs. London, Cape, 1955.
Nine Bright Shiners, illustrated by William Stobbs. London, Cape, 1955.
Vagabonds' Castle, illustrated by William Stobbs. London, Cape, 1957.
Rockets in the Dunes, illustrated by William Stobbs. London, Cape, 1958.
The Sixpenny Runner, illustrated by William Stobbs. London, Cape, 1960.
Midsummer Mountains, illustrated by William Stobbs. London, Cape, 1961.
The Rifle House Friends, illustrated by Richard Kennedy. London, Deutsch, 1965.
The Linhay on Hunter's Hill, illustrated by Laszlo Acs. London, Deutsch, 1966.
The Fur Princess and the Fir Prince, illustrated by Jocelyne Pache. London, Dent, 1969.
Mandog (adaptation of television serial). London, BBC Publications, 1972.
Sean's Leap. London, Deutsch, 1979.
The Winter Donkey. London, Deutsch, 1980.
Falcon's Tor. London, Deutsch, 1984.
Sandrabbit, illustrated by Suzanne Bailey. N.p., Wellspring, 1991.

Play

Television Series: *Honeyhill,* 1967-70.

Publications for Adults

Poetry

The Quarry Hare. Privately printed, 1976.

Other

The Stream Way (autobiography). London, Golden Galley Press, 1948.
Barnstaple: Town on the Taw. Chichester, Sussex, Phillimore, 1983.
A History of Ilfracombe. Chichester, Sussex, Phillimore, 1984.
Minehead and Dunster. Chichester, Sussex, Phillimore, 1987.
A Shadowed Man: Henry Williamson 1895-1977, illustrated by Peter Rothwell. N.p., Wellspring, 1990; revised edition, West Country Books, 1991.
Take Off from Chivenor. N.p., Badger Books, 1990.
Lundy: Island without Equal. Swimbridge, Devon, Mark Young, 1993.
A Look at the Past of Swimbridge. Privately printed, 1993.
Parson Jack Russell of Swimbridge. Privately printed, 1994.
A Book of Georgeham and the Northwest Corner of Devon. N.p., Westwell Publishing, 1995.
Ilfracombe in Old Photographs. Strond, Alan Sutton Publishing, 1996.

Television Documentary: *The Old Navigator,* 1967.

*

Manuscript Collections: de Grummond Collection, University of Southern Mississippi, Hattiesburg.

Lois Lamplugh comments:

Georgeham, in north Devon, where I grew up, was a village lived in or visited by a number of writers during the 1920s and 1930s. The most noteworthy was Henry Williamson, who in fact rented a cottage belonging to my grandmother, and wrote most, if not all, of *Tarka the Otter* there. As a result, I heard a good deal of talk of books and writing during those years, which undoubtedly encouraged my own interest in writing.

Perhaps the most noticeable aspect of my books—even one or two among the earlier ones that belong to the adventure story category—is their sense of place. Often this is some part of north Devon, although I've never used actual place names and have occasionally altered places for my purpose (the island in *Sean's Leap,* for instance, is a compound of Lundy, Skokholm, Skomer, and Tresco in the Scilly Isles). *The Rifle House Friends,* my own favourite among my books, is essentially a picture of Georgeham as it was in the late 1920s and early 1930s. The Cornish setting of *The Winter Donkey* is of great importance to the story, deriving from a four-year stay in Cornwall. *Vagabonds' Castle* was prompted by visits to Italy, and *Midsummer Mountains* by visits to France.

On the whole I prefer to write for older children, but the sequence of more than 300 very short (600-word) stories in the *Honeyhill* series, and the cat fantasy *The Fur Princess and the Fir Prince,* were written during the years when my own children were fairly small.

* * *

Lois Lamplugh writes mainly for older children about children their own age. She sees herself following in the Arthur Ransome tradition; but although her earliest books are ostensibly adventure stories, it is the faithful attention to the detail of everyday life which is the striking feature of her later writing. She has, perhaps, rather more in common with adult writers such as Alan Sillitoe ("The Loneliness of the Long Distance Runner") and the 1950s and 1960s preoccupations with self-examination and realism.

In *The Winter Donkey* Goldie, a young seaside donkey, spends the winter at the smallholding belonging to Matthew's grandfather. She soon becomes a favorite with the whole village; but Matthew becomes especially close to her and, when she runs away to have a foal, he brings her back to safety. This simple story, however, is hung around much broader issues. It is a very important year in Matthew's life; he is facing the eleven-plus exam with all its implications for change. Would he follow his remote elder brother Stephen to grammar school, or would he go to the local Secondary Modern with his friends? Would he eventually strike out into the wider world, (even "to England"), or would he stay in the little Cornish village where he and generations of his family had been born and brought up?

These are themes which recur throughout Lamplugh's writing: a small community, looking at the outside world with a mixture of indifference, wonder, and vague contempt. Matthew's uneasy awareness of both worlds coincides with his growing out of childhood into adolescence. He is pulled by loyalty to his family and friends, but, on the other hand, he is fascinated by new people and possibilities. These are ideas which are shown particularly clearly in *The Rifle House Friends,* perhaps Lamplugh's most compact and intense book. Tacker becomes friendly with the eccentric owner of the Rifle House, Miss Lumley. However, he will not admit to this because he is afraid of his village friends' ridicule. By the end of the book, he is sufficiently confident of his own identity to show open friendship for Sarah, the new occupant of the Rifle House, even though she, too, is an outsider.

The best of Lamplugh's work is about people and places she knows intimately. It is often set in the West Country where she was born and brought up. *Sean's Leap,* for example, describes how Sean, a boy in care, runs away from the Island of Brytherne; it was written after Lamplugh had worked in a special school herself. Sean's immediate attraction to the wild horses on Brytherne, who "are tame because they are free," foreshadows the success of his own treatment by the islanders.

Lamplugh concentrates on the interior life of her characters, and their complex and fragile emotions are extremely compelling. The incidents in her heroes' lives (and her main characters *are* nearly all boys) are like a collection of cinematic stills, but until we can recognise themes and patterns, their personalities are strangely blurred by the abundance of careful detail. Furthermore we sense that these boys might well not read her books: although each has an intense imagination, they are not verbal, literary children at all. This contrasts sharply with the sophisticated, even adult fashion in which they are presented and somehow makes them seem quite remote. Tacker is described as taking part in the "rollicking games of the village children," but we do not feel part of this fun.

Lamplugh's book, *Falcon's Tor,* returns to the earlier straightforward adventure story. Aidan is thrown from a horse and knocked unconscious, travels back in time, and awakes in 1915, a period he has been fascinated with. His struggle to get back to his own time and family (despite his interest in World War I) and discovery of his connection to the family in the past make for a rather predictable if satisfying read.

The Lamplugh style is not really that of a storyteller. She is much more of a weaver of themes and atmosphere. Her books are best remembered for their cameo-like descriptions and the nostalgic feelings that they can evoke. Probably best enjoyed by a contemplative child or even an adult, her books yield more on a second or even third reading.

—Alison Sage

LAMPMAN, Evelyn Sibley

Pseudonym: Lynn Bronson. **Nationality:** American. **Born:** Dallas, Oregon, 18 April 1907. **Education:** Oregon State University, Corvallis, B.S. 1929. **Family:** Married Herbert Sheldon Lampman in 1934 (died 1943); two daughters. **Career:** Continuity writer, 1929-34, and continuity chief, 1937-45, Radio KEX, Portland, Oregon; educational director, Radio KGW, Portland, 1945-52. **Awards:** Western Writers of America Spur award, 1968, 1971. **Died:** 13 June 1980.

Publications for Children

Fiction

Crazy Creek, illustrated by Grace Paull. New York, Doubleday, 1948.

Treasure Mountain, illustrated by Richard Bennett. New York, Doubleday, 1949.

The Bounces of Cynthiann', illustrated by Grace Paull. New York, Doubleday, 1950; Kingswood, Surrey, World's Work, 1960.

Elder Brother, illustrated by Richard Bennett. New York, Doubleday, 1951.

Captain Apple's Ghost, illustrated by Ninon MacKnight. New York, Doubleday, 1952; London, Hodder and Stoughton, 1953.

Tree Wagon, illustrated by Robert Frankenberg. New York, Doubleday, 1953.

Witch Doctor's Son, illustrated by Richard Bennett. New York, Doubleday, 1954.

The Shy Stegosaurus of Cricket Creek, illustrated by Hubert Buel. New York, Doubleday, 1955.

Navaho Sister, illustrated by Paul Lantz. New York, Doubleday, 1956.

Rusty's Space Ship, illustrated by Bernard Krigstein. New York, Doubleday, 1957.

Rock Hounds, illustrated by Arnold Spilka. New York, Doubleday, 1958.

Special Year, illustrated by Genia. New York, Doubleday, 1959.

The City under the Back Steps, illustrated by Honoré Valintcourt New York, Doubleday, 1960; London, Faber, 1962.

Princess of Fort Vancouver, illustrated by Douglas Gorsline. New York, Doubleday, 1962.

The Shy Stegosaurus at Indian Springs, illustrated by Paul Galdone. New York, Doubleday, 1962.

Mrs. Updaisy, illustrated by Cyndy Szekeres. New York, Doubleday, 1963.

Temple of the Sun, illustrated by Lili Réthi. New York, Doubleday, 1964.

Wheels West, illustrated by Gil Walker. New York, Doubleday, 196

The Tilted Sombrero, illustrated by Ray Cruz. New York, Doubleday, 1966.

Half-Breed, illustrated by Ann Grifalconi. New York, Doubleday, 1967.
The Bandit of Mok Hill, illustrated by Marvin Friedman. New York, Doubleday, 1969.
Cayuse Courage. New York, Harcourt Brace, 1970.
Once upon Little Big Horn, illustrated by John Gretzer. New York, Crowell, 1971.
The Year of the Small Shadow. New York, Harcourt Brace, 1971.
Go Up the Road, illustrated by Charles Robinson. New York, Atheneum, 1972.
Rattlesnake Cave, illustrated by Pamela Johnson. New York, Atheneum, 1974.
White Captives. New York, Atheneum, 1975.
The Potlatch Family. New York, Atheneum, 1976.
Bargain Bride. New York, Atheneum, 1977.
Squaw Man's Son. New York, Atheneum, 1978.
Three Knocks on the Wall. New York, Atheneum, 1980.

Fiction as Lynn Bronson

Timberland Adventure. Philadelphia, Lippincott, 1950.
Coyote Kid. Philadelphia, Lippincott, 1951.
Rogue's Valley. Philadelphia, Lippincott, 1952.
The Runaway. Philadelphia, Lippincott, 1953.
Darcy's Harvest, illustrated by Paul Galdone. New York, Doubleday, 1956.
Popular Girl. New York, Doubleday, 1957.

*

Manuscript Collections: University of Oregon Library, Eugene.

* * *

Evelyn Sibley Lampman, writing at times under the pen name of Lynn Bronson, wrote biographies, historical fiction, contemporary novels, and stories that are variously humorous, fanciful, or adventure-filled. She was primarily known, however, for fiction that deals with members of minority groups, particularly the Native American.

Among Lampman's less serious books are *The Shy Stegosaurus at Indian Springs,* the story of two children who find a friendly dinosaur, and *Captain Apple's Ghost,* in which a ghost to returns his former home and helps preserve it as a children's museum. Neither tale is wholly credible, but both are lively and amusing, with affable fantasy characters. Also cheerful, if at times contrived, is one of her earliest books, *The Bounces of Cynthiann'*; the motherless Bounce children are taken in by the town of Cynthianna in a tale that stresses the close ties among the children and that gives a good picture of small town life.

Special Year, one of the few serious books that does not concern an ethnic minority, is a remarkably perceptive story about preadolescent girls, with credible familial and peer group relationships, and with a realistic treatment of the conflict between adult standards and peer group mores. In *Elder Brother* Lampman pictured the cultural conflict within a Chinese-American family with no sons who adopt a boy from China; even at the turn of the century the girls in the family rebel against the traditional concepts of feminine role held by their new brother. The problems of Mexican-American migrants are examined in *Go Up the Road,* a book in which the plot and characterization are less effective than the exposing of the demeaning quality of migrant life and the organized efforts to improve it.

Lampman's sympathy for Native Americans and her understanding of the persecution and cultural conflict they have suffered made her stories about them, whether historical or invented, her best books. Of the historical fiction, three outstanding books are *The Tilted Sombrero, Cayuse Courage,* and *White Captives.* The first is set at the beginning of the Mexican War of Independence and describes the first Indian revolt against Spanish rule, a movement led by a priest. The setting is colorful, the historical details authentic, and the plot filled with action, but it is the picture the book gives of a stratified society and a rebellion against oppression that has major impact. *Cayuse Courage* is the story of the Whitman massacre told from the viewpoint of a young Indian boy, a book that enables readers to see the reasons for an event usually seen from a viewpoint sympathetic to the white pioneers.

Lampman's objectivity in seeing both the white and the Indian point of view was particularly evident in *White Captives,* based on a report written by Olive Oatman, who was taken captive by an Apache raiding party that had killed most of the members of a Mormon wagon train. The story has pace and poignancy, but it is most notable for the strong and varied characterization of Apache and Mohave Indians.

Of her novels that are pure fiction, *Half-Breed,* set in the past, is the story of a boy at home neither with the local Indians who spurn him because he is has a white father nor the white people who reject him because his mother is a Crow. Lampman concentrated, in such stories, on Native American children who face conflicting ways of life; in books with contemporary settings, such as *Navaho Sister,* Sad Girl must adjust to the new ways she finds in a government school—but must learn to be more tolerant herself. Whether the protagonist is white, as in *Rattlesnake Cave,* and learns to respect the dignity of the Native American traditions, or—as in *The Year of the Small Shadow*—is an Indian child thrust into a white environment, Lampman emphasized the fact that the child, resilient and courageous, can cope with change, accepting new patterns while retaining appreciation for the old.

—Zena Sutherland

LASENBY, Jack

Nationality: New Zealander. **Born:** 9 March 1931, Waharo, New Zealand. **Education:** Attended Auckland University, 1950-51. **Family:** Married first wife, Elizabeth, in 1963 (died 1969); two daughters, one stepdaughter, and one stepson. **Career:** Worked variously as a deer culler, possum trapper, and teacher, c. 1950-68; editor of *School Journal,* New Zealand Department of Education, Wellington, 1969-75; senior lecturer in English, Wellington Teachers' College, Wellington, New Zealand, 1975-87; full-time writer since 1987. **Awards:** New Zealand Library Association Esther Glen Award, 1989; Sargeson Fellowship, 1991; Victoria University of Wellington writer's fellowship, 1993; Dunedin College of Education writer's fellowship, 1995; Aim Book Award, 1995, for *The Waterfall*; New Zealand Post Book Award, 1996, for *The Battle of Pook Island.* **Address:** 6/3 Aro Street, Wellington, New Zealand.

Publications for Children

Fiction

Charlie the Cheeky Kea. New York, Golden Books, 1976.
Rewi the Red Deer. New York, Golden Books, 1976.
The Lake. South Melbourne, Oxford University Press, 1989.
The Mangrove Summer. London, Oxford University Press, 1989.
Uncle Trev. Picton, New Zealand, Cape Catley Press, 1991.
Uncle Trev and the Great South Island Plan. Picton, New Zealand, Cape Catley Press, 1991.
Uncle Trev and the Treaty of Waitangi. Picton, New Zealand, Cape Catley Press, 1992.
The Conjuror. South Melbourne, Oxford University Press, 1993.
Harry Wakatipu. Dunedin, New Zealand, McIndoe, 1993.
Dead Man's Head. Dunedin, New Zealand, McIndoe, 1994.
The Waterfall. Dunedin, New Zealand, Longacre, 1995.
The Battle of Pook Island. Dunedin, New Zealand, Longacre, 1996.
Because We Were the Travellers. Dunedin, New Zealand, Longacre, 1997.
Uncle Trev's Teeth. Picton, New Zealand, Cape Catley Press, 1997.

*

Jack Lasenby comments:

When I was young, I lost my way. A story showed me how to keep going, which direction. The story was in a book in a cousin's house which I visited each year. One year I went back, and the house had gone. I've looked for the book with that story most of my life but realise now I'll never find it again. Even if I found it how, would I still recognise the story?

I don't understand why I write for children rather than for adults. It came about as I had children of my own and began teaching. Editing for children, lecturing on children's literature, I knew I must write for them. At last, a student said to me, "Don't just tell us that story. Write it down." I did—my first novel, *The Lake.* Ten years, and a dozen books later, I'm still writing for children—from the young to the grotesquely-labelled "Young Adults". That adults also enjoy my books is a delight to me.

I don't see any essential difference between the best of children's and adults' books. On the whole, the children's are better written. I'd love to write something as good as *Huckleberry Finn,* something that defies the stupid categories of "children's" and "adults". People such as Margaret Mahy, Kipling, Arthur Ransome, Cynthia Voigt, William Mayne, and Philippa Pearce are amongst the best writers of the Twentieth Century.

Reading was such a delight to me in childhood! It retains its glamour. For ten years I was a hunter and trapper in the New Zealand bush. At first I carried books into my camps on my back and on pack-horses, then by air-drops, and by helicopter. Some of those books are still on my shelves, old friends.

In comparison, television is so trivial, I won't waste my one precious life watching it. I'm now 66 and take great pleasure in re-reading the books that have given me delight for ten and sixty years. It's as important to keep in touch with my past as it is to puzzle about the future.

I've travelled little outside New Zealand. The most fantastic journeying is in my mind. That ten years living alone in the bush taught me the habit of thinking inwards, the value of reflection. I am still happy in the company of trees and mountains. For years I slept within earshot of rivers, still like to wake and think I am listening to those voices.

Life often seems absurd to me. I've known good and bad people. I've been good and bad myself. And will be both again. Writing doesn't answer all the problems, but it has given me the chance to understand myself better, why certain things happened.

I find myself moved by what I write. Moved by what I remember, what I think I remember. And by what I imagine. Perhaps it's the releasing of the imagination that is the most wonderful thing about story. You don't even need a pen and paper. You don't even need to speak. You find the story inside your head. And when you're ready, you put it into words—speak them or write them. And that's the best thing I know. Which is why I write.

* * *

In his novels for young adults and in his short stories, Jack Lasenby draws authentically on his own experiences to celebrate both rural life in small-town New Zealand and survival in the Great Outdoors of mountain, bush, lake, river, beach, and mangrove swamp. His natural ability as a storyteller and his celebration of the New Zealand landscape to explore character and theme are of particular value to New Zealand children.

Lasenby's novels become increasingly male-slanted in their focus on universal issues of importance—incest, group dynamics, war, and totalitarian political rule. Individual freedom is threatened or denied, motivating the protagonists to escape with intentions of finding a better way of life.

The issue that drives *The Lake* is incest. After being sexually molested by her new stepfather, Ruth escapes into the Urewera country. Across its mountain-bush wilderness, she ultimately finds her way to the lake where she had spent holidays with her beloved, but recently deceased, father. Lasenby lovingly evokes the beauty, majesty, and danger of Ruth's environment, which contributes to her growth in her struggle through grief and for survival. She succeeds, showing a remarkably advanced bush-craft competence that at times challenges credibility. After two or more tough years, Ruth is ready to go home and (belatedly?) protect her little sister by confronting her stepfather.

Other stories of incest or sexual attack concern a girl at Ruth's school before Ruth runs away; Gods in Polynesian mythology; a truck driver Ruth hitch-hikes with; a revengeful, dangerous "dark man" who almost kills her; and, most essential to the plot, old Tommy, who had caused his incestuously-pregnant daughter's death, but who helps Ruth at the lake. However, the cumulative effect of these examples and Ruth's forgiveness of Tommy overloads the novel and works as a male-slanted excuse for the perpetrator. Moreover, the illness of Ruth's mother is used in mitigation for Ruth's stepfather's advances. The symbolic image of the bloated eel from the depths of the lake, representing Ruth's mother, remains one of the strongest in the novel.

More coherently controlled, *The Mangrove Summer* is set during the Second World War, after Pearl Harbor, when New Zealanders are living with petrol rationing, blackouts, the activities of the Home Guard, and fear that a Japanese invasion is imminent. George recounts how this fear sends his family (mother, aunt, siblings, cousins) to their isolated beach house on the Coromandel Peninsula. After an evocation of what would be an idyllic holiday, if it weren't for the persistent fear and graphic details of war (including the treatment of conscientious objectors), George traces the exploits of the six children, aged between seven and the mid-teens, who believe the adults cannot protect them if the Japanese reach New Zealand. Guided by manipulating, autocratic Jill they escape into the tidal creeks and mangrove swamps, where no one can find them. For a while they are happy surviving on their own. But group dynamics turn harsh in a *Lord-of-the-Flies* syndrome, ending abruptly in Jimmy's death. In particular, the recurring image of the blood-red, Christmas-time blossom of the pohutukawa tree makes a poignant, ironic foreshadowing of the tragedy to come.

The power dynamics Jill exploits in a small group in *The Mangrove Summer* are enlarged in *The Conjuror* to encompass a fully imagined, futuristic, post-cataclysmic society in an appropriately volcanic landscape. This female-dominated society is class-structured according to the colour of people's eyes—Browns over Greys and the outcast Blues. In the name of the three-headed Mother Goddess, the Conjuror and her whip-wielding Black Sisters rule through cruelty, purges, histrionics, ignorance, and superstition. Lasenby does not spare his readers the terrors of totalitarian rule, carried out here by power-corrupted women. As a contrast, Johnny gains knowledge secretly from books, the civilizing agent of mankind. Breaking tradition and influence, he escapes with Hannah, the next Conjuror-elect, to travel north. Their love flourishes in a return-to-Eden wilderness away from corrupt political rule, which, nevertheless, pursues Hannah to her death. Social balance is restored when Johnny eventually finds a community established on humane terms.

Lasenby's two picture books belong to the time when New Zealand writers were developing a competent body of children's literature relevant to this country's sense of national identity. His stories of Uncle Trev and Harry Wakatipu are well-detailed and occasionally satirical, incorporating largely amusing, impossible yarns—from plans to upturn the South Island on top of the North Island to the antics of a lying, lazy, mischief-making packhorse, companion to a deer-culler in the "Vast Untrodden Ureweras." Such humorous tall tales are rare in New Zealand children's fiction, but like his serious young adult novels they express Lasenby's commitment to the New Zealand landscape and its people.

—Diane Hebley

LASSITER, Mary. See **HOFFMAN, Mary M(argaret).**

LATTIMORE, Deborah Nourse

Nationality: American. **Address:** Scholastic, Incorporated, 555 Broadway, New York, New York 10012-3999, U.S.A.

Publications for Children

Fiction

The Flame of Peace: A Tale of the Aztecs. New York, HarperCollins, 1987.

The Prince and the Golden Ax: A Minoan Tale. New York, HarperCollins, 1987.

Why There Is No Arguing in Heaven: A Mayan Myth. New York, HarperCollins, 1989.

The Dragon's Robe. New York, HarperCollins, 1990.

The Lady with the Ship on Her Head. New York, HarperCollins, Harcourt, 1990.

The Sailor Who Captured the Sea: A Story of the Book of Kells. New York, HarperCollins, 1991.

The Winged Cat: A Tale of Ancient Egypt. New York, HarperCollins, 1992.

Punga, Goddess of Ugly. New York, Harcourt, 1993.

Frida Maria: A Story of the Old Southwest. New York, Harcourt, 1994.

Arabian Nights: Three Tales. New York, HarperCollins, 1995.

Cinderhazel. New York, Blue Sky Press, 1997.

The Fool and the Phoenix. New York, HarperCollins, 1997.

*

Illustrator: *Castaways in Lilliput* by Henry Winterfeld, 1990; *Trouble at Timpetill* by Henry Winterfeld, 1990; *Gittel's Hands,* by Erica Silverman, 1996.

Critical Studies: "Cinderhazel: The Cinderella of Halloween" by Nancy Menaldi-Scanlan, *School Library Journal,* New York, Vol. 43, No. 10, 1997, 102; "The Fool and the Phoenix: A Tale of Old Japan" by Margaret Chang, *School Library Journal,* New York, Vol. 43, No. 9, 1997, 185-186.

* * *

"I want ancient cultures to be readily accessible to kids, to be entertaining and lively," Deborah Nourse Lattimore told *Publishers Weekly* in 1987. In her books she has created since then, the author-illustrator has succeeded brilliantly in attaining this goal. To her own educational background (a degree in art history and Egyptology plus graduate work in pre-Columbian, Egyptian, and classical art), Lattimore has added extensive, independent research to write a series of mythical fictions—original stories drawing on the folklore and legends of ancient and remote cultures—and to illustrate each in a style which authentically replicates the art of the culture being explored. For example, in *The Flame of Peace,* Lattimore creates the imaginative story of a young Aztec boy who travels to the Hill of Lord Morning Star to secure the flame which will bring peace to his warring people. Enroute he must outwit nine evil demons. While the story is wholly imagined, its elements are consistent with Aztec mythology—and rooted in the historic fact of the Alliance of Cities, which ushered in a great period of peace during the time of Itzcoatal. As she would in such later books as *Why There Is No Arguing in Heaven,* and *Punga, the Goddess of Ugly,* Lattimore has created endpapers which offer a visual glossary of the symbols and images used in the illustrations, and which implicitly invite the reader to return to the body of the book for re-examination and richer understanding.

The Prince and the Golden Ax offers—in an original story of a young athlete whose overweening pride causes him to challenge the Goddess Diktynna—an imagined cause for the disappearance of the once-flourishing Minoan civilization. Sumptuous, double-page illustrations evoke the art of Aegean frescoes while enhancing and enriching the accompanying text.

In *Why There Is No Arguing in Heaven,* Lattimore offers her own imaginative and slyly humorous re-telling of a Mayan creation myth. To accompany her story the author-artist has created dramatic, lushly colored images which incorporate glyphs from Mayan ruins, while her depictions of the gods themselves have the mass and weight of pre-Columbian stone sculpture. The harmony of the respective styles of the story and the accompanying artwork make this one of Lattimore's most successful books.

Her most visually sumptuous is inarguably *The Dragon's Robe.* Set in 13th-century China, the book tells how the quiet heroism of the orphan girl Kwan Yin saves the kingdom from the invading Tartar armies. The visual style which Lattimore has employed to accompany her story is a lavish homage to the art of Chinese screen painting. The text is presented in scroll-like boxes, many of which also contain secondary images which appear to have been woven. Altogether, the book is a triumph of design and, not surprisingly, won the PEN Center USA West Award in Children's Literature.

Not all of Lattimore's work is set in ancient or non-Western cultures. *The Lady with the Ship on Her Head* has as its setting France in the eighteenth-century, a period of such elaborate style it begs to be satirized. Lattimore does this ably by creating a rollicking story about the efforts of the supremely silly Madame Pompenstance to win the Medal of Honor for the Best Headdress at the King's Fancy Dress Ball. Examining the amazingly elaborate dresses that Lattimore has created for Madame and her rivals is like touring a museum of costume. In amusing counterpoint, the almost grotesque features of the vainglorious characters evoke the pleasingly satirical spirit and style of Hogarth.

Lattimore offers similar visual amusement in *Punga, the Goddess of Ugly,* which is set in New Zealand and based on Maori culture and folklore. *Frida Maria,* which tells the story of a spirited, convention-defying young girl, is set in the Old Southwest and celebrates the art and architecture of the California missions. More serious, but equally faithful to the cultures being evoked, are *The Winged Cat,* a tale of ancient Egypt inspired by the Book of the Dead, and *The Sailor Who Captured the Sea,* which is set in ninth century Ireland and owes its visual inspiration to the Book of Kells. This title is perhaps the clearest exposition of Lattimore's amazingly painstaking attention, as an artist, to detail. Its pages are stained, for example, to look like parchment; the figures in the illustrations are subtly stylized to recall the treatment of the human figure in Medieval manuscripts, while the amazingly elaborate borders are gloriously faithful to the high art of illumination found in the Book of Kells. Like all of Lattimore's work, this book invites close and careful examination and rewards both adult scholars and young readers who may be encountering, for the first time, the cultures and peoples this splendidly accomplished author-illustrator so captivatingly celebrates.

Typically, Lattimore's research into costume and folkloric motifs are evident in her sumptuous watercolor paintings. One such picture book is set in Japan during the Tokugawa dynasty which dated from 1603 to 1868. In text and illustration, Lattimore creates a story in which goodness conquers treachery and true love prevails. Despite its elaborate, evocative illustrations, *The Fool and the Phoenix* has its flaws. The plot is, at times, illogical and difficult to follow. This is especially noticeable in Lattimore's treatment of the myth of the phoenix rising from its own ashes. This part of the story is presented in an understated, nebulous fashion that will not help children to appreciate this myth. Further, as Margaret Chang points out in *School Library Journal,* it is culturally inconsistent to refer to the magical female phoenix as a maiden when she is, according to the story, a widow. Finally, although Lattimore presents the text in frames with intricate borders and creates opulent illustrations, her attempts to pay tribute to Japanese art of the era lack the elegant simplicity of the art she strives to emulate.

Arabian Nights: Three Tales, retold and illustrated by Lattimore, is an important contribution to the body of folklore available to children since few of the Arabian tales exist in picture book format. Lattimore includes the familiar story of Aladdin and two other tales which are less well known but which have personal meaning for her—always a good motivation for sharing a story. The author's note about her contact with Nicholas Clapp, a documentary filmmaker who discovered many of the sites described in "Ubar, the Lost City of Brass," is sure to intrigue young readers. The illustrations for this book alternate between jewel tones that convey the rich opulence of the sultan's dwelling and somber hues that parallel the ominous threat the heroes must overcome. There are, however, some inconsistencies between text and illustration. The illustration on the title page shows a young man entertaining listeners with the tales that Lattimore herself attributes to Sheherazade, the sultan's wife who saved her life by telling her husband stories for 1,001 nights. In addition, the scene of Aladdin entering the four chambers of the Treasure of a Thousand Ginns bears little resemblance to the text describing the underground marvel.

Cinderhazel is another picture book written and illustrated by Lattimore. This tale is a parody, in text and illustration, of the folktale, Cinderella. The main character is known not for her beauty but for her slovenly ways. She doesn't want to go to the ball until she learns that the prince is a kindred spirit. With the help of her godmother, she goes, disgusts everyone and ends up living messily ever after with the prince. While both text and illustration are likely to tickle the funny bone of elementary school children, this picture book is an artistic disappointment. The characters lack coherence, the plot is trite and the illustrations have little to distinguish them—except their silliness.

Gittel's Hands, written by Erica Silverman, is a Jewish variant of the familiar tale, Rumpelstiltskin. As in Rumpelstiltskin, a poor father exaggerates his daughter's abilities. However, some interesting differences appear in this tale. The daughter is unable to perform the first two tasks assigned to her but performs acts of kindness, instead. She is assisted in the third task by a magical figure who she recognizes as the prophet, Elijah, who has observed the girl's goodness. In the end, the girl asserts her independence, rejecting employment by the merchant who tried to cheat her father. Instead, she goes into business for herself. Lattimore's paintings for this tale are exquisite. In the style of Chagall, the artist employs luminous blues and greens to convey the timeless message of this tale. Her illustrations convincingly portray the characters, from the wise and compassionate Elijah, to the braggart father, to the unscrupulous hay merchant and to Gittel, whose various emotions and genuine kindness are evident to the reader. Viewers will also delight in Lattimore's portrayal of the dybbuks, the little demons who embody the foolish words of Gittel's father. In this story, Lattimore is at her best. Her art captures the culture of the tale and brings to life all the narrative elements of the story.

—Michael Cart, updated by Anne Drolett Creany

LATTIMORE, Eleanor (Frances)

Nationality: American. **Born:** Shanghai, China, 30 June 1904. **Education:** California School of Arts and Crafts, Berkeley, 1920-22; Art Students' League, New York, 1924; Grand Central Art School, New York, 1927. **Family:** Married Robert Armstrong Andrews in 1934 (died 1963); two sons. **Career:** Freelance artist, 1925-30. Group shows: Doll and Richards Gallery, Boston, 1923; Anderson Gallery, New York, 1924; Gibbes Gallery, Charleston, South Carolina, 1939. **Died:** 12 May 1986.

Publications for Children (illustrated by the author)

Fiction

Little Pear. New York, Harcourt Brace, 1931; London, Museum Press, 1947.
Jerry and the Pusa. New York, Harcourt Brace, 1932.
The Seven Crowns. New York, Harcourt Brace, 1933.
Little Pear and His Friends. New York, Harcourt Brace, 1934.
The Lost Leopard. New York, Harcourt Brace, 1935.
The Clever Cat. New York, Harcourt Brace, 1936.
Junior, A Colored Boy of Charleston. New York, Harcourt Brace, 1938.
Jonny. New York, Harcourt Brace, 1939.
The Story of Lee Ling. New York, Harcourt Brace, 1940.
Storm on the Island. New York, Harcourt Brace, 1942.
The Questions of Li-fu. New York, Harcourt Brace, 1942.
Peachblossom. New York, Harcourt Brace, 1943.
First Grade. New York, Harcourt Brace, 1944.
Bayou Boy. New York, Morrow, 1946.
Jeremy's Isle. New York, Morrow, 1947.
Three Little Chinese Girls. New York, Morrow, 1948; London, Angus and Robertson, 1961.
Davy of the Everglades. New York, Morrow, 1949.
Deborah's White Winter. New York, Morrow, 1949.
Indigo Hill. New York, Morrow, 1950.
Christopher and His Turtle. New York, Morrow, 1950.
The Fig Tree. New York, Morrow, 1951.
Bells for a Chinese Donkey. New York, Morrow, 1951; London, Angus and Robertson, 1959.
Lively Victoria. New York, Morrow, 1952.
Wu, The Gatekeeper's Son. New York, Morrow, 1953; London, Angus and Robertson, 1963.
Jasper. New York, Morrow, 1953.
Holly in the Snow. New York, Morrow, 1954.
Diana in the China Shop. New York, Morrow, 1955.
Willow Tree Village. New York, Morrow, 1955; London, Angus and Robertson, 1961.
Molly in the Middle. New York, Morrow, 1956.
Little Pear and the Rabbits. New York, Morrow, 1956; London, Angus and Robertson, 1963.
The Monkey of Crofton. New York, Morrow, 1957.
The Journey of Ching Lai. New York, Morrow, 1957; London, Angus and Robertson, 1959.
Happiness for Kimi. New York, Morrow, 1958.
Fair Bay. New York, Morrow, 1958; London, Angus and Robertson, 1964.
The Fisherman's Son. New York, Morrow, 1959; London, Angus and Robertson, 1962.
The Youngest Artist. New York, Morrow, 1959.
Beachcomber Boy. New York, Morrow, 1960.
The Chinese Daughter. New York, Morrow, 1960; London, Angus and Robertson, 1962.
The Wonderful Glass House. New York, Morrow, 1961.
Cousin Melinda. New York, Morrow, 1961.
The Bittern's Nest. New York, Morrow, 1962; London, Angus and Robertson, 1964.
Laurie and Company. New York, Morrow, 1962.
Janetta's Magnet. New York, Morrow, 1963.
The Little Tumbler. New York, Morrow, 1963; London, Angus and Robertson, 1964.
Felicia. New York, Morrow, 1964; London, Angus and Robertson, 1965.
The Mexican Bird. New York, Morrow, 1965; London, Angus and Robertson, 1966.
The Bus Trip. New York, Morrow, 1965.
The Search for Christina. New York, Morrow, 1966.
The Two Helens. New York, Morrow, 1967.
Bird Song. New York, Morrow, 1968.
The Girl on the Deer. New York, Morrow, 1969.
The Three Firecrackers. New York, Morrow, 1970.
More about Little Pear. New York, Morrow, 1971.
A Smiling Face. New York, Morrow, 1973.
The Taming of Tiger. New York, Morrow, 1975.
Adam's Key, illustrated by Alan Tiegreen. New York, Morrow, 1976.
Proudfoot's Way, illustrated by Beatrice Darwin. New York, Morrow, 1978; as *Which Way, Black Cat?,* New York, Scholastic, 1980.

*

Manuscript Collections: Kerlan Collection, University of Minnesota, Minneapolis; de Grummond Collection, University of Southern Mississippi, Hattiesburg.

Illustrator: *Turkestan Reunion* by Eleanor Holgate Lattimore, 1934; *Picture Tales from the Chinese* by Berta Metzger, 1934; *Rainbow Bridge* by Florence Crannell Means, 1934; *All Around the City* by Esther Freivogel, 1938.

Eleanor Lattimore commented:

(1978) I don't know quite what to say about my books except that I enjoy writing and always have been interested in children. Since I draw as well as write, I "see" my characters as I write about them. The settings are real, the characters imaginary. My stories, with one exception, are realistic. The exception is *Felicia,* about a cat who assumes the form of a girl.

* * *

Eleanor Lattimore's first book, *Little Pear,* which introduced China to the young readers of the 1930s and 1940s, remains a classic, and is a prototype for her many books for children written during a half-century. She merged an episodic plot, a strong character, and a detailed Chinese setting to produce the delightful story, and the five-year-old hero is memorable enough to be listed in Margery Fisher's *Who's Who in Children's Books* (1975). Sequels were published decades apart, although in *Little Pear and His Friends* (1934) he is only one year older, and remains a youngster in *Little Pear and the Rabbits* (1956) and *More about Little Pear* (1971). The Chinese culture permeates the text so thoroughly that the story cannot be separated from the place. Clothing, food, games, and customs are integrated into the child's adventures. Published the same year as Pearl Buck's *The Good Earth, Little Pear* seems naive in contrast.

The plots of her books are predictable, conforming to a pattern of a search or problem resolved. *The Fig Tree* concludes with the finding of a missing cup in a miniature tea set, while *The Fisherman's Son* solves the mystery of a stolen yellow bird. *Storm on the Island* challenges the resourcefulness of a family during a hurricane and its aftermath. A more contemporary story, *The Taming of Tiger,* follows a boy moving from the inner city to a suburb. A diversion from her usual plot is *Jonny,* describing a two-year-old child's entire day.

Lattimore created other memorable characters. *Junior, A Colored Boy of Charleston* was an effective book when published in 1938, sympathetically portraying an enterprising child who earned money for the family. However, the book is long since out-of-print and is not mentioned in Augusta Baker's *The Black Experience in Children's Books* (1971) or Charlemae Rollins's *We Build Together* (1967). There is interaction between children of two cultures in *The Story of Lee Ling,* when the Chinese girl meets an American girl with "yellow hair like corn." *The Chinese Daughter* deals with a mixed racial adoption, while *Jerry and the Pusa* sees China from the point of view of an American child. Childlike competitiveness exists in *Beachcomber Boy* when Barry's shell-collecting territory on the Carolina coast is invaded by Floridians.

In addition to China, the United States and other countries provide the background for a number of books. South Carolina is the setting for *The Youngest Artist,* New Hampshire for *The Clever Cat.* Japan, Denmark, and England serve as the backdrops for *Happiness for Kimi, The Seven Crowns,* and *The Lost Leopard,* respectively. *Happiness for Kimi,* S.C. Gross wrote in the *New York Times* (2 February 1958), "opens a Japanese wing in the author's oriental gallery. It has the simplicity and truth of a proverb touched with humor."

Lattimore's success was based on her understanding of story, children, and locale. She had *Little Pear* so clearly in mind that she wrote it in one week, according to a letter to Dr. Irvin Kerlan. Writing for the reader with one or two years of experience, she usually selected characters which appeal to that age group. Each character has at least one distinguishing feature, such as the six-year-old in *Adam's Key.* His personality is molded by being the youngest of five children and the inheritor of hand-me-downs. As M.L. Becker wrote in a review, the author "has often shown her desire to bridge the gulf of interracial misunderstanding and her power to send across it filaments of good-will from one child to another."

—Karen Nelson Hoyle

LAWRENCE, Ann (Margaret)

Nationality: British. **Born:** Tring, Hertfordshire, 18 December 1942. **Education:** Hemel Hempstead Grammar School; University of Southampton, 1961-64, B.A. (honours) in English 1964. **Family:** Married Alan Smith in 1971. **Career:** Worked for the British Trust for Ornithology, Tring, 1964-66; cook, Lundy Field Society, Summer 1965; teacher, Aylesbury, Buckinghamshire, 1966-71, and Tring, 1969-71. **Died:** May 1987.

Publications for Children

Fiction

Tom Ass; or, The Second Gift, illustrated by Ionicus. London, Macmillan, 1972; New York, Walck, 1973.

The Travels of Oggy, illustrated by Hans Helweg. London, Gollancz, 1973.

The Half-Brothers, illustrated by Ionicus. London, Macmillan, and New York, Walck, 1973.

The Conjuror's Box, illustrated by Brian Aldridge. London, Kestrel, 1974.

Mr. Robertson's Hundred Pounds, illustrated by Elisabeth Trimby. London, Kestrel, 1976.

Between the Forest and the Hills, illustrated by Chris Nolan. London, Kestrel, 1977.

Oggy at Home, illustrated by Hans Helweg. London, Gollancz, 1977.

The Good Little Devil, illustrated by Ionicus. London, Macmillan, 1978.

Oggy and the Holiday, illustrated by Hans Helweg. London, Gollancz, 1979.

Mr. Fox, illustrated by Antony Maitland. London, Macmillan, 1979.

The Hawk of May, illustrated by Shirley Felts. London, Macmillan, 1980.

Beyond the Firelight (stories), illustrated by Gail Lewton. London, Macmillan, 1983.

There and Back Again (stories), illustrated by Shirley Felts. Oxford, Oxford University Press, 1985.

Summer's End: Stories of Ghostly Lovers, illustrated by Robert Kettell. Oxford, Oxford University Press, 1987.

Other (retellings)

Merlin the Wizard, illustrated by Susan Hunter. London, Methuen, and Milwaukee, Raintree, 1986.

Tales from Perrault, illustrated by Tony James Chance. Oxford and New York, Oxford University Press, 1989.

*

Ann Lawrence commented:

(1978) I write stories which amuse me and which I hope may amuse other people. Generally in the process of getting written they generate ideas, which are worked out and demonstrated through the characters and the development of the plot, but again these are ideas which interest me, and *may* interest someone else, rather than didactic pills hiding inside a coating of fiction. I have not the least intention of offering the young any assistance with their social adjustments, beyond that which comes as a matter of course when one makes the imaginative effort of putting oneself in someone else's shoes. I should think that books are to the older child what play is to the younger: an opportunity to try out all the roles and situations life offers in the safety of one's own imagination. I feel that this is something achieved as readily through a fairytale as through the most earnest of social documents; I cannot see that it is necessary for the reader to be able to identify with the *setting* of a story, as long as he or she can identify with the characters. Indeed my feeling is that it is easier to handle one's own emotions objectively when they are distanced by an historical or fanciful setting. I presume that this has always been the function of folktales, myths, fables, and legends of all kinds, and this is the tradition of storytelling in which I should like to believe that I work. I believe that all honest art is experimental, in the sense that every piece of work poses a problem of some sort which has to be worked out in its making. One cannot impose one's own solution on it, but must follow patiently the logic of the work itself.

I am concerned beyond anything with the extraordinariness of the ordinary (and following from that, with the baffling matter-o'-factness of marvels *once they have actually happened*) and with the powerful, magical clarity of any particular present moment, as soon as one becomes conscious of its unique presentness, even though nothing much may be happening—because that is the moment when *anything* could happen. I am also fascinated by people talking and the odd, revealing things they do while they are talking. Consequently I find myself trying to cast everything I write in pictures or in scenes of dialogue, so that my people and places can as far as possible speak for themselves. I do not want to explain them, I want to *show* them to you, as I see them, and let you meet them directly. I think of each book as an object, having size and shape; but also in terms of musical form, with key, rhythm, and dynamics, when regarded as a continuum, and I am always aware of having in mind some visual style which I hope to recall. However, these, like my "diagrams" of plot, characters, and ideas, are only working drawings—I do not know whether it is of any use or interest to a reader to know about them, except perhaps for the purpose of knowing that a good deal of thought may go to make even the slightest of literature.

It is my opinion that any style of which one is aware while reading is probably bad.

* * *

The death of Ann Lawrence in 1987 has deprived the children's book world of a significant writer. If her books had a common theme, it was the variety of human nature. If she had an outstanding quality, it was her unobtrusive, but always appropriate, style and her skill with dialogue.

The main body of her writing falls into the fantasy or historical genres. All her work was influenced, in one way or another, by folktale and legend and has the strength and exuberance of many folktales. Her early fantasies such as *Tom Ass, The Half-Brothers,* and *The Conjuror's Box* display her wide-ranging themes comprising, as they do, the tribulations of an overconfident youngest son in 15th-century London; a sophisticated tale of Renaissance life in Europe; and a dramatic fantasy with some thoughts about the nature of time. It was perhaps with *The Good Little Devil* that she found her own voice, creating characters and plot of much greater originality. In this, a mischievous imp appears to some monks who assume responsibility for him and try to educate him with the choirboys. Thus tamed, the imp becomes so unhappy that a compassionate Brother is moved to release him, freeing the imp to teach some necessary lessons to the boys who had persecuted him.

Lawrence has a direct and timeless style that suits the unusual settings and other times about which she writes and helps to give credibility to the fantasy she creates.

Among her historical novels, *Mr. Robertson's Hundred Pounds* is a rich novel about a boy who travels to Europe in 1595 in pursuit of a thief. Although it deals with questions of loyalty, love, religious tolerance, artistic ambition, and political ideology, the exciting plot makes this a stimulating and gripping novel for the reader of 12 and older. *The Hawk of May* is a tale of Sir Gawain, tricked into a compromising situation in order to discredit King Arthur's court. He is given a year to solve a riddle and save his life, and there is a simple perfection in the solution to the riddle and the climax of the story. The book will appeal to teenagers and possibly adults as well, because of the philosophical undertones about behaviour, choice, and freedom. The Arthurian theme was continued for much younger readers, and perhaps less successfully, in *Merlin the Wizard.* Because this tells only those parts of King Arthur's story where Merlin is directly involved, it is somewhat fragmentary and episodic. Often the most interesting part is what happens *between* Merlin's appearances and the text is full of statements like, "From then on Merlin was seldom at court" or "Merlin disappeared about his own affairs."

In her later works Lawrence turned her skill to the short story form. *Beyond the Firelight* is a title in the Flying Carpets series of Macmillan which consists of folktales and fairytales rewritten to bridge the gap between picture books and longer stories. Skilfully written, but not written down, to combine a simplicity of style with the timeless quality of folktale, *Beyond the Firelight* tells four short tales of supernatural creatures invading ordinary life: the boggart who disrupts a farm and is finally—with great difficulty—evicted by the farmer; the three strange sisters who help a girl with an impossible task of spinning fleeces; the pathetic creature who is finally liberated from service to a young man by an act of kindness. *There and Back Again* is another collection of stories and is typical of her work in that she bases them on familiar fairytale characters but creates with them something original and with universal appeal.

One of her last published works, *Summer's End,* fittingly combines many strands of Lawrence's work and is told with the style, characterisation, and wit so characteristic of all her work. Subtitled *Stories of Ghostly Lovers,* the fantasy of the traditional tales is complemented by the down-to-earth presence of the innkeeper's three daughters to whom they are told. Lawrence's writing had a quiet, subtle excellence which may have failed to make the headlines or win awards but which was directed by her own strong vision. Many of her books were more truly original and thought-provoking than those of other better-known writers.

—Valerie Brinkley-Willsher

LAWSON, Robert

Nationality: American. **Born:** New York City, 4 October 1892. **Education:** Montclair High School, New Jersey; New York School of Fine and Applied Art, 1911-14. **Military Service:** American Expeditionary Forces, 40th Engineers Camouflage Section, during World War I. **Family:** Married Marie Abrams in 1922 (died 1956). **Career:** Freelance magazine illustrator, New York, 1914-17; commercial artist, 1919-30; from 1930 freelance book illustrator. Individual shows (etchings): New York, 1932, 1933. **Awards:** Society of American Etchers John Taylor Arms prize, 1931; American Library Association Caldecott Medal, 1941, and Newbery Medal, 1945. **Died:** 26 May 1957.

PUBLICATIONS FOR CHILDREN (ILLUSTRATED BY THE AUTHOR)

Fiction

Ben and Me. Boston, Little Brown, 1939.
They Were Strong and Good. New York, Viking Press, 1940.
I Discover Columbus. Boston, Little Brown, 1941; London, Harrap, 1943.
Rabbit Hill. New York, Viking Press, 1944; London, Harrap, 1947.
Mr. Wilmer. Boston, Little Brown, 1945; London, Muller, 1946.
Mr. Twigg's Mistake. Boston, Little Brown, 1947.
Robbut: A Tale of Tails. New York, Viking Press, 1948; London, Heinemann, 1949.
The Fabulous Flight. Boston, Little Brown, 1949.
Smeller Martin. New York, Viking Press, 1950.
McWhinney's Jaunt. Boston, Little Brown, 1951.
Edward, Hoppy and Joe. New York, Knopf, 1952.
Mr. Revere and I. Boston, Little Brown, 1953.
The Tough Winter. New York, Viking Press, 1954.
Captain Kidd's Cat. Boston, Little Brown, and London, Muller, 1956.
The Great Wheel. New York, Viking Press, 1957; London, Angus and Robertson, 1967.

Other

Dick Whittington and His Cat. New York, Limited Editions Club, 1949.

Editor, *Just for Fun: A Collection of Stories and Verses.* Chicago, Rand McNally, 1940.
Editor, *Watchwords of Liberty: A Pageant of American Quotations.* Boston, Little Brown, 1943.

PUBLICATIONS FOR ADULTS (ILLUSTRATED BY THE AUTHOR)

Other

Country Colic. Boston, Little Brown, 1944.
At That Time (autobiographical). New York, Viking Press, 1947; London, Heinemann, 1949.
Robert Lawson, Illustrator: A Selection of His Characteristic Illustrations, edited by Helen L. Jones. Boston, Little Brown, 1972.

*

Manuscript Collections: Free Library, Philadelphia; May Massee Collection, Emporia State University, Kansas.

Illustrator: *The Wonderful Adventures of Little Prince Toofat* by George Randolph Chester, 1922; *The Wee Men of Ballywooden,* 1930, *The Roving Lobster,* 1931, and *From the Horn of the Moon,* 1931, all by Arthur Mason; *The Unicorn with Silver Shoes* by Ella Young, 1932; *Peik* by Barbara Ring, 1932; *The Hurdy-Gurdy Man* by Margery Williams Bianco, 1933; *Haven's End* by John P. Marquand, 1933; *Treasure of the Isle of Mist* by W.W. Tarn, 1934; *Slim* by William Wister Haines, 1934; *The Golden Horseshoe* by Elizabeth Coatsworth, 1935; *Drums of Monmouth,* 1935, and *Miranda Is a Princess,* 1937, both by Emma Gelders Sterne; *The Story of Ferdinand,* 1936, *Wee Gillis,* 1938, *The Story of Simpson and Sampson,* 1941, and *Aesop's Fables,* 1941, all by Munro Leaf; *Seven Beads of Wampum* by Elizabeth Gale, 1936; *Betsy Ross* and *Francis Scott Key* both by Helen Dixon Bates, 1936; *Four and Twenty Blackbirds* edited by Helen Dean Fish, 1937; *The Prince and the Pauper* by Mark Twain, 1937; *The Story of Jesus for Young People* by Walter Russell Bowie, 1937; *Under the Tent of Sky,* 1937, and *Gaily We Parade,* 1940, both edited by John E. Brewton; *I Hear America Singing* by Ruth Barnes, 1937; *Wind of the Vikings* by Maribelle Cormack, 1937; *Swords and Statues* by Clarence Stratton, 1937; *Mr. Popper's Penguins* by Richard and Florence Atwater, 1938; *One Foot in Fairyland* by Eleanor Farjeon, 1938; *A Tale of Two Cities* by Charles Dickens, 1938; *Pilgrim's Progress* by John Bunyan, 1939; *Poo-Poo and the Dragons* by C.S. Forester, 1942; *Prince Prigio* by Andrew Lang, 1942; *The Crock of Gold* by James Stephens, 1942; *Adam of the Road* by Elizabeth Janet Gray, 1942; *The Little Woman Wanted Noise* by Val Teal, 1943; *The Shoelace Robin* by William Hall, 1945; *Greylock and the Robins* by Tom Robinson, 1946; *Mathematics for Success* by Mary A. Potter, 1952.

* * *

The only individual to win both the Newbery and Caldecott Medals, author-illustrator Robert Lawson holds a unique position in the history of American literature for children. His works are significant not only because of the recognition they received, but also because they support the notion that art both reflects and informs the values of an era.

A successful commercial artist and etcher, Lawson became internationally known during the 1930s as an illustrator of children's books following his collaboration with Munro Leaf for *The Story of Ferdinand* in 1936. He assumed the dual role of author-illustrator in 1939 with the publication of *Ben and Me,* first of four comic fantasies in which loquacious pets revealed the foibles of their notable owners—Benjamin Franklin, Christopher Columbus, Captain Kidd, and Paul Revere.

Whether illustrating his own texts or the texts of others, his drawings, characterized by traditional composition and an emphasis on meticulous draftsmanship, had the narrative quality which Barbara Bader in *American Picturebooks from Noah's Ark to The Beast Within* (1976) identifies as a particularly American attribute. This narrative quality appears in the tales he wrote as a strong sense of story conveyed through the forms, personae, and techniques associated with American humor. The two elements—words and pictures—merge to create a particular vision of American ideals and the American national character.

The four historical fantasies, for example, employ the talking beast motif, a familiar folklore device, but adapted to a convention of American humor, the comic monologue delivered by an apparently insignificant character who would be expected to celebrate rather than ridicule his betters. Although this same motif is apparent in the Newbery Medal-winning *Rabbit Hill* as well as in *The Tough Winter* and *Edward, Hoppy and Joe,* these are primarily stories of animal communities in the tradition of *The Wind in the Willows.* Yet the characters are basically American personalities, revealed not through lengthy description but through descriptive dialogue, complemented by explicit illustrations.

More obviously reflective of mid-20th-century American values are the Caldecott Medal-winning *They Were Strong and Good,* a picture book biography of Lawson's ancestors, and *The Great Wheel,* a period romance celebrating the ideal of America as the land of opportunity. Concurrently with these tributes to American virtues, however, Lawson satirized such American institutions as merchandising and tourism in *Mr. Wilmer, Mr. Twigg's Mistake,* and *The Fabulous Flight.* Similarly, *McWhinney's Jaunt,* often compared to the stories of Baron Munchausen, could also be interpreted as a humorous warning to gullible consumers; yet it is essentially a tall tale, American in style and tone, dominated by the angular figure of the Yankee peddler in 20th-century disguise.

Undoubtedly Lawson's delineation of the homely virtues thought to be particularly American and his use of literary and visual techniques considered characteristic elements in the American cultural tradition contributed much to his popularity in the 1940s and 1950s. From a later perspective, it has been noted that his treatment of minorities failed to transcend the sociological clichés of his time. Indeed, few of his human characters have the multi-dimensional personalities of his more memorable animal creations. Essentially a fabulist, he reflected the attitudes of his own era and yet, in his historical fantasies, notably *Ben and Me,* he managed to present for children an iconoclastic version of the traditions from which many of those attitudes were derived.

—Mary Mehlman Burns

LEAF, (Wilbur) Munro

Pseudonyms: John Calvert; Mun. **Nationality:** American. **Born:** Hamilton, Maryland, 4 December 1905. **Education:** University of Maryland, College Park, A.B. 1927; Harvard University, Cambridge, Massachusetts, M.A. 1931. **Military Service:** United States Army, 1942-46: Major. **Family:** Married Margaret Butler Pope in 1926; two sons. **Career:** Teacher and coach, Belmont Hill School, Massachusetts, 1929-30; teacher, Montgomery School, Wynnewood, Pennsylvania, 1931; reader, Bobbs Merrill, publishers, Indianapolis, 1932; editor and director, Frederick A. Stokes Company, publishers, New York, 1932-39; columnist ("Watchbirds"), *Ladies' Home Journal,* 1938-60. **Died:** 21 December 1976.

Publications for Children

Fiction

Lo, The Poor Indian (as Mun), illustrated by the author. New York, Leaf Mahony Seidel and Stokes, 1934.
Robert Francis Weatherbee, illustrated by the author. New York, Stokes, 1935; London, Chatto and Windus, 1936.
The Story of Ferdinand, illustrated by Robert Lawson. New York, Viking Press, 1936; London, Hamish Hamilton, 1937.
Noodle, illustrated by Ludwig Bemelmans. New York, Stokes, 1937; London, Hamish Hamilton, 1938.
Wee Gillis, illustrated by Robert Lawson. New York, Viking Press, and London, Hamish Hamilton, 1938.
John Henry Davis, illustrated by the author. New York, Stokes, 1940.
The Story of Simpson and Sampson, illustrated by Robert Lawson. New York, Viking Press, 1941; London, Warne, 1944.
Gordon the Goat, illustrated by the author. Philadelphia, Lippincott, 1944; London, Warne, 1947.
Gwendolyn the Goose (as John Calvert), illustrated by Garrett Price. New York, Random House, 1946.
Boo, Who Used to Be Scared of the Dark, illustrated by Frances Hunter. New York, Random House, 1948; as *Boo, The Boy Who Didn't Like the Dark,* London, Publicity Products, 1954.
Sam and the Superdroop, illustrated by the author. New York, Viking Press, 1948.
The Wishing Pool, illustrated by the author. Philadelphia, Lippincott, 1960.
Turnabout. Philadelphia, Lippincott, 1967.

Other (illustrated by the author)

Grammar Can Be Fun. New York, Stokes, 1934; London, Ward Lock, 1951.
Manners Can Be Fun. New York, Stokes, 1936; London, Hamish Hamilton, 1937; revised edition, Philadelphia, Lippincott, 1958.
Safety Can Be Fun. New York, Stokes, 1938; London, Ward Lock, 1951; revised edition, Philadelphia, Lippincott, 1961.
Listen, Little Girl, Before You Come to New York, illustrated by Dick Rose. New York, Stokes, 1938.
The Watchbirds: A Picture Book of Behavior. New York, Stokes, 1939; London, Warne, 1945.
Your Library and Some People You Don't Want in It. New York, Wilson, 1939.
Fair Play. New York, Stokes, 1939; London, Warne, 1959.
More Watchbirds. New York, Stokes, 1940.
Fly Away, Watchbird! New York, Stokes, 1941.
Aesop's Fables, illustrated by Robert Lawson. New York, Heritage Press, 1941.
A War-Time Handbook for Young Americans. Philadelphia, Stokes, 1942.
Health Can Be Fun. Philadelphia, Stokes, 1943; London, Warne, 1944.
3 and 30 Watchbirds. Philadelphia, Lippincott, 1944.
Let's Do Better. Philadelphia, Lippincott, 1945; London, Warne, 1947.
How to Behave and Why. Philadelphia, Lippincott, 1946.
Arithmetic [History, Geography, Reading, Science] Can Be Fun. Philadelphia, Lippincott, 5 vols., 1949-60; London, Ward Lock, 5 vols., 1951-60; revised edition of *Geography Can Be Fun,* Lippincott, 1962.
Lucky You. Philadelphia, Lippincott, 1955.
Three Promises to You. Philadelphia, Lippincott, 1957.
Being an American Can Be Fun. Philadelphia, Lippincott, 1964.
Who Cares? I Do. Philadelphia, Lippincott, 1971.
Metric Can Be Fun. Philadelphia, Lippincott, 1976.

Publications for Adults

Other

You and Psychiatry, with William C. Menninger. New York, Scribner, 1948.

*

Illustrator: *The Danger of Hiding Our Heads* by the Committee on the Present Danger, 1951.

* * *

Munro Leaf was the author and illustrator of many stories for children—but only two of them are popular today. Of his slighter, ephemeral materials, such as the various *Watchbirds,* there is little to be said other than that they were suited to the tenor of their times, and were widely read, thanks to the *Ladies' Home Journal,* of which they were a feature between 1938 and 1960. Most of his other children's titles were more or less didactic and forgettable: he had a good-natured but inexorable urge to preach, on manners, self-improvement, patriotism, conformity. Some of the subjects he illustrated for the...*Can Be Fun* group, such as *Manners, Metrics,* and *Safety,* neither are nor require to be *Fun;* they are merely necessary. But for all that, twice in his career, Leaf struck a vein of purest gold, and producing two indisputable classics of children's literature isn't after all a bad score.

First and best is the well-loved *The Story of Ferdinand.* Ferdinand first appears as a large-eyed calf, gentle, sweet-natured, rather a worry to his loving mother for his failure to make a place for himself among the bovine roughnecks huffing and chuffing about the pasture. Ferdinand will have none of it. He likes to sit just quietly, by himself, smelling the flowers under his favourite cork tree. Time passes. Ferdinand and the rest are now stout young stock, eligible to be selected by the scouts from Madrid for that supreme honour—the bullring! The other bulls are anxiously showing off, running, leaping, butting, and snorting. Not Ferdinand. Let those who wish seek fame and glory; he wants none of it. Alas, at the worst possible moment, Ferdinand is stung by a bee in a *very* sensitive spot, and his subsequent antics arouse the admiration of the scouts. Here, they think, is a *fighter!* He is chosen, taken away to the city, and soon comes the moment of truth. Ferdinand must face the fierce, if frightened, banderilleros, picadores, and last of all, the gallant matador. Ferdinand sees nothing, is conscious of nothing, but the flowers in the lovely senoritas' hair. As before, as always, he sits quietly to smell the flowers...and they have to take Ferdinand home again. We leave him, perfectly content, under his favourite cork tree, the perfect ending for the hero of one of the most charming of all animal stories.

Wee Gillis has not quite the same universal appeal, but is in its way irresistible in its quirky charm and good humour. Wee Gillis is a half-breed of sorts: his mother was Lowland Scots, his father Highland. He spends his time alternately herding cattle in the Lowlands and stalking stags in the Highlands; but when he comes to years of discretion, both sides of his family insist that he must decide, once and for always, whether he will be High or Low. Gillis is torn between the two sides of the raging family argument, and finally goes off to make his momentous decision. As he ponders, he encounters a dejected man, who has constructed the biggest bagpipes in all of Scotland, and now hasn't got enough wind to play them. Gillis has all the lung power of a lad who has called cattle home through the Lowland mist, and who had held his breath for long minutes while stalking the wary Highland stag. He can blow the pipes, and he does. His problem is solved. He will live just between the Highlands and the Lowlands, and he will be the most famous piper in all of Scotland. Would that all problems could be so happily solved.

—Joan McGrath

LEE, Dennis (Beynon)

Nationality: Canadian. **Born:** Toronto, Ontario, 31 August 1939. **Education:** University of Toronto, B.A. 1962, M.A. in English 1964. **Family:** Married 1) Donna Youngblut in 1961 (divorced 1972), two daughters and one son; 2) Susan Ruth Perly in 1985. **Career:** Full-time writer. Taught at Victoria College, University of Toronto, 1964-67, and Rochdale College, Toronto, 1967-69; artist-in-residence, Trent University, Peterborough, Ontario, 1975. Editor, House of Anansi Press, Toronto, 1967-72; consulting editor, Macmillan of Canada, publishers, Toronto, 1973-78; poetry consultant, McClelland and Stewart, publishers, Toronto, 1981-84. Songwriter, *Fraggle Rock* television programme, Canadian Broadcasting Corporation, 1982-86. **Awards:** Governor-General's award, for verse, 1973; Canadian Library Association Book of the Year Medal, 1975, 1978; Ruth Schwartz award, 1978; Philips Information Systems prize, 1985; Vicky Metcalf award, 1986. **Address:** c/o WCA, 94 Harbord St., Toronto, Ontario, M5S 1G6, Canada.

Publications for Children

Fiction

The Ordinary Bath, illustrated by Jon McKee. Toronto, McClelland and Stewart, 1979.

Poetry

Wiggle to the Laundromat, illustrated by Charles Pachter. Toronto, New Press, 1970.
Alligator Pie, illustrated by Frank Newfeld. Toronto, Macmillan, 1974; Boston, Houghton Mifflin, 1975.
Nicholas Knock and Other People, illustrated by Frank Newfeld. Toronto, Macmillan, 1974; Boston, Houghton Mifflin, 1977.
Garbage Delight, illustrated by Frank Newfeld. Toronto, Macmillan, 1977; Boston, Houghton Mifflin, 1978.
Jelly Belly, illustrated by Juan Wijngaard. Toronto, Macmillan, and London, Blackie, 1983.
Lizzy's Lion, illustrated by Marie-Louise Gay. Toronto, Stoddart, and London, Hodder and Stoughton, 1984.
The Dennis Lee Big Book, illustrated by Barb Klunder. Toronto, Gage, 1985.
The Ice Cream Store. New York, Scholastic, 1992.
Riffs. London, Ontario, Brick Books, 1993.

Recordings: *Alligator Pie and Other Poems,* music by Don Heckman, Caedmon, 1978; *Fraggle Rock,* music by Philip Balsam, Muppet Music, 1984.

Publications for Adults

Poetry

Kingdom of Absence. Toronto, Anansi, 1967.
Civil Elegies. Toronto, Anansi, 1968.
Civil Elegies and Other Poems. Toronto, Anansi, 1972.
Not Abstract Harmonies But. Vancouver and San Francisco, Kanchenjunga, 1974.
The Death of Harold Ladoo. Vancouver and San Francisco, Kanchenjunga, 1976.
Miscellany. Privately printed, 1977.
The Gods. Vancouver and San Francisco, Kanchenjunga, 1978.
The Gods (collection). Toronto, McClelland and Stewart, 1979.
The Difficulty of Living on Other Planets: An Adult Entertainment. Toronto, Macmillan, 1987.

Other

Notes on Rochdale. Ottawa, Canadian Union of Students, 1967(?).
Savage Fields: An Essay in Literature and Cosmology. Toronto, Anansi, 1977.

Editor, with R.A. Charlesworth, *An Anthology of Verse.* Toronto, Oxford University Press, 1964.
Editor, with R.A. Charlesworth, *The Second Century Anthologies of Verse, Book 2.* Toronto, Oxford University Press, 1967.
Editor, with Howard Adelman, *The University Game.* Toronto, Anansi, 1968.
Editor, *T.O. Now: The Young Toronto Poets.* Toronto, Anansi, 1968.
Editor, *The New Canadian Poets 1970-85.* Toronto, McClelland and Stewart, 1985.

*

Manuscript Collections: Fisher Rare Book Room, University of Toronto.

Critical Studies: *Task of Passion: Dennis Lee at Mid-Career,* edited by Donna Bennett, Russell Brown, and Karen Mulhallen, Toronto, Descant, 1982.

Dennis Lee comments:

I can sum up the concerns of my children's poetry in two words: "roots" and "play." Beyond that, it sinks or swims on its own merits.

* * *

The key to Dennis Lee's poetry, both juvenile and adult, is that he is Canadian. Lee's Canadianness has two main aspects: first, his awareness of Canada as a unique place, his homeland; second, his awareness of Canada's colonial status, from which she must be liberated. In his children's poetry, these two aspects have their equivalents in the concepts of "roots" and "play." The former means literature both rooted in a particular time and place, and also articulating to the reader his own roots. The latter means literature which, in Lee's words, tries "to reanimate repressed feelings," which is emotionally released, free and joyous, full of play.

It was in response to these impulses that Lee's children's verse was written. Explaining its genesis in the epilogue to *Alligator Pie,* he writes that, when reading *Mother Goose* to his children, he began to realize the distance between the nursery rhymes and contemporary Canadian reality: "The details of *Mother Goose*—the wassails and Dobbins and pipers and pence—had become exotic; children loved them, but they were no longer home ground." At the same time, Lee recognized that Canadians "are a colonial people; leaving aside the political and economic aspects of the thing for now, we have always been a colony of the imagination, first of England and France, latterly of the United States." Lee's answer was to liberate Canadian children from the colonial mentality by creating poems rooted in the things that are part of a Canadian child's inner and outer life. And in doing so he found himself becoming liberated, regaining the ability to play.

Lee has published several volumes of children's poetry. Nursery rhymes (for preschoolers) appear in *Alligator Pie,* which includes poems playing with incantatory Canadian place names ("Tongue Twister," "Kahshe or Chicoutimi"), activity songs ("Bouncing Song," "Rattlesnake Skipping Song"), and short word-play poems ("Skyscraper," "Willoughby Wallaby Woo"). Such works contain much pure play; alliteration, onomatopoeia, rhyme, and rhythm are so strongly stressed that the words often function as music. A few poems in the latter half of the book are more for children of school-entering age; they are longer and often more serious, sensitively exploring the child's inner world ("The Special Person," "The Friend").

For the 7-10 age group, the poems in *Nicholas Knock and Other People* are most appropriate. Most of them are longer, more complex in thought, and sometimes deal with such specialized topics as the Spadina Expressway or the Mackenzie Rebellion of 1837 (both, incidentally, anti-authoritarian people's struggles). One prominent subject is the child's imaginative world ("Mister Hoobody," "The Thing"), sometimes under threat from the adult "real" world ("Nicholas Knock"). Other poems deal with the child's reaction to close relationships ("Going Up North," "With My Foot in My Mouth"); these pieces—while rooted in a sense of self—express affection clearly though indirectly. The kind of black humour that sets children chortling is also given effective expression ("Oilcan Harry"). Play, of course, has its place in all the poems; at times, as in the Ookpik poems, it even becomes the theme, a liberating force. Lee describes Ookpik as "another of the vital figures that challenge how we are. He's a dancer, an embodiment of pure lyricism: harmless, pointless, irrepressible... There are four Ookpik poems, and by the last one he has become a kind of totemic figure or tutelary god for the books. The theme of play and the theme of roots fuse in that poem, as they often do." Ookpik: the "tutelary god" for the books. How does the last Ookpik poem end? "Ookpik,/Ookpick/By your Grace,/Help us/ Live in/Our own/Space." Lee's final word, then, is directed at the need for Canadians to inhabit—both physically and imaginatively—their own space, their country.

Garbage Delight, illustrated by Frank Newfeld, is very similar in design and content to the previous two books. Unfortunately, in spite of some fine individual poems, it does not achieve as high a standard, overall, as its predecessors. The poetry is more uneven in quality; the prospective audience falls into a wider, less coherent age range; and the humour, rhyme, and rhythm are sometimes more strained. Thematically, there is less reference to political events and greater focus on one's self, including the joys afforded by play and eating—activities which literally and symbolically assert one's own imagination and taste. Technically, parody ("The Big Blue Frog and the Dirty Flannel Dog") and spoonerism ("The Big Molice Pan and the Bertie Dumb") are more apparent. Particularly prominent are Newfeld-Lee "insider" jokes, such as the cartoon strip depicting the pair, the pictures of Lee accompanying "Goofus," etc. Unfortunately, sometimes Newfeld's pictures in this volume limit the full expression of the exuberant play that Lee's words suggest. Thus Lee's "Bloody Bill" is a gory, messy tale, not adequately depicted by Newfeld's staid, neat illustrations. Similarly, Lee's "Garbage Delight" tells of a jumbled, indescribable mixture of everything gooey, sweet, and delicious, not Newfeld's ordered assortment of conventional sweets.

Such discrepancies between illustration and text are eliminated in *The Ordinary Bath.* Here Jon McKee's illustrations superbly parallel the overflowing imaginative exuberance of Lee's playful protagonist, as the child's imagination transforms his ordinary bathtub world into an extraordinary one, peopled with colorful monsters—friendly and otherwise—that pour out of the tap and join in his play. Yet even while his imagination exults in glorious freedom, the child knows its expression must be reconciled with the demands of the real world—in this case his mother's requirements that the floor be kept dry and the bath end at a certain time. The resolution of this tension, through harmonious written and pictorial techniques, provides an artful balancing of the two worlds, depicting the limits of play at the point where freedom becomes anarchy.

Lizzy's Lion is a much lesser book. In 14 quatrains superimposed on 14 double-page illustrations by Marie-Louise Gay, the narrative tells of a rotten robber who, attempting to purloin Lizzy's piggy bank, encounters her pet lion and becomes the lion's lunch. Unfortunately there is a lack of variation from picture to picture which, added to the skimpiness of the text, suggests that both author and illustrator stretched their material too far.

In 1983 Lee extended his poetic range to what he calls "foetus literature": poems written for babies and young preschoolers. In *Jelly Belly* the sound and rhythm of words are at least as marked as in *Alligator Pie,* though the more recent volume is less varied and invigorating overall. However, there are some excellent activity poems ("Three Tickles," "The Army Went A-Marching"), and witty word-play is evident ("There Was An Old Lady"). Juan Wijngaard's superb illustrations admirably complement and extend the text. Beautifully grotesque, free, imaginative, humorous: they are very appealing to children and add much to the book's continuity, resonance, and integrity.

For the other end of the age spectrum Lee has published *The Difficulty of Living on Other Planets,* subtitled *An Adult Entertainment.* Though this collection uses many of the rhymes and rhythms of his children's poetry, the tone is different: sometimes more overtly nostalgic, occasionally more mystical, and often more cynical and satirical. A few of the poems are revisions of ones in *Nicholas Knock.* The cat in "The Cat and the Wizard," for example, becomes a "She"—adding a sexual suggestiveness to her relationship with the wizard. In "Nicholas Knock" some stanzas are added, others removed—increasing the mystical element. However, the collection as a whole is neither as compelling as Lee's other adult books nor as captivating as his better illustrated children's ones.

Overall, Lee's work represents the best in children's poetry; it dances off the page and involves the reader in its world.

—John Robert Sorfleet

LE FEUVRE, Amy

Pseudonym: Mary Thurston Dodge. **Nationality:** British. **Born:** Blackheath, London. **Career:** Wrote serials for *Sunday at Home* and *Quiver* magazines, London. **Died:** 29 April 1929.

Publications for Children

Fiction

Eric's Good News (published anonymously). London, Religious Tract Society, 1894; Chicago, Revell, 1896.

Probable Sons (published anonymously). London, Religious Tract Society, 1895; Chicago, Revell, 1897.

Teddy's Button! (published anonymously). London, Religious Tract Society, and Chicago, Revell, 1896.

Dwell Deep; or, Hilda Thorne's Life Story. London, Religious Tract Society, and Chicago, Revell, 1896.

On the Edge of a Moor (published anonymously). London, Religious Tract Society, and Chicago, Revell, 1897.

Odd (published anonymously). London, Religious Tract Society, 1897; as *The Odd One,* Chicago, Revell, 1897.

A Puzzling Pair, illustrated by Eveline Lance. London, Religious Tract Society, and Chicago, Revell, 1898.

His Big Opportunity, illustrated by Sydney Cowell. London, Hodder and Stoughton, and Chicago, Revell, 1898.

Bulbs and Blossoms, illustrated by Eveline Lance. London, Religious Tract Society, and Chicago, Revell, 1898.

A Thoughtless Seven. London, Religious Tract Society, and Chicago, Revell, 1898.

The Carved Cupboard. London, Religious Tract Society, and New York, Dodd Mead, 1899.

Bunny's Friends. London, Religious Tract Society, and Chicago, Revell, 1899.

What the Wind Did. Chicago, Revell, 1899.

Roses, illustrated by Sydney Cowell. London, Hodder and Stoughton, and New York, Ketcham, 1899.

Legend-Led. London, Religious Tract Society, and New York, Dodd Mead, 1899.

Brownie, illustrated by W.H.C. Groome. London, Hodder and Stoughton, and New York, American Tract Society, 1900.

Olive Tracy. London, Hodder and Stoughton, 1900; New York, Dodd Mead, 1901.

A Cherry Tree. London, Hodder and Stoughton, 1901; as *Cherry, The Cucumber That Bore Fruit,* Chicago, Revell, 1901.

Heather's Mistress. London, Religious Tract Society, and New York, Crowell, 1901.

A Daughter of the Sea. London, Hodder and Stoughton, and New York, Crowell, 1902.

Odd Made Even, illustrated by Harold Copping. London, Religious Tract Society, 1902.

The Making of a Woman. London, Hodder and Stoughton, 1903.

Two Tramps. London, Hodder and Stoughton, and Chicago, Revell, 1903.

Jill's Red Bag, illustrated by Alfred Pearse. London, Religious Tract Society, and Chicago, Revell, 1903.

His Little Daughter. London, Religious Tract Society, 1904.

A Little Maid. London, Religious Tract Society, 1904.

Bridget's Quarter Deck. London, Hodder and Stoughton, 1905.

The Buried Ring, illustrated by Gordon Browne. London, Hodder and Stoughton, 1905.
The Children's Morning Message, illustrated by Jenny Wylie. London, Hodder and Stoughton, 1905.
Christina and the Boys, illustrated by Gordon Browne. London, Hodder and Stoughton, 1906.
The Mender, illustrated by W. Rainey. London, Religious Tract Society, 1906.
Miss Lavender's Boy and Other Sketches. London, Religious Tract Society, 1906.
Robin's Heritage, illustrated by Gordon Browne. London, Hodder and Stoughton, 1907.
Number Twa! London, Religious Tract Society, 1907.
The Chateau by the Lake. London, Hodder and Stoughton, 1907.
A Bit of Rough Road, illustrated by Percy Tarrant. London, Religious Tract Society, 1908.
Me and Nobbles. London, Religious Tract Society, 1908.
Us, and Our Donkey, illustrated by W.H.C. Groome. London, Religious Tract Society, 1909.
A Country Corner. London, Cassell, 1909.
His Birthday: A Christmas Sketch, illustrated by Eveline Lance. London, Religious Tract Society, 1909.
Joyce and the Rambler. London, Hodder and Stoughton, 1910.
A Little Listener, illustrated by W.H.C. Groome. London, Religious Tract Society, 1910.
Us, and Our Empire, illustrated by W.H.C. Groome. London, Religious Tract Society, 1911.
Tested! Philadelphia, Heidelberg Press, 1911; London, Partridge, 1912.
Four Gates. London and New York, Cassell, 1912.
Laddie's Choice, illustrated by W.H.C. Groome. London, Religious Tract Society, 1912; as Mary Thurston Dodge, New York, Dodd Mead, 1912.
Some Builders. London, Cassell, 1913.
Her Husband's Property. London, Religious Tract Society, 1913.
Herself and Her Boy. London, Cassell, 1914.
Harebell's Friend. London, Religious Tract Society, 1914.
Daddy's Sword. London, Hodder and Stoughton, 1915.
Joan's Handful. London, Cassell, 1915.
Dudley Napier's Daughters. London, Morgan and Scott, 1916.
A Madcap Family; or, Sybil's Home. London, Partridge, 1916.
Us, and Our Charge. London, Religious Tract Society, 1916.
Tomina in Retreat. London, Religious Tract Society, 1917.
Joy Cometh in the Morning, illustrated by Harold Copping. London, Religious Tract Society, 1917.
Dreamikins. London, Religious Tract Society, 1918.
A Happy Woman. London, Religious Tract Society, 1918.
Terrie's Moorland Home. London, Morgan and Scott, 1918.
Little Miss Moth. London, Partridge, 1919.
The Chisel. London, Religious Tract Society, 1919.
The Discovery of Damaris. London, Religious Tract Society, 1920.
Martin and Margot, illustrated by Gordon Browne. London, Religious Tract Society, 1921.
Oliver and the Twins, illustrated by Gordon Browne. London, Religious Tract Society, 1922.
The Children of the Crescent, illustrated by Arthur Twiddle. London, Religious Tract Society, 1923.
The Little Discoverers, illustrated by M.D. Johnston. London and New York, Oxford University Press, 1924.
My Heart's in the Highlands. London, Ward Lock, 1924.
A Girl and Her Ways. London, Ward Lock, 1925.
Granny's Fairyland. London, Sheldon Press, 1925.
Noel's Christmas Tree. London, Ward Lock, 1926.
Three Little Girls. London, Shaw, 1926.
Andy Man: A Story of Two Simple Souls. London, Pickering and Inglis, 1927.
Jock's Inheritance. London, Ward Lock, 1927.
Cousins in Devon. London, Religious Tract Society, 1928.
Adrienne. London, Ward Lock, 1928.
Alick's Corner. London, Religious Tract Society, 1929.
Around a Sundial, and Dicky's Brother. London, Pickering and Inglis, 1929.
Her Kingdom: A Story of the Westmorland Fells. London, Ward Lock, 1929.
Under a Cloud. London, Ward Lock, 1930.
Rosebuds: Choice and Original Short Stories. London, Pickering and Inglis, 1931.
A Strange Courtship. London, Ward Lock, 1931.
Mimosa's Field. London, Lutterworth Press, 1953.

Other

The Most Wonderful Story in the World: A Life of Christ for Little Children. London, Hodder and Stoughton, and Chicago, Revell, 1922; as *Little Tots' Story of Jesus,* Revell, 1928.
Chats with Children; or, Pearls for Young People Strung from the Word of Truth. London, Pickering and Inglis, 1926.
Stories of the Lord Jesus, with Lettice Bell, illustrated by E.S. Hardy. London, Shaw, 1933.

* * *

Amy Le Feuvre was one of the Religious Tract Society's more prolific authors. Her popularity, which began in the 1890s, was maintained through the first three decades of this century, and her writing was typical of the new approach of the evangelical writers to the young reader. The stern style of the earlier 19th century was now completely outmoded. In *A Puzzling Pair* she wrote of the "hell-fire" and "day of wrath" type of preaching as something marvellously old-fashioned. The street arab story, which had been the standard type of Sunday leisure reading since the late 1860s, was overworked. The new hero of the evangelical story was the artless child who brought a gospel message of love to the adult. There was much emphasis on "the strong and steadfast faith of childhood." As one of her characters remarked, "They live so near to the throne of the Eternal One that they draw those with whom they live to do the same."

Like many of her contemporaries she was particularly fond of the "quaint" child, "old-fashioned," with delicate health, a type modelled upon Paul Dombey. With their innocent prattle these children melted the cold, stern hearts of elders who had too long been preoccupied with material things. Her most popular story in this style was *Probable Sons,* in which the fragile, curly-haired little Milly—whose mispronunciation of "prodigal sons" is responsible for the title—brings her Uncle Edward back to Christ.

In a more robust manner, she wrote tales of family life, specializing in the outwardly naughty child, the odd one out, whose motives are consistently misunderstood by the adults. She made it clear that, unlike her evangelical predecessors, she thought that absent-minded disobedience and imaginative naughtiness were attractive childish traits and could well go hand in hand with an understanding of heavenly things. This is the theme of *Teddy's*

Button!, perhaps her best-known story; Teddy, whose passionate wish is to follow in his father's footsteps and be a soldier, is persuaded first to join Christ's army and fight the bad elements in his nature. The Lutterworth Press (successors to the Religious Tract Society) have kept some of Le Feuvre's tales in print and these are still used as gift books in mission schools abroad.

—Gillian Avery

L'ENGLE, Madeleine

Nationality: American. **Born:** Madeleine L'Engle Camp, New York City, 29 November 1918. **Education:** Smith College, Northampton, Massachusetts, A.B. (honors) 1941; New School for Social Research, New York, 1941-42; Columbia University, New York, 1960-61. **Family:** Married Hugh Franklin in 1946 (died 1986); two daughters and one son. **Career:** Worked in the theatre, New York, 1941-47; member of the faculty, University of Indiana, Bloomington, summers 1965-66, 1971; writer-in-residence, Ohio State University, Columbus, 1970, and University of Rochester, New York, 1972. Since 1960 teacher, St. Hilda's and St. Hugh's School, New York; since 1966 librarian, Cathedral of St. John the Divine, New York; since 1970 president, Crosswicks Ltd., New York; since 1976 Lecturer, Wheaton College, Illinois; since 1976 member, Board of Directors, Authors League Foundation; president, Authors Guild of America. **Awards:** American Library Association Newbery Medal, 1963; University of Southern Mississippi award, 1978; Smith College Medal, 1980, and Sophie award, 1984; American Book award, for paperback, 1980; *Logos* award, for adult non-fiction, 1981; Catholic Library Association Regina Medal, 1984; National Council of Teachers of English ALAN award, 1986. **Agent:** Robert Lescher, 67 Irving Place, New York, New York 10009. **Address:** Crosswicks, Goshen, Connecticut 06756, U.S.A.

Publications for Children

Fiction

The Small Rain (for adults). New York, Vanguard Press, 1945; London, Secker and Warburg, 1955; abridged edition (for children), as *Prelude,* New York, Vanguard Press, 1968; London, Gollancz, 1972.
And Both Were Young. New York, Lothrop, 1949.
Camilla Dickinson. New York, Simon and Schuster, 1951; London, Secker and Warburg, 1952; as *Camilla,* New York, Crowell, 1965.
Meet the Austins. New York, Vanguard Press, 1960; London, Collins, 1966.
Madeleine L'Engle's Time Quartet. New York, Dell, 1987.
  A Wrinkle in Time. New York, Farrar Straus, 1962; London, Constable, 1963.
  A Wind in the Door. New York, Farrar Straus, 1973; London, Methuen, 1975.
  A Swiftly Tilting Planet. New York, Farrar Straus, 1978; London, Souvenir Press, 1980.
  Many Waters. New York, Farrar Straus, 1986.
The Moon by Night. New York, Farrar Straus, 1963.
The Twenty-Four Days Before Christmas, illustrated by Inga. New York, Farrar Straus, 1964.
The Arm of the Starfish. New York, Farrar Straus, 1965.
The Young Unicorns. New York, Farrar Straus, 1968; London, Gollancz, 1969.
Dance in the Desert, illustrated by Symeon Shimin. New York, Farrar Straus, and London, Longman, 1969.
Dragons in the Waters. New York, Farrar Straus, 1976.
  The Time Trilogy (*A Wrinkle in Time, A Wind in the Door, A Swiftly Tilting Planet*). New York, Farrar Straus, 1979.
A Ring of Endless Light. New York, Farrar Straus, 1980.
The Anti-Muffins, illustrated by Gloria Ortiz. New York, Pilgrim Press, 1980.
The Sphinx at Dawn: Two Stories, illustrated by Vivian Berger. New York, Seabury Press, 1982.
A House Like a Lotus. New York, Farrar Straus, 1984.
An Acceptable Time. New York, Farrar Straus, 1989.
The Glorious Impossible, illustrated by Giotto. New York, Simon and Schuster, 1990.
Troubling a Star. New York, Farrar, Straus, Giroux, 1994.
A Live Coal in the Sea. New York, Farrar, Straus, and Giroux, 1996.

Plays

18 Washington Square, South (produced Northampton, Massachusetts, 1940). Boston, Baker, 1944.
How Now Brown Cow, with Robert Hartung (produced New York, 1949).
The Journey with Jonah, illustrated by Leonard Everett Fisher (produced New York, 1970). New York, Farrar Straus, 1967.

Poetry

Lines Scribbled on an Envelope and Other Poems. New York, Farrar Straus, 1969.

Other

Everyday Prayers, illustrated by Lucile Butel. New York, Morehouse Barlow, 1974.
Prayers for Sunday, illustrated by Lucile Butel. New York, Morehouse Barlow, 1974.
Ladder of Angels: Scenes from the Bible Illustrated by Children of the World. New York, Seabury Press, 1979.
Anytime Prayers, photography by Maria Rooney. Wheaton, Illinois, Harold Shaw Publishers, 1994.
Miracle on 10th Street, and Other Christmas Writings. Wheaton, Illinois, Harold Shaw Publishers, 1998.

Publications for Adults

Novels

Ilsa. New York, Vanguard Press, 1946.
A Winter's Love. Philadelphia, Lippincott, 1957.
The Love Letters. New York, Farrar Straus, 1966.
The Other Side of the Sun. New York, Farrar Straus, 1971; London, Eyre Methuen, 1972.

A Severed Wasp. New York, Farrar Straus, 1982; London, Faber, 1984.
Certain Women. New York, Farrar Straus, 1992.
The Other Side of the Sun: A Novel. by Madeleine L'Engle. Wheaton, Illinois, Harold Shaw Publishers, 1996.

Poetry

Weather of the Heart. Wheaton, Illinois, Shaw, 1978.
A Cry Like a Bell. Wheaton, Illinois, Shaw, 1987.

Other

A Circle of Quiet. New York, Farrar Straus, 1972.
The Summer of the Great-Grandmother. New York, Farrar Straus, 1974.
The Irrational Season. New York, Seabury Press, 1977.
Walking on Water: Reflections on Faith and Art. Wheaton, Illinois, Shaw, 1980; Tring, Hertfordshire, Lion, 1982.
And It Was Good: Reflections on Beginnings. Wheaton, Illinois, Shaw, 1983.
Dare to Be Creative. Washington, D.C., Library of Congress, 1984.
Trailing Clouds of Glory: Spiritual Values in Children's Books. Philadelphia, Westminster Press, 1985.
A Stone for a Pillow. Wheaton, Illinois, Shaw, 1986.
Two-Part Invention: The Story of a Marriage. New York, Farrar Straus, 1988.
Sold Into Egypt: Joseph's Journey into Human Being. Wheaton, Illinois, Shaw, 1989.
The Rock That Is Higher: Story as Truth. Wheaton, Illinois, Shaw, 1993.
With Carole F. Chase, *Glimpses of Grace: Daily Thoughts and Reflections.* San Francisco, HarperSanFrancisco, 1996.
With Luci Shaw, *Wintersong: Christmas Readings.* Wheaton, Illinois, Harold Shaw, 1996.
Penguins + Golden Calves: Icons and Idols. Wheaton, Illinois, Harold Shaw Publishers, 1996.
Mothers & Daughters, photography by Maria Rooney. Wheaton, Illinois, Harold Shaw Publishers, 1997.
With Luci Shaw, *Friends for the Journey: Two Extraordinary Women Celebrate Friendships Made and Sustained through the Seasons of Life.* Ann Arbor, Michigan, Vine Books/Servant Publications, 1997.
Bright Evening Star: Mystery of the Incarnation. Wheaton, Illinois, H. Shaw, 1997.
My Own Small Place: Developing the Writing Life. Wheaton, Illinois, H. Shaw Publishers, 1998.
A Winter's Love. Wheaton, Illinois, Harold Shaw Publishers, 1998.

Editor, with William B. Green, *Spirit and Light: Essays in Historical Theology.* New York, Seabury Press, 1976.

*

Media Adaptations: *A Wrinkle in Time* was recorded by Newbery Award Records, 1972, and adapted as a filmstrip with cassette by Miller-Brody, 1974; *A Wind in the Door* was recorded and adapted as a filmstrip with cassette by Miller-Brody; *Camilla* was recorded as a cassette by Listening Library; *A Ring of Endless Light* was recorded and adapted as a filmstrip with cassette by Random House. *And Both Were Young, The Arm of the Starfish, Meet the Austins, The Moon by Night, A Wrinkle in Time,* and *The Young Unicorns* have been adapted into Braille; *The Arm of the Starfish, Camilla, Dragons in the Waters, A Wind in the Door,* and *A Wrinkle in Time* have been adapted into talking books; *The Summer of the Great-Grandmother* is also available on cassette.

Manuscript Collections: Wheaton College, Illinois; Kerlan Collection, University of Minnesota, Minneapolis; de Grummond Collection, University of Southern Mississippi, Hattiesburg.

Biography: Entry in *More Junior Authors,* New York, H.W. Wilson, 1963; essay in *Authors and Artists for Young Adults,* Volume 1, Detroit, Gale, 1989; essay in *Speaking for Ourselves: Autobiographical Sketches by Notable Authors of Books for Young Adults,* Volume 1, compiled and edited by Donald R. Gallo, National Council of Teachers of English, 1990; essay in *Something about the Author Autobiography Series,* Volume 15, Detroit, Gale, 1993.

Critical Studies: *Children's Literature Review,* Detroit, Gale, Volume 1, 1976, Volume 14, 1988. *Contemporary Literary Criticism,* Volume 12, Detroit, Gale, 1980; *The Swiftly Tilting Worlds of Madeleine L'Engle: Essays in Her Honor,* edited by Luci Shaw, Wheaton, Illinois, Harold Shaw Publishers, 1998.

Madeleine L'Engle comments:

When I am asked why I write at least half of my books for children, especially since my first books were for adults, I answer, truthfully, that when I have something to say which I think is going to be too difficult for adults, I write it in a book for children. Children are excited by new ideas; they have not yet closed the doors and windows of their imaginations. Provided the story is a good story, and makes them want to keep turning the pages, nothing is too difficult for children. Most of my children's novels at least border on fantasy, and the response from children in hundreds of letters keeps me constantly stimulated. It is the children themselves who help me to move on from one book to the next.

* * *

A Wrinkle in Time, awarded the Newbery Medal of Honor three decades ago, both continues to be read by youngsters and readily stands up under critical scrutiny. Madeline L'Engle's finest novel is, first of all, a realistic family novel. The Murrys are a closely knit, affectionate, supportive, and intelligent family; and these qualities are both plausible and attractive because they derive from the family's behavior and words. The Murrys' goodness, in particular, is not innate or miraculously accounted for, but earned through hard choices and the pain of self-sacrifice. *A Wrinkle in Time* is also a serious novel that unabashedly investigates the nature of good and evil and points out how the decisions and actions of individuals contribute to or detract from, whether intended or not, society's moral and ethical well-being.

A Wrinkle in Time is also a young adult novel that honestly portrays its protagonists, Meg Murry and Calvin O'Keefe, in situations typically experienced by many young people—anxiety over physical appearance, unsettled parental relationships, peer and sibling rivalries, and the search for identity. The novel refuses to pander to the biases of the young reader or offer easy solutions. Instead, characters and, hence, readers are encouraged to look beyond themselves and their peers for answers. The characterization and prominence of Meg, incidentally, are happy anticipations of the non-sexist female protagonist of today. Finally, because *A Wrinkle in Time* features a futuristic mode of space travel and speculates about possible life elsewhere in the universe, it is science fiction. As such, it is a historically important book since it is the first juvenile SF novel admitted into the mainstream of children's literature and also honored in a significant way—thus heralding juvenile SF's coming of age.

In *Meet the Austins,* L'Engle anticipated the form and achievement of her masterpiece, *A Wrinkle in Time.* The Austins are also a warmly affectionate and close family whose obvious goodness is offset by enough failings to make the family believable and likeable. Preadolescent Vicky Austin, the main character, is an obvious predecessor of Meg Murry. Three subsequent novels narrate the further adventures of this popular family. *The Moon by Night* is a low-keyed, relatively unexciting account of a cross-country vacation trek undertaken by the family. *The Young Unicorns* describes the Austins' unwilling involvement in a plot to ferment civil turmoil in New York City. More intricately plotted and more seriously thematic than the previous Austin novels—and in these respects similar to *A Wrinkle in Time*—the novel lacks the stylistic verve, the range of allusions, and the deft and interesting characterization that makes the former superior fiction. *A Ring of Endless Light* movingly depicts the Austins' response to Grandfather's imminent death. Striking too is the exploration of current experimentation concerning ESP, in particular involving dolphins.

Several of L'Engle's other novels deserve attention. In *The Arm of the Starfish,* L'Engle altered her usual approach a bit. Instead of working outward from within the intimate family circle, she has the main character, Adam Eddington, earn his way into the O'Keefe family. Unfortunately, the rest of the plot resembles formula cloak and dagger, and the goodness of the O'Keefes is stock and unbelievable. *A Wind in the Door,* the immediate sequel to *A Wrinkle in Time,* suffers in comparison with its predecessor. Because the mixture of its elements is too contrived and predictable, it lacks freshness and interest. Highly speculative and intensely earnest, *A Swiftly Tilting Planet,* another companion volume to *A Wrinkle in Time,* involves the Murrys' becoming caught up in a "last chance" effort to avoid nuclear catastrophe in a heavily plotted story spanning many centuries and involving many characters.

More recently, in *House Like a Lotus,* we again see the well-crafted story of L'Engle, blending a multitude of issues in an artful discussion of the complexities of life. As always, L'Engle contrasts the power of faith and hope with human fallibility and the ironies of life. In this companion novel to *The Arm of the Starfish* and *Dragons in the Water,* Polly O'Keefe is troubled and alone in Athens on her way to a conference in Cypress. We discover the traumatic events leading to her running away through flashback as she records and reflects in her journal. Lack of tolerance gives way to compassion and understanding as Polly gradually recognizes the importance of loving, giving, and sharing. Multiple subplots weave together both the past and the present to create an interesting and engaging mystery. L'Engle returns to her successful combination of science fiction and fantasy in her novel, *Many Waters,* which features the Murry twins, Sandy and Dennys, in a time travel adventure that returns them to the days before the great flood. In the desert land of earthquakes and unicorns, Sandy and Dennys join the family of Noah during the building of the ark. The novel further discusses the themes of good and evil and the total interrelatedness of the universe. The twins must also learn to deal for the first time with the fact that they are separate people. In contrast with the trilogy, L'Engle assigns the narrator a lesser role and, instead, uses dialogue to convey the meaning of the novel. The twins are far more objective and less prone to inner reflecting than characters in *A Wrinkle in Time.* Both this objectivity and L'Engle's continued use of cross characterization add a freshness to the read.

Even if L'Engle had not written *A Wrinkle in Time,* she would still be counted among the relatively few novelists who manage to entertain their young readers while honestly portraying some of the problems that they face. When *A Wrinkle in Time* is added to her corpus, however, L'Engle must be ranked as one of the truly important writers of juvenile fiction in recent decades.

—Francis J. Molson and Susan B. Steffel

LENSKI, Lois (Lenore)

Nationality: American. **Born:** Springfield, Ohio, 14 October 1893. **Education:** Local schools in Anna, Ohio, and high school in Sidney, Ohio, graduated 1911; Ohio State University, Columbus, 1911-15, B.S. in education 1915; Art Students' League, New York, 1915-20; Westminster School of Art, London, 1920-21. **Family:** Married the artist Arthur Covey in 1921 (died 1960); one son and two stepchildren. **Career:** Freelance illustrator from 1920. Individual shows: Weyhe Gallery, New York, 1927 (oils); Ferargils Gallery, New York, 1932 (watercolors); group shows: Pennsylvania Water Color Show, 1922; New York Water Color Show; Detroit Art Institute. **Awards:** American Library Association Newbery Medal, 1946; Child Study Committee award, 1948; Catholic Library Association Regina Medal, 1969; University of Southern Mississippi award, 1969. Litt.D.: Wartburg College, Waverly, Iowa, 1959; Capital University, Columbus, 1966; Southwestern College, Winfield, Kansas, 1968; D.H.L.: University of North Carolina Women's College, Greensboro, 1962. **Died:** 11 September 1974.

PUBLICATIONS FOR CHILDREN (ILLUSTRATED BY THE AUTHOR)

Fiction

Skipping Village. New York, Stokes, 1927.
A Little Girl of Nineteen Hundred. New York, Stokes, 1928.
Two Brothers and Their Animal Friends. New York, Stokes, 1929.
Two Brothers and Their Baby Sister. New York, Stokes, 1930.
Spinach Boy. New York, Stokes, 1930.
Benny and His Penny. New York, Knopf, 1931.
Grandmother Tippytoe. New York, Stokes, 1931.
Arabella and Her Aunts. New York, Stokes, 1932.
Johnny Goes to the Fair. New York, Minton Balch, 1932.
The Little Family. New York, Doubleday, 1932.
Gooseberry Garden. New York, Harper, 1934.
The Little Auto. New York and London, Oxford University Press, 1934; as *The Baby Car,* London, Oxford University Press, 1937.
Surprise for Mother. New York, Stokes, 1934.
Sugarplum House. New York, Harper, 1935.

Little Baby Ann. New York and London, Oxford University Press, 1935.
The Easter Rabbit's Parade. New York and London, Oxford University Press, 1936.
Phebe Fairchild, Her Book. New York, Stokes, 1936.
The Little Sail Boat. New York, Oxford University Press, 1937; as *The Little Sailing Boat*, London, Oxford University Press, 1938.
A-Going to the Westward. New York, Stokes, 1937.
Bound Girl of Cobble Hill. New York, Stokes, 1938.
The Little Airplane. New York and London, Oxford University Press, 1938.
Ocean-Born Mary. New York, Stokes, 1939.
Blueberry Corners. New York, Stokes, 1940.
The Little Train. New York and London, Oxford University Press, 1940.
Indian Captive. New York, Stokes, 1941.
The Little Farm. New York and London, Oxford University Press, 1942.
Bayou Suzette. Philadelphia, Lippincott, 1943.
Davy's Day. New York and London, Oxford University Press, 1943.
Let's Play House. New York and London, Oxford University Press, 1944.
Puritan Adventure. Philadelphia, Lippincott, 1944.
Strawberry Girl. Philadelphia, Lippincott, 1945; London, Oxford University Press, 1951.
Blue Ridge Billy. Philadelphia, Lippincott, 1946.
The Little Fire Engine. New York, Oxford University Press, 1946; London, Oxford University Press, 1947.
Surprise for Davy. New York, Oxford University Press, 1947.
Judy's Journey. Philadelphia, Lippincott, 1947; London, Oxford University Press, 1955.
Mr. and Mrs. Noah. New York, Crowell, 1948.
Boom Town Boy. Philadelphia, Lippincott, 1948.
Cotton in My Sack. Philadelphia, Lippincott, 1949.
Cowboy Small. New York, Oxford University Press, 1949; London, Oxford University Press, 1957.
Texas Tomboy. Philadelphia, Lippincott, 1950.
Papa Small. New York, Oxford University Press, 1951; London, Oxford University Press, 1957.
Prairie School. Philadelphia, Lippincott, 1951; London, Oxford University Press, 1959.
Peanuts for Billy Ben. Philadelphia, Lippincott, 1952.
We Live in the South. Philadelphia, Lippincott, 1952.
Mama Hattie's Girl. Philadelphia, Lippincott, 1953.
Corn-Farm Boy. Philadelphia, Lippincott, 1954.
Project Boy. Philadelphia, Lippincott, 1954.
We Live in the City. Philadelphia, Lippincott, 1954.
San Francisco Boy. Philadelphia, Lippincott, 1955.
A Dog Came to School. New York and London, Oxford University Press, 1955.
Berries in the Scoop. Philadelphia, Lippincott, 1956.
Big Little Davy. New York and London, Oxford University Press, 1956.
Flood Friday. Philadelphia, Lippincott, 1956.
We Live by the River. Philadelphia, Lippincott, 1956.
Davy and His Dog. New York and London, Oxford University Press, 1957.
Houseboat Girl. Philadelphia, Lippincott, 1957.
Little Sioux Girl. Philadelphia, Lippincott, 1958.
Coal Camp Girl. Philadelphia, Lippincott, 1959.
We Live in the Country. Philadelphia, Lippincott, 1960; London, Oxford University Press, 1961.
Davy Goes Places. New York, Walck, 1961.
Policeman Small. New York, Walck, 1962.
We Live in the Southwest. Philadelphia, Lippincott, 1962.
Shoo-Fly Girl. Philadelphia, Lippincott, 1963.
We Live in the North. Philadelphia, Lippincott, 1965.
High-Rise Secret. Philadelphia, Lippincott, 1966.
Debbie and Her Grandma. New York, Walck, 1967; London, Oxford University Press, 1968.
To Be a Logger. Philadelphia, Lippincott, 1967.
Christmas Stories. Philadelphia, Lippincott, 1968.
Deer Valley Girl. Philadelphia, Lippincott, 1968.
Debbie and Her Family. New York, Walck, 1969.
Debbie Herself. New York, Walck, 1969.
Debbie and Her Dolls. New York, Walck, 1970.
Debbie Goes to Nursery School. New York, Walck, 1970.
Debbie and Her Pets. New York, Walck, 1971.

Plays

The Bean-Pickers: A Migrant Play, music by Clyde Robert Bulla. Washington, D.C., National Council of Churches, 1952.
A Change of Heart: A Migrant Play, music by Clyde Robert Bulla. Washington, D.C., National Council of Churches, 1952.
Strangers in a Strange Land: A Migrant Play, music by Clyde Robert Bulla. Washington, D.C., National Council of Churches, 1952.

Poetry

Alphabet People. New York, Harper, 1928.
Animals for Me. New York and London, Oxford University Press, 1941.
Forgetful Tommy. Harwinton, Connecticut, Greenacres Press, 1943.
Spring Is Here. New York and London, Oxford University Press, 1945.
Now It's Fall. New York, Oxford University Press, 1948.
I Like Winter. New York and London, Oxford University Press, 1950.
We Are Thy Children (hymns), music by Clyde Robert Bulla. New York, Crowell, 1952.
On a Summer Day. New York and London, Oxford University Press, 1953.
Songs of Mr. Small, music by Clyde Robert Bulla. New York, Oxford University Press, 1954.
Songs of the City, music by Clyde Robert Bulla. New York, Marks Music, 1956.
Up to Six, Book I, music by Clyde Robert Bulla. New York, Hansen Music, 1956.
I Went for a Walk, music by Clyde Robert Bulla. New York, Walck, 1958.
At Our House, music by Clyde Robert Bulla. New York, Walck, 1959; Kingswood, Surrey, World's Work, 1964.
When I Grow Up, music by Clyde Robert Bulla. New York, Walck, 1960.
The Life I Live: Collected Poems. New York, Walck, 1965.
City Poems. New York, Walck, 1971.
Sing a Song of People, illustrated by Giles Laroche. Boston, Little Brown, 1987.

Other

The Wonder City: A Picture Book of New York. New York, Coward McCann, 1929.
The Washington Picture Book. New York, Coward McCann, 1930.
My Friend the Cow. Chicago, National Dairy Council, 1946.
Ice Cream Is Good. Chicago, National Dairy Council, 1948.
Living with Others. Hartford, Connecticut Council of Churches, 1952.

Editor, *Jack Horner's Pie: A Book of Nursery Rhymes.* New York, Harper, 1927; as *Lois Lenski's Mother Goose,* n.d.
Editor, *Susie Mariar* (folk rhyme). New York and London, Oxford University Press, 1939.

PUBLICATIONS FOR ADULTS (ILLUSTRATED BY THE AUTHOR)

Poetry

Florida, My Florida. Tallahassee, Friends of the Florida State University Library, 1971.

Other

Adventures in Understanding: Talks to Parents, Teachers, and Librarians, 1944-1966. Tallahassee, Friends of the Florida State University Library, 1968.
Journey into Childhood: Autobiography of Lois Lenski. Philadelphia, Lippincott, 1972.

*

Bibliographies: by Esther G. Witcher, in *The Lois Lenski Collection in the University of Oklahoma Library,* Norman, University of Oklahoma Library and School of Library Science, 1963; *The Lois Lenski Collection in the Florida State University Library* by Nancy Bird, Tallahassee, Florida State University Press, 1966.

Manuscript Collections: University of Oklahoma Library, Norman; Florida State University Library, Tallahassee; Amos Memorial Library, Sidney, Ohio; Capital University Library, Columbus, Ohio; Illinois State University Library, Normal; Kerlan Collection, University of Minnesota, Minneapolis; State University of New York, Buffalo; Syracuse University, New York.

Illustrator: *Children's Frieze-Book,* 1918; *Dolls from the Land of Mother Goose,* 1918; *The Golden Age,* 1921, and *Dream Days,* 1922, both by Kenneth Grahame; *The Green-Faced Toad* by Vera B. Birch, 1921; *Cinderella,* 1922; *My ABC Book,* 1922; *The Peep-Show Man* by Padraic Colum, 1924; *The Monkey That Would Not Kill* by Henry Drummond, 1925; *Chimney Corner Stories,* 1925, *Chimney Corner Fairy Tales,* 1926, *Fireside Stories,* 1927, *Candle-Light Stories,* 1928, *Chimney Corner Poems,* 1930, and *Fireside Poems,* 1930, all edited by Veronica S. Hutchinson; *A Merry-Go-Round of Modern Tales,* 1927, *The Hat-Tub Tale,* 1928, and *Mr. Nip and Mr. Tuck,* 1930, all by Caroline D. Emerson; *A Book of Princess Stories,* 1927, *A Book of Enchantments,* 1928, and *There Were Giants,* 1929, all edited by Kathleen Adams and Frances Atchinson; *Prudence and Peter and Their Adventures with Pots and Pans* by Elizabeth Robins and Octavia Wilberforce, 1928; *Sing a Song of Sixpence,* 1930; *Mother Goose Rhymes,* 1930; *Little Rag Doll,* 1930, and *A Name for Obed,* 1941, both by Ethel C. Phillips; *The Twilight of Magic* by Hugh Lofting, 1930; *Rustam, Lion of Persia,* 1930, and *Odysseus, Sage of Greece,* 1931, both by Alan Lake Chidsey; *Jolly Rhymes of Mother Goose* edited by Watty Piper, 1932, and *The Little Engine That Could* retold by Piper, 1945; *Golden Tales of the Prairie States [the Far West, Canada, New England, the Southwest, the Old South],* all edited by May Becker, 6 vols., 1932-41; *A Scotch Circus* by Tom Powers, 1934; *Betsy-Tacy,* 1940, *Betsy-Tacy and Tib,* 1941, *Over the Big Hill,* 1942, and *Down Town,* 1943, all by Maud Hart Lovelace; *Twenty-Two Short Stories of America* edited by E.R. Mirrielees, 1937; *Edgar, The 7:58* by Phil Stong, 1938; *Once on Christmas* by Dorothy Thompson, 1938; *Mother Makes Christmas* by Cornelia Meigs, 1940; *Indigo Treasure* by Frances Rogers, 1941; *The First Thanksgiving* by Lena Barksdale, 1942; *A Letter to Popsey* by Mabel La Rue, 1942; *They Came from France* by Clara Ingram Judson, 1943; *Five and Ten* by Roberta Whitehead, 1943; *The Surprise Place* by Mary Graham Bonner, 1945; *The Donkey Cart* by Clyde Robert Bulla, 1946; *Pinocchio* adapted by Allen Chaffee, 1946; *Read-to-Me-Storybook* by the Child Study Association, 1947.

* * *

Lois Lenski was a prolific author of books for children for more than 40 years. Her work, much of it still in print, is aimed at children from preschool through the middle elementary school years. Lenski's writing is best described as sober, realistic, and straightforward. Her prose is easy to read, convincing but not vivid, and generally quite humorless. Had she chosen to write music, it would surely have been plainsong.

Her books for very young children form one body of work by themselves. Serious, very simply written, rather flat-footed, they have had an abiding appeal for many small children who seem to find in them a satisfying exactness, a comfortable familiarity. Lenski has a sure eye for those adult occupations most visible and interesting to young children. She writes about Mr. Small as a policeman, train engineer, farmer, boat captain, and cowboy, giving brief glimpses of his duties in each role. (Interesting occupations are exclusively male in Lenski's world.) The methodical activities of Mr. Small in whatever guise may strike some adults (and some children) as dull, but it is clear that many children identify closely with Lenski's characters and that, for them, the orderly, informative text is an aid to imaginative participation in the adult world at a level they can comprehend.

The second major part of Lenski's work comprises the so-called historical and regional series. Both sets of stories are fiction, both share the plain narrative style, the realism and the simplicity that characterize the books for younger children. Of the two, the regional series is probably the better known.

These books, as their name implies, explore American life in various parts of the country. Here, as in her books for young children, Lenski's interest in the working world is apparent; how a family gets its living is an important theme. Lenski's research is sound; the background facts are authentic and dialect is accurate. More unusual, particularly for the 1940s and 1950s, is her focus on the poorer levels of American society. Sharecroppers are depicted in *Cotton in My Sack,* Florida "crackers" in *Strawberry Girl,* and the mountain people who scratch a bare living in the Appalachians in *Blue Ridge Billy.* In all of these, Lenski presents patterns of life often invisible in children's books. For the most part, she does so with neither condescension nor sentimentality. The haphazard financial habits of the sharecropper family in *Cotton in My Sack* are given honestly, and the makeshift household arrangements of migrant worker families described sympathetically but entirely without pathos in *Judy's Journey*. Nevertheless, Lenski's values are ultimately conventional, and her literary realism has clear limits. There are problems in her stories but no tragedies; her characters face many difficulties, but few without solution. Plots generally center around a mild (sometimes mildly improbable) success story. And success usually requires that her characters trade the hand-to-mouth ways of lower-class living for something closer to middle-class behavior. The values of industry, education, sobriety, and thrift always triumph.

At their best, as in *Strawberry Girl,* the regional stories blend local color, simple plot, and uncomplicated characterization into plausible if rather predictable wholes. When Lenski is less successful, as in *To Be a Logger,* the research seems undigested, and the book remains a conglomerate of fact and message rather than a story with a shape and life of its own.

The historical stories are generally more detailed than the regional books, appealing to a slightly older audience. Otherwise, their strengths and weaknesses parallel those of the regional stories; realism is their greatest attraction (they are based on the experiences of real people); lack of humor, pat plots and sometimes an over-abundance of incident and informative detail weaken them.

—Anne Scott MacLeod

LE SIEG, Theo. See **SEUSS, Dr.**

L'ESTRANGE, C. James. See **STRANG, Herbert.**

LEVIN, Betty

Nationality: American. **Born:** Betty Lowenthal, New York City, 10 September 1927. **Education:** National Cathedral School, Washington, D.C., 1941-44; Lincoln School, New York, 1944-45; University of Rochester, New York, A.B. (high honors) 1949 (Phi Beta Kappa); Radcliffe College, Cambridge, Massachusetts, M.A. 1951; Harvard School of Education, Cambridge, Massachusetts, A.M.T. 1951. **Family:** Married Alvin Levin in 1947; three daughters. **Career:** Research assistant, Museum of Fine Arts, Boston, 1951-52; part-time teaching fellow, Harvard Graduate School of Education, 1953; creative writing fellow, Radcliffe Institute, 1968-70; Massachusetts coordinator, McCarthy Historical Archive, 1969; Instructor, Pine Manor Open College, Chestnut Hill, Massachusetts, 1971-75, and Emmanuel College, Boston, 1975; feature writer, Minute Man Publications, Lexington, Massachusetts, 1972; Special Instructor in Children's Literature, 1975-77, and Adjunct Professor of Children's Literature,1977-87, Simmons College, Boston. Member of the Faculty, Radcliffe Seminars. Founding Board Member, Children's Literature New England, until 1996. Also a sheep farmer. **Awards:** Parent's Choice Award for *Away to Me, Moss*; Children's Book of the Year, Child Study Association, for *Gift Horse.* **Address:** Old Winter Street, Lincoln, Massachusetts 01773, U.S.A.

Publications for Children

Fiction

The Zoo Conspiracy, illustrated by Marian Parry. New York, Hastings House, 1973.
The Sword of Culann. New York, Macmillan, 1973.
A Griffon's Nest. New York, Macmillan, 1975.
The Forespoken. New York, Macmillan, 1976.
Landfall. New York, Atheneum, 1979.
The Beast on the Brink, illustrated by Marian Parry. New York, Avon, 1980.
The Keeping-Room. New York, Greenwillow, 1981.
A Binding Spell. New York, Dutton, 1984.
Put on My Crown. New York, Dutton, 1985.
The Ice Bear. New York, Greenwillow, 1986; London, MacRae, 1987.
The Trouble with Gramary. New York, Greenwillow, 1988.
Brother Moose. New York, Greenwillow, 1990.
Mercy's Mill. New York, Greenwillow, 1992.
Starshine and Sunglow, illustrated by Joseph A. Smith. New York, Greenwillow, 1994.
Away to Me, Moss. New York, Greenwillow, 1994.
Fire in the Wind. New York, Greenwillow, 1995.
Gift Horse, illustrated by Jos. A. Smith. New York, Greenwillow, 1996.
Island Bound. New York, Greenwillow, 1997.
Look Back, Moss. New York, Greenwillow, 1998.
Creature Crossing. New York, Greenwillow, 1999.

*

Manuscript Collections: Kerlan Collection, University of Minnesota, Minneapolis.

Betty Levin comments:

Most of my writing reflects my early and continuing interest in agriculture and animal husbandry and in history. Through fiction I keep discovering new patterns and connections in which people are grounded in the land (or sea) that supports all life and which children very often feel and recognize most keenly. The historical element is the vertical connection or ground, linking today's reading child with those who were children, too, but in another time or age. Having begun with fantasy, I am now beginning to explore other fictional ways of spinning my yarns and knitting my fictional patterns.

* * *

Betty Levin has written realistic novels and fantasies as well as works which combine both genres. In her time-travel trilogy consisting of *The Sword of Culann, A Griffon's Nest,* and *The Forespoken* she draws on a rich background of Celtic and Norse mythologies. In each of the three books an American girl, Claudia, is drawn back through time by means of an ancient sword hilt kept by an old recluse. In *The Sword of Culann* Claudia and her stepbrother Evan find themselves in ancient Ireland as witnesses to the struggle between the fierce Queen Medb and Cuchulain (the House of Culann). In *A Griffon's Nest* the pair are brought to the Orkney Islands during medieval times. In *The Forespoken* the historical setting is the 19th-century Orkney Islands and Claudia travels there alone in pursuit of a crow belonging to the recluse.

The contemporary setting in each of the books is an island off the coast of Maine. Levin is skillful in writing of the physical realities of both worlds, especially the cold, dampness, dirt, and hard physical labour. She is less successful in integrating the stories of the large, squabbling family in Maine with the historical journeys through time. In the first book the juxtaposition of the family trying survival camping in Maine while the two youngest children are shifting backward and forward in time seems awkward. In the two later books the contemporary setting becomes less important as more of the emphasis shifts to relationships in the historical period.

Levin's more recent work has moved between fantasy and realism with a greater emphasis upon the realistic elements. *A Binding Spell,* the story of a family transplanted from a comfortable suburban life to the harshness of rural Maine, is set firmly in the here-and-now although a strand of fantasy runs through it. Young Wren finds mysterious traces of a horse in the deserted barn and around the property. A growing friendship with a neighbor who has refused to leave his house ever since tractors displaced the horses that he had loved leads to a greater involvement with the Pedersen clan, the family's nearest neighbors. The contemporary problems of family alcoholism, the difficulty of making friends in a new school, and the threat of death on the roads are blended with the story of the ghost horse which only Wren and the recluse can see. The book ends with each problem nearing solution, although none disappear with unrealistic finality. Levin's characters are well-drawn and believable, but the magical elements are not closely integrated with the realistic story, which would have stood well on its own.

The Ice Bear takes place in the mythical medieval Kingdom of Thyrne where the people are being oppressed by an evil lord during the king's absence. This situation, similar to the background of the Robin Hood stories, is brought to life through the adventures of the boy Wat, who is forced to set off with a strange young girl and an ice bear cub after the girl's father and the cub's mother have been hanged by the townspeople. While the girl longs to return to her northern homeland, Wat hopes to take the bear to the king and receive a large reward. Wat's respect for the girl, Kaila, grows as they travel, and his understanding of loyalty and duty gradually change. The book ends when Wat meets the king, but the ending leaves room for a sequel, so perhaps this will grow into another trilogy. Unencumbered by a dual time perspective, the book brings its unusual setting to vivid life and is one of Levin's strongest stories so far.

The Trouble with Gramary deals with real life in modern-day Maine. Merkka's grandmother Gramary is considered an eccentric by many townspeople. Her welding business is viewed as creating an eyesore, and the metal sculptures she makes are dismissed with ridicule. By the time the book ends Merkka has come to terms with her grandmother's need for artistic and personal integrity. Although Gramary dominates the book, Merkka and the rest of the family are also strong and believable characters. This book marks a departure from Levin's earlier writings and it remains to be seen whether this versatile writer will continue to move toward realism.

Levin is not an easy writer. Many of her early books with their preoccupation with the impingement of the past on the present and with ecological concerns and mythological predictions make difficult demands—demands which few young readers can meet. More recent books rely less on background knowledge outside the world of the book itself, but the descriptions are dense and the situations and characters complex. Time and effort are required to move into the worlds that Levin creates. Readers who are willing to immerse themselves in the strange settings and to struggle to understand the significance of mysterious events will find themselves embarking on an enriching experience. Levin's work grows in strength and scope with each book published.

In the 1990s, Betty Levin has continued toward realism, though all of her books approach the line between reality and fantasy, and some of them cross it. All acknowledge the influence of the past on the present. Sometimes this process is clearly fantastic, as in *Mercy's Mill,* where twentieth-century Sarah meets a time-traveler who enables her to experience events and people hundreds of years old; sometimes the memories and discoveries of present-day characters reveal this debt to the past, as Joellen's and Chris's do in *Island Bound.* This book, arguably Levin's best to date, smoothly narrates the real-life adventure of an ornithologist's daughter and a boy on an outward-bound type of dare as they unravel a local legend. Other frequent motifs in Levin's writing are a sense of family and of community, both human and ecological, as in *Fire in the Wind,* where a 1947 Maine community battles fire during a drought and Meg battles the fear that her backward brother Orin may be partly responsible. Levin's plots often revolve around pastoral issues that might seem minor to much of contemporary society: will the farmer in *Starshine and Sunglow* be persuaded by his neighbors to resume growing delicious corn if they help him defeat the marauding raccoons? Placing a television in the cornfield reduces the thieves to a raccoon version of couch potatoes and saves the maize. Yet the integrity of Levin's position, as well as her keen, appealing presentation of animals and the children who come to know them, elicits respect and appreciation. Some of Levin's best portrayals are her animals, whether it's the title character in *Brother Moose,* the strong-willed sheepdog in *Away to Me, Moss,* or the Norwegian Fiord horse Loki in *Gift Horse.*

—Adele M. Fasick, updated by Frieda F. Bostian

LEVY, Elizabeth

Nationality: American. **Born:** 4 April 1942, Buffalo, New York. **Education:** Brown University, Providence, Rhode Island, B.A. (magna cum laude) 1964; Columbia University, New York City, M.A.T. 1968. **Career:** Writer since 1971. Editor and researcher in news department, American Broadcasting Co., New York City, 1964-66; assistant editor, Macmillan Publishing Co., New York

City, 1967-69; writer in public relations, New York Public Library, New York City, 1969; staff writer, JPM Associates (urban affairs consultants), New York City, 1970-71. **Awards:** *New York Times* Outstanding Book of the Year, 1977, *Struggle and Lose, Struggle and Win: The United Mineworkers Story.* **Member:** Authors Guild, Authors League of America, Mystery Writers of America, PEN: Co-Chair of Children's Book Committee, 1996-97. **Agent:** Amy Berkower, Writers House, 21 West 26th Street, New York, New York 10010, U.S.A. **Address:** 344 West 23rd Street, New York, New York 10011, U.S.A. **E-mail Address:** LizMys@aol.com.

Publications for Children

Fiction

Nice Little Girls, illustrated by Mordicai Gerstein. New York, Delacorte, 1974.
Lizzie Lies a Lot, illustrated by John Wallner. New York, Dell, 1976.
Frankenstein Moved in on the Fourth Floor, illustrated by Mordicai Gerstein. New York, HarperCollins, 1979.
The Tryouts, illustrated by Jacquie Hann. New York, Four Winds Press, 1979.
Dracula Is a Pain in the Neck, illustrated by Mordicai Gerstein. New York, HarperCollins, 1983.
Running Out of Time, illustrated by W.T. Mars. New York, Knopf, 1980.
Running Out of Magic with Houdini, illustrated by Blanche Sims. New York, Knopf, 1981.
The Computer that Said Steal Me. New York, Four Winds Press, 1983.
The Shadow Nose, illustrated by Mordicai Gerstein. New York, Morrow, 1983.
Keep Ms. Sugarman in the Fourth Grade, illustrated by Dave Henderson. New York, HarperCollins, 1992.
Cheater, Cheater. New York, Scholastic, 1993.
Gorgonzola Zombies in the Park, illustrated by George Ulrich. New York, HarperCollins, 1993.
Cleo and the Coyote. illustrated by Diana Bryer. New York, HarperCollins, 1996.
Wolfman Sam, illustrated by Bill Basso. New York, HarperCollins, 1996.
My Life as a Fifth-Grade Comedian. New York, HarperCollins, 1997.
Third Grade Bullies, illustrated by Tim Barnes. New York, Hyperion, 1998.

"Something Queer" Mystery Series, illustrated by Mordicai Gerstein:
Something Queer Is Going On. New York, Delacorte, 1973.
Something Queer at the Ballpark. New York, Delacorte, 1975.
Something Queer at the Library. New York, Delacorte, 1977.
Something Queer on Vacation. New York, Delacorte, 1980.
Something Queer at the Haunted School. New York, Delacorte, 1982.
Something Queer at the Lemonade Stand. New York, Delacorte, 1982.
Something Queer in Rock 'n' Roll. New York, Delacorte, 1987.
Something Queer at the Birthday Party. New York, Delacorte, 1990.
Something Queer in Outer Space. New York, Hyperion, 1993.
Something Queer in the Cafeteria. New York, Hyperion, 1994.
Something Queer at the Scary Movie. New York, Delacorte, 1995.
Something Queer in the Wild West. New York, Hyperion, 1997.
Something Queer Under the Sea. New York, Hyperion, 1999.

"Magic Mysteries" Series, illustrated by Ellen Eagle:
The Case of the Gobbling Squash. New York, Simon & Schuster, 1988.
The Case of the Mind-Reading Mommies. New York, Simon & Schuster, 1989.
The Case of the Tattletale Heart. New York, Simon & Schuster, 1990.
The Case of the Dummy with Cold Eyes. New York, Simon & Schuster, 1991.

"The Gymnasts" Series:
The Beginners. New York, Scholastic, 1988.
First Meet. New York, Scholastic, 1988.
Nobody's Perfect. New York, Scholastic, 1988.
The Winner. New York, Scholastic, 1989.
Trouble in the Gym. New York, Scholastic, 1989.
Bad Break. New York, Scholastic, 1989.
Tumbling Ghosts. New York, Scholastic, 1989.
Captain of the Team. New York, Scholastic, 1989.
Crush on the Coach. Scholastic, 1990.
Boys in the Gym. New York, Scholastic, 1990.
Mystery at the Meet. New York, Scholastic, 1990.
Out of Control. New York, Scholastic, 1990.
First Date. New York, Scholastic, 1990.
World Class Gymnast. New York, Scholastic, 1990.
Nasty Competition. New York, Scholastic, 1991.
Fear of Falling. New York, Scholastic, 1991.
Gymnasts Commandos. New York, Scholastic, 1991.
The New Coach. New York, Scholastic, 1991.
Tough at the Top. New York, Scholastic, 1991.
The Gymnast Gift. New York, Scholastic, 1991.
Go for the Gold. New York, Scholastic, 1992.
Team Trouble. New York, Scholastic, 1992.

"Brian and Pea Brain" Series, illustrated by George Ulrich:
Rude Rowdy Rumors. New York, HarperCollins, 1994.
School Spirit Sabotage. New York, HarperCollins, 1994.
A Mammoth Mix-Up. New York, HarperCollins, 1995.

"Invisible Inc." Series, illustrated by Denise Brunkus:
The Schoolyard Mystery. New York, Scholastic, 1994.
The Mystery of the Missing Dog. New York, Scholastic, 1995.
The Snack Attack Mystery. New York, Scholastic, 1995.
The Creepy Computer Mystery. New York, Scholastic, 1996.
The Karate Class Mystery. New York, Scholastic, 1996.
Parents' Night Fright. New York, Scholastic, 1998.

Publications for Young Adults

Fiction

Come Out Smiling. New York, Delacorte, 1981.
Double Standard. New York, Avon, 1984.

The Dani Trap. New York, Morrow, 1984.
Night of Nights. New York, Ballantine, 1984.
All Shook Up. New York, Scholastic, 1986.
Cold as Ice. New York, Morrow, 1988.
The Drowned. New York, Hyperion, 1995.
"Jody and Jake Mystery" Series:
The Case of the Frightened Rock Star. New York, Pocket Books, 1980.
The Case of the Counterfeit Race Horse. New York, Pocket Books, 1980.
The Case of the Fired-Up Gang. New York, Pocket Books, 1981.
The Case of the Wild River Ride. New York, Pocket Books, 1981.
The Case of the Mile High Race. London, Hodder and Stoughton, 1982.

Nonfiction

The People Lobby: The SST Story. New York, Delacorte, 1973.
Lawyers for the People. New York, Knopf, 1974.
By-Lines: Profiles in Investigative Journalism. New York, Four Winds Press, 1975.
Before You Were Three: How You Began to Walk, Talk, Explore, and Have Feelings, with Robie H. Harris, photographs by Henry E.F. Gordillo. New York, Delacorte, 1977.
Doctors for the People: Profiles of Six Who Serve, with Mara Miller. New York, Knopf, 1977.
Elephants in the Living Room, Bears in the Canoe: The Story of the Incredible Family Who Raise and Train Wild Animals in Their Home, with Earl and Liz Hammond. New York, Delacorte, 1977.
Struggle and Lose, Struggle and Win: The United Mineworkers Story, with Tad Richards, photographic essay by Henry E.F. Gordillo. New York, Four Winds Press, 1977.
Our Animal Kingdom, with Earl Hammond and Liz Hammond. New York, Delacorte, 1977.
Politicians for the People: Six Who Stand for Change. New York, Knopf, 1979.
If You Were There When They Signed the Constitution, illustrated by Richard Rosenblum. New York, Scholastic, 1987.

Plays

Croon (one-act; produced New York City, 1976).
Never Waste a Virgin (two-act; produced New York City, 1977).
Lizzie Lies a Lot (based on her novel of the same title; produced 1978).

Other

"Fat Albert and the Cosby Kids" Series:
The Shuttered Window. New York, Dell, 1981.
Mister Big Time. New York, Dell, 1981.
Take Two, They're Small. New York, Dell, 1981.
Spare the Rod. New York, Dell, 1981.
Mom or Pop. New York, Dell, 1981.
The Runt. New York, Dell, 1981.
Marco Polo: The Historic Adventure Based on the Television Spectacular, Random House, 1982.
Father Murphy's First Miracle (based on the television series *Father Murphy*), Random House, 1983.
Return of the Jedi (based on the film of the same title), Random House, 1983.
A Different Twist. New York, Scholastic, 1984.
The Bride (based on the film of the same title), Random House, 1985.

*

Biography: Essay in *Something about the Author* Volume 69, Detroit, Gale, 1992.

Elizabeth Levy comments:

I've been writing children's books for over twenty years, and I realize that in so many of my books, I am exploring the same areas that got me in trouble as a kid. Is there such a thing as being too funny? Why do we love to tease the people we're closest too? How do we manage to keep friendships going even through rough times? Kids love jokes and kids all over the world sent me jokes for *My Life as A Fifth Grade Comedian.* I love to speak at schools and I'm a volunteer in my own neighborhood school, P.S.11. Some of the kids who write the funniest stories are the ones who get in the most trouble. I saw how their wonderful teacher, Emilyn Garrick, loved them, and wanted the best for every kid in her classroom.

For my characters to triumph they learn a lot about love and being loved. So there's a serious side to my characters and me, but I also love knowing why it's so easy to fool vampires. *Because they're suckers.* That's not a put-down. It's just a joke and it's funny.

* * *

Elizabeth Levy has written a variety of fiction and nonfiction books for children and young adults, but she is best known for her children's fiction—in particular, the *Something Queer* series. All of her books feature snappy dialogue and strong, resourceful characters. While her books are characterized by a breezy humor, Levy also displays a sympathetic understanding of the problems faced by children and teens. One of Levy's greatest strengths as a writer is that she allows her young characters to find their own paths without moralizing lectures by the narrator or adult characters.

Levy's light-hearted *Something Queer* series features two smart and appealing girl detectives named Jill and Gwen who, with the help of a faithful hound dog called Fletcher, whose spots resemble the continents, solve mysteries in locations ranging from the public library to outer space. The solutions to the mysteries might not be a surprise to adult readers, but the books are ingenious and full of unexpected twists. Although the *Something Queer* books look like picture books, beginning readers will enjoy them just as much as preschoolers. These books feature positive female images like the protagonist, Jackie, in Levy's *Nice Little Girls.* The imaginative illustrations and plots invite readers to consider the puzzling situations encountered by Jill and Gwen. This series resulted in *Learning* magazine calling Levy "the Dorothy Sayers of the elementary set."

Levy specializes in creating characters who are intelligent and resourceful, but still real kids. An example is Jackie in *Keep Ms. Sugarman in the Fourth Grade.* Rebel Jackie is furious when her favorite teacher is promoted to principal in the middle of the school year. Jackie's father has convinced her that fourth grade is the year they "separate the goats from the sheep" and she is determined to hold onto the one person who does not see her as a "goat."

Determined to hold onto her favorite teacher, Jackie handcuffs herself to Ms. Sugarman's desk—with hilarious results.

Both *Lizzie Lies a Lot* and *Cheater, Cheater* are about honesty and the consequences of dishonesty, both common themes in Levy's writing. In *Lizzie Lies a Lot,* nine-year-old Lizzie learns the hard way that regaining someone's trust can be a lot harder than telling the truth in the first place when a friendship is threatened by the outrageous lies Lizzie tells to gain attention. In *Cheater, Cheater,* Lucy learns a tough, but funny, lesson when she cheats in a game in order to impress a cute boy. Not only is the boy not impressed, but he tells everyone that she is a cheater. The situation becomes worse when a teacher accuses her of cheating on a difficult science test. In reality, Lucy had studied very hard for the test, but no one at school believes her and she is made to retake the exam. Lucy fears that she will always be known as a cheater. In both books, Levy deftly matches the tone to the girl's mood, ranging from lighthearted banter to loneliness and fear of rejection.

Dracula Is a Pain in the Neck, Frankenstein Moved in on the Fourth Floor, Gorgonzola Zombies in the Park, and *Wolfman Sam* feature the comic capers of two brothers, Sam and Robert. Together, they investigate their creepy new neighbor, unmask "Count Dracula" at summer camp, solve the mystery of the vandalized statues in Central Park, and discover the perks of puberty. Although the plots are far-fetched, strong characters and believable bickering make the wacky adventures enjoyable.

Levy has written several popular series for children. These include the *Magic Mysteries, The Gymnasts, Fat Albert and the Cosby Kids, Jody and Jake Mystery, Something Queer, Brian and Pea Brain,* and

Invisible Inc. series. While her other series are not as popular as the *Something Queer* series, they are similar in that they feature fun characters who strive to overcome the problems facing them—whether the problems are finding the perfect Mother's Day gift (*The Case of the Mind-Reading Mommies*), a friend who steals (*Take Two, They're Small*), or a crush (*Crush on the Coach*). The *Jody and Jake Mystery* series and the *Magic Mysteries* series both feature young detectives who clear up mysteries with humor and lively dialogue. As an added bonus, the characters in the *Magic Mysteries* series explain simple magic tricks for readers to try.

The *Brian and Pea Brain* series features a brother and sister who work together to solve such problems as who has spread rumors about them or stolen part of their science project. The sometimes antagonistic, often humorous relationship between Brian and his younger sister, Penny, is believable. Levy's *Invisible Inc.* series features three children: Charlene, who can be bossy and brave, Justin, who is hearing impaired, and Chip, who is invisible because of an accident. Together, they use their unique abilities to solve mysteries such as finding Chip's lost dog. The characters also utilize modern technology such as e-mail as tools to resolve problems. Levy's chapter books, whether in a series or a single title, provide adventures and characters that appeal to children at beginning reading levels, especially reluctant readers. For example, *Third Grade Bullies* shows how the new girl in school, Sally Shapiro, who is tired of moving every year, and timid Tina Kerby, and bully Jake Powell learn how to work as a team to improve themselves and stop making fun of classmates.

Similar issues are discussed in *My Life as a Fifth-Grade Comedian.* Bobby Garrick, the class clown, risks being sent to another school because of his classroom behavior. Readers learn that Bobby's father uses humor to ridicule his son and that Bobby's older brother, Jimmy, was also a troubled student. Bobby's concerned teacher, Mr. Matous, realizes that Bobby's behavior is a cry for attention and suggests that Bobby plan a "laugh-off," a school comedy contest, to learn how to use humor positively. Sharing jokes she collected from readers, Levy shows Bobby's transformation through his relationships with his father, brother, and friend Janeen as he gains self-esteem and stops teasing and demeaning others with his jokes.

Levy focuses on friendship in her picture book, *Cleo and the Coyote,* in which the text is framed by southwestern art. Cleopatra, a street-smart, stray dog, is adopted by Martin who takes her to visit his uncle in Utah. In the desert, Cleo meets Tricky, a coyote who seems to be Cleo's opposite. Cleo soon realizes that she and Tricky have much in common, including a need to love and be loved. Both dog and coyote save each other's life and explain why they are loyal to their culture. In *The Drowned,* Levy departs from her humorous fiction and presents a macabre ghost story. Lily Potter is spending the summer in Atlantic City with her aunt. To earn money for college, she researches and leads a tour of local haunts, including visiting the bed of a drowned boy that his mother keeps in her front yard. Lily meets Clark DeLuge, who seems both sinister and nurturing toward her and is vital to the plot. During the summer, Lily copes with her grief for her father who drowned at Atlantic City years earlier and attempts to resist the efforts of the drowned boy's demented mother to make Lily her annual sacrifice to the sea.

Levy's nonfiction works, such as *Struggle and Lose, Struggle and Win* (With Tad Richards), *By-Lines,* and *Politicians for the People,* are similar to her fiction books in that they are about problems people face and the ways in which they deal with these problems. *Struggle and Lose, Struggle and Win,* which was named outstanding book of the year by the *New York Times* in 1977, is a compelling book that traces the United Mine Workers union from its beginnings to its emergence as one of the most powerful labor unions in the United States.

Levy writes with humor and understanding of the problems facing young people. Her suspenseful yet often silly stories reassure children about common issues and situations they encounter at home and school and with friends. The books promote respect and acceptance of others and the importance of individual talents to teamwork. Levy's characters are funny and sassy and should appeal to readers of both sexes.

—Christine Miller and Patrick Jones,
updated by Elizabeth D. Schafer

LEWIS, C(live) S(taples)

Pseudonyms: Clive Hamilton; N. W. Clerk. **Nationality:** British. **Born:** Belfast, Northern Ireland, 29 November 1898. **Education:** Wynyard House, Watford, Hertfordshire, 1908-10; Campbell College, Belfast, 1910; Cherbourg School, Malvern, Worcestershire, 1911-13, and Malvern College, 1913-14; privately, in Great Bookham, Surrey, 1914-17; University College, Oxford (scholar; Chancellor's English Essay prize, 1921), 1917, 1919-23, B.A. (honours) 1922. **Military Service:** Somerset Light Infantry, 1917-19: First Lieutenant. **Family:** Married Joy Davidman Gresham in

1956 (died 1960); two stepsons. **Career:** Philosophy Tutor, 1924, and Lecturer in English, 1924, University College, Oxford; Fellow and Tutor in English, Magdalen College, Oxford, 1925-54; Professor of Medieval and Renaissance English, Cambridge University, 1954-63. Lecturer, University College of North Wales, Bangor, 1941; Riddell Lecturer, University of Durham, 1943; Clark Lecturer, Cambridge University, 1944. **Awards:** Gollancz prize, 1937; Library Association Carnegie Medal, 1957. D.D.: University of St. Andrews, Fife, 1946; Docteur-ès-Lettres, Laval University, Quebec, 1952; D. Litt.: University of Manchester, 1959; Hon. Dr.: University of Dijon, 1962; University of Lyon, 1963. Honorary Fellow, Magdalen College, Oxford, 1955; University College, Oxford, 1958; Magdalene College, Cambridge, 1963. Fellow, Royal Society of Literature, 1948; Fellow, British Academy, 1955. **Died:** 22 November 1963.

Publications for Children (illustrated by Pauline Baynes)

Fiction

The Chronicles of Narnia:

The Lion, The Witch, and the Wardrobe. London, Bles, and New York, Macmillan, 1950.

Prince Caspian: The Return to Narnia. London, Bles, and New York, Macmillan, 1951.

The Voyage of the "Dawn Treader." London, Bles, and New York, Macmillan, 1952.

The Silver Chair. London, Bles, and New York, Macmillan, 1953.

The Horse and His Boy. London, Bles, and New York, Macmillan, 1954.

The Magician's Nephew. London, Lane, and New York, Macmillan, 1955.

The Last Battle. London, Lane, and New York, Macmillan, 1956.

Other

Letters to Children, edited by Lyle W. Dorsett and Marjorie Lamp Mead. New York, Macmillan, and London, Collins, 1985.

Publications for Adults

Novels

Out of the Silent Planet. London, Lane, 1938; New York, Macmillan, 1943.

Perelandra. London, Lane, 1943; New York, Macmillan, 1944; as *Voyage to Venus,* London, Pan, 1953.

That Hideous Strength: A Modern Fairy-Tale for Grown-Ups. London, Lane, 1945; New York, Macmillan, 1946; abridged edition, as *The Tortured Planet,* New York, Avon, 1958.

Till We Have Faces: A Myth Retold. London, Bles, 1956; New York, Harcourt Brace, 1957.

Short Stories

Of Other Worlds: Essays and Stories, edited by Walter Hooper. London, Bles, 1966; New York, Harcourt Brace, 1967.

The Dark Tower and Other Stories, edited by Walter Hooper. London, Collins, and New York, Harcourt Brace, 1977.

Poetry

Spirits in Bondage: A Cycle of Lyrics (as Clive Hamilton). London, Heinemann, 1919.

Dymer (as Clive Hamilton). London, Dent, and New York, Dutton, 1926.

Poems, edited by Walter Hooper. London, Bles, 1964; New York, Harcourt Brace, 1965.

Narrative Poems, edited by Walter Hooper. London, Bles, 1969; New York, Harcourt Brace, 1972.

Other

The Pilgrim's Regress: An Allegorical Apology for Christianity, Reason, and Romanticism. London, Dent, 1933; New York, Sheed and Ward, 1935; revised edition, London, Bles, 1943; Sheed and Ward, 1944.

The Allegory of Love: A Study in Medieval Tradition. Oxford, Clarendon Press, and New York, Oxford University Press, 1936.

Rehabilitations and Other Essays. London and New York, Oxford University Press, 1939.

The Personal Heresy: A Controversy, with E.M.W. Tillyard. London and New York, Oxford University Press, 1939.

The Problem of Pain. London, Bles, 1940; New York, Macmillan, 1944.

The Weight of Glory. London, S.P.C.K., 1942.

The Screwtape Letters. London, Bles, 1942; New York, Macmillan, 1943; revised edition, as *The Screwtape Letters and Screwtape Proposes a Toast,* Bles, 1961; Macmillan, 1962.

Broadcast Talks: Right and Wrong: A Clue to the Meaning of the Universe, and What Christians Believe. London, Bles, 1942; as *The Case for Christianity,* New York, Macmillan, 1943.

A Preface to "Paradise Lost" (lectures). London and New York, Oxford University Press, 1942; revised edition, 1960.

Christian Behaviour: A Further Series of Broadcast Talks. London, Bles, and New York, Macmillan, 1943.

The Abolition of Man; or, Reflections on Education with Special Reference to the Teaching of English in the Upper Forms of Schools. London, Oxford University Press, 1943; New York, Macmillan, 1947.

Beyond Personality: The Christian Idea of God. London, Bles, 1944; New York, Macmillan, 1945.

The Great Divorce: A Dream. London, Bles, and New York, Macmillan, 1946.

Miracles: A Preliminary Study. London, Bles, and New York, Macmillan, 1947.

Vivisection. London, Anti-Vivisection Society, and Boston, New England Anti-Vivisection Society, 1947(?).

Transposition and Other Addresses. London, Bles, 1949; as *The Weight of Glory and Other Addresses,* New York, Macmillan, 1949.

The Literary Impact of the Authorized Version (lecture). London, Athlone Press, 1950; Philadelphia, Fortress Press, 1963.

Mere Christianity. London, Bles, and New York, Macmillan, 1952.

Hero and Leander (lecture). London, Oxford University Press, 1952.

English Literature in the Sixteenth Century, Excluding Drama. Oxford, Clarendon Press, 1954.

De Descriptione Temporum (lecture). London, Cambridge University Press, 1955.

Surprised by Joy: The Shape of My Early Life. London, Bles, 1955; New York, Harcourt Brace, 1956.

Reflections on the Psalms. London, Bles, and New York, Harcourt Brace, 1958.
Shall We Lose God in Outer Space? London, S.P.C.K., 1959.
The Four Loves. London, Bles, and New York, Harcourt Brace, 1960.
The World's Last Night and Other Essays. New York, Harcourt Brace, 1960.
Studies in Words. London, Cambridge University Press, 1960; revised edition, 1967.
An Experiment in Criticism. London, Cambridge University Press, 1961.
A Grief Observed (as N.W. Clerk; autobiography). London, Faber, 1961; Greenwich, Connecticut, Seabury Press, 1963.
They Asked for a Paper: Papers and Addresses. London, Bles, 1962.
Beyond the Bright Blur (letters). New York, Harcourt Brace, 1963.
Letters to Malcolm, Chiefly on Prayer. London, Bles, and New York, Harcourt Brace, 1964.
The Discarded Image: An Introduction to Medieval and Renaissance Literature. London, Cambridge University Press, 1964.
Screwtape Proposes a Toast and Other Pieces. London, Fontana, 1965.
Letters, edited by W.H. Lewis. London, Bles, and New York, Harcourt Brace, 1966.
Studies in Medieval and Renaissance Literature, edited by Walter Hooper. London, Cambridge University Press, 1966.
Spenser's Images of Life, edited by Alastair Fowler. London, Cambridge University Press, 1967.
Christian Reflections, edited by Walter Hooper. London, Bles, and Grand Rapids, Michigan, Eerdmans, 1967.
Letters to an American Lady, edited by Clyde S. Kilby. Grand Rapids, Michigan, Eerdmans, 1967; London, Hodder and Stoughton, 1969.
Mark vs. Tristram: Correspondence Between C.S. Lewis and Owen Barfield, edited by Walter Hooper. Cambridge, Massachusetts, Lowell House Printers, 1967.
A Mind Awake: An Anthology of C.S. Lewis, edited by Clyde S. Kilby. London, Bles, 1968; New York, Harcourt Brace, 1969.
Selected Literary Essays, edited by Walter Hooper. London, Cambridge University Press, 1969.
God in the Dock: Essays on Theology and Ethics, edited by Walter Hooper. Grand Rapids, Michigan, Eerdmans, 1970; as *Undeceptions: Essays on Theology and Ethics,* London, Bles, 1971.
The Humanitarian Theory of Punishment. Abingdon, Berkshire, Marcham Books Press, 1972.
Fern-Seed and Elephants and Other Essays on Christianity, edited by Walter Hooper. London, Fontana, 1975.
The Joyful Christian: 127 Readings, edited by William Griffin. New York, Macmillan, 1977.
They Stand Together: The Letters of C.S. Lewis to Arthur Greeves 1914-1963, edited by Walter Hooper. London, Collins, and New York, Macmillan, 1979.
C.S. Lewis at the Breakfast Table and Other Reminiscences, edited by James T. Como. New York, Macmillan, 1979; London, Collins, 1980.
The Visionary Christian: 131 Readings, edited by Chad Walsh. New York, Macmillan, 1981.
On Stories and Other Essays on Literature, edited by Walter Hooper. New York, Harcourt Brace, 1982.
Of This and Other Worlds, edited by Walter Hooper. London, Collins, 1982.
The Cretaceous Perambulator, with Owen Barfield, edited by Walter Hooper. Oxford, C.S. Lewis Society, 1983.
The Business of Heaven: Daily Readings from C.S. Lewis, edited by Walter Hooper. London, Fount, and New York, Harcourt Brace, 1984.
Boxen: The Imaginary World of the Young C.S. Lewis, edited by Walter Hooper. London, Collins, and San Diego, Harcourt Brace, 1985.
Present Concerns, edited by Walter Hooper. London, Fount, and San Diego, Harcourt Brace, 1986.
Timeless at Heart: Essays on Theology, edited by Walter Hooper. London, Fount, 1987.
The Essential C.S. Lewis, edited by Lyle W. Dorsett. New York, Macmillan, 1988.
Letters: C.S. Lewis and Don Giovanni Calabria. Ann Arbor, Michigan, Servant, 1988.
C.S. Lewis Letters: A Study in Friendship, translated by Martin Moynihan. Ann Arbor, Michigan, Servant, 1988.
Letters: C.S. Lewis and D.G. Calabria, edited and translated by Martin Moynihan. London, Collins, 1989.

Editor, *George MacDonald: An Anthology.* London, Bles, 1946; New York, Macmillan, 1947.
Editor, *Arthurian Torso, Containing the Posthumous Fragment of "The Figure of Arthur,"* by Charles Williams. London, and New York, Oxford University Press, 1948.

*

Bibliographies: "A Bibliography of the Writings of C.S. Lewis" by Walter Hooper, in *Light on C.S. Lewis* edited by Jocelyn Gibb, London, Bles, 1965; *C.S. Lewis: An Annotated Checklist of Writings about Him and His Works* by Joe R. Christopher and Joan K. Ostling, Kent, Ohio, Kent State University Press, 1974.

Manuscript Collections: Bodleian Library, Oxford; Wheaton College, Illinois.

Critical Studies (selection): *C.S. Lewis* by Roger Lancelyn Green, London, Bodley Head, and New York, Walck, 1963, revised edition, in *Three Bodley Head Monographs,* Bodley Head, 1969, *C.S. Lewis: A Biography* by Green and Walter Hooper, London, Collins, and New York, Harcourt Brace, 1974, revised edition, 1988, and *Past Watchful Dragons: The Narnian Chronicles of C.S. Lewis,* New York, Macmillan, 1979, and *Through Joy and Beyond: A Pictorial Biography of C.S. Lewis,* New York, Macmillan, 1982, both by Hooper; *Light on C.S. Lewis* edited by Jocelyn Gibb, London, Bles, 1965; *The Lion of Judah in Never-Never Land: The Theology of C.S. Lewis Expressed in His Fantasies for Children,* Grand Rapids, Michigan, Eerdmans, 1973, and *The C.S. Lewis Hoax,* Portland, Oregon, Multinomah, both by Kathryn Ann Lindskoog; *The Secret Country of C.S. Lewis* by Anne Arnott, London, Hodder and Stoughton, 1974, Grand Rapids, Michigan, Eerdmans, 1975; *The Longing for Form: Essays on the Fiction of C.S. Lewis* edited by Peter J. Schakel, Kent, Ohio, Kent State University Press, 1977, and *Reading with the Heart: The Way into Narnia* by Schakel, Grand Rapids, Michigan, Eerdmans, 1979; *The Inklings: C.S. Lewis, J.R.R. Tolkien, Charles Williams and Their Friends* by Humphrey Carpenter, London, Allen and Unwin, 1978, Boston, Houghton Mifflin, 1979; *The Literary Legacy of C.S. Lewis* by Chad Walsh, New York, Harcourt Brace, and London, Sheldon Press, 1979; *A Guide Through Narnia* by Martha C. Sammons, Wheaton, Illinois, Shaw, and London, Hodder and Stoughton, 1979; *Narnia Explored* by Paul A. Karkainen, Old Tappan, New Jersey, Revell, 1979; *Companion to Narnia* by Paul F. Ford, New York, Harper, 1980; *C.S. Lewis, Spinner of Tales: A Guide to His Fiction* by Evan K. Gibson, Grand Rapids, Michigan, Christian University Press, 1980; *C.S. Lewis* by Margaret Patterson Hannay, New York, Ungar, 1981; *C.S. Lewis: The Art of Enchantment* by Donald E. Glover, Athens, Ohio University Press, 1981; *C.S. Lewis* by Brian Murphy, Mercer Island, Washington, Starmont House, 1983; *The Politics of Fantasy: C.S. Lewis and J.R.R. Tolkien* by Lee D. Rossi, New York and Epping, Essex, Bowker, 1984; *Clive Staples Lewis: The Drama of a Life* by William Griffin, New York, Harper, 1986; *C.S. Lewis: His Literary Achievement* by C.N. Manlove, London, Macmillan, 1987; *C.S. Lewis* by Joe R. Christopher, Boston, Twayne, 1987; *C.S. Lewis, Man of Letters: A Reading of His Fiction* by Thomas Howard, Worthing, Sussex, Churchman, 1987; *Jack: C.S. Lewis and His Times* by George Sayer, London, Macmillan, 1988; *C.S. Lewis and His World* by David Barratt, Grand Rapids, Michigan, Eerdmans, 1988.

* * *

Ever since the first of the seven Narnia books appeared in 1950, C.S. Lewis has been perhaps the best-liked post-war "quality" writer for children in Britain. This success is all the more interesting because, at the time of publishing, these books ran directly across a number of attitudes and taboos in children's fiction—and in certain ways do so still. They contain violence, pain, and death. Their tone is often admonitory; they are morally and theologically didactic. It would be wrong, of course, to think these all disadvantages. Indeed, it could be said that Lewis won his readers not only by his stunning scenes and plot situations and by his manner—a well-gauged air of intimate authority—but by a deliberate *using* of large taboos, religion and death in particular.

In the autobiographical *Surprised by Joy,* and elsewhere, Lewis has valuably charted the reading, tastes, and events of his early life that led to these children's stories. "I wrote," he declared characteristically, "the books I should have liked to read. That's always been my reason for writing...no rot about 'self-expression.'" He was the younger of two brothers, born and brought up in Northern Ireland. Motherless at nine, with a moody Welsh solicitor father, he was accustomed to an inventive, dreaming, bookish solitude. "I am a product of long corridors, empty sunlit rooms, upstair indoor silences, attics explored in solitude, distant noises of gurgling cisterns and pipes, and the noise of wind under the tiles. Also of endless books." Most in the house were adult novels and of no interest to the myth-loving young romantic. What *did* make a lasting impact were E. Nesbit's three "magic" novels, *The Story of the Amulet* in particular. "It first opened my eyes to antiquity, 'the dark backward and abysm of time.' I can still reread it with delight." Gulliver was another favourite. Andersen's *Snow Queen* and Grahame's *Dream Days* must have been read about this time. At 12 he was caught by the spell of "Northernness"—Norse myths, Rackham's illustrations to *The Ring,* Morris's *Sigurd the Volsung.* At 16, under a private tutor, W.T. Kirkpatrick, he raced into Homer. "Day after day and month after month we drove gloriously onward, tearing the whole *Achilleid* out of the *Iliad*...and then reading the *Odyssey* entire, till the music of the thing and the clear bitter brightness...had become part of me." A year or so later, by way of *Phantastes,* he discovered George MacDonald—a major experience. All these and many other early-read tales go to the making of Narnia. Of all the books, the first, *The Lion, The Witch, and the Wardrobe,* remains the favourite (or the best-remembered, which may be the same thing). There are good enough reasons for this. It is usually the first one to be read, and the gateway to the rest; it also contains one of the great moments in children's fiction (in an empty room of an old vast rambling country house a wardrobe leads to a snowy forest, faun and dwarf and witch). But it was also the key book from Lewis's view, the one where he first set out precisely (as much to himself as to his readers) the Christ-role of Aslan, who dies to save Edmund, on the Stone Table, and then rises again; the pilgrimage role (fallible, favoured, leading to brightness) of the human children; and something more: his personal view that pagan myth and Christian gospel are not inimical. In the final Narnian story centaurs, fauns, real animals, and fabulous creatures pass with humans through the golden gate.

"In a certain sense," wrote Lewis, "I have never actually 'made' a story...I see pictures. Some of these pictures have a common flavour...which groups them together. Keep quiet and watch and they will begin joining themselves up.... I have no idea whether this is the usual way of writing stories.... It is the only one I know; images always come first." Where there are gaps, he added, some conscious inventing must at last be done.

Images always come first—much of the impact of the Narnian tales must come from this.

In *Prince Caspian* the four Pevensie children, already met in the first book, are drawn back, by a magic horn, to the aid of Caspian, in danger of death from his evil uncle Miraz who has usurped the throne. Advised of this by his half-dwarf tutor, Dr. Cornelius, Caspian escapes and goes (with the human children) to rally supporters and to restore the land to its original honour. Among his followers are the Old People, centaurs, fauns, squirrels, ravens, "a small but genuine giant, Wimbleweather, of Deadman's Hill," even Silenus and Bacchus. ("I wouldn't have felt very safe with Bacchus and all his wild girls if we'd met them without Aslan," murmurs Susan. "I should think not," says Lucy.) In the culminating battle, Peter fights with style. He "swung to face Sopespian, slashed his legs from under him, and with the backcut of the same stroke, walloped off his head." Lewis never fails in describing such expertise.

Though it has weaknesses (and the improbable Eustace Scrubb is the principal one), *The Voyage of the "Dawn Treader"* seems the most intoxicating (or, one might say, intoxicated) of the Narnian books. The abiding influence throughout is Homeric, clearly going back to young Lewis's "glorious" race through the *Odyssey.* Edmund, Lucy, and their unloved cousin Eustace Scrubb enter a picture (like the children in Grahame's *Dream Days*). It is of an ancient dragon-prowed vessel in towering waves—and there they are on board, with young King Caspian, carrying out his vow to search for the seven loyal lords whom Miraz despatched "to the unknown Eastern Seas, beyond the Lone Islands." Eustace becomes a dragon (but recovers and mends his ways); a Sea Serpent nearly crushes the boat in its coils; and they reach the edge of the World's End, and look into Aslan's country. Only one may step into it—Reepicheep, the Knightly Mouse: "For you," says the Lamb, "the door into Aslan's country is from your own world."

But as sheer fairytale, *The Silver Chair* should take top place of the seven. Jill and Eustace, wretched at school, call Aslan's name, and find themselves on the edge of what must be the highest cliff in all fiction. Eustace falls—but Aslan wafts him on his breath to "the west of the world," Jill follows, and the two are sent on a quest to find the lost Prince Rilian, heir to the old King of Narnia. Aslan gives four signs to Jill, which she must not forget. (She does.) A Marsh-Wiggle, Puddleglum (one of Lewis's best creations), joins the journey as guide, to the Bottom of the World, where Rilian, enslaved by a Witch Queen, sits bound in a silver chair. A superb and magical story.

The Horse and His Boy, which could seem at first glance a witty vivacious Arabian Nights pastiche, provides a new pair of human children. A fair-haired fisherman's boy in dark Calormen (in fact a foundling, cast ashore as an infant) escapes being sold into slavery and, helped by a Talking Horse called Bree (echoes of Gulliver?) and joined by a fearless runaway girl called Aravis, makes the long perilous journey to Narnia—dungeons, mountains, haunted deserts—where in fact his own identity lies. This is a first-class story and children like it well. Yet, though Aslan provides the *gravitas* (aid in crisis, admonition: three real claw-stripes for Aravis) it remains one of the lighter-weight books of the seven. The children in *The Magician's Nephew,* most Nesbit-like of the novels, live in late-Victorian London, when "Mr. Sherlock Holmes was still living in Baker Street and the Bastables were looking for treasure in the Lewisham Road"; they are Digory (father in India, mother ill) and Polly who lives next door. Uncle Andrew, who dabbles in magic, propels the two into the Other Place, where Narnia is soon (in this book, indeed) to be created. Unfortunately through inquisitiveness (or scientific interest) Digory releases Jadis, a beautiful evil witch, from a prisoning spell; she returns with the pair to London (a riotous Nesbit episode) and (symbolically) inserts herself into the new-born Narnia. Aslan sends Digory forth to collect the magic apple whose tree may help to keep her power at bay. A cabdriver and his horse (echoes of MacDonald's *North Wind*) join the return to Narnia and are given high roles in the kingdom. More contrived ("invented") than some of the books, it is not among the best. Yet the facts about Narnia's making deserve attention.

The final book, *The Last Battle,* is a curious and disturbing work, fine in passages, yet overambitious for its scope. In the last days of Narnia an ape called Shift finds a lion-skin, wraps it about his simple donkey servant, Puzzle, and claims that Aslan has returned. Through this poor puppet he orders the cutting down of the forests; he makes commercial pacts with the evil Calormenes, and sells the Narnian creatures off to work in the mines. When young Tirian, "last of the Kings of Narnia," calls for aid to "the helpers beyond the world," Jill and Eustace appear (from a railway train) and help to gather forces for the battle on Stable Hill. This gripping and terrible confrontation provides one of Lewis's best set-pieces. Aslan appears at last; the vanquished seem the victors; the frightful stable, from which no one returns alive, seems a bright and sunlit garden for Aslan-followers. The children realize that they were killed in a railway accident; Narnia disintegrates; the sun is squeezed like an orange; as we have noted, friendly creatures from all the stories pass with the humans through the golden gates; a kind of Judgment Day. "I see," says Lucy thoughtfully, "This garden is like the Stable. It is far bigger inside than it was outside." They are in Narnia, fresh and green; they are in their English home. "The dream is ended; this is the morning," Aslan says. End of the world? or end of these children's lives? It is hard to say.

One need not be a philosopher or even an adult to note the illogic and crotchets in Lewis's work. As a boy he was deeply unhappy at conventional boarding schools. Yet, it is the "progressive" school which provokes his ire. (*Did* such schools use only surnames, favour bullying?) He had real fondness for animals (excepting the ape and the wolf) and accorded them a nobler place in his books than most writers with a strong sense of hierarchy (Kipling, for instance). To eat a Talking Animal in Narnia was not to be thought of. Yet the very word "vegetarian" lashes him into fury, and he imposes on the vegetarian Eustace (who would in life need courage to hold his views) such qualities as cowardliness, meanness, greed. A loner and a dreamer himself, he commends the military virtues.

Yet readers read only what they read, and Lewis's books are outstanding witness to this fact. Without heavy prompting, what child perceives the symbolism in, say, the Stone Table episode? Would the young Lewis himself have done so? But wardrobe and lamppost are firmly lodged in every reader's mind. For all his convert's zeal he leaves a reader not so much with a dose of theology as a sensation of noble deeds, far distances, the freedom of space and time, the sure division of right and wrong. Matter of myth; matter of fairytale.

—Naomi Lewis

LEWIS, Hilda (Winifred)

Nationality: British. **Born:** London, in 1896. **Family:** Married Michael Lewis; one son. **Career:** Taught in London for a few years; lived many years in Nottingham. **Died:** February 1974.

Publications for Children

Fiction

The Ship That Flew. London, Oxford University Press, 1939; New York, Criterion, 1958.

The Gentle Falcon, illustrated by Evelyn Gibbs. London, Oxford University Press, 1952; New York, Criterion, 1957.

Here Comes Harry, illustrated by William Stobbs. London, Oxford University Press, and New York, Criterion, 1960.

Harold Was My King. London, Oxford University Press, 1968; New York, McKay, 1970.

Publications for Adults

Novels

Pegasus Yoked. London, Hurst and Blackett, 1933.
Madam Gold. London, Hurst and Blackett, 1933.
Full Circle. London, Hurst and Blackett, 1935.
Pelican Inn. London, Jarrolds, 1937.
Because I Must. London, Jarrolds, 1938.
Said Dr. Spendlove. London, Jarrolds, 1940.
Penny Lace. London, Jarrolds, 1942.
Imogen under Glass. London, Jarrolds, 1943.
Strange Story. London, Jarrolds, 1945; New York, Random House, 1947.

Gone to the Pictures. London, Jarrolds, 1946.
The Day Is Ours. London, Jarrolds, 1947.
More Glass Than Wall. London, Macdonald, 1950.
No Mate, No Comrade. London, Macdonald, 1951.
Enter a Player. London, Macdonald, 1952.
Wife to Henry V. London, Jarrolds, 1954; New York, Putnam, 1957.
The Witch and the Priest. London, Jarrolds, 1956; New York, McKay, 1970.
I, Jacqueline. London, Jarrolds, 1957.
Wife to Great Buckingham. London, Jarrolds, 1959; New York, Putnam, 1960.
Call Lady Purbeck. London, Hutchinson, 1961; New York, St. Martin's Press, 1962.
A Mortal Malice. London, Hutchinson, 1963.
Wife to Charles II. London, Hutchinson, 1965; as *Catherine,* New York, St. Martin's Press, 1966.
Wife to the Bastard. London, Hutchinson, 1966; New York, McKay, 1967.
Harlot Queen. London, Hutchinson, and New York, McKay, 1970.
I Am Mary Tudor. London, Hutchinson, 1971; New York, McKay, 1972.
Mary the Queen. London, Hutchinson, 1973.
Bloody Mary. London, Hutchinson, 1974.
Rose of England. London, Hutchinson, 1977.
Heart of a Rose. London, Hutchinson, 1978.

* * *

Out of Hilda Lewis's large output of historical novels, only four were written for children. All her books are meticulous in detail and recreation of period, and the characters full of life and colour.

In *Here Comes Harry* she gives a vivid portrait of English court life in the 15th century as she draws a parallel between the lives of Harry Rushden, 13-year-old apprentice goldsmith who really wants to be a knight fighting for his King, and the child King Henry VI, alone and surrounded by political intrigue. In *The Gentle Falcon,* the tragic tale of the French child Princess Isabella, who was married to Richard II, is similarly seen through the eyes of her namesake and lady in waiting, Isabella Clinton. *Harold Was My King* is introduced by Lewis herself thus: "My tale is told by Edmund, an English boy who loses everything through the coming of William. It is bound to be somewhat prejudiced but Edmund tries to be fair and to look beyond his own losses. In the end he comes to understand that harsh man, the Conqueror. One day you will, very likely, read the old Chronicles for yourself and make up your own mind." Lewis chose her historical interpretation of events and fashioned her account around them. The excellence of her narration inspires further reading and research, surely one of the prime intentions of historical fiction, and the best way to engender an interest.

Her classic book is the one for younger children, *The Ship That Flew.* It is a book to put alongside *Puck of Pook's Hill* and *Tom's Midnight Garden.* Peter paid all the money he had in the world—"and a bit over"—for a tiny wooden ship, not larger than six inches, that he found in the curious old shop. It is a magic ship that grows and grows until he and his brother and sisters can all sail in her—the ship that flew. But this vessel is no mere Tardis; given to Frey the norse god as a wedding present by Odin, it is only magic if one believes. While the children believe, it takes them to Asgard, to Runnymede, to the Nile, and many more places and events. They meet Chaucer, Horatius, Robin Hood, and countless others from the pageant of history. Each new scene and character is portrayed in great detail and atmosphere, and the contrasts in the various historical periods are vivid and startling. Although first published in 1939, the book itself has travelled through time and lives on as a model of its kind.

—Fiona Waters

LEXAU, Joan M.

Pseudonym: Joan L. Nodset. **Nationality:** American. **Born:** St. Paul, Minnesota. **Education:** College of St. Thomas and College of St. Catherine, both St. Paul; New School for Social Research, New York. **Career:** Has worked as a salesperson, waitress, library clerk, and office worker; editorial secretary, *Catholic Digest,* St. Paul, 1953-55; advertising production manager, *Glass Packer* magazine, New York, 1955-56; reporter, *Catholic News,* New York, 1956-57; correspondent, Religious News Service, New York, 1957; children's books production liaison, Harper and Row, publishers, New York, 1957-61. **Award:** Child Study Committee award, 1963. **Address:** c/o Harper and Row, 10 East 53rd Street, New York, New York 10022, U.S.A.

Publications for Children

Fiction

Olaf Reads, illustrated by Harvey Weiss. New York, Dial Press, 1961.
Cathy Is Company, illustrated by Aliki. New York, Dial Press, 1961.
Millicent's Ghost, illustrated by Ben Shecter. New York, Dial Press, 1962.
The Trouble with Terry, illustrated by Irene Murray. New York, Dial Press, 1962.
Olaf Is Late, illustrated by Harvey Weiss. New York, Dial Press, 1963.
That's Good, That's Bad, illustrated by Aliki. New York, Dial Press, 1963.
José's Christmas Secret, illustrated by Don Bolognese. New York, Dial Press, 1963; revised edition, as *The Christmas Secret,* New York, Scholastic, 1973.
Benjie, illustrated by Don Bolognese. New York, Dial Press 1964.
Maria, illustrated by Ernest Crichlow. New York, Dial Press, 1964
I Should Have Stayed in Bed!, illustrated by Syd Hoff. New York Harper, 1965; Kingswood, Surrey, World's Work, 1966.
More Beautiful than Flowers, illustrated by Don Bolognese. Philadelphia, Lippincott, 1966.
The Homework Caper, illustrated by Syd Hoff. New York Harper, 1966.
A Kite over Tenth Avenue, illustrated by Symeon Shimin. New York Doubleday, 1967.
Finders Keepers, Losers Weepers, illustrated by Tomie de Paola Philadelphia, Lippincott, 1967.
Every Day a Dragon, illustrated by Ben Shecter. New York Harper, 1967.

Three Wishes for Abner, illustrated by Gloria Kamen. Boston, Ginn, 1967.
Striped Ice Cream!, illustrated by John Wilson. Philadelphia, Lippincott, 1968.
The Rooftop Mystery, illustrated by Syd Hoff. New York, Harper, 1968; Kingswood, Surrey, World's Work, 1969.
A House So Big, illustrated by Fritz Siebel. New York, Harper, 1968.
Archimedes Takes a Bath, illustrated by Salvatore Murdocca. New York, Crowell, 1969.
Benjie on His Own, illustrated by Don Bolognese. New York, Dial Press, 1970.
Me Day, illustrated by Robert Weaver. New York, Dial Press, 1971.
Emily and the Klunky Baby and the Next-Door Dog, illustrated by Martha Alexander. New York, Dial Press, 1972.
I'll Tell on You, illustrated by Gail Owens. New York, Dutton, 1976.
I Hate Red Rover, illustrated by Gail Owens. New York, Dutton, 1979.
The Poison Ivy Case, illustrated by Marylin Hafner. New York, Dial Press, 1983.
Strawberry Shortcake and Sad Mr. Sun, illustrated by Pat Sustendal. Beverly, Massachusetts, Parker, 1983.
Don't Be My Valentine, illustrated by Syd Hoff. New York, Harper, 1985.
The Dog Food Caper, illustrated by Marylin Hafner. New York, Dial Press, 1985; London, A. and C. Black, 1987.
Oh, Little Rabbit!, illustrated by Kathy Wilburn. New York, Golden Books, 1989.
Trouble Will Find You, illustrated by Michael Chesworth. Boston, Houghton Mifflin, 1994.

Fiction as Joan L. Nodset

Who Took the Farmer's Hat?, illustrated by Fritz Siebel. New York, Harper, 1963.
Go Away, Dog, illustrated by Crosby Bonsall. New York, Harper, 1963.
Where Do You Go When You Run Away?, illustrated by Adriana Saviozzi. Indianapolis, Bobbs Merrill, 1964.
Come Here, Cat, illustrated by Steven Kellogg. New York, Harper, 1973.

Other (folktales)

Crocodile and Hen, illustrated by Joan Sandin. New York, Harper, 1969.
It All Began with a Drip, Drip, Drip..., illustrated by Joan Sandin. New York, McCall, 1970; Kingswood, Surrey, World's Work, 1972.
T for Tommy, illustrated by Janet Compere. Champaign, Illinois, Garrard, 1971.
That's Just Fine, and Who-o-o Did It?, illustrated by Dora Leder. Champaign, Illinois, Garrard, 1971.
The Tail of the Mouse, illustrated by Roberta Langman. Boston, Ginn, 1974.
The Spider Makes a Web, illustrated by Arabelle Wheatley. New York, Hastings House, 1979.
Jack and the Beanstalk, illustrated by Carol Nicklaus. New York, Random House, 1980.

Other

Come! Sit! Stay!, illustrated by Marsha Winborn. New York, Watts, 1984.

PUBLICATIONS FOR ADULTS

Other

Editor, *Convent Life: Roman Catholic Religious Orders for Women in North America.* New York, Dial Press, 1964.

*

Manuscript Collections: Kerlan Collection, University of Minnesota, Minneapolis; de Grummond Collection, University of Southern Mississippi, Hattiesburg.

Joan M. Lexau comments:
I like kids, have a lot of child friends and relatives, remember being a child, how it felt. I always wanted to write and was reintroduced to children's books while working at Harper and Row, so I write books for children. I do a lot of easy-to-read books because I remember vividly the explosive joy of being able to read my first real book (but nothing about the process of learning to read). I am now getting into high interest, low vocabulary books for older children who are having trouble reading.

* * *

The sweet side of harsh reality defines the sentiment and the setting of some of Joan M. Lexau's most effective endeavours. When the scene is Harlem she sketches the street gangs and the tenements, the precarious financial circumstances and the inevitable one-adult households. But such socially erosive factors never dominate. They are the foil which sets off her most telling theme—the triumph of the human spirit.

It is never an epic victory. Harlem must remain what it is, an all-too-often inescapable terrain, a cauldron forever seething and threatening to reduce solid humanity into a soft decomposing mass. But there are those who with sustained commitment to decency and ordered existence achieve a succession of modest accomplishments in the ongoing struggle against the forces of uncertainty and despair. Benjie and his grandmother are two such unlikely victors in a field of battle against unsmiling, often savage hordes who use the innocent as their prey. Granny and Benjie might occupy the fourth floor of some overcrowded apartment where hopelessness engulfs most of the inhabitants, but Granny maintains a homey sense of class which is manifest even in a picture-book presentation. The fourth floor with no elevator becomes a game not a burden as "they set off down the stairs and down the stairs and down the stairs...to the sidewalk" (*Benjie*). The sameness settles into a tradition instead of becoming a treadmill. They might share a bathroom with a virtual horde of faceless occupants of this compartment of last resort, but Granny has long since devised a lifestyle which mingles impeccable cleanliness and an unchanging routine with a wry humour that sprinkles joy into an environment which might have been expected to have dried out everything living. She scrubs and scrubs. Benjie's scuffed shoes are treated with a brown crayon. Such homely aesthetics underline the triumph of invention over poverty. Eventually the over-shy Benjie himself secures a momentary mastery over his fears in order to recover Granny's lost earring, one of her few legitimate treasures. With despair glaring down upon them, Granny and Benjie uncover a generous measure of self-reliance, a very real accomplishment whose monument too often remains hidden within the soul of the doer.

Striped Ice Cream! is a tender idyll of another single-parent black family. The importance of a proper proportion of dreams and reality spices a situation which could degenerate into a series of bland sentiments or a sociological horror story. Mama insists that in spite of financial woes the family does get by. Her son retorts, "Sure...nobody said we didn't. We were just dreaming." Mama, who like Granny knows that the blend of reality and ideals is crucial, replies, "no harm in that...as long as we know it's a dream and don't spend all our time in just dreaming." Overblown dreams had cost the family its father, as illusions led to shame and then desertion. But there are dreams which not only serve as incentive, but which, with a mite of ingenuity, can be wedded to reality. The economically deprived family does manage to get the longed-for striped ice cream for the youngest girl's birthday.

Rafer (*Me Day*) finds all the ordinary amenities of birthdays (cake, authority in selecting television shows, and exemption from chores) offset by the absence of his father who, unable to find employment, fled the face of failure. His father does make an unexpected if temporary appearance to spend the day with Rafer. It's only a day to be sure, but even the father who succumbed to conditions emerges with the reassuring words. "Look, your mother and me are divorced. Not you kids. No way! You and me are tight, buddy. Together like glue." To which Rafer replies "Don't go so fast, Daddy...I want it to be a long, long day." The artistry in prolonging substantial pleasantries—soundings of Emerson—make frequent appearances in any of number of Lexau's situations. They do not solve circumstances, but they do considerably more than make them tolerable.

Snatching jewels from ordinary places appears as an embedded theme within the wide variety of Lexau's topics. The philosopher Archimedes (*Archimedes Takes a Bath*) might be an elderly genius, but he is also the archetypical child. Preoccupied with his thoughts, he finds hygiene and personal appearance bothersome matters. His attendant, a young boy, finally coaxes him into a tub where the irrepressible philosopher uses the experience to deduce a means to figure out a principle of physics, and in the process solves a palace mystery. His bath, a confinement of sorts not unlike the Harlem tenement, yields unexpected insights. Ingenuity is the connection of a series of things known to produce the unusual. The childlike sense of discovery must be maintained in the adult behaviour if the flow of treasures is not to cease.

Even with her zany adventures there is the element of strange people supplying answers. The eccentric Miss Hepp who doesn't appear to know what she is doing (and probably doesn't) (*The Dog Food Caper*) shakes up things and a solution to the mystery emerges where stale probability had exhausted itself. No wonder she earned herself the title of witch.

Human ingenuity can arise from genius, from eccentricity, or from calm determination to remain decent. Its wisdom can drop from seeming failures in the not-so-funny comedy of humours. In the process of tracing its whereabouts, Lexau is an appealing guide. There are many answers, many sources, many unlikely sages. The quest continues along with her ever-expanding writings for the young of all ages.

—Leonard R. Mendelsohn

LIFTON, Betty Jean

Nationality: American. **Born:** Betty Jean Kirschner, New York City. **Education:** Barnard College, New York, B.A. 1948; Union Institute, Ph.D. 1992. **Family:** Married the writer Robert Jay Lifton in 1952; one son and one daughter. **Address:** 300 Central Park West, New York, New York 10024, U.S.A.

Publications for Children

Fiction

Joji and the Dragon, illustrated by Eiichi Mitsui. New York, Morrow, 1957.

Mogo the Mynah, illustrated by Anne Scott. New York, Morrow, 1958.

Joji and the Fog, illustrated by Eiichi Mitsui. New York, Morrow, 1959.

Kap the Kappa, illustrated by Eiichi Mitsui. New York, Morrow, 1960.

The Dwarf Pine Tree, illustrated by Fuku Akino. New York, Atheneum, 1963.

Joji and the Amanojaku, illustrated by Eiichi Mitsui. New York, Norton, 1965.

The Cock and the Ghost Cat, illustrated by Fuku Akino. New York, Atheneum, 1965.

The Rice-Cake Rabbit, illustrated by Eiichi Mitsui. New York, Norton, 1966.

The Many Lives of Chio and Goro, illustrated by Yasuo Segawa. New York, Norton, 1966.

Taka-Chan and I: A Dog's Journey to Japan, by Runcible, photographs by Eikoh Hosoe. New York, Norton, 1967.

Kap and the Wicked Monkey, illustrated by Eiichi Mitsui. New York, Norton, 1968.

The Secret Seller, illustrated by Etienne Delessert. New York, Norton, 1968.

The One-Legged Ghost, illustrated by Fuku Akino. New York, Atheneum, 1968.

The Mud Snail Son, illustrated by Fuku Akino. New York, Atheneum, 1971.

The Silver Crane, illustrated by Laszlo Kubinyi. New York, Seabury Press, 1971.

Good Night, Orange Monster, illustrated by Cyndy Szekeres. New York, Atheneum, 1972.

Jaguar, My Twin, illustrated by Ann Leggett. New York, Atheneum, 1976.

I'm Still Me. New York, Knopf, 1981.

Tell Me a Real Adoption Story, illustrated by Claire A. Nivola. New York, Knopf, 1994.

Play

Kap the Kappa, adaptation of her own story, in *Contemporary Children's Theater,* edited by Lifton. New York, Avon, 1974.

Other

A Dog's Guide to Tokyo, photographs by Eikoh Hosoe. New York, Norton, 1969.

Children of Vietnam, with Thomas C. Fox. New York, Atheneum, 1972.
Editor, *Contemporary Children's Theater.* New York, Avon, 1974.

PUBLICATIONS FOR ADULTS

Play

Moon Walk, music and lyrics by the Open Window (produced New York, 1970).

Other

Return to Hiroshima, photographs by Eikoh Hosoe. New York, Atheneum, 1970; revised edition, as *A Place Called Hiroshima,* New York and London, Kodansha, 1985.
Twice Born: Memoirs of an Adopted Daughter. New York, McGraw Hill, 1975; London, Penguin, 1977.
Lost and Found: The Adoption Experience. New York, Dial Press, 1979.
The King of Children: A Biography of Janusz Korczak. New York, Farrar Straus, and London, Chatto and Windus, 1988.
Journey of the Adopted Self: A Quest for Wholeness. New York, BasicBooks, 1994.

* * *

Betty Jean Lifton's prolific work as a writer reflects the influence of sojourns in the Far East. In her children's fiction such oriental themes as non-violence and the eternal recurrence of nature are accompanied by a cavalcade of strange creatures chiefly drawn from (often moralistic) Japanese folktales.

Among the folk creatures is Joji, a peace-loving scarecrow befriended by the very crows he is supposed to frighten away from a farmer's rice field. In *Joji and the Dragon* Joji's master discards him for a hired dragon. The crows scare off their would-be conqueror, thus enabling Joji to be restored to his rightful position. Captured by a rice-paddy-terrorizing demon in *Joji and the Amanojaku* he is again rescued by his crow friends who intimidate his ferocious captor. Joji, a lively espouser of non-violence, is appealing to the very young.

Another protagonist is a Kappa, a legendary Japanese river elf with a monkey's face and a turtle's back. In *Kap the Kappa* the mischievous Kap leaves his river home to be adopted by a fisherman whose family disguise him as a boy. However, his incorrigible pranks disclose his identity to all, and, after realizing he cannot be a human, he returns to the river and his true parents. An inspired creation, Kap inhabits other stories as well as a play which evinces the author's considerable skill as a playwright for children.

A mountain demon in *The Dwarf Pine Tree* grants a tiny evergreen its wish to become a dwarf pine tree beautiful enough to cure an ailing princess. The tree patiently undergoes the necessary painful transformation, is discovered and brought to the princess whose health is restored, and then it passes away to become a tree spirit. This poignant work reflecting the gentle spirit of Buddha emerges as a minor masterpiece.

Animal characters also abound in Lifton's books. A loyal rooster in the suspenseful and touching *The Cock and the Ghost Cat* sacrifices himself to protect his master from a ghost cat bent on stealing the household's provisions. The man-size title character of *The Rice-Cake Rabbit* makes the best rice-cakes in Japan but aspires to be a samurai, a profession reserved for men. He is banished to the moon when he succeeds. This gently ironic yarn is among the author's best. In *The Many Lives of Chio and Goro* the transmigrating souls of a farm couple pass through animal life back to human life with comic complications in a tale which the reader can appreciate on several levels.

Lifton's stories have an audience range of ages four to 10. They are characterized by humor, an economy of words, vivid characterizations, well-structured narratives drawn from Japanese folktales without diluting the cultural source, and handsomely imaginative and colorful brush and ink illustrations by such artists as Eiichi Mitsui and Fuku Akino. Her fiction's appeal for young children and its effectiveness in stimulating interest in oriental culture are unquestionable. These factors earn Lifton a position of prominence in juvenile literature as an imaginative, sensitive, and skillful story teller.

—Christian H. Moe

LINDSAY, Norman (Alfred William)

Nationality: Australian. **Born:** Creswick, Victoria, 22 February 1879. **Education:** Creswick State School and Creswick Grammar School. **Family:** Married 1) Kate Parkinson in 1900 (divorced 1920), three sons, including the writer Jack Lindsay; 2) Rose Soady in 1920, two daughters. **Career:** Artist and freelance illustrator: for the *Hawklet* sporting paper, after 1896, and *Tocsin,* both in Melbourne; co-editor, the *Rambler,* Melbourne, 1899; joined Sydney *Bulletin* in 1901, and chief cartoonist until 1923, and 1932-58; associated with the *Lone Hand,* Melbourne, 1907-21, and Endeavour Press, Sydney, 1932-35. Individual shows: Sydney and Melbourne, 1909; Adelaide, 1924; London, 1925; Sydney, 1968; Newcastle, New South Wales, 1969; group show: Exhibition of Australian Art, London, 1923. **Died:** 21 November 1969.

PUBLICATIONS FOR CHILDREN (ILLUSTRATED BY THE AUTHOR)

Fiction

The Magic Pudding, Being the Adventures of Bunyip Bluegum and His Friends Bill Barnacle and Sam Sawnoff. Sydney, Angus and Robertson, 1918; London, Hamish Hamilton, and New York, Farrar and Rinehart, 1936.
The Flyaway Highway. Sydney, Angus and Robertson, 1936.

Poetry

Puddin' Poems, Being the Best of the Verse from "The Magic Pudding." Sydney, Angus and Robertson, 1977.

PUBLICATIONS FOR ADULTS

Fiction

A Curate in Bohemia. Sydney, Bookstall, 1913; London, Laurie, 1937.

Hyperborea: Two Fantastic Travel Essays. London, Fanfrolico Press, 1928.
Madam Life's Lovers: A Human Narrative Embodying a Philosophy of the Artist in Dialogue Form. London, Fanfrolico Press, 1929.
Redheap. London, Faber, 1930; as *Every Mother's Son,* New York, Cosmopolitan, 1930.
The Cautious Amorist. New York, Farrar and Rinehart, 1932; London, Laurie, 1934.
Miracles by Arrangement. London, Faber, 1932; as *Mr. Gresham and Olympus,* New York, Farrar and Rinehart, 1932.
Saturdee. Sydney, Endeavour Press, 1933; London, Laurie, 1936; New York, AMS Press, 1976.
Pan in the Parlour. New York, Farrar and Rinehart, 1933; London, Laurie, 1934.
Age of Consent. London, Laurie, and New York, Farrar and Rinehart, 1938.
The Cousin from Fiji. Sydney and London, Angus and Robertson, 1945; New York, Random House, 1946.
Halfway to Anywhere. Sydney, Angus and Robertson, 1947.
Dust or Polish? Sydney and London, Angus and Robertson, 1950.
Rooms and Houses: An Autobiographical Novel. Sydney and London, Ure Smith, 1968.

Other

Norman Lindsay's Book 1-2, edited by Harold Burston. Sydney, Bookstall, 1912-15.
The Pen Drawings of Norman Lindsay, edited by Sydney Ure Smith and Bertram Stevens. Sydney, Angus and Robertson, 1918.
Creative Effort: An Essay in Affirmation. Sydney, Art in Australia, 1920; revised edition, London, Palmer, 1924.
Pen Drawings. Sydney, McQuitty, 1924.
The Etchings of Norman Lindsay. London, Constable, 1927.
Norman Lindsay's Pen Drawings. Sydney, Art in Australia, 1931.
Norman Lindsay Water Colour Book: Eighteen Reproductions in Colour from Original Watercolours, with an Appreciation of the Medium. Sydney, Springwood Press, 1939; augmented edition, Sydney and London, Ure Smith, 1969.
Paintings in Oil.... Sydney, Shepherd Press, 1945.
Bohemians of the Bulletin. Sydney, Angus and Robertson, 1965.
The Scribblings of an Idle Mind. Melbourne, Lansdowne Press, 1966.
Norman Lindsay's Ship Models. Sydney, Angus and Robertson, 1966.
Selected Pen Drawings. Sydney, Angus and Robertson, 1968; New York, Bonanza, 1970.
Pencil Drawings. Sydney, Angus and Robertson, 1969.
My Mask, for What Little I Know of the Man Behind It: An Autobiography. Sydney and London, Angus and Robertson, 1970.
Two Hundred Etchings, edited by Douglas Stewart. Sydney, Angus and Robertson, 1973.
Pen Drawings. Sydney, Ure Smith, 1974.
Norman Lindsay's Cats, edited by Douglas Stewart. Melbourne, Macmillan, 1975; revised edition, Melbourne, Sun, 1983.
Siren and Satyr: The Personal Philosophy of Norman Lindsay. Melbourne, Sun, 1976.
Favourite Etchings. Sydney, Angus and Robertson, 1977; London, Angus and Robertson, 1978; as *Etchings,* London, Angus and Robertson, 1982.
Letters of Norman Lindsay, edited by R.G. Howarth and A.W. Barker. Sydney and London, Angus and Robertson, 1979.
Norman Lindsay's War Cartoons, edited by Peter Fullerton. Melbourne and London, Melbourne University Press, 1983.
The World of Norman Lindsay, edited by Lin Bloomfield. Melbourne, Sun, 1983.
The Comic Art of Norman Lindsay, edited by Keith Wingrove. Sydney, Angus and Robertson, 1987.

Editor, *The Golden Shanty: Short Stories,* by Edward Dyson. Sydney, Angus and Robertson, 1963.

*

Critical Studies: *Norman Lindsay,* Melbourne, Lansdowne Press, 1962, and *Norman Lindsay: The Embattled Olympian,* Melbourne and London, Oxford University Press, 1973, both by John Hetherington: *Norman Lindsay: His Books, Manuscripts, and Autograph Letters in the Library of, and Annotated by, Harry F. Chaplin,* Sydney, Wentworth Press, 1969; *Norman Lindsay: A Personal Record* by Douglas Stewart, Melbourne, Nelson, 1975; *Portrait of Pa* by Jane Lindsay, Sydney, Angus and Robertson, 1983; *Norman Lindsay: Impulse to Draw* by Lin Bloomfield, Sydney, Bay, 1984.

Illustrator: *Oblation* by A.G. Stephens, 1902; *This Is the Book of Our New Selection* by Arthur H. Davis, 1903; *Satyrs and Sunlight,* 1909 and 1928, *Colombine,* 1920, and *Idyllia,* 1922, all by Hugh McCrae; *Satyricon,* 1910, and *The Complete Works of Gaius Petronius,* 1927; *Songs of a Campaign,* 1917, and *The Isle of San,* 1919, both by Leon Gellert; *The Man from Snowy River,* 1920, and *The Animals Noah Forgot,* 1933, both by A.B. Paterson; *The Inns of Greece and Rome* by W.C. Firebaugh, 1923; *Fauns and Ladies,* 1923, *The Passionate Neatherd,* 1926, and *Faces and Places,* 1974, all by Jack Lindsay, *Lysistrata,* 1925, and *Women in Parliament,* 1929, both by Aristophanes, *Propertius in Love,* 1927, and *Homage to Sappho,* 1928, all translated by Jack Lindsay, and *Loving Mad Tom,* 1927, edited by Jack Lindsay; *Thief of the Moon,* 1924, *Cuckooz Contrey,* 1932, and *Five Bells,* 1939, all by Kenneth Slessor; *The Antichrist* by Nietzsche, 1928; *As It Was in the Beginning* by Dulcie Deamer, 1929; *A Defence of Women* by John Donne, 1930; *Our Earth* by Kenneth Mackenzie, 1937; *Elegy for an Airman,* 1940, *Sonnets to an Unknown Soldier,* 1941, *Ned Kelly,* 1946, *Shipwreck,* 1947, *Sun Orchids and Other Poems,* 1952, *Fisher's Ghost,* 1960, and *The Garden of Ships,* 1962, all by Douglas Stewart; *Great Expectations* by Dickens, 1947; *A Drum for Ben Boyd* by Francis Webb, 1948; *The Letters of Rachel Henning* edited by David Adams, 1952; *The Collected Verse of A.B Paterson,* 1982.

* * *

In Norman Lindsay's *The Magic Pudding* an urbane young koala called Bunyip Bluegum leaves home because of nuisances cre ated by his Uncle Wattleberry's whiskers. Nattily dressed in Edwardian leisure-wear, Bunyip soon discovers a disadvantage of genteel strolling:

> Observe my doleful plight.
> For here am I without a crumb
> To satisfy a raging tum—
> O what an oversight!
> "As he was indulging in these melancholy reflections he came round a bend in the road, and discovered two people in the very act of having lunch. These people were none other than Bill Barnacle, the sailor, and his friend, Sam Sawnoff, the penguin bold."

These boisterous characters invite Bunyip to share their pudding, which has the advantages of being inexhaustible and as variable in kind and flavours as the eaters wish. It is also a larrikin called Albert, with sprinting ability when not being dined upon, and with unrefined speech to express contempt of all but hearty eaters:

> Eat away, chew away, munch and bolt and guzzle,
> Never leave the table till you're full up to the muzzle!

The rest of the story is a rollick of campfire feasts and roaring songs, interrupted by desperate attempts to recover Albert from puddin' thieves. These are mostly a "snooting, snouting" Possum and his accomplice, "a bulbous, boozy-looking Wombat," but there is also "a Judge who's been poisoned/By Puddin' and Port."

In these adventures Bill and Sam produce the necessary snout-bending pugilistics; Bunyip Bluegum supplies encouragement, inspirations, and tactics. The nonsense story is told in fluent colloquial prose, in uproarious verse, and in the vigorous drawings of Lindsay at the height of his great ability as an illustrator in black-and-white.

So much of the fun and fast movement depends on sound that children of nine or 10, unable to read well enough to appreciate the rollicking prose and verse, often fail to enjoy the book. Read aloud, however, it's an instant success. There seems no upward limit to its "reading age."

Lindsay is said to have written the book to back one of his multitudinous opinions: that children prefer food to fairies. It may seem that, although he rejected the phoney faerie of Victorian fiction, he accepted the talking-animal mode; but perhaps his animal characters are metaphors, rather than personifications. Certainly Lindsay, a life-long experimenter in crafts, became so involved in his essay at a book for children that the story has none of the humourless stiffness of so many first attempts. In fact, *The Magic Pudding* is the only Australian children's book that is indisputably a classic.

He tried again, in 1936, but *The Flyaway Highway* lacks the glorious spontaneity of *The Puddin'*. It depends on outdated ideas (the platitudinous themes of late-Victorian popular fiction) and on dated slang. In spite of its vigorous pen-drawings, and the presence of "the bloke with cow's hooves" (who seems to be an irreverent response to Kenneth Grahame's Pan), it fails to satisfy either children or adults.

—Dennis Hall

LINE, David

Pseudonym for Lionel Davidson. **Nationality:** British. **Born:** Hull, Yorkshire, 31 March 1922. **Military Service:** Royal Naval Submarine Service, 1941-46. **Family:** Married Fay Jacobs in 1949; two sons. **Career:** Freelance magazine journalist and editor, 1946-59. **Awards:** Crime Writers Association Gold Dagger, for adult fiction, 1961, 1967, 1979. **Agent:** Curtis Brown, 28/29 Haymarket, London SW14 4SP, England.

Publications for Children

Fiction

Soldier and Me. New York, Harper, 1965.
Run for Your Life. London, Cape, 1966.
Mike and Me. London, Cape, 1974.
Under Plum Lake (as Lionel Davidson). London, Cape, and New York, Knopf, 1980.
Screaming High. London, Cape, and Boston, Little Brown, 1985.

Publications for Adults as Lionel Davidson

Novels

The Night of Wenceslas. London, Gollancz, 1960; New York, Harper, 1961.
The Rose of Tibet. London, Gollancz, and New York, Harper, 1962.
A Long Way to Shiloh. London, Gollancz, 1966; as *The Menorah Men,* New York, Harper, 1966.
Making Good Again. London, Cape, and New York, Harper, 1968.
Smith's Gazelle. London, Cape, and New York, Knopf, 1971.
The Sun Chemist. London, Cape, and New York, Knopf, 1976.
The Chelsea Murders. London, Cape, 1978; as *Murder Games,* New York, Coward McCann, 1978.
Kolymsky Heights. London, Heinemann, and New York, St. Martin's, 1994.

* * *

"David Line" is the pseudonym of the novelist Lionel Davidson. He is an occasional writer for children—only five novels in 20 years—but a very popular and successful one, whose books are highly regarded by teachers as well as having a proven direct appeal to children. Writing as David Line, he has published four children's novels, all thrillers, and under his own name a fifth, the children's fantasy *Under Plum Lake.* Although the choice of name clearly signifies the author's own sense of a difference not just of genre but of seriousness, nevertheless there are points in common between all of the books which declare them clearly the same author's work.

The Line stories are deceptively simple both in narrative and language. In fact they belong to a scarce and valuable form of children's writing, the nature of which accounts for their popularity with educators as well as children themselves. They are taut, lean, strongly plotted thrillers, with fast-moving narratives filled with unrelenting excitement and suspense—a traditional "good read" in fact. The economy of narrative style matches the economy of unembellished action: terse sentences, short paragraphs, and concise chapters all make the stories easy to read quickly. But the books are also highly literate and intelligent; simplicity does not mean simplification, spareness and pace of language do not bring cliché, and familiar situations avoid hackneyed stereotype by their freshness of particular setting and meticulous accuracy of technical detail.

Two of the books, *Run for Your Life* and *Mike and Me,* involved the same main character, Jim Woolcott. *Run for Your Life* is like a junior version of John Buchan's *The Thirty-Nine Steps,* and Woolcott strongly resembles an English schoolboy equivalent of Buchan's Richard Hannay. Like Hannay, Woolcott comes into accidental possession of significant political information, and is unable to free himself of it by simply informing the authorities; like Hannay, he is quickly on the run, pursued by those who wish to silence him; like Hannay, he has enemies who can assume plausible disguises and official roles, and is exposed in a familiar British landscape which is suddenly dangerous and isolating; and his equivalent of Hannay's powerful friends come finally to his aid. Woolcott is in most respects a reluctant adventurer, a conformist figure who dislikes avoidable hassle, but when occasion demands he proves intelligent and resourceful, adaptable and plucky. And in his convincing first-person narrative he shows a shrewd, iconoclastic wit and humour which often cut the adult world to size.

Unlike Hannay, however, Jim Woolcott is not alone. In *Run for Your Life* his adventures are shared (indeed caused) by a less orthodox companion. The refugee Hungarian schoolboy "Soldier" is a likeable oddity with a gift for finding trouble. This is the pattern for the other books too. In *Mike and Me* the action is confined to Woolcott's home town, but again involves dangerous information, escape, and hot pursuit; and again Woolcott has an eccentric partner, his naive and trouble-prone cousin Mike. The same pattern recurs in a more intricate and ambitious story, *Screaming High,* where the bright but circumspect schoolboy Nick is led into hair-raising adventures by his friendship with a maverick and wonderfully gifted adolescent trumpet-player known as Ratbag. Nick, like Woolcott, is a model of unwilling courage and resource when crisis strikes.

In each book there is a serious political or social theme—the politics of emigré Hungarians in *Run for Your Life,* unscrupulous property developers in *Mike and Me,* international drug trafficking in *Screaming High*—but each time it is deftly understated, its seriousness indicated but not allowed to subvert the primacy of adventure.

Under Plum Lake also has an "ordinary" schoolboy hero, Barry Gordon, with an extraordinary partner, Dido, and in narrative style and method there is much in common with the other books. But the stakes are higher here. Barry's world of (not quite) accidental adventure is Egon, a parallel world beneath the seas, an enigmatic co-existent universe to which Dido has lured him. Egon is a kind of Utopia, an enormously advanced and civilised world of general happiness and transcendent youthfulness and play. It is an alternative evolutionary outcome, a vision of what our world could one day be, but in some ways it is also a place of transfigured and perpetual childhood. After Barry's visit all memory of Egon should be erased from his mind, but it isn't. Barry is explicitly left psychologically damaged, stranded between two worlds. And therein lies his peril. *Under Plum Lake* is a lyrical but disturbing book, capable of simple readings but multiple interpretation. At one level the two worlds stand for childhood and maturity. Egon may represent specific fantasy delights of childhood, delights which are real and true in their psychological time, but which we, like Barry, cannot for our peace afford to revisit or recall, once childhood is over.

—Peter Hollindale

LINKLATER, Eric (Robert Russell)

Nationality: British. **Born:** Dounby, Orkney, 8 March 1899. **Education:** Aberdeen Grammar School; studied medicine, then English at the University of Aberdeen, M.A. 1925. **Military Service:** Black Watch, 1917-19: private; Royal Engineers, commanding the Royal Engineers Orkney Fortress, 1939-41: Major; member of staff, Directorate of Public Relations, War Office, 1941-45; temporary Lieutenant-Colonel in Korea, 1951: Territorial Decoration. **Family:** Married Marjorie MacIntyre in 1933; two sons and two daughters. **Career:** Assistant editor, *Times of India,* Bombay, 1925-27; assistant to the Professor of English Literature, University of Aberdeen, 1927-28; Commonwealth Fellow, Cornell University, Ithaca, New York, and the University of California, Berkeley, 1928-30; full-time writer from 1930. Rector, University of Aberdeen, 1945-48; Deputy Lieutenant of Ross and Cromarty, Scotland, 1968-73. **Awards:** Library Association Carnegie Medal, 1945. L.L.D.: University of Aberdeen, 1946. Fellow, Royal Society of Edinburgh, 1971. C.B.E. (Commander, Order of the British Empire), 1954. **Died:** 7 November 1974.

Publications for Children

Fiction

The Wind on the Moon, illustrated by Nicolas Bentley. London and New York, Macmillan, 1944.

The Pirates in the Deep Green Sea, illustrated by William Reeves. London and New York, Macmillan, 1949.

Other

Karina with Love, photographs by Karl Werner Gullers. London, Macmillan, 1958.

Publications for Adults

Novels

White-Maa's Saga. London, Cape, and New York, Peter Smith 1929.

Poet's Pub. London, Cape, 1929; New York, Cape and Smith, 1930.

Juan in America. London, Cape, and New York, Cape and Smith 1931.

The Men of Ness: The Saga of Thorlief Coalbiter's Sons. London Cape, 1932; New York, Farrar and Rinehart, 1933.

Magnus Merriman. London, Cape, and New York, Farrar and Rinehart, 1934.

Ripeness Is All. London, Cape, and New York, Farrar and Rinehart 1935.

Juan in China. London, Cape, and New York, Farrar and Rinehart, 1937.
The Sailor's Holiday. London, Cape, 1937; New York, Farrar and Rinehart, 1938.
The Impregnable Women. London, Cape, and New York, Farrar and Rinehart, 1938.
Judas. London, Cape, and New York, Farrar and Rinehart, 1939.
Private Angelo. London, Cape, and New York, Macmillan, 1946.
A Spell for Old Bones. London, Cape, 1949; New York, Macmillan, 1950.
Mr. Byculla: A Story. London, Hart Davis, 1950; New York, Harcourt Brace, 1951.
Laxdale Hall. London, Cape, 1951; New York, Harcourt Brace, 1952.
The House of Gair. London, Cape, 1953; New York, Harcourt Brace, 1954.
The Faithful Ally. London, Cape, 1954; as *The Sultan and the Lady,* New York, Harcourt Brace, 1955.
The Dark of Summer. London, Cape, 1956; New York, Harcourt Brace, 1957.
Position at Noon. London, Cape, 1958; as *My Fathers and I,* New York, Harcourt Brace, 1959.
The Merry Muse. London, Cape, 1959; New York, Harcourt Brace, 1960.
Roll of Honour. London, Hart Davis, 1961.
Husband of Delilah. London, Macmillan, 1962; New York, Harcourt Brace, 1963.
A Man over Forty. London, Macmillan, and New York, St. Martin's Press, 1963.
A Terrible Freedom. London, Macmillan, 1966.

Short Stories

The Crusader's Key. London, White Owl Press, and New York, Knopf, 1933.
The Revolution. London, White Owl Press, 1934.
God Likes Them Plain. London, Cape, 1935.
Sealskin Trousers and Other Stories. London, Hart Davis, 1947.
A Sociable Plover and Other Stories and Conceits. London, Hart Davis, 1957.
The Stories of Eric Linklater. London, Macmillan, 1968; New York, Horizon Press, 1969.

Plays

The Devil's in the News (produced in the 1930s). London, Cape, 1934.
The Crisis in Heaven: An Elysian Comedy (produced Edinburgh and London, 1944). London, Macmillan, 1944; New York, Macmillan, 1945.
To Meet the MacGregors (produced Glasgow, 1946?). Included in *Two Comedies,* 1950.
Love in Albania (produced Glasgow, 1948; London, 1949). London, English Theatre Guild, 1950.
Two Comedies: Love in Albania and To Meet the MacGregors. London and New York, Macmillan, 1950.
The Mortimer Touch, adaptation of *The Alchemist* by Ben Jonson (as *The Atom Doctor,* produced Edinburgh, 1950; as *The Mortimer Touch,* produced London, 1952). London, French, 1952.
Breakspear in Gascony. London, Macmillan, and New York, St. Martin's Press, 1958.

Screenplay: *The Man Between,* with Harry Kurnitz, 1953.

Poetry

Poobie. Edinburgh, Porpoise Press, 1925.
A Dragon Laughed and Other Poems. London, Cape, 1930.

Other

Ben Jonson and King James: Biography and Portrait. London, Cape, 1931; New York, Cape and Smith, 1932.
Mary, Queen of Scots. London, Davies, and New York, Appleton Century, 1933.
Robert the Bruce. London, Davies, and New York, Appleton Century, 1934.
The Lion and the Unicorn; or, What England Has Meant to Scotland. London, Routledge, 1935.
The Cornerstones: A Conversation in Elysium. London and New York, Macmillan, 1941.
The Defence of Calais. London, His Majesty's Stationery Office, 1941.
The Man on My Back: An Autobiography. London and New York, Macmillan, 1941.
The Northern Garrisons: The Defence of Iceland and the Faroe, Orkney and Shetland Islands. London, His Majesty's Stationery Office, and New York, Garden City Publishing Company, 1941.
The Raft, and Socrates Asks Why: Two Conversations. London, Macmillan, 1942; New York, Macmillan, 1943.
The Highland Division. London, His Majesty's Stationery Office, 1942.
The Great Ship, and Rabelais Replies: Two Conversations. London, Macmillan, 1944; New York, Macmillan, 1945.
The Art of Adventure (essays). London, Macmillan, 1947.
The Campaign in Italy. London, Her Majesty's Stationery Office, 1951.
Our Men in Korea. London, Her Majesty's Stationery Office, 1952.
A Year of Space: A Chapter in Autobiography. London, Macmillan, and New York, Harcourt Brace, 1953.
The Ultimate Viking (essays). London, Macmillan, 1955; New York, Harcourt Brace, 1956.
Edinburgh. London, Newnes, 1960; New York, Macmillan, 1961.
Gullers' Sweden, photographs by Karl Werner Gullers. Stockholm, Almqvist och Wiksell, 1964.
Orkney and Shetland: An Historical, Geographical, Social, and Scenic Survey. London, Hale, 1965.
The Prince in the Heather. London, Hodder and Stoughton, 1965; New York, Harcourt Brace, 1966.
The Conquest of England. London, Hodder and Stoughton, and New York, Doubleday, 1966.
The Survival of Scotland: A Review of Scottish History from Roman Times to the Present Day. London, Heinemann, and New York, Doubleday, 1968.
Scotland. London, Thames and Hudson, and New York, Viking Press, 1968.
The Secret Larder; or, How a Salmon Lives and Why He Dies. London, Macmillan, 1969.
The Royal House of Scotland. London, Macmillan, 1970; as *The Royal House,* New York, Doubleday, 1970.

Fanfare for a Tin Hat: A Third Essay in Autobiography. London, Macmillan, 1970.
The Music of the North. Aberdeen, Haddo House Choral Society, 1970.
The Corpse on Clapham Common: A Tale of Sixty Years Ago. London, Macmillan, 1971.
The Voyage of the "Challenger". London, Murray, and New York, Doubleday, 1972.
The Black Watch: The History of the Royal Highland Regiment, with Andro Linklater. London, Barrie and Jenkins, 1977.

Editor, *The Thistle and the Pen: An Anthology of Modern Scottish Writers.* London, Nelson, 1950.
Editor, *John Moore's England: A Selection from His Writings.* London, Collins, 1970.

*

Critical Studies: *Eric Linklater: A Critical Biography* by Michael Parnell, London, Murray, 1985.

* * *

Eric Linklater told the story of the genesis of *The Wind on the Moon* in a letter to me which was subsequently included in *Chosen for Children,* the Library Association's book about the Carnegie Medal. Allowing for natural exuberance—he was always rather larger than life—this can be accepted as the true account of one man's approach to writing for children. It cannot be recommended as a method to aspiring writers, but every original creative mind is idiosyncratic.

The Wind on the Moon was an improvisation, born of the necessity to entertain a pair of demanding children. It belongs in fact to that important group of books, those devised for the private entertainment of individual children. Where it differs from *Alice* and *The Wind in the Willows* is that it was the work of a professional novelist, with whom it must be a rule of life that nothing goes to waste. Even as he spun the rich absurdities out of his mind, Linklater must have known that it must eventually become a book. Its extemporary origin is revealed in an episodic structure, but the episodes are linked and related expertly. *The Wind on the Moon* is a comic fantasy which plays with the idea of humans translated into animal form. One of these is the detective who longed to be able to see over walls; out of this urge came, very naturally, an elongation of neck which ended only in his becoming a giraffe. This and other strange happenings are highly diverting. However, the story was devised in wartime, and although it offered plenty of scope for humour the war was no joke and neither was Nazism. Suddenly the light-hearted and frivolous tale turns serious. The children who had frolicked so joyously as kangaroos become involved in a struggle against tyranny. They suffer hardship and extreme danger and their dearest friend dies. The transition from farce to tragedy is abrupt, but Linklater is too accomplished a writer to fail to make it convincing.

Linklater won a Carnegie Medal with *The Wind on the Moon.* The award amused him because he regarded his book as a trifle written for an occasion. The mastery of construction, the vividly realized adventures, the sharp portraiture and effervescent writing made it a book which transcends its origins.

When he returned later to writing for children Linklater's inspiration was lacking. *The Pirates in the Deep Green Sea* had some characteristic touches, particularly in the invention of grotesque characters, and the crazy story was told with a nautical heartiness. But it quite lacked the spontaneity and the underlying passion which made *The Wind on the Moon* outstanding among the children's books of the war years.

—Marcus Crouch

LIONNI, Leo

Nationality: American (originally Dutch: emigrated to the United States, 1939, naturalized citizen, 1945). **Born:** Born Leonard Lionni in Amsterdam, Netherlands, 5 May 1910. **Education:** Educated at the University of Zurich, 1928-30; University of Genoa, Ph.D. in economics 1935. **Family:** Married Nora Maffi in 1931; two sons. **Career:** Freelance designer, 1930-39; art director, N.W. Ayer and Son Inc., Philadelphia, 1939-47; design director, Olivetti Corporation, New York, 1949-59; art director, *Fortune* magazine, New York, 1949-62; co-editor, *Print,* 1950s; editor, *Panorama,* Milan, 1964-65. Head of the Graphics Design Department, Parsons School of Design, New York, 1952-54. Individual shows: Worcester Museum, Massachusetts, 1958; Philadelphia Art Alliance, 1959; Naviglio, Milan, 1963; Obelisco, Rome, 1964; Galleria dell'Ariete, Milan, 1966; Galleria del Milione, Milan, 1972; Linea 70, Verona, 1973; Il Vicolo, Genoa, 1973; Baukunst Galerie, Cologne, 1974; Klingspor Museum, Offenbach, 1974; Galleria CIAK, Rome, 1975; group shows: Museum of Modern Art, New York, 1954; Bratislava Biennale, 1967; Venice Biennale, 1972. **Awards:** National Society of Art Directors award, 1955; Architectural League Gold Medal, 1956; Bratislava Biennale Golden Apple, 1967; Teheran Film Festival award, 1970; Christopher award, 1970; George G. Stone Center for Children's Books award, 1976; American Institute of Graphic Arts Gold Medal, 1984. **Agent:** Agenzia Letteraria Internazionale, Corso Matteotti 3, Milan, Italy. **Address:** Porcignano, 53017 Radda in Chianti, Siena, Italy.

PUBLICATIONS FOR CHILDREN (ILLUSTRATED BY THE AUTHOR)

Fiction

Little Blue and Little Yellow. New York, McDowell Obolensky 1959; Leicester, Brockhampton Press, 1962.
Inch by Inch. New York, Obolensky, 1960; London, Dobson, 1967.
On My Beach There Are Many Pebbles. New York, Obolensky, 1961; London, Abelard Schuman, 1977.
Swimmy. New York, Pantheon, 1963.
Tico and the Golden Wings. New York, Pantheon, 1964.
Frederick. New York, Pantheon, 1967; London, Abelard Schuman, 1971.
The Alphabet Tree. New York, Pantheon, 1968.
The Biggest House in the World. New York, Pantheon, 1968; London, Andersen Press, 1978.
Alexander and the Wind-Up Mouse. New York, Pantheon, 196[illegible]; London, Abelard Schuman, 1971.
Fish Is Fish. New York, Pantheon, 1970; London, Abelard Schuman, 1972.

Theodore and the Talking Mushroom. New York, Pantheon, 1971; London, Abelard Schuman, 1972.
The Greentail Mouse. New York, Pantheon, 1973.
In the Rabbitgarden. New York, Pantheon, 1975; London, Abelard Schuman, 1976.
A Colour of His Own. London, Abelard Schuman, 1975; New York, Pantheon, 1976.
Pezzettino. New York, Pantheon, 1975; London, Andersen Press, 1977.
I Want to Stay Here! I Want to Go There! A Flea Story. New York, Pantheon, 1977; London, Andersen Press, 1978.
Geraldine, the Music Mouse. New York, Pantheon, and London, Andersen Press, 1979.
Mouse Days. New York, Pantheon, 1981.
Let's Make Rabbits: A Fable. New York, Pantheon, and London, Andersen Press, 1982.
Cornelius. New York, Pantheon, and London, Andersen Press, 1983.
Who? What? Where? When?, 4 vols. New York, Pantheon, 1983.
Tre Amici. Firenze, Regione Toscana, 1984.
Words, Colours, Letters, Numbers, 4 vols. New York, Pantheon, 1984.
Frederick's Fables: A Leo Lionni Treasury. New York, Pantheon, 1985; as *Frederick's Tales,* London, Andersen Press, 1986.
It's Mine! New York, Knopf, and London, Andersen Press, 1986.
Nicolas, Where Have You Been? New York, Knopf, and London, Andersen Press, 1987.
Six Crows. New York, Knopf, 1988; London, Andersen Press, 1989.
Tillie and the Wall. New York, Knopf, and London, Andersen Press, 1989.
Matthew's Dream. London, Andersen, 1991.
Mr. McMouse. New York, Knopf, 1992; London, Andersen Press, 1993.
A Busy Year. New York, Knopf, 1992.
A Color of His Own. New York, Knopf, 1993.
Let's Play. New York, Random House, 1993.
An Extraordinary Egg. New York, Knopf, 1994.

Publications for Adults

Design for the Printed Page. New York, Fortune Magazine, 1960.
Il Taccuino di Leo Lionni. Milan, Electa, 1972.
La Botanica Parallela. Milan, Adelphi, 1976; translated by Patrick Creagh, as *Parallel Botany,* New York, Knopf, 1977.
Leo Lionni at the Library of Congress: A Lecture for International Children's Book Day, presented on May 12, 1988, edited by Sybille A. Jagusch. Washington, Library of Congress, 1992.
Between Worlds: The Autobiography of Leo Lionni. New York, Knopf, 1997.

*

Illustrator: *Mouse Days Calendar 1981,* 1980; *Mouse Days: A Book of Seasons* by Hannah Solomon, 1981; *Come with Us* by Naomi Lewis, 1982.

Leo Lionni comments:

Making books for children occupies a place of prime importance in my endeavors as an artist exploring the possibilities of self-expression and communication. Here, too, are hiding places for private doubts and fantasies, and for private sensual (aesthetic) pleasures. But everything, content and form, has to be simple, explicit, and logical to the utmost. This is not only an exciting challenge but an extraordinary discipline.

I try, in fact, to reduce complex, so-called adult problems (alienation, search for identity, violence, love) to the most elementary verbal and visual structures in the hope that little by little my fables will stimulate creative interpretation on all age levels, and release questions and meanings that lie hidden in the words and pictures.

* * *

Leo Lionni is primarily an artist. He communicates through shape and colour. Because, one suspects, he does not often find a writer whose vision and message match his own, most of his glowingly colourful picture books have his own texts. Like most of the great picture-book makers—Beatrix Potter, Ardizzone, Sendak—he has made a virtue of this necessity, fashioning a literary style that is precisely matched to his images. There is a rare degree of unity in his books which greatly increases their impact on the reader. His texts are designed to be read aloud; they are accordingly rather longer than many picture-book makers (and publishers) would consider desirable, but the delicate balance between word and picture is carefully maintained. The amount of detail in each picture is calculated to occupy the child's attention just for the time that the adult reader takes to read the text aloud.

Lionni's stories are invariably brief. Each contains a single idea and message. In their conception they owe much to the ancient makers of fables; in execution they have all the artist's idiosyncratic viewpoint. *Frederick,* for example, is the reverse side of the Aesop fable the Ant and the Cricket. In Aesop the ant is brought low because he wasted the summer in idle singing. Lionni's Frederick is a mouse who sits around, observing and thinking while his friends and relations store up a harvest against the coming cold. When they rebuke him he claims that he is working, gathering sunrays and colours and words. Winter comes, and the mice tell tales and eat their stores. When the corn is "only a memory" they turn to Frederick, and he warms them with memories of sunlight, brings back the colours of summer, and comforts them with a poem evoking the moods of the seasons. They may still be hungry, but Frederick has helped them through the lean days.

If this seems a rather cosy picture of the real world, others of Lionni's stories are coloured with a tart wit. In *Theodore and the Talking Mushroom* another mouse fails to placate his friends. When Theodore discovers a mushroom that can talk (but only the single word "Quirp") he interprets this to his companions as "the mouse should be venerated above all other animals." The deception works, but not for long. Theodore loses his crown and his livelihood.

The message is usually more positive than this. *Swimmy* shows that unity can be strength: a school of small fish defeat their big enemy by sailing in convoy. In *Cornelius,* a very funny story about crocodiles, the moral—again one which would be acceptable to Aesop—is that it is right to experiment and not put up with inborn physical limitations. Cornelius chooses to walk upright while his brothers and sisters are content to crawl. He takes instruction from a monkey and learns to stand on his head and hang from his tail. When he demonstrates these new achievements to the other crocodiles, their reaction is "So what!" As he walks away disappointed, he observes that they are all trying to emulate his skills. "Life on the riverbeach would never be the same again."

The moral in *The Alphabet Tree* may be for adults only, and none the worse for that. The leaves of the alphabet tree have each a letter. Their one enemy is the wind which may blow them away. The word-bug advises them to join together to make words, and with this added strength they resist the wind. The words however are set out haphazard, and this distresses a passing caterpillar. Following his guidance they form themselves into sentences. Finally they join up to say something *really* important: PEACE ON EARTH AND GOODWILL TOWARD ALL MEN. They climb on to the caterpillar's back, and he sets off. But where? "'To the President,' said the caterpillar."

Lionni's control of words is so sure that it may pass unnoticed. Matched with these strong, richly coloured, and always humorous designs, which gain much from their bold cut-paper technique, his stories speak clearly and irresistibly to adult and child alike.

—Marcus Crouch

LIPKIND, William

Pseudonym: Will. **Nationality:** American. **Born:** New York City, 17 December 1904. **Education:** City College, New York, B.A. 1927; Columbia University Law School, New York, 1928, and Graduate School, 1934-37, Ph.D. in anthropology 1937. **Military Service:** United States Office of War Information, England and Germany, 1944-46. **Family:** Married Maria Cimino in 1937. **Career:** Studied Carajá and Javahé Indians in Brazil, 1938-40; Research Associate in Anthropology, Columbia University, 1940-42; Assistant Professor of Anthropology, Ohio State University, Columbus, 1942-44; Adjunct Assistant Professor, New York University, 1948-70. **Died:** 2 October 1974.

Publications for Children

Fiction as Will (illustrated by Nicolas Mordvinoff, as Nicolas)

The Two Reds. New York, Harcourt Brace, 1950.
Finders Keepers. New York, Harcourt Brace, 1951; Kingswood, Surrey, World's Work, 1964.
Even Steven. New York, Harcourt Brace, 1952.
The Christmas Bunny. New York, Harcourt Brace, 1953.
Circus Ruckus. New York, Harcourt Brace, 1954.
Chaga. New York, Harcourt Brace, 1955.
Perry the Imp. New York, Harcourt Brace, 1956.
Sleepyhead. New York, Harcourt Brace, 1957.
The Magic Feather Duster. New York, Harcourt Brace, 1958.
Four-Leaf Clover. New York, Harcourt Brace, 1959.
The Little Tiny Rooster. New York, Harcourt Brace, 1960.
Billy the Kid. New York, Harcourt Brace, 1961.
Russet and the Two Reds. New York, Harcourt Brace, 1962.
The Boy and the Forest. New York, Harcourt Brace, 1964.

Fiction as William Lipkind

Boy with a Harpoon, illustrated by Nicolas Mordvinoff. New York, Harcourt Brace, 1952.
Boy of the Islands, illustrated by Nicolas Mordvinoff. New York, Harcourt Brace, 1954.
Professor Bull's Umbrella, illustrated by Georges Schreiber. New York, Viking Press, 1954.
Nubber Bear, illustrated by Roger Duvoisin. New York, Harcourt Brace, 1966; London, Faber, 1968.

Other

Days to Remember: An Almanac, illustrated by Jerome Snyder. New York, Obolensky, 1961.

Publications for Adults

Poetry

Beginning Charm for the New Year. New York, Weekend Press, 1951.

Other

Winnebago Grammar. New York, Columbia University Press, 1945.

*

Manuscript Collections: Kerlan Collection, University of Minnesota, Minneapolis.

* * *

William Lipkind's reputation in children's literature was assured by the publication of *The Two Reds,* a runner-up for the Caldecott Medal in 1951, and *Finders Keepers,* the winner in 1952. The honor gained here by Nicolas Mordvinoff, the illustrator of these books, doubtless has reflected upon Lipkind, Mordvinoff's longtime collaborator. Although Mordvinoff's illustrations in their books overshadowed Lipkind's literary contributions to them, one should not dismiss his effect on their success. There seems little doubt that Lipkind well understood the conventions of writing for young children. One children's author, Robert Burch, has remarked that it was a course on writing for children taught by Lipkind that gave him a healthy respect for children's books.

In general, Lipkind used two kinds of narrative plots in his picture books. One is based on fables and other forms of traditional literature. The other takes a more modern approach. An example of the first kind is *Finders Keepers.* Here two dogs fight over a bone instead of sharing it (a common dilemma in fables). They find, however, that this attitude will end only in the loss of the bone. Hence, they agree not to be selfish (the moral of the tale). *Nubber Bear* also contains some of the major motifs of folk literature, e.g., the small person (bear) disobeying authority and journeying away from home on a quest (for honey) that turns out to be fraught with peril and punishment. This serious story falls below Lipkind's usually satisfactory offering, however, because his experiment in having Nubber speak in couplets dissolves into strained doggerel.

That Lipkind can be both serious and frolicsome is apparent. In *Even Steven* a runt of a horse, Steven, proves his merit by recapturing a herd of stolen horses. Thus, he gets "even" for the slight mistreatments he has suffered because of his size. *The Tw*

Reds is a madcap adventure, full of slapstick humor (as is *Professor Bull's Umbrella*), in which a red cat, who tried to steal a red-haired boy's fish, and the boy, find (through parallel adventures) that it is better to be friends than enemies.

The strength of Lipkind's writing is implied by these remarks. It lies for one thing in the kind of characters he chooses, the dialogue they speak, and in the understandable manner in which he describes adventure and creates humor. The weakest parts of his books (*Finders Keepers* is a notable exception) are his awkward plots. Too often Lipkind's plots turn and twist with melodramatic, even haphazard, effects, which makes for loose-jointed and irregular structures, hard to follow—and to believe. In *Professor Bull's Umbrella* the professor's lost umbrella blows around, to no determinable effect, then miraculously (and incredibly) lands back in his hand just as it starts to rain.

If Lipkind's stories for young children generally are little more than mediocre, no such negative criticism can justifiably be lodged against his longer works for older children. *Boy of the Islands,* for example, exemplifies Lipkind's ability to depict in an easy and natural yet compelling style a historical adventure in a culture far removed from his reader's experience. Lipkind creates here an entirely convincing, well-formed, honestly motivated story of the difficulties of growing up in a primitive society. *Boy of the Islands* proves the obvious paradox that Lipkind's greatest literary success was with his lesser-selling books.

—Patrick Groff

LISLE, Janet Taylor

Nationality: American. **Born:** Farmington, Connecticut, 1947. **Education:** Smith College, B.A. 1969; Georgia State University, certificate in journalism 1971. **Family:** Married 1) first husband (divorced); 2) Richard Waterman Lisle in 1976, one daughter. **Address:** c/o Orchard Books, 95 Madison Avenue, New York, New York 10016-7801, U.S.A.

Publications for Children

Fiction

The Dancing Cats of Applesap, illustrated by Joell Shefts. New York, Bradbury, 1984.
Sirens and Spies. New York, Bradbury, 1985.
The Great Dimpole Oak, illustrated by Stephen Gammell. New York, Orchard, 1987.
Afternoon of the Elves. New York, Orchard, 1989.
The Lampfish of Twill, illustrated by Wendy Anderson Halperin. New York, Orchard, 1991.
Forest. New York, Orchard, 1993.
The Gold Dust Letters. New York, Orchard, 1994.
Looking for Juliette. New York, Orchard, 1994.
A Message from the Match Girl, New York, Orchard, 1995.
Angela's Aliens, New York, Orchard, 1996.

* * *

Janet Taylor Lisle creates powerful stories in which magical worlds merge with the everyday worlds of childhood which, of course, have their own share of magic. Her first book, *The Dancing Cats of Applesap,* brings together three very unusual human characters with 100 dancing cats. Painfully shy 10-year-old Melba combines forces with crotchety old Mr. Jiggs and the even more difficult Miss Toonie who works at the fountain in Jiggs drugstore. Together they put their small town on the map and the cats in the Guinness Book of World Records.

Sirens and Spies begins with Jimmy Dee, the town drunk, hiding in the bushes beneath the violin teacher's window, hoping to hear the music. Here too are highly individualistic characters, from 14-year-old Elsie who seems to be an outsider in her family, to flamboyant Miss Fitch who teaches the violin to both Elsie and her sister Mary. Elsie is stubbornly unforgiving when she discovers that the teacher has a secret past. Ultimately, however, Elsie discovers that she and Miss Fitch are very much alike.

The Great Dimpole Oak stands at the center of the town and its history and at the center of this novel. Around it Lisle skillfully weaves many characters and their stories in what is probably her most technically ambitious work. As with all her books, there are surprises, twists of plot, beautiful language, and joyous originality.

Afternoon of the Elves convinces readers that "even without being believed, magic can begin to change things. It moves invisibly through the air, dissolving the usual ways of seeing, allowing new ways to creep in, secretly, quietly, like a stray cat sliding through bushes." Sara-Kate stomps through this story in her dirty combat boots, making younger Hillary almost believe, not only in elves who build a magnificent ferris wheel, but also in Sara-Kate's ability to survive against impossible odds. Even when Hillary's mother breaks through the magic to get help for Sara-Kate and her mother in the real world, Hillary retains a bit of magic, preserving the elves' world in her own backyard.

In *The Lampfish of Twill,* Lisle again brings readers to a place where reality and an otherworld meet. Young Eric who, like so many others, has been orphaned by the sea, ekes out a meager living from that sea with his aunt Opal. A strange older character, Ezekial Cantrip, the only survivor of a downspout into the sea, leads Eric on a mysterious adventure to a world below. Along with Eric's bedraggled pet seagull, the two are guided by the rosy-hued light of the lampfish down a whirlpool to Underwhirl where nothing ever moves, including previous human visitors now rooted as trees. Eric returns to his own world, but he is forever changed.

In *Forest,* Lisle creates the parallel worlds of Upper Forest inhabited by squirrels and Lower Forest where humans live. Only twelve-year-old Amber is perceptive enough to notice the society above, and is it she who prevents war from breaking out between the two in this imaginative mix of realism and fantasy that explores the nature of human conflict.

The Gold Dust Letters is the first of four books in the "Investigators of the Unknown" series. In it, Angela and her two friends discover the source of the "real magic" occurring in Angela's home. This book is less complex than most of the author's stories, but it retains her beauty of language and believable characters who, like most children, can still believe in what can't be explained logically.

In all of her work, Lisle's respect for young readers is evident. She is an elegant writer whose stories are carefully woven with just enough space left for readers to continue to wonder and to imagine new possibilities at the book's close.

—Kay E. Vandergrift

LITTLE, (Flora) Jean

Nationality: Canadian. **Born:** Tainan, Formosa, now Taiwan, 2 January 1932. **Education:** Schools in Guelph, Ontario; Victoria College, University of Toronto, B.A. in English 1955; Institute of Special Education, Salt Lake City. **Career:** Visiting Instructor, Florida State University, Tallahassee; specialist teacher, Beechwood School for Crippled Children, Guelph. **Awards:** Canadian Children's Book award, 1961; Vicky Metcalf award, 1974; Governor General's Literary Award for Children's Literature, Canada Council, 1977; Canada Council prize, 1979; Children's Literature prize (West Germany), 1981; Canadian Library Association Book of the Year award, 1985; Ruth Schwartz award, 1985; *Boston Globe-Horn Book* Honor Award, 1988; Order of Canada, 1993; IODE award, 1995. **Address:** 198 Glasgow Street N, Guelph, Ontario N1H 4X2, Canada.

Publications for Children

Fiction

Mine for Keeps, illustrated by Lewis Parker. Boston, Little Brown, 1962; London, Dent, 1964; Toronto, Little, Brown 1988.
Home from Far, illustrated by Jerry Lazare. Boston, Little Brown, 1965; Toronto, Little, Brown, 1988.
Take Wing, illustrated by Jerry Lazare. Boston, Little Brown, 1968.
From Anna, illustrated by Joan Sandin. New York, Harper, 1972.
Stand in the Wind, illustrated by Emily McCully. New York, Harper, 1975; Toronto and London, Puffin, 1995.
Lost and Found, illustrated by Leoung O'Young. Markham, Ontario, Penguin, and New York, Viking Kestrel, 1985.
Different Dragons, illustrated by Laura Fernandez. Markham, Ontario, New York, and London, Viking Kestrel, 1986.
With Maggie DeVries, *Once Upon a Golden Apple,* illustrated by Phoebe Gilman. New York, London, and Markham, Ontario, Viking Kestrel, 1991.
Jess Was the Brave One, illustrated by Janet Wilson. Toronto and London, Viking, 1991; New York, Viking Kestrel, 1992.
Revenge of the Small Small, illustrated by Janet Wilson. Toronto and London, Viking, 1992; New York, Viking Kestrel, 1993.
With Claire McKay, *Bats about Baseball,* illustrated by Kim LeFerve. Toronto and New York, Viking Kestrel, 1995.
His Banner Over Me. Toronto and New York, Viking Kestrel, 1995.
Jenny and the Hanukkah Queen, illustrated by Suzanne Mogensen. Toronto, Viking, 1995.
Gruntle Piggle Takes Off, illustrated by Johnny Wales. Toronto, Viking, 1996; New York, Viking Kestrel, 1996.
The Belonging Place. Toronto and New York, Viking Kestrel, 1997.
Emma's Magic Winter. New York, HarperCollins, 1998.

Poetry

It's a Wonderful World. Privately printed, 1947.
When the Pie Was Opened. Boston, Little Brown, 1968.
Hey World, Here I Am!, illustrated by Barbara Di Lella. Toronto, Kids Can Press, 1986; New York, Harper, and Oxford, Oxford University Press, 1989.

Publications for Young Adults

Fiction

Spring Begins in March, illustrated by Lewis Parker. Boston, Little Brown, 1966; Toronto, Puffin, 1996.
One to Grow On, illustrated by Jerry Lazare. Boston, Little Brown, 1969; Toronto, Puffin, 1991.
Look Through My Window, illustrated by Joan Sandin. New York, Harper, 1970; Toronto, HarperCollins, 1995.
Kate. New York, Harper, 1971.
Listen for the Singing. New York, Dutton, 1977; Toronto, Clark, Irwin, 1981.
Mama's Going to Buy You a Mockingbird. Markham, Ontario, Penguin, 1984; New York, Viking Kestrel, 1985.

Other

Zephyr. Winnipeg, J. Little, 1983.
Little by Little: A Writer's Education. Markham, Ontario, Viking, 1987.
Invitations to Joy: A Celebration of Canada's Young Readers and the Books They Love. Toronto, Canadian Children's Book Centre, 1989.
Stars Come Out Within. Markham, Ontario, Penguin, 1990.

*

Media Adaptations: *Listening for the Singing* (braille edition), Manitoba Department of Education, Special Materials Services, 1978, CNIB, 1994; *Listen for the Singing* (sound recording), Library Services Branch, 1979, CNIB, 197?; *From Anna* (sound recording), CNIB, 197?, Alberta Education, 1980, 1993, Crane Library, 1980, Canadian Broadcasting Corporation, 1984; *Kate* (sound recording), CNIB, 197?; *Stand in the Wind* (sound recording), CNIB, 197?; *Kate* (braille edition), CNIB, 197?, 1982; *One to Grown On* (braille edition), American Printing House for the Blind, 197?; *From Anna* (braille edition), CNIB, 1980, Seedlings Braille Books for Children, 1989, W. Ross MacDonald School, 1995; *Look Through My Window* (sound recording), CNIB, 1983, Alberta Education, 1980, 1991; *Look Through My Window* (braille edition), CNIB, 1983; *Home From Far* (motion picture and videorecording), Beacon Films, 1984; *Mama's Going to Buy You a Mocking Bird* (sound recording), CNIB, 1985, Manitoba Education, 1988; *Lost and Found* (sound recording), CNIB, 1986, Vancouver Library Services Branch, 1992; *Lost and Found* (braille edition), CNIB, 1986; *Different Dragons* (sound recording), CNIB, 1987; *Hey World, Here I Am!* (sound recording), CNIB, 1987; *Hey World, Here I Am*. (braille edition), CNIB, 1987; *Mama's Going to Buy You a Mocking Bird* (braille edition), CNIB, 1987; *Little By Little: A Writer's Education* (sound recording), CNIB, 1988; *Little By Little: A Writer's Education* (braille edition), CNIB, 1988; *Different Dragons* (braille edition), CNIB, 1989, Atlantic Provinces Special Education Authority Resource Centre for the Visually Impaired, 1992 *Mine For Keeps* (braille edition), Atlantic Provinces Resource Centre for the Visually Impaired, 1989; *Jess Was The Brave On* (braille edition), CNIB, 1989; *Once Upon a Golden Apple* (braill edition), CNIB, 1991; *Stars Come Out Within* (sound recording CNIB and Alberta Education, 1991; *Lost and Found* (braille edition), CNIB, 1992; *Revenge of the Small Small* (braille edition CNIB, 1992; *Stars Come Out Within* (braille edition), CNIB, 199

Manuscript Collections: Kerlan Collection, University of Minnesota, Minneapolis.

* * *

Jean Little's novels use motifs which also appear in adult Canadian literature (e.g., the immigrant experience), but she focuses on these through children's experiences. For instance, she writes of the difficulty of a child's finding his own place in a family, a school, or a country; she shows that intolerance is rooted in fear which activates both the victim and the victimizer; and she demonstrates that when people enlarge their window on the world, they can create greater humanity in themselves and others. Blind herself since birth, Little writes about "sight" in its fullest sense: insight. Philosophically, her books are infused with a deep and caring spirituality, but they are neither didactic nor sectarian. She excels in her ability to develop complexity in characters, to depict the nuances in both hostile and loving relationships, and to keep plot subordinate to character while yet maintaining an interesting story line. Her award-winning books, widely translated, draw additional power from their successful juxtaposing of the adult and child's world.

Her first book, *Mine for Keeps,* depicts every child's fear of new situations. The child, a cerebral palsy victim, indeed suffers from the cruelty of children in a new school, but she is more victimized by her fear of her own inadequacy. Only when she escapes from the prison of self-pity does she begin to develop the insight necessary for good peer relationships. In this book Little goes beyond the mere handicap to explore the feelings it imposes: self-pity, loneliness, jealousy, low self-esteem. *Home from Far* presents a family who adopts two children shortly after losing a child. The book, after revealing the resentments and split loyalties felt by both the natural and the foster children, depicts a child's terror of rejection, the necessity of discipline, and the healing power of parental love. *Spring Begins in March,* one of the several novels set in the imaginary town of Riverside, Ontario (Jean's native Guelph), gives us new perspectives on two families presented earlier. The book focuses on a child whose alienation is intensified when a cranky grandmother comes to live with them, usurping her space. Meg, the child, eventually adapts, gaining compassion and better self-discipline. *Take Wing* uses the story of a family's difficulty in accepting a son's mental retardation to illustrate the dangers of overprotecting children. Again, children's fear of peer ridicule is depicted in conjunction with the gradual revelation of some causes of the hostility.

One to Grow On tells the story of a 12-year-old girl in a large family living in "Riverside." Feeling lonely, unimportant, and unloved, she irritates her family by telling lies to get attention. After being victimized by another liar, the heroine grows beyond pettiness. *Look through My Window* tells of yet another WASP Riverside family, a relaxed one, with one happy child. This child is introduced to an introspective, angry Jewish girl from a tense and intellectual family. Juxtaposing the two lifestyles and personality types, Little shows how learning to look through another's window helps dispel prejudice and animosity. *Kate,* its sequel, explores the roles of religious and cultural heritage in one's psychological makeup. A story with many resonances, it recreates the loneliness of those who live in private internal places and shows that taking risks to expand can bring both happiness and disaster. The book's conclusion shows that while growth and change may cause loss in friendships, there is always the consolation of the memory of a shared past. *Hey World, Here I Am!,* written 15 years before publication, is a book comprised of poetry and prose sketches by "Kate"; in the book's preface, Little explains how a fictional character can take hold of an author's imagination and write through the author.

Stand in the Wind depicts the complicated relationships of various children within two families, one a bustling Canadian family with normal squabbling siblings and the other a rather anxious American family in which each parent openly favors one child. The children come to terms with each other when they are left alone for a week in a cottage in Northern Ontario. *From Anna,* one of Little's most successful and widely taught books, is the story of a German family who flees Nazi Germany to settle in Toronto. The visually handicapped heroine, Anna, is a misfit in a lively, fractious, competitive family. Cruelly teased by her talented, arrogant older brother, she nevertheless grows out of a withdrawn unhappiness into insight; in the sequel, *Listen for the Singing,* her older brother becomes kinder to her, making it possible for her to respond to his misery after he is blinded in an accident. *Mama's Going to Buy You a Mockingbird* shows how the illness and death of a much-adored father in a closely knit family causes the adolescent male protagonist to withdraw and strike out in anger; through interaction with another child who has experienced a different kind of loss—abandonment by a mother—he begins to heal. Little's subsequent books, *Lost and Found* and *Different Dragons,* are written for a younger audience. Both stories feature pets and show a child overcoming personal limitations through interaction with a dog.

In the first volume of her award-winning and highly acclaimed fictionalized autobiography, *Little by Little: A Writer's Education,* Little depicts the stages of her own social, psychological, intellectual, and artistic development. This book is an extraordinary achievement as autobiography for its portrayal of a child who was often a trial to both parents and siblings. It depicts a close family, with understanding parents. The story is lively to read because the fast-paced anecdotal structure is built on memorable anecdotes, but its artistic merits derive from the author's subtle handling of tone and point of view: its speaking voice is wry and humorous, and it shows a child who was a full-range of the feelings we are conditioned to suppress: anger, envy, jealousy, pride, fear. The dramatization of the child's behavior, often far from model, combined with the skilful presentation of the understandable feelings that produced that behaviour, produces a humorous book that is equally moving for child and adult readers. The sequel, *Stars Come Out Within,* continues her life from her first position teaching before she had any literary success to her mature years, when she has become an internationally-known writer. It details her deteriorating vision, her subsequent depression, her acquisition of a talking computer to write with, and her experiences with her first seeing eye dog, Zephyr.

Younger children are the audience for the majority of Little's most recent works of fiction. *Once Upon a Golden Apple,* co-authored with her niece, Maggie DeVries, is a picture-book in which the phrases that are traditional in well-known fairy tales are playfully mixed up. *Jess Was the Brave One* tells of a little girl beset with an "over-active imagination." *Revenge of the Small Small* is the story of a youngest child who was teased by her older siblings until she conveys her feelings to them by making a village out of paper and then buries them all in its graveyard. Her *Bats about Baseball,* co-authored with Claire MacKay, gives fast repartee between a grandmother glued to the baseball game on TV and her grandson who wants her attention.

But Little hasn't forgotten her original audience. Her two most recent longer works are historical novels for the nine to twelve-year-old set, both of which delve into the nature of family. *His Banner over Me,* a story loosely based on the life of Little's mother, relates the story of Flora, the child of missionaries, who is sent with her siblings to live with her aunt and uncle in Ontario during World War I, while *The Belonging Place,* tells of a young 19th century Scottish orphan who is plagued by doubts about whether her adopted family has truly accepted her. Forthcoming is *Emma's Magic Winter,* An I Can Read Book.

Little captures those times when ordinary children feel isolated and frightened in a threatening world. Her books follow such children as they grow in insight, and, using their newfound broader perspectives, develop greater self-esteem and the ability to give to others.

—Mary Rubio, updated by Jackie C. Horne

LITTLE, Lessie Jones

Nationality: American. **Born:** Parmele, North Carolina, 1 October 1906. **Education:** Attended North Carolina State Normal School (now Elizabeth City State University), 1924-26. **Family:** Married Weston W. Little, 17 October 1926; two sons and three daughters, including the author Eloise Greenfield (see her entry). **Career:** Elementary school teacher in rural North Carolina, 1924-29; clerk-typist, U.S.Army Office of the Surgeon General, Washington, D.C., 1956-64, coding clerk, 1964-70; writer, 1974-86. **Awards:** Child Study Association of America Children's Books of the Year, 1979; Boston Globe-Horn Book award honor book, nonfiction, 1980; Parents' Choice award, 1988. **Died:** 4 November 1986.

Publications for Children

Fiction

I Can Do It By Myself, with Eloise Greenfield; illustrated by Carole Byard. New York, Crowell, 1978.

Poetry

Children of Long Ago, illustrated by Jan Spivey Gilchrist. New York, Philomel, 1979.

Other

Childtimes: A Three-Generation Memoir, illustrated by Jerry Pinkney. New York, Philomel, 1988.

* * *

Lessie Jones Little's three books for children show that when she began writing, at age 67, she drew on a lifetime of carefully stored memories as well as empathetic observation of contemporary childhood. She was also inspired by the insights and creativity of her daughter, the well-known author Eloise Greenfield. Greenfield collaborated with her mother on two of the books, the second of which also includes a third family voice, that of Little's mother, Pattie Frances Ridley Jones. For Little, writing was very much a family enterprise, characterized by intimacy, warmth, and loving attention paid to the small details of everyday life.

I Can Do It by Myself, Little's first book, was also the first written in collaboration with her daughter. Published in picture book format with illustrations by Carole Byard, *I Can Do It by Myself* is as likely to strike a familiar chord with parents as with its intended preschool and early primary school audience. Donny, who is just old enough to have two front teeth missing, wants to buy his mother's birthday present without assistance (which he sees as interference) from his big brother, Wade. Donny insists that he can manage transporting the big plant he has chosen, and he does, by means of a wagon his father left behind for Donny when his father moved away. Donny's journey to the plant store and back illustrates the young child's simultaneous desire for independence and need for reassurance. His trip home with the plant is briefly interrupted by a dog that scares Donny into shouting for his mother, but he escapes unharmed on his own and proudly presents his gift to his equally proud mother. In its matter-of-fact treatment of the absence of Donny's father, the story clearly portrays the warmth and security of this single-parent home.

Little's next book was also written in collaboration, this time with her daughter and also material from Little's mother that the family had published privately some years earlier. *Childtimes: A Three-Generation Memoir* is divided into three sections, with Pattie Frances Ridley Jones, Lessie Jones Little, and Eloise Greenfield speaking in turn. Brief background sketches called "Landscapes" punctuate the text. They set the childhoods of these three African American women in the broader context of "black people struggling, not just to stay alive, but to live, to give of their talents, whether to many or few". Jones's narrative is the briefest. Born in 1884, she describes growing up in Parmele, North Carolina, a small mill town, where her family, like most in the African American community, lived a financially marginal existence despite hard work and ingenuity. Jones's emphasis, nevertheless, is on the events in a growing child's life: school, chores, visiting relatives, parties, church activities, her siblings' adventures (including a runaway buggy and a dramatic snakebite).

Although Parmele was no longer a mill town by the time of Little's birth in 1906, its transformation to a train town does not appear to have changed the overall tenor of childhood there a generation later. Little's narrative is almost twice as long as her mother's, but many of the small town events parallel those of an earlier era. What distinguishes her "childtime" from her mother's are her parents' separating from each other for two years (for reasons never explained in the text) and the impingement of the larger world in the form of World War I and the Spanish Flu. Greenfield's narrative, however, is the one that really brings the story into the 20th century, with the family's move to an urban life in Washington, D.C. Yet even this change has an aura of continuity, so firmly interwoven are the three generations of this memoir.

Children of Long Ago, published posthumously, is the one book Jones wrote without a collaborator. It is a collection of poems—lyrics set in an idyllic past of little country towns, where children eat supper by the light of oil-filled lamps and measure the passage of time by the bongs of mama's grandpa clock. The tone throughout is comforting, even old-fashioned, a final testament to the strength Little drew from her memories of childhood and her desire to share that childtime with future generations.

—Janice M. Alberghene

LIVELY, Penelope (Margaret)

Nationality: British (came to England, 1945). **Born:** Penelope Margaret Low, Cairo, Egypt, 17 March 1933. **Education:** Boarding school in Sussex, 1945-51; St. Anne's College, Oxford, B.A. (honours) in modern history 1956. **Family:** Married Jack Lively in 1957; one daughter and one son. **Career:** Has been presenter for BBC Radio program on children's literature; regular reviewer for newspapers and magazines in England. Fellow, Royal Society of Literature, 1985. **Awards:** Library Association Carnegie Medal, 1974; Whitbread award, 1976; Southern Arts Association prize, for adult fiction, 1979; Arts Council National Book award, for adult fiction, 1980; Booker prize, for adult fiction, 1987.

Publications for Children

Fiction

Astercote, illustrated by Antony Maitland. London, Heinemann, 1970; New York, Dutton, 1971.
The Whispering Knights, illustrated by Gareth Floyd. London, Heinemann, 1971; New York, Dutton, 1976.
The Wild Hunt of Hagworthy, illustrated by Juliet Mozley. London, Heinemann, 1971; as *The Wild Hunt of the Ghost Hounds,* New York, Dutton, 1972.
The Driftway. London, Heinemann, 1972; New York, Dutton, 1973.
The Ghost of Thomas Kempe, illustrated by Antony Maitland. London, Heinemann, and New York, Dutton, 1973.
The House in Norham Gardens. London, Heinemann, and New York, Dutton, 1974.
Going Back. London, Heinemann, and New York, Dutton, 1975.
Boy Without a Name, illustrated by Ann Dalton. London, Heinemann, and Berkeley, California, Parnassus Press, 1975.
A Stitch in Time. London, Heinemann, and New York, Dutton, 1976.
The Stained Glass Window, illustrated by Michael Pollard. London, Abelard Schuman, 1976.
Fanny's Sister, illustrated by John Lawrence. London, Heinemann, 1976; New York, Dutton, 1980.
The Voyage of QV66, illustrated by Harold Jones. London, Heinemann, 1978; New York, Dutton, 1979.
Fanny and the Monsters, illustrated by John Lawrence. London, Heinemann, 1979.
Fanny and the Battle of Potter's Piece, illustrated by John Lawrence. London, Heinemann, 1980.
The Revenge of Samuel Stokes. London, Heinemann, and New York, Dutton, 1981.
Uninvited Ghosts and Other Stories, illustrated by John Lawrence. London, Heinemann, 1984; New York, Dutton, 1985.
Dragon Trouble, illustrated by Valerie Littlewood. London, Heinemann, 1984.
Debbie and the Little Devil, illustrated by Toni Goffe. London, Heinemann, 1987.
A House Inside Out, illustrated by David Parkins. London, Deutsch, 1987; New York, Dutton, 1988.
Judy and the Martian. London, Simon and Schuster, 1992.
The Cat, the Crow, and the Banyan Tree, illustrated by Terry Milne. London, Walker, and Cambridge, Massachusetts, Candlewick Press, 1994.
Good Night, Sleep Tight, illustrated by Adriano Gon. London, Walker, 1994.
Heat Wave. New York, HarperCollins, 1996.
The Five Thousand and One Nights. Seattle, Washington, Fjord Press, 1997.

Play

Time Out of Mind (television play), 1976.

Other

The Presence of the Past: An Introduction to Landscape History. London, Collins, 1976.

Publications for Adults

Novels

The Road to Lichfield. London, Heinemann, 1977.
Treasures of Time. London, Heinemann, and New York, Doubleday, 1979.
Judgement Day. London, Heinemann, 1980; New York, Doubleday, 1981.
Next to Nature, Art. London, Heinemann, 1982.
Perfect Happiness. London, Heinemann, 1983; New York, Dial Press, 1984.
According to Mark. London, Heinemann, 1984; New York, Beaufort, 1985.
Moon Tiger. London, Deutsch, 1987; New York, Grove Press, 1988.
Passing On. London, Deutsch, 1989; New York, Grove Press, 1990.
City of the Mind. London, Deutsch, 1991; New York, Harper, 1991.
Cleopatra's Sister. London, Viking, and New York, Harper, 1993.

Short Stories

Nothing Missing But the Samovar and Other Stories. London, Heinemann, 1978.
Corruption and Other Stories. London, Heinemann, 1984.
Pack of Cards: Stories 1978-86. London, Heinemann, 1986; New York, Grove Press, 1989.

Plays

Boy Dominic (television series; 3 episodes), 1974.

Other

Oleander Jacaranda: A Childhood Perceived (memoir). London, Viking, and New York, HarperCollins, 1994.

*

Penelope Lively comments:
Most of my books for children reflect, in one way or another, my own interest in the workings of memory—whether personal or collective. They all seem to come out differently—memory fantastical, memory experimental, memory pastoral or historical or comical—but somehow, so far, the theme has persisted.

* * *

Penelope Lively's first novel was published in 1970. She rapidly established herself as one of the most interesting and rewarding of contemporary novelists for children. The books are very different, to such an extent indeed that children (who notoriously enjoy the "mixture as before") may be disappointed when they try one after enjoying another. To an adult one of the great pleasures of her work is her ability to create entirely fresh and individual books which are yet variations on the theme "we are what we have been." Lively's concern is with identity through historical continuity. She is particularly interested in place, in the English landscape (from which she was separated during her most formative years as a child in Egypt) and in houses: "A house is a preservative," she has written, "a record of the lives it has sheltered." Her *A House Inside Out* reminds children that houses shelter other creatures as well as the human families that live in them.

The first book, *Astercote,* reflected an obsession the writer had at the time with deserted medieval villages. Lively was rightly criticized for her failure to create living characters and convincing dialogue but the story was intriguing—and exciting. *The Whispering Knights* and *The Wild Hunt of Hagworthy* explore two recurrent themes in English folklore. *The Driftway* is probably her least successful novel as far as child readers are concerned, but there is a great deal in it to absorb anyone interested in Lively's view of life. In *The Driftway* she "wanted to use landscape as a channel for historical memory." She wrote about "a road, a perfectly ordinary road, the B4525 from Banbury to Northampton, but a road that is very ancient and seemed to lend itself perfectly to a double symbolism." This sounds a little pretentious and it should be made clear at once that Lively is never pretentious. She is not trying to convey to children an appreciation of their own past and throwing in a story to make the message more palatable. The stories are seamless garments. As one critic has put it: "The concern isn't added to the story; rather the story is written out of it.... There are real children, changing in relation to their experiences. The novels are dense with life, with flux and growth."

The stories are good ones. Most accessible of all is the Carnegie Medal-winner *The Ghost of Thomas Kempe.* Lively says that in this book she was indulging a taste for ghosts. "It is a light-hearted affair on the whole, but concerned with the serious matter of a child's awaking to the concept of memory." In fact, the serious matter is absorbed wholly in the comedy. It was the first book in which the writer seemed completely relaxed and in charge of her material. A lot of the fun derives from unlikely conjunctions; the ghost of a Jacobean sorcerer loose in a world of cake mixes, phone boxes, and biros.

Clever and delightful as it is, *Thomas Kempe* is a minor book compared with its successor *The House in Norham Gardens.* This is primarily the story of a quiet winter in the life of Clare Mayfield, aged 14, who lives with her great-aunts in a house in North Oxford with relics of the past. They acquire a couple of tenants: Maureen, who works for an estate agent, and John, an anthropology student from Uganda. Clare and her friend, Liz, eat baked beans and do their Latin homework together; she goes to London with John for the day; a Norfolk cousin stays the night. She has a bit part in the school *Macbeth,* and, finally, she has a bicycle accident and breaks her arm. These are the small outward events—but in Clare's mind other things are going on. This is a book about time and continuity and the relationship between the things we possess and the people we are.

Clare's great-grandfather was an anthropologist. In the attic in the house in Norham Gardens she finds one of the tamburans or ceremonial shields which he brought back from New Guinea in 1905. She becomes obsessed by this shield and the tribe it belonged to, who had no word for love in their language, no knowledge of their past, whose dead stayed with them as spirits, represented by the shields. Clare dreams about these people and feels she must return the shield. But when she does, in the hospital sleep after her accident, she knows it is too late for them. New Guinea is transformed before her eyes: the thatched huts become concrete bungalows; it is "time for Music Roundup" on the transistor radio and too late for tamburans. Clare gives the shield to the Pitt Rivers Museum. The winter is over and she chooses for her aunt's birthday not something from the antique shop (though the woman assures her "It's fashionable having old things") but a copper beech which will flourish for two hundred years. It is time to look forward.

Everything in this subtle, rich, compelling story is part of the pattern but there is nothing forced about the pattern; it seems entirely natural. Clare (a thinking, listening girl) and her aunts (early graduates, still interested in Africa and art though not in gutters or new pence) are entirely convincing—people one is glad to get to know. Lively has certainly written more exciting books, but it is a considerable achievement to write so honestly about the long Sunday afternoons, the creeping clocks, the boredom of being 14, without ever being boring. Her relaxed, flexible style copes equally well with visits to the butcher and the brisk, useless doctor and with "the shadows of another world and another time."

Going Back is another considerable achievement. Again it is centred on a house, this time Medleycott, a house in Somerset, built at the turn of the century, with rose garden and tennis lawn, goldfish pond, stables, and kitchen gardens. There is a great deal of circumstantial detail: splendid descriptions of the natural world ("clenched by frost" or "filmy with mist, the trees waist deep in it floating") and the convincing wartime background of land-girls and spam fritters, ration books, conscientious objectors, Spitfires and Hurricanes in playground games, and the knitting of balaclava helmets. But the war is incidental. It creates the situation and reinforces the alienation between Jane and Edward and their insensitive blustering father, who ultimately sends Edward away to school and precipitates the climax of the story. The suffering is real enough to make the reader weep.

The story is for the most part quiet and slow, but not easy to read. Lively makes few concessions to a young reader. Her style is often elliptical and the vocabulary difficult (she prefers "benign and munificent" to "kind and generous"). There is no clear time scale. "In the head all springs are one spring," and characters come into focus only at particular moments, and sometimes not at all. But the tension of the narrative is beautifully sustained and it is never dull. We care passionately about what happens to Jane and Edward, especially Edward. Less is expected of Jane, the narrator, as she is a girl; the class and sexist attitudes of the time are clear and painful. We are never sure that what we remember is what actually happened, as Lively says, but no one reading *Going Back* could forget it.

Again in *A Stitch in Time,* which won the Whitbread award, a house is at the centre; a rented house in Lyme Regis. "Places," she writes, are "like clocks—full of all the time there's ever been in them, and all the people, and all the things that have happened like the ammonites in the stones." The ammonite reference is not a casual one, because the place this time is Lyme Regis and fossils are, of course, part of the story.

Maria Foster, only child of quiet boring parents, is not, like Jane Austen's young people, "wild to see Lyme." In fact, she is decidedly lukewarm about their holiday destination. Indeed, in spite of an agreeable habit of talking to inanimate objects and hearing their replies, Maria is rather a lukewarm dull girl. The book is a little lukewarm and dull itself. It lacks the richness of *The House in Norham Gardens,* the flow of *Going Back,* and the atmosphere of both of them. Children will, however, find it a much easier and more straightforward book. There is much to enjoy; the pleasure in knowing names (quercus ilex, grass vetchling, gryphaea), the contrasting families on either side of the holiday fence, the descriptions of days which might have been entirely different ones, and the reminder of days long past when a girl called Harriet had reluctantly stiched a sampler, with a swing which still creaks in the garden where there is no swing, and a dog which still barks in a house where there are no dogs.

Animals come into their own in Lively's most important children's book of more recent years, *The Voyage of QV66,* an original exploration of a time after the Second Flood when Man has been wiped off the face of the earth and evolution, in some sense, has to start all over again. The immediate concern is with Stanley, the monkey in the crew of QV66, journeying to London in a search for identity. This is a book which can be enjoyed at many different levels. In spite of the assertion in a 1982 *Guardian* feature that, with her success as a novelist for adults, Lively said farewell to children's books, there has been a steady stream of children's books published in the 1980s, as well as the slightly earlier Fanny stories in Heinemann's Long Ago Children series, brought together under the title *Fanny and the Monsters* to give a satisfying picture of life in one particular Victorian family with a strong girl character. There has also been *The Revenge of Samuel Stokes,* which begins splendidly: "You may well ask how a smell of roast venison could come out of Mrs. Thornton's washing machine...." The idea behind the book—of the physical impact of the past on a contemporary housing estate—is a good one; but one has to admit, for all one's continued admiration for Lively's wit and ingenuity, that she is not quite enough at home with the denizens of Charstock Estate to make the fantasy as convincing as its most comparable predecessor, the ever-popular *Ghost of Thomas Kempe.*

Recently, Lively has written the texts of two interesting picture books, both dedicated to granddaughters. Perfectly paced for reading aloud at bed-time, *Good Night, Sleep Tight,* with its deep understanding of the ways and language of small children, could well become a classic.

—Ann Thwaite

LIVINGSTON, Myra Cohn

Nationality: American. **Born:** Omaha, Nebraska, 17 August 1926. **Education:** Sarah Lawrence College, Bronxville, New York, 1945-48, B.A. 1948. **Family:** Married Richard R. Livingston in 1952 (died 1990); two sons and one daughter. **Career:** Professional French horn player, 1940-48 (studied music with Darius Milhaud, 1944); assistant editor, *Campus* magazine, Los Angeles, 1948-50; worked in public relations for movie and musical personalities, 1949-52; instructor in creative writing for children, Dallas Public Library, 1959-64; instructor, Los Angeles County Museum of Art, 1966-67, Beverly Hills Public Library, 1966-74, and University of California Elementary School, Los Angeles, 1972; instructor, 1966-71, and poet-in-residence, 1966-84, Beverly Hills Unified School District. Since 1972 Senior Extension Instructor, University of California, Los Angeles. Has lectured on poetry and conducted writing workshops throughout the United States since 1959. Member of the Editorial Board, *New Advocate,* Needham Heights, Massachusetts; and *The Reading Teacher;* advisory board member, Reading is Important of South California. **Awards:** Texas Institute of Letters award, 1961, 1980; National Council of Teachers of English award, for verse, 1980; National Jewish Book award, 1986; University of Minnesota Kerlan award, 1994. **Agent:** McIntosh and Otis, 310 Madison Avenue, New York, New York 10017, U.S.A. **Address:** 9308 Readcrest Drive, Beverly Hills, California 90210, U.S.A.

Publications for Children

Fiction

I'm Hiding, illustrated by Erik Blegvad. New York, Harcourt Brace, 1961.
See What I Found, illustrated by Erik Blegvad. New York, Harcourt Brace, 1962.
I Talk to Elephants!, photographs by Isabel Gordon. New York, Harcourt Brace, 1962.
I'm Not Me, illustrated by Erik Blegvad. New York, Harcourt Brace, 1963.
Happy Birthday, illustrated by Erik Blegvad. New York, Harcourt Brace, 1964.
I'm Waiting, illustrated by Erik Blegvad. New York, Harcourt Brace, 1966.
Come Away, illustrated by Irene Haas. New York, Atheneum, 1974.

Poetry

Whispers and Other Poems, illustrated by Jacqueline Chwast. New York, Harcourt Brace, 1958.
Wide Awake and Other Poems, illustrated by Jacqueline Chwast. New York, Harcourt Brace, 1959.
The Moon and a Star and Other Poems, illustrated by Judith Shahn. New York, Harcourt Brace, 1965.
Old Mrs. Twindlytart and Other Rhymes, illustrated by Enrico Arno. New York, Harcourt Brace, 1967.
A Crazy Flight and Other Poems, illustrated by James Spanfeller. New York, Harcourt Brace, 1969.
The Malibu and Other Poems, illustrated by James Spanfeller. New York, Atheneum, 1974.
The Way Things Are and Other Poems, illustrated by Jenni Oliver. New York, Atheneum, 1974.
4-Way Stop and Other Poems, illustrated by James Spanfeller. New York, Atheneum, 1976.
A Lollygag of Limericks, illustrated by Joseph Low. New York, Atheneum, 1978.
O Sliver of Liver, Together with Other Triolets, Cinquains, Haiku, Verses, and a Dash of Poems, illustrated by Iris Van Rynbach. New York, Atheneum, 1979.
No Way of Knowing: Dallas Poems. New York, Atheneum, 1980.

A Circle of Seasons, illustrated by Leonard Everett Fisher. New York, Holiday House, 1982.
Sky Songs, illustrated by Leonard Everett Fisher. New York, Holiday House, 1984.
A Song I Sang to You, illustrated by Margot Tomes. New York, Harcourt Brace, 1984.
Monkey Puzzle and Other Poems, illustrated by Antonio Frasconi. New York, Atheneum, 1984.
Celebrations, illustrated by Leonard Everett Fisher. New York, Holiday House, 1985.
Worlds I Know and Other Poems, illustrated by Tim Arnold. New York, Atheneum, 1985.
Sea Songs, illustrated by Leonard Everett Fisher. New York, Holiday House, 1986.
Earth Songs, illustrated by Leonard Everett Fisher. New York, Holiday House, 1986.
Higgledy-Piggledy, illustrated by Peter Sis. New York, Macmillan, 1986.
Space Songs, illustrated by Leonard Everett Fisher. New York, Holiday House, 1988.
There Was a Place and Other Poems. New York, McElderry, 1988.
Up in the Air, illustrated by Leonard Everett Fisher. New York, Holiday House, 1989.
Birthday Poems, illustrated by Margot Tomes. New York, Holiday House, 1989.
Remembering, and other poems. New York, Macmillan, 1989.
My Head Is Red, and other Riddle Rhymes, illustrated by Tere Lo Prete. New York, Holiday House, 1990.
Let Freedom Ring: A Ballad of Martin Luther King, Jr., illustrated by Samuel Byrd. New York, Holiday House, 1992.
Light and Shadow, photographs by Barbara Rogasky. New York, Holiday House, 1992.
I Never Told, and other poems. New York, McElderry, 1992.
Abraham Lincoln: A Man for All the People, illustrated by Samuel Byrd. New York, Holiday House, 1993.
Just Keep on Singing: A Ballad of Marian Anderson, illustrated by Samuel Byrd. New York, Holiday House, 1994.
Flights of Fancy and Other Poems. New York, Margaret K. McElderry Books, 1994.
B Is for Baby: An Alphabet of Verses, photographs by Steel Stillman. New York, McElderry Books, 1996.
Festivals, illustrated by Leonard Everett Fisher. New York, Holiday House, 1996.
Cricket Never Does: A Collection of Haiku and Tanka, illustrated by Kees de Kiefte. New York, McElderry Books, 1997.

Other

Editor, *A Tune Beyond Us: A Collection of Poetry,* illustrated by James Spanfeller. New York, Harcourt Brace, 1968.
Editor, *Speak Roughly to Your Little Boy: A Collection of Parodies and Burlesques,* illustrated by Joseph Low. New York, Harcourt Brace, 1971.
Editor, *Listen, Children, Listen: An Anthology of Poems for the Very Young,* illustrated by Trina Schart Hyman. New York, Harcourt Brace, 1972.
Editor, *What a Wonderful Bird the Frog Are: An Assortment of Humorous Poetry and Verse.* New York, Harcourt Brace, 1973.
Editor, *Poems of Lewis Carroll.* New York, Crowell, 1973.
Editor, *One Little Room, An Everywhere: Poems of Love,* illustrated by Antonio Frasconi. New York, Atheneum, 1975.
Editor, *O Frabjous Day: Poetry for Holidays and Special Occasions.* New York, Atheneum, 1977.
Editor, *Callooh! Callay! Holiday Poems for Young Readers,* illustrated by Janet Stevens. New York, Atheneum, 1978.
Editor, *Poems of Christmas.* New York, Atheneum, 1980.
Editor, *Why Am I Grown So Cold? Poems of the Unknowable.* New York, Atheneum, 1982.
Editor, *How Pleasant to Know Mr. Lear! Edward Lear's Selected Works.* New York, Holiday House, 1982.
Editor, *Christmas Poems,* illustrated by Trina Schart Hyman. New York, Holiday House, 1984.
Editor, *Easter Poems,* illustrated by John Wallner. New York, Holiday House, 1985.
Editor, *A Learical Lexicon: A Magnificent Feast of Boshblobberbosh and Fun from the Works of Edward Lear,* illustrated by Joseph Low. New York, Atheneum, 1985.
Editor, *Thanksgiving Poems,* illustrated by Stephen Gammell. New York, Holiday House, 1985.
Editor, *Poems for Jewish Holidays,* illustrated by Lloyd Bloom. New York, Holiday House, 1986.
Editor, *Valentine Poems,* illustrated by Patience Brewster. New York, Holiday House, 1987.
Editor, *Cat Poems,* illustrated by Trina Schart Hyman. New York, Holiday House, 1987; Oxford, Oxford University Press, 1989.
Editor, *New Year's Poems,* illustrated by Margot Tomes. New York, Holiday House, 1987.
Editor, *I Like You, If You Like Me: Poems of Friendship.* New York, McElderry, 1987.
Editor, with Norma Farber, *These Small Stones.* New York, Harper, 1987.
Editor, *Poems for Mothers,* illustrated by Deborah Kogan Ray. New York, Holiday House, 1988.
Editor, *Poems for Fathers,* illustrated by Robert Casilla. New York, Holiday House, 1989.
Editor, *Dilly Dilly Piccalilli: Poems for the Very Young,* illustrated by Eileen Christelow. New York, McElderry, 1989.
Editor, *Halloween Poems,* illustrated by Stephen Gammell. New York, Holiday House, 1989.
Editor, *Dog Poems,* illustrated by Leslie Morrill. New York, Holiday House, 1990; Oxford, Oxford University Press, 1993.
Editor, *If the Owl Calls Again: A Collection of Owl Poems,* illustrated by Antonio Frasconi. New York, Macmillan, 1990.
Editor, *Poems for Grandmothers,* illustrated by Patricia Callen-Clark. New York, Holiday House, 1990.
Editor, *Poems for Brothers, Poems for Sisters,* illustrated by Jean Zallinger. New York, Holiday House, 1991.
Poem-Making: Ways to Begin Writing Poetry. New York, Harper and Row, 1991.
Editor, *Lots of Limericks.* New York, Macmillan, 1991.
Editor, *If You Ever Meet a Whale,* illustrated by Leonard Everett Fisher. New York, Holiday House, 1992.
Editor, *A Time to Talk: Poems of Friendship.* New York McElderry, 1992.
Translator, with Joseph F. Dominguez, *Platero,* edited by Jua R. Jimenez, illustrated by Antonio Frasconi. Boston, Houghto Mifflin, 1993.
Editor, *Read Along: Poems on Wheels.* New York, McElderry 1993.
Editor, *Riddle-me Rhymes.* New York, McElderry, 1994.
Editor, *Animal, Vegetable, Mineral: Poems about Small Thing* New York, HarperCollins, 1994.

Editor, *Call Down the Moon: Poems of Music.* New York, McElderry Books, 1995.
Editor, *I Am Writing a Poem about—a Game of Poetry.* New York, McElderry Books, 1997.

Publications for Adults

Other

When You Are Alone/It Keeps You Capone: An Approach to Creative Writing with Children. New York, Atheneum, 1973.
A Tribute to Lloyd Alexander. Philadelphia, Drexel Institute, 1976.
The Child as Poet: Myth or Reality? Boston, Horn Book, 1984.
Editor, with Zena Sutherland, *The Scott Foresman Anthology of Children's Literature.* Chicago, Scott Foresman, 1984.
Climb into the Bell Tower: Essays on Poetry. New York, HarperCollins, 1990.

*

Myra Cohn Livingston comments:

A deep respect for the emotions, sensitivities, and thoughts of young people as they differ from those of adults has always been of importance to me. *Whispers and Other Poems,* written when I was a college freshman, is a reflection of my own childhood, and although my recent poetry encompasses a more contemporary view of childhood, I feel I have never departed from the child I was; the child I know best. I am not consciously aware of writing *for* children: my poetry seems to be born of the genre of childhood. The thousands of young people with whom I share poetry and to whom I teach something of the writing of it reinforce, for me, the feeling that the early years encompass a freshness and wonder that must be nurtured, a curiosity and celebration of the simple things which each succeeding generation discovers anew. As an anthologist I am conscious of choosing those poems which speak to the young in a diction and emotional climate to which they can relate—something of the universal experience from poets of all ages and countries which may serve as an insight toward the individual growth and humanization of the reader.

* * *

In the tradition of Robert Louis Stevenson, Myra Cohn Livingston fills her poetry for children with the elements of a child's own world and experience: babbling brooks, starry skies, elephants, crocodiles, kangaroos, balloons, whispering, jumping, pretending, discovering, growing up, feathers and acorns and rubber bands and daisies, fathers and beaches and math class, bedtime and bubblegum are the subjects of her earlier work; working mothers, stepmothers, death, and divorce are (most unlike Stevenson) the more somber elements of her later poems. How our children's lives and concerns have changed since the 1950s!

Like Stevenson, Livingston transforms the everyday into the poetic through a skillful use of metre, rhyme, and imagery. Onomatopoeia and alliteration may add to the poetic effect:

> Whispers
> tickle through your ear
> telling things you like to hear.
>
> Whispers
> are as soft as skin
> letting little words curl in.
>
> Whispers
> come so they can blow
> secrets others never know.

Some of her poetry is concrete verse:

> Cold that day
> we started down
>
> tobogganing
> the snowy ground
> held our breath
> around a tree
> and Shirley Ann
> squeezed tight to me;
> Laura yelled,
> as we flew past
> one crazy kid,
> his skis half-smashed,
> and Margie steered
> around a sled
> until
> until
> I felt my head
> go spinning round
> in sprays of snow

Livingston's recent collaboration with painter Leonard Everett Fisher has resulted in songs to the earth, sea, and sky that are particularly compelling, as complex, imagistic free verse joins dramatic double-page spread paintings. On a deep blue page of moon, sea spray, and boulders, *Sea Songs* begins:

> Crashing on dark shores, drowning, pounding
> breaker swallows breaker. Tide follows
> tide. Lost in her midnight witchery
> moon watches, cresting tall waves, pushing
> through mist and blackness the cold waters.
>
> Moon, you have worked long.
> Now rest...

While Livingston's earlier verse is perhaps most effective when read aloud to small groups of young children (or, better, read by parent to child), her later poetry will stimulate the imaginations of older children.

Livingston has been an intelligent and discriminating anthologist of poetry for children as well. She has collected poems for very young children by such poets as A. A. Milne, Theodore Roethke, and Christina Rossetti (*Listen, Children, Listen*); humorous verse by W. S. Gilbert, Edward Lear, Ogden Nash, Phyllis McGinley, Robert Frost, even Ezra Pound (*What a Wonderful Bird the Frog Are*); love poems by William Butler Yeats, E. E. Cummings, Emily Dickinson, and others (*One Little Room, An Everywhere*) and poems of friendship (*I Like You, If You Like Me*); Christmas poems, Thanksgiving poems, and poems for other holidays and special occasions. She is an admirer of the work of Lewis

Carroll and Edward Lear, and has also edited collections of their work (*Poems of Lewis Carroll* and *How Pleasant to Know Mr. Lear!*).

—Marcia Welsh

LOBEL, Anita

Nationality: American (originally Polish: emigrated to the United States, 1952, became citizen, 1956). **Born:** Anita Kempler, Krakow, Poland, 3 June 1934. **Education:** At schools in Stockholm and New York City; Pratt Institute, Brooklyn, New York, B.F.A. 1955; Brooklyn Museum Art School. **Family:** Married Arnold Lobel, *q.v.,* in 1955 (died 1987); one daughter and one son. **Career:** Textile designer and freelance illustrator. Lives in Brooklyn. **Awards:** Boston *Globe-Horn Book* award, for illustration, 1982, 1984. **Address:** c/o Tundra Books of Northern New York, P.O. Box 1030, Plattsburgh, New York, 12901, U.S.A.

PUBLICATIONS FOR CHILDREN (ILLUSTRATED BY THE AUTHOR)

Fiction

Sven's Bridge. New York, Harper, 1965; London, MacRae, 1994.
The Troll Music. New York, Harper, 1966.
Potatoes, Potatoes. New York, Harper, 1967; Kingswood, Surrey, World's Work, 1969.
The Seamstress of Salzburg. New York, Harper, 1970.
Under a Mushroom. New York, Harper, 1970; Kingswood, Surrey, World's Work, 1972.
A Birthday for the Princess. New York, Harper, 1973; Kingswood, Surrey, World's Work, 1975.
Alison's Zinnia. New York, Greenwillow, 1990.
The Dwarf Giant. New York, Holiday, 1991.
Pierrot's ABC Garden. New York, Golden Book, 1992.
Away From Home. New York, Greenwillow, 1994.

Other (folktales)

King Rooster, Queen Hen. New York, Greenwillow, 1975; Kingswood, Surrey, World's Work, 1977.
The Pancake. New York, Greenwillow, 1978; Kingswood, Surrey, World's Work, 1979.
The Straw Maid. New York, Greenwillow, and London, MacRae, 1983.
No Pretty Pictures: A Child of War. New York, Greenwillow, 1998.

*

Illustrator: *Cock-a-Doodle Doo! Cock-a-Doodle Dandy!* by Paul Kapp, 1966; *Puppy Summer* by Meindert De Jong, 1966; *The Wishing Penny and Other Stories,* 1967; *Indian Summer* by F.N. Monjo, 1968; *The Little Wooden Farmer* by Alice Dalgliesh, 1968; *The Wisest Man in the World,* 1968, and *How the Tsar Drinks Tea,* 1971, both by Benjamin Elkin; *Someone Small* by Barbara Borack, 1969; *The Uproar,* 1970, and *Little John,* 1972, both by Doris Orgel; *Three Rolls and One Doughnut* edited by Mirra Ginsburg, 1970; *Soldier, Soldier, Won't You Marry Me?* edited by John Langstaff, 1972; *One for the Price of Two* by Cynthia Jameson, 1972; *Clever Kate* by Elizabeth Shub, 1973; *Christmas Crafts* by Carolyn Meyer, 1974; *Peter Penny's Dance* by Janet Quin-Harkin, 1976; *How the Rooster Saved the Day,* 1977, *A Treeful of Pigs,* 1979, *On Market Street,* 1980, and *The Rose in My Garden,* 1984, all by Arnold Lobel; *Fanny's Sister* by Penelope Lively, 1980; *Singing Bee!,* 1982, as *Sing a Song of Sixpence!,* 1983, edited by Jane Hart; *The Night Before Christmas* by Clement C. Moore, 1984; *A New Coat for Anna* by Harriet Ziefert, 1986; *Once: A Lullaby* by B.P. Nichol, 1986; *Princess Furball* by Charlotte Huck, 1989; *This Quiet Lady* by Charlotte Zolotow, 1992; *The Cat and the Cook and Other Fables of Krylov* retold by Ethel Heins, New York, Greenwillow Books, 1995; *Toads and Diamonds* retold by Charlotte Huck, New York, Greenwillow Books, 1996; *Mangaboom* by Charlotte Pomerantz. New York, Greenwillow Books, 1997; *Not Everyday an Aurora Borealis for Your Birthday* by Carl Sandburg, New York, Alfred A. Knopf, 1998; *My Day in the Garden* by Miela Ford, New York, Greenwillow Books, 1998.

Anita Lobel comments:

Writing and illustrating books for children is a form of drama for me. I approach the construction of a picture book as if it were a theatre piece to be performed, assigning dialogue, dressing the characters, and putting them into an appropriate setting. Some books take the form of zany farces (*King Rooster, Queen Hen,* and *The Pancake.*) Others, like *Peter Penny's Dance,* are a bit like *Around the World in Eighty Days,* a sort of movie or musical. *The Seamstress of Salzburg* and *A Birthday for the Princess* are more like operettas. *On Market Street* was constructed like a series of solos in a ballet, held together by a prologue and epilogue, with an implied divertimento for a score.

* * *

Humor pervades much of Anita Lobel's work, from her earliest picture book for children, *Sven's Bridge,* to *Alison's Zinnia,* a more recent alphabet book. In *Sven's Bridge,* for instance, humor is embodied in the foolish character of the king, who first orders that Sven's bridge be destroyed when his ship cannot pass through—and then demands that it be rebuilt when his carriage falls into the river. In *Under a Mushroom,* it is not so much the actions of a character but the nature of the minor characters themselves—the Glump, the Schnooze, the Gizzygonk and Dizzydonk, along with the group of Gleeps and other characters—which make the reader laugh. In *The Seamstress of Salzburg* more minor characters—the Queen and the fine ladies of the court—are humorous in their wishes to outdo one another in fine apparel and in their unskilled attempts to sew dresses for the coming marriage of the prince and the seamstress. In these works, as well as in *King Rooster, Queen Hen* and *The Pancake* (all retellings of Danish folktales), Lobel accentuates her humorous characters and situations through her illustrations, such as her depiction of the Gleeps' pointed heads and noses, the pinned together gowns of the ladies, and the dumbfounded expression on each animal's face as the pancake evades every attempt, but the last, to eat it.

While Lobel illustrated the award winning *On Market Street,* *Alison's Zinnia* is her first endeavor with both text and illustration for an alphabet book. Here, her language is as colorful as the flowers that she paints, giving the reader quite a tongue twisting ri with such alliterations as "Olga ordered an Orchid for Paulette" and "Paulette plucked a Peony for Queenie." Lobel's clever method of using alliteration is wedded with another technique, that of introducing the next letter by means of the flower recipient's name. The book comes full circle as "Zena zeroed in on a Zinnia for Alison" and the story begins again. Humor clearly emerges in this picture book through alliteration and ingenious action.

Several of Lobel's works concern more serious issues. *Potatoes, Potatoes* focuses on the brutal nature of war and its contradictory glamour, as well as on the major roles of a mother. The mother character of *Potatoes, Potatoes,* for example, not only serves to protect her sons from joining in the fighting for a number of years but also functions as a peacemaker when she reminds them, and the opposing armies they lead, of their former lives of contentment. *A Birthday for the Princess* also touches on deeper themes. In this work, the king and queen learn that material goods and strict instruction are not the best means by which to raise a child. Their daughter yearns for love and attention, but when her parents continually fail to show their affection and concern, she runs away with a young organ-grinder and his monkey to a land where they love one another and are happy together. Her parents never regain the princess they have so foolishly lost.

Whatever their particular tone might be, all of Lobel's books are characterized by their settings of long ago and their happy endings. *The Troll Music,* for instance, is set in a time of traveling musicians and a mischievous, fun-loving troll. Its story ends happily with the musicians placating the troll family with a cake and gifts, the troll removing his spell over the instruments, and the musicians playing more beautifully than ever. *The Seamstress of Salzburg* also demonstrates time-honored narrative techniques. Set in a past of royalty, promenades, and transportation by horseback, this tale recalls the traditional form of the folktale, especially in its happy ending. Not only does the seamstress marry her prince, but the ladies of the court gain the pride that comes from sewing their own gowns.

With her predominant tone of humor, occasional serious themes, settings from the past, and endings which leave the reader satisfied, Lobel ably illustrates the meaning of a statement she made to *Publishers Weekly* in 1971: "It's nice to tell a tale that is pleasant for a child to read, be diverting, and at the same time have some kind of substance to it." Her books are clearly informed by the pleasant, substantial spirit of which she speaks.

—Jacqueline L. Gmuca

LOBEL, Arnold (Stark)

Nationality: American. **Born:** Los Angeles, California, 22 May 1933. **Education:** At schools in Schenectady, New York; Pratt Institute, Brooklyn, New York, B.F.A. 1955. **Family:** Married Anita Kempler (i.e., Anita Lobel, *q.v.*) in 1955; one daughter and one son. **Career:** Worked in advertising, 1955-58. **Awards:** Christopher award, 1972, 1977; George G. Stone Center for Children's Books award, 1978; American Library Association Caldecott Medal, 1981; University of South Mississippi award, 1985; Society of Children's Book Writers Golden Kite award, for illustration, 1988. **Died:** 4 December 1987.

PUBLICATIONS FOR CHILDREN (ILLUSTRATED BY THE AUTHOR)

Fiction

A Zoo for Mister Muster. New York, Harper, 1962.
A Holiday for Mister Muster. New York, Harper, 1963.
Prince Bertram the Bad. New York, Harper, 1963; Kingswood, Surrey, World's Work, 1970.
Giant John. New York, Harper, 1964; Kingswood, Surrey, World's Work, 1965.
Lucille. New York, Harper, and Kingswood, Surrey, World's Work, 1964.
The Bears of the Air. New York, Harper, 1965; Kingswood, Surrey, World's Work, 1966.
The Great Blueness and Other Predicaments. New York, Harper, 1968; Kingswood, Surrey, World's Work, 1970.
Small Pig. New York, Harper, 1969; Kingswood, Surrey, World's Work, 1970.
Frog and Toad Are Friends. New York, Harper, 1970; Kingswood, Surrey, World's Work, 1971.
Mouse Tales. New York, Harper, 1972; Kingswood, Surrey, World's Work, 1973.
Frog and Toad Together. New York, Harper, 1972; Kingswood, Surrey, World's Work, 1973.
Owl at Home. New York, Harper, 1975; Kingswood, Surrey, World's Work, 1976.
Frog and Toad All Year. New York, Harper, 1976; Kingswood, Surrey, World's Work, 1977.
How the Rooster Saved the Day, illustrated by Anita Lobel. New York, Greenwillow, and London, Hamish Hamilton, 1977.
Mouse Soup. New York, Harper, 1977; Kingswood, Surrey, World's Work, 1978.
Grasshopper on the Road. New York, Harper, 1978; Kingswood, Surrey, World's Work, 1979.
A Treeful of Pigs, illustrated by Anita Lobel. New York, Greenwillow, 1979; London, MacRae, 1980.
Days with Frog and Toad. New York, Harper, 1979; Kingswood, Surrey, World's Work, 1980.
Frog and Toad Tales (collection). Kingswood, Surrey, World's Work, 1981.
Uncle Elephant. New York, Harper, 1981; Kingswood, Surrey, World's Work, 1982.
Ming Lo Moves the Mountain. New York, Greenwillow, and London, MacRae, 1982.

Poetry

Martha, The Movie Mouse. New York, Harper, 1966; Kingswood, Surrey, World's Work, 1967.
The Ice-Cream Cone Coot and Other Rare Birds. New York, Parents' Magazine Press, 1971.
On the Day Peter Stuyvesant Sailed into Town. New York, Harper, 1971.
The Man Who Took the Indoors Out. New York, Harper, 1974; Kingswood, Surrey, World's Work, 1976.
The Book of Pigericks: Pig Limericks. New York, Harper, 1983; London, Cape, 1984.
The Rose in My Garden, illustrated by Anita Lobel. New York, Greenwillow, and London, MacRae, 1984.
Whiskers and Rhymes. New York, Greenwillow, 1985; London, MacRae, 1986.

The Turnaround Wind. New York, Harper, 1988.
Humpty Dumpty Book and Doll Set. New York, Random House, 1988.

Other

Fables. New York, Harper, and London, Cape, 1980.
On Market Street (alphabet book), illustrated by Anita Lobel. New York, Greenwillow, and London, Benn, 1981.
Frog and Toad Coloring Book. New York, Harper, 1981.
The Frog and Toad Pop-Up Book. New York, Harper, and London, Heinemann, 1986.

Editor, *Gregory Griggs and Other Nursery Rhyme People.* New York, Greenwillow, and London, Hamish Hamilton, 1978.

*

Manuscript Collections: Kerlan Collection, University of Minnesota, Minneapolis.

Illustrator: *Bibletime, Hebrew Dictionary, Holiday Dictionary,* all by Sol Scharfstein, 1958; *Red Tag Comes Back* by Fred Phleger, 1961; *Something Old, Something New* by Susan Oneacre Rhinehart, 1961; *Little Runner of the Longhouse* by Betty Baker, 1962; *Terry and the Caterpillars,* 1962, *Greg's Microscope,* 1963, *Let's Get Turtles,* 1965, and *Benny's Animals,* 1966, all by Millicent E. Selsam; *Let's Be Indians,* 1962, *Let's Be Early Settlers with Daniel Boone,* 1967, and *Dinosaur Time,* 1974, all by Peggy Parish; *The Secret Three,* 1963, and *Ants Are Fun,* 1968, both by Mildred Myrick; *The Quarreling Book,* 1963, and *Someday,* 1965, both by Charlotte Zolotow; *Red Fox and His Canoe,* 1964, *Oscar Otter,* 1966, *The Strange Disappearance of Arthur Cluck,* 1967, and *Sam the Minuteman,* 1969, all by Nathaniel Benchley; *Miss Suzy,* 1964, *Miss Suzy's Easter Surprise,* 1972, *Miss Suzy's Christmas,* 1973, and *Miss Suzy's Birthday,* 1974, all by Miriam Young; *Dudley Pippin* by Phil Ressner, 1965; *The Witch on the Corner* by Felice Holman, 1966; *The Magic Spectacles,* 1966, and *Junk Day on Juniper Street,* 1969, both by Lilian Moore; *The Star Thief* by Andrea Di Noto, 1967; *The Four Little Children Who Went round the World,* 1968, and *The New Vestments,* 1970, both by Edward Lear; *The Microscope* by Maxine Kumin, 1968; *The Comic Adventures of Old Mother Hubbard* by Sarah Catherine Martin, 1968; *The Terrible Tiger,* 1969, *Circus,* 1974, *Nightmares,* 1976, *The Mean Old Mean Hyena,* 1978, *The Headless Horseman Rides Tonight,* 1980, and *Tyrannosaurus Was a Beast,* 1988, all by Jack Prelutsky, and *The Random House Book of Poetry for Children* edited by Prelutsky, 1983; *I'll Fix Anthony* by Judith Viorst, 1969; *Tot Botot and His Little Flute* by Laura E. Cathon, 1970; *Hansel and Gretel* by the Grimm Brothers, 1971; *The Master of Miracle* by Sulamith Ish-Kishor, 1971; *Hildilid's Night* by Cheli Ryan, 1971; *Seahorse* by Robert A. Morris, 1972; *Good Ethan* by Paula Fox, 1973; *The Clay Pot Boy* by Cynthia Jameson, 1973; *As I Was Crossing Boston Common* by Norma Farber, 1975; *As Right as Right Can Be* by Anne K. Rose, 1976; *Merry, Merry Fibruary* by Doris Orgel, 1977; *Tales* [*More Tales*] *of Oliver Pig* by Jean Van Leeuwen, 2 vols., 1979-81; *The Tale of Meshka the Kvetch* by Carol Chapman, 1980; *A Three Hat Day* by Laura Geringer, 1985; *The Random House Book of Mother Goose,* 1986, as *Arnold Lobel's Book of Mother Goose,* 1987; *Bear All Year* [*Gets Dressed, Goes Shopping*], 3 vols., 1986, *Bear's Busy Morning,* 1986, and *Where's the Guinea Pig?* [*Turtle? Dog?, Cat?*], 4 vols., 1987, all by Harriet Ziefert; *The Devil and Mother Crump* by Valerie Scho Carey, 1987.

* * *

As a creator of picture books, Arnold Lobel's achievement was enormous. Beginning in 1961 with his illustrations to Fred Phleger's *Red Tag Comes Back* and in 1962 with *A Zoo for Mister Muster,* the first work Lobel both wrote and illustrated, his 27-year career was launched. During that time Lobel was continually recognized for the quality of both his texts and illustrations. A number of his works have been included among the *New York Times* Best Illustrated Books and the Children's Book Showcase, while several have received the Christopher award and been named Caldecott Honor Books. In 1973 *Frog and Toad Together* was recognized with a Newbery Honor designation, and *Fables* was awarded the Caldecott Medal in 1981.

Undoubtedly Lobel's list of awards owes much to his memorable characters. Frog and Toad, Small Pig and Owl are readily identified with by both children and adults. Indeed, who can not see themselves in Owl, frightened of the mysterious bumps under his covers or in Toad, waiting every day for letters that never come until Frog, understanding his need, writes him a note? Clearly Lobel's characters live in the reader's memories well after the stories are told and the books put away for the next day or the next child. In Lobel's words, finely drawn characters "have a life outside of that book, so that when the child gets back to the book, he refreshes his memory, he reunites himself with it. But when he closes the book, they're still there. Those are the characters that live."

Not only are Lobel's characters memorable, but his works contain two other timeless qualities which have traditionally defined classic works of children's literature: humor and truth.

The first of these qualities takes many forms. There is the simple warmth that pervades the Christmas celebration of the two friends in *Frog and Toad All Year;* the humorous reaction to Ming Lo and his wife as they try to move their mountain and then believe that they have done so, in the literary folktale of *Ming Lo Moves the Mountain;* the absurdist nature of common objects like milk bottles and door keys as they assume the shape of birds in *The Ice-Cream Cone Coot and Other Rare Birds;* and the satirical points made in *Grasshopper on the Road* when the grasshopper meets the obsessive house- and world-cleaning fly and the three butterflies devoted to routine. Such diversity and depth of Lobel's humor underscore the importance of this quality in his work.

Universal truths abound as well. The farmer's wife in *Small Pig* discovers that she must respect, not deny, the living space of others—in this case, the favorite mudhole of Small Pig. And in *Fables,* a mouse finds out that continued perservance will end in attaining what was sought. But perhaps the greatest truth of Lobel's stories is the meaning of friendship. That theme resounds again and again in works such as *A Zoo for Mister Muster,* with its story of the animals' affection for the man who visits them each day and *On Market Street* where a boy journeys to the various vendors and buys "presents for a friend"—his beloved white cat.

Such truths emerge, Lobel told the audience during the 1983 Everychild conference, from his inner being. He found out early in his career that anticipating what children will want to read is not the answer. He needed to write, instead, "out of the middle of myself, to work out of the sadness and, of course, the joy." Sad ness exists in Lobel's work as it does in *Uncle Elephant* when the main character suffers the loss of his father and mother who are missing at sea. But laughter and happiness ultimately prevail in the character of Uncle Elephant who cares for and amuses his nephew until the parents are found.

Through his work of more than a quarter of a century, Lobel explored the many dimensions of the picture book. He illustrated the words of others, complementing and interpreting, without overshadowing, their texts. As a writer, he created narrative and nonsense poetry, limericks, and nursery rhymes; wove literary folktales and fables; and formed animal fantasies, using and extending the conventions of the controlled vocabulary, easy-to-read genre.

In this diversity and through his memorable characters, humor, and truths, one final quality emerges: Lobel's ability to merge such timeless elements.Through both his stories and illustrations, Lobel created truly unified picture books for children.

—Jacqueline L. Gmuca

LOCKE, Elsie (Violet)

Nationality: New Zealander. **Born:** Elsie Violet Farrelly, Hamilton, 17 August 1912. **Education:** Waiuku school, 1917-29; Auckland University, B.A. 1933. **Family:** Married John Gibson Locke in 1941; two sons and two daughters. **Career:** Secretary, Woman Today Society, and member of the editorial committee, *Woman Today* magazine, Wellington, 1937-39. **Member:** National Committee, New Zealand Campaign for Nuclear Disarmament, 1956-65. **Awards:** Katherine Mansfield award (*Landfall* magazine), for essay, 1958; Canterbury Council of the New Zealand Reading Association Nada Beardsley Literacy Award, 1992; Children's Literature Association award, for distinguished services to New Zealand children's literature, 1992; Honours Award, 1996, for *Joe's Ruby.* L.H.D.: University of Canterbury, Christchurch, 1987. **Address:** 392 Oxford Terrace, Christchurch 1, New Zealand.

PUBLICATIONS FOR CHILDREN

Fiction

The Runaway Settlers, illustrated by Antony Maitland. Auckland, Blackwood and Janet Paul, and London, Cape, 1965; New York, Dutton, 1966; new edition, illustrated by Gary Hebley, Christchurch, New Zealand, Hazard Press, 1993.
The End of the Harbour, illustrated by Katrina Mataira. Auckland, Blackwood and Janet Paul, and London, Cape, 1968.
Moko's Hideout, illustrated by Elisabeth Plumridge and Beatrice Foster-Barham. Christchurch, Whitcoulls, 1976.
The Boy with the Snowgrass Hair, with Ken Dawson, illustrated by Jean Oates. Christchurch, Whitcoulls, 1976.
Explorer Zach, illustrated by David Waddington. Christchurch, Pumpkin Press, 1978.
Journey under Warning. Auckland, Oxford University Press, 1983.
A Canoe in the Mist, illustrated by John Shelley. London, Cape 1984.

Other

A Land Without a Master. Wellington, Department of Education, 1962.
Viet-nam. Wellington, Department of Education, 1963.
Six Colonies in One Country, illustrated by Stephen Furlonger. Wellington, Department of Education, 1964.
Provincial Jigsaw Puzzle, illustrated by Stephen Furlonger. Wellington, Department of Education, 1965.
The Long Uphill Climb: New Zealand 1876-1891, illustrated by David A. Cowe. Wellington, Department of Education, 1966.
High Ground for a New Nation, illustrated by David A. Cowe. Wellington, Department of Education, 1967.
The Hopeful Peace and the Hopeful War, illustrated by David A. Cowe. Wellington, Department of Education, 1968.
Growing Points and Prickles: Life in New Zealand 1920-1960, illustrated by Cath Brown and R.E. Brockie. Christchurch, Whitcombe and Tombs, 1971.
It's the Same Old Earth, illustrated by Victor Ambrus. Wellington, Department of Education, 1973.
Maori King and British Queen (textbook), illustrated by Murray Grimsdale. Amersham, Buckinghamshire, Hulton, 1974.
Look under the Leaves (ecology), edited by David Young and David Ault, illustrated by David Waddington. Christchurch, Pumpkin Press, 1975.
Snow to Low Levels: Interaction in a Disaster. Christchurch, Whitcoulls, 1976.
Crayfishermen and the Sea: Interaction of Man and Environment. Christchurch, Whitcoulls, 1976.
A Land Without Taxes: New Zealand from 1800 to 1840. Wellington, Department of Education, 1979; revised edition, as *The Kauri and the Willow: How We Lived and Grew from 1801-1942,* Wellington, Government Printer, 1984.
Two Peoples, One Land: A History of Aotearoa/New Zealand, illustrated by Elisabeth Plumridge. Wellington, Government Printer, 1988.
Joe's Ruby, illustrated by Gary Hebley. Picton, Cape Catley Press, 1995.

PUBLICATIONS FOR ADULTS

Poetry

The Time of the Child: A Sequence of Poems. Privately printed, 1954.

Other

The Shepherd and the Scullery-Maid. Christchurch, New Zealand Communist Party, 1950.
The Human Conveyor Belt. Christchurch, Caxton Press, 1968.
The Roots of the Clover: The Story of the Collett Sisters and Their Families. Privately printed, 1971.
Discovering the Morrisons (and the Smiths and the Wallaces): A Pioneer Family History. Privately printed, 1976.
The Gaoler (on Henry Monson). Palmerston North, Dunmore Press, 1978.
Student at the Gates (memoir). Christchurch, Whitcoulls, 1981.
Co-Operation and Conflict: Pakeha and Maori in Historical Perspective. Auckland, New Zealand Foundation for Peace Studies, 1988.

Peace People: A History of Peace Activities in New Zealand. Christchurch, New Zealand, Hazard Press, 1992.

Editor, *Gordon Watson, New Zealander-1912-1945: His Life and Writings.* Auckland, New Zealand Communist Party, 1949.

Editor, with Janet Paul, *Mrs. Hobson's Album.* Auckland, Auckland University Press, 1990.

Editor, with Jacquie Matthews. *Stick Out, Keep Left: Memoirs of Margaret Thorn.* Auckland, Bridget Williams Books/Auckland University Press, 1997.

*

Manuscript Collections: Alexander Turnbull Library, Wellington; Canterbury Public Library, Christchurch.

Elsie Locke comments:

Although as a child I walked to school with serial stories writing themselves in my head, I did not settle down to being a writer until my own children were growing into their teens. By that time I was thoroughly hooked on children's books, and my own ideas were budding, and still keep budding from year to year. To me, writing a story for children is a way of sharing. Naturally I share those themes that stir my interest, imagination, sympathy, sense of fun, delight, and concern. History, nature, and peace get into my books because I am keen about these matters. My grandparents and great-grandparents were pioneers in the early days of New Zealand. Around the family fireside I listened to many adventurous tales and I think today's children might like to do the same. Whether my readers live in New Zealand and enjoy the familiar settings, or somewhere else and find the settings exotic, I am giving them a small piece of a big world whose glory is the great variety of places and peoples and languages and customs—not to mention all the other living things, the sky and land and the sea. My best-known work is *The Runaway Settlers.*

* * *

Elsie Locke imbues her children's historical novels with sincerity and fairness resulting from thorough research and from having learnt the Maori language in order to reflect more accurately the Maori viewpoint.

In her first novel, *The Runaway Settlers,* based on a real family, her characters in their struggle to survive make some mutually respectful and helpful contact with the Maori people. But her achievement here is in breathing life into a most remarkable pioneer woman and six lively children. In 1859, Mary Small escapes with her children from the drunken brutality of her husband, changes their name to Phipps, and finally reaches Lyttelton from Sydney. A series of incidents brings them to Governor's Bay where in time they establish themselves through hard work and determination. Yet how they sing! One son nearly perishes on the goldfields. Another contributes to the climax of the story when he goes with his mother on her amazing trek across the Southern Alps, driving 34 head of cattle for sale near Hokitika.

In the novels that follow Locke turns her attention to Maori-European relationships in friendship and war. The David-Jonathan friendship between David and Honatana is a binding symbol of hope through *The End of the Harbour,* set in the Waiuku district of 1860. Complex events, including broken promises by inefficient officials, drag settlers and Maoris into the troubles of the wars. The pity of it is that Potatau teaches "Let there be no evil between Maori and Pakeha." Yet greed and treachery add to the troubles. Land rights, today a prime political matter, and the difficulties of establishing justice and peace become central concerns.

A dispute over land rights also leads to the unfortunate Wairau Affray of 1843, subject of *Journey under Warning.* When Wakefield's Company, having bought land cheaply in Nelson, sends surveyors to the Wairau Plain, the Maoris gather their Te Rauparaha to protect the land that is still rightfully theirs. Although events are seen through the eyes of Gibby Banks, aged 15, who has to develop considerable skills and courage to survive the bloodshed, the character to make the strongest impression is Will Morrison, a Scot under Company orders, who experiences the crisis of the conflict. The passions, prejudices, and different points of view, including revenge, held by each group, are presented with sympathy, but the detailed complexity requires advanced readership.

A natural disaster, the eruption of Mount Tarawera in 1866, provides the crisis for *A Canoe in the Mist.* This highly dramatic novel clearly describes the settlement of Te Wairoa, the customs and dances of the Maori people, the beauty of the famous Pink and White Terraces, and the approaching doom, compelling the reader to believe in the waka wairua, the ghost canoe which predicts disaster. The central characters are two girls aged 11. Mattie is English, thus allowing an enlarged dimension of the world. The mixture of historical and fictional characters includes the girls' parents, uncouth tourists, the landlord Joe McRae, the schoolteacher, and Tuhoto the tohunga. They show varying degrees of courage and aroha through the long terror. Strong criticism is made by various characters of desecrating tourists and untrustworthy greedy pakehas. Perhaps the most telling moment of bi-cultural insensitivity comes when Tuhoto dies in a pakeha sanitorium after surviving four days of being buried under volcanic mud. "Pakeha ignorance had broken the tapu and killed him." In such ways in her novels, Locke has made an accumulation of statements about our needs in this country for greater understanding between races.

As well, her deeply-felt concern about environmental issues informs her shorter pieces, such as *It's the Same Old Earth* and *Look under the Leaves,* important poems and articles about ecology. Her short stories in *Moko's Hideout,* in a regrettably dismal production, are about an ugly-duckling-like paua finding his own beauty, a New Zealand gecko which is a unique baby-producing gecko, the godwits which migrate to Siberia, and two keas, "entertainers, thieves, and vandals," and birds of beauty. *Explorer Zach* is a longer short story with period details of the 1920s. Though Zach at eight is not always fully credible, his travels through the countryside with his dog Bruce are zestfully described.

Lastly, *The Boy with the Snowgrass Hair* is an episodic account of exploration in six parts linked by an interlude for planning the next trip. Tom, aged 14, recounts his adventures in mountains and river valleys with varying interesting companions. Inexperienced Lou, aged 14, is small in stature but grows in spirit. Above all, the reader is made aware of the power and beauty of this New Zealand mountain country.

—Diane Hebley

LOFTING, Hugh (John)

Nationality: American (originally British: emigrated to the United States, 1912, naturalized citizen). **Born:** Maidenhead, Berkshire, 14 January 1886. **Education:** Mount St. Mary's College, Chesterfield, Derbyshire; Massachusetts Institute of Technology, Cambridge, 1904-05; London Polytechnic, 1906-07. **Military Service:** Irish Guards in Flanders, 1916-17. **Family:** Married 1) Flora W. Small in 1912 (died 1927), one son and one daughter; 2) Katherine Harrower-Peters in 1928 (died 1928); 3) Josephine Fricker in 1935, one son. **Career:** Prospector and surveyor in Canada, 1908-09; civil engineer, Lagos Railway, West Africa, 1910-11, and United Railways, Havana, Cuba, 1912; worked for British Ministry of Information, New York, 1915. **Award:** American Library Association Newbery Medal, 1923. **Died:** 27 September 1947.

PUBLICATIONS FOR CHILDREN (ILLUSTRATED BY THE AUTHOR)

Fiction

The Story of Dr. Dolittle, Being the History of His Peculiar Life and Astonishing Adventures in Foreign Parts. New York, Stokes, 1920; as *Doctor Dolittle,* London, Cape, 1922.
The Voyages of Dr. Dolittle. New York, Stokes, 1922; London, Cape, 1923.
Dr. Dolittle's Post Office. New York, Stokes, 1923; London, Cape, 1924.
The Story of Mrs. Tubbs. New York, Stokes, 1923; London, Cape, 1924.
Dr. Dolittle's Circus. New York, Stokes, 1924; London, Cape, 1925.
Dr. Dolittle's Zoo. New York, Stokes, 1925; London, Cape, 1926.
Dr. Dolittle's Caravan. New York, Stokes, 1926; London, Cape, 1927.
Dr. Dolittle's Garden. New York, Stokes, 1927; London, Cape, 1928.
Dr. Dolittle in the Moon. New York, Stokes, 1928; London, Cape, 1929.
Noisy Nora. New York, Stokes, and London, Cape, 1929.
The Twilight of Magic, illustrated by Lois Lenski. New York, Stokes, 1930; London, Cape, 1931.
Gub Gub's Book: An Encyclopedia of Food. New York, Stokes, and London, Cape, 1932.
Dr. Dolittle's Return. New York, Stokes, and London, Cape, 1933.
Tommy, Tilly and Mrs. Tubbs. New York, Stokes, 1936; London, Cape, 1937.
Dr. Dolittle and the Secret Lake. Philadelphia, Lippincott, 1948; London, Cape, 1949.
Dr. Dolittle and the Green Canary. Philadelphia, Lippincott, 1950; London, Cape, 1951.
Dr. Dolittle's Puddleby Adventures. Philadelphia, Lippincott, 1952; London, Cape, 1953.
Dr. Dolittle: A Treasury, compiled by Olga Fricker. Phiadelphia, Lippincott, 1967.

Poetry

Porridge Poetry: Cooked, Ornamented, and Served by Hugh Lofting. New York, Stokes, 1924; London, Cape, 1925.

Other

Dr. Dolittle's Birthday Book. New York, Stokes, 1935.

PUBLICATIONS FOR ADULTS

Poetry

Victory for the Slain. London, Cape, 1942.

*

Critical Studies: *Hugh Lofting* by Edward Blishen, in *Three Bodley Head Monographs,* London, Bodley Head, 1968.

* * *

The stubby, square-nosed Dr. Dolittle, animal doctor extraordinary from Puddleby-on-the-Marsh, is one of the most popular and enduring of children's heroes. The man who invented him, Hugh Lofting, imagined a figure whose innocence and common sense anchored the most fantastic of adventures firmly within the limits of credibility. For it is the essentially pedestrian nature of the Doctor's style—from his unperturbed expression to his plain language and practical solutions—that makes the whole lunatic world he inhabits possible.

Lofting was a young soldier serving in Flanders during World War I—and much concerned about the terrible conditions and fate of the Army horses—when he conceived of Dr. Dolittle, a doctor turned animal vet who, because he learns the languages of his patients, is able to enter worlds and adventures inconceivable to others.

Neither the fantasy nor the subject were wholly alien to Lofting's character. As a child he had kept a miniature zoo and wildlife museum in his mother's linen cupboard and had enjoyed making up stories for his brothers and sisters. After an education in a Jesuit school, Lofting worked for a time as an architect, then became a civil engineer and visited Canada, Africa, and the West Indies. These facts are important. Both the nature of his work and the places he saw provided him with a rich fund of material and settings for the Doctor's voyages—he had a keen eye for detail and an obvious love of travel.

The first Dr. Dolittle stories, written from the trenches in letters home, were intended to make his two small children laugh. Dr. Dolittle was at first a comic character, a man who got into muddles. Even his appearance, as illustrations in the margins of the letters showed, was a little ludicrous; a portly, ungainly man, wearing clothes that could have been smart and yet were somehow too big and quite inappropriate. It was only in later books, perhaps as Lofting himself became older and more disillusioned by the war, that the Doctor changes. His lightheartedness gives way to seriousness, and the compassionate side to his nature is constantly emphasised in accounts of his hatred of all aggression and bullying, his growing disapproval of hunting, ill-run zoos, and pet shops.

In the first of what were to be 12 separate books on the doctor's adventures, *The Story of Dr. Dolittle,* Dr. John Dolittle is simply an ordinary doctor, with human patients. The trouble is that he keeps so many animals as pets, appearing to prefer their company, that one by one his patients, irritated and alarmed by the other occupants of his house, forsake him. Even his sister Sarah, anxious about the dwindling income, leaves.

Finally his only remaining patient is Matthew Mugg, the Cat's-Meat-Man, who suggests that the doctor should start earning his living instead as an animal doctor. Polynesia, the doctor's wise and somewhat dictatorial parrot, offers to teach him the language of the animals, starting with the ABC of birds. Before long, Puddleby-on-the-Marsh is transformed by the presence of short-sighted cart horses in spectacles. Dr. Dolittle's success is assured. Because he can actually communicate with the animals, they can tell him what is wrong with them, rather than leaving the diagnosis up to guess-work.

Dr. Dolittle's first adventure takes him to the Land of the Monkeys in Africa to cure thousands of sick gorillas, orangoutans, chimpanzees, and marmosets. The grateful patients present him with a pushmi-pullyu, a shy animal with a head at each end who eats with one mouth and talks with another, and with a marked character of his own, like the Doctor's other friends. Chee-Chee, the monkey, is nervous, and Too-Too, the owl, wise. Dabdab is a practical duck who becomes the Doctor's housekeeper. Gub Gub the pig is very greedy, and as such the natural butt of Lofting's obvious love of puns, jokes, and comic situations. Later books introduce Dobbin the horse, Sophie the seal, and a strange and unfathomable moon cat called Iffy. There are dozens more.

The books are also something of an education. While subsequent adventures take the Doctor to ever more outlandish places—the Moon, the Secret Lake—Lofting nonetheless manages to provide a good deal of practical and detailed information about geography, vegetation, species of animal, and some history, for example, references to Wilberforce and the slave trade (approximately the period in which the stories are set).

Lofting's other books for children lack the magic of Dr. Dolittle. The first of the Doctor's adventures was published, to immediate critical success, in New York in 1920. It was illustrated, as they all were, by the author's charming, somewhat dotty pen and ink drawings, which are quite as much part of the books as the stories themselves and in some ways even more memorable.

Recently Lofting has come in for attack for his use of words like "nigger" and "coon" and for his comical portrayal of the "savages" he encounters. These are uncharacteristic and thoughtless lapses in books that are otherwise so carefully designed. Recent editions of some of the books have been edited to remove offensive terminology and characterizations. Besides, these lapses should not be allowed to spoil the books' real worth: their innocence, the lack of all whimsy, and the fact that Lofting was a genuinely original writer with an unusually inventive mind and a great gift for adventure.

—Caroline Moorehead

LOURIE, Helen. See **STORR, Catherine.**

LOVELACE, Maud Hart (Palmer)

Nationality: American. **Born:** Mankato, Minnesota, 25 April 1892. **Education:** University of Minnesota, Minneapolis, 1911-12. **Family:** Married Delos W. Lovelace in 1917 (died 1967); one daughter. **Died:** 11 March 1980.

Publications for Children

Fiction

Betsy-Tacy, illustrated by Lois Lenski. New York, Crowell, 1940.
Betsy-Tacy and Tib, illustrated by Lois Lenski. New York, Crowell, 1941.
Over the Big Hill, illustrated by Lois Lenski. New York, Crowell, 1942; as *Betsy and Tacy Go over the Big Hill,* 1961 (?).
Down Town, illustrated by Lois Lenski. New York, Crowell, 1943; as *Betsy and Tacy Go Down Town,* 1961.
Heaven to Betsy, illustrated by Vera Neville. New York, Crowell, 1945.
Betsy in Spite of Herself, illustrated by Vera Neville. New York, Crowell, 1946.
Betsy Was a Junior, illustrated by Vera Neville. New York, Crowell, 1947.
Betsy and Joe, illustrated by Vera Neville. New York, Crowell, 1948.
Carney's House Party, illustrated by Vera Neville. New York, Crowell, 1949.
The Tune Is in the Tree, illustrated by Eloise Wilkin. New York, Crowell, 1950.
Emily of Deep Valley, illustrated by Vera Neville. New York, Crowell, 1950.
The Trees Kneel at Christmas, illustrated by Gertrude Howe. New York, Crowell, 1950.
Betsy and the Great World, illustrated by Vera Neville. New York, Crowell, 1952.
Winona's Pony Cart, illustrated by Vera Neville. New York, Crowell, 1953.
Betsy's Wedding, illustrated by Vera Neville. New York, Crowell, 1955.
What Cabrillo Found, illustrated by Paul Galdone. New York, Crowell, 1958.
The Valentine Box, illustrated by Ingrid Fetz. New York, Crowell, 1966.

Other

The Golden Wedge: Indian Legends of South America, with Delos W. Lovelace, illustrated by Charlotte Chase. New York, Crowell, 1942.

Publications for Adults

Novels

The Black Angels. New York, Day, 1926.
Early Candlelight. New York, Day, 1929.
Petticoat Court. New York, Day, 1930; London, Sampson Low, 1931.

The Charming Sally. New York, Day, 1932.
One Stayed at Welcome, with Delos W. Lovelace. New York, Day, 1934.
Gentlemen from England, with Delos W. Lovelace. New York, Macmillan, 1937.

*

Manuscript Collections: University of Oregon Library, Eugene.

* * *

Many authors turn to childhood memories for inspiration, but Maud Hart Lovelace knit her life and art into a particularly tight weave. Her main body of work, the 10 books that comprise the Betsy-Tacy series (plus three related titles), are recreations of the happy days she spent growing up in Mankato, Minnesota (here called Deep Valley), in the early 1900s. She did grow up in that small yellow cottage so familiar to her readers. Her father, like Betsy Ray's, owned a shoe store. And her sisters, fictionalized as Julia and Margaret, appear in the books as do many of her friends.

In *Betsy-Tacy* Betsy invites the painfully shy Tacy Kelly to her 5th birthday party. A misunderstanding distances them, but eventually the two become fast friends. In the second book, they are joined by Thelma Mueller, a fearless though not overly imaginative child. Now they are *Betsy-Tacy and Tib.* The next two books, *Over the Big Hill* and *Down Town,* find Betsy the acknowledged leader and with a burning desire to be a writer. She gets her friends involved in all sorts of schemes and plans redolent of the era: their first automobile ride, a furious fight with Julia and pals to see who will be Queen of Summer, and one memorable incident where the trio takes up the cause of a Syrian girl harassed by boys in the town. This theme of helping immigrants reappears in a later book, *Emily of Deep Valley,* in which Betsy's crowd is only mentioned peripherally.

Perhaps Lovelace's most popular books are the four that take place when Betsy and her Crowd are in high school. Anchored by yearly events and family traditions, Lovelace changes these familiar happenings in each book to enhance the particular story. These four volumes are filled with the concerns teenage girls have always had, boyfriends, school, self-doubts. Yet it is all wrapped in a cloak of nostalgia that recreates a simpler time, a happier place.

As a series, this one is particularly satisfying because it takes Betsy through her wedding to the young man the other books have foreshadowed as her true love. The readers, girls eight through 13 primarily, are taken with the completeness of it all. And while Lovelace is a believer in happy ever afters, she is a feminist as well; most of her characters succeed at lofty ambitions. Betsy becomes a writer, Julia an opera star, Carney finishes Vassar, and Tib finds a career in fashion design. That diminutive blond is particularly disdainful of men who prize her delicate looks rather than her accomplishments.

Librarians are familiar with mothers who loved this series as girls, now bringing their daughters in to meet their old friends. For friends are what the Ray family and entourage become to readers—warm, comfortable, slipped on as easily as a favorite piece of clothing. Lovelace broke no new ground, reached no dazzling heights. She did something almost as difficult, she endured.

—Ilene L. Cooper

LUNN, Janet (Louise)

Nationality: Canadian (originally American: became Canadian citizen, 1963). **Born:** Janet Louise Swoboda, Dallas, Texas, United States, 28 December 1928. **Education:** High school in Montclair, New Jersey, graduated 1946; Notre Dame Convent, Ottawa, 1947; Queen's University, Kingston, Ontario, 1947-50. **Family:** Married Richard Lunn in 1950 (died); four sons and one daughter. **Career:** Children's editor, Clarke Irwin, publishers, Toronto, 1972-75; children's book consultant, Ginn and Company, Scarborough, Ontario, 1968-78; writer-in-residence, Regina Public Library, Ontario, 1982-83. Writer-in-residence, Kitchener Public Library, Ontario, 1988, Ottawa University, 1993. Chairwoman, Writers Union of Canada, 1984-85. **Awards:** Vicky Metcalf award, 1981; Canadian Library Association award, 1982, 1987. Honorary Doctorate of Laws, Queen's University, 1992; Honorary Diploma, Loyalist College of Applied Arts and Technology, 1993; Order of Ontario, 1996; Order of Canada, 1997. **Agent:** Lee Davis Creal, 187 Browning Avenue, Toronto, Ontario M4K 1W7, Canada. **Address:** R.R. 2, Hillier, Ontario K0K 2J0, Canada.

Publications for Children

Fiction

Double Spell. Toronto, PMA Books, 1968; London, Heinemann, 1985; as *Twin Spell,* New York, Harper, 1969.
The Root Cellar. Toronto, Lester and Orpen Dennys, 1981; New York, Scribner, and London, Heinemann, 1983.
Shadow in Hawthorn Bay. Toronto, Lester and Orpen Dennys, and New York, Scribner, 1986; London, Walker, 1988.
Amos's Sweater, illustrated by Kim LaFave. Toronto, Groundwood, 1988.
One Hundred Shining Candles. Toronto, Lester and Orpen Dennys, 1989.
Duck Cakes for Sale, illustrated by Kim LaFave. Toronto, Groundwood, 1989.
Come to the Fair, illustrated by Gilles Pelletier. Toronto, Tundra, 1997.
The Hollow Tree. Toronto, Knopf Canada, 1997.

Other

Larger Than Life (Canadian history), illustrated by Emma Hesse. Victoria, British Columbia, Press Porcépic, 1979.
The Twelve Dancing Princesses (retelling), illustrated by Laszlo Gal. Toronto, London, and New York, Methuen, 1979.
The Story of Canada, with Christopher Moore, illustrated by Alan Daniel. Toronto, Lester-Key Porter, 1990.
Editor, *The Unseen.* Toronto, Lester, 1994.

Publications for Adults

Other

The County, with Richard Lunn. N.p., Prince Edward County Council, 1967.

*

Janet Lunn comments:

Most of my stories are set in—or partly in—historical times. I like how events in one time are connected to events in other times and I sometimes wonder if time mightn't flow in more than one direction—like a reversing falls. So I write about that. In *Double Spell* the main character is two people, twins. One day they are walking past an antique store when they are drawn, as if by a magnet, to an old doll in the window. From this moment the doll leads them into a mystery, that can only be solved by understanding something that happened more than 100 years earlier.

The Root Cellar is about Rose who goes back in time. Through an old root cellar she finds herself in the time of the American Civil War. The friends she makes in the 19th century lead her into an adventure that helps her to understand a lot more about herself and the people she knows in her own 1980s time.

Shadow in Hawthorn Bay is an historical novel. There's no moving back and forth in time except that Mary Urquhart, the heroine, is a seer. She sees into the future, into the past and into the present distance. When she comes to Canada from the Highlands of Scotland because she hears her cousin call her, she sets in motion a very hard time for herself.

I am a grandmother now and have had a lifetime to watch time flow and to look for the patterns in it. Sometimes, though, I leave history alone and write a small funny story; I have written stories for two picture books. One is called *Amos's Sweater* and is about an old sheep who wants his wool back. The other is about an old woman who always seems to have more on her hands than she wants—and it's always her own fault. It's called *Duck Cakes for Sale.*

I can't leave history alone, though, and I am working on one book now, a new historical novel. It's related to both *The Root Cellar* and *Shadow in Hawthorn Bay.*

* * *

As a Canadian who was born and grew up as an American, Janet Lunn is very conscious of the potential confusion of identity experienced by border crossers. In her novels for young adults, she crosses not only national borders, but also time, age, and gender borders—appropriate for readers negotiating the shift from child to adult. All of Lunn's novels contain an element of the supernormal: time-shift (in *The Root Cellar*), and second sight (visions of the past in *Double Spell* and visions of the future in *Shadow in Hawthorn Bay*). But her fictions are always woven into geographically and historically accurate settings.

In "Myth, Story and History" (the 1994 Helen E. Stubbs Memorial Lecture for the Osborne Collection in Toronto) Janet Lunn writes about her faith in the ability of stories "to help us understand what actually happened to people in other times: stories about how people felt, how they were affected by the culture they lived in, [and] how they were affected by the great events the historians chronicle." As historian and author, Janet Lunn is pre-eminent among those making cultural history vital and accessible to readers.

Both *The Canadian Children's Treasury* (1989)—which she describes as an "old-fashioned peep-show"—and *The Story of Canada* (1992) written with Christopher Moore, offer more history than what is usually taught to schoolchildren. But Lunn's main gift is as a historical novelist.

In her novel, *The Root Cellar,* Rose—an orphan who looks like Anne of Green Gables but behaves like Mary from *The Secret Garden*—feels herself out of her own time and place. It is only when she "time-shifts" into the 1860s through the root cellar of her aunt's dilapidated house that she finds her own identity. Her journey into the past takes her first to the house as it was at the time of the American Civil War, to Will whose family owned the house, and to Susan, who would eventually marry him. From there she goes with Susan from Prince Edward County in Ontario to Washington, D. C. to find Will who, in sympathy with his United Empire Loyalist roots, has gone to fight in the Civil War. The journey that Rose and Susan take, shown on a map at the front of the book, is geographically accurate—as is the time of the train they took from Oswego to New York City (Lunn held the train timetable for that date). The identity quest too is psychologically accurate: Rose finds the capacity to control her own destiny, and also finds her emotional connection with the place she lives and her adoptive family.

In *Double Spell* 12-year-old twins Jane and Elizabeth discover their family history through a mysterious connection they have with a doll they chance upon in a Toronto antique shop. Although they don't actually time-shift, they both suddenly begin to share atavistic, often vaguely frightening memories, of a time over 100 years earlier when the doll was new. The supernatural events counterpoint the finely observed details of Toronto past and present. And the genealogical table at the end of the book gives physical reality to the twins' psychic experiences.

Although *Shadow in Hawthorn Bay* is the most recent of Lunn's novels, it is set furthest back in time—1815. Instead of modern characters who find the past, this story is about Mairi, a pioneer girl who can see the future but is drawn to her past. She comes to Prince Edward County (where *The Root Cellar* is set and where Lunn lives) from Scotland, because she hears her cousin Duncan call. He had always been her twin, her shadow, her double; she has to go to him. But when she arrives, she finds him dead and his family gone back to Scotland. The story is a bizarre love triangle. Mairi is torn between her Canadian suitor's desire to marry her, and Duncan's desire—from beyond the grave—to drown her in Hawthorn Bay, as he drowned himself. Her quest involves coming to terms with herself, her relationship with Luke, her new home, Canada, and the double-edged gift of her two sights.

The gender and age borders that Lunn crosses in her novels are less marked than the temporal and spatial ones, but they are clearly visible. In *The Root Cellar* Rose manages to take a controlling role when she travels in the past partly because she crosses a gender line. Her androgynous 20th-century jeans and tee-shirt disguise her as a boy in the 19th century. The age boundary that usually inhibits children from recognizing that grown-ups, especially elderly ones, might once have been children, is crossed as well. The young Susan who goes with Rose on her journey turns up as a "shifted" old woman who appears to Rose in the 20th-century house. And it is Susan's grandmother, Mairi, who appears as a young girl in *Shadow in Hawthorn Bay.*

Although Lunn's novels, like many works of young adult fiction, are about the burning issue of an identity quest, what makes them different is her capacity to see identity as multiple, not as a single thing which can be sought and found. For the characters in her books, identity is about finding a way of integrating various parts of the individual—a redemptive, Jungian notion made visible.

Lunn's notion of identity reaches past the individual in her novel, *The Hollow Tree,* which is set farther back in time than her first two and is about the events surrounding the American Revo lution. By focusing on that critical moment in American history, Lunn brilliantly touches the pulse of local contemporary Canadian and global millennial crises: the break up of the familiar and the coalescence of a new order. Phoebe (the daughter of a man killed fighting on the side of the Revolution) embarks on a journey to Canada on behalf of her beloved cousin Gideon—hanged for being a Loyalist spy. What's clear in this story of a family divided, is that although the political outcome is inevitable (America will be its own country), Phoebe's actions are not politically motivated. She acts not as a blind ideologue, but out of compassion, humanity and belief in the value of individual lives. By setting family loyalties against political loyalties, Lunn brings the impossibility of a clearly defined national identity into sharp focus. As Canada struggles with the possibility of the separation of Quebec, Lunn speaks to our own unquiet state.

—Lissa Paul

LURGAN, Lester. See **WYNNE, May.**

LYNCH, Patricia (Nora)

Nationality: Irish. **Born:** Cork, 7 June 1898. **Education:** At a convent school, and secular schools in Ireland, Scotland, England, and Belgium. **Family:** Married Richard Michael Fox in 1922. **Career:** Feature writer, *Christian Commonwealth,* Dublin, 1918-20. **Award:** Tailteann Festival Silver Medal, 1947. **Died:** 1 September 1972.

PUBLICATIONS FOR CHILDREN

Fiction

The Green Dragon. London, Harrap, 1925.
The Cobbler's Apprentice, illustrated by M.R. Lamb. London, Shaylor, 1930.
The Turf-Cutter's Donkey, illustrated by Jack B. Yeats. London, Dent, 1934; New York, Dutton, 1935.
The Turf-Cutter's Donkey Goes Visiting, illustrated by George Altendorf. London, Dent, 1935; as *The Donkey Goes Visiting,* New York, Dutton, 1936.
King of the Tinkers, illustrated by Katherine C. Lloyd. London, Dent, and New York, Dutton, 1938.
The Turf-Cutter's Donkey Kicks Up His Heels, illustrated by Eileen Coghlan. New York, Dutton, 1939; London, Dent, 1952.
The Grey Goose of Kilnevin, illustrated by John Keating. London, Dent, 1939; New York, Dutton, 1940.
Fiddler's Quest, illustrated by Isobel Morton-Sale. London, Dent, 1941; New York, Dutton, 1943.
Long Ears: The Story of a Little Grey Donkey, illustrated by Joan Kiddell-Monroe. London, Dent, 1943.
Strangers at the Fair and Other Stories, illustrated by Eileen Coghlan. Dublin, Browne and Nolan, 1945; London, Penguin, 1949.
Lisheen at the Valley Farm and Other Stories, with Helen Staunton and Teresa Deevy. Dublin, Gayfield Press, 1945.
Brogeen of the Stepping Stones, illustrated by Alfred Kerr. London, Kerr Cross, 1947.
The Mad O'Haras, illustrated by Elizabeth Rivers. London, Dent, 1948; as *Grania of Castle O'Hara,* Boston, Page, 1952.
The Dark Sailor of Youghal, illustrated by Jerome Sullivan. London, Dent, 1951.
The Boy at the Swinging Lantern, illustrated by Joan Kiddell-Monroe. London, Dent, 1952.
Brogeen Follows the Magic Tune, illustrated by Peggy Fortnum. London, Burke, 1952; New York, Macmillan, 1968.
Delia Daly of Galloping Green, illustrated by Joan Kiddell-Monroe. London, Dent, 1953.
Brogeen and the Green Shoes, illustrated by Peggy Fortnum. London, Burke, 1953.
Brogeen and the Bronze Lizard, illustrated by Grace Golden. London, Burke, 1954; New York, Macmillan, 1970.
Orla of Burren, illustrated by Joan Kiddell-Monroe. London, Dent, 1954.
Tinker Boy, illustrated by Harry Kernoff. London, Dent, 1955.
Brogeen and the Princess of Sheen, illustrated by Christopher Brooker. London, Burke, 1955.
The Bookshop on the Quay, illustrated by Peggy Fortnum. London, Dent, 1956.
Brogeen and the Lost Castle, illustrated by Christopher Brooker. London, Burke, 1956.
Fiona Leaps the Bonfire, illustrated by Peggy Fortnum. London, Dent, 1957; as *Shane Comes to Dublin,* New York, Criterion, 1958.
Cobbler's Luck, illustrated by Christopher Brooker. London, Burke, 1957.
The Old Black Sea Chest: A Story of Bantry Bay, illustrated by Peggy Fortnum. London, Dent, 1958.
Brogeen and the Black Enchanter, illustrated by Christopher Brooker. London, Burke, 1958.
The Stone House at Kilgobbin, illustrated by Christopher Brooker. London, Burke, 1959.
Jinny the Changeling, illustrated by Peggy Fortnum. London, Dent, 1959.
The Runaways. Oxford, Blackwell, 1959.
Sally from Cork, illustrated by Elizabeth Grant. London, Dent, 1960.
The Lost Fisherman of Carrigmor, illustrated by Christopher Brooker. London, Burke, 1960.
Ryan's Fort, illustrated by Elizabeth Grant. London, Dent, 1961.
The Longest Way Round, illustrated by D.G. Valentine. London, Burke, 1961.
The Golden Caddy, illustrated by Juliette Palmer. London, Dent, 1962.
Brogeen and the Little Wind, illustrated by Beryl Sanders. London, Burke, 1962; New York, Roy, 1963.
The House by Lough Neagh, illustrated by Nina Ross. London, Dent, 1963.
Brogeen and the Red Fez, illustrated by Beryl Sanders. London, Burke, 1963.
Holiday at Rosquin, illustrated by Mary Shillabeer. London, Dent, 1964.

Guests at the Beech Tree, illustrated by Beryl Sanders. London, Burke, 1964.
The Twisted Key and Other Stories, illustrated by Joan Kiddell-Monroe. London, Harrap, 1964.
Mona of the Isle, illustrated by Mary Shillabeer. London, Dent, 1965.
Back of Beyond, illustrated by Susannah Holden. London, Dent, 1966.
The Kerry Caravan, illustrated by James Hunt. London, Dent, 1967.

Other

Knights of God: Stories of the Irish Saints, illustrated by Alfred Kerr. London, Hollis and Carter, 1945; Chicago, Regnery, 1955.
The Seventh Pig and Other Irish Fairy Tales, illustrated by Jerome Sullivan. London, Dent, 1950; revised edition, as *The Black Goat of Slievemore and Other Irish Tales,* 1959.
Tales of Irish Enchantment (legends), illustrated by Fergus O'Ryan. Dublin, Clonmore and Reynolds, and London, Burns Oates, 1952.

Publications for Adults

Other

A Story-Teller's Childhood (autobiography). London, Dent, 1947; New York, Norton, 1962.

* * *

Country gatherings like fairs and races and tinker encampments play a large part in Patricia Lynch's stories, and to the natural bustle and exuberance of these events and places a magic element is often added. At the fair in *The Turf-Cutter's Donkey,* Eileen and Seamus are followed around by a small man and a pig, and the children find that they can fly simply by jumping in the air. But Eileen's boots have been mended by a leprechaun, and this makes plausible the elaborate sequence of events that follows. In the Long Ears series, magic is unrestrained and owes a great deal to the type of Irish folktale that deals in talking animals and bewildering changes in settings and objects. Usually an odd collection of characters is brought together: a couple of children, a ballad singer, an apple woman, a leprechaun, tinker, changeling, or captain of a barge. Action is continuous and always directed towards the achievement of a moral resolution. The goal of the central characters is domestic cosiness, and often they are waifs and strays to make the point more telling.

Sheila, in *The Grey Goose of Kilnevin,* is sent on an errand to Bridgie Swallow, and at once a formal pattern is established: the ritualized quest, with tests and trials at every step. Sheila gets the three pounds of butter and much else besides; like all Lynch's heroines she is clever and spirited and always ready to share her few possessions with any strangers that she may meet along the road. A number of peculiar alliances result from the latter: a fox makes friends with the little grey goose, and a scarecrow provides a coat for the Ballad singer.

The fantasy is usually down-to-earth with a strong rough-and-tumble flavour; but sometimes the characters are taken right off the ground and swept into a mythological realm. This is not always successful. The author has made good use of the standard figures of Irish legend and myth: the wise woman of the mountain; the fool who recovers his wits; the Fianna, ancient warrior band; the salmon of knowledge; the Children of Lir who were changed into swans by a malicious stepmother; and so on. But Lynch has no sense of the numinous and sometimes the magical episodes have a picture postcard element when they aren't enlivened by sheer rumbustious humour.

Two excellent stories with no supernatural overtones appeared in the 1940s: *Fiddler's Quest* and *The Mad O'Haras.* Again, in each of these we have the movement towards emotional security. In the former, Ethne Cadogan, the fiddler of the title, comes to Ireland to search for her traditional home, Inniscoppal (the Island of Horses), and her itinerant grandfather. Unusually, the book has an urban setting, a courtyard in Dublin; it is also the only novel by Lynch to exploit the romantic aspect of Irish nationalism. Nial Desmond is a Republican on the run; at one point in the narrative Ethne and the Rafferty children drive a cartload of guns through an army barricade. Suspense is maintained admirably through a series of incidents that includes shooting and evacuation. The book has a kind of realism that is not found often in her work, and it is offset to good effect by the use of familiar stereotypes like the ballad singer and the story teller.

Ethne the fiddler is a talented child; like Grania in *The Mad O'Haras* she has plans for a career. Grania won't submit to convention, unlike her cousin Sally who longs to be a jockey but works as a hairdresser, a suitable girl's occupation. Lynch's heroines face up to opposition and overcome it. Grania means to be a painter, and wins a scholarship to a Dublin art school. First, however, she helps to solve the problems of her wild relatives in whom the ramshackle, devil-may-care quality of Irish life is embodied. The romantic O'Haras have tinker blood and live in a tumbledown castle. The perennial Irish theme of "bad blood" is indicated here, but naturally in the children's book context it is muted and easily resolved.

There is no complexity of situation or motive in Lynch's stories, and little attempt at character differentiation. The central characters are effectively interchangeable. The predominant virtue is kindness, and if its rewards are sometimes disproportionate this is acceptable in terms of the rigid fairytale structure. Even the straightforward children's novels have a simplified moral basis. The author went on producing alternate fantasy and family tales along the lines that she had laid down in the 1930s and early 1940s. In *Tinker Boy,* for instance, there is acknowledgement of the glamour of vagabond life; but the tinkers' apparent lawlessness is really an illusion. It was always easy to get the better of the dreadful King of the Tinkers with his spotted kerchief. When villainy is larger than life it ceases to be frightening and of course many of Lynch's books are for younger children who can relish without question the white pigs and mermaids and changelings and magic boots.

Jinny the Changeling employs familiar motifs: the four swans, the quest for a missing father, the swirling mists that are conjured up to mask queer goings-on. The Clerys are a poor but generous family whose fortunes begin to change when they find a baby in a clump of bushes. ("You're a dote of a Changeling," everyone says about Jinny.) As usual, when she tries to be poetic about the supernatural, Lynch descends into a kind of vulgarity: it is all pretty-pretty where it should be delicate and ethereal. There is in fact a slight sense of dislocation in the stories that move from one plane to another: those that work best are completely magical or completely prosaic (though in later books like *Tinker Boy* the dreariness of small Irish towns is beginning to make itself felt).

Lynch's reputation rests on her assured evocations of fairground and bog and fairy rath, the racy outspoken quality of her dialogue, and her ability to amalgamate the traditional folktale with the present-day children's story.

—Patricia Craig

LYONS, Mary E.

Nationality: American. **Born:** Mary E. Lyons, Macon, Georgia, 28 November 1947. **Education:** Appalachian State University, Boone, North Carolina, B.S. 1970, M.S. 1972. **Family:** Married Paul Collinge. **Career:** Reading teacher, elementary and middle schools in North Carolina and Charlottesville, Virginia,1970-1986; school librarian for elementary, middle, and high schools, Charlottesville, 1986-1993; writer, from 1993. Plays banjo with folk music band, The Chicken Heads. **Awards:** Carter G. Woodson Secondary Book Award, 1991; National Endowment for the Humanities fellowships, 1991, 1994, 1995; Golden Kite Award, Society of Children's Book Writers and Illustrators, 1992; Jane Addams Children's Book Award honor, 1993; Carter G. Woodson Elementary Book Award, 1994; Carter G. Woodson Elementary Merit Book Award, 1995; Jefferson Cup Series Award, Virginia Library Association, 1995. **Website:** http://www.comet.net/writersc/lyonsden.

Publications for Children

Nonfiction

Sorrow's Kitchen: The Life and Folklore of Zora Neale Hurston. New York, Macmillam, 1990.

Letters from a Slave Girl: The Story of Harriet Jacobs. New York, Macmillan, 1992.

Stitching Stars: The Story Quilts of Harriet Powers. New York, Macmillan, 1993.

Starting Home: The Story of Horace Pippin. New York, Macmillan, 1993.

Deep Blues: Bill Trayler, Self-Taught Artist. New York, Macmillan, 1994.

Master of Mahogany: The Story of Tom Day, Free Black Cabinetmaker. New York, Macmillan, 1994.

Painting Dreams: Minnie Evans, Visionary. Boston, Houghton Mifflin, 1996.

Catching the Fire: Philip Simmons, Blacksmith. Boston, Houghton Mifflin, 1997.

Fiction

The Butter Tree: Tales of Bruh Rabbit. New York, Henry Holt, 1995.

The Poison Place: A Novel. New York, Atheneum, 1997.

Other

Editor, *Raw Head, Bloody Bones: African-American Tales of the Supernatural.* New York, Macmillan, 1991.

Editor, *Talking with Tebe, Memory Artist.* Boston, Houghton Mifflin, 1998.

Publications for Young Adults

Nonfiction

Keeping Secrets: The Girlhood Diaries of Seven Women Writers. New York, Henry Holt, 1995.

Other

A Story of Her Own: A Resource Guide to Teaching Literature by Women.

Mary E. Lyons comments:

I was a reading specialist for seventeen years and a school librarian for six. During these years, I discovered that young readers were fascinated by the lost and forgotten stories of women and African Americans. This is not surprising, since half of my students were girls and half were African American. Now I am a full-time writer, and my books are a way to continue what I started in the classroom.

I love to uncover hidden history. For example, few people are aware that Moses Williams, an eighteenth-century silhouette cutter, may have been the first professional African-American artist in America. Researching his life and imagining it for *Poison Place: A Novel* has been the most exciting experience of my writing career so far.

Perhaps one day women and African Americans will be an integral part of American history, not merely faces on posters that we display during February and March. These months help us focus on black history and women's history, but girls are girls every day and African Americans are black all year round. We should celebrate and enjoy their history throughout the year.

* * *

Sorrow's Kitchen: The Life and Folklore of Zora Neale Hurston makes the accomplishments of this most fascinating female of the Harlem Renaissance accessible to young readers. One might speculate whether the folklore of the subtitle refers to the larger-than-life aspects of Hurston's biography or to her writing. For, indeed, Lyons's depiction of that life presents a woman of legendary proportions who seemed to delight in the outrageous and yet had the savvy and the sensitivity to sit and wait for those from whom she was attempting to collect local folklore to open up and tell her their stories. Lyons has skillfully woven excerpts from Hurston's collections of folkstories into the story of her own life to draw relationships between the two.

Zora Neale Hurston also figures prominently as the recorder of two of the fifteen stories in *Raw Head, Bloody Bones: African-American Tales of the Supernatural.* Lyons's introduction and brief notes at the end of each tale place them in the context of their origins reflected in the dialects of the original storytellers. The monstrous creatures captured here, both familiar and unfamiliar, provide rich resources for contemporary storytellers brave enough to venture into the darker regions of the human mind. Of course, through the power of story, the human spirit conquers, and even learns from, the beasts.

Two books in the "African-American Artists and Artisans" series were published in 1993. *Stitching Stars: The Story Quilts of Harriet Powers* skillfully pieces together what is known about Power's life, a more general story of slavery in Georgia prior to the Civil War, and the Biblical stories and folklore recorded in the appliqued quilts now in the Smithsonian Museum and the Boston Museum of Fine Arts. *Starting Home: The Story of Horace Pippin,* Lyons also combines the life and the work of this disabled veteran of World War I who taught himself to paint and became one of the most celebrated African-American artists. Two more books in this series, one about artist Bill Traylor and the other about cabinetmaker Tom Day, are scheduled for publication in late 1994.

Letters from a Slave Girl: The Story of Harriet Jacobs is a compelling retelling of incidents from Harriet Jacobs's 1861 autobiography. This story begins in 1825 with eleven-year-old Harriet waiting to see if her kindly mistress will set her free. Although she does not get her freedom, Harriet does have one liberty forbidden to most slaves, the ability to read and write. The first eight years of this story are told through letters to her dead mother, to her father, and to the young man she loves, none of whom receive or read them. At the end of Part I, Harriet is still avoiding the advances of her master but already has two children by another, more kindly, white man, hoping her pregnancies would keep Dr. Norcom away from her. During most of the seven years recorded in Part II, Harriet is hiding "up under the roof in a space no bigger than a few coffins." Here she pours out her feelings in letters to her uncles Joseph and Stephen and to her brother John who had already escaped from slavery and to her Aunt Betty who had died. At one point, she even writes to Dr. Norcom to convince him that she had fled to Boston. The final letter, the first Harriet ever sends, is to Gran back home to report that she has arrived in Philadelphia. In Part III, Lyons tells the rest of Harriet's story, including the writing of her autobiography which remains a classic tale of slavery from a woman's perspective.

Of special interest to teachers and librarians is Lyons's *A Story of Her Own: A Resource Guide to Teaching Literature by Women* published by the National Women's History Project in 1985. This guide includes an annotated bibliography and feminist and multicultural alternatives to established works by white males in the literary canon. Suggestions for student activities and for supplementing the existing curriculum are also included. This valuable resource reflects the author's deep concern for a multicultural and gender-fair view of history that is brought to life in her writing for young people.

Mary E. Lyons continues to produce biographical studies that are meticulously researched, impressively illustrated, and capably written. Her African-American Artists and Artisans series now includes *Painting Dreams: Minnie Evans, Visionary,* about a gatekeeper for the Airlie Gardens estate in Wilmington, North Carolina, whose primitive, other-worldly paintings have been compared to those of William Blake, and *Catching the Fire: Philip Simmons, Blacksmith* , about the man whose graceful iron gates are landmarks in Charleston, South Carolina. Like earlier books in this series, these two feature excellent full-color photographs. In *Keeping Secrets: The Girlhood Diaries of Seven Women Writers,* Lyons asserts that Louisa May Alcott, Charlotte Forten, Sarah Jane Foster, Kate Chopin, Alice Dunbar-Nelson, Ida B. Wells, and Charlotte Perkins Gilman revealed their rebellious thoughts and feelings in their diaries even when a surrounding society demanded decorum. Though this thesis is unsurprising, Lyons's presentation of the women is fresh, and she skillfully chooses and interweaves portions of their diaries with her own account of their circumstances. She has also straightforwardly retold six short stories in *The Butter Tree: Tales of Bruh Rabbit.*

Lyons's most significant recent book is *The Poison Place: A Novel,* which like *Letters from a Slave Girl* is historical fiction. Freed from the laudable but constraining demands of complete historical verification, Lyons's style blossoms gracefully. Replete with a map of Philadelphia and floor-plan of the Peale museum there, this book tells a subtle, complex story clearly and elegantly. In it, Moses Williams, a former slave of the painter Charles Willson Peale, takes his daughter Maggie on a night-time tour of the museum in 1827. This tour structures Williams's reminiscences about his well-known master and the master's son Raphael, who was Williams's boyhood friend and adult concern. The probable cause of Raphael's death offers a touch of mystery in this well-paced book.

—Kay E. Vandergrift, updated by Frieda F. Bostian

M

MACAULAY, David (Alexander)

Nationality: American. **Born:** 2 December 1946, Burton-on-Trent, England; came to the United States in 1957. **Family:** Two daughters. **Education:** Rhode Island School of Design, B.Arch. 1969. **Career:** Instructor in interior design, Rhode Island School of Design, Providence, 1969-73, instructor in two-dimensional design, 1974-76, adjunct faculty, department of illustration, 1976-90, chairman, department of illustration, 1977-79; free-lance illustrator and writer since 1979. Public school art teacher, Central Falls, Rhode Island, 1969-70, and Newton, Massachusetts, 1972-74; designer, Morris Nathanson Design, 1969-72. Visiting lecturer, Yale University, 1978-79, Simmons College, 1989-90; visiting professor of art, Wellesley College, 1985-87; visiting instructor, Brown University, 1982-86. Worked as a consultant and presenter for television shows produced by Unicorn Projects, Washington, D.C., including "Castle," 1982, "Cathedral," 1985, and "Pyramid," 1987; presenter of television show "Sense of Place," WJAR-TV, Providence, 1988. Trustee, Partners for Livable Places, Washington, DC, Slater Mill Historic Site, Pawtucket, Rhode Island, and Community Preparatory School, Providence. Works are in the permanent collections of Cooper Hewitt Museum, Toledo Museum of Art, and Museum of Art, Rhode Island School of Design. **Awards:** *New York Times* Ten Best Illustrated Books, 1973, 1980; Caldecott honor, 1974, 1978; Jugendbuchpreis Award (Germany), 1975; Silver Slate Pencil Award (Holland), 1975; Christopher Award, 1975; *New York Times* Outstanding Children's Book of the Year, 1975, 1976; *Boston Globe-Horn Book* honor, 1976, 1978; *New York Times Book Review* Outstanding Book of the Year, 1977; New York Academy of Sciences Children's Science Book Awards honorable mention, 1978; Washington Children's Book Guild Award for a body of work, 1977; American Institute of Architects Medal, for his contribution as "an outstanding illustrator and recorder of architectural accomplishment," 1978; American Library Association Best Books for Young Adults, 1980; New York Public Library's Books for the Teen Age, 1980; Parents' Choice Award for illustration in children's books, 1980; New York Academy of Sciences Awards honorable mention, 1981; English-Speaking Union Books-across-the-Sea, Ambassador of honor book, 1982; *New York Times Book Review* Notable Book of the Year, 1982; *School Library Journal* Best Books, 1983; New York Public Library's Children's Books, 1983; Hans Christian Andersen Illustrator medal nomination, 1984; *Times Educational Supplement* senior information book award, 1989; The Science Museum/Copus (London) science book prize for under sixteen, 1989; *Boston Globe-Horn Book* award for best nonfiction book, 1989; American Institute of Physics best science book of the year, 1990; Caldecott Medal, 1991, for *Black and White*; honorary Doctor of Literature, Rhode Island College, 1987; honorary Doctor of Humanities, Savannah College of Art and Design, 1987. **Address:** 146 Water St., Warren, Rhode Island 02885, U.S.A.

Publications for Children

Nonfiction (illustrated by the author)

Cathedral: The Story of Its Construction. Boston, Houghton, 1973.
City: A Story of Roman Planning and Construction. Boston, Houghton, 1974.
Pyramid. Boston, Houghton, 1975.
Underground. Boston, Houghton, 1976.
Castle. Boston, Houghton, 1977.
Great Moments in Architecture. Boston, Houghton, 1978.
Motel of the Mysteries. Boston, Houghton, 1979.
Unbuilding. Boston, Houghton, 1980.
Mill. Boston, Houghton, 1983.
BAAA. Boston, Houghton, 1985.
Why the Chicken Crossed the Road. Boston, Houghton, 1987.
The Way Things Work. Boston, Houghton, 1988.
Black and White. Boston, Houghton, 1990.
Ship. Boston, Houghton, 1993.

*

Media Adaptations: *Castle* (television film), PBS-TV, 1983; *Cathedral* (television film), PBS-TV, 1985; *Pyramid* (television film), PBS-TV, 1987.

Illustrator: David L. Porter, *Help! Let Me Out!,* Houghton, 1982; *Electricity,* Tennessee Valley Authority, 1983; Robert Ornstein and Richard F. Thompson, *The Amazing Brain,* Houghton, 1984.

* * *

David Macaulay is one of the most popular and critically acclaimed writers and illustrators of nonfiction books for children. The many awards he has received include the Caldecott medal and two Honor medals, the Christopher award, the *Boston Globe-Horn Book* award and two honorable mentions, the *Jugendbuchpreis* from Germany, and the Silver Slate Pencil award from Holland. Most of Macaulay's books help explain architecture, engineering, or technology through inventive narrative and pictures, making his subjects accessible to young readers.

In his earliest books, Macaulay draws on his own architectural training, using monochromatic drawings and fictionalized narratives to illuminate the design and construction of various architectural mysteries. His subjects include a thirteenth-century Gothic cathedral (*Cathedral: The Story of Its Construction*), a Roman city begun in 26 B.C. (*City: A Story of Roman Planning and Construction*), an ancient Egyptian pyramid (*Pyramid*), a thirteenth-century Welsh castle (*Castle*), and four nineteenth-century New England textile mills (*Mill*). These books have been praised for their attention to detail—*Castle* shows, step-by-step, how such a structure might have been built, including the original plan; the necessary workers, tools, and building materials; and its careful construction and subsequent partial destruction.

Two of Macaulay's early books demonstrate his penchant for experimenting with narrative strategies, his use of satire, and his desire to help readers look beyond surface appearances. Layer by layer, *Underground* strips away the ground of a modern city to show what lies beneath it, while *Unbuilding* literally deconstructs the Empire State Building, which Macaulay fantasizes is being torn down and rebuilt to become the headquarters for the Greater Riyadh Institute of Petroleum (GRIP).

Macaulay's most ambitious attempt to explain technology is *The Way Things Work.* The 384-page tome reveals the inner workings of such seemingly ordinary objects as a can opener, a piano, a guitar, a light bulb, and a telephone, as well as more mysterious machines and devices, including microcomputers, a space telescope, radar, and nuclear weapons.

Some critics have suggested that as Macaulay has continued to experiment, his works have become increasingly pessimistic. Certainly, *Great Moments in Architecture, Motel of the Mysteries,* and *Baaa*—in which Macaulay moves away from primarily informative books—all poke fun at human nature and contemporary culture, positing future worlds where life is markedly different. *Great Moments in Architecture,* a collection of humorous sketches, includes several pictures of future archaeologists excavating icons of contemporary culture, including a fast food restaurant, a gas station, a drive-in theater, and a mobile home. *Motel of the Mysteries* takes this idea further, relating Howard Carson's discovery of a buried motel and his erroneous theories about the importance and function of such objects as toilets and "Do Not Disturb" signs. *Baaa,* with a concept similar to that of George Orwell's *Animal Farm,* presents a future society in which sheep learn to talk and wear clothes, assuming the lifestyle of human beings.

Macaulay has continued to stretch himself, experimenting with fiction and color illustrations. *Why the Chicken Crossed the Road* is a humorous explanation of the age-old question posed by its title and features characters who later appear in *Black and White,* which won the Caldecott medal. *Black and White* lacks a linear plot and resists the conventions of traditional storytelling. The title page suggests that the book may contain not just one story, but four. Full page spreads, each featuring four illustrations in different styles and from different stories, appear upon closer observation to be interconnected. Macaulay himself has suggested that the book is subversive and an intellectual exercise, one which also attempts to help children become closer readers.

In Macaulay's most recent book, *Ship,* he again explores the planning and construction of an historical object, in this case, a fifteenth-century sailing vessel. Unlike his earliest work, however, the book employs two different artistic styles—color illustrations and a two-part narrative, one of which is a day-by-day, first-person account of the ship's construction. While Macaulay has already established a reputation for creating some of the best informational books for children, he is clearly not content with past successes, and he will likely continue to experiment as a writer and illustrator, adding to an already substantial body of work.

—Joel D. Chaston

MACDONALD, Caroline

Nationality: New Zealander. **Born:** Taranaki, 1 October 1948. **Career:** Editor of teaching materials, Deakin University, Geelong, Australia, 1984-88. **Awards:** New Zealand Literary Fund Choysa bursary, 1983; New Zealand Library Association Esther Glen Medal, 1984; New Zealand Children's Book of the Year award, 1985; Children's Book Council of Australia Book of the Year, older honor, 1989. **Died.**

Publications for Children

Fiction

Elephant Rock. Auckland, Hodder and Stoughton, 1984; London, Hodder and Stoughton, 1988.

Visitors, illustrated by Garry Meeson. Auckland, Hodder and Stoughton, 1984; London, Hodder and Stoughton, 1988.

Yellow Boarding House. Auckland, Oxford University Press, 1985.

Joseph's Boat, illustrated by Chris Gaskin. Auckland, Hodder and Stoughton, 1988.

Earthgames, illustrated by Chris Johnson and Rowena Cory. Melbourne, Rigby, 1988.

The Lake at the End of the World. Auckland, Hodder and Stoughton, 1988; New York, Dial Press, 1989.

Speaking to Miranda. Auckland, Hodder and Stoughton, 1991; New York, HarperCollins, 1992.

Hostilities: Nine Bizarre Stories. Norwood, South Australia, Omnibus Books, 1991; New York, Scholastic, 1994.

Eye Witness. Auckland, Hodder and Stoughton, 1992.

Secret Lives. Melbourne, Ashton Scholastic, 1993.

*

Caroline Macdonald comments:

Future fiction, science fiction, the supernatural and the mystical are the thematic areas I'm interested in. I like to suggest there's a strange edge to be found in a mundane world. I enjoy forming characters who are for some reason removed from the usual processes of conditioning.

* * *

Although Caroline Macdonald's novels and picture book texts have a wide range of subject matter and environments, they all demonstrate her preoccupation with young people who are in some way isolated. Their separation from normal peer groups renders them more sensitive to the unusual, be it visitors from outer space, time slips, or challenging circumstances. The child alone is inevitably more dependent on adults, and her multi-layered novels are sensitive explorations of parent-child relationships, which often suffer from a breakdown in communication.

Her first book, *Elephant Rock,* daringly and uncompromisingly examines the situation of 12-year-old Ann whose mother is dying of cancer. The pitfalls inherent in such a scenario are deftly avoided through the use of a time-slip device that enables Ann to relive her mother's youth and consequently understand and more readily accept the impending bereavement.

Kaye Webb once quoted a child who said of another novel, "I felt older after reading this." The same statement could apply to *Elephant Rock:* the reader will grow through experiencing it. Although inevitably sad, it is neither depressing nor sentimental as the spare economical prose is allowed to make its own impact.

Visitors is a counterpoint of differing cross-threads of communication. The "Visitors" are from Outer Space and have been trapped in this world for hundreds of years. Every attempt to escape has failed because they cannot find anyone to understand their messages. Finally they select Terry, a lonely boy, to help them. Terry is the classic poor little rich boy, given every luxury by his hard-working professional parents except their time and attention. He retreats into the world of the small screen and picks up pictures from the Visitors on video. He cannot understand their meaning until he is helped by Maryanne, a physically handicapped school friend who, because she herself can only communicate effectively through a word processor, has more insight into what the Visitors are trying to say and solves the puzzle. The Visitors' predicament thus highlights the human problems, and solving the one assists in easing the others. Not only is Maryanne revealed as an intelligent girl instead of an object of pity, but Terry's parents are alerted to his needs.

In addition to investing fantasy with a compelling life of its own, Macdonald demonstrates considerable scientific acumen as Maryanne and Terry have to work out various aspects of wavelengths and light refraction in order to free the Visitors.

There is a move away from fantasy in *Yellow Boarding House,* which is set in Australia where a New Zealand mother and her daughter Lyndsay are stranded in Melbourne with no money when the father fails to return from a trip to Queensland. The mother is forced to work in order to pay their way and Lyndsay, alone in a strange city, inadvertently becomes involved with a drug-smuggling gang. The mother-daughter relationship is astutely portrayed; the mother under stress still protectively treats Lyndsay like a child, while Lyndsay, emerging into adulthood, is resentful at not being given responsibility or taken into her mother's confidence.

A father and son feature in the long picture book *Joseph's Boat.* Here the isolation is through living on a small island, away from other children or any female influence. Joseph is motherless and his father, immersed in day-to-day farming, fails to realize that Joseph's pleas to accompany him on visits to the mainland stem from loneliness. It is not until Joseph takes a boat and is nearly lost at sea that communication is satisfactorily established with his father. Chris Gaskin's pictures are a particularly evocative accompaniment to this book.

Her novel *The Lake at the End of the World* is set in 2025 when the world has virtually been killed by pollution except for a lake and its environs in New Zealand. Unknown to one another two groups of people live near its shore, one a highly structured community who inhabit underground caves, the other a family consisting of father, mother, and daughter, Diana, who eke out a subsistence living above ground. The novel opens when teenage Hector from the community finds his way into the outside world and meets Diana. Their differing circumstances lead to widely divergent viewpoints but both have to cooperate when the formerly utopian underground community becomes a dystopia as its leadership degenerates into tyranny.

The book unobtrusively asks large questions about power, the direction of agricultural management, and industrial pollution. A potent contrast is drawn between the authoritarian but sheltered regime of the community and the family, vulnerable to the exigencies of weather, accident, and illness. Nevertheless, it is the family who retains the myth-making capacity, as they weave stories about the Lake that dominates their existence. In the technological environment of the caves, musical instruments lie idle and the voices of poets have been silenced.

—Betty Gilderdale

MacDONALD, Golden. See **BROWN, Margaret Wise**.

MacINTYRE, Elisabeth

Nationality: Australian. **Born:** Sydney, New South Wales, 1 November 1916. **Education:** Sydney Church of England Girls Grammar School; Bowral High School; art student at East Sydney Technical College. **Military Service:** Served in the Land Army during World War II. **Family:** Married John Roy Eldershaw in 1951; one daughter. **Career:** Designer, Lever's Advertising Agency, Lintas, 1937-42; freelance artist and feature writer, the *Age,* Melbourne, Sydney *Sunday Telegraph, Australian Woman's Weekly,* and the New South Wales Education Department *School Magazine;* devised and illustrated television cartoons for the Australian Broadcasting Commission. **Awards:** Australian Children's Book Council Picture Book of the Year award, 1965; Australian Literature Board fellowship, 1973-76; Australia-Japan Foundation fellowship, 1977. **Address:** 2/3 Pacific Street, Bronte, New South Wales 2024, Australia.

Publications for Children (illustrated by the author)

Fiction

Ambrose Kangaroo: A Story That Never Ends. Sydney, Consolidated Press, 1941; New York, Scribner, 1942.
The Handsome Duckling. Sydney, Dawfox, 1944.
The Black Lamb. Sydney, Dawfox, 1944.
The Forgetful Elephant. Sydney, Dawfox, 1944.
The Willing Donkey. Sydney, Dawfox, 1944.
Ambrose Kangaroo Has a Busy Day. Sydney, Consolidated Press, 1944.
Jane Likes Pictures. New York, Scribner, and London, Collins, 1959.
Ambrose Kangaroo Goes to Town. Sydney and London, Angus and Robertson, 1964.
Hugh's Zoo. New York, Knopf, and London, Constable, 1964.
Ninji's Magic, illustrated by Mamoru Funai. New York, Knopf, 1966; London, Angus and Robertson, 1967.
The Purple Mouse. Nashville, Nelson, 1975.
It Looks Different When You Get There. Sydney and London, Hodder and Stoughton, 1978.
Ambrose Kangaroo Delivers the Goods. Sydney, Angus and Robertson, 1978.
A Wonderful Way to Learn the Language. Sydney and London, Hodder and Stoughton, 1982.

Radio Serials

The Riddle of Rum Jungle, 1957.
The Kings of Corroboree Plains, 1960.

Poetry

Susan, Who Lives in Australia. New York, Scribner, 1944; as *Katherine,* Sydney, Australasian Publishing Company, and London, Harrap, 1946; revised edition, Sydney and London, Angus and Robertson, 1958.
Mr. Koala Bear. New York, Scribner, 1954; London, Angus and Robertson, 1966.
The Affable, Amiable Bulldozer Man. New York, Knopf, 1965; London, Angus and Robertson, 1966.

Other

Willie's Woollies: The Story of Australian Wool. Melbourne, Georgian House, 1951.

*

Manuscript Collections: Mitchell Library, Sydney; Lu Rees Collection, Canberra College of Advanced Education.

Illustrator: *Three Cheers for Piggy Grunter* by Noreen Shelley, 1959; *The Story House* by Ruth Fenner, 1960.

Elisabeth MacIntyre comments:

Simple and lighthearted as my books may be, they are a sincere attempt to say something I really believe in. A straight book about conservation might seem dull, but, as I see it, my *Affable, Amiable Bulldozer Man* sums up the whole subject painlessly. And a book about someone coping with a disability could be depressing; but I like to think that, in *The Purple Mouse,* it can still be a wryly amusing account of rising above problems that might seem insurmountable if the girl hadn't been too worried about other things to worry about them.

At first I wrote and illustrated picture books, using words sparingly. Now less interested in how things look, and more concerned in how they seem to *be,* I write full-length books, not so much for children, more for young adults—they seem to be becoming younger every year.

* * *

Elisabeth MacIntyre's reputation was made initially through her picture books, which she wrote and illustrated. Of these *Susan* (published in Australia and Britain as *Katherine*), a straightforward, amusing, uncomplicated description of a little girl "who lives in Australia/With her toys and her pets and her paraphernalia" has proved to have the most universal and lasting appeal. Two later picture books, *Hugh's Zoo* (a runner-up for the Australian Children's Book of the Year award) and *The Affable, Amiable Bulldozer Man* were produced during the 1960s, when public awareness of nature conservation was being very actively stirred; both have this "message" to put across, and neither has quite the same sense of gaiety and fun as *Katherine.* The author's first full-length novel (for the 8-11 age group) was *Ninji's Magic,* a well-coordinated story set in contemporary New Guinea. The theme, sensitively handled, is the reaction of a primitive, superstitious village community to the introduction of a school and the white man's education, exemplified in the clash, subsequently resolved, between the boy, Ninji, and his grandfather. The considerable background research behind this work is excellently assimilated.

In *The Purple Mouse* (for the 10-13 age group), the author tackles with empathy the problem of deafness, a subject with which she is personally familiar, and which she had wanted to write about for a long time. She shows how a teenage girl begins to overcome this handicap, and cope with the inevitable social problems it brings. The story is laced with a keen sense of humour—an ingredient so often missing from "social problem" novels.

More recently, MacIntyre has turned to the older teenage audience: *It Looks Different When You Get There* is concerned with a heroine who decides against an abortion for her illegitimate child. Again, the narrative is striking for its gentle humour and the heroine's own sense of the ridiculous, as well as the compassion with which the author develops this situation. This book demonstrates the most significant development of MacIntyre's skill.

—Barbara Ker Wilson

MACKAY, Claire

Nationality: Canadian. **Born:** Claire Bacchus, Toronto, Ontario, 21 December 1930. **Education:** Jarvis Collegiate Institute, graduated 1948; University of Toronto, 1948-52, B.A. (honours) in political science and economics 1952; University of British Columbia, Vancouver, 1968-69; University of Manitoba, Winnipeg, certificate in rehabilitation counselling 1971. **Family:** Married Jackson F. Mackay in 1952; three sons. **Career:** Library assistant, Polysar Corporation, Sarnia, Ontario, 1952-55; medical social worker, Wascana Hospital, Regina, Saskatchewan, 1969-71; research librarian, Steelworkers' Union, Toronto, 1972-78. Since 1978 freelance researcher and writer. Visiting writer, John Wanless School, Toronto, 1986, and Toronto libraries, 1987. Since 1986 consultant, Houghton Mifflin Canada. Member of Board of Directors, Children's Book Centre, Toronto, 1985-89. **Awards:** Ontario Arts Council grant, 1980, 1983, 1984, 1985, 1986, 1989; Ruth Schwartz award, 1982; Vicky Metcalf award, for body of work, 1983, for short story, 1988; Parenting Publications of America award of excellence, 1990, 1991; City of Toronto book prize finalist, 1991; City of Toronto award of merit, 1992. **Address:** 6 Frank Crescent, Toronto, Ontario M6G 3K5, Canada.

PUBLICATIONS FOR CHILDREN

Fiction

Mini-Bike Hero, illustrated by Merle Smith. Richmond Hill, Ontario, Scholastic, 1974.
Mini-Bike Racer, illustrated by Merle Smith. Richmond Hill, Ontario, Scholastic, 1976.
Exit Barney McGee, illustrated by David Simpson. Richmond Hill, Ontario, Scholastic, 1979.
One Proud Summer, with Marsha Hewitt. Toronto, Women's Educational Press, 1981; New York, Penguin, 1988.
Mini-Bike Rescue. Richmond Hill, Ontario, Scholastic, 1982.
The Minerva Program. Toronto, Lorimer, 1984; Oxford, Oxford University Press, 1987; Boston, Houghton Mifflin, 1993.
Bats About Baseball, with Jean Little, illustrated by Kim LaFave. Toronto and New York, Viking, 1994.

Other

Pay Cheques and Picket Lines: All About Unions in Canada. Toronto, Kids Can Press, 1987.
The Toronto Story, illustrated by Johnny Wales. Willowdale, Ontario, Firefly Books, 1991.
Touching All the Bases: Baseball for Kids of All Ages. Richmond Hill, Ontario, Boardwalk, 1994.

Compiler, *Laughs: Funny Stories.* Toronto, Tundra Books, 1997.

*

Claire Mackay comments:

I got into the field of children's writing almost by accident (the first novel was written for my son) and have continued because people (publishers and kids) keep asking me to write books. I have tried, I think, to be faithful to a pair of comments in my earliest letters from children: "I like your stories because you put all the adventures in at the right time"; and "You're on our side!"

* * *

In her six novels for young teenagers, Claire Mackay draws on her own experiences as a child growing up in an active and radical political family, as the mother of three boys, and as a social worker and counsellor. The joy of riding mini-bikes across the Canadian prairies, the dilemmas of relating to parents, and the traumas of discovering the economic forces of adult life are described in her stories with the realism of one who has been there as either teenager or adult.

Mackay's first novel, *Mini-Bike Hero,* reveals her considerable strengths as a writer for young adults. The 12-year-old hero Steve MacPherson must hide his new love of riding mini-bikes from his father, who is still grieving over the death of his own brother, killed years ago in a motorcycle accident. From a motorcycle shop owner, who had lost his son, Steve learns the skills of his new hobby, but must confront the moral dilemmas his secrecy creates. The book clearly delineates the character conflicts of the hero,

joyfully describes the pleasures of riding, and adds just enough adventure to make it a thoroughly satisfying novel. Unfortunately, two sequels—*Mini-Bike Racer,* about the conflicts between Steve and his friend Kim, and *Mini-Bike Rescue,* the story of the adventures of the boys' friend Julie, sent to Ontario to learn to become more "ladylike"—rely too heavily on such plot thrillers as kidnapping by a bank robber and a motorcycle rescue from an attacking bear.

Set in the metropolis of Toronto, *Exit Barney McGee* and *The Minerva Program* focus on the inner struggles of two troubled young adolescents. In the former, Barney McGee runs away to Toronto to

escape his mother's new husband and their new baby and to search for his father, who he discovers is a down-and-out alcoholic. In the latter, Minerva is at the point of raising her self-confidence by becoming a member of the school's computer club when she is accused of altering the grades of herself and her friends. In the struggle to prove her innocence, she also learns of the tensions and fears of her mother. In both books, the process of maturing involves not only facing the truth about oneself but also the real characters of one's parents.

Set in 1946 in an industrial town in Quebec, *One Proud Summer* (written with Marsha Hewitt) describes 13-year-old Lucille's growing involvement in a textile worker's strike. While the fears of the heroine and the intolerable conditions of the laborers are vividly described, the authors present the management and owners as stereotypes, with some characters becoming stage villains.

Mackay's skill in communicating with younger readers is also seen in her non-fiction books about various aspects of Canadian life. In *Pay Cheques and Picket Lines,* she present as history of labor unions in Canada, transforming a potentially dull subject into a very interesting one through her inclusion of sharp character portrayals and interesting anecdotes. *The Toronto Story,* about her home town, and *Touching All the Bases: Baseball for Kids of All Ages* include quotations, photographs, and cartoons that break up chapters which, although filled with information, are written in a breezy style.

Although the plots of her novels are sometimes melodramatic, with events seeming contrived devices to increase reader excitement rather than to reveal and develop character, Mackay's books, in their clear and sympathetic portrayal of young teenage boys and girls facing the difficult choices involved in growing up, have justly earned a place as important Canadian novels about contemporary life.

—Jon C. Stott

MACKAY, Constance D'Arcy

Nationality: American. **Born:** St. Paul, Minnesota. **Education:** Boston University, 1903-04. **Family:** Married Roland Holt in 1923 (died 1931). **Career:** Director of Pageantry and Drama, War Camp Community Service, 1918-19. **Died:** 21 August 1966.

Publications for Children

Plays

The Queen of Hearts (produced Boston, 1904).

The House of the Heart and Other Plays (includes *The Gooseherd and the Goblin, The Enchanted Garden, Nimble-Wit and Fingerkin, A Little Pilgrim's Progress, A Pageant of Hours, On Christmas Eve, The Elf Child, The Princess and the Pixies, The Christmas Guest*). New York, Holt, 1909.

The Silver Thread and Other Folk Plays (includes *The Forest Spring, The Foam Maiden, Troll Magic, The Three Wishes, A Brewing of Brains, Siegfried, The Snow Witch*). New York, Holt, 1910.

The Pageant of Patriotism (also director; produced Brooklyn, New York, 1911).

Patriotic Plays and Pageants for Young People (includes *Pageant of Patriots* [*Princess Pocahontas; George Washington's Fortune; Daniel Boone, Patriot; Benjamin Franklin, Journeyman; The Boston Tea Party; Abraham Lincoln, Rail Splitter*] and *The Hawthorne Pageant* [*Merrymount* and *In Witchcraft Days*]). New York, Holt, 1912.

The Pageant of Schenectady (also director; produced Schenectady, New York, 1912). Schenectady, New York, Gazette Press, 1912.

The Historical Pageant of Portland, Maine, music by Will C. Macfarlane (also director; produced Portland, 1913). Portland, Southworth, 1913.

The Beau of Bath and Other One-Act Plays of Eighteenth-Century Life (includes *The Silver Lining, Ashes of Roses, Gretna Green, Counsel Retained, The Prince of Court Painters*). New York, Holt, 1915; London, Dent, 1924.

Plays of the Pioneers (includes *The Pioneers, The Fountain of Youth, May-Day, The Vanishing Race, The Passing of Hiawatha, Dame Greel o'Portland Town*). New York, Harper, 1915.

William of Stratford: Shakespeare's Tercentenary Pageant (produced Baltimore, 1916).

The Forest Princess and Other Masques (includes *The Gift of Time, A Masque of Conservation, The Masque of Pomona, A Masque of Christmas, The Sun Goddess*). New York, Holt, 1916.
Memorial Day Pageant. New York, Harper, 1916.
Pageant of Sunshine and Shadow (produced New York, 1916). Included in *Youth's Highway and Other Plays,* 1929.
Patriotic Christmas Pageant (produced San Francisco, 1918).
Victory Pageant (produced New York, 1918).
Franklin. New York, Holt, 1921.
America Triumphant: A Pageant of Patriotism. New York, Appleton, 1926.
Youth's Highway and Other Plays (includes *In the Days of Piers Ploughman, A Calendar of Joyful Saints, The Pageant of Sunshine and Shadow, The First Noël*). New York, Holt, 1929.
Midsummer Eve: An Outdoor Fantasy (in verse). New York and London, French, 1929.
Ladies of the White House. Boston, Baker, 1948.
A Day at Nottingham: A Festival at Which All the Playgrounds of a City Can Take Part. New York, National Recreational Association, 1952.

Publications for Adults

Other

Costumes and Scenery for Amateurs. New York, Holt, 1915; revised edition, 1932.
How to Produce Children's Plays. New York, Holt, 1915.
The Little Theatre in the United States. New York, Holt, 1917.
Patriotic Drama in Your Town: A Manual of Suggestions. New York, Holt, 1918.
Play Production in Churches and Sunday Schools. New York, Playground and Recreation Association of America, 1921.
Rural Drama Bibliography. New York, Playground and Recreation Association of America, n.d.

Editor, *Suggestions for the Dramatic Celebration of the 300th Anniversary of the Purchase of Manhattan, 1626-1926.* New York, Playground and Recreation Association of America, 1926.

* * *

Constance D'Arcy Mackay was a notable early advocate and writer of community and children's drama in the United States. Also a seasoned producer, she invariably accompanied her works with instructions for their production by community and school groups. Her productive writing career, extending from 1904 to 1952, encompassed a variety of dramatic forms from folk and history plays to pageant dramas and morality plays. Believing that youth yearns for the heroic and the wonderful, she peopled her dramas with leading characters who realize heroic and humane virtues by overcoming danger and difficulty.

Based on international folktales, *The Silver Thread and Other Folk Plays* presents seven durable dramas marked by quaint superstitions and homely truths. Typical is *The Foam Maiden,* a Celtic tale in which a fisherman boy suffers retribution from capturing a mermaid. Through the other well-wrought plays march Cornish goblins, Norwegian trolls, and other creatures to captivate the youthful spectator. The plays are masterfully filled with sprightly characters and situations.

Less durable dramatic types in the Mackay canon are the morality play and the masque. Both intermix allegorical and human figures, and accent a moral. Examples of the morality play are found in a collection of 10 short verse plays, *The House of the Heart and Other Plays.* Masques, which add the element of spectacle and the intent of outdoor production, appear in *The Forest Princess and Other Masques.* Representative of the short plays contained there is *A Masque of Conservation* in which forest spirits persuade a young land owner not to sell his forest to callous woodcutters. In both anthologies the plays are imaginatively written, even if somewhat locked into their own time.

Two collections of Mackay's pageant plays reveal another aspect of her writing. Although many of the short plays were originally conceived as episodes in historical pageants (a form which recreated events in a community's past for a particular occasion), they can stand independently. *Plays of the Pioneers* embraces plays ranging in subject from western pioneers and Indians to a patriotic New England tavern mistress of 1775. *Patriotic Plays and Pageants for Young People* offers short dramas focusing on the youth of American notables like Washington, Franklin, Lincoln, and Daniel Boone, and encompassing groups like the Pilgrims and Puritans. Generally well-structured, the dramas convincingly revivify historical periods and figures.

Exemplifying the author's best biography dramas are *Franklin,* a full-length play credibly showing its hero's development from printer's apprentice to statesman, and *The Beau of Bath and Other One-Act Plays of Eighteenth-Century Life,* a collection of six short verse plays set in England and treating such personages as Edmund Burke, the actresses Kitty Clive and Peg Woffington, and the author Fanny Burney. The high quality of the dialogue and the characterizations, and the vivid credibility of the period created in these plays are theatrical strengths.

Mackay's dramas display worthy content and literary quality, imaginative theatricality, and a respect for the intelligence of the young. That her dramas are not produced today does not diminish their worth and their historical influence. She stands tall as an early leader in her field.

—Christian H. Moe

MACKEN, Walter (Augustine)

Nationality: Irish. **Born:** Galway, 3 May 1915. **Education:** Presentation Convent National School and Patrician Brothers' Secondary School, Galway. **Family:** Married Margaret Mary Kenny in 1936; two sons. **Career:** Member, Taibhdhearc, Gaelic-language theatre, Galway, 1932-36, and actor, manager, and producer, 1939-48; insurance salesperson, London, 1937-38; actor, 1948-51, government representative on Board of Directors, and assistant manager and artistic adviser, 1965 (resigned 1966), Abbey Theatre, Dublin. Full-time writer and occasional actor, 1951-64. **Died:** 22 April 1967.

Publications for Children

Fiction

Island of the Great Yellow Ox, illustrated by Charles Keeping. London, Macmillan, and New York, Macmillan, 1966.

The Flight of the Doves. London, Macmillan, and New York, Macmillan, 1968.

Play

Television Play: *Island of the Great Yellow Ox,* from his own story, 1972.

Publications for Adults

Novels

Quench the Moon. London, Macmillan, and New York, Viking Press, 1948.
I Am Alone. London, Macmillan, 1949.
Rain on the Wind. London, Macmillan, 1950; New York, Macmillan, 1951.
The Bogman. London, Macmillan, and New York, Macmillan, 1952.
Sunset on the Window-Panes. London, Macmillan, 1954; New York, St. Martin's Press, 1955.
Sullivan. London, Macmillan, and New York, Macmillan, 1957.
Seek the Fair Land. London, Macmillan, and New York, Macmillan, 1959.
The Silent People. London, Macmillan, and New York, Macmillan, 1962.
The Scorching Wind. London, Macmillan, and New York, Macmillan, 1964.
Brown Lord of the Mountain. London, Macmillan, 1967; as *Lord of the Mountain: A Novel of Ireland,* New York, Macmillan, 1967.

Short Stories

The Green Hills and Other Stories. London, Macmillan, and New York, St. Martin's Press, 1956.
God Made Sunday and Other Stories. London, Macmillan, and New York, Macmillan, 1962.
The Coll Doll and Other Stories. Dublin, Gill and Macmillan, and London, Macmillan, 1969.

Plays

Mungo's Mansion: A Play of Galway Life (produced Dublin, 1946; as *Galway Handicap,* produced London, 1947). London, Macmillan, 1947.
Vacant Possession (produced London, 1954). London, Macmillan, 1948.
Home Is the Hero (produced Dublin, 1952; New York, 1954). London, Macmillan, 1953.
Twilight of a Warrior (produced Dublin, 1955). London, Macmillan, 1956.
Look in the Looking Glass (produced Dublin, 1958).
The Voices of Doolan (produced Dublin, 1960).
Recall the Years (produced Dublin, 1966).

*

Manuscript Collections: University Library, Wuppertal, West Germany.

* * *

Walter Macken wrote only two books for children, *Island of the Great Yellow Ox* and *The Flight of the Doves.* Both show resourceful, ingenious yet innocent children in danger from wicked adults.

In *Island of the Great Yellow Ox* four boys become marooned on an island where Agnes, an archaeologist, and her husband, the Captain, are engaged in an obsessive search for a golden idol. Since the children know too much, the adults try to eliminate them. To the boys, the malice of the villains is incomprehensible, although they do share something of the excitement of the search. The problems of the youngsters are practical rather than psychological, and the account of their predicament is vivid and convincing. From our point of view, the villains are indeed explained, but their internal and mutual conflicts are not well integrated with the action of the book. Agnes is warped by her obsession and she manipulates the Captain through his guilt about drinking. We understand, but the boys, with whom we are invited to identify, do not.

If the story, to some degree, remains fantastic, the island setting, a favourite one with Macken, is firmly authentic and the natural enemies, such as storms, are more terrifying than the villains.

The Flight of the Doves is the more serious and satisfying work. Finn and Derval Dove flee across Ireland from their cruel stepfather to seek Granny. The chase allows Macken to diversify both the locations and the characters. Being themselves outside the law, the children are helped by others similarly placed. Uncle Toby, who has law on his side, is an outright villain, but most characters are capable of surprising. Mickser, a criminal, is kind to the children; Powder, a tinker, would betray them. Michael, an off-duty policeman who functions as a good fairy, is prepared to tread a legal tightrope.

The themes emerge from the interplay of character. With Finn we learn that appearances deceive, that law and justice are not necessarily identical. Most importantly, Macken explores the relationship between the rationally plausible and the intuitive. Finn inspires instinctive trust. He has a natural goodness and responsibility that certain adults lack, but he is saved from authorial idealisation to some degree by his unawareness of it. Character, in this book, is more of a piece with the action and there are splendid dramatic scenes. The final confrontation is well worthy of an author who was also a playwright.

Macken was able to observe and create the child mentality, to construct exciting narrative and to deploy a language which is direct and honest but whose terseness restrains him from overindulging his sentimental optimism.

—A.W. England

MacLACHLAN, Patricia

Nationality: American. **Born:** Cheyenne, Wyoming. **Family:** Married Robert MacLachlan; two sons and one daughter. **Career:** Has taught English and creative writing. Lives in Leeds, Massachusetts. **Awards:** Society of Children's Book Writers Golden Kite award, 1980; American Library Association Newbery Medal, 1986. **Address:** c/o Harper and Row, 10 East 53rd Street, New York, New York 10022, U.S.A.

Publications for Children

Fiction

Through Grandpa's Eyes, illustrated by Deborah Ray. New York, Harper, 1980.
Arthur, for the Very First Time, illustrated by Lloyd Bloom. New York, Harper, 1980.
Moon, Stars, Frogs, and Friends, illustrated by Tomie de Paola. New York, Pantheon, 1980.
Mama One, Mama Two, illustrated by Ruth Lercher Bornstein. New York, Harper, 1982.
Cassie Binegar. New York, Harper, 1982.
Tomorrow's Wizard, illustrated by Kathy Jacobi. New York, Harper, 1982.
Seven Kisses in a Row, illustrated by Maria Pia Marrella. New York, Harper, 1983; London, MacRae, 1989.
Unclaimed Treasures. New York, Harper, 1984.
Sarah, Plain and Tall. New York, Harper, 1985; London, MacRae, 1986.
The Facts and Fictions of Minna Pratt. New York, Harper, 1988; London, MacRae, 1989.
Baby. New York, Delacorte, 1993.
Journey. London, MacRae, 1991; New York, Dell, 1993.
All the Places to Love, illustrated by Mike Wimmer. New York, HarperCollins, 1994.
Skylark. New York, HarperCollins, and London, Lions, 1994.
Three Names, illustrated by Alexander Pertzoff. New York, HarperCollins, 1994.
What You Know First, illustrated by Barry Moser. New York, HarperCollins, 1995.

* * *

All of Patricia MacLachlan's work so far has been directed to children—not to young adults—and it shows a fine mastery of the difficult art of writing for preadolescents without flippancy, patronizing, or sentimentality. MacLachlan was a wife and a mother before she became a writer; her books are markedly autobiographical, for she feels a close connection not only to her own childhood and that of her children but, through anecdote and memory, to her family's past. "Just what is the magic," she has asked, "the literature or the life from which it grows?"

As a writer she began modestly with picture-book texts; two of them might have been dismissed as therapeutic problem novels in miniature, were it not for their calm, straightforward narrative tone. *Through Grandpa's Eyes* tells of a little boy's experiences with his blind grandfather—a sensory revelation of the way the elderly man ingeniously and independently manages to live an active and satisfying life. In *Mama One, Mama Two* a little girl is taken by a kindly social worker to live with a loving foster mother while her own unhappy mother is sent "to a place where doctors and nurses could help her."

But more important books were on the way. With a deep awareness of the child's instinctive resistance to change and healthy self-centeredness, MacLachlan views children not in isolation but in their close, though sometimes stormy, relationships with nurturing adults. Her first novel, *Arthur, for the Very First Time,* is centered on an observant, introspective, yet entirely believable child; and *Cassie Binegar* intensifies MacLachlan's theme of rebelliousness, growth, and acceptance. Both books gave early evidence of the author's originality, compassionate and non-didactic approach, droll humor, and carefully chastened yet fluent style. Already evident too was her preoccupation with intergenerational affinities and her idiosyncratic, unconventional characters.

MacLachlan's stories, unified by her recurring themes and underlying convictions, belong mainly in the realm of realism. Only once has the author created a sustained work of fantasy—*Tomorrow's Wizard*—which recounts five magical tales about a cranky wizard, his cheerful young apprentice, and a good-natured talking horse. Exhibiting again MacLachlan's inventiveness, structural skill, and lyrical, witty prose, the book is pure delight.

In *Unclaimed Treasures,* her longest, most complex, and multilayered novel, a passionate 11-year-old girl full of grandiose notions about life and love struggles to distinguish between the ordinary and the extraordinary. The ebullient story rests on artless craftsmanship and imagistic writing—a celebration of abiding love, human uniqueness, and, incidentally, of art and music. Among other memories, one finds unforgettable the recurring presence of a pair of happily determined elderly ladies, sitting in the garden playing two parts of a Beethoven trio.

Contained in *Arthur, for the Very First Time* was a hint of the story of the Newbery Medal winner *Sarah, Plain and Tall,* a spare, exquisite, diminutive novel. Into a yearning motherless pioneer family living on the prairie comes a strong, independent, vibrant woman from the coast of Maine. According to the author, the book grew out of what her mother used to call "the heroics of a common life." In its subtle unfolding the story takes on an uncommon crystalline clarity and displays two paradoxes of true art—silences that speak more eloquently than words, and a profound simplicity, which here sets forth the intricacies of human relationships.

Music and eccentricity of character become even more prominent in *The Facts and Fictions of Minna Pratt.* In a slapdash but caring household, Minna's father is a psychologist, and her bemused mother a children's book writer who never asks, like other mothers, "Did you pass your math test? What did you have for lunch?" but rather, "Do you ever think of love?" or "What is the quality of beauty?" No one is concerned that Minna's younger brother sings—in public—the newspaper headlines, or that his friend Emily plays baseball wearing enormous dangly rhinestone earrings "shaped like chandeliers." And Minna, playing her cello and longing only for a proper vibrato, finds a soulmate in the radiant Lucas, who has not only a fine, professional vibrato on the viola but also a well-hidden collection of frogs. Here MacLachlan wonderfully transmutes the ordinary into the extraordinary. And although the book is full of delicious madness and Mozart, it is also full of the clear-eyed honesty and deep wisdom that characterize her other stories about children teetering on the edge of growing up.

MacLachlan's stories quietly speak of the essential truths of life. In *What You Know First* the narrator is not the only one feeling loss at leaving their home behind, for Mamma cried and "Pappa took a long walk." But she realizes she will never forget this home she knew first and it is up to her to bring it alive for the baby who will not remember. Likewise, in *Baby,* Larkin's family takes in the year-old Sophie, found on their doorstep with a note saying her mother will be back for her. Sophie needs Larkin's family to care for her, but Larkin's family also needs Sophie to overcome the grief of a baby boy who lived only a day and whose tombstone lacks a name. The powerful story touches deep emotions.

Skylark, her sequel to *Sarah, Plain and Tall,* survives the scrutiny given sequels. It too, touches deeply on emotions of love, acceptance, and never forgetting the first home we know. In continuing the story of the mail-order bride from Maine, Sarah takes Anna and Caleb to visit her relatives in Maine when drought, fire, and unrelenting heat make life unbearable on the prairie. Jacob travels to the east coast to bring the family together again. When they return to their prairie home, Sarah writes her name in the earth, connecting her to this new life, though her roots are embedded deep within the New England coast. Like the readers, MacLachlan's characters are ordinary people living ordinary lives. They face their troubles with courage strengthened through love.

—Ethel L. Heins, updated by Lisa A. Wroble

MacVICAR, Angus

Nationality: British. **Born:** Argyll, Scotland, 28 October 1908. **Education:** Campbeltown Grammar School, 1920-26; Glasgow University, 1926-30, M.A. 1930. **Military Service:** Served in the Royal Scots Fusiliers, 1940-45: Captain; mentioned in despatches. **Family:** Married Jean Smith McKerral in 1936 (died); one son. **Career:** Reporter and assistant editor, Campbeltown *Courier,* 1931-33. Honorary Sheriff Substitute of Argyll, 1967. **Awards:** Litt.D., Stirling University, 1986. **Agent:** A.M. Heath, 79 St. Martin's Lane, London WC2N 4AA, England. **Address:** Achnamara, Southend, Campbeltown, Argyll PA28 6RW, Scotland.

Publications for Children

Fiction

The Crocodile Men. London, Art and Educational, 1948.
The Black Wherry. London, Foley House Press, 1948.
Faraway Island, illustrated by Denis Alford. London, Foley House Press, 1949.
King Abbie's Adventure, illustrated by James Clark. London, Burke, 1950.
Stubby Sees It Through, illustrated by Lunt Roberts. London, Burke, 1950.
The Grey Pilot. London, Burke, 1951.
Tiger Mountain, illustrated by Jack Matthew. London, Burke, 1952.
The Lost Planet. London, Burke, 1953.
Return to the Lost Planet. London, Burke, 1954.
Dinny Smith Comes Home. London, Burke, 1955.
Secret of the Lost Planet. London, Burke, 1955.
The Atom Chasers. London, Burke, 1956.
The Atom Chasers in Tibet. London, Burke, 1957.
Satellite 7. London, Burke, 1958.
Red Fire on the Lost Planet. London, Burke, 1959.
Peril on the Lost Planet. London, Burke, 1960.
Space Agent from the Lost Planet. London, Burke, 1961.
Space Agent and the Isles of Fire. London, Burke, 1962; New York, Roy, 1963.
Kilpatrick, Special Reporter. London, Burke, 1963.
The High Cliffs of Kersivay, illustrated by Douglas Relf. London, Harrap, 1964.
Space Agent and the Ancient Peril. London, Burke, 1964.
Life-Boat—Green to White, illustrated by Paul Sharp. Leicester, Brockhampton Press, 1965.
The Kersivay Kraken, illustrated by Douglas Relf. London, Harrap, 1966.
The Cave of the Hammers, illustrated by Hilary Abrahams. London, Kaye and Ward, 1968.
Super Nova and the Rogue Satellite [*Frozen Man*]. Leicester, Brockhampton Press, 2 vols., 1969-70.

Plays

Radio Plays: Has adapted 19 of his books into radio serials.

Television Plays: *The Lost Planet,* and *Return to the Lost Planet,* from his own stories.

Other

Let's Visit Scotland. London, Burke, 1966; revised edition, with John C. Caldwell, New York, Day, 1967.
Rescue Call: The Story of the Life-Boatmen. London, Kaye and Ward, 1967.

Publications for Adults

Novels

The Purple Rock. London, Stanley Paul, 1933.
Death by the Mistletoe. London, Stanley Paul, 1934.
The Screaming Gull. London, Stanley Paul, 1935.
The Temple Falls. London, Stanley Paul, 1935.
The Ten Green Brothers. London, Stanley Paul, 1936.
The Cavern. London, Stanley Paul, 1936.
Flowering Death. London, Stanley Paul, 1937.
The Crooked Finger. London, Stanley Paul, 1937.
Crime's Masquerader. London, Stanley Paul, 1938.
The Singing Spider. London, Stanley Paul, 1938.
11 for Danger. London, Stanley Paul, 1939.
Strangers from the Sea. London, Stanley Paul, 1939.
The Crouching Spy. London, Stanley Paul, 1941.
Commodore Norah. London, Pemberton, 1942.
Death on the Machar. London, Stanley Paul, 1947.
The Other Man. London, Pemberton, 1947.
Greybreek. London, Stanley Paul, 1947.
Fugitive's Road. London, Stanley Paul, 1949.
Escort to Adventure. London, Stanley Paul, 1952.
The Dancing Horse. London, Long, 1961.
The Killings on Kersivay. London, Long, 1962.
The Hammers of Fingal. London, Long, 1963.
The Grey Shepherds. London, Long, 1964.
Murder at the Open. London, Long, 1965.
The Canisbay Conspiracy. London, Long, 1966.
Night on the Killer Reef. London, Long, 1967.
Maniac. London, Long, 1969.
Duel in Glenfinnan. London, Long, 1969.
The Golden Venus Affair. London, Long, 1972.
The Painted Doll Affair. London, Long, 1973.

Plays

Minister's Monday. Galashiels, Selkirk, McQueen, 1957.
Final Proof. Glasgow, Brown and Ferguson, 1958.

Mercy Flight. Glasgow, Brown and Ferguson, 1959.
Storm Tide. Glasgow, Brown and Ferguson, 1960.
Under Suspicion. Glasgow, Brown and Ferguson, 1962.
Stranger at Christmas. Glasgow, Brown and Ferguson, 1964.

Radio Plays: *The Singing Spider, Strangers from the Sea, The Dancing Horse, The Hammers of Fingal, The Canisbay Conspiracy,* and *Night on Killer Reef,* from his own novels; *The Four Green Feathers; The Dragon Star; Murray of the Mercy Flight; The Glens of Glendale* series, 1954-59.

Television Series: *Confessions of a Minister's Son,* 1965-70.

Other

Salt in My Porridge: Confessions of a Minister's Son. London, Jarrolds, 1971.
Heather in My Ears: More Confessions of a Minister's Son. London, Hutchinson, 1974.
Rocks in My Scotch: Still More Confessions of a Minister's Son. London, Hutchinson, 1977.
Silver in My Sporran: Confessions of a Writing Man. London, Hutchinson, 1979.
Bees in My Bonnet. London, Hutchinson, 1982.
Golf in My Gallowses: Confessions of a Fairway Fanatic, with Jock MacVicar. London, Hutchinson, 1983.
Gremlins in My Garden: Confessions of a Harassed Horticulturalist. London, Hutchinson, 1985.
Capers in My Kirk: Confessions of a Would-Be Christian. London, Hutchinson, 1987.
A Highlands Omnibus. London, Arrow, 1991.

*

Angus MacVicar comments:
I found myself with one talent—the ability to tell a story. For more than sixty years I have been trying hard to develop it (along with my golf swing).

* * *

Angus MacVicar's range is wide, including schoolboy stories, adventure tales, and science fiction. It is perhaps unfortunate that, in Britain at least, his books are out of print.

The Grey Pilot is based on a true story about Bonnie Prince Charlie's adventure after the Battle of Culloden but it is, as the author states, an adventure story, not an historical work, and the exciting part of the book is certainly the account of how Donald McLeod, the Grey Pilot, and his son Murdoch became involved in helping the Prince to escape. As in that book, so too in books like *Stubby Sees It Through* and *Kilpatrick, Special Reporter* the author is at his best when involved in fast-moving adventure with plenty of action and dialogue and with the characters only lightly sketched. The settings vary, Scotland frequently but sometimes abroad, but the approach is predictable—a group of characters, united in their love for adventure and mystery solving, lots of fast-moving action, plenty of dialogue, and a minimum of descriptive writing, all of which result in books which appeal to many children.

Oddly enough, it is in his science-fiction books that MacVicar produces his most descriptive writing both of scenery and human beings—"the red, pear-shaped fruit on the trees, growing upwards like fat candle-sticks, the salmon-pink rocks, sharp and unweathered like crystal, the green turf that was composed not of grass, but of fine spongy moss." It is almost as if his concentration on the scientific aspect of these books has sharpened his awareness of the countryside and its people. His characterisations are sharper, more clearly defined, and much better developed. These are the kind of people who *could* be going on rocket flights.

Since it is many years since the Lost Planet books were written and present-day children are now quite blasé about moon flights, it is remarkable that MacVicar's science-fiction books still have the power to interest and excite. Familiarity with count-downs does not prevent the reader becoming quite tense as the moment of blast-off approaches. Obviously the author enjoyed writing these books and the challenge they presented brought forth his best writing. Although science fiction is not my favourite theme, I find MacVicar's handling of the subject quite rivetting and much more powerful than his other stories. The books pulsate with action and the atmosphere crackles with tension.

MacVicar is not a sophisticated writer but he is a worthy successor to his Highland forebears, a storyteller who knows the essence of good storytelling.

—Margaret Walker

MAGUIRE, Gregory

Nationality: American. **Born:** Albany, New York, 9 June 1954. **Education:** State University of New York, Albany, 1972-76, B.A. 1976; Simmons College, Boston, 1977-78, M.A. 1978; Tufts University, Ph.D. 1990. **Career:** English teacher, Vincentian Elementary School, Albany, 1976-77; staff member, 1979-83, and Associate Director and Assistant Professor, 1983-87, Center for the Study of Children's Literature, Simmons College, Boston; founding board member and codirector, Children's Literature New England, since 1987. **Awards:** Bread Loaf Writers' Conference fellowship, 1978; Blue Mountain Center fellowship, 1986-1990, 1995; Artist-in-Residence, Isabella Stewart Gardner Museum, 1994; American Library Association Notable Children's Book, 1994, for *Seven Spiders Spinning*; Parents' Choice Award, 1994, for *Missing Sisters.*

PUBLICATIONS FOR CHILDREN

Fiction

The Lightning Time. New York, Farrar Straus, 1978; London, Chatto and Windus, 1979.
The Daughter of the Moon. New York, Farrar Straus, 1980.
Lights on the Lake. New York, Farrar Straus, 1981.
The Dream Stealer. New York, Harper, 1983.
I Feel Like the Morning Star. New York, Harper, 1989.
The Peace and Quiet Diner, illustrated by David Perry. New York, Parents' Magazine Press, 1989.
Lucas Fishbone, illustrated by Frank Gargiulo. New York, Harper, 1990.
Seven Spiders Spinning, illustrated Dirk Zimmer. New York, Clarion, 1994.

Missing Sisters. New York, M. K. McElderry Books, and Toronto, Macmillan, 1994.
Six Haunted Hairdos, illustrated by Elaine Clayton. New York, Clarion, 1997.
Five Alien Elves. New York, Clarion, 1998.

Publications for Young Adults

Fiction

"The Honorary Shepherds," in *Am I Blue? Coming Out of the Silence* (short story). New York, HarperCollins, 1994.
The Good Liar. Dublin, O'Brien Press, 1995.
Oasis. New York, Clarion, 1996.

Publications for Adults

Fiction

Wicked: The Life and Times of the Wicked Witch of the West. New York, HarperCollins, 1995.

Other

Editor, with Barbara Harrison, *Innocence and Experience: Essays and Conversations on Children's Literature.* New York, Lothrop, 1987.

*

Manuscript Collection: Kerlan Collection, University of Minnesota, Minneapolis.

Biography: Entry in *Something about the Author,* Vol. 84, Detroit, Gale, 1997, 154-159.

Gregory Maguire comments:

While a number of my books are set in the Adirondack mountains of upstate New York, which is not far from where I was born and raised, I think that the magic of a particular geographical place is only part of the compulsion which sets me writing. The other part—to the extent I can identify it—is rooted in a fascination for the healing and prophetic power of both poetry and dreams. There are sections of each one of my books which were suggested by my own dreams; also, I often read poetry before sitting down to write—it helps magnify my sympathies and focus my intentions.

* * *

Gregory Maguire is a fantasy writer whose early work used the traditions of British fantasy writing for the young in American settings. His first novel, *The Lightning Time,* is highly derivative, yet crisp and fresh in execution. It is suffused with a pantheistic sense of the sacredness of beautiful places, in this case a mountainside overlooking Canaan Lake, in New York State, where young Daniel Rider has been sent to stay with his grandmother. The story contains magic lightning, a walking stone lion from Europe, talking beasts, an episode in which the hero and heroine change sizes and enter the burrow of "a small furry animal," a very well-worn and implausible story line—children and Grandma defeat wicked developer—and a surprise ending—Daniel's "cousin," his companion in adventure, is really an apparition from the past, his grandmother as a child—a motif which bears more than a passing resemblance to Philippa Pearce's *Tom's Midnight Garden.* For all its faults, *The Lightning Time* is full of promise and the author's evident delight in his material; Maguire is already well able technically and stylistically to achieve his effects.

Lights on the Lake, Maguire's third book, returns to Canaan Lake and Daniel Rider. Unhampered this time by stage villains imposed by the plot, the book offers the loving and witty evocation both of the landscape and the small-town community in which Daniel is now living, and the process of making friends and settling in. There is a strong fantasy element in the story, in which Daniel is drawn into the dreams of neighbours, and into danger on the frozen lake. In the heart of the story is a traumatized poet, Nikos Griskas, dumped on the doorstep of a retreat house in the village, and acting like a zombie. Nobody knows how to help Nikos. The answer lies in the strange lights that play uncannily on the lake and suspend time.

Between these two titles came *The Daughter of the Moon,* set in an ugly street in Chicago, where Erikka makes friends with a bookshop owner and a boy from an orphanage. Her family life is crowded and desperately humdrum, and the bookshop is a refuge for her. When she annoys some customers (a wicked rich couple) the bookshop is threatened, and a plot concerning the theft and retheft of an autographed copy of Walt Whitman's poems is set in motion. Another thread of the story concerns a watercolour landscape, painted for her by her aunt, into which she can step, to be transported to Canaan Lake. This space-shift fantasy leads to the reuniting of the bookseller and his long lost sweetheart.

At this stage Maguire's scope seemed predictable; he was a charming writer, full of human warmth and exuberance, deeply attached to a single place, and a little liable to preciosity. Nobody could have expected *The Dream Stealer.* Robust, touching, funny, and profound, *The Dream Stealer* is the work of a writer finding his voice, and putting not a foot wrong. As in his earlier work he happily raids earlier literature for elements of the story, which makes liberal use of Russian folktale. As in his earlier work a wonderfully detailed, warm, and humorous picture of a little community, young and old, bright and grumpy, emerges. And this time there is a powerful story line both magical—what does the terrible wolf want?—and realistic—how will the village survive the winter if the trains don't bring passengers to buy their goods, because the wolf is scaring everyone away? As well as the wit and skill of the narrator there is an underlying resonant meditation on the meaning of dreams, memory, and desire.

With *I Feel Like the Morning Star* Maguire changed tack. Although it is set in the future, in a fallout shelter, it is the first of his books not to involve any element of fantasy in the plot. In a mode deeply unlike most science fiction, the interest of this book is entirely in the portrayal of character, this time of three teenagers, two boys and a girl, living in a community under stress. Their lives are regulated by a committee supposedly democratic, but actually getting above itself; those who ask questions are "treated" to silence them. The oppression is doubly sinister because the committee is probably well-meaning. Nobody knows what is happening above ground. Among the imprisoned is a one-time campaigning folk singer, who won't sing. In an extraordinary climax the singer sings at last, while the teenagers acting pied piper to a group of children escape pursuit and emerge above ground to find themselves gazing at a living tree. The whiff of whimsy and of implausibility that weakened Maguire's early work has entirely disappeared, and *I Feel Like the Morning Star* is powerful and authoritative; his belief in the central importance of dreams and of story-telling is now openly articulated.

Gregory Maguire's formidable talents have developed impressively in at least three directions since his early work. His new works of realistic young adult fiction are each true and poignant. According to *Something About the Author, The Good Liar,* "set in occupied France in 1942 and written in epistolatory style, it tells the story of three brothers who have a fibbing contest that ultimately becomes a matter of life and death." The title of *Missing Sisters* works doubly, referring first to Alice Colossus, a speech- and hearing-impaired twelve-year old orphan who accidentally discovers her twin sister, Miami, with whom she plots cleverly but unsuccessfully to be taken in by Miami's adoptive family. The title's second reference is to Sister St. Vincent de Paul, who befriends Alice until a kitchen fire burns the elderly nun. Alice's successful search for this hospitalized Sister frames and becomes a foil for her other search in this compelling book, whose characters Maguire portrays with wry affection.

In *Oasis,* thirteen-year-old Hand (Mohandas Gandhi Gunther) discovers his father dead from a heart attack in the book's first sentence. In the remainder of the book, Hand struggles with his own guilt and grief about his father, as well as mistrust and anger toward his mother, who returns after a three-year absence. Though some elements of the book might seem trendy and disparate when catalogued—an Iranian refugee family, an uncle dying of AIDS, an artsy older sister, and the Oasis motel itself—Maguire centers the book in Hand and writes about him with grace and humor. The portrayal evokes understanding and pleasure.

Maguire's second direction is the light-hearted Hamlet Chronicles, so called for the Vermont town where they are set. The precocious students in Miss Earth's middle-school classroom join the Tattletales if they're girls and the Copycats if they're boys, but they all compete and meet fantastic creatures with literate verve. In *Seven Spiders Spinning,* Siberian snow spiders from the Ice Age being flown to a research lab at Harvard land in Hamlet, and their juvenile affection and adult antipathy become grist for Miss Earth's charges. In *Six Haunted Hairdos,* the Tattletales don costumes to spook the Copycats, only to be spooked themselves by the ghost of a baby elephant whom they all aid in finding a surrogate ghost mother.

Maguire's third direction, adult fiction as represented by *Wicked: The Life and Times of the Wicked Witch of the West,* is beyond the scope of this volume, but noteworthy because of its inspiration from Frank Baum's *The Wizard of Oz.* As a mature writer, Maguire has delivered handsomely on his earlier promise.

—Jill Paton Walsh, updated by Frieda F. Bostian

MAHY, Margaret

Nationality: New Zealander. **Born:** Whakatane, New Zealand, 21 March 1936. **Education:** University of Auckland, B.A. 1957, Diploma of Librarianship 1958. **Family:** Two daughters. **Career:** Writer. Petone Public Library, New Zealand, assistant librarian, 1958-59; School Library Service, Christchurch, New Zealand, librarian in charge, 1967-76; Canterbury Public Library, Christchurch, children's librarian, 1976-80. Writer in Residence, Canterbury University, 1984, and Western Australian College of Advanced Education, 1985. **Awards:** Esther Glenn award, New Zealand Library Association, 1970, for *A Lion in the Meadow,* 1973, for *The First Margaret Mahy Story Book,* 1983, for *The Haunting;* New Zealand Literary Fund grant, 1975; *School Library Journal* Best Book citation, 1982, for *The Haunting;* Carnegie Medals, British Library Association, 1983, for *The Haunting,* 1985, for *The Changeover: A Supernatural Romance,* and 1987, for *Memory;* Notable Children's Book citation, 1984, Association for Library Service to Children, Children's Book of the Year citation, and Best Books for Young Adults award, American Library Association, all 1986, for *The Changeover;* Honor List citation, *Horn Book,* 1985, for *The Changeover,* and 1987, for *The Catalogue of the Universe; Observer* prize, 1987; Books of 1987 citation, ALA Young Adult Services Division, for *The Tricksters,* and 1989, for *Memory;* Society of School Libraries International Book award, and *Boston Globe/Horn Book* award, both 1988, for *Memory.* May Hill Arbuthnot Lecturer, ALSC, 1989. **Agent:** Vanessa Hamilton, The Summer House, Woodend, West Stoke Chichester, West Sussex PO18 9BP, England. **Address:** 23 Merlincote Crescent, Governor's Bay, Lyttelton Harbor, Canterbury, South Island, New Zealand

Publications for Children

Fiction

The Dragon of an Ordinary Family, illustrated by Helen Oxenbury. New York, Watts, and London, Heinemann, 1969.

A Lion in the Meadow, illustrated by Jenny Williams. New York, Watts, and London, Dent, 1969; augmented edition, as *A Lion in the Meadow and Five Other Favorites,* London, Dent, 1976.

Mrs. Discombobulous, illustrated by Jan Brychta. New York, Watts, and London, Dent, 1969.

Pillycock's Shop, illustrated by Carol Barker. New York, Watts, and London, Dobson, 1969.

The Procession, illustrated by Charles Mozley. New York, Watts, and London, Dent, 1969.

The Little Witch, illustrated by Charles Mozley. New York, Watts, and London, Dent, 1970.

Sailor Jack and the 20 Orphans, illustrated by Robert Bartelt. New York, Watts, and London, Dent, 1970.

The Boy with Two Shadows, illustrated by Jenny Williams. New York, Watts, and London, Dent, 1971.

The Princess and the Clown, illustrated by Carol Barker. New York, Watts, and London, Dobson, 1971.

The Man Whose Mother Was a Pirate, illustrated by Brian Froud. London, Dent, 1972; New York, Atheneum, 1973; revised edition illustrated by Margaret Chamberlain, New York, Viking, 1986.

The Railway Engine and the Hairy Brigands, illustrated by Brian Froud. London, Dent, 1973.

Clancy's Cabin, illustrated by Trevor Stubley. London, Dent, 1974.

The Rare Spotted Birthday Party, illustrated by Belinda Lyon. London, Watts, 1974.

Rooms to Rent, illustrated by Jenny Williams. New York, Watts, 1974; as *Rooms to Let,* London, Dent, 1975.

Stepmother, illustrated by Terry Burton. London, Watts, 1974.
The Witch in the Cherry Tree, illustrated by Jenny Williams. London, Dent, and New York, Parents' Magazine Press, 1974.
The Boy Who Was Followed Home, illustrated by Steven Kellogg. New York, Watts, 1975; London, Dent, 1977.
The Bus Under the Leaves, illustrated by Margery Gill. London, Dent, 1975.
The Great Millionaire Kidnap, illustrated by Jan Brychta. London, Dent, 1975.
Ultra-Violet Catastrophe! or, The Unexpected Walk with Great-Uncle Mangus Pringle, illustrated by Brian Froud. London, Dent, and New York, Parents' Magazine Press, 1975.
David's Witch Doctor, illustrated by Jim Russell. London, Watts, 1976.
Leaf Magic, illustrated by Jenny Williams. London, Dent, 1976; New York, Parents' Magazine Press, 1977.
The Wind Between the Stars, illustrated by Brian Froud. London, Dent, 1976.
The Nonstop Nonsense Book, illustrated by Quentin Blake. London, Dent, 1977; New York, McElderry, 1989.
The Pirate Uncle, illustrated by Mary Dinsdale. London, Dent, 1977.
The Great Piratical Rumbustification, and The Librarian and the Robbers, illustrated by Quentin Blake. London, Dent, 1978; Boston, Godine, 1986.
Raging Robots and Unruly Uncles, illustrated by Peter Stevenson. London, Dent, 1981.
Cooking Pot, with Joy Cowley and June Melser, illustrated by Deidre Gardiner. Auckland, Shortland, 1982; Leeds, Arnold Wheaton, 1985.
The Crocodile's Christmas Sandals, illustrated by Deidre Gardiner. Wellington, Department of Education School Publications Branch, 1982; as *The Crocodile's Christmas Thongs,* Melbourne, Nelson, 1985.
Fast and Funny, with Joy Cowley and June Melser, illustrated by Lynette Vondruska. Auckland, Shortland, 1982; Leeds, Arnold Wheaton, 1985.
Roly-Poly, with Joy Cowley and June Melser, illustrated by Deidre Gardiner. Auckland, Shortland, 1982; Leeds, Arnold Wheaton, 1985.
Sing to the Moon, with Joy Cowley and June Melser, illustrated by Isabel Lowe. Auckland, Shortland, 1982; Leeds, Arnold Wheaton, 1985.
Tiddalik, with Joy Cowley and June Melser, illustrated by Philip Webb. Auckland, Shortland, 1982; Leeds, Arnold Wheaton, 1985.
The Bubbling Crocodile, illustrated by Deidre Gardiner. Wellington, Department of Education School Publications Branch, 1983.
A Crocodile in the Library, illustrated by Deidre Gardiner. Wellington, Department of Education School Publications Branch, 1983.
Mrs. Bubble's Baby. Wellington, Department of Education School Publications Branch, 1983.
The Pirates' Mixed-Up Voyage: Dark Doings in the Thousand Islands, illustrated by Margaret Chamberlain. London, Dent, 1983.
Shopping with a Crocodile. Wellington, Department of Education School Publications Branch, 1983.
The Birthday Burglar, and A Very Wicked Headmistress, illustrated by Margaret Chamberlain. London, Dent, 1984; Boston, Godine, 1988.
The Dragon's Birthday, illustrated by Philip Webb. Auckland, Shortland, 1984.
Fantail, Fantail, illustrated by Bruce Phillips. Wellington, Department of Education School Publications Branch, 1984.
Going to the Beach, illustrated by Dick Frizzell. Wellington, Department of Education School Publications Branch, 1984.
The Great Grumbler and the Wonder Tree, illustrated by Diane Perham. Wellington, Department of Education School Publications Branch, 1984.
The Spider in the Shower, illustrated by Rodney McRae. Auckland, Shortland, 1984.
Ups and Downs and Other Stories, illustrated by Philip Webb. Auckland, Shortland, 1984.
Wibble Wobble and Other Stories. Auckland, Shortland. 1984.
The Adventures of a Kite, illustrated by David Cowe. Auckland, Shortland, 1985; Leeds, Arnold Wheaton, 1986.
The Cake, illustrated by David Cowe. Auckland, Shortland, 1985; Leeds, Arnold Wheaton, 1986.
The Catten, illustrated by Jo Davies. Auckland, Shortland, 1985; Leeds, Arnold Wheaton, 1986.
Clever Hamburger, illustrated by Rodney McRae. Auckland, Shortland, 1985; Leeds, Arnold Wheaton, 1986.
A Crocodile in the Garden, illustrated by Deidre Gardiner. Wellington, Department of Education of Education School Publications Branch, 1985.
The Earthquake, illustrated by Dianne Perham. Auckland, Shortland, 1985; Leeds, Arnold Wheaton, 1986.
Horrakopotchin. Wellington, Department of Education School Publications Branch, 1985.
Jam: A True Story, illustrated by Helen Craig. London, Dent, 1985; Boston, Atlantic Monthly Press, 1986.
Out in the Big Wild World, illustrated by Rodney McRae. Auckland, Shortland, 1985.
Rain, illustrated by Elizabeth Fuller. Auckland, Shortland, 1985.
Sophie's Singing Mother, illustrated by Jo Davies. Auckland, Shortland, 1985; Leeds, Arnold Wheaton, 1986.
Arguments, illustrated by Kelvin Hawley. Auckland, Shortland, 1986.
Baby's Breakfast, illustrated by Madeline Beasley. Auckland, Heinemann, 1986.
Beautiful Pig. Auckland, Shortland, 1986; Leeds, Arnold Wheaton, 1987.
An Elephant in the House, illustrated by Elizabeth Fuller. Auckland, Shortland, 1986.
Feeling Funny, illustrated by Rodney McRae. Auckland, Heinemann, 1986.
The Fight on the Hill, illustrated by Jan van der Voo. Auckland, Shortland, 1986; Leeds, Arnold Wheaton, 1987.
The Funny Funny Clown Face, illustrated by Miranda Whitford. Auckland, Heinemann, 1986.
The Garden Party, illustrated by Rodney McRae. Auckland, Heinemann, 1986.
Grow Up Sally Sue. Auckland, Heinemann, 1986.
Jacko, The Junk Shop Man, illustrated by Jo Davies. Auckland, Shortland, 1986.
The King's Treasure. Auckland, Heinemann, 1986.
The Long Grass of Tumbledown Road. Auckland, Shortland, 1986; Leeds, Arnold Wheaton, 1987.
The Man Who Enjoyed Grumbling, illustrated by Wendy Hodder. Auckland, Heinemann, 1986.
Mr. Rooster's Dilemma, illustrated by Elizabeth Fuller. Auckland, Shortland, 1986; as *How Mr. Rooster Didn't Get Married,* Leeds, Arnold Wheaton, 1986.

Mr. Rumfitt, illustrated by Nick Price. Auckland, Heinemann, 1986.
The Mouse Wedding, illustrated by Elizabeth Fuller. Auckland, Shortland, 1986.
Muppy's Ball, illustrated by Jan van der Voo. Auckland, Heinemann, 1986.
My Wonderful Aunt, illustrated by Dierdre Gardiner. Auckland, Heinemann, 4 vols., 1986; revised edition, Chicago, Children's Press, 1988.
The New House Villain, illustrated by Elizabeth Fuller. Auckland, Heinemann, 1986.
A Pet to the Vet, illustrated by Philip Webb. Auckland, Heinemann, 1986.
The Pop Group, illustrated by Madeline Beasley. Auckland, Heinemann, 1986.
The Robber Pig and the Ginger Beer [Green Eggs], illustrated by Rodney McRae. Auckland, Shortland, 2 vols., 1986; Leeds, Arnold Wheaton, 2 vols., 1987.
Shuttle 4. Auckland, Heinemann, 1986.
Squeak in the Gate, illustrated by Jo Davies. Auckland, Shortland, 1986.
The Terrible Topsy-Turvy, Tissy-Tossy Tangle, illustrated by Vicki Smillie-McItoull. Auckland, Heinemann, 1986.
The Three Wishes, with others, illustrated by Rodney McRae and others. Auckland, Shortland, 1986.
Tinny Tiny Tinker, illustrated by David Cowe. Auckland, Shortland, 1986.
The Tree Doctor, illustrated by Wendy Hodder. Auckland, Heinemann, 1986.
Trouble on the Bus, illustrated by Wendy Hodder. Auckland, Heinemann, 1986.
The Trouble with Heathrow, illustrated by Rodney McRae. Auckland, Heinemann, 1986.
A Very Happy Birthday, illustrated by Elizabeth Fuller. Auckland, Shortland, and Leeds, Arnold Wheaton, 1986.
Tai Taylor and His Education, illustrated by Nick Price. Auckland, Heinemann, 1986-87.
Tai Taylor and the Sweet Annie, illustrated by Nick Price. Auckland, Heinemann, 1986-87.
Tai Taylor Goes to School, illustrated by Nick Price. Auckland, Heinemann, 1986-87.
Tai Taylor Is Born, illustrated by Nick Price. Auckland, Heinemann, 1986-87.
Elliott and the Cats Eating Out. Auckland, Heinemann, 1987.
The Girl Who Washed in Moonlight, illustrated by Robyn Belton. Auckland, Heinemann, 1987.
Guinea Pig Grass, illustrated by Kelvin Hawley. Auckland, Shortland, 1987.
The Haunting of Miss Cardamon, illustrated by Korky Paul. Auckland, Heinemann, 1987.
Iris La Bonga and the Helpful Taxi Driver, illustrated by Vicki Smillie-McItoull. Auckland, Heinemann, 1987.
The Mad Puppet, illustrated by Jon Davis. Auckland, Heinemann, 1987.
The Man Who Walked on His Hands, illustrated by Martin Bailey. Auckland, Shortland, 1987.
No Dinner for Sally, illustrated by John Tarlton. Auckland, Shortland, 1987.
As Luck Would Have It, illustrated by Deidre Gardiner. Auckland, Shortland, 1988.
A Not-So-Quiet Evening, illustrated by Glenda Jones. Auckland, Shortland, 1988.
Sarah, The Bear and the Kangaroo, illustrated by Elizabeth Fuller. Auckland, Shortland, 1988.
When the King Rides By. Glasgow, Thornes, 1988.
The Blood and Thunder Adventure on Hurricane Peak, illustrated by Wendy Smith. London, Dent, 1989.
The Great White Man-Eating Shark: A Cautionary Tale, illustrated by Jonathan Allen. New York, Dial, 1990.
Making Friends, illustrated by Wendy Smith. New York, McElderry, 1990.
Seven Chinese Brothers, illustrated by Jean and Mou-sien Tseng. New York, Scholastic, 1990.
Dangerous Spaces. New York, Viking, 1991.
Keeping House. New York, Macmillan, 1991.
Pumpkin Man and the Crafty Creeper. New York, Greenwillow, 1991.
The Queen's Goat, illustrated by Emma Chichester Clark. New York, Dial Press, 1991.
The Horrendous Hullabaloo, illustrated by Patricia MacCarthy. New York, Viking, 1992.
Underrunners. New York, Viking, 1992.
The Good Fortunes Gang, illustrated by Marion Young. New York, Delacorte, 1993.
A Busy Day for a Good Grandmother, illustrated by Margaret Chamberlain. London, Hamish Hamilton, and New York, Margaret K. McElderry Books, 1993.
The Rattlebang Picnic, illustrated by Steven Kellogg. New York, Dial Books for Young Readers, 1994.
The Christmas Tree Tangle, illustrated by Anthony Kerins. New York, Margaret K. McElderry Books, and Toronto, Maxwell Macmillan Canada, 1994.
The Greatest Show Off Earth, illustrated by Wendy Smith. New York, Viking, 1994.
Tick Tock Tales: Stories to Read around the Clock, illustrated by Wendy Smith. New York, Margaret K. McElderry Books, 1994.
Tingleberries, Tuckertubs and Telephones: A Tale of Love and Ice-cream, illustrated by Robert Staermose. New York, Viking, 1995.
The Five Sisters, illustrated by Patricia MacCarthy. New York, Viking, 1996.
Boom, Baby, Boom, Boom, illustrated by Patricia MacCarthy. New York, Viking, 1997.
The Horribly Haunted School. London, Hamish Hamilton, 1997.
Operation Terror. London, Puffin, 1997.

Screenplays: Adaptor, *The Haunting of Barrey Palmer* (based on *The Haunting*). New Zealand, 1987.

Television Scripts: *A Land Called Happy Wooly Valley, Once upon a Story,* and *The Margaret Mahy Story Book Theatre.*

Poetry

Seventeen Kings and Forty Two Elephants, illustrated by Charles Mozley. London, Dent, 1972; revised edition edited by Phyllis J. Fogelman with illustrations by Patricia MacCarthy, New York, Dial Press, 1987.
The Tin Can Band and Other Poems, illustrated by Honey de Lacey. London, Dent, 1989.

Collections

The First Margaret Mahy Story Book: Stories and Poems, illustrated by Shirley Hughes. London, Dent, 1972.

The Second Margaret Mahy Story Book: Stories and Poems, illustrated by Shirley Hughes. London, Dent, 1973.
The Third Margaret Mahy Story Book: Stories and Poems, illustrated by Shirley Hughes. London, Dent, 1975.
The Great Chewing-Gum Rescue and Other Stories, illustrated by Jan Ormerod. London, Dent, 1982.
Leaf Magic and Five Other Favourites, illustrated by Margaret Chamberlain. London, Dent, 1984.
The Downhill Crocodile Whizz and Other Stories, illustrated by Ian Newsham. London, Dent, 1986.
Mahy Magic: A Collection of the Most Magical Stories from the Margaret Mahy Story Books, illustrated by Shirley Hughes. London, Dent, 3 vols., 1986.
The Horrible Story and Others, illustrated by Shirley Hughes. London, Dent, 1987.
The Door in the Air and Other Stories, illustrated by Diana Catchpole. London, Dent, 1988; New York, Delacorte, 1991.
Chocolate Porridge and Other Stories, illustrated by Shirley Hughes. London, Puffin, 1989.
Bubble Trouble and Other Poems and Stories, illustrated by Margaret Mahy. New York, Macmillan, 1992.
The Girl With the Green Ear: Stories About Magic in Nature, illustrated by Shirley Hughes. New York, Knopf, 1992.
A Tall Story and Other Tales, illustrated by Jan Nesbitt. New York, Macmillan, 1992.

Nonfiction

New Zealand: Yesterday and Today. London, Watts, 1975.
Look under V, illustrated by Deidre Gardiner. Wellington, Department of Education School Publications Branch, 1977.

PUBLICATIONS FOR YOUNG ADULTS

Novels

The Haunting, illustrated by Bruce Hogarth. London, Dent, 1982; New York, Atheneum, 1983.
The Changeover: A Supernatural Romance. London, Dent, and New York, Atheneum, 1984.
The Catalogue of the Universe. London, Dent, 1985; New York, Atheneum, 1986.
Aliens in the Family. London, Methuen, and New York, Scholastic, 1986.
The Tricksters. London, Dent, 1986; New York, McElderry, 1987.
Memory. London, Dent, and New York, McElderry, 1987.
The Other Side of Silence. New York, Viking, 1995.

Other

My Mysterious World (autobiography), photographs by David Alexander. Katonah, New York, R.C. Owen Publishers, 1995.

*

Media Adaptations: *The Haunting* (cassette), G.K. Hall, 1986; *The Chewing Gum Rescue and Other Stories* (cassette), G.K. Hall, 1988; *The Pirate's Mixed-Up Voyage* (cassette), G.K. Hall; *Nonstop Nonsense* (cassette), G.K. Hall.

Biography: *Introducing Margaret Mahy* by Betty Gilderdale, Auckland, Viking and Puffin, 1987; essay in *Introducing 21 New Zealand Children's Writers* by Betty Gilderdale, Auckland, Hodder & Stoughton, 1991; essay in *Authors and Artists for Young Adults,* Volume 8, Detroit, Gale, 1992.

Manuscript Collections: J.M. Dent and Sons Ltd., London.

Critical Studies: Entry in *Children's Literature Review,* Volume 7, Detroit, Gale, 1984.

* * *

Margaret Mahy is one of the most distinguished contemporary writers for children. Her success has been built upon humour, upon an outstanding command of language, and an exuberant vitality which matches children's own energy. The great strength of her work is that it is multi-layered. She noted in the *Children's Literature Association of New Zealand Yearbook:*

> "I have come to see my stories as shadows cast in the conscious world by unconscious actions and journeys, the crests of icebergs shining in the sun while their greater part remains drowned in green water.... And some children are able by a mysterious process or faculty that we roughly call "imagination' to apprehend that part of the story that is hidden and use it to illuminate their own hidden experiences."

Her early work, initially short stories which were later made into picture books, owed much to fairy tale archetypes which had fired her own imagination, figures such as heroes, lions, witches and wizards. But she does not see the last two as sinister, rather as forms of energy which enter into people's lives, whirl them around and leave them irrevocably altered. Like her pirates, witches and wizards are free spirits, untrammeled by the demands of convention. But how can the demands of creative, adventurous living be reconciled with everyday constraints? The conflict involved in balancing differing demands of left and right hemispheres of the brain is one of the most persistent themes in Mahy's work—it is no coincidence that many of her protagonists are jugglers.

But the humdrum and ordinary are often defeated by adventurous voyaging into uncharted territory. In *The Man Whose Mother Was a Pirate* a conventional little man relinquishes his safe office job and takes his pirate mother to sea. In *The Pirates Mixed-Up Voyage* Lionel Wafer disagrees with his gloomy deterministic parrot who believes that, "everything that happens in the Universe is part of a vast mysterious plan". On the contrary Lionel declares that, "... in the heroic life things are simple, free and unplanned," and off he goes to sail the ocean.

Release from the everyday is a major theme in the collection of stories *The Door in the Air.* In one tale, "The Magician in the Tower", a magician is freed from his tower to move on. In "The Bridge Builder" the aging builder's youngest child, Merlin, knows the world "of release and remaking" which "allows people to become their true selves". In "The Two Sisters" one sister has "a song of release" which enables their elderly mother to die in peace.

One story in *The Door in the Air* first appeared as a picture book, *The Wind Between the Stars.* It tells of Phoebe, first as a young dancing girl, then as a wife and mother, and finally as an impoverished old lady who has to go out cleaning to earn a living.

On two occasions in her life she had heard the "Wind Between the Stars" but had not gone with it, but this time when it comes she sees it as a release, and she is taken with the Wind, joining the procession of peacocks, mermaids, princesses and lions. The Wind takes "all things that flow and are free ... and if anyone wants to go with it, it will take them, but they mustn't hope to come back again."

The story can be interpreted either as following the creative imagination, or as Phoebe's death, but it shows extraordinary compassion for an elderly women. When Phoebe sees herself in a mirror after a long interval without one, she is astonished at how she has aged, "Yet", she thought, "I don't feel so different, I'm still the same. Here I am. But who is there to remember me by my name Phoebe, to know who I really am, to see the real me looking out from behind all these wrinkles?"

It is a compassion for the elderly which flowered in her book for older readers, *Memory,* in which Sophie, in spite of suffering from Alzheimers disease, still retains her dignity. In the picture book *Making Friends* two lonely old people are brought together by their dogs. In *The Ultra Violet Catastrophe* an elderly man resents being cosseted like a pot plant, and escapes with his great niece to have an adventurous walk.

More recently the elderly have appeared as intrepid grandmothers. In *The Rattlebang Picnic* the grandmother is not a marvelous cook, but her exceedingly tough pizzas save the family from being overtaken by an erupting volcano when they lose a car wheel but are able to replace it with one of the pizzas. But in *A Busy Day for a Good Grandmother* the grandmother is a splendid cook who goes by trail bike, skateboard, plane and raft to visit a teething grandchild who can only by soothed by her cock-a-hoop-honey cake. In the junior novel *Tingleberries, Tuckertubs and Telephones* Saracen's formidable grandmother is a detective inspector. Kindly, but overpowering, she may be the reason that Saracen is so shy that he refuses to talk on the telephone. It is a younger version of the novel *The Other Side of Silence,* which also features communication difficulties engendered by the effect of forceful mothers upon their children.

Strong and memorable women, in fact, are major players amongst Mahy's "dramatis personnae". One of the earliest was the formidable *Mrs. Discombobulous,* others appear as witches or female pirates. Then there are the scientists such as the mother in *Jam* who can "whip up a pot of atomic porridge. She can tuck a computer into bed and sing it to sleep with a lullabye." But while she is preoccupied with developing an electronic medicine to cure sunspots, a plum tree in the garden produces so prolific a crop that the family is constrained to make, then eat, plum jam for the next year.

If underlying Mahy's stories are hidden philosophic depths, on the surface there is a great deal of food—undoubtedly something which endears her to her child readers. People eat fruit, make cakes, go for picnics and have parties which, like the one in *The Great Piratical Rumbustification,* resemble, "fireworks, whizzing and buzzing and going off bang, filling the air with rainbows and parrot feathers."

Cakes and parties are associated with birthdays, as in *The Rare Spotted Birthday Party* and, indeed, birthdays are seen to be sufficiently important to be stolen, as they are in *The Birthday Burglar,* a story which bubbles with alliteration almost as much as the poems in *Bubble Trouble.* A party, or a procession, is often the happy finale in her books, and her latest junior novel *The Horribly Haunted School* is no exception. Here Monty is the son of a government philosopher who works in the Department of National Despair. His clever mother is a jig-saw champion and both these logical parents are horrified to discover that their son is sensitive to ghosts. To correct this fault he is sent to the "Brinsley Codd School of Sensible Thought", (one of several restrictive schools such as that in *A Very Wicked Headmistress*). But once there he causes chaos when he discovers the ghost of a former headmaster. The main message of the novel is that sometimes an imaginative and unusual approach turns out to be better than strictly logical methods.

In Mahy's terms ghosts are perceptions at the edge of vision, always present, waiting to be discovered but seen only by the sensitive. In the remarkable novel *The Haunting,* a ghost acts as a catalyst in the family, and is finally responsible for the revelation that an old grandmother was a magician (not a witch), but that she had rejected her powers in favour of "ordering and tidying everything, ... to crush the magic right out of her life, to wipe out her own specialness". She had placed "a false order on things around her" because she feared that her imagination, or creativity, would lead her away from the ordinary and the predictable.

Ghosts are more threatening in the novel *Dangerous Spaces.* "Dangerous spaces" have opened up in the emotional life of recently orphaned Anthea. She retreats into the imaginary world of Viridian where she meets a great uncle who had died in childhood and who tries to lure her into his world, a world from which there would be no return. She is only rescued from this frightening situation by the warmth and love of her foster family.

Mahy's style, exuberant in her fantasy stories, becomes more spare and controlled in her novels of social realism. *Underrunners* is the story of Tristam, whose mother has deserted him, but who finds comfort in the imaginary games he plays in shallow underrunning tunnels beneath tussock land. One day he is joined there by Winola, a girl from the local children's home, who insists that she is threatened by a man who is looking for her. At first Tristam thinks she is inventing her story, but he soon realizes that this is harsh reality and their lives become as tense and exciting as any of his make-believe games.

Social realism is less harsh in the four books about the Fortune family which form *The Cousins Quartet.* Each novel focuses on one of a group of cousins, who live conveniently close to one another, and who form a close-knit "gang". But in the first book, *The Good Fortunes Gang* one of the cousins, Peter, returns from living in Australia and has difficulty being accepted by the others. As an "invitation" trial he is required to sleep overnight in the graveyard. Mahy resists the tempation to introduce a ghost, bu Peter is startled to find that he is sleeping on the grave of ar ancester who bears his own name.

The three following novels of the quartet feature a girl in *A Fortune Branches Out* who is determined to become a rich corporat executive, and close twins in *Tangled Fortunes* who find that grow ing up places more distance between them. The books portra instantly recognizable late twentieth century children. Younge ones play with Barbie dolls, their older brothers play in gigs. Bu family dynamics are unchanging. Breakfast time in Fortune house holds evokes amused recognition. Pereniel too, is the secret inne life of children whose individual dreams and uncertainties cease t be solitary burdens when they are shared with their families.

Mahy's own interests in science and astronomy often find ec oes in her books. Although much of her writing uses tradition themes they are always invested with some of the latest techno ogy. In *Raging Robots and Unruly Uncles,* two sets of cousi construct robots to send as presents to one another. One lot of robots behaves in an exemplary manner, but the other runs riot, with hilarious results. Her science ficiton novel *Aliens in the Family* depicts a huge volcanic eruption and although Mahy's work is international, it must be remembered that she is a New Zealander and her landscapes are those of her native country. She grew up within sight of an active volcano, she has lived all her life in a seismic area—if earthquakes are frequent occurrences in her stories, so they are in reality.

Like all good scientists Mahy asks "What if?" In the story "The Wonderful Memory Stretch-Wool Socks" in the collection *The Downhill Crocodile Whizz,* she wonders what would happen if "memory stretch wool socks" got muddled in the wash, so that a son put on his father's stretch wool socks, and vice versa. The result is that the son is taken by the socks to his father's office, while the father is taken to school, with some predictable and unpredictable—outcomes. In the same collection the story "Thunderstorms and Rainbows" asks "what if?" the rainiest town in the country started advertising its rain and thunderstorms as an asset rather than a liability. In the young adult novel *The Tricksters* she explores the Quantum theory in which the Observer affects the Observed.

Recent scientific philosophy sees little in the universe that is fixed, and the element of surprise, or unpredictability, is another central theme in Mahy's work. Aspiring astronomer Tycho in *The Catalogue of the Universe* discovers that "only common sense is tidy, Truth wobbles and hides." *A Horribly Haunted School* ends with the wisdom that "surprises were lurking in the heart of everything, and even a sensible life could be unexpectedly full of ghosts, jokes, stories, puzzles and astonishment, and that way was the best way for any sensible life to be."

It is a philosophy which is in tune with children, whose lives are often unpredictable and out of their own control. In spite of a playful approach in humour and language, Mahy takes children very seriously. She is never condescending but simply invites them to accompany her on imaginative journeys like Merlin's in "The Bridge Builder" which winds, "Over hills, across cities, along seashores and through shrouded forests, crossing my father's bridges and the bridges of other men, as well as all the infinitely divided roads and splintered pathways that lie between them."

—Betty Gilderdale

MANN, Josephine. See **PULLEIN-THOMPSON, Josephine.**

MANNING, Rosemary (Joy)

Pseudonyms: Sarah Davys; Mary Voyle. **Nationality:** British. **Born:** Weymouth, Dorset, 9 December 1911. **Education:** Royal Holloway College, University of London, 1930-33, B.A. in classics 1933. **Career:** Worked as a shop assistant and secretary; from late 1930s teacher. **Died.**

Publications for Children

Fiction

Green Smoke, illustrated by Constance Marshall. London, Constable, and New York, Doubleday, 1957.
Dragon in Danger, illustrated by Constance Marshall. London, Constable, 1959; New York, Doubleday, 1960.
The Dragon's Quest, illustrated by Constance Marshall. London, Constable, 1961; New York, Doubleday, 1962.
Arripay, illustrated by Victor Ambrus. London, Constable, 1963; New York, Farrar Straus, 1964.
Boney Was a Warrior, illustrated by Lynette Hemmant. London, Hamish Hamilton, 1966.
The Rocking Horse, illustrated by Lynette Hemmant. London, Hamish Hamilton, 1970.
Dragon in the Harbour, illustrated by Peter Rush. London, Kestrel, 1980.

Other

Heraldry, illustrated by Janet Price. London, A. and C. Black, 1966.
Railways and Railwaymen. London, Kestrel, 1977.

Editor, *The Shepherd's Play, and Noah and the Flood: Two Miracle Plays.* Glasgow, Grant, 1955.
Editor, *A Grain of Sand: Poems,* by William Blake, illustrated by Blake. London, Bodley Head, 1967; New York, Watts, 1968.
Editor, *Great Expectations,* by Charles Dickens, illustrated by Gareth Floyd. London, Collins, 1970.

Publications for Adults

Novels

Remaining a Stranger (as Mary Voyle). London, Heinemann, 1953.
A Change of Direction (as Mary Voyle). London, Heinemann, 1955.
Look, Stranger. London, Cape, 1960; as *The Shape of Innocence,* New York, Doubleday, 1961.
The Chinese Garden. London, Cape, 1962; New York, Farrar Straus, 1963.
Man on a Tower. London, Cape, 1965.
Open the Door. London, Cape, 1983.

Other

From Holst to Britten: A Study of Modern Choral Music. London, Worker's Music Association, 1949.
A Time and a Time: An Autobiography (as Sarah Davys). London, Calder and Boyars, 1971; as Rosemary Manning, London, Boyars, 1986.
A Corridor of Mirrors (autobiography). London, Women's Press, 1987.

*

Rosemary Manning comments:

My first three children's books, all still in print, were written for Sue, the small daughter of a friend. Perhaps this gives them a personal quality which comes out in the relationship between the green Dragon and Sue. Now grown up, Sue does not figure in the fourth "dragon book," which is dedicated to my friends.

* * *

The puzzle for outsiders is to find the link between Rosemary Manning, the academic, business-like woman who had considerable professional success outside writing, and the author of the bedtime stories of R. Dragon, 1,500 years old, with a weakness for almond buns.

The first three Dragon stories appeared between 1957 and 1961, dedicated to Susan Elisabeth Astle, who may have been their inspiration. Certainly the books appear to have roots in a familiar landscape and a close relationship with a child listener. The opening of the first book, *Green Smoke,* establishes the associations very clearly: "This is a story about a girl called Susan, or Sue for short, who went for a seaside holiday to Constantine Bay in Cornwall." The immediate, unpretentious style is maintained. Not for Manning's readers the puzzle of sorting out detailed landscape instructions: "Just think of the rockiest rocks, the sandiest sand, the greenest sea and the bluest sky you can possibly imagine and you will have some idea of Constantine Bay."

Susan finds a dragon in a secret cove, a dragon with a fund of stories which he is willing to share—of Cornish giants and magical creatures and, especially, of King Arthur. The Arthurian theme is continued in *The Dragon's Quest,* where the dragon is missing, gone on a visit, but leaves Sue his account of his adventures at Arthur's court to keep her company. The technique is of stories within a story, a framework elaborated by Paul Biegel in *The King of the Copper Mountains,* and one could complain that it provides here neither the satisfaction of an old tale retold well nor the originality of new tales. *Dragon in Danger* changes the pattern, telling what happened when R. Dragon decided to visit Sue's home near London. The Dragon stories were out of print for many years until the Puffin editions of 1967-74, and in some ways they rate as period pieces, with their cosy background of Mummy and Daddy and workmen who say "Thank you kindly mum." Their strength is the intimate storytelling voice which immediately commands attention. R. Dragon reappeared in 1980 after a hibernation of some 20 years in a tale set in present-day Weymouth, *Dragon in the Harbour,* which retained the light touch and persuasive tone of the three early stories.

Endearing as the stories of Sue and R. Dragon are, Manning's most impressive children's book is *Arripay,* a story of Harry Paye, the 15th-century privateer who sailed the Dorset coast in the reign of Henry IV. In this novel, firmly founded on historical fact, Manning tackles a theme worthy of Rosemary Sutcliff. Against a precisely realised setting of Poole harbour is a robust tale of piracy, greed, and betrayal through which we follow Adam, a boy out of sorts with his family and neighbours, with no stomach for violence, nor yet the temperament for a monk's life, until he finds eventually a role which he can accept.

It is ironical that today *Arripay* is largely forgotten, lost in the anti-historical swing which followed the vogue for historical stories in the 1950s, while *Green Smoke* is in its fifth Puffin reprint. Thoughts on this paradox may well have inspired Manning's much-quoted article, "Whatever Happened to Onion John" (*The Times Literary Supplement,* 4 December 1969) but in later years the fickleness of literary fashion was of only marginal interest to an author whose writing for children ceased as Susan Elisabeth Astle grew to adulthood.

—Peggy Heeks

MANNING-SANDERS, Ruth

Nationality: British. **Born:** Swansea, Glamorgan, in 1888. **Education:** Schools in Sheffield and Manchester; Channing House boarding school, London; Manchester University. **Family:** Married George Sanders (died 1952); one son and one daughter. **Career:** Travelled for two years with Rosaire's Circus. **Awards:** Blindman International Poetry prize, 1926. **Died:** 12 October 1988.

Publications for Children

Fiction

Children by the Sea, illustrated by Mary Shepard. London, Collins, 1938; as *Adventure May Be Anywhere,* New York, Stokes, 1939.

Elephant. New York, Stokes, 1938; London, Collins, 1940.

Mystery at Penmarth, illustrated by Anne Bullen. London, Collins, 1940; New York, McBride, 1941.

Circus Book. London, Collins, 1947; as *The Circus,* New York, Chanticleer Press, 1948.

Circus Boy, illustrated by Annette Macarthur-Onslow. London, Oxford University Press, 1960.

The Smugglers, illustrated by William Stobbs. London, Oxford University Press, 1962.

The Crow's Nest, illustrated by Lynette Hemmant. London, Hamish Hamilton, 1965.

Slippery Shiney, illustrated by Constance Marshall. London, Hamish Hamilton, 1965.

The Extraordinary Margaret Catchpole. London, Heinemann, 1966.

The Magic Squid, illustrated by Eileen Armitage. London, Methuen, 1968.

The Spaniards Are Coming!, illustrated by Jacqueline Riszi. London, Heinemann, 1969; New York, Watts, 1970.

Ram and Goat, illustrated by Robin Jacques. London, Methuen, 1974.

Young Gabby Goose, illustrated by James Hodgson. London, Methuen, 1975.

Boastful Rabbit, illustrated by James Hodgson. London, Methuen, 1978.

Oh Really, Rabbit!, illustrated by James Hodgson. London, Methuen, 1980.

Hedgehog and Puppy Dog Tales. London, Methuen, 1982.

Other

Swan of Denmark: The Story of Hans Christian Andersen, illustrated by Astrid Walford. London, Heinemann, 1949; New York, McBride, 1950.

Peter and the Piskies: Cornish Folk and Fairy Tales, illustrated by Raymond Briggs. London, Oxford University Press, 1958 New York, Roy, 1966.

Red Indian Folk and Fairy Tales, illustrated by C. Walter Hodges London, Oxford University Press, 1960; New York, Roy, 1962

Animal Stories, illustrated by Annette Macarthur-Onslow. London, Oxford University Press, 1961; New York, Roy, 1962.

A Book of Giants [*Dwarfs, Dragons, Witches, Wizards, Mermaids Ghosts and Goblins, Princes and Princesses, Devils and Demons, Charms and Changelings, Ogres and Trolls, Sorcerer and Spells, Magic Animals, Monsters, Enchantments and Curses, Kings and Queens, Spooks and Spectres, Cats and Creatures, Heroes and Heroines, Marvels and Magic, Magic Adventures, Magic Horses*], illustrated by Robin Jacques. London, Methuen, 22 vols., 1962-84; New York, Dutton, 22 vols., 1964-84.

Damian and the Dragon: Modern Greek Folk-Tales, illustrated by William Papas. London, Oxford University Press, 1965; New York, Roy, 1966.

Stories from the English and Scottish Ballads, illustrated by Trevor Ridley. London, Heinemann, and New York, Dutton, 1968.

The Glass Man and the Golden Bird: Hungarian Folk and Fairy Tales, illustrated by Victor Ambrus. London, Oxford University Press, and New York, Roy, 1968.

Jonnikin and the Flying Basket: French Folk and Fairy Tales, illustrated by Victor Ambrus. London, Oxford University Press, and New York, Dutton, 1969.

Gianni and the Ogre, illustrated by William Stobbs. London, Methuen, 1970; New York, Dutton, 1971.

A Choice of Magic, illustrated by Robin Jacques. London, Methuen, and New York, Dutton, 1971.

The Three Witch Maidens, illustrated by William Stobbs. London, Methuen, 1972.

Tortoise Tales, illustrated by Donald Chaffin. London, Methuen, 1972; Nashville, Nelson, 1974.

Sir Green Hat and the Wizard, illustrated by William Stobbs. London, Methuen, 1974.

Grandad and the Magic Barrel, illustrated by Robin Jacques. London, Methuen, 1974.

Old Dog Sirko: A Ukrainian Tale, illustrated by Leon Shtainmets. London, Methuen, 1974.

Stumpy: A Russian Tale, illustrated by Leon Shtainmets. London, Methuen, 1974.

Fox Tales, illustrated by James Hodgson. London, Methuen, 1976.

Scottish Folk Tales, illustrated by William Stobbs. London, Methuen, 1976.

The Town Mouse and the Country Mouse: Aesop's Fable Retold, illustrated by Harold Jones. London, Angus and Robertson, 1977.

Robin Hood and Little John, illustrated by Jo Chesterman. London, Methuen, 1977.

Old Witch Boneyleg, illustrated by Kilmeny Niland. London, Angus and Robertson, 1978.

The Cock and the Fox, illustrated by Jenny Williams. London, Angus and Robertson, 1978.

Folk and Fairy Tales (collection), illustrated by Robin Jacques. London, Methuen, 1978.

The Haunted Castle, illustrated by Kilmeny Niland. London, Angus and Robertson, 1979.

Robin Hood and the Gold Arrow, illustrated by Jo Chesterman. London, Methuen, 1979.

Tales of Magic and Mystery, illustrated by Christopher Quaile. London, Methuen, 1985.

Editor, *A Bundle of Ballads,* illustrated by William Stobbs. London, Oxford University Press, 1959; Philadelphia, Lippincott, 1961.

Editor, *Birds, Beasts and Fishes* (poetry anthology), illustrated by Rita Parsons. London, Oxford University Press, 1962.

Editor, *The Red King and the Witch: Gypsy Folk and Fairy Tales,* illustrated by Victor Ambrus. London, Oxford University Press, 1964; New York, Roy, 1965.

Editor, *The Hamish Hamilton Book of Magical Beasts,* illustrated by Raymond Briggs. London, Hamish Hamilton, 1965; as *A Book of Magical Beasts,* New York, Nelson, 1970.

Editor, *Festivals,* illustrated by Raymond Briggs. London, Heinemann, 1972; New York, Dutton, 1973.

Editor, *A Cauldron of Witches,* illustrated by Scoular Anderson. London, Methuen, 1988.

Publications for Adults

Novels

The Twelve Saints. London, Christophers, 1925; New York, Clode, 1926.

Selina Pennaluna. London, Christophers, 1927.

Waste Corner. London, Christophers, 1927; New York, Clode, 1928.

Hucca's Moor. London, Faber, 1929.

The Crochet Woman. London, Faber, and New York, Coward McCann, 1930.

The Growing Trees. London, Faber, and New York, Morrow, 1931.

She Was Sophia. London, Cobden Sanderson, 1932.

Run Away. London, Cassell, 1934.

Mermaid's Mirror. London, Cassell, 1935.

The Girl Who Made an Angel. London, Cassell, 1936.

Luke's Circus. London, Collins, 1939; Boston, Little Brown, 1940.

Mr. Portal's Little Lions. London, Hale, 1952.

The Golden Ball. London, Hale, 1954.

Melissa. London, Hale, 1957.

Poetry

The Pedlar and Other Poems. London, Selwyn and Blount, 1919.

Karn. Richmond, Surrey, Leonard and Virginia Woolf, 1922.

Pages from the History of Zachy Trenoy. London, Christophers, 1923.

The City. London, Benn, and New York, Dial Press, 1927.

Other

The West of England. London, Batsford, 1949.

Seaside England. London, Batsford, 1951.

The River Dart. London, Westaway, 1951.

The English Circus. London, Laurie, 1952.

* * *

To note that Ruth Manning-Sanders, undoubtedly best-known for her retellings of folktales from all over the world, also produced original work may be misleading, since the successful handling of folk material calls in itself for a high degree of creativity: a sympathy for the traditional themes and a feeling for language which enabled Manning-Sanders to present her tales in a vigorous style which is neither old-fashioned nor anachronistically modernized. And it is interesting to find folk themes cropping up time and again in those stories she wrote which are not retellings of traditional material, and which range from mystery adventure, through historical novels, to simple but attractive stories for younger readers.

Even *Mystery at Penmarth,* first published in 1940 and bearing many of the hallmarks of a dated prewar genre with its ponies, children's secret societies, comic servants, and Vicar, has stories of historical Cornwall and accounts of Cornish customs woven into the plot. Cornwall is again the setting for *The Smugglers,* a first-person narrative by the local Squire's son Ned of smuggling at the period when that activity seemed romantic; the revenue men are the villains of the piece, and all ends well for Ned and his much admired hero, the dashing smuggler Zach. It is the author's feeling for her Cornish background that counts here.

The ethics of smuggling are seen from a more sombre viewpoint in *The Extraordinary Margaret Catchpole,* a novel based on the real-life story of the Suffolk farm girl who took up, disastrously, with a smuggler named William Laud, was twice condemned to death—for horse-stealing and for escaping from prison—and finally transported to Australia, where she made good. The social conditions of hardship in which the agricultural poor of the late 18th-century lived are well realized, and Margaret herself makes an attractive heroine.

However, perhaps the best of Manning-Sanders's historical novels is *Circus Boy,* another first-person narrative, presenting the world of the travelling showmen of Victorian times through the eyes of Tommy Gough. With his father's circus he travels the English and Irish countryside, and the family suffer a fairytale reversal of fortune when they are engaged to perform at the Crystal Palace. There is plenty of verve in this story; the background detail is excellent, and the author enters into the spirit of circus life as lived by the artistes themselves.

For younger readers, *The Spaniards Are Coming!,* written as part of the Long Ago Children series, follows the fortunes of Simon and Beth, who are peripherally involved with the Spanish Armada: a good introduction to the subject and the period. Two little stories for young children just beyond the picture book and reading primer stage are *The Magic Squid* and *The Crow's Nest.* Yet again it is interesting that even in these simple stories with their modern settings—the former in the Channel Islands, the latter in Scotland—the author makes telling use of such traditional themes as the magical sea creature, which must eventually be returned to its native element, and the thieving-magpie motif. The adult reader will be reminded of Manning-Sanders's feeling for traditional folk material and skill in handling it, and the child reader of these books will be led on to her fine collections of folktales and ballads.

—Anthea Bell

MARCH, Carl. See **FLEISCHMAN, (Albert) Sid(ney).**

MARCHANT, Bessie

Nationality: British. **Born:** Petham, Kent, 12 December 1862. **Education:** Educated privately. **Family:** Married Jabez Ambrose Comfort in 1889; one daughter. Lived in Charlbury, Oxfordshire. **Died:** 10 November 1941.

Publications for Children

Fiction

The Old House by the Water. London, Religious Tract Society, 1894.

In the Cradle of the North Wind. Edinburgh, Nimmo, 1896.

Weasel Tim. London, Culley, 1897.

Among the Torches of the Andes. Edinburgh, Nimmo, 1898; as *On the Track,* London, Sampson Low, 1924.

The Bonded Three, illustrated by William Rainey. London, Blackie, 1898.

Yuppie. London, Culley, 1898.

The Girl Captives, illustrated by William Rainey. London, Blackie, 1899.

The Humbling of Mark Lester. London, Simpkin Marshall, 1899.

Winning His Way. London, Gall and Inglis, 1899.

The Rajah's Daughter; or, The Half-Moon Girl. London, Partridge, 1899; as *The Half-Moon Girl,* 1924.

Tell-Tale-Tit. London, Culley, 1899.

The Ghost of Rock Grange. London, S.P.C.K., 1900.

Held at Ransom. London, Blackie, 1900.

Cicely Frome, The Captain's Daughter. Edinburgh, Nimmo, 1900.

In the Toils of the Tribesmen. London, Gall and Inglis, 1900.

From the Scourge of the Tongue. London, Melrose, 1900.

Among Hostile Hordes. London, Gall and Inglis, 1901.

The Fun o' the Fair. London, Culley, 1901.

In Perilous Times. London, Gall and Inglis, 1901.

That Dreadful Boy! London, Culley, 1901.

Three Girls on a Ranch [*in Morocco, in Mexico*], illustrated by William Rainey. London, Blackie, 3 vols., 1901-11.

Tommy's Trek. London, Blackie, 1901.

The Bertrams of Ladywell, illustrated by John Jellicoe. London, Wells Gardner, 1902.

A Brave Little Cousin. London, S.P.C.K., 1902.

Fleckie. London, Blackie, 1902.

The House at Brambling Minster. London, S.P.C.K., 1902.

Leonard's Temptation. London, Culley, 1902.

The Secret of the Everglades. London, Blackie, 1902; New York, Mershon, 1915.

A Heroine of the Sea. London, Blackie, 1903.

Lost on the Saguenay. London, Collins, 1903.

The Owner of Rushcote. London, Culley, 1903.

The Captives of the Kaid. London, Collins, 1904.

Chupsie. London, Culley, 1904.

The Girls of Wakenside. London, Collins, 1904.

Hope's Tryst. London, Blackie, 1904.

Yew Tree Farm. London, S.P.C.K., 1904.

Caspar's Find. London, Culley, 1905.

A Daughter of the Ranges, illustrated by A.A. Dixon. London, Blackie, 1905.

The Debt of the Damerals. London, Clarke, 1905.

The Mysterious City, illustrated by W.S. Stacey. London, S.P.C.K. 1905.

The Queen of Shindy Flat, illustrated by Charles Sheldon. London, Wells Gardner, 1905.

Athabasca Bill. London, S.P.C.K., 1906.

A Girl of the Fortunate Isles, illustrated by Paul Hardy. London Blackie, 1906.

Kenealy's Ride. London, Gall and Inglis, 1906.

Maisie's Discovery, illustrated by R. Tod. London, Collins, 1906.

Uncle Greg's Man Hunt. London, Culley, 1906.
Darling of Sandy Point, illustrated by Harold Piffard. London, S.P.C.K., 1907.
Juliette, The Mail Carrier, illustrated by R. Tod. London, Collins, 1907.
The Mystery of the Silver Run. London, Wells Gardner, 1907.
No Ordinary Girl, illustrated by Frances Ewan. London, Blackie, 1907; New York, Caldwell, 1911.
Sisters of Silver Creek, illustrated by Robert Hope. London, Blackie, 1907.
The Apple Lady, illustrated by G. Soper. London, Collins, 1908.
A Courageous Girl, illustrated by William Rainey. London, Blackie, 1908.
Daughters of the Dominion. London, Blackie, 1908.
Rolf the Rebel, illustrated by W.S. Stacey. London, S.P.C.K., 1908.
An Island Heroine, illustrated by W.H. Margetson. London, Collins, 1909.
Jenny's Adventure. London, Butcher, 1909.
The Adventures of Phyllis, illustrated by F. Whiting. London, Cassell, 1910.
The Black Cockatoo, illustrated by Lancelot Speed. London, Religious Tract Society, 1910.
A Countess from Canada, illustrated by Cyrus Cuneo. London, Blackie, 1910.
Greta's Domain, illustrated by William Rainey. London, Blackie, 1910.
Molly of One Tree Bend. London, Butcher, 1910.
The Deputy Boss, illustrated by Oscar Wilson. London, S.P.C.K., 1910.
The Ferry House Girls, illustrated by W.R.S. Stott. London, Blackie, 1911.
A Girl of Distinction, illustrated by William Rainey. London, Blackie, 1911.
Redwood Ranch, illustrated by Harold Piffard. London, S.P.C.K., 1911.
A Girl of the Northland, illustrated by N. Tenison. London, Hodder and Stoughton, 1912.
His Great Surrender, illustrated by Gordon Browne. London, S.P.C.K., 1912.
A Princess of Servia, illustrated by William Rainey. London, Blackie, 1912.
The Sibyl of St. Pierre, illustrated by William Rainey. London, Wells Gardner, 1912.
The Western Scout, illustrated by W.S. Stacey. London, S.P.C.K., 1912.
The Youngest Sister, illustrated by William Rainey. London, Blackie, 1912.
The Adventurous Seven, illustrated by W.R.S. Stott. London, Blackie, 1913.
The Heroine of the Ranch, illustrated by Cyrus Cuneo. London, Blackie, 1913.
Denver Wilson's Double, illustrated by W. Douglas Almond. London, Blackie, 1914.
Helen of the Black Mountain. London, Blackie, 1914.
The Loyalty of Hester Hope, illustrated by William Rainey. London, Blackie, 1914.
A Mysterious Inheritance. London, Blackie, 1914.
A Girl and a Caravan. London, Blackie, 1915.
Joyce Harrington's Trust. London, Blackie, 1915.
Molly Angel's Adventures. London, Blackie, 1915.
A Canadian Farm Mystery; or, Pam the Pioneer. London, Blackie, 1916.
A Girl Munition Worker. London, Blackie, 1916.
The Unknown Island. London, Blackie, 1916.
The Gold-Marked Charm. London, Blackie, 1917.
Lois in Charge; or, A Girl of Grit, illustrated by Cyrus Cuneo. London, Blackie, 1917.
A V.A.D. in Salonika. London, Blackie, 1917.
Cynthia Wins, illustrated by John E. Sutcliffe. London, Blackie, 1918.
A Dangerous Mission, illustrated by Wal Paget. London, Blackie, 1918.
Norah to the Rescue, illustrated by W.R.S. Stott. London, Blackie, 1919.
A Transport Girl in France. London, Blackie, 1919.
Sally Makes Good, illustrated by Leo Bates. London, Blackie, 1920.
The Girl of the Pampas. London, Blackie, 1921.
Island Born, illustrated by Leo Bates. London, Blackie, 1921.
The Mistress of Purity Gap. London, Cassell, 1921; New York, Funk and Wagnalls, 1922.
Harriet Goes a-Roaming. London, Blackie, 1922.
The Fortunes of Prue. London, Ward Lock, 1923.
Rachel Out West, illustrated by Henry Coller. London, Blackie, 1923.
A Bid for Safety. London, Ward Lock, 1924.
Diana Carries On. London, Nelson, 1924.
The Most Popular Girl in the School. London, Partridge, 1924.
Sylvia's Secret, illustrated by W.E. Wightman. London, Blackie, 1924.
By Honour Bound. London, Nelson, 1925.
Her Own Kin. London, Blackie, 1925.
To Save Her School, illustrated by H.L. Bacon. London, Partridge, 1925.
Delmayne's Adventures. London, Collins, 1925.
Cousin Peter's Money. London, Sheldon, 1926.
Di the Dauntless, illustrated by W.E. Wightman. London, Blackie, 1926.
Millicent Gwent, Schoolgirl. London, Warne, 1926.
Molly in the West, illustrated by F.E. Hiley. London, Blackie, 1927.
The Two New Girls. London, Warne, 1927.
Glenallan's Daughters. London, Nelson, 1928.
Lucie's Luck, illustrated by F.E. Hiley. London, Blackie, 1928.
The Bannister Twins, illustrated by E. Brier. London, Nelson, 1929.
Hilda Holds On, illustrated by F.E. Hiley. London, Blackie, 1929.
How Nell Scored. London, Nelson, 1929.
Laurel the Leader. London, Blackie, 1930.
Cuckoo of the Log Raft. London, Newnes, 1931.
Two on Their Own, illustrated by F.E. Hiley. London, Blackie, 1931.
The Homesteader Girl, illustrated by V. Cooley. London, Nelson, 1932.
Jane Fills the Breach, illustrated by F.E. Hiley. London, Blackie, 1932.
Silla the Seventh. London, Newnes, 1932.
Deborah's Find, illustrated by Henry Coller. London, Blackie, 1933.
The Courage of Katrine. London, Warne, 1934.
Erica's Ranch. London, Blackie, 1934.
Lesbia's Little Blunder. London, Warne, 1934.
Hosea's Girl. London, Hutchinson, 1934.
Anna of Tenterford, illustrated by F.E. Hiley. London, Blackie, 1935.

Felicity's Fortune. London, Blackie, 1936.
Nancy Afloat. London, Nelson, 1936.
A Daughter of the Desert. London, Blackie, 1937.
Miss Wilmer's Gang, illustrated by J.A. May. London, Blackie, 1938.
Waifs of Woollamoo. London, Warne, 1938.
A Girl Undaunted; or, The Honey Queen, illustrated by J.A. May. London, Blackie, 1939.
Marta the Mainstay. London, Blackie, 1940.
Two of a Kind. London, Blackie, 1941.
The Triumphs of Three. London, Blackie, 1942.

* * *

Bessie Marchant was important in the history of girls' adventure stories as one of the first writers to allow her female characters real adventure in settings from Canada to South Africa, Brazil to Borneo. The heroines meet many dangers but triumph through hard work and indomitable spirit. Typical is *Di the Dauntless* in which Di treks into the Moroccan desert to search for her father. She escapes from a band of Riffs, avoids being sold into slavery, and returns home safely, to be drawn into the arms of a handsome young pilot.

This introduces another common element. Despite the independence and intrepid natures of Marchant's heroines, domestic matters are very much part of their lives. After playing a prominent part in an undertaking involving diamond mines and bandits, the heroine of *Held at Ransom* is told, "But you can do so many things that no boy or man can ever manage, housekeeping and all that sort of work." Similarly one of the heroines of *Three Girls in Mexico* "had come to her woman's kingdom of loving and being loved," and some now unfashionable advice is given to Hester in *The Loyalty of Hester Hope:* "There is a lot of nonsense talked in these days about the emancipation of women and that sort of thing...the only chance of married happiness is for man to be what his Maker intended he should be—the head of the house."

It is easy to laugh at synopses of Marchant's plots, but she upholds universal virtues. Her books are in the tradition of the happy family story with brothers and sisters bound together by mutual affection, exhibiting unselfishness, courage, self-sacrifice and cheerfulness. Barbara, in *The Triumphs of Three,* gives up the chance of a good post as a teacher to look after the elderly couple who had made sacrifices to give her a chance in life. *The Courage of Katrine* is full of pious comments, such as, "It was to his credit that he had mastered the temptation and held firmly to what he knew to be his duty."

The stories were also important in showing that brains and scientific ability were an asset for a girl. In *Di the Dauntless* two girls make a wireless receiver; Hester Dayrell in *The Rajah's Daughter* joins an expedition to Borneo in search of the missing Darwinian link; and many crises are averted by the heroines' abilities to speak the local language.

World War I gave many girls an opportunity to break out of domestic restrictions, and Marchant reflected this in *A Girl Munition Worker* in which the heroine, working in a cordite factory, defeats a spy. Although *Sally Makes Good* is set in post-war Tasmania, Sally's two sisters had been a departmental manager in a munition factory and a WAAS driver in France. Sally's skills are rather different—sweeping, dusting, cooking and washing—and her form of "making good" is to fall in love and marry before her accomplished but rather silly older sisters.

The plots are certainly implausible and marred by the colossal coincidences by which most of them are resolved. Typically, when Audrey comes to London, in *The Gold-Marked Charm,* the first person she meets is a man she had known long before in the Soudan; and in *The Loyalty of Hester Hope* there is a terrible inevitability when the Russian who is sent to help Hester run the farm turns out to be the long-lost father of a child who had earlier been taken into the household. However, the stories must have been a very liberating and escapist experience for young readers earlier this century. The struggles of the young heroines to survive and accomplish daring undertakings, the fast action, and the promise of domestic bliss to come would have carried them through the moralising and the improbabilities.

—Valerie Brinkley-Willsher

MARKOOSIE (Patsauq)

Nationality: Canadian. **Born:** Port Harrison, Quebec, 19 June 1942. **Education:** Port Harrison Elementary School and a high school in Yellowknife, Northwest Territories; earned commercial pilot's licence, and carpentry diploma. **Family:** Married Zipporah Kudluk in 1961 (divorced 1974); one son and four daughters. **Career:** Pilot, Atlas Aviation, Resolute, Northwest Territories, 1969-75; translator, Northern Quebec Innuit Association, Montreal and Port Harrison, 1975-76; since 1976 manager of the Community Council, Inukjuak, Quebec; since 1978 administrator of Public Services, Government of Quebec. **Address:** c/o McGill-Queen's University Press, 855 Sherbrooke Street West, Montreal, Quebec H3A 2T7, Canada.

Publications for Children

Fiction

Harpoon of the Hunter, illustrated by Germaine Arnaktauyok. Montreal and London, McGill-Queen's University Press, 1970.

* * *

The publication of *Harpoon of the Hunter* was significant in the history of Canadian publishing since it marked the first ap- pearance of an Eskimo fiction story published in English. After the tale was serialized in the Eskimo newsletter *Inuttituut* Markoosie was urged to make an English translation in order to give the story the wide audience it deserved.

Markoosie writes of the difficult struggle for survival in an in- hospitable environment and the courage and indomitable fortitud displayed by the inhabitants of a bleak, forbidding land. The stor begins in a dramatic fashion as a small settlement is attacked du ing the night by a rabid polar bear. Sixteen-year-old Kamik ac companies the small band of hunters who plan to track down an destroy this potential threat to the entire group. Their missio ends in tragedy and Kamik, the sole survivor of another attack b the now-wounded bear, is left to make his way home. He is foun by searchers after suffering incredible hardships and all seems we as he and his tribe embark on a move to a larger settlement. Du ing the move, his mother and future wife are killed and Kamik, bereft, chooses to end his life and find the peace of which his dying father had spoken.

Markoosie's spare, unembellished language gives the story the heightened impact of a Greek drama. The tragic tale has a fitting setting—the stark and silent landscape provides a contrast to the constant motion of the characters across it. The writing reminds one that the oral tradition is still very much a part of the Eskimo way of life. The story has the immediacy of the spoken word due to Markoosie's use of simple sentence structure and avoidance of descriptive passages. The writing is characterized, above all, by action. Something is continually happening or about to happen and the reader is led swiftly to the tale's conclusion. Tension is emphasized by the author's technique of shifting from one scene to another. The single-minded hatred of the wounded bear is juxtaposed effectively against the group of hunters whose hunger and inadequate weapons render them horribly vulnerable. Ooramik's dream of disaster provides an ominous hint of the death of the hunters.

Harpoon of the Hunter is a brilliantly successful portrayal of courage in the face of impossible odds.

—Fran Ashdown

MARSHALL, Edward. See **MARSHALL, James.**

MARSHALL, James (Edward)

Also wrote as Edward Marshall. **Nationality:** American. **Born:** San Antonio, Texas, 10 October 1942. **Education:** New England Conservatory of Music, Boston, 1960-61; Southern Connecticut State College, New Haven, B.A. in history 1967; Trinity College, Hartford, Connecticut, 1967-68. **Career:** French and Spanish teacher, Cathedral High School, Boston, 1968-70. After 1970 freelance writer and illustrator. **Died:** 1992.

PUBLICATIONS FOR CHILDREN (ILLUSTRATED BY THE AUTHOR)

Fiction

George and Martha. Boston, Houghton Mifflin, 1972; London, Methuen, 1974.
What's the Matter with Carruthers? Boston, Houghton Mifflin, 1972.
Yummers! Boston, Houghton Mifflin, 1972; London, Methuen, 1974.
George and Martha Encore. Boston, Houghton Mifflin, 1973.
Miss Dog's Christmas Treat. Boston, Houghton Mifflin, 1973.
The Stupids Step Out, with Harry Allard. Boston, Houghton Mifflin, 1974; London, Methuen, 1976.
Willis. Boston, Houghton Mifflin, 1974.
The Guest. Boston, Houghton Mifflin, 1975.
Eugene. Boston, Houghton Mifflin, 1975.
Sing Out, Irene. Boston, Houghton Mifflin, 1975.
Snake, His Story. Boston, Houghton Mifflin, 1975.
Speedboat. Boston, Houghton Mifflin, 1976.
George and Martha Rise and Shine. Boston, Houghton Mifflin, 1976.
Miss Nelson Is Missing! [*Back, Has a Field Day*], with Harry Allard. Boston, Houghton Mifflin, 3 vols., 1977-85.
A Summer in the South. Boston, Houghton Mifflin, 1977; London, Evans, 1979.
The Stupids Have a Ball, with Harry Allard. Boston, Houghton Mifflin, 1978.
George and Martha One Fine Day. Boston, Houghton Mifflin, 1978; London, Kestrel, 1981.
Portly McSwine. Boston, Houghton Mifflin, 1979; London, Dent, 1981.
George and Martha, Tons of Fun. Boston, Houghton Mifflin, 1980.
The Stupids Die, with Harry Allard. Boston, Houghton Mifflin, 1981.
Taking Care of Carruthers. Boston, Houghton Mifflin, 1981; London, Bodley Head, 1983.
Rapscallion Jones. New York, Viking Press, 1983; London, Bodley Head, 1984.
George and Martha Back in Town. Boston, Houghton Mifflin, 1984.
The Cut-Ups. New York, Viking Kestrel, 1984; London, Bodley Head, 1985.
Wings: A Tale of Two Chickens. New York, Viking Kestrel, 1986; London, A. and C. Black, 1987.
Three Up a Tree. New York, Dial Press, and London, A. and C. Black, 1986.
Merry Christmas, Space Case. New York, Dial Press, 1986.
Yummers Too: The Second Course. Boston, Houghton Mifflin, 1986.
The Cut-Ups Cut Loose. New York, Viking Kestrel, 1987.
George and Martha Round and Round. Boston, Houghton Mifflin, 1988.
Fox on the Job. New York, Dial Press, 1988; as *Fox at Work,* London, Bodley Head, 1991.
The Cut-Ups at Camp Custer. New York, Viking Kestrel, 1989.
The Stupids Take Off. Boston, Houghton Mifflin, 1989.
The Cut-Ups Carry On. New York, Puffin, 1990.
Fox Be Nimble. London, Bodley Head, 1991; New York, Dial Press, 1990.
Rats on the Roof. London, Hamish Hamilton, 1991.
Rats on the Range and Other Stories. New York, Dial Press, 1993.
Fox on Stage. New York, Dial Press, 1993.
The Cut-Ups Crack Up. New York, Puffin, 1994.

Fiction as Edward Marshall

Troll Country. New York, Dial Press, 1980; London, Bodley Head, 1981.
Space Case. New York, Dial Press, 1980.
Three by the Sea. New York, Dial Press, 1981; London, Bodley Head, 1982.
Fox in Love. New York, Dial Press, 1982; London, Bodley Head, 1983.
Fox and His Friends. New York, Dial Press, and London, Bodley Head, 1982.

Fox at School. New York, Dial Press, 1983; London, Bodley Head, 1984.
Fox on Wheels. New York, Dial Press, 1983; London, Bodley Head, 1992.
Fox All Week. New York, Dial Press, and London, Bodley Head, 1984.
Four on the Shore. New York, Dial Press, and London, A. and C. Black, 1985.

Other (retellings)

Mother Goose. New York, Farrar Straus, 1979.
Red Riding Hood. New York, Dial Press, 1987; as *Little Red Riding Hood,* London, Collins, 1987.
Goldilocks and the Three Bears. New York, Dial Press, 1988; as *Goldilocks,* London, Collins, 1988.
The Three Little Pigs. London, Collins, 1990.
Hansel and Gretel. London, HarperCollins, 1991.
Pocketful of Nonsense. New York, Golden Books, 1993.
Old Mother Hubbard and Her Wonderful Dog. New York, Farrar Straus, 1993.

*

Manuscript Collections: Kerlan Collection, University of Minnesota, Minneapolis; University of Oregon Library, Eugene.

Illustrator: *Plink, Plink, Plink* by Byrd Baylor, 1971; *All the Way Home* by Lore Segal, 1973; *Dinosaur's Housewarming Party* by Norma Klein, 1974; *The Piggy in the Puddle* by Charlotte Pomerantz, 1974; *The Tutti-Frutti Case,* 1975, *It's So Nice to Have a Wolf Around the House,* 1977, *Bumps in the Night,* 1979, *I Will Not Go to Market Today,* 1979, and *There's a Party at Mona's Tonight,* 1981, all by Harry Allard; *The Frog Prince* retold by Edith Tarcov, 1974; *Mary Alice,* 1975, *Bonzini!,* 1976, *Nosey Mrs. Rat,* 1985, and *Mary Alice Returns,* 1986, all by Jeffrey Allen; *Dinner at Alberta's* by Russell Hoban, 1975; *Someone Is Talking about Hortense* by Laurette Murdock, 1975; *A Day with Whisker Wickles* by Cynthia Jameson, 1975; *The Boy Who Cried Wolf* by Freya Littledale, 1976; *Lazy Stories* retold by Diane Wolkstein, 1976; *Carrot Nose* by Jan Wahl, 1978; *MacGoose's Grocery* by Frank Asch, 1978; *How Beastly!: A Menagerie of Nonsense Poems* by Jane Yolen, 1980; *The Exploding Frog and Other Fables* retold by John McFarland, 1981; *Roger's Umbrella* by Daniel Pinkwater, 1982; *The Night Before Christmas* by Clement C. Moore, 1985; *Haunted House Jokes* by Louis Phillips, 1987; *Cinderella* retold by Barbara Karlin, 1989.

James Marshall comments:

I have literally hundreds of notebooks and sketchbooks, and I always carry one with me. My published books grow out of these.

* * *

James Marshall, the prolific author-illustrator of more than 40 books principally for very young children (grades 1-5), illustrated nearly an equal number by others since his career began in 1971. His books use wit and humor to convey themes suitable for the young: respect, kindness, and friendship. His illustrations likewise mix bold colors and simple outlines with visual puns. An acknowledged debt to such different artists as Maurice Sendak and Edward Gorey shows in his work, to whom he has dedicated a book each. His stories often paradoxically link opposites: adult sophistication and novelty meld with the traditional format of stories for children. In story and illustration, he intends to give the reader, as he said, "two diverse elements that shouldn't go together, but when they do it clicks." His better stories do click for both parent and child.

The series of seven George and Martha books, the fifth of which was dedicated to Sendak, shows these qualities best. In these short vignettes, a pair of hippos, named after the protagonists of Edward Albee's *Who's Afraid of Virginia Woolf,* demonstrate their mutual affection, tolerance, and forgiveness of each other's foibles and failings. Each book consists of five very short and often linked stories, in which, for example, George looms over the refrigerators he's raiding, Martha incongruously walks a tightrope, the two take turns scaring each other, or Martha lends George the irritating cuckoo clock which he had bought for her present.

Another series which he illustrated and wrote with Harry Allard chronicles the inane adventures of the Stupid family. These satirize the antics of the nuclear American family in the mass media of the 1950s and feature Stanley Q. Stupid, Mrs. Stupid, their children Buster and Petunia, dog Kitty, cat Xylophone, and assorted Stupid kin. These are calculated to amuse adults and children, though on different levels; for example, in *The Stupids Have a Ball,* the Stupids celebrate their children's failing report cards.

The popular series of Miss Nelson books, also co-authored with Harry Allard, deal with the adventures of grade-school children in relating to their sweet teacher Miss Nelson and her alter-ego Miss Viola Swamp. In Marshall's own series about grade-school friends, Spider, Lolly, and Sam try to top each other's scary stories in *Three by the Sea, Four on the Shore,* and *Three Up a Tree.* Other books feature the cross bear Carruthers and his friends Emily Pig and Eugene Turtle. *What's the Matter with Carruthers?* and *Taking Care of Carruthers* emphasize mutual responsibility among these friends. Emily and Eugene appear also in *Yummers!* and the sequel *Yummers Too* gentle satires on Emily's frequent lapses from her diet. The later series, six easy readers begun under the pen name of Edward Marshall, features Fox, named from Fassbinder's film, who is often outfoxed by his younger sister Louise or by fate. But this adolescent hero fumbles on to success. An adult version of this inept unfoxy hero bumbles his way through *Rapscallion Jones.*

Other books about diverse friendships include *Willis,* wherein Bird, Lobster, and Snake put on a show at the beach to buy sun glasses for their friend Willis the Alligator. In *The Guest* the unlikely friends are moose Mona and a snail, Maurice. *Speedboat* celebrates the unlikely friendship of the dog Jasper Raisintoast, an irresponsible adventurer, and his stay-at-home friend Tweedy Jones. In *Portly McSwine* a worrywart pig, despite his friends' reassurances, anticipates endlessly the misadventures possible at his party on National Snout Day. He even gets a swine flu shot. *Space Case* shows how people trivialize the extraordinary. A flying saucer found by Buddy McGee is just another gadget to his family; to those at school an electronic calculator; and to those out on the streets at Halloween, just another kid in costume. In *Merry Christmas, Space*

Case the flying saucer keeps its promise to return at Christmas despite being stopped for speeding and lingering at a science-fiction movie. It rescues Buddy from the rotten, rich Goober twins by turning them into snowmen. Similarly in *Troll Country* a little girl defeats the real trolls that her mother believes in but that her stolid father ignores. Marshall's books occasionally play with the format of the adult mystery story. In *Miss Dog's Christmas Treat* the reader is to find the missing box of candy. *A Summer in the South,* spoofing Agatha Christie, features detective Eleanor Owl, her assistant Mr. Paws (a cat), and various eccentrics such as Don Coyote, a reclusive hypochondriac, at an island's resort hotel where a stolen Egyptian treasure is retrieved. His illustrations grace similar spoofs such as Harry Allard's *Bumps in the Night,* which are clever imitations of Edward Gorey's sets and costumes for the New York production of *Dracula.*

Marshall also illustrated or retold versions of classical children's stories, such as Edith Tarcov's *The Frog Prince;* John McFarland's *The Exploding Frog and Other Fables,* retold from Aesop; and Clement C. Moore's *The Night Before Christmas.* These have amusing touches in the unusual selections chosen or the illustrations; for example one line-up of characters in Marshall's own retelling of *Mother Goose* recalls a familar scene from TV's *Muppet Show.* But with his witty retelling and illustrations for *Red Riding Hood* and *Goldilocks and the Three Bears,* Marshall went further to make these familiar stories his own. Red Riding Hood's house was copied from the author's house in Connecticut, even to its number 93. Grannie, who lies in bed reading from a pile of books, was modeled after a neighbor and scholar of children's literature. The heroine is a brunette innocent who is misled by the courteous wolf in the forest. But at the end of the story, she has learned her lesson well and avoids a charming alligator who beckons to her with hat and cane in hand. In contrast, the little blond heroine of *Goldilocks and the Three Bears* is a pest, notorious among her neighbors. She reminds readers of the two bad boys in *The Cut-Ups* and *The Cut-Ups Cut Loose.* She deliberately ignores signs warning against the short cut through the forest. She breaks into the charming Victorian cottage (modeled after quaint 19th-century summer homes in a church campground near the author's Connecticut home) of the very civilized and courteous bears. She eats up or spills the porridge, breaks chairs, and beds, after replying to her own invitation "I don't mind if I do." She mistakes the brown fur in the cottage for signs of a kitty. She chooses the Baby Bear's toy-cluttered bed for sleep when she is "quite tuckered out." When the bears return, she jumps out the window and they hope never to see this rude interloper again. Both of these books have been acclaimed by reviewers and librarians for their fresh approaches to familiar stories. They demonstrate that Marshall developed into a confident reteller of classic stories.

Marshall's own original stories, parodies, and retellings, along with their clever but simple illustrations, offer humor, wit, and occasionally sophistication. He takes the perennial concerns of young children and balances them against the greater virtues of that age—being infinitely forgiving, trusting, and loving, totally honest, eager to learn (even French in the case of George), and unfailingly supportive of friends despite their obvious faults. Thus life in many of Marshall's stories, especially the George and Martha books, resolves itself through "mini-farces," artful stories told and illustrated in a seemingly artless style.

—Hugh T. Keenan

MARTIN, David

Has written as Spinifex. **Nationality:** British. **Born:** Ludwig Detsinyi in Budapest, Hungary, 22 December 1915. **Education:** Schools in Germany. **Military Service:** Served as a first-aid orderly in the International Brigade, Spain, 1937-38. **Family:** Married Elizabeth Richenda Powell in 1941; one son. **Career:** Worked for European Service, BBC, and the *Daily Express,* 1938-47, and literary editor, *Reynolds News,* 1945-47, all in London; foreign correspondent in India, 1948-49; Hindu Madras correspondent in Australia, 1949-69. Writer-in-residence, Western Australian Institute of Technology, Bentley, 1981. **Awards:** Australian Council Senior fellowship, 1973, 1975, 1979, 1981; A.M. (Member, Order of Australia), 1988; Patrick White Award, 1991; Emeretus Award, 1996. **Died:** 1 July 1997.

Publications for Children

Fiction

Hughie, illustrated by Ron Brooks. Melbourne, Nelson, and New York, St. Martin's Press, 1971; London, Blackie, 1972.
Frank and Francesca. Melbourne, Nelson, 1972; London, Blackie, 1973.
Gary, illustrated by Con Aslanis. Melbourne, Cassell, 1972; London, Cassell, 1975.
The Chinese Boy. Sydney, Hodder and Stoughton, and Leicester, Brockhampton Press, 1973.
The Cabby's Daughter. Sydney, Hodder and Stoughton, and Leicester, Brockhampton Press, 1974.
Katie, with Richenda Martin, illustrated by Noela Young. Sydney, Hodder and Stoughton, and Leicester, Brockhampton Press, 1974.
Mister P and His Remarkable Flight, illustrated by Astra Lacis. Sydney, Hodder and Stoughton, 1975; as *Mister P Street Pigeon,* London, Macdonald, 1988.
The Devilish Mystery of the Flying Mum. Melbourne, Nelson, 1977.
The Mermaid Attack. Collingwood, Victoria, Outback Press, 1978.
The Man in the Red Turban, illustrated by Genevieve Rees. Richmond, Victoria, Hutchinson, 1978.
Peppino Says Goodbye. Adelaide, Rigby, 1980.
Peppino Turns His Luck. Adelaide, Rigby, and Leeds, Edward Arnold, 1982.
Peppino and the Tobacco War. Adelaide, Rigby, 1984.
The Girl Who Didn't Know Kelly. Richmond, Victoria, Hutchinson, 1985.
Clowning Sim, illustrated by Jan Martin. Blackburn, Victoria, Collins Dove, 1988.

Poetry

I Rhyme My Time: A Selection of Poems for Young People, illustrated by Robert Ingpen. Milton, Queensland, Jacaranda Press, 1980.
The Kitten Who Wouldn't Purr, illustrated by Mark Payne. Melbourne, Macmillan, 1987; London, Macmillan, 1988.

Other

Fox on My Door (autobiography). Blackburn, Victoria, Collins Dove, 1987.

Publications for Adults

Novels

Tiger Bay. London, Martin and Reid, 1946.
The Stones of Bombay. London, Wingate, 1949.
The Young Wife. London, Macmillan, 1962.
The Hero of Too. London, Cassell, 1965; as *The Hero of the Town,* New York, Morrow, 1965.
The King Between. Melbourne and London, Cassell, 1966; as *The Littlest Neutral,* New York, Crown, 1966.
Where a Man Belongs. Melbourne and London, Cassell, 1969.

Short Stories

The Shoes Men Walk In. London, Pilot Press, 1946.
Foreigners. Adelaide, Rigby, 1981.

Plays

The Shepherd and the Hunter (produced London, 1945). London, Wingate, 1946.
The Young Wife (produced Melbourne, 1966).

Poetry

Battlefields and Girls. Glasgow, Maclellan, 1942.
Trident, with Hubert Nicholson and John Manifold. London, Fore, 1944.
From Life: Selected Poems. Sydney, Current, 1953.
Rob the Robber, His Life and Vindication (as Spinifex). Melbourne, Waters, 1954.
Poems 1938-1958. Sydney, Edwards and Shaw, 1958.
Spiegel the Cat: A Story-Poem. Melbourne, Cheshire, 1961; London, Cassell, 1969; New York, Potter, 1971.
The Gift: Poems 1959-1965. Brisbane, Jacaranda Press, 1966.
The Idealist. Brisbane, Jacaranda Press, 1968.
David Martin's Beechworth Book. David Lovell, 1995.

Other

Psychological Effects of the "Western" Film, with F.E. Emery. Melbourne, University of Melbourne Department of Visual Aids, 1957.
Television Tension Programmes. Canberra, Australian Broadcasting Control Board, 1963.
On the Road to Sydney (travel), illustrated by Jan Martin. Melbourne, Nelson, 1970.
I'll Take Australia, photographs by Georg Lindström. Milton, Queensland, Jacaranda Press, 1978.
Armed Neutrality for Australia. Blackburn, Victoria, Collins Dove, 1984.

Editor, *Rhyme and Reason: 34 Poems.* London, Fore, 1944.
Editor, *New World, New Song: A Selection of Poems from the Left.* Sydney, Current, 1955.

*

Manuscript Collection: National Library of Australia, Canberra.

David Martin comments:

I make no sharp distinction between writing for young readers and other readers. My "young novels" are often concerned with the struggle of outsiders (Australian aborigines, Chinese on the Australian goldfields, etc.). I came to young fiction fairly late in life, and don't intend to concentrate on it exclusively. I like writing for teenagers because they respond honestly to an honest story: they do not require attention-whipping novelty at any price. I write about girls with as much sincerity and pleasure as I do about boys.

* * *

David Martin, described by one critic as "the most improbable Australian writer who ever existed," had origins both European and Jewish. His contribution to Australian children's literature has thus been distinguished by a somewhat exotic quality. He understandably chose to espouse the cause of neglected minority groups in his adopted country, and has enriched its literature for the young in terms of content if not in style.

In his first children's book, *Hughie,* he took as his theme the plight of the Aborigines, ironically treated as aliens in their own country. In *The Chinese Boy* he showed how Chinese goldminers were persecuted during the goldrushes of the 1860s at Kiandra and Lambing Flat, in New South Wales. *The Man in the Red Turban* is the story of one of the conspicuous itinerant Indian hawkers who plied their wares in suspicious and conservative white rural Australia during the Great Depression of the 1930s. This book also reflects the author's repugnance towards capitalist exploitation of the working classes.

Martin could handle raw humour with gusto and is at his best in exploring the thoughts, fears, hopes, and preoccupations of children, rather than what they actually say. His particular themes are the value of love and the necessity for struggle, as exemplified in his best work, such as *The Cabby's Daughter,* set in the Victorian gold-mining town of Beechworth in 1902, or *Mister P and His Remarkable Flight,* which examines the same theme in the life of an "outsider" pigeon, rather than an alienated human—such as the famous bushranger outlaw, Ned Kelly, in *The Girl Who Didn't Know Kelly.* His Peppino books, for younger readers, about an immigrant boy's experiences in Italy and Australia, are also about the need to stand up for one's rights in the face of opposition, bullying, and conflict.

The didacticism in Martin's early novels for children seems heavy-handed today, as does their old-fashioned *Boy's Weekly* flavour, which relies on colourful and spectacular incident rather than strong characterisation or fully thought-out thematic treatment. His books are seldom totally satisfying because of this dichotomy; plot and propaganda do not grow naturally out of one another with any sense of unity. His habit of fragmenting families, sometimes by death (as in *The Cabby's Daughter* and *Frank and Francesca*) or desertion (the hero of *Clowning Sim* has a succession of foster parents) may at first seem a melodramatic device, but it reflects something of the state of the author's own childhood (he was raised by a stepmother in what was, to him, a foreign country).

Generally, Martin was at his weakest in portraying major characters—his are mainly types. His minor characters, sometimes only glimpsed, are often more memorable than his improbable heroes or his dastardly villains. Sim, the boy who can't stop clowning (*Clowning Sim*) is probably his most rounded and interesting character.

In spite of his stylistic shortcomings and excesses, Martin was a writer of life, zest, and humour who shared strong personal emotions with his readers. In *Fox on My Door,* he also shares with them his reminiscences of an eventful life, and his thoughts (not at all morbid) about death—even down to the preparations he has carefully made for it! It is this kind of "improbability" which makes Martin unique among Australian writers for children.

—Walter McVitty

MATHERS, Petra

Nationality: German. **Born:** Todtmoos, Black Forest Region, Germany, 25 March 1945. **Education:** Apprenticeship in the book business. **Family:** Married to Michael Mathers; one son. **Career:** has worked in bookstores, for Brockhaus (German encyclopedia company), as a waitress and nightclub hostess; author, illustrator, and freelance artist. **Awards:** Ezra Jack Keats Award, 1985, for *Maria Theresa*; *New York Times* Ten Best Illustrated Children's Books, 1986, for *Molly's New Washing Machine,* and 1988, for *Theodor and Mr. Balbini*; *New York Times* Best Illustrated Children's Book and *Reading Rainbow* Review Book, 1990, for *I'm Flying*; Reading Rainbow Selection and *School Library Journal* Best Book, 1991, for *Borreguita and the Coyote*; *Boston Globe/Horn Book* award and *Reading Rainbow* selection, 1991, for *Sophie and Lou*; Parents' Choice Award, 1993, for *When It Snowed That Night*; *School Library Journal* Best Book, 1994, for *Mrs. Merriwether's Musical Cat*; Society of Illustrators Silver Medal and Parents' Choice Award, 1995, for *Kisses from Rosa*; Hungry Mind Review Award and *School Library Journal* Best Book, 1996, for *Grandmother Bryant's Pocket.* **Address:** c/o Simon and Schuster Children's Publishing Division, 1230 Avenue of the Americas, New York, New York 10020, U.S.A.

Publications for Children (illustrated by the author)

Maria Theresa. New York, Harper, 1985.
Theodor and Mr. Balbini. New York, Harper, 1988.
Sophie and Lou. New York, HarperCollins, 1991.
Victor and Christabel. New York, Knopf, 1993.
Kisses from Rosa. New York, Knopf, 1995.
Lottie's New Beach Towel. New York, Atheneum, 1998.

*

Critical Studies: Review of *Sophie and Lou* in "Picture Books for Children" by Donnarae MacCann and Olga Richard, in *Wilson Library Bulletin,* September 1991, 107; "The Artist at Work" by Petra Mathers, in *Horn Book,* March/April 1992, 171-77; "Petra Mathers" in *Children's Book Illustration and Design,* edited by Julie Cummings, New York, Library of Applied Design, 1992, 114-17; review of *Victor and Christabel* in "Picture Books for Children" by Donnarae MacCann and Olga Richard, *Wilson Library Bulletin,* May 1994, 94-95; "Petra Mathers" by Claudia Logan, in *Children's Books and Their Creators,* edited by Anita Silvey, Boston, Houghton Mifflin, 1995, 438-39; *Myth, Magic and Mystery* by Michael Patrick Hearn, Trinkett Clark, and Nicholas B. Clark, Roberts Rinehart Publishers in cooperation with the Chrysler Museum of Art, 1996, 41, 43, 105, 114-115.

Illustrator: *How Yossi Beat the Evil Urge,* 1983, and *Yossi Asks the Angels for Help,* 1985, by Miriam Chaikin; *Molly's New Washing Machine* by Laura Geringer, 1986; *Frannie's Fruits* by Leslie Kimmelman, 1989; *Block Book* by Susan Arkin Couture, 1990; *I'm Flying* by Alan Wade, 1990; *Borreguita and the Coyote: A Tale from Ayutla, Mexico* retold by Verna Aardema, 1991; *Little Love Song* by Richard Kennedy, 1992; *Aunt Elaine Does the Dance from Spain* by Leah Komaiko, 1992; *When It Snowed that Night* by Norma Farber, 1993; *Mrs. Merriwether's Musical Cat* by Carol Purdy, 1994; *Patchwork Island* by Karla Kuskin, 1994; *Grandmother Bryant's Pocket* by Jacqueline Briggs Martin, 1996; *Mommy Go Away,* 1997, and *I Need a Snake,* 1998, by Lynne Jonell; *Tell Me a Season* by Mary McKenna Siddals, 1997; *On Ramon's Farm: Five Tales of Mexico* by Campbell Geeslin, 1998; *It's My Birthday, Too* by Lynne Jonell, 1998.

Petra Mathers comments:

I don't enjoy starting out on a new book. It makes me fidget. I get up a lot and groan, or I vacuum, then I go to the mirror to see if I'm still there.

When it looks like it's all falling apart I feel found out. any moment the children's book patrol will drive up and take all my stuff away and seal off my studio.

But all the while, slowly, a story comes together, crude and on wobbly legs, but with a beginning, middle and end. From then on it gets easier. Now it's improvement. I love improving; crummy houses, used cars, second hand pets, anything.

I am doing exactly what I want to be doing with plenty of room for improvement.

* * *

Petra Mathers is the illustrator and author/illustrator of several highly praised picture books. Words frequently used to describe her illustrations include surrealistic, naive, flat, clean-edged, original, folkloric, and quirky. In 1985, Mathers published *Maria Theresa,* the first book she both wrote and illustrated, the story of an adventurous hen and her owner, Signora Rinaldo. Signora Rinaldo is an older woman who lives alone in New York City and keeps chickens on the roof of her high-rise building. Her life is well-ordered, with quiet breakfasts of fresh eggs accompanied by the *New York Times* and recordings of opera music. Signora Rinaldo, her stockings drying on the side of the stove, keeps an orderly kitchen. Several varieties of canned Italian tomatoes and a collection of cook books, ranging from the *Joy of Cooking* to books by Adele Davis and M.F.K. Fisher, intershelved with some opera books, reveal her interest in cooking. Maria Theresa (Signora Rinaldo's favorite and her only hen not named after an opera heroine) perches apart from the others and looks out the window while the other hens doze. She also sometimes appears to listen to "faraway voices," so it is not surprising that one day when Signora Rinaldo forgets to close the gate, Maria Theresa flies the coop, and after an adventurous journey finds herself in the country, where there are lots of worms and seeds and the distant mountains "look like giant blue eggs." Maria Theresa joins a circus, and with Miss Lola, a bareback-riding juggler, and Esmeralda, the cow on which she rides, becomes one of a trio called "Three Who Dare." Meanwhile, Signora Rinaldo is distraught over the loss of her hen, but finally is persuaded to visit the country cottage of her opera star friend Salvatore, where they one night go to the circus and the Signora and her hen are reunited. There is a huge celebration with dancing, champagne, and fireworks, and Salvatore and Signora Rinaldo announce their engagement. Maria Theresa makes plans to meet the happy couple in Vermont for Christmas, where she wants to take skiing lessons.

Many of the predominant themes in *Maria Theresa* also appear in Mathers's next three books, and to a lesser extent in her autobiographical *Kisses from Rosa.* These include isolated, apparently ordinary, rather lonely, even shy characters who live alone and who, despite their seeming ordinariness, have an inner strength that leads them to pursue their goals and to find happiness and love or companionship. There is pathos in these books, and a psychological depth enhanced by brilliantly executed illustrations that manage to be simultaneously dreamlike and matter-of-fact, spare yet containing significant, telling details. Mathers writes in "An Artist at Work" that she admires William Steig "as a storyteller and an illustrator" and that she also loves the work of Vera Williams. It is easy to see affinities between Mathers's work and Steig's tales of humorous and rather bizarre adventures and underlying psychological depth, and Williams's rich colors and celebration of unconventional characters and the warmth of human relationships.

Like Signora Rinaldo, Mr. Balbini in *Theodor and Mr. Balbini* (1988) lives a happy, orderly life alone, with only his dog Theodor for company. "Theodor seemed happy too," but the accompanying picture foreshadows changes to come. As Mr. Balbini throws a stick, Theodor is looking in another direction. Like Maria Theresa, he has (perhaps unrecognized) ambitions. When Theodor suddenly begins to talk, he begins to take over Mr. Balbini's life. Mr. Balbini has a brilliantly illustrated dream, that includes Theodor wearing a Napoleon hat and an image of a dogfood can with Mr. Balbini's face on it, revealing the extent to which the natural order has been disturbed.

Theodor not only learns to speak English, but he demands to learn French. The exuberant French teacher, Madame Poulet ("All of my students are special, Monsieur"), is delighted with Theodor, and to Mr. Balbini's relief invites him home with her. Although pleased with the peace and quiet, Mr. Balbini finds he misses Theodor "the way he was before he talked." He sits alone, an untouched sandwich beside him, a silent telephone on the windowsill, and a lovely view of egrets wading in the water in the sunset beyond his window. When the phone rings it is the cheery Madame Poulet, inviting him to dinner the next evening. It turns out to be Josephine, Madame Poulet's sweet poodle who is feeling displaced by Theodor, who is most delighted to see him. Mr. Balbini and Madame Poulet find they have much in common, and Josephine happily goes home with Mr. Balbini, while Theodor stays with Madame Poulet. They all agree to get together for a picnic the next week. All four characters have found happiness and fulfillment in keeping with their individual natures, and there is a promise of a continuing friendship, and perhaps even a romance, between Mr. Balbini and Madame Poulet.

Sophie and Lou (1991) provides an even more fascinating articulation between text and pictures than *Maria Theresa* and *Theodor and Mr. Balbini.* Lou, a dapper mouse, is scarcely mentioned in the story, but he shadows Sophie in the pictures, and Sophie is aware of him. We see him reading a book entitled *Love Poems for Mice* at the bookmobile, and when Sophie sees him on the street she says to herself, "I like his face." The "mousy" Sophie, who reads books about piloting airplanes and practices dancing by herself in her living room across the street from the new dance studio, becomes braver and braver, until one moonlit night when Lou rings her doorbell, she dances out onto the lawn with him without missing a beat. "'My name is Lou,' he said bowing from the waist. 'May I have this dance?' 'You bet,' said Sophie and stepped into his arms."

Victor and Christabel (1993) is a love story, like *Sophie and Lou,* and involves a magical transformation as in *Theodor and Mr. Balbini.* It is the story of two alligators, Victor, a guard in an art museum, and the lovely Christabel, who is imposed upon and abused by her diabolical cousin Anatole Fidibus who then casts a magic spell transforming her into a painting, based on an actual Renaissance painting, "Saint Ursula's Dream" by Vittore Carpaccio. Some reviewers have pointed out that the story has resemblances to "Sleeping Beauty," but it also has resemblances to "Snow White" and to "Cinderella." Needless to say, love wins out in the end, and Christabel returns to life.

In all of her books, including those she has illustrated for other writers, Mathers creates stunning, highly original, surreal, richly detailed illustrations that perfectly complement, enhance, and extend the stories. *Kisses from Rosa* (1995), based on her own experience of being separated from her parents as a young child, is warm and richly detailed, and although it has humor and a bit of fantasy, is less fanciful and whimsical than her other books. Especially in her illustrations of books by other writers, Mathers has experimented with variations in style, incorporating Mexican folk traditions in *Borreguita and the Coyote* (1991), techniques of the patchwork quilt in *Patchwork Island* (1994), early American folk traditions in *Grandmother Bryant's Pocket* (1996), and childlike colored pencil art in *Mommy Go Away* (1997), a departure from her usual pencil and watercolor technique.

—Linnea Hendrickson

MATTINGLEY, Christobel (Rosemary)

Nationality: Australian. **Born:** Christobel Rosemary Shepley, Adelaide, South Australia, 26 October 1931. **Education:** Presbyterian Ladies College, Pymble, New South Wales, 1940-45; The Friends' School, Hobart, Tasmania, 1945-47; University of Tasmania, Hobart, 1948-51, B.A. (honours) 1951; Public Library of Victoria Training College, 1952, Certificate of Proficiency 1952; Associate, Library Association of Australia, 1972. **Family:** Married Cecil David Mattingley in 1953; one daughter and two sons **Career:** Librarian, Department of Immigration, Canberra, 1951 Latrobe Valley Libraries, Victoria, 1953, in England, 1954-55 Prince Alfred College, Adelaide, 1956-57, and St. Peter's Girls School, Adelaide, 1966-70; acquisitions librarian, 1971, and reade services librarian, 1972, Wattle Park Teachers' College, Adelaide reader services librarian, Murray Park College of Advanced Education, Adelaide, 1973-74. Presenter, *Children's Books to Enjo* program (TV), 1973-74. Writer-in-residence, West Australian Co lege of Advanced Education, Churchlands, 1982. **Awards:** Au tralia Council fellowship, 1975, 1983; International Youth Librar scholarship, 1976; Children's Book Council Junior Book of th Year award, 1982; National Parks and Wildlife Services awar 1983; Australian Christian Children's Book of the Year Award f

The Miracle Tree, 1986; City of South Perth WA inaugurated annual Christobel Mattingley Awards for Young Writers, 1987; Advance Australia Award for service to literature, 1990;Honorary Doctorate of the University of South Australia, 1995; Member of the Order of Australia, 1996. **Agent:** Hickson Associates, 128 Queen St., Woollahra, NSW 2025, Australia. **Address:** 10 Rosebark Tee, Stonyfell, South Australia 5066, Australia.

Publications for Children

Fiction

The Picnic Dog, illustrated by Carolyn Dinan. London, Hamish Hamilton, 1970.
Windmill at Magpie Creek, illustrated by Gavin Rowe. Leicester, Brockhampton Press, 1971.
Worm Weather, illustrated by Carolyn Dinan. London, Hamish Hamilton, 1971.
Emu Kite, illustrated by Gavin Rowe. London, Hamish Hamilton, 1972.
Queen of the Wheat Castles, illustrated by Gavin Rowe. Leicester, Brockhampton Press, 1973.
The Battle of the Galah Trees, illustrated by Gareth Floyd. Leicester, Brockhampton Press, 1973.
Show and Tell, illustrated by Helen Sallis. Sydney, Hodder and Stoughton, and Leicester, Brockhampton Press, 1974.
Tiger's Milk, illustrated by Anne Ferguson. Sydney and London, Angus and Robertson, 1974.
The Surprise Mouse, illustrated by Carolyn Dinan. London, Hamish Hamilton, 1974.
Lizard Log, illustrated by Helen Sallis. Sydney, Hodder and Stoughton, 1975.
The Great Ballagundi Damper Bake, illustrated by Will Mahony. Sydney and London, Angus and Robertson, 1975.
The Long Walk, illustrated by Helen Sallis. Melbourne, Nelson, 1976; London, Hamish Hamilton, 1977.
The Special Present and Other Stories, illustrated by Noela Young. Sydney, Collins, 1976; London, Collins, 1977.
New Patches for Old. London, Hodder and Stoughton, 1977.
The Big Swim, illustrated by Elizabeth Honey. Melbourne, Nelson, 1977; London, Hamish Hamilton, 1978.
Budgerigar Blue, illustrated by Tony Oliver. Sydney, Hodder and Stoughton, 1977; London, Hodder and Stoughton, 1978.
The Jetty, illustrated by Gavin Rowe. London, Hodder and Stoughton, 1978.
Black Dog, illustrated by Craig Smith. Sydney, Collins, 1979; London, Bodley Head, 1980.
Rummage, illustrated by Patricia Mullins. Sydney and London, Angus and Robertson, 1981.
Brave with Ben, illustrated by Elizabeth Honey. Melbourne, Nelson, 1982; London, Hamish Hamilton, 1983.
Lexl and the Lion Party, illustrated by Astra Lacis. Sydney, Hodder and Stroughton, 1982.
Duck Boy, illustrated by Patricia Mullins. Sydney and London, Angus and Robertson, 1983; New York, Atheneum, 1986.
Southerly Buster. Sydney and London, Hodder and Stoughton, 1983.
The Magic Saddle, illustrated by Patricia Mullins. Sydney, Hodder and Stoughton, 1983; London, Hodder and Stoughton, 1984.
The Angel with a Mouth-Organ, illustrated by Astra Lacis. Sydney and London, Hodder and Stoughton, 1984; New York, Holiday House, 1986.
Ghost Sitter, illustrated by Christina Brimage. London, Hardy, 1984.
The Miracle Tree, illustrated by Marianne Yamaguchi. Sydney, Hodder and Stoughton, and San Diego, Harcourt Brace, 1985.
McGruer and the Goat, illustrated by Carol McLean-Carr. Sydney and London, Angus and Robertson, 1987.
The Butcher, the Beagle, and the Dog Catcher, illustrated by Carol McLean-Carr, Sydney, Hodder and Stoughton, 1991.
Tucker's Mob, illustrated by Jeanie Adams. Adelaide, Omnibus Books, 1992.
The Sack, illustrated by Simon Kneebone. Puffin Books, 1993.
The Secret, Puffin Books, 1994.
Dance with Didgeridoo, Adelaide, Omnibus Books, 1995.
The Race, illustrated by Anne Spudvilas. Sydney, Ashton Scholastic, 1995.
Daniel's Secret, illustrated by Mark Wilson. Sydney, Scholastic, 1997.
Ginger. Puffin Books, 1997.
Big Sister, Little Sister, Puffin Books, forthcoming.
Poppy Peeker, Puffin Books, forthcoming.

Nonfiction

No Gun for Asmir, illustrated by Elizabeth Honey. Melbourne, Puffin Books, 1993.
Asmir in Vienna, illustrated by Elizabeth Honey. Ringwood, Penguin, 1995.
Escape from Sarajevo, Ringwood, Penguin, 1996.

Plays

The Long Walk (television play), from her own novel, 1978.
Come to the Party! Children's Libraries (screenplay), South Australian Film Corp., 1980.
Social Development Series—for Junior Primary (screenplay), South Australian Film Corp., 1980.
Women Artists of Australia, South Australian Film Corp. (screenplay), 1980.
Rummage (television play), from her own novel, 1983.
Brave with Ben (television play), 1989.
Windmill at Magpie Creek (television play), 1992.

Publications for Adults

Other

Editor, *Survival in Our Own Land: Aboriginal Experience in South Australia since 1836.* Netley, South Australia, Wakefield Press, 1988.

*

Biography: Essay 'You Can't Count the Beans in a Book' in *The Early Dreaming: Australian Children's Authors on Childhood,* edited by Michael Dugan, Milton, Jacaranda Press, 1980

Christobel Mattingley comments:

My memories of childhood are intense and vivid, and my development as a writer began at an early age. The power of words and the magic of books had already enthralled me before I started school, and by the age of eight I was reading widely, writing poetry, and making up stories and plays. I was always conscious of an affinity with nature and at nine was introduced to serious nature study by an enlightened teacher and began keeping copious diaries of careful observations. At 10 I had my first publishing acceptance, in a natural history magazine. My father's work as a civil engineer building dams and bridges in various parts of Australia made me aware of the need for harmony between man and nature and intensified my love for wilderness areas. Experiencing childhood again with my own family acted as a catalyst for writing, and my stories have evolved as a combination of everyday events, places and personalities reinforcing my own emotions of childhood.

As I grew up during World War II and worked after graduation from university with refugees, I developed an empathy with displaced persons. A number of my books tell of the impact of war and dispossession, the first being *The Angel with a Mouth Organ.*

Experiences while visiting our children now grown up and living in other countries also inspired stories. I wrote *The Miracle Tree* in Nagasaki, while our daughter lived in Japan. And more recently I wrote *No Gun for Asmir, Asmir in Vienna,* and *Escape from Sarajevo,* when our older son living in Vienna helped several Bosnian families escape. This trilogy follows the true story of those families' traumas of separation and anguish through the recent war.

At home in Australia I spent eight years at the request of Aboriginal people on the book *Survival in Our Own Land: "Aboriginal" Experiences in "South Australia" Since 1836* which presents the viewpoint of the dispossessed and is a landmark in Australian history.

Two of my recent children's novels, *The Sack* and *WORK WANTED,* deal with the problems of unemployment and its impact on families. Currently I am working on memoirs and a biography of two remarkable Tasmanian pioneers.

* * *

Christobel Mattingley's versatility is her strength. Mattingley's career has spanned picture story books, novellas, full-length novels, books for young children, middling children, teenagers, young adults and adult readers. Her early books, for younger readers, derived from her own childhood memories and observations of her growing family. The events in these books are always of the ordinary, everyday kind—such as a kite-flying contest in *Warm Weather*—and the problems are commonplace and believable. In *Queen of the Wheat Castles,* Cathy tries to save the lives of unwanted kittens by finding owners for them. The under-sized Antony in *Tiger's Milk* just wants to grow bigger and stronger. (The book's solution is a recipe that any child can try at home.)

Some of these early books dwell on the common fears of ordinary children. In *The Long Walk,* Michael finds his bus trip to and from school an intimidating ordeal. Brad needs to come to terms with his fear of the sea in *The Jetty,* and Peter undergoes his own ordeal by water in *The Big Swim.* In *Brave with Ben,* the young hero overcomes his fear of dense bushland with the help of a friendly dog. In *Windmill at Magpie Creek,* Tim develops an aversion for heights and to aggressive magpies. In each case, the solutions are natural and unforced.

In the adolescent novels *New Patches for Old* and *Southerly Buster,* conflict with peer groups and adults is an important issue. In *New Patches for Old,* Patricia struggles to cope with total dislocation and relocation of her family, and the death of her grandfather back in England. She finds everything strange and puzzling in Australia, a dry land, where every drop of water is precious. Everything seems upside down like the ordinary things she sees reflected in the bowl of a tablespoon, torn apart like shreds of pastry from the pie grandma is baking, or the scraps from a rag-bag. Yet somehow remoulded into a pastry leaf, or pieced together in a totally new quilt; pastry and patchwork serve as metaphors for Patricia's new life. In *Southerly Buster,* Julie is challenged by her own developing sexuality and the emotional shock she experiences when her mother becomes pregnant late in life. Nature conservation is central to *Battle for the Galah Trees* and *Lizard Log,* as are other social issues, such as the boy's undiagnosed handicap in *The Race.* Her work as oral historian for the Australian Aboriginal people of South Australia, which led to the documentary account *Survival in Our Own Land,* and later the children's story *Tucker's Mob,* takes her involvement even further.

Overseas travel led to a broadening of Mattingley's range and a move away from domestic dramas in everyday Australian settings. *Rummage* is the story of a London street-market junk dealer who learns the futility of denying his own nature in order to conform to the perceived expectations of others. An extended stay in Germany (including a period spent in residence at Munich while attached to the International Youth Library) resulted in *Lexl and the Lion Party,* which describes the delight of a young boy when his favourite carved stone lions, from the buildings and monuments in the city in which he lives, come to life one midnight. *The Angel with a Mouth-Organ* is a poignant story of the struggle of a closely knit refugee family to stay together during World War II, while *No Gun for Asmir* tells of a Sarajevo refugee family escaping the civil war in the former Yugoslavia. Separation from loved ones by war is also the theme of *The Miracle Tree.* For 20 years Taro, a gardener, has hoped for a miracle that would see him united once more with his beautiful wife—missing since the atomic bomb blast in her city of Nagasaki. As in the other stories of this period, there is pathos and sentiment, and the wishes do come true. This story resulted from a visit the author made to Japan in 1981 to be with her daughter, who was living there as an exchange student. Similarly, *Mr. McGruer and the Goat,* a comic tale of a retired sea captain and his pet octopus, had its beginnings in a lecture tour of New Zealand. Set in the 1930s Depression in Australia, *The Sack* is a return to the theme of family hardships and poverty caused by unemployment. Throughout the great variety of her work, Mattingley illustrates the importance of common, everyday experiences.

—Walter McVitty, updated by John Gough

MAYER, Mercer

Nationality: American. **Born:** Little Rock, Arkansas, 30 December 1943. **Education:** Theodore Roosevelt High School, Honolulu, Hawaii; Honolulu Academy of Arts; Art Students League, New York City. **Family:** Married 1) Marianna, in 1963 (divorced 1978); 2) Jo in 1979; one son (adopted), one daughter. **Career**

Political cartoonist, International Brotherhood of Teamsters, Hawaii; painter, Kahala Hilton Hotel; artist with an advertising agency in Connecticut; since 1967, children's book author and illustrator. **Awards:** Society of Illustrators Annual National Exhibit Citation, 1970, and Brooklyn Art Books Citation, 1973, for *A Boy, a Dog and a Frog*; AIGA Children's Book Award, 1970-71, for *A Special Trick*; Association for Childhood Education International Books for Children Award, 1974, for *A Boy, a Dog, and a Frog* and *A Boy, a Dog, a Frog, and a Friend*; Brooklyn Art Books for Children Citation, 1975, for *What Do You Do with a Kangaroo?*; Brooklyn Art Books Citation, 1976, for *Frog Goes to Dinner*; Irma Simonton Black Award, 1976, and *New York Times* Best Illustrated Children's Books of the Year, for *Everyone Knows What a Dragon Looks Like* by Jay Williams. **Address:** 16 Judds Bridge Road, Roxbury, Connecticut 06783, U.S.A.

Publications for Children

Fiction (illustrated by the author)

A Boy, a Dog, and a Frog. New York, Dial, 1967.
If I Had. New York, Dial, 1968.
The Terrible Troll. New York, Dial, 1968.
There's a Nightmare in My Closet. New York, Dial, 1968.
Frog, Where Are You? New York, Dial, 1969.
I Am a Hunter. New York, Dial, 1969.
A Special Trick. New York, Dial, 1970.
With Marianna Mayer, *Mine.* New York, Simon & Schuster, 1970.
The Queen Always Wanted to Dance. New York, Simon & Schuster, 1971.
With Marianna Mayer, *A Boy, a Dog, a Frog, and a Friend.* New York, Dial, 1971.
With Marianna Mayer, *Me and My Flying Machine.* New York, Four Winds, 1971.
A Silly Story. New York, Parents' Magazine Press, 1973.
Bubble, Bubble. New York, Parents' Magazine Press, 1973.
Frog on His Own. New York, Dial, 1973.
Mrs. Beggs and the Wizard. New York, Parents' Magazine Press, 1973.
Frog Goes to Dinner. New York, Dial, 1974.
One Monster After Another. New York, Golden Press, 1974.
Two Moral Tales. New York, Four Winds, 1974.
Two More Moral Tales. New York, Four Winds, 1974.
What Do You Do with a Kangaroo? New York, Four Winds, 1974.
You're the Scaredy-Cat. New York, Parents' Magazine Press, 1974.
The Great Cat Chase. New York, Four Winds, 1974.
Walk, Robot, Walk. Lexington, Massachussetts, Ginn, 1974.
Just for You. New York, Golden Press, 1975.
With Marianna Mayer, *One Frog Too Many.* New York, Dial, 1975.
Ah-Choo. New York, Dial, 1976.
Hiccup. New York, Dial, 1976.
Liza Lou and the Yeller Belly Swamp. New York, Parents' Magazine Press, 1976.
Just Me and My Dad. New York, Golden Press, 1977.
Little Monster's Word Book. New York, Golden Press, 1977.
Mercer's Monsters. New York, Golden Press, 1977.
Oops. New York, Dial, 1977.
Professor Wormbog in Search for the Zipperump-a-Zoo. New York, Golden Press, 1977.
Professor Wormbog's Gloomy Kerploppus: A Book of Great Smells (and a Heart-Warming Story, Besides). New York, Golden Press, 1977.
Little Monster at Home. New York, Golden Press, 1978.
Little Monster at School. New York, Golden Press, 1978.
Little Monster at Work. New York, Golden Press, 1978.
Little Monster's Alphabet Book. New York, Golden Press, 1978.
Little Monster's Bedtime Book. New York, Golden Press, 1978.
Little Monster's Counting Book. New York, Golden Press, 1978.
Little Monster's Neighborhood. New York, Golden Press, 1978.
Little Monster's You-Can-Make-It Book. New York, Golden Press, 1978.
How the Trollusk Got His Hat. New York, Golden Press, 1979.
Little Monster's Mother Goose. New York, Golden Press, 1979.
East of the Sun & West of the Moon. New York, Four Winds, 1980.
Herbert, the Timid Dragon. New York, Golden Press, 1980.
Little Monster's Scratch and Sniff Mystery. New York, Golden Press, 1980.
Professor Wormbog's Crazy Cut-Ups. New York, Golden Press, 1980.
Merry Christmas, Mom and Dad. New York, Golden Press, 1982.
Play with Me. New York, Golden Press, 1982.
Just a Snowy Day. New York, Golden Press, 1983.
Malcom's Race. New York, Scholastic, 1983.
Gator Cleans House. New York, Scholastic, 1983.
Just Go to Bed. New York, Golden Press, 1983.
Too's Bracelet. New York, Scholastic, 1983.
Sweetmeat's Birthday. New York, Scholastic, 1983.
Possum Child Goes Shopping. New York, Scholastic, 1983.
When I Get Bigger. New York, Golden Press, 1983.
Bat Child's Haunted House. New York, Scholastic, 1983.
All by Myself. New York, Golden Press, 1983.
I Was So Mad. New York, Golden Press, 1983.
Just Grandma and Me. New York, Golden Press, 1983.
Me Too! New York, Golden Press, 1983.
The New Baby. New York, Golden Press, 1983.
Tuk Takes a Trip. New York, Bantam, 1984.
Teep and Beep, Go to Sleep. New York, Bantam, 1984.
Tink Goes Fishing. New York, Bantam, 1984.
Tinka Bakes a Cake. New York, Bantam, 1984.
Little Critter's Day at the Farm. New York, Scholastic, 1984.
Little Critter's Holiday Fun. New York, Scholastic, 1984.
Little Monster's Moving Day. New York, Scholastic, 1984.
Little Monster's Sports Fun. New York, Scholastic, 1984.
Trouble in Tinktonk Land. New York, Bantam, 1985.
The Tinktonks Find a Home. New York, Bantam, 1985.
Just Me and My Puppy. New York, Golden Press, 1985.
Tonk Gives a Magic Show. New York, Bantam, 1985.
Zoomer Builds a Racing Car. New York, Bantam, 1985.
Just Grandpa and Me. New York, Golden Press, 1985.
Policeman Critter. New York, Simon & Schuster, 1986.
Fireman Critter. New York, Simon & Schuster, 1986.
Cowboy Critter. New York, Simon & Schuster, 1986.
Astronaut Critter. New York, Simon & Schuster, 1986.
Just Me and My Little Sister. New York, Golden Press, 1986.
Just Me and My Babysitter. New York, Golden Press, 1986.
Whinnie the Lovesick Dragon. New York, Macmillan, and London, Collier Macmillan, 1986.
There's an Alligator Under My Bed. New York, Dial, 1987.
Construction Critter. New York, Simon & Schuster, 1987.
Doctor Critter. New York, Simon & Schuster, 1987.

Mail Critter. New York, Simon & Schuster, 1987.
Sailor Critter. New York, Simon & Schuster, 1987.
Just a Mess. Racine, Wisconsin, Western Publishing Company, 1987.
Baby Sister Says No! Racine, Wisconsin, Western Publishing Company, 1987.
Happy Easter, Little Critter. Racine, Wisconsin, Western Publishing Company, 1988.
Little Critter's Staying Overnight. New York, Golden Press, 1988.
Little Critter's This Is My House. New York, Golden Press, 1988.
Little Critter's These Are My Pets. New York, Golden Press, 1988.
Little Critter's The Trip. New York, Golden Press, 1988.
Little Critter's The Picnic. New York, Golden Press, 1988.
Little Critter's Little Sister's Birthday. Racine, Wisconsin, Western Publishing Company, 1988.
I Just Forgot. New York, Golden Press, and Racine, Wisconsin, Western Publishing Company, 1988.
Just My Friend and Me. New York, Golden Press, and Racine, Wisconsin, Western Publishing Company, 1988.
Little Critter's The Fussy Princess. New York, Golden Press, and Racine, Wisconsin, Western Publishing Company, 1989.
Just a Daydream. New York, Golden Press, and Racine, Wisconsin, Western Publishing Company, 1989.
Just Shopping with Mom. Racine, Wisconsin, Western Publishing Company, 1989.
Just Camping Out. New York, Golden Press, and Racine, Wisconsin, Western Publishing Company, 1989.
Little Critter's Christmas Book. New York, Golden Press, and Racine, Wisconsin, Western Publishing Company, 1989.
Little Critter's This Is My Friend. New York, Golden Press, and Racine, Wisconsin, Western Publishing Company, 1989.
Just a Nap. New York, Golden Press, and Racine, Wisconsin, Western Publishing Company, 1989.
Mercer Mayer's Little Critter at Play. New York, Golden Press, and Racine, Wisconsin, Western Publishing Company, 1989.
Mercer Mayer's Little Critter's Day. New York, Golden Press, and Racine, Wisconsin, Western Publishing Company, 1989.
There's Something Spooky in My Attic. New York, Macmillan, 1989.
Little Critter's This Is My School. Racine, Wisconsin, Western Publishing Company, 1990.
Just Going to the Dentist. Racine, Wisconsin, Western Publishing Company, 1990.
Just Me and My Mom. Racine, Wisconsin, Western Publishing Company, 1990.
Just a Rainy Day. Racine, Wisconsin, Western Publishing Company, 1990.
Just Me and My Little Brother. Racine, Wisconsin, Western Publishing Company, 1991.
Little Critter's Jack and the Beanstalk. New York, Random House, B. Dalton, 1991.
Little Critter's Little Red Riding Hood. New York, Random House, B. Dalton, 1991.
When I Grow Up. New York, Golden Press, 1991.
Mercer Mayer's Herbert the Timid Dragon. New York, Golden Press, and Racine, Wisconsin, Western Publishing Company, 1991.
Little Critter's Hansel and Gretel. New York, Green Frog Publishers, 1991.
Little Critter's Where Is My Frog? New York, Random House, B. Dalton, 1991.
Little Critter's Where's Kitty? New York, Random House, B. Dalton, 1991.
Where's My Sneaker? New York, Green Frog Publishers, 1991.
Super Critter to the Rescue. Racine, Wisconsin, Western Publishing Company, 1991.
I Am Helping. New York, Random House, 1992.
I Am Sharing. New York, Random House, 1992.
I Am Hiding. New York, Random House, 1992.
I Am Playing. New York, Random House, 1992.
Little Critter's The Night Before Christmas. New York, Green Frog Publishers, 1992.
Little Critter's ABCs. New York, Random House, 1992.
Little Critter's Shapes. New York, Random House, 1992.
Little Critter's Colors. New York, Random House, 1992.
Little Critter's Numbers. New York, Random House, 1992.
Little Critter's Read-it-Yourself Storybook: Six Funny Easy-to-Read Stories. Racine, Wisconsin, Western Publishing Company, 1993.
Little Critter in Search of the Beautiful Princess. New York, Green Frog Publishers, 1993.
Little Critter's Joke Book. Racine, Wisconsin, Western Publishing Company, 1993.
Little Critter's Camp Out. Racine, Wisconsin, Western Publishing Company, 1993.
Little Critter's Favorite Things. Racine, Wisconsin, Western Publishing Company, 1994.
If I Had a Gorilla. Inchelium, Washington, Rainbird Press, 1994.
To Catch a Little Fish. New York, Random House, 1996.
Old Howl Hall. New York, Random House, 1996.

Fiction

Appelard and Liverwurst, illustrated by Steven Kellogg. New York, Four Winds, 1978.
Liverwurst Is Missing, illustrated by Steven Kellogg. New York, Four Winds, 1981.

Other

Abridger, *A Christmas Carol* by Charles Dickens. New York, Macmillan, 1986.

Editor, *The Poison Tree and Other Poems.* New York, Scribner's, 1977.
Editor and reteller, *The Sleeping Beauty.* New York, Macmillan, 1984; London, Collier Macmillan, 1984.

*

Biography: Entry in *Something About the Author,* Detroit, Gale, Vol. 32, 1983, Vol. 73, 138-144; entry in *Major Authors and Illustrators for Children and Young Adults: A Selection of Sketches from Something About the Author,* edited by Laurie Collier and Joyce Nakamura, Gale, 1993, 1597-1601.

Critical Studies: "Mercer Mayer" by P. Gila Reinstein, in *Dictionary of Literary Biography,* Vol. 61, Detroit, Gale, 1987, 200-209.

Illustrator: *The Great Brain,* 1967, *More Adventures of the Grea Brain,* 1969, *Me and My Little Brain,* 1971, *The Great Brain a the Academy,* 1972, *The Great Brain Reforms,* 1973, *Return of th Great Brain,* 1974, and *The Great Brain Does It Again,* 1975, al by John D. Fitzgerald; *The Boy Who Made a Million* by Sidne Offit, 1968; *The Crack in the Wall and Other Terribly Weird Tale* and *The Gillygoofang* by George Mendoza, 1968; *Outside My Window* by Liesel M. Skorpen, 1968; *Boy, Was I Mad!* by Kathryn Hitte, 1969; *Golden Butter* by Sheila La Farge, 1969; *Good-Bye Kitchen* by Mildred Kantrowitz, 1969; *The Mousechildren and the Famous Collector* by Warren Fine, 1970; *Jack Tar* by Jean Russell Larson, 1970; *Me and My Flying Machine,* 1971, and *Beauty and the Beast,* 1978, by Marianna Mayer; *Let Me Fall Before I Fly,* 1971, and *Amanda Dreaming,* 1973, by Barbara Wersba; *The Bird of Time* by Jane Yolen, 1971; *Margaret's Birthday* 1971, and *Grandmother Told Me,* 1972, by Jan Wahl; *Kim Ann and the Yellow Machine* by Candida Palmer, 1972; *While the Horses Galloped to London* by Mabel Watts, 1973; *The Figure in the Shadows* by John Bellairs, 1975; *Everyone Knows What a Dragon Looks Like,* 1976, and *The Reward Worth Having,* 1977, by Jay Williams; *Just Me and My Cousin,* 1992, *Rosie's Mouse,* 1992, *A Very Special Critter,* 1992, *Trick or Treat, Little Critter,* 1993, *Just Like Dad,* 1993, *Just Say Please,* 1993, *Just a Gum Wrapper,* 1993, *That's Not Fair,* 1993, *It's Mine,* 1993, *This Is My Body,* 1993, *Going to the Races,* 1993, *Taking Care of Mom,* 1993, *Just Me in the Tub,* 1994, *Just Too Little,* 1994, *Just Lost,* 1994, *Just Me and My Bicycle,* 1994, *I Didn't Mean To,* 1995, *I Was So Sick,* 1995, *Just a Bad Day,* 1995, *Just a Little Different,* 1995, *Just an Airplane,* 1995, *The Loose Tooth,* 1995, *My Big Sister,* 1995, *The School Play,* 1995, and *I'm Sorry,* 1996, all by Gina Mayer; *The Cat's Meow,* 1994, *The Purple Kiss,* 1994, *The Alien,* 1995, *The E-mail Mystery,* 1995, *The Swamp Thing,* 1995, *The Prince,* 1995, *The Golden Eagle,* 1995, *Jaguar Paw,* 1995, *The Goblin's Birthday Party,* 1996, *If You Dream a Dragon,* 1996, all by Erica Farber.

* * *

Mercer Mayer is the creator of several extensive popular series of picture books for young children. The first series, which began with *A Boy, a Dog and a Frog* in 1976, consists of witty stories told entirely by pictures. The *Frog* series, influenced a bit by Maurice Sendak's cross-hatching techniques, shows the adventures of a boy and his frog in a variety of settings. Done with brown ink on a plain white background, the five-by-seven-inch books tell amusing tales with wordless images. Much of the humor of the stories comes from Frog's leaping into unexpected places and causing havoc for unsuspecting humans. The expressive faces of the boy, his pets, and the adults in the illustrations furnish much of the interest in these books as well. Thus, in *Frog Goes to Dinner* (1974), one of the best, and best-known, of the series, the frog's gleeful innocence, the restaurant patrons' dismay and outrage, the waiter's hauteur, and the parents' disgruntlement are conveyed with dramatic expression. The boy and his frog have a close connection with each other, and the frog can be seen as displaying the mischievous spirit the boy has to suppress in order to be properly behaved. After the frog escapes from his pocket at the restaurant and creates chaos by finding his way into places such as the mouth of the saxophone or the salad of a diner, the boy identifies the frog as his own before he and his family are thrown out by an enraged maitre'd. Though the boy and his frog look gloomy and downcast on the ride home, chastened by the disapproval of the rest of the family, when they are alone together in the boy's bedroom they share a big laugh.

As the stories of the boy, the frog, and the dog progress, the brown ink lines become bolder and darker. It is also evident that Mayer refines the art of telling coherent and exciting stories through images alone, employing the dramatic potential of the two-page panels and the revelations made possible by the turning of the page.

Another of Mayer's successful series is the long list of *Little Critter* books. Little Critter (a registered trademark of Mercer Mayer) is a child-like creature who looks like a cross between a beaver and a dog, with an unruly mop of hair. He has a big, wide nose, a single tooth in the middle of his upper lip, large eyes, and a broad grin. He is, like many anthropomorphic animals in children's literature, a symbolic child. Little Critter is full of mischief, but somewhat innocent at the same time. In many of his stories, the written text, which is usually Little Critter's own account of events, contradicts or complicates what we see in the pictures. Sometimes, as in *Just Me and My Babysitter,* what we see is the opposite of what we're told. Little Critter says, "I eat everything she gives me, even if I don't like it," but what we see is that Little Critter is offering his plate to the puppy to clean off, hidden from the babysitter's view. Little Critter says, "I go right to bed when my babysitter tells me to," but what we see is Little Critter refusing to put on his pajamas as the TV screen displays "The Real Real Late Show." Little Critter pretends to fulfill his Mom's belief that "I'm the babysitter's big helper," and the joke running through the book is that, whether he thinks he's being a big help or not, he isn't actually. In other Little Critter books, such as *Just Grandpa and Me,* the joke is at least partly on the child figure himself. When he and his Grandpa go to the movies, Little Critter tells us that "I sat close to Grandpa in the scary parts so he wouldn't be afraid," but what we actually see is a very frightened Little Critter clinging to his Grandpa for dear life.

Little Critter is a character who allows Mayer to explore the fears, frustrations, desires, and problems of being a child. P. Gila Reinstein argues that the books in which Little Critter appears "are easier for adults to live with [than other works by Mayer] because they omit the strongly rebellious, vengeful, terrified feelings that are brought forward in many of Mayer's other books. Not that these books deny all negative emotions: frustration, loneliness, and embarrassment, for example, are included, but characters display these feelings to a rather mild degree and are brought to emotional comfort within each book." The art work varies in luminosity and mood somewhat from book to book, but the general effect is bold, lively, and humorous.

Two books that break the pattern of the series books in Mayer's production are the folktale books *Beauty and the Beast,* retold by Marianna Mayer (1978), and *East of the Sun & West of the Moon* (1980). These are ornate and ambitious illustrations of serious folktale material. In the latter book, Mayer retells the Scandinavian tale but also interweaves elements of the story of the Frog Prince and inventions of his own. Both books are lush and visually detailed interpretations of the stories they tell.

Several other books of Mercer Mayer's that deserve mention are *There's a Nightmare in My Closet, There's an Alligator Under My Bed, Mrs. Beggs and the Wizard,* and *What Do You Do With a Kangaroo?* The first two of these deal with a child's fears in symbolic form: creatures live in the child's vicinity and frighten him, but he learns to tame and subdue them. In these books, the monsters are real enough to the main character, but can also be amusing to a child reader. The pictures are done with clean, dark ink strokes and bright, colorful watercolor washes. The second set of these books, *Mrs. Beggs and the Wizard,* and *What Do You Do With a Kangaroo?,* deals with a child's hostilities and aggressions. In *Mrs. Beggs* adult characters enact a child's angry fantasies, which end in the punishment of the antagonist. As Reinstein has pointed out, *What Do You Do With a Kangaroo?* is "a more playful treatment of the same theme.... *Kangaroo* closes with a young girl taking several obstreperous, demanding animals to bed with her, accepting them as parts of herself."

In the *Appelard and Liverwurst* books, Mayer presents the zany highjinks of Appelard the farmer, his group of barnyard animals, a "baby rhinosterwurst," and a cast of crazy characters. These books were illustrated by Steven Kellogg.

It is interesting to note that Mercer Mayer spent a good deal of time as a child in Hawaii hunting snakes and lizards in the the swamps near the Navy base where his family lived. In his work as an adult, he has transformed the search for swamp reptiles and other animals into explorations of the swampy topography of childhood emotions, represented through creatures that are symbolic hybrids of human and animal traits. His humor and honesty have served to enrich the imaginative realm of picture books for children.

—J. D. Stahl

McBRATNEY, Sam

Nationality: British/Irish. **Born:** Belfast, 1 March 1943. **Education:** Lisburn Central School, to 1954; Friends' School, Lisburn, 1954-61; Trinity College Dublin, B.A. in History and Political Science 1965. **Family:** Married Maralyn Green in 1964; three children; **Career:** Teacher in Primary and Grammar Schools and at a Further Education College, 1965-1991; writer, from 1992. **Awards:** Bass Ireland Arts Prize. 1979; Bisto Book of the Year, teenage fiction category, 1992-93, and merit award, 1993-94; Kurt Maschler Award shortlist, 1994; British Book Award shortlist, 1994; Silveren Griffel, Holland, 1995; American Bookseller Book of the Year Award, 1996. **Agent:** Caroline Walsh, David Higham Associates Ltd., 5-8 Lower John Street, London, W1R 4HA. **Address:** 17 Ballymote Road, Glenavy, Co. Antrim, BT29 4NS Northern Ireland.

Publications for Children

Fiction

A Dip of the Antlers. London, Abelard-Schuman, 1977.
The Final Correction. London, Abelard-Schuman, 1978.
Boy Blue. London, Abelard, 1979.
From the Thorenson Dykes. London, Abelard, 1980.
The Hanging Man, illustrated by Bruce Symons. London, Cassell, 1980.
The Man Who Tried to Fly, illustrated by Bruce Symons. London, Cassell, 1980.
The Pigeon Killer, illustrated by Bruce Symons. London, Cassell, 1980.
The Stolen Honda, illustrated by Bruce Symons. London, Cassell, 1980.
Jimmy Zest, illustrated by Thelma Lambert. London, Hamish Hamilton, 1982.
The Jimmy Zest All-Stars, illustrated by Thelma Lambert. London, Hamilton, 1985.
Colvin and the Snake Basket, illustrated by Carol Holmes. London, Methuen, 1985.
Zesty, illustrated by Susan Hellard. London, Methuen, 1985.
The Missing Lollipop, illustrated by Linda Birch. London, Hamilton, 1986.
Uncle Charlie Weasel and the Cuckoo Bird. London, Methuen, 1986.
Claudius Bald Eagle, illustrated by Joanna Carey. London, Methuen, 1987.
Uncle Charlie Weasel's Winter, illustrated by Mike Daley. London, Methuen, 1988.
The Ghosts of Hungryhouse Lane. London, Hippo, 1988, and New York, Holt, 1989.
Funny How the Magic Starts. London, Methuen, 1989.
Zesty Goes Cooking. London, Hamilton, 1989.
The Secret of Bone Island. London, Hippo, 1989.
Bones and the Monster. Aylesbury, Ginn, 1990.
Bones at the Pet Show. Aylesbury, Ginn, 1990.
Bones and the Beast. Aylesbury, Ginn, 1990.
Pip Goes to Africa. Aylesbury, Ginn, 1990.
The Thursday Creature. London, Heinemann, 1990.
Noah Sorts the Animals. Aylesbury, Ginn, 1990.
Jill Has Three Pets. Aylesbury, Ginn, 1990.
Cyclops and the Greenbeans, illustrated by Terry McKenna. Aylesbury, Ginn, 1990.
Jealous Jools and Dominique. London, Puffin, 1991.
Something Big, illustrated by Tessa Richardson-Jones. London, Heinemann, 1992.
Art You're Magic! London, Walker, 1992 and Dublin, O'Brien, 1994.
The Green Kids. London, Walker, 1992.
A Case of Blue Murder. London, Heinemann, 1993.
The Stranger from Somewhere in Time, illustrated by Steve Cox. London, Heinemann, 1994.
The Lough Neagh Monster, illustrated by Donald Teskey. Dublin, O'Brien, 1994.
Guess How Much I Love You, illustrated by Anita Jeram. London, Walker, 1994; Cambridge, Massachusetts, Candlewick, 1995; as *Guess How Much I Love You Board Book,* London, Walker, 1996.
Henry Seamouse. London, Longman, 1994.
Flash Eddie and the Big Bad Wolf, illustrated by Hunt Emerson. London, Walker, 1994.
The Ghastly Gerty Swindle, with the Ghosts of Hungryhouse Lane, illustrated by Lisa Thiesing. New York, Holt, 1994.
Hurray for Monty Ray!. Hemel Hempstead, Simon & Schuster, 1994.
Francis Fry Private Eye, illustrated by Kim Blundell. London, Collins, 1995.
Firetail Cat. London, Macdonald Young Books, 1995.
In Crack Willow Wood, illustrated by Ivan Bates. London, Walker 1995.
Suzuki Goodbye, illustrated by Peter Dennis. London, Collins Educational, 1995.
Oliver Sundew, Tooth Fairy, illustrated by Dom Mansell. London, Walker, 1995.
The Dark at the Top of the Stairs, illustrated by Ivan Bates. London, Walker, 1996, and Cambridge, Massachusetts, Candlewick 1996.
The Caterpillow Fight, illustrated by Jill Barton. London, Walker and Cambridge, Massachusetts, Candlewick, 1996.
Francis Fry and the O.T.G., illustrated by Kim Blundell. London Collins, 1996.

Little Red Riding Hood, illustrated by Emma Chichester Clark. London, Macdonald Young Books, 1996.
Celtic Myths, illustrated by Stephen Player. Hove, Macdonald Young Books, 1997, and New York, Bedrick, 1998.
Just One, illustrated by Ivan Bates. Cambridge, Massachusetts, Candlewick, 1997.
Just You and Me, illustrated by Ivan Bates. London, Walker and Cambridge, Massachusetts, Candlewick, 1998.

Publications for Young Adults

Fiction

Mark Time. London, Abelard-Schuman, 1976
Put a Saddle on the Pig. London, Methuen, 1992; as *You Just Don't Listen,* London, Mammoth, 1994.
The Chieftain's Daughter. Dublin, O'Brien, 1993, and Nimot, Colorado, Irish American Books, 1997.
"Blind Chance" in *First Times,* edited by Robert Dunbar. Dublin, Poolbeg, 1997.

Nonfiction

Cassell Discovery Books. Set 6: People. London, Cassell, 1981.
How We Travelled Long Ago. Aylesbury, Ginn, 1990.
Who Likes Work? Aylesbury, Ginn, 1991.
Animals at Work. Aylesbury, Ginn, 1991.

Other

Lagan Valley Details (short stories). Belfast, Blackstaff, 1980.
Breakfast with Ublob (play), illustrated by Nick Schon. Aylesbury, Ginn, 1993.
Bananas (play). Aylesbury, Ginn, 1993.
Long, Tall, Short and Hairy Poems. London, Hodder, 1996.

Editor, *What's Time to a Pig and Other Stories* (with teacher's notes). Belfast, Northern Ireland Centre for Learning Resources, 1991.
Editor, *Today & Yesterday: A Selection of Stories from BBC Northern Ireland Schools' Radio* (with teacher's notes), illustrated by Liam McComish. Belfast, Northern Ireland Centre for Learning Resources, 1992.
Editor, *People, Places & Ideas: A Selection of Stories from BBC Northern Ireland Schools' Radio* (with teacher's notes). Belfast, Northern Ireland Centre for Learning Resources, 1993.

*

Media Adaptations: *The Ghosts of Hungryhouse Lane* (sound recording), G.K. Hall, 1991; *Jimmy Zest* (sound recording), Chivers Audio Books, 1993.

Sam McBratney comments:

When my first book was published in 1976, I had no idea that I would go on and write so many others. To see them set out in a list like that quite amazes me.

Children often ask me why do I write books. It sounds like an easy question, but actually it isn't, and each time I am asked I give a different answer. This could mean that I don't really know why I write books, but it's more likely that there are lots and lots of reasons and that I haven't thought of them all yet.

I put a lot of it down to an over-active brain! My head never gives me peace, and although I'm very happy being who I am, I love wondering what life would be like if I were somebody else, or in a different place. I like to tell children that we all have an imagination. An imagination is your very own friendly monster. I try to keep mine well fed on books and ideas. *You* can feed yours by reading, and also by writing your own stories. You'll have a lot of fun, and one day you might get some of them published.

* * *

Sam McBratney is one of the most accomplished writers for children in Ireland in the late 1990s. His first book *Mark Time,* though written in the late sixties, was only published in 1976 after "the Troubles" broke out. It is an attempt to write for and about teenagers living the reality of the strife in Northern Ireland. Since that first publication he has written more than seventy titles for children across the complete age range, from international best-selling picture book *Guess How Much I Love You* to *Put a Saddle on the Pig,* a deeply moving young adult novel. He is particularly adept at writing bright, funny, shining texts for the young first time reader or the just established reader. McBratney told Pat Donlon "my views on books and children is that children in schools are given books which are too difficult for them. It happens with Dickens, Shakespeare, and Heaney and at all other levels as well.... [E]njoyment of a book is what comes first—would you be turned on by something that was difficult to read?"

McBratney's style is never difficult or boring, writing as he does with a breezy, individual style that is both funny and assured. His characters are convincing and familiar and stories like *The Thursday Creature* are constructed and written in such a way that the reluctant reader would be hooked without feeling patronised or looked down upon. McBratney is a master of the first line, that hook which catches a reader and holds them for the rest of the book. His books have featured such beginnings as: "Fear is catching. Did you know that?"; "There are times when mothers can be strange and impulsive creatures"; "There are good monsters, there are monsters who are not so good and there are monsters who are downright pests"; and "Apart from the smile he wore, the stranger was unarmed."

In *Something Big* we meet Ben Dubarry, who has made the longest painting in his class. This painting includes everybody who is important in Ben's life: all his friends, family, and teachers, with one exception—Rosalind Cruickshank. "After thinking deeply for some moments," however, Ben "saw what he must do," and he found space in his drawing between a passing cloud and his dad's crash helmet for his pencilled-in "spider woman." But Ben is no saint, for we learn that "he drew her quite small".

In *The Lough Neagh Monster,* McBratney tells of the time Nessy, the Lough Ness Monster, decides to visit her cousin Noblett, the Lough Neagh Monster, and misbehaves. This tale is a perfect vehicle for the author's off-beat and slightly zany sense of humour. "It wasn't long before the headlines began IS THERE A PLESIOSAUR IN LOUGH NEAGH? asked *The Irish Times* or A DINOSAUR CHEWED MY OAR SAYS BOATMAN wrote *The Belfast Telegraph.* People began to take notice, officials in the tourist board licked their lips and thought about flocks of American tourists." A real treat for the beginner reader is *Francis Fry Private Eye* and *Francis Fry and the O.T.G.,* which introduce us to the laconic, slick sleuth Francis Fry—a latter day Humphrey

Bogart who solves mystery after mystery whilst chewing liquorice, and turning to us from time to time to urge "Think about it".

Put a Saddle on the Pig is a *tour de force,* a double-sided narrative of a watershed moment in the lives of Laura and Victoria Clements, mother and daughter. So well depicted are the characters and the emotional dilemma they face that it is impossible to read the book without being torn in two, now siding with the young adult, now with her mother. There is a deep vein of pity and melancholy throughout this book despite, McBratney's humorous garnishes. Only in the end, when both have suffered and made sacrifices, do they reach a peaceful solution, one that finds Laura decidedly more mature.

McBratney is a distinctively Irish writer in his use of language and many of his books have an Irish setting. Apart from *Mark Time,* however, he has not sought to explain his troubled land through his books, believing that writers should be careful of "tackling the raw aspects of life here without being able to call upon the complete range of adult concepts which help us make sense of what is happening. Themes involving violence, bigotry, sex, religion and death are bound to be tricky territory for writers of children's books." Despite this caveat McBratney in *The Chieftain's Daughter* has written a most powerful historical novel with an Irish setting. This novel is set at the time of the first Christian missionaries to Ireland and is written in a sparse and mythic style. It is a story within a story both complex and moving despite its stark, simple style. The story is uncovered layer by layer by the old Chief Dinn Keene recounts his tale for Patrick of the Pens, the great man of speech. When he was but a boy, Dinn Keene was brought to a village by the priest Corag Mor, whom we learn is someone whose face "was always on guard in case his lips were surprised by that warm, too human thing called a smile." The message of this story has a resonance in Ireland today, where people still live with the consequences of a feud that, once started, "becomes a thing apart—it selects its own victims and you have no control over it."

It is somewhat ironic that having served his young readers well for over twenty years with his thoughtful and insightful writings, it was a picture book which brought him international fame and recognition. The concept behind *Guess How Much I Love You* is simple, universal and timeless. Generations of people, young and old, have played the game of seeking to measure and compete in expressing the extent of their love. In alternating double-page spreads, sensitively illustrated by Anita Jeram, Little Nutbrown Hare and Big Nutbrown Hare playfully compete in physical feats to mark the boundaries of their love. Finally, sleepy and contented with his declaration "I love you right up to the MOON" and Big Nutbrown Hare's response "Oh, that's far. that is very far," the little hare falls asleep. But the last word goes to Big Nutbrown Hare as he whispers "I love you right up to the MOON AND BACK."

McBratney is an author of many moods and *the Caterpillow Fight* finds him at his most playful. It too is an end of day story:

"When the caterpillars went / to their caterpillar beds / They all had caterpillows / for their caterpillar heads." A caterpillow fight ends in a flurry of feathers with big caterpillar arriving on the scene uttering the immortal admonition, "This caterpillar laughing will end in caterpillar tears."

—Pat Donlon

McCAUGHREN, Tom

Nationality: Irish. **Born:** Ballymena, County Antrim, Northern Ireland, 11 August 1936. **Education:** Ballymena Technical High School, 1949-51; Millar's Academy, Ballymena, 1952-53. **Family:** Married Frances Byrne in 1970; four daughters. **Career:** Reporter, Dungannon *Courier and News,* County Tyrone, 1954, Ballymena *Weekly Telegraph* and Belfast *Telegraph,* 1954-55; reporter and defence correspondent, *Irish Times,* Dublin, 1955-68. Reporter, 1968-75, assistant news editor, 1975-76, and since 1977 security correspondent, RTE Radio and Television, Dublin. **Awards:** Reading Association of Ireland Children's Book award, 1985; Irish Book award, 1987; Irish Children's Book Trust Book of the Decade Award (1980-1990); Oscar Wilde Literary Recognition Award, 1992. **Address:** c/o The Children's Press, 90 Lower Baggot Street, Dublin 2, Ireland.

Publications for Children

Fiction

The Legend of the Golden Key, illustrated by Terry Myler. Dublin, Children's Press, 1983.

The Legend of the Phantom Highwayman, illustrated by Terry Myler. Dublin, Children's Press, 1983.

Run with the Wind, illustrated by Jeanette Dunne. Dublin, Wolfhound Press, 1983.

The Legend of the Corrib King, illustrated by Terry Myler. Dublin, Children's Press, 1984.

Run to Earth, illustrated by Jeanette Dunne. Dublin, Wolfhound Press, 1984.

The Children of the Forge, illustrated by Terry Myler. Dublin, Children's Press, 1985.

Run Swift, Run Free, illustrated by Jeanette Dunne. Dublin, Wolfhound Press, 1986.

The Silent Sea, illustrated by Terry Myler. Dublin, Children's Press, 1987.

Rainbows of the Moon. Dublin, Anvil Books, 1989.

Run to the Ark. Dublin, Wolfhound Press, 1991.

Run Wild. Dublin, Wolfhound Press, 1993.

Run to the Wild Wood, illustrated by Jeannette Dunne. Dublin, Wolfhound, 1996.

Other

The Peacemakers of Niemba. Dublin, Browne and Nolan, 1966.

*

Tom McCaughren comments:

For many years a gap existed in Irish literature. For some rea son children's fiction had virtually ceased to be produced. Th few children's books that were being produced were being pub lished elsewhere. It was for that reason that I began writin children's fiction. Other writers had also come to notice this laps in our literary tradition, and in 1981, with the help of the Ar Council, the first children's books in many years began to appea My first book, *The Legend of the Golden Key,* was published 1983, and like several of those that were to follow, was an adve ture story involving some aspect of our history or folklore. I had also noticed that while good wildlife fiction had been produced elsewhere, it had not appeared in Ireland. And so came my three books on the fox. With them, my books took on an international dimension, as editions have now appeared in other countries and other languages.

* * *

Since he began writing for children in 1983, Tom McCaughren has become one of the most popular and successful of Irish children's writers. His works can be divided into two separate categories, his adventure stories and his wildlife trilogy. His first book *The Legend of the Golden Key* and its sequels *The Legend of the Phantom Highwayman* and *The Legend of the Corrib King* are lively adventure stories which were published in a short uniform format. Despite this limitation, however, their contemporary portrayal of the traditional adventure story was a welcome addition to the Irish scene. A distinctive feature of these books is their affectionate sense of people and places. This helps to stimulate in children an interest in their local environment and folk tradition at a time when they are particularly receptive. The first two are set in McCaughren's home area of County Antrim and the third in the west of Ireland. *The Children of the Forge* is very much in the same style. Its slightly greater length allows more scope for a variety of themes to be introduced. An added international dimension to this story draws on McCaughren's experience in Lebanon as security correspondent for Irish television.

It was with the first volume of his wildlife trilogy *Run with the Wind* that McCaughren received serious critical attention. This book perfectly exemplifies the best of the genre. It is the story of a fox colony fighting for survival, told vividly and unsentimentally. The personalities of the individual foxes are carefully drawn, yet they remain true to their animal natures. The later volumes *Run to Earth* and *Run Swift, Run Free* further develop the characters and give us a picture of the animal world that is particularly detailed and fascinating. These books provide a thoughtful and thought-provoking picture of the environment. They are written in a style that flows easily and fluently; McCaughren never allows his detailed knowledge of and obvious commitment to the environment to overwhelm his story.

His latest book, *The Silent Sea,* is a return to the adventure story and is his most successful to date in this genre. In all of McCaughren's books the place and ambience are captured most skilfully, but in none is the landscape and wildlife more evocatively drawn. The plot is plausible, contemporary, and relevant and he introduces us to an engaging and well-drawn cast of characters. As increasing international recognition shows, McCaughren is developing as a skilful and confident writer.

—Sheila Flanagan

McCLOSKEY, (John) Robert

Nationality: American. **Born:** Hamilton, Ohio, 15 September 1914. **Education:** Vesper George Art School, Boston, 1932-34; National Academy of Design, New York (President's award, 1936), 1934-36; American Academy in Rome (fellow), 1939. **Military Service:** United States Army Infantry, 1942-45; Sergeant. **Family:** Married Margaret Durand in 1940; two daughters. **Career:** Artist and illustrator; sculpted a bas relief in Hamilton, 1935, and painted a mural in Boston. Group shows: National Academy and Tiffany Foundation, both New York; Society of Independent Artists, Boston. **Awards:** American Library Association Caldecott Medal, 1942, 1958; Catholic Library Association Regina Medal, 1974; D.Litt.: Miami University, Oxford, Ohio, 1964; Mount Holyoke College, South Hadley, Massachusetts, 1967; University of Maine, 1990. **Address:** Little Deer Isle, Maine 04650, U.S.A.

Publications for Children (illustrated by the author)

Fiction

Lentil. New York, Viking Press, 1940.
Make Way for Ducklings. New York, Viking Press, 1941; Oxford, Blackwell, 1944.
Homer Price. New York, Viking Press, 1943; London, Penguin, 1976.
Blueberries for Sal. New York, Viking Press, 1948; London, Angus and Robertson, 1967.
Centerburg Tales. New York, Viking Press, 1951; abridged edition, as *More Homer Price,* New York, Scholastic, 1963.
One Morning in Maine. New York, Viking Press, 1952; London, Penguin, 1976.
Time of Wonder. New York, Viking Press, 1957; London, Penguin, 1977.
Burt Dow, Deep-Water Man. New York, Viking Press, 1963.

*

Manuscript Collection: May Massee Collection, Emporia State University, Kansas.

Illustrator: *Yankee Doodle's Cousins* by Anne Burnett Malcolmson, 1941; *Tree Toad* by Robert Hobart Davis, 1942; *The Man Who Lost His Head* by Claire Huchet Bishop, 1942; *Trigger John's Son* by Tom Robinson, 1949; *Journey Cake, Ho!* by Ruth Sawyer, 1953; *Junket* by Anne H. White, 1955; *Henry Reed, Inc.,* 1955, *Henry Reed's Journey,* 1963, *Henry Reed's Baby-Sitting Service,* 1966, and *Henry Reed's Big Show,* 1970, all by Keith Robertson.

* * *

I once read a fifth-grade book report that ended with the sentence: "Robert McCloskey is a Yankee Doodle Dandy of a writer." And I thought then, and think now, that no other author for children over the past 50 years fits that description so well.

The fifth grader was writing about the book *Homer Price,* a story of a boy growing up in the small midwestern American town of McCloskey's boyhood 70 years ago. There is a lot of McCloskey in Homer, who loves to invent and tinker with all sorts of gadgets, and in Lentil, his other boy hero, who loves to play the harmonica. Like Twain's Tom Sawyer, McCloskey's boys have the knack of getting themselves into and out of fantastic adventures and misadventures. The incidents in these books are authentically shaped out of actual experience and touched with the gentle humor of a grown-up's remembrance. As McCloskey says of his work: "I have one foot resting on reality and the other foot planted firmly on a banana peel."

McCloskey's stories also have the distinct quality of the grand exaggeration and broad humor that one finds in the tall tales of traditional American folklore. The episode of the doughnut machine in *Homer Price* is as well-known to American children today as any of the adventures of folk characters like Paul Bunyan and Pecos Bill, and it would seem as much at home in a collection of American folklore as it would in an anthology of fiction. James Daugherty found McCloskey's "boy" books to be "America laughing at itself with a broad and genial humanity, without bitterness or sourness or sophistication." Through these books young readers today and in the future can be in touch with the folk America of their grandparents and great-grandparents.

McCloskey's picture books for younger children usually grow out of real incidents that have occurred in actual families, either his own, as in *One Morning in Maine, Blueberries for Sal,* and *Time of Wonder,* or that of Mr. and Mrs. Mallard in *Make Way for Ducklings.* These books have won great acclaim for the illustrations, but one should not overlook the writing. McCloskey, like Daugherty and Kate Seredy, was one of those illustrators who, at the urging of that remarkable children's editor May Massee, discovered that he had a talent for writing as well as for drawing. And he brought to that writing the same painstaking integrity that marks his illustration. As he says: "It's a good feeling to be able to put down a line and know that it's right."

In the picture books McCloskey usually employs a straightforward matter-of-fact style, except for *Time of Wonder,* which is more like a prose poem, uniquely written in second-person narrative. Though he admittedly "thinks in pictures," McCloskey's stories are always skillfully tuned for the ear, so that they are particularly suited for reading aloud. They are also especially suited for the young child because they are full of gentle wisdom and reassurance, while always focussing on what's right in the world.

In almost 50 years of writing and illustrating books for children McCloskey has not once produced anything that is not of the highest quality. To repeat my fifth-grade friend, he is indeed "a Yankee Doodle Dandy of a writer."

—James E. Higgins

McCORD, David (Thompson Watson)

Nationality: American. **Born:** New York City, 15 November 1897. **Education:** Lincoln High School, Portland, Oregon, graduated 1917; Harvard University, Cambridge, Massachusetts, A.B. in physics 1921, A.M. in romance languages 1922. **Military Service:** Served in the Field Artillery, United States Army, 1918: Second Lieutenant. **Career:** Associate editor, 1923-25, and editor, 1940-46, *Harvard Alumni Bulletin;* member of the drama staff, Boston *Evening Transcript,* 1923-28. Executive director, Harvard Fund Council, 1925-63; Phi Beta Kappa Poet, Harvard University, 1938, Tufts College, Medford, Massachusetts, 1938 and 1978, College of William and Mary, Williamsburg, Virginia, 1950, Massachusetts Institute of Technology, Cambridge, 1973, and Colby College, Waterville, Maine, 1979; lecturer, Lowell Institute, Boston, 1950; staff member, Bread Loaf Writers Conference, Vermont, 1958, 1960, 1962, 1964; Instructor in Creative Writing, Harvard University, summers 1963, 1965, 1966; Visiting Professor, Framingham State College, Massachusetts, 1974; councilor, Harvard Society of Advanced Study and Research, 1967-72; member, Overseers' Visiting Committee, Department of Astronomy, Harvard University. Painter: several individual shows of water colors. Honorary member, Phi Beta Kappa, 1938; honorary life associate, Dudley House, Harvard University; honorary member, Senior Common Room, Lowell House, Harvard University. **Awards:** New England Poetry Club Golden Rose, 1941; William Rose Benét award, 1952; Guggenheim fellowship, 1954; American Academy grant, 1961; Sarah Josepha Hale award, 1962; Miriam Kallen award, 1976; National Council of Teachers of English award, for verse, 1977; Littauer Foundation grant, 1983; Harvard Medal, 1984. Litt.D.: Northeastern University, Boston, 1954; University of New Brunswick, Fredericton, 1963; Williams College, Williamstown, Massachusetts, 1971; Keene State College, New Hampshire, 1983; Skidmore College, Saratoga Springs, New York, 1986; LL.D.: Washington and Jefferson College, Washington, Pennsylvania, 1955; L.H.D.: Harvard University, 1956; Colby College, 1968; Framingham State College, 1975; Fitchburg State College, Massachusetts, 1986; Art.D.: New England College, Henniker, New Hampshire, 1956; Ed.D.: Suffolk University, Boston, 1979; D.C.L.: Simmons College, Boston, 1983. Fellow, American Academy of Arts and Sciences; Benjamin Franklin fellow, Royal Society of Arts, London. **Died:** May 1997.

PUBLICATIONS FOR CHILDREN

Poetry

Far and Few, illustrated by Henry B. Kane. Boston, Little Brown, 1952.

Take Sky (single poem). Privately printed, 1961.

Take Sky (collection), illustrated by Henry B. Kane. Boston, Little Brown, 1962.

Books Fall Open (bookmark). New York, Children's Book Council, 1964.

All Day Long, illustrated by Henry B. Kane. Boston, Little Brown, 1966.

Every Time I Climb a Tree, illustrated by Marc Simont. Boston, Little Brown, 1967.

For Me to Say, illustrated by Henry B. Kane. Boston, Little Brown, 1970.

Mr. Bidery's Spidery Garden, illustrated by Henry B. Kane. London, Harrap, 1972.

Pen, Paper and Poem. New York, Holt Rinehart, 1973.

Away and Ago, illustrated by Leslie Morrill. Boston, Little Brown, 1974.

The Star in the Pail, illustrated by Marc Simont. Boston, Little Brown, 1975.

One at a Time: His Collected Poems for the Young, illustrated by Henry B. Kane. Boston, Little Brown, 1977.

Speak Up, illustrated by Marc Simont. Boston, Little Brown, 1980.

All Small, illustrated by Madelaine Gill Linden. Boston, Little Brown, 1986.

Recordings: *The Pickety Fence and 51 Other Poems,* Pathways of Sound.

Publications for Adults

Short Story

The Camp at Lockjaw. New York, Doubleday, 1952.

Play

Alice in Botolphland. Boston, St. Botolph Club, 1932.

Poetry (includes broadsheets)

Floodgate. Cambridge, Massachusetts, Washburn and Thomas, 1927.
Oxford Nearly Visited: A Fantasy. Cambridge, Massachusetts, Cygnet Press, 1929.
Fiftieth Anniversary Ode. Boston, St. Botolph Club, 1930.
Chocorua. Privately printed, 1932.
The Crows. New York, Scribner, 1934.
Bay Window Ballads. New York, Scribner, 1935.
The Stretch. Privately printed, 1937.
Twelve Verses from XII Night. Privately printed, 1938.
The Knowing. Privately printed, 1938.
Reflection in Blue. Privately printed, 1939.
And What's More. New York, Coward McCann, 1941.
The Legend of St. Botolph. Privately printed, 1942.
Christmas 1943. Privately printed, 1943.
On Occasion. Cambridge, Massachusetts, Harvard University Press, 1943.
Remembrance of Things Passed. Boston, Club of Odd Volumes, 1947.
Midway in This Middle Year of the Twentieth Century. Privately printed, 1950.
A Star by Day. New York, Doubleday, 1950.
Poet Always Next But One. Williamsburg, Virginia, College of William and Mary, 1951.
Blue Reflections on the Merchants Limited. Boston, Club of Odd Volumes, 1952.
The Old Bateau and Other Poems. Boston, Little Brown, 1953.
Ten Limericks. Privately printed, 1953.
Odds Without Ends. Boston, Little Brown, 1954.
By Swancote Pool. Privately printed, 1954.
Whereas to Mr. Franklin. Boston, Old South Association, 1954.
60 Lines for Three-Score Hatch. Boston, India Wharf Rats Club, 1957.
Sonnets to Baedecker. Meriden, Connecticut, Meriden Gravure Company, 1965.
In Memory of Sir Winston Churchill, 25 January 1965. Privately printed, 1965.
H.R.H. H.H.R. Privately printed, 1965.
Observation Tower. Boston, Club of Odd Volumes, 1966.
Roland Hayes. Privately printed, 1967.
Poem for the Occasion. Boston, Colonial Society of Massachusetts, 1970.
Spree Fever. Privately printed, 1970.
Thomas Dudley Cabot. Privately printed, 1972.
R.R.: Lines, Sharp as Serifs, on the By-Passing of His Ninetieth Birthday. Privately printed, 1973.
Sestina for the Queen. Boston, Bostonian Society, 1976.
The Children's World. Privately printed, 1979.

Other

Oddly Enough (essays). Cambridge, Massachusetts, Washburn and Thomas, 1926.
Stirabout (essays). Cambridge, Massachusetts, Washburn and Thomas, 1928.
H.T.P.: Portrait of a Critic (on Henry Taylor Parker). New York, Coward McCann, 1935.
Notes on the Harvard Tercentenary. Cambridge, Massachusetts, Harvard University Press, 1936.
An Acre for Education, Being Notes on the History of Radcliffe College. Cambridge, Massachusetts, Radcliffe College, 1938; revised edition, 1954, 1958, 1963.
About Boston: Sight, Sound, Flavor and Inflection, illustrated by the author. New York, Doubleday, 1948.
...as Built with Second Thoughts. Boston, Centennial Commission of the Boston Public Library, 1953.
The Related Man. Boston, American Academy of Arts and Sciences, 1953.
David McCord's Oregon. Boston, Massachusetts Historical Society, 1959.
On the Frontier of Understanding (address). Fredericton, University of New Brunswick, 1959.
The Language of Request: Fishing with a Barbless Hook (essays). Washington, D.C., American Alumni Council, 1961.
The Fabrick of Man: Fifty Years of the Peter Bent Brigham Hospital. Boston, Hospital Celebration Committee, 1963.
In Sight of Sever: Essays from Harvard. Cambridge, Massachusetts, Harvard University Press, 1963.
Art and Education (lecture), with David B. Little and Sinclair H. Hitchings. Boston, Boston Public Library, 1966.
Children and Poetry (lecture). Chicago, University of Chicago Press, 1966.
Notes from Four Cities 1927-1953. Worcester, Massachusetts, A.J. St. Onge, 1969.
Celebration: 1925-1975 (history of Harvard College Fund). Privately printed, 1975.

Editor, *Once and For All* (essays). New York, Coward McCann, 1929.
Editor, *What Cheer: An Anthology of American and British Humorous and Witty Verse.* New York, Coward McCann, 1945; as *The Pocket Book of Humorous Verse,* New York, Pocket Books, 1946; as *The Modern Treasury of Humorous Verse,* New York, Doubleday, 1951.
Editor, *Bibliotheca Medica: Physician for Tomorrow.* Boston, Harvard Medical School, 1966.
Editor, *New England Revisited,* by Arthur Griffin. Boston, Houghton Mifflin, 1966.
Editor, *Stow Wengenroth's New England.* Barre, Massachusetts, Barre Publishers, 1969.

*

Manuscript Collections: Boston Public Library; Houghton Library, Harvard University, Cambridge, Massachusetts; and other collections.

David McCord comments:

Giving a rather long talk to a group of children's librarians gathered at the University of Chicago a dozen years ago, I was forced to come to grips with myself over the natural question: Why does one write for children? The most generous and general answer, I suppose, is simply: Why not? But perhaps I had a special reason.

For me the small years, as Frank Kendon calls them, were never lonely, though I had neither brother nor sister nor much of anyone to play with. Childhood, and even most of my boyhood, marred by recurring malaria but not by the resulting large amount of solitude and freedom from school, left me with time to read, work with my hands, and raise chickens. I very early built and operated, with unmalarial fever, a licensed wireless telegraph station, not unaware that the dot-dash code itself is language of pure rhythm and a kind of haunting poetry in isolation. Above all, I soon became a countryman at heart: learned to look on the sky with as much affection as on the land; to walk in silence, listen, notice things and to explore with almost equal young delight the wonders of the backyard or the wilderness. That is literally true, for I began all this in Woodmere on Long Island, New York, adjacent to a poultry farm, and finished it out west beside the wild Rogue River on my uncle's ranch in Oregon: a slice of frontier life as yet unvanished, where a boy could pan for gold for pocket money, with little chance to spend it. Thrill enough it was to have it weighed out on the big brass scales of an old bank in a town about as old as 1849.

I read and was read to aloud. And into the far west I took remembrance of my Presbyterian grandmother Reed's lovely voice and the rhythm of the King James version of the Bible. My own reading wavered on another kind of scale between the Oz books, Dickens, Ralph Henry Barbour, Mark Twain, Jules Verne; Lear, Carroll, and Gilbert; W.W. Jacobs, Jack London, and such. I also read three equally indispensable magazines: *St. Nicholas,* Gernsback's *Modern Electrics,* and *The Reliable Poultry Journal.* By the time I was 10 I had read five or six books by the New Brunswick writer, Charles G.D. Roberts, from cover to cover. I still consider *Red Fox* one of the two greatest animal stories ever written. The other one for me—of course, years later—is *Tarka the Otter* by Henry Williamson. Another thing: because I was read aloud to when very young, I came to love the sound of words as well as the look of them on paper.

I began to write verse when I was 15, and verse for children when just out of Graduate School at Harvard. Now, some 400 poems-for-children later, I dare to offer one or two rules for the conduct of this seemingly simple but dangerously abstruse art.

First, just be a child before you grow up and let nothing interfere with the process. Write it all *out* of yourself and *for* yourself as you remember that weasel body with the eagle eyes. Next, never take the phrase "writing verse *for* children" seriously. If you write *for* them you are lost. Ask your brain's computer what you know about a child's mind and what goes on inside it. The answer is zero. What do they think of this calamitous new world which you don't even pretend to understand? They do not compare it with the past. It is the only world they know. Don't ever even pretend you are *looking* at the young; just make sure the young are *looking* at you. Make your readers believe you are letting them into your own dark life, into your own serene confusion, not you into theirs. Never talk down; and if for weeks at a time you have absolutely nothing to say, fight the uphill fight and do not say it.

* * *

David McCord has often been called an acrobat with language—an apt description of this poet whose verses are filled with surprising rhythm and sound effects and inventive rhyming twists, all done with acrobatic grace and playfulness. Typical of McCord, for instance, is the characterization of a little bat as not "flight able" (to rhyme with "gable"); and description of three flying geese as making a V "with two in the caboose and one in the/a-po-gee"; and a combination of poem and picture in which a dangling rope and long narrow line of print force the reader to read up the page about the grasshopper who is climbing up out of a well (all three poems in *Far and Few*).

A playful tone permeates almost all of the poems, whatever the subject matter, because exploration of the textures of language is so paramount an aim for this poet. Remembering this, one can still group the subjects loosely into five major categories: 1) poems about small creatures—a newt, bats, frogs, crickets, ants, and many others; 2) poems written in the first person about the thoughts and feelings of a child who is flying kites, fishing, eating, drawing pictures, skating, taking castor oil, going to the dentist, making a snowman, jumping in autumn leaves—all in the course of daily living indoors and out; 3) a few poems for or about children, written from the vantage point of an adult looking back; 4) poems primarily of language exploration and word play ("You *know* the word *cathedral,*/How about *Tetartohedral?*" from "The Look and Sound of Words" in *For Me to Say*); 5) two groups of poems, in *Take Sky* and *For Me to Say,* demonstrating the writing of 10 verse-forms, beginning with couplet and ending with haiku.

It is interesting to note which poems—out of this array of more than 200—are most often reprinted by anthologists and writers of children's literature texts. My informal survey indicates that there are two top favorites, appearing over and over again: the chant about the pickety fence from "Five Chants" and "This Is My Rock" (both in *Far and Few*). The chant catches the pickety, lickety sounds and the quick, brittle rhythm of the childhood game of running along and clicking a stick on a fence. This is one of the simpler language-play poems, easy to read without stumbling on rhythm or syntax. "This Is My Rock" is also an easily read poem, but serious in tone and without word-play. In fact, it is one of the least typical of McCord's poems. In it a child simply speaks about a rock where he likes to sit and watch the sun and sky and the coming of the evening. Are these two poems first choices because of their simplicity and readability, as well as their charm? Children undoubtedly turn away from many of the more complex poems because of the language difficulties—unless, of course, an adult is helping with the interpretation. What, for instance, is an uninitiated child to make of the tricky algebra here (from "Exit *x*" in *For Me to Say*):

> If *vex*
> is *x*2, <EIUC0%24>ex<DC255%0>
> will equal one-no-three.

Also difficult are lines like these from the poem "O-U-G-H" in *All Day Long:* "Supposing *Though's not tho,* but more like *thoff,*/ and *sough's sow's* not a pig that sows, but *soff?*"

McCord should be read aloud to young children who are just discovering him—read aloud by adults who enjoy the rhythms and won't trip up on the word-play. A good book to begin on is *Every Time I Climb a Tree,* a collection of 25 of the earlier poems, produced as a picture book with large bright water-color illustrations. Here are not only "This Is My Rock", the pickety fence poem, and the grasshopper poem mentioned earlier, but two short ones that show McCord at his best in the game of inventing rhymes: "Glowworm" with its rhyming "knowworm", "down belowworm", "slowworm", and "Helloworm!"; and "I Want You to Meet" in which "Lady-bug" is rhymed with "Sadiebug," "Mrs. Gradybug," "oldmaidybug," and "fraidybug." Also there are winter poems, food poems (one especially for lovers of bananas and cream), Halloween and Christmas poems, and of course the title poem about pleasures of climbing a tree (good for ants though not for pants). Almost all are just for fun and surprise and present little reading difficulty. Not strictly for fun are "This Is My Rock" and the five-line poem "Cocoon," perhaps even more moving for adults than for children, about the little caterpillar who has three good tries before it dies.

Another collection of earlier poems for the youngest readers is *The Star in the Pail,* this one also colorfully illustrated and presented as a picture book. Here, too, are easily read poems. Most readers, however, would probably vote for *Every Time I Climb a Tree*—so full of old favorites—if a choice had to be made between the two collections.

Though a great many of McCord's poems have been in print for over 40 years, few of them are what contemporary children might consider old-fashioned. True, there's the reference (in "The Trouble Was Simply That" in *For Me to Say*) to a boy's hat with its good crown and lining and brim. "*What?*" a boy today might wonder. And readers who are girls might wish there were more girls in the poems, and might even take offense at the attitude toward girls revealed in the lines "Little boys out for trout,/Little girls flumped about" (from "Dr. Klimwell's Fall" in *Take Sky*). But wit with words is for both girls and boys and does not go out of date. McCord's ingenious and crisp inventions will doubtless go on pleasing readers for years to come. Might as well expect Edward Lear to move into oblivion.

Now that McCord's recent death has brought to an end his long and productive career, it is perhaps unrealistic to hope that unpublished manuscripts will be found and brought into print. But there may be new editions in paper, and already readers can enjoy the 1992 small paperback of one of the favorite collections: *All Day Long: Fifty Rhymes of the Never Was and Always Is* (Little, Brown). "Always Is"—just the write words for David McCord

—Claudia Lewis

MCCULLY, Emily Arnold

Nationality: American. **Born:** Emily Arnold, Galesburg, Illinois, 1 July 1939. **Education:** Brown University, A.B. 1961; Columbia University, M.A. 1964. **Family:** Married George McCully in 1961 (divorced 1975); two sons. **Career:** Freelance magazine and advertising artist, 1961-67; illustrator of books for children, from 1966; writer, from 1975. Teacher of workshops at Brown University, Boston University, St. Clements, Cummington Community of the Arts, and Rockland Center for the Arts. **Awards:** Gold medal, Philadelphia Art Directors, 1968; Showcase Title citation, Children's Book Council, 1972, for *Hurray for Captain Jane!*; Art Books for Children citation, Brooklyn Museum and New York Public Library, for *MA nDA LA*; Juvenile Award, Council of Wisconsin Writers, 1979, for *Edward Troy and the Witch Cat*; National Endowment for the Arts grant in creative writing, 1980; New York State Council on Arts fiction grant, 1982; American Book Award nomination, 1983, for *A Craving*; Best Book of the Year citation, *School Library Journal,* 1984, American Library Association Notable Book citation, 1984, Christopher Award, 1985, and inclusion in International Biennale at Bratislava, 1985, all for *Picnic*; Caldecott Medal, and *New York Times* Ten Best Illustrated Books citation, both 1993, for *Mirette on the High Wire.* **Agent:** Harriet Wasserman, Literary Agency, Inc., 137 East 36th Street, New York, New York 10016. **Address:** 3 Washington Square Village, New York, New York 10012, U.S.A.

Publications for Children

Fiction (illustrated by the author)

The Playground. New York, Golden, 1983.
Picnic. New York, Harper, 1985.
First Snow. New York, Harper, 1985.
The Show Must Go On. Racine, Wisconsin, Western Publishing, 1987.
School. New York, Harper, 1987.
New Baby. New York, Harper, 1988.
Christmas Gift. New York, Harper, 1988.
You Lucky Duck! Racine, Wisconsin, Western Publishing, 1988.
The Grandma Mixup. New York, Harper,1988.
Zaza's Big Break. New York, HarperCollins, 1989.
The Evil Spell. New York, HarperCollins, 1990.
Grandmas at the Lake. New York, HarperCollins, 1990.
Speak Up, Blanche! New York, HarperCollins, 1991.
Mirette on the High Wire. New York, Putnam, 1992.
Grandmas at Bat. New York, HarperCollins, 1993.
Crossing the New Bridge. New York, Putnam, 1994.
My Real Family. San Diego, Harcourt, 1994.
Little Kit, or The Industrious Flea Circus Girl. New York, Dial, 1995.
The Pirate Queen. New York, Putnam, 1995.
The Ballot Box Battle. New York, Knopf, 1996.
The Bobbin Girl. New York, Dial, 1996.
Starring Mirette & Bellini. New York, Putnam, 1997.
Popcorn at the Palace. San Diego, Harcourt, 1997.
Beautiful Warrior. New York, Arthur A. Levine Books, 1998.
Kung Fu Nun. New York, Scholastic, 1998.
An Outlaw Thanksgiving. New York, Dial, 1998.

Publications for Adults

Fiction

"How's Your Vacuum Cleaner Working?" (short story), in *The O. Henry Collection: Best Short Stories.* New York, Doubleday, 1976.
A Craving. New York, Avon, 1982.
Life Drawing. New York, Delacorte and Dell, 1987.

*

Media Adaptations: "Picnic," in *Max's Chocolate Chicken and Other Stories for Young Children* (video), Weston Woods Studios, 1993.

Biography: Entry in *Something about the Author,* Vol. 76, Detroit, Gale, 1994.

Critical Studies: Review of *Mirette on the High Wire,* in *Horn Book,* October 1992; review of *Mirette on the High Wire* by Jean Van Leeuwen, in *New York Times Book Review,* 8 November 1992.

Illustrator: *Sea Beach Express* by George Panetta, 1966; *The Seventeenth Street Gang* by Emily Cheney Neville, 1966; *Rex* by Marjorie W. Sharmat, 1967; *Luigi of the Streets* by Natalie S. Carlson, 1967; *That Mean Man* by Liesel M. Skorpen, 1968; *Gooney* by Barbara Borack, 1968; *Animals in Field and Laboratory: Science Project in Animal Behavior* by Seymour Simon, 1968; *Journey from Peppermint Street* by Meindert De Jong, 1968; *The Mouse and the Elephant* by Barbara K. Wheeler and Naki Tezel, New York, 1969; *The Fisherman* by Jan Wahl, 1969; *Tales from the Rue Broca* by Pierre Gripari, translated by Doriane Grutman, 1969; *Here I Am! An Anthology of Poems Written by Young People in Some of America's Minority Groups* edited by Virginia O. Baron, 1969; *Twin Spell* by Janet Louise and Swoboda Lunn, 1969; *Hobo Toad and the Motorcycle Gang* by Jane H. Yolen, 1970; *Slip! Slop! Gobble!* and *The Cat and the Parrot* by Jeanne B. Hardendorff, 1970; *Friday Night Is Papa Night* by Ruth A. Sonneborn, 1970; *Maxie,* 1970, and *When Violet Died,* 1973, by Mildred Kantrowitz; *Steffie and Me* by Phyllis M. Hoffman, 1970; *Go and Hush the Baby* by Betsy Byars, 1971; *Finders Keepers* by Alix Shulman, 1971; *MA nDA LA,* 1971, *Black Is Brown Is Tan,* 1973, *Where Wild Willie,* 1978, by Arnold Adoff; *Hurray for Captain Jane!* by Sam Reavin, 1971; *Michael Is Brave* by Helen E. Buckley, 1971; *Finding Out with Your Senses* by Seymour Simon, 1971; *Henry's Pennies* by Louise McNamara, 1972; *Jane's Blanket* by Arthur Miller, 1972; *Grandpa's Long Red Underwear* by Lynn Schoettle, 1972; *Girls Can Too!* by Lee Bennett Hopkins, 1972; *The Boyhood of Grace Jones,* 1972, and *Her Majesty, Grace Jones,* 1974, by Jane Langton; *Isabelle the Itch* by Constance C. Greene, 1973; *That New Boy* by Mary Lystad, 1973; *How to Eat Fried Worms* by Thomas Rockwell, 1973; *Jenny's Revenge* by Anne Norris Baldwin, 1974; *Tree House Town* by Miska Miles, 1974; *I Want Mama* by Marjorie W. Sharmat, 1974; *Stand in the Wind* by Jean Little, 1975; *Amanda, the Panda and the Redhead* by Susan Terris, 1975; *The Bed Book* by Sylvia Plath, 1976; *My Street's a Morning Cool Street* by Ianthe Thomas, 1977; *Martha's Mad Day* by Miranda Hapgood, 1977; *That's Mine* by Elizabeth Winthrop, 1977; *No Help at All* and *Partners* by Betty Baker, 1978; *The Twenty–Elephant Restaurant* by Russell Hoban, 1978; *What I Did Last Summer* by Glory St. John, 1978; *The Highest Hit* by Nancy Willard, 1978; *I and Sproggy* by Constance C. Greene, 1978; *Edward Troy and the Witch Cat* by Sarah Sargent, 1978; *Whatever Happened to Beverly Bigler's Birthday?* by Barbara Williams, 1979; *Last Look* by Clyde Robert Bulla, 1979; *Ookie-Spooky* by Mirra Ginsburg, 1979; *The Black Dog Who Went into the Woods,* 1980, and *I Dance in My Red Pajamas,* 1982, by Edith Thatcher Hurd; *How I Found Myself at the Fair* by Pat Rhoads Mauser, 1980; *Oliver and Allison's Week* by Jane Breskin Zalben, 1980; *How We Got Our First Cat* by Tobi Tobias, 1980; *Play and Sing, It's Christmas! A Piano Book of Easy-to-Play Carols* compiled by Brooke M. Varnum, 1980; *Pajama Walking* by Vicki Kimmel Artis, 1981; *The April Fool* by Alice Schertle, 1981; *Joseph on the Subway Trains* by Kathleen Benson, 1981; *Mail-Order Wings,* 1981, *Fifth Grade Magic,* 1982, *Best Friend Insurance,* 1983, *The Ghastly Glasses,* 1985, *Richard and the Vratch,* 1988, *The Magic Mean Machine,* 1989, *More Fifth Grade Magic,* 1989, *Wanted, UFO,* 1990, *Sky Guys to White Cat,* 1991, by Beatrice Gormley; *The Seeing Summer* by Jeannette Everly, 1981; *The New Friend* by Charlotte Zolotow, 1981; *The Halloween Candy Mystery,* 1982, and *The Christmas Present Mystery,* 1984, by Marion M. Markham; *Mitzi and the Terrible Tyrannosaurus Rex,* 1982, *Mitzi's Honeymoon with Nana Potts,* 1983, *Mitzi and Frederick the Great,* 1984, *Mitzi and the Elephants,* 1985, by Barbara Williams; *Alice and the Boa Constrictor* by Laurie Adams and Allison Coudert, 1983; *Good Dog, Bad Dog* by Corrine Gerson, 1983; *For I Will Consider My Cat Jeoffry* by Christopher Smart, 1984; *The Playground,* 1984; *Gertrude's Pocket* by Miska Miles, 1984; *The Thing in Kat's Attic* by Charlotte T. Graeber, 1985; *The Explorer of Barkham Street* by Mary Stolz, 1985; *Fourth of July,* 1985, *Jam Day,* 1987, *Dinah's Mad, Bad Wishes,* 1989, by Barbara M. Joosse; *Lulu and the Witch Baby* by Jane O'Connor, 1986; *Wheels* by Jane R. Thomas, 1986; *Lulu Goes to Witch School* by Jane O'Connor, 1987; *Molly,* 1987, *Molly Goes Hiking,* 1987, *Molly Goes to the Library,* 1988, *Breakfast by Molly,* 1988, by Ruth Shaw Radlauer; *The Boston Coffee Party* by Doreen Rappaport, 1987; *Ridin' That Strawberry Roan* by Marcia Sewall, 1987; *The Baby Bubble Book* by Rhoda Josephs, 1988; *It Always Happens to Leona* by Juanita Havill, 1989; *The Grandpa Days* by Joan W. Bloss, 1989; *Selene Goes Home* by Lucy Diggs, 1989; *The Take-Along Dog* by Barbara A. Porte, 1989; *The Day Chubby Became Charles* by Achim Broger, translated by Rene Vera Cafiero, 1990; *Stepbrother Sabotage* by Sally Wittman, 1990; *Leona and Ike* by Juanita Havill, 1991; *Meatball* by Phyllis Hoffman, 1991; *The Butterfly Birthday* by Ann Bixby Herold, 1991; *Beavers Beware* by Barbara Brenner, 1992; *In My Tent* by Marilyn Singer, 1992; *Isabelle the Itch* by Constance Green, 1992; *Meet the Lincoln Lions Marching Band* and *Yankee Doodle Drumsticks,* both 1992, and *The Great Shamrock Disaster,* 1993, by Patricia Reilly Giff; *Annie's Birthday Bike* by Crescent Dragonwagon, 1993; *Amzat and His Brothers: Three Italian Tales* by Paula Fox, 1993; *If You Grew Up with George Washington* by Ruth Belov Gross, 1993; *Leo the Magnificent* by Ann Martin, 1996; *Old Home Day* by Donald Hall, 1996; *The Divide* by Michael Bedard, 1997.

Emily Arnold McCully comments:

Picture books offer me a chance to unite two powerful impulses—to write and to draw. Although I was pulled into children's books by a visionary editor, and didn't think of it myself, the field has given me a chance to tell stories in a way that uniquely satisfies this pair of urges.

As a child, I couldn't find stories about girls who were adventurous, persevering, brave, so I'm trying to fill that void now. I love reading history and find lots of ideas there, as well as in memory. As an untrained artist, I learn on the job and in every book try to extend my skills a little further. I try to put life into the pictures, not to make meticulous representations. I hope that in vigorous "sketchy" illustrations, readers will find ways to enter into the story.

*   *   *

Emily Arnold McCully is a gifted storyteller and illustrator. She began writing and illustrating stories as a young child, and her early drawings showed considerable skill in depiction of the human form. When contemporaries were doing finger painting, she was, at age five, drawing people in fancy dress.

Her family moved to Long Island during her childhood. As a teenager she enjoyed visiting her father, a documentary writer and producer, at work in New York's Rockefeller Center, walking through the Museum of Modern Art, and sketching people in Union Square Park. She particularly admired the works of the "Ashcan" group of eight American artists distinctive for their depictions of everyday life. At Brown University McCully studied art and art history; later, at Columbia University, she majored in art history. When she and her husband moved to Belgium she again concentrated on drawing.

Upon returning from Europe McCully did book review illustrations for the *New York Herald Tribune* and other free lance work, which came to the attention of a New York children's book editor. The editor asked her if she would care to illustrate a book for children. She did, and went on to illustrate 73 books for children written by other people before she wrote and illustrated a book of her own. Since then she has illustrated many books of her own as well as many books for other writers. Her output is prodigious.

Her first book for children, *Picnic,* is about a mouse family's outing on a beautiful sunny day. Grandparents, parents, and nine little mice go bouncing down the country road, on their way to the lake, in their old red truck. When they arrive at the lake, they take out the picnic hamper, the bat and ball, the banjo. But as the children leap out of the truck, there are only eight of them. The ninth child bounced out of the truck a few pages earlier. The search for the missing mouse, and his excellent survival skills, form the core of the book. The book is a tour de force because there are no words, only soft watercolor pictures to tell the tale. McCully created four other wordless picture books about this mouse family: *First Snow, School, New Baby,* and *Christmas Gift.*

McCully won the Caldecott Award for her *Mirette on the High Wire,* a story about a spirited young girl of nineteenth century Paris. Mirette helps her mother run a boarding house for traveling performers. When Bellini (formerly the Great Bellini), comes to stay with them and practices his high-wire walk in their courtyard, Mirette is entranced and asks him to teach her the walk. He refuses, for he has retired because he has lost his nerve. It is Mirette who teaches herself to wire-walk and teaches Bellini how to have courage again. The characters of Mirette and Bellini, imaginative and determined people, are beautifully drawn. And the watercolor paintings of Paris, from the cobblestone streets below to the rooftops above, are enchanting. The pictures do indeed add drama and depth to the tale.

A sequel, *Starring Mirette and Bellini,* presents the two as a performing team, seeing the world from their high wire. They make a grand tour of the great cities of Europe—Milan, Budapest, Vienna, Paris—and then they go on to St. Petersburg. Such exciting adventures for Mirette! But when they get to St. Petersburg and Bellini speaks out for freedom, he is jailed. Mirette is called upon to show exceptional courage to set him free. The pictures of European and Russian towns are wonderful; they give the reader a grand tour of their own.

McCully has written a series of beginner readers about a boy's two grandmothers. Grandma Nan and Grandma Sal are not at all alike, one being old fashioned, the other quite new fashioned. And they tend to disagree with each other about a number of things. But one thing they always agree on is their responsibility to do the right thing for their grandson Pip. In *Grandmas at Bat,* Pip's baseball team will not be allowed to play in Saturday's game because the coach has the chicken pox. So Grandma Nan and Grandma Sal decide to take on the coaching job. It is clear that neither grandmother knows much about baseball. They argue with each other and they hog the field. Pip suggests that they just sit on the bench and watch the team practice. But the grandmothers feel left out until they think of another way to support the team: as cheerleaders. They don't look like cheerleaders, even in their fancy clothes, but they wave their pom-poms wildly and in the end Pip's team wins the game.

McCully has published other picture books with rich European settings and stories of independent and courageous children. In *The Amazing Felix,* a young boy wants to live up to the expectations of his famous pianist father, but really doesn't enjoy the piano and doesn't practice as he should. "Practice, practice, practice," his father tells him. When Felix and his mother and sister sail from New York to London to meet father, Felix meets up with and is enchanted by a magician on the boat. He wants to be a magician. The magician shows Felix the first magic trick, and then says, "Practice, practice, practice." Felix does practice. When he gets to London, he shows his father his magic trick, and finds out that his father has loved magic since a boy. Felix explains to his father how to make a coin vanish. "You must practice, practice, practice," he tells his father. The charm of the story line is enhanced by romantic scenes of boat travel and castle exploration.

Little Kit, or The Industrious Flea Circus Girl, is the story of an orphan looking for a home. Kit lives in an alley in Victorian London and sells flowers on the street from dawn to dusk to obtain food. Professor Malefetta, owner of The Industrious Flea Circus, comes into the alley looking for a helper. Kit agrees to go with him, in hope of a better life. But the Professor treats Kit as cruelly as he treats his performing fleas. Kit is resourceful enough to find an escape in the night, and she brings the tortured fleas with her. The characters in this book are sharply drawn; the somber watercolors allow a tale of exploitation and violence to be dramatically told.

McCully's illustrations for the works of others are also lyrical, and they show the same attention to the blending of words and pictures to form an artistic whole. She has illustrated books of distinguished writers of both prose and poetry.

McCully's works for adults deal with pain and courage and hope. Her novel, *A Craving,* is the story of an alcoholic artist's struggle with a failing marriage and alienated children. In addition to writing and painting, McCully also acts in off-Broadway plays. Her interest in the performing arts is vividly reflected in her writings and illustrations of wire-walkers, magicians, pianists, dreamers of all sorts. Her books are likely to encourage others to dream.

—Mary Lystad

MCDERMOTT, Gerald (Edward)

Nationality: American. **Born:** Detroit, Michigan, 31 January 1941. **Education:** Pratt Institute of Design, B.F.A. 1964. **Family:** Married Beverly Brodsky, 1969 (divorced). **Career:** Filmmaker, illustrator, reteller of folktales. Graphic designer for public television station, New York City, 1962; producer and designer of original films, including *The Stonecutter, Anansi the Spider, The Magic Tree,* and *Arrow to the Sun.* Exhibitions include "Film as Art,"

San Francisco Film Festival, 1966; "Best Short Films," American Film Festival, New York City, 1969; "Contemporary Animated Films," Annecy International Film Festival, France, 1971; "Illustrating Myth and Legend," Everson Museum, Syracuse, New York, 1975; "Illustrating Picture Books," Children's Museum, Indianapolis, 1979; "Best American Animators," Whitney Museum, New York City, 1980. **Awards:** Blue Ribbon, Educational Film Library Association, 1969; Silver Lion, Italian Government, 1970; American Film Festival Blue Ribbon, 1970, for *Anansi the Spider* (film); Caldecott Honor Book, 1973, for *Anansi the Spider*; *Boston Globe/Horn Book* Honor Book, for *The Magic Tree*; Caldecott Medal, 1975, for *Arrow to the Sun.*

Publications for Children

Folktales (retold and illustrated by the author)

Anansi the Spider: A Tale from the Ashanti. New York, Holt, 1972.
The Magic Tree: A Tale from the Congo. New York, Holt, 1973.
Arrow to the Sun: A Pueblo Indian Tale. New York, Viking, 1974.
The Stonecutter: A Japanese Folk Tale. New York, Viking, 1975.
The Voyage of Osiris: A Myth of Ancient Egypt. New York, Dutton, 1977.
The Knight of the Lion. New York, Four Winds, 1978.
Papagayo the Mischief Maker. New York, Dutton, 1978.
Sun Flight. New York, Four Winds, 1980.
Daughter of Earth: A Roman Myth. New York, Delacorte, 1984.
Daniel O'Rourke: An Irish Tale. New York, Viking, 1986.
Tim O'Toole and the Wee Folk: An Irish Tale. New York, Viking, 1990.
Musicians of the Sun: An Aztec Myth. New York, Delacorte, 1991.
Zomo the Rabbit: A Trickster Tale from West Africa. New York, Harcourt, 1992.
Raven: A Trickster Tale from the Pacific Northwest. New York, Harcourt, 1993.
Coyote: A Trickster Tale from the American Southwest. San Diego, Harcourt, 1994.
Musicians of the Sun. New York, Simon and Schuster, 1997.
The Light of the World: The Story of the Nativity. New York, Simon and Schuster, 1998.

*

Biography: "Caldecott Award Acceptance," in *Horn Book,* August 1975; entry in *Something about the Author,* Vol. 74, Detroit, Gale, 1993.

Critical Studies: Entry in *Children's Literature Review,* Vol. 9, Detroit, Gale, 1985.

Illustrator: *Carlo Collodi's The Adventures of Pinocchio* translated and adapted by Marianna Mayer, 1981; *Aladdin and the Enchanted Lamp,* 1985, and *The Spirit of the Blue Light,* 1987, retold by Marianna Mayer; *Alley Oop!,* 1985, *The Brambleberrys Animal Book of Alphabet,* 1991, *The Brambleberrys Animal Book of Colors,* 1991, *The Brambleberrys Animal Book of Counting,* 1991, *The Brambleberrys Animal Book of Shapes,* 1991, *Marcel the Pastry Chef,* 1991, and *Marcel at War,* 1991, all by Marianna Mayer.

* * *

Gerald McDermott has distinguished himself in several artistic fields: as a filmmaker, a reteller of folk tales, and an illustrator. McDermott was born in Detroit, Michigan, and very early showed artistic interests and talent. At age four his parents enrolled him in the Detroit Institute of Art, and he spent the Saturdays of his childhood and early adolescence at the Institute, drawing, painting, and studying their collection. He also as a child became interested in films and filmmaking. At age nine he became a regular actor on "Storytime," a Detroit TV program which dramatized folktales and legends. Working with actors and filmmakers furthered his interest in becoming a professional in this field. Unable to find film classes, he went to study art and design at Cass Technical High School in Detroit. He also experimented with making his own films. After graduation he received a Scholastic Publications National Scholarship to attend the Pratt Institute in New York City. While in New York he worked as a graphic designer for New York's public television station. There he began to experiment with animated films. He wanted to design films that were highly stylized in color and form. He eschewed conventional cartoons, turning to folktales as source material for more dramatic works. His first major film was *The Stonecutter,* based on a Japanese fable of a man's foolish longing for power. Borrowing from design motifs of old Japanese prints, McDermott used traditional animation techniques to set the design in motion.

After he finished *The Stonecutter,* he met Joseph Campbell, a distinguished mythologist who viewed myths as suppliers of symbols to carry forward the human spirit of a culture. Buoyed by Campbell's work, McDermott's next two films were based on African folk tales. *Anansi the Spider* is taken from a Ghanaian fable, one of many about a mischief maker who gets into a lot of trouble. Here McDermott borrowed designs from the colorful Ashanti people of Ghana, whose expressive sculpture and colorful woven cloths have been admired for generations. The highly expressive film won the 1970 Blue Ribbon at the American Film Festival.

McDermott's next film, *The Magic Tree,* was a retelling of a tale from the Congo. This is a tale of two brothers, one handsome and one ugly, and of the magic that turned the ugly brother's life around. Its graphic style reflects the austere stylized carvings of Central Africa. The book version of *The Magic Tree* follows the ugly brother who, while traveling on a river, comes to a great tree with magical leaves. Suddenly all he wishes for—beauty, wealth, strength, love—are his, but only if he keeps the secret of the magic tree. The brilliant designs and color of this book are juxtaposed with a sparse text to make a dramatic story.

After making these films McDermott moved to France to study the techniques of European filmmakers. Before leaving he was offered a contract to adapt his films into picture books for children. While abroad he sought to produce a book version of his film, *Anansi the Spider.* He found the task difficult, for he no longer had a captive audience in a darkened room, no longer had music and sound effects. The reader was in control. McDermott's book version of *Anansi the Spider* was runner-up for the Caldecott Medal. It is a humorous story of how the mischief maker Anansi is saved from terrible fates by his more responsible sons. Before composing the book McDermott studied carefully the language rhythms as well as the design patterns of the Ashanti.

McDermott began his first simultaneous film and book project with *Arrow to the Sun.* The book won the Caldecott Medal in 1975. In this tale sun sends a spark of life to earth, into the home of a young maiden. In this way, a boy comes into the world of men. The boy, mocked by other boys because he has no father, leaves home to find his father. When he goes to the arrow maker for help, this wise man sees that the boy has come from the sun. He creates a special arrow; the boy becomes the arrow and the arrow maker fits the boy to his bow and draws it. The boy flies into the heavens, to the sun, and the sun calls on the boy to endure four trials to prove himself. After the boy does so, father and son rejoice, and son returns to earth to bring sun's spirit to the world of men. On the last double page spread the Dance of Life is celebrated. The art work for this book was rendered in gouache and ink; the black line was preseparated, and the art was reproduced in four-color process. This text is sparse, in deference to the blazing colors and stylized Pueblo forms. The forms leap off of each page, in one direction, then another, as if in a highly choreographed dance.

McDermott's two Irish tales, *Daniel O'Rourke* and *Tim O'Toole and the Wee Folk,* are much more conventional in style. They also abound in magic, but the stories are merry and free, with traditional representational art.

McDermott is fascinated by trickster tales, wherever they are from. Zomo the Rabbit is a member of the family of animal tricksters who inhabit traditional tales of West Africa. Zomo, from the Hausa people of Nigeria, has links to Cunny Rabbit of the Caribbean and Brer Rabbit of the United States. Like tricksters around the world, Zomo outwits larger foes with guile and trickery, and like his African cousin, Anansi the spider, uses his wit to gain wisdom. In the book *Zomo the Rabbit* all sorts of animals run and jump, climb and roll, in rapid motions, and the African designs that accompany them on each page do the same. *Raven* is a trickster tale from the Pacific Northwest. In this book Raven, the trickster, wants to give people the gift of light. But he first has to find out where Sky Chief keeps it. Again McDermott uses spectacular drawings, reflective of Indian totems, and simple, rhythmic language, to tell his story.

McDermott has also illustrated works of Marianna Mayer, most of which are for younger children. But it is his own works, wise and witty, rich in storytelling and bold in form, that are his special gift to children's literature.

—Mary Lystad

McFARLANE, Sheryl

Nationality: Canadian. **Born:** Ottawa, Ontario, 20 January 1954. **Family:** Married; three daughters. **Awards:** CNL Notable Book, National IODE Book Award, 1992, for *Waiting for the Whales.* **Address:** Vancouver Island, British Columbia, Canada.

PUBLICATIONS FOR CHILDREN

Picture Books

Waiting for the Whales, illustrated by Ron Lightburn. Victoria, British Columbia, Orca Books, 1991; Philomel, 1992.

Jessie's Island, illustrated by Sheena Lott. Victoria, British Columbia, Orca Books, 1992.

Moonsnail Song, illustrated by Sheena Lott. Victoria, British Columbia, Orca Books, 1994.

Eagle Dreams, illustrated by Ron Lightburn. Victoria, British Columbia, Orca Books, 1994.

Tides of Change: Faces of the Northwest Coast, illustrated by Ken Campbell. Victoria, British Columbia, Orca Books, 1995.

Going to the Fair, illustrated by Sheena Lott. Victoria, British Columbia, Orca Books, 1996.

* * *

The picture books of Sheryl McFarlane are lyrical and reflective: they take seriously their young readers or listeners, speaking to their awareness of nature, of seasons, of family love and responsibility, and of the cycle of life and death. Despite the seriousness of these themes, MaFarlane's writing never preaches: it tells stories or describes feelings in a gentle mood that draws us in but leaves us free to take what we wish from them. Her picture books are mainly set on or around Vancouver Island, off the west coast of Canada, where McFarlane herself lives. Her deep love and appreciation of the island landscape and its wildlife is evident in each of the books; although writing about the opposite side of the continent, McFarlane's work resembles the picture books of Robert McCloskey, about Maine, in conveying with similar intensity a child's absorption in the sounds, smells, and colours, vegetation, weather, and atmosphere of island life, and linking these to a perception of the greater mysteries of the cycle of life itself.

Waiting for the Whales, McFarlane's first and award-winning book, is a moving story of family love which, like the greatest picture books, implies much more than it actually says. An old man's love for his seashore garden and for the whales who annually return to the bay where he lives does not keep him from loneliness; when his daughter comes to live with him, bringing a small granddaughter, he is able to share what he cares for with the child, who grows to help him tend the garden and watch for the return of the whales. In time, the grandfather dies, but he lives on in the little girl through the things he has taught her to love. McFarlane conveys this meaning through the actions of the story, through the tending and hoeing and waiting and sighting, rather than through any overt moralizing or philosophizing. Ron Lightburn's illustrations also play their part on underlining implicit meanings; the old man's hat, for example, at first conceals his face from the viewer, later is removed when the old man is unable to continue his tasks, and then finally is put on by the child as she takes on her grandfather's life and work. The book is both simple and deep—one of the outstanding Canadian achievements in the genre.

Few picture books make use of letters as their texts, but *Jessie's Island* takes the form of a defence of her rural way of life by young Jessie in response to the letter from her city cousin noting how bored she must be to live on an island away from the bright lights and activities available to the city child. In this appealing version of the Town Mouse/Country Mouse story, Jessie gives a very persuasive assertion of the pleasures of island life, so complete that she doesn't have to resort to criticizing the city. McFarlane's strong sense of place and vivid appeals to the senses again gives conviction to the story. *Moonsnail Song* hymns the charm of the sea and seashore even more directly, in a prose poem describing the rhythms and atmosphere of the sea as they are brought to the memory and imagination of a little girl listening to the curved shell of a moonsnail she has found on the beach. The sounds and feelings brought to her by the shell are more real to her than the noisy distractions of everyday life, and they echo through her own movements and carry her at the end of the day into dreams.

Eagle Dreams is set on a farm, though the sea shore is not far off, and concerns a dreamy farmer's son who gains a sense of responsibility through caring for an injured eagle. The eagle here, like the whales in the first book, seems clearly representative of more than itself, although the story works well on a purely literal level. Awe-inspiring and utterly wild, the eagle is eventually released to freedom, confirming the boy in his sense of the value of the dreaming, imaginative side of his nature as well as the practical, hard-working side he has learned to develop.

The Tides of Change once again reflects McFarlane's love of the area where she lives as she explores the people, the history, and the beauty of the natural environment of the northwest coast. In this non-fiction book, McFarlane's text provides information at the same time as it encourages curiousity and reflection with the use of questions.

Going to the Fair, her most recent book, once again tells a story, although this time located in a more generic rural setting. From the perspective of a young girl, Erin, who has entered her pumpkin in a fall fair contest, McFarlane evokes the sensuous experience of attending a country fall fair.

Sheryl McFarlane has been well-treated by her publisher, Orca Books, in being matched with illustrators who respond to the lyrical and evocative qualities of her work. In her skillful use of simple words and subtle rhythms of language, and her understanding of the young child's intense sensory awareness of the world and concern for the mysteries of life, McFarlane is one of Canada's most promising picture book authors.

—Gwyneth Evans

McGINLEY, Phyllis (Louise)

Nationality: American. **Born:** Ontario, Oregon, 21 March 1905. **Education:** Attended school in Iliff, Colorado; Sacred Heart Academy, Ogden, Utah; Ogden High School; University of Utah, Salt Lake City, graduated 1927; University of Southern California, Los Angeles. **Family:** Married Charles L. Hayden in 1937 (died 1972); two daughters. **Career:** Schoolteacher in Utah, 1928, and New Rochelle, New York, 1929-34; worked for an advertising agency, New York, 1930s; staff writer, *Town and Country,* New York, 1937. Member, Advisory Board, *American Scholar,* Washington, D.C. **Awards:** Christopher award, 1955; Poetry Society award, 1955; Catholic Writers Guild award, 1955; Edna St. Vincent Millay award, 1955; St. Catherine de Siena Medal, 1956; Catholic Institute of the Press award, 1960; Pulitzer Prize, 1961; Catholic Poetry Society Spirit Gold Medal, 1962; Laetare Medal, Notre Dame University, 1964; Campion award, 1967. D.Litt.: Wheaton College, Illinois, 1956; St. Mary's College, Notre Dame, Indiana, 1958; Marquette University, Milwaukee, 1960; Dartmouth College, Hanover, New Hampshire, 1961; Boston College, 1962; Wilson College, Chambersburg, Pennsylvania, 1964; Smith College, Northampton, Massachusetts, 1964; St. John's University, Jamaica, New York, 1964. Member, American Academy, 1955. **Died:** 22 February 1978.

PUBLICATIONS FOR CHILDREN

Fiction

The Horse Who Lived Upstairs, illustrated by Helen Stone. Philadelphia, Lippincott, 1944.
The Plain Princess, illustrated by Helen Stone. Philadelphia, Lippincott, 1945.
A Name for Kitty, illustrated by Feodor Rojankovsky. New York, Simon and Schuster, 1948; London, Muller, 1950.
The Most Wonderful Doll in the World, illustrated by Helen Stone. Philadelphia, Lippincott, 1950.
The Horse Who Had His Picture in the Paper, illustrated by Helen Stone. Philadelphia, Lippincott, 1951.
Blunderbus, illustrated by William Wiesner. Philadelphia, Lippincott, 1951.
The Make-Believe Twins, illustrated by Roberta MacDonald. Philadelphia, Lippincott, 1953.
The B Book, illustrated by Robert Jones. New York, Crowell Collier, 1962; London, Collier Macmillan, 1968.

Plays

Walk the Plank! A Pirate Squall, music by Gladys Rich. New York, Schirmer, 1928.
Garden Magic: A Flower Fantasy, music by Gladys Rich. New York, Fischer, 1931.

Poetry

All Around the Town, illustrated by Helen Stone. Philadelphia, Lippincott, 1948.
The Year Without a Santa Claus, illustrated by Kurt Werth. Philadelphia, Lippincott, 1957; Leicester, Brockhampton Press, 1960.
Lucy McLockett, illustrated by Helen Stone. Philadelphia, Lippincott, 1959; Leicester, Brockhampton Press, 1961.
Sugar and Spice: The ABC of Being a Girl, illustrated by Colleen Browning. New York, Watts, 1960.
Mince Pie and Mistletoe, illustrated by Harold Berson. Philadelphia, Lippincott, 1961.
Boys Are Awful, illustrated by Ati Forberg. New York, Watts, 1962.
How Mrs. Santa Claus Saved Christmas, illustrated by Kurt Werth. Philadelphia, Lippincott, 1963; Kingswood, Surrey, World's Work, 1964.
A Girl and Her Room, illustrated by Ati Forberg. New York, Watts, 1963.
Wonderful Time, illustrated by John Alcorn. Philadelphia, Lippincott, 1966.
A Wreath of Christmas Legends, illustrated by Leonard Weisgard. New York, Macmillan, 1967.

Other

Wonders and Surprises: A Collection of Poems. Philadelphia, Lippincott, 1968.

PUBLICATIONS FOR ADULTS

Plays

Small Wonder (revue), with others, music by Baldwin Bergersen and Albert Selden (produced New York, 1948).

Screenplay (English narration): *The Emperor's Nightingale,* 1951.

Poetry

On the Contrary. New York, Doubleday, 1934.
One More Manhattan. New York, Harcourt Brace, 1937.
A Pocketful of Wry. New York, Duell, 1940; revised edition, New York, Grosset and Dunlap, 1959.
Husbands are Difficult; or, The Book of Oliver Ames. New York, Duell, 1941.
Stones from a Glass House: New Poems. New York, Viking Press, 1946.
A Short Walk from the Station. New York, Viking Press, 1951.
The Love Letters of Phyllis McGinley. New York, Viking Press, 1954; London, Dent, 1955.
Merry Christmas, Happy New Year. New York, Viking Press, 1958; London, Secker and Warburg, 1959.
Times Three: Selected Verse from Three Decades. New York, Viking Press, 1960; as *Times Three: Selected Verse from Three Decades with Seventy New Poems,* London, Secker and Warburg, 1961.
Christmas con and pro. Berkeley, California, Hart Press, 1971.
Confessions of a Reluctant Optimist, edited by Barbara Wells Price. Kansas City, Missouri, Hallmark Editions, 1973.

Other

The Province of the Heart (essays). New York, Viking Press, 1959; Kingswood, Surrey, World's Work, 1961.
Sixpence in Her Shoe (autobiography). New York, Macmillan, 1964; London, Dent, 1966.
Saint-Watching. New York, Viking Press, 1969; London, Collins, 1970.

*

Manuscript Collections: Syracuse University Library, New York.

Critical Studies: *Phyllis McGinley* by Linda Welshimer Wagner, New York, Twayne, 1971.

* * *

Best known for her light verse for adults (which won her a Pulitzer Prize in 1961), Phyllis McGinley wrote outstanding and memorable fiction and poetry for children as well. Here, her light touch and tender heart are enhanced by moral lessons and happy endings: characters like Esmeralda, the "Plain Princess," live happily ever after, "or at least as happily as is possible in this mortal world."

McGinley's first book for children, *The Horse Who Lived Upstairs,* was inspired by a set of drawings of horses done by her friend Helen Stone, whose old-fashioned, lively, and realistic drawings grace many of McGinley's books for children. *The Horse Who Lived Upstairs* is about Joey, who lives in a fourth-floor stall in a big brick building in New York City and pulls a fruit and vegetable wagon for Mr. Polaski. But Joey is discontented. He wants to live in the country, "in a red barn with a weathervane," with a meadow where he can "run and kick up his heels." Then Mr. Polaski gets a truck, and Joey's dream comes true: he is sent to a farm. However, he soon discovers that he is no happier in the country. His barn is cold in winter and hot in summer; he must work pulling a plow from dawn to dusk; and he is lonely for his city friends: "I don't think I belong in the country after all....I am now more discontented than ever." When Mr. Polaski is unable to get new tires for his truck, he returns for Joey and brings him back home to the city. "How did you like the country?" Joey's New York friends ask. "The country is all right for country animals," he replies, "but I guess I am just a City horse at heart." Joey has learned his lesson, and is "never discontented again." (He even becomes quite a celebrity in *The Horse Who Had His Picture in the Paper.*)

The Plain Princess is a "once upon a time, in a distant kingdom" fairytale about eight-year-old princess Esmeralda, who has everything: golden hair, a fair complexion, excellent posture and grace, even golden braces for her teeth. Yet, she is plain. And, like some plain princesses, she's a snob. But when she learns to stop turning her nose up at the world, to be proud of the work of her own hands, and to be unselfish—her nose turns down, her mouth turns up, and her eyes start to glow. Now beautiful, in appearance as well as in character, she lives happily ever after (with the aforementioned proviso).

Dulcy, the six-going-on-seven heroine of *The Most Wonderful Doll in the World,* like equine Joey, finds it hard to be satisfied with "Things as They Are." She is always wishing "her fly-away hair could be ringlets or that she lived on a farm instead of a pretty village or that she were tall and slim instead of plump and rosy-round." She feels the same about her dolls, "always wishing things were a little different or a little better." When, one winter, Dulcy loses her new doll, Angela, in the snow, the plain little doll grows in Dulcy's imagination, far prettier than all her other dolls. Naturally, when Dulcy finds Angela in the Spring, she has a hard but important lesson to learn: "Everybody has a dream," said Dulcy's mother. "And sometimes people get mixed up about what is dream and what is real. That's how it happened with Angela. You remembered your dream of her."

All Around the Town is a clever alphabet book, in verse, of "the gay things/The stray things/That city children see," from aeroplanes (that "advertise/And write amusing messages/Across the city skies") to "a million winking Windows/When the dusk is coming down," "'Xcavations," and the city Zoo. *Lucy McLockett,* in pictures, prose, and verse, tells us about Lucy, a five-year-old, "plump/And curly/And good as gold" who loses a tooth, and then begins to lose other things—mittens, grocery lists, even herself in a large department store—until Mr. Repairs screws her head on straight and she learns to *think. A Girl and Her Room* is a nostalgic look in verse at the stage of a girl's life as reflected in the changes in her bedroom: from a baby's room of crib, bottles, and talcum powder, to that of a teenager, with diaries, invitations to football games, and shoes with heels:

> Jump ropes, Mother Goose,
> All forgot.
> But the room remembered
> If she did not.
> And someday, maybe,
> After a bit,
> Another little girl
> May live in it.

Wonderful Time is about minutes, hours, night, day, sun, moon, the four seasons, and clocks.

McGinley's books for children are books to treasure, for a child's delight and an adult's pleasure.

—Marcia G. Fuchs

McGOUGH, Roger

Nationality: British. **Born:** Liverpool, Lancashire, 9 November 1937. **Education:** St. Mary's College, Crosby, Lancashire; Hull University, Yorkshire, B.A. in French and geography 1957, Cert. Ed. 1960. **Family:** Married 1) Thelma Monaghan in 1970 (marriage dissolved 1980), two sons; 2) Hilary Clough in 1986, one son, one daughter. **Career:** Schoolteacher, Liverpool, 1960-64; lecturer, Liverpool College of Art, 1969-70; poetry fellow, University of Loughborough, Leicestershire, 1973-75. Formerly, member of the performing group The Scaffold. Free-lance writer and performer. **Awards:** *Signal* award, 1984; BAFTA award, for television play, 1985; honorary professor, Thames Valley University, 1993; award O.B.E. for Services to Poetry, 1997. **Agent:** A.D. Peters, 5th Floor, The Chambers, Chelsea Harbour, Lots Road, London SW10 0XF, England.

Publications for Children

Fiction

The Great Smile Robbery, illustrated by Tony Blundell. London, Kestrel, 1982.
The Stowaways, illustrated by Tony Blundell. London, Viking Kestrel, 1986.
The Lighthouse That Ran Away. London, Bodley Head, 1991.
Another Custard Pie, illustrated by Graham Percy. London, Collins, 1993.
Stinkers Ahoy!, illustrated by Tony Blundell. London, Viking, 1994.
The Magic Fountain, illustrated by Philip Hopman. London, Bodley Head, 1995.
The Kite and Caitlin, illustrated by John Prater. London, Bodley Head, 1996.

Plays

Wind in the Willows (lyrics only, with William Perry), book by Jane Iredale, music by Perry, adaptation of the story by Kenneth Grahame (produced Washington, D.C., 1984; New York, 1985).
Fast Forward (television play). 1986.

Poetry

Mr. Noselighter, illustrated by André François. London, G. Whizzard, 1976.
You Tell Me, with Michael Rosen, illustrated by Sara Midda. London, Kestrel, 1979.
Sky in the Pie, illustrated by Satoshi Kitamura. London, Kestrel, 1983.
Nailing the Shadow, illustrated by Marketa Prachatická. London, Viking Kestrel, 1987.
An Imaginary Menagerie, illustrated by Tony Blundell. London, Viking Kestrel, 1988.
Helen Highwater: A Shropshire Lass, illustrated by Martin Chatterton. London, Viking Kestrel, 1989.
Pillow Talk. London, Viking Kestral, 1990.
My Dad's a Fire-eater. London, Puffin, 1992.
Lucky, illustrated by Sally Kindberg. London, Viking, 1993.
Bad, Bad Cats, illustrated by Lydia Monks. London, Viking, 1997.

Other

Noah's Ark, illustrated by Ljiljana Rylands. London, Dinosaur, 1986.
Counting by Numbers. London, Viking Kestrel, 1989.
The Oxford ABC Picture Dictionary. Oxford, Oxford University Press, 1990.

Editor, *Strictly Private: An Anthology of Poetry,* illustrated by Graham Dean. London, Kestrel, 1981.
Editor, *The Kingfisher Book of Comic Verse,* illustrated by Caroline Holden. London, Kingfisher, 1986.
Editor, *The Oxford 123 Book of Number Rhymes.* Oxford, Oxford University Press, 1992.
Until I Met Dudley (How Everyday Things Really Work). New York, Walker & Co, 1997.
Editor, *The Kingfisher Book of Poems about Love,* illustrated by Chloe Cleese. London, Kingfisher, 1997.

Publications for Adults

Plays

Birds, Marriages and Deaths, with others (produced London, 1964).
The Chauffeur-Driven Rolls (produced Liverpool, 1966).
The Commission (produced Liverpool, 1967).
The Puny Little Life Show (produced London, 1969). Published in *Open Space Plays,* edited by Charles Marowitz, London, Penguin, 1974.
Zones (produced Edinburgh, 1969).
Stuff (produced London, 1970).
P.C. Plod (produced London, 1971).
Plod (screenplay), 1972.
Wordplay (produced London, 1975).
The Lifeswappers (television play), 1976.
Gruff: A TV Commercial (radio play), 1977.
Summer with Monika, music by Andy Roberts (produced London, 1978).
Watchwords (produced Nottingham, 1979).
Like Father, Like Son, Like (produced Nottingham, 1980).
Lifeswappers (produced Edinburgh and London, 1980).
All the Trimmings, music by Peter Brewis (produced London, 1980).
Golden Nights and Golden Days (produced on tour, 1980).
Walking the Dog (radio play), 1981.
Behind the Lines (revue), with Brian Patten (produced London, 1982).
The Mouthtrap, with Brian Patten (produced Edinburgh and London, 1982).
Kurt, B.P. Mungo, and Me (television play), 1983.
The Narrator (radio play), 1985.

A Matter of Chance, adaptation of a story by Nabokov (produced Edinburgh and London, 1988).
Falling Angels (dance play; produced in India, 1997).

Poetry

The Mersey Sound: Penguin Modern Poets 10, with Adrian Henri and Brian Patten. London, Penguin, 1967; revised edition, 1974, 1983.
Frinck, A Life in the Day of, and Summer with Monika: Poems (novel and verse). London, Joseph, and New York, Ballantine, 1967.
Watchwords. London, Cape, 1969.
After the Merrymaking. London, Cape, 1971.
Out of Sequence. London, Turret, 1973.
Gig. London, Cape, 1973.
Sporting Relations. London, Eyre Methuen, 1974; revised with illustrations by the author, London, Viking, 1996.
In the Glassroom. London, Cape, 1976.
Summer with Monika, revised edition. London, Deutsch, 1978; revised, London, Penguin, 1990.
Holiday on Death Row. London, Cape, 1979.
Unlucky for Some. London, Bernard Stone, 1980.
Waving at Trains. London, Cape, 1982.
New Volume, with Adrian Henri and Brian Patten. London, Penguin, 1983.
Crocodile Puddles. London, Pyramid, 1984.
Melting into the Foreground. London, Viking, 1986.
Selected Poems 1967-1987. London, Cape, 1989; as *Blazing Fruit: Selected Poems 1967-1987.* London, Penguin, 1990.
You at the Back Selected Poems 1967-1987. London, Penguin, 1991.
Defying Gravity. London, Viking, 1992.

Recordings: *The Incredible New Liverpool Scene,* CBS, 1967; *McGough McGear,* Parlophone; *"Scaffold" Live at Queen Elizabeth Hall,* Parlophone; *"Scaffold" L. The P.,* Parlophone; *Grimms,* Island; *Fresh Liver,* Island; *Sleepers,* DJM; *McGough/Patten,* Argo; *Summer with Monika,* Island, 1978; *Gifted Wreckage,* with Brian Patten and Adrian Henri, Talking Tape, 1984; *Jelly Pie,* with Brian Patten, Puffin, 1987; *Blazing Fruit,* Random House, 1991; *Pillow Talk,* Collins, 1992; *The Magic Fountain,* Random House, 1996; *Bad, Bad Cats,* Penguin Audio, 1997.

*

Manuscript Collection: University of Hull.

* * *

Roger McGough is a performer and his poems show a comic's inventiveness, sense of timing, and delivery. For some years he appeared with the group *The Scaffold,* remarking wryly in a later poem that "I was somebody then (the one on the right with glasses) singing Lily the Pink." He has made a number of recordings of his own work, and has written for stage, television, film, and radio. His work contains frequent echoes of popular entertainment: music hall, stand-up comedy, and pantomime (as revealed in works like "Pantomime Poem," "Cinema Poem," or the ventriloquial "A Gottle of Geer"). This concern for reaching an audience, combined with his wit and verbal ingenuity, has meant that there is no firm division between his prolific writing for children and his work for adults. Volumes like *Sporting Relations* seem divided between pieces for young readers and others that are not; numbers of his poems have been printed in collections for both audiences, and frequently they can be read in different ways at different ages. He is repeatedly concerned to subvert conventional thinking about poetry, as in "Take a poem, Miss Jones," when a bored poet dictates a stock of worn-out cliches to his secretary, or in "I don't like the poems", or in the boy's verdict that "I like a good poem / one with lots of fighting in it." He sardonically undermines his own role in "The Poet Inspired," "When I am Dead," or "The Examination".

His prose works are perhaps less effective than his verse, although comic tales like *The Great Smile Robbery* and the more recent *Stinkers Ahoy!* are ingeniously told and well-integrated with Tony Blundell's illustrations. They deal with the chaotic adventures of a broadly drawn group of characters like Billy Bogie, King Pong, and Mrs. Wobblebottom. McGough's concern for school runs from his early volume *In the Glassroom,* which included "The Lesson," in which the teacher cheerfully butchers a troublesome class, to the more recent "Class warfare." The early poems showed an empathetic sympathy with figures like the child just starting school, the boy in the bottom stream, the rebel ("I'm a nooligan"), or the football freak. This may help to explain his success as an anthologist for young readers; *Strictly Private* was for a decade the outstanding selection of modern verse for older schoolchildren.

The title of his volume *Sky in the Pie* conveys something of McGough's enjoyment of word-play and his lightheartedly surrealist view of the world. His poems display a love of puns and revitalising cliches ("When people ask: 'How are you?' / I say, 'Bits of me are fine.'") There are occasional lyrical passages, and beneath the jauntiness and conversational wit there is sometimes a serious concern for values. His concerns have always been broadly humanitarian, with an awareness of the frailties of human nature, rather than narrowly political. A strong social concern is nearly always worked out in terms of particular individuals, as in "Beatings," with its record of "domestic daily cruelty," or in the sequence "Unlucky for Some" and *Melting into the Foreground.*

McGough has always had a weakness for strange creations like the Skwerp and Poltergeese, and *An Imaginary Menagerie* is full of creatures like the Duffle Goat and the Brushbaby, who "lives under the stairs / on a diet of dust and old dog hairs" while "dreaming of beauty parlours and stardom." Some of the sly allusions now seem too dated for a young audience. He has gone on to produce *Pillow Talk,* with its insistent rhymes and playing with words aimed at younger children, and *Lucky,* which covers a remarkable range from the comic and silly to the thoughtful and moving. Here, as in the earlier work, there is the enjoyment of evocative words like the namecalling of "Prayer to St. Grobianus," the patron saint of coarse people, with its "fuzzdutties and cullions / dunderwhelps and trollybags." By implicitly prompting children to respond in their own talking and writing and to employ forms like his "Indefinite definitions," McGough gives language a twist that provokes his readers into fresh thinking and feeling.

The Bad, Bad Cats that give the title to his 1997 volume are the subject of the opening poems in this collection: the Mafia cats with their protection racket, kidnapping of kittens, and demands to be paid off with cans of tuna. The volume ends with a dozen pieces grouped as "Carnival of the Animals," loosely based on the Saint-Saens performance piece, and making an interesting comparison with the earlier collection *An Imaginary Menagerie.* Between these two sections come a variety of his carefully artless poems. As usual there are frequent echoes of popular entertainment, of his sardonic concern for school ("Concise Hints for New Teachers" and "Here Come the Dinner Ladies"), and an empathetic sympathy with children's experiences like "The Going Pains." Significantly the epigraph to the volume says that the poems "need reading, So over to you," and in more than one place he urges that they should be read aloud.

Even in his works for children, McGough is more than simply a light-hearted entertainer. Beneath the jauntiness and conversational wit there is sometimes a nightmarish grimness ("Late Night News"). In "The Identification," a distraught father, brought to identify the charred body of his son, struggles to explain why the boy was carrying cigarettes when he had been forbidden to smoke. The scene is described with a wry detachment that avoids sentimentality, but also with a strong sense of compassion. Often a light-hearted mood is subverted by an ironic or sad ending, as in "The Pet," where the ten-year-old reveals the death of his father. *My Dad's a Fire-eater* is a rollicking description of bonfire night excitements, when the local fire engines cannot get to the hospital and fire-eater dad saves the situation, but in a sobering twist it is revealed that the narrator suffers from leukemia. In *The Kite and Caitlin,* with illustrations by John Prater, McGough makes a sensitive approach to the disturbing situation of a dying child. Caitlin has spent two years in and out of hospital, is unable to walk, and knows that she is going to die. She is given a kite that has been passed on from other, more active, children who have not valued it, and "what Caitlin loved about the kite was its sadness." She dreams of being able to fly away with it over the highest mountains in the world. McGough presents her eventual death in terms of release and freedom, picturing Caitlin and the kite travelling ever higher until "the earth is just a pebble" from the great mountain of light, "where happiness ever after waits for Caitlin and the kite."

—Robert Protherough

McGREGOR, Iona

Nationality: British. **Born:** Aldershot, Hampshire, 7 February 1929. **Education:** Monmouth School for Girls; University of Bristol, B.A. (honours) 1950. **Career:** Sub-editor, *Dictionary of the Older Scottish Tongue,* Edinburgh University Press, 1951-57; classics teacher, Simon Langton Girls' School, Canterbury, 1958-62, and Beaverwood School, Chislehurst, Kent, 1962-69. Classics teacher, St. George's School for Girls, Edinburgh, from 1969. **Address:** 9 Saxe Coburg Street, Edinburgh EH3 5BN, Scotland.

Publications for Children

Fiction

An Edinburgh Reel. London, Faber, 1968.
The Popinjay. London, Faber, 1969.
The Burning Hill. London, Faber, 1970.
The Tree of Liberty. London, Faber, 1972.
The Snake and the Olive. London, Faber, 1974.

Other

Edinburgh and the Eastern Lowlands: Lothian, Fife, and the Borders. London, Faber, 1979.
Wallace and Bruce (textbook). Edinburgh, Oliver and Boyd, 1986.
Bairns: Scottish Children in Photographs, photographs selected by Helen Kemp and Liz Robertson, captions by Dorothy I. Kidd. Edinburgh, National Museums of Scotland, 1994.

Publications for Adults

Novel

Death Wore a Diadem. London, Women's Press, 1989.
Alice in Shadowtime. Edinburgh, Polygon, 1992.

Play

Radio Play: *A Kind of Glory,* 1971.

Other (study notes)

The Importance of Being Earnest. London, Penguin, 1987.
Mark Twain, The Adventures of Huckleberry Finn. London, Penguin, 1988.

*

Iona McGregor comments:

As a writer I have always needed the stimulus of "history" to set an edge on my imagination, although by this I mean the minutiae of daily living and the impatience of new ideas rather than great events or the people who initiated them. Eastern Scotland, the background I most enjoy writing about, is visually still close to its past. I could say that in a very small way I am searching for lost time, since it is the effort to strip these scenes and places of modern accretions which brings my characters alive for me.

* * *

When reading Iona McGregor's books one is reminded of the drawings by Hogarth and Rowlandson—the scene is a mass of people. Her aim is to interpret these characters as flesh and blood realities, and she succeeds very well. She is at her best when dealing with her native Scotland, and her interest in history is the peg on which many of her stories are hung. However, she has to thank her training in the classics for her exactness in speech.

In *The Popinjay* we are immediately introduced to the central character, 16-year-old David Lindsay, the popinjay of the title. David is summoned from Bordeaux in 1546 by the Cardinal Archbishop Beaton to St. Andrews; his future looks rosy and his insolence is matched only by his dreams. However, soon all is changed, the Archbishop murdered, David a wounded fugitive—and it is at this point that McGregor really gets to grips with her characters. David begins to learn what life is like in the terror-stricken and plague-infested town, and his development to maturity through his involvement with the fishergirl, Elspeth, and Father Anthony from the Priory, shows evidence of the author's acute understanding of human nature. The whole story rings true and the reader is completely involved throughout.

No doubt it is because the author is so interested in the 18th century that she writes about it so confidently and convincingly, especially in her recreation of Edinburgh at this time. Her touch is so sensitive and the writing so vivid that the reader can almost smell the stench and hear the noises of the crowds and carriages in the Lawnmarket and Canongate. This is the setting which inspires McGregor to some of her finest writing, and *An Edinburgh Reel* is as lively as the dance itself. Christine's father, embittered by his experience as a prisoner after Culloden, returns to Edinburgh vowing vengeance on his unknown betrayer after the battle, whereas his daughter wants him to forgive and forget. The pages are scattered with fascinating characters—Lord Balmuir, the elderly judge, Lucky Robertson who owns the pie shop, Ewan McDonnell who tries to tempt Christine's father back into Jacobite plotting, and many more. McGregor blends them all into a colorful picture of Edinburgh life, pulsating with vigour and vitality. Everything in the book echoes the authenticity of her writing, the marvelous dialogue, the jostling crowds, the personal hatreds and hopes, and the contrasting natures of the main protagonists. It is a glorious piece of writing, compulsive and exhilarating and a fine example of McGregor at her best.

—Margaret Walker

MCKAY, Hilary

Nationality: British. **Born:** Boston, Lincolnshire. **Education:** St. Andrews University, M.Sc. in Botany and Zoology. **Family:** Married; one son. **Awards:** *Guardian* Children's Fiction Award, 1992, for *The Exiles*; Smarties Overall Winner, 1993, for *The Exiles at Home*. **Address:** c/o Hodder & Stoughton, 338 Euston Road, London NW1 3BH, England.

Publications for Children

Fiction

The Exiles. London, Gollancz, 1992.
The Exiles at Home. London, Gollancz, 1993.
Dog Friday. London, Gollancz, 1994.
The Amber Cat. London, Gollancz, 1995.
Why Didn't You Tell Me? illustrated by John Eastwood. London, Piccadilly Press, 1996.
Exiles in Love. London, Gollancz, 1996.
Happy and Glorious, illustrated by Hilda Offen. London, Hodder and Stoughton, 1996.
Practically Perfect, illustrated by Hilda Offen. London, Hodder and Stoughton, 1997.

"Paradise House" Series (illustrated by Tony Kenyon)

Magic in the Mirror. London, Gollancz, 1996.
Zoo in the Attic. London, Gollancz, 1996.
Treasure in the Garden. London, Gollancz, 1996.
The Echo in the Chimney. London, Gollancz, 1996.

* * *

Hilary McKay's style of writing is refreshingly traditional. She immediately established herself as a major force in children's literature, grabbing the attention of book prize judges, with her first book. *The Exiles* won the *Guardian* Children's Fiction Award and its sequel, *The Exiles at Home*, won the Smarties Children's Book Award.

McKay's books do not rely on gimmicks, fantastic settings, zany characters, wacky situations, or state-of-the-art technology. Instead they have all the hallmarks of classic children's literature—credible characters with strong personalities, convincing, well-plotted storylines with acceptable outcomes, excellent characterisation with well-developed relationships between the characters, and an abundance of humour. The dialogue between characters is genuinely funny with a good stock of one-liners and the adults in her books demonstrate as much stimulating repartee as the children. In many of her books she depicts rather disordered but generally happy family life with harassed parents trying to juggle the demands of work and children.

The Exiles is the first of three books about four spirited sisters: Naomi, Ruth, Rachel, and Phoebe Conroy. It starts with them dreading the summer holidays which they are being forced to spend with Big Grandma, who they feel is disapproving of them. They love reading and Big Grandma hides all the books, so that they have to amuse themselves out of doors. In spite of this they manage to have a surprisingly good time, discovering old-fashioned ways of entertaining themselves and gaining a certain amount of independence and insight into themselves in the process. They rediscover the "great outdoors," experimenting with cooking for themselves and relishing the freedom from adult intervention and organisation. There are echoes of bygone days here and idyllic summers spent doing nothing.

The girls return in *Exiles at Home*, in which further domestic chaos ensues when Ruth rather magnanimously agrees to sponsor a child in Africa. This causes problems when she realises that £10 is a lot of money to find every month, especially when no-one else must know that she has lied about being eighteen. Eventually, her sisters find out and join her in trying to raise the money each month. Their ever-more inventive ways of finding things to do that they can be paid for arouses the suspicions of Big Grandma, who guesses what they are up to. The ending, in which the girls inherit enough money to sponsor the African child for life and for the four of them and big Grandma to visit him, ties up all the ends neatly. One forgives it being a trifle contrived because it is so immensely satisfying. The generosity of spirit engendered by the girls' good intentions makes this an uplifting book.

The next book in the series sees Ruth, now fifteen, prone to falling hopelessly in love, which Big Grandma describes as the "family failing." Naomi soon follows suit as she and Ruth both develop a crush on their Temporary English Teacher and Naomi takes to wandering about reciting poetry in a dreamy voice. Meanwhile Rachel is desperate to be elected May Queen and the rest of the family wait with baited breath as they are certain she will be disappointed, and Phoebe is training to become an international spy. Once again Big Grandma comes to the rescue with the idea of inviting a French boy to stay, and once again it does not have quite the effect that she intended. The book ends with Big Grandma taking them all to Brittany to see the boy's grandfather and demonstrating that she, too, is a victim of the "family failing." Phoebe's spying results in misunderstandings galore, which are cleverly constructed to produce some marvellous scenes of pure farce.

Hilary McKay has a gift for making her readers empathise totally with her characters. The girls in these books live life to the absolute limits of their emotions, which are so accurately portrayed that the reader feels almost physically exhausted by the sheer intensity of it all. Girls particularly identify strongly with these feisty role models.

In two novels for a slightly younger age group, Hilary McKay creates two more likeable families. In *Dog Friday* Robin Brogan is living a quiet life with his mother in a large house by the sea, which she is running as a bed and breakfast business. Then the Robinson family moves in next door with three boisterous children and a dog and everything changes. Most of the things they do to help end in near disaster. When Robin finds a stray dog on the beach, and overcomes his initial fear of dogs, he wants to keep it. The Robinson children come up with a plan to ensure the dog's real owner does not claim him back. The well-observed characters are once again bursting with energy, humour, and warmth and their wild antics are hugely entertaining.

In the sequel, *The Amber Cat,* the characters continue to have the exciting and engaging escapades, inspired by Mrs. Brogan's reminiscences about her own childhood spent on the beach. Underneath are more sensitive issues, like being able to talk about Robin's father, who has died, and remembering happier times. There is a great deal of poignancy in the appearance of a mysterious girl on the beach, who it is rumoured is the ghost of a child.

In spite of the high-spirited humour in all Hilary McKay's books she deals with some serious ethical issues. To say that they go unnoticed would be wrong, but she introduces them in such a light-handed way that readers may not be consciously aware of them. For example, with the issue of sponsoring the child in Africa in *Exiles at Home,* she throws in a line from the mother that she doesn't all together approve of singling out individual children in Africa and expecting them to be grateful. The issue is not raised again, but the point has been made and will provoke thought among children.

In a slight departure from the realistic family story are two books about a palace where the Queen is a child and consequently some unlikely things happen. The first book, *Happy and Glorious,* sees the Queen waking up on her tenth birthday, bouncing on her bed, and demanding presents, even though it is her Unofficial Birthday. Michael the gardener's boy procures a donkey for her, by mistake rather than design, and some farcical episodes ensue with and without the Royal Donkey. Much of the humour is derived from the fact that the Ladies in Waiting, the Prime Minister and his wife, and the Treasurer must all obey the ten-year-old Queen, even when her ideas are less than sensible. There is more of the same in the sequel, *Practically Perfect,* in which the Ladies in Waiting have had enough and decide that they would have a more peaceful existence if the Queen were married off.

Although her forte is in developing characters and plot in full-length novels, Hilary McKay has also successfully written books for younger readers that demonstrate all the humour and quality of writing of her longer books. These include *Why Didn't You Tell Me?,* in which only child Nicholas Brown decides that another baby would stop his mother fussing over him. Slightly longer and for fluent readers is the "Paradise Road" series, which centres round a large house that has been converted into flats. The stories are primarily about the everyday adventures of the children who live in the flats. As in all Hilary McKay's books, the characters are believable and the situations well developed.

—Fiona Lafferty

McKEE, David (John)

Nationality: British. **Military Service:** British Army, Royal Army Education Corps, instructor 1956-58; became sergeant. **Career:** Freelance painter, illustrator, cartoonist, and children's television filmmaker. **Awards:** Children's Literature prize (West Germany), 1987. **Address:** c/o Andersen Press, Random House, 20 Vauxhall Bridge Road, London SW1, England.

PUBLICATIONS FOR CHILDREN (ILLUSTRATED BY THE AUTHOR)

Fiction

Bronto's Wings. London, Dobson, 1964.
Two Can Toucan. London, Abelard Schuman, 1964; New York, Abelard Shuman, 1965.
Mr. Benn, Red Knight. London, Dobson, 1967; New York, McGraw Hill, 1968.
Mark and the Monocycle. London and New York, Abelard Shuman, 1968.
Elmer: The Story of a Patchwork Elephant. London, Dobson, and New York, McGraw Hill, 1968; revised edition, London, Andersen Press, and New York, Lothrop, 1989.
123456789 Benn. London, Dobson, and New York, McGraw Hill, 1970.
The Magician Who Lost His Magic. London and New York, Abelard Schuman, 1970.
Six Men. Montchaldorf, Switzerland, Nord-Sud Verlag, 1971; London, A. and C. Black, 1972.
Lord Rex, The Lion Who Wished. London and New York, Abelard Schuman, 1973.
The Magician and the Sorcerer. London, Abelard Schuman, and New York, Parents' Magazine Press, 1974; as *Melric and the Sorcerer,* London, Methuen, 1987.
The Day the Tide Went Out, and Out, and Out.... London, Abelard Schuman, 1975; New York, Abelard Schuman, 1976.
Elmer Again and Again. London, Dobson, 1975.
The Magician and the Petnapping. London, Abelard Schuman, and Boston, Houghton Mifflin, 1976.
Two Admirals. London, Andersen Press, and Boston, Houghton Mifflin, 1977.
The Magician and the Balloon. London, Abelard Schuman, 1978; New York, Bedrick, 1986.
Tusk Tusk. London, Andersen Press, 1978; Woodbury, New York, Barron's, 1979.
The Magician and the Dragon. London, Abelard Schuman, 1979; as *Melric and the Dragon,* London, Methuen, 1987.
Big Game Benn. London, Dobson, 1979.
King Rollo and the Bread [*Birthday, New Shoes, Tree, Dishes, Balloons, Bath, King Frank, Search*]. London, Andersen Press, 9 vols., 1979-81; first 3 vols. published Boston, Little Brown, 1979; first 4 vols. published as *The Adventures of King Rollo,* New York, Penguin, 1 vol., 1986, London, Andersen, 1996.
Big Top Benn. London, Dobson, 1980.
Not Now, Bernard. London, Andersen Press, 1980.
The Magician and Double Trouble, illustrated by David Hope. London, Abelard Schuman, 1981.
I Hate My Teddy Bear. London, Andersen Press, 1982; New York, Clarion, 1984.

King Rollo's Playroom and Other Stories. London, Andersen Press, 1983.
The Hill and the Rock. London, Andersen Press, 1984; New York, Clarion, 1985.
King Rollo's Letter and Other Stories. London, Andersen Press, 1984.
Two Monsters. London, Andersen Press, 1985; New York, Bradbury Press, 1986.
King Rollo's Spring [*Summer, Autumn, Winter*]. London, Andersen Press, 4 vols., 1986.
The Sad Story of Veronica Who Played the Violin. London, Andersen Press, 1987; Brooklyn, New York, Kane-Miller, 1991.
The Magician's Apprentice. London, Blackie, 1987.
Snow Woman. London, Andersen Press, 1987; New York, Lothrop, 1988.
Who's a Clever Baby, Then? London, Andersen Press, 1988; New York, Lothrop, 1989.
The Magician and the King's Crown. London, Blackie, 1988.
The Monster and the Teddy Bear. London, Andersen, 1989.
King Rollo's Letter and Other Stories. London, Trafalgar Square, 1989.
King Rollo and Santa's Beard. London, Andersen, 1990.
Annabelle Pig and the Travellers [and] Benjamin Pig and the Apple Thiefs. London, Macmillan, 1990.
Tales of Melric the Magician. London, Treasure, 1991.
Elmer Again. London, Andersen, 1991; New York, Lothrop, 1992.
Zebra's Hiccups. London, Andersen, 1991; Simon & Schuster, 1993.
The Schoolbus Comes at Eight O'Clock. London, Andersen, 1993; New York, Hyperion, 1994.
Elmer on Stilts. London, Andersen, 1993; New York, Lothrop, 1995.
Caveman. London, Hodder and Stoughton, 1993.
Diver. London, Hodder and Stoughton, 1993.
Spaceman. London, Hodder and Stoughton, 1993.
Red Knight. London, Hodder and Stoughton, 1993.
Our Favorite Rhymes. Harlow, Longmann, 1994.
Elmer and Wilbur. London, Andersen, 1994; New York, Lothrop, 1996.
Elmer's Colors. London, Andersen, and New York, Lothrop, 1994.
Elmer's Weather. London, Andersen, and New York, Lothrop, 1994.
Elmer's Day. London, Andersen, and New York, Lothrop, 1994.
Elmer's Friends. London, Andersen, and New York, Lothrop, 1994.
Elmer in the Snow. New York, Lothrop, 1995.
Isabel's Noisy Tummy. London, Andersen, 1995.
Charlotte's Piggy Bank. London, Andersen, 1996.
I Can, Too! An Elmer Pop-Up Book. New York, Lothrop, 1997.
Prince Peter and the Teddy Bear. London, Andersen and New York, Farrar, 1997.
Elmer Takes Off. New York, Lothrop, 1998.

Plays

Greenback Hell (screenplay), 1974.
Mr. Benn (television series).

Other

Hans in Luck. London and New York, Abelard Schuman, 1967.
Mathematics Everywhere. London, Longman, 1969.
The Man Who Was Going to Mind the House: A Norwegian Folk-Tale. London, Abelard Schuman, 1972; New York, Abelard Schuman, 1973.
Mr. Benn Annual. London, Argus Press, 1972.

*

Illustrator: *The Poor Farmer and the Robber Knights* by Walter Kreye, 1969; *Hector's House Annual*, 1969-73; *Bertha the Tanker* by Liane Smith, 1969; *Vamos Amigos* by Heloise Lewis, 1971; *Mr. Drackle and His Dragons* by Elizabeth Hull Froman, 1971; *Joseph the Border Guard*, 1972, *Joachim the Dustman*, 1974, and *Joachim the Policeman*, 1975, all by Kurt Baumann; *Kids' London* by Elizabeth Holt, 1972; *Fire*, 1973, *The Day We Went to the Seaside*, 1973, and *What in the World*, 1979, all by David Mackay; *Piccolo Book of Parties and Party Games* by Deborah Manley, 1973; *The Follyfoot Pony Quiz Book* by Christine Pullein-Thompson, 1974; *Yan and the Gold Mountain Robbers*, 1974, and *Yan and the Firemonsters*, 1976, both by Sydney Paulden; *Cook for Your Kids!* by Merry Archard, 1975; *Fiery Frederica* by Christine N'stlinger, 1975; *Helping* by Caroline Moorehead, 1975; *Tomfoolery*, 1975, *Witcracks*, 1975, and *A Twister of Twists, A Tangler of Tongues: Tongue Twisters*, 1976, all edited by Alvin Schwartz; *Okki-Tokki-Unga: Action Stories* edited by Beatrice Harrop, 1976, and *Harlequin* edited by Harrop and David Gadsby, 1981; *A Book of Elephants* edited by Katie Wales, 1977; *The King of Quizzical Island* by Gordon Snell, 1978; *Albert's World Tour* by Rosemary Weir, 1978; *Super Gran*, 1978, *Super Gran Rules, O.K.!*, 1981, *Super Gran Superstar*, 1982, *More Television Adventures of Super Gran*, 1984, *Super Gran on Holiday*, 1985, and *Super Gran at the Circus*, 1987, *Super Gran is Magic*, 1990, *Super Gran to the Rescue*, 1992, *Super Gran Abroad*, 1991, all by Forrest Wilson; *A Book of Pig Tales*, 1979, *A Book of Bears*, 1981, *A Book of Cats*, 1983, *Stories for a Prince*, 1983, and *A Book of Mice*, 1987, all edited by Rosemary Debnam; *Abracadabra Guitar!* by Hilary Bell, 1980; *Jeffy, The Burglar's Cat*, 1981, and *Spid*, 1985, both by Ursula Moray Williams; *Blue Bell Hill Games* edited by R.A. Smith, 1982; *The Speckled Panic*, 1982, *The Choking Peril*, 1985, *One Green Bottle*, 1987, and *Gary Who?*, 1988, *Hot Stuff*, 1991, *Who's Afraid of the Evil Eye?*, 1994, all by Hazel Townson; *The Wizard of Oz*, 1982, and *The Marvellous Land of Oz*, 1985, both by L. Frank Baum; *Game-Songs with Professor Dogg's Troupe* edited by Harriet Powell, 1983; *Paddington and the Knickerbocker Rainbow* [*at the Zoo, at the Fair, and the Marmalade Maze*], 4 vols., 1984-87, *Paddington's Painting Exhibition*, 1985, as *Paddington's Art Exhibition*, 1986, and *Paddington's Busy Day* [*Magical Christmas*], 2 vols., 1987-88, all by Michael Bond; *A Book of Dragons* edited by Joan Cass, 1985; *Hands On, Hands Off* by Christopher Schenk, 1986; *Something New for Bear to Do*, 1986, and *A Special Place for Edward James*, 1988, both by Shirley Isherwood; *Pudmuddle Jumps In: Poems* edited by Beverly Mathias and Jill Bennett, 1987; *The Scourge of the Dinner Ladies*, 1987, and *The Dinner Ladies Clean Up!*, 1990, both by David Tinkler; *Bags of Trouble*, 1988, and *Trouble Abroad*, 1990, both by Michael Harrison; *Uncle Ambrosio's Helper* by Jose Luis Olaizola, 1989; *The Mystery of the Blue Arrows* by Chuck McKee, 1990; *Revenge of the Dinner Ladies* by David Tinkler, 1991; *Henry's Most Unusual Birthday* by Elizabeth Hawkins, 1991; *Out of the Blue: Poems about Color* by Hiawyn Oram, 1992; *The Toffees From Zongaba* by Valerie Stillwell, 1992; *A Book of Dragons* compiled by Joan Cass, 1993; *Rolf and Rosie* by Robert

Swindells, 1993; *Willy and the Semolina Pudding and Other Stories* by Roger Collinson, 1994; *Disaster Bag, The One-Day Millionaires,* and *Rumpus on the Roof,* all by Hazel Townson, 1995; *Willie and the UPF and Other Stories* by Roger Collinson, 1995.

* * *

A seamless bond between illustrations and text characterises David McKee's picture books. Readers can also be certain that his books will be laced with both wit and humor. He employs a spectrum of styles from the lyrical, especially when animals are featured, to the semi-realistic, when children are the main focus, to the comic-strip, as in the King Rollo series or in *Two Monsters.* All are recognisably his work, direct and appealing to children. He is on their side.

Just as he calls on a variety of styles in his considerable output, so McKee returns to certain themes. Most obviously, he uses specific characters in whole series, King Rollo for one and Mr. Benn for another. King Rollo underpins the least demanding of his work—Rollo is no older than the early readers he addresses but, being a king, can do all the things that young children would like to do themselves like scaring grown-ups. There are even tiny books, such as *King Rollo and King Frank,* for tiny hands.

The Mr. Benn series moves beyond the nursery into a large and fantastic world. Mr. Benn is a meek sort of chap, but he has only to go to the costume shop and don another outfit to be transported into the appropriate place and time to become involved in a wild and wonderful adventure with dragons, perhaps, or elephants or even entire circuses. When all is satisfactorily resolved, he trots out of the shop attired once more in his dark suit and bowler hat, always with a souvenir of his expedition and the promise of more adventures in future. The series featuring Melric the Magician has a Camelot-style setting but the characters, including the hero, behave much like contemporary mortals, though helped with convenient powers.

McKee is closely in touch with young children and, in works that seek to help them explore ideas and values, he draws often on folktales and offers his own interpretations. *Two Can Toucan, Tusk Tusk,* and his early Elmer books all have echoes of traditional tales and address personal aspirations and conflict. The message of *Tusk Tusk* is in fact a dismal one, suggesting that so long as there is difference there must inevitably be conflict. White and black elephants fight to the death of all except the few pacifists, who slide off into the forests, from which emerge a generation later only grey elephants...but lately, the last line tells us "the little ears and the big ears have been giving each other strange looks." *Two Monsters* offers a happier resolution and an important lesson. The monsters fight so bitterly over whose view is correct that they demolish the intervening mountain—and learn that one sees things differently if one looks in different directions.

So (justly) confident is McKee of the unity between his two media that he occasionally pulls off a book in which the pictures say a good deal more than, and sometimes something quite different from, the line or so of text per page. In *Not Now, Bernard* the text speaks for Bernard's parents, always too busy doing things to give Bernard the attention he wants. But the pictures tell the story through a child's eyes and the reader is compelled to pay attention to the monster who gobbles Bernard up! Equally preoccupied are the parents in *Snow Woman,* though they do insist on the term "snowperson," while demonstrating non-sexist distribution of their own domestic tasks. The children, however, are not convinced nor is the matter satisfactorily resolved: when the snow couple disappear, the children decide to build a genderless snow bear.

The divergence of text and picture in *I Hate My Teddy Bear* is practically subversive. Parents are likely to find themselves out of control of reading the book as their preliterate children, instead of merely listening appreciatively, tell them the story from the bizarre activities in the pictures. Nothing could be more calculated to instill in young children a real love of books than enabling them to interpret and enjoy them for themselves, with sharing them as an optional extra.

In the 1990s McKee focused again on a character he created in 1968—the lovable patchwork elephant, Elmer. In *Elmer and Wilbur,* Elmer and his black-and-white cousin Wilbur indulge their love of practical joking, while Elmer shows his fellow jungle dwellers that hot and cold are relative terms when he takes them on a jaunt to the mountains in *Elmer in the Snow.* Can an elephant fly? Elmer can't believe that a creature as heavy as himself can be blown away, even by the strongest wind, but he just may be surprised in *Elmer Takes Off.* In addition to picture books, the perennially popular pachyderm has appeared in a series of concept board books devoted to colors, friendship, weather, and everyday events, as well as his very own pop-up book, *I Can, Too!* With his gentle sense of humor, subtle but obvious love of irony, and illustrations packed with visual appeal, McKee has created in Elmer a character children around the world have taken to heart.

—Gillian Klein, updated by Jackie C. Horne.

MCKISSACK, Patricia C. and Fredrick L(emuel)

Nationality: American. **Born:** (Fredrick) 12 August 1939, Nashville, Tennessee; (Patricia) 9 August 1944, Nashville, Tennessee. **Education:** Both educated at Tennessee Agricultural and Industrial State University (now Tennessee State University), B.S. 1964 (Fredrick) and B.A. 1964 (Patricia). **Military Service:** (Fredrick) United States Marine Corps, 1957-60. **Family:** Married 12 December 1964; three sons. **Career:** (Fredrick) Civil engineer for city and federal governments, 1964-74; owner of general contracting company, St. Louis, Missouri, 1974-82; writer since 1982. (Patricia) English teacher, junior high school, Kirkwood, Missouri, 1968-75; part-time instructor in English, Forest Park College, St. Louis, Missouri, since 1975; Children's book editor, Concordia Publishing, since 1984. Both co-owners, All-Writing Services. **Awards:** (Both) C.S. Lewis Silver Medal awards, Christian Educators Association, 1985, for *Abram, Abram, Where are We Going?*; Jane Addams Children's Book Award, Women's International League for Peace and Freedom, and Coretta Scott King Award, both 1990, for *A Long Hard Journey: the Story of the Pullman Porter*; Coretta Scott King Honor Award, 1993, for *Sojourner Truth: Ain't I a Woman?*; (Patricia) Newbery Honor Award and Coretta Scott King Author Award, both 1993, for *The Dark-Thirty: Southern Tales of the Supernatural.* **Address:** P.O. Box 967, Chesterfield, Missouri 63006-0967, U.S.A. *Office:* All-Writing Services, 14629 Timberlake Manor Ct., Chesterfield, Missouri 63017, U.S.A.

Publications for Children

Fiction

Look What You've Done Now, Moses, illustrated by Joe Boddy. Chicago, David C. Cook, 1984.
Abram, Abram, Where Are We Going?, illustrated by Boddy. Chicago, David C. Cook, 1984.
Cinderella, illustrated by Tom Dunnington. Chicago, Children's Press, 1985.
Country Mouse and City Mouse, illustrated by Anne Sikorski. Chicago, Children's Press, 1985.
The Little Red Hen, illustrated by Dennis Hockerman. Chicago, Children's Press, 1985.
The Three Bears, illustrated by Virginia Bala. Chicago, Children's Press, 1985.
The Ugly Little Duck, illustrated by Peggy Perry Anderson. Chicago, Children's Press, 1986.
When Do You Talk to God? Prayers for Small Children, illustrated by Gary Gumble. Minneapolis, Augsburg, 1986.
King Midas and His Gold, illustrated by Tom Dunnington. Chicago, Children's Press, 1986.
A Real Winner, illustrated by Quentin Thompson and Ken Jones. St. Louis, Missouri, Milliken, 1987.
The King's New Clothes, illustrated by Gwen Connelly. Chicago, Children's Press, 1987.
Tall Phil and Small Bill, illustrated by Kathy Mitter. St. Louis, Missouri, Milliken, 1987.
Three Billy Goats Gruff, illustrated by Tom Dunnington. Chicago, Children's Press, 1987.
My Bible ABC Book, illustrated by Reed Merrill. Minneapolis, Augsburg, 1987.
All Paths Lead to Bethlehem, illustrated by Kathryn E. Shoemaker. Minneapolis, Augsburg, 1987.
Messy Bessey, illustrated by Richard Hackney. Chicago, Children's Press, 1987.
The Big Bug Book of Counting, illustrated by Bartholomew. St. Louis, Missouri, Milliken, 1987.
The Big Bug Book of Opposites, illustrated by Bartholomew. St. Louis, Missouri, Milliken, 1987.
The Big Bug Book of Places to Go, illustrated by Bartholomew. St. Louis, Missouri, Milliken, 1987.
The Big Bug Book of the Alphabet, illustrated by Bartholomew. St. Louis, Missouri, Milliken, 1987.
Bugs! illustrated by Martin. Chicago, Children's Press, 1988.
The Big Bug Book of Things to Do, illustrated by Bartholomew. St. Louis, Missouri, Milliken, 1987.
The Children's ABC Christmas, illustrated by Kathy Rogers. Minneapolis, Augsburg, 1988.
Constance Stumbles, illustrated by Dunnington. Chicago, Children's Press, 1988.
Oh, Happy, Happy Day! A Child's Easter in Story, Song, and Prayer, illustrated by Elizabeth Swisher. Minneapolis, Augsburg, 1989.
God Made Something Wonderful, illustrated by Ching. Minneapolis, Augsburg, 1989.
Messy Bessey's Closet, illustrated by Richard Hackney. Chicago, Children's Press, 1990.
Messy Bessey's Garden, illustrated by Martin. Chicago, Children's Press, 1991.
From Heaven Above: The Story of Christmas Proclaimed by the Angels, illustrated by Barbara Knutson. Minneapolis, Augsburg, 1992.
God Makes All Things New, illustrated by Ching. Minneapolis, Augsburg, 1993.
Messy Bessey's School Desk, illustrated by Dana Regan. Danbury, Connecticut, Children's Press, 1998.
Let My People Go: Bible Stories of Faith, Hope, and Love as told by Price Jefferies, A Free Man of Color to His Daughter, Charlotte, in Charleston, South Carolina, 1806-1816, illustrated by James Ransome. New York, Atheneum Books for Children, 1998.
Messy Bessey and the Birthday Overnight, illustrated by Dana Regan. Danbury, Connecticut, Children's Press, 1998.

Fiction by Patricia McKissack

It's the Truth, Christopher, illustrated by Bartholomew. Minneapolis, Augsburg, 1984.
Lights Out, Christopher, illustrated by Bartholomew. Minneapolis, Augsburg, 1984.
Flossie and the Fox, illustrated by Rachel Isadora. New York, Dial, 1986.
Who Is Coming? illustrated by Clovis Martin. Chicago, Children's Press, 1986.
Give It with Love, Christopher: Christopher Learns about Gifts and Giving, illustrated by Bartholomew. Minneapolis, Augsburg, 1988.
Speak Up, Christopher: Christopher Learns the Difference between Right and Wrong, illustrated by Bartholomew. Minneapolis, Augsburg, 1988.
A Troll in a Hole, St. Louis, Missouri, Milliken, 1988.
Nettie Jo's Friends, illustrated by Scott Cook. New York, Knopf, 1988.
Mirandy and Brother Wind, illustrated by Jerry Pinkney. New York, Knopf, 1988.
Monkey-Monkey's Trick: Based on an African Folk-Tale, illustrated by Paul Meisel. New York, Random House, 1989.
With Ruthilde Kronberg, *A Piece of the Wind and Other Stories to Tell.* New York, Harper, 1990.
No Ned for Alarm. St. Louis, Missouri, Milliken, 1990.
A Million Fish—More or Less, illustrated by Dena Schutzer. New York, Knopf, 1992.
The Dark Thirty: Southern Tales of the Supernatural, illustrated by Brian Pinkney. New York, Knopf, 1992.

Nonfiction

Fredrick Douglas: A Biography. Chicago, Children's Press, 1986.
Frederick Douglass: The Black Lion. Chicago, Children's Press, 1987.
The Civil Rights Movement in America from 1865 to the Present. Chicago, Children's Press, 1987, 2nd edition, 1991.
James Weldon Johnson: "Lift Every Voice and Sing." Chicago, Children's Press, 1990.
A Long Hard Journey: The Story of the Pullman Porter. New York, Walker & Co., 1990.
History of the Civil Rights Movement. Chicago, Children's Press, 1990.
Taking a Stand against Racism and Racial Discrimination. New York, Franklin Watts, 1990.
W.E.B. DuBois. New York, Franklin Watts, 1990.
The Story of Booker T. Washington. Chicago, Children's Press, 1991.

Carter G. Woodson: The Father of Black History, illustrated by Ned Ostendorf. New Jersey, Enslow, 1991.
Frederick Douglass: Leader Against Slavery, illustrated by Ned Ostendorf. New Jersey, Enslow, 1991.
George Washington Carver: The Peanut Scientist, illustrated by Ned Ostendorf. New Jersey, Enslow, 1991.
Ida B. Wells-Barnett: A Voice Against Violence. New Jersey, Enslow, 1991.
Louis Armstrong: Jazz Musician, illustrated by Ned Ostendorf. New Jersey, Enslow, 1991.
Marian Anderson: A Great Singer. New Jersey, Enslow, 1991.
Martin Luther King Jr.: Man of Peace. New Jersey, Enslow, 1991.
Mary Church Terrell: Leader for Equality, illustrated by Ned Ostendorf. New Jersey, Enslow, 1991.
Mary McLeod Bethune: A Great Teacher, illustrated by Ned Ostendorf. New Jersey, Enslow, 1991.
Ralph J. Bunche: Peacemaker. New Jersey, Enslow, 1991.
Jesse Owens. New Jersey, Enslow, 1992.
From Heaven Above. Minneapolis, Augsburg, 1992.
Langston Hughes. New Jersey, Enslow, 1992.
Sojourner Truth. New Jersey, Enslow, 1992.
Zora Neale Hurston: Writer and Storyteller. New Jersey, Enslow, 1992.
Satchel Paige. New Jersey, Enslow, 1992.
Sojourner Truth: Ain't I a Woman? New York, Scholastic, 1992.
Madam C.J. Walker: Self-Made Millionaire. New Jersey, Enslow, 1992.
Paul Robeson: A Voice to Remember, illustrated by Michael David Biegel. New Jersey, Enslow, 1992.
Booker T. Washington: Leader and Educator, illustrated by Michael Bryant. New Jersey, Enslow, 1992.
Christmas in the Big House, Christmas in the Quarters, illustrated by John Thompson. New York, Scholastic, 1994.
The Royal Kingdoms of Ghana, Mali, and Songhay: Life in Medieval Africa. New York, Henry Holt, 1994.
African-American Scientists. Brookfield, Connecticut, Millbrook Press, 1994.
With Frederick McKissack, Jr., *Black Diamond: The Story of the Negro Baseball Leagues.* New York, Scholastic, 1994.
African-American Inventors. Brookfield, Connecticut, Millbrook Press, 1994.
Red-tail Angels: The Story of the Tuskegee Airmen of World War II. New York, Walker and Co., 1995.
Rebels Against Slavery. New York, Scholastic, 1996.
Young, Black, and Determined: A Biography of Lorraine Hansberry. New York, Holiday House, 1998.

Nonfiction by Patricia McKissack

As L'Ann Carwell, *Good Shepherd Prayer.* St. Louis, Mississippi, Concordia, 1978.
As L'Ann Carwell, *God Gives New Life.* St. Louis, Mississippi, Concordia, 1979.
Ask the Kids. St. Louis, Mississippi, Concordia, 1979.
Who Is Who? Chicago, Children's Press, 1983.
Martin Luther King, Jr.: A Man to Remember. Chicago, Children's Press, 1984.
Paul Lawrence Dunbar: A Poet to Remember. Chicago, Children's Press, 1984.
Michael Jackson, Superstar. Chicago, Children's Press, 1984.
The Apache. Chicago, Children's Press, 1984.
Mary McLeod Bethune: A Great American Educator. Chicago, Children's Press, 1985.
Aztec Indians. Chicago, Children's Press, 1985.
The Inca. Chicago, Children's Press, 1985.
The Maya. Chicago, Children's Press, 1985.
Our Martin Luther King Book, illustrated by Rachel Isadora. Chanhassen, Minnesota, Child's World, 1986.
Jesse Jackson: A Biography. New York, Scholastic, 1989.

*

Biography: *Something about the Author,* Detroit, Gale Research, Vol. 73, 1992.

* * *

Patricia and Fredrick McKissack were married twenty years before they decided to write books together. Separately Fredrick, a general contractor, and Patricia, an editor and teacher, had successfully written books, mostly for younger readers. When they became a writing team they at first wrote mostly fiction and then biographies. They now specialize in nonfiction for children about African-American history. Together they have written over seventy-five books for a broad range of readers, from elementary-aged to upper junior high readers. Adults, too, have found many of the their books to be interesting, and covering areas in which information is lacking, such as the Tuskegee airmen, the history of black baseball leagues, and biographies of notable African-American scientists and inventors. Their names have become synonymous with quality biographies and histories that fully and accurately address the African-American experience. Two of these books, a biography on Sojourner Truth, and a history of Pullman Porters and the union they established, have each won several awards.

Though the two grew up in the same town, they did not really come to know each other until they attended college together. Fredrick had served three years in the Marines before attending college so they graduated together in 1964 and were married that same year. Their experiences growing up in the south during the 1950s and 1960s became fodder for their future writing careers, from the Vietnam War to the Civil Rights Movement, from church bombings to violent racial incidents. In their early adult life the McKissacks were affected by the assassinations of President John F. Kennedy, Senator Robert Kennedy, Martin Luther King, Jr, and Malcolm X. "The reason we write for children is to tell them about these things and to get them to internalize the information, to feel just a little of the hurt, the tremendous amount of hurt and sadness that racism and discrimination cause—for all people, regardless of race," Fredrick said in *Something About the Author.*

Their biography subjects include well-known African-Americans such as Martin Luther King, Jr. and Booker T. Washington, as well as lesser-known subjects. Satchel Paige, for example, was a black baseball star in the early twentieth century; Mary Church Terrell fought for equality for blacks and women; Ida B. Wells-Barnett spoke out against violence. And the African-American contribution to the arts is not overlooked with biographies on Louis Armstrong, Langston Hughes, and singer Marian Anderson. One of the outstanding features of these biographies is the McKissacks' ability to make the information accessible to the lower elementary grades. They also portray the subjects as people with such strong convictions that the obstacles of their racially-biased society would not deter them from following these convictions. In *Sojourner Truth: Ain't I a Woman?* (1992) the McKissacks not only portray the life of this woman who was born a slave and given her freedom at the age of thirty, but her need to speak out against slavery, often winning over hostile audiences. They show how their subject's opinion often differed from other abolitionists and how Truth was influenced by other prominent people of the time, including her former master who also became an abolitionist.

Their attention to detail and portrayal of facts in an interesting, entertaining, and appropriate manner for the targeted age level has given the McKissacks' other works on the African-American experience a prominent place on library shelves. *A Long Hard Journey: The Story of the Pullman Porter* (1990) won the 1990 Coretta Scott King Award. It covers not only the history of the Pullman Porters, but the saga behind the Brotherhood of Sleeping Car Porters, the first major black labor union to be admitted into the American Federation of Labor (AFL) whose struggle helped pave the way for labor and civil rights in America. Their books often include songs, poetry, historical photos, and personal reminiscences to better convey the story and to bring it alive for the readers.

Red-Tail Angels: The Story of the Tuskegee Airmen of World War II (1995) sheds light on another area of history given marginal space in history texts. The McKissack's interviewed surviving pilots and researched personal accounts of these black aviation pioneers who gained a reputation for their aerial dogfighting and who, combined, brought home 150 Distinguished Flying Crosses and Legions of Merit at the close of World War II. The book begins with a brief history of black soldiers in the American military, and an account of the beginnings of aviation and the role of women and blacks in this arena, before moving into the "experiment" to establish an all-black fighter squadron at Tuskegee. Historical photographs and personal snapshots of the airmen bring these men alive to the readers. The firsthand accounts of the exploits of the 332nd Fighter Group reveal the men's courage and extraordinary determination to survive.

The same depth of research, peppered with personal accounts, enlivens *Black Diamond: The Story of the Negro Baseball Leagues* (1994). Readers feel the emotion behind the history of a league whose players often went to Cuba, Mexico, and South America to find the respect so easily granted to white players in the United States. Italic type sets off the personal accounts and numerous photographs range from the various teams in the league to players waiting in bus terminals—a grim reminder of how discrimination made the success of the leagues difficult and travel for games less than glamorous for the players.

In *Something About the Author,* Patricia McKissack said, "Writing has allowed us to do something positive with our experiences although some of our experiences have been very negative. We try to enlighten, to change attitudes, to form new attitudes—to build bridges with our books." For many children, the bridge has been built, not only in understanding these many important aspects of history, but in reading nonfiction as well as fiction for the enjoyment of the words and the emotions and inner understanding the "story" invokes. The McKissacks have set an example for other nonfiction authors to follow in their informative and lively books used as a bridge to learning and opening the mind.

—Lisa A. Wroble

McLEAN, Allan Campbell

Nationality: British. **Born:** Walney Island, Lancashire, 18 November 1922. **Education:** Walney Island Elementary School and Barrow-in-Furness Junior Technical School, Lancashire. **Military Service:** Served in the Royal Air Force in North Africa, Sicily, and Italy, 1941-46. **Family:** Married Margaret Elizabeth White in 1946; two sons and one daughter. **Career:** Clerk, J.F. Dobson, accountants, Barrow-in-Furness, 1938-41. **Awards:** Frederick Niven award, for fiction, 1962; Scottish Arts Council award, 1972. **Agent:** A.M. Heath, 79 St. Martin's Lane, London WC2N 4AA, England; or, Brandt and Brandt, 1501 Broadway, New York, New York 10036, U.S.A.

Publications for Children

Fiction

The Hill of the Red Fox. London, Collins, 1955; New York, Dutton, 1956.
The Man of the House, illustrated by Shirley Hughes. London, Collins, 1956; as *Storm over Skye,* New York, Harcourt Brace, 1957.
Master of Morgana. New York, Harcourt Brace, 1959; London, Collins, 1960.
Ribbon of Fire. London, Collins, and New York, Harcourt Brace, 1962.
A Sound of Trumpets. New York, Harcourt Brace, 1966; London, Collins, 1967.
The Year of the Stranger. London, Collins, 1971; New York, Walck, 1972.

Publications for Adults

Novels

The Carpet-Slipper Murder. London, Ward Lock, 1956; New York, Washburn, 1957.
Death on All Hallows. London, Ward Lock, and New York, Washburn, 1958.
Deadly Honeymoon. London, Ward Lock, 1958.
Murder by Invitation. London, Ward Lock, 1959.
Stand-In for Murder. London, Ward Lock, 1960.
The Islander. London, Collins, 1962; as *The Gates of Eden,* New York, Harcourt Brace, 1962.
The Glasshouse. New York, Harcourt Brace, 1968; London, Calder and Boyars, 1969.

Other

Explore the Highlands and Islands. Inverness, Highlands and Islands Development Board, 1972.
The Highlands and Islands of Scotland. London, Collins, 1976; New York, Crown, 1977.

*

Allan Campbell McLean comments:

All my historical novels for young people—*Ribbon of Fire, A Sound of Trumpets, The Year of the Stranger*—are based upon actual historical happenings in the Isle of Skye. My aim has been to present the young reader with a picture of the 19th-century life in the Scottish Highlands that he or she would be unlikely to acquire from school textbooks.

* * *

To read Allan Campbell McLean's novels is to be transported straightway into the Highlands and islands of Scotland which provide the authentic background to his full-blooded adventure stories. He uses the main character as narrator, and this personal involvement adds realism and excitement to the tales. An Englishman who has lived many years in Scotland, McLean has a poet's ear for language, and his attention to the cadences and rhythms of the speech of the people results in truly authentic dialogue. His writing is frequently centered on social injustice and hardship, but this is historically true of the period and setting of his books and reinforces the impact of his writing.

Master of Morgana is probably the book least inspired by his social conscience, but it is a vehicle for powerfully dramatic descriptions of the lives of fishermen in Skye. Niall is seeking the man responsible for his brother's near-fatal accident, and his adventures are gripping and exciting. Yet it is frequently the drama of the boy and his fellow fishermen struggling with the stormy sea which makes the greatest impression. Salmon fishing technique is minutely described, and the power of the sea in all its fury is fully equalled by the author's descriptive prose and skill in creating atmosphere. However, it is in *The Year of the Stranger* that McLean's writing reaches its height. A tale of injustice and harshness, it grips the reader from the very first sentence: "Something wet and cold hit me across the belly, jerking me awake...." Tension and excitement build up though interspersed with passages of poetic beauty, and soon the story becomes an allegory with visionary splendour breathtaking in its effect. Here is an ideal mixture of harshness and gentleness, excitement and peace, history and hope, all skillfully interwoven to produce a thought-provoking story.

McLean is a writer so attuned to his background and environment that his writing always rings true. Description and action are finely balanced to produce first-rate adventure stories which linger in the memory for a long time.

—Margaret Walker

McNEILL, Janet

Nationality: British. **Born:** Dublin, Ireland, 14 September 1907. **Education:** Birkenhead School, Cheshire, 1914-24; St. Andrews University, Scotland, M.A. in classics 1929. **Family:** Married Robert P. Alexander in 1933 (died 1973); three sons (one deceased) and one daughter. **Career:** Secretary, Belfast *Telegraph,* 1930-33. **Agent:** A.P. Watt Ltd., 20 John Street, London WC1N 2DL. **Address:** St. Monica's, Cote Lane, Westbury-on-Trym, Bristol BS9 3UN, England.

PUBLICATIONS FOR CHILDREN

Fiction

My Friend Specs McCann, illustrated by Rowel Friers. London, Faber, 1955.

A Pinch of Salt, illustrated by Rowel Friers. London, Faber, 1956.

A Light Dozen: Eleven More Stories, illustrated by Rowel Friers. London, Faber, 1957.

Specs Fortissimo, illustrated by Rowel Friers. London, Faber, 1958.

This Happy Morning, illustrated by Rowel Friers. London, Faber, 1959.

Special Occasions: Eleven More Stories, illustrated by Rowel Friers. London, Faber, 1960.

Various Specs, illustrated by Rowel Friers. London, Faber, 1961; New York, Nelson, 1971.

Try These for Size, illustrated by Rowel Friers. London, Faber, 1963.

The Giant's Birthday, illustrated by Walter Erhard. New York, Walck, 1964.

Tom's Tower, illustrated by Mary Russon. London, Faber, 1965; Boston, Little Brown, 1967.

The Mouse and the Mirage, illustrated by Walter Erhard. New York, Walck, 1966.

The Battle of St. George Without, illustrated by Mary Russon. London, Faber, and Boston, Little Brown, 1966.

I Didn't Invite You to My Party, illustrated by Jane Paton. London, Hamish Hamilton, 1967.

The Run-Around Robins, illustrated by Monica Brasier-Creagh. London, Hamish Hamilton, 1967.

Goodbye, Dove Square, illustrated by Mary Russon. London, Faber, and Boston, Little Brown, 1969.

Dragons, Come Home! and Other Stories, illustrated by John Lawrence. London, Hamish Hamilton, 1969.

Umbrella Thursday, illustrated by Carolyn Dinan. London, Hamish Hamilton, 1969.

Best Specs: His Most Remarkable Adventures, illustrated by Rowel Friers. London, Faber, 1970.

The Other People. Boston, Little Brown, 1970; London, Chatto and Windus, 1973.

The Youngest Kite, illustrated by Elizabeth Haines. London, Hamish Hamilton, 1970.

The Prisoner in the Park. London, Faber, and Boston, Little Brown, 1971.

Much Too Much Magic, illustrated by Carolyn Harrison. London, Hamish Hamilton, 1971.

A Helping Hand, illustrated by Jane Paton. London, Hamish Hamilton, 1971.

Wait for It and Other Stories. London, Faber, 1972.

A Monster Too Many, illustrated by Ingrid Fetz. Boston, Little Brown, 1972.

A Snow-Clean Pinny, illustrated by Krystyna Turska. London, Hamish Hamilton, 1973.

A Fairy Called Andy Perks, illustrated by John Lawrence. London, Hamish Hamilton, 1973.

We Three Kings. London, Faber, and Boston, Little Brown, 1974.

Ever After. London, Chatto and Windus, and Boston, Little Brown, 1975.

The Magic Lollipop, illustrated by Linda Birch. Leicester, Brockhampton Press, 1975; Chicago, Children's Press, 1976.

The Three Crowns of King Hullabaloo, illustrated by Mike Cole. Leicester, Brockhampton Press, 1975; Chicago, Children's Press, 1976.

Just Turn the Key and Other Stories, illustrated by Douglas Hall. London, Hamish Hamilton, 1976; as *Free Parking and Other Stories,* London, Beaver, 1978.

Plays

Finn and the Black Hag, music by Raymond Warren. London, Novello, 1962.
Switch On—Switch Off and Other Plays (includes *Can I Help You?, There's a Man in That Tree, Clothes-Line, Three from Four Leaves One, Burning Topic*). London, Faber, 1968.
Graduation Ode, music by Raymond Warren (produced Belfast, 1968).

Other (readers)

It's Snowing Outside, illustrated by Carol Barker. London, Macmillan, 1968.
The Day They Lost Grandad, illustrated by Julius. London, Macmillan, 1968.
The Nest Spotters, illustrated by Geraldine Spence. London, Macmillan, 1972.
The Family Upstairs, illustrated by Trevor Stubley. London, Macmillan, 1973.
My Auntie, illustrated by George Him. London, Macmillan, 1975.
Go On, Then, illustrated by Terry Reid. London, Macmillan, 1975.
Growlings, illustrated by Richard Rose. London, Macmillan, 1975.
The Day Mum Came Home, illustrated by Prudence Seward. London, Macmillan, 1976.
Look Who's Here, illustrated by Gerald Rose. London, Macmillan, 1976.
The Hermit's Purple Shirts. London, Macmillan, 1976.
Billy Brewer Goes on Tour. London, Macmillan, 1976.

Publications for Adults

Novels

A Child in the House. London, Hodder and Stoughton, 1955.
Tea at Four O'Clock. London, Hodder and Stoughton, 1956.
The Other Side of the Wall. London, Hodder and Stoughton, 1956.
A Furnished Room. London, Hodder and Stoughton, 1958.
Search Party. London, Hodder and Stoughton, 1959.
As Strangers Here. London, Hodder and Stoughton, 1960.
The Early Harvest. London, Bles, 1962.
The Maiden Dinosaur. London, Bles, 1964; as *The Belfast Friends,* Boston, Houghton Mifflin, 1966.
Talk to Me. London, Bles, 1965.
The Small Widow. London, Bles, 1967; New York, Atheneum, 1968.

Plays

Gospel Truth. Belfast, Carter, 1951.

Also author of more than 20 radio plays.

*

Janet McNeill comments:

I began writing fantasy for children because an active and agile imagination is a great help to a child confronted by the facts of a largely materialistic world. I then found it possible, and interesting, to write of the children in this world and their reaction to it. I am always glad if I can make a child laugh and remember laughing.

* * *

Janet McNeill is a godsend equally to adults who advocate reading for enjoyment and to children who want to enjoy what they read. She has a special brand of quirky humour and lightness of touch, even when writing about intrinsically serious subjects. Few authors have such empathy with children, from the very young to confused adolescents.

In the books for younger readers—even in those tailored to the demands and format of a particular series—all the children show a perceptiveness typified by little Madge in *A Helping Hand.* Though led by naive logic to some odd conclusions about the characteristics of old age, she creates a satisfying relationship with the crotchety couple next door.

For preadolescents, there is the ludicrous world of Specs McCann and his friend Curly, the close-knit society of schoolboys, with their in-jokes and their extraordinary speech patterns. The hazards and misfortunes of being a growing boy in a world controlled by (to him) unpredictable and prejudiced adults have never been better portrayed. Likewise, Matt and his friends, in *The Battle of St. George Without,* are involved with eccentric yet believable adults. McNeill sees oddities of character with the child's eye, that perception which is so devastating in the classroom; yet the comic element sharpens perspective, especially when the largely make-believe gang-life of adolescents impinges on the adult world of real crime and danger.

The same characters, grown older, reappear in *Goodbye, Dove Square,* coping with typically urban stress and change. Rehoused in a high-rise flat, Matt looks back nostalgically to the warm untidy life when walls were thicker and people "took things the way they were." The environment is constricting and nasty, the gang is splitting up, Matt alone is still at school. Internal adjustments are difficult; his mates now enjoy enviable wealth and freedom; for them, displacement is alleviated by compensations which he cannot share. Everything exacerbates his feeling that there are many things he cannot understand, even about himself, much less about other people and their bewildering relationships.

Kate, in *The Other People,* also has problems of coming to terms with a new life. Her difficulty is more a matter of adjusting to a reality which proves entirely different from her rosy expectations. Like Matt, she finds a way of piecing together the complicated jigsaws of adult life. Each of them reaches some understanding of the separateness and of the individual importance of other people.

McNeill not only has her own distinctive way of writing "realistic" stories. She has a gift, too, for letting elements of fantasy creep into tales firmly set in the everyday world. The vivid evocation of school life in *Tom's Tower,* for example, slides convincingly into the realms of fancy. Many of her short stories, too, contain some twist of circumstance, some unexpected slant. Even the commonplace is never banal, and what *seems* quite ordinary turns out to be rather odd—not far-fetched, not forced, but perceived as more-than-ordinary by an author who makes a truth of the truism that some people can see more than meets the eye.

—Cecilia Gordon

MEADER, Stephen W(arren)

Nationality: American. **Born:** Providence, Rhode Island, 2 May 1892. **Education:** Rochester High School; Moses Brown School, Providence; Haverford College, Pennsylvania, A.B. 1913. **Family:** Married 1) Elizabeth White Hoyt in 1916 (died 1962), two sons and two daughters; 2) Patience R. Ludlam in 1963. **Career:** Case worker, Children's Aid Society, Newark, New Jersey, 1913-14; secretary, Essex County Big Brother Movement, Newark, 1915; member of the publicity department, Reilly and Britton, publishers, Chicago, 1916; assistant editor, *Country Gentleman* magazine, Philadelphia, 1916-21; advertising writer, Holmes Press, Philadelphia, 1921-27; copy writer, 1927-57, and associate copy director, 1941-57, N.W. Ayer and Son, Philadelphia. **Died:** 18 July 1977.

Publications for Children

Fiction

The Black Buccaneer, illustrated by the author. New York, Harcourt Brace, 1920.
Down the Big River, illustrated by the author. New York, Harcourt Brace, 1924.
Longshanks, illustrated by Edward Caswell. New York, Harcourt Brace, 1928.
Red Horse Hill, illustrated by Lee Townsend. New York, Harcourt Brace, 1930.
Away to Sea, illustrated by Clinton Balmer. New York, Harcourt Brace, 1931.
King of the Hills, illustrated by Lee Townsend. New York, Harcourt Brace, 1933.
Lumberjack, illustrated by Henry Pitz. New York, Harcourt Brace, 1934; London, Bell, 1955.
The Will to Win and Other Stories, illustrated by John Gincano. New York, Harcourt Brace, 1936.
Who Rides in the Dark?, illustrated by James MacDonald. New York, Harcourt Brace, 1937; Oxford, Blackwell, 1938.
T-Model Tommy, illustrated by Edward Shenton. New York, Harcourt Brace, 1938.
Boy with a Pack, illustrated by Edward Shenton. New York, Harcourt Brace, 1939.
Bat, The Story of a Bull Terrier, illustrated by Edward Shenton. New York, Harcourt Brace, 1939.
Clear for Action!, illustrated by Frank Beaudouin. New York, Harcourt Brace, 1940.
Blueberry Mountain, illustrated by Edward Shenton. New York, Harcourt Brace, 1941; London, Bell, 1960.
Shadow in the Pines, illustrated by Edward Shenton. New York, Harcourt Brace, 1942.
The Sea Snake, illustrated by Edward Shenton. New York, Harcourt Brace, 1943.
The Long Trains Roll, illustrated by Edward Shenton. New York, Harcourt Brace, 1944.
Skippy's Family, illustrated by Elizabeth Korn. New York, Harcourt Brace, 1945.
Jonathan Goes West, illustrated by Edward Shenton. New York, Harcourt Brace, 1946.
Behind the Ranges, illustrated by Edward Shenton. New York, Harcourt Brace, 1947.
River of the Wolves, illustrated by Edward Shenton. New York, Harcourt Brace, 1948.
Cedar's Boy, illustrated by Lee Townsend. New York, Harcourt Brace, 1949.
Whaler 'round the Horn, illustrated by Edward Shenton. New York, Harcourt Brace, 1950; London, Museum Press, 1953.
Bulldozer, illustrated by Edwin Schmidt. New York, Harcourt Brace, 1951.
The Fish Hawk's Nest, illustrated by Edward Shenton. New York, Harcourt Brace, 1952.
Sparkplug of the Hornets, illustrated by Don Sibley. New York, Harcourt Brace, 1953.
The Buckboard Stranger, illustrated by Paul Calle. New York, Harcourt Brace, 1954.
Guns for the Saratoga, illustrated by John Cosgrave. New York, Harcourt Brace, 1955.
Sabre Pilot, illustrated by John Polgreen. New York, Harcourt Brace, 1956.
Everglades Adventure, illustrated by Charles Beck. New York, Harcourt Brace, 1957.
The Commodore's Cup, illustrated by Don Sibley. New York, Harcourt Brace, 1958.
The Voyage of the Javelin, illustrated by John Cosgrave. New York, Harcourt Brace, 1959.
Wild Pony Island, illustrated by Charles Beck. New York, Harcourt Brace, 1959.
Buffalo and Beaver, illustrated by Charles Beck. New York, Harcourt Brace, 1960.
Snow on Blueberry Mountain, illustrated by Don Sibley. New York, Harcourt Brace, 1961.
Phantom of the Blockade, illustrated by Victor Mays. New York, Harcourt Brace, 1962.
The Muddy Road to Glory, illustrated by George Hughes. New York, Harcourt Brace, 1963.
Stranger on Big Hickory, illustrated by Don Lambo. New York, Harcourt Brace, 1964.
A Blow for Liberty, illustrated by Victor Mays. New York, Harcourt Brace, 1965.
Topsail Island Treasure, illustrated by Marbury Brown. New York, Harcourt Brace, 1966.
Keep 'em Rolling, illustrated by Al Savitt. New York, Harcourt Brace, 1967.
Lonesome End, illustrated by Ned Butterfield. New York, Harcourt Brace, 1968.
The Cape May Packet, illustrated by Robert Frankenberg. New York, Harcourt Brace, 1969.

Other

Trap Lines North. New York, Dodd Mead, and London, Harrap, 1936.

* * *

Stephen W. Meader lived his first 12 years in Providence, Rhode Island, where his father taught at a religious school. His family then moved to rural New Hampshire, where his father was a timber cutter. Two important childhood influences were books and the outdoor life near the timber camps. After college, doing social work with both the Children's Aid Society and the Big Brother Movement gave him particular knowledge of the interests and needs of boys.

An incredibly prolific author for almost 50 years, Meader was one of a number of writers who concentrated on adolescent and young adult male characters, their enterprises and their dreams. He wrote fast-moving and fast-reading mysteries, adventure and sports stories, and stories of young boys making the transition into adulthood. Among the more suspenseful of his mysteries are *Red Horse Hill,* a cracking story of a boy and his horses which focuses on a lost will; *Who Rides in the Dark?,* featuring a masked rider whose identity is finally solved by an orphaned stable boy; and *Shadow in the Pines,* about a young country boy, highly knowledgeable about his rural environment, who helps the FBI in rounding up a gang of saboteurs. These adolescent characters are spirited and curious, which indeed they need to be in order to meet the exciting challenges all around them.

Meader's adventure stories often revolve about American expansion and war. He is exceptionally able to interpret the culture of ethnic regions at times of American expansion. *Buffalo and Beaver* is a story of western adventure in the days of the mountain men. *Everglades Adventure* is a tale of action and suspense set in Fort Dallas, Florida. Meader is also skilled in his war stories, presenting fairly and accurately the arguments of all sides. *Guns for the Saratoga* is an authentic story of privateering during the Revolutionary War. *Phantom of the Blockade* concerns life aboard a Confederate blockade runner in the Civil War. *The Sea Snake* is about a Nazi agent on the North Carolina Coast during World War II. *Sabre Pilot* concerns a jet fighter pilot in the Korean War.

Meader's sports stories and his stories of early occupational success concentrate on the needs of adolescents to excel and be independent. He wrote about a small high school basketball team and its uphill fight for the State championship (*Sparkplug of the Hornets*), sailing for the yacht club fleet (*The Commodore's Cup*), the story of a Maine boy who starts a contracting business with a reconditioned bulldozer (*Bulldozer*), and the story of two boys in the Pocono Mountains of Pennsylvania who discover that they can grow blueberries commercially (*Blueberry Mountain*).

Meader was successful in writing of young people facing problems of growing up, adapting to new environments, choosing careers, and achieving goals in spite of initial obstacles and setbacks. He did this with understanding of human needs, concern for human development, and unshakeable belief in American growth and opportunity.

—Mary Lystad

MELWOOD, Mary

Pseudonym for Eileen Mary Lewis. **Nationality:** British. **Born:** Eileen Mary Hall, Carlton-in-Lindrick, Nottinghamshire. **Education:** Retford County High School for Girls, Nottinghamshire. Married Morris Lewis in 1939; two sons. **Awards:** First Arts Council award for a children's play, 1964, 1966; *Observer*-Rank Organisation ficiton prize, 1982. **Agent:** Europa Books, 6 Park Street, Kemptown, Brighton, Sussex BN2 2BS; or Patricia Whitton, New Plays Inc., Box 273, Rowayton, Connecticut 06853, U.S.A. **Address:** 5 Hove Lodge Mansions, Hove Street, Hove, Sussex BN3 2TS, England.

Publications for Children

Fiction

Nettlewood. London, Deutsch, 1974; New York, Seabury Press, 1975.
The Watcher Bee. London, Deutsch, 1982.

Plays

The Tingalary Bird (produced London, 1964). New York, New Plays, 1964.
Five Minutes to Morning (produced London, 1965). New York, New Plays, 1966.
Masquerade (produced Nottingham, 1970).
The Small Blue Hoping Stone, music by Nancy Kelel (produced Detroit, 1976).

Radio Play: *It Isn't Enough,* BBC, 1957; adapted for television, 1959.

Publications for Adults

Novel

Reflections in Black Glass. London, Deutsch, 1987.

* * *.

Mary Melwood's first play, *The Tingalary Bird,* arrived in an unpromising world. For a form of entertainment that is so much appreciated there is remarkably little demand for children's theatre. Certainly there is none from its audience. A high percentage of children in England don't know what theatre is and those that do would surely not be capable of registering a protest were all children's theatre to disappear overnight. Such demand as exists is manufactured by a few adults working in the field or by the occasional parent looking for something to take the kids to as a change from the zoo. If children's theatre is at the mercy of this handful of adults, naturally its playwrights are too. *The Tingalary Bird* had a lot of surviving to do.

Since 1945 children's theatre had been dominated by small heroic touring companies taking their work into schools with desperately limited facilities. Inevitably they looked for small-cast plays with no technical requirements whatever. Writers had to provide this kind of play or not be performed at all. Circumstances created a very restricted art form which those who cared came to regard as the only thing children wanted. In the 1960s, when Theatre in Education got under way, custom-built plays were wanted and were frequently assembled by the companies themselves, thus cutting out the playwright entirely. Any playwright with ambitions to write a work for children with a quarter of the staging difficulties of *Peter Pan* was doomed. Children's theatre began to petrify. John Osborne had happened in adult theatre, but children's plays had scarcely put a toe out of the fairy ring.

By some miracle, Melwood, a teacher in Nottingham, knew none of this and blithely sent her play, with a small cast but with massive technical needs, to Caryl Jenner, who had the good sense to hire a theatre and put it on. The play was successful, the Arts Council of Great Britain granted it an award (the first ever for a children's play), and children's theatre had taken a great leap forward.

As the curtain went up on a pleasant sailor singing an equally pleasant song, the audience in 1964 could not have the slightest idea that Melwood was going to ask seven-year-olds to examine with her the breakdown of a marriage.

An ancient couple living in a failed inn are terrified to discover a huge caged bird has arrived in their living room during a thunder storm. Through this electrifying visitor, Melwood looks at the causes of their shattered relationship. At first they seem very simple; plainly the old woman is nasty, plainly the old man is nice. A subtler conflict emerges as one realises that each character holds a different version of the truth; the old man sees the bird's eyes are golden, the old woman says they are green. Both are correct. The audience begins to see that each has driven the other into these extremes of their personalities and, since nobody leaves, a suspicion that each finds their bitter tussle necessary is confirmed by the old woman's line, of her husband, "I should have missed him if he'd got away."

All stormy night the battle goes on. By dawn the beautiful bird has gone, the old man is heartbroken and the old woman utterly routed. Her horde of gold has been revealed, her dusty doll's cradle, kept for a child she never had, is broken, the key to her bare food cupboard is in her husband's possession and, believe it or not, it has been funny lots of the time. The old woman throws down her broomstick, symbol of her authority, opts out of trying to keep the forest tidy, and goes to bed. But as she sneaks back to recover the doll occupant of the cradle one feels she is not so much defeated as diminished, and that this is all to the good. She is no longer frantically being clean enough and thrifty enough or selfish enough for two. The Tingalary Bird has set her husband free from her, but it has also set her free from having to compensate for the old man's delightful deficiencies. The relationship will never be reasonable but it has been reasoned. The audience leaves her wiser and well entertained.

Thereafter Melwood began to write specifically for Caryl Jenner's Unicorn company and particularly for Matyelok Gibbs, its artistic director, who created all Melwood's dashing unsentimentalised old ladies and for whom *The Small Blue Hoping Stone* was written.

Five Minutes to Morning is resolved by another "all nighter." Set in a ruined schoolroom, the play involves a boy who has recently inherited the property, and who resists his clear duty to allow Mrs. Venny, the old school teacher, to continue to occupy the premises. The second act reworks, in a dream sequence, the struggle within himself between enlightenment and chaos as represented by Mrs. Venny and Tom Skinch, the would-be buyer of the property. With this play Melwood is suggesting to her audience that the true excitement in our lives lies not in that furtively thrilling, brutal side of us but in the more dangerous area of our flights of fancy (at one point the schoolroom apparently takes off and flies) and, more sombrely, in learning. Not a fashionable theme.

To convey this theme, Melwood deliberately confuses vision with perception. Significantly, Jolyon, the boy, loses his spectacles at old Mrs. Venny's front door and doesn't get them back till the end of the play. From there on it is the schoolmarm's surprisingly racy and tart version of the world that he must adopt. During his nightmare he sometimes magnifies things to clarify the truth for himself. A vast squirrel cavorts with a football-size hazel nut, the cat is a sleek, affectionate giantess, but the wild white pony, a sort of fierce, living grail, is a reversal of itself and comes tamely to Mrs. Venny's door to be fed. Skinch, in the first act a belligerent landowner, turns total killer and becomes the Unruly Creature. Everything has a changed perspective so that Jolyon can understand and decide. He does—at five minutes to morning. He chooses Mrs. Venny while yet acknowledging that the tension and balance between the Venny and Skinch in him is his fundamental vitality.

In my experience, the danger of this play is that Skinch's naughty boy act and his very amusing flouting of authority in the early stages of the nightmare sequence so endears him to the children that they are inclined to see him as a sort of William grown up, not as the malignant destroyer of us all that Melwood intends. The play loses direction.

Still, Melwood remains a writer for children of the first order. My one regret is that she is English, though it has been left to America to perform *The Small Blue Hoping Stone.* It is always an adventure to be involved in a Melwood production. I envy my colleagues across the water.

—Ursula M. Jones

MERRILL, Jean (Fairbanks)

Nationality: American. **Born:** Rochester, New York, 27 January 1923. **Education:** Allegheny College, Meadville, Pennsylvania, B.A. in English 1944 (Phi Beta Kappa); Wellesley College, Massachusetts, M.A. 1945; University of Madras (Fulbright fellow), 1952-53. **Career:** Assistant feature editor, 1945-46, and feature editor, 1946-49, *Scholastic* Magazines, New York; associate editor, 1950-51, and editor, 1956-57, *Literary Cavalcade,* New York; associate editor, 1965-66, and consultant, 1969-71, Bank Street College of Education Publications Division, New York; contributor of short stories to anthologies and magazines. **Agent:** Dorothy Markinko, McIntosh and Otis, 310 Madison Avenue, New York, New York 10017. **Address:** Angel's Ark, 29 South Main Street, Randolph, Vermont 05060, U.S.A.

Publications for Children

Fiction

Henry, The Hand-Painted Mouse, illustrated by Ronni Solbert. New York, Coward McCann, 1951.

The Woover, illustrated by Ronni Solbert. New York, Coward McCann, 1952.

Boxes, illustrated by Ronni Solbert. New York, Coward McCann, 1953.

The Tree House of Jimmy Domino, illustrated by Ronni Solbert. New York and London, Oxford University Press, 1955.

The Travels of Marco, illustrated by Ronni Solbert. New York, Knopf, 1956.

A Song for Gar, illustrated by Ronni Solbert. New York, McGraw Hill, 1957.

The Very Nice Things, illustrated by Ronni Solbert. New York, Harper, 1959.

Blue's Broken Heart, illustrated by Ronni Solbert. New York, McGraw Hill, 1960.

Tell about the Cowbarn, Daddy, illustrated by Lili Wronker. New York, Scott, 1963.

The Pushcart War, illustrated by Ronni Solbert. New York, Scott, 1964; London, Hamish Hamilton, 1973.
The Elephant Who Liked to Smash Small Cars, illustrated by Ronni Solbert. New York, Pantheon, 1967.
Red Riding, illustrated by Ronni Solbert. New York, Pantheon, 1968.
The Black Sheep, illustrated by Ronni Solbert. New York, Pantheon, 1969.
Mary, Come Running, illustrated by Ronni Solbert. New York, McCall, 1970.
Here I Come—Ready or Not!, illustrated by Frances Scott. Chicago, Whitman, 1970.
How Many Kids Are Hiding on My Block?, illustrated by Frances Scott. Chicago, Whitman, 1970.
Please, Don't Eat My Cabin, illustrated by Frances Scott. Chicago, Whitman, 1971.
The Second Greatest Clown in the World. Boston, Houghton Mifflin, 1971.
The Jackpot. Boston, Houghton Mifflin, 1971.
The Toothpaste Millionaire, illustrated by Jan Palmer. Boston, Houghton Mifflin, 1972.
Maria's House, illustrated by Frances Scott. New York, Atheneum, 1974.
The Girl Who Loved Caterpillars, illustrated by Floyd Cooper. New York, Philomel, 1992.

Plays

Tightrope Act, in *Isn't That What Friends Are For?,* edited by Bank Street College of Education. Boston, Houghton Mifflin, 1972.
Mary Come Running (libretto), music by Gwyneth Walker (produced Randolph, Vermont, Hartford, Connecticut, and Bethesda, Maryland, 1983).
The Claws in the Cat's Paw (television play). 1956.

Poetry

Emily Emerson's Moon, illustrated by Ronni Solbert. Boston, Little Brown, 1960.

Other

Shan's Lucky Knife: A Burmese Folk Tale, illustrated by Ronni Solbert. New York, Scott, 1960; Kingswood, Surrey, World's Work, 1961.
The Superlative Horse: A Tale of Ancient China, illustrated by Ronni Solbert. New York, Scott, 1961.
High, Wide and Handsome and Their Three Tall Tales: A Burmese Folk Tale, illustrated by Ronni Solbert. New York, Scott, 1964.
The Bumper Sticker Book, illustrated by Frances Scott. Chicago, Whitman, 1973.

Editor, with Ronni Solbert, *A Few Flies and I* (haiku), by Issa Kobayashi, translated by R.H. Blyth and Nobuyuki Yuasa. New York, Pantheon, 1969.

PUBLICATIONS FOR ADULTS

Helping Hummingbirds. Montpelier, Vermont Life, 1968.

*

Manuscript Collections: Rare Book Division, University of Wyoming Library, Laramie; de Grummond Collection, University of Southern Mississippi, Hattiesburg; Kerlan Collection, University of Minnesota, Minneapolis; Rutgers University, New Brunswick, New Jersey.

Jean Merrill comments:

As to my general motivation as a writer, I would say that it is to celebrate those aspects of the human experience that affirm the creative and life-reverencing instinct in man. To the extent that a writer for children occasionally glimpses himself, as does any adult directing his concern to children, I am conscious of more specific motivations, among them:

—*to educate*—in the sense of socializing the child in the direction of a constructive use of his potential;

—*to entertain*—to encourage the capacity for joy by enticing the free play of a child's curiosity, humor, and inventiveness;

—*to liberate*—by opening up the child to emotional as well as to intellectual experience.

Though I am referring to "the child" as if he were a receptacle, the child for whom one essentially writes is oneself, and at base writing is motivated by one's own need to resolve the enigma of life. I am always the imagined reader, as well as writer, of my books.

Writers for children are often asked whether they feel limitations on subject matter or theme in writing for children. I have never felt constrained in writing for children about anything that concerned me as an adult; what I perceive as touchstones of the human experience are as appropriate, indeed essential, to books for very young readers as to books for the literate 14-year-old.

One must obviously be selective of the language and metaphor that will most readily translate one's perceptions to children of various ages, but this necessity is no more a limitation than trying to converse with adults of background or experience different from one's own. And finding the word or symbol that will translate my feeling into a form accessible to a child is to me the essential challenge of writing.

My interest in writing children's books may have derived from the impact certain books had on me as a child and a wish to recreate the quality of that experience. Certainly, one of the satisfactions of writing for children is the intensity that caring young readers lavish on the books they like.

It is often the books we read as children that stay with us the longest, whose titles, characters, plots, and emotional tone we never forget. Their significance with repeated readings is imprinted on memory until they are as much a part of the landscape that forever colors our perception and expectation of the world as the faces of our parents and the look and smell of the houses we grew up in.

Given this extra durability that may attach to what children read, whatever a writer feels may be worth communicating seems to me to be additionally worth communicating to children. And seems also to require of those of us who write for children that we be uncompromising enemies of the shoddy, meretricious, or sentimental in our work.

* * *

Jean Merrill has earned her solid reputation as a children's writer by the consistently fine quality of her books. Her themes and formats are varied. Her interest in the Far East has produced some fine books such as *High, Wide and Handsome, Shan's Lucky Knife,* and *The Superlative Horse.* Her picture books are clever, original, and appealing to young listeners. One good example of this genre is *The Elephant Who Liked to Smash Small Cars. Elephant* presents the conflicts between "doing your own thing" and harming others; it is also a story of growing up, of becoming aware of others' needs. While some adults worry about the violence—i.e., the elephant's delight in smashing small cars and the "tit-for-tat" treatment he receives—young children seem to be deeply satisfied both by the portrayal of Elephant's antisocial drives and the resolution of them.

Merrill writes equally effectively for older children. Though one of her earlier and most famous books, *The Pushcart War,* is identified as for children 9 to 12, it really is for ages 9 to 90. The humorous wisdom and courageous actions of the pushcart owners in resisting the onslaughts of the powerful trucking concerns appeal to adults as well as children.

The Pushcart War exemplifies a favorite theme of Merrill—the struggle of the small and weak against the strong and mighty. In a delightful book for older readers, *The Toothpaste Millionaire* (also shown on film as a television special), a young black boy, Rufus, invents an effective toothpaste from simple materials. As his product oversells the established brands by nearly 100 percent, the enraged manufacturers try to put him out of business. As in *The Pushcart War,* the big corporations meet their comeuppance, even though Rufus is already dreaming up new enterprises.

Merrill's humanistic concerns are evident in all her books. In *The Superlative Horse* merit doesn't depend on outward trappings but on inward ability. In *The Black Sheep,* a book for younger children, there is gentle insight into the worth of the "different" individual.

Merrill not only catches the flow and flavor of real children's language but structures it in such naturalistic speech that even poor readers become absorbed in her stories. She blends long and short sentences, sentence fragments, phrases, and dialogue so skillfully that it reads as "real talk written down"; and the young reader immediately identifies with the characters. She has mastered the subtle art of "immediacy"—the reader is there and the adventure is happening to him or her.

One last observation: Merrill is also intrigued by mathematics. Her pleasure in this science often makes it more meaningful to the reader than most textbooks on the subject. Rufus can become a toothpaste millionaire because he can understand cost and profit; in *The Pushcart War* a professor carries percentage to its ultimate absurdity; in "The Seventeen Horses of Ali" (a story in *Discoveries: An Individualized Approach to Reading*), she presents a playful puzzle in fractions that might well awaken delight in mathematics.

A craftsman with words, a prolific and creative writer, a humorous mathematician, and a fine storyteller—Merrill is all these things; but above all, she is a tender but strong affirmer of human rights.

—Betty Boegehold

MEYNELL, Laurence (Walter)

Pseudonyms: Valerie Baxter; Robert Eton; Geoffrey Ludlow; A. Stephen Tring. **Nationality:** British. Born in Wolverhampton, Staffordshire, 9 August 1899. **Education:** St. Edmund's College, Ware, Hertfordshire. **Military Service:** Served in the Honourable Artillery Company during World War I; Royal Air Force, 1939-45: mentioned in despatches. **Family:** Married 1) Shirley Ruth Darbyshire in 1932 (died 1955), one daughter; 2) Joan Belfrage in 1956 (died 1986). **Career:** Articled pupil in a land agency, 1920s; worked as a schoolteacher and an estate agent. General editor, Men of the Counties series, Bodley Head, publishers, London, 1955-57; literary editor, *Time and Tide,* London, 1958-60. **Died:** 14 April 1989.

Publications for Children

Fiction

Smoky Joe, illustrated by Charlotte Hough. London, Lane, 1952.
Smoky Joe in Trouble, illustrated by Charlotte Hough. London, Lane, 1953.
Policeman in the Family, illustrated by Neville Dear. London, Oxford University Press, 1953.
Under the Hollies, illustrated by Ian Ribbons. London, Oxford University Press, 1954.
Bridge under the Water, illustrated by John S. Goodall. London, Phoenix House, 1954; New York, Roy, 1957.
Animal Doctor, illustrated by Raymond Sheppard. London, Oxford University Press, 1956.
Smoky Joe Goes to School, illustrated by Charlotte Hough. London, Lane, 1956.
Sonia Back Stage. London, Chatto and Windus, 1957.
The Young Architect, illustrated by David Knight. London, Oxford University Press, 1958.
District Nurse Carter. London, Chatto and Windus, 1958.
Nurse Ross Takes Over. London, Hamish Hamilton, 1958.
The Hunted King. London, Bodley Head, 1959.
Nurse Ross Shows the Way. London, Hamish Hamilton, 1959.
Monica Anson, Travel Agent. London, Chatto and Windus, 1959.
Nurse Ross Saves the Day. London, Hamish Hamilton, 1960.
Bandaberry. London, Bodley Head, 1960.
Nurse Ross and the Doctor. London, Hamish Hamilton, 1962.
The Dancers in the Reeds. London, Hamish Hamilton, 1963.
Good Luck, Nurse Ross. London, Hamish Hamilton, 1963.
Scoop. London, Hamish Hamilton, 1964.
The Empty Saddle. London, Hamish Hamilton, 1965.
Break for Summer. London, Hamish Hamilton, 1965.
Shadow in the Sun. London, Hamish Hamilton, 1966.
The Suspect Scientist. London, Hamish Hamilton, 1966.
The Man in the Hut, illustrated by Tony Hart. London, Kaye and Ward, 1967.
Peter and the Picture Thief, illustrated by Tony Hart. London Kaye and Ward, 1969.
Jimmy and the Election, illustrated by Tony Hart. London, Kaye and Ward, 1970.
Tony Trotter and the Kitten, illustrated by Peter Edwards. London, Kaye and Ward, 1971.
The Great Cup Tie, illustrated by Gareth Floyd. London, Kaye and Ward, 1974.

Fiction as A. Stephen Tring

The Old Gang, illustrated by John Camp. London, Oxford University Press, 1947.

Penny Dreadful, illustrated by T.R. Freeman. London, Oxford University Press, 1949.
The Cave by the Sea, illustrated by T.R. Freeman. London, Oxford University Press, 1950.
Barry's Exciting Year, illustrated by Charlotte Hough. London, Oxford University Press, 1951.
Barry Gets His Wish, illustrated by Charlotte Hough. London, Oxford University Press, 1952.
Young Master Carver: A Boy in the Reign of Edward III, illustrated by Alan Jessett. London, Phoenix House, 1952; New York, Roy, 1957.
Penny Triumphant, illustrated by T.R. Freeman. London, Oxford University Press, 1953.
Penny Penitent, illustrated by T.R. Freeman. London, Oxford University Press, 1953.
Barry's Great Day, illustrated by Charlotte Hough. London, Oxford University Press, 1954.
Penny Puzzled, illustrated by T.R. Freeman. London, Oxford University Press, 1955.
The Kite Man. Oxford, Blackwell, 1955.
Penny Dramatic, illustrated by T.R. Freeman. London, Oxford University Press, 1956.
Penny in Italy, illustrated by T.R. Freeman. London, Oxford University Press, 1957.
Frankie and the Green Umbrella, illustrated by Richard Kennedy. London, Hamish Hamilton, 1957.
Pictures for Sale, illustrated by Christopher Brooker. London, Hamish Hamilton, 1958.
Penny and the Pageant, illustrated by Kathleen Gell. London, Oxford University Press, 1959.
Peter's Busy Day, illustrated by Raymond Briggs. London, Hamish Hamilton, 1959.
Ted's Lucky Ball, illustrated by James Russell. London, Hamish Hamilton, 1961.
Penny Says Good-bye, illustrated by Kathleen Gell. London, Oxford University Press, 1961.
The Man with the Sack, illustrated by Peter Booth. London, Hamish Hamilton, 1963.
Chad, illustrated by Joseph Acheson. London, Hamish Hamilton, 1966.

Fiction as Valerie Baxter

Jane: Young Author. London, Lane, 1954.
Elizabeth: Young Policewoman. London, Lane, 1955.
Shirley: Young Bookseller. London, Lane, 1956.
Hester: Ship's Officer. London, Hamish Hamilton, 1957.

Other

Builder and Dreamer: A Life of Isambard Kingdom Brunel, illustrated by Lee Kenyon. London, Lane, 1952; revised edition, as *Isambard Kingdom Brunel,* London, Newnes, 1955.
Rolls, Man of Speed: A Life of Charles Stewart Rolls. London, Lane, 1953; revised edition, as *The Hon. C.S. Rolls,* London, Newnes, 1955.
Great Men of Staffordshire. London, Lane, 1955.
The First Men to Fly: A Short History of Wilbur and Orville Wright. London, Laurie, 1955.
James Brindley: The Pioneer of Canals. London, Laurie, 1956.
Our Patron Saints, illustrated by John Turner. London, Acorn Press, 1957.
Thomas Telford: The Life Story of a Great Engineer, illustrated by Donald Forster. London, Lane, 1957.
Farm Animals, illustrated by Jennifer Miles. London, Ward, 1958.
Airmen on the Run: True Stories of Evasion and Escape by British Airmen of World War II, illustrated by Richard Kennedy. London, Odhams Press, 1963.
The Beginning of Words: How English Grew, with Colin Pickles. London, Blond, 1970; New York, Putnam, 1971.

Publications for Adults

Novels

Mockbeggar. London, Harrap, 1924; New York, Appleton, 1925.
Lois. London, Harrap, and New York, Appleton, 1927.
Bluefeather. London, Harrap, and New York, Appleton, 1928.
Death's Eye. London, Harrap, 1929; as *The Shadow and the Stone,* New York, Appleton, 1929.
Camouflage. London, Harrap, 1930; as *Mystery at Newton Ferry,* Philadelphia, Lippincott, 1930.
Asking for Trouble. London, Ward Lock, 1931.
Consummate Rose. London, Hutchinson, 1931.
Storm Against the Wall. London, Hutchinson, and Philadelphia, Lippincott, 1931.
The House on the Cliff. London, Hutchinson, and Philadelphia, Lippincott, 1932.
Paid in Full. London, Harrap, 1933; as *So Many Doors,* Philadelphia, Lippincott, 1933.
Watch the Wall. London, Harrap, 1933; as *The Gentlemen Go By,* Philadelphia, Lippincott, 1934.
Odds on Bluefeather. London, Harrap, 1934; Philadelphia, Lippincott, 1935.
Inside Out! or, Mad as a Hatter (as Geoffrey Ludlow). London, Harrap, 1934.
Third Time Unlucky! London, Harrap, 1935.
On the Night of the 18th.... London, Nicholson and Watson, and New York, Harper, 1936.
Women Had to Do It! (as Geoffrey Ludlow). London, Nicholson and Watson, 1936.
The Door in the Wall. London, Nicholson and Watson, and New York, Harper, 1937.
The House in the Hills. London, Nicholson and Watson, 1937; New York, Harper, 1938.
The Dandy. London, Nicholson and Watson, 1938.
The Hut. London, Nicholson and Watson, 1938.
His Aunt Came Late. London, Nicholson and Watson, 1939.
And Be a Villain. London, Nicholson and Watson, 1939.
The Creaking Chair. London, Collins, 1941.
The Dark Square. London, Collins, 1941.
Strange Landing. London, Collins, 1946.
The Evil Hour. London, Collins, 1947.
The Bright Face of Danger. London, Collins, 1948.
The Echo in the Cave. London, Collins, 1949.
The Lady on Platform One. London, Collins, 1950.
Party of Eight. London, Collins, 1950.
The Man No One Knew. London, Collins, 1951.
The Frightened Man. London, Collins, 1952.
Danger round the Corner. London, Collins, 1952.
Too Clever by Half. London, Collins, 1953.
Give Me the Knife. London, Collins, 1954.

Where Is She Now? London, Collins, 1955.
Saturday Out. London, Collins, 1956; New York, Walker, 1962.
The Sun Will Shine. London, Transworld, 1956.
The Breaking Point. London, Collins, 1957.
One Step from Murder. London, Collins, 1958.
The Abandoned Doll. London, Collins, 1960.
The House in Marsh Road. London, Collins, 1960.
The Pit in the Garden. London, Collins, 1961.
Moon over Ebury Square. London, Hale, 1962.
Virgin Luck. London, Collins, 1963; New York, Simon and Schuster, 1964.
Sleep of the Unjust. London, Collins, 1963.
More Deadly Than the Male. London, Collins, 1964.
Double Fault. London, Collins, 1965.
Die by the Book. London, Collins, 1966.
The Imperfect Aunt. London, Hale, 1966.
Week-end in the Scampi Belt. London, Hale, 1967.
The Mauve Front Door. London, Collins, 1967.
Death of a Philanderer. London, Collins, 1968; New York, Doubleday, 1969.
Of Malicous Intent. London, Collins, 1969.
The Shelter. London, Hale, 1970.
The Curious Crime of Miss Julia Blossom. London, Macmillan, 1970.
The End of the Long Hot Summer. London, Hale, 1972.
Death by Arrangement. London, Macmillan, and New York, McKay, 1972.
A Little Matter of Arson. London, Macmillan, 1972.
A View from the Terrace. London, Hale, 1972.
The Fatal Flaw. London, Macmillan, 1973; New York, Stein and Day, 1978.
The Thirteen Trumpeters. London, Macmillan, 1973; New York, Stein and Day, 1978.
The Fortunate Miss East. London, Hale, 1973; New York, Coward McCann, 1974.
The Woman in Number Five. London, Hale, 1974; as *Burlington Square,* New York, Coward McCann, 1975.
The Fairly Innocent Little Man. London, Macmillan, 1974; New York, Stein and Day, 1977.
The Footpath. London, Hale, 1975.
Don't Stop for Hooky Hefferman. London, Macmillan, 1975; New York, Stein and Day, 1977.
Hooky and the Crock of Gold. London, Macmillan, 1975.
The Lost Half Hour. London, Macmillan, 1976; New York, Stein and Day, 1977.
The Vision Splendid. London, Hale, 1976.
The Folly of Henrietta Dale. London, Hale, 1976.
The Little Kingdom. London, Hale, 1977.
Folly to Be Wise. London, Hale, 1977.
Hooky Gets the Wooden Spoon. London, Macmillan, and New York, Stein and Day, 1977.
Papersnake. London, Macmillan, 1978.
The Dangerous Year. London, Hale, 1978.
The Sisters. London, Hale, 1979.
Hooky and the Villainous Chauffeur. London, Macmillan, 1979.
The Lady Who Wasn't. London, Hale, 1980.
Hooky and the Prancing Horse. London, Macmillan, 1980.
Hooky Goes to Blazes. London, Macmillan, 1981.
Parasol in the Park. London, Hale, 1981.
The Blue Door. London, Hale, 1982.
The Secret of the Pit. London, Macmillan, 1982.
The Visitor. London, Hale, 1983.
Silver Guilt. London, Macmillan, 1983.
False Gods. London, Hale, 1984.
The Open Door. London, Macmillan, 1984.
Quenells. London, Hale, 1985.
Affair at Barwold. London, Macmillan, 1985.
Hooky Catches a Tartar. London, Macmillan, 1986.
The Abiding Thing. London, Hale, 1986.
The Rivals. London, Hale, 1987.
Hooky on Loan. London, Macmillan, 1987.
Hooky Hooked. London, Macmillan, 1988.

Novels as Robert Eton

The Pattern. London, Harrap, 1934.
The Dividing Air. London, Harrap, 1935.
The Bus Leaves for the Village. London, Nicholson and Watson, 1936.
Not in Our Stars. London, Nicholson and Watson, 1937.
The Journey. London, Nicholson and Watson, 1938.
Palace Pier. London, Nicholson and Watson, 1938.
The Legacy. London, Nicholson and Watson, 1939.
The Faithful Years. London, Nicholson and Watson, 1939.
The Corner of Paradise Place. London, Nicholson and Watson, 1940.
St. Lynn's Advertiser. London, Nicholson and Watson, 1947.
The Dragon at the Gate. London, Nicholson and Watson, 1949.

Screenplay: *The Umbrella,* with H. Fowler Mear, 1933.

Poetry

The Ballad of Pen Fields, with a Plan of the Battlefield. Privately printed, 1927.

Other

Bedfordshire. London, Hale, 1950.
Famous Cricket Grounds. London, Phoenix House, 1951.
"Plum" Warner. London, Phoenix House, 1951.
Exmoor. London, Hale, 1953.

*

Manuscript Collection: Mugar Memorial Library, Boston University.

* * *

A. Stephen Tring, better known as Laurence Meynell, deserves to be ranked with Geoffrey Trease and E.W. Hildick for his endeavours to introduce realism and vitality into stories for boys.

His first boy's school story, *The Old Gang,* follows traditional formulae although he abandons the prestigious boarding-school setting to deal with grammar school and secondary modern school rivalries. This racy novel is told in the first person by a member of "the old gang," Frank Dilmot. It is highly readable, packed with incident, with a strong emphasis on various sports and feuds, rivalries and pranks. Authenticity is reduced by the introduction of an incredible mystery, and unacceptable attitudes tend to prevail but regardless of such faults *The Old Gang* remains in print with its lively, convincing dialogue, its quick humour, and its notable schoolboy trio, Frank, Joe, and Mickey.

In the three books about Barry Briggs, Tring breaks free from the accepted patterns of an earlier period to create a strong central character, whose hopes, fears, and fantasies are vividly presented to the reader in a highly realistic framework particularly of family life on a council housing estate. This series shows more originality and realism than *The Old Gang* and was unusual in the 1950s for its rounded portrayal of parents. In this series the mystery elements are more feasible than in some of Tring's other books, but the introduction of upper-class characters detracts from the otherwise excellent realism of this series.

The Penny series for girls is less memorable than either *The Old Gang* or the Barry series. *Penny Dreadful* shows a degree of originality and zest not maintained in later titles of the series. The young heroine and her family are reasonably well-drawn and plots are packed with action, but the fairly affluent background of the series has little relevance to the readership of a later period. As in *The Old Gang,* rather incredible mystery situations are introduced and unacceptable attitudes persist.

As an experienced writer of stories for both adults and for children Tring proved willing to use his expertise to cater for particular contemporary needs: no easy task. His success is partly due to his readable, sometimes deceptively easy style of writing, and also to his combination of action with realism. His most successful work in this area is without doubt the series of books about Barry Briggs.

—Anne W. Ellis

MILNE, A(lan) A(lexander)

Nationality: British. **Born:** London, 18 January 1882. **Education:** Westminster School, London (Queen's scholar), 1893-1900; Trinity College, Cambridge (editor, *Granta,* 1902), 1900-03, B.A. (honours) in mathematics 1903. **Military Service:** Royal Warwickshire Regiment, 1914-18. **Family:** Married Dorothy de Sélincourt in 1913; one son, Christopher Robin Milne. **Career:** Freelance journalist, 1903-06; assistant editor, *Punch,* London, 1906-14. **Died:** 31 January 1956.

Publications for Children

Fiction

Once on a Time, illustrated by H.M. Brock. London, Hodder and Stoughton, 1917; New York, Putnam, 1922.
A Gallery of Children, illustrated by Saida. London, Stanley Paul, and Philadelphia, McKay, 1925.
Winnie-the-Pooh, illustrated by Ernest Shepard. London, Methuen, and New York, Dutton, 1926.
The House at Pooh Corner, illustrated by Ernest Shepard. London, Methuen, and New York, Dutton, 1928.
Prince Rabbit, and the Princess Who Could Not Laugh, illustrated by Mary Shepard. London, Ward, and New York, Dutton, 1966.

Plays

Make-Believe (includes *The Princess and the Woodcutter, Oliver's Island, Father Christmas and the Hubbard Family*), music by George Dorlay, lyrics by C.E. Burton (produced London, 1918). Included in *Second Plays,* 1921.
The Man in the Bowler Hat: A Terribly Exciting Affair (produced New York, 1924; London, 1925). London and New York, French, 1923.
King Hilary and the Beggarman (produced London, 1926).
Toad of Toad Hall, music by H. Fraser-Simson, adaptation of the story *The Wind in the Willows* by Kenneth Grahame (produced Liverpool, 1929; London, 1930). London, Methuen, and New York, Scribner, 1929.
The Ugly Duckling (for children). London, French, 1941; in *Twenty-Four Favorite One-Act Plays,* edited by Bennett Cerf and Van H. Cartmell, New York, Doubleday, 1958.

Poetry (illustrated by Ernest Shepard)

When We Were Very Young. London, Methuen, and New York, Dutton, 1924.
Now We Are Six. London, Methuen, and New York, Dutton, 1927.

Publications for Adults

Novels

Lovers in London. London, Alston Rivers, 1905.
Mr. Pim. London, Hodder and Stoughton, 1921; New York, Doran, 1922; as *Mr. Pim Passes By,* London, Methuen, 1929.
The Red House Mystery. London, Methuen, and New York, Dutton, 1922.
Two People. London, Methuen, and New York, Dutton, 1931.
Four Days' Wonder. London, Methuen, and New York, Dutton, 1933.
One Year's Time. London, Methuen, 1942.
Chloe Marr. London, Methuen, and New York, Dutton, 1946.

Short Stories

The Secret and Other Stories. London, Methuen, and New York, Fountain Press, 1929.
Birthday Party and Other Stories. New York, Dutton, 1948; London, Methuen, 1949.
A Table near the Band and Other Stories. London, Methuen, and New York, Dutton, 1950.

Plays

Wurzel-Flummery (produced London, 1917). London and New York, French, 1922; revised version, in *First Plays,* 1919.
Belinda: An April Folly (produced London and New York, 1918). Included in *First Plays,* 1919.
The Boy Comes Home (produced London, 1918). Included in *First Plays,* 1919.
First Plays (includes *Wurzel-Flummery, The Lucky One, The Boy Comes Home, Belinda, The Red Feathers*). London, Chatto and Windus, and New York, Knopf, 1919.
The Red Feathers (produced Leeds, 1920; London, 1921). Included in *First Plays,* 1919.

The Lucky One (produced New York, 1922; Cambridge, 1923; London, 1924). Included in *First Plays,* 1919; as *Let's All Talk about Gerald* (produced London, 1928).
The Camberley Triangle (produced London, 1919). Included in *Second Plays,* 1921.
Mr. Pim Passes By (produced Manchester, 1919; London, 1920; New York, 1921). Included in *Second Plays,* 1921.
The Romantic Age (produced London, 1920; New York, 1922). Included in *Second Plays,* 1921.
The Stepmother (produced London, 1920). Included in *Second Plays,* 1921.
Second Plays (includes *Make-Believe, Mr. Pim Passes By, The Camberley Triangle, The Romantic Age, The Stepmother*). London, Chatto and Windus, 1921; New York, Knopf, 1922.
The Great Broxopp: Four Chapters in Her Life (produced New York, 1921; London, 1923). Included in *Three Plays,* 1922.
The Truth about Blayds (produced London, 1921; New York, 1922). Included in *Three Plays,* 1922.
The Dover Road (produced New York, 1921; London, 1922). Included in *Three Plays,* 1922.
Three Plays (includes *The Dover Road, The Truth about Blayds, The Great Broxopp*). New York, Putnam, 1922; London, Chatto and Windus, 1923.
Berlud, Unlimited (produced London and New York, 1922).
Success (produced London, 1923; as *Give Me Yesterday,* produced New York, 1931). London, Chatto and Windus, 1923; New York, French, 1924.
The Artist: A Duologue. London and New York, French, 1923.
To Have the Honour (produced London, 1924; as *To Meet the Prince,* produced New York, 1929). London and New York, French, 1925.
Ariadne; or, Business First (produced New York and London, 1925). London and New York, French, 1925.
Portrait of a Gentleman in Slippers: A Fairy Tale (produced Liverpool, 1926; London, 1927). London and New York, French, 1926.
Four Plays (includes *To Have the Honour, Ariadne, Portrait of a Gentleman in Slippers, Success*). London, Chatto and Windus, 1926.
Miss Marlow at Play (produced London, 1927; New York, 1940). London and New York, French, 1936.
The Ivory Door: A Legend (produced New York, 1927; London, 1929). New York, Putnam, 1928; London, Chatto and Windus, 1929.
The Fourth Wall: A Detective Story (produced London, 1928; as *The Perfect Alibi,* produced New York, 1928). New York, French, 1929; London, French, 1930.
Michael and Mary (produced New York, 1929; London, 1930). London, Chatto and Windus, 1930; New York, French, 1932.
They Don't Mean Any Harm (produced London and New York, 1932).
Four Plays (includes *Michael and Mary, To Meet the Prince, The Perfect Alibi, Portrait of a Gentleman in Slippers*). New York, Putnam, 1932.
Other People's Lives (produced London, 1932). London and New York, French, 1935.
More Plays (includes *The Ivory Door, The Fourth Wall, Other People's Lives*). London, Chatto and Windus, 1935.
Miss Elizabeth Bennet, adaptation of the novel *Pride and Prejudice* by Jane Austen (produced London, 1938). London, Chatto and Windus, 1936.
Sarah Simple (produced London, 1937; New York, 1940). London, French, 1939.
Gentleman Unknown (produced London, 1938).
Before the Flood. London and New York, French, 1951.

Screenplays: *The Bump,* 1920; *Five Pounds Reward,* 1920; *Bookworms,* 1920; *Twice Two,* 1920; *Birds of Prey* (*The Perfect Alibi*), with Basil Dean, 1930.

Poetry

For the Luncheon Interval: Cricket and Other Verses. London, Methuen, and New York, Dutton, 1925.
Behind the Lines. London, Methuen, and New York, Dutton, 1940.
The Norman Church. London, Methuen, 1948.

Other

The Day's Play (*Punch* sketches). London, Methuen, 1910; New York, Dutton, 1925.
The Holiday Round (*Punch* sketches). London, Methuen, 1912; New York, Dutton, 1925.
Once a Week (*Punch* sketches). London, Methuen, 1914; New York, Dutton, 1925.
Happy Days (*Punch* sketches). New York, Doran, 1915.
Not That It Matters. London, Methuen, 1919; New York, Dutton, 1920.
If I May. London, Methuen, 1920; New York, Dutton, 1921.
The Sunny Side. London, Methuen, 1921; New York, Dutton, 1922.
(*Selected Works*). London, Library Press, 7 vols., 1926.
The Ascent of Man. London, Benn, and New York, Dutton, 1928.
By Way of Introduction. London, Methuen, and New York, Dutton, 1929.
Those Were the Days: The Day's Play, The Holiday Round, Once a Week, The Sunny Side. London, Methuen, and New York, Dutton, 1929.
When I Was Very Young (autobiography). London, Methuen, and New York, Fountain Press, 1930.
A.A. Milne (selections). London, Methuen, 1933.
Peace with Honour: An Enquiry into the War Convention. London, Methuen, and New York, Dutton, 1934; revised edition, 1935.
It's Too Late Now: The Autobiography of a Writer. London, Methuen, 1939; as *Autobiography,* New York, Dutton, 1939.
War with Honour. London, Macmillan, 1940.
War Aims Unlimited. London, Methuen, 1941.
Going Abroad? London, Council for Education in World Citizenship, 1947.
Books for Children: A Reader's Guide. London, Cambridge University Press, 1948.
Year In, Year Out. London, Methuen, and New York, Dutton, 1952.

*

Bibliographies: *A.A. Milne: A Handlist of His Writings for Children* by Brian Sibley, Chislehurst Common, Kent, Henry Pootle Press, 1976; *A.A. Milne: A Critical Bibliography* by Tori Haring-Smith, New York, Garland, 1982.

Manuscript Collections: Humanities Research Center, University of Texas, Austin.

Critical Studies: *A.A. Milne* by Thomas Burnett Swann, New York, Twayne, 1971; *The Enchanted Places* by Christopher Milne, London, Eyre Methuen, 1974, New York, Dutton, 1975; *The Pooh Perplex* by Frederick C. Crews, Milton Keynes, Buckinghamshire, Clark, 1979; *Winnie-the-Pooh, Capitalist Lackey?* by Simon Colverson, Andoversford, Gloucestershire, Whittington Press, n.d.; *The Tao of Pooh* by Benjamin Hoff, London, Methuen, 1982.

* * *

A.A. Milne was a successful writer and dramatist for many years before and after the publication of the children's books for which he is famous. Even in children's literature, the Christopher Robin stories and verses were not his only achievement; his other work included *Once on a Time,* a comic fantasy about the war between Euralia and Barodia, and *Toad of Toad Hall,* a play based on Kenneth Grahame's *The Wind in the Willows.* But Milne's reputation rests immovably on the four Christopher Robin books: two of stories, *Winnie-the-Pooh* and *The House at Pooh Corner,* and two of verses, *When We Were Very Young* and *Now We Are Six.*

All four were published in the space of five years, while Milne's son Christopher was a small boy. Clearly Christopher was the inspiration; and Pooh and Piglet, Tigger and Eeyore, Kanga and Roo were originally his toys. Mrs. Milne had already brought them to life and given them individual voices, said Milne in his autobiography, and the artist Ernest Shepard "drew them as one might say from the living model." It should be said, incidentally, that this is one of the few, exceptional cases—the Alice books are another—where the illustrator could claim to rank as co-creator. Christopher Robin, Pooh, Piglet, and the rest are Shepard's characters as well as Milne's.

The setting of the stories that make up *Winnie-the-Pooh* and *The House at Pooh Corner* is the Hundred-Acre Wood: a happy, self-contained Arcadian world in which all animals are equal and none more equal than others, a reassuring world in which nobody will ever come to any harm. For the child reader or hearer, there is pleasant scope for condescension towards Pooh, the Bear of Very Little Brain, or towards Owl, whose wisdom and spelling fall so far short of his pretensions; whereas the child can identify contentedly with Christopher Robin, who always knows what to do, and to whom the animals go for help as if to an adult. The characters themselves are drawn with two or three simple strokes: Piglet is small, squeaky, and timid, Eeyore the donkey is gloomy, Tigger bouncy, Kanga maternal; and Pooh—admitted by the author to be the favourite among them all—is slow-witted, vain, greedy, and yet, in the way of teddy bears, extremely lovable. The incidents are not only funny but curiously memorable. Few adults who grew up on *Winnie-the-Pooh* can have forgotten Pooh dangling from a sky-blue balloon and pretending to be a cloud, or Pooh and Piglet trying to trap a Heffalump or tracking a Woozle round the spinney in the snow. The Expotition to the North Pole, the problem of What Tiggers Like to Eat, and the game of Poohsticks are lodged by now in what could almost be called the folk-memories of the 20th century.

One of the pleasures of these books is the way they move effortlessly into verse from time to time; Pooh is constantly singing a song or humming a hum. Milne was an extremely accomplished versifier. The two books of poems, *When We Were Very Young* and *Now We Are Six,* are notable for their ingenuity. Stanza forms and rhyme schemes are handled with such mastery that one hardly notices how intricate they often are. Milne was well aware of this: whatever else his verses lacked, he said, they were technically good.

Many of the verses are extremely funny: for example "The King's Breakfast" ("I do like a little bit of butter to my bread") or "The Little Black Hen" or "The Knight Whose Armour Didn't Squeak." Others are pitched precisely at the small child's eye level ("John had/Great big/Waterproof/Boots on" or "Halfway down the stairs/Is a stair/Where I sit./There isn't any/Other stair/quite like/It."). Charges of sentimentality have been levelled at Milne, especially over "Vespers" ("Little Boy kneels at the foot of the bed") but, interestingly, he himself said in a "preface to parents" that in his poems he had tried to indicate "the uncharming part of a child's nature: the egotism and the heartlessness"; and he pointed out that in "Vespers" it was not "God bless Mummy, because I love her so," but "God bless Mummy, I know that's right"; not "God bless Daddy because he buys me food and clothes," but "God bless Daddy, I quite forgot." Admittedly, when Milne goes on to say that "the truth about a child is also that, fresh from its bath, newly powdered and curled, it is a lovely thing, God wot," one is reminded that from a good deal of internal evidence it seems unlikely that he ever bathed the baby himself; and the world of Pooh and Christopher Robin is undoubtedly a comfortable, bourgeois, nanny-protected world. But then, that was the world in which, 70 years ago, Christopher Milne was a small boy.

The four books have one essential quality that makes children's books last; they appeal both to the child and to the adult who has pleasure in reading them aloud; indeed, they are never really outgrown. They have bubbling humour, easy and skilful craftsmanship, quick, light characterisation, and the much-maligned but genuine quality of charm.

—John Rowe Townsend

MINARIK, Else (Holmelund)

Nationality: American (originally Danish: emigrated to the United States, 1925). **Born:** Denmark, 13 September 1920. **Education:** Queens College, New York. **Family:** Married 1) Walter Minarik (died 1963), one daughter; 2) the journalist Homer Bigart in 1970. **Career:** Reporter, *Daily Sentinel,* Rome, New York; teacher, Commack, Long Island, 1940s. **Address:** c/o Greenwillow Books, 1350 Avenue of the Americas, New York, New York 10019, U.S.A.

Publications for Children

Fiction

Little Bear, illustrated by Maurice Sendak. New York, Harper, 1957; Kingswood, Surrey, World's Work, 1965.

No Fighting, No Biting!, illustrated by Maurice Sendak. New York, Harper, 1958; Kingswood, Surrey, World's Work, 1969.

Father Bear Comes Home, illustrated by Maurice Sendak. New York, Harper, 1959; Kingswood, Surrey, World's Work, 1960.

Cat and Dog, illustrated by Fritz Siebel. New York, Harper, 1960; Kingswood, Surrey, World's Work, 1969.

Little Bear's Friend, illustrated by Maurice Sendak. New York, Harper, 1960; Kingswood, Surrey, World's Work, 1961.
Little Bear's Visit, illustrated by Maurice Sendak. New York, Harper, 1961; Kingswood, Surrey, World's Work, 1962.
Little Giant Girl and the Elf Boy, illustrated by Garth Williams. New York, Harper, 1963.
A Kiss for Little Bear, illustrated by Maurice Sendak. New York, Harper, 1968; Kingswood, Surrey, World's Work, 1969.
What If?, illustrated by Margaret Bloy Graham. New York, Greenwillow, 1987.
It's Spring!, illustrated by Margaret Bloy Graham. New York, Greenwillow, 1989.
Percy and the Five Houses, illustrated by James Stevenson. New York, Greenwillow, 1989.
Am I Beautiful?, pictures by Yossi Abolafia. New York, Greenwillow, 1992.

Poetry

The Winds That Come from Far Away and Other Poems, illustrated by Joan Berg. New York, Harper, 1964.

Other

Translator, *My Grandpa Is a Pirate,* by Jan Lööf. New York, Harper, 1968.

* * *

While recently she has written some charming picture books with a variety of characters, Else Minarik is still best-known for her series of books about Little Bear, an appealing cub who resembles a preschool child. Minarik's genius lies in her ability to create three-dimensional characters and humorous plots within the limits of a very simple text, accessible to beginning readers. In the Little Bear books, she focuses on the crucial concerns of young children: the tug and pull between the need for independence and taking risks and the need for reassurance and security; the interplay between the real world and the child's imaginary world; the need for acceptance and for friendship. Minarik's insight and emotional accuracy, coupled with her gentle humor, make these miniature stories rich and satisfying.

Little Bear is a thoroughly likeable character. He is imaginative, affectionate, and adventurous. He concocts fantasy games and tales, begs for stories, enjoys his friends and family. His world is secure and loving. He never ventures too far from home; his excursions are lighthearted. Play is his main occupation. No cares or responsibilities weigh him down.

In *Little Bear,* the first book in the series and the most satisfying because of the resolution, unity, and completeness of the stories, Mother Bear is the stable, constant center of Little Bear's world. He ventures away from her to explore and play, but returns to her again and again for reassurance and affection. She never disappoints him, even in "Birthday Soup" when she arrives just in time with the cake. And she promises to be this dependable forever: "I never did forget your birthday, and I never will."

In *Father Bear Comes Home* Father Bear is less central to Little Bear's life, more exotic, but still gently accepting of Little Bear's imagination: "if you find a mermaid," said Father Bear, "ask her to picnic with us." Little Bear's world expands in *Little Bear's Friend:* "I climbed to a treetop and I saw the wide world." The first human character enters the series, a little girl named Emily. She becomes Little Bear's friend and joins the other animals in play. When Emily goes to school at the end of the book, Little Bear, left behind, cries. Once again, it is Mother Bear who gives comfort. "My goodness, Little Bear," she said. "You will be going to school, too, and you will learn to write. Then you can write to Emily." And so we learn that Little Bear is growing up.

Grandmother and Grandfather Bear are introduced in *Little Bear's Visit,* giving just the sort of wholehearted acceptance and love that grandparents are so good at. Little Bear "had some bread and jam, cake and cookies, milk and honey, and an apple. 'Have some more,' said Grandmother. 'Yes, thank you,' said Little Bear. 'I am not eating too much, am I?' 'Oh no, no!' said his grandmother." Both Grandmother and Grandfather tell stories, and the visit ends predictably with a sleeping Little Bear being carried home on his father's shoulder. It is no wonder that Little Bear decides to send Grandmother a present in *A Kiss for Little Bear.* He sends her a drawing and she sends him a kiss that gets passed from friend to friend before it finally reaches Little Bear. The story brings all the animals together for a festive celebration at the skunks' wedding.

The Little Bear books are notable for the graceful simplicity of the language, which avoids the choppy repetition characteristic of most books for beginning readers. And they are remarkable for their wealth of warmth, humor, and understanding. Although their format makes them accessible to new independent readers, it is the preschool child, hearing them read aloud, who will enjoy them most. They capture his world and highlight his concerns with clarity, insight, and love.

—Christine McDonnell

MINOR, Wendell G.

Nationality: American. **Born:** Aurora, Illinois, 17 March 1944. **Education:** Graduated from Ringling School of Art and Design, Sarasota, Florida, 1966; attended Kansas City Art Institute, 1967. **Family:** Married Florence Friedmann Minor, 1978. **Career:** Illustrator for Hallmark Cards, 1966-67; illustrator with Paul Bacon, New York City, 1968-70; freelance illustrator, since 1970; exhibitor in many one-man shows; designer of nearly two thousand book jackets, including those for David McCullough's *Truman,* Toni Morrison's *Sula,* and Pat Conroy's *The Prince of Tides.* **Awards:** Winner of over two hundred professional awards for his work, including the California Library Association award, 1992, for *Sierra*; John and Patricia Beatty Award; silver medals from the Society of Illustrators and the New York Art Directors Club; gold medal, Creativity Exhibition, for *Shaker Hearts*; Notable Children's Trade Books in Social Studies; ALA Booklist Children's Choices; International Reading Association Teacher's Choices; Parents Choice Foundation "Silver Honor"; Smithsonian's Notable Books for Children; John Burroughs List of Nature Books for Young Readers. **Address:** 15 Old North Rd., P.O. Box 1135, Washington, Connecticut 06793, U.S.A. **Website:** http://www.minorart.com. **E-mail Address:** minorart@aol.com.

Publications for Children (illustrated by the author)

Grand Canyon: Exploring a Natural Wonder. New York, Scholastic, 1998.

Publications for Adults

With Florence Friedmann Minor, *Art for the Written Word: Twenty-Five Years of Book Cover Art,* illustrated by Wendell Minor. New York, Harcourt Brace, 1995.

Contributor, *On the Wings of Peace: Writers and Illustrators Speak out for Peace, In Memory of Hiroshima and Nagasaki.* New York, Houghton Mifflin, 1995.

Minor's work has been included in the following books: *Two Hundred Years of American Illustration* by Henry Pitz and Bob Crozier, Random House, 1977; *Contemporary Western Artists* by P. Samuels and Harold Samuels, Southwest Art Publishing, 1991; *Art for Survival: The Illustrator and the Environment,* edited by Joy Aquilino, Graphis Press Corp., 1992; *Children's Book Illustration and Design* by Julie Cummins, PBC International, Inc., 1992; *The Very Best of Children's Book Illustration* by the Society of Illustrators Staff, North Light Books, 1993; *Speak! Children's Book Illustrators Brag About Their Favorite Dogs,* edited by Michael J. Rosen, Harcourt Brace, 1993; *Purr! Children's Book Illustrators Brag About Their Cats,* edited by Michael J. Rosen, Harcourt Brace, 1996; *The Fantastic Vision of Science Fiction Art* by Vincent Di Fate, Viking Penguin, 1998.

*

Biography: Unpublished interview with Christine Doyle-Stott, 26 April 1998.

Illustrator: *Eleanor Roosevelt* by Jane Goodsell, 1970; *The Greenlander* (for adults) by Mark Adlard, 1978; *Mojave,* 1988, *Heartland,* 1989, and *Sierra,* 1991, all by Diane Siebert; *The Seashore Book* by Charlotte Zolotow, 1992; *The Moon of the Owls,* 1993, *Everglades,* 1994, *Julie,* 1994, *Julie's Wolf-Pack,* 1997, *Arctic Son,* 1997, and *Morning, Noon, and Night,* forthcoming, all by Jean Craighead George; *Red Fox Running* by Eve Bunting, 1993; *Shaker Hearts* by Ann Turner, 1997; *Scratching the Woodchuck: Nature on an Amish Farm* (for adults) by David Kline, 1997; (paintings) *Grassroots* by Carl Sandburg, 1998; *Call of the Wild* by Jack London, forthcoming; *A Lucky Thing: Poems by Alice Schertle,* forthcoming.

Wendell Minor comments:

My mission as an artist is to try to record the best of my childhood memories—the sense of time and place, and especially of *belonging to* a time and place—in order to develop in children a sensitivity to their time and place—their environment—and the desire to preserve and protect it.

* * *

When Wendell Minor was a boy, his father used to take him along as he pursued two of his favorite hobbies, hunting and fishing. For the young Wendell, this essentially meant long hours of quiet watching and waiting. But while his father watched and waited for game to appear or fish to bite, the future artist intently observed his surroundings, absorbing the sights and sounds of the environment. When he actually began to study art, he became enamored of nineteenth-century American wildlife and landscape painters such as John James Audubon and Thomas Moran, who, before the development of photography, were "the eyes of the country," bringing the limitless variety of the American continent, as they observed it, to people who had not experienced it for themselves. It is this highly developed power of observation that intrigues Minor, and that he seeks to encourage in children through the art of the picture book.

Although Minor has been a professional artist since 1966 when he began working for Hallmark Cards, he only began turning his talents seriously toward children's books in 1986, when he created the paintings that accompany Diane Siebert's desert poem published as *Mojave* in 1988. His books typically carry the announcement, "Paintings by..." rather than the more common "Illustrations by...." Minor consciously works to break down the barriers between painting and illustration. To his mind, the illustrations in a picture book should "honor" the written text, but not seek to duplicate it; rather, they should stand on their own in communicating an idea, and be so well-crafted as to be worthy of framing and hanging on the wall. In a good picture book, he says, the text tells a story, the art tells what may be a slightly different story, and the reader putting text and art together creates yet another story. Consider *Grassroots,* in which Minor's paintings accompany his selection of poems by Carl Sandburg. One poem, "Pearl Horizons," concerns a "fog moon" on the prairie, and alludes to "lonesome dogs." No dogs appear in Minor's painting, and the moon only shines in reflected light in a pasture occupied by a single cow. Yet both poem and painting highlight the fog, and together they evoke the loneliness of this particular midnight on the prairie more intensely than either does alone. Picture books, Minor insists, "afford the opportunity to expose children to art in a grander sense." The more sophisticated picture book can, in fact, be the young observer's introduction to fine art in a world where visual art more often takes the form of video games or television cartoons. Thus, whether a picture book painting becomes the impetus for thoughtful consideration of the relationships between different modes of expression or possibly for further explorations and even creative efforts in the world of art, it always has that possibility of going beyond the purpose for which it originally was conceived.

A picture book that works at the level of art requires harmony between author and illustrator. Two of Minor's most fulfilling author/artist partnerships thus far have been with writers Diane Siebert and Jean Craighead George. Minor said that, for him, Siebert's poem "Mojave" was a sort of "landscape painting in words"; it evoked the same kind of wonder, vastness, and richly observant detail as did his paintings, thus making the resultant book combining the two a powerfully artistic experience. They collaborated on two further books paying tribute to American landscapes, *Heartland* and *Sierra.*

Minor's relationship with Jean Craighead George began when he was asked to re-illustrate the cover of George's famous novel, *Julie of the Wolves,* in 1985. However, he actually met George for the first time at the United Nations on Earth Day, 1990. The two committed environmentalists found they had much in common, and Minor became the illustrator for the two sequels to *Julie of the Wolves* as well as providing paintings for *Moon of the Owls,* one of the books in George's *Thirteen Moons* series, and harmonizing with her texts for *Everglades* and *Arctic Son.* These last two, as well as the *Julie* books, have strong environmentalist themes, an important issue for both George and Minor.

The first children's book for which Minor provides both text and pictures is *Grand Canyon: Exploring a Natural Wonder.* Having read that the average Grand Canyon tourist spends a total of only about three to four hours there, Minor wanted to create a sense of closely observed moments over a period of several days at the Canyon. The text provides verbal expression of the observations in a journal format influenced by John Muir's detailed wilderness writings, while the paintings do it visually.

While Minor created the *Grand Canyon* paintings "on the spot" while visiting the Canyon for about two weeks, he typically takes anywhere from five hundred to a thousand photographs while he visits sites for research purposes when planning a book. When a series of paintings is completed, he has only begun the process of actual design of the book, which includes work on the cover, title page, end papers, and overall arrangement of the series of paintings. Viewing the pictures in their final order, he believes, should produce the effect of a continuous journey through the book. The successful artist can use shifting perspectives as a writer uses language, to tell a particular story and to manipulate the reader/observers' emotions as they move through the entire series of pictures. With Wendell Minor paintings, this often means shifting from small animals foregrounded against vast landscapes, to larger animals against even vaster landscapes (a whale on the beach in *Arctic Son,* for example), to animals that match their landscapes (a tortoise with a huge tortoise-shaped rock behind him in *Mojave*), to animals whose faces fill an entire page, dwarfing even mountain ranges in the background (a black bear in *Sierra*). For Minor, the purpose is not only to shape the observer's point of view in a particular way, to provide a specific rhythm for a book, but also to suggest that an animal *has* a point of view, a perspective—and to call attention to the fact that, too often in our world, animals *are* considered insignificant.

Whether he is presenting spectacular visions of the Florida Everglades or Arctic ice floes, Wendell Minor's evocative paintings bring the child reader into contact with the extraordinary, urging him or her to explore the extraordinary in the ordinary world through close and careful observation, and ultimately to preserve and protect that extraordinary world of natural wonder.

—Christine Doyle-Stott

MITCHELL, (Sibyl) Elyne (Keith)

Nationality: British and Australian. **Born:** (Sibyl) Elyne (Keith) Chauvel, Melbourne, Victoria, 30 December 1913. **Education:** St. Catherines, Melbourne and Radcliffe University, United States. **Family:** Married Thomas Walter Mitchell in 1935 (died 1984); two daughters and two sons (one deceased). **Awards:** Order of Australia medal, for services to children's literature, 1991. D. Litt.: Charles Sturt University, 1993. **Agent:** Curtis Brown, 162-168 Regent Street, London W1R 5TB, England, or P.O. Box 19, Paddington, Sydney, New South Wales 2021. **Address:** Towong Hill, Corryong, Victoria 3707, Australia.

Publications for Children

Fiction

The Silver Brumby, illustrated by Ralph Thompson. London, Hutchinson, 1958; New York, Dutton, 1959.

Silver Brumby's Daughter, illustrated by Grace Huxtable. London, Hutchinson, 1960; as *The Snow Filly,* New York, Dutton, 1961.

Kingfisher Feather, illustrated by Grace Huxtable. London, Hutchinson, 1962.

Winged Skis, illustrated by Annette Macarthur-Onslow. London, Hutchinson, 1964.

Silver Brumbies of the South, illustrated by Annette Macarthur-Onslow. London, Hutchinson, 1965.

Silver Brumby Kingdom, illustrated by Annette Macarthur-Onslow. London, Hutchinson, 1966.

Moon Filly, illustrated by Robert Hales. London, Hutchinson, 1968.

Jinki, Dingo of the Snows, illustrated by Michael Cole. London, Hutchinson, 1970.

Light Horse to Damascus, illustrated by Victor Ambrus. London, Hutchinson, 1971.

Silver Brumby Whirlwind, illustrated by Victor Ambrus. London, Hutchinson, 1973.

The Colt at Taparoo, illustrated by Victor Ambrus. Richmond, Victoria, Hutchinson, 1975; London, Hutchinson, 1976.

Son of the Whirlwind, illustrated by Victor Ambrus. Richmond, Victoria, and London, Hutchinson, 1976.

The Colt from Snowy River, illustrated by Victor Ambrus. Richmond, Victoria, Hutchinson, 1979; London, Hutchinson, 1980.

Snowy River Brumby, illustrated by Victor Ambrus. Richmond, Victoria, Hutchinson, 1980; London, Hutchinson, 1981.

Brumby Racer, illustrated by Victor Ambrus. Richmond, Victoria, Hutchinson, 1981; London, Hutchinson, 1982.

Silver Brumby Silver Dingo, illustrated by Victor Ambrus. Sydney, HarperCollins, 1993.

Dancing Brumby. New York, HaperCollins, 1995.

Brumbies of the Night. New York, HarperCollins, 1997.

Publications for Adults

Novels

Flow River, Blow Wind. Sydney, Australasian Publishing Company, and London, Harrap, 1953.

Black Cockatoos Mean Snow. London, Hodder and Stoughton, 1956.

The Man from Snowy River (novelization of screenplay). Sydney and London, Angus and Robertson, 1982.

Discoverers of the Snowy Mountains. Melbourne, Macmillan, 1985.

The Lighthorse Men (novelization of screenplay). Melbourne, Penguin, 1987.

Other

Australia's Alps. Sydney and London, Angus and Robertson, 1942.

Speak to the Earth. Sydney and London, Angus and Robertson, 1945.

Soil and Civilization. Sydney and London, Angus and Robertson 1946.

Images in Water. Sydney, Angus and Robertson, 1947.

Australian Treescape: A Photographic Study. Sydney, Ure Smith 1950.

Light Horse: The Story of Australia's Mounted Troops. Melbourn and London, Macmillan, 1978.

The Snowy Mountains, photographs by Mike James. Adelaide Rigby, 1980.

Chauvel Country: The Story of a Great Australian Pioneering Family. Melbourne, Macmillan, 1983.
Discoverers of the Snowy Mountains. Melbourne, Macmillan, 1985.
A Vision of Snowy Mountains. Melbourne, Macmillan, 1988.
Towong Hill, Fifty Years on an Upper Murray Cattle Station. Melbourne, Macmillan, 1989.

*

Media Adaptation: *Silver Brumby* (film adaptation of her book of the same title), 1993.

Elyne Mitchell comments:

The children's books simply grew out of the life we led. I had had six adult books published, and a growing family. The children were on Correspondence School work, which I had to teach. So *The Silver Brumby* was written for the eldest—something exciting about wild horses to introduce her to the mountain world which I loved so much. Very soon after it was written, the first road was built through the mountains, the Silver Brumby country. Some of the wilderness was no longer wilderness, but it was possible to take very young children skiing and walking, and the whole family grew to love the snow country. More Brumby stories were written, and a ski story for Harry, then a dingo story, and the story of World War I, in which the hero is a horse in my father's Light Horse, and more brumby stories.

* * *

In the Australian Alps where the Granite Tors of the Ramshead Range stretch between Mt. Kosciusko and the icy waters of the Crackenback River, the wind roars as it flattens the springy snowgrass, dark storms sweep across the skyline, and snow falls in silent flakes or comes in wild tremendous blizzards. In summer the gums and tussocks bow to the breezes and sunset turns every ridge and hill-top into gold and the valleys into "long fingers of blue shadow." This is the home country of Elyne Mitchell which she loves as passionately as she does her own horses and the wild horses who roam free. She writes lovingly of brumbies who move across the landscape together or alone, the colts who run together and fight for a herd of their own as each young stallion establishes a claim to his own mares.

This is the country in which Bel Bel, the cream brumby mare, "gave birth to a colt foal, pale like herself or paler in a wild, black storm." So Thowra, the silver brumby, whose name means wind, born in the wind and as fleet as the wind, begins a long fight for supremacy over man and fellow beast. The initial story, *The Silver Brumby,* is written with a deeply lyrical feeling for the wild horses and the territory over which they roam, and was highly commended by the judges of the Australian Children's Book of the Year award in 1959, and the sequel, *Silver Brumby's Daughter,* was commended in 1961. *Winged Skis,* a mystery adventure set in the ski resorts of the Australian Alps, was highly commended in 1965.

Mitchell has been criticised in her own country for the anthropomorphism of her horses who, in the earlier stories, talk together in human terms. However, her brumby stories are widely read not only by children in Australia but have been translated into Spanish, German and Finnish, and are published both in Britain and the United States. They are strongly felt regional novels, connected as a series by the struggle for survival of each generation in freedom and dignity. There are savage and bloody battles between stallions, tender and loyal familial relationships between sire and progeny, the sexual pursuit of his mate by the male, and, in *Silver Brumby Whirlwind,* a mystical farewell and a sense of destiny fulfilled as Thowra bids farewell to his true friend Benni, the kangaroo. Then the whirlwind of the south encircles him, and he returns to his own country forever.

In the later Brumby books, which become a coda to the Silver Brumby saga, there is a strong sense of interaction between the humans from the homesteads of the Monaro and their horses. But always the primary human world is subsumed by the free-flowing secondary world of the silver brumby's progeny. The author's style now is less mannered than it was in the "middle" Brumby books and in *Jinki* where there is no circling dance of the brumbies to justify her elliptical use of language. *Light Horse to Damascus* is the story of a Queenslander, Dick Osborne, and his horse Karloo who with the Australian Light Horse beat their way across the desert to war and to Damascus. Literary techniques which succeeded when the author was writing from personal involvement are no longer valid. It is for her Silver Brumby that Mitchell will be remembered as a writer.

—H.M. Saxby

MITCHISON, Naomi (Margaret)

Nationality: British. **Born:** Naomi Margaret Haldane, Edinburgh, 1 November 1897; daughter of the scientist John Scott Haldane; sister of J. B. S. Haldane, *q.v.* **Education:** at Lynam's School, Oxford; St. Anne's College, Oxford. **Military Service:** Volunteer nurse, 1915. **Family:** Married G. R. Mitchison (who became Lord Mitchison, 1964) in 1916 (died 1970); three sons and two daughters. **Career:** Labour candidate for Parliament, Scottish Universities constituency, 1935; member, Argyll County Council, 1945-66; member, Highland Panel, 1947-64, and Highlands and Islands Development Council, 1966-76. Tribal adviser, and Mmarona (Mother), to the Bakgatla of Botswana, 1963-89. **Awards:** D. Univ.: University of Stirling, Scotland, 1976; University of Dundee, Scotland, 1985; D. Litt.: University of Strathclyde, Glasgow, 1983. Honorary Fellow, St. Anne's College, 1980, and Wolfson College, 1983, both Oxford. Officer, French Academy, 1924. C. B. E. (Commander, Order of the British Empire), 1985. **Address:** Carradale House, Carradale, Campbeltown, Scotland.

Publications for Children

Fiction

The Hostages and Other Stories for Boys and Girls, illustrated by Logi Southby. London, Cape, 1930; New York, Harcourt Brace, 1931.
Boys and Girls and Gods. London, Watts, 1931.
The Big House. London, Faber, 1950.
Graeme and the Dragon, illustrated by Pauline Baynes. London, Faber, 1954.
The Land the Ravens Found, illustrated by Brian Allderidge. London, Collins, 1955.

Little Boxes, illustrated by Louise Annand. London, Faber, 1956.
The Far Harbour, illustrated by Martin Thomas. London, Collins, 1957.
Judy and Lakshmi, illustrated by Avinash Chandra. London, Collins, 1959.
The Rib of the Green Umbrella, illustrated by Edward Ardizzone. London, Collins, 1960.
The Fairy Who Couldn't Tell a Lie, illustrated by Jane Paton. London, Collins, 1963.
Henny and Crispies. Wellington, New Zealand, Department of Education, 1964.
Ketse and the Chief, illustrated by Christine Bloomer. London, Nelson, 1965; New York, Nelson, 1967.
Friends and Enemies, illustrated by Caroline Sassoon. London, Collins, 1966; New York, Day, 1968.
The Big Surprise. London, Kaye and Ward, 1967.
Don't Look Back, illustrated by Laszlo Acs. London, Kaye and Ward, 1969.
The Family at Ditlabeng, illustrated by Joanna Stubbs. London, Collins, 1969; New York, Farrar Straus, 1970.
Sun and Moon, illustrated by Barry Wilkinson. London, Bodley Head, 1970; Nashville, Nelson, 1973.
Sunrise Tomorrow. London, Collins, and New York, Farrar Straus, 1973.
The Danish Teapot, illustrated by Patricia Frost. London, Kaye and Ward, 1973.
Snake!, illustrated by Polly Loxton. London, Collins, 1976.
The Little Sister, with works by Ian Kirby and Keetla Masogo, illustrated by Angela Marrow. Cape Town, Oxford University Press, 1976.
The Wild Dogs, with works by Megan Biesele, illustrated by Polly Loxton. Cape Town, Oxford University Press, 1977.
The Brave Nurse and Other Stories, illustrated by Polly Loxton. Cape Town, Oxford University Press, 1977.
The Two Magicians, with Dick Mitchison, illustrated by Danuta Laskowska. London, Dobson, 1978.
The Vegetable War, illustrated by Polly Loxton. London, Hamish Hamilton, 1980.
A Girl Must Live. Glasgow, Drew, 1990.
The Oath-takers. Nairn, Balnain, 1991.
Sea-green Ribbons. Nairn, Balnain, 1991.

Plays

Nix-Nought-Nothing: Four Plays for Children (includes *My Ain Sel', Hobyah! Hobyah!, Elfen Hill*). London, Cape, 1928; New York, Harcourt Brace, 1929.
Kate Crackernuts: A Fairy Play. Oxford, Alden Press, 1931.
An End and a Beginning and Other Plays (includes *The City and the Citizens, For This Man Is a Roman, In the Time of Constantine, Wild Men Invade the Roman Empire, Charlemagne and His Court, The Thing That Is Plain, Cortez in Mexico, Akbar, But Still It Moves, The New Calendar, American Britons*). London, Constable, 1937; as *Historical Plays for Schools,* 2 vols., 1939.

Other

The Swan's Road (on the Vikings), illustrated by Leonard Huskinson. London, Naldrett Press, 1954.
The Young Alexander the Great, illustrated by Betty Middleton-Sandford. London, Parrish, 1960; New York, Roy, 1961.
Karensgaard: The Story of a Danish Farm. London, Collins, 1961.
The Young Alfred the Great, illustrated by Shirley Farrow. London, Parrish, 1962; New York, Roy, 1963.
Alexander the Great, illustrated by Rosemary Grimble. London, Longman, 1964.
A Mochudi Family, illustrated by Stephen John. Wellington, New Zealand, Department of Education, 1965.
Highland Holiday, photographs by John K. Wilkie. Wellington, New Zealand, Department of Education, 1967.
African Heroes, illustrated by William Stobbs. London, Bodley Head, 1968; New York, Farrar Straus, 1969.

Editor, *An Outline for Boys and Girls and Their Parents.* London, Gollancz, 1932.

Publications for Adults

Novels

The Conquered. London, Cape, and New York, Harcourt Brace, 1923.
Cloud Cuckoo Land. London, Cape, 1925; New York, Harcourt Brace, 1926.
The Corn King and the Spring Queen. London, Cape, and New York, Harcourt Brace, 1931; as *The Barbarian,* New York, Cameron, 1961.
The Powers of Light. London, Cape, and New York, Peter Smith, 1932.
Beyond This Limit. London, Cape, 1935.
We Have Been Warned. London, Constable, 1935; New York, Vanguard Press, 1936.
The Blood of the Martyrs. London, Constable, 1939; New York, McGraw Hill, 1948.
The Bull Calves. London, Cape, 1947.
Lobsters on the Agenda. London, Gollancz, 1952.
Travel Light. London, Faber, 1952.
To the Chapel Perilous. London, Allen and Unwin, 1955.
Behold Your King. London, Muller, 1957.
Memoirs of a Spacewoman. London, Gollancz, 1962.
When We Become Men. London, Collins, 1965.
Cleopatra's People. London, Heinemann, 1972.
Solution Three. London, Dobson, and New York, Warner, 1975.
Not by Bread Alone. London, Boyars, 1983.
Early in Orcadia. Glasgow, Drew, 1987.

Short Stories

When the Bough Breaks and Other Stories. London, Cape, and New York, Harcourt Brace, 1924.
Black Sparta: Greek Stories. London, Cape, and New York, Harcourt Brace, 1928.
Barbarian Stories. London, Cape, and New York, Harcourt Brace, 1929.
The Delicate Fire: Short Stories and Poems. London, Cape, and New York, Harcourt Brace, 1933.
The Fourth Pig: Stories and Verses. London, Constable, 1936.
Five Men and a Swan: Short Stories and Poems. London, Allen and Unwin, 1958.
Images of Africa. Edinburgh, Canongate, 1980.

What Do You Think Yourself? Scottish Short Stories. Edinburgh, Harris, 1982.
Beyond This Limit: Selected Shorter Fiction of Naomi Mitchison, edited by Isobel Murray. Edinburgh, Scottish Academic Press, 1986.

Plays

The Price of Freedom, with L. E. Gielgud (produced Cheltenham, 1949). London, Cape, 1931.
Full Fathom Five, with L.E. Gielgud (produced London, 1932).
As It Was in the Beginning, with L. E. Gielgud. London, Cape, 1939.
The Corn King, music by Brian Easdale, adaptation of the novel by Mitchison (produced London, 1950).
Spindrift, with Denis Macintosh (produced Glasgow, 1951). London, French, 1951.

Poetry

The Laburnum Branch. London, Cape, 1926.
The Alban Goes Out. Harrow, Middlesex, Raven Press, 1939.
The Cleansing of the Knife and Other Poems. Edinburgh, Canongate, 1978.

Other

Anna Comnena. London, Howe, 1928.
Comments on Birth Control. London, Faber, 1930.
The Home and a Changing Civilisation. London, Lane, 1934.
Vienna Diary. London, Gollancz, and New York, Smith and Haas, 1934.
Socrates, with Richard Crossman. London, Hogarth Press, 1937; Harrisburg, Pennsylvania, Stackpole, 1938.
The Moral Basis of Politics. London, Constable, 1938; Port Washington, New York, Kennikat Press, 1971.
The Kingdom of Heaven. London, Heinemann, 1939.
Men and Herring: A Documentary, with Denis Macintosh. Edinburgh, Serif, 1949.
Other People's Worlds (travel). London, Secker and Warburg, 1958.
A Fishing Village on the Clyde, with G. W. L. Patterson. London, Oxford University Press, 1960.
Presenting Other People's Children. London, Hamlyn, 1961.
Return to the Fairy Hill (autobiography and sociology). London, Heinemann, and New York, Day, 1966.
The Africans: A History. London, Blond, 1970.
Small Talk: Memories of an Edwardian Childhood. London, Bodley Head, 1973.
A Life for Africa: The Story of Bram Fischer. London, Merlin Press, and Boston, Carrier Pigeon, 1973.
Oil for the Highlands? London, Fabian Society, 1974.
All Change Here: Girlhood and Marriage (autobiography). London, Bodley Head, 1975.
Sittlichkeit (lecture). London, Birkbeck College, 1975.
You May Well Ask: A Memoir 1920-1940. London, Gollancz, 1979.
Mucking Around: Five Continents over Fifty Years. London, Gollancz, 1981.
Margaret Cole 1893-1980. London, Fabian Society, 1982.
Among You, Taking Notes: The Wartime Diary of Naomi Mitchison 1939-1945, edited by Dorothy Sheridan. London, Gollancz, 1985.
Naomi Mitchison (autobiographical sketch). Edinburgh, Saltire Society, 1986.

Editor, *An Outline for Boys and Girls and Their Parents.* London, Gollancz, 1932.
Editor, with Robert Britton and George Kilgour, *Re-Educating Scotland.* Glasgow, Scoop, 1944.
Editor, *What the Human Race Is Up To.* London, Gollancz, 1962.

*

Manuscript Collections: National Library of Scotland, Edinburgh; University of Texas, Austin.

Naomi Mitchison comments:

I like writing for children because it means writing straight: not putting in clever bits or the kind of passage which is only there to impress and perhaps confuse the reader. Children are very critical and they want a good story. I think I am essentially a story teller, not an observer of manners or morals. I hope young people will get from my stories what I got from E. Nesbit's. I have been lucky to have a critical audience—children of my own and later grandchildren—who have kept me on my toes. I like reading my books aloud and they have been willing to listen and tell me, for instance, what I have left out and ought to have told the reader.

One big pleasure of writing children's books is that I need not be ashamed of having a happy ending, something I like increasingly as real life gets further away from it.

* * *

Naomi Mitchison's books have brought to many children in our epoch what feel like direct experiences of living at other times, in other places, and in alien cultures, among people with strange customs, clothes, festivals, beliefs, and assumptions about the world; people who yet remain vivid characters, with recognizable, sharable feelings—love, grief, homesickness, fear, anger, loyalty, and conflicts of loyalty.

Most of her stories are set in periods of deep collective changes, sudden or gradual, seen as they shape the lives of individuals and families. They may happen when great civilizations clash, or interact, or crossfertilize one another; or when industrial culture burns into some traditional way of life; or in the midst of modern war, when small groups lose their hostility to one another and unite against one great enemy, as in the enchanting *The Rib of the Green Umbrella,* whose hero is a boy in the Italian Resistance movement.

Among my own favourites is *The Hostages.* Though it contains brief historical sketches linking each tale with its predecessor along a thousand years, these stories are lively and concrete, untainted by the useful dreary hold-all abstractions of the textbook. And each story, wherever or whenever it takes place, has an extraordinarily vivid sensory quality. The details of landscapes, roads, houses, clothes, kitchens, all kinds of work are shown with a clarity which extends even to smells—of flowers or food or horses or sweaty crowds or blood. Such sensations, surviving through centuries of historical change, make every scene actual to the reader. So does Mitchison's quick awareness of moods and feelings and emotional reactions, whether in a tired young Etruscan boy captive made to walk, full of sadness and shame, along hot interminable streets in a Roman Triumph; in the chilly terror of a prehistoric girl child lost in British mountain mists near a sacred stone; in a modern misunderstanding between an English and an Indian schoolfriend (as in *Judy and Lakshmi*); or in the allegiances, divided between past wisdom and future change, of children growing up in Africa (where the author was in fact the adoptive mother of a Botswana tribe). Her own deep roots in Scottish history and folklore with its wizards and elves and nixies flowered as early as 1928 in *Nix-Nought-Nothing,* and underline her living understanding of such beliefs at any time.

Mitchison's work has not only given a great deal of enjoyment and opened many new horizons to readers and read-to; it has above all extended human sympathy to understand and to feel with and for "all sorts and conditions of men."

—Renée Haynes

MOLLEL, Tololwa M(arti)

Nationality: Canadian. **Born:** Arusha, Tanzania, 25 June 1952; emigrated to Canada in 1986; became a Canadian citizen in 1993. **Family:** Married Obianuju Olisa in 1978; two sons. **Education:** University of Dar-es-Salaam, B.A. in Literature and Theater 1972; University of Alberta, M.A. in Drama 1979. **Career:** University lecturer, director of children's theater, and actor in Tanzania, 1979-86; writer, storyteller, and lecturer in Canada, since 1986. **Awards:** Pick of the Lists citation, American Bookseller Association, 1991-92; Notable Book citation, American Library Association, 1991-92; honorable mention, Annual California Children's Media Awards, 1992; Florida Reading Association award, 1993. **Agent:** Joanne Kellock, 11017-80 Avenue, Edmonton, Alberta, T6G OR2. **Address:** 354 King's Court, Edmonton, Alberta T6J 2E4, Canada.

Publications for Children

Picture Books

Rhino's Boy: A Maasai Legend. Auckland, New Zealand, Outriggers Publishers, 1988.
The Orphan Boy, illustrated by Paul Morin. Toronto, Oxford University Press, 1990; New York, Clarion, 1991.
Rhinos for Lunch and Elephants for Supper!, illustrated by Barbara Spurll. Toronto, Oxford University Press, 1991; New York, Clarion, 1992.
A Promise to the Sun: An African Story, illustrated by Beatriz Vidal. Toronto and Boston, Little, Brown, 1992.
The Princess Who Lost Her Hair: An Akamba Legend, illustrated by Charles Reasoner. Mahwah, New Jersey, Troll Associates, 1993.
The King and the Tortoise, illustrated by Kathy Blankley. Toronto, Lester, and New York, Clarion, 1993.
The Flying Tortoise: An Igbo Tale, illustrated by Barbara Spurll. Toronto, Oxford University Press, 1993; New York, Clarion Books, 1994.
Big Boy, illustrated by E. B. Lewis. Toronto, Stoddart, and New York, Clarion Books, 1995.
Ananse's Feast: An Ashanti Tale, illustrated by Andrew Glass. New York, Clarion Books, 1997.
Dume's Roar, illustrated by Kathy Blankley Roman. Toronto and Buffalo, New York, Stoddart Kids, 1997.
Kele's Secret, illustrated by Catherine Stock. Toronto, Stoddart Kids, and New York, Lodestar, 1997.
Kitoto the Mighty, illustrated by Kristi Frost. Toronto, Stoddart, 1998.
Shadow Dance, illustrated by Donna Perrone. New York, Clarion Books, 1998.

*

Media Adaptations: *The Orphan Boy: A Maasai Story* and *Rhinos for Lunch and Elephants for Supper!* (recordings by Tololwa M. Mollel), Toronto, Oxford University Press, 1992.

Critical Studies: "Bordering the Mainstream: The Writing of Tololwa Mollel" by Louise Saldanha, in *Canadian Children's Literature* (Guelph, Ontario), Vol. 22, No. 1, 1996, 24-30; interview with Tololwa M. Mollel by Raymond E. Jones, January, 1998.

* * *

Tololwa Mollel has received international recognition as a narrative artist who makes African materials accessible to children from other cultures. In an interview with Raymond E. Jones, he said that he blends two traditions: "I see myself as both a storyteller and an author." As part of what he calls "the continuum of storytellers," Mollel passes on tales from the oral traditions of Africa. As an author belonging to a literary tradition, however, Mollel emphasizes originality: "I add my own themes or amplify the themes of the original tales." The resulting picture books, whether retellings of tribal tales or original stories incorporating traditional motifs, have narrative economy, verbal polish, and thematic focus.

Mollel's first major, *The Orphan Boy,* is a retelling of a *pour quoi* tale about the planet Venus, which the Maasai call Kiliken, the orphan boy. Its theme connects love and trust. The tale first focuses on the magic of love, recounting how an orphan named Kiliken comes to live with a poor, lonely old man. Kiliken mysteriously performs the man's chores in impossibly brief amounts of time. Even when drought strikes, Kiliken ensures that the cattle remain fat and that the man prospers. No longer poor or lonely, the happy old man loves Kiliken as his son. Uncontrolled curiosity, however, leads him to betray Kiliken's trust. Although warned that he will lose everything if he learns the secret of Kiliken's power, the old man follows the advice of his shadow, a symbol of unrepressed curiosity, and trails Kiliken when he goes off with the cattle. Kiliken sees the old man, explodes into a star, and ascends into the sky. The old man again becomes poor and lonely. This cautionary tale reflects Maasai beliefs that one must not seek some forms of knowledge, but it also implies that lack of trust will destroy anyone's love and happiness.

Many of Mollel's subsequent books also feature ironic reversals, but they are lighter in mood because they employ the comic trickster figure. Mollel is fond of this figure, he told Jones, because, "Something has to make things happen in a children's story and the trickster makes things happen, for better or worse." His first published trickster tale, *Rhinos for Lunch and Elephants for Supper!,* employs two tricksters and shows the discrepancy between appearance and reality. When hare hears a voice coming from her cave, she seeks help from a succession of larger animals

Each is frightened away by the booming voice, which declares that it is a monster that eats rhinos for lunch and elephants for supper. A clever frog finally tricks the monster by shouting that she eats rhinos, elephants, and monsters: farcically, the monster that then emerges is merely a trickster, a caterpillar who has used the echo in the cave to make himself seem ferocious. In addition to showing that appearances are deceptive, this cumulative tale suggests that wit is more effective than brawn in solving problems.

Several of Mollel's other tales also pit tricksters against each other. In *The King and the Tortoise,* Tortoise, a major trickster figure in African tales, outwits a proud king, who tries to establish his own cleverness by challenging his subjects to make a robe of smoke. Exacting a promise that the king will provide any necessary materials, Tortoise demonstrates his superior wit and earns the king's appreciative laughter by requesting a thread of fire. The revenge tale *Ananse's Feast* contains two parallel comic episodes. First, Ananse the Spider, another major African trickster, fools Akye the Turtle, who visits his house hoping for food. Ananse slyly insists that politeness demands that Akye wash his hands before eating. Because he walks on all fours, however, Akye dirties his hands immediately after washing. Greedy Ananse therefore repeatedly sends him away to wash and thus avoids sharing his food. Later, Akye exacts revenge and humiliates his adversary. Inviting Ananse to his house for a feast, he insists that politeness requires Ananse to remove his robe. Because Ananse has weighted his pockets with stones in order to keep himself submerged in the turtle's underwater home, Ananse floats to the surface and is unable to share the meal. Mollel does not rely exclusively on traditional tricksters. In *Shadow Dance,* for example, Crocodile, stranded in a gully after floodwaters recede, tricks a little girl, Salome, into releasing him and taking him to the river. When he then seizes her, Salome uses wit to survive: she tricks the vain Crocodile into returning to the gully to prove that he was truly trapped and was not merely pretending. When the Crocodile again strands himself, Salome wisely abandons him to his fate.

Mollel's other books include both adaptations of oral tales, such as *The Princess Who Lost Her Hair, The Flying Tortoise,* and *Kitoto the Mighty,* and original stories presented in the style of folk tales, such as *A Promise to the Sun* and *Dume's Roar.* Of these, only the elegantly economical *Dume's Roar,* about a tortoise who tricks a scared lion into frightening hunters and reforming his selfish character, ranks with Mollel's best work. Mollel has also written two books about contemporary Africa. According to its author's note, *Big Boy* uses the African motif of the prodigious child, but its plot follows the familiar pattern of the therapeutic dream journey. Told that he is too small to do what his big brother does, little Oli sneaks out of the house. A magic bird grants his wish, transforming Oli into a giant who travels around the country. Oli falls asleep, only to awaken as a small boy surrounded by his worried family. Because his mother carries him home but his brother must walk, Oli cheerfully accepts that being small has advantages. *Kele's Secret,* inspired by Mollel's experiences on his grandfather's farm, is a simple first-person account of the pride a little boy feels when he helps his family by discovering where Kele the hen hides her eggs. A new direction for a writer known for adapting traditional materials, these contemporary stories suggest that Mollel can point to the universal in African experience without sacrificing its exotic qualities.

—Raymond E. Jones

MONJO, F(erdinand) N(icolas, III)

Nationality: American. **Born:** Stamford, Connecticut, 28 August 1924. **Education:** Stamford High School; Columbia University, New York, B.A. 1946. **Family:** Married Louise Elaine Lyczak in 1950; three sons and one daughter. **Career:** Editor, Golden Books, Simon and Schuster, 1953-58, and American Heritage Junior Library, 1958-61, both New York; assistant director, Books for Boys and Girls, Harper and Row, New York, 1961-69; vice-president and editorial director, Books for Boys and Girls, Coward McCann and Geoghegan, New York, 1969-78. **Died:** 9 October 1978.

Publications for Children

Fiction

Indian Summer, illustrated by Anita Lobel. New York, Harper, 1968; Kingswood, Surrey, World's Work, 1969.

The Drinking Gourd, illustrated by Fred Brenner. New York, Harper, 1970; Kingswood, Surrey, World's Work, 1971.

The One Bad Thing about Father, illustrated by Rocco Negri. New York, Harper, 1970.

Pirates in Panama, illustrated by Wallace Tripp. New York, Simon and Schuster, 1970.

The Jezebel Wolf, illustrated by John Schoenherr. New York, Simon and Schuster, 1971; London, Dent, 1973.

The Vicksburg Veteran, illustrated by Douglas Gorsline. New York, Simon and Schuster, 1971.

Slater's Mill, illustrated by Laszlo Kubinyi. New York, Simon and Schuster, 1972.

Rudi and the Distelfink, illustrated by George Kraus. New York, Windmill, 1972.

The Secret of the Sachem's Tree, illustrated by Margot Tomes. New York, Coward McCann, 1972.

Poor Richard in France, illustrated by Brinton Turkle. New York, Holt Rinehart, 1973.

Me and Willie and Pa, illustrated by Douglas Gorsline. New York, Simon and Schuster, 1973.

Grand Papa and Ellen Aroon, illustrated by Richard Cuffari. New York, Holt Rinehart, 1974.

The Sea-Beggar's Son, illustrated by C. Walter Hodges. New York, Coward McCann, and London, Chatto and Windus, 1974.

King George's Head Was Made of Lead, illustrated by Margot Tomes. New York, Coward McCann, 1974.

Letters to Horseface, illustrated by Don Bolognese and Elaine Raphael. New York, Viking Press, 1975.

Gettysburg: Tad Lincoln's Story, illustrated by Douglas Gorsline. New York, Windmill, 1976.

Willie Jasper's Golden Eagle, illustrated by Douglas Gorsline. New York, Doubleday, 1976.

Zenas and the Shaving Mill, illustrated by Richard Cuffari. New York, Coward McCann, 1976.

The Porcelain Pagoda, illustrated by Richard Egielski. New York, Viking Press, 1976.

A Namesake for Nathan, illustrated by Eros Keith. New York, Coward McCann, 1977.

The House on Stink Alley: A Story about the Pilgrims in Holland, illustrated by Robert Quackenbush. New York, Holt Rinehart, 1977.

Prisoners of the Scrambling Dragon, illustrated by Arthur Geisert. New York, Holt Rinehart, 1980.

Other

Clarence and the Burglar, illustrated by Paul Galdone. New York, Coward McCann, 1973; Kingswood, Surrey, World's Work, 1975.

Translator, with Nina Ignatowicz, *The Crane,* by Reiner Zimnik illustrated by Zimnik. New York, Harper, 1970; London, Penguin, 1974.

*

Manuscript Collections: Kerlan Collection, University of Minnesota, Minneapolis.

* * *

F.N. Monjo's sense of history was people-centered. His historical books, novels, novelettes, easy-reading history books, and young biographies revolve around both the great and the near-great of the past. His own sense of family history was equally people-centered. He grew up surrounded by Americana in the stories his family told of his father's fur-merchant ancestors and his mother's plantation-bred forebears. Monjo determined his own writing course, having noted as an editor that "most of the fun of history lay in the details most children's books seemed to omit."

Monjo's ability to capture those detailed glimpses and transmit them to eager readers can be measured by the success of three of his many books: *The Drinking Gourd, Indian Summer,* and his extremely popular *Poor Richard in France.*

The Drinking Gourd is both fact and fiction in an easy-to-read format. Written in a straightforward, unadorned style, it is Monjo's second book, and it established both his reputation and the direction of his work. The story of an Underground Railway stop and the young minister's son who helps a family of black fugitives, the book appeals to both head and heart of the young reader. Monjo is not patronizing to either.

His first book, *Indian Summer,* was also well-received. But events in American publishing and the awareness of librarians have made the book a problem for Monjo. It is the story of a pioneer family and the mother and children who fight off an attack by cowardly marauding Indians. Monjo's talent for frill-less, direct storytelling was already very apparent in this story. But organizations like the Council on Interracial Books have been critical of the tale. And in her introduction to a selected bibliography, *American Indian Authors for Young Readers,* Mary Gloyne Byler escalated the attack. Monjo countered in a persuasive article in *School Library Journal* saying that an author has an obligation to inform himself on a topic but has the right to choose that topic and its point of view. Still, the controversy has not died.

In his National Book award nominee, *Poor Richard in France,* Monjo is at his unassailable best. Here his sense of humor—slightly impish and impious—can be plainly seen. In the five years between this book and his first, Monjo perfected his simple style. There is not a loose word or unnecessary phrase in the book, a charming anecdotal view of Franklin through his grandson's eyes. It is a technique Monjo used again and again in later books to great advantage. The use of the child narrator is a common juvenile book technique, but Monjo made the child's voice authentically his own. And his gimlet eye, slightly softened by the child's lens through which he peers, gives us a fresh and appealing look at any number of otherwise overworked periods of history.

Except for his friend and colleague Jean Fritz, Monjo had no peer in the writing of easy-reading history books.

—Jane Yolen

MONTGOMERY, L(ucy) M(aud)

Nationality: Canadian. **Born:** Clifton (now New London), Prince Edward Island, 30 November 1874. **Education:** Schools in Cavendish, Prince Edward Island, and Prince Albert, Saskatchewan; Prince of Wales College, Charlottetown, Prince Edward Island, teacher's certificate 1894, teacher's license 1895; Dalhousie College, Halifax, Nova Scotia, 1895-96. **Family:** Married Ewan Macdonald in 1911; two sons. **Career:** Schoolteacher, Bideford, 1894-95, 1896-97, and Lower Bedeque, 1897-98, both in Prince Edward Island; assistant postmistress, Cavendish, 1898-1911; staff member, Halifax *Echo,* 1901-02. **Awards:** Fellow, Royal Society of Arts, 1923. O.B.E. (Officer, Order of the British Empire), 1935. **Died:** 24 April 1942.

Publications for Children

Fiction

Anne of Green Gables, illustrated by M.A. and W.A. Claus. Boston, Page, and London, Pitman, 1908.
Anne of Avonlea. Boston, Page, and London, Pitman, 1909.
Kilmeny of the Orchard, illustrated by George Gibbs. Boston, Page, and London, Pitman, 1910.
The Story Girl. Boston, Page, and London, Pitman, 1911.
Chronicles of Avonlea. Boston, Page, and London, Sampson Low, 1912.
The Golden Road. Boston, Page, 1913; London, Cassell, 1914.
Anne of the Island. Boston, Page, and London, Pitman, 1915.
Anne's House of Dreams. New York, Stokes, and London, Constable, 1917.
Rainbow Valley. Toronto, McClelland and Stewart, and New York, Stokes, 1919; London, Constable, 1920.
Further Chronicles of Avonlea..., illustrated by John Goss. Boston, Page, 1920; London, Harrap, 1953.
Rilla of Ingleside. Toronto, McClelland and Stewart, New York, Stokes, and London, Hodder and Stoughton, 1921.
Emily of New Moon. New York, Stokes, and London, Hodder and Stoughton, 1923.
Emily Climbs. New York, Stokes, and London, Hodder and Stoughton, 1925.
The Blue Castle. Toronto, McClelland and Stewart, New York, Stokes, and London, Hodder and Stoughton, 1926.
Emily's Quest. New York, Stokes, and London, Hodder and Stoughton, 1927.
Magic for Marigold. Toronto, McClelland and Stewart, New York Stokes, and London, Hodder and Stoughton, 1929.
A Tangled Web. New York, Stokes, 1931; as *Aunt Becky Began It* London, Hodder and Stoughton, 1931.

Pat of Silver Bush. New York, Stokes, and London, Hodder and Stoughton, 1933.
Mistress Pat: A Novel of Silver Bush. New York, Stokes, and London, Harrap, 1935.
Anne of Windy Poplars. New York, Stokes, 1936; as *Anne of Windy Willows,* London, Harrap, 1936.
Jane of Lantern Hill. Toronto, McClelland and Stewart, New York, Stokes, and London, Harrap, 1937.
Anne of Ingleside. New York, Stokes, and London, Harrap, 1939.
The Road to Yesterday. Toronto, McGraw Hill Ryerson, 1974; London, Angus and Robertson, 1975.
The Doctor's Sweetheart and Other Stories, edited by Catherine McLay. Toronto, McGraw Hill Ryerson, and London, Harrap, 1979.
Akin to Anne: Tales of Other Orphans, edited by Rea Wilmshurst. Toronto, McClelland and Stewart, 1988.
Along the Shore: Tales by the Sea, edited by Rea Wilmhurst. Toronto, McClelland and Stewart, 1989.
Among the Shadows: Tales from the Darker Side, edited by Rea Wilmhurst. Toronto, McClelland and Stewart, 1990.
Days of Dreams and Laughter: The Story Girl and Other Tales (includes *The Story Girl, The Golden Road,* and *Kilmeny of the Orchard*). Avenel, 1990.

Publications for Adults

Poetry

The Watchman and Other Poems. Toronto, McClelland and Stewart, 1916; New York, Stokes, 1917; London, Constable, 1920.
The Poetry of Lucy Maud Montgomery, edited by Kevin McCabe and John Ferns. Markham, Ontario, Fitzhenry and Whiteside, 1987.

Other

Courageous Women, with Marian Keith and Mabel Burns McKinley. Toronto, McClelland and Stewart, 1934.
The Green Gables Letters to Ephraim Weber 1905-1909, edited by Wilfrid Eggleston. Toronto, Ryerson Press, 1960.
The Alpine Path: The Story of My Career. Don Mills, Ontario, Fitzhenry and Whiteside, 1974.
My Dear Mr. M.: Letters to G.B. MacMillan, edited by Francis W.P. Bolger and Elizabeth R. Epperly. Toronto, McGraw Hill Ryerson, 1980.
Spirit of Place: L.M. Montgomery and Prince Edward Island, edited by Francis W. P. Bolger. Toronto, Oxford University Press, 1982.
The Selected Journals 1: 1889-1910 [2: 1910-1921], edited by Mary Rubio and Elizabeth Waterston. Toronto, Oxford University Press, 2 vols., 1985-87.
After Many Days, New York, Bantam, 1992.

*

Critical Studies: *The Years Before "Anne"* by Francis W.P. Bolger, Charlottetown, Prince Edward Island Heritage Foundation, 1975; *The Wheel of Things: A Biography of L.M. Montgomery* by Mollie Gillen, Don Mills, Ontario, Fitzhenry and Whiteside, 1975, London, Harrap, 1976; *L.M. Montgomery: An Assessment* edited by John Robert Sorfleet, Guelph, Ontario, Canadian Children's Press, 1976; *L.M. Montgomery: A Preliminary Biography* by Ruth Weber Russell, Waterloo, Ontario, University of Waterloo Library, 1986.

* * *

At times, L.M. Montgomery's work challenges conventional opinion about what makes a children's book. Is it a child or adolescent protagonist? Then what does one do with such books as *Anne's House of Dreams* and *Anne of Ingleside,* wherein Anne is a married mother with, eventually, five children? Is it comparatively innocuous subject matter? Then what does one do with the bitterness and jealousies evident in extended family relationships in many of the novels, or the marital hatred of Olivia and Peter Kirk in *Anne of Ingleside,* or the actual separation of the protagonist's parents in *Jane of Lantern Hill*—not to mention the frequent deaths of children and adults in the books? In fact, virtually all of Montgomery's fiction—including *The Blue Castle* and *A Tangled Web,* sometimes termed "adult" novels—is read and enjoyed by children and adolescents. This is because Montgomery deals with the psychological realities and conflicts of childhood and adolescence: need for an independent identity and for respect in an unjust and repressive world run by adults; flare-ups of hatred as well as love for family, relatives, and others; cross-sex hostility as well as affection; stirrings of passion versus fear of the changes it implies and inner perspectives it reveals; and so on. Indeed, a Freudian analysis of Montgomery's work, related to what we know of her inner life, could be at least as interesting—and revealing—as existing analyses of Lewis Carroll's *Alice in Wonderland.*

Her best-known book is *Anne of Green Gables,* first of a long series. This tale of an orphaned girl, sent by mistake to an elderly brother and sister who expect a boy, was enormously successful, and its heroine was termed by Mark Twain "the dearest, and most lovable child in fiction since the immortal Alice." The novel counterpoises child and adult perspectives, and this provides the basis for much of the novel's humour as well as some pathos. Anne is childhood spontaneity and imagination confronting adult conventionalism and dogmatism—both social and religious. Her words and actions effectively undermine the hypocrisy of the adult world and deflate its pretensions, while at the same time asserting the value of imaginative reality in a society which tends to deny it. And, while portraying Anne and the other characters—not to mention the land and the psychological relationships—realistically, Montgomery adds force to her depiction by drawing on the powers of fairytale archetype: the orphaned heroine coming to an unknown land, where she is involved in a case of mistaken identity, gains protectors, demonstrates her worth, defeats her enemies, and is finally reconciled with her Prince Charming, Gilbert Blythe.

Anne of Green Gables was followed by five other Anne books plus associated works such as *Rainbow Valley* and *Rilla of Ingleside* in which she appears. These later books show a considerable falling-away from the qualities of the first, as the original inspiration, a red-haired hoyden, inevitably growing up, encounters the more stringent social pressures and realities facing a young woman. Only *Anne of the Island,* which focuses on the exciting period of Anne's college years and her various courtships, comes anywhere near the readability of the first Anne book.

With *Emily of New Moon,* Montgomery initiated her second series. The Emily trilogy presents what might be called a "Portrait of the Artist" in the successive stages of girl, teenager, and young woman. As might be expected, these novels draw upon Montgomery's own childhood experiences even more extensively than her other books. The first novel reveals that, like Anne, Emily is an orphan, though her father's death is not antecedent to the book's beginning but occurs in the third chapter. Besides being a writer by nature and circumstance, Emily is notable for her "flashes" of mystical insight and moments of second sight. As for literary considerations, *Emily of New Moon*—like its sequels, *Emily Climbs* and *Emily's Quest*—competently relates symbolism, characterization, irony, and other stylistic concerns to a coherent and consistent exposition of theme and plot. In fact, except for a slightly over-rich effect in some of the passages representing Emily's thoughts, as a group this trilogy is better integrated and more satisfying than the Anne series.

Among Montgomery's later novels are *The Blue Castle* and *A Tangled Web,* appealing especially to adolescent girls. The former is clearly the better: except for some momentary falterings, it's a good, enjoyable book of its type—the identity crisis *cum* love story—which has a solid technical underpinning (e.g., the symbolism) as well. Reading it leads one to wonder—with reason, according to the Montgomery journals—about the state of Montgomery's own mind and marriage at the time. *A Tangled Web,* by contrast, has the defects its title implies; there are too many threads of plot and unbelievable situations, resulting in a not really satisfactory book.

In the fiction of Montgomery's final decade, two new protagonists are introduced. The first is Pat Gardiner—unusual in Montgomery's work because she has both parents living—who appears in *Pat of Silver Bush* and its sequel *Mistress Pat.* The earlier of the two is slightly the better. Its theme is the child's fear of change in the face of its inevitability. There are a few tear-jerking passages, and children might laugh at Judy Plum's Irish dialect when the novel is read aloud, but overall it is not a memorable book, perhaps because Pat is an Anne without spirit, an Emily without ability.

Montgomery's final heroine is Jane Stuart in *Jane of Lantern Hill.* Though with no outstanding talents, Jane has a hard core of selfhood which enables her to survive the bitter hostility of a tyrannical grandmother whose interference has maintained a ten-year marital separation between Jane's parents. Further, eventually Jane's self-directed actions enable her to become the instrument for her parents' reconciliation. This tale of tyranny, self-identity, and reunion is one that rewards psychological analysis. Also suggestive are the settings, rural Prince Edward Island and urban Toronto—the latter a notable innovation in Montgomery's novels. It's a book well worth a child's reading.

Overall, Montgomery's work is marked by a succession of unforgettable heroines seen against the backdrop of the beautiful Prince Edward Island landscape. Within them their isolated selves struggle to flourish against a set of outside pressures that urge conformity and denial of selfhood as the price of social acceptance. Yet they do not submit, and eventually their struggles are rewarded by their acceptance as them*selves,* not as mere specious semblances. And further, the outer Island landscape tends to operate in parallel to the heroines' inner lives, bringing comfort when needed, as it did for Montgomery herself. Indeed, in showing the importance of heroic inner struggle at the same time as stressing the outer physical landscape, Montgomery reveals herself to be operating within the mainstream of the Canadian literary tradition.

—John Robert Sorfleet

MOORE, Dorothea (Mary)

Nationality: British. **Born:** London in 1881. **Education:** Godolphin School, Salisbury; Cheltenham Ladies College. **Military Service:** Voluntary Aid Detachment, 1914. **Career:** Actress on tour with the Alex Maclean Company, 1911-12. **Died:** 19 May 1933.

Publications for Children

Fiction

Mistress Dorothy. London, National Society, 1902.
Evelyn. London, Nelson, 1904.
God's Bairn. London, Blackie, 1904; as *Marlowe of the Fens,* 1934.
Brown. London, Nisbet, 1905; New York, Eaton and Mains, 1907; as *Three Feet of Valour,* Nisbet, 1921.
Sydney Lisle, illustrated by Wal Paget. London, Partridge, 1905; Philadelphia, McKay, 1910; as *A Golden Dawn,* Partridge, 1925.
Jepthah's Lass. London, Partridge, 1907.
Elizabeth's Angel and Other Stories. London, National Society, 1907.
Knights of the Red Cross. London, Nelson, 1907.
Pamela's Hero, illustrated by A.A. Dixon. London, Blackie, 1907.
A Plucky School-Girl. London, Nisbet, 1908.
The Christmas Children. London, Partridge, 1909; as *The Children of the Marshes,* 1927.
The Luck of Ledge Point, illustrated by C. Horrell. London, Blackie, 1909.
A Lady of Mettle. London, Partridge, 1910.
The Making of Ursula. London, Partridge, 1910.
The Lucas Girls, illustrated by Tom Peddie. London, Partridge, 1911.
Under the Wolf's Fell. London, Partridge, 1911.
Nadia to the Rescue. London, Nisbet, 1912.
A Runaway Princess. London, Partridge, 1912.
Terry the Girl-Guide, illustrated by A.A. Dixon. London, Nisbet, 1912.
A Brave Little Royalist, illustrated by John Campbell. London, Nisbet, 1913.
Only a Girl! London, Partridge, 1913.
Rosemary the Rebel. London, Partridge, 1913.
Captain Nancy. London, Nisbet, 1914.
Cecily's Highwayman, illustrated by John Campbell. London, Nisbet, 1914.
Septima, Schoolgirl. London, Cassell, 1915.
Wanted, An English Girl: The Adventures of an English Schoolgirl in Germany. London, Partridge, 1916.
The New Girl. London, Nisbet, 1917.
The Head Girl's Sister. London, Nisbet, 1918.
Tam of Tiffany's. London, Partridge, 1918.
Her Schoolgirl Majesty. London, Partridge, 1918.
Head of the Lower School. London, Nisbet, 1919; New York, Putnam, 1920.
A Nest of Malignants. London, S.P.C.K., 1919; New York, Macmillan, 1920.
The Right Kind of Girl. London, Nisbet, 1920.
The New Prefect. London, Nisbet, 1921.
An Adventurous Schoolgirl, illustrated by Archibald Webb. London, Cassell, 1921; New York, Funk and Wagnalls, 1922.

Greta of the Guides. London, Partridge, 1921.
Guide Gilly, Adventurer. London, Nisbet, 1922.
The New Girl at Pen-y-Gant. London, Nisbet, 1922.
The Only Day-Girl. London, Nisbet, 1923.
A Young Pretender. London, Nisbet, 1924.
Fen's First Term. London, Cassell, 1924.
In the Reign of the Red Cap, illustrated by Archibald Webb. London, Sheldon Press, 1924.
Smuggler's Way, illustrated by H.M. Brock. London, Cassell, 1924.
A Rough Night. London, Partridge, 1925.
"Z" House. London, Nisbet, 1925.
My Lady Venturesome. London, Sheldon Press, 1926.
Perdita, Prisoner of War. London, Cassell, 1926.
A Schoolgirl Adventurer. London, A. and C. Black, 1927.
Tenth at Trinder's. London, Cassell, 1927.
Adventurers All!, illustrated by P. Walford. London, Partridge, 1927.
Brenda of Beech House. London, Nisbet, 1927.
Seraphine-Di Goes to School. London, Religious Tract Society, 1927.
Darry the Dauntless. London, Cassell, 1928.
A Rebel of the Third. London, Nisbet, 1929.
Adventurers Two. London, Sheldon Press, 1929.
The Wrenford Tradition. London, Nisbet, 1929.
Judy, Patrol Leader [*Lends a Hand*]. London, Collins, 2 vols., 1930-32.
Nicky of Nine Schools. London, Oxford University Press, 1932.
Sara to the Rescue. London, Nisbet, 1932.
At Friendship's Call. London, Oxford University Press, 1932.
Dick of the Day-Girls. London, Nisbet, 1933.
Queens for Choice. London, Oxford University Press, 1934.
Babs Goes to Court. London, Sheldon Press, 1936.
The Crooked Headstone. London, Pearson, 1939.

Publications for Adults

Novels

My Lady Bellamy. London, Nisbet, 1909.
When the Moon Is Green. London, Partridge, 1917.

Plays

My Lady Bellamy (produced Margate, Kent, and London, 1910).
The Grey Mask, with Alexander Maclean (produced Margate, Kent, 1912).
By the King's Leave, with Alexander Maclean (produced Margate, Kent, 1912).
Lilies and Lavender (produced London, 1929).

* * *

Like Bessie Marchant, Angela Brazil, and others who were writing at the start of the 20th century, Dorothea Moore endeavoured to produce a more robust type of fiction than the unexciting domestic stories that had hitherto been staple reading matter for girls. Her books were popular for almost four decades and her range was wide. She contributed poems, plays, and well-structured short stories to several children's magazines, including *Little Folks* and *The Girls' Own Paper*, and to *Blackie's*, the *Oxford*, and *British Girls'* annuals. The liveliness of her short stories, however, was not always conveyed in her novels which, particularly after the 1920s, sometimes lacked style and inventiveness.

Some of her school stories feature rebellious characters like the heroine of *Tenth at Trinder's*, who initially resist discipline and conformity but are nudged by staunch chums, admired prefects, and fearfully understanding headmistresses into acceptance of team-spiritedness and loyalty to the school. Moore makes strong use of the customary alarms and accidents of the genre (girls rescuing schoolmates from burning, drowning, or literal cliff-hanging, etc.). But she is at her best when describing lower key aspects of school life in a series of persuasive images of girls cycling to school in broad-brimmed felt hats and well-brushed blue serge gymslips, or changing into white frocks for "exuberantly cooked" suppers, and dutifully awaiting their turns on bathroom rotas, and so on. These vignettes not only convey the rhythms of school routines but a greater sense of period (the 1920s) than Moore managed to achieve in her historical stories. *Cecily's Highwayman, In the Reign of the Red Cap, The Luck of Ledge Point,* and several other of her historical novels lack this integral feeling for period, although, with plenty of peripheral excitement and atmosphere, they succeed at the romance level.

A Girl Guide Commissioner, Moore made her most significant contribution to girls' fiction with *Terry the Girl-Guide* in 1912. This was the first full-length guiding novel to be published, and its authentic re-creation of the pioneering mood set a pattern that other authors were to follow for some 30 years. Moore produced colourful variations on the theme in several stories of teenage princesses from vaguely Ruritanian backgrounds who were redeemed—either physically or psychologically—by contact with the idealism, resourcefulness, and grit of the typical British Girl Guide (*A Young Pretender, Brenda of Beech House,* etc.). By 1930, however, she seemed at last to have exhausted guiding as a story writing stimulus, and *Judy, Patrol Leader* is no more than a disappointing rehash of the ingredients that made her vigorous early books on the theme so memorable.

Many of Moore's heroines experience engaging flashes of wry self-awareness, but the main characteristic of her stories is that they have an overall charm that has ensured their long-lasting appeal to girls—and to women who now read them nostalgically.

—Mary Cadogan

MORAY WILLIAMS, Ursula

Nationality: British. **Born:** Petersfield, Hampshire, 19 April 1911. **Education:** Privately and at schools in Annecy, France, and Winchester. **Family:** Married Peter John in 1935 (died 1974); four sons. **Agent:** Curtis Brown Ltd., 162-168 Regent Street, London W1R 5TA. **Address:** Court Farm House, Beckford, near Tewkesbury, Gloucestershire GL20 9AA, England.

Publications for Children

Fiction

Jean-Pierre, illustrated by the author. London, A. and C. Black, 1931.

The Pettabomination, illustrated by the author. London, Archer, 1933; revised edition, London, Lane, 1948.
Kelpie, The Gipsies' Pony, illustrated by the author and Barbara Moray Williams. London, Harrap, 1934; Philadelphia, Lippincott, 1935.
Anders and Marta, illustrated by the author. London, Harrap, 1935.
Adventures of Anne, illustrated by the author. London, Harrap, 1935.
The Twins and Their Ponies, illustrated by the author. London, Harrap, 1936.
Sandy-on-the-Shore, illustrated by the author. London, Harrap, 1936.
Tales for the Sixes and Sevens, illustrated by the author. London, Harrap, 1936.
Dumpling, illustrated by the author. London, Harrap, 1937.
Elaine of La Signe, illustrated by the author and Barbara Moray Williams. London, Harrap, 1937; as *Elaine of the Mountains,* Philadelphia, Lippincott, 1939.
Adventures of Boss and Dingbat, photographs by Peter John. London, Harrap, 1937.
Adventures of the Little Wooden Horse, illustrated by Joyce Lankester Brisley. London, Harrap, 1938; Philadelphia, Lippincott, 1939.
Adventures of Puffin, illustrated by Mary Shillabeer. London, Harrap, 1939.
Peter and the Wanderlust, illustrated by Jack Matthew. London, Harrap, 1939; Philadelphia, Lippincott, 1940; revised edition, as *Peter on the Road,* London, Hamish Hamilton, 1963.
Pretenders' Island, illustrated by Joyce Lankester Brisley. London, Harrap, 1940; New York, Knopf, 1942.
A Castle for John-Peter, illustrated by Eileen Soper. London, Harrap, 1941.
Gobbolino the Witch's Cat. London, Harrap, 1942.
The Good Little Christmas Tree, illustrated by the author. London, Harrap, 1943.
The Three Toymakers, illustrated by the author. London, Harrap, 1945; revised edition, London, Hamish Hamilton, 1970; New York, Nelson, 1971.
The House of Happiness, illustrated by the author. London, Harrap, 1946.
Malkin's Mountain, illustrated by the author. London, Harrap, 1948; revised edition, London, Hamish Hamilton, 1970; New York, Nelson, 1972.
The Story of Laughing Dandino, illustrated by the author. London, Harrap, 1948.
Jockin the Jester, illustrated by Barbara Moray Williams. London, Chatto and Windus, 1951; Nashville, Nelson, 1973.
The Binklebys at Home, illustrated by the author. London, Harrap, 1951.
The Binklebys on the Farm, illustrated by the author. London, Harrap, 1953.
The Secrets of the Wood, illustrated by the author. London, Harrap, 1955.
Grumpa, illustrated by the author. Leicester, Brockhampton Press, 1955.
Goodbody's Puppet Show, illustrated by the author. London, Hamish Hamilton, 1956.
Golden Horse with a Silver Tail, illustrated by the author. London, Hamish Hamilton, 1957.
Hobbie, illustrated by the author. Leicester, Brockhampton Press, 1958.
The Moonball, illustrated by the author. London, Hamish Hamilton, 1958; New York, Meredith Press, 1967.
The Noble Hawks. London, Hamish Hamilton, 1959; as *The Earl's Falconer,* New York, Morrow, 1961.
The Nine Lives of Island Mackenzie, illustrated by Edward Ardizzone. London, Chatto and Windus, 1959; as *Island Mackenzie,* New York, Morrow, 1960.
Beware of the Animal, illustrated by Jane Paton. London, Hamish Hamilton, 1964; New York, Dial Press, 1965.
Johnnie Tigerskin, illustrated by Diana Johns. London, Harrap, 1964; New York, Duell, 1966.
O for a Mouseless House!, illustrated by the author. London, Chatto and Windus, 1964.
High Adventure, illustrated by Prudence Seward. London, Nelson, 1965.
Cruise of the "Happy-Go-Gay," illustrated by Gunvor Edwards. London, Hamish Hamilton, 1967; New York, Meredith Press, 1968.
A Crown for a Queen, illustrated by Shirley Hughes. London, Hamish Hamilton, and New York, Meredith Press, 1968.
The Toymaker's Daughter, illustrated by Shirley Hughes. London, Hamish Hamilton, 1968; New York, Meredith Press, 1969.
Mog, illustrated by Faith Jaques. London, Allen and Unwin, 1969.
Boy in a Barn, illustrated by Terence Dalley. London, Allen and Unwin, and New York, Nelson, 1970.
Johnnie Golightly and His Crocodile, illustrated by Faith Jaques. London, Chatto Boyd and Oliver, 1970; New York, Harvey House, 1971.
Traffic Jam, illustrated by Robert Hales. London, Chatto and Windus, 1971.
Man on a Steeple, illustrated by Mary Dinsdale. London, Chatto and Windus, 1971.
Mrs. Townsend's Robber, illustrated by Gavin Rowe. London, Chatto and Windus, 1971.
Out of the Shadows, illustrated by Gavin Rowe. London, Chatto and Windus, 1971.
Castle Merlin. London, Allen and Unwin, and Nashville, Nelson, 1972.
A Picnic with the Aunts, illustrated by Faith Jaques. London, Chatto and Windus, 1972.
The Kidnapping of My Grandmother, illustrated by Mike Jackson. London, Heinemann, 1972.
Tiger-Nanny, illustrated by Gunvor Edwards. Leicester, Brockhampton Press, 1973; Nashville, Nelson, 1974.
Grandpapa's Folly and the Woodworm-Bookworm, illustrated by Faith Jaques. London, Chatto and Windus, 1974.
The Line, illustrated by Barry Wilkinson. London, Penguin, 1974.
No Ponies for Miss Pobjoy, illustrated by Pat Marriott. London, Chatto and Windus, 1975; Nashville, Nelson, 1976.
Bogwoppit, illustrated by Shirley Hughes. London, Hamish Hamilton, and Nashville, Nelson, 1978.
Jeffy, The Burglar's Cat, illustrated by David McKee. London, Andersen Press, 1981.
Bellabelinda and the No-Good Angel, illustrated by Glenys Ambrus. London, Chatto and Windus, 1982.
The Further Adventures of Gobbolino and the Little Wooden Horse, illustrated by Pauline Baynes. London, Penguin, 1984.
Spid, illustrated by David McKee. London, Andersen Press, 1985.
Grandma and the Ghowlies, illustrated by Susan Varley. London, Andersen Press, 1986.

Paddy on the Island, illustrated by Tor Morisse. London, Andersen Press, 1987.

Plays

The Autumn Sweepers and Other Plays (includes *Mother Josephine Bakes Bread, Forfeits, Tavi of Gold, The Organ Grinder: A Mime, A Sea Ballet*), illustrated by the author. London, A. and C. Black, 1933.
The Good Little Christmas Tree. London, French, 1951.
The House of Happiness. London, French, 1951.
The Pettabomination. London, French, 1951.

Poetry

Grandfather, illustrated by the author. London, Allen and Unwin, 1933.

Other

For Brownies: Stories and Games for the Pack and Everybody Else, illustrated by the author. London, Harrap, 1932.
More for Brownies, illustrated by the author. London, Harrap, 1934.
Children's Parties, and Games for a Rainy Day. London, Corgi, 1972.

*

Ursula Moray Williams comments:

I began to write in 1930 and *Jean-Pierre* was published in 1931. Of course I had written all my life, but this was my first published work, and there has been a steady flow ever since. I have only written childrens' books (not *for* children, but they seem to like them!).

We were read aloud to all our childhood, and now that I am in my eighties I often dip into those old books with great enjoyment.

I've no idea why I write or wrote what I did. Ask a hen why it lays an egg.

* * *

Ursula Moray Williams has written over 60 children's stories and plays, notable for the variety of their appeal to a range of ages from three to 13; and though some of the earlier stories may now seem old-fashioned, she continues to write with unabated zest. A good storyline, a simple and compelling lucidity of language, a firm though not overpowering moral attitude, and an irrepressible sense of fun are common to all her stories. Kindness, compassion, and concern for others are almost invariably set against selfish greed, heartlessness, trickery, and violence, a confrontation which is most explicit in three stories about a beautiful but heartless and often maliciously spiteful doll, Marta. *The Three Toymakers, Malkin's Mountain,* and *The Toymaker's Daughter* are set in a fantasy kingdom of peasants, mountain scenery and magic with a strong folklore element in the telling, though they are less astringent than the traditional folktale. Akin to these tales are *Adventures of the Little Wooden Horse* and *Gobbolino the Witch's Cat.* They share the fantasy folktale element, but the observation of the complexities of good and evil is sharper and less sentimental. As the stories are episodic they are well-suited to reading aloud in installments to six or seven-year-olds, and the two main characters, the "quiet little horse" and the unhappy witch's cat, still have charm and sure appeal for children. In a pleasantly alarming and adventurous sequel, *The Further Adventures of Gobbolino and the Little Wooden Horse,* these two characters combine to rescue Gobbolino's wicked sister Sootica from the witch, demonstrating incidentally the values of a kind heart and faithfulness and that even witches deserve loyalty and compassion.

In a different, lighthearted, and amusing vein of fantasy are two picture books with an Edwardian flavour, the ingenious *Grandpapa's Folly and the Woodworm-Bookworm* and *A Picnic with the Aunts;* the absurdly lunatic *Johnnie Golightly and His Crocodile; Tiger-Nanny,* the story of a tiger-cub who loves children—to look after, not to eat; *The Kidnapping of My Grandmother,* a Parisian adventure with a Paul Berna flavour; and *Mog,* a zany story of two eccentric old ladies.

There is an impish delight in mischief in some more recent books for seven to 10-year-olds. In *Jeffy, The Burglar's Cat* Miss Amity's enjoyment of her criminal activities is almost too much for Jeffy's reforming zeal; in *Bogwoppit* there is no taming either the determined young heroine or the extraordinary marshy and mischievous bogwoppits she encounters; and though the work ethic triumphs in the girls' boarding-school story *No Ponies for Miss Pobjoy,* there is strong sympathy for the pony-mad rebels as well. The youngest ghowlie in *Grandma and the Ghowlies* is full of mischief too, a determinedly disruptive poltergeist, who sets everyone by the ears, but really only needs to be loved. This is a lively and amusing ghost story, with some touching little scenes as well as a variety of problems and trials for Grandma in her attempt to find new homes for the five waif-like ghostlings. In *Spid,* on the other hand, the eponymous spider-hero creates his own welcome, ingratiating himself so ingeniously and effectively even with spider-haters that in the end he has to assert his independence. He wants to live his own life, not be anyone's pet. *Bellabelinda and the No-Good Angel* tells how an unsuccessful guardian angel finally makes the grade with the help of three mischievous boys and a lollipop lady who claims descent from a witch; while *Paddy on the Island* is a quietly amusing little story of a boy who escapes from his overbearing family to a desert island, where he finds at first some of the peace he seeks, but also the adventures and the mixture of good and bad fortune a wishing stone can be expected to bring.

For older readers, *Boy in a Barn* is an adventure story with a mountain peasant background similar to that of the earlier fantasies, but set in postwar Europe; *The Noble Hawks* an historical story of a 14th-century yeoman's son who longs to be a falconer. *Castle Merlin* is a story of the present day, but exploiting the continuing popularity of time fantasies, and *The Line* is an imaginative story of a magical modern invention. There are some uncertainties in handling the more complex plots of these stories, and some stereotyping in the minor characters; but the main characters are seen to develop in self-awareness and maturity, and there are witty and satirical undertones to the writing which, while bearing affinity to the slyly wicked humour of the stories for younger children, add a further dimension to Moray Williams's story-telling. She is an inventive as well as a prolific writer, and in their different ways her books are well-written, pleasantly intriguing, and occasionally achieve a haunting power and a delightfully sharp and witty observation of the foibles of mankind.

—Winifred Whitehead

MOREY, Walt(er Nelson)

Nationality: American. **Born:** Hoquiam, Washington, 3 February 1907. **Education:** Benkhe Walker Business College, 1927. **Family:** Married 1) Rosalind Alice Ogden in 1934 (died 1977); 2) Peggy Kilburn in 1978. **Career:** Construction worker, millworker, and theatre manager in Oregon and Washington, 1930s; burner foreman and superintendent, Kaiser Shipyards, Vancouver, Washington, 1940-45; deep-sea diver and fish trap inspector, Alaska, 1951; director, Oregon Nut Cooperative, Newberg, 1960-61. Filbert farmer, from 1937. **Agent:** Lenniger Literary Agency, 104 East 40th Street, New York, New York 10016, U.S.A.

Publications for Children

Fiction

Gentle Ben, illustrated by John Schoenherr. New York, Dutton, 1965; London, Dent, 1966.
Home Is the North, illustrated by Robert Shore. New York, Dutton, 1967; London, Dent, 1968.
Kävik, The Wolf Dog, illustrated by Peter Parnall. New York, Dutton, 1968; London, Dent, 1969.
Angry Waters, illustrated by Richard Cuffari. New York, Dutton, 1969; London, Dent, 1970.
Gloomy Gus. New York, Dutton, 1970; as *The Bear at Friday Creek,* London, Dent, 1971.
Deep Trouble. New York, Dutton, 1971; London, Dent, 1972.
Scrub Dog of Alaska. New York, Dutton, 1971; London, Sidgwick and Jackson, 1975.
Canyon Winter. New York, Dutton, 1972; London, Dent, 1974.
Runaway Stallion. New York, Dutton, 1973.
Run Far, Run Fast. New York, Dutton, 1974.
Year of the Black Pony. New York, Dutton, 1976; London, Collins, 1977.
Sandy and the Rock Star. New York, Dutton, 1979.
The Lemon Meringue Dog. New York, Dutton, 1980.
Death Walk, illustrated by Fredrika Spillman. Blue Heron, 1991.
Hero. New York, Puffin Books, 1995.

Other

Operation Blue Bear. New York, Dutton, 1975.

Publications for Adults

Other

North to Danger, with Virgil Burford. New York, Day, 1954; revised edition, Caldwell, Idaho, Caxton, 1969.

*

Manuscript Collections: University of Oregon Library, Eugene.

* * *

Walt Morey is a writer in the Jack London tradition; many of his books are animals stories set in Alaska. Morey's Alaska is that of the 1950s, the years just before the territory achieved statehood, and he writes from his experience of living and working there, primarily in the occupations concerning salmon-fishing on which the economy of the area depended. Life in small settlements like Orca City is rough and tough; many of the people are as migrant as the salmon on their annual run, and while qualities such as courage and endurance are valued, ruthless exploitation is equally a condition of survival. The message of many of Morey's novels is a questioning of this situation; their formula is often that of an adolescent boy who is for some reason a "loner"; he befriends an animal whom he has to defend from adults who would use or kill it. These stories do not stay long on library shelves; their vivid descriptions of icy wastes combined with the warmth of their emotional tone make them popular reading.

Gentle Ben is still one of the best-loved. Ben, contrary to generally held opinions of the nature of bears, especially those soured by ill-treatment in captivity, becomes the pet of young Mark Andersen and is saved by him not only from the villagers of Orca City but also from big-game hunters from the outside world.

Home Is the North and *Kävik, The Wolf Dog* both have Malamute dogs as their animal heroes, and both contrast the land of the wild and free with civilisation as represented by Seattle, the port of embarkation for Alaska. In the first, the orphan Brad fights to stay and work on the fishing boats rather than join his aunt in Seattle, especially as this means giving up his dog, Mickie. In the second, Kävik survives ill treatment and privation in his attempts to make the long journey home to the north. The latter, perhaps because it centres on the animal's reactions rather than humans', is the better book; it is both moving and powerful.

In *Gloomy Gus* Eric Strong's pet bear is sold by his elders to a circus and filial loyalty leads him to accept this, much as he dislikes it. *Scrub Dog of Alaska* is another story of making good. Dave Martin, son of an Indian mother and a white father, has to stand up to the racist sneers of his father's relatives in the States. His dog Scrub develops from being the weakest of the litter to being the leader of the pack. *Canyon Winter* is an exciting survival story of a boy who is marooned by a plane crash in the Cascade Mountains over the winter. This experience and the influence of the old recluse who saves him make him, on his return to civilisation, a fierce conservationist.

In *Canyon Winter,* and in all his later books, Morey takes as his setting not the Alaska of his young maturity, but the Oregon of his childhood and retirement, which he describes vividly from memory and from research of earlier pioneer days. *Runaway Stallion* is his first book to have a horse as its main animal character in a story of a racehorse running wild until adopted by a boy on an isolated ranch. His best book in this genre, though, is *Year of the Black Pony,* which draws more deeply on autobiographical sources and which has a well-sustained climax in the boy hero's being carried home safely by his horse when lost in a Christmas blizzard. Morey's heroes are often boys and young men who achieve maturity by protecting animals against predatory adults; those in *Sandy and the Rock Star* and *The Lemon Meringue Dog* are contemporary youths, a pop singer and a young coastguard in a "drug bust" programme.

Respect and concern for wild life and the wild places of the earth are Morey's themes; his message is the conservationist one of a proper balance between man and nature.

—Mary Croxson

MORGAN, Alison (Mary)

Nationality: British. **Born:** Alison Mary Raikes, Bexley, Kent, 2 March 1930. **Education:** St. Helen's School, Northwood, Middlesex, 1943-47; Somerville College, Oxford, 1949-52, B.A. (honours) 1952; University of London, 1952-53, Cert. Ed. 1953. **Family:** Married John Morgan in 1960; two sons. **Career:** Taught in secondary modern school, Malvern, Worcestershire, 1953-54, and in girls' grammar school, Newtown, Montgomery, 1954-59. Justice of the Peace, from 1964. **Awards:** Welsh Arts Council award, 1973. **Agent:** A.P. Watt Ltd., 20 John Street, London WC1N 2DL. **Address:** Talcoed, Llanafan, near Builth Wells, Powys, Wales.

Publications for Children

Fiction

Fish, illustrated by John Sergeant. London, Chatto and Windus, 1971; as *A Boy Called Fish,* New York, Harper, 1973.
Pete. London, Chatto and Windus, 1972; New York, Harper, 1973.
Ruth Crane. London, Chatto and Windus, 1973; New York, Harper, 1974.
The Raft, illustrated by Trevor Parkin. London, Abelard Schuman, 1974.
At Willie Tucker's Place, illustrated by Trevor Stubley. London, Chatto and Windus, 1975; Nashville, Nelson, 1976.
River Song, illustrated by John Schoenherr. New York, Harper, 1975; London, Chatto and Windus, 1976.
Leaving Home. London, Chatto and Windus, 1979; as *All Sorts of Prickles,* New York, Elsevier Nelson, 1979.
Paul's Kite, illustrated by Vanessa Julian-Ottie. London, Chatto and Windus, 1981; New York, Atheneum, 1982.
Christabel, illustrated by Mariella Jennings. London, MacRae, 1984.
Bright-Eye, illustrated by Vanessa Julian-Ottie. London, Viking Kestrel, 1984.
Staples for Amos, illustrated by Charles Front. London, MacRae, 1986.
The Eyes of the Blind. Oxford, Oxford University Press, 1986.
The Wild Morgans, illustrated by Liz Roberts. London, Viking Kestrel, 1988.
The Biggest Birthday Card in the World. London, MacRae, 1989.
Smudge and the Danger Lion. London, MacRae, 1989.
A Walk with Smudge. London, MacRae, 1989.
Dante and the Medieval other World. New York, Cambridge University Press, 1990.
Caroline's Coat. London, MacRae, 1991.
Smudge. London, Walker, 1992.

*

Alison Morgan comments:

Fish, Pete, Ruth Crane, and *At Willie Tucker's Place* form a quartet of stories set in a hypothetical mid-Wales with different children from the village community as major characters in each case. *The Raft* is a short story concerned with two boys, one disabled and the other afraid of water, who in the course of a dangerous adventure learn to understand something of each other's problems. *River Song* traces a year in the life of a group of riverside birds.

In *Leaving Home* and its sequel, *Paul's Kite,* although the main character has come from a mid-Wales setting similar to that of the earlier books, the stories concern his new life, first in a South Wales seaside town and later in London.

* * *

Alison Morgan's books fall into distinct categories but each shares common themes and a common attitude to life. Whether overtly or as an underlying issue, her novels are always concerned with children being tested, or testing themselves, and in the process learning about themselves or about other people.

She writes with an admirable lack of sentimentality and even in her shortest pre-novels she contrives to create a past and a future for her characters and a continuity for the countryside. Life is going on all around and the incident at the heart of each book is not plucked out and written as a self-contained episode. This strong feeling for the countryside and the community must come from Morgan's own view of life and yet she manages to write objectively, keeping herself out of the book and letting characters and events speak for themselves.

Her first group of novels is set in a small Welsh village. *Fish,* which immediately established her as a significant new writer for children, began a thread which was to run through many of her novels—that of the outsider who gradually gains acceptance. Three other books also chronicle events in LLanwern: *Pete, At Willie Tucker's Place,* and *Ruth Crane,* which is aimed at a slightly older reader and introduces an American teenager. Perhaps because of the dramatic nature of this story—Ruth's mother and sister are badly injured in a car accident which kills her father—and the older readership, it does not fit entirely happily into the group but it still raises some thought-provoking questions about outsiders and about changes imposed from without. Two later books, *Leaving Home* and *Paul's Kite,* also deal with the adjustments which have to be made when changes are imposed concerning, as they do, a boy sent from his home to live with relatives in London.

All of Morgan's stories show a deep awareness of the environment, particularly of the continuity of nature, and this is the subject matter of two of her books: *River Song,* which describes a year in the life of a colony of birds, and *Bright-Eye.* The latter is perhaps the more successful because of its format as a short story in the Kestrel Kites series aimed at early readers of seven-to-nine years who are not yet ready for the complexity of a full-length novel. The length is appropriate for what is essentially a small incident in which Amanda struggles to hatch and rear a wild duck when an egg is rescued from the plough by her father. The conservation theme is lightly handled and, despite offering a lot of information about wildlife, it never becomes a tract. Morgan's accurate ear for the rhythms of speech is evident in creating a warm family story, strong on domestic life, seeming to recreate real—if economical—speech and always told from a child's-eye view.

Another relatively short book for the middle years is *Staples for Amos* which, in the same way that *Bright-Eye* tells a self-contained chapter from Amanda's life, describes an episode in a boy's life as he searches for the right sort of staples so that antagonistic Amos will mend the fence and stop the bullocks coming through. As so often in Morgan's work, this superficially self-contained incident touches on deeper themes, in this case racial prejudice. As well as a search for staples, it is a search for acceptance in the local community by the part West Indian boy and his mother.

The Eyes of the Blind is a totally different book, suitable for confident teenage readers. Benjamin (grandson of the prophet Isaiah) is caught up in an Assyrian seige and the novel tells the events of his flight to Jerusalem, initially in the convoy of women and children, largely in the company of Adad, blind son of the Assyrian general. It is a demanding read, full of detail, but the rewards are in proportion to the demands made on the reader. At the heart of the book are universal themes and personal relationships which are as relevant today as 2000 years ago. As in her other books, the two boys learn much about each other as they pass through dangers and stirring times together and, in this respect, it is not unlike a much shorter book, *The Raft,* where two boys facing danger together learn to appreciate something of what it is like to be the other—one disabled, one with a disabling fear of water.

—Valerie Brinkley-Willsher

MORGAN, Helen (Gertrude Louise)

Nationality: British. **Born:** Helen Gertrude Louise Axford, Ilford, Essex, 11 April 1921. **Education:** Barking Abbey Grammar School, Essex, 1932-37; Royal National College for the Blind, London, 1938-42. **Family:** Married Tudor Meredydd Morgan in 1954; three daughters. **Career:** Lived in Wales. **Agent:** Rosemary Bromley, Juvenilia Literary Agency, Avington Lodge, Avington, near Winchester, Hampshire SO21 1DB. **Died:** 1990.

Publications for Children

Fiction

The Little Old Lady: Four Stories, illustrated by Irene Hawkins. London, Faber, 1961.
Tales of Tigg's Farm, illustrated by Shirley Hughes. London, Faber, 1963.
Meet Mary Kate, illustrated by Shirley Hughes. London, Faber, 1963.
A Mouthful of Magic, illustrated by W.J. Gale. London, Harrap, 1963.
Two in the Garden [*in the House, on the Farm, by the Sea*], illustrated by Jillian Willett. Leicester, Brockhampton Press, 4 vols., 1964-67.
The Tailor and the Sailor and the Small Black Cat, illustrated by Michael Hoare. London, Nelson, 1964.
A Dream of Dragons and Other Tales, illustrated by Shirley Hughes. London, Faber, 1965.
Satchkin Patchkin, illustrated by Shirley Hughes. London, Faber, 1966; Philadelphia, Macrae Smith, 1970.
Mary Kate and the Jumble Bear and Other Stories, illustrated by Shirley Hughes. London, Faber, 1967.
Mrs. Pinny and the Blowing Day [*Sudden Snow, Salty Sea Day*], illustrated by Shirley Hughes. London, Faber, 3 vols., 1968-72.
Mary Kate and the School Bus and Other Stories, illustrated by Shirley Hughes. London, Faber, 1970; as *Mary Kate,* Nashville, Nelson, 1972.
Mother Farthing's Luck, illustrated by Shirley Hughes. London, Faber, 1971.
The Sketchbook Crime, illustrated by Jim Russell. Exeter, Wheaton, 1980.
The Witch Doll. New York, Viking, 1991.

*

Helen Morgan comments:

I write for children because I like children. I like to make them laugh and to stimulate their imaginations and to make them feel safe. Childhood doesn't last long. It ought to be happy.

* * *

To appraise the achievement of a gifted writer whose implied readers are always the very young is to seek out the ways in which the plot, theme, narrative, and form all combine to show something which is significant, precursory, and new.

Helen Morgan's work is often rooted in the homely and the accessible, the here-and-now of young childhood that criticism used misguidedly to call "realism." The Mary Kate tales and "Two" books slow down and turn into art the action, sounds, sights, feelings, of childhood. The universal experiences—birthdays, bonfires, losing a tooth, starting school—need space for reflection. Deceptively simple techniques of form like the length of chapters and the interplay of episodes help a storyteller who never seems to be in a hurry catch the quintessential *slowness* of childhood time.

Stories such as those about the indomitable washerwoman Mrs. Pinny link the rustic ordinary with the fabulous, so encouraging reading as venture and possibility. The passing of time is important in her stories: events often happen all in a day and can be held in the head. Her first pages tend to be crucial parts of the invitation. "It was a beautiful bright and blowing day—a windy, wonderful washing day. The clouds were splashes of frothy suds and the sun was a piece of yellow soap in the deep blue bowl of the sky." The young reader has the cohesion of theme, plot, image, and action.

Her original fairytales are miniature masterpieces. The stories of *Satchkin Patchkin,* the little green Magic Man, and Jasper Dark, the anti-hero of *Mother Farthing's Luck,* make folk worlds with their own music, motifs, and potentiality for both order and misrule.

In all Morgan's writing, there is a craftswoman's care for what language can achieve. We find a poetic resonance too rare in writing for the very young ("the fluttering, twittering, golden, glittering morning made her forget the Workday Wednesday") and at times ("Long, long ago, when days were slow and there was time for looking...") an extraordinary musicality.

—Colin Mills

MORRIS, (Margaret) Jean

Pseudonym: Kenneth O'Hara. **Nationality:** British. **Born:** Sevenoaks, Kent, 15 January 1924. **Education:** Bromley High School, Kent; University of London, honours graduate. **Family:** Has one daughter. **Awards:** Arts Council bursary, for drama, 1955. **Address:** Flat 1, 56 Pevensey Road, Eastbourne, East Sussex, BN21 3HT, England.

Publications for Children

Fiction

The Path of the Dragons. London, Hutchinson, 1980.
Twist of Eight, illustrated by Jolyne Knox. London, Chatto and Windus, 1981.
The Donkey's Crusade. London, Bodley Head, 1983.
The Song under the Water. London, Bodley Head, 1985.
The Troy Game. London, Bodley Head, 1987.
The Paper Canoe. London, Bodley Head, 1988.
A New Calling. London, Bodley Head, 1992.

Play

The Spongees, in *Eight Plays 1,* edited by Malcolm Stuart Fellows. London, Cassell, 1965.

Publications for Adults

Novels

Man and Two Gods. London, Cassell, 1953; as *A Man and Two Gods,* New York, Viking Press, 1954.
Half of a Story. London, Cassell, 1957.
The Adversary. London, Cassell, 1959.
The Blackamoor's Urn. London, Cassell, 1962.
A Dream of Fair Children. London, Cassell, 1966.

Novels as Kenneth O'Hara

A View to a Death. London, Cassell, 1958.
Sleeping Dogs Lying. London, Cassell, 1960; New York, Macmillan, 1962.
Underhandover. London, Cassell, 1961; New York, Macmillan, 1963.
Double Cross Purposes. London, Cassell, 1962.
Unknown Man, Seen in Profile. London, Gollancz, 1967.
The Bird-Cage. London, Gollancz, 1968; New York, Random House, 1969.
The Company of St. George. London, Gollancz, 1972.
The Delta Knife. London, Gollancz, 1976.
The Ghost of Thomas Penry. London, Gollancz, 1977.
The Searchers of the Dead. London, Gollancz, 1979.
Nightmares' Nest. London, Gollancz, 1982.

Plays

Island of Gulls (produced Guildford, Surrey, 1956).
Anne of Cleves (televised 1970). Published in *The Six Wives of Henry VIII,* edited by J.C. Trewin, London, Elek, 1972.

Radio Plays: *Safety of the City,* 1961; *The Heretic,* 1962; *Sonata Form of Words,* 1962; *Royal Hunt and Storm,* 1963; *The Mislaid Cause,* 1964; *The Singing Bird,* 1964; *Explosions,* 1965; *Travelling in Winter,* 1971; *The Road to Oxford,* 1976.

Television Play: *Anne of Cleves,* 1970.

Other

The Monarchs of England. New York, Charterhouse, 1975.

Translator, with Radost Pridham, *The Peach Thief and Other Bulgarian Stories.* London, Cassell, 1968.

* * *

Jean Morris is, quite possibly, the most interesting fantasy writer of the 1980s. Her use of magic is so reasoned and practical, so basic to life as she presents it, that it seems natural rather than supernatural—something which she may owe to Ursula K. Le Guin (*Earthsea* trilogy). This is not cancelled out by episodes of powerful eeriness, nor by the fact that her animals use human language occasionally, but they do so sparingly, and they speak sense.

The Path of the Dragons is by far the most complex and demanding of her novels. If you know nothing at all about old Greek and northern myths, if you have never heard of Atlantis, you will lose much of its point. Her views though are not conventional, nor do they taste of the schoolroom. Her Atlantids (inhabitants of Atlantis) are exceptionally gifted: they have computers, air-transport, radio communication; they can also read thoughts. They have no servants, they eat no meat, and they usefully carry their skills—toned down to local level—to needy tribes elsewhere. But can this advanced society last? The assigned dragon-roads in the sky are disturbed. Vast, sage, and splendid, "the most intelligent life-form known to the Atlantids," may also owe a little to Le Guin. The tale will take in much before the island finally vanishes. A gross fellow, Heracles, with a club and a dead lion's skin, sad and stinking, over his shoulder, comes to reconnoitre. The Hyperion/Apollo story (not in the least like Keats's version) is played out. Atlas's burden is both of knowledge and of ignorance. Ideas abound. The dialogue entertains. All these things keep a laden but remarkable vessel buoyant and afloat.

Twist of Eight contains eight tales, each casting a fresh glance at certain legendary stereotypes (Cinderella, Perseus, True Thomas). This is easily the most accessible of Morris's books, even to quite young children; its ideas have wit and sense for anyone. The most original story is about a conscientious horse who, hired for a brief ride, refuses to take part in the Andromeda exploit. He sees no reason why he should prefer princesses to sea-monsters. "If the princess were rescued," he asks, "would the sea-monster have anything *else* to eat?"

Newcomers to Morris should start with *The Donkey's Crusade* which shows her individual quality at its best. Thomas, 15, a novice in an Antioch monastery but by birth and teaching (and desire) a "traveller" or guide, is summoned by the Abbot to conduct a certain Brother James to the distant East, on a wild quixotic mission to the legendary Prester John. (Did he not once offer help in rescuing the Holy City from the infidel?) They are joined by a Frankish flute-playing urchin Aubery—but the wisest member is the fourth, a sage and sometimes cynical donkey, who carries the loads, speaks human language (only when he must), and is perhaps the conscience of the band. As a traveller's tale, the book stands up to anything in that genre for detail, landscape, characters, wonders. As a quest tale alone it should endure, a notable reminder that the search is rather more than the finding.

The Troy Game, another striking Morris original, is again a quest. Brannock, younger son of a king (chief king of a group of seven smallish kingdoms), is sent on a journey by the Merlin-like Mennor. "There is far more to this errand than knowing every path in the Seven Kingdoms...I need you to go to a place to which there is no path: to go to the hall of my Order." Few people have ever seen this hall. Mennor gives the boy a golden brooch, worn and scratched, but engraved with lines that are in fact the paths of the old troy maze, long overgrown with grass and brambles in the grounds. Heading as directed into the eastern wild, Brannock very soon loses his fine horse, his scarlet tunic, and his arrogance (but not his dog, Goldeneye), and acquires a companion, his girl cousin Eilian. She (and her cat) will be indispensable on the long and teasing journey, with its terrors, joys, and marvels. A time comes when the only hope is to summon the Wild Hunt, and to do this you must give all—perhaps lose all. A tremendous episode; the Hunt does not select its victims. Magic is not imposed on this thrilling book; it is intrinsic.

Water is the prevailing element of *The Song under the Water.* It works Jem's father's mill. Jem himself loves to swim, in secret, in the forest pools. It can be a danger, when floods invade the village. The villagers speak with dread of the ominous Water Horse. And it holds the strange water-boy Thorn, who becomes Jem's friend, and seems perhaps a reflection of himself. Thorn, he finds, has a link with the great chateau, where the mysterious Lady Esclairemont lives in solitude. And the water draws all the characters together when, as the floods rise, the Lady opens her doors to the villagers. The book has some fine passages as well as plenty of Morris expertise. But the plot runs obscurely, and the magic isn't wholly absorbed; as a sum of the parts it is probably the least successful of her books.

The Paper Canoe is also commended to all Morris-followers. It has its oddities, its journey too; but in place of the supernatural, we find ourselves in in a powerful daydream. The girl Carly ("a pale resentful shrimp of a girl") has a holiday job in a garden centre with two older boys: Jonathan, handsome, bossy, and humourless, and Raff, a kindly country boy from a long line of Hardyan skilled farmworkers. All three are awaiting exam results, and Carly, clever enough in many things, is the most troubled. Her father's recent death (which brought the family back from Kenya to dull and rainy England) hasn't broken his domination. Will she have failed him in the geography papers—*his* special subject, not hers? Absorbed in Mary Kingsley's *Travels in West Africa,* she starts on a vivid daydream journey down a great African river, leading, she believes, to the sea. The interlinking of the girl's two lives during this week of waiting is most skilfully done; every (literate) teenager should give a recognising nod.

Morris is always an entertaining writer, witty and quotable. Her serious underlying ideas are usually voiced, thought, or discussed by the characters themselves. Her books are not widely popular, but they are a young (or older) connoisseur's discovery, and they gain more and more with each rereading. This can be said of very few works of junior fiction today.

—Naomi Lewis

MUKERJI, Dhan Gopal

Nationality: Indian: emigrated to the United States, 1910. **Born:** Near Calcutta, 6 July 1890. **Education:** Indian schools; Hindu priest-initiate, 1904-06; University of Calcutta, 1908; Tokyo University, 1909; University of California, Berkeley, 1910-13; Stanford University, California, Ph. B. 1914. **Family:** Married Ethel Ray Dugan in 1918; one son. **Career:** Lecturer. Lived in New Milford, Connecticut. **Awards:** American Library Association Newbery medal, 1928. **Died:** Suicide, 14 July 1936.

Publications for Children

Fiction

Kari the Elephant, illustrated by J.E. Allen. New York, Dutton, 1922; London, Dent, 1923.
Jungle Beasts and Men, illustrated by J.E. Allen. New York, Dutton, 1923; London, Dent, 1924.
Hari the Jungle Lad, illustrated by Morgan Stinemetz. New York, Dutton, 1924.
Gay-Neck: The Story of a Pigeon, illustrated by Boris Artzybasheff. New York, Dutton, 1927; London, Dent, 1928.
Ghond the Hunter, illustrated by Boris Artzybasheff. New York, Dutton, 1928; London, Dent, 1929.
The Chief of the Herd, illustrated by Mahlon Blaine. New York, Dutton, and London, Dent, 1929.
Bunny, Hound and Clown, illustrated by Kurt Wiese. New York, Dutton, 1931.
The Master Monkey, illustrated by Florence Weber. New York, Dutton, 1932.
Fierce-Face: The Story of a Tiger, illustrated by Dorothy P. Lathrop. New York, Dutton, 1936.

Other

Hindu Fables for Little Children, illustrated by Kurt Wiese. New York, Dutton, 1929.
Rama, The Hero of India: Valmiki's "Ramayana" Done into a Short English Version, illustrated by Edgar Parin d'Aulaire. New York, Dutton, 1930; London, Dent, 1931.

Publications for Adults

Novel

The Secret Listeners of the East. New York, Dutton, 1926.

Plays

Chintamini: A Symbolic Drama, with Mary Carolyn Davies, adaptation of a play by Girish C. Ghose. Boston, Badger, 1914.
Layla-Majnu. San Francisco, Paul Elder, 1916.
The Judgment of Indra, in *Drama,* edited by A.D. Dickinson. New York, Doubleday, 1922; in *Fifty One-Act Plays,* edited by Constance M. Martin, London, Gollancz, 1934.

Poetry

Rajani: Songs of the Night. San Francisco, Paul Elder, 1916.
Sandhya: Songs of Twilight. San Francisco, Paul Elder, 1917.

Other

Caste and Outcast (autobiography). New York, Dutton, and London, Dent, 1923.

My Brother's Face. New York, Dutton, 1924; London, Butterworth, 1925.
The Face of Silence (on Ramakrishna). New York, Dutton, 1926; London, Wassenaar, 1973.
A Son of Mother India Answers. New York, Dutton, 1928.
Visit India with Me. New York, Dutton, 1929.
Devotional Passages from the Hindu Bible. New York, Dutton, 1929.
Disillusioned India. New York, Dutton, 1930.
Daily Meditation; or, The Practice of Repose. New York, Dutton, 1933.
The Path of Prayer. New York, Dutton, 1934.

Editor, *Hindu Scriptures: Hymns from the Rigveda, Five Upanishads, the Bhagavadgita.* New York, Dutton, 1938.

Editor and Translator, *The Song of God: Translation of the Bhagavad-Gita.* New York, Dutton, 1931; London, Dent, 1932.

* * *

Dhan Gopal Mukerji wrote the kind of books for children first made popular by Ernest Thompson Seton, stories of wildlife in which the landscape plays almost as important a part as the animals and birds whose lives are described. "Grey Owl" is another writer in the same genre, and was Mukerji's contemporary.

For the most part his books are anecdotal, a stringing together of incidents from his boyhood in Northern India. For example, in *Ghond the Hunter* Ghond describes village life and ceremonies, recalls journeys to Agra, Delhi, and Kashmir, and tells stories of various animals he had befriended—a mongoose, a pet panther. *Kari the Elephant* and *Jungle Beasts and Men* consist of similar assorted incidents.

The Chief of the Herd is in the classic animal-story mould. It tells the life of Sirdar the elephant, leader of the herd: election as leader, a mate, a son, a forest fire, a flood. The book is packed with interesting observations on animal lore. Mukerji writes in a clear prose which occasionally topples over into lushness—"heavy kine throbbing with fat draw their silken flanks through the grain fields"—but which is in the main vivid and lively in its evocation of the Indian scene.

His prize-winning book *Gay-Neck* lacks the narrative power of a Kipling or a Henry Williamson, but must have had for its readers the charm of an exotic setting and the excitement of patriotic sentiment. Gay-Neck the pigeon is trained by his young master in Calcutta, travels to the Himalayas, and is then loaned during the 1914-18 War to the Indian army. He carries vital messages across the trenches from behind enemy lines, survives his ordeal, and is returned, wounded and frightened, to his beloved master in India where the healing powers of the Lama in the Himalayan monastery set him once more at peace and give him courage to fly again.

Mukerji's creatures are not credited with as much human sentiment as Kipling's in *The Jungle Book.* It is illuminating to contrast the two: the outsider Englishman's exotic Jungle with its animals each addressing each other in a curious stylised biblical language, each animal strongly characterised as an individual but nevertheless obeying the Law of the Jungle, an invention of Kipling's, older of course than man-made laws but still an evolved code with, one cannot help but suspect, affinities with English law; and the native-born Mukerji's more accurately observed jungle where the animals when they speak utter a plainer prose but where the natural world fits into a divine scheme of things, where "you cannot destroy one species of animal without upsetting the balance of life. Life is a whole. There is no escape from this." These words were written in 1929. Mukerji, with a view of life arising out of the same oriental philosophy that, however diluted, produced the hippie trail to Katmandu, foresaw dangers which the west is only now choosing to recognise.

—Mary Rayner

MULLEN, Michael

Nationality: Irish. **Born:** 5 December 1937, Castlebar, Ireland. **Education:** Attended Waterford de La Salle Teacher's College, 1958; National University of Ireland, University College, Dublin, B.A. 1962; Dublin University, H.D.P. 1967. **Family:** Married Deirdre McLoughlin, 31 March 1973. **Career:** Teacher of English, St. Joseph's College, Mauritius, 1962-66; taught English and French, 1962-85; writer. **Agent:** Bill Hamilton, A. M. Heath & Co. Ltd., 40-42 William IV St., London WC2N 4DD, England. **Address:** Rathbawn Dr., Castlebar, County Mayo, Ireland. **E-mail Address:** mullen@jazzybee.ie.

Publications for Children

Fiction

Magus the Lollipop Man. Edinburgh, Canongate, 1981; Dublin, Wolfhound Press, 1983.
Sea Wolves from the North. Edinburgh, Canongate, and Dublin, Wolfhound Press, 1982.
Barney the Hedgehog. Dublin, Children's Press, 1988.
The Viking Princess. Dublin, Wolfhound Press, 1988.
The Little Drummer Boy. Dublin, Poolbeg, 1989.
The Caravan. Dublin, Poolbeg, 1990.
The Long March. Dublin, Poolbeg, 1990.
The Flight of the Earls. Dublin, Poolbeg, 1991.
Glor na Mara (in Gaelic). Dublin, Coisceim, 1991.
The Four Masters. Dublin, Poolbeg, 1992.
The First Christmas. Dublin, Poolbeg, 1993.
Marcus the School Mouse. Dublin, Poolbeg, 1993.
Na Saoithe Anoir (in Gaelic). Dublin, Coisceim, 1993.
An tOilean Orga (in Gaelic). Dublin, Coisceim, 1994.
To Hell or Connaught. Dublin, Poolbeg, 1994.
Michaelangelo. Dublin, Poolbeg, 1994.
The Last Days of the Romanovs. Dublin, Poolbeg, 1995.
Flight from Toledo. Dublin, Poolbeg, 1996.
Pillars of Fire. Dublin, Blackwater Press, 1997.
Scath na nAingeal (in Gaelic). Dublin, Coisceim, 1997.

Nonfiction

The Darkest Years: A Famine Story. Cavendish House Publications, 1997.

Publications for Adults

Novels

Kelly. Dublin, Wolfhound Press, 1981.
The Festival of Fools. Dublin, Wolfhound Press, 1984.
The Hungry Land. London, Corgi, 1986; Dublin, Poolbeg, 1992.
Rites of Inheritance. London, Corgi, 1990.
The House of Mirrors. London, HarperCollins, 1992.
The Midnight Country. London, HarperCollins, 1995.

Michael Mullen comments:

Originally I worked on two mythological novels which were published by Wolfhound Press. I wished to return to my roots and seek out the basic heroic qualities which is the stuff of my imagination and from which I draw both strength and integrity. Later I moved into historical fiction. Ireland had moved into the third sector of the twentieth century and I believed that many key issues and key errors had to be addressed. The best vehicle at my command was the historical novel. I dealt with the battle of the Boyne in *The Little Drummer Boy,* the origin of *The Book of Kells* in *Sea Wolves from the North,* the duality of culture in Ireland both in *The Four Masters* and *To Hell or Connaught.*

On a wider canvas I wrote a Trilogy on the Nineteenth Century in order to give readers a view of our complicated and tragic history.

I have now completed this task and I have moved now to more European themes. *The Last Days of the Romanovs* speaks for itself. *Flight from Toledo* deals with the Spanish Inquisition, *Michelangelo* on the Renaissance Movement and *Pillars of Fire* deals with the Holocaust.

I also write in Irish in order to set my roots in my own culture and I feel that Irish writers should make more use of this medium.

Writing is uncertain and themes suggest themselves. When I get the kernel of an idea I let it root a little and then at a certain time I sit down and write the novel. I never over plan a novel. I believe that it should be organic rather than structured.

I have an interest in computers and the new technology and some basic knowledge of how it works. I believe that part of my creativity may be channelled in this direction at some future date.

* * *

Michael Mullen has made one of the most significant contributions to children's literature in Ireland over the past dozen years. His appeal is wide reaching and is not limited to a particular age group. He is, above all, a storyteller and all his books bear the hallmark of this tradition. He has created a gallery of vivid and memorable characters. A common thread runs through all his works. His books emphasize, time and time again, the importance of a cultural identity and this theme and the twin themes of friendship and loyalty is present in all his books.

The greatest body of his work for children has been devoted to the historical novel. Mullen has mined a rich tradition of Irish history and culture. He has recognised its importance in an Ireland that is changing and developing where the deeds and events of the past can easily become submerged by the tidal wave of late twentieth century life. His knowledge, affection, and respect for the landscape is evident in all his books. In his novels Mullen presents a vivid and accessible portrait of our cultural heritage and tradition, while preserving the integrity of the past. He has an impressive sense of time and place and conjures up for his readers the often bleak and tragic events of Irish history. A young fictional character is introduced as an observer to a significant event in Irish history. Although Mullen introduces fictional child characters for his readers to identify with, his main objective is the telling of historical event. These events are interpreted for the children by the creation of a knowledgeable and protective adult and this device also deepens the historical perspective for the reader. The historical character often features as largely as the fictional one and is certainly never reduced by the introduction of a fictional element.

The Flight of the Earls is a classic example of how Mullen treats the historical theme. The story begins with the death of the Earl of Tyrone (Hugh O'Neill) in exile in Rome. He is attended by his nephew Rory through whom the events are recounted. The tragedy of the story never overwhelms the plot. Mullen is very fair and balanced interpreter of Irish history. The story moves at a lively pace and yet there is an impressive attention to historical detail and vigorous evocation of seventeenth century life.

The Long March covers the same historical period as *The Flight of the Earls.* It tells the story of O'Sullivan Beare and his thousand followers who, after the Battle of Kinsale, attempted to march from Cork to Leitrim. Mullen takes another tragic episode in Irish history and brings it to life in all its savagery, sorrow, and heroism. The horrors of the march are seen through the eyes of two young people whose mother is one of the victims. Once more the relationship between the fictional and the historical characters is delicately balanced. Although less dramatic than Mullen's other historical novels, *The Long March* contains the themes which are constant through his books—friendship, loyalty, and fortitude in the face of adversity.

The Four Masters takes the reader away from the battlefield. It is the story of the Irish annalists and scribes who lovingly transcribed the history of Ireland. Around this event Mullen creates a lively and dramatic narrative, peopled with untraditional heroes in the form of monks and scribes. Taking an unlikely topic with unlikely heroes, Mullen brings alive the creation of the manuscripts. The text is richly informative and descriptive but the strands of the story are so well woven that the resulting drama is never weighed down by historical detail. *Seawolves from the North* shows Mullen at his most skilful and realistic. In a fast moving, strong narrative Mullen manages to interweave the history and traditions of the Vikings and the life and work of the monks and scribes on the island of Iona. Mullen's skill is in making the labours and hardships of the scribes and illuminators as graphic and realistic as the adventures and battles of the Viking warriors. *The Viking Princess* is set in Dublin and draws from recent archaeological and historical findings to bring an immediacy and excitement to the complexity of subject. A strong and resourceful heroine adds another dimension to a male dominated world.

Mullen's balanced and fair approach to historical events is clearly seen in *The Little Drummer Boy* which presents a vision of history that is unclouded by prejudice. The story of the Battle of the Boyne is seen through the eyes of young protagonists from both sides. Mullen's approach is uncomplex but he paints a realistic picture with an impressive attention to detail. In this as in all of Mullen's books the violence and brutality of war is not minimized. *Magus the Lollipop Man* is a complete contrast, a fairy tale written with an unerring touch. This warm and gentle story introduces us to a magical world full of memorable characters. The resolution is as satisfying as it is delightful. *Barney the Hedgehog* is Mullen's plea for the protection of the modern Irish environment. It is perhaps his least successful book. Although it moves at a fast pace and has all of Mullen's inventive characterisation it lacks his usual sureness and evenness of tone. The complex issues he tries to tackle in the end overwhelm the story. *The Caravan* another contemporary novel is very much more successful as it deals with themes similar to those in his historical novels. It tells the story of a fatherless family on a soulless Dublin housing estate who are terrorised by a loan shark. Mullen paints a telling picture of the bleakness and loneliness of the family's urban surroundings. The mother acquires a caravan and they travel across Ireland to the safety of her home in the West. As the family draws nearer its roots it becomes more potent and more in control of its own destiny. At one level an exciting chase, Mullen's belief in the importance of home and identity is very much at the core of the book.

—Sheila Flanagan and Rachel O'Flanagan

MULLER, (Lester) Robin

Nationality: Canadian. **Born:** Toronto, Ontario, 30 October 1953. **Education:** Algonquin College, B.F.A. 1979; attended George Brown College, 1982. **Career:** Fine artist, editorial illustrator, and set designer. Studio coordinator, University of Toronto, Fine Art Department, 1977-83; art director, Graph Em, Toronto, 1984. **Awards:** Toronto Art Directors Award, 1982; New York Art Directors Award, 1984; I.O.D.E. Award, 1986; Alquin Award, 1986; Ezra Jack Keats Memorial Medal, 1986. **Member:** Canadian Writers Union. **Address:** 587 Logan Ave., Toronto, Ontario, Canada.

Publications for Children

Fiction (retold folktales, illustrated by the author)

Mollie Whuppie and the Giant. Richmond Hill, Ontario, Scholastic, 1982.
Tatterhood. Richmond Hill, Ontario, Scholastic, 1984.
The Sorcerer's Apprentice. Toronto, Kids Can Press, 1985.
The Lucky Old Woman. Toronto, Kids Can Press, 1987.
Little Kay. Richmond Hill, Ontario, Scholastic, 1988.
The Magic Paintbrush. Toronto, Doubleday, 1989; New York, Viking, 1992.
The Nightwood. Toronto, Doubleday, 1991.

Other

Hickory, Dickory, Dock, illustrated by Suzanne Duranceau. Richmond Hill, Ontario, Scholastic, 1992.
Row, Row, Row Your Boat. Richmond Hill, Ontario, Scholastic, 1993.
Little Wonder. Richmond Hill, Ontario, Scholastic, 1994.
The Angel Tree. Toronto, Doubleday Canada, 1997.

* * *

Like all good adaptors of traditional narratives, Robin Muller discovers the contemporary relevance of old motifs and tale types and, in the timeless essences of the stories, themes that speak to young readers of the late twentieth century. From *Mollie Whuppie and the Giant,* in which the feisty English folk hero displays qualities of character that make her like a very capable liberated modern woman, to *The Magic Paintbrush,* in which a very old Chinese tale, moved to a nineteenth century European setting, reveals much about modern economic and political tyranny, the author-illustrator uses old story conventions to present contemporary messages.

With one exception, *The Lucky Old Woman* (about a hardworking and poor but unselfish and cheerful peasant), Muller's narratives are about young men and women who must set out into the world to find better lives than those they leave behind. Mollie Whuppie must look out for herself and her two hapless older sisters after their impoverished parents abandon them in the forest. In *Tatterhood,* the less-favored of two sisters frees her sibling from a curse caused by their mother's carelessness and finds them both royal husbands. Robin, the sorcerer's apprentice, is an orphan who uses his ability to read and write to free a princess trapped by an evil magician. The title hero of *Little Kay,* the youngest of three sisters, is brave, clever, and determined, and saves her sonless father from being shamed by a male chauvinist sultan. Nib, of *The Magic Paintbrush,* is a homeless orphan with great artistic talent, which he uses to rid the country of a despotic monarch. Elaine, in *The Nightwood* (an adaptation of the Scottish ballad "Tamlynne"), is repressed by her autocratic father and seeks fulfillment by running to the enchanted nightwood. Only when she faces her inner strengths and limitations is she able to rescue and then marry a handsome young man.

Each of Muller's young heroes is marginalized and, in a sense, imprisoned—by age, gender, economic status, physical appearance, or place within the family. Those who restrict them are adults with power: a cannibalistic giant in *Mollie Whuppie,* witches who seek to control the two princesses' destinies in *Tatterhood,* a sorcerer who would be king, a king who enslaves a child who can help him fulfill his greed and desire for wider political power in *The Magic Paintbrush,* a father who will not accept his daughter's becoming a woman in *The Nightwood,* and a sultan who considers females of little consequence in *Little Kay.* The heroes achieve freedom and empowerment because they already possess within themselves qualities that can lead them to success. These usually include courage, cleverness, and selflessness, characteristics that, in Muller's books, are to be found equally in both genders. At the end of four of the stories, the heroes are married to people of noble or royal blood, and, as it is explicitly stated in two of the stories, they share power equally, using it for the good of all their subjects.

Two of the heroes are, perhaps, slightly autobiographical. Robin has the ability to read and write, language talents he uses to destroy his master, who misuses words, and to liberate the princess and a kingdom. Nib, a superb artist, becomes fully successful when he learns to paint from the heart and in so doing rids the kingdom of tyranny and saves the life of his best friend. Perhaps these two characters embody Muller's view of the role of the artist and his works: to use his talents to delight people, but more important to show them the ways to personal freedom and fulfilling relationships.

Little Wonder, Muller's original story for younger readers, also examines the theme of power and the use of talents. A timid little pup displays his hidden talents—a profoundly loud howl—to alert police about a burglar who has forced his way into his master's apartment. Muller has also freely adapted two traditional songs for younger readers. *Row, Row, Row Your Boat* joins the familiar refrain to a number of verses in which a badger takes on more and more passengers until a disaster leads him to abandon the river for railroad travel. In *Hickory, Dickory, Dock* a group of animals creates chaos in the search for a missing clock.

—Jon C. Stott

MUN. See **LEAF, Munro.**

MUNSCH, Robert

Nationality: Canadian; became Canadian citizen, 1983. **Born:** Pittsburgh, Pennsylvania, 11 June 1945. **Education:** Fordham University, Bronx, New York, 1965-69, B.A. in history 1969; Boston University, 1969-70, M.A. in anthropology 1971; Tufts University, Medford, Massachusetts, 1971-72, M.Ed. in child studies 1973; studied for the Jesuit priesthood for 7 years. **Family:** Married Ann Beeler in 1973; two daughters and one son. **Career:** Teacher, Bay Area Childcare, Coos Bay, Oregon, 1973-75. Head Teacher, Family Studies Laboratory Preschool, 1975-84, Assistant Professor, 1980-84, University of Guelph, Ontario; full-time writer, since 1984. Professional storyteller. **Awards:** Ruth Schwartz award, 1985; Juno award, for recording, 1985; North Dakota Children's Choice (Picture Book), 1989; Author of the Year, Canadian Booksellers Association, 1991. **Address:** c/o Writers Union, 24 Ryerson Avenue, Toronto, Ontario M5T 2P3, Canada.

Publications for Children

Fiction

Mud Puddle, illustrated by Sami Suomalainen. Toronto, Annick Press, 1979.
The Dark, illustrated by Sami Suomalainen. Toronto, Annick Press, 1979.
The Paper Bag Princess, illustrated by Michael Martchenko. Toronto, Annick Press, 1980; London, Hippo, 1982.
Jonathan Cleaned Up, Then He Heard a Sound, illustrated by Michael Martchenko. Toronto, Annick Press, 1981.
The Boy in the Drawer, illustrated by Michael Martchenko. Toronto, Annick Press, 1982.
Murmel, Murmel, Murmel, illustrated by Michael Martchenko. Toronto, Annick Press, 1982.
Angela's Airplane, illustrated by Michael Martchenko. Toronto, Annick Press, 1983.
David's Father, illustrated by Michael Martchenko. Toronto, Annick Press, 1983.
The Fire Station, illustrated by Michael Martchenko. Toronto, Annick Press, 1983.
Mortimer, illustrated by Michael Martchenko. Toronto, Annick Press, 1983; Oxford, Oxford University Press, 1985.
Millicent and the Wind, illustrated by Suzanne Duranceau. Toronto, Annick Press, 1984.
Thomas's Snowsuit, illustrated by Michael Martchenko. Toronto, Annick Press, 1985.
50 Below Zero, illustrated by Michael Martchenko. Toronto, Annick Press, 1985.
Love You Forever, illustrated by Sheila McGraw. Scarborough, Ontario, Firefly, 1986.
I Have to Go!, illustrated by Michael Martchenko. Toronto, Annick Press, 1987.
Moira's Birthday, illustrated by Michael Martchenko. Toronto, Annick Press, 1987.
A Promise Is a Promise, illustrated by Vladyana Krykorka. Toronto, Annick Press, 1988.
Pigs, illustrated by Michael Martchenko. Toronto, Annick Press, 1989.
Giant; or, Waiting for the Thursday Boat, illustrated by Gilles Tibo. Toronto, Annick Press, 1989.
Something Good, illustrated by Michael Martchenko. Toronto, Annick Press, 1990.
Good Families Don't, illustrated by Alan Daniel. New York, Doubleday, 1990.
Show and Tell, illustrated by Michael Martchenko. Toronto, Annick Press, 1991.
Get Me Another One, illustrated by Shawn Steffler. Toronto, Doubleday, 1992.
Purple, Green and Yellow, illustrated by Helene Desputeaux. Toronto, Annick Press, 1992.
Wait and See, illustrated by Michael Martchenko. Toronto, Annick Press, 1993.
Where Is Gah-Ning?, illustrated by Helen Desputeaux. Toronto, Annick Press, 1994.
From Far Away, illustrated by Michael Martchenko. Toronto, Annick Press, 1995.
Something Good, illustrated by Michael Martchenko. Toronto, Annick Press, 1995.
Stephanie's Ponytail, illustrated by Michael Martchenko. Toronto, Annick Press, 1996.
Alligator Baby, illustrated by Michael Martchenko. New York, Scholastic, 1997.
Get Out of Bed, illustrated by Alan Daniel. New York, Scholastic, 1998.
Andrew's Loose Tooth, illustrated by Michael Martchenko. Richmond Hill, Ontario, Scholastic Canada, 1998.
A Promise is a Promise, Holly Harris (play). Woodstock, Illinois, Dramatic Publishing, 1995.

Recordings: *Munsch: Favourite Stories,* Kids' Records, 1983; *Murmel, Murmel, Munsch: More Outrageous Stories,* Kids' Records, 1985; *Love You Forever,* Kids' Records, 1987.

*

Critical Studies: *Meet the Author: Robert Munsch* (videocassette), School Services of Canada, 1993.

Robert Munsch comments:

My stories all develop through storytelling to groups of children. My goal when I make them up is to keep an audience happy.

* * *

Long popular as a storyteller, Robert Munsch's first published work appeared in 1979. Since then, he has become Canada's best selling children's writer. His earliest books grew from story-telling sessions with preschoolers in the University of Guelph's Child Studies laboratory school, and his books' popularity with children draws from his continuing method of composition—telling and retelling stories to children hundreds of times before enshrining the stories in print. His books, which have been translated into nine languages, have also appeared in sound recording and animated film format.

As pure entertainment, a Munsch story often begins with an ordinary child, going about his or her daily business, who is suddenly enmeshed in a situation of disorder or chaos. The forces responsible for the upset are variously presented as fantastic, mythic, or melodramatic, though these forces are invariably drawn from the child's ordinary world, one in which dirt, fears, stubbornness, or childish enthusiasms can bring upset into the orderly adult world. Speaking from the child's viewpoint, the narrative persona heightens the ordinary into a zany situation which, through exaggeration, becomes humorous. In the end, order is usually restored—frequently by the child itself—but a moral is never drawn. In fact, the adults who were upset by the disorder are sometimes made to look comical through one of Munsch's puckish lines.

A good example of this occurs in *Alligator Baby.* Kristen's comically confused parents don't seem to notice that instead of the baby brother they say they have for Kristen, they present her first with a baby alligator, then a baby seal, and finally a baby gorilla. It is up to the little girl herself to restore the normal order, which she most handily does by going to the zoo and finding her baby brother. Then, when the zoo mothers come to her house to claim their babies, she reunites the zoo babies with their mothers to create the happy ending.

In stories like *Mud Puddle, Jonathan Cleaned Up, Then He Heard a Sound,* and *The Boy in the Drawer,* the child protagonist does not consciously get dirty or create the mess: an outside force is responsible. However, the child must cope with the consequences. In *Mud Puddle,* for instance, little Jule Ann, freshly scrubbed and put in the back yard by her mother, stands helpless as a mud puddle jumps all over her. After various repetitions of this situation, Jule throws soap and water on the mud puddle, which then runs away. In *Jonathan Cleaned Up,* a little boy who is left in a clean living room watches as the wall opens and a subway of people appear and disappear, leaving the room in disarray. Held guilty for the mess, Jonathan finds the mayor and gets the subway rerouted. In *The Boy in the Drawer,* a little girl finds untidiness in her room being created by a "bad boy" who lives in her drawer, but she quells his destructive tendencies by being kind to him. Munsch shows a subtle understanding of how little children feel when they find themselves in messes which they did not intend to create; on a psychological level, these stories undoubtedly mirror a child's natural desire to displace guilt onto a "bad" force outside itself, and then restore equilibrium to a cross parent, without losing face, by dispelling its anarchic "double."

Another grouping of stories depicts children creating mayhem in the adult world by ordinary ornery behaviour. Mortimer (of *Mortimer*) sings his naughty song when he doesn't want to go to sleep; Thomas (of *Thomas's Snowsuit*) doesn't want to put on his snowsuit before playing in the snow; and Andrew (of *I Have to Go!*) refuses to "go pee" before getting into the car for a long trip. In each case the comedy results from Munsch's hammed-up depiction of how a small determined child can disrupt the adult world. Just when the adults think they have re-established order, there is usually a comic denouement. Stories in this vein include *Moira's Birthday,* a comic account of what happens when a little girl's birthday invitation list gets out of hand, and *Pigs,* which opens the gate to chaos at home and school when Megan lets her father's pigs out of their pen.

Munsch also pleases his young audience by occasionally highlighting words and behaviors normally considered mildly inappropriate in stories for children. Focusing as they do on bodily functions usually considered private, these stories sometimes upset an adult sense of propriety every bit as much as they tickle the fancy of Munsch's young audience. One example is the previously mentioned *I Have to Go!* which provides a comedic rendition of the way one clever small boy exercises control over adults. In episodes of *Pigs,* readers are told that the errant pigs are "peeing" on the shoes of Megan's father and principal. Children, whether readers or listeners, respond with great glee to this piggy challenge to two of the most authoritative figures in their young lives. *Good Families Don't* pushes boundaries even further by depicting a rollicking story about Carmen's experience with "a great big purple, green and yellow fart" she discovers "lying on her bed." As is typical in a Munsch story, the child can restore order when, in this case, neither parents nor police can.

One of Munsch's earliest successes was *The Paper Bag Princess,* a story which reverses the situation in Andersen's *The Little Swineherd* (where the princess is too superficial to realize the value of the prince's gifts when he is dressed like a swineherd). The little girl in Munsch's feminist tale uses her wits against the dragon's strength, saving the prince who has been carried away, only to be told by the rescued prince that her singed dress looks a "mess." Adding an "adult hook," Munsch concludes, "They didn't get married after all." In the phenomenally successful *Love You Forever,* Munsch has written a book which appeals equally to children, mothers, and grandmothers—but for totally different reasons. The storyline is simple: a baby is born, grows up, has his own child, and loves it as well as the aged mother who looked after him. Children respond to the repetitions and ludicrous situations (like seeing a mother rock a grown-up man), whereas adults respond to the message that cycles of love cement family ties, remaining constant amid the change and loss in human life. Published in 1986, this book sold over four million copies in its first six years.

Munsch's small picture books are as simple as fables, but they have no overt moral, despite the fact that the stories operate within a reassuring cultural framework, showing that children (even girls) can exert control over their environment; that fear can create its own demons; that neatness and order are approved by parents; that tolerance and understanding of others' differences are desirable; and that love is the single most abiding force in human life. Munsch's presentation of anarchy and use of taboo words like "pee" and "fart" sometimes draw negative responses from adults, but children merely delight in Munsch's zany exaggerations, his skill as a storyteller, and his ability to dramatize a child's way of feeling.

—Mary Rubio, updated by Linda Benson

MURPHY, Jill (Frances)

Nationality: British. **Born:** London, 5 July 1949. **Education:** Chelsea, Croydon, and Camberwell schools of art. **Family:** Divorced; one child. **Career:** Worked in a children's home for four years, and as a nanny for one year. Freelance writer and illustrator. **Awards:** *Parents* Best Books for Babies award, 1987. **Agent:** A.P. Watt Ltd., 20 John Street, London WC1N 2DL, England.

Publications for Children (illustrated by the author)

Fiction

The Worst Witch. London, Allison and Busby, 1974; New York, Schocken, 1980.
The Worst Witch Strikes Again. London, Allison and Busby, and New York, Schocken, 1980.
Peace at Last. London, Macmillan, and New York, Dial Press, 1980.
A Bad Spell for the Worst Witch. London, Kestrel, 1982.
On the Way Home. London, Macmillan, 1982.
Whatever Next! London, Macmillan, 1983; as *What Next, Baby Bear!,* New York, Dial Press, 1984.
Five Minutes' Peace. London, Walker, and New York, Putnam, 1986.
All in One Piece. London, Walker, and New York, Putnam, 1987.
Peace at Last—In Miniature! London, Macmillan, 1987.
Worlds Apart. London, Walker, 1988.
A Piece of Cake. New York, Putnam, 1989.
Geoffrey Strangeways. London, Walker, 1990; as *Jeffrey Strangeways,* Cambridge, Candlewick Press, 1992.
A Quiet Night In. London, Walker, 1993; Cambridge, Candlewick Press, 1994.
The Worst Witch All at Sea. London, Viking, 1993.
The Last Noo-Noo. London, Walker, 1995.

*

Illustrator: *The Duke Who Had Too Many Giraffes* by Fiona Macdonald, 1977; *The Witch in Our Attic* by Brian Ball, 1979.

Jill Murphy comments:

I have always drawn since I can remember, and written stories from an early age (four to be exact): the two skills were automatically linked. I still feel more comfortable in the company of children, so it's natural I should like to write about things they appreciate.

* * *

Jill Murphy has a particular talent for writing stories that appeal to children who have learned the basic skill of reading, and want something bright and enticing to make them enjoy books thenceforward—an art more difficult than it might seem.

Her stories about Mildred Hubble, the worst witch, take themes relevant to all children—school, pets, friends, magic, getting into trouble—and by placing them in a school for witches she can allow herself a degree of exaggeration and funny invention which makes them immensely attractive.

Some of the same ability to understand what children like can be seen in her novel, *Worlds Apart,* which must represent every 10-year-old girl's dream. Susan Hunter finds that her long-lost father is a famous TV star: she tracks him down and there's a reconciliation between her parents so they may all live happily ever after. Adults will see some important unanswered questions in this book, but children will read it with unalloyed pleasure.

Murphy's lively style as a writer is matched by her ability as an artist. In a succession of popular picture books her glowing colour and attention to domestic detail have produced highly attractive pictures. These accompany texts in which contemporary situations that will be recognised by every family are handled with humour and affection. Using animal characters for the most part, she again allows herself the scope for pleasant exaggeration. How one sympathises with Father Bear in *Peace at Last*—and with Mrs. Large in *Five Minutes' Peace!* Yet one also understands exactly the need for the young elephants to be with their mother—and the visual joke which concludes *All in One Piece* (a further adventure of the Large family) will appeal to parents and children alike.

Murphy knows and gets on well with children, and perhaps that is the secret of her greatest strength—her accessibility. She reaches out to the reader, parent or child, and draws that reader straight into the book. That's a talent that many would envy enormously, and which must place her work high in the ranks of books children actually enjoy.

—Felicity Trotman

MURPHY, Jim

Nationality: American. **Born:** 25 September 1947, Newark, New Jersey. **Education:** Rutgers University, New Jersey, B.A. 1970; graduate study, Radcliffe College, 1970. **Family:** Married Elaine A. Kelso, 12 November 1970; one son. **Career:** Various positions, Seabury Press (later Clarion), juvenile division, 1970-77; full-time writer, from 1977. **Awards:** Children's Choice, International Reading Association, 1979, *for Weird and Wacky Inventions*; ALA Notable Book listing, 1982, for *Death Run*; Golden Kite Award, 1990, for *The Boys' War,* and 1992, for *Long Road to Gettysburg*; Orbis Pictus Award, 1993, for *Across America on an Emigrant Train*; *Dictionary of Literary Biography Yearbook* Award for a Distinguished Children's Book Published in 1995, and *Boston Globe/Horn Book* Honor Book designation, 1995, for *The Great Fire.*

Publications for Children

Fiction

Rat's Christmas illustrated by Dick Gackenbach. Englewood Cliffs, Prentice-Hall, 1979.
Harold Thinks Big. New York, Crown, 1980.
Death Run. New York, Clarion, 1982.
The Last Dinosaur, illustrated by Mark Alan Weatherby, III. New York, Scholastic, 1988; translated into French as *Le dernier dinosaure,* Paris, Ecole des loisirs, 1989.

The Call of the Wolves, illustrated by Mark Alan Weatherby, III. New York, Scholastic, 1989; translated into French as *L'appel des loups,* Paris Ecole des loisirs, 1989.
Backyard Bear, illustrated by Jeffrey Greene. New York, Scholastic, 1992.
West to a Land of Plenty: The Diary of Teresa Angelino Viscardi. New York, Scholastic, 1998.

Short Stories

Night Terrors. New York, Scholastic, 1993.

Nonfiction

Weird and Wacky Inventions. New York, Crown, 1978.
Two Hundred Years of Bicycles. New York, Lippincott, 1983.
The Indy 500. New York, Clarion, 1983.
Baseball's All-time All-stars. New York, Clarion, 1984.
Tractors: From Yesterday's Steam Engines to Today's Turbo-charged Giants. New York, Lippincott, 1984.
Guess Again: More Weird and Wacky Inventions. New York, Bradbury, 1986.
Custom Car: A Nuts and Bolts Guide to Creating One. New York, Clarion, 1989.
A Little Book of Animal Riddles. New York, Scholastic, 1988.
The Boys' War: Confederate and Union Soldiers Talk about the Civil War. New York, Clarion, 1990.
Dinosaur for a Day, illustrated by Mark Alan Weatherby, III. New York, Scholastic, 1992.
The Long Road to Gettysburg. New York, Clarion, 1992.
Across America on an Emigrant Train. New York, Clarion, 1993.
Into the Deep Forest with Henry David Thoreau, illustrated by Kate Kiesler. New York, Clarion, 1995.
The Great Fire. New York, Scholastic, 1995.
A Young Patriot: The American Revolution as Experienced by One Boy. New York, Clarion, 1996.
Gone A-Whaling: The Lure of the Sea and the Hunt for the Great Whale. New York, Clarion, 1998.

*

Biography: Essay in *Something about the Author,* edited by Ann Commire, Gale, 1994, Vol. 77, 139-42.

* * *

From his debut with *Weird and Wacky Inventions,* Jim Murphy has consistently made fact more interesting than any fiction. His own fascination with motorized and other transportation shows plainly in many of his earlier books such as *Two Hundred Years of Bicycles, The Indy 500, Tractors,* and *Custom Car*; Murphy himself actually restored a junked car exactly as he describes in *Custom Car.* All are painstakingly researched and splendidly illustrated in what has become the characteristic Murphy manner.

Some of his earlier books came closer to fiction in effect, though still solid in their research. Even in the overcrowded field of dinosaur books, Murphy's *Dinosaur for a Day,* about the little-known Hypsilophodon, is a model of what science books for younger children should be (like most of Murphy's books, it includes a carefully selected bibliography). *The Last Dinosaur,* which crosses the line into fiction, examines similar material from a different perspective. In between the two is *Backyard Bear,* based on a true story, which describes a young bear's accidental intrusion into the suburbs as humans and their dwellings encroach on its habitat.

Murphy's breakthrough in writing for the middle grades and above came with *The Boys' War,* an account of the Civil War drawn from the diaries and letters of the youngest participants; since its publication, historical nonfiction, using primary sources as much as possible, has become Murphy's most important contribution to children's and young adult literature. *The Boys' War* follows the fortunes of teenaged (and sometimes younger) participants, from recruitment to return or death. Murphy carefully points out the mixed motives of many young recruits, as well as the relative ease of passing for an older person in an age before drivers' licenses and computerized records. He describes the drum corps, the chief employment for boys in both armies, and daily life in makeshift uniforms, without adequate food or shelter. Remarkable photographs include one of a curiously serene-looking young man lying in a shallow ditch with the simple caption, "fourteen-year-old soldier killed by bayonet at Fort Mahone." Other photographs depict twelve-year-old William Black, the youngest known soldier to have been wounded in the war, and Johnny Clem, also twelve.

The Long Road to Gettysburg followed *The Boys' War,* again using more primary material than is common in juvenile nonfiction, but focusing this time on a time and a place, rather than on a single group of people. The use of young officers as the two central figures guarantees reader appeal: Lieutenant John Dooley's diary from the Confederate standpoint, and Corporal Thomas Galway's from the Union one, help to personalize the costly struggle that was Gettysburg. Photographs and other archival illustrations are appropriately grim.

Even when treating a war without photographs, Murphy is not at a loss. *A Young Patriot* follows the military career of Joseph Plumb Martin from his enlistment at fifteen to his discharge at twenty-two; in between lie training in New York, Joseph's first action at the Battle of Long Island, later battles including Germantown, and the grim winter at Valley Forge. Murphy uses engravings and other archival materials, showing how quickly battles can become romanticized: one "highly imaginative French engraving," as his ironic caption puts it, shows "the Battle of Yorktown as a classic siege of a walled castle." Another image, nearly a century after the war, depicts "the image of the American soldier ... polished to a romantic glow. He is well fed and wears a clean, new uniform" (unlike the real soldiers in the book).

Not all of Murphy's historical nonfiction concerns war. Other facets of nineteenth-century American life appear in *Across America on an Emigrant Train, The Great Fire,* and *Gone A-Whaling: The Lure of the Sea and the Hunt for the Great Whale.* The first of these, *Across America on an Emigrant Train,* follows a transcontinental journey made by Robert Louis Stevenson in 1879; short of funds, Stevenson traveled with emigrants as they crossed the ocean and then the continent. Because emigration attracted fewer photographers than the Civil War, *Across America by Emigrant Train* is illustrated with an ingenious combination of photographs, lithographs, and engravings. *The Great Fire,* a beautifully produced volume, originated in Murphy's chance acquisition of an 1871 book, *The Great Conflagration,* containing many first-hand accounts of the fire. Using many first-hand accounts from *The Great Conflagration* and elsewhere, Murphy describes the fire and its aftermath from the point of view of ordinary people, including a young girl terrifyingly separated from her family. The maps and other geographical aids are another outstanding feature of this book. *Gone A-Whaling: The Lure of the Sea and the Hunt for the Great Whale,* Murphy's most recent non-fiction, returns to the approach of his war books in its focus on boys and young men engaged in whaling, rather than a wide spectrum of people as in *Across America on an Emigrant Train* and *The Great Fire.* Murphy includes accounts of African Americans involved in whaling, as well as the part played by women. The final chapters bring whaling up to the present with a description of factory whaling ships and a list of endangered whales.

Murphy continues to explore the boundary between fiction and nonfiction. *Into the Deep Forest with Henry David Thoreau* uses excerpts from Thoreau's own works but weaves them into a specific journey that, at least in the form recorded in the book, never took place. Since the target audience is somewhat younger than in some of his other books, Murphy also softens a few of Thoreau's notes; moose that the naturalist describes being shot get a reprieve from Murphy, who simply has them escape into the trees. Kate Kiesler's paintings of Maine scenes complement Murphy's text nicely. Another fictionalized presentation of history, Murphy's *West to a Land of Plenty: The Diary of Teresa Angelino Viscardi,* forms part of the Dear America series. Like its companion volumes, *West to a Land of Plenty* takes the form of a diary, that of a young Italian-American girl travelling westward from New Jersey with her family.

—Caroline C. Hunt

N

NAUGHTON, Bill

Nationality: British. **Born:** William John Francis Naughton, Ballyhaunis, County Mayo, Ireland, 12 June 1910; grew up in Lancashire, England. **Education:** St. Peter and St. Paul School, Bolton, Lancashire. **Military Service:** Civil Defence driver in London during World War II. **Family:** Married to Ernestine Pirolt. **Career:** Has worked as a lorry driver, weaver, and coal-bagger. **Awards:** Screenwriters Guild award, 1967, 1968; Italia prize, for radio play, 1974; Children's Rights Workshop Other award, 1978. **Died:** 9 January 1992, Isle of Man, United Kingdom.

PUBLICATIONS FOR CHILDREN

Fiction

Pony Boy. London, Pilot Press, 1946.
The Goalkeeper's Revenge and Other Stories, illustrated by Dick De Wilde. London, Harrap, 1961.
The Goalkeeper's Revenge, and Spit Nolan, illustrated by Trevor Stubley. London, Macmillan, 1974; new edition of *Spit Nolan,* illustrated by Kate Brennan Hall. Mankato, Minnesota, Creative Education, 1988.
A Dog Called Nelson, illustrated by Charles Mozley. London, Dent, 1976.
My Pal Spadger, illustrated by Charles Mozley. London, Dent, 1977.

PUBLICATIONS FOR ADULTS

Novels

Rafe Granite. London, Pilot Press, 1947.
One Small Boy. London, MacGibbon and Kee, 1957.
Alfie. London, MacGibbon and Kee, and New York, Ballantine, 1966.
Alfie, Darling. London, MacGibbon and Kee, 1970; New York, Simon and Schuster, 1971.

Short Stories

Late Night on Watling Street and Other Stories. London, MacGibbon and Kee, 1959; New York, Ballantine, 1966.
The Bees Have Stopped Working and Other Stories. Exeter, Wheaton, 1976.

Plays

My Flesh, My Blood (broadcast 1957). London, French, 1959; revised version, as *Spring and Port Wine* (produced Birmingham, 1964; London, 1965; as *Keep It in the Family,* produced New York, 1967), London, French, 1967.
She'll Make Trouble (broadcast 1958). Published in *Worth a Hearing: A Collection of Radio Plays,* edited by Alfred Bradley, London, Blackie, 1967.
June Evening (broadcast 1958; produced Birmingham, 1966). London, French, 1973.
All in Good Time (as *Honeymoon Postponed,* televised 1961; as *All in Good Time,* produced London, 1963; New York, 1965). London, French, 1964.
Alfie (as *Alfie Elkins and His Little Life,* broadcast 1962; as *Alfie,* produced London, 1963; New York, 1964). London, French, 1964.
He Was Gone When We Got There, music by Leonard Salzedo (produced London, 1966).
Annie and Fanny (produced Bolton, Lancashire, 1967).
Lighthearted Intercourse (produced Liverpool, 1971).

Screenplays: *Alfie,* 1966; *The Family Way,* with Roy Boulting and Jeffrey Dell, 1966; *Spring and Port Wine,* 1970.

Radio Plays: *Timothy,* 1956; *My Flesh, My Blood,* 1957; *She'll Make Trouble,* 1958; *June Evening,* 1958; *Late Night on Watling Street,* 1959; *The Long Carry,* 1959; *Seeing a Beauty Queen Home,* 1960; *On the Run,* 1960; *Wigan to Rome,* 1960; *'30-'60,* 1960; *Jackie Crowe,* 1962; *Alfie Elkins and His Little Life,* 1962; *November Day,* 1963; *The Mystery,* 1973; *A Special Occasion,* 1982.

Television Plays: *Nathaniel Titlark* series, 1957; *Starr and Company* series, 1958; *Yorky* series, with Allan Prior, 1960-61; *Looking for Frankie,* 1961; *Honeymoon Postponed,* 1961; *Somewhere for the Night,* 1962; *It's Your Move,* 1967.

Other

A Roof over Your Head (autobiography). London, Pilot Press, 1945.
On the Pig's Back: An Autobiographical Excursion. Oxford and New York, Oxford University Press, 1987.
Saintly Billy: A Catholic Boyhood. Oxford, Oxford University Press, 1988.

* * *

Bill Naughton was not so much a children's writer as a writer about childhood and young manhood whose books appeal greatly to young as well as adult readers.

Naughton was largely self-educated in public libraries during the depression years. His first book, *A Roof over Your Head,* was written while he was working as a Civil Defence driver in wartime London. It takes the form of a series of autobiographical sketches which do not follow on chronologically and which end in an unsatisfactory, tailing-off way. However, this book, despite its clumsy construction and occasionally uncertain style, already demonstrates Naughton's power as a writer and chronicler of life in the working class industrial Lancashire of the 1930s. Naughton's ear for dialogue and ironic humour are already in evidence. But, above all, the intensity of feeling that Naughton evokes in writing about poverty and hardship and their effect on the family, and in writing about love between man and woman, parent and child, are conveyed with a rawness in this first book that has become his hallmark, albeit somewhat overlaid with nostalgia in his later, more polished writings.

Closest in form to *A Roof over Your Head, One Small Boy* takes the form of a novel yet it is clearly based on Naughton's own life. Events are seen from the point of view of the boy Michael, who starts life in Ireland and then moves to an industrial town in the north of England with his family (Bolton?). The reader follows Michael's *rites de passage* through school days (often very funny), relationships with parents and friends, and later on with girls. Irish dialect words, colloquialisms, and regionalisms lend Naughton's dialogue a precise and robust sense of place.

Pony Boy and *Alfie* are novels set mainly in London. *Pony Boy* tells of the adventures of two boys, Corky and Ginger, who have just left school. *Alfie,* Naughton's most well-known novel, was first written as a radio play (*Alfie Elkins and His Little Life*) and was also made into a film. It relates, with much situation comedy, the amorous adventures of a young man with a succession of girl friends, only to find that a crucial success is to elude him. As in all Naughton's writing, the world depicted is a male-dominated one in which female characters are seen only in relation to the hero, which gives a rather dated feel to these books.

Naughton's collections of short stories—*Late Night on Watling Street, The Goalkeeper's Revenge,* and *My Pal Spadger*—are in the main "street corner" stories (i.e., they treat the interactions and adventures of the groups of boys who gathered on street corners in the days before radio and television). Other stories are set in particular work places. As always, Naughton's exact detail of northern community and working life lends credibility and interest to his writing. Economy and clarity of construction combine with humour and sensitivity in the best of these stories, which appear simple and direct and yet imply much about people and situations.

At the center of the stage, always, in Naughton's work is the everyday life of the ordinary working-class youth, presented in its complexity, with depth, feeling, and sincerity. Naughton's influence in putting working-class characters on the literary map has been considerable, for children's books and for books written for adults. As Naughton himself said: "I write mostly about the life I have known."

—Rosemary Stones

NAYLOR, Phyllis Reynolds

Nationality: American. **Born:** Anderson, Indiana, 4 January 1933. **Education:** Joliet Junior College, Illinois, 1951-53, diploma 1953; American University, Washington, D.C., 1959-63, B.A. in psychology 1963. **Family:** Married Rex V. Naylor in 1960 (second marriage); two sons. **Career:** Clinical secretary, Billings Hospital, Chicago, 1953-56; teacher in elementary schools, Hazelcrest, Illinois, 1956; assistant executive secretary, Montgomery County Education Association, Rockville, Maryland, 1958-59; editorial assistant, National Education Association *NEA Journal,* Washington, D.C., 1959-60. Since 1960 freelance writer. **Awards:** Society of Children's Book Writers Golden Kite award, 1978; Child Study Committee award, 1983; Mystery Writers of America Edgar Allan Poe award, 1985; National Endowment for the Arts fellowship, 1987; Society of School Librarians International Book award, 1988; Christopher Award, 1989; Newbery Award, 1992; Kerlan Award, University of Minnesota, 1995; Appalachian Medallion, University of Charleston (WV), 1997; plus 27 different state awards. **Agent:** Bill Reiss, John Hawkins and Associates, Suite 1600, 71 West 23rd Street, New York, New York 10010. U.S.A. **Address:** 9910 Holmhurst Road, Bethesda, Maryland 20817, U.S.A.

Publications for Children

Fiction

The Galloping Goat and Other Stories, illustrated by Robert Jefferson. Nashville, Abingdon Press, 1965.

Jennifer Jean, The Cross-Eyed Queen (as Phyllis Naylor), illustrated by Harold K. Lamson. Minneapolis, Lerner, 1967.

The New Schoolmaster, illustrated by Mamoru Funai. Morristown, New Jersey, Silver Burdett, 1967.

A New Year's Surprise, illustrated by Jack Endewelt. Morristown, New Jersey, Silver Burdett, 1967.

What the Gulls Were Singing, illustrated by Jack Smith. Chicago, Follett, 1967.

Meet Murdock, illustrated by Gioia Fiammenghi. Chicago, Follett, 1969.

To Make a Wee Moon, illustrated by Beth and Jo Krush. Chicago, Follett, 1969.

Wrestle the Mountain, illustrated by Paul Giovanopoulos. Chicago, Follett, 1971.

To Walk the Sky Path, illustrated by Jack Endewelt. Chicago, Follett, 1973.

Witch's Sister, illustrated by Gail Owens. New York, Atheneum, 1975.

Witch Water, illustrated by Gail Owens. New York, Atheneum, 1977; London, W.H. Allen, 1979.

The Witch Herself, illustrated by Gail Owens. New York, Atheneum, 1978; London, W.H. Allen, 1979.

How Lazy Can You Get?, illustrated by Alan Daniel. New York, Atheneum, 1979; London, Hamish Hamilton, 1980.

Eddie, Incorporated, illustrated by Blanche Sims. New York, Atheneum, 1980.

All Because I'm Older, illustrated by Leslie Morrill. New York, Atheneum, 1981.

The Boy with the Helium Head, illustrated by Kay Chorao. New York, Atheneum, 1982.

The Mad Gasser of Bessledorf Street, illustrated by Andrew Rhodes. New York, Atheneum, 1983.

Old Sadie and the Christmas Bear, illustrated by Patricia Montgomery Newton. New York, Atheneum, 1984.

The Agony of Alice, illustrated by Blanche Sims. New York, Atheneum, 1985.

The Bodies in the Bessledorf Hotel, illustrated by Gail Owens. New York, Atheneum, 1986.

The Baby, the Bed, and the Rose, illustrated by Mary Szilagyi. New York, Clarion, 1987.

Beetles, Lightly Toasted, illustrated by Melodye Rosales. New York, Atheneum, 1987.

Maudie in the Middle, with Lura Schield Reynolds, illustrated by Judith Gwyn Brown. New York, Atheneum, 1988.

One of the Third Grade Thonkers, illustrated by Walter Gaffney-Kessell. New York, Atheneum, 1988.

Alice in Rapture, Sort Of, illustrated by Blanche Sims. New York, Atheneum, 1989.

Keeping a Christmas Secret, illustrated by Lena Shiffman. New York, Atheneum, 1989.
Bernie and the Bessledorf Ghost. New York, Atheneum, 1990.
Witch's Eye. New York, Delacorte, 1990.
Reluctantly Alice. New York, Atheneum, 1991.
Shiloh. New York, Atheneum, 1991.
King of the Playground, illustrated by Nola Langner Malone. New York, Atheneum, 1991.
Witch Weed. New York, Delacorte, 1991.
Josie's Troubles. New York, Atheneum, 1992.
The Witch Returns. New York, Delacorte, 1992.
All But Alice. New York, Atheneum, 1992.
The Grand Escape. New York, Atheneum, 1993.
The Face in the Bessledorf Funeral Parlor. New York, Atheneum, 1993.
The Boys Start the War. New York, Delacorte, 1993.
The Girls Get Even. New York, Delacorte, 1993.
Boys Against Girls. New York, Delacorte, 1994.
Being Danny's Dog. New York, Atheneum, 1995.
Ice. New York, Atheneum, 1995.
Shiloh Season. New York, Atheneum, 1996.
The Bomb in the Bessledorf Bus Depot. New York, Atheneum, 1996.
The Healing of Texas Jake, illustrated by Alan Daniel. New York, Atheneum, 1997.
I Can't Take You Anywhere, illustrated by Jef Kaminsky. New York, Atheneum, 1997.
Saving Shiloh. New York, Atheneum, 1997.
Danny's Desert Rats. New York, Atheneum, 1998.
The Treasure of Bessledorf Hill. New York, Atheneum, 1998.
The Girls' Revenge. New York, Atheneum, 1998.

Other

Getting Along in Your Family, illustrated by Rick Cooley. Nashville, Abingdon Press, 1976.
How I Came to Be a Writer, illustrated by Lou Carbone. New York, Atheneum, 1978.
Getting Along with Your Friends, illustrated by Rick Cooley. Nashville, Abingdon Press, 1980.
Getting Along with Your Teachers, illustrated by Rick Cooley. Nashville, Abingdon Press, 1981.
Ducks Disappearing, pictures by Tony Maddox. New York, Atheneum, 1997.
Strawberries. New York, Atheneum, 1999.

PUBLICATIONS FOR YOUNG ADULTS

Fiction

To Shake a Shadow, illustrated by Gloria Kamen. Nashville, Abingdon, 1967.
When Rivers Meet, illustrated by Allan Eitzen. New York, Friendship, 1968.
Making It Happen, illustrated by Joe De Velasco. Chicago, Follett, 1970.
No Easy Circle, illustrated by Lou Aronson. Chicago, Follett, 1972.
Walking through the Dark, illustrated by James and Ruth McCrea. New York, Atheneum, 1976.
Shadows on the Wall, illustrated by Ruth Sanderson. New York, Atheneum, 1980.
Faces in the Water, illustrated by Ruth Sanderson. New York, Atheneum, 1981.
Footprints at the Window, illustrated by Ruth Sanderson. New York, Atheneum, 1981.
A String of Chances, illustrated by Ruth Sanderson. New York, Atheneum, 1982.
The Solomon System, illustrated by Ronald Himler. New York, Atheneum, 1983.
Night Cry, illustrated by Ruth Sanderson. New York, Atheneum, 1984.
The Dark of the Tunnel, illustrated by Ronald Himler. New York, Atheneum, 1985.
The Keeper, illustrated by Ronald Himler. New York, Atheneum, 1986.
The Year of the Gopher, illustrated by John Steven Gurney. New York, Atheneum, 1987.
Send No Blessings. New York, Atheneum, 1990.
Alice in Between. New York, Atheneum, 1994.
The Fear Place. New York, Atheneum, 1994.
Alice the Brave. New York, Atheneum, 1995.
Alice in Lace. New York, Atheneum, 1996.
Outrageously Alice. New York, Atheneum, 1997.
Achingly Alice. New York, Atheneum, 1997.
Sang Spell. New York, Atheneum, 1998.
Alice on the Outside. New York, Atheneum, 1999.
Jade Green: A Ghost Story. New York, Atheneum, 1999.

Nonfiction

How to Find Your Wonderful Someone, How to Keep Him/Her If You Do, How to Survive If You Don't. Philadelphia, Fortress, 1972.
An Amish Family, illustrated by George Armstrong. Chicago, O'Hara, 1974.

Short Stories

Grasshoppers in the Soup: Short Stories for Teen-agers, illustrated by Elsa Bailey. Philadelphia, Fortress, 1965.
Knee Deep in Ice Cream and Other Stories, illustrated by Johanna Sperl. Philadelphia, Fortress, 1967.
The Dark Side of the Moon, illustrated by Joseph Papin. Philadelphia, Fortress, 1969.
The Private I and Other Stories, illustrated by Elsa Bailey. Philadelphia, Fortress, 1969.
Ships in the Night, illustrated by Otto Reinhardt. Philadelphia, Fortress, 1970.
Change in the Wind. Minneapolis, Augsburg Press, 1980.
Never Born a Hero. Minneapolis, Augsburg Press, 1982.
A Triangle Has Four Sides. Minneapolis, Augsburg Press, 1984.

PUBLICATIONS FOR ADULTS

Novels as Phyllis Naylor

Revelations. New York, St. Martin's Press, 1979; London, Sphere, 1981.
Unexpected Pleasures. New York, Putnam, 1986.

Other (as Phyllis Naylor)

Crazy Love: An Autobiographical Account of Marriage and Madness. New York, Morrow, 1977.
In Small Doses (essays). New York, Atheneum, 1979.
The Craft of Writing the Novel. Boston, The Writer, 1989.

*

Manuscript Collections: Kerlan Collection, University of Minnesota, Minneapolis; de Grummond Collection, University of Southern Mississippi, Hattiesburg.

Critical Studies: *Contemporary Authors, Vols. 21-22.* Detroit, Gale Research, 1969; *Something About the Author, Vol. 6.* Detroit, Gale Research, 1977; *Vol. 66,* 1991. *Children's Literature Review,* Volume 17, Detroit, Gale, 1989. *Something About the Author, Autobiography Series, Vol. 10.* Detroit, Gale Research, 1990. *Authors and Artists for Young Adults, Vol. 4.* Detroit, Gale Research, 1990. *Meet the Authors and Illustrators, Vol. 2.* Scholastic, 1993. *Children's Books and Their Creators,* Boston, Houghton Mifflin, 1995. *Presenting Phyllis Naylor* by Lois Thomas Stover, New York, Twayne, 1997.

Phyllis Reynolds Naylor comments:

I love to get up in the morning, but I also like going to bed at night. I enjoy being around people, but thrive on solitude as well. A worrier, I am, at the same time, a happy person. In fact, I'm one of the luckiest people I know, because I write.

If it's still dark when I open my eyes, I wonder, "Is it time yet?" If it's not, and I begin thinking about where in a manuscript I left off the day before, sleep becomes impossible. I creep quietly out of bed and head for my big comfortable chair in the living room.

A book begins with a feeling of intense excitement. And because there is always a book in my head, I live in a chronic state of anticipation: with me, it's always the week before Christmas. I never start writing a book until the characters or setting or theme or plot ignites something special in me. Then everything I see and hear seems to relate somehow to the work at hand, and I am constantly putting things together like the pieces of a puzzle—something old, something new, something borrowed, something blue. My books are made up of things both imagined and remembered.

As soon as I finish writing a mystery, I want to do a humorous book, a realistic novel, or an adventure story. Because life is like that—exciting, boring, scary, thrilling, wonderful, terrible, and always changing from day to day. When there is a crisis in my novels, I am working out problems on paper where they aren't quite so threatening, deciding how and even whether I could cope. My characters are old and young, wealthy and poor, uneducated and privileged, because I want to experience everything. And the only way I know how to do this is to become the people in my books.

* * *

Phyllis Reynolds Naylor is a prolific, versatile writer of books for widely divergent audiences ranging from preschoolers to adults. She writes well in a variety of forms and styles, including comic adventure stories, philosophical time-travel fantasies, realistic novels about adolescents maturing, dark problem novels, and various kinds of nonfiction.

Naylor has a talent for humorous invention. In stories such as *The Bodies in the Bessledorf Hotel* and *Beetles, Lightly Toasted,* she creates funny predicaments that appeal to children's sense of humor. Sometimes this humor becomes routine or merely silly, but often it contains threads of genuine anxiety or uncertainty that lead to deeper insights.

The York Trilogy, a fantasy series consisting of *Shadows on the Wall, Faces in the Water,* and *Footprints at the Window,* won acclaim for its convincing characterizations, complex and intriguing plot, and challenging philosophical explorations. In these novels the central character Dan Roberts confronts difficulties in 4th- and 14th-century England as well as in 20th-century Pennsylvania. Hereditary disease, war, plague, and the nature of chance are some of the themes treated.

In her realistic novels about adolescents, Naylor reveals the growth and dilemmas of authentically drawn young people.

In *A String of Chances,* one of her best, 16-year-old Evie experiences a summer away from home, living with a cousin and the cousin's husband, who are expecting a baby. She has her first serious romance, gains insights into her family's patterns of behavior, and struggles with her longstanding dislike of a boy who is living at her parents' home for the summer. Evie's father is a country preacher, and she confronts her own religious doubts and questions, especially when the beloved baby Joshua suddenly dies. What might easily have become trite and stereotypical is not at all so: Evie's father is loving and genuine and has a sense of humor; the baby's death and the consequent grief of all involved are presented with truthfulness and depth; and Evie emerges stronger and wiser but without easy resolutions to her religious questions or to her difficulties in romance. The milieu of small-town life is aptly brought to life, and even the minor characters are intriguing and vital.

The Year of the Gopher is narrated by 17-year-old George Richards, whose well-to-do suburban Minneapolis family suffers from performance expectations that have ruled family behavior for three generations. George revolts against these expectations by refusing to go to college (his lawyer father would prefer that he go to an Ivy League school as he himself did) and chooses to find blue-collar work instead, at least for a year. Naylor draws the world of George's teenage peers with observant, accurate detail. George's first sexual relationship, his relationship with his siblings, and his maturing realizations about life are all presented without clichés or sensationalism.

Some of Naylor's books might accurately be described as problem novels, since a difficult social or psychological issue forms the central theme of these works. *The Keeper,* which deals with the recognition and consequences of mental illness in a boy's father, is an example of such a novel. But Naylor's approach to the problems treated in these novels is not narrow or didactic. The characters are shown struggling with painful realities of life in ways that do not set them apart from other human beings, though their situations may be unusually complex or hard to bear.

In such books as *An Amish Family* and *Maudie in the Middle* (the latter co-authored with Lura Schield Reynolds, the writer's mother), Naylor weaves together factual information with fictional elements. It is noteworthy how thoroughly Naylor imbues all of her work—not only the nonfiction or semi-autobiographical fiction—with the particularity of place, family, and ethnic culture.

There is a sense in Naylor's work that she trusts children and young people to understand the complexities of the larger world, and to form their own responsible views. In *Shiloh Season,* her sequel to *Shiloh,* she continues the story of a West Virginia boy who has taken possession of an abused dog through subterfuge. In the earlier book, Marty had blackmailed the hard-drinking Judd Travers to give him Shiloh, and now he must face the results of his actions. There is nothing easy about the ethical dilemma presented here: on the one hand, the dog was being abused, and Marty is clearly a better master and friend to Shiloh; but his methods are questionable, and Naylor does not attempt to decide the question for her readers.

The Bomb in the Bessledorf Bus Depot, on the other hand, is pure lighthearted fun. With the help of friends Weasel and Georgene, Bernie Magruder, 11-year-old son of the Bessledorf Hotel manager, pursues the mystery of a bomber who has detonated blasts in the bus depot, the swimming pool, and other places. *School Library Journal,* criticized the book as "unfortunately untimely," commenting that "in Naylor's cartoon creation nobody ever gets hurt as bombs go off...." Naylor's story and its lack of realism was published in the world of the Unabomber and the Oklahoma City explosion. However, her purpose was not to instruct, but to entertain, and in that regard *Bomb* may not be a megablast, but it's not an absolute dud either.

Naylor's work is distinguished by her skill at diversity. From comedy to tragedy, from books for younger children to books for older young adults, in novels with rural settings or urban landscapes, from fantasy to realism, she reveals a fine sense of the unexpected difficulties and rewards of life. Her characters have depth, individuality, and complexity, and Naylor has the power to make them matter to us. She treats her characters with an admirable mixture of sympathy and critical insight. Symptomatic of Naylor's vision is her willingness to present religious, ethical, and psychological issues without a hidden—or, for that matter, obvious—agenda, but simply with honesty and sensitivity.

—John D. Stahl, updated by Judson Knight

NEEDHAM, (Amy) Violet

Nationality: British. **Born:** London, 5 June 1876. **Education:** At home. **Died:** 8 June 1967.

Publications for Children

Fiction

The Black Riders, illustrated by Anne Bullen. London, Collins, 1939.

The Emerald Crown, illustrated by Anne Bullen. London, Collins, 1940.

The Stormy Petrel, illustrated by Joyce Bruce. London, Collins, 1942.

The Horn of Merlyns, illustrated by Joyce Bruce. London, Collins, 1943.

The Woods of Windri, illustrated by Joyce Bruce. London, Collins, 1944.

The House of the Paladin, illustrated by Joyce Bruce. London, Collins, 1945.

The Changeling of Monte Lucio, illustrated by Joyce Bruce. London, Collins, 1946.

The Bell of the Four Evangelists, illustrated by Joyce Bruce. London, Collins, 1947.

The Boy in Red, illustrated by Joyce Bruce. London, Collins, 1948.

The Betrayer, illustrated by Joyce Bruce. London, Collins, 1950.

Pandora of Parrham Royal, illustrated by Joyce Bruce. London, Collins, 1951.

The Avenue, illustrated by Joyce Bruce. London, Collins, 1952.

How Many Miles to Babylon?, illustrated by Joyce Bruce. London, Collins, 1953.

Adventures at Hampton Court, illustrated by Will Nickless. London, Lutterworth Press, 1954.

Richard and the Golden Horse Shoe, illustrated by Joyce Bruce. London, Collins, 1954.

The Great House of Estraville, illustrated by Joyce Bruce. London, Collins, 1955.

The Secret of the White Peacock, illustrated by Joyce Bruce. London, Collins, 1956.

The Red Rose of Ruvina, illustrated by Richard Kennedy. London, Collins, 1957.

Adventures at Windsor Castle, illustrated by David Walsh. London, Lutterworth Press, 1957.

* * *

Violet Needham's first book, *The Black Riders,* was published in 1939, at a time when the action of most books for children revolved around ponies, dormitories, and secret passages. She avoided all the conventions of the genre by setting many of her own books in an imaginary European Empire and its satellite kingdoms and principalities. Yet, despite their Ruritanian background, Needham's novels are refreshingly free of the jangling of spurs and the clashing of sabres. Her heroes may sometimes be kings—boy-kings, in fact—but the regal trappings are always subordinate to the development of plot and character, and the royal heroes are recognisable and convincing children who, by virtue of the setting and their rank, can be subjected to dangers which would seem excessive in more realistic circumstances. Few children, even in the more lurid adventure stories, can be subjected to assassination attempts or slow poisoning without some suspension of the reader's belief, but high drama of this kind is acceptable in a setting of acknowledged romantic fantasy.

Above all, though, Needham was concerned with character. Her heroes may be kings but they are often reluctant ones. *The Emerald Crown* is set in the kingdom of Flavonia, which is ruled by a usurper. The people hope for the return of a legendary lost heir who will restore the most legitimate line to the throne, but in the end the true king turns out to be an English schoolboy who doesn't want to be "a rotten little king of a rotten little country." He overcomes his reluctance eventually but his struggle is typical of those confronting Needham's heroes. They must all face unbearable decisions, and choose between the call of duty and their own wills, or between loyalty to their country and loyalty to their friends. In *The Stormy Petrel,* young Carol becomes Emperor after the sudden death of his grandfather and is totally unprepared for the threatened revolution and assassination attempts which accompany his accession. Dick, "The Stormy Petrel" and hero of many of the books, must, in *The Betrayer,* decide between loyalty to his emperor and country, and his devotion to a friend who threatens the security of both.

Not all Needham's books were concerned with political intrigue in fictitious kingdoms. She wrote four conventional stories with English settings, among them *The Bell of the Four Evangelists* and *The Horn of Merlyns,* which centred on the finding of long-lost treasure, the ending of family feuds, and similar stock ingredients of children's books of the period. Her finest work, though, is to be found in her historical novels, especially *The Woods of Windri* and *The Changeling of Monte Lucio,* absorbing linked adventure stories which take place in imaginary countries, and *The Boy in Red,* a richly detailed novel set in the Netherlands during the revolt against the Spanish. In this book, and her only other straightforward historical story, *The Avenue,* Needham drew upon the family background of her Dutch mother for inspiration.

Needham holds a unique position among British writers for children. Apart from one or two isolated examples, no other writer has attempted to create the same brand of romantic adventure. She was in her sixties when her first book was published (*The Black Riders* had been written 20 years before and rejected by publishers as being too difficult for children) and perhaps this may explain why her style and themes were so different from those of other writers of the period. Whatever the reason, her books enjoyed enormous popularity and are still regarded with fanatical devotion by those adults who enjoyed her work when they were young.

—Lance Salway

NESBIT, E(dith)

Pseudonyms: E. Bland; Fabian Bland. **Nationality:** British. **Born:** London, 15 August 1858. **Education:** Attended an Ursuline convent in Dinan, France, 1869, and schools in Germany and Brighton. **Family:** Married 1) the writer Hubert Bland in 1880 (died 1914), two sons, one daughter, one adopted daughter, and one adopted son; 2) Thomas Terry Tucker in 1917. **Career:** Journalist, elocutionist, greeting cards decorator; poetry critic, *Athenaeum* magazine, London, 1890s; co-editor, *Neolith* magazine, London, 1907-08; general editor, Children's Bookcase series, Oxford University Press and Hodder and Stoughton, 1908-11. Granted a Civil List pension, 1915. **Member:** Founding member, 1884, and member of the Pamphlet Committee, Fabian Society. **Died:** 4 May 1924.

Publications for Children

Fiction

Listen Long and Listen Well, with others. London, Tuck, 1893.
Sunny Tales for Snowy Days, with others. London, Tuck, 1893.
Told by Sunbeams and Me, with others. London, Tuck, 1893.
Fur and Feathers: Tales for All Weathers, with others. London, Tuck, 1894.
Lads and Lassies, with others. London, Tuck, 1894.
Tales That Are True, for Brown Eyes and Blue, with others, edited by Edric Vredenburg, illustrated by M. Goodman. London, Tuck, 1894.
Tales to Delight from Morning till Night, with others, edited by Edric Vredenburg, illustrated by M. Goodman. London, Tuck, 1894.
Hours in Many Lands: Stories and Poems, with others, edited by Edric Vredenburg, illustrated by Frances Brundage. London, Tuck, 1894.
Doggy Tales, illustrated by Lucy Kemp-Welch. London, Ward, 1895.
Pussy Tales, illustrated by Lucy Kemp-Welch. London, Ward, 1895.
Tales of the Clock, illustrated by Helen Jackson. London, Tuck, 1895.
Dulcie's Lantern and Other Stories, with Theo Gift and Mrs. Worthington Bliss. London, Griffith Farran, 1895.
Treasures from Storyland, with others. London, Tuck, 1895.
Tales Told in Twilight: A Volume of Very Short Stories. London, Nister, 1897.
Dog Tales, and Other Tales, with A. Guest and Emily R. Watson, edited by Edric Vredenburg, illustrated by R.K. Mounsey. London, Tuck, 1898.
Pussy and Doggy Tales, illustrated by Lucy Kemp-Welch. London, Dent, 1899; New York, Dutton, 1900.
The Story of the Treasure Seekers, Being the Adventures of the Bastable Children in Search of a Fortune, illustrated by Gordon Browne and Lewis Baumer. London, Unwin, and New York, Stokes, 1899.
The Book of Dragons, illustrated by H.R. Millar. London and New York, Harper, 1900.
Nine Unlikely Tales for Children, illustrated by H.R. Millar and Claude Shepperson. London, Unwin, and New York, Dutton, 1901.
The Wouldbegoods, Being the Further Adventures of the Treasure Seekers, illustrated by Arthur H. Buckland and John Hassell. London, Unwin, 1901; New York, Harper, 1902.
Five Children and It, illustrated by H.R. Millar. London, Unwin, 1902; New York, Dodd Mead, 1905.
The Revolt of the Toys and What Comes of Quarrelling, illustrated by Ambrose Dudley. London, Nister, and New York, Dutton, 1902.
Playtime Stories. London, Tuck, 1903.
The Rainbow Queen and Other Stories. London, Tuck, 1903.
The Phoenix and the Carpet, illustrated by H.R. Millar. London, Newnes, and New York, Macmillan, 1904.
The Story of the Five Rebellious Dolls. London, Nister, 1904.
The New Treasure Seekers, illustrated by Gordon Browne and Lewis Baumer. London, Unwin, and New York, Stokes, 1904.
Cat Tales, with Rosamund Bland, illustrated by Isabel Watkin. London, Nister, and New York, Dutton, 1904.
Pug Peter: King of Mouseland, Marquis of Barkshire, D.O.G., P.C. 1906, Knight of the Order of the Gold Dog Collar, Author of Doggerel Lays and Days..., illustrated by Harry Rountree. Leeds, Alf Cooke, 1905.
Oswald Bastable and Others, illustrated by C.E. Brock and H.R. Millar. London, Wells Gardner, 1905; New York, Coward McCann, 1960.
The Story of the Amulet, illustrated by H.R. Millar. London, Unwin, 1906; New York, Dutton, 1907.
The Railway Children, illustrated by C.E. Brock. London, Wells Gardner, and New York, Macmillan, 1906.
The Enchanted Castle, illustrated by H.R. Millar. London, Unwin, 1907; New York, Harper, 1908.
The House of Arden, illustrated by H.R. Millar. London, Unwin, 1908; New York, Dutton, 1909.
Harding's Luck, illustrated by H.R. Millar. London, Hodder and Stoughton, 1909; New York, Stokes, 1910.

The Magic City, illustrated by H.R. Millar. London, Macmillan, 1910; New York, Coward McCann, 1958.
The Wonderful Garden; or The Three C's, illustrated by H.R. Millar. London, Macmillan, 1911; New York, Coward McCann, 1935.
The Magic World, illustrated by H.R. Millar and Spencer Pryse. London and New York, Macmillan, 1912.
Wet Magic, illustrated by H.R. Millar. London, Laurie, 1913; New York, Coward McCann, 1937.
Our New Story Book, with others, illustrated by Elsie Wood and Louis Wain. London, Nister, and New York, Dutton, 1913.
The New World Literary Series, Book Two, edited by Henry Cecil Wyld. London, Collins, 1921.
Five of Us—And Madeline, edited by Mrs. Clifford Sharp, illustrated by Nora S. Unwin. London, Unwin, 1925; New York, Adelphi, 1926.
Fairy Stories, edited by Naomi Lewis, illustrated by Brian Robb. London, Benn, 1977.

Plays

Cinderella (produced London, 1892). London, Sidgwick and Jackson, 1909.
The Magician's Heart (produced London, 1907).

Poetry

Songs of Two Seasons, illustrated by J. MacIntyre. London, Tuck, 1890.
The Voyage of Columbus, 1492: The Discovery of America, illustrated by Will and Frances Brundage. London, Tuck, 1892.
Our Friends and All about Them. London, Tuck, 1893.
As Happy as a King, illustrated by S. Rosamund Praeger. London, Ward, 1896.
Dinna Forget, with G.C. Bingham. London, Nister, 1897; New York, Dutton, 1898.
To Wish You Every Joy. London, Tuck, 1901.

Other

The Children's Shakespeare, edited by Edric Vredenburg, illustrated by Frances Brundage. London, Tuck, 1897; Philadelphia, Altemus, 1900.
Royal Children of English History, illustrated by Frances Brundage. London, Tuck, 1897.
Twenty Beautiful Stories from Shakespeare: A Home Study Course, edited by E.T. Roe, illustrated by Max Bihn. Chicago, Hertel and Jenkins, 1907.
The Old Nursery Stories, illustrated by W.H. Margetson. London, Oxford University Press-Hodder and Stoughton, 1908.
My Sea-Side Book, with George Manville Fenn. London, Nister, and New York, Dutton, 1911.
Children's Stories from Shakespeare, with *When Shakespeare Was a Boy,* by F.J. Furnivall. Philadelphia, McKay, 1912.
Children's Stories from English History, with Doris Ashley, edited by Edric Vredenburg, illustrated by John H. Bacon and Howard Davie. London, Tuck, 1914.
Long Ago When I Was Young, illustrated by Edward Ardizzone. London, Whiting and Wheaton, and New York, Watts, 1966.

Editor, with Robert Ellice Mack, *Spring* [*Summer, Autumn, Winter*] *Songs and Sketches.* London, Griffith Farran, and New York, Dutton, 4 vols., 1886.
Editor, with Robert Ellice Mack, *Eventide Songs and Sketches.* London, Griffith Farran, 1887; as *Night Songs and Sketches,* New York, Dutton, 1887.
Editor, with Robert Ellice Mack, *Morning Songs and Sketches.* London, Griffith Farran, 1887; as *Noon Songs and Sketches,* New York, Dutton, 1887.
Editor, with Robert Ellice Mack, *Lilies and Heartsease: Songs and Sketches.* New York, Dutton, 1888(?).
Editor, *The Girl's Own Birthday Book.* London, Drane, 1894.
Editor, *Poet's Whispers: A Birthday Book.* London, Drane, 1895.
Editor, *A Book of Dogs, Being a Discourse on Them, with Many Tales and Wonders...,* illustrated by Winifred Austin. London, Dent, and New York, Dutton, 1898.
Editor, *Winter-Snow,* illustrated by H. Bellingham Smith. New York, Dutton, 1898(?).

PUBLICATIONS FOR ADULTS

Novels

The Prophet's Mantle (as Fabian Bland, with Hubert Bland). London, Drane, 1885; Chicago, Belford Clarke, 1889.
The Secret of the Kyriels. London, Hurst and Blackett, and Philadelphia, Lippincott, 1899.
The Red House. London, Methuen, and New York, Harper, 1902.
The Incomplete Amorist. London, Constable, and New York, Doubleday, 1906.
Daphne in Fitzroy Street. London, George Allen, and New York, Doubleday, 1909.
Salome and the Head: A Modern Melodrama. London, Alston Rivers, 1909; as *The House with No Address,* New York, Doubleday, 1909.
Dormant. London, Methuen, 1911; as *Rose Royal,* New York, Dodd Mead, 1912.
The Incredible Honeymoon. New York, Harper, 1916; London, Hutchinson, 1921.
The Lark. London, Hutchinson, 1922.

Short Stories

Something Wrong. London, Innes, 1893.
Grim Tales. London, Innes, 1893.
The Butler in Bohemia, with Oswald Barron. London, Drane, 1894.
In Homespun. London, Lane, and Boston, Roberts, 1896.
Thirteen Ways Home. London, Treherne, 1901.
The Literary Sense. London, Methuen, and New York, Macmillan, 1903.
Man and Maid. London, Unwin, 1906.
These Little Ones. London, George Allen, 1909.
Fear. London, Stanley Paul, 1910.
To the Adventurous. London, Hutchinson, 1923.
Tales of Terror, edited by Hugh Lamb. London, Methuen, 1983.
In the Dark: Tales of Terror, edited by Hugh Lamb. Wellingborough, Northamptonshire, Thorsons, 1988.

Plays

A Family Novelette, with Oswald Barron (produced London, 1894).
The King's Highway (produced London, 1905).
The Philandrist; or, The Lady Fortune-Teller, with Dorothea Deakin (produced London, 1905).
Unexceptionable References (produced London, 1912).

Poetry

Lays and Legends. London and New York, Longman, 2 vols., 1886-92.
The Lily and the Cross. London, Griffith Farran, and New York, Dutton, 1887.
The Star of Bethlehem. London, Nister, 1887.
Leaves of Life. London and New York, Longman, 1888.
The Better Part and Other Poems. London, Drane, 1888.
Easter-Tide: Poems, with Caris Brooke. London, Drane, and New York, Dutton, 1888.
The Time of Roses, with Caris Brooke and others. London, Drane, 1888.
By Land and Sea. London, Drane, 1888.
Landscape and Song. London, Drane, and New York, Dutton, 1888.
The Message of the Dove: An Easter Poem. London, Drane, and New York, Dutton, 1888.
The Lilies Round the Cross: An Easter Memorial, with Helen J. Wood. London, Nister, and New York, Dutton, 1889.
Corals and Sea Songs. London, Nister, 1889.
Life's Sunny Side, with others. London, Nister, 1890.
Sweet Lavender. London, Nister, 1892.
Flowers I Bring and Songs I Sing (as E. Bland), with H.M. Burnside and A. Scanes. London, Tuck, 1893.
Holly and Mistletoe: A Book of Christmas Verse, with Norman Gale and Richard Le Gallienne. London, Ward, 1895.
A Pomander of Verse. London, Lane, and Chicago, McClurg, 1895.
Rose Leaves. London, Nister, 1895.
Songs of Love and Empire. London, Constable, 1898.
The Rainbow and the Rose. London and New York, Longman, 1905.
Ballads and Lyrics of Socialism 1883-1908. London, Fabian Society, 1908.
Jesus in London: A Poem. London, Fifield, 1908.
Ballads and Verses of the Spiritual Life. London, Elkin Mathews, 1911.
Garden Poems. London, Collins, 1912.
Many Voices. London, Hutchinson, 1922.

Other

Wings and the Child; or, The Building of Magic Cities. London, Hodder and Stoughton, and New York, Doran, 1913.

Editor, *Battle Songs.* London, Max Goschen, 1914.
Editor, *Essays,* by Hubert Bland. London, Max Goschen, 1914.

*

Critical Studies: *E. Nesbit: A Biography* by Doris Langley Moore, London, Benn, 1933, revised edition, Philadelphia, Chilton, 1966, Benn, 1967; *Magic and the Magician: E. Nesbit and Her Children's Books* by Noel Streatfield, London, Benn, and New York, Abelard Schuman, 1958; *E. Nesbit* by Anthea Bell, London, Bodley Head, 1960, New York, Walck, 1964; *A Woman of Passion: The Life of E. Nesbit* by Julia Briggs, London, Hutchinson, 1987.

* * *

E. Nesbit was one of those writers who do not perceive when they have found their level, and repine for the career they think they should have had in some other field of literature. She believed in herself primarily as a poet, but her quite numerous books of verse are now wholly neglected while the tales she wrote for children "to keep the house going" are recognized as little masterpieces of ingenuity and humour.

They fall into two categories, those based on magic and fantasy as in fairy tales from time immemorial, and those which are realistic and credible comedies of juvenile behaviour. To the first group belongs the trilogy which comprises *Five Children and It, The Phoenix and the Carpet,* and *The Story of the Amulet.* The major works in the second group also form a trilogy, *The Story of the Treasure Seekers, The Wouldbegoods,* and *The New Treasure Seekers.* Each volume can be read independently of the others. It is hard to choose between the two genres, in both of which, though imitated, Nesbit remains inimitable.

The protagonists, whether the plot hinges on magic or the adventures and misadventures of the human child, are usually families of what was then average size—four or five—with parents who are often got out of the way by absence abroad or some other simple expedient for leaving the children to their own world. Since they are differentiated by age as well as character, young readers can identify either with the eldest, aged about 11 to 14, or the little ones from six upwards. The smallest may be an infant. With no trace of priggishness, the elder ones, whether girls or boys, feel protective responsibility towards the others. Nesbit has little interest in school life and her *dramatis personae* seldom appear in situations where conformity and discipline are admired. Their virtues are courage, kindliness, a high sense of honour, and good manners, on which she lays particular stress.

Unlike most of her Victorian predecessors, she never intrudes religion, there are no pious death-bed scenes, no conversions or serious repentances. Wrongdoers are assigned only minor parts. "She was not a nice woman, and I am glad to say that she goes out of this story almost at once"—such is her typical way of dismissing a necessary but dislikable instrument of the story in *Harding's Luck.* Except when they can be given amusing roles, of which fortunately she creates many, her grown-ups tend to be somewhat sentimentalized.

The children's background is in general a rather hard-up section of the middle class. There is little pocket money, and treats that have to be paid for are scarce. Nesbit was an active pioneering socialist and a founder member of the Fabian Society, but she was able to combine its tenets, not very consistently, with unashamed imperialism and conventional, though unobtrusive, patriotism. In this respect her children are as truly Edwardian as the clothes they wear in the delightful illustrations, chiefly by H.R. Millar.

Although she occasionally touches with sympathy on the overworked and underprivileged, she does not allow political creeds to shape her narratives, and indeed she is more inclined to idealize the pre-industrial past than to look forward to a progressive future. The hero of *Harding's Luck,* a sequel to *The House of Arden,* is a crippled boy from the slums of Deptford. She describes both him and his squalid home with down-to-earth conviction, for she knew the living conditions of the poor through the charities she organized, but she provides him with aristocratic ancestors and noble aspirations, nor, when she has her youthful audience in view, does she recommend any subversion of the existing social order. She took a pride in not preaching at children and never writing down to them. Her prose, lucid and unpretentious but not over-simplified, lends itself perfectly to being read aloud.

The authors who influenced her most were probably Dickens, to whom she was devoted, though, in her youth, he had been decidedly out of fashion, Rudyard Kipling, and F. Anstey. The last-named certainly inspired the turn her imagination took when she depicted normal, everyday people caught up in amazing supernatural situations. Like him, she dealt with such manifestations humorously and avoided—at least in stories for juveniles—anything that might be frightening. Her magical creatures, the Psammead, the Phoenix, and the Mouldiwarp, are all endearing personalities in their own right. When she introduced historic scenes or distant lands, she took considerable trouble over the correctness of local colour but always with a light touch and a knack for singling out features entertaining to a child.

After her comic sense, perhaps Nesbit's greatest strength is her keen memory for the details which catch the eyes and ears of childhood, and which somehow she contrives to bring copiously into every tale without in the least slowing up her answers to the eager question: "What happens next?"

—Doris Langley Moore

NESS, Evaline

Nationality: American. **Born:** Evaline Michelow, Union City, Ohio, 24 April 1911. **Education:** Ball State Teachers College, Muncie, Indiana, 1931-32; Chicago Art Institute, 1933-35; Corcoran School of Art, Washington, D.C., 1943-45; Art Students' League, New York, 1947; Accademia di Belle Arti, Rome, 1951-52. **Family:** Married 1) the law enforcement officer Eliot Ness in 1938 (divorced 1946); 2) Arnold Bayard in 1959. **Career:** Teacher of children's art classes, Corcoran School of Art, 1945-46, and Parsons School of Design, New York, 1959-60; fashion illustrator, Saks Fifth Avenue, New York, and magazine illustrator, 1946-49. From 1959 freelance illustrator. **Award:** American Library Association Caldecott Medal, 1967. **Died:** 12 August 1986.

PUBLICATIONS FOR CHILDREN (ILLUSTRATED BY THE AUTHOR)

Fiction

A Gift for Sula Sula. New York, Scribner, 1963.
Josefina February. New York, Scribner, 1963; London, Chatto Boyd and Oliver, 1970.
Exactly Alike. New York, Scribner, 1964; Edinburgh, Oliver and Boyd, 1968.
Pavo and the Princess. New York, Scribner, 1964.
A Double Discovery. New York, Scribner, 1965.
Sam, Bangs, and Moonshine. New York, Holt Rinehart, 1966; London, Bodley Head, 1967.
The Girl and the Goatherd; or, This and That and Thus and So. New York, Dutton, 1970.
Do You Have the Time, Lydia? New York, Dutton, 1971; London, Bodley Head, 1972.
Yeck Eck. New York, Dutton, 1974.
Marcella's Guardian Angel. New York, Holiday House, 1979.
Fierce the Lion. New York, Holiday House, 1980.

Other

Long, Broad, and Quickeye. New York, Scribner, 1969; London, Chatto Boyd and Oliver, 1971.
An American Colonial Paper House: To Cut Out and Color. New York, Scribner, 1975.
This Is a Paper Palace: To Cut Out and Color. New York, Scribner, 1976.
Four Rooms from the Metropolitan Museum of Art: To Cut Out and Color. New York, Scribner, 1977.
A Victorian Paper House: To Cut Out and Color. New York, Scribner, 1978.
A Shaker Paper House: To Cut Out and Color. New York, Scribner, 1979.

Editor, *Amelia Mixed the Mustard and Other Poems* (anthology). New York, Scribner, 1975.

*

Manuscript Collections: Kerlan Collection, University of Minnesota, Minneapolis.

Illustrator: *The Story of Ophelia* by Mary J. Gibbons, 1954; *The Bridge* by Charlton Ogburn, Jr., 1957; *The Sherwood Ring* by Elizabeth Pope, 1958; *Lonely Maria,* 1960, and *The Princess and the Lion,* 1963, both by Elizabeth Coatsworth; *Ondine* by Maurice Osborne, 1960; *Listen—The Birds* by Mary Britton Miller, 1961; *Across from Indian Shore* by Barbara Robinson, 1962; *Where Did Josie Go?,* 1962, *Some Cheese for Charles,* 1963, *Josie and the Snow,* 1964, *Josie's Buttercup,* 1967, and *Too Many Crackers,* 1971, all by Helen Buckley; *Thistle and Thyme,* 1962, and *A Scottish Songbook,* 1969, both edited by Sorche Nic Leodhas, and *All in a Morning Early,* 1963, and *Kellyburn Braes,* 1968, both by Nic Leodhas; *Macaroon,* 1962, and *Candle Tales,* 1968, both by Julia W. Cunningham; *Funny Town* by Eve Merriam, 1963; *A Pocketful of Cricket* by Rebecca Caudill, 1964; *Coll and His White Pig,* 1965, and *The Truthful Harp,* 1967, both by Lloyd Alexander; *Favorite Fairy Tales Told in Italy* edited by Virginia Haviland, 1965; *Tom Tit Tot: An English Folk Tale,* 1965, and *Mr. Miacca: An English Folk Tale,* 1967, both edited by Joseph Jacobs; *Pierino and the Bell* by Sylvia Cassedy, 1966; *Some of the Days of Everett Anderson,* 1970, *Everett Anderson's Christmas Coming,* 1971, and *Don't You Remember?,* 1973, all by Lucille Clifton; *Joey and the Birthday Present,* 1971, and *The Wizard's Tears,* 1975, both by Maxine Kumin and Anne Sexton, and *What Color Is Caesar?,* by Kumin, 1978; *Old Mother Hubbard and Her Dog* by Sarah Catherine Martin, 1972; *The Woman of the Wood* by Algernon Black, 1973; *The Steamroller* by Margaret Wise Brown, 1974; *The Lives of My Cat Alfred* by Nathan Zimelman, 1976; *The Warmint* by Walter de la Mare, 1976; *The Devil's Bridge* by Charles Scribner, Jr., 1978; *The Hand-Me-Down Doll* by Steven Kroll, 1983.

* * *

Evaline Ness was, in my opinion, the most brilliant and original illustrator of children's books in America in recent times. But she also wrote as well as illustrated several books, created books on doll houses, and assembled a collection of children's poetry called *Amelia Mixed the Mustard and Other Poems.*

Each of her own books is for younger children, and each is an excellent example of that category. Like another writer-illustrator, Maurice Sendak, who is usually billed above her (but not by me), her texts are as carefully conceived as is her artwork; and both are blended into so satisfactory a whole that it's difficult to consider them separately.

Take *Yeck Eck,* for example. It begins, "This small person, Tana Jones, had everything she wanted except the thing she wanted most, A BABY." As the humorous fantasy unfolds, a friend with numerous younger siblings donates a baby to Tana (which she promptly names Agift). Agift cries, "Yeck, Eck!"—words interpreted by Tana to mean, "Take me!" As more and more babies are donated to her, the text spills over onto the bibs and dresses and walls—the words become part of the art. But even dream wishes end, when the babies prefer an adult caregiver to Tana. Now hearing their burbling cries, Tana sadly asks herself, "What does Yeck-Eck mean?" And herself answers, "Only a baby knows."

If the art and text interweave here to create a charming whole, what of the message? In the age of Women's Lib, how did Ness dare to create a heroine who wants to play with babies rather than paints, skates, or trucks? (Shh! Many children still agree with Tana!) The answer is, Ness never cut her cloth—or her stories—to fit the fad of the moment; but, on the other hand, she was often in advance of the current trend. In a book called *The Girl and the Goatherd,* written before the Women's Movement gained public notice, a girl seeks the traditional gift of beauty. But before she receives that desired beauty, she wins the love of the Goatherd who likes her as she is; and beauty, once attained, proves worthless. A crotchety, stubborn heroine who comes to comprehend the superficial value of physical perfection? An unlikely theme for those days!

Or consider *Do You Have the Time, Lydia?* A hectic activist, Lydia races from one non-traditional interest to another. Yet, unlike that of the present crop of feminist writers, the activism here is only the background of the story, which focuses rather on Lydia's inability to finish a job and her insensitivity to her younger brother. Though the story's theme is a universal one of changing values, the background images may well linger longer in young readers' memories than the more strident messages received from some feminist presses.

All Ness's protagonists are girls except one—the boy in her illustrations to the scary English folktale, *Mr. Miacca.* And each girl is a unique creation both in character and in the problems she faces; perhaps, considering the interchangeability of more prolific authors' characters, in Ness's case, less is more. And not only do the girls assume a three-dimensional reality, the adults too, when present, are unique individuals. The only three families shown are single-parent families. The girl in *Exactly Alike* lives with younger twin brothers and a mother constantly busy with sewing to sustain the family. The girl must take care of the naughty, teasing twins, a job that would tax an adult's patience. But she learns to cope with the situation by persistence and initiative. In *Yeck Eck* Tana lives with a father who drives a taxicab; Josefina, in *Josefina February,* lives with a poor farmer uncle; and in Ness's most famous book, *Sam, Bangs, and Moonshine* (a Caldecott Medal winner), the young Samantha, called Sam, lives with a fisherman father.

Sam has "the reckless habit of lying." Or, as her father implores her, "Talk real, not moonshine....Moonshine is flummadiddle. Real is the opposite." Sam's mother is dead—but not to Sam. In the "moonshine" she spins to her cat Bangs, to her friend Thomas, and to herself, she sees her mother as a mermaid. Then she sends Thomas on a quest for an imaginary kangaroo which has gone to live with her mermaid mother in a seacave; and she ignores her conscience, which speaks through Bangs, of the dangers of the incoming tide. Bangs goes after Thomas, and both seem lost when a sudden storm hits the coast.

At this point, a dedicated feminist might have Sam involved in the active rescue work; but Ness gives Sam the harder job—that of waiting alone with her suffering. And in that suffering (which all of us sometimes endure), Sam finally recognizes that "real" is Thomas, is Bangs, is no mother. But her perceptive father reassures her that "there is good moonshine and bad moonshine—it's just important to know the difference." And Sam, like Josefina February, is able to make a hard choice to help a friend.

Ness's words speak for themselves; their poetry, their clarity, their honesty well match her subtle but straightforward portraits of children. Unlike the present trend of presenting "ugly" children under the guise of reality, Ness gave us, in both words and pictures, children as they really are—beautiful, straight, and honest, involved in the pleasures and problems of life.

—Betty Boegehold

NEWMAN, Robert (Howard)

Nationality: American. **Born:** New York City, 3 June 1909. **Education:** Ethical Culture School, New York; Brown University, Providence, Rhode Island, 1927-28. **Military Service:** Served in the Office of War Information, New York, 1942-44: Chief, Radio Outpost Division. **Family:** Married Dorothy Crayder in 1936; one daughter. **Career:** Radio writer, 1936-42: created *City Hospital* series. **Died:** 7 December 1988.

Publications for Children

Fiction

The Boy Who Could Fly, illustrated by Paul Sagsoorian. New York, Atheneum, 1967; London, Hutchinson, 1968.

Merlin's Mistake, illustrated by Richard Lebenson. New York, Atheneum, 1970; London, Hutchinson, 1971.

The Testing of Tertius, illustrated by Richard Cuffari. New York, Atheneum, 1973; London, Hutchinson, 1974.

The Shattered Stone, illustrated by John Gretzer. New York, Atheneum, 1975; London, Hutchinson, 1976.

Night Spell, illustrated by Peter Burchard. New York, Atheneum, 1977.

The Case of the Baker Street Irregular, illustrated by David Stone. New York, Atheneum, 1978; as *A Puzzle for Sherlock Holmes,* London, Hutchinson, 1979.

The Case of the Vanishing Corpse, illustrated by David Stone. New York, Atheneum, 1980; London, Hutchinson, 1981.

The Case of the Somerville Secret, illustrated by David Stone. New York, Atheneum, 1981.

The Case of the Threatened King, illustrated by David Stone. New York, Atheneum, 1982.

The Case of the Etruscan Treasure. New York, Atheneum, 1983.

The Case of the Frightened Friend. New York, Atheneum, 1984.

The Case of the Murdered Players. New York, Atheneum, 1985.

The Case of the Indian Curse. New York, Atheneum, 1986.

The Case of the Watching Boy. New York, Atheneum, 1987.

Other

The Japanese: People of the Three Treasures, illustrated by Mamoru Funai. New York, Atheneum, 1964.
Grettir the Strong, illustrated by John Gretzer. New York, Crowell, 1968.
The Twelve Labors of Hercules, illustrated by Charles Keeping. New York, Crowell, 1972; London, Hutchinson, 1973.

PUBLICATIONS FOR ADULTS

Novels

Identity Unknown. Chicago, Ziff Davis, 1945.
The Enchanter. Boston, Houghton Mifflin, 1962.
Corbie. New York, Harcourt Brace, 1966; London, Hutchinson, 1967.

Radio Plays: *Inner Sanctum Mysteries,* 1938-42; *Adventures of the Thin Man,* 1939; *Big Sister,* 1945-52.

Television Plays: *City Hospital,* 1950-52; *Search for Tomorrow,* 1968-70; *Another World,* 1970-72; *Return to Peyton Place,* 1973-74.

*

Manuscript Collections: Mugar Memorial Library, Boston University.

* * *

Robert Newman was an author for whom the classics had great appeal. *The Twelve Labors of Hercules* is an excellent introduction to the Greek legends, and his "sequels" to the Sherlock Holmes stories (starting with *The Case of the Baker Street Irregular*) make good reading. However, his particular appeal for children is to be found in his three books about the world of Arthurian legend (*Merlin's Mistake, The Testing of Tertius,* and *The Shattered Stone*). He has a strong feel for the period, but does not regard it as sacrosanct, since he is able to poke gentle fun at its style. The very concept of *Merlin's Mistake* is comic. At the birth of Tertius, his godfather Merlin endows him with the gift of all possible knowledge. However, since the wizard was already under the spell of the enchantress Nimue, his intentions got muddled and Tertius was blessed with all *future* knowledge, but not even the simple ability to cure warts. In his teens the boy sets off on a quest to remedy this defect, and is joined by Brian, in search of knightly adventures. Various odd characters attach themselves to the travellers and Tertius's knowledge proves useful when he circumvents fire and steel by using a burning-glass to light a fire, and gets the goldsmith to grind lenses to make spectacles and a telescope. To get them out of a tight spot he "invents" gunpowder, incurring the wrath of Nimue for upsetting history, but as he finds her using a computer to aid her witchery she cannot really complain. In the second book Tertius, at last apprenticed to Merlin, calls again on Brian, now happily married, to join him in France to help defend Europe from the Mongol hordes. There is a superb mix of ancient and modern when Tertius calls up the Tank Corps and a fighter squadron to help defeat the Tartars.

Newman's language is splendidly varied, and the tongue of High Chivalry, where "varlets" and "paynims" abound, is given an affectionate parody, which can only be done successfully by someone who really cares for what he mocks. Children appreciate good "tongue-in-cheek" humour, and that they will get in plenty here.

His last books continued with the detective/mystery theme, and are less successful than the mediaeval "spoofs." Too many other books of this type are on the market already, and he did not seem to have been able to transfer his zany humour and mastery of language.

—Ann G. Hay

NICHOLS, Ruth (Joanne)

Nationality: Canadian. **Born:** Toronto, Ontario, 4 March 1948. **Education:** University of British Columbia, Vancouver, B.A. (honours) 1969; McMaster University, Hamilton, Ontario (Woodrow Wilson fellow) M.A. 1972, Ph.D. 1977. **Family:** Married William Norman Houston in 1974. **Career:** Lecturer, Carleton University, Ottawa, 1974. **Awards:** Canada Council Fellowship, 1972, 1973, 1974; Canadian Library Association award, 1973. **Address:** c/o Gage Educational Publishing Company, 164 Commander Boulevard, Agincourt, Ontario M1S 3C7, Canada.

PUBLICATIONS FOR CHILDREN

Fiction

A Walk Out of the World, illustrated by Trina Schart Hyman. Toronto, Longman, and New York, Harcourt Brace, 1969.
The Marrow of the World, illustrated by Trina Schart Hyman. Toronto, Macmillan, and New York, Atheneum, 1972.
Song of the Pearl. Toronto, Macmillan, and New York, Atheneum, 1976.
The Left-Handed Spirit. Toronto, Macmillan, and New York, Atheneum, 1978.

PUBLICATIONS FOR ADULTS

Novels

Ceremony of Innocence. London, Faber, 1969.
The Burning of the Rose. New York, St. Martin's Press, 1989.
What Dangers Deep. Headline, 1992.

Other

Framework for Reading, with Joan Dean. London, Evans, 1974.

*

Manuscript Collections: Mills Memorial Library, McMaster University, Hamilton, Ontario.

Ruth Nichols comments:

The process of my development can be followed in print since my earliest published book, *A Walk Out of the World,* was published when I was 21, and other books have followed at regular intervals. Most of these are fantasy. I believe fantasy provides a valid and important means of examining the human passions and the nature of our relationship to reality.

*   *   *

For its readers fantasy embodies the will's ability to transcend the known. But the rationale for that metaphysical act must be expressed in a time-tested formula that leads the way through the labyrinths of fantasy to a satisfying conclusion. If the body cannot follow the mind in its passage through eons of time past, time to come, and worlds in space, the compensation for this lack lies in the reality of words to say that it can be done.

In her autobiographical novel, *Ceremony of Innocence,* Ruth Nichols traces her precocious contact with her memory of eternity: she professes a metaphysical contact that gives her stories the roots of reality and the limbs of fantasy. Her almost total recall of childhood encounters and conversations allows her to develop her plot on several planes, one of which is the intuitive. This novel seems to state the apologia for her familiarity with the psychic world.

Nichols writes about what she knows, the first principle of convincing composition. She begins her two fantasies for children in places known to her: in Ontario's Georgian Bay cottage country in *The Marrow of the World; A Walk Out of the World* is into a Vancouver park out of a crowded apartment house. But she intuits so much more than the given physical settings that place her books in Canada. She is first of this world, then of another, a remembered one in which her second self finds a friendly ambience to range metaphysically.

She understands the majesty of ritual, and she initiates her heroes in ritual. She tells the reader too that there is a way that things are done, and that way has an almost fateful logic. Her disciplined pen hews to the moral line as good vanquishes evil; she is quite sure what good is. The other-worldly characters are all her own wishes come true—they do as she bids, even in the delicious pursuit of evil. For it is never in question, the ending. The way however must be strewn with pitfalls so that the good can be fully and finally appreciated. But even it has a bitter sweetness. This world must be borne yet a space, while the untranscended life measures out its days on earth. Then the promised second walk out of the world for Tobit and Judith will be the last one. In *The Marrow of the World* Philip and Linda carry tangible marks of their time travel; their promised gift they will carry even during their terrestrial life.

These chosen earthlings feel emotion and sensations like pain, but they intuit more than they understand of their roles through the uncharted forests of fantasy. They only know they must be good people. Judith and Tobit are more sympathetic characters than Philip and Linda in *The Marrow;* they are not so remote from the readers' longing for the impossible. In *The Marrow* the author has perfected the stylization of her quest fantasy and the characters are altogether more decisive, colder. And their readers fear the shadows more, and do not trust the author as totally.

Nichols wrote *A Walk Out of the World* when she was 18, and won the Canadian Association of Children's Librarians' Bronze Medal for the best book of the year in 1972 for *The Marrow of the World.* These first works are exemplars of style; she learned the rudiments early. Now only the elements will be expanded as she matures, and she may yet develop into Canada's very best fantasist.

—Irma McDonough Milnes

NICHOLSON, (Sir) William (Newzam Prior)

Nationality: British. **Born:** Newark-on-Trent, Nottinghamshire, 5 February 1872. **Education:** Magnus Grammar School, Newark; Hubert von Herkomer's art school, Bushey, Hertfordshire, two years; Académie Julian, Paris. **Family:** Married 1) Mabel Pryde in 1893, three sons, including the painter Ben Nicholson, and one daughter; 2) Edith Phillips in 1919, one daughter. **Career:** Artist: collaborated with James Pryde on posters as the "Beggarstaff Brothers"; also stage designer. **Award:** Knighted, 1936. **Died:** 16 May 1949.

PUBLICATIONS FOR CHILDREN (ILLUSTRATED BY THE AUTHOR)

Fiction

Clever Bill. London, Heinemann, and New York, Doubleday, 1926.

The Pirate Twins. London, Faber, and New York, Coward McCann, 1929.

Other

An Alphabet. London, Heinemann, and New York, Russell, 1898.

PUBLICATIONS FOR ADULTS

Other

Characters of Romance (lithographs). London, Heinemann, and New York, Russell, 1900.

Twelve Portraits. London, Heinemann, and New York, Russell, 2 vols., 1900-02.

The Book of Blokes. London, Faber, 1929.

William Nicholson (illustrations). London, Penguin, 1948.

*

Illustrator: *An Almanac of Twelve Sports* by Rudyard Kipling, 1898; *London Types* by William Ernest Henley, 1898; *The Square Book of Animals* by Arthur Waugh, 1899; *The Velveteen Rabbit* by Margery Williams Bianco, 1922; *The Hour of Magic,* 1922, *True Travellers,* 1923, and *Moss and Feather,* 1928, all by W. H. Davies; *Polly* by John Gay, 1923; *Memoirs of a Fox-Hunting Man* by Siegfried Sassoon, 1929.

Critical Studies: *William Nicholson* by Marguerite Steen, London, Collins, 1943; *William Nicholson* by Lillian Browse, London, Hart Davis, 1956; *William Nicholson, Drawings and Prints* (exhibition catalogue) by Duncan Robinson, London, Arts Council, 1980.

* * *

As artist only, William Nicholson would not qualify for the present book—though his illustrations for Margery Bianco's *The Velveteen Rabbit* still make that story memorable. But as artist-author of two distinguished picture books for the very young, *Clever Bill* and *The Pirate Twins,* he holds an unquestioned place. Quite apart from the technical interest of the art itself, both books show an absolute ease and mastery in the linking of text and pictures; each little drama speeds along with a blithe assurance, and the turns and twists engage us to the end. In *Clever Bill* the little girl Mary is invited to visit her Aunt (we are shown the actual letter of reply); she excitedly plans what to take—then forgets to pack her favourite doll, the soldier bandsman Bill. But "he ran/and he ran/and he ran/and he ran so fast that/he was just in time to meet her train at Dover./'Clever Bill!'" (So run the last six pages.) A perfect story.

Better than a summary, though, is a text itself in full. *The Pirate Twins* runs thus: "One evening on the sands/Mary found/the Pirate Twins./She took them Home/and bathed them/and fed them/on this/and that/and the other./She taught them how to dress/what the S stands for/where to find Jamaica/and the Milky Way/how to dance/and how to play" [one is shown clashing cymbals, the other with bagpipes] "but they didn't care/they bit their nails and sucked their thumbs,/put things into the cat's milk,/played dominoes in bed. UNTIL/one fine day/they left a note and/stole a boat/and sailed away/to sea/but they never forgot their Home/and always came back/in time for/Mary's birthday." The note—see back a few pages—says: "Dear Mary, we have gone for ever. Don't worry. Back soon. Love from B and A/xxxx."

These picture books belong to a later period than Nicholson's striking poster work with James Pryde (as "the Beggarstaff Brothers") and his series of coloured woodcuts which Whistler persuaded the publisher Heinemann to commission at the turn of the century. But they retain the flavour of this earlier work in their bold and jaunty line, clear light colours, and exciting masses of black. The interwoven pictures and words are as fresh and current today as when the books were first devised for Nicholson's young daughter over 60 years ago.

—Naomi Lewis

NIC LEODHAS, Sorche

Pseudonym for Leclaire Alger. **Nationality:** American. **Born:** Leclaire Gowans, 20 May 1898, Youngstown, Ohio. **Education:** Carnegie Library School, graduated 1929. **Family:** Married 1) Amos Risser Hoffman in 1916 (died 1918), one son; 2) second husband several years later. **Career:** Author and librarian. Began writing as a child; started as a page with the Carnegie Library of Pittsburgh, 1915; worked for the New York Public Library, 1921-25; librarian with several branches of the Carnegie Library of Pittsburgh, 1929-66; retired to devote full time to writing in 1966. **Awards:** Lewis Carroll Shelf Award runner-up, 1962; Newbery honor, 1963. **Died:** 14 November 1969.

PUBLICATIONS FOR CHILDREN

Fiction as Leclaire Alger

Jan and the Wonderful Mouth Organ, illustrated by Charlotte Becker. New York, Harper, 1939.
Dougal's Wish, illustrated by Marc Simont. New York, Harper, 1942.
The Golden Summer, illustrated by Aldren Watson. New York, Harper, 1942.

Fiction as Sorche Nic Leodhas

All in the Morning Early, illustrated by Evaline Ness. New York, Holt, 1963.
Gaelic Ghosts, illustrated by Nonny Hogrogian. New York, Holt, 1963.
Ghosts Go Haunting, illustrated by N. Hogrogian. New York, Holt, 1965.
Always Room for One More, illustrated by N. Hogrogian. New York, Holt, 1965.
Sea-Spell and Moor Magic: Tales of the Western Isles, illustrated by Vera Bock. New York, Holt, 1969.
Kellyburn Braes, illustrated by E. Ness. New York, Holt, 1969.
The Laird of Cockpen, illustrated by Adrienne Adams. New York, Holt, 1969.

Other as Sorche Nic Leodhas

Twelve Great Black Cats, and Other Eerie Scottish Tales, illustrated by V. Bock. New York, Dutton, 1971.

Editor, *Heather and Broom: Tales of the Scottish Highland,* illustrated by Consuelo Jones. New York, Holt, 1961.
Editor, *Thistle and Thyme: Tales and Legends from Scotland,* illustrated by E. Ness. New York, Holt, 1963.
Editor, *Claymore and Kilt: Tales of Scottish Kings and Castles,* illustrated by Leo and Diane Dillon. New York, Holt, 1967.
Editor, *A Scottish Song Book,* illustrated by E. Ness. New York, Holt, 1969.
Editor, *By Loch and by Lin: Tales from Scottish Ballads,* illustrated by V. Bock. New York, Holt, 1969.

* * *

Sorche Nic Leodhas was the pen name chosen by Leclaire Gowans Alger, an American children's librarian from Pittsburgh, for the bulk of her work. Under her own name, Leclaire Alger wrote three books, published in the years 1939-42. *Jan and the Wonderful Mouth-Organ, The Golden Summer,* and *Dougal's Wish* are full-length children's adventures that give clear evidence of the author's ability to tell a story.

They also provide firm evidence of her interest in folk material—for it was as a reteller of folk material that Nic Leodhas made her name. *Jan and the Wonderful Mouth-Organ* and *The Golden Summer* are both set in Slovakia—though at the end of *The Golden Summer* Andrusik and Fanya must emigrate to America—and they are full of details about the traditional way of life in a small Slovakian community before the second World War. *Dougal's Wish* brings us nearer to Nic Leodhas: it concerns a small boy, immensely proud of his Scottish ancestry, who buys a book of old Scottish legends on his way home from school, and details all the extraordinary and magical things that happen as a result.

It was some years after these novels, when Nic Leodhas turned to the stories of Scotland themselves, that she found her true place as a writer. Scottish oral tradition is enormously rich, and she had heard many stories told the proper way—aloud—in her parents' home; for not only was she of Scottish descent herself, but many Scottish relatives travelling to America came to stay with the family and delighted in telling stories from home.

In Scotland, the seanachie, or storyteller, holds an honoured position, and represents a long tradition. The first of these storytellers were bards and harpers, then monks, anxious to find out and preserve what they thought was "history." There was also a special kind of story, a sgeulachdan, which was never written down. They were told at special times of the year, such as Hallowe'en, or at ceilidhs—parties and festival gatherings—celebrating great events, such as a christening or a wedding, and the accomplished practitioner would bring in the names of people listening as characters in the stories.

One of the features of this kind of story is that it is generally short, or shortish, so as not to lose the attention of the crowd. To be able to write down such tales, and retain all the character of the spoken word, whatever the variety of story, was no mean gift. Nic Leodhas, in a series of books, tells ghost stories—some very funny—historical stories, romances, legends, trickster tales, stories about honour, strength, clan loyalties, and even ballad material so vividly and with such skill it is as though there is a voice in the room as one reads. She is never guilty of padding, neither does she skimp if detail is necessary. The stories are absolutely authentic, but there is never any feeling of heavy-handed scholarship about them. They are light, lively, full of atmosphere and action. There is fun where it's needed, and a shiver when supernatural matters are the subject. She even manages to impart the sound of a Scottish voice without adding off-putting and incomprehensible dialect—a trap many retellers fall into.

Sometimes there are surprises, even for those used to reading folk material. The Lochmaben harper, who features in a story in *Claymore and Kilt,* stole the English King Henry's horse from him as a bet. He received not only a reward from the King for returning the horse, but money and land for winning the bet—alas, however, how he did it was his wife's idea!

In "The Lay of the Smithy," a very old story indeed, Lon Lonnrach the smith, who first brings the secrets of metalworking to Scotland, is a female giant! In "The Gaberlunzie Man," it's not such a surprise that the beggar in the blue coat turns out to be the king—but the easy relationship between the king and the farmer, whom the king calls his friend, is not so usual. This is one of the special aspects of Scottish stories: "To a Scottish crofter or villager, kings and nobles, in spite of their high estate, are only men, after all." At the other end of the scale, it's a surprise to find stories with comparatively modern settings, like "The Man Who Missed the Tay Bridge Train," which appears in *Twelve Great Black Cats.*

Nic Leodhas was a prize-winner: her book *Heather and Broom* was voted a Notable book of 1960 by the American Library Association, and *Thistle and Thyme* was a runner-up for the John Newbery Award in 1963. Of her picture-book texts, *All in the Morning Early,* with artwork by Evaline Ness, was a Caldecott Medal runner-up, and *Always Room for One More,* with pictures by Nonny Hogrogrian, won the Caldecott Medal in 1966. Such honours are not given lightly, and it is a tribute to the excellence of the author's work that so many of her collections are featured in lists of outstanding children's books.

Nic Leodhas found a rich lode of ore, which she mined and refined into precious metal. The stories are still good metal, for those who enjoy beautifully told folk-tales, or even for those who simply enjoy a good story. "S dh'imich an sgeul marsin" ("and so passeth the old tale away"), the story-teller would say at the end of the narration. With retellings of the quality of Nic Leodhas's available, there should be no danger of the old tales passing away and being forgotten, to the detriment of all.

—Felicity Trotman

NICOLL, Helen

Nationality: British. **Born:** Natland, Westmorland, 10 October 1937. **Education:** Attended schools in Bristol; Dartington Hall, Devon; Froebel Education Institute, London. **Family:** Married Robert Kime in 1970; one daughter and one son. **Career:** Producer of children's programmes, BBC television, 1967-71; editor, *The Egg* magazine, 1977-79; producer, Cover to Cover Cassettes, Wiltshire, since 1983. **Address:** c/o Walker Books Ltd., 87 Vauxhall Walk, London SE11 5HJ, England.

Publications for Children

Fiction (illustrated by Jan Pienkowski)

Meg and Mog. London, Heinemann, 1972; New York, Atheneum, 1973.
Meg's Eggs. London, Heinemann, 1972; New York, Atheneum, 1973.
Meg at Sea. London, Heinemann, 1973; New York, Harvey House, 1976.
Meg on the Moon. London, Heinemann, 1973; New York, Harvey House, 1976.
Meg's Car. London, Heinemann, 1975.
Meg's Castle. London, Heinemann, 1975.
Meg's Veg. London, Heinemann, 1976.
Mog's Mumps. London, Heinemann, 1976; New York, Penguin, 1982.
Quest for the Gloop: The Exploits of Murfy and PHIX. London, Heinemann, 1980.
Mog at the Zoo. London, Heinemann, 1982; New York, Penguin, 1984.
Mog in the Fog. London, Heinemann, 1984.
Owl at School. London, Heinemann, 1984; New York, Penguin, 1985.
Mog's Box. London, Heinemann, 1987.
Owl at the Vet. London, Heinemann, 1991.

Other

Editor, *Poems for Seven Year Olds and Under,* illustrated by Michael Foreman. London, Kestrel, 1983.

* * *

The simple but richly coloured line drawings of Jan Pienkowski have blended with Helen Nicoll's brief sharp text to give the Meg and Mog books the impact of good strip cartoons. The principal characters, the witch Meg, her cat Mog, and their familiar Owl are clearly figures from the dark moonlit side of life; but the author has, as it were, transferred their scene of action to the common daylight. Indeed, written at a level suitable for the very young, the stories are actually an artless and effective example of situation comedy. When the trio make their excursion into outer space in *Meg on the Moon,* or in *Meg's Castle* into the mediaeval world, such a trip is not so much the product of a naturally fantastic order as a diversion sought out to alleviate the tedium of suburban isolation. Other characters are rare and, curiously, nearly always faceless, their features masked by a space helmet or a knight's visor or, in *Meg at Sea,* behind helicopter glass. While Meg retains the cauldron, the flying besom, the tattered widow's weeds, and conical hat—the full uniform and equipment of any properly accredited witch—her magic is only shakily controlled and applied with some misgivings. Nor can a beneficial outcome be predicted with much confidence. The broiling sun conjured up to aid the crops in *Meg's Veg* and the wind invoked to speed the becalmed ship in *Meg at Sea* both overfulfil their magical contract to produce respectively drought and storm. The eggs summoned as a teatime treat are enormous and inedible; in the night they hatch dinosaurs (*Meg's Eggs*). The same spell which releases Mog from captivity in *Mog at the Zoo* imprisons Meg herself.

To young children uncertain of their own powers and the power of household implements, Meg's hit-or-miss spells must be particularly compelling. As it imitates life's habit of presenting desired ends in undesirable form Meg's magic displays an effortless didactic charm. However it is notable that in a real crisis the heroine will as often and more unerringly choose a practical solution. After self-inflicted witchcraft has marooned Meg and her entourage on a tiny island (*Meg at Sea*), she reveals the attributes of an accomplished Girl Guide, first employing a magnifying glass to make fire and then her cape to telegraph SOS smoke signals in morse code. It is resourcefulness of this kind, combined with Meg's skill at piloting spaceships and growing vegetables, which has presumably placed these books on lists of those recommended as showing women in a more positive and active light. Certainly these brief and amusing stories abound in practical detail. In *Mog in the Fog* a sherpa offers Mog a cup of tea with butter in it. Within its limits *Meg's Veg* is a faultless gardening manual. But as the series progresses something of the aura of Tony Hancock's weary home life in Railway Cuttings gathers itself about the domestic threesome; a slight depression insinuates itself as the extravagance of moon jaunts gives way to the more rueful and mundane humour of *Mog's Mumps.*

In the very latest tales Meg shows some concern to exercise more properly her responsibility as the head of a one-parent family. Owl is lovingly packed off to school with a lunch box to learn soaring and swooping with the other owls (*Owl at School*). When Mog puts in his trade union claim for a lunch box too in *Mog's Box,* a spell quickly delivers one the size of a suitcase; with a characteristic sting in the tail it contains nothing more nourishing than a caterpillar.

With the first eight stories coming thick and fast between 1972 and 1976, then just four more appearing from 1982 until the present, it seems Nicoll has waning or only intermittent interest in these delightful characters. In other hands one can imagine them syndicated in comic strips all around the globe. Nor, perhaps more wisely, has *Quest for the Gloop,* a confusing science-fantasy farrago in which a little green man and his robot complete a successful intergalactic search for the life-saving Gloop, been followed by a sequel.

—John Churcher

NÍ DHUIBHNE, Éilís

Also writes as Elizabeth O'Hara. **Nationality:** Irish. **Born:** Dublin, 22 February 1954. **Education:** Attended University College, Dublin; University of Copenhagen, B.A., M. Phil., Ph.D. **Family:** Married Bo Almquist in 1982; two sons. **Career:** Part-time lecturer, assistant keeper, National Library of Ireland, Dublin. **Member:** Irish Writers Union (chair, 1994-95). **Awards:** Listowel Writers Weeks Poetry Award, 1989; shortlisted Bisto Book of the Year 1990-91; shortlisted Bisto Book of the Year 1993-94; Bisto Book of the Year 1994-95;Reading Association of Ireland Book Award 1995.

Publications for Children

Fiction

The Uncommon Cormorant. Dublin, Poolbeg, 1990.
Hugo and the Sunshine Girl. Dublin, Poolbeg, 1991.
The Hiring Fair. Dublin, Poolbeg, 1993.
Blaeberry Sunday. Dublin, Poolbeg, 1994.
Penny-farthing Sally. Dublin, Poolbeg, 1996.

Publications for Adults

Fiction

The Bray House. Dublin, Attic Press, 1990.

Short Stories

Blood and Water. Dublin, Attic Press, 1988.
Eating Women Is Not Recommended. Dublin, Attic Press, 1991.
The Inland Ice. Belfast, Blackstaff, 1997.

Plays

Dun Na Mban Tri Thine (in Irish; produced Dublin, 1994).
Milseog an tSamhraidh (in Irish; produced Dublin, 1997).

*

Éilís Ní Dhuibhne comments:

I began writing short stories and novels for adults when I was about twenty and these continue to be an important part of my output. I began writing for children when I had children (boys) myself, partly in response to their request for books which they could read. My first two children's books, *The Uncommon Cormorant* and *Hugo and the Sunshine Girl* are written for younger children, and are to some extent books about boys. As I became more seriously committed to children's literature, however, I have begun to write for older children, and my last two books have been historical novels about a teenage girl. I feel that in the last book in particular, the distinction between adult and children's literature is becoming blurred. I am becoming more interested in adolescence, as a phase in human experience, but I feel that when writing for adolescents I wish to introduce themes—loss, betrayal, joy, love, tolerance—and styles of writing which are not emphatically juvenile. In *Blaeberry Sunday,* for instance, I have risked using two tenses, both the past and the present, and have used some symbolism. I feel that readers from the age of 11 or 12 can be introduced, gently, to the techniques as well as some of the themes of mature literary fiction, and indeed that it is important that they should be. Although it is difficult to make predictions about the future, I hope to continue to write for older children in a way which is not totally different from the way in which I write for adults.

As a child books were the most important thing in my life. I read without any guidance whatsoever, as was the norm in Ireland in the 1960s, and so had a mixed diet of popular fiction, by Enid Blyton, Elinor Brent-Dyer, and so on. Insofar as I had favourite authors they were Louisa May Alcott, Johanna Spyri, Susan Coolidge, and Richmal Compton. In my early teenage years I became fond of G.K. Chesterton and Somerset Maugham—writers whom I would seldom if ever read now. I think that all writers one reads repeatedly and with love, particularly in childhood and adolescence, influence not only one's style of writing but one's style of thinking. I believe they shape one's personality and attitudes as strongly as "reality" does. This is one reason why it is important to write truthfully (in the broadcast sense) for children.

* * *

Éilís Ní Dhuibhne takes her place amongst a group of writers of the 1990s in Ireland who have found an eager audience for their stories. Her first two books are fantasy stories for younger readers *The Uncommon Cormorant,* and *Hugo and the Sunshine Girl.* Many of the traits and characteristics of Ní Dhuibhne's writing are present in the *Uncommon Cormorant.* Her matter of fact merge of fantasy and reality, her wry social comment and gentle humour are distinctive traits. Every day Ragnar travels to school with his Mum on the DART (Dublin Area Rapid Transport) and in the introductory paragraph we learn something of the locale and the people as Ní Dhuibhne gives us a litany or chant of the sea world along the coasts, the "seagulls, seawalls, seaweeds, seaside hotels and seaside huts and seaside bungalows" with a special comment reserved for "seadogs and seapeople." In a lovely aside or social comment on fitness freaks we get the following description: "They strolled along that strand every single morning, even if it rained, even if it snowed, even if the wind was howling so that the waves lashed in and almost swallowed up the train. Absolutely nothing deterred them." This interesting first novel is somewhat contrived and even derivative of Eileen O'Faolain's *Miss Pennyfeather,* or P. L. Travers' *Mary Poppins.* Nevertheless its author's understanding of children and her ability to tell a story keeps the reader turning pages to the very end.

For her second novel, Ní Dhuibhne takes an international folktale "The Girl as Helper in the Hero's Flight" in its Irish variant as recorded by her as a student on field work in County Donegal. The author tells us in an introduction that the plot and motifs are unchanged but that she tells it in her own language and develops the character. She also points to the unusual balance in the folktale of equal roles played by both hero and heroine. This is a much more assured novel than *The Uncommon Cormorant* and Ní Dhuibhne is a gentle feminist who pokes fun at fairy tale conventions. The story has all the conventional fairy tale ingredients—wicked stepmother, kindly old woman, magic wishes, promises to be fulfilled in a year and a day and on and on—but all of them are woven together with a very strong thread of reality. These are no cardboard cut-out figures so common of folk and fairy tale but people whom you believe you know and certainly by the end of the story whom you have come to love. There is a very contemporary tone to the story which gives it this added layer of reality. When the castle is built overnight by magic, Hugo is understandably delighted and somewhat puzzled when next morning he faces the wrath of the stonemasons. He listens bemusedly to mutterings of "Have you ever heard of a trade union?" or "Getting in other contractors to do the work." When he finally placates them by offering work at the castle, it is to grumbles of "re-deployment."

Ní Dhuibhne as narrator takes her readers outside the story from time to time to comment, to reassure, or simply to note that this is usually the kind of thing you read about in story books, adding another layer of reality creating a literary *trompe d'oeil.* The reader too is occasionally questioned and implicitly applauded for getting it right. Hugo after six dreadful years of harsh treatment by his stepmother who fed him porridge and water runs away. After a day and night of escape he finally stops at a cottage where he is invited to breakfast and the author asks with anticipation, "What do you think they were having for breakfast?" And of course instantly the reader knows the answer—porridge and water. There is a gentle vein of feminism which runs right through this folktale so it's no surprise that it is in fact the Sunshine Girl who pops the question and the dazed Hugo who replies, "But that's exactly what I want to do too."

In *The Hiring Fair,* the first of a trilogy, Ní Dhuibhne has written under the pseudonym of Elizabeth O'Hara and in a genre new to her—historical fiction. For older children it is a rite of passage story of scatterbrained Sally who lives a comfortable life on a small Donegal farm, dreaming dreams of an exciting future and losing herself in books such as *Little Women* or *Uncle Tom's Cabin.* Sally, who "could be dim sometimes especially where housework was concerned," was "quite clever at things you did sitting down." When Sally's father is drowned while out fishing, life changes dramatically for Sally and her younger sister, Katie. The sisters find themselves going to the Hiring Fair to seek employment in order to help prevent the family's eviction from their farmhouse. The author's background in folklore and folk tradition ensures that we are given an accurate and vivid picture of life in rural Ireland at the end of the last century. The historical realities impinge only slightly on our young heroine in asides, and sermons, and headlines but they have little to do with the worries and realities that Sally faces. If this was a 19th-century novel, and there are many elements similar, our young heroine would have been hired by cruel harsh masters and set to endure unspeakable hardships. As it is they are treated fairly but with the standards and realities faced by all servants at that period. Homesickness, missing her mother and her odd old granny and little sister and "the sound of people talking her own language ... she was missing the sound of Irish now. Like the sound of the sea it had been in her ears since the moment she was born. It's hard to get used to a set of new sounds," are the real trials to be endured. These are the kind of realities that Sally faces and endures. The author conveys a true historical perspective without a trace of didacticism in the vulnerability of the tenant farmer, the superstitions of a divided community, and the growing mutual respect of employer and employee.

Blaeberry Sunday continues the story of Sally Gallagher and her family with the book opening in the summer of 1893 as Sally and her sister return home from their stint as hired girls. Sally's reaction at the sight of her homestead is an echo of many emigrant songs and letters from America. Time has brought changes for Sally to deal with—the marriage of her widowed mother, the changes in her old friends, and her growing love for Manus. The turmoil Sally experiences is mirrored in the events—the excitement of the touring fair with its acrobats, the anguish of standing by while old neighbours are evicted, the loss of Manus to the doctor's daughter. Outsiders often act as commentators or filters on Sally's life putting it in focus—quite literally as in the scene where the author describes the arrival of the famous Dublin photographic firm Lawrence with their photographer Robin French. Ní Dhuibhne uses a well-known historical portrait of an unknown peasant girl and through Sally breathes life into the dim negative. In the final part of the trilogy *Penny-farthing Sally* she is in Dublin, working as governess. It is an exciting time to be in the capital as the old century nears its end and the movement to revive Gaelic Ireland gains momentum. With a toss of her independent head Sally Gallagher—Irish to her marrow—joins Jo March and Ann of Green Gables in the ranks of feisty young women.

—Pat Donlon

NIMMO, Jenny

Nationality: British. **Born:** Windsor, Berkshire, 15 January 1944. **Education:** Private boarding schools, 1950-60. **Family:** Married David Wynn Millward in 1974; two daughters and one son. **Career:** Actress and assistant stage manager, Theatre Southeast, Sussex and Kent, 1960-63; governess, Amalfi, Italy, 1963; photographic researcher, 1964-66, assistant floor manager, 1966-68 and 1971-74, and director and writer of children's programs, 1970, all BBC Television, London; full-time writer, since 1975. **Awards:** Smarties prize, 1986; Welsh Arts Council Tir na n'Og award, 1987. **Address:** Henllan Mill, Llangynyw, Welshpool, Powys SY21 9EN, Wales.

Publications for Children

Fiction

The Bronze Trumpeter, illustrated by Caroline Scrace. London, Angus and Robertson, 1975.
Tatty Apple, illustrated by Priscilla Lamont. London, Methuen, 1984.
The Snow Spider, illustrated by Joanna Carey. London, Methuen, 1986; New York, Dutton, 1987.
Emlyn's Moon, illustrated by Joanna Carey. London, Methuen, 1987; as *Orchard of the Crescent Moon,* New York, Dutton, 1989.
The Red Secret, illustrated by Maureen Bradley. London, Hamish Hamilton, 1989.
The Chestnut Soldier. London, Methuen, 1989.
The Bears Will Get You! London, Methuen, 1990.
Jupiter Boots. London, Heinemann, 1990.
Ultramarine. London, Methuen, 1990.
Delilah and the Dogspell. London, Methuen, 1991.
Rainbow and Mr. Zed. London, Methuen, 1992.
The Witches and the Singing Mice, illustrated by Angela Barrett. New York, Dial, 1993.
The Stone Mouse, illustrated by Helen Craig. London, Walker, 1993.
The Breadwitch, illustrated by Ben Cort. London, Heinemann, 1993.
Delilah and the Dishwasher Dogs, illustrated by Ben Cort. London, Methuen, 1993.
The Starlight Cloak, illustrated by Justin Todd. London, Collins, 1994.
Griffin's Castle. London, Mammoth, 1994.
Wilfred's Wolf, illustrated by David Wynn Millward. London, Red Fox, 1994.
Ronnie and the Giant Millipede, illustrated by David Parkins. London, Walker, 1995.
Granny Grimm's Gruesome Glasses, illustrated by David Wynn Millward. London, A. & C. Black, 1995.
Alien on the 99th Floor, illustrated by Martin Chatterton. London, Heinemann, 1996.
The Witch's Tears, illustrated by Paul Howard. London, Collins Children's Books, 1996.
Gwion and the Witch, illustrated by Jac Jones. Llandysul, Pont, 1996.
Delilah Alone, illustrated by Georgien Overwater. London, Mammoth, 1997.

*

Jenny Nimmo comments:

I live and work in a rural community in Wales where my three bilingual children are growing into an old but vigorous culture. Here place names hark back to legend and it seems to me that the past is still part of the rhythm of everyday life. My books are concerned with the very real problem of growing children, and most of them are set in a landscape which is undeniably magical; they are described as fantasies.

* * *

Writers who live in Wales have a special responsibility as well as rare opportunities, both of which come from the ageless tradition of mysticism, magic, and quirky humour natural to the Celtic world. Richly imaginative, and possibly explosive, material lies all around on the hills, in the huddled stone cottages, in the playground and the butcher's shop. Here is the source of Jenny Nimmo's highly individual books.

For a writer of such potential Nimmo's debut was modest in scale. Her first notable book was *Tatty Apple,* 90-odd pages of large print in Methuen's Read Aloud series. Into this pint pot she poured, with all the exuberance of the beginner, a gallon or two of sparkling ideas. The scene is her own Mid Wales, the central character Owen-Owen, a small boy of indomitable spirit and high humour. Owen-Owen wants to have a ride on the little railway that carries tourists and local shoppers down the valley to Welshpool. He is too young to go alone, Mam is too busy, and sister Elin, who has been before, remembers too well the pain of the bumpy ride. Owen-Owen bribes Elin with a little hen, got from irascible Mr. Evans, and while he is at Mr. Evans's farm he finds Tatty Apple, a green rabbit. Tatty Apple is magical. Nimmo holds the magic firmly in check, and allows most of the action, which is lively and very amusing, to come out of the characters and their situation.

Joyous as the book is, it did not prepare the reader for what was to follow. *The Snow Spider,* although still governed by the physical limitations of publication in a series, is a big book in its theme and its implications. Every Welsh writer must come under the influence of *The Mabinogion,* that extraordinary mixture of medieval romances, hero tales, Arthurian legends, and wry humour which is the foundation stone of Welsh literature. The theme of *The Snow Spider* comes directly from that book. Gwyn, at nine, is a reluctant magician. His scatty Nain has hailed him as the reincarnation of Math, Lord of Gwynedd, and given him a most unpromising collection of junk as his birthday present. With these in hand Gwyn sets out to solve the mystery of Bethan, the sister who disappeared from the mountain. His quest brings him many marvellous experiences, some of them dangerous, for among the forces ranged against him is the spirit of Efnisien, the most inexplicably malignant figure in the medieval saga. Gwyn's task has to be performed while he continues with his normal life of school and farm and his on/off relationships with his neighbours. Nimmo brings off her complicated story with much skill, blending the wonderful and the ordinary with a sure hand and maintaining the right atmosphere with some unobtrusively lovely descriptions of landscape and (a basic element in the Welsh scene) weather.

The setting and some of the characters of *The Snow Spider* are carried over into *Emlyn's Moon,* another story of magic and of personal and family dilemmas. This time the focus is on Nia, a member of the numerous Lloyd family who are Gwyn's neighbours. The Lloyd farm has foundered, and Mr. Lloyd and his brood move to the town where he runs the butcher's shop. Nia ("Nia-can't-do-nothing" to her insensitive family) suffers at home and school from a sense of inadequacy, from which she is rescued by Emlyn and his artist father (who have troubles enough of their own). Gwyn's magic plays a part too. There are deeper implications in this story, and Nimmo explores them confidently. Again the writing is sensitive and evocative, and the eloquence is always at the service of the story. Nia in her plight is a touching figure and her salvation is something to be taken very seriously, but the book is also full of humour and sharply drawn portraits.

Nimmo is a living example of the basic formula for success in an author: write what you know. She works in big ideas on a small canvas, which she fills with the figures of her own rural community. Magic or no magic, hers is a real world, viewed with a keen and understanding eye and with rich appreciation of its fun and its folly.

Nimmo brought her "Snow Spider" trilogy to a powerful conclusion with *The Chestnut Soldier,* the first story in the sequence to escape from the physical limitations of an Easy Reader series. The new novel demands space in which to deploy a complicated plot and mature and complex characters. Four years have gone by since Gwyn reluctantly accepted that he was by heredity a magician, and he hopes deeply that the powers will soon leave him. "To be average was Gwyn's greatest wish." One more challenge awaits him, and this again comes from Efnisien, the malign prince from the remote past whose symbol, among the miscellaneous objects given to Gwyn by his Nain, is the mutilated horse that bears the warning—"Dim hon" ["Not this"]. It is not altogether Gwyn's fault that the evil spirit of Efnisien is released and finds a new home in Evan Llyr, a soldier cousin of the Lloyds who is recovering from injuries sustained in Northern Ireland (but why are there no scars on his handsome body?).

Although Gwyn and Nia are again important actors in this drama, parts of the story are focussed upon sixteen-year-old Catrin Lloyd, a lovely girl who comes under the spell of her grown-up cousin. With her characteristic touch, Nimmo blends the magic and the sinister elements in her creation with the quiet, funny, and commonplace events of everyday life.

Nimmo has not found it easy to put aside her Mabinogion sources and turn to new scenes and themes. The two major novels that followed *The Chestnut Soldier—Ultramarine* and *Rainbow and Mr. Zed*—leave behind the homeliness of Mid-Wales and the familiar patterns of village life. The seaside settings of both books are vitally important, but they remain undefined topographically. The principal characters—Ned and Nell in the first book, Nell in the sequel—are children whose lives are dominated by the sights and sounds of the sea, and so is Nimmo's writing, which spills over with the imagery of water and ocean. The action of these books is too complex for summary, but the theme, to express it crudely, is the preservation of land and sea from abuse and exploitation.

The confrontation between Nell's father and her uncle Mr. Zed, which forms the climax of the latter story, presents the issues in dramatic terms, but they lie at the heart of both stories. With such vital matters at stake, there is little room for Nimmo's usual humor, and the contexts are remote from normal experience. In compensation Nimmo offers superb seascapes and a handful of vivid portraits, of which the most successful is Nell (aka Rainbow), a shy and unworldly girl who rises most splendidly to meet her crisis. A third volume is promised.

As her major work grows in scale and complexity, Nimmo has turned to the creation of small, simpler worlds. Of her little books, the finest is unquestionably *The Stone Mouse.* Aunt Maria leaves the Stone Mouse in charge of her house, but his position as guardian is jeopardized by the hostility of Ted, an angry small boy who comes on holiday with his sister Elly. To Ted, the Stone Mouse is "a dirty old pebble," and he resents Elly's devotion to it. "In a rage" he steals the mouse and buries it too deep even for the claws of Moss and Minnie, the house cats. It is the Stone Mouse nevertheless who helps Ted to identify the source of his anger, and it is the Stone Mouse, who cannot speak, who has the last word. This slight book, exquisite in form, quietly eloquent in style, demands recognition for its authority and its wisdom.

—Marcus Crouch

NOONAN, Diana

Nationality: New Zealander. **Born:** Dunedin, New Zealand, 7 January 1960. **Education:** Tokomairiro High School, Otago University, B.A. in English; Auckland Secondary Teachers College. **Family:** Married artist Keith Olsen, 1984; one son. **Career:** Secondary school teacher, until 1986; writer, since 1986. Appointed editor of the New Zealand School Journals 1996. **Awards:** Queen Elizabeth II Arts Council Children's Writer's Bursary, 1991; Writer in Residence, Dunedin College of Education, 1993; White Raven Award, International Library of Munich, 1992, for *Leaving the Snow Country,* and 1993, for *A Sonnet for the City*; AIM Children's Book Award, junior Fiction, 1994, for *A Dolphin in the* Bay, 1994; AIM Children's Book Award, picture book, 1995, for *The Best Loved Bear*; New Zealand Library and Information Association Book Award, nonfiction, 1997, for *I Spy Wildlife, The Field.*

Publications for Children

The Silent People. Dunedin, John McIndoe, 1990.
Leaving the Snow Country. Dunedin, John McIndoe, 1991.
A Sonnet for the City. Dunedin, John McIndoe, 1992.
A Dolphin in the Bay. Norwood South Australia, Omnibus, 1993.
Goodbye Toss. Auckland, HarperCollins, 1993.
The Whalers' Garden. Dunedin, John McIndoe, 1994.
Room 4 at Cattle Creek. Auckland, HarperCollins, 1994.
The Deer. Auckland, Ashton Scholastic, 1994.
The Best Loved Bear, illustrated by Elizabeth Fuller. Auckland, Ashton Scholastic, 1994.
Kangaroo Bill and the Forest Behind the Bay. Auckland, Reed, 1994.
A Touch of Jungle Fever. Auckland, HarperCollins, 1995.
Danny to the Rescue. Auckland, HarperCollins, 1995.
The Last Steam Train, illustrated by Brent Putze. Auckland, Ashton Scholastic, 1995.
I Spy Wildlife. Auckland, Heinemann Education, 1996.
Hercules. Norwood, South Australia, Omnibus, 1996.
The Know, Sow and Grow Kids Book of Plants. Alexandra, Bridge Hill Publishing, 1997.

*

Critical Studies: *Personal Best,* edited by Tessa Duder and P. McFarlane, Auckland, Reed, 1997.

Diana Noonan comments:

Some authors have wanted, from a very young age, to be writers. I had no plans to write until I shifted to the remote Catlins in 1986 and discovered that I wanted to paint the magnificent scenery I saw all about me. Frustration led me to write about what I saw instead and so I completed my first novel.

Since then I have published over one hundred pieces of work, picture books for young children, novels, educational and School Journal pieces. With my family I live as simple a lifestyle as possible. We grow most of our own food, keep bees, preserve for the winter, and generally aim to have a minimum impact on the Earth. I am an ardent conservationist and whenever I have time, I plant trees.

My interests necessarily revolve around my daily life—bee keeping, harvester gardening, and sewing. They also include the environment around us—I walk on the beach and in the forest, tramp, swim, bird watch, enjoy the company of our two donkeys and spend as much time as possible with our son Max.

I am also a dedicated traveller and whenever possible, my family and I visit other countries. We once stayed in a Greek village for three months but I have also cycled around much of the world. I enjoy writing because words take me to places I have never visited before.

* * *

In a relatively short career Diana Noonan has achieved outstanding success in every field of writing for children. All her work is underpinned by a strong sense of place and her novels vividly depict the beautiful area of Otago in southern New Zealand where she lives. Protecting it from exploitation is the theme of her first book, *The Silent People.* Here Jenny worries that the local council may soon build a road which will not only involve cutting down native forest but which will also desecrate an ancient burial ground. She then discovers that poachers are stealing rare yellow-eyed penguins from the beaches, but her concern for the fragile environment leads her into danger.

Noonan's protagonists are always thoughtful, a condition often bred through sheer physical isolation. Noonan said in *Personal Best,* "I am fascinated by the brave decisions and amazing achievements young people can make when they are freed from the influence of their peers. For that reason my characters are often alone or socially isolated."

Seventeen-year-old Penny, the main character in *Leaving the Snow Country,* is certainly isolated. She has lived all her live on a high-country Otago farm, attaining her education through correspondence school. She is articulate and intelligent and she wins a scholarship to university. Her parents are delighted, but she does not want to leave the "Snow Country" where she wanders on her donkey, romantically named "Heathcliff." When a newly-arrived young doctor persuades her to accompany him on his rounds, however, she discovers that even within her own beloved district there are neuroses, infidelity, illness and death. The recognition shakes her idealized notions of society and she realizes that she may best serve it by going to university and gaining qualifications.

In the sequel *A Sonnet for the City* Penny has arrived at Otago University, where her idealism leads her into radical student politics. But when she is told to kidnap a local member of Parliament she is faced with the age-old dilemma of whether questionable means are justified to achieve laudable ends.

Another teenage protagonist, Virginia, is shaken into re-assessing her own values in *The Whalers' Garden.* The novel is set in 1970 when Virginia goes to stay with her aunt Bernadette, who is a nun in a remote Otago community. Bernadette is an unorthodox free spirit who interprets the teaching of St. Francis in contemporary ecological terms. But other people in the settlement are less idealistic and Virginia must make up her own mind. Her conclusions are implicit in the epilogue set twenty years later when she has become a Presbyterian minister. All three novels are refreshingly different from many condescending books for young adults. Noonan's teenagers are fortunate in enjoying basically happy human relationships. Unimpeded by self-pity and introspection they are free to explore important aspects of politics and of philosophy.

A Dolphin in the Bay is for rather younger readers. Seb, the central character, is isolated by shortsightedness which prevents him from going out with his father and brother when they are on holiday. Left alone in the rented house he discovers a recorder with manuscript music. He plays it and is reminded of the call he had heard when he saw a dolphin just off the beach. But there is a mystery about the dolphin: does it rescue people in distress, does it assume female form? He discovers the answers in a climax which sees him grow in confidence and self-esteem. This is a multi-faceted story which poetically weaves together the threads of seascape, music, conservation, and human relationships.

Friendship is the theme in *Goodbye Toss,* a sensitive exploration of the adjustments called for when one of two close friends moves out of the district. Noonan moves to a lively vein of satire, however, in *A Touch of Jungle Fever,* another novel for the 8-to-11-year-olds. Here Jay suffers from a "New Age" mother who takes him on a "Whole Life Enrichment" residential holiday. Jay's life is boring rather than enriched until he discovers an old book which explains that the accompanying packet of seed contains "immortalis juvenis" (eternal youth). The effect of this find on a community not over-endowed with common sense is joyfully exploited in this very amusing novel.

Both *Kangaroo Bill and the Forest Behind the Bay* and *The Deer* are for beginner readers and both return to the theme of conservation. In the first the Government's intentions to log a scenic reserve are thwarted by Kangaroo Bill. In the second the young protagonist is determined to free a wild deer which has been penned in order to be shot for sport.

Noonan's picture books for young children move to more general topics. *The Last Steam Train* paints a compassionate portrait of a former stationmaster who has become very forgetful but still retains a fund of stories to tell his grandchildren. When he is invited to raise the signal for the last steam train the children fear that his memory will lapse, but he acquits himself admirably.

In the much acclaimed *The Best Loved Bear* Tim worries that his bear will never succeed in a "Best Loved Bear" competition. Its ear is torn, it is bald in places, and sticky from ice-cream. He is so ashamed of it that he takes it to school in a bag. But a perceptive judge sees that this bear has been very much loved and it returns home in triumph on Tim's shoulder. The simple story, well within the experience of every child, is beautifully illustrated by Elizabeth Fuller.

Noonan exhibits a shrewd understanding of children of all ages and she is never condescending to her readers. Her subject matter is interesting, her plots are well-managed and her style is always elegant, whether writing nonfiction, early readers, or novels for young adults. The exploration of large issues is made credible by her exact observation of every-day activities and conversations. Her characters may be inspired by ideals but they are well-rounded flesh-and-blood people who linger in the memory long after the book is closed.

—Betty Gilderdale

NORMAN, Lilith

Nationality: Australian. **Born:** Sydney, New South Wales, 27 November 1927. **Education:** Sydney Girls' High School, 1940-44. **Career:** Library assistant, Newtown Library, Sydney, 1947-49; telephonist, Bonnington Hotel, London, 1950-51; sales assistant, Angus and Robertson Books, Sydney, 1952-53; nurse, Balmain District Hospital, Sydney, 1953-56; library assistant, 1956-58, research officer, 1958-66, and children's librarian, 1966-70, Sydney Public Library; assistant editor, 1970-76, and editor, 1976-78, New South Wales Department of Education *School Magazine.* Since 1978 freelance writer. **Awards:** Queen's Silver Jubilee Medal, 1977. **Agent:** Margaret Connelly & Associates, 37 Ormond St., Paddington, New South Wales, 2021, Australia.

PUBLICATIONS FOR CHILDREN

Fiction

Climb a Lonely Hill. London, Collins, 1970; New York, Walck, 1972.
The Shape of Three. London, Collins, 1971; New York, Walck, 1972.
The Flame Takers. Sydney and London, Collins, 1973.
A Dream of Seas, illustrated by Edwina Bell. Sydney and London, Collins, 1978.
My Simple Little Brother, illustrated by David Rae. Sydney and London, Collins, 1979.
The Laurel & Hardy Kids. Sydney, Random House, 1989.
The Paddock: A Story in Praise of the Earth, illustrated by Robert Roennfeldt. Milsons Point, New South Wales, Random House, 1992; London, J. MacRae, and New York, Knopf, 1993.
Aphanasy, illustrated by Maxim Svetlanov, Sydney, Random House, 1994.
Hans Christian Andersen's The Beetle, illustrated by Maxim Svetlanov. Milsons Point, New South Wales, Random House Australia, 1995.

Plays

Contributor of television play to *Catch Kandy* series, 1973; short plays published in *School Magazine,* Sydney.

Other

Mocking-Bird Man (reader), illustrated by Astra Lacis. Sydney and London, Hodder and Stoughton, 1977.

PUBLICATIONS FOR ADULTS

The Brown and Yellow: Sydney Girls' High School 1883-1983. Melbourne, Oxford University Press, 1983.

Other

The City of Sydney: Official Guide. Sydney, City Council, 1959.
Facts about Sydney. Sydney, City Council, 1959.
Asia: A Select Reading List. Sydney, City Council, 1959.
Some Notes on the Early Land Grants at Potts Point. Sydney, City Council, 1959.
A History of the City of Sydney Public Library. Sydney, City Council, 1960.
Notes on the Glebe. Sydney, City Council, 1960.
Historical Notes on Paddington. Sydney, City Council, 1961.
Historical Notes on Newtown. Sydney, City Council, 1962.

*

Lilith Norman comments:

I managed to avoid becoming a writer for quite a long time, mainly, I think, because it seemed like very hard work for a very speculative result. It wasn't until I started working as a children's librarian that I realised *these* were the books I wanted to write. I was lucky, for as well as being perhaps the most rewarding and personal form of writing, it was also one of the most disciplined. And I believe discipline is the forgotten word of our times. Discipline in writing, to me, means honing your style, your rhythm and, most of all, your own thinking, 'til everything has a true sharp edge, as precise and delicate as a craftsman's tool. I like to write about ordinary children trying to cope, for I believe that most of us can cope with whatever is thrown at us, *if we really have to*—otherwise we'd all be living in caves still. I've written about realistic situations in *Climb a Lonely Hill* and *The Shape of Three* but I've written fantasy in *The Flame Takers*. And there's the rub! Having put a tentative toe in the great ocean of fantasy, everything else seems flat and commonplace. More recently I've discovered the deep satisfaction of writing picture book texts, where one has the opportunity of polishing the words as fully as one can.

* * *

If there is any theme common to Lilith Norman's very diverse books, it is the effect of environment on character. Her children are products of their backgrounds, which are quite different in every novel.

In *Climb a Lonely Hill* there is an almost totally deprived home where the mother's early death caused the father to squander what little money he had on drink. Jack, his teenage son, reacts to this by being conformist and reluctant to make decisions, whereas Susan, his daughter, is sharp and resourceful beyond her years. Yet when the children have to survive in the harsh outback after a car crash that kills their uncle, it is Jack who has to take command because Susan's foot is injured, and in the fight against heat, dust, thirst, and flies he finally learns initiative and with it self-respect.

The exploration of heredity and environment is central to *The Shape of Three.* Here fraternal twins Shane and Greg Herbert accidentally meet Bruce Cunningham, who is the exact replica of Greg. Subsequent investigation reveals that they were all born in Sydney on the same night but a hospital emergency had caused the babies to be muddled. Greg and Bruce are the true identical twins and Shane is the Cunningham. The climax of the story comes when the children are restored to their rightful families and bewildered Bruce finds himself in the hurly-burly of a large warm Roman Catholic lower-middle class home, whereas the bereft Shane has to adjust to being the only child of a wealthy Protestant estate-agent father and neurotic perfectionist mother. The convincing contrast drawn between the Herbert and Cunningham households highlights the poignancy of Bruce and Shane's dilemmas as they struggle not only with uprooting but with vague feelings of hereditary kinship for their new-found relatives.

The background of *The Flame Takers* is different again, and there is another original theme—that of the sudden and inexplicable dying of talent. Here not only professional actor parents but also their musical son suddenly lose their inspirational flame and become bourgeois and materialistic. These changes are somehow connected with a sadistic schoolmaster and a fat chess-playing German, but no real explanation is given, and the book's strengths lie less in plot than in the exploration of yet another type of family and of central Sydney rather than the suburbs of the previous novel.

A Dream of Seas is a totally different type of fantasy in which Norman sees legendary selkie—seal people—folklore in terms of the present-day Sydney surf-riding scene. A boy—whose real name is never given and who is known only by his nickname of "Seasick"—feels drawn towards the sea, in which his father had drowned. In his daydreams seals and surfies are indistinguishable and when he himself gets a surfboard he paddles out to sea, feeling free of his mother who has re-married and is expecting another child. Throughout the book there are flashes to a young shadow seal and its mother that echo the relationship between the boy and his mother, until the final pages when the boy and the shadow seal become one and a child cries, "Look, Mum. Look at the sea!"

There could hardly be a stronger contrast than between this book and *My Simple Little Brother,* humorously written in the first-person Australian vernacular by the elder brother of five-year-old Fieldsy. Fieldsy's problem is that he takes metaphorical sayings literally and each chapter is a separate episode of his interpretation of such sayings as "turning the tables," "the wrong end of the stick," or "throwing the baby away with the bath water."

The Laurel & Hardy Kids continues Norman's exploration of different families when the daughter of a solo mother finds herself involved with the son of a large and impecunious family. The story's main theme is the love/hate relationship between the two, but there are considerable digressions into the feminist life of the mother and the "trendy" assumptions of her companions.

With *The Paddock* comes a return to Norman's love of the Australian landscape. This poetically written picture book looks at a plot of land from its initial formation from lava, through the times of the dinosaurs, to the hunting, then pastoral, and finally urban usage. The soil of the paddock is soured and killed, but time is on its side and it will ultimately regenerate.

Norman has shown courage and originality in tackling unusual subjects. She has a keen ear for Australian speech patterns and dialogue. She is an astute observer, and whether depicting people or places, she accurately portrays the diversity of an emerging nation in a time-worn continent.

—Betty Gilderdale

NORTH, Sterling

Nationality: American. **Born:** Near Edgerton, Wisconsin, 4 November 1906. **Education:** University of Chicago, A.B. 1929. **Family:** Married Gladys Buchanan in 1927; one son and one daughter. **Career:** Reporter, 1929-31, and literary editor, 1932-43, Chicago *Daily News;* literary editor, New York *Post,* 1943-49, and New York *World Telegram and Sun,* 1949-56; founding editor, North Star Books, Houghton Mifflin, publishers, Boston, 1957-64. **Died:** 21 December 1974.

Publications for Children

Fiction

The Five Little Bears, illustrated by Clarence Biers and Hazel Frazee. Chicago, Rand McNally, 1935; London, Shaw, 1940.

The Zipper ABC Book, illustrated by Keith Ward. Chicago, Rand McNally, 1937.

Greased Lightning, illustrated by Kurt Wiese. Philadelphia, Winston, 1940.

Midnight and Jeremiah, illustrated by Kurt Wiese. Philadelphia, Winston, 1943.

The Birthday of Little Jesus, illustrated by Valenti Angelo. New York, Grosset and Dunlap, 1952; Manchester, World Distributors, 1953.

Son of the Lamp-Maker: The Story of a Boy Who Knew Jesus, illustrated by Manning Lee. Chicago, Rand McNally, 1956.

Rascal: A Memoir of a Better Era, illustrated by John Schoenherr. New York, Dutton, 1963; as *Rascal: The True Story of a Pet Raccoon,* London, Hodder and Stoughton, 1963; abridged edition, as *Little Rascal,* New York, Dutton, 1965; Leicester, Brockhampton Press, 1966.

The Wolfling, illustrated by John Schoenherr. New York, Dutton, 1969; London, Heinemann, 1970.

Other

Abe Lincoln: Log Cabin to White House, illustrated by Lee Ames. New York, Random House, 1956.

George Washington, Frontier Colonel, illustrated by Lee Ames. New York, Random House, 1957.

Young Thomas Edison, illustrated by William Barss. Boston, Houghton Mifflin, 1958.

Thoreau of Walden Pond, illustrated by Harve Stein. Boston, Houghton Mifflin, 1959.

Captured by the Mohawks and Other Adventures of Radisson, illustrated by Victor Mays. Boston, Houghton Mifflin, 1960.

Mark Twain and the River, illustrated by Victor Mays. Boston, Houghton Mifflin, 1961.

The First Steamboat on the Mississippi, illustrated by Victor Mays. Boston, Houghton Mifflin, 1962.

PUBLICATIONS FOR ADULTS

Novels

Midsummer Madness. New York, Grosset and Dunlap, 1933.

Tiger. Chicago, Reilly and Lee, 1933.

Plowing on Sunday. New York, Macmillan, 1934.

Night Outlasts the Whippoorwill. New York, Macmillan, 1936; London, Cobden Sanderson, 1937.

Seven Against the Years. New York, Macmillan, 1939.

So Dear to My Heart. New York, Doubleday, 1947; London, Odhams Press, 1949.

Reunion on the Wabash. New York, Doubleday, 1952.

Poetry

(*Poems*). Chicago, University of Chicago Press, 1925.

Other

The Pedro Gorino: The Adventures of a Negro Sea-Captain in Africa, with Harry Dean. Boston, Houghton Mifflin, 1929; as *Umbala,* London, Harrap, 1929.

The Writings of Mazo De La Roche. Boston, Little Brown, n.d.

Being a Literary Map of These United States Depicting a Renaissance No Less Astonishing Than That of Periclean Athens or Elizabethan London, with Gladys North, map by Frederic J. Donseif. New York, Putnam, 1942.

Hurry Spring! New York, Dutton, 1966.

Raccoons Are the Brightest People. New York, Dutton, 1966; as *The Raccoons of My Life,* London, Hodder and Stoughton, 1967.

Editor, with Carl Kroch, *So Red the Nose; or, Breath in the Afternoon: Literary Cocktails* (recipes). New York, Farrar and Rinehart, 1935.

Editor, with C.B. Boutell, *Speak of the Devil: An Anthology of the Appearances of the Devil in the Literature of the Western World.* New York, Doubleday, 1945.

*

Manuscript Collections: Boston University Library.

* * *

Exceptional children's books are often by authors who do not customarily write for young audiences. Sterling North's *Rascal* and *The Wolfling* are prime examples. The latter touches upon the hardships of frontier life, but stresses its pleasures, especially the pleasures of companioning with a creature who is part wolf, part dog. This well-crafted "documentary novel" is as idyllic in tone as the author's masterpiece, *Rascal,* but less complex in its overall texture. *Rascal* is a pastoral drama about a child and a raccoon; but, more important, the surface plot is a means for picturing a region, an era, and an unusual family. The simplified edition, *Little Rascal,* is too attenuated to be anything more than a mundane memoir.

The narration of *Rascal* is a shrewd mixture of child and adult points of view. A raccoon kit is captured by two Wisconsin boys during World War I. Both the diction and action convey the perspective of childhood as Sterling warns his friend, "You'll get a licking when you get home," and Oscar puts up a bold front: "Ishkabibble, I should worry!" When Sterling describes his Saint Bernard, time has subtly shifted and we see an adult perspective and prose style: "Wowser never started a fight, but after being challenged, badgered, and insulted, he eventually would turn his worried face and great sad eyes upon his tormenter, and more in sorrow than in anger, grab the intruder by the scruff of the neck, and toss him into the gutter." The parallel between human and animal offspring has symbolic as well as dramatic importance. Sterling is indulged by his father to the point where he can build his 18-foot canoe in the living room; Rascal is pampered as a baby would be pampered (dining with the adults, sharing Sterling's bed). In adulthood, Rascal leaves his human family to find a mate, while the boy faces a more demanding kind of maturity—even the subordination of his own desires for the sake of others. The reader feels the simultaneous sadness and triumph in growing up when Sterling is able to say finally: "Do as you please, my little Raccoon; it's your life."

The language of the novel underpins the symbolic comparisons. Animals are personified (as when Wowser has a "worried face") and, conversely, the boy is depicted as very close to the animal world. Sterling's deceased mother schooled him as a naturalist, and the meticulous training of pets helps the child deal with his bereavement. Characterization is developed through surface action and in deeper ways. The protagonist puzzles over his mother's death, but the reader is able to fill out the family portraits with information that the boy is not himself conscious of. For example, we learn that his father removed himself from the premises when each of his four children were born. Sterling doesn't see this as a clue to his father's overall personality, but the reader relates this information to the scenes in which Sterling is left alone with his pet. Indirectly we see the father's compulsion to withdraw from his parental role. The pressures on the father are not stated explicitly. The general cultural setting suggests what they might be: a war that sends one son to the trenches; a burgeoning industrial ization that places commerce at the hub of existence; a rigidly conformist tendency in some neighbors and family members.

The textural complexity in *Rascal* is developed through a mixture of modes—a blend of the realistic, romantic, and local color traditions. Countervailing moods enrich the story because it is both a celebration and a lamentation. After evoking the bliss of childhood freedom, North subtly separates the naive realm of nature from the enigmatic realm of human history. By the time Sterling and Rascal are separated in a literal sense, the reader has enjoyed the thematic depth and psychological veracity which make a novel memorable.

—Donnarae MacCann

NORTON, Mary

Nationality: British. **Born:** Mary Pearson, London, 10 December 1903. **Education:** St. Margaret's Convent, East Grinstead, Sussex. **Family:** Married 1) Robert C. Norton in 1926, two daughters and two sons; 2) Lionel Bonsey in 1970. **Career:** Actress, Old Vic Theatre Company, London, 1925-26; lived in Portugal, 1926-39; worked for the BBC, 1940, and the British Purchasing Company, New York, 1941; from 1942 actress in London. **Award:** Library Association Carnegie Medal, 1953. **Died:** 1992.

Publications for Children

Fiction

The Magic Bed-Knob; or, How to Become a Witch in Ten Easy Lessons, illustrated by Waldo Peirce. New York, Hyperion Press, 1943.

The Magic Bed-Knob, illustrated by Joan Kiddell-Monroe. London, Dent, 1945.

Bonfires and Broomsticks, illustrated by Mary Adshead. London, Dent, 1947.

The Borrowers, illustrated by Diana Stanley. London, Dent, 1952; New York, Harcourt Brace, 1953.

The Borrowers Afield, illustrated by Diana Stanley. London, Dent, and New York, Harcourt Brace, 1955.

Bedknob and Broomstick (revised versions of *The Magic Bed-Knob* and *Bonfires and Broomsticks*), illustrated by Erik Blegvad. London, Dent, and New York, Harcourt Brace, 1957.

The Borrowers Afloat, illustrated by Diana Stanley. London, Dent, and New York, Harcourt Brace, 1959.

The Borrowers Aloft, illustrated by Diana Stanley. London, Dent, and New York, Harcourt Brace, 1961.

Poor Stainless, illustrated by Diana Stanley. London, Dent, and New York, Harcourt Brace, 1971.

Are All the Giants Dead?, illustrated by Brian Froud. London, Dent, and New York, Harcourt Brace, 1975.

The Borrowers Avenged, illustrated by Pauline Baynes. London, Kestrel, and New York, Harcourt Brace, 1982.

The Borrowers Omnibus. London, Dent, 1990.

The Borrower's Activity Book. New York, Puffin, 1993.

* * *

With the Borrowers Mary Norton created a powerful mythology, which she clad in such circumstantial detail that these creatures now seem always to have been part of English folklore. This minuscule race, entirely dependent upon human beings, whom they suppose to have been created for their benefit—"Human beans are *for* borrowers—like bread's for butter"—are not fairies; they are earthly, practical material beings, who live by "borrowing" the morsels that careless humans leave around. "They thought," says the old woman who tells the child Kate their story, "that human beings were just invented to do the dirty work—great slaves put there for them to use. At least, that's what they told each other. But my brother said that, underneath, he thought they were frightened. It was because they were frightened, he thought, that they had grown so small. Each generation had become smaller and smaller, and more and more hidden." By the time Kate hears their story they have vanished forever.

Pod, Homily and Arrietty, Uncle Hendreary, Aunt Lupy, the cousins Timmis and Eggletina—their very names are borrowed, and oddly changed in the borrowing. They echo human follies and delusions (though Norton achieves her object without Swiftian savagery), and ultimately, in their never-ending quest for permanency, the human predicament. "I only wanted her to know we were *safe,*" Arrietty says of her human friend at the end of *The Borrowers Avenged.* "Peagreen looked back at her. He was smiling his quizzical, one-sided smile. 'Are we?' he said gently. 'Are we? Ever?'"

Adults may read the five books as a parable of the human condition or of the wanderings of the homeless and stateless of this century; children, while probably recognizing their poignance, read them for the excellence of the stories, and for the marvellous ingenuity of the practical detail, for a world observed from the height of six inches. We never see the Borrowers achieve the stability for which they crave. At the end of *The Borrowers* they are driven out from their home under the kitchen floorboards in the big old house by all the terror that humans can devise—gas, dogs, ferrets—and are last seen fleeing through the fields. *The Borrowers Afield* takes up the story of their flight, describes their life in the open air with the winter closing in on them as they vainly look for Borrower relations to give them shelter. In *The Borrowers Afloat* they have to leave the gamekeeper's cottage where they have taken refuge because the house is to be shut up, and without its occupants they would starve. Escaping by a drain they voyage downstream in an old kettle looking again for shelter. In *The Borrowers Aloft* they have settled in a model village but are wrenched away by greedy humans who observe them moving among the village's plaster residents, and hope to make a fortune out of putting them on show. They escape by means of a balloon contrived out of the materials they find in their attic-prison, but though they make their way home to Little Fordham they know that there is no longer safety there, that once more they must set out on their quest. 21 years after this last was written *The Borrowers Avenged* takes up their story at the moment when they are leaving their village. They find a new resting-place behind a grate in the nearby Old Rectory. But the reader knows, as do the Borrowers, that it cannot last.

The characters of the three Borrowers, the parents Pod and Homily, their daughter Arrietty, 13 at the beginning of the saga, nearly 17 when it ends, are subtly drawn: Pod the bread-winner, sturdy, brave, dependable, but limited in his outlook by lack of learning and a profound conservatism; Homily the home-maker, anxiously genteel, looking on with shocked horror, tinged with no little envy, at such Borrower families as the Overmantels with their wild and worldly ways, terrified of the world beyond the floorboards; and Arrietty, the questing spirit, who, though loyal and affectionate, has aspirations and longings that her scandalized parents find unnatural, longings for the blue sky, and open air, and space where she can climb and run, and, even more dangerous, an urge to talk to, and even befriend, human beings. She wants to tell her father, but in his view and that of her mother it was still a disgrace, almost a tragedy, to be "seen"; to them it meant broken homes, wearisome treks across unexplored country, and the labour of building anew. "No good never really came to no one from any human bean," says Pod roundly, though it is typical of the humour of the books that in *The Borrowers* he does show himself regularly to bed-ridden Aunt Sophy who drinks a decanter of Fine Old Pale Madeira every night and after the first three glasses never believes in anything she sees.

This sort of humour also pervades *Bedknob and Broomstick,* the story of Miss Price, that excellent English gentlewoman who is also an amateur witch but rather undecided about the ethics of what she is doing, and *Are All the Giants Dead?,* a fantasy about the hereafter of fairytale characters, both entertaining stories but without the depth of the Borrower books.

—Gillian Avery

NWAPA, Flora

Nationality: Nigerian. **Born:** Florence Nwanzuruahu Nkiru Nwapa, Ogutu, East Central State, 18 January 1931. **Education:** Archdeacon Crowther's Memorial Girls' School, Elelenwa, 1945-48; Church Missionary Society Girls' School, Lagos, 1949-50; Queen's College, Lagos, 1951; University College, Ibadan, 1953-57; University of Edinburgh, 1957-58, B.A. (London) 1957, Dip. Ed. (Edinburgh) 1958. **Family:** Married Gogo Nwakuche in 1967; three children. **Career:** Woman education officer, Calabar, 1958; teacher, Queen's School, Enugu, 1959-62; assistant registrar (public relations), University of Lagos, 1962-67; commissioner and member of the Executive Council, East Central State, 1970-75: with ministries of Health and Social Welfare; Lands, Survey, and Urban Development; and Establishments. Since 1978 managing director, Tana Press Ltd. and Flora Nwapa and Company, Enugu. **Agent:** David Bolt Associates, 12 Heath Drive, Send, Surrey GU23 7EP, England. **Address:** Tana Press Ltd., 2-A Menkiti Lane, Ogui, Enugu, Nigeria.

Publications for Children

Fiction

Emeka, Driver's Guard, illustrated by Roslyn Isaacs. London, University of London Press, 1972.
Mammywater, illustrated by Obiora Udechukwu. Enugu, Tana Press, 1979.
Journey to Space, illustrated by Chinwe Orieke. Enugu, Tana Press, 1980.
The Miracle Kittens, illustrated by Emeka Onwudinjo. Enugu, Tana Press, 1980.
The Adventures of Deke, illustrated by Obiora Udechukwu. Enugu, Tana Press, 1980.

Other

My Tana Colouring Book, illustrated by P.S.C. Igboanugo. Enugu, Tana Press, 1979.
My Animal Number Book, illustrated by Emeka Onwudinjo. Enugu, Tana Press, 1981.

Publications for Adults

Novels

Efuru. London, Heinemann, 1966.
Idu. London, Heinemann, 1970.
Never Again. Enugu, Nwamife, 1974.
One Is Enough. Enugu, Tana Press, 1982.
Women Are Different. Enugu, Tana Press, 1986.

Short Stories

This Is Lagos and Other Stories. Enugu, Nwankwo Ifejika, 1971.
Wives at War and Other Stories. Enugu, Tana Press, 1980.

Poetry

Cassava Song and Rice Song. Enugu, Tana Press, 1986.

* * *

Flora Nwapa began her literary career by writing stories for young girls. These stories were never published, but were developed into the novels about Nigerian women for which she has earned an international reputation as a fiction writer. Following the Nigerian Civil War, Nwapa resumed writing stories for children and founded a publishing company devoted to producing literature for children. As a publisher she has encouraged the writing of easy books for new readers and commissioned Nigerian artists to create picture books with Nigerian content that will teach Nigerian children to read and count.

Emeka, Driver's Guard, the first of Nwapa's children's books, appeared in the Modern English Readers Series. Like all stories in this series, it is didactic and moralistic. It educates children about the duties of a driver's guard and emphasizes the value of attending school and succeeding at academic studies. The plot about childhood hardships includes themes common to stories about orphans written by authors from all parts of the world. As in most African fiction published in Europe, the illustrations do not depict the Nigerian setting of the story.

All of Nwapa's other children's stories have been published in Nigeria. They incorporate, without explanation, facets of eastern Nigerian culture, including folklore, which are familiar to Nigerian children and include drawings by Nigerian artists that are integral to telling the stories.

Most of Nwapa's stories are in the Read It Yourself Series. As is characteristic of stories for new readers, Nwapa's are very simple and sometimes are little more than superficial Nigerian adaptations of common western types. *The Miracle Kittens* is such a story in which a cat and her kittens rid a house of rats after diverse human attempts all fail. It is the illustrations more than the words that give this story its Nigerian content. *Journey to Space,* in contrast, is a fantasy which incorporates elements of folklore about two Nigerian children who are carried by a lift through the roof of their apartment to the sky, where they meet a talking dog and fairies from the moon. Although the children never reach their goal, the moon, they enjoy their adventures in space before the fairies return them to their apartment and warn them not to play in the lift in the future.

Mammywater is Nwapa's only children's book in which the creative powers so evident in her adult fiction are fully utilized. The story is based on oral traditions about Mammy Water that are widely known in southern Nigeria and Cameroon. Like the female deities in Nwapa's novels, Mammy Water is a deity who resides in a lake. The story includes common themes about such deities: Mammywater takes humans to live with her, changes herself into many different forms, and has a home famous for its riches at the bottom of a lake. The fast-moving story told primarily in dialogue by two Nigerian children has a moral, too—humility is a valuable human characteristic.

As both a writer and publisher Nwapa is helping the development of Nigerian children's literature.

—Nancy J. Schmidt

NYE, Robert

Nationality: British. **Born:** London, 15 March 1939. **Education:** Dormans Land, Surrey; Hamlet Court, Westcliff, Essex; Southend High School, Essex. **Family:** Married 1) Judith Pratt in 1959 (divorced 1967); three sons; 2) Aileen Campbell in 1968; one daughter, one stepdaughter, and one stepson. **Career:** Freelance writer, since 1961; poetry editor, the *Scotsman,* since 1967; poetry critic, *The Times,* since 1971; writer-in-residence, University of Edinburgh, 1976-77. **Awards:** Eric Gregory award, 1963, for *Juvenilia 2*; Scottish Arts Council bursary, 1970, 1973, and publication award, 1970, 1976; James Kennaway Memorial award, 1970, for *Tales I Told My Mother*; *Guardian* Fiction prize, 1976, and Hawthornden prize, 1977, both for *Falstaff*; Fellow, Royal Society of Literature, 1977; Society of Authors Travel Scholarship, 1991. **Agent:** Giles Gordon, Curtis Brown Ltd., 6 Ann Street, Edinburgh EH4 1PJ, Scotland. **Address:** Thornfield, Kingsland, Ballinhassig, County Cork, Ireland.

Publications for Children

Fiction

Taliesin, illustrated by Sheila Hawkins. London, Faber, 1966; New York, Hill and Wang, 1967.

Wishing Gold, illustrated by Helen Craig. London, Macmillan, 1970; New York, Hill and Wang, 1971.

Poor Pumpkin, illustrated by Derek Collard. London, Macmillan, 1971; as *The Mathematical Princess and Other Stories,* New York, Hill and Wang, 1972.

Out of the World and Back Again, illustrated by Joanna Troughton. London, Collins, 1977; as *Out of This World and Back Again,* Indianapolis, Bobbs Merrill, 1978.

The Bird of the Golden Land, illustrated by Krystyna Turska. London, Hamish Hamilton, 1980.

Harry Pay the Pirate. London, Hamish Hamilton, 1981.

Three Tales (includes *Beowulf, Wishing Gold, Taliesin*). London, Hamish Hamilton, 1983.

Lord Fox and Other Spine-Chilling Tales, illustrated by Sophy Williams. London, Orion, 1997.

Other (retellings)

March Has Horse's Ears, illustrated by Sheila Hawkins. London, Faber, 1966; New York, Hill and Wang, 1967.

Bee Hunter: Adventures of Beowulf, illustrated by Aileen Campbell. London, Faber, 1968; as *Beowulf: A New Telling,* illustrated by Alan E. Cober, New York, Hill and Wang, 1968, and Turtleback/Demco Medea, 1990; as *Beowulf, The Bee Hunter,* Faber, 1972; as *Beowulf,* New York, Dell, 1982, and London, Orion, 1994.

Cricket: Three Stories, illustrated by Shelley Freshman. Indianapolis, Bobbs Merrill, 1975; as *Once upon Three Times,* London, Benn, 1978.

Publications for Adults

Novels

Doubtfire. London, Calder and Boyars, and New York, Hill and Wang, 1968.

Falstaff. London, Hamish Hamilton, and Boston, Little Brown, 1976.

Merlin. London, Hamish Hamilton, 1978; New York, Putnam, 1979.

Faust. London, Hamish Hamilton, 1980; New York, Putnam, 1981.

The Voyage of the Destiny. London, Hamish Hamilton, and New York, Putnam, 1982.

The Memoirs of Lord Byron: A Novel. London, Hamish Hamilton, 1989.

The Life and Death of My Lord Gilles de Rais. London, Hamish Hamilton, 1990.

Mrs. Shakespeare: The Complete Works. London, Sinclair-Stevenson, 1993.

The Late Mr. Shakespeare. London, Chatto & Windus, 1998.

Short Stories

Tales I Told My Mother. London, Calder and Boyars, 1969; New York, Hill and Wang, 1970; London, Marion Boyars, 1992.

Penguin Modern Stories 6, with others. London, Penguin, 1970.

The Facts of Life and Other Fictions. London, Hamish Hamilton, 1983.

Plays

Sawney Bean, with William Watson (produced Edinburgh, 1969; London, 1972; New York, 1982). London, Calder and Boyars, 1970.

Sisters (broadcast, 1969; produced Edinburgh, 1973). Included in *Penthesilea, Fugue, and Sisters,* 1975.

Penthesilea, adaptation of the play by Heinrich von Kleist (broadcast, 1971; produced London, 1983). Included in *Penthesilea, Fugue, and Sisters,* 1975.

The Seven Deadly Sins: A Mask, music by James Douglas (produced Stirling and Edinburgh, 1973). Rushden, Northamptonshire, Omphalos Press, 1974.

Mr. Poe (produced Edinburgh and London, 1974).
Penthesilea, Fugue, and Sisters. London, Calder and Boyars, 1975.

Radio Plays: *Sisters,* 1969; *A Bloody Stupit Hole,* 1970; *Reynolds, Reynolds,* 1971; *Penthesilea,* 1971; *The Devil's Jig,* with Humphrey Searle, from a work by Thomas Mann, 1980.

Poetry

Juvenilia 1. Northwood, Middlesex, Scorpion Press, 1961.
Juvenilia 2. Lowestoft, Suffolk, Scorpion Press, 1963.
Darker Ends. London, Calder and Boyars, and New York, Hill and Wang, 1969.
Agnus Dei. Rushden, Northamptonshire, Sceptre Press, 1973.
Two Prayers. Richmond, Surrey, Keepsake Press, 1974.
Five Dreams. Rushden, Northamptonshire, Sceptre Press, 1974.
Divisions on a Ground. Manchester, Carcanet, 1976.
A Collection of Poems, 1955-1988. London, Hamish Hamilton, 1989.
Collected Poems 1995. London, Sinclair-Stevenson, 1995.
Henry James and Other Poems. Manchester, Carcanet Press, and Edgewood, Kentucky, R. L. Barth, 1995.

Other

Editor, *A Choice of Sir Walter Ralegh's Verse.* London, Faber, 1972.
Editor, *William Barnes: A Selection of His Poems.* Cheadle, Cheshire, Carcanet, 1972.
Editor, *A Choice of Swinburne's Verse.* London, Faber, 1973.
Editor, *The Faber Book of Sonnets.* London, Faber, 1976; as *A Book of Sonnets,* New York, Oxford University Press, 1976.
Editor, *The English Sermon 1750-1850.* Manchester, Carcanet, 1976.
Editor, *The English Sermon.* Vol. 3, Manchester, Carcarnet, 1981.
Editor, *PEN New Poetry.* London, Quartet, 1986.
Editor, with Elizabeth Friedmann and Alan J. Clark, *First Awakenings: The Early Poems of Laura Riding.* New York, Persea Books, 1992; Manchester, Carcanet, 1992.
Editor, *A Selection of the Poems of Laura Riding.* Manchester, Carcanet, 1994; New York, Persea Books, 1997.

*

Manuscript Collections: University of Edinburgh; University of Texas, Austin; National Library of Scotland, Edinburgh; Colgate University, Hamilton, New York.

Robert Nye comments:

I started to write stories to amuse myself when I was not writing poems. These stories were always intended to amuse others besides myself, although in effect I have noticed that it is mostly poets who tend to be amused by them. This might be because, plain or purl, they are so much storytelling stuff, tales rather than "short stories," and poets preserve a liking for such simplicities, or because they are composed upon certain verbal principles and patterns not all that different from some of the procedures of poetic composition. I have also tried my hand at the same kind of telling for children, sometimes in direct translation or interpretation, as in *Beowulf* (1968), sometimes by reworking old material to make it new, as with *Wishing Gold* (1970). My task as a writer of stories I take to be the writing of a single story which might amuse poets *and* children.

* * *

Robert Nye is a Rabelaisian storyteller of reckless heroes, feckless kings, vampire-ridden fens, and headless horses. Widows play chess with blackbirds, a king grows horse's ears, and failed suitors get beheaded. His abiding interest in ancient, usually Welsh and Celtic, myths and legends has produced imaginative retellings of Beowulf, Merlin, and Taliesin. Enormous respect for the possibilities of words pervades his work, and his imagery is simple but vivid, conveying the joys of climbing, sailing, dreaming, loving, and becoming a hare. Both qualities compel the reader to think imaginatively about quotidian life. In one instance, "Even the light had a brief look about it, as though it were a trespasser." In another, a boy sees a buzzard, flying high, "like a full-stop scratched on the sun."

The plots of Nye's retellings, so essential to young readers, are carefully preserved and straightforward. Creativity comes in his ability to make Taliesin's story both powerful and humorous, and to render Beowulf an accessible hero to modern readers. Indeed, by a small twist of narrative or an unexpected line of dialogue, old heroes are given more humanity and realism, most notably in *Bee Hunter* and *March Has Horse's Ears.* Magic has its place, but is generally kept in check by elementary human needs. The villainous Unferth "began gnawing at his finger nails. They tasted of dirt and where he had been poking at his boil. Unferth hated the taste of himself, but he had to have it." Such figures relate to recognizable loneliness, unpopularity, and the humor and tensions of family and communal life, even in the midst of the most grandiose exploits. Panting from slaying the dragon, for instance, Beowulf develops toothache; the great poet Taliesin shows sly, schoolboy mischief. A dragon may have a legitimate grievance, a villain or monster have pathos, and a golden warrior reveal flaws. The rhythms, adroit repetitions, and the unusual words carefully planted, make these stories excellent for reading aloud. *Wishing Gold* perfectly confirms this.

—Peter Vansittart, updated by Rebecca R. Saulsbury

O

OAKLEY, Graham

Nationality: British. **Born:** Shrewsbury, Shropshire, 27 August 1929. **Education:** At a grammar school; Warrington Art School, Lancashire, 1950. **Career:** Scenic artist in various repertory companies, 1950-55, and at Royal Opera House, London, 1955-57; staff member, Crawford Advertising Agency, 1960-62; designer, BBC Television, London, 1962-77. Since 1977 freelance writer and illustrator. **Address:** c/o Macmillan Children's Books, 4 Little Essex Street, London WC2R 3LF, England.

Publications for Children (illustrated by the author)

Fiction

The Church Mouse. London, Macmillan, and New York, Atheneum, 1972.
The Church Cat Abroad. London, Macmillan, and New York, Atheneum, 1973.
The Church Mice and the Moon. London, Macmillan, and New York, Atheneum, 1974.
The Church Mice Spread Their Wings. London, Macmillan, 1975; New York, Atheneum, 1976.
The Church Mice Adrift. London, Macmillan, 1976; New York, Atheneum, 1977.
The Church Mice at Bay. London, Macmillan, 1978; New York, Atheneum, 1979.
Magical Changes. London, Macmillan, 1979; New York, Atheneum, 1980.
The Church Mice at Christmas. London, Macmillan, and New York, Atheneum, 1980.
Hetty and Harriet. London, Macmillan, 1981; New York, Atheneum, 1982.
The Church Mice in Action. London, Macmillan, 1982; New York, Atheneum, 1983.
Henry's Quest. London, Macmillan, and New York, Atheneum, 1986.
The Diary of a Church Mouse. London, Macmillan, 1986; New York, Atheneum, 1987.
The Church Mice Chronicles. London, Macmillan, 1986.
Once Upon a Time: A Prince's Fantastic Journey. London, Macmillan, 1990.
More Church Mice Chronicles. London, Macmillan, 1990.
The Church Mice and the Ring. London, Macmillan, and New York, Atheneum, 1992.
The Foxbury Force. London, Macmillan, 1994.

*

Illustrator: *Monsters and Marlinspikes* by Hugh Popham, 1958; *Kidnapped* by Robert Louis Stevenson, 1960; *Discovering the Bible* by David Scott Daniell, 1961; *The King of the Golden River* by John Ruskin, 1961; *White Horizons* by Charles Kervern, 1962; *The Three Feathers,* 1963, *Skillywidden,* 1965, and *The Bird-Catcher and the Crow-Peri,* 1968, all by Mollie Clarke; *The White Dragon,* 1963, and *Jack of Dover,* 1966, both by Richard Garnett; *Grandmother's Footsteps* by Patricia Ledward, 1966; *Stories Told round the World* by Taya Zinkin, 1968; *The Ancient World* by Robert Ogilvie, 1969; *The Water Wheel* by Brian Read, 1970; *The Dragon Hoard* by Tanith Lee, 1971; *The Two Sisters* by Elizabeth MacDonald, 1975.

* * *

Graham Oakley belongs to the growing band of author/artists whose books are conceived as a single entity, words and pictures sharing the burden of the story. Unusually for one who is an artist first and a writer second, he does not make the mistake of simply trying to get away with as few words as possible, regardless of their quality. Such deceptive simplicity is as difficult to carry off successfully as anything a writer can be asked to do. Instead, Oakley writes as he draws, with a wealth of incidental detail and asides. Pictures and text are used equally to embellish and advance the tale he has to tell, his one guiding principle being never to repeat the identical joke in both media.

Except for one excursion into total wordlessness with *Magical Changes,* where the pages are divided horizontally on the time-honoured principle of "heads, bodies, and legs," to produce a set of fantastic variations on the original pictures, he has remained faithful to the setting ad characters introduced in his first book, *The Church Mouse.* Arthur, the mouse of the title, inhabits a splendid church, filled with Victorian gothic ornament. "Sampson, the church cat, had listened to so many sermons about the meek being blessed and everybody really being brothers that he had grown quite frighteningly meek and treated Arthur just like a brother." But, though in no danger, Arthur is lonely and tired of a diet of choirboys' sweets. He solves this problem by persuading the vicar to let him bring in the rest of the town's mice, with a promise that the mice will keep the church tidy in return for a weekly ration of cheese. Their ensuing adventures range from trapping a burglar (Sampson helps the mice tie his shoelaces together and roll him in the carpet) to sabotaging the Wortlethorpe Municipal Moon Programme (*The Church Mice and the Moon*) and getting rid of an undesirable curate (*The Church Mice at Bay*). Inevitably in a series of this kind, not all the books reach the consistently high standard of the first. Some of the plots strain credulity too far. *The Church Cat Abroad* even sees Sampson and two of the mice marooned on a desert island. But in every case the narrative and pictures combine to give the books an enjoyable satirical edge, appreciated by adults as well as children. The scientists of WOMUMP are horrified when their television screen apparently reveals an archangel with a trumpet on the way to the moon—really a tombstone glimpsed overhead as Sampson and the mice tow the rescued astronauts back to the vestry—and delighted when the moon itself seems actually to be made of cheese. Festive television screens, in *The Church Mice at Christmas,* show nothing but violence. A captured burglar reclines at ease in his cell, being fed tea and Christmas cake by a paper-hatted copper. All these details, adding richness and interest to the main story, are an integral part of Oakley's distinctive style and help to give his books a more long-lasting appeal than the general run of picture books.

—Anne Carter

ODAGA, Asenath (Bole)

Nationality: Kenyan. **Born:** Rarieda, 5 July 1938. **Education:** Ngiya Girls School, 1950-52; Alliance Girls High School, Kikuyu, 1953-54; Kikuyu Teacher Training College, 1955-56; University of Nairobi, 1971-74, B.A. (honours) in literature 1974, Dip. Ed. 1974, M.A. 1981. **Family:** Married James Charles Odaga in 1958; five children. **Career:** Tutor, Church Missionary Society Teacher Training College, Ngiya, 1957-58; teacher, Butere Girls School, 1959-60; founder and first headmistress, Nyakach Girls School, 1961-63; assistant secretary, Kenya Dairy Board, Nairobi, 1965-67; secretary, Kenya Library Services, Nairobi, 1968; advertising assistant, *East African Standard* newspaper and Kerr Downey and Selby Safaris, both Nairobi, 1969-70; assistant director of the curriculum development programme, Christian Churches Educational Association, Nairobi, 1974- 75; research fellow, Institute of African Studies, University of Nairobi, 1976-82. Professional writer, editor, Lake publisher, and researcher, from 1982. Founding member of Writers Association of Kenya; chairperson, Children's Literature Association of Kenya, from 1988; affiliated to International Board on Books for Young People. **Addresses:** P.O. Box 1743, Kisumu, Kenya; Chairperson, Gender and Development Centre, P.O. Box 1588, Kisumu, Kenya.

Publications for Children

Fiction

Jande's Ambition, illustrated by Adrienne Moore. Nairoi, East African Publishing House, 1966.
The Secret of the Monkey Rock, illustrated by William Agutu. London, Nelson, 1966.
The Diamond Ring, illustrated by Adrienne Moore. Nairobi, East African Publishing House, 1967.
The Angry Flames, illustrated by Adrienne Moore. Nairobi, East African Publishing House, 1968.
Sweets and Sugar Cane (short stories), illustrated by Beryl Moore. Nairobi, East African Publishing House, 1969.
The Villager's Son, illustrated by Shyam Varma. London, Heinemann, 1971.
Kip on the Farm, illustrated by Beryl Moore. Nairobi, East African Publishing House, 1972.
Kip at the Coast, illustrated by Gay Galsworthy. London, Evans, 1977.
Kip Goes to the City, illustrated by Gay Galsworthy. London, Evans, 1977.
The Storm, illustrated by Njoroge. Kisumu, Lake, 1986.
The Rag Ball, illustrated by Jos Odaga. Kisumu, Lake, 1987.
Munde Goes to the Market, illustrated by Peter Odaga. Kisumu, Lake, 1987.
Munde and His Friends, illustrated by Peter Odaga. Kisumu, Lake, 1987.
The Silver Cup, illustrated by Peter Odaga. Kisumu, Lake, 1988.
A Night on a Tree, illustrated by Jos Odaga. Kisumu, Lake, 1991.
Ogilo and the Hippo, illustrated by Kirui. Nairobi, Heinemann, 1991.
The Cloud Boy. Kisumu, Lake, 1994.
The Honey River. Kisumu, Lake, 1994.
The Night Runners, illustrated by Alice Ahelo, Kisumu, Lake, 1998.

Other (in Luo language)

Poko Nyar Mugumba (Poko Mugumba's Daughter), illustrated by Sophia Ojienda. Nairobi, Foundation, 1978.
Sigendini gi Timbe Luo Moko (Stories and Some Customs of the Luo), illustrated by Alice Odaga. Kisumu, Lake, 1982.
Ogilo Nungo Piny Kirom. Nairobi, Heinemann, 1983.
Kisera (Courtship; novel). Kisumu, Lake, 1997.

Other (folktales)

The Hare's Blanket and Other Tales, illustrated by Adrienne Moore. Nairobi, East African Publishing House, 1967.
Thu Tinda: Stories from Kenya. Nairobi, Uzima Press, 1980.
The Two Friends, illustrated by Barrack Omondi. Nairobi, Bookwise, 1981.
Kenyan Folk Tales, illustrated by Margaret Humphries. Caithness, Scotland, Humphries, 1981.

Editor, with David Kirui and David Crippen, *God, Myself, and Others.* Nairobi, Evangel, 1976.

Publications for Adults

Novels

The Shade Changes. Kisumu, Lake, 1984.
Between the Years. Kisumu, Lake, 1987.
A Bridge in Time. Kisumu, Lake, 1987.
Riana. Kisumu, Lake, 1988.
Love Tale. Kisumu, Lake, 1994.
Endless Road, Kisumu, Lake, 1995.

Short Stories

Rosa, Love, Ash, With Other Stories. Kisumu, Lake, 1982.

Plays

Miaha (The Bride; produced Nairobi, 1981; Luo language only).
Simbi Nyaima (The Sunken Village; produced Kisumu, 1982). Kisumu, Lake, 1983 (Luo and English languages).
African Radio Plays, with others, edited by Woffram Frommlet. (English language only) N.p., Nomos, 1991.
Nyaimgondho the Son of Oubere (Luo and English). Kisumu, Lake, 1996.

Other

Nyathini Koa e Nyuolne Nyaka Higni Adek (in Luo: Your Child from Birth to Age Three). Nairobi, Evangel, 1976.
Oral Literature: A School Certificate Course, with A. Bole Odaga and S. Kichamu Akivaga. Nairobi, Heinemann, 1982.
Yesterday's Today: The Study of Oral Literature. Kisumu, Lake 1984.
Literature for Children and Young People in Kenya. Nairobi, Kenya Literature Bureau, 1985.
Basic Luo-English Words and Phrases, Kisumu, Lake, 1993.
Luo-English, English-Luo Dictionary. Kisumu, Lake, 1994.
Luo Sayings and Proverbs, Kisumu, Lake, 1995.

Asenath Odaga comments:

My writing is for members of my society: adults and children. It is about their daily experiences and involvement with life. The bits and pieces that fit into the stream of their existence and make their life whole are interesting to read about, and it is from these bits that I try to create realistic and objective work. Apart from entertaining my readers, I also try to be true to the African belief that art is never indulged in just for its aesthetic value, but is seen as something with practical uses to the people. I therefore believe my readers can also benefit from my works in these other ways.

For children, apart from writing about what they are familiar and can identify with, I collect stories that were told and still are told orally among the various peoples of Kenya. These oral narratives are interesting and entertaining, but they are also educative and instructive. They embody the wisdom and philosophy of our ancestors which are our children's heritage, a heritage to which children should have access through the written word, since it is no longer possible to follow the traditional methods of telling and preserving that heritage.

Many young people are often eager to find out from me how I began to write and how I get all those things I write about and whether I can teach them how to write. In fact, some of them imagine writers to be extraordinary and totally different from normal human beings. As a result they are surprised when they find me to be a very ordinary person.

Writing is skill and like other skills it can be taught, but probably more easily to those with a flair of writing. All they need is a few lessons on writing techniques and cetain important guidelines to be observed while writing. One other thing I often tell my young readers who wish to become writers is that writing like all the other skills needs practice consistently in order to be improved. My guiding rule over the years has been to read all sorts of writing: good, bad, trash, and so forth, from all kinds of writers. In this way I am able to learn what topics and issues different writers tackle from the East, West, North, and South and, of course, from my own country, Kenya, and the continent of Africa.

* * *

Asenath Odaga is a prominent Kenyan children's writer and publisher of materials in English and Luo. She believes that Kenyan children should start their education by reading literature about "the close and familiar things forming their lives." Her fiction for younger children focuses on children's daily activities at home or school and especially on oral traditions, many of which she has collected, whereas her young adult fiction concentrates on urban settings, social issues, and value conflicts that are commonplace in Africa.

Several of Odaga's children's books focus on Kenyan oral traditions. *Yesterday's Today* includes a broad selection of oral literature (tales, proverbs, riddles, tongue twisters, and songs) that Odaga collected throughout Kenya. This volume, intended for older children and the general public, is illustrated with photographs and includes exercises to increase the reader's understanding of oral literature. *The Hare's Blanket and Other Tales,* written for younger children, includes four rabbit trickster tales which are simple summaries of the original tales told largely in dialogue. In contrast, *Thu Tinda* includes fictionalized folktales that incorporate songs, extensive dialogue, and a patterned ending, retold for older children. Odaga has used her imagination in "modernizing" these tales. Odaga also writes adventure stories. Some, like *The Diamond Ring,* blend oral traditions with experiences from contemporary life. When the hero, a herd boy, goes to visit his grandfather, he obtains a protective charm from Black Wizard and a magic song from his mother. On his journey the hero encounters dwarves, giants, snakes, and dangerous animals, and passes through a town that has cars, lorries, and houses similar to those he is familiar with, but the people speak a strange language and hold him prisoner. He escapes from all dangers through wit, cunning, protective charms, and his magic song. The hero wonders if he has been dreaming, but his grandfather confirms that the strange people are Kande, and tells him about their activities in the old days.

Other adventure stories, especially those for young adults, focus on contemporary urban life, but incorporate traditional customs and lifestyles. *The Shade Changes,* for example, is a detective story set in Mombasa, about a marriage of convenience of a young woman to an older man who is her father's business partner, in which the bride is kidnapped and her father's house is robbed of wealth gained illegally. The characters are motivated by conflicting sets of values that focus on "traditional" family values and contemporary urban values of wealth and status which are familiar to young adults in Africa. Like all Odaga's fiction, this story has lessons to teach, but it is not explicitly didactic. It is a well- crafted adventure story.Most of Odaga's fiction written for younger children *is* explicitly didactic. The short stories collected in *Sweets and Sugar Cane* and the series of Kip books are educational stories that describe such adventures as helping on the farm, going to market, molding clay figures, playing games, and taking trips to Nairobi by car or train. *Jande's Ambition* is an autobiographical schoolgirl story that describes the life of a western Kenyan girl from early childhood until she enrolls in teacher training college. Experiences familiar to Kenyan and other African school children such as difficulty earning school fees, failing exams, and conflict between family responsibilities and attending school are included in this fast-moving story told largely in dialogue.

Odaga writes a wide variety of literature for children of all ages. The popularity of her books in Kenya reflects her skill at creating interesting and exciting stories based on people, places, events, and traditions with which they are familiar.

—Nancy J. Schmidt

O'FAOLAIN, Eileen

Nationality: Irish. **Born:** Eileen Gould, Cork in 1902. **Education:** University College, Cork. **Family:** Married the writer Sean O'Faolain in 1928; one daughter (the writer Julia O'Faolain) and one son. **Died:** 1988.

PUBLICATIONS FOR CHILDREN

Fiction

The Little Black Hen, illustrated by Trefor Jones. London, Oxford University Press, and New York, Random House, 1940; as *The Fairy Hen,* Dublin, Parkside Press, 1945.

The King of the Cats, illustrated by Nano Reid. Dublin, Talbot Press, 1941; New York, Morrow, 1942.
Miss Pennyfeather and the Pooka, illustrated by Nora McGuinness. Dublin, Browne and Nolan, 1942; New York, Random House, 1946.
The Children of Crooked Castle. Dublin, Browne and Nolan, 1945.
May Eve in Fairyland. Dublin, Parkside Press, 1945.
Miss Pennyfeather in the Springtime, illustrated by Muriel Brandt. Dublin, Browne and Nolan, 1946.
The Shadowy Man, illustrated by Phoebe Llewellyn Smith. London, Longman, 1949.
The White Rabbit's Road, illustrated by Phoebe Llewellyn Smith. London, Longman, 1950.
High Sang the Sword, illustrated by Brian Wildsmith. London, Oxford University Press, 1959.

Other (retellings)

Irish Sagas an Folk-Tales, illustrated by Joan Kiddell-Monroe. London, Oxford University Press, and New York, Walck, 1954.
Children of the Salmon and Other Irish Folktales, illustrated by Trina Schart Hyman. London, Longman, and Boston, Little Brown, 1965.

* * *

Eileen O'Faolain's output is almost entirely in the realms of fairytale, fantasy, and retellings of old sagas and myths from Irish folklore. It is not a large output, but in the context of Irish children's literature it is significant. It spans several decades and provided during World War II and the immediate post-war period in Ireland a literature which spoke to children in a familiar language and showed them that adventure and fairy are only just around the corner. Like some of the very best of children's stories, they were written with a specific child in mind—Julia, the author's daughter.All of her stories have an element of fantasy and in every instance the fantasy and magic are wrought through the animal world. Enchanted animals are the link between the real world and that of fairy—hens, cats, dogs, donkeys, and foals are the key to a magic world, a world which even they fear and respect. Even in the Miss Pennyfeather stories, which revolve around an eccentric old lady living by the River Lee in Cork, animals are important and can act and speak as humans some of the time. Like Patricia Lynch, by whom she was overshadowed, O'Faolain was attuned to the rhythms and lore of the old storytellers. She recounted how the core of the story of *The Little Black Hen,* long a firm favourite with her readers, was given to her by an old shanchie or storyteller. He was in conversation with the author one day and pointing to distant hills commented, "The fairies are in a bad way this long time. The Queen is dead. Ah, but that Cliona was always a bad queen." From this chance comment came the story of Cossey Darg who is captured by Cliona and made to work in the royal kitchens beneath the fairy fort, and of the children Julie and Garret who set about rescuing her and the other bewitched creatures. By the end of the story all that remains from the fairy world is the little mob cap which in her excitement the little hen forgets to remove. Finding it the old woman Biddy comments: "They believe it now. But later on, when they grow up, they won't believe it. I'll keep this little cap to show them, then—and they will know that it all really happened, and that it wasn't just one of old Biddy's silly fairy-stories after all, but the true story of Cossey Darg and the Queen of the Muskerry fairies." She has that little cap to this very day.

—Pat Donlon

O'HARA, Elizabeth. See **NÍ DHUIBHNE, Éilís.**

O'HARA (Alsop), Mary

Nationality: American. **Born:** Cape May Point, New Jersey, 10 July 1885. **Education:** Packer Institute, Brooklyn, New York. **Family:** Married 1) Kent K. Parrot in 1905 (divorced 1922), one daughter and one son; 2) Helge Sture-Vasa in 1922 (divorced 1947). **Career:** Writer and composer. **Died:** 15 October 1980.

Publications for Children

Fiction

My Friend Flicka. Philadelphia, Lippincott, 1941; London, Eyre and Spottiswoode, 1943.
Thunderhead. Philadelphia, Lippincott, 1943; London, Eyre and Spottiswoode, 1945.
Green Grass of Wyoming. Philadelphia, Lippincott, 1946; London, Eyre and Spottiswoode, 1947.
The Catch Colt (fictionalization of her stage play). London, Methuen, 1979.

Play

The Catch Colt, music by O'Hara (produced Washington D.C.). New York, Dramatists Play Service, 1964.

Publications for Adults

Novels

The Son of Adam Wingate. New York, McKay, and London, Eyre and Spottiswoode, 1952.
Wyoming Summer. New York, Doubleday, 1963.

Screenplays: *The Last Card,* with Molly Parro, 1921; *Life's Darn Funny,* with Arthur Ripley, 1921; *There Are No Villains,* 1921; *Turn to the Right,* with June Mathis, 1922; *The Prisoner of Zenda,* 1922; *Peg o' My Heart,* 1922; *The Age of Desire,* with Lenore Coffee and Dixie Willson, 1923; *Merry Go-Round,* with Finis Fox and Harvey Gates, 1923; *The Woman on the Jury,* 1924; *Braveheart,* 1925; *The Home Maker,* 1925; *The Honeymoon Express,* 1926; *Frames,* 1927; *Perch of the Devil,* 1927.

Other

Let Us Say Grace (as Mary Sture-Vasa). Boston, Christopher, 1930.
Novel-in-the-Making. New York, McKay, 1954.
A Musical in the Making. Chevy Chase, Maryland, Markane Publishing, 1966.
Flicka's Friend: The Autobiography of Mary O'Hara. New York, Putnam, 1982.

*

Music: *Esperan,* 1943; *May God Keep You,* 1946; *Wyoming Suite,* 1946; *Windharp;* and other works for piano.

* * *

Mary O'Hara's reputation as a children's author rests upon her trilogy of American ranch life, *My Friend Flicka, Thunderhead,* and *Green Grass of Wyoming.* Based on the author's experiences as a Wyoming rancher, the novels record seven years in the life of Ken McLaughlin, the younger son of Rob McLaughlin, a West Point graduate who has left the Army to raise thoroughbred horses, and his wife, Nell, an artistic Bryn Mawr graduate. The three books are unified by their account of Ken's recurring clashes with his strong-willed father, the boy's gradual maturing and reconciliation with Rob, and the adult McLaughlins' long-standing financial troubles at their Goose Bar Ranch.

The works are closely linked. *My Friend Flicka* introduces the McLaughlin family, establishes their financial straits, and relates 10-year-old Ken's efforts to tame his colt, Flicka, a descendant of a wild white range stallion, the Albino. *Thunderhead* resumes the narrative two years later, telling of the birth and training of Flicka's first foal, a white colt resembling the Albino. The story of Ken's two-year-long opposition to his father's determination to geld the fractious Thunderhead is intensified by a growing estrangement between Rob and Nell; the tensions, however, are eased by the family's achieving a degree of financial security and by Nell's pregnancy. *Green Grass of Wyoming,* the most traditionally constructed of the books, tells two stories: that of Rob McLaughlin's grudging but eventual acceptance of Thunderhead as the Goose Bar stud and that of the developing romance between 17-year-old Ken and the grandniece of a wealthy horse-breeder.

Although working within the conventions of the realistic animal story, O'Hara avoids the usual pitfalls of the genre. She does not blink at the biological facts of life, but she sets reproduction and the transmission of genetic types at the heart of the novels. Nor does she gloss over the occasional conflicts of family life. She makes the subtle antagonisms between Rob and Nell and the quarrels between the day-dreaming Ken and the determined Rob as much a part of the books as the genuine love that all three share. She deals, in fact, with all of the facets of life, from the impact of climate and space to that of politics and economics, making the works accounts of believably fallible persons who are trying, at considerable cost to themselves, to live the life of their dreams.

—Fred Erisman

O HUIGIN, sean

Nationality: Canadian. **Born:** John Higgins in Brampton, Ontario, 27 June 1942; changed name in the 1960s and always spells it in lower case. **Career:** Performance artist and poet; minor partner in Toronto's Bohemian Embassy, 1960; co-founder of Toronto's New Writers' Workshop, 1967; member of Toronto Inner City Angels, giving readings at inner city schools, 1969; recipient of Ontario Arts Council Artists in the Schools grant to conduct school poetry readings, 1969; Poet-in-Residence, Vauxhall Manor Secondary School, London, England, 1974-76; writer. **Awards:** Canada Council Children's Literature Prize, 1983. **Address:** c/o Black Moss Press, 2450 Byng Rd., Windsor, Ontario N8W SE8, Canada.

Publications for Children

Poetry

The Trouble with Stitches, illustrated by Anthony LeBaron. Windsor,
Ontario, Black Moss Press, 1981.
Scary Poems for Rotten Kids, illustrated by Anthony LeBaron. Windsor, Ontario, Black Moss Press, 1982.
The Ghost Horse of the Mounties, illustrated by Phil McLeod. Windsor, Ontario, Black Moss Press, 1983; illustrated by Barry Moser, Boston, D. R. Godine, 1991.
Well, You Can Imagine, illustrated by John Fraser. Windsor, Ontario, Black Moss Press, 1983.
The Dinner Party, illustrated by Maureen Paxton. Windsor, Ontario, Black Moss Press, 1984.
Blink: (a strange book for children), illustrated by Barbara Di Lella. Windsor, Ontario, Black Moss Press, 1984.
Atmosfear, illustrated by Barbara Di Lella. Windsor, Ontario, Black Moss Press, 1985.
I'll Belly Your Button in a Minute!, illustrated by Barbara Di Lella. Windsor, Ontario, Black Moss Press, 1985.
Monsters He Mumbled, illustrated by John Fraser and Scott Hughes. Windsor, Ontario, Black Moss Press, 1989.
King of the Birds, illustrated by Tim Dixon. Windsor, Ontario, Black Moss Press, 1991.
A Dozen Million Spills and Other Disasters: Poems New and Old, illustrated by John Fraser. Windsor, Ontario, Black Moss Press, 1993.

Fiction

Pickles, Street Dog of Windsor, illustrated by Phil McLeod. Windsor, Ontario, Black Moss Press, 1982.
Pickles and the Dog Nappers, illustrated by Phil McLeod. Windsor, Ontario, Black Moss Press, 1986.

Publications for Adults

Poe-Tree: A Simple Introduction to Experimental Poetry. Windsor, Ontario, Black Moss Press, 1978.

*

Media Adaptations: *The Ghost Horse of the Mounties* (sound recording), Kids' Records, 1986; *Acid Rain* (animated motion picture), National Film Board of Canada, 1987.

* * *

The first children's poet ever awarded the Canada Council Children's Literature Prize, sean o huigin openly challenges traditional assumptions about children's poetry. In *Poe-Tree: A Simple Introduction to Experimental Poetry* (an essay that is also reprinted in *Well, You Can Imagine*), o huigin argues that experimental poetry is valuable because it forces people to face the problems of language, makes readers active participants in the creation of meaning, and instills an appreciation of poetic techniques. He himself, therefore, avoids capitalization and punctuation, which he believes to be conventions that prevent children from directly experiencing poems and from exploring the various meanings a single poem may contain.

Despite its experimental veneer, however, much of o huigin's work is essentially traditional light verse. For example, *The Trouble with Stitches,* his first book, and *A Dozen Million Spells,* which reprints the first collection's better poems along with some new ones, humorously describe such common childhood experiences as getting stitches, having an urgent need to go to the bathroom, and fearing a vaccination. Frequently, o huigin adds a touch of the bizarre to common events. *I'll Belly Your Button in a Minute!* describes a boy examining changes in the shape of his navel. Suddenly, he sees a little man crawl out of it. Another person crawls out of that man's navel, and so on, until the room fills with strange little people. The boy finally gets the people to go back to their proper places, but he worries that his navel is again changing. *Blink: (a strange book for children)* makes better thematic and structural use of a strange situation. Describing a child who imagines herself in two places at once, the poem cleverly uses a double-column format: one column describes the city scenes that the girl sees with her left eye, and the other column describes the corresponding country scenes that she sees with her right eye. The resolution is equally clever and thoroughly satisfying. When the girl stops imagining that she is in two places and her father lovingly hugs her, both columns of poetry become identical, thus suggesting that she is no longer divided about her identity, that she is now certain of who she is and where she belongs.

O huigin's most popular books, those containing poems about ghosts and monsters, also have a light verse heritage: their poems resemble Hilaire Belloc's cautionary verses because of their comical warnings and exaggerated violence. For example, in *Scary Poems for Rotten Kids,* "The Day the Mosquitoes Ate Angela Jane" warns against meanness by describing the fate of a bad girl. Her face becomes so red because of her yelling that mosquitoes, believing that her blood will make them meaner, suck her dry. Ironically, the mosquitoes also die because her temper has made her blood nasty. Most of these poems, however, raise goosebumps by expressing familiar childhood fears about concealed monsters. "The Body" thus cautions children that if they close their eyes in the dark, a boneless beast might eat their flesh. Similarly, in *Monsters He Mumbled,* the narrator of "My Monster" warns people away from his house by declaring that a hideous child-eating monster lives under its floorboards. Part of the appeal in many of these poems of comic terror comes from their grotesque and disgusting images, elements that subvert traditional poetics of the beautiful. *The Dinner Party,* originally a picture book but reprinted in *Monsters He Mumbled,* thus describes a meal that begins with raw bits of skin that might contain rats.

In addition to his comic verse, o huigin has also written two comical prose works that contain some verse. *Pickles, Street Dog of Windsor,* recounts the narrator's surprised discovery of a dog who speaks in free verse. *Pickles and the Dog Nappers* continues the tale by telling of a time when Pickles and other dogs were captured by aliens who forced them to work in the salt mines. It concludes by casting doubt on the narrator's belief that he dreamed the events, but the question of ambiguity seems as irrelevant as the pointlessly meandering plot.

Although he is most popular as a comic writer, o huigin has produced some relatively more serious verse. *Atmosfear,* a picture book poem reprinted in *Monsters He Mumbled,* issues a serious warning that pollution will eventually destroy the world. The poem claims, however, that the destruction will come because the pollution will eventually melt the ice that has imprisoned a monster for centuries. By thus personifying the monster of global warming, the poem blunts its message that all pollution is ruinous. *King of the Birds,* an unjustifiably long *pour quoi* tale explaining why wrens fly close to the ground, suffers because its frame makes no meaningful contribution to the tale and its verse is awkward.

The Ghost Horse of the Mounties, o huigin's most ambitious book, is based on an historical event. In 1874 a lengthy and violent thunderstorm stampeded the horses of the first Mounties in Manitoba; one horse never returned, and one Mountie was seriously wounded. In this account of the episode, however, the narrator is more concerned with evoking an atmosphere than with recounting dramatic events. The narrator therefore uses repetition, rhythm, and sound to create a dream-like state that compels the reader to imagine himself alternately a horse and a Mountie. The descriptions of the separate deaths of the horse and the Mountie then evoke pathos, whereas the brief description of their apotheosis, in which the ghostly horse carries the rider into the sky, closes the poem on a muted note of triumph.

o huigin has not always been successful in his use of experimental verse forms. Some of his poems composed for oral presentation depend upon sound devices that simply do not work on the printed page. Sometimes his poems seem to be divided into extremely short lines for absolutely arbitrary or quirky reasons. Nevertheless, o huigin has also shown that rhyme, repetition, and parataxis can make free verse effective in provoking laughter or evoking serious feelings.

—Raymond E. Jones

OKORO, Anezi

Nationality: Nigerian. **Born:** Arondizuogu, 17 May 1929. **Education:** Methodist College, Uzuakoli, 1941-45; Dennis Memorial Grammar School, Onitsha, 1946-47; University College, Ibadan, 1948-52; University of Bristol, England, 1953-56, M.B., Ch.B. 1956; University of Edinburgh, F.R.C.P. 1977. **Family:** Married Eseohe Olumese; five children. **Career:** House surgeon, University College Hospital, Ibadan, 1956-57; medical officer, 1957-64, and consultant dermatologist, 1965-66, Ministry of Health, Lagos; Associate Lecturer, College of Medicine, University of Lagos, 1964-66; consultant dermatologist, Ministry of Health, Enugu

1966-74; Senior Lecturer, 1967-74, Reader, 1974-75, and since 1975 Professor of Medicine, University of Nigeria, Nsukka. Director, Nigerian National Petroleum Corporation, Lagos, 1977-81. Visiting Professor, Medical College of Georgia, Augusta, 1987, and University of Minnesota, Minneapolis, 1988. President, African Association for Dermatology, 1986-1991. **Address:** Skin Clinic, University of Nigeria Teaching Hospital, P.M.B. 01129, Enugu, Nigeria.

Publications for Children

Fiction

The Village School, illustrated by Frances Effiong. Lagos, African Universities Press, 1966.
The Village Headmaster, illustrated by Frances Effiong. Ibadan, African Universities Press, 1967.
Febechi in Cave Adventure, illustrated by Emma Okoro. Enugu, Nwamife, 1971.
One Week One Trouble, illustrated by Charles Ohu. Ibadan, African Universities Press, 1973.
Dr. Amadi's Postings, illustrated by the author. Benin City, Ethiope, 1975.
Febechi down the Niger, illustrated by Monica Eloji. Enugu, Nwamife, 1975.
Education Is Great, illustrated by Emma Okereke. Enugu, Fourth Dimension, 1986.
Double Trouble. Lagos, African Universities Press, 1990.

Other

Pictorial Handbook of Common Skin Diseases. London, Macmillan, 1981.
I Do (television play), 1988
Pariah Earth and Other Stories. Durham, United Kingdom, Pentland Press Ltd., 1994.

*

Anezi Okoro comments:
My books, aimed at children 10-14 years, are simple stories, spiced with innocent but hair-raising adventure. They lack the more popular twists of blatant violence and rampant sex. The setting is African, but some of the characters are widely travelled. The heroes, heroines, and villains are irrepressible and young.

* * *

Set in the colonial period in the Nigerian village, Amanzu, Anezi Okoro's *The Village School* is one particular school, the Central School. In addition, *The Village School* depicts a very rigid and somewhat hostile school system and its effect on African children. The village primary school comes alive from the moment the roll is called in the morning to the moment when the end of term brings an exciting change—going for holiday. In *The Village School* Mr. Offor the headmaster and his staff believe strongly that the cane for whipping pupils is a very important part of the teaching method, and use the young children as laborers on their farms and in their various household chores.The iron discipline of Mr. Offor and his staff creates distance between the school authority and the African pupils. When Mr. Offor is transfered to another school the adult community is sad but quite a good number of the African children do not feel the same—"Why waste goodwill on an old man who bullied everybody?" This cold relationship between staff and pupils gives way to a warm and cordial one with the arrival of Mr. Mozie who does not believe in caning just for the fun of it. The adventures in these two books essentially deal with rumors about the coming and arrival of a new headmaster, a boy getting lost, and a variety of pranks Nigerian pupils play in school. School life routines, various weekend activities, and Amanzu community activities provide the background for the adventures.

The thrust of *Febechi down the Niger* and *Febechi in Cave Adventure* is one of the adventures of young Febechi. In *Double Trouble,* living up to his nickname, "Willie in Trouble," Wilson Tagboe steals out of school one night to be initiated into a secret cult. But this adventure leads him into far more serious trouble than he had ever imagined. *One Week One Trouble* is about Wilson Tagboe's various problems in adjusting to high school life.

In all Okoro's works for children, beside the series of adventures that sustain reading zest, especially among Nigerian children, there are elements of didacticism: school rules to be followed, obedience to authority (the prefects, teachers, and headmaster), regular study habits, and work in the school garden. Not strong in technique, Okoro's works are generally shorter than African young adult and adult literary works. Because of their brevity, these fictional works—mainly adventure stories—can be completed and in most cases understood in less time, giving the primary school pupil a positive feeling of achievement. With due regard to the emotional and intellectual development of the Nigerian child, the action in Okoro's works moves in a simple chronological manner. He does not use complex sentences or sophisticated literary allusions because children are not yet mature enough to grapple with these concepts. These works do not proclaim any complex psychological theme or philosophical position. Yet for all their simplicity and apparent transparency, they offer a logical starting point in literary education for Nigerian school children.

—Osayimwense Osa

OLDFIELD, Pamela

Nationality: British. **Born:** London, 1931. **Family:** Has one son and one daughter. **Career:** Has worked as a teacher and secretary.

Publications for Children

Fiction

Melanie Brown Goes to School, illustrated by Carolyn Dinan. London, Faber, 1970.
Melanie Brown Climbs a Tree, illustrated by Carolyn Dinan. London, Faber, 1972.

The Adventures of Sarah and Theodore Bodgitt. Leicester, Brockhampton Press, 1974.
The Halloween Pumpkin, illustrated by Ferelith Eccles Williams. London, Hodder and Stoughton, 1974; Chicago, Children's Press, 1976.
Melanie Brown and the Jar of Sweets, illustrated by Carolyn Dinan. London, Faber, 1974.
Simon's Extra Gran, illustrated by Derek Lucas. London, Kight, 1974; Chicago, Children's Press, 1976.
A Witch in the Summer House, illustrated by Susan Hunter. London, Hodder and Stoughton, 1976.
The Terribly Plain Princess and Other Stories, illustrated by Glenys Ambrus. London, Hodder and Stoughton, 1977.
The Adventures of the Gumby Gang, illustrated by Lesley Smith. London, Blackie, 1978.
The Gumby Gang Again, illustrated by Lesley Smith. London, Blackie, 1978.
Katy and Dom, illustrated by Jane Paton. Brighton, Angus and Robertson, 1978.
Children of the Plague, illustrated by Janet Duchesne. London, Hamish Hamilton, 1979.
More About the Gumby Gang, illustrated by Lesley Smith. London, Blackie, 1979.
The Princess Well-I-May, illustrated by Glenys Ambrus. London, Hodder and Stoughton, 1979.
The Gumby Gang Strikes Again, illustrated by Lesley Smith. London, Blackie, 1980.
The Rising of the Wain, illustrated by Thelma Lambert. London, Abelard, 1980.
The Riverside Cat, illustrated by Charlotte Voake. London, Hamish Hamilton, 1980.
Cloppity, illustrated by Linda Birch. London, Hamish Hamilton, 1981.
The Willerbys and the Burglar [*Haunted Mill, Old Castle, Sad Clown, Bank Robbers, Mystery Man*], illustrated by Shirley Bellwood. London, Blackie, 6 vols., 1981-84.
Parkin's Storm, illustrated by Peter Westcott. London, Abelard, 1982.
The Gumby Gang on Holiday, illustrated by Lesley Smith. London, Blackie, 1983.
Tommy Dobbie and the Witch-Next-Door, illustrated by Glenys Ambrus. London, Hodder and Stoughton, 1983.
Ghost Stories, illustrated by Gavin Rowe. London, Blackie, 1984.
Barnaby and Bell and the Birthday Cake, illustrated by Jenny Williams. London, Piccadilly, 1985.
Barnaby and Bell and the Lost Button, illustrated by Jenny Williams. London, Piccadilly, 1985.
The Christmas Ghost, illustrated by Vanessa Julian-Ottie. London, Blackie, 1985.
Ginger's Nine Lives, illustrated by Linda Birch. London, Blackie, 1986.
The Return of the Gumby Gang, illustrated by Kate Rogers. London, Blackie, 1986.
Toby and the Donkey, illustrated by Linda Birch. London, Methuen, 1986.
The Ghosts of Bellering Oast, illustrated by Vanessa Julian-Ottie. London, Blackie, 1987.
Spine Chillers, illustrated by Colin Robinson. London, Blackie, 1987.
Sam, Sue and Cinderella, illustrated by Jenny Williams. London, Methuen, 1989.
Bomb Alert. London, Armada, 1989.
Secret Persuader. London, Armada, 1989.
A Shaggy Dog Story. London, Blackie, 1990.
A Ginger Cat and a Shaggy Dog. London, Puffin, 1992.
Cat with No Name, illustrated by Linda Birch. London, Blackie, 1994.

Other

Stories from Ancient Greece (retellings), illustrated by Nick Harris. London, Kingfisher, and New York, Doubleday, 1988.
The Mill Pond Ghost and Other Stories. London, Lions, 1991.
The Haunting of Wayne Briggs and Other Spinechilling Stories. London, Lions, 1993.
The Marvellous Magical Storybook, with others. N.p., Dean, 1993.

Editor, *Helter-Skelter: Stories for Six-Year-Olds,* illustrated by Linda Birch. London, Blackie, 1983.
Editor, *Hurdy Gurdy,* illustrated by Linda Birch. London, Blackie, 1984; as *Merry-Go-Round: Stories for Seven-Year-Olds,* Sevenoaks, Kent, Knight, 1985.
Editor, *Roller Coaster,* illustrated by Linda Birch. London, Blackie, 1986.

Publications for Adults

Novels

The Heron Saga:
The Rich Earth. London, Futura, 1980.
This Ravished Land. London, Futura, 1980.
After the Storm. London, Futura, 1981.
White Water. London, Futura, 1982.
Green Harvest. London, Century Hutchinson, 1983.
Summer Song. London, Century Hutchinson, 1984; Guilford, Connecticut, 1993.
Golden Tally. London, Century Hutchinson, 1985.
The Gooding Girl. London, Century Hutchinson, 1985.
The Stationmaster's Daughter. London, Century Hutchinson, 1986.
Lily Golightly. London, Century Hutchinson, 1987.
Turn of the Tide. London, Century Hutchinson, 1988.
A Dutiful Wife. London, Joseph, 1989.
Sweet Sally Lunn. London, Joseph, 1990.
The Halliday Girls. London, Jospeh, 1991; Guilford, Connecticut, Ulverscroft, 1993.
Long Dark Summer. London, Joseph, 1992; Guilford, Connecticut, Ulverscroft, 1993.
Passionate Exile. London, Joseph, 1993.

* * *

Pamela Oldfield maintains a remarkably consistent standard throughout her many books for children. Her assured knowledge of the primary school age group for which she writes leads to confident handling of her always appropriate themes. Her style is unobtrusive, suited to her subjects and comfortably within the abilities of her intended readers. She provides ephemerally absorbing entertainment to hook young children on to the idea of books for enjoyment—essential carbohydrate in the reading diet.

Her earliest books, about Melanie Brown, were cosy stories for four- to six-year-olds full of small domestic preoccupations and ideal for reading aloud. More recent titles show the same skill in appealing to preschool children and leading them on to an enjoyment of longer texts. The Barnaby and Bell stories are small dramas concerning a rag doll and a teddy, while in *Tommy Dobbie and the Witch-Next-Door* Oldfield takes the familiar situation of the small child who cannot get his mother's attention. On a very small canvas she skillfully contrasts the domesticity of the setting with the farcical appearance of an elephant, a tiger, and a pig (conjured up by a helpful neighbourhood witch) until the boy finally gains his mother's attention when he appears as a mouse. This is a fantasy which most small children would recognize as true to life in one sense, hilariously fantastic in others.

When young readers are gaining in confidence and beginning to read voraciously, there is something to be said for books in a series that provide a familiar framework for the development of reading skills. The series of mysteries in which the Willerbys feature provides such a framework, as do the books about the Gumby Gang. In these, three children, hindered by four-and-a-half-year-old Bet and Buster the dog, plan excitements and good deeds (which always turn out wrong) with all the paraphernalia of passwords and secret meeting places. They are not memorable stories but they are well-crafted and appeal to six- to eight-year-olds.

The Halloween Pumpkin is another lively story for younger readers in which a pumpkin face originally made to scare witches frightens almost everyone else until it is finally dispatched by a pig. Also for six- to eight-year-olds is *Children of the Plague,* a rare foray for Oldfield into the straightforward historical setting. This is quite a strong story about an undaunted small girl who is left to fend for herself as members of her family die in the plague of 1665—or are unavoidably elsewhere. It gives a good flavour of the period within its brief framework.

For older readers of eight to 11, Oldfield writes undemandingly of ghosts and witches. They offer no real threat; no deep emotions are stirred but she creates good, exciting or amusing tales, well-plotted with believable main characters. Secondary characters like Miss Timms, the librarian in *A Witch in the Summer House,* are frequently caricatured and there are stereotyped situations: absent parents, absentminded uncles. It is, however, easy to see the attractions for the young reader of stories in which 10-year-olds cope single-handedly with time-travelling witches or misplaced ghosts. In *A Witch in the Summer House* Emma inadvertantly "summons" a witch across four centuries and has trouble in finding the dismissing spell to return her to her own time. Meanwhile the witch causes mild chaos to village life. In *The Ghosts of Bellering Oast* twins Cathy and Paul get involved in a present-day mystery connected with a tragedy in the past. The resolution comes through cooperation between the twins and two perky ghosts who missed their chance to leave this world when they died and must now wait for another opportunity. Finally both old and new mysteries are resolved, although not before another near-tragedy occurs. In *Ghost Stories* Oldfield writes about ghosts who are, on the whole, gentle and helpful in their interaction with children. It is perhaps the fact that her stories are told sympathetically from the child's point of view that both stops the ghosts and witches from appearing threatening and accounts for the book's appeal with younger readers.

Oldfield writes with an easy prose style, an ear for dialogue, and minimum description. There is also accurate observation of children and their relationships with adults (even when the adults are largely absent). The plot is all important but many of her stories are thought-provoking for those who look beneath the surface.

—Valerie Brinkley-Willsher

OPIE, Iona and Peter

Nationality: British.

OPIE, Iona: Born: 13 October 1923, Colchester, England. **Education:** Attended schools in England. **Military Service:** Women's Auxiliary Air Force, meteorological section, 1941-43; became sergeant. **Family:** Married Peter Opie 2 September 1943; two sons and one daughter. **Career:** May Hill Arbuthnot Lecturer, 1991. **Awards:** Joint recipient with Peter Opie: Coote Lake esearch Medal, 1960; M.A., Oxford University, 1962; European Prize of the City of Caorle, 1964; Chicago Folklore Prize, 1970; Child Study Association of America's Children's Book of the Year, 1973, 1974; *Redbook* Children's Picturebook Award, 1988. D.Litt., Southampton University, 1987; Nottingham University, 1991; Surrey University, 1997. **Address:** Westerfield House, West Liss, Hampshire GU33 6JQ, England.

OPIE, Peter: Born: 25 November 1918, Cairo, Egypt. **Education:** Attended Eton College. **Military Service:** Royal Fusiliers, Royal Sussex Regiment, 1939-41; became lieutenant. **Career:** Author and folklorist. **Member:** Folklore Society (president, 1963-64), British Association for the Advancement of Science (president of anthropology section, 1962-63). **Awards:** Chosen Book Competition (joint winner), 1944; Silver Medal from the Royal Society of Arts, 1953; M.A., Oxford University, 1962. **Died:** 5 February 1982.

Publications for Children

Works by Iona and Peter Opie

Christmas Party Games. New York, Oxford University Press, 1957.
The Lore and Language of Schoolchildren. Oxford, Clarendon Press, 1959.
Children's Games in Street and Playground: Chasing, Catching, Seeking, Hunting, Racing, Duelling, Exerting, Daring, Guessing, Acting, Pretending. Oxford, Clarendon Press, 1969.
A Nursery Companion. London, Oxford University Press, 1980.
The Singing Game. London, Oxford University Press, 1985.
The Treasures of Childhood: Books, Toys, and Games from the Opie Collection, with son, Robert Opie, and Brian Alderson. New York, Little, Brown, 1989.
Children's Games with Things, London, Oxford University Press, 1997.

Compilers, *I Saw Esau.* London, Williams & Norgate, 1947.
Compilers, *The Oxford Nursery Rhyme Book,* illustrated by Joan Hassall and others. Oxford, Clarendon, 1955.
Compilers, *The Puffin Book of Nursery Rhymes,* illustrated by Pauline Baynes. London, Penguin, 1963; as *A Family Book of Nursery Rhymes,* New York, Oxford University Press, 1964.

Compilers, *The Classic Fairy Tales.* London, Oxford University Press, 1974.
Compilers, *The Oxford Book of Narrative Verse.* London, Oxford University Press, 1983.

Editors, *The Oxford Dictionary of Nursery Rhymes.* Oxford, Clarendon Press, 1951.
Editor (Iona Opie), *Ditties for the Nursery,* illustrated by Monica Walker. London, Oxford University Press, 1954.
Editors, *Three Centuries of Poetry and Nursery Rhymes for Children* (exhibition catalogue). London, Oxford University Press, 1973; J. G. Schiller, 1977.
Editors, *The Oxford Book of Children's Verse.* London, Oxford University Press, 1973.
Editors, *Tail Feathers from Mother Goose: The Opie Rhyme Book.* New York, Little, Brown, 1988.

Other

Compilers, *The Opie Collection of Children's Literature: A Guide to the Microfiche Collection.* Ann Arbor, Michigan, University Microfilms, 1992.
Compilers, *Babies: Unsentimental Anthology.* London, Trafalgar Square, 1991.

Works by Iona Opie

The People in the Playground, London, Oxford UniversityPress, 1993.

Editor, *A Dictionary of Superstitions,* with Moira Tatem. London, Oxford University Press, 1989.

Works by Peter Opie

I Want to Be a Success (autobiography), M. Joseph, 1939.
Having Held the Nettle, Torchstream Books, 1945.
The Case of Being a Young Man, Wells Gardner, Darton, 1946.

*

Media Adaptations: "The Lore and Language of Schoolchildren" (also hosts), British Broadcasting Corp., 1960.

Manuscript Collections: The Opie Collection of Children's Literature, Bodleian Library, University of Oxford.

Critical Studies: *Children and Their Books: A Celebration of the Work of Iona and Peter Opie,* edited by Gillian Avery, London, Oxford University Press, 1990.

* * *

Although they would not have thought of themselves as "children's writers," the husband and wife partnership of Iona and Peter Opie made an outstanding contribution to our understanding of writing for children and can claim a major share in establishing it as a legitimate field for scholarship. Their work made nonsense of rigid academic boundaries, skilfully combining literary, historical, cultural and anthropological approaches. It was the birth of the couple's first child in 1944 that seems to have prompted their interest in studying the folklore tradition within which children grew up.

The Oxford Dictionary of Nursery Rhymes (1951), defined by the authors as "those verses which are traditionally passed on to a child while it is still of nursery age," brought a century's serious interest in these rhymes to its culmination and established a scholarly collection on which others have built. The volume aimed to print the earliest recorded version of each rhyme, to discuss its origins, to illustrate variants through the years, and to relate it to cognate forms in other countries. The Opies were able to show that probably half of the rhymes were more than two hundred years old. The admiration (with a trace of condescension) that originally greeted this work is summed up by one reviewer's judgement that this would be "the standard encyclopedic tome on the little art." The Opies' own later compilations produced specifically for children include *The Oxford Nursery Rhyme Book* and *The Puffin Book of Nursery Rhymes.*

For *I Saw Esau* they made a first collection of rhymes known to schoolchildren but rarely printed. This, the beginning of an original research project for which Iona Opie did the fieldwork and Peter most of the writing, led to two seminal works—*The Lore and Language of Schoolchildren* (1959), and *Children's Games in Street and Playground* (1969). Unlike the nursery rhymes, transmitted by adults, these riddles, nicknames, parodies and pranks were not intended for adult ears. As the authors wrote, they came from a "thriving unselfconscious culture" as unnoticed by the sophisticated world as if they belonged to some "dwindling aboriginal tribe." The Opies drew directly on a continuing oral tradition by observing 5,000 children from seventy schools, but by also relating this evidence at times to printed sources, showing, for example, how one playground rhyme had run through twelve versions between 1725 and 1954. By listening to children in very different parts of Britain they were able to show how the terms used to claim first turn or to demand a truce varied from region to region. A third related book, *The Singing Game,* was the last joint work of the couple. A record of 133 games, arranged according to type, the book presented each with details of texts and variants from Britain and abroad.

While working on nursery rhymes, the Opies had become collectors of early children's books and games, gathering materials that at first many people considered rubbish. This interest developed with such speed that by the mid-1970s their home-based *Collection of Child Life and Literature* was unmatched in Britain and possibly in the world. At the time of Peter's death in 1982 their library amounted to some 20,000 titles, and an appeal in the 1980s ensured its survival intact in the Bodleian Library in Oxford. The collection, which became better known through exhibition catalogues and a later descriptive volume, *The Treasures of Childhood,* also formed the basis for much of the Opies' later work, such as *A Nursery Companion* (1980), which consisted of coloured facsimiles of almost thirty illustrated children's books from the early nineteenth century. The Opies' *Oxford Book of Children's Verse* (1973), a chronological arrangement of what were felt to be "the classics of children's poetry," was a scrupulous record of how children have been addressed in verse over five centuries—but was criticised by some for being an adult-centred book that would not attract children as readers.

By contrast, their volume of *The Classic Fairy Tales* (1974 was extremely well received. When, in their preface, they were able to record that "fairy tales are now considered a reputabl subject for research," readers were well aware that this was i large measure because of the Opies' own work. They printed th earliest surviving English texts of 24 selected stories, together wit notes on their history and details of variants and analogues. These stories awoke many to the grotesqueness and cruel force of the early versions that had progressively been softened and bowdlerised. A final book that Iona had planned with Peter, and eventually completed with Moira Tatem, was *A Dictionary of Superstitions* (1990), another innovative work which attempted a systematic presentation by organising the material chronologically within each major theme, illustrating each by quotations.

Iona and Peter Opie have been called "the Frazers of the tribal life of children." Their work has been marked by thoroughness of observation and enquiry, a highly readable and vivid style of writing, and an engaging sense of humour. It is no exaggeration to say that their work has changed the way in which we now think of children and of children's writing.

—Robert Protherough

ORAM, Hiawyn

Nationality: British **Born:** Johannesburg, South Africa. **Education:** University of Natal, B.A. in English and Drama, 1968. **Family:** Divorced; two sons. **Career:** Advertising copywriter, Johannesburg and London, 1969-73; children's author, from 1974. Has also written for television, theatre, and film. **Awards:** Mother Goose Award, 1983, and Japanese Picture Book Award, 1988, for *Angry Arthur*; Prix du Livre Culturel, 1989, for *Just Like Us*; Smarties Prize shortlist, 1994, for *The Second Princess.* **Address:** c/o Andersen Press, 20 Vauxhall Bridge Road, London SW1V 2SA, England; 4 Quarry Road, London SW18 2QJ, England.

Publications for Children

Skittlewonder and the Wizard. London, Andersen Press, 1979.
Angry Arthur, illustrated by Satoshi Kitamura. London, Andersen Press, 1982.
Ned and the Joybaloo, illustrated by Satoshi Kitamura. London, Andersen Press, 1983.
What Stanley Knew, illustrated by Lesley Arkless. London, Andersen Press, 1983.
In the Attic, illustrated by Satoshi Kitamura. London, Andersen Press, 1984.
Jenna and the Troublemaker, illustrated by Tony Ross. London, Andersen Press, 1986.
Anyone Seen Harry Lately? illustrated by Tony Ross. London, Andersen Press, 1988.
A Boy Wants a Dinosaur, illustrated by Satoshi Kitamura. London, Andersen Press, 1990.
Just Like Us. London, Orchard Books, 1990.
Mine!, illustrated by Mary Rees. London, Frances Lincoln, 1992.
Reckless Ruby, illustrated by Tony Ross. London, Andersen Press, 1992.
The Second Princess, illustrated by Tony Ross. London, Andersen Press, 1994.
Badger's Bring Something Party, illustrated by Susan Varley. London, Andersen Press, 1994; in paperback as *Badger's Party,* London, Picture Lions, 1996.
Billy and the Brilliant Babysitter. London, Orchard Books, 1994.
A Message for Santa, illustrated by Tony Ross. London, Andersen Press, 1995.
Counting Leopard's Spots, illustrated by Tim Warnes. London, Orchard Books, 1996.
Mole's Moon, illustrated by Susan Varley. London, Andersen Press, 1997.
Badger's Bad Mood, illustrated by Susan Varley. London, Andersen Press, 1997.
Not So Grizzly Bear Stories, illustrated by Tim Warnes. London, Orchard Books, 1997.
Wise Doll, illustrated by Ruth Brown. London, Andersen Press, 1997.
Camomile Gets Her Way, illustrated by Susan Varley. London, Andersen Press, 1998.
Just Dog, illustrated by Lisa Flather. London, Orchard Books, 1998.
Little Giant and Jabber-Jabber, illustrated by Ken Brown. London, Andersen Press, 1998.
The Wrong Overcoat, illustrated by March Burchell. London, Andersen Press, 1999.
All-Better Bears, illustrated by Frederick Joos. London, Andersen Press, 1999.
Where Are You Hiding, Little Lamb?, illustrated by Jonathan Langley. London, Harper Collins, 1999.
Little Brother and the Cough, illustrated by Mary Rees. London, Frances Lincoln, 1999.
Gerda the Goose, illustrated by David Melling. London, Hodder Children's, 2000.

"Chillers" Series

Wilf and the Black Hole. London, Puffin, 1994.
Wilf, the Black Hole and the Poisonous Marigold. London, A. & C. Black, 1994.

"Beetle and Bug" Series (illustrated by Sonia Holleyman)

Beetle and Bug. London, Orchard Books, 1994.
Beetle and Bug Go to Town. London, Orchard Books, 1994.
Beetle and Bug and the Haunted House. London, Orchard Books, 1995.
Beetle and Bug and the Pharaoh's Tomb. London, Orchard Books, 1995.
Beetle and Bug and their Magic Rug. London, Orchard Books, 1995.
Beetle and Bug at Croak Castle. London, Orchard Books, 1996.

"Mona the Vampire" Series (illustrated by Sonia Holleyman)

Mona the Vampire and the Big Brown Bap Monster. London, Orchard Books, 1995.
Mona the Vampire and the Hairy Hands. London, Orchard Books, 1995.
Mona the Vampire and the Jackpot Disaster. London, Orchard Books, 1997.
Mona the Vampire and the Tinned Poltergeist. London, Orchard Books, 1997.

"Animal Heroes" Series (illustrated by Judith Lawton)

Cat in the Corner. London, Orchard Books, 1996.
Dog in Danger. London, Orchard Books, 1996.

Dolphin SOS! London, Orchard Books, 1996.
Monkey in Space. London, Orchard Books, 1996.
Horse of the Year. London, Orchard Books, 1997.
Pig Detective. London, Orchard Books, 1997.
Dog to the Rescue. London, Orchard Books, 1998.
Donkey Leads the Way. London, Orchard Books, 1998.

Other

Speaking for Ourselves (poems). London, Methuen, 1990.
Out of the Blue (poems), illustrated by David McKee. London, Andersen Press, 1992.
The Vackees (musical), music by Carl Davis. London, Josef Weinberger, 1993.
A Creepy Crawly Songbook (poems). London, Andersen Press, 1993.
Good-time Boys (play). London, A. & C. Black, 1998.
Marvellous Milly (animated series for television). Germany, Alexandra Schatz Filmproduktion, 1998.

*

Hiawyn Oram comments:

I have had and am having a wonderful time writing children's books and now children's animated TV series and feature films, of which several are in development in the United Kingdom and in Europe. My ideas and motives in all my work in this field are to "confirm" children as well, of course, as to interest and entertain children—and their adult carers, if I can!

* * *

Hiawyn Oram writes picture book texts that have a rare quality. She manages to get inside the heads of young children and to verbalise a problem and find a way of solving it through a story. She does it so subtly, however, that children are blissfully unaware of having their doubts and worries dealt with in this way. Her books have a variety of different tones that have been interpreted brilliantly by several illustrators.

Her collaborations with Satoshi Kitamura have a surreal perspective, exploring ideas of feelings in fantastic, but nevertheless concrete terms. *Angry Arthur* is a perfect example of this. Arthur's anger escalates, building up into a storm cloud, then a typhoon and so on, devastating more and more of the world. Finally, we see Arthur sitting on a piece of Mars, wondering what he was angry about in the first place. This is a perceptive observation of a young child having a tantrum that gets out of control so quickly, but, equally, is over and forgotten just as soon. *Out of the Deep* explores the fear of the unknown as Ben imagines a monster lurking in the deep, but once again there is a reassuring and logical conclusion.

In the Attic is a story about a boy who is bored with his toys. He climbs the ladder on his fire engine and disappears into the attic where he has lots of fun. It is not until the final page, when the mother says they do not have an attic, that the reader realises it is a figment of the boy's imagination. Even then a ladder up against the wall leaves a lingering doubt. *Ned and the Joybaloo* and *A Boy Wants a Dinosaur* have at their core imaginary pets. Every Friday night Ned plays with an imaginary creature called the Joybaloo, who lives in the airing cupboard, but as he makes more demands on it, it gradually disappears. *A Boy Wants a Dinosaur* looks at the literal consequences of having a dinosaur as a pet, before deciding that perhaps a rabbit would be more suitable. Children can see themselves in these subtle and humorous stories, which can provide a way of them working through their desires or insecurities.

The books that have been illustrated by Tony Ross adopt a more down to earth approach, but again focus on insecurities of childhood. In *Jenna and the Troublemaker* Jenna worries about feeling different or left out, or wanting things. When the Troublemaker allows her to swap her troubles for someone else's she realises her own aren't so bad after all. In *Anyone Seen Harry Lately?* Harry demonstrates his aggressive behaviour in a variety of disguises, as "Harrylion," "Harrystrictor," "Harrytank," and so on. Each guise mirrors some of the negative and irrational feelings and moods young children commonly experience.

Many of Oram's books have strong, determined, and independent female characters. *Reckless Ruby* attacks overprotective parents in light-hearted vein. Ruby's parents want their precious daughter to grow up to marry a prince and be wrapped in cotton wool, but Ruby has very different ideas and becomes very, very reckless. After numerous dangerous stunts she ends up in hospital, with her parents bemoaning the fact that she will never marry a prince—to Ruby's great relief.

The Second Princess looks at jealousy between siblings. The second princess does not like being second and will do anything to get rid of her sister—even hiring someone to kill her. When she is discovered her parents are models of restraint and understanding and come to a satisfactory arrangement for everyone. This book acknowledges and deals with these quite shocking thoughts within the safe context of a larger-than-life situation.

A Message for Santa recognises a fear of Santa Claus, another common anxiety in children. Emily forbids Santa to come down the chimney, but allows him to come in the kitchen door—but only as far as the table. In this enlightened book Santa perfectly understands this fear and respects her wishes, thus recognising that admitting fear is perfectly acceptable.

In collaboration with Susan Varley, Hiawyn Oram has produced gentle books with measured responses to powerful emotions. *Badger's Bring Something Party* is about making people feel good. Mole turns up by himself to Badger's "bring something party." The others make him feel bad for not making more effort until Badger persuades him to stop feeling sorry for himself and enjoy the party. *Badger's Bad Mood* sees Badger suffering from depression until Mole has an idea for making him feel loved and wanted. Featuring the same woodland characters, *Mole's Moon* is a more straightforward story about Mole seeing the reflection of the moon in water.

Recently, Hiawyn Oram has branched out from picture books and created several series of books for a slightly older audience. She clearly delights in inventing and developing unconventional characters and situations and the stories go along at a brisk pace. One such series features Beetle and Bug and other insect characters in some wacky escapades. Written in rollicking verse, these books are simple enough for beginner readers and fun to read aloud, with the emphasis on humour. Her Mona the Vampire stories, meant for reading alone, are a variation on the superhero theme, as the protagonist, a small girl with a big imagination, turns into Mona the Vampire. Aided by Fang the Vampire cat and her friend Charley-Knees as Zapman, she gets into some amusing scrapes. In "Animal Heroes," another series for beginners, the stories are of unconventional things that have happened to animals in rea life. In these she demonstrates her ability to tell a good story, whatever the subject.

—Fiona Lafferty

ORMONDROYD, Edward

Nationality: American. **Born:** Wilkinsburg, Pennsylvania, 8 October 1925. **Education:** University of California, Berkeley (Phi Beta Kappa, 1951), A.B. 1951, M.L.S. 1958. **Military Service:** United States Naval Reserve, 1943-45. **Family:** Married Joan Ormondroyd; four stepchildren and three children from previous marriage. **Career:** Has worked as merchant seaman, bookstore clerk, paper factory machine operator; technical services librarian, Finger Lakes Library System, Ithaca, New York. **Address:** 5258 Curry Road, Trumansburg, New York 14886, U.S.A.

Publications for Children

Fiction

David and the Phoenix, illustrated by Joan Raysor. Chicago, Follett, 1957.

The Tale of Alain, illustrated by Robert Frankenberg. Chicago, Follett, 1960.

Time at the Top, illustrated by Peggie Bach. Berkeley, California, Parnassus Press, 1963; London, Heinemann, 1976.

Theodore, illustrated by John Larrecq. Berkeley, California, Parnassus Press, 1966.

Michael, The Upstairs Dog, illustrated by Cyndy Szekeres. New York, Dial Press, 1967.

Broderick, illustrated by John Larrecq. Berkeley, California, Parnassus Press, 1969.

Theodore's Rival, illustrated by John Larrecq. Berkeley, California, Parnassus Press, 1971.

Castaways on Long Ago, illustrated by Ruth Robbins. Berkeley, California, Parnassus Press, 1973.

Imagination Greene, illustrated by John Lewis. Berkeley, California, Parnassus Press, 1973.

All in Good Time, illustrated by Ruth Robbins. Berkeley, California, Parnassus Press, 1975.

Johnny Castleseed, illustrated by Diana Thewlis. Boston, Houghton Mifflin, 1985.

Poetry

Jonathan Frederick Aloysius Brown, illustrated by Suzi Spector. San Carlos, California, Golden Gate Books, 1964.

*

Edward Ormondroyd comments:

The child I once was, and still am, somewhere, loved certain kinds of books. I try to write those kinds of books to please him. I am delighted when I succeed in beguiling not only him, and myself, but other children as well.

* * *

Edward Ormondroyd is best known for his contribution to the genre of time-travel fiction. His novels with the most lasting appeal, *Time at the Top* and its sequel, *All in Good Time,* approach the subject in a unique and intriguing way by employing an unusual and sophisticated narrative style. In both, Ormondroyd makes himself a character who supplies needed information from another time period and therefore helps to advance the plot. In the first book young Susan Shaw, seeking solitude after a particularly trying day, wants to escape to the seventh floor of her apartment building to admire the view but "The elevator kept on going." Susan has been delivered into the Victorian household of the Walker family, whose home had been in the same location 100 years earlier. Susan quickly becomes involved in a plot to rescue Victoria and Robert Walker's mother from an evil man who marries widows and subsequently absconds with their money. Most time-travel novels for young people conclude with the main character returning to the book's original time period or setting in possession of increased insights into global or personal problems, but Ormondroyd's Susan, who has become enamored of the sights and fragrances of the previous century, resolves to use the last of her three trips in the elevator to return once again to 1881 with her father in tow; she is sure a marriage between Mr. Shaw and Mrs. Walker will result and she will subsequently be able to stay with her new friends in their time. In *All in Good Time* Susan, with the help of the Walker children, succeeds in the final defeat of the villainous Mr. Sweeney and the joyous pairing of the two adults.

In his novels Ormondroyd creates characters that are blievable and then places them in incredible situations that defy reality; he judiciously offers fragments of evidence—an old photograph, a diary, newspapers—that mount until young readers must ask the question: "Did this really happen?" These books, replete with mystery, adventure, slapstick, and intrigue, are fun to read yet challenging because of the time-shift possibilities.

Ormondroyd has additionally turned his talents to the field of picture books and, at various times during his career, has produced books which appeal to a younger audience. *Theodore* is "...an old experienced bear, comfortably smudgy..." who is sometimes forgotten by his owner Lucy; he is philosophical about her carelessness because "...she understands bears." After the stuffed bear accidently suffers the indignity and discomfort of a tumble in the washing machine and dryer and is then jolted out of the wagon on his trip home, he is discovered by Lucy who does not recognize him in his "...shiny and golden and fluffy..." new fur. Some dogs and cats and a boy with a sticky taffy sucker help Theodore to return to his comfortable rumpled old self. Theodore's reunion with Lucy is heartwarming and reinforces his faith in Lucy as someone with a perception of what makes stuffed bears happy. In *Theodore's Rival* Theodore feels displaced by one of Lucy's new birthday presents, a musical panda. "Not—not another—bear? It can't be! *I'm* the bear in this family!" Theodore's jealous response strikes a familiar chord with children who feel threatened by a sibling or a new child in the classroom. When panda Benjamin disappears in the supermarket, Theodore seizes the opportunity to engineer his rescue which delights Lucy and reinforces his perception that Lucy truly understands bears "And pandas too, of course." Theodore's relationship with Lucy echoes the reality of a parent-child relationship and children are reassured by the forgive-and-forget attitude demonstrated by both Lucy and her stuffed bear. In *Broderick* an extremely literate mouse with a burning ambition to make his mark in the world becomes the most accomplished and renowned surfer in mouse history. Using elements of humor and adventure, Ormondroyd again offers children a book they can take to heart. Ormondroyd's most recent picture book, *Johnny Castleseed,* leaves behind the fantasy of his previous books and breaks new ground for the author. A father and son, during their visit to a California beach, build an elaborate sand castle using only their hands. Their glorious creation inspires many other families to try their hands at sand castle construction and sand castles soon sprout along the beach in much the same way that Johnny Appleseed's trees germinated because of his seed planting efforts. The instructions for making the sand castle are delivered by Evan's father in such a straightforward and concise way that they could actually be used on the beach as a simple manual.

Ormondroyd approaches themes and subjects that interest young people, such as time travel, activities at the beach, and teddy bears, in an original and direct fashion. His books are never precious or coy but speak in a clear and childlike voice to young readers. It is for this no-nonsense approach to writing for children that he is most appreciated.

—Ellen G. Fader

O'SHEA, Pat

Nationality: Irish. **Born:** Pat Shiels, Galway, 22 January 1931. **Education:** Presentation Convent, 1935-44, and Convent of Mercy, 1945-47, both Galway. **Family:** Married J.J. O'Shea in 1953 (separated); one son. **Awards:** British Arts Council drama bursary, 1967. **Address:** 19 Chandos Rd., Chorlton-cum-Hardy, Manchester M21 1SS, England.

Publications for Children

Fiction

The Hounds of the Morrigan, illustrated by Stephen Lavis. Oxford, Oxford University Press, 1985; New York, Holiday House, 1986.

Other

Finn MacCool and the Small Men of Deeds (retelling), illustrated by Stephen Lavis. Oxford, Oxford University Press, and New York, Holiday House, 1987.

*

Pat O'Shea comments:

The Hounds of the Morrigan, although set in the present, is built on the scaffolding of Irish mythology. It is a comic fantasy in which two children, Pidge and Brigit, are asked to go on a quest—by the Irish God, the Dagda—to recover a blood-stained pebble and prevent it falling into the hands of the Morrigan, the goddess of death and destruction. Their journey is epic and during it they meet and are helped by many diverse characters: an earwig who thinks he's Napoleon, a comic watchfrog named Puddeneen Whelan, a wise fox named Cooroo, and many others including the hero Cuchulain, Gods in various guises, and a Garda (police) sergeant who plays a key role. As a backdrop I drew on my knowledge of the countryside and folk customs that I absorbed as a child during summer holidays at Cregmore and Kilbannon in County Galway. I grew up knowing a good deal of the mythology from fireside stories and my school primers. Further mythological background material I garnered from books collected over the years and from the reference section in Manchester Central Library.

The second book *Finn MacCool and the Small Men of Deeds* is much smaller in scale—a humorous retelling of an Irish folktale in my own style. Every Seanachie (traditional storyteller) in Ireland has his or her own interpretation of tales from the common treasure chest. So in the story I was simply following the old tradition, using up-to-date language and contemporary attitudes here and there, as people have always done in the intervening centuries since the stories were first conceived.

In this story, Finn, assisted by eight small men with special and individual talents, solves the mystery of who is stealing the children of the King of the Giants and restores the children to a grateful Daddy!

* * *

It is rare that an author emerges with a first novel with such style and assurance as did Pat O'Shea. *The Hounds of the Morrigan* is the fruit of 10 years' labour and is a richly woven fabric of fantasy in a definite Celtic pattern.

The book has a huge cast of characters, human, fairy, and animal. The basic theme of the book is of Pidge and his sister Brigit's somewhat unwilling journey and quest that ultimately conquers the evil Morrigan and dispels the power of Olc Glas, the snake who wants to bring destruction to the world.

As fantasy it obeys all the rules, creating a world that is solid, safe, and believable. Pidge and Brigit are the channels and instigators of the fantasy and are themselves caught up and perplexed by the rapidly changing landscapes they pass on their quest. The borders between reality and fantasy are smudged but, as one of the wise ones explains: "You are still in Ireland, but you are in Faery too. Here it is like, and it is unlike, the same and not the same...Our frontiers are made of mists and dreams and tender waters: thresholds are crossed from time to time...the two worlds go hand in hand." With great skill and deftness O'Shea takes us on a complex journey with as many twists and loops and devices as a piece of Celtic interlace border on an old book. Indeed, it is not surprising that it is one such old manuscript, discovered by Pidge in a Galway bookshop, that is the key which unlocks the old magic of the Morrigan and her pack of hounds. Brigit must surely be speaking for every reader when she confesses "I like being afraid, but not too much."

The twists and turns of the plot, with many breath-holding Hitchcock-like moments of suspense and fear keep the reader turning the pages of this generous novel. With great assurance the author handles the moments of genuine fear and provides light relief in the ground-level world of frogs, spiders, and ear-wigs, all of whom speak their own highly idiosyncratic, colourful, and infectious language. The local cadences and use of words are well observed, being distinctly Irish without any trace of the "Shure-and-begorrah" brogue so beloved of writers in the 1940s and 1950s. Everyone speaks with his or her own precise language—so that the iron weathervane utters a type of Newspeak Bureaucratic:

"Dear sir, or madam, business as unusual. Insomuch as, heretofore and notwithstanding, please excuse brevity of reply. Yours cordially." This is the first major work of fantasy since Patricia Lynch which harnesses the wealth of Celtic myth and legend and creates from it a credible and exciting narrative of universal appeal.

The same humour and inventiveness is used with success in the retelling of the traditional story of Finn in *Finn MacCool and the Small Men of Deeds.*

—Pat Donlon

OVERTON, Jenny (Margaret Mary)

Nationality: British. **Born:** Cranleigh, Surrey, 22 January 1942. **Education:** Guildford County Grammar School, Surrey, 1953-60; Girton College, Cambridge, B.A. (honours) 1964, M.A. 1966. **Career:** Appeals secretary, 1965-66, and Principal's private secretary, 1966-67, Newnham College, Cambridge; assistant editor, Aluminium Federation, London, 1967-69; editor, Macmillan, Basingstoke, Hampshire, 1969-71; editor, Lutterworth Press, Guildford, Surrey, 1971-84; freelance editor, from 1984.

Publications for Children

Fiction

Creed Country. London, Faber, 1969; New York, Macmillan, 1970.
The Thirteen Days of Christmas, illustrated by Shirley Hughes. London, Faber, 1972; Nashville, Nelson, 1974.
The Nightwatch Winter. London, Faber, 1973.
The Ship from Simnel Street. London, Faber, and New York, Greenwillow, 1986.

* * *

With a small output of work to date, Jenny Overton has established herself as an original and gifted novelist. Her skill lies in capturing all aspects of family life, often spanning an age range from mid-childhood to early adult independence. The forced coexistence of touchy, competitive, and vulnerable young people, each at his or her own uniquely stressful stage of growth, each with individual doubts, problems, and ambitions, formed the background to all of her first three books, though in other respects *The Thirteen Days of Christmas* seemed an unlikely product of the same imagination as *Creed Country* and its sequel *The Nightwatch Winter.*

The Thirteen Days of Christmas is a comic fantasy, enjoyed by children across a wide age range. Its subject is a crazily improbable version of the carol "The Twelve Days of Christmas." The carol is interpreted literally, with truly awesome implications for the sheer number of presents cast upon the besieged heroine. At the centre of the fantasy is a highly practical domestic situation—the desire of two young boys to marry off their elder sister, whose household accomplishments unfortunately exclude the gift of cookery, to an ardent lover who is so rich that the defect will not matter. The story is imaginatively conceived and wittily told.

Overton's most recent book, *The Ship from Simnel Street,* shares much in imaginative conception with *The Thirteen Days of Christmas.* Again a familiar song, in this case the folk song "Polly Oliver," supplies the basis for a fanciful extravaganza rooted in the affections of family life, the practicalities of food and baking, and the calendar of festival, which marks out the year. Polly Oliver is a baker's daughter in a southern English naval town in the early 19th century, and she runs away to join her soldier lover who is fighting in the Peninsular War. While Polly's father vainly searches Portugal to find her, her mother conceives the idea of sending off a mammoth load of cakes to the army there, quite literally enough to feed a regiment. The vast and wonderful baking that ensues, just like the spate of presents in the earlier book, combines warm and extravagant comedy with a serious point about family life and loyalty.

Overton's eye and ear for family drama, as shown in these straightforward tales, are also at work in the more complex and realistic situations of *Creed Country* and *The Nightwatch Winter,* novels of some difficulty which require an older, more sophisticated reader. In these books the humour works in counterpoint against the explosive emotional tensions of adolescence. In *Creed Country,* for example, evidence of Sarah's first emotional entanglement is the subject of banter and mockery in her crowded family circle, and we are made aware how funny it is to adolescents who are callously uninvolved; but the story also brings out fully her embarrassment, uncertainty, and pain.

Other elements are common to all four novels: a remarkable (and very rare) ability to communicate the wonder and the communal delight of music; an often playful and sardonic but nonetheless serious concern with religious belief and observance; and a sense of cycle, change, and festival, both in the seasonal landscape and in human society, with all its periodic rituals of school and home. *Creed Country* and *The Nightwatch Winter* are, in part, stories of tension and crisis, but their distinction lies especially in their humour and psychological insight, in their rich sense of place and history, and in the highly professional control of demanding and intricate plots.

—Peter Hollindale

OWEN, (John) Gareth

Nationality: British. **Born:** Ainsdale, Lancashire, 15 March 1936. **Education:** Merchant Taylors' School, Crosby, Lancashire, 1949-52; Bretton Hall College of Education, Bretton, Yorkshire, 1958-60, certificate in education (University of Leeds); Goldsmiths' College, University of London, 1960-61. **Family:** Divorced. **Career:** Teacher, Downshall Secondary Modern School, Ilford, Essex, 1961-65; Lecturer and Senior Lecturer, Bordesley College of Education, Birmingham, 1965-82. Owner and manager of independent record company, 1976-83; Presenter, writer for BBC Radio's "Verse Universe" program, 1991-94; Regular reader of verse on various BBC poetry programs including "Poetry Please!", 1995-97; Performed as Conrad in BBC R4 production of *Much Ado About Nothing,* 1993; Performed voice-over narration for BBC 2 television production of "Excalibur," 1994, and "Reel Truth," 1998. **Award:** *Signal* award, for poetry, 1986; winner, John Tripp Welsh Academy Competition for Spoken Poetry; winner, B.P. Speak a Poem

Award, 1992; prizewinner, W.H. Smith/West Yorkshire Playhouse Plays for Children Competition, 1992. **Agent:** Rogers Coleridge and White, 20 Powis Mews, London W11 1JN, England.

Publications for Children

Fiction

The Final Test, illustrated by Paul Wright. London, Gollancz, 1985.
The Man with Eyes like Windows. London, Collins, 1987.
Douglas the Drummer, illustrated by Paul Dowling. London, Fontana, 1989.
Ruby and the Dragon, illustrated by Bob Wilson. London, Fontana, 1989.
Saving Grace. London, Collins, 1989; as *Never Walk Alone.* London, Lions, 1991.
Omelette: A Chicken in Peril. London, Bodley Head, 1990.
"A Cake Called Albert," (included in anthology *Stories for 6-Year-Olds,* Harper Collins, 1993).
Rosie No-Name and the Forest of Forgetting. Oxford, Oxford University Press, 1996.
Say Cheese! London, Corgi, 1996.

Plays

Mr. Clips and the Silver Chicken (pantomime; produced Birmingham, 1977).
Alice in Dreamsville (musical; produced Birmingham, 1979).
Voices, in *Drama 1,* edited by John Foster. London, Macmillan, 1987.
Don't Look Down, in *Drama 2,* edited by John Foster. London, Macmillan, 1987.
The Race (verse drama; produced for BBC Radio, 1985, 1991).
Voices (produced for BBC Radio, 1992).
The Game (featuring Owen as the lead; produced for BBC Radio, 1993).
Lessons in Italian (produced for BBC Radio, 1994).

Poetry

Salford Road, illustrated by Mike Hurlow. Privately printed, 1976.
Song of the City, illustrated by Jonathan Hills. London, Fontana, 1985.
Bright Lights Blaze Out, with Alan Bold and Julie O'Callaghan. Oxford, Oxford University Press, 1986.
My Granny Is a Sumo Wrestler. Fontana, 1994.
The Fox on the Roundabout. London, HarperCollins, 1995.

Publications for Adults

Plays

Wedding Breakfast (produced Birmingham, 1972).
A Play Called George (produced Birmingham, 1973).
Margaret Born (produced Birmingham, 1973; New York, 1982).
The Confessions of Jon-Jack Crusoe (also director; produced Edinburgh, 1973).
Penalty (produced Birmingham, 1975).
Traveller (produced Birmingham, 1975).
Mandog (produced Birmingham, 1975; New York, 1978).
Rumpus (musical; produced Birmingham, 1976).
Double Exposure (produced Birmingham, 1976).
In and Out the Windows (produced Birmingham, 1976).
Widowmaker (produced Birmingham, 1977).
Silver Chicken (produced Birmingham, 1977).
Salford Road, music by Richard Isen (produced New York and Edinburgh, 1979).
The Ladder Gag (produced Edinburgh and London, 1980).
The House of Mr. Vanzetti (produced Birmingham, 1982).

Poetry

Nineteen Fragments. Birmingham, Birmingham Arts Lab Press, 1974.

Contributor, *Cambridge Contemporary Poets,* edited by Wes Magee. Cambridge, Cambridge University Press, 1992.

*

Gareth Owen comments:
My novels and poems aren't children's books but are about childhood. I try to see the world through the mind of the child that once was me but I use the skill and experience of an adult totry to make the vision significant, interesting or funny. I suppose I'm a romantic about the real and the commonplace. I write so that things won't pass away entirely. I'm shoring up a dyke against Time. Always too, in the further recesses of my mind, I have a hope that there's another soul out there who will say, "That's how it was for me." Writing is much more to do with memory and recognition than with mere invention.

* * *

The range of Gareth Owen's writing covers poetry, novels, and illustrated stories for young children. He is still probably best remembered for his first collection of poems, *Salford Road,* which became widely known in the 1980s, particularly through the many individual poems which appeared in anthologies for use in schools. It is a collection which catches the nature of childhood experiences without sentimentality or condescension. Several of the poems are written from the standpoint of an adult looking back, like the title poem which nostalgically recreates the suburban street of childhood and reflects on the passing of youth. In many poems Owen succeeds in the difficult attempt to speak and write in the voices of children themselves. There is a range of both theme and tone in the collection, including the humour of "Jonah and the Whale"; the vivid description which brings alive an ordinary scene in "The Building Site", and the gentle parody of adventure stories in "Real Life". "Growing Up" expresses a young adolescent's bemusement about the changes in himself over which he seems to have no control; "Our School" and "Sitting on Trev's Back Wall on the Last Day of the Holidays" show both the writer's ear for the language of children and his understanding of their concerns, attitudes, and humour. Owen employs a variety of forms in the collection, ranging from the rhymed regularity of the title poem to colloquial monologues like "My Sister Betty". The same qualities of directness and understanding of children's lives are shown in Owen's later collection, *Song of the City,* in which recognisable experiences are again brought to life.

Gareth Owen's novels are informed by his knowledge of children and their reading interests, gained from his frequent visits to schools to work with pupils on their own writing. In *The Final Test* and *Saving Grace,* stories about sport are given unexpected ingredients. The "sports genre" story of a boy who qualifies to play cricket for the County in *The Final Test* has the expected action details—but these are less absorbing than the central relationship in the novel. Taters, an uncomplicated boy, is drawn, through a new and intense friendship, into contact with an unusual family and powerful emotions which eclipse the satisfactions and pleasures of his success at cricket. His reactions and feelings are believably evoked, although the characterisation of Skipper, Tater's crippled friend, is less convincing. Football is the starting point of *Saving Grace,* but expectations are overturned when the central character proves to be a strong, independent girl. Frankie, a star footballer, is encouraged in her ambitions by a grandfather who was once a star player himself. The plot of the novel revolves around Frankie and her friends' battle to preserve the penalty spot at Grace Park, where Grandpa once scored, from powerful developers. The school scenes which make up the body of the novel have authentic atmosphere and humour.

With a more serious theme, but no less humour in the narration, *The Man With Eyes Like Windows* follows Louie's attempts to find his wandering, ex-film extra father before his mother marries "Uncle Edgar". An eventual happy reunion confronts both son and father with truths they have to face up to and accept. There are some disturbing and powerful moments in the novel, such as the opening dream sequence and some of Louie's encounters during his search.

Owen's stories for younger readers are characterised by lively action and humour. *Ruby and the Dragon,* for example, is a cartoon-style illustrated story of the triumphs and disasters of the lively, irrepressible Ruby, who is to play the dragon in her school's play. In *Douglas the Drummer,* the appealing relationship between young boy and grandfather is introduced when Douglas uses his grandfather's drum kit to summon the fire brigade to save him from burning.

Young readers respond with enjoyment to Gareth Owen's work, but particularly to the directness and empathetic understanding shown in his poetry.

—Judith Atkinson

OXENBURY, Helen

Nationality: British. **Born:** Suffolk, England, 2 June 1938. **Education:** Studied at Ipswich School of Art and Central School of Arts and Crafts, London. **Family:** Married John Burningham (see his entry) in 1964; two daughters and one son. **Career:** Writer and illustrator of children's books. Stage designer in Colchester, England, 1960, and Tel-Aviv, Israel, 1961; television designer in London, England, 1963. **Awards:** British Library Association Kate Greenaway Medal, 1969 (two); Kurt Maschler Award runner-up, 1985; Kate Greenaway Medal highly commended, 1989 and 1991; Smarties Book Prize, 1989, for *We're Going on a Bear Hunt,* 1991, for *Farmer Duck,* British Book Award (Illustrated), 1991; Kurt Maschler Award and Smarties Book Prize, both 1994, and Smith Under 5's Prize and Kate Greenaway Medal, both 1995, all for *So Much.* **Agent:** Greene and Heaton, Ltd., 37 Goldhawk Rd., London W12 8QQ, England.

Publications for Children

Picture Books (illustrated by the author)

Numbers of Things. New York, F. Watts, 1968; as *Helen Oxenbury's Numbers of Things,* London, Delacorte, 1983.

Helen Oxenbury's ABC of Things. London, Heinemann, 1971; as *ABC of Things,* New York, F. Watts, 1972.

Pig Tale. London, Heinemann, and New York, Morrow, 1973.

The Queen and Rosie Randall (from an idea by Jill Buttfield-Campbell). New York, Morrow, 1979.

729 Curious Creatures. New York, Harper, 1980; as *Curious Creatures,* HarperCollins, 1985.

729 Merry Mix-ups. New York, Harper, 1980; as *Merry Mix-ups,* HarperCollins, 1985; as *729 Animal Allsorts,* London, Methuen, 1980.

729 Puzzle People. New York, Harper, 1980; as *Puzzle People,* New York, HarperCollins, 1985,

Bill and Stanley. London, Benn, 1981.

Dressing. New York, Simon and Schuster, 1981.

Family. New York, Simon and Schuster, 1981.

Friends. New York, Simon and Schuster, 1981.

Playing. New York, Simon and Schuster, 1981.

Working. New York, Simon and Schuster, 1981.

Tiny Tim: Verses for Children, selected by Jill Bennett. New York, Delacorte, 1982; London, Mammoth, 1993.

Bedtime. London, Walker, 1982.

Mother's Helper. London, Walker, and New York, Dial Books for Young Readers, 1982.

Shopping Trip. London, Walker, and New York, Dial Books for Young Readers, 1982.

Good Night, Good Morning. London, Walker, and New York, Dial Books for Young Readers, 1982.

Beach Day. London, Walker, and New York, Dial Books for Young Readers, 1982.

The Birthday Party. London, Walker, and New York, Dial Books for Young Readers, 1983.

The Car Trip. New York, Dial Books for Young Readers, 1983; as *The Drive,* London, Walker, 1983.

The Checkup. New York, Dial Books for Young Readers, 1983; as *The First Check-Up,* London, Walker, 1983.

The Dancing Class. London, Walker, and New York, Dial Books for Young Readers, 1983.

Eating Out. London, Walker, and New York, Dial Books for Young Readers, 1983.

First Day of School. New York, Dial Books for Young Readers, 1983; as *Playschool,* London, Walker, 1983.

Grandma and Grandpa. New York, Dial Books for Young Readers, 1984; as *Gran and Granpa,* London, Walker, 1984.

The Important Visitor. New York, Dial Books for Young Readers, 1984; as *The Visitor,* London, Walker, 1984.

Our Dog. London, Walker, and New York, Dial Books for Young Readers, 1984.

Reteller, *The Helen Oxenbury Nursery Story Book.* London, Walker, and New York, Random House, 1985.

I Can. London, Walker, and New York, Random House, 1986.

I Hear. London, Walker, and New York, Random House, 1986.

I See. London, Walker, and New York, Random House, 1986.
I Touch. London, Walker, and New York, Random House, 1986.
Baby's First Book and Doll. London, Walker, and New York, Simon and Schuster, 1986.
All Fall Down. London, Walker, and New York, Aladdin Books, 1987.
Say Goodnight. London, Walker, and New York, Aladdin Books, 1987.
Tickle, Tickle. London, Walker, and New York, Aladdin Books, 1987.
Clap Hands. London, Walker, and New York, Aladdin Books, 1987.
Monkey See, Monkey Do. London, Walker, and New York, Dial Books for Young Readers, 1991.
Reteller, *The Helen Oxenbury Nursery Treasury.* London, Heinemann, 1992.
The Three Little Wolves and the Big, Bad Pig. London, Heinemann, 1993.
It's My Birthday. London, Walker, and New York, Candlewick Press, 1994.

Tom and Pippo Series

Tom and Pippo Go for a Walk. London, Walker, and New York, Aladdin Books, 1988.
Tom and Pippo Make a Mess. London, Walker, and New York, Aladdin Books, 1988.
Tom and Pippo Read a Story. London, Walker, and New York, Aladdin Books, 1988.
Tom and Pippo and the Washing Machine. London, Walker, and New York, Aladdin Books, 1988.
Tom and Pippo Go Shopping. London, Walker, and New York, Aladdin Books, 1989.
Tom and Pippo See the Moon. London, Walker, and New York, Aladdin Books, 1989.
Tom and Pippo's Day. London, Walker, and New York, Aladdin Books, 1989.
Tom and Pippo in the Garden. London, Walker, and New York, Aladdin Books, 1989.
Tom and Pippo in the Snow. London, Walker, and New York, Aladdin Books, 1989.
Tom and Pippo Make a Friend. London, Walker, and New York, Aladdin Books, 1989.
Pippo Gets Lost. London, Walker, and New York, Aladdin Books, 1989.
Tom and Pippo and the Dog. London, Walker, and New York, Aladdin Books, 1989.

*

Illustrator: *The Great Big Enormous Turnip* by Alexei Tolstoy, translated by E. Scimanskaya, F. Watts, 1968; *The Quangle-Wangle's Hat* by Edward Lear, Heinemann, 1969, F. Watts, 1970; *Letters of Thanks* by Manghanita Kempadoo, Simon and Schuster, 1969; *The Dragon of an Ordinary Family* by Margaret Mahy, F. Watts, 1969; *The Hunting of the Snark* by Lewis Carroll, F. Watts, 1970; *Meal One* by Ivor Cutler, F. Watts, 1971; *Cakes and Custard* compiled by Brian Anderson, Heinemann, 1974, Morrow, 1975, revised abridged version with new illustrations published as *The Helen Oxenbury Nursery Rhyme Book,* Morrow, 1987; *Balooky Klujypop* by Cutler, Heinemann, 1975; *Elephant Girl* by Cutler, Morrow, 1976; *The Animal House* by Cutler, Heinemann, 1976, Morrow, 1977; *A Child's Book of Manners* by Fay Maschler, J. Cape, 1978, Atheneum, 1979; *We're Going on a Bear Hunt* by Michael Rosen, Macmillan, 1989; *Farmer Duck* by Martin Waddell, Heinemann, 1991; *The Three Little Wolves and the Big Bad Pig* by Eugene Trivizias, Reed, 1993; *So Much* by Trish Cooke, Walker, 1994; *The Growing Story* by Ruth Krauss, HarperCollins, 2000; *Franny B. Kranny, There's a Bird in Your Hair* by Harriet Lerner and Susan Goldhor, HarperCollins, 2000.

* * *

Helen Oxenbury belongs to the top rank of children's artists, and is certainly one of the best known in Britain today. As an illustrator she has worked on books for different age groups, but her own books have been restricted to the youngest age range. The robust and expressive simplicity of her style is immediately appealing.

Her first book in 1967, *Number of Things,* and its companion *ABC of Things,* made their mark with their wittily incongruous juxtapositions. But it was the three series of board books which she did for Walker Books in the early 1980s which established her as a household name. They were published at a time when the idea that books could, and should, be used with babies and toddlers—first mooted by Dorothy Butler in her book *Babies Need Books*—was very new, and Oxenbury gave board books a distinctive "designer" look of artful simplicity which gets to the essence of babies' lives. One of the series was produced for the Sainsburys supermarket chain, which pioneered the selling of quality children's books in supermarkets, and proved phenomenally successful. Later, the larger format big board books, ideal for using with play groups, were probably the first to be "multicultural," featuring bouncing and energetic babies of different races in titles such as *Clap Hands* and *All Fall Down.* Oxenbury put board books as a genre on the map of children's publishing, and it opened up a whole market.

One of her inspirations for doing the books had been that there was nothing around at the time to use with her own baby daughter; as the latter grew up, so Oxenbury's books "grew up" too. Her first picture books, for children starting out in the world, are based on close observation of children and adults: titles such as *The Dancing Class, Playschool,* and *The Check-up* seem to encapsulate every child's experiences in a humorous way.

Oxenbury's books have been very successful in the co-edition market, gaining publishers in numerous different countries, and it has had a snowball effect with commissions sometimes coming from abroad. Her work is very highly regarded in France for instance, and a comic strip she did for a French children's magazine led to the Tom and Pippo books. Tom is the archetypal toddler, and Pippo his soft-toy monkey, there to share in all Tom's activities. Tom reads a book to Pippo after his father has read it to him; he makes Pippo dress up warmly when they go for a walk on a cold day; and is distressed when a muddy Pippo has to take a tumble in the washing machine. But equally he is very ready to blame Pippo when things go wrong: "Pippo wanted to run with me, but we fell over. I'm sure Pippo made me run too fast," as in *Tom and Pippo Go for a Walk.* With their large type and card pages, the fourteen books in this series are ideal for reading to a toddler; one of the delights is Pippo's eloquent range of expressions.

Her more recent book, *It's My Birthday,* features a toddler who asks his animal friends to help him make a cake for his birthday, and then of course they all help him to eat it.

One of Oxenbury's hallmarks as an illustrator is the wonderfully expressive faces of her animals, very much in evidence in her lively retelling of ten nursery tales in *The Helen Oxenbury Nursery Story Book.* But she produced masterly watercolour landscapes in *We're Going on a Bear Hunt,* illustrating a text by Michael Rosen, while *Farmer Duck* (by Martin Waddell) combines both character in her brilliant portrayal of the put-upon duck, and the coarse figure of the tyrannical farmer, with softly dappled landscapes; both books won the Smarties award, in 1989 and 1991 respectively, and represent her most impressive artistic achievements to date.

—Jennifer Taylor

P

PAGE, Eleanor. See **COERR, Eleanor.**

PALMER, C(yril) Everard

Nationality: Canadian. **Born:** Kendal, Jamaica, 15 October 1930. **Education:** Mico Training College, Jamaica, teaching diploma 1955; Lakehead University, Thunder Bay, Ontario, B.A. 1973. **Career:** Teacher, Red Rock, Ontario, since 1971. **Address:** 2590 Argyle Road, #1109, Mississauga, Ontario L5B 1V3, Canada.

Publications for Children (illustrated by Laszlo Acs)

Fiction

The Cloud with the Silver Lining. London, Deutsch, 1966; New York, Pantheon, 1967.

Big Doc Bitteroot. London, Deutsch, 1968; Indianapolis, Bobbs Merrill, 1971.

The Sun Salutes You. London, Deutsch, 1970; Indianapolis, Bobbs Merrill, 1971.

The Hummingbird People. London, Deutsch, 1971.

A Cow Called Boy, illustrated by Charles Gaines. Indianapolis, Bobbs Merrill, 1972; London, Deutsch, 1973.

The Wooing of Beppo Tate. London, Deutsch, 1972.

Baba and Mr. Big, illustrated by Lorenzo Lynch. Indianapolis, Bobbs Merrill, 1972; London, Deutsch, 1974.

My Father, Sun-Sun Johnson. London, Deutsch, 1974.

A Dog Called Houdini, illustrated by Maurice Wilson. London, Deutsch, 1978.

Beppo Tate and Roy Penner; The Runaway Marriage Brokers: Two Stories. London, Deutsch, 1980.

Houdini, Come Home, illustrated by Gavin Rowe. London, Deutsch, 1981.

Publications for Adults

Novel

A Broken Vessel. Kingston, Jamaica, Pioneer Press, 1960.

* * *

The Jamaican village of Kendal is the setting for C. Everard Palmer's rich studies of West Indian life. Of his early work he has written, "These books are intended to revive for adults fast-disappearing or totally extinct aspects of Jamaican life and for children creating them because they have missed them." Kendal, Palmer's own birthplace, is remote in place as well as time: it is 130 miles from Kingston and 4 miles up the hill road from the coastal hamlet of Green Island. It is rural and largely self-sufficient; it is easy to see from these books why a West Indian calls his village "my community." The rise and fall of reputations, the feuds and the power struggles provide the plot dynamics, and each story culminates in a set-piece—a hurricane, a fire, a trial, or some village festivity—which re-affirms the bonds of the community. The stories have strong characterisation, racing narratives, and abundant and colourful detail. Palmer has a vivid and exuberant humour and a highly individual style; he makes full use of dialect. Except to West Indian readers, who will appreciate these novels as literature of their heritage, the setting may appear strange and exotic. But their ambience, the world of the village, is universal.

The Cloud with the Silver Lining is a warm and gentle story of two boys who keep the family smallholding going when the breadwinner, their grandfather, is immobilized by an accident. *Big Doc Bitteroot* contains Palmer's most memorable character, Kelso Crane. He is a larger-than-life itinerant quack doctor who dazzles the unsophisticated villagers until one of his cures goes wrong and he is brought to trial. *The Sun Salutes You* again treats of village politics when Mike Johnson challenges Matt Southern's control not only of the trucking business but also of the villagers' lives. While Matt corrupts the police to stay in power, Mike enlists the aid of superstition in the person of a Pocomanian prophetess, Shepherdess Annie. *The Hummingbird People* tells of rival villages' plans to celebrate the return from war of three airmen. The "jollifying" of their plans and counter-plans has the book humming with exuberance. *The Wooing of Beppo Tate* is a comedy of courtship between Mr. Tate and Mrs. Belmont and between the latter's daughter, Daphne, and the former's adopted son, Beppo. Beppo has enough trouble in his new role without falling in love. But all ends happily in this successful story for older children. *A Cow Called Boy* is a simple anecdotal tale of Josh whose pet calf follows him to school and causes chaos in the classroom. The enforced sale of Boy which results involves the whole village. *Baba and Mr. Big* tells of the kinship between an old man and a hawk. It is Jim Anderson, a newcomer, who brings them together, for capturing the hawk is the price of his initiation into the village gang; but in the process he learns new values.

My Father, Sun-Sun Johnson is Palmer's best book so far and is again for older readers. Rami Johnson takes his father's side when his parents part and his mother marries Jake, a man with a driving need for success. But Sun-Sun Johnson and his son too have their success in rebuilding their lives and conquering adversity.

Apart from *Beppo Tate and Roy Penner,* Palmer's latest work reflects not the West Indies of his youth but the Canada of his present home. In two animal stories for younger readers, *A Dog Called Houdini* and *Houdini, Come Home,* the setting is the Arctic north rather than the tropical south. But the warmth, humour, and insight into the pressures of life in small communities, which are the characteristic features of Palmer's work, are still to be found.

—Mary Croxson

PARDOE, M(argot Mary)

Nationality: British. **Born:** London, 7 August 1902. **Education:** Privately; at Abbots Hill, Hemel Hempstead, Hertfordshire; Mademoiselle Fontaine's finishing school, Neuilly, France; studied music and singing in London and Paris. **Family:** Married John Francis Swift in 1934; one son. **Career:** Proprietor, Crossacres Hotel, Selworthy, Somerset, 1937-47. **Died:** 5 January 1996.

Publications for Children

Fiction

The Far Island, illustrated by R.M. Turvey. London, Routledge, 1936.

Four Plus Bunkle, illustrated by J.D. Evans. London, Routledge, 1939.

Bunkle Began It [*Butts In, Bought It, Breaks Away, and Belinda, Baffles Them, Went for Six, Gets Busy*], illustrated by Julie Neild. London, Routledge, 8 vols., 1942-51.

The Ghost Boat, with Howard Biggs, illustrated by Webster Murray. London, Hodder and Stoughton, 1951.

Bunkle's Brainwave, illustrated by Mary Smith. London, Routledge, 1952.

Bunkle Scents a Clue, illustrated by Pamela Kemp. London, Routledge, 1953.

The Boat Seekers, illustrated by B. Kay. London, Hodder and Stoughton, 1953.

Charles Arriving, illustrated by Leslie Atkinson. London, Routledge, 1954.

The Dutch Boat, illustrated by Leslie Atkinson. London, Hodder and Stoughton, 1955.

May Madrigal, illustrated by Leslie Atkinson. London, Routledge, 1955.

Argle's Mist, illustrated by Leslie Atkinson. London, Routledge, 1956; as *Curtain of Mist,* New York, Funk and Wagnalls, 1957.

The Nameless Boat, illustrated by Leslie Atkinson. London, Hodder and Stoughton, 1957.

Argle's Causeway, illustrated by Leslie Atkinson. London, Routledge, 1958.

Argle's Oracle, illustrated by Audrey Fawley. London, Routledge, 1959.

The Greek Boat Mystery. London, Hodder and Stoughton, 1960.

Bunkle Brings It Off, illustrated by Audrey Fawley. London, Routledge, 1961.

* * *

Although M. Pardoe wrote other adventure stories and time fantasies, it is the series of books about Bunkle which made her such a popular writer during the 1940s and 1950s, and which are still remembered with affection. Bunkle is the nickname given to young Billy de Salis by his elder brother and sister because, as they say, he talks "a lot of bunk." And it is Bunkle's skill at talking his way out of dangerous situations which carries him breathlessly through a succession of adventures, beginning in 1939 with *Four Plus Bunkle.* This book tells how he and his brother and sister, while on holiday in France, are entrusted with the task of delivering a secret document into the hands of the British Secret Service. Later adventures involve the de Salis children with German spies in Devon, black marketeers in Hampshire, and Communist kidnappers in the Pyrenees, but, although the plots may be melodramatic, Pardoe's stories were far superior to similar adventure stories of the period. Unlike other writers of the time, she placed her characters very firmly in the real world. Bunkle may go to school at Winchester and have a father in the Secret Service, but, like other children, he has to endure the wartime discomforts of rationing, the blackout, and bombing. The de Salis family may take tea at Gunter's but the cream in the cakes is mock, and they are well aware that their way of life is under threat. "When this war ends," muses Mrs. de Salis in *Bunkle Butts In,* "I don't think that any of us are going to be able to go back to the sort of life we used to lead." It is this awareness of wider issues which lifts Pardoe's stories out of the conventional holiday-adventure rut.

The Bunkle books are also distinguished by realistic observation of character. While the children in comparable books remain marooned in an ageless limbo, the de Salis family mature and develop as the series progresses. Bunkle is 10 years old in *Four Plus Bunkle,* his first adventure. By the time the series ends, he is 17, and his elder sister is married and has a child. And, unlike other children's book heroes of the period, the de Salises have an existence below the waist. "What are we to do?" asks Bunkle's sister in *Four Plus Bunkle,* as she and her brothers emerge from a hiding place in a small French town, desperate to relieve themselves. "Why didn't we think of this? It's another of the things we didn't think of. How *do* they manage in books?"

It is realistic detail like this, coupled with exact description of place, which make the Bunkle books so memorable. The settings of the stories range from the French Riviera, the Pyrenees, and Switzerland to Guernsey, The Orkneys, and Chichester Harbour, but, in each case, the landscape is accurately observed, and the various journeys of the de Salis family can be followed on a map. In the later books, the geographical precision can become tedious, and the plots of *Bunkle Baffles Them* and *Bunkle Scents a Clue* sink almost without trace beneath thick blankets of inconsequential local colour. The earlier books, though, are rich in atmospheric description, and one remembers them not so much for their plots as for their settings: the dismal out-of-season seaside resort in war time that is the background for *Bunkle Began It,* the marshy coastal creeks of *Bunkle Butts In,* the rain-sodden second-rate riverside hotel in *Bunkle Breaks Away,* perhaps the best book in the series. Few authors of the time conveyed so subtly and yet so vividly the gloom and austerity of wartime and post-war Britain.

Despite Pardoe's skill at evocative description—or possibly because of it—the Bunkle books remain period pieces. The upper-middle-class milieu and the dated dialogue are out of step with today's taste, and political and scientific changes have blunted the relevance of the plots. Yet the books are well worth reading, if only for the character of Bunkle himself. Lively, resourceful, insolent, clever, exasperating—he is a memorable creation, and Pardoe deserves credit for investing a familiar fictional formula with such an engaging hero.

—Lance Salway

PARISH, Peggy

Nationality: American. **Born:** Margaret Cecile Parish, Manning, South Carolina, 14 July 1927. **Education:** University of South Carolina, Columbia, B.A. in English 1948; Peabody College (now Vanderbilt University), Nashville, 1950. **Career:** Teacher in Kentucky and Oklahoma, and at Dalton School, New York, 1948-67. **Died:** 19 November 1988.

PUBLICATIONS FOR CHILDREN

Fiction

Good Hunting, Little Indian, illustrated by Leonard Weisgard. New York, Scott, 1962.
Willy Is My Brother, illustrated by Shirley Hughes. New York, Scott, and London, Gollancz, 1963.
Amelia Bedelia, illustrated by Fritz Siebel. New York, Harper, 1963; Kingswood, Surrey, World's Work, 1964.
Thank You, Amelia Bedelia, illustrated by Fritz Siebel. New York, Harper, 1964; Kingswood, Surrey, World's Work, 1965.
Amelia Bedelia and the Surprise Shower, illustrated by Fritz Siebel. New York, Harper, 1966; Kingswood, Surrey, World's Work, 1967.
Key to the Treasure, illustrated by Paul Frame. New York, Macmillan, 1966.
Clues in the Woods, illustrated by Paul Frame. New York, Macmillan, and London, Collier Macmillan, 1968.
Little Indian, illustrated by John E. Johnson. New York, Simon and Schuster, 1968.
A Beastly Circus, illustrated by Peter Parnall. New York, Simon and Schuster, 1969.
Granny and the Indians, illustrated by Brinton Turkle. New York, Macmillan, 1969.
Jumper Goes to School, illustrated by Cyndy Szekeres. New York, Simon and Schuster, 1969.
Granny and the Desperadoes, illustrated by Steven Kellogg. New York, Macmillan, 1970.
Ootah's Lucky Day, illustrated by Mamoru Funai. New York, Harper, 1970; Kingswood, Surrey, World's Work, 1971.
Snapping Turtle's All-Wrong Day, illustrated by John E. Johnson. New York, Simon and Schuster, 1970.
Come Back, Amelia Bedelia, illustrated by Wallace Tripp. New York, Harper, 1971; Kingswood, Surrey, World's Work, 1973.
Haunted House, illustrated by Paul Frame. New York, Macmillan, and London, Collier Macmillan, 1971.
Granny, The Baby, and the Big Gray Thing, illustrated by Lynn Sweat. New York, Macmillan, 1972; Kingswood, Surrey, World's Work, 1973.
Play Ball, Amelia Bedelia, illustrated by Wallace Tripp. New York, Harper, 1972; Kingswood, Surrey, World's Work, 1973.
Too Many Rabbits, illustrated by Leonard Kessler. New York, Macmillan, 1974; Kingswood, Surrey, World's Work, 1975.
Pirate Island Adventure, illustrated by Paul Frame. New York, Macmillan, 1975.
Good Work, Amelia Bedelia, illustrated by Lynn Sweat. New York, Greenwillow, 1976; Kingswood, Surrey, World's Work, 1977.
Teach Us, Amelia Bedelia, illustrated by Lynn Sweat. New York, Greenwillow, 1977; Kingswood, Surrey, World's Work, 1978.
Hermit Dan, illustrated by Paul Frame. New York, Macmillan, 1977.
Zed and the Monsters, illustrated by Paul Galdone. New York, Doubleday, 1979; Kingswood, Surrey, World's Work, 1980.
Be Ready at Eight, illustrated by Leonard Kessler. New York, Macmillan, 1979.
Amelia Bedelia Helps Out, illustrated by Lynn Sweat. New York, Greenwillow, 1979; Kingswood, Surrey, World's Work, 1981.
Amelia Bedelia and the Baby, illustrated by Lynn Sweat. New York, Greenwillow, 1981.
No More Monsters for Me!, illustrated by Marc Simont. New York, Harper, 1981.
Mr. Adams's Mistake, illustrated by Gail Owen. New York, Macmillan, 1982; London, Macmillan, 1983.
The Cats' Burglar, illustrated by Lynn Sweat. New York, Greenwillow, 1983.
Amelia Bedelia Goes Camping, illustrated by Lynn Sweat. New York, Greenwillow, 1985.
Merry Christmas, Amelia Bedelia, illustrated by Lynn Sweat. New York, Greenwillow, 1986.
The Ghosts of Cougar Island. New York, Dell, 1986.
Amelia Bedelia's Family Album, illustrated by Lynn Sweat. New York, Greenwillow, 1988.
Scruffy, illustrated by Kelly Oechsli. New York, Harper, 1988.
Good Hunting, Blue Sky, illustrated by James Watts. New York, Harper, 1988.

Other

My Golden Book of Manners, illustrated by Richard Scarry. New York, Golden Press, 1962; London, Golden Pleasure Books, 1963.
Let's Be Indians, illustrated by Arnold Lobel. New York, Harper, 1962.
The Story of Grains: Wheat, Corn, and Rice, with W.W. Crowder, illustrated by William Moyers. New York, Grosset and Dunlap, 1965.
Let's Be Early Settlers with Daniel Boone, illustrated by Arnold Lobel. New York, Harper, 1967.
Costumes to Make, illustrated by Lynn Sweat. New York, Macmillan, 1970; London, Collier Macmillan, 1971.
Sheet Magic: Games, Toys and Gifts from Old Sheets, illustrated by Lynn Sweat. New York, Macmillan, and London, Collier Macmillan, 1971.
Dinosaur Time, illustrated by Arnold Lobel. New York, Harper, 1974; Kingswood, Surrey, World's Work, 1975.
December Decorations: A Holiday How-To Book, illustrated by Barbara Wolff. New York, Macmillan, 1975.
Let's Celebrate: Holiday Decorations You Can Make, illustrated by Lynn Sweat. New York, Greenwillow, 1976.
Mind Your Manners!, illustrated by Marylin Hafner. New York, Greenwillow, 1978.
Beginning Mobiles, illustrated by Lynn Sweat. New York, Macmillan, 1979.
I Can—Can You? (readers), illustrated by Marylin Hafner. New York, Greenwillow, 4 vols., 1980; as *See and Do Book Bag,* London, MacRae, 4 vols., 1980.

*

Manuscript Collections: Kerlan Collection, University of Minnesota, Minneapolis.

* * *

Peggy Parish had the formula for combining humor and wordplay in a way that fulfills a child's need for the obvious. She wrote several successful series of which Amelia Bedelia is best-known. Introduced in *Amelia Bedelia,* the character amazes her audience with ridiculous episodes. Amelia Bedelia is quite literal in her interpretation of everyday events. Her first day as the maid for the Rogers family, she dusts with dusting powder, draws the drapes by sketching, and dresses the chicken in trousers and socks. Her delicious lemon meringue pie rescues her from dismissal. In *Amelia Bedelia and the Surprise Shower* she and Cousin Alcolu help throw a bridal shower complete with gifts and garden hose. Following her dismissal, in *Come Back, Amelia Bedelia* she pounds the pavement looking for a job while leaving havoc in her wake. Her outrageous interpretation of baseball terminology in *Play Ball, Amelia Bedelia* runs the gamut from stealing bases to running home. Her predicaments are obvious enough to allow early readers the enjoyment of a play on words.

Granny and the Indians introduces another unique and likable character. Alone with a gun that doesn't shoot, Granny Guntry proves competent in dealing with Indians, desperadoes, and wolves. Granny's a nice, sweet, tough, and independent old lady who wants things done her way. Her casual brushes with danger are just close enough to be exciting. The action never ceases until things are settled to her liking.

The mystery series involving Jed, Liza, and Bill Roberts are longer but provide enough action to maintain interest and enjoyment. The children always manage to keep the adults in suspense while unraveling the mysteries. Grandpa Roberts provides the initial clues for two of the mysteries that involve word scrambles, secret codes, and picture clues. Though easy to read, deciphering the clues becomes absorbing and draws the reader into the intrigue.

In contrast to her other work, Parish's stories about Little Indian are stereotypical. The lack of names for the characters in *Good Hunting, Little Indian* is offensive. Many readers today will be insulted by the implication that all Indians are called "Little Indian" while earning a name.

Parish showed great skill in combining an ever-popular subject, monsters, with an easy reader format. *No More Monsters for Me!* and *Zed and the Monsters* provide humorous and involving situations with a flowing text—the dynamics for enjoyable stories.

—Martha J. Fick

PARKER, Richard

Nationality: British. **Born:** Stanmore, Middlesex, 15 February 1915. **Education:** Kingsbury County Training College, London. **Military Service:** British Army during World War II. **Family:** Married Kathleen Hook in 1939; five children. **Career:** Library assistant, Maidstone Public Library, Kent, 1934-36; secretary to Rupert Croft-Cooke, 1937-38; reporter, *Kent Messenger;* primary school teacher for many years. **Died:** September, 1990.

Publications for Children

Fiction

Escape from the Zoo, illustrated by Val Biro. London, Sylvan Press, 1945.

A Camel from the Desert, illustrated by Val Biro. London, Sylvan Press, 1947.

The Penguin Goes Home, illustrated by Val Biro. London, Chatto and Windus, 1951.

A Moor of Spain: The Story of a Rogue, illustrated by John Harwood. London, Penguin, 1953.

The Three Pebbles, illustrated by Prudence Seward. London, Collins, 1954; New York, McKay, 1956.

The Sword of Ganelon. London, Collins, 1957; New York, McKay, 1958.

Lion at Large, illustrated by Paul Hogarth. Leicester, Brockhampton Press, 1959; New York, Nelson, 1961; as *Midnight Beast,* New York, Scholastic, n.d.

More Snakes than Ladders, illustrated by Jillian Willett. Leicester, Brockhampton Press, 1960; as *Almost Lost,* New York, Nelson, 1962.

New Home South, illustrated by Prudence Seward. Leicester, Brockhampton Press, 1961; as *Voyage to Tasmania,* Indianapolis, Bobbs Merrill, 1961.

A Valley Full of Pipers, illustrated by Richard Kennedy. London, Gollancz, 1962; Indianapolis, Bobbs Merrill, 1963.

The House That Guilda Drew, illustrated by Prudence Seward. Leicester, Brockhampton Press, 1963; Indianapolis, Bobbs Merrill, 1964.

The Boy Who Wasn't Lonely, illustrated by Prudence Seward. Leicester, Brockhampton Press, 1964; Indianapolis, Bobbs Merrill, 1965.

Perversity of Pipers, illustrated by Richard Kennedy. London, Gollancz, and Princeton, New Jersey, Van Nostrand, 1964.

Private Beach, illustrated by Victor Ambrus. London, Harrap, 1964; New York, Duell, 1965.

Second-Hand Family, illustrated by Gareth Floyd. Leicester, Brockhampton Press, 1965; Indianapolis, Bobbs Merrill, 1966.

M for Mischief, illustrated by Juan Ballesta. London, Constable, 1965; New York, Duell, 1966.

The Punch Back Gang, illustrated by John Plant. London, Harrap, 1966; as *New in the Neighborhood,* New York, Duell, 1966.

One White Mouse, illustrated by Rene Hummerstone. Leicester, Brockhampton Press, 1966; as *No House for a Mouse,* Chicago, Follett, 1968.

The Hendon Fungus. London, Gollancz, 1967; New York, Meredith Press, 1968.

A Sheltering Tree. New York, Meredith Press, 1969; London, Gollancz, 1970.

Spell Seven, illustrated by Trevor Ridley. London, Longman, and New York, Nelson, 1971.

The Old Powder Line. London, Gollancz, and New York, Nelson, 1971.

Paul and Etta, illustrated by Gavin Rowe. Leicester, Brockhampton Press, 1972; Nashville, Nelson, 1973.

Frank's Fire. London, Macmillan, 1972.

John Morris's Mermaid. London, Macmillan, 1972.

Not at Home. London, Macmillan, 1972.

One Green Bottle, illustrated by Michael Jackson. London, Heinemann, 1973.

A Time to Choose. London, Hutchinson, 1973; New York, Harper, 1974.

He Is Your Brother, illustrated by Gareth Floyd. Leicester, Brockhampton Press, 1974; Nashville, Nelson, 1976.

Snatched, illustrated by Peter Kesteven. Newton Abbot, Devon, David and Charles, 1974; as *Three by Mistake,* Nashville, Nelson, 1974.

Beyond the Back Gate, illustrated by Peter Dennis. London, Abelard Schuman, 1975.

Boy into Action, illustrated by Trevor Parkin. London, Abelard Schuman, 1975.
The Fire Curse, illustrated by Trevor Stubley. London, Heinemann, 1975.
Hugo Takes Off, illustrated by Trevor Stubley. London, Hodder and Stoughton, 1976; as *The Runaway,* Nashville, Nelson, 1977.
Quarter Boy. London, Heinemann, and Nashville, Nelson, 1976.
In and Out the Window. London, Hutchinson, 1976.

Plays

Six Plays for Boys (includes *The New Football Boots, The Rabbit Hutch, The Wish, The Medicine Man, The Raft, No Excitement*). London, Methuen, 1951.
Seven Plays for Boys (includes *The Rehearsal, The Hut, The Waxworks, Lazy Jack, The Dilemma, A Message to the Kite, The Coconut Shy*). London, Methuen, 1953.

Other (readers)

Brother Turgar and the Vikings, illustrated by Joan Milroy. London, Ginn, 1959.
The Kidnapped Crusaders, illustrated by Richard Kennedy. London, Ginn, 1959.
The Green Highwayman, illustrated by Richard Kennedy. London, Ginn, 1960.
Goodbye to the Bush, illustrated by Kenneth Brown. London, Ginn, 1963.
Lost in a Shop, illustrated by Carol Barker. London, Macmillan, 1968.
Me and My Boots, illustrated by George Adamson. London, Macmillan, 1968.
Keeping Time, illustrated by Jane Hickson. London, Heinemann, 1973.
Digging for Treasure, illustrated by Trevor Stubley. London, Benn, 1976.
Flood, illustrated by Trevor Stubley. London, Benn, 1976.
Sausages on the Shore, illustrated by Trevor Stubley. London, Benn, 1976.
The Sunday Papers, illustrated by Trevor Stubley. London, Benn, 1976.

Publications for Adults

Novels

Only Some Had Guns. London, Collins, 1952.
The Gingerbread Man. London, Collins, 1953; New York, Scribner, 1954.
A Kind of Misfortune. London, Collins, 1954; New York, Scribner, 1955.
Draughts in the Sun. London, Collins, 1955.
Harm Intended. New York, Scribner, 1956; London, Secker and Warburg, 1957.
Fiddler's Place. London, Davies, 1961.
Boy on a Chain. London, Davies, 1964; as *Killer,* New York, Doubleday, 1964.

*

Richard Parker comments:

(1989) I began writing for children when I became a teacher, and to begin with the stories were largely a by-product. They were written to give enjoyment to or to help some particular group of children, sometimes technically and sometimes emotionally. Some stories were written for individuals, some for the class I happened to be teaching at the time. After two years (1959-61) in the Australian education system, however, I became less interested in education and more concerned with writing as a profession. Nowadays I find myself writing a story because it seems a good one and presents interesting problems, and worry far less about who will read it.

* * *

Over-zealous pigeon-holing of writers and writing for the young often ceases to be useful when appreciation of the prolific and dedicated like the late Richard Parker is supplanted by a genre approach which makes "boys adventure" (or "the teenage novel") do for all. His books are mainly for adolescents, or slightly younger readers; most of his protagonists are boys. But the thematic underpinning of his work is the reader's pleasure in a tale well-structured and narrated.

An astute awareness of a readership which likes to be drawn in early, and carried by plots with pace and tailored episodes, informs all his work. Central characters are often lonely, insecure, uncertain, in between: recently orphaned and bound for a foreign country in *New Home South;* rootless, nomadic in *The House That Guilda Drew;* fostered unlovingly in *Second-Hand Family.* The pitfalls of over-dramatising or voyeurism are always avoided. The adults are often well-meaning but unhelpful. Parker's strong storylines make his readers secure enough to face the potentially trying such as the pressures brought upon children by an autistic sibling (and an insensitive father) in *He Is Your Brother.* His dialogue is vivid, especially when family tensions are below the surface of domestic small talk. The uneasy conversations between the moody girl and her unwelcome foster-brother in *Paul and Etta,* the half-understood bickering of unhappy parents in *Hugo Takes Off* often foster in his teenage readers a new kind of reading—to discern atmosphere and relationships. Parker was able to deal unobtrusively with the often-fraught hinterland between childhood and young adulthood.

He never used fictional devices for mere effect, always for a refining of plot and ideas. The clever time-shift in *The Old Powder Line* reveals to the young that the old were once young, too. A loss of memory at a pop festival enables the young hero in *In and Out the Window* to see himself and his surroundings afresh. Books which range widely in geographical and historical contexts still keep the story in the foreground so that, invited in, the young gain a sense of place and period. The vivid Australian backcloth of the Pipers books adds vigour and a rough edge to plots and characters. The absorbing portrayal of the Anglo-Saxon boy's quest in *The Sword of Ganelon* and the superb smuggling story set in 19th-century Kent—*A Sheltering Tree*—display a genuine talent for coherent historical writing. In his last writings, Parker showed a willingness to tackle contemporary themes without being ingratiating or trendy. There is in all his work a concern for technique which is solid, but never dull, a respect for the young which is not overbearing.

—Colin Mills

PARKINSON, Siobhán

Nationality: Irish. **Born:** Dublin, 23 November 1954. **Education:** Scoil Mhuire gan Smal and Loreto Convent, Letterkenny, Co. Donegal, Leaving Certificate 1972; Trinity College Dublin, B.A. in English and German 1976, Ph.D. in English Literature 1981. **Family:** Married Roger Bennett in 1978; one son. **Career:** Assistant editor, Royal Irish Academy, 1980-83; freelance editor, 1983-87; editor, C.J. Fallon Ltd. (educational publishers), 1987-89; head of technical writing, CBT Systems, 1989-95; editor and writer, Focus Ireland (a major Irish charity working on behalf of homeless people), 1995-97; managing editor, Town House publishers, from 1998; writer and freelance editorial consultant. **Awards:** Bisto Book of the Year shortlist, 1993-94 and 1995-96; Bisto Book of the Year 1996-97. **Address:** 7 Kenilworth Park, Dublin, 6, Ireland.

Publications for Children

Off We Go ... The Dublin Adventure. Dublin, O'Brien, 1992.
Off We Go ... The Country Adventure. Dublin, O'Brien, 1992.
The Leprechaun Who Wished He Wasn't, illustrated by Donal Teskey. Dublin, O'Brien, 1993.
All Shining in the Spring, illustrated by Donal Teskey. Dublin, O'Brien, 1995.

Publications for Young Adults

Amelia. Dublin, O'Brien, 1993.
No Peace for Amelia. Dublin, O'Brien, 1994.
Sisters ... No Way! Dublin, O'Brien, and Nimot, Irish American Book Company, 1996.
*Four Kids, Three Cats, Two Cows, One Witch (Maybe).*Dublin, O'Brien, and Nimot, Irish American Book Company, 1997.
"Damson Jam," in *First Times,* edited by Robert Dunbar. Dublin, Poolbeg, 1997.

Other

Editor, *Home: An Anthology of Modern Irish Writing.* Dublin, A.&.A. Farmar, 1996.
Editor, *A Part of Ourselves: Laments for Lives that Ended Too Soon.* Dublin, A.& A. Farmar, 1997.

*

Siobhán Parkinson comments:

As a child I wanted to be a writer "when I grew up." Being a child I wanted to write for children, naturally enough. My parents thought this an amusing little idea.

Then I did grow up (well, sort of), but by now, I rather agreed with my parents that wanting to be an author was an amusing little idea. To tell the truth, the feeling that I mightn't be all that good at it was really what kept me for so long from embarking on a literary career, together with a horror of all the competition out there and of the exposing of one's inner self that writing involves. I suppose I needed to do a lot more growing up before I was ready to take that plunge.

It's an old cliche, isn't it, that people come to writing for children when they have children themselves. When my son was born, even when he started to take an interest in books, when I started to read to him, when he started to read back ... none of these things moved me to want to be a children's writer. It never crossed my mind. But then something happened in our family, and I desperately needed a book to help my son (then five years old) to understand what was going on, but no such book existed. That's when I wrote my first children's book.

What happened was that I discovered, late in my second pregnancy, that the child I was carrying was not going to survive birth. My small son had followed the progress of the pregnancy eagerly and was very excited about this big event in our lives. So how to break this dreadfully disappointing, even disturbing news to him? Being a literary sort of person, my first instinct was to reach for a book, but the books I found, although I was able to bend them to my purpose, were quite unsuitable for our unusual (but not unique) situation. I found the available books on death for children were sentimental and rather poorly produced, and none of the ones I could find at any rate dealt with such a taboo idea as baby-death. In the end, I wrote the book I was looking for myself.

The publisher I sent it to did eventually publish it several years later (as *All Shining in the Spring*), but in the meantime they called me in and announced that they thought I was a children's writer, and asked me when I could produce my next manuscript. I laughed. Amusing little idea, I thought. And that was how I came to be a children's writer. When I am feeling particularly spiritual (which is only occasionally), I like to think that little Daniel brought gifts with him, though he didn't stay long, and one of those gifts was my becoming a children's writer, because if it hadn't been for him, I don't think I would ever have dreamt of doing such a thing.

* * *

Although her first book was for young children and was followed by several other successful books for the under tens, it is Parkinson's writings for young adults which have brought her recognition and success. This writer's sense of irony and laconic view of life is obvious even in her early work such as *The Leprechaun Who Wished He Wasn't.* For most Irish people leprechauns belong in the folklore of past times or as tacky souvenirs to be sold to gullible tourists. From the first sentences of the book you know that this is a gentle send-up of another icon: "Laurence was fed up with being a leprechaun. He was tired of sitting under a boring old rainbow, guarding a mouldy old crock of gold and making endless shoes. He wanted to be a human being."

Parkinson's skill at telling a good story in clear, sometimes funny, almost always compelling prose is evident in most of her books. In a mere sixty pages of text and images in *All Shining in the Spring* she tells poignantly and honestly of the devastation and lack of comprehension of a young boy at the untimely death of his baby brother. In a narrative that is neither harrowing nor maudlin she simply states the reality. With one of the loveliest book titles ever, we know that Matthew will recall each year his short-lived baby brother as he and his parents visit the flower-studded grave "all-shining in the spring."

In the late 1980s and 1990s in Ireland there has been a dramatic change in both the number and quality of books published for children and young adults. Irish people have a great interest in and obsession with history, so it is not surprising that in their writings, many of the best contemporary authors eventually are drawn to this genre. Parkinson too has given us some interesting work in this area with *Amelia* and *No Peace for Amelia.* She draws an accurate and compelling picture of Dublin in the 1914-16 period without bogging the reader down in historical detail. When we meet her, Amelia, the daughter of a well-to-do Quaker family, is preparing to celebrate her fourteenth birthday. Against this background is played out the social tensions of a changing society, the rumours of an impending insurrection, and the threat of War in Europe. At its simplest this is a riches-to-rags story of the declining fortunes of the Pim family, and the reactions of all involved. All is changing for the bewildered Amelia as she is deserted by her former classmates and friends, but befriended by the young servant girl Mary Ann. Parkinson is at her best when describing apparently mundane happenings. When Amelia first tries to use that new-fangled invention the telephone the scene in the General Post Office is so written that the reader too suffers the embarrassment of snooty officials, the terror of new technology, the overriding fear of looking foolish.

In the sequel *No Peace for Amelia* we have moved on a little in time—and whilst the family fortunes have not exactly been restored, through diligence and hard work Amelia's father has regained a small foothold on the social ladder. Amelia falls in love and is forced to reconcile her love for the soldier Frederick with the Quaker abhorrence of violence. The divided world of early twentieth-century Ireland is epitomised neatly in the anxieties of the two young women: Amelia, with her young man going to fight for King and country, and Mary Ann, the servant girl, with her brother fighting a very different fight for the cause of Irish freedom. The uneasy alliance and understanding serves as a microcosm of the wider historical and social realities.

Parkinson's young people are refreshingly normal and relatively angst free. *Sisters ... No Way!* is a cleverly conceived flip-over book. Two diaries of two very different young women thrown together by the marriage of their parents, one separated, one recently-widowed, are printed back-to-back. The reader is immediately confronted with the dilemma of which diary to read first and in that choice inevitably becomes embroiled in that sister's particular perspective of the world. This is a clever, thought-provoking book which uses the interplay of the two narratives to counterpoint different life styles. Readers must constantly reassess as they finally come to the recognition that there is no one truth, no one reality, only life as viewed through different eyes. Parkinson has an acute ear for the euphemisms society adopts to hide embarrassment, as when Aishling, the more conservative of the "sisters," rails against her father because he introduces his daughters to newcomers as "My daughters, from before, you know." It is Cindy, the outwardly punk, rebellious daughter who comes the closest to the reality of her situation as she moans confidingly to her diary about her new family: "Not that they're mean or horrible or anything—just plain boring and neurotic and silly and, oh, just not like us. Of course we're neurotic too, everyone is, but I think our neuroses are more creative."

In an author's note at the beginning of *Four Kids, Three Cats, Two Cows, One Witch (Maybe)*—ostensibly a summer holiday adventure trip to an island—Parkinson gives us a clue to the underlying symbolism of the journey: "In some cultures young people who are approaching adulthood have to undergo some sort of test or ordeal.... They might have to go off by themselves into the forest, for example, and survive on their own initiative. In other cultures the transition is marked by the older people telling the children the secret stories of their tribe. Once they have these stories, they are no longer children, but grown-up members of the tribe. But no matter what form these ceremonies and rituals take (and in some cultures they are pretty nasty) every child has to make the journey from childhood to young adulthood for himself or herself."

Snobby Beverly, extremely self-contained (at least on the surface), constantly looking down her nose at the local youth Kevin from her sophisticated stance, has her rite of passage when on a cliff edge she suffers an attack of vertigo. In a stunning *tour de force* Parkinson details the panic and fright she suffers and her resigned acceptance of help and ultimately friendship from the heretofore despised Kevin. The catalyst in the story, as in so many young adult novels, is an outsider, an older person—the eccentric and possibly insane Dymphna, rumoured by the mainlanders to be a witch. Her presence haunts the entire book, at first only through the knowledge of the local boy Kevin, but later as a presence felt by all of the four protagonists. Yet the story is well-advanced before we actually get to meet Dymphna as she comes home to her ramshackle cottage to find the four sheltering there from the impending storm. Interwoven throughout the book are the tales told by the young people under the spell of Lady Island, tales that are allegorical, sometimes surprising even the tellers themselves by their unexpected twists and always with the ghost presence of the strange listener. This is Parkinson's most complex and sophisticated book to date and is a story which can be enjoyed at many levels.

—Pat Donlon

PARRISH, Anne

Nationality: American. **Born:** Colorado Springs, Colorado, 12 November 1888. **Education:** Misses Ferris's School and San Luis School, Colorado Springs; Misses Hebb's School, Claymont, Delaware; Philadelphia School of Design. **Family:** Married 1) Charles Albert Corliss in 1915 (died 1936); 2) Josiah Titzell in 1938 (died 1943). **Awards:** Harper prize, 1925. **Died:** 5 September 1957.

Publications for Children

Fiction

Knee-High to a Grasshopper, with Dillwyn Parrish, illustrated by the authors. New York, Macmillan, 1923.

The Dream Coach, with Dillwyn Parrish, illustrated by the authors. New York, Macmillan, 1924.

The Story of Appleby Capple, illustrated by the author. New York, Harper, 1950.

Poetry

Floating Island, illustrated by the author. New York, Harper, and London, Benn, 1930.

Publications for Adults

Novels

A Pocketful of Poses. New York, Doran, and London, Hodder and Stoughton, 1923.
Semi-Attached. New York, Doran, 1924; London, Brentano's, 1926.
The Perennial Bachelor. New York, Harper, 1925; London, Heinemann, 1926.
To-morrow Morning. New York, Harper, and London, Heinemann, 1927.
All Kneeling. New York, Harper, 1928; London, Benn, 1929.
The Methodist Faun. New York, Harper, 1929; London, Benn, 1930.
Loads of Love. New York, Harper, and London, Benn, 1932.
Sea Level. New York, Harper, and London, Hamish Hamilton, 1934.
Golden Wedding. New York, Harper, and London, Hamish Hamilton, 1936.
Mr. Despondency's Daughter. New York, Harper, and London, Hamish Hamilton, 1938.
Pray for Tomorrow. New York, Harper, 1941.
Poor Child. New York, Harper, 1945; London, Heinemann, 1947.
A Clouded Star. New York, Harper, 1948; London, Heinemann, 1949.
And Have Not Love. New York, Harper, 1954; as *And Have Not Charity,* London, Hutchinson, 1955.
The Lucky One. New York, Harper, 1958.

Short Stories

Lustres. New York, Doran, 1924.

* * *

Anne Parrish, born into a family of painters, took naturally to a deep appreciation of people and of nature. She and her brother created fantasy stories and games about both during their childhood, and later collaborated as authors/illustrators of several children's books where fantasy, mystery, and adventure are paramount.

Parrish became well-known for her adult novels, some of which were bestsellers. As an author of books for children, she is best remembered for *Floating Island* and *The Story of Appleby Capple.* Both of these books are dream-like and witty, expressing very human emotions in non-human disguises. *Floating Island,* told in verse, is one of a number of books about dolls and other toys popular in the early part of this century. It was the author's favorite of her books. The doll family—consisting of Mr. and Mrs. Doll, William Doll, Annabel Doll, Baby Doll, and Dinah the Cook—live in a proper doll house in a proper toy store. When they are bought by a devoted uncle and shipped across the seas to his niece, they, fortunately or unfortunately, are shipwrecked and find themselves on a tropical island. The family members are scattered on the island, and each has to react alone to unknown beauty and unknown terror. Their reactions to the special wonders of ferns and sea shells and wild blossoms, and to the special threats of crabs and monkeys and large birds, are told strictly through the eyes of small dolls, some of whom are unbendable. The Dolls make very intelligent use of their stay on the island and they enjoy its surprises; but all except Dinah ultimately leave it for a proper existence again. The book is imaginative and wistful and gentle, but somewhat outdated in its stereotypical approach to family life and to sex and racial differences. *The Story of Appleby Capple* grew out of a letter game the author and her brother invented as children. It indicates the author's awareness of the delight children receive from playing with unusual, multicolored, and splendid words.

Parrish once said that "for pure joy there is nothing like working on a book for children." Her joy is communicated in these works, with their combination of reverence for nature and understanding of human foibles.

—Mary Lystad

PATCHETT, Mary Elwyn (Osborne)

Pseudonym: David Bruce. **Nationality:** Australian. **Born:** Sydney, New South Wales, 2 December 1897. **Education:** New England Girls' School, Armidale; Church of England Girls' Grammar School, Sydney. **Family:** Married Stanser Patchett (died); one son and one daughter (deceased). **Career:** Journalist, *Sun* group of newspapers, Sydney, 1926-31, then freelance writer in England and Europe; ran beauty salon in London; lived in the Caribbean in the 1930s, and in London from 1946. **Address:** c/o Abelard Schuman, 7 Leicester Place, London WC2H 7BP, England.

Publications for Children

Fiction

Ajax, The Warrior, illustrated by Eric Tansley. London, Lutterworth Press, 1953; as *Ajax, Golden Dog of the Australian Bush,* Indianapolis, Bobbs Merrill, 1953.
Kidnappers of Space. London, Lutterworth Press, 1953; as *Space Captives of the Golden Men,* Indianapolis, Bobbs Merrill, 1953.
The Lee Twins, Beauty Students. London, Lane, 1953.
Tam the Untamed, illustrated by Joan Kiddell-Monroe. London, Lutterworth Press, 1954; Indianapolis, Bobbs Merrill, 1955.
Lost on Venus. London, Lutterworth Press, 1954; as *Flight to the Misty Planet,* Indianapolis, Bobbs Merrill, 1956.
Evening Star, illustrated by Olga Lehmann. London, Lutterworth Press, 1954.
Adam Troy, Astroman. London, Lutterworth Press, 1954.
"Your Call, Miss Gaynor," illustrated by Bill Martin. London, Lutterworth Press, 1955.
Treasure of the Reef, illustrated by Joan Kiddell-Monroe. London, Lutterworth Press, 1955; as *The Great Barrier Reef,* Indianapolis, Bobbs Merrill, 1958.
Undersea Treasure Hunters, illustrated by Joan Kiddell-Monroe. London, Lutterworth Press, 1955; as *The Chance of Treasure,* Indianapolis, Bobbs Merrill, 1957.
Send for Johnny Danger. London, Lutterworth Press, 1956; New York, McGraw Hill, 1958.
Return to the Reef, illustrated by Joan Kiddell-Monroe. London, Lutterworth Press, 1956.
Sally's Zoo, illustrated by Pat Marriott. London, Hamish Hamilton, 1957.

Outback Adventure, illustrated by Joan Kiddell-Monroe. London, Lutterworth Press, 1957.
Caribbean Adventurers, illustrated by William Stobbs. London, Lutterworth Press, 1957.
The Mysterious Pool, illustrated by Pat Marriott. London, Hamish Hamilton, 1958.
The Brumby, illustrated by Juliet McLeod. London, Lutterworth Press, 1958; as *Brumby, The Wild White Stallion,* Indianapolis, Bobbs Merrill, 1959.
The Call of the Bush, illustrated by Brian Wildsmith. London, Lutterworth Press, 1959.
The Quest of Ati Manu, illustrated by Stuart Tresilian. London, Lutterworth Press, 1960; Indianapolis, Bobbs Merrill, 1962.
Warrimoo, illustrated by Roger Payne. Leicester, Brockhampton Press, 1961; Indianapolis, Bobbs Merrill, 1963.
Come Home, Brumby, illustrated by Stuart Tresilian. London, Lutterworth Press, 1961; as *Brumby, Come Home,* Indianapolis, Bobbs Merrill, 1962.
The End of the Outlaws, illustrated by Roger Payne. London, Lutterworth Press, 1961; Indianapolis, Bobbs Merrill, 1963.
Dangerous Assignment, illustrated by Roger Payne. Leicester, Brockhampton Press, 1962; Indianapolis, Bobbs Merrill, 1964.
The Golden Wolf, illustrated by Roger Payne. London, Lutterworth Press, 1962; Indianapolis, Bobbs Merrill, 1965.
Circus Brumby, illustrated by Stuart Tresilian. London, Lutterworth Press, 1963.
The Venus Project, illustrated by Roger Payne. Leicester, Brockhampton Press, 1963.
Ajax and the Haunted Mountain, illustrated by Roger Payne. London, Lutterworth Press, 1963; Indianapolis, Bobbs Merrill, 1966.
Tiger in the Dark, illustrated by Roger Payne. Leicester, Brockhampton Press, 1964; New York, Duell, 1966.
Ajax and the Drovers, illustrated by Roger Payne. London, Lutterworth Press, 1964.
Stranger in the Herd, illustrated by Stuart Tresilian. London, Lutterworth Press, 1964; New York, Duell, 1966.
The White Dingo, illustrated by Peter Kesteven. London, Lutterworth Press, 1965.
Brumby Foal, illustrated by Victor Ambrus. London, Lutterworth Press, 1965.
Summer on Wild Horse Island, illustrated by Roger Payne. Leicester, Brockhampton Press, 1965; New York, Meredith Press, 1967.
The Terror of Manooka, illustrated by Roger Payne. London, Lutterworth Press, 1966.
Summer on Boomerang Beach, illustrated by Roger Payne. Leicester, Brockhampton Press, 1967.
Festival of Jewels, illustrated by Roger Payne. Leicester, Brockhampton Press, 1968.
Farm Beneath the Sea, illustrated by H. Johns. London, Harrap, 1969.
Quarter Horse Boy, illustrated by Roger Payne. London, Harrap, 1970.
The Long Ride, illustrated by Michael Charlton. London, Lutterworth Press, 1970.
Rebel Brumby, illustrated by Roger Payne. Guildford, Surrey, Lutterworth Press, 1972.
Roar of the Lion, illustrated by Douglas Phillips. Guildford, Surrey, Lutterworth Press, 1973.
Hunting Cat. London, Abelard Schuman, 1976.

Publications for Adults

Novels

Wild Brother. London, Collins, 1954.
Cry of the Heart. London, Collins, 1956; New York, Abelard Schuman, 1957.
The Saffron Woman. London, Heinemann, 1958.
Brit. London, Hodder and Stoughton, 1961.
In a Wilderness. London, Hodder and Stoughton, 1962; as *Dingo,* New York, Doubleday, 1963.
The Last Warrior. London, Hodder and Stoughton, 1965; New York, Doubleday, 1966.

Other

The Proud Eagles. London, Heinemann, 1960; Cleveland, World, 1961.
A Budgie Called Fred. London, Barker, 1964.
Bird of Jove (as David Bruce). New York, Putnam, 1971.

*

Mary Elwyn Patchett comments:

All my books, for adults and for children, concern my main interests—animals, falconry, undersea exploration, interplanetary flight, history—and almost all are factual adventure. The animals concerned range from a great Berkut eagle from Central Asia to a small hunting cat from Trinidad. I often use Australian background and animals, and I work on accuracy.

If I had another life to live it would be spent with animals; not to tame them, or to sentimentalize over them, nor to make them replicas of myself or improve their love-lives, but simply to understand them and, if I could, to compensate a little for the hideous things which man has done, and is doing, to them.

I don't think I write especially for children, with the exception of a few books for small children. I just think of an idea and write the book in the best way I can.

* * *

Though some of her early books are on other subjects, Mary Elwyn Patchett's main theme, and her best, is animal life. She makes an attempt to understand the natures of animals as themselves and not merely as adjuncts to human life. This sympathy, together with her concern for their often threatened lives and her intimate knowledge of their surroundings, gives her books vision and vigour. The movement and freedom of her writing, the independence of her characters, and their ability to deal with the unexpected and dangerous, could well be the inheritance from an Australian birth and an upbringing in the bush.

Her best book by most counts is *Tiger in the Dark,* a quest in the Australian interior for the supposedly extinct Australian marsupial tiger-wolf. A blind Aboriginal child serves as guide. *Roar of the Lion,* an African story, is about a boy's struggle to come to terms with the inevitable separation from his pet lioness cub when, at maturity, she must return to her life in the wild. In the Brumbies books, a series about wild horses in Australia, Joey Muhan tries, against great odds, to protect the brumbies from hunters and to build up a herd in a place where they can live in safety. The Ajax books describe the life of a girl on a cattle station in the Australian outback. *Quarter Horse Boy,* also a story of the outback, is about an Aboriginal boy's skill with horses and his affectionate adoption by the human family for whom he works.

Other books include *Farm Beneath the Sea,* which combines science fiction with facts about marine life and some evocative descriptions. The Dexter family, having undergone a lung operation to make them breathe like fish, descend a hundred feet below the surface of the Pacific among the "incredible blaze of multicolored corals. They looked almost lush in the way flowers do. The small fishey-life swarmed about them like bees around spring flowers." Here they live and set up an experimental attempt to farm the sea bed. A friendly dolphin helps. *Summer on Wild Horse Island* is, again, set beside the Great Barrier Reef among the sharks and barracudas.

—Nancy Shepherdson

PATERSON, Katherine

Nationality: American (originally Chinese: came to the United States, 1940). **Born:** Katherine Womeldorf, Qing Jiang, China, 31 October 1932. **Education:** King College, Bristol, Tennessee, 1950-54, A.B. (summa cum laude) 1954; Presbyterian School of Christian Education, Richmond, Virginia, 1955-57, M.A. 1957; Kobe School of the Japanese Language, Japan, 1957-59; Union Theological Seminary, New York, 1961-62, M.R.E. 1962. **Family:** Married John Barstow Paterson in 1962; two sons and two adopted daughters. **Career:** Teacher, Lovettsville Elementary School, Virginia, 1954-55; missionary, Presbyterian Church Board of World Missions, Shikoku Island, Japan, 1957-61; master of Sacred Studies and English, Pennington School for Boys, New Jersey, 1963-65. Lives in Barre, Vermont. **Awards:** National Book award, 1977, 1979; American Library Association Newbery medal, 1978, 1981; Christopher award, 1979; University of Southern Mississippi award, 1983; University of Minnesota Kerlan award, 1983; Catholic Library Association Regina medal, 1988. Litt.D.: King College, 1978; Saint Mary-of-the-Woods College, Indiana, 1981; University of Maryland, College Park, 1982; Washington and Lee University, Lexington, Virginia, 1982; D.H.L.: Otterbein College, Westerville, Ohio, 1980; Shenandoah College, Winchester, Virginia, 1986. **Address:** c/o E.P. Dutton, 2 Park Avenue, New York, New York 10016, U.S.A.

Publications for Children

Fiction

The Sign of the Chrysanthemum, illustrated by Peter Landa. New York, Crowell, 1973; London, Kestrel, 1975.
Of Nightingales That Weep, illustrated by Haru Wells. New York, Crowell, 1974; London, Kestrel, 1976.
The Master Puppeteer, illustrated by Haru Wells. New York, Crowell, 1975.
Bridge to Terabithia, illustrated by Donna Diamond. New York, Crowell, 1977; London, Gollancz, 1978.
The Great Gilly Hopkins. New York, Crowell, 1978; London, Gollancz, 1979.
Angels and Other Strangers: Family Christmas Stories. New York, Crowell, 1979; as *Star of Night,* London, Gollancz, 1980.
Jacob Have I Loved. New York, Crowell, 1980; London, Gollancz, 1981.
Rebels of the Heavenly Kingdom. New York, Dutton, and London, Gollancz, 1983.
Come Sing, Jimmy Jo. New York, Dutton, 1985; London, Gollancz, 1986.
Park's Quest. New York, Dutton, 1988; London, Gollancz, 1989.
The Tale of the Mandarin Ducks, illustrated by Leo and Diane Dillon. New York, Dutton, 1990.
Lyddie. New York, Dutton, 1991.
The King's Equal. New York, HarperCollins, 1992.
Smallest Cow in the World. New York, HarperCollins, 1993.
Flip-flop Girl. New York, Dutton, 1994.
A Midnight Clear: Stories for the Christmas Season. New York, Lodestar Books, 1995.
Jip: His Story. New York, Lodestar Books, 1996.
The Angel and the Donkey, illustrated by Alexander Koshkin. New York, Clarion Books, 1996.
Marvin's Best Christmas Present Ever, illustrated by Jane Clark Brown. New York, HarperCollins, 1997.
Celia and the Sweet, Sweet Water, illustrated by Vladimir Vagin. New York, Clarion Books, 1998.
Parzival: The Quest of the Grail Knight. New York, Lodestar Books, 1998.

Other

Who Am I?, illustrated by David Stone. Richmond, C.L.C. Press, 1966.
To Make Men Free: Learning Center Box. Richmond, John Knox Press, 1973.
Justice for All People. New York, Friendship Press, 1973.
Consider the Lilies: Plants of the Bible, with John Paterson, illustrated by Anne Ophelia Dowden. New York, Crowell, 1986.

Editor with others, *The Big Book for the Planet.* New York, Dutton, 1993.

Translator, *The Crane Wife,* by Sumiko Yagawa, illustrated by Suekichi Akaba. New York, Morrow, 1981.
Translator, *The Tongue-Cut Sparrow* (Japanese folktale), retold by Momoko Ishii, illustrated by Suekichi Akaba. New York, Dutton, 1987.

Publications for Adults

Other

Gates of Excellence: On Reading and Writing Books for Children. New York, Elsevier Nelson, 1981.
The Spying Heart: More Thoughts on Reading and Writing Books for Children. New York, Dutton, 1989.
A Sense of Wonder: On Reading and Writing Books for Children. New York, Plume, 1995.
Images of God: Views of the Invisible, with John Paterson. New York, Clarion Books, 1998.

*

Media Adaptations: *Bridge to Terabithia* (play), music by Steve Liebman New York, Samuel French, 1992.

Manuscript Collections: Kerlan Collection, University of Minnesota, Minneapolis.

Katherine Paterson comments:

My aim as a writer is to engage young readers in the life of a story that came out of me, but which is not mine, but ours. I don't just want my readers' time or attention, I want their lives. I want their senses, imagination, intellect, emotions, and all the experiences they have known breathing life into the words upon the page. I hope to do my part so well that young readers will delight to join me as co-authors.

* * *

The quest for the father—or the mother—is a recurrent theme and structural pattern in the novels of Katherine Paterson. Under one guise or another, Paterson's protagonists, with the exception of her two most recent, Lydia Worthen and Vinnie Matthews, are searching not only for self but also, in Joseph Campbell's terms, for the Father/Mother. Whether it is paramount or subordinate in any given story, whether its object is living or dead, a known actual presence or a fantasy, that quest infuses Paterson's stories with a metaphysical meaning, reflective of her values as well as providing her work with a principle of unity. A particular family, however impaired, provides a framework that anchors each novel in concrete reality, simultaneously enabling meaning to transcend the limitations of historical time and cultural locale. In Paterson's fictions the bruised or broken family and the search for the father become milieu and metaphor for the archetypal heroic quest, the end of which, according to Campbell's theory of the monomyth, is that moment of enlightenment when the hero attains "transpersonal centeredness"—that is, when he or she penetrates to the source of life, rises above the individual self and achieves atonement (at-one-ment) with the Universal will, a ubiquitous power out of which all things rise (i.e. the father or mother).

For Paterson's protagonists the quest for the father/mother on the human level becomes a metaphor for the soul's journey, for attempts to understand the human being's relationship with God, a point the author herself seems to affirm: "The hero," she says, "must leave home, confront fabulous dangers, and return the victor to grant boons to his fellows. Or a wandering nobody must go out from bondage through the wilderness and by the grace of God become truly someone who can give back something of what she has been given." Such, Paterson says, is the story of her own life and those of her characters (*Spying Heart*). Because the quest is an archetypal pattern, and because Paterson is adroit at fusing several levels of story, her novels are powerful dramas, never overtly didactic nor sectarian, both eliciting and restraining heartfelt emotion. Because the possible combination of characters and incidents is infinite, the search for the father provides the author with an inexhaustible story lode, which she mines with variety and verve, whether her stories are set in twelfth or eighteenth-century Japan, nineteenth-century China, or the United States of the 1840s, 1940s, or 1990s.

Though the quest for the father permeates Paterson's canon, individual novels explore unique characters and situations, as well as different aspects and implications of the quest and its fulfillment. The quest for the father is most overt in Paterson's first novel, *The Sign of the Chrysanthemum* (1973) and *Park's Quest* (1988). The protagonists of both books—the orphaned Muna in twelfth-century Heiankyo (significantly, the Japanese for "City of Eternal Peace"), and the semi-orphaned Parkington Waddell Broughton the Fifth in post-Vietnam Washington, D.C.—deliberately set out to find their biological fathers of whom they know almost nothing. Through a painful passage each comes to know a spiritual father-guide and protector, the sword maker Fukuji and Uncle Frank respectively. In the latter novel, allusion and imagery specifically connect Park's quest with those of Parzival and the Arthurian knights' search for the Holy Grail. Thus *Park's Quest,* like *Jacob Have I Loved* (1980), emphasizes the mythological and metaphysical dimensions that make each so much more than realistic problem novels. *Jacob Have I Loved* explores within a family setting the mystery of God's love, coexistent with a kind of impersonality, a love which breaks through even self-inflicted blinders. Initiated and enlightened through their trials, both Park Broughton and Louise Bradshaw become like the merciful father: through them compassion and healing flow out to others.

The Master Puppeteer (1975) depicts two heroes, Jiro and Kinshi, who, despite knowing their biological fathers (Hanji the puppet maker and Yoshida the puppeteer), struggle to reconcile in those parents their cruel, destructive sides with their humane, beneficent qualities. *Bridge to Terabithia* (1977) subsumes the quest for the father in the theme of friendship that conquers death. Nonetheless, the parents of both Jesse Aarons and Leslie Burke, and the relationships between them and their children, are intrinsic to the story, and the revelation of the usually abstracted Mr. Aarons as an understanding and compassionate father images a universal power who cares that children die and that others cannot comprehend why. Gilly Hopkins has to surrender the vision of her biological mother as a true parent and to recognize "god" and "home" in the huge-lapped Maime Trotter, who loves the child as she is. Having achieved union with this mother-god, Gilly is able to return to the real world of her biological grandmother, and like Park Broughton and Louise Bradshaw, to give and accept love.

The dissolution of the families of both protagonists of *Rebels of the Heavenly Kingdom* (1983) calls forth Mei Lin and Wang Lee on their journeys. Mei Lin's father is the archetypal ogre who figuratively chews her up by selling her to the army for the soldiers' pleasure. Wang Lee's father is weak, can only stand by, helpless to prevent his son's enslavement. Finally, after the betrayal and slaughter wreaked by a war of zealotry, Mei Lin and Wang Lee marry, their union symbolizing that they have beheld the face of the Father, that is, they have attained a glimpse of a world united in justice and peace. Their vision is translated into action in their own immediate domestic sphere through subsequent cultivation of the land and the raising of their male and female children with equal rights and responsibilities, both acts of healing of the "great angry wound[s] upon the flesh of the earth."

In *Of Nightingales That Weep* (1974) and *Come Sing, Jimmy Jo* (1985), the protagonists' search for the father is more involved, complicated in the former by the fusion of a father figure and a bridegroom into the same character, and in the latter by the exigency of the protagonist's choice between the biological father he never knew and the step-father who has raised him. In the Japanese historical romance, when the dwarf Goro marries Takiko's widowed mother, he invades the child's paradisal relationship with her mother and the memory of her hero father. For several turbulent years Takiko regards Goro, in turn, as a misshapen monster, tolerable step-father and mentor, then ogre-father whom she can neither conquer nor conciliate. Ultimately recognizing the "little god" in Goro, she realizes he is her love and heartsease. Thus, for Takiko, discovery of the father is one with finding a husband and becoming a mother.

When James Johnson's quest in *Come Sing, Jimmy Jo* discloses that the gentle Jerry Lee is not his biological father, the boy feels betrayed, abandoned. After James has courageously disavowed the cowardly, opportunist Flem Keeser, he comes face to face with the mother-god figure, in this novel Grandma, who has come to take him to his Family. James's decision to acknowledge Jerry Lee as his real father reflects his atonement (repentance for his self-centeredness) and his at-one-ment with the father. Lyddie (*Lyddie,* 1991) and Vinnie Matthews (*Flip-Flop Girl,* 1994) are different from their literary predecessors. Unlike earlier female heroes Takiko, Sara Louise, and Mei Lin, Lyddie rejects love and marriage as the path to fulfillment, the way to happiness and security, and chooses knowledge and independence. Couched in terms of the novel's major theme of deliverance out of slavery into freedom, Lyddie's quest is an attempt to free herself from the father—and the obligations with which he has encumbered her—in order to discover her authentic self. She must come to terms with her betrayal as a woman by the father and by masculine institutions, to learn that she is not dependent on any Father for her sense of her own value as a person and as a woman. Lyddie's rejection of Luke Stevens, her decision to go to Oberlin, and her final epigrammatic words "We can still hop," indicate that she has the courage to venture alone into untried, and, in the 1840s, unconventional, experiences as a "wandering nobody must go out from bondage through the wilderness." She has become aware that until she knows who she is as a person, reunion with the other—the Father/Mother—and attainment of "transpersonal centeredness," symbolized in marriage, is neither desirable nor possible. Vinnie Matthews' story focuses on her grief and dislocation at the death of her father. Like Lyddie (though she is much younger and her story simpler), she comes to accept the death of the father she remembers fondly, and to take upon herself responsibility for her actions, looking to herself to redress the wrongs she has wrought.

After their moments of enlightenment, none of Paterson's heroes refuses to return to society. Each moves out to share the fruits of a life-centering, life-renewing vision with others, be they a little sister or brother, a husband and children, a lonely grandmother, the inhabitants of a mountain hamlet, hungry and clamoring fans, or through education the evils of social institutions. Thus, Paterson's heroes become, in a sense, saviors of their people, channels of grace, and her novels provide readers with experiences of healing and a sense of hope.

Setting is a multi-functional constituent of Paterson's novels. The specific time in history and the actual geographical location, carefully researched and finely detailed, incite the protagonists' dreams and influence the kinds of persons they become. The famine of 1783-87 has reduced the populace of Osaka to bestial scavengers plundering and burning their city in *Master Puppeteer.* The movement back and forth, in and out from the streets of Osaka and the disciplined world of the Hanaza, the theater compound, provides the novel with a structural framework, creates and controls the dramatic and emotional tension, and incorporates a major theme, that life and art reflect each other. In *Bridge to Terabithia,* the scene shifts to contemporary America. Although *Bridge* is more immediately about place—those special places that entice children into secret realms where they become kings and queens and heroic defenders against giants of evil—the specific places are not so fully depicted as the Japanese city and countryscapes. Evocatively outlined, they invite readers to paint in details from their own experiences. Setting engenders major images and symbols knit smoothly into the pattern of each novel. The binding images of a novel often become symbols of the main characters and their relationships, as do fire and the sword in *The Sign of the Chrysanthemum,* the potter's clay and the koto Takiko plays in *Nightingales,* the songs the Johnson Family performs solo or in harmony in *Come Sing, Jimmy Jo,* the coconut shell from which Park, Thanh, and the Grandfather drink the water in the springhouse in *Park's Quest,* and the bear and the machines that symbolize the beasts from without and within that threaten Lyddie.

A significant source of additional images and symbols is literary allusion, a particularly distinctive characteristic of Paterson's narrative technique. Allusions serve Paterson also as a structural and thematic device. Not only do they indicate a continuity among Paterson's stories and the literatures of a variety of cultures, they also connect the stories of her humble characters with similar stories of more eminent figures, and, thus, heighten the significance of the ordinary and extend meaning beyond the individual to the universal. Each of Paterson's novels except her most recent, *Flip-Flop Girl* (1994), is couched within references to other literary works—fairy tales, Japanese and Biblical myth, heroic epic, poetry, drama, song lyrics. Even this latest novel nods to the popularity of subliterary texts, the "knock-knock" jokes, among eight-to-ten year-olds, probably its largest audience. For the author, committed to both her Christian faith and to honest, unblinking confrontation of contemporary reality, literary allusion is particularly useful, for it permits the disclosure of authorial values without narrative commentary, an attribute appealing to a writer whose style is characteristically spare and who eschews didacticism in favor of the imaginative and emotional power of story. Literary allusion allows the author to communicate revealed truths, which she perceives as offering hope and joy in realistic fictions that explore the meanings and *modus operandi* of those truths in concrete worlds of suffering, fear, and hopelessness. Literary allusion contributes to the explicability and credibility of the transformation of tragedy into romance in Paterson's earliest fictions, and into comedy in her later fictions.

In *Of Nightingales That Weep,* the epigraph from a No play suggests the archetypal theme that human love partakes of the divine in its power to transform the bestial into the beautiful. The novel affirms the verity of the epigraph, which states that the meeting of human hearts can change a "fragile dream of joy/ Into the lasting love of waking life!" Subsequent novels are less romantic, more ironic, perhaps none more complex than *Jacob Have I Loved,* in which the controlling referents are the traditional Appalachian carol "I Wonder as I Wander" and the Bible story of God's preference for an apparently undeserving but favored younger twin. The meaning of the Biblical myth is explored, finally ironically overturned in its literal sense, and only ambiguously reaffirmed by an ending in which allusion and Paterson's fiction coalesce swiftly and brilliantly. In *Come Sing, Jimmy Jo,* the song lyrics, which comprise the dominant allusions—to mention only three: "Keep on the Sunny Side," "Way-faring Stranger," and "Will the Circle Be Unbroken?"—are clues to the tensions and theme of the story: people are sojourners on earth, scourged by life's disjunctions, but journeying to a state of unity and bliss. The two paramount sources of allusion in *The Great Gilly Hopkins* are fairy tales, including Tolkien's trilogy, and Wordsworth's "Intimations of Immortality" ode. Both function primarily to accentuate the development of the protagonist and to articulate an age-old—and a fundamental Patersonian—theme: the great myth of unification, of reconciliation of separate and isolated entities in an eternal synthesis. Dickens' *Oliver Twist* provides the overt allusive frame for *Lyddie,* highlighting the demons of impersonal and impoverishing institutions, dominated by cruel male agents, and opening Lyddie's imagination and insight into story and life; however, the implicit and more significant undercurrent throughout *Lyddie* is the myth of Artemis, the goddess who, according to Christine Downing, beckons from the future to call a woman to the person she is to become. The strongest beckoning voice within the novel is actually called Diana, and Lyddie, at the end, is ready for the "wilderness of Arcadia," for college at Oberlin, where a different logic prevails and where she can develop the parts of herself suppressed during her quest in the textile mills. More than any of the novels, *Park's Quest,* the basic story pattern and theme of which are reminiscent of *Gilly Hopkins,* seems consciously shaped by its dominant referents, the exploits of the Arthurian Round Table, particularly Parzival's quest for the Holy Grail. In a last deft allusion to the Grail story, Paterson accomplishes what she does so often at the end of her novels. She draws together various levels of story, disparate images and themes, in a final consummate image so that fictional elements overlap, intertwine, and subtly take on the ambience of one another. Beyond this, the allusion with which each of Paterson's novels closes becomes an objective correlative of the protagonists' assent to the fundamental truth of the earlier literary work, despite the continual challenging and undercutting of that truth throughout their fictions. Paterson's novels customarily end with such an allusion in scenes that symbolically reveal that their heroes, in beholding the face of the Father, have attained a glimpse of the source and meaning of life and have become ripe to understand, in Campbell's words, "how the sickening and insane tragedies of this vast and ruthless cosmos are completely validated in the majesty of Being."

Paterson's imagination has obviously been shaped by literature, notably by various mythologies, particularly the Bible. It is natural, then, that her original and provocative stories reflect archetypal patterns amplified by meaning accrued to them in subsequent literary classics. For, as Campbell again reminds us, mythological figures that come down to us are "controlled and intended statements of certain spiritual principles." Muna, Takiko, Jiro and Kinshi, Jesse Aarons and Leslie Burke, Gilly Hopkins, Louise Bradshaw, Wang Lee and Mei Lin, James Johnson, and Parkington Waddell Broughton V are twelve of the thousand faces of the archetypal hero finely crafted by Katherine Paterson. In Lydia and Lavinia Matthews, Paterson makes explicit a feminist note that has been minor in many of her earlier novels. Theirs are not quests for the "other" to complete and fulfill them. Rather, Vinnie and especially Lyddie are more like today's heroine, who, as defined by Maureen Murdock "must release resentment toward the mother, put aside blame and idolization of the father, and find the courage to face her own darkness. Her shadow is hers to name and embrace" (*The Heroine's Journey*). While Lyddie's final choice may not actually set her apart from other Paterson heroes, it does distinguish her story from theirs because in it the author dramatizes a story in the hero's life that she may only allude to in earlier ones.

—M. Sarah Smedman

PATTEN, Brian

Nationality: British. **Born:** Liverpool, Lancashire, 7 February 1946. **Education:** Sefton Park Secondary School, Liverpool. **Career:** Formerly reporter, *Bootle Times,* and editor, *Underdog,* both Liverpool. Regents Lecturer, University of California, San Diego, 1985. **Awards:** Eric Gregory award, 1967; Arts Council grant, 1969; Mystery Writers of America special award, 1976; English Arts Council award, 1997. **Agent:** Rogers, Coleridge & White, 20 Powis Mews, London, W11 1JN. **Address:** c/o Puffin Books, 27 Wrights Lane, London W8 5TZ, England.

Publications for Children

Fiction

The Elephant and the Flower: Almost-Fables, illustrated by Meg Rutherford. London, Allen and Unwin, 1970.
Manchild. London, Covent Garden Press, 1973.
Two Stories. London, Covent Garden Press, 1973.
Mr. Moon's Last Case, illustrated by Mary Moore. London, Allen and Unwin, 1975; New York, Scribner, 1976.
Emma's Doll, illustrated by Mary Moore. London, Allen and Unwin, 1976.
Jimmy Tag-Along, illustrated by David Mostyn. London, Viking Kestrel, 1988.
Grizzelda Frizzle and Other Stories. London, Viking, 1992.
The Magic Bicycle, illustrated by Arthur Robins. New York, Walker, 1993.
Impossible Parents. London, Walker, 1992.

Plays

The Pig and the Junkle (produced Nottingham, 1975; London, 1977).
The Sly Cormorant (produced London, 1977).
The Ghosts of Riddle Me Heights (produced Birmingham, 1980).
Gargling with Jelly, adaptation of his own poems (produced Hull, 1988; playscript published by Samuel French, London, 1991).

Radio Play: *The Hypnotic Island,* 1977.

Television Plays: *The Man Who Hated Children,* 1978; *Mr. Moon's Last Case,* from his own story, 1983.

Poetry

The Sly Cormorant and the Fishes: New Adaptations into Poetry of the Aesop Fables, illustrated by Errol Le Cain. London, Kestrel, 1977.
Gargling with Jelly, illustrated by David Mostyn. London, Viking Kestrel, 1985.
Thawing Frozen Frogs. London, Viking, 1990.
The Utter Nutters, illustrated by David Mostyn. London, Viking, 1994.

Other

Jumping Mouse (American Indian tale), illustrated by Mary Moore. London, Allen and Unwin, 1972.

Editor, *Gangsters, Ghosts, and Dragonflies: A Book of Story Poems,* illustrated by Terry Oakes. London, Allen and Unwin, 1981.
Editor, *The Puffin Book of Twentieth-Century Children's Verse.* London, Penguin Children's Books/Viking, 1991.

PUBLICATIONS FOR ADULTS

Plays

Behind the Lines (revue), with Roger McGough (produced London, 1982).
The Mouthtrap, with Roger McGough (produced Edinburgh and London, 1982).
Films of Fire: The Dying of the Light, (television play; Chanel 4, British television, 1997).

Radio Play: *Blind Love,* 1983.

Poetry

Portraits. Privately printed, 1962.
The Mersey Sound: Penguin Modern Poets 10, with Adrian Henri and Roger McGough. London, Penguin, 1967; revised edition, 1974, 1983.
Little Johnny's Confession. London, Allen and Unwin, 1967; New York, Hill and Wang, 1968.
Atomic Adam. London, Fulham Gallery, 1967.
Notes to the Hurrying Man: Poems Winter '66-Summer '68. London, Allen and Unwin, and New York, Hill and Wang, 1969.
The Homecoming. London, Turret, 1969.
The Irrelevant Song. Frensham, Surrey, Sceptre Press, 1970.
Little Johnny's Foolish Invention: A Poem (bilingual edition), translated by Robert Sanesi. Milan, M'Arte, 1970.
Walking Out: The Early Poems of Brian Patten. Leicester, Transican, 1970.
At Four O'Clock in the Morning. Frensham, Surrey, Sceptre Press, 1971.
The Irrelevant Song and Other Poems. London, Allen and Unwin, 1971; revised edition, 1975.
When You Wake Tomorrow. London, Turret, 1971.
And Sometimes It Happens. London, Steam Press, 1972.
The Eminent Professors and the Nature of Poetry as Enacted Out by Members of the Poetry Seminar One Rainy Evening. London, Poem-of-the-Month Club, 1972.
Double Image, with Michael Baldwin and John Fairfax. London, Longman, 1972.
The Unreliable Nightingale. London, Rota, 1973.
Vanishing Trick. London, Allen and Unwin, 1976.
Grave Gossip. London, Allen and Unwin, 1979.
Love Poems. London, Allen and Unwin, 1981.
New Volume, with Adrian Henri and Roger McGough. London, Penguin, 1983.
Storm Damage. London, Unwin Hyman, 1988.
Grinning Jack. London, Allen and Unwin, 1990.
ARMADA. London, HarperCollins and Flamingo Books, 1996.

Recordings: *Selections from Little Johnny's Confession and Notes to the Hurrying Man and New Poems,* Caedmon, 1969; *Vanishing Trick,* Tangent, 1976; *The Sly Cormorant,* Argo, 1977; *Gifted Wreckage,* with Roger McGough and Adrian Henri, Talking Tape, 1984; *Jelly Pie,* with Roger McGough, Puffin, 1987; *Grizzelda Frizzle and Other Stories* (double cassette), London, Chivers, 1994.

Other

Editor, with Pat Krett, *The House That Jack Built: Poems for Shelter.* London, Allen and Unwin, 1973.
Editor, *Clare's Countryside: Natural History Poetry and Prose,* by John Clare. London, Heinemann, 1981.

Brian Patten comments:

My chief aim in writing poetry for children is to delight, in writing poetry for adults, to remind them of what they forgot they knew.

* * *

From his early precocious success as a poet, Brian Patten has combined a childlike curiosity and clarity of vision with a more sophisticated poetic imagination. Most of his many published volumes for adults contain at least some poems that are accessible to children. His early work (like the *Little Johnny* poems and "Schoolboy") is grounded in schooldays and their associations. There are images of lollipops and toffees, overflowing inkwells, "an old rocking-horse in Woolworth's," cinema matinees. Although he queries the youthful icons ("Where are you now Superman?")—Winnie-the-Pooh, Mr. Toad, Alice, and Brer Rabbit still exert a bookish nostalgic charm: "Soon you will climb into a bus full of schoolchildren/ and ask for a single back to innocence." Patten has described his intense childhood memories of a neighbour's book-filled house which "contained many worlds.... In it I felt free of the restraints imposed on me by adults, it became a sanctuary from the crowded and claustrophobic world in which I lived." That experience of the potentially liberating power of books seems to underlie his sardonic contempt for the English teacher who does not read books, saying, "I'm too busy for literature, that's the problem" ("Dead Thick"), or the academic critic's negative concern for what poems do *not* do ("The Critics' Chorus or What the Poem Lacked"). These sentiments also seem to motivate the way in which Patten himself writes for children.

Patten has a delight in retelling fables and folk tales, not always with a conventional moral. One of his early works for children, *Jumping Mouse,* draws on an American Plains Indian creation myth about the inevitability with which all living creatures are interrelated. It tells of an innocent mouse who jumped high enough to see the distant world and resolved to travel. The mouse's song expresses a hope that, if he is to be eaten by some predator, the eater will enjoy him: "One of us must reap some benefit from such drastic action!" In fact he is ultimately metamorphosed into an eagle, and the fable can be read at a series of different natural and symbolic levels. *The Sly Cormorant and the Fishes* has a similar emphasis on the constant interaction between hunters and hunted in a volume of verses that adapt some of Aesop's *Fables* (in their race, the hare beats the tortoise) and creates some new ones. Patten describes the stories that make up *The Elephant and the Flower* as "almost fables." They combine realism and fantasy in a jungle world where a talking flower and a tiny elephant are involved with friendly birds and animals.

In his introduction to *The Puffin Book of Twentieth-Century Children's Verse* (1991)—an excellent anthology—Patten expresses a conviction that while most adult poems age badly, "poems written for children retain their freshness. The best have a sense of wonder, mystery and mischief that their older brothers and sisters often seem to lose." Certainly the best of his own work combines a precise, almost clinical, awareness of the realities of the world with a sense of some magical power that can transmute them. *Gargling with Jelly* spent some time high on the best seller lists, sold well on audiotape, and became a popular stage show at Hull Truck Theatre. Many of the poems seem like deliberate answers to children who say "I don"t like poetry," challenging them by being unusual (the repeated missing word in "Someone Stole the"), by their comic virtuosity ("The Trouble with My Sister" and its counterpart about brothers), sometimes aggressive or challenging ("The Newcomer" and "Burying the Dog in the Garden") and sometimes serious or inspiring ("Last of my Kind" and "The Apple-Flavoured Worm"). The end of his poem on "Rules" is the golden rule: "If you do not like the rules, OPEN YOUR MOUTH AND SHOUT!" "The Saga of the Doomed Cyclist" (also published as *The Magic Bicycle*, a picture book with maps for younger children) tells of Harry Harris, who is unfortunate enough to knock over a woman who turns out to be a witch. She puts a spell on his bicycle, which forces him to go on a non-stop bike journey round the world, including some less obvious destinations. In a bewildering mixture of subjects and styles, striking, inventive lines jostle with others that are flat or sentimental. At his best, Patten has the power to make young people look again at the familiar world around them and to see something new in it.

—Robert Protherough

PEARCE, (Ann) Philippa

Has also written as Warrener. **Nationality:** British. **Born:** Great Shelford, Cambridgeshire. **Education:** Perse Girls' School, Cambridge, 1929-39; Girton College, Cambridge, B.A. (honours) in English and history 1942, M.A. **Family:** Married Martin Christie in 1963 (died 1965); one daughter. **Career:** Civil servant, 1942-45; scriptwriter and producer, 1945-58, and freelance producer, 1960-62, BBC Radio, London; assistant editor, Educational Department, Clarendon Press, Oxford, 1958-60; children's editor, André Deutsch Ltd., publishers, London, 1960-67. Freelance reviewer and lecturer. **Awards:** Library Association Carnegie medal, 1959; New York Herald Tribune Spring Festival Award, 1963; Whitbread award, 1978; Honorary Doctorate, Hull University, 1995; Officer of the British Empire, 1997. **Agent:** Laura Cecil, 17 Alwyne Villas, London N1 2HG, England.

PUBLICATIONS FOR CHILDREN

Fiction

Minnow on the Say, illustrated by Edward Ardizzone. London, Oxford University Press, 1955; as *The Minnow Leads to Treasure*, Cleveland, World, 1958.

Tom's Midnight Garden, illustrated by Susan Einzig. London, Oxford University Press, and Philadelphia, Lippincott, 1958.

Mrs. Cockle's Cat, illustrated by Antony Maitland. London, Constable, 1961; Philadelphia, Lippincott, 1962.

A Dog So Small, illustrated by Antony Maitland. London, Constable, 1962; Philadelphia, Lippincott, 1963.

The Strange Sunflower, illustrated by Kathleen Williams. London, Nelson, 1966.

The Children of the House, with Brian Fairfax-Lucy, illustrated by John Sergeant. Harmondsworth, Kestrel, and Philadelphia, Lippincott, 1968; as *The Children of Charlecote*, London, Gollancz, 1989.

The Elm Street Lot, illustrated by Mina Martinez. London, BBC Publications, 1969; augmented edition, London, Kestrel, 1979.

The Squirrel Wife, illustrated by Derek Collard. London, Longman, 1971; New York, Crowell, 1972.

What the Neighbours Did and Other Stories, illustrated by Faith Jaques. London, Longman, 1972; New York, Crowell, 1973.

The Battle of Bubble and Squeak, illustrated by Alan Baker. London, Deutsch, 1978.

The Way to Sattin Shore, illustrated by Charlotte Voake. London, Kestrel, and New York, Greenwillow, 1983.

Lion at School and Other Stories, illustrated by Caroline Sharpe. London, Viking Kestrel, 1985; New York, Greenwillow, 1986.

Who's Afraid and Other Strange Stories, illustrated by Peter Melnyczuk. London, Viking Kestrel, 1986; New York, Greenwillow, 1987.

Emily's Own Elephant, illustrated by John Lawrence. London, MacRae, 1987; New York, Greenwillow, 1988.

The Tooth Ball, illustrated by Helen Ganly. London, Deutsch, 1987.

Freddy, illustrated by David Armitage. London, Deutsch, 1988.

Old Belle's Summer Holiday, illustrated by William Geldart. London, Deutsch, 1989.

Here Comes Tod! Cambridge, Massachusetts, Candlewick Press, 1992; London, Walker, 1992.

Picture Books as Warrener

A Picnic for Bunnykins, illustrated by Walter Hayward. Harmondsworth, Viking, 1984.

Two Bunnykins Out for Tea, illustrated by Glenys Corkery. Harmondsworth, Viking, 1984.

Bunnykins in the Snow, illustrated by Walter Hayward. Harmondsworth, Viking, 1985.

Other

Beauty and the Beast, illustrated by Alan Barrett. London, Longman, and New York, Crowell, 1972.

What the Neighbours Did and Other Stories (collection of short stories). London, Kestrel/PEnguin, 1972.

The Shadow-Cage and Other Tales of the Supernatural (short stories), illustrated by Janet Archer. London, Kestrel, and New York, Crowell, 1977; excerpts reissued as *At the River-gates and Other Stories*, London, Penguin, 1996.

Editor, *Stories from Hans Christian Andersen*, illustrated by Pauline Baynes. London, Collins, 1972.

Editor, *Dread and Delight: A Century of Children's Ghost Stories*. Oxford and New York, Oxford, 1995; reissued as *A Century of Children's Ghost Stories: Tales of Dread and Delight*, 1996.

Translator, *Wings of Courage* by George Sand, illustrated by Hilary Abrahams. London, Kestrel, 1982.

*

Biography: "Philippa Pearce" by Judith Gero John, in *Dictionary of Literary Biography,* Vol. 161, *British Children's Writers since 1960, First Series,* edited by Caroline C. Hunt, Detroit, Gale, 1996, 258-267.

Critical Studies: "Philippa Pearce" by John Rowe Townsend, in *A Sense of Story: Essays on Contemporary Writers for Children,* London, Longman, 1971, 163-171; "Achieving One's Heart's Desires" by David Rees, in *The Marble in the Water: Essays on Contemporary Writers of Fiction for Children and Young Adults,* Boston, Horn Book, 1980; "Philippa Pearce's *Tom's Midnight Garden:* Finding and Losing Eden" by Raymond E. Jones, in *Touchstones: Reflections on the Best in Children's Literature,* edited by Perry Nodelman, West Lafayette, Children's Literature Association, 1985, 212-221.

* * *

Philippa Pearce's works, whether fantastic or realistic, are most memorable for their observation and presentation of individual children's thoughts and feelings, and their sometimes troubled relationships with other people. Often isolated by personality or circumstances, these children take refuge in daydreams or passionate quests. The often surprising resolutions of stories show them coming to terms, gradually, with the realities they must accept. Pearce's tales, whether full length novels or short stories, appeal to readers through their gentle humour, their range of characterisation, their lively dialogue and clear, direct style. She has also written for very young readers, with her characteristic blend of directness, humour, and fantasy.

In *Minnow on the Say,* Philippa Pearce's first published novel for children, David and Adam, owners of the canoe "Minnow," are involved in a traditional "treasure hunt" plot, but the novel is principally interesting for its picture of David learning to understand a family different from his own. A similar contrast between families and households is the starting point for *Tom's Midnight Garden,* which has proved to be Philippa Pearce's most enduring success. Banished from home by measles, Tom spends his quarantine with childless relatives in their flat in a converted house where, bored by his new life, he explores at midnight and opens a door onto the garden and house as they were in Victorian times. Invisible to everyone except Hatty, an equally lonely child who becomes Tom's friend, he makes nightly visits to the garden that last for only minutes in real time. The visits become a secret and almost obsessive pleasure, but the reader realizes before Tom that Hatty is becoming a young woman. When he is excluded from the garden the novel is brought to a dramatic and unexpected conclusion, when all questions are answered and Tom is helped to understand his feelings. The atmosphere of the garden episodes is both dreamlike and vividly concrete, and the sense of time throughout the novel is mysterious and challenging. Both the reader and Tom ask questions so that the skillfully plotted conclusion is satisfying emotionally and intellectually. The novel has been called "perfect" by John Rowe Townsend, an assessment with which most readers enthusiastically agree.

Like Tom, the central character of *A Dog So Small* is a lonely child filled with a private longing. Ben, a quiet boy in a big family, longs for a dog but knows that this is impossible in their London flat. When his grandparents send him a consolatory picture of a chihuahua, his yearning dreams the dog into existence. He is eventually given a puppy and must then come to terms with a real dog, rather than the exotic dog of his dreams. The familiar theme of the novel, a child's longing for a pet, is handled with unusual subtlety. The novel quietly points to the dangers of living in the imagination rather than the real world—and through its vivid portrayals of family life suggests the common sense and love that Ben seems to be rejecting.

The two strands of Philippa Pearce's story-telling, naturalism and a sense of mystery beneath the surface of ordinary life, are separately represented in her two collections of short stories. In *What the Neighbours Did,* stories of unremarkable happenings that children can easily identify with lead readers to think about feelings and situations they might take for granted. The supernatural in *The Shadow Cage* appears in different forms in stories which are intriguing and enjoyably chilling.

In *The Battle of Bubble and Squeak,* winner of a Whitbread award, Pearce again depicts family life with humour and sensitivity. The simple plot of children's struggle to keep two gerbils in the face of their mother's refusal is the vehicle for a picture of a family coming to terms with itself. Relationships within the family develop through the disasters of the "battle," as Mrs. Sparrow tries to expel the gerbils while the children, supported quietly by their stepfather, resist with determination. The climax of the novel, in which Mrs. Sparrow instinctively acts to defend the gerbils, marks both of her acceptance of them and the family's new-found unity. The story is told with simple directness and well-observed details.

The most recent novel, *The Way to Sattin Shore,* breaks new ground in having a girl as its central character—but also in introducing powerful adult emotions, as seen through lonely, observant Kate's eyes. Her single-minded search to find out the truth about her missing father's disappearance leads to the family's happy reunion, but not before Kate has been forced to confront some uncomfortable discoveries about adult behaviour. The child's loneliness and uncertain feelings about family and friends are explored with sensitivity. The novel seems less successful, however, in the plot's resolution, which lacks the direct impact of Pearce's earlier books.

—Judith Atkinson, updated by Caroline C. Hunt

PEASE, Howard

Nationality: American. **Born:** Stockton, California, 6 September 1894. **Education:** Stanford University, California, A.B. 1923. **Military Service:** American Expeditionary Forces at Base Hospital 3, France, 1918-19. **Family:** Married 1) Pauline Nott in 1927 (died), one son; 2) Rossie Ferrier in 1956. **Career:** Merchant seaman, early 1920s; teacher in public and private schools, California, 1924-25, 1928-34; Instructor in English, Vassar College, Poughkeepsie, New York, 1926-27. **Award:** Child Study Committee award, 1947. **Died:** 14 April 1974.

Publications for Children

Fiction

The Tattooed Man, illustrated by Mahlon Blaine. New York, Doubleday, and London, Heinemann, 1926.
The Jinx Ship, illustrated by Mahlon Blaine. New York, Doubleday, and London, Heinemann, 1927.
Shanghai Passage, illustrated by Paul Forster. New York, Doubleday, 1929.
The Gypsy Caravan, illustrated by Harrie Wood. New York, Doubleday, 1930.
Secret Cargo, illustrated by Paul Forster. New York, Doubleday, 1931.
The Ship Without a Crew. New York, Doubleday, 1934.
Wind in the Rigging. New York, Doubleday, 1935.
Hurricane Weather. New York, Doubleday, 1936.
Foghorns, illustrated by Anton Otto Fischer. New York, Doubleday, 1937.
Captain Binnacle, illustrated by Charles E. Pont. New York, Dodd Mead, 1938; London, Harrap, 1939.
Jungle River, illustrated by Armstrong Sperry. New York, Doubleday, 1938.
Highroad to Adventure, illustrated by Frank Dobias. New York, Doubleday, 1939.
Long Wharf. New York, Doubleday, 1939.
The Black Tanker. New York, Doubleday, 1941.
Night Boat and Other Tod Moran Mysteries. New York, Doubleday, 1942.
Thunderbolt House, illustrated by Armstrong Sperry. New York, Doubleday, 1944.
Heart of Danger. New York, Doubleday, 1946.
Bound for Singapore. New York, Doubleday, 1948.
The Dark Adventure. New York, Doubleday, 1950.
Captain of the "Araby." New York, Doubleday, 1953.
Shipwreck. New York, Doubleday, 1957.
Mystery on Telegraph Hill. New York, Doubleday, 1961.

* * *

Howard Pease's World War I service in France as well as his merchant marine experience in the Pacific provided him with first-hand experiences with adventure. He translated a love of travel and fascination with intrigue into over 20 mysteries featuring, and aimed at, young men. Pease's plots are predictable only in terms of their surprise turns; his characters are persons with real feelings and real abilities at solving curious human problems.

The Tod Moran mysteries consist of over a dozen titles, from *The Tattooed Man* (1926) to *Mystery on Telegraph Hill* (1961). Tod Moran, Third Mate, has an enviable career on trading vessels which go across the Pacific as far as Manila and Hong Kong. Tod is a young lad who keeps his cool in the face of typhoons and earthquakes, murder and deception in faraway places. Even on a simple overnight vacation voyage out of San Francisco Bay, though, he finds strange events to pique his interest and stir him into action for the cause of social order.

Typical of Pease's sea tales is *Secret Cargo,* a story about Larry Mathews, a poor boy who sets off to earn his own living somehow. He ships out from New Orleans on an old trading vessel bound for the South Seas. There is a death on board which Larry believes is not accidental; he then goes about solving the mystery of what was actually a murder. *Jungle River* features Don Carter who travels into the New Guinea jungle in search of his father, lost in an airplane accident.

Pease's writing is swift and concise. His characters, whether from industrial United States or primitive jungle societies, are carefully drawn, and interactions between peoples of different cultures—such as American plantation owners and Philippine laborers, American soldiers and Japanese captors—show understanding of human groups and human needs. The author was at ease writing about major North and South American ports and cities and a wide variety of Pacific Islands under colonial rules. He carried into the 20th century the American boy's dreams of independence and opportunity, which are satisfied primarily in unusual places doing unusual things, all for the cause of human justice. Fantasy, yes. Capital fantasy.

—Mary Lystad

PEET, Bill

Nationality: American. **Born:** William Bartlett Peet, Grandview, Indiana, 29 January 1915. **Education:** John Herron Art Institute, Indianapolis, 1933-37. **Family:** Married Margaret Brunst in 1937; two sons. **Career:** Writer-illustrator, Walt Disney Studio, Hollywood, 1937-64. **Awards:** Named outstanding Hoosier author of children's literature, 1967; California Reading Association's Significant Author Award, 1983; George C. Stone Center for Children's Books award, 1985; Caldecott honor book, 1989, for *Bill Peet: An Autobiography*; Annie Award for distinguished contribution to the art of animation. **Address:** 11478 Laurelcrest Road, Studio City, California 91604, U.S.A.

Publications for Children (illustrated by the author)

Fiction

Goliath II. New York, Golden Press, 1959.
Chester the Worldly Pig. Boston, Houghton Mifflin, 1965; London, Deutsch, 1985.
Farewell to Shady Glade. Boston, Houghton Mifflin, 1966; London, Deutsch, 1967.
Capyboppy. Boston, Houghton Mifflin, 1966; London, Deutsch, 1969.
Buford the Little Bighorn. Boston, Houghton Mifflin, 1967; London, Deutsch, 1968.
Jennifer and Josephine. Boston, Houghton Mifflin, 1967; London, Deutsch, 1970.
Fly Homer Fly. Boston, Houghton Mifflin, 1969; London, Deutsch, 1974.
The Whingdingdilly. Boston, Houghton Mifflin, and London, Deutsch, 1970.
The Wump World. Boston, Houghton Mifflin, 1970; London, Deutsch, 1976.
How Droofus the Dragon Lost His Head. Boston, Houghton Mifflin, 1971; London, Deutsch, 1972.
The Ant and the Elephant. Boston, Houghton Mifflin, 1970; London, Deutsch, 1975.

The Spooky Tail of Prewitt Peacock. Boston, Houghton Mifflin, 1972; London, Deutsch, 1978.
Merle the High Flying Squirrel. Boston, Houghton Mifflin, 1974; London, Deutsch, 1978.
Cyrus the Unsinkable Sea Serpent. Boston, Houghton Mifflin, 1975; London, Deutsch, 1977.
The Gnats of Knotty Pine. Boston, Houghton Mifflin, 1975; London, Deutsch, 1977.
Big Bad Bruce. Boston, Houghton Mifflin, 1977; London, Deutsch, 1979.
Eli. Boston, Houghton Mifflin, 1978; London, Deutsch, 1980.
Cowardly Clyde. Boston, Houghton Mifflin, 1979; London, Deutsch, 1980.
Encore for Eleanor. Boston, Houghton Mifflin, 1981; London, Deutsch, 1982.
Pamela Camel. Boston, Houghton Mifflin, 1984; London, Deutsch, 1985.
Jethro and Joel Were a Troll. Boston, Houghton Mifflin, 1987.
Cock-a-Doodle Dudley. Boston, Houghton Mifflin, Houghton, 1990.

Plays

Screenplays (with others): *Pinocchio,* 1940; *Dumbo,* 1941; *Fantasia,* 1941; *Song of the South,* 1946; *Cinderella,* 1950; *Alice in Wonderland,* 1951; *Peter Pan,* 1953; *Sleeping Beauty,* 1959; *One Hundred and One Dalmatians,* 1961; *The Sword in the Stone,* 1963; and short subjects.

Poetry

Hubert's Hair-Raising Adventure. Boston, Houghton Mifflin, 1959; London, Deutsch, 1960.
Huge Harold. Boston, Houghton Mifflin, 1961; London, Deutsch, 1964.
Smokey. Boston, Houghton Mifflin, 1962; London, Deutsch, 1964.
The Pinkish Purplish Bluish Egg. Boston, Houghton Mifflin, 1963; London, Deutsch, 1967.
Randy's Dandy Lions. Boston, Houghton Mifflin, 1964.
Ella. Boston, Houghton Mifflin, 1964; London, Deutsch, 1966.
Kermit the Hermit. Boston, Houghton Mifflin, 1965; London, Deutsch, 1967.
The Caboose Who Got Loose. Boston, Houghton Mifflin, 1971; London, Deutsch, 1974.
Countdown to Christmas. San Carlos, California, Golden Gate Books, 1972.
The Luckiest One of All. Boston, Houghton Mifflin, 1982; London, Deutsch, 1983.
No Such Things. Boston, Houghton Mifflin, 1983.
The Kweeks of Kookatumdee. Boston, Houghton Mifflin, 1985; London, Deutsch, 1986.
Zella, Zack, and Zodiac. Boston, Houghton Mifflin, 1986; London, Deutsch, 1987.

Other

Bill Peet: An Autobiography. Boston, Houghton Mifflin, 1989.

*

Bill Peet comments:

Many years ago I illustrated the works of others, but found it to be frustrating. In writing my own stories I am able to choose the subject matter, the things I enjoy drawing, which is far more satisfactory, and far more creative. I am not an author who illustrates, but an illustrator who writes. Such freedom is a luxury after working for over 27 years at the Disney Studio where so many cooks can spoil the broth.

Of all the responses in letters from the kids, their comments about the humor in my books please me most—"Your books are funny and make us laugh." Reading should be fun for the young ones (and for everyone).

* * *

Bill Peet's widely read picture books for young children have an exotic patina of fantasy and realistic detail with simple but imaginatively sympathetic illustrations by the author. Although the majority of Peet's texts are in prose, he uses a number of poetic devices to enhance his text, namely alliteration, assonance, consonance, and internal rhyme. Also, the texts have a balance and poise that are characteristic of the work of an author who gives attention to rhythm and the crystallizing properties of good versification, even though he is writing in prose. While his play of words and sounds may be a bit saccharine for an adult audience, children love it; and while many children forget titles of stories that have been read to them, because of Peet's repetition of sound few forget *Kermit the Hermit, The Whingdingdilly, Huge Harold,* or *The Caboose Who Got Loose.* Peet's characters are equally memorable because they all have a peculiarity or singularity that takes them off the level of stereotypes. Droofus, in *How Droofus the Dragon Lost His Head,* is a grass-eating dragon, not just a kind and good one. Scamp, the dog in *The Whingdingdilly,* wants to be a horse, but "Not just any horse. Scamp wanted to be a great horse like Palomar the giant Percheron who lived on the farm just across the road." Zack is an abandoned ostrich chick who gets a zebra foster mother. The structural pattern of most of Peet's works is consistent. The main character is introduced, there is enough exposition to set the scene before conflict is introduced, and then follows a straightforward, lively, and suspense-filled narration. The climax comes swiftly and the resolution is satisfying. Typical emotions are fear and anticipation coupled with gratification at the end of the story.

Peet's illustrations fit very well with his texts. There is a slight sense of exaggeration and elongation, even awkwardness or gawkiness in the characters that is charming rather than demeaning. Perhaps the most appealing quality in the pictures of main characters, however, is their eyes and mouths, both of which are highly expressive and not without a sense of irony, perspective, and introspection. Peet's stories for children are eminently readable, and the pictures are strong enough to stand on their own.

—Rachel Fordyce

PETERSHAM, Maud and Miska

Nationality: Americans. **PETERSHAM, Maud (Sylvia). Born** Maud Sylvia Fuller, Kingston, New York, 5 August 1889. **Education:** Vassar College, Poughkeepsie, New York, graduated 1912; New York School of Fine and Applied Arts. **Family:** Married

Miska Petersham in 1917; one son. **Career:** Worked for International Art Service, New York. **Died:** 29 November 1971. **PETERSHAM, Miska. Born:** Mikaly Petrezselyem in Törökszentmiklós, Hungary, 20 September 1888; emigrated to England, 1911, and to the United States, 1912. **Education:** Royal Academy of Art, Budapest. **Career:** Commercial artist; worked for International Art Service, New York. **Died:** 15 May 1960. **Award:** American Library Association Caldecott medal, 1946.

Publications for Children (illustrated by the authors)

Fiction

Miki. New York, Doubleday, 1929.
The Ark of Father Noah and Mother Noah. New York, Doubleday, 1930.
Auntie and Celia Jane and Miki. New York, Doubleday, 1932.
Get-a-Way, and Háry János. New York, Viking Press, 1933; London, Lovat Dickson, 1935.
Miki and Mary: Their Search for Treasure. New York, Viking Press, 1934; London, Lovat Dickson, 1935.
My Very First Book. New York, Macmillan, 1948.
The Box with Red Wheels. New York, Macmillan, 1949; London, Macmillan, 1958.
The Circus Baby. New York, Macmillan, 1950; London, Macmillan, 1958.
Off to Bed: Seven Stories for Wide-Awakes. New York, Macmillan, 1954.
The Boy Who Had No Heart. New York, Macmillan, 1955.
The Peppernuts. New York, Macmillan, and London, Macmillan, 1958.

Other

The Story Book of Clothes [*Food, Houses, Things We Use, Transportation, Earth's Treasures, Gold, Iron and Steel, Oil, Ships, Trains, Wheels, Coal, Aircraft, Foods from the Field, Rice, Sugar, Wheat, Corn, Cotton, Rayon, Silk, Things We Wear, Wool*]. Philadelphia, Winston, 24 vols., 1933-39; *Coal, Iron and Steel, Oil, Houses, Food, Clothes, Gold, Transportation, Wheels, Aircraft, Ships, Trains,* London, Dent, 12 vols., 1936-38; *Cotton, Rayon, Rice, Wheat, Wool, Corn,* London, Wells Gardner Darton, 6 vols., 1947-48.
David. Philadelphia, Winston, and London, Dent, 1938.
Joseph and His Brothers. Philadelphia, Winston, and London, Dent, 1938.
Moses. Philadelphia, Winston, and London, Dent, 1938.
Ruth. Philadelphia, Winston, and London, Dent, 1938.
An American ABC. New York, Macmillan, 1941.
America's Stamps: The Story of One Hundred Years of United States Postage Stamps. New York, Macmillan, 1947.
The Story of the Presidents of the United States of America. New York, Macmillan, 1953; revised edition, 1966.
The Silver Mace: A Story of Williamsburg. New York, Macmillan, 1956.

*

Manuscript Collections: May Massee Collection, Emporia State University, Kansas; University of Oregon Library, Eugene; Kerlan Collection, University of Minnesota, Minneapolis.

Illustrators: *The Cambridge Book of Poetry for Children* (illustrated by Maud alone) edited by Kenneth Grahame, 1916; *Everyday Classics: Primer—Second Reader* by Franklin T. Baker and Ashley H. Thorndike, 1917; *A Child's Own Book of Verse* edited by Ada Maria Skinner and Frances Wickes, 3 vols., 1917; *Fil and Filippa* by John Stuart Thomson, 1917; *Guld the Cavern King* by Mary L.B. Branch, 1918; *History Stories for Primary Grades,* 1919, and *History Stories,* 1925, both by John Wayland; *Tales of Enchantment from Spain* by Elsie S. Eells, 1920; *Enchanted Forest* by William Bowen, 1920; *Children of Ancient Britain* by Louise Lamprey, 1921; *Twenty-Four Unusual Stories for Boys and Girls* edited by Anna Cogswell Tyler, 1921; *The Broom Fairies* by Ethel May Gate, 1922; *Rootabaga Stories,* 1922, and *Rootabaga Pigeons,* 1923, both by Carl Sandburg; *Tales from Shakespeare* by Charles and Mary Lamb, 1923; *Under the Story Tree,* 1923, *The F-U-N Book,* 1923, *In Animal Land,* 1924, *Billy Bang Book,* 1927, *Little Indians,* 1930, and *Zip the Toy Mule and Other Stories,* 1932, all by Mabel La Rue; *The Language Garden,* 1924, and *Number Friends,* 1927, both by Inez M. Howard and others; *The Poppy Seed Cakes* by Margery Clark, 1924; *Marquette Readers,* 1924; *Nursery Friends from France,* 1925, and *Tales Told in Holland,* 1926, both by Olive B. Miller; *The Pathway to Reading* by Bessie Coleman and others, 1925; *Little Ugly Face* by Florence Coolidge, 1925; *Philippine National Literature Book Two* by Harriet Fansler and Isidoro Panlasigui, 1925; *The Easy Book,* 1926, and *The Picnic Book,* 1934, both by Jean Y. Ayer, and *Everyday Stories* by Ayer and others, 1929; *Children of the Mountain Eagle,* 1927, *Pran of Albania,* 1929, and *Young Trajan,* 1931, all by Elizabeth Cleveland Miller; *Where Was Bobby?* by Marguerite Clément, 1928; *Everyday Canadian Primer,* 1928; *Pleasant Pathways,* 1928; *Winding Roads,* 1928, *Faraway Hills,* 1929, and *Heights and Highways,* 1929, all edited by Wilhelmina Harper and A.J. Hamilton; *The Magic Doll of Roumania* by Marie, Queen of Romania, 1929; *New Trails,* 1930, and *Beckoning Road, Rich Cargoes, Treasure Trove,* and *Wings of Adventure,* 4 vols., 1931, all edited by S. V. Rowland, W.D. Lewis, and E.J. Marshall; *The Christ Child,* 1931; *Martin the Goose Boy,* 1932, and *The Four and Lena,* 1938, both by Marie Barringer; *Heidi* by Johanna Spyri, 1932; *Pinocchio* by Carlo Collodi, 1932; *Albanian Wonder Tales* by Post Wheeler, 1936; *Susannah the Pioneer Cow,* 1941, and *Miss Posy Longlegs,* 1955, both by Miriam Evangeline Mason; *A Little Book of Prayers* by Emilie Johnson, 1941; *Jesus' Story,* 1942; *Literature* edited by E.A. Cross and Elizabeth Lehr, 7 vols., 1943-48; *The Rooster Crows: A Book of American Rhymes and Jingles,* 1945; *Told under the Christmas Tree,* 1948; *A Bird in the Hand: Sayings from Poor Richard's Almanack* by Benjamin Franklin, 1951; *Rip van Winkle, and The Legend of Sleepy Hollow* by Washington Irving, 1951; *In Clean Hay* by Eric Kelly, 1953; *The Shepherd Psalm* (illustrated by Maud alone), 1962.

* * *

"I don't think any American can appreciate this country as I do," Miska Petersham stated during his acceptance speech for the Caldecott Medal in 1946. This remark was properly directed towards adults, for what did it matter to a child poring over the books of the Petershams in the 1920s, 1930s, and even today that Miska came from Hungary and Maud was born in the United States?

Yet, the adventures of *Miki* and his trip to Hungary—climbing into a feather pillow bed, dancing to gypsy music, warming himself against a white clay stove, listening to shepherds' tales of warriors who raced across the Milky Way, watching Sari, the goose, dressed in strudel dough—this was the magic, the touchstone to another world that the Petershams' own backgrounds made possible. So it was with *Miki and Mary*—children boarding a ship to visit distant lands—as well as a seemingly forgotten book, *Auntie.* There were children like Celia Jane, Flossie, and Trailing Arbutus in America's multi-racial world, with stern Puritan figures like Grandfather and Auntie, the schoolteacher: the Petershams mixed a sense of haunting mystery about adults with touches of levity—the magic table and a schoolroom scene bordering on hilarity.

The child, it seems to me, is not concerned with who writes the text or illustrates any given book, but rather that both words and pictures enrich as a whole. It was the Petershams' talent that their backgrounds and interests spurred them to bridge many worlds, places and themes, whether illustrating the story of *The Christ Child,* which reflected the deeply religious aspect of their being, or using Benjamin Franklin's wisdom as the text for *A Bird in the Hand,* or satisfying a young reader's curiosity for facts in their *Story Books of Things We Use.*

Their love for animals is omnipresent in all of their books, yet dominant in such as *Off to Bed* or *The Circus Baby.* The animals in *Miki* and *Auntie,* however, seem more credible than in the later books where they often become almost cartoon-like and a bit too precious. *The Rooster Crows: A Book of American Rhymes and Jingles* (a questionable subtitle, for many of the verses originated in England) brings together many elements of the Petershams' art, yet seems less successful to me than their earlier books, where their own sense of story, of broadening worlds with an appropriate dash of dignity, discovery, and humor, prevails.

Certainly in dozens of books Miska Petersham showed his appreciation for America and Maud her religious background in a blending which showed respect for other cultures and races, with a regard for the child who wished his facts to be presented with visual accompaniment. Although the Petersham texts may appear to be somewhat simplistic today, it is well to remember that their concern for multi-ethnic and racial consciousness made its first appearance in book form in 1929, many years before other authors and illustrators took into account this important aspect of books for the young reader.

—Myra Cohn Livingston

PEVSNER, Stella

Nationality: American. **Born:** Lincoln, Illinois. **Education:** Illinois University and Northwestern University. **Family:** Married; four children. **Career:** Teacher; advertising copy writer for a drugstore chain and for various advertising agencies; promotion director, Dana Perfumes; fee-lance writer of articles, commercial film strips, and reading texts; writer for children, from 1969. **Awards:** First annual award for children's literature, Chicago Women in Publishing, 1973, for *Call Me Heller, That's My Name*; Dorothy Canfield Fisher Award, Vermont Congress of Parents and Teachers, 1977, and Junior Literary Guild outstanding book, both for *A Smart Kid Like You*; Notable Children's Trade Book in the Field of Social Studies, 1977, for *Keep Stompin' till the Music Stops*; Golden Kite Award, Society of Children's Book Writers, and Clara Ingram Judson Award, both 1978, both for *And You Give Me a Pain, Elaine*; Carl Sandburg Award, Friends of the Chicago Public Library, 1980, for *Cute is a Four-Letter Word*; American Library Association Best Books for Young Adults list, 1989, for *How Could You Do It, Diane?* **Address:** c/o Authors Guild, 330 West 42nd Street, 29th Floor, New York, New York 10036, U.S.A.

Publications for Children

Fiction

Break a Leg!, illustrated by Barbara Seuling. New York, Crown, 1969.
Footsteps on the Stairs, illustrated by Barbara Seuling. New York, Crown, 1970.
Call Me Heller, That's My Name, illustrated by Richard Cuffari. New York, Seabury, 1973.
A Smart Kid Like You. New York, Seabury, 1975.
Keep Stompin' till the Music Stops. New York, Seabury, 1977.
Me, My Goat, and My Sister's Wedding. New York, Clarion, 1985.
The Night the Whole Class Slept Over. New York, Clarion, 1991.
Jon, Flora, and the Odd-Eyed Cat. New York, Clarion, 1994.
Would My Fortune Cookie Lie? New York, Clarion, 1996.

Publications for Young Adults

Fiction

And You Give Me a Pain, Elaine. New York, Seabury, 1978.
Cute Is a Four-Letter Word. New York, Clarion, 1980.
I'll Always Remember You ... Maybe. New York, Clarion, 1981.
Lindsay, Lindsay, Fly Away Home. New York, Clarion, 1983.
Sister of the Quints. New York, Clarion, 1987.
How Could You Do It, Diane? New York, Clarion, 1989.
I'm Emma, I'm a Quint. New York, Clarion, 1993.
With Fay Tang, *Sing for Your Father, Su Phan.* New York, Clarion, 1997.

Plays

The Young Brontés: A Play in One Act. Boston, Baker's Plays, 1967.

*

Media Adaptations: *Me and Dad's New Wife* (television drama), ABC Afterschool Special, 1976; *Illinois Reads: Talks with Illinois Authors, #5: Stella Pevsner and Berniece Rabe* (video recording), Wheeling, Illinois, Library Cable Network, 1986.

Biography: Entry in *Something about the Author,* edited by Kevin S. Hile and Diane Telgen, Detroit, Gale, 1994, 156-160; *Speaking for Ourselves: Autobiographical Sketches by Notable Authors of Books for Young Adults,* edited by Donald Gallo, Urbana, Illinois, National Council of Teachers of English, 1990, 171-172; entry in *Something about the Author Autobiography Series,* Detroit, Gale, 1992, 183-193.

Critical Studies: Review of *How Could You Do It, Diane?* by Zena Sutherland, in *Bulletin of the Center for Children's Books,* September 1989, 14; "Families: Who They Are and What They Mean" by Deborah Abbott, in *Book Links,* February 15, 1991, 1217; review of *The Night the Whole Class Slept Over* by Carolyn Phelan, in *Booklist,* October 1991, 331; review of *The Night the Whole Class Slept Over* by Cindy Darling Codell, in *School Library Journal,* November 1991, 124; review of *I'm Emma: I'm a Quint* by Cindy Darling Codell, in *School Library Journal,* December 1993, 116; review of *Sing for Your Father, Su Phan,* in *Kirkus Reviews,* October 1997.

* * *

Stella Pevsner's works imaginatively recreate what it is like to be a child or a young adult, caught up in turmoil, fantasy, real life, friendship, problems at school and at home, crises or comedy. Sometimes her characters are living in the midst of several of these at once. With a sound ear for how children and young adults actually speak, a sympathetic and intelligent grasp of character, and a strong sense of plot, Pevsner creates novels that address young readers where they are at.

Pevsner did not set out early to become a writer. In fact, her early ambitions were to become a tap dancer, an actress, or a singer. As a child, she would force her brothers to play "show" with her, performing for them on an improvised stage while they unwillingly watched. As she has said, "their rude remarks ... were good practice for rejection slips that would come my way in the future, as they do to most beginning writers."

In high school, a teacher asked her to write a humor column for the school magazine. When she told him that she didn't know how, he gave her a book of Thurber's essays to read and encouraged her to "go to it." "I did, and loved the experience," she later said. Through her voracious reading as a child and her imaginative flights away from her ordinary reality, she was unconsciously preparing for her later career as a writer.

It wasn't until her son challenged her to "write a funny book that kids can enjoy" that she began writing for children. The first product of her efforts was *Break a Leg!,* for which her own children were her first and most enthusiastic audience. In *Break a Leg!,* not surprisingly, amateur theatricals help a young girl overcome her shyness. Similarly, *Footsteps on the Stairs,* her second novel, is a mystery in which a boy discovers that he can conquer fears of a different kind.

"My very early books, written as they were, at the behest of my children, were fairly light," Pevsner has written. Eventually, however, her themes became more serious and complex. *A Smart Kid Like You* is an ingenious exploration of the feelings of a girl, Nina, whose parents are divorced and who is living with her mother. Nina gets a tremendous shock at school when she discovers that her math teacher is her father's new wife. Her friends and classmates think it's a terrible thing for her to endure, so they concoct a scheme to torment the new teacher. Gradually, however, Nina begins to have her doubts about this plan, and as she gets acquainted with her teacher, she slowly changes her mind. Told from Nina's perspective, this book sympathetically traces the feelings of a child bewildered and hurt by her parents' divorce, but it also makes it quite clear that Nina's parents are much happier now that they are no longer married to each other, and that her parents' new and more fulfilling partnerships, though not easy for her to accept, will be beneficial to Nina in the long run.

Another of Stella Pevsner's noteworthy books is *And You Give Me a Pain, Elaine.* Thirteen-year-old Andrea considers herself ordinary. "'Me? I don't have any problems,'" she thinks. "'All I have is a wacko sister, a brother who no longer loves me best of all, a mother who takes me for granted, and a father who's headed for an ulcer. Not to mention slipping grades'" (37). She struggles with feelings of worthlessness, but she does have a lot of good things going for her, despite a sister who, from her perspective, behaves "like a rat in a snake pit," and gets all their mother's attention for it. It's hard to live with a sister who is naturally elegant-looking, acts spoiled and mean, and treats you as if you were scum. Andrea's best friend and ally is her brother Joe, but he has gone off to college and besides, he's in love with Cassandra, a charming and kind young woman, so he's not there whenever she needs him. Andrea has a clever and sympathetic friend, Robyn, who is starting an advice column in the school paper under the pseudonym "Iris." But writing a letter to "Iris" turns out to be a dangerous thing, when you complain about a teacher who has it in for you, and the note gets lost—perhaps to fall into his hands.

Elaine behaves worse and worse, eventually running off to Arizona with a boy named Steve and a rag-tag crew, causing her parents terrible anxiety. Andrea suffers because even when her mother depends on her for comfort, she knows she's just a substitute for glamorous Elaine, who was the child of her mother's dreams.

And You Give Me a Pain, Elaine explores the hopes and anxieties of Andrea from her point of view. Joe provides a loving and sensible perspective on the chaos and conflict in the family, as well as encouragement and support for Andy, despite—or perhaps in part because of—his distance. Andrea's dad is a somewhat vague figure, less present or well developed than her mother, whose troubled relationship with Elaine appears to be the axis of the family. At school, Andrea finds unexpected satisfaction in working on the technical end of a production of the play *Dracula,* an unsought-for assignment that leads her to a friendship with a boy named Chris, which might lead to more. But then a terrible thing happens. Andrea's maturity is put to the stress test through agony and grief, and everything looks different from the other end of this experience.

What Pevsner does well in this novel is to capture the small and large anxieties and the incremental growth of an insecure young person wavering between childhood and young adulthood. Particularly intriguing are the subtle hints here and there that Andrea's perceptions of her sister are not the whole truth, though they remain in the foreground; specifically, that their mother's expectations of a vicarious second adolescence through Elaine have caused her headlong rebellion. Interesting also is the realization that Cassie, who seemed to be a rival for Joe's affection, has a healing insight to offer, though things don't turn out at all as Andrea expected. Not significantly dated despite occasional references to the 1970s when it was written, this novel values steadiness and strength over glamour and self-absorption.

In *Sister of the Quints,* Natalie, a smart and athletic girl, finds herself overwhelmed by having to care for her five half-sisters, her father's quintuplets with his second wife, Jean. At first the idea of five little babies seemed cute and appealing, but soon the chaos and hard work required to keep them diapered, fed, and happy becomes too much. Even worse, Natalie's dad, a pilot who has taken a desk job to be closer to home so that he can look after the quints, seems to care more about them than he does about Natalie. He even forgets about her birthday in the excitement of planning for the quints' birthday. Jean, her step-mother, is terrific and she's not to blame, but even she finds the demands of this huge new family almost too much.

Natalie has just met an attractive and intriguing boy when the novel begins, a handsome Canadian newcomer named Noel. Natalie has a circle of dependable friends, but she hates the fact that even they mention the quints every time she is introduced. Natalie chose to live with her dad; she could have gone to live with her mother in Colorado. Why in the world didn't she, she begins to wonder, as the pressure of life with the quints gets worse. She is a conscientious helper at home, but she resents the inroads the babies are making on her athletics and on her social life. When the TV stations and newspaper reporters begin hounding the family, Natalie dreads all the attention focused on the quints, while she is on the sidelines, just the "sister of the quints." She decides to leave and go to live with her mother, but that turns out not to be as easy as she thought, either. It's a tough decision to leave all her friends and her familiar environment, even if she wants to escape from a tough situation.

This insightful and well-written novel tells with convincing detail what it might be like to be the sibling of multiple babies born in a set. As she does in other novels, Pevsner recreates the milieu of school and teenage social life, and shows the oddities and shortcomings of parents and teachers from a young adult's perspective. Natalie's dad, step-mother, and especially her mother are drawn with fine shadings. Her mother is a person of strong feeling and self-possessed integrity: she is the kind of person who does not attempt to persuade or manipulate anyone. It takes Natalie some time and effort to realize that her mother wants her to choose to come and live with her, not to escape a demanding situation, but because she wants to reciprocate her mother's love. That is the moving insight at the climax of this novel. Natalie matures through the freedom her mother enables her to have, and through her concern for the quints, whom she begins to see as individuals who will have an even greater struggle with their need for separate identities than she, the "sister of the quints," has had.

This theme is pursued from a different angle in the book *I'm Emma, I'm a Quint,* which *School Library Journal* called "a well-constructed sequel ... written in Pevsner's breezy, yet intimate style that adolescents love." Here, with humor and insight, Pevsner develops the theme of Emma's realization that she is an individual who must make her own decisions.

The ability to treat young people's anxieties and adventures with a skillful blend of humor and seriousness is a hallmark of Pevsner's writing. This achievement is notable in *The Night the Whole Class Slept Over,* a novel about a boy whose family is planning to move—yet again. A reviewer in *Booklist* noted that "the conversational style and consistent viewpoint make Dan's narrative convincing as well as humorous." This ability to express humor through a distinctive point of view is also represented in *Me, My Goat, & My Sister's Wedding,* a mostly lighthearted romp.

Sometimes, as in her novel about teen suicide, *How Could You Do It, Diane?,* the emphasis is more heavily on the serious. Bethany finds her stepsister Diane dead of an overdose of barbiturates at the beginning of the story, which is told through Beth's memories of Diane and her search for the causes of this terrible event. But even in this novel, hope and recovery begin to balance out the grief and suffering in the end.

In a recent venture, Pevsner worked with a refugee from Vietnam to tell the story of a girl's life during the war. *Kirkus Reviews* calls *Sing for Your Father, Su Phan,* co-authored with Fay Tang, "a compelling portrait of the life of a child for whom terrible hardship was an accepted part of reality."

Pevsner's writings probe the inner worlds of believable children and young adults whose lives are, like those of their readers, frequently unpredictable, disconcerting, and stressful—yet also often funny, complicated, absorbing and rewarding. Pevsner is particularly good at creating interesting children and adolescents whose lives are interdependent with those of adults. She is able to suggest the complexity of those adults' lives without losing her primary focus of telling us what the world looks like from the perspective of her main characters. She also understands friendship, its vicissitudes and its rewards, exceptionally well. Perhaps best of all, Pevsner is a writer whose funny bone is connected to her heart.

—J. D. Stahl

PICARD, Barbara Leonie

Nationality: British. **Born:** Richmond, Surrey, 4 December 1917. **Education:** St. Katharine's School, Wantage, Berkshire, 1930-34. **Address:** c/o Oxford University Press, Walton Street, Oxford OX2 6DP, England.

Publications for Children

Fiction

The Mermaid and the Simpleton, illustrated by Philip Gough. London, Oxford University Press, 1949; New York, Criterion, 1970.

The Faun and the Woodcutter's Daughter, illustrated by Charles Stewart. London, Oxford University Press, 1951; New York, Criterion, 1964.

The Lady of the Linden Tree, illustrated by Charles Stewart. London, Oxford University Press, 1954; New York, Criterion, 1962.

Ransom for a Knight, illustrated by C. Walter Hodges. London, Oxford University Press, 1956; New York, Walck, 1967.

Lost John, illustrated by Charles Keeping. London, Oxford University Press, 1962; New York, Criterion, 1963.

The Goldfinch Garden: Seven Tales, illustrated by Anne Linton. London, Harrap, 1963; New York, Criterion, 1965.

One Is One, illustrated by Victor Ambrus. London, Oxford University Press, 1965; New York, Holt Rinehart, 1966.

The Young Pretenders, illustrated by Victor Ambrus. London, Ward, and New York, Criterion, 1966.

Twice Seven Tales, illustrated by Victor Ambrus. London, Kaye and Ward, 1968.

Selected Fairy Tales, illustrated by Julia Cobbold, Oxford University Press, 1994.

The Deceivers. London, Janus, 1996.

Other

The Odyssey of Homer, illustrated by Joan Kiddell-Monroe. London, Oxford University Press, and New York, Walck, 1952.

Tales of the Norse Gods and Heroes, illustrated by Joan Kiddell Monroe. London, Oxford University Press, 1953; revised a *Tales of the Norse Gods,* illustrated by Joan Kiddell-Monroe London, Oxford University Press, 1994.

French Legends, Tales, and Fairy Stories, illustrated by Joan Kiddell-Monroe. London, Oxford University Press, and New York, Walck, 1955.
Stories of King Arthur and His Knights, illustrated by Roy Morgan. London, Oxford University Press, 1955; New York, Walck, 1966.
German Hero-Sagas and Folk-Tales, illustrated by Joan Kiddell-Monroe. London, Oxford University Press, and New York, Walck, 1958.
The Iliad of Homer, illustrated by Joan Kiddell-Monroe. London, Oxford University Press, and New York, Walck, 1960.
The Story of Rama and Sita, illustrated by Charles Stewart. London, Harrap, 1960.
Tales of the British People, illustrated by Eric Fraser. London, Ward, and New York, Criterion, 1961.
The Tower and the Traitors (history), illustrated by William Stobbs. London, Batsford, and New York, Putnam, 1961.
Hero-Tales from the British Isles, illustrated by Gay Galsworthy. London, Ward, and New York, Criterion, 1963.
Celtic Tales: Legends of Tall Warriors and Old Enchantments, illustrated by Gay Galsworthy. London, Ward, 1964; New York, Criterion, 1965.
The Story of the Pandavas, Retold from the Mahabharata, illustrated by Charles Stewart. London, Dobson, 1968.
William Tell and His Son, from a translation by Bettina Hürlimann, illustrated by Paul Nussbaumer. London, Sadler, 1969.
Three Ancient Kings: Gilgamesh, Hrolf Kraki, Conary, illustrated by Philip Gough. London, Kaye and Ward, and New York, Warne, 1972.
Tales of Ancient Persia, Retold from the Shah-Nama of Firdausi, illustrated by Victor Ambrus. London, Oxford University Press, 1972; New York, Walck, 1973.
The Iliad and Odyssey of Homer, illustrated by Joan Kiddell-Monroe. Chancellor Press, 1986.

Editor, *Encyclopaedia of Myths and Legends of All Nations,* revised edition. London, Ward, 1962.

*

Barbara Leonie Picard comments:

From very early years I had intended to be a writer—but I came to be a children's writer by accident. My first books were original fairy stories told in the traditional vein, and were written entirely for my own amusement. When they were published, their success encouraged my publishers to persuade me to continue writing for young people on the subjects which held most interest for me: mythology, legends, and folklore. I have also written several historical novels for older children and teenagers on themes which attracted me. I never write any book unless it is to please myself.

* * *

Not surprisingly, because of her experience as a reteller of old tales, Barbara Leonie Picard's original writing lies in the two fields of the invented fairy story and the historical novel.

The collections of fairytales—*The Mermaid and the Simpleton, The Faun and the Woodcutter's Daughter,* and *Twice Seven Tales* (which includes *The Lady of the Linden Tree*)—derive from the main traditions of Europe and the East, but courtly romance preponderates. The motifs of the true folktale are often used but generally the themes are more orderly. The setting of court or castle is less idealized, with considerable descriptive detail, the product of research rather than the peasant's imagination. Maidens, except when enchanted, are always good and beautiful, and heroes, whether peasant or king, are deserving of whatever good fortune they gain. Moral virtues are always stressed, though trickery is permitted when it is the only way of overcoming evil. Some stories, in the Andersen tradition, lack a happy ending.

The historical novels are fine pieces of writing, considerably longer than the average children's book. *Ransom for a Knight* has a single-strand plot, but the determined little Alys and the not-very-bright Hugh, the serf's child, come through as satisfactory characters. All shades of medieval society are included: the baronial hall, the rich merchant's house, the peasant's hovel with its fleas. Alys's childish eagerness wins over most of the people she meets, and kind and unkind hearts are found among the wealthy and the poor, the honest and the dishonest, the Scots and the English. *Lost John* is an absorbing story of conflicting loyalties. Fighting is for killing, not for the exercise of knightly arts: the outlaws with whom John throws in his lot are not romantic Robin Hood figures. Too often, as in real life, motives are misunderstood and the wrong reactions follow. The ending may sound contrived, but does not seem so.

In *One Is One* Stephen fulfills all his ambitions, but is the cost worth it? The sensitive, artistic boy, rejected by his family, learns three times to love, in each case to lose its object through death. In its stress on knightly combat the book owes much to Picard's own retelling of Malory. Sir Pagan is too idealised to be real, yet this is how Stephen sees him. Through the three tragedies Stephen learns where his own future lies and that his prayers were after all answered. The "great house" setting of *The Young Pretenders* is attractive. The depiction of the main characters is remarkably acute. The theme is unusual—a rogue masquerading as a fleeing Jacobite to save his life. The children are never found out, but the story ends rather sadly because life goes on just as it did before Seumas came into it. Historical details are worked in effortlessly and understandably and never obtrude as they did just occasionally in *Ransom for a Knight.*

—Margaret M. Tye

PILLING, Ann

Pseudonym: Ann Cheetham. **Nationality:** British. **Born:** Warrington, Lancashire, 17 October 1944. **Education:** King's College, University of London, 1964-69, B.A. (honours) 1967, M.Phil. in English 1971. **Family:** Married Joe Pilling in 1968; two sons. **Career:** Has taught English in secondary schools. Publications officer, Federation of Children's Book Groups, 1978-81. **Award:** *Guardian* award, 1986. **Agent:** Gina Pollinger, 222 Old Brompton Rd, London SW5 0BZ, England. **Address:** 22 Norham Gardens, Oxford OX2 6QD, England.

Publications for Children

Fiction

The Year of the Worm, illustrated by Ian Newsham. London, Viking Kestrel, 1984.
Henry's Leg, illustrated by Rowan Clifford. London, Viking Kestrel, 1985.

The Friday Parcel, illustrated by Robert Bartelt. London, Blackie, 1986.
No Guns, No Oranges, illustrated by Jolyne Knox. London, Heinemann, 1986.
The Big Pink. London, Viking Kestrel, 1987.
The Beast in the Basement, illustrated by Jolyne Knox. London, Heinemann, 1988.
Dustbin Charlie, illustrated by Jean Baylis. London, Viking Kestrel, 1988.
On the Lion's Side. London, Heinemann, 1988.
Stan. London, Viking Kestrel, 1988.
The Big Biscuit, illustrated by Linda Birch. London, Hodder and Stoughton, 1989.
The Jungle Sale, illustrated by Robert Bartelt. London, Blackie, 1989.
Our Kid. London, Viking Kestrel, 1989.
The Donkey's Day Out. London, Lion, 1990.
The Boy with His Leg in the Air. London, Heinemann, 1991.
Vote for Baz. London, Viking Kestrel, 1992.
The Baked Bean Kids. London, Walker, 1993.
Dustbin Charlie Cleans Up, illustrated by Jean Baylis. London, Viking, 1993.
Mother's Daily Scream. London, Viking, 1995.

Fiction as Ann Cheetham

Black Harvest. London, Collins, 1983.
The Beggar's Curse. London, Collins, 1984.
The Witch of Lagg. London, Collins, 1986.
The Pit. London, Collins, 1987.

Other

Compiler, *Love Stories,* illustrated by Aafke Brouwer. London, Kingfisher, 1997.

Editor, with Anne Wood, *Our Best Stories,* illustrated by Mairi Hedderwick. London, Hodder and Stoughton, 1986.
Editor, *Something to Do with Love.* Oxford, Lion, 1996.

Reteller, *Before I Go to Sleep: Bible Stories, Poems, and Prayers for Children,* illustrated by Kady MacDonald Denton. New York, Crown, 1990.
Reteller, *The Kingfisher Children's Bible: Stories from the Old and New Testaments,* illustrated by Kady MacDonald Denton. New York, Kingfisher, 1993.
Reteller, *Realms of Gold: Myths & Legends from around the World,* illustrated by Kady MacDonald Denton. New York, Kingfisher, 1993.
Reteller, *The Life of Jesus, Bible Stories, Poems and Prayers,* illustrated by Kady Macdonald Denton. London, Kingfisher, 1996.
Reteller, *Noah's Ark, Bible Stories, Poems and Prayers,* illustrated by Kady MacDonald Denton. London, Kingfisher, 1996.

PUBLICATIONS FOR ADULTS

Fiction

A Broken Path. London, New English Library, 1991.
Considering Helen. London, Hodder and Stoughton, 1993.

*

Ann Pilling comments:

Although I have written for younger children, and have enjoyed doing so, I regard myself as a children's novelist; and although when writing for children one's scope is limited in some ways, it is a mistake ever to talk down to them, or to think they deserve less than the best (poor style, flabby plot construction, two-dimensional characters).

I have two "hats." As Ann Cheetham I have written a quartet of ghost stories, sometimes called the *Black Harvest* series. These are ambitious, semi-fantastic stories involving children of the 1980s who are swept back into the past, to solve some kind of mystery. For each I did a considerable amount of research, e.g. *Black Harvest* deals with the Irish potato famine of the 1840s, *The Pit* is about the London Plague of 1665. I regard them as my most powerful books.

As Ann Pilling I have written a collection (all different) of much lighter, contemporary novels, set mainly in the north of England where I was brought up, though *On the Lion's Side* is set in Wales. Whatever my subject I have always aimed to tell a story well, and to fill my canvas with living, breathing human beings. Adults enjoy my books, which is a compliment. They are valued for their humour, their authenticity and in some cases (*Stan*) for their breathless pace.

As a Christian I believe in hope. Even in the ghost stories there is a peaceful, if not always totally happy, resolution of events. I feel we have been dogged too long in the world of children's literature by "the problem novel." Whatever misfortunes my characters suffer—and they are many—courage, hope, and cheerfulness shine through, I trust. I feel I can write no other way. If a child is deprived of hope, and of what D. H. Lawrence called "the wonder of life" then he is deprived of everything that makes living worthwhile.

* * *

Ann Pilling is an original and effective writer of stories for young people, ranging from infants to adolescents. She established her reputation with three lively novels centring on children who were very different from the conventional heroes of juvenile fiction. Peter Wrigley in *The Year of the Worm* is an undersized, nervous boy, tormented by other children and misunderstood by teachers. Henry Hooper in *Henry's Leg* is a quirky original, a compulsive hoarder of discarded junk, including a plastic leg that he finds outside a dress shop. Angela Collis-Browne is an awkward, self-conscious girl with a weight problem who gets nicknamed *The Big Pink* (the novel's title) after the boarding-school dormitory she lives in.

These central characters in Pillings stories are placed in odd or embarrassing situations. Peter longs to be a hero but his efforts only make him look ridiculous. Henry tries to make money by collecting recently dead hedgehogs to sell to the local polytechnic. Angela's attempts to trampoline on her bed end in a spectacular crash, and she nearly pops out of her dress when performing on stage. However, each of the novels moves toward a conventional happy ending. The Worm does at last become a hero, saving the life of an injured companion on a hostelling trip. Henry survives the attention of local crooks, wins a reward, and sees his junk collection turned into sculpture. Angela excels at music, gains recognition, and is awarded a special prize.

Pilling's books for younger children similarly combine unusual ideas and comic situations with credible young characters and positive conclusions. In *The Beast in the Basement*, Neil and Terry (the terrible twins) discover an old man, living in a basement flat, who turns out to be a hedgehog enthusiast and makes friends with the boys' darts-playing grandmother. *The Baked Bean Kids* are Joss and her aggravating little copy-cat brother. When she collects fifty labels from baked bean cans to win a prize, he does the same, and the book tells the story of how they then cope with a hundred tins of beans.

All Pilling's books encourage readers to reassess immediate judgements about people and situations; her recurrent theme explores how young people can learn to come to terms with themselves and others. Re-evaluation of the three boys in *The Year of the Worm* is partly achieved by seeing them through the eyes of the intelligent Millicent. Henry's mixture of love and irritation for his incompetent mother is a more important element of the story than the stock narrative about crooks, and the real happy ending is the return of his father, who had gone off with a new girlfriend. Angela has to learn to adjust both her feelings of fear for her Auntie Pat, the cool progressive head of the school, and her crush on the teenage Seb Barrington-Ward. These shifting relationships are handled with warmth and sensitivity, and the scenes in which they are described carry conviction.

Pilling's thrillers for adolescent readers, such as *Stan* and *On the Lion's Side,* set gripping events (escape and pursuit, a hunt for treasure) in dangerous contemporary settings. The backdrops of these stories—the risky hitchhiking, demolition sites, and terrorist hide-out in *Stan,* and the lonely Welsh cottage and disused mineshaft of *On the Lion's Side*—are meticulously realised. In *Stan,* for instance, the title character plans to escape from the last of a series of unsatisfactory foster homes to join his elder brother in Ireland. In a rather contrived though exciting opening, a packet of drugs is planted in Stan's rucksack and he realises that a dangerous criminal is pursuing him. The two come face to face on the Irish ferry, where Stan flings the rucksack and the drugs into the sea. In Belfast he is plunged into a separate series of adventures with a terrorist gang, escaping from ambush and explosion, crossing the border in a gun battle, and eventually being reunited with his brother, though "nothing was as he'd planned."

Pilling's Christianity is explicit in her skilful retelling of stories in *The Kingfisher Children's Bible,* and in *The Donkey's Day Out,* which describes Fred the donkey as he carries Jesus into Jerusalem. But her moral principles are implicit in all her works, carrying the suggestion that children can relate to their own, and that it is possible for them to come through misfortunes and disappointments. Ultimately, what remains in the mind after reading *Stan* are less the dramatic events and more the series of odd encounters, the unexpected kindnesses of ordinary people, and the presentation of moral choices that caused one reviewer to liken the book to the work of Graham Greene.

Ann Pilling has also written ghost stories under the name Ann Cheetham and, in *Realms of Gold,* has retold in a simple but imaginative way myths and legends from a variety of cultures, ranging through classical, Nigerian, and Iroquois sources. She is a lively, original, sensitive author who manages to write books that appeal both to young readers and to their parents and teachers.

—Robert Protherough

PINKNEY, Andrea Davis

Nationality: American. **Born:** Washington, D.C., 25 September 1963. **Education:** Syracuse University, New York, B.A. in journalism. **Family:** Married to J. Brian Pinkney, children's book illustrator and son of Jerry and Gloria Pinkney; one child. **Career:** Editor at various magazines; editor at Scholastic, Inc.; senior editor, *Essence* Magazine; children's book editor, Simon and Schuster Books for Young Readers; senior editor and head of Jump at the Sun imprint, Hyperion Books for Children, from 1997. **Awards:** Best Arts Feature award, Highlights for Children Foundation, 1992; Parenting Publication award, 1993; "Pick of the List," American Bookseller's, 1993; Notable Children's Trade Book in the Field of Social Studies, NCSS-CBS, 1994; Notable Book citation, Society of School Librarians International, 1996; Notable Book citation, American Library Association, 1996.

PUBLICATIONS FOR CHILDREN

Fiction

I Smell Honey. New York, Red Wagon Books, Harcourt Brace, 1997.
Pretty Brown Face. New York, Red Wagon Books, Harcourt Brace, 1997.
Solo Girl. New York, Hyperion, 1997.
Shake Shake Shake. San Diego, Harcourt Brace, 1997.
Watch Me Dance. San Diego, Harcourt Brace, 1997.

Nonfiction

Seven Candles for Kwanzaa. New York, Dial, 1993.

Biography

Alvin Ailey. New York, Hyperion, 1993.
Dear Benjamin Banneker. San Diego, Harcourt Brace, 1994.
Bill Pickett: Rodeo-Ridin' Cowboy. San Diego, Harcourt Brace, 1996.
Duke Ellington. New York, Hyperion, 1998.

PUBLICATIONS FOR YOUNG ADULTS

Hold Fast to Dreams. New York, Hyperion, 1996.
Raven in a Dove House. San Diego, Harcourt Brace, 1998.

*

Critical Sources: "The Rhythm of Writing and Art" by Diana L. Winarski, in *Teaching K-8,* Vol. 28, No. 2, 1997, 38-40.

* * *

Andrea Davis Pinkney's contributions to children's literature are significant. As a senior editor at Hyperion Books for Children, she directs the Jump at the Sun imprint, which focuses on the celebration of the beauties of Black culture. As a writer, she focuses on topics that are relevant to her own heritage. "A writer is just who I am," Andrea Pinkney told Diana Winarski of *Teaching K-8* magazine. "And I've always been a voracious reader, and I love to tell stories."

Pinkney's biographies of influential African-Americans impress upon readers of any ethnic background the significant contributions of these individuals to society. The intensity of her research brings life to her publications. In addition to reading printed text, she experiences her subject's art, interviews close family members or acquaintances, and places her subjects within the larger context of African-American experience. Her rich descriptions of people, historical and geographical eras, the movement and emotional quality of various arts, and the use of colorful language variations vividly convey her message. Without sacrificing the complexity or authenticity of the lives she shares, Pinkney makes her work accessible to young readers.

Pinkney's family is deeply involved in the making of children's books. And many of her works are collaborative efforts with her husband artist Brian Pinkney, son of Jerry and Gloria Pinkney who also create books for children. Together Andrea and Brian research topics, meet as colleagues to collaborate and critique their processes. Andrea's select descriptions, dialogue and imagery are complemented by the scratchboard technique of Brian as the artistry of each is interwoven with the other in powerful ways throughout each book.

Alvin Ailey and *Seven Candles for Kwanzaa* are the first collaborative works by the Pinkneys. *Seven Candles for Kwanzaa* explains this African-American celebration through bright pictures and simplistic but precisely selected words. *Alvin Ailey* begins a series of life stories of African-Americans whose contributions will forever be part of our nation's history and of international significance. In preparing to write this story, both author and illustrator participated in classes teaching the modern-dance technique of Ailey. The grace, vibrancy, and rhythm of the African-American cultural experience which Ailey's career sought to portray is found in both the art and language of this book. Describing Ailey's modern dance, Andrea Pinkney described how "He flung his arms and shim-shammed his middle to express jubilation" and wrote that "His dips and slides could even show anger and pain". While elaborating on how Ailey's choreography depicted the story of his heritage through blues, jazz, and gospel, Pinkney explained that he captured "that weepy sadness all folks feel now and then." And she put Ailey's contributions in a larger cultural context with such phrases as "*Revelations* honored the heart and the dignity of black people while showing that hope and joy are for everyone." In addition to her own text, Pinkney included valuable author's insights at the end of the story (as she has in several other books) to further elaborate on her subject's career.

In *Dear Benjamin Banneker* Pinkney highlights the contributions of a person of historical significance who is not found in history books. She introduces young readers to a self-taught mathematician and astronomer who spoke out against racism and slavery, even in writing to Thomas Jefferson. She also describes the struggles of Banneker to share his findings with a society where black people, even if free, were not regarded as equal in abilities and rights. Pinkney's text celebrates his persistence and accomplishments, and her cultural perspective make this book a valuable addition to the study of early American history.

The cowboy community of the 1800s comes alive in *Bill Pickett.* Young Bill discovers a bulldog biting a cow's lip—bulldogging—and naively decides to use this to enter the world of cowhands and later rodeos. Pinkney expresses the curiosity and excitement of a child who is fascinated with his environment and uses it to introduce the reader to the geography and lifestyle of the old West as she follows Pickett along his career as a popular cowboy hero. Following the story is an informative author's note containing further information about black cowboys in United States history.

In the biography of Duke Ellington, Andrea Pinkney takes the reader from Ellington's childhood days through his journey to become a "master maestro." The rhythmic quality of her words and phrases set the tone of the story. Individual instruments come alive with her descriptions. "Toby let loose on his sleek brass sax, curling his notes like a kite tail in the wind. A musical loop-de-loop, with a serious twist." The reader experiences the blending of art, music, and words in such phrases as, "He could swirl the butterscotch tones of Tricky Sam's horn with the silver notes of the alto saxophones." *Duke Ellington* honors not only the "King of Keys" but also this musical era and its contribution to the world. Andrea Pinkney's celebration of art and music through language also flows through her other picture books for children. *Shake Shake Shake* and *Watch Me Dance* continue sharing her love of music with young readers.

Pinkney also writes about the struggles and achievements of young adolescents as they seek personal identity and the fulfillment of ambitions. The isolation and sensitive situations in *Hold Fast To Dreams* and *Raven in a Dove House,* can be appreciated by all readers even though she has recreated experiences of young people who do not identify with the dominant culture of a community.

Pinkney's books have a place in every classroom. They enhance the appreciation of notable Americans, celebrate diversity, integrate the curriculum, and provide rich examples of language use and writing scholarship. As a result they nurture a delight in reading.

—Janelle B. Mathis

PINKNEY, (Jerry) Brian

Nationality: American. **Born:** Boston, Massachusetts, 1961. **Education:** Philadelphia College of Art, B.F.A. 1983; School of Visual Arts, M.F.A. 1990. **Family:** Married Andrea Davis, 1991. **Career:** Writer and Illustrator. Taught at the Children's Art Carnival in Harlem, New York, and the School of Visual Arts, New York City. Exhibitions include Society of Illustrators Annual Show, 1990, 1991, School of Visual Arts Student Galleries and Society of Illustrators Annual Show, 1992. **Awards:** National Arts Club Award of Distinction, 1990; Parents' Choice Honor Award for Illustration, 1990, for *The Boy and the Ghost*; Parents' Choice Honor Award for Story Books, 1990, for *The Ballad of Belle Dorcus*; Parents' Choice Picture Book award, 1991, for *Where Does This Trail Lead?* and *A Wave in Her Pocket*; Golden Kite Honor Award, 1991, for *Where Does This Trail Lead?*; Coretta Scott King Honor Book award for illustration, American Library Association Notable Book, American Bookseller Pick of the Lists, International Reading Association Teacher's Choice, *Booklist* Editor's Choice, *School Library Journal* Best Book, and Bulletin Blue Ribbon, all 1992, all for *Sukey and the Mermaid*; Caldecott Honor Book, 1995, for *The Faithful Friend.* **Address:** Brooklyn, New York, U.S.A.

Publications for Children

Fiction (illustrated by author)

Max Found Two Sticks. New York, Simon and Schuster, 1994.
Jojo's Flying Side Kick. New York, Simon and Schuster, 1995.
The Adventures of Sparrow Boy. New York, Simon and Schuster, 1997.

*

Biography: Entry in *Something about the Author,* Detroit, Gale Research, Vol. 74, 1993, 191-193.

Illustrator: (As J. Brian Pinkney) *Shipwrecked on Mystery Island* by Roy Wandelmaier, 1985; (as J. Brian Pinkney) *Julie Brown: Racing with the World* by R. Rozanne Knudson, 1988; (as J. Brian Pinkney) *The Boy and the Ghost,* 1989, *Sukey and the Mermaid,* 1992, *Cut from the Same Cloth,* 1993, and *The Faithful Friend,* 1995, *Cendrillon: A Creole Cinderella,* 1998, by Robert D. San Souci; *The Ballad of Belle Dorcus* by William H. Hooks, 1990; *Harriet Tubman and Black History Month* by Polly Carter, 1990; *Where Does This Trail Lead?* by Burton Albert, 1991; *A Wave in Her Pocket: Stories from Trinidad* by Lynn Joseph, 1991; *The Lost Zoo* by Christopher Cat and Countee Cullin, 1992; *The Dark-Thirty: Southern Tales of the Supernatural* by Patricia C. McKissack, 1992; *The Elephant's Wrestling Match* by Judy Sierra, 1992; *Alvin,* 1993, *Seven Candles for Kwanzaa,* 1993, *Dear Benjamin Banneker,* 1994, *Bill Pickett, Rodeo Ridin' Cowboy,* 1996, *Pretty Brown Face,* 1997, *I Smell Honey,* 1997, *Watch Me Dance,* 1997, and *Duke Ellington: The Piano Prince and His Orchestra,* 1998, by Andrea Davis Pinkney; (as J. Brian Pinkney) *Happy Birthday, Martin Luther King* by Jean Marzollo, 1993; *The Dream Keeper and Other Poems* by Langston Hughes, 1994; *Day of Delight: A Jewish Sabbath in Ethiopia,* 1994, and *I Left My Village,* 1996, by Maxine Schur; *Wiley and the Hairy Man* by Judy Sierra, 1996.

Brian Pinkney comments:

I always knew I wanted to be an illustrator because my father is an illustrator, and I wanted to be just like him. I did everything he did. My desk was a miniature version of his desk. The paintbrushes and pencils I used were often the ones from his studio that were too old or too small for him to use. I had a paint set like his and a studio like his. Except my studio was a walk-in closet, which made it the perfect size for me.

When I began writing for my own children's books, I used my childhood experiences as the inspiration for my stories. For *Max Found Two Sticks,* I remembered what it felt like to play the drums for the first time and how I used drumbeats to express myself. When I wrote *Jojo's Flying Side Kick,* I recalled the feeling I had as a beginner in tae kwon do. *The Adventures of Sparrow Boy* was inspired by three ideas: the paper route I had as a kid, my fascination with wanting to fly, and my love of adventure stories and comic books.

* * *

Brian Pinkney is from a family of picture book writers and illustrators. His father, Jerry Pinkney, has illustrated distinguished books for children, some of which were written by his mother, Gloria Pinkney. His wife, Andrea Davis Pinkney, is a writer who increasingly collaborates with him. Pinkney has written and illustrated his own picture books, and he has illustrated picture books, folk tales, and poetry of others. The works of this family of artists often appear on selected lists of children's books by African heritage writers and artists.

Pinkney was always drawing, painting, or building something as a child. He discovered his favorite artistic medium while experimenting with scratchboard at the School of Visual Arts. Scratchboard is a technique, much like engraving, in which a white board is covered with black ink. The ink is then scratched off with a sharp tool to reveal white underneath. Pinkney likes to work in scratchboard because it allows him to sculpt the image. When he etches the drawing out of the board, he develops a rhythm with his lines which feels like sculpture to him. And indeed, his illustrations of human beings seem three dimensional, coming out of the page into the space surrounding it.

Pinkney enjoys being involved in the subject matter about which he is working. The first book he both wrote and illustrated, *Max Found Two Sticks,* is based on his own enjoyment in playing the drums. The book he illustrated for his wife about Alvin Ailey, *Alvin,* prompted him to take dance lessons, which he also relished. And he continues to illustrate folk tales from Africa and from the West Indies because through the tales he learns about his own cultural heritage.

Pinkney has illustrated several picture books relating to African-American history. *Seven Candles for Kwanzaa* celebrates traditional African harvest festivals. *Happy Birthday, Martin Luther King,* describes King's struggle to change discriminatory laws in this country. Martin Luther King, giving his "I have a dream" speech in front of the Washington Monument in our country's capital, is eloquently illustrated in a double page spread. Pinkney's use of the scratchboard technique allowed him to draw powerful images of the large crowd with few strokes.

Pinkney's illustrations for the folk tale *Sukey and the Mermaid* have won many awards. Pinkney drew pictures of enormous movement, showing the powerful sea washing into a little island off the coast of South Carolina. The colors are muted, dark greens and reds. The island vegetation blowing in the wind, the sea's waves pounding on the shore, achieve a rhythmic whole. In this story, a poor girl finds her wishes answered, not by the treasures of the sea or the magic of its mermaid, but by goodness and love of human beings. This is one of the few authenticated African-American folktales which have mermaids as central characters. Pinkney has adorned his mermaid with jewels of West African designs.

In *Cut From the Same Cloth: American Women of Myth, Legend, and Tall Tale,* Pinkney uses only black and white (except for the book jacket), and each full-page illustration is framed, increasing its impact. This collection of tales, 15 in all, is about strong-willed American women of the northeast, south, midwest, southwest, and west. There is the tale of "Bess Call," an Anglo-American girl of Essex County, New York. Bess's brother Joe was reported to be the strongest man in America, and though Bess was younger and slightly shorter than he was, she was just as sturdy. When Joe tired of wrestling, Bess took on those who wanted to challenge him. After she finished wrestling, she took hold of one victim, threw him over the fence, then threw his horse over too, so he could go on home. "Old Sally Cato" is about an African-American widow in the Missouri hill country. The story has numerous African antecedents, which usually involve a flesh-eating elephant that swallows people whole until an old woman, with knife and digging stick, lets herself be swallowed up. She then finishes off the elephant from within, cutting away for all those inside the elephant to gain their freedom. In this version, Old Sally Cato does the same to Billy Bally Bully, the name of a giant who lives beyond the hill.

Wiley and the Hairy Man is a popular Alabama folktale. The Hairy Man is a mean, ugly ogre who captures children and puts them in a sack. Wiley manages to escape once, but his mama, who knows conjure magic, finds a way to keep Hairy Man away from her boy forever. Hairy Man is an American mixture of European devil, African ogre, and conjure doctor. The author has been telling it orally for twenty years. This artful retelling, and Pinkney's vibrant oil paintings on scratchboard of a very scary Hairy Man, provide an unforgettable read.

The Dream Keeper and Other Poems, written by Langston Hughes, includes lyrical, wonderful illustrations by Pinkney. Pinkney's small, black-and-white scratchboard drawings eloquently illustrate Hughes' exquisite poems. For the poem titled "The Dream Keeper" Pinkney provides an oval picture of a young boy seated at the trunk of a tree, looking in the distance. For "The Weary Blues" he gives us a jazz pianist swaying to and fro as he makes his piano moan. For "African Dance," Pinkney shows a lady who swings back her arms and brings forward her feet as she responds to the rhythm of the drums. Pinkney has pictures of a mother cradling her baby, of an old man praying, of sunbursts and flowers, that are beautiful and moving. In companionship with Langston Hughes' poems, he provides a celebration of life. The book is not large, and there are only 80 pages. One can enjoy it, cover to cover, over and over again. It is a treat for children and for adults.

—Mary Lystad

PLOWMAN, Stephanie

Nationality: British. **Born:** 28 December 1922. **Education:** University of London, B.A. (honours) in history 1944; graduate study, 1948-50, Ph.D. **Family:** Married A.R. Hamilton-Dee (died 1957). **Career:** Has taught in England, South Africa, and Ghana; Gulbenkian Research fellow, Lucy Cavendish College, Cambridge, 1969-72. **Address:** 12 Lower Meddon St., Bideford, Devonshire, England.

Publications for Children

Fiction

Sixteen Sail in Aboukir Bay, illustrated by Richard Kennedy. London, Methuen, 1956.
To Spare the Conquered. London, Methuen, 1960.
The Road to Sardis. London, Bodley Head, 1965; Boston, Houghton Mifflin, 1966.
Three Lives for the Czar. London, Bodley Head, 1969; Boston, Houghton Mifflin, 1970.
My Kingdom for a Grave. London, Bodley Head, 1970; Boston, Houghton Mifflin, 1971.
A Time to Be Born and a Time to Die. London, Bodley Head, 1975.
The Leaping Song. London, Bodley Head, 1976.

Other

Nelson, illustrated by Richard Kennedy. London, Methuen, 1955.

Publications for Adults

Play

Radio Play: *The Royal Exiles,* 1953.

*

Stephanie Plowman comments:

The gestation period of my becoming a writer of historical fiction began when, as a 16-year-old, I was required to write an essay criticising the policy of Napoleon after 1807. The sheer lunacy of this made me start working out privately why I wanted to go on learning history—certainly not to be able to pontificate on the "mistakes" made by the greatest military intelligence of modern times when I myself possibly couldn't run a village post office. To learn people, then? What it was like to live during certain happenings? To make the past present?

Nowadays there are two stages. An age or incident takes possession, and the obsessive reading begins. And in the course of this, a sentence, or even a few words, call a character into being, i.e., a young officer who rode with his squadron from Novgorod in a futile attempt to save the Tsar, a single title among the list of books left by the Imperial children at Ekaterinburg. After this the manuscript writes itself.

* * *

The distinction between adult and children's literature is fine enough to encourage many people, including some of the most notable of writers of children's books, to believe that the distinction does not exist. Certainly it is difficult to think of Stephanie Plowman except as a novelist whose appeal is to a certain kind of reader, not to readers of a certain age. Her blend of passion and scholarship is so rare and precious that adults and children who are able to meet its demands are richer for the experience.

Plowman's major books fall into groups, those of classical Greece and those dealing with the last days of Imperial Russia. The latter are perhaps the more successful, but both groups show the same qualities of historical irony and personal involvement. It is the essence of these stories that they deal with historical figures, even though the central characters are invented. Seeing the real people through fictional eyes somehow gives them a sharper reality. There is a good example of this in *The Road to Sardis* where, at the lowest point of Athens's degradation, the hero sees a stranger examining the dismantled Long Walls with a professional eye. This is Thucydides, balancing despair at the destruction of his city against a historian's concern to prove the theory that Themistocles had built the walls in haste. There are equally telling portraits of Euripides and Socrates and a brilliant hostile thumb-nail sketch of Xenophon.

The Road to Sardis is mainly the story of the war between Athens and Sparta and the decline of democracy. Plowman showed

Athens in her glory in *The Leaping Song,* which begins with Marathon and ends with Salamis when the Persian fleet was destroyed in the narrow seas. This is a more mature work, particularly in the control of narrative (which is occasionally difficult to follow in the earlier book), but the blend of fiction and history is similar and as effective.

Between the two Greek stories Plowman studied the Russian Revolution and wrote the novels *Three Lives for the Czar* and *My Kingdom for a Grave.* In these a young Russo-Scotsman witnesses the decline and fall of the Romanov dynasty and the outbreak of revolution. Alexei Hamilton is committed by traditional loyalty and personal affection to the Russian royal family, but neither blinds him to the fatal weakness which has doomed them. These are deeply moving novels, in which major research has been completely digested so that, although the writer's authority is never in question, the story is nearer to Greek tragedy than to modern history. The reader, with the narrator, is the helpless witness of world-shaking events. One hesitates, so near the time of publication, to prophesy classic status, but here, if anywhere in modern children's literature, one is in the presence of greatness.

—Marcus Crouch

POLACCO, Patricia

Nationality: American. **Born:** Patricia Barber, 11 July 1944, Lansing, Michigan. **Education:** Attended California College of Arts and Crafts and Laney College; Monash University, B.A. 1974; University of Melbourne, M.A., Ph.D., 1978. **Family:** Married Enzo Mario Polacco 19 August 1979; two daughters and one son. **Career:** Author and illustrator, since 1986. Worked previously as an art historian consultant for local museums; speaker at schools and reading organizations. **Awards:** International Reading Association best picture book award, 1989; Sydney Taylor Award, 1989; Educators for Social Responsibility Award, 1991; Society of Children's Book Writers and Illustrators Golden Kite Award for illustration, 1992; Jane Addams Children's Book Award, picture book honor, 1993. **Member:** Center for US/USSR Initiatives, since 1984; Citizens Exchange Council, 1988-91. **Agent:** Edythea Selman, 14 Washington Place, New York, New York, 10003.

PUBLICATIONS FOR CHILDREN (ILLUSTRATED BY THE AUTHOR)

Picture Books

Meteor! New York, Dodd, 1987.
Rechenka's Eggs. New York, Philomel, 1988.
Boatride with Lillian Two Blossom. New York, Philomel, 1988.
The Keeping Quilt. New York, Simon and Schuster, 1988.
Uncle Vova's Tree. New York, Philomel, 1989.
Babushka's Doll. New York, Simon and Schuster, 1990.
Just Plain Fancy. New York, Bantam, 1990.
Thunder Cake. New York, Philomel, 1990.
Some Birthday! Simon and Schuster, 1991.
Appelemando's Dreams. New York, Philomel, 1991.
Chicken Sunday. New York, Philomel, 1992.
Mrs. Katz and Tush. New York, Bantam, 1992.
Picnic at Mudsock Meadow. New York, Putnam, 1992.
Babushka Baba Yaga. New York, Philomel, 1993.
The Bee Tree. New York, Putnam, 1993.
My Rotten, Redheaded, Older Brother. New York, Simon and Schuster, 1994.
Pink and Say. New York, Philomel, 1994.
Tikvah Means Hope. New York, Doubleday, 1994.
Babushka's Mother Goose. New York, Philomel, 1995.
My Ol' Man. New York, Philomel, 1995.
Aunt Chip and the Great Triple Creek Dam Affair. New York, Philomel Books, 1996.
I Can Hear the Sun: A Modern Myth. New York, Philomel Books, 1996.
The Trees of the Dancing Goats. New York, Simon and Schuster, 1996.
In Enzo's Splendid Gardens. New York, Philomel Books, 1997.
Uncle Isaaco. New York, Philomel Books, 1997.
Mrs. Mack. New York, Philomel Books, 1998.
Thank you, Mr. Falker. New York, Philomel Books, 1998.

Other

Firetalking, photographs by Lawrence Migdale. Katonah, New York, R.C. Owen, 1994.

Adapter, *Casey at the Bat.* New York, Putnam, 1988.

* * *

In *Firetalking,* her photo-autobiography, Patricia Polacco speaks of her stories as being true, "but they may not have happened." She is a consummate storyteller who draws upon family history and ritual for many of her tales. Her enthusiastic artwork captures the spirit of her stories through choices of color and energetic displays of movement.

The Keeping Quilt reveals the voices of four generations of women who make, treasure, and hand down a quilt that serves as a Sabbath tablecloth, a baby quilt, a play tent, and a huppa for a wedding, and, more importantly, as a family keepsake. Polacco's sepia-colored drawings with the quilt in bright cheery reds, yellows, and blues forces the eye to focus on the quilt as central to the story.

Drawing again on Russian family tradition, *Rechenka's Eggs* is a tale of a goose who was healed by a caring babushka and then accidentally destroys the healer's precious beautifully designed, hand-painted eggs. But Rechenka repays her by leaving exquisite eggs each day which win the first prize for her friend. The face of Baba is very old and warm, and the colors and costumes are traditional. Unlike most tales of Baba Yaga, Polacco, both in this story and in *Babuska,* Baba Yaga presents the old woman from an alternative and more positive point of view. Polacco's stories often relate directly to a childhood fear and explore that fear in a humorous and intelligent fashion.

Thunder Cake, a model solution for a day with a thunderstorm, is a perfect device for intensifying the event while lessening the fear. With so many things to do before the thunder cake is finished, the balance between fear and bravery makes this tale work. In *The Bee Tree,* Mary Ellen learns a wondrous lesson on the importance of reading from her grandfather who decides that they must find a bee tree and thus begins a chase through many pages. Placing honey on the book brings the story full circle and firmly sets the lesson of the tale. Repeatedly, Polacco's tales involve multigenerational families. In *Chicken Sunday,* the importance of values and a sense of responsibility are revealed in the Eula Mae Walker story of a hat in the window and the presentation of painted eggs to Mr. Kodinski. Chicken soup symbolically touches the heart and makes the relationship among the characters real. Eula Mae's voice in the Baptist church choir is as pure as sunlight, and the illustrations convey that warmth and glory.

Differing in many ways from her other illustrations, *Appelemando's Dreams* tells of a child whose dreams pop from his head and turn into paintings on the walls of his village. When the elders see the wildly colored paintings, they believe the children are mischief-making. The children, on the other hand, are more concerned that Appelemando can't dream anymore, and they become lost on the way home. But Appelemando dreams and the dreams are seen by the villagers as they appear above the forest, leading to the rescue of the children. The lesson is clear: dreams, no matter how bizarre, are to be valued.

Just Plain Fancy is a story from the Amish culture in which Naomi and Ruth are learning responsibility in caring for their chickens. Naomi finds a beautifully marked egg and takes it back to Henny's nest. When it hatches, it is very different from the other chicks, and the children worry that it is too fancy for their culture. As their strange bird grows, Naomi despairs that it will cost her even more than her white cap, representing responsibility; she might be shunned. During the summer working bee, Fancy escapes and their secret is out. An elder explains that shunning is for going against the laws of their people. Naomi gets her white cap and learns that raising a peacock is indeed a responsibility.

Pink and Say is a story of the Civil War in which a young white soldier is saved by a young black soldier whose mother nurses them both back to health. Polacco demonstrates her love for cats in both *Tikvah Means Hope* and in *Mrs. Katz and Tush.* Each cat is the focal point of the story, Tikvah survives a devastating fire and a community comes together to celebrate the miracle. Tush brings life and heart to Mrs. Katz and her young friend.

Polacco combines wonderful subtleties in her illustration, often placing multicultural images within her frame and mixing strong sepia and/or black line images with highlights of color in skirts or hats or decorations. Thus, she focuses the eye of the reader in intriguing ways and sometimes offers a new perspective on the text. Often Polacco ends a story with attention to its continuation so that when someone has died, that person's influence and memory lives on.

—Kay E. Vandergrift

POLAND, Marguerite

Nationality: South African. **Born:** Johannesburg, Transvaal, 3 April 1950. **Education:** Rhodes University, Grahamstown, 1968-70, B.A.; Stellenbosch University, Cape Province, 1971, honours degree in African languages; Natal University, Durban, 1976, M.A. **Family:** Married Martin Oosthuizen in 1973; two daughters. **Career:** Assistant, South African Museum, Cape Town, 1972; research assistant, Institute for Social Research, Natal University, 1973-75. **Awards:** Percy Fitzpatrick award, 1979, 1984; Sankei Honourable Award, 1989, for translated edition of *The Mantis and the Moon.* **Address:** 6 Robertson Avenue, Kloof 3610, KwaZulu-Natal, South Africa.

Publications for Children

Fiction

The Mantis and the Moon: Stories for the Children of Africa, illustrated by Leigh Voigt. Johannesburg, Ravan Press, 1979.
Nqalu, The Mouse with No Whiskers, illustrated by Cora Coetzee. Cape Town, Tafelberg, 1979.
Once at KwaFubesi, illustrated by Leigh Voigt. Johannesburg, Ravan Press, 1981.
The Bush Shrike. Johannesburg, Ravan Press, 1982.
The Fiery-Necked Nightjar: A Christmas Story, illustrated by Leigh Voigt. Johannesburg, Ravan Press, 1983.
The Wood-Ash Stars, illustrated by Shanne Altshuler. Cape Town, Philip, 1983.
Marcus and the Boxing Gloves [*Go-Kart*], illustrated by Cora Coetzee. Cape Town, Tafelberg, 2 vols., 1984-88.
Shadow of the Wild Hare, illustrated by Leigh Voigt. Cape Town, Philip, 1986.
The Small Clay Bull, illustrated by Shanne Altshuler. Cape Town, Philip, 1986.
Sambane's Dream. New York, Penguin, 1990.

Publications for Adults

Novel

Train to Doringbult. London, Bodley Head, 1987.
Shades. New York, Viking/Penguin, 1993.

*

Manuscript Collections: Killie Campbell Africana Library, Durban; National English Literary Museum, Grahamstown.

Marguerite Poland comments:

When I was a child there were very few books available which were set in South Africa, none which gave a sense of "belonging." I have tried to rectify this lack. I was fortunate to have had the opportunity to study African folklore and various African languages. From these studies I developed an abiding interest in the African folk tradition. However, I do *not* reproduce folktales in any way but create original stories which draw inspiration from this rich tradition. I hope to raise both social and environmental issues. I write primarily to entertain, but hope too to give children insights into the complex past and present of my fascinating but tragic country. I hope, in some small way, to encourage children to hold dear that which is good and beautiful from the past but to aspire to a society that is just and equal for all.

* * *

Marguerite Poland's animal stories are highly regarded in South Africa but as yet little known elsewhere. Some have European forerunners, but most have been influenced by various African traditions in storytelling. All are notable for a lucid style and an acute and detailed observation of the natural life of the East Cape countryside where she once lived.

Nqalu, The Mouse with No Whiskers, is a finely illustrated story of a journey of self-discovery which bears comparison with Bria

Patten's creation myth, *Jumping Mouse*—though on the simpler level of a charming moral tale extolling the virtues of modesty and courage.

Like Kipling's *Just So Stories,* the brief title story of *The Mantis and the Moon* is a *pourquoi* tale. The mantis tries to capture the moon in its journey across the sky, and is briefly blinded for his audacity, but he obtains the forgiveness he prays for. This is why his descendants still pray to the moon. The next and longer story is quite different in style and appeal. Ntini, a small otter, is swept away with his grandfather in the flood that follows when men have dammed the river. But his adventures are those of any wilful, mischievous small boy, who is nevertheless desperately in need of the assistance of the various small creatures (including a mouse and an owl) who rescue him from his enemies and reunite him with his grandfather. This variety of type and complexity of story within the same volume is refreshing but can also be disconcerting. Fortunately most of these tales can be read and enjoyed at different levels of understanding, at any age from eight upwards.

This is certainly true of "The Windflower" in *Once at KwaFubesi.* Lwembu the brown jumping spider is lured from her quiet country home to the town, where she lives on a squalid overcrowded rubbish heap, the prey of marauders and *tsotsis* like the big Zindlavini spiders, or the cockroaches, the Maphela. This can be read straightforwardly as an adventure story but it can also be read as a satirical story of the unhealthy and danger-ridden existence in South African black townships. In the same volume, "Sidenge's Potion," a trickster story in the vein of the Brer Rabbit or Anansi folktales, is comparatively sophisticated at all levels in its working out of the spring hare's complex attempts to become a "whistling diviner."

Other books contain traditional-type stories of the lives of Southern African peoples: San, Xhosa, Tsonga, and Zulu. *The Wood-Ash Stars* and *The Small Clay Bull* each contain four such lively tales incorporating folk beliefs, and telling of the adventures of children or the concerns of older people as they herd their animals, hunt, encounter hyenas, long for a child, or escape from the guns of the first white settlers.

There are also stories of white children. Round the simple activities of a 10-year-old country boy Poland has created two pleasant little books, of particular interest and value to South African youngsters, but typical of children's interests anywhere. In *Marcus and the Boxing Gloves* Marcus dreams of defeating the school bully and becoming champion, but learns that keeping promises is more important than winning fame. In *Marcus and the Go-Kart* he has adventures in town with new friends.

Shadow of the Wild Hare is a story for slightly older readers. Rosie frees a riverine rabbit which the Xhosa trapper is using as bait to catch jackals. Through her concern for this rare wild creature she learns to value both its individuality and need for freedom and the trapper's knowledge and wisdom.

There is evident respect and affection in most of these stories for African folklore and family life, but save for the bleak portrait of black townships already mentioned, there is little direct reference in them to racial inequalities within South Africa. *The Bush Shrike,* however, is a delicate and poignant teenage novel which reveals anew Poland's skill in conveying character and situation, but contains in addition an implicit protest against racial prejudice. 14-year-old Anna becomes interested in the storeman's son, Josh, a lonely, aloof boy. Together they explore the countryside, observing the wildlife for the nature records Josh is keeping. But their developing friendship comes to an abrupt end when Anna's parents discover that Josh has coloured blood and promptly send their daughter away to boarding school. Uneasy relationships under apartheid are also explored in a searching adult novel, *Train to Doringbult.* Here one is reminded of Doris Lessing's Rhodesian stories of black and white children growing up together in harmony and friendship, until the relationship changes inevitably into the distant one of master and servant.

Though readers outside South Africa may have some initial trouble with vernacular names of people, vegetation, and animals (the striking accompanying illustrations are often helpful here), and with the scattering of words and phrases from Afrikaans, Xhosa, Zulu, and other African languages, Poland's books are varied and interesting and deserve a wider audience.

—Winifred Whitehead

POLLAND, Madeleine A(ngela)

Pseudonym: Frances Adrian. **Nationality:** British. **Born:** Madeleine Angela Cahill, Kinsale, County Cork, Ireland, 31 May 1918. **Education:** Hitchin Girls' Grammar School, Hertfordshire, 1929-37. **Military Service:** Women's Auxiliary Air Force, 1942-45. **Family:** Married Arthur Joseph Polland in 1946; one daughter and one son. **Career:** Assistant librarian, Letchworth Public Library, Hertfordshire, 1939-42 and 1945-46. **Address:** Edificio Hercules 634, Avenida Gamonal, Arroyo de la Miel, Malaga, Spain.

Publications for Children

Fiction

Children of the Red King, illustrated by Annette Macarthur-Onslow. London, Constable, 1960; New York, Holt Rinehart, 1961.

The Town Across the Water, illustrated by Brian Wildsmith. London, Constable, 1961; New York, Holt Rinehart, 1963.

Beorn the Proud, illustrated by William Stobbs. London, Constable, 1961; New York, Holt Rinehart, 1962.

Fingal's Quest, illustrated by W.T. Mars. New York, Doubleday, and London, Burns Oates, 1961.

The White Twilight, illustrated by William Stobbs. London, Constable, 1962; New York, Holt Rinehart, 1965.

Chuiraquimba and the Black Robes, illustrated by Juan Carlos Barberis. New York, Doubleday, and London, Burns Oates, 1962.

City of the Golden House, illustrated by Leo Summers. New York, Doubleday, 1963; Kingswood, Surrey, World's Work, 1964.

The Queen's Blessing, illustrated by William Stobbs. London, Constable, 1963; New York, Holt Rinehart, 1964.

Flame over Tara, illustrated by Omar Davis. New York, Doubleday, 1964; Kingswood, Surrey, World's Work, 1965.

Mission to Cathay, illustrated by Peter Landa. New York, Doubleday, 1965; Kingswood, Surrey, World's Work, 1966.

Queen Without Crown, illustrated by William Stobbs. London, Constable, 1965; New York, Holt Rinehart, 1966.

Deirdre, illustrated by Sean Morrison. New York, Doubleday, and Kingswood, Surrey, World's Work, 1967.
To Tell My People, illustrated by John Holder. London, Hutchinson, and New York, Holt Rinehart, 1968.
Stranger in the Hills, illustrated by Victor Ambrus. New York, Doubleday, 1968; London, Hutchinson, 1969.
To Kill a King, illustrated by John Holder. London, Hutchinson, 1970; New York, Holt Rinehart, 1971.
Alhambra, illustrated by Mary Frances Gaaze. New York, Doubleday, 1970; London, Hutchinson, 1971.
A Family Affair, illustrated by Trevor Stubley. London, Hutchinson, 1971.
Daughter to Poseidon, illustrated by John Holder. London, Hutchinson, 1972; as *Daughter of the Sea,* New York, Doubleday, 1972.
Prince of the Double Axe, illustrated by Gareth Floyd. London, Abelard Schuman, 1976.

Publications for Adults

Novels

Thicker than Water. New York, Holt Rinehart, 1965; London, Hutchinson, 1967.
The Little Spot of Bother. London, Hutchinson, 1967; as *Minutes of a Murder,* New York, Holt Rinehart, 1967.
Random Army. London, Hutchinson, 1969; as *Shattered Summer,* New York, Doubleday, 1970.
Package to Spain. London, Hutchinson, and New York, Walker, 1971.
Double Shadow (as Frances Adrian). New York, Fawcett, and London, Macdonald and Jane's, 1977.
Sabrina. New York, Delacorte Press, and London, Collins, 1979.
All Their Kingdoms. New York, Delacorte Press, and London, Collins, 1981.
The Heart Speaks Many Ways. New York, Delacorte Press, and London, Collins, 1982.
No Price Too High. New York, Delacorte Press, 1984; London, Piatkus, 1985.
As It Was in the Beginning. London, Piatkus, 1987.
Rich Man's Flowers. London, Piatkus, 1990.
The Pomegranate House. London, Piatkus, 1992.

*

Manuscript Collection: Mugar Memorial Library, Boston University.

Madeleine A. Polland comments:

(1978) Almost without exception my books for children may be said to be the product of my own intense consciousness of the reality of history, and the reality of historical figures as people. It has always been my idea to try to portray events in which children become involved in the dramatic past. And it is, of course, infinitely more plausible to create dramatic adventures for children in past centuries, when it was perfectly possible for them to be abandoned with the need to look after themselves. Except in times of war, which television presents in all its heartbreaking contemporary detail (leaving no imagination necessary), children's lives at the present tend to run on more scheduled lines, leaving adventure to the days of history.

(1983) I would add that if I have forsaken the children for the moment, it is with a preoccupation with people of all times and all ages. Although I would admit to a sneaking affection for the period of *Sabrina*—1912 onwards.

* * *

Madeleine A. Polland is noted for her impressive list of historical novels with backgrounds as various as her own native Ireland, China, Viking Denmark, Norman England, mediaeval Scotland, Moorish Spain, and ancient Crete. However, two recent books are contemporary, and one is a mixture of ancient and modern. If we take her books published in the 1970s as representative of her skill in writing for young people, we may conclude that she offers, whether historical or contemporary, a cultivated and thickly textured species of adolescent romantic fiction. These books illustrate what Frank Eyre may have had in mind when he included Polland in a small group of modern children's writers who "have produced books that in a less demanding age would have been outstanding."

Although the narrative of *To Kill a King* hinges on a Saxon plot to assassinate William the Conqueror, the main interest lies in the love of Merca and Edward which blossoms during the dangers of their flight to Scotland. Edward's love "saves" Merca from the contemplative life towards which her misery following her parents' slaughter by the Normans has led her. In *Alhambra* the dramatic conflict is supplied by the young Juanito's longing for Princess Nahid despite his fiercely patriotic rejection of the Moors with whom he has lived since early childhood. In *A Family Affair,* it is true, the incipient teenage romantic attachment of Alex, the English girl, to Christian, the Danish boy, during the annual family holiday in Copenhagen, is muted to allow more prominence to the improbable mystery thriller involving eccentric aunts and inept thefts from picture galleries. But young love is the principal theme in *Daughter to Poseidon,* both in the contemporary framework story of Saran's dependence upon the love of Miklos, the Greek student, in assuaging her grief and feelings of guilt over her parents' death in a car crash, and also in the parallel though much bulkier historical narrative in which Saran is rescued from the sea by Mikolai, the Cretan youth who with Saran's resolute support saves Knossos from infiltration by the Hellenes. The interweaving of these two levels is imaginatively done, as is the exciting build-up to the earthquake and the overthrow of Paradocles.

Polland's historical researchers may seldom provide more than a vivid romanticised background to the drama she unfolds, and her plots on occasion may slip into the implausible. In her concern to convey emotion and describe mental states she may at times prolong the agony at the expense of narrative pace and indulge in slightly inflated prose, often marked by a trick of repeating names or other words, as in "she would be safer, safer against the threat of war" and "Saran felt the soft, soft touch of the fine linen on her legs." But she portrays her characters in bitter conflict, cruel dilemmas; they suffer pain and permanent injury on the road to self-knowledge. To the older reader who has not yet fully entered the world of adult fiction she may well provide a not inconsiderable bridge.

—Graham Hammond

POMERANTZ, Charlotte

Nationality: American. **Born:** Brooklyn, New York, 24 July 1930. **Education:** Sarah Lawrence College, B.A. 1953. **Family:** Married Carl Marzani, 1966; one son, one daughter. **Career:** Writer; has worked as a salesperson, waitress, researcher, copy editor, and editor. **Awards:** Outstanding Picture Book of the Year Citation, *New York Times,* 1972, and one of ten U.S. books chosen for the International Year of the Child, International Board on Books for Young People, 1978, both for *The Day They Parachuted Cats on Borneo*; Outstanding Book of the Year Citation, *New York Times,* 1974, and Reading Rainbow selection, 1992, both for *The Piggy in the Puddle*; Jane Addams Children's Book award, Jane Addams Peace Association, 1975, for *The Princess and the Admiral,* and Honor Award, 1983, for *If I Had a Paka*; Notable Book Citation, American Library Association, 1980, and Reading Rainbow selection, 1985, both for *The Tamarindo Puppy and Other Poems*; Christopher Award, 1984, for *Posy*; Top Ten Picture Books of 1989 Citation, *Boston Globe,* and Parent's Choice Award, 1990, both for *The Chalk Doll*; Children's Book of the Year Citation, Library of Congress, 1991, for *How Many Trucks Can a Tow Truck Tow?*; Top 100 Book Citation, New York Public Library, 1993, for *The Outside Dog.* **Address:** 261 West 21st Street, New York, New York 10011, U.S.A.

PUBLICATIONS FOR CHILDREN

Fiction

The Bear Who Couldn't Sleep, illustrated by Meg Wohlberg. New York, Morrow, 1965.
The Moon Pony, illustrated by Loretta Trezzo. New York, Young Scott Books, 1967.
Ask the Windy Sea, illustrated by Nancy Grossman and Anita Siegel. New York, Young Scott Books, 1968.
Why You Look Like You Whereas I Tend to Look Like Me, illustrated by Rosemary Wells and Susan Jeffers. New York, Young Scott Books, 1969.
The Princess and the Admiral (folktale), illustrated by Tony Chen. New York, Addison-Wesley, 1974.
Detective Poufy's First Case; or, The Missing Battery-Operated Pepper Grinder, illustrated by Marty Norman. New York, Addison-Wesley, 1976.
The Mango Tooth, illustrated by Marylin Hafner. New York, Greenwillow, 1977.
The Downtown Fairy Godmother, illustrated by Susanna Natti. New York, Addison-Wesley, 1978.
Noah and Namah's Ark, illustrated by Kelly Carson. New York, Holt, 1981.
Buffy and Albert, illustrated by Yossi Abolafia. New York, Greenwillow, 1982.
Posy, illustrated by Catherine Stock. New York, Greenwillow, 1983.
The Half-Birthday Party, illustrated by DyAnne DiSalvo-Ryan. New York, Clarion, 1984.
One Duck, Another Duck, illustrated by Jose Aruego and Ariane Dewey. New York, Greenwillow, 1984.
Where's the Bear?, illustrated by Byron Barton. New York, Greenwillow, 1984.
Whiff, Sniff, Nibble, and Chew: The Gingerbread Boy Retold, illustrated by Monica Incisa. New York, Greenwillow, 1984.
Timothy Tall Feather, illustrated by Catherine Stock. New York, Greenwillow, 1986.
How Many Trucks Can a Tow Truck Tow?, illustrated by R.W. Alley. New York, Random House, 1987.
The Chalk Doll, illustrated by Frané Lessac. New York, Lippincott, 1989.
Serena Katz, illustrated by R.W. Alley. New York, Macmillan, 1992.
The Outside Dog, illustrated by Jennifer Plecas. New York, HarperCollins, 1993.
Here Comes Henny, illustrated by Nancy Winslow Parker. New York, Greenwillow, 1994.
You're Not My Best Friend Anymore, illustrated by David Soman. New York, Dial, 1997.
Mangaboom, illustrated by Anita Lobel. New York, Greenwillow, 1997.

Poetry

The Piggy in the Puddle, illustrated by James Marshall. New York, Macmillan, 1974.
The Tamarindo Puppy and Other Poems, illustrated by Byron Barton. New York, Greenwillow, 1980.
If I Had a Paka: Poems in Eleven Languages, illustrated by Nancy Tafuri. New York, Greenwillow, 1982.
All Asleep: Poems and Lullabies, illustrated by Nancy Tafuri. New York, Greenwillow, 1984.
Flap Your Wings and Try, illustrated by Nancy Tafuri. New York, Greenwillow, 1989.
Halfway to Your House, illustrated by Gabrielle Vincent. New York, Greenwillow, 1993.

Other

The Day They Parachuted Cats on Borneo: A Drama of Ecology (play), illustrated by Jose Aruego. New York, Young Scott Books, 1971.

Lyricist and co-author with Jennifer Dent, *Eureka!* (musical based on the legend of Archimedes, 1996-97).

Also contributor to anthologies, including *Sound of A Distant Drum,* New York, Holt, 1967, *Read-Aloud Rhymes for the Very Young,* edited by Jack Prelutsky, New York, Knopf, 1986, and *To the Moon and Back,* compiled by Nancy Larrick, New York, Delacorte, 1991.

*

Media Adaptations: *Rap, Snap: The Electric Gingerbreak Boy* (rap play adapted from *Whiff, Sniff, Nibble, and Chew: The Gingerbread Boy Retold*), produced at Children's Dance Theater, 1984; *Piggy in the Puddle,* featured in claymation on Reading Rainbow, from 1993; *The Day They Parachuted Cats on Borneo* and *The Princess and the Admiral* have been produced as children's plays at public schools.

Biography: Entry in *Something about the Author,* Detroit, Gale Research, Vol. 80, 1995, 179-184.

* * *

Charlotte Pomerantz writes engaging books in prose and poetry for the pre-schooler and for the beginner reader. Her plots are fun, with unexpected twists and turns. Her characters are quite diverse, including elderly people of wit and wisdom and little children just beginning to stand; boys who are caring and girls who are daring; comfortable urban Americans and poor islanders from Jamaica and Puerto Rico; and children speaking different languages from several parts of the world. Pomerantz welcomes and enjoys a number of populations.

Her fiction for children includes several books about grandparents and grandchildren. In her counting book, *One Duck, Another Duck,* a boy and his grandmother go to the pond to inspect the ducks. "One duck, another duck" counts Danny. "No," says his Grandmother; "You know how to count. Count them again." And with grandmother's gentle encouragement, Danny does count from one all the way to ten. Another book, *Buffy and Albert,* is the story of friendship between grandchildren and a grandfather. With the grandchildren's gentle encouragement, grandfather accepts the infirmities of old age, and gets on with life.

In *The Half-Birthday Party,* a big brother named Daniel is so excited when his six-month-old sister Katie stands on her own for the first time that he decides to give her a half-birthday party, complete with half-presents and a half-cake. Daniel's own half-present to Katie comes at night time: it is a glorious half-moon.

The Chalk Doll is a mother's tale of an impoverished childhood, told to her daughter. Rose's mother grew up in Jamaica, too poor to have a chalk doll or birthday parties or birthday presents. She made her own rag doll out of a piece of material, folded over once, and stuffed with rags. Rose is comfortably situated in America; she has many chalk dolls and stuffed animals. Now she asks her mother for a rag doll, and together they make one.

Two of Pomerantz's books which show strong heroines are *Posy* and *The Princess and the Admiral.* Posy is a young girl who bites into a mango pit and loses her first tooth. She is rewarded with ten cents for this mango tooth. So she looks forward to losing more teeth and earning more money. She loses a chicken bone tooth and a tootsie pop tooth. When she persuades her mother to pay her twenty cents for an elephant tooth, she wisely eats elephant animal crackers rather than biting into the real thing. *The Princess and the Admiral* is based on Kublai Khan's invasion of Vietnam in the thirteenth century. It begins as the kingdom is about to celebrate one hundred years of peace. Princess Mat Mat is advised that attackers are moving into the harbor; she defends her kingdom with courage and ingenuity.

One of Pomerantz's plays, *The Day They Parachuted Cats on Borneo,* is a story of ecological devastation. It tells how the insecticide DDT, sprayed on the Island of Borneo to kill the mosquitoes that breed malaria, was ingested by roaches. The roaches were eaten by geckoes, and the cats that ate the geckoes were poisoned and killed. When rats, unchecked by cats, infested the island, ecologists saved the environment by parachuting cats onto Borneo. This play has been produced at public schools throughout the country.

Pomerantz has lived both in New York City and in Puerto Rico. Well aware that many American children speak two languages, she has produced several books of poetry which incorporate more than English. *The Tamarindo Puppy and Other Poems* is written in English and in Spanish. The title poem begins: "The Tamarindo puppy/Is a very nice puppy/Is a muy lindo puppy/Whom we visit every day."

The inclusion of simple words in each language allows a reader of one language to understand the poetry without translation. The poem "Fire House" provides an account of firemen rescuing animals from a burning barn. "My Fat Cat" is a funny poem about a fat cat, snoozing in the hay, dreaming about a yummy mouse who got away. Byron Barton's delightful illustrations for this book are bold in line and filled with color.

If I Had a Paka is a book of poems in eleven languages: Swahili, Serbo-Croatian, Native American, English, Samoan, Dutch, Vietnamese, Japanese, Indonesian, Spanish, and Yiddish. The title poem, incorporating Swahili words, begins:

> If I had a paka
> meow, meow,
> meow, meow
> I would want a mm-bwa
> bow wow wow wow
> If I had a mm-bwa
> bow wow wow wow
> I would want a simba
> roar, roar, roar, roar.

What fun for a child to listen to or to read such words! Nancy Tafuri's graphic designs, filled with rhythm, add to the enjoyment of this book.

Pomerantz enriches the child's world by presenting many types of relationships between peoples and cultures in clear and unassuming fashion. She focuses primarily on familiar settings for the child. But she also deals directly with problems of living: elderly infirmities, war between nations, ecological imbalance. She describes social issues with intelligence and insight, and her imaginative use of languages broaden a child's experiences and understanding.

—Mary Lystad

POOLE, (Jane Penelope) Josephine

Nationality: British. **Born:** Jane Penelope Josephine Cumpston, London, 12 February 1933. **Education:** Fyling Hall School, Cumberland, 1941-45; Queensgate School, London, 1945-50. **Family:** Married 1) Timothy Ruscombe Poole in 1956, four daughters; 2) Vincent John Hawker Helyar in 1975, one daughter and one son. **Career:** Solicitor's secretary, London, 1951-54; secretary, BBC Features Department, London, 1954-56. **Agent:** Gina Pollinger, 222 Old Brompton Rd., London SW5 0BZ, England. **Address:** Poundisford Lodge, Poundisford, Taunton, Somerset TA3 7AE, England.

Publications for Children

Fiction

A Dream in the House, illustrated by Peggy Fortnum. London, Hutchinson, 1961.

Moon Eyes. London, Hutchinson, 1965; Boston, Little Brown, 1967.

Catch as Catch Can. London, Hutchinson, 1969; New York, Harper, 1970.
Billy Buck. London, Hutchinson, 1972; as *The Visitor,* New York, Harper, 1972.
Touch and Go. London, Hutchinson, and New York, Harper, 1976.
The Open Grave, illustrated by Tony Kerins. London, Benn, 1979.
The Forbidden Room, illustrated by Tony Kerins. London, Benn, 1979.
Hannah Chance. London, Hutchinson, 1980.
Diamond Jack. London, Methuen, 1983.
Three for Luck, illustrated by Barrie Thorpe. London, Hutchinson, 1985.
Wildlife Tales, illustrated by Douglas Hall. London, Hutchinson, 1986.
The Loving Ghosts. London, Hutchinson, 1988.
Angel. London, Hutchinson, 1989.
This Is Me Speaking. London, Hutchinson, 1990, Random House, 1991.
Paul Loves Amy Loves Christo. London, Hutchinson, 1992.
Deadly Inheritance. London, Hutchinson, 1995.
Hero. London, Hodder, 1997.

Plays

Caractacus, music by Michael Dyer (produced 1986).

Television Plays: *The Inheritance* (*Shadows* series), 1976; *Ring a Rosie,* 1982; *With Love, Belinda,* 1982; *The Animal Lover,* 1982; *Three in the Wild: Fox, Buzzard, Dartmoor Pony,* 1984.

Other

When Fishes Flew: A Selection of Legends and Old Wives' Tales from the West Country, illustrated by Barbara Swiderska. London, Benn, 1978; as *Kings, Ghosts, and Highwaymen,* London, Carousel, 1981.
Golden Classics (*Puss in Boots, The Sleeping Beauty*), illustrated by Edmund Morin. London, Hutchinson, 2 vols., 1988; New York, Barron's, 1988.
Pinocchio, illustrated by James Mayhew, Simon & Schuster, 1994.
Joan of Arc, illustrated by Angela Barrett. New York, Knopf, 1998.

Reteller, *Snow White,* illustrated by Angela Barrett. London, Hutchinson, and New York, Knopf, 1992.
Reteller, *The Water Babies* by Charles Kingsley, illustrated by Jan Omerod. London, MacDonald Young, 1996; Brookfield, Connecticut, Millbrook Press, 1998.

Publications for Adults

Novels

The Lilywhite Boys. London, Hart Davis, 1968.
Yokeham. London, Murray, 1970.

Short Stories

West Country Tales (based on television plays), with others. Exeter, Webb and Bower, 1981.
Scared to Death and Other Ghostly Stories. London, Hutchinson, 1994.

Plays

Television Plays: *The Harbourer* (*Country Tales* series), 1975; *The Sabbatical, The Breakdown,* and *Miss Constantine* (*West Country Tales* series), 1981.

Other

The Country Diary Companion. Exeter, Webb and Bower, 1984.

*

Media Adaptations: *Catch as Catch Can* (audio cassette), Listening Library, 1979.

Josephine Poole comments:

The main influences on the creative part of my life:

I was very small when the Second World War began and we went noth to live with my father's aunt in a huge, old house surrounded by garden and a wood. It was very dark and cold and damp, with open fires even in the bedrooms, and no electricity. It was often alarming, and very beautiful. In the evenings my mother read to us, her four daughters—not "children's" books, but the classics—*Wuthering Heights, Jane Eyre, Vanity Fair, David Copperfield, Nicholas Nickleby, Dombey & Son, Great Expectations, Kim, The Jungle Books,* and poetry. She was a natural actress and read with passion. Later we moved to a farm cottage, very wild and also most beautiful, but not frightening except for the bull which often roamed at will, and the occasional convoy of tanks if one met them with the pony and trap.

My mother herself loved to read widely, so did I, and when I began to write, no one was more encouraging than she. She was a professional artist, illustrating children's books. Even if it was a story she disliked, she always worked to the best of her (considerable) ability. She never deliverd an inferior piece of work, and in this way was an invaluable example for any young creative person. She was entirely professional.

* * *

Josephine Poole is a writer specialising in mystery: supernatural, in *Moon Eyes,* criminal, in *Catch as Catch Can,* and, all-pervadingly, in everything she does, the mystifying nature of life itself. She has a talent for building tension out of small details and creating menace in an apparently normal, friendly scene. In her handling of *la chasse humaine* she rivals Geoffrey Household, with whom she has much in common. The scene in *Touch and Go,* probably her most accomplished work to date, in which the heroine is hunted by unknown attackers round unfamiliar farm buildings in the dark and fog, is a masterpiece of its kind.

The story of *Touch and Go,* racy, outrageous, and just plausible enough to suspend disbelief, is characteristic Poole country. Teenage Emily and her with-it, intellectual mother—Poole also has a knack of brief, astringent pen portraits as merciless as they are funny—have booked for a "farmhouse" holiday in Devon. On the way they crash the car and Emily, recovering overnight in hospital, stumbles on the first clue in a sequence which leads her, with the help of her friend, Charles, to a gang of terrorists planning an explosion in the local naval college. The narrative ranges between the creepily sinister and the downright hilarious: the dialogue is crisp and realistic. In addition, there is the added ingredient which lifts Poole's writing a long way above the common. This is her treatment of her characters, and it is a thread which runs consistently through all her books. It sustains the occasional weaknesses of plot and gives an added depth to what would otherwise be no more than light entertainment. Emily is plump and unsophisticated for her age, the heroine of *Moon Eyes* imaginative but intellectually idle, yet both are intensely real, and, witches and smugglers notwithstanding, so are the worlds in which they live.

This psychological element is carried even further in *Hannah Chance*. Here the heroine is actually an adult, a youngish schoolteacher, emotionally undeveloped, living with her clergyman father. Nor is her life made easier by her unfortunate name of Miss Chance. When a fellow-teacher disappears, she is badgered by a teenage boy into following up his conviction that the man has been murdered. But the real interest of the book lies less in the slightly contrived twists of the plot than in the growing relationship between the two: the retiring, self-critical woman and the intelligent, determined boy whose apparent confidence hides an equal need for reassurance. It is typical of Poole's way of thought that in both cases it is not years but intensity of living which brings maturity.

Poole's growth as a writer can been seen in the broadened range of her work in the 1980s and 1990s. While still writing mysteries for younger readers (*Three for Luck*) she has also begun writing young adult mysteries such as *Diamond Jack, The Loving Ghosts,* and *Deadly Inheritance,* where romance takes a more prominent place beside mystery. She has also tried her hand at carefully researched short stories about animals in *Wildlife Tales.* And she has shown her versatility by writing for the picture book audience, with retellings of such classic tales as *Snow White, Pinocchio,* and the story of French heroine *Joan of Arc.* An adaptation of of Charles Kingsley's beloved tale *The Water Babies* proves her still wonderfully adept at writing for her original audience.

—Anne Carter, updated by Jackie C. Horne

PORTER, Gene Stratton

Nationality: American. **Born:** Geneva Grace Stratton Porter, Wabash County, Indiana, 17 August 1863. **Education:** Attended public schools. **Family:** Married Charles Darwin Porter in 1886; one daughter. **Career:** Regular contributor, *McCall's Magazine;* photographic editor, *Recreation* magazine; member of the natural history department, *Outing* magazine; natural history photography specialist, *Photographic Times Annual Almanac,* four years. Founded Gene Stratton Porter Productions film company, 1922. **Died:** 6 December 1924.

PUBLICATIONS FOR CHILDREN

Fiction

Freckles, illustrated by E. Stetson Crawford. New York, Doubleday, 1904; London, Murray, 1905.

A Girl of the Limberlost, illustrated by Wladyslaw T. Benda. New York, Doubleday, 1909; London, Hodder and Stoughton, 1911.

The Magic Garden, illustrated by Lee Thayer. New York, Doubleday, and London, Hutchinson, 1927.

Other

Morning Face (poetry), illustrated by the author. New York, Doubleday, and London, Murray, 1916.

A Girl of the Limberlost (screenplay). 1924.

PUBLICATIONS FOR ADULTS

Novels

The Song of the Cardinal: A Love Story. Indianapolis, Bobbs Merrill, 1903; London, Hodder and Stoughton, 1913.

At the Foot of the Rainbow. New York, Outing Publishing Company, 1907; London, Hodder and Stoughton, 1913.

The Harvester. New York, Doubleday, and London, Hodder and Stoughton, 1911.

Laddie: A True-Blue Story. New York, Doubleday, and London, Murray, 1913.

Michael O'Halloran. New York, Doubleday, and London, Murray, 1915.

A Daughter of the Land. New York, Doubleday, and London, Murray, 1918.

Her Father's Daughter. New York, Doubleday, and London, Murray, 1921.

The White Flag. New York, Doubleday, and London, Murray, 1923.

The Keeper of the Bees. New York, Doubleday, and London, Hutchinson, 1925.

Poetry

The Fire Bird. New York, Doubleday, and London, Murray, 1922.

Jesus of the Emerald. New York, Doubleday, and London, Murray, 1923.

Other

What I Have Done with Birds: Character Studies of Native American Birds. Indianapolis, Bobbs Merrill, 1907; revised edition, New York, Doubleday, 1917; as *Friends in Feathers,* London, Curtis Brown, 1917.

Birds of the Bible. Cincinnati, Jennings and Graham, 1909; London, Hodder and Stoughton, 1910.

Music of the Wild, illustrated by the author. Cincinnati, Jennings and Graham, and London, Hodder and Stoughton, 1910.

Moths of the Limberlost, illustrated by the author. New York, Doubleday, 1912; London, Hodder and Stoughton, 1913.

After the Flood. Indianapolis, Bobbs Merrill, 1912.

Birds of the Limberlost. New York, Doubleday, 1914.

Homing with the Birds. New York, Doubleday, and London, Murray, 1919.

Wings. New York, Doubleday, 1923.

Tales You Won't Believe (natural history). New York, Doubleday and London, Heinemann, 1925.

Let Us Highly Resolve (essays). New York, Doubleday, and London, Heinemann, 1927.

*

Critical Studies: *The Lady of the Limberlost: The Life and Letters of Gene Stratton Porter* by Jeanette Porter Meehan, New York, Doubleday, 1928, as *Life and Letters of Gene Stratton Porter,* London, Hutchinson, 1928; *Gene Stratton Porter* by Bernard F. Richards, Boston, Twayne, 1980.

* * *

Although Gene Stratton Porter's novels might now be called old-fashioned, they have several timeless qualities. Porter was a naturalist and a resident of the Limberlost area of northern Indiana; her motive was first of all to interest readers in the world of nature. Her books are filled with description of birds and moths particularly. The focal significance of the lives of some of her characters is the wilderness in which Elnora Comstock, the Bird Woman, and Freckles, in her best known books, *A Girl of the Limberlost* and *Freckles,* observe and collect, make notes and entice converts to nature study.

Characters like Elnora Comstock and Freckles seem perhaps to contemporary readers incredibly dedicated to the Golden Rule; they behave in an idealized manner, their anger shortlived and responding to reason, their selfishness recognized and yielding to love. Surprisingly, however, many of these characters are memorable, most significantly those who, like McLean the lumber boss in *Freckles,* live close to a natural environment. The city dwellers are more flat and therefore less believable, but Porter makes even them transcend their sinful natures for late conversions to goodness.

Two themes seem apparent in Porter's writing: first, a thematic reverence for nature and a Christian mystic's appreciation for a world that God has made perfect; and second, her optimism about human behavior and its perfectability. This latter theme is particularly evident in *A Girl of the Limberlost* wherein Elnora earns her way through high school by hunting rare moths. Her emergence in radiant maturity is echoed by her mother's change from sour to sweet.

Porter's nonfiction about birds and moths is accompanied by her own photographic illustrations, painstakingly filmed and meticulously accurate in color effects. In her fiction Porter's word pictures are equally carefully painted; her words clothe in natural detail the romantic stories of love that wins despite hardship and of vicious hatred that turns to incredible generosity. Sentimental as they seem to readers of today, and called both "saccharine" and "appealing" by her contemporaries, Porter's novels had great readership during the early years of the century.

—Rebecca J. Lukens

PORTER, Sheena

Nationality: British. **Born:** Melton Mowbray, Leicestershire, 19 September 1935. **Education:** King Edward VII Grammar School, Melton Mowbray, 1947-54; Loughborough College School of Librarianship, Leicestershire, 1955-56. **Family:** Married Patrick Lane in 1966; two daughters. **Career:** Library assistant, Leicester City Library, 1954-57; regional children's librarian, Nottinghamshire County Library, 1957-60; editorial assistant, Oxford University Press, London, 1960-61; regional children's librarian, Shropshire County Library, 1961-62. **Award:** Library Association Carnegie medal, 1965. **Address:** 7 St. Mary's Mews, Ludlow, Shropshire, England.

Publications for Children

Fiction

The Bronze Chrysanthemum, illustrated by Shirley Hughes. London, Oxford University Press, 1961; Princeton, New Jersey, Van Nostrand, 1965.

Hills and Hollows, illustrated by Victor Ambrus. London, Oxford University Press, 1962.

Jacob's Ladder, illustrated by Victor Ambrus. London, Oxford University Press, 1963.

Nordy Bank, illustrated by Annette Macarthur-Onslow. London, Oxford University Press, 1964; New York, Roy, 1967.

The Knockers, illustrated by Gareth Floyd. London, Oxford University Press, 1965.

Deerfold, illustrated by Victor Ambrus. London, Oxford University Press, 1966.

The Scapegoat, illustrated by Doreen Roberts. London, Oxford University Press, 1968.

The Valley of Carreg-Wen, illustrated by Doreen Roberts. London, Oxford University Press, 1971.

The Hospital, illustrated by Robin Jacques. London, Oxford University Press, 1973.

* * *

Sheena Porter's stories are those of an author with impressive skills and a deep sense of history. She received the Carnegie Medal for *Nordy Bank,* a haunting holiday adventure story set in Shropshire. In this book, Bron, the main character, is not gifted with heroine-like qualities, but is shy, quiet, and introverted. In the course of the story she becomes difficult, aggressive, and withdrawn under the influence of the historic atmosphere pervading Nordy Bank. This strong awareness of place and past is subtly blended with down-to-earth factual detail of the minutiae of camping: a combination which enables different types of reader to enjoy this book at various levels. Porter adds to a sound setting peopled with convincing characters the intense drama of an escaped Alsatian dog. Bron successfully captures the dog, and in winning his confidence regains her own. The reader shares Bron's anguish over the fate of Griff, a deaf army dog in need of retraining, but the climax of the book is reached with the choice which Bron has to make: a decision which involves conflicting loyalties and which is finally made for her by her parents.

Nordy Bank has qualities of other books by Porter: the authentic, identifiable background; the evolution of the leading character; relationships with parents and friends; convincing detail of family life and its various ramifications. *The Bronze Chrysanthemum* showed considerable potential, and this was fulfilled with *Jacob's Ladder* and *Nordy Bank.* Unlike many writers Porter has not been content to find a successful formula and slavishly repeat it. Her plots are remarkable for their wide range of location and of theme. By the late 1960s an increasing number of writers tended to deal with contemporary problems: a trend now in danger of being carried to extremes. Porter is perhaps marginally less successful in her novels on such themes, but she handles the serious problem of mental illness with acute sensitivity in *The Hospital,* environmental problems with awareness in *The Valley of Carreg-Wen,* and the timeless stepmother problem with understanding in *The Scapegoat.*

Porter, more than many contemporary writers for children, covers widely different themes. She wrote initially with the deliberate intention of providing a bridge between the easy adventure story and the more demanding material of writers like Lucy Boston and William Mayne, but she has developed as a distinguished writer for children in her own right. Children's literature is the richer for her contribution.

—Anne W. Ellis

POTTER, (Helen) Beatrix

Nationality: British. **Born:** London, 28 July 1866. **Education:** Privately. **Family:** Married William Heelis in 1913. **Career:** Settled in Sawrey, Lancashire as a farmer and sheep-breeder. Chairman, Herdwick Breeders' Association. Artist: Drawings Exhibition, Victoria and Albert Museum, London, 1972; National Book League, London, 1976; Abbott Hall Art Gallery, Kendal, Cumbria, 1983; Tate Gallery, London, 1987; Pierpont Morgan Library, New York, 1988. **Died:** 22 December 1943.

Publications for Children (illustrated by the author)

Fiction

The Tale of Peter Rabbit. Privately printed, 1900; revised edition, London and New York, Warne, 1902.
The Tailor of Gloucester. Privately printed, 1902; revised edition, London and New York, Warne, 1903; as *The Tailor of Gloucester from the Original Manuscript,* 1969.
The Tale of Squirrel Nutkin. London and New York, Warne, 1903.
The Tale of Benjamin Bunny. London and New York, Warne, 1904.
The Tale of Two Bad Mice. London and New York, Warne, 1904.
The Tale of Mrs. Tiggy-Winkle. London and New York, Warne, 1905.
The Pie and the Patty-Pan. London and New York, Warne, 1905.
The Tale of Mr. Jeremy Fisher. London and New York, Warne, 1906.
The Story of a Fierce Bad Rabbit. London and New York, Warne, 1906.
The Story of Miss Moppet. London and New York, Warne, 1906.
The Tale of Tom Kitten. London and New York, Warne, 1907.
The Tale of Jemima Puddle-Duck. London and New York, Warne, 1908.
The Roly-Poly Pudding. London and New York, Warne, 1908; as *The Tale of Samuel Whiskers; or, The Roly-Poly Pudding,* London, Warne, 1926.
The Tale of the Flopsy Bunnies. London and New York, Warne, 1909.
Ginger and Pickles. London and New York, Warne, 1909.
The Tale of Mrs. Tittlemouse. London and New York, Warne, 1910.
The Tale of Timmy Tiptoes. London and New York, Warne, 1911.
The Tale of Mr. Tod. London and New York, Warne, 1912.
The Tale of Pigling Bland. London and New York, Warne, 1913.
The Tale of Johnny Town-Mouse. London and New York, Warne, 1918.
The Fairy Caravan. London, privately printed, and Philadelphia, McKay, 1929.
The Tale of Little Pig Robinson. Philadelphia, McKay, and London, Warne, 1930.
Sister Anne, illustrated by Katharine Sturges. Philadelphia, McKay, 1932.
Wag-by-Wall. London, Warne, and Boston, Horn Book, 1944.
The Tale of the Faithful Dove, illustrated by Marie Angel. London, Warne, 1955; New York, Warne, 1956.
The Sly Old Cat. London and New York, Warne, 1971.
The Tale of Tuppenny, illustrated by Marie Angel. London and New York, Warne, 1973.

Poetry

Appley Dapply's Nursery Rhymes. London and New York, Warne, 1917.
Cecily Parsley's Nursery Rhymes. London and New York, Warne, 1922.
Beatrix Potter's Nursery Rhyme Book. London and New York, Warne, 1984.

Other

Peter Rabbit's Painting Book. London and New York, Warne, 1911.
Tom Kitten's Painting Book. London and New York, Warne, 1917.
Jemima Puddle-Duck's Painting Book. London and New York, Warne, 1925.
Peter Rabbit's Almanac for 1929. London and New York, Warne, 1928.
Yours Affectionately, Peter Rabbit: Miniature Letters by Beatrix Potter, edited by Anne Emerson. London and New York, Warne, 1983.

Publications for Adults

Other

The Art of Beatrix Potter: Direct Reproductions of Beatrix Potter's Preliminary Studies and Finished Drawings, Also Examples of Her Original Manuscript, edited by Leslie Linder and W.A. Herring. London and New York, Warne, 1955; revised edition, 1972.
The Journal of Beatrix Potter from 1881 to 1897, Transcribed from Her Code Writing by Leslie Linder. London and New York, Warne, 1966.
Letters to Children. Cambridge, Massachusetts, Harvard College Library Department of Printing and Graphic Arts, 1967.
Beatrix Potter's Birthday Book, edited by Enid Linder. London and New York, Warne, 1974.
Dear Ivy, Dear June: Letters from Beatrix Potter, edited by Margaret Crawford Maloney. Toronto, Other Press, 1977.
Beatrix Potter's Americans: Selected Letters, edited by Jane Crowel Morse. Boston, Horn Book, 1981; London, Warne, 1982.

*

Manuscript Collections: Leslie Linder Bequest (include watercolours and sketches), National Book League, London; Fre Library, Philadelphia.

Critical Studies: *The Tale of Beatrix Potter: A Biography,* London and New York, Warne, 1946, revised edition, 1968, 1985, and *The Magic Years of Beatrix Potter,* London and New York, Warne, 1978, both by Margaret Lane; *Beatrix Potter* by Marcus Crouch, London, Bodley Head, 1960, New York, Walck, 1961; *The History of "The Tale of Peter Rabbit,"* London and New York, Warne, 1976; *Cousin Beatie: A Memory of Beatrix Potter* by Ulla Hyde Parker, London, Warne, 1981; *Beatrix Potter in Scotland* by Deborah Rolland, London, Warne, 1981; *The Art of Beatrix Potter 1866-1943* (exhibition catalogue), Kendal, Cumbria, Abbot Hall Art Gallery, 1983; *Beatrix Potter: The Victoria and Albert Collection Catalogue* edited by Anne S. Hobbs and Joyce Irene Whalley, London, Victoria and Albert Museum, 1985, New York, Warne, 1986; *Beatrix Potter: Artist, Storyteller and Countrywoman,* London and New York, Warne, 1986, and *That Naughty Rabbit: Beatrix Potter and Peter Rabbit,* London and New York, Warne, 1987, both by Judy Taylor; *The Real World of Beatrix Potter* by Elizabeth M. Battrick, Norwich, Jarrold, 1986; *Beatrix Potter* by Ruth MacDonald, Boston, Twayne, 1986; *Beatrix Potter* by Elizabeth Buchan, London, Hamish Hamilton, 1987; *Beatrix Potter 1866-1943: The Artist and Her World* by Judy Taylor, Joyce Irene Whalley, Anne Hobbs, and Elizabeth M. Battrick, London, Warne, 1987, New York, Warne, 1988; *Beatrix Potter's Derwentwater* by Wynne Bartlett and Joyce Irene Whalley, London, Warne, 1988.

Illustrator: *A Happy Pair* by F.E. Weatherley, 1893(?); *Comical Customers,* 1894(?); *Wayside and Woodland Fungi* by W.P.K. Findlay, 1967.

* * *

Beatrix Potter's tales for children are remarkable in that few of them include any children—or indeed any humans at all. Other writers for children had of course used animals as the main protagonists of their stories, and indeed by the time that Potter started writing at the beginning of the 20th century, the tradition of the animal story was well-established. But most stories were quite obviously about humans in animal form, with human attitudes and behaviour—a genre that goes back to Aesop. What particularly distinguished Potter's work was that her animals were primarily animals, in a world where the human was intrusive and unnecessary. Her natural history drawings are the key to her later work, for from a child she had shown great interest in the natural world, and had recorded it as she saw it, from the hesitant flower sketches of her childhood to the competent microscopic drawings of her late teens. She studied her own pet rabbit meticulously, and likewise the other creatures that aroused her interest: spiders, flies, ducks, mice. She made many scientifically accurate drawings, including a remarkable series of fungi, which astonish those who only know her from her Peter Rabbit books. She also had a great feeling for place, and her interest in landscape was heightened by a further interest in photography, a pursuit which she shared with her father on many a countryside photographic expedition. All this made her a careful and precise recorder of the natural scene and the little creatures that inhabit it.

With such a background she could have developed into a good artist and illustrator, but would not necessarily have become a good writer. However, it is quite obvious that for Potter the word and the picture were complementary. We can see this from the fact that some of the famous stories originated in pictorial letters, sent earlier in her life to children of her acquaintance. For she saw even as she wrote, and the picture and the tale made a coherent whole. Only later in life, when the imaginative faculty was weakening did she attempt to write round her pictures, while the fragmentary scraps of original writing not allied to illustrations show how bereft of inspiration she became when the cohesion of the word and its visual counterpart were lacking. Her drawings were made originally for her own pleasure, but she wasted nothing. She borrowed back the picture letters she had originally sent to the Moore children and reworked them to make her books; she remembered the story she had been told about an old tailor in Gloucester; even the mice that sat down to spin did so on chairs she had seen in her grandmother's house. She could see, both in her mind's eye and with her pencil, so accurately that readers who know the stories well can go about the countryside she knew and loved and say "That is in *Peter Rabbit,*" or "That is the path in *Tom Kitten.*" In the same way, the staff of the Textile Department in the Victoria and Albert Museum, London, were able to recognize the 18th-century costumes which she drew there many years before for use in *The Tailor of Gloucester.*

Nevertheless, out of these remembered incidents and re-used sketches, Potter created a whole new world of characters who are as alive today as they were more than 80 years ago, when Peter Rabbit first appeared. For many of us, Jemima Puddleduck, Mrs. Tiggy-Winkle, and Jeremy Fisher have personalities that transcend time and place, and how much, we may wonder, have the Potter tales affected the attitude to mice and rabbits of several generations of children! For the adult, faced with repeated requests for re-reading a favourite tale, it is also important that the language in which Potter chose to write her children's books was both simple and direct, with no attempt to write down to the young listener—indeed her use of the word "soporific" in *The Flopsy Bunnies* is notorious. As a result, her stories are as easy to read aloud as to listen to.

Potter was always very concerned about the actual appearance of her books, the text as much as the illustrations. She herself occasionally altered the amount of text appearing on the printed page, moving a word or two overleaf if she felt it would produce the page appearance that she desired. The format of the Peter Rabbit books was quite distinctive at the time when they made their first appearance, and in spite of changes in the style of children's books during the century, they remain much the same as when they were first published. An attempt to issue *The Pie and the Patty Pan* and *The Roly-Poly Pudding* in a larger format was not a success and they too eventually conformed to the established pattern of a size which fits so comfortably into small hands. The length of the stories too is right for the young child, being fairly short, with simple uncrowded events which can be understood by the very youngest listener.

If is difficult to sum up the reason for the popularity which Potter has enjoyed for more than three-quarters of a century—a popularity which shows no sign of diminishing in any of the many countries where her works have been published. Moreover, as recent exhibitions of her works have shown, she appeals equally to all ages, if for varying reasons, and has become something of a cult on both sides of the Atlantic. Undoubtedly part of the attraction must lie in the aptness of her illustrations to the text, and the perfection of the art work itself. But in the end the stories must stand or fall by the writing, and there is no doubt that as a storyteller she was able to create a complete world in which the characters go about their normal daily life, and into which we are allowed merely a brief peep. They inhabit a twilight world between reality and imagination, in which the very young child can also share. But for those long past their childhood she offers a gallery of characters whose personalities are so fixed in our minds that Benjamin Bunny, Squirrel Nutkin, and the rest exist forever in the timeless countryside of her own beloved Lakeland.

—Joyce Irene Whalley

POWER, Rhoda (Dolores le Poer)

Nationality: British. **Born:** Altrincham, Cheshire, in 1890. **Education:** Oxford High School for Girls, 1903-09; Girton College, Cambridge, 1909-12. **Career:** Director of Children's Broadcasting, BBC Radio, London, 1920s and 1930s. **Died:** 9 March 1957.

PUBLICATIONS FOR CHILDREN

Fiction

Boys and Girls of History, with Eileen Power. London, Cambridge University Press, 1926; New York, Macmillan, 1927; revised edition, London, Dobson, 1968; New York, Roy, 1970.

More Boys and Girls of History, with Eileen Power. London, Cambridge University Press, and New York, Macmillan, 1928.

Ten Minute Tales and Dialogue Stories, illustrated by Gwen White. London, Evans, 1943.

Here and There Stories, illustrated by Phyllis Bray. London, Evans, 1945.

Redcap Runs Away, illustrated by C. Walter Hodges. London, Cape, 1952; Boston, Houghton Mifflin, 1953.

We Were There, illustrated by Charl. London, Allen and Unwin, 1955.

We Too Were There: More Stories from History, illustrated by Charl. London, Allen and Unwin, 1956.

From the Fury of the Norsemen and Other Stories, illustrated by Pauline Baynes. Boston, Houghton Mifflin, 1957.

Other

Union Jack Saints: Legends, with others. London, Constable, 1920.

Twenty Centuries of Travel: A Simple Survey of British History, with Eileen Power. London, Pitman, 1926.

Cities and Their Stories: An Introduction to the Study of European History, with Eileen Power. London, A. and C. Black, and Boston, Houghton Mifflin, 1927.

The Age of Discovery from Marco Polo to Henry Hudson. London and New York, Putnam, 1927.

How It Happened: Myths and Folktales, illustrated by Agnes Miller Parker. Cambridge, University Press, 1930; Boston, Houghton Mifflin, 1936.

Richard the Lionheart and the Third Crusade, edited by Eileen Power. London and New York, Putnam, 1931.

Stories from Everywhere, illustrated by Nina K. Brisley. London, Evans, and New York, Macmillan, 1931; as *The Big Book of Stories from Many Lands,* New York, Watts, 1970.

Great People of the Past (*Ancient Times, A.D. 600-1600, Modern Times*). London, Cambridge University Press, 3 vols., 1932; New York, Macmillan, 1 vol., 1933.

The Kingsway Histories for Juniors (*From Early Days to Norman Times, Norman Times and the Middle Ages, The Peasants' Revolt to James I, From James I to Modern Times*), illustrated by E. Hamilton Thompson. London, Evans, 4 vols., 1937-38.

PUBLICATIONS FOR ADULTS

Other

Under Cossack and Bolshevik. London, Methuen, 1919; as *Under the Bolshevik Reign of Terror,* New York, McBride, 1919.

* * *

In the 1930s intelligent school librarians and parents were always on the lookout for a new book by Rhoda Power. She could give young readers an interest in history which would last and take them on to serious study. Her *Boys and Girls of History,* written in collaboration with her sister, Eileen, the historian, were outstanding of their kind. They were halfway between fiction and solid history. She told her stories of these boys and girls through minor characters mostly, unless there happened to be a very well-documented child, like, for example, the young Mary Queen of Scots. On the whole they are the stories of apprentices, of children on the outskirts of some great event: the Bristol lad or the Burmese child attaching himself first to the extraordinary stranger Ralph Fitch, first Englishman to visit Burma, but deserting him for the greater honour of tending a white elephant.

By today's standards these are long stories with no talking down or easy vocabulary, but they are compulsive reading for anyone interested in the past and must have helped many a history teacher as well as her pupils. They range the world with endpaper maps showing the voyages; and they are packed with authentic detail described so vividly that they are never boring. In the voyage to the Bermudas in 1609 everyone is bailing the ships after a storm: "The richer ones looking strangely bedraggled for the colours in their silk doublets were running and the stuffing in their bombasted britches was so clogged with water that it smelt of wet hay." This I think gives a taste of her writing. When I collaborated with her in a BBC series she always knew exactly where I could get the right reference; she would never let me guess! Her *How It Happened* ranged the world of folklore (and has outstanding illustrations by Agnes Miller Parker), and here equally there is no talking down. She never sets herself above her child audience but expects them to be her equals. This was her strength.

—Naomi Mitchison

POWLING, Chris

Nationality: British. **Born:** London, 16 February 1943. **Education:** Bromley Grammar School, Kent; St. Catherine's College, Oxford, M.A. 1965; King's College, University of London, postgraduate certificate in education 1966; Royal Academy of Music, diploma in speech and drama 1968; Institute of Education, London, advanced diploma in education, 1970; University of Sussex, Brighton, M.A. 1984. **Family:** Married Janet Smith in 1966; two daughters. **Career:** Primary school teacher, 1966-75, and head teacher, 1975-85, London. Since 1985 Senior Lecturer in English, King Alfred's College, Winchester. Since 1976 occasional contributor and presenter, BBC Radio 4. Editor, *Books for Keeps* (bimonthly journal on children's books), 1989-96. **Address:** 9 Guildford Grove, Greenwich, London, SE10 8JY, England.

PUBLICATIONS FOR CHILDREN

Fiction

Daredevils or Scaredycats, illustrated by Frank Rodgers. London, Abelard, 1979.
Mog and the Rectifier, illustrated by Stephen Lavis. London, Abelard, 1980.
The Mustang Machine. London, Abelard, 1981.
Uncle Neptune. London, Abelard, 1982.
The Conker as Hard as a Diamond, illustrated by Jon Riley. London, Viking Kestrel, 1984.
Stuntkid, illustrated by Stephen Lavis. London, Blackie, 1985.
The Phantom Carwash, illustrated by Jean Baylis. London, Heinemann, 1986.
Fingers Crossed, illustrated by Jean Baylis. London, Blackie, 1987.
Flyaway Frankie, illustrated by Robert Bartelt. London, Blackie, 1987.
Bella's Dragon, illustrated by Robert Bartelt. London, Blackie, 1988.
Hiccup Harry, illustrated by Scoular Anderson. London, A. and C. Black, 1988.
Hoppity-Gap, illustrated by Maureen Bradley. London, Hamish Hamilton, 1988.
Ziggy and the Ice Ogre, illustrated by Peter Furmin. London, Heinemann, 1988.
Harry's Party, illustrated by Scoular Anderson. London, A. and C. Black 1989.
ELF 61. London, Hamish Hamilton, 1990.
Harry with Spots on, illustrated by Scoular Anderson. London, A. and C. Black, 1990.
A Spook at the Superstore, illustrated by Liz Summers. London, Heinemann, 1990.
Butterfingers. London, Blackie, 1991.
Dracula in Sunlight. London, Young Lions, 1992.
Wesley at the Water Park. London, Blackie, 1992.
Where the Quaggy Bends. New York, Harper Collins, 1992.
Harry Moves House, illustrated by Scoular Anderson. London, Young Lions, 1993.
It's That Dragon Again, illustrated by Alan Marks. London, Hamish Hamilton, 1993.
Razzle Dazzle Rainbow, illustrated by Alan Marks. London, Viking Kestrel, 1993.
Faces in the Dark: A Book of Scary Stories, illustrated by Peter Bailey. New York, Kingfisher, 1994.
Famous with Smokey Joe, illustrated by Alan Marks. London, Heinemann, 1995.
Kit's Castle, illustrated by Peter Bailey. New York, Kingfisher, 1996.
Harry the Superhero, illustrated by Scoular Anderson. London, A & C Black, 1996.
Harry on Holiday, illustrated by Scoular Anderson. London, A & C Black, 1997.
Gorgeous George. London, Orchard, 1998.

Other

Roald Dahl, illustrated by Stephen Gulbis. London, Hamish Hamilton, 1983; picture book version, Evans, 1997.
Jan Hoy: A Personnel Manager. London, Ginn, 1990.
Michael Rosen: A Poet. London, Ginn, 1990.
Quentin Blake: An Illustrator. London, Ginn, 1990.
Trish Cooke: A Television Presenter. London, Ginn, 1990.

*

Chris Powling comments:

There are two kinds of bad faith for a children's author. One is to write "down" to the child reader; the other is to write "up" for the adult critic. I try very hard to avoid both errors in my books—and to remember always that children's books belong to *children* not to the adult who writes them or mediates them.

For me what matters most in my work is plot, humour, and a narrating voice as close as the text allows to that of a storyteller improvising out loud about his/her characters. If I can also capture something of the freshness, enthusiasm, and ruthless honesty of children at their best, so much the better. Children see the world from the viewpoint of someone who hasn't lived very long ... and it's not a bad viewpoint. Certainly none of us becomes so wise we can afford to dispense with sheer astonishment at existence and what it entails. This is why writing for children seems to me to be just as serious as writing for adults—and a lot more fun.

* * *

"So long as a story is sparky I'll be hooked." Chris Powling's words about himself as a reader could equally stand as a comment on his own writing for children, which is always lively, energetic, and full of action. His young characters, usually 11 years-old and from varied racial backgrounds, are often known only by the nicknames children enjoy bestowing. They are city children at home in streets, old buildings, and derelict wasteland, usually in small gangs, often led by tough, independent girls, and very aware of the dangers of older bullies or officious adults. The plots of the stories involve dares, mischief, and occasionally the possibility of real danger. Many of the plot resolutions are securely happy, and although bullies of different ages come near to succeeding, the central characters learn from their experiences how to overcome threats and their own fears. The fast-paced stories, often narrated by children, are written in a lively, colloquial style with dialogue which Chris Powling takes pains to match to his young characters.

The short stories in *Daredevils or Scaredycats* were readers' first introduction to Powling's distinctive world. Enjoyable mischief appears alongside deeper feelings, and children share a sense of humour which some adult readers have found disturbingly cruel. This is illustrated by "Thingy," a story involving other children's reactions to a girl born with a stump for an arm. In *Mog and the Rectifier,* the first of Powling's strong female characters is at the centre of a plot to outwit the monstrously rich Howard and his father, and in doing so to imitate the Rectifier, a mysterious Robin Hood figure who tracks down the rich who cheat the Inland Revenue. Mog, the leader of the gang, is an intrepid, agile, and intelligent girl whose betrayal by the boy narrator suggests an interesting relationship which is never fully worked through. The tension between male and female gang leaders is returned to in *Stuntkid,* when Andy's leadership is challenged by Vicky, the Stuntkid. The basic idea for the novel, of a stunt double for children who will stand in for situations which seem frightening or impossible, is appealing, and the climax, when the children collaborate to complete the final reel of a film for Vicky's Errol Flynn-style father, is ingenious, if implausible.

At the heart of both *The Mustang Machine* and *Where the Quaggy Bends* is bullying, a theme which Powling recognises is of more immediate interest to children than to adult readers. One reviewer found it "disconcerting" to think that the author, the Principal of an English primary school, "has probably drawn from life the bullying abuses he describes with such relish". The plot of *Where the Quaggy Bends* has traditional ingredients of children defending a vulnerable old man who has a fortune carelessly stored in a drawer. More interesting is the picture of Skip and Ren's home life—with their highly successful, but absent, mother, and their father absorbed in his novel-writing. Although the 13 year-old Ren, with her lethal catapult, is perhaps difficult to believe, her relationship with the local gang of bullies suggests the mixture of fascination and repulsion their cruelty might inspire in such a girl.

Chris Powling's writing for younger readers gives the author the opportunity to explore his enjoyment of language—and of exciting, obviously implausible happenings—in ways which older readers might not accept. A magic conker in *The Conker as Hard as a Diamond,* for example, takes Alpesh through a series of increasingly grand adventures, culminating in the Conker Championship of the Universe. The story is told with gusto and enjoyable sound effects. A multi-coloured rope in *Razzle-Dazzle Rainbow* also invests the central character, Yen, with magic powers in a story full of inventive language and literary echoes.

Insight into Chris Powling's priorities as a writer can be found in his profile, written for children, of the author Roald Dahl. Here, Powling advises children to consider which of Dahl's books "has the most thrilling story, uses the most exciting language and is the most fun."

—Judith Atkinson

PRATCHETT, Terry

Nationality: British. **Born:** Beaconsfield, 24 April 1948. **Education:** Attended Wycombe Technical High School. **Family:** Married; one daughter. **Career:** Journalist in Buckinghamshire, Bristol, and Bath, 1965-80; press officer, Central Electricity Board Western Region, 1980-87; writer, since 1987. **Awards:** British Science Fiction award, 1989, for "Discworld" series, and 1990, for *Good Omens.* **Agent:** Colin Smythe Ltd., P.O. Box 6, Gerrards Cross, Buckinghamshire SL9 8XA, England.

Publications for Children

Science Fiction

Carpet People. Gerrards Cross, Buckinghamshire, Smythe, 1971; revised edition, London, Doubleday, 1992.

Truckers (Truckers/Bromeliad series). London, Doubleday, 1989; New York, Delacorte, 1990.

Diggers (Truckers/Bromeliad series). London, Doubleday, and New York, Delacorte, 1990.

Wings (Truckers/Bromeliad series). London, Doubleday, 1990; New York, Delacorte, 1991.

Terry Pratchett's Truckers (picture book based on the animated television series). London, Corgi, 1992.

Only You Can Save Mankind. London, Doubleday, 1992.

Johnny and the Dead. London, Doubleday, 1993.

Johnny and the Bomb. London, Doubleday, 1995.

The Johnny Maxwell Trilogy, (includes *Only You Can Save Mankind, Johnny and the Dead,* and *Johnny and the Bomb*). New York, Literary Guild, 1998.

Short Stories

Contributor, *Hidden Turnings: A Collection of Stories through Time and Space,* edited by Diana Wynne Jones. London, Methuen, 1989; New York, Greenwillow, 1990.

Publications for Adults

Science Fiction

The Dark Side of the Sun. Gerrards Cross, Buckinghamshire, Smythe, and New York, St. Martin's, 1976.

Strata. Gerrards Cross, Buckinghamshire, Smythe, and New York, St. Martin's Press, 1981.

The Colour of Magic (Discworld). Gerrards Cross, Buckinghamshire, Smythe, and New York, St. Martin's Press, 1983.

The Light Fantastic (Discworld). Gerrard's Cross, Buckinghamshire, Smythe, and New York, St. Martin's Press, 1986.

Equal Rites (Discworld). London, Gollancz, 1986; New York, New American Library, 1987.

Mort (Discworld). London, Gollancz, and New York, New American Library, 1987.

Sourcery (Discworld). London, Gollancz, 1988; New York, New American Library, 1989.

Wyrd Sisters (Discworld). London, Gollancz, and New York, Roc, 1988.

Pyramids (Discworld). London, Gollancz, and New York, Roc, 1989.

Guards! Guards! (Discworld). London, Gollancz, 1989; New York, Roc, 1991.

Eric (Discworld), illustrated by Josh Kirby. London, Gollancz, 1989; revised edition, with no illustrations, London, Gollancz, 1990. New York, Roc, 1995.

Good Omens: The Nice and Accurate Predictions of Agnes Nutter, Witch, with Neil Gaiman. London, Gollancz, and New York, Workman, 1990.

Moving Pictures (Discworld). London, Gollancz, 1990; New York, Roc, 1992.

Reaper Man (Discworld). London, Gollancz, 1991; New York, Roc, 1992.

Witches Abroad (Discworld). London, Gollancz, 1991; New York, Roc, 1993.

Small Gods (Discworld). London, Gollancz, 1992; New York, HarperCollins, 1994.

Lords and Ladies (Discworld). London, Gollancz, 1992; New York, HarperPrism, 1994.

Men at Arms (Discworld). London, Gollancz, 1993; New York, HarperPrism, 1993.
The Streets of Ankh-Morpork, with Stephen Briggs. London, Corgi, 1993.
Soul Music (Discworld). London, Gollancz, and New York, HarperCollins, 1994.
The Discworld Companion, with Stephen Briggs. London, Gollancz, 1994.
Interesting Times (Discworld). London, Gollancz, 1994; New York, HarperPrism, 1997.
Hogfather (Discworld). London, Gollancz, 1996.
Feet of Clay (Discworld). New York, HarperPrism, 1996.
Maskerade (Discworld). London, Gollancz, 1995; New York, HarperPrism, 1997.
Jingo (Discworld). New York, HarperPrism, 1998.

Other

The Unadulterated Cat, with illustrations by Gray Jolliffe. London, Gollancz, 1989.
The Discworld Map, with Stephen Briggs. London, Corgi, 1995.
Discworld's Unseen University Diary 1998, with Stephen Briggs, illustrated by Paul Kidby. London, Gollancz, 1997.

*

Media Adaptations: *Truckers* (television series by Cosgrove Hall) Thames Video, 1992, 1997; *Music from the Discworld* (music based on his series), composed and performed by Dave Greenslade, Virgin Records, 1994; "Discworld" and "Discworld II: Missing Presumed ..." (video games based on his series), Sony/Psygnosis, 1994, 1996; *Johnny and the Dead* (television series), London Weekend Television, 1995, Warner Vision International, 1995, adapted for the stage by Stephen Briggs, Oxford, Oxford University Press, 1996; *Wyrd Sisters* (adapted for the stage by Stephen Briggs), London, Corgi, 1996; *Mort* (adapted for the stage by Stephen Briggs), London, Corgi, 1996; *Guards! Guards!* (adapted for the stage by Stephen Briggs), London, Corgi, 1997; *Men at Arms* (adapted for the stage by Stephen Briggs), London, Corgi, 1997; *Wyrd Sisters* (television series by Cosgrove Hall Films), Channel 4, 1997 and on video; *Soul Music* (television series by Cosgrove Hall Films), Channel 4, 1997, and on video.

* * *

Terry Pratchett is a successful author in a genre few writers have tackled—comic fantasy—and is the co-creator, with Douglas Adams, of a kind of science fantasy where the anachronistic jokes refer back to contemporary Britain. First a cult author among science-fiction fans, he broke through to the general public in the late 1980s with his sixth book in the *Discworld* sequence, *Wyrd Sisters*, a parody of Shakespearean tragedy, among other things. Soon after, he published his first children's book with a mainstream publisher, *Truckers*. (However, his very first book, written when he was 17, was a children's fantasy, *The Carpet People*.)

The premise of *Truckers*, first in a trilogy, that tiny people live in hiding among us is a classic children's book theme, and Pratchett's "nomes" have much in common with Mary Norton's Borrowers. They know they must keep their existence secret from humans, but they have much less awareness of human achievements and civilisation. Like the Borrowers, they are non-magical; very much unlike them, they originally came from space, which makes the trilogy science-fiction, not fantasy.

Masklin, four inches high and the trilogy's hero, leads a small tribe of countryside nomes. After defeating a fox, he decides the tribe must move away; they climb on a lorry and arrive in the garage of a department store that, they discover, has been populated with nomes since its foundation in 1905. These nomes are happy living secretly among the departments: they have shelter, clothes, and free food. Tribes rule each department, and Masklin's special allies are Dorcas, a nome who understands electricity, and Gurder, the leader of the Stationeri, the all-male monkish caste who can read.

Humour is derived from aspects of the store nomes' life that are unknown to Masklin. They have written the Book of Nome, in the style of the Authorised Version of the Bible: "And Arnold Bros (est.1905) said, Let there be a Store, And Let it be a Store such as the World has not Seen hitherto." They believe that Arnold Bros (est.1905) is their personal god, and that the signs around the store, which they usually misinterpret, are his messages to them: Fire Sale, Prices Slashed, Bargains Galore. It takes Masklin's extra initiative, with the help of a black cube his tribe inherited, which has been silent for thousands of years but now suddenly speaks, in contact with the store's electricity, to find out that the store is closing down, and that the nomes' spaceship is "still up there somewhere."

The rest of the trilogy describes how the nomes learn to read, to drive a lorry by coordinated string-pulling, to manipulate a JCB during their stay in a quarry, and to travel to NASA in Florida, with the cube, in order to communicate with their spaceship. Throughout, Pratchett sprinkles sly digs at human society: "(Driving a lorry) can't be very difficult, otherwise humans wouldn't be able to do it"; and there is the serious message that reading is too important to be left to menfolk, and that society can't afford to neglect women's talents.

The *Truckers* trilogy became an instant best-seller, and Pratchett received so much fan mail requesting the reprinting of *The Carpet People* that he decided to revise it. Benefiting from new satirical observations about human nature, it is revealed as a delightful quest fantasy in the style of *The Hobbit*. The carpet people are very tiny indeed: their city is the size of a full stop and they live under the threat of Fray. They revere peculiar artefacts that fell out of the sky, like a penny and a matchstick. The saga concerns tribal conflict and a ruling Empire, rather like Britain and Gaul under the Romans, and also introduces the threat of mouls riding on snargs, rather like Tolkien's goblins on their wargs.

Pratchett has also written two supernatural novels about Johnny Maxwell, a young teenager growing up in today's Britain and bewildered by adult behaviour. His parents are quarrelling and might divorce, and he retreats to computer games. Trying out a new game, "Only you can save mankind," with a space-war theme, he finds the aliens sending him a message that they surrender and want to escape. Johnny takes on the burden of somehow enabling them to escape "game space" and go home. His ally is a girl computer addict who idolises Sigourney Weaver in the *Alien* films. The book is set during the 1991 Gulf War, which accentuates the anti-war message.

In the sequel, *Johnny and the Dead*, Johnny discovers that the local council has sold its public cemetery for a few pennies to a property developer. The tombstones will be pulled down and the remains reburied. Johnny finds that he can see and speak to the dead, who come out of their graves, first to protest, then to find out what has been going on in Britain since they died: advances in women's rights, a new shopping mall, even films about ghosts like *Ghostbusters. Johnny and the Dead* is a unique comic-horror novel. In the final novel in the Johnny Maxwell trilogy, *Johnny and the Bomb,* Johnny and his friends discover the local bag-lady, Mrs. Tachyon, is a time traveler and Johnny ends up adventuring in 1941—the time of the Blitz.

Much of Pratchett's adult fantasy appeals to young adults, especially the Discworld series. Its humor is irreverent and ironic with identifiable bits of ancient history repackaged in the realm of Discworld. In *Small Gods* the main character is an adolescent novice in the corrupt religious hierarchy with parellels to the era of the Inquisition and crusades of the medieval Eurpean church. Risking death for heresy, Brutha follows the voice of the turtle who falls into his life in the gardens of the Citadel. The turtle claims to be the great god Om trapped in the body of a lesser god because of the indifference and corruption of his followers. Brutha may be the next prophet and Om may be the next "big" god.

It is unlikely that Pratchett will desert adult fantasy for children's literature. He only writes for children when an original idea strikes and he can give of his best. As he says in "Let There Be Dragons," his speech to the Booksellers' Association, "Fantasy ... is the compost for a healthy mind ... a rich internal fantasy life is as good and necessary for a child as healthy soil is for a plant."

—Jessica Yates, updated by Lisa A. Wroble

PRELUTSKY, Jack

Nationality: American. **Born:** Brooklyn, New York, 8 September 1940. **Education:** High School of Music and Art, New York; Hunter College, New York. **Family:** Married. **Career:** Has worked as store assistant, cab driver, bus boy, photographer, furniture mover, potter, folksinger, and actor. **Awards:** A Children's Choice, International Reading Association/Children's Book Council award, 1978; *New York Times* Outstanding Book of the Year award, 1980; Child Study Association Children's Book of the Year award, 1983; Library of Congress Book of the Year, 1983; Parent's Choice Award, 1986; Garden State Children's Book Award, 1986; Association for Library Services Notable Book, 1990. **Address:** c/o Greenwillow Books, 1350 Avenue of the Americas, New York, New York 10019, U.S.A.

PUBLICATIONS FOR CHILDREN

Poetry

A Gopher in the Garden and Other Animal Poems, illustrated by Robert Leydenfrost. New York, Macmillan, 1967.

Lazy Blackbird and Other Verses, illustrated by Janosch. New York, Macmillan, 1969.

Three Saxon Nobles and Other Verses, illustrated by Eva Rubin. New York, Macmillan, 1969.

The Terrible Tiger, illustrated by Arnold Lobel. New York, Macmillan, 1969; London, Bodley Head, 1975.

Toucans Two and Other Poems, illustrated by Jose Aruego. New York, Macmillan, 1970; as *Zoo Doings,* London, Hamish Hamilton, 1971.

Circus, illustrated by Arnold Lobel. New York, Macmillan, 1974; London, Hamish Hamilton, 1975.

The Pack Rat's Day and Other Poems, illustrated by Margaret Bloy Graham. New York, Macmillan, 1974.

Nightmares: Poems to Trouble Your Sleep, illustrated by Arnold Lobel. New York, Greenwillow, 1976; London, A. and C. Black, 1978.

It's Halloween [*Christmas, Thanksgiving*], illustrated by Marylin Hafner. New York, Greenwillow, 3 vols., 1977-82; *It's Halloween* published Kingswood, Surrey, World's Work, 1978.

The Snopp on the Sidewalk and Other Poems, illustrated by Byron Barton. New York, Greenwillow, 1977.

The Mean Old Mean Hyena, illustrated by Arnold Lobel. New York, Greenwillow, 1978.

The Queen of Eene, illustrated by Victoria Chess. New York, Greenwillow, 1978.

The Headless Horseman Rides Tonight: More Poems to Trouble Your Sleep, illustrated by Arnold Lobel. New York, Greenwillow, 1980; London, A. and C. Black, 1984.

Rainy Rainy Saturday, illustrated by Marylin Hafner. New York, Greenwillow, 1980.

Rolling Harvey Down the Hill, illustrated by Victoria Chess. New York, Greenwillow, 1980.

The Sheriff of Rottenshot, illustrated by Victoria Chess. New York, Greenwillow, 1982.

Kermit's Garden of Verses, illustrated by Brucy McNally. New York, Random House, 1982.

The Baby Uggs Are Hatching, illustrated by James Stevenson. New York, Greenwillow, 1982.

Zoo Doings: Animal Poems (includes *A Gopher in the Garden, Toucans Two,* and *The Pack Rat's Day*), illustrated by Paul O. Zelinsky. New York, Greenwillow, 1983.

It's Valentine's Day, illustrated by Yossi Abolafia. New York, Greenwillow, 1983.

It's Snowing! It's Snowing!, illustrated by Jeanne Titherington. New York, Greenwillow, 1984.

What I Did Last Summer, illustrated by Yossi Abolafia. New York, Greenwillow, 1984.

The New Kid on the Block, illustrated by James Stevenson. New York, Greenwillow, 1984; London, Heinemann, 1986.

My Parents Think I'm Sleeping, illustrated by Yossi Abolafia. New York, Greenwillow, 1985.

Ride a Purple Pelican, illustrated by Garth Williams. New York, Greenwillow, 1986.

Tyrannosaurus Was a Beast, illustrated by Arnold Lobel. New York, Greenwillow and London, Julia MacRae, 1988.

Beneath a Blue Umbrella, illustrated by Garth Williams. New York, Greenwillow, 1990.

Something Big Has Been Here, illustrated by James Stevenson. New York, Greenwillow, 1990; London, Heinemann, 1991.

Twickham Tweer (from *The Sheriff of Rottenshot*), illustrated by Eldon Doty. DLM, 1991.

There'll Be A Slight Delay: And Other Poems for Grown-Ups, illustrated by Jack Ziegler. William Morrow & Co., 1991.

Sweet & Silly Muppet Poems, illustrated by Joe Ewers. New York, Western, 1992.

The Dragons Are Singing Tonight, pictures by Peter Sis. New York, Greenwillow, 1993.

Monday's Troll, illustrated by Peter Sis. New York, Greenwillow, 1996.

A Pizza the Size of the Sun, illustrated by James Stevenson. New York, Greenwillow, 1996.
With Dr. Seuss, *Hooray for Diffendoofer Day!,* illustrated by Lane Smith. New York, Knopf, 1998.

Other

Collector, *Poems of A. Nonny Mouse,* illustrated by Henrik Drescher. New York, Knopf, 1989; London, Orchard, 1992.

Compiler, *For Laughing Out Loud: Poems to Tickle Your Funnybone,* illustrated by Marjorie Priceman. New York, Knopf, 1991; London, Hutchinson, 1992.
Compiler, *For Laughing Out Louder: More Poems to Tickle Your Funnybone,* illustrated by Marjorie Priceman. New York, Knopf, 1995.
Compiler, *A. Nonny Mouse Writes Again!* illustrated by Marjorie Priceman. New York, Knopf, 1993.
Compiler, *Beauty of the Beast: Poems from the Animal Kingdom,* illustrated by Mielo So. New York, Knopf, 1997.
Compiler, *Dinosaur Dinner (with a Slice of Alligator Pie): Favorite Poems by Dennis Lee,* illustrated by Debbie Tilley. New York, Knopf, 1997.
Compiler, *Imagine That: Poems of Never-Was,* illustrated by Kevin Hawkes. New York, Random House, 1998.

Editor, *The Random House Book of Poetry for Children,* illustrated by Arnold Lobel. New York, Random House, 1983; as *The Walker Book of Poetry for Children,* London, Walker, 1984.
Editor, *Read-Aloud Rhymes for the Very Young,* illustrated by Marc Brown. New York, Knopf, 1986.

Translator, *The Mountain Bounder* by Heinrich Hoffman-Donner. New York, Macmillan, 1967.
Translator, *The Bad Bear,* by Rudolf Neumann, illustrated by Eva Rubin. New York, Macmillan, 1967.
Translator, *No End of Nonsense: Humorous Verses,* illustrated by Wilfried Blecher. New York, Macmillan, 1968; London, Abelard Schuman, 1970.
Translator, *The Wild Baby* [*Goes to Sea, Gets a Puppy*], by Barbro Lindgren, illustrated by Eva Eriksson. New York, Greenwillow, 3 vols., 1981-88.
Translator, *Brave Little Pete of Geranium Street,* by Rose and Samuel Lagercrantz, illustrated by Eva Eriksson. New York, Greenwillow, 1986.
Translator, *Jumping Jacks: Six Humorous Songs* by Stefania Maria De Kennessey. Bryn Mawr, Pennsylvania, Hildegard Pubilshing Company, 1994.

*

Media Adaptations: *Nightmares and Other Poems to Trouble Your Sleep* (record, audio cassette), Children's Books and Music, 1985; *It's Thanksgiving* (audio cassette), Listening Library, 1985; *The New Kid on the Block* (audio cassette), Listening Library, 1986; *It's Halloween* (audio cassette), Scholastic, 1987; *It's Christmas* (audio cassette), Scholastic, 1987; *Ride a Purple Pelican* (audio cassette), Listening Library, 1988; *Read-Aloud Rhymes for the Very Young* (audio cassette), Knopf, 1988; *It's Valentine's Day* (audio cassette), Scholastic, 1988; *Something Big Has Been Here* (audio cassette), Listening Library, 1991; *Rolling Harvey Down the Hill* (audio cassette), Listening Library, 1993; *The New Kid on the Block* (CD-ROM), Living Books and William Morrow, 1993; *The Dragons are Singing Tonight* (audio cassette), Listening Library, 1994; *Monday's Troll* (audio cassette), Listening Library, 1996.

Manuscript Collections: DeGrummond Collection, University of Southern Mississippi; Kerlan Collection, University of Minnesota.

Biography: *Meet Jack Prelutsky* (VHS Video), Rhache Publishers Ltd., 1994.

Critical Studies: *Poetry Fun by the Ton with Jack Prelutsky* by Cheryl Potts, Fort Atkinson, Wisconsin, Alleyside Press, 1995.

* * *

Frequent among the adjectives used by critics and reviewers to describe the work of Jack Prelutsky are "irreverent," "tongue-in-cheek," "delightfully fiendish," and just plain "gross." With their often grotty subject matter, Prelutsky's poems crash through the boundaries of classical light verse, which stresses wit, decorum, and elegance. It is the style, rather than content, of his verse which links him to the genre: his use of traditional form, a keen ear for lively anapestic rhythm, and a penchant for neologisms and rollicking alliteration. His craftsmanship, as well as his appreciation for the absurd and the disgusting, has made him one of the most popular poets for children of his generation.

Prelutsky's verse is often characterized by a fascination with the aberrations of human physiology and behavior, a taste for the macabre, and a delight in the baser side of human nature. This is felt in his almost obsessive concern with gluttony and obesity, a greed that goes beyond familiar foods and dwells on a never-ending variety of non-edibles. Gretcher's pot contains "A lizard's gizzard, lightly mashed,/and ogre's backbone, slightly smashed." The wozzit eats clothes, Herbert Glerbert eats 50 pounds of lemon sherbert and turns into "a thing that is a ghastly green,/a thing a world has never seen,/a puddle thing, a gooey pile/of something strange that does not smile." Pies made of nuts and bolts, of shoe polish and candied eyeballs, are typical staples. Pumberly Pott's niece devours his automobile piece by piece. Many of Prelutsky's characters eat each other—the fonster, floober, flummie and flakker, the frummick and freely. Others squash one another by sheer force of overweight.

Added to all this sheer nonsense is an element of what for some readers is tantalizing, for others fright-inducing, terror. For in Prelutsky's verse, the reader is often threatened directly—the grobbles, It, lurpp, and preternatural creatures, Prelutsky warns, may also eat *you.* In *Nightmares: Poems to Trouble Your Sleep* and *The Headless Horseman Rides Tonight,* a catalog of supernatural beings wallow in blood and death. The bogeyman will "crumple your bones in his bogey embrace," and the ghoul, having eaten other boys and girls, waits outside school "perhaps for you." Here are echoes of the German school, of *Struwwelpeter* with cautionary tales to frighten, things that exist physically to attack beyond the limits of the page, of a world inhabited by children in which no adults exist, either through word of illustration, for guidance or protection—a wonderfully thrilling idea for many young readers, a frightful one for others. *Rolling Harvey Down the Hill* is another instance of the darker side of human nature. Harvey is nasty, selfish, a cheat and braggart, a "tub of lard," a sadist who ties up his friends, and, although he is rolled down the hill for punishment, the reader has learned that boys who dress neatly and "dumb" girls are outside of Harvey's accepted circle.

Prelutsky's belief in verse as quick, accessible entertainment is felt in many of his later books, such as *Ride a Purple Pelican, What I Did Last Summer, It's Valentine's Day, It's Snowing! It's Snowing!,* and others. Prelutsky seems at his best in such books as *Tyrannosaurus Was a Beast, The Dragons Are Singing Tonight,* and *Monday's Troll,* for here the nature of the beast, as it were, dictates Prelutsky's own predilection of nastiness and odd eating habits. With their focus on wordplay, wit, and above all, gross humor, his ebullient collaborations with illustrator James Stevenson—*The New Kid on the Block, Something Big Has Been Here,* and *A Pizza the Size of the Sun*—led *Publishers Weekly* to dub the duo "poetry's bad boys."

Prelutsky has some lighter moments with word-play. In *The Sheriff of Rottenshot* there is a bicycling centipede who "merits medals, working all those centipedals" and an ocelot who likes to "toss a lot" and "fuss a lot." As a craftsman Prelutsky knows the power of the anapestic line and alliteration; he is also keenly aware of children of a certain age who delight in the grosser aspects of life.

A great many writers of light verse have sought to imitate Prelutsky both in subject and form. None have succeeded. He is certainly head and shoulders above them in originality and craftsmanship. As an anthologist, he has also shown his skill for recognizing the talents of other gifted writers. His early collections—*The Random House Book of Poetry for Children, Read-Aloud Rhymes for the Very Young, Poems of A. Nonny Mouse*—bypass the serious in favor of light verse that emphasizes wordplay and the pleasures of language. His later work—*For Laughing Out Loud* and *For Laughing Out Louder, The Beauty of the Beast,* and *Imagine That*—prove equally entertaining, packed with visceral, never stuffy, verse and vibrant illustrations by some of the most noted artists working in the field today.

There can be no question that Jack Prelutsky is an immensely popular writer and "has appeared in more libraries and schools than he can count," as a jacket blurb attests. While his "bad boy" reputation and penchant for the disgusting may give some readers pause, it is clear that for the majority, Prelutsky is the author to turn to for poetry with guaranteed child-appeal.

—Myra Cohn Livingston, updated by Jackie C. Horne.

PRICE, Evadne

Pseudonym: Helen Zenna Smith. **Nationality:** British. **Born:** At sea, in 1896. **Education:** West Maitland, New South Wales, and in Belgium. **Military Service:** Worked for the Air Ministry during World War I. **Family:** Married 1) C.A. Fletcher (died); 2) Kenneth A. Attiwill in 1929. **Career:** Actress from 1906. Columnist, *Sunday Chronicle* and *Sunday Graphic;* feature writer, *Daily Sketch;* war correspondent, the *People,* 1943-45; astrology columnist, *She* magazine, and *Vogue Australia,* Sydney. **Award:** Severigne prize (France), for adult novel. **Died:** 17 April 1985.

PUBLICATIONS FOR CHILDREN

Fiction

Just Jane. London, John Hamilton, 1928.
Meet Jane. London, Marriott, 1930.
Enter—Jane. London, Newnes, 1932.
Jane the Fourth. London, Hale, 1937.
Jane the Sleuth. London, Hale, 1939.
Jane the Unlucky, illustrated by Frank R. Grey. London, Hale, 1939.
Jane the Popular. London, Hale, 1939.
Jane the Patient. London, Hale, 1940.
Jane Gets Busy. London, Hale, 1940.
Jane at War. London, Hale, 1947.
Jane and Co. (omnibus), edited by Mary Cadogan. London, Macmillan, 1985.

PUBLICATIONS FOR ADULTS

Novels

Diary of a Red-Haired Girl. London, Long, 1932.
The Haunted Light. London, Long, 1933.
Strip Girl. London, Hurst and Blackett, 1934.
Probationer! London, Hurst and Blackett, 1934.
Society Girl. London, Harrap, 1935.
Red for Danger! London, Long, 1936.
Glamour Girl. London, Harrap, 1937.
The Dishonoured Wife. London, Jenkins, 1951.
Escape to Marriage. London, Jenkins, 1952.
My Pretty Sister. London, Jenkins, 1952.
Her Stolen Life. London, Milestone, 1954.
What the Heart Says. London, Hale, 1956.
The Love Trap. London, Hale, 1958.
Air Hostess in Love. London, Gresham, 1962.

Novels as Helen Zenna Smith

Not So Quiet...: Stepdaughters of War. London, Marriott, 1930; as *Stepdaughters of War,* New York, Dutton, 1930.
Women of the Aftermath. London, Long, 1931; as *One Woman's Freedom,* New York, Longman, 1932.
Shadow Women. London, Long, 1932.
Luxury Ladies. London, Long, 1933.
They Lived with Me. London, Long, 1934.

Plays

The Phantom Light, with Joan Roy-Byford (as *The Haunted Light,* produced London, 1928; as *The Phantom Light,* produced London, 1937). London, French, 1949.
Red for Danger (produced Richmond, Surrey, 1938).
Big Ben, with Ruby Miller (produced Malvern, Worcestershire, 1939).
Once a Crook, with Kenneth Attiwill (produced London, 1940). London, French, 1943.
Who Killed My Sister?, with Kenneth Attiwill (produced London, 1942).
Three Wives Called Roland, with Kenneth Attiwill (produced London, 1943).

Through the Door (also director: produced London, 1946).
What Lies Beyond (also director: produced Margate, Kent, 1948).
Cabin for Three, with Kenneth Attiwill (produced Southsea, Hampshire, 1949).
Blonde for Danger (produced London, 1949).
Wanted on Voyage, with Kenneth Attiwill (produced Wimbledon, 1949).

Screenplays: *Wolf's Clothing,* with Brock Williams, 1936; *When the Poppies Bloom Again,* with Herbert Ayres, 1937; *Merry Comes to Town,* with Brock Williams, 1937; *Silver Top,* with Gerald Elliott and Dorothy Greenhill, 1938; *Lightning Conductor,* with J. Jefferson Farjeon and Ivor McLaren, 1938; *Not Wanted on Voyage,* with others, 1957.

Other

She Stargazes (on astrology). London, Ebury Press, 1965.

*

Theatrical Activities:
Director: **Plays**—*Through the Door,* London, 1946; *What Lies Beyond,* Margate, Kent, 1948.

Actress: **Plays**—In *Peter Pan* by J.M. Barrie, Sydney, 1906; Nang Ping in *Mr. Wu* by H.M. Vernon and Harold Owen, tour 1914; toured in South Africa, and in *Oh, I Say* and *Within the Law,* 1915; Suzee in *Five Nights,* tour, 1919; Liliha in *The Bird of Paradise,* London, 1919, 1922; Sua-See in *The Dragon,* London, 1920; Tessie Kearns in *Merton of the Movies* by George S. Kaufman and Marc Connelly, London, 1923; Princess Angelica in *The Rose and the Ring,* London, 1923.

* * *

Evadne Price's series for children, the 10 Jane books (1928-47), was written as part of a long and varied career which ranged from actress to astrologer. I find it very curious that there is no extended analysis of Jane, and that she should have been called a literary curiosity like Fanny Hill! Jane is a mid-20th-century version of that motif in literature, "the little monster," the naughty child, which is at least as old as classical Greek mime. Her more immediate literary ancestor, however, may be sought for in the "pickles" and "scamps" of the nurseries of children's fiction of the 1880s onward, whose main characteristics are high-spiritedness and kind hearts, untainted by any element of malice, exemplifying that post-Dickensian vision of the child in literature as the embodiment of "original innocence" rather than original sin.

Price has categorically denied that the adventures of Jane were in any way modelled upon those of Richmal Crompton's William, of whom she said she had never heard until a critic had taken for granted that such was the case. This would serve as a warning against over-hasty ascriptions of influence. However, the comparison is almost an inevitable one, since the Jane books are contemporary with the William series, which continued to be written and to be in print many decades after the last Jane book had been published. The similarities are obvious. The high-spirited middle-class child, leader of a small group of cohorts, the background of English village or suburban life, the setting up of an opposition between the "natural," naughty child on the one hand, the whited sepulchre on the other, the stock adult characters in the background (stern fathers, angular spinsters, comic servants, the local aristocracy), and the short, episodic narrative pieces, whose nature allows for neither aging nor development, the child characters merely being repeatedly put through their paces, are common to both. The basic pattern is to display again and again the havoc wrought by the group of children in the midst of such adult activities as love-affairs, amateur theatricals, public meetings and fetes, sometimes during the trials of civilian life during the Second World War. Both authors attempted to write "full-length" novels about their characters as well as collections of short stories, but these are in the nature of occasional experiments only.

Too much, however, can be made of the Jane/William affinity. It is to be hoped that one day Price's individual qualities will be recognized in their own right, without external reference. She seems to me radically original in a number of ways. First, historically, Jane is among the first female leader of boys in children's literature, providing a positive, active female model for the readers. Second, Price's depiction of adults in books for children is "subversive": the manipulations and adsurdities of Jane's mother, the will-to-power of her grandparents, and the tone of sensible camaraderie between narrative voice and reader are rare in fiction for children even today. Third, despite occasional lapses into very 19th-century sentimentality in the stories, the strategy for survival advocated by Vilet the Cockney cook ("Lay low, Miss Jane love, and don't 'arp") is not a version of "suffer and be still," but commonsensical in a way both comforting and refreshing. Finally, Price's sophisticated parody of and literary reference to various narrative styles, modes, and conventions, and her use of cacorthography, in badly-spelt letter-narratives ostensibly by the child-protagonist herself, reveal the artistry with which these books are constructed. It is a great pity that copies of them are so rare.

—Sanjay Sircar

PRICE, Susan

Nationality: British. **Born:** Round's Green, Staffordshire, 8 July 1955. **Education:** Tividale Comprehensive School. **Career:** Shop assistant, Co-operative Society Grocery, Dudley, Worcestershire, 1972-74; guide, Open Air Black Country Museum, 1979; writer-in-residence, North Riding College of Education, Scarborough, 1980, and Worcester Central Library, 1986. **Awards:** Children's Rights Workshop Other award, 1975; Library Association Carnegie medal, 1988. **Agent:** Michael Thomas, A.M. Heath, 79 St. Martin's Lane, London WC2N 4AA. **Address:** c/o Faber and Faber Ltd., 3 Queen Square, London WC1N 3AU, England.

Publications for Children

Fiction

The Devil's Piper. London, Faber, 1973; New York, Greenwillow, 1976.
Twopence a Tub. London, Faber, 1975.
Sticks and Stones. London, Faber, 1976.
Home from Home. London, Faber, 1977.
Christopher Uptake. London, Faber, 1981.

In a Nutshell, illustrated by Alison Price. London, Faber, 1983.
From Where I Stand. London, Faber, 1984.
Ghosts at Large, illustrated by Alison Price. London, Faber, 1984.
Odin's Monster, illustrated by Patrick Lynch. London, A. and C. Black, 1986.
The Ghost Drum. London, Faber, and New York, Farrar Straus, 1987.
Ghostly Tales. Loughborough, Leicestershire, Ladybird, 1987.
Here Lies Price. London, Faber, 1987.
The Bone Dog. London, Scholastic, 1988.
Master Thomas Katt. London, A. and C. Black, 1988.
Phantom from the Past. London, Paperbird, 1989.
Crack-a-Story. London, Faber, 1989.
A Feasting of Trolls. London, A. and C. Black, 1990.
Thunderpumps. London, Heinemann, 1990.
Forbidden Doors. London, Faber, 1991.
Ghost Song. New York, Farrar Straus, 1992.
Heads and Tales. London, Faber, 1993.
Ghost Dance. New York, Farrar Straus, 1994; London, Faber, 1994.
Coming Down to Earth. London, HarperCollins, 1994.
Foiling the Dragons. London, Scholastic, 1994.
Elfgift. London, Scholastic, 1995.
Hauntings. London, Hodder Children's Books, 1995.

Other

The Carpenter and Other Stories (retellings). London, Faber, 1981.
Jack and the Beanstalk and Other Stories (retellings), illustrated by Colin and Moira Maclean. New York, Kingfisher, 1990.
Little Red Riding Hood and Other Stories (retellings), illustrated by Colin and Moira Maclean. New York, Kingfisher, 1990.
The Three Bears and Other Stories (retellings), illustrated by Colin and Moira Maclean. New York, Kingfisher, 1990.

Compiler, *Horror Stories,* illustrated by Harry Horse. London, Kingfisher 1995.

*

Susan Price comments:

The more I write, the less I feel I want to make any "personal statement." I write for money; it's my living. I try to do my job as well as I can. That's all.

* * *

Susan Price is an instinctive writer with the ability to get inside her characters and make their stories real and immediate whether they are in fantasy, historical, or contemporary settings.

The Devil's Piper was written when she was only 16 and showed the confidence and originality which have developed in subsequent books. It is an exciting story with lively dialogue and convincing characters which give solidity to the enchanted world into which an evil-tempered leprechaun leads the four children.

Her second novel was very different. In *Twopence a Tub* she turned from fantasy to the very real problems facing the miners who were involved in the disastrous pit strike in Dudley in 1851. Her considerable achievement in recreating this situation was recognized by the Children's Rights Workshop which named *Twopence a Tub* winner of the Other award. Price draws on family records and memories to help her recreate the squalid poverty of the miners' lives, their spirit, and their brutality, and contrasts this with the affluence of the pit owners. Lesser writers might have been trapped into manufacturing a happy ending, but Price does not shirk the bitterness and frustration when the miners are forced to return to work accepting a reduction in their wages.

A number of Price's early books deal with similar theme of the struggles of a teenage boy to shake off the constraints of his home background or environment. 16-year-old Graeme, in *Sticks and Stones,* struggles to direct his own life despite the well-meaning but unimaginative care of his parents. In *Home from Home* Paul forms a close relationship with an elderly lady who provides a warmth and interest in him which is lacking in his own charmless home. In a very different book, *Christopher Uptake,* the central character is also a young man who wants only to be left in peace to get on with his own life. Set in Elizabethan England, it presents a chilling picture of religious tolerance and persecution, loyalty and betrayal, but Christopher's dilemma could be applied to any contemporary conflict and will speak directly to the thoughtful teenager.

In her more recent books Price has largely turned from realism to stories of ghosts and other fantasy themes. The exception is *From Where I Stand* which deals with the very real problems of racism and bullying in an urban school. Maybe because the theme is so important, this book is a little less successful as a novel but it is a deeply felt statement on an issue of real concern in the lives of many young people.

Like all the best writers of fantasy, Price plots her novels and short stories with great logic and confident story-telling. Frequently she has a strong vein of humour, as in *In a Nutshell* where she contrives to write a moral parable which is funny. Two tiny beings (in the Thumbelina and Tom Thumb tradition) come into the world and, after a great struggle to be reunited, become "humans" and healers. Ghosts feature in *Ghosts at Large* and *Here Lies Price,* both of which contain stories of very varied moods: moving and macabre, frightening and funny. Much of her success lies in her down-to-earth style and her skill in describing the details and creating the atmosphere which make the supernatural nature of her stories so believable, whether she is writing of a scary headless boggart or of Fearless Mary who sets herself up for life in her dealings with ghosts.

Perhaps Price's major achievement has been her Carnegie Medal-winning novel *The Ghost Drum,* which tells an exotic tale of the stunting imprisonment of a young Czarevich and the training of a witch's apprentice. Her confident, economic style is fitted to the folktale basis of the story and she manages to adapt her style to each changing mood of the story. Her descriptions, though spare, bring each scene vividly to life ("the cold is so fierce the frost can be heard crackling and snapping as it travels through the air"). Each word works hard for its place in the narrative but, although it is so well-crafted, the story—like much of her recent work—lacks the passion evident in her early writing.

—Valerie Brinkley-Willsher

PRICE, Willard

Nationality: American (originally Canadian: moved to the United States, 1901). **Born:** Peterborough, Ontario, Canada, 28 July 1887. **Education:** Western Reserve University, Cleveland, B.A. 1909;

New York School of Philanthropy, 1911-12; Columbia University, New York, M.A. 1914. **Family:** Married 1) Eugenia Reeve in 1914 (died 1929), one son; 2) Mary Selden in 1932. **Career:** Member of the editorial staff, the *Survey,* New York, 1912-13; editorial secretary, Methodist Episcopal Church Board of Foreign Missions, 1915-19; editor, *World Outlook,* New York, 1915-20. Traveled on many expeditions for the National Geographic Society and the American Museum of Natural History, 1920-67. **Award:** Litt.D.: Columbia University, 1930. **Died:** 14 October 1983.

PUBLICATIONS FOR CHILDREN

Fiction

Amazon Adventure, illustrated by Georg Hartmann. New York, Day, 1949; London, Cape, 1951.
South Sea Adventure. New York, Day, and London, Cape, 1952.
Underwater Adventure. New York, Day, 1954; London, Cape, 1955.
Volcano Adventure. New York, Day, and London, Cape, 1956.
Whale Adventure. New York, Day, and London, Cape, 1960.
African Adventure. New York, Day, and London, Cape, 1963.
Elephant Adventure. New York, Day, and London, Cape, 1964.
Safari Adventure. New York, Day, and London, Cape, 1966.
Lion Adventure. New York, Day, and London, Cape, 1967.
Gorilla Adventure. New York, Day, and London, Cape, 1969.
Diving Adventure. New York, Day, and London, Cape, 1970.
Cannibal Adventure, illustrated by Pat Marriott. London, Cape, 1972; New York, Day, 1973.
Tiger Adventure, illustrated by Pat Marriott. London, Cape, 1979.
Arctic Adventure, illustrated by Pat Marriott. London, Cape, 1980.

Other

My Own Life of Adventure: Travels in 148 Lands. London, Cape, 1982.

PUBLICATIONS FOR ADULTS

Novel

Barbarian. New York, Day, 1941; London, Heinemann, 1942.

Other

Ancient Peoples at New Tasks. New York, Missionary Education Movement, 1918.
The Negro Around the World. New York, Doran, 1925.
The South Sea Adventure: Through Japan's Equatorial Empire. Tokyo, Hokuseido Press, 1936; as *Pacific Adventure,* New York, Reynal, 1936; as *Rip Tide in the South Seas,* London, Heinemann, 1936.
Japan's New Horizons. Tokyo, Hokuseido Press, 1938; as *Children of the Rising Sun,* New York, Reynal, 1938; as *Where Are You Going Japan?,* London, Heinemann, 1938; as *Japan Reaches Out,* Sydney, Angus and Robertson, 1938.
Japan Rides the Tiger. New York, Day, 1942.
Japan's Islands of Mystery. New York, Day, and London, Heinemann, 1944.
Japan and the Son of Heaven. New York, Duell, 1945; as *The Son of Heaven: The Problem of the Mikado,* London, Heinemann, 1945.
Key to Japan. New York, Day, and London, Heinemann, 1946.
Roving South: Rio Grande to Patagonia. New York, Day, 1948; as *Tropic Adventure,* London, Heinemann, 1949.
I Cannot Rest from Travel: An Autobiography of Adventure in Seventy Lands. New York, Day, and London, Heinemann, 1951.
The Amazing Amazon. New York, Day, and London, Heinemann, 1952.
Journey by Junk: Japan after MacArthur. New York, Day, 1953; London, Heinemann, 1954.
Adventures in Paradise: Tahiti and Beyond. New York, Day, 1955; London, Heinemann, 1956.
Roaming Britain: 8000 Miles Through England, Scotland, and Wales. New York, Day, 1958; as *Innocents in Britain,* London, Heinemann, 1958.
Incredible Africa. London, Heinemann, 1961; New York, Day, 1962.
The Amazing Mississippi. London, Heinemann, 1962; New York, Day, 1963.
Rivers I Have Known. New York, Day, 1965.
America's Paradise Lost. New York, Day, 1966.
Odd Way round the World. New York, Day, 1969.
The Japanese Miracle and Peril. New York, Day, and London, Heinemann, 1971.

Editor, *The Voice and the Book.* New York, American Bible Society, 1926.

*

Manuscript Collection: Syracuse University Library, New York.

Willard Price commented:

(1983) My aim in writing the "Adventure" series for young people was to lead them to read by making reading exciting and full of adventure. At the same time I want to inspire an interest in wild animals and their behavior. Judging from the letters I receive from boys and girls around the world, I believe I have helped open to them the worlds of books and natural history.

* * *

Willard Price's highly improbable adventures of Hal and Roger Hunt have all the ingredients of Superman except the boys wear safari suits and save animals rather than humans.

In the first of the adventures, *Amazon Adventure,* the framework is set for all the following books. John Hunt had "studied and collected animals for twenty years, supplying zoos, circuses and museums," and was planning a trip to South America accompanied by his sons, Hal and Roger. "No man could want better pals on a jungle journey. Hal, finished with school and about to go to college was as tall and strong as his father. Roger did not run to length, but he was alert and wiry, and brave enough." Hal and Roger, at 19 and 15, never seem to age and so remain conveniently popular with the widest age range of readers possible. Equally, there is never any real development in the two characters, Hal steady and almost a man, Roger endowed with great courage but not much common sense. The plot is always simple, a search for whatever kind of animal is required, but well endowed with feats of endurance and dramatic episodes, and the pages quite crammed with factual detail on the animals which the boys appear ever to have at their encyclopaedic finger tips. They also possess a remarkable facility for picking up scientific and technical detail relevant to the current project, and are therefore able to take on board ballooning, underwater diving or diamond mining without any hesitation or pause for training. Most of all they do have an extraordinary amount of luck. In *Gorilla Adventure* they survive between them a charge by an infuriated gorilla, fire in their cabin and a fight with their local guide, an attack by a mamba and then a spitting cobra, a 20-foot fall followed by a fight with a black leopard—all the while managing to collect 22 animals for their father, to find enough diamonds to maintain an ailing bush hospital, and to capture a python and a gorilla together with one rope.

The exploits may be fiction, but the facts and settings could only have come from real life; Price's tales are based on his own tumultuous and action-packed life. The detail in these adventure books is all accurate and undoubtedly has an enormous appeal to his wide following. Nothing gets in the way of the narration, of the boys' exploits and the constant stream of information—no time is wasted on philosophizing or theorizing, all is action and very successful.

—Fiona Waters

PRINCE, Alison

Nationality: British. **Born:** Beckenham, Kent, 26 March 1931. **Education:** Beckenham Grammar School, Kent, 1940-48; Slade School of Fine Art, London, diploma in fine art 1948-51; Goldsmiths' College, University of London, art teachers' certificate 1953-54. **Family:** Married Goronwy Siriol Parry in 1957 (separated); one daughter and two sons. **Career:** Head of art department, Elliott Comprehensive School, London, 1954-58. **Award:** Fellow in creative writing, Jordanhill College of Education, Glasgow, 1988. **Address:** Burnfoot House, Whiting Bay, Isle of Arran KA27 8QL, Scotland.

Publications for Children

Fiction

The House on the Common, illustrated by the author. London, Methuen, 1969; New York, Farrar Straus, 1970.
The Red Alfa, illustrated by the author. London, Methuen, 1971; as *The Red Jaguar,* New York, Atheneum, 1972.
Ben's Fish, with Chris Connor, illustrated by Connor. London, Benn, 1972.
The Doubting Kind. London, Methuen, 1975; New York, Morrow, 1977.
The Night I Sold My Boots. London, Heinemann, 1979.
The Turkey's Nest. London, Methuen, 1979; New York, Morrow, 1980; as *Willow Farm.* New York, Ace, 1980.
Haunted Children (stories), illustrated by Michael Bragg. London, Methuen, 1982.
Mill Green on Fire. London, Armada, 1982.
Mill Green on Stage. London, Armada, 1982.
The Sinister Airfield, illustrated by Edward Mortelmans. London, Methuen, 1982; New York, Morrow, 1983.
Goodbye Summer. London, Methuen, 1983.
Night Landings, illustrated by Edward Mortelmans. London, Methuen, 1983; New York, Morrow, 1984.
A Spy at Mill Green. London, Armada, 1983.
The Ghost Within (stories). London, Methuen, 1984.
Hands Off Mill Green! London, Armada, 1984.
The Others. London, Methuen, 1984.
Scramble!, illustrated by Anne Knight. London, Methuen, 1984.
Rock On, Mill Green. London, Armada, 1985.
A Job for Merv, illustrated by David Higham. London, Deutsch, 1986.
Nick's October. London, Methuen, 1986.
The Type One Super Robot, illustrated by the author. London, Deutsch, 1986; New York, Four Winds Press, 1988.
How's Business, illustrated by the author. London, Deutsch, 1987; New York, Four Winds Press, 1988.
The Blue Moon Day, illustrated by the author. London, Deutsch, 1988.
A Haunting Refrain (stories). London, Methuen, 1988.
A Dog Called You. London, Pan Macmillan, 1993.
Merv on the Road. London, Young Piper, 1993.
Kenneth Grahame: An Innocent in the Wild Wood. London, Allison and Busby, 1994.
On Arran. Glendaruel, Argyll, 1994.
The Witching Tree. London, Busby, 1996.
Magic Dad, illustrated by Magda Van Tilburg. London, Piccadilly, 1997.

Plays

Ellie Bagg's Account (radio play), 1984.
Joe (television series), 1968-71.
War Stories (television play), 1970.
Trumpton (television play), 1970.
Watch with Mother (television series scripts).

Other (illustrated by the author)

Whosaurus? Dinosaurus!, with Jane Hickson. London, Studio Vista, 1975.
Who Wants Pets? London, Methuen, 1988.
The Necessary Goat and Other Essays on Formative Thinking. Glasgow, Taranis, 1992.
Having Been in the City. Edinburgh, Taranis Books, 1994.

Publications for Adults

Other

The Good Pets Guide. London, Armada, 1981.

*

Illustrator: *Don't Panic!,* 1975, *Keeping Time,* 1976, and *Get Well Soon,* 1978, all by Audrey Coppard; *Hello to Ponies,* 1979, and *Hello to Riding,* 1980, both by Jane Allen and Mary Danby.

Alison Prince comments:

Childhood seems to me to hold the key to the whole of a person's life, being the time when awareness is most acute, and most free from the pressures of convention which overlay it in later years. For this reason, children are the most vital section of the community to write for, and I would like to think my books supply interest for them throughout their growing years, right into their adult life. In the future, I very much want to write for the adult market, to provide a further continuity, for we are all at heart no more than grown-up children, and we never lose our dreams.

* * *

Alison Prince's career began by collaborating with a friend in writing and illustrating the story of a small boy living in a transport cafe in the early 1960s and which was produced as a BBC television series for the under-five age group. A writer of great versatility, her work covers poetry, novels for both children and adults, biography and journalism. Prince also illustrates her own books, in addition to contributing illustrations for other author's works.

A genre in which Prince has had considerable success is that of the short story—in particular, forays into the supernatural and fantasy world. *The Ghost Within* contains some macabre characters who seem to have been crafted with a malevolent delight. One example is *The Fire Escape* which contains Victorian melodrama linked to the modern-day taste for horror. A *Haunting Refrain* also has a supernatural theme, only these stories are devoid of horror and have a more gentle flavour. Music links the present to the past and recalls events which intrude upon the present. The reader is left to ponder the consequences as in *Josef's Carol,* a poignant story of a boy and his imaginary friend whose lives, both real and imaginary, are linked to a sad, white-haired old man, locked in his silent world.

Prince's teenage novels are perhaps the most accurately observed—language, sexuality, and unconventional lifestyles are accurately and perceptively described. The dialogue is honest, fresh, and often humorous, and controversial subjects such as pregnancy are handled in a sympathetic and straightforward manner. *Goodbye Summer,* and the sequel, *Nick's October* charts the unpredictable, stormy, yet loving relationship between Nick and Sasha, whose families do little to encourage the liaison. The book highlights the uncertainty and insecurity of young people and explore their fears with friends and parents. They also portray the pressures of parental manipulation—all refreshingly realistic.

Prince's most interesting book, however, is *How's Business*—an unusual novel in that it was written with the active participation of twenty-one 7- to 11-year-olds in a Lincolnshire primary school. The children suggested the story line, developed the characters, and involved the whole community in their project. Set in war-time England, the plot is conventional enough, a London evacuee is sent to live in the Fens and who is determined to return to London at the earliest opportunity. But the story totally absorbs the reader as the character of young How Grainger comes to life along with the other children and adults in the Fenland village. The war-time atmosphere is successfully created by its young authors who were born many years after that time. Their imaginations have no doubt been fuelled by other books and films about this period. Nevertheless, they have captured the pleasures and hardships in a surprisingly accurate way. To weld together so many young and inexperienced writers and produce such an excellent product is a great accomplishment on its originator's part.

Prince now lives on the island of Arran, off the west coast of Scotland where she takes an active role in island life playing in the local brass band and contributing a regular column for the *Arran Banner,* the local newspaper. The articles are wonderfully idiosyncratic, ranging widely over such diverse subjects as sewage disposal, the provision of vandal-proof toilets and a regular campaign against the detritus left by tourists in wild places. She has recently published an acclaimed biography of Kenneth Grahame, creator of *The Wind in the Willows* and is currently working on an adult novel, a collection of poetry, and another children's book *The Sherwood Hero.*

—Valerie Bierman

PRINGLE, Laurence P(atrick)

Has also written as Sean Edmund. **Nationality:** American. **Born:** Rochester, New York, 26 November 1935. **Education:** One-room schoolhouse in rural Mendon, New York, 1940-45; Honeoye Falls, New York, public schools, 1945-1953; Cornell University 1954-58, B.S. 1958; University of Massachusetts, M.S. 1961; attended Syracuse University, 1960-62. **Family:** Married 1) Judith Malanowicz in 1962 (divorced 1970); one daughter and two sons; married Alison Newhouse in 1971 (divorced 1974); married Susan Klein in 1983; one son and one daughter. **Career:** Science teacher, Lima Central School, Lima, New York, 1961-62; writer and editor, American Museum of Natural History children's magazine *Nature and Science,* New York City, 1963-70; faculty member, New School for Social Research, New York City, 1976-78; writer-in-residence, Kean College of New Jersey, Union, 1985-86; faculty member, *Highlights for Children* Writers Workshop, 1987-98; free-lance writer and photographer, since 1970. **Awards:** Numerous Notable Book citations, American Library Association; Special Conservation Award, National Wildlife Federation, 1978; Eva L. Gordon Award, American Nature Society, 1983; Orbis Pictus honor award, 1996, for *Dolphin Man,* and 1998, for *An Extraordinary Life: The Story of a Monarch Butterfly,* 1998. **Address:** P.O. Box 252, West Nyack, New York 10994, U.S.A.

Publications for Children

Nonfiction

Dinosaurs and Their World. New York, Harcourt, 1968.
The Only Earth We Have. New York, Macmillan, 1969.
From Field to Forest: How Plants and Animals Change the Land, photographs by the author. New York, World Publishers, 1970.
In a Beaver Valley: How Beavers Change the Land, photographs by the author. New York, World Publishers, 1970.
One Earth, Many People: The Challenge of Human Population Growth. New York, Macmillan, 1971.
Ecology: Science of Survival. New York and London, Macmillan, 1971.
Cockroaches: Here, There, and Everywhere, illustrated by James McCrea and Ruth McCrea. New York, Crowell, 1971.
This Is a River: Exploring an Ecosystem. New York, Macmillan, 1972.

From Pond to Prairie: The Changing World of a Pond and Its Life, illustrated by Karl W. Stuecklen. New York, Macmillan, 1972.

Pests and People: The Search for Sensible Pest Control. New York, Macmillan, 1972.

Estuaries: Where Rivers Meet the Sea. New York, Macmillan, 1973.

Into the Woods: Exploring the Forest Ecosystem. New York, Macmillan, 1973.

Follow a Fisher, illustrated by Tony Chen. New York, Crowell, 1973.

Twist, Wiggle, and Squirm: A Book about Earthworms, illustrated by Peter Parnall. New York, Crowell, 1973.

Recycling Resources. New York, Macmillan, 1974.

Energy: Power for People. New York, Macmillan, 1975.

City and Suburb: Exploring an Ecosystem. New York, Macmillan, 1975.

Chains, Webs, and Pyramids: The Flow of Energy in Nature, illustrated by Jan Adkins. New York, Crowell, 1975.

Water Plants, illustrated by Kazue Mizumura. New York, Crowell, 1975.

The Minnow Family: Chubs, Dace, Minnows, and Shiners, illustrated by Dot Barlowe and Sy Barlowe. New York, Morrow, 1976.

Listen to the Crows, illustrated by Ted Lewin. New York, Crowell, 1976.

Our Hungry Earth: The World Food Crisis. New York, Macmillan, 1976.

Death Is Natural. New York, Four Winds, 1977.

The Hidden World: Life under a Rock, illustrated by Erick Ingraham. New York, Macmillan, 1977.

The Controversial Coyote: Predation, Politics, and Ecology. New York, Harcourt, 1977.

The Gentle Desert: Exploring an Ecosystem. New York, Macmillan, 1977.

Animals and Their Niches: How Species Share Resources, illustrated by Leslie Morrill. New York, Morrow, 1977.

The Economic Growth Debate: Are There Limits to Growth? New York and London, Franklin Watts, 1978.

Dinosaurs and People: Fossils, Facts, and Fantasies. New York, Harcourt, 1978.

Wild Foods: A Beginner's Guide to Identifying, Harvesting, and Cooking Safe and Tasty Plants from the Outdoors, photographs by the author and illustrations by Paul Breeden. New York, Four Winds, 1978.

Nuclear Power: From Physics to Politics. New York, Macmillan, 1979.

Natural Fire: Its Ecology in Forests. New York, Morrow, 1979.

Lives at Stake: The Science and Politics of Environmental Health. New York, Macmillan, 1980.

What Shall We Do with the Land? Choices for America. New York, Crowell, 1981.

Frost Hollows and Other Microclimates. New York, Morrow, 1981.

Vampire Bats. New York, Morrow, 1981.

Water: The Next Great Resource Battle. New York and London, Macmillan, 1982.

Radiation: Waves and Particles, Benefits and Risks. Hillside, New Jersey, Enslow, 1983.

Wolfman: Exploring the World of Wolves. New York, Scribner, 1983.

Feral: Tame Animals Gone Wild. New York, Macmillan, 1983.

"The Earth Is Flat," and Other Great Mistakes, illustrated by Steve Miller. New York, Morrow, 1983.

Being a Plant, illustrated by Robin Brickman. New York, Crowell, 1983.

Animals at Play. San Diego, Harcourt, 1985.

Nuclear War: From Hiroshima to Nuclear Winter. Hillside, New Jersey, Enslow, 1985.

Here Come the Killer Bees. New York, Morrow, 1986, revised edition published as *Killer Bees,* 1990.

Throwing Things Away: From Middens to Resource Recovery. New York, Crowell, 1986.

Home: How Animals Find Comfort and Safety. New York, Scribner, 1987.

Restoring Our Earth. Hillside, New Jersey, Enslow, 1987.

Rain of Troubles: The Science and Politics of Acid Rain. New York, Macmillan, 1988.

The Animal Rights Controversy. New York, Harcourt, 1989.

Bearman: Exploring the World of Black Bears, photographs by Lynn Rogers. New York, Scribner, 1989.

Nuclear Energy: Troubled Past, Uncertain Future. New York, Macmillan, 1989.

Living in a Risky World. New York, Morrow, 1989.

The Golden Book of Insects and Spiders, illustrated by James Spence. New York, Western Publishing, 1990.

Global Warming: Assessing the Greenhouse Threat. New York, Arcade, 1990.

Saving Our Wildlife. Hillside, New Jersey, Enslow, 1990.

Batman: Exploring the World of Bats, photographs by Merlin D. Tuttle. New York, Scribner, 1991.

Living Treasure: Saving Earth's Threatened Biodiversity, illustrated by Irene Brady. New York, Morrow, 1991.

Antarctica: The Last Unspoiled Continent. New York, Simon and Schuster, 1992.

The Golden Book of Volcanoes, Earthquakes, and Powerful Storms, illustrated by Tom LaPadula. New York, Western Publishing, 1992.

Jackal Woman: Exploring the World of Jackals, photographs by Patricia Des Roses Moehlman. New York, Scribner, 1993.

Chemical and Biological Warfare: The Cruelest Weapons. Hillside, New Jersey, Enslow, 1993.

Oil Spills: Damage, Recovery, and Prevention. New York, Morrow, 1993.

Scorpion Man: Exploring the World of Scorpions. New York, Scribner, 1994.

Coral Reefs: Earth's Undersea Treasures. New York, Simon and Schuster, 1995.

Dinosaurs!: Strange and Wonderful, illustrated by Carol Heyer. Honesdale, Pennsylvania, Boyds Mills Press, 1995.

Dolphin Man: Exploring the World of Dolphins, photographs by Randall S. Wells. New York, Atheneum, 1995.

Fire in the Forest: A Cycle of Growth and Renewal, illustrated by Bob Marstall. New York, Atheneum, 1995.

Vanishing Ozone: Protecting Earth from Ultraviolet Radiation. New York, Morrow, 1995.

Smoking: A Risky Business. New York, Morrow, 1996.

Taking Care of the Earth: Kids in Action. Honesdale, Pennsylvania, Boyds Mills Press, 1996.

Animal Monsters: The Truth about Scary Creatures. New York, Marshall Cavendish, 1997.

Drinking: A Risky Business. New York, Morrow, 1997.

An Extraordinary Life: The Story of a Monarch Butterfly, illustrated by Bob Marstall. New York, Orchard, 1997.

Elephant Woman: Cynthia Moss Explores the World of Elephants, photographs by Cynthia Moss. New York, Atheneum, 1997.

Everybody Has a Belly Button: Your Life Before You Were Born, illustrated by Clare Wood. Honesdale, Pennsylvania, Boyds Mills Press, 1997.
Nature!: Wild and Wonderful, photographs by Tim Holmstrom. Katonah, New York, Richard C. Owen, 1997.
One Room School, illustrated by Barbara Garrison. Honesdale, Pennsylvania, Boyds Mills Press, 1998.

Fiction

Jesse Builds a Road, illustrated by Leslie Morrill. New York, Macmillan, 1989; as *Simon Builds a Road,* London, Blackie, 1990.
Octopus Hug, illustrated by Kate Salley Palmer. Honesdale, Pennsylvania, Boyds Mills Press, 1993.
Naming the Cat, illustrated by Katherine Potter. New York, Walker, 1997.

Compiler

Discovering the Outdoors: A Nature and Science Guide to Investigating Life in Fields, Forest, and Ponds. Garden City, New York, Natural History Press, 1969.
Discovering Nature Indoors: A Nature and Science Guide to Investigations with Small Animals. Garden City, New York, Natural History Press, 1970.
Highlights Ecology Handbook. Columbus, Ohio, Highlights for Children, 1973.
Introduccion a la ecologia; ciencia de la vida. Buenos Aires, Ediciones Marymar, 1976.

PUBLICATIONS FOR ADULTS

Wild River (nonfiction, photographs by the author). Philadelphia, Lippincott, 1972.
With editors of Time-Life Books, *Rivers and Lakes* (nonfiction). New York, Time-Life Books, 1985.

Contributor to books and periodicals, including *Audubon, Highlights for Children, Open Road, Ranger Rick's Nature Magazine,* and *Smithsonian,* sometimes under the pseudonym Sean Edmund.

*

Critical Studies: *Children's Literature Review,* Detroit, Gale, Vol. 4, 1984, Vol. 68, 1991; *Something About the Author Autobiography Series,* Gale, Vol. 6, 1988; "A Voice for Nature" by Laurence Pringle, in *The Voice of the Narrator in Children's Literature,* edited by Charlotte Otten and Garry Schmidt, New York, Greenwood, 1989, 277-82; *Nature!: Wild and Wonderful* by Laurence Pringle, Katonah, New York, Richard C. Owen, 1997.

Laurence Pringle comments:

As is often the case, E. B. White, author of *Charlotte's Web,* said it best. When asked why he wrote for children, he responded: "All that I ever hope to say in books is that I love the world."

That sounds right to me. *Charlotte's Web* and White's other books for children were fiction, but he carefully researched his subjects. He observed spiders and read about them. He wrote about animals with respect; Charlotte did not apologize for her eating habits.

Somehow, as a lonely boy growing up in rural western New York, I also developed a respect for nature, a burning curiosity about it, and perhaps even the ambition to urge others to share these feelings. There is no space here to explore the "somehow." All writers have values and feelings that shape their work, and some of mine originate in the Hopper Hills of Mendon and Ionia, south of Rochester.

With my strong curiosity, I enjoy research more than writing. I also like to challenge popular but incorrect notions about the natural world, and have done so in books about forest fires, dinosaurs, bats, wolves, jackals, and killer bees. When I tackle natural resource issues, I feel it vital to write about the economic and political factors as well as the science and technology. And, since I am a hopeful person, I offer hope. I feel strongly that writers of both fiction and nonfiction must offer hope to young readers.

I am fascinated by how things are interconnected, and that fascination is expressed in countless ways, for example, in connecting the ancient middens that anthropologists study to today's landfills (in *Throwing Things Away*), and in connecting the loss of wild pigs in a Brazilian forest with the loss of the frogs that reproduced in the pigs' wallows (in *Living Treasure*). I suppose one of the most extraordinary interconnections I've written about is a simple, everyday one. In *Death is Natural,* I traced the path of some carbon atoms from a dead rabbit through the process of decay, through the soil, into a raspberry bush, through the process of becoming part of sugar molecules in raspberries that a boy ate. This prompts people to think about their food: Where in earth history have these atoms been?

In order to feel a kinship with the living and nonliving world around us, we must have some knowledge about it. Kids are hungry to know. What is that animal's name and why does it behave that way? What are these critters and why are they living under this rock? Some of my books encourage readers to investigate their backyard and nearby environment. Sometimes, in visits to schools, I tell about the fascinating world of microclimates, including the little climates on our own bodies—"the desert of the forearm, the cool woods of the scalp, the tropical forest of the armpit."

In one school a girl asked if I'd ever written any books that were fun. I was taken aback; most nonfiction offers few laughs. Kids do love funny books, but does having fun always mean jokes and giggles? Sometimes it is fun to have your curiosity tickled. Sometimes it is fun to suddenly grasp an important idea that may influence you all the rest of your life. Sometimes it is fun to meet a historical character or a contemporary scientist and learn something about their lives, including their childhoods. Sometimes it is fun to be lured into making your own observations, about soap bubbles or tadpoles. And sometimes it is fun to learn about a bat or a butterfly that does this amazing thing—like the female monarch that flies from Massachusetts to Mexico in *An Extraordinary Life.*

It is fun to learn about the beauty, the intricacy, and the connectedness of life, and that's what I write about.

* * *

Laurence Pringle is best-known for his outstanding books on nature, biology, and often-controversial environmental topics. His books cover a wide range of topics, making it difficult to collect all of them from library shelves to obtain an overview of his work. Yet, perseverance is rewarded, for they are as skillful, artful, and imaginative as any works of fiction.

Pringle began his writing career as an editor for *Nature and Science,* a magazine for children published by the American Museum of Natural History. In an autobiographical sketch in the *Fourth Book of Junior Authors and Illustrators* he wrote, "At *Nature and Science* we took great care that both text and illustrations were clear and accurate, and I apply the same standards to my books." This attention to accuracy and detail is evident throughout Pringle's work. Nearly every book contains an acknowledgement of assistance from an expert who has read the book for accuracy. Nearly every one contains an index, a glossary, and a bibliography of sources or suggestions for further reading. All are clearly written and appropriately illustrated. Pringle is also a photographer, and many of his own photographs illustrate his books.

Pringle also brings his experience as a high school science teacher to his books. "My approach to writing a book is like that of a teacher planning to present a subject to students—not 'how many facts, dates, and definitions can I jam into their heads,' but 'what are the key ideas and how can I spark some enthusiasm about them,'" he wrote in the *Something about the Author Autobiography Series.*

However, despite his experience as a teacher, science editor, and writer of short articles, Pringle's first book, *Dinosaurs and Their World* (1968) faced two years of rejection before it was published. It carries many of the hallmarks of Pringle's writing, his emphasis on science as a process of discovery, his belief that knowledge is something that is constantly evolving, his debunking of common misconceptions, and his emphasis on people and the human connection. The book jacket advertises that "clues have been put together to give us a picture of life on our earth millions of years ago." Pringle begins by involving the reader in the mysteries of the duckbill dinosaurs and describing early theories that attempted to explain the fossils. He then engages the reader with the story of how John Ostrom gathered evidence from all over the world and through careful observation proved these earlier theories wrong. Pringle concludes by asking a question even greater than those he has answered: "The duckbills and their crests are still big riddles, but dinosaurs have left the world an even greater mystery. That is the question: Why did the dinosaurs die out?" In this way he engages the reader in the continuing process of discovery and stimulates further exploration.

Many of Pringle's books emphasize the relatedness of all life and the complex interactions of communities. In *Water Plants* (1975), the reader follows a frog to the shore of a pond and then into the water, and along the way sees detailed pictures of the plants and learns fascinating details about them and the animals and insects that live in or near the water. The frog is swallowed by a pickerel, whose journey the reader then follows among fanworts and coontails and plants that grow at the bottom of the pond. Finally, in shallow water among some arrowheads, the pickerel is swallowed by a great blue heron. "Gulp—the pickerel was gone. Hunting was good among the water plants." No sentimentality or anthropomorphism here, but a strong sense of the complex web of life surrounding a pond. The soft, yet detailed drawings by Kizue Mizumura are a perfect complement to the text.

Pringle has not hesitated to write about difficult and controversial subjects. *Death Is Natural* (1977), a Children's Notable Book and Outstanding Science Trade Book for Children, sensitively and imaginatively treats a difficult topic that "has special meanings for us.... the only animal that is able to think ahead to the end of life." The final chapter of this short book discusses extinction, or the death of species, and concludes with the sobering and unwelcome thought that "the extinction of a whole species is as natural as the death of an individual animal or plant," and that "humans can become extinct, too." Yet, "There is beauty, variety, and change, and death helps make it all possible."

In books for older children and young adults, Pringle has explored such controversial topics as population growth, nuclear power, acid rain, animal rights, global warming, chemical and biological warfare, oil spills, the vanishing ozone layer, smoking, and drinking. He does not hesitate to make forthright statements or criticize existing policies. In *Oil Spills,* for example, he writes: "The U.S. government has no official energy policy, but unofficially it encourages extravagant use of gasoline and other petroleum products. Thanks in part to the politically powerful oil industry and automobile manufacturers, the United States is the world's most car- and oil-dependent nation."

In *Smoking: A Risky Business,* he presents the arguments of the tobacco industry as well as the results of research on nicotine addiction, but he makes clear that the weight of the evidence is against the claims of the tobacco industry: "A pack of twenty cigarettes provides about two hundred little jolts or 'hits' of nicotine." Pringle does not hesitate to describe the tobacco industry's efforts to recruit new smokers among young people: "With older customers dying and others managing to quit, young people represent the tobacco industry's main hope of maintaining sales in the United States. Teenagers are the primary source of new smokers." In his essay in the *Something about the Author Autobiography Series,* Pringle says, "My books about controversial issues are not balanced—in a sense of equal space and weight applied to all sides—but are balanced by presenting arguments from the opposing interests, and a reading list that includes a diversity of views for those who want to explore the subject further." In some of his books, however, such as *The Animal Rights Controversy* (1989), Pringle's presentation of multiple points of view is so even-handed and open-ended that one almost wishes he would take sides.

In the 1990s, Pringle began to move in some new directions. More of his books began to be published with spectacular full-color illustrations, including additional titles in the popular series that began with *Wolfman* (1983). These books combine stunning photographs taken by the subjects, with personal information and biographical background on the scientists, as well as discussions of their research and the problems that fascinate them. In addition, perhaps inspired by fathering a second family of young children in mid life, Pringle wrote *Everybody Has a Belly Button: Your Life Before You Were Born* (1997) for young children, began publishing fiction picture books, and wrote an autobiography for young children. With two books illustrated by Bob Marstall, *Fire in the Forest* (1995), and *An Extraordinary Life: The Story of a Monarch Butterfly* (1997), Pringle's work received, perhaps for the first time, the kind of lavish full-color illustrations and innovative book design that his excellent texts have long-deserved. Both of these books touch on the underlying themes found throughout Pringle's work: natural patterns of life, death, and change; the interrelatedness of all things; the importance of questioning and clear thinking; the debunking of myths and misconceptions; the process of discovery; and perhaps most of all, a sense of love and respect for the natural world.

—Linnea Hendrickson

PULLEIN-THOMPSON, Christine

Pseudonym: Christine Keir. **Nationality:** British. **Born:** Wimbledon, Surrey, 1 October 1930; daughter of the writer Joanna Cannan, *q.v.;* twin sister of Diana Pullein-Thompson, *q.v.*, and sister of Josephine Pullein-Thompson, *q.v.*, and the writer Denis Cannan. **Education:** Wychwood School, Oxford. **Family:** Married Julian Popescu in 1954; two sons and two daughters. **Career:** Director, Grove Riding Schools, Oxfordshire, 1945-55. **Agent:** Jennifer Luithlen Agency, 88 Holmfield Road, Leicester LE2 1SB, England. **Address:** The Old Parsonage, Mellis, Eye, Suffolk IP23 8EE, England.

Publications for Children

Fiction

It Began with Picotee, with Diana and Josephine Pullein-Thompson, illustrated by Rosemary Robinson. London, A. and C. Black, 1946.
We Rode to the Sea, illustrated by Mil Brown. London, Collins, 1948.
We Hunted Hounds, illustrated by Marcia Lane Foster. London, Collins, 1949.
I Carried the Horn, illustrated by Charlotte Hough. London, Collins, 1951.
Goodbye to Hounds, illustrated by Charlotte Hough. London, Collins, 1952.
Riders from Afar, illustrated by Charlotte Hough. London, Collins, 1954.
Phantom Horse, illustrated by Sheila Rose. London, Collins, 1955.
A Day to Go Hunting, illustrated by Sheila Rose. London, Collins, 1956.
The First Rosette, illustrated by Sheila Rose. London, Burke, 1956.
Stolen Ponies, illustrated by Sheila Rose. London, Collins, 1957.
The Impossible Horse (as Christine Keir), illustrated by Maurice Tulloch. London, Evans, 1957.
The Second Mount, illustrated by Sheila Rose. London, Burke, 1957.
Three to Ride, illustrated by Sheila Rose. London, Burke, 1958.
The Lost Pony, illustrated by Sheila Rose. London, Burke, 1959.
Ride by Night, illustrated by Sheila Rose. London, Collins, 1960.
The Horse Sale, illustrated by Sheila Rose. London, Collins, 1960.
Giles and the Elephant [*Greyhound, Canal*], illustrated by Dorothy Clark. 3 Vols., London, Burke, 1960.
For Want of a Saddle, illustrated by Anne Bullen. London, Burke, 1960.
Giles and the Greyhound, illustrated by Dorothy Clark. London, Burke, 1961.
The Empty Field, illustrated by Anne Bullen. London, Burke, 1961.
Giles and the Canal, illustrated by Dorothy Clark. London, Burke, 1961.
The Open Gate, illustrated by Barbara Crocker. London, Burke, 1962.
Bandits in the Hills, illustrated by Janet Duchesne. London, Hamish Hamilton, 1962.
The Gipsy Children, illustrated by Janet Duchesne. London, Hamish Hamilton, 1962.
The Doping Affair, illustrated by Enid Ash. London, Burke, 1963; as *The Pony Dopers,* London, Atlantic, 1968.
Homeless Katie, illustrated by Prudence Seward. London, Hamish Hamilton, 1964.
No-One at Home, illustrated by C.R. Evans. London, Hamish Hamilton, 1964.
The Eastmans in Brittany, illustrated by Dorothy Clark. London, Burke, 1964.
Granny Comes to Stay, illustrated by Christine Marsh. London, Hamish Hamilton, 1964.
The Eastmans Move House, illustrated by Susan Broadley. London, Burke, 1965.
The Boys from the Café, illustrated by Mary Russon. London, Hamish Hamilton, 1965.
The Eastmans Find a Boy, illustrated by Joan Calvert. London, Burke, 1966.
The Stolen Car, illustrated by Elizabeth Grant. London, Hamish Hamilton, 1966.
The Lost Cow, illustrated by Lynette Hemmant. London, Hamish Hamilton, 1966.
A Day to Remember, illustrated by Lynette Hemmant. London, Hamish Hamilton, 1966.
Little Black Pony, illustrated by Lynette Hemmant. London, Hamish Hamilton, 1967.
Robbers in the Night, illustrated by Andrew Sier. London, Hamish Hamilton, 1967.
Room to Let, illustrated by Lynette Hemmant. London, Hamish Hamilton, 1968.
Dog in a Pram, illustrated by Prudence Seward. London, Hamish Hamilton, 1969.
Nigel Eats His Words, illustrated by Dorothy Clark. London, Burke, 1969.
Phantom Horse Comes Home. London, Armada, 1970.
Riders on the March. London, Armada, 1970.
They Rode to Victory. London, Armada, 1970.
Phantom Horse Goes to Ireland. London, Armada, 1972.
I Rode a Winner. London, Armada, 1973; New York, Scholastic, 1978.
Black Beauty's Clan, with Diana and Josephine Pullein-Thompson. Leicester, Brockhampton Press, 1975.
Mystery at Black Pony Inn, illustrated by Gareth Floyd. London, Pan, 1976.
Strange Riders at Black Pony Inn, illustrated by Gareth Floyd. London, Pan, 1976.
Pony Patrol. St. Albans, Dragon, 1977.
Pony Patrol SOS. St. Albans, Dragon, 1977.
Pony Patrol Fights Back. London, Dragon, 1977.
Prince at Black Pony Inn, illustrated by Gareth Floyd. London, Pan, 1978.
Secrets at Black Pony Inn, illustrated by Gareth Floyd. London, Pan, 1978.
Black Beauty's Family, with Diana and Josephine Pullein-Thompson, illustrated by Elisabeth Grant. London, Hodder and Stoughton, 1978; New York, McGraw Hill, 1980.
Phantom Horse in Danger. London, Armada, 1980.
Phantom Horse Goes to Scotland. London, Armada, 1981.
Pony Patrol and the Mystery Horse. London, Severn, 1981; New York, Simon & Schuster, 1992.
Father Unknown. London, Dobson, 1982.
Black Beauty's Family 2, with Diana and Josephine Pullein-Thompson. London, Hamlyn Beaver, 1982.

Ponies in the Park, illustrated by Tony Morris. London, Beaver, 1982.
Ponies in the Forest. London, Beaver, 1983.
Ponies in the Blizzard. London, Beaver, 1984.
Wait for Me, Phantom Horse. London, Severn House, 1985.
A Home for Jessie, illustrated by Sheila Ratcliffe. Aylesbury, Buckinghamshire, Goodchild, 1986.
Stay at Home Ben, illustrated by Kate Rodgers. London, Hamish Hamilton, 1987.
Please Save Jessie, illustrated by Sheila Ratcliffe. Aylesbury, Buckinghamshire, Goodchild, 1987.
The Big Storm, illustrated by Lesley Smith. London, Hodder and Stoughton, 1988.
Careless Ben, illustrated by Kate Rogers. London, Hamish Hamilton, 1988.
The Road Through the Hills, illustrated by Gavin Rowe. London, Hodder and Stoughton, 1988.
A Home for Jessie. London, Scholastic; U.S., Willowslip, 1988.
Candy Goes to the Gymkhana. Loughborough, Leics, Ladybird, 1989.
Candy Stops a Train. N.p., Paperbird, 1989.
Smoke in the Hills. London, Hodder and Stoughton, 1989.
Across the Frontier. London, Andersen Press, 1990.
Catastrophe at Black Pony Inn. Southampton, Swift, 1990.
Runaway Ben. London, Hamish Hamilton, 1990.
Good Deeds at Black Pony Inn. Southampton, Swift, 1991.
Come Home Jessie. London, Scholastic; U.S., Willowslip, 1991.
The Long Search. London, Andersen Press, 1991; New York, Bradbury, 1993.
I Want That Pony. Hemel Hempsted, Simon and Schuster, 1993.
The Best Pony for Me. Hemel Hempsted, Simon and Schuster, 1995.
Horsehaven. Upavon, Cavalier, 1996.
A Pony in Distress. Warminster, Cavalier, 1997.
The Pony Test. Hemel Hempsted, Simon and Schuster, 1997.
The Pony Picnic. Hemel Hempsted, Simon and Schuster, 1998.

Other

The Follyfoot Pony Quiz Book, illustrated by David McKee. London, Pan, 1974.
A Pony to Love, illustrated by Claude Kailer and others. London, Pan, 1975.
Good Riding, illustrated by Christine Bousfield. London, Armada, 1975.
Riding for Fun, illustrated by Christine Bousfield. London, Armada, 1976.
Improve Your Riding, illustrated by Christine Bousfield. London, Armada, 1979.
Riding (as Christine Keir), illustrated by Glenn Steward. London, Granada, 1983.
Bedtime Pony Stories, illustrated by Mark Smallman. Upavon, Cavalier, 1997.

Editor, *A Pony Scrap Book.* London, Pan, 1972.
Editor, *A Second Pony Scrap Book.* London, Pan, 1973.
Editor, *Christine Pullein-Thompson's Book of Pony Stories,* illustrated by Gareth Floyd. London, Pan, 1975.
Editor, *The Second Book of Pony Stories,* illustrated by Ron Stenberg. London, Pan, 1977.
Editor, *Pony Parade.* London, Dragon, 1978.
Editor, *Horse and Pony Stories,* illustrated by Victor Ambrus. London, Kingfisher, 1992.
Editor, *Thundering Hooves,* illustrated by Victor Ambrus. London, Kingfisher, and New York, Kingfisher, 1996; reissued (London) as *More Horse and Pony Stories,* 1998.
Editor, *More Bedtime Pony Stories,* illustrated by Mark Smallman. Upavon, Cavalier, 1997.

*

Christine Pullein-Thompson comments:

I have written books since I was in my teens—all are for children varying from ages five to 16. Most concern ponies but more than 40 are for younger children without a pony to be seen. They are easy to read and, I hope, exciting.

I love animals so I usually write about them. At the moment I am writing for younger children because I am a little out of touch with teenagers. I love travelling and have been to most of Europe, Thailand, Japan, and Malaysia. I have also worked in the United States and have visited Canada several times.

My husband is half Romanian so I know the Balkans quite well. But I think I love Scotland most of all, which is where my mother's family came from.

* * *

Christine Pullein-Thompson has been writing children's pony stories for more than 40 years, and her books demonstrate a consistency and professionalism not always found in children's books. Although none of her work qualifies as major children's literature, her books deserve to be recognized for what they are, lightweight entertainment and escapism for children of 9-12 years—particularly those who are obsessed with horses.

Pullein-Thompson excels in plot construction, even if sometimes the story becomes rather farfetched. In her adventure stories, she can delay the climax with considerable skill—not a common gift. *Phantom Horse* is a good example of this, and *Ride by Night* produces unexpected and dramatic complications with Romanian dissidents on the west coast of Scotland when they are least expected. Even in her more mundane pony books, she places her young heroes and heroines in unusual (though plausible) situations.

It is easy to criticize the writing of so prolific an author. She tends to fall back on several standard phrases to get a quick effect: "I was so happy I felt like singing" is one, and whenever hunting is involved "a glorious burst of music" crops up. But if the style is rather slapdash, it is also readable, and the dialogue is generally realistic. The dated colloquialisms of her earlier books has given way to more modern language, beginning in the 1980s. Some of her more recent books, *Pony Patrol* and *Ponies in the Park,* for instance, show Pullein-Thompson to be up-to-date with contemporary comments, terminology, and situations.

In addition to her trademark mid-grades fiction, Pullein-Thompson has also written for younger children. Her short books for the Antelope and Reindeer series demonstrate thoughtful, more careful writing and considerable powers of observation and understanding of human situations. She has also produced a number of informative non-fiction books about horses. *Good Riding* and *Riding for Fun,* for instance, are excellent, well planned, and imaginative, offering useful information—like how to run a gymkhana—not easily found in other pony books. Her edited collections of horse and pony stories have sold steadily and well.

In recent years, Pullein-Thompson has developed some new themes. In *The Long Search,* for instance, twelve-year-old Ion Radu seeks his parents, political prisoners in an Eastern European country (clearly modeled on Romania). The appalling conditions of wartime life, and the excitement of the 1989 revolution, make this a worthwhile experiment in spite of its sometimes wooden prose. Even in more horse-oriented tales, new concerns appear: *Horsehaven* deals with an animal sanctuary and *A Pony in Distress* hints at more serious problems than those that befell horses in the author's earliest books.

Christine Pullein-Thompson clearly writes for children, without much attention to reviewers, and she has been rewarded by steady sales and continuity in print which few authors can match. Perhaps adults should not dismiss these books as easily as they do, giving a child an all-too-often guilty feeling for enjoying what has been written simply to be enjoyed.

—Linda Yeatman, updated by Caroline C. Hunt

PULLEIN-THOMPSON, Diana

Has also written as Diana Farr. **Nationality:** British. **Born:** Wimbledon, Surrey, 1 October 1930; daughter of the writer Joanna Cannan, *q.v.;* twin sister of Christine Pullein-Thompson, *q.v.,* and sister of Josephine Pullein-Thompson, *q.v.,* and the writer Denis Cannan. **Education:** Wychwood School, Oxford. **Family:** Married the museum director Dennis Farr in 1959; one son and one daughter. **Career:** Staff member, Rosica Colin Ltd., literary agency, London, 1950-52; editorial assistant, Faith Press, London, 1958-59; director, Grove Riding Schools, Oxfordshire, 15 years. **Address:** 35 Esmond Road, London W4 1JG, England.

Publications for Children

Fiction

It Began with Picotee, with Christine and Josephine Pullein-Thompson, illustrated by Rosemary Robinson. London, A. and C. Black, 1946.
I Wanted a Pony, illustrated by Anne Bullen. London, Collins, 1946.
Three Ponies and Shannan, illustrated by Anne Bullen. London, Collins, 1947.
The Pennyfields. London, Collins, 1949.
A Pony to School, illustrated by Anne Bullen. London, Collins, 1950.
A Pony for Sale, illustrated by Sheila Rose. London, Collins, 1951.
Janet Must Ride, illustrated by Mary Gernat. London, Collins, 1953.
Horses at Home, and Friends Must Part, illustrated by Sheila Rose. London, Collins, 1954.
Riding with the Lyntons, illustrated by Sheila Rose. London, Collins, 1956.
The Boy and the Donkey, illustrated by Shirley Hughes. London, Collins, and New York, Criterion, 1958; as *The Donkey Race,* London, Armada, 1970.
The Secret Dog, illustrated by Geraldine Spence. London, Collins, 1959.
The Hidden River, illustrated by Sheila Rose. London, Hamish Hamilton, 1960.
The Boy Who Came to Stay, illustrated by Alan Breese. London, Faith Press, 1960.
The Battle of Clapham Common. London, Parrish, 1962.
Bindi Must Go, illustrated by Sheila Rose. London, Harrap, 1962.
Hermit's Horse. London, Armada, 1974.
Black Beauty's Clan, with Christine and Josephine Pullein-Thompson. Leicester, Brockhampton Press, 1975.
Ponies in the Valley. London, Collins, 1976.
Black Beauty's Family, with Christine and Josephine Pullein-Thompson, illustrated by Elisabeth Grant. London, Hodder and Stoughton, 1978; New York, McGraw Hill, 1980.
Ponies on the Trail. London, Armada, 1978.
Ponies in Peril. London, Armada, 1979.
Cassidy in Danger. London, Dent, 1979.
Only a Pony. London, Armada, 1980.
A Foal for Candy. London, Sparrow, 1981.
The Pony Seekers. London, Sparrow, 1981.
Black Beauty's Family 2, with Christine and Josephine Pullein-Thompson. London, Hamlyn Beaver, 1982.
A Pony Found. London, Sparrow, 1983.
Dear Pup: Letters to a Young Dog, illustrated by William Rushton. London, Barrie and Jenkins, 1988.
This Pony is Dangerous. New York, State Mutual Book and Periodical Service, 1990.

Other

Riding for Children. London, Foyle, 1957.
Fair Girls on Grey Horses: Memories of a Country Childhood, with Christine and Diana Pullein-Thompson. London, Allison & Busby, 1996.

Editor, *True Horse and Pony Stories.* London, Armada, 1976.

Publications for Adults as Diana Farr

Novel

Choosing. London, Bodley Head, 1988.

Other

Gilbert Cannan: A Georgian Prodigy. London, Chatto and Windus, 1978.
Five at 10: Prime Ministers' Consorts since 1957. London, Deutsch, 1985.

*

Diana Pullein-Thompson comments:

My children's stories are written specifically for young people, not for book-buying parents or literary critics. The most favourably reviewed sell the least well. My first book, *I Wanted a Pony,* is probably my most popular work; yet much of it seems to me now over-dramatised and trivial. My own favourites are *Cassidy in Danger* and *Ponies in Peril.* Because the financial rewards of writing are so poor and there are always bills to be paid I tend to write too much and too often. The most encouraging remark ever made to me by a fan is, "I love your books so much that I keep them on a shelf by my pillow."

* * *

Diana Pullein-Thompson is a better writer than the pony book image she is associated with would lead most people to expect. Whether this has worked for or against her readers and more or fewer children have read her books because of the "pony tag" is hard to assess. But for those who have read her books, whatever the reason, the story tends to live on for a while after it has been finished, as is the way with all good books. This is because she really writes about people, and people situations, not just about ponies and riding situations. Her child characters are plausible, there are always plenty of ways to identify with the main character, and the emotional complications are graphically drawn.

Her first solo book, *I Wanted a Pony,* was written when, as she puts it, she was nearly a child herself, and her observations on grown-ups and family situations are shrewd. The commentary by the unhappy heroine on her cousins and on the horsey world they all live in is both perceptive and amusing. This, coupled with a good story told in an artless, almost naive style, makes the book memorable. It has been read by two generations of children and is still in demand.

After such a good start it might have been hard to go on, but she has continued to develop with great effect the human and emotional situations in her books. *Riding with the Lyntons* and *Three Ponies and Shannan* are two examples where the children in the stories are involved with ponies and riding, but it is the personal misfortunes of the children that carry the reader along. *Friends Must Part* is a story many will warm to as it tells of a foolish disagreement between two great friends and their ensuing quarrel, painful to all, quite senseless and described so well. She is also able to convey the really nasty side of the horsey world, which so many children, tentative riders or outsiders, have witnessed or experienced, yet not often articulated.

Pullein-Thompson has not confined her writing to pony books. She has written for a religious publisher (*The Boy Who Came to Stay*), and several stories are set in London, which she knows as well as the horse world. *The Boy and the Donkey* is a good example of an urban story with its lonely child in a rundown street, gang warfare, and the unpredictability of town life. It is a well-written, touching book. *The Hidden River* and *The Secret Dog* are other examples of her sympathy with the loner, the child in a town, and the child whose world presents problems he can't contain.

Her contributions to the *Black Beauty* series, which she and her sisters wrote as sequels to Anna Sewell's *Black Beauty,* are imaginative and poignant. Black Princess, one of her creations, even found herself in France at the front during World War I.

Cassidy in Danger, one of Pullein-Thompson's more recent books, is perhaps her best. There is a pony in the story, but the heart of the matter is a girl whose upbringing has been so unsettled she has never learnt to read. As the story unfolds one warms not only to all the characters in the book, but to the author too for highlighting what can be a nightmare to so many children and conveying the problem in a sympathetic light to those who can read.

Some of the books appear dated now, for they are full of details (sums of money, social comments, children's slang, clothes, etc.) which have changed with the times. Her own suggestion that in reprints the date the book was written should be inserted in the opening sentence is a good one, for if a reader knows they are reading about 1956 or 1947 they are more prepared for the period slant—indeed, it can add interest to the story.

None of Diana Pullein-Thompson's books can be called profound, but they are perceptive and entertaining, and offer a genuinely good read to a young reader.

—Linda Yeatman

PULLEIN-THOMPSON, Josephine (Mary Wedderburn)

Pseudonym: Josephine Mann. **Nationality:** British. **Born:** Wimbledon, Surrey; daughter of the writer Joanna Cannan, *q.v.;* sister of Christine and Diana Pullein-Thompson, *qq.v.,* and the writer Denis Cannan. **Education:** Wychwood School, Oxford. **Career:** PEN English Centre, General Secretary, 1976-93, President, 1993-97. **Award:** M.B.E. (Member, Order of the British Empire), 1984. **Address:** 16 Knivet Road, London SW6 1JH, England.

Publications for Children

Fiction

It Began with Picotee, with Christine and Diana Pullein-Thompson, illustrated by Rosemary Robinson. London, A. and C. Black, 1946.

Six Ponies, illustrated by Anne Bullen. London, Collins, 1946.

I Had Two Ponies, illustrated by Anne Bullen. London, Collins, 1947.

Plenty of Ponies, illustrated by Anne Bullen. London, Collins, 1949.

Pony Club Team, illustrated by Sheila Rose. London, Collins, 1950.

The Radney Riding Club, illustrated by Sheila Rose. London, Collins, 1951.

Prince among Ponies, illustrated by Charlotte Hough. London, Collins, 1952.

One Day Event, illustrated by Sheila Rose. London, Collins, 1954.

Show Jumping Secret, illustrated by Sheila Rose. London, Collins, 1955.

Patrick's Pony, illustrated by Geoffrey Whittam. Leicester, Brockhampton Press, 1957.

Pony Club Camp, illustrated by Sheila Rose. London, Collins, 1957.

The Trick Jumpers, illustrated by Sheila Rose. London, Collins, 1958.

All Change, illustrated by Sheila Rose. London, Benn, 1961; as *The Hidden Horse,* London, Armada, 1982; London, J.A. Allen, 1989.

Race Horse Holiday. London, Armada, 1971.

Black Beauty's Clan, with Christine and Diana Pullein-Thompson. Leicester, Brockhampton Press, 1975.

Star-Riders of the Moor, illustrated by Elisabeth Grant. London, Hodder and Stoughton, 1976; London, J.A. Allen, 1990.

Black Beauty's Family, with Christine and Diana Pullein-Thompson, illustrated by Elisabeth Grant. London, Hodder and Stoughton, 1978; New York, McGraw Hill, 1980.
Fear Treks the Moor. London, Hodder and Stoughton, 1979.
Ride to the Rescue, illustrated by Elisabeth Grant. London, Hodder and Stoughton, 1979.
Ghost Horse on the Moor, illustrated by Eric Rowe. London, Hodder and Stoughton, 1980.
The No-Good Pony. London, Sparrow, 1981.
Treasure on the Moor, illustrated by Jon Davis. London, Hodder and Stoughton, 1982.
The Prize Pony. London, Sparrow, 1982.
The Hidden Horse, illustrated by Sheila Rose. London, Armada, 1982; London, J.A. Allen.
Black Beauty's Family 2, with Christine and Diana Pullein-Thompson. London, Hamlyn Beaver, 1982.
Pony Club Cup. London, Armada, 1983; London, Read International, 1994.
Save the Ponies! London, Sparrow, 1983.
Mystery on the Moor, illustrated by Chris Rothero. London, Hodder and Stoughton, 1984.
Pony Club Challenge. London, Fontana, 1984; London, Read International, 1994.
Pony Club Trek. London, Armada, 1985.
Suspicion Stalks the Moor, illustrated by Glenn Steward. London, Hodder and Stoughton, 1986.
Black Swift. Edinburgh, Canongate, 1991.
A Job with Horses. London, J.A. Allen, 1994.

Other

How Horses Are Trained. London, Routledge, 1961.
Ponies in Colour, photographs by Nicholas Meyjes. London, Batsford, and New York, Viking Press, 1962.
Learn to Ride Well. London, Routledge, 1966; as *How to Ride Well,* Upavon, Wiltshire, Cavalier, 1997.
Ride Better and Better. London, Blackie, 1974.
Fair Girls on Grey Horses: Memories of a Country Childhood, with Christine and Diana Pullein-Thompson. London, Allison & Busby, 1996.

Editor, *Horses and Their Owners.* London, Nelson, 1970.
Editor, *Proud Riders: Horse and Pony Stories.* Leicester, Brockhampton Press, 1973.

PUBLICATIONS FOR ADULTS

Novels

Gin and Murder. London, Hammond, 1959.
They Died in the Spring. London, Hammond, 1960.
Murder Strikes Pink. London, Hammond, 1963.
A Place with Two Faces (as Josephine Mann). London, Coronet, 1972; New York, Pocket Books, 1974.

*   *   *

Pony-mad readers make one basic demand. Their favourite writers must share with them an idealization of everything equine, believe that the clatter of hooves is the world's sweetest music, the smell of a stable more intoxicating than the finest perfume, and the possession of a pony the highest state of bliss. No writer has fulfilled these demands more satisfactorily than Josephine Pullein-Thompson. Every story she has written reveals her single-minded passion for horses. What makes her a dominant figure in the field of pony books, however, is that mere adoration is never enough for her. She writes with the serious purpose of turning her readers into better horsemen.

For her mother, Joanna Cannan, the ability to ride was something one scrambled into among the other delights of country life; her heroines learn horsemanship from their mistakes. By contrast Josephine's approach was much more professional. Her experiences as a riding instructor and Pony Club worker persuaded her that standards of riding needed to be raised, and she set about using the pony story, with its well-tried themes of struggle and achievement, as a vehicle for instruction. All her early books, from *Six Ponies* to *One Day Event,* show groups of children, or individuals, mastering the skills of horsemanship through various pony-centered events; and her readers are encouraged to identify with the most dedicated and persevering characters, as they school their ponies and improve their riding. Passages of direct technical instruction are boldly included, perhaps as advice given at a Pony Club rally; but these—acceptable, in any case to pony devotees—are made palatable to the general reader by the vitality of the style.

This brisk, cheerful style is one of Josephine Pullein-Thompson's assets. Her books are consistently readable. The Pullein-Thompsons were said to derive their dialogue from conversations they overheard among their riding school pupils, and Josephine's books are full of lively, realistic dialogue, swinging from grumbles to raptures, jokes to quarrels. Her characters, human and equine, are drawn on fairly basic and simple lines, but she handles her large casts with humour and ease.

In the 1960s Josephine Pullein-Thompson wrote mostly for adults, and when she returned to children's books in the 1970s she unfortunately plunged into a world of kidnappers, drug-smugglers, and horse thieves to which she was not suited. At the same time she used her considerable historical knowledge in her contributions to the tales of Black Beauty's imaginary descendants, in which she collaborated with her sisters. Her material is interesting, but comparison reveals the flatness of these modern versions beside the passion of the original Black Beauty.

In the 1980s she again took up the straightforward instructional story, and *The Prize Pony,* with its sympathetic treatment of an inexperienced young rider trying to manage a difficult pony, reaches the high levels of her first books. It offers the blend of clear advice and skilful story-telling that remains her distinctive contribution to the pony book.

—Angela Bull

PYE, Virginia (Frances Kennedy)

Nationality: British. **Born:** London, 27 October 1901; sister of the writer Margaret Kennedy. **Education:** Private. **Family:** Married Sir David Pye in 1926; one daughter and two sons. **Died:** 12 April 1994.

PUBLICATIONS FOR CHILDREN (ILLUSTRATED BY RICHARD KENNEDY)

Fiction

Red-Letter Holiday, illustrated by Gwen Raverat. London, Faber, 1940.
Snow Bird. London, Faber, 1941.
Primrose Polly. London, Faber, 1942.
Half-Term Holiday. London, Faber, 1943.
The Prices Return. London, Faber, 1946.
The Stolen Jewels. London, Faber, 1948.
Johanna and the Prices. London, Faber, 1951.
Holiday Exchange. London, Faber, 1953.

PUBLICATIONS FOR ADULTS

Short Stories

St. Martin's Summer. London, Heinemann, 1930.

*

Virginia Pye comments:

I wrote my children's books during and after World War II. They have, therefore, the background of war time and post-war England and in this sense they are dated. I reread them recently and thought them even funnier than when I wrote them. The application for translation into German was made because "they give such a true picture for English family life." I believe this aspect is entirely undated and the relationship and interplay between the four children and their adult contacts is as true now as it was then and was in the books of E. Nesbit.

I am enchanted by most of the drawings by my cousin Richard Kennedy, particularly the small expressive ones which recapture perfectly the humour of a situation (for example, each child's rosy vision of the prospective return to London after the war in *The Prices Return*).

The Prices Return is my favourite. *Half-Term Holiday* is hilarious, but dated. *The Stolen Jewels* was written at the request of a children's librarian and was intended to be a carrot for slow readers; it didn't really come off. *Red-Letter Holiday* has a splendid ending and would make an excellent television episode. *Johanna and the Prices* (short stories) would make a nice paperback for a long journey or measles: very popular. *Primrose Polly* has a goodish, rather romantic, plot. *Snow Bird* and *Holiday Exchange* are, I think, averagely entertaining reading.

* * *

Virginia Pye's books were published between 1940 and 1953, and it is hard to believe that the modern holiday adventure story, inspired by Ransome's *Swallows and Amazons,* was only ten years old when the first of them, *Red-Letter Holiday,* was published. By 1940 the holiday adventure formula was in danger of being abused and stereotyped, but Pye, while using the conventions of the formula, provided a refreshing element of humour. Published during what was, for children's books, a rather bleak period because of wartime shortages and restrictions, it is not surprising that the Pye books were warmly welcomed by children's librarians and are uniformly praised in articles and conference papers of the period. What is surprising is that the books have been allowed to go out of print, particularly as they are hardly dated by internal references.

Pye's most striking gifts are for portrayal of character and humour. Most of the books are concerned with the holiday adventures of the Price family—Susan, Tom, and Alan with the occasional involvement of their friend Johanna Allard. These four children come over as very real personalities. Alan, the youngest, is inclined to act without thinking, which sometimes involves the family in unexpected situations, as when he decides to improve on the idea of running a tea garden by displaying a notice "licensed to sell wines, spirits and tobacco" (*Red-Letter Holiday*), or, on a grander scale, to arrange with his Swiss pen-friend that their families should exchange houses (*Holiday Exchange*). However, when he is rendered *hors de combat* in *Primrose Polly,* Tom and Susan become involved in adventures without his help. Tom, though competent, is far from being the know-all elder brother, while Susan is well ahead of her time (except that she wears a skirt instead of jeans) in that she does not automatically assume the female role of feeding, and generally ministering to the wants of, her brothers. Johanna is even more unconventional, providing an outside catalyst for those adventures in which she features. Introduced to the Price family (*Red-Letter Holiday*) through a photograph which shows her wearing a white dress and playing a violin, she seems determined to give the lie to this image. Having acquired a black eye and a cut lip before setting out for Cornwall to join the Prices, she manages to lose the train en route and consequently arrives later then expected. She is also ready with the original suggestion which turns the action in a new direction.

The plot of *Red-Letter Holiday* was also well ahead of its time in that the central incident is concerned with finding the skeleton of a prehistoric monster—the kind of theme which was to become popular twenty years later. This book, like the other Pye stories, is packed with incident and moves quickly from one unlikely situation to another; but the succession of events is made credible by the observed detail of life around and the attention paid to the minor figures.

The characters, their conversations, and the humour stay in the mind long after the details of the adventures are forgotten.

—Sheila G. Ray

Q-R

QUINN, John

Nationality: Irish. **Born:** Ballivor, County Meath. **Education:** Attended local schools; Patrician College, Ballyfin, County Laois; St. Patrick's College, Drumcondra, graduated 1961. **Family:** Married; three children. **Career:** Primary school teacher for seven years, Finglas, Dublin; secondary school teacher, County Sligo and Navan, County Meath; editor and compiler, C.J. Fallon Ltd., Educational Publishers, 1970-75. Education officer, RTE, 1975-77, and radio producer in the education department since 1977. **Awards:** Japan Prize Awards (Radio) 1981; Jacobs Award, 1987; Japan Prize Awards (Radio) 1990; BISTO Book of the Year, 1992; Jacobs Award 1992; short listed Reading Association of Ireland Book Award, 1993.

PUBLICATIONS FOR CHILDREN

Fiction

The Summer of Lily and Esme. Dublin, Poolbeg, 1991.
The Gold Cross of Killadoo. Dublin, Poolbeg, 1992.
Duck and Swan. Dublin, Poolbeg, 1993.
One Fine Day. Dublin, Poolbeg, 1995.

PUBLICATIONS FOR ADULTS

Generations of the Moon. Dublin, Poolbeg, 1995.

Other

Editor, *A Portrait of the Artist as a Young Girl* (adapted from his radio series of the same name). London, Methuen, 1985.
Editor, *My Education* (adapted from his radio series). Dublin, Town House, 1997.

Radio Series: *Learning to Read,* 1981; *Children Reading,* 1982; *A Portrait of the Artist as a Young Girl,* 1985; *Ewan and Peggy,* 1987.

*

John Quinn comments:
Where did it come from, the idea for the story of Lily and Esme? I don't know. No, that's not true. Where does anything creative come from—from experiences, from shards of memory that pierce the sub-conscious, from the people, the places that formed one. From all that—and in this case—from an intrigue with the affinity that exists between the young and the very old. To what or to whom else do I owe a debt? To the splintered mirror of one's own childhood—fragments of memory that are sharp enough to pierce the sub-conscious. A day on the bog...a lonely woman who provided tea...adults who established a ready and easy rapport with a young boy...a photograph in the family album which showed a dog in the middle of the read looking at a retreating figure on a bike ... expressions people used to use (like, 'How is every bit of you?') ... football matches ... the whole quiet certitude of living in a small village (excerpted from Quinn's comments in *Children's Literature in Ireland*).

* * *

John Quinn, a highly respected broadcaster and educationalist, brings all his communication skills to the fore in his first prize-winning novel *The Summer of Lily and Esme.* From the first page we are deftly and stealthily carried to the heart of the narration: the journey to a new home, the tensions between Alan's dominant Father and over fussy Mother, the sense of unease, uncertainty, unfamiliar, of dislocation. Then some seven pages into the story someone mentions a ghost and the strangeness is intensified. This is a beautifully written book that has claimed many adult readers as well as its intended young audience. It is at times lyrical, funny, and poignant and the author weaves a rich tapestry of rural life seen through the eyes of a former city dweller, Alan. This rural setting is peopled with a whole range of characters, but none so memorable as the elderly twins Lily and Esme, whose memories are frozen to a time of childhood. Quinn's books are peopled by decent people, youngsters not yet alienated from their nuclear family or fighting against the status quo. By no means goody goody, yet they are ready to do the decent thing. The author captures the exaggerated mocking banter of his young protagonists and depicts them in honest relationships with the adult community. Loneliness is a spur to Alan's friendship with the elderly Lily and Esme as it is with Emer in *Duck and Swan.* Alan's attempt to cocoon the elderly duo in their fantasy world leads them to adopt the persona of "Albert" and to the unravelling of the mystery surrounding this ghost boy—the Glebe House and the poetry of Francis Ledwidge. Francis Ledwidge was a rural poet from County Meath, killed in action in World War I and Quinn links his life to that of Lily and Esme's father and uses his poetry as a haunting background theme. The bewilderment and confusion of the two sisters is treated honestly as is the ultimate death of one of them. History, traditions, and different generations share the same space and merge into an almost lyrical invocation of summertime. By the end of the story, Alan has learned much about the frailties and vulnerabilities of adults and come to appreciate the value of friendships with his peers, with his parents and with kindred spirits of whatever age. The story is rounded and complete yet leaves the reader wishing for more and hunting for Ledwidge's *Collected Poems.*

In his second book for children, *The Gold Cross of Killadoo,* Quinn gives a very different narrative and different setting. It is the Ireland of 990 suffering at the hands of Viking raiders and the story is as much the tale of adventure as an historic novel. Quinn is an award-winning radio producer and some of his skill at grafting sounds and setting scenes translates to the printed page.

Duck and Swan is closer to the mood and emotion of *The Summer of Lily and Esme* yet without the different time frames. It too is about loneliness and alienation: Emer a middle child worried about her mother's health and missing her best friend literally stumbles across Martin "Duck" Oduki. Duck is a misfit, abandoned by a Nigerian father and Irish mother who has just run away from a care centre. This black boy and Galway girl form an unlikely friendship and gradually the runaway learns how to be part of a team, a family, and a community. Again, the theme of friendship across the years is used most effectively through the bond which grows between old man Tom and Nan Flynn and Duck. Nan's understanding and sympathy for Duck is heightened by the fact that she too was a home child, an outsider banished from society. Both are people who have been out of step with the rest of the gang and, in his treatment of the bond between Lily and Esme and young Alan, the author steers a confident course between sentimentality and sensitivity. Quinn is not afraid to tackle life in all its aspects and in so doing earns the respect of his readers.

In *One Fine Day* Quinn has written a densely-woven book, a moving story of human endurance and hope. Set in 1974 it centres around Rossa, recently uprooted from his home in Belfast as he tries to adjust to his new environment in a remote village in County Clare. All the main characters in *One Fine Day* are victims, each is damaged by life in a variety of ways: Rossa's young autistic brother, his mother Maureen fleeing the devastation of bombs in Belfast and her husband's involvement with the terrorist organisation the IRA, Margie—Rossa's only friend suffering the silent fear of the sexually abused. The catalyst for all of them is Lissy,—the strange gypsy woman, half-Irish, half-Italian, whose only friends are the bevy of odd animals and whose tumbled-down shack in the bog becomes the focus of community attempts to halt a refuse site in their area. The book is drama-filled and the pace never slackens, yet for all the action this is a deeply reflective work. The story ends with a resolution of many of the dilemma teasing the reader at the beginning, but with enough left unsaid to keep you wondering long after the pages have been closed. Above all you care about the youngsters as they face life already bruised but not without hope nor bereft of courage.

—Pat Donlon

RAE, Gwynedd

Nationality: British. **Born:** London, 23 July 1892. **Education:** Manor House School, Brondesbury, London, 1907-09; Villa St. George's School, Paris, 1909-10. **Military Service:** Voluntary Aid Detachment during World War I. **Career:** Social worker. **Died:** 14 November 1977.

PUBLICATIONS FOR CHILDREN (ILLUSTRATED BY IRENE WILLIAMSON, EXCEPT AS NOTED)

Fiction

Mostly Mary, illustrated by Harry Rountree. London, Mathews and Marrot, 1930; New York, Morrow, 1931.
All Mary, illustrated by Harry Rountree. London, Mathews and Marrot, 1931.
Mary Plain in Town. London, Cobden Sanderson, 1935.
Mary Plain on Holiday. London, Cobden Sanderson, 1937.
Mary Plain in Trouble. London, Routledge, 1940.
Mary Plain in War-Time. London, Routledge, 1942; as *Mary Plain Lends a Paw,* 1949.
Mary Plain's Big Adventure. London, Routledge, 1944.
Mary Plain Home Again. London, Routledge, 1949.
Mary Plain to the Rescue. London, Routledge, 1950.
Mary Plain and the Twins. London, Routledge, 1952.
Mary Plain Goes Bob-a-Jobbing. London, Routledge, 1954.
Mary Plain Goes to America. London, Routledge, 1957.
Mary Plain, V.I.P. London, Routledge, 1961.
Mary Plain's Whodunit. London, Routledge, 1965.

PUBLICATIONS FOR ADULTS

Novels

And Timothy Too. London, Blackie, 1934.
Leap Year Born. London, Blackie, 1935.

* * *

The continuing popularity of Gwynedd Rae's Mary Plain, "an unusual first-class bear from the bear-pits at Berne," is shown by the publication in 1976 of an omnibus edition of four of the early stories. Although she has never achieved the fame of other bears such as Paddington or Winnie-the-Pooh, Mary has always had her admirers among several generations of readers.

The books were given early publicity by broadcast readings in the BBC Radio programme *Children's Hour,* but there are also qualities inherent in the books which have ensured their lasting popularity: the warm, appealing character of the bear cub, the fun for children in decoding Mary's pictographic writing, and the humour which, without ever being unkind, often arises because the reader is cleverer than Mary. The animals, of course, are anthropomorphic, but children recognise the cub's behavior as that of a naughty small girl who can enjoy mischief denied to the young reader. The other bears also have their own natures: fussy, ineffectual Friska, greedy Bunch, and revered Big Wool.

Many of the stories were topical and some, such as those set in wartime, may now seem dated to adults but perhaps historical to the child. The domestic incidents are usually more successful than the wilder fantasies, such as Mary's starring role in a Hollywood film, but the universal nature of the young bear's behavior gives her something to say to each generation. Although superficially the stories are suitable for very young children, the skills needed to read the quite long texts and to appreciate the jokes make the books most suitable for 8 to 10-year-olds.

—Valerie Brinkley-Willsher

RANSOME, Arthur (Michell)

Nationality: British. **Born:** Leeds, Yorkshire, 18 January 1884. **Education:** Old College, Windermere, 1893-97; Rugby College, Warwickshire, 1897-1901; Yorkshire College (now Leeds University), 1901. **Family:** Married 1) Ivy Walker in 1909 (divorced 1924), one daughter; 2) Evgenia Shelepin in 1924. **Career:** Office boy, Grant Richards, publishers, London, 1901-02; assistant, Unicorn Press, London, 1902-03; freelance writer, ghost writer, and publisher's reader, after 1903; assistant editor, *Temple Bar* magazine, London, 1905-06; moved to Russia in 1913; correspondent, *Daily News,* 1915-19, and the *Observer,* 1917-19; correspondent in the Soviet Union, 1919-24, Egypt, 1924-25, 1929-30, and China, 1926-27; correspondent, 1921-29, and columnist, 1925-28, Manchester *Guardian.* **Awards:** Library Association Carnegie medal, 1937. Litt.D.: University of Leeds, 1952; M.A.: University of Durham. C.B.E. (Commander, Order of the British Empire), 1953. **Died:** 3 June 1967.

Publications for Children

Fiction

Swallows and Amazons, illustrated by Helene Carter. London, Cape, 1930; Philadelphia, Lippincott, 1931.
Swallowdale, illustrated by Clifford Webb. London, Cape, 1931; Philadelphia, Lippincott, 1932.
Peter Duck, illustrated by the author. London, Cape, 1932; Philadelphia, Lippincott, 1933.
Winter Holiday, illustrated by the author. London, Cape, 1933; Philadelphia, Lippincott, 1934.
Coot Club, illustrated by the author and Helene Carter. London, Cape, 1934; Philadelphia, Lippincott, 1935.
Pigeon Post, illustrated by the author. London, Cape, 1936; Philadelphia, Lippincott, 1937.
We Didn't Mean to Go to Sea, illustrated by the author. London, Cape, 1937; New York, Macmillan, 1938.
Secret Water, illustrated by the author. London, Cape, 1939; New York, Macmillan, 1940.
The Big Six, illustrated by the author. London, Cape, 1940; New York, Macmillan, 1941.
Missee Lee, illustrated by the author. London, Cape, 1941; New York, Macmillan, 1942.
The Picts and the Martyrs; or, Not Welcome at All, illustrated by the author. London, Cape, and New York, Macmillan, 1943.
Great Northern? London, Cape, 1947; New York, Macmillan, 1948.
Coots in the North and Other Stories, edited by Hugh Brogan. London, Cape, 1988.

Poetry

Aladdin and His Wonderful Lamp, illustrated by Mackenzie. London, Nisbet, 1919; New York, Brentano's 1920.

Other

The Child's Book of the Seasons. London, Treherne, 1906.
The Things in Our Garden. London, Treherne, 1906.
Pond and Stream. London, Treherne, 1906.
Highways and Byways in Fairyland. London, Alston Rivers, 1906; New York, McBride, 1909.
The Imp and the Elf and the Ogre. London, Nisbet, 1910.
Old Peter's Russian Tales, illustrated by Dmitri Mitrokhin. London, Jack, 1916; New York, Stokes, 1917.
The Soldier and Death: A Russian Folk Tale Told in English. London, Wilson, 1920; New York, Huebsch, 1922.
The War of the Birds and the Beasts and Other Russian Tales, edited by Hugh Brogan, illustrated by Faith Jaques. London, Cape, 1984.

Publications for Adults

Novel

The Elixir of Life. London, Methuen, 1915.

Short Stories

The Hoofmarks of the Faun. London, Secker, 1911.

Other

The ABC of Physical Culture. London, Henry Drane, 1904.
The Souls of the Streets and Other Little Papers. London, Brown Langham, 1904.
The Stone Lady, Ten Little Papers, and Two Mad Stories. London, Brown Langham, 1905.
Bohemia in London. London, Chapman and Hall, and New York, Dodd Mead, 1907.
A History of Story-Telling: Studies in the Development of Narrative. London, Jack, 1909; New York, Stokes, 1910.
Edgar Allan Poe: A Critical Study. London, Secker, and New York, Kennerley, 1910.
Oscar Wilde: A Critical Study. London, Secker, 1912; New York, Kennerley, 1913.
Portraits and Speculations. London, Macmillan, 1913.
Radek and Ransome on Russia, Being Arthur Ransome's "Open Letter to America" with a New Preface by Karl Radek. New York, Socialist Publication Society, 1918.
Six Weeks in Russia in 1919. London, Allen and Unwin, 1919; as *Russia in 1919,* New York, Huebsch, 1919.
The Crisis in Russia. London, Allen and Unwin, and New York, Huebsch, 1921.
Racundra's First Cruise. London, Allen and Unwin, and New York, Huebsch, 1923.
The Chinese Puzzle. London, Allen and Unwin, 1927.
Rod and Line: Essays, Together with Aksakov on Fishing. London, Cape, 1929.
Fishing. Cambridge, University Press, 1955.
Mainly about Fishing. London, A. and C. Black, 1959.
The Autobiography of Arthur Ransome, edited by Rupert Hart-Davis. London, Cape, 1976.

Editor, *The World's Story Tellers.* London, Jack, and New York, Dutton, 12 vols., 1908-09.
Editor, *The Book of Friendship* [and *Love*]: *Essays, Poems, Maxims, and Prose Passages.* London, Jack, 2 vols., 1909-10; New York, Stokes, 2 vols., 1910-11.

Translator, *A Night in the Luxembourg,* by Rémy de Gourmont. London, Stephen Swift, 1912.
Translator, *A Week,* by Y.N. Libedinsky. London, Allen and Unwin, 1923.

*

Manuscript Collection: Brotherton Collection, Leeds.

Critical Studies: *Arthur Ransome* by Hugh Shelley, London, Bodley Head, 1960, New York, Walck, 1964; *The Life of Arthur Ransome* by Hugh Brogan, London, Cape, 1984; *Arthur Ransome* *and Captain Flint's Trunk* by Christina Hardyment, London, Cape, 1984; *Arthur Ransome's Lakeland: A Quest for the Real "Swallow and Amazons" Country* by Roger Wardale, Clapham, Yorkshire, Dalesman, 1986.

Illustrator: his own books *Swallowdale,* 1938, and *Swallows and Amazons,* 1938.

* * *

"It always rained on that day, both indoors and out of doors," wrote Arthur Ransome in his autobiography, recalling the mournful ending of the summer holidays, the return to Leeds from the farm in the Lakes where, until his father died when Arthur was 13, the Ransome family settled themselves for the Long Vacation. "The rain would stream down the window outside, and we with our noses pressed to the glass were blinded by our tears."

Besides this holiday everything else in his childhood was shadowy, it seemed, and when he came, late in life, to write his children's books it was only the holidays that he chose to record, recalling the intensity of delight of the sight of the lakeside farm at last, the ritual dipping of the hand in the water to prove that one had indeed "come home," the greeting of the familiar faces, all to find a place in the books: the kind farmer's daughter (a Swainson there, as she was in real life) who darned threadbare knickerbockers "in situ," the charcoal burners in the woods, the woodcutters, the friendly postman.

Of his 12 books for children only five concern the Lakes, but for most readers this is the background with which they identify Ransome. In *Coot Club, Secret Water, The Big Six,* and *Great Northern?,* the Norfolk Broads and Hebridean scenery is real enough, but one senses that for the author it has not the magic that sent him, during his bohemian years in London, hurrying to Euston whenever he could scrape together the fare to the north.

When the Swallows and Amazons sail Lake Windermere we are in landscape with all the elements that a child most wants, a lake like an inland sea, with islands in it where nobody goes, hills, streams, woods, places to light your own fires without interference. One can wander on the fells all day and meet nothing more than a crag-fast sheep. The natives churn up and down the lakes in their steamers in the distance, but they have no real existence in the children's minds. The characters exist in their holidays only; we are told nothing else of them and nothing else matters. It would be a betrayal to try to imagine them at school; they move for us in their own world where they are Authority. In so far as adult authority—their parents—exists, they co-operate, but their parents tacitly admit their children's holiday supremacy, and make no demands that the children cannot recognize as valid. When unjust authority descends in the shape of great-aunt, then children and mother and uncle are united in silent resistance. It is a dreamworld thought up by a writer who still remembered with resentment how inadequate he had been throughout his school career, slow, stupid, pitifully short-sighted, the butt of both masters and boys.

Perfectly Ransome recaptures the child's deep absorption in himself and his doings, and succeeds in conveying the intense importance and excitement of day-to-day details when one is fending for oneself. He can recall it minutely, so that he can describe the ascent of a tree foothold by foothold, naming the branches that call for particular care. Success blended with occasional failure. Certainly the children manipulate their camps and their boats with serene efficiency; when they set out to divine water they find it; they can build a hut that does not fall down; their signalling systems work, their homing pigeons really do carry messages to reassure the grownups. But now and then even these children are fallible; the *Swallow* is wrecked and all the ecstatic holiday happiness temporarily with it: "it was if the summer itself had been the cargo of the little ship and had gone with her to the bottom of the lake."

The children themselves are a blend of fantasy and reality. Captain Nancy, bold and swashbuckling and defiant, could have no existence outside a story, but the Walker family are all aspects of the author himself. Roger, "ship's boy," is the child Arthur, enthusiastic, unthinking, confident that his elders will sort everything out; Titty, a rather older Arthur, fanciful, a worrier, but often the unexpected victor; John, the calm and business-like captain whom Arthur would have liked to have been, the boy whose commands are unquestioningly obeyed (as no elder brother's ever are). Susan, the brisk school matron, stands alone, Arthur Ransome's concession to the mothers of the 1930s anxious for the dry feet, clean teeth, and proper bedtime of their young. No one quarrels with Susan's dictatorial fussiness; to quarrel would be undignified. Ransome has given to his child characters a dignity and a stature that real children would dearly like to possess; it is one of the elements of his eternal appeal.

—Gillian Avery

RATHMANN, Peggy

Nationality: American. **Born:** Margaret Crosby Rathmann, St. Paul, Minnesota, 4 March 1953. **Education:** University of Minnesota, B.A.; studied art at American Academy, Chicago, Atelier Lack, Minneapolis, and Otis Parsons School of Design, Los Angeles. **Family:** Married John Wick. **Career:** Author, illustrator. **Awards:** Cuffie Award, *Publisher's Weekly,* 1991, for *Ruby the Copycat*; American Library Association Notable Children's Book and a *Parenting Magazine*'s Best Children's Book, 1994, for *Good Night, Gorilla*; Caldecott Medal, and Children's Choice Award Winner in Pennsylvania and Wisconsin, 1996, for *Officer Buckle and Gloria.* **Address:** c/o G.P. Putnam's Sons, 200 Madison Avenue, New York, New York 10016, U.S.A.

PUBLICATIONS FOR CHILDREN

Fiction (illustrated by author)

Ruby the Copycat. New York, Scholastic, 1991.
Goodnight, Gorilla. New York, Putnam, 1994.
Officer Buckle and Gloria. New York, Putnam, 1995.
Ten Minutes till Bed. New York, Putnam, 1998.

*

Biography: "Aunt Peggy" by Robin Rathmann-Noonan, in *Horn Book,* July/August 1996, 429; "Peggy Rathmann: Going Where the Laughter Takes Her" by Donna Freedman, in *Children's Writer*

Guide to 1997, edited by Susan M. Tierney, West Redding, Connecticut, 1997, 187-189.

Illustrator: *Bootsie Barker Bites* by Barbara Bottner, 1992.

* * *

Peggy Rathmann took a while to decide what she would do when she grew up. She started out as a psychology major in college, then switched to biology and pre-med. But what she really liked was to draw. Pre-med showed her a potential application: structural drawings of the body for teaching purposes. After college she took art lessons at three different art schools: for commercial art, for fine art, and for children's book writing and illustration. She fell into children's book writing and illustration because of her interest in adding words to the pictures she drew, and because of a growing number of nieces and nephews who sat around her, just waiting to be entertained.

One of her nieces, Robin Rathmann-Noonan, wrote in *Horn Book* that her Aunt Peggy looks like an adult and acts like an adult. But she understands children, and in her words and pictures she entertains, teaches, and cares for them. Rathmann-Noonan says that the most important thing she has learned from her Aunt Peggy is that you should do something you really enjoy. It took Rathmann a while to find out what she enjoyed most, and now she is doing it.

Rathmann says she gets her ideas for her books from her own life. She has a funny story about every book she has written. Her first, *Ruby the Copycat,* was written at the Otis Parsons School of Design. She spent the first three weeks at the school copying characters from the other students in the class. The teacher urged her to be original, to create a character driven by something secret in herself. That did it. She wrote a story about a copycat and she made the character look like her sister, because she didn't want anyone to know who the character really was.

Bootsie Barker Bites was a collaboration between Rathmann and her teacher at the Otis Parsons School, Barbara Bottner. The terrible tempered Bootsie, who threatens the daughter of her mother's best friend every time she is brought to visit her, has orange hair and a toothy smile; she is much bigger than the girl she comes to visit. How the smaller girl finds a way to intimidate Bootsie Barker is the core of the story. On the last page Bootsie Barker is no longer in the house of the daughter of her Mother's best friend, but far away on the moon, her teeth biting hard on a star in the sky. The dust jacket claims that Bootsie Barker looks a lot like Peggy Rathmann's baby pictures. Why? Because Ms. Rathmann did not wish to offend anyone else.

A homework assignment resulted in the next book, an almost wordless story, *Good Night, Gorilla.* This board book is about a gorilla who takes the zookeeper's keys and follows him home with other zoo animals. The story came from Rathmann's childhood memory of summers running barefoot through the grass in the dark, staring into other people's picture windows, wondering what it would be like to go home to someone else's house. The original story was only 19 pages, and the ending, everyone thought, didn't work. Two years and ten endings later, *Good Night, Gorilla* was published.

Next came the Caldecott Medal winner, *Officer Buckle and Gloria.* The story features Officer Buckle, of the Napville Police Department. Officer Buckle tours Napville Elementary Schools to talk about safety, but his boring lectures often put children to sleep. One day the Napville Police Department gets a police dog named Gloria, who travels with Officer Buckle to the schools. He shows the children how Gloria sits obediently beside him, and begins his discussion of 100 safety tips—say no to drugs; never put anything in your ear; never accept rides from strangers; never tilt your chair back on two legs; on and on and on. Officer Buckle is serious about his serious message, but now the children appreciate his message. They clap and cheer and even write him thank you letters.

But, alas, when Officer Buckle sees a video tape of one of his lectures, he realizes that it isn't him that the children are clapping and cheering for. They are clapping and cheering for Gloria, who is waving, standing on her head, and doing somersaults behind Officer Buckle. Officer Buckle feels betrayed and refuses to do any more lectures. Gloria goes to the schools alone, but Gloria alone is as boring as was Officer Buckle when he was alone. It takes the two of them to promote safety, and provides Buckle with Safety Tip No. 101: "Always stick with your buddy."

The pictures in this book are cartoon-like. Sometimes they run off the page. And they are hilarious in their portrayal of a school where the Principal stands on a swivel chair to tack up a sign, where children trip over their untied shoe laces, where banana pudding falls out of a lunch box onto the floor, where a pile of books carried upstairs by one child falls over on the head of the child climbing the stairs behind her. The Principal is very careless about safety and so are her students.

Rathmann feels that a good picture book is an entertaining one. If you don't entertain, she reasons, the reader is not going to bother finishing the book. She feels now that she has received the Caldecott Medal for *Officer Buckle and Gloria,* critics may be more accepting of humorous works. Many of the Caldecott Medal winners are earnest stories about courage, social problems, major historical events. And in most of the Caldecott books the text and the pictures work in perfect synchrony. In *Officer Buckle* the text gives Officer Buckle's serious safety presentation to the children and the art work provides Gloria's acrobatic presentation to the children, and they are not in sync, which delights the children in the book and the child reader of the book. This book, done in bright water colors and ink, in the style of old fashioned cartoons, is a slapstick comedy. It reminds one of some of the early movies of the Marx Brothers. But it also has serious messages about safety. And it has a message about friendship; Officer Buckle and Gloria need each other.

Rathmann even has a personal story about this book, and the personal story is no less humorous than the book itself. It concerns a family breakfast and her parents' dog Skippy. A video of the gathering in the dining room reveals Rathmann's mother chatting with her guests while, unnoticed by her or the cameraman, Skippy is licking every poached egg on the buffet. The video resumes when everyone is seated around the dining room table, complimenting Rathmann's mother on the delicious eggs. Only after the meal, when the family looks at the video, do they see what occurred; Skippy did not tell.

Rathmann believes that a picture book is a special medium because the pictures don't work without the words, and the words don't work without the pictures. For her the challenge is putting the two together for good entertainment. She is living up to the challenge in any number of innovative ways.

—Mary Lystad

RAY, Mary (Eva Pedder)

Nationality: British. **Born:** Rugby, Warwickshire, 14 March 1932. **Education:** Rugby High School, 1937-50; College of Arts and Crafts, Birmingham, 1950-52; College of the Ascension, Birmingham, 1952-57, London Diploma of Social Studies and Cambridge Certificate of Religious Knowledge; University of Kent, Canterbury, 1988, Hons B.A. in classical civilisation, 1991, Lambeth M.A. in church history, 1994. **Career:** Parish worker, Sheffield Diocese, 1958-61; assistant matron, Warwickshire County Council Old People's Homes, Solihull, 1961-62; civil servant, Export Credits Guarantee Department, Birmingham, 1962-64, 1965-78; staff member, Amphenol Ltd., Whitstable, 1980-82; doctor's receptionist 1984-88. **Address:** 2 Harcourt Drive, Canterbury, Kent CT2 8DP, England.

Publications for Children

Fiction

The Voice of Apollo, illustrated by John Cooper. London, Cape, 1964; New York, Farrar Straus, 1965.
The Eastern Beacon, illustrated by Janet Duchesne. London, Cape, 1965; New York, Farrar Straus, 1966.
Standing Lions, illustrated by Janet Duchesne. London, Faber, 1968; New York, Meredith Press, 1969.
Spring Tide, illustrated by Janet Duchesne. London, Faber, 1969.
Shout Against the Wind, illustrated by Peter Branfield. London, Faber, 1970.
A Tent for the Sun. London, Faber, 1971.
The Ides of April. London, Faber, 1974; New York, Farrar Straus, 1975.
Sword Sleep. London, Faber, 1975.
Beyond the Desert Gate. London, Faber, 1977.
Song of Thunder. London, Faber, 1978.
Rain from the West. London, Faber, 1980.
The Windows of Elissa. London, Faber, 1982.
The Golden Bees, illustrated by Lynda Gray. London, Faber, 1984.

Plays

The Mary Rose, music by Sydney Sagar (produced Rugby, 1983).
Dragons and Dinosaurs, music by Sydney Sagar (produced Cheltenham, 1985).
The Dolphin Boy, music by Sydney Sagar (produced Cheltenham, 1985).

Other

Living in Earliest Greece, illustrated by Peter Branfield. London, Faber, 1969.

*

Mary Ray comments:

After a gap since my early teens (when I had produced very horrific historical fiction and poetry), I began to write again quite suddenly in my late twenties when a friend told me that she had started a book and I could think of no good reason why I shouldn't too. It seemed obvious to me that I should write for children, as I was still very much under the influence of books that I had read as a child, and also that the books should have a classical setting. Since about the age of six I had never felt any strangeness or distance about what I had learned of the people of Greece and Rome and of earlier civilisations; I was at home in the period in the way that some people are at home in a place or a country. I started with Roman Britain, because I knew what the places looked like, and for me it is important that the three strands of the actual geographical first-hand knowledge, historical research, and imagination should all be as strong as I can make them. After I was able to go to Greece regularly I particularly enjoyed writing about people who lived there. I became fascinated by what was the same for me—smells and weather and mountains and ants—and what was quite different because the way that earlier people thought and the things they expected and accepted were different—slavery, pain, and the worship of different gods.

Looking back I can see that certain themes are usually important in my books. Creative people have a habit of turning up as characters, because making things, from jam to fine art, is very important to me, and my creative people often have to fight to be able to practice their skills as one does in real life. I also enjoy writing about the very old and the very young, which is a hangover from working in residential homes for mothers and babies and the old when I was a social science student. I am also obsessed by a theme very common in children's books—how and when you become able to come to terms with what life brings. I suppose this is because to children's writers their own childhood is still very alive. We remember what it hurt to learn, what we had to fight for and what we had to accept; the characters in our books follow where we went, or go the way we wish we had gone.

* * *

The historical novels of Mary Ray bear witness to a passionate interest in early western civilisation, as manifested in ancient Greece, Rome, and Britain, especially at times of turbulence and cultural change such as the birth of Christianity. Concepts which might be thought too complex for children's reading are bravely tackled by this committed writer who often hints at far more that she can express within the confines of a children's book.

Her attitude to the classical world is ambivalent. Although she is attracted to—even obsessed with—ancient culture, as shown in her detailed, loving descriptions of the landscape and the daily life, there are terrible drawbacks. Life is rigidly stratified and many of her characters are poor, enslaved, condemned to drudgery or forced marriage. Women are especially powerless. Although Roman civilisation is a highly organised creation, it needs Christian philosophy to perfect it.

Ray has written of the Mycenean period in *Standing Lions* and *Shout Against the Wind.* In the former she uses the theories of Robert Graves and others about the Mother Goddess and the annual sacrifice of the King in a tale of invasion and court intrigue *Shout Against the Wind* is about refugees from the Dorian invasions, a group of people of different social class who sink these differences to make a new life.

Religion is an important element in her work, and all her main characters feel the need to communicate with some external power, to find the right god and make the right offering. Sh has written a cycle of novels about the early days of Christianity when it was a secret underground cult. The first book, *A Tent for the Sun,* about St. Paul's visits to Corinth, makes one feel the excitement and complete surrender of the soul demanded by the new faith.

Two stories about Camillus and the slave Hylas continue the theme of conversion to Christianity. In *The Ides of April,* set in Rome, Hylas is suspected of murder and Camillus helps him to freedom. Hylas is sheltered by a secret Christian, and it is suggested that Christ's power has brought the truth to light. In *Sword Sleep,* set in Athens, their friendship has become closer and more romantic. Hylas is now a Christian, and Flavius, the unhappy boy befriended by them both, makes a third in their emotional bond. Themes which inspired Mary Renault are also dear to Ray: in her earlier books, Mycenean Greece and the cult of the Mother Goddess, and now the Athenian setting with its flashbacks to the wars of Alexander and its intense male friendships which could be described as quasi-love affairs.

The fourth book, *Beyond the Desert Gate,* takes Hylas to Palestine during the Jewish revolt against Roman rule. The quintet concludes with *Rain from the West,* when Camillus, Hylas, and Flavius are reunited in Roman Britain, and Hylas eventually marries Pyrrha (a character from *A Tent for the Sun,* who has travelled to Britain from Corinth).

Apart from this linked sequence, Ray has continued to write novels set in the turbulent times of the ancient world. *Song of Thunder* is about the eruption of Santorini in 1450 B.C., *The Golden Bees* about the peaceful time on Crete just prior to that eruption, and *The Windows of Elissa* about the siege of Carthage in 310 B.C. Her characters continue to be faced with life-and-death decisions, at the mercy of others who fear and need to propitiate capricious deities. Elissa's sister Sophi is threatened with sacrifice to Baal to save Carthage from destruction. There is no doubt about the evil side of human nature presented by Ray, just as true today as in the ancient world. Against this evil, her characters bravely uphold their faith in a greater force for good.

Having specialised in a particular theme and period, and chosen a formal, metaphoric style of writing, has inevitably endeared her to critics rather than the majority of children, but her Roman Empire sequence is still to be regarded as an important achievement in the field of the historical novel for children.

—Jessica Yates

RAYNER, Mary (Yoma)

Nationality: British. **Born:** Mary Yoma Grigson, Mandalay, Burma, 30 December 1933. **Education:** Nazareth Convent, Ootacamund, India, 1943-45; St. Swithun's School, Winchester, 1945-51; University of St. Andrews, Fife, 1952-56, M.A. (honours) in English 1956. **Family:** Married 1) E.H. Rayner in 1960 (divorced 1982), one daughter and two sons; 2) A.C.T. Hawksley in 1985. **Career:** Editorial and production assistant, Hammond Hammond, publishers, London; copywriter, Longmans Green, publishers, London, 1959-62. Free-lance writer and illustrator. Lives in Wiltshire. **Agent:** Laura Cecil, 17 Alwyne Villas, London N1 2HG, England.

Publications for Children (illustrated by the author, except where noted)

Fiction

The Witch-Finder. London, Macmillan, 1975; New York, Morrow, 1976.
Mr. and Mrs. Pig's Evening Out. London, Macmillan, and New York, Atheneum, 1976.
Garth Pig and the Icecream Lady. London, Macmillan, and New York, Atheneum, 1977.
The Rain Cloud. London, Macmillan, and New York, Atheneum, 1980.
Mrs. Pig's Bulk Buy. London, Macmillan, and New York, Atheneum, 1981.
Crocodarling. London, Collins, 1985; New York, Bradbury Press, 1986.
Mrs. Pig Gets Cross and Other Stories. London, Collins, 1986; New York, Dutton, 1987; as *Mr. Pig Gets Cross,* London, Macmillan, 1996.
Reilly. London, Gollancz, 1987.
Oh Paul! London, Heinemann, 1988; New York, Barron, 1989.
Bathtime for Garth Pig. London, Picture Lions, 1989.
Marathon and Steve. New York, Dutton, 1989.
Rug. London, Collins, and Lake Forest, Illinois, Forest House, 1989.
Open Wide, illustrated by Kate Simpson. London, Longman, 1990.
The Echoing Green, illustrated by Michael Foreman. London, Viking, 1992.
Garth Pig Steals the Show. London, Macmillan, and New York, Dutton, 1993.
One by One, Garth Pig's Rain Song. London, Macmillan, and New York, Dutton, 1994.
Ten Pink Piglets, Garth Pig's Wall Song. London, Macmillan, and New York, Dutton, 1994.
Wicked William. London, Macmillan, 1996.
The Small Good Wolf. London, Macmillan, 1997.
Shark Sunday. London, Viking, 1997.

*

Illustrator: *Harry* by Daphne Ghose, 1973; *The White Rabbit* by Stella Nowell, 1975; *Because of Blunder,* 1977, *Cass the Brave,* 1978, *Silver's Day,* 1980, and *Revenge of the Wildcat,* all by Griselda Gifford; *Dog Detective Ranjha* by Partap Sharma, 1978; *The Boggart* by Emma Tennant, 1980; *Daggie Dogfoot,* 1980, *Magnus Powermouse,* 1982, and *The Sheep-Pig,* 1983 (published in the United States as *Babe: The Gallant Pig,* 1993), all by Dick King-Smith; *The Dead Letter Box* by Jan Mark, 1982; *Mr. Weller's Long March* by Anthea Colbert, 1983; *Lost and Found* by Jill Paton Walsh, 1984; *Thank You for the Tadpole* by Pat Thomson, 1987.

Media Adaptations: *Babe: A Little Pig Goes a Long Way* (film) Universal, 1995.

* * *

The emergence of significant author-artists like Mary Rayner in the 1970s stimulated a refined critical appreciation. Their particular contribution to children's literature requires an evaluative language which can accommodate both the craft of the story teller and the literary possibilities available to the young.

In her picture books about the Pig family, narrative patterns as old as story-telling, in which terror is resolved, greed receives its desserts, and the elements harmonise with the world, are firmly located within a contemporary universe of babysitters, supermarket trips, bunk beds, and ice-cream vans. Her pictures of Garth and his siblings, life-abundant and characterful, evoke bustle and *esprit de corps* in a way that lets the young reader in on the games, rhyme chanting, TV viewing, bathtime frolics, and bedtime exhaustion. Wryly humanised through movement, expression, gesture, and dress, the piglets enable children to be onlookers, revelling in both the fun and the form of early childhood.

The integration of the visual and the verbal makes available to the young particular kinds of pleasure and competence that school reading lessons too often leave out. Varying tones of colour in *The Rain Cloud* show changing weather and landscape while also shifting the pace of the plot. Children see the rites of passage being played out during the early days in school by looking at the ways the protagonists draw their pictures (and fight over the toys) in *Crocodarling.* Children look at Rayner's pictures to build up an expectation of what will happen next: an important thing to do in the suspense-laden stories of *Mr. and Mrs. Pig's Evening Out* and *Garth Pig and the Ice Cream Lady.* There is a sophisticated enjoyment which even her youngest readers gain from the gap between pictures and text: what's left unsaid when Mrs. Pig innocently welcomes the new babysitter (a Mrs. Wolf) or when Mr. Pig, left to mind the children, settles down obliviously with his reading (*The New Porker*). The artistry that combines pathos and irony with laughter, an oral tradition with witty realism, is a constant challenge to long-held notions of the picture book as mere preparation for "real" literary experience.

Rayner's work for older readers has established her as a versatile talent. *Oh Paul!,* for six-to-nine year olds, is saved from what could be a formulaic story in the "little boy who cannot get it right" mould by the writer's ability to catch the essence of a community within a short narrative span. Her ear for classroom talk is particularly acute. Similarly, in *Reilly,* readers of 10 and over are treated to sharply contemporary social observation as a stray cat observes the foibles and petty jealousies based on subtle social differentiations within his adopted territory. Chilling motives echo off ordinary domestic events in *The Witch-Finder,* where strange, even unspeakable, fears are folded within a simple-seeming surface story for young adolescents.

Though Mary Rayner's illustrations of Dick King-Smith's *The Sheep Pig* had been known in England since the book's 1983 publication, they were unfamiliar to North American readers until the book was published in 1993 as *Babe: The Gallant Pig.* Adapted by Universal Studios, the book was the basis for its 1995 film *Babe: A Little Pig Goes a Long Way.* Rayner's charming pen-and-ink drawings echo in the movie's combination of live animals and computer animation (dubbed "robotechnology"). This blend of reality and fantasy works well to represent the story of a piglet who learns to herd sheep from a motherly collie, then earns Farmer Hogget a perfect score at the Grand Challenge Sheepdog Trials. This extremely popular film earned seven Academy Award nominations, including Best Picture.

—Colin Mills, updated by Frieda Bostian

REES, David (Bartlett)

Nationality: British. **Born:** London, 18 May 1936. **Education:** King's College School, Wimbledon, 1946-54; Queens' College, Cambridge, 1955-58, B.A. 1958, M.A. 1961. **Family:** Married Jenny Lee Watkins in 1966; two sons. **Career:** Lived in France, 1958-59; schoolmaster, Wilson's Grammar School, London, 1960-65; Head of the Department of English, Vyners School, Ickenham, Middlesex, 1965-68; Lecturer, 1968-73, and Senior Lecturer 1973-78, St. Luke's College, Exeter, Devon; Lecturer in Education, University of Exeter, 1978-84. Lived in the United States, 1982-83. **Awards:** Library Association Carnegie Medal, 1979; Children's Rights Workshop Other award, 1980. **Died:** 22 May 1993.

Publications for Children

Fiction

Storm Surge, illustrated by Trevor Stubley. Guildford, Surrey, Lutterworth Press, 1975.
Quintin's Man. London, Dobson, 1976; New York, Elsevier Nelson, 1979.
The Missing German. London, Dobson, 1976.
Landslip, illustrated by Gavin Rowe. London, Hamish Hamilton, 1977.
The Spectrum. London, Dobson, 1977.
The Ferryman. London, Dobson, 1977.
Risks. London, Heinemann, 1977; Nashville, Nelson, 1978.
The Exeter Blitz. London, Hamish Hamilton, 1978; New York, Elsevier Nelson, 1980.
The House That Moved, illustrated by Laszlo Acs. London, Hamish Hamilton, 1978.
In the Tent. London, Dobson, 1979; Boston, Alyson, 1985.
Silence. London, Dobson, 1979; New York, Elsevier Nelson, 1981.
The Green Bough of Liberty. London, Dobson, 1979.
The Lighthouse. London, Dobson, 1980.
The Night Before Christmas Eve, illustrated by Peter Kesteven. Exeter, Wheaton, 1980.
Miss Duffy Is Still with Us. London, Dobson, 1980.
A Beacon for the Romans, illustrated by Peter Kesteven. Exeter, Wheaton, 1981.
Holly, Mud and Whisky, illustrated by David Grosvenor. London, Dobson, 1981.
The Milkman's on His Way. London, Gay Men's Press, 1982.
The Mysterious Rattle, illustrated by Maureen Bradley. London, Hamish Hamilton, 1982.
Waves. London, Longman, 1983.
The Burglar, illustrated by Ursula Sieger. Leeds, Arnold Wheaton, 1986.
Friends and Neighbours, illustrated by Clare Herroneau. Leeds, Arnold Wheaton, 1986.
The Flying Island. London, Third House, 1988.

Publications for Adults

Novels

The Estuary. London, Gay Men's Press, 1983.
Out of the Winter Gardens. London, Olive Press, 1984.

A Better Class of Blond. London, Olive Press, 1985.
Watershed. Stamford, Connecticut, Knights Press, 1986.
The Hunger. London, Gay Men's Press, 1986.
Twos and Threes. London, Third House, 1987.
The Wrong Apple. Stamford, Connecticut, Knights Press, 1988.
Quince. London, Third House, 1988.
The Colour of His Hair. London, Third House, 1989.
Letters to Dorothy. London, Third House, 1990.
Odds, Sods and Last Things. London, Third House, 1993.

Short Stories

Islands. Stamford, Connecticut, Knights Press, 1985.
Flux. London, Third House, 1988.

Other

The Marble in the Water: Essays on Contemporary Writers of Fiction for Children and Young People. Boston, Horn Book, 1980.
Painted Desert, Green Shade: Essays on Contemporary Writers for Children and Young Adults. Boston, Horn Book, 1984.
What Do Draculas Do?: Essays on Contemporary Writers for Children and Young Adults. London, Scarecrow, 1990.
Fabulous Tricks, with Peter Robins. East Haven, Connecticut, Inbook, 1991.
Dog Days, White Nights. London, Third House, 1991.
Not for Your Hands: An Autobiography. London, Third House, 1992.
Packing It In. N.p., Millivres, 1992; East Haven, Connecticut, Inbook, 1993.
Words and Music, edited by Peter Burton. N.p., Millivres, and East Haven, Connecticut, Inbook, 1993.

Editor, with Peter Robins, *Oranges and Lemons: Stories by Gay Men.* London, Third House, 1987.
Editor, with Peter Robins, *The Freezer Counter.* London, Third House, 1989.

*

Manuscript Collection: School of Education Library, University of Exeter.

David Rees commented:

(1989) Although I don't write much in a directly autobiographical way in my books for children and teenagers, I find the material comes from rearranging the patterns of my own childhood and adolescence. But I've said everything I have to say about the teenage years; my most recent books are for adults. These are more directly autobiographical and current work in progress is in fact a full-length autobiography.

* * *

David Rees's first book, *Storm Surge,* was runner-up for the *Guardian* award; in 1979 he took the Carnegie Medal with *The Exeter Blitz,* and in 1980 the Other award for *The Green Bough of Liberty.* These successes perhaps exemplified his virtues and vices as a writer.

He had an unexceptional journeyman prose style, combined with a good eye for subject matter that was relevant (coping with adolescence, sexuality, death) or intriguing and naturalistic (historical incidents, disasters natural and man-made); he was clearly concerned with the emotional, educational, and narrative needs of his audience. On the other hand, he tended towards the ready-made in language and character ("it made his head spin..."), his plots could be contrived (this is particularly true of *The Exeter Blitz,* where history is moved around for the sake of the story), with *The House That Moved* perhaps overlocal.

Rees's early work is notable for considerable energy, and some uncertainty about the limits of the children's book. *Storm Surge,* about floods on the east coast of England, has impressive atmosphere and action, successfully confronts death and early marriage, although few characters are fully developed. *The Spectrum* is a rich mixture of sexuality and superstition, centred on an historically documented Devon poltergeist, and shows clearly Rees's juxtaposition of the sensual and the prescriptive. *The Exeter Blitz* is possibly the least distinguished of his books, using continual abstraction which allows little involvement with character; more impressive is the low-keyed *Landslip,* a more controlled story of minor upheavals in 19th-century East Anglia.

The status of *The Milkman's on His Way* as a children's book will doubtless remain questionable, but it is probably Rees's best work. It is a very explicit, and often painfully moving, account of homosexual adolescence (which he had touched on in *Quintin's Man* and *In the Tent*). Although it has the faults of the evangelical—stridency of tone and the intrusion of scarcely disguised textbook information—its commitment and certainty of purpose produce a fluidity and involvement which outweigh the occasional melodramatic contrivance.

Rees's collection of critical pieces on children's books, *The Marble in the Water,* was disappointingly uneven in critical stance and tone. Both as writer and critic he seemed unsure of his methods and medium, while remaining adventurous in his ideas for children's books.

—Peter Hunt

REES, (George) Leslie (Clarence)

Nationality: Australian. **Born:** Perth, Western Australia, 28 December 1905. **Education:** Perth Modern School; University of Western Australia, Nedlands (editor, *Black Swan*), 1924-29, B.A.; University College, London University, 1930. **Family:** Married Coralie Clarke in 1931 (died 1972); two daughters. **Career:** Drama critic, *Era,* London, 1931-35; co-founder, 1937, and honorary chairman, 1938-63, Playwrights Advisory Board, Sydney; federal play editor, 1937-57, and deputy director of drama, 1957-66, Australian Broadcasting Commission. Writer-in-residence, Mt. Lawley College of Advanced Education, Perth, 1975, and Curtin University, Perth, 1988. President, Sydney Centre of International PEN, 1967-75. **Awards:** Australian Children's Book award, 1946; Townsville Foundation Literature award, 1978. A.M. (Member, Order of Australia), 1981. **Address:** 4/5 The Esplanade, Balmoral Beach, New South Wales 2088, Australia.

Publications for Children

Fiction

Digit Dick on the Great Barrier Reef [*and the Tasmanian Devil, in Black Swan Land, and the Lost Opals, and the Magic Jabiru, and the Zoo Plot*], illustrated by Walter Cunningham, Latif Hutchings, and others. Sydney, Sands, 4 vols., 1942-57, Ure Smith, 1 vol., 1979, Angus and Robertson, 1 vol., 1982.
The Story of Shy the Platypus, illustrated by Walter Cunningham. Sydney, Sands, 1944; London, Angus and Robertson, 1958.
Gecko, The Lizard Who Lost His Tail, illustrated by Walter Cunningham. Sydney, Sands, 1944; London, Angus and Robertson, 1958.
The Story of Karrawingi the Emu, illustrated by Walter Cunningham. Sydney, Sands, 1946.
The Story of Sarli the Barrier Reef Turtle, illustrated by Walter Cunningham. Sydney, Sands, 1947.
Mates of the Kurlalong, illustrated by Alfred Wood. Sydney, Sands, 1948.
The Story of Shadow the Rock Wallaby, illustrated by Walter Cunningham. Sydney, Sands, 1948.
Bluecap and Bimbi, The Blue Wrens, illustrated by Walter Cunningham. Sydney, Trinity House, 1948.
The Story of Kurri Kurri the Kookaburra, illustrated by Margaret Senior. Sydney, Sands, 1950; London, Angus and Robertson, 1958.
Quokka Island, illustrated by Arthur Horowicz. London, Collins, 1951.
The Story of Aroora the Red Kangaroo, illustrated by John Singleton. Sydney, Sands, 1952.
Two-Thumbs: The Story of a Koala, illustrated by Margaret Senior. Sydney, Sands, 1953.
Danger Patrol. Sydney and London, Collins, 1954.
The Story of Koonaworra the Black Swan, illustrated by Margaret Senior. Sydney, Sands, 1957; London, Angus and Robertson, 1959.
The Story of Wy-Lah the Cockatoo, illustrated by Walter Cunningham. Sydney, Sands, and London, Angus and Robertson, 1960.
The Story of Russ the Australian Tree Kangaroo, illustrated by Walter Cunningham. Sydney, Sands, 1964.
Boy Lost on Tropic Coast, illustrated by Frank Beck. Sydney, Ure Smith, 1968.
Mokee the White Possum, illustrated by Tony Oliver. Sydney, Hamlyn, 1973.
Panic in the Cattle Country. Adelaide, Rigby, 1974.
Billa the Wombat Who Had a Bad Dream, illustrated by Penny Walton. Sydney, Child, 1988.
The Seagull Who Liked Cricket, illustrated by Margaret Wilson. University Western Australia Press, 1997.

Publications for Adults

Novel

Here's to Shane. Sydney, Wentworth, 1977.

Plays

Sub-Editor's Room (televised 1956), in *Best Australian One-Act Plays,* edited by William Moore and T. Inglis Moore. Sydney, Angus and Robertson, 1937.
Mother's Day, in *Six Australian One-Act Plays.* Sydney, Mulga, 1944.
The Harp in the South, with Ruth Park, adaptation of the novel by Park (produced 1949). Montmorency, Victoria, Yackandandah, 1987.

Other

Towards an Australian Drama. Sydney and London, Angus and Robertson, 1953.
Spinifex Walkabout: Hitch-Hiking in Remote North Australia, with Coralie Rees. Sydney, Australasian Publishing Company, and London, Harrap, 1953.
Westward from Cocos: Indian Ocean Travels, with Coralie Rees. Sydney, Australasian Publishing Company, and London, Harrap, 1956.
Coasts of Cape York: Travels Around Australia's Pearl-Tipped Peninsula, with Coralie Rees. Sydney, Angus and Robertson, 1960.
People of the Big Sky Country, with Coralie Rees. Sydney, Ure Smith, 1970.
A History of Australian Drama:
The Making of Australian Drama: A Historical and Critical Survey from the 1830s to the Late 1960s. Sydney, Angus and Robertson, 1973; revised edition, 1978; London, Angus and Robertson, 1979.
Australian Drama in the 1970s: A Historical and Critical Survey. Sydney, Angus and Robertson, 1978; London, Angus and Robertson, 1979; revised edition, as *The History of Australian Drama 1970-85,* Sydney and London, Angus and Robertson, 1987.
Hold Fast to Dreams: Fifty Years in Theatre, Radio, Television, and Books. Sydney, Alternative Publishing Co-operative, 1982.

Editor, *Australian Radio Plays.* Sydney, Angus and Robertson, 1946.
Editor, *Modern Short Plays.* Sydney and London, Angus and Robertson, 1951.
Editor, *Mask and Microphone: Plays.* Sydney, Angus and Robertson, 1963.

*

Manuscript Collections: Mitchell Library, Sydney; University of Western Australia, Nedlands.

Leslie Rees comments:
I think children like exploring, recognising, discovering; they like adventure, meeting strange and interesting people, animals, and birds, they like laughing, play-acting, narrow escapes; but in the long run feeling secure with someone and something to put their faith in. I like these things too, because there's still a child and still a boy in me. I also like sharing with children the fun and excitement I've had in travelling and getting to know Australian creatures of the wild, and reaching unusual Australian places. And with this emphasis and this incentive I go to work finding a method and an idiom that will catch the interest of the young. I am gratified to find that some of my books have reached child audiences in most English-speaking countries, and in some non-English-speaking countries, with especially large audiences in Russia.

For me one important thing about writing a children's book was not merely the joy of writing it, not merely the satisfaction of reaching contact with the mind of young readers, but the fact that it started new patterns of living for me. I was invited to write a series of life-stories about Australian animals and birds, one book for each creature. Walter Cunnignham was to do the pictures. With him I visited gullies, forests, and streams in the Blue Mountains area, noting detail in words while he make authentic sketches for *The Story of Shy the Platypus.*

Suddenly I, who had had no success with adult storytelling, became aware of a continued capacity to communicate through story with innumerable children, and this opportunity for self-expression was being luckily provided with fresh base material, assimilated from all around me. The full variety of indigenous creature-life of our continent, so different from that of all other lands, had hardly begun in the 1940s to be transmuted by writers and artists into agreeable forms for new generations who ought, so I believed, to have the chance of knowing and accepting all this Australian life as their essential heritage. Here, with the aid of a willing publisher who had the latest technologies of printing at hand, and a clever and sympathetic artist, was a chance to do something new and worthwhile.

Shy the Platypus was nature lore in narrative form, *Digit Dick* was fantasy. So was *Mates of Kurlalong,* my longer story of animals taking charge of a ferry on Sydney Harbour. The "junior novel" called *Quokka Island* was literal adventure seen through the eyes of the unsuppressed boy still inside me.

Among these ways of writing, I had—still have—a special fondness for fantasy. It gives me infinite pleasure that younger children, at least, share my enthusiasm. I think that a total imaginative mergence with fantasy is every child's right as well as joy.

* * *

The contribution of Leslie Rees to Australian children's literature has been threefold: the development of fantasy for young readers; a loving concern for the wildlife of his country; and the keeping alive of the fast-moving adventure story for boys.

Digit Dick, an Australian Tom Thumb, has the universal appeal of diminutive creatures as well as an engaging personality of his own. In that Digit Dick's adventures take him to the Great Barrier Reef and other remote areas of the continent, Rees introduces his readers to an exotic landscape which he peoples with strangely exciting but authentic sea and bush creatures. Inseparable from the Digit Dick stories are the somewhat cartoon-like illustrations of Walter Cunningham which elaborate the author's wordplay and verbal exaggeration. But it was with *Mates of the Kurlalong* that Rees made his most significant contribution to the development of nonsense fantasy in Australia. Here he is less didactic than in his other stories for young children, and he exploits an hilarious central situation in which the hero "not exactly a wombat although he looked like one" and "not exactly a boy although he always behaved like one" commandeers a Sydney Harbour ferry. With an animal crew from Taronga Park Zoo a gloriously fantastic day of freedom begins, to end in a glorification of the endlessly possible adventures of uninhibited childhood.

It is in his series of Nature Tales, also faithfully and beautifully illustrated by Walter Cunningham, from *The Story of Shy the Platypus* through *The Story of Karrawingi the Emu,* the first recipient of the Australian Children's Book of the Year Award, to *Mokee the White Possum,* that Rees has made his most serious contribution to writing for children. Each story is a carefully detailed and authentic study of wildlife in which the title character moves inevitably and dramatically through his cycle of life. The writing is clearer, cleaner, and less wordy than in the Digit Dick stories. Developing readers easily identify with the struggle to survive and to maintain an ordained life-style of Shy the platypus, who "with the consciousness of motherhood upon her" turns from her cherished pool to the dark entrances of her tunnel under the surface of the earth. There is ready sympathy, too, for Karrawingi, the emu, who races through the bush at midnight, proclaiming his fatherhood—of eighteen oval eggs.

Rees has also written full-blooded, tense adventure stories for older boys such as *Danger Patrol,* based on a young Patrol Officer's adventures in a still primitive New Guinea and *Panic in the Cattle Country,* which explores the mystery of cattle in the Outback slaughtered and left with huge tearing wounds, by persons or creatures unknown. Rees's fascination with a geologically ancient continent, its aboriginal inhabitants and the white men who live in its remote vastness, its wildlife and the sweep of its rugged scenery, gives a peculiarly Australian flavour to a yarn belonging firmly in the tradition of the robust boys' adventure story.

—H. M. Saxby

REEVES, James

Pseudonym for John Morris Reeves. **Nationality:** British. **Born:** London, 1 July 1909; brother of Joyce Gard, *q.v.* **Education:** Stowe School, Buckinghamshire; Cambridge University, M.A. (honours) in English 1931. **Family:** Married Mary Phillips in 1936 (died 1966); one son and two daughters. **Career:** Taught in schools and colleges of education, 1933-52; from 1951 general editor, Poetry Bookshelf series, William Heinemann Ltd., London; from 1960 general editor, Unicorn Books, London. Fellow, Royal Society of Literature. **Died:** 1 May 1978.

Publications for Children

Fiction

Pigeons and Princesses, illustrated by Edward Ardizzone. London, Heinemann, 1956.

Mulbridge Manor, illustrated by Geraldine Spence. London, Heinemann, 1958.

Titus in Trouble, illustrated by Edward Ardizzone. London, Bodley Head, 1959; New York, Walck, 1960.

Sailor Rumbelow and Britannia, illustrated by Edward Ardizzone. London, Heinemann, 1962.

Sailor Rumbelow and Other Stories (includes *Pigeons and Princesses* and *Sailor Rumbelow and Britannia*), illustrated by Edward Ardizzone. New York, Dutton, 1962.

The Strange Light, illustrated by Lynton Lamb. London, Heinemann, 1964; Chicago, Rand McNally, 1966.

The Pillar-Box Thieves, illustrated by Dick Hart. London, Nelson, 1965.

Rhyming Will, illustrated by Edward Ardizzone. London, Hamish Hamilton, 1967; New York, McGraw Hill, 1968.

Mr. Horrox and the Gratch, illustrated by Quentin Blake. London, Abelard Schuman, 1969.
The Path of Gold, illustrated by Krystyna Turska. London, Hamish Hamilton, 1972.
The Lion That Flew, illustrated by Edward Ardizzone. London, Chatto and Windus, 1974.
The Clever Mouse, illustrated by Barbara Swiderska. London, Chatto and Windus, 1976.
Eggtime Stories, illustrated by Colin McNaughton. London, Blackie, 1978.
The James Reeves Storybook, illustrated by Edward Ardizzone. London, Heinemann, 1978; as *The Gnome Factory and Other Stories,* London, Penguin, 1986.
A Prince in Danger, illustrated by Gareth Floyd. London, Kaye and Ward, 1979.

Plays

Mulcaster Market: Three Plays for Young People (includes *Mulcaster Market, The Pedlar's Dream, The Stolen Boy*), illustrated by Dudley Cutler. London, Heinemann, 1951; as *The Peddler's Dream and Other Plays,* New York, Dutton, 1963.
The King Who Took Sunshine. London, Heinemann, 1954.
A Health to John Patch: A Ballad Operetta. London, Boosey, 1957.

Poetry

The Wandering Moon, illustrated by Evadne Rowan. London, Heinemann, 1950; New York, Dutton, 1960.
The Blackbird in the Lilac: Verses, illustrated by Edward Ardizzone. London, Oxford University Press, 1952; New York, Dutton, 1959.
A Puffin Quartet of Poets, with others, edited by Eleanor Graham, illustrated by Diana Bloomfield. London, Penguin, 1958.
Prefabulous Animiles, illustrated by Edward Ardizzone. London, Heinemann, 1957; New York, Dutton, 1960.
Ragged Robin, illustrated by Jane Paton. London, Heinemann, and New York, Dutton, 1961.
Hurdy-Gurdy: Selected Poems for Children, illustrated by Edward Ardizzone. London, Heinemann, 1961.
The Story of Jackie Thimble, illustrated by Edward Ardizzone. New York, Dutton, 1964; London, Chatto and Windus, 1965.
Complete Poems for Children, illustrated by Edward Ardizzone. London, Heinemann, 1973.
More Prefabulous Animiles, illustrated by Edward Ardizzone. London, Heinemann, 1975.

Other

English Fables and Fairy Stories, Retold, illustrated by Joan Kiddell-Monroe. London, Oxford University Press, 1954; New York, Walck, 1966(?).
Exploits of Don Quixote, Retold, illustrated by Edward Ardizzone. London, Blackie, 1959; New York, Walck, 1960.
Fables from Aesop, Retold, illustrated by Maurice Wilson. London, Blackie, 1961; New York, Walck, 1962.
Three Tall Tales, Chosen from Traditional Sources, illustrated by Edward Ardizzone. London and New York, Abelard Schuman, 1964.
The Road to a Kingdom: Stories from the Old and New Testaments, illustrated by Richard Kennedy. London, Heinemann, 1965.
The Secret Shoemakers and Other Stories, illustrated by Edward Ardizzone. London and New York, Abelard Schuman, 1966.
The Cold Flame, Based on a Tale from the Collection of the Brothers Grimm, illustrated by Charles Keeping. London, Hamish Hamilton, 1967; New York, Meredith Press, 1969.
The Trojan Horse, illustrated by Krystyna Turska. London, Hamish Hamilton, 1968; New York, Watts, 1969.
Heroes and Monsters: Legends of Ancient Greece Retold, illustrated by Sarah Nechamkin:
Gods and Voyagers. London, Blackie, 1969; New York, Two Continents, 1978.
Islands and Palaces. London, Blackie, 1971; as *Giants and Warriors,* Blackie, 1977; New York, Two Continents, 1978.
The Angel and the Donkey, illustrated by Edward Ardizzone. London, Hamish Hamilton, 1969; New York, McGraw Hill, 1970.
Maildun the Voyager, illustrated by John Lawrence. London, Hamish Hamilton, 1971; New York, Walck, 1972.
How the Moon Began, illustrated by Edward Ardizzone. London, Abelard Schuman, 1971.
The Forbidden Forest and Other Stories, illustrated by Raymond Briggs. London, Heinemann, 1973.
The Voyage of Odysseus: Homer's Odyssey Retold. London, Blackie, 1973.
Two Greedy Bears (Persian folktale), illustrated by Gareth Floyd. London, Hamish Hamilton, 1974.
Quest and Conquest: Pilgrim's Progress Retold, illustrated by Joanna Troughton. London, Blackie, 1976.
Snow-White and Rose-Red, illustrated by Jenny Rodwell. London, Andersen Press, 1979.

Editor, *Orpheus: A Junior Anthology of English Poetry.* London, Heinemann, 2 vols., 1949-50.
Editor, *Heinemann Junior Poetry Books.* London, Heinemann, 4 vols., 1954.
Editor, *The Merry-Go-Round: A Collection of Rhymes and Poems for Children,* illustrated by John Mackay. London, Heinemann, 1955.
Editor, *A Golden Land: Stories, Poems, Songs New and Old,* illustrated by Gillian Conway and others. London, Constable, and New York, Hastings House, 1958.
Editor, *A First Bible: An Abridgement for Young Readers,* illustrated by Geoffrey Fraser. London, Heinemann, 1962.
Editor, *The Christmas Book,* illustrated by Raymond Briggs. London, Heinemann, and New York, Dutton, 1968.
Editor, *One's None: Old Rhymes for New Tongues,* illustrated by Bernadette Watts. London, Heinemann, 1968; New York, Watts, 1969.
Editor, *The Springtime Book: A Collection of Prose and Poetry,* illustrated by Colin McNaughton. London, Heinemann, 1976.
Editor, *The Autumn Book: A Collection of Prose and Poetry,* illustrated by Colin McNaughton. London, Heinemann, 1977.

Translator, *Primrose and the Winter Witch,* by Frantisek Hrubín, illustrated by Jirí Trnka. London, Hamlyn, 1964.
Translator, *The Golden Cockerel and Other Stories,* by Alexander Pushkin, illustrated by Ján Lebis. London, Dent, and New York Watts, 1969.
Translator, *The Shadow of the Hawk and Other Stories,* by Marie de France, illustrated by Anne Dalton. London, Collins, 1975; New York, Seabury Press, 1977.

PUBLICATIONS FOR ADULTS

Play

A.D. One: A Masque for Christmas. Privately printed, 1974.

Poetry

The Natural Need. Deyá, Mallorca, Seizin Press, and London, Constable, 1935.
The Imprisoned Sea. London, Editions Poetry London, 1949.
XIII Poems. Privately printed, 1950.
The Password and Other Poems. London, Heinemann, 1952.
The Talking Skull. London, Heinemann, 1958.
Collected Poems 1929-1959. London, Heinemann, 1960.
The Questioning Tiger. London, Heinemann, 1964.
Selected Poems. London, Allison and Busby, 1967; revised edition, 1977.
Subsong. London, Heinemann, 1969.
Poems and Paraphrases. London, Heinemann, 1972.
Collected Poems 1929-1974. London, Heinemann, 1974.
Arcadian Ballads, illustrated by Edward Ardizzone. Andoversford, Gloucestershire, Whittington Press, 1977.
The Closed Door. Sidcot, Somerset, Gruffyground Press, and Brookston, Indiana, Twinrocker, 1977.

Other

Man Friday: A Primer of English Composition and Grammar. London, Heinemann, 1953.
The Critical Sense: Practical Criticism of Prose and Poetry. London, Heinemann, 1956.
Teaching Poetry: Poetry in Class Five to Fifteen. London, Heinemann, 1958.
A Short History of English Poetry 1340-1940. London, Heinemann, 1961; New York, Dutton, 1962.
Understanding Poetry. London, Heinemann, 1965; New York, Barnes and Noble, 1968.
Commitment to Poetry. London, Heinemann, and New York, Barnes and Noble, 1969.
Inside Poetry, with Martin Seymour-Smith. London, Heinemann, and New York, Barnes and Noble, 1970.
How to Write Poems for Children. London, Heinemann, 1971.
The Reputation and Writings of Alexander Pope. London, Heinemann, and New York, Barnes and Noble, 1976.
The Writer's Approach to the Ballad. London, Harrap, 1976.

Editor, with Denys Thompson, *The Quality of Education: Methods and Purposes in the Secondary Curriculum.* London, Muller, 1947.
Editor, *The Poets' World: An Anthology of English Poetry.* London, Heinemann, 1948; revised edition, as *The Modern Poets' World,* 1957.
Editor, *The Writer's Way: An Anthology of English Prose.* London, Christophers, 1948.
Editor, with Norman Culpan, *Dialogue and Drama.* London, Heinemann, 1950; Boston, Plays Inc., 1968.
Editor, *Selected Poems,* by D. H. Lawrence. London, Heinemann, 1951.
Editor, *The Speaking Oak: English Poetry and Prose: A Selection.* London, Heinemann, 1951.
Editor, *Selected Poems,* by John Donne. London, Heinemann, 1952; New York, Macmillan, 1958.
Editor, *The Bible in Brief: Selections from the Text of the Authorised Version of 1611.* London, Wingate, 1954; as *The Holy Bible in Brief,* New York, Messner, 1954.
Editor, *Selected Poems,* by John Clare. London, Heinemann, 1954; New York, Macmillan, 1957.
Editor, *Gulliver's Travels: The First Three Parts.* London, Heinemann, 1955.
Editor, *Selected Poems,* by Gerard Manley Hopkins. London, Heinemann, 1956; New York, Macmillan, 1957.
Editor, *Selected Poems,* by Robert Browning. London, Heinemann, 1956; New York, Macmillan, 1957.
Editor, *The Idiom of the People: English Traditional Verse from the Manuscripts of Cecil J. Sharp.* London, Heinemann, and New York, Macmillan, 1958.
Editor, *Selected Poems of Emily Dickinson.* London, Heinemann, 1959; New York, Barnes and Noble, 1966.
Editor, *Selected Poems,* by Samuel Taylor Coleridge. London, Heinemann, 1959.
Editor, *The Personal Vision....* London, Poetry Book Supplement, 1959.
Editor, *The Rhyming River: An Anthology of Verse.* London, Heinemann, 4 vols., 1959.
Editor, with William Vincent Aughterson, *Over the Ranges.* Melbourne, Heinemann, 1959.
Editor, *The Everlasting Circle: English Traditional Verse.* London, Heinemann, and New York, Macmillan, 1960.
Editor, with Desmond Flower, *The War 1939-1945.* London, Cassell, 1960; as *The Taste of Courage,* New York, Harper, 1960.
Editor, *The Unicorn Leacock,* by Stephen Leacock. London, Heinemann, 1960.
Editor, *Great English Essays.* London, Cassell, 1961.
Editor, *Selected Poetry and Prose of Robert Graves.* London, Hutchinson, 1961.
Editor, *Georgian Poetry.* London, Penguin, 1962.
Editor, *Gulliver's Travels: Parts I-IV.* London, Heinemann, 1964.
Editor, *The Cassell Book of English Poetry.* London, Cassell, and New York, Harper, 1965.
Editor, *Selected Poems,* by Jonathan Swift. London, Heinemann, and New York, Barnes and Noble, 1967.
Editor, with Martin Seymour-Smith, *A New Canon of English Poetry.* London, Heinemann, and New York, Barnes and Noble, 1967.
Editor, *An Anthology of Free Verse.* Oxford, Blackwell, 1968.
Editor, *The Reader's Bible.* London, Tandem, 1968.
Editor, *The Sayings of Dr. Johnson.* London, Baker, 1968.
Editor, with Seán Haldane, *Homage to Trumbull Stickney: Poems.* London, Heinemann, 1968.
Editor, *Poets and Their Critics 3: Arnold to Auden.* London, Hutchinson, 1969.
Editor, with Martin Seymour-Smith, *The Poems of Andrew Marvell.* London, Heinemann, and New York, Barnes and Noble, 1969.
Editor, *Chaucer: Lyric and Allegory.* London, Heinemann, 1970.
Editor, *A Vein of Mockery: Twentieth-Century Verse Satire.* London, Heinemann, 1973.
Editor, *Selected Poems,* by Thomas Gray. London, Heinemann, 1973; as *The Complete English Poems of Thomas Gray,* New York, Barnes and Noble, 1973.
Editor, *Five Late Romantic Poets.* London, Heinemann, 1974.

Editor, with Martin Seymour-Smith, *Selected Poems of Walt Whitman.* London, Heinemann, 1976.

Editor, with Robert Gittings, *Selected Poems of Thomas Hardy.* London, Heinemann, 1981.

* * *

"We must always provide poetry in such a way that it creates and nourishes a continuing craving for poetry and does not kill it by making poetry seem something childish," said James Reeves once at a conference, condemning cosy and sloppy verse and praising nursery rhymes and Walter de la Mare. He succeeded in keeping that advice in mind in his own poems, of which the humorous ones are most often quoted, like "Cows" from *The Blackbird in the Lilac:*

> Half the time they munched the grass, and all the time
> they lay
> Down in the water-meadows, the lazy month of May
> A-chewing
> A-chewing
> To pass the hours away
> "Nice weather," said the brown cow
> "Ah," said the white.
> "Grass is very tasty
> Grass is all right."

All of the poems are short with a dancing rhythm and plenty of nonsense. They catch a mood quickly and lightly, like these examples from *The Wandering Moon:*

> So grim and gloomy
> Are the caves beneath the sea
> Oh, rare but roomy
> And bare and boomy
> Those soft sea caverns be.

or

> Waiting, waiting, waiting
> For the party to begin
> Waiting, waiting, waiting
> For the laughter and the din.
> Waiting, waiting, waiting
> With hair just so
> And clothes trim and tidy
> From topknot to toe.

or

> Slowly the hands move round the clock,
> Slowly the dew dies on the dock.
> Slow is the snail—but slowest of all
> The green moss spreads on the old brick wall.

When the poet turned to stories for younger children, he created unusual characters and backgrounds, like sailor Rumbelow, the little figure on the ship in a bottle, who loved Britannia in the glass ball, or Foo the clumsy Chinese potter, as well as the more usual royal families with Queens who bake cakes and Kings who hunt. Human failings, particularly pomposity or bad temper, are suitably mocked; kindness always wins in the end. Magic appears now and again, as in "The Old Woman and the Four Noises," in which friendly elves reassure the old country woman that they cause the noises in her cottage: "Don't be afraid...you cannot see me but I live in your front door and I bring you luck. Every time the door is opened or closed, I squeak just to remind you I am here." "What an odd thing," said the old woman, "I never knew before that there was such a thing as a door elf that squeaked, but now I come to think about it, I see no reason why there shouldn't be."

The Strange Light is a longer fantasy about a small girl who discovers, on the other side of a hedge in a field of sunshine, all the characters who are waiting for writers to use them in their books, an ingenious idea. Their faces take on a strange purple glow when an author is thinking of them. This fades when he changes his mind or becomes brighter when they are summoned to go off into a story. One unattractive boy, who is never chosen, leads a revolt, but the heroine rushes back through the hedge to her uncle, who then writes a story about him and his gang, so all is well.

Mulbridge Manor is also set in the English country in summer but has a longer plot for older readers. A group of village children, led by the doctor's son, befriend an eccentric old lady at the Manor, help find a will, and defeat a criminal. Events move swiftly and unexpectedly, and, as in the short stories, virtue is rewarded with a happy ending, but fate plays some funny tricks on the way. The background and the characters are all briefly introduced; no words are wasted: "Mulcaster...was a sleepy place at the best of times...the bells in the cathedral tower dropped four notes on the silent air, almost apologetically, as if sorry to disturb the city in its sleep." The children enter at once on their bicycles, each with a characteristic gesture.

Reeves, besides writing his own very original verse and fiction, retold old fairy stories, Aesop's Fables, and the Bible. In *Sailor Rumbelow* he included the folk tales Rapunzel and Simple Jack, adding some spirited touches; in *The Forbidden Forest and Other Stories* he rescued ten of the lesser known of the Grimm brothers' collection. His short crisp sentences get swiftly to the point; none of the characters bandies words or minces matters.

When Reeves tackled *Exploits of Don Quixote,* he kept closer to the original Spanish text than do most English versions and obviously enjoyed the humour. In his introduction he wrote: "Knight and squire represent two sides of human nature—the desire to lead and the desire to serve, the need for a spiritual aim and the need for material well-being; the balance between madness and commonsense, illusion and reality, courage and prudence."

Perhaps Reeves welcomed Cervantes's creations as fitting companions to some of his own. But the last words on his talent must come from one of his poems:

> The sea is a hungry dog
> Giant and grey
> He rolls on the beach all day.
> With his clashing teeth and shaggy jaws
> Hour upon hour he gnaws
> The rumbling, tumbling stones,
> And "Bones, bones, bones, bones,"
> The giant sea-dog moans,
> Licking his greasy paws.
>
> But on quiet days in May or June
> When even the grasses on the dune

Play no more their reedy tune,
With his head between his paws
He lies on the sandy shores
So quiet, so quiet, he scarcely snores.

—Margaret Campbell

REID, Meta Mayne

Nationality: British. **Born:** Woodlesford, Yorkshire, 23 January 1905. **Education:** Leeds Girls' High School; Manchester University, 1924-27, B.A. (honours) in English. **Family:** Married E. Mayne Reid in 1935; two sons. **Career:** Chairwoman, Belfast PEN, 1960-61; President, Irish PEN, Dublin, 1970-72. **Award:** Listowel Festival trophy, for verse, 1974. **Died:** 8 December 1991.

Publications for Children

Fiction

Phelim and the Creatures, illustrated by Sydney Passmore. London, Chatto and Windus, 1952.
Carrigmore Castle, illustrated by Richard Kennedy. London, Faber, 1954.
All Because of Dawks, illustrated by Geoffrey Whittam. London, Macmillan, and New York, St. Martin's Press, 1955.
Dawks Does It Again, illustrated by Geoffrey Whittam. London, Macmillan, and New York, St. Martin's Press, 1956.
Tiffany and the Swallow Rhyme, illustrated by Richard Kennedy. London, Faber, 1956.
The Cuckoo at Coolnean, illustrated by Richard Kennedy. London, Faber, 1956.
Dawks on Robbers' Mountain, illustrated by Geoffrey Whittam. London, Macmillan, and New York, St. Martin's Press, 1957.
Strangers in Carrigmore, illustrated by Richard Kennedy. London, Faber, 1958.
Dawks and the Duchess. London, Macmillan, 1958.
The McNeills at Rathcapple, illustrated by Brian Wildsmith. London, Faber, 1959.
Storm on Kildoney, illustrated by Geoffrey Whittam. London, Macmillan, and New York, St. Martin's Press, 1961.
Sandy and the Hollow Book, illustrated by Richard Kennedy. London, Faber, 1961.
The Tobermillin Oracle, illustrated by Richard Kennedy. London, Faber, 1962.
With Angus in the Forest, illustrated by Zelma Blakely. London, Faber, 1963.
The Tinkers' Summer, illustrated by Peggy Fortnum. London, Faber, 1965.
The Silver Fighting Cocks. London, Faber, 1966.
The House at Spaniard's Bay. London, Faber, 1967.
The Glen Beyond the Door. London, Faber, 1968.
The Two Rebels. London, Faber, 1969.
Beyond the Wide World's End, illustrated by Antony Maitland. Guildford, Surrey, Lutterworth Press, 1972.
The Plotters of Pollnashee, illustrated by Gareth Floyd. Guildford, Surrey, Lutterworth Press, 1973.
Snowbound by the Whitewater, illustrated by Peter Dennis. London, Abelard Schuman, 1975.
The Noguls and the Horse, illustrated by Tony Morris. London, Abelard Schuman, 1976.
A Dog Called Scampi, illustrated by John Laing. London, Abelard Schuman, 1980.

Publications for Adults

Novels

The Land Is Dear. London, Melrose, 1936.
Far-off Fields Are Green. London, Melrose, 1937.

Poetry

No Ivory Tower. Walton-on-Thames, Surrey, Outposts, 1974.

*

Manuscript Collection: de Grummond Collection, University of Southern Mississippi, Hattiesburg.

Meta Mayne Reid commented:

(1989) Although all the literary tradition is on my husband's side of the family I have written since I was very young. I am fortunate in being able to write any time and any place—at the station, on the bus, with my back to the TV set, among family talk. Poetry, perhaps, gives the greatest pleasure, but writing for children aged 8 to 12 is a kind of poetry. It must transfix the moment, heighten the sense of wonder, and all the time allow the narrative to leap ahead on the backs of firmly drawn characters. I have written straightforward adventure stories, but I prefer fantasy or history as they present the challenge of making a new world.

My tales move on an Irish country background, and, since my family has lived in Northern Ireland for centuries, much of my detail springs from family stories. To be happy I must write something every day, which accounts for the 400-500 letters I send every year, most of them based on daily minutiae—a rich source of material since both fantasy and history demand practical foundations. My own favourites are *With Angus in the Forest* (Viking period) and *The Silver Fighting Cocks* (Napoleonic period).

* * *

Meta Mayne Reid's fiction is set in Ulster, usually in Down or Derry, and the books fall roughly into two categories: the straightforward historical novel and the present-day story with a basis of fantasy. Of the two, the former is the more successful. The time-traveling, magical, or symbolical formula usually produced an element of contrivance: the parallel episodes were not always successfully integrated. Sometimes the author simply went too far: the children turned into animals in the Carrigmore series, for instance, are not convincing.

The House at Spaniard's Bay is one modern story that does not rely too heavily on the supernatural. A lively tale of illicit distilling, adolescent ambition, and infatuation, it has one exotic character—the tinker Judith—to embody the fey Irish quality that distinguished the books. But the author could not resist introducing a figure from the past—the mythical Gráinne—who makes a rather theatrical appearance in a mountain cave. In *The Glen Beyond the Door,* past and present are interwined in an episodic, unsatisfactory way.

A story for 10 to 12 year-olds, *The Noguls and the Horse* uses the topical theme of a terrorist bombing to show how a child can come to terms with her shaken sense of personal security. Reid was at her best, however, when she wrote about the Planter community of the years between 1798 and 1810. The industry of the Scottish Presbyterian settlers in Ulster is posited as an alternative to the traditional fecklessness of the native Irish hill farmer. But the author was well aware of the potent romantic aspects of dispossession and insurrection. *The Two Rebels* gives an excellent account of the aftermath of the '98 Rebellion, when the countryside was swarming with soldiers and men on the run. The rebels of the title are typical insurgents: a young Presbyterian farmer and a liberal Protestant aristocrat.

Red-coats and revenue officers are the blustering authoritarian figures outwitted incessantly by resourceful children. The historical context gives point and vigour to the unoriginal themes, and domestic detail adds credibility. Complex social and racial distinctions are simplified effectively. The heroine is usually a well-adjusted but naturally exuberant girl who has been allowed to run wild: Priscilla McCurdy, for instance (in *The Silver Fighting Cocks*) thinks sadly that "she must stop pretending that she [is] a boy...and be a demure young miss, learning how to be a good wife in five years' time or so." Her friend Jamie is Catholic, and therefore in a lower social class: in *The Plotters of Pollnashee* the 11-year-old farmer's daughter is befriended by a gentleman's son—the point made about natural affinities is still valid.

In *Beyond the Wide World's End* a couple of ragamuffins set off on a quest for emotional security—and find it, though there is a twist in the end. The year is 1810, and the author's research as usual was meticulous. Ulster has an intricate and sometimes romantic history that seems to offer enormous scope for the children's novelist—but Reid was the only author to exploit it.

—Patricia Craig

REY, H.A. and Margret

Nationality: Americans (originally German: emigrated to the United States, 1940; became citizen, 1946). **REY, H.A.:** Also wrote as Uncle Gus. **Born:** Hans Augusto Reyersbach in Hamburg, Germany, 16 September 1898. **Education:** University of Munich, 1919-20; University of Hamburg, 1920-23. **Military Service:** German Infantry and Medical Corps, France and Russia, 1916-19. **Family:** Married Margret Waldstein in 1935. **Career:** Salesman for import firm, Rio de Janeiro, 1924-36. **Career:** Freelance writer and illustrator in Paris, 1936-40, New York, 1940-63, and from 1963 in Cambridge, Massachusetts. Also taught astronomy at Cambridge Center for Adult Education. **Died:** 26 August 1977. **REY, Margret (Elisabeth). Born:** Margret Elisabeth Waldstein, Hamburg, Germany, May 1906. **Education:** Bauhaus, Dessau, 1927; Dusseldorf Academy of Art, 1928-29; University of Munich, 1930-31. **Career:** Reporter and advertising copywriter, Berlin, 1928-29; photographer in London, Hamburg, and Brazil, 1930-35. Individual shows (watercolors): Berlin, 1929-34. Freelance writer in Paris, 1936-40, New York, 1940-63, and since 1963 in Cambridge, Massachusetts; from 1979 Professor of Creative Writing, Brandeis University, Waltham, Massachusetts. **Agent:** A.P. Watt Ltd., 20 John Street, London WC1N 2DL, England. **Address:** 14 Hilliard Street, Cambridge, Massachusetts 02138, U.S.A.

PUBLICATIONS FOR CHILDREN (ILLUSTRATED BY H.A. REY)

Fiction

How the Flying Fishes Came into Being. London, Chatto and Windus, 1938.
Raffy and the Nine Monkeys. London, Chatto and Windus, 1939; as *Cecily G. and the Nine Monkeys,* Boston, Houghton Mifflin, 1942.
How Do You Get There? Boston, Houghton Mifflin, 1941; London, Folding Books, 1951.
Curious George. Boston, Houghton Mifflin, 1941; as *Zozo,* London, Chatto and Windus, 1942.
Elizabite: The Adventures of a Carnivorous Plant. New York, Harper, 1942; London, Chatto and Windus, 1964.
Tommy Helps, Too. Boston, Houghton Mifflin, 1943.
Curious George Takes a Job [Rides a Bike, Gets a Medal, Flies a Kite, Learns the Alphabet, Goes to the Hospital]. Boston, Houghton Mifflin, 6 vols., 1947-66; as *Zozo Takes a Job [Rides a Bike, Gets a Medal, Flies a Kite, Learns the Alphabet, Goes to the Hospital]*, London, Chatto and Windus, 6 vols., 1954-67.
With introduction by Margret Rey, *The Adventures of Curious George* (includes *Curious George, Curious George Takes a Job, Curious George Rides a Bike, Curious George Gets a Medal, Curious George Flies a Kite, Curious George Learns the Alphabet, Curious George Goes to the Hospital*). New York, Book-of-the-Month Club, 1994.

Fiction by Margret Rey

Pretzel. New York, Harper, 1944; London, Folding Books, 1950.
Spotty. New York, Harper, 1945; London, Folding Books, 1950.
Pretzel and the Puppies. New York, Harper, 1946.
Billy's Picture. New York, Harper, 1948; London, Chatto and Windus, 1964.

Poetry

Anybody at Home? London, Chatto and Windus, 1939; Boston, Houghton Mifflin, 1943.
Tit for Tat. New York, Harper, 1942.
Where's My Baby? Boston, Houghton Mifflin, 1943; London, Folding Books, 1950.
Feed the Animals. Boston, Houghton Mifflin, 1944; London, Folding Books, 1950.
See the Circus. Boston, Houghton Mifflin, and London, Chatto and Windus, 1956.

Other by H.A. Rey

Zebrology (drawings). London, Chatto and Windus, 1937.
Aerodrome for Scissors and Paint. London, Chatto and Windus, 1939.

Au Clair de la Lune and Other French Nursery Songs. New York, Greystone Press, 1941.
Look for the Letters: A Hide-and-Seek Alphabet. New York, Harper, 1945.
Mary Had a Little Lamb, with Margret Rey. London, Penguin, 1951.
Find the Constellations. Boston, Houghton Mifflin, 1954; revised edition, 1976.

Editor, *Humpty Dumpty and Other Mother Goose Songs.* New York, Harper, 1943.

Other by H.A. Rey (as Uncle Gus)

Farm. Boston, Houghton Mifflin, 1942.
Circus. Boston, Houghton Mifflin, 1942; London, Folding Books, 1950.
Christmas Manger. Boston, Houghton Mifflin, 1942.

Other by Margret Rey

Editor, with Alan J. Shalleck, *Curious George and the Dump Truck [Goes to the Circus, Goes Sledding, Goes Fishing, Goes to a Costume Party, Plays Baseball, Visits a Police Station, Walks the Pets, Goes to the Aquarium, and the Pizza, at the Fire Station, Goes Hiking, Goes to an Ice Cream Shop, Visits the Zoo, at the Ballet, at the Airport, at the Laundromat]* (adapted from the *Curious George* film series). Boston, Houghton Mifflin, 16 vols., 1984-87.

PUBLICATIONS FOR ADULTS BY H.A. REY

Other

The Stars: A New Way to See Them. Boston, Houghton Mifflin, 1952; as *A New Way to See the Stars,* London, Hamlyn, 1966; revised edition, Houghton Mifflin, 1967; as *The Stars,* London, Chatto and Windus, 1975.

*

Illustrator (H.A. Rey): *The Polite Penguin,* 1941, and *Don't Frighten the Lion!,* 1942, both by Margaret Wise Brown; *Katy No-Pocket* by Emmy Payne, 1944; *The Park Book* by Charlotte Zolotow, 1944; *We Three Kings and Other Christmas Carols,* 1944; *Egbert and His Marvellous Adventures* by Paul T. Gilbert, 1944; *The Daytime Lamp and Other Poems* by Christian Morgenstern, 1973.

Media Adaptations: *Curious George Bakes a Cake* (motion picture); *Curious George Bakes a Cake,* edited by Margret Rey and Alan J. Shalleck, Boston, Houghton Mifflin, 1990; *Curious George Goes to a Chocolate Factory* and *Curious George and the Puppies,* Boston, Houghton Mifflin, 1998.

* * *

It matters little that the names Margret and H.A. Rey are practically unknown among the kindergarten set; what does matter is that their fictional offspring, Curious George, or Zozo in Great Britain, is instantaneously recognized and applauded by millions of children throughout the world. George, the curious little monkey, first saw light of day in the early 1940s when the world was wracked by war, and he immediately gained superstar status in the picture book world, maintaining it to this day.

It is easy, perhaps, for a critic to pass glibly over books like *Curious George* and its sequels when he is considering classic works in the field of children's literature. Such a critic might feel that there is an abyss between the comic strip and "the book," and that his job is to point out those elements which basically separate the two. For there is no denying that the Reys' work has strong links with the traditional comic strip, but therein one finds not only its energy and unique attraction to young children, but also the very subtle craftmanship of its creators. (Yes, *subtle*—for the best practitioners in broad physical humor achieve their effects in a seemingly effortless fashion.)

Since *Curious George* consistently heads the popularity list of what children themselves call "funny books," it is worth our attention to see if we can identify those components in *George* which help it maintain that high rank. As already mentioned, much of the humor in the *George* books is found in physical situations. This is the slapstick humor to be found not only in the comic strips and cartoon films, but in the traditional tall tales as well, and in the films of such comic greats as Chaplin. The humor is the same: a comic character steps into an everyday, ordinary situation and the world immediately turns topsy-turvy. The difference is that George is a child character who gets involved in the everyday incidents in which children often find themselves.

George is always simply introduced on the opening page (as in *Curious George Goes to the Hospital*):

> This is George.
> He lived with his friend, the man with the yellow hat.
> He was a good little monkey, but he was always curious.
> Today George was curious about the big box on the man's desk.

The child audience half knows and half waits to be surprised by the mischief and hilarity that will follow. It is indeed a simple story formula, but one that demands a writer (in this case a team) with a gifted sense of childlike humor and an endless inventiveness.

One last point about these books that adults should not miss—from children's responses to the *George* books it is evident that the man with the yellow hat is the kind of grownup that they most admire and respect. They constantly look for his yellow hat in the crowd, especially when George is center stage and up to his ears in trouble. They know that though he never intrudes, George's grownup friend is always there when he's needed.

—James E. Higgins

RICE, Alice (Caldwell) Hegan

Nationality: American. **Born:** Shelbyville, Kentucky, 11 January 1870. **Education:** Private schools. **Family:** Married Cale Young Rice in 1902. **Career:** Co-founder, Cabbage Patch Settlement House, Louisville, Kentucky. **Awards:** D. Litt.: Rollins College, Winter Park, Florida, 1928; University of Louisville, 1937. **Died:** 10 February 1942.

Publications for Children

Fiction

Mrs. Wiggs of the Cabbage Patch (as Alice Caldwell Hegan). New York, Century, 1901; London, Hodder and Stoughton, 1902.
Lovey Mary. New York, Century, and London, Hodder and Stoughton, 1903.
Captain June, illustrated by C.D. Weldon. New York, Century, and London, Hodder and Stoughton, 1907.

Publications for Adults

Novels

Sandy. New York, Century, and London, Hodder and Stoughton, 1905.
Mr. Opp. New York, Century, and London, Hodder and Stoughton, 1909.
A Romance of Billy-Goat Hill. New York, Century, and London, Hodder and Stoughton, 1912.
The Honorable Percival. New York, Century, and London, Hodder and Stoughton, 1914.
Calvary Alley. New York, Century, and London, Hodder and Stoughton, 1917.
Quin. New York, Century, and London, Hodder and Stoughton, 1921.
The Buffer. New York, Century, and London, Hodder and Stroughton, 1929.
Mr. Pete & Co. New York, Appleton Century, and London, Hodder and Stoughton, 1933.
The Lark Legacy. New York, Appleton Century, and London, Hodder and Stoughton, 1935.
Our Ernie. New York, Appleton Century, and London, Hodder and Stoughton, 1939.

Short Stories

Miss Mink's Soldier and Other Stories. New York, Century, and London, Hodder and Stoughton, 1918.
Turn About Tales, with Cale Young Rice. New York, Century, and London, Hodder and Stoughton, 1920.
Winners and Losers, with Cale Young Rice. New York, Century, and London, Hodder and Stoughton, 1925.
Passionate Follies: Alternate Tales, with Cale Young Rice. New York, Appleton Century, and London, Hodder and Stoughton, 1936.

Other

On Being Clinnicked: A Bit of a Talk over the Alley Fence. Franklin, Ohio, Eldridge, 1931.
My Pillow Book. New York, Appleton Century, 1937.
The Inky Way (autobiography). New York, Appleton Century, 1940.
Happiness Road. New York, Appleton Century, 1942.

* * *

Alice Hegan Rice is remembered now as the creator of Mrs. Wiggs, the purveyor of homespun philosophy: "The way to git cheerful is to smile when you feel bad, to think about somebody else's headache when yer own is 'most bustin', to keep on believin' the sun is a-shinin' when the clouds is thick enough to cut." *Mrs. Wiggs of the Cabbage Patch* is an example of a book which has not so much been taken over by children as passed down to them. It was aimed originally at adult readers, and contains, as well as its account of the Wiggs family, their ups and downs and the way they cope with misfortune (from which no doubt the prosperous reader was expected to derive salutary lessons), the sub-plot of a chequered romance between their two benefactors. The Wiggs family is indeed poor, and Alice Hegan Rice, while allowing them to be "quaint"—addicts always recall how the girls Asia, Australia, and Europena have their pigtails ironed, five plaits to each head before they go for a wonderful first visit to the theatre—does not attempt to gloss over or prettify the desperate straits in which they find themselves when the rent can't be paid, the children cry with hunger, and the eldest boy, the bread-winner, dies from cold and lack of food. The book ends on a modest note of happiness with the lovers' quarrel sorted out and two of the children with settled jobs, but the author provides no fairy tale solution for the problems of the Mrs. Wiggses of this world. We meet her again in *Lovey Mary* where a little girl runs away from an orphanage with the small boy whom she tends and finds refuge with Mrs. Wiggs ("There ain't no hole so deep can't somebody pull you out"). With the large-hearted generosity with which readers by now identify her, Mrs. Wiggs takes them in and shelters them, and not only Mary and Tommy but Tommy's real mother too.

Captain June, unlike the Mrs. Wiggs books, was written specifically for children. The story of a little American boy's stay in Japan, it lacks the warmth and interest of the stories of the Cabbage Patch.

—Gillian Avery

RICHARDS, Frank

Pseudonym: Charles Harold St. John Hamilton. **Nationality:** British. **Born:** Ealing, Middlesex, 8 August 1876. **Education:** Schools in Ealing and Chiswick, including Thorn House School, Ealing. **Career:** Songwriter, with Percy Harrison. Freelance journalist, and staff member, as Martin Clifford, for *Pluck,* 1906, and *The Gem,* 1907-39; as Frank Richards, for *The Magnet,* 1908-40; as Owen Conquest and Ralph Redway, for *Boys' Friend,* from 1915; as Hilda Richards, for *School Friend,* and *The Magnet,* 1919-40; as Charles Hamilton, for *Modern Boy,* from 1928. Also contributed to *The Popular, Empire Library, Schoolboys' Own Library, Boys' Friend Library, The Marvel, Dreadnought, Boys' Journal, Boys' Herald, Vanguard Library,* and *The Nugget Library.* **Died:** 24 December 1961.

Publications for Children

Fiction

Schoolboy series (*The Secret of the School, The Black Sheep of Sparshott, First Man In, Looking after Lamb, The Hero of Sparshott, Pluck Will Tell*). London, Merrett, 6 vols., 1946.

Billy Bunter of Greyfriars School, illustrated by R.J. Macdonald. London, Skilton, 1947.
Mascot Schoolboy series (*Top Study at Topham, Bunny Binks on the War-Path, The Dandy of Topham, Sent to Coventry*). London, John Matthew, 4 vols., 1947.
Billy Bunter's Barring-Out, illustrated by R.J. Macdonald. London, Skilton, 1948.
Billy Bunter's Banknote. London, Skilton, 1948.
Billy Bunter in Brazil. London, Skilton, 1949.
Billy Bunter's Christmas Party, illustrated by R.J. Macdonald. London, Skilton, 1949.
Billy Bunter among the Cannibals, illustrated by R.J. Macdonald. London, Skilton, 1950.
Billy Bunter's Benefit, illustrated by R.J. Macdonald. London, Skilton, 1950.
Jack of All Trades. London, Mandeville, 1950.
Billy Bunter Butts In, illustrated by R.J. Macdonald. London, Skilton, 1951.
Billy Bunter's Postal Order, illustrated by R.J. Macdonald. London, Skilton, 1951.
The Rivals of Rookwood School (as Owen Conquest). London, Mandeville, 1951.
Billy Bunter and the Blue Mauritius, illustrated by R.J. Macdonald. London, Skilton, 1952.
Billy Bunter's Beanfeast, illustrated by R.J. Macdonald. London, Cassell, 1952.
Billy Bunter's Brain-Wave, illustrated by R.J. Macdonald. London, Cassell, 1953.
Billy Bunter's First Case, illustrated by R.J. Macdonald. London, Cassell, 1953.
Billy Bunter the Bold, illustrated by R.J. Macdonald. London, Cassell, 1954.
Bunter Does His Best, illustrated by R.J. Macdonald. London, Cassell, 1954.
The Lone Texan. London, Atlantic, 1954.
Backing Up Billy Bunter, illustrated by C.H. Chapman. London, Cassell, 1955.
Billy Bunter's Double, illustrated by R.J. Macdonald. London, Cassell, 1955.
The Banishing of Billy Bunter, illustrated by C.H. Chapman. London, Cassell, 1956.
Lord Billy Bunter. London, Cassell, 1956.
Billy Bunter Afloat, illustrated by C.H. Chapman. London, Cassell, 1957.
Billy Bunter's Bolt, illustrated by C.H. Chapman. London, Cassell, 1957.
Billy Bunter the Hiker, illustrated by C.H. Chapman. London, Cassell, 1958.
Billy Bunter's Bargain, illustrated by C.H. Chapman. London, Cassell, 1958.
Bunter Comes for Christmas, illustrated by C.H. Chapman. London, Cassell, 1959.
Bunter Out of Bounds, illustrated by C.H. Chapman. London, Cassell, 1959.
Bunter Keeps It Dark, illustrated by C.H. Chapman. London, Cassell, 1960.
Bunter the Bad Lad. London, Cassell, 1960.
Billy Bunter at Butlin's, illustrated by C.H. Chapman. London, Cassell, 1961.
Billy Bunter's Treasure-Hunt, illustrated by C.H. Chapman. London, Cassell, 1961.
Bunter the Ventriloquist, illustrated by C.H. Chapman. London, Cassell, 1961.
Billy Bunter's Bodyguard, illustrated by C.H. Chapman. London, Cassell, 1962.
Bunter the Caravanner, illustrated by C.H. Chapman. London, Cassell, 1962.
Just Like Bunter, illustrated by C.H. Chapman. London, Cassell, 1963.
Big Chief Bunter, illustrated by C.H. Chapman. London, Cassell, 1963.
Bunter the Stowaway, illustrated by C.H. Chapman. London, Cassell, 1964.
Thanks to Bunter, illustrated by C.H. Chapman. London, Cassell, 1964.
Bunter and the Phantom of the Towers. London, Armada, 1965.
Bunter the Racketeer. London, Armada, 1965.
Bunter the Sportsman, illustrated by C.H. Chapman. London, Cassell, 1965.
Bunter the Tough Guy of Greyfriars. London, Armada, 1965.
Bunter's Holiday Cruise. London, Armada, 1965.
Bunter's Last Fling, illustrated by C.H. Chapman. London, Cassell, 1965.
Billy Bunter and the Man from South America. London, Hamlyn, 1967.
Billy Bunter and the School Rebellion. London, Hamlyn, 1967.
Billy Bunter and the Secret Enemy. London, Hamlyn, 1967.
Billy Bunter's Big Top. London, Hamlyn, 1967.
Billy Bunter and the Bank Robber. London, Hamlyn, 1968.
Billy Bunter, Sportsman. London, Hamlyn, 1968.
Billy Bunter and the Crooked Captain. London, Hamlyn, 1968.
Billy Bunter's Convict. London, Hamlyn, 1968.
Yarooh! A Feast of Frank Richards, edited by Gyles Brandreth. London, Eyre Methuen, 1976.
A New Anthology from the Works of Charles Hamilton, edited by John Wernham. Maidstone, Kent, Museum Press, 1977.

Fiction as Hilda Richards

Headland House series (*Winifred on the Warpath, The Girls of Headland House, Under Becky's Thumb*). London, Merrett, 3 vols., 1946.
Mascot Schoolgirl series (*Pamela of St. Olive's, The Stranded Schoolgirls, The Jape of the Term*). London, John Matthew, 3 vols., 1947.
Bessie Bunter of Cliff House School, illustrated by R.J. Macdonald. London, Skilton, 1949.

Fiction as Martin Clifford

The Secret of the Study. London, Mandeville, 1949.
Tom Merry and Co. of St. Jim's. London, Mandeville, 1949.
Rallying round Gussy. London, Mandeville, 1950.
The Scapegrace of St. Jim's. London, Mandeville, 1951.
Talbot's Secret. London, Mandeville, 1951.
Gold Hawk series (*Tom Merry's Secret, Tom Merry's Rival, The Man from the Past, Who Ragged Railton?, Skimpole's Snapshot, Trouble for Trimble, D'Arcy in Danger, D'Arcy on the War-path, D'Arcy's Disappearance, D'Arcy the Reformer, D'Arcy's Day Off*). London, Hamilton, 11 vols., 1952.
A Strange Secret. Maidstone, Kent, Old Boys Book Club, 1968.

Other

Tom Merry's Own (annual; as Martin Clifford and Frank Richards). London, Mandeville, 4 vols., 1952-55.
Billy Bunter's Own (annual). London, Mandeville, 7 vols., 1953-59; London, Oxonhoath, 1 vol., 1960.

Publications for Adults

Other

As Charles Hamilton, *On the Ball!* (song). Canvey Island, Essex, Woodford, 1908.
Plus ça Change; or, The 8:45 from Surbiton (radio play). 1945.
The Autobiography of Frank Richards. London, Skilton, 1952.

*

Critical Studies: *The Charles Hamilton Companion* by John Wernham, Mary Cadogan, Eric Fayne, and Roger Jenkins, Maidstone, Kent, Museum Press, 7 vols., 1972-84; *The World of Frank Richards* by W.O.G. Lofts and Derek J. Adley, London, Baker, 1975; "Across Six Reigns" by Mary Cadogan and Patricia Craig, in *Howard Baker Greyfriars Annual,* 1978; *Greyfriars for Grown-Ups* by Lawrence Sutton, London, Howard Baker Press, 1980; *Frank Richards: The Chap Behind the Chums* by Mary Cadogan, London, Viking, 1988.

*   *   *

According to published statistics Charles Hamilton is the most prolific writer in the English language. He produced over 72 million words of published fiction, the equivalent of 2,000 novels. Under his 20 or so pen names he created many characters who have remained popular for decades with successive generations of readers. At least one of these seems likely to attain literary immortality; the name of Billy Bunter, the "Fat Owl" of the Greyfriars Remove, has become part of the language, synonymous with gluttonous obesity.

Hamilton is best remembered as Frank Richards for his stories of Greyfriars School in *The Magnet,* and as Martin Clifford writing of St. Jim's in *Pluck* and *The Gem.* For a fairly long period, in addition to producing 20,000 words each week for both *The Magnet* and *The Gem,* Hamilton, as Owen Conquest, wrote regular 5,000-word stories of Rookwood School for *Boys' Friend.* He was the original Hilda Richards, creating Cliff House School and Bessie Bunter for *School Friend.* Apart from school stories Hamilton's output included tales of romance, travel, the Wild West, detection, and adventure. He created over 100 fictional schools and new examples of his work are still coming to light.

Hamilton's school stories were addictive from the beginning though the quality of his writing improved over a period of 20 years, reaching a climax of style and presentation in the early 1930s. He perfected a fairly elaborate structure of interlocking episodes and plots, held together by an inner logic and consistency. Like some other children's authors (E. Nesbit, Richmal Crompton, etc.) Hamilton has more than a merely nostalgic appeal for many adults. The stories that are savoured uncritically by children can be appreciated by older readers for their technical accomplishment.

George Orwell's essay on boys' weeklies in the March 1940 issue of *Horizon* criticised the Frank Richards stories on both literary and sociological grounds. The essay contained several errors of fact, including Orwell's statement that the main body of the stories could not represent the output of one man. He conceded that Bunter was "a really first-rate character" but condemned the stories as tautological, artificial, facetiously padded, chauvinistic, and out of date. He also dismissed Richards's style as trite and easily imitated. Orwell here showed less discernment than many bright schoolboy readers of the 1920s and 1930s who wrote indignantly to *The Magnet*'s editor, when substitute authors were used, to demand stories from "the real Frank Richards." In fact Hamilton's style is a highly individual blend of cosiness, satirical comment, and classical allusion that is deceptively difficult to analyse or imitate.

Orwell's major criticism, however, was that the stories were likely to persuade working-class boys to accept the established social structure of society. He condemned what he called the unreal and glamorized atmosphere of Hamilton's public schools and the gulf between this and the quality of life experienced by proletarian boys who enjoyed *The Magnet* and *The Gem.* Of course, if Orwell's sociological assessments were accepted as valid literary criticism, the writers of fairy stories, thrillers, and fantasy fiction could equally be indicted for creating worlds removed from the limited "reality" known to readers from underprivileged homes.

Hamilton's spirited reply to these criticisms was published in the next issue of *Horizon.* He wrote that Orwell's idea of realism would destroy rather than edify the working-class readers about whom the critic showed so much concern: "Mr. Orwell would have told him that he is a shabby little blighter, his father an ill-used serf, his world a dirty, muddled, rotten sort of show!" Hamilton commented that he preferred to inject humour and warmth into his young readers' lives, on the assumption that "Happiness is the best preparation for adult misery if misery must come!"

A contrasting view from Orwell's of the influence of *The Magnet* and *The Gem* is expressed by Professor Robert Roberts in *The Classic Slum* (1971), his survey of Salford life in the early part of this century. According to Roberts, Hamilton's work "set ideals and standards. These our own tutors, religious and secular, had signally failed to do. In the final estimate it may well be found that Frank Richards during the first quarter of the twentieth century had more influence on the mind and outlook of young working-class England than any other single person, not excluding Baden-Powell."

Although Hamilton is celebrated for his manly and wholesome heroes like Harry Wharton and Bob Cherry, he is often at his most skilful with adolescent characters of a complex disposition, who flout adult authority and ideals of esprit de corps. Typical examples of these "outsiders" are the cynical and fastidious Cardew of St. Jim's, or Vernon-Smith, the flamboyant but resolute "Bounder" of Greyfriars. Hamilton's ironic humour counterbalances melodrama, contrivance, and repetition in his stories. Like P.G. Wodehouse, he could use a hackneyed or high-flown phrase and give it a comic, sophisticated flavour. There is also, of course, plenty of crude comedy—Bunter's perpetual tuck-pilfering, the whoopings and "yaroohs," the ghastly gurgles of masters struggling under the soot and glue of schoolboys' booby traps. However there is an overall subtlety of approach that has not always been acknowledged by critics. Hamilton is unsurpassed as a school story writer and remains the most resilient contributor to this minor but intriguing branch of English fiction.

After *The Magnet* ended, Hamilton wrote a series of 38 hardcover Greyfriars books (*Billy Bunter of Greyfriars School,* etc.), numerous annuals (*Billy Bunter's Own, Tom Merry's Own*), and paperbacks. Greyfriars School was featured in a series of BBC television programmes and Christmas plays in London's West End. Since 1969 Howard Baker has been regularly republishing Hamilton's boys' paper stories in facsimile editions. These have proved so popular that now over three-quarters of the 1,683 original stories from *The Magnet* have been reprinted, as well as many stories from *The Gem* and the annuals.

—Mary Cadogan

RICHARDS, Laura E(lizabeth)

Nationality: American. **Born:** Boston, Massachusetts, 27 February 1850; daughter of the poet Julia Ward Howe and the educator Samuel Gridley Howe. **Education:** Miss Caroline Wilby's School, Boston. **Family:** Married Henry Richards in 1871; five daughters and two sons. **Career:** Lived in Gardiner, Maine, after 1876. Associated with District Nurse Association and the National Child Labor Committee; founder, 1895, and president for 26 years, Woman's Philanthropic Union. Founded and with her husband ran Camp Merryweather (boys' summer camp), Lake Cobbosseecontee, 1900-30; president, Maine Consumers League, 1905-11. **Awards:** Pulitzer prize, for biography, 1915. D.H.L.: University of Maine, Orono, 1936. **Died:** 14 January 1943.

Publications for Children

Fiction

Five Mice in a Mouse-Trap, by the Man in the Moon, Done in Vernacular, from the Lunacular, illustrated by Kate Greenaway and others. Boston, Estes, 1880.
Little Tyrant. Boston, Estes, 1880.
Our Baby's Favorite. Boston, Estes, 1881.
The Joyous Story of Toto, illustrated by E.H. Garrett. Boston, Roberts, 1885; London, Blackie, 1886.
Toto's Merry Winter. Boston, Roberts, 1887.
Queen Hildegarde. Boston, Estes, and London, Gay and Bird, 1889.
Hildegarde's Holiday. Boston, Estes, and London, Gay and Bird, 1891.
Captain January. Boston, Estes, and London, Gay and Bird, 1891.
Hildegarde's Home. Boston, Estes, 1892.
Melody. Boston, Estes, 1893; London, Gay and Bird, 1895.
Marie. Boston, Estes, 1894.
Narcissa; or, The Road to Rome, and In Verona: Two Tales. Boston, Estes, 1894.
Nautilus. Boston, Estes, 1895.
Five Minute Stories, illustrated by A.R. Whelan and Etheldred Barry. Boston, Estes, 1895; London, Allenson, 1906.
Hildegarde's Neighbors. Boston, Estes, 1895.
Jim of Hellas; or, In Durance Vile, and Bethesda Pool. Boston, Estes, 1895.
Isla Heron, illustrated by Frank Merrill. Boston, Estes, 1896.
"Some Say," and Neighbors in Cyrus. Boston, Estes, 1896.
Three Margarets, illustrated by Etheldred Barry. Boston, Estes, 1897.
Hildegarde's Harvest. Boston, Estes, 1897.
Rosin the Beau. Boston, Estes, 1898.
Margaret Montfort, illustrated by Etheldred Barry. Boston, Estes, 1898.
Peggy, illustrated by Etheldred Barry. Boston, Estes, 1899.
Quicksilver Sue, illustrated by W.D. Stevens. New York, Century, 1899.
Chop-Chin and the Golden Dragon. Boston, Little Brown, 1899.
The Golden-Breasted Koo-Too. Boston, Little Brown, 1899.
Rita, illustrated by Etheldred Barry. Boston, Estes, 1900.
Fernley House, illustrated by Etheldred Barry. Boston, Estes, 1901.
The Green Satin Gown, illustrated by Etheldred Barry. Boston, Estes, 1903.
More Five-Minute Stories, illustrated by Wallace Goldsmith. Boston, Estes, 1903.
The Golden Windows: A Book of Fables for Young and Old. Boston, Little Brown, 1903; London, Allenson, 1904.
The Merryweathers, illustrated by Julia Ward Richards. Boston, Estes, 1904.
The Armstrongs, illustrated by Julia Ward Richards. Boston, Estes, 1905.
The Silver Crown: Another Book of Fables. Boston, Little Brown, and London, Allenson, 1906.
The Pig Brother and Other Fables and Stories. Boston, Little Brown, 1908.
A Happy Little Time. Boston, Estes, 1910.
The Naughty Comet and Other Fables and Stories. London, Allenson, 1910; revised edition, 1925.
The Little Master. Boston, Estes, 1913; as *Our Little Feudal Cousin of Long Ago,* Boston, Page, 1922.
Three Minute Stories, illustrated by Josephine Bruce. Boston, Page, 1914.
Honor Bright, illustrated by Frank Merrill. Boston, Page, 1920.
Honor Bright's New Adventure, illustrated by Elizabeth Withington. Boston, Page, 1925.
Star Bright: A Sequel to Captain January, illustrated by Frank Merrill. Boston, Page, 1927.
Harry in England, illustrated by Reginald Birch. New York, Appleton Century, 1937.

Plays

The Pig Brother Play-Book (includes *The Pig Brother; The Shadow; For You and Me; The Useful Coal; The Sailor Man; The Cooky; Oh, Dear!; "Go" and "Come"; Child's Play; The Naughty Comet; The Tangled Skein; The Cake; Hokey Pokey; About Angels; The Great Feast; The Wheat-Field*). Boston, Little Brown, 1915.
Fairy Operattas (includes *Cinderella, The Babes in the Wood, Beauty and the Beast, Bluebeard, The Three Bears, Good King Arthur, Puss in Boots, The Sleeping Beauty*), illustrated by Mary Robertson Bassett. Boston, Little Brown, 1916.

Poetry

Sketches and Scraps, illustrated by Henry Richards. Boston, Estes, 1881.
Tell-Tale from Hill and Dale, illustrated by A. Hochstein. Troy, New York, Nims, 1886.

Kasper Kroak's Kaleidoscope, with Henry Baldwin, illustrated by A. Hochstein. Troy, New York, Nims, 1886.
In My Nursery. Boston, Roberts, 1890.
Sundown Songs. Boston, Little Brown, 1899.
The Hurdy-Gurdy. Boston, Estes, 1902.
The Piccolo. Boston, Estes, 1906.
Jolly Jingles. Boston, Estes, 1912.
Tirra Lirra: Rhymes Old and New, illustrated by Marguerite Davis. Boston, Little Brown, 1932; London, Harrap, 1933.
Merry-Go-Round: New Rhymes and Old, illustrated by Winifred Lefferts. New York, Appleton Century, 1935.
I Have a Song to Sing to You, illustrated by Reginald Birch. New York, Appleton Century, 1938.
Drawings by Kate Greenaway, Verses by Laura E. Richards from the Ladies' Home Journal 1895 and 1896, edited by Lucile Rasmussen. Berkeley, California, Rasmussen Press, 1974.

Other

The Old Fairy Tales (*Beauty and the Beast* and *Hop o' My Thumb*), illustrated by Gordon Browne. Boston, Roberts, and London, Blackie, 2 vols., 1886.
When I Was Your Age (autobiography). Boston, Estes, 1894.
Snow-White; or, The House in the Wood. Boston, Estes, 1900.
Florence Nightingale, The Angel of the Crimea. New York, Appleton, 1909.
Two Noble Lives: Samuel Gridley Howe, Julia Ward Howe. Boston, Estes, 1911.
Elizabeth Fry, The Angel of the Prisons. New York, Appleton, 1916.
Abigail Adams and Her Times. New York, Appleton, 1917.
Joan of Arc. New York, Appleton, 1919.
Laura Bridgman: The Story of an Opened Door. New York, Appleton, 1928.

Editor, *Baby's Rhyme* [*Story*] *Book.* Boston, Estes, 2 vols., 1878-79.
Editor, *Four Feet, Two Feet, and No Feet; or, Furry and Feathery Pets and How They Live.* Boston, Estes, 1885.

PUBLICATIONS FOR ADULTS

Novels

Love and Rocks. Boston, Estes, 1898.
Geoffrey Strong. Boston, Estes, 1901; London, Simpkin, 1912.
Mrs. Tree. Boston, Estes, 1902; London, Simpkin, 1912.
Mrs. Tree's Will. Boston, Estes, 1905.
Grandmother: The Story of a Life That Never Was Lived. Boston, Estes, 1907.
The Wooing of Calvin Parks. Boston, Estes, 1908.
"Up to Calvin's." Boston, Estes, 1910.
On Board the Mary Sands. Boston, Estes, 1911.
Miss Jimmy. Boston, Estes, 1913.
Pippin, A Wandering Flame. New York, Appleton, 1917.
A Daughter of Jehu. New York, Appleton, 1918.
In Blessed Cyrus. New York, Appleton, 1921.
The Squire. New York, Appleton, 1923.

Short Stories

For Tommy and Other Stories. Boston, Estes, 1900.

Plays

Seven Oriental Operettas (includes *A Royal Wooing, Abou Hassan the Wag, The Forty Thieves, Pretty Perilla, Aladdin, The Enchanted Birds, The Statue Prince*). Boston, Baker, 1924.
Acting Charades. Boston, Baker, 1924.

Poetry

To Arms! Songs of the Great War. Boston, Page, 1918.
The Hottentot and Other Ditties, music by Twining Lynes. New York, Schirmer, 1939.

Other

Glimpses of the French Court: Sketches from French History. Boston, Estes, 1893.
Julia Ward Howe, 1819-1910, with Maud Howe Elliott. Boston, Houghton Mifflin, 2 vols., 1915.
Stepping Westward (autobiography). New York, Appleton, 1931.
Samuel Gridley Howe. New York, Appleton Century, 1935.
E.A.R. (on Edwin Arlington Robinson). Cambridge, Massachusetts, Harvard University Press, 1936.
"Please." Privately printed, 1936.
What Shall the Children Read? New York, Appleton Century, 1939.
Laura E. Richards and Gardiner (collection). Augusta, Maine, Gannett, 1940.

Editor, *Letters and Journals of Samuel Gridley Howe.* Boston, Estes, 2 vols., 1906-09; London, Lane, 2 vols., 1907-09.
Editor, *The Walk with God,* by Julia Ward Howe. New York, Dutton, 1919.

*

Manuscript Collections: Colby College Library, Waterville, Maine; Gardiner Public Library, Maine.

* * *

Laura E. Richards was a successful writer of both prose and poetry for children during the "golden age" of children's literature in the late 19th and early 20th centuries. Her work was widely published, but she is probably best remembered for her association with the famous *St. Nicholas* magazine, in which many of her verses appeared.

Except for a very few reprint editions, Richards's prose works for children are unavailable today. She wrote a number of biographies, mostly of women (Abigail Adams, Florence Nightingale, Elizabeth I, and others) using the semi-fictional approach common to most biographies for children of the time. Though she strengthened her accounts with excerpts from diaries, letters, and journals, Richards also greatly oversimplified both the characters of her subjects and the historical context of their lives. This, together with an old-fashioned style, has dated the biographies, and they are unlikely to be revived. The same must be said for such fiction as the Queen Hildegarde and Three Margarets series, both very popular in their time but now of interest mainly as period pieces.

It is in fact only her verse that has kept Richards's name alive in the field of children's literature. *Tirra Lirra* is included in most library poetry collections for children. The dominant mood of the verses in *Tirra Lirra* is cheerful and humorous. Lightheartedness was generally characteristic of the author, though some of Richards's verse published in *St. Nicholas* before the turn of the century reflected the sentimental attitudes of that period.

On the whole, however, Richards was a good deal less sentimental in her approach to children and poetry than were many of her contemporaries. Indeed, a slight acidity, surely welcome in the customarily earnest atmosphere of the late 19th century, often flavors her work. The wicked mockingbird whose practical joke caused the frog of Okefenokee to break his lovely green neck does not get off scot-free: "I'm happy to say/He was drowned the next day/In the waters of Okefenokee." Similarly, the aged cook dispatches without a quaver of remorse one of the seven little tigers who propose to eat him. No high-minded conclusions are ever drawn; Richards was not inclined to moralize.

Technically, Richards was a competent and facile versifier. She used a variety of rhyme schemes, mostly strong, unsubtle tetrameters, ballad forms, and limericks, though she never handled them with the intricacy of interest that, say, A.A. Milne could produce at his best. (On the other hand, she was never as far away from a child's point of view as Milne at his nostalgic worst.) She was fond—perhaps overfond—of nonsense words and repetition, certainly reflecting the influence of Edward Lear and Lewis Carroll. And while her made-up words were neither as witty as Carroll's nor as unselfconscious as Lear's, such inventions as the wigglewasticus and the ichthyosnortoryx gave her poems a nice sense of freedom. "Eletelephony," undoubtedly her best-known nonsense poem, is a truly funny play on tangled words, and "An elderly lady named Mackintosh/[who] set out to ride in a hackintosh" anticipates Ogden Nash.

Richards deserves her niche in children's literature. If she was never highly original, still she was humorous, irreverent, and pleasant to the ear. Unlike her prose, her verse is surprisingly undated.

—Anne Scott MacLeod

RICHLER, Mordecai

Nationality: Canadian. **Born:** Montreal, Quebec, 27 January 1931. **Education:** Sir George Williams University, 1949-51. **Family:** Married Catherine Boudreau (divorced); married Florence Wood, 1960; five children. **Career:** Author and screen writer; writer in residence, Sir George Williams University, Montreal, Canada, 1968-69; visiting professor, Carleton University, Ottawa, Canada, 1972-74. **Awards:** Canadian Governor General's Award for fiction, 1972, for *St. Urbain's Horseman*; Canadian Association of Children's Librarians Book of the Year Medal, 1976, for *Jacob Two-Two Meets the Hooded Fang*. **Address:** c/o McClelland and Stewart, 481 University Avenue, Toronto, Ontario M5G 2E9, Canada; P.O. Box 100, Austin, Quebec J0B 1B0, Canada.

Publications for Children

Fiction

Jacob Two-Two Meets the Hooded Fang. Toronto, McClelland and Stewart, 1975.
Jacob Two-Two and the Dinosaur. Toronto, McClelland and Stewart, 1987.
Jacob Two-Two's First Spy Case. Toronto, McClelland and Stewart, 1995.

Publications for Adults

Fiction

The Acrobats. New York, Putnam, 1954.
Son of a Smaller Hero. Toronto, Collins, 1955.
A Choice of Enemies. Toronto, Collins, 1957.
The Apprenticeship of Duddy Kravitz. Toronto, McClelland and Stewart, 1959.
The Incomparable Atuk. Toronto, McClelland and Stewart, 1963; as *Stick Your Neck Out.* New York, Simon and Schuster, 1963.
Cocksure. New York, Simon and Schuster, 1968.
The Street: Stories. Toronto, McClelland and Stewart, 1969.
St. Urbain's Horseman. New York, Knopf, 1971.
Joshua Then and Now. New York, Knopf, 1980.
Solomon Gursky Was Here. Toronto, McClelland and Stewart, 1989.
Barney's Version. Toronto, McClelland and Stewart, 1997.

Nonfiction

Shoveling Trouble. Toronto, McClelland and Stewart, 1973.
Notes on an Endangered Species and Others. New York, Knopf, 1974.
Images of Spain, photographs by Peter Christopher. New York, Norton, 1977.
The Great Comic Book Heroes and Other Essays. Toronto, McClelland and Stewart, 1976.
Home Sweet Home: My Canadian Album. New York, Knopf, 1984.

Plays

Screenplays: With Nicholas Phipps, *No Love for Johnnie,* Embassy, 1962; with Geoffrey Cotterell and Ian Foxwell, *Tiara Tahiti,* Rank, 1962; with Phipps, *The Wild and the Willing,*. Rank, 1962, released in the United States as *Young and Willing,* Universal, 1965; *Life at the Top,* Royal International, 1965; *The Apprenticeship of Duddy Kravitz,* Paramont, 1974; with David Giler and Jerry Belson, *Fun with Dick and Jane,* Bart/Palevsky, 1977; *Joshua Then and Now,* Twentieth Century-Fox, 1985.

Television and Radio Scripts: "The Acrobats," Canadian Broadcasting Corporation, 1956 (radio), 1957 (television); "Friend of the People," CBC-TV, 1957; "Paid in Full," ATV (England), 1958; "Benny, the War in Europe, and Myerson's Daughter Bella," CBC-Radio, 1958; "The Trouble with Benny," ABC (England), 1959; "The Apprenticeship of Duddy Kravitz," CBC-TV, 1960; "The Spare Room," CBC-Radio, 1961; "Q for Quest," CBC-Radio, 1963; "The Fall of Mendel Krick," BBC-TV, 1963; "It's Harder to be Anybody," CBC-Radio, 1965; "Such Was St. Urbain Street," CBC-Radio, 1966; "The Wordsmith," CBC-Radio, 1979.

Other

"The Suit" (animated filmstrip). National Film Board of Canada, 1976.

*

Media Adaptations: *Duddy* (play; based on novel *The Apprenticeship of Duddy Kravitz*), first produced in Edmonton, Alberta, 1984.

Manuscript Collections: University of Calgary Library, Alberta, Canada.

* * *

Although Mordecai Richler's reputation is based on his comic novels and satiric, often acerbic commentaries written for adults, his three novels about Jacob Two-Two, so named because he repeats himself in order to gain attention in his family, have earned him a significant place in Canadian children's literature. In these books, a young boy who feels insignificant as the youngest member of his family achieves a sense of self-worth because of heroic actions in his adventures, some pure fantasy, some realistic although exaggerated.

Jacob Two-Two Meets the Hooded Fang follows the conventions of the dream-journey narrative as the two-plus-two-plus-two-year-old hero, troubled by his rejection by brothers and sisters and criticism from adults, dreams that he is sent to the Child's Prison, where he encounters, in exaggerated form, many people from his waking world. He becomes a hero by freeing other children and exposing the foolishness of the irrational, dominating, and often cruel adults and their fear of children's spontaneity. The book, which draws on the characters and activities of the author's own children, succeeds because of the vitality of the characterization and the humor infused into the narrative. Richler is also particularly adept at presenting a child's view of adults and presenting the wish fulfillment of a young person's achieving control over them. In many ways, his treatment of child-adult relationships resembles similar portrayals in Lewis Carroll's *Alice in Wonderland* and several novels by Charles Dickens.

A sequel published twelve years later is less successful. In *Jacob Two-Two and the Dinosaur,* the hero, who has added two years to his age, receives a pet lizard from his parents. However, it turns out to be a talking dinosaur that grows to enormous size. The boy and his pet/friend travel across Canada in search of a hiding place and a mage for the beast. The plot of the book seems forced, the characterization flat, and the satire—much of it on Canadian politics—irrelevant.

Jacob Two-Two's First Spy Case is closer in tone to the first book, the language and situations of which it often deliberately echoes. Jacob, who does not seem as old as he was in the second book, still considers himself insignificant in his family. The new head master and the caterer of his exclusive private school seek only to make money off the institution and are hostile to Jacob and the other children, whom they set out to repress. However, with the aid of an eccentric old spy who befriends him, Jacob uncovers the illegal activities of the school officials and, as in the first book, becomes a hero to the other children, his older siblings, and his parents. The satire is less politically topical and more directed at the meanness and pettiness of many adults. The hero, who is more fully developed than in the second novel, is still insecure, but displays considerable courage as he rights the wrongs at his school and, as he did in the first book, unmasks the villainous, tyrannous adults.

Although Richler's satire, which is much milder than that in his adult works, will appeal to older children, his portrayal of the young hero along with his clear perception of the hypocrisy of the adults he encounters will delight younger readers. Only *Jacob Two-Two Meets the Hooded Fang* has achieved the status of a Canadian classic; however, Richler's three children's novels are important in their perceptive portrayals of young children establishing their identities in a world controlled by bigger, more powerful adults.

—Jon C. Stott

RIDGE, Antonia (Florence)

Nationality: British. **Born:** Amsterdam, Netherlands, 7 October 1895. **Education:** Schools in the Netherlands and England. **Family:** Married James Henry Ridge in 1926; one daughter and one son. **Career:** Writer and freelance broadcaster. **Award:** Writer's Guild award, for radio play, 1969. **Died:** June 1981.

Publications for Children

Fiction

The Handy Elephant and Other Stories, illustrated by A.E. Kennedy. London, Faber, 1946.
Rom-Bom-Bom and Other Stories, illustrated by A.E. Kennedy. London, Faber, 1946.
Hurrah for Muggins and Other Stories, illustrated by Francis Gower. London, Faber, 1947.
Endless and Co., illustrated by A.E. Kennedy. London, Faber, 1948.
Galloping Fred, illustrated by A.E. Kennedy. London, Faber, 1950.
Leave It to Brooks!, illustrated by Nora S. Unwin. London, National Magazine Company, 1950.
Jan and His Clogs, illustrated by Barbara C. Freeman. London, Faber, 1951; New York, Roy, 1952.
Stories from France (*The Market, The Station, The Village, The Farm, The Mountain, The Seaside*). Leicester, Brockhampton Press, 6 vols., 1956-57.
The Little Red Pony, with Mies Bouhuys, illustrated by Dick De Wilde. London, Harrap, 1960; Indianapolis, Bobbs Merrill, 1962.

Hurrah for a Dutch Birthday, with Mies Bouhuys, illustrated by Jillian Willett. London, Faber, 1964.
Melodia: A Story from Holland, with Mies Bouhuys, illustrated by Leslie Wood. London, Faber, 1969.

Plays

Puppet Plays for Children (includes *Spring Magic, Melodious Mixture, The Tropical Island, Blue Beans, A Cure for Lions, All Aboard the "Bookworm Bell"*), illustrated by Barbara C. Freeman. London, Faber, 1953.
Six Radio Plays (includes *Under the Monkey-Bread Tree, Hare and the Field of Millet, Three Mice for the Abbot, Emhammed of the Red Slippers, The Legend of Saint Basil, Saint Martha and the Tarasque of Tarascon*). Leeds, E.J. Arnold, 1954.
The Poppenkast; or, How Jan Klaassen Cured the Sick King. London, Faber, 1958; as *How Jan Klaassen Cured the King,* 1969.

Other

Jan Klaassen Cures the King: An Old Dutch Story, illustrated by Barbara C. Freeman. London, Faber, 1952.
Never Run from the Lion and Another Story (Algerian folk-tales), illustrated by Barbara C. Freeman. London, Faber, 1958; New York, Walck, 1959.

Translator, Père Castor Books (*Singing Bird House, Three Little Goats, The Moon Game, My Son Scamp, The Sun Box, Three Little Pigs, Me and My Master, The Good Friends, The Story of a Mouse, Little Goat Goes to Market, The Three Little Cats, The Breadcrumbs, The Animals Who Went Looking for Summer, A Rabbit Story, A Dog's Life, The Story of a Baby Lion Who Wasn't Hungry, Some Strange Animals, Come On, Neddy!, Snowball, Kathy's New Dress, The Old Grey Mare and the Little White Hen*), illustrated by Albertine Deletaille, Gerda Muller, and Lucile Butel. London, Harrap, 21 vols., 1960-70.
Translator, *Mission Underground,* by Norbert Casteret, illustrated by H. Johns. London, Harrap, 1968.

Publications for Adults

Novels

Family Album. London, Faber, and New York, Harper, 1952.
Cousin Jan. London, Faber, 1954.
Grandma Went to Russia. London, Faber, 1959.
The Thirteenth Child. London, Faber, 1962; as *The Royal Pawn,* New York, Appleton Century Crofts, 1963.
The Man Who Painted Roses: The Story of Pierre-Joseph Redouté. London, Faber, 1974.

Short Stories

By Special Request. London, Faber, 1958.

Plays

Radio Plays: With Edith Saunders, *Maria Lafarge,* 1968; *The Little French Clock,* 1969; *Au Clair de la Lune,* 1970; *Gentleman's Agreement,* 1972; and others.

Other

For Love of a Rose. London, Faber, 1965.

Editor, *A String of Beads,* by Dorothy McCall. London, Faber, 1960.

* * *

Antonia Ridge was one of the best short story writers that we had. To quote one reviewer, "she knows how to turn a tale well—as juicy as pippins in autumn." Her output was prolific, and in the children's field alone she was the author of many broadcast scripts as well as amusing and entertaining volumes of short stories such as *Rom-Bom-Bom, Hurrah for Muggins, Endless and Co.,* and *Galloping Fred.* These stories feature the animal characters with which she is associated—Fred the donkey, Muggins the dog, and Endless who is of course a Manx cat. A different kind of tale appears in *Never Run from the Lion,* which consists of two traditional folk-tales based on the theme of courage, admirable choices for reading aloud.

Much of Ridge's work revealed her Dutch inheritance. This is particularly so in the case of her best-known play, *The Poppenkast; or, How Jan Klaassen Cured the Sick King,* adapted from an old Dutch puppet play.

During the 1960s Ridge collaborated with the Dutch author Mies Bouhuys in producing a picture book illustrating the stress laid in Dutch family life on a child's birthday, called appropriately enough *Hurrah for a Dutch Birthday.* Bouhuys was also her co-author in the writing of *Melodia,* the story of a Dutch street organ. The scene is well set, the Dutch landscape with its dykes and windmills. Grandpa Brack, who owns Melodia, is a great favorite with the local children, but he and his wife are always hoping to visit their own six grandchildren in faraway America. The fairytale theme of the rich American visitor who makes it possible for this to happen is a well-worn one but very satisfying in the context of this story. The text is slightly marred, however, by a conversational style, wholly suitable for reading aloud, which becomes condescending in print.

Although Ridge was particularly good when writing for very young children—the English text to the Père Castor series of young picture books proves this—it is also true to say that her stories for adults, such as *The Thirteenth Child* and *Family Album,* are much enjoyed by older children. Their values are very sound, and they can be heartily recommended.

—Berna C. Clark

RIDLEY, Philip

Nationality: English. **Born:** 1964. **Education:** St. Martin's School of Art, B.A (Honours) 1986. **Career:** Novelist, painter, playwright, screenwriter, film director, stage director, lyricist. **Awards:** Smarites award and W. H. Smiths Mind Boggling Book award, 1992, for *Krindlekrax*; Whitbread Best Children's Novel award shortlist, 1995, for *Kasper in the Glitter*; Nasen Special Education Needs Book award commendation, 1998, for *Scribbleboy.* **Agent:** c/o Caradoc King, A.P. Watt Literary Agents, 20 John Street, London WC1 2DR England.

Publications for Children

Fiction

Mercedes Ice. London, Collins, 1989; illustrated by Chris Riddell, London, Viking, 1995.
Dakota of the White Flats. London, Collins, 1989; New York, Knopf, 1991; illustrated by Chris Riddell, London, Viking, 1995.
Krindlekrax. London, Cape, 1991; New York, Knopf, 1992.
Kasper in the Glitter. London, Viking, 1994; New York, Dutton, 1997.
Meteorite Spoon, illustrated by Chris Riddell. London, Viking, 1994.
Dreamboat Zing. London, Puffin, 1996.
Hooligan's Shampoo. London, Penguin, 1996.
Scribbleboy. London, Viking, 1997.
Zinderzunder. London, Puffin, 1998.

Plays

Two Plays for Young People: Fairytaleheart and Sparkleshark. London, Faber and Faber, 1998.

Publications for Adults

Fiction

Crocodilia. London, Brilliance, 1988.
In the Eyes of Mr. Fury. London, Penguin, 1989.
Flamingoes in Orbit. London, Penguin, 1991.

Plays

The Pitchfork Disney. London, Methuen, 1991.
The Fastest Clock in the Universe. London, Methuen, 1992.
Ghost from a Perfect Place. London, Methuen, 1994.
The Krays (screenplay). London, Methuen, 1997.
The American Dreams: The Reflecting Skin and the Passion of Darkly Noon (screenplay). London, Methuen, 1997.
Ridley: Plays One (collection). London, Methuen, 1997.

*

Media Adaptations: *The Krays* (film), United Kingdom, Rank, and United States, Miramax, 1990; *The Reflecting Skin* (film), United Kingdom, Virgin, and United States, Miramax, 1991; *The Passion of Darkly Noon* (film), United Kingdom, Entertainment, 1995.

Philip Ridley comments:

Read! This will prepare you! For what? For the perception of magic, of course. Look! That old building you've always been told is a slum—it's magical! The junkyard—wonderful! That run-down street—amazing! These are new myths and legends—urban fairytales to help you make sense of things. Feel it? The words are part of you! Images whiz through your mind! You are magical, wonderful, amazing! Let the story take over—oh, faster, brighter, louder, zappier, fizzier, funkier, jazzier.

* * *

Much has been made of Philip Ridley's varied talents. He has been successful in a number of art forms: painting, film scripts, writing and directing films, plays, novels and short stories for adults, and novels for children. In all of these works there is a very obvious use of the urban landscape as a setting for any number of fantastical excursions. Ridley was born in London's East End and still lives there and the atmosphere of this most urban of settings is a strong influence on his work. He also has great flair in the use of words which may also belong to part of his urban background.

The urban setting is paramount from his first books for children. *Mercedes Ice* is a modern folk tale told across several generations. The dominant feature in the book is a huge tower block of flats which is being built at the beginning and which is the setting for much of the rest of the book, where it remains huge and monolithic and gradually disintegrating, just as so many tower blocks did which were seen as the dawn of a new housing era in the post-World War II period. Rosie Glow's ambition is to live at the very top of this block of flats despite the fact that its building has claimed the life of one of the builders who has befriended her. She gets her wish but becomes so grossly fat that she is not able to leave the disintegrating building. Her son, Mercedes Ice, is overindulged by his mother and in turn dominated by the building until he accidentally helps to bring about its destruction. Similarly in *Dakota of the White Flats* the urban landscape plays an important part. A jewelled turtle is stolen from a Miss Haversham type character and Dakota and her friend set out to find it. To get to the broken glass fortress where the turtle is being kept, however, they have to navigate a polluted canal filled with mutant eels.

The main child characters in these books are strong ones but the hero of *Krindlekrax,* Ridley's next book, is initially a bullied loner. Nine-year-old Ruskin's only real friend is the school caretaker, Corky, whose death provides the hero with the impetus to seek out Krindlekrax, the overgrown crocodile who lives in the sewers. Ruskin's new found confidence enables him to stand up to Elvis, the school bully, and to achieve his ultimate aim of starring in the school play. *Krindlekrax* is notable also for its strong array of adult characters who populate the street where Ruskin lives and who each have their own catchphrases or quirks. The book builds a strong picture of community.

Adult characters also figure prominently in *Meteorite Spoon.* Ridley has often been compared to Roald Dahl and this is probably his most Dahlesque work. Two children, Filly and Fergal, live with their continually arguing parents, appropriately called Mr. and Mrs. Thunder. Each member of the couple is constantly irritated by the actions of the other, an action graphically demonstrated by Ridley's prose and also by the striking illustrations of Chris Riddell, who began a strong partnership with the writer with this book. The two children are transported by the use of the magical meteorite spoon to a fantasy island where they encounter Mr. and Mrs. Love, who they assume to be their parents earlier in their lives. An erupting volcano helps them to get home where their newly subdued parents greet them with glee. *Meteorite Spoon* demonstrates Ridley's love of words and of different ways of expressing emotions. His sentences, sometime deliberately short, sometimes long and complex, help to almost paint the page as they snake in and out among Riddell's striking illustrations.

Ridley's more recent books have used his familiar devices—a strong and varied collection of characters and his delight in the use of language—but because of their length they sometimes attempt too vast a canvas and can become tedious in their use of repetition. *Kasper in the Glitter* tells of another journey. Kasper lives on the edge of a large city, which he has not been allowed to visit, with his mother, the resplendently beautiful Pumpkin. When a stranger from the city steals Pumpkin's brooch, Kasper sets off through the unknown dangers of the city where he encounters the exciting but dangerous world of King Streetwise. Despite the fact that Kasper and Pumpkin eventually defeat Streetwise there is still the threat that the king will eventually carry out his plan to control all the children in the world. *Scribbleboy* uses graffiti as a main theme. A mysterious stranger is decorating the walls of buildings in the same way that they were decorated years ago by a creature called Scribbleboy. The identity of the modern day Scribbleboy and his predecessor are established by the end of the book. In the meantime the reader is introduced to a galaxy of characters including the wheelchair bound Ziggy Fuzz.

Ridley's books leave a huge impression on any reader. They are big and bold, with fantastic settings and characters. The dialogue plays around with language in a highly distinctive way. Their settings will be familiar to many city children: sprawling urban landscapes full of the dangers and excitements of town life. Ridley has achieved a great deal in the relatively small number of titles he has produced for children. To judge from his most recent work, however, he needs to take care in keeping his many themes and characters in check. A successor to Dahl? Only time will tell.

—Keith Barker

RIEU, E(mile) V(ictor)

Nationality: British. **Born:** London, 10 February 1887. **Education:** St. Paul's School, London; Balliol College, Oxford, 1906-08. **Military Service:** 105th Mahratta Light Infantry, 1918: 2nd lieutenant; served in the Home Guard, 1943: major. **Family:** Married Nelly Lewis in 1914; two sons and two daughters. **Career:** Manager, Oxford University Press, Bombay, 1912-19; educational manager, 1923-33, managing director, 1933-36, and adviser from 1936, Methuen, publishers, London; editor, Penguin Classics series, 1944-64. **Member:** Committee for New Translation of the Bible, from 1951. **Awards:** Royal Society of Literature Benson medal, 1968. D. Litt.: University of Leeds, 1949. Fellow, Royal Society of Literature (vice-president, 1958). C.B.E. (Commander, Order of the British Empire), 1953. **Died:** 11 May 1972.

Publications for Children

Poetry

Cuckoo Calling: A Book of Verse for Youthful People, illustrated by Violet M. Guy. London, Methuen, 1933.

A Puffin Quartet of Poets, with others, edited by Eleanor Graham, illustrated by Diana Bloomfield. London, Penguin, 1958.

The Flattered Flying Fish and Other Poems, illustrated by Ernest Shepard. London, Methuen, and New York, Dutton, 1962.

Publications for Adults

Poetry

The Tryst and Other Poems. London, Oxford University Press, 1917.

Other

The Logic of Christian Faith. Goring, Berkshire, Layman, 1954.

Editor, with H.C. Bradley, *Letters de mon Moulin,* by Alphonse Daudet. London, Oxford University Press, 1912.

Editor, *The Prisoner of Zenda* (abridgement), by Anthony Hope. London, Frowde, 1915.

Editor, *A Book of Latin Poetry, from Ennius to Hadrian.* London, Methuen, 1925; 4th edition, New York, St. Martin's Press, 1953.

Editor, *Essays* [*More Essays*] *by Modern Masters.* London, Methuen, 2 vols., 1926-34.

Editor, with Peter Wait, *Modern Masters of Wit and Laughter.* London, Methuen, 1938.

Translator, *The Odyssey,* by Homer. London, Penguin, 1946.

Translator, *The Pastoral Poems,* by Virgil. London, Penguin, 1949.

Translator, *The Iliad,* by Homer. London, Penguin, 1950.

Translator, *The Four Gospels.* London, Penguin, 1952.

Translator, *The Voyage of Argo,* by Apollonius of Rhodes. London, Penguin, 1959.

Translator, *The Word: A Synthesis of the Four Gospels.* London, Faith Press, 1965.

* * *

Before 1958 E.V. Rieu was known to the general public, if at all, as the editor of Penguin Classics and as the highly successful and idiosyncratic translator of Homer and Virgil. A very intelligent and humorous writer with a flexible turn of mind, one might have thought, but one who was essentially "adult." His book of verse *Cuckoo Calling* (1933) should have corrected this picture, but this book made little impact on readers. In 1958 Eleanor Graham included Rieu as one of her *Puffin Quartet of Poets.* She knew him professionally through her connections with Penguin Books and with Methuen (Rieu had been at one time managing director of the latter), and had been privileged to penetrate the facade of the business man and academic to the very private person who wrote verses for his own satisfaction. The *Quartet* set him in the company of his peers, his older contemporary Eleanor Farjeon and the much younger Reeves and Serraillier. Since then his poems have appeared from time to time in anthologies, but he has remained a secret, enigmatic figure.

The 29 poems selected by Eleanor Graham give an accurate impression of the range and quality of Rieu's work. He may play with fantastic ideas, but he is not a maker of fantasy worlds. For him the real world is fantasy enough, and his favourite method is to take an ordinary situation, turn it this way and that, upside-down if need be, and find in it some paradox or absurdity which will illuminate its ordinariness. Even the rhymes about such exotic creatures as flying-fish and hippopotami are gentle reflexions on human weaknesses. Mostly the objective is fun, but not the robust loud laugh, rather the inward glow that comes from a point suddenly taken or a truth revealed. He is a master of tenderness too, with sympathy wide enough to embrace the widowed mouse and the insomniac tortoise as well as the more obviously appealing domestic tabby. There is anguish in "The Lost Cat" and an elegiac resignation in "Cat's Funeral." All his verse is strongly formal. He is a craftsman who loves to polish and prune. So successfully does he cut out the inessential that some of his lapidary verses are briefer than their titles!

Rieu came nearest to giving away his secret in a most self-revealing poem called "The Paint Box." The poet urges the painter to paint "somebody utterly new." The dialogue continues:

> "I have painted the cook and a camel in blue
> And a panther in purple." "You painted them true.
>
> Now mix me a colour that nobody knows,
> And paint me a country where nobody goes.
> And put in it people a little like you,
> Watching a unicorn drinking the dew."

—Marcus Crouch

RINGGOLD, Faith

Nationality: American. **Born:** 8 October 1930, New York City. **Family:** Married 1) Robert Earl Wallace in 1950 (divorced 1956), two daughters; 2) Burdette Ringgold in 1962. **Education:** City College of the City University of New York, B.S. 1955, M.A. 1959. **Career:** Painter, mixed media sculptor, performance artist, and writer. Art teacher in public schools, New York City, 1955-73; professor of art, University of California, San Diego, since 1984. In 1960s, after trip to Europe, completed first political paintings and held first one-person show. In 1972, began making paintings framed in cloth (called tankas), soft sculptures, costumes, and masks, later using these media in masked performances of the early and mid 1970s. In 1980, produced first painted quilt and in 1983, created first story quilt. Visiting lecturer, performer, and artist at art centers, universities, and museums, including Mills College, 1987, Museum of Modern Art, 1988, University of West Florida, 1989, San Diego Museum, 1990, Museum of African American Art, 1991, and Atlantic Center for the Arts, 1992. Artwork has been nationally exhibited in museums and galleries throughout the world, including Boston Museum of Fine Art, Chase Manhattan Bank Collection, Clark Museum, Guggenheim Museum, High Museum, Metropolitan Museum of Art, Museum of Modern Art, Newark Museum, Phillip Morris Collection, and Studio Museum in Harlem. "Faith Ringgold: A 25 Year Survey," a nationally touring retrospective exhibition, curated by the Fine Arts Museum of Long Island, 1990-93. **Awards:** Coretta Scott King Award, illustrator, 1992; Caldecott honor award, 1992; Jane Addams Children's Book award, picture book, 1992. **Agent:** Marie Brown Associates, Room 902, 625 Broadway, New York, New York 10012, U.S.A.

Publications for Children

Fiction (illustrated by the author)

Tar Beach. New York, Crown, 1991.
Aunt Harriet's Underground Railroad in the Sky. New York, Crown, 1993.
Dinner at Aunt Connie's House. New York, Crown, 1994.
My Dream of Martin Luther King. New York, Crown, 1995.
Bonjour, Lonnie. New York, Hyperion, 1996.

Publications for Adults

Other

Faith Ringgold: A 25 Year Survey (catalog). Fine Arts Museum of Long Island, 1990.
We Flew Over the Bridge: The Memoirs of Faith Ringgold. Boston, Little Brown, 1995.
Talking to Faith Ringgold, with Linda Freeman and Nancy Roucher. New York, Crown, 1996.

*

Biography: Entry in *Contemporary Black Biography,* Detroit, Gale, Vol. 4, 1993; *Faith Ringgold* by Robyn Montana Turner, Boston, Little, Brown, 1993.

Critical Studies: Entry in *Contemporary Authors,* Detroit, Gale, Vol. 54, 1997; entry in *Authors & Artists for Young Adults,* Detroit, Gale, Vol. 19, 1997.

* * *

Few artists combine painting, quiltmaking, and storytelling to create their works of art. When such an artist then adapts her work to create picture books for children, the result is both visually arresting and thematically nuanced. Faith Ringgold's books in this genre, *Tar Beach* and *Dinner at Aunt Connie's House,* together with *Aunt Harriet's Underground Railroad in the Sky,* an original work for children, draw upon family tradition, autobiography, and history to portray inspiring African-American heroines, both real and imagined.

Ringgold's first book, *Tar Beach,* is adapted from a quilt painting—in this case, one of five in her *Woman on a Bridge* series. The original quilt involves a central scene painted on unstretched canvas and framed by quilted strips as well as fabric strips of printed text. The words in the book differ only slightly from those on the quilt. It is the story these words tell that inspired Ringgold's illustrations for *Tar Beach,* and the quilt's central scene serves as the cover for the book.

The protagonist and narrator of *Tar Beach* is eight-year-old Cassie Louise Lightfoot. Cassie tells the reader that she can fly, and by flying over something, it is hers forever. Chief among the possessions she has acquired this way is the George Washington Bridge, on which her father worked and which was completed the day she was born in 1931. The bridge can also be seen from Tar Beach, the real yet magical rooftop of the building in which Cassie lives with baby brother Be Be, her parents, and their neighbors Mr. and Mrs. Honey. They all climb up there at night to share a meal, and while the adults socialize, Cassie plans to fly over more objects, not for personal gain, but to acquire them for her father, who is not allowed to join the union because he is "colored" and a "half-breed Indian." Then he will not have to leave the family to look for work in the winter.

A long note included at the end of the book stresses that *Tar Beach* is a work of the imagination, a "transformation of Ringgold's memories of childhood." Ringgold combines hot summer nights spent on the roof of her building in Harlem; the African-American folk motif of flying to freedom; and the historical fact of the exclusion of minorities from unions to present a young girl who can fulfill her own dreams as well as those of her family.

Aunt Harriet's Underground Railroad in the Sky also makes extensive use of the motif of flying to freedom. Baby brother Be Be, who appears as a bit player in *Tar Beach,* is central to the action in this story. While out flying with Cassie, Be Be jumps aboard a "ramshackled" train that moves off before Cassie can grab him or climb aboard herself. A very frightened Cassie is calmed and instructed by the whispers in her ear from the woman conductor, Harriet Tubman, who is called Aunt Harriet by the people whom she helps. Referring to Tubman as "Aunt" underscores the ties Cassie, a twentieth-century child, will discover with enslaved African-Americans who made the arduous journey to freedom on the Underground Railroad—which in Ringgold's treatment becomes a literal railroad. Always one stop behind Be Be's train, Cassie experiences the same perils facing her brother and his fellow passengers as they elude slave catchers and bounty hunters.

Cassie is eventually reunited with Be Be in Canada, but not before she is transported in a coffin to Niagara Falls. This last stage of the trek reflects not only the stratagems escaping slaves had to employ, but it signals, too, their approaching rebirth as free persons, as does the survival of Baby Freedom, a little girl born during the journey who makes the trip tied to Be Be's back. Also present are Aunt Harriet, an angel-like women dressed in white, and the other passengers on the Underground Railroad. What Cassie and Be Be have experienced is a centenary re-creation and celebration of Harriet Tubman's first successful flight on the Underground Railroad, and what they have learned is the importance of freedom and their great-great-grandparents' struggle to achieve it.

Dinner at Aunt Connie's House, Ringgold's third book for young readers, is dedicated to "all the risk takers and great women in history." It, too, celebrates Harriet Tubman, but this time as one of 12 African-American women whose achievements are featured. Once again, a spirited young girl narrates the story. Melody is joined in her adventures by cousin Lonnie. His mother, Aunt Connie, is an artist who invites the extended family to a special dinner and showing of her artwork every summer. While playing hide and seek, Melody and Lonnie discover Aunt Connie's paintings before they have been brought out for viewing. Each painting is of an African-American woman whose painted image literally speaks to the two children about her accomplishments. After listening to the paintings, Melody is determined to become President of the United States, and Lonnie decides to be a famous opera singer. The children also resolve to marry each other; in Ringgold's feminist and egalitarian vision, Lonnie's admiration of great women extends to his choice of spouse as well.

Lonnie reappears in *Bonjour, Lonnie,* which tackles problems challenging to younger readers—not just the pronunciation of French words, but a closer look at a favorite Ringgold theme, the biracial experience. As in her earlier book about Harriet Tubman, with *My Dream of Martin Luther King* Ringgold creates a tale involving a Civil Rights leader and some rather surreal twists of space and time. Hence a living King is seen standing hand in hand with two boys, one black and one white, in front of a school named for him—something that didn't exist until after he was dead. Critics suggested that the King book did not work as well as the Tubman piece, because Ringgold tried to cover too many difficult subjects at once. Perhaps Ringgold's error was an excess of authorial ambition, hardly a fatal flaw.

A composite view of Ringgold's picture books suggests that Aunt Connie is a particularly appropriate alter ego for the artist herself. Like Aunt Connie, Ringgold has created lively female characters who are proud of their rich heritage as African-Americans and are determined to make their dreams come true.

—Janice M. Alberghene, updated by Judson Knight

ROBERTS, (Sir) Charles G(eorge) D(ouglas)

Nationality: Canadian. **Born:** Douglas, New Brunswick, 10 January 1860. **Education:** Collegiate School, Fredericton, New Brunswick, 1874-76; University of New Brunswick, Fredericton (Douglas medal in Latin and Greek; Alumni Gold medal for Latin Essay), 1876-81, B.A. (honours) in mental and moral science and political economy 1879, M.A. 1881. **Military Service:** British Army, 1914-15: captain; transferred to the Canadian Army, 1916: major; subsequently worked with Lord Beaverbrook in the Canadian War Records Office, London. **Family:** Married 1) Mary Isabel Fenety in 1880 (died 1930), three sons and one daughter; 2) Joan Montgomery in 1943. **Career:** Headmaster, Chatham Grammar School, New Brunswick, 1879-81, and York Street School, Fredericton, 1881-83; editor, *This Week,* Toronto, 1883-84; Professor of English and French, 1885-88, and Professor of English and Economics, 1888-95, King's College, Windsor, Nova Scotia; associate editor, *Illustrated American,* New York, 1897-98; co-editor, Nineteenth Century series, 1900-05; lived in England, 1911-25. **Awards:** Lorne Pierce medal, 1926. LL.D.: University of New Brunswick, 1906. Fellow, 1890, and president of Section 2, 1933, Royal Society of Canada; fellow, Royal Society of Literature, 1892; member, American Academy, 1898. Knighted, 1935. **Died:** 26 November 1943.

PUBLICATIONS FOR CHILDREN

Fiction

The Raid from Beauséjour, and How the Carter Boys Lifted the Mortgage: Two Stories of Acadie. New York, Hunt and Eaton, 1894; *The Raid from Beauséjour* published as *The Young Acadian,* Boston, Page, 1907.

Reube Dare's Shad Boat: A Tale of the Tide Country. New York, Hunt and Eaton, 1895; as *The Cruise of the Yacht "Dido": A Tale of the Tide Country,* Boston, Page, 1906.

Around the Campfire, illustrated by Charles Copeland. New York, Crowell, 1896; London, Harrap, 1906.

Earth's Enigmas: A Book of Animal and Nature Life, illustrated by Charles Livingston Bull. Boston, Lamson Wolffe, 1896; revised edition, Boston, Page, 1903; London, Duckworth, 1904.

The Kindred of the Wild: A Book of Animal Life, illustrated by Charles Livingston Bull. Boston, Page, 1902; London, Duckworth, 1903.

The Watchers of the Trails: A Book of Animal Life, illustrated by Charles Livingston Bull. Boston, Page, and London, Duckworth, 1904.
Red Fox: The Story of His Adventurous Career in the Ringwaak Wilds, and of His Final Triumph over the Enemies of His Kind, illustrated by Charles Livingston Bull. Boston, Page, and London, Duckworth, 1905.
The Haunters of the Silences: A Book of Animal Life, illustrated by Charles Livingston Bull. Boston, Page, and London, Duckworth, 1907.
In the Deep of the Snow, illustrated by Denman Fink. New York, Crowell, 1907.
The House in the Water: A Book of Animal Life, illustrated by Charles Livingston Bull and Frank Vining Smith. Boston, Page, 1908; London, Ward Lock, 1909.
The Backwoodsmen. New York, Macmillan, and London, Ward Lock, 1909.
Kings in Exile, illustrated by Paul Bransom and Charles Livingston Bull. London, Ward Lock, 1909; New York, Macmillan, 1910.
Neighbours Unknown, illustrated by Paul Bransom. London, Ward Lock, 1910; New York, Macmillan, 1911.
More Kindred of the Wild, illustrated by Paul Bransom. London, Ward Lock, and New York, Macmillan, 1911.
Babes of the Wild, illustrated by Warwick Reynolds. London and New York, Cassell, 1912; as *Children of the Wild,* New York, Macmillan, 1913.
The Feet of the Furtive, illustrated by Paul Bransom. London, Ward Lock, 1912; New York, Macmillan, 1913.
Hoof and Claw, illustrated by Paul Bransom. London, Ward Lock, 1913; New York, Macmillan, 1914.
The Secret Trails, illustrated by Paul Bransom and Warwick Reynolds. New York, Macmillan, and London, Ward Lock, 1916.
The Ledge on Bald Face, illustrated by Paul Bransom. London, Ward Lock, 1918; as *Jim: The Story of a Backwoods Police Dog,* New York, Macmillan, 1919.
Wisdom of the Wilderness. London, Dent, and New York, Dutton, 1922.
They Who Walk in the Wild, illustrated by Charles Livingston Bull. New York, Macmillan, 1924; as *They That Walk in the Wild,* London, Dent, 1924.
Eyes of the Wilderness, illustrated by Dorothy Burroughes. New York, Macmillan, and London, Dent, 1933.
Further Animal Stories. London, Dent, 1935.
Thirteen Bears, edited by Ethel Hume Bennett, illustrated by John A. Hall. Toronto, Ryerson Press, 1947.
Forest Folk, edited by Ethel Hume Bennett, illustrated by John A. Hall. Toronto, Ryerson Press, 1949.
King of Beasts and Other Stories, edited by Joseph Gold. Toronto, Ryerson Press, 1967.
Eyes of the Wilderness and Other Stories: A New Collection, illustrated by Brian Carter. London, Dent, 1980.
The Lure of the Wild: The Last Three Animal Stories, edited by John C. Adams. Ottawa, Borealis, 1980.

Other

A History of Canada for High Schools and Academies. Boston, Lamson Wolffe, 1897; London, Kegan Paul, 1898.

Publications for Adults

Fiction

The Forge in the Forest, Being the Narrative of the Acadian Ranger, Jean de Mer. Boston, Lamson Wolffe, 1896.
A Sister to Evangeline, Being the Story of Yvonne de Lamourie. Boston, Lamson Wolffe, 1898; London, Lane, 1900; as *Lovers in Acadie,* London, Dent, 1924.
The Heart of the Ancient Wood. New York, Silver Burdett, 1900; London, Methuen, 1902.
Barbara Ladd. Boston, Page, and London, Constable, 1902.
The Prisoner of Mademoiselle: A Love Story. Boston, Page, and London, Constable 1904.
The Heart That Knows. Boston, Page, and London, Duckworth, 1906.
A Balkan Prince. London, Everett, 1913.

Short Stories

By the Marshes of Minas. New York, Silver Burdett, 1900.
The Red Oxen of Bonval. New York, Dodd Mead, 1908.
Cock Crow. New York, Federal Printers, 1913.
In the Morning of Time. London, Hutchinson, and New York, Stokes, 1919.
The Last Barrier and Other Stories. Toronto, McClelland and Stewart, 1958.

Poetry

Orion and Other Poems. Philadelphia, Lippincott, 1880.
Later Poems. Privately printed, 1881.
Later Poems. Fredericton, Crockett, 1882.
In Divers Tones. Boston, Lothrop, 1886.
Autotochthon. Privately printed, 1889.
Ave: An Ode for the Centenary of the Birth of Percy Bysshe Shelley, 4th August, 1792. Toronto, Williamson, 1892.
Songs of the Common Day, and Ave: An Ode for the Shelley Centenary. London, Longman, 1893.
The Book of the Native. Toronto, Copp Clark, and Boston, Lamson Wolffe, 1896.
New York Nocturnes and Other Poems. Boston, Lamson Wolffe, 1898.
Poems. New York, Silver Burdett, 1901; London, Constable, 1903.
The Book of the Rose. Boston, Page, 1903; London, R. Brimley Johnson, 1904.
Poems. Boston, Page, 1907.
New Poems. London, Constable, 1919.
The Sweet o' the Year and Other Poems. Toronto, Ryerson Press, 1925.
The Vagrant of Time. Toronto, Ryerson Press, 1927; revised edition, 1927.
Be Quiet Wind; Unsaid. Privately printed, 1929.
The Iceberg and Other Poems. Toronto, Ryerson Press, 1934.
Selected Poems. Toronto, Ryerson Press, 1936.
Twilight over Shaugamauk and Three Other Poems. Toronto, Ryerson Press, 1937.
Canada Speaks of Britain and Other Poems of the War. Toronto, Ryerson Press, 1941.
Selected Poems, edited by Desmond Pacey. Toronto, Ryerson Press, 1956.

Poets of the Confederation, with others, edited by Malcolm Mackenzie Ross. Toronto, McClelland and Stewart, 1960.
The Collected Poems of Charles G.D. Roberts, edited by Desmond Pacey and Graham Adams. Wolfville, Nova Scotia, Wombat Press, 1985.

Other

The Canadian Guide-Book: The Tourist's and Sportsman's Guide to Eastern Canada and Newfoundland. New York, Appleton, 1891; London, Heinemann, 1892.
The Land of Evangeline and the Gateways Thither...for Sportsman and Tourist. Kentville, Nova Scotia, Dominion Atlantic Railway Company, 1894.
Discoveries and Explorations in the Century (nineteenth century series). London, Chambers, 1903; Philadelphia, Linscott, 1904.
Canada in Flanders, vol. 3. London, Hodder and Stoughton, 1918.
Selected Poetry and Critical Prose, edited by W.J. Keith. Toronto, University of Toronto Press, 1974.

Editor, *Poems of Wild Life.* London, Scott, 1888.
Editor, *Northland Lyrics,* by William Carman Roberts, Theodore Roberts, and Elizabeth Roberts Macdonald. Boston, Small Maynard, 1899.
Editor, *Shelley's Adonais and Alastor.* Boston, Silver Burdett, 1902.
Editor, with Arthur L. Tunnell, *A Standard Dictionary of Canadian Biography: The Canadian Who Was Who.* Toronto, Trans-Canada Press, 2 vols., 1934-38.
Editor, with Arthur L. Tunnell, *The Canadian Who's Who,* vols. II and III. Toronto, Trans-Canada Press, 1936-39.
Editor, *Flying Colours: An Anthology.* Toronto, Ryerson Press, 1942.

Translator, *The Canadians of Old,* by Philippe Aubert de Gaspé. New York, Appleton, 1890; as *Cameron of Lochiel,* Boston, Page, 1905.

*

Critical Studies: *Sir Charles G.D. Roberts: A Biography* by Elsie M. Pomeroy, Toronto, Ryerson Press, 1943; *Charles G.D. Roberts* by W.J. Keith, Toronto, Copp Clark, 1969; *The Proceedings of the Charles G.D. Roberts Symposium,* Sackville, New Brunswick, Mount Allison University, 1984; *Sir Charles God Damn: The Life of Charles G.D. Roberts* by John Coldwell Adams, Toronto, University of Toronto Press, 1986.

* * *

Charles G.D. Roberts, one of the first three Canadians to be knighted (1935), probably received that honor because he was well known as a poet, possibly even deserving the title "father of Canadian poetry." In *Ten Canadian Poets* Desmond Pacey analyzes the achievement of Roberts solely as a poet, critically and with skill. But he makes no more than a passing note of what to me and to thousands of Roberts's readers at the end of the old century and the first of this was inescapable: Roberts stood head and shoulders above his few North American contemporaries, such as Ernest Thompson Seton, as a nature writer who made the wild animals, birds, fish, and even dragonflies of back-woods New Brunswick come alive on the printed page. He despised any anthropomorphic approach: fox was fox, lynx lynx, porcupine porcupine, bear bear, eagle eagle, grouse grouse, owl owl, a wise old trout a wise old trout. No nicknames; no concealing of nature's cruelty, the disaster of sub-zero weather or forest fire. He wrote the prose of a poet: color in his words, economy in style, drama in his action, rhythm in the wilderness life of hunter and hunted. Beyond all this, what set Roberts's stories apart was his unwavering respect for the dignity of life—the dignity of death—among these creatures of the wild.

Of his dozen books which gathered these stories together five or six stand out: *Red Fox* (a novel), *The Kindred of the Wild, The Watchers of the Trails, The Haunters of the Silences, The Feet of the Furtive, Kings in Exile.* The masterpiece is *Red Fox,* surely the one wild animal story in English to stand beside Henry Williamson's *Tarka the Otter* (the gem of them all) and Jack London's *The Call of the Wild.* But there is a purity about *Red Fox,* a spareness, a kind of breathlessness, isolation from human creatures, which it alone possesses. Are these books for children? They are for all ages, just as much as *The Wind in the Willows, The Jungle Books,* Hudson's *Far Away and Long Ago,* Sally Carrighar's *One Day on Beetle Rock,* H.M. Tomlinson's *The Brown Owl.*

Roberts was fortunate in his two illustrators: Charles Livingston Bull and Paul Bransom, and fortunate in his typographers too. The original books were (and remain) works of art to look at, a delight to handle. Could any child who has never paddled a canoe, camped in the wilderness, worn snowshoes, seen a raccoon fishing in a stream, or watched a dragonfly emerge from her private cellophane on a rock in the sun by a river fail to be enchanted by one of these books alone? I doubt it.

Let me close by saying that three years on my uncle's ranch in the old frontier by the wild Rogue River in Oregon when I was 12 to 15 gave me a chance to verify some of the things I had read about earlier in *Red Fox* and the other books. Two short stories in *The Watchers of the Trails,* "The Little Wolf of the Pool" (about the larva of the dragonfly) and "The Little Wolf of the Air" (about the dragonfly itself), have a timeless pure magic in their fascination for young readers; they bring the wilderness to one's back door. They have the very look of everlastingness.

Years later, when I began to write poems for children I, too, was fortunate in my illustrator. For the naturalist-artist Henry B. Kane had read Roberts when *he* was a boy. *Red Fox* had made me wish to try to become a writer. The illustrations by Charles Livingston Bull had made Kane wish to become an artist.

—David McCord

ROBERTS, Elizabeth Madox

Nationality: American. **Born:** Perryville, Kentucky, 30 October 1881. **Education:** Covington Institute, Springfield, Kentucky; Covington High School, Kentucky, 1896-1900; attended State College of Kentucky (now University of Kentucky), Lexington, 1900-01, 1916; University of Chicago (McLaughlin prize; Fiske prize, 1921), 1917-21, Ph.B. in English, 1921 (Phi Beta Kappa). **Career:** Private tutor and teacher in public schools, Springfield, 1901-10. **Awards:** O. Henry award, 1930. L.H.D.: Russell Sage College, Troy, New York, 1933. **Member:** American Academy, 1940. **Died:** 13 March 1941.

Publications for Children

Poetry

Under the Tree. New York, Huebsch, 1922; London, Cape, 1928; revised edition, New York, Viking Press, 1930.

Publications for Adults

Novels

The Time of Man. New York, Viking Press, 1926; London, Cape, 1927.

My Heart and My Flesh. New York, Viking Press, 1927; London, Cape, 1928.

Jingling in the Wind. New York, Viking Press, 1928; London, Cape, 1929.

The Great Meadow. New York, Viking Press, and London, Cape, 1930.

A Buried Treasure. New York, Viking Press, 1931; London, Cape, 1932.

He Sent Forth a Raven. New York, Viking Press, and London, Cape, 1935.

Black Is My Truelove's Hair. New York, Viking Press, 1938; London, Hale, 1939.

Short Stories

The Haunted Mirror. New York, Viking Press, 1932; London, Cape, 1933.

Not by Strange Gods. New York, Viking Press, 1941.

Poetry

In the Great Steep's Garden. Colorado Springs, Gowdy Simmons, 1915.

Song in the Meadow. New York, Viking Press, 1940.

*

Manuscript Collection: Library of Congress, Washington, D.C.

Critical Studies: *Elizabeth Madox Roberts: A Personal Note* by Glenway Wescott, New York, Viking Press, 1930; *Elizabeth Madox Roberts: An Appraisal* by J. Donald Adams and others, New York, Viking Press, 1938; *Elizabeth Madox Roberts, American Novelist* by Harry Modean Campbell and Ruel E. Foster, Norman, University of Oklahoma Press, 1956; *Herald to Chaos: The Novels of Elizabeth Madox Roberts* by Earl Rovit, Lexington, University Press of Kentucky, 1960; *Elizabeth Madox Roberts* by Frederick P.W. McDowell, New York, Twayne, 1963 (includes bibliography).

* * *

Elizabeth Madox Roberts, Kentucky-born novelist and poet who died in 1941, is best remembered for two of her several distinguished novels: *The Time of Man* (1926) and *The Great Meadow* (1930). In 1940 she published an uneven book of poems called *Song in the Meadow.* But way back in 1922 she had already produced her one undoubted masterpiece: a gentle, quiet book of verse for children, called very gently and quietly *Under the Tree.* It was revised and reissued in 1930 with enchanting illustrations by F.D. Bedford. Any discussion of her merit as a writer for children centers entirely on this collection, even though three or four of the poems included in the early part of *Song in the Meadow* sound like worthy echoes from the 1922 volume. And very clear as well as worthy echoes too.

So what does one say of this undiminished book, until recently still in print in hard cover? For Roberts, without question, remains absolutely unique in the field of verse for children. To me she is the only poet, man or woman, writing in the English language who possessed and consistently used the undisguised, uninterrupted voice of childhood. Excepting Emily Dickinson, not Blake, nor Lear, Carroll, Stevenson, Eugene Field, Christina Rossetti, Laura E. Richards, Eleanor Farjeon, Milne, Eve Merriam, Norma Farber, Marchette Chute, Aileen Fisher, Myra Cohn Livingston, Reeves, or Serraillier—no one who wrote or writes poems for children commanded or commands, as she did, not only the vocabulary but the attitude and voice-inflection of a small girl lost in wonder:

A little light is going by,
Is going up to see the sky,
A little light with wings.

I never could have thought of it,
To have a little bug all lit
And made to go on wings.

She was born to notice things and actions. The world implied, and she was already to infer. When her small brother Clarence begins his country school days, what does she do?

We climb up on the fence and gate
And watch until he's small and dim,
Far up the street, and he looks back
To see if we keep on watching him.

The average post-Georgian poet, I think, would have said, "To see if we keep watching him," omitting the "on." But not a child; not Roberts; not a poet of her special genius. Could the Greek and Latin poets with their gifts for onomatopoeia manage to describe the unexisting *sound* of a silent vanishing dirt Kentucky road as she does here?

The road was going on and on
Beyond to reach some other place....

Or look back into all the brook poetry you can think of, including Tennyson and Robert Frost, and try to match the flawless order of these first three lines of the fourth and last stanza of "The Branch," so settled in their utter calm that in the fourth line not one syllable and certainly not the magic of the perfect adjective "rough" will escape you:

And where it is smooth there is moss on a stone,
And where it is shallow and almost dry
The rocks are broken and hot in the sun,
And a rough little water goes hurrying by.

Two other things. In the total assembly of poems about Christmas, save for Thomas Hardy's "The Oxen," I can think of none to equal Roberts's "Christmas Morning"—her wondrous imaginary visit to Bethlehem. Length forbids quoting all 10 stanzas. Here is the last one:

While Mary put the blankets back
The gentle talk would soon begin.
And when I'd tiptoe softly out
I'd meet the wise men going in.

Twice in the course of the 59 poems in *Under the Tree* there appears a certain small boy named with a certain not-quite-hidden tone of secret admiration. He's not called Tiny Tim or Huckleberry Finn or Christopher Robin. He has the far more romantic handle of Joe B. Kirk. Through many rereadings of this book I have often wondered about him: did he live to grow up? and what has he done with his life? His one big moment in the poems is in (or at) "The Picnic" when Miss Kate-Marie, the Sunday school teacher, kisses all the children. How marvellous, how real, how visible is Joe B. Kirk's reaction:

She kissed us all and Joe B. Kirk;
But Joe B. didn't mind a bit.
He walked around and swung his arms
And seemed to be very glad of it.

Among my personal desert island books I include a copy of *Under the Tree* to go with *The Wind in the Willows.*

—David McCord

ROBERTSON, Keith (Carlton)

Pseudonym: Carlton Keith. **Nationality:** American. **Born:** Dows, Iowa, 9 May 1914. **Education:** United States Naval Academy, Annapolis, Maryland, B.S. 1937. **Military Service:** United States Navy: radioman on a battleship, 1930-33; officer, on destroyers, 1941-45; Captain, United States Naval Reserve. **Family:** Married Elisabeth Hexter in 1946; two daughters and one son. **Career:** Refrigeration engineer, 1937-41; worked for a publisher, 1945-47; free-lance writer, 1947-58 and since 1968. Lives in Hopewell, New Jersey. **Died:** 23 September 1991.

Publications for Children

Fiction

Ticktock and Jim, illustrated by Wesley Dennis. Philadelphia, Winston, 1948; as *Watch for a Pony,* London, Heinemann, 1949.
Ticktock and Jim, Deputy Sheriffs, illustrated by Everett Stahl. Philadelphia, Winston, 1949.
The Dog Next Door, illustrated by Morgan Dennis. New York, Viking Press, 1950.
The Missing Brother, illustrated by Rafaello Busoni. New York, Viking Press, 1950; London, Faber, 1952.
The Lonesome Sorrel, illustrated by Taylor Oughton. Philadelphia, Winston, 1952.
The Mystery of Burnt Hill, illustrated by Rafaello Busoni. New York, Viking Press, 1952.
Mascot of the Melroy, illustrated by Jack Weaver. New York, Viking Press, 1953.
Outlaws of the Sourland, illustrated by Isami Kashiwagi. New York, Viking Press, 1953.
Three Stuffed Owls, illustrated by Jack Weaver. New York, Viking Press, 1954.
Ice to India, illustrated by Jack Weaver. New York, Viking Press, 1955.
The Phantom Rider, illustrated by Jack Weaver. New York, Viking Press, 1955.
The Pilgrim Goose, illustrated by Erick Berry. New York, Viking Press, 1956.
The Pinto Deer, illustrated by Isami Kashiwagi. New York, Viking Press, 1956.
The Crow and the Castle, illustrated by Robert Grenier. New York, Viking Press, 1957.
Henry Reed Inc., illustrated by Robert McCloskey. New York, Viking Press, 1958.
If Wishes Were Horses, illustrated by Paul Kennedy. New York, Harper, 1958.
Henry Reed's Journey [*Baby-Sitting Service, Big Show*], illustrated by Robert McCloskey. New York, Viking Press, 3 vols., 1963-70.
The Year of the Jeep, illustrated by W.T. Mars. New York, Viking Press, 1968.
The Money Machine, illustrated by George Porter. New York, Viking Press, 1969.
In Search of a Sandhill Crane, illustrated by Richard Cuffari. New York, Viking Press, 1973.
Tales of Myrtle the Turtle, illustrated by Peter Parnall. New York, Viking Press, 1974.
Henry Reed's Think Tank. New York, Viking Kestrel, 1986.

Other

The Wreck of the Saginaw, illustrated by Jack Weaver. New York, Viking Press, 1954.
The Navy: From Civilian to Sailor, illustrated by Charles Geer. New York, Viking Press, 1958.
New Jersey. New York, Coward McCann, 1969.

Publications for Adults as Carlton Keith

Novels

The Diamond-Studded Typewriter. New York, Macmillan, 1958; London, Heinemann, 1960; as *A Gem of a Murder,* New York, Dell, 1959.
Missing, Presumed Dead. New York, Doubleday, 1961.
Rich Uncle. New York, Doubleday, 1963; London, Hale, 1965.
The Hiding Place. New York, Doubleday, 1965; London, Hale, 1966.
The Crayfish Dinner. New York, Doubleday, 1966; as *The Elusive Epicure,* London, Hale, 1968.
A Taste of Sangria. New York, Doubleday, 1968; as *The Missing Book-Keeper,* London, Hale, 1969.

*

Manuscript Collection: May Massee Collection, Emporia State University, Kansas.

* * *

Keith Robertson's boys are the natural descendants of Tom Sawyer and Penrod: bright, ambitious, inquisitive, and inventive; never still for a moment; often in hot water but safely out again before there is serious cause for alarm. They are boys who never grow up, just as Tom Sawyer remains a boy forever. Not in the magical sense of Peter Pan's Never Never Land agelessness, but simply because boyishness is their very essence.

Henry Reed always has some enterprises on hand; his world is divided between those who understand the necessity of rabbit-keeping and running small businesses having to do with earthworm culture, babysitting, or rodeo organization, and those of the older generation or even unsympathetic young people who object to such undertakings on trumped-up adult grounds such as trespass and game laws. All the Henry Reed books hang on some plot peg such as a babysitting agency (whose clients can only be described as fiendish), or a cross-country motor trip; but they are usually episodic and rambling; one harmless complication follows another, with never a dull moment spent on the boring business of life as most of us live it. No one could wish that Henry's sunny existence should change in any particular; he's such a contented young man it does one's heart good to meet him even in print.

Robertson's alternate heroes, the young Carson Street Detectives Neil and Swede, are, like Henry Reed, model American boys of about 1950 vintage, clean-cut, wholesome, bright young fellows with short haircuts who would do credit to any senior Boy Scout Troop. It is a restful pleasure to encounter these uncomplicated kids, after struggling through various tomes dealing with the tortured life and psyche of the typical mixed-up young hero of today's often harrowing fiction for children.

Henry, Neil, and Swede are not milksops; they encounter more adventures in a chapter than most of us do in a lifetime: but they are untroubled by problems beyond their power to solve. Their temporary difficulties may be complex in the extreme, but they *always* come out all right in the end: Mom is usually busy whipping up a batch of pies, and Dad has never yet failed to come through in a pinch. This is the mythical middle-America upon which nostalgia for a golden past is built. Home was never like this—but how nice if it had been! No wonder young readers enjoy the adventures of Henry Reed and the Carson Street Detectives. They leave you feeling that it isn't such a bad old world after all. An uncommonly pleasant sensation.

—Joan McGrath

ROBINSON, Joan (Mary) G(ale)

Also wrote as Joan Gale Thomas. **Nationality:** British. **Born:** Joan Mary Gale Thomas, Gerrard's Cross, Buckinghamshire, in 1910. **Education:** Educated privately, and at Chelsea Illustrators' Studio, London. **Family:** Married Richard Gavin Robinson in 1941 (second marriage); two daughters. **Died:** 20 August 1988.

PUBLICATIONS FOR CHILDREN (ILLUSTRATED BY THE AUTHOR, EXCEPT AS NOTED)

Fiction

My Book about Christmas (as Joan Gale Thomas). London, Mowbray, 1946; New York, Morehouse, 1947.
My Garden Book (as Joan Gale Thomas). London, Mowbray, 1947.
Debbie Robbie's Day Nursery. London, University of London Press, 1950.
Susie at Home. London, Harrap, 1953.
Teddy Robinson. London, Harrap, 1953.
More about Teddy Robinson. London, Harrap, 1954.
Teddy Robinson's Book. London, Harrap, 1955.
Dear Teddy Robinson. London, Harrap, 1956.
Mary-Mary. London, Harrap, 1957.
Teddy Robinson Himself. London, Harrap, 1957.
More Mary-Mary. London, Harrap, 1958.
Another Teddy Robinson. London, Harrap, 1960.
Madam Mary-Mary. London, Harrap, 1960.
Keeping Up with Teddy Robinson. London, Harrap, 1964.
Mary-Mary Stories (from *Mary-Mary, More Mary-Mary, Madam Mary-Mary*). London, Harrap, 1965; New York, Coward McCann, 1968.
When Marnie Was There, illustrated by Peggy Fortnum. London, Collins, 1967; New York, Coward McCann, 1968.
Charley, illustrated by Prudence Seward. London, Collins, 1969; New York, Coward McCann, 1970.
The House in the Square, illustrated by Shirley Hughes. London, Collins, 1972.
The Summer Surprise, illustrated by Glenys Ambrus. London, Collins, 1977.
Meg and Maxie. London, Gollancz, 1978; as *The Dark House of the Sea Witch,* New York, Coward McCann, 1979; as *The Sea Witch,* London, Beaver, 1981.

Poetry as Joan Gale Thomas

A Stands for Angel. London, Mowbray, 1939; as *A Is for Angel,* New York, Lothrop, 1953.
Our Father. London, Mowbray, 1940; New York, Lothrop, 1952.
If Jesus Came to My House. London, Mowbray, 1941; New York, Lothrop, 1951.
God of All Things. London, Mowbray, 1948.
One Little Baby. London, Mowbray, 1950; New York, Lothrop, 1956.
Little Angels. London, Mowbray, 1951.
The Happy Year. London, Mowbray, 1953.
If I'd Been Born in Bethlehem. London, Mowbray, 1953; New York, Lothrop, 1954.
I Ask a Blessing. London, Mowbray, 1955.
Where Is God? London, Mowbray, 1957; New York, Lothrop, 1959.
The Christmas Angel. London, Mowbray, 1961.
Seven Days. London, Mowbray, 1964.

Other

Monsieur Charbon, défense de fumer (reader), with Gale Young, illustrated by Dick Robinson. London, Harrap, 1962.

*

Illustrator: *Tales of Betsy-May* by Enid Blyton, 1940; *The Dip Bucket,* 1941, *Lift Up the Latch,* 1942, *When the Fire Burns Blue,* 1944, and *Shadows on the Stairs,* 1946, all by Dorothy Ann Lovell; *Beryl's Wonderful Week* by Madeleine Collier, 1944; *Janey,* 1953, and *Janey and Her Friends,* 1953, both by Irene Pearl; *Jonathan on the Farm,* 1954, and *Jonathan and Felicity,* 1955, both by Mary Cockett; *The House under the Tree,* 1954, and *The House in Hyde Park,* 1956, both by Jennifer Ford; *The Carol Book,* 1959.

Joan G. Robinson commented:

(1978) I write slowly and laboriously, always hoping to achieve that final "spontaneity and simplicity" that I remember once being credited with in some review. I try to write from a child's-eye-view without going down on all fours; to entertain not only the child but, in stories for younger children, the patient adult reading aloud—but never at the child's expense.

The Joan Gale Thomas books stemmed from originally designing Christmas cards for Mowbrays, and then as material to illustrate. The longer books for older children came as a welcome escape from the strict discipline of vocabulary and subject matter which governs the earlier books. These longer books were also an opportunity to write about the loner, the odd one out, the not-so-jolly—though not entirely without humour, I hope. This writing, too, proved to have its own discipline.

* * *

Joan G. Robinson wrote many well-crafted tales for the very young, including the Teddy Robinson and the slightly more sophisticated Mary-Mary series. Teddy Robinson the Bear, humorous, with make-believe but no magic, must have entered much family folklore. Nevertheless, her three novels for older children, *When Marnie Was There, Charley,* and *The House in the Square,* really established her serious reputation.

All these books are realised through a lonely, sensitive girl in a strange place, the loner, non-joiner, reticent and perforce ungiving, who "spoils everything," wanting both too little and too much, painfully enduring the dreamy poetry of growing up. One gets a direct feel of the child's day, the moments of wanting to be injured and misunderstood, the vindictive retorts stored up for defence, the puzzled resentment when only others get invited to the party, the expectation of disappointment. There is a sense of firelit rooms with a single mute figure in the dark outside, or a solitary mysterious human shadow at a high window. But also the joys of sudden acceptance in a big, cheerful family or of unexpected intimacies with a stranger, glamorous, strangely sympathetic, who may become the legendary, exclusive "best friend." Happiness exists, even if too often beyond reach. Life and people are exciting but unreliable. Robinson's careful observation often contains a drop of fantasy, a hint of fairy-tale glimmering among solid adventure, practical problems, the quarrels and thoughtlessness. Sudden betrayals can crack the world. An adopted child is shocked to discover that foster-parents are paid to love, that generous friendly adults can cheat and lie. The novels have strong awareness of place: wide Norfolk landscapes where creeks and marshes lie silent but alive, and a windmill is uncannily stark against the sky; and a London of tall soundless houses, empty gardens, statues that sometimes seem to breathe.

—Peter Vansittart

ROCKWELL, Anne

Nationality: American. **Born:** Anne Foote, Memphis, Tennessee, 8 February 1934. **Education:** Sculpture Center, New York, 3 years; Pratt Institute, Brooklyn. **Family:** Married Harlow Rockwell in 1955 (died); two daughters and one son. **Career:** Member of production department, Silver Burdett, publishers, Morristown, New Jersey, 1952; secretary, Young and Rubicam, advertising, New York, 1953; assistant recreation leader, Goldwater Memorial Hospital, New York, 1954-56. **Address:** P.O. Box 379, Old Greenwich, Connecticut 06870, U.S.A.

Publications for Children (illustrated by the author)

Fiction

Paul and Arthur Search for an Egg. New York, Doubleday, 1964.
Gypsy Girl's Best Shoes. New York, Parents' Magazine Press, 1966.
Sally's Caterpillar, illustrated by Harlow Rockwell. New York, Parents' Magazine Press, 1966.
Molly's Woodland Garden. New York, Doubleday, 1971.
Paul and Arthur and the Little Explorer. New York, Parents' Magazine Press, 1972.
Thruway, with Harlow Rockwell. New York, Macmillan, 1972.
The Awful Mess. New York, Parents' Magazine Press, 1973.
Gift for a Gift. New York, Parents' Magazine Press, 1974.
The Gollywhopper Egg. New York, Macmillan, 1974; Kingswood, Surrey, World's Work, 1977.
The Story Snail. New York, Macmillan, 1974; Kingswood, Surrey, World's Work, 1977.
Big Boss. New York, Macmillan, 1975; Kingswood, Surrey, World's Work, 1977.
No More Work. New York, Greenwillow, 1976; Kingswood, Surrey, World's Work, 1978.
Albert B. Cub and Zebra: An Alphabet Storybook. New York, Crowell, 1977.
A Bear, A Bobcat, and Three Ghosts. New York, Macmillan, 1977.
Buster and the Bogeyman. New York, Four Winds Press, 1978.
Gogo's Car Breaks Down. New York, Doubleday, 1978.
Gogo's Pay Day. New York, Doubleday, 1978.
Timothy Todd's Good Things Are Gone. New York, Macmillan, 1978.
Willy Runs Away. New York, Dutton, 1978.
Blackout, with Harlow Rockwell. New York, Macmillan, 1979.
The Bump in the Night. New York, Greenwillow, 1979; London, Hamish Hamilton, 1983.
Henry the Cat and the Big Sneeze. New York, Greenwillow, 1980.
Honk Honk! New York, Dutton, 1980.
Out to Sea, with Harlow Rockwell. New York, Macmillan, 1980.
Walking Shoes. New York, Doubleday, 1980.
Happy Birthday to Me, with Harlow Rockwell. New York, Macmillan, 1981.
My Barber, with Harlow Rockwell. New York, Macmillan, 1981.
I Play in My Room, with Harlow Rockwell. New York, Macmillan, 1981.
Thump! Thump! Thump! New York, Dutton, 1981.
Big Bad Goat. New York, Dutton, 1982.
Can I Help? with Harlow Rockwell. New York, Macmillan, 1982.

How My Garden Grew, with Harlow Rockwell. New York, Macmillan, 1982.
I Love My Pets, with Harlow Rockwell. New York, Macmillan, 1982.
Sick in Bed, with Harlow Rockwell. New York, Macmillan, 1982.
The Night We Slept Outside, with Harlow Rockwell. New York, Macmillan, 1983.
My Backyard, with Harlow Rockwell. New York, Macmillan, 1984.
Our Garage Sale, with Harlow Rockwell. New York, Greenwillow, 1984.
When I Go Visiting, with Harlow Rockwell. New York, Macmillan, 1984.
First Comes Spring. New York, Crowell, 1985.
In Our House. New York, Crowell, 1985; London, Heinemann, 1986.
My Babysitter. New York, Crowell, 1985.
At Night. New York, Crowell, 1986.
At the Playground. New York, Crowell, 1986.
In the Morning. New York, Crowell, 1986.
In the Rain. New York, Crowell, 1986.
Come to Town. New York, Crowell, and London, Heinemann, 1987.
Around the Day. London, Heinemann, 1988.
Handy Hank Will Fix It. New York, Holt Rinehart, 1988.
Hugo at the Window. New York, Macmillan, and London, Macmillan, 1988.
Things to Play With. New York, Macmillan, 1988; London, Heinemann, 1991.
My Spring Robin, illustrated by Harlow Rockwell and Lizzy Rockwell. New York, Macmillan, 1989.
On Our Vacation. New York, Dutton, 1989.
Apple and Pumpkins, illustrated by Lizzy Rockwell. New York, Macmillan, 1989.
Willy Can Count. New York, Arcade, 1989.
On Our Holiday. London, Heinemann, 1990.
Root-a-Toot-Toot. New York, Macmillan, 1991.
Mr. Panda's Painting. New York, Macmillan, 1993.
Busy Bear's Big Word Book. N.p., Dean, 1993.
Ducklings and Polliwogs, illustrated by Lizzy Rockwell. New York, Macmillan, 1994.
The Way to Captain Yankee's. New York, Macmillan, 1994.
Our Stars. San Diego, Harcourt Brace, 1999.
Thanksgiving Day, illustrated by Lizzy Rockwell. New York, HarperCollins, 1999.

Other

Filippo's Dome. New York, Atheneum, 1967; London, Macmillan, 1968.
Glass, Stones and Crown: The Abbé Suger and the Building of St. Denis. New York, Atheneum, and London, Macmillan, 1968.
The Good Llama. Cleveland, World, 1968.
The Stolen Necklace: A Picture Story from India. Cleveland, World, 1968.
Temple on a Hill: The Building of the Parthenon. New York, Atheneum, 1968.
The Wonderful Eggs of Furicchia (retelling). Cleveland, World, 1969.
Olly's Polliwogs, with Harlow Rockwell. New York, Doubleday, 1970.
When the Drum Sang: An African Folktale. New York, Parents' Magazine Press, 1970.
The Monkey's Whiskers: A Brazilian Folktale. New York, Parents' Magazine Press, 1971.
Paintbrush and Peacepipe: The Story of George Catlin. New York, Atheneum, 1971.
The Toolbox, with Harlow Rockwell. New York, Macmillan, 1971.
Tuhurahura and the Whale (Maori legend). New York, Parents' Magazine Press, 1971.
What Bobolino Knew (retelling). New York, McCall, 1971.
The Dancing Stars: An Iroquois Legend. New York, Crowell, 1972.
Machines. New York, Macmillan, 1972.
Toad, with Harlow Rockwell. New York, Doubleday, 1972.
The Boy Who Drew Sheep. New York, Atheneum, 1973.
Games (and How to Play Them). New York, Crowell, 1973.
Head to Toe, with Harlow Rockwell. New York, Doubleday, 1973.
The Wolf Who Had a Wonderful Dream: A French Folktale. New York, Crowell, 1973.
Befana: A Christmas Story (retelling). New York, Atheneum, 1974.
Poor Goose: A French Folktale. New York, Crowell, 1976.
I Like the Library. New York, Dutton, 1977.
The Girl with a Donkey Tail. New York, Dutton, 1979.
The Old Woman and Her Pig, and 10 Other Stories (retelling). New York, Crowell, 1979.
The Supermarket, with Harlow Rockwell. New York, Macmillan, 1979.
Up a Tall Tree, illustrated by Jim Arnosky. New York, Doubleday, 1981.
When We Grow Up. New York, Dutton, 1981.
Boats. New York, Dutton, 1982; London, Hamish Hamilton, 1983.
Cars. New York, Dutton, and London, Hamish Hamilton, 1984.
Nice and Clean, with Harlow Rockwell. New York, Macmillan, 1984.
Trucks. New York, Dutton, and London, Hamish Hamilton, 1984.
The Emergency Room, with Harlow Rockwell. New York, Macmillan, 1985; as *Going to Casualty,* London, Hamish Hamilton, 1987.
Planes. New York, Dutton, and London, Hamish Hamilton, 1985.
Big Wheels. New York, Dutton, and London, Hamish Hamilton, 1986.
Fire Engines. New York, Dutton, and London, Viking Kestrel, 1986.
Things That Go. New York, Dutton, and London, Hamish Hamilton, 1986.
At the Beach, with Harlow Rockwell. New York, Macmillan, and London, Macmillan, 1987.
Bear Child's Book of Hours. New York, Crowell, 1987.
Bikes. New York, Dutton, and London, Viking Kestrel, 1987.
The First Snowfall, with Harlow Rockwell. New York, Macmillan, 1987; London, Hamish Hamilton, 1988.
Puss in Boots and Other Stories. New York, Macmillan, 1988.
Trains. New York, Dutton, and London, Hamish Hamilton, 1988.
Bear Child's Book of Special Days. New York, Dutton, 1989.
Pots and Pans, illustrated by Lizzy Rockwell. New York, Macmillan, 1993.
Space Vehicles, with David Brion. New York, Dutton, 1994.

The Storm, illustrated by Robert Sauber. New York, Hyperion, 1994.
The Robber Baby: Stories from the Greek Myths. New York, Greenwillow, 1994.

Editor, *Savez-Vous Planter les Choux? and Other French Songs.* Cleveland, World, 1962; London, Hamish Hamilton, 1972.
Editor, *The Three Bears and 15 Other Stories.* New York, Crowell, 1975; London, Hamish Hamilton, 1976.

*

Manuscript Collection: Kerlan Collection, University of Minnesota, Minneapolis.

Illustrator: *Eric and the Little Canal Boat* by Lillian Bason, 1967; *The Three Visitors,* 1967, *The Glass Valentine,* 1968, and *A Gift for Tolum,* 1972, all by Marjorie Hopkins; *The Minstrel and the Mountain* by Jane Yolen, 1967; *Mexicali Soup* by Kathryn Hitte, 1970; *Munachar and Munachar,* 1970, and *Master of All Masters,* 1972, both by Joseph Jacobs; *Legends of the Saints* by Ann Petry, 1970; *What Happens to a Hamburger* by Paul Showers, 1970; *The Dancers* by Walter Dean Myers, 1972; *Cunningham's Rooster* by Barbara Brenner, 1975; *Never Hit a Porcupine* by Barbara Williams, 1977; *Bing Bong Bang and Fiddle Dee Dee* by Gerda Mantinband, 1979; *The Stubborn Old Women* by Clyde Robert Bulla, 1980; *Gray Goose and Gander and Other Mother Goose Rhymes,* 1980; *The Turtle and the Two Ducks* by Patricia Plante, 1981; *The Emperor's New Clothes* by Hans Christian Andersen, 1982; *Toot! Toot!* by Steven Kroll, 1983.

Anne Rockwell comments:

My books are for the youngest of children. I loved, and still love, young children's picture books. I feel fortunate to have retained a sense of how young children see the world which enables me to do books for them. My own children reinforced this way of seeing in me so that I can focus on what most small children notice. I see that they are visually very alert and that illustrations can communicate where words are still difficult. In pictures they *see* everything.

* * *

In her 35 years of writing books for children, Anne Rockwell has directed her efforts toward a progressively younger audience. Having concentrated in earlier works on scientific and historical books for school-aged children, and on retellings of folktales from all over the world, she has more recently used her talents to create picture books and even board books for very young children. Yet she maintains in her creative work the best aspects of the earlier books: her interest in and talent for the telling of folktales, and a simplicity within diversity in her "true" stories which both satisfies and stimulates young readers.

Rockwell's books for beginning readers capture the flavor of the folktale so well, one easily forgets these are controlled-vocabulary stories. Two of the best of them are *The Story Snail* and *Big Boss.* In the former, a young boy sets out on a journey which is initiated by his encounter with a story-telling snail. He must use his wits and considerable determination to discover that what he most seeks is within him already. The language is simple but captivating; Rockwell even creates a magic word ("Fuzzbuzzoncetherewas") which becomes the hero's version of "Once upon a time."

In *Big Boss* a frog manages to outwit both a tiger and a fox who seek to eat him, and eventually becomes a most unlikely ruler of the forest. Again a seemingly powerless creature uses his imagination and determination, this time to triumph over more powerful adversaries. The clarity and brightness of Rockwell's illustrations is mirrored by that same clarity in her use of language. The folktale convention of word repetition lends itself well to the language limits of the controlled reader. When used by Rockwell, even controlled language has an imaginative, lilting quality.

Rockwell displays her knack for uncomplicated but interesting text in her books for preschool children as well. Sometimes teaming with husband Harlow, sometimes independently, she brings before children a wide range of experiences, always beginning with something common to most children and moving out from it. *Trucks,* for instance, starts with animal children playing with toy trucks, then moves beyond the toy trucks to describe a variety of other trucks and their functions. In the opening of *Planes,* two people stand outside, watching a plane fly overhead; again the child reader is provided with an almost universal experience as a point of departure for the rest of the book. Whether or not the child has ever seen a plane close up or has had the experience of flying, common ground has been provided as a starting point. In both books, Rockwell uses the effective technique of returning to the original scene at the end, which provides a satisfying closure.

In her books for slightly older preschoolers, Rockwell immediately engages children's interest with the adoption of a first-person point of view, in which the narrator is a young child moving through an experience described in great detail. Whether the experience is totally familiar to most children (*Sick in Bed, The Supermarket*), or possibly less familiar (*Our Garage Sale,* or *When I Go Visiting,* which details a boy's overnight stay with his grandparents), there is a basis of familiarity produced by the first-person perspective, which encourages the reader to follow along into possibly less familiar but always varied and interesting territory.

Two Rockwell books which could be enjoyed by children up to first-grade level are also worthy of note. *When We Grow Up* features members of a class talking about their ambitions for the future. It is refreshing in its non-sexist attitudes and jobs which include the typical and the more unusual as well. Her *First Comes Spring* follows Bear Child through all the seasons—ending, as she so often does, where she begins, and depicting a great variety of activities for each season. Unlike many books of this type which overwhelm young senses with too many images, Rockwell's text and illustrations give an overall view, then break the larger view into its smaller components. Again, the featured activities include some that are very familiar, some less common. Both of these books are interesting in themselves and also useful for stimulating thought beyond the confines of the specific texts.

From the realistic world of children's everyday experiences to the more imaginative world of the folktale, Rockwell's fine talent lies in her ability to endow her imaginary stories with realistic detail, and her realistic stories with enough variety to capture interest and stimulate imagination. In both types of stories, she combines surface simplicity with underlying diversity to create eminently worthwhile works for young children.

—Christine Doyle Stott

RODGERS, Mary

Nationality: American. **Born:** New York City, 11 January 1931; daughter of the composer Richard Rodgers. **Education:** Brearley School, New York, graduated 1948; Mannes College of Music, New York, 1943-48; Wellesley College, Massachusetts, 1948-51. **Family:** Married 1) Julian B. Beaty, Jr., in 1951 (divorced 1957), one son and two daughters; 2) Henry Guettel in 1961, two sons. **Career:** Script editor and assistant to the producer, New York Philharmonic Young People's Concerts, CBS-TV, 1957-71; script writer, Hunter College Little Orchestra Society, New York, 1958-59; columnist ("Of Two Minds"), with Dorothy Rodgers, *McCall's* magazine, New York, 1971-78. Composer and lyricist. **Awards:** Christopher award, 1973, 1975. **Agent:** Flora Roberts Inc., 157 West 57 Street, New York, New York 10019. **Address:** 211 Central Park West, New York, New York 10024, U.S.A.

PUBLICATIONS FOR CHILDREN

Fiction

The Rotten Book, illustrated by Steven Kellogg. New York, Harper, 1969.

Freaky Friday. New York, Harper, 1972; London, Hamish Hamilton, 1973.

A Billion for Boris. New York, Harper, 1974; London, Hamish Hamilton, 1975.

Summer Switch. New York, Harper, 1982; London, Hamish Hamilton, 1983.

Plays

Davy Jones' Locker (for marionettes; music and lyrics only), book by Arthur Birnkrant and Waldo Salt (produced New York, 1959).

Three to Make Music, music by Linda Rodgers Melnick, lyrics by Rodgers (produced New York, 1959).

Pinocchio (for marionettes), music by Rodgers, lyrics by Sheldon Harnick (produced New York, 1973).

Freaky Friday, music by Rodger, lyrics by Sheldon Harnick (produced New York, 1992).

Plays

Screenplays: *Freaky Friday,* 1977; *The Devil and Max Devlin,* with Jimmy Sangster, 1980.

PUBLICATIONS FOR ADULTS

Other

A Word to the Wives, with Dorothy Rodgers. New York, Knopf, 1970.

*

Manuscript Collection: Kerlan Collection, University of Minnesota, Minneapolis.

Music: Plays—*Once upon a Mattress* by Jay Thompson, Marshall Barer, and Dean Fuller, 1958; *Hot Spot* by Jack Weinstock and Willie Gilbert, 1963; *Young Mark Twain,* 1964; *The Mad Show* by Larry Siegel and Stan Hart, 1966; **Television**—*Mary Martin Spectacular,* 1959; *Feathertop,* 1961.

* * *

Humor is a scarce but precious commodity in contemporary technological society. Mary Rodgers breathes laughter into the situations, the characters, and the language of her books.

A child's imagination runs rampant in *The Rotten Book,* as Simon thinks of ways of being naughty. Fantasy is superimposed on a realistic background in *Freaky Friday* and its sequel, *A Billion for Boris.* Annabel Andrews awakens to find she has the body of her mother, while the ordinary events of life transpire. She witnesses the washing machine overflowing, and she mistakenly identifies her boyfriend Boris's mother as a cleaning lady, but she also participates in the parent-teacher conference in which she herself is discussed. Near tragedy is averted in *A Billion for Boris* when the television set projects tomorrow's news: the soup suspected of botulism can be destroyed, and people are persuaded to divert their plans.

The characters themselves are hilarious. Boris's eccentric artist mother has no organizational or financial skills, and he has balanced her checkbook since his ninth year. The participants in the school conference are caricatures of every child's teacher. Teenage Virginia has "theatrical aspirations, and correct grammar." Language and dialogue are wrought for their entertaining qualities. Even the dedication of the third book gives insight into the author's humor—"to my small sons, Adam and Alec, without whom I was finally able to finish it." According to the critic Betsy Wade, the author "appears to have a sharp ear for the particular tone adults use on children." Yet when the parents disagree about camp and a raincoat for Annabel, they use contemporary sophisticated adult expressions. The latter two books are narrated in the first person by 13 and then 14-year-old Annabel Andrews, and parentheses are used generously for asides directed to the reader.

Jane Langton noted in her review of *Freaky Friday* that "the pages rush by, right now in 1972, and it might all be happening in the apartment next door." The very incidents and phrases which make the books so specific will unfortunately also date them. Teenage pranks go in and out of fashion, and burning kleenex in the toilet is now passé. The advertising slogan "let your fingers do the walking" and reference to the noted criminal lawyer, F. Lee Bailey, will fall dead on the ears of the next reading generation. Even now "hi-fi" has been replaced by "cds" and the "hoover" is rarely used in America to refer to the vacuum cleaner. Slang such as "zing one of those carts" and alluding to the "monthly excuse" will contribute to the eventual demise of the books except as representatives of an era.

Nevertheless, the books are very popular. Alix Nelson, in the *New York Times Book Review* (24 November 1974), noted that *A Billion for Boris* "assumes an urban and sophisticated frame of reference on the part of the reader, and it evokes so much New York City local color (from the Village to 125th Street by way of Central Park West, Lord & Taylor, and a walk-up on West 53rd) that it really is the perfect New York City book."

Mary Rodgers, the daughter of Richard Rodgers, has also composed children's musicals. These include *Davy Jones' Locker, Young Mark Twain,* and *Pinocchio.*

—Karen Nelson Hoyle

ROSEN, Michael (Wayne)

Nationality: British. **Born:** Harrow, Middlesex, 7 May 1946. **Education:** Harrow Weald County School, 1957-62; Watford Grammar School, Hertfordshire, 1962-64; Middlesex Hospital Medical School, London, 1964-65; Wadham College, Oxford, 1965-69, B.A. (honours) in English 1969; National Film School, 1973-76; Reading University, M.A. 1993; University of North London/Worcester College of Higher Education, Ph.D. studies. **Family:** Married 1) Susanna Steele, 1976 (divorced 1987); 2) Geraldine Clark, 1987 (divorced 1997); five children. **Career:** Freelance writer and broadcaster: created Everybody Here television series, Channel 4, London, 1982-83. **Awards:** Sunday Times-National Union of Students Drama Festival award, 1968; Greater London Arts Association C. Day Lewis fellowship, 1976; Signal poetry award, 1982; Children's Rights Workshop Other Award, 1983; *Boston Globe/Horn Book* award, 1990; Smarties Book of the Year Award, 1990; Japanese Picture Book Award, Mainichi Newspapers, 1991; Cuffie Award, *Publisher's Weekly,* 1992, for best anthology; National Association of Parenting Publications Best Book Award, 1993. **Agent:** Peters Fraser and Dunlop, Fifth Floor, The Chambers, Chelsea Harbour, Lots Road, London SW10 0XF. **Address:** 49 Parkholme Road, London E8 3AQ, England.

PUBLICATIONS FOR CHILDREN

Fiction

Once There Was a King Who Promised He Would Never Chop Anyone's Head Off, illustrated by Kathy Henderson. London, Deutsch, 1976.
She Even Called Me Garibaldi. London, BBC Books, 1977.
Nasty!, illustrated by Amanda Macphail. London, Longman, 1982; revised edition, London, Penguin, 1984.
Hairy Tales and Nursery Crimes, illustrated by Alan Baker. London, Deutsch, 1985.
You're Thinking about Doughnuts, illustrated by Tony Pinchuck. London, Deutsch, 1987.
The Horribles (stories), illustrated by John Watson. London, Walker, 1988.
Norma and the Washing Machine, illustrated by David Higham. London, Deutsch, 1988.
The Class Two Monster, illustrated by Maggie Ling. London, Heinemann, 1989.
The Deadman Tapes. London, Deutsch, 1989.
The Royal Huddle and *The Royal Muddle,* illustrated by Colin West. London, Macmillan, 1990.
Freckly Feet and Itchy Knees, illustrated by Sami Sweeten. London, Collins, and New York, Doubleday, 1990.
Clever Cakes. London, Walker, 1991.
Moving, illustrated by Sophy Williams. London and New York, Viking, 1993.
Songbird Story, illustrated by Jill Dow. London, Lincoln, 1993.
Burping Bertha, illustrated by Tony Ross. London, Andersen, 1993.
Moving, illustrated by Sophy Williams. New York, Viking, 1993.
Songbird Story, illustrated by Peggy Dow. London, Lincoln, 1993.
Norma's Notebook, illustrated by Tony Ross. Harlow, Longman, 1994.
Dad, illustrated by Tony Ross. Harlow, Longman, 1994.
Lisa's Letter, illustrated by Tony Ross. Harlow, Longman, 1994.
The Arabian Frights and Other Gories, illustrated by Chris Fisher. New York, Scholastic, Inc., 1994.
Even Stevens. London, Collins, 1995.
This Is Our House, illustrated by Bob Graham. London, Walker Books, 1996.
Snore!, illustrated by Jonathan Langley. London, HarperCollins, 1998.

Poetry

Mind Your Own Business, illustrated by Quentin Blake. London, Deutsch, and New York, Phillips, 1974.
Wouldn't You Like to Know, illustrated by Quentin Blake. London, Deutsch, 1977; revised edition, London, Penguin, 1981.
You Tell Me, with Roger McGough, illustrated by Sara Midda. London, Kestrel, 1979.
Bathtime. London, BBC Books, 1979.
You Can't Catch Me!, illustrated by Quentin Blake. London, Deutsch, 1981.
Quick, Let's Get Out of Here, illustrated by Quentin Blake. London, Deutsch, 1983.
Don't Put Mustard in the Custard, illustrated by Quentin Blake. London, Deutsch, 1985.
When Did You Last Wash Your Feet?, illustrated by Tony Pinchuck. London, Deutsch, 1986.
Chocolate Cake, illustrated by Amelia Rosato. London, BBC Books, 1986.
The Hypnotiser, illustrated by Andrew Tiffen. London, Deutsch, 1988.
Never Mind!, London, BBC, 1990.
Little Rabbit Foo Foo, illustrated by Arthur Robins. London, Walker, and New York, Simon and Schuster, 1990.
Who Drew on the Baby's Head, illustrated by Riana Duncan. London, Deutsch, 1991.
We're Going on a Bear Hunt, illustrated by Helen Oxenbury. London, Walker, 1989; New York, Aladdin, 1992.
Mind the Gap, illustrated by Caroline Holden. New York, Scholastic, 1992.
Nuts about Nuts, illustrated by Sami Sweeten. London, Collins, 1993.
Michael Rosen's ABC, illustrated by Bee Willey. London, Macdonald Young Books, 1995.
The Best of Michael Rosen, illustrated by Quentin Blake. London, RDR Books, 1995.
You Wait Till I'm Older Than You, illustrated by Shoo Rayner. London, Penguin, 1996.
Tea in my Sugar Bowl, illustrated by Quentin Blake. London, Walker, 1997.
The Michael Rosen Book of Nonsense, illustrated by Clare Mackie. Brighton, Wayland Macdonald, 1997.

Editor

Everybody Here (miscellany). London, Bodley Head, 1982.
Inky Pinky Ponky: Children's Playground Rhymes, with Susanna Steele, illustrated by Dan Jones. London, Granada, 1982.
With David Jackson, *Speaking to You.* London, Macmillan, 1984.
With Joan Griffiths, *That'd Be Telling.* Cambridge, Cambridge University Press, 1985.

The Kingfisher Book of Children's Poetry. London, Kingfisher, 1985.

A Spider Bought a Bicycle and Other Poems, illustrated by Inga Moore. London, Kingfisher, 1986.

The Kingfisher Book of Funny Stories, illustrated by Tony Blundell. London, Kingfisher, 1988; New York, Kingfisher, 1993.

Culture Shock. London, Viking, 1990.

Give Me Shelter: Young Homelessness, Impressions in Words and Pictures. London, Bodley Head, 1991.

Mini Beasties, illustrated by Alan Baker. Sussex, Firefly, 1991.

A World of Poetry. London, Kingfisher, 1991.

Itsy-Bitsy Beasties: Poems from around the World, illustrated by Alan Baker. Minneapolis, Carolrhoda Books, 1992.

Sonsense Nongs, illustrated by Shoo Rayner. London, A. & C. Black, 1992.

South and North, East and West: The Oxfam Book of Children's Stories. London, Walker, and Cambridge, Candlewick, 1992.

The Kingfisher Book of Children's Poetry, illustrated by Alice Englander. New York, Kingfisher, 1993.

Poems for the Very Young, illustrated by Bob Graham. London, and New York, Kingfisher, 1993.

A Different Story: Poems from the Past. London, The English and Media Centre, 1994.

Pilly Soems: Michael Rosen's Book of Very Silly Poems, illustrated by Rayner. London, A&C Black, 1994.

Walking the Bridge of Your Nose, illustrated by Chloe Cheese. London, Kingfisher, 1995.

Folk Tales and Retellings

A Cat and Mouse Story, illustrated by William Rushton. London, Deutsch, 1982.

The Wicked Tricks of Till Owlyglass, illustrated by Fritz Wegner. London, Walker, 1989.

Tell Tales (*Peter Pan, Aladdin, Alice in Wonderland, Cinderella, Goldilocks and the Three Bears, Hansel and Gretel, Little Red Riding Hood, The Little Tin Soldier, The Princess and the Pea, Sinbad the Sailor, Snow White*). Hove, Firefly, 11 vols., 1989-90.

The Golem of Old Prague, illustrated by Val Biro. London, Deutsch, 1990.

How the Animals Got Their Colours: Animal Myths from Around the World, illustrated by John Clementson. London, Studio Editions, and San Diego, Harcourt Brace, 1991.

The First Giraffe, illustrated by John Clementson. London, Studio Editions, 1993; as *How Giraffe Got Such a Long Neck—And Why Rhino is So Grumpy,* New York, Dial, 1993.

The Old Woman and the Pumpkin, illustrated by Bob Hewis. London, Learning by Design, 1994.

The Man with No Shadow, illustrated by Reg Cartwright. Harlow, Longmans, 1994.

Crow and Hawk, illustrated by John Clementson. New York, Harcourt Brace, 1994.

Nonfiction

I See a Voice (on poetry). London, Thames Television-Hutchinson, 1981.

Experiences (*The Attic: Fear, The Oar: Friendship, The Tree: Imagination, The Formula: Intelligence, Isabel: Shyness, The Nose: Lying*). Hove, Firefly, 6 vols., 1989.

Other

The Bakerloo Flea, illustrated by Quentin Blake. London, Longman, 1979.

How to Get Out of the Bath and Other Problems, illustrated by Graham Round. London, Scholastic, 1984.

Scrapbooks series (*Smelly Jelly Smelly Fish, Under the Bed, Hard-Boiled Legs, Spollyollydiddilytiddlyitis*), illustrated by Quentin Blake. London, Walker, 4 vols., 1986-87; first 3 vols. published Englewood Cliffs, New Jersey, Prentice Hall, 1986-87; last vol. published as *Down at the Doctor's,* New York, Simon and Schuster, 1987.

Silly Stories (jokes), illustrated by Mik Brown. London, Kingfisher, 1988; revised as *Michael Rosen's Horribly Silly Stories,* London, Kingfisher, 1994, and as *Off the Wall: A Very Silly Joke Book,* New York, Kingfisher, 1994.

Jokes and Verses, illustrated by Quentin Blake. London, BBC Books. 1988.

Publications for Adults

Plays

Backbone (produced Oxford, 1967; London, 1968). London, Faber, 1968.

Stewed Figs (produced Durham, 1968).

Regis Debray (radio play). BBC Radio 4, 1971.

Mordecai Vanunu: A Reconstruction (produced Hackney Empire Theatre, October 1993).

Nonfiction

Did I Hear You Write?, illustrated by Tony Pinchuck. London, Deutsch, 1989.

Goodies and Daddies: An A-Z Guide to Fatherhood. London, Murray, 1991.

Holocaust Denial: The New Nazi Lie. Anti-Nazi League, 1992.

With Jill Burridge, *Treasure Islands 2: An Adult Guide to Children's Writers and Illustrators.* London, BBC Books, 1993.

Editor

Rude Rhymes, illustrated by Riana Duncan. London, Deutsch, 1989.

Dirty Ditties, illustrated by Riana Duncan. London, Deutsch, 1990.

Vulgar Verses, illustrated by Riana Duncan. London, Deutsch, 1991.

With David Widgery, *The Chatto Book of Dissent.* London, Chatto and Windus, 1991.

Rude Rhymes (revised edition of *Rude Rhymes,* combining it with *Dirty Ditties* and *Vulgar Verses*). London, Signet, 1992.

The Penguin Book of Childhood. London, Penguin, 1994.

Rude Rhymes 2. London, Signet, 1994.

With Myar Barrs, *A Year with Poetry: Teachers Write About Teaching Poetry.* London, Centre for Language in Primary Education.

Poetry

Bloody L.I.A.R.S., illustrated by Alan Gilbey. Privately printed, 1984.

You Are, Aren't You? Nottingham, Jewish Socialist Group/Mushroom Bookshop, 1993.
The Skin of Your Back. Nottingham, Five Leaves Press, 1996.

*

Media Adaptations: *The Bakerloo Flea, Never Mind, You Can't Catch Me, Quick, Let's Get Out of Here, Hairy Tales and Nursery Crimes, Don't Put the Mustard in the Custard, The Michael Rosen Rap, Right Class 6, Poems for the Very Young, Sonsense Nongs, The Wicked Tricks of Till Owlyglass,* and *You Wait Till I'm Older Than You* have all been recorded on audiocassette; *Mike Rosen* (video), ICA Video; *Count to Five and Say I'm Alive, Why Poetry?, A Poet's Life,* and *Poetry Workshop* (videos), edited by Rosen, Team Video.

Critical Studies: *What It's Like to Be Michael Rosen* by Chris Powling, Aylesbury, Ginn, 1990.

Michael Rosen comments:

Mostly I write about myself. This is potentially very boring, but I try to make sure it isn't by meeting children in schools and libraries, and informally. I try to discover where my experiences overlap with theirs. Some people are worried about whether what I write is "poetry." If they are worried, let them call it something else, e.g., "stuff."

* * *

When Michael Rosen's first book of poetry for children, *Mind Your Own Business,* appeared, it was clear that here was a new, individual, and highly accessible voice. His subsequent phenomenal popularity with children and their teachers alike was no surprise. The reasons are not hard to find. Here is verse very close to the rhythms of everyday speech, which echoes and builds on children's playground rhymes, mimics child and adult thought processes with uncanny empathy, selectively identifies the poetic, rhythmic, and humorous energy of common speech patterns. Rosen's verse is poetic just as Harold Pinter's dialogue is poetic. It has attracted the criticism that it is too throwaway, too slapdash, too prone to identify with the child and eschew the difficult path of the true poet. However, analysis of almost any poem will show how conscious Rosen's art is, how carefully wrought the effects are, what perfect microcosmic unity his verse exhibits.

An example is the untitled poem beginning "If you don't put your shoes on...." in *Mind Your Own Business.* Here, in the guise of a parent counting up to fifteen (via fourteen and a half, three quarters and fifteen sixteenths) while the child finds, puts on, and does up first socks, then shoes, is a perfect little domestic drama. A relationship is deftly established, childhood processes are reproduced, adult combination of discipline and indulgence is exactly caught, not a word is wasted, a satisfying emotional and aesthetic experience is communicated. All these elements are brought out best by performance aloud. The poem is a tour de force and an achievement repeated many times in the stream of poetry books for children which have appeared since 1974.

In *Moving,* Rosen depicts the anxiety of a large tabby cat whose routine is upset when her owners decide to move to a new home. Proud of her ability to come and go as she pleases ("No one knows what I do./No one knows where I go"), the tabby is distraught when she is confined to the backseat of the family's car and decides that nothing will induce her to enter the new house ... nothing that is, except the scent of a delicious fish dinner. Although the story is written from the perspective of a house pet, Rosen introduces a number of fears that children have when they are forced to move, a strategy that allows a child reader to identify with the cat without having to directly admit his/her own anxieties.

For the most part, Rosen is a master not so much of conventional forms as of informal though settled idiomatic conventions. An example is his ability to extract huge point and humor from *Rap,* as in "The Michael Rosen Rap" in *The Hypnotiser,* and the explosively funny "Rap Baby" in *Rap with Rap.* This leads to another preoccupation which lends strength both to his poetry and his work in schools, his understanding of and empathy with many different cultures. In *Michael Rosen's ABC,* the author's attention to diverse cultural sources is also apparent. For the letter "L," for example, Rosen writes: "Little Red Riding Hood lost her lunch and the letter for the Lady of the Lake," a passage which invites parents to explain the literary and historical antecedents for Germanic fairy tales and Arthurian legends. Bee Willey's illustrations provide portraits of children from a variety of racial and ethnic backgrounds, enabling all readers to identify with the characters and ideas present in the text.

Over the last three decades, Rosen's poetry has become almost a school institution. Its effect on the profile of poetry generally in British schools should not be minimized. Its humor, accessibility, and child's-eye view has not only brought children into its spell but has enabled them to enter the world of poetry more widely. One of his functions has been to lay the foundation of a high art form in everyday experience. That poetry's profile is now higher in schools than in the past, despite the odds currently stacked against it, is due in no small measure to him.

He is also an anthologiser and editor—*Culture Shock, The Kingfisher Book of Children's Poetry,* and *Action Replay,* a wide-ranging collection of "found" poetry, epigrams, and highly-wrought short works encapsulating single, significant moments. His book for teachers, *Did I Hear You Write?,* expressed a philosophy and methodology for teachers of language and literature based on his own experience which has been influential in many primary schools.

Rosen has written effectively for young adults. His precise narrative skill was honed by his poetry. In the intriguing *The Deadman Tapes,* eight tapes made by young people recount highly-charged episodes which may or may not be connected. The book is ambiguous and resonant, formally challenging, thematically tightly constructed. The narrative elisions, hard for some adults, are clear to young people brought up on the elisions of television. The *Golem of Old Prague,* retellings of central European Jewish folktales, have a darkly medieval yet strangely contemporary feel to them. His retelling of von Chamisso's version of the Faust legend, *The Man with No Shadow* is equally effective.

Rosen's interests also extend to folklore, and he has chosen to retell stories that have a contemporary edge to them. For instance, in *Crow and Hawk,* Rosen uses as his source a Cochiti Pueblo tale in which a mother Hawk takes in and raises a nestful of Crow babies. When the Crow returns and demands her children back, the judge, a wise Eagle, allows the Hawk to retain custody, noting that the children prefer the faithful Hawk to the inconstant Crow. Given that so many young children are faced with issues of custody, the story is timely and sensitively rendered.

Obviously, Rosen's is a many-sided achievement. His significance for poetry for children extends beyond his own writing. His is an essential voice.

—Dennis Hamley, updated by Gwen Athene Tarbox

ROSEN, Michael J(oel)

Nationality: American. **Born:** Columbus, Ohio, 20 September 1954. **Education:** Kent State University, Kent, Ohio, 1972-73; Ohio State University, Columbus, Ohio, B.S. 1976, graduate study 1976-77; St. George's School of Medicine, Grenada, West Indies, 1978; Columbia University, M.F.A. 1981. **Career:** Instructor, 1978-84, and lecturer, 1983, 1985, Ohio State University, Columbus; free-lance illustrator and designer, since 1981; literary director and program director, The Thurber House, Columbus, Ohio, since 1982; associate poetry editor, 1987-89, poetry editor, since 1990, *High Plains Literary Review.* Youth services director, program coordinator, and administrator of children's services, Leo Yassenoff Jewish Center, 1973-78; assistant, Bread Loaf Writers Conference, 1977-79; design consultant, Jefferson Center for Learning and the Arts, since 1982; founder and director, The Company of Animals Fund, since 1990; member of board of directors, Share Our Strength, since 1993; teacher and guest artist, various schools, young author conferences, and teacher workshops. Contributor of articles, poems, stories, illustrations, and reviews to magazines, including *Atlantic Monthly, Gourmet, House & Garden, New Yorker, New York Times Book Review. Paris Review, Prairie Schooner,* and *Salmagundi*; columnist for *Canine Press.* **Awards:** Ohio Arts Council fellow, 1979, 1981, 1985, and 1987; Ingram Merrill fellow, 1982-83 and 1989; National Endowment for the Arts fellow, 1984; Gustav Davison Award, Poetry Society of America, 1985, for "The Map of Emotions"; Ohioana Library Award for poetry and Ohio Poetry Day Award, both 1985, for *A Drink at the Mirage*; grants from Jefferson Center for Learning and the Arts, 1988 and 1989; National Jewish Book Award for children's picture book, Living the Dream Award, and Indiana Author's Day Award, all 1993, for *Elijah's Angel: A Story for Chanukah and Christmas*; Simon Wiesenthal Museum of Tolerance Once Upon a Book Award, 1996, for *A School for Pompey Walker*; Alice Wood Memorial Award, Ohioana Library, for children's literature, 1997; Ohioana Award for juvenile books, 1998. **Address:** The Thurber House, 77 Jefferson Ave., Columbus, Ohio 43215, U.S.A.

Publications for Children

Fiction

Elijah's Angel: A Story for Chanukah and Christmas, illustrated by Aminah Brenda Lynn Robinson. San Diego, Harcourt Brace, 1992.
Bonesy and Isabel, illustrated by James Ransome. San Diego, Harcourt Brace, 1995.
A School for Pompey Walker, illustrated by Robinson. San Diego, Harcourt Brace, 1995.
The Heart Is Big Enough: Five Stories, illustrated by Matthew Valiquette. San Diego, Harcourt Brace, 1997.
The Dog Who Walked With God, illustrated by Stan Fellows. Cambridge, Massachusetts, Candlewick Press, 1998.
Bubbe's Wishbones, illustrated by John Thompson. New York, Blue Sky Books, 1999.

Poetry

50 Odd Jobs: A Wild and Wacky Rhyming Guide to One-of-a-Kind Careers. St. Petersburg, Florida, Willowisp Press, 1988.
The Greatest Table: A Banquet to Fight Against Hunger. San Diego, Harcourt Brace, 1994.
All Eyes on the Pond, illustrated by Tom Leonard. New York, Hyperion, 1994.
Fishing with Dad, illustrated by Will Shively. New York, Artisan, 1996.
Avalanche, illustrated by David Butler. Cambridge, Massachusetts, Candlewick, 1998.

Other

The Kids' Book of Fishing. New York, Workman Publishing, 1991.
Kids' Best Dog Book. New York, Workman Publishing, 1993.

Editor, *Home: A Collaboration of Thirty Distinguished Authors and Illustrators of Children's Books to Aid the Homeless.* New York, HarperCollins, 1992.Editor, *SPEAK!: Children's Book Illustrators Brag about Their Dogs.* San Diego, Harcourt Brace, 1993.
Editor and illustrator, *Food Fight: Poets Join the Fight against Hunger with Poems to Their Favorite Foods.* San Diego, Harcourt Brace, 1996.
Editor, *Purr... Children's Book Illustrators Brag about Their Cats.* San Diego, Harcourt Brace, 1996.
Editor and illustrator, *Down to Earth.* San Diego, Harcourt Brace, 1998.

Publications for Adults

Poetry

A Drink at the Mirage. Princeton, New Jersey, Princeton University Press, 1985.
Traveling in Notions: The Stories of Gordon Penn, Poems. Columbia, University of South Carolina Press, 1996.
Telling Things: Poems. New York, Harcourt Brace, 1997.

Other

With Rosemary O. Joyce and Donn F. Vickers, *Of Thurber and Columbustown.* New York, Thurber House, 1984.

Editor, *Collecting Himself: James Thurber on Writing and Writers, Humor and Himself.* New York, HarperCollins, 1989.
Editor, *The Company of Dogs: Twenty-one Stories by Contemporary Masters.* New York, Doubleday, 1990.
Editor, *The Company of Cats: Twenty Contemporary Stories of Family Cats.* New York, Doubleday, 1992.
Editor, *The Company of Animals: Twenty Stories of Alliance and Encounter.* New York, Doubleday, 1993.
Editor, *People Have More Fun Than Anybody: A James Thurber Centennial Collection.* New York, Harcourt, 1994.
Editor, *Dog People: Writers and Artists on Canine Companionship.* New York, Artisan, 1995.

Editor, *The Genius of James Thurber.* London, the Folio Society, 1997.

Editor, *Horse People: Writers and Artisits on the Horses They Love.* New York, Artisan, 1998.

*

Critical Studies: Review of *Elijah's Angel: A Story for Chanukah and Christmas* by Ari L. Goldman, in *New York Times Book Review,* 13 December 1992, 35; "Interview: An Artful Bridge Uniting Faiths and Generations" by Richard Scheinin, in *San Jose Mercury News,* 26 December 1992; review of *The Greatest Table: A Banquet to Fight Against Hunger* by Marcia Hupp, in *School Library Journal,* April 1995, 128; National Jewish Book Award acceptance speech by Michael J. Rosen, in *Horn Book,* November 1993, 714-16; Interview with Leonard Kniffel, *Booklinks,* January 1997; Interview with Connie Zitlow and Tobie Sanders, *Ohio Journal of the English Language Arts,* winter, 1998; "Michael J. Rosen, Children's Book Author & Illustrator," brochure prepared and distributed by the author.

Michael J. Rosen comments:

When I was a kid, I wondered if I could earn a living by writing and drawing. (I also thought I might be a doctor, but a few months of medical school got that notion out of my system.) It took me years to realize that what I most like about these arts is the very fact that they are hard for me. I assumed that writing and art are about doing something perfectly, that there are two ways to do things: perfectly and wrong. I didn't realize that art is really imperfection—the crazily individual ways that our own personalities and abilities try to make sense of the beauties, challenges, and desperations our lives inherit and create.

Now I understand that some artists use realistic lines (that's the kind of talent I thought I had to have) to create works that closely resemble their subjects. But other artists can better capture the spirit, humor, confusion, or frustrations of their subjects—and their versions may not be so exacting and realistic. The same concepts apply to the art of writing. So, gradually, because I was fortunate to have mentors who would listen to version after version of my young efforts—because I read and, indeed, imitated what I envied in so many authors—I grew confident enough to appreciate some of my own writing. Gradually, I began to detect something like a voice or style, which I define as all the things a person can do in one medium, combined with all the things a person can't do.

In stories, I'm fixed on finding the small differences in the common things we share. And because we all have such differences, difference is something we have in common. Why read a book about a person of another age or race or nationality or time period (even the future) if not for the chance to find the shadows of our own stories—like a highlighter's trails, transparent and bright—among those pages? If we weren't blessed with the gift of empathy—and I do believe empathy is a survival tactic, something we gained in evolution to offset our aggressiveness—we'd never read anything, never worry about friends, never shed a tear or a bead of sweat for anyone else. No, we read because within others' stories we recognize our own. All stories are brethren. When we read or tell or hear stories, we admit ourselves to this kinship, linking arms in a blockade against fear and indifference.

* * *

As author, editor, and illustrator of children's books, Michael J. Rosen has sensitively and uniquely created stories that gently cradle those issues, experiences, and beliefs of everyday life that he most cares about. For readers of children's literature he invents characters, plots, contexts, and artistic formats that provide powerful connections to his books and reveal his concerns and experiences. During these personal connections to Rosen's books, connections that involve both heart and mind, the things he cares about emerge. Three general categories can be used to further describe the illuminating writing of Michael J. Rosen: beliefs about writing, including the use of art and print, relationships among diverse people, and issues of a social nature that he embeds in natural contexts.

Acknowledging the uniquely individual characteristic of art, Michael J. Rosen states "now I know that we need to describe our world in every possible way, with every sort of language. Sure, some artists use realistic lines ... and create art that closely matches its subject. But other talents are better at capturing the spirit, humor, confusion or feeling of their subjects." Rosen's beliefs about writing are evident in his work. He tries to capture the detail and irony of the stories, characters, and issues that most concern him through the use of a variety of artistic forms in illustration, language, book format and story structure. Poetry, short stories, accordion style books, and edited books with a diversity of impressive artistic styles are precisely chosen to tell stories that house delicate ideas and issues people care about. The touching narrative in *Bonesy and Isabel,* for example, contrasts with the poetic and scientific perspective offered in *All Eyes on the Pond.* Both differ from Rosen's edited books, which not only have a style and format of their own but are inclusive of a variety of author and illustrator experiences.

Likewise, as he extends his professional life teaching and encouraging young writers in school visits or Young Authors conferences, Michael J. Rosen continues to share his beliefs about writing. He uses his stories, such as *SPEAK!* or *Purr,* to elicit children's own stories about their pets. When sharing *The Greatest Table,* a story of Thanksgiving illustrated by 16 children's artists, Michael Rosen asks children to think of their own unique meals and how they would illustrate their own contribution to such a book. Rosen says, "I want kids to find the one answer that no one else would ever suggest, one that isn't in the common, familiar, lazy pool, but one that comes from the honestly exceptional territory of each person's experiences." He also encourages students to go beyond their question of where ideas come from, to how can one imagine a "... believable, convincing story for each idea to inhabit."

Elijah's Angel: A Story for Chanukah and Christmas is a significant example of relationships among people in Michael J. Rosen's books. This autobiographical story is about nine-year-old Michael, who is Jewish, and eighty-year-old African American wood carver Elijah Pierce, who gives Michael a hand carved angel at Christmas. Michael is uncomfortable with this as he has been taught that graven images are forbidden in Judaism. His understanding parents help him realize that the angel means friendship, and Michael in turn shares Chanukah by giving Elijah a menorah he made. This friendship was the impetus for a story that goes across cultural boundaries of age, race, and religion. How better to create an environment for young and old readers to contemplate culture?

A story about love, friendship, adoption, and death, *Bonesy and Isabel* is the story of a newly adopted child from El Salvador who, like the many animals on the old farm where she now lives, finds love and a home with her new parents. As she becomes accustomed to the strange language and different life style, the animals are her friends. The death of Bonesy, an older dog, serves to bond Isabel and her new parents as they share the loss of a friend and face a new life together. The differences of the individuals within the story represent diverse life experiences and cultures; however, the grief experienced over Bonesy's death reminds us that emotions are universal and transcend these differences. Rosen continues this thought with his question, "Why read a book about a person of another age or race or nationality or time period (even the future) if not for the chance to find the shadows of our own stories?"

A third category descriptive of Michael J. Rosen's writing is that of social issues. Rosen's books focus on those issues that are important to him, human dilemmas like homelessness and divorce or human wrongs toward other people and animals. While not claiming to be an activist, Rosen's efforts as an author have been extended to create not only a sense of "moral citizenship" in the contributing authors but to create greater support for certain organizations. After publishing his first collaborative project, *Home,* followed by *The Greatest Table* and *Food Fight: Poets Join the Fight Against Hunger with Poems to Favorite Foods,* he became involved with Share Our Strength, one of the nation's largest private hunger relief organizations. The proceeds from these books have gone to support efforts of this organization to suppress domestic hunger. As a result of his involvement with Share Our Strength, Rosen began an animal welfare project which was funded by the royalties from the books *The Company of Dogs, The Company of Cats, The Company of Animals, Dog People, SPEAK!: Children's Book Illustrators Brag about Their Dogs* and *Purr ... Children's Book Illustrators Brag About Their Cats.* Each of these edited books are a delight for animal lovers and elicit personal stories. Humorous and moving essays, stories and poems are found in *Home.* While each contribution is characteristic of the children's author who wrote it, collectively it invites the reader to consider what home means to them.

The Greatest Table: A Banquet to Fight Against Hunger is illustrated by a variety of artists with each illustration depicting a different eating situation—banquet, feast, family meal, school cafeteria, picnic. The accordion format is eye catching and allows for the illustrations to be displayed. To celebrate one's own life experiences is also to reflect on the meaning it has for each individual, however simplistic, and the reasons to support efforts to assist those whose life experiences are not so fortunate.

Michael J. Rosen's work has contributed to the field of children's literature in many ways. The use of a variety of artistic forms selectively chosen to carry significant ideas provides rich reading experiences and fine examples of the art of writing. His inclusion of a diversity of people interacting in natural contexts provides authentic stories of the similarities and differences that connect people to each other. Finally, by providing stories and illustrations on topics of interest to many, readers can add their own stories and contemplate the value of each situation for them individually.

—Janelle B. Mathis

ROSS, Tony

Nationality: British. **Born:** London, 10 August 1938. **Education:** Liverpool Regional College of Art, 1958-61. **Family:** Married 1) Carol Dawn D'Arcy in 1961 (divorced); 2) Joan Lillian Spokes in 1971 (divorced); 3) Zoë Ash in 1979, one son and two daughters. **Career:** Graphic designer, Littlewoods, Liverpool, 1961-62, and Smith Kline and French Pharmaceuticals, Welwyn Garden City, Hertfordshire, 1962-64; art director, Brunnings Advertising, Manchester, 1964-65; lecturer in illustration, Manchester Polytechnic, 1965-86. **Awards:** Silver Pencil award (Netherlands) (twice); Silver Paintbrush award (Netherlands) (twice); Children's Literature prize (Germany). **Address:** c/o Andersen Press, 20 Vauxhall Bridge Road, London SW1V 2SA England; Lake House, Leek Old Road, Sutton, Macclesfield, Cheshire SK11 0HZ, England.

PUBLICATIONS FOR CHILDREN (ILLUSTRATED BY THE AUTHOR)

Fiction

Tales from Mr. Toffy's Circus (*Big Ethel, Blodwen, Bop, Mr. Toffy, Samuel, Tiger Harry*). London, Fabbri, 6 vols., 1973.

Hugo and the Man Who Stole Colours. London, Andersen Press, and Chicago, Follett, 1977.

Hugo and the Wicked Winter. London, Sidgwick and Jackson, 1977.

Norman and Flop Meet the Toy Bandit. London, Thurman, 1977.

Hugo and Oddsock. London, Andersen Press, 1978; Windermere, Florida, Rourke, 1982.

The Greedy Little Cobbler. London, Andersen Press, 1979; Woodbury, New York, Barrons, 1980.

The True Story of Mother Goose and Her Son Jack. London, Andersen Press, 1979; Windermere, Florida, Rourke, 1982.

Hugo and the Ministry of Holidays. London, Andersen Press, 1980; as *Hugo and the Bureau of Holidays,* Windermere, Florida, Rourke, 1982.

Naughty Nigel. London, Andersen Press, 1982; as *Naughty Nicky,* New York, Holt Rinehart, 1983.

Jack the Giantkiller. London, Andersen Press, 1983.

I'm Coming to Get You. London, Andersen Press, and New York, Dial Press, 1984.

Towser and the Terrible Thing [*Water Rats, Sadie's Birthday, Haunted House, Funny Face, Magic Apple, the Monster Egg,* and *Tower's Party*]. London, Andersen Press, 8 vols., 1984-85, 1995; first 3 vols. published New York, Pantheon, 1984.

Lazy Jack. London, Andersen Press, 1985; New York, Dial Press, 1986.

I Want My Potty. London, Andersen Press, and New York, Kane Miller, 1986.

Oscar Got the Blame. London, Andersen Press, 1987; New York, Dial Press, 1988.

Super Dooper Jezebel. London, Andersen Press, and New York, Farrar Straus, 1988.

I Want a Cat. London, Andersen Press, 1988; New York, Farrar Straus, 1989.

The Treasure of Cosy Cove, or, The Voyage of the "Kipper". London, Andersen Press, 1989; New York, Farrar Straus, 1990.

The Happy Rag. London, Andersen Press, 1990.

Mrs. Goat and Her Seven Little Kids. London, Andersen Press, 1990.

Don't Do That. London, Andersen Press, 1991.
Big, Bad Barney Bear. London, Andersen Press, 1992.
I Want to Be. London, Andersen Press, and Brooklyn, New York, Kane Miller, 1993.
Animals. London, Moonlight, 1994.
Bedtime. London, Andersen, 1994.
Paintings. London, Moonlight, 1994.
Pets. London, Andersen, 1994.
Portraits. London, Moonlight, 1994.
Shapes. London, Andersen, 1994.
Weather. London, Andersen, 1994.
I Want My Dinner. London, Andersen, 1995.
The Shop of Ghosts. London, Trafalgar Square, 1995.
Let's Visit the Louvre. London, Moonlight, 1995.
Nicky. London, Andersen, 1997.
Silly, Silly. London, Andersen, 1998.

Plays

What's in a Name, King of All the Birds, Oscar Buys the Biscuits, Muddy Milly, Spacemare (all *Time for a Story* television series), 1985-86.
Towser (television series).
Hello, 21st Century. (Blue Peter television play), 1993.

Other (retellings)

Goldilocks and the Three Bears. London, Andersen Press, 1976; Woodstock, New York, Overlook, 1992.
The Pied Piper of Hamelin. London, Andersen Press, 1977; New York, Lothrop, 1978.
Little Red Riding Hood. London, Andersen Press, 1978; New York, Doubleday, 1979.
Jack and the Beanstalk. London, Andersen Press, 1980; New York, Delacorte Press, 1981.
Puss in Boots. London, Andersen Press, and New York, Delacorte Press, 1981.
The Enchanted Pig. London, Andersen Press, 1982; New York, Bedrick, 1983.
The Three Pigs. London, Andersen Press, and New York, Pantheon, 1983.
The Boy Who Cried Wolf. London, Andersen Press, and New York, Dial Press, 1985.
Foxy Fables. London, Andersen Press, and New York, Kane Miller, 1986.
Stone Soup. London, Andersen Press, and New York, Dial Press, 1987.
Hansel and Gretel. London, Andersen Press, and Woodstock, New York, Overlook, 1989.
Five Favourite Tales. London, Andersen Press, 1990.
Jack and the Beanstalk. London, Puffin, 1991.
A Fairy Tale. London, Little Brown, 1992.

*

Illustrator: *Did I Ever Tell You* series by Iris Grender, 6 vols., 1978-85; *Mr. Browser* series, 11 vols., 1979-89, *Chaos Comes to Chivvy Chase,* 1988, *Mr. Browser and the Space Maggots,* 1990, and *Pen Friend from Another Planet,* 1990, *Welcome to the Giants,* 1991, all by Philip Curtis; *Whizz Bang: Two Monkey Tales* by Patricia Gray and David Mackay, 1979; *The Charge of the Mouse Brigade,* 1979, and *The Tale of Admiral Mouse,* 1981, both by Bernard Stone; *Hare and Badger Go to Town* by Naomi Lewis, 1981; *The Methuen Book of Strange Tales,* 1981, and *The Methuen Book of Sinister Stories,* 1982, both edited by Jean Russell; *Clement Aplati* by Jeff Brown, 1982; *Kaspar and the Iron Poodle* by J.K. Hooper, 1982; *The Reluctant Vampire,* 1982, and *The Vampire's Revenge,* 1983, both by Eric Morecambe; *Le Plaisir des Mots* by Georges Jean, 1982; *Le Livre des Marins* by Dominique Duviard, 1983; *Le Livre de la Peinture* by Adrian Sington, 1983; *Paper Flags and Penny Ices,* 1984, and *Hanky-Panky,* 1986, both by Roger Collinson; *Marmalade Jim and the Fox* by Alan Sillitoe, 1984; *The Shrieking Face,* 1984, *Terrible Tuesday,* 1985, *Pilkie's Progress,* 1986, *Through the Witch's Window,* 1989, *Victor's Party,* 1990, *Amos Shrike, the School Ghost,* 1990, and *Snakes Alive!,* 1991, all by Hazel Townson; *The End of the Tale and Other Stories,* 1985, *Dear Grumble,* 1989, *Toby's Iceberg,* 1990, *Little Elephant,* 1991, *Duck Soup Farm,* 1992, and *The Grandson Boy,* 1993, all by W.J. Corbett; *Limericks* by Michael Palin, 1985; *William,* 1986, and *Just William,* 1987, both by Richmal Crompton; *Alfonso Bonzo* by Andrew Davies, 1986; *The Phantom Lollipop Lady,* 1986, *Rhinestone Rhino,* 1989, and *Dinner with the Spratts,* 1994, all by Adrian Henri; *Jenna and the Troublemaker,* 1986, *The Trouble with Harry,* 1987, *Anyone Seen Harry Lately?,* 1988, *The Second Princess,* 1994, *Reckless Ruby,* 1994, and *A Message for Santa,* 1997, all by Hiawyn Oram; *The Treasure Sock* by Pat Thompson, 1986; *The King Bird* by A.H. Benjamin, 1987; *Dangleboots,* by Dennis Hamley, 1987; *Open Door: Bill's Old Banger and Other Stories* by Elizabeth Lawrence, 1987; *Wesley and the Dinosaurs,* 1987, and *Wesley and the Dragons of Stonewade,* 1991, both by David Mackay; *Dixie's Demon,* 1987, *Wolf Pie,* 1987, *The Quiet Pirate,* 1988, *S. Claus—The Truth!,* 1989, *Dr. Monsoon Taggert's Amazing Finishing Academy,* 1989, *Mallory Cox and his Magic Socks,* 1990, *Mistress Moonwater,* 1990, *Wickedoz,* 1990, *Loads of Trouble,* 1991, *Mallory Cox and the Viking Box,* 1991, *Wickedoz and the Dragons of Stonewade,* 1991, *Mallory Cox and His Interstellar Socks,* 1993, and *Silly Stories,* 1994, all by Andrew Matthews; *Meanwhile Back at the Ranch* by Trinka Noble, 1987; *Playschool Book of Songs,* 1987; *La Grande Bretagne,* 1987; *Fantastic Mr. Fox,* 1988, and *The Magic Finger,* 1993, both by Roald Dahl; *The Whipping Boy,* 1988, and *The Midnight Horse,* 1991, both by Sid Fleischman; *The Fantora Family Files,* 1988, *The Fantora Family Photographs,* 1993, *Blossom's Revenge,* 1997, *Picasso Perkins,* 1997, and *Callie's Kitten,* 1998, all by Adèle Geras; *The Clever Potato,* 1988, *Love Shouts and Whispers,* 1990, *Travelling Light,* 1991, and *On Your Cycle, Michael,* 1992, all by Vernon Scannell; *Well I Never!* by Heather Eyles, 1988; *The Knight Who Was Afraid of the Dark* by Barbara Shook Hazen, 1989; *Your Dad's a Monkey* by Judy Corbalis, 1989; *The Pop-Up Book of Nonsense Verse,* 1989; *First Dictionary* compiled by Dee Reid, 1989; *Dr. Xargle's Book of Earth Hounds,* 1989, *Earthlets, As Explained by Professor Xargle,* 1989, *Dr. Xargle's Book of Earth Tiggers,* 1990, *Earth Weather, As Explained by Professor Xargle,* 1991, *Earth Mobiles, As Explained by Professor Xargle,* 1992, *Dr. Xargle's Book of Earth Relations,* 1993, and *Relativity, As Explained by Professor Xargle,* 1994, *The Pet Person,* 1996, and *Sloth's Shoes,* 1997, all by Jeanne Willis; *Naughty Stories,* 1990, *Even Naughtier Stories,* 1990, and *Naughtiest Stories,* 1993, all compiled by Barbara Ireson; *The Young Green Consumer Guide* by John Elkington and Julia Hailes with Douglas Hill, 1990; *Michael* by Tony Bradman, 1990; *James and the Dragon,* 1990, and *Molly and the Giant,* 1990, both by Julia

Jarman; *The Joke Machine,* 1990; *Monty the Monster Mouse* by Sheila Lavelle, 1990; *This Old Man,* 1990; *A Brontosaurus Chorus* edited by Catherine Baker, 1991; *Animals Matter,* 1991; *Bubble Trouble* by Margaret Mahy, 1991; *Space Dog and Roy,* 1991, *Space Dog and the Pet Show,* 1991, *Space Dog in Trouble,* 1991, and *Space Dog the Hero,* 1991, all by Natalie Standiford; *Tracey-Ann and the Buffalo* by Kara May, 1991; *The Bad Child's Book of Beasts* by Hilaire Belloc, 1992; *How to Be a Little Sod,* 1992, *Look Who's Walking!: Further Adventures of a Little Sod,* 1994, and *Not Another Little Sod!,* 1997, all by Simon Brett; *If Cats Could Fly* by Robert Westall, 1992; *Sir Gadabout,* 1992, *Sir Gadabout Gets Worse,* 1993, and *Sir Gadabout and the Ghost,* 1994, all by Martyn Beardsley; *You Can't Say I'm Crazy* by Robert Swindells, 1992; *Burping Bertha* by Michael Rosen, 1993; *Carrot Tops and Cotton Tails,* by Jan Mark, 1993; *Who Invented Peanut Butter?* by Alexander McCall Smith, 1993; *Through the Looking-Glass,* 1993, and *Alice's Adventures in Wonderland,* 1994, both by Lewis Carroll; *Le Bestiare,* 1993; *Les Portraits,* 1993; *Les Tableaux,* 1993; *Les Paysages,* 1993; *It Came Through the Wall,* by Tim Healey, 1993; *Amber Brown Is Not A Crayon,* 1994, *You Can't Eat Your Chicken Pox, Amber Brown,* 1995, *Amber Brown Goes Fourth,* 1995, *Forever Amber Brown,* 1996, and *Amber Brown Sees Red,* 1997, all by Paula Danziger; *Cabbages from Outer Space,* 1994, and *The Midnight Feast,* 1996, both by Lindsay Camp; *The Shop of Ghosts* by G.K. Chesterton, 1994; *The Vampire's Christmas,* 1994, *The Vampire's Revenge,* 1994, *The Vampire Vanishes,* 1995, *Vampire Park,* 1997, all by Willis Hall; *John Midas and the Vampires,* 1994, and *John Midas and the Rock Star,* 1995, by Patrick Skene Catling; *I'm Running Away* by Miriam Simon, 1994; *Something in the Fridge* by Julia Jarman, 1994; *Little Princess* board books series, 1994; *Norma's Notebook, Lisa's Letter, Dad, Figgy Roll* by Michael Rosen, 1994; *Horrid Henry and the Secret Club,* 1995, *Horrid Henry and the Tooth Fairy,* 1996, *Horrid Henry's Nits,* 1997, *Horrid Henry Strikes It Rich,* 1998, all by Francesca Simon; *The Treasure Hunt* by Tony Mitton, 1995; *Telling Tales* compiled by Barbara Ireson, 1995; *Stinky Cynthia* by Heather Eyles, 1995; *Little Wolf's Book of Badness,* 1995, and *Little Wolf's Diary of Daring Deeds,* 1997, by Ian Whybrow; *Paws and Claws,* 1995; *Stone Me!,* 1995, *Mind the Door!,* 1996, *A Touch of Wind!,* 1997, by Steve Barlow and Steve Skidmore; *4 Storie Sulle Route* by Graham Greene, 1996; *Horrid Henry and the Tooth Fairy* by Francesca Simon, 1996; *Seeing Red* by Sarah Garland, 1996; *The Pet Person* by Jeanne Willis, 1996; *Ms. Wiz* series by Terence Blacker, 1996-97; *The Family Who Won a Million* by Alison Sage, 1996; *Sticky Fingers* by Roger Collinson, 1996; *Harry the Poisonous Centipede* by Lynne Reid Banks, 1996; *Miss Dirt the Dustman's Daughter* by Allan Ahlberg, 1996; *The Greek Myths* series by Geraldine McCaughrean, 1996; *Unlocking Christ's Parables* by Rogie Spon, 1996; *Balloon Lagoon* by Adrian Mitchell, 1997; *Ghouls Rule,* 1997, *Ace Ghosts,* 1997, and *Funky Phantoms,* 1998, all by Karen Wallace; *Red Eyes at Night* by Michael Morpurgo, 1997; *Animal Stories for Seven Year Olds* edited by Helen Paiba, 1998; *Dogbird* by Paul Stewart, 1998.

Tony Ross comments:

My main, and original interest in illustrating children's books, both in colour and black and white, gives way slightly to an interest in the words. I am happy to leave teaching to the teachers and philosophy to the philosophers, both of which abound in children's books. I try to entertain. Most of my aims and ambitions are private ones, and are better staying that way.

Trying to understand children, though, is proving to be a fascinating and enlightening experience.

The motivation, of course, is the enjoyment a pen and a sheet of blank paper brings—certainly to me, every time, hopefully to others.

* * *

Tony Ross is a prolific writer-illustrator, who has created a succession of memorable protagonists, from Hugo the Mouse, who meets interesting characters on his strange adventures; Naughty Nigel, a boy who deliberately mishears everything said to him; Towser the dog, whose admirable qualities include kindness and generosity; to Super Dooper Jezebel, the model child who gets snapped up by a crocodile. Ross is equally well-known for his updating of traditional folk- and fairytales in picture-book format, which cast a powerful charm upon children, parents, and teachers alike.

As for the first group, Ross successfully identifies the concerns and fantasy life of children. For example, how may a child reconcile the Santa story with the strong possibility, or certainty, that it is Mother or Father who fills the Christmas stocking? In *Hugo and the Ministry of Holidays* Ross offers a gratifying solution to the puzzle; his over-worked Santas enlist the aid of parents to resolve the delivery problems. Again, who is to say whether an imaginary friend conceived to act as a substitute for oneself in every awkward situation is any less "real" than one of flesh and blood, as in *Oscar Got the Blame*? Ross also touches the adult nerve; we all recognise the single-mindedness of Jessy in *I Want a Cat,* who takes her campaign to the extremes of wearing a cat suit and behaving in a feline manner; her parents finally capitulate whereupon she declares she hates cats and wants a dog; in their turn children have no difficulty in identifying with Jessy's wiles, and her fantasy of actually being the object of her own desires. A darker tale, *I'm Coming to Get You,* addresses a child's fear of the unknown, externally projected as a monster, and with a witty twist shows how easily and naturally fear is reduced and squashed in daylight.

Ross's literary tale-telling favours a deadpan humour and aims to establish intimacy with the reader. His visual style varies considerably, but whatever he does, he always displays a strong sense of page design, and a masterly control of his media. Deceptively sketchy at times, his pen romps along, in the tradition of English narrative illustration. However whiskery fine, feathery light, frothy, bold, or meticulously incised, the line has unquenchable vitality. Ross varies the medium to enhance the tone of the text. Watercolour might be lightly applied, in dip and skimming washes upon rapidly executed drawings as in *I Want My Potty,* a tale in which time is of essence. Jessy's story is pictured in crayon scribble as physically determined and full of purpose as the child herself. The magical world of *Hugo and the Man Who Stole Colours* is made more mysterious by shadowy cross hatching, which settles the images on the page.

Ross is an outstanding colourist. In his comic rural folktale world uninhibited colour floats across the skies—sharp lemon, sandy pinks, and melting conjunctions of unlikely green, cerulean, and rose. Though Ross uses a wide palette he often organises a painting in a limited range of close hues to create a particular mood, as in *Puss in Boots,* when he denotes Puss stopping the king's coach, and exemplifies the animal's nerves of steel by picturing it all in controlled cool hues of blue and grey. Witty visual metaphors reward close readings. Goldilocks stumps into her story in her oversize track shoes, about to "put her foot in it" almost continuously. Puss has his wild gold eyes set upon a fortune, and Lazy Jack is too idle to take his hands out of his pockets. Ross's cast is of generally genial grotesques. The most pleasant are only rarely sentimental, and the most loathsome are too bizarre to evoke any real horror. However stylised the figures, their poses are full of conviction, and there are little stories to be made from the details of appearance of even minor characters.

Ross's excellence as an artist is easy to demonstrate; his role as an interpreter of traditional tales is much more difficult to assess. There is no doubt that his pictorial interpretation always interlocks successfully with his own texts, but the relationship of his own text and the established one gives rise to very complex questions: how a writer may strike a sound balance between retelling and remaining true to the established text, or indeed, if he should attempt to do so. Ross does not take a radical line, but like many other retellers and civilisers of tales, he seems unaware of the nature of the deeper content. This does not matter when the updating is confined to surface details, as in *Goldilocks and the Three Bears,* or *Puss in Boots,* but surely it matters very much when he tinkers with so many elements that he actually affects the prime burden, diminishing what it offers in traditional terms without compensating by adding new positive content. Ross's updating of *The Enchanted Pig* is the perfect example of how easy it is to be dazzled by his richly inventive illustration, yet his interpretation reduces the spirit of what is one of the most moving tributes to the powers of human endurance and love in the fairytale canon. *The Three Pigs* also suffers a change of emphasis as Ross brings his version to a close in misplaced irony. His sad, isolated surviving pig is certainly not a more satisfying model for a child to behold than the robust victor of the established text. Ross is not so much a gifted interpreter of the tales, as a gifted interpreter of his own versions, and in general, new tales or old, an adroit, manipulative, and often inspired maker of aesthetically rewarding picture books.

In the 1990s Tony Ross has been active in many different areas of illustration, including books on art appreciation for children. His own pictures are instantly recognisable, with their jaunty, humorously sketched lines and bright, clear colour washes. Within this distinctive style, however, Ross has some breadth of emotion, ranging from the saucy or comically bewildered figures who typify much of his work to an expressive tenderness in, for example, the last picture for *Camp's The Midnight Feast.* The 1994 "Little Princess" series of board books for babies allows Ross to reveal his strength as a colourist and designer working with very simple elements. In *Pets,* however, his mordant humour resurfaces as the various animals the Princess has been feeding all come running towards her for more, and she flees with a cry of "Help!" By the mid-1990s, Ross moved away from folk tales and into the illustration of chapter books such as the Amber Brown series by Paula Danziger and Terrence Blacker's tales of Ms. Wiz. His witty sketches set into the text enhance the stories with their inimitable sense of fun and absurdity, helping young readers bridge the gap from picture books.

—Jane Doonan, updated by Gwyneth Evans

ROUGHSEY, Dick

Tribal name: Goobalathaldin. **Nationality:** Australian. **Born:** On Langunarnji Island, Gulf of Carpentaria, Queensland, in 1924. **Education:** Mornington Island Mission School. **Family:** Married Elsie Roughsey; six children. **Career:** Stockman at Gregory Downs, Lorraine, and other cattle stations, Northern Territory, 1943-50; deckhand on the coastal ship *Cora,* early 1950s; yardman, Karumba lodge, 1962-63. From 1962 freelance artist: individual shows of bark paintings at Cairns School of Arts, Queensland, 1962, and galleries in Brisbane and Canberra. From 1973 Chairman, Aboriginal Arts Board. **Awards:** Australian Children's Book Council Picture Book of the Year award, 1976, 1979; Weickhardt award, 1976. **Died:** 20 October 1985.

Publications for Children (illustrated by the author)

Fiction

The Giant Devil Dingo. Sydney and London, Collins, 1973; New York, Macmillan, 1975.

The Rainbow Serpent. Sydney and London, Collins, 1975.

The Quinkins, with Percy Trezise. Sydney and London, Collins, 1978.

Banana Bird and the Snake Men, with Percy Trezise. Sydney, Collins, 1980.

Turramulli the Giant Quinkin, with Percy Trezise. Sydney, Collins, 1982.

The Magic Firesticks, with Percy Trezise. Sydney, Collins, 1983.

Gidja, with Percy Trezise. Sydney, Collins, 1984.

The Flying Fox Warriors, with Percy Trezise. Sydney, Collins, 1985.

Publications for Adults

Other

Moon and Rainbow: The Autobiography of an Aboriginal. Sydney, Reed, 1971.

*

Illustrator (as Goobalathaldin Roughsey): *The Turkey and the Emu* by Labamu Roughsey, 1978.

* * *

Dick Roughsey was a full-blood Australian aborigine, an elder of the Lardil tribe. His tribal name was Goobalathaldin, which meant "rough seas," hence his adopted English surname. He was making tree-bark pictures in the traditional aboriginal way when in 1962 he met Percy Trezise, a retired pilot, who encouraged him to adapt his bark paintings using techniques more appropriate to European landscape painting. His first children's picture books—the first published works written and illustrated by an Australian aboriginal—resulted from this friendship. Through his unique and arresting picture-book versions of aboriginal myths, Roughsey offered the world something of the directness, dignity, and rhythms of the language of his people, the stark strength, boldness, and colour of their art, and something of their spiritual and practical affinity with the timeless land itself.

Gradually Trezise began sharing in the making of these books: "We first wrote a description of each scene, then I did the landscapes and Dick added the figures." Both men were dedicated to preserving aspects of the disappearing traditional aboriginal culture, feeling that the picture-book medium would bring these ancient myths to a universal audience through visual images that would create lasting impressions.

The Rainbow Serpent is one of the basic creation myths, central to traditional aboriginal beliefs. *The Quinkins* are ancient spirit people of the Yalangi tribe. Some were "small, fat-bellied creatures, with large ugly heads, long teeth and claws." This Cape York story is about a Quinkin attempt to steal two children and how it was foiled by rival Quinkins. *The Giant Devil Dingo* tells of the evil Eelgin, the grasshopper woman who taught Gaiya, the giant dingo, to hunt and kill men for food. Eventually the dingo is ambushed and killed and from his bones the medicine man makes two small dingoes to be man's friend and helper. *Banana Bird and the Snake Men* illustrates an Olculla clan myth which explains the creation of a desert plateau and five particular rivers in Cape York, and subsequently the five clans of the Snake-language people.

All these books contain simple texts which have the quiet ring of authenticity, while the bold paintings are most impressive, powerful, and striking visual images. Each represents a splendid opportunity to help bridge cultures and promote understanding.

Since Roughsey's death, Percy Trezise has continued to produce books in the same spirit as the first attempts by his talented colleague.

—Walter McVitty

ROUNDS, Glen (Harold)

Nationality: American. **Born:** Near Wall, South Dakota, 4 April 1906. **Education:** Kansas City Art Institute, 1926-27; Art Students' League, New York, 1930-31. **Military Service:** United States Army Coast Artillery and Infantry, 1942-45: Staff Sergeant. **Family:** Married 1) Mary Lucas in 1928 (divorced 1937); 2) Margaret Olmsted in 1938 (died 1968); one son. **Career:** Worked as cowboy, baker, sign painter, textile designer; full-time writer since 1936. **Awards:** American Association of University Women award, 1961, 1967, 1969, 1981; University of Minnesota Kerlan award, 1980. **Address:** Box 763, Southern Pines, North Carolina 28387, U.S.A.

PUBLICATIONS FOR CHILDREN (ILLUSTRATED BY THE AUTHOR)

Fiction

Lumbercamp. New York, Holiday House, 1937; as *The Whistle Punk of Camp 15,* 1959.
Pay Dirt. New York, Holiday House, 1938.
The Blind Colt. New York, Holiday House, 1941.
Whitey's First Round-Up. New York, Grosset and Dunlap, 1942.
Whitey's Sunday Horse. New York, Grosset and Dunlap, 1943.
Whitey Looks for a Job. New York, Grosset and Dunlap, 1944.
Whitey and Jinglebob. New York, Grosset and Dunlap, 1946.
Stolen Pony. New York, Holiday House, 1948; revised edition, 1969.
Whitey and the Rustlers. New York, Holiday House, 1951.
Hunted Horses. New York, Holiday House, 1951.
Whitey and the Blizzard. New York, Holiday House, 1952.
Buffalo Harvest. New York, Holiday House, 1952.
Lone Muskrat. New York, Holiday House, 1953.
Whitey Takes a Trip. New York, Holiday House, 1954.
Whitey Ropes and Rides. New York, Holiday House, 1956.
Whitey and the Wild Horse. New York, Holiday House, 1958.
Wild Orphan. New York, Holiday House, 1961.
Whitey and the Colt-Killer. New York, Holiday House, 1962.
Whitey's New Saddle. New York, Holiday House, 1963.
The Snake Tree. Cleveland, World, 1966.
Once We Had a Horse. New York, Holiday House, 1971.
The Day the Circus Came to Lone Tree. New York, Holiday House, 1973.
Mr. Yowder and the Lion Roar Capsules. New York, Holiday House, 1976.
Mr. Yowder and the Steamboat. New York, Holiday House, 1977.
Mr. Yowder and the Giant Bull Snake. New York, Holiday House, 1978.
Blind Outlaw. New York, Holiday House, 1980.
Mr. Yowder, The Peripatetic Sign Painter (omnibus). New York, Holiday House, 1980.
Mr. Yowder and the Train Robbers. New York, Holiday House, 1981.
Wild Appaloosa. New York, Holiday House, 1983.
Mr. Yowder and the Windwagon. New York, Holiday House, 1983.
The Morning the Sun Refused to Rise: An Original Paul Bunyan Tale. New York, Holiday House, 1984.
Washday on Noah's Ark. New York, Holiday House, 1985.
Cowboys. New York, Holiday House, 1991.

Plays

Radio Scripts: *School of the Air,* 1938-39.

Other

Ol' Paul, The Mighty Logger. New York, Holiday House, 1936; revised edition, 1949, 1976.
Rodeo: Bulls, Broncs, and Buckaroos. New York, Holiday House, 1949.
Swamp Life: An Almanac. Englewood Cliffs, New Jersey, Prentice Hall, 1957.
Wildlife at Your Doorstep: An Illustrated Almanac. Englewood Cliffs, New Jersey, Prentice Hall, 1958.
Beaver Business: An Almanac. Englewood Cliffs, New Jersey, Prentice Hall, 1960.
Rain in the Woods and Other Small Matters. Cleveland, World, 1964.
The Treeless Plains. New York, Holiday House, 1967.
The Prairie Schooners. New York, Holiday House, 1968.
Wild Horses of the Red Desert. New York, Holiday House, 1969; as *Wild Horses,* New York, Holiday House, 1993.
The Cowboy Trade. New York, Holiday House, 1972.
The Beaver: How He Works. New York, Holiday House, 1976.

Old MacDonald Had a Farm (retelling). New York, Holiday House, 1989.
I Know an Old Lady Who Swallowed a Fly (retelling). New York, Holiday House, 1990.
The Three Little Pigs and the Big Bad Wolf (retelling). New York, Holiday House, 1992.
Sod Houses on the Great Plains. New York, Holiday House, 1995.

Editor, *Trail Drive,* from *Log of a Cowboy,* by Andy Adams. New York, Holiday House, 1965; London, Whiting and Wheaton, 1966.
Editor, *Mountain Men,* by George F. Ruxton. New York, Holiday House, 1966.
Editor, *The Boll Weevil.* San Carlos, California, Golden Gate Books, 1967.
Editor, *Casey Jones.* San Carlos, California, Golden Gate Books, 1968.
Editor, *The Strawberry Roan.* San Carlos, California, Golden Gate Books, 1970.
Editor, *Sweet Betsy from Pike.* Chicago, Children's Press, 1973.
Editor, *The Three Billy Goats Gruff.* New York, Holiday House, 1993.

*

Manuscript Collections: Kerlan Collection, University of Minnesota, Minneapolis.

Illustrator: *Flipper, A Sea-Lion* by Irma S. Black, 1940; *Tall Tale America* by Walter Blair, 1944; *"E" Company* by Frank O'Rourke, 1945; *Tatoosh* by Martha Hardy, 1947; *Uncle Swithin's Inventions* by Wheaton P. Webb, 1947; *Aesop's Fables,* 1949; *We Always Lie to Strangers,* 1951, *Who Blowed Up the Church House?,* 1952, *The Devil's Pretty Daughter,* 1955, *The Talking Turtle,* 1957, and *Sticks in the Knapsack,* 1958, all by Vance Randolph; *Grass, Our Greatest Crop* by Sarah J. Riedman, 1952; *Haunt Fox* by Jim Kjelgaard, 1954; *Those Glorious Mornings* by Paul Hyde Bonner, 1954; *Fire-Fly* by Paul M. Sears, 1956; *In the Arms of the Mountain* by Elizabeth Seeman, 1961; *A Wild Goose Tale,* 1961, *Dan and the Miranda,* 1962, *Big Blue Island,* 1964, *Mike's Toads,* 1970, *Squash Pie,* 1976, and *Down in the Boondocks,* 1977, all by Wilson Gage; *The Crocodile's Mouth,* 1966, and *American Tall Tale Animals,* 1968, both by Adrien Stoutenburg; *Billy Boy* edited by Richard Chase, 1966; *How the People Sang the Mountains Up* by Maria Leach, 1967; *Lucky Ladybugs,* 1968, *Tarantula, The Giant Spider,* 1972, and *Praying Mantis,* 1978, all by Gladys Conklin; *Contrary Jenkins* by Rebecca Caudill and James Ayars, 1969; *Folklore of the Great West* by John Greenway, 1969; *Ballads of the Great West* by Austin and Alta Fife, 1970; *Go Find Hanka!* by Alexander L. Crosby, 1970; *Farmer Hoo and the Baboons* by Ida Chittum, 1971; *A Twister of Twists, A Tangler of Tongues,* 1972, *Witcracks,* 1973, *Cross Your Fingers, Spit in Your Hat,* 1974, and *Kickle Snifters,* 1976, all edited by Alvin Schwartz, and *Tomfoolery,* 1973, and *Whoppers, Tall Tales, and Other Lies,* 1975, both by Schwartz; *I'm Going on a Bear Hunt* by Sandra S. Sivulich, 1973; *Jennie Jenkins* by Mark Taylor, 1975; *Three Fools and a Horse* by Betty Baker, 1975; *Lizard Lying in the Sun,* 1975, *The Happy Dromedary,* 1977, *Little Black Bear Goes for a Walk,* 1977, and *Elephant and Friends,* 1978, all by Berniece Freschet; *Tony, Granny, and George,* 1976, and *The Saving of P.S.,* 1977, both by Robbie Branscum; *Halfway Up the Mountain* by Theo E. Gilchrist, 1978; *The Lucky Man* by Mary Blount Christian, 1979; *Hush Up!,* 1980, *Shenandoah Noah,* 1985, and *Hanna's Hog,* 1988, all by Jim Aylesworth; *The Amazing Voyage of the New Orleans* by Judith St. George, 1980; *Uncle Lemon's Spring* by Jane Yolen, 1981; *The Old Woman and the Willy Nilly Man,* 1987, and *The Old Woman and the Jar of Umms,* 1989, both by Jill Wright; *Wild Pill Hickok and Other Old West Riddles* by David A. Adler, 1988; *Charlie Drives the Stage,* 1989, and *Four Dollars and Fifty Cents,* 1993, both by Eric A. Kimmel; *Soap! Soap! Don't Forget the Soap!: An AppalachianFolktale,* edited by Tom Birdseye, 1993.

* * *

Glen Rounds specializes in subject matter with which he is completely acquainted, and expresses himself distinctively and authoritatively. For a number of years, the author "drifted" around the country, and did a great many jobs. His book *Pay Dirt* tells of mining; *Lumbercamp* focuses on lumbering, and several books depict the life of a cowboy. *The Cowboy Trade,* in contrast to glamorous versions of life in the west, is authentic, based in part on his childhood.

Rounds's realistic books are invariably set in two regions—the plains, particularly a ranch near Ekalaka, Montana, and near Southern Pines, North Carolina. His 11 Whitey books are reminiscent of his relationship with the cowboys on his father's ranch. *The Treeless Plains* is based on homesteaders' memories and his return to the territory as an adult. Even his single book about the American Indian, *Buffalo Harvest,* limits itself to the tribe in his area.

Rounds describes wildlife with sensitivity and an authenticity based on hours spent at an abandoned farm and a swamp in North Carolina. *Wild Orphan* is a documentary of the first year of a beaver kit whose parents fell prey to traps; *Lone Muskrat* follows an aging animal. *Rain in the Woods and Other Small Matters* is more ecological, describing inter-relationships of flora and fauna.

While most of his books are realistic, the tall tales of his first book, *Ol' Paul,* come from Rounds's imagination, for the Paul Bunyan character was a device created for a lumber company's advertising campaign. The author is a good listener, and weaves anecdotes in his humorous books such as *The Day the Circus Came to Lone Tree* and *Mr. Yowder and the Lion Roar Capsules.*

Mr. Xenon Zebulon Yowder, "the World's Bestest and Fastest Sign Painter," covering the territory of Missouri, Kansas, Texas, and the Dakotas, is Rounds's lasting contribution to tall-tale characters. *Mr. Yowder, The Peripatetic Sign Painter* incorporates three tales published earlier, but with a more appropriate format for child readers. This "chapter book" surpasses the picture book usually associated with youngsters too young to assimilate the droll details, such as policemen "blowing their whistles and looking in rule books," which abound. The mangy lion, the sign-painter who "talked snake," and the pilot and captain who forsook card playing are unforgettable. At the conclusion of each tale, Rounds notes the disappearance of characters from that particular territory.

Rounds writes succinctly and effectively. Like a cowboy who must minimize his motions to save energy, the author is a master at economy of words. *Wild Horses of the Red Desert* opens with the sentence, "The Desert is a barren land of high rocky ridges and dusty sagebrush flats, where men seldom go." He uses the vernacular in the dialogue of his characters. Whitey wanted the "purtiest" colt on the ranch for his "Sunday" horse. In *Lumbercamp,* a paragraph in the chapter "Whiffler" reads, "Right away a gangling swamper by the name of Shikepoke spoke up. 'Reckon thet's a Sidehill Whiffler, Bub,' he said. 'They's quite a lot of 'em round right now. Yuh wanta be on the lookout for 'em.'" His robust folk humor is evident in the tall tales, but also in the dialogue of the characters. Because his books have a simple and direct approach, they are read by 7 to 10-year-old children, while adolescents needing "high interest low vocabulary" books also read them. Reviewers inevitably remind the adult that Rounds's ecology books such as *The Snake Tree* and books about the west should not be relegated only to the child's shelf.

—Karen Nelson Hoyle

RUSH, Philip

Nationality: British. **Born:** Palmers Green, London, 24 February 1908. **Education:** Southgate Grammar School; London School of Economics. **Family:** Married Geraldine Gould in 1931; one son and two daughters. **Career:** Local government officer, East Ham, London, 1930-63; chief inspector of weights and measures, East Ham, 1963-65, and Borough of Bexley, London, 1965-68. **Died:** 1996.

Publications for Children

Fiction

He Sailed with Dampier, illustrated by Richard Ogle. London, Boardman, 1947.
A Cage of Falcons, illustrated by Serena Chance. London, Collins, 1954.
Queen's Treason, illustrated by F. Partridge. London, Collins, 1955.
The Minstrel Knight, illustrated by Martin Thomas. London, Collins, 1955; Indianapolis, Bobbs Merrill, 1956.
King of the Castle, illustrated by Martin Thomas. London, Collins, 1956.
Red Man's Country, illustrated by Brian Keogh. London, Collins, 1957.
My Brother Lambert, illustrated by David Walsh. London, Phoenix House, and New York, Roy, 1957.
He Went with Dampier, illustrated by P.A. Jobson. London, Harrap, 1957; New York, Roy, 1958.
He Went with Franklin, illustrated by Anthony Douthwaite. London, Harrap, 1960.
Apprentice at Arms, illustrated by Christopher Brooker. London, Collins, 1960.
The Castle and the Harp, illustrated by Charles Keeping. London, Collins, 1963; New York, McGraw Hill, 1964.
Frost Fair, illustrated by Philip Gough. London, Collins, 1965; New York, Roy, 1967.
That Fool of a Priest and Other Tales of Early Canterbury, illustrated by David Knight. Oxford, Pergamon Press, 1970.
A Face of Stone, illustrated by David Harris. Leicester, Brockhampton Press, 1973.
Guns for the Armada, illustrated by Sheila Bewley. London, Hodder and Stoughton, 1975.
Death to the Strangers!, illustrated by Val Biro. London, Hodder and Stoughton, 1977.

Other

Great Men of Sussex, illustrated by Peter Rush. London, Lane, 1956.
Strange People: The Later Hanoverians 1760-1837, illustrated by Peter Rush. London, Hutchinson, 1958.
More Strange People: The Early Hanoverians 1714-1760, illustrated by Peter Rush. London, Hutchinson, 1958.
London's Wonderful Bridge, illustrated by Nancy Sayer. London, Harrap, 1959.
Strange Stuarts 1603-1714, illustrated by Peter Rush. London, Hutchinson, 1959.
How Roads Have Grown, illustrated by Caroline Norton. London, Routledge, 1960.
The Young Shelley, illustrated by Anne Linton. London, Parrish, 1961; New York, Roy, 1962.
Weights and Measures, with John A. O'Keefe. London, Methuen, 1962; New York, Roy, 1964.
The Book of Duels, illustrated by Peter Rush. London, Harrap, 1964.

Publications for Adults

Novels

Rogue's Lute. London, Dakers, 1944.
Mary Read, Buccaneer. London, Boardman, 1945.
Freedom Is the Man. London, Dakers, 1946.
Crispin's Apprentice. London, Dakers, 1948.
Pierce Allard. London, Hale, 1981.
Quayle. London, Hale, 1982.

*

Philip Rush comments:
The past has always fascinated me and my published work has always been historical.

* * *

Most of Philip Rush's stories are set in the Middle Ages, often in the area round Canterbury, and all centre on a particular historical event or character, generally seen through the eyes of a young person. An author's note identifies sources and separates fiction from fact, though Rush's attitude, particularly where social class is involved in conflict, is often ambivalent. Historical details are given plentifully and generally palatably.

Red Man's Country (which could have been called *He Went with Captain John Smith), He Went with Dampier,* and *He Went with Franklin* are successful pieces of formula writing. *He Went with Franklin,* which has no invented young hero, reads like a particularly gripping travel book rather than a novel. Always the characters are clearly differentiated, and racial prejudice (towards Indians and Eskimos) is shown to be misguided. *The Young Shelley* and *My Brother Lambert* present equally convincing and psychologically accurate portraits.

Other stories are more variable. In *Apprentice at Arms* and *The Castle and the Harp* fact reads like fiction, and *Frost Fair* is totally unconvincing. *King of the Castle* and *A Face of Stone* are both accounts of the Wat Tyler rebellion, the later book showing a real improvement of quality; Adam, the apprentice stonemason, is a likelier character than the callous and unattractive Sylvester.

The worst violence—the murder of the garrison of Bedford Castle in *The Castle and the Harp*—is shown off-stage, but in general battle and killing are plentiful. Hardship, particularly in the *He Went with...*stories, is related unflinchingly, and young readers are given an unglamourised picture. The same is also true of mediaeval life in the one book of short stories, *That Fool of a Priest.*

Philosophical and religious topics are dealt with openly—in the Tudor stories *Apprentice at Arms* and *Guns for the Armada* and in *The Minstrel Knight,* a retelling of an Anglo-Norman family history poem. Often, as in *Queen's Treason* and *A Face of Stone,* discussion of religious topics is a prominent feature.

Happy endings prevail because these are books for children, but where fortunate chance does not intervene there is always a slight melancholy.

—Margaret M. Tye

RUTHIN, Margaret. See **CATHERALL, Arthur.**

RYDER, Joanne (Rose)

Nationality: American. **Born:** 16 September 1946, Lake Hiawatha, New Jersey. **Education:** Marquette University, degree in journalism, 1968; University of Chicago, graduate study, 1968-69. **Family:** Married to the writer Lawrence Yep. **Career:** Editor of children's books, Harper & Row Publishers, Inc., New York City, 1970-80; full-time writer since 1980. Docent (tour guide), San Francisco Zoo; lecturer at schools and conferences. **Awards:** Children's Book Showcase, 1977; New Jersey Institute of Technology, New Jersey Author's Award, 1978, 1980, 1988, 1989; National Science Teachers Association Outstanding Science Trade Book of the Year for Children, 1979 and 1985; Parents' Choice Book, 1982; New York Academy of Sciences Children's Science Book Award (younger category), 1982; National Council of Teachers of English Outstanding Book of the Year for Children, 1985; Commonwealth Club of Northern California Children's Book Medal, 1988. **Member:** Society of Children's Book Writers, California Academy of Sciences, San Francisco Zoological Society. **Address:** 921 Populus Place, Sunnyvale, California 94086, U.S.A.

Publications for Children

Nonfiction (nature and science)

Simon Underground, illustrated by John Schoenherr. New York, Harper, 1976.

A Wet and Sandy Day, illustrated by Donald Carrick. New York, Harper, 1977.

Fireflies, illustrated by Don Bolognese. New York, Harper, 1977.

Fog in the Meadow, illustrated by Gail Owens. New York, Harper, 1979.

Snail in the Woods, with Harold S. Feinberg, illustrated by Jo Polseno. New York, Harper, 1979.

The Spiders Dance, illustrated by Robert Blake. New York, Harper, 1981.

Beach Party, illustrated by Diane Stanley. New York, F. Warne, 1982.

The Snail's Spell, illustrated by Lynne Cherry. New York, F. Warne, 1982.

The Incredible Space Machines, illustrated by Gerry Daly. New York, Random House, 1982.

C-3PO's Book about Robots, illustrated by John Gampert. New York, Random House, 1983.

Inside Turtle's Shell, and Other Poems of the Field, illustrated by Susan Bonners. New York, Macmillan, 1985.

The Evening Walk, illustrated by Julie Durrell. Racine, Wisconsin, Western Publishing, 1985.

Old Friends, New Friends, illustrated by Jane Chambless-Rigie. Racine, Wisconsin, Western Publishing, 1986.

Chipmunk Song, illustrated by L. Cherry. New York, Lodestar, 1987.

Animals in the Woods, illustrated by Lisa Bonforte. Racine, Wisconsin, Western Publishing, 1987; as *Animals in the Wild,* Racine, Wisconsin, Western Publishing, 1989.

Step into the Night, illustrated by Dennis Nolan. New York, Four Winds Press, 1988.

My Little Golden Book about Cats, illustrated by Dora Leder. Racine, Wisconsin, Western Publishing, 1988.

Puppies Are Special Friends, illustrated by James Spence. Racine, Wisconsin, Western Publishing, 1988.

White Bear, Ice Bear, illustrated by Michael Rothman. New York, Morrow, 1989.

Catching the Wind, illustrated by M. Rothman. New York, Morrow, 1989.

Mockingbird Morning, illustrated by D. Nolan. New York, Four Winds Press, 1989.

Where Butterflies Grow, illustrated by L. Cherry. New York, Lodestar, 1989.

Under the Moon, illustrated by Cheryl Harness. New York, Random House, 1989.

Lizard in the Sun, illustrated by M. Rothman. New York, Morrow, 1990.

Under Your Feet, illustrated by D. Nolan. New York, Four Winds Press, 1990.

When the Woods Hum, illustrated by Catherine Stock. New York, Morrow, 1991.

The Bear on the Moon, illustrated by Carol Lacey. New York, Morrow, 1991.

Hello, Tree!, illustrated by Michael Hays. New York, Lodestar, 1991.

Winter Whale, illustrated by M. Rothman. New York, Morrow, 1991.

Dancers in the Garden. San Francisco, Sierra, 1992.

First Grade Elves. Mahwah, New Jersey, Troll, 1993.

First Grade Ladybugs. Mahwah, New Jersey, Troll, 1993.

Hello, First Grade. Mahwah, New Jersey, Troll, 1993.

The Goodbye Walk. New York, Lodestar, 1993.

One Small Fish. New York, Morrow, 1993.

Sea Elf, illustrated by Michael Rothman. New York, Morrow, 1993.

Earthdance. New York, Holt, 1994.

A House by the Sea, illustrated by Melissa Sweet. New York, Morrow, 1994.

My Father's Hands, illustrated by Mark Graham. New York, Morrow, 1994.

Without Words, illustrated by Barbara Sonneborn. San Francisco, Sierra, 1995.

Jaguar in the Rain Forest, illustrated by Michael Rothman. New York, Morrow, 1996.

Winter White, illustrated by Carol Lacey. New York, Morrow, 1996.

Night Gliders, illustrated by Melissa Bay Mathias. Mahwah, New Jersey, BridgeWater Books, 1996.

Earth Dance, illustrated by Norman Gorbaty. New York, Holt, 1996.

Pondwater Faces, illustrated by Susan Ford. San Francisco, Chronicle Books, 1997.

Shark in the Sea, illustrated by Michael Rothman. New York, Morrow, 1997.

Other

The Night Flight (fiction), illustrated by Amy Schwartz. New York, Four Winds Press, 1985.

Adapter, *Little Toot,* by Hardie Gramatky, illustrated by Larry Ross. New York, Platt, 1988.

Adapter, *A Christmas Carol,* by Charles Dickens, illustrated by John O'Brien. New York, Platt, 1989.

Adapter, *Walt Disney's Bambi.* New York, Disney Press, 1993.

Adapter, *Walt Disney's Bambi's Forest: A Year in the Life of the Forest.* New York, Disney Press, 1993.

* * *

In many respects, *Simon Underground,* Joanne Ryder's first book for children, demonstrates the qualities that have continued to make her a leading writer of nature books for children for nearly 20 years. The story of Simon, a mole whose activities the book follows from fall to spring, exquisitely combines scientific accuracy with poetic expression. Young readers not only learn abstract facts about a mole; they are brought into such close contact with the details of its life that they must actively consider what it feels like, smells like, looks like, sounds like, to be a mole. Ryder imagines aspects of the mole's underground winter life and renders them so vividly that the reader cannot help imagining them also: the joy of his solitary existence in his secret place in the "deep-down," the loss of his sense of time as he remains there during the winter, and the experience of the above-ground field as "empty" after the closeness of his underground tunnels.

Ryder followed Simon's story with controlled and easy readers (*Fireflies, Snail in the Woods, Fog in the Meadow*) that invite identification with creatures of nature through the same kind of intense imaginative detail that characterizes the story of Simon. Her careful observations of the creatures about which she writes provide fascinating data about unlikely animals such as snails, whose eyes can move up and down their feelers, as well as the drama involved in the food chain, even at the level of insects. In one passage, a female firefly tricks a male not of her species into approaching her by imitating his particular light, but when he comes close, she devours him instead of mating with him.

The reader involvement that these early books encourage gradually evolved into the structure that characterizes Ryder's more recent work: second-person narratives that not only invite close observation of nature, but put the child reader into the position of actually becoming the creature in question. Her fine collaborations with illustrator Lynne Cherry (*The Snail's Spell, Chipmunk Song, Where Butterflies Grow*) begin by asking the reader to "imagine you are" a snail, a chipmunk, a caterpillar. The recent series of "Just for a Day" books depict boys (also "you") exploring animals' lives by actually becoming them for a day, then changing back into themselves at the end of the tale. In *Step into the Night,* the "you" in question becomes several of the creatures a young girl hears and sees on a nighttime walk. In these shapeshifting books, Ryder selects fascinating details of the animals' behavior for the child reader to explore, but also demonstrates sensitivity regarding the depiction of eating and mating habits, clearly keeping in mind that the child has *become* the creature. Whereas the third-person *Snail in the Woods* includes one snail being eaten by a shrew, another narrowly escaping a similar fate by a mouse, and a mating scene, the second-person *The Snail's Spell* wisely confines dietary considerations to the snail/child munching on lettuce in the garden and eschews mating altogether. In fact, the necessity of soft-pedalling the food-chain aspects of these books makes the polar bear of *White Bear, Ice Bear* a questionable choice for a "Just for a Day" subject. The child reader who becomes a bear does not have to deal with the prospect of killing and eating an adorable seal, because the one he stalks suddenly senses danger and escapes; unfortunately, the book leaves the reader with a fine sense of the bear's majesty but little of its characteristic ferocity.

Although Ryder has only published one nature book classified as poetry (*Inside Turtle's Shell and Other Poems of the Field*), one of the remarkable things about all her work, and a reason for her consistent popularity, is her extraordinary use of language that is at once simple, poetic, and vividly descriptive. In *Turtle's Shell,* one encounters berries that are "eat-me-red," wild geese that rise into the sky as though "climbing stairs no one can see," and a wonderfully alliterative black snake that "slides up stealing the sitting rock's sun." Evocative language is not confined to the volume of poetry, however, but enhances her other books as well. The bees in *Mockingbird Morning* wear "fat fuzzy suits" as they "wander like astronauts from moon to moon," and *Winter Whale* resonates with songs from the ocean depths. The language piques the imagination, urging the reader to regard the natural world with wonder.

Ryder's experiments outside the non-fiction animal genre have not been wholly successful. Ironically, *The Night Flight,* a fantasy flight to a city park after dark, captures the imagination less fully than does the non-fictional *Step into the Night*—and *Hello, Tree!* never comes to life the way Ryder's animal books do. Readers of the latter book learn to befriend a special tree, but not to *be* the tree in the way her other books demand. These less intriguing efforts aside, however, Joanne Ryder's work stands among the finest nature books of the past twenty years. The scientific accuracy of detail and the beauty of language for which her books are known ensure their welcome in the science and language arts classrooms as well as on the home bookshelf.

—Christine Doyle Stott

RYLANT, Cynthia

Nationality: American. **Born:** Hopewell, Virginia, 6 June 1954. **Education:** Morris Harvey College (now University of Charleston), West Virginia, 1973-75, B.A. in English 1975; Marshall University, Huntington, West Virginia, 1975-76, M.A. in English 1976; Kent State University, Kent, Ohio, 1980-81, M.L.S. 1982. **Family:** Has one son. **Career:** Writer. Part-time English instructor, Marshall University, Huntington, West Virginia, 1979-80; children's librarian, Akron Public Library, Akron, Ohio, 1983; part-time English lecturer, University of Akron, Akron, 1983-84; part-time lecturer, Northeast Ohio Universities College of Medicine, Rootstown, Ohio, since 1991. **Awards:** Named a *Booklist* reviewer's choice, 1982, Caldecott Honor Book, American Library Association (ALA) notable book, and Reading Rainbow selection, all 1983, all for *When I Was Young in the Mountains;* American Book award nomination, 1983, and English Speaking Union Book-across-the-Sea Ambassador of Honor award, 1984, both for *When I Was Young in the Mountains;* named an ALA notable book, a *School Library Journal* best book of 1984, a National Council for Social Studies best book, 1984, and a Society of Midland Authors best children's book, 1985, all for *Waiting to Waltz: A Childhood;* named a *New York Times* best illustrated, a *Horn Book* honor book, a Child Study Association of America's children's book of the year, all 1985, and a Caldecott Honor Book, 1986, all for *The Relatives Came;* named a Child Study Association of America's children's book of the year, 1985, for *A Blue-eyed Daisy;* named a *School Library Journal* best book, 1985, for *Every Living Thing;* named a *Parents' Choice* selection, 1986, and a Newbery Honor Book, 1987, for *A Fine White Dust; Boston Globe/Horn Book* award for nonfiction, 1991, for *Appalachia: The Voices of Sleeping Birds;* Garden State Children's Book award, Children's Services Section of the New Jersey Library Association, 1992, for *Henry and Mudge Get the Cold Shivers; Boston Globe/Horn Book* award, 1992, Newbery medal, 1993, both for *Missing May.*

Publications for Children

Fiction

When I Was Young in the Mountains, illustrated by Diane Goode. New York, Dutton, 1982.

Miss Maggie, illustrated by Thomas DiGrazia. New York, Dutton. 1983.

This Year's Garden, illustrated by Mary Szilagyi. New York, Bradbury, 1984.

Every Living Thing (stories). New York, Bradbury, 1985.

The Relatives Came, illustrated by Stephen Gammell. New York, Bradbury, 1985.

Night in the Country, illustrated by Mary Szilagyi. New York, Bradbury, 1986.

Birthday Presents, illustrated by Sucie Stevenson. New York, Orchard Books, 1987.

Children of Christmas: Stories for the Season, illustrated by Stephen D. Schindler. New York, Orchard Books, 1987; as *Silver Packages and Other Stories,* London, Orchard Books, 1987; as *Silver Packages: An Appalachian Christmas Story,* illustrated by Chris K. Soentpiet. New York, Orchard Books, 1997.

All I See, illustrated by Peter Catalanotto. New York, Orchard Books, 1988.

Mr. Griggs' Work, illustrated by Julie Downing. New York, Orchard Books, 1989.

An Angel for Solomon Singer, illustrated by Peter Catalanotto. New York, Orchard Books, 1992.

The Everyday Books series: *The Everyday Children, The Everyday Garden, The Everyday House, The Everyday School, The Everyday Town, The Everyday Pets,* illustrated by the author. New York, Bradbury, 5 vols., 1993.

Mr. Putter and Tabby series: *Mr. Putter and Tabby Bake the Cake* [*Pour the Tea, Walk the Dog, Pick the Pears, Fly the Plane, Row the Boat, Take the Train, Toot the Horn*], illustrated by Arthur Howard. San Diego, Harcourt Brace, 8 vols., 1994-99; first vol. published San Diego, Harcourt Brace, 1994.

Dog Heaven, illustrated by the author. New York, Blue Sky Press, 1995.

Gooseberry Park, illustrated by Arthur Howard. San Diego, Harcourt Brace, 1995.

The Van Gogh Cafe. San Diego, Harcourt Brace, 1995.

The Old Woman Who Named Things, illustrated by Kathryn Brown. San Diego, Harcourt Brace, 1996.

The Bookshop Dog. New York, Blue Sky Press/Scholastic, 1996.

The Whales. New York, Blue Sky Press, 1996.

The Blue Hill Meadows, illustrated by Ellen Beier. San Diego, Harcourt Brace, 1997.

The Blue Hill Meadows and the Much-loved Dog, illustrated by Ellen Beier. San Diego, Harcourt Brace, 1997.

Cat Heaven, illustrated by the author. New York, Blue Sky Press, 1997.

Poppleton series: *Poppleton, Poppleton and Friends, Poppleton Everyday, Poppleton Forever, Poppleton in Spring,* illustrated by Mark Teague. New York, Blue Sky Press, 1997.

Scarecrow, illustrated by Lauren Stringer. San Diego, Harcourt Brace, 1997.

An Everyday Book. New York, Simon & Schuster Books, 1997.

Bear Day, illustrated by Jennifer Selby. San Diego, Harcourt Brace, 1998.

Bless Us All: A Child's Yearbook of Blessings, illustrated by the author. New York, Simon & Schuster, 1998.

The Bird House, illustrated by Barry Moser. New York, Blue Sky Press, 1998.

The Cobble Street Cousins series: *The Cobble Street Cousins: A Little Shopping,* [*In Aunt Lucy's Kitchen, Some Good News, Special Gifts*], illustrated by Wendy Anderson Halperin. New York, Simon & Schuster, 4 vols., 1998-99.

The Islander. New York, DK Ink, 1998.

Tulip Sees America, illustrated by Lisa Desimini. New York, Blue Sky Press, 1998.

The Cookie-store Cat. New York, Blue Sky Press, 1999.

Bunny Bungalow, illustrated by Nancy Hayashi. San Diego, Harcourt Brace, 1999.

In November, illustrated by Jill Kastner. San Diego, Harcourt Brace, 1999.

Thimbleberry Stories, illustrated by Maggie Kneen. San Diego, Harcourt Brace, 2000.

The Ticky-tacky Doll, illustrated by Harvey Stevenson. San Diego, Harcourt Brace, 2000.

Other (readers)

Henry and Mudge [in Puddle Trouble, in the Green Time, under the Yellow Moon, in the Sparkle Days, and the Forever Sea, Get the Cold Shivers, and the Happy Cat, and the Bedtime Thumps, Take the Big Test, and the Long Weekend, and the Wild Wind, and the Careful Cousin, and the Best Day of All, in the Family Trees, and the Sneaky Crackers, and the Starry Night, and Annie's Good Move, and the Snowman Plan, and Annie's Perfect Pet, and the Funny Lunch, and the Tall Tree House, and Mrs. Hopper's house, and the Great Grandpas, a Very Special Merry Christmas, and the Wild Goose Chase, and the Big Sleepover, and the Tumbling Trip], illustrated by Sucie Stevenson. New York, Bradbury Press, 28 vols., 1987-99; first vol. published London, Gollancz, 1989.

PUBLICATIONS FOR YOUNG ADULTS

Fiction

A Blue-eyed Daisy. New York, Bradbury, 1985; as *Some Year for Ellie,* illustrated by Kate Rogers, Viking Kestrel, 1986.
A Fine White Dust. New York, Bradbury, 1986.
A Kindness. New York, Orchard Books, 1989.
A Couple of Kooks: And Other Stories about Love. New York, Orchard Books, 1990.
Missing May. New York, Orchard Books, 1992.
I Had Seen Castles. San Diego, Harcourt Brace, 1993.
The Dreamer, illustrated by Barry Moser. New York, Blue Sky Press, 1993.

Poetry

Waiting to Waltz: A Childhood, illustrated by Stephen Gammell. New York, Bradbury, 1984.
Soda Jerk, illustrated by Peter Catalanotto. New York, Orchard Books, 1990.
Something Permanent, photographs by Walker Evans. San Diego, Harcourt Brace, 1994.

Other

But I'll Be Back Again: An Album. New York, Orchard Books, 1989.
Appalachia: The Voices of Sleeping Birds, illustrated by Barry Moser. New York, Harcourt, 1991.
Best Wishes, photographs by Carlo Ontal. New York, Owen, 1992.
Margaret, Frank, and Andy: Three Writers' Stories. San Diego, Harcourt Brace, 1996.

*

Media Adaptations: *When I Was Young in the Mountains* (filmstrip), Random House, 1983; *This Year's Garden* (filmstrip), Random House, 1983; *The Relatives Came* (filmstrip), Random House, 1986. Several of Rylant's books are available on film through American School Publishers.

Biography: Entry in *Sixth Book of Junior Authors,* New York, H.W. Wilson, 1989; essay in *Something about the Author Autobiography Series,* Volume 13, Detroit, Gale, 1991; essay in *Speaking for Ourselves, Too* compiled and edited by Donald R. Gallo, National Council of Teachers of English, 1993; essay in *Authors and Artists for Young Adults,* Volume 10, Detroit, Gale, 1993.

Manuscript Collections: Special Collections, Kent State University, Ohio.

Critical Studies: Entry in *Children's Literature Review,* Volume 15, Detroit, Gale, 1988, pp. 167-174.

Cynthia Rylant comments:

Most of my books are based on my childhood in southern West Virginia with its rural Appalachian coal-mining towns and townsfolk influencing both the tone and theme of my work. Writers who have influenced me most are James Agee and William Maxwell. When I write I try to center down gut-level and put words to *feelings* rather than toward descriptive or action-filled passages. It is the interior I'm most interested in, and the poetry of the simple things.

* * *

Cynthia Rylant's work for children and young adults ranges from picture books to poetry, from short stories to novels. No matter what shape her work takes, however, what one remembers is Rylant's use of language, bringing settings and characters to life.

Through the imagery of her language, setting becomes memorable in the picture book story *Night in the Country.* Using very few words, Rylant has us listen to the sweep of owl wings, the clink of dog chains, and "the groans and thumps and squeaks that houses make when they are trying, like you, to sleep." Style extols setting in the author's very first work, *When I Was Young in the Mountains,* recognized as a Notable Children's Book for Young Readers by the American Library Association. This work captures the tenor of a young girl's life in the West Virginia mountains: the smell of cornbread and beans; the coolness of the swimming hole; the power of baptism; and the loving warmth of summer evenings. Rylant's lyrical use of language explains why the main character never dreamed of a world beyond the mountains, for it was there that love, adventure, and security wrapped her close. The uniqueness of the Appalachian mountains is revisited in the picture book *Appalachia: The Voices of Sleeping Birds.* Honored with the 1991 *Boston Globe-Horn Book* award for non-fiction, *Appalachia* delineates a landscape of mountains and coal camps, hospitality, and a closeness to God.

Characters are just as strongly evoked by Rylant's use of dialect and figurative language. *A Blue-Eyed Daisy,* an episodic novel for the middle-school child, has the sensation of a story told out loud, relayed in a mountain dialect that reflects its main character, Ellie. Through the third-person limited narrative, Ellie's everyday life as well as her yearnings and fears are revealed. Like every child, Ellie wants her father's love and almost is willing to shoot a beautiful doe to gain his admiration. She yearns for a bedroom of her own and, after seeing a classmate overcome with a seizure worries about whether she, too, will become an epileptic.

Equally well depicted, this time through a first-person narrative, is Pete in Rylant's second novel for the middle-school child *A Fine White Dust.* This work begins and ends with a symbol—broken pieces of a ceramic cross. Through much of the book, those pieces signify Pete's disillusionment with religion, for he has bee deserted by the evangelist preacher for whom he left his own family and friends. By the end of the story, Pete realizes that the pieces can be thrown away; he is ready for a new understanding of God. Applauded by reviewers for its focus on intense religious feelings, *A Fine White Dust* was named a Newbery Honor book for 1987.

Rylant continues her exploration of religion in *Missing May,* which received the 1992 *Boston Globe-Horn Book* award and the 1993 Newbery medal. Told in the first-person narrative, the novel graphically depicts the grief of 12-year-old Summer upon the death of her Aunt May, who for six years had been a mother to her. Her Uncle Ob's loneliness and sorrow are so intense that they almost lead to his emotional death, but the belief that May's spirit has passed by and the ill-fated search to communicate with her soul finally lead him back to life. By novel's end, he realizes how much Summer needs him and that May's spirit will always remain with the two of them. As in *A Fine White Dust,* a symbol frames the novel—whirligigs represent Ob's visions of storms and heaven, death and love, and, most importantly, May's soul. With the movement of the whirligigs from the trailer to May's garden, Ob's healing has begun, and Summer finds herself surrounded by love again.

Just as distinctive to Rylant's work are her depictions of adult characters. Ellie's father is prominent in *A Blue-Eyed Daisy.* Like other coal miners, Oakey Farley used to drink when he needed "to scare away the coming week," but due to an accident, he is unable to work and begins drinking every day. The novel traces Oakey's healing process, furthered by Ellie's love and Bullet, a hunting dog.

Parents are not the only adult characters presented in a fully drawn manner. Rylant has become well known for her portrayal of the elderly, especially those who are isolated and alone. Such portraits are found in her short story collections *Children of Christmas* and *A Couple of Kooks: And Other Stories about Love* as well as in the picture book *An Angel for Solomon Singer.*

Her latest novel, *I Had Seen Castles,* moves Rylant's work into the genre of historical fiction. In this work, 67-year-old John Dante looks back on the way World War II and the war effort transformed the lives of his family members and others. Enlisting in the service causes John to lose his sweetheart, but he survives combat through her memory. Upon returning to post-war America, however, he feels out of place, unable to find people with whom he can share the suffering he has felt.

Since the 1980s, Rylant has become known for her significant contributions as both a picture book author for young children and a powerful writer for the middle-school child. She is especially recognized for her memorable language as well as her fully delineated characters and settings.

—Jacqueline L. Gmuca

S

SACHAR, Louis

Nationality: American. **Born:** East Meadow, New York, 20 March 1954. **Education:** University of California, Berkeley, B.A. 1976; University of California, San Francisco, J.D. 1980. **Family:** Married Carla Askew in 1985; one daughter. **Career:** Shipping manager, Beldoch Industries (manufacturers of women's sweaters), Norwalk, Connecticut, 1976-77; writer since 1977; attorney since 1981. **Awards:** Ethical Culture School Book Award, 1978; Parents' Choice Foundation Parents' Choice Award, 1987; Arkansas Elementary School Council, Charlie May Simon Book Award, 1987; University of Georgia College of Education, Georgia Children's Book Award, 1987; Indian Paintbrush Book Award (Wyoming), 1987; New Mexico Library Association, Land of Enchantment Children's Book Award, 1987; Missouri Association of School Librarians Mark Twain Award, 1987; Friends of the Atlanta-Fulton Public Library (Georgia), Milner Award, 1987; Nevada Young Reader's Award, 1987; Wise Library, West Virginia University, West Virginia Book Award, 1987; Texas Library Association Texas Bluebonnet Award, 1990. **Member:** Authors Guild, Society of Children's Book Writers and Illustrators. **Address:** c/o Alfred A. Knopf Books for Young Readers, 201 E. 50th St., New York, New York, 10022, U.S.A.

Publications for Children

Fiction

Sideways Stories from Wayside School, illustrated by Dennis Hockerman. Chicago, Follett, 1978; new edition, illustrated by Julie Brinkloe, New York, Avon, 1985.
Johnny's in the Basement. New York, Avon, 1981.
Someday Angeline, illustrated by Barbara Samuels. New York, Avon, 1983.
There's a Boy in the Girls' Bathroom. New York, Knopf, 1987.
Sixth Grade Secrets. New York, Scholastic, 1987.
Wayside School Is Falling Down, illustrated by Joel Schick. New York, Lothrop, 1989.
Sideways Arithmetic from Wayside School. New York, Scholastic, 1989.
The Boy Who Lost His Face. New York, Knopf, 1989.
Dogs Don't Tell Jokes. New York, Knopf, 1991.
Monkey Soup. New York, Knopf, 1992.
"Marvin Redpost" Series:
Marvin Redpost: Kidnapped at Birth? Random House, New York, 1992.
Marvin Redpost: Is He a Girl? New York, Random House, 1993.
Marvin Redpost: Why Pick on Me? New York, Random House, 1993.
Marvin Redpost: Alone in His Teacher's House New York, Random House, 1994.
Holes. New York, Farrar, Straus and Giroux, 1998.

* * *

Louis Sachar's struggle with professional identity began when the manuscript for *Sideways Stories from Wayside School* was accepted for publication; that same week he began law school at the University of California, and the balancing act between Sachar, the children's writer, and Sachar, the attorney, had begun. *Sideways Stories from Wayside School* was the result of an undergraduate experience Sachar had as a teacher's aide in a nearby elementary school. Sachar became "Louis, the yard teacher" to his charges, and he consequently appears by that name as a character in his own *Wayside School* series. The third book in the series, *Sideways Math from Wayside School,* is a collection of entertaining math problems for children in the lower grades. The first two books in the *Wayside School* series have become immensely popular with younger readers and particular favorites among elementary school teachers, who treasure them for their read-aloud value.

Although Sachar claims to have written *Sideways Stories from Wayside School* more as a hobby than with serious literary intent, he effectively engages his readers with whimsical characters and unusual situations. Further strengths of this first effort are its extremely short chapters and the satisfying surety of resolution in each. Its sequel, *Wayside School Is Falling Down,* is an even more polished work, demonstrating a steadier pace and a tighter focus while maintaining the short-chapter and guaranteed-punch-line format. One unifying thread through this later work, in which the characters of the earlier book also appear, is the new character Benjamin Nushmutt, whose continuing identity crises humorously parallel Sachar's own as an aspiring lawyer *cum* author. Mrs. Jewls, the nicest teacher at Wayside School, mistakenly introduces her new student as Mark Miller, and before Benjamin can muster the nerve to correct the error, he has become accepted and even respected as Mark; furthermore, he evinces in that identity capabilities for which Benjamin had never dared hope. Finally, Benjamin publicly renounces his Mark-ness in a gesture with which Sachar, who had renounced his steady lawyer self to take on full-time writing, would certainly identify. The reward for Benjamin's honesty is the realization that his decision to resume his true identity has made him even more a part of the weird but happy goings-on at Wayside School. On the other hand, Louis Sachar's decision to abandon his legal identity for a career in writing has rewarded readers with a lively and perceptive string of popular favorites for young people in which, not surprisingly, Sachar's themes dwell on the efforts of his characters to discover and assert fledgling identities.

Sachar recognizes *There's a Boy in the Girls' Bathroom* as his most popular book, but its editing history points to an additional identity trauma for the author that is in turn reflected in his protagonist. Sachar's initial plan was to divide the book's point-of-view between Jeff Fishkin, the straight-arrow transfer student to Red Hill School, and Bradley Chalkers, a troubled, undermotivated failure and butt of jokes for students and teachers alike. Editors, however, insisted that Sachar write primarily from Bradley's point of view, and therein lies the book's strength: in executing this difficult characterization, Sachar gives his reader the poignant and frequently unsettling opportunity to look at the world through the eyes of a student whom every teacher dreads to see—a child to whom success, even if it were possible, would be terrifying. Carla, a school counselor, offers Bradley unqualifed acceptance and encourages him to believe that he really can be the person that he has fantasized about: a bright, creative, brave, and loving little boy. Bradley's recognition and acceptance of himself lead to his eventual acceptance by teachers and fellow students alike, and readers frankly cheer for the "monster" who is permitted to find the good inside himself. Every element of Sachar's skill in creating plot, characterization, and humorously realistic situations shows to its best advantage in *There's a Boy in the Girls' Bathroom.*

Books such as his *Sixth Grade Secrets* and *The Boy Who Lost His Face* again demonstrate Sachar's certain knowledge of the processes of discovering and establishing identity. For example, Laura Sibbie, the protagonist of *Sixth Grade Secrets,* defines herself in terms of her "Pig City" hat and her extremely long hair: one symbolizes her sense of individuality and her need for rebellion and the other her desire to remain her parents' obedient little girl. Individuality sought through rebellion, however, results in Laura's taking greater responsibility not only for herself but for her relationships as well; when Laura graduates from the sixth grade, she is poised to make the even more meaningful transition from childhood to young adulthood.

In *The Boy Who Lost His Face,* David Ballinger's one experience with the "cool" guys is enough to convince him that no worthwhile identity is ever established by following the crowd. As a result, David drifts far from the security of an old childhood friendship and his little brother's hero worship of him to the questionable status he achieves when he begins to hang out with Larry, his new friend with the blue sunglasses, and his tough-talking shop partner, Maureen, otherwise known as Mo. David's old buddy Scott and Scott's popular new friends call them the Three Stooges, but that unfortunate nickname is the least of David's worries when he begins to suspect that a witch's curse is manifesting itself in unsettling ways in what had once been his happily uneventful life.

The quality and success of Louis Sachar's books for young people confirm the wisdom of his decision to favor his identity as a children's writer over his legal career. Before recommending Sachar's books in the classroom or for a child's personal reading, however, teachers and parents alike should take note that while the *Wayside School* series and *There's a Boy in the Girls' Bathroom* are definitely children's fare and Sachar's best, the language and subject matter of *Sixth Grade Secrets* and *The Boy Who Lost His Face* may be considered more suitable for preteens and young adults.

—Patricia L. Bradley

SANTOS, Helen. See **GRIFFITHS, Helen**.

SAUER, Julia (Lina)

Nationality: American. **Born:** Rochester, New York, in 1891. **Education:** University of Rochester; New York State Library School, Albany. **Career:** Head of children's department, Rochester Public Library, 1921-58. **Died:** 26 June 1983.

Publications for Children

Fiction

Fog Magic. New York, Viking Press, 1943; London, Woodfield, 1960.

The Light at Tern Rock, illustrated by Georges Schreiber. New York, Viking Press, 1951.

Mike's House, illustrated by Don Freeman. New York, Viking Press, 1954.

Other

Editor, *Radio Roads to Reading: Library Book Talks Broadcast to Girls and Boys.* New York, Wilson, 1939.

*

Manuscript Collection: Kerlan Collection, University of Minnesota, Minneapolis.

* * *

In Julia Sauer's picture book for young people, *Mike's House,* as well as in her books for older children, *Fog Magic* and *The Light at Tern Rock,* she shows a love of nature, place, and people. Sauer is meticulous in her handling of nature, in particular its less enjoyable aspects, such as blizzards and dense fogs. She is sensitive to place (for instance North Mountain in Nova Scotia, the setting for *Fog Magic*), providing details about a town or a building or a room which make them vividly three-dimensional. And most of all she cares about people, their inner fantasies and their outer behavior. The coexistence of fantasy and reality, especially among her child characters, is seen most clearly in *Fog Magic.* In this book Sauer states that most of us live in two worlds, our real world and the one we build for ourselves out of the books we read, the heroes we admire, the things we hope to do. This book's heroine, 11-year-old Greta, lives in a modern world on one side of the mountain, but is obsessed with another world, a lost fishing village on the other side of the mountain. The story goes back and forth from the real present to the conjured-up past, pointing out the thin line between a person's reality and his fantasy, and the need for an acceptance of the two.

Mike's House, a book for much younger children, is also concerned with human needs and dreams, and, importantly, human interdependence. Four-year-old Robert sees the public library as a second home, and a fictional character as his best friend. He does not wish to share this best friend with others, but as others reach out to help him, he is finally able to respond to them.

Sauer's understanding of human nature and human development comes through clearly in her works. She has an excellent command of words and imagery. Her style, though, is didactic, and her message is labored by today's standards. Nevertheless, her obvious caring for nature, place, and especially people contributes to her continued appeal.

—Mary Lystad

SAWYER, Ruth

Nationality: American. **Born:** Boston, Massachusetts, 5 August 1880. **Education:** Mrs. Brackett's School, New York, 1887; Garland Kindergarten Normal School, graduated 1900; Columbia University, New York, B.S. 1904. **Family:** Married Albert C. Durand in 1911; one son and one daughter. **Career:** Helped organize kindergartens in Cuba, 1900; correspondent in Ireland for New York *Sun,* 1905, 1907; from 1908 professional storyteller and lecturer. Lived in Spain, 1931-32. **Awards:** American Library Association Newbery Medal, 1937, and Laura Ingalls Wilder award, 1965; Catholic Library Association Regina Medal, 1965. **Died:** 3 June 1970.

Publications for Children

Fiction

The Tale of the Enchanted Bunnies. New York, Harper, 1923.
Toño Antonio, illustrated by F. Luis Mora. New York, Viking Press, 1934.
Roller Skates, illustrated by Valenti Angelo. New York, Viking Press, 1936; London, Bodley Head, 1964.
The Year of Jubilo, illustrated by Edward Shenton. New York, Viking Press, 1940; as *Lucinda's Year of Jubilo,* London, Bodley Head, 1965.
The Least One, illustrated by Leo Politi. New York, Viking Press, 1941.
The Christmas Anna Angel, illustrated by Kate Seredy. New York, Viking Press, 1944; London, Cassell, 1948.
Old Con and Patrick, illustrated by Cathal O'Toole. New York, Viking Press, 1946.
The Little Red Horse, illustrated by Jay Hyde Barnum. New York, Viking Press, 1950.
Maggie Rose, Her Birthday Christmas, illustrated by Maurice Sendak. New York, Harper, 1952.
The Gold of Bernardino. Privately printed, 1952.
A Cottage for Betsy, illustrated by Vera Bock. New York, Harper, 1954.
The Enchanted Schoolhouse, illustrated by Hugh Troy. New York, Viking Press, 1956; Leicester, Brockhampton Press, 1958.
The Year of the Christmas Dragon, illustrated by Hugh Troy. New York, Viking Press, 1960.
Daddles: The Story of a Plain Hound-Dog, illustrated by Robert Frankenberg. Boston, Little Brown, 1964.

Poetry

A Child's Year-Book, illustrated by the author. New York, Harper, 1917.

Other

This Way to Christmas. New York, Harper, 1916; revised edition, 1967.
Picture Tales from Spain, illustrated by Carlos Sanchez. New York, Stokes, 1936.
The Long Christmas, illustrated by Valenti Angelo. New York, Viking Press, 1941; London, Bodley Head, 1964.
This Is the Christmas: A Serbian Folk Tale. Boston, Horn Book, 1945.
Journey Cake, Ho!, illustrated by Robert McCloskey. New York, Viking Press, 1953.
Dietrich of Berne and the Dwarf-King Laurin: Hero Tales of the Austrian Tirol, with Emmy Mollès, illustrated by Frederick Chapman. New York, Viking Press, 1963.
Ruth Sawyer, Storyteller (sound recording). 1965.
Joy to the World: Christmas Legends, illustrated by Trina Schart Hyman. Boston, Little Brown, 1966.
My Spain: A Story-Teller's Year of Collecting. New York, Viking Press, 1967.

Publications for Adults

Novels

The Primrose Ring. New York, Harper, 1915.
Seven Miles to Arden. New York, Harper, 1916.
Herself, Himself, and Myself: A Romance. New York, Harper, 1917.
Leerie. New York, Harper, 1920.
The Silver Sixpence. New York, Harper, 1921.
Gladiola Murphy. New York, Harper, 1923.
Four Ducks on a Pond. New York, Harper, 1928.
Folkhouse: The Autobiography of a Home. New York, Appleton, 1932.
The Luck of the Road. New York, Appleton Century, 1934.
Gallant: The Story of Storm Veblen. New York, Appleton Century, 1936.

Short Stories

Doctor Danny. New York, Harper, 1918.

Plays

The Sidhe of Ben-Mor: An Irish Folk Play. Boston, Badger, 1910.
The Awakening (produced New York, 1918).

Other

The Way of the Storyteller. New York, Viking Press, 1942; London, Harrap, 1944; revised edition, Viking Press, 1962; London, Penguin, 1976.
How to Tell a Story. Chicago, Compton, 1962.

*

Manuscript Collections: College of Sainte Catherine Library, St. Paul, Minnesota.

Critical Studies: *Ruth Sawyer* by Virginia Haviland, London, Bodley Head, and New York, Walck, 1965.

* * *

For most of her adult life a storyteller with consummate gifts—whose tales both oral and written could be characterized as living folk-art—Ruth Sawyer received both the Laura Ingalls Wilder and the Regina Medals for her numerous distinguished contributions to children's literature. Something of her strong positive personality and her unlimited creative power are conveyed by Virginia Haviland in her delightfully intimate and revealing monograph, *Ruth Sawyer.* In one characterization, Haviland says of her: "Sentences flowed full and colorful, projected in the still rich and vibrant voice—one more revelation of the teller's oral gifts. She was ever the story-teller, 'the way' shining through everything she had to say."

The procession of Sawyer's work had several emphases: stories she drew from her remembered childhood, legends and tales she collected from several countries, including some she visited for extended periods, e.g. Cuba, Ireland, Spain (the setting for *Toño Antonio* and *Picture Tales from Spain*), and finally works related to the festival of Christmas which she used as both a strong spiritual symbol and the focus for warm human ingathering.

Drawn from the recollections of her growing years is *Roller Skates,* Newbery Medal winner, featuring a 10-year-old tomboy, Lucinda Wyman, in an 1890 New York City setting. We see Lucinda's "higgledy-piggledy" life during a tremendous year of growth and learning. Its sequel, *The Year of Jubilo,* follows Lucinda after her father's death when she and her family resettle in their summer cottage in Maine. In this volume are more "impetuosities, brutal honesties, crudities" and examples of "cock-sure independence." Especially noteworthy are the letters written by Lucinda to those left behind in New York.

The author's rich and loving humor and her warmth—together with her appreciation of the richness of commonality as well as the festival quality in Christmas—are reflected in *This Way to Christmas,* real stories told to a lonesome boy stranded in northern New York. *The Long Christmas* contains Christmas legends and carols from around the world, together with a song of Saint Stephen with music. *The Christmas Anna Angel* follows the preparations of a Hungarian family during World War II for a bare Christmas, but the young heroine is resolute in her belief that her angel will provide cake for their tree. *This Is the Christmas,* a Serbian folktale, is told by a Serbian grandmother and features a blind boy shepherd who pipes to a carol. *Maggie Rose, Her Birthday Christmas* follows the daughter of an impoverished family in Maine who tries to raise some money so that her family can enjoy a birthday Christmas party. *The Year of the Christmas Dragon,* also set in Maine, presents a charming story, contrasting the long ago ancient times with "the time called now" and offering a wonderful spring promise. Referred to as "woven magic," *Joy to the World: Christmas Legends* contains a group of legends from ancient Arabia, Serbia, and Spain, as well as Christmas carols.

Journey Cake, Ho! is a lovely version of the old folktale. *The Enchanted Schoolhouse* is the story of a young immigrant from Ireland. Eager to carry a bit of his beloved country with him, he captures "a wee fairyman" and conceals him in a teapot all the way to "Maine, USA where the two of them turned Lobster Cove topsy-turvy." Something of the relationship emerges in the fairyman's plea: "Laddy, laddy, let me loose. This is no country to be coming to. All the wizards in the world must have made it." The hero tales *Dietrich of Berne and the Dwarf-King Laurin* are drawn from the mountain people of the Austrian Tyrol. In life the hero Dietrich becomes Theodoric the Great, on whose shield the Red Lion rested. *My Spain: A Story-Teller's Year of Collecting* can be enjoyed by young people as well as adults for its picture of Spain and the charming adventures and people Sawyer encountered there.

Sawyer's composite work is "gloriously alive; all the warmth and delightful chuckliness of her personality flood through the stories she tells....She writes as a jongleur might speak, in a fashion much more intense and exalted and heightened than is usual." Her long and productive life and the treasured writing she left behind provide multiple and richly varied examples of "the way of the storyteller." As Sawyer remembered her Irish nurse Johanna's influence on her, she herself succeeded in handling words so that they "join hands and dance, making a fairy ring that completely encircled" her readers.

—Clara O. Jackson

SAY, Allen

Nationality: Japanese. **Born:** Yokohama, 28 August 1937; moved to the United States, 1953. **Education:** Studied at Aoyama Gakuin, Tokyo, Japan, three years; Chouinard Art Institute, one year; Los Angeles Art Center School, one year; University of California, Berkeley, two years; San Francisco Art Institute, one year. **Military Service:** Served in U.S. Army. **Family:** Divorced; one daughter, Yuriko. **Career:** Worked at a variety of jobs, including commercial photographer; publisher, EIZO Press, 1968; photographer and illustrator, 1969-89; writer and illustrator. **Awards:** American Library Association Notable Book and Best Book for Young Adults awards, both 1979, for *The Ink-Keeper's Apprentice*; *New York Times* Best Illustrated Book award, 1980, for *The Lucky Yak*; *Horn Book* honor list, 1984, Christopher Medal and Reading Rainbow selection, both 1985, all for *How My Parents Learned to Eat*; *New York Times* Ten Best Illustrated Children's Books, 1988, for *A River Dream*; *Boston Globe/Horn Book* Award and American Library Association Notable Children's Book award, both 1988, and Caldecott Honor Medal, 1989, all for illustrations for *The Boy of the Three-Year Nap*; Caldecott Medal, 1994, for *Grandfather's Journey.* **Address:** c/o Houghton Mifflin Co., 222 Berkeley St., Boston, Massachusetts 02116-3764, U.S.A.

Publications for Children

Dr. Smith's Safari. New York, Harper, 1972.
Once under the Cherry Blossom Tree: An Old Japanese Tale. New York, Harper, 1974.
The Feast of Lanterns. New York, Harper, 1976.
The Bicycle Man. Boston, Houghton, 1982.
A River Dream. Boston, Houghton, 1988.
The Lost Lake. Boston, Houghton, 1989.
El Chino. Boston, Houghton, 1990.
Tree of Cranes. Boston, Houghton, 1991.
Grandfather's Journey. Boston, Houghton, 1993.
Stranger in the Mirror. Boston, Houghton, 1995.
Emma's Rug. Boston, Houghton, 1996.
Allison. Boston, Houghton, 1997.

Publication for Young Adults

The Ink-Keeper's Apprentice. New York, Harper, 1979.

*

Biography: Essay in *Something about the Author,* Vol. 69, Detroit, Gale, 1992; entry in *Major Authors and Illustrators for Children and Young Adults: A Selection of Sketches from Something about the Author,* Detroit, Gale, 1993; entry in *Notable Asian Americans,* Detroit, Gale, 1995.

Critical Studies: "Olé, Billy Wong!" by Liz Rosenberg, in *New York Times,* 11 November 1990, sec. 7, 51; "Mama Brought Christmas With Her" by Norma Field, in *New York Times,* 10 November 1991, sec. 7, 33; "Author Study Teacher Guide: Allen Say" by Leslie Cefali & Valerie Lewis, in *Instructor,* July/August 1993, 98-100; "The *Booklist* Interview: Allen Say" by Hazel Rochman, in *Booklist,* Vol. 90, 1 October 1993, 350-351; "An Interview with Allen Say, 1994 Caldecott Award Winner" by Jackie Peck and Judy Hendershot, in *Reading Teacher,* Vol. 48, No. 4, December 1994/January 1995, 304-306; "Parents Picks" in *Parents Magazine,* December 1995; review of *Emma's Rug* by Maria B. Salvadore, in *Horn Book,* Vol. 72, No. 5, September 1996, 586-587; review of *Emma's Rug* by Constance Decker Thompson, in *New York Times Book Review,* 13 April 1997, sec. 7, 271; review of *Allison* in *Publishers Weekly,* 4 August 1997; review of *Allison* by Susan Dove Lempke, in *Booklist,* Vol. 94, No. 8, 15 December 1997, 693; "Interview with Allen Say" by Stephanie Loer, on "Allen Say Home Page," 1997 (http://www.eduplace.com/rdg/author/say/question.html); review of *Allison,* in *Horn Book,* Vol. 7, No. 1, January 1998, 69.

Illustrator: *A Canticle to the Waterbirds* by Brother Antoninus, 1968; *Two Ways of Seeing,* edited by Wilson Pinney, 1971; *Magic and Night River* by Eve Bunting, 1978; *The Lucky Yak* by Annetta Lawson, 1980; *The Secret Cross of Lorraine* by Thea Brow, 1981; *How My Parents Learned to Eat* by Ina R. Friedman, 1984; *The Boy of the Three Year Nap* by Dianne Snyder, 1988.

* * *

Allen Say's picture books have been lauded by critics for their masterful illustrations and thoughtful approach to sensitive topics. Frequent themes in his works are the search for identity and one's place in the world, non-violence, respect for the environment, and friendship that overcomes boundaries of geography, culture, and age. Say's own life experience shows in his work, in autobiographical plot elements and in the artistic techniques he uses. From his early mentor, famed Japanese cartoonist Noro Shinpei, he learned the value of action in drawings and gained training in classical Japanese and French art styles. From his twenty-year career as a photographer, Say learned about lighting, and his illustrations often display a photographic quality. Unlike most picture book writers/illustrators, Say starts with pictures, doing them in sequence and letting the story develop from the illustrations. This method allows him to pare the written text to a minimum.

In his 1994 Caldecott-Medal-winning book *Grandfather's Journey,* Say's illustrations celebrate both the beauty of Japan and the richness and vastness of the American landscape as the story moves between the two countries. The pictures' varied styles show the influence of very different artists, from Claude Monet to Georgia O'Keeffe, Andrew Wyeth to Ansel Adams. The story is based on experiences of both his maternal grandfather and Say himself as they came to terms with their adopted land, the United States. Born in Japan to a Korean father and a Japanese-American mother who separated when he was 12, the author lived briefly but unhappily with a grandmother, then was allowed to have his own apartment. It was during this time that he became Shinpei's assistant. When Say was 16, his father brought him to America and made him attend military school. After high school, Say returned to Japan because he hated Southern California, but found he couldn't live there either. In *Grandfather's Journey,* Say explores the idea of rootlessness, of being what he called in *Booklist* a "cultural hybrid." His narrator in the picture book expresses this feeling thus: "... the moment I am in one country, I am homesick for the other."

Cross-cultural elements abound in Say's books. In *The Bicycle Man,* set in post-World War II Japan, Japanese children are initially frightened when two American soldiers—one white, one black—appear at their school's Sportsday. The fear evaporates when they see the soldiers perform feats on the principal's bicycle. Charming pen-and-ink and watercolor illustrations enhance the book's theme of coming together in friendship.

The importance of caring for the environment is a theme of *A River Dream* and *The Lost Lake.* In the former, a sick boy recalls happy times spent with his uncle learning the art of fly-fishing, one of Say's hobbies. In a dream sequence, the lad learns a valuable lesson about coexisting with nature. Its full-page illustrations earned the book a place on the *New York Times'* list of Ten Best Illustrated Children's Books of 1988. *A Tree of Cranes* is based on an experience of Say's at the age of six, when his American-born mother taught him the customs of American Christmases. The book clearly shows Say's use of action in pictures, and scenes of Japanese life introduce readers to the country's art forms and culture.

Perhaps the most clearly autobiographical of Say's books is his young adult novel *The Ink-Keeper's Apprentice.* It gives what he calls, in *The Reading Teacher,* "a fairly accurate account of my boyhood in Japan and how I began as an artist when I was 12 years old." In the picture book he recreates his relationship with Noro Shinpei, who at Say's request took him in, becoming both his teacher and his spiritual father. In an interview in *Booklist,* Say told of his continuing relationship with the great cartoonist and of shedding joyful tears on receiving approving critiques of his books from Shinpei.

El Chino tells the true story of a Chinese American who became a bullfighter in Spain. At first, when Bong Way Wong is searching for direction in life, the book's illustrations are sepia half-tones. Later, when he finds his identity as El Chino, they change to vibrant water colors. Although Liz Rosenberg wrote in the *New York Times* that the author "belabors his point" about Wong's transformation and thereby may confuse young readers, Say claimed in *Booklist* that the story is really that of his own search. When he recognized that fact, the author said, "I put *El Chino* into first-person narrative."

The protagonist in *The Stranger in the Mirror* is an eight-year-old boy who wakes one morning to see his own reflection in a mirror transformed into that of a 70-year-old man. Subsequent events in the boy's life, including getting teased by schoolmates, explore the experience of being thought "a freak." A reviewer in *Parents Magazine* called the tale a "provocative lesson about age and understanding." The illustrations also garnered praise as "exquisite watercolors, realistic and filled with light," according to Hazel Rochman in *Booklist.*

In *Emma's Rug,* an Asian-American child becomes so attached to a rug given her at birth that she carries it everywhere, using it as inspiration for her prize-winning art work. When her mother thoughtlessly washes the rug, Emma feels bereft, unable to create. However, she ultimately realizes that true inspiration comes from within and from the whole world around us. Constance Decker Thompson in a review for the *New York Times* wrote: "Powerful and haunting, Mr. Say's story is complemented to perfection by his ... [s]imple realistic watercolors, luminous with creamy shafts of light,... spare but remarkably expressive...."

In *Allison,* a young Asian-American girl is so distressed when she learns she has been adopted by her Caucasian parents that she angrily destroys mementoes of her adoptive parents' childhoods. But after she "adopts" a stray cat, Allison learns individuals can be families even if they aren't related. Though *Horn Book* reviewer Roger Sutton found the happy ending "less earned than bibliotherapeutic," Susan Dove Lempke in *Booklist* remarked that the book "deals honestly with the confused feelings all children experience when the world they know unexpectedly shifts." Lempke called Say's illustrations "poignant, exquisite paintings."

The author told *The Reading Teacher* interviewers Jackie Peck and Judy Hendershot that in his early books he was "consciously trying to entertain young people...." But in *Grandfather's Journey,* "I was trying to entertain myself. The appeal this book is enjoying comes to me as almost a shock." Whatever Say's conscious intent in producing his books, they nevertheless entertain and touch children and adults alike. Evocative illustrations and gentle, understated prose let the characters' emotions shine through, startling the reader into new awareness.

—Elbert R. Hill

SCANNELL, Vernon

Nationality: British. **Born:** Spilsby, Lincolnshire, 23 January 1922. **Education:** Queen's Park School, Aylesbury, Buckinghamshire; University of Leeds, Yorkshire, 1946-47. **Military Service:** Gordon Highlanders, 1941-45. **Family:** Married Josephine Higson in 1954; two daughters and three sons. **Career:** Professional boxer, 1945-46; English teacher, Hazelwood School, Limpsfield, Surrey, 1955-62. Freelance writer and broadcaster, from 1962. Resident poet, village of Berinsfield, Oxfordshire, 1978; visiting poet, Shrewsbury School, Shropshire, 1978-79, and King's School, Canterbury, 1979. **Awards:** Heinemann award, 1961; Arts Council grant, 1967, 1970; Cholmondeley award, 1974; Southern Arts Writers fellowship, 1975; Society of Authors travelling scholarship, 1987. Fellow, Royal Society of Literature, 1960. Granted Civil List pension, 1981. **Address:** 51 North Street, Otley, West Yorkshire LS21 1AH, England.

Publications for Children

Fiction

The Dangerous Ones. Oxford, Pergamon Press, 1970.
A Lonely Game. Exeter, Wheaton, 1979.

Poetry

Mastering the Craft. Oxford, Pergamon Press, 1970.
The Apple-Raid and Other Poems. London, Chatto and Windus, 1974.
Catch the Light, with Gregory Harrison and Laurence Smith. Oxford, Oxford University Press, 1982; New York, Oxford University Press, 1983.
The Clever Potato, illustrated by Tony Ross. London, Hutchinson, 1988.
Love Shouts and Whispers. London, Hutchinson, 1990; North Pomfret, Vermont, Trafalgar Square, 1992.
Travelling Light, illustrated by Tony Ross. London, Bodley Head, 1991.
On Your Cycle, Michael. N.p., Red Fox, 1992.

Publications for Adults

Novels

The Fight. London, Peter Nevill, 1953.
The Wound and the Scar. London, Peter Nevill, 1953.
The Big Chance. London, Long, 1960.
The Shadowed Place. London, Long, 1961.
The Face of the Enemy. London, Putnam, 1961.
The Dividing Night. London, Putnam, 1962.
The Big Time. London, Longman, 1965.
Ring of Truth. London, Robson, 1983.

Plays

Radio Plays: *A Man's Game,* 1962; *A Door with One Eye,* 1963; *The Cancelling Dark,* music by Christopher Whelen, 1965.

Poetry

Graves and Resurrections. London, Fortune Press, 1948.
A Mortal Pitch. London, Villiers, 1957.
The Masks of Love. London, Putnam, 1960.
A Sense of Danger. London, Putnam, 1962.
Walking Wounded. London, Eyre and Spottiswoode, 1965.
Epithets of War: Poems 1965-1969. London, Eyre and Spottiswoode, 1969.
Pergamon Poets 8, with Jon Silkin, edited by Dennis Butts. Oxford, Pergamon Press, 1970.
Selected Poems. London, Allison and Busby, 1971.
Company of Women. Frensham, Surrey, Sceptre Press, 1971.
Corgi Modern Poets in Focus 4, with others, edited by Jeremy Robson. London, Corgi, 1971.
Incident at West Bay. Richmond, Surrey, Keepsake Press, 1972.
The Winter Man: New Poems. London, Allison and Busby, 1973.
Meeting in Manchester. Rushden, Northamptonshire, Sceptre Press, 1974.
The Loving Game. London, Robson, 1975.
An Ilkley Quintet. Privately printed, 1975(?).
A Morden Tower Reading 1, with Alexis Lykiard. Newcastle upon Tyne, Morden Tower, 1976.
New and Collected Poems 1950-1980. London, Robson, 1980.
Of Love and Music. N.p., Mapletree, 1980.
Winterlude. London, Robson, 1982.
Funeral Games and Other Poems. London, Robson, 1987.
Soldiering On: Poems of Military Life. London, Robson, 1989.
A Time for Fires. London, Robson, 1991.
Drums of Morning: Growing Up In The Thirties. London, Robson, 1992.

Collected Poems 1950-93. London, Robson, 1993.
The Black and White Days. London, Robson, 1996.

Other

Edward Thomas. London, Longman, 1963.
The Tiger and the Rose: An Autobiography. London, Hamish Hamilton, 1971.
Three Poets, Two Children, with Dannie Abse and Leonard Clark, edited by Desmond Badham-Thornhill. Gloucester, Thornhill Press, 1975.
Not Without Glory: Poets of the Second World War. London, Woburn Press, 1976.
A Proper Gentleman. London, Robson, 1977.
How to Enjoy Poetry. Loughton, Essex, Piatkus, 1983.
How to Enjoy Novels. London, Piatkus, 1984.
Argument of Kings: An Autobiography. London, Robson, 1987; New York, Parkwest, 1989.

Editor, with Patricia Beer and Ted Hughes, *New Poems 1962.* London, Hutchinson, 1962.
Editor, *Your Attention Please: An Anthology from the Open University Poets.* Winchester, Hampshire, Hesperus, 1983.
Editor, *Sporting Literature.* Oxford, Oxford University Press, 1987.

*

Manuscript Collections: British Library, London.

Vernon Scannell comments:
I strongly agree with W.H. Auden who said that while there are some good poems which are only for adults because they presuppose adult experience in their readers, there are no good poems which are only for children. In other words I hope that none of my children's poems condescends or patronizes the young reader and that each one would give pleasure to a reader of any age.

* * *

The range of Vernon Scannell's talents—whether exemplified in his life or his art—is wide and consistently impressive. He has been a boxer, amateur and professional, a soldier with the Gordon Highlanders, serving in France and the Middle East during World War II, and has also worked in the fairground. As far as his literary career is concerned, he is perhaps best known for his many collections of poetry for adults; he has also published an autobiography and written criticism and plays for the radio. His work for children includes two novels and several collections of verse.

One of Scannell's most remarkable qualities as a poet for children, and it is one which he has himself identified as being of prime importance in his own criticism, is an ability not merely to describe an action, a mood, an experience, but to enter into it through the medium of his writing, which means that when the reader comes into contact with it, the experience of reading is remarkably similar to actually participating in that which is described. It is a poetry of direct presentation, a poetry of happenings, a poetry that does not merely concern itself with the abstract reportage of events, but gets to the living roots of the events themselves. Something about the physical quality of the language impresses itself upon us, and perhaps this relates directly to the fact that Scannell has been in his life as much a man of action as one of reflection—the qualities that Yeats thought were antagonistic to each other, eternally irreconcilable.

Scannell's poetry for children uses a wide range of subject matter and a variety of techniques. He seems to be very much at home in a balladic stanza. Consider, for example, "The Ballad of Wee Duncan and Red John," in which a young boy, Wee Duncan Bain, is assisted back to his home in the thick of a raging storm by a stranger who proves to be, we are left in no doubt, the wraith of his father, who was himself lost in a storm off the Isle of Wight. There is a surging strength and a vividness in the simplicity of this ballad, a perfect matching of striding metre and clear, bold words, that leaves us in no doubt that the poet is very much at ease in this particular country of the mind. But his talents seem to suit other clothes just as well. The fascinating poem "Junk," for example, might be described as the barebones of a science-fiction novel set in verse. A father and his son peer into a shop window crowded with strange relics from the past, including primitive machines that were once operated manually, the skins of extinct animals that were once worn as clothes, and something "shaped/ Like an oblong box, its lifted lid/ Showed no interior but solid stuff/ In slender layers...." The poem beautifully points up the essential strangeness of so much that we take for granted in our lives, and helps children to perceive things anew as they come to grips with the meaning of the poem—something that happens slowly, but all the more profoundly precisely because of that fact. The strange object is, of course, a book....

—Michael Glover

SCARLETT, Susan. See **STREATFEILD, (Mary) Noel.**

SCARRY, Richard (McClure)

Nationality: American. **Born:** Boston, Massachusetts, 5 June 1919. **Education:** Boston Museum School of Fine Arts, 1939-42, 1969-71. **Military Service:** United States Army in North Africa and the Mediterranean, 1942-46: Captain. **Family:** Married Patricia Murphy in 1948; one son. **Career:** Freelance artist and writer, New York, 1946-49, Connecticut, 1949-68, and Switzerland since 1968. **Award:** Mystery Writers of America Edgar Allan Poe Special award, 1976. **Died:** 30 April 1994.

PUBLICATIONS FOR CHILDREN (ILLUSTRATED BY THE AUTHOR)

Fiction

The Great Big Car and Truck Book. New York, Simon and Schuster, 1951.
Rabbit and His Friends. New York, Simon and Schuster, 1953; London, Muller, 1954.

Naughty Bunny. New York, Golden Press, and London, Muller, 1959.
Tinker and Tanker. New York, Doubleday, 1960; London, Hamlyn, 1969.
Tinker and Tanker Out West. New York, Doubleday, 1961; London, Hamlyn, 1969.
Tinker and Tanker and Their Space Ship. New York, Doubleday, 1961; as *Tinker and Tanker Journey to Tootletown and Build a Spaceship,* New York, Golden Press, 1978.
Tinker and Tanker and the Pirates. New York, Doubleday, 1961.
Tinker and Tanker, Knights of the Round Table. New York, Doubleday, 1963; London, Hamlyn, 1969.
Tinker and Tanker in Africa. New York, Doubleday, 1963; London, Hamlyn, 1969.
Best Word Book Ever. New York, Golden Press, 1963; London, Hamlyn, 1964; revised edition, Golden Press, 1980; as *A Scarry Wordbook,* Hamlyn, 1979.
Polite Elephant. New York, Golden Press, 1964.
Is This the House of Mistress Mouse? New York, Golden Press, 1964.
Feed the Hippo His ABC's. New York, Golden Press, 1964.
Teeny Tiny Tales. New York, Golden Press, 1965; London, Hamlyn, 1970.
The Santa Claus Book. New York, Golden Press, 1965.
The Bunny Book. New York, Golden Press, 1965; London, Golden Pleasure Books, 1966.
Busy Busy World. New York, Golden Press, 1965; London, Hamlyn, 1966.
Egg in the Hole Book. New York, Golden Press, 1967.
Best Storybook Ever. New York, Golden Press, 1968; London, Hamlyn, 1969.
The Early Bird. New York, Random House, 1968; London, Collins, 1970.
The Great Pie Robbery. New York, Random House, and London, Collins, 1969.
The Supermarket Mystery. New York, Random House, and London, Collins, 1969.
Great Big Schoolhouse. New York, Random House, and London, Collins, 1969.
Great Big Air Book. New York, Random House, and London, Collins, 1971.
Best Stories Ever. New York, Golden Press, 1971.
Funniest Storybook Ever. New York, Random House, and London, Collins, 1972; selections, as *Little Bedtime Book* and *Mr. Fixit,* Random House and Collins, 2 vols., 1978.
Nicky Goes to the Doctor. New York, Golden Press, and London, Hamlyn, 1972.
Silly Stories. New York, Golden Press, 1973; London, Hamlyn, 1974.
Babykins and His Family. New York, Golden Press, 1973; London, Hamlyn, 1974.
Great Steamboat Mystery. New York, Random House, 1975; London, Collins, 1976.
Favorite Storybook. New York, Random House, and London, Collins, 1976.
Busy Town, Busy People. New York, Random House, and London, Collins, 1976.
Storytime. London, Collins, 1976; New York, Random House, 1978.
Lowly Worm Story Book. New York, Random House, 1977; London, Collins, 1979.
Busy, Busy Word Book. New York, Random House, 1977; as *Little Word Book,* 1978.
Postman Pig and His Busy Neighbors. New York, Random House, 1978; London, Fontana, 1979.
Toy Book. New York, Random House, 1978; London, Collins, 1979.
Bedtime Stories. New York, Random House, 1978.
Tinker and Tanker Tales of Pirates and Knights. New York, Golden Press, 1979.
To Market, To Market. New York, Golden Press, 1979.
Holiday Book. London, Collins, 1979.
Work and Play Book. London, Collins, 1979.
Mix or Match Storybook. New York, Random House, 1979; London, Collins, 1980.
Best First Book Ever. New York, Random House, 1979; London, Collins, 1980; revised edition as *Board Books* (*Colours, My House,* and *Things I Do*), London, Collins, 3 vols., 1982.
Huckle's Book. New York, Random House, and London, Collins, 1979.
Peasant Pig and the Terrible Dragon. New York, Random House, 1980; London, Collins, 1981.
Christmas Mice. New York, Golden Press, 1981.
Best Christmas Book Ever. New York, Random House, and London, Collins, 1981.
Busy Houses. New York, Random House, 1981; London, Collins, 1982.
Four Busy Word Books. New York, Random House, 1982.
The Best Mistake Ever! and Other Stories. New York, Random House, 1984; London, Collins, 1985.
Best Bumper Book Ever. London, Collins, 1984.
Biggest Word Book Ever! New York, Random House, 1985; London, Hamlyn, 1986.
Big and Little. Racine, Wisconsin, Golden Press, 1986.
My First Word Book. New York, Random House, 1986.
Best Music Book Ever. London, Hamlyn, 1987.
Things That Go. New York, Golden Press, 1987.
Things to Love. New York, Golden Press, 1987.
Busy Workers. New York, Golden Press, 1987.
Best Bedtime Book Ever. London, Hamlyn, 1988.
Best Read and Learn Book Ever. London, Hamlyn, 1988.
Biggest First Book Ever. London, Collins, 1990.
Busy Busy Word Book. N.p., Carnival, 1988.
Dr. Doctor. Racine, Wisconsin, Western, 1988.
Farmer Patrick Pig. Racine, Wisconsin, Western, 1988.
Frances Fix-It. Racine, Wisconsin, Western, 1988.
Harry and Larry the Fishermen. Racine, Wisconsin, Western, 1988.
Play Day. Racine, Wisconsin, Western, 1988.
Smokey the Fireman. Racine, Wisconsin, Western, 1988.
Sniff the Detective. Racine, Wisconsin, Western, 1988.
Splish Splash Sounds. New York, Golden Press, 1988.
All About Cars. Racine, Wisconsin, Western, 1989.
Best Friend Ever. Racine, Wisconsin, Western, 1989.
Best Ride Ever. Racine, Wisconsin, Western, 1989.
Best Two-Minute Stories Ever! New York, Golden Press, 1989.
Mother Goose Scratch and Sniff Book. Racine, Wisconsin, Western, 1989.
Scarry's Best Ever. New York, Random House, 1989.
Tinker and Tanker Storybook. N.p., Treasure, 1989.
Just Right Word Book. N.p., McKay, 1990.
Be Careful, Mr. Frumble. New York, Random House, 1990.
Best Read It Yourself Book Ever. Racine, Wisconsin, Western, 1990.
Best Story Book Ever. London, Hamlyn, 1991.
Watch Your Step, Mr. Rabbit! New York, Random House, 1991.
Best Year Ever. Racine, Wisconsin, Western, 1991.

The Cat Family Takes a Trip. N.p., World International, 1991; Racine, Wisconsin, Western, 1992.
The Cat Family's Busy Day. N.p., World International, 1991; Racine, Wisconsin, Western, 1992.
Mr. Frumble's Worst Day Ever! N.p., World International, 1991; New York, Random House, 1992.
Sergeant Murphy's Busiest Day Ever. Racine, Wisconsin, Western, 1992.
Best Fairytales Ever. N.p., World International, 1992.
Best Little Word Book Ever! Racine, Wisconsin, Western, 1992.
Biggest Pop-up Book Ever! N.p., World International, and Racine, Wisconsin, Western, 1992.
Bananas Gorilla: Richard Scarry's Smallest Pop-up Book Ever! N.p., World International, and Racine, Wisconsin, Western, 1992.
Mr. Fix-It: Richard Scarry's Smallest Pop-up Book Ever! N.p., World International, and Racine, Wisconsin, Wetsern, 1992.
Mr. Frumble: Richard Scarry's Smallest Pop-up Book Ever! N.p., World International, and Racine, Wisconsin, Western, 1992.
Little Red Riding Hood. Racine, Wisconsin, Western, 1993.
The Little Red Hen. Racine, Wisconsin, Western, 1993.
The Three Bears. Racine, Wisconsin, Western, 1993.
The Three Little Pigs. Racine, Wisconsin, Western, 1993.
Huckle Cat's Busiest Day Ever. N.p., World International, 1992; New York, Random House, 1993.
Story Book. N.p., Dean, 1993.
Pie Rats Ahoy! New York, Random House, 1994.

Poetry

The Hickory Dickory Clock Book. New York, Doubleday, 1961.

Other

Nursery Tales. New York, Simon and Schuster, 1958.
Manners. New York, Golden Press, 1962.
What Animals Do. New York, Golden Press, 1963.
A Tinker and Tanker Coloring Book. New York, Doubleday, 1963.
The Rooster Struts. New York, Golden Press, 1963; as *The Golden Happy Book of Animals,* 1964; as *Animals,* London, Hamlyn, 1964.
Animal Mother Goose. New York, Golden Press, 1964; London, Hamlyn, 1965.
Best Nursery Rhymes Ever. New York, Golden Press, 1964; London, Hamlyn, 1971.
Storybook Dictionary. New York, Golden Press, 1966; N.p., Dean, 1992
Planes. New York, Golden Press, 1967.
Trains. New York, Golden Press, 1967; with *Cars,* London, Golden Pleasure Books, 1969.
Boats. New York, Golden Press, 1967; with *Planes,* London, Hamlyn, 1969.
Cars. New York, Golden Press, 1967.
What Do People Do All Day? New York, Random House, 1968; London, Collins, 1969.
What Animals Do. New York, Golden Press, 1968.
ABC Word Book. New York, Random House, 1971; London, Collins, 1972.
Look and Learn Library (*Best Stories Ever, Fun with Words, Going Places, Things to Know*). New York, Golden Press, 4 vols., 1971; last vol. published, London, Collins, 1976.
Hop Aboard, Here We Go! New York, Golden Press, and London, Hamlyn, 1972.
Find Your ABC's. New York, Random House, 1973.
Please and Thank You Book. New York, Random House, and London, Collins, 1973.
Best Rainy Day Book Ever. New York, Random House, 1974; London, Hamlyn, 1975.
European Word Book. London, Hamlyn, 1974.
Cars and Trucks and Things That Go. New York, Golden Press, and London, Collins, 1974.
Animal Nursery Tales. New York, Golden Press, and London, Collins, 1975.
Best Counting Book Ever. New York, Random House, 1975; London, Collins, 1976.
Busiest People Ever. New York, Random House, 1976; London, Collins, 1977.
Look-Look Books (*All Day Long, All Year Long, In My Town, Learn to Count, About Animals, At Work, My House, On the Farm, On Vacation* [*On Holiday*], *Short and Tall*). New York, Golden Press, 10 vols., 1976; London, Hamlyn, 10 vols., 1977.
Early Words. New York, Random House, 1976; London, Collins, 1977.
Color Book. New York, Random House, 1976; London, Collins, 1977.
Laugh and Learn Library. New York, Random House, and London, Collins, 4 vols., 1976.
Picture Dictionary. London, Collins, 1976.
Teeny Tiny ABC. New York, Golden Press, and London, Hamlyn, 1976.
Little ABC. New York, Random House, and London, Collins, 1976.
Learn to Count. New York, Golden Press, 1976.
Best Make-It Book Ever. New York, Random House, 1977; London, Collins, 1978.
Busy-Busy Counting Book. London, Collins, 1977; as *Little Counting Book,* New York, Random House, 1978.
Stories to Color. New York, Random House, 1978; London, Collins, 1979.
Little Word Book. New York, Random House, 1978.
Punch-Out Toy Book. New York, Random House, 1978.
Things to Learn. New York, Golden Press, 1978.
Little ABC. New York, Random House, 1978.
Lowly Worm Sniffy [*Word, Coloring, Car and Truck, Bath*] *Book.* New York, Random House, 5 vols., 1978-84; 1 vol. published as *Words,* London, Collins, 1982.
Busytown Pop-Up Book. New York, Random House, 1979; London, Collins, 1980.
Can You Count. London, Collins, 1979.
Lowly Worm Things on Wheels [*Where Does It Come From?, Tell-Time*] *Book.* London, Collins, 3 vols., 1979; New York, Random House, 3 vols., 1980.
Busytown Shape Book. London, Collins, 1982.
Sticker Books (*On Holiday, At School, I Can Count to Eleven*). London, Collins, 3 vols., 1982.
Pig Will and Pig Won't: A Book of Manners. New York, Random House, and London, Collins, 1984.
Busy Fun and Learn Book. Racine, Wisconsin, Golden Press, 1984; London, Hamlyn, 1987.
Best Workbooks Ever! (*Fun with Letters* [*Words, Reading, Sounds*]). New York, Random House, 4 vols., 1986.
Best Workbooks Ever! (*Fun with Numbers*). New York, Random House, 3 vols., 1986.
Going Places on the Water [*in the Air, in the Car, with Goldbug*]. London, Collins, 4 vols., 1987.

Lowly Worm's Schoolbag (*Words, Colors, ABC's, Numbers*). New York, Random House, 4 vols., 1987.
Getting Ready for School [*Writing, Numbers, Reading*]. New York, Random House, 4 vols., 1987.
Activity Book. London, Collins, 1988.
Best Times Ever: A Book about Seasons and Holidays. Racine, Wisconsin, Western, 1988.
Busy Busy Sticker Book. N.p., Carnival, 1988.
Giant Colouring Book. N.p., Carnival, 1988.
Learning How Sticker Book. N.p., Carnival, 1988.
Welcome to Scarrytown. London, Hamlyn, 1989.
Best Puzzle Word Book Ever. London, Hamlyn, 1989.
Counting Book. Racine, Wisconsin, Western, 1990.
ABC's. Racine, Wisconsin, Western, 1991.
Biggest Make-It Book Ever. New York, Random House, 1993.
Colors. New York, Golden Books, 1993.
First Words. Racine, Wisconsin, Western, 1993.
Word Book with Huckle Cat and Lowly Worm. Racine, Wisconsin, Western, 1993.

Editor, *Fables,* by Jean de La Fontaine. New York, Doubleday, 1963.

*

Illustrator: *The Boss of the Barnyard* by Joan Hubbard, 1949; *Two Little Miners* by Margaret Wise Brown and Edith Thacher Hurd, 1949, and *Little Indian* by Brown, 1954; *Let's Go Fishing,* 1949, *Mouse's House,* 1949, *Duck and His Friends,* 1949, *Brave Cowboy Bill,* 1950, and *The Party Pig,* 1954, all by Kathryn and Byron Jackson, and *The Animals' Merry Christmas,* 1950, *Here Comes the Parade,* 1951, *The New Golden Almanac,* 1952, *The Golden Bedtime Book,* 1955, and *Best House Ever,* 1989, all by Kathryn Jackson, and *My Nursery Tale Book,* 1961, by Jackson and Patsy Scarry; *Little Benny Wanted a Pony* by Oliver Barrett, 1950; *The Animals of Farmer Jones* by Leah Gale, 1953; *Danny Beaver's Secret,* 1953, *Pierre Bear,* 1954, *The Bunny Book,* 1955, and *Just For Fun,* 1960, all by Patricia Scarry; *Smokey the Bear* by Jane Werner, 1955; *My First Golden Dictionary* by Mary Reed and Edith Osswald, 1956; *My Golden Book of Manners* by Peggy Parish, 1962; *Tommy Visits the Doctor* by Jean Selligman and Levine Milton, 1962; *Nonsense Alphabet* by Edward Lear, 1962; *I Am a Bunny* by Ole Risom, 1963; *Rudolph the Red-Nosed Reindeer* by Barbara Shook Hazen, 1964; *The Golden Book of 365 Stories,* 1966; *Best Mother Goose Ever,* 1970; *Mother Goose,* 1972; *With the Animals,* 1975 (as *Meet the Animals,* 1982), *All Day Long,* 1975 (as *My Day,* 1984), *My House,* 1975, and *On Holiday,* n.d., all by J.D. Bevington; *Chipmunk's ABC* by Roberta Miller, 1976; *The Gingerbread Man,* 1981; *Little Red Riding Hood,* 1981; *Old Mother Hubbard,* 1983; *This Little Pig Went to Market,* 1983; *One, Two, Buckle My Shoe,* 1983; *Little Miss Muffet,* 1983; *My First Golden Dictionary,* 1983; *The Golden Treasury of Fairy Tales,* 1985; *Simple Simon and Other Rhymes,* 1988; *Little Miss Muffet and Other Rhymes,* 1988; *Cars and Trucks from A to Z,* 1990.

* * *

Richard Scarry's literary output enjoys a huge following among today's children. Part of his success may be attributed to the fact that his works are closely related in style to the medium of film or television in their emphasis on action. *What Do People Do All Day?,* a typical Scarry title, contains pages crammed with drawings depicting everyday activities in minute detail. The accompanying text is usually limited to a description of the particular action taking place. Occasionally, flip comments give the straightforward explanations an added dimension. Scarry's characters are both human and animal. In many cases animal figures intended to represent people and human figures are used in the same drawing, a technique which provides humor (e.g., a schoolbus loaded with owl pupils) and interest. The illustrations tend to have an air of cosiness and cuteness due to Scarry's use of rounded angles and a perspective which makes the characters appear to be operating in a miniature setting. All the characters smile, even in such unlikely situations as the fire brigade rescue in *Hop Aboard, Here We Go!*

Scarry's books are usually lacking in plot—rather they are a cumulation of bits of information in various spheres of knowledge. A typical Scarry title, *Great Big Schoolhouse,* contains a series of some 20 two-three page vignettes centred on the theme of school activities. The author details in chronological order the events and activities in which school children are apt to be involved. The text is very like the dialogue one would expect to find in an educational television program—questions are asked, admonitions are made (with regard to dangerous objects, for example), and comments are made on the behaviour of the illustrated characters. Humor is often derived from a straightforward comment juxtaposed against a ridiculous drawing.

Like Dr. Seuss, Scarry hit on a formula for success which he used repeatedly. His books with their endearing characters have a certain charm. However, in exchange for commercial success he probably forfeited any real creative development as an artist and as a writer.

—Fran Ashdown

SCHAEFER, Jack (Warner)

Nationality: American. **Born:** Cleveland, Ohio, 19 November 1907. **Education:** Oberlin College, Ohio, A.B. in English 1929; Columbia University, New York, 1929-30. **Family:** Married 1) Eugenia Hammond Ives in 1931 (divorced 1948), three sons and one daughter; 2) Louise Wilhide Deans in 1949, three stepchildren. **Career:** Reporter, United Press, New Haven, Connecticut, 1930-31; assistant director of education, Connecticut State Reformatory, Cheshire, 1931-38; associate editor, 1932-39, and editor, 1939-42, New Haven *Journal-Courier*; editorial writer, Baltimore *Sun,* 1942-44; associate editor, Norfolk *Virginian-Pilot,* 1944-48; associate, Lindsay Advertising Company, 1949. Editor and publisher, *Theatre News,* 1935-40, *The Movies,* 1939-41, and *Shoreliner,* 1949, all New Haven. **Award:** Western Literature Association Distinguished Achievement award, 1975. **Died:** 24 January 1991.

Publications for Children

Fiction

Shane. Boston, Houghton Mifflin, 1949; London, Deutsch, 1954; edited by James C. Work, Lincoln, University of Nebraska Press, 1984.

First Blood. Boston, Houghton Mifflin, 1953; London, Deutsch, 1954.
The Canyon. Boston, Houghton Mifflin, 1953; augmented edition, as *The Canyon and Other Stories,* London, Deutsch, 1955.
Old Ramon, illustrated by Harold West. Boston, Houghton Mifflin, 1960; London, Deutsch, 1962.
The Plainsmen, illustrated by Lorence Bjorklund. Boston, Houghton Mifflin, 1963.
Stubby Pringle's Christmas, illustrated by Lorence Bjorklund. Boston, Houghton Mifflin, 1964.
Mavericks, illustrated by Lorence Bjorklund. Boston, Houghton Mifflin, 1967; London, Deutsch, 1968.

Other

New Mexico. New York, Coward McCann, 1967.

Publications for Adults

Novels

The Pioneers. Boston, Houghton Mifflin, 1954; London, Deutsch, 1957.
Company of Cowards. Boston, Houghton Mifflin, 1957; London, Deutsch, 1958.
Monte Walsh. Boston, Houghton Mifflin, 1963; London, Deutsch, 1965.
The Short Novels of Jack Schaefer. Boston, Houghton Mifflin, 1967.

Short Stories

The Big Range. Boston, Houghton Mifflin, 1953; London, Deutsch, 1955.
The Kean Land and Other Stories. Boston, Houghton Mifflin, 1959; London, Deutsch, 1960.
Tales from the West. London, Hamish Hamilton, 1961.
Incident on the Trail. London, Corgi, 1962.
Collected Stories. Boston, Houghton Mifflin, 1966.
Jack Schaefer and the American West: Eight Stories, edited by C.E.J. Smith. London, Longman, 1978.
Conversations with a Pocket Gopher and Other Outspoken Neighbors, illustrated by Irene Brady. Santa Barbara, California, Capra Press, 1978.
The Collected Short Stories of Jack Schaefer. New York, Arbor House, 1985.
First Blood and Other Stories. New York, Bantam, 1988.

Other

The Great Endurance Horse Race: 600 Miles on a Single Mount, 1908, from Evanston, Wyoming, to Denver. Santa Fe, New Mexico, Stagecoach Press, 1963.
Heroes Without Glory: Some Goodmen of the Old West. Boston, Houghton Mifflin, 1965; London, Deutsch, 1966.
Adolphe Francis Alphonse Bandelier. Santa Fe, New Mexico, Press of the Territorian, 1966.
Hal West: Western Gallery. Santa Fe, Museum of New Mexico Press, 1971.
An American Bestiary. Boston, Houghton Mifflin, 1975.
Editor, *Out West: An Anthology of Stories.* Boston, Houghton Mifflin, 1955; London, Deutsch, 1959.

*

Manuscript Collections: Western History Research Center, University of Wyoming, Laramie.

Critical Studies: *Jack Schaefer* by Gerald W. Haslam, Boise, Idaho, Boise State University, 1975.

Jack Schaefer commented:

(1989) I have never deliberately and consciously written stories for children. I do not believe anyone should do so—except a writer aiming at youngsters just learning to read. I have always written my stories for people, for readers, regardless of age, doing the best job I could in each instance according to the tune and the tone and the possibilities of the material I was using. None of my books is solely for children—or solely for adults. My mail through the years has shown that the books have done what I hoped they would do: attracted readers of all ages.

* * *

Jack Schaefer's fiction-writing career began in 1949 with *Shane,* an understated tale of a gunman's involvement with a homesteading family in Wyoming, told from the point of view of their son. It ended in 1967 with *Mavericks,* the movingly evocative reminiscences of Old Jake Hanlon, a dying cowboy lost in his memories of the long-extinct American west. These two books typify Schaefer's writings for many readers; they are the terminal points of a group of works uniformly concerned with the theme of growing up and stressing the responsibility that comes with experience and maturity.

Shane, although not originally written for a youthful audience, has grown increasingly popular with young readers. Its story is simple, its point clear. The book's first-person narration gives immediacy to the emotional tensions between Shane and the Starrett family. Young Bob Starrett, the narrator, is torn between his admiration for Shane and his love for his parents, and gradually learns of the complex responsibilities of adulthood. And Shane himself, a reformed gunfighter who reluctantly resumes his violent craft to preserve the stable lives of Joe and Marion Starrett, is a poignant, dignified personification of the responsible individual.

Old Ramon continues the theme of growing up. As Ramon, an aged Mexican sheepherder, leads his patron's son through a summer's work in the pastures, the boy comes to see that independence and responsibility go hand-in-hand, and the truly mature person is the one who accepts them both. Less substantial is *Stubby Pringle's Christmas,* a tall tale about a cowpoke who substitutes for Santa Claus. Even this slight work, however, reveals Schaefer's view of responsibility, for Pringle gives up a night's festivities to make gifts for a penniless family.

Mavericks is the ultimate extension of Schaefer's recurring theme. Jake Hanlon, recalling his 70-odd years as ranch-hand and cowboy, discovers that he has contributed to the destruction of the west that he loves. He sees at last the cost of progress, and is sickened by his vision. The responsible person, Schaefer implies, must see what Jake sees: that actions have consequences, and that modern comforts come at the expense of a cruder but more vital world. Maturity, therefore, means accepting one's responsibilities to the world, the environment, and one's self. Schaefer heeded his own advice; from 1967 until his death he devoted himself to writing of mankind's effect upon the western environment and its inhabitants.

—Fred Erisman

SCHLEIN, Miriam

Pseudonyms: Susan Dorrit and Miriam Weiss. **Nationality:** American. **Born:** New York City, 1926. **Education:** Brooklyn College (now of the City University of New York), received degree. **Family:** one daughter and one son. **Awards:** Junior Book Award Medal, Boys' Clubs of America, 1953, for *Fast Is Not a Ladybug: A Book about Fast and Slow Things*; Herald Tribune Honor Book, 1954, for *Elephant Herd*; Children's Spring Book Festival Honor Book, 1955, for *Little Red Nose*; Kirkus Reviews 100 Best citation, 1974, and Westchester Library Best books citation, 1974-75, both for *What's Wrong with Being a Skunk?*; Outstanding Science Trade Book for Children citation, National Science Teachers Association/Children's Book Council, 1976, and Showcase Title selection, Children's Book Council, 1977, for *Giraffe: The Silent Giant*; Outstanding Science Trade Book for Children citations, 1979, for *Snake Fights, Rabbit Fights, and More: A Book about Animal Fighting,* 1980, for *Lucky Porcupine!,* 1982, for *Billions of Bats,* 1986, for *The Dangerous Life of the Sea Horse,* and 1991, for *Discovering Dinosaur Babies*; Honor Book citation, New York Academy of Sciences, 1984, for *Project Panda Watch*; Children's Books of the Year citation, Child Study Association, 1989, for *Pigeons*; Outstanding Science Trade Book for Children citation, 1990, and Sunshine State Young Readers Award list and Nebraska Golden Sower Award nominee, both 1992-93, all for *The Year of the Panda*; "Pick of the Lists" citation, American Booksellers Association, 1991, for *I Sailed with Columbus*; Several of Schlein's books have been selections of the Junior Library Guild and other book clubs. **Address:** 19 East 95th Street, New York, New York 10128, U.S.A.

Publications for Children

Fiction

A Day at the Playground, illustrated by Eloise Wilkin. New York, Simon and Schuster, 1951.
Tony's Pony, illustrated by Van Kaufman. New York, Simon and Schuster, 1952.
Go with the Sun, illustrated by Symeon Shimin. New York, Scott, 1952.
The Four Little Foxes, illustrated by Luis Quintanilla. New York, Scott, 1953.
When Will the World Be Mine?, illustrated by Jean Charlot. New York, Scott, 1953.
Elephant Herd, illustrated by Symeon Shimin. New York, Scott, 1954; Kingswood, Surrey, World's Work, 1967.
Oomi, The New Hunter, illustrated by George Mason. New York, Abelard Schuman, 1955; London, Abelard Schuman, 1958.
Little Red Nose, illustrated by Roger Duvoisin. New York and London, Abelard Schuman, 1955.
Puppy's House, illustrated by Katherine Evans. Chicago, Whitman, 1955; Edinburgh, Chambers, 1969.
Big Talk, illustrated by Harvey Weiss. New York, Scott, 1955; illustrated by Joan Auclair, Scarsdale, New York, Bradbury, 1990.
Lazy Day, illustrated by Harvey Weiss. New York, Scott, 1955.
Henry's Ride, illustrated by Vane Earle. Nashville, Abingdon Press, 1956.
Deer in the Snow, illustrated by Leonard Kessler. New York and London, Abelard Schuman, 1956.
Something for Now, Something for Later, illustrated by Leonard Weisgard. New York, Harper, 1956.
Little Rabbit, The High Jumper, illustrated by Theresa Sherman. New York, Scott, 1957; as *Just Like Me,* illustrated by Marilyn Janovitz, New York, Hyperion, 1993.
Amazing Mr. Pelgrew, illustrated by Harvey Weiss. New York and London, Abelard Schuman, 1957.
Here Comes Night, illustrated by Harvey Weiss. Chicago, Whitman, 1957; Edinburgh, Chambers, 1967.
The Big Cheese, illustrated by Joseph Low. New York, Scott, 1958; London, Hamish Hamilton, 1965.
The Bumblebee's Secret, illustrated by Harvey Weiss. New York and London, Abelard Schuman, 1958.
Home, The Tale of a Mouse, illustrated by E. Harper Johnson. New York, Abelard Schuman, 1958.
Herman McGregor's World, illustrated by Harvey Weiss. Chicago, Whitman, 1958; Kingswood, Surrey, World's Work, 1972.
The Fisherman's Day, illustrated by Harvey Weiss. Chicago, Whitman, 1959.
Kittens, Cubs, and Babies, illustrated by Jean Charlot. W. R. Scott, 1959.
Big Lion, Little Lion, illustrated by Joe Lasker, Chicago, Whitman, 1964; Edinburgh, Chambers, 1966.
Little Dog Little, illustrated by Hertha Depper. New York, Abelard Schuman, 1959.
The Raggle Taggle Fellow, illustrated by Harvey Weiss. New York and London, Abelard Schuman, 1959.
The Sun, The Wind, The Sea, and the Rain, illustrated by Joe Lasker. New York and London, Abelard Schuman, 1960.
Laurie's New Brother (as Susan Dorritt), illustrated by Elizabeth Donald. New York and London, Abelard Schuman, 1961.
Amuny, Boy of Old Egypt, illustrated by Thea Dupays. New York and London, Abelard Schuman, 1961.
The Pile of Junk, illustrated by Harvey Weiss. New York and London, Abelard Schuman, 1962.
The Snake in the Carpool, illustrated by N.M. Bodecker. New York and London, Abelard Schuman, 1963.
The Way Mothers Are, illustrated by Joe Lasker. Chicago, Whitman, 1963; revised edition, 1993.
Who?, illustrated by Harvey Weiss. New York, Walck, 1963.
The Big Green Thing, illustrated by Elizabeth Dauber. New York, Grosset and Dunlap, 1963; London, Muller, 1968.
Billy, The Littlest One, illustrated by Lucy Hawkinson. Chicago, Whitman, 1966; Edinburgh, Chambers, 1969.
The Best Place, illustrated by Erica Merkling. Chicago, Whitman, 1968.
My House, illustrated by Joe Lasker. Chicago, Whitman, 1971.
The Rabbit's World, illustrated by Peter Parnall. New York, Four Winds Press, 1973.

The Girl Who Would Rather Climb Trees, illustrated by Judith Gwyn Brown. New York, Harcourt Brace, 1975.
Bobo the Troublemaker, illustrated by Ray Cruz. New York, Four Winds Press, 1976.
That's Not Goldie!, illustrated by Susan Gough Magurn. New York, Simon and Schuster, 1990.
The Year of the Panda, illustrated by Kim Mak. New York, Crowell, 1990.
I Sailed with Columbus, illustrated by Tom Newsom. New York, Harper, 1991.
Secret Land of the Past, illustrated by Kees de Kiefte. New York, Scholastic, 1992.

Nonfiction

Metric: The Modern Way to Measure, illustrated by Jan Pyk. New York, Harcourt Brace, 1975.
Rosh Hashanah and Yom Kippur, illustrated by Erika Weihs. New York, Behrman House, 1983.
Hanukkah, illustrated by Katherine Kahn. New York, Behrman House, 1983.
Shavuot, illustrated by Erika Weihs. New York, Behrman House, 1983.
Shabbat, illustrated by Amy Blake. New York, Behrman House, 1983.
Prayers and Blessings, illustrated by Amye Rosenberg. New York, Behrman House, 1983.
Passover, illustrated by Katherine Kahn. New York, Behrman House, 1983.
Sukkot and Simhat Torah, illustrated by Amye Rosenberg. New York, Behrman House, 1983.
Purim, illustrated by Ruth Heller. New York, Behrman House, 1983.

Other

Shapes, illustrated by Sam Berman. New York, Scott, 1952.
Fast Is Not a Ladybug: A Book about Fast and Slow Things. New York, Scott, 1953; as *Fast Is Not a Ladybird,* Kingswood, Surrey, World's Work, 1961.
Heavy Is a Hippopotamus, illustrated by Leonard Kessler. New York, Scott, 1954.
The Sun Looks Down, illustrated by Abner Graboff. New York, Abelard Schuman, 1954; London, Abelard Schuman, 1958.
How Do You Travel?, illustrated by Paul Galdone. Nashville, Abingdon Press, 1954.
It's about Time, illustrated by Leonard Kessler. New York, Scott, 1955.
City Boy, Country Boy, illustrated by Katherine Evans. Chicago, Children's Press, 1955.
A Bunny, A Bird, A Funny Cat, illustrated by Abner Graboff. London and New York, Abelard Schuman, 1957.
My Family, illustrated by Harvey Weiss. New York, Abelard Schuman, 1960; London, Abelard Schuman, 1964.
Snow Time, illustrated by Joe Lasker. Chicago, Whitman, 1962; Edinburgh, Chambers, 1966.
Moon-Months and Sun-Days (folktales), illustrated by Shelly Sacks. New York, Scott, 1972.
Juju-Sheep and the Python's Moonstone, and Other Moon Stories from Different Times and Different Places (folktales), illustrated by Joe Lasker. Chicago, Whitman, 1973.
What's Wrong with Being a Skunk?, illustrated by Ray Cruz. New York, Four Winds Press, 1974.
Giraffe: The Silent Giant, illustrated by Betty Fraser. New York, Four Winds Press, 1976.
I Hate It, illustrated by Judith Gwyn Brown. Chicago, Whitman, 1978.
On the Track of the Mystery Animal: The Story of the Discovery of the Okapi, illustrated by Ruth Sanderson. New York, Four Winds Press, 1978.
I, Tut: The Boy Who Became Pharaoh, illustrated by Erik Hilgerdt. New York, Four Winds Press, 1979.
Snake Fights, Rabbit Fights, and More: A Book about Animal Fighting, illustrated by Sue Thompson. New York, Crown, 1979.
Antarctica: The Great White Continent. New York, Hastings House, 1980.
Lucky Porcupine!, illustrated by Martha Weston. New York, Four Winds Press, 1980.
Billions of Bats, illustrated by Walter Kessell. New York, Lippincott, 1982.
Project Panda Watch, illustrated by Robert Shetterly. New York, Atheneum, 1984.
What the Elephant Was: Strange Prehistoric Elephants. New York, Atheneum, 1985.
The Dangerous Life of the Sea Horse, illustrated by Gwen Cole. New York, Atheneum, 1986.
Jane Goodall's Animal World [*Hippos, Pandas, Elephants, Gorillas*]. New York, Atheneum, 4 vols., 1989-90.
Pigeons, photographs by Margaret Miller. New York, Crowell, 1989.
Discovering Dinosaur Babies, illustrated by Margaret Colbert. New York, Four Winds, 1991.
Let's Go Dinosaur Tracking!, illustrated by Kate Duke. New York, Harper, 1991.
Squirrel Watching, photographs by Marjorie Pillar. New York, Harper, 1992.
The Dino Quiz Book, illustrated by Nate Evans. New York, Scholastic, 1995.
More Than One, illustrated by Donald Crew. New York, Greenwillow, 1996.
Before the Dinosaurs, illustrated by Michael Rothman. New York, Scholastic, 1996.
The Puzzle of the Dinosaur-Bird: The Story of Archaeopteryx, illustrated by Mark Hallett. New York, Dial, 1996.
Sleep Safe, Little Whale: A Lullaby, pictures by Peter Sis. New York, Greenwillow, 1997.
What's a Penguin Doing in a Place Like This? Brookfield, Connecticut, Millbrook Press, 1997.
What the Dinosaurs Saw, illustrated by Carol Schwartz. New York, Scholastic, 1998.
Wait Till Sunday (as Susan Dorritt), illustrated by Roger Duvoisin. New York, Abelard-Schuman, n.d.
Jason's Lucky Day (as Susan Dorritt), illustrated by John Strickland Goodall. New York, Abelard-Schuman, n.d.
Jellybean, the Puppy Who Was Born in the Time of the Snow, (as Susan Dorritt), illustrated by Pat Marriott. New York, Abelard-Schuman, n.d.

* * *

Those who write for adults, or even for older children, can safely make certain assumptions about the understanding and abilities of their chosen audiences. Those who, like Miriam Schlein, write for beginning readers, can take very little for granted. Their little people are just setting out on the reader's voyage, and for this reason, their writer's responsibility is an especially heavy and exacting one. It is at this crucial time that lifelong readers and lovers of literature are so often made (and perhaps, who can tell, sometimes are lost as well). So much depends upon the materials offered them. If those first unsteady steps carry the reader into a land of enchantment and rich welcome, the chances are that he or she will return soon and frequently.

As Schlein so well understands, it is not merely a question of a small reading vocabulary that may impede that first important reading experience; a great part of the difficulty lies in the complex matter of grasping *concepts.* Here, though not only here, Schlein is an extremely important and influential writer for the beginner, for she has made the difficult explication of concepts for the beginning reader her province. Such deceptively simple works as *Fast Is Not a Lady Bug* and *Shapes* provide some basis for the understanding of intangibles, so baffling to readers who can readily grasp the meanings of words that lend themselves to concrete illustration.

Schlein's especial talent lies in her ability to explain while entertaining. Hers are works of charm and simplicity that have stood the tests of time and of many more or less successful attempts at emulation, none of which so far have surpassed her impressive achievement, for she is represented in most well-equipped libraries for young people, as well as in many classrooms and school science and supplementary reading collections. At a more advanced level of readership, her studies of animals and their distinctive behavior patterns have proved a treasure trove to young naturalists. From the giraffe to the humble skunk (as she so rightly points out, there is nothing wrong with being a skunk, but a lot wrong with human judgmental attitudes about skunkishness), her interest and enthusiasm for her subjects, and her passionate conservationism, shine through her words.

Though most of Schlein's books are truly "slim volumes," placed side by side they would fill a very wide shelf indeed—possibly the most important shelf in any library, for she is the welcoming lady holding open a door for the very youngest, most impressionable, arguably most important reader to enter.

—Joan McGrath

SCIESZKA, Jon

Nationality: American. **Born:** Flint, Michigan, 8 September 1954. **Education:** Albion College, B.A. 1976; Columbia University, M.F.A. 1980. **Family:** Married Jerilyn Hansen; children: one daughter and one son. **Career:** Writer; The Day School, New York City, elementary school teacher since 1980. Worked variously as a painter, lifeguard, and magazine writer, among other odd jobs.

Publications for Children

Fiction

The True Story of the Three Little Pigs, illustrated by Lane Smith. New York, Viking, 1989.

The Frog Prince, Continued, illustrated by Steve Johnson. New York, Viking, 1991.

The Stinky Cheeseman and Other Fairly Stupid Tales, illustrated by Lane Smith. New York, Viking, 1992.

The Book that Jack Wrote (poetry), illustrated by Daniel Adel. New York, Viking, 1994.

Math Curse, illustrated by Lane Smith. New York, Viking, 1995.

Tut, Tut, illustrated by Lane Smith. New York, Viking, 1996.

Summer Reading Is Killing Me!, illustrated by Lane Smith. New York, Viking, 1998.

Time Warp Trio series:

- *Knights of the Kitchen Table,* illustrated by Lane Smith. New York, Viking, 1991.
- *The Not-So-Jolly Roger,* illustrated by Lane Smith. New York, Viking, 1991.
- *The Good, the Bad, and the Goofy,* illustrated by Lane Smith. New York, Viking, 1992.
- *Your Mother Was a Neanderthal,* illustrated by Lane Smith. New York, Viking, 1993.
- *2095,* illustrated by Lane Smith. New York, Viking, 1995.

* * *

Speaking about his book with illustrator Lane Smith, *The Stinky Cheese Man and Other Fairly Stupid Tales,* Jon Scieszka told *Publishers Weekly:* "Our audience is hard-core silly kids. And there are lot of 'em out there." Scieszka's work appeals straight to the funny bone with his "fractured fairy tale" picture books and his *Time Warp Trio* chapter books. Because humor works on different levels, Scieszka's books are popular not only with the intended juvenile market, but with audiences of all ages. In fact, *The Stinky Cheese Man* was both a Caldecott honor book and a Recommended Book for Reluctant Teen Readers choice. In addition, the majority of his reviews has been positive—with two titles reviewed in the *New York Times Book Review.*

It is no surprise that the *New York Times Book Review* picked up on Scieszka, because his books are sophisticated. You can't laugh at the joke if you don't get it and some of his jokes require if not sophistication, then at least knowledge or experience. A fractured fairy tale means little to the reader who doesn't know the original one. Time warp adventures aren't as spine chilling if the reader isn't familiar with the dangers of the past. Yet, Scieszka's sophistication is like that of British comedy troupe Monty Python—dumb jokes about smart things; such as a warning at the beginning of *The Stinky Cheese Man* telling readers that "it has been determined that these tales are fairly stupid and probably dangerous to your health."

Scieszka's first book, also with Smith, *The True Story of the Three Little Pigs,* is a one joke wonder—letting the wolf tell his side of this famous story. From this point of view, the wolf is only trying to borrow a cup of sugar from the pigs, so he's not responsible for their badly constructed houses collapsing. The punch line of the book—"That's It. The Real Story. I Was Framed"—is clever for kids, and for adults another reflection on the power of the press on public trials.

After fracturing a fairy tale, Scieszka (with illustrator Steve Johnson) set about to extend one in *The Frog Prince Continued.* Taking the basic comedy riff—what if—Scieszka imagines what if the kiss didn't lead the prince to life happily every after. Thus, the prince seeks out someone to turn him back into a frog. Scieszka dances through fairy tale fandom having the prince run into the witches from Sleeping Beauty, Snow White, and Hansel and Gretel, and the fairy godmother from Cinderella. There's another great punch line, and even a happy ending.

Finally, after breaking and bending the genre, Scieszka and Smith exploded it with *The Stinky Cheese Man.* Refined after many school visits, Scieszka and Smith succeeded in making the book itself the joke—is there another book which has the table of contents page crush characters, or to have the words "Title Page" in huge letters as the title page? There is wackiness abounding through out—fairy tales with no morals ("The Really Ugly Duckling"), or no end ("The Tortoise and the Hair"). The title story "The Stinky Cheese Man" is the best of the bunch; a fractured fairy tale with references to bad odors. Scieszka seems to have a knack for knowing what makes third graders giggle. Take something serious and well known, then lampoon it for all its worth. It's hardly a new idea in comedy, but one never done quite so well for children.

Scieszka's other product line, also done in collaboration with Smith, is the *Time Warp Trio.* Each book is the same: the trio uses the magical book called "the book" to get transported in time—so far they've visited pirates (*The Not So Jolly Roger*), King Arthur (*Knights of the Kitchen Table*), the old west (*The Good, the Bad, and the Goofy*), prehistoric times (*Your Mother Was a Neanderthal*), and have travelled into the future (*2095*). The trip consists of three goofy, yet real boys—Joe, Sam, Fred—who find themselves time travelling with little but their wits. Its a comedy gold mine, as cultures clash, classical, and pop culture allusions bounce off each other, and dialogue sounds authentic right down to the terrible puns. The first two titles, *Knights* and *Jolly Roger,* came in at 55 pages, while the last two have been longer. All four are jam packed with jokes; many of them of the *Back to the Future*/ anachronism variety, but others quite clever.

In *Your Mother Was a Neanderthal,* Scieszka plops the boys naked in prehistoric times (funny), has them encounter what turns out to be a fake dinosaur head (funnier), communicate with cave men (funniest), and dress up as the "meanest two-horned, three headed, straw honking beast on the planet" (too funny). There's also a tip of the hat to television action shows where the boys apply science (how a fulcrum works) to solve a problem. The crux of Scieszka's humor is found in the pop quiz following the last chapter—here readers are asked a variety of questions like one would find on a math test, only to have an answer for each question be "I can't tell you because I was just run over by a woolly mammoth." That's smart humor: repetition of an outrageous image.

What Scieszka has done is make a book equivalent of a happy meal—taking the things that most kids like in books like humor, adventure, fairy tales, and plain old silliness, and combining them into easy to read tomes which will indeed appeal to an audience of all ages.

—Patrick Jones and Christine Miller

SCOTT, Ann. See **FRITZ, Jean.**

SCOTT, Bill

Has also written as W. N. Scott. **Nationality:** Australian. **Born:** William Neville Scott, Bundaberg, Queensland, 4 October 1923. **Education:** Caboolture State Primary School. **Military Service:** Royal Australian Navy, 1942-46. **Family:** Married Mavis Richards in 1949; one son. **Career:** Worked as a bookseller, publisher, and editor during the 1950s and 1960s. Currently a full-time writer. **Awards:** Mary Gilmore award, 1964; Australian Council fellowship, 1977, 1980, 1981; medal of the Order of Australia, 1992. **Address:** 157 Pratten Street, Warwick, Queensland 4370, Australia.

Publications for Children

Fiction (illustrated by A. M. Hicks except where noted)

Boori. Melbourne and New York, Oxford University Press, 1978; London, Abelard Schuman, 1979.
Darkness under the Hills. Melbourne, Oxford, and New York, Oxford University Press, 1980.
Shadows among the Leaves. Melbourne and London, Heinemann, 1984.
Many Kinds of Magic: Tales of Mystery, Myth and Enchantment (short stories), illustrated by Lisa Herriman. Melbourne, Penguin, and New York, Viking, 1988.
The Currency Lad. Montville, Queensland, Walter McVitty Books, 1994.

Poetry

Following the Gold, illustrated by Kerry Argent. Adelaide, Omnibus, 1989.

Recordings: *Hey Rain,* Stanthorpe, Restless Music, 1992; *Songbird in Your Pocket,* Stanthorpe, Restless Music, 1994.

Other

Editor, *Reading 360* series (*The Blooming Queensland Side, On the Shores of Botany Bay, The Golden West, Bound for South Australia, Upon Van Diemen's Land, The Victorian Bunyip, Australian Childhoods, Call of the Sea, From Nearby Lands, Going Bush, Success!, A Thousand Miles Away, Big Towns Little Towns, Ghosts Ghouls and Scary Things, Mirrors, Moments to Reme the Thing, Then and Now, Tales of the Territory*). Melbourne, Longman Cheshire, 19 vols., 1981-84.
Pelicans and Chihuahuas. Brisbane, University of Queensland Press, 1996.

Publications for Adults (earlier books as W. N. Scott)

Short Stories

Some People. Brisbane, Jacaranda Press, 1968.
My Uncle Arch and Other People. Adelaide, Rigby, 1977.
The Banshee and the Bullocky. Brisbane, University of Queensland Press, 1996.

Poetry

Brother and Brother. Brisbane, Jacaranda Press, 1972.

Other

Focus on Judith Wright. Brisbane, University of Queensland Press, 1967.

Portrait of Brisbane, paintings by Cedric Emanuel. Adelaide, Rigby, 1976.

Tough in the Old Days (autobiography). Adelaide, Rigby, 1979.

Ned Kelly after a Century of Acrimony, with John Meredith. Sydney, Lansdowne Press, 1980.

Australian Bushrangers. Sydney, Child and Henry, 1983.

The Long and the Short and the Tall: A Collection of Australian Yarns. Sydney, Western Plains, 1985.

Brisbane Sketchbook. Brisbane, Herron, 1988.

Editor, *The Continual Singing: An Anthology of World Poetry.* Brisbane, Jacaranda Press, 1973.

Editor, *The Complete Book of Australian Folklore.* Sydney, Ure Smith, 1976.

Editor, *Bushranger Ballads.* Sydney, Ure Smith, 1976.

Editor, *The Second Penguin Australian Songbook.* Melbourne, Penguin Australia, 1980.

Editor, *Impressions on a Continent: A Collection of Australian Short Stories.* Melbourne, Heinemann, 1983.

Editor, *Penguin Book of Australian Humorous Verse.* Melbourne, Penguin, 1984.

*

Bill Scott comments:

My first three novels for young people were written almost by request. An Aboriginal friend mentioned in conversation that there had been little fiction for children describing aspects of tribal society prior to European settlement in Australia. *Boori* and *Darkness under the Hills* were my response to her suggestion. Both books were Highly Commended in the annual Children's Book of the Year Awards by the Australian Children's Book Council following publication. *Shadows Among the Leaves* was written in response to a request from young people who said they wanted books about "... the country, not the city; with adventures and spooky things and a happy family, not a broken home ...." I dedicated the book to them when it was published. And being a folklorist I let the magic enter the stories when it wanted to do so. *The Currency Lad* adventure is as close to reality as life was lived in Australia just prior to and during the first gold rushes in New South Wales in the middle years of the 19th century as I could make it. *Many Kinds of Magic* is a selection of stories, mostly original, from many lands. An attempt was made to use the traditional style of story-telling from each country when the stories were written. The collection of poems for children, *Following the Gold,* was made at the suggestion of Jane Covernton, chief editor of Omnibus Books, from work I had done over a number of years. It too was short-listed by the Children's Book Council in their annual awards.

* * *

To hear Bill Scott singing or reciting his poems, especially those collected in *Following the Gold,* is to come close to the heart of Australia. This bushman, philosopher, a true son of his country, records in his verse the multi-faceted nature of Australian life. From the landscape with its peculiar beauty and unique birds and animals, to the colorful characters—including bullockies and bushrangers—to the tall stories and philosophical roots, Scott touches upon it all.

While his interests are wide-ranging, Scott is perhaps best known as a folklorist. Such poems as "The Dog's Ghost Story" and "The Cheeky Bushranger" stem from this bushman's fascination with yarn, with story. It is the same impulse from which folktales all over the world have sprung, so it is not surprising that Scott has produced his own volume of folktales, *Many Kinds of Magic: Tales of Mystery, Myth and Enchantment,* told with grace and literary discernment. The stories range in setting from Ireland to China to Australia. The collection points up the universality of myth and archetype; although Scott's novels for children are derived "largely from aboriginal myth and custom" as well as his passionate attachment to Australia, they spring also from his world view of humanity. He is a magi steeped in "many kinds of magic."

In *Boori* and its sequel *Darkness under the Hills,* Bill Scott pays tribute to the spiritual dimensions of the post-Dreamtime life of Australian aborigines. Essential to the narrative are the people's bond with the Land, their strict code of interpersonal and intertribal relationships, and, in particular, the demands of the Law, which says that people are responsible for what they do, not what they intend to do. Transgression of the Law demands atonement to restore harmony and balance to the individual and to Nature. Boori, the title character of the first book, was not born as other men but created at the bidding of Ganba, chief among the tribes of the spirits. Boori is a Goundir, a man of magical powers, who has his own spirit friend, Jaree, living in a small leather bag around his neck. The flashes of humour in Scott's book come from the friendly, though sometimes testy or even astringent, bantering of Boori and his Jaree, a kind of alter-ego who occasionally acts as Boori's spiritual scout.

Both novels concern the resolution of Boori's destiny as a Messenger. First, however, he has to bring into his friendship and service the yellow dog, Dingo, spirit chief among the dingo people. Dingo's ability to change into human form aids Boori in both stories as he pursues the heroic tasks of subduing first the Melong, the great water spirit, then, in *Darkness under the Hills,* the totally evil Rakasha who broods as a blight over the Land. In the course of his odyssey Boori weaves spells, makes magic—even sending out his spirit from his body—and invokes the aid of the local spirits of the Land of his labours. He defeats a wily old magician; helps Perentie, the lizard spirit, regain opals stolen by the Puk-wudgies of the desert; and wrests from a malicious ghost, Cooran, a magic and deadly pointing bone before releasing the shade to the eternal campfires. The stories contain moments of warmth, as when Boori establishes loving relationships with warriors whom he defeats and then befriends. These are coupled with occasional deep psychological insights—Boori allows Cooran to sense one more time the aromas, sounds, and tastes the greedy, grey ghost knew as a man. Deftly woven into the framework of the narrative are fragments of song, dance-drama, and aboriginal legend (why the crow is black, the origin of the Milky Way).

Scott writes in an heroic style in keeping with his theme, evoking the land, the law, and people in lyric and measured prose. At his best he creates terrifying images of horrific evil and apocalyptic battles. *Shadows among the Leaves* is a children's novel in a minor key in which the Shadows are formless Aboriginal Old Things or spirits, which have the force of an invisible storm and work to destroy those who would desecrate their jungle environment for personal gain.

In a note to *Boori* and in his glossaries, Scott has voiced his belief that the same animating spirits are extant in the folklore of all cultures. The Puk-wudgies, for example, equate to the dwarfs of western myth; the Christian sign of the cross is implicitly coupled with the aboriginal sign of the rainbow. Tales of water sirens, crystal balls, and a warrior pinned to the earth by Lilliputian creatures belong to many cultures. By invoking these myths Scott, the Australian bushman, scholar, poet, and storyteller, proves to be a true citizen of the world.

—Maurice Saxby

SCOTT, W. N. See **SCOTT, Bill.**

SEED, Jenny

Nationality: South African. **Born:** Cecile Eugenie Booysen, Cape Town, 18 May 1930. **Education:** Ellerslie High School, Cape Town. **Family:** Married Edward (Ted) Robert Seed in 1953; one daughter and three sons. **Career:** Worked in Roads Department, Town Planning Department, Pietermaritzburg, South Africa, 1947-53; free-lance writer, from 1965. **Awards:** M.E.R. Award (South Africa), 1987, *Place Among the Stones*; Runner-up Noma Award, *Ntombi's Song*. **Address:** 10 Pioneer Crescent, Northdene, Queensburgh Kwazulu Natal 4093, South Africa.

Publications for Children

Fiction

The Dancing Mule, illustrated by Joan Sirr. London, Nelson, 1964.
The Always-late Train, illustrated by Pieter de Weerdt. Parow, South Africa, Nasionale Boekhandel, 1965.
Small House, Big Garden, illustrated by Lynette Hemmant. London, Hamish Hamilton, 1965.
Peter the Gardener, illustrated by Mary Russon. London, Hamish Hamilton, 1966.
Tombi's Song, illustrated by Dugald MacDougall. London, Hamish Hamilton, 1966; Chicago, Rand McNally, 1968; as *Ntombi's Song,* Johannesburg, Ravan Press, 1988; illustrated by Anno Berry, Boston, Beacon Press Night Lights, 1989.
To the Rescue, illustrated by Constance Marshall. London, Hamish Hamilton, 1966.
Stop Those Children!, illustrated by Mary Russon. London, Hamish Hamilton, 1966.
Timothy and Tinker, illustrated by Lynette Hemmant. London, Hamish Hamilton, 1967.
The River Man, illustrated by Dugald MacDougall. London, Hamish Hamilton, 1968.
The Voice of the Great Elephant, illustrated by Trevor Stubley. London, Hamish Hamilton, 1968; New York, Pantheon, 1969.
Canvas City, illustrated by Lynette Hemmant. London, Hamish Hamilton, 1968.
The Red Dust Soldiers, illustrated by Andrew Sier. London, Heinemann, 1968.
The Prince of the Bay, illustrated by Trevor Stubley. London, Hamish Hamilton, 1970, and Cape Town, Tafelberg, 1989; as *Vengeance of the Zulu King,* New York, Pantheon, 1971.
The Great Thirst, illustrated by Trevor Stubley. London, Hamish Hamilton, 1971; Scarsdale, New York, Bradbury Press, 1973.
The Broken Spear, illustrated by Trevor Stubley. London, Hamish Hamilton, 1972.
Warriors on the Hills, illustrated by Pat Ludlow. London, Abelard Schuman, 1975.
The Unknown Land, illustrated by Jael Jordan. London, Heinemann, 1976.
Strangers in the Land, illustrated by Trevor Stubley. London, Hamish Hamilton, 1977.
The Year One, illustrated by Susan Sansome. London, Hamish Hamilton, 1981.
The Policeman's Button, illustrated by Joy Pritchard. Cape Town, Human & Rousseau, 1981.
Gold Dust, illustrated by Bill le Fever. London, Hamish Hamilton, 1982.
The New Fire, illustrated by Mario Sickle. Cape Town, Human & Rousseau, 1983.
The 59 Cats, illustrated by Alida Carpenter. Pretoria, Daan Retief, 1983.
The Shell, illustrated by Ann Walton. Pretoria, Daan Retief, 1983.
The Sad Cat, illustrated by Marlize Groenewald. Pretoria, Daan Retief, 1984.
The Karoo Hen, illustrated by A. Venter. Pretoria, Daan Retief, 1984.
The Disappearing Rabbit, illustrated by Ann Walton. Pretoria, Daan Retief, 1984.
Big Boy's Work, illustrated by Paula Collins. Pretoria, Daan Retief, 1984.
The Spy Hill, illustrated by Nelda Vermaak. Cape Town, Human & Rousseau, 1984.
The Lost Prince, illustrated by Ann Walton. Pretoria, Daan Retief, 1985.
Day of the Dragon, illustrated by Paula Collins. Pretoria, Daan Retief, 1985.
Bouncy Lizzie, illustrated by Esther Boshoff. Pretoria, Daan Retief, 1985.
The Strange Blackbird, illustrated by Hettie Saaiman. Pretoria, Daan Retief, 1986.
The Far-Away Valley, illustrated by Joan Rankin. Pretoria, Daan Retief, 1987.
The Christmas Bells, illustrated by Hettie Saaiman. Pretoria, Daan Retief, 1987.
Place Among the Stones, illustrated by Helmut Starcke. Cape Town, Tafelberg, 1987.
The Station-Master's Hen, illustrated by Elizabeth de Villiers. Cape Town, Human & Rousseau, 1987.
The Corner Cat, illustrated by Elizabeth de Villiers. Cape Town, Human & Rousseau, 1987.
Hurry, Hurry, Sibusiso, illustrated by Cornelia Holm. Pretoria, Daan Retief, 1988.
The Big Pumpkin, illustrated by Anno Berry. Cape Town, Human & Rousseau, 1989.

Stowaway to Nowhere. Cape Town, Tafelberg, 1990.
Nobody's Cat, illustrated by Alida Bothma. Cape Town, Human & Rousseau, 1990.
The Wind's Song, illustrated by Joan Rankin. Pretoria, Daan Tetief, 1991.
The Hungry People. Cape Town, Tafelberg, 1992.
Old Grandfather Mantis: Tales of the San, illustrated by Joan Rankin. Cape Town, Tafelberg, 1992.
Tom's Garden, illustrated by Kathy Pienaar. Pretoria, Daan Retief, 1992.
A Time to Scatter Stones. Johannesburg, Macmillan, 1993.
Eyes of a Toad. Johannesburg, Macmillan, 1993.
Run, Run, White Hen. Cape Town, Oxford University Press, 1994.
Lucky Boy. Empangeni, Excellentia Publishers, 1996.
The Strange Large Egg, illustrated by Lyn Gilbert. Durban, Gecko Books, 1996.

Other

Kulumi the Brave: A Zulu Tale, illustrated by Trevor Stubley. London, Hamish Hamilton, and New York, World, 1970.
The Sly Green Lizard (Zulu folktale), illustrated by Graham Humphreys. London, Hamish Hamilton, 1973.
The Bushman's Dream: African Tales of the Creation, illustrated by Bernard Brett. London, Hamish Hamilton, 1974; Scarsdale, New York, Bradbury Press, 1975.

*

Biography: "South African Children's Literature, I: Jenny Seed" by Jay Heale, in *Crux: A Journal on the Teaching of English* (Pretoria), February 1987, 3-5; Essay in *Something About the Author* Volume 86, Detroit, Gale, 1996; Profile in *The International Authors and Writers Who's Who* 14th edition, Cambridge, England, 1996, and *Who's Who in the World* 15th edition, New Providence, NJ, 1998.

Jenny Seed comments:

My mother was a wonderful teller of tales, especially bedtime stories, and my father was a writer whose hand-written manuscripts filled the cupboards of his bedroom. Bearing these two facts in mind, it is not surprising that from an early age I too had a great desire to work with words, and that later, after my marriage when I began to try to write in earnest, my inclination was towards stories for children.

In some ways any writing career must be like a snowball rolling down a hill, gathering momentum and increasing in size the further it goes. Soon short snippets for the children's pages in newspapers and magazines lengthened out into small novels for younger readers, and as the books grew I found myself wanting not only an exciting plot but a deeper and more meaningful theme as well. I was aware of the tremendous influence an author of children's books may have on a young and impressionable mind, and I gave much thought and soul searching in an attempt to find answers that were at once simple enough for the reader and yet as honest as I could make them. Later when I turned to historical novels for the early teens this seeking became more accentuated. Though I did not realize it at the time my novels were probably an expression of my own need to find the reality of God.

It has been said that history is His Story. For me this was true. The more I delved into and became absorbed in the shattering and dramatic events of African history, the more I came to see that all was not just meaningless chaos. Behind the human triumphs and tragedies there was a great hand holding all together with unswerving purpose and uncompromising truth. For me personally the searching came to an end in 1974 when I became a Christian. For my books, the quest continues, but with a difference. I seem now to be able to write from a firmer standpoint, not seeking after what is unknown, but rather reaching forward into a new country which is somehow already known.

*   *   *

Jenny Seed writes primarily historical fiction focusing on South African whites and secondarily folklore and fiction about South African blacks and stories for younger readers. She gives voice to both indigenous and immigrant South African children and creates vivid descriptions of South African settings and cultures. Her retellings of folklore provide insight about native tribes, primarily the Zulu, through written stories about oral legends and myths collected by early European settlers. Because of her religious convictions, Seed is especially interested in creation tales, such as those presented in *The Bushman's Dream: African Tales of the Creation,* and expresses empathy for the Bushman's affinity for nature. Recognizing the complexities of South African history, Seed attempts to find and depict truth and reality through her writing. She gathers knowledge through research in library and archival sources and presents history through the experiences and feelings of young characters as they struggle with living in new places and with unfamiliar people while developing their own identities and self-perceptions, such as the children of Boers on the Great Trek in *Unknown Land.* Seed wants to make South African history accessible and interesting to readers, providing appealing characters, details, vocabulary, and environments to advance plots. Her stories often have subtle moral messages and usually have satisfactory conclusions.

In introductions or prefaces to most of her historical fiction she provides information about the setting and sources she uses as background for the story. The historical sources include diaries, letters, and documents written by European explorers, traders, miners, missionaries, and government officials. Seed's historical fiction for younger children is usually set in the 19th century in a specific historical context, but the action of the story focuses on a child's adventure. For example, *The Year One* takes place in Natal in 1850 when a British family arrives with a group of settlers, who are left impoverished by a dishonest settlement organizer. The action focuses on the family's struggle to survive, the heroine's fear of the strange new surroundings, and the rescue of her baby sister from an enraged monkey.

The Policeman's Button also takes place in Natal, in 1890 when wars between Pondo clans were a threat to the white farmers. The 10-year-old hero admires the Natal Mounted Police who come to protect the farmers and their property. He endangers his own life and that of others when he sneaks out at night to see what the police are doing, but is rescued by them. After the police have negotiated peace and left the area, the hero has a policeman's button, given to him by one of the police, to remind him of his experience and realization of the importance of knowing when to be obedient or courageous.

Many of Seeds books portray how war affects populations especially children, and offer anti-violence themes countering glorified violent images readers are exposed to in popular culture

The Red Dust Soldiers deals with the siege of Ladysmith during the second Anglo-Boer War, and the protagonist learns about the varying points of view and motivations of each side. Similarly, in *The Spy Hill,* a young boy excited about being present at the Battle of Spionkop in 1900 soon realizes new perspectives about war, including horror and fear. In *Warriors on the Hills,* settlers at Grahamstown in 1834 encounter Xhosa warriors as told through the perspective of a boy.

Several stories focus on mining, including *Gold Dust* about a young girl who works hard with her family at Pilgrim's Rest during the Transvaal gold rush of 1874 and bravely rescues a miner who is ill with malaria during a storm, and *Canvas City,* a family's attempt to become rich during the 1866 diamond "fever" at New Rush, which eventually became Kimberley, and their being cheated by their mining foreman. Both stories focus on the physical hardships of mining life and the importance of family solidarity in overcoming hardships. Technology is also present in the six stories about the successes of transportation in *The Always-late Train.*

Most of Seed's fiction for older children also is set in the 19th century. It incorporates real historical characters and details of historical events as presented in the sources used to create the background. Seed's attitude toward South African history is stated in the introduction to *The Broken Spear.* The fall of the Zulu kings at the hands of the Boer Trekkers is viewed as part of a larger conflict between "savages" and "civilization" and the wars that occurred as part of a worldwide conflict in which "primitive weapons" were pitted against firearms. She contrasts the "despotism" of Dingane the Zulu leader with the "enormous courage and determination" of the Boers. There is no mention of the Zulu perspective of defending their land, cattle, and people against encroachment by uncompromising foreigners.

The Broken Spear is about the Boer Trek of the 1830s, while *Strangers in the Land* is about British settlement in the Cape in the 1830s. Both stories present the physical hardships of travel and settlement in considerable detail and religion as an important factor enabling perseverance against forces of man and nature. Change and adjustment are major themes, such as the Thompson family in *Strangers in the Land* learning to be farmers in the Cape Colony after working as traders in London. Although *The Prince of the Bay* is told by an African boy, Bongiseni, in 1824 when Henry Francis Fynn and other whites went to open up ivory trade with the Zulu, the use of Fynn's diaries as a source leads to Eurocentric, negative descriptions of the Zulu. The real hero of the story is the white man who protects the narrator and other Africans from the treachery of their own people. Seed features the tyrannical Zulu chief, Shaka, that Fynn encounters in *The Voice of the Great Elephant,* depicting Shaka's rise to power and murder by terrorized tribesmen. The hero of *The Great Thirst,* which takes place in the 1830s in South West Africa (Namibia), is also an African boy named Nama who is confused by his copeans and the behavior of Jonker Afrikaner, a real historical person condemned for his "bad" deeds. This adventure story about African warriors and the triumph of Christianity provides primarily negative depictions of Africans because of the focus on Jonker Afrikaner from a Eurocentric perspective. Seed does note how white traders affected Namibian culture, instigating alcoholism and poverty as some natives became addicted to imported goods. Although there are statements sympathetic to African perspectives in some of Seed's historical fiction, especially in the fiction for older children, these positive statements are overshadowed by negative stereotypes taken from the biased historical sources she used.

Some of Seed's fiction written for younger children, such as *Tombi's Song,* is more empathetic toward African characters. Tombi (called Ntombi in reprinted editions), a six-year-old Zulu girl who must walk to market through a forest as a test of maturity, is fearful of a monster who lives there. She sings a special song her mother sang to her as an infant, which gives her courage and emphasizes her individualism. Admiring her older cousin Zanele, Tombi yearns to be grown up. When she jumps out of the way of a bus, she spills sugar she bought at the market, and decides to sell plums to earn enough money to buy more sugar. Tombi resourcefully folds a banana leaf to carry the plums, but no buyers are interested in her fruit. To comfort herself, she dances while she sings her mother's song, and a pair of tourists give her a coin. Tombi replaces the sugar with her earnings and bravely returns home through the forest. Critics protested that the tourists were white, suggesting colonial paternalism, in the first edition, and, as a result, in the 1989 reprinted version, the couple are black. Also, the illustrations reveal external influences on South African culture such as a Coca-Cola sign at the store.

Kulumi the Brave is based on oral literature. The hero, the son of a Zulu chief who fears Kulumi will take his kingdom, is forced to leave. Kulumi proves his bravery by defeating monsters, learning magic, and surviving other tests, and gets to marry the girl of his choice by tricking an ogress who is holding her captive. Leaving home and rebuilding lives are often themes of Seed's books as characters develop self-confidence through misfortunes. In *The New Fire,* the protagonist must adjust to a new home with his grandfather and sister after white settlers kill his parents and other Bushmen. The new fire is Seed's metaphor for home, security, and self-acceptance. Alice settles in Natal with her parents in *The Year One* but as their plans abruptly change, she learns to survive and thrive in her new environment. Bruce stays with his Uncle Raymond, a glaciologist, in England while his parents work in Europe in *The Strange Large Egg.* A strange egg that Raymond found under an ice sheet in the Antarctic sits on his mantel and intrigues the curious Bruce, especially when one day he discovers the broken shell on the floor and explores this mystery.

Seed is skilled at writing stories that appeal to children of different ages. Her simple stories reveal profound realism whether the characters are historic figures, fictional children, or mythical animals. Her rhythmic language in picture books can be read aloud to young children or introduced to early readers. Seed enlivens dull historical facts and interests readers, even if her interpretations at times seem biased and questionable. The popularity of her stories is evident from many of them being reprinted and reissued in new editions and broadcasted in England, Canada, America, Australia, New Zealand, and Rhodesia, as well as in South Africa. Unfortunately, many of her books are out of print and difficult to obtain. South African English teacher and author Jay Heale says, "Jenny Seed is the mother—perhaps by now the grandmother—of South African children's literature." He notes that not only was she the first South African children's writer published internationally, but also that she is the most prolific. Reading her work in addition to that of other gifted writers, such as Cape Town author Niki Daly and Port Elizabeth native Margaret Sacks, provides a more balanced glimpse into South African culture and the variety of its people and heritages.

—Nancy J. Schmidt, updated by Elizabeth D. Schafer

SEFTON, Catherine. See **WADDELL, Martin.**

SEGUN, Mabel D(orothy)

Nationality: Nigerian. **Born:** Mabel Dorothy Aig-Imoukhuede, Ondo, 18 February 1930. **Education:** St. Peter's School, Edunabon, 1936-38; Akoko Jubilee Central School, Ikare, 1938; St. Paul's School, Ikole, 1939; St. David's School, Akure, 1939-41; C.M.S. Girls' School, Lagos, 1942-47; University College, Ibadan, 1949-53. **Family:** Married 1) Olujimi Jolaoso in 1951 (divorced); 2) Oludotun Segun in 1960 (divorced); two sons and one daughter. **Career:** Teacher, St. Anne's School, Ibadan, 1953, and Methodist Girls' High School, Lagos, 1954; education officer, Edo College, Benin-City, 1954-55, and Government Teacher Training College, Abraka, 1955; teacher, Ahmadiyya Grammar School, Ibadan, 1956; education officer, Government Teacher Training College, Ibadan, 1957; teacher, Ibadan Boys' High School, Ibadan, 1958-59; editor, *Hansard,* Western Nigeria Legislature, Ibadan, 1959-61; information officer, Western Nigeria Ministry of Information, Ibadan, 1961-63; copywriter, Lintas West Africa Ltd., Lagos, 1964; trainee editor, Silver Burdett, publishers, Morristown, New Jersey, 1965, and Harper and Row, publishers, New York, 1966; editor, *Modern Woman,* Lagos, 1965-67, and Franklin Book Programmes, Lagos, 1967; education officer, 1967-68, and head, 1969-70, Federal Ministry of Education Broadcasting Unit, Lagos; head, Department of English and Social Studies, 1971-73 and 1974-79, and acting vice-principal, 1978-79, National Technical Teachers College, Lagos; executive secretary, Nigerian book Development Council, Federal Ministry of Education, Lagos, 1974-76; deputy permanent delegate of Nigeria to Unesco, Federal Ministry of External Affairs, Paris, 1979-81; chief federal inspector of education, Federal Ministry of Education, Lagos, 1981-82; senior research fellow, Institute of African Studies, University of Ibadan, 1982-89; director, Children's Literature Documentation and Research Centre, Ibadan, from 1990. President, Children's Literature Association of Nigeria, Ibadan, 1978-91; consultant, African Children's Literature Programme, Nairobi, 1983-87; contributing editor, *Education Guardian 2,* Lagos, 1986-88, and *Junior Guardian,* Lagos, 1989-90; trustee, Association of Nigerian Authors, from 1987, Nigerian Book Foundation, from 1993; member of book reviews panel, African Book Publishing Record, Oxford, from 1988. **Awards:** Nigerian National Festival of the Arts Literature prize, 1954; *Radio Nigeria* Artiste of the Year, 1977. **Address:** Children's Literature Documentation and Research Centre, 18A Solel Boneh Way, Ikolaba, new Bodija, U.I.P.O. Box 20744, Ibadan, Oyo State, Nigeria.

Publications for Children

Fiction

Youth Day Parade. Ibadan, Daystar Press, 1983.
Olu and the Broken Statue, illustrated by Olu Byron. Ibadan, New Horn Press, 1985.
The First Corn, illustrated by Amarquaye Adom. Ibadan, Longman Nigeria, 1989.
The Twins and the Tree Spirits, illustrated by Yetunde Adenle. Ibadan, Children's Literature Documentation and Research Centre, 1991.

Other

My Father's Daughter (autobiography), illustrated by Prue Theobalds. Lagos, African Universities Press, 1965.
My Mother's Daughter (autobiography), illustrated by Olu Byron. Ibadan, African Universities Press, 1987.

Editor, with Neville Grant, *Under the Mango Tree* (verse), illustrated by Maureen and Gordon Gray. Lagos, Longman, 2 Vols., 1980.
Editor, *Respect for Life* (stories, poems, and plays), illustrated by Ahmed Noah, Ibadan, Amnesty International, Nigeria, 1997.

Publications for Adults

Friends, Nigerians, Countrymen (essays). Oxford, Oxford University Press, 1977; as *Sorry No Vacancy,* Ibadan, University Press, 1985.
Conflict and Other Poems (poetry). Ibadan, New Horn Press, 1986.
Ping Pong: Twenty-Five Years of Table Tennis. Ibadan, Daystar Press, 1989.
The Surrender and Other Stories. London, Longman, 1995.

Editor, *Illustrating for Children.* Ibadan, Children's Literature Association of Nigeria, 1988.

*

Mabel D. Segun comments:

The literary tradition is very strong in my family. My two brothers are writers; one is a novelist while the other was the first to write pidgin English poetry. My elder sister wrote and produced television scripts for children's programmes before she retired and my daughter, Omowunmi, won the Association of Nigerian Authors award with her very first novel which was also shortlisted for the Commonwealth Prose Prize for first books. The 'doyen' of us all, my father, Reverend Isaiah Aig-Imoukhuede, who died at 39, way back in 1938 had already written three works; viz. the history of our hometown, Sabongidda Ora, in Edo State in the midwest of the country; a mother tongue primer whose play on words and onomatopoeic effects indicated his leanings towards poetry and possession of a delightful sense of humour. He also composed the words of a now very popular song, *Iwe Kiko* which extols the dignity of labour, and was translating the Anglican hymn book into Ora when he died. I was only eight when he was taken from us, but I had been so close to him that he became my role model for hard work, creativity and service to humanity. My very first publication for children, *My Father's Daughter,* is our story. I had a very happy childhood and wanted other children to share in that happiness.

I was introduced to books much earlier than most Nigerians of my time with our British missionary guests bringing us books and father buying books each time he went to the synod meetings in Lagos. In secondary school, I became a voracious reader, pestering the teacher-librarian to let me borrow books oftener than the stipulated once a week and finding even the twice-a-week concession inadequate so that she eventually handed over the keys of the library to me and I became the first pupil librarian of C.M.S.

Girls' School, Lagos. When I left school the following year, I became the first paid school librarian.

Since I had unlimited access to books, I began to nurse the ambition of becoming a writer myself Indeed, my school certificate essay on 'My Ambition' proclaimed this to my examiners, embellished with dreams of 'a cottage in the woods beside a bubbling brook with birds singing by my window'. I still have not got my cottage but there are birds singing on the branches of an orange tree beside the house where I live in lbadan.

I had another role model—my mother—whose vision and tenacity ensured that I had a good education. As I record in my book *My Mother's Daughter,* written in 1970 but not published until 1987, she fought against those traditional gender discriminatory practices which militated against the development of women and girls, refusing to be absorbed into her brother-in-law's polygamous household and adopting a ploy which got me into secondary school contrary to my uncle's plans that I should become a trainee nurse at eleven.

My secondary school English teachers had made literature, especially poetry, so lively and enjoyable that I was determined to improve the lot of less fortunate children who were put off poetry by dull teaching which laid emphasis on memorisation. My teaching of the English language on educational television had shown me the possibilities of using creative methods in winning children to an appreciation of good literature. So when I was invited by Longman to collaborate with Neville Grant in editing a two volume poetry anthology, *Under the Mango Tree,* I jumped at the chance. In the two volumes, we dramatised poems, sang some, and turned others into a game. Since the poems were chosen from all parts of Africa and the diaspora, they promoted cultural identity, one of my concerns for African children who had been in danger of losing their cultural heritage after decades of cultural imperialism. Folktales, riddles and proverbs were turned into verse. What we could not find within existing material, we wrote ourselves.

Some of my other concerns in writing for children are global concerns such as, human rights, the environment, and peaceful coexistence. These themes are dealt with in *The Twins and the Tree Spirits* and *Respect for Life.* In all my writings I try to pass on to children my own values and standards some of which I imbibed from my parents.

I write in a simple style which almost three decades of broadcasting has helped to forge. I have always enjoyed the company of young people with literary, broadcasting and sporting activities giving me the opportunity of regular interaction with them. For example, my mixed doubles partner in my final serious international table tennis tournament in 1970 was a fourteen-year-old boy, Fatai Ayinde. I was then forty!

* * *

In children's literature Mabel D. Segun is at her best in autobiography. Her autobiographical reader for children, *My Father's Daughter,* deals with the narrator's growth in a rural village and her interaction with her father, the village pastor and disciplinarian who eventually dominates her world view. When her father dies at the end of the novel the narrator is only eight, but her emerging personality has been strongly influenced by her strong kind clergyman father: "If father left us poor in money he did not leave us poor in the things which matter most in life. He taught us to sympathize with others, to place no premium on money, to be humble in office, and above all to lead useful lives." His death essentially brings about a sudden change of fortune in the narrator's life as she and her two brothers are sent from the cozy parsonage to live with a paternal uncle—"a journey into the unknown." *My Mother's Daughter,* the sequel to *My Father's Daughter* published 22 years later, essentially narrates the change of fortune in the narrator's life—separation from her mother, living with all sorts of relations and friends in circumstances quite different from what she was used to at the parsonage. Her life in a monogamous home in the parsonage gives way to life in a polygamous home of her uncle, with all the social problems associated with an African polygamous home—jealousy, suspicion, and unhealthy rivalry among the wives and among their offspring.

Both books are set during the colonial period, back when Nigerian schools celebrated the British Empire Day on May 24, and describe some events associated with World War II—especially British propaganda against Hitler as enemy of the God-fearing British nation, and enlistment of some Nigerians as part of the British empire to fight in faraway places like Burma and India. The language of these autobiographical works is quite simple and straightforward, avoiding abstract allusions.

My Father's Daughter and *My Mother's Daughter* are one story of a Nigerian woman who looks back on the joys, fears, trials, tribulations, and sorrows of her childhood and early adolescent days with an implicit depth of gratitude to her widowed mother to whom she feels overwhelmingly indebted for struggling to put her on the path of success. Written with childlike honesty and simplicity, alloyed with the maturity of the author's present adult disposition, this autobiography is interwoven with reflections on the cultural and social life in parts of Western Nigeria during colonial days.

Leaving looking back at her childhood days, Segun concentrates on present-day children's activities in Nigeria in *Youth Day Parade* and *Olu and the Broken Statue. Youth Day Parade* deals with a group of Zuma primary school children led by Tunde toward success—putting on a super performance on the parade day. Having been directed to lead the youth day parade by the headmaster, Tunde, after some initial fear of the onerous task, pools his resources in organization, making do with what is available locally and whipping up enthusiasm in his school mates. This short story demonstrates that the virtues of unity, patriotism, and determination are indispensable in any worthwhile achievement. The selection of the characters names, Tunde (Yoruba), Audu (Hausa), Ekpo (Efik), Chike Wachukwu (Igbo), is deliberately meant to reflect the ethnic plurality of Nigeria, and subtly to indicate that setting aside ethnic differences for a cause especially in a multi-ethnic country like Nigeria will always produce positive results.

This use of diverse names to reflect the country's ethnic plurality is also apparent in *Olu and the Broken Statue:* Olu (Yoruba), Aigbe (Edo), and Ikem (Igbo) are friends from three ethnic groups. In order to raise funds to purchase new musical instruments for the school band, the headmaster asks the students to go out into the community to work for money. The prize for the group with the largest money collection is a silver cup. The various groups work and there are inter-team rivalries and inter-team cooperation. When Olu and his friends find a broken bronze statue they think of selling it for money rather than giving it to the national museum. Their sense of patriotism however comes to the fore and they do take it to the museum. In appreciation of their patriotism, the director of the museum makes a donation of 500 naira in addition to their own collection of 302 naira. The combined total of 802 naira wins them the first prize. The didactic thrust of this novel is patriotism. At a time when Nigeria's ancient artifacts are sold for exorbitant sums of money, Olu's group's decision to send their rare find to the museum is unique and is what Segun wants other children to emulate. Their major interest is not to have money from the sale of the broken statue but to help in their small way to preserve the ancient artifacts and cultural heritage of their nation.

Segun and Neville Grant have edited a two-volume collection of poems, *Under the Mango Tree.* The books essentially present a stimulating new course in reading and studying poetry at primary school level. Some old favourite songs and poems are included but the major emphasis is on new material related to the experience of children in Africa.

Segun's works for children are meant to teach Nigerian children acceptable Nigerian ways of life. In terms of accessibility, Segun's literary works for children do not pose much difficulty for African readers because quite a significant proportion of the content is rooted in the socio-cultural milieu of African children.

—Osayimwense Osa

SELDEN, George

Pseudonym for George Selden Thompson. **Nationality:** American. **Born:** Hartford, Connecticut, 14 May 1929. **Education:** Loomis School, 1943-47; Yale University, New Haven, Connecticut, B.A. 1951; University of Rome (Fulbright Fellow), 1951. **Award:** Christopher award, 1970. **Died:** 5 December 1989.

Publications for Children

Fiction

The Dog That Could Swim under Water, illustrated by Morgan Dennis. New York, Viking Press, 1956.

The Garden under the Sea, illustrated by Garry MacKenzie. New York, Viking Press, 1957; as *Oscar Lobster's Fair Exchange,* New York, Harper, 1966.

The Cricket in Times Square, illustrated by Garth Williams. New York, Farrar Straus, 1960; London, Dent, 1961.

I See What I See!, illustrated by Robert Galster. New York, Farrar Straus, 1962.

The Mice, the Monks, and the Christmas Tree, illustrated by Jan Balet. New York, Macmillan, and London, Collier Macmillan, 1963.

Sparrow Socks, illustrated by Peter Lippman. New York, Harper, 1965.

The Dunkard, illustrated by Peter Lippman. New York, Harper, 1968.

Tucker's Countryside, illustrated by Garth Williams. New York, Farrar Straus, 1969; London, Dent, 1971.

The Genie of Sutton Place. New York, Farrar Straus, 1973.

Harry Cat's Pet Puppy, illustrated by Garth Williams. New York, Farrar Straus, 1974; London, Dent, 1978.

Chester Cricket's Pigeon Ride, illustrated by Garth Williams. New York, Farrar Straus, 1981.

Irma and Jerry, illustrated by Leslie Morrill. New York, Avon, 1982.

Chester Cricket's New Home, illustrated by Garth Williams. New York, Farrar Straus, and London, Dent, 1983.

Harry Kitten and Tucker Mouse, illustrated by Garth Williams. New York, Farrar Straus, 1986.

The Old Meadow, illustrated by Garth Williams. New York, Farrar Straus, 1987.

Plays

The Children's Story, adaptation of the work by James Clavell. New York, Dramatists Play Service, 1966.

Also author of *The Genie of Sutton Place* (television play).

Other

Heinrich Schliemann, Discoverer of Buried Treasure, illustrated by Lorence Bjorklund. New York, Macmillan, and London, Collier Macmillan, 1964.

Sir Arthur Evans, Discoverer of Knossos, illustrated by Lee Ames. New York, Macmillan, and London, Collier Macmillan, 1964.

* * *

George Selden's interest in archaeology and anthropology—aesthetic as well as historical confirmation of society—found its place in his fiction for children as well as in his books on the archaeologists Heinrich Schliemann and Arthur Evans. Selden's best-known character, Chester Cricket (*The Cricket in Times Square*), in a manner of thinking, is himself a type of cultural anthropologist. By chance he alights in a culture and environment quite foreign if not downright antithetical to his being. It does not take him long, however, to achieve intense interest and concern for the civilization he happened upon. He plumbs the excavations upon which the modern epic known as Manhattan arose. Chester views the subway system less as a means of travel than as a cultural phenomenon. It does bring diverse peoples together, and is a social and economic medium. More specifically it is a means of support for a family of Italian immigrants who eke out a precarious living from a newsstand where Chester is to make his erstwhile home. The newsstand also furnishes the element of the aesthetic as the Italian vendor, even faced with financial ruin, persists in stocking a sophisticated music periodical—an act which he knows to be of questionable commercial value, but which serves as a statement of a commitment to the arts. After all, without the arts not only the newsstand, but civilization itself is likely to fold.

The cricket becomes adopted as a pet, although some unintended misdemeanors threaten his imminent expulsion. Later he becomes an omen of good fortune, then the connective factor between the animal and human realms. Finally he himself becomes an artist and in this role brings about the salvation of the family. Even as his cultural and economic utility becomes increasingly pronounced, he remains, like the anthropologist, an outsider to the society he serves and observes. It is inevitable that he must return to his own indigenous realm.

Through the agency of Chester, Selden connected art and commerce, the natural and the artificial, the city and the country, the animal and the human. It is no wonder that this seemingly frail creature became too valuable to relinquish. Accordingly, Chester resurfaces in a number of sequels. In one he tours Manhattan on the back of a pigeon, gaining for himself and the reader a bird's-eye view of the metropolis. But it is back in his native environs (*Chester Cricket's New Home*) that the connectives between urban and rural life become most pronounced. The stump which is Chester's residence is described as if it were a mid-city penthouse. It is a place with a view, several of them in point of fact. To the front there is water, to the rear a footpath where he can watch the humans undertake their strolls. But his lease upon this idyllic spot soon lapses when a corpulent woman rests her rump upon the rotted stump and it collapses. The quest to find a new home brings him in touch with the rest of the pastoral dwellers. Even so, Chester's search has much in common with that of the frantic urbanite looking for a place to hang his hat.

Communication between all forms of life reverberates throughout Selden's works. *The Garden under the Sea*, an early book, is an underwater idyll, although much of the exchange is with the mortals above. *The Genie of Sutton Place* experiments with changing forms, and the unexpected discourse between the disparate parties is both suggestive and funny. The young protagonist's pet dog rescued from the pound re-enters the home from which he had been banished transformed into one of human kind. He has the body of a man, and he can talk, but his mind is still that of a dog. His canine manners produce some comic postures. The gift of speech notwithstanding, he is enormously gratified by the prospect of an imminent return to dogdom. Communication is wondrous, transformation horrendous, at least on a long-term basis.

For all his charm, Chester Cricket's most enduring stance is that of the impresario who heightens the roles of others and brings them into appreciative contact with each other. Even his brief stint as an operatic tenor, and hence an object of veneration and wonderment, never causes him to relinquish his position as the one who connects forms of nature. Those who expect another Disney-style Jiminy Cricket, that vaudevillian replacement of Carlo Collodi's tauntingly somber embodiment of conscience, will be disappointed for a moment. Then they will be elated upon discovering a more essential if less endearing figure. Selden's world had many characters, a number of them intriguing in their own way. But his manner was similar to that of Chester, to bring together the forms and the figures in active discourse and interchange with each other—and not to isolate them with idiosyncrasy.

—Leonard R. Mendelsohn

SENDAK, Maurice (Bernard)

Nationality: American. **Born:** Brooklyn, New York, 10 June 1928. **Education:** Lafayette High School, New York (cartoonist, *Lafayette News*), graduated 1946; Art Students' League, New York, 1949-51. **Career:** Illustrator of the *Mutt and Jeff* comic strip, All American Comics, New York, 1944-45; worked for Timely Service window display firm, New York, 1946-48, and in window display department of F.A.O. Schwarz, New York, 1948-51. Since 1951 freelance illustrator and writer. Instructor in Children's Literature, Yale University, New Haven, Connecticut, 1974-75; Instructor, Parsons School of Design, New York, 1974-79. Individual shows: Gallery of Visual Arts, New York, 1964; Rosenbach Foundation, Philadelphia, 1970, 1975; Trinity College, Hartford, Connecticut, 1972; Galerie Daniel Keel, Zurich, 1974; Ashmolean Museum, Oxford, 1975; American Cultural Center, Paris, 1978. **Awards:** American Library Association Caldecott medal, 1964, and Laura Ingalls Wilder award, 1983; Hans Christian Andersen International medal, 1970; University of Southern Mississippi award, 1981; Boston *Globe-Horn Book* award, 1981; American Book award, 1982. L.H.D.: Boston University, 1977; D.F.A.: Princeton University, New Jersey, 1984. Honorary Royal Designer for Industry, Royal Society of Arts (London), 1986. **Address:** 200 Chestnut Hill Road, Ridgefield, Connecticut 06877, U.S.A.

PUBLICATIONS FOR CHILDREN (ILLUSTRATED BY THE AUTHOR)

Fiction

Kenny's Window. New York, Harper, 1956.
Very Far Away. New York, Harper, 1957; Kingswood, Surrey, World's Work, 1959.
The Sign on Rosie's Door. New York, Harper, 1960; London, Bodley Head, 1969.
Where the Wild Things Are. New York, Harper, 1963; London, Bodley Head, 1967.
Higglety Pigglety Pop! or, There Must Be More to Life. New York, Harper, 1967; London, Bodley Head, 1969.
In the Night Kitchen. New York, Harper, 1970; London, Bodley Head, 1971.
Outside over There. New York, Harper, and London, Bodley Head, 1981.
We Are All in the Dumps with Jack & Guy. New York, HarperCollins, 1993.

Plays

Really Rosie, adaptation of his own stories *The Sign on Rosie's Door* and *Nutshell Library* (televised, 1975). New York, Harper, 1975; revised version, music by Carole King (produced London and Washington, D.C., 1978; New York, 1980), New York, French, 1985.
Where the Wild Things Are, adaptation of his own story, music by Oliver Knussen (produced Brussels, 1980; London, 1984).

Poetry

The Nutshell Library (*Alligators All Around, Chicken Soup with Rice, One Was Johnny, Pierre: A Cautionary Tale*). New York, Harper, 4 vols., 1962; London, Collins, 4 vols., 1964.
Seven Little Monsters. New York, Harper, 1976; London, Bodley Head, 1977.

Other

The Acrobat. Privately printed, 1959.
The Magician: A Counting Book. Philadelphia, Rosenbach Foundation, 1971.
Pictures. New York, Harper, 1971; London, Bodley Head, 1972.
Some Swell Pup; or, Are You Sure You Want a Dog?, with Matthew Margolis. New York, Farrar Straus, and London, Bodley Head, 1976.

Publications for Adults

Other

Fantasy Sketches. Philadelphia, Rosenbach Foundation, 1970.
Questions to an Artist Who Is Also an Author: A Conversation Between Virginia Haviland and Maurice Sendak. Washington, D.C., Library of Congress, 1972.
A Conversation with Maurice Sendak, by Jeffrey Jon Smith. Elmhurst, Illinois, Smith, 1975.
Collection of Books, Posters and Original Drawings. New York, Schiller, 1984.
Posters. New York, Crown, 1986; London, Bodley Head, 1987.
Caldecott and Co.: Notes on Books and Pictures. New York, Farrar Straus, 1988; London, Reinhardt, 1989.
Maurice Sendak Book and Poster Package: Wild Things. New York, Harper, 1991.

*

Manuscript Collections: Rosenbach Foundation, Philadelphia; Kerlan Collection, University of Minnesota, Minneapolis.

Critical Studies: *Catalogue for an Exhibition of Pictures by Maurice Sendak at the Ashmolean Museum, Oxford, December 16-February 29, 1975-76* edited by Brian Alderson, London, Bodley Head, 1975; *The Art of Maurice Sendak* by Selma G. Lanes, New York, Abrams, 1980, London, Bodley Head, 1981; *Sendak at the Rosenbach: An Exhibition Held at the Rosenbach Museum & Library, April 28-October 30, 1995,* curated by Maurice Sendak and Vincent Giroud, Philadelphia, Rosenbach Museum & Library, 1995; *Sendak in Asia: Exhibition and Sale of Original Artwork.* Tokyo, Maruzen, and, Kingston, New York, Battledore, 1996.

Theatrical Activities:
Director: **Television**—*Really Rosie,* 1975.

Designer: **Theater**—*The Magic Flute,* Houston, 1980; *Where the Wild Things Are,* Brussels, 1980, and London, 1984; *The Cunning Little Vixen,* New York, 1981; *L'Amour des Trois Oranges,* Glyndebourne, Sussex, 1982; *L'enfant et les Sortilèges,* Glyndbourne, Sussex, 1987; *The Animal Family,* New York, HarperCollins, 1996; *Frank & Joey Go to Work;* New York, HarperFestival, 1996.

Illustrator: *Atomics for the Millions* by M.C. Eidinoff and others, 1947; *The Wonderful Farm,* 1951, and *The Magic Pictures,* 1954, both by Marcel Aymé; *Good Shabbos, Everybody!* by Robert Garvey, 1951; *A Hole Is to Dig,* 1952, *A Very Special House,* 1953, *I'll Be You and You Be Me,* 1954, *Charlotte and the White Horse,* 1955, *I Want to Paint My Bathroom Blue,* 1956, *The Birthday Party,* 1957, *Somebody Else's Nut Tree,* 1958, and *Open House for Butterflies,* 1960, all by Ruth Krauss; *Maggie Rose* by Ruth Sawyer, 1952; *The Giant Story,* 1953, and *What Can You Do with a Shoe?,* 1955, both by Beatrice Schenk de Regniers; *Shadrach,* 1953, *Hurry Home, Candy,* 1953, *The Wheel on the School,* 1954, *The Little Cow and the Turtle,* 1955, *The House of Sixty Fathers,* 1956, *Along Came a Dog,* 1958, and *The Singing Hill,* 1962, all by Meindert De Jong; *The Tin Fiddle* by Edward Tripp, 1954; *Mrs. Piggle-Wiggle's Farm* by Betty MacDonald, 1954; *Happy Hanukah, Everybody* by Hyman and Alice Chanover, 1955; *Seven Little Stories on Big Subjects* by Gladys Baker Bond, 1955; *The Singing Family of the Cumberlands* by Jean Ritchie, 1955; *The Happy Rain,* 1956, and *Circus Girl,* 1957, both by Jack Sendak; *Little Bear,* 1957, *No Fighting, No Biting!,* 1958, *Father Bear Comes Home,* 1959, *Little Bear's Friend,* 1960, *Little Bear's Visit,* 1961, and *A Kiss for Little Bear,* 1968, all by Else Minarik; *What Do You Say, Dear?,* 1958, and *What Do You Do, Dear?,* 1961, both by Sesyle Joslin; *Seven Tales* by Hans Christian Andersen, 1959; *The Moon Jumpers,* 1959, and *Let's Be Enemies,* 1961, both by Janice Udry; *Dwarf Long-Nose,* 1960, *The Tale of Gockel, Hinkel, and Gackeliah,* 1961, and *Schoolmaster Whackwell's Wonderful Sons,* 1962, all translated by Doris Orgel, and *Sarah's Room,* by Orgel, 1963; *The Big Green Book* by Robert Graves, 1962; *Mr. Rabbit and the Lovely Present* by Charlotte Zolotow, 1962; *She Loves Me, She Loves Me Not!* by Robert Keeshan, 1963; *The Griffin and the Minor Canon,* 1963, and *The Bee-Man of Orn,* 1964, both by Frank R. Stockton; *Nikolenka's Childhood* by Leo Tolstoy, 1963; *How Little Lori Visited Times Square* by Amos Vogel, 1963; *Pleasant Fieldmouse* by Jan Wahl, 1964; *The Bat-Poet,* 1964, *The Animal Family,* 1965, *Fly by Night,* 1976, and (with Garth Williams) *The Children's Books of Randall Jarrell,* 1988, all by Randall Jarrell; *Hector Protector, and As I Went over the Water: Two Nursery Rhymes,* 1965; *Lullabies and Night Songs* edited by William Engvick, 1965; *Zlateh the Goat* by Isaac Bashevis Singer, 1966; *Poems from William Blake's Songs of Innocence,* 1967; *The Golden Key,* 1967, and *The Light Princess,* 1969, both by George MacDonald; *King Grisly-Beard,* 1973, and *The Juniper Tree and Other Tales,* 1973, by the Grimm Brothers; *Fortunia* by Marie Catherine Aulnoy, 1974; *The Love for Three Oranges: The Glyndebourne Version* by Frank Corsaro, 1984; *You Can't Get There from Here* by Ogden Nash, 1984; *The Nutcracker* by E.T.A. Hoffmann, 1984; *The Cunning Little Vixen* by Rudolf Tesnohlidek, 1985; *In Grandpa's House* by Philip Sendak, 1985; *Dear Mili* by Wilhelm Grimm, 1988; *I Saw Esau: The Schoolchild's Pocket Book,* edited by Iona and Peter Opie, Cambridge, Massachusetts, Candlewick Press, 1992; *The Ubiquitous Pig* by Marilyn Nissenson, 1992; *The Wonderful Farm,* by Marcel Ayme, New York, HarperCollins, 1994; *The Miami Giant,* by Arthur Yorinks, New York, HarperCollins Publishers, 1995; *Pierre, or, The Ambiguities,* by Herman Melville, edited by Hershel Parker, New York, HarperCollins, 1995; *What Can You Do with a Shoe?,* by Beatrice Schenk de Regniers, New York, M.K. McElderry Books, 1997.

Animator: *Seven Monsters* and *Bumble-Ardy* (*Sesame Street* television series), 1970.

* * *

During his distinguished career in children's books, Maurice Sendak has provided richly varied pictures for more than 80 works. Of this number, 11 have been stories that the artist himself has written. As might be expected, these works provide telling insights into those qualities of head and heart that have helped to make Sendak an international figure, possibly the pre-eminent children's picture-book practitioner of our time.

Sendak is often credited with being the first author-artist to deal openly with the feelings of young children. Of his own particular gifts, he has said, "If I have an unusual talent, it's not that I draw particularly better, or write particularly better, than other people. I've never fooled myself about that. Rather, it's that I remember things other people don't recall: the sounds and feelings and images—the emotional quality—of particular moments in childhood." Certainly each of Sendak's own stories is characterized by a loving observation of, and familiarity with, the ways of real children. He has also said, "To me, illustrating means having a passionate affair with the words," and this intensity of approach goes far toward explaining his uncanny ability to make palpable the emotional reality in which his tales take place.

Kenny's Window, the first book that Sendak wrote as well as illustrated, was published when the artist was 27 and already an established illustrator of such innovative works as Ruth Krauss's *A Hole Is to Dig.* An overly long and diffuse tale about an imaginative child eager to discover more about the world beyond his front door, *Kenny's Window* constitues a treasure trove of the themes, characters, and psychological excursions that would become the core of Sendak's mature work. Undergoing psychoanalysis at the time, Sendak had become increasingly aware of the wellsprings in childhood of our deepest fears and desires. He had also just finished reading *One Little Boy,* a clinical study of a disturbed child by the psychologist Dorothy Baruch. To these influences he attributes the discovery of his prototypical child hero—and the subject that has engaged his talent and sensibility from that moment on: children who, in his own words, "are held back by life and, one way or other, manage miraculously to find release from their troubles." More introspective than any of his future heroes, Kenny escapes into dreams and fantasy to discover significant—occasionally even painful—truths about his own life.

In his next book, *Very Far Away,* Sendak tells a modest, affecting story about small Martin, who must come to terms with an unexpectedly painful home truth: his mother is so busy caring for a new baby that she has no time for him when he most craves her attention. Martin opts to run off "very far away," which, in Sendakian terms, is "many times around the block and two cellar windows from the corner." There Martin and three new friends—a bird, a horse, and a cat—live together very happily "for an hour and a half." (Clearly the author knows how children reckon endless stretches of time and distance.) At story's end, a less sulky Martin returns home in the hope that his mother may now be free to answer at least a few of his questions.

The Sign on Rosie's Door finds a more exuberant and confident author lovingly recreating the Brooklyn of his own 1930s childhood. His irrepressible Rosie, based on a real-life child Sendak once spent months observing from his Brooklyn apartment window, is a heroine capable of carrying her less imaginative cronies aloft on flights of therapeutic fancy. In this way they can happily pass summer days otherwise filled with "nothing to do."

Sendak's next work was his perennially popular *The Nutshell Library,* a medley of four minature volumes: a reptilian alphabet, *Alligators All Around;* a rhymed romp through the months of the year, *Chicken Soup with Rice*; a forward-backwards counting book, *One Was Johnny*; and a contemporary cautionary tale done with wit and irrestible charm, *Pierre* ("The moral of Pierre is: CARE!"). Revealing the author at his most fanciful, this quartet has been referred to by one critic as a young listener's "Compleat Companion into literacy," and shows just how much a gifted writer could expand upon conventional nursery themes.

With the work that won him the Caldecott Medal, *Where the Wild Things Are,* Sendak felt himself at "the end of a long apprenticeship in children's books." The story represented the culmination of his attempts to portray a child mastering "the uncontrollable and frightening aspects of his life" through the help of fantasy. Unlike Sendak's earlier protagonists, who tended to use fantasy and daydreams as escapes from real-world emotional confrontations, the intrepid Max has a temper-tantrum when his mother calls him "Wild Thing!" He then sails off to tame Wild Things of his own imagining, and returns home purged, even victorious—since the supper he didn't expect to get is waiting for him at his bedside. Though countless librarians and educators worried about the book's frightening aspects for young children—raw rage and monstrous fantasy figures—the work was an immediate success. Children seemed to find solace in a hero who could be angry with his mother and triumph over his own rage.

In the Night Kitchen is a less accessible, more personal picture-book fantasy. Beginning with another angry hero, Mickey, who has been rudely awakened by things that go bump in the night, Sendak conjures up a dream sequence about three look-alike bakers who pursue their culinary art while most children are fast asleep. If there are Freudian undercurrents in this work celebrating the sensual joys of early childhood, most young listeners are entranced by the trio of cooks, dead ringers for the movie comedian Oliver Hardy, and their mysterious incantation: "MILK IN THE BATTER! WE BAKE THE CAKE! AND NOTHING'S THE MATTER!"

The intriguing and decidedly American fairytale, *Higglety Pigglety Pop! or, There Must Be More to Life* begins where traditional fairytales leave off, at "And they lived happily ever after." Jennie, the story's dog heroine, has everything—a loving master, two windows from which to enjoy the view, two pillows (one for upstairs, one for down), and two eating bowls. Yet, she announces at the story's start: "I am discontented. There must be more to life than having everything." The voracious Jennie, who looms so large in this most personal and mystifying Sendak tale, is no garden-variety fictional heroine. In real life, she was for 15 years the author's beloved pet Sealyham. When he was working on *Higglety,* Jennie's health was failing and his own mother was dying; Sendak felt disquieting intimations of mortality, and he wanted to immortalize Jennie, perhaps himself as well, in "the World Mother Goose Theatre." Many of Sendak's admirers feel that this is his most ambitious and poetic work. Certainly, it is the one tale in which the words have as much resonance and power as the pictures.

Sendak's third volume in the self-styled picture-book trilogy, which began with *Wild Things* and was followed by *Night Kitchen,* is *Outside Over There,* a beautiful work pictorially but the most arcane in terms of story. Its beginnings lay in earlier illustrations Sendak had done for *The Juniper Tree,* a two-volume selection of tales from the Brothers Grimm. One of those tales, "The Goblins," dealt with the substitution of a changeling for a real child, and the situation's ambiguities so intrigued Sendak that he made a kidnapping by goblins the central drama of this work. What links the trio of picture books in the author's mind is that "they are all variations on a single theme: an examination of how children master various feelings—anger, boredom, fear, frustration, jealousy, to name a few—and manage to come to grips with the reality of their lives." Woven into this dark tale are real-life happenings from Sendak's own childhood: the birth of the Dionne quintuplets, the kidnapping of the Lindbergh baby. Though Ida, Sendak's plucky 9-year-old heroine, ultimately triumphs over her burdens in this grandly operatic costume drama, the victory is somehow unsatisfying. The richness of Sendak's illustrations is not matched by a sufficiently substantial story.

After designing sets and costumes for several operas and a ballet in the 1980s, Sendak joined forces with a children's book protege and colleague, Arthur Yorkins, to found a children's theater called *The Night Kitchen.* The artist's latest picture book, *We Are All in the Dumps with Jack & Guy,* is an apocalyptic improvization on two little-known English nursery rhymes. With the help of an interracial cast of parentless waifs who inhabit a haunting city slum, Sendak does battle with the big bad wolves of our time—Poverty, Violence, AIDS, and Human Indifference. When the book's two heroes, Jack and Guy, manage to rescue a "poor little kid" and a sackful of kittens from the clutches of two unregeneratively evil rats, they affirm their creator's lifelong view that children, with their unblinkingly honest acceptance of harsh realities and their miraculous resilience, still offer humanity's best (and possibly only) hope for redemption.

—Selma G. Lanes

SEREDY, Kate

Nationality: American (originally Hungarian: immigrated to the United States, 1922). **Born:** Budapest, Hungary, 10 November 1899. **Education:** Academy of Arts, Budapest, art teacher's diploma. **Military Service:** Nurse during World War I. **Career:** Ran a children's bookstore, 1933-34; owned a farm near Montgomery, New York, 1936-mid-1950s. Commercial artist and freelance illustrator. **Award:** American Library Association Newbery medal, 1938. **Died:** 7 March 1975.

Publications for Children (illustrated by the author)

Fiction

The Good Master. New York, Viking Press, 1935; London, Harrap, 1937.
Listening. New York, Viking Press, 1936.
The Singing Tree. New York, Viking Press, 1939; London, Harrap, 1940.
A Tree for Peter. New York, Viking Press, 1941.
The Open Gate. New York, Viking Press, 1943; London, Harrap, 1947.
The Chestry Oak. New York, Viking Press, 1948; London, Harrap, 1957.
Gypsy. New York, Viking Press, 1951; London, Harrap, 1952.
Philomena. New York, Viking Press, 1955; London, Harrap, 1957.
The Tenement Tree. New York, Viking Press, 1959; London, Harrap, 1960.
A Brand-New Uncle. New York, Viking Press, 1961.
Lazy Tinka. New York, Viking Press, 1962; London, Harrap, 1964.

Other

The White Stag. New York, Viking Press, 1937; London, Harrap, 1938.

Translator, *Who Is Johnny?,* by Leopold Gedö, illustrated by Gedö. New York, Viking Press, 1939.

*

Manuscript Collections: May Massee Collection, Emporia State University, Kansas; University of Oregon Library, Eugene.

Illustrator: *The Prince Commands* by Andre Norton, 1934; *Broken Son* by Sonia Daugherty, 1934; *The Selfish Giant,* 1935, and *The Gunniwolf,* 1936, both edited by Wilhelmina Harper; *Caddie Woodlawn,* 1935, and *Mademoiselle Misfortune,* 1936, both by Carol Ryrie Brink; *With Harp and Lute,* 1935, *The Oldest Story,* 1943, and *A Candle Burns for France,* 1946, all by Blanche Thompson, and *Bible Children,* 1937, edited by Thompson; *Winterbound* by Margery Williams Bianco, 1936; *Smiling Hill Farm,* 1937, and *A House for Ten,* 1949, both by Miriam Mason; *An Ear for Uncle Emil* by E.R. Gaggin, 1939; *Michel's Island* by Mabel Leigh Hunt, 1940; *The Christmas Anna Angel* by Ruth Sawyer, 1944; *Living Together at Home and at School* by Prudence Cutright and others, 1944; *Fun at the Playground* by Bernice Osler Frissell and Mary Louise Friebele, 1946; *The Wonderful Year* by Nancy Barnes, 1946; *Hoot-Owl* by Mabel La Rue, 1946; *Adopted Jane,* 1947, *Mary Montgomery, Rebel,* 1948, and *Pilgrim Kate,* 1949, all by Helen Daringer; *Little Vic* by Doris Gates, 1951; *Finnegan II* by Carolyn Sherwin Bailey, 1953; *A Dog Named Penny* by Clyde Robert Bulla, 1955.

* * *

Kate Seredy first made her mark as a writer in 1935 when May Massee, the children's editor at Doubleday, suggested that she write a book about her childhood in Hungary. Seredy did just that, and *The Good Master* was the result. Not only did May Massee become one of the outstanding children's book editors of her time, but Seredy went on to win the Newbery Medal in 1938 for *The White Stag* and to make many distinguished contributions to the field of children's literature.

The Good Master is set on a farm on the great Hungarian plains, the home of the "good master," his son Jancsi, and Jancsi's turbulent cousin Kate. Since Seredy spent most of her summers on the plains, she is able to describe vividly the people and customs of Hungary. Harvest festivals, household crafts, and even the local cooking add colour to the warm family story. Seredy's first training was as an artist, and she contributed sensitive and detailed illustrations to all her own and to other people's books. Her stories depict the human situation, the hopes and beliefs of mankind. *The Good Master* was followed by *The Singing Tree,* which tells about the effects of war on the "good master's" household. The Magyar legends she heard as a child inspired *The White Stag* and, though it was a prize-winning book, many people regard *The Good Master* as her best book.

Seredy is one of the first children's writers to have dealt with the problems of the alien. *The Singing Tree* tells of the life of Russian prisoners in Hungary during the war, as well as German refugee children who arrive to be restored to health. In *The Chestry Oak* a homeless little boy from Hungary is sent to America where he struggles to become part of that country. Although the hero is young the ideas are adult and explore the ways in which children are affected by the tragedy of war.

Although Seredy was Hungarian by birth and upbringing, she wrote English prose with no trace of foreign idiom. Her books explore values and characteristics familiar to us all, but freshly interesting against an unfamiliar background. In being both author and artist she gave her books an authenticity which is rare.

—Ann Bartholomew

SEUSS, Dr.

Pseudonym for Theodor Seuss Geisel. **Other Pseudonyms:** Theo Le Sieg; Rosetta Stone. **Nationality:** American. **Born:** Springfield, Massachusetts, 2 March 1904. **Education:** Schools in Springfield; Dartmouth College, Hanover, New Hampshire (editor, *Jack-o-Lantern*), A.B. 1925; Lincoln College, Oxford, 1925-26. **Military Service:** United States Army Signal Corps and Information and Education Division, 1943-46: Lieutenant-Colonel; Legion of Merit. **Family:** Married 1) Helen Marion Palmer in 1927 (died 1967); 2) Audrey Stone Dimond in 1968. **Career:** Freelance magazine humorist and cartoonist from 1927; advertising illustrator, Standard Oil Company of New Jersey, 1928-41, and for Ford Motor Company; editorial cartoonist, *PM* magazine, New York, 1940-42; publicist, War Production Board, 1940-42; correspondent, *Life* magazine, Japan, 1954. Since 1957 founding president and editor-in-chief, Beginner Books, Random House Inc., New York. Individual shows: San Diego Fine Arts Museum, 1950; Dartmouth College, 1975; Toledo Museum of Art, Ohio, 1975; La Jolla Museum of Contemporary Arts, 1976. **Awards:** Oscar, for documentary, 1946, 1947, for animated cartoon, 1951; Peabody award, for television cartoon, 1971 (twice); Zagreb International Cartoon Festival award, 1972; Emmy award, for television, 1977, 1982; American Library Association Laura Ingalls Wilder award, 1980; Catholic Library Association Regina medal, 1982; Pulitzer Prize special citation, 1984. L.H.D.: Dartmouth College, 1956; American International College, Springfield, Massachusetts, 1968; Lake Forest College, Illinois, 1977; Brown University, Providence, Rhode Island, 1987; D. Litt.: Whittier College, California, 1980; John F. Kennedy University, 1983; University of Hartford, Connecticut, 1986; D.F.A.: Princeton University, New Jersey, 1985. **Died:** 25 September 1991.

PUBLICATIONS FOR CHILDREN

Poetry (illustrated by the author)

And to Think That I Saw It on Mulberry Street. New York, Vanguard Press, 1937; London, Country Life, 1939.
The 500 Hats of Bartholomew Cubbins. New York, Vanguard Press, 1938; London, Oxford University Press, 1940.
The King's Stilts. New York, Random House, 1939; London, Hamish Hamilton, 1942.
Horton Hatches the Egg. New York, Random House, 1940; London, Hamish Hamilton, 1942.
McElligot's Pool. New York, Random House, 1947; London, Collins, 1975.
Thidwick, The Big-Hearted Moose. New York, Random House, 1948; London, Collins, 1968.
Bartholomew and the Oobleck. New York, Random House, 1949.
If I Ran the Zoo. New York, Random House, 1950.
Scrambled Eggs Super! New York, Random House, 1953; in *Dr. Seuss Storybook,* London, Collins, 1979.
Horton Hears a Who! New York, Random House, 1954; London, Collins, 1976.
On Beyond Zebra. New York, Random House, 1955.
If I Ran the Circus. New York, Random House, 1956; London, Collins, 1969.
The Cat in the Hat. New York, Random House, 1957; London, Hutchinson, 1958.
How the Grinch Stole Christmas. New York, Random House, 1957.
The Cat in the Hat Comes Back! New York, Random House, 1958; London, Collins, 1961.
Yertle the Turtle and Other Stories. New York, Random House, 1958; London, Collins, 1963.
Happy Birthday to You! New York, Random House, 1959.
One Fish, Two Fish, Red Fish, Blue Fish. New York, Random House, 1960; London, Collins, 1962.
Green Eggs and Ham. New York, Random House, 1960; London, Collins, 1962.
The Sneetches and Other Stories. New York, Random House, 1961; London, Collins, 1965.
Sleep Book. New York, Random House, 1962; London, Collins, 1964.
Hop on Pop. New York, Random House, 1963; London, Collins, 1964.
ABC. New York, Random House, 1963; London, Collins, 1964.
Fox in Socks. New York, Random House, 1965; London, Collins, 1966.
I Had Trouble in Getting to Solla Sollew. New York, Random House, 1965; London, Collins, 1967.
The Foot Book. New York, Random House, 1968; London, Collins, 1969.
I Can Lick 30 Tigers Today and Other Stories. New York, Random House, 1969; London, Collins, 1970.
Mr. Brown Can Moo! Can You? New York, Random House, 1970; London, Collins, 1971.
The Lorax. New York, Random House, 1971; London, Collins, 1972.
Marvin K. Mooney, Will You Please Go Now? New York, Random House, 1972; London, Collins, 1973.
Did I Ever Tell You How Lucky You Are? New York, Random House, 1973; London, Collins, 1974.
The Shape of Me and Other Stuff. New York, Random House, 1973; London, Collins, 1974.
There's a Wocket in My Pocket! New York, Random House, 1974; London, Collins, 1975.
Great Day for Up!, illustrated by Quentin Blake. New York, Random House, 1974; London, Collins, 1975.
Oh, The Thinks You Can Think. New York, Random House, 1975; London, Collins, 1976.
Because a Little Bug Went Ka-Choo! (as Rosetta Stone), with Michael Frith. New York, Random House, 1975.
Hooper Humperdink...? Not Him!, illustrated by Charles Martin. New York, Random House, 1976; London, Collins, 1977.
Oh Say Can You Say? New York, Random House, 1979; London, Collins, 1980.
Hunches in Bunches. New York, Random House, 1982.
The Butter Battle Book. New York, Random House, and London, Collins, 1984.
I Am Not Going to Get Up Today!, illustrated by James Stevenson. New York, Random House, 1987; London, Collins, 1988.
Daisy-Head Mayzie. New York, Random House, forthcoming (posthumously).

Poetry as Theo Le Sieg

Ten Apples Up on Top!, illustrated by Roy McKie. New York, Random House, 1961; London, Collins, 1963.

I Wish That I Had Duck Feet, illustrated by B. Tobey. New York, Random House, 1965; London, Collins, 1967.
Come Over to My House, illustrated by Richard Erdoes. New York, Random House, 1966; London, Collins, 1967.
The Eye Book, illustrated by Roy McKie. New York, Random House, 1968; London, Collins, 1969.
In a People House, illustrated by Roy McKie. New York, Random House, 1972; London, Collins, 1973.
The Many Mice of Mr. Brice, illustrated by Roy McKie. New York, Random House, 1973; London, Collins, 1974.
Wacky Wednesday, illustrated by George Booth. New York, Random House, 1974; London, Collins, 1975.
Would You Rather Be a Bullfrog?, illustrated by Roy McKie. New York, Random House, 1975; London, Collins, 1976.
Please Try to Remember the First of Octember, illustrated by Arthur Cumings. New York, Random House, 1977; London, Collins, 1978.
Maybe You Should Fly a Jet! Maybe You Should Be a Vet!, illustrated by Michael Smollin. New York, Random House, 1980; London, Collins, 1981.
The Tooth Book, illustrated by Roy McKie. New York, Random House, 1981.

Plays

Gerald McBoing-Boing (cartoon screenplay), 1951.

Television Plays (animated cartoons): *How the Grinch Stole Christmas,* 1966; *Horton Hears a Who,* 1970; *The Cat in the Hat,* 1971; *The Lorax; Dr. Seuss on the Loose,* 1973; *Hoober Bloob Highway,* 1975; *Halloween Is Grinch Night; Pontoffel Pock Where Are You,* 1980; *The Grinch Grinches the Cat in the Hat.*

Other (illustrated by the author)

The Cat in the Hat Dictionary, by the Cat Himself, with Philip D. Eastman. New York, Random House, 1964.
The Cat in the Hat Songbook. New York, Random House, 1967.
My Book about Me—By Me, Myself. I Wrote It! I Drew It!, illustrated by Roy McKie. New York, Random House, 1969.
I Can Draw It Myself. New York, Random House, 1970.
I Can Write—By Me, Myself (as Theo Le Sieg). New York, Random House, 1971.
The Cat's Quizzer. New York, Random House, 1976; London, Collins, 1977.
I Can Read with My Eyes Shut! New York, Random House, 1978; London, Collins, 1979.

PUBLICATIONS FOR ADULTS

Short Stories

The Seven Lady Godivas. New York, Random House, 1939.

Screenplays

Your Job in Germany (*Hitler Lives*), 1946.
Design for Death, with Helen Palmer Geisel, 1947.
The 5000 Fingers of Dr. T., with Allan Scott, 1953.

Other

Signs of Civilization! (as Seuss). La Jolla, California, La Jolla Town Council, 1956.
Lost World Revisited: A Forward-Looking Backward Glance. New York, Award Books, 1967.
You're Only Old Once. New York, Random House, 1986.
The Tough Coughs as He Ploughs the Dough: Early Writings and Cartoons by Dr. Seuss, edited by Richard Marschall. New York, Morrow, 1986.
Oh, the Places You'll Go! New York, Random House, 1990.
Six by Seuss: A Treasury of Dr. Seuss Classics (includes *And to Think That I Saw It on Mulberry Street, The 500 Hats of Bartholomew Cubbins, Horton Hatches the Egg, How the Grinch Stole Christmas, The Lorax,* and *Yertle the Turtle*). New York, Random House, 1991.

*

Manuscript Collections: Special Collections, University of California Library, Los Angeles.

Critical Studies: *Dr. Seuss from Then to Now: A Catalogue of the Retrospective Exhibition* by Mary Stofflet, New York, Random House, 1986; *Dr. Seuss* edited by Ruth K. MacDonald, New York, Twayne, 1988.

Illustrator: *Boners* and *More Boners,* both 1931.

* * *

A whole library of entertaining books has been created by Theodor Geisel, commonly known as Dr. Seuss. Fanciful invention characterizes all the stories, yet there is variety. *How the Grinch Stole Christmas* is a seasonal book, *Sleep Book* is a bedtime story, and *Fox in Socks* is a collection of such tongue twisters as "Through three cheese trees three free fleas flew." *The Sneetches, The Lorax,* and *Horton Hears a Who!* are moral tales, and *The 500 Hats of Bartholomew Cubbins* resembles a folktale. Seuss also varies his style with the use of verse and prose, as well as limited and unlimited vocabularies.

The Cat in the Hat (with 223 words) and *Green Eggs and Ham* (with 50) represent the beginning of a relatively new genre: publications designed not as textbooks intended to increase skill, but as a form of pleasurable literature for beginners. In 1957 Seuss introduced the beguiling "cat in the hat" and demonstrated a remarkably high standard of readability in books the first grader could be expected to read independently.

In his earliest children's book, *And to Think That I Saw It on Mulberry Street,* Seuss established the pattern for books which consist of loosely joined imaginative scenes. Being constructed as daydreams, they lack a dynamic progression; but each scene is an ingenious improvisation that highlights the author's interest in word play. Narratives of this sort include *McElligot's Pool, Scrambled Eggs Super!, Sleep Book, If I Ran the Circus, If I Ran the Zoo, On Beyond Zebra,* and *Oh, The Places You'll Go!*

Seuss's passion for words is exuberant but not reckless. In *If I Ran the Circus* he describes trapeze artists with a blend of grammatical logic and foolishness: "My Zoom-a-Zoop Troupe from West Upper Ben-Deezing/Who never quite know, while they zoop and they zoom,/Whether which will catch what one, or who will catch whom/Or if who will catch which by the what and just where,/Or just when and just how in which part of the air!"

Inventing new eccentrics is one of Seuss's most singular achievements, and the pages of the daydream books are crowded with odd creatures. One eats hot pebbles in order to blow smoke from his ears. Another bites his over-long tail before bedtime, and the sensation wakes him up exactly eight hours later.

In the *Sleep Book,* everyday experiences are intermixed with the fantastic: "Sleep thoughts/Are spreading/Throughout the whole land./The time for night-brushing of teeth is at hand./Up at Herk-Heimer Falls, where the great river rushes/And crashes down crags in great gargling gushes,/The Herk-Heimer Sisters are using their brushes./Those falls are just grand for tooth-brushing beneath/If you happen to be up that way with your teeth."

Seuss sustains a nice balance between characterization, incident, and thematic concerns in his folkloristic tales. *The 500 Hats of Bartholomew Cubbins* includes a peasant hero, an unscrupulous duke, and a magic hat. A key feature is the logic underlying the encounter of the hero with a king's official executioner. With spooked hats reproducing themselves, the protagonist cannot obey the protocol—"hats off to the king"—nor remove his hat to be beheaded (a rule in the Royal Executioner's book). These bureaucratic realities anchor the story to human experience, while at the same time the magic is unrestrained. Stylistically, the many parallel phrases and happenings add decorative and structural strength.

Themes in the moral tales revolve around such problems as greed, prejudice, and environmental irresponsibility. The heroic elephant in *Horton Hears a Who!* finds a dust speck which turns out to be a tiny world populated by "Whos." Since Who voices are audible to elephant ears exclusively, the jungle is full of nonbelievers. Human worth is highlighted as the mob tries to crush a microscopic community.

The Butter Battle Book repeats Seuss's concerns about intolerance while adding a theme of great import: the arms race. And on a subtler level, he satirizes aggressive nationalism. Differences about the "proper" way to butter bread leads to war. Seuss mocks behaviors that excite nationalistic fervor—e.g., marching bands and fancy uniforms. Most insidious is the acculturation of the young: "But we Yooks, as you know,/when we breakfast or sup,/spread our bread," Grandpa said,/"with the butter side *up.*"

Seuss in his last years revisited the genres that made him famous. *I Am Not Going to Get Up Today!* is a superbly witty, limited vocabulary treatise on idleness. *Oh, The Places You'll Go!* fittingly presents Seuss's last blessing upon the young. He assures their triumph in the "Great Balancing Act" of Life: "On you will go/though the weather be foul./On you will go/though your enemies prowl/. . . Onward up many/a frightening creek,/ though your arms may get sore/and your sneekers may leak/. . . KID, YOU'LL MOVE MOUNTAINS!"

Dr. Seuss was a well-disciplined nonsense poet, his work alive with wit, rhythm, eccentric characters, and substantial themes. Sometimes he drew upon the well-tested motifs of tall tales. Often he created a theme and variations on the quirkiness of human nature. We may find it difficult to fathom the full secret of his childlike humor, but the depth of his affection for children was unmistakable. Moreover, he had that rare gift that distinguishes the geniuses of children's literature: a deeply intuitive grasp of the child's perspective and free spirit.

—Donnarae MacCann

SEVERN, David

Pseudonym for David Storr Unwin. **Nationality:** British. **Born:** London, England, 3 December 1918; son of the publisher Sir Stanley Unwin. **Education:** Abbotsholme School, Derbyshire, 1933-36. **Family:** Married Bridget Mary Herbert in 1945; twin daughter and son. **Career:** Editorial assistant, League of Nations Secretariat, Geneva, 1938; worked for Unwin Brothers, printers, Woking, Surrey, 1939, and Basil Blackwell, booksellers, Oxford, 1940; member of the production department, George Allen and Unwin, publishers, London, 1941-43. **Address:** Garden Flat, 31 Belsize Park, London N.W.3, England.

Publications for Children

Fiction

Rick Afire!, illustrated by Joan Kiddell-Monroe. London, Lane, 1942.

A Cabin for Crusoe, illustrated by Joan Kiddell-Monroe. London, Lane, 1943; Boston, Houghton Mifflin, 1946.

Waggon for Five, illustrated by Joan Kiddell-Monroe. London, Lane, 1944; Boston, Houghton Mifflin, 1947.

Hermit in the Hills, illustrated by Joan Kiddell-Monroe. London, Lane, 1945.

Forest Holiday, illustrated by Joan Kiddell-Monroe. London, Lane, 1946.

Ponies and Poachers, illustrated by Joan Kiddell-Monroe. London, Lane, 1947.

Bill Badger and the Pine Martens [*Bathing Pool, Buried Treasure*], illustrated by Geoffrey Higham. London, Lane, 3 vols., 1947-50.

Wily Fox and the Baby Show [*Christmas Party, Missing Fireworks*], illustrated by Geoffrey Higham. London, Lane, 3 vols., 1947-50.

The Cruise of the "Maiden Castle," illustrated by Joan Kiddell-Monroe. London, Lane, 1948; New York, Macmillan, 1949.

Treasure for Three, illustrated by Joan Kiddell-Monroe. London, Lane, 1949; New York, Macmillan, 1950.

Dream Gold, illustrated by A.K. Lee. London, Lane, 1949; New York, Viking Press, 1952.

Crazy Castle, illustrated by Joan Kiddell-Monroe. London, Lane, 1951; New York, Macmillan, 1952.

Burglars and Bandicoots, illustrated by Joan Kiddell-Monroe. London, Lane, 1952.

Drumbeats!, illustrated by Richard Kennedy. London, Lane, 1953.

Blaze of Broadfurrow Farm, illustrated by Kiff and Wilmore. London, Lane, 1955.

Walnut Tree Meadow, illustrated by Kiff and Wilmore. London, Lane, 1955.

The Future Took Us, illustrated by Jillian Richards. London, Lane, 1958.

The Green-Eyed Gryphon, illustrated by Prudence Seward. London, Hamish Hamilton, 1958.

Foxy-Boy, illustrated by Lynton Lamb. London, Bodley Head, 1959; as *The Wild Valley,* New York, Dutton, 1963.

Three at the Sea, illustrated by Margery Gill. London, Bodley Head, 1959.

Jeff Dickson, Cowhand, illustrated by Patrick Williams. London, Cape, 1963.

Clouds over the Alberhorn. London, Hamish Hamilton, 1963.
A Dog for a Day, illustrated by Joseph Acheson. London, Hamish Hamilton, 1965.
The Girl in the Grove. London, Allen and Unwin, and New York, Harper, 1974.
The Wishing Bone, illustrated by Shirley Felts. London, Allen and Unwin, 1977.

Other

My Foreign Correspondent Through Africa, illustrated by Peter White. London, Meiklejohn, 1951.

PUBLICATIONS FOR ADULTS AS DAVID UNWIN

Novels

The Governor's Wife. London, Joseph, 1954; New York, Dutton, 1955.
A View of the Heath. London, Joseph, 1956.

Other

Fifty Years with Father. London, Allen and Unwin, 1982.

*

David Severn comments:

The series of straightforward adventure stories, with which I made my name in the 1940s, provided entertainment in their time, but I would choose to be remembered not for them but for a handful of off-beat works: *Dream Gold, Drumbeats!, Foxy-Boy,* and *The Girl in the Grove.* I feel that my fantasies are the most interesting—and certainly the most original—of all my books.

* * *

David Severn has published children's books in a space of nearly 40 years, and in that time his style and the kind of book he writes have changed as he and his life have developed.

His early books, which established him as a writer, are all domestic adventures about four children and Crusoe (a young writer) on a farm in southern England. They reflect the low-key life so many people lived during and just after the war, when a day out with sandwiches or a trip to the local town in the pony cart was an event which could turn into an adventure. *Rick Afire!* was the first of this series and it set the pace for the others, notably *A Cabin for Crusoe,* which includes some good gypsy-lore and insight into their way of life, and *Forest Holiday.* All are told in a straightforward enjoyable style with the enthusiasm of a writer in his early twenties who has a touch of the boy scout about him. They are dated now, but when they were published they had a freshness and directness which appealed strongly to young readers.

Since then Severn has turned to writing books with some supernatural element in them. *Dream Gold* is about two boys who share an identical dream which takes them to the Pacific Islands where they are caught up in a tale of piracy and treasure, and *Drumbeats!* uses the medium of an African drum to transport children from a progressive co-educational school in England into an ill-fated expedition in Africa 30 years earlier. The technique is good, but the writing is at times rather heavy. A storm is coming, for instance, and he says, "But even as we watched, the clouds expanded, sprouting new buttresses, lifting visibly into the summer's sky." *The Future Took Us* is an adventure story of two boys who are taken into the future. Here the book carries more conviction because, as in *Dream Gold,* the main character is a boy, and Severn seems to be more at ease when writing about the emotions and reactions of his own sex. This point is confirmed by *The Girl in the Grove* where the heroine is a teenage girl. Although the story of an unhappy ghost and the modern adults is carefully constructed, the emotional turmoil of the girl is overwritten and the book lacks impact. It is not really a children's book.

Foxy-Boy, on the other hand, is a fantasy for younger children which holds their attention. A lonely little girl befriends a wild boy who has been brought up by foxes, and despite the total improbability the book reads well. The secret of his success here is that it is for younger children and has less emotion loaded in. Severn's latest book, *The Wishing Bone,* is one of his best. He is writing again for a younger age group where he has scored successes in the past, not only with *Foxy-Boy* but with his Bill Badger stories and his Antelope books, notably *The Green-Eyed Gryphon,* where again a magic talisman changes children's lives. In *The Wishing Bone* some children get caught in a life-sized fort which grew from a toy fort built by one of them, and the ensuing adventures are not only well told, but the humour behind the complications of "only one wish per person" and the mis-wishes is good. The characters are all well portrayed, and the magic element is used successfully. This book has the freshness and fun that his earlier stories had, although the children in *The Wishing Bone* are far more sophisticated than the children of the Crusoe adventure stories.

Severn's imagination and fascination with magical powers have been potent forces in his children's books, but his best books derive from his ability to tell a good story rather than from his introduction of the supernatural. His prose and his dialogue are not outstanding, but his descriptions of the countryside are, and most important of all, he can capture the mood and the exuberance of children.

—Linda Yeatman

SEWELL, Helen (Moore)

Nationality: American. **Born:** Mare Island, California, 27 June 1896. **Education:** Packer Institute; Pratt Institute Art School, New York. Studied with the painter Archipenko. **Career:** Freelance illustrator. **Died:** 24 February 1957.

PUBLICATIONS FOR CHILDREN (ILLUSTRATED BY THE AUTHOR)

Fiction

A Head for Happy. New York, Macmillan, 1931.
Blue Barns. New York, Macmillan, 1933; London, Woodfield, 1955.
Ming and Mehitable. New York, Macmillan, 1936.
Peggy and the Pony. New York and London, Oxford University Press, 1937.
Jimmy and Jemima. New York, Macmillan, 1940.

Peggy and the Pup. New York and London, Oxford University Press, 1941.
Birthdays for Robin. New York, Macmillan, 1943; London, Hale, 1947.
Belinda the Mouse. New York and London, Oxford University Press, 1944.
Three Tall Tales, with Elena Eleska. New York, Macmillan, 1947.
The Golden Christmas Manger (cut-out book). New York, Simon & Schuster, 1948.

Other

ABC for Everyday. New York, Macmillan, 1930.

Editor, *Words to the Wise: A Book of Proverbs.* New York, Dodd Mead, 1932.

*

Manuscript Collections: May Massee Collection, Emporia State University, Kansas.

Illustrator: *The Cruise of the Little Dipper* by Susanne Langer, 1924; *Menagerie* by Mary Britton Miller, 1928; *Sally Gabble and the Fairies* by Miriam S. Potter, 1929; *Mr. Hermit Crab* by Mimsey Rhys, 1929; *A Round of Carols* by Thomas Noble, 1929; *Building a House in Sweden* by Marjorie Cautley, 1931; *The Dreamkeeper and Other Poems* by Langston Hughes, 1932; *The Christmas Tree in the Woods* by Susan Smith, 1932; *Little House in the Big Woods,* 1932, *Farmer Boy,* 1933; *Little House on the Prairie,* 1935, *On the Banks of Plum Creek,* 1937, *By the Shores of Silver Lake,* 1939, *The Long Winter,* 1940, and *Little Town on the Prairie,* 1941, all by Laura Ingalls Wilder; *Broomstick and Snowflake* by Johan Falkberget, 1933; *Where is Adelaide?,* 1933, and *Ann Frances,* 1935, both by Eliza Orne White; *A First Bible,* 1934; *Cinderella,* 1934; *Away Goes Sally,* 1934, *Five Bushel Farm,* 1939, *The Fair American,* 1940, *The White Horse,* 1942, *The Big Green Umbrella,* 1944, and *The Wonderful Day,* 1946, all by Elizabeth Coatsworth; *Bluebonnets for Lucinda,* 1934, and *Tagalong Tooloo,* 1941, both by Frances Clarke Sayers; *Peter and Gretchen of Old Nuremberg* by Viola May Jones, 1935; *Pinocchio* by Carlo Collodi, 1935; *Ten Saints* by Eleanor Farjeon, 1936; *Old John* by Máirín Cregan, 1936; *The Magic Hill and Other Stories,* 1937, and *The Princess and the Apple Tree and Other Stories,* 1937, both by A.A. Milne; *Baby Island* by Carol Ryrie Brink, 1937; *Jane Eyre* by Charlotte Brontë, 1938; *The Young Brontës* by Mary Louise Jarden, 1938; *Pride and Prejudice,* 1940, and *Sense and Sensibility,* 1957, both by Jane Austen; *The Blue-Eyed Lady* by Ferenc Molnar, 1942; *Book of Myths* by Thomas Bulfinch, 1942; *Christmas Magic* by James S. Tippett, 1944; *A Bee in Her Bonnet* by Eva Kristoffersen, 1944; *Boat Children of Canton* by Marion B. Ward, 1944; *Once There Was a Little Boy* by Dorothy Kunhardt, 1946; *The Brave Bantam* by Louise Seaman, 1946; *Azor,* 1948, *Azor and the Haddock,* 1949, and *Azor and the Blue-Eyed Cow,* 1951, all by Maude Cowley; *Secrets and Surprises* by Irmengarde Eberle, 1951; *Mrs. McThing* by Mary Chase, 1952; *The Bears on Hemlock Mountain,* 1952, and *The Thanksgiving Story,* 1954, both by Alice Dalgliesh; *Poems* by Emily Dickinson, 1952; *The Colonel's Squad,* 1952, *In the Beginning,* 1954, and *The Three Kings of Saba,* 1955, all by Alf Evers; *Grimm's Tales,* 1954.

* * *

Helen Sewell's contributions to children's literature have invariably been favorably commented on by her critics. It is virtually impossible, therefore, to discover a serious discussion of children's books that does not deal with her offerings on positive terms. This well-deserved high regard, which places Sewell in the upper echelon of the field of children's books, has come about, however, because of her illustrations for these books rather than for her efforts as a writer. In the latter half of her career, from roughly the mid-1940s onward, Sewell gave up almost entirely the writing of picture books. She concentrated on illustrations, to become one of the most honored of her profession, and very famous writers for children vied for her services as the illustrator of their texts. She remains, as well, one of the most adaptable. She revealed in one instance how she used the attractions children find in comic books to her advantage (in *Three Tall Tales* she imitated as nearly as possible the layout for the words as they are used in comics).

Far less familiar, even to the critics of children's literature, are the writings she did for children in the first half of her career. These books have never received the honors nor the attention of her illustrations. And rightly so, one must admit, since while the language of the studiously abbreviated picture books which Sewell both wrote and illustrated is by and large thoughtfully pleasant, clear in the way it relates concepts, and even at times amusing, it is not distinguished in either the themes or in their dramatic effects.

All of her early books are now obscure and out of print (with the exception of *Blue Barns*). *A Head for Happy* is told with few words, indeed. In fact, some of its pictures are given no explanation at all. The words Sewell uses are there to punctuate a story line of three little sisters who make a doll and then go around the world searching for a proper head to fit its body. *Blue Barns* is an amusing, gentle, and true story of a farm, a funny gander, and some wild geese. It is a small picture book, for beginning readers, whose brief text prohibits any remarkable literary effect by its author. The slight plot of *Ming and Mehitable* (a "closet drama," as one critic called it) illustrated another theme which would concern only a very young child. Here the heroine's dog runs away after being pestered by being dressed up in baby clothes. Since after a search its master can find no animal so friendly, she promises the dog freedom from such minor mistreatment if he will return. *Peggy and the Pony* likewise is a story of a preoccupation only a young child would appreciate, the unrequited wish for a pony. After a number of frustrations the girl in this tale does get her request. These quiet stories, very feminine in tone, have few psychological involvements.

But Sewell's attempts at rather more complicated plots of an obviously greater psychological nature, as in *Jimmy and Jemima* and in *Belinda the Mouse,* do little to advance her reputation as a distinctive writer. The ordinary language found here fails for that purpose. As noted, it was at about this point in her life that Sewell probably wisely decided to limit her work almost entirely to the illustration of works of writers more talented than she. It is important to note, as well, that the girlish stories of this outstanding illustrator, but rather ordinary writer, happily have lost little of their original attractiveness by the passage of time. They can still be enjoyed by today's children.

—Patrick Groff

SHANNON, Monica

Nationality: American (originally Canadian: moved to the United States as an infant). **Born:** Belleville, Ontario, Canada. **Education:** Schools in Seattle and Idaho; Bachelor of Library Science from school in California. **Family:** Married. **Career:** Worked in the Los Angeles Public Library, 1916-25. **Award:** American Library Association Newbery medal, 1935. **Died:** 13 August 1965.

PUBLICATIONS FOR CHILDREN

Fiction

California Fairy Tales, illustrated by C.E. Millard. New York, Doubleday, and London, Heinemann, 1926.

Eyes for the Dark, illustrated by C.E. Millard. New York, Doubleday, 1928; as *More Tales from California,* 1935.

Tawnymore, illustrated by Jean Charlot. New York, Doubleday, 1931.

Dobry, illustrated by Atanas Katchamakoff. New York, Viking Press, 1934; London Harrap, 1936.

Poetry

Goose Grass Rhymes, illustrated by Neva Kanaga Brown. New York, Doubleday, 1930.

PUBLICATIONS FOR ADULTS

Other

Editor, *California in Print.* Los Angeles, Los Angeles Public Library, 1919.

* * *

Monica Shannon wrote five children's books—*California Fairy Tales, Eyes for the Dark, Goose Grass Rhymes, Tawnymore,* and *Dobry.* The first two are books of artistic fairytales; the third, a book of light-hearted verse; the fourth, a pirate story of a half-breed boy; and the fifth, the story of a Bulgarian peasant boy with aspirations to become a great artist.

Collectively Shannon's books attest to her intense appreciation of nature and environment; her respect for human, plant, and animal life; and her regard for the cultural traditions in her own family background and that of others. Traces of Shannon's pleasant childhood spent in the mountains of Montana and California are evident in *Tawnymore, Dobry,* and the fairytales. From the Bulgarian immigrants who worked on her father's ranch young Monica learned about Bulgarian customs and folkways, and from the extensive mountain ranch lands over which she roamed freely during her childhood, she learned about animals, plants, and other natural life. Her keen eye for observing nature and the environment around her and her penchant for descriptive, colorful, and figurative language are clearly at work in all her writings. In "It's Going to Rain" from *Goose Grass Rhymes,* for example, Shannon describes in pictorial words and with poetic ease sun and shade playing tag, winds running races, and linen dancing on the clotheslines. In "The Tree Toad," with equal ease, the poet shows readers a neat creature "with tidy rubbers on his feet," a creature who knows nothing but embarrassment. She knows the toad is embarrassed because "his color comes, his color goes." And as to the lowly caterpillar, Shannon is of the opinion that "he giggles, as he wiggles, across a hairy leaf."

The delightful tales published in *California Fairy Tales* and *Eyes for the Dark* are numerous and varied—an amalgamation of Spain, America, Ireland, and Fairyland itself. The tales begin with such interest-capturing openers as "Now it is true that three old witch women did live under a Judas tree, right where two parts of Kaweah River ran together like jabbering gossips" or "Now, once upon a time, when the Elder Berries were very young Berries and the Sierra Nevada Mountains were still down under the Pacific Ocean, a certain Pigwidgeon lived alongside the sea." Tales beginning in such a fashion lend themselves well to oral telling and/or reading, and it is not surprising that a number of them have been recorded.

Dobry, by far the most widely known of Shannon's works, is the inspiring story of a young Bulgarian peasant boy who determines to be a great sculptor; many of the incidents are based on the experiences of Atanas Katchamakoff, the Bulgarian-born sculptor who provided the illustrations for the book. Dobry lives with his mother, Roda, and his grandfather in a peaceful Bulgarian village. Dobry's father has been killed in war, and the mother's only ambition for her son is that "he be learning to take his father's place in the fields one day." Being too hard-working and practical-minded herself to understand her son's artistic bent, Roda is prone to remind Dobry that the big peasant he will grow up to be will have no time for picture making. But Dobry's grandfather, whose personal philosophy is that people should wish to be different rather than alike, gently coaxes Roda to an understanding that her son must be allowed to develop in directions other than those she has dreamed. It is this development that constitutes the narrative of the book, through which readers learn not only about Dobry but also about Bulgarian village life and the stability and strength of people who live close to the soil. The major characters in *Dobry* are strong and well-delineated, Grandfather being one of the chief among them. He is something of a homespun philosopher and storyteller, admired not only by his grandson but by everyone. Several of Grandfather's tales, such as the "Poplar Tree Story" and "The Story of Hadutzi-Dare" are cleverly interwoven into the fabric of *Dobry.* The pages which reveal the artistic, as well as the physical, development of Dobry are filled with colorful descriptions and imagery.

Although Shannon's literary works for children were all published between 1926 and 1934, the fact that three of them, *Dobry, California Fairy Tales,* and *More Tales from California* (originally *Eyes for the Dark*), still remain in print attests to their literary quality and universality of appeal.

—Charity Chang

SHARMAT, Marjorie Weinman

Pseudonym: Wendy Andrews. **Nationality:** American. **Born:** Portland, Maine, 12 November 1928. **Education:** Lasell Junior College, Auburndale, Massachusetts, 1946-47; Westbrook Junior

College, Portland, 1947-48, graduated 1948. **Family:** Married Mitchell B. Sharmat in 1957; two sons. **Career:** Served on the circulation staff, Yale University Library, 1951-54, and Yale Law Library, 1954-55, New Haven, Connecticut. Currently full-time author of children's books. **Agent:** Harold Ober Associates, 425 Madison Avenue, New York, New York 10017, U.S.A.

PUBLICATIONS FOR CHILDREN

Fiction

Rex, illustrated by Emily McCully. New York, Harper, 1967.
Goodnight Andrew Goodnight Craig, illustrated by Mary Chalmers. New York, Harper, 1969.
Gladys Told Me to Meet Her Here, illustrated by Edward Frascino. New York, Harper, 1970.
A Hot Thirsty Day, illustrated by Rosemary Wells. New York, Macmillan, and London, Collier Macmillan, 1971.
51 Sycamore Lane, illustrated by Lisl Weil. New York, Macmillan, and London, Collier Macmillan, 1971; as *The Spy in the Neighborhood,* New York, Collier, 1974.
Getting Something on Maggie Marmelstein, illustrated by Ben Shecter. New York, Harper, 1971; London, Abelard Schuman, 1974.
A Visit with Rosalind, illustrated by Lisl Weil. New York, Macmillan, 1972.
Sophie and Gussie, illustrated by Lillian Hoban. New York, Macmillan, 1973; Kingswood, Surrey, World's Work, 1974.
Morris Brookside, A Dog, illustrated by Ronald Himler. New York, Holiday House, 1973.
Morris Brookside Is Missing, illustrated by Ronald Himler. New York, Holiday House, 1974.
I Want Mama, illustrated by Emily McCully. New York, Harper, 1974.
Walter the Wolf, illustrated by Kelly Oechsli. New York, Holiday House, 1975.
I'm Not Oscar's Friend Anymore, illustrated by Tony DeLuna. New York, Dutton, 1975.
Burton and Dudley, illustrated by Barbara Cooney. New York, Holiday House, 1975.
Maggie Marmelstein for President, illustrated by Ben Shecter. New York, Harper, 1975.
The Lancelot Closes at Five, illustrated by Lisl Weil. New York, Macmillan, 1976.
The Trip and Other Sophie and Gussie Stories, illustrated by Lillian Hoban. New York, Macmillan, 1976; Kingswood, Surrey, World's Work, 1978.
Edgemont, illustrated by Cyndy Szekeres. New York, Coward McCann, 1976.
Mooch the Messy, illustrated by Ben Shecter. New York, Harper, 1976; Kingswood, Surrey, World's Work, 1978.
I'm Terrific, illustrated by Kay Chorao. New York, Holiday House, 1977.
I Don't Care, illustrated by Lillian Hoban. New York, Macmillan, 1977.
A Big Fat Enormous Lie, illustrated by David McPhail. New York, Dutton, 1978.
Mitchell Is Moving, illustrated by Jose Aruego and Ariane Dewey. New York, Macmillan, 1978.
Thornton the Worrier, illustrated by Kay Chorao. New York, Holiday House, 1978.
Uncle Boris and Maude, illustrated by Sammis McLean. New York, Doubleday, 1979.
Mooch the Messy Meets Prudence the Neat, illustrated by Ben Shecter. New York, Coward McCann, 1979; Kingswood, Surrey, World's Work, 1980.
I Am Not a Pest, with Mitchell Sharmat, illustrated by Diane Dawson. New York, Dutton, 1979.
The 329th Friend, illustrated by Cyndy Szekeres. New York, Four Winds Press, 1979.
Scarlet Monster Lives Here, illustrated by Dennis Kendrick. New York, Harper, 1979.
Mr. Jameson and Mr. Phillips, illustrated by Bruce Degen. New York, Harper, and London, Harper & Row, 1979.
The Trolls of Twelfth Street, illustrated by Ben Shecter. New York, Coward McCann, 1979.
Octavia Told Me a Secret, illustrated by Roseanne Litzinger. New York, Four Winds Press, 1979.
Griselda's New Year, illustrated by Norman Chartier. New York, Macmillan, 1979.
Say Hello, Vanessa, illustrated by Lillian Hoban. New York, Holiday House, and Leamington Spa, Warwickshire, Scholastic, 1979.
Little Devil Gets Sick, illustrated by Marylin Hafner. New York, Doubleday, 1980.
What Are We Going to Do about Andrew?, illustrated by Ray Cruz. New York, Macmillan, 1980.
Sometimes Mama and Papa Fight, illustrated by Kay Chorao. New York, Harper, 1980.
Taking Care of Melvin, illustrated by Victoria Chess. New York, Holiday House, 1980.
The Day I Was Born, with Mitchell Sharmat, illustrated by Diane Dawson. New York, Dutton, 1980.
Grumley the Grouch, illustrated by Kay Chorao. New York, Holiday House, 1980.
Gila Monsters Meet You at the Airport, illustrated by Byron Barton. New York, Macmillan, 1980.
Twitchell the Wishful, illustrated by Janet Stevens. New York, Holiday House, 1981.
Chasing after Annie, illustrated by Marc Simont. New York, Harper, 1981.
Lucretia the Unbearable, illustrated by Janet Stevens. New York, Holiday House, 1981.
Rollo and Juliet, Forever!, illustrated by Marylin Hafner. New York, Doubleday, 1981.
The Best Valentine in the World, illustrated by Lillian Obligado. New York, Holiday House, 1982.
Two Ghosts on a Beach, illustrated by Nola Langner. New York, Harper, 1982.
Mysteriously Yours, Maggie Marmelstein, illustrated by Ben Shecter. New York, Harper, 1982.
Square Pegs (novelization of a television series). New York, Dell, 1982.
I Saw Him First. New York, Delacorte Press, and London, Transworld, 1983.
How to Meet a Gorgeous Guy. New York, Delacorte Press, and London, Transworld, 1983.
Frizzy the Fearful, illustrated by John Wallner. New York, Holiday House, 1983.
Rich Mitch, illustrated by Loretta Lustig. New York, Morrow, and Leamington Spa, Warwickshire, Scholastic, 1983.
Sasha the Silly, illustrated by Janet Stevens. New York, Holiday House, 1984.

Bartholomew the Bossy, illustrated by Normand Chartier. New York, Macmillan, 1984.
How to Meet a Gorgeous Girl. New York, Delacorte Press, 1984.
The Story of Bentley Beaver, illustrated by Lillian Hoban. New York, Harper, 1984; Kingswood, Surrey, World's Work, 1986.
He Noticed I'm Alive...And Other Hopeful Signs. New York, Delacorte Press, and London, Transworld, 1984.
My Mother Never Listens to Me, illustrated by Lynn Munsinger. Chicago, Whitman, 1984.
Attila the Angry, illustrated by Lillian Hoban. New York, Holiday House, 1985.
Two Guys Noticed Me...And Other Miracles. New York, Delacorte Press, and London, Transworld, 1985.
How to Have a Gorgeous Wedding. New York, Dell, 1985.
Get Rich Mitch!, illustrated by Loretta Lustig. New York, Morrow, 1985.
One Terrific Thanksgiving, illustrated Lillian Obligado. New York, Holiday House, 1985.
The Son of the Slime that Ate Cleveland, illustrated by Rodney Pate. New York, Dell, 1985.
Who's Afraid of Ernestine?, illustrated by Maxie Chambliss. New York, Coward McCann, 1986.
Sorority Sisters series: (*For Members Only; Snobs, Beware; I Think I'm Falling in Love; Fighting over Me; Nobody Knows How Scared I Am; Here Comes Mr. Right; Getting Closer; I'm Going to Get Your Boyfriend*). New York, Dell, 8 vols., 1986-87.
Hooray for Mother's Day! (*Father's Day!*), illustrated by John Wallner. New York, Holiday House, 2 vols., 1986-87.
Helga High-Up, illustrated by David Neuhaus. New York, Scholastic, 1987.
Go to Sleep, Nicholas Joe, illustrated by John Himmelman. New York, Harper, 1988.
The Pizza Monster, with Mitchell Sharmat, illustrated by Denise Brunkus. New York, Delacorte, and London, Pan Macmillan, 1989.
The Princess of the Fillmore Street School, with Mitchell Sharmat. New York, Delacorte, and London, Pan Macmillan, 1989.
School Bus Cat, with Andrew Sharmat. New York, HarperCollins, 1990.
The Cooking Class, with Andrew Sharmat. New York, HarperCollins, 1990.
The Sly Spy, with Mitchell Sharmat, illustrated by Denise Brunkus. New York, Delacorte, and London, Pan Macmillan, 1990.
I'm Santa Claus and I'm Famous, illustrated by Marilyn Hafner. New York, Holiday House, 1990.
Bully on the Bus, with Andrew Sharmat. New York, HarperCollins, 1991.
The Field Day Mix-up, with Andrew Sharmat. New York, HarperCollins, 1991.
The Green Toenails Gang, with Mitchell Sharmat, illustrated by Denise Brunkus. New York, Delacorte, and London, Pan Macmillan, 1991.
The Haunted Bus, with Andrew Sharmat. New York, HarperCollins, 1991.
I'm the Best! illustrated by Will Hillenbrand. New York, Holiday House, 1991.
The Secret Notebook, with Andrew Sharmat. New York, HarperCollins, 1991.
The Great Genghis Khan Look-alike Contest, illustrated by Mitchell Rigie. New York, Random House, 1993.
Genghis Khan: A Dog Star Is Born, illustrated by Mitchell Rigie. New York, Random House, 1994.
Genghis Khan: Dog-Gone Hollywood, illustrated by Mitchell Rigie. New York, Random House, 1995.
Tiffany Dino Works Out, illustrated by Nate Evans. New York, Simon & Schuster, 1995.

Nate the Great series:
Nate the Great, illustrated by Marc Simont. New York, Coward McCann, 1972; Kingswood, Surrey, World's Work, 1974.
Nate the Great Goes Undercover, illustrated by Marc Simont. New York, Coward McCann, 1974.
Nate the Great and the Lost List, illustrated by Marc Simont. New York, Coward McCann, 1975; Kingswood, Surrey, World's Work, 1977.
Nate the Great and the Phony Clue, illustrated by Marc Simont. New York, Coward McCann, 1977; Kingswood, Surrey, World's Work, 1979.
Nate the Great and the Sticky Case, illustrated by Marc Simont. New York, Coward McCann, 1978.
Nate the Great and the Missing Key, illustrated by Marc Simont. New York, Coward McCann, and Leamington Spa, Warwickshire, Scholastic, 1981.
Nate the Great and the Snowy Trail, illustrated by Marc Simont. New York, Coward McCann, 1982.
Nate the Great and the Fishy Prize, illustrated by Marc Simont. New York, Coward McCann, 1985.
Nate the Great Stalks Stupidweed, illustrated by Marc Simont. New York, Coward McCann, 1986.
Nate the Great and the Boring Beach Bag, illustrated by Marc Simont. New York, Coward McCann, 1987.
Nate the Great Goes down in the Dumps, illustrated by Marc Simont. New York, Putnam, 1989.
Nate the Great and the Halloween Hunt, illustrated by Marc Simont. New York, Coward McCann, 1989.
Nate the Great and the Musical Note, with Craig Sharmat, illustrated by Marc Simont. New York, Coward McCann, 1990.
Nate the Great and the Stolen Base, illustrated by Marc Simont. New York, Coward McCann, 1992.
Nate the Great and the Pillowcase, with Rosalind Weinman, illustrated by Marc Simont. New York, Delacorte, 1993.
Nate the Great and the Mushy Valentine, illustrated by Marc Simont. New York, Delacorte, 1994.
Nate the Great and the Tardy Tortoise, with Craig Sharmat, illustrated by Marc Simont. New York, Delacorte, 1995.
Nate the Great and the Crunchy Christmas, with Craig Sharmat, illustrated by Marc Simont. New York, Delacorte, 1996.
Nate the Great Saves the King of Sweden, illustrated by Marc Simont. New York, Delacorte, 1997.

Fiction as Wendy Andrews

Vacation Fever! New York, Putnam, 1984.
Supergirl Storybook (novelization of screenplay). New York, Putnam, 1984.
Are We There Yet? New York, Putnam, 1985.

Other

The Sign, illustrated by Pat Wong. Boston, Houghton Mifflin, 1981.

Surprises (reader), with Mitchell Sharmat. New York, Holt Rinehart, 1989.
Treasures (reader), with Mitchell Sharmat. New York, Holt Rinehart, 1989.
Kingdoms (reader), with Mitchell Sharmat. New York, Holt Rinehart, 1989.
The Perfects, illustrated by Mark Cocoran. New York, Macmillan/McGraw-Hill, 1995.

*

Biography: Entries in *Contemporary Authors, New Revision Series,* Detroit, Gale, Volume 39, 1992; *Something About the Author,* Detroit, Gale, Volume 74, 1993.

Manuscript Collections: Maine Women Writers Collection, Westbrook College, Portland, Maine; de Grummond Collection, University of Southern Mississippi, Hattiesburg.

Marjorie Weinman Sharmat comments:

I write picture books, easy readers, and novels for children and young adults. I have a resident pest in my head and that's why I'm a writer. This pest is never satisfied and constantly furnishes me with new ideas and nags me to get them on paper. I like to write funny books because I think that life is basically a serious business and needs a humorous counterbalance.

* * *

Marjorie Weinman Sharmat writes humorous stories for three age groups. Her first book, *Rex,* is a droll and imaginative tale of a small boy who has decided to be a dog and who is willing to bring the man next door his newspaper and slippers in his teeth to prove it. The gentle humor of her first story for preschoolers foreshadowed some of Sharmat's strongest features: a real originality in story concept, and the ability to work within the constraints of a simplified vocabulary list in a fresh and original manner. *Nate the Great,* a tale with echoes of James Bond's Secret Agent 007, tells of a nine-year-old detective, Nate, who can solve any case, from finding a lost cat to unearthing a purloined picture. Nate's dry humor engages readers while his actions give children lessons in deductive reasoning. Nate takes notes, interviews people, follows leads, keeps up his energy with plenty of pancakes, and takes time to think things through. But Nate is no Bond: he always leaves a note for his mother at the beginning of each case and he is glad, as he walks off into the rain at the end of the book, that he has taken his mother's advice and worn his rubbers. Nate is Sharmat's most enduring character; he has been solving mysteries for more than two decades.

Children who like the humor of *Nate the Great* also enjoy *Walter the Wolf,* a slyly humorous tale of a perfect young wolf who after years of practicing his violin, writing poetry, and never biting anybody decides to go into the biting business professionally. After his first "victim" bites him back, he decides that, although he is through trying to be perfect, biting is probably not the best way to make a living. *What Are We Going to Do about Andrew?* is a tale of a versatile lad whose parents find his ability to turn himself into a flying hippopotamus disconcerting. Written with deadpan humor not at all dampened by the controlled vocabulary, the book's unexpected ending will delight the child who feels that his parents do not appreciate his real worth.

I'm Not Oscar's Friend Anymore is representative of another literary genre exploited successfully in several of Sharmat's books for young children. In this juvenile stream-of-consciousness tale, Oscar's "former friend" thinks of all his reasons for being mad at Oscar and thinks how sad Oscar must be feeling now that he has just lost his best friend. He finally decides he will do Oscar a big favor and make up. Sharmat's attempt to re-create the thought process of a young child is handled with charm and wit and has the ring of truth about it. For children in the middle grades, Sharmat's books about urban sixth-grader Maggie Marmelstein and her sometime friend Thad Smith portray in a light-hearted and realistic manner the trials of being a sub-teenager.

Sharmat's novels for young adults include the ongoing *Sorority Sisters* series. These fast-paced and well-plotted short novels are characterized by Sharmat's humor and witty dialogue. However, although Sharmat writes successfully for both children and young adults, she is at her best when she is writing for the youngest children. The droll humor and the subtle charm of the best of her little books set them off as minor classics for preschoolers.

—Margaret F. Maxwell, updated by Judson Knight

SHARP, Margery

Nationality: British. **Born:** 25 January 1905. **Education:** Streatham Hill High School, London; Bedford College, University of London, B.A. (honours) in French. **Family:** Married Major Geoffrey Castle (died in 1990) in 1938. **Military Service:** Army education lecturer in World War II. **Died:** 14 March 1991.

PUBLICATIONS FOR CHILDREN

Fiction

The Rescuers, illustrated by Judith Brook. London, Collins, and Boston, Little Brown, 1959.
Miss Bianca, illustrated by Garth Williams. London, Collins, and Boston, Little Brown, 1962.
The Turret, illustrated by Garth Williams. Boston, Little Brown, 1963; London, Collins, 1964.
Lost at the Fair, illustrated by Rosalind Fry. Boston, Little Brown, 1965; London, Heinemann, 1967.
Miss Bianca in the Salt Mines, illustrated by Garth Williams. London, Heinemann, and Boston, Little Brown, 1966.
Miss Bianca in the Orient, illustrated by Erik Blegvad. London, Heinemann, and Boston, Little Brown, 1970.
Miss Bianca in the Antarctic, illustrated by Erik Blegvad. London, Heinemann, 1970; Boston, Little Brown, 1971.
Miss Bianca and the Bridesmaid, illustrated by Erik Blegvad. London, Heinemann, and Boston, Little Brown, 1972.
The Magical Cockatoo, illustrated by Faith Jaques. London, Heinemann, 1974.
The Children Next Door, illustrated by Hilary Abrahams. London, Heinemann, 1974.

Bernard the Brave, illustrated by Faith Jaques. London, Heinemann, 1976; Boston, Little Brown, 1977.
Bernard into Battle, illustrated by Leslie Morrill. London, Heinemann, and Boston, Little Brown, 1979.
The Rescuers Down Under. London, Boxtree, 1991.

Other

Mélisande, illustrated by Roy McKie. London, Collins, and Boston, Little Brown, 1960.

Publications for Adults

Novels

Rhododendron Pie. London, Chatto and Windus, and New York, Appleton, 1930.
Fanfare for Tin Trumpets. London, Barker, 1932; New York, Putnam, 1933.
The Nymph and the Nobleman. London, Barker, 1932.
The Flowering Thorn. London, Barker, 1933; New York, Putnam, 1934.
Sophy Cassmajor. London, Barker, and New York, Putnam, 1934.
Four Gardens. London, Barker, and New York, Putnam, 1935.
The Nutmeg Tree. London, Barker, and Boston, Little Brown, 1937.
Harlequin House. London, Collins, and Boston, Little Brown, 1939.
The Stone of Chastity. London, Collins, and Boston, Little Brown, 1940.
Three Companion Pieces: Sophy Cassmajor, The Tigress on the Hearth, and The Nymph and the Nobleman. Boston, Little Brown, 1941; *The Tigress on the Hearth* published separately, London, Collins, 1955.
Cluny Brown. London, Collins, and Boston, Little Brown, 1944.
Britannia Mews. London, Collins, and Boston, Little Brown, 1946.
The Foolish Gentlewoman. London, Collins, and Boston, Little Brown, 1948.
Lise Lillywhite. London, Collins, and Boston, Little Brown, 1951.
The Gipsy in the Parlour. London, Collins, 1953; Boston, Little Brown, 1954.
The Eye of Love. London, Collins, and Boston, Little Brown, 1957; as *Martha and the Eye of Love,* London, New English Library, 1969.
Something Light. London, Collins, 1960; Boston, Little Brown, 1961.
Martha in Paris. London, Collins, 1962; Boston, Little Brown, 1963.
Martha, Eric, and George. London, Collins, and Boston, Little Brown, 1964.
The Sun in Scorpio. London, Heinemann, and Boston, Little Brown, 1965.
In Pious Memory. Boston, Little Brown, 1967; London, Heinemann, 1968.
Rosa. London, Heinemann, 1969; Boston, Little Brown, 1970.
The Innocents. London, Heinemann, 1971; Boston, Little Brown, 1972.
The Faithful Servants. London, Heinemann, and Boston, Little Brown, 1975.
Summer Visits. London, Heinemann, 1977; Boston, Little Brown, 1978.

Short Stories

The Lost Chapel Picnic and Other Stories. London, Heinemann, and Boston, Little Brown, 1973.

Plays

Meeting at Night (produced London, 1934).
Lady in Waiting, adaptation of her novel *The Nutmeg Tree* (produced New York, 1940; as *The Nutmeg Tree,* produced London, 1941). New York, French, 1941.
The Foolish Gentlewoman, adaptation of her own novel (produced London, 1949). London, French, 1950.
The Birdcage Room (television play), 1954.

*

Manuscript Collections: Houghton Library, Harvard University, Cambridge, Massachusetts.

* * *

Margery Sharp, as a children's writer, was primarily the creator of Miss Bianca. When, in *The Magical Cockatoo,* she abandoned this enchanting mouse for the adventures of a little Victorian girl, her work seemed thinner. Although the book has Sharp's usual wit and some entertaining social satire, Lally's adventures are mostly too trivial to arouse much suspense or sympathy. But the Miss Bianca series is caviare for any age—a sophisticated taste, addictive to those who acquire it.

The first of them, *The Rescuers,* is still for many readers the most delightful of all. It is here we first see the Mouse Prisoners' Aid Society in action, when Miss Bianca, the white mouse from the Embassy (later the Society's President), sets out with the plebeian Bernard and the nautical Norwegian mouse Nils, to rescue a poet from the Black Castle. Their horrific encounters with the warder's cat arouse real suspense and excitement.

In the later stories we are often reminded of the minute size of the mice, but in other respects they are more anthropomorphic than rodent. The characters remain unchanged, except that the low-born Bernard's devotion to Miss Bianca, originally rather touching, becomes imperceptibly a satirical absurdity. But Sharp's inventiveness was inexhaustible. Miss Bianca finds herself in the most dramatic and exciting situations, whether freezing in Antarctic wastes, lost in a salt-mine, exploring the main drain of the Embassy, or playing the harp to a cruel Ranee whose attendants are all too frequently condemned to be trampled to death by elephants. Her hairbreadth escapes from these dangers are as wittily contrived as they are unexpected. Bernard's mackintosh is inflated as a raft and wafted by cheerful gangs of juvenile delinquent bats; Miss Bianca captivates an elephant; they encounter a group of marble angels in a crypt, dispossessed from an old churchyard but consoling themselves with a rendering of "All Things Bright and Beautiful"—naturally in the manner of "a perfectly trained ladies-voice choir" with harp accompaniment.

Much of the humour derives from ironic contrast—the elegant sophistication of Miss Bianca's life and surroundings, mouse though she is, or her aristocratic culture set against Bernard's worthy but innocently vulgar tastes.

Only a child who reads well can fully enjoy these books, for their subtlest appeal is that of language itself, a delight in words and the rhythm of words for their own sake, a pleasure in a consciously mannered and elaborate diction akin to the pleasures of social ceremony, and the satirist's pleasure in impish and unexpected bathos:

> "What traces could there be but of blood upon these bricks, from the child's tender, bare feet? If only she had her bedroom slippers!" sighed Miss Bianca. "To be unshod makes for one danger more."
>
> "You mean she might pick up athlete's foot?" suggested Bernard sympathetically.

These are books for the connoisseur, and blessedly have no design at all upon the reader except that of entertainment.

—Margaret Greaves

SHERRY, Sylvia

Nationality: British. **Born:** Newcastle-upon-Tyne, Northumberland. **Education:** Heaton High School, and Kenton Lodge College of Education, both Newcastle-, King's College, University of Durham (Spence Watson prize), B,A. in English. **Family:** Married to Norman Sherry. **Career:** Assistant mistress, Primary School and Girls' High School, and Lecturer, College of Education, 1955-60, all Newcastle; lived in Singapore, 1960-64. **Agent:** Jonathan Clowes Ltd., 22 Prince Albert Road, London NW1 7ST, England.

Publications for Children

Fiction

Street of the Small Night Market. London, Cape, 1966; as *Secret of the Jade Pavilion,* Philadelphia, Lippincott, 1967.
Frog in a Coconut Shell. London, Cape, and Philadelphia, Lippincott, 1968.
A Pair of Jesus-Boots. London, Cape, 1969; as *The Liverpool Cats,* Philadelphia, Lippincott, 1969.
The Loss of the "Night Wind". London, Cape, 1970; as *The Haven Screamers,* Philadelphia, Lippincott, 1970.
A Snake in the Old Hut. London, Cape, 1972; Nashville, Nelson, 1973.
Dark River, Dark Mountain. London, Cape, 1975.
Mat, The Little Monkey, illustrated by Janusz Grabianski. London, Dent, and New York, Crane Russak, 1977.
A Pair of Desert-Wellies. London, Cape, 1985.
Rocky and the Ratman. London, Cape, 1988.
Rocky and the Black Eye Mystery. London, Cape, 1992.
Elephants Have Right of Way, illustrated by Quentin Blake. London, Cape, 1995.

Plays

Little Pig (television series), 1976.
It's Our Turn (television series), 1977.

Publications for Adults

Novels

Girl in a Blue Shawl. London, Hamish Hamilton, 1978.
South of Red River. London, Hamish Hamilton, 1981.

*

Sylvia Sherry comments:

A novel for me begins with a place—a village, town, or particular area—and I do a lot of work finding out about the place and the people who live there. I hope to find the people I will write about in that setting. For example, Ah Wong, hero of my first novel, derived from a boy I saw working at a food stall in a street in Singapore at midnight. He was about 12 and was walking along the street tapping two pieces of bamboo together to tell people the noodle dish his stall made was ready. I hope also that the story will come out of the setting and will be an adventure that could happen only there. *The Loss of the "Night Wind"* was based on the loss of an actual fishing boat off the Northumberland coast. I like to travel and so my novels have a variety of settings. My aim is to create authentic characters in an authentic setting with an adventure plot. However, my four novels about Rocky O'Rourke, all set in Liverpool, have been the most popular of my children's fiction, and I hope this is because of their authenticity and adventure and their reflection of the true Liverpool atmosphere.

* * *

The consistent strength of Sylvia Sherry's novels from 1965 onwards has been the evocation of a distinctive place and period, whether it be contemporary Liverpool, the Lancashire moors in 1940, or a Malaysian coastal village at the time of the post-war Indonesian incursion. In all the full-length novels—which have tended to become more complex over the years—the central character is an enterprising boy aged 12 to 15, who overcomes some daunting peril by luck, courage, or blundering recklessness. The other characters are mainly adults, often hostile or unsympathetic to the hero, and rarely displaying any of the exemplary qualities which used to be normal in writings for children. Sherry does show considerable skill in building up tension gradually through several short chapters while setting the scene, but her denouements and endings are apt to be disappointing.

Three of Sherry's eleven books for children seem to require little comment. One, *Mat, The Little Monkey,* is a collection of picture stories for six to eight year-olds. Two others, *The Loss of the "Night Wind"* and *Dark River, Dark Mountain,* may be described as good average mystery stories with strong local colour. The former has an interesting background of fishing boats and birdwatching in the Lindisfame area, and the early development of its plot is both plausible and intriguing; but the explanation depends too much on an unlikely conspiracy of silence and an even stranger suppression of evidence by the hero and his friend. *Dark River, Dark Mountain* is more consistently credible, with the atmosphere of suspicion and spy-fever in a remote community, after Dunkirk, ringing absolutely true. The characters, however, are particularly unlikable and the ending is likely to leave many readers dissatisfied.

In the 1990s Sherry is certainly best known for her four Liverpool-based stories, *A Pair of Jesus-Boots,* televised in the 1970s, and the three sequels which have followed it after a long interval. The first story introduces 13-year-old Rocky O'Rourke and his ill-assorted gang of friends, together with his far from idyllic family; his mother comes across as a dim-witted slut, his brother is a boastful, cowardly rogue, while his small stepsister is severely disturbed and almost speechless. The use of an undiluted Liverpudlian dialect by all the characters presents another possible stumbling block, yet the story has enough pace and vivacity to keep one reading. The ending is hopeful, with Rocky rewarded for heroism and showing signs of a wiser outlook. Surprisingly, when we meet him again in the first sequel, *A Pair of Desert-Wellies,* he is as reckless as ever, and apparently dedicated to shoplifting and petty theft.

Here and in the two further sequels he triumphs over real villains more through luck and impulsive courage than by taking thought. The sinister villain of the third story, the ratman, is a particularly striking creation. In the fourth story Rocky foils a kidnapping plot and at the end has the prospect of financial security, but it seems that the author wishes us to feel that he, like the slum-culture of Liverpool itself, is virtually incorrigible.

Sherry has been rightly acclaimed for her skill in portraying an English inner-city milieu through teenage eyes, but her success in applying the same technique to overseas settings has perhaps been undervalued. Her first two books, set in Singapore and Malaysia respectively, have conventional plots and predictable happy endings, but they also do full justice to her remarkable grasp of a community's social mechanisms and changing lifestyles. This facility is equally impressive in Sherry's 1972 novel, *A Snake in the Old Hut,* which in my opinion is also her finest achievement in the way of a gripping and stimulating narrative. The place this time is Kenya and the theme that of divided loyalties, treachery, and vengeance in a climate of violence. Among adventure stories which both inform the reader and invite him to think about moral issues, this little-known novel will stand comparison with the best.

In 1995 Sherry wrote again about Kenya, but with a very different approach. *Elephants Have Right of Way* is a short, unpretentious tale about Kamau and Mr Singh, the one a humble country boy with the ambition to better himself, the other a garage owner in Nairobi who dreams of running a Rolls Royce. Their chequered progress towards success makes for lively reading, with an effective climax. Presented in the format of a picture-book, this is clearly not intended for the youngest age range, but would probably appeal most to ten-plus readers with an interest in Africa.

—Alasdair K. D. Campbell

SHULEVITZ, Uri

Nationality: Polish. **Born:** Warsaw, Poland, 27 February 1935; became naturalized American citizen. **Education:** Teacher's College, Israel, teacher's degree, 1956; attended Tel-Aviv Art Institute, 1953-55, and Brooklyn Museum Art School, 1959-61. **Family:** Married Helene Weiss, 1961 (divorced). **Military Service:** Israeli Army 1956-1959. **Career:** Kibbutz Ein Geddi, Israel, member, 1957-58; art director of youth magazine in Israel, 1958-59; illustrator of children's books, since 1961; author of children's books, since 1962. Instructor in art, School of Visual Arts, New York City, 1967-68, and Pratt Institute, Brooklyn, New York, 1970-71; instructor in art and in writing and illustrating children's books, New School for Social Research, 1970-86; director of summer workshop in writing and illustrating children's books, Hartwick College, Oneonta, New York, 1974-1992. Work has been exhibited in numerous galleries and museums, including Tel Aviv Museum, A.M. Sachs Gallery, New York City, Metropolitan Museum of Art, New York City, and New York Public Library. **Awards:** Children's Book Award, American Institute of Graphic Arts, 1963-64, for *Charley Sang a Song,* 1965-66, for *The Second Witch,* and 1967-68, for *One Monday Morning*; Certificate of Excellence, American Institute of Graphic Arts, 1973-74, for *The Magician* and *The Fools of Chelm and Their History,* and 1979, for *The Treasure*; Certificate of Merit, Society of Illustrators, New York, 1965, for *Charlie Sang a Song*; Caldecott Medal, American Library Association, and American Booksellers Gift to the Nation from the Library of the White House, both 1969, both for *The Fool of the World and the Flying Ship*; Children's Book of the Year, Child Study Association of America, 1969, for *Rain Rain Rivers,* 1972, for *Soldier and Tsar in the Forest: A Russian Tale,* 1974, for *Dawn,* and 1976, for *The Touchstone*; Bronze Medal, Leipzig International Book Exhibition, 1970, for *Rain Rain Rivers*; *Book World*'s Children's Spring Book Festival Picture Book honor, 1972, for *Soldier and Tsar in the Forest: A Russian Tale,* and 1973, for *The Magician*; *New York Times* Outstanding Books of the Year list, 1973, and Children's Book Showcase of the Children's Book Council, 1974, for *The Magician*; *New York Times* Outstanding Books of the Year list, 1974, Christopher Award, 1975, Children's Book Showcase of the Children's Book Council, 1975, International Board of Books for Young People honor list, 1976, and Brooklyn Art Books for Children Citation, 1976, 1977, and 1978, all for *Dawn*; *New York Times* Best Illustrated Books of the Year list, 1978, for *Hanukah Money,* 1979, for *The Treasure,* and 1997, for *Hosni the Dreamer*; certificate from Graphic Arts Awards of the Printing Industries of America, 1979, and Caldecott Honor Book, 1980, both for *The Treasure*; *New York Times* Outstanding Books of the Year list, *School Library Journal*'s Best Children's Books, both 1982, and Parents' Choice Award, Parents' Choice Foundation, 1983, all for *The Golem.* **Address:** c/o Farrar, Straus and Giroux, Inc., 19 Union Square West, New York, New York 10003, U.S.A.

Publications for Children

Fiction (illustrated by author)

The Moon in My Room. New York, Harper, 1963.
One Monday Morning. New York, Scribner, 1967.
Rain Rain Rivers. New York, Farrar, Straus, and Giroux, 1969.
The Magician. New York, Macmillan, 1973.
Dawn. New York, Farrar, Straus and Giroux, 1974.
The Treasure. New York, Farrar, Straus, and Giroux, 1979.
The Strange and Exciting Adventures of Jeremiah Hush. New York, Farrar, Straus and Giroux, 1986.
Toddlecreek Post Office. New York, Farrar, Straus and Giroux, 1990.
The Secret Room. New York, Farrar, Straus and Giroux, 1993.
Snow. New York, Farrar, Straus and Giroux, 1998.

Reteller, *The Golden Goose,* by the Brothers Grimm. New York, Farrar, Straus, and Giroux, 1995.

Publication for Adults

Writing with Pictures: How to Write and Illustrate Children's Books. Watson-Guptill, 1985.

*

Media Adaptations: *One Monday Morning* (film), Weston, Connecticut, Weston Woods, 1972, (filmstrip), 1973; *The Fool of the World and the Flying Ship* (cassette), Weston Woods, 1980; *The Treasure,* Weston Woods, 1980; *Dawn* (filmstrip with cassette), Weston Woods, 1982.

Biography: *Critical Studies: Newbery and Caldecott Medal Books: 1966-1975,* edited by Lee Kingman, Boston, Horn Book, 1975; *Illustrators of Children's Books: 1967-1976,* compiled by Lee Kingman and others, Boston, Horn Book, 1978; entry *Something about the Author,* Detroit, Gale Research, Vol. 50, 1988, 189-203.

Illustrator: *A Rose, a Bridge, and a Wild Black Horse* by Charlotte Zolotow, 1964; *The Mystery of the Woods* by Mary Stolz, 1964; *Charley Sang a Song* by H.R. Hays and Daniel Hays, 1964; *The Second Witch* by Jack Sendak, 1965; *Who Knows Ten? Children's Tales of the Ten Commandments,* 1965; *The Twelve Dancing Princesses* by Jacob Grimm and Wilhelm Grimm, translated by Elizabeth Shub, 1966; *Maximilian's World* by Mary Stolz, 1966; *The Silkspinners* by Jean Russell Larson, 1967; *The Month Brothers* by Dorothy Nathan, 1967; *My Kind of Verse,* edited by John Smith, 1968; *Runaway Jonah and Other Tales* by Jan Wahl, 1968; *The Fool of the World and the Flying Ship: A Russian Tale,* adapted by Arthur Ransome, 1968; *The Wonderful Kite* by Jan Wahl, 1971; *Treasure of the Turkish Pasha* by Yehoash Biber, translated from Hebrew by Baruch Hochman, 1971; *The Soldier and Tsar in the Forest: A Russian Tale,* translated by Richard Lourie, 1972; *The Fools of Chelm and Their History* by Isaac Bashevis Singer, 1973; *The Touchstone* by Robert Louis Stevenson, 1976; *Hanukah Money* by Sholem Aleichem, 1978; *The Lost Kingdom of Karnica* by Richard Kennedy, 1979; *The Golem* by Isaac Bashevis Singer, 1982; *Lilith's Cave: Jewish Tales of the Supernatural* by Howard Schwartz, 1988; *The Diamond Tree: Jewish Tales from Around the World,* selected and retold by Howard Schwartz and Barbara Rush, 1991; *Hosni the Dreamer: An Arabian Tale* by Ehud Ben-Ezer, 1997.

Uri Shulevitz comments:

I eventually understood that my initial fear that I could not write was based on a preconception that writing was strictly related to words and to spoken language. I had assumed that using many words skillfully was central to writing. I was overlooking what was of primary importance—*what* I had to say. And I was overwhelmed by what was of secondary importance—*how* to say it.

Once I understood that *what* I had to say was of primary importance, I began to concentrate on what would happen in my story. First I visualized the action, and then I thought of how to say it in words. I realized that all I had to do was communicate the action as simply as possible. The few words necessary to communicate the story fell into place on their own. It was all so simple and natural.

It also dawned on me that I could channel my natural inclination to visualize into my writing. Assuming that each of us has a preference for one of the sense perceptions, we can capitalize on that preference in our writing. Since I am inclined to see pictures, a visual approach makes sense. That is how I wrote my first book, *The Moon in My Room*; the story unfolded in my head like a movie. I was the camera seeing the action conveyed by pictures.

Furthermore, the use of this visual approach, with which I have always felt at ease, released a flow of images I hadn't experienced before. There was no doubt, *writing with pictures* was my way. Years later, I learned that when writing, C. S. Lewis saw pictures, too; that with him, "images always come first."

The approach I used for the illustrations for *The Moon in My Room* was derived from drawings I did one day while talking on the telephone. As I talked I doodled, and I noticed they had a fresh look; the lines appeared to be moving across the page. Looking back, I am amazed that this happened so unexpectedly, for in addition to my preconception about writing, I also had a preconceived idea of how an illustration evolves. I had assumed it would require much effort. But instead, while my mind was busy with the phone conversation, I let the lines flow effortlessly through my hand onto the paper; they seemed to have a life and an intelligence of their own. The lines led my hand, and my hand followed without imposing my desires on those lines. True, it subsequently took considerable work and effort to develop the doodles into appropriate illustrations, but that was at a later stage.

* * *

Warsaw-born Uri Shulevitz began drawing at the age of three, encouraged by his mother, who was an artist herself. The Warsaw blitz of World War II occurred when Shulevitz was four years old, and he remembers all too well streets caving in, buildings burning. Soon after the bombing his family fled and for the next eight years they were wanderers, settling in Paris in 1947. Shulevitz went to college and art school in Israel and then in 1959 he came to the United States, becoming a U.S. citizen a few years later. For two years he attended the Brooklyn Museum Art School, and he has lived in and around New York City ever since.

Early in his career Shulevitz won the Caldecott Medal for his illustrations of the Russian folktale *The Fool of the World and the Flying Ship.* He has consistently won praise for his works through decades of productivity.

In his book on how to write and illustrate children's books, Shulevitz encourages experimentation. In his own work he experiments with the use of pen and ink, watercolor, Japanese reed pen, and Chinese brush. Some books use a strong palette of rainbow colors; others, equally compelling, are in black and white. Some books bring to life ancient folk tales that are in essence morality plays; others describe the joys of a rainfall or a dawn breaking. Shulevitz views creating a picture book much like composing a painting; you have to arrange the parts into a unified whole. Storyboard and book dummy need to complement each other to transform the pages into a book. Shulevitz's approach to the task has changed since he first started illustrating books. For his first book he made actual size, finished dummies; for later books he made small rough dummies and storyboards only. He makes as many storyboards and small dummies as necessary and goes back and forth from one to another to plan the book.

Shulevitz cautions the would-be illustrator not to strive for a perfect picture but to concentrate on making the picture come alive. If the picture is worked on too long, he observes, the end product may be more polished but the spontaneity of the original sketch may disappear.

Shulevitz's works do have enormous energy and wit, whether he is telling his own tale or illustrating the tale of another master storyteller. *One Monday Morning* is his adaptation of an old French folksong. It is the story of a young boy who lives in a bleak tenement and who daydreams that one Monday morning the King, the Queen, and the little Prince come to visit him. It is a happy dream, with gorgeous playing-card-type King, Queen, and Prince, marching through the child's own drab home.

The Fool of the World and the Flying Ship is an ancient Russian folk tale. The Fool, a peasant looked down upon by his parents, wins the hand of the Czar's daughter by his own cleverness. The draftsmanship in this book is superb, and the bold colors—reds, blues, yellows, greens—leap out of the pages. The lyrical movements of the flying ship also command attention.

Rain Rain Rivers and *Dawn* are celebrations of nature from the vantage point of the child. The illustrations, with their quiet shapes and soft pastels, herald the beauty of the world around. In *Rain Rain Rivers,* a little girl, snug inside her home, sees and hears the rain and imagines what she can do in the puddles when it is over. In *Dawn* a young boy and his grandfather awake from their sleep under a tree by the lake. The moon goes down, and a slow dawn appears. The two take their rowboat and move into the lake. Shulevitz has illustrated Isaac Bashevis Singer's wise and witty story *The Fools of Chelm and Their History* with simple black-and-white line drawings. His humorous and lively illustrations provide a perfect backdrop for the droll story.

Another folktale retold and illustrated by Shulevitz is *The Treasure.* There once was an old man by the name of Isaac who was very poor. In a dream he is told to go to the capital city and look for a treasure under the bridge by the Royal Palace. When Isaac explains to the Captain of the Royal Guards why he is on the bridge, the man advises him to go back home and look for a treasure under his own stove. When he gets home he finds the treasure. "Sometimes one must travel far to discover what is near." The old man's journey is shown in quiet pastels, with rhythmic movement and careful detail.

More recently Shulevitz has illustrated *The Diamond Tree: Jewish Tales from Around the World,* selected and retold by Schwartz and Rush. Here his full page illustrations show the breadth of his artistic range. Some of the pictures are in soft colors, others are in loud, vibrant colors. His picture of the giant Og who helped Noah save one pair of every kind of animal to bring to the ark, and then gets to sit on the roof of the ark as reward, is hilarious. His picture of another giant who cut down the tree whose top branches touched the sky shows a mighty force whose muscular strength bulges out from head to feet. His picture of the people of Chelm has all the colors of the rainbow present in their clothing. Shulevitz displays a wonderful sense of humor and drama when he tackles a folk tale.

The Grimm story *The Golden Goose* has brilliant pictures, including one of a big ship that can sail on both water and land. This ship looks much like his flying ship of almost thirty years earlier. Like the former, it is an elegant vessel, a vessel anyone would be proud to own, a vessel that just might take you anywhere you would like to go.

Shulevitz brings magic and joy to a book. He gets to the heart of the matter with folk tales, and he enlivens and enriches new tales. His adroit combination of text and pictures provides a fine read.

—Mary Lystad

SILLY, E.S. See **KRAUS, Robert.**

SILVERSTEIN, Shel(by)

Pseudonym: Uncle Shelby. **Nationality:** American. **Born:** Chicago, Illinois, in 1932. **Military Service:** United States forces, Japan and Korea, 1950s. **Family:** Divorced; one daughter. **Career:** Former correspondent for *Pacific Stars and Stripes.* Freelance cartoonist and writer for *Playboy,* Chicago, since 1956, and other magazines; also composer and songwriter. **Awards:** George C. Stone Center for Children's Books award, 1984 (twice). **Address:** c/o HarperCollins, 10 East 53rd Street, New York, New York 10022, U.S.A.

PUBLICATIONS FOR CHILDREN (ILLUSTRATED BY THE AUTHOR)

Fiction

Uncle Shelby's ABZ Book: A Primer for Tender Young Minds. New York, Simon and Schuster, 1961.
Uncle Shelby's Story of Lafcadio, The Lion Who Shot Back. New York, Harper, 1963.
Who Wants a Cheap Rhinoceros? (as Uncle Shelby). New York, Macmillan, 1964; revised edition, 1983; London, Cape, 1988.
The Giving Tree. New York, Harper, 1964; London, Cape, 1987.
The Missing Piece. New York, Harper, 1976.
The Missing Piece Meets the Big O. New York, Harper, 1981.

Poetry

Uncle Shelby's a Giraffe and a Half. New York, Harper, 1964; as *A Giraffe and a Half,* London, Cape, 1988.
Uncle Shelby's Zoo: Don't Bump the Glump! New York, Simon and Schuster, and London, W.H. Allen, 1964.
Where the Sidewalk Ends: The Poems and Drawings of Shel Silverstein. New York, Harper, 1974; London, Cape, 1984.
A Light in the Attic: Poems and Drawings. New York, Harper, 1981; London, Cape, 1982.
Falling Up: Poems and Drawings. New York, HarperCollins, 1996.

Recording: *Where the Sidewalk Ends,* Columbia, 1984.

PUBLICATIONS FOR ADULTS

Plays

Gorilla (also director: produced Chicago, 1983).
Wild Life (includes *I'm Good to My Doggies, Chicken Suit Optional, The Lady or the Tiger Show*; produced New York, 1983).
Remember Crazy Zelda? (produced New York, 1984).
The Happy Hour (produced New York, 1985).
The Crate (produced New York, 1985).
One Tennis Shoe (produced New York, 1985).
Wash and Dry (produced New York, 1986).

Little Feet (produced New York, 1986).
Things Change (screenplay), with David Mamet. New York, Grove Press, 1988.
The Devil and Billy Markham (produced London, 1991).
Oh, Hell! (two one-act plays), with David Mamet. New York and London, French, 1991.

Contributor, *The Best American Short Plays 1992-1993: The Theatre Annual since 1937.* Applause Theatre Book Publishers, 1993.

Other (drawings)

Now Here's My Plan: A Book of Futilities. New York, Simon and Schuster, 1960.
Playboy's Teevee Jeebies. Chicago, Playboy Press, 1963.
More Playboy Teevee Jeebies. Chicago, Playboy Press, 1965.
Different Dances. New York, Harper, 1979.

*

Theatrical Activities:
Director: **Play**—*Gorilla*, Chicago, 1983.

Actor: **Film**—*Who Is Harry Kellerman and Why Is He Saying Those Terrible Things about Me?* (film), 1971.

Media Adaptations: *Things Change,* Columbia Pictures, 1988.

* * *

It is easy to dismiss Shel Silverstein as a facile versifier with the knack of combining just the right amount of sentiment and impudence to assure mass appeal, but that would not be doing him justice. Literary merit aside, Silverstein, like Dr. Seuss and Judy Blume, is a force to be reckoned with. He can be weirdly idiosyncratic and even blatantly commercial. Yet the oddities among his collected works should not be allowed to mask a body of solid achievement in the form of three books well on their way to becoming classics: *The Giving Tree, Where the Sidewalk Ends,* and *A Light in the Attic.*

The Giving Tree is a deceptively simple parable about a tree that gives all it has to the little boy it loves. The text is as spare as Silverstein's drawings, which call to mind the cerebral cartoons of Jules Feiffer. In the end the tree is a stump and the boy an embittered old man. Critical interpretations are contradictory, telling more about the reader than the book. Ministers have read it from the pulpit as an allegory of Christian self-sacrifice; feminists have denounced it as advocating the exploitation of women. Uncle Shelby's only comment is that it is a story about a tree and a boy. One suspects him laughing in his beard.

No discussion of children's poetry can ignore *Where the Sidewalk Ends* and *A Light in the Attic.* For better or worse, the monumental success of these two books has transformed the way poetry is taught in American schools. What was once pretty and safe has now become wicked and nasty. Silverstein has spawned a host of imitators, most notably Jack Prelutsky. Jim Trelease, with Silverstein in mind, maintains that the first requirement of children's verse is that it be funny. Myra Cohn Livingston and other critics have protested against the crudity, violence, and mediocre writing currently passing itself off as children's poetry. However the worst of this is usually the work of imitators rather than of Silverstein himself.

Silverstein is by no stretch of the imagination a great poet. His verse reflects his background as a country songwriter. Plodding meters carry his rhymes and couplets. He alternates between naughtiness and sentimentality. He finds his best imagery in the garbage can: "Sarah Cynthia Sylvia Stout Would Not Take the Garbage Out." Nothing in Silverstein's work compares to the originality, lyric sense, and genuine feeling of Karla Kuskin, Valerie Worth, Myra Cohn Livingston, and Eve Merriam. Even so, it is hard to say whether this is the best Silverstein can do or if he is keeping a canny eye on his audience. His poems read like those a fourth grader would write in the back of his notebook when the teacher's eye was turned. That may be precisely their appeal.

Silverstein continued his entertaining versifying and comical line drawings in *Falling Up.* The collection contains plenty of nonsense, both in language and in situations: puns ("Little Hoarse"), naughtiness ("Gardener"), and other humor, magnified by his exaggerated, bold drawings. One drawing, for "Hungry Kid Island," is a departure from the rest because its humor is more subtle than usual. Although grammarians may shudder from time to time, children will find this collection of unusual people and situations a welcome addition to his earlier work.

Whatever his literary shortcomings, by convincing millions of children that poetry is neither difficult nor threatening, Silverstein has earned himself an honorable place among the great names in writing for children.

—Eric A. Kimmel, updated by Marilyn F. Apseloff

SINGER, Isaac Bashevis

Nationality: American (originally Polish: immigrated to the United States, 1935; became citizen, 1943). **Born:** Icek-Hersz Zynger in Leoncin, Poland, 14 July 1904. **Education:** Religious primary schools in Radzymin and, from 1908, Warsaw, and schools in Bilgorny, 1917-20; Tachkemoni Rabbinical Seminary, Warsaw, 1921-22. **Family:** Married Alma Haimann in 1940; one son from earlier marriage. **Career:** Proofreader and translator, *Literarishe Bleter,* Warsaw, 1923-33; associate editor, *Globus,* Warsaw, 1933-35; journalist, *Vorwärts* (*Jewish Daily Forward*) Yiddish newspaper, New York, from 1935. Founder, *Svivah* literary magazine. **Awards:** Louis Lamed prize, 1950, 1956; American Academy grant, 1959; Daroff Memorial award, 1963; Foreign Book prize (France), 1965; two National Endowment for the Arts grants, 1966; Bancarella prize (Italy), 1968; Brandeis University Creative Arts award, 1969; National Book award, 1970, and for fiction, 1974; Association of Jewish Libraries Sydney Taylor award, 1971; Nobel Prize for Literature, 1978; Kenneth Smilen Present Tense award, 1980. D.H.L.: Hebrew Union College, Los Angeles, 1963; D.Lit.: Colgate University, Hamilton, New York, 1972; D.Litt.: Texas Christian University, Fort Worth, 1972; Ph.D.: Hebrew University, Jerusalem, 1973; Litt.D.: Bard College, Annandale-on-Hudson, New York, 1974; Long Island University, Greenvale, New York, 1979. **Member:** American Academy, 1965; American Academy of Arts and Sciences, 1969; Jewish Academy of Arts and Sciences; Polish Institute of Arts and Sciences. **Died:** 24 July 1991.

Publications for Children (translated by the author and Elizabeth Shub)

Fiction

Zlateh the Goat and Other Stories, illustrated by Maurice Sendak. New York, Harper, 1966; London, Longman, 1970.
Mazel and Shlimazel; or, The Milk of a Lioness, illustrated by Margot Zemach. New York, Farrar Straus, 1967; London, Cape, 1979.
The Fearsome Inn, illustrated by Nonny Hogrogian. New York, Scribner, 1967; London, Collins, 1970.
When Shlemiel Went to Warsaw and Other Stories, translated by Channah Kleinerman-Goldstein and others, illustrated by Margot Zemach. New York, Farrar Straus, 1968; London, Longman, 1974.
Joseph and Koza; or, The Sacrifice to the Vistula, illustrated by Symeon Shimin. New York, Farrar Straus, 1970; London, Hamish Hamilton, 1984.
Alone in the Wild Forest, illustrated by Margot Zemach. New York, Farrar Straus, 1971; Edinburgh, Canongate, 1980.
The Topsy-Turvy Emperor of China, illustrated by William Pène du Bois. New York, Harper, 1971.
The Fools of Chelm and Their History, illustrated by Uri Shulevitz. New York, Farrar Straus, 1973.
A Tale of Three Wishes, illustrated by Irene Lieblich. New York, Farrar Straus, 1976.
Naftali the Storyteller and His Horse, Sus, and Other Stories, translated by the author and others, illustrated by Margot Zemach. New York, Farrar Straus, 1976; London, Oxford University Press, 1977.
The Power of Light: Eight Stories for Hanukkah, illustrated by Irene Lieblich. New York, Farrar Straus, 1980; London, Robson, 1983.
The Golem, illustrated by Uri Shulevitz. New York, Farrar Straus, 1982; London, Deutsch, 1983.
Stories for Children. New York, Farrar Straus, 1984.
Meshugah, translated by the author and Nili Wachtel. New York, Farrar, Straus, 1994.

Other

A Day of Pleasure: Stories of a Boy Growing Up in Warsaw (autobiographical), translated by Channah Kleinerman-Goldstein and others, photographs by Roman Vishniac. New York, Farrar Straus, 1969; London, MacRae, 1980.
Elijah the Slave: A Hebrew Legend Retold, illustrated by Antonio Frasconi. New York, Farrar Straus, 1970.
The Wicked City, illustrated by Leonard Everett Fisher. New York, Farrar Straus, 1972.
Why Noah Chose the Dove, illustrated by Eric Carle. New York, Farrar Straus, 1974.

Publications for Adults

Novels

The Family Moskat, translated by A.H. Gross. New York, Knopf, 1950; London, Secker and Warburg, 1966.
Satan in Goray, translated by Jacob Sloan. New York, Farrar Straus, 1955; London, Owen, 1958.
The Magician of Lublin, translated by Elaine Gottlieb and Joseph Singer. New York, Farrar Straus, 1960; London, Secker and Warburg, 1961.
The Slave, translated by the author and Cecil Hemley. New York, Farrar Straus, 1962; London, Secker and Warburg, 1963.
The Manor, translated by Elaine Gottlieb and Joseph Singer. New York, Farrar Straus, 1967; London, Secker and Warburg, 1968.
The Estate, translated by Joseph Singer, Elaine Gottlieb, and Elizabeth Shub. New York, Farrar Straus, 1969; London, Cape, 1970.
Enemies: A Love Story, translated by Aliza Shevrin and Elizabeth Shub. New York, Farrar Straus, and London, Cape, 1972.
Shosha, translated by Joseph Singer. New York, Farrar Straus, 1978; London, Cape, 1979.
Reaches of Heaven. New York, Farrar Straus, 1980; London, Faber, 1982.
The Penitent. New York, Farrar Straus, 1983; London, Cape, 1984.
King of the Fields. New York, Farrar Straus, 1988; London, Cape, 1989.
Scum, translated by Rosaline D. Schwartz. New York, Farrar, Straus, and London, Cape, 1991.

Short Stories

Gimpel the Fool and Other Stories, translated by Saul Bellow and others. New York, Farrar Straus, 1957; London, Owen, 1958.
The Spinoza of Market Street and Other Stories, translated by Elaine Gottlieb and others. New York, Farrar Straus, 1961; London, Secker and Warburg, 1962.
Short Friday and Other Stories, translated by Ruth Whitman and others. New York, Farrar Straus, 1964; London, Secker and Warburg, 1967.
Selected Short Stories, edited by Irving Howe. New York, Modern Library, 1966.
The Séance and Other Stories, translated by Ruth Whitman and others. New York, Farrar Straus, 1968; London, Cape, 1970.
A Friend of Kafka and Other Stories, translated by the author and others. New York, Farrar Straus, 1970; London, Cape, 1972.
A Crown of Feathers and Other Stories, translated by the author and others. New York, Farrar Straus, 1973; London, Cape, 1974.
Passions and Other Stories. New York, Farrar Straus, 1975; London, Cape, 1976.
Old Love. New York, Farrar Straus, 1979; London, Cape, 1980.
The Collected Stories. New York, Farrar Straus, and London, Cape, 1982.
The Image and Other Stories. New York, Farrar Straus, 1985; London, Cape, 1986.
Gifts. Philadelphia, Jewish Publication Society, 1985.
The Death of Methuselah and Other Stories. New York, Farrar Straus, and London, Cape, 1988.

Plays

The Mirror (produced New Haven, Connecticut, 1973).
Shlemiel the First (produced New Haven, Connecticut, 1974).
Yentl, The Yeshiva Boy, with Leah Napolin, adaptation of a story by Singer (produced New York, 1974). New York, French, 1979.
Teibele and Her Demon, with Eve Friedman (produced Minneapolis, 1978; New York, 1979). New York and London, French, 1984.
A Play for the Devil (based on his short story "The Unseen," produced in New York City at the Folksbiene Theatre, 1984).

Other

In My Father's Court (autobiography), translated by Channah Kleinerman-Goldstein and others. New York, Farrar Straus, 1966; London, Secker and Warburg, 1967.
An Isaac Bashevis Singer Reader. New York, Farrar Straus, 1971.
The Hasidim: Paintings, Drawings, and Etchings, with Ira Moskowitz. New York, Crown, 1973.
Love and Exile: The Early Years: A Memoir. New York, Doubleday, 1984; London, Cape, 1985.
A Little Boy in Search of God: Mysticism in a Personal Light, illustrated by Ira Moskowitz. New York, Doubleday, 1976.
A Young Man in Search of Love, translated by Joseph Singer. New York, Doubleday, 1978.
Lost in America, translated by Joseph Singer. New York, Doubleday, 1981.
Nobel Lecture. New York, Farrar Straus, and London, Cape, 1979.
Isaac Bashevis Singer on Literature and Life: An Interview, with Paul Rosenblatt and Gene Koppel. Tucson, University of Arizona Press, 1979.
The Meaning of Freedom. West Point, New York, United States Military Academy, 1981.
My Personal Conception of Religion. Lafayette, University of Southwestern Louisiana Press, 1982.
One Day of Happiness. New York, Red Ozier Press, 1982.
Conversations with Isaac Bashevis Singer, with Richard Burgin. New York, Doubleday, 1985.
The Safe Deposit and Other Stories about Grandparents, Old Lovers and Crazy Old Men ("Masterworks of Modern Jewish Writing" series), edited by Kerry M. Orlitzky. Princeton, New Jersey, Wiener, Markus, 1989.
The Certificate, translated by Leonard Wolf. New York, Farrar, Straus, 1992.
Shrewd Todie and Lyzer the Miser and Other Children's Stories, illustrated by Margot Zemach. Boston, Barefoot Books, 1994.

Editor, with Elaine Gottlieb, *Prism 2.* New York, Twayne, 1965.

Translator, *Pan,* by Knut Hamsun. Vilna, Kletzkian, 1928.
Translator, *Di Vogler* (The Vagabonds), by Knut Hamsun. Vilna, Kletzkian, 1928.
Translator, *In Opgrunt Fun Tayve* (In Passion's Abyss), by Gabriele D'Annunzio. Warsaw, Goldfarb, 1929.
Translator, *Mete Trap* (Mette Trap), by Karin Michäelis. Warsaw, Goldfarb, 1929.
Translator, *Roman Rolan* (Romain Rolland), by Stefan Zweig. Warsaw, Bikher, 1929.
Translator, *Viktorya* (Victoria), by Knut Hamsun. Vilna, Kletzkian, 1929.
Translator, *Oyfn Mayrev-Front Keyn Nayes* (All Quiet on the Western Front), by Erich Maria Remarque. Vilna, Kletzkian, 1930.
Translator, *Der Tsoyberbarg* (The Magic Mountain), by Thomas Mann. Vilna, Kletzkian, 4 vols., 1930.
Translator, *Der Veg oyf Tsurik* (The Road Back), by Erich Maria Remarque. Vilna, Kletzkian, 1931.
Translator, *Araber: Folkstimlekhe Geshikhtn* (Arabs: Stories of the People), by Moshe Smilansky. Warsaw, Farn Folk, 1932.
Translator, *Fun Moskve biz Yerusholayim* (From Moscow to Jerusalem), by Leon S. Glaser. New York, Jankowitz, 1938.

*

Bibliography: By Bonnie Jean M. Christensen, in *Bulletin of Bibliography 26* (Boston), January-March, 1969; *A Bibliography of Isaac Bashevis Singer 1924-1949* by David Neal Miller, Bern, Switzerland and New York, Lang, 1983.

Manuscript Collections: Butler Library, Columbia University, New York.

Critical Studies: *Isaac Bashevis Singer and the Eternal Past* by Irving Buchen, New York, New York University Press, 1968; *The Achievement of Isaac Bashevis Singer* edited by Marcia Allentuck, Carbondale, Southern Illinois University Press, 1969; *Critical Views of Isaac Bashevis Singer* edited by Irving Malin, New York, New York University Press, 1969, and *Isaac Bashevis Singer* by Malin, New York, Ungar, 1972; *Isaac Bashevis Singer* by Ben Siegel, Minneapolis, University of Minnesota Press, 1969; *Isaac Bashevis Singer and His Art* by Askel Schiotz, New York, Harper, 1970; *Isaac Bashevis Singer, The Magician of West 86th Street* by Paul Kresh, New York, Dial Press, 1979; *The Brothers Singer* by Clive Sinclair, London, Allison and Busby, 1983; *Fear of Fiction: Narrative Strategies in the Works of Isaac Bashevis Singer* by David Neal Miller, Albany, State University of New York Press, 1985, and *Recovering the Canon: Essays on Isaac Bashevis Singer* edited by Miller, Leiden, Brill, 1986; *From Exile to Redemption: The Fiction of Isaac Bashevis Singer* by Grace Farrell Lee, Carbondale, Southern Illinois University Press, 1987; *Understanding Isaac Bashevis Singer* by Lawrence S. Friedman, Columbia, South Carolina University Press, 1988.

* * *

The observation is frequently made that all great authors somehow stand apart. Few modern writers embody that assertion as completely as Isaac Bashevis Singer who, among numerous other honors, has been awarded the National Book award and the Nobel Prize for Literature. Yet an outsider he remained: a Jew among Gentiles; a European in America; an old man living in a world that glorifies youth. In a scientific age he admitted to believing in ghosts and demons. He wrote in a nearly dead language for an audience that could not read his work except in translation. And he wrote for children, for whom kabbalistic mysteries, tales of wonder rabbis who lived in Poland two hundred years ago, and the musings of refugee littérateurs are as remote as the fertility rites of Hottentots. Why? Because, as Singer himself explained, "they still believe in God, the family, angels, devils, witches, goblins...and other obsolete stuff. They don't expect their beloved writer to redeem humanity. Young as they are, they know that it is not in his power. Only the adults have such childish illusions."

Singer may not have believed in the power of writers to change the world, but, as one reared in the Hasidic tradition, he firmly believed in the power of stories, and in the ability of children to understand the most profound ideas if presented to them in the form of a tale. This intense respect for the child's ability to understand marks the best of Singer's juvenile work, just as it marks the work of Andersen, Carroll, Lewis, and Grahame. In fact a comparison with Singer's adult work frequently reveals the same themes—and often the same stories—written once for an audience of adults and, in a slightly different way, for an audience of children. The picture book *Joseph and Koza* deals with a Jewish goldsmith among Slavic pagans who falls in love and rescues a pagan girl. Similar situations, though of course treated at much greater length and with greater depth, form the plots of two adult novels, *The Slave* and *King of the Fields.* Kabbalistic speculations about reincarnation, demons, and the Messiah are major elements in Singer's writing and are as important in appreciating juvenile works such as *The Fearsome Inn, Mazel and Shlimazel,* and *Alone in the Wild Forest* as they are in understanding such adult writings as *Satan in Goray, The Spinoza of Market Street,* and *Gimpel the Fool.* Finally, *A Day of Pleasure* is simply a smaller, selected edition of Singer's adult autobiography *In My Father's Court.*

Equally important to any consideration of Singer's work is understanding where his roots as a writer lie. They run through the Yiddish masters I.L. Peretz and Sholem Aleichem to the great Russian writers of the 19th century who inspired them: Gogol, Dostoevsky, Chekhov, and Tolstoy. These influences shape the patterns of *Zlateh the Goat* and Singer's subsequent story collections down to his most recent, *The Power of Light.* Rollicking tales of the fools of Chelm rub elbows with stories of ghosts and demons. And then there are those like "Zlateh the Goat," "Menashe and Rachel," and "Naftali the Storyteller and His Horse, Sus," where nothing actually happens, but whose smells and textures are so rich they might have been wafted from the Cherry Orchard.

The inspired fabric of Singer's writing brings out the best in the artists chosen to illustrate it. Margot Zemach's rough figures capture the humor and sighs of ghetto folk. Irene Lieblich's paintings for *The Power of Light* are a shining tapestry of color. The stories in *Zlateh the Goat* reveal a warmth in Maurice Sendak that seems lacking in most of his recent major work. But it is in Singer's most recent book, *The Golem,* with pictures by Uri Shulevitz, that artist and writer capture the soul of a story.

The legend of the Golem is at least five hundred years old, and various elements of it can be traced all the way back to the time of the Talmud. The story appeared in several novelized treatments in the late 19th and early 20th centuries. H. Leivick's play, *The Golem,* is one of the masterpieces of the Yiddish theater. In the tale which has emerged from these varied traditional, romantic, and impressionistic elements, Rabbi Judah Leib of Prague is commanded by God to fashion a figure of a man from clay and bring it to life. This creature, the Golem, of enormous strength and size but of no intelligence whatsoever, saves the Jewish community from destruction. But the Golem lingers beyond his time; his powers are inadvertently misused and he becomes a rampaging menace that must somehow be confronted and laid to rest. Singer's version incorporates all the familiar elements of this powerful story: the ritual murder accusation; the Golem as Sorceror's apprentice; his love-lust for a lovely girl; his mindless pain in being alive and his fear of death. One idea, however, is new. The Emperor's decision to draft the Golem into his army makes it imperative for Rabbi Leib to end the creature's life. A Golem running wild in the streets is menacing enough, but a Golem accoutered with weapons of war and taught to fight in the service of an earthly monarch is an image of overwhelming horror. Singer does not elaborate, but the modern implications are not hard to see. Our world has its own Golem—nuclear energy—which men of science brought out of the earth to serve the forces of good in a time of danger. Now we are faced with an arsenal of Golems, all out of control, subject to no authority but the whims of generals, dictators, and politicians. To lay his Golem to rest Rabbi Leib must erase the holy name on its forehead. Will we be rid of our own Golems so easily? Shulevitz's mindless Golem in his gay landesknecht's costume capering goggle-eyed through the somber streets of the ghetto is as much a symbol of our age as Picasso's Guernica.

The greatest children's writers are great writers by any standard: Defoe, Carroll, Stevenson, Twain. The 20th century will add no more than a handful of names to that number. One of them, however, will surely be that of Isaac Bashevis Singer.

—Eric A. Kimmel

SLEIGH, Barbara (de Riemer)

Nationality: British. **Born:** Acock's Green, Worcestershire, 9 January 1906. **Education:** St. Catherine's School, Bramley, Surrey; West Bromwich School of Art, Birmingham, 1922-25; Clapham High School Art Teacher's Training College, London, 1925-28, Art Teacher's Diploma. **Family:** Married David Davis in 1935; one son and two daughters. **Career:** Art teacher, Smethwick High School, Staffordshire, 1927-29; Lecturer, Goldsmiths' Teacher Training College, London, 1929-32; assistant, *Children's Hour* program, BBC Radio, London, 1932-35. Freelance broadcaster and radio writer from 1935. **Died:** 13 February 1982.

Publications for Children

Fiction

Carbonel, illustrated by V.H. Drummond. London, Parrish, 1955; Indianapolis, Bobbs Merrill, 1957.

Patchwork Quilt, illustrated by Mary Shillabeer. London, Parrish, 1956.

The Singing Wreath and Other Stories, illustrated by Julia Comper. London, Parrish, 1957.

The Seven Days, illustrated by Susan Einzig. London, Parrish, 1958; New York, Meredith Press, 1968.

The Kingdom of Carbonel, illustrated by D.M. Leonard. London, Parrish, 1959; Indianapolis, Bobbs Merrill, 1960.

No One Must Know, illustrated by Jillian Willett. London, Collins, 1962; Indianapolis, Bobbs Merrill, 1963.

Jessamy, illustrated by Philip Gough. London, Collins, and Indianapolis, Bobbs Merrill, 1967.

Pen, Penny, Tuppence, illustrated by Meg Stevens. London, Hamish Hamilton, 1968.

The Snowball, illustrated by Patricia Drew. Leicester, Brockhampton Press, 1969.

West of Widdershins: A Gallimaufry of Stories Brewed in Her Own Cauldron, illustrated by Victor Ambrus. London, Collins, 1971; as *Stirabout Stories,* Indianapolis, Bobbs Merrill, 1971.

Ninety-Nine Dragons, illustrated by Gunvor Edwards. Leicester, Brockhampton Press, 1974.

Charlie Chumbles, illustrated by Frank Franus. London, Knight, 1977.

Grimblegraw and the Wuthering Witch, illustrated by Glenys Ambrus. London, Hodder and Stoughton, 1978; revised edition, London, Penguin, 1979.

Carbonel and Calidor, illustrated by Charles Front. London, Kestrel, 1978.

Other

North of Nowhere: Stories and Legends from Many Lands, illustrated by Victor Ambrus. London, Collins, 1964; New York, Coward McCann, 1966.
Funny Peculiar: An Anthology, illustrated by Jennie Garratt. Newton Abbot, Devon, David and Charles, 1975.
Winged Magic: Legends and Stories from Many Lands Concerning Things That Fly, illustrated by John Patience. London, Hodder and Stoughton, 1979.

Editor, *Broomsticks and Beasticles: Stories and Verse about Witches and Strange Creatures,* illustrated by John Patience. London, Hodder and Stoughton, 1981.
Editor, *The Wind in the Willows,* by Kenneth Grahame, illustrated by Philip Mendoza. London, Hodder and Stoughton, 1983.

Also author of numerous radio plays.

PUBLICATIONS FOR ADULTS

Other

The Smell of Privet (autobiography). London, Hutchinson, 1971.

*

Barbara Sleigh commented:
(1978) I largely write fantasy, but, I hope, of a down-to-earth kind, avoiding mere whimsy. I feel strongly this leads young readers to wider horizons, and later to imaginative adult reading.

* * *

Like many talented and versatile writers, Barbara Sleigh suffered the irritating injustice of being associated too exclusively with one outstanding creation, in her case *Carbonel,* a splendid and brilliantly observed character. But with all due respect to Carbonel (emphatically a cat demanding respect) Sleigh as a writer stands for a good deal more.

She produced her first book only after a long apprenticeship as a storyteller for the BBC during the best years of sound radio, in which the word was all-important, before television destroyed the famous daily *Children's Hour* with an alternative making less mental demand. She learned what demands *could* safely be made on a child in subject matter and vocabulary, if the storyteller knew his job. That she knew hers is demonstrated not only in *Carbonel* and its sequels—the last, *Carbonel and Calidor,* 23 years later, displaying an undiminished fertility of fancy—but in her numerous other volumes.

These vary from short story collections, such as *West of Widdershins,* and an anthology, *Broomsticks and Beasticles,* in which her own verses and folktale retellings are joined with similar pieces from other hands, to full-length books like *Jessamy,* in which a favourite old theme—the child who slips back in time, 1914 in this case—is developed with originality. Her personal attitude to magic and fantasy is stated in a brief introduction to *West of Widdershins,* a book which exemplifies her deft verbal economy and prodigality of ingenious ideas. One of its stories, "Miss Peabody," set in a prosaic school classroom, illustrates her preference for rooting these fantasies firmly in everyday life. Humour runs strongly through all her work. *Ninety-Nine Dragons* is especially full of it, and, though the good-natured, rather than fearsome, dragon has become almost a stereotype in children's fiction, Sleigh revealed once more her flair for giving a new brightness to whatever material she handled.

In what has proved to be, with Mary Norton, Alan Garner, and many others, something of a golden age of fantasy, Sleigh earned a high place.

—Geoffrey Trease

SLOBODKIN, Louis

Nationality: American. **Born:** Albany, New York, 19 February 1903. **Education:** Beaux Arts Institute of Design, New York, 1918-23. **Family:** Married Florence Gersh in 1927; two sons. **Career:** Sculptor in studios in U.S.A. and France, 1931-35; Head of the Sculpture Department, Master Institute of United Arts, Roerich Museum, New York, 1934-37; Instructor in Sculpture, Art League, New York, 1935-36; Head of Sculpture Division, New York City Art Project, 1941-42. Awarded commissions and executed sculptures, reliefs, and statues for buildings in New York, Washington, D.C., Johnstown, Pennsylvania, and North Adams, Massachusetts, 1935-39. Numerous museum exhibitions. Member of the Board of Directors, Sculptors Guild, 1939-41; president, National Sculpture Society American Group, 1940-42; chairman, American Institute of Graphic Arts Artists Committee, 1946. **Award:** American Library Association Caldecott Medal, for illustration, 1944. **Died:** 8 May 1975.

PUBLICATIONS FOR CHILDREN (ILLUSTRATED BY THE AUTHOR)

Fiction

The Friendly Animals. New York, Vanguard Press, 1944.
Clear the Track for Michael's Magic Train. New York, Macmillan, 1945.
The Adventures of Arab. New York, Macmillan, 1946.
Hustle and Bustle. New York, Macmillan, 1948.
Bixxy and the Secret Message. New York, Macmillan, 1949.
Mr. Mushroom. New York, Macmillan, 1950.
Dinny and Danny. New York, Macmillan, 1951.
The Space Ship under the Apple Tree. New York, Macmillan, 1952.
Circus, April 1st. New York, Macmillan, 1953.
The Horse with High-Heeled Shoes. New York, Vanguard Press, 1954.
Mr. Petersand's Cats and Kittens. New York, Macmillan, 1954.
The Amiable Giant. New York, Macmillan, 1955; London, Macmillan, 1958.
The Little Mermaid Who Could Not Sing. New York, Macmillan, 1956.
Melvin the Moose Child. New York, Macmillan, 1957; London, Macmillan, 1958.
The Space Ship Returns to the Apple Tree. New York and London, Macmillan, 1958.
The Wide-Awake Owl. New York, Macmillan, 1958.

Trick or Treat. New York and London, Macmillan, 1959.
Gogo, The French Sea Gull. New York, Macmillan, 1960.
A Good Place to Hide. New York, Macmillan, 1961.
Picco, The Sad Italian Pony. New York, Vanguard Press, 1961.
The Three-Seated Space Ship. New York, Macmillan, 1962.
The Late Cuckoo. New York, Vanguard Press, 1962.
Luigi and the Long-Nosed Soldier. New York, Macmillan, and London, Collier Macmillan, 1963.
Moon Blossom and the Golden Penny. New York, Vanguard Press, 1963.
The Polka-Dot Goat. New York, Macmillan, and London, Collier Macmillan, 1964.
Colette and the Princess. New York, Dutton, 1965.
Yasu and the Strangers. New York, Macmillan, and London, Collier Macmillan, 1965.
Round Trip Space Ship. New York, Macmillan, and London, Collier Macmillan, 1968.
The Space Ship in the Park. New York, Macmillan, and London, Collier Macmillan, 1972.
Wilbur the Warrior. New York, Vanguard Press, 1972.

Poetry

Magic Michael. New York, Macmillan, 1944.
The Seaweed Hat. New York, Macmillan, 1947.
Our Friendly Friends. New York, Vanguard Press, 1951.
Millions and Millions and Millions! New York, Vanguard Press, 1955.
One Is Good but Two Are Better. New York, Vanguard Press, 1956.
Nomi and the Lovely Animals. New York, Vanguard Press, 1960.
Up High and Down Low. New York, Macmillan, 1960.

Other

Thank You—You're Welcome. New York, Vanguard Press, 1957.
The First Book of Drawing. New York, Watts, 1958.
Excuse Me! Certainly! New York, Vanguard Press, 1959.
Read about the Policeman [*Postman, Busman, Fireman*]. New York, Watts, 4 vols., 1966-67.

Publications for Adults

Other

Fo'castle Waltz. New York, Vanguard Press, 1945.
Sculpture: Principles and Practice. Cleveland, World, 1949.

*

Manuscript Collections: University of Oregon Library, Eugene.

Illustrator: *The Moffats,* 1941, *The Middle Moffat,* 1942, *Rufus M,* 1943, *The Sun and the Wind and Mr. Todd,* 1943, *The Hundred Dresses,* 1944, and *Ginger Pye,* 1951, all by Eleanor Estes; *Many Moons* by James Thurber, 1943; *Peter the Great,* 1943, *Garibaldi,* 1944, and *Lenin,* 1945, all by Nina Baker; *Young Man of the House* by Mabel Leigh Hunt, 1944; *Russia and America* by Delia Goetz, 1945; *Robin Hood* by J. Walker McSpadden, 1946; *The Adventures of Tom Sawyer* by Mark Twain, 1946; *Jonathan and the Rainbow,* 1948, and *The King and the Noble Blacksmith,* 1950, both by Jacob Blanck; *Gertie and the Horse Who Thought and Thought* by Margarite Glendinning, 1951; *Red Head* by Edward Eager, 1951; *The Magic Fishbone* by Charles Dickens, 1953; *The Alhambra* by Washington Irving, 1953; *Evie and the Wonderful Kangaroo,* 1955, and *Evie and Cooky,* 1957, both by Irmengarde Eberle; *Pysen,* 1955, *The Saucepan Journey,* 1955, and *Little O,* 1957, all by Edith Unnerstad; *Shoes Fit for a King* by Helen E. Bill, 1956; *Love and Knishes,* 1956, and *Mazel Tov Y'all,* 1968, both by Sara Kasdan; *The Warm-Hearted Polar Bear* by Robert Murphy, 1957; *Upside Down Town* by F. Amerson Andrews, 1958; *Too Many Mittens,* 1958, *The Cowboy Twins,* 1960, *Io Sono/I Am,* 1962, *Mr. Papadilly and Willy,* 1964, and *Sarah Somebody,* 1969, all by Florence Slobodkin; *Martin's Dinosaur* by Reda Davis, 1959; *Clean Clarence,* 1959, and *Marshmallow Ghost,* 1960, both by Priscilla and Otto Friedrich; *Mr. Spindles and the Spiders* by Andrew Packard, 1961; *The Lovely Culpeppers* by Martha Uppington, 1963.

* * *

Louis Slobodkin was a prolific children's book author and illustrator who began to publish in the 1940s. He is best known for books which he both wrote and illustrated, though his illustrations for James Thurber's *Many Moons* and the work he did with his wife Florence should be noted.

Slobodkin's picture books are representative of a broad range of types within a category. The early picture books are faintly didactic, the emphasis being on an instructive lesson (*Dinny and Danny*) or an implied moral (*Magic Michael*). The use of the picture book as *exemplum,* however, is played down, and the illustrations do not accentuate the moral aspect of his works. Slobodkin also wrote obviously and intentionally didactic works, such as the courtesy books *Thank You—You're Welcome* and *Excuse Me! Certainly!,* as well as a "Read About" series on busmen, postmen, firemen, and policemen. This series contains narrative histories of the various professions accompanied by episodic vignettes related to a child's perception of the profession. Slobodkin's primary text for children who are interested in learning to illustrate is held in high repute by teachers of art, and the illustrations for Florence Slobodkin's dual language text *Io Sono/I Am* enhance the instructive level of the work.

Slobodkin is also noted for a series of juvenile fiction books on the themes of space travel, space inhabitants, and a child's imaginative relationship with his world and other-worldliness. Representative titles are *The Space Ship under the Apple Tree, The Space Ship in the Park,* and *The Three-Seated Space Ship.* Most of these works are centered on a peripatetic hero called Eddie and his friend from the planet Martinea.

Slobodkin's illustrations are very simple and functional—rarely more than suggestive of the actions discussed in the text. Yet the fact that Slobodkin was a sculptor obviously influenced his illustrating; movement, tension, and the dynamics of living figures read clearly through his illustration. Slobodkin's role as illustrator reached an apex in Eleanor Estes's stories about the Moffats and James Thurber's *Many Moons,* for which he received the Caldecott Medal.

—Rachel Fordyce

SLOBODKINA, Esphyr

Nationality: American. **Born:** Siberia, Russia, 22 September 1908; immigrated to the United States, 1928; became citizen, 1935. **Education:** Attended a Russian high school, Harbin, Manchuria; National Academy of Design, New York. **Family:** Married 1) Ilya Bolotowsky in 1933 (divorced 1936); 2) William L. Urquhart in 1960 (died 1963). **Career:** President, Art Development Co., New York, 1945-68; assistant export manager, CBS/Hytron, Denver and New York, 1948-57. Since 1976 president, Urquhart-Slobodkina Inc. **Awards:** Two Yaddo fellowships; three MacDowell fellowships. **Address:** 309 Southwest 8th Street, Hallandale, Florida 33009, U.S.A.

Publications for Children (illustrated by the author)

Fiction

Caps for Sale. New York, Scott, 1940; Kingswood, Surrey, World's Work, 1959.
The Wonderful Feast. New York, Lothrop, 1955.
Little Dog Lost, Little Dog Found. New York, Abelard Schuman, 1956.
The Clock. New York and London, Abelard Schuman, 1956.
The Little Dinghy. New York and London, Abelard Schuman, 1958.
Behind the Dark Window Shade. New York, Lothrop, 1958.
Billie, illustrated by Meg Wohlberg. New York, Lothrop, 1959.
Pinky and the Petunias. New York, Abelard Schuman, 1959; London, Abelard Schuman, 1962.
Moving Day for the Middlemans. New York and London, Abelard Schuman, 1960.
Jack and Jim. New York and London, Abelard Schuman, 1961.
The Long Island Ducklings. New York, Lantern Press, 1961.
Boris and His Balalaika, illustrated by Vladimir Bobri. New York and London, Abelard Schuman, 1964.
Pezzo the Peddler and the Circus Elephant [*and the Thirteen Silly Thieves*]. New York and London, Abelard Schuman, 2 vols., 1967-70.
The Flame, The Breeze, and the Shadow. Chicago, Rand McNally, 1969.
Billy, The Condominium Cat. Reading, Massachusetts, Addison Wesley, 1980.
A Portable Library of Slobodkina Children's Books. Hallandale, Florida, Urquhart Slobodkina, 1988.

Play

Caps for Sale, music and lyrics by Tamara Schildkraut, adaptation of the book by Slobodkina. Hallandale, Florida, Urquhart Slobodkina, 1981.

Publications for Adults

Other

Notes for a Biographer. Great Neck, New York, Urquhart Slobodkina, 3 vols., 1976-85.
American Abstract Artists: Its Publications, Catalogs, and Membership. Great Neck, New York, Urquhart Slobodkina, 2 vols., 1976-80.
Ilya Bolotowsky: Letters and Drawings 1930-47. Hallandale, Florida, Urquhart Slobodkina, 1987.

*

Illustrator: *The Little Fireman,* 1938, *The Little Farmer,* 1948, *The Little Cowboy,* 1949, and *Sleepy ABC,* 1953, all by Margaret Wise Brown; *Hiding Places* by Louise Woodcock, 1943.

* * *

In her picture books Esphyr Slobodkina often uses for her purposes the "functions," as they are called, that appear in traditional folk literature. Slobodkina, born in old Russia, practices her dependency on this aged genre by relying on these old tales for the general structures of many of her stories. She borrows the essentials found in their accumulative plot schemes, their repetitive actions, and their mounting sense of suspense. Then she combines all these factors with a reduced form of language that very young children can comprehend. The resultant product proves to have a merit that exceeds the praise that she has received for this work. Her picture books do have a distinctive integrity that is hers alone, although her work is sometimes confused (in name only) with that of the more highly successful Louis Slobodkin.

Slobodkina's most distinguished effort, without any doubt, has been *Caps for Sale.* The sales of this book testify that it is among the most popular of any of its kind written so far. Reported to have sold over a million copies, it easily has found its place on the all-time best-seller list. Young children are smitten by this uncomplicated yet intriguing tale of a simple cap seller, who after a disappointing day takes a rest under a tree. As soon as he dozes off, however, a band of monkeys descends and steals his caps. No amount of scolding on his part can get them back, he later finds. When he shakes his fist the monkeys merely return the gesture. Finally, in total exasperation he throws his own cap to the ground, and lo, so do all the monkeys—which nicely ends the story.

None of Slobodkina's later picture books have reached this exceptional level of success. This does not mean they are lacking in merit, however. On the contrary, some of her books for the very young are near-perfect examples of the cumulative tale, a format fancied by many picture-book writers, many of whom do not carry it off as well as she does. *The Wonderful Feast* is a prime example of Slobodkina's success with this "house-that-Jack-built" type of story. Here a farmer gives his horse some feed. Then, in order, a goat ate what the horse left; a hen what the goat left; a mouse what the hen left; and an ant ate the very last grain. All thought it a "wonderful feast." Highly simplistic stories of this nature need illustrations of notable excellence. Since Slobodkina is an artist of undoubted ability (her abstract art has been given much praise) she is able to infuse the simple words of her cumulative tales with a vigor far beyond that which they inherently contain. Instead of the art work in her books overshadowing their literary content, it magnifies and focuses it.

This arrangement seems to work the best (see *The Clock*), however, when Slobodkina stays with the very short text required for the cumulative story. In some of her longer displays of verbal text her limited ability to sustain a satisfactory fictional drama is apparent. In her *Pezzo the Peddler* books, for example, she tries to concoct spin-offs of *Caps for Sale.* Here a cap peddler loses and retrieves his caps in various ways. Even Slobodkina's use of many short sentences, a great deal of dialogue, and explicit descriptions cannot overcome the repetitive plots, which are simply too weak to sustain these books. On the other hand, Slobodkina has demonstrated, as in *Boris and His Balalaika,* that when she depends on her imagination rather than her past success she is fully able to write admirable longer plots.

—Patrick Groff

SLOTE, Alfred

Pseudonym: A.H. Garnet. **Nationality:** American. **Career:** Has worked as an educational television producer, journalist, and teacher. Lives in Ann Arbor, Michigan. **Address:** c/o Lippincott, 10 East 53rd Street, New York, New York 10022, U.S.A.

Publications for Children

Fiction

The Princess Who Wouldn't Talk, illustrated by Ursula Arndt. Indianapolis, Bobbs Merrill, 1964; Kingswood, Surrey, World's Work, 1966.
Stranger on the Ball Club. Philadelphia, Lippincott, 1970.
Jake. Philadelphia, Lippincott, 1971.
The Biggest Victory. Philadelphia, Lippincott, 1972.
My Father, The Coach. Philadelphia, Lippincott, 1972.
Hang Tough, Paul Mather. Philadelphia, Lippincott, 1973.
Tony and Me. Philadelphia, Lippincott, 1974.
Matt Gargan's Boy. Philadelphia, Lippincott, 1975.
My Robot Buddy, illustrated by Joel Schick. Philadelphia, Lippincott, 1975.
The Hot Shot, photographs by William LaCrosse. New York, Watts, 1977.
My Trip to Alpha I, illustrated by Harold Berson. New York, Lippincott, 1978.
Love and Tennis. New York, Macmillan, 1979.
The Devil Rides with Me and Other Fantastic Stories. New York, Methuen, 1980.
C.O.L.A.R.: A Tale of Outer Space, illustrated by Anthony Kramer. New York, Lippincott, 1981.
Clone Catcher, illustrated by Elizabeth Slote. New York, Lippincott, 1982.
Rabbit Ears. New York, Lippincott, 1982.
Omega Station, illustrated by Anthony Kramer. New York, Lippincott, 1983.
The Trouble on Janus. New York, Lippincott, 1985.
Moving In. New York, Lippincott, 1988.
A Friend Like That. New York, Lippincott, 1988.
Make-Believe Ballplayer, illustrated by Tom Newsom. New York, Lippincott, 1989.
The Trading Game. New York, HarperCollins, 1990.
Finding Buck McHenry. New York, HarperCollins, 1991.

Other

The Moon in Fact and Fancy, illustrated by John Kaufmann. Cleveland, World, 1967; revised edition, 1971.
Air in Fact and Fancy, illustrated by Dan Dickas. Cleveland, World, 1968.

Publications for Adults

Novels

Denham Proper. New York, Putnam, 1953.
Lazarus in Vienna. New York, McGraw Hill, 1956.
Strangers and Comrades. New York, Simon and Schuster, 1964; London, W.H. Allen, 1965.

Novels as A.H. Garnet

The Santa Claus Killer, with Garnet Garrison. New Haven, Connecticut, Ticknor and Fields, 1981; London, Gollancz, 1982.
Maze, with Garnet Garrison. New Haven, Connecticut, Ticknor and Fields, 1982; London, Gollancz, 1983.

Short Stories

Preparation for Retirement, with Woodrow W. Hunter. Ann Arbor, University of Michigan Press, 1968.

Other

Termination: The Closing at Baker Plant. Indianapolis, Bobbs Merrill, 1969.

* * *

The books of Alfred Slote, appropriate for children ages seven to 12, are mainly sports fiction and science fiction. Characteristics of Slote's books are action-filled plots centered on male characters.

Baseball is the topic of most of the Slote's sports books. These works deal with two common themes: developing team work and becoming a winning team. They are unlike typical sports books, however, because they include plot elements beyond the realm of sports and provide a view that keeps sports in perspective.

In *Stranger on the Ball Club,* central character Tim Foster is the new kid in town. In addition to adjusting to that status, he is also coping with the death of his mother. Tim finds a baseball mitt and keeps it, even though it is marked with a boy's name. The reader gets involved in the tangled web of stealing, lying, and trying to make things right again. Similarly complicated plots unfold in other baseball stories. In *Jake,* an orphan boy must deal with living with an uncle whose only interest is music. In *Hang Tough, Paul Mather* a 12-year-old pitcher faces an incurable blood disease. Henry Smith, the central character of *Make-Believe Ball Player,* must face the fact that his baseball prowess is all in his imagination. Sibling rivalry is well developed in this book, but at the recommendation of his sister, Henry accepts his limited athletic ability and directs his talents into acting. The importance and contributions of the Negro baseball leagues are explored in *Finding Buck McHenry,* which includes complex personal relationships and a mystery.

The father-son relationship is the major focus of two of Slote's baseball books. In *My Father, The Coach,* Ezell Corkins is embarrassed by the bungling efforts his father makes at coaching his team. Ezell is ashamed of his father: his job, his clothes, his forgetfulness, and his demeanor. In the course of a season, Ezell has time to reassess his feelings for his father and confirms his love for him. Danny Gargan in *Matt Gargan's Boy* has a very different situation. His father, a major league player, is divorced from his mother. Danny must deal with his father's expectations of him, as well as the father's absence.

Through all of the sports action, these books manage to keep sports in perspective. In *Stranger on the Ball Club,* Tim Foster's dad speaks for many of the characters in other books as well: "Tim, I'm happy you made the team, happy you're making friends and liking it here. You don't have to be a baseball player as far as I'm concerned. Playing ball is fun, but there are more important things in life." Andy Harris, in *The Trading Game,* also must question the place baseball has in his life. He is sure of many things at the beginning of the story: he loves baseball, he likes collecting baseball cards, he thinks his little league team has the worst possible coach, and he wishes his grandfather would coach his team. Andy lives with his mother; his parents are divorced. Then Andy's father dies suddenly and we realize the father-son conflict that existed between Andy's father and Andy's grandfather. In a series of events, he comes to question almost everything he had been sure of. These two books remind us that sports are fun and exciting and enrich life, but they are not life itself; only part of it.

Slote's science-fiction stories differ in theme. Here the characters become involved in battles of good and evil and learn to appreciate both human qualities and the beauty of the earth. Of the six future-oriented, science-fiction books, four revolve around Jack Jameson and his look-alike robot, Danny One. In the first story, *My Robot Buddy,* Jack is given Danny as a birthday present. Together, they foil a "robot-napper's" attempt to steal Danny. In subsequent adventures, Jack and Danny come to sympathize with the rights of robots programmed only to work in *C.O.L.A.R.* They later risk their own safety to save Earth from Dr. Drago who is intent on blowing up the world in *Omega Station* and uncover the plot of a would-be deceiver about to overtake the throne on a faraway planet in *The Trouble on Janus.*

All of the stories about Jack Jameson put young people in charge of their adventures as they do in the two other science-fiction adventures. In *My Trip to Alpha I,* the hero thwarts a plot to trap his Aunt Katherine forever in her look-alike "dummy" while her fortune is stolen. And, in *Clone Catcher,* Arthur Dunn helps people understand the rights of clones who had been created only to be used as spare parts in the master's body.

A secondary theme in these books is an appreciation of the treasures of the earth. Jack asks in *My Robot Buddy* if his robot could be programmed for happiness and is told "No...I'm afraid you have to be born a human being to be able to feel happiness for free: a nice day, a pretty sunset, a birdcall...important things like this, people get just being alive."

In two novels written in the late 1980s, Slote departs from sports fiction and science-fiction topics. Father-child relationships are explored in *Moving In,* a story about 11-year-old Robby, his sister Peggy, and their recently widowed father. Fearing his father is becoming interested in a female business associate, Robby hopes to interfere by ruining their business. In a sequel, *A Friend Like That,* Robby becomes worried about future romances of his father. In the end the conflict is resolved through improved father-son communication.

Considering the works of Slote, it is apparent the questions that he is asking: What is the role of sports in life experience? What makes up the relationship of father and son? What are a father's expectations? How can a son live up to them? Slote continues to develop plots to explore these questions.

—Mary J. Lickteig

SMITH, William Jay

Nationality: American. **Born:** Winnfield, Louisiana, 22 April 1918. **Education:** Blow School, St. Louis, 1924-31; Cleveland High School, 1931-35; Washington University, St. Louis, 1935-41, B.A. 1939, M.A. in French 1941; Institut de Touraine, Tours, France, 1938; Columbia University, New York, 1946-47; Wadham College, Oxford (Rhodes Scholar), 1947-48; University of Florence, 1948-50. **Family:** Married 1) the poet Barbara Howes in 1947 (divorced 1965), two sons; 2) Sonja Haussmann in 1966, one stepson. **Military Service:** United States Naval Reserve, 1941-45; Lieutenant. **Career:** Assistant in French, Washington University, 1939-41; Instructor in English and French, 1946-47, and Visiting Professor of Writing, School of the Arts, and Acting Chairman, Writing Division, 1973-75, Columbia University; Instructor in English, 1951, and poet-in-residence and Lecturer in English, 1959-64, 1966-67, Williams College, Williamstown, Massachusetts. Writer-in-residence, 1965-66, Professor of English, 1967-68 and 1970-80, and Professor Emeritus, since 1980, Hollins College, Virginia. Consultant in Poetry, 1968-70, and Honorary Consultant, 1970-76, Library of Congress, Washington, D.C.; Lecturer, Salzburg Seminar in American Studies, 1974; Fulbright Lecturer, Moscow State University, 1981; poet-in-residence, Cathedral of St. John the Divine, New York, 1986-89. Editorial consultant, Grove Press, New York, 1958-60; poetry reviewer, *Harper's,* New York, 1962-66. Democratic Member, Vermont House of Representatives, 1960-62. **Awards:** Young Poets prize, 1945, and Union League Civic and Arts Foundation prize, 1964 (*Poetry,* Chicago); Alumni citation, Washington University, 1963; Ford fellowship, for drama, 1964; Henry Bellamann Major award, 1970; Loines award, 1972; National Endowment for the Arts grant, 1972; National Endowment for the Humanities grant, 1975; Gold Medal of Labor (Hungary), 1978; New England Poetry Club Golden Rose, 1980; Ingram Merrill Foundation grant, 1982; Médaille de Vermeil, French Academy, 1991; Pro Cultura Hungaria medal, Hungary, 1993; D.Litt.: New England College, Henniker, New Hampshire, 1973. **Agent:** George Nicholson, Sterling Lord Literistic, 65 Bleecker Street, New York, New York 10012, U.S.A. **Address:** 63 Luther Shaw Road, Cummington, Massachusetts 01026-9787, U.S.A.

Publications for Children

Poetry

Laughing Time, illustrated by Juliet Kepes. Boston, Little Brown, 1955; London, Faber, 1956.

Boy Blue's Book of Beasts, illustrated by Juliet Kepes. Boston, Little Brown, 1957.

Puptents and Pebbles: A Nonsense ABC, illustrated by Juliet Kepes. Boston, Little Brown, 1959; London, Faber, 1960.
Typewriter Town, illustrated by the author. New York, Dutton, 1960.
What Did I See?, illustrated by Don Almquist. New York, Crowell Collier, 1962.
My Little Book of Big and Little (*Little Dimity, Big Gumbo, Big and Little*), illustrated by Don Bolognese. Riverside, New Jersey, Routledge, 3 vols., 1963.
Ho for a Hat!, illustrated by Ivan Chermayeff. Boston, Little Brown, 1964; revised edition, illustrated by Lynn Munsinger, 1989.
If I Had a Boat, illustrated by Don Bolognese. New York, Macmillan, 1966; Kingswood, Surrey, World's Work, 1967.
Mr. Smith and Other Nonsense, illustrated by Don Bolognese. New York, Delacorte Press, 1968.
Around My Room and Other Poems, illustrated by Don Madden. New York, Lancelot Press, 1969.
Laughing Time and Other Poems, illustrated by Don Madden. New York, Lancelot Press, 1969.
Grandmother Ostrich and Other Poems, illustrated by Don Madden. New York, Lancelot Press, 1969.
Laughing Time: Nonsense Poems, illustrated by Fernando Krahn. New York, Delacorte, 1980.
The Key. New York, Children's Book Council, 1982.
Birds and Beasts, illustrated by Jacques Hnizdovsky. Boston, Godine, 1990.
Laughing Time: Collected Nonsense, illustrated by Fernando Krahn. New York, Farrar Straus, 1990.
Big and Little, illustrated by Don Bolognese. Boyds Mills Press, 1992.

Other

Editor, with Louise Bogan, *The Golden Journey: Poems for Young People,* illustrated by Fritz Kredel. Chicago, Reilly and Lee, 1965; London, Evans, 1967; revised, Chicago, Contemporary Books, 1990.
Editor, *Poems from France,* illustrated by Roger Duvoisin. New York, Crowell, 1967.
Editor, *Poems from Italy,* illustrated by Elaine Raphael. New York, Crowell, 1972.
Editor, *A Green Place: Modern Poems,* illustrated by Jacques Hnizdovsky. New York, Delacorte Press, 1982.
Editor, with Carol Ra, *Behind the King's Kitchen: A Roster of Rhyming Riddles,* illustrated by Jacques Hnizdovsky. Honesdale, Pennsylvania, Boyds Mills Press, 1992.
Editor, with Carol Ra, *The Sun Is Up: A Child's Year of Poems,* illustrated by Jane Chambliss Wright. Boyds Mills Press, 1996.

Translator, *Children of the Forest,* by Elsa Beskow, illustrated by Beskow. New York, Delacorte Press, 1970.
Translator, *The Pirate Book,* by Lennart Hellsing, illustrated by Poul Ströyer. New York, Delacorte Press, and London, Benn, 1972.
Translator, with Max Hayward, *The Telephone,* by Kornei Chukovsky, illustrated by Blair Lent. New York, Delacorte Press, 1977.
Translator, *Songs of Childhood,* by Federico Garcia Lorca, illustrated by John DePol. Stone House Press, 1994.

Publications for Adults

Plays

The Straw Market (comedy), music by the author (produced Washington, D.C., 1965; New York, 1969).
Army Brat: A Dramatic Narrative for Three Voices (based on Smith's *Army Brat: A Memoir*), (produced New York City, 1980).

Poetry

Poems. New York, Banyan Press, 1947.
Celebration at Dark. London, Hamish Hamilton, and New York, Farrar Straus, 1950.
Snow. Schlosser Paper Corp., 1953.
The Stork: A Poem Announcing the Safe Arrival of Gregory Smith. New York, Caliban Press, 1954.
Typewriter Birds. New York, Caliban Press, 1954.
The Old Man on the Isthmus. Privately printed. 1957.
The Bead Curtain: Calligrams. Privately printed, 1957.
Poems 1947-1957. Boston, Little Brown, 1957.
Two Poems. Pownal, Vermont, Mason Hill Press, 1959.
A Minor Ode to the Morgan House. Privately printed, 1961.
Prince Souvanna Phouma: An Exchange Between Richard Wilbur and William Jay Smith. Williamstown, Massachusetts, Chapel Press, 1963.
Morels. Privately printed, 1964.
Quail in Autumn. Privately printed, 1965.
A Clutch of Clerihews. Privately printed, 1966.
The Tin Can and Other Poems. New York, Delacorte Press, 1966.
Winter Morning. Privately printed, 1967.
Imaginary Dialogue. Privately printed, 1968.
Hull Boy, St. Thomas. Privately printed, 1970.
New and Selected Poems. New York, Delacorte Press, 1970.
A Rose for Katherine Anne Porter. New York, Albondocani Press, 1970.
At Delphi: For Allen Tate on His Seventy-Fifth Birthday, 19 November 1974. Williamstown, Massachusetts, Chapel Press, 1974.
Venice in the Fog. Greensboro, North Carolina, Unicorn Press, 1975.
Song for a Country Wedding. Privately printed, 1976.
Verses on the Times, with Richard Wilbur. New York, Gutenberg Press, 1978.
Journey to the Dead Sea: A Poem. Omaha, Abattoir, 1979.
The Tall Poets. Winston-Salem, North Carolina, Palaemon Press, 1979.
Mr. Smith. New York, Delacorte, 1980.
The Traveler's Tree: New and Selected Poems. New York, Persea, 1980; Manchester, Carcanet, 1981.
Oxford Doggerel. Privately printed, 1983.
Collected Translations: Italian, French, Spanish, Portuguese. St. Paul, Minnesota, New Rivers Press, 1985.
The Tin Can. Roslyn, New York, Stone House Press, 1988.
Journey to the Interior. Roslyn, New York, Stone House Press, 1988.
Plain Talk: Epitaphs, Satires, Nonsense, Occasional, Concrete and Quotidian Poems. New York, Center for Book Arts, 1988.
Collected Poems, 1939-1989. New York, Macmillan, 1990.
The Cyclist. Stone House Press, 1995.

Christmas Card Poems (with Barbara Howes): *Lachrymae Christi and In the Old Country,* 1948; *Poems: The Homecoming and The Piazza,* 1949; *Two French Poems: The Roses of Saadi and Five Minute Watercolor,* 1950—all privately printed.

Other

The Spectra Hoax (criticism). Middletown, Connecticut, Wesleyan University Press, 1961.
The Skies of Venice. N.p., Andre Emmerich Gallery, 1961.
Children and Poetry: A Selective, Annotated Bibliography, with Virginia Haviland. Washington, D.C., Library of Congress, 1969; revised edition, 1979.
Louise Bogan: A Woman's Words. Washington, D.C., Library of Congress, 1972.
The Streaks of the Tulip: Selected Criticism. New York, Delacorte Press, 1972.
Army Brat: A Memoir. New York, Persea, 1980; London, Penguin, 1982.

Editor and Translator, *Selected Writings of Jules Laforgue.* New York, Grove Press, 1956.
Editor, *Herrick.* New York, Dell, 1962.
Editor, *Light Verse and Satires,* by Witter Bynner. New York, Farrar Straus, and London, Faber, 1978.
Editor, with Emanuel Brasil, *Brazilian Poetry 1950-1980.* Middletown, Connecticut, Wesleyan University Press, 1983; London, Harper, 1984.
Editor, with J.S. Holmes, *Dutch Interior: Post-War Poetry of the Netherlands and Flanders.* New York, Columbia University Press, 1984.
Editor, with Dana Gioia, *Poems from Italy.* St. Paul, Minnesota, New Rivers Press, 1985.
Editor, with F.D. Reeve, *An Arrow in the Wall: Selected Poetry and Prose of Andrei Voznesensky.* New York, Holt, and London, Secker and Warburg, 1987.
Editor, *Life Sentence,* by Nina Cassian. London, Anvil Press, 1990.

Translator, *Scirroco,* by Romualdo Romano. New York, Farrar Straus, 1951.
Translator, *Poems of a Multimillionaire,* by Valery Larbaud. New York, Bonaccio and Saul, 1955.
Translator, *Two Plays by Charles Bertin: Christopher Columbus and Don Juan.* Minneapolis, University of Minnesota Press, 1970.
Translator, *Chairs above the Danube,* by Szabolcs Várady. Privately printed, 1976.
Translator, *Saga,* by Andrei Voznesensky. Privately printed, 1977.
Translator, with Leif Sjöberg, *Agadir,* by Artur Lundkvist. Pittsburgh, International Poetry Forum, 1979.
Translator, with Ingvar Schousboe, *The Pact: My Friendship with Isak Dinesen,* by Thorkild Bjørnvig. Baton Rouge, Louisiana State University Press, 1983.
Translator, *Moral Tales,* by Jules Laforgue. New York, New Directions, 1985; London, Picador, 1987.
Translator, with Leif Sjöberg, *Wild Bouquet: Nature Poems,* by Henry Martinson. Kansas City, Missouri, Bookmark Press, 1985.
Translator, with Edwin Morgan and others, *Eternal Moment: Selected Poems,* by Sandor Weöres. St. Paul, Minnesota, New Rivers Press, and London, Anvil Press, 1988.
Translator, with Sonja Haussmann Smith, *The Madman and the Medusa,* by Tchicaya U Tam'Si. Charlottesville, Virginia, University Press of Virginia, 1989.
Translator, *Christopher Columbus,* illustrated by John DePol. New York, Stone House Press, 1992.
Translator, with others, *Window on the Black Sea: Bulgarian Poetry in Translation,* 2nd edition. Pittsburgh, Pennsylvania, Carnegie-Mellon University Press, 1992.

*

Manuscript Collection: Washington University, St. Louis.

* * *

William Jay Smith represents an unusual phenomenon, that of a serious poet for adults trying to be funny—for children. It is understandable, then, that when this prize-winning poet showed a colleague his first attempts he was greeted with hoots of surprise bordering on reproach. This does not mean that Smith went into this new venture half-cocked, however. Smith was also a critic of poetry, and had given much thought as to what poetry should be and do. Smith's contributions to children's literature, therefore, present a rare opportunity to find out if a writer's work lives up to his expectations. There is a further interest, since Smith tells us that writing children's poems has given him the chance to explore themes he developed in his works for adults.

In Smith's books of poetry for children it can be seen, first, that his writing does fulfill to a large extent one of his major goals, to "risk everything and play for the highest stakes." It is clear that Smith's books of poetry for children offer many cleverly written bits of infectious nonsense on a wide range of topics. From page to page there is no telling what Smith will do next.

Second, most of Smith's poems for children reflect the technical soundness of good adult poetry, a standard which Smith has set for poems for the young. In general, his rhymes are usually bright and strong, his topics are the kind with appeal for children, and his figures of speech are far from clichés, yet well within the intellectual grasp of his readers (e.g. "Toaster": "a silver-scaled Dragon with Jaws of flaming red"). In Smith's collections of adult poetry he has been praised for "much leaving out, and stern self-correction." While there are bewildering exceptions to this seen in his poems for children, by and large they do reflect his studious effort. While some of his lines diminish into simple chatter, often of a playground variety (e.g. "Over and under/Over and under/Crack the whip/And hear it thunder"), and while Smith reverts at times to practical matters (e.g. in his poem "Dictionary"), his offerings to children usually aim to explore and try out new things and to maintain a sense of poesy.

Another goal Smith has set for poetry is that variety is everything. His poems for children certainly do explore a wide range of unexpected topics. The exasperation one often feels in reading conventional anthologies of poetry for children, with their seemingly endless items on nature and goodness ("sentimental drivel," Smith calls them), never applies to Smith. His heterogeneous offerings are a buffer against this. This exemption is also partly achieved from a fulfillment of another of his precepts for poetry, that it should be humorous. The chuckles abound in his books, almost on every page.

Finally, it is also true that in general Smith gets to his poem-making for children with "directness and élan—and without fuss," as he has said it should be done. His poems are playfully graphic, full of imagery, and song-like. This aspect of his writing is enhanced by his intensive use of verbs and nouns to carry the impact of what he says. Smith's direct approach to his task is also shown by his lack of pretension and condescension: he is obviously excited about experimenting with language for children, and the excitement shows.

—Patrick Groff

SMUCKER, Barbara Claassen

Nationality: American; Canadian landed immigrant. **Born:** Newton, Kansas, 1 September 1915. **Education:** Bethel College, North Newton, Kansas, 1932-33; Kansas State University, Manhattan, 1933-36, B.S. in journalism 1936; Rosary College Library School, River Forest, Illinois, 1963-65; University of Waterloo, Ontario, 1975-77. **Family:** Married Donovan E. Smucker in 1939; two sons and one daughter. **Career:** Teacher of journalism and English, Harper High School, Kansas, 1937-38; reporter, Newton *Evening Kansan,* 1939-41; teacher, Ferry Hall School, Lake Forest, Illinois, 1960-63; bookseller, Lake Forest Bookstore, 1963-67; children's librarian, Kitchener Public Library, Ontario, 1969-77; head librarian, 1977-82, and since 1982 senior fellow, Renison College, University of Waterloo. **Awards:** Ruth Schwartz award, 1980; Canada Council prize, 1980; Kansas State University Distinguished Service award, 1980; Vicky Metcalf award, 1988. Litt.D.: University of Waterloo, 1986. Honorary fellow, Renison College, 1982. **Address:** c/o Penguin Books Canada, #10 Alcorn Ave., Ste. 300, Toronto, Ontario, M4V 3B2 Canada.

Publications for Children

Fiction

Henry's Red Sea, illustrated by Allan Eitzen. Scottdale, Pennsylvania, Herald Press, 1955.
Cherokee Run, illustrated by Allan Eitzen. Scottdale, Pennsylvania, Herald Press, 1957.
Wigwam in the City, illustrated by Gil Miret. New York, Dutton, 1966; as *Susan,* New York, Scholastic, 1972.
Underground to Canada, illustrated by Tom McNeely. Toronto, Clarke Irwin, 1977; London, Penguin, 1978; as *Runaway to Freedom,* New York, Harper, 1977.
Days of Terror, illustrated by Kim La Fave. Toronto, Clarke Irwin, and Scottdale, Pennsylvania, Herald Press, 1979; London, Penguin, 1981.
Amish Adventure. Toronto, Irwin, and Scottdale, Pennsylvania, Herald Press, 1983; London, Penguin, 1984.
White Mist. Toronto, Irwin, 1985.
Jacob's Little Giant. Markham, Ontario, Penguin, 1987; New York, Viking Kestrel, 1988.
Jumbo. Toronto, Doubleday, 1989; as *Incredible Jumbo,* New York, Viking, 1989.
Garth and the Mermaid. Toronto, Viking, 1992.
Selina and the Bear Paw. Toronto, Viking, 1994.

Publications for Adults

Play

The Abiding Place (oratorio), music by Ester Wiebe (produced Strasbourg, France, 1984). Winnipeg, Manitoba, Canadian Mennonite College, 1984.

*

Manuscript Collections: Kerlan Collection, University of Minnesota, Minneapolis.

Barbara Claassen Smucker comments:
Ideas for my books come in many ways. When they come it is with a pinch of magic, a drop of inspiration, and a great deal of excitement. I write for young people because I like their fresh response, buoyant enthusiasm, and honest frankness. I like my story heroes to have difficult goals to win and to strive for values that are the very best in our society.

* * *

Barbara Claassen Smucker's books treat issues of contemporary relevance within the framework of well-researched fiction based on specific historic events. Her books, informed by a compassionate understanding of human nature borne of her own Mennonite heritage, frequently show two ideologies, cultures, or power groups in conflict with each other. The focus is on the child who has bruising encounters within this larger context, and it allows for a satisfying resolution of the particular situation while giving the child reader insight into the causes of human fallibility or social injustice in a contemporary world. Her books have dealt with political oppression, racial and class discrimination, religious intolerance, cultural clashes, and the destruction of natural resources.

Two of her books deal with the Mennonites. *Henry's Red Sea,* an early account of the Mennonite exodus from Europe, primarily conveys historical and factual information about this religious sect. *Days of Terror,* her later treatment of the same narrative field, has much greater scope and psychological depth. It depicts the mass migration of Mennonites from the Russian Ukraine to Canada and the United States, and it records, through the eyes of a 10-year-old boy, the injustice suffered by the peaceful and hardworking Mennonites during the terror imposed by the anarchy and famine during the 1917 Russian Revolution. *Underground to Canada* presents a much different kind of victimization, that of 19th-century American blacks. The heroine, a courageous young black girl, makes her way to Ontario, Canada, through the "underground railway," seeking freedom and the promise of a happier life. *Wigwam in the City* portrays the cultural differences and social disharmony between American Indians and whites when the family of a young Indian girl moves from the reservation to Chicago so her father can find work. Though the events and psychological twists occasionally seem forced, the story has a true cultural basis. *White Mist,* a later book which treats Indian-white relations within the larger framework of current concerns over the death of forests because of acid rain, is skillfully handled time fantasy. *Jacob's Little Giant,* a book for younger children, continues the theme of the natural environment by focusing on a little boy's attachment to a giant Canada goose family that is recolonized on his father's farm by the Department of Natural Resources.

Amish Adventure is a compelling and complex story of the encounter between two groups in contemporary Canadian society—the predominant empire-building Scots-Canadian and the minority Canadian-Amish who eschew modernization, maintaining 19th-century farming and living practices. Written from the perspective of a 12-year-old Scottish-Canadian boy who was riding in a speeding car that crashed into a horse and buggy on a country road, the story treats the boy's attempts to counteract the ensuing devastation. Like Smucker's other books, this one gives in-depth treatment to psychological, generational, and cultural forces which cause human intolerance and conflict. Her next two novels depict with sensitivity and subtlety a child's yearning for a dead and/or absent parent: the first, *Incredible Jumbo,* weaves the appealing and true story of P. T. Barnam's famous circus elephant into a fictional story about a lonely young boy whose dead father and hospitalized mother are partially replaced by the affectionate and sometimes cantankerous elephant. The second, *Garth and the Mermaid,* is a skilful time-travel fantasy which begins with a very modern problem—a young person having to accept a new step-parent who is not wanted—and reframes this in 14th century England where he encounters parallel but intensified versions of his modern difficulties. Smucker's carefully researched historical books both teach history and how to live in the present.

—Mary Henley Rubio

SOBOL, Donald J.

Nationality: American. **Born:** New York City, 4 October 1924. **Education:** Fieldston School, New York, 1942; Oberlin College, Ohio, B.A. 1948; New School for Social Research, New York, 1949-51. **Military Service:** United States Army Corps of Engineers, 1943-46. **Family:** Married Rose Tiplitz in 1955; one daughter and three sons (one deceased). **Career:** Reporter, New York *Sun,* 1948, and *Long Island Daily Press,* New York, 1949-51; buyer, R.H. Macy's, New York, 1953-54. Wrote "Two-Minute Mystery" syndicated newspaper series, 1959-68. Lives in Miami. **Awards:** Young Readers Choice award, 1972; Mystery Writers of America Edgar Allan Poe award, 1975; Garden State Children's Book Award, 1979. **Agent:** McIntosh and Otis Inc., 310 Madison Avenue, New York, New York 10017, U.S.A.

PUBLICATIONS FOR CHILDREN

Fiction

The Double Quest, illustrated by Lili Réthi. New York, Watts, 1957.

The Lost Dispatch, illustrated by Anthony Palumbo. New York, Watts, 1958.

Encyclopedia Brown, Boy Detective, [*and the Case of the Secret Pitch, Finds the Clues, Gets His Man, Solves Them All, Keeps the Peace, Saves the Day, Tracks Them Down, Shows the Way, Takes the Case, Lends a Hand, and the Case of the Dead Eagles, and the Case of the Midnight Visitor, Carries On, Sets the Pace, and the Case of the Mysterious Handprints, and the Case of the Treasure Hunt, and the Case of the Disgusting Sneakers*], illustrated by Leonard Shortall, Lillian Bradi, Ib Ohlsson, and Gail Owens. New York and Nashville, Nelson, 13 vols., 1963-77; New York, Four Winds Press, 2 vols., 1980-81; New York, Morrow, 3 vols., 1985-90; London, Hamish Hamilton, 6 vols., 1980.

Secret Agents Four, illustrated by Leonard Shortall. New York, Four Winds Press, 1967.

Two-Minute Mysteries [*More* and *Still More Two-Minute Mysteries*]. New York, Scholastic, 3 vols., 1967-75.

Greta the Strong, illustrated by Trina Schart Hyman. Chicago, Follett, 1970.

Milton, The Model A, illustrated by Joan Drescher. Irvington-on-Hudson, New York, Harvey House, 1971.

Angie's First Case, illustrated by Gail Owens. New York, Four Winds Press, 1981.

Encyclopedia Brown (omnibus), illustrated by Leonard Shortall. London, Angus and Robertson, 1983.

Encyclopedia Brown Takes the Cake!, with Glenn Andrews, illustrated by Ib Ohlsson. New York, Four Winds Press, 1983.

The Amazing Power of Ashur Fine. New York, Macmillan, 1986.

Encyclopedia Brown's Book of Strange but True Crimes, with Rose Sobol. New York, Scholastic, 1992.

The Best of Encyclopedia Brown, illustrated by Ib Ohlsson. New York, Scholastic, 1993.

Encyclopedia Brown and the Case of the Two Spies, illustrated by Eric Velasquez. New York, Delacorte, 1994.

My Name is Amelia. New York, Atheneum, 1994.

Encyclopedia Brown and the Case of Pablo's Nose, illustrated by Eric Velasquez. New York, Delacorte, 1996.

Other

The First Book of Medieval Man, illustrated by Lili Réthi. New York, Watts, 1959; revised edition, as *The First Book of Medieval Britain,* London, Mayflower, 1960.

Two Flags Flying (biographies of Civil War leaders), illustrated by Jerry Robinson. New York, Platt and Munk, 1960.

The Wright Brothers at Kitty Hawk, illustrated by Stuart Mackenzie. New York, Nelson, 1961.

The First Book of the Barbarian Invaders, A.D. 375-511, illustrated by W. Kirtman Plummer. New York, Watts, 1962; London, Ward, 1963.

The First Book of Stocks and Bonds, with Rose Sobol. New York, Watts, 1963.

Lock, Stock, and Barrel (biographies of American Revolutionary War leaders), illustrated by Edward J. Smith. Philadelphia, Westminster Press, 1965.

The Amazons of Greek Mythology. South Brunswick, New Jersey, A.S. Barnes, and London, Yoseloff, 1972.

Strange but True. New York, Scholastic, 1973.

True Sea Adventures. Nashville, Nelson, 1975.

Disaster. New York, Pocket Books, 1979.

Encyclopedia Brown's [*Second, Third*] *Record Book of Weird and Wonderful Facts,* illustrated by Sal Murdocca and Bruce Degen. New York, Delacorte Press, 3 vols., 1979-85.

Encyclopedia Brown's Book of Wacky Crimes [*Spies, Sports, Animals, Cars, Outdoors*], illustrated by Ted Enik. New York, Lodestar, 1 vol., 1982; New York, Morrow, 5 vols., 1984-87.

Editor, *A Civil War Sampler,* illustrated by Henry S. Gillette. New York, Watts, 1961.

Editor, *An American Revolutionary War Reader.* New York, Watts, 1964.
Editor, *The Strongest Man in the World,* illustrated by Cliff Schule. Philadelphia, Westminster Press, 1967.
Editor, *The Best Animal Stories of Science Fiction and Fantasy.* New York, Warne, 1979.

*

Manuscript Collection: Kerlan Collection, University of Minnesota, Minneapolis.

Donald J. Sobol comments:

I am totally unqualified to be a writer. My childhood was unimpoverished and joyful. Even worse, I loved and admired my parents, and I got along well with my brother and sister. Thus I never felt the need to have a "message," which is not quite the same as writing without a theme. My themes are brotherhood and honor. For me, the primary function of juvenile fiction is to entertain. I am devoted to plot, pace, and humor, normally in that order. The meandering exploration and illumination of character so favored by critics as "literary" and "uplifting" I leave to others.

* * *

Donald J. Sobol's Encyclopedia Brown series is well loved by middle-grade readers. Each book contains 10 mysteries, all solved by the boy detective, Encyclopedia Brown, son of the Chief of Police. The reader is also able to solve the mysteries; solutions are printed in the back of each book. The books are simply written in short, clear sentences. Each chapter is self-contained and quite brief. No time is wasted on description or character development. Idaville, Encyclopedia's home town, is a thinly sketched Anywhere, U.S.A. The people in Idaville are all two-dimensional, and easily divided into good guys and bad guys. This simplicity, brevity, and clarity are all a boon to the reluctant or shaky reader.

Complexity in writing style is not Sobol's intent, nor is it required for the success of these books. Although the stories are simply written, they are clever and fresh, and seldom obvious or easy to solve. The twist comes in the thinking, not in the vocabulary or the sentence structure. Each mystery is unpredictable and cannot be solved with the same techniques or logic that solve other cases. Sometimes we are looking at motive, sometimes at contradiction, sometimes at physical evidence. The logic and the type of clues are always changing. What is required to solve these is careful, meticulous reading. The hesitant, painstaking reader is rewarded. He has a distinct advantage over the skimmer. The tortoise wins the race.

In addition to the clever twists in the clues, these mysteries are funny in a goofy, childlike way that matches the simple writing style. They are loaded with puns and funny phrases. They also contain eccentric characters and outrageous situations which alternate with everyday events: the ordinary and the extraordinary mix.

In a sense these are formula books; the design of each is the same. This standardized structure might give the hesitant reader a sense of familiarity and therefore, confidence. But these books are not formula stories in their plot and logic. The uniformity in design is coupled with originality in thinking. Sobol's books have been translated into fourteen foreign languages and most have gone into paperback editions. He is represented in more than seventy anthologies.

The key to Encyclopedia Brown's enormous popularity is enjoyment. The books are easy to read and fun to solve. They star a child who is the smartest person in town. And, as if that wasn't satisfying enough, the children who read and solve these prove that they are just as smart as Encyclopedia Brown himself.

—Christine McDonnell

SOFTLY, Barbara

Nationality: English. **Born:** Barbara Frewin, Ewell, Surrey, 12 March 1924. **Education:** Nonsuch County Grammar School, Cheam, Surrey, 1938-42; Froebel Teachers Training College, London, 1942-44. **Family:** Married Alan Softly in 1951. **Career:** English and history teacher, Manor House School, Little Bookham, Surrey, 1944-55. **Address:** Bundels, Ridgway, Sidbury, Devon EX10 0SF, England.

Publications for Children

Fiction

Plain Jane, illustrated by Shirley Hughes. London, Macmillan, 1961; New York, St. Martin's Press, 1962.
Place Mill, illustrated by Shirley Hughes. London, Macmillan, and New York, St. Martin's Press, 1962.
A Stone in a Pool, illustrated by Shirley Hughes. London, Macmillan, and New York, St. Martin's Press, 1964.
Ponder and William [*on Holiday, at Home, at the Weekend*], illustrated by Diana John. London, Penguin, 2 vols., and London, Longman, 2 vols., 1966-74.
Hippo, Potta and Muss, illustrated by Tony Veale. London, Chatto Boyd and Oliver, 1969; New York, Harvey House, 1970.
A Lemon-Yellow Elephant Called Trunk, illustrated by Tony Veale. London, Chatto Boyd and Oliver, and New York, Harvey House, 1971.
Geranium, illustrated by Margaret Wetherbee. London, Hutchinson, 1972.

Other

Magic People, illustrated by Gunvor Edwards. Edinburgh, Oliver and Boyd, 1966; New York, Holt Rinehart, 1967.
More Magic People, illustrated by Gunvor Edwards. London, Chatto Boyd and Oliver, 1969; as *Magic People Around the World,* New York, Holt Rinehart, 1970.
Another Child's Garden of Verses, illustrated by Molly Brett and Alan Softly. Privately printed, 1994.

Publications for Adults

Other

The Queens of England. Newton Abbot, Devon, David and Charles, and New York, Stein and Day, 1976.
Victorian Childhood, Edwardian Youth 1888-1900. N.p., 1992.

Tapping at the Garden Gate: The Village of Sidbury in the 19th Century: Based on the Diary of Eliza Clarke, 1867. West Country Books, 1995.
Tales from Sidbury Village: 20th Century Village Life. Halsgrove House, 1998.

*

Barbara Softly comments:

At seven years old I wanted to be a poet, but on visiting Westminster Abbey and seeing where poets were buried, I decided against it and to write stories instead! Historical novels were scribbled, written properly, and published after I finished teaching. Ponder the panda pyjama-case followed in stories originally written for a small nephew. Now, with a large garden that is open to the public and five cats, my husband and I have become joint Hon. Archivists for village of Sidbury—a fascinating and very time-consuming hobby, which has brought us into contact with many overseas people who were researching their forebears. The song used as the title for *Tapping* came from America in 1869, was heard by Eliza Clarke here in 1870, and was found in the Library of Congress by an American who was looking for her ancestors in Sidbury a few years ago.

My historical novels for children were started when I was 13 and I felt I had read all the books in my parents' house and decided to write my own. The picture books were based on posters sent to me by a publisher who asked if I could write a story about them. Why not try this—you can have great fun.

* * *

Barbara Softly is perhaps best loved for her Ponder and William stories. William's cousin Winifred has a panda pyjama-case which she lends him whenever he comes to stay. He calls it Ponder and it talks to him, making interesting things happen, though grown-ups might see them as very ordinary—making jelly, for instance, and using the garden hose. One of the major attractions of these tales is the way that Ponder, the "imaginary friend" of so many solitary children, gives William a viewpoint on the adult world. All the things they do together and find so absorbing are the very ones we take for granted or find annoying. We look at a power outage and the resulting need to use candles as an irritant, whereas Ponder helps William see this as a thrill. These are ideal stories for reading aloud to the very young, and—more than most bedtime tales—they can be enjoyed by the parental reader. Ponder opens for us a window into the child's world and gives us ideas of experiences we might not otherwise have thought of sharing.

Softly's other books for the young, such as *Magic People,* also maintain the wonderment and delight of the world in which the young child finds himself. For older children, her love of history comes to the fore, particularly in her very sensitive collection of biographies, *The Queens of England.* Whether they are dynamic leaders, loving wives and mothers, tragically misguided characters, or just shadowy, nebulous figures eclipsed by dominant husbands, these women are brought to life, and we see them as real people, playing their part in shaping the affairs of the country. Surely the best way of getting children hooked on history is to offer them someone with whom to empathize. Every girl reader should find someone whose personality attracts, and of whose life and times she would like to find out more.

—Ann G. Hay, updated by Judson Knight

SORENSEN, Virginia

Nationality: American. **Born:** Virginia Eggertsen, Provo, Utah, 17 February 1912. **Education:** Brigham Young University, Provo, A.B. 1934; Stanford University, California. **Family:** Married 1) Frederick C. Sorensen in 1933 (divorced), one daughter and one son; 2) the writer Alec Waugh in 1969 (died 1981). **Career:** Writer-in-residence, State University of Oklahoma, Edmond, 1966-67. **Awards:** Guggenheim fellowship, 1946, 1954; Child Study Committee award, 1956; American Library Association Newbery Medal, 1957. Fellow, Phi Beta Kappa. **Died:** 24 December 1991.

Publications for Children

Fiction

Curious Missie, illustrated by Marilyn Miller. New York, Harcourt Brace, 1953.
The House Next Door: Utah 1896, illustrated by Lili Cassel. New York, Scribners, 1954.
Plain Girl, illustrated by Charles Geer. New York, Harcourt Brace, 1955.
Miracles on Maple Hill, illustrated by Beth and Joe Krush. New York, Harcourt Brace, 1956; Leicester, Brockhampton Press, 1967.
Lotte's Locket, illustrated by Fermin Rocker. New York, Harcourt Brace, 1964.
Around the Corner, illustrated by Robert Weaver. New York, Harcourt Brace, 1971.
Friends of the Road. New York, Atheneum, 1978.

Publications for Adults

Novels

A Little Lower Than the Angels. New York, Knopf, 1942.
On This Star. New York, Reynal, 1946.
The Neighbors. New York, Reynal, 1947.
The Evening and the Morning. New York, Harcourt Brace, 1949.
The Proper Gods. New York, Harcourt Brace, 1951.
Many Heavens. New York, Harcourt Brace, 1954.
Kingdom Come. New York, Harcourt Brace, 1960.
The Man with the Key. New York, Harcourt Brace, 1974.

Short Stories

Where Nothing Is Long Ago: Memories of a Mormon Childhood. New York, Harcourt Brace, 1963.

*

Manuscript Collections: Special Collections, Boston University Library; Kerlan Collection, University of Minnesota, Minneapolis.

Critical Studies: *Virginia Sorensen* by L.L. and Sylvia B. Lee, Boise, Idaho, Boise State University, 1978.

* * *

Virginia Sorensen's strong sense of family wins a warm response from her readers, and her best-loved work, the Newbery Medal-winning *Miracles on Maple Hill,* most successfully brings to life a family and a community. Father has returned at last from the war to a family that never gave up hope, but the time he has spent in prison camp has changed him. The whole family becomes tense and uneasy with Father's tension. Little things—voices, noises, small frustrations—cause trouble. Mother becomes convinced that the cure can be found in the country, at Grandmother's old place in Maple Hill. Father is not optimistic—the whole idea of retreat to the country strikes him as far-fetched and simplistic—but, unwillingly, he agrees: and the miracles begin. They are the simple miracles of nature, of healing and growth: but they seem miraculous indeed to city children. When at last trouble comes, as it will do even in Maple Hill, can the city family, so new to country ways and work, save the precious crop? Predictably enough they can and do, but the story is surprisingly suspenseful. Throughout, there is the warm strength of caring—for family, for neighbours, for the lonely old hermit living nearby among his goats. The message that people matter is one that bears repeating and remembering.

Plain Girl shares the same warmth, with even more respect for old country traditions. Esther is the only daughter in a family of Plain People—the Amish. Esther feels sadly like an only child, for her brother Daniel has flouted the strict ways of the People and gone off to see the world. He has cut his hair, wears buttons on his clothes—even drives a car! Esther is shocked but at the same time curious. When the time comes for her to go to school as the law dictates, she becomes friends with a little girl who is the very opposite of Plain, who wears pink frilly dresses and ribbons in her hair. Esther longs to try these pretty, different unPlain garments, to trade clothes with her friend Mary. But Daniel's return, saddened by his contact with the world and eager to be Plain once more, teaches her the value of her Amish ways.

In *Lotte's Locket* Danish Lotte is the eighth in her family to bear her historic name. When war-widowed mother marries an American, Lotte is torn between love of her "Mor" and devotion to her homeland: but the locket, a precious family heirloom, allows her to carry a little of her Danish heritage over the seas to her new home in America. In *Around the Corner* Junie (short for Junior) is forbidden to go where the "hillbillys" have moved into a condemned shack: but after curiosity lures him there, neighbourliness keeps bringing him back to visit the friendly family from West Virginia; and good things begin to happen.

Not as winning as others of her works, *Friends of the Road* is the sentimental story of two girls whose parents are in the foreign service, and who meet in Morocco. Though parted by circumstances, they keep their friendship alive through their letters. Sorensen's books are filled with a wholesome philosophy of love and caring. They are mild, even quaint, in contrast with the hard-hitting, no-holds-barred children's literature so prevalent today, but it will be a sad world when there is no place left in it for gentle kindliness.

—Joan McGrath

SPERRY, Armstrong

Nationality: American. **Born:** New Haven, Connecticut, 7 November 1897. **Education:** Yale School of Fine Arts, New Haven, 1918; Art Students' League, New York, 1919-21; Académie Colarossis, Paris, 1922. **Military Service:** United States Navy, 1917. **Family:** Married Margaret Mitchell in 1930; one son and one daughter. **Career:** Assistant ethnologist, *Kaimiloa* expedition to the South Pacific, 1925-26; commercial artist and illustrator. **Award:** American Library Association Newbery Medal, 1941. **Died:** 28 April 1976.

PUBLICATIONS FOR CHILDREN (ILLUSTRATED BY THE AUTHOR)

Fiction

One Day with Manu. Philadelphia, Winston, 1933.
One Day with Jambi in Sumatra. Philadelphia, Winston, 1934.
One Day with Tuktu, An Eskimo Boy. Philadelphia, Winston, 1935.
All Sail Set. Philadelphia, Winston, 1935; London, Lane, 1946.
Wagons Westward: The Old Trail to Santa Fe. Philadelphia, Winston, 1936; London, Lane, 1948.
Little Eagle, A Navajo Boy. Philadelphia, Winston, 1938.
Lost Lagoon. New York, Doubleday, 1939; London, Lane, 1943.
Call It Courage. New York, Macmillan, 1940; as *The Boy Who Was Afraid,* London, Lane, 1942.
Coconut, The Wonder Tree. New York, Macmillan, 1942; London, Lane, 1946.
Bamboo, The Grass Tree. New York, Macmillan, 1942; London, Lane, 1946.
No Brighter Glory. New York, Macmillan, 1942; London, Hutchinson, 1944.
Storm Canvas. Philadelphia, Winston, 1944.
Hull-Down for Action. New York, Doubleday, 1945; London, Lane, 1948.
The Rain Forest. New York, Macmillan, 1947; London, Lane, 1950.
Danger to Windward. Philadelphia, Winston, 1947; London, Lane, 1952.
Black Falcon. Philadelphia, Winston, 1949.
River of the West, illustrated by Henry Pitz. Philadelphia, Winston, 1952; London, Lane, 1954.
Thunder Country. New York, Macmillan, 1952; London, Lane, 1953.
Frozen Fire. New York, Doubleday, 1956; London, Lane, 1957.
South of Cape Horn. Philadelphia, Winston, 1958.

Other

The Voyages of Christopher Columbus. New York, Random House, 1950.
John Paul Jones, Fighting Sailor. New York, Random House, 1953.
Pacific Islands Speaking. New York, Macmillan, 1955.
Captain Cook Explores the South Seas. New York, Random House, 1955; revised edition, as *All about Captain Cook,* London, W.H. Allen, 1960.
All about the Arctic and Antarctic. New York, Random House, 1957.
All about the Jungle. New York, Random House, 1959; London, W.H. Allen, 1960.
The Amazon, River Sea of Brazil. Champaign, Illinois, Garrard, 1961; London, Muller, 1962.
Great River, Wide Land: The Rio Grande Through History. New York, Macmillan, and London, Collier Macmillan, 1967.

Editor, *Story Parade: A Collection of Modern Stories for Boys and Girls.* Philadelphia, Winston, 5 vols., 1938-42.

*

Illustrator: *Stars to Steer By,* 1934, and *House Afire!,* 1941, both by Helen T. Follett; *The Codfish Market* by Agnes D. Hewes, 1936; *Shuttered Windows* by Florence Crannell Means, 1938; *Jungle River,* 1938, and *Thunderbolt House,* 1944, both by Howard Pease; *Boat Builder* by Clara Ingram Judson, 1940; *Teri Taro from Bora Bora* by William S. Stone, 1940; *Two Children of Brazil* by Rosa Brown, 1940; *Nicholas Arnold, Toolmaker* by Marion Hansing, 1941; *Winabojo, Master of Life* by James Clyde Bowman, 1941; *Dogie Boy* by Edith Heal, 1943; *Clipper Ship Men* by Alexander Laing, 1944; *Courage over the Andes* by Frederic Kummer, 1944; *Sky Highways* by Trevor Lloyd, 1945; *Story of Hiawatha* edited by Allen Chaffee, 1951.

* * *

Two of Armstrong Sperry's interests shaped the course of his writings for children. As an ethnologist in the South Pacific, he developed a deep and abiding interest in the life and culture of the island peoples. His service in the U.S. Navy gave an added dimension to his love of the sea and things nautical. Together, these two loves, plus his talent as an artist, gave shape and direction to his work.

His early works, such as the tales of Manu, Jambi, and Tuktu, are unlikely to be found in library collections of today, in an era rendered more sensitive to the feelings of minority cultures and racial pride than the 1930s. Coloured as they were by the prevailing attitudes of his day, Sperry's ethnological works for young readers would by critics of today be stigmatized as condescending in their approach: it is all too easy to lose the historical perspective that would credit him with enlightenment and objectivity, given their date of publication. A similar change of perspective has effectively ended the usefulness of such later titles as *Lost Lagoon* and *Hull-Down for Action.* They partake of the fierce emotions of World War II, specifically of the highly charged Pearl Harbor era, and naturally enough reflect the rage and rancour of that unhappy time. As with any "boys' book" produced in wartime, stereotypes of the antagonists as unredeemed villains are predictably two-dimensional.

Where Sperry shone, and continues to shine, and where he earned a place in the galaxy of notable children's writers, is with the timeless tale, in particular, with *Call It Courage.* It is the story of a Polynesian youth, Mafatu, a child of the sea people who fears the sea. As a tiny child, just old enough to remember, he suffered the loss of his mother in a hurricane at sea, and was rescued barely alive after the ordeal. Now, when the young men of the island are eager for the challenge of the deep, Mafatu hangs back, busying himself with net mending. He is pitied and despised by his people, and is the despair of his father, the chief. At last life becomes unendurable to Mafatu. He determines to face that which he fears—and if he must die, it will at least be a man's death. In a frail outrigger canoe, Mafatu sets out to find his fate, accompanied only by a dog, and without the knowledge or consent of his people. There follows a gripping account of adventure and survival with a veritable boyish Robinson Crusoe, alone on a remote island that is sometimes visited by a terrifying cannibal tribe. Of course Mafatu returns at last to his people in glorious triumph. His father, who had mourned him as dead, now sees his son wearing a necklace of boar's teeth, and carrying a spear, a man's weapon he has earned and now deserves. It is a tremendously satisfying story—the epic struggle of child-man against the elements, yet written well within the grasp of young readers not yet ready for full-length adult stories of survival. It is written unaffectedly, yet in the language of myth and legend.

Sperry's own illustrations admirably support the simple power of his heroic theme. Sperry's ethnological materials have come to honourable retirement, and his style of sentimental fictionalized biography is no longer much admired, but Sperry's achievement in *Call It Courage* ensures his continued presence in the best of children's collections.

—Joan McGrath

SPIER, Peter (Edward)

Nationality: American (became citizen, 1958). **Born:** Amsterdam, Netherlands, 6 June 1927; came to the United States, 1951. **Education:** Rijksacademie voor beeldende kunsten, 1945-47. **Family:** Married Kathryn Pallister, 1958; one son, one daughter. **Military Service:** Royal Netherlands Navy, 1947-51; Lieutenant. **Career:** Junior editor, Elsevier's Weekblad, Paris, France, 1949-51; junior editor, Elsevier Publishing, Houston, Texas, 1951-52; author and illustrator, since 1952. **Awards:** Caldecott Honor Book, 1962 for *The Fox Went Out on a Chilly Night*; *Boston Globe/Horn Book* Award for Illustration, 1967, for *London Bridge Is Falling Down!,* and Honor Book, 1967, for *To Market! To Market!*; Child Study Association of America's Children's Books of the Year, 1968, for *Hurrah, We're Outward Bound!,* 1969, for *And So My Garden Grows,* 1970, for *The Erie Canal,* 1972, for *Crash! Bang! Boom!,* 1975, for *Tin Lizzie,* 1979, for *The Legend of New Amsterdam,* and 1987, for *Dreams*; Christopher Award, 1971, for *The Erie Canal*; *New York Times* Outstanding Books of the Year, 1971, for *Gobble, Growl, Grunt,* 1973, for *The Star-Spangled Banner,* 1977, for *Noah's Ark,* and 1978, for *Bored, Nothing to Do*; New York Academy of Science's Children's Science Book Award, 1972, for *Gobble, Growl, Grunt*; Christopher Award, 1977, Caldecott Medal and Lewis Carroll Shelf Award, both 1978, International Board on Books for Young People Honor List, 1980, and American Book Award finalist for paperback picture book, 1982, all for *Noah's Ark*; American Library Association Notable Book, 1978, for *Oh, Were They Ever Happy!,* 1982, for *Rain*; Christopher Award and American Book Award finalist for children's hardcover nonfiction, both 1980, and Mass Media Award from the Conference of Christians and Jews, all for *People*; University of Southern Mississippi Silver Medallion, 1984, in recognition of his distinguished career as an author and illustrator of books for children. **Address:** P.O. Box 566, 5 Warden Cliff Road, Shoreham, New York 11786-0566, U.S.A.

Publications for Children

Fiction (illustrated by the author)

The Fox Went Out on a Chilly Night: An Old Song. New York, Doubleday, 1961.
London Bridge Is Falling Down! New York, Doubleday, 1967.
To Market! To Market! New York, Doubleday, 1967.
Hurrah, We're Outward Bound! New York, Doubleday, 1968.
And So My Garden Grows. New York, Doubleday, 1969.
Noah's Ark. New York, Doubleday, 1977; published in England as *The Great Flood,* London, World's Work, 1978.
Oh, Were They Ever Happy! New York, Doubleday, 1978; published in *England as Nothing Like a Fresh Coat of Paint,* London, World's Work, 1981.
Bored, Nothing to Do! New York, Doubleday, 1978.
Peter Spier's Christmas! New York, Doubleday, 1983.
Peter Spier's Little Bible Storybooks. New York, Doubleday, 1983.
Reteller, *The Book of Jonah.* New York, Doubleday, 1985.
Dreams. New York, Doubleday, 1986.
Peter Spier's Circus! New York, Doubleday, 1992.
Father, May I Come? New York, Doubleday, 1993.

Nonfiction

Of Dikes and Windmills. New York, Doubleday, 1970.
The Erie Canal. New York, Doubleday, 1970.
Gobble, Growl, Grunt. New York, Doubleday, 1971.
Crash! Bang! Boom! New York, Doubleday, 1972.
Fast-Slow, High-Low: A Book of Opposites. New York, Doubleday, 1972.
The Star-Spangled Banner. New York, Doubleday, 1973.
Tin Lizzie. New York, Doubleday, 1975.
The Legend of New Amsterdam. New York, Doubleday, 1979.
People. New York, Doubleday, 1980.
The Pet Store. New York, Doubleday, 1981.
My School. New York, Doubleday, 1981.
The Fire House. New York, Doubleday, 1981.
The Food Market. New York, Doubleday, 1981.
The Toy Shop. New York, Doubleday, 1981.
Bill's Service Station. New York, Doubleday, 1981; as *Bill's Garage,* London, Collins, 1981.
Rain. New York, Doubleday, 1982.
Peter Spier's Little Cats. New York, Doubleday, 1984.
Peter Spier's Little Dogs. New York, Doubleday, 1984.
Peter Spier's Little Ducks. New York, Doubleday, 1984.
Peter Spier's Little Rabbits. New York, Doubleday, 1984.
We the People: The Story of the U.S. Constitution. New York, Doubleday, 1987.
Fast Cars, Slow Cars. New York, Random House, 1988.
Here Come the Fire Trucks. New York, Random House, 1988.
Trucks that Dig and Dump. New York, Random House, 1988,
Big Trucks, Little Trucks. New York, Random House, 1988.

*

Media Adaptations: *The Cow Who Fell in the Canal* (cassette; sound filmstrip), Weston, Connecticut, Weston Woods, 1965, (feature film), 1970; *The Fox Went Out on a Chilly Night* (cassette; sound filmstrip), Weston Woods, 1965; *London Bridge is Falling Down* (feature film), Weston Woods, 1969, (cassette; sound filmstrip), 1971; *The Erie Canal* (cassette, sound filmstrip), Weston Woods, 1971, (feature film), 1976; *The Star-Spangled Banner* (feature film; cassette; filmstrip), Weston Woods, 1975; *Oh, Were They Ever Happy!* (filmstrip with cassette), New York, Random House, 1976; *Noah's Ark* (filmstrip), Weston Woods, 1978; *Bored, Nothing to Do* (filmstrip), New Rochelle, New York, Spoken Arts,Inc. 1982; *Tin Lizzie* (filmstrip), Spoken Arts, Inc. 1982; *Rain* (filmstrip), Spoken Arts Inc., 1985; *Christmas* (film strip), Spoken Arts, Inc., 1985; *Little Bible Stories* (filmstrip), Spoken Arts, Inc., 1985; *Noah's Ark* (sound recording), New York, Lightyear Entertainment, 1990; *People* (videorecording), New York, Lightyear Entertainment, 1995.

Biography: Entry in *Something about the Author,* Vol. 54, Detroit, Gale Research, 1989, 119-123.

Critical Studies: "The Illustrations of Peter Spier," in *American Artist* (New York), 1969; *Down the Rabbit Hole: Adventures and Misadventures in the Realm of Children's Literature* by Selma Lanes, New York, Atheneum, 1976; *Newbery and Caldecott Medal Books: 1976-1985,* edited by Lee Kingman, New York, Horn Book, 1986.

Illustrator: *Thunder Hill* by Elmer Reynolds, 1953; *Adventurers All* by Louis Untermeyer, 1953; *Tam Morgan, the Liveliest Girl in Salem* by Ruth Langland Holberg, 1953; *Cocoa* by Margaret G. Otto, 1953; *Wonders of the World* by H.J. Berkhard, 1953; *Last Hurdle* by Frieda K. Brown, 1953; *Cargo for Jennifer* by Marjorie Vetter, 1954; *Little Lord Fauntleroy* by Frances H. Burnett, 1954; *The Prince and the Pauper* by Mark Twain, 1954; *The Cow Who Fell in the Canal* by Phyllis Krasilovsky, 1957; *Favorite Christmas Carols: Fifty-Nine Yuletide Songs Both Old and New* compiled by Margaret B. Boni, 1957; *Hans Brinker; or, the Silver Skates* by Mary Mapes Dodge, 1958; *Jessica's Journal* by Jessica Reynolds, 1958; *Lions Fed the Tigers* by Douglas Angus, 1958; *Hector the Stowaway Dog: A True Story* by Kenneth Dodson, 1958; *Esmeralda Ahoy!* by Elizabeth Fairholme and Pamela Powell, 1959; *Island City: Adventures in Old New York* by Lavina Davis, 1961; *Boy Overboard!* by George H. Grant, 1961; *Golden Book Encyclopedia,* Vol. 1, 1970; *The Little Riders* by Margaretha Shemin, 1988; *Last Hurdle* by F.K. Brown, 1988.

* * *

Though he was born and attended schools in the Netherlands, Peter Spier came to the United States after serving in the Royal Netherlands Navy and has lived for some decades in New York. Spier's works are varied in subject matter but similar in illustrative style. For works that he writes or adapts, he draws on folk tales, Mother Goose rhymes, bible stories, and historical events. He also has turned his attention to people around the world and their cultures, and to animals and noisy machines. He approaches this array of subject matter in ways to interest and entertain a child.

Early in his career he conceived of The Mother Goose Library, a series of books which blend traditional rhymes with colorful art. The first book of the series, *London Bridge Is Falling Down!,* is a sprightly story of historical London. Spier's two page illustrative spreads are remarkable in their detail. He portrays the sprawling town filled with people and animals and boats and carriages. The bridge construction scenes, the boat traffic on the

Thames River, and the town mercantile area are packed with people working and playing, making plans and making mistakes. At the end of the book a short historical account of London Bridges through the centuries is provided. A subsequent book in the series, *Hurrah, We're Outward Bound!,* charts the maiden voyage of an early-nineteenth-century sailing vessel. From the shipyards of Honfleur, France, the ship *La Jeune Francaise* goes to New York City and back again to France by way of Dartmouth, England. At the end of this book a short historical account of the port of Honfleur and its place in France's history is provided.

Noah's Ark begins with Jacobus Revius seventeenth-century poem "The Flood," translated from the Dutch by Spier. Spier provides magnificent two page spreads of animals in all shapes and sizes as they climb on board the ark with Noah and his kin to escape the Great Flood. When they are safely aboard the huge vessel, the rain waters cover the world. When the flood subsides, the animals and people return to dry land, and under the sign of the rainbow, they make their peace with the Lord, and begin life all over again.

The enormity of the flood, the carefulness of Noah and his kin, the patience of the animals, and the final redemption are shown in careful pen and ink scratches and pastel wash. There are no words after the poem, and none are needed as the lyrical illustrations carry the story to conclusion. Spier won the Caldecott Medal for *Noah's Ark.*

Besides nursery rhymes and historical tales, Spier has written and illustrated thoroughly modern tales such as *Bored, Nothing to Do!* In this book two brothers look for a way to keep busy one bright day. They decide to build an airplane, using mother's clothesline, father's Volkswagen car engine, the wheel from baby's carriage, and some other odd objects from around the house. The plane does fly, the parents do sigh, but somehow by evening everything has been put back in its proper place again. But since the boys no longer have their airplane, they are bored again.

People is perhaps Spier's most ambitious work. It is a book large in size and scope, with a large number of pictures of peoples and cultures. It has appeal to both adults and children, and can be studied from beginning to end, over and over again. The book looks at the differences among the billions of people who inhabit the earth. Spier states on the first page that each and every one of us is different from all others, unique in his or her own right. He then describes some differences and some similarities among people around the world. He begins with physical sizes and shapes and colors. Then he tackles peculiarities: some people with straight hair want theirs to be wavy, and others with little curls want their hair straight. What is considered beautiful in one place may be considered ugly or ridiculous elsewhere. He describes games and dwellings and artistic tastes and celebrations. He does this with humor: reporting that Eskimos find blubber a delicacy, Africans like elephant meat, Frenchmen like frog legs. He reminds us that some people are rich and some are desperately poor. People around the globe are different; how dull the world would be if we all looked and acted the same! There is a message here, gently told.

Spier's *Christmas* is a wordless picture book. The first double page spread shows people shopping in a mall that boasts a dozen Christmas wreaths, seven decorated Christmas trees, and one live Santa, reminding shoppers that there are only a few days until Christmas. We journey through the days: buying a Christmas tree, getting the decorations down from the attic, on to Christmas day and preparing the turkey, grandparents arriving, children at the table with favorite toys by their chairs, and lots of dishes to clean after the party is over. The last page continues the humor; it shows not-so-neat mounds of Christmas boxes, ribbons, paper on the curb for pick-up. The pictures so graphically tell the story that a pre-school child can go through the events by himself, over and over.

We the People: The Constitution of the United States of America is Spier's special gift to his adopted country. It is an artistic celebration of the document, including the Bill of Rights and all the amendments. It dwells on the roots of American freedom and the changes that have taken place as a result of the Constitution. Spier's careful research shows the actual programs that have resulted from the Constitution to promote the general welfare: the Library of Congress, National Wildlife Refuge, Army Corps of Engineers, Federal Aviation Administration, United States Public Health Service, Environmental Protection Agency, Social Security, and on.

Later Spier turns again to pure entertainment. In *Circus!* he shows the inner workings of Circus McNulty, with its 14 acres of canvas, 100 miles of ropes and wires, seven miles of electrical cables, and 2,200 seats. Feeding time involves 250 pounds of fish, tons of hay and grains, meats, bananas, apples, carrots, and fresh fruit for the animals. The high wire artists are awesome, the clowns are funny, the elephants are large, and the human cannonball is truly spectacular. The illustrations in this book have energy and excitement. Children will pour over the pictures before they see the real circus, and after they come back home from the circus they'll pour over the pictures again.

Because of his enormous talent in line drawing, Spier has been recruited to illustrate a number of books for adults: books on gardens, architecture, furniture. His output is prodigious. In addition to his illustrations and his writings, he finds time to build model ships, including Dutch seagoing vessels, and to sail real boats in the waters near his home.

—Mary Lystad

SPIRIN, G(ennady)

Also known as Gennadii or Gennadij. **Nationality:** Russian. **Born:** Orekhovo-Zuevo, U.S.S.R., 25 December 1948. **Education:** Attended Moscow Art School and Moscow Strogonov Academy of Fine Arts. **Family:** Married Raisa; three sons. **Career:** Artist and illustrator in New Jersey, from 1991. **Awards:** Golden Apple Award, International Biennale of Illustration, Czechoslovakia, 1983 for *Marissa and the Gnomes*; Outstanding Science Trade Book for Children, National Science Teachers Association/Children's Book Council, 1985, for *Once There Was a Tree*; Best Illustrated Books, New York Times, 1990 for *The Fool and the Fish: A Tale from Russia,* 1993, for *Gulliver's Adventures in Lilliput,* and 1995, for *Kashtanka*; Fiera Di Bologna honor, 1991, for *Sorotchintzy Fair*; VI Premio Internacional Catalonia d'Illustracio del Libres per a Infants, 1995 for *Kashtanka;* Gold Medal, New York Society of Illustrators, 1992, for *Boots and the Glass Mountain,* 1993, for *The Children of Lir,* 1994, for *The Frog Princess,* and 1996, for *The Tale of Tsar Saltan.*

*

Illustrator: *Once There Was a Tree* by Natalia Romanova, New York, Dial, 1985; *The Mysterious Tale of Gentle Jack and Lord Bumblebee* by George Sand, New York, Dial 1988; *The Tale of the Unicorn* by Otfried Preussler, New York, Dial, 1989; *The White Cat: An Old French Fairy Tale* by Madame d'Aulnoy retold by Robert D. Sans Souci, New York, Orchard, 1990; *The Fool and the Fish: A Tale from Russia* by Alexander N. Afanasyev retold by Lenny Hort, New York, Dial, 1990; *Sorotchintzy Fair* by Nikolai Gogol, Boston, David Godine, 1991; *Rumpelstiltskin* by Wilhelm and Jacob Grimm retold by Alison Sage, Great Britain, A & C Black, 1990; New York, 1991; *Boots and the Glass Mountain* retold by Claire Martin, New York, Dial, 1992; *Snow White and Rose Red* by Wilhelm and Jacob Grimm, New York, Philomel, 1992; *The Nose* by Nikolai Gogol, David Godine, 1993; *Gulliver's Adventures in Lilliput* by Jonathan Swift retold by Ann Keay Beneduce, New York, Putnam, 1993; *The Children of Lir* by Sheila MacGill-Callahan, New York, Dial, 1993; *The Frog Princess: A Russian Folktale* retold by Patrick Lewis, New York, Dial, 1994; *Kashtanka* by Anton Chekhov, Germany, J. F. Schreiber, 1994 and New York, Harcourt, 1995; *The Nutcracker* by E. T. A. Hoffman, Stewart, Tabori & Chang, 1996; *The Tale of the Tsar Saltan* by Alexander S. Pushkin; New York, Dial, 1996; *The Tempest* by William Shakespeare retold by Ann Keay Beneduce, New York, Putnam, 1996; *The Sea King's Daughter: A Russian Legend* retold by Aaron Shepard, New York, Atheneum, 1997.

Critical Studies: *Seventh Book of Junior Authors and Illustrators,* edited by Sally Holmes Holtze, Dublin and New York, H.W. Wilson, 1996, 304-306; "Gennady Spirin" by Barbara Elleman, in *Booklinks,* Chicago, March, 1995, 6-7; *Something about the Author,* edited by Alan Hedblaad, Detroit, Gale Research, Inc., 1998, 195-199.

* * *

Art in children's picture books plays many roles: to extend, to explain, to elaborate upon an author's text, and to advance the narrative line of the story. Gennady Spirin's illustrations fill all of these roles and more—they breathe life into the storyline, capturing moods and emotions, drawing the viewer into sumptuous scenes the illustrator creates. Few artists capture the essence of a culture in such exquisite detail as does Spirin.

Spirin's work in children's book illustration first received recognition with the publication of *Marissa and the Gnomes* in 1983. In that year, he captured the world's attention, receiving the Golden Apple Award at the Biennale of Illustration in Bratislava. Spirin continues to dazzle readers with his elaborate, elegant illustrations which he executes primarily in tempera and watercolor because of an allergy he developed to oil paints while in Art school in Moscow. Many of the books Spirin illustrates are folktales and classic stories from Europe and several of the stories originate in his native Russia.

One of Spirin's early works, *Once There Was a Tree,* was published first in Russia in 1983. The story delivers an environmental message that revolves around the life cycle of a tree in the forest that has died, is cut down and visited by various inhabitants that subsequently claim the tree's stump as their own Eventually a new tree grows and it "belongs to all, because it grows from the earth that is home for all." The artist utilizes rich earth tones of brown and rust and gold to imbue this simple story with a sense of lush vitality. Several of Spirin's distinctive design elements are included in this book. Each illustration appears in its own stylized frame; the text on the adjacent page is identically framed and elements of the illustration serve as decorative additions to the framed text.

Spirin's talent seems especially suited to the illustration of folklore. *The Children of Lir* is based on an Irish myth about an evil stepmother whose jealousy drives her to transform her twin stepsons and stepdaughters into swans. Full page watercolor illustrations and double page spreads that gleam with the crisp greens and blues of the Northern coast of Ireland are the perfect backdrop for this story that many consider the basis for Shakespeare's *King Lear.* Spirin adds illuminated page numbers and Celtic-inspired designs enhance several of the borders of his illustrations.

Boots and the Glass Mountain is a Cinderella variant from Norway. The hero is the youngest brother, Boots, abused by his older siblings but blessed by the gift of his dead mother's tinderbox and her words of wisdom. His courage and cleverness enable him to tame and secretly keep the three magnificent stallions who appear on consecutive midsummer's eves to eat his father's grain and they, in turn, make it possible for him to conquer the glass mountain and win the hand of the princess who already loves him for his goodness. Spirin infuses golden overtones throughout scenes of pomp and splendor as contestants gather to challenge the glass mountain. His characters are expressive, filled with vitality and robust good humor. Boots' older brothers are oafish; the trolls are suitably repulsive; the horses are splendid steeds and the princess and her hero are a match destined to live happily ever after. Again, Spirin frames both illustration and text with borders that are decorated with elements from the storyline. Several cameo pictures add decorative and narrative details to the story.

A similar storyline is found in the Russian folktale, *The Fool and the Fish.* Once again, it is the youngest brother who wins the hand of the princess but the protagonist in this story is lazy albeit lucky. When sent to fetch water, he has the good fortune to capture a magic fish who, in return for his freedom, grants the fool's wishes. Spirin creates drama in his illustrations, juxtaposing rich crimsons and blues against a cool white and silver palette. The detail in his characters' costumes is reminiscent of Renaissance paintings.

Elegant costuming and elaborate settings are the most striking aspects of Spirin's illustrations for *The Frog Princess.* In this distinctly Russian tale, the tsar orders his three sons to shoot an arrow "into the heart of Russia. Whoever finds your arrow will be your bride." When Ivan, the youngest son's arrow is found by a frog, he believes he has been cursed but he soon learns that this is no ordinary frog but the frog princess, Vasilisa the Wise. The characters Spirin depicts in this story are expressively portrayed. The antagonists are chillingly evil, Vasilisa and Ivan radiate goodness, and the tsar is resplendent in his power. Elleman noted in *Booklinks,* that Spirin's use of textured layering gives dimension to the pictures while unique design elements provide the perfect ambience for this book. The texture and ambience are evident in the gold embroidered fabric Spirin employs to border the text and illustrations that take place in the palace. In contrast, he surrounds the scenes in the woods with fabric that is adorned by wildflowers. In the cor ner of each page is an illuminated page number, next to a frog with an arrow in its mouth.

Another classic Russian tale which Spirin illuminated with his drawings is *The Sea King's Daughter: A Russian Legend.* Spirin devises a medieval setting for this celebration of the power of music and dancing both on land and below the sea. The colors he uses to create this story of love and the difficult choices it sometimes entails glitter. The crowd scenes both above and below the waves are a visual feast. Expressive faces, hands and body postures lend a sense of gaiety and vitality to this legendary story.

Folklore is not the only genre upon which Spirin has impressed his distinctive style. He has also lent his considerable talent to the illustration of classic tales which have been adapted as picture books. One such tale is *The Tale of Tsar Saltan* written by the renowned Russian poet, Alexander Pushkin. In a story of love, jealousy, betrayal, and retribution, Spirin employs a comparatively neutral palette which serves as a splendid foil when he incorporates the gleaming gold of thirty-three knights in shining armor that rise from the ocean or the scene reuniting the tsar with his wife and his son and his new daughter-in-law, the swan maiden who made their reunion possible. Arching over every illustration, in repetition of the curve of the barrel that carried the tsarina and her son out to sea, is a panel that establishes the setting for the action taking place. Robust, expressive figures abound in this story as do embroidered costumes that are almost palpable in their opulent embroidery.

Another classic story which Spirin enlivens with his artwork is *Gulliver's Adventures in Lilliput.* In an editorial note, the reader learns that *Gulliver's Travels* was Spirin's favorite story as a youngster and that illustrating this book fulfilled a lifelong dream. To the viewer of his lavish illustrations, Spirin's affection for this story is quite evident. It is easy to become lost in the intricate details of his drawings as Spirin chronicles the Herculean endeavors of the Lilliputians to capture, subdue, feed, transport and clothe their visitor. The artist uses lush color to create an elaborate Renaissance setting peopled with characters who are revealed as individuals with distinct personalities and a measure of hubris, despite their diminutive size. He portrays Gulliver as the splendid giant he appears to be in Lilliput, responding to his tiny captors with puzzlement, indulgence, gentleness, and, eventually, disappointment. Spirin uses full page illustrations for this classic tale and includes double page spreads to emphasize the disparity in size between Gulliver and the Lilliputians. The text is incorporated into the illustration, presented in frames that reflect the action or setting of the storyline. On several pages, the Lilliputians are in the process of constructing or securing the framework for the text. On other pages, the text appears framed by Renaissance buildings. The overall effect of Spirin's paintings and design is as enervating and exciting as the plot of this enduring classic. The artwork of Gennady Spirin makes a remarkable contribution to the field of children's literature. Children, as well as adults, who are introduced to his work will delight in his opulent settings, well defined characters, wealth of details and intriguing elements of design. Whether Spirin illustrates stories set in nature, in palaces, in medieval cities, or under the sea, he is able to extend, embellish and enhance a story and frequently adds to the narrative with his spectacular art.

—Anne Drolett Creany

SPYKMAN, E(lizabeth) C(hoate)

Nationality: American. **Born:** Southboro, Massachusetts, 17 July 1896. **Education:** Westover School, Middlebury, Connecticut, graduated 1914. **Family:** Married Nicholas John Spykman in 1931 (died 1943); two daughters. **Died:** 7 August 1965.

Publications for Children

Fiction

A Lemon and a Star. New York, Harcourt Brace, 1955; London, Macmillan, 1956.

The Wild Angel. New York, Harcourt Brace, 1957; London, Macmillan, 1958.

Terrible, Horrible Edie. New York, Harcourt Brace, 1960; London, Macmillan, 1961.

Edie on the Warpath. New York, Harcourt Brace, 1966; London, Macmillan, 1967.

Publications for Adults

Other

Westover. Middlebury, Connecticut, Westover School, 1959.

* * *

E.C. Spykman's four novels—the turn-of-the-century saga of the Cares family of Summerton, Massachusetts—are one of the treasures of children's literature. The four younger Cares, Ted, Jane, Hubert, and Edie, are independent, argumentative, and intelligent. They live in a comfortably well-off world of servants, sailboats, summers by the sea, and exciting new motor cars. Reminiscent of E. Nesbit's Bastable children, they spend most of their time plotting adventures and figuring out ways to circumvent the unreasonable rules and regulations of the adult world.

Though all four children are vivid and highly individualistic characters, Edie, the youngest, emerges as Spykman's most finely drawn portrait. In the first book—*A Lemon and a Star*—10-year-old Jane is the central figure while 5-year-old Edie is merely an annoying younger sibling. But in the course of the next three books, Edie moves to center stage. Impetuous, self reliant, always on the lookout for adventure, Edie Cares is one of the most spirited heroines ever to live between the covers of a children's book. She lops off her long hair and rides with the boys in a sheep round-up. She plots to capture an imagined kidnapper. She marches with the suffragettes. Yet throughout she maintains an inner tenderness and sensitivity which marks her as a fully developed—though not fully grown—human being, rather than a sterotypical "tomboy" character.

The great achievement of Spykman was this ability to create full and utterly believable characters, while at the same time presenting a richly evocative picture of the time and place in which they lived. With no sense of nostalgia, she presents in equal portions the joys and the sorrows of being young. The books live, for both children and adults, because they remain consistently true to the child's perception of the world. A concern for fairness and justice is ever present, but adult moralizing is absent. Humor, lightheartedness, and moments of tenderness make reading the books a delight. An underlying recognition of the fact that, in spite of the fun, growing up is a serious business, makes the memory of them linger long after the covers are closed.

—Susan Meyers

STANLEY, Diane

Has also written as Diane Stanley Zuromskis and Diane Zuromskis. **Nationality:** American. **Born:** Abilene, Texas, 27 December 1943. **Education:** Trinity University, San Antonio, Texas, B.A. 1965; Edinburgh College of Art, 1966-67; Johns Hopkins University, Baltimore, Maryland, M.A. 1970. **Family:** Married 1) Peter Zuromskis in 1970 (divorced 1979); two daughters; 2) Peter Vennema in 1979; one son. **Career:** Freelance medical illustrator, 1970-74; graphic designer, Dell Publishing, New York City, 1977; art director of children's books, G.P. Putnam's Sons and Coward, McCann & Geoghegan, New York City, 1977-79; author and illustrator of books for children, since 1978. Exhibition: Bush Galleries, Norwich, Vermont, 1987. **Awards:** American Reading Association Children's Choice award, 1979, for *The Farmer in the Dell*; *School Library Journal* Best Book selection, 1983, for *The Month Brothers: A Slavic Tale*; Outstanding Science Trade Book for Children, Children's Book Council-National Science Teachers Association, 1985, for *All Wet! All Wet!*; Notable Children's Trade Book in the Field of Social Studies, 1983, for *The Month Brothers: A Slavic Tale* and *The Conversation Club,* 1985, for *A Country Tale,* 1986, for *Peter the Great* and *Captain Whiz-Bang,* 1988, for *Shaka: King of the Zulus,* 1990, for *Fortune,* 1991, for *The Last Princess: The Story of Princess Kai'iulani of Hawai'i,* and 1992, for *Bard of Avon: The Story of William Shakespeare*; American Library Association Notable Book, 1986, for *Peter the Great,* 1990, for *Good Queen Bess: The Story of Elizabeth I of England,* 1992, for *Bard of Avon: The Story of William Shakespeare,* 1994, for *Cleopatra,* 1997, for *Leonardo da Vinci,* and 1998, for *Rumpelstiltskin's Daughter*; Golden Kite Award Honor Book, Society of Children's Book Writers, 1987, for *Peter the Great,* and 1997, for *Saving Sweetness*; *New York Times Book Review* ten best illustrated books of 1988 and notable book of 1988 selections, both for *Shaka: King of the Zulus*; *Parenting Magazine* Reading Magic Award, *Boston Globe/Horn Book* Honor Book for Nonfiction, *Parent's Magazine* Best Kids' Books of 1990, all 1990, all for *Good Queen Bess: The Story of Elizabeth I of England*; *Parents Magazine* Best Kids' Books of 1991 selection, *Booklist* Editor's Choice selection, 1991, and Carter G. Woodson Award, National Council for the Social Studies, 1992, all for *The Last Princess: The Story of Princess Kai'iulani of Hawai'i*; Children's Choices for 1992, International Reading Association-Children's Book Council, for *Siegfried*; Horn Book Twenty-five Best Nonfiction Books of the Year selection, *Publisher's Weekly* Fifty Best Books selection, *Booklist* Editor's Choice, *School Library Journal* Best Books selection, and *Parenting Magazine* Reading Magic Award, all 1992, and Notable Children's Book in the Language Arts, 1993, all for *Bard of Avon: The Story of William Shakespeare*; *Parenting Magazine* Best Books of 1993 selection, and American Bookseller Pick of the Lists, 1993, both for *Charles Dickens: The Man Who Had Great Expectations*; *Publisher's Weekly* Best Books of 1994 selection, *Parenting Magazine*'s Best Books of 1994 selection, and *Booklist* Children's Editors' Choice selection, 1994, all for *Cleopatra*; *Boston Globe/Horn Book* Honor Book for Nonfiction, 1997, for *Leonardo da Vinci.* **Address:** 2120 Tangley, Houston, Texas 77005, U.S.A.

Publications for Children

Fiction (illustrated by the author)

The Conversation Club. New York, Macmillan, 1983.
Birdsong Lullaby. New York, Morrow, 1985.
Captain Whiz-Bang. New York, Morrow, 1987.
Fortune. New York, Morrow, 1990.
Rumpelstiltskin's Daughter. New York, Morrow, 1997.

Biographies (illustrated by the author)

Peter the Great. New York, Aladdin, 1986.
With Peter Vennema, *Shaka: King of the Zulus.* New York, Morrow, 1988.
With Peter Vennema, *Good Queen Bess: The Story of Elizabeth I of England.* New York, Four Winds, 1990.
With Peter Vennema, *Bard of Avon: The Story of William Shakespeare.* New York, Morrow, 1992.
With Peter Vennema, *Charles Dickens: The Man Who Had Great Expectations.* New York, Morrow, 1993.
With Peter Vennema, *Cleopatra.* New York, Morrow, 1994.
Leonardo da Vinci. New York, Morrow, 1996.
Joan of Arc. New York, Morrow, 1998.

Fiction

The Good-Luck Pencil, illustrated by Bruce Degen. New York, Four Winds, 1986.
Siegfried, illustrated by John Sandford. New York, Bantam, 1991.
Moe the Dog in Tropical Paradise, illustrated by Elise Primavera. New York, Putnam, 1992.
The Gentleman and the Kitchen Maid, illustrated by Dennis Nolan. New York, Dial, 1994.
Saving Sweetness, illustrated by G. Brian Karas. New York, Putnam's, 1996.

Other

Elena. New York, Hyperion, 1996.

*

Media Adaptations: *Moe the Dog in Tropical Paradise* (videorecording), MCA/Universal Home Video, 1994.

Critical Studies: Review of *Bard of Avon: The Story of William Shakespeare* by Phillis Sidorsky, in *Washington Post Book World,* 6 December 1972, 18; entry in *Something About the Author,* Detroit, Gale, Vol. 80, 1995, 215-220; "Diane Stanley: Illustrating a Life" by Elizabeth Devereaux, in *Publisher's Weekly,* 22 July 1996, 216-217.

Illustrator: (Under name Diane Zuromskis) *The Farmer in the Dell,* 1978; *Fiddle-I Fee: A Traditional American Chant,* 1979; (under name Diane Stanley Zuromskis) *Half-a-Ball-of-Kenki: An Ashanti Tale* retold by Verna Aardema, 1979; *Little Mouse Nibbling* by Tony Johnston, 1979; *The Man Whose Name Was Not Thomas* by M. Jean Craig, 1981; *Onions, Onions* by Toni Hormann, 1981; *Petrosinella, a Neopolitan Rapunzel* by Giambattista Basile, adapted from the translation by John Edward Taylor, 1981; *Sleeping Ugly* by Jane Yolen, 1981; *Robin of Bray* by Jean Marzollo and Claudio Marzollo, 1982; *Beach Party* by Joanne Ryder, 1982; *Little Orphant Annie* by James Whitcomb Riley, 1983; *The Month Brothers: A Slavic Tale* by Samuel Marshak, translated by Thomas P. Whitney, 1983; *All Wet! All Wet!* by James Skofield, 1984; *The Last Princess: The Story of Princess Kai'iulani of Hawai'i* by Fay Stanley, 1991.

* * *

There is a touch of the fairy tale in the real-life story of Diane Stanley and her husband-collaborator Peter Vennema: they met after Stanley had graduated from college and got a job at a medical lab in Houston; they dated but drifted apart, both marrying others and eventually divorcing; then Diane moved with her two young daughters to New York and got a job in publishing—in an office that turned out to be just next door to Peter's parents' brownstone—and the rest is history.

Stanley's work in publishing was in design and art direction (always talented in art, she had studied medical illustration after Peter encouraged her to do more with her life than work in the "dead-end" job she had in Houston), and her first published books were illustrations of works by others, including a folktale by Verna Aardema, Giambattista Basile's Neopolitan version of *Rapunzel,* a Slavic tale by Samuel Marshak, and James Whitcomb Riley's fairy tale-like story-poem of *Little Orphant Annie.*

Stanley soon began to write her own stories. *The Conversation Club,* her first effort at writing and illustrating, is the story of a club of mice who get together for conversation—all talking at the same time, resulting in terrible headaches—until newcomer Peter Fieldmouse ingeniously solves the problem by starting a listening club. *Birdsong Lullaby,* Stanley's next book, is a dream-like tale of a little girl who imagines all the wonderful things she could do if she were a bird: soar through the air, fly off to exotic places, float on the wind and touch the clouds, fly into a rainbow and come out full of colors. *A Country Tale* is Stanley's imaginative and elegant retelling of the tale of the country mouse and the city mouse, but with cats instead of mice as the protagonists!

It was at this point that Stanley started writing and illustrating the notable biographies for which she has become perhaps most acclaimed. Her first subject, like the hero of her first storybook, was named Peter—this time, the greatest Peter of them all, Peter the Great. This was followed by biographies of the Zulu king Shaka, Queen Elizabeth I, William Shakespeare, Charles Dickens, Cleopatra, and, finally, Leonardo da Vinci. "I don't know why I didn't do Leonardo earlier. He has been my hero for as long as I can remember," Stanley told Elizabeth Devereaux in her interview for *Publisher's Weekly.*

All challenging subjects for children, to be sure, but Stanley has met the challenge by culling colorful anecdotes from Peter Vennema's in-depth research to enliven the basic facts of her subjects' lives and achievements: the young, pre-bankruptcy Charles Dickens in his white beaver top hat playing with his school friends Giles's cats; Cleopatra hiding from Octavian's invading armies in the tomb she'd prepared for herself next to that of Alexander the Great; Elizabeth cleverly using her wits to avoid entering into a number of proposed political marriages in which a husband might try to tell her how to run her country ("She didn't say no, she didn't say yes, she said maybe"). Her illustrations add to the authenticity and lively detail of the text: Elizabeth's lace collars, Dickens' cobblestone streets, the fragments of Leonardo's drawings. She also includes bibliographies of special interest to young people as well as maps and pronunciation guides where appropriate. "What a lucky day for young readers when Diane Stanley and her husband Peter Vennema produce one of their distinguished biographies," exclaimed Phyllis Sidorsky in her review of *Bard of Avon: The Story of William Shakespeare* for the *Washington Post Book World.*

With her latest book, Stanley has returned to the fairy tale world, taking a step into the future by imagining how Rumpelstiltskin's daughter might have dealt with the greedy king's demands. In this totally modern version, the miller's daughter married the charming Rumpelstiltskin when he agreed to spin the straw into gold in return for her firstborn child ("I promise I'll be an excellent father. I know all the lullabies. I'll read to the child every day. I'll even coach Little League."). And when their daughter is captured by the king, she devises a solution that will satisfy the king as well as better the lives of all of his subjects. "Oh, and I forgot to tell you, " Stanley concludes her tale, "Rumpelstiltskin's daughter had a name, too. It was Hope."

—Marcia Welsh

STEELE, Mary Q(uintard)

Pseudonym: Wilson Gage. **Nationality:** American. **Born:** Mary Quintard Govan, Chattanooga, Tennessee, 8 May 1922. **Education:** University of Chattanooga, B.S. 1943. **Family:** Married William O. Steele, *q.v.*, in 1943 (died 1979); two daughters and one son. **Address:** 329 Crestway Drive, Chattanooga, Tennessee 37411, U.S.A.

Publications for Children

Fiction

Journey Outside, illustrated by Rocco Negri. New York, Viking Press, 1969; London, Macmillan, 1970.

The First of the Penguins, illustrated by Susan Jeffers. New York, Macmillan, 1973; London, Macmillan, 1974.

Because of the Sand Witches There, illustrated by Paul Galdone. New York, Greenwillow, 1975; London, Macmillan, 1976.

The Eye in the Forest, with William O. Steele. New York, Dutton, 1975.

The True Men. New York, Greenwillow, 1976.

The Owl's Kiss: Three Stories. New York, Greenwillow, 1978.

Wish, Come True, illustrated by Muriel Batherman. New York, Greenwillow, 1979.

The Life (and Death) of Sarah Elizabeth Harwood. New York, Greenwillow, 1980.

Fiction as Wilson Gage

The Secret of the Indian Mound, illustrated by Mary Stevens. Cleveland, World, 1958.
The Secret of the Crossbone Hill, illustrated by Mary Stevens. Cleveland, World, 1959.
The Secret of the Fiery Gorge, illustrated by Mary Stevens. Cleveland, World, 1960.
A Wild Goose Tale, illustrated by Glen Rounds. Cleveland, World, 1961.
Dan and the Miranda, illustrated by Glen Rounds. Cleveland, World, 1962.
Miss Osborne-the-Mop, illustrated by Paul Galdone. Cleveland, World, 1963.
Big Blue Island, illustrated by Glen Rounds. Cleveland, World, 1964.
The Ghost of Five Owl Farm, illustrated by Paul Galdone. Cleveland, World, 1966; London, Faber, 1967.
Mike's Toads, illustrated by Glen Rounds. New York, World, 1970.
Squash Pie, illustrated by Glen Rounds. New York, Greenwillow, 1976.
Down in the Boondocks, illustrated by Glen Rounds. New York, Greenwillow, 1977.
Mrs. Gaddy and the Ghost, illustrated by Marylin Hafner. New York, Greenwillow, 1979; London, Bodley Head, 1981.
Cully Cully and the Bear, illustrated by James Stevenson. New York, Greenwillow, and London, Bodley Head, 1983.
The Crow and Mrs. Gaddy, illustrated by Marylin Hafner. New York, Greenwillow, and London, Bodley Head, 1984.
Mrs. Gaddy and the Fast-Growing Vine, illustrated by Marylin Hafner. New York, Greenwillow, 1985; London, Bodley Head, 1986.

Poetry

Anna's Summer Songs [*Garden Songs*], illustrated by Lena Anderson. New York, Greenwillow, 2 vols., 1988-89.

Other

Editor, *The Fifth Day* (poetry anthology), illustrated by Janina Domanska. New York, Greenwillow, 1978.
Editor, *Traditional Tales.* Stroud, Thimble, 1989.

PUBLICATIONS FOR ADULTS

Other

The Living Year: An Almanac for My Survivors (essays). New York, Viking Press, 1972.

*

Manuscript Collections: Kerlan Collection, University of Minnesota, Minneapolis.

Mary Q. Steele comments:
My primary interest is in natural history, and especially birds. And the puzzle of humanity's place in the scheme of things follows as the night the day, and I suppose this is what I am talking about in my books, however light-hearted they may be. Which sounds a little pompous and I pray forgiveness.

I would hope my books would be enjoyed; I like to think the books make readers laugh. But I would hope too for the occasional reader who closes one of my books and ever after looks at the world of living things with some small measure of my own sense of astonishment and gratitude.

* * *

Mary Q. Steele is most noted for her Newbery Honor Book *Journey Outside* and for her enormously popular *Miss Osborne-the-Mop.* However, Steele has written a variety of children's books from simple stories for younger children such as *Mike's Toads,* to more complex considerations of death and suicide in *The Life (and Death) of Sarah Elizabeth Harwood.* The most common theme in Steele's books is an appreciation for nature. In *Mike's Toads* a young boy learns that taking small creatures out of their natural environment is not a good idea; in *The Life (and Death) of Sarah Elizabeth Harwood* one of the characters rescues and revives insects, and in *Dan and the Miranda* spiders cause humorous problems for a young scientist. While the natural history in these books is interesting and sometimes amusing, it does not always compensate for rather dated dialogue and unexciting storylines. In *Mike's Toad,* for instance, Mike's tendency to volunteer other people without asking their permission happens so frequently in the first few pages of the book that by the time the toads are introduced the story has become silly and predictable. It is hard to feel sympathy for a character who persists in an activity that invariably gets him into pointless trouble—or for parents who continue to bail him out.

It is Steele's second theme that has made stories such as *Miss Osborne-the-Mop* so popular. In these books Steele combines a child's eye view of magic and witchcraft with childlike wackiness. Not all of these books have been critically successful but they have been very popular with children who are just moving into "chapter" books. These stories are just strange and silly enough to be really appealing and to keep young readers reading.

A third theme in Steele's work has been an interest in placing characters in situations that require them to come to terms with some of the difficulties of living. In *The Life (and Death) of Sarah Elizabeth Harwood* a young girl contemplates suicide. Sarah lives in what her father describes as an eccentric family. Her brother calculates the nutritional levels of every food that he consumes, her sister traps herself in a tree while trying to study the sleeping habits of birds, and her mother celebrates the rebirth of a plant by screaming to raise the dead. Not surprisingly, Sarah feels out of place, and unable to do anything right. After she misplaces a valuable album belonging to a friend, she becomes increasingly distraught. Her initial conclusion that suicide is her only way out is thwarted, and a visit to her aging grandmother helps Sarah gain some perspective on her problems. In *Wish, Come True,* two children enliven a three-week visit to Great Aunt's "small, rather dark, old-fashioned" apartment by learning to make their own entertainment—with a little magic. *Big Blue Island* takes a similar theme—a move from Detroit to an island on a Tennessee river—and traces a boy's growing self-reliance and appreciation for his unusual uncle.

The most interesting of Steele's books, however, is *Journey Outside.* In this short novel, Steele's attention to the environment is linked with an adolescent's quest for something more than the life that his people accept. Dilar of the Raft People has been raised on a string of rafts continuously moving along an underground river, searching for a "Better Place." Convinced that his people merely travel in circles, Dilar jumps off his family's raft, clambers through a cleft in the rock face, and discovers a world of "day" and "green." As Dilar searches the new world he has found, Steele builds an allegory in which common assumptions about how people "should" live are questioned. Is it better to store up for the future, or live for the moment? Dilar's search for wisdom leads him inevitably to himself. He decides to bring his people up into the world again. *Journey Outside* is fascinating on several levels, and could be read as a simple fantasy-adventure story, as well as an allegory. As with other award-winning books, however, this book probably has less child-appeal than Steele's lighter, more straightforward stories.

—Linda S. Levstik

STEELE, William O(wen)

Nationality: American. **Born:** Franklin, Tennessee, 22 December 1917. **Education:** Cumberland University, Lebanon, Tennessee, 1936-40, B.A. 1940; University of Chattanooga, Tennessee, 1951. **Military Service:** United States Army Air Corps during World War II. **Family:** Married Mary Quintard Govan (i.e., Mary Q. Steele, *q.v.*) in 1943; two daughters and one son. **Award:** Women's International League for Peace and Freedom Jane Addams award, 1958. **Died:** 25 June 1979.

Publications for Children

Fiction

The Golden Root, illustrated by Fritz Kredel. New York, Aladdin, 1951.
The Buffalo Knife, illustrated by Paul Galdone. New York, Harcourt Brace, 1952.
Over-Mountain Boy, illustrated by Fritz Kredel. New York, Aladdin, 1952.
Wilderness Journey, illustrated by Paul Galdone. New York, Harcourt Brace, 1953.
Winter Danger, illustrated by Paul Galdone. New York, Harcourt Brace, 1954; London, Macmillan, 1963.
Tomahawks and Trouble, illustrated by Paul Galdone. New York, Harcourt Brace, 1955.
We Were There on the Oregon Trail, illustrated by Jo Polseno. New York, Grosset and Dunlap, 1955.
David Crockett's Earthquake, illustrated by Nicolas. New York, Harcourt Brace, 1956.
We Were There with the Pony Express, illustrated by Frank Vaughn. New York, Grosset and Dunlap, 1956.
The Lone Hunt, illustrated by Paul Galdone. New York, Harcourt Brace, 1956; London, Macmillan, 1957.
Flaming Arrows, illustrated by Paul Galdone. New York, Harcourt Brace, 1957; London, Macmillan, 1958.
Daniel Boone's Echo, illustrated by Nicolas. New York, Harcourt Brace, 1957.
The Perilous Road, illustrated by Paul Galdone. New York, Harcourt Brace, 1958; London, Macmillan, 1960.
Andy Jackson's Water Well, illustrated by Michael Ramus. New York, Harcourt Brace, 1959.
The Far Frontier, illustrated by Paul Galdone. New York, Harcourt Brace, 1959; London, Macmillan, 1960.
The Spooky Thing, illustrated by Paul Coker. New York, Harcourt Brace, 1960.
The Year of the Bloody Sevens, illustrated by Charles Beck. New York, Harcourt Brace, 1963.
Wayah of the Real People, illustrated by Isa Barnett. Williamsburg, Virginia, Colonial Williamsburg Inc., 1964.
The No-Name Man of the Mountain, illustrated by Jack Davis. New York, Harcourt Brace, 1964.
Trail Through Danger, illustrated by Charles Beck. New York, Harcourt Brace, 1965.
Tomahawk Border, illustrated by Vernon Wooten. Williamsburg, Virginia, Colonial Williamsburg Inc., 1966.
Hound Dog Zip to the Rescue, illustrated by Mimi Korach. Champaign, Illinois, Garrard, 1970.
Triple Trouble for Hound Dog Zip, illustrated by Mimi Korach. Champaign, Illinois, Garrard, 1972.
John's Secret Treasure, illustrated by R. Dennis. New York, Macmillan, 1975.
The Eye in the Forest, with Mary Q. Steele. New York, Dutton, 1975.
The Man with the Silver Eyes. New York, Harcourt Brace, 1976.
The War Party, illustrated by Lorinda Bryan Cauley. New York, Harcourt Brace, 1978.
The Magic Amulet. New York, Harcourt Brace, 1979.

Other

John Sevier, Pioneer Boy, illustrated by Sandra James. Indianapolis, Bobbs Merrill, 1953.
The Story of Daniel Boone, illustrated by Warren Baumgartner. New York, Grosset and Dunlap, 1953; London, Muller, 1957.
Francis Marion: Young Swamp Fox, illustrated by Dick Gringhuis. Indianapolis, Bobbs Merrill, 1954.
The Story of Leif Ericson, illustrated by Pranas Lapé. New York, Grosset and Dunlap, 1954; London, Sampson Low, 1960.
De Soto: Child of the Sun, illustrated by Lorence Bjorklund. New York, Aladdin, 1956.
Westward Adventure: The True Stories of Six Pioneers. New York, Harcourt Brace, 1962.
The Old Wilderness Road: An American Journey. New York, Harcourt Brace, 1968.
The Wilderness Tattoo: A Narrative of Juan Ortiz. New York, Harcourt Brace, 1972.
Henry Woodward of Carolina: Surgeon, Trader, Indian Chief, illustrated by Hoyt Simmons. Columbia, South Carolina, Sandlapper Press, 1972.
The Cherokee Crown of Tannassy. Winston-Salem, North Carolina, Blair, 1977.
Talking Bones: Secrets of Indian Burial Mounds, illustrated by Carlos Llerena-Aguirre. New York, Harper, 1978.

*

Manuscript Collections: Kerlan Collection, University of Minnesota, Minneapolis; Special Collections, John Brister Library, Memphis State University, Tennessee.

William O. Steele commented:

(1978) My fiction for the 8- to 12-year-old reader has mostly been concerned with pioneer and Indian struggles in the southeastern U.S. during the 18th century when the red and white cultures clashed at the cutting edge of the frontier. I try always to see the past as it was, to put into books, not 20th-century characters with a fake pioneer dress of split cowhide, but 18th-century boys and men with buckskin shirts rubbing against their shoulder blades, and the smell of sweat and woodsmoke around them, and their bellies only half-full of dried deer meat and gritty ashcakes. What I am trying to get over to my readers is not events but people who make the events. History textbooks can give a reader the high spots—but it takes more than textbooks to give you the heart-squeezed hopelessness and fear that sounds of Indian warwhoops can cause.

In my books I try to give a true picture of what the unspoiled frontier country was like when it began to be settled, of the dangers and hardships and rewards of settling it. Above all I try to convey something of the real essence of the times, something of the restless, tough-bodied, forward-looking pioneer who pushes further and further into the wilderness. And I try to accomplish this in as entertaining a fashion as I can.

In the 1950s and 1960s I could write historical fiction from the white pioneer's viewpoint and not be criticised as slighting the Indian's side. Now in the 1970s I would not want to write that kind of book and probably would find no publisher if I did on account of today's ethnic sensitivity. In the future, so as to not waste a quarter of a century of research on the frontier period, I may switch to the Indian viewpoint in his struggles against the whites on the frontier. I would prefer, however, to go back in time to the fascinating prehistoric Indian groups of eastern America. It will be a challenge, but it seems to be a wide open field.

* * *

William O. Steele wrote what used to be confidently called "boys' books." Vigorous novels of pioneering, wilderness travel, and Indian fighting, written for readers of the middle years but strong enough for "reluctant readers" of 12 to 14, are his main stock in trade. Steele provides for maximum reader involvement: the major protagonist is always a young boy of 10 to 12 who is portrayed as staunch and resourceful, but never unrealistically brave or infallible. Most stories are set in the Tennessee wilderness during the pioneering period of American history, a background all but guaranteeing adventure.

The overarching theme of the novels usually involves a step by the young protagonist toward maturity; in the course of his adventures, he learns something important about himself and about life. In *Flaming Arrows* young Chad Rabun learns tolerance of others; in *The Buffalo Knife* Andy gains confidence in his own courage. At the very least, the outlook of the young hero is expanded: the Indian boy in *Wayah of the Real People* discards some of his superstitious fear of whites, as does Talatu in *The Man with the Silver Eyes.* But Steele never allows such themes to interfere with his central purpose, which is to tell a fast-moving, exciting story. In some books, indeed, the growing-and-learning motif is nearly smothered under an avalanche of physical adventure. In more thoughtful novels, like *Winter Danger* and *The Man with the Silver Eyes,* the elements are better balanced.

Characterization in Steele's stories centers on the young protagonist and is fairly simple. The boys are meant to be typical; one can be distinguished from the other mainly by the particular fear with which he comes to terms in the story. Adults, especially parents, are usually stock figures, brave, kind, supportive, but generalized. There are occasional exceptions: Caje's father, in *Winter Danger,* is a footloose "woodsy" whose character is briefly but sharply sketched; Camp Green, the Daniel Boone-like "Long Hunter" and Mr. Rhea, the dolorous trader, both of *Wilderness Journey,* are memorable.

After the mid-1960s, Steele from time to time shifted the viewpoint in his stories, giving Indian-white encounters from the Indian's side. *Wayah of the Real People* shows white society in the Williamsburg of 1752 through the eyes of a young Cherokee boy sent to Brafferton Hall for a year of schooling. Adventure is minor, but the point of view is fresh. *The Man with the Silver Eyes,* a far more somber story of an Indian boy who discovers that he is half-white, acknowledges the inherent tragedy in the clash of cultures. Though its climax is overly theatrical, this book is a welcome departure from the simplistic view of Indian-as-enemy that prevails in most of Steele's early books.

Steele's novels are credible in period detail, lively in incident, and colorful with vernacular speech. They are sometimes glib and unconvincing at any deeper level; character change is often accomplished with unrealistic ease, and incidents of physical peril and violence frequently seem contrived or gratuitous.

Steele also wrote several tall tales drawn from Tennessee mountain lore. *Andy Jackson's Water Well, The No-Name Man of the Mountain,* and several other short books tell exaggerated tales with proper deadpan style and expressive local language. The language and humor of these tales are richer and livelier than those of the adventure fiction, but for young readers, they lack the strong narrative power and the sense of identification provided by the adventure novels.

—Anne Scott MacLeod

STEIG, William

Nationality: American. **Born:** New York City, 14 November 1907. **Education:** City College, New York, 1923-25; National Academy of Design, New York, 1925-29. **Family:** Married 1) Elizabeth Mead in 1936 (divorced), one daughter and one son; 2) Karl Homestead in 1950 (divorced 1963), one daughter; 3) Stephanie Healey in 1964 (divorced 1966); 4) Jeanne Doron in 1969. **Career:** Since 1930, freelance humorous artist. Individual shows: Downtown Gallery, New York, 1939; Smith College, Northampton, Massachusetts, 1940. **Awards:** American Library Association Caldecott Medal, 1970; Christopher award, 1973; American Book award, for picture book, 1983; New England Book award, 1993. **Address:** 301 Berkeley St., #4, Boston, Massachusetts 02116, U.S.A.

PUBLICATIONS FOR CHILDREN (ILLUSTRATED BY THE AUTHOR)

Fiction

Roland, The Minstrel Pig. New York, Windmill, 1968; London, Hamish Hamilton, 1974.

Sylvester and the Magic Pebble. New York, Windmill, 1969; London, Abelard Schuman, 1972.

The Bad Island. New York, Windmill, 1969; revised edition, as *Rotten Island,* New York, Godine, 1984, London, Viking Kestrel, 1986.
Amos and Boris. New York, Farrar Straus, 1971; London, Hamish Hamilton, 1972.
Dominic. New York, Farrar Straus, 1972; London, Hamish Hamilton, 1973.
The Real Thief. New York, Farrar Straus, 1973; London, Hamish Hamilton, 1974.
Farmer Palmer's Wagon Ride. New York, Farrar Straus, 1974; London, Hamish Hamilton, 1975.
Abel's Island. New York, Farrar Straus, 1976; London, Hamish Hamilton, 1977.
The Amazing Bone. New York, Farrar Straus, 1976; London, Hamish Hamilton, 1978.
Caleb and Kate. New York, Farrar Straus, 1977; London, Hamish Hamilton, 1980.
Tiffky Doofky. New York, Farrar Straus, 1978; London, Hamish Hamilton, 1980.
Gorky Rises. New York, Farrar Straus, 1980; London, Gollancz, 1989.
Doctor De Soto. New York, Farrar Straus, 1982; London, Andersen Press, 1983.
Yellow and Pink. New York, Farrar Straus, 1984; London, Gollancz, 1986.
Solomon the Rusty Nail. New York, Farrar Straus, 1985; London, Gollancz, 1987.
Brave Irene. New York, Farrar Straus, 1986; London, Gollancz, 1988.
The Zabajaba Jungle. New York, Farrar Straus, 1987.
Spinky Sulks. New York, Farrar Straus, 1988.
Shrek! New York, Farrar Straus, 1989; London, Gollancz, 1990.
Doctor De Soto Goes to Africa. New York, HarperCollins, 1992.
Zeke Pippin. New York, HarperCollins, 1994.
Grown-ups Get to Do All the Driving. New York, HarperCollins, 1995.
Toby, Where Are You?, illustrated by Teryl Euvremer. New York, HarperCollins, 1997.

Poetry

An Eye for Elephants. New York, Windmill, 1970.

Other

C D B! (word games), New York, Windmill, 1968.
The Bad Speller (reader). New York, Windmill, 1970.
C D C? New York, Farrar Straus, 1984.

PUBLICATIONS FOR ADULTS

Other (drawings)

Man about Town. New York, Long and Smith, 1932.
About People: A Book of Symbolical Drawings. New York, Random House, 1939.
The Lonely Ones. New York, Duell, 1942.
All Embarrassed. New York, Duell, 1944.
Small Fry (*New Yorker* cartoons). New York, Duell, 1944; London, Phoenix House, 1947.
Persistent Faces. New York, Duell, 1945.
Till Death Do Us Part: Some Ballet Notes on Marriage. New York, Duell, 1947.
The Agony in the Kindergarten. New York, Duell, 1950.
The Rejected Lovers. New York, Knopf, 1951.
Dreams of Glory and Other Drawings. New York, Knopf, 1953.
The Steig Album. New York, Duell, 1953.
Continuous Performance (cartoons). New York, Duell, 1963.
Male/Female. New York, Farrar Straus, 1971.
Drawings. New York, Farrar Straus, 1979; London, Faber, 1980.
Ruminations. New York, Farrar Straus, 1984.
Our Miserable Life. New York, Farrar Straus, 1990.
Strutters & Fretters, or, The Inescapable Self. New York, HarperCollins, 1992.
Collected Drawings. Wakefield, Rhode Island, Moyer Bell, 1994.

*

Illustrator: *How to Become Extinct,* 1941, and *The Decline and Fall of Practically Everybody,* 1950, both by Will Cuppy; *Mr. Blandings Builds His Dream House* by Eric Hodgins, 1947; *Listen Little Man! A Document from the Archives of the Orgone Institute* by William Reich, 1948; *Giggle Box* edited by Phyllis R. Fenner, 1950; *Poker for Fun and Profit* by Irwin Steig, 1959; *Consider the Lemming,* 1988, *The Old Testament Made Easy,* 1990, and *Alpha Beta Chowder,* 1992, all by Jeanne Steig.

* * *

In 1968 when William Steig published his first children's book, *Roland, The Minstrel Pig,* he was 61 and had already enjoyed a successful career beginning in 1930 when he became a cartoonist and cover designer for the *New Yorker.* Since the publication of his first children's book, Steig has continued to make significant contributions to American children's literature with such distinguished picture books as *Sylvester and the Magic Pebble,* his two award-winning novels *Dominic* and *Abel's Island,* his readers *C D B!, C D C?,* and *The Bad Speller,* and a book of children's verse, *An Eye for Elephants.*

Steig's books feature such themes as the lost child who is saved from evil and reunited with the family; the hero whose quest includes time for friendship, community, art, and music, as well as weapons; a beneficent and deeply romantic conception of the natural world; such resonant archetypes as initiation, death, and rebirth; and magical transformations. Steig's themes are rendered in elegant, sometimes self-consciously literary language. The presiding voice in these works is urbane and witty, yet never condescending; rather it invites the young reader to participate in this humorous, sophisticated view of the world. Steig's books often reflect his childhood reading of *Grimms' Fairy Tales,* "Hansel and Gretel," *Pinocchio, Tales of King Arthur,* the Katzenjammer Kids, and his love of Charlie Chaplin films. For example, Steig's marvelous character Sylvester Duncan, the wondrous donkey who is turned into stone when he uses a magic pebble to escape from a hungry lion, reminds the reader of Pinocchio; as Pinocchio is locked into the wooden body of a puppet and yearns to be a real boy, so Sylvester, physically and spiritually paralyzed in the rock, longs for speech, for mobility, family, and community. In *The Amazing Bone* Steig draws upon the Grimms' story of fratricide in "The Singing Bone." Steig's amazing bone acts as a protective magical talisman for the innocent and vulnerable child, Pearl the pig.

In *Roland, The Minstrel Pig* Steig introduced many motifs and structural devices which have recurred in his work during the last 20 years: the use of droll anthropomorphized animals; the quest as a structural device; the celebration of art, nature, and community; and a felicitous mixture of art styles (primarily cartoon and impressionism). With full color cartoon illustrations, Steig introduces his readers to Roland, a pig who enjoys a safe and civilized community in which he plays his lute and sings for the gratified entertainment of his friends. In this innocent pastoral place dogs, cats, a cow, goat, monkey, goose, deer, bear, and even a parrot dance in harmonious delight. Eventually Roland's friends convince him that his talent deserves a wider audience. On his journey to find fame Roland confronts loneliness for the first time. More seriously, he encounters evil in the form of the scheming fox, Sebastion, who plans to eat him at an opportune moment. Sebastion nearly succeeds, but the King hears Roland singing and saves him to become the royal minstrel. Thus, Roland achieves the fame for which he longed, while the villainous fox is thrown into a dungeon to live the rest of his days "on nothing but stale bread with sour grapes and water."

While Roland finds happiness in a new home, many of Steig's childlike animal characters return home to celebrate a joyous reunion with their families. Among the most notable of these circular journeys are *Sylvester and the Magic Pebble, The Amazing Bone,* and the novel-length survival story *Abel's Island.*

Sylvester and the Magic Pebble justly deserves its wide recognition as one of the most distinguished works in contemporary American picture books. The opening scene shows Sylvester at home with his parents, happy and secure. Soon thereafter Sylvester finds a magic pebble and accidentally transforms himself into a rock to escape a ferocious lion. Mr. and Mrs. Donkey search everywhere and finally seek help from their local police (controversially depicted as rather befuddled pigs). The police and indeed the entire community turn out to search for the lost Sylvester but fail to locate him because he looks and smells like a rock instead of Sylvester. While Sylvester's parents grieve for their missing son, he undergoes a deathlike sleep as summer turns to autumn, and autumn yields to the isolation and frozen waste of winter. With spring's rebirth, Mr. and Mrs. Duncan try to revive their spirits by going on a picnic amid flowering trees, lush grass, and a profusion of impressionistic flowers. Luckily they use the rock that is Sylvester for a table. Mr. Duncan spies the shiny red pebble and places it on the rock, just as Sylvester exclaims, "I wish I were my real self again!" Instantly the Duncans are reunited amid the scattered picnic. The final illustration shows Sylvester at home curled securely between his parents on a rounded cozy sofa.

In this picture book Steig addresses children's fears of separation from their parents, as well as their fears and terrors and even wishes for radical transformations. He also reveals the power of nature as a healing force and introduces magic as a significant element.

In *The Amazing Bone* Steig portrays an innocent young female pig, Pearl, who dawdles in the woods after school and finds a talking bone, which first saves her from a band of robbers but fails to dupe a clever fox. The fox takes Pearl home to roast for dinner. As the fox tosses a salad and sharpens his cutlery, the bone begins to utter magic words that transform the fox into a tiny mouse-sized creature. Pearl and the bone go home to rejoicing parents.

Steig's two longer fantasies for children, *Abel's Island* and *Dominic,* also feature feisty animal characters as heroes. Abel, an Edwardian mouse in a velvet smoking jacket, is washed away in a storm as he gallantly tries to retrieve his wife's handkerchief. He takes shelter at last on an island, where he learns to fight for survival. Not only does he learn to survive physically; he also learns to create art and to appreciate nature in all of its moods. When he finally returns to his wife, Abel is much more resourceful than the mama's boy who had been washed away a year earlier. *Abel's Island* is a delightful addition to the long tradition of *Robinsonades* which appeared in the aftermath of *Robinson Crusoe.* Abel manages to maintain his elegant and civilized manners even as he must struggle against overwhelming odds to survive.

Dominic, the redoubtable dog hero, in the fantasy of the same title, finds himself discontent with existence and departs on the road to adventure. In this fantasy Steig delights in gentle parody of the heroic tradition. Unlike King Arthur, who receives his sword from the Lady in the Lake, Dominic receives his speare from a catfish in the pond. He also enjoys interludes in his heroic quest when he plays his piccolo and feels his romantic spirit resonate in tune with the rhythms of the universe. Dominic saves several victims of the evil Doomsday Gang along the way, undergoes a death and rebirth or spiritual transformation in the woods, and eventually awakes his own sleeping beauteous dog in a palace amid exquisite gardens. The two continue their adventures together. *Dominic* is a beautifully crafted, highly lyrical wish fulfillment fantasy. Yet Steig's humorous drawings and delicately satirical prose counter what would otherwise be a hopelessly sentimental story.

Many of Steig's picture books incorporate wish-fulfillment childhood fantasies. An adventurous frog in *Gorky Rises* concocts a magical potion enabling him to soar to the stars, break free of adult constraints, and yet return home safely with concrete and indisputable proof that his adventures have actually happened. In *Doctor De Soto* a mouse dentist outwits the crafty fox who poses as a patient. In *Solomon the Rusty Nail* Steig again features the theme of transformation and the child's concern with identity. When Solomon the rabbit wishes, he can transform himself into a rusty nail. Eventually this trick saves him from a hungry cat but backfires when the cat nails him into the house, where he is trapped in the wood. Later, he is released when the house burns, and Solomon becomes himself again and runs home to ecstatic parents. Change, though terrifying, Steig seems to imply, is finally a good and beneficent thing.

Most of Steig's children's picture books feature charming animal characters. With *Caleb and Kate* Steig uses human beings as central characters. Caleb, a carpenter, and Kate, a weaver, love each other, but "not every single minute." A marital spat sends Caleb into the woods where an evil witch, Yedida, changes him into a dog, who then consoles and protects Kate in her grief. Eventually the evil spell is broken, and the couple is reunited. Steig's odd little book *Yellow and Pink* appears to be an allegory about the artist's relationship to his creations. Two small wooden figures, one yellow and one pink, explore the great philosophical issues, "Who am I?" and "Where did I come from?" Their ontological deliberations are interrupted when the artist checks to see whether their paint is dry. In *Brave Irene* Steig reveals the virtues of loyalty and friendship.

Steig is quite simply one of America's finest artists. His witty humorous books celebrate the powers of imagination, art, language, and nature. His comic works are deeply humane and appeal to children and adult critics alike. He has created enduring gifts for the world's children and has reminded all of his readers that laughter helps us to survive.

—Anita Moss

STEPTOE, John (Lewis)

Nationality: American. **Born:** Brooklyn, New York, 14 September 1950. **Education:** New York School of Art and Design, 1964-67. **Family:** One daughter and one son. **Career:** Freelance illustrator; teacher, Brooklyn Museum School, Summer 1970. **Awards:** Society of Illustrators Gold Medal, 1970; American Library Association Newcott award, 1976, and Coretta Scott King award, 1982, for illustration, 1988; Boston *Globe-Horn Book* award, 1987; Milner award, 1989. **Died:** 28 August 1989.

Publications for Children (illustrated by the author)

Fiction

Stevie. New York, Harper, 1969; London, Longman, 1970.
Uptown. New York, Harper, 1970.
Train Ride. New York, Harper, 1971.
Birthday. New York, Holt Rinehart, 1972.
My Special Best Words. New York, Viking Press, 1974.
Marcia. New York, Viking Press, 1976.
Daddy Is a Monster...Sometimes. Philadelphia, Lippincott, 1980.
Jeffrey Bear Cleans Up His Act. New York, Lothrop, 1983.
Baby Says. New York, Lothrop, 1988.

Other (retellings)

The Story of Jumping Mouse. New York, Lothrop, 1984.
Mufaro's Beautiful Daughters: An African Tale. New York, Lothrop, 1987; London, Hamish Hamilton, 1988.

*

Illustrator: *All Us Come Cross the Water* by Lucille Clifton, 1973; *She Come Bringing Me That Little Baby Girl* by Eloise Greenfield, 1974; *Mother Crocodile* translated by Rosa Guy, 1981; *OUTside/INside Poems,* 1981, and *All the Colors of the Race,* 1982, both by Arnold Adoff; *Roses* by Barbara Cohen, 1984.

* * *

John Steptoe, a black writer who wrote and illustrated *Stevie* when he was only 17, filled his early books with the children and neighborhoods of his own life. Except for the idealized community in *Birthday,* these neighborhoods are ghettoes, but Steptoe's pictures of them, suggesting Rouault in their shapes and colors, are glowing, and his children are coping well with their lives.

Uptown and *Train Ride* are sketches from life, with the grammar and vocabulary of urban black children, usually understandable to any reader. In *Uptown,* however, the words used by the two boys as they talk about the clothing they like—playboys, beavers, bad silks—could baffle the uninitiated.

Stevie has remained the most popular of these early books. Its situation is universal—the jealousy and annoyance of a boy of seven or eight—Robert—whose mother helps out a neighbor by taking in her little son for a few weeks. This could happen to a black or white family and the language is colloquial in a way that is hard to identify as strictly "black." What happens to Robert in the end has universality, too. After all the irritation has been expressed, positive feelings find their way in. Stevie is missed when he is gone.

In *Birthday, My Special Best Words,* and *Marcia,* Steptoe changes the scene. *Birthday* details the celebration of a black boy's eighth birthday in an imagined rural community where the warm spirit of cooperation and intimacy becomes the main point of the story. In *My Special Best Words* Steptoe writes a book for the young about three-year-old Bweela and her year-old brother, Javaka, who lived alone with their father. Bweela tells in black baby talk—not always easily read aloud—about the events of daily life, including attempts to toilet-train Javaka. The scenes are intimate, honest, and loving. In *Marcia* Steptoe moves up into teenage territory, writing a gentle love story with a sex problem at the center. Here, too, the language is the natural speech of the black characters, the tone is hopeful—so hopeful, in fact, that the story rises in the end toward an almost declamatory pitch.

Recently Steptoe has moved in new directions with his two large picture books that are retellings of old legends. *The Story of Jumping Mouse,* based on a Native American legend, tells of the courageous small mouse who successfully makes a journey to "the far-off land" though giving away her sight and sense of smell to others more in need. The pictures here are a new departure also—abundant nature scenes in muted black and white. *Mufaro's Beautiful Daughters,* on the other hand, is painted in glowing colors and takes the reader to the Africa of the ancient Zimbabwe region. Based on an African folktale, it tells of two daughters, one of whom is greedy and jealous, and the other kind to all. Of course it is the kind one who becomes the wife of the king.

Also unlike Steptoe's early work are two recent short picture books. In *Jeffrey Bear Cleans Up His Act,* Jeffrey (a humanized bear) is bored with school and the visiting speaker on garbage, and daydreams about how he would manage the class. In *Baby Says,* a short picture book for the very young with few words and large pictures, a toddler in a playpen tries to get the attention of an older brother. The relationship between these two small black children is a warm one, and the clear, bright pictures reflect the mood.

Steptoe's untimely death in 1989, the year *Baby Says* was published, brings to an end the Steptoe books—a fact a little hard to believe. But readers will now be able to find two large and beautiful picture books, *The Story of Jumping Mouse* and *Mufaro's Beautiful Daughters,* available in paperback. Perhaps as times passes, more of his books will appear in paper.

—Claudia Lewis

STEVENSON, James

Nationality: American. **Born:** New York City, 11 July 1929. **Education:** Yale University, New Haven, Connecticut, B.A. 1951. **Military Service:** United States Marine Corps, 1951-53. **Family:** Married 1) Jane Walker in 1953 (died); five sons and four daughters; 2) Josephine Merck, 1993. **Career:** Reporter, *Life* magazine, New York, 1955; cartoonist and writer for "Talk of the Town," *New Yorker* magazine, New York, 1956-1963; creator of "Capitol Games" (syndicated political comic strip); writer and illustrator, from 1962. **Awards:** *New York Times* Outstanding Children's Book of the Year and *School Library Journal* Best

Books for Spring honor, both 1977, for *"Could Be Worse!"*; American Library Association (ALA) Notable Book designation, 1978, for *The Sea View Hotel,* 1979, for *Fast Friends: Two Stories,* 1980, for *That Terrible Halloween Night School Library Journal* Best Books for Spring honor, 1979, for *Monty Children's Choice Award, International Reading Association, 1979, for The Worst Person in the World,* 1980, for *That Terrible Halloween Night,* 1982, for *The Night after Christmas,* 1989, for *The Supreme Souvenir Factory,* and 1990, for *Oh No, It's Waylon's Birthday!*; Best Illustrated Book and Outstanding Book honors, both *New York Times,* 1980, for *Howard School Library Journal* Best Books of 1981 honor, for *The Wish Card Ran Out!*; *Boston Globe/Horn Book* honor list, 1981, for *The Night after Christmas*; Christopher Award, 1982, for *We Can't Sleep*; Parents Choice Award, 1982, for *Oliver, Clarence, and Violet*; *Boston Globe/Horn Book* honor list, ALA Notable Book designation, *School Library Journal* Best Books of 1983 honor, all 1983, for *What's under My Bed?*; Garden State Children's Book Award, New Jersey Library Association, 1983, for *Clams Can't Sing*; ALA Notable Book designation, 1986, for *When I Was Nine*; Redbook award, 1987, for *Higher on the Door.*

Publications for Children (illustrated by the author)

Fiction

Walker, The Witch, and the Striped Flying Saucer. Boston, Little Brown, 1969.
The Bear Who Had No Place to Go. New York, Harper, 1972.
Here Comes Herb's Hurricane! New York, Harper, 1973.
Could Be Worse! New York, Greenwillow, 1977.
Wilfred the Rat. New York, Greenwillow, 1977.
Help! Yelled Maxwell, with Edwina Stevenson. New York, Greenwillow, 1978.
The Sea View Hotel. New York, Greenwillow, 1978; London, Gollancz, 1979.
Winston, Newton, Elton, and Ed. New York, Greenwillow, 1978.
The Worst Person in the World. New York, Greenwillow, and London, Kestrel, 1978.
Fast Friends: Two Stories. New York, Greenwillow, 1979.
Monty. New York, Greenwillow, and London, Gollancz, 1979.
Clams Can't Sing. New York, Greenwillow, 1980.
Howard. New York, Greenwillow, 1980; London, Gollancz, 1981.
That Terrible Halloween Night. New York, Greenwillow, 1980.
The Night after Christmas. New York, Greenwillow, 1981; London, Gollancz, 1982.
The Wish Card Ran Out! New York, Greenwillow, 1981.
Oliver, Clarence, and Violet. New York, Greenwillow, 1982.
We Can't Sleep. New York, Greenwillow, 1982.
Barbara's Birthday. New York, Greenwillow, and London, Bodley Head, 1983.
Grandpa's Great City Tour. New York, Greenwillow, 1983.
The Great Big Especially Beautiful Easter Egg. New York, Greenwillow, and London, Gollancz, 1983.
What's under My Bed? New York, Greenwillow, 1983; London, Gollancz, 1984.
Worse than Willy! New York, Greenwillow, 1984; London, Gollancz, 1985.
Yuck! New York, Greenwillow, 1984; London, Gollancz, 1985.
Are We Almost There? New York, Greenwillow, 1985.
Emma. New York, Greenwillow, 1985; London, Gollancz, 1986.
That Dreadful Day. New York, Greenwillow, 1985.
Fried Feathers for Thanksgiving. New York, Greenwillow, 1986.
No Friends. New York, Greenwillow, 1986; London, Gollancz, 1987.
There's Nothing to Do! New York, Greenwillow, and London, Gollancz, 1986.
When I Was Nine. New York, Greenwillow, 1986.
Higher on the Door. New York, Greenwillow, 1987.
Happy Valentine's Day, Emma! New York, Greenwillow, 1987.
No Need for Monty. New York, Greenwillow, 1987.
Will You Please Feed Our Cat? New York, Greenwillow, and London, Gollancz, 1987.
The Supreme Souvenir Factory. New York, Greenwillow, 1988.
We Hate Rain! New York, Greenwillow, 1988.
The Worst Person in the World at Crab Beach. New York Greenwillow, 1988.
Oh No, It's Waylon's Birthday! New York, Greenwillow, 1989.
Un-Happy New Year, Emma! New York, Greenwillow, 1989.
Emma at the Beach. New York, Greenwillow, 1990.
July. New York, Greenwillow, 1990.
Mr. Hacker, illustrated by Frank Modell. New York, Greenwillow, 1990.
National Worm Day. New York, Greenwillow, 1990.
Quick! Turn the Page! New York, Greenwillow, 1990.
The Stowaway. New York, Greenwillow, 1990.
Which One Is Whitney? New York, Greenwillow, 1990.
Brrr! New York, Greenwillow, 1991.
Rolling Rose. New York, Greenwillow, 1991.
That's Exactly the Way It Wasn't. New York, Greenwillow, 1991.
The Worst Person's Christmas. New York, Greenwillow, 1991.
And Then What? New York, Greenwillow, 1992.
Don't You Know There's a War On? New York, Greenwillow, 1992.
The Flying Acorns. New York, Greenwillow, 1993.
The Pattaconk Brook. New York, Greenwillow, 1993.
Fun/No Fun. New York, Greenwillow, 1994.
The Mud Flat Olympics. New York, Greenwillow, 1994.
Worse Than the Worst. New York, Greenwillow, 1994.
All Aboard!, New York, Greenwillow, 1995.
Sweet Corn: Poems, New York, Greenwillow, 1995.
I Had A Lot Of Wishes, New York, Greenwillow, 1995.
The Worst Goes South, New York, Greenwillow, 1995.
The Bones in the Cliff, New York, Greenwillow, 1995.
A Village Full of Valentines, Greenwillow, 1995.
The Oldest Elf, New York, Greenwillow, 1995.
I Meant To Tell You, New York, Greenwillow, 1996.
Yard Sale, New York, Greenwillow, 1996.
The Unprotected Witness, New York, Greenwillow, 1997.
Heat Wave at Mud Flat, New York, Greenwillow, 1997.
The Mud Flat Mystery, New York, Greenwillow, 1997.
Mud Flat April Fool, New York, Greenwillow, 1998.
Popcorn, New York, Greenwillow, 1998.
Sam the Zamboni Man, pictures By Harvey Stevenson, New York, Greenwillow, 1998.

Publications for Adults

Novels

Do Yourself a Favor, Kid. New York, Macmillan, 1962.
The Summer Houses. New York, Macmillan, 1963.

Sometimes, But Not Always. Boston, Little Brown, 1967.
Cool Jack and the Beanstalk (comic strip novel). New York, Penguin, 1976.

Other

Sorry, Lady—This Beach Is Private! (cartoons). New York, Macmillan, 1963.
Something Marvelous Is About to Happen. New York, Harper, 1971.
Let's Boogie! (cartoons). New York, Dodd Mead, 1978.
Uptown Local, Downtown Express. New York, Viking Press, 1983.

*

Illustrator: *Weekend Guests* by William Zinsser, 1963; *If I Owned a Candy Factory* by James Walker Stevenson, 1968; *Tony and the Toll Collector* by Eric Stevenson, 1969; *Tony's Hard Work Day* by Alan Arkin, 1972; *Alec's Sand Castle* by Lavinia Ross, 1972; *Good Old James* by John Donovan, 1975; *What's a Father For?* by Sara D. Gilbert, 1975; *Jack the Bum and the Haunted House,* 1977, *Jack the Bum and the Halloween Handout,* 1977, and *Jack the Bum and the UFO,* 1978, all by Janet Schulman; *Say It!,* 1980, and *I Know a Lady,* 1984, both by Charlotte Zolotow; *The Baby Uggs Are Hatching,* 1982, *The New Kid on the Block,* 1984, and *Something Big Has Been Here* (poetry), 1990, all by Jack Prelutsky; *How Do You Get a Horse Out of the Bathtub?,* 1983, *263 Brain Busters,* 1985, and *How Do You Lift a Walrus with One Hand?,* 1988, all by Louis Phillips; *Cully Cully and the Bear* by Wilson Gage, 1983; *Otto Is Different* by Franz Brandenberg, 1985; *Georgia Music,* 1986, *Grandaddy's Place,* 1987, and *Grandaddy and Janetta,* 1993, all by Helen V. Griffith; *I Am Not Going to Get up Today!* by Dr. Seuss, 1987; *Percy and the Five Houses* by Else Minarik, 1989; *Explorer* by Rupert Matthews, 1991; *The Armchair Book of Baseball: A Lavish Celebration of the National Pastime from an All-Star Lineup of Writers, Reporters, & Raconteurs* edited by John Thorn, Macmillan, 1992; photographer, *Boat* by Eric Kentley, 1992; *Loop the Loop* by Barbara Dugan, 1992; photographer, *Volcano & Earthquake* by Susanna van Rose, 1992; *Bun* by William Maxwell, 1994; *The Royal Nap* by Charles C. Black, 1995; *Grandaddy's Stars* by Helen V. Griffith, 1995; *Mrs. Donald's Dog Bun and His Home Away from Home* by William Maxwell, 1995; *A Pizza the Size of the Sun: Poems* by Jack Prelutsky, 1996; *Happily Ever After* by Anna Quindlen, 1997; *Hooper Humperdink—? Not Him!* by Dr. Seuss, 1997.

*   *   *

Author and illustrator James Stevenson's picture books are among the most engaging in children's literature. And his witty *New Yorker* cartoons are a pleasure to adults. Stevenson's inventiveness and zany logic, make his moral lessons pleasing to children. *Monty,* one of his earliest books, is a good example. Every day Monty the alligator ferries Arthur, Doris, and Tom over the stream to school and back in the afternoon. (They are, as it happens, rabbit, duck, and frog, but that is the idiom.) Yet the cheeky three are not very grateful; indeed, they are quite rude at times. One morning Monty declares that he is on vacation. The three try to devise other means of crossing the water, all ludicrously unsuccessful, until they realise how much old Monty is needed. The moment they voice this, Monty appears. "I thought you were on vacation," says one. "I am, but sometimes when I am on vacation I take a day off." In *Howard,* a young wild duck gets left behind in the city when the others fly south for the winter. With newfound friends (a frog, a mouse) and after various mishaps, he (and they) find shelter in a derelict theatre. Other creatures join the community, visit museums, and produce their own plays and concerts—really, a well-spent winter. When spring arrives, and Howard's "group" returns, he says goodbye. But is it to the birds or to his friends? Ah, that's the clever bit—friendships and loyalties matter.

Stevenson is at his best in the moving yet hilarious *Clams Can't Sing.* Here, the seashore creatures are planning a gala festival: singing, dancing, reciting. Only the clams aren't asked to perform; for what can clams do? What indeed? The two little clams devise an extraordinary contribution to the show. (We too can see it in detail.) Yes, everyone can do something.

In *Yuck!* and *Happy Valentine's Day, Emma!* Stevenson, still in high form, offers a modish witch theme. Two wonderfully disgusting old sorceresses ("Stencheroo, Dolores!" cries one as she stirs her noxious brew) throw scorn at good little Emma, a witchlet who can't manage spells but has a nice nature and plenty of animal friends. With their help she deceives the awful pair into thinking that she has a spell or two up her sleeve. And everyone gets the right valentine.

Stevenson has a group of books in which a grandfather soothes his grandson and granddaughter with stories of how he and his infant brother Wainie dealt with similar problems to those that trouble his grandchildren. The titles may suggest the themes—*No Friends* (they have moved to a new neighborhood), *There's Nothing to Do!, Worse than Willy!* (coping with a new baby brother), *Will You Please Feed Our Cat?*—but not the mad range of events that grandfather plucks out of his resourceful head, sped along by the wildly euphoric Stevenson pictures and cartoons.

Stevenson is a prolific worker—possibly too prolific (not all of his published works have crossed the Atlantic), but the verve and assurance of his line remains unchanged. At his best he is very hard to match.

—Naomi Lewis

STEWART, A(gnes) C(harlotte)

Nationality: British. **Born:** Liverpool, Lancashire, 9 March. **Education:** Private schools. **Family:** Married to Robert Frederick Stewart; one daughter. **Award:** Scottish Arts Council award, 1977. **Address:** Knowetop, Corsock, Castle Douglas, Kirkcudbrightshire DG7 3EB, Scotland.

Publications for Children

Fiction

The Boat in the Reeds, illustrated by Christopher Brooker. London, Blackie, 1960; Englewood Cliffs, New Jersey, Bradbury Press, 1970.
Falcon's Crag. London, Blackie, 1969.
The Quarry Line Mystery. London, Faber, 1971; Nashville, Nelson, 1973.

Elizabeth's Tower. London, Faber, and New York, Phillips, 1972.
Dark Dove. New York, Phillips, 1974; London, Macmillan, 1975.
Ossian House. London, Blackie, 1974; New York, Phillips, 1976.
Beyond the Boundary. London, Blackie, 1976.
Silas and Con. London, Blackie, and New York, Atheneum, 1977.
Brother Raimon Returns. London, Blackie, 1978.
Biddy Grant of Craigengill. London, Blackie, 1979.

Publications for Adults

Novel

Wandering Star. London, Hale, 1981.

*

A.C. Stewart comments:

I find it very difficult to write about my books: for any author so much of what goes into his books is unconscious and so when one comes to analyse them they are full of surprises. My chief concern is to tell a good story that will entertain; this is, I believe, what writing novels is about. Into my stories is bound to go much of what I believe in and care about, but if at the same time any form of advice to children gets in it is because it is part of the story and belongs in it—not as a lecture to the reader. I never meant to write for children but it has come about that way and now I find a greater interest and satisfaction in doing so than when writing for adults.

* * *

In A.C. Stewart's novels the narrative is much less significant than the setting. Place and character are fully and sensitively evoked as the narrative unfolds, at times almost somnolently. These are books about enduring human values rooted in the spirits of time and place, and to absorb these values her young heroes and heroines must learn to own with the heart. There are adventures to be sure, and gripping ones at that, told with arresting skill, but they rest less on the meeting of adversaries than on human struggle against the vicissitudes of nature in lonely and remote places.

Ian eventually sails the Shearwater of *The Boat in the Reeds,* and indeed sails it close to disaster over the bar. But this is no ordinary tale of courage at sea. He has earned his right to sail the boat in rebuilding it with loving care. The sailing is almost incidental to the owning, and the reader will remember the child pouring his heart and imagination into the derelict dinghy long after he forgets the near-fatal sailing. Similarly, a few adventures befall John in *Ossian House* as he roams his grandfather's lands, but as the slow tale unfolds the boy becomes a part of the continuity of the world of fells and glens, linking past, present, and foreseeable future in his growing love for his heritage. In *Dark Dove* Margaret draws strength from her roots in the Highlands, turning always to home exactly as her pigeons return to the loft.

If setting and the slow unfolding of character are central concerns of Stewart's novels, a distinguishing and recurring theme is the child-adult relationship. Each of her books brings a child and an adult together in mutual respect. And it is a remarkable quality of her writing that, though the child's perceptions are consistently at the centre, the principal grown-up characters are sensitively and fully adult. Child and adult complement each other while each remains true to his own station. There is nothing either patronizing or whimsical here. Adults are totally uncondescending; children are never precociously wise. Elizabeth leans on the crippled Lawrence in *Elizabeth's Tower* even as he draws strength from her mixture of practical good sense and child-like dependence. In each novel a similar relationship is developed; John and Duncan the shepherd in *Ossian House*; Margaret and Callum, the local laird, in *Dark Dove*; Ian and Tim the idler in *The Boat in the Reeds.* In *Brother Raimon Returns* Major Carpenter's affection for Alice is as generous as it is genuine while he and Michael share a wary antagonism of mutual respect.

It is in *Falcon's Crag* and its belated sequel, *Biddy Grant of Craigengill,* that Stewart's recurring concern with place and character and relationships is expressed at its most profound. Biddy grows to understand her Uncle Neil and Great Uncle Dermot as through her growing love for Craigengill she becomes attuned to the spirit of the place and its morose history. In these most absorbing of Stewart's novels she expresses perhaps most deeply what her other excellent novels have sought to clarify, that human values, like life, are found in the living, and are assayed as much in the heart as in the head.

—Myles McDowell

STOREY, Margaret

Pseudonym: Elizabeth Eyre. **Nationality:** British. **Born:** London, 27 June 1926. **Education:** Sutton High School, Surrey; Samuel King's School, Alston, Cumbria; St. Paul's Girls' School, London; Girton College, Cambridge, B.A. (honours) in English 1948, M.A. 1953. **Career:** Private tutor, 1956-59; English teacher, Miss Ironside's School, London, 1959-69; senior teacher, Vale School, London, 1969-72; senior English teacher, The Study, Wimbledon, 1972-77, and Putney Park School, London, 1977-87. **Agent:** A.M. Heath, 79 St. Martin's Lane, London WC2N 4AA, England.

Publications for Children

Fiction

Kate and the Family Tree, illustrated by Shirley Hughes. London, Bodley Head, 1965; as *The Family Tree,* Nashville, Nelson, 1973.
Pauline. London, Faber, 1965; New York, Doubleday, 1967.
The Smallest Doll, illustrated by Shirley Hughes. London, Faber, 1966.
The Smallest Bridesmaid, illustrated by Shirley Hughes. London, Faber, 1966.
Timothy and Two Witches, illustrated by Charles Stewart. London, Faber, 1966; New York, Dell, 1973.
The Stone Sorcerer, illustrated by Charles Stewart. London, Faber, 1967; as *The Stone Wizard,* 1979.
The Dragon's Sister, and Timothy Travels, illustrated by Charles Stewart. London, Faber, 1967; New York, Dell, 1974.
A Quarrel of Witches, illustrated by Doreen Roberts. London, Faber, 1970.
The Mollyday Holiday, illustrated by Janina Ede. London, Faber, 1971.

The Sleeping Witch, illustrated by Janina Ede. London, Faber, 1971.
Wrong Gear. London, Faber, 1973.
Keep Running. London, Faber, 1974; as *Ask Me No Questions,* New York, Dutton, 1975.
A War of Wizards, illustrated by Janina Ede. London, Faber, 1976.
The Double Wizard, illustrated by June Jackson. London, Faber, 1979.

Publications for Adults

Novels

Goodbye, Nanny Gray, with Jill Staynes. London, Bodley Head, 1987.
Body of Opinion, with Jill Staynes. London, Bodley Head, 1988.
A Knife at the Opera, with Jill Staynes. London, Bodley Head, 1988.
Grave Responsibility, with Jill Staynes. London, Barrie & Jenkins, 1990.
Death of a Duchess (as Elizabeth Eyre), with Jill Staynes. London, Headline, 1991.
Curtains for the Cardinal (as Elizabeth Eyre), with Jill Staynes. London, Headline, 1992.
The Late Lady, with Jill Staynes. London, Century, 1992.
Bone Idle, with Jill Staynes. London, Century, 1993.
Poison for the Prince (as Elizabeth Eyre) with Jill Staynes. London, Headline, 1993.
Bravo for the Bride (as Elizabeth Eyre) with Jill Staynes. London, Headline, 1994.

*

Margaret Storey comments:

I write because I like writing; it's communicating ideas that interests me. No one in my books is a portrait of anyone I know, but places are often real ones. I have an acute recall of much of my childhood, a memory of frustrations, triumphs, failure to be understood, pleasures, and friends.

* * *

Margaret Storey began by writing for younger children. She has a great enthusiasm for wizardry and magic, and tales like *The Stone Sorcerer* and, most recently, *The Double Wizard,* show this clearly. She carefully defuses situations that could become frightening to the young reader, though a cleverly measured frisson of fear is allowed to creep up the spine, just enough to be enjoyable.

Her collections of tales about witches and magic, such as *The Dragon's Sister* and *A Quarrel of Witches,* balance excitement and humour. *The Smallest Bridesmaid* and *The Mollyday Holiday* are true-to-life stories of a little girl's joy when at last she is chosen to be a bridesmaid and, in the second story, when she goes on her long-awaited holiday. The drawings by Shirley Hughes are delightful. Most children will find something with which to identify in these stories of events which, at their age, are redletter days.

Her later books are for older girls, and invite them to identify with real-life situations which may be troubling them. *Pauline* is the story of a recently orphaned girl growing up with unsympathetic foster-parents who disapprove of her new friends. Storey does not talk down to her readers, nor does she resort to glib solutions to the problems she poses. The adolescent girl reading her books has to put something of herself into the situation.

In *Wrong Gear* a child of divorced parents is torn between loves and loyalties. She runs away from her father and his new wife to her mother, who is unable to take her in. Unexpected help comes from school, and she learns to grow up more happily. *Keep Running* is also a case of divided loyalty. A kidnapped girl builds up a complex relationship with her captor. While wanting to escape, she feels that because he has given her parole she owes him something and does not want to cause him trouble.

Since most teenagers at times feel torn between "want" and "ought," these books by an author who views their problems with sympathetic insight may well have a cathartic effect and prove helpful.

—Ann G. Hay

STORR, Catherine

Pseudonyms: Irene Adler; Helen Lourie. **Nationality:** British. **Born:** Catherine Cole, London, 21 July 1913. **Education:** St. Paul's Girls' School, London; Newnham College, Cambridge, 1932-36, 1939-41, B.A. (honours) in English 1935; West London Hospital, 1941-44, qualified medical practitioner 1944; Licensee, Royal College of Physicians; Member, Royal College of Surgeons. **Family:** Married 1) the writer and psychiatrist Anthony Storr in 1942, three daughters; 2) Thomas Balogh in 1970. **Career:** Assistant psychiatrist, West London Hospital, 1948-50; senior hospital medical officer, Department of Psychological Medicine, Middlesex Hospital, London, 1950-62; assistant editor, Penguin Books Ltd., London, 1966-70. **Agent:** A.D. Peters Ltd., 5th Floor, The Chambers, Chelsea Harbour, Lots Road, London SW10 0XF. **Address:** 12 Frognal Gardens, Flat 5, London NW3 6UX, England.

Publications for Children

Fiction

Ingeborg and Ruthy. London, Harrap, 1940.
Clever Polly and Other Stories, illustrated by Dorothy Craigie. London, Faber, 1952.
Stories for Jane, illustrated by Peggy Jeremy. London, Faber, 1952.
Clever Polly and the Stupid Wolf, illustrated by Marjorie-Ann Watts. London, Faber, 1955.
Polly, The Giant's Bride, illustrated by Marjorie-Ann Watts. London, Faber, 1956.
The Adventures of Polly and the Wolf, illustrated by Marjorie-Ann Watts. London, Faber, 1957; Philadelphia, Macrae Smith, 1970.
Marianne Dreams, illustrated by Marjorie-Ann Watts. London, Faber, 1958; as *The Magic Drawing Pencil,* New York, A.S. Barnes, 1960; revised edition, as *Marianne Dreams,* London, Penguin, 1964.
Marianne and Mark, illustrated by Marjorie-Ann Watts. London, Faber, 1960.
Lucy, illustrated by Dick Hart. London, Bodley Head, 1961; Englewood Cliffs, New Jersey, Prentice Hall, 1968.
Lucy Runs Away, illustrated by Dick Hart. London, Bodley Head, 1962; Englewood Cliffs, New Jersey, Prentice Hall, 1969.

Robin, illustrated by Peggy Fortnum. London, Faber, 1962; as *The Freedom of the Seas,* New York, Duell, 1965.
The Catchpole Story. London, Faber, 1965.
Rufus, illustrated by Peggy Fortnum. London, Faber, and Boston, Gambit, 1969.
Puss and Cat, illustrated by Carolyn Dinan. London, Faber, 1969.
Thursday. London, Faber, 1971; New York, Harper, 1972.
Kate and the Island, illustrated by Gareth Floyd. London, Faber, 1972.
The Painter and the Fish, illustrated by Alan Howard. London, Faber, 1975.
The Chinese Egg. London, Faber, and New York, McGraw Hill, 1975.
The Story of the Terrible Scar, illustrated by Gerald Rose. London, Faber, 1976.
Who's Bill? London, Macmillan, 1976.
Hugo and His Grandma, illustrated by Nita Sowter. Cambridge, Dinosaur, 1977.
Hugo and His Grandma's Washing Day, illustrated by Nita Sowter. Cambridge, Dinosaur, 1978.
Winter's End. London, Macmillan, 1978; New York, Harper, 1979.
Tales of Polly and the Hungry Wolf, illustrated by Jill Bennett. London, Faber, 1980.
Vicky. London, Faber, 1981.
The Bugbear, illustrated by Elaine McGregor Turney. London, Hamish Hamilton, 1981.
It Couldn't Happen to Me. Cambridge, Dinosaur, 1982.
February Yowler, illustrated by Gareth Floyd. London, Faber, 1982.
The Castle Boy. London, Faber, 1983.
Two's Company. London, Hardy, 1984.
It Shouldn't Happen to a Frog. London, Macmillan, 1984.
Wagga Storybooks (*Enter Wagga, Lost and Found Wagga, Wagga's Magic Ears, Watchdog Wagga*), illustrated by Colin Caket. London, Hamlyn, 4 vols., 1984.
Cold Marble and Other Ghost Stories. London, Faber, 1985.
The Underground Conspiracy. London, Faber, 1987.
The Boy and the Swan, illustrated by Laszlo Acs. London, Deutsch, 1987; translated into Welsh as *Y bachgen a'r alarch,* Llandysul, Gomer, 1991.
Not Too Young and Other Stories, with Griselda Gifford and Jill Kent. London, Macmillan, 1987.
Mrs. Circumference. London, Deutsch, 1989.
Daljit and the Unqualified Wizard. London, Heinemann, 1989.
The Spy before Yesterday. London, Hamish Hamilton, 1990.
We Didn't Think of Ostriches. New York, Longman, 1990.
Babybug, illustrated by Fiona Dunbar, Hemel Hempstead, Simon & Schuster, 1992.
Finn's Animal. London, Heinemann, 1992.
The Mirror Image Ghost. London, Faber, 1994.
Watcher at the Window, illustrated by Judith Lawton. Harlow, Longman, 1995.
Stephen and the Family Nose, illustrated by Ken Cox. Aylesbury, Ginn, 1885.

Plays

Flax into Gold: The Story of Rumpelstiltskin (libretto), music by Hugo Cole. London, Chappell, 1964.
Starting Out (television series), 1973-78.

Other

Pebble (reader). London, Macmillan, 1979.
Pen Friends (reader), illustrated by Charles Front. London, Macmillan, 1980.
People of the Bible series (*Noah and His Ark, Joseph and His Brothers, The Birth of Jesus, Jesus Begins His Work, Adam and Eve, Jonah and the Whale, The Prodigal Son, Miracles by the Sea, Moses of the Bulrushes, Joseph the Dreamteller, The First Easter, The Good Samaritan, Abraham and Isaac, Moses and the Plagues of Egypt, David and Goliath, St. Peter and St. Paul, Jesus and John the Baptist, Joseph the Long Lost Brother, Moses Leads His People, The Trials of Daniel, King David, Sampson and Delilah, Ruth's Story, Jesus the Healer*). London, Watts, and Milwaukee, Raintree, 24 vols., 1982-86.
Feasts and Festivals, illustrated by Jenny Rhodes. London, Hardy, 1983.
Great Tales from Long Ago (*Robin Hood, Hiawatha, The Pied Piper of Hamelin, Rip Van Winkle, Joan of Arc, King Midas and His Gold, King Arthur's Sword, Odysseus and the Enchanters, Theseus and the Minotaur, Dick Whittington, Androcles and the Lion, The Wooden Horse, Richard the Lionheart*). London, Methuen, 13 vols., 1984-87; Milwaukee, Raintree, 12 vols., 1984-89; *The Wooden Horse* published as *The Trojan Horse,* Milwaukee, Raintree, 1985. Selections translated into Chinese: *Joan of Arc* as *Sheng nu Chen-te: ai kuo ti nung chia shao nu*; *King Arthur=s Sword* as *Ya-se wang: pa chu shih chung chien ti jen; The Pied Piper of Hamelin as Pan i chui ti jen: shen huai mo fa ti chu hai che; Dick Whittington* as *Ti-ko Hui-ting-tun: hsing yun ti hsiang hsia nan hai; Androcles and the Lion* as *An-cho-ko-li ssu: yu shih tzu wei yu ti nu li*; *Theseus and the Minotaur* as *Hsi-hsiu-ssu: yung wu ti Ya-tien ying hsiung*; *Odysseus and the Enchanters* as *Ao-ti-sai: liu lang hai shang ti ying hsiung; The Trojan Horse* as *Te-lo-i mu ma: Hsi-la jen po ti ti miao chi*; *Rip Van Winkle* as *Li-pu Wen-ko: i shui erh shih nien ti jen; The Flying Dutchman* as *Piao po ti Ho-lan jen: yu ling chuan ti chuan chang*; all volumes published at Tai-pei by Lu chiao wen hua shih yeh yu hsien kung ssu, 1991. Selections (*Androcles and the Lion, Theseus and the Minotaur, Midas and His Gold, Odysseus and the Enchanters)* translated into Russion as *Geroi drevnego mira,* Moscow, DOM, 1993. Excerpts (*Merlin the Wizard, King Arthur's Sword, Sir Gawain and the Green Knight, Richard the Lionheart, Robin Hood, Dick Whittington, Chanticleer)* translated into German as *Englishche Sagen (Great Tales from Long Ago),* Munich, Deutscher Tagenbuch Verlag, 1993.
Easy Piano Picture Books (*Swan Lake, The Nutcracker, The Sleeping Beauty, Hansel and Gretel, Peter & the Wolf*), first vol. with Dianne Jackson. London, Faber, 5 vols., 1987-92.
Let's Read Together series (*A Fast Move, Find the Specs, Grandpa's Birthday, Gran Builds a House*), illustrated by Toni Goffe. London, Macdonald, 4 vols., 1987; Morristown, New Jersey, Silver Burdett, 3 vols., 1987; last vol. published as *Building a House,* Morristown, New Jersey, Silver Burdett, 1987.
Competitions and Ponies. London, Macmillan, 1987.

Publications for Adults

Novels

A Question of Abortion (as Helen Lourie). London, Bodley Head, 1962.

Freud for the Jung; or, Three Hundred and Sixty Six Hours on the Couch (as Irene Adler). London, Cresset Press, 1963.
The Merciful Jew. London, Barrie and Rockliff, 1968.
Black God, White God. London, Barrie and Jenkins, 1972.
Unnatural Fathers. London, Quartet, 1976.

Short Stories

Tales from the Psychiatrist's Couch. London, Quartet, 1977.

Plays

Bevil (radio play), 1984.

Other

Cook's Quick Reference: Essential Information on Cards. London, Penguin, 1971.
Growing Up: A Practical Guide to Adolescence for Parents and Children. London, Arrow, 1975.

Editor, *On Children's Literature,* by Isabelle Jan. London, Allen Lane, 1973; New York, Schocken, 1974.

*

Manuscript Collections: Kerlan Collection, University of Minnesota Minneapolis.

Catherine Storr comments:

I am a compulsive writer and a natural storyteller, which is why I'm better and more successful at writing for children, who want a story above everything else, than I am at writing fiction for adults. I'm mainly interested in the area of the different faces of reality; hence the preoccupation with the possibilities of explaining events in more than one way—the "scientific" and "magical" explanations. I'm often classed as a writer of fantasy, but I prefer to think that I write in a sort of symbolic language which is no more obscure or pompous than that of folk or fairy stories.

I write for myself, only secondarily for a particular child, and then only if the child happens to want something I want to write. I consider writing to be for me a kind of auto-psycho-therapy, for which I'm fortunate enough to get paid by other people's money as well as by what it does for me.

* * *

With any novelists, the fact of their profession is incidental: relevant, certainly, but not the main thing. Catherine Storr is widely known by the adults who buy her books approvingly to be a psychologist, and indeed there are details in her books which come from psychological interests, together with larger structures—the systematic duality of her stories, for instance, such that appearance and reality for the heroines run in clear and separate parallel throughout the narrative—which are surely the product of the analytic psychologist's frame of mind. Far more to the point, however, are the richly human characteristics of an unusually modest writer—modest in that one has constantly the sense that these books are lightly and easily written. The modesty belies great gifts: with greater ambitions, Storr could surely write as brilliantly and beautifully as the very best of children's novelists—do something as good as Philippa Pearce's *Tom's Midnight Garden,* say, or Joan Aiken's *The Whispering Mountain.* As it is, these bold, direct, continent tales are most stylishly directed to a few particular points of attention which are filled in with greater detail while the surrounding narrative moves briskly and briefly to the conclusion.

The duality I mentioned comes out most straightforwardly in the excellent Polly books. She takes the deeply traditional—if you like, Freudian-traditional—big bad wolf of fairy tale and makes him, in a rich, comic implausibility, into the inept, relentlessly stupid marauder of clever Polly's amiable suburban life. Persistent, gullible, dim, unfailingly goofy, the wolf pads round Chislehurst or Altrincham or Sutton Coldfield or wherever Polly lives, and—always promising to do his wolfish duty and gobble her up—is always outwitted by Polly's serene and patronizingly imperturbable good sense. One's only objection might be that Storr anaesthetizes the terrors which fairy tales embody so conveniently in any old big, bad, black omnivore rather too comfortably. Terrors still do walk abroad, after all, and if you don't call them "wolf," what name can they have? But little girls, it may be replied, have plenty to be frightened of, and it can only be exhilarating and strengthening to follow an example of such calm and affectionate (the heroine is often sorry for her wolf) resolution and adequacy as Polly.

The Polly books perfectly fit a congruence of tone, vocabulary, structure of sentiment and suspense to that of a normally impressionable little girl of, say, seven years old. The Lucy books move at the same gentle but variously paced walk. To adapt a phrase, these stories walk like a child; they show a child's variety of attention, now closely focussed, now darting on to tell you what happens next, now coming comfortably to a close. The Lucy books would be an excellent first experience of reading a whole novel, but while making that rather limp developmental point of praise, I would also emphasize their warm sympathy, their recognisability, their loving faithfulness to the facts of a 7 or 8 year old's way of making up fictions in her head. The first Lucy book is perhaps a touch weaker than *Lucy Runs Away.* The duality here is between the real, tomboy, Lucy, who very believably wants nothing better than to *be* a boy, and her own lived fiction, Lew the detective. The brief little tale in which Lucy stows away in a robber's furniture van and effects the thieves' capture may even be found by a child to be less touching and to my mind certainly less real than the sequel in which the heroine carries out her threat to run away from her fantasy life into the real world, sounds the alarm to save a swimmer in trouble, and, sometimes frightened, sometimes tired, always indomitable, comes safely home. The best of this endearing, graceful tale, as it is of *Rufus,* is the delicate registration of railway journey and seaside, the sense Storr has of child's eye clarity of vision and child's pace which never fails her. I think it is best put by saying that hers are stories *told to listeners,* rather than novels written for readers.

This is true of the books written in a more major key, *Thursday* and the Marianne books, which mark the point at which the adult reader finds her enjoying larger and more demanding themes. A thriller like *The Catchpole Story* is thoroughly well done—a reworking of *Lucy* perhaps—where the moral interest is largely focussed on the interplay of 13-year-old girl and 7-year-old brother, and the way in which his perfectly spontaneous cheerfulness and tearfulness require her to maintain a grown-up courage and steadiness which she can, in a scarey adventure, only just manage. But the significance of neither novel lies in characterization, but rather in the truths to be learned about and from a reality which appears to be merely fantastic. In *Marianne Dreams* Marianne's long convalescence is the opportunity for entering the intense and vivid world of the dream house in which she constructs a model of the process of convalescence itself, and constructs it moreover on behalf of the invalid boy Mark, and in the face of the threats of death and destruction themselves. So the story is a metaphor for nursing, itself the noblest symbol in our pictures of femininity: of altruism, patience, gentleness—and gentleness, as the novel makes clear, is in no way incompatible with a tough insistence on self-determination. I think it is her best book, although the sequel moves into an altogether larger and more populated world and is the longest of Storr's novels. It is good of course, but shrewd rather than fine, gingerly rather than delicate about adolescent love and softness. *Marianne Dreams* has gravity and power (for all that it overworks suspense), and it correctly interweaves the psyche and morality.

None of these books is thin; each, like their heroines and heroes, is small and solid, and if Storr is an occasional rather than a dedicated writer, a good storyteller rather than an artist, and wholesome rather than really creative, her gifts and qualities are strong, humorous, motherly, and indispensable. The three fiction titles published after Storr turned eighty continue these same trends, though *The Mirror Image Ghost* and *Watcher at the Window* have not been as well received critically as most of Storr's earlier titles for older children. This estimate of Storr's qualities is not to sell her cheaply. *Marianne Dreams* is unquestionably a classic; with *Tom's Midnight Garden* and Gillian Avery's *The Warden's Niece* it may be taken to have initiated the remarkable flowering of children's novels we enjoyed in Britain for the twenty years after their publication. Polly and her Wolf are, by the same token, by now unshakeably settled in the galaxies of the primary school heavens: there are very few assemblies or storytimes in which they are not regularly acclaimed. The heroes of old, in Storr's brisk retellings, continue to be popular not only in English-speaking lands but in various translations. Storr, in a way surprising but admirable in a clinical analyst, makes heroism out of great good sense and the kind of greatness and goodness only made possible by a sense of humour.

—Fred Inglis, updated by Caroline C. Hunt

STRANG, Herbert

Joint pseudonym for George Herbert Ely and C. James L'Estrange. **Nationality:** British. **ELY, George Herbert: Born:** London, 1866. **Family:** Married Margaret Ashworth. **Career:** Worked for Oxford University Press from 1920. **Died:** 17 September 1958. **L'ESTRANGE, C. James: Born:** London, 1867. **Family:** Married Maude L'Estrange. **Career:** Worked for Oxford University Press from 1920. **Died:** 8 January 1947. **Career:** Both writers edited, with others, many books and annuals as Mrs. Herbert Strang.

Publications for Children

Fiction

Tom Burnaby. London, Blackie, 1904; as *Young Tom Burnaby,* New York, Street and Smith, n.d.

Boys of the Light Brigade, illustrated by William Rainey. London, Blackie, 1904; as *The Light Brigade in Spain,* New York, Putnam, 1904.

Kobo, illustrated by William Rainey. London, Blackie, 1904; New York, Putnam, 1905.

Brown of Moukden, illustrated by William Rainey. London, Blackie, 1905; New York, Putnam, 1906; as *Jack Brown, The Hero,* New York, Street and Smith, n.d.; as *Jack Brown in China,* London, Oxford University Press, 1923.

The Adventures of Harry Rochester, illustrated by William Rainey. London, Blackie, and New York, Putnam, 1905.

Jack Hardy, illustrated by William Rainey. London, Hodder and Stoughton, 1906; Indianapolis, Bobbs Merrill, 1907.

One of Clive's Heroes, illustrated by William Rainey. London, Hodder and Stoughton, 1906; as *In Clive's Command,* Indianapolis, Bobbs Merrill, 1906.

Samba, illustrated by William Rainey. London, Hodder and Stoughton, 1906; as *Fighting on the Congo,* Indianapolis, Bobbs Merrill, 1906.

Rob the Ranger, illustrated by W.H. Margetson. London, Hodder and Stoughton, and Indianapolis, Bobbs Merrill, 1907.

With Drake on the Spanish Main, illustrated by Archibald Webb. London, Hodder and Stoughton, 1907; as *On the Spanish Main,* Indianapolis, Bobbs Merrill, 1909.

King of the Air, illustrated by W.E. Webster. London, Hodder and Stoughton, and Indianapolis, Bobbs Merrill, 1907.

On the Trail of the Arabs, illustrated by Charles Sheldon. Indianapolis, Bobbs Merrill, 1907.

Herbert Strang's Historical Series (*With Marlborough to Malplaquet, With the Black Prince, A Mariner of England, One of Rupert's Horse,* and *Lion-Heart,* all with Richard Stead; *Claud the Archer* and *In the New Forest,* both with John Aston; *Roger the Scout* and *For the White Rose,* both with George Lawrence). London, Hodder and Stoughton, 9 vols., 1907-12.

Humphrey Bold. London, Hodder and Stoughton, 1908; Indianapolis, Bobbs Merrill, 1909.

Barclay of the Guides, illustrated by H.W. Koekkoek. London, Hodder and Stoughton, 1908; New York, Doran, 1909.

Lord of the Seas, illustrated by C. Fleming Williams. London, Hodder and Stoughton, 1908; New York, Doran, 1910.

Palm Tree Island, illustrated by Archibald Webb and Alan Wright. London, Hodder and Stoughton, 1909; New York, Doran, 1910.

Settlers and Scouts, illustrated by T.C. Dugdale. London, Hodder and Stoughton, 1909; New York, Doran, 1910.

Swift and Sure. London, Hodder and Stoughton, 1909; New York, Doran, 1910.

The Cruise of the Gyro-Car, illustrated by A.C. Michael. London, Hodder and Stoughton, 1910.

The Adventures of Dick Trevanion, illustrated by William Rainey. London, Hodder and Stoughton, 1910.

Round the World in Seven Days, illustrated by A.C. Michael. London, Hodder and Stoughton, and New York, Doran, 1910.

The Flying Boat, illustrated by T.C. Dugdale. London, Hodder and Stoughton, 1911.

The Air Scout, illustrated by W.R.S. Stott. London, Hodder and Stoughton, 1911.

The Motor Scout, illustrated by Cyrus Cuneo. London, Hodder and Stoughton, 1912.

The Air Patrol, illustrated by Cyrus Cuneo. London, Hodder and Stoughton, 1912.

Cerdic the Saxon, with L.L. Weedon. London, Hodder and Stoughton, 1913.
A Little Norman Maid. London, Hodder and Stoughton, 1913; New York, Doran, n.d.
Sultan Jim, Empire Builder. London, Hodder and Stoughton, 1913.
A Gentleman-at-Arms. London, Hodder and Stoughton, 1914.
A Hero of Liège. London, Hodder and Stoughton, 1914.
Fighting with French. London, Hodder and Stoughton, 1915.
The Boy Who Would Not Learn. London, Oxford University Press, 1915; New York, Oxford University Press, 1921.
The Silver Shot. London, Oxford University Press, 1915; New York, Oxford University Press, 1921.
In Trafalgar's Bay. London, Oxford University Press, 1915; New York, Oxford University Press, 1921.
Burton of the Flying Corps. London, Hodder and Stoughton, 1916.
Frank Forester. London, Hodder and Stoughton, 1916.
The Old Man of the Mountain, illustrated by René Bull. London, Hodder and Stoughton, 1916.
Through the Enemy's Lines, illustrated by H.E. Elcock. London, Hodder and Stoughton, 1916.
Carry On!, illustrated by H.E. Elcock and H. Evison. London, Hodder and Stoughton, 1917.
With Haig on the Somme. London, Oxford University Press, 1917.
Steady, Boys, Steady. London, Hodder and Stoughton, 1917.
The Long Trail. London, Oxford University Press, 1918.
Tom Willoughby's Scouts. London, Oxford University Press, 1919.
The Blue Raider. London, Oxford University Press, 1919.
Bright Ideas, illustrated by C.E. Brock. London, Oxford University Press, 1920.
No Man's Island, illustrated by C.E. Brock. London, Oxford University Press, 1921.
The Cave in the Hills. London, Oxford University Press, 1922.
Bastable Cove. London, Oxford University Press, 1922.
Winning His Name, illustrated by C.E. Brock. London, Oxford University Press, 1922.
Honour First, illustrated by W.E. Wightman. London, Oxford University Press, 1923.
True as Steel, illustrated by C.E. Brock. London, Oxford University Press, 1923.
A Thousand Miles an Hour. London, Oxford University Press, 1924.
The Heir of a Hundred Kings. London, Oxford University Press, 1924.
Young Jack. London, Oxford University Press, 1924.
Martin of Old London. London, Oxford University Press, 1925.
Olwyn's Secret. London, Oxford University Press, 1925.
Dan Bolton's Discovery. London, Oxford University Press, 1926.
Strang's Penny Books (*Three Boys at the Fair, Kitty's Kitten, The Cinema Dog, Bill Sawyer's V.C., The Game of Brownies, Jenny's Ark, Baa-Baa and the Wide World, Tom Leaves School, The Mischief-Making Magpie, A Ride with Robin Hood, Pete's Elephant, Ten Pounds Reward, Adolf's Dog, The Adventures of a Penny Stamp, Don't Be Too Sure, Jack and Jocko, The Princess and the Robbers, The Christmas Fairy, The Seven Sons, The Red Candle, The Miller's Daughter, The Grey Goose Feathers, The Birthday Present, There Was a Little Pig, The Magic Smoke, The Children of the Ferry, Sugar Candy Town, Little Mr. Pixie, The Little Sea Horse, The Little Blue-Grey Hare*). London, Oxford University Press, 30 vols., 1926-27.
Lost in London. London, Oxford University Press, 1927.
The River Pirates. London, Oxford University Press, 1927.
The Riders. London, Oxford University Press, 1928.
On London River. London, Oxford University Press, 1929.
Ships and Their Story: Scouting Stories. London, Oxford University Press, 1931.
Dickon of the Chase. London, Oxford University Press, 1931.
A Servant of John Company. London, Oxford University Press, 1932.

Other

The Boyhood of the King. London, Hodder and Stoughton, 1911.
Our Great Adventure. London, Hodder and Stoughton, 1913; New York, Oxford University Press, 1921.
The British Army [*Navy*] *in War.* London, Hodder and Stoughton, 2 vols., 1916.
The Empire in Arms. London, Hodder and Stoughton, 1916.
Great Britain and the War. London, Hodder and Stoughton, 1916; revised edition, 1918.
The Story of Daniel [*Joseph*]. London, Oxford University Press, 2 vols., 1927.
The Splendid Book for Boys. London, Oxford University Press, 1931.

Editor, *Herbert Strang's Annual.* London, Hodder and Stoughton, 10 vols., 1908-17, and London, Oxford University Press, 9 vols., 1918-26; continued as *The Oxford Annual for Boys,* Oxford University Press, 15 vols., 1927-41.
Editor, *Herbert Strang's Library.* London, Hodder and Stoughton and Oxford University Press, 56 vols., 1909-39.
Editor, *The Boys' Holiday* [*Story*] *Book.* London, Hodder and Stoughton, 2 vols., 1910.
Editor, *The Romance of the World.* London, Hodder and Stoughton, 23 vols., 1910-15.
Editor, *By Land and Sea.* London, Hodder and Stoughton, 1911.
Editor, *In School and Camp.* London, Hodder and Stoughton, 1911.
Editor, *The Red* [*Green, Blue, Brown, Purple, Orange, Scarlet*] *Book for Boys.* London, Hodder and Stoughton and Oxford University Press, 7 vols., 1911-20.
Editor, *Stirring Tales.* London, Hodder and Stoughton, 1911.
Editor, *Treasure Trove.* London, Hodder and Stoughton, 1911.
Editor, *Daring Deeds.* London, Hodder and Stoughton, 1912.
Editor, *Peril and Adventure.* London, Hodder and Stoughton, 1912.
Editor, *The Red Book of British Battles* [*the War*]. London, Hodder and Stoughton, 2 vols., 1914-15.
Editor, *The Blue Book of British Naval Battles* [*the War*]. London, Hodder and Stoughton, 2 vols., 1914-16.
Editor, *Herbert Strang's Book of Adventure Stories.* London, Hodder and Stoughton, 1914.
Editor, *Herbert Strang's Readers.* London, Hodder and Stoughton, 76 vols., 1914-41.
Editor, *This Year's Book for Boys.* New York, Doran, 1914.
Editor, *The Children's Hour.* London, Hodder and Stoughton, 6 vols., 1915.
Editor, *Little Talks about Birds and Beasts.* London, Hodder and Stoughton, 1915.
Editor, *The Battle and the Breeze.* London, Hodder and Stoughton, 1915.
Editor, *For the Flag.* London, Hodder and Stoughton, 1915.
Editor, *Shoulder to Shoulder.* London, Hodder and Stoughton, 1915.
Editor, *The Boys' Treasury.* London, Hodder and Stoughton, 1915.

Editor, *The Bugle Call.* London, Hodder and Stoughton, 1915.
Editor, *Play the Game.* London, Hodder and Stoughton, 1915.
Editor, *Hearts of Oak.* London, Hodder and Stoughton, 1915.
Editor, *Ready, Aye Ready!* London, Hodder and Stoughton, 1915.
Editor, *Great Battles of the British Army.* London, Hodder and Stoughton, 1915.
Editor, *Every Boy's Book of the War.* New York, Doran, 1916.
Editor, *With Our Brave Allies* [*the British Army, the British Navy*]. London, Hodder and Stoughton, 3 vols., 1916.
Editor, *Our Allies and Enemies.* London, Hodder and Stoughton, 1916.
Editor, *The War at Sea* [*on Land*]. London, Hodder and Stoughton, 2 vols., 1916.
Editor, *The Clarion Call.* London, Hodder and Stoughton, 1917.
Editor, *Fall In!* London, Hodder and Stoughton, 1917.
Editor, *Fife and Drum.* London, Hodder and Stoughton, 1917.
Editor, *The Oxford Annual for Scouts.* London, Oxford University Press, 5 vols., 1919-23.
Editor, *The Red Book for Scouts.* London, Oxford University Press, 1921.
Editor, *The Golden Book for Boys.* London, Oxford University Press, 1922.
Editor, *The Big Books.* London, Oxford University Press, 10 vols., 1923-29.
Editor, with Mrs. Herbert Strang, *The Great Books.* London, Oxford University Press, 10 vols., 1925-30.
Editor, *One Hundred Poems for Boys* [*Children, Girls*]. London, Oxford University Press, 3 vols., 1925.
Editor, *Half Holiday Tales.* London, Oxford University Press, 1926.
Editor, *Fifty Poems for Infants.* London, Oxford University Press, 1927.
Editor, *Little Books of the Bible.* London, Oxford University Press, 12 vols., 1927-36.
Editor, *Stories from the Bible.* London, Oxford University Press, 6 vols., 1927.
Editor, with Mrs. Herbert Strang, *The Grand Books.* London, Oxford University Press, 3 vols., 1928.
Editor, *Two Hundred Poems for Boys and Girls.* London, Oxford University Press, 1928.
Editor, *The Happy Readers.* London, Oxford University Press, 6 vols., 1929.
Editor, *Stories for the Class-Room.* London, Oxford University Press, 6 vols., 1930.
Editor, *Scouting Stories.* London, Oxford University Press, 1931.
Editor, with Mrs. Herbert Strang, *The Golden Story Books.* London, Oxford University Press, 10 vols., 1931-36.
Editor, with Mrs. Herbert Strang, *The Golden Treasure Book for Boys.* London, Oxford University Press, 1931.
Editor, *Toddles Own Book.* London, Oxford University Press, 1931.
Editor, *A Treasury of English Prose for Schools.* London, Oxford University Press, 1932.
Editor, *The Bright Books for Boys.* London, Oxford University Press, 4 vols., 1933-36.
Editor, *The New Blue* [*Buff*] *Book for Boys.* London, Oxford University Press, 2 vols., 1934.
Editor, *The New Red Book for Scouts.* London, Oxford University Press, 1935.
Editor, *The Rainbow Readers.* London, Oxford University Press, 16 vols., 1936.
Editor, *The Giant Book for Boys.* London, Oxford University Press, 2 vols., 1937-38.
Editor, *The Happy Days Series,* by John Anderson. London, Oxford University Press, 2 vols., 1937.
Editor, *The Picture Story Books,* by John Anderson. London, Oxford University Press, 15 vols., 1937-39.
Editor, *Round the World Series,* by John Anderson. London, Oxford University Press, 5 vols., 1937-39.
Editor, *Gateway to Adventure* [*Romance*]: *Fifteen Stories for Boys* [*Girls*]. London, Oxford University Press, 2 vols., 1938.
Editor, *Jolly Days for Boys.* London, Oxford University Press, 1939.
Editor, *Stories for Boys.* London, Oxford University Press, 1940.

Other by George Herbert Ely

History of England from 1603 to the Present Time. London, Blackie, 1896.

Editor, with others, *Blackie's Junior School Shakespeare.* London, Blackie, 1893.

Publications for Adults

Other by C. James L'Estrange

Familiar London. London, Nister, 1890.

Other by George Herbert Ely

Translator, *Songs of Béranger.* London, Blackie, 1899.
Translator, *The Women of the Renaissance: A Study of Feminism,* by René de Maulde-la-Clavière. London, Swan Sonnenschein, 1900.
Translator, *The Art of Life,* by René de Maulde-la-Clavière. London, Swan Sonnenschein, 1902.
Translator, *Saint Cajetan,* by René de Maulde-la-Clavière. London, Duckworth, 1902.

* * *

Herbert Strang, a synthetic name derived from two collaborators, George Herbert Ely and James L'Estrange, was one of those authors regarded in the early years of the 20th century as the likely successor to G.A. Henty as the master of boys' adventure stories. Nor is this view surprising, for Strang's first publisher, Blackie, had been Henty's, and many of Strang's titles, such as *With Drake on the Spanish Main* or *One of Clive's Heroes* almost echo those of the popular Victorian's. Like Henty, furthermore, Strang was able and willing to turn his hand to many different kinds of work, and in addition to producing over 50 full-length tales was responsible for School Readers, for retellings of Biblical stories, for editing a famous *Annual* for many years as well as anthologies of poetry and prose, and also collaborated with various scholars on a *Historical Series* with such titles as *One of Rupert's Horse.*

Most of the full-length tales follow a predictable pattern, where a young hero, usually in a foreign setting, encounters an immediate crisis, such as a shipwreck or a minor skirmish, from which he escapes only to become engaged in a more urgent mission, to gather secret information in *Barclay of the Guides,* or to warn of a threatened ambush in *Tom Burnaby,* but which in the performance involves the hero in even graver matters, the Indian Mutiny, the Slave Trade, the '45 Rebellion, to give three examples. Needless to say, the hero acquits himself valiantly and is ultimately rewarded with material success.

Strang's execution of this kind of formulaic plot is very limited, however. The heroes are endowed with little individuality, and other characters, especially foreigners, are treated as predictable stereotypes. The geographical backgrounds, sometimes attributed to the travels of L'Estrange, have a kind of vitality, especially the African Congo in *Tom Burnaby,* but the historical background is often only peripheral, and has little of Henty's thorough, if dull, documentation, even in the *Historical Series.*

Like Westerman, Strang made some attempts to update his material, and in addition to his historical stories and tales of contemporary adventure in exotic parts, wrote several books about World War I, though works such as *With Haig on the Somme* are embarrassing to read now because of their overall lack of taste as well as depth. More interesting are a series of books in which Strang uses pseudo-scientific inventions as the background for his heroes' adventures, somewhat in the manner of Jules Verne.

King of the Air, for example, tells the story of young Tom Dorrell who designs and builds a strange airship, shaped like a bird but power-fuelled, which, because of its extraordinary capacity to hover, and to land vertically, is able not only to rescue sailors from drowning, but also to land on the flat roof of a Moroccan Kasbah and rescue a British diplomat, held hostage by rebel tribesmen! There is some attempt at comedy in the portrayal of Tom's rich eccentric patron, and a cowardly German salesman, Herr Schwab, but the book also reveals a disturbing anti-semitism. If Strang's books survive, it is likely to be because of the curiosity-value of their technology than because of their literary values.

—Dennis Butts

STRANGER, Joyce

Nationality: British. **Born:** Joyce Muriel Judson, Forest Gate, London, 26 May. **Education:** County School for Girls, Dartford, Kent; University College, London, B.Sc. 1942. **Family:** Married Kenneth B. Wilson in 1944; two sons and one daughter. **Career:** Research chemist, Imperial Chemical Industries, Manchester, 1942-46. Lecturer and writer on dog training. Lives in Anglesey, Wales. **Agent:** Aitken, Stone & Wylie, 29 Fernshaw Road, London SW10 0TG, England. **Address:** Anglesey; Glanllyn, Dwyran, Anglesey, Gwynedd, North Wales.

Publications for Children

Fiction

Wild Cat Island, illustrated by Joe Acheson. London, Methuen, 1961.
Circus All Alone, illustrated by Sheila Rose. London, Harrap, 1965.
Jason—Nobody's Dog, illustrated by Douglas Phillips. London, Dent, 1970.
The Honeywell Badger, illustrated by Douglas Phillips. London, Dent, 1972.
Paddy Joe. London, Collins, 1973.
The Hare at Dark Hollow, illustrated by Charles Pickard. London, Dent, 1973.
Trouble for Paddy Joe. London, Collins, 1973.
The Secret Herds: Animal Stories, illustrated by Douglas Reay. London, Dent, 1974.
Paddy Joe at Deep Hollow Farm. London, Collins, 1975.
The Fox at Drummer's Darkness, illustrated by William Geldart. London, Dent, 1976; New York, Farrar Straus, 1977.
The Wild Ponies, illustrated by Robert Rothero. London, Kaye and Ward, 1976.
Paddy Joe and Thomson's Folly. London, Pelham, 1979.
The Curse of Seal Valley. London, Dent, 1979.
Vet on Call. London, Carousel, 1981.
Double Trouble. London, Carousel, 1981.
Vet Riding High. London, Carousel, 1982.
No More Horses. London, Carousel, 1982.
Dial V.E.T. London, Carousel, 1982.
Marooned! London, Kaye and Ward, 1982.
The Hound of Darkness. London, Dent, 1983.
Shadows in the Dark. London, Kaye and Ward, 1984.
The Family at Fools' Farm. London, Dent, 1985.
Spy, the No-Good Pup. London, Dent, 1989.
Midnight Magic. London, Lions, 1991.
Animal Park Trilogy. London, Lions, 1992.
The Runaway. London, Lions, 1992.
The Secret of Hunter's Keep. London, Lions, 1993.
The House of Secrets Trilogy. London, Lions, 1994.
Bran's Secret. London, Lions, 1994.
Georgie's Secret. London, Lions, 1994.
Liam's Secret. London, Lions, 1994.
A Cry on the Wind. London, Souvenir, 1995.
Simon's Island, illustrated by David O'Conner. London, Collins, 1996.

Poetry

Joyce Stranger's Book of Hanák's Animals, illustrated by Mirko Hanák. London, Dent, 1976.

Publications for Adults

Novels

The Running Foxes. London, Hammond, 1965; New York, Viking Press, 1966.
Breed of Giants. London, Hammond, 1966; New York, Viking Press, 1967.
Rex. London, Harvill Press, 1967; New York, Viking Press, 1968.
Casey. London, Harvill Press, 1968; as *Born to Trouble,* New York, Viking Press, 1968.
Rusty. London, Harvill Press, 1969; as *The Wind on the Dragon,* New York, Viking Press, 1969.
One for Sorrow. London, Corgi, 1969.
Zara. London, Harvill Press, and New York, Viking Press, 1970.
Chia, The Wildcat. London, Harvill Press, 1971.
Lakeland Vet. London, Harvill Press, and New York, Viking Press, 1972.

Walk a Lonely Road. London, Harvill Press, 1973.
Never Count Apples. London, Harvill Press, 1974.
Never Tell a Secret. London, Harvill Press, 1975.
Flash. London, Harvill Press, 1976.
Khazan, The Horse That Came Out of the Sea. London, Harvill Press, 1977.
A Walk in the Dark. London, Joseph, 1978.
The January Queen. London, Joseph, 1979.
The Stallion. London, Joseph, 1981.
Josse. London, Joseph, 1983.
The Hounds of Hades. London, Joseph, 1985.
The Hills Are Lonely. London, Souvenir, 1993.
Thursday's Child. London, Souvenir, 1994.

Short Stories

A Dog Called Gelert and Other Stories. London, Corgi, 1973.
The Monastery Cat and Other Stories. London, Corgi, 1982.

Other

Kym: The True Story of a Siamese Cat. London, Joseph, 1976; New York, Coward McCann, 1977.
Two's Company. London, Joseph, 1977.
Three's a Pack. London, Joseph, 1980.
All about Your Pet Puppy. London, Pelham, 1980.
How to Own a Sensible Dog. London, Corgi, 1981.
Two for Joy. London, Joseph, 1982.
Stranger Than Fiction: The Biography of Elspeth Bryce-Smith. London, Joseph, 1984.
A Dog in a Million. London, Joseph, 1984.
Dog Days. London, Joseph, 1986.
Double or Quit. London, Joseph, 1987.

*

Manuscript Collections: Boston University.

Joyce Stranger comments:

I trained as a biologist. I have always spent my spare time watching animals, as I specialised in animal behaviour. Many books, especially those for children, are inaccurate, or sentimentalise or humanise the animal. Animals exist in their own right, live in worlds which impinge on ours but in no way are similar to ours. I try to show how (as far as a human can) animals live in a world that is real to *them.* In my adult books I am portraying country life in a state of change—the old ways and the little farms, the country sports that over-civilised urban people may end forever—to our great loss, as human and animal need to co-exist for balance, sanity, and to improve the quality of life. Man in an urban surrounding is doomed to increasing lack of mental stability. Those who retain the link with nature remain balanced—even the presence of a dog in the house restores proportion, if the dog is studied. No one is a hero or a great man to his dog—it speedily removes delusions of grandeur. The human-animal partnership is vital to all of us—but too many of us have lost the knowledge of this.

Too many believe the human is above the animals. We are animals. We experience pain, fear, panic; the expression in the eyes of a mouse with her young is that of a mother with her child. The reaction to danger is the same. We need to marvel at the intricacies of creation, the immense variety in the animal world, and we need to fight for the right to inherit wildlife in variety and not to reduce the marvels of creation to human tidiness and concrete prisons away from sun and trees and flowers. Suburban gardens and the cult of the family pet show men's needs—yet how many children's writers are aware of the tremendous bond between a boy who cares about animals and his dog, or the girl and her horse (and not on pony club levels)?

Training people to train their dogs reveals an enormous gap in understanding animals. Many failed relationships are due to the human partner believing the animal thinks on human terms. My books are intended as part educational, in that they are aimed at trying to show in a light readable way, to people who would not read nonfiction, just how an animal's mind does work. When an animal is understood, the ensuing partnership is far more rewarding to both partners, in a way that most people would not understand as they have never experienced the total trust and obedience of an animal that works with them as opposed to being dependent on them. This is the theme of many of my books; for many people, an animal can provide a harmony lacking in day-to-day relationships with people; the animal asks little and gives all the time. I train people to train their dogs and understand them.

Over the years my feelings about the human/animal bond have become stronger. We lose humanity when we ignore the normal balance and eliminate species, or we spread like a plague over the world. Population explosion can only result in war, death, famine, and a lack of all normal resources.

* * *

Joyce Stranger's work has a wide appeal. Many of her adult novels, especially those that are about animals, are enjoyed by children too. She has a knack with storylines that is hard to define. Indeed, how define the qualities that make a best-seller? *The Running Foxes,* which first established her reputation, was a best-seller, and many of her other novels share the same simplicity of outline and the same sympathetic insight into animal nature. A favourite theme is friendship between a person and an animal—no new theme, granted, but nevertheless given lively renewal in many of her books: *Jason—Nobody's Dog,* the Paddy Joe books, *Walk a Lonely Road,* and *Spy, the No-Good Pup.*

Stranger is keenly aware of the destructiveness of humankind. This defines a moral sense that runs through all her work. It sometimes means that a rather depressing tone pervades the story when the human protagonists feel guilty and remorseful. *The Honeywell Badger,* for instance, is about a boy and girl who are so keen to have a badger for a pet they pay a poacher for one and learn too late what problems they have brought upon themselves and the poor animal. In *Trouble for Paddy Joe* the boy has neglected the training of his young Alsatian, Storm. Consequently the dog, ignoring Paddy Joe's call, wanders off and gets lost in a Scottish wilderness. Everything that happens during the boy's long search for the dog makes a convincing and interesting narrative—the finding of an old diary confirming a legend, the exploring of the island, the storm, and the solitary boat trip—but the reader is all this time in the company of Paddy Joe who is no coward but desperately sad, lonely, and guilty; his thoughtless launching of the boat in which he nearly dies from exposure is like a beckoning to death.

With *The Hare at Dark Hollow,* on the other hand, we can enjoy watching an animal's intelligence and resilience as it adapts to a series of changes in its habitat. In the rich area of "animal biography" in English literature this is a book of real distinction. It tells a year in the life of a young hare entirely from the animal's point of view. The reader learns that Dark Hollow is to be developed as building land. We see the emigration or destruction of wildlife, the chain reaction in a habitat once busy with small creatures, the new fears and dangers for survivors. The ending, a happy one, is also true: hares find refuge from human hunters and other predators on the grassy expanses of airfields. The tension, always present in Stranger's books, between animals' right to live and mankind's careless destructiveness provides a current of controlled feeling and mounting suspense throughout the book.

In *The Fox at Drummer's Darkness* Stranger found artistic form and expression that resolve the conflicting elements in her talent. It is an extraordinary achievement, transcending all the problems that dogged her earlier efforts to relate man and beast in one literary frame. Conceived, it seems, in one daemonic impulse of creation, it has something of the epic, something of the ballad. Its few human characters are simple, unchanging figures like statues; the constantly recurring themes of burning drought, ghostly army, threat of industrial poison, give the book a structural rhythm that works inexorably towards its climax. The farmer projects all his primitive fears upon the fox, the senile huntsman lives a fantasy of hunts that never will be, and Johnny Toosmall, nightwatchman at the factory, befriends the starving, scavenging animal. But it is the animal, the fox itself, who is at the centre, alive in every detail, its intelligence and endurance stretched to the utmost and described with loving insight and understanding.

> Men were asleep. The glowing street lamps showed nothing but the fox's shadow, growing eerily long, shrinking uncannily, fading, and re-appearing on the opposite side of him, worrying him. He was used to sun shadow and moon shadow, predictable as dusk and starset, but he had never seen ranked lamps before, nor watched the change as he ran between them.
>
> At first, as the shadow flashed along the ground, he froze, watching the unnerving shape freeze with him. Then, as he ran, it began to play again, first large, then small, a fleeting silent darkness glued to his paws by a magic that he never understood.
>
> A cat sped in front of him, turned, horrified, and swiftly slashed his face in quick daring. It knew the free ways better than he, so that it leaped, lightning fast, over a wall and vanished under a garden shed...

We find the same poetic style in the short pieces she has written for Hanák's animals. She has been refining this vivid, flowing language all her professional life.

Stranger's books in the 1990s—all for children—continue to give sound family backgrounds and characters and a seemingly inexhaustible richness of animal lore new-minted. *Midnight Magic,* 1991, and *The Secret of Hunter's Keep,* 1993, have particular claims to excellence.

Midnight Magic is in the romantic mode: the romantic element is the beautiful black stallion of the title, a ghost horse glimpsed by Mandy and few others when she and her father come to buy Hunt Cottage. Mandy, 12, is keen to ride well but a fall has made her nervous. The first half of the story is a series of setbacks culminating in the closing of her much loved riding school and her own family's move to another part of the country. Here, things take an intriguing turn for the better, thanks to Kristy, the elderly horsewoman who gives Mandy lessons. Mandy learns to respond to each horse as an individual, its different paces, temperament, and needs. She loses her fear and she is rewarded for her hard work and devotion by being given Midnight Magic's great great grandson to ride. Any young horse lover would easily absorb the wisdom of Kristy's approach; it builds the essential rapport between human and animal. This fictional instruction is a remarkable *tour de force* even from a writer whose feeling for animals has always been her greatest strength.

In *The Secret of Hunter's Keep* the setting is important to both plot and atmosphere and to the theme of conservation. Daniel's father is head gamekeeper on a large old estate where pheasants are reared for the shoot. The old Lord has a modern house but Daniel and his parents have a flat in what remains of a very old mansion complete with priest hole and tunnel to the outside world. The boy keeps the chance discovery of this secret place to himself; he uses it for his night excursions to visit a vixen and her cubs. His dream is to have a cub of his own and he pursues this wish with determination. There is an element of bravado in this for he is not on good terms with his father—who, of course, must shoot the foxes. Daniel thinks him harsh and fears his temper.

After a long and dangerous vigil the boy does succeed in catching one cub who escaped the guns. But no sooner has his dream come true than he begins to realize how irresponsible he and his friend Anna have been in trying in secret to save animals that they haven't the means to care for properly. He is burdened with problems. Then, in an expansive moment the father talks to his son about his work, his concern for the native animals and threatened wild plants, and his deep knowledge of nature and what conserving it really means, and Daniel's perspective changes.

A young poacher tries to steal the cub and a pup. The little animals get trapped in a pipe, and in freeing them Daniel unearths a valuable statue, one of many that had been hidden during the War and lost. The sale of these will save the old Lord from having to sell the estate and part with his gamekeeper. The lesser problems of the children fall into place, and Daniel has taken a big step in growing up, his feeling for his father much happier.

—Gwen Marsh

STREATFEILD, (Mary) Noel

Pseudonym: Susan Scarlett. **Nationality:** British. **Born:** Amberley, Sussex, 24 December 1895. **Education:** Schools in St. Leonard's on Sea, Sussex; Laleham School, Eastbourne, Sussex; Academy of Dramatic Art, London. **Career:** Actress in England, South Africa, and Australia, 1920s; joined Women's Voluntary Services in 1939. **Awards:** Library Association Carnegie medal, 1939. O.B.E. (Officer, Order of the British Empire), 1983. **Died:** 11 September 1986.

Publications for Children

Fiction

Ballet Shoes, illustrated by Ruth Gervis. London, Dent, 1936; New York, Random House, 1937.

Tennis Shoes, illustrated by D.L. Mays. London, Dent, 1937; New York, Random House, 1938.
The Circus Is Coming, illustrated by Steven Spurrier. London, Dent, 1938; revised edition, 1948, 1960; as *Circus Shoes,* New York, Random House, 1939.
Dennis the Dragon, illustrated by Ruth Gervis. London, Dent, 1939.
The House in Cornwall, illustrated by D.L. Mays. London, Dent, 1940; as *The Secret of the Lodge,* New York, Random House, 1940.
The Children of Primrose Lane, illustrated by Marcia Lane Foster. London, Dent, 1941; as *The Stranger in Primrose Lane,* New York, Random House, 1941.
Harlequinade, illustrated by Clarke Hutton. London, Chatto and Windus, 1943.
Curtain Up, illustrated by D.L. Mays. London, Dent, 1944; as *Theater Shoes; or, Other People's Shoes,* New York, Random House, 1945.
Party Frock, illustrated by Anna Zinkeisen. London, Collins, 1946; as *Party Shoes,* New York, Random House, 1947.
The Painted Garden, illustrated by Ley Kenyon. London, Collins, 1949; revised edition, London, Penguin, 1961; as *Movie Shoes,* New York, Random House, 1949.
Osbert, illustrated by Susanne Suba. Chicago, Rand McNally, 1950.
The Theater Cat, illustrated by Susanne Suba. Chicago, Rand McNally, 1951.
White Boots, illustrated by Milein Cosman. London, Collins, 1951; as *Skating Shoes,* New York, Random House, 1951.
The Fearless Treasure, illustrated by Dorothy Braby. London, Joseph, 1952.
The Bell Family, illustrated by Shirley Hughes. London, Collins, 1954; as *Family Shoes,* New York, Random House, 1954.
The Grey Family, illustrated by Pat Marriott. London, Hamish Hamilton, 1956.
Wintle's Wonders, illustrated by Richard Kennedy. London, Collins, 1957; as *Dancing Shoes,* New York, Random House, 1958.
Bertram, illustrated by Margery Gill. London, Hamish Hamilton, 1959.
New Town, illustrated by Shirley Hughes. London, Collins, 1960; as *New Shoes,* New York, Random House, 1960.
Apple Bough, illustrated by Margery Gill. London, Collins, 1962; as *Traveling Shoes,* New York, Random House, 1962.
Lisa Goes to Russia, illustrated by Geraldine Spence. London, Collins, 1963.
The Children on the Top Floor, illustrated by Jillian Willett. London, Collins, 1964; New York, Random House, 1965.
Let's Go Coaching, illustrated by Peter Warner. London, Hamish Hamilton, 1965.
The Growing Summer, illustrated by Edward Ardizzone. London, Collins, 1966; as *The Magic Summer,* New York, Random House, 1967.
Old Chairs to Mend, illustrated by Barry Wilkinson. London, Hamish Hamilton, 1966.
Caldicott Place, illustrated by Betty Maxey. London, Collins, 1967; as *The Family at Caldicott Place,* New York, Random House, 1968.
Gemma, illustrated by Betty Maxey. London, Armada, 1968.
Gemma and Sisters, illustrated by Betty Maxey. London, Armada, 1968.
The Barrow Lane Gang. London, BBC Publications, 1968.
Gemma Alone. London, Armada, 1969.
Goodbye Gemma. London, Armada, 1969.
Thursday's Child, illustrated by Peggy Fortnum. London, Collins, and New York, Random House, 1970.
Ballet Shoes for Anna, illustrated by Mary Dinsdale. London, Collins, 1972.
When the Siren Wailed, illustrated by Margery Gill. London, Collins, 1974; New York, Random House, 1977.
Far to Go, illustrated by Charles Mozley. London, Collins, 1976.
Meet the Maitlands, illustrated by Antony Maitland. London, W.H. Allen, 1978.
The Maitlands: All Change at Cuckly Place, illustrated by Antony Maitland. London, W.H. Allen, 1979.

Plays

The Children's Matinee, illustrated by Ruth Gervis (includes *The Fourum, Me-ow, Olympus, The Princess and the Pea, The Cat, The Lily, Gentlemen of the Road, The Thirteenth Fairy*). London, Heinemann, 1934.

Radio Plays: *The Bell Family* series, 1949-51; *New Town* series; *Kick Off,* 1973, and others.

Other

The Picture Show of Britain, illustrated by Ursula Koering. Drexel Hill, Pennsylvania, Bell, 1951.
The First Book of Ballet. New York, Watts, 1953; revised edition, London, Ward, 1963.
The First Book of England, illustrated by Gioia Fiammenghi. New York, Watts, 1958; revised edition, London, Ward, 1963.
Queen Victoria, illustrated by Robert Frankenberg. New York, Random House, 1958; London, W.H. Allen, 1961.
The Royal Ballet School. London, Collins, 1959.
Ballet Annual. London, Collins, 1959.
The January [*February, March, April, May, June, July, August, September, October, November, December*] *Baby.* London, Barker, 12 vols., 1959.
Look at the Circus, illustrated by Constance Marshall. London, Hamish Hamilton, 1960.
The Thames: London's River. Champaign, Illinois, Garrard, 1964; London, Muller, 1966.
Enjoying Opera, illustrated by Hilary Abrahams. London, Dobson, 1966; as *The First Book of the Opera,* New York, Watts, 1966.
Before Confirmation. London, Heinemann, 1967.
The First Book of Shoes, illustrated by Jacqueline Tomes. New York, Watts, 1967; London, Watts, 1971.
Red Riding Hood, illustrated by Svend Otto S. London, Benn, 1970.
The Boy Pharaoh, Tutankhamen. London, Joseph, 1972.
A Young Person's Guide to Ballet, illustrated by Georgette Borbier. London and New York, Warne, 1975.

Editor, *The Years of Grace* (essays). London, Evans, 1950; revised edition, 1956.
Editor, *By Special Request: New Stories for Girls.* London, Collins, 1953.
Editor, *Growing Up Gracefully,* illustrated by John Dugan. London, Barker, 1955.

Editor, *Confirmation and After.* London, Heinemann, 1963.
Editor, *Priska,* by Merja Otava, translated by Elizabeth Portch. London, Benn, 1964.
Editor, *Nicholas,* by Marlie Brande, translated by Elizabeth Boas. London, Benn, and Chicago, Follett, 1968.
Editor, *Sleepy Nicholas,* by Marlie Brande, translated by Elizabeth Boas. London, Benn, and Chicago, Follett, 1970.
Editor, *The Christmas Holiday [Summer Holiday, Easter Holiday, Birthday Story, Weekend Story] Book,* illustrated by Sara Silcock. London, Dent, 5 vols., 1973-77.

PUBLICATIONS FOR ADULTS

Novels

The Whicharts. London, Heinemann, 1931; New York, Brentano's, 1932.
Parson's Nine. London, Heinemann, 1932; New York, Doubleday, 1933.
Tops and Bottoms. London, Heinemann, and New York, Doubleday, 1933.
Shepherdess of Sheep. London, Heinemann, 1934; New York, Reynal, 1935.
It Pays to Be Good. London, Heinemann, 1936.
Caroline England. London, Heinemann, 1937; New York, Reynal, 1938.
Luke. London, Heinemann, 1939.
The Winter Is Past. London, Collins, 1940.
I Ordered a Table for Six. London, Collins, 1942.
Myra Carrol. London, Collins, 1944.
Saplings. London, Collins, 1945.
Grass in Piccadilly. London, Collins, 1947.
Mothering Sunday. London, Collins, and New York, Coward McCann, 1950.
Aunt Clara. London, Collins, 1952.
Judith. London, Collins, 1956.
The Silent Speaker. London, Collins, 1961.
Gran-Nannie. London, Joseph, 1976.

Novels as Susan Scarlett

Clothes-Pegs. London, Hodder and Stoughton, 1939.
Sally-Ann. London, Hodder and Stoughton, 1939.
Peter and Paul. London, Hodder and Stoughton, 1940.
Ten Way Street. London, Hodder and Stoughton, 1940.
The Man in the Dark. London, Hodder and Stoughton, 1941.
Baddacombe's. London, Hodder and Stoughton, 1941.
Under the Rainbow. London, Hodder and Stoughton, 1942.
Summer Pudding. London, Hodder and Stoughton, 1943.
Murder While You Work. London, Hodder and Stoughton, 1944.
Poppies for England. London, Hodder and Stoughton, 1948.
Pirouette. London, Hodder and Stoughton, 1948.
Love in a Mist. London, Hodder and Stoughton, 1951.

Plays

Them Wings (also director: produced London, 1933).
Wisdom Teeth (produced London, 1936). London, French, 1936.
Welcome Mr. Washington (screenplay), with Jack Whittingham, 1944.
Many Happy Returns, with Roland Pertwee (produced Windsor, 1950). London, English Theatre Guild, 1953.

Other

Magic and the Magician: E. Nesbit and Her Children's Books. London, Benn, and New York, Abelard Schuman, 1958.
A Vicarage Family (autobiographical). London, Collins, and New York, Watts, 1963.
Away from the Vicarage (autobiographical). London, Collins, 1965; as *On Tour,* New York, Watts, 1965.
Beyond the Vicarage (autobiographical). London, Collins, 1971; New York, Watts, 1972.

Editor, *The Day Before Yesterday: Firsthand Stories of Fifty Years Ago.* London, Collins, 1956.

*

Critical Studies: *Noel Streatfeild* by Barbara Ker Wilson, London, Bodley Head, 1961, New York, Walck, 1964; *Noel Streatfeild: A Biography* by Angela Bull, London, Collins, 1984.

* * *

Noel Streatfeild frequently claimed that a "blotting paper memory" was the secret of her success as a children's writer. She had, she said, a capacity to think herself back into childhood, recalling vividly the delights of pets and holidays and Christmas, and the miseries of being snubbed, overlooked, and excluded. In her best books the reader has the experience of living intensely with the child characters, understanding exactly how they feel about things, and why; and this sense of complete identification is one reason for her books still seeming alive to child readers 50 years after they were written.

Surprisingly she spent her early years as an adult trying to forget her childhood. She was the second daughter of an Anglican clergyman; and, sandwiched between a pretty, delicate elder sister, and a sharp-witted, attractive younger one, she was bitterly conscious of being considered plain and naughty. The naughtiness was, at least partly, cultivated—it was the best way of making her personality felt; but nobody understood her craving to be important. Only in the plays she and her sisters put on for parish causes did she shine; and so, after making munitions at Woolwich Arsenal during World War I, it was a natural step for her to train as an actress.

Her 10 years on the stage were not, in themselves, very successful, but they left her with an intimate knowledge of theatre life which she used in her first adult novel, *The Whicharts,* the story of three girls struggling in the underworld of second-rate show business. Other novels followed, and critics were quick to notice how many contained striking portraits of child characters. Nevertheless it came as a surprise to Streatfeild when Mabel Carey, the newly appointed editor at Dents, sent for her, and suggested she should write about children in the theatre. Somewhat unenthusiastically Streatfeild agreed, and in a very short time rehashed *The Whicharts* to produce a child's version, *Ballet Shoes,* the story of three adopted sisters who train for stage and ballet careers.

Its immediate success astonished her. Knowing little about contemporary children's books, she had no idea she had done anything unusual; but the immense success of *Ballet Shoes* came from its being so original. She had both unveiled the romantic world of the theatre, hardly touched on in children's books before, and introduced hard-working, money-conscious, professional children of an entirely different breed from the amateurish, country-house heroes and heroines of most current stories. The Fossils are lively, well-drawn characters, and the charming illustrations of them by Streatfeild's sister, Ruth Gervis, have left them firmly imprinted in her readers' imaginations.

Two other books of equal brilliance followed quickly. The first, *Tennis Shoes,* was Streatfeild's favourite, for its heroine, Nicky, was something of a self-portrait. The story contrasts two sisters—Susan, pretty and popular, apparently an ideal heroine, and Nicky, difficult, uncooperative, and conceited. Yet by an extraordinary reversal of the usual standards in children's books, it is Nicky who proves to be the tennis star, while Susan is left on the sidelines. Geniuses, Streatfeild suggests, will inevitably be misfits, and a temperamental law unto themselves. Among her many portraits of child stars, none is more convincing than Nicky.

The Circus Is Coming, which won the Carnegie Medal, is probably her most outstanding book. Once again she took immense risks with her characters, and pulled them off. The plot concerns two orphan children who run away to the circus where their uncle works. The circus is shown as a tough world, in which the highest standards are expected, and the overprotected children find adjustment extremely taxing. All their pretensions are ruthlessly exposed, from Santa's violin playing to Peter's spurious gentlemanliness. The trials inflicted on them may seem excessively hard to some child readers, but the book is written with great integrity and reaches a completely satisfying solution.

Between 1939 and 1946 Streatfeild was too much occupied with war work and with adult novels to spend much time on her children's books. *The House in Cornwall* and *The Children of Primrose Lane* are run-of-the-mill adventure stories. *Curtain Up,* her most detailed look at the serious theatre, lacks proper organization and is rather shapeless. Much the best of her war books is *Party Frock,* an original story and a splendid piece of craftsmanship. Streatfeild chose the difficult subject of a village pageant, and handled both its development and her huge cast with astonishing ease.

For 20 years after the war Streatfeild was the leading figure in the British children's book world. She lectured on children's books, reviewed them, campaigned against trashy "juveniles" and horror comics, and appeared in the first children's television book programmes. Her output, in fiction and nonfiction, was enormous, and if no single book quite reached the standard of her pre-war trio, her level remained high. *White Boots,* with its skating heroine, Lalla, who finally has the courage to say "I can't do it"; *The Growing Summer,* a celebration of the magic of Ireland, a country she knew and loved; and *Thursday's Child,* the story of an Edwardian orphan of invincible determination, are perhaps the best known; but her tales of the Bell family, originally written for radio; *The Fearless Treasure,* a social history of England worked into a fantasy framework; *Apple Bough,* with its gentle Victorian overtones; and the brilliantly written *The Boy Pharaoh, Tutankhamen* also give some idea of her great range and versatility. In later years she complained that reviewers took her for granted, as a "national monument," but this was a tribute to her prestige and her immense sales.

Streatfeild's talent was to present life as dramatic and colourful, without resorting to artificial adventures; to draw lively, convincing characters; and to write in a flowing, easy style, laced with humour, that was immediately acceptable to children. Her stories are valuable as paths, luring inexperienced readers pleasantly onward into the world of books.

—Angela Bull

SUDBERY, Rodie

Nationality: British. **Born:** Rodie Tutton, Chelmsford, Essex, 2 April 1943. **Education:** Girton College, Cambridge, B.A. in mathematics 1964. **Family:** Married Anthony Sudbery in 1964; two daughters. **Address:** 5 Heslington Croft, Fulford, York YO1 4NB, England.

Publications for Children

Fiction

The House in the Wood. London, Deutsch, 1968; as *A Sound of Crying,* New York, McCall, 1970.
Cowls. London, Deutsch, 1969.
Rich and Famous and Bad. London, Deutsch, 1970.
The Pigsleg. London, Deutsch, 1971.
Warts and All. London, Deutsch, 1972.
A Curious Place. London, Deutsch, 1973.
Inside the Walls, illustrated by Sally Long. London, Deutsch, 1973.
Ducks and Drakes. London, Deutsch, 1975.
Lightning Cliff, illustrated by Sally Long. London, Deutsch, 1975.
The Silk and the Skin. London, Deutsch, 1976.
Long Way Round, illustrated by Sally Long. London, Deutsch, 1977.
Somewhere Else. London, Deutsch, 1978.
A Tunnel with Problems. London, Deutsch, 1979.
The Village Secret. London, Deutsch, 1980.
Night Music. London, Gollancz, 1983.
Grandmother's Footsteps, illustrated by Vanessa Julian-Ottie. London, Hamish Hamilton, 1984.

* * *

Rodie Sudbery's novels are all based in family life, and her outstanding skill is to explore the relationships among children and between children and adults without letting the adult's perception creep into the story. She has the ability to get under the skins of the children she writes about and enable the reader to feel what the characters are feeling. Rarely are the children in real danger (*Lightning Cliff* is perhaps an exception), nor are they underprivileged at home, and yet the problems and dilemmas they encounter are nonetheless real, and many young readers would identify with, and find comfort in, the situations.

Among her books for older readers are the five about the Devenish family. Polly is 12 in the first book *The House in the Wood* which, as well as being Sudbery's first published book, was a rare excursion for her into fantasy. The interaction of the past and the present are interestingly handled. The series continues with *Cowls* (a haunted house mystery), *Rich and Famous and Bad, Warts and All,* and *Ducks and Drakes,* in which Polly Devenish is an undergraduate. Sudbery is less successful in describing adolescent relationships than those of younger children, but the series as a whole is both interesting and readable, with a refreshingly varied approach in each book.

Long Way Round stands out among her stories for 8-10-year-olds. Typically, the plot centers on a single situation of the sort which can seem trivial to an adult but overwhelming to a child. Simon and Jeremy resent having to take a new girl with them on their journey to school but in the end, after some unobtrusive manipulation by their teacher, the three become friends. It is not every adult who can empathise with children as Sudbery seems to. Celia's abject misery at having to eat her packed lunch in Miss Jane's kitchen is tangible, as is her shy inability to admit that she made a mistake in getting off the school bus at the wrong stop. This skill at getting inside the children's heads and transmitting their thoughts and feelings makes her books full of relevance for young readers. *Inside the Walls* is another ordinary everyday story, but her understanding of children lifts it above the ordinary. She makes natural use of dialogue, leaning on it heavily to carry her plots along and recreating accurately the direct and economical speech of young children talking among themselves. In *Lightning Cliff* her understanding of the dilemmas of childhood again lifts an unexceptional adventure story into something with more substance and quality which opens up questions of behaviour and morality.

In Cressida, the central character of *The Pigsleg,* Sudbery has created a powerful and dominating leader of a gang of children—all the offspring of university dons. As usual, she writes about the world that she knows, which could lead her to be accused of writing cosily about middle-class children from privileged, or at least comfortable, backgrounds. There is, however, nothing cosy about the outcome of the dares in which Cressida's gang indulge. When things begin to get out of hand, the adults are finally involved and Cressida is cut down to size. It is part of Sudbery's success that she contrives to make Cressida an attractive character despite her unhealthy domination over the others and also to weave a very complex but clear picture of the relationships between four families.

Sudbery's contribution to the Antelope series is aimed broadly at 6-8-year-olds who are just ready to enjoy a full-length story. The constraints of writing to a specific brief seem to have restricted her natural freedom to write the story she wants to write. Although her writing is as good as ever and her dialogue largely carries the story of *Grandmother's Footsteps* along in the children's words, there are none of the more subtle undertones which lift her other books above the level of the mundane, and there is a feeling about it of unconcluded business. Nevertheless, young readers will enjoy the story about three children trying—not always successfully—to ensure that their grandmother's visit goes well, and perhaps it is unfair to ask more of a book for this age group than that it should be read with enjoyment.

—Valerie Brinkley-Willsher

SUTTON, Eve(lyn Mary)

Nationality: New Zealander (originally British: immigrated to New Zealand, 1949; became citizen, 1955). **Born:** Evelyn Mary Breakell, Preston, Lancashire, England, 14 September 1906. **Education:** Park School, Preston, 1917-24; Goldsmiths' College, University of London, 1925-27, teachers' training diploma. **Family:** Married Alfred Sutton in 1931; two sons. **Career:** Primary school teacher, Deepdale, Lancashire, 1927-31. **Award:** New Zealand Library Association Esther Glen award, 1975. **Died.**

Publications for Children

Fiction

Green Gold, illustrated by Paul Wright. London, Hamish Hamilton, 1976.
Tuppenny Brown, illustrated by Paul Wright. London, Hamish Hamilton, 1977.
Johnny Sweep, illustrated by Paul Wright. London, Hamish Hamilton, 1977.
Moa Hunter, illustrated by Bernard Brett. London, Hamish Hamilton, 1978.
Skip for the Huntaway, illustrated by Ernest Papps. Wellington, Price Milburn, 1983.
Surgeon's Boy. Wellington, Mallinson Rendel, 1983; Barnstaple, Devon, Spindlewood, 1984.
Kidnapped by Blackbirders, illustrated by Fiona Kelly. Wellington, Mallinson Rendel, and Barnstaple, Devon, Spindlewood, 1984.
Valley of Heavenly Gold, illustrated by Doss. Wellington, Mallinson Rendel, 1987.

Poetry

My Cat Likes to Hide in Boxes, illustrated by Lynley Dodd. London, Hamish Hamilton, 1973; New York, Parents' Magazine Press, 1974.

*

Eve Sutton comments:

My first venture into the field of children's literature, the picture book *My Cat Likes to Hide in Boxes,* came as the result of an amiable conversation with my cousin Lynley Dodd—"Wouldn't it be fun to do a book together?" But I like the actual writing and plotting, so it seemed natural to turn to books for older children. The early New Zealand scene has interested me ever since we came here and makes a natural background for my stories.

* * *

Eve Sutton's preferred field is a problematical one, that which caters, simultaneously, for able readers of seven and over, and slower readers of 11 and 12. Its requirements are exacting. The principal character must fall within the upper age group and yet be accessible to the sympathies of the younger, a limiting consideration by which few writers would care to be bound. Emotional exploration of character is virtually prohibited, the resultant hero usually emerging as a somewhat vacuous personality, independent and resourceful on the one hand, but inclined to excessive virtue on the other. But there are advantages; intelligent seven-year-olds are likely to be bored by stories about their peers, who are all too likely to be bound by the very constraints of overprotected family life which they themselves find so irksome. And less able 12-year-olds, if they can be reached, provide a ready ear for stories which are exciting, uncomplicated, and simply told.

Sutton contrives to avoid the pitfalls, while capitalising on the advantages. Certainly not one of her three youthful heroes, each obliged to make his own way alone in the wild young colony that was New Zealand in the mid-19th century, lacks individuality. Her use of the first person contributes to this success. Adam, Tuppenny, and Johnny emerge, in their different ways, as real boys, credible products of the backgrounds from which they have been plucked in England, and exposed to a bombardment of new impressions on the other side of the world. The story, in each case, is engrossing.

The apparent simplicity of the text of these short novels conceals, to some extent, Sutton's capacity for establishing place and character, and for managing a pace which is both swift enough to ensure interest and deliberate enough to avoid confusion. A surprising amount of detail is included: the horrors of the outward voyage, the brash jauntiness of the early colony, the rigours of breaking in virgin land for farming, the thrilling yet sickening experience of whaling, the backbreaking toil of gum-digging—and through it all, the pervasive sense of hope, of beginning, of man's willingness to risk death and face hardship in search of freedom.

Sutton's only book for very young children, *My Cat Likes to Hide in Boxes,* reveals a facility with language, rhythm, and rhyme, and a sure feeling for the nonsense-humour of early childhood. Its competence is undoubted; but the author's real aptitude—and preference—seems to be in books for older children.

—Dorothy Butler

SWEENEY, Matthew

Nationality: Irish. **Born:** County Donegal, 1952. **Family:** Married; two children. **Career:** Writer-in-Residence, Farnham College, Surrey, 1984, 1985; University of East Anglia Writing Fellowship, 1986; external advisor in creative writing, West Surrey College of Aart and Design, Farnham, 1986-89; publicist and events assistant, Poetry Society, London, 1988-90; Poet in Residence Hereford & Worcester, 1991; Writer in Residence, South Bank Centre, London, 1994-95. **Awards:** Prudence Farmer Award, 1984; Cholmondeley Award, 1987; Arts Council of Great Britain Bursary in creative Writing, 1992. **Address:** 11 Dombey St., London WC1N 3PB, England.

Publications for Children

Fiction

The Chinese Dressing Gown. London, Raven Arts Press, 1987.
The Snow Vulture. London, Faber and Faber, 1992.

Poetry

The Blue Taps. London, Prospero Poets, 1994.
Fatso in the Red Suit. London, Faber and Faber, 1995.
The Bridal Suite. London, Cape, 1997.

Editor, *One for Jimmy: An Anthology from the Hereford and Worcester Poetry Project.* England, Hereford and Worcester County Council, 1992

Publications for Adults

Poetry

A Dream of Maps. London, Raven Arts Press, 1981.
A Round House. London, Allison and Busby, 1983.
The Lame Waltzer. London, Allison and Busby, 1985.
Blue Shoes. London, Secker and Warburg, 1989.
Cacti. London, Secker and Warburg, 1992.

* * *

As a writer Matthew Sweeney does not fit easily into any category. His works are not in the mainstream and are characterised by a somewhat bleak vision of life and a downbeat atmosphere. The intensity of his writing is in no way modified when he addresses children. His poetry for children is distinguished by the same characteristics that have made his adult poetry so arresting. His collection, *The Flying Spring Onion,* is in many ways deceptively accessible; although often short and sparse in style, his poems encapsulate all of the storyteller's tradition. They have all of the qualities that attract children to poetry; brevity, lucidity, language that is everyday and undaunting, and a story. Some of the poems have a similar appeal to that of the traditional cautionary tale. In "Into the Mixer" the "noisy boy" who climbs into the cement mixer comes out

> "Onto the road made of the same
> quick setting stuff.
> He looked rough
> and he had only himself to blame."

But this is not simply a mundane or prosaic collection of humorous verse. A macabre and occasionally menacing humour permeates the collection. This humour is sharp but never throwaway. Almost without exception the poems have a challenging edge. There is a bleak and downbeat element in Sweeney's poetry. The optimistic aspirations of the "Cows on the Beach" "fed up with grass, field, farmer" who think that they have found "a better place to be" are brutally quashed by the farmer:

> "This is no place for cows to be,
> he shouted, and slapped them
> with seaweed, all the way home."

The bright expectations at the start of the poem are soundly demolished by the ending. This is a pattern which is repeated in other poems in the collection. In "Worrying Days" the old donkey thinks he is safe from the slaughter house:

> When his owner stopped to stare
> at his rump, and shout 'Salami!'—
> whatever that meant. 'Salami!'

There is a dark atmosphere and resonance in the brutal and graphic image of the fishbones:

> ...in the smelly bin
> he was a head a backbone and a tail
> soon the cats would be in for him.

This is offset by Sweeney's humour and deftness of touch which occasionally lightens the tone of the collection in the form of such poems as "The Burglar":

when the Burglar burgled
he didn't know
that another burglar
was inside *his* house.

and the confident Flying Spring Onion who defiantly announces to the tomatoes that he won't go

In a salad bowl with you,
stung by lemon,
greased by oil,
and nothing at all to do
except wait to be eaten.

The resonance of Sweeney's poetry for children lasts long after the reading. His verse stimulates and excites. This is true also of his fiction. *The Chinese Dressing Gown* was Sweeney's first venture into children's fiction. It is a story made memorable by a subtle and interesting concept. Too subtle perhaps, as it is not a concept young children can readily address. A young girl, Boo, cannot understand who is taking her dressing gown every night and leaving it in her parent's bedroom. Her parents being "lazy as well as liars" are no help in solving the mystery. Boo however, like other Sweeney child characters is tough and self-reliant. The dressing gown thief turns out to be a young boy and Boo discovers that her ghostly playmate is her own father as a child. The resolution of the story may bemuse young readers, and yet it is a haunting tale. *The Snow Vulture* is more accessible. A short novel written for older children, it tells the story of rival twin brothers Clive and Carl. Whereas Clive is good and well-behaved, Carl is nasty, moody, and uncooperative. Carl creates a snow sculpture that takes on a menacing life of its own. The snow vulture becomes indestructible and thrives on Carl's badness, but soon Carl must turn to Clive for help to destroy his own creation. The brothers have to resolve their differences and overcome their divisive competitiveness in their efforts to defeat it.

As in Sweeney's other works there is an underlying darkness and bleakness to the novel. The fantasy element is in sharp contrast to the stark realism of the rest of the plot. Once again parents are distant and seemingly detached. It is up to the boys themselves to solve their problem and rid themselves of the evil snow vulture.

—Sheila Flanagan and Rachel O'Flanagan

SYME, (Neville) Ronald

Nationality: Irish. **Born:** Lancashire, England, 13 March 1910. **Education:** Durham School, 1924-26; Collegiate School, Wanganui, New Zealand, 1926-29. **Military Service:** British Army Intelligence Corps, 1940-45: major. **Family:** Married Ngamarama Heiarii Feena Amoa in 1960; one daughter. **Career:** Cadet and officer, 1930-34, and gunner, 1939-40, British Merchant Service; reporter and foreign correspondent, 1934-39; assistant editor, John Westhouse and Peter Lunn Ltd., publishers, London, 1946-48; public relations officer, British Road Federation, London, 1948-50. Public relations officer and parliamentary correspondent, Cook Islands Government, 1979-83. **Died:** 19 December 1992.

Publications for Children

Fiction

That Must Be Julian, illustrated by William Stobbs. London, Lunn, 1947.
Julian's River War, illustrated by John Harris. London, Heinemann, 1949.
Ben of the Barrier, illustrated by J. Nicholson. London, Evans, 1949.
The Settlers of Carriacou. London, Hodder and Stoughton, 1953.
Gipsy Michael, illustrated by William Stobbs. London, Hodder and Stoughton, 1954.
They Came to an Island, illustrated by William Stobbs. London, Hodder and Stoughton, 1955.
Isle of Revolt, illustrated by William Stobbs. London, Hodder and Stoughton, 1956.
Ice Fighter, illustrated by William Stobbs. London, Hodder and Stoughton, 1956.
The Amateur Company. London, Hodder and Stoughton, 1957.
The Great Canoe. London, Hodder and Stoughton, 1957.
The Forest Fighters, illustrated by William Stobbs. London, Hodder and Stoughton, 1958.
River of No Return, illustrated by William Stobbs. London, Hodder and Stoughton, 1958.
The Spaniards Came at Dawn, illustrated by William Stobbs. London, Hodder and Stoughton, 1959.
Thunder Knoll, illustrated by William Stobbs. London, Hodder and Stoughton, 1960.
The Buccaneer Explorer, illustrated by William Stobbs. London, Hodder and Stoughton, 1960.
The Mountainy Men, illustrated by Richard Payne. London, Hodder and Stoughton, 1961.
Coast of Danger, illustrated by Richard Payne. London, Hodder and Stoughton, 1961.
Nose-Cap Astray, illustrated by Roger Payne. London, Hodder and Stoughton, 1962.
Two Passengers for Spanish Fork, illustrated by Brian Keogh. London, Hodder and Stoughton, 1963.
Switch Points at Kamlin, illustrated by Brian Keogh. London, Hodder and Stoughton, 1964.
The Dunes and the Diamonds, illustrated by Brian Keogh. London, Hodder and Stoughton, 1964.
The Missing Witness. London, Hodder and Stoughton, 1965.
The Saving of the Fair East Wind, illustrated by A.R. Whitear. London, Dent, 1967.

Other (illustrated by William Stobbs)

Full Fathom Five (not illustrated). London, Lunn, 1946.
Hakluyt's Sea Stories. London, Heinemann, 1948.
Bay of the North: The Story of Pierre Radisson, illustrated by Ralph Ray. New York, Morrow, 1950; London, Hodder and Stoughton, 1951.
Cortes of Mexico. New York, Morrow, 1951; as *Cortez, Conqueror of Mexico,* London, Hodder and Stoughton, 1952.

I, Mungo Park [*Captain Anson, Gordon of Khartoum*]. London, Burke, 3 vols., 1951-53.
Champlain of the St. Lawrence. New York, Morrow, 1952; London, Hodder and Stoughton, 1953.
Columbus, Finder of the New World. New York, Morrow, 1952.
The Story of Britain's Highways (not illustrated). London, Pitman, 1952.
La Salle of the Mississippi. New York, Morrow, and London, Hodder and Stoughton, 1953.
Magellan, First Around the World. New York, Morrow, 1953.
John Smith of Virginia. New York, Morrow, and London, Hodder and Stoughton, 1954.
Henry Hudson. New York, Morrow, 1955; as *Hudson of the Bay,* London, Hodder and Stoughton, 1955.
Balboa, Finder of the Pacific. New York, Morrow, 1956.
De Soto, Finder of the Mississippi. New York, Morrow, 1957.
The Man Who Discovered the Amazon (on Pizarro). New York, Morrow, 1958.
Cartier, Finder of the St. Lawrence. New York, Morrow, 1958.
On Foot to the Arctic: The Story of Samuel Hearne. New York, Morrow, 1959; as *Trail to the North,* London, Hodder and Stoughton, 1959.
Vasco Da Gama, Sailor Towards the Sunrise. New York, Morrow, 1959.
Captain Cook, Pacific Explorer. New York, Morrow, 1960.
Francis Drake, Sailor of the Unknown Seas. New York, Morrow, 1961.
First Man to Cross America: The Story of Cabeza de Vaca. New York, Morrow, 1961.
Walter Raleigh. New York, Morrow, 1962.
The Young Nelson, illustrated by Susan Groom and Trevor Parkin. London, Parrish, 1962; New York, Roy, 1963.
African Traveler: The Story of Mary Kingsley, illustrated by Jacqueline Tomes. New York, Morrow, 1962.
Francisco Pizarro, Finder of Peru. New York, Morrow, 1963.
Invaders and Invasions. London, Batsford, 1964; New York, Norton, 1965.
Nigerian Pioneer: The Story of Mary Slessor, illustrated by Jacqueline Tomes. New York, Morrow, 1964.
Alexander Mackenzie, Canadian Explorer. New York, Morrow, 1964.
Sir Henry Morgan, Buccaneer. New York, Morrow, 1965.
Francisco Coronado and the Seven Cities of Gold. New York, Morrow, 1965.
Quesada of Colombia. New York, Morrow, 1966.
William Penn, Founder of Pennsylvania. New York, Morrow, 1966.
Garibaldi, The Man Who Made a Nation. New York, Morrow, 1967.
Bolivar, The Liberator. New York, Morrow, 1968.
Captain John Paul Jones, America's Fighting Seaman. New York, Morrow, 1968.
Amerigo Vespucci, Scientist and Sailor. New York, Morrow, 1969.
Frontenac of New France. New York, Morrow, 1969.
Benedict Arnold, Traitor of the Revolution. New York, Morrow, 1970.
Vancouver, Explorer of the Pacific Coast. New York, Morrow, 1970.
Toussaint, The Black Liberator. New York, Morrow, 1971.
Zapata, Mexican Rebel. New York, Morrow, 1971.
John Cabot and His Son Sebastian. New York, Morrow, 1972.
Juarez, The Founder of Modern Mexico, illustrated by Richard Cuffari. New York, Morrow, 1972.
Verrazano, Explorer of the Atlantic Coast. New York, Morrow, 1973.
Fur Trader of the North: The Story of Pierre de la Verendrye, illustrated by Richard Cuffari. New York, Morrow, 1973.
John Charles Frémont, The Last American Explorer, illustrated by Richard Cuffari. New York, Morrow, 1974.
Marquette and Joliet, Voyagers on the Mississippi. New York, Morrow, 1974.
Geronimo, The Fighting Apache, illustrated by Ben Stahl. New York, Morrow, 1975.
Osceola, Seminole Leader, illustrated by Ben Stahl. New York, Morrow, 1976.

Publications for Adults

Other

The Story of British Roads. London, British Road Federation, 1951.
The Windward Islands (*Frontiers of the Caribbean, Islands of the Sun, A Schooner Voyage in the West Indies*), photographs by the author. London, Pitman, 3 vols., 1953.
The Story of New Zealand (*We Dip into the Past, Life in New Zealand Today, A Tour of New Zealand*). London, Pitman, 3 vols., 1954.
The Cook Islands (*The Coming of Man, Life in the Islands Today, A Tour of the Islands*). London, Pitman, 3 vols., 1955.
The Travels of Captain Cook, photographs by Werner Forman. New York, McGraw Hill, 1971; London, Joseph, 1972.
Isles of the Frigate Bird (autobiographical). London, Joseph, 1975.
The Lagoon Is Lonely Now (autobiographical). Wellington, Millwood Press, 1979.
Fictional History Old and New Hadrian. Oxford, Somerville College, 1986.
Roman Papers, edited by Anthony R. Birley. Oxford, Clarendon, 1988.
The Augustan Aristocracy. Oxford, Clarendon Press, and New York, Oxford University Press, 1989.

* * *

Ronald Syme is best known for his exciting adventure stories for boys, moving at a fast pace and set in remote parts of the globe—although when the mood takes him, he is clearly capable of investing his plots with serious themes. *The Amateur Company,* for example, tells how Joe and Uncle Ben develop the natural resources of the island of Arorangi in the South Seas. When they depart, leaving behind them the destruction of a simple but tranquil and contented Arcadian community, both of them are troubled by some nagging doubts as to the lasting benefits of the changes arriving in the wake of their alien energy and technical know-how. And in *They Came to an Island* the same theme of the impact of an alien culture upon a primitive people is again discernible in the incident-packed story of mutiny and shipwreck, exploration and treasure hunting, but it is never obtrusive; the reader is not distracted.

If Syme has a fault it is the continuous piling up of climax upon climax. No sooner is one stirring episode out of the way than another is looming up; there is no time for reflection, and the story jerks along, breathless and impatient. But who would deny the inventiveness that allows the author this luxury? Nobody, certainly, has ever heard his readers complain.

The South Seas is often the locale of Syme's fiction: *Nose-Cap Astray,* the recovery of a space rocket by two boys, white and native, and *The Saving of the Fair East Wind,* the salvaging of an overloaded and abandoned cargo vessel, both feature the entertaining Prince Oro of Manapoa. But Syme is equally at home in the Caribbean of the 18th century. *Isle of Revolt* concerns a negro revolt against the English planters, and is seen through the eyes of Bill Holdsworth, the 15-year-old son of a planter, and his cousin Harry fresh out from England, while *The Settlers of Carriacou* relates the struggles of a small band of English colonists against powerful French attacks on the tiny island of Dominica. Another English cousin pops up in *Julian's River War,* in which Julian is a young Australian inventor who, with his assistant Snoddy, his sister Jannine, Percival Pomeroy the English cousin, and Uncle Eric, becomes involved in all sorts of mechanical contrivances, notably a car that sprouts wings and flies. At its own level this is a delightful book although the cast is really no more than a collection of stock characters.

But Syme no doubt realised that young readers welcome easily recognizable characters and situations. At this stage reading should essentially be full of fun and excitement, and these Syme provides in plenty.

—Alan Edwin Day

SYMONDS, John

Nationality: British. **Born:** 1914. **Address:** c/o Pindar Press, 66 Lyncroft Gardens, London NW6 1JY, England.

Publications for Children

Fiction

William Waste, illustrated by André François. London, Sampson Low, 1947.
The Magic Currant Bun, illustrated by André François. Philadelphia, Lippincott, 1952; London, Faber, 1953.
Travellers Three, illustrated by André François. Philadelphia, Lippincott, 1953.
The Isle of Cats, with Gerard Hoffnung. London, Laurie, 1955; revised edition, London, Scolar Press, 1979.
Away to the Moon, illustrated by Pamela Bianco. Philadelphia, Lippincott, 1956.
Lottie, illustrated by Edward Ardizzone. London, Lane, 1957.
Elfrida and the Pig, illustrated by Edward Ardizzone. London, Harrap, 1959; New York, Watts, 1960.
Dapple Grey: The Story of a Rocking-Horse, illustrated by James Boswell. London, Harrap, 1962.
The Story George Told Me, illustrated by André François. London, Harrap, 1963; New York, Pantheon, 1964.
Tom and Tabby, illustrated by André François. New York, Universe, 1964.
Grodge-Cat and the Window Cleaner, illustrated by André François. New York, Pantheon, 1965.
The Stuffed Dog, illustrated by Edward Ardizzone. London, Dent, 1967.
Harold: The Story of a Friendship, illustrated by Pauline Baynes. London, Dent, 1973.

Publications for Adults

Novels

The Lady in the Tower. London, Chapman and Hall, 1951.
The Bright Blue Sky. London, Chapman and Hall, 1956.
A Girl among Poets. London, Chapman and Hall, 1957.
The Only Thing That Matters. London, Unicorn Press, 1960; New York, Horizon Press, 1961.
Bezill. London, Unicorn Press, 1962.
Light over Water. London, Unicorn Press, 1963.
With a View on the Palace. London, Baker, 1966.
The Hurt Runner. London, Baker, 1968; New York, Day, 1969.
Prophecy and Parasites. London, Duckworth, 1973; New York, Braziller, 1975.
The Shaven Head. London, Duckworth, 1974.
Letters from England. London, Duckworth, 1975.
The Child: Prologue to an Earthquake. London, Duckworth, 1976.
The Guardian of the Threshold. London, Pindar Press, 1980.
Zélide. London, Pindar Press, 1984.
Sidony. London, Pindar Press, 1987.
The Poison-Maker. London, Pindar Press, 1990.
The White Fox. London, Pindar Press, 1991.
The Trickster and the Devil. London, Pindar Press, 1992.
White Dove, Black Raven. London, Pindar Press, 1992.
A Lady of Suffolk. London, Pindar Press, 1993.
Oldcastle. London, Pindar Press, 1994.
Tower above the Clouds: An Extravaganza. London, Pindar Press, 1994.
Lenin and the Tsar. London, Pindar Press, 1995.

Short Story

A Christmas Story. North Walsham, Norfolk, Warren House Press, 1977.

Plays

Sheila (produced London, 1953).
I, Having Dreamt, Awake (television play), 1961.
The Other House (radio play), 1963.
The Bicycle Play, and The Winter Forest. London, Duckworth, 1976.
The Bicycle Play (collection). London, Pindar Press, 1981.
The Lunatic Asylum Is on Fire!; Zilpah. London, Pindar Press, 1982.
The Revolutionary. London, Pindar Press, 1984.
The Soldier and the Werewolf. London, Pindar Press, 1985.
The Wall. London, Pindar Press, 1986.
The Great Happiness. London, Pindar Press, 1987.

Other

The Great Beast: The Life of Aleister Crowley. London, Rider, 1951; New York, Roy, 1952; revised edition, London, Macdonald, 1971.

The Magic of Aleister Crowley. London, Muller, 1958.
Madame Blavatsky, Medium and Magician. London, Odhams Press, 1959; as *The Lady with the Magic Eyes,* New York, Yoseloff, 1960; as *In the Astral Light,* London, Panther, 1965.
Thomas Brown and the Angels: A Study in Enthusiasm. London, Hutchinson, 1961.
Conversations with Gerald (on G.B.F. Hamilton). London, Duckworth, 1974.
Julia Daughter of Claudius: A Comedy in Twenty Scenes. London, Pindar Press, 1989.
The King of the Shadow Realm: Aleister Crowley, His Life, and Magic. London, Duckworth, 1989.
Poems. London, Pindar Press, 1994.

Editor, with Kenneth Grant, *The Confessions of Aleister Crowley: An Autohagiography,* abridged edition. London, Cape, 1969; New York, Bantam, 1971; revised edition, London, Routledge, 1979.
Editor, with Kenneth Grant, *The Magical Record of Beast 666: The Diaries of Aleister Crowley 1914-1920.* London, Duckworth, 1972.
Editor, with Kenneth Grant, *Magick,* by Aleister Crowley. London, Routledge, 1973.
Editor, with Kenneth Grant, *White Stains,* by Aleister Crowley. London, Duckworth, 1973.
Editor, with Kenneth Grant, *The Complete Astrological Writings of Aleister Crowley.* London, Duckworth, 1974.
Editor, with Kenneth Grant, *Moonchild,* by Aleister Crowley. London, Sphere, 1974.
Editor, with Kenneth Grant, *Magical and Philosophical Commentaries on the Book of the Law,* by Aleister Crowley. Montreal, 93 Publishing, 1974.

* * *

John Symonds's fantasies are shorter than most novels for older children, and his stories move quickly: they can be enjoyed by anyone over the age of about seven. Toys speak and have problems; children or playthings from the past meet children from this century and create a mutual understanding. *Lottie* is about the adventures of a doll and a dog in the 18th century; *Dapple Grey* is about a rocking horse trying to find his way home. The tone is always cheerful, often witty, and the endings satisfactory.

In *The Stuffed Dog* two modern schoolgirls, exploring an attic full of a miscellaneous collection of things bought at auction sales, discover a ventriloquist's doll a hundred years old. She tells the girls how the ventriloquist bullied her—so she stole his voice and ran away to hide in a box and fell asleep, but she is now repentant and wants to return his voice. The girls give her tea and take her to see the ventriloquist's house, where the doll is horrified to see that his dog has been stuffed. In the churchyard they find the grave with a carved headstone reading: "Poor Gerald is no more. Died dumb October 25, 1867." So they know it is all true. The doll asks to be returned to the box, where she lies looking so beautiful and peaceful.

This slightly eerie tale is told in a matter-of-fact way. The doll over tea remarks: "They're all dead, dead, dead," then fetches a deep sigh and says: "Please may I have another slice of cake?" The description of the tea table is original: "a gorgeous green cake raising its head proudly and a plate of bread and butter which crouched low with envy." The modern children have quite an adventure in the attic: the trunk that houses the doll's box is so large that one of them falls inside; she discovers a telescope through which she can see "pancakes and what looked like the prow of a ship painted pink. Gosh! It was Daisy's nose and the pancakes were her freckles and what appeared to be great white rocks were her teeth."

Harold is a story of a friendship between 20th-century Octavius, an only child, and an 18th-century ghost. Octavius's parents are always busy; he is left on his own. During their holiday in a house by the sea he meets a very old lady, Agnes Golightly, who has always lived in the attic and only comes down at night. She introduces him to Harold, who was killed falling off the church tower while looking at the gargoyles. Harold's punishment is that he must wander around until he can spend a week playing with another boy, so he and Octavius enjoy exploring a shipwreck together, and Octavius is tremendously happy at having helped him. Agnes Golightly's observations on all the inhabitants of the house provide the humour. The descriptions are all short but effective: "And the sea. It was as blue as the nose of a frozen child."

—Margaret Campbell

SYMONS, (Dorothy) Geraldine

Pseudonym: Georgina Groves. **Nationality:** British. **Born:** Newera Eliya, Ceylon, 13 August 1909. **Education:** Godolphin School, Salisbury, Wiltshire, 1920-27. **Military Service:** Red Cross, 1939-42; Voluntary Aid Detachment, 1943-46; Monitoring Department, British Broadcasting Corporation and YWCA. **Career:** Has worked as a secretary, waitress, chambermaid, cook, and historic house guide, 1950-69. **Died.**

Publications for Children

Fiction

Minnie the Minnow, illustrated by the author. Ewell, Surrey, Tally Ho Books, n.d.
The Rose Window, illustrated by F.R. Exell. London, Heinemann, 1964; New York, Duell, 1966.
Morning Glory (as Georgina Groves), illustrated by Carol Barker. London, Whiting and Wheaton, 1966.
The Quarantine Child, illustrated by F.R. Exell. London, Heinemann, 1966.
The Workhouse Child, illustrated by Alexy Pendle. London, Macmillan, 1969; New York, Macmillan, 1971.
Miss Rivers and Miss Bridges, illustrated by Alexy Pendle. London, Macmillan, 1971; New York, Macmillan, 1972.
Mademoiselle, illustrated by Alexy Pendle. London, Macmillan, 1973.
Now and Then. London, Faber, 1977; as *Crocuses Were Over, Hitler Was Dead,* Philadelphia, Lippincott, 1978.
Second Cousins, Once Removed. London, Macmillan, 1978.

Publications for Adults

Novels

All Souls. London and New York, Longman, 1950.
French Windows. London and New York, Longman, 1952.
The Suckling. London, Macmillan, 1969.

Other

Children in the Close (autobiography), illustrated by Helen Symons. London, Batsford, 1959.

* * *

Geraldine Symons wrote several books for children, five in a sequence that covers the years 1909-14. In these the central characters are Pansy and Atalanta, a complementary pair whose exploits are chronicled with rationality and gusto. Pansy on her own is less impressive, as *The Rose Window* shows; she is a conventional heroine without the formidable presence of Atalanta to set her off.

Atalanta is a triumph of characterization. She is stolid, logical, and down-to-earth without being in the least bit priggish. She is well-informed, rather blasé in manner and slapdash in appearance, and speaks with the gruff precision of a bored don. Pansy is more impressionable and frivolous: the combination of the two girls is enough to spark off the alarming or amusing events that the novels relate. In *The Workhouse Child* Pansy flees from the terrible matron of an orphanage and is forced to take refuge on the bloody floor of a butcher's shop. After a rather exciting afternoon, she finds Atalanta sitting calmly "on a molehill by a gorse bush reading *The Wide Wide World.*" She goes on reading.

Miss Rivers and Miss Bridges, in the book of that title, are Atalanta and Pansy disguised as a couple of middle-aged suffragettes. This is the most remarkable and effective novel of the series: its surface humour doesn't detract in the least from the seriousness of the theme. It was published in 1971; it took roughly 60 years for the suffragette movement to get sympathetic treatment in children's literature. "If the Government persists in its pigheaded policy, I have no intention of stopping at a brick," Atalanta states. In fact she jumps off Westminister Bridge, and the two schoolgirls are later detained briefly in a prison cell. "Gross inefficiency," Atalanta concludes after looking around. She becomes interested in prison reform.

In *Mademoiselle* the friends are staying in Paris just before the outbreak of war. *Mademoiselle* is really *fräulein,* a German spy who has walked into a diplomatic trap. In fact the whole spy genre is subtly parodied in this book. A faint mocking detachment is evident in the dedication ("To all patriotic sleuths"), but *Mademoiselle* is also an excellent adventure story. The precision of its detail raises the farcical moments to high comedy. And it has Atalanta to keep it firmly based on the ground. "Don't be so melodramatic and silly," she tells Pansy repressively.

The heroine of *Now and Then* is called Jassy, and she is one of those uncanny fictional children who can step into another era. She has only to walk down the garden to find herself back in 1940, digging a grave for two dogs that have been killed by enemy action or helping to apprehend a German pilot in a wood. The book is in a lower key than the Pansy and Atalanta stories, but it is nonetheless a distinguished addition to "time-travelling" fiction.

—Patricia Craig

SZEKERES, Cyndy

Nationality: American. **Born:** 31 October 1933, Bridgeport, Connecticut. **Family:** Married Gennaro Prozzo in 1958; two sons. **Education:** Pratt Institute, certificate, 1954. **Address:** P.O. Box 280, RFD 3, Putney, Vermont 05346, U.S.A.

Publications for Children

Picture Books (illustrated by the author)

Long Ago. New York, McGraw, 1977.
A Child's First Book of Poems. New York, Golden Books, 1981; as *Cyndy Szekeres' ABC,* New York, Golden Books, 1983.
Puppy Too Small. New York, Golden Books, 1984.
Scaredy Cat! New York, Golden Books, 1984.
Thumpity Thump Gets Dressed. New York, Golden Books, 1984.
Baby Bear's Surprise. New York, Golden Books, 1984.
Cyndy Szekeres' Counting Book 1 to 10. New York, Golden Books, 1984.
Suppertime for Frieda Fuzzypaws. New York, Golden Books, 1985.
Hide-and-Seek Duck. New York, Golden Books, 1985.
Nothing-to-Do Puppy. New York, Golden Books, 1985.
Good Night, Sammy. New York, Golden Books, 1986.
Puppy Lost. New York, Golden Books, 1986.
Sammy's Special Day. New York, Golden Books, 1986.
Little Bear Counts His Favorite Things. New York, Golden Books, 1986.
Melanie Mouse's Moving Day. New York, Golden Books, 1986.
Good Night, Sweet Mouse. New York, Golden Books, 1988.
Cyndy Szekeres' Favorite Two-Minute Stories. New York, Golden Books, 1989.
Things Bunny Sees. Racine, Wisconsin, Western Publishing, 1990.
What Bunny Loves. Racine, Wisconsin, Western Publishing, 1990.
Cyndy Szekeres' Nice Animals. Racine, Wisconsin, Western Publishing, 1990.
Cyndy Szekeres' Hugs. Racine, Wisconsin, Western Publishing, 1990.
Puppy Learns to Share. Racine, Wisconsin, Western Publishing, 1990.
Ladybug, Where Are You? Racine, Wisconsin, Western Publishing, 1991.
Fluffy Duckling. Racine, Wisconsin, Western Publishing, 1992.
Teeny Mouse Counts Herself. Racine, Wisconsin, Western Publishing, 1992.
Cyndy Szekeres' Colors. Racine, Wisconsin, Western Publishing, 1992.
Cyndy Szekeres' Kisses. Racine, Wisconsin, Western Publishing, 1993.
Puppy Dear. Racine, Wisconsin, Western Publishing, 1993.
Cyndy Szekeres' Baby Animals. Racine, Wisconsin, Western Publishing, 1994.
Cyndy Szekeres' I Am a Puppy. Racine, Wisconsin, Western Publishing, 1994.
Little Puppy Cleans His Room. Racine, Wisconsin, Western Publishing, 1994.
Cyndy Szekeres' Christmas Mouse. New York, Golden Book, and Racine, Wisconsin, Western Publishing, 1995.
Cyndy Szekeres' Giggles. Racine, Wisconsin, Western Publishing, 1996.

The Mouse that Jack Built. New York, Scholastic, 1997.

Reteller, *Yes, Virginia, There Is a Santa Claus.* New York, Scholastic, 1997.

Cyndy Szekeres' I Love My Busy Book. New York, Scholastic, 1997.

The Deep Blue Sky Twinkles with Stars. New York, Scholastic, 1998.

I Can Count 100 Bunnies, and So Can You! New York, Scholastic, 1998.

"Tiny Paw Library" Series:

A Busy Day. New York, Golden Books, 1989.

The New Baby. New York, Golden Books, 1989.

Moving Day. New York, Golden Books, 1989.

A Fine Mouse Band. New York, Golden Books, 1989.

A Mouse Mess. Racine, Wisconsin, Western Publishing, 1990.

Compiler, *Cyndy Szekeres' Book of Poems.* Racine, Wisconsin, Western Publishing, 1987.

Compiler, *Cyndy Szekeres' Mother Goose Rhymes.* New York, Golden Books, 1987.

Compiler, *Cyndy Szekeres' Book of Fairy Tales.* New York, Golden Books, 1988.

Compiler, *Cyndy Szekeres' Favorite Fairy Tales.* Racine, Wisconsin, Western Publishing, 1992.

Compiler, *Cyndy Szekeres' Favorite Mother Goose Rhymes.* Racine, Wisconsin, Western Publishing, 1992.

*

Illustrator: Sam Vaughan, *New Shoes,* Doubleday, 1961; Jean Latham and Bee Lewi, *When Homer Honked,* Macmillan, 1961; Marjorie Flack, *Walter, the Lazy Mouse,* Doubleday, 1963; Evelyn Sibley Lampman, *Mrs. Updaisy,* Doubleday, 1963; Phyllis Krasilovsky, *Girl Who Was a Cowboy,* Doubleday, 1965; (With others) Alvin Tresselt, editor, *Humpty Dumpty's Storybook,* Parents Magazine Press, 1966; Edward Ormondroyd, *Michael, the Upstairs Dog,* Dial, 1967; Nancy Faulkner, *Small Clown and Tiger,* Doubleday, 1968; Kathleen Lombardo, *Macaroni,* Random House, 1968; Peggy Parrish, *Jumper Goes to School,* Simon & Schuster, 1969; Adelaide Holl, *Moon Mouse,* Random House, 1969; Barbara Robinson, *Fattest Bear in the First Grade,* Random House, 1969; John Peterson, *Mystery in the Night Woods,* Scholastic Book Services, 1969; Joy Lonergan, *Brian's Secret Errand,* Doubleday, 1969; Patsy Scarry, *Little Richard,* McGraw, 1970; P. Scarry, *Waggy and His Friends,* McGraw, 1970; Kathryn Hitte, *What Can You Do without a Place to Play?,* Parents Magazine Press, 1971; Lois Myller, *No! No!,* Simon & Schuster, 1971; P. Scarry, *Little Richard and Prickles,* McGraw, 1971; Betty Jean Lifton, *Good Night, Orange Monster,* Atheneum, 1972; Mary Lystad, *James, the Jaguar,* Putnam, 1972; Betty Boegehold, *Pippa Mouse,* Knopf, 1973; A. Holl, *Bedtime for Bears,* Garrard, 1973; P. Scarry, *More about Waggy,* American Heritage Press, 1973; Miriam Anne Bourne, *Four-Ring Three,* Coward, 1973; Albert Bigelow Paine, "Hollow Tree" series, three volumes, Avon, 1973; M. Lystad, *The Halloween Parade,* Putnam, 1973; Kathy Darling, *Little Bat's Secret,* Garrard, 1974; Robert Welber, *Goodbye, Hello,* Pantheon, 1974; Julia Cunningham, *Maybe, a Mole,* Pantheon, 1974; Albert Bigelow Paine, *Snowed-in Book,* Avon, 1974; Jan Wahl, *The Muffletumps' Christmas Party,* Follett, 1975; J. Wahl, *The Muffletumps' Storybook,* Follett, 1975; Carolyn S. Bailey, *A Christmas Party,* Pantheon, 1975; B. Boegehold, *Here's Pippa Again!,* Knopf, 1975; J. Wahl, *The Clumpets Go Sailing,* Parents Magazine Press, 1975; J. Wahl, *The Muffletumps' Halloween Scare,* Follett, 1977; J. Wahl, *Doctor Rabbit's Foundling,* Pantheon, 1977; Tony Johnston, *Night Noises, and Other Mole and Troll Stories,* Putnam, 1977; Mary D. Kwitz, *Little Chick's Story,* Harper, 1978; J. Wahl, *Who Will Believe Tim Kitten?,* Pantheon, 1978; A. Holl, *Small Bear Builds a Playhouse,* Garrard, 1978; Judy Delton, *Brimhall Comes to Stay,* Lothrop, 1978; Marjorie W. Sharmat, *The 329th Friend,* Four Winds Press, 1979; T. Johnston, *Happy Birthday, Mole and Troll,* Putnam, 1979; Catherine Hiller, *Argentaybee and the Boonie,* Coward, 1979; J. Wahl, *Doctor Rabbit's Lost Scout,* Pantheon, 1979; B. Boegehold, *Pippa Pops Out!,* Knopf, 1979; B. Boegehold, *Hurray for Pippa!,* Knopf, 1980; P. Scarry, *Patsy Scarry's Big Bedtime Storybook,* Random House, 1980; Polly B. Berends, *Ladybug and Dog and the Night Walk,* Random House, 1980; Marci Ridion, *Woodsey Log Library,* four volumes, Random House, 1981; Margo Hopkins, *Honey Rabbit,* Golden Books, 1982; Marci McGill, *The Six Little Possums: A Birthday ABC,* Golden Press, 1982; M. McGill, *The Six Little Possums and the Baby Sitter,* Golden Press, 1982; M. McGill, *The Six Little Possums at Home,* Golden Press, 1982; M. McGill, *The Six Little Possums: Pepper's Good and Bad Day,* Golden Press, 1982; Clement C. Moore, *The Night before Christmas,* Golden Books, 1982; Selma Lanes, selector, *A Child's First Book of Nursery Tales,* Golden Books, 1983, published as *Cyndy Szekeres' Book of Nursery Tales,* 1987; T. Johnston, *Five Little Foxes and the Snow,* HarperCollins, 1987; B. Boegehold, *Here's Pippa!,* Knopf, 1989; Margaret Wise Brown, *Whispering Rabbit,* Western Publishing, 1992; Ole Risom, *I Am a Kitten,* Western Publishing, 1993; Beatrix Potter, *Peter Rabbit,* Western Publishing, 1993.

Also creator of calendars, including *Cyndy's Animal Calendar, 1973,* McGraw, 1973, *Cyndy's Animal Calendar, 1975,* McGraw, 1974, and *Long Ago,* McGraw, 1976; and of *My Workbook Diary, 1973,* McGraw, 1972, and *My Workbook Diary, 1975,* McGraw, 1974.

* * *

Cyndy Szekeres began her career in picture books in 1961 with drawings for *New Shoes* by Sam Vaughan, and she has illustrated at least two books annually ever since. She attributes her love for illustrating tales to a first visit to the Metropolitan Opera in New York while she was still in grade school: the magical contribution of costumes, stage sets, and musical accompaniment to the telling of a story proved "overwhelming" and made her aspire to life as an artist. She found her particular gift in "speaking with pictures," a talent that held her in good stead, since, in the beginning, she often got less than choice manuscripts to illustrate. Szekeres soon learned to develop characters and settings that could provide a life and clarity that the words sometimes lacked.

By the late 1960s, with the encouragement of her then-Random House editor, Polly Berends, she discovered that her drawings in pencil were "fuller and richer" than her pictures in ink. Starting with her illustrations for Adelaide Hall's *Moon Mouse,* she did all her finished drawings in pencil. She then painted over them in guache and added finishing touches in colored pencil. She also began to concentrate on what she liked to draw best: anthropomorphic animals in completely believable settings and costumes.

It is no surprise, then, that when Szekeres came to illustrate a selection of *Mother Goose Rhymes,* her Mother Goose would be just that: a warm, matronly goose sporting a straw-boater hat and wearing a strand of pearls around her lace-trimmed blouse. Garth

Williams is one of her all-time favorite illustrators, and what she most admires in his work is that "Nobody, NOBODY has achieved broadcasting the presence of heart and soul in animal characters as well as he."

Szekeres's illustrations for Clement Moore's *The Night Before Christmas* provide a telling insight into her modus operandi. She creates a richly realized and totally believable woodland setting—a cozily furnished home in the trunk of an old tree—for her family of three mice children and their parents. Father and Mother Mouse share an old sardine can as their double bed, its key-wound tin cover providing an inspired decorative headboard. A rumpled dollar bill makes for a perfect scatter rug beneath it. And the mouse family has thoughtfully left a platter of toll-house cookies and a glass of milk on a thread-spool table as a snack for Santa when he calls. The Moore poem springs to new and convincing life with the artist's animal casting and detailed milieu. In defense of her predilection for animal protagonists, Szekeres points out that when an artist draws a blond child, the picture is of that particular child only, but a small mouse or rabbit in overalls can represent Everychild.

Among the artist's best-known books are Barbara Robinson's *The Fattest Bear in First Grade, Patsy Scarry's Big Bedtime Storybook,* and Betty Boegehold's *Pippa Mouse.* The artist's own favorite among her books is Jan Wahl's *Doctor Rabbit's Foundling,* a somewhat sentimental story about separation and loss, and the pain of love. It is Szekeres' wondrously warm and convincing pictures that render the text both deeply moving and memorable. The affection and family feeling her animal protagonists exhibit for one another is palpable in her every picture and reflect Szekeres's firm belief that "children thrive on an abundance of love."

For more than a dozen years, beginning in the early 1980s, the artist agreed to work exclusively for Western Publishing Company, illustrating a wide variety of picture books for their Golden Books imprint. With a forthrightness that is typical of her, she says of this arrangement that "My titles subtly moved from what I do best to what needs to be done."

She worries occasionally that her fondness for small, fuzzy young animals translates into "cute," but this is never her intention. She lives in the country and, when she draws, like Beatrix Potter before her, she uses live animal models whenever possible. She still looks on each new assignment as a singular opportunity and confesses with pride that she is "still learning how to illustrate effectively and still making mistakes."

—Selma G. Lanes

T

TAFURI, Nancy

Nationality: American. **Born:** 14 November 1946, Brooklyn, New York. **Education:** Graduated from School of Visual Arts, New York City, 1967. **Family:** Married Thomas Michael Tafuri in 1969; one daughter. **Career:** Assistant art director, Simon & Schuster (publisher), New York City, 1967-69; co-founder, graphic designer, and illustrator, One Plus One Studio (graphic design firm), Roxbury, Connecticut, since 1971. Work exhibited by Society of Illustrators, 1977, 1990-93. **Awards:** *School Library Journal* Best Books, 1983; Caldecott honor book, 1985. **Address:** One Plus One Studio, 44 Tophet Rd., Roxbury, Connecticut 06783, U.S.A.

PUBLICATIONS FOR CHILDREN

Picture Books (illustrated by the author)

All Year Long. New York, Greenwillow, 1983.
Early Morning in the Barn. New York, Greenwillow, 1983.
Have You Seen My Duckling? New York, Greenwillow, 1984.
Rabbit's Morning. New York, Greenwillow, 1985.
Who's Counting. New York, Greenwillow, 1986.
In a Red House. New York, Greenwillow, 1987.
Where We Sleep. New York, Greenwillow, 1987.
My Friends. New York, Greenwillow, 1987.
Do Not Disturb. New York, Greenwillow, 1987.
Spots, Feathers, and Curly Tails. New York, Greenwillow, 1988.
Two New Sneakers. New York, Greenwillow, 1988.
One Wet Jacket. New York, Greenwillow, 1988.
Junglewalk. New York, Greenwillow, 1988.
The Ball Bounced. New York, Greenwillow, 1989.
Follow Me! New York, Greenwillow, 1990.
This Is the Farmer. New York, Greenwillow, 1994.
What the Sun Sees, What the Moon Sees. New York, Greenwillow Books, 1997.
I Love You, Little One. New York, Scholastic Press, 1997.
Counting to Christmas. New York, Scholastic Press, 1998.
The Barn Party. New York, Greenwillow, forthcoming.

*

Illustrator: Jean Holzenthaler, *My Hands Can,* Dutton, 1977; George Shannon, *The Piney Woods Peddler,* Greenwillow, 1981; Charlotte Zolotow, *The Song,* Greenwillow, 1982; Mirra Ginsburg, *Across the Stream,* Greenwillow, 1982; Charlotte Pomerantz, *If I Had a Paka: Poems in Eleven Languages,* Greenwillow, 1982; Pomerantz, *All Asleep,* Greenwillow, 1984; Crescent Dragonwagon, *Coconut,* Harper, 1984; Helen V. Griffith, *Nata,* Greenwillow, 1985; Ginsburg, *Four Brave Sailors,* Greenwillow, 1987; Pomerantz, *Flap Your Wings and Try,* Greenwillow, 1989; Mirra Ginsburg, *Asleep, Asleep,* 1992; Lilly Patricia, *Everything Has a Place,* 1993.

*   *   *

Clear and crisp images fill Nancy Tafuri's books. She subtley teaches child readers to look around and see all kinds of things going on within their visual reach. For the most part Tafuri does not use many words in her books, often only an opening and closing. It is the pictures that carry the reader, and those pictures many times evoke a story. One of her most careful considerations is the jacket art that invites the reader into the pages of her stories. On the cover of *Follow Me!,* she paints a curious baby seal, who within the book follows a tiny red crab scurrying through the sand. Of course, the baby seal's mother protectively follows along. The followers move through the pages, passing brown pelicans, anemones, sea otters, and starfish along the way. Clearly Tafuri portrays curiosity but also demonstrates the continuing, although at a distance, care of the mother.

In *Rabbit's Morning,* the author shares the morning walk of a rabbit around the countryside. Although the rabbit is pleased to see porcupines, opossums, pheasants, and even a ladybug, coming home is warm and good. Characteristically, Tafuri places a small image in different sections of her pages to force the reader to look very closely and help build the evidence that the main character is moving. In this book it is the pheasant in the upper corners who later is the full-page pheasant as Rabbit passes by to visit the next animal.

Junglewalk demonstrates Tafuri's ability to encourage the imagination of a child to blossom and, at the same time, to preserve the feelings of safety a child needs. This wordless adventure story takes a child from reading about animals into the dream world of a jungle. Animals pass through the jungle as does the young child. The colors are vibrant, and the eye concentrates on the main animal but returns to find details scattered throughout. Again, movement is shown as the child is pictured in different places in the jungle as the pages turn. The animals are the focus of the eye, and finally the child awakes as his cat jumps onto his bed in the morning. Tafuri has the ability to soothe and calm the reader but, at the same time, to inform the reader with each picture. She provides help inside the back of the bookjacket to the adult sharing the book with a child, giving a list of all the jungle animals pictured with their place of origin. This helps the adult teach the child names and places. Tafuri also uses this same technique in many of her other books.

In *Do Not Disturb,* Tafuri teaches by observation. She shows a family camping, playing, and eating while unaware that they are disturbing all of the animals, fish, and birds in their vicinity. Although the family doesn't see this or even hear the quick escapes of their neighbors, the animals turn the tables at night and the climax page is a double-spread of animals voicing their cries and a wide-eyed family peeking out of a tent.

In her book *Who's Counting?,* Tafuri takes a simple approach to counting, using different animals to represent the numbers one through ten. Carefully selected lettering makes reading the numbers easy for young readers. She employs a nice touch on number 10, showing ten puppies who are eating from numerically labeled bowls on the pages that follow.

Have You Seen My Duckling? demonstrates the caring for an apparently lost baby—in this case, one of the mallard's chicks. Mama is anxious, but baby is finally reunited, never really having been too far off from mother. Tafuri's *This Is the Farmer* is a delightful domino tale. When the farmer leaves and kisses his wife, she pats the dog and then a series of unobserved things continue to happen. As a special added touch, Tafuri has a tiny brown mouse scurrying from page to page watching the action.

Tafuri deals gently with her reader, painting large and color-filled pages that move the eye to see feelings and to think about larger things. She illustrates for other writers with care, but it is her own books that reveal her sensitivity for the young reader.

—Kay E. Vandergrift

TAKASHIMA, Shizuye

Nationality: Canadian. **Born:** 12 June 1928, Vancouver, British Columbia. **Education:** Ontario College of Art, associate degree 1953; attended Pratt Institute, New York City, 1966. **Career:** Painter and writer. Has exhibited paintings in galleries in the U.S. and Canada. Guest instructor, Ontario College of Art, 1971. **Awards:** Canada Council award, 1971; Canadian Association of Children's Librarians Gold Medal, 1971, for best illustrated book; Look of Books award, 1972, for best designed and produced book in Canada; Sankai Shinbun juvenile literary award, 1975.

Publications for Children

A Child in Prison Camp (partially fictionalized autobiographical account). Plattsburg, New York, Tundra, 1971.

* * *

Comparatively few authors have acquired an international reputation on the merits of a single book. Japanese-Canadian artist and writer Shizuye Takashima is one who has. Her book, *A Child in Prison Camp,* is a partially fictionalized autobiographical account of her early teenage years in the New Denver relocation camp, one of eight camps where Japanese-Canadians suffered internment during World War II.

A Child in Prison Camp belongs to the comparatively rare class of books that have no clearly defined audience but communicate effectively and memorably with readers of all ages. Originally intended for adults and quickly co-opted by adolescents, the book is now rather widely used in elementary schools in the United States and Canada, especially those where Asian-American students comprise a significant percentage of the student body. When used with students in grades one through four, the book is commonly excerpted rather than taught (or read) in full; slightly older students, especially those who are mature readers, are equipped to read the book in its entirety.

The usefulness and appeal of the text are closely aligned and are dependent upon some important characteristics. First, Takashima's narrative is simple yet richly poetic, evoking vivid sensory perceptions of a time and place that are utterly foreign to most contemporary readers. Second, the book is structured as a journal, where the writer's voice is believably that of Shichan, a likeable, sensitive, and sensible youngster with whom the reader quickly identifies—the journal format increases the reality and immediacy of Shichan's situation while allowing greater fluidity in moving into and out of the situations the book describes. Third, as a consequence of its child narrator, the book enjoys the "Anne Frank effect," by which, paradoxically, surrounding events seem both harsher and less harsh than they would if an adult were recounting the history—and the book is thus richer than it otherwise might be. Fourth, while Shichan is a consistently admirable guide, she is (at least in the beginning) also imperfect and naive. Read as a growing-up story, the book has marvelous universal appeal. Finally, in terms of its pedagogical applications, the book is versatile and powerful. Excerpts from the book can be used to introduce cultural studies units, to stimulate student writing, to preface discussions of ideologies and contemporary political/social issues, and to deconstruct cultural and political norms.

Eight watercolor plates (also by Takashima) illustrate key scenes of the narrative; they are convincing, moving embodiments of the spirit of the narrative and of the historical experience itself.

—Keith Lawrence

TALBOT, Ethel

Nationality: British. **Born:** London, 1888. **Family:** Married Herman Scheffauer about 1912; one daughter. **Died:** 1976.

Publications for Children

Fiction

Billy the Scout and His Day of Adventures, illustrated by Harold Earnshaw. London, Nelson, 1918.
The School on the Moor, illustrated by Noel Harrold. London, Cassell, 1919.
The Cosy-Comfy Book, illustrated by Anne Anderson. London, Collins, 1920.
Peggy's Last Term, illustrated by C.E. Brock. London, Nelson, 1920.
Farmyard Fun, illustrated by M. Morris. London, Collins, 1922.
Holiday Chums. London, Sheldon Press, 1923.
The Island Camp. London, Sheldon Press, 1923.
The Adventures of Woodeny and Other Stories, with Harold Avery and Ada Holman. London, Nelson, 1923.
Neighbours at School. London, Nelson, 1923.
The New Girl at the Priory. London, Ward Lock, 1923.
The Sport of the School, illustrated by J.R. Burgess. London, Chambers, 1923.
Two on an Island and Other Stories. London, Nelson, 1923.
Betty at St. Benedick's [*Holds the Reins*]. London, Nelson, 2 vols., 1924-29.
Billy at St. Bede's. London, Nelson, 1924.
The Bravest Girl in the School. London, Cassell, 1924.
The Luck of the School, illustrated by Molly Benatar. London, Chambers, 1924.
Sally at School. London, Nelson, 1924.
Scout Island. London, Nelson, 1924.
While Mother Was Away. London, Sheldon Press, 1924.
The Best of All Schools. London, Jarrolds, 1924.
Between Two Terms. London, Ward Lock, 1925.

Fellow Fags, illustrated by P. Walford. London, Sheldon Press, 1925.
The Girls of the Rookery School. London, Nelson, 1925.
Patricia, Prefect. London, Nelson, 1925.
The Stranger in the Train and Other Stories, illustrated by R.H. Brock. London, Sheldon Press, 1925.
That Wild Australian Schoolgirl. London, South, 1925.
An Unexpected Schoolgirl. London, Cassell, 1925.
Bringing Back the Frasers and Other Stories. London, Nelson, 1926.
The Camp in the Wood. London, Epworth Press, 1926.
Jane and the Beanstalks, illustrated by R.B. Ogle. London, Pearson, 1926.
Little Black Tumgo's Tale and Other Stories. London, Epworth Press, 1926.
The Luckiest Girl at St. Chad's. London, Jarrolds, 1926.
The Magic Island. London, Children's Companion, 1926.
Rags: The Pranks of a Little Doggie. London, Epworth Press, 1926.
The School of None-Go-By, illustrated by Margaret Forbes. London, Ward Lock, 1926.
Aunt Mary. London, Sheldon Press, 1927.
Bunch at Boarding-School, illustrated by T. Heath Robinson. London, Warne, 1927.
The Family Next Door. London, Sheldon Press, 1927.
Jan at Island School, illustrated by E. Brier. London, Nelson, 1927.
Jill, Lone Guide, illustrated by R.B. Ogle. London, Pearson, 1927.
Just the Girl for St. Jude's. London, Cassell, 1927.
Let's Pretend Tales. London, Epworth Press, 1927.
Priscilla the Prefect. London, Sheldon Press, 1927.
Twenty-Six Ethel Talbot Tales for Girls, illustrated by R.H. Stone. London, Religious Tract Society, 1927.
Listening-in and Other Stories for Girls, with others. London, Nelson, 1927.
Adventures of Skurry the Scout. London, Epworth Press, 1928.
At School with Morag. London, Warne, 1928.
Baby Animals, illustrated by A.E. Kennedy. London, Nelson, 1928.
Brownies at St. Bride's. London, Warne, 1928.
Carol's Second Term, illustrated by W.B. Hamilton. London, Nelson, 1928.
The Half-and-Half Schoolgirl, illustrated by R.F.C. Waudby. London, Nelson, 1928.
Ranger Rose. London, Nelson, 1928.
Schoolgirl Rose. London, Cassell, 1928.
The New Centre-Forward, illustrated by R.H. Brock. London, Collins, 1929; as *Meta, The New Girl; Meta, Centre-Forward;* and *Meta's Last Term,* 3 vols., 1930-31.
The Peppercorn Patrol. London, Cassell, 1929.
Ranger Jo. London, Pearson, 1929.
Rhona Runs Away. London, Pilgrim Press, 1929.
Skipper & Co. London, Warne, 1929.
The Smiths of Silver Lane, illustrated by R.F.C. Waudby. London, Nelson, 1929.
Billy of the Wolf Cubs and Other "Good Turn" Tales. London, Epworth Press, 1930.
Jean's Two Schools, illustrated by E. Brier. London, Nelson, 1930.
Meggy at St. Monica's. London, Ward Lock, 1930.
Nancy, New Girl, and The Girl Who Was Different. London, Warne, 1930.
The Mystery of the Manor. London, Sheldon Press, 1930.
Little Books (*How Golly Grew Good, The Story of Little Bo-Peep, The Story of Mother Hubbard and the Silver Sixpence, The Adventure of Mary Contrary, The Adventures of Noah and Poll in Fairyland, The Ark Animal Scouts*). London, Religious Tract Society, 6 vols., 1931.
Brownies All! London, Warne, 1931.
The Foolish Phillimores. London, Nelson, 1931.
"Good Turn Tales" for Wolf Cubs. London, Epworth Press, 1931.
Anne of Queen Anne's. London, Warne, 1932.
The Brownie Pack and Other Good Turn Tales. London, Epworth Press, 1932.
Dearly Bought. London, Leng, 1932.
A Girl Die-Hard. London, Thomson, 1932.
Phoebe of the Fourth. London, Nelson, 1932.
Red Caps at School. London, Sheldon Press, 1932.
Anne-on-Her-Own. London, Ward Lock, 1933.
Fairy Tales for Brownie Folk. London, Epworth Press, 1933.
Paul and Pam: The Twins' Holiday Adventure. London, Warne, 1933.
Surprise Island. London, Blackie, 1933.
The Upper Hand. London, Leng, 1933.
Betty and the Brownies. London, Warne, 1934.
The Middletons Make Good. London, Nelson, 1934.
Mascot of the School. London, Hutchinson, 1934.
Brownie Island. London, Warne, 1935.
Fifty-Two Thrilling Stories for Girls, illustrated by Glossop. London, Hutchinson, 1935.
The Girls of the Big House. London, Nelson, 1935.
Pioneer Pat. London, Ward Lock, 1935.
Pluck at St. Cyprian's. London, Pilgrim Press, 1935.
Schoolgirl by Chance. London, Hutchinson, 1935.
Sea Rangers All. London, Warne, 1935.
Old House. London, Nelson, 1936.
Sea Rangers' Holiday. London, Warne, 1937.
Diana the Daring. London, Ward Lock, 1938.
Guide's Luck. London, Pearson, 1938.
Nesta on Her Own, illustrated by J.R. Burgess. London, Nelson, 1938.
Rangers and Strangers and Other Stories. London, Nelson, 1938.
Sadie Sees It Through. London, Ward Lock, 1939.
Terry's Only Term, illustrated by F.G. Moorson. London, Blackie, 1939.
The Warringtons in War-Time. London, Nelson, 1940.
Gerda Gets There. London, Ward Lock, 1940.
Jane Steps Out. London, Ward Lock, 1948.

Verse

London Windows. London, Swift, 1912.
Baby Fluff. London, Oxford University Press, 1921.

Other

The Story Natural History. London, Nelson, 1919; New York, Nelson, 1920.
My Picture Book of the Circus. London, Ward Lock, 1930.

* * *

For most of the 1920s and 1930s, Ethel Talbot was remarkably prolific as a writer of juvenile poetry and prose. She covered a wide range of themes and skillfully adapted her style for different age groups. As E. Talbot she wrote several school and adventure stories for boys in *Chums, Little Folks,* and the *Boy's Own Paper,* but she is best known for her full-length school and Girl Guide novels for girls.

Her achievements are somewhat overshadowed by more celebrated writers of the period (Brazil, Bruce, etc.), and she never succeeded in creating characters who became as popular as theirs. Nevertheless, she wrote with similar zest and, at times, rather more imagination. Many of Talbot's stories are spiced with touches of magic and fantasy that are associated with symbolic places or objectives, like the old, protective tower in *Carol's Second Term* and the shepherdess tapestry that dominates the school hall in *Patricia, Prefect.* She is possibly the only "schoolgirl" author who managed successfully to combine the disparate themes of down-to-earth school routines and elusive woodland magic ("The Girl Who Found the Fairies" in *Little Folks,* 1919).

In keeping with the traditions of the genre, her heroines are usually "blade straight," "gamey," "comradey," and passionately concerned with *esprit de corps* and the honour of their schools. (The greatest compliment one Talbot girl can "gulp" out to another in her more emotional moments is "You're Chads!" or "You're Cyprians!") However, Talbot also considers the problems of the talented, artistic individualist forced by the confines of school life into prolonged uncongenial associations with ordinary or "philistine" girls. With more frankness than other school-story writers, too, in *Patricia, Prefect* she explores in depth the even trickier subject of a really intense relationship between a senior and a junior girl.

Her Girl Guide stories contain the expected excitements and demonstrations of adolescent pluck—spy-spotting while picking sphagnum moss on the moors during World War I, for example, in "Luck" (*British Girls' Annual,* 1919). But as well as conveying the expansive spirit of the early days of the movement, she produced some entertaining vignettes of over-enthusiastic tenderfoots whose approach to the business of Guiding was bizarrely removed from that of Baden-Powell.

Despite her versatility and occasionally challenging approach, Talbot is now remembered mainly for her conventional school stories about energetic chums who enjoy experiencing "the extreme joy of aching muscles after a topping afternoon's hockey," and who wholesomely follow this up by dancing foxtrots and Charlestons to gramophone accompaniments in the gym!

—Mary Cadogan

TARKINGTON, (Newton) Booth

Nationality: American. **Born:** Indianapolis, Indiana, 29 July 1869. **Education:** Phillips Exeter Academy, New Hampshire; Purdue University, Lafayette, Indiana, 1888-89; Princeton University, New Jersey, 1891-93. **Family:** Married 1) Laurel Louisa Fletcher in 1902 (divorced 1911), one daughter; 2) Susannah Robinson in 1912. **Career:** Writer from 1893; also an artist: illustrated *Character Sketches* by James Whitcomb Riley and other works; member of the Indiana House of Representatives, 1902-03. **Awards:** Pulitzer Prize, 1919, 1922; American Academy Gold Medal, 1933, and Howells Medal, 1945; Roosevelt Distinguished Service Medal, 1942. A.M.: Princeton University, 1899; Litt.D.: Princeton University, 1918; De Pauw University, Greencastle, Indiana, 1923; Columbia University, New York, 1924; L.H.D.: Purdue University, 1939. **Member:** American Academy. **Died:** 19 May 1946.

Publications for Children

Fiction

Seventeen. New York, Harper, and London, Hodder and Stoughton, 1916.

Penrod. New York, Doubleday, and London, Hodder and Stoughton, 1914.

Penrod and Sam. New York, Doubleday, 1916; London, Hodder and Stoughton, 1917.

Penrod Jashber. New York, Doubleday, and London, Heinemann, 1929.

Penrod: His Complete Story. New York, Doubleday, 1931.

Play

The Ghost Story (produced 1922). Boston, Baker, 1922.

Publications for Adults

Novels

The Gentleman from Indiana. New York, Doubleday, 1899; London, Richards, 1900.

Monsieur Beaucaire. New York, McClure Phillips, 1900; London, Murray, 1901.

The Two Vanrevels. New York, McClure Phillips, and London, Richards, 1902.

Cherry. New York, Harper, 1903.

The Beautiful Lady. New York, McClure Phillips, and London, Murray, 1905.

The Conquest of Canaan. New York, Harper, 1905; London, Hodder and Stoughton, 1917.

His Own People. New York, Doubleday, and London, Murray, 1907.

The Guest of Quesnay. New York, McClure Phillips, and London, Heinemann, 1908.

Beasley's Christmas Party. New York, Harper, 1909.

The Flirt. New York, Doubleday, and London, Hodder and Stoughton, 1913.

Growth. New York, Doubleday, and London, Heinemann, 1927.

- *The Turmoil.* New York, Harper, 1914; London, Hodder and Stoughton, 1915.
- *The Magnificent Ambersons.* New York, Doubleday, and London, Hodder and Stoughton, 1918.
- *The Midlander.* New York, Doubleday, 1923; London, Heinemann, 1924.

Ramsey Milholland. New York, and London, Hodder and Stoughton, Doubleday, 1919.

Alice Adams. New York, Doubleday, and London, Hodder and Stoughton, 1921.

Gentle Julia. New York, Doubleday, and London, Hodder and Stoughton, 1922.

Women. New York, Doubleday, and London, Heinemann, 1925.

The Plutocrat. New York, Doubleday, and London, Heinemann, 1927.
Claire Ambler. New York, Doubleday, and London, Heinemann, 1928.
Young Mrs. Greeley. New York, Doubleday, and London, Heinemann, 1929.
Mirthful Haven. New York, Doubleday, and London, Heinemann, 1930.
Mary's Neck. New York, Doubleday, and London, Heinemann, 1932.
Wanton Mally. New York, Doubleday, 1932; London, Heinemann, 1933.
Presenting Lily Mars. New York, Doubleday, 1933; London, Heinemann, 1934.
Little Orvie. New York, Doubleday, 1934; London, Heinemann, 1935.
Mr. White, The Red Barn, Hell, and Bridewater. New York, Doubleday, 1935; London, Heinemann, 1937.
The Lorenzo Bunch. New York, Doubleday, and London, Heinemann, 1936.
Rumbin Galleries. New York, Doubleday, 1937; London, Heinemann, 1938.
The Heritage of Hatcher Ide. New York, Doubleday, and London, Heinemann, 1941.
The Fighting Littles. New York, Doubleday, 1941; London, Heinemann, 1942.
Kate Fennigate. New York, Doubleday, 1943; London, Hammond, 1946.
Image of Josephine. New York, Doubleday, 1945; London, Hammond, 1948.
The Show Piece (unfinished). New York, Doubleday, 1947; London, Hammond, 1951.
Three Selected Short Novels (includes *Walterson, Uncertain Molly Collicut,* and *Rennie Peddigoe*). New York, Doubleday, 1947.

Short Stories

In the Arena: Stories of Political Life. New York, McClure Phillips, and London, Murray, 1905.
The Spring Concert. New York, Ridgeway, 1910.
Harlequin and Columbine and Other Stories. New York, Doubleday, 1918; London, Heinemann, 1923.
The Fascinating Stranger and Other Stories. New York, Doubleday, and London, Brown, 1923.
Selections from Booth Tarkington's Stories, edited by Lilian Holmes Strack. Boston, Baker, 1926.

Plays

The Guardian, with Harry Leon Wilson. Privately printed, 1907; as *The Man from Home* (produced Chicago, 1907; New York, 1908), New York, Harper, 1908; revised edition, New York and London, French, 1934.
Cameo Kirby, with Harry Leon Wilson (produced New York, 1908).
Foreign Exchange, with Harry Leon Wilson (produced New York, 1909).
If I Had Money, with Harry Leon Wilson (produced New York, 1909); as *Getting a Polish* (produced New York, 1909).
Springtime (produced New York, 1909).
Your Humble Servant, with Harry Leon Wilson (produced New York, 1910). New York, Rosenfield, 1910.
Beauty and the Jacobin: An Interlude of the French Revolution (produced 1912). New York and London, Harper, 1912.
The Man on Horseback (produced 1912).
The Ohio Lady, with Julian Street. Privately printed, 1916; as *The Country Cousin* (produced New York, 1917), New York and London, French, 1921.
Mister Antonio (produced New York, 1916). New York, French, 1925; London, French, 1935.
Up from Nowhere, with Harry Leon Wilson (produced New York, 1919).
Clarence (produced New York, 1919). New York and London, French, 1921.
The Gibson Upright, with Harry Leon Wilson (produced Indianapolis, 1919). New York, Doubleday, 1919.
Poldekin (produced New York, 1920).
The Wren (produced Boston and New York, 1921). New York and London, French, 1922.
The Intimate Strangers (produced Washington, D.C. and New York, 1921). New York and London, French, 1921.
Rose Briar (produced New York, 1922).
The Trysting Place (produced 1923). New York and London, French, 1923.
Tweedles, with Harry Leon Wilson (as *Bristol Glass,* produced Cleveland, 1923; as *Tweedles,* produced New York, 1923). New York and London, French, 1924.
Magnolia (produced New York, 1923).
Bimbo, The Pirate (produced 1926). New York, French, 1924.
The Travelers (produced 1927). New York and London, French, 1927.
Station YYYY (produced 1927). New York, French, 1927.
How's Your Health?, with Harry Leon Wilson (produced New York, 1929). New York and London, French, 1930.
Colonel Satan (produced New York, 1931).
The Help Each Other Club (produced 1933). New York, Appleton, 1934.
Lady Hamilton and Her Nelson (produced 1945). New York, House of Books, 1945.

Screenplays: *Edgar and the Teacher's Pet,* 1920; *Edgar's Hamlet,* 1920; *Edgar's Little Saw,* 1920; *Edgar, The Explorer,* 1921; *Get Rich Quick Edgar,* 1921; *Pied Piper Malone,* with Tom Geraghty, 1924; *The Man Who Found Himself,* with Tom Geraghty, 1925.

Radio Plays: *Maud and Cousin Bill* series, 1932-33 (75 episodes).

Other

The Works of Booth Tarkington (Autograph Edition). New York, Doubleday, 27 vols., 1918-32.
The Works of Booth Tarkington (Seaweed Edition). New York, Doubleday, 27 vols., 1922-32.
The Collector's Whatnot, with Hugh Kahler and Kenneth Roberts. Boston, Houghton Mifflin, 1923.
Looking Forward and Others (essays). New York, Doubleday, and London, Heinemann, 1926.
The World Does Move (reminiscences). New York, Doubleday, 1928; London, Heinemann, 1929.
Some Old Portraits: A Book about Art and Human Beings. New York, Doubleday, 1939.
As I Seem to Me (essays). Philadelphia, Curtis, 1941.

Your Amiable Uncle: Letters to His Nephews. Indianapolis, Bobbs Merrill, 1949.

On Plays, Playwrights, and Playgoers: Selections from the Letters of Booth Tarkington to George C. Tyler and John Peter Toohey 1918-1925, edited by Alan S. Downer. Princeton, Princeton University Library, 1959.

*

Bibliography: *A Bibliography of Booth Tarkington* by Dorothy Ritter Russo and Thelma L. Sullivan, Indianapolis, Indiana Historical Society, 1949, supplement in *Princeton University Library Chronicle 16,* 1955.

Critical Studies: *Booth Tarkington: Gentleman from Indiana* by James Woodress, Philadelphia, Lippincott, 1955; *Booth Tarkington* by Keith J. Fennimore, New York, Twayne, 1974; *My Amiable Uncle: Recollections about Booth Tarkington* by Susanah Mayberry, West Lafayette, Indiana, Purdue University Press, 1983.

Illustrator: *Antiquamania* by Kenneth Roberts, 1928.

* * *

Booth Tarkington's *Penrod* stories must be of particular interest to English readers in that they appear to be the inspiration for Richmal Crompton's William. Though Crompton always denied reading them, the similarities are surely too close to be accidental. Both Penrod and William feel that the adult cards are hopelessly stacked against them; their story is the farcical havoc that boys can cause while intending to do good. "This is a boy's lot: anything he does, anything whatever, may afterwards turn out to have been a crime—he never knows." There is the same interruption to the elder sister's courtship, the same bribery by suitors: "The serious poetry of all languages has omitted the little brother; and yet he is one of the great trials of love—the immemorial burden of courtship" says the author in *Penrod,* amplifying this in *Seventeen* with: "During the glamours of early love, if there be a creature more deadly than the little brother of a budding woman, that creature is the little sister of a budding man."

Many of the characters are parallel; the good boy, for instance (Georgie Bassett in the Penrod books is designed to be a minister—always clean and devoted to his mother). Though whereas William has three supporting Outlaws, Penrod has only Sam. There are whole episodes that are similar, such as the debacle of the children's pageant into which both are pressed by well-meaning ladies. And the hearts of both boys turn to melting ice cream when confronted by violet eyes and amber curls—this was habitual with American Bad Boys from Tom Sawyer on, but was almost the first time the young English male had been shown so susceptible. *Penrod* indeed ends on this note, on the eve of the boy's 12th birthday, when, as he sits on the garden fence in the setting sun, there is a gleam of amber curls, a tremulous laugh, and footsteps retreating: "in the grass, between Duke's forepaws, there lay a white note...'Your my Bow.'"

Penrod and its sequel, *Penrod and Sam,* come toward the end of the American celebration of Bad Boyhood that began in 1870 with Thomas Bailey Aldrich's account of his youthful exploits in Portsmouth, New Hampshire. All the writers who looked back with such nostalgia to a vanished golden age seem agreed that the optimum age was 12. As Tarkington put it: "A boy just 12 is like a Frenchman just elected to the Academy. Distinction and honor wait upon him....11 is not quite satisfactory; it is only an approach...13 is embarrassed by the beginnings of a new colthood. But 12 is the top of boyhood." But whereas the chronicle of William Brown is all farce, *Penrod* and *Penrod and Sam* swing between farce and autobiography, sandwiched with a certain amount of sentimentality. There is, in addition, some shrewd observation: "There is no boredom (not even an invalid's) comparable to that of a boy who has nothing to do." And Tarkington can combine a richly comic account of the mayhem initiated by Penrod and his cronies at a children's party with insight into what caused it: "Underneath the surface, nearly all children's parties contain a group of outlaws who wait only for a leader to hoist the black flag. The group consists mainly of boys too shy to be at ease with the girls, but who wish to distinguish themselves in some way; and there are others, ordinarily well behaved, whom the mere actuality of a party makes drunken."

Seventeen shows how Penrod might have turned out in adolescence, only the subject is William Sylvanus Baxter, no longer in command of events but being tripped up by them as he courts Miss Pratt and suffers the agonies of first love. To outside observers he is pathetic and irritating, but "to himself he is sometimes exalted to almost divine heights." As funny, but sadder than *Penrod,* it has the same insight into how it feels to be young.

—Gillian Avery

TATE, Eleanora E(laine)

Nationality: American. **Born:** Canton, Missouri, 16 April 1948. **Education:** Drake University, Des Moines, Iowa, B.A. 1973. **Family:** Married Zack E. Hamlett III in 1972; one daughter. **Career:** News editor, *Iowa Bystander,* West Des Moines, 1966-68; staff writer, *Des Moines Register and Tribune,* Des Moines, Iowa, 1968-76; writer and researcher, Kreative Koncepts, Inc., Myrtle Beach, South Carolina, 1979-81; president and co-owner (with her husband), Positive Images, Inc., 1983-92. Guest speaker at schools, colleges, and universities, 1968 to present. Member, Iowa Arts Council Writers in the Schools program, 1969-76, 1986-89; member, South Carolina Arts Commission, Artists in Education, 1987-92; founding member, Board of Governors, South Carolina Academy of Authors, 1986-90; Secretary, 1986-87, vice-president, 1988-89, president, 1990-91, Horry County [South Carolina] Cultural Arts Council, and helped to implement its Artists in Education program; invited writer, 1998 North Carolina Writers Network Blumenthal Readers and Writers Series; former board member, North Carolina Writers Network. **Awards:** Fifth Annual Council on Interracial Books for Children's Third World Writing Contest finalist, 1973; Unity award from Lincoln University, 1974, for educational reporting; Community Lifestyles award from Tennessee Press Association, 1977; Mary Louise Kennedy-Weekly Reader Children's Book Club Fellowship for *Just an Overnight Guest,* enabling the author to receive a Bread Loaf Writer's Fellowship, 1981; *Just an Overnight Guest* (film adaptation), shown on the PBS *Wonderworks* series and on Nickelodeon, was placed on the "Selected Films for Young Adults 1985" list by the Young Adult Committee of the American Library Association; *The Se-*

cret of Gumbo Grove won a Parents' Choice Gold Seal Award, 1987, was named to *USA Today*'s 1991 list of top ten recommended books for adolescents, and was a California Young Reader Medal nominee, 1991-92; *Thank You, Dr. Martin Luther King, Jr.!* was named an NCSS-CBC Notable Children's Trade Book in the field of Social Studies, 1990; a 1990 Child Study Children's Book Committee "Children's Book of the Year," a 1992-93 Maryland Black-Eyed Susan Children's Book nominee, and a South Carolina School Librarians Children's Book nominee, 1992-93. *Front Porch Stories at the One-Room School* was named a 1992 American Bookseller "Pick of the Lists," an Indiana Young Hoosier and a Sequoya [Oklahoma] Children's Book nominee, named to CBS's *This Morning*'s 1994 List of Recommended Books for Summer Reading for Kids, and a 1994-95 North Carolina Children's Junior Book Award nominee. *A Blessing in Disguise* was named an American Bookseller Pick of the Lists, 1996. **Agent:** Charlotte Sheedy, Sheedy Literary Agency, 65 Bleecker Street, New York, New York 10012, U.S.A. **Address:** P. O. Box 3581, Morehead City, North Carolina 28557, U.S.A.

Publications for Children

Fiction

Just an Overnight Guest. New York, Dial, 1980; reprint, East Orange, New Jersey, Just Us Books, 1997.
The Secret of Gumbo Grove. New York, F. Watts, 1987.
Thank You, Dr. Martin Luther King, Jr! New York, F. Watts, 1990.
Front Porch Stories at the One-Room School, illustrated by Eric Velasquez. New York, Bantam, 1992.
Retold African Myths, illustrated by Don Tate. Logan, Iowa, Perfection Learning Corporation, 1993.
A Blessing in Disguise. New York, Delacorte, 1995.
Don't Split the Pole: Tales of Down-Home Folk Wisdom, illustrated by Cornelius Van Wright and Ying-Hwa Hu. New York, Delacorte, 1997.

Other

"I'm Life," essay in *Children of Longing,* edited by Rosa Guy. New York, Bantam, 1970.
"African Violets, Part Four: Feet," poem in *Broadside Annual 1972.* Detroit, Broadside Press, 1972.
"An Ounce of Sand," short story in *Impossible?* Boston, Houghton, 1972.
"Bobby Griffin," short story in *Off-Beat.* New York, Macmillan, 1974.
Poetry in *Sprays of Rubies.* Ragnarok, 1975.
Poetry in *Valhalla Four.* Ragnarok, 1977.
"Hawkeye Hatty Rides Again," short story in *Success Stories* [anthology]. Institute of Children's Literature, 1994.
"Ethel's Story," adapted for *Storyworks Magazine,* Scholastic, Inc., fall 1992.
"Momma's Kitchen Table," personal essay, *In Praise of Our Fathers and Our Mothers: A Black Family Treasury by Outstanding Authors and Artists.* East Orange, New Jersey, Just Us Books, 1997.

Contributor, *Communications.* Lexington, Massachusetts, Heath, 1973.
Editor and contributor, *Eclipsed,* with husband Zack E. Hamlett, III. [Privately printed chapbook], 1975.
Editor and contributor, *Wanjiru: A Collection of Blackwomanworth.* [Privately printed chapbook], 1976.

Foreword, *Lil Muddy Waters* [picture book] by Ronald Daise. Beaufort, South Carolina, GOG Enterprises, 1997.

*

Media Adaptations: *Just an Overnight Guest* (film, starring Fran Robinson, Tiffany Hill, Rosalind Cash, and Richard Roundtree), Phoenix/B.F.A. Films & Videos, 1983; *The Secret of Gumbo Grove* (audiobook), Recorded Books, Inc., 1997; *Thank You, Dr. Martin Luther King, Jr.!* (audiobook), Recorded Books, Inc., 1998.

Eleanora E. Tate comments:

I like to write books for folks age 9 through 99, and I like to write about African Americans so that readers of all colors can get a truer viewpoint of who we are, and how important our history, past and present, is to America and to the world.

* * *

Children achieve greater self-esteem and pride in their family, their community, and their culture in Eleanora E. Tate's books. By engaging her readers' imaginations, Tate encourages readers to satisfy their intellectual curiosity, have a positive self-image, show compassion, explore their heritage, and share their stories with others.

In *Just an Overnight Guest* a middle-class African-American family living in Missouri confronts sudden change. The once-comfortable life that Margie Carson, nine, had enjoyed with her parents and older sister is turned upside-down when a four-year-old misfit, Ethel Hardisen, intrudes as an unwelcome "overnight guest." Abandoned by her mother, Ethel is an ill-mannered, bed-wetting, half-white, half-Black, "trashy little kid," as far as Margie is concerned. Ethel's intrusion is even more bitterly resented when Margie learns that Ethel is her cousin and will be living with them permanently. Mr. Carson explains that some situations will not change, so people must change in accepting them; in fact, the *New York Times Book Review* praises this sensitive presentation of life's moral ambiguities. The novel's film version has reached large television audiences on Nickelodeon and the Public Broadcasting System's *Wonderworks.*

Front Porch Stories at the One-Room School, the sequel to *Just an Overnight Guest* celebrates of storytelling and family unity. Three years after Ethel crashed into her family, Margie has not fully accepted her. Margie loves to tease Ethel unmercifully and still wonders about her own father's affection toward his niece. But this puzzlement ends one hot summer night Margie and Ethel sit on the front steps of the abandoned one-room school, listening to Mr. Carson's interesting tales about history and his scary ghost stories. Margie then shares a true story an 8'4" woman, and Ethel tells her own heartbreaking story about an abandoned little girl. Deeply touched by this pitiful tale of parental neglect, Margie finally accepts her cousin in her family.

The Secret of Gumbo Grove depicts a close-knit South Carolina family. Raisin Stackhouse, eleven, hates hearing her history teacher say that local African Americans never did anything worth mentioning, because Raisin desperately wants local heroes, people like Harriet Tubman and Sojourner Truth. When she accepts the challenge of 88-year-old Miz Effie Pfluggins, the recording secretary of Raisin's church, to restore an abandoned church cemetery, she discovers Gumbo Grove's "secret": the city's founder, assumed to be white, lies buried in the Black cemetery. Fascinating tales of Black ancestors and pioneers eventually enable Raisin and her friends to take pride in their heritage. Honored as the first recipient of a community service award, Raisin feels proud of finally knowing her community's history. Writing such a convincing work resulted from Tate's research into the Black community in Myrtle Beach, South Carolina; she also helped to renovate a run-down Black cemetery because she was inspired by voices from those neglected headstones. She firmly believes that involving youth in history connects them to their roots and instills pride.

In *Thank You, Dr. Martin Luther King, Jr.!* (a sequel to *The Secret of Gumbo Grove*), Mary Elouise Avery, nine, laments her dark skin and dreads hearing her white teacher and classmates discuss Black history with negative, stereotyped images of slavery that make her ashamed of her race. The teacher uses books, filmstrips, and movies showing "dead Black people hanging from tree limbs, or German shepherd dogs biting on them" or "starving Africans . . . with flies crawling on their faces, white crud around their mouths, and big bellies. Nasty!" Mary Elouise wonders if these people somehow deserved to be so abused. However, after a visiting Black storyteller encourages Mary Elouise to take pride in her African ancestors, she is no longer as embarrassed to be Black as she confidently narrates a school play about Black history. She thanks Dr. King and other African American heroes for inspiring her to achieve anything she wants.

Completing Tate's South Carolina trilogy, *A Blessing in Disguise* dramatically shows how people can unite to stop drugs from destroying families and communities. Zambia Brown, twelve, unhappily lives with her aunt and uncle because her mother is hospitalized (ravaged by AIDS, prostitution, and drug and alcohol abuse) and her drug-dealing father, who has another family, refuses responsibility for her. Zambia envies her half-sisters' lifestyle of fine clothes and fancy cars. Thus, turning away from her adopted family's love and moral values, Zambia enters her father's world of illicit drugs and violence and ignores her uncle's warning, "Anybody who lies down with dogs will get up with fleas." Shocked by the tragic consequences of a drug deal gone bad, the community bonds together to get rid of drugs; consequently, even the worst thing can be a blessing in disguise.

Besides these novels, Tate has two collections of tales. *Retold African Myths* adapts 18 myths about creation, death, gods, mortals, tricksters, and moral dilemmas. Readers are encouraged to add sound effects and read parts aloud to better appreciate the African storytelling tradition. Learning about the continent's rich storytelling tradition becomes easy and fun with illustrations, a map of Africa noting the various cultural groups, insights about diverse cultures, vocabulary words defined and highlighted in context, and lists of main characters. Also entertaining and instructive, *Don't Split the Pole: Tales of Down-Home Folk Wisdom* presents seven stories showing how youngsters learn the truth of popular sayings such as "What goes around comes around," You can't teach an old dog new tricks," "A hard head makes a soft behind," and "Big things come in small packages." Complemented by black-and-white illustrations, these engaging stories present a wonderfully diverse cast of characters—not only Black and white children but also talking dogs.

Tate's multicultural stories, aimed at third- through sixth-grade readers, celebrate the strong moral values needed for today's children to survive the destructive forces tearing families and communities apart. Indeed, learning about family traditions and cultural heritage empowers not only her characters but also, as one would hope, her young readers.

—Laura M. Zaidman

TATE, Joan

Nationality: British. **Born:** Tonbridge, Kent, 23 September 1922. **Family:** Married; two daughters and one son. **Career:** Freelance writer, translator, and publishers reader. **Address:** 7 College Hill, Shrewsbury, Shropshire SY1 1LZ, England.

Publications for Children

Fiction

Jenny, illustrated by Charles Keeping. London, Heinemann, 1964.

The Crane, illustrated by Richard Wilson. London, Heinemann, 1964.

The Rabbit Boy, illustrated by Hugh Marshall. London, Heinemann, 1964.

Coal Hoppy, illustrated by J. Yunge-Bateman. London, Heinemann, 1964.

The Next-Doors, illustrated by Charles Keeping. London, Heinemann, 1964; New York, Scholastic, 1976.

The Silver Grill, illustrated by Hugh Marshall. London, Heinemann, 1964; New York, Scholastic, 1976.

Picture Charlie, illustrated by Laszlo Acs. London, Heinemann, 1964.

Lucy, illustrated by Richard Willson. London, Heinemann, 1964.

The Tree, illustrated by George Tuckwell. London, Heinemann, 1966; as *Tina and David,* Nashville, Nelson, 1973.

The Holiday, illustrated by Leo Walmsley. London, Heinemann, 1966.

Tad, illustrated by Leo Walmsley. London, Heinemann, 1966.

Bill, illustrated by George Tuckwell. London, Heinemann, 1966.

Mrs. Jenny, illustrated by Charles Keeping. London, Heinemann, 1966.

Bits and Pieces, illustrated by Quentin Blake. London, Heinemann, 1967.

The New House. Stockholm, Almqvist & Wiksell, 1967; London, Pelham, 1976.

The Soap Box Car. Stockholm, Almqvist & Wiksell, 1967.

The Old Car. Stockholm, Almqvist & Wiksell, 1967.

The Great Birds. Stockholm, Almqvist & Wiksell, 1967; London, Blackie, 1976.

The Train. Stockholm, Almqvist & Wiksell, 1967.

Polly. Stockholm, Almqvist & Wiksell, 1967; London, Cassell, 1976.

The Circus and Other Stories, illustrated by Timothy Jacques. London, Heinemann, 1967.

Letters to Chris, illustrated by Mary Russon. London, Heinemann, 1967.

Wild Martin, and The Crow, illustrated by Richard Kennedy. London, Heinemann, 1967.

Luke's Garden, illustrated by Quentin Blake. London, Heinemann, 1967; revised edition, London, Longman, 1976.
Sam and Me. London, Macmillan, 1968; New York, Coward McCann, 1969.
Out of the Sun. London, Heinemann, 1969.
Whizz Kid. London, Macmillan, 1969; as *Not the Usual Kind of Girl,* New York, Scholastic, 1974.
The Letter. Stockholm, Almqvist & Wiksell, 1969.
Puddle's Tiger. Stockholm, Almqvist & Wiksell, 1969.
The Caravan. Stockholm, Almqvist & Wiksell, 1969.
Edward and the Uncles. Stockholm, Almqvist & Wiksell, 1969.
The Secret. Stockholm, Almqvist & Wiksell, 1969.
Varieties:
1. *The Ball, The Lollipop Man, The Nest,* illustrated by Mary Dinsdale, John Dyke, and Prudence Seward. London, Macmillan, 1969.
2. *The Cheapjack Man, The Gobblydock, The Treehouse,* illustrated by Richard Rose, Jenny Williams, and Mary Dinsdale. London, Macmillan, 1969.

Clipper. London, Macmillan, 1969; as *Ring on My Finger,* 1971; New York, Scholastic, 1976.
The Long Road Home. London, Heinemann, 1971.
Gramp, illustrated by Robert Geary. London, Chatto Boyd and Oliver, 1971; revised edition, London, Pelham, 1979.
Wild Boy, illustrated by Trevor Stubley. London, Chatto Boyd and Oliver, 1972; New York, Harper, 1973.
Wump Day, illustrated by John Storey. London, Heinemann, 1972.
Ben and Annie, illustrated by Mary Dinsdale. Leicester, Brockhampton Press, 1973; New York, Doubleday, 1974.
Dad's Camel, illustrated by Margaret Power. London, Heinemann, 1973.
Jock and the Rock Cakes, illustrated by Carolyn Dinan. Leicester, Brockhampton Press, 1973; Chicago, Children's Press, 1976.
Grandpa and My Sister Bee, illustrated by Leslie Wood. Leicester, Brockhampton Press, 1973; Chicago, Children's Press, 1976.
Taxi! Paderborn, Schöningh, 1973.
Night Out. Stockholm, Almqvist & Wiksell, 1973.
The Match. Stockholm, Almqvist & Wiksell, 1973.
Dinah. Stockholm, Almqvist & Wiksell, 1973.
Journal for One. Stockholm, Almqvist & Wiksell, 1973.
The Man Who Rang the Bell. Stockholm, Almqvist & Wiksell, 1973.
Ginger Mick. London, Heinemann, 1974; revised edition, London, Longman, 1975.
The Runners, illustrated by Douglas Phillips. Newton Abbot, Devon, David and Charles, 1974; revised edition, London, Longman, 1977.
Dirty Dan. Stockholm, Almqvist & Wiksell, 1974.
Sandy's Trumpet. Stockholm, Almqvist & Wiksell, 1974.
Zena. Stockholm, Almqvist & Wiksell, 1974.
The Thinking Box. Stockholm, Almqvist & Wiksell, 1974.
Your Dog. London, Pelham, 1975.
Turn Again Whittington. London, Pelham, 1976.
The House That Jack Built. London, Pelham, 1976.
Crow and the Brown Boy, illustrated by Gay Galsworthy. London, Cassell, 1976.
Polly and the Barrow Boy, illustrated by Gay Galsworthy. London, Cassell, 1976.
Billoggs, illustrated by Trevor Stubley. London, Pelham, 1976.
You Can't Explain Everything. London, Longman, 1976.
See You and Other Stories. London, Longman, 1977.
See How They Run. London, Pelham, 1978.
Cat Country. Godalming, Surrey, Ram, 1979.
Luke's Garden, and Gramp: Two Short Novels. New York, Harper, 1981.
Jumping Jo the Joker, illustrated by Maggie Dawson. London, Macmillan, 1984.
Clee and Nibs. London, Penguin, 1990.

Other

Going Up. Stockholm, Almqvist & Wiksell, 3 vols., 1969-74.
Your Town, illustrated by Virginia Smith. Newton Abbot, Devon, David and Charles, 1972.
How Do You Do? Paderborn, Schöningh, 3 vols., 1973-76.
The Living River, illustrated by David Harris. London, Dent, 1974.
Your Dog, illustrated by Babette Cole. London, Pelham, 1975.
Disco Books (*Big Fish, Tom's Trip, The Day I Got the Sack, Girl in the Window, Supermarket, Gren, Day Off, Moped*), illustrated by Gay Galsworthy, Jill Cox, and George Craig. London, Cassell, 8 vols., 1975.
On Your Own 1-2. Exeter, Devon, Wheaton, 2 vols., 1977-78.
Frankie Flies. London, Macmillan, 1980.
Club Books (*The Jimjob, The Totter Man, Trip to Liverpool, New Shoes*), illustrated by George Craig and Jill Cox. London, Cassell, 4 vols., 1981.
The Fox and the Stork and Other Fables (retellings from Aesop), illustrated by Svend Otto S. London, Pelham, 1985.
The Donkey and the Dog (retelling from Aesop), illustrated by Svend Otto S. London, Pelham, 1987.
Twenty Tales of Aesop, illustrated by Svend Otto S. London, Pelham, 1987.
Avalanche!, illustrated by Svend Otto S. London, Pelham, 1987.
Dad's Camel. Red Fox/Andersen Press, 1991.

Translator of more than 120 books for children by Gunnel Beckman, Astrid Lindgren, Svend Otto S., Gun and Ingvar Björk, Irmelin Sandman Lilius, and others; also translator of over 150 books for adults by Maj Sjöwall and Per Wahlöö, Maria Lang, Elisabeth Söderström, Carl Nylander, Thomas Dinesen, and others.

*

Manuscript Collections: Kerlan Collection, University of Minnesota, Minneapolis.

Joan Tate comments:
It is impossible to explain what inspires me in simple terms, but I suppose it could be said that everything about life inspires a writer, anyhow this one. I used to jot down notes onto handy pieces of paper and shove them into a file euphemistically called the Ideas File, then leave them there for sometimes months or even years, then forget all about them. When asked for another "story," or the time had come to write one, I would riffle through this scruffy collection of bits of paper, torn-off newspaper, backs of menus, old cards, etc., and read some of them. I had always completely forgotten what was written on them, but the moment I read them again, I remembered with crystal clarity what they had been about, and that became the core of a story, the initial idea.

* * *

There are many children who for various reasons cannot or do not wish to read, and it is for this group that Joan Tate writes the majority of her books. Not all these children have actual reading problems, but many are bored by the majority of books they see. Tate writes books like *Whizz Kid*—short, topical, full of snappy dialogue, and with a plot that is relevant and interesting to teenagers. These are the books which many reluctant readers will pick up; they are designed to be read by the 12-16 age group, but have an actual reading age of 9-10 years. The vivid stories have a simple vocabulary, an easy style, and are set in a working-class area with teenage motor mechanics, shop assistants (*The Rabbit Boy*), and nurses (*Letters to Chris*) as their main characters.

The everyday problems of urban living are tackled in a straightforward way which can capture the imagination of both boys and girls: the young marrieds in *Sam and Me;* the problem neighbours in *The Next-Doors;* the young West Indian couple in *Mrs. Jenny* coping with housing difficulties and the strange winter cold. The majority of these books have attractive, often dramatic covers designed to catch the eye. The type is big and bold, well-spaced but still looking like the good long read to be found in other paperbacks for teenagers. It is this physical attractiveness and boldness which help to popularise the books among teenage readers.

Wild Boy, first published as a short story in *Wild Martin, and The Crow,* has a strong storyline. After Will finds a wild boy living on the Yorkshire Moors above his home, the reader is intrigued enough to read on to find out what happens. There are never too many characters in her books to confuse the plot, and the reader always feels drawn to identify with the hero and heroine. The expanded version has a deeper plot and more finely drawn characters than the short story.

Tate has also written a number of books for younger children; *Grandpa and My Sister Bee* and *Jock and the Rock Cakes* are examples of her simple picture stories with domestic settings and realistic dialogue for the 5- to 7-year-olds. In books such as *The New House* and *Billoggs,* the author uses everyday settings but allows her characters more flights of fancy and more imagination than exists in some stories. In *Billoggs* the old tramp decides that the scrap car will make an ideal home without realising that Susan, George, and Ester have used it as a base for their adventures.

Tate is a prolific writer who has specialised in that very difficult area of writing for a specific audience rather than children at large. She has reached out to those young people who are not by instinct readers. She has also used the environment as a theme; *The Living River* is a leisurely and attractive look at the River Severn with a strong conservation message.

—Jean Russell

TAYLOR, Cora (Lorraine)

Nationality: Canadian. **Born:** Cora Lorraine Traub in Fort Qu'Appelle, Saskatchewan, 14 January 1936. **Family:** Married 1) Durward Thomas in 1953 (divorced), one daughter and one son; 2) Don Livingston in 1958 (divorced), two sons; 3) Russell Taylor. **Education:** University of Alberta, B.A., Teaching Certificate, 1973. **Career:** Medical secretary, University of Alberta, University Hospital, Edmonton, 1964-68; theatre critic, Allied Bulletin, 1967; teacher, Duffield School, Duffield, Alberta, 1973-75; writer since 1975. Member: Canadian Authors Association (Alberta vice-president, 1980-86; national award chairman, 1987). **Awards:** Alberta Writers Guild R. Ross Annett Award; Canadian Library Association Book of the Year Award; and Canada Council Award, all 1985, for *Julie*; City of Edmonton Arts Award, 1987;Ruth Schwartz Children's Book Award, 1988, for *The Doll*; Austrian Youth Book Prize, 1991, for *Julie* (in translation); White Ravens Selection of the International Youth Library, Munich, 1992, for *Julie's Secret*; Canadian Library Association Book of the Year Award, 1995, for *Summer of the Mad Monk.* **Address:** R.R.1, Winterburn, Alberta TOE 2NO, Canada.

Publications for Children

Fiction

Julie. Saskatoon, Vancouver, Douglas & McIntyre, 1985.
The Doll. Saskatoon, Vancouver, Douglas & McIntyre, 1992.
Julie's Secret. Saskatoon, Vancouver, Douglas & McIntyre, 1991.
Ghost Voyages. Richmond Hill, Ontario, Scholastic, 1992.
The Summer of the Mad Monk. Vancouver, Greystone Books, 1994.
Vanishing Act. Red Deer, Alberta, Red Deer College Press, 1997.

* * *

Cora Taylor burst on the Canadian juvenile literature scene in 1985 when her first novel, *Julie,* was nominated for three national children's literature prizes and won two of them. Since then, Taylor has produced five other titles for middle school audiences with the critical response being divided among them.

Julie tells a haunting story of loneliness, in particular the isolation that can come from being different. The seventh child of a seventh child, Julie Morgan is described as a "sensitive child" by Granny Goderich, an old woman with a local reputation for being able to read tea leaves with uncanny accuracy. Initially, the vivid stories Julie told were attributed to her imagination and were a source of amazement to her siblings and of amusement for her parents, but gradually family members began to find Julie's behaviour disquieting. By age six, Julie had stopped sharing her "visions/stories" with her family and had retreated into herself. Among the few who offer Julie solace is Granny Goderich, who speaks to Julie regarding her talent to see things that others do not. Though the visions stop for a period, a situation that allows Julie to feel "normal," they return when she is 10. While Julie realized that she could know many things without knowing how she knew, she questioned the worth of such an ability. In the book's concluding portion, Julie's capability to see into the future places her in a situation wherein she must determine whether or not to change what is to happen.

Taylor's second book, *The Doll,* an award-winning time slip fantasy, is built around a real, century-old china doll, Jessie, which had belonged to Taylor's homesteading grandmother. In the story, while 10-year-old Meg is recovering from rheumatic fever at her grandmother's home, her parents are preparing to separate and divorce. A china doll, a Shearer family heirloom, becomes the key for a sleeping Meg to drift into the past and assume the identity of Morag, a child in a pioneer family travelling west from Ontario via the Carlton Trail. Because Meg's life as Morag is more appealing than her disintegrating life in the present, she spends increasing time asleep—with her pioneer family. Only when a deadly prairie grass fire frees Meg to live entirely in the present does she finally confront her contemporary problems.

Julie's Secret and *Ghost Voyages* are both competently written, but they do not meet the standards Taylor had established with her initial books. As the title suggests, *Julie's Secret* is a sequel. Taking shelter from an unexpected spring blizzard in a barn on an abandoned neighbouring farm, Julie senses that some horrific happenings have occurred there; subsequent investigations by the Royal Canadian Mounted Police uncover the recently-disposed-of body of a teenager, plus evidence of an old double murder. When Billy, Julie's brother, is later kidnapped, Julie helps to facilitate his rescue by reluctantly acquiescing to her father's request to use her "gift" to discover Billy's whereabouts. While *Julie*'s more slow-moving plot had a mystical flavour, *Julie's Secret* simply comes across as an action-adventure story.

Ghost Voyages, another time travel fantasy, opens with Jeremy, aged nine, perusing an old stamp album that had belonged to his now deceased granddad. When Jeremy uses his grandfather's magnifying glass to examine some Canadian stamps featuring historic ships, he twice finds himself transported to the decks of the ship portrayed on the stamp. There he becomes a participant observer in the significant historical event connected to that vessel. In the first instance, Jeremy boards the Northcote, which is transporting government troops dispatched to suppress the Riel Rebellion; in the second, the Nonsuch is carrying fur traders into Hudson Bay. Though the historical portions of the book exhibit some life, the contemporary sections are flat, as is the plot's resolution.

The Summer of the Mad Monk, set in rural 1932 Alberta, again evidences the fine quality of Taylor's earlier works. The principal storyline involves the well-read Philip "Pip" Tyler, 12, who becomes convinced that the nearby community's new blacksmith, a Russian called Raspinsky, is really the Mad Monk Rasputin. When Pip discovers that Raspinsky is hiding an injured man in his shop, that person can only be the Tsarvich Alexei who has somehow escaped the Russian royal family's execution. While Pip fantasizes about some day being welcomed to the restored Russian court by a grateful Tsar Alexei, in the present Pip must cope with the town bully, Pete McKnight, 14, who treats the children of poor farmers with contempt. In addition to devising a strong story with good characterization, Taylor also graphically recreates the horrendous wind and dust storms that relentlessly struck the arid prairies during the Depression—and reveals the emotionally eroding effects these storms had on homesteaders like Pip's parents.

The fantastic element in *Vanishing Act* is introduced early in the story when 13-year-old Jennifer discovers a spell that makes her invisible. Along with her twin sister, Maggie, and friend Sam, Jennifer refines her ability to disappear and reappear and contemplates the use of such ability in her amateur detective work. Jennifer ultimately uses her power, along with the help of the other children and her grandmother, to find her father, who had been kidnapped, and to help him escape from Turkey. *Vanishing Act* is set firmly in 1997 and the travel of the characters depends solidly on very real tickets, planes, ships, and schedules; this is not the magical time travel of Taylor's earlier works. While engaging, this story is closer to the action-adventure genre of *Julie's Secret,* and lacks the subtleties in tone and character development that distinguish Taylor's strongest works.

—David H. Jenkinson, updated by Alexandra MacLennan

TAYLOR, Sydney

Nationality: American. **Born:** Sydney Brenner, New York City, 31 October 1904. **Education:** New York University. **Family:** Married Ralph Taylor in 1925; one daughter. **Career:** Actress, Lenox Hill Players, New York, 1925-29; dancer, Martha Graham Dance Company, New York, 1930-35; instructor in dance and dramatics, Cejwin Camps, Port Jervis, New York, from 1942. **Awards:** Jewish Book Council of America Isaac Siegel Memorial award, 1952; Association of Jewish Libraries award, 1979. **Died:** 12 February 1978.

PUBLICATIONS FOR CHILDREN

Fiction

All-of-a-Kind Family, illustrated by Helen John. Chicago, Wilcox and Follett, 1951; London, Blackie, 1961.

More All-of-a-Kind Family, illustrated by Mary Stevens. Chicago, Follett, 1954; London, Blackie, 1967.

All-of-a-Kind Family Uptown, illustrated by Mary Stevens. Chicago, Follett, 1958.

Mr. Barney's Beard, illustrated by Charles Geer. Chicago, Follett, 1961.

Now That You Are Eight, illustrated by Ingrid Fetz. New York, Association Press, 1963.

A Papa Like Every One Else, illustrated by George Porter. Chicago, Follett, 1966.

The Dog Who Came to Dinner, illustrated by John E. Johnson. Chicago, Follett, 1966.

All-of-a-Kind Family Downtown, illustrated by Beth and Joe Krush. Chicago, Follett, 1972.

Ella of All-of-a-Kind Family, illustrated by Gail Owens. New York, Dutton, 1978.

Danny Loves a Holiday, illustrated by Gail Owens. New York, Dutton, 1980.

Author, director, and choreographer of many plays for children's camps.

*

Manuscript Collections: Kerlan Collection, University of Minnesota, Minneapolis.

* * *

An amateur writer, Sydney Taylor initially told the story of her own childhood in an orthodox Jewish family to her daughter at bedtime. Her books are purposeful, but despite soaring moments of brilliance, they lack the careful development of plot, character, setting, and style.

The intent of the series books is to describe a family in New York City at the turn of the century and to instill an attitude of pride in the reader. *All-of-a-Kind Family* introduces the reader to six siblings and to Jewish customs and holidays. The author writes knowingly, as she was herself the Sarah in the stories. Stimulated by letters from readers, she wrote chronologically about the blossoming family; the series covers five years, but was published over a period of 21 years. Taylor also wrote two beginning-to-read books with vocabularies of 150 words, *Mr. Barney's Beard* and *The Dog Who Came to Dinner.*

Taylor's method of creating plot is episodic: Mama places 12 buttons around the room for the child to find while dusting, or Henny charges her friends a penny each to see the baby bathed. Connections between the books are limited, as the author did not originally plan to write a series. There is some foreshadowing, though, as in *All-of-a-Kind Family* when Charlie finds his long lost love, the library lady whom the children already know. Bachelor Uncle Hiram marries the woman who rescued the little brother in *More All-of-a-Kind Family.*

Characters mature chronologically rather than by inner growth. The five sisters and brother, born at the close of the first book, father, mother, uncle and aunt have stable characteristics and change little. Henrietta is consistently mischievous and is reprimanded at school as well as at home. In *All-of-a-Kind Family Uptown,* Ella does state, "guess this is what growing up really means, Grace. Standing on your own two feet and being your own mountain." Aunt Lena becomes morose after falling victim to polio, but returns to her cheerful self following a single lecture from Mama.

The specific setting of the books is well handled. New York's east side, uptown, downtown, and the beach are the areas in which the children move, and the junk shop, library, market, and school are sketched in detail. References to the Fourth of July, settlement houses, and knitting for the Red Cross support the uniqueness of place and time, and there are constant examples of Jewish foods in the home: "Teiglech are fried balls of dough soaked in honey" and gefilte fish on Friday are important on the menu.

Anecdotes are expanded into entire chapters, and are spiced with humor. When Henny wore her sister's dress without permission and spilled tea on it, she dyed the entire garment in tea. Yiddish words and the word order of immigrants are interspersed throughout the text: "Schlumper (untidy one)" and "get away from the sink already." Mama states adages, like "do your work with good will and it'll get done twice as fast" or "there's nothing like keeping busy to help a person over a bad time." The point-of-view is inconsistent, as the narrator may relate the thoughts of one person, such as the library lady, but not another, such as Charlie. Taylor keeps the story moving swiftly in the All-of-a-Kind series, but uses the cumulative tale pattern in *Mr. Barney's Beard.*

Taylor's All-of-a-Kind Family books have remained in print in the United States since their initial publication. They have been compared to Margaret Sidney's *The Five Little Peppers* and Herman Wouk's *City Boy.* The author has endeared herself to librarians by providing stories in which the library is a focal point, while at the same time introducing children to an ethnic group in a pluralistic society.

—Karen Nelson Hoyle

TAYLOR, William

Nationality: New Zealander. **Born:** Wellington, 11 October 1938. **Family:** Divorced; two sons. **Career:** Schoolteacher in New Zealand, 1960-84; principal, Ohakune School, 1978-84. Since 1984 full-time writer. Mayor of Ohakune, 1980-88. **Address:** RD 2, Owhango, New Zealand.

PUBLICATIONS FOR CHILDREN

Fiction

Pack Up Pick Up and Off. Petone, Price Milburn, 1981.
My Summer of the Lions. Auckland, Reed Methuen, 1986.
Shooting Through. Auckland, Reed Methuen, 1986.
Break a Leg! Auckland, Reed Methuen, 1987; London, Penguin, 1989.
Possum Perkins. Auckland, Ashton Scholastic, 1987; as *Paradise Lane,* London, Century Hutchinson, and New York, Scholastic, 1987.
The Worst Soccer Team Ever! Auckland, Reed Methuen, 1987; London, Penguin, 1989.
Making Big Bucks. Auckland, Reed Methuen, 1987.
The Kidnap of Jessie Parker. Auckland, Heinemann Reed, 1989.
I Hate My Brother Maxwell Potter. Auckland, Heinemann Reed, 1989.
Agnes the Sheep. Auckland, Ashton Scholastic, 1989.
Knitwits. New York, Scholastic, 1992.
Secret Lives. London, Scholastic, 1994.
The Porter Brothers. Auckland, Harper Collins, 1991.
Supermum and Spike the Dog. Auckland, Harper Collins, 1992.
S.W.A.T. Auckland, Harper Collins, 1993.
The Blue Lawn. Auckland, Harper Collins, 1994.

Other

The Third Day (reader), illustrated by Nan Reid. Wellington, Department of Education, 1982.

PUBLICATIONS FOR ADULTS

Novels

Episode. London, Hale, 1970.
The Mask of the Clown. London, Hale, 1970.
The Plekhov Place. London, Hale, 1971.
Pieces in a Jigsaw. London, Hale, 1972.
The Persimmon Tree. London, Hale, 1972.
The Chrysalis. London, Hale, 1974.

Other

Burnt Carrots Don't Have Legs. Palmerston, Dunmore Press, 1976.

*

William Taylor comments:

I write fiction for young people—11-15 years. While reflective of New Zealand, my work has a "universality" that appears to make it increasingly popular overseas, with publication in the United Kingdom, United States, and a number of European translations.

My work ranges from the humorous to the serious—and most points in-between. I imagine my prime aim is to tell a story and, secondly, to tell it as well as I can.

* * *

Because William Taylor has served an apprenticeship in writing adult fiction, he brings a professionalism and an ability to slice deeply and quickly into the heart of things. Since, also, he has taught enthusiastically in primary and intermediate schools and has served as a principal, he brings a wide knowledge of children from many different backgrounds. He shows a keen sympathy for them, especially for those suffering hurt, deprivation, or harassment because of poverty, race, sex, or prejudice.

Taylor's knowledge of New Zealand children is immediately obvious. The boys and girls of his dramas show great energy whether they are pursuing their sport or evading the law, running away, searching for the wrong-doer, putting on a play, organising a soccer team, or "making big bucks."

All the various types are there, individualised. Thirteen-year-old Marty Smith attempts to come to terms with his grief at the sudden death of his mother by petty theft with his reluctant friend, the Samoan boy Ioane. Rosie Perkins is saved from the hopelessness of her family life by the warmth of the Geraghty family. The escaping boys in *Shooting Through* find the respite they need and the encouragement to make a new start from their experience with a Maori family in the remote mountain area of the North Island. The gang who dominate the pages of the trilogy beginning with *The Worst Soccer Team Ever!* humorously clown their way through their experiences of very early adolescence at the Greenhill Intermediate School.

There is a marked difference in tone and subject matter between the first four novels and the Greenhill trilogy. In the former, the author captures the sense of place very exactly, and the characters find their salvation amid a network of conflicting forces. The rabbiter's family in *Pack Up Pick Up and Off* finds itself vulnerable to the condescension and suspicion of rigid landowning settlement. The one-teacher school is at the centre—its children, activities, and workings beautifully observed.

In *Shooting Through,* the desolation of the ghost town symbolises the wretchedness of the boys' lives. In this story and in the other two of this group, *My Summer of the Lions* and *Possum Perkins,* animals play an important role in the healing process. The two lions Felix and Felicity are a constant delight in this story.

Soccer matches, school plays, and the business of making money for the holidays are the chief motivating forces of the trilogy. The children, mostly preadolescents, are slangy, at times earthy, curious, and cheeky, but are always cheerful. They handle their teachers and parents and parents' friends with good-natured casualness, grumbling when they have to do their jobs, trying to avoid work, but generally showing respect and concern for parents and teachers. Not only do the child characters show vitality and liveliness such as the redoubtable Lavender and Griller, so also do the adult characters.

Taylor's novels skim along, the narrative carried by the speed and vigour of the dialogue which is idiomatic and individualised. At the start of a match we hear, "'We're gonna waste ya,' says one. 'We're gonna waste ya,' said another. 'Can't wait,' and he grinned evilly." Tom Colman, Lavender Gibson, and their gang may be harum-scarum at times, they may not be angels, and because they are yet children there is an innocence even when they are headstrong. The trauma of adolescence is just around the corner.

Taylor has demonstrated his power of imagination in constructing such an exuberant world. When he broadens his scope to encompass other genres, possibly for age groups both younger and older than that of 11-14, he could call on his many gifts as a writer to entertain and continue to enrich New Zealand writing in the deepest way.

—Tom Fitzgibbon

TERHUNE, Albert Payson

Nationality: American. **Born:** Newark, New Jersey, 21 December 1872; son of the writer Mary Virginia Terhune (pseudonym: Marion Harland). **Education:** Columbia University, New York, A.B. 1893. **Family:** Married 1) Lorraine Marguerite Bryson in 1898 (died), one daughter; 2) Anice Morris Stockton. **Career:** Journalist, New York *Evening World,* 1894-1916; freelance writer from 1916. Park commissioner, State of New Jersey, from 1925. **Award:** Columbia University Medal of Excellence, 1933. **Died:** 18 February 1942.

Publications for Children

Fiction

Lad, A Dog. New York, Dutton, 1919; London, Dent, 1920.
Bruce. New York, Dutton, 1920.
Buff, A Collie and Other Dog Stories. New York, Doran, and London, Hodder and Stoughton, 1921.
Further Adventures of Lad. New York, Doran, 1922; London, Hodder and Stoughton, 1923; as *Dog Stories Every Child Should Know,* New York, Doubleday, 1941.
His Dog. New York, Dutton, and London, Dent, 1922.
Lochinvar Luck. New York, Doran, 1923; London, Hodder and Stoughton, 1924.
Treve. New York, Doran, and London, Hodder and Stoughton, 1924.
The Heart of a Dog, illustrated by Marguerite Kirmse. New York, Doran, 1924; London, Hodder and Stoughton, 1925.
Wolf. New York, Doran, 1925; London, Hodder and Stoughton, 1926.
My Friend the Dog, illustrated by Marguerite Kirmse. New York, Harper, 1926; London, Hutchinson, 1927.
Treasure. New York, Harper, 1926; London, Hutchinson, 1927; as *The Faith of a Collie,* New York, Grosset and Dunlap, 1949.
Gray Dawn. New York, Harper, 1927; London, Hutchinson, 1928.
The Luck of the Laird. New York, Harper, 1927; London, Hutchinson, 1929; as *A Highland Collie,* New York, Grosset and Dunlap, 1950.
Lad of Sunnybank. New York, Harper, 1929; London, Chapman and Hall, 1930.
A Dog Named Chips. New York, Harper, 1931; London, Chapman and Hall, 1932.
The Way of a Dog, Being Further Adventures of Gray Dawn and Some Others. New York, Harper, 1932; London, Chapman and Hall, 1933.
The Critter and Other Dogs. New York, Harper, 1936.
The Terhune Omnibus, edited by Max J. Herzberg, photographs by Margaret Bourke-White. New York, Harper, 1937; as *The Best-Loved Dog Stories,* New York, Grosset and Dunlap, 1954.

Grudge Mountain. New York, Harper, 1939; as *The Mystery of Grudge Mountain,* London, Chapman and Hall, 1939; as *Dog of the High Sierras,* New York, Grosset and Dunlap, 1951.
Loot! New York, Harper, 1940; as *Collie to the Rescue,* New York, Grosset and Dunlap, 1952.

Other

The Dog Book, illustrated by Diana Thorne. Akron, Ohio, Saalfield, 1932.
Real Tales of Real Dogs, illustrated by Diana Thorne. Akron, Ohio, Saalfield, 1935.
True Dog Stories, illustrated by Diana Thorne. Akron, Ohio, Saalfield, 1936.
A Book of Famous Dogs, illustrated by Robert Dickey. New York, Doubleday, 1937.
Dogs, illustrated by Kurt Wiese. Akron, Ohio, Saalfield, 1940.

Publications for Adults

Novels

Dr. Dale: A Story Without a Moral, with Marion Harland. New York, Dodd Mead, 1900.
Caleb Conover, Railroader. New York, Authors and Newspapers Association, and London, Cassell, 1907.
The New Mayor (novelization of play). New York, Ogilvie, 1908.
The Fighter. New York, Lovell, 1910; London, Methuen, 1919.
The Woman (novelization of play). Indianapolis, Bobbs Merrill, 1912.
Dad (3 chapters by Sinclair Lewis). New York, Watts, 1914; London, Methuen, 1920.
The Story of Damon and Pythias (novelization of screenplay). New York, Grosset and Dunlap, 1915.
The Years of the Locust. New York, Shores, 1917.
Dollars and Cents. New York, Shores, 1917.
Fortune. New York, Doubleday, 1918.
The Man in the Dark. New York, Dutton, 1921.
Black Gold. New York, Doran, and London, Hodder and Stoughton, 1922.
Black Caesar's Clan. New York, Doran, 1922; London, Hodder and Stoughton, 1924.
The Amateur Inn. New York, Doran, 1923; London, Hodder and Stoughton, 1924.
The Pest. New York, Dutton, 1923.
The Tiger's Claw. New York, Doran, 1924; London, Hodder and Stoughton, 1925.
Najib. New York, Doran, 1925; London, Hodder and Stoughton, 1926.
The Runaway Bag. New York, Doran, 1925.
Blundell's Last Guest. New York, Chelsea House, 1927.
Water! New York, Harper, 1928; London, Hutchinson, 1929.
The Secret of Sea-Dream House. New York, Harper, and London, Butterworth, 1929.
Letters of Marque. New York, Harper, 1934.
Unseen! New York, Harper, 1937.

Short Stories

Columbia Stories. New York, Dillingham, 1897.

Plays

Nero, with William C. de Mille (produced 1904).
Around the World in Thirty Days; or, The Greatest Trip Ever Made. New York, Street and Smith, 1914.
Black Wings. New York, Allen, 1928.

Screenplays: *The Night of the Pub,* 1920; *The Lotus Eater,* with Marion Fairfax, 1921; *Grand Larceny,* with Bess Meredyth and Charles Kenyon, 1922.

Poetry

Bumps. New York, Harper, 1927.

Other

Syria from the Saddle. New York, Silver Burdett, 1896.
The World's Great Events. New York, Dodd Mead, 1908.
Superwoman. New York, Moffat, 1916; as *Famous Hussies of History,* Cleveland, World, 1943.
Wonder Women in History. London, Cassell, 1918.
Now That I'm Fifty (autobiography). New York, Doran, 1924.
To the Best of My Memory (autobiography). New York, Harper, 1930.
Proving Nothing. New York, Harper, 1930.
The Son of God. New York, Harper, 1932.
The Book of Sunnybank, photographs by Margaret Bourke-White. New York, Harper, 1934; as *Sunnybank, Home of Lad,* New York, Grosset and Dunlap, 1953.
Across the Line, edited by Anice Terhune. New York, Dryden Press, 1945.

*

Manuscript Collections: Library of Congress, Washington, D.C.; Central Connecticut State College, New Britain; Columbia University, New York.

* * *

Albert Payson Terhune was a prolific writer of popular literature in a number of different fields. He spent more than 20 years as an editor and feature and sportswriter for the New York *Evening World.* Outside of his newspaper work, he wrote voluminously as well, producing travel accounts, fiction, popular history, and verse.

Though Terhune was not by intention a "children's writer," his most enduring popularity rests on his famous dog stories, which found a wide, if not an exclusive, audience among young readers. *Lad, A Dog* was published in 1919. Its immediate popularity inspired a second dog story, *Bruce,* which was in turn followed by *Buff, A Collie, Further Adventures of Lad,* and others at the rate of about one a year until 1937.

They were all quite successful and all very much alike. The protagonist in each case is a collie (Terhune bred collies for years) whose adventures are the basis for a loosely gathered series of episodes that make up the book. These canine heroes (Terhune sometimes even calls Lad "the hero dog") embody the author's ideas of high personal virtue: they are brave, loyal, loving, understanding, honorable, and unfailingly obedient to The Law as laid down by The Master. Moreover, they feel every human emotion, including romantic love; Terhune's portrayal of animals is entirely sentimental and anthropomorphic. The analogy between the animal—"brute," as Terhune terms it—and the human world extends to the social order. Terhune makes constant reference to the differences between thoroughbreds and curs, with equally constant comment on the parallels with human behavior.

Terhune's popularity has dimmed over the past 25 years or so; only a few of his books remain in print, mostly the dog stories. Though he had the newspaperman's knack for making his work readable, much of it is by today's standards stilted in language, repetitious in plot, and sentimental in outlook. While it is not inconceivable that some young readers might still enjoy Terhune's dog stories, more naturalistic writing about animals, like Kjelgaard's or Gipson's, has proved to have better staying power.

—Anne Scott MacLeod

THURBER, James (Grover)

Nationality: American. **Born:** Columbus, Ohio, 8 December 1894. **Education:** Ohio State University, Columbus, 1913-14, 1915-18. **Family:** Married 1) Althea Adams in 1922 (divorced 1935), one daughter; 2) Helen Wismer in 1935. **Career:** Code clerk, American Embassy, Paris, 1918-20; reporter, Columbus *Dispatch,* 1920-24, Paris edition of Chicago *Tribune,* 1925-26, and New York *Evening Post,* 1926-27; editor, 1927, writer, 1927-38, then freelance contributor, *New Yorker*; also an illustrator from 1929: several individual shows. **Awards:** Litt.D.: Kenyon College, Gambier, Ohio, 1950; Yale University, New Haven, Connecticut, 1953; L.H.D.: Williams College, Williamstown, Massachusetts, 1951. **Died:** 2 November 1961.

Publications for Children

Fiction

Many Moons, illustrated by Louis Slobodkin. New York, Harcourt Brace, 1943; London, Hamish Hamilton, 1945.
The Great Quillow, illustrated by Doris Lee. New York, Harcourt Brace, 1944.
The White Deer, illustrated by the author and Don Freeman. New York, Harcourt Brace, 1945; London, Hamish Hamilton, 1946.
The 13 Clocks, illustrated by Marc Simont. New York, Simon and Schuster, 1950; London, Hamish Hamilton, 1951.
The Wonderful O, illustrated by Marc Simont. New York, Simon and Schuster, and London, Hamish Hamilton, 1955.

Publications for Adults

Short Stories and Sketches (illustrated by the author)

The Owl in the Attic and Other Perplexities. New York, Harper, 1931.
The Seal in the Bedroom and Other Predicaments. New York, Harper, 1932.
My Life and Hard Times. New York, Harper, 1933.
The Middle-Aged Man on the Flying Trapeze: A Collection of Short Pieces. New York, Harper, and London, Hamish Hamilton, 1935.
Let Your Mind Alone! and Other More or Less Inspirational Pieces. New York, Harper, and London, Hamish Hamilton, 1937.
Cream of Thurber.... London, Hamish Hamilton, 1939.
The Last Flower: A Parable in Pictures. New York, Harper, and London, Hamish Hamilton, 1939.
Fables for Our Time and Famous Poems Illustrated. New York, Harper, and London, Hamish Hamilton, 1940.
My World—and Welcome to It. New York, Harcourt Brace, and London, Hamish Hamilton, 1942.
Men, Women, and Dogs: A Book of Drawings. New York, Harcourt Brace, 1943; London, Hamish Hamilton, 1945.
The Thurber Carnival. New York, Harper, and London, Hamish Hamilton, 1945.
The Beast in Me, and Other Animals: A New Collection of Pieces and Drawings about Human Beings and Less Alarming Creatures. New York, Harcourt Brace, 1948; London, Hamish Hamilton, 1949.
The Thurber Album: A New Collection of Pieces about People. New York, Simon and Schuster, and London, Hamish Hamilton, 1952.
Thurber Country: A New Collection of Pieces about Males and Females, Mainly of Our Own Species. New York, Simon and Schuster, and London, Hamish Hamilton, 1953.
Thurber's Dogs: A Collection of the Master's Dogs, Written and Drawn, Real and Imaginary, Living and Long Ago. New York, Simon and Schuster, and London, Hamish Hamilton, 1955.
A Thurber Garland. London, Hamish Hamilton, 1955.
Further Fables for Our Time. New York, Simon and Schuster, and London, Hamish Hamilton, 1956.
Alarms and Diversions. New York, Harper, and London, Hamish Hamilton, 1957.
Lanterns and Lances. New York, Harper, and London, Hamish Hamilton, 1961.
Credos and Curios. New York, Harper, and London, Hamish Hamilton, 1962.
Vintage Thurber: A Collection...of the Best Writings and Drawings of James Thurber. London, Hamish Hamilton, 2 vols., 1963.
Thurber and Company. New York, Harper, 1966; London, Hamish Hamilton, 1967.
92 Stories. New York, Avenel, 1985.
The Works of James Thurber (selected stories). New York, Longmeadow Press, 1986.

Plays

The Male Animal, with Elliott Nugent (produced New York, 1940; London, 1949). New York, Random House, 1940; London, Hamish Hamilton, 1950.
A Thurber Carnival, adaptation of his own stories (produced Columbus and New York, 1960). New York, French, 1962.

Wrote the books for the following college musical comedies: *Oh My! Omar,* with Hayward M. Anderson, 1921; *Psychomania,* 1922; *Many Moons,* 1922; *A Twin Fix,* with Hayward M. Anderson, 1923; *The Cat and the Riddle,* 1924; *Nightingale,* 1924; *Tell Me Not,* 1924.

Other

Is Sex Necessary? or, Why You Feel the Way You Do, with E.B. White. New York, Harper, 1929; London, Heinemann, 1930.

Thurber on Humor. Columbus, Martha Kinney Cooper Ohioana Library Association, 1953.
The Years with Ross. Boston, Little Brown, and London, Hamish Hamilton, 1959.
Selected Letters, edited by Helen Thurber and Edward Weeks. Boston, Little Brown, 1981; London, Hamish Hamilton, 1982.
Conversations with James Thurber, edited by Thomas French. University Press of Mississippi, 1989.
Collecting Himself: James Thurber on Writing and Writers, edited by Michael Rosen, New York, Harper, and London, Hamish Hamilton, 1989.

*

Bibliographies: *James Thurber: A Bibliography* by Edwin T. Bowden, Columbus, Ohio State University Press, 1968; *James Thurber: An Annotated Bibliography of Criticism* by Sarah Eleanora Toombs, New York, Garland, 1987.

Manuscript Collections: Ohio State University Library, Columbus.

Critical Studies: *James Thurber* by Robert E. Morsberger, New York, Twayne, 1964; *The Art of James Thurber* by Richard C. Tobias, Athens, Ohio University Press, 1969; *James Thurber, His Masquerades: A Critical Study* by Stephen A. Black, The Hague, Mouton, 1970; *The Clocks of Columbus: The Literary Career of James Thurber* by Charles S. Holmes, New York, Atheneum, and London, Secker and Warburg, 1973, and *Thurber: A Collection of Critical Essays* edited by Holmes, Englewood Cliffs, New Jersey, Prentice Hall, 1974; *Thurber: A Biography* by Burton Bernstein, New York, Dodd Mead, and London, Gollancz, 1975; *Thurber's Anatomy of Confusion* by Catherine McGehee Kenney, Hamden, Connecticut, Shoe String Press, 1984; *James Thurber* by Robert Emmet Long, New York, Ungar, 1988.

Illustrator: *No Nice Girl Swears* by Alice Leone Moates, 1933; *Her Foot Is on the Brass Rail* by Don Marquis, 1935; *How to Raise a Dog...* by James R. Kinney and Ann Honeycutt, 1938; *Men Can Take It* by Elizabeth Hawes, 1939; *In a Word* by Margaret Samuels, 1939.

*   *   *

James Thurber, an American original in humor, satire, nonsense, drawing, and patently a wild tyrannothesaurus type when on the hunt for words, slipped into the field of children's literature by the back front gate, like a cat "walking on velvet"—an expression of his own. By 1943 he was well established through the *New Yorker:* (a) in prose; (b) in his childlike drawings of dominant women, dominated men, and semisomnolent dogs; and (c) apart from the *New Yorker,* for such wry pieces of psychological foolery as "The Secret Life of Walter Mitty" and "The Night the Bed Fell." In that year, without any warning, *Many Moons* appeared: a very slight but delicately enchanting fairytale involving royalty and an itemized royal retinue in the royal pecking order of a Lord High Chamberlain, Royal Wizard, Royal Mathematician, Court Jester, and Royal Goldsmith. The King's daughter had fallen ill and wanted the moon. It takes but half an hour to tell you how she got it.

Many Moons was followed by *The Great Quillow,* designed perhaps for a somewhat older group, if one stops to consider its plot and the generous play of its language. And then, though surely *not* aimed just at children, came a trinity: *The White Deer, The 13 Clocks,* and *The Wonderful O.* Call them fairytales, or parodies of fairytales or pseudo fables; they are, it seems, entirely suitable for all readers between 9 and 99 who have imagination and a true sense of the ridiculous. The anatomy of these five books is interchangeable: impossible tasks, indomitable courage, improbable solutions, appropriate wizardry, and nothing so serious or warped as not to be funny.

The Great Quillow, a first-rate tale in concept and execution, offers an outsized giant (instead of a king) who plumps himself down on the edge of a village and not in it. To get rid of him and his crippling daily demands for food and entertainment is the problem facing the village council—tailor, butcher, candymaker, blacksmith, baker, candlemaker, lamplighter, cobbler, carpenter, and locksmith. The toymaker, not of the council, is the David of the story—with a mind more useful than a slingshot, and a blueprint of action which only a Thurber could have given him.

The White Deer follows the old fairytale prescription of tasks set by a princess, and three princes (rated A, D minus, and E) to accomplish them. *The 13 Clocks,* by all odds the one masterpiece of the quintet, was written in Bermuda instead of whatever it was that Thurber went there to write. Delightfully complex, dexterously sinister, mathematically proportional, *The Wonderful O* is all about disappointed pirates on the Island of Ooreo who set about removing the o's from all words that contain them. An attenuated tale, as if the life work of an oölogist (lgist) were reduced t chas befre yur eyes r rbs.

Auden once said he would test a prospective poet by asking if he (or she) likes to make lists of things. No need to ask this of Thurber, who comes across with endless lists so curious they would have delighted Lear, Carroll, Rabelais, and Herman Melville. He loves to ring vowel changes—Rango, Rengo, Ringo, Rongo, Rungo, for example—in dozens of concatenations livelier than the catalogues of ships and whales. And at times he outdoes even L. Frank Baum in nonsense names, words, and phrases: Mok-Mok, Tocko, Duff of the Dolorous Doom, Thag, Wag, Gag; Prince Jorn, Hunder, St. Nillin's Day; Lobo, Bolo, Olob, Obol; Woddly; Golux, Zorn of Zorna, Xingu, the Todal who gleeped; puppybabble, whupple, thrug; "I'll slit you from your guggle to your zatch"; a blob of glup.

Another conspicuous hallmark of Thurber the fairytale teller is an increasing use, in the last three of these books, of rhyme *written as prose,* swimming like the scum on cocoa: "'I like the taste of wine,' he said, 'the feel of leather. I'll ride or drink your father down in any weather.'" You will find this going on more lyrically in E.B. White's *Stuart Little,* published in the same year as Thurber's *The White Deer.* White writes (as in straight prose): "She comes from fields once tall with wheat, from pastures deep in fern and thistle; she comes from vales of meadowsweet, and she loves to whistle." This is not a new trick, but Thurber makes much of it—perhaps too much of it: "'A bell of triumph, or a knell?' 'Time,' the old man said, 'will tell.'"

But his own best trick is a solitary one in that marvelous book *The 13 Clocks:* a couple of limericks done in an inverted style original with him:

> There was an old coddle so molly,
> He talked in a glot that was poly,

His gaws were so gew
That his laps became dew,
And he ate only pops that were lolly.

Two of these books—*The 13 Clocks* and *The Wonderful O*—are illustrated in color by Marc Simont, winner of the 1957 Caldecott Medal. This reader considers Simont's work in *The 13 Clocks* his absolute masterpiece, inseparable from the text as Tenniel's from *Alice.*

—David McCord

THWAITE, Ann (Barbara)

Nationality: British. **Born:** Ann Barbara Harrop, London, 4 October 1932. **Education:** Marsden Collegiate School, Wellington, New Zealand, 1942-45; Queen Elizabeth's Girls' Grammar School, Barnet, Hertfordshire, 1945-51; St. Hilda's College, Oxford, B.A. 1955, M.A. 1959. **Family:** Married the writer Anthony Thwaite in 1955; four daughters. **Career:** Lecturer, 1956-57, and Visiting Professor, 1985-86, Tokyo Women's University; publishers reader, 1958-65. Regular reviewer for *Times Literary Supplement,* London, and other publications, 1963-84; since 1974 member of the Editorial Board, *Cricket* magazine, La Salle, Illinois. **Awards:** Duff Cooper Memorial prize, for nonfiction, 1985. Whitbread Biography of the Year, 1990. **Agent:** Michael Shaw, Curtis Brown, 162-168 Regent Street, London W1R 5TB. **Address:** The Mill House, Low Tharston, Norfolk NR15 2YN, England.

PUBLICATIONS FOR CHILDREN

Fiction

The House in Turner Square, illustrated by Robin Jacques. London, Constable, 1960; New York, Harcourt Brace, 1961.
A Seaside Holiday for Jane and Toby, illustrated by Janet Martin. London, Constable, 1962.
Toby Stays with Jane, illustrated by Janet Martin. London, Constable, 1962.
Jane and Toby Start School, illustrated by Janet Martin. London, Constable, 1965.
Toby Moves House, illustrated by Janet Martin. London, Constable, 1965.
Home and Away, illustrated by Shirley Hughes. Leicester, Brockhampton Press, 1967; as *The Holiday Map,* Chicago, Follett, 1969.
The Travelling Tooth, illustrated by George Thompson. Leicester, Brockhampton Press, 1968.
The Day with the Duke, illustrated by George Him. Leicester, Brockhampton Press, and New York, World, 1969.
The Camelthorn Papers. London, Macmillan, 1969.
The Only Treasure, illustrated by Glenys Ambrus. Leicester, Brockhampton Press, 1970.
The Poor Pigeon, illustrated by Glenys Ambrus. Leicester, Brockhampton Press, 1974; Chicago, Children's Press, 1976.
Rose in the River, illustrated by John Dyke. Leicester, Brockhampton Press, 1974; Chicago, Children's Press, 1976.
Horrible Boy, illustrated by Glenys Ambrus. Leicester, Brockhampton Press, 1975; Chicago, Children's Press, 1976.
The Chatterbox, illustrated by Glenys Ambrus. London, Deutsch, 1978.
Tracks, illustrated by Gavin Rowe. London, Methuen, 1978.
A Piece of Parkin: A True Story from the Autobiography of Frances Hodgson Burnett, illustrated by Glenys Ambrus. London, Deutsch, 1980.
Pennies for the Dog, illustrated by Margery Gill. London, Deutsch, 1985.
Gilbert and the Birthday Cake, illustrated by Jack Harvey. London, Hutchinson, 1986.
Amy and the Night-Time Visits, illustrated by J.C. Skinner. London, Deutsch, 1987.
The Ashton Affair. London, Scholastic, 1995.
The Horse at Hilly Fields, illustrated by Elaine Mills. London, Scholastic, 1995.

Other

The Young Traveller in Japan. London, Phoenix House, 1958.

Editor, *Allsorts 1-7.* London, Macmillan, 5 vols., 1969-72, and Methuen, 2 vols., 1974-75.
Editor, *All Sorts of Poems.* London, Angus and Robertson, 1978.

PUBLICATIONS FOR ADULTS

Other

Waiting for the Party: The Life of Frances Hodgson Burnett 1849-1924. London, Secker and Warburg, and New York, Scribner, 1974; new and revised edition, Boston, Godine, 1991, and London, Faber, 1994.
Edmund Gosse: A Literary Landscape 1849-1928. London, Secker and Warburg, and Chicago, University of Chicago Press, 1984.
A.A. Milne: His Life. London, Faber, and Boston, Faber, 1990.
The Brilliant Career of Winnie-the-Pooh. London, Methuen, 1992, and New York, Dutton, 1994.

Editor, *My Oxford.* London, Robson, 1977; with *My Cambridge,* edited by Ronald Hayman, New York, Taplinger, 1979.
Editor, *Portraits from Life* by Edmund Gosse. London, Scolar Press, 1991.

*

Ann Thwaite comments:

My work over 25 years was almost entirely devoted to children's books—reviewing, editing, talking about them, writing them. My main interests have been in bringing good reading and children together, and in preserving in fictional form my own experiences of children and places. My interest in children's writers of the past led me to spend four years writing a definitive biography of Frances Hodgson Burnett, and this book has taken me at last outside the field of children's books. I have now written a full-scale biography of Edmund Gosse, but I am still involved in many different ways with children's reading. My biography of A.A. Milne was published in 1990 and was followed by a scrapbook devoted to his most famous characters. Now I am working on a biography of Emily Tennyson, the poet's wife, but I am happy to have written my first children's novel for many years and also the text of a picture book for my grandchildren.

* * *

What marks Ann Thwaite's work—her own and the selections for the *Allsorts* anthologies—is her acute understanding of contemporary sensibilities. Her eye unerringly selects the stories of daily life that are the stuff of fiction. Her ear is tuned to the rhythms of everyday speech and to the finer diction of contemporary poetry.

From her picture books to her junior novels, Thwaite chooses stories that apparently play within conventional forms of children's literature but ultimately subvert them. *The Chatterbox,* a picture book, is a "cautionary tale for teachers" as Thwaite says—rather than the more usual caution for children. The story is about the virtue of talking in a primary school, rather than the virtue of silence.

Both *The Only Treasure* and *The Camelthorn Papers,* for older children, look like they ought to be conventional adventure stories of the kind that take in everything from *Treasure Island* to *The Famous Five.* But they're not. *The Only Treasure,* set in Jersey, does include the requisite map, notes on caves, and a mysterious warning to "Watch out for the only treasure." The heroine, Anna, does set out on what she imagines is a storybook adventure. She also thinks that the elegant Felicity, daughter of the local hotel owners, can help her. Instead it is Felicity who puts Anna in danger, and who is the "only treasure" of the warning.

The Camelthorn Papers, set in Libya, chronicles the adventures of English sisters Kate and Jessica and their half-English, half-Egyptian friend Gamal. It too begins as an apparently traditional adventure. Kate promises grocer Derek Lister, father of her best friend in England, that she will try to find the metal box of poems and journals he buried near Benghazi, under a camelthorn tree, just before he was taken prisoner during World War II. Kate, like Anna, does not find the treasure she was looking for. Instead she finds a story of loss: Derek Lister's lost youth and lost opportunity to be a poet; and the graves of the lost young men from England, Europe, and the Middle East who lie dead in the cemeteries. But there are other signs of loss in the story. There are, for example, snatches of poetry about loss from Philip Larkin and Wilfred Owen. In one remarkable scene, the children come upon a young man who appears to be drowned. Kate gives him artificial respiration. In a garden-variety children's story, the man is supposed to revive. In *The Camelthorn Papers* he doesn't. So by the time Kate finds Derek Lister's tin box under the camelthorn tree, the fact that the papers have crumbled to dust is not unexpected. The story Thwaite tells is not one of happily-ever-after fairytales, but a contemporary story of choices and possibilities, coded in the refrain that runs through the book: "He who does not keep moving is lost."

In her fiction, Thwaite's ear for contemporary language often appears in the way she captures uncomfortable exchanges between parents and children. In *The Camelthorn Papers,* it is in Kate's embarrassment at the banality of her mother's conversation. In *Tracks* Julie finds herself in the awkward position of arriving just as Ross is having an argument with his father about clothes. Ross, a typical teenager, wants to wear a comfortably tattered tee-shirt for a hike on the mountain. His father tells him to "go and change immediately"—a standard response. Thwaite's skill in the weaving of plot and language is evident in the story: proper mountain-climbing clothes become an integral part of the plot of the novel when Ross suffers from hypothermia.

It is inappropriate to close without mentioning *Allsorts,* an annual anthology of poems, stories, puzzles, and the like (in the tradition of the sort popular in the 19th century) she edited between 1969 and 1975. Thwaite commissioned new material for the anthologies, and each one is a tribute to the excellence of her literary taste. Children who received her *Allsorts* annuals were exposed very early to the likes of Vernon Scannell, X. J. Kennedy, Roy Fuller, Philip Larkin, Anthony Thwaite, Stevie Smith, Ted Hughes, James Fenton, Dannie Abse, Ian Serraillier, and Charles Causley. The list goes on, but it certainly includes most of the finest poets of our time, some of whom were chosen just as they were beginning to establish their reputations. What better introduction, for children (or grown-ups for that matter) to pleasures of contemporary literature?

—Lissa Paul

TITUS, Eve

Pseudonym: Nancy Lord. **Nationality:** American. **Born:** New York City, 16 July 1922. **Education:** New York University. **Family:** Divorced; one son. **Career:** Professional pianist. **Agent:** McIntosh and Otis Inc., 310 Madison Avenue, New York, New York 10017, U.S.A.

Publications for Children

Fiction (illustrated by Paul Galdone)

Anatole. New York, McGraw Hill, 1956; London, Lane, 1957.
Anatole and the Cat. New York, McGraw Hill, 1957; London, Lane, 1958.
Basil of Baker Street. New York, McGraw Hill, 1958.
My Dog and I (as Nancy Lord). New York, McGraw Hill, 1958.
Anatole and the Robot. New York, McGraw Hill, 1960; London, Bodley Head, 1961.
Anatole over Paris. New York, McGraw Hill, 1961; London, Bodley Head, 1962.
Basil and the Lost Colony. New York, McGraw Hill, 1964; London, Hodder and Stoughton, 1975.
Anatole and the Poodle. New York, McGraw Hill, 1965; London, Bodley Head, 1966.
Anatole and the Piano. New York, McGraw Hill, 1966; London, Bodley Head, 1967.
Anatole and the Thirty Thieves. New York, McGraw Hill, and London, Bodley Head, 1969.
Anatole and the Toyshop. New York, McGraw Hill, 1970.
Basil and the Pygmy Cats. New York, McGraw Hill, 1971; London, Hodder and Stoughton, 1977.
Anatole in Italy. New York, McGraw Hill, 1973; London, Bodley Head, 1974.
Basil in Mexico. New York, McGraw Hill, 1976.
Anatole and the Pied Piper. New York, McGraw Hill, 1979.
Basil in the Wild West. New York, McGraw Hill, 1981.

Other

The Mouse and the Lion, illustrated by Leonard Weisgard. New York, Parents' Magazine Press, 1962.
The Two Stonecutters, illustrated by Yoko Mitsuhashi. New York, Doubleday, 1967.
Mr. Shaw's Shipshape Shoeshop, illustrated by Larry Ross. New York, Parents' Magazine Press, 1970.
Why the Wind God Wept, illustrated by James Barkley. New York, Doubleday, 1972.
The Kitten Who Couldn't Purr, illustrated by Amrei Fechner. New York, Morrow, 1991.

*

Manuscript Collections: Case Collection, Wayne State University, Detroit.

* * *

Eve Titus is known primarily for her Anatole and Basil books, but she has written several individual stories for magazines and in book form. The series stories maintain a high standard in plot and style and have the precision and rhythm expected of a musician.

Anatole was her first published book, and it has remained the most prominent. Anatole is a French mouse whose occupation is cheese tasting for M'sieu Duval. Either the cheese factory or Anatole's family is threatened in a different manner in each book, and the mouse *magnifique* comes to the rescue. The specific character or situation is obvious from the title. The belling of the cat is the classical theme used for the second story, while the robot Cheezak provides the challenge in the third book. The next six books deal with his family stranded on the Eiffel tower, the kidnapping of the model poodle Juliette, the salvaging of pearls from a grand piano, the foiling of thieves, the rescuing of his family from the clutches of a toyshop owner, and his visit to a cheese factory in Italy. *Anatole and the Toyshop* is the most dramatic, for the proprietor forces his six youngsters to ride their bicycles around the window display continually to attract an audience of shoppers.

The swiftly moving stories are sprinkled with French phrases and words. Repetition is used in introducing Anatole's wife Doucette, and their children, Paul, Paulette, Claude, Claudette, Georges, and Georgette. The three suspects in the Great Cheese Robbery are Baptiste the Baker, Blanchard the Barber, and Bernard the Bookseller. Titus uses rhythmical phrasing ("Concerning cheese, the world agrees a mouse's nose is better than a policeman's") and her sense of humor is revealed both in the situations and in the language, such as "And be quiet as mice!"

While Anatole is French, Basil is British and the books about him are written in the style of Arthur Conan Doyle's *Sherlock Holmes.* Basil lives at Baker Street, Number 221-B and solves mysteries with his doctor companion, David Q. Dawson. Plots, characters, and language have parallels with the Sherlockian canon. The introductory paragraphs tantalize, digress, and then proceed to the basic story. Conclusions invariably point to another adventure, as in *Basil and the Pygmy Cats* where there is reference to a Mexican adventure, and in *Basil and the Lost Colony* a mysterious note arrives. In the latter book, the detective and companion visit Tellmice, in which the inhabitants are unaware that Switzerland has regained her freedom in 1291. "Relda" the mouse opera star is introduced in the book, while Professor Ratigan, leader of the mouse underworld, captures the adventures in *Basil and the Pygmy Cats.*

The language used alludes to both mice and to Holmes. "Pawhand" and "shortpaw" refer to writing, while "Mouseland Yard" and "Mousemoor Prison" are locations; and after a heroic episode, Basil is elected to lifetime membership in the Royal Academy of Mousology. In Holmesian tradition, Basil uses his deductive powers, wears a Persian robe, plays the violin, and enjoys Mrs. Judson's cheese soufflé. There is even the identification, "'Basil of Baker Street, I presume?'" Inconsistencies are rare, but Basil's pipe is described as being both "berrywood" and "meerwood" in *Basil of Baker Street.*

Titus has written other stories, but they don't have the inventiveness of those about Anatole and Basil. *My Dog and I,* written under the pseudonym Nancy Lord, is a slight picture book. *The Two Stonecutters* is a free adaptation from the Japanese, and too elaborate for a folktale. There is only a reference to the historic meeting in *The Mouse and the Lion,* a "Reading Readiness book" in which the lion visits the world of people and the mouse has almost no role. *Mr. Shaw's Shipshape Shoeshop* has rhythm and a strong plot, but is too long. The Anatole and Basil books far outweigh the others in impact and popularity. The two characters are important enough to be represented by entries in Margery Fisher's *Who's Who in Children's Books.* Since the audience reading Basil books is considerably younger than those reading the Sherlock Holmes books, they may be seen as preparation for the Victorian detective rather than as a pastiche.

—Karen Nelson Hoyle

TODD, Barbara Euphan

Has also written as Barbara Bower; Euphan. **Nationality:** British. **Born:** Arksey, Yorkshire, 9 January 1890(?). **Education:** St. Catherine's School, Bramley, Surrey. **Military Service:** Voluntary Aid Detachment, 1914-18. **Family:** Married John Graham Bower in 1932 (died 1940). **Career:** Regular contributor to *Punch,* London. **Died:** 2 February 1976.

Publications for Children

Fiction

The 'normous Saturday Fairy Book, with Marjory Royce and Moira Meighn. London, Stanley Paul, 1924.
The 'normous Sunday Story Book, with Marjory Royce and Moira Meighn. London, Stanley Paul, 1925.
The Very Good Walkers, with Marjory Royce, illustrated by H.R. Millar. London, Methuen, 1925.
Mr. Blossom's Shop. London, Nelson, 1929.
Happy Cottage, with Marjory Royce. London, Collins, 1930.
South Country Secrets (as Euphan), with Klaxon. London, Burns Oates, 1935.
The Touchstone, with Klaxon. London, Burns Oates, 1935.

Worzel Gummidge; or, The Scarecrow of Scatterbrook, illustrated by Elizabeth Alldridge. London, Burns Oates, 1936.
Worzel Gummidge Again, illustrated by Elizabeth Alldridge. London, Burns Oates, 1937.
The Mystery Train. London, University of London Press, 1937.
The Splendid Picnic. London, University of London Press, 1937.
More about Worzel Gummidge. London, Burns Oates, 1938.
Mr. Dock's Garden, illustrated by Ruth Westcott. Leeds, E.J. Arnold, 1939.
Gertrude the Greedy Goose, illustrated by Benjamin Rabier. London, Muller, 1939.
The House That Ran Behind, with Esther Boumphrey. London, Muller, 1943.
Worzel Gummidge, The Scarecrow of Scatterbrook Farm (from *Worzel Gummidge; or, The Scarecrow of Scatterbrook* and *Worzel Gummidge Again*), illustrated by Ursula Koering. New York, Putnam, 1947.
Worzel Gummidge and Saucy Nancy, illustrated by Will Nickless. London, Hollis and Carter, 1947.
Worzel Gummidge Takes a Holiday, illustrated by Will Nickless. London, Hollis and Carter, 1949.
Aloysius Let Loose, with Klaxon, illustrated by A.E. Batchelor. London, Collins, 1950.
Earthy Mangold and Worzel Gummidge, illustrated by Jill Crockford. London, Hollis and Carter, 1954.
Worzel Gummidge and the Railway Scarecrows, illustrated by Jill Crockford. London, Evans, 1955.
Worzel Gummidge at the Circus, illustrated by Jill Crockford. London, Evans, 1956.
The Boy with the Green Thumb, illustrated by Charlotte Hough. London, Hamish Hamilton, 1956.
The Wizard and the Unicorn, illustrated by Prudence Seward. London, Hamish Hamilton, 1957.
Worzel Gummidge and the Treasure Ship, illustrated by Jill Crockford. London, Evans, 1958.
The Shop Around the Corner, illustrated by Olive Coughlan. London, Hamish Hamilton, 1959.
Detective Worzel Gummidge, illustrated by Jill Crockford. London, Evans, 1963.
The Shop by the Sea, illustrated by Sarah Garland. London, Hamish Hamilton, 1966.
The Clock Shop, illustrated by Jill Crockford. Kingswood, Surrey, World's Work, 1967.
The Shop on Wheels, illustrated by Jill Crockford. Kingswood, Surrey, World's Work, 1968.
The Box in the Attic, illustrated by Lynette Hemmant. Kingswood, Surrey, World's Work, 1970.
The Wand from France, illustrated by Lynette Hemmant. Kingswood, Surrey, World's Work, 1972.

Plays

The Frog Prince, with Mabel Constanduros. London, French, 1956.
The Sleeping Beauty, with Mabel Constanduros. London, French, 1956.

Poetry

Hither and Thither. London, Harrap, 1927.
The Seventh Daughter (as Euphan). London, Burns Oates, 1935.

Other

Stories of the Coronations (as Euphan), with Klaxon. London, Burns Oates, 1937.

PUBLICATIONS FOR ADULTS

Novels

Miss Ranskill Comes Home (as Barbara Bower). London, Chapman and Hall, and New York, Putnam, 1946.

* * *

The fame of Barbara Euphan Todd will rest on the stories that feature Worzel Gummidge and his fellow scarecrows. Typically, in *Worzel Gummidge; or, The Scarecrow of Scatterbrook,* John and Susan, aged 10 and 12, spend holidays at Scatterbrook Farm where they have hilarious and singularly credible adventures, protecting the nature and escapades of these walking, talking scarecrows from discovery by adults. These stories are for sharing and are excellent for reading aloud to children of eight or nine in chapters sufficiently self-contained to make satisfactory reading units. The dialogue of the scarecrows, such as "'Tain't disgustin'" will present problems to some children who try to read the stories for themselves, but there is a strong incentive to succeed.

The older people, especially the patronising though well-meaning Mrs. Bloomsbury-Barton, tend to be caricatures of "not-understanding" adults. But they are merely foils: the scarecrows themselves are strongly individualised and have real life breathed into them. Chief among these is Worzel Gummidge himself, with his turnip head, broomstick arms, and bottle-straw boots; he is full of professional pride, unpredictable, and almost always irritatingly right. Earthy Mangold is not very bright and is professionally most inept, but she "allus tries to be comfortin'"; it is typical of her that she shoos away the hens so that the sparrows may get the grain, and that she cannot think of her hedgerow origin without aching once more to shelter the nests of the small birds and feel their wings flutter among her boughs. Little Upsidaisy, made from a milking stool, isn't very bright either, but she is always cheerful, while valetudinarian Hannah Harrow suffers from a variety of extraordinary complaints, from the "damping off" to "the mice"—for which complaint she is advised by her friends to swallow a mousetrap.

In all these stories, the excitement lies in the adventures and the fun in the dialogue, especially in the scarecrows' irrefutable logic from quaint premises. Here is Gummidge's justification for his threat to wish that all human beings were turned into earwigs: "Nobody wouldn't think as grass could turn into milk, but it does," argued Gummidge. "And humans is more the shape o' earwigs than grass is the shape o'milk. Stands to reason."

The stories without Gummidge in the title have no scarecrows in them, and so lack their author's most magic touch, though they are mostly about magic. For instance, Fred has a Green Thumb, which brings to life a donkey cut in a hedge and causes a red hot poker plant to set fire to a sweet shop, while candytuft becomes real candy to replace lost sweets. These books, also, are good for reading aloud in convenient chapter units and are easier than the Gummidge books for younger children to read for themselves.

—Norman Culpan

TOLKIEN, J(ohn) R(onald) R(euel)

Nationality: British. **Born:** Bloemfontein, South Africa, 3 January 1892; came to England, 1895. **Education:** King Edward's School, Birmingham, 1900-02, 1903-11; St. Philip's School, Birmingham, 1902-03; Exeter College, Oxford (open classical exhibitioner; Skeat prize, 1914), 1911-15, B.A. (honours), 1915, M.A. 1919. **Military Service:** Lancashire Fusiliers, 1915-18: Lieutenant. **Family:** Married Edith Mary Bratt in 1916 (died 1971); three sons and one daughter. **Career:** Assistant, Oxford English Dictionary, 1919-20; Reader in English, 1920-23, and Professor of the English Language, 1924-25, University of Leeds, Yorkshire. At Oxford University: Rawlinson and Bosworth Professor of Anglo-Saxon, 1925-45; Fellow, Pembroke College, 1926-45; Leverhulme Research Fellow, 1934-36; Merton Professor of English Language and Literature, 1945-59; Honorary Fellow, Exeter College, 1963; Emeritus Fellow, Merton College. Andrew Lang Lecturer, University of St. Andrews, Fife, 1939; W.P. Ker Lecturer, University of Glasgow, 1953. Artist: individual show, Ashmolean Museum, Oxford, 1977. **Awards:** International Fantasy Award, 1957; Royal Society of Literature Benson Medal, 1966; Foreign Book Prize (France), 1973; World Science Fiction Convention Gandalf Award, 1974; Hugo Award, 1978. D.Litt.: University College, Dublin, 1954; University of Nottingham, 1970; Oxford University, 1972; Dr. en Phil et Lettres: Liège, 1954; honorary degree: University of Edinburgh, 1973. Fellow, Royal Society of Literature, 1957. C.B.E. (Commander, Order of the British Empire), 1972. **Died:** 2 September 1973.

Publications for Children

Fiction

The Hobbit; or, There and Back Again, illustrated by the author. London, Allen and Unwin, 1937; Boston, Houghton Mifflin, 1938; revised edition, 1951; revised edition, 1966; *The Annotated Hobbit,* edited by Douglas A. Anderson, London, Unwin Hyman, and Boston, Houghton Mifflin, 1989.

Farmer Giles of Ham, illustrated by Pauline Baynes. London, Allen and Unwin, 1949; Boston, Houghton Mifflin, 1950.

Smith of Wootton Major, illustrated by Pauline Baynes. London, Allen and Unwin, and Boston, Houghton Mifflin, 1967.

The Father Christmas Letters, edited by Baillie Tolkien, illustrated by the author. London, Allen and Unwin, and Boston, Houghton Mifflin, 1976.

Mr. Bliss, illustrated by the author. London, Allen and Unwin, 1982.

Roverandom, illustrated by the author and edited by Christina Scull and Wayne G. Hammond. London, HarperCollins, 1998.

Poetry

The Adventures of Tom Bombadil and Other Verses from the Red Book, illustrated by Pauline Baynes. London, Allen and Unwin, 1962; Boston, Houghton Mifflin, 1963.

Bilbo's Last Song, illustrated by Pauline Baynes. London, Allen and Unwin, and Boston, Houghton Mifflin, 1974.

Oliphaunt, illustrated by Hank Hinton. Chicago, Contemporary Books, 1989.

Publications for Adults

Novels

The Lord of the Rings:

The Fellowship of the Ring. London, Allen and Unwin, and Boston, Houghton Mifflin, 1954; revised edition, Allen and Unwin, 1966; Houghton Mifflin, 1967.

The Two Towers. London, Allen and Unwin, 1954; Boston, Houghton Mifflin, 1955; revised edition, Allen and Unwin, 1966; Houghton Mifflin, 1967.

The Return of the King. London, Allen and Unwin, 1955; Boston, Houghton Mifflin, 1956; revised edition, Allen and Unwin, 1966; Houghton Mifflin, 1967.

The Silmarillion, edited by Christopher Tolkien. London, Allen and Unwin, and Boston, Houghton Mifflin, 1977.

Morgoth's Ring. London, HarperCollins, 1993.

The War of the Jewels. London, HarperCollins, 1994.

The Peoples of Middle-Earth. London, HarperCollins, 1996.

Short Stories

Unfinished Tales of Númenór and Middle-Earth, edited by Christopher Tolkien. London, Allen and Unwin, and Boston, Houghton Mifflin, 1980.

Play

The Homecoming of Beorhtnoth Beorhthelm's Son (radio broadcast, 1954). Included in *The Tolkien Reader,* 1966; in *Tree and Leaf, Smith of Wootton Major, The Homecoming of Beorhtnoth Beorhthelm's Son,* 1975.

Poetry

Songs for the Philologists, with others. Privately printed, 1936.

The Road Goes Ever On: A Song Cycle, music by Donald Swann. Boston, Houghton Mifflin, 1967; London, Allen and Unwin, 1968; revised edition, Houghton Mifflin, 1978.

Poems and Stories. London, Allen and Unwin, 1980.

Other

A Middle English Vocabulary. Oxford, Clarendon Press, and New York, Oxford University Press, 1922.

Beowulf: The Monsters and the Critics. London, Oxford University Press, 1937.

Tree and Leaf (includes short story "Leaf by Niggle" and essay "On Fairy-Stories"). London, Allen and Unwin, 1964; Boston, Houghton Mifflin, 1965; revised edition, London, Unwin Hyman, 1988.

The Tolkien Reader. New York, Ballantine, 1966.

Tree and Leaf, Smith of Wootton Major, The Homecoming of Beorhtnoth Beorhthelm's Son. London, Allen and Unwin, 1975.

Pictures. London, Allen and Unwin, and Boston, Houghton Mifflin, 1979.

The Letters of J.R.R. Tolkien, edited by Humphrey Carpenter. London, Allen and Unwin, and Boston, Houghton Mifflin, 1981.

Finn and Hengest: The Fragment and the Episode, edited by Alan Bliss. London, Allen and Unwin, and Boston, Houghton Mifflin, 1983.

The Monsters and the Critics and Other Essays, edited by Christopher Tolkien. London, Allen and Unwin, 1983; Boston, Houghton Mifflin, 1984.
The History of Middle-Earth, edited by Christopher Tolkien:
The Book of Lost Tales 1-2. London, Allen and Unwin, 2 vols., 1983-84; Boston, Houghton Mifflin, 2 vols., 1984.
The Lays of Beleriand. London, Allen and Unwin, and Boston, Houghton Mifflin, 1985.
The Shaping of Middle-Earth. London, Allen and Unwin, and Boston, Houghton Mifflin, 1986.
The Lost Road and Other Writings. London, Unwin Hyman, and Boston, Houghton Mifflin, 1987.
The Return of the Shadow. London, Unwin Hyman, 1988; Boston, Houghton Mifflin, 1989.
The Treason of Isengard: The History of The Lord of the Rings, Part 2. Boston, Houghton Mifflin, 1989.
The War of the Ring: The History of The Lord of the Rings, Part 3. Boston, Houghton Mifflin, 1990.
Sauron Defeated: The History of The Lord of the Rings, Part 4. Boston, Houghton Mifflin, 1992.

Editor, with E. V. Gordon, *Sir Gawain and the Green Knight.* Oxford, Clarendon Press, and New York, Oxford University Press, 1925.
Editor, *Ancrene Wisse.* London, Oxford University Press, 1962; New York, Oxford University Press, 1963.

Translator, *Sir Gawain and the Green Knight, Pearl, and Sir Orfeo,* edited by Christopher Tolkien. London, Allen and Unwin, and Boston, Houghton Mifflin, 1975.
Translator, *The Old English Exodus,* edited by Joan Turville-Petre. Oxford, Clarendon Press, 1981.

*

Bibliography: *Tolkien Criticism: An Annotated Checklist* by Richard C. West, Kent, Ohio, Kent State University Press, 1970; revised edition, 1981.

Manuscript Collections: Wade Collection, Wheaton College, Illinois; Marquette University, Milwaukee.

Critical Studies (selection): *Master of Middle-Earth: The Fiction of J.R.R. Tolkien* by Paul Kocher, Boston, Houghton Mifflin, 1972, London, Thames and Hudson, 1973; *Tolkien's World,* London, Thames and Hudson, and Boston, Houghton Mifflin, 1974, and *Tolkien and the Silmarils,* Thames and Hudson, 1981, both by Randel Helms; *J.R.R. Tolkien: A Biography* (includes bibliography) by Humphrey Carpenter, London, Allen and Unwin, and Boston, Houghton Mifflin, 1977; *The Mythology of Middle-Earth* by Ruth S. Noel, London, Thames and Hudson, and Boston, Houghton Mifflin, 1977; *The Complete Guide to Middle-Earth* by Robert Foster, London, Allen and Unwin, and New York, Ballantine, 1978; *Tolkien's Art: A Mythology for England* by Jane C. Nitzche, London, Macmillan, 1979; *Tolkien: New Critical Perspectives* edited by Neil D. Isaacs and Rose A. Zimbardo, Lexington, University Press of Kentucky, 1981; *The Road to Middle-Earth* by T.A. Shippey, London, Allen and Unwin, 1982, Boston, Houghton Mifflin, 1983; *J.R.R. Tolkien: This Far Land* edited by Robert Giddings, London, Vision, 1983; *The Song of Middle-Earth: J.R.R. Tolkien's Themes, Symbols, and Myths* by David Harvey, London, Allen and Unwin, 1985.

* * *

The fantasy world of J.R.R. Tolkien, scholar and professor of mediaeval literature, had its base in stories he told to himself during his adolescence, which he elaborated during World War I into the saga of *The Silmarillion,* the love story of a beautiful Elf-woman and a mortal man. The story gave substance to a language he had invented—Elvish—and was inspired by his own love affair with his future wife. *The Silmarillion* remained unpublished until 1977, but other stories about his imaginary world of Middle-earth became world-famous. Although Tolkien's Middle-earth is based on our world, a new geography of mountain ranges and coastlines has been superimposed. In this essay, I will deal with the Middle-earth fantasies *The Hobbit* and *The Lord of the Rings* (a work, probably, for adults, but one which is certainly enjoyed by many children) and the children's stories *Farmer Giles of Ham, Smith of Wootton Major,* "Leaf by Niggle," *The Father Christmas Letters,* and *Mr. Bliss.*

In the traditional English way, Tolkien's first published story came about as a family tale told to his children in the 1930s. The word "hobbit" swam into his head, and soon he had invented the genus of hole-dwelling manikins, 3-4 feet high, domesticated yet tough—idealised versions of the Olde English countryman. Published in 1937, *The Hobbit* was an extraordinary book for its time. The mood of children's books was realistic and anti-magical; critics and teachers demanded books about working-class urban life and thought magic was babyish. The fact that attitudes have changed so much over the years is due in no small measure to Tolkien. Those who enjoyed his books had to justify themselves. Inspired by his own essay "On Fairy-Stories," his readers found good reasons for reading fairytales in anthropological theories of human development. The human psyche, according to Jung, needed the emotional nourishment of tales of Quest, Victory of the Youngest Son, and Defeat of the Dragon if it was ever to mature. Primitive tribes knew this instinctively; modern man needed to relearn it.

The Hobbit is a comic and tragic tale, rich in magical adventure. Characters like the cantankerous old wizard Gandalf, the dragon Smaug, evil Gollum, and the 13 dwarves are all famous now. Bilbo, the Hobbit, undergoes great trials to discover courage and maturity. Although the climax is a terrible battle, the moral crux of the book comes earlier. Thorin, the chief dwarf, owes his treasure to the hero who slew the dragon, but refuses to give him any reward, although he and his fellow Lake-men are made homeless when the dragon dies. Thorin fails the test, but Bilbo redeems him by giving the men an ancestral treasure of the dwarves to help their bargaining. One can only marvel at the imagination which created the sequence of exciting adventures in which elements from Norse and Teutonic myth have been blended—trolls, elves, giant spiders, a were-bear, dragon, wild wolves, and goblins all appear.

A sequel to *The Hobbit* was demanded, and for years Tolkien laboured to fit this story into the framework of Middle-earth history he had begun with *The Silmarillion.* To continue the story of the magic ring of invisibility which Bilbo "stole" from Gollum, Tolkien would have to start thousands of years after *The Silmarillion* takes place. The main characters would still be elves and men, and they would fight Sauron, servant of Morgoth who stole the silmarils of the earlier book. But he now had his hobbits as well, as comic commentary on the epic situation, and so his theme could be, as with *The Hobbit,* the triumph of weak over strong.

The Lord of the Rings tells how Frodo, Bilbo's nephew, inherits Bilbo's magic invisible ring, and with it a great burden. The ring can make its owner Ruler of the World (as in Wagner's Ring Cycle) and so it must be destroyed before Sauron, Lord of the Rings, who made it, can find it again. Frodo has to make the long and desperately dangerous journey to Sauron's country, Mordor, to throw the Ring into the Cracks of Doom.

Once more we marvel at the author's imagination, as the narrative is sustained through three long volumes. New adventures, heroes, and horrors meet us in every chapter. After volume 1, the fellowship of the Ring divides, and we follow the fortunes of three separate groups. We encounter terrors like the Mines of Moria, Shelob the Spider, and the invisible Black Riders; beauty in Goldberry the River's daughter, Lórien the hidden forest; and fight the battles of Helm's Deep and the Pelennor Fields.

With a book so strong in plot, other elements must be weaker. There is no subtle characterisation: just good and evil, white and black. Moral choices are easily perceived, though not so easily made for all that: Boromir, for instance, makes the wrong choice, though basically a good man, and both Gollum and Saruman have a chance to repent. One cannot criticise Tolkien, however, for keeping to the laws of his genre and failing to give us the complex character analysis of the 20th-century novel. In a prose epic modelled on fairytale, many characters are unrounded because they are essentially archetypal. And so we have Aragorn the Hero, Arwen the Princess, Éowyn the Amazon, Galadriel the Enchantress, and Gandalf the Wizard.

In an epic where good must eventually triumph, fate and luck often work on the side of Good. Tolkien occasionally hints that a Power is influencing events, though the characters still have the free will to take or reject these opportunities. So coincidence is frequently used: rescues happen in the nick of time, people meet by chance—yet those in tune with higher powers, such as Gandalf and Tom Bombadil, question whether chance is really the right word, if a Higher Power is at work.

Tolkien's epic style is often a stumbling-block to his critics. *The Lord of the Rings* is far from completely epic in diction, and the hobbits' conversation and jokes are informal enough, but when Heroes talk with Elves and Wizards, an antique style is used in which the language derives from Old English. "Verily," said Gandalf, "...that way lies our hope, where sits our greatest fear. Doom hangs still on a thread." The society of the horse-riders of Rohan is deliberately modeled on Anglo-Saxon culture, and their poetry, which Tolkien quotes, paraphrases Old English verse. However, while some critics complain of hackneyed clichés, others welcome the historical insight the style affords—especially teachers who have found Tolkien a great inspiration to students to return to the original sagas and epics. Certainly where children are concerned, *The Lord of the Rings* is a book which opens the door to adult literature. (It can be read by good readers from the age of eight upward.)

Tolkien's shorter tales also became bestsellers. There was *Farmer Giles of Ham,* about a dragon less successful than Smaug, which also gave the supposed origins of the Oxfordshire villages of Thame and Worminghall. Two shorter stories, *Smith of Wootton Major* and "Leaf by Niggle," are really parables about Tolkien at the end of his career, the former about giving up trips to fairyland and the latter about facing death with his work unfinished. For *The Silmarillion,* the first child of his imagination, was still unpublished, pestering from fans continually interrupted him, and since *The Lord of the Rings* was published there had been many inconsistencies to correct.

The first fictional work to be published since his death was *The Father Christmas Letters* written yearly to his children in the guise of Father Christmas. Illustrated by the author, they are destined to become a children's classic. Father Christmas is helped, and hindered, by accident-prone Polar Bear, a new kind of comic character for Tolkien.

Mr. Bliss reproduces the manuscript of an unpublished story Tolkien wrote and illustrated for his children in the early 1930s; in its modern publication a printed text has been provided on facing pages, although Tolkien's graceful handwriting is still legible. It is a nonsense-tale about an eccentric man who has adventures with his new car, and has some affinities with Beatrix Potter's work. It also looks forward to the Shire of the hobbits in its portrayal of a Cotswold village at the turn of the century.

Tolkien left so many unpublished drafts of his Middle-earth tales that his son Christopher has continued to sort and transcribe them, with the possibility of working right through until the end of *The Lord of the Rings.* The first five volumes of *The History of Middle-earth* deal with early versions of *The Silmarillion,* which began as *The Book of Lost Tales* in 1917, when Tolkien was convalescing after the battle of the Somme. Volume 3, *The Lays of Beleriand,* contains poetic versions of two of the tales, and is probably the most accessible of these five books. With volume 6, *The Return of the Shadow,* Christopher began to transcribe early versions of *The Lord of the Rings,* and therefore this book is of absorbing interest to any lover of *The Fellowship of the Ring.* In first draft it appears to be much more of a "children's book," with its hero Bingo and the mysterious Trotter, and its informal, slangy dialogue; and one gradually notes, as chapters are redrafted, its evolution towards epic quality, taking on a more formal literary style and doom-laden theme.

Critics have argued since Edmund Wilson's criticism in 1956 about whether *The Lord of the Rings* is a great book. *The Lord of the Rings* has also inspired many children's and adult authors to write heroic fantasy, especially in trilogy form. Children's authors who have acknowledged a debt to Tolkien include Lloyd Alexander, C.S. Lewis, and Susan Cooper; others who feel they must react against his influence include Alan Garner, Robert Westall, and Ursula Le Guin. Adult fantasy authors modelling themselves partly on Tolkien, and partly on the American "pulp" magazine tradition of "sword-and-sorcery," seem to be proliferating even more now than in the years of the Tolkien cult (1965-75), and the Tolkien influence also lies behind the popular computer games set in fantasy worlds, and Fighting Fantasy programmed adventure books.

The Tolkien cult itself has passed through its phase of intense growth and publicity, to be revived among small groups of readers whenever they discover a common interest in Tolkien's world. As a classic of world literature, *The Lord of the Rings* will bear out Stanley Unwin's prophecy and be read for years to come.

—Jessica Yates

TOMALIN, Ruth

Has also written as Ruth Leaver. **Nationality:** British. **Born:** Piltown, County Kilkenny, Ireland. **Education:** Chichester High School, Sussex; King's College, University of London, Diploma of Journalism 1939. **Military Service:** Women's Land Army, 1941-42. **Family:** Married 1) Vernon Leaver in 1942 (divorced), one son; 2) William N. Ross in 1971. **Career:** Reporter for newspapers in Hampshire, Sussex, Dorset, and Hertfordshire, 1942-61; part-time press reporter, London Magistrates' Courts and Crown Courts, since 1961. **Address:** c/o Barclays Bank, 15 Langham Place, London, W.1, England.

Publications for Children

Fiction

Green Ink (as Ruth Leaver). London, Harrap, 1951.
The Sound of Pens (as Ruth Leaver), illustrated by Betty Ladler. London, Blackie, 1955.
The Daffodil Bird, illustrated by Brian Wildsmith. London, Faber, 1959; New York, A.S. Barnes, 1960.
The Sea Mice, illustrated by Sheila Rose. London, Faber, 1962.
A Green Wishbone, illustrated by Gavin Rowe. London, Faber, 1975.
A Stranger Thing, illustrated by Robin Jacques. London, Faber, 1975.
The Snake Crook, illustrated by Shirley Hughes. London, Faber, 1976.
Gone Away. London, Faber, 1979.
Little Nasty, illustrated by Sue Scullard. London, Faber, 1985.
A Summer Ghost. London, Faber, 1986.
Another Day. London, Faber, 1988.

Publications for Adults

Novels

All Souls. London, Faber, 1952.
The Garden House. London, Faber, 1964.
The Spring House. London, Faber, 1968.
Away to the West. London, Faber, 1972.
Long Since. London, Faber, 1989.

Verse

Threnody for Dormice. London, Fortune Press, 1947.
Deer's Cry. London, Fortune Press, 1952.

Other

The Day of the Rose: Essays and Portraits. London, Fortune Press, 1947.
W.H. Hudson (short biography). London, Witherby, and New York, Philosophical Library, 1954.
W.H. Hudson: A Biography. London, Faber, 1982.

Editor, *Best Country Stories.* London, Faber, 1969.

*

Ruth Tomalin comments:

Most of my stories are about people and things of the English countryside. All are set in places well known to me at different times, ranging from a copse full of wild life (*The Daffodil Bird*) to Broadcasting House, London (*The Sea Mice*); and from a glass "watch-house" in a nature reserve (*A Stranger Thing*) to a reporters' room on a provincial evening paper (*Green Ink*).

* * *

Ruth Tomalin's work falls into two distinct categories. There are a number of short novels for children of 9 to 10, the best of which are *A Stranger Thing* and *A Summer Ghost.* There is also a group of novels concerned with the childhood and youth of Ralph Oliver and latterly his young cousin Rowan—*The Garden House, The Spring House,* and *Away to the West;* these are longer and far more demanding works, so difficult to classify that in the judgment of some critics they are adult novels and cannot be regarded as children's books at all.

Certainly the Ralph Oliver novels are far beyond the comprehension of the small children who will enjoy *The Sea Mice, The Daffodil Bird,* or *A Stranger Thing. The Garden House,* with its subtle vision of early childhood, is thematically recondite for adolescent readers and best regarded as an adult novel. But *The Spring House* and *Away to the West* are admirable stories for the right teenage reader, though their appeal is highly specialised. Unless readers share Tomalin's intimate knowledge and love of wildlife, her care for the English countryside, and her concern for the impact of humanity on landscape and fauna alike, the novels cannot be understood at their deepest imaginative level. But for those who do share these affections and concerns, they have much to offer. They are also, after all, about young people growing up—the problems of choosing a career, of coping with uncomprehending parents, of living through the anguish of first love. These are important themes in the novels, treated with sympathy, tact, and humour, and with acute, uncondescending insight.

The stories for younger readers are essentially miniatures—very brief and sharply focused, characteristically preoccupied with the private, often secret world of a single child. Although the range of plots and settings is quite wide, the best and most typical of the stories involve intimate meetings between children and wild creatures, and delicate suggestions of magic and ghostliness. A deceptive simplicity of narrative allows subtle exploration of the clandestine childhood territory between fear and wonder, and the most successful stories contrive to place children in situations of enforced solitude, where apprehension and nervous self-reliance prove to be the starting point for magical discovery.

The formula is a fragile one, and *Another Day* is an instance of a book which breaks it. This story engages with the themes of a full-length children's novel within the narrow compass of the short book. One half of the plot realistically traces Francie's effort to cope with the isolating effects of sudden promotion in her school in 1934 and her struggles with the jealousy, ostracism, and resentment of her peers. The other half is a ghost story, in which with the aid of a magic Celtic whistle Francie summons a "ghost from the future," who is finally identified as her grandson-to-be. *Another Day* attempts to be school story, pony story, ghost story, and even historical novel within a hundred pages, and not surprisingly emerges as cryptic and sketchy.

This is a rare technical misjudgement on the part of a writer who is usually in immaculate control of her chosen medium. In the short novels, precision of setting is all-important. The settings can be urban and public (even Broadcasting House, in *The Sea Mice*) but transformed to privacy by the secret life of a child. More commonly they are rural and secluded, offering shelter to fugitive children escaping from an uncongenial world; the most memorable of such sanctuaries are the wintry gazebo in *A Stranger Thing* and the haunted beech wood in *A Summer Ghost.* The beech wood in this excellent story stands for many of Tomalin's locales: it is "haunted" by the presence of a long-dead girl who loved it, but also by a family of red squirrels, newly released by modern naturalists to repopulate their former "haunts."

Solitary days in secret places, encounters and friendships between child and animals, and nuances of the supernatural, combine in these stories to give strength and nurture to vulnerable children. The real-life, natural world assumes its own magic in these books. They are the product of a richly sensitive imagination and an infectious zest for the sheer diversity of life.

—Peter Hollindale

TOZER, Katharine

Nationality: British. **Born:** Katharine Alison Demuth, Bishops Tawton, near Barnstable, Devon, 31 July 1907. **Education:** St. Mary's College, London, 1922-24; Slade College of Fine Art, London, 1928-32. **Family:** Married James McCallum Tozer in 1932; one son. **Career:** Writer. **Died:** 1943.

Publications for Children (illustrated by the author)

Fiction

The Wanderings of Mumfie. London, Murray, 1935.
Here Comes Mumfie. London, Murray, 1936.
Mumfie the Admiral. London, Murray, 1937.
Mumfie's Magic Box. London, Murray, 1938.
Mumfie's Uncle Samuel. London, Murray, 1939.
Noah: The Story of Another Ark. London, Murray, 1940.
Adventures of Alfie. London, Murray, 1941.
Mumfie Marches On. London, Murray, 1942.
Mumfie's Picture Book, edited by Eiluned Lewis. London, Murray, 1947.

*

Illustrator: *Paladins in Spain* by Eleanor Farjeon, 1937; *The Man Who Asked Questions* by L.A.G. Strong, 1937; *The Chinese Children Next Door* by Pearl S. Buck, 1943.

* * *

Margery Fisher has remarked that "stories about toys give children a wonderful chance to be naughty by proxy," and one might add that they also give plenty of scope for earnest authors to lecture and warn by proxy. Certainly the great majority of stories in this genre which survive from the hundred years or so up to World War II are unashamedly didactic and immovably rooted in conventional middle-class morality—Masefield's *The Midnight Folk* and its sequel being among the very few exceptions. Writing at the very end of this period, Katharine Tozer can hardly be said to have shown particular originality or any ability to break the mould of racial, social, and professional stereotypes. Her central characters, Mumfie the toy elephant and his companion Scarecrow, always have a certain charm and in the later stories are effectively developed with contrasting personalities. Their assortment of friends or enemies from the nursery and fairyland are generally no better than stylized puppets. In the first book there is a deplorable scene in which the golliwog Jack Gingerbread is needlessly humiliated; and even in the jollier atmosphere of *Mumfie the Admiral,* the author's attitude towards Alabama the negro cook, whose reward at the end is to receive the "Illustrious Order of the Sit in the Sun and eat Melons," is crudely patronizing.

Assuredly, then, the secret of Tozer's success is not to be found in character-drawing, nor indeed in her plot construction, for by adult standards her central situations are generally of the tritest, and developed without the slightest hint of subtlety. Nevertheless her Mumfie books have been regularly reprinted and otherwise publicised during the last 50 years—and for several perfectly good reasons. First, she was able to apply most expertly the principle of "never a dull moment," with a new heading at the top of every page of text to indicate the unbroken run of action. Second, she had obviously identified the sort of things that small children really enjoy around their own homes, such as climbing trees or gorging themselves at tea-parties, and made sure that these activities were well to the fore in her fictional settings. Third, she did show a real imaginative power, which even mature readers can appreciate, in describing such things as Night's icefloored palace in *Mumfie's Magic Box,* or the climbing of the giant's mountain in *Mumfie's Uncle Samuel.* And last, but by no means least, as a talented artist she was able to illustrate almost every single incident with an appropriate full-page or inset drawing.

Tozer wrote eight stories before she died at age 36 while giving birth to her son. In addition to her Mumfie books, she wrote one about an American boy called Noah and one about an animated puppet. Only the first five Mumfie books have survived, but a reading of them suggests that she was improving her technique all the time. *Magic Box* is perhaps the most imaginative and *Uncle Samuel* the best constructed and most entertaining.

—Alasdair K.D. Campbell

TRAVERS, P(amela) L(yndon)

Nationality: British. **Born:** Queensland, Australia, in 1906. **Education:** Private schools. **Career:** Journalist, actress, and dancer, 1920s; regular contributor to the *Irish Statesman,* Dublin, 1920s and 1930s; worked for the British Ministry of Information in the United States during World War II. Writer-in-residence, Radcliffe College, Cambridge, Massachusetts, 1965-66; Smith College, Northampton, Massachusetts, 1966-67; Scripps College, Claremont, California, 1970. **Awards:** Focus Award, 1985. D.H.: Chatham College, Pittsburgh, 1978. O.B.E. (Officer, Order of the British Empire), 1977. **Agent:** David Higham Associates Ltd., 5-8 Lower John Street, London W1R 4HA.

Publications for Children

Fiction

Mary Poppins, illustrated by Mary Shepard. London, Howe, and New York, Reynal, 1934; revised edition, New York, Harcourt Brace, 1981.
Mary Poppins Comes Back, illustrated by Mary Shepard. London, Dickson and Thompson, and New York, Reynal, 1935.
Happy Ever After, illustrated by Mary Shepard. Privately printed, 1940.
I Go by Sea, I Go by Land, illustrated by Gertrude Hermes. London, Davies, and New York, Harper, 1941.
Mary Poppins Opens the Door, illustrated by Mary Shepard and Agnes Sims. New York, Reynal, 1943; London, Davies, 1944.
Mary Poppins in the Park, illustrated by Mary Shepard. London, Davies, and New York, Harcourt Brace, 1952.
The Fox at the Manger, illustrated by Thomas Bewick. New York, Norton, 1962; London, Collins, 1963.
Mary Poppins from A to Z, illustrated by Mary Shepard. New York, Harcourt Brace, 1962; London, Collins, 1963.
Friend Monkey. New York, Harcourt Brace, 1971; London, Collins, 1972.
Mary Poppins in Cherry Tree Lane, illustrated by Mary Shepard. London, Collins, and New York, Delacorte Press, 1982.
Mary Poppins and the House Next Door, illustrated by Mary Shepard. New York, Delacorte Press, 1989.

Other

About the Sleeping Beauty, illustrated by Charles Keeping. New York, McGraw Hill, 1975; London, Collins, 1977.
Mary Poppins in the Kitchen: A Cookery Book with a Story, with Maurice Moore-Betty, illustrated by Mary Shepard. New York, Harcourt Brace, 1975; London, Collins, 1977.
Two Pairs of Shoes (folktales), illustrated by Leo and Diane Dillon. New York, Viking Press, 1980.

Publications for Adults

Other

Moscow Excursion. London, Dickson and Thompson, and New York, Reynal, 1935.
Aunt Sass. Privately printed, 1941.
Ah Wong. Privately printed, 1943.
Johnny Delaney. Privately printed, 1944.
In Search of the Hero: The Continuing Relevance of Myth and Fairy Tale (lecture). Claremont, California, Scripps College, 1970.
Translator, with Ruth Lewinnek, *The Way of Transformation: Daily Life as a Spiritual Exercise,* by Karlfried Dürckheim Montmartin. London, Allen and Unwin, 1971.
George Ivanovitch Gurdjieff. Toronto, Traditional Studies Press, 1973.
What the Bee Knows: Reflections on Myth, Symbol and Story. Wellingborough, Northamptonshire, Thorsons, 1989.

*

Critical Studies: *Mary Poppins and Myth* by Staffan Bergsten, Stockholm, Almqvist & Wiksell, 1978.

P.L. Travers comments:

I have always said that I don't think I write for children specially. After all, my early writing was mostly poetry and I imagine that *Mary Poppins* stems from that. I am not a great one for seeking personal publicity and agree with C.S. Lewis when he says, in a letter, "There is only one creator and we merely mix the elements He gives us."

* * *

Before Mary Poppins—that most intriguing of English nannies—blew into children's fiction on an east wind in 1934, her author's reputation as a poet and dramatic critic had already been established. P.L. Travers's ability to combine poetic insight with a feeling for dramatic situation brought a balance and an inner intensity to her stories.

Mary Poppins is a many-faceted character. Superficially she seems the prim, archetypal nannie, reading "Everything a Lady Should Know" and exuding a competent aura of boot polish and Sunlight Soap. She crackles, however, not only with starch but with an elemental and challenging magic: the startlingly blue eyes of her Dutch Doll face can see "over the rim of the world" as well as into the minds of her charges. The children of the Banks family find that in Mary's company their fantasy exploits often find exciting expression. Magical adventures might arise at any moment from commonplace circumstances. For instance, Mary Poppins can casually pick up a plum painted on the pavement by a street artist and take a bite from it. Travers firmly believes that in children's stories an ordinary environment is an essential background for magic. "To climb or to fly you need a solid basis from which to take off; otherwise everything becomes too fey."

Certainly there is nothing sentimental or amorphous about Mary Poppins. She can be imaginative or sternly practical as occasion demands. Her actions often have a catalytic effect. The magic which she brings into the lives of the Banks children sharpens their understanding of themselves and reality: it is exuberant but not escapist. Unlike many other fictional immortals Mary never makes "happily ever after" promises. She implies that the only security is an ability to accept constant change; the temporary nature of her own presence in the Banks household is stressed by the fact of her sleeping on a camp bed. Her ever present parrot-headed umbrella and capacious carpet bag too are reminders that she is always ready to travel at a moment's notice.

The original *Mary Poppins* in 1934 was quickly followed by *Mary Poppins Comes Back. Mary Poppins Opens the Door* was intended as the last of the series. In its final pages Mary leaves the Banks family forever, although "the gifts she had brought would remain...." However in response to readers' demands, a further volume, *Mary Poppins in the Park,* was produced in 1952, but its action takes place during the visits of Mary Poppins that were chronicled in the three previous books. This is true too of *Mary Poppins in the Kitchen,* published as recently as 1975. Mary becomes temporary cook for the Banks family and teaches the children to prepare attractive meals. The book consists of a story and some recipes for each day of the week.

The series was written over several years, but always firmly set against a background of nursery cosiness common to many English homes in the 1930s. (In the Walt Disney film there was a transposition to the Edwardian period, but a similar atmosphere was conveyed.) Yet in the Mary Poppins stories, something of the timeless appeal of the classic fairy tales exists.

In 1982, after a gap of 30 years, Travers produced another novel in the Mary Poppins saga. Like its predecessors, *Mary Poppins in Cherry Tree Lane* works on several levels. It can be read simply as a description of a huge, midsummer's eve romp spiced by plenty of zany happenings; but the serious mystical quality that found subtle expression in the earlier books is now stronger and more persuasive than ever.

A companion volume to *Mary Poppins in Cherry Tree Lane* came in 1989 with *Mary Poppins and the House Next Door.* Again the catalytic magic of the Banks family's nannie has suffered no toning down, and the author's inventiveness is still evident (notably in the episode dealing with the children's visit to the Man in the Moon). A brown and beautiful boy from the South Seas, temporarily residing in Cherry Tree Lane, is perhaps a little too golden to be true, but Mary Poppins and the other regular characters are conveyed with Travers's customary flair.

There are no magical overtones in *I Go by Sea, I Go by Land.* This account of two English children's wartime evacuation to the United States catches the atmosphere of the period—a grim acceptance of the "backs to the wall" situation coupled with a dogged optimism. For Sabrina and James, there is also the excitement and apprehension of the U-boat-menaced sea trip to America and a new life far away from home and parents. Their responses to change and challenge make lively reading. The wonders of the World's Fair and the Statue of Liberty possibly impress them less than the sophistication of American children—like their hostess's daughter who has permanently waved hair; or the satisfaction of having constant supplies of Coca-Cola, sweet corn, and out-of-season strawberries: "You can't wonder that the Americans are proud of their country." But underlying all the new discoveries and fulfillments is the fear about what might be happening to their parents left behind in England, exposed to the Blitz and the threat of invasion. Travers does not gloss over the severely disrupting effect on many young people of this wartime break-up of family life; but, as in the Mary Poppins books, her fictional children are nudged by circumstances into an acceptance of their responsibilities and an ability to cope with difficulties.

In *The Fox at the Manger* and *Friend Monkey,* Travers brings together her interest in mythology and religion and her appreciation of nature. In her stories, animals are more likely to be wild than domestic, as she considers that the latter have often been debased and made sycophantic by man. It is characteristic of her unsentimental attitude toward animals that the fox who joins the domesticated animals at the manger should give the Christ-child the rather surprising gift of his cunning—and that the child appreciates this above all the other gifts which are showered upon him.

In *Friend Monkey* the animal hero is equally robust. He is based upon Hanuman, the monkey lord of Hindu mythology, and his engaging efforts to help the human family who have adopted him usually result in chaos. Like most of Travers's stories, this book implies that life cannot be tied up into neat packages. Monkey gives his friends no resting place, no panaceas. He opens their eyes frequently to deeper and more challenging aspects of life.

About the Sleeping Beauty is a re-telling of a traditional story. This suggests that fairyland "intersects our mortal world at every point and at every second. The two of them together make one web woven fine." The literal and symbolic immortality of Mary Poppins—Travers's most famous character—underlines the truth of this.

—Mary Cadogan

TREADGOLD, Mary

Nationality: British. **Born:** London, 16 April 1910. **Education:** Ginner-Mawer School of Dance and Drama, 1916-22; Challoner School, London, 1921-23; St. Paul's Girls' School, London, 1923-28; Bedford College, University of London, 1930-36, M.A. (honours) in English. **Career:** Children's editor, William Heinemann Ltd., London, 1938-40; producer and literary editor, BBC, London, 1940-60. **Award:** Library Association Carnegie Medal, 1942. **Address:** c/o Jonathan Cape, Random Century House, 20 Vauxhall Bridge Rd., London SW1V 2SA, England.

Publications for Children

Fiction

We Couldn't Leave Dinah, illustrated by Stuart Tresilian. London, Cape, 1941; as *Left till Called For,* New York, Doubleday, 1941.
No Ponies, illustrated by Ruth Gervis. London, Cape, 1946.
The "Polly Harris." London, Cape, 1949; as *The Mystery of the "Polly Harris,"* New York, Doubleday, 1951; revised edition, as *The "Polly Harris,"* London, Hamish Hamilton, 1968; New York, Nelson, 1970.
The Heron Ride, illustrated by Victor Ambrus. London, Cape, 1962.
The Winter Princess, illustrated by Pearl Falconer. Leicester, Brockhampton Press, 1962; Princeton, New Jersey, Van Nostrand, 1964.
Return to the Heron, illustrated by Victor Ambrus. London, Cape, 1963.
The Weather Boy, illustrated by Robert Geary. Leicester, Brockhampton Press, 1964; Princeton, New Jersey, Van Nostrand, 1965.
Maids' Ribbons, illustrated by Susannah Holden. London, Nelson, 1965; New York, Nelson, 1967.
Elegant Patty, illustrated by Lynette Hemmant. London, Hamish Hamilton, 1967.
Poor Patty, illustrated by Lynette Hemmant. London, Hamish Hamilton, 1968.
This Summer, Last Summer, illustrated by Mary Russon. London, Hamish Hamilton, 1968.
The Humbugs, illustrated by Faith Jaques. London, Hamish Hamilton, 1968.
The Rum Day of the Vanishing Pony. Leicester, Brockhampton Press, 1970.
Journey from the Heron. London, Cape, 1981.

Publications for Adults

Novel

The Running Child. London, Cape, 1951.

*

Mary Treadgold comments:

(1978) I regard myself as a good example of the "hobby-writer"—writing is something I've enjoyed doing, never taken over-seriously. I am delighted when people take me seriously and when anyone tells me he or she has enjoyed what I've written!

(1983) As I grow older, I find it increasingly important to write books that a child will remember—at any rate something of—when he or she is grown-up. Perhaps only a character, or a landscape, or something outstanding somebody said—as I myself nearly 70 years later remember at odd moments scenes that at the time must have made some impression from that immortal book *The Secret Garden.* I think this writing for a child's *imaginative* future is of greater moment than I at first realised.

* * *

Mary Treadgold's first novel, *We Couldn't Leave Dinah,* won the Carnegie Medal for 1941, which lifts her well above the run of pony-adventure story writers. In fact, she is a novelist of very considerable power, and while both ponies and adventure have continued to feature prominently in her books, they have never come near to monopolising them or blurring a shrewd eye for character and relationships.

Both *We Couldn't Leave Dinah* and its successor, *No Ponies,* are essentially war stories. In the first, which deals with the Nazi invasion of a mythical Channel island, Clerinel, Mick and Caroline Templeton are confronted with adult problems of collaboration and divided loyalties, as well as the more ordinary excitements of a spy story. The second opens just after the war when the London-bred Atherleys travel to their aunt's lovely pre-war home in the south of France. Their happiness at being abroad is only marred by the thought of the ponies and the riding that awaits them when their athletic cousins arrive. But when they reach Beaubassin, the ponies are not there. The subsequent adventure proves to the children that wars are not always over with the fighting, and that the damage to people's minds may be harder to cure.

Compared with more recent books about the war, *We Couldn't Leave Dinah* and *No Ponies* still stand up extremely well. Some things have dated—child-adult relationships seem oddly formal, the triplets are said to be 14 but could be 12—yet in other ways there is a greater maturity than we have grown used to, a kind of objectivity, perfectly convincing, that makes these children seem older.

The same lack of self-centredness is felt in *The "Polly Harris"* which finds the reluctant Templetons enrolled at a London crammer's. The sensitive Caroline is both aware and highly critical of her own childishness. The plot here is in some ways much ahead of its time, with terrorists as well as smugglers (but no ponies). Running through the book at a deeper level is the idea of loneliness, one of Treadgold's haunting themes. This recurs in more overt form in the later "Heron" books, especially in her most recent, *Journey from the Heron,* where it is combined with the reassessments brought about by the war of 1914-18, but it is in *The "Polly Harris"* that the theme is most clearly expressed:

> For the first time [Caroline] was appalled to her soul at the way people could fail other people—could misunderstand their very nature, wound the delicate structure of their human spirit, and then send them back about their ways, uncomforted and quite alone...To her now came the knowledge that people could also misunderstand her as she had misunderstood David—could fail her, wound her and even destroy her. Not yet—there was no one yet to do it, but she knew that she had a long life before her. As she reached the lower landing, the burden of her long life lay on her, heavy as frost.

—Anne Carter

TRESSELT, Alvin

Nationality: American. **Born:** Passaic, New Jersey, 30 September 1916. **Education:** Passaic High School, graduated 1934. **Family:** Married Blossom Budney in 1949; two daughters. **Career:** Worked in a defense plant, Connecticut, 1943-46; display designer and advertising copywriter, B. Altman Co., New York, 1946-52; editor, *Humpty Dumpty's Magazine,* New York, 1952-65; editor, 1965-67, and executive editor and vice-president, 1967-74, Parents' Magazine Press, New York. Since 1974 Instructor and Dean of Faculty, Institute of Children's Literature, Redding Ridge, Connecticut.

Publications for Children

Fiction

Rain Drop Splash, illustrated by Leonard Weisgard. New York, Lothrop, 1946.

White Snow Bright Snow, illustrated by Roger Duvoisin. New York, Lothrop, 1947.

Johnny Maple-Leaf, illustrated by Roger Duvoisin. New York, Lothrop, 1948.

The Wind and Peter, illustrated by Gary MacKenzie. New York, Oxford University Press, 1948.

Bonnie Bess, The Weathervane Horse, illustrated by Marylin Hafner. New York, Lothrop, 1949.

Sun Up, illustrated by Roger Duvoisin. New York, Lothrop, 1949; Kingswood, Surrey, World's Work, 1966.

The Little Lost Squirrel, illustrated by Leonard Weisgard. New York, Grosset and Dunlap, 1950.

Follow the Wind, illustrated by Roger Duvoisin. New York, Lothrop, 1950.

Hi, Mr. Robin!, illustrated by Roger Duvoisin. New York, Lothrop, 1950.

Autumn Harvest, illustrated by Roger Duvoisin. New York, Lothrop, 1951.

A Day with Daddy, photographs by Helen Heller. New York, Lothrop, 1953.

Follow the Road, illustrated by Roger Duvoisin. New York, Lothrop, 1953.

I Saw the Sea Come In, illustrated by Roger Duvoisin. New York, Lothrop, 1954; Kingswood, Surrey, World's Work, 1967.

Wake Up, Farm!, illustrated by Roger Duvoisin. New York, Lothrop, 1955; Kingswood Surrey, World's Work, 1966.

Wake Up, City!, illustrated by Roger Duvoisin. New York, Lothrop, 1957; revised edition, illustrated by Carol Ewing, 1990.

The Rabbit Story, illustrated by Leonard Weisgard. New York, Lothrop, 1957.

The Frog in the Well, illustrated by Roger Duvoisin. New York, Lothrop, 1958; Edinburgh, Oliver and Boyd, 1966.

The Smallest Elephant in the World, illustrated by Milton Glaser. New York, Knopf, 1959.
Timothy Robbins Climbs the Mountain, illustrated by Roger Duvoisin. New York, Lothrop, 1960; Kingswood, Surrey, World's Work, 1967.
An Elephant Is Not a Cat, with Wilbur Wheaton, illustrated by Tom Vroman. New York, Parents' Magazine Press, 1962.
Hide and Seek Fog, illustrated by Roger Duvoisin. New York, Lothrop, 1965; Kingswood, Surrey, World's Work, 1966.
The Old Man and the Tiger, illustrated by Albert Aquino. New York, Grosset and Dunlap, 1965; London, Muller, 1970.
A Thousand Lights and Fireflies, illustrated by John Moodie. New York, Parents' Magazine Press, 1965.
The World in the Candy Egg, illustrated by Roger Duvoisin. New York, Lothrop, 1967.
The Fox Who Travelled, illustrated by Nancy Sears. New York, Grosset and Dunlap, 1968.
It's Time Now!, illustrated by Roger Duvoisin. New York, Lothrop, 1969; Kingswood, Surrey, World's Work, 1971.
What Did You Leave Behind?, illustrated by Roger Duvoisin. New York, Lothrop, 1978; Kingswood, Surrey, World's Work, 1979.
The Gift of the Tree, illustrated by Henri Sorenson. New York, Lothrop, Lee and Shepard, 1992.

Other (folktales)

Under the Trees and Through the Grass (ecology), illustrated by Roger Duvoisin. New York, Lothrop, 1962.
The Mitten: An Old Ukrainian Folktale, illustrated by Yaroslava. New York, Lothrop, 1964; Kingswood, Surrey, World's Work, 1965.
How Far Is Far? (science), illustrated by Ward Brackett. New York, Parents' Magazine Press, 1964.
The Tears of the Dragon, illustrated by Chihiro Iwasaki. New York, Parents' Magazine Press, 1967.
Legend of the Willow Plate, with Nancy Cleaver, illustrated by Joseph Low. New York, Parents' Magazine Press, 1968; London, Hamish Hamilton, 1969.
The Crane Maiden, illustrated by Chihiro Iwasaki. New York, Parents' Magazine Press, 1968.
Helpful Mr. Bear, illustrated by Kozo Kakimoto. New York, Parents' Magazine Press, 1968.
Ma Lien and the Magic Brush, illustrated by Kei Wakana. New York, Parents' Magazine Press, 1968.
How Rabbit Tricked His Friends, illustrated by Yasuo Segawa. New York, Parents' Magazine Press, 1969.
The Rolling Rice Ball, illustrated by Saburo Watanabe. New York, Parents' Magazine Press, 1969.
The Fisherman under the Sea, illustrated by Chihiro Iwasaki. New York, Parents' Magazine Press, 1969.
The Land of Lost Buttons, illustrated by Kayako Nishimaki. New York, Parents' Magazine Press, 1970.
Eleven Hungry Cats, illustrated by Noboru Baba. New York, Parents' Magazine Press, 1970.
Gengoroh and the Thunder God, illustrated by Yasuo Segawa. New York, Parents' Magazine Press, 1970.
The Beaver Pond (ecology), illustrated by Roger Duvoisin. New York, Lothrop, 1970; Kingswood, Surrey, World's Work, 1971.
A Sparrow's Magic, illustrated by Fuyuji Yamanaka. New York, Parents' Magazine Press, 1970.
The Hare and the Bear and Other Stories, illustrated by Yoshiharu Suzuki. New York, Parents' Magazine Press, 1971.
Stories from the Bible, illustrated by Lynd Ward. New York, Coward McCann, 1971.
Ogre and His Bride, illustrated by Shosuke Fukuda. New York, Parents' Magazine Press, 1971.
Lum Fu and the Golden Mountain, illustrated by Daihacki Ohta. New York, Parents' Magazine Press, 1971.
The Little Mouse Who Tarried, illustrated by Kozo Kakimoto. New York, Parents' Magazine Press, 1971.
Wonder-Fish from the Sea, illustrated by Irmgard Lucht. New York, Parents' Magazine Press, 1971.
The Dead Tree (ecology), illustrated by Charles Robinson. New York, Parents' Magazine Press, 1972.
The Little Green Man, illustrated by Maurice Kenelski. New York, Parents' Magazine Press, 1972.
The Nutcracker, illustrated by Seiichi Horiuchi. New York, Parents' Magazine Press, 1974.

*

Manuscript Collections: Kerlan Collection, University of Minnesota, Minneapolis.

Alvin Tresselt comments:

My books are mostly about nature, the weather and seasons, although I have also written fantasy, humor, and here-and-now stories as well as a number of free adaptations of Japanese folktales. In my nature stories I have avoided a didactic approach and striven for a poetic prose style that would nurture in children a feeling for words and language, even while they were reading about the journey of rain to the sea, the mysteries of fog, or the importance of a dead tree. I generally use a cyclical plot when writing these stories, letting the progressions of a natural phenomenon dictate the form rather than casting the event within the confines of a conventional story.

All of my books have been in the four to eight picture book range.

* * *

White snow, bright snow, smooth and deep.
Light snow, night snow, quiet as sleep.
Down, down, without a sound;
Down, down, to the frozen ground.

Covering roads and hiding fences.
Sifting in cracks and filling up trenches.
Millions of snowflakes, tiny and light.
Softly, gently, in the secret night.

Those two stanzas from the prologue to his *White Snow Bright Snow* suggest why Alvin Tresselt was one of the pathbreaking American picture book authors of the late 1940s and early 1950s. Along with Margaret Wise Brown and others, he helped to establish the patterns of the "mood" picture book that sought to catch and hold the attention of young listeners and readers by projecting the essence of a familiar experience in vivid yet simple language.

White Snow Bright Snow, for which illustrator Roger Duvoisin won the Caldecott Medal, is a prime example of the Tresselt technique. Although there is no central character, and no plot in the classic sense, Tresselt does introduce representative characters—the postman, the farmer, the policeman—who recur throughout the narrative. And he structures the text in a dramatic way, starting with the low gray sky that presages the snow-storm and ending with the first spring robin that signals the season of snow is over.

Tresselt pioneered this approach to nature subjects in an earlier picture book, *Rain Drop Splash,* in which he traced the path of a raindrop from a puddle to the ocean. He continued it in such books as *Hi, Mr. Robin!, Wake Up, Farm!,* and *Hide and Seek Fog,* which details the impact of a thick fog that blankets a Cape Cod fishing village for three days.

Not surprisingly, the Tresselt mood nature books spawned a horde of imitators. They seemed so simple to write—after all, who hadn't observed some process of nature, whether a butterfly emerging from a chrysalis or a pair of wrens building a nest, hatching eggs, and raising a new family. Why not write a picture book text about it? Hundreds if not thousands of writers tried their hand at such manuscripts. The great majority were never published, but many others did get into print. They inevitably tended to lessen the impact of some of Tresselt's own later books, especially when he seemed to repeat himself in books like *Under the Trees and Through the Grass.*

At this juncture, Tresselt happily widened his range by turning to folktales and fantasy. *The Mitten* was his delightful rendition of the Ukrainian tale about all the shivering forest animals that tried to crowd for warmth into the little boy's lost mitten. And even though it suffered from an uncertain point-of-view, *The World in the Candy Egg* contained some of Tresselt's loveliest writing, like this climactic extract:

> Magic world, little world, made for a child's delight,
> Where time doesn't pass and it never gets cold,
> And the shepherd and shepherdess never grow old...
> The sheep nibble grass and crows fly away, fly away,
>
> fly away,
> In the make-believe world of the egg.

Then, in the late 1960s and early 1970s, Tresselt returned to nature themes. *It's Time Now!, The Dead Tree,* and *The Beaver Pond* proved that his touch was as sure as ever. Like the beavers who built first one dam and then another, he could still take the most ordinary material from nature and shape it into something fresh and special for children.

—James Cross Giblin

TREVOR, (Lucy) Meriol

Nationality: British. **Born:** London, 15 April 1919. **Education:** Perse School, Cambridge; St. Hugh's College, Oxford, 1938-42, B.A. 1942. **Career:** Worked in wartime nurseries, London, 1943-44, and steerer on Grand Union Canal, 1944-45; relief worker, UNRRA, Italy, 1946-47. **Awards:** James Tait Black Memorial award, for biography, 1963; Fellow, Royal Society of Literature. **Address:** 41 Fitzroy House, Pulteney Street, Bath BA2 4DW, England.

Publications for Children

Fiction

The Forest and the Kingdom, illustrated by Philip Hepworth. London, Faber, 1949.
Hunt the King, Hide the Fox, illustrated by Philip Hepworth. London, Faber, 1950.
The Fires and the Stars, illustrated by Philip Hepworth. London, Faber, 1951.
Sun Slower, Sun Faster, illustrated by Edward Ardizzone. London, Collins, 1955; New York, Sheed and Ward, 1957.
The Other Side of the Moon, illustrated by Martin Thomas. London, Collins, 1956; New York, Sheed and Ward, 1957.
Merlin's Ring, illustrated by Martin Thomas. London, Collins, 1957.
The Treasure Hunt, illustrated by Constance Marshall. London, Hamish Hamilton, 1957.
The Caravan War, illustrated by Janet Pullan. London, Hamish Hamilton, 1958.
Four Odd Ones, illustrated by Martin Thomas. London, Collins, 1958.
The Sparrow Child, illustrated by Martin Thomas. London, Collins, 1958.
The Rose Round. London, Hamish Hamilton, 1963; New York, Dutton, 1964; San Francisco, Ignatius Press, 1995.
William's Wild Day Out, illustrated by Raymond Briggs. London, Hamish Hamilton, 1963.
The Midsummer Maze, illustrated by Hugh Marshall. London, Macmillan, and New York, St. Martin's Press, 1964.
Lights in a Dark Town, illustrated by Hilda Offen. London, Macmillan, 1964.
The King of the Castle, illustrated by Hugh Marshall. London, Macmillan, 1966.
The Crystal Snowstorm. San Francisco, Ignatius Press, and Bethlehem Books, 1997.
Following the Phoenix. San Francisco, Ignatius Press, and Bethlehem Books, 1998.

Publications for Adults

Novels

The Last of Britain. London, Macmillan, and New York, St. Martin's Press, 1956.
The New People. London, Macmillan, and New York, St. Martin's Press, 1957.
A Narrow Place. London, Macmillan, 1958.
Shadows and Images. London, Macmillan, 1960; New York, McKay, 1962.
The City and the World. London, Dent, 1970.
The Holy Images. London, Dent, 1971.
The Two Kingdoms. London, Constable, 1973.
The Sun with a Face. New York, Fawcett, 1982; London, Hale, 1984.
The Golden Palaces. Frome, Somerset, Bran's Head, 1985.

Luxembourg Novels

The Fugitives. London, Hodder and Stoughton, 1973; New York, Pocket Books, 1974.

The Marked Man. London, Hodder and Stoughton, and New York, Pocket Books, 1974.
The Enemy at Home. London, Hodder and Stoughton, and New York, Pocket Books, 1974.
The Forgotten Country. London, Hodder and Stoughton, 1975.
The Treacherous Paths. London, Hodder and Stoughton, 1976.
The Fortunes of Peace. London, Hodder and Stoughton, 1978.

English Novels

The Fortunate Marriage. London, Hodder and Stoughton, and New York, Dutton, 1976.
The Civil Prisoners. London, Hodder and Stoughton, and New York, Dutton, 1977.
The Wanton Fires. London, Hodder and Stoughton, and New York, Dutton, 1979.

Verse

Midsummer, Midwinter. Aldington, Kent, Hand and Flower Press, 1957.

Other

Newman: Pillar of the Cloud [and] *Light in Winter* (biography). London, Macmillan, 2 vols., 1962; New York, Doubleday, 2 vols., 1962-63; abridged edition, as *Newman's Journey,* London, Fontana, 1974; Huntingdon, Indiana, Our Sunday Visitor, 1985; with new introduction, New York, HarperCollins Fount Classics, 1996.
Newman Today. London, Catholic Truth Society, 1963.
Newman, A Portrait Restored: An Ecumenical Revaluation, with John Coulson and A.M. Allchin. London, Sheed and Ward, 1965.
Apostle of Rome: A Life of Philip Neri, 1515-1595. London, Macmillan, 1966.
Pope John. London, Macmillan, and New York, Doubleday, 1967.
Prophets and Guardians: Renewal and Tradition in the Church. London, Hollis and Carter, and New York, Doubleday, 1969.
The Arnolds: Thomas Arnold and His Family. London, Bodley Head, and New York, Scribner, 1973.
The Shadow of a Crown: The Life Story of James II of England and VII of Scotland. London, Constable, 1988.

*

Meriol Trevor comments:

I wrote some children's books because I wanted to, and I dedicated them to the children of friends, who all seemed to enjoy reading them. I still sometimes hear from children who have read and enjoyed my books. In all my stories I have tried to involve the children in the lives and problems of sympathetic young adults often by putting the loves and hates among and between the generations at one remove, because I think this makes it easier for children to understand, or to recognize, their own emotions.

* * *

Meriol Trevor has written books for children in several different genres. Her favourite medium is a kind of fantasy that is peculiarly her own, mixing myth, magic, traditional folklore, and Christian allegory. A number of these books, such as *The Forest and the Kingdom* and *Hunt the King, Hide the Fox,* derive from a fictitious world, The World Dionysus, which the author and a friend, Margaret Priestley, invented when they were children. Together and separately the two women have written several World Dionysus stories rather as the Brontë sisters invented and wrote about Gondal. Trevor has also produced realistic novels—*The Sparrow Child* and *The Rose Round* are examples—and stories for younger children in the Antelope and Reindeer series.

Nearly all Trevor's writing is suffused by her deeply held Roman Catholic beliefs. This means that her books often have a specialist interest, being perhaps more easily appreciated by people of that religious persuasion than by Protestant or agnostic readers. At times, the didactic intention shows through too much, as in *The Sparrow Child,* where the story becomes somewhat implausible when the Christian myth of the grail is given too much prominence in the closing chapters.

The structure of her novels is always competent—*The Rose Round* is an interesting example of a complex story that is handled skillfully enough for the plot to seem quite simple—and there is a heavy reliance on dialogue, which is not always so convincing, sometimes failing to portray the differences of thought and feeling between the characters adequately. Perhaps her most successful books are the short novels for young readers, *William's Wild Day Out, The Treasure Hunt,* and *The Caravan War,* which, slight though they may be, are distinguished by a lively sense of humour and an assurance of tone in the writing that do not always appear in the longer, more serious novels.

—David Rees

TREZISE, Percy (James)

Nationality: Australian. **Born:** Tallangatta, Australia, 28 January 1923. **Military Service:** Royal Australian Air Force, pilot, 1941-45. **Family:** Married Beverley Elizabeth English, 25 October 1950; two sons and two daughters. **Career:** Pilot, Ansett Airlines of Australia, 1950-74; writer. **Awards:** Advance Australia Award; Australian Children's Book Award (picture book), 1979 and 1983; Order of Australia, 1996. **Member:** Australian Institute of Aboriginal Studies. **Address:** 5 Fulton Close, Whitfield, Cairns, Queensland 4870, Australia.

PUBLICATIONS FOR CHILDREN

Picture Books

The Quinkins, with Dick Roughsey. North Ryde, Australia, Collins, 1978.
Banana Bird and the Snakemen. North Ryde, Collins, 1980.
Turramulli the Giant Quinkin, with D. Roughsey. North Ryde, Collins, 1982.
The Magic Firesticks, with D. Roughsey. North Ryde, Collins, 1983.
Gidja the Moon, with D. Roughsey. North Ryde, Collins, 1984.
The Flying Fox Warriors, with D. Roughsey. North Ryde, Collins, 1985.
Ngalculli, the Red Kangaroo. North Ryde, Collins, 1986.

The Owl People. Pymble, New South Wales, HarperCollins, 1987.
The Cave Painters. Pymble, New South Wales, HarperCollins, 1988.
Black Duck and Water Rat, with Mary Haginikitas. Pymble, New South Wales, Gareth Stevens, 1989.
The Peopling of Australia. Pymble, New South Wales, Gareth Stevens, 1989.
Lasca and Her Pups. Pymble, New South Wales, HarperCollins, 1990.
Mungoon-Gali the Giant Goanna. Pymble, New South Wales, HarperCollins, 1991.
Children of the Lake. Pymble, New South Wales, HarperCollins, 1992.
Nungadin and Willijen, with Mary Haginikitas. Pymble, New South Wales, HarperCollins, 1992.
Quinkin Mountain. Pymble, New South Wales, HarperCollins, 1995.
Journey of the Great Lake series:
Home of the Kadimakara People. Pymble, New South Wales, HarperCollins, 1996.
Land of the Dingo People. Pymble, New South Wales, HarperCollins, 1997.
Land of the Magpie Goose People. Pymble, New South Wales, HarperCollins, 1997.
Land of the Emu People. Pymble, New South Wales, HarperCollins, 1998.
Land of the Snake People. Pymble, New South Wales, HarperCollins, 1998.

Publications for Adults

Other

Quinkin Country: Adventures in Search of Aboriginal Rock Art. A. H. and A. W. Reed, 1969.
The Rock Art of South-East Cape. Australian Institute of Aboriginal Studies, 1971.
Last Days of a Wilderness. Collins, 1973.
Dream Road. St. Leonards, New South Wales, Allen and Unwin, 1993.

*

Illustrator, with Mary Haginikitas: *Platypus and Kookaburra* by Rex Ingamells, 1987; *The Last of His Tribe* by Henry Kendall, 1989.

* * *

Percy James Trezise was born in Tallangatta, located near the Murray River in northeastern Victoria, Australia. Growing up on a farm, he attended primary school in the Australian bush. Trezise received his secondary education at Albury High School. He later served as a pilot in the Air Force during the Second World War. Following the war, Trezise worked as an Ansett Airlines pilot for 24 years. It was in 1962 that he met and became associated with Dick Roughsey, an Aboriginal artist of the Lardil people of Mornington Island, off the North Queensland coast. A strong friendship developed between the two men, leading to a richly rewarding professional relationship for both. All of the work Trezise has engaged in during his 25-year writing and artistic career has been connected with Aboriginal interests.

Trezise's first three books *Quinkin Country: Adventures in Search of Aboriginal Rock Art* (1969), *Rock Art of South-East Cape York* (1972), and *Last Days of a Wilderness* (1973) are adult works based upon his explorations of Aboriginal cave galleries of the Cape York Peninsula area. Roughsey joined him in some of these explorations. The two men made contacts among the elderly native men of the area, who shared with them concerns that with their passing traditional Dreamtime stories might not be preserved. Trezise and Roughsey promised them that they would preserve the stories through publication. Dreamtime stories tell of the ancestors of the Aboriginal people during the period of creation. Trezise and Roughsey selected the format of the picture book as the vehicle for their publications.

Trezise and Roughsey's first official collaboration took place in the writing and illustrating of *The Quinkins* (1978), winner of the 1979 Australian Picture Book of the Year Award, a story that set the model for the collaborations that followed. In this story, readers are introduced to some of the creatures and beings of Dreamtime Australia. The illustrations are powerful, depicting tension and movement. Dramatic landscapes are highlighted by dynamic earth colors.

Trezise and Roughsey subsequently wrote and illustrated five additional works: *Banana Bird and the Snakemen* (1980), *Turramulli the Giant Quinkin* (1982), *The Magic Firesticks* (1983), *Gidja* (1984), and *Flying Fox Warriors* (1985; shortlisted for the 1984 Picture Book of the Year), all of which were based upon the Dreamtime stories. All feature strong dramatic elements, vividly drawn Aboriginal characters, and detailed depictions of local flora and fauna of the Cape York area—with an eye toward preserving basic likenesses within distinctly artistic renderings. In these collaborations, Trezise has maintained that he had general responsibility for the drawing of the landscapes while Roughsey drew the figures. The medium in all of the works (as has been the case in Trezise's books done after Roughsey's death in 1985) is acrylic paint.

Of all of the collaborations, *Turramulli the Giant Quinkin* is perhaps the most striking. Two children, Moonbi and Leealin, first introduced in *The Quinkins,* are pursued by the terrible Turramulli, a Dreamtime creature with an Abominable Snowman-like appearance. Perspective is deftly utilized in this story, an excellent example occurring when the children, taking refuge in a log to escape the monster, see his huge foot directly outside their hiding place. This, juxtaposed against the fragile appearance of the background trees and the terrifyingly active gait of a distant fleeing Timara Quinkin, emphasizes the dramatic impact of the scene. All of the stories, in general, attempt to accurately reflect the traditional concerns and fears of the native people and their spiritual relationship to the land. These stories have achieved popularity in Australia. They have been less well accepted in the United States, where knowledge of Aboriginal culture is far less widespread. Even so, the stunning quality of the work has been noted in the United States; *Turramulli the Giant Quinkin* was listed as an ALA Notable Book for 1989.

Following Roughsey's death, Trezise has continued to produce books, all based upon Aboriginal themes, most of which bear a look similar to that developed through the collaborations of the two men. Some of these books have been done by Trezise alone, while others have been done in collaboration with Mary Haginikitas, Henry Kendall, and Rex Ingamells. Single-authored works include *Ngalculli the Red Kangaroo* (1986), *The Owl People* (1987), *The Peopling of Australia* (1987), *The Cave Painters*

(1988), *Lasca and Her Pups* (1990), *Mungoon-Gali the Giant Goanna* (1991) and *Children of the Lake* (1992).

Works done in collaboration with Haginikitas include *Platypus and Kookaburra* (by Rex Ingamells and illustrated by Trezise and Haginikitas, 1987), *The Last of His Tribe* (by Henry Kendall and illustrated by Trezise and Haginikitas, 1989), *Black Duck and Water Rat* (1988) and *Nungadin and Willijen* (1992).

In the works Trezise has single authored, one notes less emphasis on details of human features and a more stylized approach to the drawing of the human body. Trezise has also sought to place more emphasis upon stories of prehistoric Australian creatures and traditions, utilizing a less fanciful presentation in stories like *The Cave Painters* than was earlier seen in the Roughsey-Trezise collaborative works. The stories done in collaboration with Haginikitas, Ingamell and Kendall offer greater diversification in approach, employing such devices as verse, and paintings including larger and more detailed figures.

Trezise maintains his writing and illustrating career in addition to heading a company that offers tours of the Cape York area. Through his work he, both singly and in collaboration, has made important contributions in enhancing the understandings and appreciations of young people for Aboriginal traditional stories.

—Karen Patricia Smith

TRING, A. Stephen. See **MEYNELL, Laurence**.

TUBBY, I.M. See **KRAUS, Robert.**

TURKLE, Brinton (Cassady)

Nationality: American. **Born:** Alliance, Ohio, 15 August 1915. **Education:** Carnegie Institute of Technology (now Carnegie-Mellon University), Pittsburgh, 1933-36; Museum of Fine Arts School, Boston, 1938-40. **Family:** Married Yvonne Foulston in 1948; one daughter and two sons. **Career:** Freelance illustrator. **Award:** Christopher award, 1973. **Address:** c/o E.P. Dutton and Co., 375 Hudson St., New York, New York 10014, U.S.A.

PUBLICATIONS FOR CHILDREN (ILLUSTRATED BY THE AUTHOR)

Fiction

Obadiah the Bold. New York, Viking Press, 1965.
The Magic of Millicent Musgrave. New York, Viking Press, 1967.
The Fiddler of High Lonesome. New York, Viking Press, 1968.
Thy Friend, Obadiah. New York, Viking Press, 1969.
The Sky Dog. New York, Viking Press, 1969.
Mooncoin Castle; or, Skulduggery Rewarded. New York, Viking Press, 1970.
The Adventures of Obadiah. New York, Viking Press, 1972.
It's Only Arnold. New York, Viking Press, 1973.
Deep in the Forest. New York, Dutton, 1976.
Rachel and Obadiah. New York, Dutton, 1978.
Do Not Open. New York, Dutton, 1981.

*

Illustrator: *Timber Line Treasure* by Adrien Stoutenburg, 1951; *Miracle of Sage Valley* by Janet Randall, 1958; *You Say You Saw a Camel!* by Elizabeth Coatsworth, 1959; *Danny Dunn on the Ocean Floor,* 1960, and *Danny Dunn and the Fossil Cave,* 1961, both by Jay Williams and Raymond Abrashkin; *War Cry of the West* by Nathaniel Burt, 1964; *Indian Children of America* by Margaret Farquhar, 1964; *If You Lived in Colonial Times,* 1964, and *If You Grew up with Abraham Lincoln,* 1992, both by Ann McGovern; *The Far-Off Land* by Rebecca Caudill, 1964; *Four Paws into Adventure* by Claude Cenac, 1965; *The Doll in the Bakeshop* by Carol Beach York, 1965; *How Joe the Bear and Sam the Mouse Got Together,* 1965, and *Catch a Little Fox,* 1970, both by Beatrice Schenk de Regniers; *The Story of Ben Franklin* by Eve Merriam, 1965; *The Mystery of the Red Tide* by Frank Bonham, 1966; *Belinda and Me* by Bettye Hill Braucher, 1966; *High-Noon Rocket* by Charles May, 1966; *A Special Birthday Party for Someone Very Special,* 1966, *Sam and the Impossible Thing,* 1967, and *Jake,* 1969, all by Tamara Kitt; *The Lollipop Party* by Ruth A. Sonneborn, 1967; *The Troublesome Tuba* by Barbara Rinkoff, 1967; *That's What Friends Are For* by Florence Parry Heide and Sylvia W. Van Clief, 1968; *Granny and the Indians* by Peggy Parish, 1969; *Yvette* by Leon Harris, 1970; *Anna and the Baby Buzzard* by Helga Sandburg, 1970; *C Is for Circus* by Bernice Chardiet, 1971; *Who Likes It Hot?* by Mary Garelick, 1972; *The Ballad of William Sycamore* by Stephen Vincent Benét, 1972; *The Boy Who Didn't Believe in Spring* by Lucille Clifton, 1973; *Poor Richard in France* by F.N. Monjo, 1973; *Over the River and Through the Wood* by Lydia Child, 1974; *The Elves and the Shoemaker* by Freya Littledale, 1975; *Island Time* by Betty Lamont, 1976.

* * *

Through the books that he has written and illustrated, Brinton Turkle has shown his depth and originality as a writer both for younger and for older readers. In his picture books, most noticeably the four about Obadiah, through text and illustrations he has brought 19th-century Nantucket and the Quaker Starbuck family vividly to life. Obadiah has the old-fashioned speech and dress of the period and of his religion, but his antics and feelings are those of any era. He is embarrassed by the seagull who follows him in *Thy Friend, Obadiah;* he dreams of becoming a pirate in *Obadiah the Bold;* and he turns the tables on disbelieving adults in *The Adventures of Obadiah.* In *Rachel and Obadiah,* the last of the four books, the focus has shifted to Obadiah's younger sister, Rachel, in a tale with overtones of "The Tortoise and the Hare." In all of the books, the expressive, homey illustrations, full of accurate details about Nantucket, and the warmth of the family brought out in the writing capture the hearts of children.

In Turkle's most memorable story for older readers, *The Fiddler of High Lonesome,* the mood is far different from the picture books. Here dark, brooding illustrations set the mood although the American mountain dialect and exaggerations are humorous at first. When gentle Lysander Bochamp joins the wild Fogles because they are the only "kin" he believes he has left, they accept him when they discover that he can play the fiddle. However, what seems to have the makings of a merry tale changes dramatically at the climax, and the reader is left with a hauntingly sad feeling.

Mooncoin Castle, another book for older readers, is a complete turn-about from *Fiddler.* The setting is Ireland instead of the American mountains, and the narrator is Jeremy, a jackdaw, who, along with a ghost named Patrick and a witch named Maude, attempts to save Mooncoin Castle from destruction: an American-style concrete and glass shopping center is to be erected in its place. In the story Turkle satirizes pop singing groups and hilariously characterizes the unlikely trio of defenders. There is much tongue-in-cheek humor in this comical tale.

His picture book, *Do Not Open,* for younger readers, has folktale origins. Miss Moody and her cat, Captain Kid, live by the sea, collecting various treasures deposited on the beach by storms. A special find is a purple bottle marked DO NOT OPEN, but Miss Moody cannot resist the child-like voice appealing to her from within. The somewhat predictable results are offset by the highly expressive illustrations in rich colors.

—Marilyn F. Apseloff

TURNER, Ann (Warren)

Nationality: American. **Born:** Northampton, Massachusetts, 10 December 1945. **Education:** Bates College, B.A. 1967; attended Oxford University; University of Massachusetts, M.A.T. 1968. **Family:** Married Richard E. Turner in 1967; one daughter and one son. **Career:** High school English teacher, Great Barrington, Massachusetts, 1968-69; writer, since 1970; assistant director, Antioch University, Northampton, Massachusetts, 1978-80; instructor of writing at University of Massachusetts, 1987-90. **Awards:** *Atlantic Monthly* college creative writing contest, 1967; New York Academy of Sciences honor book citation, 1976; American Library Association notable children's book citations, 1980 and 1985; International Reading Association children's choice, 1988; National Council of Social Studies Notable Book citation, 1989, 1990, 1991; School Library Journal Best Book Selection, 1991. **Address:** 60 Briar Hill Road, Williamsburg, Massachusetts 01096, U.S.A.

Publications for Children

Fiction

A Hunter Comes Home. New York, Crown, 1980.
The Way Home. New York, Crown, 1982.
Third Girl from the Left. New York, Macmillan, 1986.
Time of the Bison. New York, Macmillan, 1987.
Nettie's Trip South. New York, Simon & Schuster, 1987.
Hedgehog for Breakfast. New York, Simon & Schuster, 1989.
Heron Street. New York, HarperCollins, 1989.
Through Moon and Stars and Night Skies. New York, HarperCollins, 1990.
Katie's Trunk. New York, Simon & Schuster, 1991.
Rosemary's Witch. New York, HarperCollins, 1991.
Stars for Sarah. New York, HarperCollins, 1991.
Apple Valley Year. New York, Simon & Schuster, 1993.
A Moon for Seasons. New York, Simon & Schuster Children's, 1994.
Sewing Quilts. New York, Simon & Schuster, 1994.
One Brave Summer. New York, World Publications, 1995.
Dust for Dinner. New York, HarperCollins, 1995.
Elfsong. San Diego, Harcourt Brace, 1995.
Nettie's Trip South. New York, Simon & Schuster, 1995.
Grasshopper Summer. New York, Simon & Schuster, 1997.
Finding Walter. San Diego, Harcourt, Brace, 1997.
Drummer Boy: Marching to the Civil War. New York, HarperCollins, 1998.
Angel Hide & Seek, illustrated by Lois Ehlert. New York, HarperCollins, 1998.
Let's Be Animals. New York, Harper Festival, 1998.

Poetry

Tickle a Pickle. New York, Macmillan, 1986.
Dakota Dugout. New York, Simon & Schuster, 1989.
Street Talk. Boston, Houghton Mifflin Company, 1992.
Rainflowers. New York, HarperCollins, 1992.
Grass Songs: Poems. San Diego, Harcourt Brace & Company, 1993.
The Christmas House. New York, HarperCollins, 1994.
Mississippi Mud: 3 Prairie Journals. New York, HarperCollins, 1997.
Shaker Hearts. New York, HarperCollins Children's Books, 1997.
A Lion's Hunger: Poems of First Love. New York, Marshall Cavendish, 1998.

Nonfiction

Vultures. New York, HarperCollins, 1976.
Houses for the Dead. New York, David McKay, 1976.
Rites of Birth. New York, David McKay, 1978.

*

Critical Studies: Entry in *Contemporary Authors, New Revision Series,* edited by James Lesniak, Vol. 31, Detroit, Gale Research, 1990, 437-38; entry in *Something about the Author,* edited by Kevin S. Hile and Diane Telgen, Vol. 77, Detroit, Gale Research, 1994, 218-221; review of *Finding Walter,* in *Kirkus Reviews,* 1 August 1997; review of *Angel Hide and Seek,* in *Kirkus Reviews,* 11 May 1998.

Ann Turner comments:

The queerest thing about writing is how a story chooses you, instead of you choosing it. I often feel as if I am walking along quietly, minding my own business, when a story creeps up behind me and taps me on the shoulder. "Tell me, show me, write me!" it whispers in my ear. And if I don't tell that story, it wakes me up in the morning, shakes me out of my favorite afternoon nap, and insists upon being told.

Writers write for the same reasons readers read—to find out the end of the story. I never know the endings of my stories when I start out; I must wrestle my way through them, punching out unnecessary words, arguing with self-important paragraphs, until I arrive at the end—thirsty, tired, but victorious. This tells you, of course, that writing is not easy for me. Once in a blue moon it is, but most of the time it is hard, hard work. And I work every day. I sit down at my computer and write. It could be about anything, of course—my husband, Rick, my children Ben and Charlotte, or the woods that surround our house in Williamsburg, Massachusetts.

Remember that you have stories to tell, too. Remember that you have a voice that is worth being heard. Write your stories down, keep journals. Learn to be a spy. I am a nosy, curious spy who eavesdrops on people at the beach, or as they stroll along at the mall. I always wonder; "Why is she walking so fast? Is she mad? How come his mouth looks like that? What is that lady saying to her child?" If you keep your eyes and ears open, you will see that you are surrounded by drama and astonishing things, even in the midst of everyday life. Notice it; write it down, and who knows, maybe someday you will be a writer, too.

* * *

Growing up with a father who continuously provided library books to satisfy her desire to read, Ann Turner says she cannot remember not wanting to write. At the same time, she said in *Contemporary Authors* that her artist mother gave her ... "an eye for beauty and interest in what others might think ugly or dull: dead weeds, old men and women, fat ladies at the beach, ancient and venerable crows, and vultures." Such an upbringing has helped Ann Turner create a body of literature characterized by rich imagery of language, sensitive insights into the human experience, a desire to understand the past and extend that understanding to her readers, and a search for meaningful and realistic endings to stories that have their beginnings in something she knows, such as a story inspired by family history. The themes and topics that characterize her work are diverse and cut across the genres of fiction, nonfiction, fantasy and poetry.

Turner claims that poetry will always be her first love, and her several collections of poetry are a testament to that love. Silly poems, such as in *Tickle a Pickle,* reflect childhood experiences such as throwing Daddy's shoes into the toilet. This collection of nonsense poems, like the free verse in *Street Talk,* is full of energy, in-line rhyme and alliteration, and imagery that appeals to all the senses. The poetic text of *Angel Hide and Seek* complements the unique illustrative designs of Lois Ehlert as both author and artist involve the reader in a search for angels in nature.

Though Turner has the ability to entertain through nonsense, she is also able to carve lasting impressions of the struggles individuals have faced during trying times within our country's history. *Nettie's Trip South* describes a young girl's visit to the South and her first confrontation and questioning of slavery. In the form of a letter to a friend, the smells, sights, sounds, and emotional feelings that engulf Nettie are shared as she witnesses the inhuman treatment of slaves in the South. Turner captures the feeling of "sickness" and provides a voice for the complexity of unanswered questions as to how and why such a practice could be condoned. *Drummer Boy: Marching to the Civil War* creates yet another impression of this historical era.

The poetic text of *Dakota Dugout* shares with the reader the joys, uncertainties, and heartaches of a young bride's first years on the Dakota prairie a century ago. Told in first person from the perspective of the woman to her granddaughter, the narrative is filled with sensitive imagery that describes the relationship of the early pioneers with nature. Both their dependency on nature for survival and their struggle to survive despite natural phenomenon such as icy winters and burning hot summers contribute to the memories of the earthen home in which they began. Using letters and diaries of pioneer women, Turner has written *Grass Songs,* poetry about the struggles of pioneer women. *Shaker Hearts* uses the Shaker motto "Hands to work, hearts to God" to describe in rhyming verse the simple life of the Shakers. In addition to celebrating the beauty and simplicity of their life, an introduction to the verse describes the history of the Shakers and a concluding section addresses their contributions to our present society.

In addition to a sensitive command of language, Turner has also used themes of survival to create authentic literary experiences for readers. This is seen in her more serious poetry, but also appears in her works of fiction. *Katie's Trunk* portrays for young readers the determination of a young girl caught in a community newly divided by the beliefs that began the American Revolution. Unsure of why Rebel neighbors were suddenly not speaking and calling her Tory, Katie attempts to defend her home during a rebel raid. This perspective on the beginnings of war is based on an incident that happened to one of Turner's ancestors. Told in simple prose, the story reminds us that elements of goodness remain, even in times of unrest.

For older readers, *A Hunter Comes Home* and *Third Girl From the Left* reflect the struggle to survive that Turner addresses out of an interest, she says, in what qualities lead people to have happy lives in spite of the struggles they endure. *A Hunter Comes Home* is the story of a fifteen-year-old Eskimo boy's struggle between the modern European-American culture he has learned at boarding school and the traditional culture of his people. *Third Girl From the Left* tells the story of a young girl's decision to leave Maine for Montana to become a "mail order bride." Sarah's struggles against freezing weather, loneliness, and unfulfilled expectations are met with humor and determination as she realizes her love for the western land.

Rosemary's Witch includes elements of fantasy as well as historical fiction in the story of a young girl who finds a witch living in the woods near her family's old New England house. Rosemary is agitated with the pranks the witch plays for attention, and the interaction between the witch and child are humorous at times. While the reader is drawn in by the dual perspectives within the story, Rosemary learns about herself through the witch. Fantasy is also the genre that frames *Finding Walter.* All children delight in the idea that their toys might actually come alive. Emily and Rose are no different as they share in the dilemma of her doll family who cannot find one member. The allegorical quality of this story is evident as the problems facing the doll family reflect the real life problems of Emily and Rose. The gentle, old-fashioned personalities of the doll family provide a perspective on love, family, and change that soothes the tension between the two sisters.

Ann Turner's ability to recreate an array of emotions experienced by people across time, genre, and situation invites her readers to make personal connections to many historical contexts. Her insights into the universality of people's needs, feelings, and desires within diverse social and historical settings provide a comprehensive understanding of events in history.

—Janelle B. Mathis

TURNER, Philip (William)

Pseudonym: Stephen Chance. **Nationality:** British (came to England in 1926). **Born:** Rossland, British Columbia, Canada, 3 December 1925. **Education:** Hinckley Grammar School, Leicestershire; Worcester College, Oxford, 1946-49, B.A. 1950, M.A. 1962; Chichester Theological College, Sussex, 1949-51, ordained priest, Church of England, 1951. **Military Service:** Served in the Royal Naval Volunteer Reserve, 1943-46: Sub-Lieutenant. **Family:** Married Margaret Diana Samson in 1950; two sons and one daughter. **Career:** Anglican parish priest, St. Bartholomew's, Armley, Leeds, 1951-56, St. Peter's, Crawley, Sussex, 1956-60, and St. Matthew's, Northampton, 1962-65; head of religious broadcasting, BBC Midland Region, Birmingham, 1965-70; teacher, Droitwich High School, Worcestershire, 1970-73; chaplain, Eton College, Buckinghamshire, 1973-75. From 1975 part-time teacher, Malvern College, Worcestershire. **Awards:** Library Association Carnegie Medal, 1966. **Agent:** Watson Little Ltd., Suite 8, 26 Charing Cross Road, London WC2H 0DG. **Address:** 181 West Malvern Road, Malvern, Worcestershire, England.

Publications for Children

Fiction

Colonel Sheperton's Clock, illustrated by Philip Gough. London, Oxford University Press, 1964; Cleveland, World, 1966; as *The Mystery of the Colonel's Clock,* Aylesbury, Buckinghamshire, Goodchild, 1984.
The Grange at High Force, illustrated by William Papas. London, Oxford University Press, 1965; Cleveland, World, 1967; as *The Adventure at High Force,* Aylesbury, Buckinghamshire, Goodchild, 1984.
Sea Peril, illustrated by Ian Ribbons. London, Oxford University Press, 1966; Cleveland, World, 1968.
Steam on the Line, illustrated by Trevor Ridley. London, Oxford University Press, and Cleveland, World, 1968.
War on the Darnel, illustrated by Doreen Roberts. London, Oxford University Press, and New York, World, 1969.
Wig-wig and Homer, illustrated by Graham Humphreys. London, Oxford University Press, 1969; New York, World, 1970.
Devil's Nob. London, Hamish Hamilton, 1970; Nashville, Nelson, 1973.
Powder Quay. London, Hamish Hamilton, 1971.
Dunkirk Summer. London, Hamish Hamilton, 1973.
Skull Island. London, Dent, 1977.
Decision in the Dark: Tales of Mystery. London, Dent, 1978.
Rookoo and Bree, illustrated by Terry Riley. London, Dent, 1979.
The Candlemass Treasure. Cambridge, Lutterworth Press, 1988.

Fiction as Stephen Chance

Septimus and the Danedyke Mystery. London, Bodley Head, 1971; Nashville, Nelson, 1973.
Septimus and the Minster Ghost. London, Bodley Head, 1972; as *Septimus and the Minster Ghost Mystery,* Nashville, Nelson, 1974.
Septimus and the Stone of Offering. London, Bodley Head, 1976; as *The Stone of Offering,* Nashville, Nelson, 1977.
Septimus and the Spy Ring. London, Bodley Head, 1979.

Other

The Christmas Story: A Carol Service for Children. London, Church Information Office, 1964.
The Bible Story, illustrated by Brian Wildsmith. London, Oxford University Press, 1968; as *Illustrated Bible Stories,* New York, Watts, 1969.
The Good Shepherd (retelling), illustrated by Bunshu Iguchi. London, Dent, 1986.

Publications for Adults

Plays

Christ in the Concrete City (produced Hinckley, Yorkshire, 1953). London, S.P.C.K., 1956; revised edition, 1960; Boston, Baker, 1965.
Mann's End (produced Armley, Yorkshire, 1953). Included in *Tell It with Trumpets,* 1959.
Passion in Paradise Street (produced Armley, Yorkshire, 1954). Included in *Tell It with Trumpets,* 1959.
How Many Miles to Bethlehem? in *Three One-Act Plays.* London, British Council of Churches, 1957; published separately, Boston, Baker, 1986.
Cry Dawn in Dark Babylon: A Dramatic Meditation (as *Benny Death and His Old Bones,* produced Durham, 1957). London, S.P.C.K., 1959.
Tell It with Trumpets: Three Experiments in Drama and Evangelism (includes *Mann's End, Passion in Paradise Street, Six-Fifteen to Eternity,* with Jack Windross). London, S.P.C.K., 1959.
Casey: A Dramatic Meditation on the Passion (produced Crawley, Sussex, 1961). London, S.P.C.K., 1962.
This Is the Word, and Word Made Flesh. London, S.P.C.K., 1962.
So Long at the Fair. Melbourne, Board of Christian Education of Australia and New Zealand, 1966.
Men in Stone. Boston, Baker, 1966.
Cantata for Derelicts. London, S.P.C.K., 1967.
Madonna in Concrete. London, S.P.C.K., and Boston, Baker, 1971.
The Pantomime of Septimus Totter. Privately printed, n.d.
Watch at the World's End. Boston, Baker, 1980.

Other

Peter Was His Nickname. London, Waltham Forest Books, 1965.

*

Philip Turner comments:

It has never seemed to me that writing for children is different from writing for anyone else—except that there are some (not many) parts of adult experience that are of no interest to children because they are not yet old enough to have come across them. I write about what interests me and about what I enjoy. If other people—whether 7 or 70—enjoy it as well, that is splendid. In prose most of what I write comes out as children's stories because of the common interest in "the wonderful oddity of things." In drama I tend to get a bit long-faced and theological for the young.

* * *

Philip Turner is an able but uneven writer, whose gifts have never, perhaps, been fused with complete success in a single book. Occasional failures of tone, weakening of imaginative stamina, and lapses of characterisation occur as minor blemishes in otherwise spirited and enjoyable stories. On the other hand, he has major qualities which are infrequently found in more technically consistent novelists and lift his work far above the ordinary. Turner's lapses seem due to some uncertainty about his own role and purposes, and especially to sporadic retreat from the seriousness that his themes demand. Inopportune humour explains certain failures of psychological conviction: he has a strange technique of transferred detachment, attributing to his young characters—often at incongruous moments of intense responsibility and crisis—a wry and amused perspective on their perils which is properly the author's own. Turner is an accomplished humorist, and hilarious episodes abound in his stories of present-day adventure, but the humour sometimes jars against a more sombre prevailing mood.

Despite the blemishes, Turner's holiday adventures are a considerable achievement. He has created his own distinctive landscape. It reaches from the little seaport of Darnley Mills, inland and up-river across a country estate, to the hill quarries and bleak open moors. Much of its length is traversed and linked by a narrow-gauge railway, which figures largely both as a focus of adventure and as an index of social history in several novels set in previous generations, and is revived in the modern adventure *War on the Darnel.* This is the setting for Turner's present-day adventures, in which three schoolboys, very different in character but close friends, play and work and grow up.

The Grange at High Force and *War on the Darnel* are good examples of these books, which follow a similar pattern. There are comedy and high jinks, and there is also a serious crisis in which play is forgotten and the boys' responsibility tested. In *The Grange at High Force* there is much fun with the firing of an 18th-century cannon and a reconstructed Roman ballista, but there is also an appalling blizzard which sends the boys out to rescue the sheep from the high fells and a middle-aged recluse from her snow-bound cottage. In *War on the Darnel* there is mock warfare between rival groups of Christian aid collectors, but there is also a dangerous flood in which lives are threatened. The natural rhythm of boyhood is here, in which games and horseplay and ingenious technical experiment prepare for the demands of adult life, recreation and duty can overlap at any time, and childlike pleasure be swamped by emergency.

The fifth story in this sequence, *Skull Island,* is another holiday adventure but is set in unfamiliar terrain, a remote and uninhabited offshore island. For the three schoolboys, now almost grown up, the holiday journey to this isolated place marks the exploration of a widening future, while for the adults with them it is a quest or pilgrimage to the scene of long-past wartime tragedy. It forms a most effective conclusion to the series. These are good stories, full of vigorous action, but they also successfully depict Christian worship as a natural part of life, and pause at times in reverent stillness before the natural world.

More serious, and more uniformly successful, are the books that explore the adventures of former generations in this same landscape, *Steam on the Line, Devil's Nob,* and *Powder Quay.* In these three books, the changing fortunes of the little railway are the focus of wider movements of social change and historical experience. Turner admirably catches the lift and decline of lives and ways of life, of families and generations. These books have an emotional and political dimension which is missing in the present-day stories. *Devil's Nob* and *Powder Quay* both describe adolescent love, each with a moving realism, honesty, and tenderness. The books are concerned with class differences, the realities of poverty and social injustice, the harshness of economic catastrophe or war. Turner approaches these with evident discomfort and indignation: he is a traditionalist writer, affirming established values which his individual sympathies at times compel him to dispute. The result is some loss of ideological cohesion but a great gain in emotional force and complexity. The books have a manifest urgency and relevance which historical novels do not commonly achieve.

Turner's crime-and-adventure novel *The Candlemass Treasure* shows the same attractive blend of firm moral values, exciting action, and vividly realised locations, in this case East Anglia and Holy Island.

Turner has written for younger children, notably a charming story of two runaway piglets, *Wig-wig and Homer.* And under the name Stephen Chance he has published several stories of crime and mayhem for older readers. In *Septimus and the Danedyke Mystery* the chief character is a retired London detective who, having somewhat improbably turned country parson, finds even more improbably that his former concerns refuse to desert him. The books are an amusing and modestly successful attempt to fill in an evident gap in adolescent fiction, but they do not seriously rival the achievement of the Darnley Mills stories.

—Peter Hollindale

U-V

UCHIDA, Yoshiko

Nationality: American. **Born:** Born in Alameda, California, 24 November 1921. **Education:** University of California, Berkeley, A.B. (cum laude) 1942; Smith College, Northampton, Massachusetts (graduate fellow), M.Ed. 1944. **Career:** Teacher, Japanese relocation center, Utah, 1942-43, and Frankford Friends School, Philadelphia, 1944-45; secretary, Institute of Pacific Relations, New York, 1946-47, United Student Christian Council, New York, 1947-52, and Lawrence Radiation Laboratory, University of California, Berkeley, 1957-62. Wrote series of articles on folk arts and crafts for *Nippon Times,* Tokyo, 1953-54; columnist ("Letter from San Francisco"), *Craft Horizons,* New York, 1955-64. **Awards:** Ford Foundation fellowship, 1952; University of Oregon award, 1981. **Died:** 21 June 1992.

Publications for Children

Fiction

New Friends for Susan, illustrated by Henry Sugimoto. New York, Scribner, 1951.
The Full Circle, illustrated by the author. New York, Friendship Press, 1957.
Takao and Grandfather's Sword, illustrated by William Hutchinson. New York, Harcourt Brace, 1958; Edinburgh, Oliver and Boyd, 1966.
The Promised Year, illustrated by William Hutchinson. New York, Harcourt Brace, 1959.
Mik and the Prowler, illustrated by William Hutchinson. New York, Harcourt Brace, 1960.
Rokubei and the Thousand Rice Bowls, illustrated by Kazue Mizumura. New York, Scribner, 1962.
The Forever Christmas Tree, illustrated by Kazue Mizumura. New York, Scribner, 1963.
Sumi's Prize, illustrated by Kazue Mizumura. New York, Scribner, 1964.
Sumi's Special Happening, illustrated by Kazue Mizumura. New York, Scribner, 1966.
In-Between Miya, illustrated by Susan Bennett. New York, Scribner, 1967; London, Angus and Robertson, 1968.
Sumi and the Goat and the Tokyo Express, illustrated by Kazue Mizumura. New York, Scribner, 1969.
Hisako's Mysteries, illustrated by Susan Bennett. New York, Scribner, 1969.
Makoto, The Smallest Boy, illustrated by Akihito Shirakawa. New York, Crowell, 1970.
Journey to Topaz, illustrated by Donald Carrick. New York, Scribner, 1971.
Samurai of Gold Hill, illustrated by Ati Forberg. New York, Scribner, 1972.
The Birthday Visitor, illustrated by Charles Robinson. New York, Scribner, 1975.
The Rooster Who Understood Japanese, illustrated by Charles Robinson. New York, Scribner, 1976.
Journey Home, illustrated by Charles Robinson. New York, Atheneum, 1978.
A Jar of Dreams. New York, Atheneum, 1981.
The Best Bad Thing. New York, Atheneum, 1983.
The Happiest Ending. New York, Atheneum, 1985.
The Magic Purse, illustrated by Keiko Narahashi. New York, Macmillan, 1993.
The Bracelet, illustrated by Joanna Yardley. New York, Philomel Books, 1993.

Other

The Dancing Kettle and Other Japanese Folk Tales, illustrated by Richard Jones. New York, Harcourt Brace, 1949.
The Magic Listening Cap: More Folk Tales from Japan, illustrated by the author. New York, Harcourt Brace, 1955.
The Sea of Gold and Other Tales from Japan, illustrated by Marianne Yamaguchi. New York, Scribner, 1965.
Tabi: Journey Through Time: Stories of the Japanese in America. El Cerrito, California, Sycamore Congregational Church Board of Education, 1981.
The Two Foolish Cats (retelling), illustrated by Margot Zemach. New York, McElderry, 1987.
The Invisible Thread: A Memoir. Morristown, New Jersey, Silver Burdett Press, 1991.
Bird Song (poems), illustrated by the author. Privately printed, 1992.
The Wise Old Woman (retelling), illustrated by Martin Springett. New York, McElderry, 1994.

Publications for Adults

Novel

Picture Bride. Flagstaff, Arizona, Northland Press, 1987.

Other

We Do Not Work Alone: The Thoughts of Kanjiro Kawai. Kyoto, Folk Art Society, 1953.
The History of Sycamore Church. Privately printed, 1974.
Margaret de Patta (exhibition catalogue). Oakland, California, Oakland Museum, 1976.
Desert Exile: The Uprooting of a Japanese American Family. Seattle, University of Washington Press, 1982.

*

Manuscript Collections: University of Oregon Library, Eugene; Bancroft Library, University of California, Berkeley.

Yoshiko Uchida comments:

Because I felt I could make the best contribution by writing from my own cultural heritage, all my books have been about Japanese or Japanese-Americans. In my earlier books I wrote about Japan in the hope that American children would not only learn to understand and respect its culture, but would identify with the Japanese people as fellow human beings. Because of the growing awareness of the various ethnic groups in the United States, however, I am now writing books based on the relatively unexplored history of Japanese-Americans. I hope these books will help dispel long-existing stereotypic images and also increase among Japanese-American young people an understanding of their own history and pride in their identity. Ultimately, however, I try to write of meaningful relationships between human beings, to celebrate our common humanity.

* * *

The talented and prolific author of nearly three dozen books, Yoshiko Uchida was one of the most important pioneers of Japanese-American children's literature. Her graceful retellings of Japanese folk tales, her autobiographical and fictional renditions of the Japanese-American relocation camp experience during World War II, and her explorations of the world through the eyes of Japanese and Japanese-American pre-teens delighted young readers for more than four decades.

As a rule, Uchida's literary themes correspond with the three categories into which her works are often divided. The Japanese folk tales, predictably, extol traditional Japanese virtues deriving from Taoist and Buddhist precepts: respect for the wisdom and forbearance accompanying age; the dangers of greed and materialism; the importance of patience and endurance; the kinship between humans and animals; and the predominance of intellect over physical prowess. The works based on the Japanese-American camp experience examine and condemn white prejudice (while insisting that such prejudice was not universal); these works also suggest the attitudes, behaviors, and attributes which, from Uchida's perspective, enable a person to overcome—and even deflate—the racism of others. Finally, Uchida's contemporary stories of childhood imply that the efforts of a "soundhearted" protagonist will, in the long run, work to her advantage and to the advantage of her circle, even if such efforts appear naive or misguided in the short term.

Naturally, some overlapping of themes occurs. Stories like *A Jar of Dreams* deal with various kinds of racism; such stories also extol traditional Japanese values. The child protagonists of works based on the Second World War camp experience are naive and unknowing; their stories are concerned as much with the universal path to maturity as with the often disheartening facts of American history. And the folk tales seem colored by Uchida's contemporary experience, appropriately emphasizing gender equality and featuring redrawn protagonists who, by traditional Japanese standards, are brash, independent, and even rebellious.

Of Uchida's works especially for young children, virtually all are picture books written on the second-grade level (though many first and third graders enjoy these same books). And of these, the most timeless in their appeal are the retold folk tales featuring the captivating illustrations of Kazue Mizumura, Keiko Narahashi, and Martin Springett: *Rokubei and the Thousand Rice Bowls, The Man Who Bought a Dream, The Two Foolish Cats, The Terrible Leak, The Magic Purse,* and *The Wise Old Woman.* Among the most entertaining of these is the story of Rokubei, which tells of a Japanese potter who loves to make earthenware but hates the business of selling it; of special thematic significance (and equally delightful in the view of many readers) are *Foolish Cats,* which argues that survival is dependent upon harmony and cooperation, and *Wise Old Woman,* the protagonist of which outwits a vengeful warlord and thereby preserves her community. These and other Japanese folk tales are collected in Uchida's *The Dancing Kettle, The Magic Listening Cap* and *The Sea of Gold,* volumes most suited to third, fourth, and fifth graders.

Uchida's contemporary stories for young children also enjoy a wide and appreciative readership. The best of these are *The Forever Christmas Tree,* which offers poignant Japanese perspectives on the significance of Christmas; *Sumi and the Goat and the Tokyo Express,* the third story in the "Sumi trilogy," this one telling how a mischievous goat brings recognition to Sumi and excitement to her small village; *Makoto, the Smallest Boy,* which argues that self-confidence is the only true security; and *The Rooster Who Understood Japanese,* whose young protagonist finds a home for her neighbor's rooster, thereby bringing harmony and a spirit of cooperation to her neighborhood.

Uchida's only attempt to portray the relocation camp experience in picture book form is *The Bracelet,* a largely unsatisfying venture. While the book's heart is in the right place (it attempts to define racism and explore its consequences in terms children can understand, and suggests, too, that friendship is based on feelings and memories, not material things), it has no real plot. More crucially, while young readers understand that the book's protagonist has ended up in some kind of prison, they don't know why she is there and they worry about what will become of her. True, the book can provoke rich discussion in the classroom or between a parent and child. But a child reading the book alone is apt to find it incoherent and troubling.

While Uchida's short novels seem intended for readers who are 11 or older, many fourth and fifth graders enjoy them as well. Especially popular among young girls is the "Rinko trilogy"—*The Jar of Dreams, The Best Bad Thing,* and *The Happiest Ending*—although some readers complain that they cannot really identify with Rinko, a girl growing up in a rather idealized Berkeley during the 1930s. Young boys find subdued yet engaging adventure in *Takao and Grandfather's Sword* and *Samurai of Gold Hill.* Mature fourth and fifth graders also enjoy the relocation camp novels written for young adolescents: *Journey to Topaz, Desert Exile,* and *Journey Home.*

—Keith Lawrence

UNGERER, Tomi

Nationality: French. **Born:** Jean Thomas Ungerer, Strasbourg, 28 November 1931. **Education:** Ecole Municipale des Arts Décoratifs, Strasbourg, 1953-54. **Family:** Married 1) Miriam Lancaster in 1959 (marriage dissolved); 2) Yvonne Deborah Wright in 1971; three daughters. **Career:** Freelance illustrator and commercial artist; founder, Wild Oats Film Company. Individual shows: Haus am Lutzowplatz, Berlin, 1962; D'Arcy Galleries, New York, 1963; Galerie Daniel Keel, Zurich, 1969, 1972-75; Waddel Gallery, New York, 1970; Kestner Gesellschaft, Hannover, Germany, 1972; Galerie Wolfgang Gurlitt, Munich, 1972; Taxis Palais, Innsbruck, 1973; Museum des 20 Jahrhunderts, Vienna, 1973; Galerie Bloch, Innsbruck, 1975; Musée d'Art Moderne, Strasbourg, 1975; Musée des Arts Décoratifs, Paris (retrospective), 1981; Royal Festival Hall, London (retrospective), 1985; and others. Lived in the United States, 1956-71, in Canada, 1971-76, and in Ireland since 1976. **Awards:** Society of Illustrators Gold Medal, 1960; *New York*

Times award, for illustration, 1962, 1971, 1974; American Institute of Graphic Arts award, 1969. Commander, Order of Arts and Letters (France). **Address:** c/o Diogenes Verlag, Sprecherstrasse 8, CH-8032 Zurich, Switzerland.

Publications for Children (illustrated by the author)

Fiction

The Mellops Go Flying. New York, Harper, 1957; London, Methuen, 1962.
The Mellops Go Diving for Treasure. New York, Harper, 1957.
The Mellops Strike Oil. New York, Harper, 1958.
Crictor. New York, Harper, 1958; London, Methuen, 1959.
Adelaide. New York, Harper, 1959.
Emile. New York, Harper, 1960.
Christmas Eve at the Mellops'. New York, Harper, and London, Hamish Hamilton, 1960.
Rufus. New York, Harper, 1961.
Snail, Where Are You? New York, Harper, 1962.
The Three Robbers. New York, Atheneum, and London, Methuen, 1962.
The Mellops Go Spelunking. New York and London, Harper, 1963.
Orlando the Brave Vulture. New York, Harper, 1966; London, Methuen, 1967.
Moon Man. London, Whiting and Wheaton, 1966; New York, Harper, 1967.
Zeralda's Ogre. New York, Harper, 1967; London, Bodley Head, 1970.
Basil Ratski. Zurich, Diogenes, 1967.
Ask Me a Question. New York, Harper, 1968.
The Hat. New York, Parents' Magazine Press, 1970; London, Bodley Head, 1971.
The Beast of Monsieur Racine. New York, Farrar Straus, 1971; London, Bodley Head, 1972.
I Am Papa Snap and These Are My Favorite No-Such Stories. New York, Harper, 1971; London, Methuen, 1973.
No Kiss for Mother. New York, Harper, 1973; London, Methuen, 1974.
Allumette: A Fable, with Due Respect to Hans Christian Andersen, the Grimm Brothers, and the Honorable Ambrose Bierce. New York, Parents' Magazine Press, 1974; London, Methuen, 1975.
Flix. Boulder, Colorado, Roberts Rinehart Publishers, 1998.

Poetry

One, Two, Where's My Shoe? New York and London, Harper, 1964.

Other

Editor, *A Storybook from Tomi Ungerer.* New York, Watts, and London, Collins, 1974.

Publications for Adults (drawings)

Other

Inside Marriage: Wedding Pictures. New York, Grove Press, 1960.
Horrible: An Account of the Sad Achievements of Progress. New York, Atheneum, and London, Hamish Hamilton, 1960.
Der Herzinfarkt. Zurich, Diogenes, 1962.
A Television Notebook. New York, CBS, 1963.
The Underground Sketch Book of Tomi Ungerer. New York, Viking Press, and London, Bodley Head, 1964.
The Party. New York, Paragraphic, 1966.
Fornicon. New York, Rhinoceros Press, 1969.
Portfolio. Zurich, Diogenes, 1970.
Compromises. New York, Farrar Straus, and London, Bodley Head, 1970.
The Poster Art of Tomi Ungerer, edited by Jack Rennert. New York, Darien House, 1970; London, Constable, 1973.
Der Sexmaniak. Zurich, Diogenes, 1971.
Der Spiegelmensch. Zurich, Diogenes, 1973.
Adam and Eve: A Collection of Cartoons. Zurich, Diogenes, 1974; London, Cape, 1976.
America: Zeichnungen 1956-1971. Zurich, Diogenes, 1974.
Freut Euch des Lebens. Zurich, Diogenes, 1975.
Das grosse Liederbuch. Zurich, Diogenes, 1975.
Das kleine Liederbuch. Zurich, Diogenes, 1975.
Hopp Hopp Hopp (erotica). Privately printed, 1975.
Totempole: Erotische Zeichnungen 1968-1975. Zurich, Diogenes, 1976.
Babylon. Zurich, Diogenes, 1979.
Abracadabra. Cologne, Argos Verlag, 1979.
Politricks. Zurich, Diogenes, 1980.
Der Furz. Cologne, Argos Verlag, 1980.
Symptomatics. Zurich, Diogenes, 1982.
Das Kamasutra der Frösche. Zurich, Diogenes, 1982; as *The Joy of Frogs,* London, Souvenir Press, 1984; New York, Grove Press, 1985.
Here Today—Gone Tomorrow (reportage). Zurich, Diogenes, 1983; as *Far Out Isn't Far Enough,* New York, Grove Press, and London, Methuen, 1984.
Slow Agony. Zurich, Diogenes, 1983.
1911—(erotica). Zurich, Diogenes, 1983.
Rigor Mortis. Zurich, Diogenes, 1983.
Once in a Lifetime. London, Cape, 1984.
Tomi Ungerers Frauen. Zurich, Diogenes, 1984.
Testament: A Collection of Satirical Drawings 1960-80. London, Cape, 1985.
Frisch, Frosch, Fröhlich, Frei. Zurich, Diogenes, 1985.
Warteraum. Zurich, Diogenes, 1985.
Schutzengel der Hölle. Zurich, Diogenes, 1986.
Derby. Zurich, Diogenes, 1987.
A la Guerre Comme a la Guerre. Nuee Bleue, France, Strasbourg, 1991.
Tomi Ungerer im Gesprach fur Europa. Elster, West Germany, Baden-Baden, 1992.

*

Manuscript Collections: Free Library, Philadelphia.

Illustrator: *The Brave Coward* by Art Buchwald, 1957; *Agee on Film* by James Agee, 1958; *Seeds and More Seeds* by Millicent E. Selsam, 1959; *Amerika für Angänger* by Paul Rothenhäusler, 1960; *The Backside of Washington* by Dick West, 1961; *Comfortable Words* by Bergen Evans, 1962; *The Book of Gambling* edited by David Newman, 1962; *Riddle Dee Dee* by Bennett Cerf, 1962; *Frédou* by Mary Stolz, 1962; *Frances Face-Maker,* 1963, and *That Pest, Jonathan,* 1970, both by William Cole, and *A Cat-Hater's*

Handbook, 1963, *Beastly Boys and Ghastly Girls,* 1964, *Oh, What Nonsense!,* 1966, *A Case of the Giggles,* 1966, *What's Good for a Four-Year-Old,* 1967, *This Is Ridiculous,* 1967, *Oh, How Silly!,* 1970, *The Book of Giggles,* 1970, and *Oh, That's Ridiculous!,* 1972, all edited by Cole; *Owls and More Owls* by John Hollander, 1963; *Come into My Parlor,* 1963, and *The Too Hot to Cook Book,* 1966, both by Miriam Ungerer; *The Girls We Leave Behind,* 1963, and *The Clambake Mutiny,* 1964, both by Jerome Beatty; *Der Spottsdrossel* by Ambrose Bierce, 1963; *All about Women* edited by Saul Maloff, 1963; *Erlesene Verbrechen and Makellose Morde,* 1964; *Ein Bündel Geschichten für Lüsterne Leser,* 1967, both by Henry Slesar; *Games, Anyone?* by Robert Thomson, 1964; *Dear N.A.S.A., Please Send Me a Rocket* by Tait Trussel and Paul Hencke, 1964; *Flat Stanley* by Jeff Brown, 1964; *A Collection of French Poetry,* 1966; *Warwick's Three Bottles,* 1966, and *Cleopatra Goes Sledding,* 1968, both by André Hodeir; *Mr. Tall and Mr. Small* by Barbara Brenner, 1966; *The Donkey Ride* by Jean B. Showalter, 1967; *Nonsense Verses* by Edward Lear, 1967; *The Sorcerer's Apprentice* by Barbara Shook Hazen, 1969; *New York für Anfänger* by Herbert Feuerstein, 1969; *Der Gestohlene Bazillus* by H.G. Wells, 1969; *The Consumer in American Society* by A.W. Troelstrup, 1970; *School Life in Paris,* 1970; *Kneipenlieder* by Rainer Brambach and Frank Geerk, 1974; *Liebesdienste* by Ben Witter, 1976; *The Great Song Book* edited by Timothy John, 1978; *Heidi* retold by Rosemary Harris, 1983; *School Life in Paris, and Lovely Nights of Young Girls,* 1984; *Das Grosse Buch der Kleinen Tiere* by Bernhard Lassahn, 1989; *Tomi Ungerer's Heidi: The Classic Novel* translated by Helen B. Dole, 1990; *Les Caretes Postales de Tomi Ungerer* by Patrick Hamm, 1991; *Eva Demskis Katzenbuch mit Zeichnungen von Tomi Ungerer* by Eva Demski, 1992; *Marianne Moore* by Dave Page, 1994.

* * *

One of Tomi Ungerer's many talents is that of lending charm and appeal to various denizens of the human or animal population not generally loved or admired by the public. Among his host of unlikely animal heroes are to be found Emile the octopus, Rufus the bat, Crictor the heroic boa constrictor, the Mellops family of handsome and amiable pigs, and Orlando the brave vulture. In more or less human guise come the child-devouring ogre who is eventually humanized into marriageability by sweet Zeralda, the three grim robbers of the black capes and ominous eyes, and M. Racine's friend the peculiar looking and unidentifiable Beast, to name but a few. Each represents some form of life or fantastic order of being usually regarded as repulsive, threatening, or disgusting, yet in Ungerer's light-hearted picture stories all are transformed into the World's Valentines.

That this is so must be attributed at least in part to the winning way in which Ungerer has drawn them: it is quite impossible to think of Ungerer's text without reference to his pictures, for the two are inseparable. (When Crictor's acrobatic body forms letters of the alphabet, should the result be described as art or literature?) Pictures give point to his spare and economical prose, while his wickedly sly text underscores his pictorial wit. His work is dotted with "visual puns," a little piggy-boy has (of course) a human-shaped penny bank; Emile at the grand piano plays "La Mer" in concert style.

If Ungerer's animal and reptile heroes are almost-human creatures of fantasy, his human creations, however fantastic their adventures, are solidly down-to-earth. Young Zeralda, the ogre-tamer, has the self-possession of an Alice in Wonderland: no matter how bizarre the situation in which she finds herself, she holds firmly to the one essential principle that a hungry man (or ogre) must be fed. Her businesslike, matter-of-fact behaviour makes her a memorably charming young heroine. Little orphan Tiffany is made of the same sturdy stuff. Kidnapped by three fierce robbers, she remains poised and in control of the situation. Her reasonable inquiries as to the purpose of their activities lead the robbers to reconsider their antisocial behaviour and become philanthropists. Allumette, the ragged match girl suddenly deluged by inexplicable treasure from the sky, is not stunned by the situation as we should be: she immediately opens a welfare office in order to distribute largess in an orderly fashion. Their unruffled, reasonable behavior is the secret of Ungerer's little people's charm. He can take a tired old theme, give it a twist no-one else could have dreamt of—and the end result is both unpredictable and somehow inevitable and satisfying. Ungerer's is an unprejudiced eye, able to discover admirable qualities in unlikely places, and, better still, he is able to make his readers do the same.

—Joan McGrath

UTTLEY, Alison

Nationality: British. **Born:** Alice Jane Taylor, Cromford, Derbyshire, 17 December 1884. **Education:** Lady Manners School, Bakewell, Derbyshire; Manchester University, B.Sc. (honours) in physics, 1906; Cambridge University, 1907. **Family:** Married James A. Uttley in 1911 (died 1930); one son. **Career:** Science teacher, Fulham Secondary School for Girls, London, 1908-11. Litt.D: Manchester University, 1970. **Died:** 7 May 1976.

Publications for Children

Fiction

The Squirrel, The Hare, and the Little Grey Rabbit, illustrated by Margaret Tempest. London, Heinemann, 1929.
How Little Grey Rabbit Got Back Her Tail, illustrated by Margaret Tempest. London, Heinemann, 1930.
The Great Adventure of Hare, illustrated by Margaret Tempest. London, Heinemann, 1931.
Moonshine and Magic, illustrated by Will Townsend. London, Faber, 1932.
The Story of Fuzzypeg the Hedgehog, illustrated by Margaret Tempest. London, Heinemann, 1932.
Squirrel Goes Skating, illustrated by Margaret Tempest. London, Collins, 1934.
Wise Owl's Story, illustrated by Margaret Tempest. London, Collins, 1935.
The Adventures of Peter and Judy in Bunnyland, illustrated by L. Young. London, Collins, 1935.
Candlelight Tales, illustrated by Elinor Bellingham-Smith. London, Faber, 1936.
Little Grey Rabbit's Party, illustrated by Margaret Tempest. London, Collins, 1936.

The Knot Squirrel Tied, illustrated by Margaret Tempest. London, Collins, 1937.
The Adventures of No Ordinary Rabbit, illustrated by Alec Buckels. London, Faber, 1937.
Mustard, Pepper, and Salt, illustrated by Gwen Raverat. London, Faber, 1938.
Fuzzypeg Goes to School, illustrated by Margaret Tempest. London, Collins, 1938.
A Traveller in Time. London, Faber, 1939; New York, Putnam, 1940.
Tales of the Four Pigs and Brock the Badger, illustrated by Alec Buckels. London, Faber, 1939.
Little Grey Rabbit's Christmas, illustrated by Margaret Tempest. London, Collins, 1939.
Moldy Warp, The Mole, illustrated by Margaret Tempest. London, Collins, 1940.
The Adventures of Sam Pig, illustrated by Francis Gower. London, Faber, 1940.
Sam Pig Goes to Market, illustrated by A.E. Kennedy. London, Faber, 1941.
Six Tales of Brock the Badger, illustrated by Alec Buckels and Francis Gower. London, Faber, 1941.
Six Tales of Sam Pig, illustrated by Alec Buckels and Francis Gower. London, Faber, 1941.
Six Tales of the Four Pigs, illustrated by Alec Buckels. London, Faber, 1941.
Ten Tales of Tim Rabbit, illustrated by Alec Buckels and Francis Gower. London, Faber, 1941.
Hare Joins the Home Guard, illustrated by Margaret Tempest. London, Collins, 1942.
Little Grey Rabbit's Washing-Day, illustrated by Margaret Tempest. London, Collins, 1942.
Nine Starlight Tales, illustrated by Irene Hawkins. London, Faber, 1942.
Sam Pig and Sally, illustrated by A.E. Kennedy. London, Faber, 1942.
Cuckoo Cherry-Tree, illustrated by Irene Hawkins. London, Faber, 1943.
Sam Pig at the Circus, illustrated by A.E. Kennedy. London, Faber, 1943.
Water-Rat's Picnic, illustrated by Margaret Tempest. London, Collins, 1943.
Little Grey Rabbit's Birthday, illustrated by Margaret Tempest. London, Collins, 1944.
The Spice Woman's Basket and Other Tales, illustrated by Irene Hawkins. London, Faber, 1944.
Mrs. Nimble and Mr. Bumble, illustrated by Horace Knowles. London, James, 1944.
Some Moonshine Tales, illustrated by Sarah Nechamkin. London, Faber, 1945.
The Adventures of Tim Rabbit, illustrated by A.E. Kennedy. London, Faber, 1945.
The Weather Cock and Other Stories, illustrated by Nancy Innes. London, Faber, 1945.
The Speckledy Hen, illustrated by Margaret Tempest. London, Faber, 1946.
Little Grey Rabbit and the Weasels, illustrated by Margaret Tempest. London, Collins, 1947.
Grey Rabbit and the Wandering Hedgehog, illustrated by Margaret Tempest. London, Collins, 1948.
John Barleycorn: Twelve Tales of Fairy and Magic, illustrated by Philip Hepworth. London, Faber, 1948.
Sam Pig in Trouble, illustrated by A.E. Kennedy. London, Faber, 1948.
The Cobbler's Shop and Other Tales, illustrated by Irene Hawkins. London, Faber, 1950.
Macduff, illustrated by A.E. Kennedy. London, Faber, 1950.
Little Grey Rabbit Makes Lace, illustrated by Margaret Tempest. London, Collins, 1950.
The Little Brown Mouse Books (Snug and Serena Meet a Queen, Snug and Serena Pick Cowslips, Going to the Fair, Toad's Castle, Mrs. Mouse Spring-Cleans, Christmas at the Rose and Crown, The Gypsy Hedgehogs, Snug and the Chimney-Sweeper, The Mouse Telegrams, The Flower Show, Snug and the Silver Spoon, Mr. Stoat Walks In), illustrated by Katherine Wigglesworth. London, Heinemann, 12 vols., 1950-57.
Yours Ever, Sam Pig, illustrated by A.E. Kennedy. London, Faber, 1951.
Hare and the Easter Eggs, illustrated by Margaret Tempest. London, Collins, 1952.
Little Grey Rabbit Goes to Sea, illustrated by Margaret Tempest. London, Collins, 1954.
Little Red Fox and the Wicked Uncle, illustrated by Katherine Wigglesworth. London, Heinemann, 1954; Indianapolis, Bobbs Merrill, 1962.
Sam Pig and the Singing Gate, illustrated by A.E. Kennedy. London, Faber, 1955.
Hare and Guy Fawkes, illustrated by Margaret Tempest. London, Collins, 1956.
Little Red Fox and Cinderella, illustrated by Katherine Wigglesworth. London, Heinemann, 1956.
Magic in My Pocket: A Selection of Tales, illustrated by Judith Brook. London, Penguin, 1957.
Little Grey Rabbit's Paint-Box, illustrated by Margaret Tempest. London, Collins, 1958.
Little Grey Rabbit and the Magic Moon, illustrated by Katherine Wigglesworth. London, Heinemann, 1958.
Snug and Serena Count Twelve, illustrated by Katherine Wigglesworth. London, Heinemann, 1959; Indianapolis, Bobbs Merrill, 1962.
Tim Rabbit and Company, illustrated by A.E. Kennedy. London, Faber, 1959.
Sam Pig Goes to the Seaside: Sixteen Stories, illustrated by A.E. Kennedy. London, Faber, 1960.
Grey Rabbit Finds a Shoe, illustrated by Margaret Tempest. London, Collins, 1960.
John at the Old Farm, illustrated by Jennifer Miles. London, Heinemann, 1960.
Grey Rabbit and the Circus, illustrated by Margaret Tempest. London, Collins, 1961.
Snug and Serena Go to Town, illustrated by Katherine Wigglesworth. London, Heinemann, 1961; Indianapolis, Bobbs Merrill, 1963.
Little Red Fox and the Unicorn, illustrated by Katherine Wigglesworth. London, Heinemann, 1962.
The Little Knife Who Did All the Work: Twelve Tales of Magic, illustrated by Pauline Baynes. London, Faber, 1962.
Grey Rabbit's May Day, illustrated by Margaret Tempest. London, Collins, 1963.
Tim Rabbit's Dozen, illustrated by Shirley Hughes. London, Faber, 1964.
Hare Goes Shopping, illustrated by Margaret Tempest. London, Collins, 1965.

The Sam Pig Storybook, illustrated by Cecil Leslie. London, Faber, 1965.
The Mouse, The Rabbit, and the Little White Hen, illustrated by Jennie Corbett. London, Heinemann, 1966.
Enchantment, illustrated by Jennie Corbett. London, Heinemann, 1966.
Little Grey Rabbit's Pancake Day, illustrated by Margaret Tempest. London, Collins, 1967.
The Little Red Fox and the Big Big Tree, illustrated by Jennie Corbett. London, Heinemann, 1968.
Little Grey Rabbit Goes to the North Pole, illustrated by Katherine Wigglesworth. London, Collins, 1970.
Lavender Shoes: Eight Tales of Enchantment, illustrated by Janina Ede. London, Faber, 1970.
The Brown Mouse Book: Magical Tales of Two Little Mice, illustrated by Katherine Wigglesworth. London, Heinemann, 1971.
Fuzzypeg's Brother, illustrated by Katherine Wigglesworth. London, Heinemann, 1971.
Little Grey Rabbit's Spring Cleaning Party, illustrated by Katherine Wigglesworth. London, Collins, 1972.
Little Grey Rabbit and the Snow-Baby, illustrated by Katherine Wigglesworth. London, Collins, 1973.
Fairy Tales, edited by Kathleen Lines, illustrated by Ann Strugnell. London, Faber, 1975.
Hare and the Rainbow, illustrated by Katherine Wigglesworth. London, Collins, 1975.
Stories for Christmas, edited by Kathleen Lines, illustrated by Gavin Rowe. London, Faber, 1977.
From Spring to Spring: Stories of the Four Seasons, edited by Kathleen Lines, illustrated by Shirley Hughes. London, Faber, 1978.
Foxglove Tales, edited by Lucy Meredith, illustrated by Shirley Felts. London, Faber, 1984.

Plays

Little Grey Rabbit to the Rescue, illustrated by Margaret Tempest. London, Collins, 1946.
The Washerwoman's Child: A Play on the Life and Stories of Hans Christian Andersen, illustrated by Irene Hawkins. London, Faber, 1946.
Three Little Grey Rabbit Plays (includes *Grey Rabbit's Hospital, The Robber, A Christmas Story*). London, Heinemann, 1961.

Publications for Adults

Novels

High Meadows. London, Faber, 1938.
When All Is Done. London, Faber, 1945.

Other

The Country Child. London, Faber, and New York, Macmillan, 1931.
Ambush of Young Days. London, Faber, 1937.
The Farm on the Hill. London, Faber, 1941.
Country Hoard. London, Faber, 1943.
Country Things. London, Faber, 1946.
Carts and Candlesticks. London, Faber, 1948.
Buckinghamshire. London, Faber, 1950.
Plowmen's Clocks. London, Faber, 1952.
The Stuff of Dreams. London, Faber, 1953.
Here's a New Day. London, Faber, 1956.
A Year in the Country. London, Faber, 1957.
The Swans Fly Over. London, Faber, 1959.
Something for Nothing. London, Faber, 1960.
Wild Honey. London, Faber, 1962.
Cuckoo in June. London, Faber, 1964.
A Peck of Gold. London, Faber, 1966.
Recipes from an Old Farmhouse. London, Faber, 1966.
The Button Box and Other Essays. London, Faber, 1968.
A Ten O'Clock Scholar and Other Essays. London, Faber, 1970.
Secret Places and Other Essays. London, Faber, 1972.
Country World: Memories of Childhood, edited by Lucy Meredith. London, Faber, 1984.
Our Village: Alison Uttley's Cromford, edited by Jacqueline Mitchell. Cromford, Derbyshire, Scarthin, 1984.

Editor, *In Praise of Country Life: An Anthology.* London, Muller, 1949.

*

Manuscript Collections: Kerlan Collection, University of Minnesota, Minneapolis.

Critical Studies: *The World of Alison Uttley* by Elizabeth Saintsbury, London, Baker, 1980; *The Country Child: A Biography of Alison Uttley* by Denis Judd, London, Joseph, 1986.

* * *

Like most if not all creative writers Alison Uttley drew extensively on memories of her childhood; she found in them an inexhaustible source of inspiration and of the facts of country life that she needed to provide the right setting for her stories.

She is probably best known as the author of the Little Grey Rabbit books and there is a lot of Uttley herself in the character of Grey Rabbit: the resourceful countrywoman, the lover of traditional customs and festivals, the sensitive observer who enjoyed all the signs and sounds and smells of the countryside. In fact in one special foreword she made the clear statement: "The country ways of Grey Rabbit were the country ways known to the author." But Grey Rabbit has her own character and so do her companions, boastful but basically kind Hare, timid and sometimes rather foolish Squirrel, and all the friends who visit them, Wise Owl, Fuzzypeg, and the rest. Uttley was fortunate in her main illustrator, Margaret Tempest, whose pictures gave visible form to the group of animal characters.

But one set of stories was by no means enough for Uttley who kept three publishers busy. More or less simultaneously with Grey Rabbit, Sam Pig came to life, with a quite separate collection of farmyard characters: Sally the mare, several other little pigs, and their knowledgeable friend Brock the Badger. Sam Pig became very popular, reflecting perhaps Uttley's experience of small boys she knew. And at about the same time Tim Rabbit appeared, "No Ordinary Rabbit," who had some rather extraordinary experiences. But this was not all. Two further groups of characters appeared later: Snug and Serena (in the Little Brown Mouse books) and Little Red Fox, who had quite a substantial series of his own.

In addition there are the charming books of fairytales. But it should not be thought that there is a clear-cut division between these and the animal stories. It is characteristic of Uttley that magic and fantasy play a part in all her writing. This element was a fundamental part of her mind and her imagination, with the result that throughout the animal stories, though they are soundly based on direct knowledge of country life, there is always the possibility that the characters will be faced with some fantastic experience which is accepted without any questioning. There is continuity between the stories about animals and the stories that can be regarded as fairytales proper, and the connection works both ways. As Kathleen Lines says in her introduction to a selection of fairytales: "The stories...reveal to the willing eye and ear, the usually unsuspected magic in the countryside and in the lives of humble village people." And Uttley herself is quoted as saying: "So each and every tale holds everyday magic, and each is connected with awareness of everyday life, where reality is made visible, and one sees what goes on with new eyes." Here is the essence of much of Uttley's writing for children.

The Washerwoman's Child is a play written round the life of Hans Andersen, introducing versions of seven of his fairytales. Hans Andersen's stories clearly had a special appeal for Uttley, as on the one hand they were often concerned with everyday things and simple people—a pair of scissors or an iron, a chimney sweep or a shepherdess—and on the other told of those traditional characters almost equally familiar to Uttley as a storyteller, such as the Snow Queen, or imaginary Princes and Princesses and Emperors. But for her these characters were often seen in a more homely setting. To quote Kathleen Lines again: "The traditional 'princess' is a beautiful country maiden, the 'prince' a fine, upstanding shepherd or farm labourer, whose rival in love is either a member of the fairy folk or a manifestation of some natural force."

But once, and in her most original and important work of fiction, she wrote about a real queen. The stories described above are for younger children: *A Traveller in Time* is for those who are older, perhaps particularly girls (though the book is gripping for anyone) as the protagonist is a young schoolgirl, surely Uttley herself, in spite of the fact that the heroine is called Penelope and the name Alison is given to Penelope's elder sister. Here all Uttley's skills and special qualities are seen at their best. The scene is the Derbyshire farm where she was born and brought up, but woven into this simple background is the dream world which always meant a very great deal to her: and the core of the story is the girl's journeys in time to the period when Mary Queen of Scots spent part of her imprisonment in a nearby Derbyshire manor house. The girl, Penelope, moves in fantasy, or in dream, between the farm she knows in her real contemporary life and the 16th-century drama enacted by the Babington family in their attempts to rescue the imprisoned Queen. Anthony Babington, later to go to his death on account of the Babington plot, is the leading character in this side of the story, but it is his younger brother Francis whom Penelope specially loves with a romantic affection which seems to have caught hold of the writer herself. By the skill of her writing Uttley manages to make the story of the Babingtons and Mary Queen of Scots more "real" than the simple story of Penelope's visits to the farm. This is Uttley's finest achievement and an outstandingly imaginative work that is uniquely her own.

—Peter du Sautoy

VAN ALLSBURG, Chris

Nationality: American. **Born:** Grand Rapids, Michigan, 18 June 1949. **Education:** University of Michigan, Ann Arbor, B.F.A.; Rhode Island School of Design, Providence, M.F.A. in sculpture 1974. **Family:** Married Lisa Van Allsburg. **Career:** Artist: numerous individual shows. Teacher of drawing and poster design, Rhode Island School of Design. **Awards:** Boston *Globe-Horn Book* award 1980; American Book award, 1982; American Library Association Caldecott Medal, 1982, 1986. **Address:** Lives in Providence.

PUBLICATIONS FOR CHILDREN (ILLUSTRATED BY THE AUTHOR)

Fiction

The Garden of Abdul Gasazi. Boston, Houghton Mifflin, 1979; London, Hamish Hamilton, 1981.
Jumanji. Boston, Houghton Mifflin, 1981.
Ben's Dream. Boston, Houghton Mifflin, 1982.
The Wreck of the Zephyr. Boston, Houghton Mifflin, and London, Andersen Press, 1983.
The Mysteries of Harris Burdick. Boston, Houghton Mifflin, 1984; London, Andersen Press, 1985.
The Polar Express. Boston, Houghton Mifflin, 1985; London, Andersen Press, 1986.
The Stranger. Boston, Houghton Mifflin, 1986.
The Alphabet Theater Proudly Presents the Z Was Zapped. Boston, Houghton Mifflin, 1987.
Two Bad Ants. Boston, Houghton Mifflin, 1988.
Just a Dream. Boston, Houghton Mifflin, 1990.
The Wretched Stone. Boston, Houghton Mifflin, 1991.
The Widow's Broom. Boston, Houghton Mifflin, 1992.
The Sweetest Fig. Boston, Houghton Mifflin, 1993.
Bad Day at Riverbend. Boston, Houghton Mifflin, 1995.

*

Illustrator: *Swan Lake* by Mark Helprin, 1989; *A City in Winter* by Mark Helprin, 1996; *The Veil of Snows* by Mark Helprin, 1997.

* * *

Chris Van Allsburg represents something of a phenomenon in children's literature, given his prolific output of quality works so early in his career. Since 1979 he has averaged one book a year, though not all his later works are as effective as the early ones. Van Allsburg's children books seem to fall into two types: picture storybooks of a full narrative treating imaginatively tantalizing occurrences, and books short on text that might better be termed imagistic puzzles. For example, *The Alphabet Theater Proudly Presents the Z was Zapped,* an alphabet book, portrays a pictorial puzzle for each letter, which is then textually solved when one turns the page: "The F was firmly Flattened," "The C was Cut to ribbons." The fate of the letters is violent yet amusing in its depiction and play upon perspective. *The Mysteries of Harris Burdick* is presented as a puzzle-within-a-puzzle; in his introduction Van Allsburg tells of a Harris Burdick who left 14 drawings with a publisher, but who failed to return with their accompanying stories. Van Allsburg proffers these drawings along with their respective titles and captions to his audience "in the hope that other children will be inspired by them" to create their own stories. Brevity is all in this instance. Titles such as "Under The Rug" and "The Third-Floor Bedroom" carry teasing captions like "Two weeks passed and it happened again," or, "It all began when someone left the window open"—reminiscent of Edward Gorey's pregnant lines. The pictures are themselves visual riddles, often portraying physical impossibilities or suggesting pictorial puns and allusions.

This puzzle motif continues in Van Allsburg's picture storybooks. *The Garden of Abdul Gasazi* conjures with the possibility that the lost dog Fritz was turned into a fowl by the mysterious neighbor, Abdul Gasazi. *Jumanji* overtly shows a puzzle in the form of the boardgame Peter and Judy find under a tree (How did it get there? Whose is it? What sort of game waits within the box?). Van Allsburg's clever premise, converting the words on the board to actual realities inside the children's home, extends the puzzle as we wonder what the next turn will bring: "Lion attacks, move back two spaces"; "Monsoon season begins, lose one turn"; "Python sneaks into camp..." Further suspense attends the conditions of the game, which must be played through to its end. Pandora's box has never been so well served.

The Wreck of the Zephyr, Van Allsburg's first book employing color, likewise mystifies its narrator with the remains of a wrecked sailboat high up on the cliffs; the solution to this mystery leaves both narrator and reader wondering whether the old man has told a "tall tale" of flying ships or a variant of the truth. Reminiscent of this work in its illustration and nautical material, *The Wretched Stone,* though less successful, presents the puzzle of just what that uncanny stone, never shown, is; here, the narrative assumes the form of terse, "just the facts" entries in the captain's log, all the more teasing for what is left unsaid.

Vaporous truth suffuses *Ben's Dream,* a visual cruise through real geography and history, with its ending query: was it a dream? Puzzle and dream go hand in indistinct hand in Van Allsburg's works. The dream motif helps craft *Just A Dream* and *The Polar Express,* with the latter appearing to show the boy's Christmas dream while the jingling denouement suggests that this fantasy has some footing in fact. *The Stranger,* a tender fable personifying and contemporizing frost, the advent of winter, gives us an amnesiac stranger as the puzzle to be solved. A different sort of fable is spun in *The Widow's Broom,* which on the surface is an amusing, sepia-tinged tale of a magical witch's broom and the widow's rescuing it from her superstitious neighbors via a visual trick of her own. Yet there is a gravity beneath the surface, a dark pull of history, witch-hunts, prejudice and human intolerance, which makes this one of Van Allsburg's more noticeably serious works. On a lighter though equally violent note, *Two Bad Ants* charts the ants' high adventure inside a kitchen, where they endure the trials of such human commonplaces as a toaster and garbage disposer, all unidentified in the text and drawn from the ants' point of view—a realistic and more credible variant of the popular motif of shrinking humans and shrunken kids, and one which affords direct plays upon physical scale and perspective.

The puzzling, the mysterious, the uncertain boundary between reality and dream, substance and smoke, experience and perception, constitute the playground of Van Allsburg's imagination and creation. Often his works recreate the experience of one's straddling the threshold between fact and fantasy, logic and feeling, the doubting mind and affirming senses, with liminality suffusing both storyline and its pictorial translation. Paradoxically, this dreamlike quality is sustained with the aid of Van Allsburg's considerable skills as an illustrator. His early artistic training and work as a sculptor are evidenced in his overall style of illustration: one that values form and curve and solidity, one that utilizes chiaroscuro like a sculpting blade, one that plays upon the apparently infinite possibilities of perspective. Not surprisingly, Van Allsburg has been the recipient of numerous awards, including two Caldecott Medals (*Jumanji, The Polar Express*).

The success of Van Allsburg's children's books lies in his artistic mastery and skill as a teller of intriguing, riddle-rich tales. He applies an alchemical imagination to rather mundane bits of matter (a boardgame, a geography/history lesson, ants in the sugarbowl, a stone, a broom). His storylines tend toward one fairly simple action, though the rippling possibilities they cast are never simplistic. Likewise, characters are flat, one-dimensional means to the plot's end; narrative style is straightforward, unadorned, clean. Such characteristics suggest an affinity with the folktale and fairytale, as does the magical aura of so many of his works. One is especially reminded of those elder tales treating a human's sojourn in the fairy world; the experience is real enough at the time it occurs, then shifts like a dream upon one's return to the human world, only to have doubt arise as some nugget of fairy gold spills from one's turned-out pocket—which world is the dream, which the reality?

Van Allsburg's use of motifs such as the journey, the quest, the mythic cosmogonic cycle, the presence of some boon as a confirming sign of one's adventure—all such elements help flesh out the bare bones of plot, style, and characterization to convey a sense of depth and texture, of substance and meaning, which is in turn reinforced by his substantive style of illustration. In his finest works—*The Garden of Abdul Gasazi, Jumanji, The Wreck of the Zephyr, The Polar Express*—puzzle, riddle, dream, and mystery dissolve into the liminal quality of life itself, and one senses how interlaced what we experience is with what we perceive. Thus, altered perception yields altered experience; imagination and dream transmute what we think we know and see as reality. At his best, through the felicitous confluence of his words and art, Van Allsburg gives us truly transforming experience.

—Joyce Thomas

VAN STOCKUM, Hilda (Gerarda)

Nationality: American (originally Dutch: emigrated to the United States, 1934, became citizen, 1936). **Born:** Rotterdam, Netherlands, 9 February 1908. **Education:** Amsterdam Academy of Art; Dublin School of Art; Corcoran School of Art, Washington, D.C., 1936-37; Andre Lhote Studio, Paris. **Family:** Married Ervin R. Marlin in 1932; four daughters and two sons. **Career:** Art teacher in Ireland and illustrator for Browne and Nolan, publishers, Dublin, late 1920s; Montessori instructor, Child Education Foundation, New York, 1934; Instructor in Art and Creative Writing, Institute of Lifetime Learning, Washington, D.C., 1965-74. Individual shows: Painters Gallery, Dublin, 1953; Difas Gallery, Geneva, 1964; De Kuyl Gallery, Bilthoven, Netherlands, 1964; Venables Gallery, Washington, D.C., 1974; Den Arts Gallery, Ottawa, 1974; group shows: Montreal Museum of Fine Arts, 1957; Royal Academy, London, 1961, 1977; van der Straeten Gallery, New York, 1973, and many others. President, Children's Book Guild, Washington, D.C., 1972-74; retrospective, Royal Hibernian Academy, 1991. **Awards:** Honorary member, Royal Hibernian Academy, 1984. **Address:** 8 Castle Hill, Berkhamsted, Hertfordshire, England.

Publications for Children

Fiction (illustrated by the author)

A Day on Skates. New York, Harper, 1934; reissued, with illustrations and a new introduction by the author, Vancouver, Washington, Bethlehem Books, 1994.
The Cottage at Bantry Bay. New York, Viking Press, 1938; London, Muller, 1946.
Francie on the Run. New York, Viking Press, 1939; London, Muller, 1941.
Kersti and Saint Nicholas. New York, Viking Press, 1940; London, Muller, 1944.
Pegeen. New York, Viking Press, 1941; London, Muller, 1944.
Andries. New York, Viking Press, 1942; London, Muller, 1946.
Gerrit and the Organ. New York, Viking Press, 1943; London, Muller, 1948.
The Mitchells. New York, Viking Press, 1945.
Canadian Summer. New York, Viking Press, 1948.
Patsy and the Pup. New York, Viking Press, 1950.
King Oberon's Forest, illustrated by Brigid Marlin. New York, Viking Press, 1957; London, Constable, 1958.
Friendly Gables. New York, Viking Press, 1960.
Little Old Bear. New York, Viking Press, 1962; London, Constable, 1963.
The Winged Watchman. New York, Farrar Straus, 1962; London, Constable, 1964.
Jeremy Bear. London, Constable, 1963.
Bennie and the New Baby. London, Constable, 1964.
New Baby Is Lost. London, Constable, 1964.
Mogo's Flute, illustrated by Robin Jacques. New York, Viking Press, 1966; London, Constable, 1967.
Penengro. New York, Farrar Straus, 1972.
Rufus Round and Round, illustrated by Joanna Worth. London, Longman, 1973.
The Borrowed House. New York, Farrar Straus, 1975; London, Collins, 1977.

Poetry

The Angel's Alphabet. New York, Viking Press, 1948.

Other

Translator, *Tilio, A Boy of Papua,* by Rudolf Voorhoeve, illustrated by Van Stockum. Philadelphia, Lippincott, 1937; London, Hutchinson, 1939.
Translator, *Marian and Marion,* by J.M. Selleger-Elout, illustrated by B. Midderigh-Bokhurst. New York, Viking Press, 1949.
Translator, *Corso the Donkey,* by Christina Pothast-Gimberg, illustrated by Elly van Beek. London, Constable, 1962.
Translator, *The Curse of Laguna Grande,* by Siny R. van Iterson. New York, Morrow, 1973.
Translator, *The Smugglers of Buenaventura,* by Siny R. van Iterson. New York, Morrow, 1974.
Translator, *In the Spell of the Past,* by Siny R. van Iterson. New York, Morrow, 1975.
Translator, *Bruno,* by Achim Bröger, illustrated by Ronald Himler. New York, Morrow, 1975.
Translator, *Kasimir,* by Achim Bröger. New York, Morrow, 1976.
Translator, *The Spirits of Chocamata,* by Siny R. van Iterson. New York, Morrow, 1977.

*

Manuscript Collections: de Grummond Collection, University of Southern Mississippi, Hattiesburg; May Massee Collection, Emporia State University, Kansas; Kerlan Collection, University of Minnesota, Minneapolis.

Illustrator: *Afke's Ten* by Sjoukhe Troelstra, 1936; *Beggar's Penny,* 1943, and *The Bells of Leyden Sing,* 1944, both by Catherine Coblentz; *The Burro of Barnegat Road* by Delia Goetz, 1945; *Hans Brinker* by Mary Mapes Dodge, 1946; *Little Women,* 1946, and *Little Men,* 1950, both by Louisa May Alcott; *Willow Brook Farm* by Katherine D. Christ, 1948; *The Rainbow Book of Bible Stories* edited by May Becker, 1948; *Stryd voor een molen* by Jan den Tex, 1952.

Critical Studies: *Authors of Books for Young People,* Metuchen, New Jersey, Scarecrow Press, 1990.

Hilda van Stockum comments:

I am delighted that my books are available again—they are like children of mine, and bring back so many memories. When I first started to write, I was just married and we did not have much money. We were living in Ireland, and it was 1932—the worst year of the Depression in America. So I thought I'd write a book about my skating memories in Holland, and when my husband went to America, he could sell it there. And that is what happened: Harper's took it and the advance paid for my first baby.

And as more books followed, so did more babies. We had a sort of race with the Taxman. We didn't earn enough to be taxable yet—and whenever we earned enough, we had another baby and were still tax-free! But there was always a book again, too. So we had great fun living like that, but in the end, the Taxman caught up with us. The books went on when the babies stopped!

* * *

Hilda van Stockum spent her childhood in Holland and Ireland, and her married life in Canada and the United States, experiences reflected in her stories for young and older children. She focuses on family life, on day-to-day tasks and concerns as well as on the extraordinary events which bring family members together—or push them apart. *The Winged Watchman* concerns the Verhagen family—10-year-old Joris, his older brother Dirk Jan, their parents, and the children and young adults to whom they give asylum during the German occupation of Holland in World War II. Their relationships with each other, with their Dutch underground neighbors, and with the feared enemy are described vividly and compassionately. Van Stockum portrays human frailties and strengths—often in the same individual at the same time—and also shows the horrors of war, which can last long after the truce.

In a series of stories that includes *The Cottage at Bantry Bay, Francie on the Run,* and *Pegeen,* van Stockum introduces the O'Sullivan family of Ireland: Mother and Father; two responsible older children, Michael and Brigid; and the irrepressible twins, Francie and Liam. Francie has a club foot, and in the first book there is no money to have it cared for. In the second book he goes to a hospital to have it treated, but before being discharged he walks out, headed in the wrong direction, and enjoys weeks of great adventure all over Ireland.

The Mitchells is a warm and witty picture of family life in the United States during World War II. Van Stockum has also set stories in Canada (*Canadian Summer*) and Kenya (*Mogo's Flute*). Her own six children and their high spirits must have provided her with much material for these tales, but the finely delineated characters and social settings are her special artistic gift. She is never sentimental about the age-old conflicts between parent and child, and between child and his inner self. Instead she personalizes these conflicts with sharp insights, skill, and generous bits of humor.

Van Stockum has also made a contribution to English literature for children through her translations of a number of stories from other cultures. She is also a distinguished artist, and illustrated many of her own children's tales with delicate line drawings.

In the 1990s, Bethlehem Books, based in Ft. Collins, Colorado, began reprinting van Stockum's books and making them available through Spring Arbor book distributors. Reissued books include the Bantry Bay and Mitchells series, *Night Watchman, A Day on Skates,* and a color edition of *The Angel's Alphabet.*

—Mary Lystad, updated by Judson Knight

VERNEY, (Sir) John

Second Baronet; succeeded to the baronetcy, 1959. **Nationality:** British. **Born:** London, 30 September 1913. **Education:** Eton College, Buckinghamshire; Christ Church, Oxford, B.A. (honours) in history 1935. **Military Service:** North Somerset Yeomanry, Special Air Service: mentioned in despatches; Military Cross, 1944; Legion of Honour (France), 1945. **Family:** Married Lucinda Musgrave in 1939; two sons (one deceased) and five daughters. **Career:** Painter and illustrator: group shows at Royal Society of British Artists, London; London Group; Leicester, Redfern, and Zwemmer galleries, London. **Member:** Farnham Urban District Council, 1968-74. **Died:** 2 February 1993.

Publications for Children

Fiction

Friday's Tunnel, illustrated by the author. London, Collins, 1959; revised edition, London, Penguin, 1962; New York, Holt Rinehart, 1966.
February's Road, illustrated by the author. London, Collins, 1961; New York, Holt Rinehart, 1966.
The Mad King of Chichiboo, illustrated by the author. London, Collins, and New York, Watts, 1963.
ismo, illustrated by the author. London, Collins, 1964; New York, Holt Rinehart, 1967.
Seven Sunflower Seeds. London, Collins, 1968; New York, Holt Rinehart, 1969.
Samson's Hoard. London, Collins, 1973.

Other

Look at Houses, illustrated by the author. London, Hamish Hamilton, 1959; revised edition, London, Mayflower, 1970.
A John Verney Collection. N.p., Alastair, 1989.

Editor, with Patricia Campbell, *Under the Sun: Stories, Poems, Articles from Elizabethan and Other Sources.* London, Constable, 1964.

Publications for Adults

Novels

Every Advantage. London, Collins, 1961.
Fine Day for a Picnic. London, Hodder and Stoughton, 1968.

Other

Verney Abroad, illustrated by the author. London, Collins, 1954.
Going to the Wars: A Journey in Various Directions. London, Collins, and New York, Dodd Mead, 1955.
A Dinner of Herbs (autobiographical). London, Collins, 1966.

*

Illustrator: *The Odyssey* translated by George P. Kerr, 1958; *The Trampoline* by John Pudney, 1959; *James Without Thomas,* 1959, *The Elephant War,* 1960, *To Tame a Sister,* 1961, *The Greatest Gresham,* 1962, *The Peacock House,* 1963, and *The Italian Spring,* 1964, all by Gillian Avery, and *Unforgettable Journeys,* 1965, and *School Remembered,* 1967, both edited by Avery; *Diary of an Old Man* by Chaim Bermant, 1966; *Our Friend Jennings* by Anthony Buckeridge, 1967; *The Puffin Book of Horses* edited by Susan Chitty and Anne Parry, 1975; *Travels with Lionel* by Hart Massey, 1988; *The Dodo-Pad* (annual telephone table journal).

John Verney commented:

(1989) Having six children, much of my life has been occupied with trying to amuse, and thereby educate, the young, one way or another. My novels for the young are really aimed at all who are young in heart, of whatever age. They are essentially about family life as it is affected by events in the adult world (e.g., a world crisis in *Friday's Tunnel,* a plot to assassinate President de Gaulle in *ismo*).

* * *

John Verney's chronicles of the huge Callendar family have never really achieved the runaway popular success they merit. At the back of the mind lurks the suspicion that it only needs one slight, unforseen chance and Gus Callendar, his wife, and his children, Friday, February, Gail, Barry, Des and Chrys, and Hildbrand, would become as familiar figures in the world of children's books as the Famous Five or the Secret Seven. There are drawbacks, of course; the stories are witty, literate, original, ingenious, and deserve and repay careful reading, but no other author writing for children approaches Verney's mastery in capturing the precise manner in which children become enmeshed in their parents' affairs and activities. Above all he wrote naturally and can in no way be charged with that awful air of condescension that afflicts so many children's writers.

Gus Callendar, the *paterfamilias,* is a famous newspaper correspondent, a convenient career from the author's point of view in that he will be attracted in the normal course of events to odd incidents and will become closely involved in successive local, national, and even international issues. This implies in turn that his lively and likeable family are accustomed to being drawn in.

There is too an air of plausibility about each episode no matter how inherently implausible a situation really is. In *Friday's Tunnel,* for example, the action is centred round a sudden political crisis in the Mediterranean and the discovery of a very-much-in-demand mineral. The whole family find themselves inextricably bound up in this; they meet the personalities directly involved, and yet, at the end of the day, the problem is resolved in the tunnel Friday is digging in the paddock of their home on the Sussex downs. To maintain the narrative on these two levels, homely familiar Sussex and exotic Mediterranean, demands a high level of technical competence in novel writing, to say nothing of an imperturbable aplomb.

February's Road, arguably the best in the series, concerns a new London-Portsmouth trunk road which threatens to run straight through the bottom of their garden, and in this case it is February Callendar who pits her wits against the whole complex machinery of local politics and ministerial policy. In *Seven Sunflower Seeds* it is Barry who suspects that these are somehow mixed up in simultaneous plots to "fix" the Grand National steeplechase and to edge Britain into the Common Market. And in *Samson's Hoard* they all become heavily embroiled in local elections, a treasure hunt, business deals, and conservation, when Mr. Callendar stands as Independent candidate for the council. These are recognizeable situations confronting the members of one family who perhaps because of their own individual qualities appear as old friends as their continuing saga unfolds.

—Alan Edwin Day

VIORST, Judith

Nationality: American. **Born:** Judith Stahl, Newark, New Jersey, 2 February 1931. **Education:** Rutgers University, New Brunswick, New Jersey, B.A. in history 1952 (Phi Beta Kappa); Washington Psychoanalytic Institute, Washington, D.C., 1975-81. **Family:** Married Milton Viorst in 1960; three sons. **Career:** Children's book editor, New York, 1957-60; science book editor, Washington, D.C., 1960-63; columnist, *Redbook* magazine, New York, 1968-1996; columnist, Washington Star Syndicate, 1970-72. **Awards:** Emmy award, for television script, 1970; Albert Einstein College of Medicine award, 1975; Christopher award, 1988. **Agent:** Lescher and Lescher, 67 Irving Place, New York, New York 10003. **Address:** 3432 Ashley Terrace N.W., Washington, D.C. 20008, U.S.A.

Publications for Children

Fiction

Sunday Morning, illustrated by Hilary Knight. New York, Harper, 1968.
I'll Fix Anthony, illustrated by Arnold Lobel. New York, Harper, 1969.
Try It Again, Sam, illustrated by Paul Galdone. New York, Lothrop, 1970.
The Tenth Good Thing about Barney, illustrated by Erik Blegvad. New York, Atheneum, 1971; London, Collins, 1972.
Alexander and the Terrible, Horrible, No Good, Very Bad Day, illustrated by Ray Cruz. New York, Atheneum, 1972; London, Angus and Robertson, 1973.
My Mama Says There Aren't Any Zombies, Ghosts, Vampires, Creatures, Demons, Monsters, Fiends, Goblins, or Things, illustrated by Kay Chorao. New York, Atheneum, 1973.
Rosie and Michael, illustrated by Lorna Tomei. New York, Atheneum, 1974.
Alexander, Who Used to Be Rich Last Sunday, illustrated by Ray Cruz. New York, Atheneum, 1978; London, Angus and Robertson, 1979.
The Good-Bye Book, illustrated by Kay Chorao. New York, Macmillan, 1988.
Earrings!, illustrated by Nola L. Malone. New York, Macmillan, 1993.
The Alphabet from A to Z (with much confusion on the way), illustrated by Richard Hull. New York, Atheneum, 1993.
Alexander, Who's Not (Do You Hear Me? I Mean It!) Going to Move, illustrated by Robin Preiss-Glasser. New York, Atheneum, 1995.

Poetry

If I Were in Charge of the World and Other Worries: Poems for Children and Their Parents, illustrated by Lynne Cherry. New York, Atheneum, 1981.
Sad Underwear and Other Complications: More Poems for Children and their Parents, illustrated by Richard Hull. New York, Atheneum, 1995.

Other

Projects: Space. New York, Washington Square Press, 1962.
150 Science Experiments Step-by-Step, illustrated by Dennis Telesford. New York, Bantam, 1963.
The Natural World: A Guide to North American Wildlife. New York, Bantam, 1965.
The Changing Earth, illustrated by Feodor Rimsky. New York, Bantam, 1967.

Editor, with Shirley Moore, *Wonderful World of Science,* illustrated by Don Trawin. New York, Bantam, 1961.

Publications for Adults

Poetry

The Village Square. New York, Coward McCann, 1965.
It's Hard to Be Hip over Thirty and Other Tragedies of Married Life. Cleveland, World, 1968; London, Angus and Robertson, 1973.

People and Other Aggravations. New York, World, 1971; London, Angus and Robertson, 1973.
How Did I Get to Be Forty and Other Atrocities. New York, Simon and Schuster, 1976.
A Visit from St. Nicholas (To a Liberated Household). New York, Simon and Schuster, 1977.
When Did I Stop Being Twenty and Other Injustices: Selected Poems from Single to Mid-Life. New York, Simon and Schuster, 1987.
Forever Fifty and Other Negotiations. New York, Simon and Schuster, 1989.

Other

The Washington, D.C., Underground Gourmet, with Milton Viorst. New York, Simon and Schuster, 1970.
Yes, Married: A Saga of Love and Complaint (collected prose). New York, Saturday Review Press, 1972.
Love and Guilt and the Meaning of Life, etc. New York, Simon and Schuster, 1979.
Necessary Losses. New York and London, Simon and Schuster, 1987.
Murdering Mr. Monti: A Merry Little Tale of Sex and Violence. New York, Simon & Schuster, 1994.
Imperfect Control: Our Lifelong Struggle with Power and Surrender. New York, Simon & Schuster, 1998.

*

Critical Studies: *Contemporary Authors, New Revision Series,* Detroit, Gale Research, 1989; *Authors of Books for Young People,* Metuchen, New Jersey, Scarecrow Press, 1990; *Major Authors and Illustrators for Children and Young Adults,* Detroit, Gale Research, 1993; *Something About the Author,* Detroit, Gale Research, 1993; *Twentieth Century Children's Writers,* Detroit, St. James, 1995; Jill C. Wheeler, *Judith Viorst,* Minneapolis, ABDO & Daughters, 1997.

Judith Viorst comments:

I've been writing just about always—starting at seven or eight. Since second grade, I wanted to be a writer. I liked to take all my feelings and thoughts and put them down in different ways on paper. I liked having other people read them, too. So I wrote them down, and I sent them out, hoping to have them published. But for years and years and years and years, and more years after that, every person I sent them to said "No."

I learned that there are a thousand ways to say "No." But I kept writing. In fact, I didn't know how to *not* keep writing. I wrote when I was sad and when I was happy and when I was worried and even when I was furious, and even when I was totally mixed up. I wrote, I sent out, I got back. I kept getting back. I think I got back a whole bedroom full of "No's." And then one day, when I was least expecting it, I opened my mail and found an astonishing "Yes!"

I have now published more than two dozen books, about half of them for children and half for adults. I'm often asked how I feel about being a writer. The answer—you've probably figured this out—is VERY VERY glad.

* * *

Judith Viorst chronicles the phenomenon of parents' and children's attempts to gain mutual understanding, a syndrome known all too well to adults who live and work with young children. Viorst has continuously tackled what were once considered "difficult" subjects of children's emotional stress in her books for children, and her nonsexist stories balance humor and pathos, without losing the central message. This is especially true of her picture-book stories, whether the subject be a pet's death (*The Tenth Good Thing about Barney*), bad days (*Alexander and the Terrible, Horrible, No Good, Very Bad Day*), boy-girl friendship (*Rosie and Michael*), or nighttime fears (*My Mama Says There Aren't Any Zombies, Ghosts, Vampires, Creatures, Demons, Monsters, Fiends, Goblins, or Things.*)

Her character Alexander, with his pessimistic sense of humor, is enormously entertaining. And in the increasingly mobile life of American society, a book such as *Alexander, Who's Not (Do You Hear Me? I Mean It!) Going to Move* has a great deal to offer to children whose parents are moving them to another town and another school. On the other hand, *Sad Underwear and Other Complications: More Poems for Children and Their Parents*—a companion piece to the earlier *If I Were in Charge of the World and Other Worries*—is just plain good fun.

Viorst has based most of her juveniles on actual people and experiences inside her family. Her boy characters do not suffer the less for demonstrating affection, fears, or tears; in fact, they become all the more human because of this portrayal. This is especially true in *The Good-Bye Book,* in which a young boy implores his parents not to leave for the evening until his babysitter—a male—arrives. Viorst's girl characters, like the boys, also run counter to societal stereotypes. They are often seen as aggressive, open, physically strong, and at times even vengeful. Instead of losing their femininity, they actually gain in growth.

Viorst handles her subjects with depth and perception, never taking sides on an issue; instead, she brings out both sides—adult and juvenile—leading the reader to make his or her own judgment. Viorst can be viewed as a sophisticated and impartial recorder of human drama for children. In her books—adult and juvenile—no one loses; rather, everyone wins, especially the reader.

—Jim Roginski, updated by Judson Knight

VIPONT, Charles. See **VIPONT, Elfrida.**

VIPONT, Elfrida

Pseudonym: Charles Vipont. Has also written as E.V. Foulds. **Nationality:** British. **Born:** Manchester, Lancashire, 3 July 1902. **Education:** Manchester High School for Girls; Mount School, York. **Family:** Married Robinson Percy Foulds in 1926 (died 1954); four daughters. **Career:** Headmistress, Quaker Evacuation School, Yealand Manor, Lancashire, 1939-45. **Awards:** Library Association Carnegie Medal, 1951. D.H.L.: Earlham College, Richmond, Indiana, 1984. **Died:** 15 March 1992.

Publications for Children

Fiction

Blow the Man Down (as Charles Vipont), illustrated by Norman Hepple. London, Oxford University Press, 1939; Philadelphia, Lippincott, 1952.
The Lark in the Morn, illustrated by T.R. Freeman. London, Oxford University Press, 1948; Indianapolis, Bobbs Merrill, 1951.
The Lark on the Wing, illustrated by T.R. Freeman. London, Oxford University Press, 1950; Indianapolis, Bobbs Merrill, 1951.
The Family at Dowbiggins, illustrated by T.R. Freeman. London, Lutterworth Press, and Indianapolis, Bobbs Merrill, 1955.
The Heir of Craigs (as Charles Vipont), illustrated by Tessa Theobald. London, Oxford University Press, 1955.
The Spring of the Year, illustrated by T.R. Freeman. London, Oxford University Press, 1957.
The Secret of Orra, illustrated by D.J. Watkins-Pitchford. Oxford, Blackwell, 1957.
More about Dowbiggins, illustrated by T.R. Freeman. London, Lutterworth Press, 1958; as *A Win for Henry Conyers*, London, Hamish Hamilton, 1968.
Changes at Dowbiggins, illustrated by T.R. Freeman. London, Lutterworth Press, 1960; as *Boggarts and Dreams*, London, Hamish Hamilton, 1969.
Flowering Spring, illustrated by Shirley Hughes. London, Oxford University Press, 1960.
Search for a Song, illustrated by Peter Edwards. London, Oxford University Press, 1962.
Stevie, illustrated by Raymond Briggs. London, Hamish Hamilton, 1965.
Larry Lopkins, illustrated by Pat Marriott. London, Hamish Hamilton, 1965.
Rescue for Mittens, illustrated by Jane Paton. London, Hamish Hamilton, 1965.
The Offcomers, illustrated by Janet Duchesne. London, Hamish Hamilton, 1965; New York, McGraw Hill, 1967.
Terror by Night: A Book of Strange Stories. London, Hamish Hamilton, 1966; as *Ghosts' High Noon*, New York, Walck, 1967.
The China Dog, illustrated by Constance Marshall. London, Hamish Hamilton, 1967.
The Secret Passage, illustrated by Ian Ribbons. London, Hamish Hamilton, 1967.
The Pavilion, illustrated by Prudence Seward. London, Oxford University Press, 1969; New York, Holt Rinehart, 1970.
Michael and the Dogs, illustrated by Pat Marriott. London, Hamish Hamilton, 1969.
The Elephant and the Bad Baby, illustrated by Raymond Briggs. London, Hamish Hamilton, and New York, Coward McCann, 1969.
Children of the Mayflower, illustrated by Evadne Rowan. London, Heinemann, 1969; New York, Watts, 1970.
Swarthmoor Hall. London, Friends Home Service Committee, 1979.
The Candle of the Lord. Wallingford, Pennsylvania, Pendle Hill, 1983.

Plays

A True Tale (radio play), 1952.
John Crook, Quaker (radio play), 1954.
Dr. Dinsdale in Russia (radio play), 1956.
Kitty Wilkinson (radio play), 1956.

Other

Good Adventure: The Quest of Music in England, illustrated by Estella Canziani. Manchester, Heywood, 1931.
Colin Writes to Friends House, illustrated by Elisabeth Brockbank. London, Friends' Book Centre, 1934; revised edition, London, Bannisdale Press, 1946.
A Lily among Thorns: Some Passages in the Life of Margaret Fell of Swarthmoor Hall. London, Friends Home Service Committee, 1950.
Sparks among the Stubble, illustrated by Patricia Lambe. London, Oxford University Press, 1950.
Henry Purcell and His Times, illustrated by L.J. Broderick. London, Lutterworth Press, 1959.
The Story of Christianity in Britain, illustrated by Gaynor Chapman. London, Joseph, 1961.
What about Religion?, illustrated by Peter Roberson. London, Museum Press, 1961.
Some Christian Festivals. London, Joseph, 1963; New York, Roy, 1964.
Weaver of Dreams: The Girlhood of Charlotte Brontë. London, Hamish Hamilton, and New York, Walck, 1966.
A Child of the Chapel Royal, illustrated by John Lawrence. London, Oxford University Press, 1967.
Towards a High Attic: The Early Life of George Eliot. London, Hamish Hamilton, 1970; New York, Holt Rinehart, 1971.
A Little Bit of Ivory: A Life of Jane Austen. London, Hamish Hamilton, 1977.

Editor, *The High Way: An Anthology*. London, Oxford University Press, 1957.
Editor, *Bless This Day: A Book of Prayer*, illustrated by Harold Jones. London, Collins, and New York, Harcourt Brace, 1958.
Editor, *The Bridge: An Anthology*, illustrated by Trevor Brierley Lofthouse. London, Oxford University Press, 1962.

Publications for Adults

Novel

Bed in Hell. London, Hamish Hamilton, 1974; New York, St. Martin's Press, 1975.

Other

The Story of Quakerism 1652-1952. London, Bannisdale Press, 1954; as *The Story of Quakerism Through Three Centuries*, 1960; revised edition, Richmond, Indiana, Friends United Press, 1977.
Arnold Rowntree: A Life. London, Bannisdale Press, 1955.
Ackworth School, From Its Foundation in 1779 to the Introduction of Co-Education in 1946. London, Lutterworth Press, 1959.
A Faith to Live By. Philadelphia, Friends General Conference, 1962; as *Quakerism: A Faith to Live By*, London, Bannisdale Press, 1966.
George Fox and the Valiant Sixty. London, Hamish Hamilton, 1975.

Other as E.V. Foulds

Quakerism: An International Way of Life. Manchester, 1930 Committee, 1930.
Lift Up Your Lamps: The Pageant of a Friends' Meeting. Manchester, 1930 Committee, 1939.
The Birthplace of Quakerism: A Handbook for the 1652 Country. London, Friends Home Service Committee, 1952; revised edition, 1968, 1973, 1987.
Let Your Lives Speak: A Key to the Quaker Experience. Wallingford, Pennsylvania, Pendle Hill, 1953; London, Friends Home Service Committee, 1954.
Living in the Kingdom. Philadelphia, Young Friends Movement, 1955.
The Quaker Witness: Yesterday and Today. Richmond, Indiana, Friends United Press, 1955.

*

Manuscript Collections: Kerlan Collection, University of Minnesota, Minneapolis; Lancaster Library, Lancashire.

Elfrida Vipont commented:

(1989) When people learn that I am a writer, they often ask, "What do you write?" When I reply, "Mainly books for children and young people," they say "Oh" rather sadly, as if to imply, "Poor thing, obviously she can't write for adults." Personally, I think writing for children is one of the most rewarding jobs imaginable. Lascelles Abercrombie used to speak of the "significant world"—"the world we never quite get except in art." If we do no more than offer a key to that significant world, our work will be well worth while. It is, of course, perfectly possible to offer a key to an ephemeral world instead, a world peopled by puppets in contrived situations, but most children's writers would rather fail in an attempt to create a living world, peopled by living characters, than succeed in presenting an artificial "readymix."

* * *

Though she has written many books, historical as well as modern, Elfrida Vipont is best known for *The Lark in the Morn,* its Carnegie Medal-winning sequel *The Lark on the Wing,* and the two other loosely connected stories, *The Spring of the Year* and *Flowering Spring,* continuing the Haverard family saga. Even of these, it is the first two that enjoy a particular popularity. Perhaps they reveal the deepest feeling. For, along with their Quakerism (which pervades all Vipont's writing), they are about music, the other interest closest to her heart. She trained and performed as a professional singer, and readers are quick to recognise the authenticity of these books. Also, they broke new ground, appearing at a time when the girls' school story still mainly followed the pattern cut by Angela Brazil, and children's fiction in general was only starting that subtler exploration of emotions and relationships which is now expected of any good junior novel. Finally, *The Lark in the Morn* had the special freshness of an early work, drawing on an author's untapped reservoir of experience, rich in this case since, when the book was published, its creator was already in her mid-forties and had four daughters. The book is no flawless masterpiece, but it bids fair to survive as a classic, loved for the "naturalness and sincerity" which caused as perceptive a critic as Kathleen Lines to bracket it with *Little Women.*

If a writer should be judged by her best books, so should those books be assessed more on their excellences than on their minor blemishes. For all their originality, the *Lark* stories carry traces of the Brazilian model from which they were breaking free. There is an admired senior girl whose "mop of fair curls" and "elfin face" are mentioned more than once, and critics have justifiably deprecated the way in which characters "rap out," "explode," and otherwise deliver dialogue which is itself well written and full of character. Others have found the books a little sentimental—occasionally true, but far outweighed by the genuinely intense feeling of most passages—while others again, unsympathetic to the Quakerism, have accused them of "cultural snobbery" and "exclusiveness." These objections seem overstated but not entirely incomprehensible.

Yet when the stylistic blemishes are admitted, and it is conceded that the uncompromising moral values are unfashionable in some quarters today, there remains a memorable and moving story, full of vivid characters—especially the elder ones, with a dedicated young heroine who involves our sympathy. If the education of the emotions is a function of the junior novel, Vipont's achievement must be rated high.

—Geoffrey Trease

W

WABER, Bernard

Nationality: American. **Born:** Philadelphia, Pennsylvania, 27 September 1924. **Education:** University of Pennsylvania, Philadelphia; Museum School of Fine Art, Philadelphia, 1946-50; Pennsylvania Academy of Fine Arts, Philadelphia, 1950-51. **Military Service:** United States Army, Panama Canal Zone, 1942-45: Staff Sergeant. **Family:** Married Ethel Bernstein in 1952; three children. **Career:** Commercial artist, Condé Nast Publications, New York, and *Seventeen* magazine, New York, 1952-54; graphic designer, *Life* magazine, New York, 1955-72. Since 1974 graphic designer, *People* magazine, New York. **Address:** Houghton Mifflin Co., 222 Berkley St., Boston, Nassachusetts 02116, U.S.A.

PUBLICATIONS FOR CHILDREN (ILLUSTRATED BY THE AUTHOR)

Fiction

Lorenzo. Boston, Houghton Mifflin, 1961.
The House on East 88th Street. Boston, Houghton Mifflin, 1962; as *Welcome, Lyle,* London, Chatto Boyd and Oliver, 1969.
Rich Cat, Poor Cat. Boston, Houghton Mifflin, 1963.
How to Go About Laying an Egg. Boston, Houghton Mifflin, 1963.
Lyle, Lyle, Crocodile. Boston, Houghton Mifflin, 1965; Edinburgh, Oliver and Boyd, 1966.
Lyle and the Birthday Party. Boston, Houghton Mifflin, 1966; Edinburgh, Oliver and Boyd, 1967.
"You Look Ridiculous," Said the Rhinoceros to the Hippopotamus. Boston, Houghton Mifflin, 1966; London, Hamish Hamilton, 1967.
An Anteater Named Arthur. Boston, Houghton Mifflin, 1967; London, Chatto Boyd and Oliver, 1969.
Cheese. Boston, Houghton Mifflin, 1967.
A Rose for Mr. Bloom. Boston, Houghton Mifflin, 1968.
Lovable Lyle. Boston, Houghton Mifflin, 1969; London, Chatto Boyd and Oliver, 1970.
A Firefly Named Torchy. Boston, Houghton Mifflin, 1970.
Ira Sleeps Over. Boston, Houghton Mifflin, 1972; as *Good Night Ben,* Leicester, Brockhampton Press, 1974.
Lyle Finds His Mother. Boston, Houghton Mifflin, 1974; London, Chatto and Windus, 1976.
I Was All Thumbs. Boston, Houghton Mifflin, 1975.
But Names Will Never Hurt Me. Boston, Houghton Mifflin, 1976.
Goodbye, Funny Dumpy-Lumpy. Boston, Houghton Mifflin, 1977.
Mice on My Mind. Boston, Houghton Mifflin, 1977.
The Snake: A Very Long Story. Boston, Houghton Mifflin, 1978.
You're a Little Kid with a Big Heart. Boston, Houghton Mifflin, 1980.
Dear Hildegarde. Boston, Houghton Mifflin, 1980.
Bernard. Boston, Houghton Mifflin, 1982.
Funny, Funny Lyle. Boston, Houghton Mifflin, 1987.
Ira Says Goodbye. Boston, Houghton Mifflin, 1988.
Lyle at the Office. Boston, Houghton Mifflin, 1994.
Do You See a Mouse?, Boston, Houghton Mifflin, 1995.
Bearsie Bear and the Surprise Sleepover Party, Boston, Houghton Mifflin, 1997.

Other

Just Like Abraham Lincoln. Boston, Houghton Mifflin, 1964.
Nobody Is Perfick (cartoons). Boston, Houghton Mifflin, 1971; London, Angus and Robertson, 1973.

*

Manuscript Collections: Kerlan Collection, University of Minnesota, Minneapolis.

Bernard Waber comments:

My involvement with children's books originated with some illustrations of children I carried in my art portfolio. Several art directors suggested that my drawings seemed suited for children's books. At the same time, I was also having read-aloud sessions with my own three children. I am afraid my enthusiasm for "their" books began, in fact, to cause them occasional discomfort. "Daddy, why don't you look at the grown-ups' books," they once chided as I trailed after them into the children's room of our local library. Before long I was mailing out stories and ideas to publishers. Rejections followed, but after a time cheery encouragement arrived from Houghton Mifflin Company, and to my delight a contract was offered for *Lorenzo.*

* * *

Bernard Waber infuses his work with warmth, a freshness of style, and a disarmingly ready wit. He is equally capable in the realms of fantasy and reality. Most amusing are the adventures involving Lyle, an endearing and whimsical crocodile, who materializes in a bathtub in *The House on East 88th Street.* With aplomb and dazzling showmanship, Lyle entertains and enchants the inhabitants, the Primms. In *Lyle, Lyle, Crocodile,* his removal to the local zoo is orchestrated by the irascible Mr. Grumps and his terrified cat, Loretta. Hector P. Valenti ensnares Lyle and lures him away on a money-making scheme in *Lyle Finds his Mother.* Lyle prevails and finally reunites with his mother. Laughter and humor abound coupled with a fast pace, ridiculous antics, and the casual acceptance of the crocodiles' absurd and preposterous existence. Text and illustrations merge dynamically to balance fantasy with the exploration of feelings and relationships. Culminating the series, *Funny, Funny Lyle* spotlights Lyle's relationship with his mother as he shares in her adventures.

Similarly, *An Anteater Named Arthur* is a charming and delightful look at a mother and son relationship with a slightly different slant. Using a conversational format in five short tableaux, Waber gently pokes fun at the inherent problems in their relationship. Reading it aloud heightens audience enjoyment and appreciation. Contrasting his fantasy, *Just Like Abraham Lincoln* is an attempt to enliven biography. Mr. Potts, a modern look-alike, relates anecdotes and stories which labor in parts where the similarities between Potts and Lincoln seem overdrawn.

Ira Sleeps Over captures the mood of a little boy wrestling with the decision to take his teddy bear on his overnight adventure to his friend Reggie's house. The story is an insightful probe into the ambivalence this attachment represents. The sibling rivalry and indecision build to a climax through his faithful reproduction of children's jibes, taunts, and harassing remarks. Magically, Ira and the reader seem to reach a decision together. A gentle touch of irony is revealed by the disclosure that Reggie lives next door. *Ira Says Goodbye* draws Ira and Reggie together in the trauma of best friends saying goodbye. Reggie is moving, and Waber deftly enables the reader to feel the impact. The conversations and illustrations mesh, drawing us into the mood to share the moment with Ira and Reggie.

But Names Will Never Hurt Me is amusing but slight, lacking the impact and involvement of the Ira series. Alison Wonderland resents her name. Some of the force of her discomfort is lost on an audience too young to appreciate the significance. The word play is more successful in *Nobody is Perfick* and *A Rose for Mr. Bloom. The Snake* is a rare disappointment, combining an overdrawn story with a tiresome moral in an easy reader. *Dear Hildegarde* blends humorous puns and a unique comical style with sage advice and owlish wisdom. *Bernard* is amusingly effective at portraying a dog's perspective on his fate, resulting from his owners' separation and property split.

—Martha J. Fick

WADDELL, Martin

Pseudonym: Catherine Sefton. **Nationality:** Irish. **Born:** Belfast, Northern Ireland, 10 April 1941. **Education:** Primary and secondary schools. **Family:** Married Rosaleen Carragher in 1969; three sons. **Awards:** Arts Council of Northern Ireland bursary, 1971, 1974, 1981; Children's Rights Workshop Other award, 1986; Smarties prize, 1988, 1991; shortlist for Smarties Prize, 1992.

Publications for Children

Fiction

Ernie's Chemistry Set [*Flying Trousers*], illustrated by Ronnie Baird. Belfast, Blackstaff Press, 2 vols., 1978.

Napper Goes for Goal [*Strikes Again*], illustrated by Barrie Mitchell. London, Penguin, 2 vols., 1981.

The Great Green Mouse Disaster, illustrated by Philippe Dupasquier. London, Andersen Press, 1981.

Harriet and the Crocodiles. London, Abelard Schuman, 1982; Boston, Little Brown, 1984.

The House under the Stairs. London, Methuen, 1983.

Going West, illustrated by Philippe Dupasquier. London, Andersen Press, 1983; New York, Harper, 1984.

Solve-It-Yourself Mysteries (*The Mystery Squad and the Dead Man's Message* [*the Artful Dodger, The Whistling Teeth, Mr. Midnight, the Creeping Castle, the Candid Camera, the Cannonball Kid, the Robot's Revenge, the Gemini Job*]), illustrated by Terry McKenna. London, Blackie, 9 vols., 1984-86.

Napper's Golden Goals, illustrated by Barrie Mitchell. London, Penguin, 1984.

Harriet and the Haunted School, illustrated by Mark Burgess. London, Abelard, 1984; Boston, Little Brown, 1985.

Big Bad Bertie, illustrated by Glenys Ambrus. London, Methuen, 1984.

Harriet and the Robot, illustrated by Mark Burgess. London, Blackie, 1985; Boston, Little Brown, 1987.

The Budgie Said Grrrrrr, illustrated by Glenys Ambrus. London, Methuen, 1985.

The Day It Rained Elephants, illustrated by Glenys Ambrus. London, Methuen, 1986.

Owl and Billy [*and the Space Days*]. London, Methuen, 2 vols., 1986-88.

Our Wild Weekend. London, Methuen, 1986.

Little Dracula's First Bite [*Christmas*], illustrated by Joseph Wright. London, Walker, and New York, Viking, 2 vols., 1986.

The Tough Princess, illustrated by Patrick Benson. London, Walker, 1986; New York, Putnam, 1987.

The Tall Story of Wilbur Small. London, Blackie, 1987.

Harriet and the Flying Teachers, illustrated by Mark Burgess. London, Blackie, 1987.

Alice the Artist, illustrated by Jonathan Langley. London, Methuen, and New York, Dutton, 1988.

Class Three and the Beanstalk, illustrated by Toni Goffe. London, Blackie, 1988.

Tales from the Shop That Never Shuts, illustrated by Maureen Bradley. London, Viking Kestrel, 1988.

Can't You Sleep, Little Bear?, illustrated by Barbara Firth. London, Walker, 1988; Cambridge, Massachusetts, Candlewick Press, 1992.

Little Dracula Goes to School [*at the Seaside*], illustrated by Joseph Wright. London, Walker, 2 vols., 1987; Cambridge, Massachusetts, Candlewick Press, 2 vols., 1992.

Joe's Gang. Aylesbury, Ginn and Bothell, Washington, Wright Group, 1988.

Our Sleepysaurus. London, Walker, 1988.

Great Gran Gorilla to the Rescue [*and the Robbers*], illustrated by Dom Mansell. London, Walker, 2 vols., 1988.

The Park in the Dark, illustrated by Barbara Firth. London, Walker, 1989; Cambridge, Massachusetts, Candlewick Press, 1996.

Fred the Angel. London, Walker, 1989.

Judy the Bad Fairy. London, Walker, 1989.

Once There Were Giants, illustrated by Penny Dale. London, Walker, 1989; Cambridge, Massachusetts, Candlewick Press, 1995.

My Great Grandpa, illustrated by Dom Mansell, London, Walker, and New York, Putnam, 1990.

Amy Said. London, Walker, and Boston, Joy Street, 1990.

Candy Can-do and the Dragon Doors [*and the King's Diamond, Goes to Spy Island*]. Aylesbury, Bucks, Ginn, 3 vols., 1990.

Daisy's Christmas. London, Methuen, 1990; New York, Dell, 1993.

The Ghost Family Robinson. London, Viking Kestrel, 1990.

Grandma's Bill. London and New York, Simon and Schuster, 1990.

The Hidden House, with Angela Barrett. London, Walker, 1990; Cambridge, Massachusetts, Candlewick Press, 1997.

We Love Them. London, Walker, 1990; Cambridge, Massachusetts, Candlewick Press, 1997.

Super Pet. Aylesbury, Bucks, Ginn, 1990.

Rosie's Babies. London, Walker, 1990.

Wild Cat, with Gini Wade. Aylesbury, Ginn, 1990.
Coming Home, with Neil Reed. Hemel Hempstead, Simon and Schuster, 1991.
Daisy's Christmas. Little Mammoth, 1991; New York, Dell, 1993.
Farmer Duck, illustrated by Helen Oxenbury. London, Walker, 1991; Cambridge, Massachusetts, Candlewick Press, 1992.
The Ghost Family Robinson at the Seaside. London, Viking Kestrel, 1991.
The Happy Hedgehog Band, illustrated by Jill Barton. London, Walker, and Cambridge, Massachusetts, Candlewick Press, 1991.
Herbies Whistle. London, Viking Kestrel, 1991.
Let's Go Home, Little Bear, illustrated by Barbara Firth. London, Walker, and Cambridge, Massachusetts, Candlewick Press, 1991.
Little Obie and the Flood [*and the Kidnap*], illustrated by Elsie Lennox. London, Walker, 2 vols., 1991; Cambridge, Massachusetts, Candlewick Press, 1992-94.
Man Mountain. London, Viking Kestrel, 1991.
Squeak-a-lot, illustrated by Virginia Miller. London, Walker and New York, Greenwillow, 1991.
The Toymaker: A Story in Two Parts, illustrated by Terry Milne. London, Walker, 1991; Cambridge, Massachusetts, Candlewick Press, 1992.
Sailor Bear, illustrated by Virginia Austin. London, Walker, and Cambridge, Massachusetts, Candlewick Press, 1992.
The Pig in the Pond, illustrated by Jill Barton. London, Walker, and Cambridge, Massachusetts, Candlewick Press, 1992.
Sam Vole and his Brothers, illustrated by Barbara Firth. London, Walker, and Cambridge, Massachusetts, Candlewick Press, 1992.
Owl Babies, illustrated by Patrick Benson. London, Walker, and Cambridge, Massachusetts, Candlewick Press, 1992.
Owl and Billy Stories, illustrated by C. Dinan. Mammoth, 1994.
Baby's Hammer. London, Walker, 1993.
The Big Bad Mole's Coming! London, Walker, 1993.
The Fishface Feud, illustrated by Arthur Robins. Dublin, O'Brien, 1993.
Little Mo, illustrated by Jill Barton. London, Walker, and Cambridge, Massachusetts, Candlewick Press, 1993.
The Lucky Duck Song. London, Puffin, 1993.
Napper's Big Match, illustrated by Richard Berridge. London, Puffin, 1993.
Napper's Luck, illustrated by Richard Berridge. London, Puffin, 1993.
Napper Super-Sub, illustrated by Richard Berridge. London, Puffin, 1993.
Rubberneck's Revenge, illustrated by Arthur Robins. Dublin, O'Brien, 1993.
The School That Went To Sea, illustrated by Leo Hartas. Dublin, O'Brien, 1993.
The Big, Big Sea, illustrated by Jennifer Eachus. London, Walker, and Cambridge, Massachusetts, Candlewick Press, 1994.
Big Bad Bill, illustrated by Graham Philpot. Aylesbury, Ginn, 1994.
Billy Fishbone and Other Sea Stories. Harlow, Longman, 1994.
A Frog in the Throat. Harlow, Longman, 1994.
The Get-Away Hen, illustrated by Susie Jenkin-Pearce. London, Puffin, 1995.
Granny Big Boots, illustrated by Jane Gedye. Aylesbury, Ginn, 1994.
The Hairy Canaries And Other Nonsense, illustrated by Alan Case. Harlow, Longman, 1994.
Kangaroos, illustrated by Frank James. Aylesbury, Ginn, 1994.
The Kidnapping of Suzie Q. London, Hamish Hamilton, 1994; Cambridge, Massachusetts, Candlewick Press, 1996.
Little Frog and the Dog. Harlow, Longman, 1994.
Little Frog and the Olympics. Harlow, Longman, 1994.
Little Frog and the Tadpoles. Harlow, Longman, 1994.
Old Jelly's Egg-Laying Cow. Aylesbury, Ginn, 1994.
The Shadow Dance. Harlow, Longman, 1994.
Shipwreck at Old Jelly's Farm. Aylesbury, Ginn, 1994.
Upside Down Harry Brown. Aylesbury, Ginn, 1994.
When the Teddy Bears Came, illustrated by Penny Dale. London, Walker, 1994; Cambridge, Massachusetts, Candlewick Press, 1995.
The Dump Gang, illustrated by Paul Sample. London, Walker, 1995.
John Joe and the Big Hen, illustrated by Paul Howard. Cambridge, Massachusetts, Candlewick Press, 1995.
Mimi and the Dream House, illustrated by Leo Hartas. Dublin, O'Brien Press, 1995; Cambridge, Massachusetts, Candlewick Press, 1998.
Tango's Baby. London, Walker, and Cambridge, Massachusetts, Candlewick Press, 1995.
Bears Everywhere, illustrated by Margaret Chamberlain. Cambridge, Massachusetts, Candlewick Press, 1996.
My Auntie Sal and the Mega-Sized Moose, illustrated by Helen Craig. London, Walker, 1996.
Small Bear Lost, illustrated by Virginia Austin. Cambridge, Massachusetts, Candlewick Press, 1996.
What Use Is a Moose?, illustrated by Arthur Robins. Cambridge, Massachusetts, Candlewick Press, 1996.
You and Me, Little Bear, illustrated by Barbara Firth. London, Walker and Cambridge, Massachusetts, Candlewick Press, 1996.
Mimi's Christmas, illustrated byLeo Hartas. Cambridge, Massachusetts, Candlewick Press, 1997.
Mimi and the Picnic, illustrated by Leo Hartas. Cambridge, Massachusetts, Candlewick Press, 1998.
Yum, Yum, Yummy, illustrated by John Bendall-Brunello. Cambridge, Massachusetts, Candlewick Press, 1998.

Fiction as Catherine Sefton

In a Blue Velvet Dress: Almost a Ghost Story, illustrated by Gareth Floyd. London, Faber, 1972; New York, Harper, 1973.
The Sleepers on the Hill. London, Faber, 1973.
The Back House Ghosts. London, Faber, 1974; as *The Haunting of Ellen,* New York, Harper, 1975.
The Ghost and Bertie Boggin, illustrated by Jill Bennett. London, Faber, 1980.
Emer's Ghost. London, Hamish Hamilton, 1981.
The Finn Gang, illustrated by Sally Holmes. London, Hamish Hamilton, 1981.
A Puff of Smoke, illustrated by Thelma Lambert. London, Hamish Hamilton, 1982.
The Emma Dilemma, illustrated by Jill Bennett. London, Faber, 1982.
Island of the Strangers. London, Hamish Hamilton, 1983; San Diego, Harcourt Brace, 1985.
My Gang, illustrated by Catherine Bradbury. London, Hamish Hamilton, 1984.
The Blue Misty Monsters, illustrated by Elaine McGregor Turney. London, Faber, 1985.
The Ghost Girl. London, Hamish Hamilton, 1985.

The Ghost Ship, illustrated by Martin Ursell. London, Hamish Hamilton, 1985.
Starry Night. London, Hamish Hamilton, 1986.
Flying Sam, illustrated by Margaret Chamberlain. London, Hamish Hamilton, 1986.
Shadows on the Lake. London, Hamish Hamilton, 1987.
Bertie Boggin and the Ghost Again! London, Faber, 1988.
Frankie's Story. London, Hamish Hamilton, 1988.
The Day the Smells Went Wrong, illustrated by John Rogan. London, Hamish Hamilton, 1988.
The Haunted Schoolbag. London, Hamish Hamilton, 1989.
The Beat of the Drum. London, Hamish Hamilton, 1989.
Along a Lonely Road. London, Hamish Hamilton, 1991.
The Boggart in the Barrel. London, Hamish Hamilton, 1991.
Horace the Ghost. London, Hamish Hamilton, 1991.
The Ghosts of Cobweb [and the Skully Bones Mystery, and the Circus Star, and the TV Battle], illustrated by Jean Baylis. London, Hamish Hamilton, 1992-94.
The Cast-Off. London, Hamish Hamilton, 1993.
The Pocket Elephant, illustrated by Andy Ellis. London, Hamish Hamilton, 1995.
The Skeleton Club, illustrated by Maureen Bradley. London, Hamish Hamilton, 1995.
Watch Out, Fred's About, illustrated by Caroline Crossland. London, Hamish Hamilton, 1996.

Plays

Radio Plays: *The Fleas and Mr. Morgan,* 1969; *Bazaar* series, from 1974; *One Potato, Two Potato* series, from 1975.

Other

Diz and the Big Fat Burglar and Other Stories, with Margaret Stuart Barry. London, Puffin, N.d.
Stories from the Bible: Old Testament Stories (retelling), illustrated by Geoffffrey Patterson. London, Frances Lincoln, and New York, Ticknor and Fields, 1993.

Editor, *A Tale to Tell: Stories by Young People from Northern Ireland.* Belfast, Arts Council of Northern Ireland, 1982.

Publications for Adults

Novels

Otley. London, Hodder and Stoughton, and New York, Stein and Day, 1966.
Otley Pursued. London, Hodder and Stoughton, and New York, Stein and Day, 1967.
Otley Forever. London, Hodder and Stoughton, and New York, Stein and Day, 1968.
Otley Victorious. London, Hodder and Stoughton, and New York, Stein and Day, 1969.
Come Back When I'm Sober. London, Hodder and Stoughton, 1969.
A Little Bit British, Being the Diary of an Ulsterman. London, Stacey, 1970.

*

Media Adaptations: *Otley* (motion picture), Columbia, 1969; *In a Blue Velvet Dress* (television), BBC-TV, 1974; *The Sleepers on the Hill* (television), BBC-TV, 1976; *Fred the Angel* (television), BBC-TV, n. d., *Island of the Strangers* (television), Thames TV, n. d.

Manuscript Collections: Linen Hall Library, Belfast.

Martin Waddell comments:

I try to write with clarity and brevity, with the aim of entertaining and amusing children, rather than instructing them. My "Catherine Sefton" work is based largely on the idea of family and is very much concerned with the emotions of the characters, always within the framework of an amusing story. I am strongly against the idea of "problem" novels, as I feel these reflect adult interests. To date I have written only one book for children which could be classed as a "problem" book (*The Island of the Strangers*), but the treatment of the "problem" therein clearly subordinates it to the story and the people.

I write against the political background of Northern Ireland, but not usually about it. My children are subjected to it every day in terms of stereotype.... I try to write in terms of individuals and their emotions.

Most of my "Martin Waddell" books are for amusement only.

* * *

For most of his career, Martin Waddell has been leading a double life—publishing books for young and middle grade readers under his own name, and books for young adults under the pen name Catherine Sefton. Waddell was writing before Sefton, with the adult Otley series and other work. But he soon turned to works for children, publishing his first young adult novel in 1972. Because of his reputation as a writer of comedies and thrillers for adults, Waddell decided to take a pseudonym based on his grandmother's maiden name. Sefton's first book, *In a Blue Velvet Dress,* is subtitled, rather coyly, *Almost a Ghost Story.* In fact it definitely is a ghost story, a very good one, predating Penelope Lively's classic *The Ghost of Thomas Kempe* by one year. Shorter and gentler than Lively's, it has a similar sense of comedy. Already in this first book there are the elements which are to become so familiar in Sefton's novels: wit, slapstick, acute dialogue, caring families under strain, Irish Protestants and Catholics, sensitive curious children—and ghosts!

Almost all of Sefton's novels have ghosts. But with any kind of ghost story, it is valuable to ask why? The better the reason for the haunting, the more convincing is the story. Less convincing or satisfying as literature are what can be called "spook" stories which use the supernatural just to give a thrill or drive the narrative. The ghost in *In a Blue Velvet Dress* is haunting in order to help the living. This ghost, like the living heroine of the novel, is (or was) a lonely bookworm. Occasionally, however, it is the ghost who needs help, as in *The Back House Ghosts.* Such stories are hauntings with a purpose, set within a personal relationship between haunter and hauntee. In these situations the living characters have room to feel and develop. Matters from the past can meaningfully impinge on and interact with the present. In all her ghost stories, it is to Sefton's credit that she has never written a "spook" story. But sometimes the haunting can seem unjustified or weakly motivated.

The Back House Ghosts is a very satisfactory summer holida ghost story—solid characters, strong setting, robust plot. Ghost can usually be relied on for a good yarn. But there is some weakness in the reason for the haunting. The desire of a ghost to communicate an important message to the living is used more convincingly in *Emer's Ghost,* where young Emer accidentally discovers a lost doll that had once belonged to a girl who died keeping a secret from Cromwell's invading Protestant army. What had been a matter of love in *The Back House Ghosts* becomes a matter of religious politics, with particular relevance in modern Northern Ireland.

The Ghost Girl is a development of both *In a Blue Velvet Dress* and *The Back House Ghosts,* with an interesting twist. On a summer holiday, a sensitive young Protestant girl finds herself haunted, she believes, by a sad gentle ghost girl. The retired Catholic Canon she tries to confide in remarks significantly, "If you think there's someone watching you, what's there to watch?" The motivation for the haunting and the relation between the ghost and the person being haunted are subtly highlighted.

Sefton has written many other kinds of hauntings, for different age levels. *The Ghost Ship* is a picture book in which the ship and the ghost pirate boy are probably the invention of the imaginative young hero. In *The Emma Dilemma* young Emma finds herself "haunted" by a shadowy *doppelganger* of herself as a result of concussion—a mixture of poltergeist and out-of-body experience. *The Ghost and Bertie Boggin* is a domestic farce for young readers on the pattern of the films *Topper* and *Harvey* where one character can see the ghost but no one else believes in it.

There are also several novels with no haunting, and virtually no explicit politics, although increasingly in Sefton's novels the background recognises the political tensions of Northern Ireland. These include *Shadows on the Lake* and *Island of the Strangers*—satisfying stories of social and domestic conflict in which the central characters must confront their own prejudices and overcome them by personal growth.

In 1986 Sefton won the Other award for *Starry Night,* the first volume of a trilogy that includes *Frankie's Story* and *The Beat of the Drum.* These (like *Shadows on the Lake*) are wholly realistic, not a hint of a ghost. They are about young girls growing up in Protestant Northern Ireland during the recent tragic sectarian violence. There are echoes here of Edna O'Brien and Joan Lingard. But Sefton writes very convincingly and individually about Irish people caught in family problems and in the undeclared civil war between the Provisional IRA and British Ulster. When Sefton's ghost stories are good they are very good. But in the trilogy with no ghosts she is tremendous!

Waddell published his first book for children under his own name in 1978. Unlike his Catherine Sefton books, these titles are aimed at a younger audience, and are, in his words, "for amusement only." This is true of many of his early efforts, for example, of *Ernie's Flying Trousers*—they really fly, and it is all a rather silly story based on a silly gimmick. But even this has a very strong sense of visual humour that exceeds the cartoon style of the illustrations, and really cries out for a good television production. Waddell found an outstanding illustrator in Philippe Dupasquier. *The Great Green Mouse Disaster* is an almost wordless triumph of visual slapstick. *Going West* has a very spare text, but enough to make a strong narrative of a family in a covered wagon struggling to cross to Oregon in the days of the Old West of America. Writing for a slightly older audience, Waddell produced several series—the *Napper* books, based on his own experiences as a soccer goalkeeper; the *Mystery Squad* series; the *Harriet* books; and several *Little Dracula* titles—each marked by a strong dose of lighthearted fun.

Waddell's works of the past decade, while still marked by an emphasis on amusement and entertainment, have also included several books with more lasting value, stories that have provided a series of talented illustrators with wonderful vehicles for their art. His *Little Bear* books, illustrated by Barbara Firth, are characterized by an affectionate humor and comforting warmth that few readers (young or old) can resist. *Sailor Bear* and *Small Bear Lost* relate the adventures of a small but plucky stuffed animal, a bear brought to charmingly old-fashioned life in the artwork of Virginia Austin. Waddell spins a modern fable in *Farmer Duck,* the story of a hardworking bird (brought to endearing life by Helen Oxenbury) who must tend the fields because the farmer himself is too lazy to do his job. And when a new baby comes to Tom's house, so do the bears, in *When the Teddy Bears Came,* a simple, reassuring story of adjusting to a new sibling graced by soft, soothing illustrations by Penny Dale.

While still publishing an occasional title under the Sefton name, the majority of his recent titles have been all Waddell, even those for older readers. *The Kidnapping of Susie Q* is a suspenseful tale of a teen taken hostage during a grocery store robbery, perfect for reluctant readers. Noteworthy for its wry humor and strong plotting and characterization, *Tango's Baby* recounts Brian Tangello's attempts to hold onto his girlfriend and to the baby born to them. Waddell has also contributed many titles to several educational publishers' reading series.

The output of Waddell and Sefton can be seen as that of a prolific writer who needs two names to be able to publish fast enough. But both are always entertaining, and at their best very rewarding at several different levels.

—John Gough, updated by Jackie C. Horne

WAGNER, Jenny

Nationality: Australian. **Born:** United Kingdom 1939; moved with her family to Australia in 1948. **Awards:** Australian Children's Book Council award, for picture book, 1974, 1977; Zilveren Griffel Award (Netherlands), 1978; New South Wales Premier's Literary Award, 1979. **Address:** c/o Penguin Books Australia, P.O. Box 257, 487 Maroondah Highway, Ringwood, Victoria 3134, Australia.

PUBLICATIONS FOR CHILDREN

Fiction

The Werewolf Knight, illustrated by Karl Homes. Melbourne and London, Macmillan, 1972; revised edition, illustrated by Robert Roennfeldt, Milsons Point, New South Wales, Random House, 1995.

The Bunyip of Berkeley's Creek, illustrated by Ron Brooks. Melbourne, Childerset, and London, Longman, 1973; Scarsdale, New York, Bradbury Press, 1977.

Peter and the Zauberleaf, illustrated by Giulietta Stomann. Sydney, Hamlyn, 1973.

Aranea: A Story about a Spider, illustrated by Ron Brooks. Melbourne, Childerset, and London, Kestrel, 1975; Scarsdale, New York, Bradbury Press, 1978.

Hannibal, illustrated by Karl Homes. Melbourne, Childerset, 1976.
John Brown, Rose, and the Midnight Cat, illustrated by Ron Brooks. London, Kestrel, 1977; Scarsdale, New York, Bradbury Press, 1978.
The Nimbin, illustrated by Inga Moore. Melbourne, Nelson, 1978; London, Penguin, 1980.
Jo-Jo and Mike, illustrated by Ann James. Melbourne, Nelson, 1982.
The Machine at the Heart of the World, illustrated by Jeff Fisher. Ringwood, Victoria and London, Kestrel, 1983.
Goanna, illustrated by Noela Hills. Ringwood, Victoria and London, Viking Kestrel, 1988.
The Windmill in the Paddock, illustrated by Valerie Carter. Canberra, Curriculum Development Centre, 1988.
Amy's Monster, illustrated by Terry Denton. Ringwood, Victoria, and New York, Viking, 1990.
Message from Avalon. Nundah, Queensland, Jam Roll Press, 1990; St. Lucia, Queensland, University of Queensland Press, 1994.
Motor Bill and the Lovely Caroline, illustrated by Ron Brooks. Ringwood, Victoria, Viking, 1994; New York, Ticknor & Fields Books for Young Readers, 1995.

Other

On Writing Books for Children. St Leonards, New South Wales, Allen & Unwin, 1992; Middlesex, Independent Publishers, 1993.

* * *

Jenny Wagner is best known for two highly acclaimed picture books, both illustrated by Australian artist and author Ron Brooks, *The Bunyip of Berkeley's Creek* and *John Brown, Rose, and the Midnight Cat.* These books have provoked considerable discussion amongst critics because of the profound nature of their themes based on notions of reality, perception, human relationships, and death. These themes are also evident in *Motor Bill and the Lovely Caroline,* the fourth book from the famous partnership of Wagner and Brooks. In her other picture books Wagner has considered cycles and change (*Peter and the Zauberleaf*), individual survival and creativity (*Aranea: A Story about a Spider*), political control and personal choice (*Jo-Jo and Mike*), and the effect of human greed on the environment (*The Machine at the Heart of the World* and *Goanna*).

Wagner's particular skill lies in incorporating such weighty themes into highly entertaining narratives. In *The Bunyip of Berkeley's Creek,* a benign bunyip (a usually fearful monster from Aboriginal lore said to inhabit billabongs and other inland pools and waterways) climbs out of black mud and asks "What am I?" The Bunyip's search for identity is an exemplification of Bishop George Berkeley's proposition of the relationship between perception and being. All the animals the Bunyip meets and questions describe only the creature of myth, and a man who "looked right through him" said "Bunyips simply don't exist." Saddened, Bunyip goes away, but all ends happily when another bunyip climbs out of the mud and Bunyip is able to answer her question, "What am I?"

The Bunyip of Berkeley's Creek can be read and enjoyed without knowing anything of Bishop Berkeley. In essence the story is about the pleasures of companionship. Similarly Wagner's best book, *John Brown, Rose, and the Midnight Cat* is a text with meaning for readers of all ages. Rose, a widow, lives with her dog, John Brown. It is apparent from the text and illustrations that they live a quiet, well-ordered life, "'We are all right, John Brown,' said Rose. 'Just the two of us, you and me.'" However, one night Rose sees the midnight cat and wants to give it some milk. John Brown is jealous and won't let it in. After a while Rose becomes ill and goes to bed "forever." John Brown opens the door to the midnight cat, Rose gets out of bed, and the three sit by the fire. It is not easy to describe in words the charm and power of this book. The author herself felt the story "so strange" she was reluctant to send it to a publisher. The nature of relationships, particularly the need to let love flourish rather than be restrictive is in the foreground, but colouring this theme is the suggestion of mysterious things beyond our ken, most particularly the mystery of death. Indeed these two themes—of individual autonomy, and the possibilities of things beyond human intelligence—are the principal concerns apparent in all of Wagner's writing.

In Wagner's short novels, *The Nimbin* and *Return of the Nimbin,* a young girl has to care for a loveable but troublesome creature who comes and goes with the phases of the moon. *Message from Avalon,* a novel for somewhat older readers, features an eccentric family, a lottery win, a romantic ramshackle house, a ghost, and a mystery.

In *Aranea,* a spider patiently builds and rebuilds her web despite harassment from schoolboys and threats from changing weather. Mike, the sign-painter in *Jo-Jo and Mike,* leaves his job in a growing town, but before he leaves he changes all the "Don't" signs he has had to make to more positive messages as a protest against officious and petty bureaucracy. *The Machine at the Heart of the World* lacks the easy rhythm and resonance of Wagner's other writing. The pale illustrations detract from the text, and although the tale is a comment on how the world survives human greed, the intention of the message is unclear. Rather more earthy is *Amy's Monster* in which nasty bullies, Meredith and Jocasta, try to scare their cousin Amy, but the worm turns and Amy, making friends with a monster under the bed, asks him kindly to terrify her cousins! *Motor Bill and the Lovely Caroline* is an amusing tale about love that has echoes of the concerns of earlier works by Wagner and Brooks. Bill has a motor car, or so he claims, and his friend Caroline trusts him despite the ridicule of others.

Another love story is the re-illustrated and substantially re-written edition of Wagner's first book, *The Werewolf Knight.* Feolf is a gentle knight, destined to marry the king's daughter Fioran, but some nights he is a werewolf. In both guises he is noble, but when Fioran finds out she is worried about marrying a wolf and asks advice from a magician. He wants to marry her himself and gives advice that leaves Feolf stranded in the forest. After a hard winter a king's grace saves Feolf and the lover's are reunited. A fantasy with real heart to it, treading as it does on the edges of our own subconscious.

—Kerry White

WAHL, Jan (Boyer)

Nationality: American. **Born:** Columbus, Ohio, 1 April 1933. **Education:** Cornell University, Ithaca, New York, 1950-53, B.A. 1953; University of Copenhagen (Fulbright fellow), 1953-54, M.A.

1954; University of Michigan, Ann Arbor (Avery Hopwood prize), 1955-58, M.A. 1958; Bowling Green State University, Bowling Green, Ohio, Ph.D. 1996. **Career:** Worked in Denmark for the film director Carl T. Dreyer, 1954-55, and as secretary to the writer Isak Dinesen, 1957-58. **Agent:** Rogers Coleridge and White, 20 Powis Mews, London W11 1JN, England. **Address:** 6766 Carrietowne Lane, Toledo, Ohio 43617, U.S.A.

Publications for Children

Fiction

Pleasant Fieldmouse, illustrated by Maurice Sendak. New York, Harper, 1964; Kingswood, Surrey, World's Work, 1969.
The Howards Go Sledding, illustrated by John E. Johnson. New York, Holt Rinehart, 1964.
Hello, Elephant, illustrated by Edward Ardizzone. New York, Holt Rinehart, 1964.
Cabbage Moon, illustrated by Adrienne Adams. New York, Holt Rinehart, 1965.
The Muffletumps: The Story of Four Dolls, illustrated by Edward Ardizzone. New York, Holt Rinehart, 1966.
Christmas in the Forest, illustrated by Eleanor Schick. New York, Macmillan, 1967.
Pocahontas in London, illustrated by John Alcorn. New York, Delacorte Press, 1967.
The Furious Flycycle, illustrated by Fernando Krahn. New York, Delacorte Press, 1968; London, Longman, 1970.
Push Kitty, illustrated by Garth Williams. New York, Harper, 1968.
Cobweb Castle, illustrated by Edward Gorey. New York, Holt Rinehart, 1968.
Rickety Rackety Rooster, illustrated by John E. Johnson. New York, Simon and Schuster, 1968.
A Wolf of My Own, illustrated by Lillian Hoban. New York, Macmillan, 1969.
How the Children Stopped the Wars, illustrated by Mitchell Miller. New York, Farrar Straus, 1969; London, Abelard Schuman, 1975; revised edition, illustrated by Maureen O'Keefe, Berkeley, Tricycle Press, 1993.
The Fishermen, illustrated by Emily McCully. New York, Norton, 1969.
May Horses, illustrated by Blair Lent. New York, Delacorte Press, 1969.
The Norman Rockwell Storybook, illustrated by Rockwell. New York, Windmill, 1969.
The Prince Who Was a Fish, illustrated by Robin Jacques. New York, Simon and Schuster, 1970.
The Mulberry Tree, illustrated by Feodor Rojankovsky. New York, Grosset and Dunlap, 1970.
Doctor Rabbit, illustrated by Peter Parnall. New York, Delacorte Press, 1970; London, Longman, 1972.
The Animals' Peace Day, illustrated by Victoria Chess. New York, Crown, 1970.
The Wonderful Kite, illustrated by Uri Shulevitz. New York, Delacorte Press, 1971.
Abe Lincoln's Beard, illustrated by Fernando Krahn. New York, Delacorte Press, 1971.
Anna Help Ginger, illustrated by Lawrence Di Fiori. New York, Putnam, 1971.
Crabapple Night, illustrated by Steven Kellogg. New York, Holt Rinehart, 1971.
Margaret's Birthday, illustrated by Mercer Mayer. New York, Four Winds Press, 1971.
The Six Voyages of Pleasant Fieldmouse, illustrated by Peter Parnall. New York, Delacorte Press, 1971; revised edition, illustrated by Tim Bowers, New York, Tor Books, 1994.
Lorenzo Bear & Company, illustrated by Fernando Krahn. New York, Putnam, 1971.
The Very Peculiar Tunnel, illustrated by Steven Kellogg. New York, Putnam, 1972.
Magic Heart, illustrated by Trina Schart Hyman. New York, Seabury Press, 1972; Kingswood, Surrey, World's Work, 1973.
Grandmother Told Me, illustrated by Mercer Mayer. Boston, Little Brown, 1972.
Cristóbal and the Witch, illustrated by Janet McCaffery. New York, Putnam, 1972.
S.O.S. Bobomobile! or, The Further Adventures of Melvin Spitznagle and Professor Mickimecki, illustrated by Fernando Krahn. New York, Delacorte Press, 1973; London, Kestrel, 1975.
The Five in the Forest, illustrated by Erik Blegvad. Chicago, Follett, 1974.
Pleasant Fieldmouse's Halloween Party, illustrated by Wallace Tripp. New York, Putnam, 1974; Kingswood, Surrey, World's Work, 1976.
Mooga Mega Mekki, illustrated by Fernando Krahn. Chicago, O'Hara, 1974.
Jeremiah Knucklebones, illustrated by Jane Breskin Zalben. New York, Holt Rinehart, 1974.
The Muffletump Storybook, illustrated by Cyndy Szekeres. Chicago, Follett, 1975.
The Clumpets Go Sailing, illustrated by Cyndy Szekeres. New York, Parents' Magazine Press, 1975; Kingswood, Surrey, World's Work, 1977.
Bear, Wolf, and Mouse, illustrated by Kinuko Kraft. Chicago, Follett, 1975.
The Screeching Door; or, What Happened at the Elephant Hotel, illustrated by J. Winslow Higginbottom. New York, Four Winds Press, 1975.
The Muffletumps' Christmas Party, illustrated by Cyndy Szekeres. Chicago, Follett, 1975; Kingswood, Surrey, World's Work, 1977.
Great-Grandmother Cat Tales, illustrated by Cyndy Szekeres. New York, Pantheon, 1976.
Grandpa's Indian Summer, illustrated by Joanne Scribner. Englewood Cliffs, New Jersey, Prentice Hall, 1976.
The Pleasant Fieldmouse Storybook, illustrated by Erik Blegvad. Englewood Cliffs, New Jersey, Prentice Hall, and Kingswood, Surrey, World's Work, 1977.
Doctor Rabbit's Foundling, illustrated by Cyndy Szekeres. New York, Pantheon, 1977; Kingswood, Surrey, World's Work, 1979.
Frankenstein's Dog, illustrated by Kay Chorao. Englewood Cliffs, New Jersey, Prentice Hall, 1977; London, Hutchinson, 1980.
The Muffletumps' Halloween Scare, illustrated by Cyndy Szekeres. Chicago, Follett, 1977; Kingswood, Surrey, World's Work, 1979.
Pleasant Fieldmouse's Valentine Trick, illustrated by Marc Brown. New York, Windmill, 1977; Kingswood, Surrey, World's Work, 1979.
Carrot Nose, illustrated by James Marshall. New York, Farrar Straus, 1978.
Dracula's Cat, illustrated by Kay Chorao. Englewood Cliffs, New Jersey, Prentice Hall, 1978.

Who Will Believe Tim Kitten?, illustrated by Cyndy Szekeres. New York, Pantheon, 1978; Kingswood, Surrey, World's Work, 1980.
Jamie's Tiger, illustrated by Tomie de Paola. New York, Harcourt Brace, 1978.
Youth's Magic Horn: Seven Stories. Nashville, Nelson, 1978.
The Teeny, Tiny Witches, illustrated by Margot Tomes. New York, Putnam, 1979.
Doctor Rabbit's Lost Scout, illustrated by Cyndy Szekeres. New York, Pantheon, 1979.
Sylvester Bear Overslept, illustrated by Lee Lorenz. New York, Parents' Magazine Press, 1979; Kingswood, Surrey, World's Work, 1981.
Old Hippo's Easter Egg, illustrated by Lorinda Bryan Cauley. New York, Harcourt Brace, 1980.
Button Eye's Orange, illustrated by Wendy Watson. New York, Warne, 1980.
The Cucumber Princess, illustrated by Caren Caraway. Owings Mills, Maryland, Stemmer House, 1981.
The Little Blind Goat, illustrated by Antonio Frasconi. Owings Mills, Maryland, Stemmer House, 1981.
Grandpa Gus's Birthday Cake, illustrated by John Wallner. Englewood Cliffs, New Jersey, Prentice Hall, 1981.
Tiger Watch, illustrated by Charles Mikolaycak. New York, Harcourt Brace, 1982.
The Pipkins Go Camping, illustrated by John Wallner. Englewood Cliffs, New Jersey, Prentice Hall, 1982.
More Room for the Pipkins, illustrated by John Wallner. Englewood Cliffs, New Jersey, Prentice Hall, 1983.
Peter and the Troll Baby, illustrated by Erik Blegvad. Racine, Wisconsin, Golden Press, 1984.
So Many Raccoons, illustrated by Beth Lee Weiner. New York, Cademon, 1985.
Cheltenham's Party, illustrated by Lucinda McQueen. Racine, Wisconsin, Golden Press, 1985.
Runaway Jonah, illustrated by Jane Conteh-Morgan. New York, Caedmon, 1985.
Rabbits on Roller Skates!, illustrated by David Allender. New York, Crown, 1986.
Humphrey's Bear, illustrated by William Joyce. New York, Holt, 1987; London, Gollancz, 1988.
Let's Go Fishing!, illustrated by Bruce Lemorise. Racine, Wisconsin, Golden Press, 1987.
Timothy Tiger's Terrible Toothache, illustrated by Lisa McCue. Racine, Wisconsin, Golden Press, 1988.
Little Dragon's Grandmother, illustrated by Lucinda McQueen. Racine, Wisconsin, Golden Press, 1988.
Tim Kitten and the Red Cupboard, illustrated by Bruce Degen. New York, Simon and Schuster, 1988.
The Golden Christmas Tree, illustrated by Leonard Weisgard. Racine, Wisconsin, Golden Press, 1988.
Tales of Fuzzy Mouse, illustrated by Lillian Hoban. Racine, Wisconsin, Golden Press, 1988.
The Adventures of Underwater Dog, illustrated by Tim Bowers. New York, Grosset and Dunlap, 1989.
Little Eight John, illustrated by Will Clay. New York, Lodestar Books, 1992.
My Cat Ginger, illustrated by Naava. New York, Tambourine Books, 1992.
The Sleepytime Book, illustrated by Arden Johnson. New York, Tambourine Books, 1992.
Suzy and the Mouse King, illustrated by Catherine A. Macaro. Monroe, Michigan, Monroe County Library System, 1992.
Little Gray One, illustrated by Frane Lessac. New York, Tambourine Books, 1993.
How the Children Stopped the Wars, illustrated by Maureen O'Keefe. Berkeley, California, Tricycle Press, 1993.
Will Santa Come? illustrated by Catherine A. Macaro. Monroe, Michigan, Monroe County Library System, 1993.
"I Remember!," Cried Grandma Pinky, illustrated by Arden Johnson. Mahwah, New Jersey, Bridgewater, 1994.
The Furious Flycycle, illustrated by Ted Enik. New York, Tor Books, 1994.
S.O.S. Bobomobile!, illustrated by Ted Enik. New York, Tor Books, 1995.
Cats and Robbers, illustrated by Dolores Avendaño. New York, Tambourine Books, 1995.
Emily and the Snowflake, illustrated by Carolyn Ewing. Mahwah, New Jersey, Troll Books, 1995.
Once When the World Was Green, illustrated by Fabricio Vanden Broeck. Berkeley, California, Tricycle Press, 1996.
Jack Rabbit and the Giant, illustrated by Katie Macaro. Monroe, Michigan, Monroe County Library System, 1996.
The Singing Geese, illustrated by Sterling Brown. New York, Lodestar Books, 1998.
Cabbage Moon, illustrated by Arden Johnson. Honesdale, Pennsylvania, Boyds Mills Press, 1998.

Verse

The Beast Book, illustrated by E.W. Eichel. New York, Harper, 1964.
Follow Me, Cried Bee, illustrated by John Wallner. New York, Crown, 1976.
The Toy Circus, illustrated by Tim Bowers. San Diego, Harcourt Brace, 1986.
I Met a Dinosaur, illustrated by Chris Sheban. Mankato, Minnesota, Creative Editions, 1997.

Other

Runaway Jonah and Other Tales, illustrated by Uri Shulevitz. New York, Macmillan, 1968.
Crazy Brobobalou, illustrated by Paula Winter. New York, Putnam, 1973.
The Woman with the Eggs, illustrated by Ray Cruz. New York, Crown, 1974.
Juan Diego and the Lady, illustrated by Leonard Everett Fisher. New York, Putnam, 1974.
Drakestail (folktale), illustrated by Byron Barton. New York, Greenwillow, 1978; Kingswood, Surrey, World's Work, 1980.
Needle Noodle and Other Silly Stories (English folktales), illustrated by Stan Mack. New York, Pantheon, 1979.
The Wizard of Oz Movie Storybook. Racine, Wisconsin, Golden Press, 1989.

Publications for Adults

Play

Paradiso! Paradiso! (produced Ithaca, New York, 1954).

*

Manuscript Collections: Jan Wahl Collection, University of Wyoming, Laramie; Kerlan Collection, University of Minnesota, Minneapolis; Bowling Green State University, Bowling Green, Ohio.

Jan Wahl comments:

The first most vivid memory I have is of a drawing by my great-grandmother, made for me when I was four years old. I was fascinated by her pencil moving across the sheet of paper. So I do not find it odd that I am perfectly happy to have my stories accompanied by magical pictures.

One of my brothers once asked me *when* was I going to grow up? When was I going to stop writing my "little" books? I found those astonishing questions. There are two ways to grow up or to grow older. One is as most people (including my brother) do: rushing as a train does, from station to station, leaving things behind, speeding to the next stop. The other and preferable way, I think, is to grow as a tree does; that is, to grow rings each and every year, become young and old at the same time. At least this is what an artist or writer must do and since I find it a perfectly sensible arrangement, I have no plans to change it.

Even in my so-called adult fiction—stories printed in various magazines—I realized I was writing about the qualities of childhood. Therefore it occurred to me to write directly for children, that is, for the child in *me,* by means of fables and picture-book stories. I see picture books themselves as small films. Several artists I've worked with (Maurice Sendak and Uri Shulevitz) have agreed with me. I try to follow no trends but to write what I would wish to read if I, today, were a child. I find it a satisfying, exciting occupation.

* * *

> The bright sun, the pride of spring, popped into the sky like a flying orange. The forest stirred, then morning began, shaking its new green shades. Red cardinals and yellow finches darted among the trees like bold-painted arrows.
>
> Somebody was hammering a sign beside the thick black oak. This somebody was Pleasant Fieldmouse, who lived inside the oak, at the bottom. *I Am a Fireman* it said on the sign. Pleasant Fieldmouse was wearing a fine red hat which was really a cap from a bottle. *Tipsy Cola,* the cap was labeled, but you were not supposed to look at him from the top.

Those opening paragraphs from Jan Wahl's first book for children, *Pleasant Fieldmouse,* inadvertently reveal some of the main strengths and weaknesses that run through much of his writing. On the positive side stand imagination, a gentle whimsicality, humor, and fresh imagery. But balancing and sometimes outweighing these good qualities are the author's tendency to strain too hard for the unusual word or phrase, and his frequent descents into archness.

Wahl has published a wide range of books in the last two decades, from brief picture-book texts like *Drakestail, A Wolf of My Own,* and *Follow Me, Cried Bee,* to original fairytales (*The Cucumber Princess, Cobweb Castle, Magic Heart*), to unusual short biographies (*Abe Lincoln's Beard, Pocahontas in London*), to humorous novels for the 8 to twelve-year-old audience (*The Furious Flycycle, The Screeching Door*). He has even written a collection of contemporary short stories for young adults, *Youth's Magic Horn,* which combines echoes of Flannery O'Connor's eccentric humor with a pathos reminiscent of Sherwood Anderson. However, the majority of his published work falls into the picture book category.

Wahl's picture-book output slackened somewhat in the 1980s. But his gift for humor touched with feeling lent distinction to *Humphrey's Bear,* and his imagination literally ran wild in the rollicking text for *Rabbits on Rollerskates!*

All of Wahl's picture books are filled with surprises—an unusual word that juts out from the text, a fantastic character who suddenly enters the scene, a startling new situation that develops unexpectedly. Accompanying the surprises, though, is what often seems like a lack of control over the material and the narrative as a whole. Storylines wander off on colorful but inconclusive tangents; interesting characters appear, take center stage for a while and then vanish, never to reappear again. Sometimes the texts actually read like dreams that Wahl wrote down as soon as he awoke in the morning and then never touched again.

In a sense Wahl could probably be described as a victim of the boom in children's book publishing that flared up in the United States during the years of President Lyndon B. Johnson's so-called "Great Society" (1964-69). That was the period when generous appropriations of federal funds were being spent on the creation and expansion of school libraries all across the country. A prolific author like Wahl could—and did—sell just about everything he wrote to one publisher or another, even fragmentary pieces like *Pocahontas in London* and *May Horses.* Inevitably these slight books diminished Wahl's reputation, and there came a time in the 1970s when critics seemed to be on the verge of dismissing some of his richer and more unified books along with his weaker ones.

If that had happened, it would have been a shame—not only for Wahl but for the field of children's literature. Uneven, unsatisfying, and exasperating as Wahl's stories sometimes are, he can still come through with marvelous new approaches and insights as in *Runaway Jonah,* his retelling of five Old Testament stories. And he also has to his credit a true modern classic in *Push Kitty,* which dramatizes the ultimate in smothering love as the little girl narrator describes how she dresses up her kitten and tries to make him into her baby. "Baby, you are pretty lucky to have a mama like me, DON'T YOU AGREE?"

If only for *Push Kitty* and *Pleasant Fieldmouse,* Wahl would have a secure niche in any chronicle of American children's books from the 1960s onwards.

—James Cross Giblin

WALKER, David (Harry)

Nationality: Canadian (originally Scottish: became Canadian citizen, 1957). **Born:** Angus, Scotland, 9 February 1911. **Education:** Shrewsbury School, Shropshire, 1924-29; Royal Military College, Sandhurst, Surrey, 1929-30. **Family:** Married Willa Magee in 1939; five sons (one deceased). **Military Service:** British Army, in the Black Watch, 1931-47: served in India, 1932-36, and in the

Sudan, 1936-38; aide-de-camp to the Governor-General of Canada, 1938-39; prisoner-of-war in Germany, 1940-45; Instructor at the Staff College, Camberley, Surrey, 1945-46; comptroller to the Viceroy of India, 1946-47; retired as Major, 1947; M.B.E (Member, Order of the British Empire), 1946. **Career:** Since 1947 full-time writer. Canadian commissioner since 1965, and chairman, 1970-72, Roosevelt Campobello International Park Commission. **Member:** Canada Council, 1957-61. **Awards:** Governor-General's award, for novel, 1953, 1954. D. Litt.: University of New Brunswick, Fredericton, 1955. Fellow, Royal Society of Literature, 1950; member, Queen's Body guard for Scotland; member, Order of Canada. **Died:** 5 March 1992.

Publications for Children

Fiction

Sandy Was a Soldier's Boy, illustrated by Dobson Broadhead. London, Collins, and Boston, Houghton Mifflin, 1957; as *Sandy,* Collins, 1961.
Dragon Hill, illustrated by Ray Keane. Boston, Houghton Mifflin, 1962; London, Collins, 1963.
Pirate Rock, illustrated by Victor Mays. London, Collins, and Boston, Houghton Mifflin, 1969.
Big Ben, illustrated by Victor Ambrus. Boston, Houghton Mifflin, 1969; London, Collins, 1970.

Publications for Adults

Novels

The Storm and the Silence. Boston, Houghton Mifflin, 1949; London, Cape, 1950.
Geordie. Boston, Houghton Mifflin, and London, Collins, 1950.
The Pillar. Boston, Houghton Mifflin, and London, Collins, 1952; as *The Wire,* New York, Permabooks, 1953.
Digby. London, Collins, and Boston, Houghton Mifflin, 1953.
Harry Black. London, Collins, and Boston, Houghton Mifflin, 1956.
Where the High Winds Blow. London, Collins, and Boston, Houghton Mifflin, 1960.
Winter of Madness. London, Collins, and Boston, Houghton Mifflin, 1964.
Mallabec. London, Collins, and Boston, Houghton Mifflin, 1965.
Come Back, Geordie. London, Collins, and Boston, Houghton Mifflin, 1966.
Devil's Plunge. London, Collins, 1968; as *CAB-Intersec,* Boston, Houghton Mifflin, 1968.
The Lord's Pink Ocean. London, Collins, and Boston, Houghton Mifflin, 1972.
Black Dougal. London, Collins, 1973; Boston, Houghton Mifflin, 1974.
Ash. London, Collins, and Boston, Houghton Mifflin, 1976.
Pot of Gold. London, Collins, 1977.

Short Stories

Storms of Our Journey and Other Stories. Boston, Houghton Mifflin, 1962; London, Collins, 1963.

Other

Lean, Wind, Lean: A Few Times Remembered (memoirs). London, Collins, 1984.

* * *

David Walker was born in Scotland, but having adventured his way around the world, settled at last in Canada. His eventful personal history, which provided him with the material for prize-winning adult works, lends his children's books a ring of authenticity few of the genre can match.

Dragon Hill is the story of a "growing summer." Young William is unwilling to have his plans for the holiday spoiled by the intrusion of Mary, an unknown and unwanted remote relation from Scotland, whose widowed mother is off honeymooning with a second husband. Bad enough, thinks William, to be lumbered with a girl; but a girl in *her* frame of mind....After a poor start, the youngsters strike an uneasy truce, cemented in the usual way by getting into mischief together. They decide to brave Dragon Hill, the strictly forbidden ground belonging to Old Dragon, otherwise Captain McDurgan, a crusty curmudgeon with a grudge against the world. As the summer unfolds, so does the Dragon's withered spirit under the influence of the two children, and during the hurricane which is the story's climax, the old man who "hates everybody" rises to the occasion to become the hero of the hour. The brief and charming *Big Ben* is the story of a family and its huge, lovable St. Bernard, who though known affectionately as Ben, really labours under the appellation Hospice Excelsior. When the gentle giant is wrongfully accused of killing sheep and summarily condemned, Tim and Jinny, his young owners, go to extreme lengths to save him from a trigger-happy neighbour and to prove his innocence, in a story to warm a dog lover's heart.

Most ambitious of Walker's books for children is *Pirate Rock,* which tells of adventure in the Bay of Fundy, the meeting place of Canada and the United States. Teenagers Keith and Nelson are eager to take a summer job crewing a lavish speedboat for the ostentatiously rich newcomer in town. While in his employ, the boys discover evidence of mysterious, clandestine activities; and as their curiosity grows, so does their danger. This is a fairly complex tale of tangled personal and patriotic loyalties, and the eventual dramatic solution of the mystery, as so often in real life, is painful and difficult to accept for all concerned.

Although his "Mom and Dad" characters are an unattractive crew, Walker's young people compensate for their elders' charmlessness. It is notable that he has added some engaging and spirited girls to the traditional "boys' book" format. As breezy as the summers in which, one suspects, they were written, Walker's adventures are robustly fast-paced and readable.

—Joan McGrath

WALL, Dorothy

Nationality: Australian. **Born:** Wellington, New Zealand, in 1894. **Education:** Studied art in New Zealand. **Family:** Married Andrew Delfosse Badgery; one son. **Career:** Lived in Australia from 1914. **Died:** 1942.

Publications for Children (illustrated by the author)

Fiction

Tommy Bear and the Zookies. Sydney, Triumph, 1920.
The Complete Adventures of Blinky Bill. Sydney, Angus and Robertson, 1939.
Blinky Bill, The Quaint Little Australian. Sydney, Angus and Robertson, 1933.
Blinky Bill Grows Up. Sydney, Angus and Robertson, 1934.
Blinky Bill and Nutsy: Two Little Australians. Sydney, Angus and Robertson, 1937.
The Tale of Bridget and the Bees. London, Methuen, 1934; Poughkeepsie, New York, Artists and Writers Guild, 1935.
Brownie: The Story of a Naughty Little Rabbit. Sydney, Angus and Robertson, 1935; London, Angus and Robertson, 1977.
Stout Fellows: Chum, Angelina Wallaby, Um-Pig, and Flip. Sydney, Angus and Robertson, 1936.
Blinky Bill Joins the Army. Sydney, Angus and Robertson, 1940.
A Tiny Story of Blinky Bill. Sydney, Offset Printing, n.d.
Fun with Blinky Bill. Sydney, Angus and Robertson, 1953.
Horrie Kiwi and the Kids. London, Angus and Robertson, 1984.
The Blinky Bill Connection, edited by Walter McVitty. Sydney, Angus and Robertson, 2 vols., 1988.

Other

Blinky Bill Dress-Up Book. Sydney, Offset Printing, 1944 (?).
Blinky Bill's ABC Book. Sydney, Offset Printing, 1947.

*

Illustrator: *The Crystal Bowl* by J.J. Hall, 1921; *Jacko the Broadcasting Kookaburra,* 1933, and *The Amazing Adventures of Billy Penguin,* 1934, both by Brooke Nicholls; *Australians All: Bush Folk in Rhyme* by Nelle Grant Cooper, 1934.

* * *

Blinky Bill, the jaunty little koala bear, is one of the best-known characters in the world of Australia's childhood. Dorothy Wall created him in 1933, inspired by her own young son, and children have eagerly identified with the mischievous and appealing bear who has most of the characteristics of a small boy.

Wall died at a comparatively young age over 40 years ago, but her Blinky Bill stories have retained their wide popularity. Her career began as an illustrator and her fine technique can be seen in the books she illustrated for other authors. It was not until she created her first Blinky Bill story for her own small son that text and illustrations combined to give children a truly imaginative story which had an immediate appeal. *Blinky Bill, The Quaint Little Australian* was quickly followed by two sequels, and all three books were reprinted more or less yearly until the three were combined into one volume in 1939; it has remained in print ever since. The charm of the stories lies in the fact that the bear behaves just like a lively little boy, and his exploits occur in an imaginary urbanized bush setting, all the characters being humans disguised as bush creatures. Adults may sometimes query Wall's taste, but the books are enjoyed by children for their humour and incident. Their warmth and spontaneity make them ideal to read aloud to young primary school children, the stories consisting of episodes with engaging illustrations printed alongside the text. Throughout the stories Blinky Bill and his companions get into trouble through disobedience to their mother's instructions, and through their curiosity. This naughty behaviour and the suspense over its consequences is irresistible to young readers and listeners. And yet undoubtedly the particular strength of the books lies in the vibrant and imaginative black and white illustrations.

The Australian setting with other Australian animal characters gave the books great appeal at a time when most children's books emanated from England, and occasional informative paragraphs briefly give some facts about the particular animal mentioned. The books are very much in the style of animal tales in fashion in the 1930s and 1940s and their reputation is enhanced by their long popularity. The exuberance of the stories and the author's wish to amuse occasionally produce a forced humour and sentimentality which at times rather dates them.

Although some cheap publications using Wall's characters with new illustrations roughly based on the original books have been produced and are sold widely, Wall's own books are also in print. An impressive and well-produced set comprising a compendium volume of all her stories, together with a full-length biography containing many previously unpublished drawings has just been published and should enhance her reputation and ensure her continued popularity.

—Marcie Muir

WALLACE, Ian

Nationality: Canadian. **Born:** Niagara Falls, Ontario, 31 March 1950. **Education:** Ontario College of Art, Toronto, 1969-74, A.A. 1974. **Family:** Married Debra Wiedman in 1988. **Career:** Staff writer and illustrator, Kids Can Press, Toronto, 1974-76; information officer, Art Gallery of Ontario, Toronto, 1976-80. **Award:** Canadian Library Association Amelia Frances Howard-Gibbon medal, 1985, for illustration; American Library Association Notable Book, 1986; Mr. Christie's Book award for illustration, 1990; Elizabeth Mrazik-Cleaver Canadian Picture Book Award, 1990; Hans Christian Andersen award nomination, 1994; IODE book award, for *A Winter's Tale,* 1998. **Address:** 184 Major Street, Toronto, Ontario M5S 2L3, Canada.

Publications for Children (illustrated by the author)

Fiction

Julie News. Toronto, Kids Can Press, 1974.
The Sandwich, with Angela Wood, illustrated by the authors. Toronto, Kids Can Press, 1975.
The Christmas Tree House. Toronto, Kids Can Press, 1976.
Chin Chiang and the Dragon's Dance. Toronto, Groundwood, New York, Margaret K. McElderry Books, and London, Methuen, 1984.
The Sparrow's Song. Markham, Ontario, Viking Kestrel, 1986; New York, Viking Kestrel, 1987.
Morgan the Magnificent. Toronto, Groundwood, 1987; New York, Margaret K. McElderry Books, and London, Hamish Hamilton, 1988.

Mr. Kneebone's New Digs. Toronto, Groundwood, 1991.
A Winter's Tale. Toronto, Groundwood, 1997.

*

Illustrator: *Very Last First Time* by Jan Andrews, 1985; *Architect of the Moon* by Tim Wynne-Jones, 1988; *The Name of the Tree: A Bantu Folktale* by Celia Barker, 1990; *The Year of Fire* by Teddy Jam, 1992; *The Mummer's Song* by Bud Davidge, 1993; *Hansel and Gretel* by the Brothers Grimm, 1994; *Sarah and the People of Sand River,* W. D. Valgardsen, 1996.

Ian Wallace comments:

In my work as an author I do not sit down to write stories, nor do I consciously choose stories to illustrate because they will be distinguished as being multi-cultural or Canadian or whatever flag one chooses to wave over them. I write or illustrate stories because first and foremost they are stories that will intrigue, inspire, and touch young readers. The characters who inhabit these tales are people who have earned my sympathy and are ones with whom I can empathize on a personal level. They are universal characters with universal emotions and universal experiences that make us human. They are characters whom I respect for their dignity of spirit and purpose of life, characters who struggle, who test limits, and who endure. But most importantly they are characters who through the story go through some kind of change. At the end of a good story, a reader comes away with the confidence that the protagonist will never be the same and will treasure the memory. It is my hope that the reader of my books will never be the same either.

* * *

Very Last First Time is the title of a work illustrated by Ian Wallace that embodies the major theme of his works—the initiation experience by which a child moves to understanding of self and the larger world. In words and pictures, Wallace presents boys and girls from a variety of places and times, each involved in the difficult process of growing up. He has also sensitively portrayed the lives of the aged poor.

Wallace's first two stories, published in the mid 1970s, are apprentice works introducing themes most fully explored in his later books. In *The Sandwich,* Vincenzo, taking his lunch to school for the first time, feels ashamed when his friends laugh at the mortadella and provolone sandwich his father had made. However, on his return home he learns that "you are who you are and you have nothing to be ashamed of." Nick, central character in *The Christmas Tree House,* makes a friend of Don Valley Rose, who he discovers is not the dreaded witch of local rumor.

In *Chin Chiang and the Dragon's Dance,* the title hero runs away on the morning of his first performance of the New Year's dance, fearing he will fail. With the help and encouragement of a wise old woman, he returns in time to take his part in the dance and, by extension, his place within his culture. Katie, the central character in *The Sparrow's Song,* tends a fledgling bird whose mother had been killed by his brother Charles. She learns forgiveness and he, repentance, and the two experience the mystic powers of nature present in the gorge of the Niagara River. *A Winter's Tale* also deals with a girl's relationship to nature. On her first winter camping trip with her father and brother, Abigail discovers a trapped fawn which, with her family's help, she sets free. *Morgan the Magnificent,* inspired by the author's love of circus art and equipment, is a new version of the old tale of a child running away to the circus. Morgan, a young girl living with her single parent father, sneaks into the star performer's tent, dons one of her costumes, climbs to the high-wire, starts across, and freezes in panic. Like Chin Chiang, she requires the help of a wise adult, in this case the Amazing Anastasia. Like Chin, Katie, and Charles, she completes her adventure more aware of her strengths and limitations and of her relationship to the worlds in which she lives.

In *Mr. Kneebone's New Digs,* Wallace returns to a character type first examined in *The Christmas Tree House:* the poor, lonely old person. With her dog, Mr. Kneebone, April Moth leaves her rundown, one-room flat in search of a new, better home. Only at the story's conclusion is she happy, having found "new digs" in a cave in the park, away from the dirt, noise, big buildings, and impersonality of the metropolis. Under the apparently happy ending, Wallace implies disturbing questions: "What will happen when April Moth is discovered by park officials? Will the cave be warm and dry enough when winter comes?"

Wallace's texts for these stories are given expanded meanings by his illustrations. Each book has an appropriate major color: the red of the dominant Chinese dragon and symbol of health and prosperity in *Chin Chiang*; the greens of nature in which the children learn and the sparrow is healed in *The Sparrow's Song*; and gold, the hue not only of the gilded circus wagons, but also of the realm of wonder in *Morgan.* In *Mr. Kneebone's New Digs,* the colors are muted, even dingy, suggesting the dirty and dreary life of the big city. Even the green of the park at the end is not vibrant, perhaps symbolic of April Moth's uncertain future. In *A Winter's Tale,* the red of Abigail's mittens contrasts the cold blues and whites of winter and symbolizes her caring nature.

Visual style is also varied from book to book: formal patterns reflect Chinese ceremony in *Chin Chiang*; free flowing depictions of water, rocks, and trees symbolize the ever-changing panorama of nature in *The Sparrow's Song*; and circus designs are on all the pages of Morgan. Like Maurice Sendak, whose work has influenced him, Wallace varies picture sizes to reinforce his themes, most notably in *The Sparrow's Song,* where the pictures of the children in the gorge are bled to the edge of the page to indicate their expanded consciousness in nature, and in *Very Last First Time,* when illustrations expand to double-spreads reflecting the heroine's new knowledge as she explores the worlds below the sea ice.

Wallace's illustrations for other's stories add to conflict, theme, and tone. For example, in *Very Last First Time* by Jan Andrews, the shadowy figures behind Eva as she walks under the ice emphasize not only the danger she is in, but also the dangers facing her mother, who waits on the surface. In *Hansel and Gretel,* the powerful evil of the witch is emphasized by an aerial view of the forest, which contains the shape of her face. The luminescence of the grays and yellows in the illustrations for *Sarah and the People of Sand River,* by W. D. Valgardson, suggest the supernatural powers that are aiding the girl.

Although Wallace's output is relatively small, his status in Canadian children's literature is great. He has treated the universal theme of initiation and portrayed the lives of the aged poor, has presented these in deceptively simple stories, and through the color, design, and details of his illustrations has expanded events to symbolic dimensions.

—Jon C. Stott

WALTER, Mildred Pitts

Nationality: American. **Born:** Sweetville, Louisiana, 9 September 1922. **Education:** Southern University, Louisiana, B.A. 1944; University of California, Los Angeles; California State College, 1950-52; University of Southern California, Los Angeles; Antioch College, Yellow Springs, Ohio, M.Ed. 1977. **Family:** Married Earl Lloyd Walter in 1947 (died 1965); two sons. **Career:** Shipwright helper in Vancouver, Washington, 1943-44; salesperson, City Dye Works, Los Angeles, California, 1944-48; personnel clerk, 1949-52, elementary schoolteacher, 1952-70, Los Angeles Public Schools; educational consultant and lecturer on cultural diversity for educational institutions, 1971-73. Civil rights activist for Congress of Racial Equality (CORE), during 1950s and 1960s. Northeast Women's Center, Denver, Colorado, cofounder and administrator, 1982-86. Delegate to Second World Black and African Festival of the Arts and Culture, Lagos, Nigeria, 1977. **Awards:** Runner-up for Irma Simonton Black award, 1981, for *Ty's One-Man Band; Parents' Choice* awards, 1984, for *Because We Are,* and 1985, for *Brother to the Wind;* Coretta Scott King awards from Social Responsibility Round Table of American Library Association, honorable mention, 1984, for *Because We Are,* honorable mention, 1986, for *Trouble's Child,* winner 1987, for *Justin and the Best Biscuits in the World,* for *Mississippi Challenge,* Honor award 1993; Best Book Christopher award, for *Mississippi Challenge,* 1992; Carter G. Woodson Secondary Book award, for *Mississippi Challenge,* 1993; Jane Addams Honor Book award and Virginia Library Association Jefferson Cup Worthy of Special Note award, for *Second Daughter,* 1997.

Publications for Children

Fiction

Ty's One-Man Band, illustrated by Margot Tomes. New York, Four Winds Press, 1980.
My Mama Needs Me, illustrated by Pat Cummings. New York, Lothrop, 1983.
Brother to the Wind, illustrated by Diane and Leo Dillon. New York, Lothrop, 1985.
Justin and the Best Biscuits in the World, illustrated by Catherine Stock. New York, Lothrop, 1986.
Have a Happy..., illustrated by Carole Byard. New York, Lothrop, 1989.
Two and Too Much, illustrated by Pat Cummings. New York, Bradbury, 1990.
Tiger Ride. New York, Macmillan, 1994.
Darkness, illustrated by Marcia Jameson, New York, Simon & Schuster, 1995.

Publications for Young Adults

Fiction

Lillie of Watts: A Birthday Discovery, illustrated by Leonora E. Prince. Los Angeles, Ward Ritchie Press, 1969.
Lillie of Watts Takes a Giant Step, illustrated by Bonnie Helene Johnson. New York, Doubleday, 1971.
The Girl on the Outside. New York, Lothrop, 1982.
Because We Are. New York, Lothrop, 1983.
Trouble's Child. New York, Lothrop, 1985.
Mariah Loves Rock. New York, Bradbury Press, 1988.
Mariah Keeps Cool, illustrated by Pat Cummings. New York, Bradbury, 1990.
Second Daughter, New York, Scholastic, 1996.

Nonfiction

Mississippi Challenge. New York, Bradbury Press, 1992.

* * *

The small but growing body of work by Mildred Pitts Walter brims with metamorphosis. When Martha of *Trouble's Child* realizes at the close of the book that "she was on the threshold of searching, learning, knowing, of stretching her mind," not only do her thoughts pay tribute to her own growing recognition of a self-identity, but they also exemplify the transformations that occur in all of Walter's black characters. Walter writes with power, determination, and truth about black children and young adults who come to a sense of self-awareness in a unique cultural and social environment within the United States. She writes not of the cultural deprivation of black Americans, but of their cultural defamation, and the struggle to face the realities of their racial heritage to become fully connected human beings. One of the greatest strengths of Walter's work is that although she writes about blacks, her books transcend that particular experience to become books about people—people of all colors, all races, all creeds. In the end, the importance of the human connection is what makes the difference.

Lillie of Watts, the perceptively written story of 11-year-old Lillie, details her efforts to make meaning in a world where racial differences parallel social and economic privileges. Advertisements bombard Lillie with the message that to be white is more desirable than to be black. Over the course of the story Lillie learns that "people are more important than cats, sweaters, and cars." Her mother's demonstration of unconditional love moves Lillie toward appreciation and understanding that it is not what you have that makes you complete, but what you are.

Justin and the Best Biscuits in the World, a 1987 Coretta Scott King award winner and an intergenerational story that cuts across gender stereotypes, introduces the reader to 10-year-old Justin, a lover of basketball and a hater of all that smacks of "women's work." On a visit to his grandpa's Missouri ranch, Justin hears stories of famous black cowboys and learns to "ride fence," clean fish, make a bed, pick up after himself, and finally, to make the best biscuits in the world. Justin also becomes aware of his racial heritage, some of the horrors his ancestors lived through, and the implications of that legacy for his life. Under Grandpa's sage guidance, Justin learns that he must know where he's come from to find the way to where he wants to go.

A young adult novel, *Trouble's Child* is a coming-of-age story set in the lush Louisiana bayou community of Blue Isle. Martha, the main protagonist, nurtures a wish to finish her high school education while grappling to free herself from the binding ties of her community and its expectation that she marry and follow in her grandmother's footsteps as midwife. Martha's aspirations finally come to fruition when she finds the courage to face her community and follow her dreams. Rich in detail, and written in the soft cadence of Louisiana speech, the book strongly but tenderly portrays a universal adolescent dilemma.

Like all of Walter's books, *The Girl on the Outside* is written with honesty and integrity. A fictional recreation of the 1957 integration of Central High School in Little Rock, Arkansas, it focuses on the experiences of two students—Sophie, a white girl, and Eva, a black girl. The story speaks movingly and forcefully about the problems, fears, and prejudices that must be dealt with in the acceptance of integration.

Mariah Loves Rock also confronts the problem of integration—the integration of her daddy's daughter from his first marriage into Mariah's family. Mariah worries that with the arrival of Denise, not only will her daddy love Mariah less, but also she will have to sacrifice her bedroom, decorated with posters of her beloved rock star, the Sheik. With keen insight into the psyche of the family unit, Walter chronicles the transformation in Mariah as she moves from resentment of Denise as a rival, to acceptance of her as a sister.

Metamorphosis also characterizes *Ty's One-Man Band,* a picture-book folktale illustrated by Margot Tomes. Ty, restless and bored on a steamy summer's day, meets Andro, a peg-legged man who calls himself a one-man band. Using a washboard, two wooden spoons, a tin pail, and a comb, Andro turns everyday objects into the music of dancing horses, gurgling streams, dripping faucets, and puffing freight trains. In a succinct, lyrical evocation of the transforming power of the imagination, Ty broadens his scope of vision, learning that the ordinary can often become the extraordinary.

From the picture book to the middle reader to the young adult novel, Walter's writing resonates with feeling and conviction of purpose. Her work celebrates change—by times frightening, comforting, exhilarating, and perplexing—as essential in coming to terms with oneself and one's society. Wellsprings of hope, Walter's books embrace life even as they acknowledge the sometimes seemingly insurmountable difficulties of living.

—Carolyn Shute

WARDELL, Phyl(lis)

Nationality: New Zealander. **Born:** Phyllis Robinson, Christchurch, 21 October 1909. **Education:** Avonside Girls High School; Christchurch Girls High School. **Family:** Married Rae Wardell in 1935; one son and one daughter. **Career:** Secretary, Jewell Skinner advertising agency, Christchurch, 1928-37. **Agent:** Richards Literary Agency, P.O. Box 31240, Milford, Auckland 9. **Address:** 192 Salisbury Street, Christchurch, New Zealand.

Publications for Children

Fiction

Gold at Kapai, illustrated by Douglas F. Maxted. Wellington, Reed, and London, Harrap, 1960.
The Secret of the Lost Tribe of Te Anau, illustrated by Keith Money. Wellington, Reed, and London, Harrap, 1961.
Passage to Dusky, illustrated by Garrick Palmer. London, Parrish, 1967.
Hazard Island, illustrated by Albert Wagenvoort. Christchurch, Whitcoulls, 1976.
The Nelson Treasure, illustrated by Alan Gilderdale. Auckland, Hodder and Stoughton, 1983.
Beyond the Narrows, illustrated by Gary Meeson. Auckland and London, Hodder and Stoughton, 1985.

Plays

Radio Plays: *Gold at Kapai, The Secret of the Lost Tribe of Te Anau,* and *Passage to Dusky,* from her own stories, 1959-66; *The Missing Skindiver,* 1966.

*

Manuscript Collections: Canterbury Public Library, Christchurch.

Phyl Wardell comments:

I began writing in the 1950s when I was 40. I tried a couple of romantic novels which, halfway through, turned into murder mysteries. They did not sell.

I was planning a third murder story when an editor asked me to write a children's magazine serial full of action, adventure, and cliffhangers. This resulted in my first children's novel, *Gold at Kapai.* Writing for children was so satisfying that I stayed with it.

* * *

For sound straight-out action stories with a New Zealand setting Phyl Wardell has few rivals. She attempts no maudlin sentiment or quasi-psychology but writes lucidly and produces unpretentious but absorbing novels. All six of her books, written over a period of 25 years, have a strong element of detection and in all of them some aspect of the New Zealand heritage, flora, or fauna are under threat. Living as she does in Christchurch, she is within easy travelling distance of the Southern Alps and of the South Western fiords, and apart from the strong storyline which keeps the pages turning, her work could be seen as an evocation of the New Zealand landscape.

Her settings move from gold fields in *Gold at Kapai,* where a group of young people investigate a murder attempt on an old miner, to Fiordland in *The Secret of the Lost Tribe of Te Anau,* in which a film company hopes to track down and film a lost Maori tribe. It is based on a legend which relates how the Ngati Mamoe tribe withdrew into the dense bush and mountains after losing a battle. The book sets the pattern for her subsequent interest in conservation—typically, although the lost tribe is discovered it is decided to leave them in peace and not intrude the 20th century upon them. In *Passage to Dusky,* again set in the Sounds, Maori greenstone artifacts are rescued. *Hazard Island* sees an investigation into the disappearance of a diver, which leads to the discovery of paua shell smuggling. *The Nelson Treasure,* the only book set in the North Island, has as its theme the conservation of native bush and of the rediscovery of the rare huia bird, thought to be extinct. It exists in an area which has been carefully protected from tourists by an unusual man, Matt, who, in a surprise ending, turns out to be a woman, one of the early aviators who was assumed killed when her gipsy moth plane crashed after she had crossed the Tasman singlehandedly 40 years ago.

Another extinct bird features in the latest novel *Beyond the Narrows* when there are reported sightings of a moa in Fiordland. Through investigating these rumours the young protagonists uncover the misuse of a drug which, initially intended to increase sheep's wool production, has had the effect of causing animals that were given experimental doses to grow to giant proportions. Thus Canada geese have become as large as moas.

Wardell's books have carefully constructed plots, there are no extraneous episodes, the action is fast, and one event leads logically to another. It is in the story, rather than in character development, that her main interest lies. Her enterprising young people have little time for introspection; they are too involved with the immediacy of the task in hand. In this they are true descendants of the early settlers, but unlike them, their concern is to preserve the land rather than to dominate it.

—Betty Gilderdale

WARRENER. See **PEARCE, (Ann) Philippa.**

WATKINS-PITCHFORD, D(enys) J(ames)

Pseudonyms: BB; Michael Traherne. **Nationality:** British. **Born:** Lamport, Northamptonshire, 25 July 1905. **Education:** Private; studied art in Paris, 1924, and at the Royal College of Art, London; associate, Royal College of Art Painting School, 1926-28. **Military Service:** City of London Yeomanry Royal Horse Artillery, 1926-29 (King's Cup Medal); served in the Home Guard, 1940-46: Captain. **Family:** Married Cecily Mary Adnitt in 1939 (died 1974); one daughter and one son (deceased). **Career:** Assistant art master, Rugby School, Warwickshire, 1930-47. Since 1947 freelance author and illustrator. **Awards:** Library Association Carnegie Medal, 1943. M.A.: Leicester University, 1986. Fellow, Royal Society of Arts. **Died:** 8 September 1990.

PUBLICATIONS FOR CHILDREN (AS BB; ILLUSTRATED BY THE AUTHOR)

Fiction

Wild Lone. London, Eyre and Spottiswoode, and New York, Scribner, 1938.
Sky Gipsy: The Story of a Wild Goose. London, Eyre and Spottiswoode, 1939; as *Manka, The Sky Gipsy,* New York, Scribner, 1939.
The Little Grey Men. London, Eyre and Spottiswoode, 1942; New York, Scribner, 1949.
Brendon Chase. London, Hollis and Carter, 1944; New York, Scribner, 1945.
Down the Bright Stream. London, Eyre and Spottiswoode, 1948.
The Forest of Boland Light Railway. London, Eyre and Spottiswoode, 1955; as *The Forest of the Railway,* New York, Dodd Mead, 1957.
Monty Woodpig's Caravan. London, Ward, 1957.
Ben the Bullfinch. London, Hamish Hamilton, 1957.
Wandering Wind. London, Hamish Hamilton, 1957; as *Bill Badger and the Wandering Wind,* London, Methuen, 1981.
Alexander. Oxford, Blackwell, 1957.
Monty Woodpig and His Bumblebuzz Car. London, Ward, 1958.
Mr. Bumstead. London, Eyre and Spottiswoode, 1958.
The Wizard of Boland. London, Ward, 1959.
Bill Badger's Winter Cruise. London, Hamish Hamilton, 1959.
Bill Badger and the Pirates. London, Hamish Hamilton, 1960.
Bill Badger's Finest Hour. London, Hamish Hamilton, 1961.
Bill Badger's Whispering Reeds Adventure. London, Hamish Hamilton, 1962.
Lepus, The Brown Hare. London, Benn, 1962.
Bill Badger's Big Mistake. London, Hamish Hamilton, 1963.
Bill Badger and the Big Store Robbery. London, Hamish Hamilton, 1967.
The Whopper. London, Benn, 1967.
At the Back o' Ben Dee. London, Benn, 1968.
Bill Badger's Voyage to the World's End. London, Kaye and Ward, 1969.
The Tyger Tray. London, Methuen, 1971.
The Pool of the Black Witch. London, Methuen, 1974.
Lord of the Forest. London, Methuen, 1975.
Stories of the Wild, with A.L.E. Fenton and A. Windsor-Richards. London, Benn, 1975.
More Stories of the Wild, with A. Windsor-Richards. London, Benn, 1977.
Bill Badger and the Secret Weapon. London, Methuen, 1983.

Other

Meeting Hill: BB's Fairy Book. London, Hollis and Carter, 1948.
The Wind in the Wood. London, Hollis and Carter, 1952.
The Badgers of Bearshanks. London, Benn, 1961.
The Pegasus Book of the Countryside. London, Dobson, 1964.

PUBLICATIONS FOR ADULTS (AS BB; ILLUSTRATED BY THE AUTHOR)

Short Stories

5 More Stories, with others. Oxford, Blackwell, 1957.

Other

The Idle Countryman. London, Eyre and Spottiswoode, 1943.
The Wayfaring Tree. London, Hollis and Carter, 1945.
A Stream in Your Garden. London, Eyre and Spottiswoode, 1948.
Be Quiet and Go A-Angling (as Michael Traherne). London, Lutterworth Press, 1949.
Confessions of a Carp Fisher. London, Eyre and Spottiswoode, 1950; revised edition, London, Witherby, 1970.
Tide's Ending. London, Hollis and Carter, and New York, Scribner, 1950.
Letters from Compton Deverell. London, Eyre and Spottiswoode, 1950.
Dark Estuary. London, Hollis and Carter, 1953; Chicago, Academy, 1984.

A Carp Water: Wood Pool and How to Fish It. London, Putnam, 1958.
The Autumn Road to the Isles. London, Kaye, 1959.
The White Road Westwards. London, Kaye, 1961.
September Road to Caithness and the Western Sea. London, Kaye, 1962.
The Summer Road to Wales. London, Kaye, 1964.
A Summer on the Nene. London, Kaye and Ward, 1967.
Recollections of a 'longshore Gunner. Ipswich, Suffolk, Boydell Press, 1976.
A Child Alone: The Memoirs of BB. London, Joseph, 1978.
Ramblings of a Sportsman-Naturalist. London, Joseph, 1979.
The Naturalist's Bedside Book. London, Joseph, 1980.
The Quiet Fields. London, Joseph, 1981.
Indian Summer. London, Joseph, 1984.
The Best of BB. London, Joseph, 1985.
Fisherman's Folly. Woodbridge, Suffolk, Boydell and Brewer, 1987.

Editor, *The Sportsman's Bedside Book.* London, Eyre and Spottiswoode, 1937.
Editor, *The Countryman's Bedside Book.* London, Eyre and Spottiswoode, 1941.
Editor, *The Fisherman's Bedside Book.* London, Eyre and Spottiswoode, 1945; New York, Scribner, 1946.
Editor, *The Shooting Man's Bedside Book.* London, Eyre and Spottiswoode, and New York, Scribner, 1948.

*

Illustrator: *Sport in Wildest Britain* by H.V. Prichard, 1936; *Winged Company* by R.G. Walmsley, 1940; *England Is a Village* by Clarence H. Warren, 1940; *Southern English* by Eric Benfield, 1942; *Narrow Boat* by L.T.C. Rolt, 1944; *Red Vagabond* by Gerald D. Adams, 1946; *It's My Delight* by Brian V. Fitzgerald, 1947; *Philandering Angler* by Arthur Applin, 1948; *A Sportsman Looks at Eire* by J.B. Drought, 1949; *Landmarks* by Arthur G. Street, 1949; *Fairy Tales of Long Ago* edited by Mabel C. Carey, 1952; *The White Foxes of Gorfenletch,* 1954, *Beasts of the North Country,* 1961, and *To Do With Birds,* 1965, all by Henry S. Tegner; *The Secret of Orra* by Elfrida Vipont, 1957; *The Long Night,* 1958, and *Thirteen O'Clock,* 1960, both by William Mayne; *Vix,* 1960, *Birds of the Lonely Lake,* 1961, *The Cabin in the Woods,* 1963, and *The Wild White Swan,* 1965, all by Arthur Richards; *Prince Prigio and Prince Ricardo* by Andrew Lang, 1961; *The Rogue Elephant,* 1962, *Red Ivory,* 1964, and *Jungle Rescue,* 1967, all by Arthur Catherall; *Granny's Wonderful Chair* by Frances Browne, 1963; *King Todd* by Norah Burke, 1963; *The Lost Princess* by George MacDonald, 1965; *Where Vultures Fly* by Gerald Summers, 1974.

D.J. Watkins-Pitchford commented:

(1989) Though some of my best-selling books were written for young people, most—if not all—are appreciated equally by adults and I take this as a great compliment! A keen observation is essential to a successful author. I write because I find it an intensely rewarding thing, and it is fun to illustrate my own books.

* * *

More familiar to us as BB, D.J. Watkins-Pitchford is known above all for his wildlife books. An enthusiastic natural historian, he was able to convey vividly his wide knowledge and deep love of the countryside. *Sky Gipsy* is the story of a wild goose, telling with sympathetic insight of the beautiful but harsh life of these birds. *Wild Lone* is a moving but unsentimental account of the life of a fox in the Pytchley Hunt country. *Brendon Chase* is also about survival in the wild, but here it is two boys playing truant to live in the woods and finding that open-air living has its disadvantages.

For younger children he created the enchanted forest of Boland, a place where anything can happen. Absurd humour which tickles the palates of the under-tens predominates in *The Wizard of Boland,* where incompetence in high places produces hilarious results. *The Forest of Boland Light Railway* is similarly delightful. Watkins-Pitchford's animal heroes Bill Badger and the hedgehog Monty Woodpig have adventures in the woodland and by the canal which appeal greatly to sixes and sevens and are splendid for reading aloud.

The Little Grey Men won the Carnegie Medal in 1943, and is still a prime favourite. Its sequel, *Down the Bright Stream,* was illustrated by the author in scraperboard, though in later editions he painted in oils. These are truly delightful tales and make ideal bedtime stories. They deal with three dwarves, Dodder, Balemoney, and Sneezewort (all old country wildflower names) and their quest for their long-lost brother, using a clockwork toy boat which they find.

In all of D.J. Watkins-Pitchford's books, the English countryside is not merely supportive but a leading character, making them pleasurable reading for all ages.

—Ann G. Hay

WATSON, Clyde

Nationality: American. **Born:** New York City, 25 July 1947. **Education:** Smith College, Northampton, Massachusetts, A.B. in music 1968. **Family:** Married Denis Devlin in 1978; one son and one daughter. **Career:** Professional violinist and violin teacher: teacher, The Common School, Amherst, Massachusetts, 1968-70, and Indian Township School, Maine, 1971-73. **Address:** 7 Low Road, Hanover, New Hampshire 03755, U.S.A.

PUBLICATIONS FOR CHILDREN (ILLUSTRATED BY WENDY WATSON)

Fiction

Tom Fox and the Apple Pie. New York, Crowell, 1972; London, Macmillan, 1973.
How Brown Mouse Kept Christmas. New York, Farrar Straus 1980; London, Hamish Hamilton, 1981.
Valentine Foxes, illustrated by Wendy Watson. New York, Orchard, 1989.

Verse

Father Fox's Pennyrhymes. New York, Crowell, 1971; London, Macmillan, 1972.
Hickory Stick Rag. New York, Crowell, 1976.

Catch Me and Kiss Me and Say It Again. New York, Collins World, and London, Collins, 1978.
Midnight Moon, illustrated by Susanna Natti. New York, Collins, 1979.
Applebet: An ABC. New York, Farrar Straus, 1982.
Father Fox's Feast of Songs, music by the author, illustrated by Wendy Watson. New York, Philomel, 1983.
Valentine Foxes. New York, Orchard, 1989; Oxford, Heinemann, 1990.
How Brown Mouse Kept Christmas. New York, Farrar Straus, 1992.
Mister Toad, illustrated by N. Cameron Watson. New York, Macmillan, 1992.
Love's a Sweet. New York, Viking, N.d.

Other

Quips and Quirks (collection of epithets). New York, Crowell, 1975.
Binary Numbers. New York, Crowell, 1977.

Recording: *Father Fox's Feast of Songs and Three Stories,* Hanover, New Hampshire, Sassafras, 1986.

*

Illustrator: *How Does It Feel to Be a Tree?* by Flo Morse, 1976.

Music: *Fisherman Lullabies,* by Wendy Watson, 1968; *Carol to a Child,* lyrics by Nancy Dingman Watson, 1969; *Father Fox's Feast of Songs,* illustrated by Wendy Watson, 1983.

* * *

The key to Clyde Watson's writing is the fact that she is a musician. Her poems are often song lyrics; her prose has a musical ring. She writes quasi-Mother Goose rhyme that is influenced by three things: the old poems, her New England background, and her musical ability.

Her first works were the straightforward musical arrangements for her sister's *Fisherman Lullabies* and her mother's *Carol to a Child.* She seemed to be riding into the publishing world on her family's coattails.

However, with *Father Fox's Pennyrhymes* Watson came into her own. It is the best of all the Watson family's many books. The book is a collection of short, simple, spirited, and highly original nonsense rhymes, many of which are actually lyrics to songs Clyde composed. The impeccable rhythms, the melodic flow of the full and slant rhymes all bespeak the author's musical background:

The sky is dark, there blows a storm,
Our cider is hot, the fire is warm,
The snow is deep and the night is long:
Old Father Fox, will you sing us a song?

The poems obviously come from a folkloric tradition—Mother Goose, English ballads, lullabies, and jump-rope rhymes. But instead of the 17th-century English countryside or the streets of London, they celebrate New England and especially rural Vermont where Watson was brought up. The verses range from the decidedly impish to the boisterously aggressive to some that are as soft as a cradle song. They are instantly memorized by young listeners. The pictures in the book, again by her sister, are colorful and inventive, in a comic strip format. The details in both the rhymes and the illustrations are both personal (family jokes are enshrined, the Putney farm is pictured) and universal. The book, in fact, was recognized as a modern classic on publication, winning, among other prizes, a National Book award nomination. Quite simply, it is a beautiful, individual volume, certainly one of the few in the 1970s that is destined to outlast its decade—and even its century.

Tom Fox and the Apple Pie (a simple prose sequel), *Quips and Quirks* (a witty assemblage of name-calling epithets), *Hickory Stick Rag* (rhyming verse immortalizing the turn-of-the-century rural school house and its denizens), and *Catch Me and Kiss Me and Say It Again* (gentle poems for pre-schoolers) are all clever and childlike and full of appealing mischief. But none of them reaches the depth of *Father Fox's Pennyrhymes* nor do any of them have its range of color, tone, and musical appeal.

—Jane Yolen

WATSON, James

Nationality: British. **Born:** Darwen, Lancashire, 8 November 1936.**Education:** University of Nottingham, B.A. (honours) in history 1958; University of Sussex, Brighton, 1977-78, M.A. in education 1979. **Military Service:** Royal Army Education Corps, 1958-60: Lieutenant. **Family:** Married Catherine Downey in 1963; three daughters,two granddaughters. **Career:** English teacher, British Council, Milan, Italy, 1960-61; journalist and art critic, *North East Evening Gazette,* Middlesbrough, Yorkshire, 1961-63; education officer, Dunlop Company, London, 1963-65. Currently Senior Lecturer in Communication, West Kent College, Tonbridge, and course director of media and communication programme of study, in partnership with the University of Greenwich. **Awards:** Children's Rights Workshop Other Award, 1983; Walter Hines Page scholarship, 1987; Buxtehuder Bulle Prize (Germany), 1987. **Address:** 9 Farmcombe Close, Tunbridge Wells, Kent TN2 5DG, England.

PUBLICATIONS FOR CHILDREN

Fiction

Sign of the Swallow. London, Nelson, 1967.
The Bull Leapers. London, Gollancz, 1970; New York, Coward McCann, 1970.
Legion of the White Tiger. London, Gollancz, 1973.
The Freedom Tree. London, Gollancz, 1976.
Talking in Whispers. London, Gollancz, 1983; New York, Knopf, 1983.
Where Nobody Sees. London, Gollancz, 1987.
Make Your Move (stories). London, Gollancz, 1988.
No Surrender. London, Gollancz, 1991.
The Noisy Ducks of Buxtehude. Buxtehude, Germany, Verlag an der Este, 1992.

Ticket to Prague. London, Gollancz, 1993.
Justice of the Dagger. London, Penguin, 1997.

Plays

Gilbert Makepeace Lives! (radio plays), BBC, 1972.
Venus Rising from the Sea (radio plays), BBC, 1977.
A Slight Insurrection (radio plays), BBC, 1980.
What a Little Moonlight Can Do (radio plays), BBC, 1982.
No Surrender (radio play, adapted from his book of the same title), BBC, 1993.

Publications for Adults

Liberal Studies in Further Education. Windsor, National Foundation for Educational Research, 1973.
The Loneliness of Long Distance Innovation: General Studies in a College of Further Education: A Document for the Future. Nottingham, Association for Liberal Education, 1980.
With Anne Hill, *A Dictionary of Communication and Media Studies.* London, Arnold, 1984; revised editions, 1989, 1993, 1996.
What Is Communication Studies? London, Arnold, 1985.
Media Communication: An Introduction to Theory and Process. London, Macmillan, 1998.

James Watson comments:

After beginning my writing career with books exploring my interest in history, I moved to themes that stirred interest but also a more involved concern. *The Freedom Tree,* set in the Spanish Civil War, its climax the bombing of Guernica, led on to the world of here and now. *Talking in Whispers* is about the Chile of the generals—it seems to have struck a particularly resonant note in the hearts and minds of young readers. *Where Nobody Sees* returns me to home ground, telling the story of two teenagers who discover the illegal dumping of nuclear waste and the peril this places them in when they attempt to make the matter public. My first collection of stories, *Make Your Move* ranges from a tale set in the Chaco War in Bolivia to the kind of problems faced by teenagers in modern Britain. *No Surrender* is set in the forgotten war in Angola, while in *Ticket to Prague* Amy Douglas meets a forgotten Czech poet in an English mental hospital. Their friendship transforms them both, he to a poet reborn and returning to the land of his birth, she discovering a new world in herself and one reborn in the enchanting and enchanted city of Prague. In *Justice of the Dagger* I return to issues that one pressing, and global, telling a tale, set in East Timor and describing the genocide of native tribes and the destruction of the forests which have been their home since the beginning of time. The story focuses on the struggle for survival of young people subject to the tyranny of "Distant Masters," and of the timber companies whose activities threaten to destroy the ecology of the island.

* * *

Writers of books for young people are not renowned for their interest in overtly political situations. This is not to say that these writers do not write in a political way: for example, it would not be difficult to guess the political stance of an Imperialist writer like Henty or to ascertain the amount of liberal feeling a writer like Enid Blyton shows when discussing her social inferiors. James Watson is first and foremost a political writer but one who, in his most important work, is able to display this political feeling in a powerful and telling manner.

Watson's early work consists of three historical novels. *Sign of the Swallow* is set in the Renaissance, *The Bull Leapers* is an interpretation of the Theseus and the Minotaur legend, while *Legion of the White Tiger* presents the contrast between the Roman culture and that of the Huns. Although all three are of interest to students of Watson's work, none of them could be considered more than apprentice pieces.

The Freedom Tree marks a transition in Watson's writing. It is also an historical novel but one more concerned with recent history, and it contains the beginnings of the political themes running through Watson's later books. It is set during the Spanish Civil War, which coincides with the Depression in 1930s England. Will Viljoen, whose father has died fighting for the Republicans in Spain, comes to London from Jarrow in the hope of travelling to Spain also. In London he teams up with Griff and later with the painter Candy Sam, who adds them to his group of friends travelling to Spain, where Sam's sister, Molly, is a nurse. After a series of adventures in France, they arrive to find themselves in a badly organised war. Most of Will's friends are killed, but Will and Molly eventually reach Guernica where they witness the destruction of the village by the Fascists. Although *The Freedom Tree* is a novel of power in places, particularly towards its climax, there is a feeling that Watson is unsure at this point in his career of the difference between a history textbook and a novel. Skillfully plotted though the book is, none of the characters apart from Will seem real: they range from the saintly Molly to the caricatured Basque Federico ("I speak the Enn-glish like the cannibal, eh?").

Talking in Whispers is a convincing and powerful story with political depth and credible characters. The novel is set in Chile, "sometime between the present and the future," although a reader with a rudimentary knowledge of South American history will recognise some of the situations. Andres, son of an anti-establishment singer, escapes when his father's car is ambushed. He is helped by a brother and sister, twin puppeteers. The main political opponent of the Junta is also shot prior to an election which would put him in power, and Andres receives the photographic evidence which shows a member of the Secret Service carrying out the shooting. Watson describes Andres' attempts to bring the truth to the world in an exciting and absorbing way. Watson highlights the anger in his voice by keeping it in reserve. But he does not shirk from showing the darker side of an inhuman regime, as in the episode of Andres's torture in the infamous House of Laughter. *Talking in Whispers* is widely read, discussed, and enjoyed by teenage readers.

Where Nobody Sees brings Watson's work firmly back to his own country and time. Vicar's son Luke discovers sinister happenings in woods near his home. The appearance of Petra, a member of a community theatre group whom Luke's mother has encountered at a peace camp, leads to the revelation that nuclear waste is being dumped in the woods. Petra's determination to expose this in a theatrical performance brings on the exciting climatic events of the novel. Watson is a much more confident writer in this novel, showing skill in both plot and characterisation. The characters are not merely mouthpieces for the author's views but show human qualities and failings: Luke's parents, for instance, although both rightminded, have obvious faults, as have Luke and Petra. The facts about nuclear waste are eased into the story in a subtle way that makes them more memorable and telling.

No Surrender is set in Angola at the time of free elections in Namibia. Two young people, Hamish, a white South African deserter, and Malenga, the black daughter of a local politician, are captured by a band of guerrillas. Their understanding of each other grows as they are faced with danger, a danger made more tangible by Watson's skillful use of tension. The characters, however, are presented very much in black and white, with the heroine associated with poetry and healing while the guerrillas are very obviously evil.

Ticket to Prague returns to Europe, with an intriguing contrast between Amy, forced to do community service in a mental institution, and Josef, a Czech exile who has not spoken for more than 20 years. Amy breaks down Josef's mental barriers to discover that he is a famous dissident poet. A trip to modern Czechoslovakia, accompanied by a television crew, is the catalyst for a series of unusual events which are bound to keep the book's readers intrigued.

Watson's strengths and flaws can be seen to good effect in his short story collection, *Make Your Move.* While some of the earlier are too wordy and didactic, Watson curbed that tendency in his later writing. Yet the majority of the stories have an uncompromising and realistic attitude to both public and private life that goes far deeper than much writing for teenagers.

Although most of his books contain disturbing material, Watson still has room for hope, which comes through his young protagonists. Despite the hardships Andres suffers at the hands of the Junta in *Talking in Whispers,* he is last seen handing out copies of the photograph that may destroy the regime. As one of the mercenaries involved in the dumping of nuclear waste says near the end of *Where Nobody Sees,* "We make the cash, but they make the hope."

—Keith Barker

WAUGH, Sylvia

Nationality: British. **Born:** Gateshead, 1935. **Education:** Grammar School, Gateshead; Durham University, B.A. in English; King's College, Newcastle, Diploma of Education. **Family:** Married; three children. **Career:** English Literature teacher. **Awards:** *Guardian* Fiction Award, 1993. **Address:** c/o Random House Children's Books, 20 Vauxhall Bridge Road, London SW1V 2SA, England.

Publications for Children

Fiction

The Mennyms. London, Julia MacRae, 1993.
Mennyms in the Wilderness. London, Julia MacRae, 1994.
Mennyms Under Siege. London, Julia MacRae, 1995.
Mennyms Alone. London, Julia MacRae, 1996.
Mennyms Alive. London, Julia MacRae, 1996.

* * *

Sylvia Waugh is a fascinating publishing phenomenon. A retired teacher whose children are grown up, she had her first novel published to immediate and overwhelming critical acclaim. It seemed that in *The Mennyms* she had written the equivalent of an oasis in the desert. At the time children's books appeared to be full of divorce, depression, and drugs, with stories about children bullied at school, abused at home, running away or living in squalor. *The Mennyms* is a fantasy, along the lines of *The Borrowers,* the publication of which was both refreshing and brave. The overriding reason it was so successful is because it is minutely detailed and meticulously constructed in every way, and, of course, it is a good story.

The Mennyms appear to be an ordinary family who keep to themselves. There are grandparents, Sir Magnus and Granny Tulip, son and daughter-in-law, Joshua and Vinetta, and their five children—teenagers Soobie and Appleby, ten-year-old twins Wimpey and Poopie, and Baby Googles—and Miss Quigley, who starts life as an occasional visitor and becomes the baby's nanny. But the Mennyms are in fact life-size rag dolls who have managed to live as humans without being discovered since their creator died, over forty years before the story opens. Then one day a letter from Australia brings the disturbing news that one Albert Pond has inherited the house from his uncle Chesney and intends to visit them, thus threatening their existence. After a series of letters describing his travels he finally decides against coming after all and the family breathes a sigh of relief. They are immediately thrown into further upset and confusion by another letter, this time from a solicitor, telling them that on the death of Mr. Chesney one Loftus Sir Magnus has inherited the house. It turns out that the original letters and Albert Pond are the creation of Appleby, who just wanted to inject some excitement into their lives. As a result of the family's outrage at this discovery Appleby runs away.

There are constant gentle reminders that the characters are dolls and not human. For example when Appleby returns she is so dirty that she has to have a bath and then spends some weeks drying out in the airing cupboard. In the first book another rag-doll is found unfinished in the attic, is completed and becomes part of the family, fitting in as Soobie's twin. These are just some of the many incidents that add intrigue and suspense to the saga. It is this delicate balance between reality and pretence, and between the enclosed world inside the house and the many dangers presented by the outside world, that keep readers completely involved in the lives of these extraordinary characters.

Having created the character of Albert Pond, and dismissed him as a figment of Appleby's imagination, Sylvia Waugh starts the second book in the series with another letter from another "Albert Pond." In an artful device Albert Pond has been brought into the secret by the ghost of the Mennyms' creator, Kate Penshaw, who turns out to have been his great, great aunt. With his help the Mennyms move out of their house and into a house in the country, when their home is threatened with demolition to make way for a new bypass.

The third title *Mennyms under Siege* finds the Mennyms under scrutiny from a nosy neighbour. Then, to avoid a neighbour looking too closely at the baby in its pram, Miss Quigly panics and says that the baby has whooping cough. The authorities start to get interested in the family and Sir Magnus decides that they must not venture out again, so starts the siege. This creates an unbearable tension in the house and relationships are severely strained. At the height of the drama the ghost of their creator, Kate Penshaw, appears to Appleby to warn her about opening a door in the attic. She cannot resist, however, and discovers a force that is beyond their control. As the door is opened everyone is immobilised. As she shuts it the rest of the family comes to life again, but Appleby dies, heralding yet another phase in their existence.

In the fourth book the Mennyms are once again in danger of discovery. The family that is to inherit their house when they die starts to wonder how old Sir Magnus is, as logically he should have already died. The rag dolls manage to stall them, but they must ultimately find a way of leaving their house before they are discovered. They decide that they must use the device of the attic door to immobilise them and make them really appear to be lifeless dolls, sacrificing life rather than facing discovery. This is indeed what happens and they are re-housed above an antique shop owned by an old lady called Daisy.

In the fifth and final book Sylvia Waugh's inventive powers do not diminish. The Mennyms come to life again, and attempt to continue their uncertain existence. This time though they are discovered to be alive by a young boy who visits his great aunt Daisy and plays with the life-size "rag-dolls." Daisy and the boy implicitly become part of the pretence, which is in itself sensitively handled, and Daisy helps to effect their eventual survival by keeping their secret. The five books together form an exquisitely crafted and captivating saga that represents an astonishing literary achievement.

—Fiona Lafferty

WAYNE, (Anne) Jenifer

Nationality: British. **Born:** London, 1917. **Education:** Blackheath High School, London; Somerville College, Oxford, 1936-39, B.A. (honours) 1939. **Family:** Married C.R. Hewitt in 1948; two daughters and one son. **Career:** Worked for the London Ambulance Service, 1939; junior English mistress, Newark High School, Nottinghamshire, 1940-41; writer and producer, BBC Radio Features Department, London, 1941-48. **Died:** 10 December 1982.

Publications for Children

Fiction (illustrated by Margaret Palmer)

Clemence and Ginger, illustrated by Patricia Humphreys. London, Heinemann, 1960.
The Day the Ceiling Fell Down, illustrated by Dodie Masterman. London, Heinemann, 1961.
The Night the Rain Came In, illustrated by Dodie Masterman. London, Heinemann, 1963.
Kitchen People. London, Heinemann, 1963; Indianapolis, Bobbs Merrill, 1965.
Merry by Name. London, Heinemann, 1964.
The Ghost Next Door. London, Heinemann, 1965.
Saturday and the Irish Aunt. London, Heinemann, 1966.
Someone in the Attic. London, Heinemann, 1967.
Ollie. London, Heinemann, 1969.
Sprout. London, Heinemann, 1970; New York, McGraw Hill, 1976.
Something in the Barn. London, Heinemann, 1971.
Sprout's Window-Cleaner. London, Heinemann, 1971; New York, McGraw Hill, 1976.
Sprout and the Dog-Sitter. London, Heinemann, 1972; New York, McGraw Hill, 1977.
The Smoke in Albert's Garden. London, Heinemann, 1974.
Sprout and the Helicopter. London, Heinemann, 1975; New York, McGraw Hill, 1977.
Sprout and the Conjuror. London, Heinemann, 1976; as *Sprout and the Magician,* New York, McGraw Hill, 1977.
John Brown, Rose and the Midnight Cat. New York, Kestrel, 1978.

Publications for Adults

Play

The Queen of the Castle (screenplay), 1969.

Poetry

The Shadows and Other Poems. London, Secker and Warburg, 1959.

Other

This Is the Law: Stories of Wrongdoers by Fault or Folly. London, Sylvan Press, 1948.
Brown Bread and Butter in the Basement: A Twenties Childhood. London, Gollancz, 1973.
The Purple Dress: Growing Up in the Thirties. London, Gollancz, 1979.

* * *

To everyone who has been reading children's books during the last 25 years or so, the name of Jenifer Wayne must be synonymous with the memory of a rollicking family story, which before many pages have been read becomes hilarious.

Always a family of individualists, always a harassed mother, always a "Wayne" unexpected development in the plot, which in less capable hands would be almost unbelievable. Wayne was also able to draw first-class character studies of people in her stories whose activities are amusing to read about, but who might be termed minor characters in the plot. An example is Mr. Kim the gardener in *The Ghost Next Door.* In the same book she depicts the bogus Royal Navy Commander who successfully fools everyone, thus striking a warning note to her readers to take nothing for granted. These stories are relaxing, splendid, and true to life—at least as far as some families are concerned. Wayne wrote several stories of this kind—the titles alone reveal their nature—*The Day the Ceiling Fell Down, The Night the Rain Came In, The Smoke in Albert's Garden.*

Perhaps, however, her greatest creation was the hero of a series of books for younger children—the little boy called Sprout. Sprout is so named because of a lock of his hair that refuses to lie down. Sprout—and sometimes his young sister Tilly as well—get up to the most extraordinary adventures in an innocent sort of way. Sprout goes carol-singing after a bout of flu, gets lost in the snow, and wakes up to find what he thought was a polar bear standing over him. Actually, it is a sheepdog called Chops who is Sprout's devoted companion forevermore. Sprout wins a dinghy in a seaside competition, and when his name, Rupert E. Smith, is announced, Sprout almost fails to realize that he is the winner.

Possessed of a very strong imagination, Wayne wrote stories that are a tonic to read.

—Berna C. Clark

WEBSTER, Jean (Alice Jane Chandler Webster)

Nationality: American. **Born:** Fredonia, New York, 24 July 1876; grandniece of the writer Mark Twain. **Education:** Schools in Fredonia; Lady Jane Grey School, Binghamton, New York, graduated 1896; Vassar College, Poughkeepsie, New York, B.A. in English and economics 1901. **Family:** Married Glenn Ford McKinney in 1915; one daughter. **Died:** 11 June 1916.

Publications for Children

Fiction (illustrated by the author)

Daddy-Long-Legs. New York, Century, 1912; London, Hodder and Stoughton, 1913.

Dear Enemy. New York, Century, and London, Hodder and Stoughton, 1915.

Play

Daddy Long-Legs, adaptation of her own novel (produced New York, 1914; London, 1916). New York, French, 1922; London, French, 1927.

Publications for Adults

Novels

The Wheat Princess. New York, Century, 1905; London, Hodder and Stoughton, 1916.

Jerry, Junior. New York, Century, and London, Gay and Bird, 1907; as *Jerry,* London, Hodder and Stoughton, 1916.

The Four-Pools Mystery (published anonymously). New York, Century, 1908; as Jean Webster, London, Hodder and Stoughton, 1916.

Much Ado about Peter. New York, Doubleday, 1909; London, Hodder and Stoughton, 1916.

Short Stories

When Patty Went to College. New York, Century, 1903; as *Patty and Priscilla,* London, Hodder and Stoughton, 1915.

Just Patty. New York, Century, 1911; London, Hodder and Stoughton, 1915.

Verse

Vitriol and Lilacs. Cleveland, Press of Flozari, 1943.

* * *

Two books only—one and its sequel—keep us aware of Jean Webster's name today. But these two, *Daddy-Long-Legs* and *Dear Enemy,* have stayed in print through the century; they have even slipped into modern mythology, and they entertain us still. Lighthearted and effervescent though they are, they grew from a serious thought. In the author's student days at Vassar in the late 19th century, as part of an economics course, she had visited orphanages and other grim institutions. It was then that her belief began to grow that, however unlucky a start a boy or girl might have, the chance of success should be possible for all. She worked this out at last in the two books here. Because of her sudden early death they were her final stories.

In *Daddy-Long-Legs* Judy (Jerusha Abbott, named from a tombstone and a telephone book) has spent all her life in the bleak and regimented John Grier Orphanage. At 17 she is still there as general help. A youngish trustee (30-ish as we later find), rich but unconventional, is amused by one of her essays and arranges to send her to college. All that is required of her is to write a monthly letter, via his secretary, to "Mr. John Smith," and not to expect a reply. John Smith? What a name to choose, thinks the audacious girl. She addresses her letters to Daddy-Long-Legs, after the long thin shadow she once saw of the unknown trustee-benefactor. The letters, with all their problems, joys, discoveries, secrets, are the book, and they delight the recipient as much as they please us. In his own persona (he's related to her haughty patrician room-mate Julia Pendleton) he makes acquaintance with Judy. He becomes jealous enough to try to use his authority (as Trustee Mr. Smith) to prevent her meeting brothers of her friends. Ah, complications....

Why was this book such a triumph? What still keeps it alive? For one thing, an orphan is the heroine, and orphans, whether Jane Eyre or Heathcliff, Oliver Twist or Anne of Green Gables, Froggy and his sad little brother or any of those foundlings in legend, have always had a special power in story. The more sheltered the reader's life the more the romantic appeal. Then, too, the book is a neat variation of that favourite of fairy tales, Cinderella. For readers of 1912 (Webster's young ladies are reading Shaw and Wells) this version had a particularly modern twist: the waif is to do so well in her new life that the prince is in danger of losing her. And another irresistible theme is woven in—that of a newcomer from another place, time, or social order discovering with astonishment the reader's familiar scene. Much piquancy comes from the fact that Judy has never had letters or birthday presents; that she has never been on a train journey, never even inside a private house.

The letter writing formula itself has a curious charm (note the success of the recent American *84 Charing Cross Road*). Letters have immediacy; they reveal; they make rapport with the reader. But *Daddy-Long-Legs* has another point of interest—the college curriculum: literature, Latin, French, mathematics, physiology, philosophy, history of art—Webster doesn't skimp details. We almost take the course ourselves. There are also all those basic books which Judy must secretly add to her mind's furniture—*Alice, Jane Eyre*—a fascinating list. Never underrate the fictional interest of facts.

True, you may observe that Judy is not a fair example. She has looks and charm (Jervis Pendleton is not her only admirer); she is clever enough to learn all those new college subjects; she can also "room" easily with girls from the top families in New York, and please their parents when she visits their homes. But in fact, as today's world shows, her progress is not as unlikely as it might seem. Indeed, whatever in the plot is preposterous (and there are many points for quibbling over) the book has the truth of fiction—more exactly, of fairy tale.

Dear Enemy still, happily, keeps the letter formula, but the writer is now the red-haired Sally McBride, Judy's college roommate and best friend. The now-married Judy and Jervis are determined to reform the John Grier Home, and have imposed on Sally, idling away in socialite Massachusetts, the task of doing so. In her letters to the elusive pair she rebels, she protests, but—for the time being—she stays. She continues to stay. She also writes now and then to Gordon, a rich, debonair young man who obediently sends gifts and equipment to the Home while waiting for Sally to tire of this latest whim. But for practical reasons more (if shorter) notes go to the dour Scottish orphanage doctor, "Dear Enemy," so vexing, so baffling, yet such a pillar of strength in a crisis. Meanwhile, against all possible problems (not to mention dramas of individual orphans) reforms advance.

Webster's orphanage theories (as put into practice by Sally) are modern enough: the setting up of cottage family homes ("As long as the family is the unit of society, children should be hardened early to family life"), the choosing of personal clothes, the admission of pets, the experience of spending or saving money. Surprisingly, she does not add a library; books (and these were pre-television days) are never mentioned at all. Her ideas on diet might need revising too. "You would never dream of all the delightful surprises we are going to have," writes Sally: "brown bread, corn pone, graham muffins, samp, rice pudding with *lots* of raisins, thick vegetable soup, macaroni Italian fashion, polenta cake with molasses, apple dumplings, gingerbread—oh, an endless list!" There are greater differences. Children outnumbered adopters—and adopters call the tune. They can specify that a child must be not only blue-eyed but of legitimate birth. Old ladies (especially when rich) are welcomed. One senses, too (perhaps from the nice scribbly pictures), that the ethnic minglings so much part of our Homes and schools today, had not reached the John Grier. Most arrivals (like Sally herself) are Irish. Yet is not fiction the readiest teacher of history—of social history certainly? These books still make rewarding reading.

—Naomi Lewis

WEIR, Rosemary

Pseudonym: Catherine Bell. **Nationality:** British. **Born:** Rosemary Green, Kimberley, South Africa, 22 July 1905. **Education:** Schools in South Africa and England. **Military Service:** First Aid Nursing Yeomanry during World War II. **Family:** Married Napier Weir in 1931 (died 1973); one daughter. **Career:** Has worked as an actress, farmer, teacher, and cook. **Address:** Ford Farm, Holcombe Rogus, Wellington, Somerset, England.

PUBLICATIONS FOR CHILDREN

Fiction

The Secret Journey. London, Parrish, 1957.
The Secret of Cobbetts Farm. London, Parrish, 1957.
No. 10 Green Street. London, Parrish, 1958.
Island of Birds. London, Parrish, 1959.
The Honeysuckle Line. London, Parrish, 1959; as *Robert's Rescued Railway,* New York, Watts, 1960.
The Hunt for Harry. London, Parrish, 1959.
Great Days in Green Street. London, Parrish, 1960.
Pineapple Farm, illustrated by Hugh Marshall. London, Parrish, 1960.
Little Lion's Real Island, illustrated by W.F. Phillipps. London, Harrap, 1960.
The House in the Middle of the Road. London, Parrish, 1961.
Albert the Dragon, illustrated by Quentin Blake. London and New York, Abelard Schuman, 1961.
What a Lark, illustrated by Val Biro. Leicester, Brockhampton Press, 1961.
Tania Takes the Stage. London, Hutchinson, 1961.
Top Secret. London, Parrish, 1962.
The Star and the Flame, illustrated by William Stobbs. London, Faber, 1962; New York, Farrar Straus, 1964.
Soap Box Derby, illustrated by Val Biro. Leicester, Brockhampton Press, 1962; Princeton, New Jersey, Van Nostrand, 1965.
Black Sheep. London, Parrish, 1963; as *Mystery of the Black Sheep,* New York, Criterion, 1964.
The Smallest Dog on Earth, illustrated by Charles Pickard. London, Abelard Schuman, 1963; New York, Abelard Schuman, 1964.
Further Adventures of Albert the Dragon, illustrated by Quentin Blake. London and New York, Abelard Schuman, 1964.
Mike's Gang, illustrated by Charles Pickard. London and New York, Abelard Schuman, 1965.
A Patch of Green. London, Parrish, 1965.
Devon Venture (as Catherine Bell). London, Collins, 1965.
The Real Game, illustrated by Aedwin Darroll. Leicester, Brockhampton Press, 1965; as *The Heirs of Ashton Manor,* New York, Dial Press, 1966.
The Boy from Nowhere, illustrated by Dennis Turner. London and New York, Abelard Schuman, 1966.
High Courage, illustrated by Ian Ribbons. London, Faber, and New York, Farrar Straus, 1967.
Pyewacket, illustrated by Charles Pickard. London and New York, Abelard Schuman, 1967.
Boy on a Brown Horse. London, Hamish Hamilton, 1967; New York, Hawthorn, 1971.
The Foxwood Flyer, illustrated by Robert Hales. London, Hamish Hamilton, 1968.
Albert the Dragon and the Centaur, illustrated by Quentin Blake. London and New York, Abelard Schuman, 1968.
No Sleep for Angus, illustrated by Elisabeth Grant. London and New York, Abelard Schuman, 1969.
Summer of the Silent Hands, illustrated by Lynette Hemmant. Leicester, Brockhampton Press, 1969.
The Lion and the Rose, illustrated by Richard Cuffari. New York, Farrar Straus, 1970; London, Abelard Schuman, 1972.
The Three Red Herrings. Nashville, Nelson, 1972.
Blood Royal, illustrated by Richard Cuffari. New York, Farrar Straus, 1973.
Uncle Barney and the Sleep-Destroyer, illustrated by Carolyn Dinan. London, Abelard Schuman, 1974.
Uncle Barney and the Shrink-Drink, illustrated by Carolyn Dinan. London, Abelard Schuman, 1977.
Albert and the Dragonettes, illustrated by Gerald Rose. London, Abelard Schuman, 1977.

Albert's World Tour, illustrated by David McKee. London, Abelard Schuman, 1978.
Pyewacket & Son, illustrated by Charles Pickard. London, Abelard Schuman, 1980.

Other

The Off-White Elephant (radio play; for adults). 1958.
A Dog of Your Own: or, Dogs Without Tears: Do's and Don't's for Young Dog Owners, illustrated by K.F. Barker. London, Harrap, 1960.
The Young David Garrick, illustrated by Anne Linton. London, Parrish, 1963; New York, Roy, 1964.
The Man Who Built a City: A Life of Sir Christopher Wren. New York, Farrar Straus, 1971.

*

Rosemary Weir comments:

I began to write for children when my own daughter was grown up and I myself was over 50. I remembered my own childhood very clearly and perhaps my books for children were a way of returning to a happy time of my life. On the whole I have most enjoyed writing for younger children, *The Smallest Dog on Earth* being my own favourite.

* * *

Rosemary Weir's books are for a wide range of readers, from very simple stories to straight historical adventures and novels for much older children.

Albert, the peaceful dragon, and Pyewacket, the ferocious old alley-cat, have adventures original and entertaining enough to lure the inexperienced reader to books. The humour and interest depend almost wholly upon external situation, but they are excellent for their purpose. Longer books, still for young children, such as *What a Lark* and *Soap Box Derby,* are cheerful, convincing, and undemanding. One feels they may have been written to meet the demand by some librarians and teachers for "neighborhood stories," and many children will enjoy them.

The historical adventures offer far more. They are well researched but not too heavily cumbered with details of contemporary events or manners. They remain stories, not history lessons. *High Courage,* set in the time of Simon de Montfort, brings alive the violence and tragedy of civil wars, the constricting life of a mediaeval castle, the contrasts of wealth and poverty. *The Lion and the Rose* tells of a lad ambitious to be a master stone-carver, who works on the rebuilding of St. Paul's. The feeling for the quality of stone itself, and the impressions of St. Paul's and the Portland quarries, are lively and memorable. These novels tell a good straightforward story with pace and interest. They are more concerned with events than character; the persons are satisfactorily rounded but not studied in any depth.

Weir's best work is in the novels for older readers. *The Real Game* tells of two children from the Australian outback who discover that their father is the heir to an earldom. Their own knowledge of the English aristocracy is derived from a battered copy of *Little Lord Fauntleroy,* found by mere chance; but when they are sent home to Ashton Court the slow adjustment from dream to reality is both funny and touching. Sebastian, shy, nervous, always too dependent on his loving but bossy sister, is deeply troubled until at last he discovers his true gift and becomes a person in his own right. This is a book full of warmth and humour and kindness, with a very sensitive understanding of the anxieties and uncertainties and embarrassments of childhood. The same ability to probe and interpret experience is seen in *Summer of the Silent Hands,* which concerns a brilliant boy pianist suddenly deprived by an accident of his gift and of the only life he knows. Through loneliness and anxiety, friendship and laughter, he has slowly to find his way in the uncharted world of family life and ordinary childhood.

It is these books for older readers that show Weir as an original and perceptive writer. The characterization is strong and clear, including satisfactory and fruitful relationships with adults as well as children. She stimulates interest by developing an unusual situation, but through it she explores the emotional experiences common to most children. She is concerned with the problems of growing up, but she makes them the material of art and not of social therapy.

—Margaret Greaves

WEISS, Miriam. See **SCHLEIN, Miriam.**

WELCH, Ronald

Pseudonym for Ronald Oliver Felton. **Nationality:** British. **Born:** Aberavon, Glamorganshire, 14 December 1909. **Education:** Berkhamsted School, Hertfordshire, 1922-28; Clare College, Cambridge, M.A. (honours) in history 1931. **Military Service:** Territorial Army, 1933-39; Welch Regiment during World War II: Company Commander and Staff Major. **Family:** Married Betty Llewellyn Evans in 1934; one daughter. **Career:** Assistant history master, Berkhamsted School, 1931-33; senior teacher, Bedford Modern School, 1933; headmaster, Okehampton Grammar School, Devon, 1947-63. **Award:** Library Association Carnegie Medal, 1955. **Died:** 5 February 1982.

PUBLICATIONS FOR CHILDREN

Fiction

The Black Car Mystery. London, Pitman, 1950.
The Clock Stood Still. London, Pitman, 1951.
The Gauntlet, illustrated by T.R. Freeman. London, Oxford University Press, 1951.
Knight Crusader, illustrated by William Stobbs. London, Oxford University Press, 1954; New York, Oxford University Press, 1979.
Sker House (as Ronald Felton). London, Hutchinson, 1954.

Captain of Dragoons, illustrated by William Stobbs. London, Oxford University Press, 1956; New York, Oxford University Press, 1957.
The Long Bow. Oxford, Blackwell, 1957.
Mohawk Valley, illustrated by William Stobbs. London, Oxford University Press, and New York, Criterion, 1958.
Captain of Foot, illustrated by William Stobbs. London, Oxford University Press, 1959.
Escape from France, illustrated by William Stobbs. London, Oxford University Press, 1960; New York, Criterion, 1961.
For the King, illustrated by William Stobbs. London, Oxford University Press, 1961; New York, Criterion, 1962.
Nicholas Carey, illustrated by William Stobbs. London, Oxford University Press, and New York, Criterion, 1963.
Bowman of Crécy, illustrated by Ian Ribbons. London, Oxford University Press, 1966; New York, Criterion, 1967.
The Hawk, illustrated by Gareth Floyd. London, Oxford University Press, 1967; New York, Criterion, 1969.
Sun of York, illustrated by Doreen Roberts. London, Oxford University Press, 1970.
The Galleon, illustrated by Victor Ambrus. London, Oxford University Press, 1971.
Tank Commander, illustrated by Victor Ambrus. London, Oxford University Press, 1972; Nashville, Nelson, 1974.
Zulu Warrior, illustrated by David Harris. Newton Abbot, Devon, David and Charles, 1974.
Ensign Carey, illustrated by Victor Ambrus. London, Oxford University Press, 1976.

Other

Ferdinand Magellan, illustrated by William Stobbs. London, Oxford University Press, 1955; New York, Criterion, 1956.

* * *

In his historical novels, Ronald Welch took one aspect of the past, military history, and made it his own. No other historical novelist for children is as good on battles as he is. His books are extremely well-researched, full of authentic detail, and always excitingly plotted.

The Gauntlet is a time-slip story in which Welch was feeling his way—a modern boy experiences his ancestors' adventures in a Welsh castle in the 14th century—but with *Knight Crusader* (a well-deserved Carnegie Medal winner) Welch had found his metier and his style. It tells the adventures of a young crusading knight, Philip d'Aubigny, in the Holy Land in the 12th century who, at the end of the book, goes home to Wales to take up his inheritance and to found the Carey family, whose fortunes Welch followed in many of his books.

Charles Carey fights with Marlborough's army in *Captain of Dragoons,* Alan Carey is with Wolfe at Quebec in *Mohawk Valley,* Richard Carey helps to rescue French kinsmen from the revolution in *Escape from France,* Neil Carey is a Royalist soldier in the Civil War in *For the King,* Nicholas Carey fights in the Crimea in *Nicholas Carey,* and Harry Carey takes to the sea in Elizabethan England in *The Hawk.* Best of the Carey books are *Tank Commander,* with its superb evocation of World War I, and *Captain of Foot,* in which Christopher Carey serves under Wellington in the Peninsular. In this book the famous diarists of the period, George Simmons and John Kincaid, are drawn upon, giving this book characters more rounded than usual.

Not Carey stories, but with jumping off points in the Welsh border country, were an Elizabethan story, *The Galleon,* and *Bowman of Crécy,* an enthralling story, full of authentic detail about the Hundred Years War. Less successful, perhaps, is another Carey book, *Zulu Warrior,* which is not only pedestrian but expresses the Jingoistic sentiments of the characters which are right for the times portrayed but out of mesh with today's attitudes both to Africa and to war.

Welch's great achievement was to produce stories full of accurate information about the weapons and warfare of the times he was writing about; he never glorified war, but made it quite clear that mud and discomfort, wounds and death were part of soldiering as well as comradeship and adventure. Welch was a soldier as well as a history teacher, and he drew on both experiences in making his historical novels for boys.

—Pamela Cleaver

WELLS, Rosemary

Nationality: American. **Born:** New York City, 29 January 1943. **Education:** Red Bank High School, New Jersey; Museum School, Boston. **Family:** Married Thomas Moore Wells in 1963; two daughters. **Career:** Worked in a store in Austin, Massachusetts, and in publishing in Boston and New York. Since 1968, freelance illustrator and writer. **Awards:** Children's Book Showcase award, Children's Book Council, 1974, for *Noisy Nora*; Art Book for Children citation, Brooklyn Museum and Brooklyn Public Library, 1975, 1976, 1977, for *Benjamin and Tulip*; Irma Simonton Black award, for *Benjamin and Tulip,* and 1975, for *Morris's Disappearing Bag: A Christmas Story*; runner-up for Edgar Allan Poe award, Mystery Writers of America, for *Through the Hidden Door,* and 1981, for *When No One Was Looking*; *Hazel's Amazing Mother* was named one of the *New York Times* Best Illustrated Books, 1985; Washington Irving Children's Book Choice award, Westchester Library Association, 1986, for *Peabody,* and 1988, for *Max's Christmas*; *Boston Globe-Horn Book* award, 1989, for *Shy Charles*; *Noisy Nora, Morris's Disappearing Bag, Leave Well Enough Alone, Stanley and Rhoda, Max's Toys, Max's Breakfast, Max's Bedtime, Max's Bath, When No One Was Looking, Max's Christmas, Shy Charles,* and *Max's Chocolate Chicken* were named among the best books of the year by *School Library Journal*; American Library Association (ALA) Notable Book citations for *Noisy Nora, Benjamin and Tulip, Morris's Disappearing Bag, Max's Breakfast, Max's Christmas, Max's Chocolate Chicken,* and *Max's Dragon Shirt*; ALA Best Books for Young Adults citation for *Through the Hidden Door*; *Bulletin of the Center for Children's Books* Blue Ribbon for *The Little Lame Prince*; *American Bookseller* Pick of the Lists citations for *Abdul, Stanley and Rhoda, Goodnight Fred, Timothy Goes to School, A Lion for Lewis, Forest of Dreams,* and *Max's Chocolate Chicken*; *Booklist* Children's Editor's Choice citations for *Max's Toys, Timothy Goes to School,* and *Through the Hidden Door*; Child Study Association Children's Books of the Year citations for *Morris's Disappearing Bag* and *Don't Spill It Again, James*; *Horn Book* Fanfare citation and West Australian Young Readers' Book award, both for *When No One*

Was Looking; Virginia Young Readers award and New York Public Library Books for Teenagers citation, both for *The Man in the Woods*; Parents' Choice award, Parents' Choice Foundation, for *Shy Charles*; Golden Kite award, Society of Children's Book Writers, and International Reading Association Teacher's Choices List, both for *Forest of Dreams*; International Reading Association Children's Choices citation for *Max's Chocolate Chicken*; International Reading Association/Children's Book Council Children's Choice citations for *Timothy Goes to School, A Lion for Lewis,* and *Peabody*; Cooperative Children's Book Center citation for *Max's Bedtime.* **Address:** c/o Doubleday and Co., 666 Fifth Ave., New York, New York 10103, U.S.A.

PUBLICATIONS FOR CHILDREN (ILLUSTRATED BY THE AUTHOR UNLESS OTHERWISE INDICATED)

Fiction

John and the Rarey. New York, Funk and Wagnalls, 1969.
Michael and the Mitten Test. Englewood Cliffs, New Jersey, Bradbury Press, 1969.
The First Child. New York, Hawthorn, 1970.
Martha's Birthday. Englewood Cliffs, New Jersey, Bradbury Press, 1970.
Miranda's Pilgrims. Englewood Cliffs, New Jersey, Bradbury Press, 1970.
Unfortunately Harriet. New York, Dial Press, 1972.
Benjamin and Tulip. New York, Dial Press, 1973; London, Kestrel, 1977.
Abdul. New York, Dial Press, 1975.
Morris's Disappearing Bag: A Christmas Story. New York, Dial Press, 1975; London, Kestrel, 1977.
Stanley and Rhoda. New York, Dial Press, 1978; London, Kestrel, 1980.
Max's First Word [*New Suit, Ride, Toys, Bedtime, Bath, Birthday, Hooray for Max, Breakfast, Christmas, Chocolate Chicken, Dragon Shirt*]. New York, Dial Press, 12 vols., 1979-91; London, Benn, 4 vols., 1980; London, Collins, 5 vols., 1985-86.
Timothy Goes to School. New York, Dial Press, and London, Kestrel, 1981.
Good Night, Fred. New York, Dial Press, 1981; London, Macmillan, 1982.
A Lion for Lewis. New York, Dial Press, and London, Macmillan, 1982.
Peabody. New York, Dial Press, 1983; London, Macmillan, 1984.
Hazel's Amazing Mother. New York, Dial Press, 1985; London, Collins, 1986.
Through the Hidden Door. New York, Dial Press, 1987.
Shy Charles. New York, Dial Press, and London, Collins, 1988.
Forest of Dreams, illustrated by Susan Jeffers. New York, Dial Press, and London, Collins, 1988.
The Little Lame Prince. New York, Dial Press, 1990.
Fritz and the Mess Fairy. New York, Dial Press, 1991.
Voyage to the Bunny Planet. New York, Dial Press, 1992.
First Tomato. New York, Dial, 1992.
The Island Light. New York, Dial, 1992.
Lucy's Come to Stay, pictures by Patricia Cullen-Clark. New York, Dial, 1992.
Moss Pillows. New York, Dial, 1992.
Max and Ruby's First Greek Myth: Pandora's Box. New York, Dial, 1993.
Reteller, *Lassie Come Home* by Eric Knight, illustrated by Susan Jeffers. New York, Holt, 1995.
Edward's Overwhelming Overnight. New York, Dial, 1995.
Edward in Deep Water. New York, Dial, 1995.
Edward Unready for School. New York, Dial, 1995.
The Language of Doves, illustrated by Greg Shed. New York, Dial, 1996.
Bunny Cakes. New York, Dial, 1997.
Bunny Money. New York, Dial, 1997.
McDuff and the Baby, illustrated by Susan Jeffers. New York, Hyperion, 1997.
Jack and the Beanstalk, illustrated by Norman Messenger. New York, Dorling Kindersley, 1997.
Max's Ride. New York, Dial, 1998.
Read to Your Bunny. New York, Scholastic, 1998.
Max's Breakfast. Rosemary Wells. New York, Dial, 1998.
McDuff's New Friend, illustrated by Susan Jeffers. New York, Hyperion, 1998.
Old MacDonald. New York, Scholastic, 1998.
The Bear Went Over the Mountain. New York, Scholastic, 1998.
Bingo. New York, Scholastic, 1998.
Itsy Bitsy Spider. New York, Scholastic, 1998.
Yoko. New York, Hyperion, 1998.
Rachel Field's Hitty: Her First Hundred Years with New Adventures, illustrated by Susan Jeffers. New York, Simon & Schuster, 1999.

Poetry

Noisy Nora. New York, Dial Press, 1973; London, Collins, 1976; with new illustrations by Rosemary Wells, New York, Dial, 1997.
Don't Spill It Again, James. New York, Dial Press, 1977.

Other

Contributor, *So I Shall Tell You a Story: The Magic World of Beatrix Potter.* New York, Warne, 1993.

PUBLICATIONS FOR YOUNG ADULTS (ILLUSTRATED BY THE AUTHOR UNLESS OTHERWISE INDICATED)

The Fog Comes on Little Pig Feet. New York, Dial, 1972.
None of the Above. New York, Dial, 1974.
Leave Well Enough Alone. New York, Dial, 1977.
When No One Was Looking. New York, Dial, 1980; London, Deutsch, 1984.
The Man in the Woods. New York, Dial, 1984; London, Deutsch, 1985.
Waiting for the Evening Star, paintings by Susan Jeffers. New York, Dial, 1993.
Mary on Horseback. New York, Dial, 1997.
Streets of Gold (based on Mary Antin's memoir, *The Promised Land*), illustrated by Dan Andreasen. New York, Dial, 1999.

PUBLICATIONS FOR ADULTS

Other

Cooking for Nitwits, with Joanna Hurley. New York, Dutton, 1989.

*

Media Adaptations: *Max's Christmas* and *Morris's Disappearing Bag* have been adapted as short films by Weston Woods.

Biography: Essay in *Something about the Author Autobiography Series,* Vol. 1, Detroit, Gale, 1986.

Critical Studies: Entry in *Children's Literature Review,* Vol. 16, Detroit, Gale, 1989; entry in *Contemporary Literary Criticism,* Vol. 12, Detroit, Gale, 1980.

Illustrator: *A Song to Sing, O!,* 1968, and *The Duke of Plaza Toro,* 1969, both by W.S. Gilbert; *Hungry Fred* by Paula Fox, 1969; *Why You Look Like You Whereas I Tend to Look Like Me* by Charlotte Pomerantz, 1969; *The Shooting of Dan McGrew and The Cremation of Sam McGee* by Robert Service, 1969; *The Cat That Walked by Himself* by Rudyard Kipling, 1970; *Marvin's Manhole* by Winifred Rosen, 1970; *Impossible, Possum* by Ellen Conford, 1971; *A Hot Thirsty Day* by Marjorie Weinman Sharmat, 1971; *Two Sisters and Some Hornets* by Beryl Epstein and Dorrit Davis, 1972; *With a Deep Sea Smile* edited by Virginia A. Tashjian, 1974; *Tell Me a Trudy* by Lore Segal, 1977; *The Christmas Mystery* by Jostein Gaarder (translated by Elizabeth Rokkan), 1996; *My Very First Mother Goose,* edited by Iona Opie, 1996.

* * *

Although Rosemary Wells is known principally for her entertaining series of picture books about animal characters with remarkably human characteristics, she has also ventured into other genres with as much success. She has given to the children's book world an array of inimitable personalities: Noisy Nora, Stanley and Rhoda, Morris, Max, beautifully observed anthropomorphic creatures who are strong on human feelings such as sibling rivalry. *Noisy Nora,* for instance, is the middle child in a mouse family who tries to attract attention from parents who are too concerned with her young brother Jack. While Nora's sister laconically tells her she is "so dumb," the author uses rollicking verse to show how the situation is resolved after Nora walks out on her parents. She returns to the family home, to be loved and appreciated, "with a monumental crash."

As in all good picture books, Wells's illustrations tell as much of the story as the words. This is particularly true of *Stanley and Rhoda,* another perceptive study of siblings. A mouse brother and sister share a group of situations wittily observed by the author. In one of these episodes, for instance, Rhoda is supposedly stung on the foot by a bee and is apparently distraught until Stanley suggests that the best method for easing the foot is to soak it in boiling butter. "'It's better now, Stanley' said Rhoda." *Morris's Disappearing Bag* is set at Christmas. Morris's older brother and sisters are unwilling to let him use their presents until Morris discovers one gift left under the tree. This is a bag that makes its owner disappear on climbing into it. Needless to say, this proves more attractive to Morris's family, giving him a free rein of the other presents. This book contains a nicely attuned move towards anti-sexism as does *Benjamin and Tulip,* which has a positive, if not to say dominant, heroine. Affinity between the sexes is also shown in *Timothy Goes to School,* in which Timothy discovers that his dislike for the perfect Claude is only matched by that felt by Violet for Grace because "She sings. She dances. She counts up to a thousand and she sits next to me."

These are probably the most successful of Wells's picture books, although she has also produced other memorable creations such as Max, a rabbit who has appeared in a series of board books and who discovers Father Christmas in *Max's Christmas.* Other characters are less memorable, however: the teddy bear *Peabody,* for instance, whose story is little different from that of many other teddy characters in children's literature. Even typically Wells creations such as *Hazel's Amazing Mother* or *Shy Charles* lack the quintessential Wells magic.

However, the author has also developed another area of creativity: thrillers written for a teenage audience. *When No One Was Looking* is an Edgar Allan Poe Award runner-up. Kathy is a tennis champion with a determination to win and a fierce temper. However, when one of her opponents is murdered, Kathy has to discover who has drowned the girl. This is a book which is intriguing in its detection and also shows insights into teenage friendships. More intricately plotted and suitably tense is *The Man in the Woods,* in which Helen discovers a mysterious man in the woods who is supposed to be throwing rocks at car windscreens, a discovery that leads Helen and her friend Pinky into a deeper mystery involving drug trafficking.

These thrillers help to demonstrate Wells's versatility, as does her simple, almost naive text for Susan Jeffers's evocative paintings in *Forest of Dreams.* Whichever directions Wells's talent leads her in future years, thousands of children will be grateful to her for her creations of Nora, Morris, and all those other characters with sibling problems.

—Keith Barker

WEST, Joyce (Tarlton)

Pseudonym: Manu Gilbert. **Nationality:** British. **Born:** Auckland, New Zealand. **Education:** Maori schools and by correspondence courses. **Career:** Worked as an accounting clerk. **Died:** 1985.

Publications for Children (illustrated by author)

Fiction

Drovers Road. London, Dent, 1953.
The Year of the Shining Cuckoo. Hamilton, Paul's Book Arcade, 1961; London, Dent, 1963; New York, Roy, 1964.
Cape Lost. Auckland, Paul's Book Arcade, and London, Dent, 1963.
The Golden Country. Hamilton, Blackwood and Janet Paul, and London, Dent, 1965.
The Sea Islanders. London, Dent, and New York, Roy, 1970.
The River Road. London, Dent, 1980.

Publications for Adults

Novels

Sheep Kings. Wellington, Tombs, 1936.
Fatal Lady, with Mary Scott. Hamilton, Paul's Book Arcade, 1960.

Such Nice People, with Mary Scott. Hamilton, Paul's Book Arcade, 1962.
The Mangrove Murder, with Mary Scott. Auckland, Paul's Book Arcade, and London, Angus and Robertson, 1963.
No Red Herrings, with Mary Scott. London, Angus and Robertson, 1964.
Who Put It There?, with Mary Scott. Hamilton, Blackwood and Janet Paul, and London, Angus and Robertson, 1965.
Lineman's Ticket (as Manu Gilbert). Hamilton, Blackwood and Janet Paul, 1967.

*

Joyce West commented:

(1978) My own childhood was spent in the remote country districts of New Zealand where my parents were teachers in the Maori schools. We lived far from towns, in a world of bush roads and river crossings; we rode horseback everywhere, and kept a large menagerie of dogs, cats, kittens, ducks, turkeys, pet lambs, and goats. It always seemed to be summertime. When I began to write, it was with the wish that I might save a little of the charm and flavour of those times and places for the children of today.

* * *

In New Zealand, Joyce West is best known for an early work, *Drovers Road,* which describes in episodic form the humorous adventures of Gay, who, though deserted by both her parents, enjoys a happy and secure life with her Aunt Belle, her uncle Dunsany, and several cousins on a rather isolated sheep station on the East Coast of the North Island of New Zealand. In many ways the book demonstrated the best qualities of this author. There are the warmth and love of a united family, a deep feeling and a sensitivity to nature and to animals. Despite some sentimentality, West, with her shrewd characterisation, her gift for comedy, and her racy style, very satisfyingly demonstrates one type of New Zealand child who lives still very much in the English tradition.

We meet the characters of *Drovers Road* in further novels. In *The Golden Country,* for example, the former schoolgirl who had appeared in an intervening novel entitled *Cape Lost* is now the owner of an old homestead and coastal station at Cape Lost. While the book is still blemished by the element of fairy tale, the writing is confident and compelling, the characterisation realistic and memorable with, unfortunately, some instances of mawkishness. Gay's tenacious search for independence and her agonising over the choice of Mr. Right takes place in the context of the hardships and the isolation of hill country sheep farming.

The Year of the Shining Cuckoo is set in another inaccessible spot: this time in dairying country bordering a tidal harbour. In this story of a boy's efforts to buy a filly, the chief interest lies in the adult characters, Grandfather and Aunt Garance, both larger than life, lovable and memorable. The themes of loneliness and the compensating warmth of family and community life are accompanied by scenes, such as that at the horse fair, which reveal West's comic gifts and acute observation. The same delight in all living things, and in the bush, the sea, and the hills, gives her writing a flavour of the appeal of the backblocks. *The Sea Islanders,* in presenting a group of children in a Robinson Crusoe setting, allows West plenty of freedom to explore flora and fauna of a tiny island.

West illustrated all her books, and these illustrations, along with her sensitive descriptions, make her contribution to children's literature something very special. Along with these qualities are her ability to create a comic scene and her strength in the observation of the delightful quirks of all the country characters whom she describes. These qualities more than make up for any weaknesses in plot and sentimentality of character.

—Tom Fitzgibbon

WESTERMAN, Percy (Francis)

Nationality: British. **Born:** Portsmouth, Hampshire, in 1876. **Education:** Portsmouth Grammar School. **Military Service:** Royal Navy and Royal Flying Corps during World War I, and in Dorset Home Guard during World War II. **Family:** Married Florence Wager in 1900. **Career:** Admiralty clerk, Portsmouth Dockyard, 1896-1911. Lived many years in Wareham, Dorset. **Died:** 22 February 1959.

PUBLICATIONS FOR CHILDREN

Fiction

A Lad of Grit, illustrated by E.S. Hodgson. London, Blackie, 1908.
The Winning of Golden Spurs. London, Nisbet, 1911.
The Young Cavalier, illustrated by Gordon Browne. London, Pearson, 1911.
The Quest of the "Golden Hope," illustrated by Frank Wiles. London, Blackie, 1911.
The Flying Submarine. London, Nisbet, 1912.
Captured at Tripoli, illustrated by Charles Sheldon. London, Blackie, 1912.
The Sea Monarch, illustrated by E.S. Hodgson. London, A. and C. Black, 1912.
The Scouts of Seal Island, illustrated by Ernest Prater. London, A. and C. Black, 1913; New York, Macmillan, 1922.
The Rival Submarines, illustrated by C. Fleming Williams. London, Partridge, 1913.
The Stolen Cruiser. London, Jarrolds, 1913.
When East Meets West, illustrated by C.M. Padday. London, Blackie, 1913.
Under King Henry's Banners, illustrated by John Campbell. London, Pilgrim Press, 1913.
The Sea-Girt Fortress, illustrated by W.E. Wigfull. London, Blackie, 1914.
The Sea Scouts of the "Petrel." London, A. and C. Black, 1914; New York, Macmillan, 1924.
The Log of a Snob, illustrated by W.E. Wigfull. London, Chapman and Hall, 1914.
'Gainst the Might of Spain. London, Pilgrim Press, 1914.
Building the Empire. London, Jarrolds, 1914.
The Dreadnought of the Air. London, Partridge, 1914.
The Dispatch-Riders. London, Blackie, 1915.
The Fight for Constantinople. London, Blackie, 1915.
The Nameless Island. London, Pearson, 1915.
A Sub. of the R.N.R. London, Partridge, 1915.

Rounding Up the Raider, illustrated by E.S. Hodgson. London, Blackie, 1916.
The Secret Battleplane. London, Blackie, 1916.
The Treasures of the "San Philipo." London, Religious Tract Society, 1916.
A Watch-Dog of the North Sea. London, Partridge, 1916.
Deeds of Pluck and Daring in the Great War. London, Blackie, 1917.
To the Fore with the Tanks!, illustrated by Dudley Tennant. London, Partridge, 1917.
Under the White Ensign. London, Blackie, 1917.
The Fritz Strafers. London, Partridge, 1918; as *The Keepers of the Narrow Seas,* 1931.
Billy Barcroft, R.N.A.S. London, Partridge, 1918.
A Lively Bit of the Front, illustrated by Wal Paget. London, Blackie, 1918.
The Secret Channel and Other Stories. London, A. and C. Black, 1918; New York, Macmillan, 1919.
The Submarine Hunters. London, Blackie, 1918.
A Sub and a Submarine. London, Blackie, 1918.
With Beatty off Jutland. London, Blackie, 1918.
Wilmshurst of the Frontier Force. London, Patridge, 1919.
Winning His Wings, illustrated by E.S. Hodgson. London, Blackie, 1919.
The Thick of the Fray at Zeebruge, April 1918, illustrated by W.E. Wigfull. London, Blackie, 1919.
'Midst Arctic Perils. London, Pearson, 1919.
The Airship "Golden Hind." London, Partridge, 1920.
The Mystery Ship. London, Partridge, 1920.
The Salving of the "Fusi Yama," illustrated by E.S. Hodgson. London, Blackie, 1920.
Sea Scouts All, illustrated by Charles Pears. London, Blackie, 1920.
Sea Scouts Abroad, illustrated by Charles Pears. London, Blackie, 1921.
The Third Officer, illustrated by E.S. Hodgson. London, Blackie, 1921.
Sea Scouts Up-Channel, illustrated by C.M. Padday. London, Blackie, 1922.
The Wireless Officer, illustrated by W.E. Wigfull. London, Blackie, 1922.
The War of the Wireless Waves, illustrated by W.E. Wightman. London, Oxford University Press, 1923.
The Pirate Submarine. London, Nisbet, 1923.
A Cadet of the Mercantile Marine, illustrated by W.E. Wigfull. London, Blackie, 1923.
Clipped Wings, illustrated by E.S. Hodgson. London, Blackie, 1923.
The Mystery of Stockmere School. London, Partridge, 1923.
Sinclair's Luck. London, Partridge, 1923.
Captain Cain. London, Nisbet, 1924.
The Good Ship "Golden Effort," illustrated by W.E. Wigfull. London, Blackie, 1924.
The Treasure of the Sacred Lake. London, Pearson, 1924.
Unconquered Wings, illustrated by E.S. Hodgson. London, Blackie, 1924.
Clinton's Quest, illustrated by R.B. Ogle. London, Pearson, 1925.
East in the "Golden Gain," illustrated by Rowland Hilder. London, Blackie, 1925.
The Boys of the "Puffin," illustrated by G.W. Goss. London, Partridge, 1925.
The Buccaneers of Boya, illustrated by William Rainey. London, Blackie, 1925.
The Sea Scouts of the "Kestrel." London, Seeley, 1925.
Annesley's Double. London, A. and C. Black, and New York, Macmillan, 1926.
King of Kilba. London, Ward Lock, 1926.
The Luck of the "Golden Dawn," illustrated by Rowland Hilder. London, Blackie, 1926.
The Riddle of the Air, illustrated by Rowland Hilder. London, Blackie, 1926.
Tireless Wings. London, Blackie, 1926.
The Terror of the Seas. London, Ward Lock, 1927.
Mystery Island. London, Oxford University Press, 1927.
Captain Blundell's Treasure, illustrated by J. Cameron. London, Blackie, 1927.
Chums of the "Golden Vanity," illustrated by Rowland Hilder. London, Blackie, 1927.
In the Clutches of the Dyaks, illustrated by F. Marston. London, Partridge, 1927.
The Junior Cadet, illustrated by Rowland Hilder. London, Blackie, 1928.
On the Wings of the Wind, illustrated by W.E. Wigfull. London, Blackie, 1928.
A Shanghai Adventure, illustrated by Leo Bates. London, Blackie, 1928.
Pat Stobart in the "Golden Dawn," illustrated by Rowland Hilder. London, Blackie, 1929.
Rivals of the Reef, illustrated by Kenneth Inns. London, Blackie, 1929.
Captain Starlight, illustrated by W.E. Wigfull. London, Blackie, 1929.
Captain Sang. London, Blackie, 1930.
Leslie Dexter, Cadet. London, Blackie, 1930.
A Mystery of the Broads, illustrated by E.A. Cox. London, Blackie, 1930.
The Secret of the Plateau, illustrated by W.E. Wigfull. London, Blackie, 1931.
The Senior Cadet, illustrated by Rowland Hilder. London, Blackie, 1931.
In Defiance of the Ban, illustrated by E.S. Hodgson. London, Blackie, 1931.
All Hands to the Boats!, illustrated by Rowland Hilder. London, Blackie, 1932.
The Amir's Ruby, illustrated by W.E. Wigfull. London, Blackie, 1932.
Captain Fosdyke's Gold, illustrated by E.S. Hodgson. London, Blackie, 1932.
King for a Month, illustrated by Comerford Watson. London, Blackie, 1933.
Rocks Ahead!, illustrated by D.L. Mays. London, Blackie, 1933.
The White Arab, illustrated by Henry Coller. London, Blackie, 1933.
The Disappearing Dhow, illustrated by D.L. Mays. London, Blackie, 1933.
Chasing the "Pleiad." London, Blackie, 1933.
Tales of the Sea, with others, illustrated by Terence Cuneo. London, Tuck, 1933.
The Westow Talisman, illustrated by W.E. Wigfull. London, Blackie, 1934.
Andy-All-Alone, illustrated by D.L. Mays. London, Blackie, 1934.
The Black Hawk, illustrated by Rowland Hilder. London, Blackie, 1934.
Standish of the Air Police. London, Blackie, 1935.

The Red Pirate, illustrated by Rowland Hilder. London, Blackie, 1935.
Sleuths of the Air, illustrated by Comerford Watson. London, Blackie, 1935.
On Board the "Golden Effort." London, Blackie, 1935.
The Call of the Sea, illustrated by D.L. Mays. London, Blackie, 1935.
Captain Flick, illustrated by E.S. Hodgson. London, Blackie, 1936.
His First Ship. London, Blackie, 1936.
Midshipman Raxworthy. London, Blackie, 1936.
Ringed by Fire. London, Blackie, 1936.
Winged Might. London, Blackie, 1937.
Under Fire in Spain, illustrated by Ernest Prater. London, Blackie, 1937.
The Last of the Buccaneers. London, Blackie, 1937.
Haunted Harbour, illustrated by John de Walton. London, Blackie, 1937.
His Unfinished Voyage, illustrated by D.L. Mays. London, Blackie, 1937.
Cadet Alan Carr, illustrated by D.L. Mays. London, Blackie, 1938.
Midshipman Webb's Treasure, illustrated by D.L. Mays. London, Blackie, 1938.
Standish Gets His Man, illustrated by W.E. Wigfull. London, Blackie, 1938.
Sea Scouts Alert! London, Blackie, 1938.
Standish Loses His Man, illustrated by W.E. Wigfull. London, Blackie, 1939.
In Eastern Seas. London, Blackie, 1939.
The Bulldog Breed, illustrated by E. Boye Uden. London, Blackie, 1939.
At Grips with the Swastika, illustrated by Leo Bates. London, Blackie, 1940.
Eagles' Talons. London, Blackie, 1940.
In Dangerous Waters. London, Blackie, 1940.
When the Allies Swept the Seas, illustrated by J.C.B. Knight. London, Blackie, 1940.
Standish Pulls It Off. London, Blackie, 1940.
The War—And Alan Carr, illustrated by E. Boye Uden. London, Blackie, 1940.
War Cargo. London, Blackie, 1941.
Sea Scouts at Dunkirk. London, Blackie, 1941.
Standish Holds On. London, Blackie, 1941.
Fighting for Freedom. London, Blackie, 1941.
Alan Carr in the Near East. London, Blackie, 1942.
Destroyer's Luck. London, Blackie, 1942.
On Guard for England, illustrated by J.C.B. Knight. London, Blackie, 1942.
Secret Flight. London, Blackie, 1942.
With the Commandoes, illustrated by S. Van Abbe. London, Blackie, 1943.
Sub-Lieutenant John Cloche, illustrated by H. Pym. London, Blackie, 1943.
Alan Carr in Command, illustrated by Terence Cuneo. London, Blackie, 1943.
Alan Carr in the Arctic, illustrated by E. Boye Uden. London, Blackie, 1943.
Combined Operations, illustrated by S. Van Abbe. London, Blackie, 1944.
Engage the Enemy Closely, illustrated by Terence Cuneo. London, Blackie, 1944.
Secret Convoy, illustrated by Terence Cuneo. London, Blackie, 1944.
One of the Many, illustrated by Ellis Silas. London, Blackie, 1945.
Operations Successfully Executed, illustrated by S. Drigin. London, Blackie, 1945.
By Luck and Pluck, illustrated by Terence Cuneo. London, Blackie, 1946.
Return to Base, illustrated by Leslie Wilcox. London, Blackie, 1946.
Squadron Leader, illustrated by Terence Cuneo. London, Blackie, 1946.
Unfettered Night, illustrated by S. Jezzard. London, Blackie, 1947.
Trapped in the Jungle, illustrated by A.S. Forrest. London, Blackie, 1947.
The Phantom Submarine, illustrated by J.C.B. Knight. London, Blackie, 1947.
The "Golden Gleaner," illustrated by M. Mackinlay. London, Blackie, 1948.
First Over, illustrated by Ellis Silas. London, Blackie, 1948.
Mystery of the Key, illustrated by Ellis Silas. London, Blackie, 1948.
Missing, Believed Lost, illustrated by Will Nickless. London, Blackie, 1949.
Contraband, illustrated by A. Barclay. London, Blackie, 1949.
Beyond the Burma Road, illustrated by Victor Bertoglio. London, Blackie, 1949.
Sabarinda Island, illustrated by A. Barclay. London, Blackie, 1950.
Mystery of Nix Hall, illustrated by D.C. Eyles. London, Blackie, 1950.
By Sea and Air. London, Blackie, 1950.
Desolation Island, illustrated by W. Gale. London, Blackie, 1950.
Held to Ransom, illustrated by Ellis Silas. London, Blackie, 1951.
The Isle of Mystery, illustrated by Philip. London, Blackie, 1951.
Working Their Passage, illustrated by Ellis Silas. London, Blackie, 1951.
Sabotage!, illustrated by Ellis Silas. London, Blackie, 1952.
Round the World in the "Golden Gleaner," illustrated by Jack Matthew. London, Blackie, 1952.
Dangerous Cargo, illustrated by W. Gale. London, Blackie, 1952.
Bob Strickland's Log, illustrated by Jack Matthew. London, Blackie, 1953.
The Missing Diplomat, illustrated by R.G. Campbell. London, Blackie, 1953.
Rolling Down to Rio, illustrated by R.G. Campbell. London, Blackie, 1953.
Wrested from the Deep, illustrated by Robert Johnston. London, Blackie, 1954.
A Midshipman of the Fleet, illustrated by P.A. Jobson. London, Blackie, 1954.
The Ju-Ju Hand. London, Blackie, 1954.
The Dark Scout, illustrated by Victor Bertoglio. London, Blackie, 1954.
Daventry's Quest, illustrated by P.A. Jobson. London, Blackie, 1955.
The Lure of the Lagoon, illustrated by E. Kearon. London, Blackie, 1955.
Held in the Frozen North, illustrated by Edward Osmond. London, Blackie, 1956.
The Mystery of the "Sempione," illustrated by P.B. Batchelor. London, Blackie, 1957.
Jack Craddock's Commission, illustrated by Edward Osmond. London, Blackie, 1958.

Mistaken Identity, illustrated by Robert Johnston. London, Blackie, 1959.

* * *

Between the wars Percy Westerman was a popular writer of boys' adventure stories: inside the cover of *Standish of the Air Police,* for example, 60 titles are listed. Yet today he is out of print in both England and America. He owed his popularity to skill as "a spinner of yarns," usually with a nautical or flying background, with strong suspense elements involving clashes with unspecified foreign enemies of law and order. This mixture today spells total neglect. Writing of an attempt to land an airship on a tropical island, Westerman wrote, "It was a sort of gamble—everything depended on foresight and chance, and a fortunate combination of the two alone could bring success." In his own case foresight was lacking and chance has been unkind. In storytelling, foresight does not depend on an ability to supply market calculations, but on the quality of an author's imaginative sympathy for his fictions.

Westerman's writing falls too easily into cliché and his characters into stereotypes. Thus swindles are invariably "barefaced," meals are usually "square" and civilian life is "full of pitfalls" for unsuspecting servicemen. And the heroic character depends as much on the force of muscle as of mind. McAlastair in *The Bulldog Breed* is typical, "Although long-limbed he possessed enormous muscular development...." Intelligence is properly limited to resourceful action in dealing with such everyday situations as piloting ships through typhoons and airships through mid-air collisions. Likewise the villains fall naturally into stock situations: "The occupant of the tent turned. He held a hair brush in each hand. His glossy black hair reeked of perfumed oil." In these matters Westerman falls short of the proper demands of his trade. But change of fashion has also deprived him of his readership. His accounts of machinery and "inventions," like the Crophelium gas which powers the airship Black Comet II, have been left behind by the commonplaces of post-war technology. In the same way the actions which asserted the self-assurance of imperialism, the unquestioning obedience to authority, the stress on courage and clean-living were inappropriate to England's declining economic power during the years of depression. It is not that the heroes and their deeds are unworthy within their own limits, but in showing themselves unaware of large areas of the life of their time, they have come to stand for those values which an anti-heroic age finds least bearable.

—Kenneth J. Sterck

WHEATLEY, Nadia

Nationality: Australian. **Born:** Sydney, New South Wales, 30 April 1949. **Education:** Sydney University, 1966-70, B.A. (honours) in history 1970; Macquarie University, Sydney, M.A. (honours) 1976. **Awards:** Australian Children's Book Council Book of the Year award, 1988; Eve Pownell award, 1988. **Agent:** Barbara Mobbs, P. O. Box 126, Edgecliff, New South Wales 2027, Australia.

PUBLICATIONS FOR CHILDREN

Fiction

Five Times Dizzy, illustrated by Neil Phillips. Melbourne, Oxford University Press, 1982.
Dancing in the Anzac Deli, illustrated by Waldemar Buczynski. Melbourne, Oxford University Press, 1984.
The House That Was Eureka. Melbourne, Viking Kestrel, 1984.
My Place, with Donna Rawlins. Melbourne, Collins, 1987.
The Blooding. Melbourne, Viking Kestrel, 1987; London, Viking Kestrel, 1988.
Lucy in the Leap Year, illustrated by Ken Searle. Melbourne, Omnibus, 1993.
The Night Tolkien Died (short stories). Melbourne, Random House Australia, 1994.
The Greatest Treasure of Charlemagne the King, illustrated by Deborah Klein, Scholastic, 1997.
Highway, illustrated by Andrew McLean, Melbourne, Omnibus, 1998.

Plays

Lucy in the Leap Year (Produced by Theatre South, 1996).

Television Series: *Five Times Dizzy,* with Terry Larsen, 1986.

Other

1 Is for One, illustrated by Helen Leitch. Melbourne, Oxford University Press, 1985.

Editor, *Children and Family Problems: Books for Young Children.* Melbourne, Australian Institute of Family Studies, 1988.
Editor, *Adolescents and Family Problems: Books for Young Children.* Melbourne, Australian Institute of Family Studies, 1988.
Editor, *Trouble in Lotus Land,* by Charmian Clift. North Ryde, Angus & Robertson, 1990.
Editor, *Being Alone with Oneself,* by Charmain Clift, Melbourne, HarperCollins, 1991.
Editor, *Landmarks.* London, Penguin, 1993.

*

Nadia Wheatley comments:

The main influences on my work as a children's book writer have probably been: (1) the children's book writers of my own childhood of the 1950s, and particularly the Australian writers; (2) the work of E.P. Thompson, and particularly his emphasis on recording the history of "ordinary" people; (3) George Orwell's essay, "Boys' Weeklies," in which it is shown how ruling-class propaganda can imbue the fiction which working-class children read.

Thus in my stories I have tried to write for and about ordinary Australian people.

* * *

Running through Nadia Wheatley's writing: her junior novels; her picture book, *My Place;* her short stories; and her young adult novels is a strong sense of Wheatley's perspective that the past gives to the present. This is most apparent in *My Place,* the story of a house and its occupants of various nationalities, moving backwards in decades from 1988 to 1788. Both the original landowners and the present residents are Aborigines. Changes in Australia's social fabric are subtly traced with the passing decades.

Wheatley's five years living in Greece and her familiarity with Sydney, Australia's inner suburbs, along with her study of history and her social and political viewpoint have enabled her to write sympathetically of life in working-class suburbs with their large migrant populations. But Wheatley is equally at ease in Australian mining towns, the pastoral countryside, or a rural logging community.

Her first two novels, *Five Times Dizzy* and *Dancing in the Anzac Deli,* are about a Greek family living in the inner-Sydney suburb of Newtown, and especially the problems of the non-English speaking Yaya. In the first book, Mareka, the granddaughter, brings about a miracle, a "resurrection," a change of perspective, for Yaya who, uprooted from her native land, can now accept her new community and be accepted by it. In *Dancing in the Anzac Deli,* Yaya's "born again" experience is paralleled by the images of her past involvement in the guerilla warfare that took place in Greece during World War II.

Lucy, who, in *Lucy in the Leap Year,* lives with her taxi driver father in an inner-city suburb, has lost her mother, is prone to natural fears and anxieties, and is lonely in her inner being. The Leap Year of the story is marked by a series of small leaps by Lucy toward maturity. Anzac Day, Mother's Day and a series of occasions bring her into a closer relationship with her neighbours and her father; and when spring comes, a bare tree sprouting is an epiphany: a small realisation of life's wonders and its continuity.

Wheatley is acutely aware of caste and social distinction. Written without undue bitterness or a propagandist message, *The House That Was Eureka* is the story of two terrace houses—201/203 Liberty Street, Newtown—and their occupants in 1931, at the height of the Great Depression, and 1981, when unemployment was again rife. In the house at 201 Liberty lives Mrs. Weston, the Despot, who owns both dwellings and lets out 203. An Irish family, the Cruises, rented it in 1931. The Despot's warrant to have the unemployed Paddy evicted arouses the support of the Unemployed Workers' Movement. The house is picketed against bailiffs and turned into a Eureka Stockade, to become the scene of a gun battle between police and workers. Another battle is waged in 1981. The plot is free of manipulation and hysteria, yet Wheatley makes it clear that no side has a "monopoly on morality" but that "struggle never fails."

The Blooding is set in a fictitious, isolated, frontier township where the greenies have moved in to protest against the logging which is the lifeblood of the precarious outpost. Colum, the 17-year-old son of one of the loggers, tells the story in a journal from his hospital bed where he lies with broken bones after a run-in between the timber workers and the conservationists. Wheatley is careful to present both sides of this fundamental issue impartially, yet without letting the reader off the hook.

Wheatley commands attention and respect for her ideas; she also structures her books compellingly and has extended the technique of the novel for young people in Australia. Because she sees parallels and analogies in history, and time present often as a replay of time past, her books abound in parallels: the past with the present; opposing but parallel points of view; lives which run together and then diverge.

This is the structure of many of the short stories collected in *The Night Tolkien Died.* The stories themselves are as varied as contemporary Australian life: city, coastal, and country living; religious, political, and social diversity. The point of view fluctuates between male and female, young and old. Running throughout is the theme of developing a wider viewpoint, of taking a step toward self-understanding and establishing mature relationships. An introverted young man in "Land/Scape" begins to understand his father; in "The Prodigal" a selfish runaway provides her sister with the perspective needed for a piece of art. Through the quicksand of memory a girl who once owned a blue dress comes to see herself more clearly ("Quicksand"); time brings a new perspective and understanding of the people and events of the past ("Women's Business"). "The Most Unforgettable Character I Have Ever Met" is a powerful statement as to how far best friends can drift apart; and not only because one is gay and one is straight in every sense.

Wheatley's wide-ranging social vision is matched by the scope of her writing techniques. Along with conventional narration and stream of consciousness, she reproduces handwritten letters in *Dancing in the Anzac Deli,* news reports and references to historical figures in *Eureka,* and reports, oral history, songs, and letters, along with Colum's pungent asides and flashbacks, as he maintains his first-person journal in *The Blooding.* Short stories such as "Land/Scape," "Melting Point," and "The Night Tolkien Died" extend the form through pungent paragraph headings, definitions, passages of Latin with a translation, type set in the form of a concrete poem, and even multiple choice boxes. Yet these devices are never ostentatious, and form is always in accord with content. Wheatley is one of the most modest but thought-provoking writers in Australia today.

—H.M. Saxby

WHITE, Eliza Orne

Nationality: American. **Born:** Keene, New Hampshire, 2 August 1856. **Education:** Schools in Keene, and at Miss Hall's School for Girls, Roxbury, Massachusetts. **Career:** Lived in Brookline, Massachusetts, 1881-1947. **Died:** 23 January 1947.

Publications for Children

Fiction

When Molly Was Six, illustrated by Katharine Pyle. Boston, Houghton Mifflin, 1894.

A Little Girl of Long Ago. Boston, Houghton Mifflin, 1896.

Ednah and Her Brothers, illustrated by Margaret Bush-Brown. Boston, Houghton Mifflin, 1900.

An Only Child, illustrated by Katharine Pyle. Boston, Houghton Mifflin, 1905.

A Borrowed Sister, illustrated by Katharine Pyle. Boston, Houghton Mifflin, 1906.

Brothers in Fur. Boston, Houghton Mifflin, 1910.

The Enchanted Mountain, illustrated by E. Pollak-Ottendorff. Boston, Houghton, Mifflin, 1911.
The Blue Aunt, illustrated by Katharine Pyle. Boston, Houghton, Mifflin, 1918.
The Strange Year, illustrated by Alice Preston. Boston, Houghton Mifflin, 1920.
Peggy in Her Blue Frock, illustrated by Alice Preston. Boston, Houghton Mifflin, 1921.
Tony, illustrated by Alice Preston. Boston, Houghton Mifflin, 1924.
Joan Morse, illustrated by M.A. Benjamin. Boston, Houghton Mifflin, 1926.
Diana's Rosebush, illustrated by Constance Whittemore. Boston, Houghton Mifflin, 1927.
The Adventures of Andrew. Boston, Houghton Mifflin, 1928.
Sally in Her Fur Coat, illustrated by Lisl Hummel. Boston, Houghton Mifflin, 1929.
The Green Door, illustrated by Lisl Hummel. Boston, Houghton Mifflin, 1930.
When Abigail Was Seven, illustrated by Lisl Hummel. Boston, Houghton Mifflin, 1931.
The Four Young Kendalls, illustrated by Lisl Hummel. Boston, Houghton Mifflin, 1932.
Where Is Adelaide?, illustrated by Helen Sewell. Boston, Houghton Mifflin, 1933.
Lending Mary, illustrated by Grace Paull. Boston, Houghton Mifflin, 1934.
Ann Frances, illustrated by Helen Sewell. Boston, Houghton Mifflin, 1935.
Nancy Alden, illustrated by Mildred Boyle. Boston, Houghton Mifflin, 1936.
The Farm Beyond the Town, illustrated by Mildred Boyle. Boston, Houghton, Mifflin, 1937.
Helen's Gift House, illustrated by Helen Blair. Boston, Houghton Mifflin, 1938.
Patty Makes a Visit, illustrated by Helen Blair. Boston, Houghton Mifflin, 1939.
The House Across the Way, illustrated by Lois Maloy. Boston, Houghton Mifflin, 1940.
I: The Autobiography of a Cat, illustrated by Clarke Hutton. Boston, Houghton Mifflin, 1941.
Training Sylvia, illustrated by Dorothy Bayley. Boston, Houghton Mifflin, 1942.
When Esther Was a Little Girl, illustrated by Connie Moran. Boston, Houghton Mifflin, 1944.

PUBLICATIONS FOR ADULTS

Novels

Miss Brooks. Boston, Roberts, 1890.
Winterborough. Boston, Houghton Mifflin, 1892.
The Coming of Theodora. Boston, Houghton Mifflin, and London, Smith and Elder, 1895.
A Lover of Truth. Boston, Houghton Mifflin, and London, Smith and Elder, 1898.
John Forsyth's Aunts. New York, McClure Phillips, 1901.
Lesley Chilton. Boston, Houghton Mifflin, 1903.
The Wares of Edgefield. Boston, Houghton Mifflin, 1909.
The First Step. Boston, Houghton Mifflin, 1914.

Short Stories

A Browning Courtship and Other Stories. Boston, Houghton Mifflin, and London, Smith and Elder, 1897.

Other

Editor, *William Orne White: A Record of Ninety Years* (letters). Boston, Houghton Mifflin, 1917.

* * *

Most writers of successful books for children have found—though never conceivably in anything like perfect balance—an ongoing audience of boys and girls, girls and boys. Boys of my own dim day could stomach those Five Little Peppers, including Phronsie, through all their serial growing pains. We read the Pepper books, but we didn't boast about it. So what of the currently enchanting Miss Bianca and her four-foot Women's Lib? I for one read every Margery Sharp book just as fast as it comes off the press. Why not? After all, isn't Louisa May Alcott really but a younger edition of Jane Austen, working in the same old vineyard? For do not *Emma* and *Little Women* share in common the unfailing readership of full-grown men? Common? Surely Virginia Woolf's "common reader" is not divided, cell-like, sex by sex. Neither is the youthful "common reader" of *Alice,* the Oz books, *The Wind in the Willows, Martin Pippin in the Apple Orchard, Charlotte's Web, Millions of Cats, Tom, Dick, and Harriet, Peacock Pie,* Howard Pyle's *The Wonder Clock,* Henry Beston's *The Starlight Wonder Book.* Beyond that, it is more than (worse than) idle, in listing such books, to set up these silly horizontal milestones for the age groups: fourth grade, sixth grade, pre- and post-teenagers. Aren't we always in our separate lives alike in easy reach of the cookie jar as well as of Bernard Shaw, Henry James, Wallace Stevens, Thoreau, Hudson, Proust, *The Road to Xanadu*?

And so we come to Eliza Orne White, a now faded figure in children's literature: an American Victorian writer whose father had a parish, and whose maternal grandfather was Chester Harding, the well-known painter. She appears to have been popular enough in her day (1856-1947) to have published in all some 25 novels and stories for the very young. And most specifically, in her case, stories for very young girls, *not* boys. All her life she dearly loved little girls and cats. Her cats were characters in themselves. Her two most popular books were *When Molly Was Six* and *A Little Girl of Long Ago.* The young of today, however, could not and would not enter the world of unbelievable innocence that she describes.

She was born in Keene, New Hampshire, a pleasant town through which I have often driven: a pretty, partially industrial town whose Main Street is surely the widest in all New England. It was a town which obviously should have produced at least one literary figure. It produced White, who lived there until she was 22. Let her describe it:

> It was just the right sort of a place for a little girl to live in who was to write stories for other little girls when she grew up, for there were all the things to be found there that children most like. The town was very beautiful, with the hills around it, and Monadnock to be seen from the lower end of Main Street, and the Ashuelot River and

Beaver Brook, with the woods near them, made splendid places for picnics or drives.

In the winter, like Molly, "when she was six," my father would take me and some small friend coasting on a big black sled, down a snowy hill and across an icy pond, and we had sleigh-rides to the accompaniment of jingling sleigh-bells, and less speedy rides when we fastened our sleds to slowly moving ox teams.

She was from first to last a period piece. Her style, a sweet stillwater as old-fashioned as the flowers in her garden, as respectful as my own Presbyterian grandmother who always spoke of my Pennsylvania grandfather as "Mr. Reed." You may learn (in *When Molly Was Six*) of the difference between cows and bossies; of "pink-and-white dyaletras"; of hanging "over the *balusters,*" not "banisters"; of playing jackstraws—a game of my own youth; of words like rowboats and ponycarts spelled with a hyphen; of Mammá, not Mámma or Mom; of a time when one ran *into* and not *in* the house. That is, we are told, through little twists and tags of speech, of an almost insufferable formality of deportment and confected give-and-take. Most of these books' adventures seem tame enough—as though the lives of little girls of 80 years ago were lived in greater part in a doll's house. Hence "a pew-door seemed made on purpose for little children." In *A Little Girl of Long Ago* when a somewhat older and more gregarious heroine than Molly, along with her younger sister and brother, struggles to help another young brother free his head which he had squeezed through the back of his chair, we find the victim wailing, "Oh, dear, how you hurt!" Take a look at the prose of E. Nesbit in *The Railway Children:* it is not at all like that. But at least there is scarcely any moralizing; and when White, in one of her rare didactic moments, says a word about cheating, or abandons reality to show the child reader the dreadful danger of (a) deep water or (b) setting one's clothes and hair accidently on fire, she does not labor the message; nor does she repeat it. White's obvious lack is a sense of humor to leaven all her gentleness, kindness, and Sehnsucht. And, as Ethel Heins more importantly points out, her *real* failure (unlike E. Nesbit, for example) is not dealing in any way with fantasy pure and simple. Fantasy is what lasts.

—David McCord

WIER, Ester (Alberti)

Nationality: American. **Born:** Seattle, Washington, 17 October 1910. **Education:** Southeastern Teachers College, Durant, Oklahoma, 1929-30; University of California, Los Angeles, 1931-32. **Family:** Married Henry Robert Wier in 1934; one son and one daughter.

Publications for Children

Fiction

The Loner, illustrated by Christine Price. Philadelphia, McKay, 1963; London, Constable, 1966.

Gift of the Mountains, illustrated by Richard Lewis. Philadelphia, McKay, 1963.

The Rumptydoolers, illustrated by W.T. Mars. New York, Vanguard Press, 1964.

Easy Does It, illustrated by W.T. Mars. New York, Vanguard Press, 1965.

The Barrel, illustrated by Carl Kidwell. Philadelphia, McKay, 1966.

The Wind Chasers, illustrated by Kurt Werth. Philadelphia, McKay, 1967; London, Constable, 1968.

The Winners, illustrated by Ursula Koering. Philadelphia, McKay, 1967.

The Space Hut, illustrated by Leo Summers. Harrisburg, Pennsylvania, Stackpole, 1967.

Action at Paradise Marsh, illustrated by Earl Blust. Harrisburg, Pennsylvania, Stackpole, 1968.

The Long Year, illustrated by Ursula Koering. Philadelphia, McKay, 1969.

The Straggler, illustrated by Leonard Vosburgh. Philadelphia, McKay, 1970.

The White Oak, illustrated by Anne Marie Jauss. Philadelphia, McKay, 1971.

The Partners, illustrated by Anna Maria Ahl. Philadelphia, McKay, 1972.

The Hunting Trail, illustrated by Richard Cuffari. New York, Walck, 1974.

King of the Mountain. New York, Walck, 1975.

Publications for Adults

With Dorothy Hickey, *The Answer Book on Naval Social Customs* and *Air Force Social Customs,* 2 Vols. Harrisburg, Pennsylvania, Military Service Publishing, 1956-57.

Army Social Customs. Harrisburg, Pennsylvania, Military Service Publishing, 1958.

What Every Air Force Wife Should Know. Harrisburg, Pennsylvania, Military Service Publishing, 1958.

*

Manuscript Collections: Kerlan Collection, University of Minnesota, Minneapolis; de Grummond Collection, University of Southern Mississippi, Hattiesburg.

Ester Wier comments:

I have tried to make my books understandable and acceptable to young readers. Each event in each story could have happened to some child somewhere in the course of his everyday existence. The backgrounds have been of great importance to me since here was my chance to acquaint children with other places while allowing them to see that life goes on pretty much the same no matter where you are. If I have aroused curiosity in them about peers living in other locations and led them to search out more about different places, then I have succeeded in what I have intended. And if I have been able to instill in them a love and feeling of responsibility for animals, then I am content.

* * *

Writer of many stories, Ester Wier has developed her skills considerably beyond the point of her first excellent book, *The*

Loner, runner-up for the 1963 Newbery award. The body of her work contains many stories of children, primarily boys, who are seeking acceptance by themselves or others. Wier shows strong understanding of youth's efforts to stand on its own, and yet she accepts its real needs to belong to someone else somewhere. The need to achieve and to be accepted motivates her characters, whether they live in the southwest of the United States and are surrounded by plains and plateaus like Whit in *The Rumptydoolers,* or live in the Everglades of Florida like Chance Reedy in *The Barrel* and are surrounded by alligators and razorbacks.

Perhaps the best of Wier's stories are those with nature settings, in sheep country or shellfish shorelands. Her depictions of the natural environment are detailed without becoming boring, integrated with the story, and yet vivid enough to convince the reader of their reality. Research must surely be part of Wier's preparation, for many of the stories capture the flavor of regional speech. Although early Wier books are filled with telling rather than showing, telling the reader the thoughts and feelings of the protagonist rather than showing the action that results from feelings and thoughts, later stories contain well-drawn and believable characters like Jesse growing up in *The Long Year.* When the subject of Wier's story is a wild creature, as it occasionally is, the scientific facts are evident without being obtrusive. *The White Oak,* for example, traces effectively 150 years of ecological forest life.

Wier's skills lie in her ability to interweave imagery with action and dialogue. Regionalism, much of it tropical or subtropical Florida, shows the way of life, the influence of environment upon people, the motivations that make the characters local and yet universal.

—Rebecca J. Lukens

WIESNER, David

Nationality: American. **Born:** Bridgewater, New Jersey, 5 February 1956. **Education:** Rhode Island School of Design, B.F.A. 1978. **Family:** Married Kim Kahng, 1983; one son and one daughter. **Career:** Author and illustrator of children's books. Exhibitions include Metropolitan Museum of Art, New York City, 1982, Master Eagle Gallery, New York City, 1980-89, Museum of Art, Rhode Island School of Design, Providence, 1989, Brooklyn Public Library, New York, 1990, Muscarele Museum of Art, College of William and Mary, Williamsburg, Virginia, 1990, and Society of Illustrators, New York City, 1991 and 1992. **Awards:** Children's Picturebook Award, *Redbook,* 1987 for *The Loathsome Dragon*; Caldecott Honor Book, 1989, for *Free Fall*; American Bookseller "Pick of the List" and *School Library Journal* "Best Books of 1990," for *Hurricane*; 1991 Reviewer's choice by Sesame Street Parents Guide; "Ten Best Books of 1991" list, *Parenting Magazine,* American Bookseller "Pick of the List," *School Library Journal* "Best Books of the Year," all 1991, and Caldecott Medal, 1992, all for *Tuesday*; ALA Notable Book, *Reading Rainbow* selection, and Parents' Choice citation, 1992, all for *June 29, 1999.* **Address:** c/o Clarion Books, 215 Park Ave. S., New York, New York 10003, U.S.A.

PUBLICATIONS FOR CHILDREN

Fiction (illustrated by the author)

Retelling, with Kim Kahng, *The Loathsome Dragon.* New York, Putnam, 1987.
Free Fall. New York, Lothrop, 1988.
Hurricane. New York, Clarion Books, 1990.
Tuesday. New York, Clarion Books, 1991.
June 29, 1999. New York, Clarion Books, 1992.
Sector 7. New York, Clarion Books, 1999.

*

Media Adaptations: *Tuesday* (videorecording), Hightstown, New Jersey, American School Publication, 1992.

Biography: *Something about the Author,* Vol. 72, Detroit, Gale Research, 1993, 245-254; "Caldecott Acceptance Speech" by David Wiesner, in *Horn Book,* July/August 1992, 416-422.

Critical Studies: *Horn Book,* January/February 1992, 84.

Illustrator: *Honest Andrew* by Gloria Skurzynski, 1980; *Man from the Sky* by Avi, 1980; *The Ugly Princess* by Nancy Luenn, 1981; *The One Bad Thing about Birthdays* by David R. Collins, 1981; *The Boy Who Spoke Chimp,* 1981, and *Neptune's Rising: Songs and Tales of the Undersea Folk,* 1982, by Jane Yolen; *Owly* by Mike Thaler, 1982; *Miranty and the Alchemist,* 1983; *The Dark Green Tunnel* by Allen W. Eckert, 1984; *E.T.: The Storybook of the Green Planet* by William Kotzwinkle, based on a story by Steven Spielberg, 1985; *The Wand: The Return to Mesmeria* by Allan W. Eckert, 1985; *Kite Flier* by Dennis Haseley, 1986; *Firebrat* by Nancy Willard, 1988; *The Sorcerer's Apprentice: A Greek Fable* retold by Marianna Mayer, 1989; *The Rainbow People,* 1989, and *Tongues of Jade,* 1991, retold by Laurence Yep; *Night of the Gargoyles* by Eve Bunting, 1994; *Looking for Merlin* by Dilys Evans, forthcoming.

* * *

David Wiesner's interest in art began in early childhood. His family encouraged him to draw by providing him with art supplies on Christmas and birthdays, and his older siblings gave him their old art supplies as well. When he reached high school, Wiesner became intrigued with two art movements: the Renaissance movement of the fifteenth and sixteenth centuries, as exemplified by the superb draftsmanship of Michelangelo and Leonardo da Vinci, and Surrealism of the twentieth century, which also boasted superb draftsmen whose drawings presented a distorted portrayal of reality. Wiesner was also influenced by sci-fi films, such as Stanley Kubrick's *2001: A Space Odyssey.* Such films fit into his interest in an extraordinary world.

While attending the Rhode Island School of Design Wiesner thought he might work as an illustrator for some kind of an adult fantasy magazine. Though he hadn't thought of children's books, one of his college instructors suggested he show his work to author-illustrator Trina Schart Hyman, art director for the children's magazine *Cricket.* Hyman offered him the opportunity to do a magazine cover and thus began his journey into children's literature. After finishing art school, Wiesner did freelance work illustrating textbooks before he moved on to illustrating children's books. Since that time he has illustrated a number of books written by others, most of them fantasy stories or folk tales.

The first book which he wrote (with his wife) and illustrated was *The Loathsome Dragon.* Based on the English fairy tale, "The Laidly Worm of Spindleston Huegh," it is the tale of a beautiful Princess who is trapped inside the body of a scaly dragon through the sorcery of her jealous stepmother. The medieval settings of dreamy landscapes, sprawling castles, and a very big, though gentle, dragon, provide a lyrical depiction of the Middle Ages.

Free Fall is a wordless picture book about a young boy who falls asleep while reading a book of maps. He dreams of a journey, and his bedspread becomes a landscape in which he is transported to a chessboard with live people, to a medieval castle with knights and a scaly dragon, to a sea of swans and fishes, and finally back to his own bed. The events and characters of the dream reflect real objects in the youngster's bedroom, such as goldfish and chessmen on the table next to his bed. Wiesner saw that *Free Fall* was all the more powerful without words; he felt he was now doing the kind of illustrations he wanted to do.

Hurricane is a story with words that tells of two brothers experiencing a hurricane. The fierceness of the wind and the relentlessness of the rain are dramatically illustrated. A favorite elm tree is toppled in the yard, and the next day when the brothers examine it, it looks like a big sleeping giant. The limbs and branches are as a jungle, so the boys play safari and have a fearless expedition into the heart of the jungle, catching up with elephant herds and stalking some mighty leopards. That afternoon they ride the seven seas, searching the horizon for pirate ships. Their imaginative play comes alive with glorious pictures of nature as it moves and changes.

Wiesner won the Caldecott Medal for his next book, *Tuesday,* a nearly wordless picture book. On Tuesday evening at eight frogs leap out of the quiet pond. They travel to the city, knocking down clothes lines, entering houses through open windows and chimneys, watching TV, and then in the early morning returning to their quiet ponds. This book is a visual comedy; its antecedents include animated cartoons, silent movies, and superhero comic books of the 1960s. The leaping pale green frogs are funny, and even though they are bigger than the frogs you are used to, you would enjoy having them invade your home.

June 29, 1999 is a date that Holly Evans of Ho-Ho-Kus, New Jersey, will never forget. Holly has great hopes for her science project, sending seedlings aloft into the ionosphere. But she does not anticipate the consequences: all over the country skies fill with vegetables, huge turnips, cabbages, broccoli, and red peppers. Big vegetables become big business in America. But then other huge vegetables come down: arugula, eggplant, avocado, rutabaga. Holly did not plant them, but who did? The story concludes with a picture of the Arcturian starcruiser, Alula Borealis, cruising in the ionosphere and it may have the answer. The reader gets to decide on his own.

The pictures in all of the books Wiesner writes show superb draftsmanship and weird happenings. The happenings may at times be a little frightening, but they are also funny and very entertaining. And they encourage the reader to think of further strange things that might happen, that could happen, and of the strange consequences they would bring to a commonplace world. The happenings reflect quite well Wiesner's early interest in the surreal.

It is not surprising that Wiesner illustrated William Kotzwinkle's *E.T.: The Storybook of the Green Planet,* based on Steven Spielberg's story. He has also illustrated a number of books of old folk tales from around the world. These include two books of Chinese tales as told by Laurence Yep: *The Rainbow People* and *Tongues of Jade.* His illustrations for these books include small black and white drawings which are visually stunning but traditional in content.

Wiesner brings life to old as well as to new fantasies, the new ones being mostly those he himself creates. His books are fun, and his wordless books are especially fun, because the reader has to enter into the conclusion of the story. Each reader has to look closely at the fantastic pictures, to carefully figure out what is in them, so that he can complete the tale for himself. Wiesner's books should elicit grand group discussions as readers pool their insights and theories. Wiesner invites dreamers to dream on.

—Mary Lystad

WIGGIN, Kate Douglas

Nationality: American. **Born:** Kate Douglas Smith, Philadelphia, Pennsylvania, 28 September 1856. **Education:** Schools in Portland, Hollis, and Buxton, Maine; Gorham Female Seminary, Hollis; Morison Academy, Baltimore; Abbot Academy, Andover, Massachusetts; Mrs. Severance's Kindergarten Training School, Los Angeles, 1877. **Family:** Married 1) Samuel Wiggin in 1881 (died 1889); 2) George Christopher Riggs in 1895. **Career:** Head of a private kindergarten, Santa Barbara, California, 1877; founder, with Felix Adler, Silver Street Free Kindergarten, San Francisco, 1878; founder, with Nora A. Smith, California Kindergarten Training School, San Francisco, 1880. Litt.D.: Bowdoin College, Brunswick, Maine, 1904. **Died:** 24 August 1923.

Publications for Children

Fiction

The Story of Patsy: A Reminiscence. San Francisco, Murdock, 1883; revised edition, Boston, Houghton Mifflin, and London, Gay and Bird, 1889.

The Birds' Christmas Carol. San Francisco, Murdock, 1887; London, Gay and Bird, 1891.

A Summer in a Cañon. Boston, Houghton Mifflin, 1889; London, Gay and Bird, 1893.

Timothy's Quest. Boston, Houghton Mifflin, 1890; London, Gay and Bird, 1892.

The Story Hour, with Nora A. Smith. Boston, Houghton Mifflin, 1890; London, Gay and Bird, 1893.

Polly Oliver's Problem. Boston, Houghton Mifflin, and London, Gay and Bird, 1893.

A Cathedral Courtship, and Penelope's English Experiences, illustrated by Clifford Carleton. Boston, Houghton Mifflin, and London, Gay and Bird, 1893.

Penelope's Progress. Boston, Houghton Mifflin, 1898; as *Penelope's Experiences in Scotland,* London, Gay and Bird, 1898.

Penelope's Irish Experiences. Boston, Houghton Mifflin, and London, Gay and Bird, 1901.

The Diary of a Goose Girl, illustrated by Claude Shepperson. Boston, Houghton Mifflin, and London, Gay and Bird, 1902.
Rebecca of Sunnybrook Farm. Boston, Houghton Mifflin, and London, Gay and Bird, 1903.
Half-a-Dozen Housekeepers, illustrated by Mills Thompson. Philadelphia, Altemus, and London, Kelly, 1903.
A Village Stradivarius. London, Gay and Bird, 1904.
Rose o' the River, illustrated by George Wright. Boston, Houghton Mifflin, and London, Constable, 1905.
New Chronicles of Rebecca. Boston, Houghton Mifflin, and London, Constable, 1907; as *More about Rebecca of Sunnybrook Farm,* London, A. and C. Black, 1930.
Finding a Home. Boston, Houghton Mifflin, 1907.
Mother Carey's Chickens. Boston, Houghton Mifflin, 1911; as *Mother Carey,* London, Hodder and Stoughton, 1911.
A Child's Journey with Dickens. Boston, Houghton Mifflin, and London, Hodder and Stoughton, 1912.
Penelope's Postscripts: Switzerland, Venice, Wales, Devon, Home. Boston, Houghton Mifflin, and London, Hodder and Stoughton, 1915.
The Romance of a Christmas Card, illustrated by Alice Hunt. Boston, Houghton Mifflin, and London, Hodder and Stoughton, 1916.
The Spirit of Christmas. Boston, Houghton Mifflin, 1927.

Plays

Rebecca of Sunnybrook Farm, with Charlotte Thompson, adaptation of the story by Wiggin (produced Springfield, Massachusetts, 1909; New York, 1910; London, 1912). New York and London, French, 1932.
The Birds' Christmas Carol, with Helen Ingersoll, adaptation of the story by Wiggin. Boston, Houghton Mifflin, 1914.
Bluebeard: A Musical Fantasy. New York, Harper, 1914.
Mother Carey's Chickens, with Rachel Crothers, adaptation of the story by Wiggin (produced Poughkeepsie, New York, and New York City, 1917). New York and London, French, 1925.

Other

Kindergarten Chimes: A Collection of Songs and Games. Boston, Ditson, 1885; revised edition, 1887.
The Arabian Nights Retold, with Nora A. Smith, illustrated by Maxfield Parrish. New York, Scribner, and London, Laurie, 1909.

Editor, with Nora A. Smith, *Hymns for Kindergartners.* San Francisco, Froebel Society, 1881.
Editor, with Nora A. Smith, *Golden Numbers: A Book of Verse.* New York, McClure, 1902.
Editor, with Nora A. Smith, *The Posy Ring: A Book of Verse.* New York, McClure, 1903; as *Poems Every Child Should Know,* New York, Doubleday, 1942.
Editor, with Nora A. Smith, *The Library of Fairy Literature* (*The Fairy Ring, Magic Casements, Tales of Laughter, Tales of Wonder, The Talking Beasts*). New York, McClure, 3 vols., 1906-08; last 2 vols., published, New York, Doubleday, 1909-11; *The Fairy Ring* published as *Fairy Stories Every Child Should Know,* New York, Doubleday, 1942.
Editor, with Nora A. Smith, *Pinafore Palace: A Book of Rhymes for the Nursery.* New York, McClure, 1907; as *Pinafore Palace: Baby's Friend and Nursery Heroes and Heroines,* New York, Doubleday, 1923.
Editor, with Nora A. Smith, *An Hour with the Fairies.* New York, Doubleday, 1911.
Editor, with Nora A. Smith, *Christmas Stories.* New York, Grosset and Dunlap, 1916.
Editor, with Nora A. Smith, *Stories and Poems,* by Rudyard Kipling. New York, Grosset and Dunlap, 1916.
Editor, with Nora A. Smith, *The Scottish Chiefs,* by Jane Porter, illustrated by N.C. Wyeth. New York, Scribner, and London, Hodder and Stoughton, 1921.
Editor, with Nora A. Smith, *Pinafore Palace Series* (*Baby's Plays and Journeys, Nursery Nonsense, Palace Bedtime, Palace Playtime*), illustrated by Ruth Hambridge. New York, Doubleday, 4 vols., 1923.
Editor, with Nora A. Smith, *Twilight Stories,* illustrated by Kathryn Draper. Boston, Houghton Mifflin, 1925.

Publications for Adults

Novels

The Village Watch-Tower. Boston, Houghton Mifflin, and London, Gay and Bird, 1895.
Marm Lisa. Boston, Houghton Mifflin, and London, Gay and Bird, 1896.
The Affair at the Inn, with others. Boston, Houghton Mifflin, and London, Gay and Bird, 1904.
The Old Peabody Pew: A Christmas Romance of a Country Church. Boston, Houghton Mifflin, and London, Constable, 1907.
Susanna and Sue. Boston, Houghton Mifflin, and London, Hodder and Stoughton, 1909.
Robinetta, with others. Boston, Houghton Mifflin, and London, Gay and Hancock, 1911.
The Story of Waitstill Baxter. Boston, Houghton Mifflin, and London, Hodder and Stoughton, 1913.
Ladies in Waiting. Boston, Houghton Mifflin, and London, Hodder and Stoughton, 1919.
The Quilt of Happiness. Boston, Houghton Mifflin, 1923.
Love by Express. Privately printed, 1924.

Short Stories

Creeping Jenny and Other New England Stories. Boston, Houghton Mifflin, 1924.

Plays

The Old Peabody Pew, adaptation of her own novel (produced Buxton, Maine, 1916). New York, French, 1917.
A Thorn in the Flesh: A Monologue, adaptation of a play by Ernest Legouvé. Boston, Badger, 1925; London, French, 1926.
Fragments of a Play, in *Poet Lore 40* (Boston), 1929.

Verse

Nine Love Songs and a Carol. Boston, Houghton Mifflin, and London, Gay and Bird, 1896.

Other

The Relation of the Kindergarten to the Public School. San Francisco, Murdock, 1891.

Children's Rights: A Book of Nursery Logic, with Nora A. Smith. Boston, Houghton Mifflin, and London, Gay and Bird, 1892.
The Republic of Childhood (*Froebel's Gifts, Froebel's Occupations, Kindergarten Principles and Practice*), with Nora A. Smith. Boston, Houghton Mifflin, 3 vols., 1895-96; London, Gay and Bird, 3 vols., 1896.
The Girl and the Kingdom: Learning to Teach. Los Angeles, City Teachers' Club, 1915.
The Writings of Kate Douglas Wiggin. Boston, Houghton Mifflin, 9 vols., 1917.
My Garden of Memory: An Autobiography. Boston, Houghton Mifflin, 1923; London, Hodder and Stoughton, 1924.
A Thanksgiving Retrospect; or, Simplicity of Life in Old New England. Boston, Houghton Mifflin, 1928.

Editor, *The Kindergarten.* New York, Harper, 1893.
Editor, *A Book of Dorcas Dishes: Family Recipes Contributed by the Dorcas Society of Hollis and Buxton.* Privately printed, 1911.

*

Critical Studies: *Kate Douglas Wiggin as Her Sister Knew Her* by Nora A. Smith, Boston, Houghton Mifflin, and London, Gay and Hancock, 1925; *Kate Douglas Wiggin's Country of Childhood* by Helen F. Benner, Orono, University of Maine Press, 1956.

* * *

Kate Douglas Wiggin is a quintessential example of the genteel, turn-of-the-century author of books for children. She was well, if spottily, educated, literate, and easily, pleasantly articulate as a writer. Neither a rebel nor a radical, she was nevertheless a confident, forward-looking woman who clearly expected to "do something" with her life and talents—as she did. She joined the kindergarten movement early, first as a student of the Froebel method, then as a highly successful teacher and promoter of kindergartens, and finally, as author of several books on the Froebel approach. Her pleasure in working with children, the amusement and interest she found in their characters (all well recorded in her autobiography, *My Garden of Memory*), provided a natural avenue to her career as a writer of children's books.

One of her first books was *The Birds' Christmas Carol,* a brief, gracefully written tale of a charming invalid girl, who extends charity to the numerous children of a poor Irish family and who dies, happy in her generosity, on Christmas Day. Everything about the story reflects its time: the idealized child, her affluent, genteel family, the sentimental mood, the message of joy in charity. It was immensely popular for many years.

Though she wrote a number of other successful children's stories, the books for which she is best remembered are *Rebecca of Sunnybrook Farm* and its later companion, *New Chronicles of Rebecca.* The flavor of these stories is strongly regional. Like her older contemporary, Sarah Orne Jewett, Wiggin knew Maine and its people well, and described them fondly but perceptively in a number of books. She recognized both the strengths and the narrowness of the rural character; while she shared the widespread American conviction about the moral value of country life, she also knew how heavily its limitations could weigh upon an ambitious mind or an unconventional personality. The books are notably less sentimental than *The Birds' Christmas Carol,* as though the chill winds of Maine had a bracing effect on Wiggin's romantic nature even at a writer's remove.

The Rebecca books are first and foremost a character study of their heroine. Rebecca, who is 10 at the beginning of her story and 17 at the end, clearly represents Wiggin's ideal of childhood and young girlhood, with her warm heart, quick intelligence, and free-flying spirit. It is an attractive, amusing portrait, interesting for what it says about the qualities of heart and mind that Wiggin (and many of her contemporaries) admired in children, interesting, too, for what she saw as reasonable expectations for a girl of such qualities. According to Wiggin's own account, the original Rebecca story grew from a single glimpse of a little girl she never met, but those who read *A Child's Journey with Dickens* may be tempted to see the young Rebecca as a self portrait by Wiggin. In any case, the image is glowingly painted, though not so romanticized as to make it a bad fit within the authentic realism of its setting. The charm of the books has not eroded with the years; they are still engaging and often funny, especially on Rebecca's younger years. Had their reputation not been blighted by the Hollywood film that borrowed the name (but nothing more) from the first book, they might find more readers today.

Wiggin belonged to the great age of children's literature that flourished on either side of the century's turn; she was, in fact, one of its shining lights. Though largely neglected today, her work helped to set a creditable standard of literary competence for children's books. She deserves her place in any critical history of literature for the young.

—Anne Scott MacLeod

WILDER, Laura (Elizabeth) Ingalls

Nationality: American. **Born:** Pepin, Wisconsin, 7 February 1867. **Education:** Schools in Walnut Grove, Minnesota, Burr Oak, Iowa, and De Smet, Dakota Territory. **Family:** Married Almanzo James Wilder in 1885 (died 1949); one daughter. **Career:** Schoolteacher, De Smet, 1882-85; farmer in De Smet, 1885-90 and 1892-94, and from 1894 in Mansfield, Missouri; lived in Florida, 1890-92. Columnist, *Missouri Ruralist,* 1911-24; poultry editor, St. Louis *Star*; secretary-treasurer, Mansfield Farm Loan Association, 1919-27. **Award:** American Library Association Laura Ingalls Wilder award, 1954. **Died:** 10 February 1957.

Publications for Children

Fiction

Little House in the Big Woods, illustrated by Helen Sewell. New York, Harper, 1932; London, Methuen, 1956.
Farmer Boy, illustrated by Helen Sewell. New York, Harper, 1933; London, Lutterworth Press, 1965.
Little House on the Prairie, illustrated by Helen Sewell. New York, Harper, 1935; London, Methuen, 1957.
On the Banks of Plum Creek, illustrated by Helen Sewell and Mildred Boyle. New York, Harper, 1937; London, Methuen, 1958.

By the Shores of Silver Lake, illustrated by Helen Sewell and Mildred Boyle. New York, Harper, 1939; London, Lutterworth Press, 1961.
The Long Winter, illustrated by Helen Sewell and Mildred Boyle. New York, Harper, 1940; London, Lutterworth Press, 1962.
Little Town on the Prairie, illustrated by Helen Sewell and Mildred Boyle. New York, Harper, 1941; London, Lutterworth Press, 1963.
These Happy Golden Years, illustrated by Helen Sewell and Mildred Boyle. New York, Harper, 1943; London, Lutterworth Press, 1964.
The First Four Years, illustrated by Garth Williams. New York, Harper, 1971; Guildford, Surrey, Lutterworth Press, 1973.

PUBLICATIONS FOR ADULTS

Other

On the Way Home: The Diary of a Trip from South Dakota to Mansfield, Missouri, in 1894, with Rose Wilder Lane. New York, Harper, 1962.
West from Home: Letters from Laura Ingalls Wilder to Almanzo Wilder, San Francisco 1915, edited by Roger Lea MacBride. New York, Harper, 1974; Guildford, Surrey, Lutterworth Press, 1976.
A Little House Sampler, with Rose Wilder Lane, edited by William T. Anderson. Lincoln, University of Nebraska Press, 1988.
Little House in the Ozarks: A Laura Ingalls Wilder Sampler, the Rediscovered Writings (nonfiction), edited by Stephen W. Hines. London, Nelson, 1991.
Going to Town, illustrated by Renee Graef. New York, HarperCollins, 1994.
Winter Days in the Big Woods, illustrated by Renee Graef. New York, HarperCollins, 1994.

*

Bibliography: *Laura Ingalls Wilder: A Bibliography* by Mary J. Mooney-Getoff, Southold, New York, Wise Owl Press, 1980.

Manuscript Collections: Laura Ingalls Wilder Home and Museum, Mansfield, Missouri; Pomona Public Library, California; Detroit Public Library.

Critical Studies: *The Life of Laura Ingalls Wilder* by Donald Zochert, New York, Avon, 1977; *Laura Ingalls Wilder: American Authoress* by Sheila Black, New York, Kipling Press, 1987; *The Plum Creek Story of Laura Ingalls Wilder* by William T. Anderson, Davison, Michigan, Anderson, 1987, and *The Horn Book's Laura Ingalls Wilder* edited by Anderson, Davison, Michigan, Anderson, 1987; *Laura Ingalls Wilder* by Janet Spaeth, Boston, Twayne, 1987.

* * *

Laura Ingalls Wilder was in her 60s when, at her daughter's urging, she began to set down in written form her extraordinarily vivid memories of childhood during the 1870s and 1880s in the pioneer middle west. The result was not a simple autobiography but a cycle of shorter books whose third-person device gave them the agreeable perspective of fiction. Published in America in the 1930s and 1940s they soon achieved classic status both as history and as narrative—a superb set of stories, most of them as apt for the very young as for other readers. Though, oddly, they did not appear in England until well after World War II (which blocked so much publication), the Wilder books are as much admired today on this side of the Atlantic as on the other.

The first of the books, *Little House in the Big Woods,* establishes the characters if not the essential intimate solitude of the best of the later tales. The family—parents and three little girls, Mary, Laura, and baby Carrie—live in a log cabin in the Wisconsin woods. The children have never seen a town or store, but they know how cheese and butter are made, how skins are turned into leather, how an old-fashioned rifle is cleaned and reloaded—a long slow business, so the first shot has to kill. Mary is golden-haired, obedient, and good. Laura, even at five years old, is restless, fearless, inquisitive, quick to turn thought into action; she is often in trouble, and discipline is stern. But behind the rules is father (Pa) who, with only an axe and some trees, can make houses, tables, beds; who can please Laura by refraining from shooting a wolf or even an animal needed for food when its behaviour interests him; who will take down his fiddle each night and teach them songs and dances. We are made aware too of the uncomplaining resourceful mother, ready to take up her roots again and again, and create an orderly home wherever they next alight.

For even now too many people are settling near the woods for Pa's liking. And so, in *Little House on the Prairie* (one of the best of all the books) the westward journeying starts. They leave in the chill and early spring, for their covered wagon, drawn by two horses, must cross the Mississippi before the ice can thaw. And indeed, once they are over the ominous cracks are heard. Another river is crossed on a raft; at a flooded fording place father has to swim with the terrified horses, the wagon sagging, half-submerged, behind. A site for a home is found; log by log (carefully watched by Laura) Pa builds house and furniture. A reader could do the same (on model scale, at least) from the description. Cowboys drive their huge herds past the door; Pa helps, and earns a cow and calf. The family are all struck down by "fever and ague" (malaria); the dog, which normally hates strangers, goes out to look for help. And Mr. Edwards, their bachelor neighbour, turns up on Christmas Eve. Like one of those Bret Harte characters at Roaring Camp he has gone to the town, 40 miles away, to find presents for the children, and has swum with them through the creek. (This, with Edwards's account of his meeting with Santa Claus, is a splendid episode.)

But never far from the doorstep, or from the family's thoughts, are the Indians, whose land it really is. Of course, as Pa says, "when white settlers move into a country the Indians have to move on." Or is this too simple? A threatened attack on the house is quelled only by the intervention of an Indian chief, one of the Osage people, a noble and enigmatic warrior known as Soldat du Chene. And yet, the Ingalls family must move on, for the new line drawn by the government sets them in Indian territory.

On the Banks of Plum Creek takes the family to Minnesota, after the usual long slow journey; now they are near enough to a town for Laura and Mary to walk each day to school. They timidly go to a party given by the storekeeper's vulgar and spoilt little daughter. (What clothes should one wear? how behave?) All their new security now lies with the wheat, a magnificent crop which is soon to be harvested. Pa will be able to have new boots at last, Laura reflects. But why is the light so queer? A cloud seems to be blotting out the sun:

> It was not like any cloud they had ever seen before. It was a cloud of something like snowflakes, but they were larger than snowflakes, and thin and glittering. Light shone through each flickering particle. There was no wind. The grasses were still and the hot air did not stir but the edge of the cloud came on across the sky faster than wind. The hair stood up on dog Jack's neck.

Something hits Laura's head and falls to the ground; it is a grasshopper, in the van of a vast invasion. The creatures ravage all growing things for scores of miles; then they lay their eggs in the fields for the following season. There can be no more school that year for the girls; no boots for Pa. *By the Shores of Silver Lake* tells, at the start, of a new baby, Grace. But Mary is now blind, after scarlet fever, and the land has been so weakened by locusts that they move on again. Pa takes a timekeeper's job at a railway camp in Dakota Territory, and when the camp is closed for the winter the family stays alone on the shores of the lake, 60 miles away from human dwellings. Spring will be time enough to trek to the town to file the claim for the perfect piece of land that Pa has found. Or *will* he be in time?

The Long Winter, which follows, is surely the most memorable of all the Wilder books. An October Indian summer changes overnight to ice and blizzard—and the ice and blizzard continue for an incredible seven months. The train with supplies is blocked in a mountain of hard-packed snow, and must stay there until spring. The inhabitants of the little town survive as well as they can on what they have. When fuel gives out in the Ingalls home, Pa and the girls endlessly plait hard twists of hay for burning. Wheat grains are continually ground in the coffee mill to make a kind of bread, almost their only food. In the "dark twilight" of the day, Laura feels that she can never escape from:

> the hateful ceaseless pounding of the storm. The coffee mill's handle ground round and round, it must not stop. It seemed to make her part of the whirling winds driving the snow round and round over the earth and in the air, whirling and beating at Pa on the way to the stable, whirling and shrieking at the lonely houses, whirling the snow between them and up to the sky and far away, whirling forever over the endless prairie.

Then, when the last of the wheat gives out, two young men, Almanzo Wilder and his equally reckless friend Cap Garland, set out over 20 miles of trackless wastes to find a rumoured settler who *might* have a hoard of grain. Their journey and the return, horses and sacks constantly falling into holes and airpockets, are described in characteristic unstressed detail. It is a miniature epic, none the less.

Little Town on the Prairie covers the years when Laura is 14 and 15, a schoolgirl hoping to qualify for being a teacher at 16 and so help to pay towards Mary's fees at a college for the blind. The dashing Almanzo Wilder, whom all the girls admire, sees her home. Though still under age, she is offered her first schoolteaching post, at a settlement some 12 miles of prairie away. And so, at the start of *These Happy Golden Years* she leaves home for the first time. Some of the pupils at the tiny school, boys as well as girls, are older than she is herself (she is not yet 16). Her lodgings are with a half-deranged slatternly housewife who desperately longs to be back in town; the weather is bitterly cold. Yet on Friday afternoon she hears the sound of sleigh bells; Almanzo has come to take her home (and brings her back on the Sunday); so he continues to do, in the worst of weathers, until the term's contract ends. And the book closes with a fresh beginning, as Laura, at 18, now Mrs. Wilder, steps into her new home on "the tree claim." To avoid an expensive family wedding they have married without fuss in the local minister's parlour, she in her new homemade black cashmere and old blue-lined poke bonnet. Characteristically, she has asked for the word "obey" not to be used. "I cannot make a promise that I will not keep." (Almanzo's early story can be found in *Farmer Boy,* actually the second book written in the series.) Finally, *The First Four Years,* a curiously moving book, tells how the marriage took shape. Those years were hard—sickness, accidents, poverty, farming disasters. Two children were born; one died. But, the four years over, Laura knows that after all, for good or ill, she and Almanzo will live their lives on the land.

What are the qualities that keep these books alive? As tales in the "family" genre they have, of course, immense appeal—yet readers drawn to themes of solitude find them of no less interest. For one thing, they present a small close group of people alone in ranges of uninhabited country, a geographical isolation that gives peculiar intensity to the compact sheltering home, where both necessities and luxuries (including birthday and Christmas gifts)—pastimes too—must so often be made, found, grown, or improvised. (This is the atmosphere that television versions have signally failed to understand or present.) In our overcrowded scene today, the Ingalls' life seems less like fact than fantasy. What must be said is that Laura Ingalls Wilder was a more gifted writer than she knew. Her power of exact recall is matched by her ability, long years after, to fix in words what was seen, heard, felt by the observing child. At the end of the first book Laura voices something of the immediacy that is her most shining trait:

> She was glad that the cosy house, and Pa and Ma, and the firelight and the music, were now. They could not be forgotten she thought, because now is now. It can never be a long time ago.

—Naomi Lewis

WILLARD, Nancy (Margaret)

Nationality: American. **Born:** Ann Arbor, Michigan, 26 June 1936. **Education:** University of Michigan, Ann Arbor (five Hopwood awards), B.A. 1958, Ph.D. in English 1963; Stanford University, California (Woodrow Wilson fellow), M.A. 1960. **Family:** Married Eric Lindbloom in 1964; one son. **Career:** Since 1965 Lecturer in English, Vassar College, Poughkeepsie, New York; since 1975 Instructor, Bread Loaf Writers Conference. **Awards:** Devins Memorial award, for poetry, 1967; O. Henry award, for short story, 1970; National Endowment for the Arts grant, 1976, 1987; Creative Artists Public Service award, 1977; Lewis Carroll Shelf Award, 1977, 1979; *New York Times* Outstanding Book award, 1981; Golden Kite Fiction Honor award, 1981; American Library Association Newbery Medal, 1982; American Book Award nominee, 1982; National Book Critics Circle Award nomination, 1989; Michigan Author award, 1994. **Agent:** Jean V. Naggar

Literary Agency, 216 E 75th Street, New York, NY 10021, U.S.A. **Address:** Vassar College, Department of English, Raymond Avenue, Poughkeepsie, New York 12601, U.S.A.

PUBLICATIONS FOR CHILDREN

Fiction

Sailing to Cythera and Other Anatole Stories, illustrated by David McPhail. New York, Harcourt Brace, 1974.
The Snow Rabbit, illustrated by Laura Lydecker. New York, Putnam, 1975.
Shoes Without Leather, illustrated by Laura Lydecker. New York, Putnam, 1976.
The Well-Mannered Balloon, illustrated by Haig and Regina Shekerjian. New York, Harcourt Brace, 1976.
Strangers' Bread, illustrated by David McPhail. New York, Harcourt Brace, 1977.
Simple Pictures Are Best, illustrated by Tomie de Paola. New York, Harcourt Brace, 1977; London, Collins, 1978.
The Highest Hit, illustrated by Emily McCully. New York, Harcourt Brace, 1978.
Papa's Panda, illustrated by Lillian Hoban. New York, Harcourt Brace, 1979.
The Island of the Grass King: The Further Adventures of Anatole, illustrated by David McPhail. New York, Harcourt Brace, 1979.
The Marzipan Moon, illustrated by Marcia Sewall. New York, Harcourt Brace, 1981.
Uncle Terrible: More Adventures of Anatole, illustrated by David McPhail. New York, Harcourt Brace, 1982.
The Nightgown of the Sullen Moon, illustrated by David McPhail. New York, Harcourt Brace, 1983.
The Mountains of Quilt, illustrated by Tomie de Paola. San Diego, Harcourt Brace, 1987.
Firebrat, illustrated by David Wiesner. New York, Knopf, 1988.
The High Rise Glorious Skittle Skat Roarious Sky Pie Angel Food Cake, illustrated by Richard Jesse Watson. New York, Harcourt, 1990.
The Magic Cornfield. San Diego, Harcourt, 1997.
The Tortilla Cat, illustrated by Jeanette Winter. San Diego, Harcourt, 1998.

Reteller, *Beauty and the Beast,* illustrated by Barry Moser. New York, Harcourt, 1992.

Play

East of the Sun and West of the Moon, illustrated by Bruce Moser. San Diego, Harcourt, 1989.

Poetry

The Merry History of a Christmas Pie, with a Delicious Description of a Christmas Soup, illustrated by Haig and Regina Shekerjian. New York, Putnam, 1974.
All on a May Morning, illustrated by Haig and Regina Shekerjian. New York, Putnam, 1975.
A Visit to William Blake's Inn: Poems for Innocent and Experienced Travelers, illustrated by Alice and Martin Provensen. New York, Harcourt, 1981; London, Methuen, 1982.
Night Story, illustrated by Ilse Plume. San Diego, Harcourt, and London, Methuen, 1986.
The Voyage of the Ludgate Hill: Travels with Robert Louis Stevenson, illustrated by Alice and Martin Provensen. San Diego, Harcourt, 1987.
Pish Posh, Said Hieronymus Bosch, illustrated by Leo and Diane Dillon. New York, Harcourt, 1992.
A Starlit Somersault Downhill, illustrated by Jerry Pinkney. Boston, Little Brown, 1992.
The Sorcerer's Apprentice, illustrated by Leo, Diane, and Lee Dillon. New York, Scholastic, 1993.
An Alphabet of Angels, illustrated by the author. New York, Scholastic, 1994.
The Good-Night Blessing Book, illustrated by the author. New York, Scholastic, 1996.
Gutenberg's Gift: A Book Lover's Pop-up Book, illustrated by Bryan Leister. San Diego, Harcourt, 1996.

Nonfiction

Cracked Corn and Snow Ice Cream: A Family Almanac, illustrated by Jane Dyer. San Diego, Harcourt, 1997.

PUBLICATIONS FOR ADULTS

Novel

Things Invisible to See. New York, Knopf, 1984.
Sister Water. New York, Knopf, 1993.

Short Stories

The Lively Anatomy of God. New York, Eakins Press, 1968.
Childhood of the Magician. New York, Liveright, 1973.
Angel in the Parlor: Five Stories and Eight Essays. New York, Harcourt, 1983.

Poetry

In His Country. Ann Arbor, Michigan, Generation, 1966.
Skin of Grace. Columbia, University of Missouri Press, 1967.
A New Herball. Baltimore, Ferdinand Roten Galleries, 1968.
19 Masks for the Naked Poet. Santa Cruz, California, Kayak, 1971.
Carpenter of the Sun. New York, Liveright, 1974.
Household Tales of Moon and Water. New York, Harcourt Brace, 1982.
The Ballad of Biddy Early, illustrated by Barry Moser. New York, Knopf, 1989.
Water Walker. New York, Knopf, 1989.
Among Angels, with Jane Yolen, illustrated by S. Saelig Gallagher. San Diego, Harcourt, 1995.
Swimming Lessons: New and Selected Poems. New York, Knopf, 1998.

Other

Testimony of the Invisible Man: William Carlos Williams, Francis Ponge, Rainer Maria Rilke, Pablo Neruda. Columbia, University of Missouri Press, 1970.

A Nancy Willard Reader: Selected Poetry and Prose, edited by Robert Pack and Jay Parini. Hanover, New Hampshire, University Press of New England, 1991.

Telling Time: Angels, Ancestors, and Stories (essays). San Diego, Harcourt, 1993.

Editor, *Step Lightly: Poems for the Journey.* San Diego, Harcourt, 1998.

*

Media Adaptations: *The Nightgown of the Sullen Moon* (filmstrip), Random House, 1983; *A Visit to William Blake's Inn* (audio cassette recording), American School Publishing, 1985; *The Voyage of the Ludgate Hill* (videorecording), Random House, 1988; *A Visit to William Blake's Inn* (filmstrip), Random House, 1992.

Manuscript Collections: Kerlan Collection, University of Minnesota, Minneapolis; Special Collections, University of Michigan.

Biography: *Talk with Nancy Willard* (VHS Video), Tompkins Associates, 1993.

Illustrator: *The Letter of John to James,* 1981, and *Another Letter of John to James about Church and the Eucharist,* 1982, both by John Kater; *The Octopus Who Wanted to Juggle,* by Robert Pack, 1990.

* * *

"We need poets: to sing the hidden side of things," poet, novelist, and children's author Nancy Willard wrote in her 1988 essay "Telling Time." In her many outstanding books for children, Willard indeed explores the hidden side of things—the magical mystery worlds of night, dream, Biddy Early ("the wise woman of Clare"), poet/painter/mystic William Blake, singularly eccentric artist Hieronymus Bosch, an enchanted ocean voyage, a magic carpet quilt, even a wondrous angel food cake—with gentle sensibility, poetic vision, and lyrical expression.

Simple Pictures Are Best, one of Nancy Willard's first books for children, is a simple story of a simple shoemaker and his wife who decide to have their picture taken on their wedding anniversary. Although the photographer repeatedly advises them that "simple pictures are best", the picture becomes more and more complicated as the couple thinks of important things to include in the picture—the squash and colorful carrots from their garden, the wife's red and blue hats, the shoemaker's favorite old shoes and his newest ones, his fiddle, her spoons, and of course Puss, their one-eyed cat—until the local bull arrives, stands in front of the clicking camera, and simplifies everything!

Grandmother's patchwork quilt is transformed into a magic carpet, taking her on a fantastic voyage, in *The Mountains of Quilt,* another incremental tale. When it finally brings her back home, the quilt is no longer just a quilt or a flying carpet, but "a country of marvelous beauty: ferns, waterfalls, and green fields tufted with poppies as red as embers, where the golden cows and silver sheep grazed and gamboled together".

Come along now to the world of William Blake:
"Will you come?" said the Sun.
"Soon," said the Moon.
"How far?" said the the Star.
"I'm there," said the Air.

Blake's tigers, lambs, and sunflowers are all here, as are two mighty dragons who bake the bread, two patient angels who wash and shake the featherbeds, a shaggy old bear, a wise cow, a sullen rat, and a rabbit guide. In her Newbery Medal acceptance speech for *A Visit to William Blake's Inn: Poems for Innocent and Experienced Travelers,* Willard wrote, "The poet writes poems for people to listen to, poems to be heard as well as read." These wonderfully imaginative poems, inspired by Blake's own writing, are indeed poems to be heard as well as read as they depict scenes in the life at this imaginary inn run by William Blake.

Night Story is a quietly reassuring story poem in which a young boy takes "the night train to the country where nothing lasts," encounters cheese that shines "like a blue moon", which is eaten by a dream-mouse, which is in turn eaten by a dream-cat, and so on. Finally, the boy returns to his own country and his very own room—"where nothing changes".

Robert Louis Stevenson's 1887 Atlantic crossing inspired *The Voyage of the Ludgate Hill.* In this story poem, we again encounter birds and beasts: a card-playing baboon, an ape in a gabardine cape, five monkeys twitching their tails, stallions and mares, and a cat named Huntingtokill. "I was so happy on board that ship, I could not have believed it possible....My heart literally sang," wrote Stevenson in a letter. One hundred years later, Nancy Willard brings back the heart-song to contemporary readers—and listeners.

The Ballad of Biddy Early is a collection of "songs and poems, limericks and ballads" based on the life of the "wise woman of Clare", who lived between 1798 and 1874 and used her magical powers to heal and help: "I want to live...with crickets and cats and stones,/and when I die, I shall give back to Earth/all her gifts for the healing of hurts and ills./I shall come back in water and words and leaves". And in the vividly evocative poems of Nancy Willard.

The complex world of fifteenth-century Dutch painter Hieronymus Bosch, with its wildly fantastic birds, beasts, and everyday objects, is brought to incredible light and life in Willard's humorous story poem *Pish, Posh Said Hieronymus Bosch. Grandmother's High Rise Glorious Skittle Skat Roarious Sky Pie Angel Food Cake* is the subject of Willard's "roarious" but gentle tale by that title.

Many of Willard's titles showcase her innovation, her idiosyncratic style, and her penchant for creative risk-taking. *An Alphabet of Angels* and its companion volume, *The Good-Night Blessing Book,* feature photographs (taken by Willard) of angels and folk art, juxtaposed against her ethereal verse. In *Gutenberg's Gift,* a pop-up book, she seamlessly weaves information about the life and work of Johann Gutenberg, the inventor of movable type, into a fictionalized verse story about his struggle to complete his first printed Bible in time to give it as a Christmas gift to his wife, Anna. A series of witty postcards (illustrated with real postcards with authentic stamps and postmarks) sent by Tottem to his cousin Bottom after he becomes lost on his way to Bottom's 100th birthday party form the substance of *The Magic Cornfield.* Magic appears in the form of a cat in the picture book *The Tortilla Cat,* about a creature who appears in the night to cure the five Romero children of their fevers.

Throughout her career, Willard has been fortunate to have had illustrators—exceptional artists like David McPhail, Marcia Sewall, Tomie de Paola, Alice and Martin Provensen, Leo Dillon and Diane Dillon, and Barry Moser—who have been able to perfectly capture her unique and exceptional sensibility. And in Willard's most personal book to date, *Cracked Corn and Snow Ice Cream: A Family Almanac,* artist Jane Dyer is as much a collaborator as an illustrator. She and Willard draw upon the stories and memories of their own relatives to present folk wisdom, fun facts, garden tips, recipes, jokes, and stories in a month-by-month format that evokes the feel of country life in bygone times.

In her adult poem "Little Elegy with Books and Beasts," written in memory of Martin Provensen, Nancy Willard wrote of "that light by which we read, while he was here,/the chapter called Joy in the Book of Creation". Willard has surely made significant contributions to that chapter with her joyous books for children.

—Marcia Welsh, updated by Jackie C. Horne

WILLIAMS, Margery. See **BIANCO, Margery Williams.**

WILLIAMS, Vera B.

Nationality: American. **Born:** Vera Baker, Hollywood, California, 28 January 1927. **Education:** Attended public schools, including the High School of Music and Art in New York City; studied art with Florence Cane; Black Mountain College, North Carolina, 1945-49, B.F.A. in graphic art 1949; attended Boston Museum School. **Family:** Married Paul Williams (divorced); two daughters and one son. **Career:** Writer, graphic artist, educator, political activist; co-founder, teacher, and member Gate Hill Cooperative Community and Collaberg (Barker) alternative school for children, Stony Point, New York, 1953-1970; cook, teacher and baker, Everdale School, Ontario, Canada, 1970-73; instructor, Goddard College, Plainfield, Vermont, 1980-82; executive committee War Resisters League, 1984-87; author and illustrator of children's books since 1975. **Awards:** Parents' Choice Award for illustrations, 1981, for *Three Days on a River in a Red Canoe*; *School Library Journal* Best Children's Books list, 1982, for *A Chair for My Mother,* and 1983, for *Something Special for Me*; Caldecott Honor and *Boston Globe-Horn Book* Award for Illustration, 1983, and the Other Award from the *Children's Book Bulletin,* 1984, for *A Chair for My Mother*; Jane Addams Children's Book Award Honor, 1985, Parents' Choice Award in Literature Notable Book, and Child Study Association of America's Children's Books of the Year, 1986, all for *Music, Music for Everyone*; *New York Times* Best Illustrated Books of the Year and *Boston Globe-Horn Book* Honor Award for Illustration for *Cherries and Cherry Pits,* 1987; Caldecott Honor, 1991, for *"More More More" Said the Baby*; *Boston Globe-Horn Book* Award for Fiction, 1994, for *Scooter*; Charlotte Zolotow Award, 1998, for *Lucky Song.* **Address:** c/o Greenwillow Books, 1350 Avenue of the Americas, New York, New York 10019.

Publications for Children (illustrated by the author)

Fiction

The Great Watermelon Birthday. New York, Greenwillow, 1980.
Three Days on a River in a Red Canoe. New York, Morrow, 1981.
A Chair for My Mother. New York, Greenwillow, 1982; London, MacRae, 1984.
Something Special for Me. New York, Greenwillow, 1983; London, MacRae, 1985.
Cherries and Cherry Pits. New York, Greenwillow, 1986; as *Cherries and Cherry Stones,* London, MacRae, 1987.
Stringbean's Trip to the Shining Sea, illustrated by the author and Jennifer Williams. New York, Greenwillow, 1988.
"More More More," Said the Baby: 3 Love Stories. New York, Greenwillow, 1990.
Scooter. New York, Greenwillow, 1993.
Lucky Song. New York, Greenwillow, 1997.

Other

It's a Gingerbread House: Bake It, Build It, Eat It! New York, Greenwillow, 1978.

*

Critical Studies: *Children's Literature Review,* Vol. 9, Detroit, Gale, 1985; *Something about the Author,* Vol. 53, Detroit, Gale, 1988; review of *"More More More" Said the Baby,* in *Horn Book,* November/December 1990, 736; "The Work of Keeping Writing Play: A View through Children's Literature" by George Shannon, in *Children's Literature in Education,* Vol. 21, No. 1, March 1990, 37-43; "Inside Story: Vera Williams' *Scooter*" by Barbara Elleman, and "On Words and Wheels" by Vera B. Williams, in *Book Links,* November 1994, 42-44; "Vera B. Williams" by Pat Cummings, in *Talking With Artists,* Vol. 2, New York, Simon and Schuster, 1995, 76-81; "Scooter Is Us," *Horn Book,* January/February 1995, 22-29.

Illustrator: *Hooray for Me!* by Remy Charlip and Lilian Moore, 1975; *Our Class Presents Ostrich Feathers: A Play in Two Acts* by Barbara Brenner, 1978; *365 Reasons Not to Have Another War* (peace calendar), 1989; *Long Walks and Intimate Talks* by Grace Paley, 1991.

Vera B. Williams comments:

At various times I have helped start a cooperative housing community, an alternative school, a peace center, and a bakery where young people could work. I have worked to end nuclear power and weapons, and for women's rights. I have demonstrated and been jailed. I have produced posters, leaflets, magazine covers, drawings, paintings, short stories, and poems, as well as books.

* * *

Certain descriptors continue to surface in reviews of Vera B. Williams's work as picture-book author-illustrator: childlike, spontaneous, vibrant, joyous, fresh, loving. As appropriate as these attributes are, they often belie the careful attention and skill, as well as the consciously realized world view, that goes into each of her books. Williams's background as an experimental educator, political activist, feminist, and environmentalist has found a new but altogether consistent forum in her fiction for children.

Williams may be best known for the three picture books which make up the Rosa Trilogy (*A Chair for My Mother, Something Special for Me,* and *Music, Music for Everyone*). These books have been compared to Ezra Jack Keats's Peter books with their energetic, expressionistic illustrations and non-traditional treatment of minority children in urban settings. But Williams brings to the picture-book genre a uniquely honest and celebratory portrait of working-class culture which has seldom been executed so successfully. Williams conveys a strong sense of working-class life without glossing over the hardships or adjustments her economically disadvantaged characters face. Her books express a strong sense of solidarity, portraying loving and supportive families in which the child is not the center, but an integral, working member of a larger unit. This connectedness is the source of security and potential power; with it comes also a sense of responsibility to others.

One of the first of Williams's books to gain wide attention, *Three Days on a River in a Red Canoe,* combines techniques of fiction and nonfiction in an innovative manner. Written in the style of a journal, with diagrams, recipes, maps, and hand-drawn illustrations created by the young girl narrator, the book tells the story of the narrator, her cousin, and their two mothers as they wind their way down the river, over falls, through mishaps and adventures. Williams says, "*Three Days on a River* isn't a social issue book but I feel that my devotion to a full life for women and to an unpolluted nature and to adventure for children are all in there somehow." A later work, *Stringbean's Trip to the Shining Sea,* uses pages from a photo album and postcards, complete with carefully designed stamps, to chronicle a trip from Kansas to the Pacific Ocean taken by young Stringbean and his older brother.

The highly acclaimed *A Chair for My Mother,* the first of three books featuring Rosa, a young girl who lives with her waitress mother and grandmother, tells the story of how the three women save all their spare change in a large jar until they have enough to buy Rosa's overworked mother a "wonderful, beautiful, fat, soft armchair," to replace the chairs and sofa lost in a fire. The armchair becomes not only a much-needed resting place, it is also an object of beauty, a place of protection, a throne for three, a symbol of female solidarity.

Rosa's story continues in *Something Special for Me.* This time the coins accumulating in the jar are to be used for Rosa's birthday present. After lengthy deliberation, Rosa decides on an accordion, a gift which brings with it the heritage of her accordion-playing grandmother and the promise of future shared music making. Rosa's dilemma underscores a common Williams theme: community over individualism. With the help of her patient, playful mother, Rosa finds a way to give a present to her family as well as to herself. Again, Williams sensitizes the reader to the struggles and decisions inherent in being poor, while not romanticizing that state.

Williams's usually vibrant watercolors become especially intense and emotionally charged when the element of music is added, as it is in *Music, Music for Everyone.* The jar is empty again, and is unlikely to be replenished as long as Rosa's grandmother is sick and needs medical attention. Rosa and friends decide to earn money by performing with the band they have formed. With the help of a music teacher and lots of practice, their first appearance—at the 50th anniversary celebration of the corner grocery store—is a triumph.

In *Cherries and Cherry Pits* Williams deals with the power of creative imagination as a potential force for change. The story is framed by a narrator who relates the tales of her young artist friend, Bidemmi. The work uses two distinct styles of art to tell the story, juxtaposing the author-narrator's accomplished paintings with Bidemmi's childlike drawings made with markers. Bidemmi draws stories of people who eat cherries, ending with a vision of how she, Bidemmi, plants lots of seeds in her "junky, old yard," transforming urban blight into a glorious Garden of Eden.

Aimed at a younger audience than her previous books, the brief text in *"More More More" Said the Baby: 3 Love Stories* is rainbow-hued and integrated with the vibrant illustrations. Williams states in *Talking with Artists* that she created this book "When I was just in love with my new grandchild. I could hardly *not* write." These truly are love stories, showing 3 small children of different races being chased, held, hugged, and loved by a daddy, a grandma, and a mama. Each story vividly expresses in both words and text the love that little children elicits in adults. As Nancy Vasilakis wrote in *Horn Book,* "The rhythmic language begs to be read aloud, and young listeners are sure to wriggle with delight at all the many ways their favorite grown-ups have of saying 'I love you.'" *Lucky Song,* similar in conception and design to *"More More More," Said the Baby,* is a simple story of sequential actions. Here Williams plays with the idea of beginnings and endings by directing the reader back to the beginning at the end of her "song."

Scooter, perhaps the most original and captivating novel for younger readers since *Charlotte's Web,* marked Williams's move beyond the picture-book. Recipient of the prestigious *Boston Globe/Horn Book* award for children's fiction, it is the exuberant story of Elana Rose Rosen, her blue scooter, and her friends of all ages at Melon Hill Houses, a story and setting inspired by Williams's own childhood in the Bronx and her reading of Ruth Sawyer's *Roller Skates.* As in Williams's earlier books, the themes of individuality and community are prominent, and like *The Great Watermelon Birthday* and *Music, Music for Everyone* the story concludes with a community celebration. The book is decorated in the margins and throughout with Elana Rose's acrostics and red and black drawings, while the track of her scooter tires flow through the text (Williams says she used a Lego wheel to make the scooter tracks). Williams's award acceptance speech characteristically takes both a highly individual and communal form. All the characters in *Scooter,* Williams says, wanted to come to accept the award, but since that posed logistical problems, she instead allowed them each of them to "have their say" in individual messages, which she then delivered in her speech. They also, in true Williams fashion, appear in print in the various styles of handwriting, printing, and typefaces in which they were originally written. Elana Rose writes, "I want to say my own special *Thank You* to *My Author* for making a really long book where I could talk and talk." Vera Williams is an author who has consistently given voices to memorable characters representative of groups seldom heard.

—Nancy Tillman Romalov, updated by Linnea Hendrickson

WILLIAMSON, Henry

Nationality: British. **Born:** Parkstone, Dorset, 1 December 1895. **Education:** Colfe's Grammar School, Lewisham, London. **Mili-**

tary Service: Infantryman and officer in the Bedfordshire Regiment of the British Army, 1914-19. **Family:** Married Ida Letitia Hibbert in 1925 (divorced 1947), four sons and one daughter; remarried in 1948, one son. **Career:** Worked in the advertising department of *The Times,* London, 1919-20; broadcaster, on farming and country life, for the Western Region of the BBC, Bristol, 1930s. Briefly interned at the outbreak of World War II for Fascist sympathies. **Award:** Hawthornden prize, 1928. **Died:** 13 August 1977.

PUBLICATIONS FOR CHILDREN

Fiction

Tarka the Otter, Being His Joyful Water-Life and Death in the Country of the Two Rivers. London, Putnam, 1927; New York, Dutton, 1928.
Salar the Salmon. London, Faber, 1935; Boston, Little Brown, 1936.
Scribbling Lark. London, Faber, 1949.
The Henry Williamson Animal Saga (stories). London, Macdonald, 1960.
The Scandaroon, illustrated by Ken Lilly. London, Macdonald, 1972; New York, Saturday Review Press, 1973.

PUBLICATIONS FOR ADULTS

Novels

The Flax of Dream. London, Faber, 1936.
The Beautiful Years. London, Collins, 1921; revised edition, London, Faber, and New York, Dutton, 1929.
Dandelion Days. London, Collins, 1922; revised edition, London, Faber, and New York, Dutton, 1930.
The Dream of Fair Women. London, Collins, and New York, Dutton, 1924; revised edition, London, Faber, and Dutton, 1931.
The Pathway. London, Cape, 1928; revised edition, London, Faber, and New York, Dutton, 1929.
The Patriot's Progress, Being the Vicissitudes of Pte. John Bullock. London, Bles, and New York, Dutton, 1930.
The Gold Falcon; or, The Haggard of Love (published anonymously). London, Faber, and New York, Smith, 1933; revised edition, as Henry Williamson, Faber, 1947.
The Star-Born. London, Faber, 1933; revised edition, 1948.
The Sun in the Sands. London, Faber, 1945.
The Phasian Bird. London, Faber, 1948; Boston, Little Brown, 1950.
A Chronicle of Ancient Sunlight:
The Dark Lantern. London, Macdonald, 1951.
Donkey Boy. London, Macdonald, 1952.
Young Phillip Maddison. London, Macdonald, 1953.
How Dear Is Life. London, Macdonald, 1954.
A Fox under My Cloak. London, Macdonald, 1955.
The Golden Virgin. London, Macdonald, 1957.
Love and the Loveless: A Soldier's Tale. London, Macdonald, 1958.
A Test to Destruction. London, Macdonald, 1960.
The Innocent Moon. London, Macdonald, 1961.
It Was the Nightingale. London, Macdonald, 1962.
The Power of the Dead. London, Macdonald, 1963.
The Phoenix Generation. London, Macdonald, 1965.
A Solitary War. London, Macdonald, 1966.
Lucifer Before Sunrise. London, Macdonald, 1967.
The Gale of the World. London, Macdonald, 1969.

Short Stories and Sketches

The Peregrine's Saga and Other Stories of the Country Green. London, Collins, 1923; as *Sun Brothers,* New York, Dutton, 1925.
The Old Stag. London, Putnam, 1926; New York, Dutton, 1927.
The Linhay on the Downs. London, Mathews and Marrot, 1929.
The Ackymals. San Francisco, Windsor Press, 1929.
The Village Book. London, Cape, and New York, Dutton, 1930.
The Labouring Life. London, Cape, 1932; as *As the Sun Shines,* New York, Dutton, 1933.
On Foot in Devon; or, Guidance and Gossip, Being a Monologue in Two Reels. London, Maclehose, 1933.
The Linhay on the Downs and Other Adventures in the Old and New World. London, Cape, 1934.
Life in a Devon Village (based on material in *The Village Book* and *The Labouring Life*). London, Faber, 1945.
Tales of a Devon Village (based on material in *The Village Book* and *The Labouring Life*). London, Faber, 1945.
Tales of Moorland and Estuary. London, Macdonald, 1953.
In the Woods. Llandeilo, Wales, St. Albert's Press, 1960.
Collected Nature Stories. London, Macdonald, 1970.

Play

Television Documentary: *The Vanishing Hedgerow,* 1972.

Other

The Lone Swallows. London, Collins, 1922; New York, Dutton, 1926; revised edition, as *The Lone Swallows and Other Essays of Boyhood and Youth,* London and New York, Putnam, 1933.
The Wet Flanders Plain. London, Beaumont Press, and New York, Dutton, 1929; revised edition, London, Faber, 1929.
The Wild Red Deer of Exmoor: A Digression on the Logic and Ethics and Economics of Stag-Hunting in England Today. London, Faber, 1931.
Devon Holiday. London, Cape, 1935.
Goodbye, West Country (diary). London, Putnam, 1937; Boston, Little Brown, 1938.
The Children of Shallowford (autobiography). London, Faber, 1939; revised edition, 1959.
As the Sun Shines: Selections. London, Faber, 1941.
The Story of a Norfolk Farm (autobiography). London, Faber, 1941.
Genius of Friendship: "T.E. Lawrence". London, Faber, 1941.
Norfolk Life, with L.R. Haggard. London, Faber, 1943.
A Clear Water Stream (autobiography). London, Faber, 1958; New York, Washburn, 1959; revised edition, London, Macdonald and Jane's, 1975.
The Weekly Despatch: Articles Contributed by Henry Williamson in the Years 1920-21. N.p., Henry Williamson Society, 1983.
Days of Wonder (essays). N.p., Henry Williamson Society, 1987.

Editor, *A Soldier's Diary of the Great War,* by Douglas Herbert Bell. London, Faber, 1929.
Editor, *An Anthology of Modern Nature Writing.* London, Nelson, 1936.
Editor, *Richard Jefferies: Selections of His Work.* London, Faber, 1937.
Editor, *Hodge and His Masters,* by Richard Jefferies. London, Methuen, 1937.
Editor, *Unreturning Spring, Being the Poems, Sketches, Stories and Letters of James Farrar.* London, Williams and Norgate, 1950.
Editor, *My Favourite Country Stories.* London, Lutterworth Press, 1966.

*

Bibliography: *A Bibliography and a Critical Survey of the Works of Henry Williamson* by I. Waveney Girvan, Chipping Campden, Gloucestershire, Alcuin Press, 1931.

Critical Studies: *Henry Williamson: A Tribute* by Ted Hughes, London, Rainbow Press, 1979; *Henry Williamson: The Man, The Writings* edited by Brocard Sewell, Padstow, Cornwall, Tabb House, 1980; *An Appreciation of Henry Williamson* by Daniel Farson, London, Joseph, 1982; *The Novels of Henry Williamson* by John M. Murry, n.p., Henry Williamson Society, 1986; *Henry Williamson: A Portrait* by Daniel Farson, London, Robinson, 1986.

* * *

Henry Williamson's *Tarka the Otter* was not written for children. But, like other notable works in this genre (such as *Red Fox* by Charles G.D. Roberts and *Abandoned* by G.D. Griffiths), it belongs as naturally to the junior library as to the adult. This branch of fiction—the factual (i.e., non-fantastic) animal narrative, imaginatively seen from the animal view—has no age barriers.

The book grew out of a happening in North Devon where the young Williamson, unsettled after his war experiences, had come to rediscover himself. He had managed to rear an infant otter cub whose mother had been shot by a farmer; it grew to be a playful, close companion. But it was caught in a gin trap and, though released, fled in terror. For many weeks Williamson looked for its maimed footprint, following the two rivers Taw and Torridge, from the estuary where they met to the Dartmoor source of each, but he never found his protégé again. However, this close continual searching of earth and plant and water brought him almost inside the otter's world, and that of other wild creatures. (He extended this knowledge, it must be said, by going out with the local otter hunt.) That wild two-rivered region, from Dartmoor to the sea, is the country of the book.

Williamson's claim to have rewritten *Tarka* 17 times can well be believed, so vivid and meticulous are the writing and the detail. In theme it follows the customary plan of such books: a wild creature's birth, education, journeyings, mating; the hazards of nature (the winter chapter is a classic); the direr hazards brought by man—gun, snare, gin trap, poison, prongs, the hunter and the hounds. It is the human hand that brings in tragedy—that adds to fact (if you like) the dimension of fiction. To read the book is a complete experience, for reader, like writer, lives and perceives at otter level. In this richly inhabited scene, everything has its story. Open the pages anywhere:

> A stain began to move in the water, and a plaice flapped off the bottom and swam in what it thought was the beginning of a flood, when worms came swirling into the Junction Pool. This sea-fish had lived a strange and lonely life in fresh water ever since it had been swallowed in the estuary by a heron and ejected alive from the crop a quarter of an hour afterwards when the bird, flying up the valley, had been shot by a water-bailiff. The shape of an otter loomed in the water, and the plaice swam down again in a rapid, waving slant, perceived by a one-eyed eel that was lying with its tail inside a bullock's skull, wedged in a cleft of rock. Thrust through the eel's blank socket was the rusty barbed point of a hook, the shank of which stuck out of its mouth—a hook almost straightened before the line had broken. Tarka swam up....

What an abundance of narrative is here!

Chance—and the impetus of success (it won the prestigious Hawthornden Prize)—have made *Tarka* the best-known work of its kind. It also contains the best of Williamson's writing. He always disputed this. But his later fiction (outside the other "nature" books written in *Tarka's* wake—*Salar the Salmon,* for instance) is too often flawed by obsessions that can't be overlooked in any assessment: vanity and self-pity (animals know neither); a perverse attraction to power and cruelty which made him a besotted admirer of Hitler. The alibi of his own war experiences, valid at first, long became threadbare as cover for this mania. *Tarka,* written between 1923 and 1927, often in conditions of extreme domestic hardship and poverty, a book where plant and animal life hold the foreground, is still clear of these maladies.

Except perhaps for one point, already hinted at. In 1927 (his biographer relates) Williamson called on Hardy, boasting of all the praise he had had for the novel. Hardy mildly asked if he did not think otter hunting rather cruel. Disconcerted, Williamson murmured that it might be, but that he did not want to take sides. And yet—in this case the writer surpassed the man. In his exact describing the truth comes through about a particularly gross and ugly "sport"; the facts carry their own indictment.

Nevertheless, the irony remains that the first edition of *Tarka* was dedicated to the Master of the local Hunt. The dedicatee's name remains in modern editions, but the embarrassing detail of his occupation is usually removed.

—Naomi Lewis

WILSON, Barbara Ker

Nationality: British. **Born:** Sunderland, County Durham, 24 September 1929. **Education:** North London Collegiate School, 1938-48. **Family:** Married Peter Richard Tahourdin in 1956; two daughters. **Career:** Assistant editor, Oxford University Press, London, 1949-54; children's books editor, Bodley Head, London, 1954-57, William Collins, London, 1957-62, Angus and Robertson, Sydney, 1965-73, and Hodder and Stoughton, Sydney, 1973-76. Since 1978 editor, Readers Digest Condensed Books, Sydney. **Address:** 1/10 Harnett Avenue, Mosman Bay, New South Wales 2088, Australia.

Publications for Children

Fiction

Path-Through-the-Woods, illustrated by Charles Stewart. London, Constable, and New York, Criterion, 1958.
The Wonderful Cornet, illustrated by Raymond Briggs. London, Hamish Hamilton, 1958.
The Lovely Summer, illustrated by Marina Hoffer. London, Constable, and New York, Dodd Mead, 1960.
Last Year's Broken Toys. London, Constable, 1962; as *In Love and War,* Cleveland, World, 1963.
Ann and Peter in Paris [and *in London*], illustrated by Harry and Ilse Toothill. London, Muller, 2 vols., 1963-65.
A Story to Tell: Thirty Tales for Little Children, illustrated by Sheila Sancha. London, J. Garnet Miller, 1964.
Beloved of the Gods. London, Constable, 1965; as *In the Shadow of Vesuvius,* Cleveland, World, 1965.
A Family Likeness, illustrated by Astra Lacis Dick. London, Constable, 1967; as *The Biscuit-Tin Family,* Cleveland, World, 1968.
Hiccups and Other Stories: Thirty Tales for Little Children, illustrated by Richard Kennedy. London, J. Garnet Miller, 1971.
The Persian Carpet Story, with Jacques Cadry, illustrated by Nyorie Bungey. Sydney, Methuen, 1981; London, Methuen, 1982.
Kelly the Sleepy Koala, illustrated by Lorraine Itannay. Sydney, Golden Press, 1983.
Molly. Sydney, Golden Press, 1983.
Kevin the Kookaburra, illustrated by Sue Price. Sydney, Golden Press, 1983.
Acacia Terrace, illustrated by David Fielding. Sydney, Ashton, 1988.

Other

Scottish Folk Tales and Legends, illustrated by Joan Kiddell-Monroe. London, Oxford University Press, and New York, Walck, 1954.
Fairy Tales of Germany, illustrated by Gertrude Mittelmann, (*Ireland, Mexico,* and *Persia,* all illustrated by G.W. Miller, *India,* illustrated by Rene Mackensie, *Russia,* illustrated by Jacqueline Athram, *France,* illustrated by William McLaren, *England,* illustrated by John S. Goodall). London, Cassell, and New York, Dutton, 8 vols., 1959-61.
Look at Books, illustrated by John Woodcock. London, Hamish Hamilton, 1960.
Legends of the Round Table, illustrated by Marra Calati. London, Hamlyn, 1966.
Greek Fairy Tales, illustrated by Harry Toothill. London, Muller, 1966; Chicago, Follett, 1968.
Animal Folk Tales, illustrated by Mirko Hanák. London, Hamlyn, 1968; New York, Grosset and Dunlap, 1971.
Australia, Wonderland Down Under. New York, Dodd Mead, 1969.
Tales Told to Kabbarli: Aboriginal Legends Collected by Daisy Bates, illustrated by Harold Thomas. Sydney and London, Angus and Robertson, and New York, Crown, 1972.
The Magic Fishbones and Other Fabulous Tales of Asia, illustrated by Susanne Dolesch. Sydney, Angus and Robertson, 1973; London, Angus and Robertson, 1975.
The Magic Bird and Other Fabulous Tales from Europe, illustrated by Susanne Dolesch. Sydney, Angus and Robertson, 1973; London, Angus and Robertson, 1975.
Just for a Joyride (reader). Sydney, Holt Rinehart, 1977.
The Turtle and the Island: Folk Tales from Papua New Guinea, edited by Donald S. Stokes, illustrated by Tony Oliver. Sydney and London, Hodder and Stoughton, 1978.
The Willow Pattern Story (Chinese tale), illustrated by Lucienne Fontannaz. Sydney and London, Angus and Robertson, 1978.
Wishbones: A Folk Tale from China, illustrated by Meilo So. New York, Macmillan, 1993.

Editor, *The Second Young Eve.* London, Blackie, 1962.
Editor, *What a Girl* [and *Boy*] *Should Know about Sex,* by Bernhardt Gottlieb. London, Constable, 2 vols., 1962.
Editor, *Australian Kaleidoscope,* illustrated by Margery Gill. Sydney and London, Collins, 1968; New York, Meredith Press, 1969.
Editor, *A Handful of Ghosts: Thirteen Eerie Tales by Australian Authors.* Sydney, Hodder and Stoughton, 1976; London, Hodder and Stoughton, 1977.
Editor, *Alice's Adventures in Wonderland,* by Lewis Carroll, translated into Pitjantjatjara by Nancy Sheppard, illustrated by Byron Sewell. Adelaide, Adelaide University Press, 1976.
Editor, *Illustrated Treasury of Australian Stories and Verses for Children.* Melbourne, Nelson, 1987.

Publications for Adults

Novels

Jane Austen in Australia. London, Secker and Warburg, 1984; as *Antipodes Jane,* New York, Viking, 1985.
The Quade Inheritance. Richmond, Victoria, Heinemann, and London, Secker and Warburg, 1988; New York, St. Martin's Press, 1989.

Other

Writing for Children. London, Boardman, 1960; New York, Watts, 1961.
Noel Streatfeild. London, Bodley Head, 1961; New York, Walck, 1964.

*

Barbara Ker Wilson comments:
Social history, with a special background interest in the historical position of women, seems, in retrospect, to have formed the springboard for my teenage-reader novels: *Path-Through-the-Woods, The Lovely Summer, Last Year's Broken Toys,* and *A Family Likeness.* My main aim, however, was and will for future work remain to tell a *story.* This enjoyment in storytelling extends, too, to collections of stories for very young children, and most of the tales in my two collections *A Story to Tell* and *Hiccups* are often broadcast and televised. My other very strong interest is in folklore where I feel the often artificial borderline between literature for the young and for the adult most satisfyingly disappears.

* * *

Barbara Ker Wilson's background is part English, part Australian, and though most of the stories in *A Story to Tell* and *Hiccups* would be acceptable to the under-fives from either country, some depend on Australian setting. Some are short invented fairytales, but most are designed to stimulate imaginative parents who make up stories for and about their own small children.

Ann and Peter in Paris and *Ann and Peter in London* are formula writing, but with enough plot to make the information palatable. Ann and Peter, like most natives, know less about London than the average visitor, an ingenious device which gives Peter the opportunity to read up the guide book before their journeys.

Path-Through-the-Woods is the story behind a patchwork quilt. In a series of pictures of the life of a Victorian family—unusual because the eldest sister breaks from convention and becomes a pioneer woman doctor—the middle-class atmosphere is well conveyed. Jemima's death coincides with the launching of the Great Eastern and generally facts are conveyed incidentally.

The Lovely Summer is really several summers, just before and during World War I. The campaign for women's suffrage and implicitly the feminist movement is shown in the lives of three girls of different social classes. This is a convincing and readable book, with a fairly broad-minded approach to its theme—violence versus non-violence.

Probably the best book she will ever write, *Last Year's Broken Toys* reflects the author's own childhood before and during the last war. In a sense the war is the "hero." There are dozens of characters but however brief the glimpses they are all real people. There is no straight plot, boy and girl friendships change, odd coincidences happen though the participants are not always aware of them. Some die, most survive. All the ends are tied up for the reader but not for the people involved—this is real life.

Beloved of the Gods is a competent and thoroughly researched novel about ancient Rome and the destruction of Pompeii, but there is perhaps too much concern with historical detail so that the characters come alive only occasionally.

A Family Likeness is an Australian story paralleling and contrasting the lives of the present-day girl and her mid-19th-century forebears. The switches are cleverly done, but one feels that the Victorian episodes were thought of first and that therefore the modern Debbie is less alive and less interesting. The history seems to intrude more than it did in *Last Year's Broken Toys* although there was so much more of it in the earlier book. Perhaps there is more need to "explain" things of a century ago, especially in Australia.

—Margaret M. Tye

WILSON, Gina

Nationality: British. **Born:** Gina Jones, Abergele, North Wales, 1 April 1943. **Education:** Manchester High School for Girls, 1955-61; University of Edinburgh, 1961-65, M.A. (honours) in English 1965; Mount Holyoke College, South Hadley, Massachusetts, 1965-66. **Family:** Married Edward Wilson in 1972; two daughters and one son. **Career:** Assistant editor, *Scottish National Dictionary,* 1967-73, and *Dictionary of the Older Scottish Tongue,* 1972-73, Edinburgh. **Agent:** Gina Pollinger, 222 Old Brompton Road, London SW5 0B2, England.

Publications for Children

Fiction

Cora Ravenwing. London, Faber, and New York, Atheneum, 1980.
A Friendship of Equals. London, Faber, 1981.
The Whisper. London, Faber, 1982.
All Ends Up. London, Faber, 1984.
Family Feeling. London, Faber, 1986.
Just Us. London, Faber, 1988.
Polly Pipes Up, illustrated by Jacqui Thomas. London, Heinemann, 1989.
Wompus Galumpus, illustrated by Clive Scruton. London, Walker, 1989.
I Hope You Know..., illustrated by Alison Catley. London, Hutchinson, 1989.
Riding the Great White. London, Bodley Head, 1992.
Prowlpuss, illustrated by David Parkins. London, Walker, and Cambridge, Massachusetts, Candlewick, 1994.

Verse

Jim-Jam Pyjamas, illustrated by Sally Anne Lambert. London, Cape, 1989.

* * *

Gina Wilson's chief strengths lie in accurate delineation of character development within small groups—gang, family, school—and the difficult transition from child to adult understanding.

Her first novel, *Cora Ravenwing,* contained several themes which were to be developed later. The narrative is presented as a reminiscence of childhood set down by an adult: the action takes place in an English Village in the 1950s. Rebecca's family comes to Okefield. Rebecca recounts her clash of loyalties. On the one hand is the majority village society her parents wish to enter and the school peer group—Hermione, Susan, and Barbara—with whom Rebecca identifies. On the other is Cora, the ambiguous outsider, living with her father, surrounded by suspicion after her mother's death—"a little stick-like figure ... beady eyes and jerky little head with the flapping black fringe." The cost of keeping in with the peer group and maintaining friendship with the outcast is too great: Rebecca loses both. But, in a process crucial to Wilson's novels, she gains self-knowledge, grows through the experience, and takes on valuable insights for life.

The struggle involves other clashes: honesty and artifice, reality and falsity. A key character is Hermione—rich, pretty, self-regarding—a would-be sensitive poet. But her work, compared with the spare honesty of Cora's mother's observations and the artless purity of Cora's own voice, is hollow, indulgent, in the end worthless. Another key character is the egregious Mrs. Briggs, main fomenter of feeling against Cora. In a superbly ambiguous—even frightening—moment towards the story's climax, she is suddenly seen as a witch.

A Friendship of Equals and *The Whisper* reinforced Wilson's reputation as chronicler of friendship, jealousy, and attainment of self-understanding. In the first named novel, Stella is rich but physically handicapped: Louise lives at the village shop. The friendship is seen by some as ill-assorted: adult attitudes are important in this narrative—especially the ambiguous Agnes, long-serving nurse to Stella. *The Whisper* also deals with a difficult relationship, when Lily has to cope with her "cuckoo-in-the-nest" cousin Marie, seemingly supplanting her in her parent's affections.

The influence of adults—sometimes constructive, sometimes baneful—looms large in her next books. The fallible, dishonest conduct of three sets of parents in *All Ends Up* causes great difficulties for Claudia, Sylvie, and Anna. In *Family Feeling,* the clash between the generations is overt and powerful. Alice Mather's father dies and her mother remarries. Donald is divorced, has a brilliant but withdrawn son, Edwin, and a lonely, volatile—even disturbed—younger daughter Corinna. Alice begins a difficult period of adjustment in her new home. Her school friendship with Josie Stapleton is firmly based though it leads to alarming, dangerous experiences with boys. However, the crisis comes at home. She and Edwin develop a tentative but profound relationship which can only be called love. Corinna, racked with jealousy at what she regards as Alice's treachery, becomes an agent of destruction: the family group cannot contain this unlooked-for, explosive situation. Meanwhile, Josie's mother, quiet and unremarked, dies in a superbly-worked subplot throwing into sharp relief the novel's central scale of values. *Family Feeling* is a book of rare power dealing confidently and honestly with urgent adolescent themes.

After *Just Us,* Wilson wrote the remarkable *Riding the Great White,* like *Cora Ravenwing* a first person reminiscence of a formative time in a Buckinghamshire village. Gin looks back to when their gang, the Thakers, despite her efforts, finally broke up. Ironically, the main agent of disintegration is Gav, a visitor oddly reminiscent of Cora—"a tall, thin figure, stiff as a scarecrow ... dressed all in black, picking his way spikily." Gav is urban, dangerous, and to Gin—entirely fascinating. Their doomed relationship develops frighteningly quickly, causing fraught feelings among the other Thakers. It evaporates with similar speed, leaving Gin grown-up and desolate. But she comes to terms with Haz (Aunt Hazel, with whom she lives) and her right to a settled relationship, with the inevitability of change and the taking-on of new experience. *Riding the Great White* is a complex, subtle, fascinating novel. The title refers to a roller coaster ride which serves as an appropriate image for Gin's experiences.

Significantly, Wilson's present preoccupation is towards writing for adults. However, 1989 saw a new departure; picture-book texts couched in memorable, rhythmic language: *I Hope You Know...*, *Wompus Golumpus,* and the narrative poem *Prowlpuss.* Her poetry collection, *Jim-Jam Pyjamas,* contains finely-crafted, filigree verse representing many moods.

Wilson's achievement and range are impressive. She stands as a vivid and accurate portrayer of adolescent understanding.

—Dennis Hamley

WILSON, Jacqueline

Nationality: British. **Born:** Bath, Somerset, 17 December 1945. **Education:** Coombe Girls School, Surrey; Carshalton Technical College, Surrey. **Family:** Married William Millar Wilson in 1965; one daughter. **Career:** Staff member, D.C. Thomson, Dundee, Scotland, 1963-65. Freelance journalist. **Awards:** Smarties Award, 1995; Children's Book Award, 1996; Young Telegraph Award, 1995. **Agent:** Caroline Walsh, David Higham Associates, 5-8 Lower John Street, Golden Square, London W1R 4HA, England. **Address:** 1-B Beaufort Road, Kingston-on-Thames, Surrey KT1 2TH, England.

Publications for Children

Fiction

Ricky's Birthday, illustrated by Margaret Belsky. London, Macmillan, 1973.
Nobody's Perfect. Oxford, Oxford University Press, 1982.
Waiting for the Sky to Fall. Oxford, Oxford University Press, 1983.
The Killer Tadpole, illustrated by Rebecca Campbell-Grey. London, Hamish Hamilton, 1984.
The Other Side. Oxford, Oxford University Press, 1984.
The School Trip, illustrated by Sally Holmes. London, Hamish Hamilton, 1984.
How to Survive Summer Camp, illustrated by Bob Dewar. Oxford, Oxford University Press, 1985.
Amber. Oxford, Oxford University Press, 1986.
The Monster in the Cupboard, illustrated by Kate Rogers. London, Blackie, 1986.
Glubbslyme, illustrated by Jane Cope. Oxford, Oxford University Press, 1987.
The Power of the Shade. Oxford, Oxford University Press, 1987.
Stevie Day series (*Lonelyhearts, Supersleuth, Rat Race, Vampire*). London, Armada, 4 vols., 1987-88.
This Girl. Oxford, Oxford University Press, 1988.
The Left-Outs. London, Blackie, 1989.
The Party in the Lift. London, Blackie, 1989.
Falling Apart. Oxford, Oxford University Press, 1989.
Is There Anybody There? (*Spirit Raising, Crystal Gazing*). London, Armada, 2 vols., 1990.
The Story of Tracy Beaker. London, Doubleday, 1991.
Take a Good Look. London, Blackie, 1991.
The Werepuppy. London, Blackie, 1991.
The Dream Palace. Oxford, Oxford University Press, 1991.
The Suitcase Kid, illustrated by Nick Sharratt. London, Doubleday, 1992.
Video Rose. London, Blackie, 1992.
Mark Spark, illustrated by Bethan Matthews. London, Hamish Hamilton, 1992.
Mark Spark in the Dark. London, Hamish Hamilton, 1993.
The Mum-Minder, illustrated by Nick Sharratt. London, Doubleday, 1993.
Deep Blue. Oxford, Oxford University Press, 1993.
The Bed and Breakfast Star. London, Doubleday, 1994.
Come Back Teddy!, Freddy's Teddy, Teddy at the Fair, and *Teddy Goes Swimming.* London, Longman Book Project, 1994.
Twin Trouble, illustrated by Philippe Dupasquier. London, Methuen, 1994.
The Werepuppy on Holiday, illustrated by Janet Robertson. London, Blackie, 1994.
Cliffhanger, illustrated by Nick Sharratt. London, Yearling, 1995.
The Dinosaur's Packed Lunch, illustrated by Nick Sharratt. London, Doubleday, 1995.
Double Act, illustrated by Nick Sharratt and Sue Heap. London, Doubleday, 1995.
Jimmy Jelly. London, Piccadilly Press, 1995.
My Brother Bernadette. London, Heinemann Young Books, 1995.
Bad Girls, illustrated by Nick Sharratt. London, Doubleday, 1996.

Connie and the Water Babies, illustrated by Georgien Overwater. London, Methuen, 1996.
Mr. Cool. London, Kingfisher, 1996.
Girls in Love, illustrated by Nick Sharratt. London, Doubleday, 1997.
The Lottie Project, illustrated by Nick Sharratt. London, Doubleday, 1997.
The Monster Story-teller, illustrated by Nick Sharratt. London, Doubleday, 1997.
Buried Alive. London, Doubleday, 1998.
Girls Under Pressure. London, Doubleday, 1998.

Play

Beauty and the Beast. London, A. & C. Black, 1996.

PUBLICATIONS FOR ADULTS

Novels

Hide and Seek. London, Macmillan, 1972; New York, Doubleday, 1973.
Truth or Dare. London, Macmillan, 1973; New York, Doubleday, 1974.
Snap. London, Macmillan, 1974.
Let's Pretend. London, Macmillan, 1976.
Making Hate. London, Macmillan, 1977; New York, St. Martin's Press, 1978.

Plays

Radio Plays: *Are You Listening?* 1981; *It's Disgusting at Your Age,* 1982; *Ask a Silly Question,* 1983.

*

Media Adaptations: *Cliffhanger* has been adapted for educational television.

Jacqueline Wilson comments:
When I was nine years old I bought myself an out-of-date paper pattern book and for years it was my favourite possession. I didn't care about fashion—I snipped out hundreds of "models," naming them all and playing endless games with these paper dolls. Writing novels is really a grown-up version of these pretend games. I name and sort and sift my imaginary girls until they come to life. And when they do, they generally turn out to be the sort of girls who'd play similar games. They daydream, they run bizarre cartoons inside their heads, they embroider, they write stories. They have more than their fair share of problems in their real lives but they generally cope by escaping into their own inner world of imagination. They're still my paper dolls—and yet by the end of each book they seem real flesh and blood friends.

* * *

Initially seen as a writer for young teenagers, since the publication of *The Story of Tracy Beaker* in 1991 Jacqueline Wilson has become a very popular writer for children in the 8-12 age group. Her stories portray the variety of the family situations in which children live today—with single parents, with older parents, with stepfamilies, in a children's home or a foster home. Most of her novels are illustrated by Nick Sharratt in a way which is integral to the story, mood, theme, and most importantly, the humour. This partnership between author and illustrator is one of the hallmarks of Wilson's more recent novels. The themes she selects, the liveliness of the writing, and the overall presentation of the books entice the reluctant as well as the committed reader.

Wilson uses a variety of devices such as diaries and letters to structure her first person narratives. In *The Story of Tracy Beaker,* the first book which marked her departure from fiction for older children, the eponymous Tracy Beaker lives in a children's home and fantasises about the day her mother will come to reclaim her. Letters, notes, word games, and Tracy's "My Book about Me" are all incorporated within the text.

The Suitcase Kid is Andy, the daughter of divorced parents, who spends one week with her mother's new family, the next with her father's. She dreams of the time when she lived with both her parents in Mulberry Cottage. Each chapter is headed by a letter of the alphabet, seemingly a contrivance, but one which works very well in moving the reader on through the book.

The Mum Minder takes the form of a diary account of the week when Sadie has to help her mother, who works as a childminder, by assisting the parents to look after all the children usually in her care, when her mother is ill.

In *Bad Girls,* each chapter heading is named after a colour until we arrive at the final rainbow end. This story causes the reader to question who the real "bad girls" are—Tanya the foster child next door who gives Mandy new confidence in herself despite getting them both into trouble with the police, or the girls in Mandy's school who bully.

The Lottie Project is slightly different as it includes an historical element, but otherwise it handles similar themes to much of Wilson's other work. Charlie (short for Charlotte) and her mother live happily alone until her mother's potential new partner looks as though he will change their lives and Charlie perceives him as a threat. Running parallel to this narrative is the diary of Victorian servant girl Lottie which Charlie is writing for a school project.

In *Double Act,* twins Garnet and Ruby come to terms with their differences and similarities. An interesting feature of this book is that the twins are each drawn by a different illustrator, one by Jacqueline Wilson's regular collaborator Nick Sharratt, the other by Sue Heap, who has a similar style. Twins feature in some of her other books, this time for a slightly younger age group, *Twin Trouble* and its sequel, *Connie and the Water Babies.* Unlike *Double Act,* which is a first person, or perhaps dual person narrative, these stories describe Connie's feelings on being presented with twin baby siblings rather than the story being told by Connie herself. An element of magic is present, facilitated by Nurse Meade and her blue beads.

Fantasy features in other Jacqueline Wilson stories, especially those for the newly independent reader. In *The Dinosaur's Packed Lunch,* Dinah turns into an iguanadon on a school visit to a natural history museum, while in *The Monster Storyteller,* Natalie shrinks in size and takes a trip on a flying saucer with a little monster to his planet, which is not so very different from her own.

Jacqueline Wilson has recently widened the range of her writing once again by producing another novel for young teenagers, *Girls in Love,* the first in a proposed trilogy. It retains the distinctive humour which has endeared her to younger readers and has a different, more light-hearted tone from her earlier teenage novels published during the 1980s.

Most of Jacqueline Wilson's popular novels have featured a girl as the main character. An exception is *Cliffhanger,* which has been dramatised for educational television. This story concerns a boy who has been sent to an adventure camp by his parents to toughen him up, much against his will. A sequel, *Buried Alive,* has recently been published.

The themes Jacqueline Wilson chooses are serious, yet she always invests her tales of modern life with a childlike humour while never condescending to her young readers. The family of Elsa, in *The Bed and Breakfast Star,* are homeless and she suffers physical abuse at the hands of her stepfather, yet the reader is never left with a feeling of hopelessness at the end of a Jacqueline Wilson book. On the contrary, her resilient heroines always bounce back with a zest for life.

Jacqueline Wilson's books have been shortlisted for many awards including the Carnegie Medal. Her books have been particularly favoured by judging panels where children have a voice in the selection, such as the Children's Book Award.

—Ann Lazim

WISNIEWSKI, David

Nationality: American. **Born:** Middlesex, England, 21 March 1953. **Education:** Attended University of Maryland, 1971; Ringling Brothers and Barnum and Bailey Clown College, 1972. **Family:** Married Donna Harris, 1976; one son and one daughter. **Career:** Clown, Ringling Brothers and Barnum and Bailey Circus, 1973-75; clown, Circus Vargas, 1975-76; puppeteer, Maryland National Park and Planning Commission, 1977-80; co-director, Clarion Shadow Theatre, Laurel, Maryland, from 1980; vice-president, designer, and illustrator, Clarion Graphics, from 1987; author and illustrator of children's books, from 1989. **Awards:** Henson Foundation grants, 1983-85; citation of excellence, Union Internationale de Marionette, 1984; Notable Children's Trade Book in the Field of Social Studies, National Council on the Social Studies and the Children's Book Council, 1990, for *Elfwyn's Saga*; American Library Association Notable Book, and Notable Children's Trade Book in the Field of Social Studies, National Council on the Social Studies and the Children's Book Council, 1992, for *Sundiata, Lion King of Mali*; Notable Children's Trade Book in the Field of Social Studies, and one of *New York Times* 10 Best Illustrated Books of the Year, 1994, for *The Wave of the Sea-Wolf*; Caldecott Medal, 1997, for *Golem.*

Publications for Children

Fiction (illustrated by author)

The Warrior and the Wise Man. New York, Lothrop, 1989.
Elfwyn's Saga. New York, Lothrop, 1990.
Rain Player. New York, Clarion Books, 1991.
Sundiata: Lion King of Mali. New York, Clarion Books, 1992.
The Wave of the Sea-Wolf. New York, Clarion, 1994.
Golem. New York, Clarion, 1996.
A Kid's Guide to the Secret Knowledge of Grown-ups. New York, Lothrop, 1998.

Publications for Adults

With Donna Wisniewski, *Worlds of Shadow: Teaching with Shadow Puppetry* (nonfiction). Englewood, Colorado, Teacher Ideas Press, 1997.

*

Critical Study: *Horn Book,* Vol. 18, no. 1, Spring 1997, 106.

Illustrator: *Sing Your Sillies Out: A Music Handbook for Head Start Teachers* (for adults) by Michele Valerie, 1985; *American Holidays and Special Days* (for adults) by George and Virginia Schaun, 1986; *Ducky* by Eve Bunting, 1997; *Workshop* by Andrew Clements, 1998.

* * *

David Wisniewski was born in England, the son of a U.S. Air Force father and a British mother. The family traveled often, with stations in the United States, England, and Germany. Wisniewsksi's mother encouraged his early interest in drawing; in the beginning he relished copying superheroes from comic books. He became an ardent reader, attracted to science fiction and other fantasy type stories. In high school he developed an interest in theatre and speech. This latter required presentation, and Wisniewski became adroit at performing in public.

After high school, Wisniewski enrolled in the drama department at the University of Maryland. While there, a clown for Ringling Brothers and Barnum and Bailey Circus came to talk about the Ringling Clown College. Wisniewski applied for admission to the Clown College, and was accepted. He later worked for Ringling Brothers Circus and Circus Vargas. Then he returned to Maryland and applied for a puppeteer's position with the Maryland National Capital Park and Planning Commission. The person who hired him was Donna Harris, and she became his wife six months later. In a few years they formed their own touring company, Clarion Shadow Theatre.

Wisniewski's work as a puppeteer provided valuable experience in the creation and presentation of a good story. Wisniewski became accomplished at paper cutting while making shadow puppets and now uses cut paper as his primary illustration medium.

The illustrations for his first book, *The Warrior and the Wise Man,* were cut from art papers and adhered with double-stick photo mountings. Each figure's silhouette was then transformed to the back of a sheet of black paper. The outline was inked with a technical pen and then cut out with an X-Acto knife. Colored papers were cut in the same way for backgrounds and buildings. More than 800 blades were used to produce the startling, highly energized illustrations.

This book was the first of several original folk tales, set in ancient cultures, that Wisniewski has completed. The story dramatizes two approaches to solving a problem: one which relies on blind force, another which relies on reasoned action. The setting is 12th century Japan, a society that had clearly defined classes of warriors and wise men. In this book it is Toemon, the wise man, rather than his twin brother Tozaemon, the warrior, who is able to save his country. Profile cut-outs of humans and animals and demons come to life in front of the brilliant backgrounds of land and sea and sky. The illustrations are rich in color and movement, and the details reflect careful research into Japanese decorative arts. On the last page the author provides information on both Japanese culture and art contained within.

For his next book, *Elfwyn's Saga,* Wisniewski turns to 10th century Iceland in the Viking age, to tell a tale of evil and good. Some Vikings came to Iceland merely for adventure and plunder, but others came for better homes and richer farms. Despite difficulties, the latter managed to form a republic and instituted the world's first parliament. Here too the illustrations were cut from art papers and an X-Acto knife; over 1000 sharp blades were used to produce the illustrations. The brilliant blues and purples evoke the atmosphere of the cold northern areas and the Northern Lights. Again, an author's note on the last page provides cultural and artistic explanations of the text and the pictures.

Rain Player takes us to another part of the world and another time period: the Classical Period of the Maya, A.D. 300 to 900. The ancient Maya believed that the future was divinely decreed and could not be changed. The Mayan civilization is the setting for this original tale of a boy who challenges that traditional belief by taking his fate, and that of his people, into his own hands. The cut-outs of majestic Mayan temples, stylized personal ornamentation, and decorative headdresses are spectacular in form and color; the lush scenery leaps out of the pages. Again, an author's note provides background for the book, excellent for classroom discussion.

Sundiata: Lion King of Mali takes us to West Africa in the 13th century. It is the story of Sundiata, son of the King of Mali, during the time of the great trading empires of Africa. As a boy, Sundiata was unable to speak or walk. He overcame these obstacles, and was made his father's heir, only to be driven into exile by a rival queen. A few years later, Mali was overrun by the forces of a sorcerer king, and eighteen-year-old Sundiata returned to his homeland to defeat the intruder and claim his rightful throne. The oranges and reds and greens, the geometric patterning of the people's dress, reflect very old textile patterns of the area. For this book, Wisniewski consulted the library of the Smithsonian's National Museum of African Art, as well as African art scholars. The richness of the culture and the pride of its people are shown in page after page of handsome illustrations.

The Wave of the Sea-Wolf takes us to the Pacific Northwest in the late 18th century, at the time the Tlinget Indians first made contact with European adventurers, who wanted to buy their sea otter fur. The Europeans were interested in amassing great wealth; the Tlinget were interested in wealth, but they also were concerned about protecting the environment around them. In telling this tale of Indian courage and wisdom, Wisniewski makes wonderful use of their colorful designs, with repeated motifs in red, white, blue, and black. The illustration of the sea-wolf itself, on the book cover and on the title page, is a particularly striking expression of Pacific Northwest Indian art.

With *Golem,* Wisniewski takes us to Prague in the late 16th century. According to legend, some four hundred years ago a revered Jewish scholar, Rabbi Loew, shaped a giant man of clay, a golem, and brought him to life. The golem's task was to vanquish those who persecuted the Jews of Prague. In this story he performs the task well. The author's note explains that repression has been all too typical of Jewish experience for centuries. In modern times, after the Holocaust, the nation of Israel, was founded. Like the Golem, Israel was created to protect the physical safety of Jews through the use of physical power. The pictures in this book are primarily dark ones; browns and blacks and grays predominate, reinforcing the harshness of the story being told.

Wisniewski's next work of fiction reflects his original career of clowning. *A Kid's Guide to the Secret Knowledge of Grown-Ups* is a tongue-in-cheek revelation of the real reasons why adults tell children to do things such as: eat your vegetables, comb your hair, don't blow bubbles in your milk. The humor here is good for adults as well as children. *Worlds of Shadow: Teaching with Shadow Puppetry* is a how-to book which compliments Wisniewski's picture books. Designed for teachers, it describes in clear and concise language the basic elements of shadow puppetry: a light, a screen, and something to put between them to cast a shadow. It offers suggestions on how to teach shadow puppetry to different age groups. Though written for teachers, older children with an interest in the technique can benefit from the book's illustrations. And after performing shadow puppetry, the child will certainly appreciate even more the incredible cut paper illustrations in Wisniewski's picture books.

Wisniewski has illustrated a music handbook for teachers, *Sing Your Sillies Out,* and he has illustrated a historical piece, *American Holidays and Special Days.* Both of these books are useful for classroom projects.

Wisniewski is a marvelous artist and entertainer. The books that he writes and illustrates show real concern for the human condition; they are works of beauty and strength. His willingness to share his wit and wisdom with teachers and performing arts groups is another gift he gives to children.

—Mary Lystad

WOOD, David

Nationality: British. **Born:** Sutton, Surrey, 21 February 1944. **Education:** Chichester High School for Boys, 1957-63; Worcester College, Oxford, 1963-66, B.A. (honours) in English 1966. **Family:** Married 1) Sheila Ruskin in 1966 (marriage dissolved 1970); 2) Jacqueline Stanbury in 1975, two daughters. **Career:** Since 1966 director, W.S.G. Productions; since 1979 director, Whirligig Theatre; since 1983 director, Verronmead Limited television production company; since 1986 director, Westwood Theatre Productions; since 1995 director, W2 Productions Ltd. **Awards:** Nottinghamshire Children's Book of the Year Award, 1990, for *Sidney the Monster.* **Agent:** (for plays) Casarotto Ramsay Ltd., National House, 60-66 Wardour Street, London W1V 3HP, England; (for children's books) Eunice McMullen, 38, Clewer Hill Road, Windsor, Berkshire SL4 4BW, England.

PUBLICATIONS FOR CHILDREN

Fiction

The Operats of Rodent Garden, illustrated by Geoffrey Beitz. London, Methuen, 1984.

The Gingerbread Man, from his own play, illustrated by Sally Anne Lambert. London, Pavilion, and Manchester, New Hampshire, Salem House, 1985.
The Discorats, illustrated by Geoffrey Beitz. London, Methuen, 1985.
Chish 'n' Fips, with Don Seed. London, Boxtree, 1987.
Sidney the Monster, illustrated by Clive Scruton. London, Walker, 1988.
Save the Human, with Tony Husband. London, Hamish Hamilton, 1991.

Plays

The Tinder Box, adaptation of a story by Hans Christian Andersen (produced Worcester, 1967).
Cinderella (lyrics only), book by Sid Colin, music by John Gould (produced Glasgow, 1968).
The Owl and the Pussycat Went to See..., with Sheila Ruskin, music and lyrics by Wood, adaptation of works by Edward Lear (produced Worcester, 1968; London, 1969). London, French, 1970.
Larry the Lamb in Toytown, with Sheila Ruskin, music and lyrics by Wood, adaptation of stories by S.G. Hulme Beaman (produced Worcester, 1969; London, 1973). London, French, 1977.
The Plotters of Cabbage Patch Corner, music by Wood (produced Worcester, 1970; London, 1971). London, French, 1972.
Flibberty and the Penguin, music by Wood (produced Worcester, 1971; London, 1977). London, French, 1974.
Tickle (produced on tour, 1972; London, 1977). London, French, 1978.
The Papertown Paperchase, music by Wood (produced Worcester, 1972; London, 1973). London, French, 1976.
Hijack over Hygenia, music by Wood (produced Worcester, 1973). London, French, 1974.
Swallows and Amazons (screenplay). 1974.
Old Mother Hubbard, music by Wood (produced Hornchurch, Essex, 1975). London, French, 1976.
Old Father Time, music by Wood (produced Hornchurch, Essex, 1976). London, French, 1978.
The Gingerbread Man, music by Wood (produced Basildon, Essex, 1976; London, 1977). London, French, 1977.
Nutcracker Sweet, music by Wood (produced Farnham, Surrey, 1977; London, 1980). London, French, 1981.
Mother Goose's Golden Christmas, music by Wood (produced Hornchurch, Essex, 1977). London, French, 1978.
Babes in the Magic Wood, music by Wood (produced Hornchurch, Essex, 1979). London, French, 1980.
There Was an Old Woman, music by Wood (produced Leicester, 1979). London, French, 1980.
Cinderella, music by Wood (produced Hornchurch, Essex, 1980). London, French, 1981.
The Ideal Gnome Expedition, music by Wood (as *Chish and Fips,* produced Liverpool, 1980; as *The Ideal Gnome Expedition,* produced on tour and London, 1981). London, French, 1982.
Aladdin, music by Wood (produced Hornchurch, Essex, 1980). London, French, 1981.
Robin Hood, with Dave and Toni Arthur, music by Wood (produced Nottingham, 1981; London, 1982). London, French, 1985.
Meg and Mog Show, music by Wood, adaptation of stories by Helen Nicoll (produced London, 1981).
Dick Whittington and Wondercat, music by Wood (produced Hornchurch, Essex, 1981). London, French, 1982.
Jack and the Giant (produced Hornchurch, Essex, 1982). London, French, 1987.
Magic and Music Show (produced London, 1983).
The Selfish Shellfish (produced Farnham, Surrey, and London, 1983). Oxford, Amber Lane Press, 1983.
Jack the Lad, with Dave and Toni Arthur, music by Wood (produced Manchester, 1984).
The Old Man of Lochnagar, adaptation of the story by Prince Charles (produced Aberdeen and London, 1986). Oxford, Amber Lane Press, 1986.
Dinosaurs and All That Rubbish, music by Peter Pontzen, adaptation of the story by Michael Foreman (produced Denbigh, Wales, 1986; London, 1988). Oxford, Amber Lane Press, 1986.
The See-Saw Tree (produced Farnham, Surrey, 1986; London, 1987).
Robin Hood and Friar Tuck and *Marian and the Witches' Charm,* in *Playstages,* edited by John Alcock. London, Methuen, 1987.
Save the Human (produced Cambridge and London, 1990). London, French, 1990.
The BFG (Big Friendly Giant), by Roald Dahl, adapted for the stage by Wood. London, and New York, Samuel French, 1991.
The Pied Piper, with Dave and Toni Arthur, based on the tale by Robert Browning. London, and New York, Samuel French, 1991.
The BFG: Plays for Children, adapted from the book by Roald Dahl and the play by David Wood. London, Puffin, 1993.
Noddy, adapted from stories by Enid Blyton (produced Wimbledon and London, 1993). London, French, 1995.
Rupert and the Dragon, adapted from the "Rupert" stories by Mary Tourtel and Alfred Bestall (produced Leatherhead, 1993). London, French, 1997.
The Witches, adapted from the story by Roald Dahl. London and New York, Samuel French, 1994.
Meg and Nog: Four Plays for Children, adapted from the books by Helen Nicoll and Jan Pienkowski. London, Puffin, 1994.
More Adventures of Noddy, adapted from stories by Enid Blyton (produced Wimbledon, 1995). London, French, 1998.
The Christmas Story (nativity play). London, A. & C. Black, 1996.
Babe, the Sheep-Pig, based on the book *The Sheep-Pig* by Dick King-Smith (produced Woking and London, 1997). London, French, 1997.

Television Writing: *Playaway* series, 1973-77; *Emu's Christmas Adventure,* 1977; *Chish 'n' Fips,* 1984; *Chips' Comic,* 1984; *Seeing and Doing,* 1986; *Back Home,* adaptation of the story by Michelle Magorian, 1989; *Tide Race,* 1989; *Watch,* 1992.

Novelty Books (created with and illustrated by Richard Fowler)

Play Theatre (*Nativity Play* and *Jack and the Beanstalk*). London, Pavilion, and New York, Holt, 2 vols., 1987.
Happy Birthday, Mouse!: A First Counting Book. London, Hodder, and New York, Grosset, 1990.
Baby Bear's Buggy Ride (*To the Shops* and *To the Park*). London, Hazar, 1993.
Pop-up Theatre: Cinderella. London, Kingfisher, 1994.
Bedtime Story. London, Transworld, and New York, Western, 1995.
The Magic Show. London, Hazar, 1995.
Mole's Summer Story. London, Transworld, 1997.
Owl's Birthday Party. London, Hazar, 1998.

Silly Spider. London, Transworld, and New York, Harcourt Brace, 1998.
Mole's Winter Story. London, Transworld, 1998.

Publications for Adults

Plays

Hang Down Your Head and Die, with David Wright (produced Oxford, London, and New York, 1964).
Sketches, with John Gould, in *Four Degrees Over* (produced Edinburgh and London, 1966).
And Was Jerusalem, with Mick Sadler and John Gould (produced Oxford, 1966; as *A Present from the Corporation,* produced Worcester and London, 1967).
A Life in Bedrooms, with David Wright (produced Edinburgh, 1967; as *The Stiffkey Scandals of 1932,* produced London, 1968).
Three to One On, with John Gould (produced Edinburgh, 1968).
Postscripts, with John Gould (produced London, 1969).
Down Upper Street, with John Gould (produced London, 1971).
Just the Ticket, with John Gould (produced Leatherhead, Surrey, 1973).
Rock Nativity, music by Tony Hatch and Jackie Trent, lyrics by Wood (produced Newcastle-upon-Tyne, 1974; as *A New Tomorrow,* produced Wimbledon, 1976). London, Weinberger, 1977.
Maudie, with Iwan Williams (produced Leatherhead, Surrey, 1974).
Chi-Chestnuts, with Bernard Price and Julian Sluggett (produced Chichester, 1975).
Think of a Number, with John Gould (produced Peterborough, 1975).
Bars of Gould, with John Gould (revue; produced Exeter, 1977).
The Luck of the Bodkins, with John Gould, adaptation of a work by P.G. Wodehouse (produced Windsor, 1978).
Abbacadabra, music by Björn Ulvaeus and Benny Andersson, lyrics by Don Black, Mike Batt, and Ulvaeus (produced London, 1983).

Other

With Janet Grant, *Theatre for Children: Guide to Writing, Adapting, Directing and Acting.* London, Faber and Faber, 1997.

*

Media Adaptations: *Noddy* (video production of the author's stage adaptation of Enid Blyton's books), BBC Video, 1994.

Theatrical Activities:
Director: Most of his own plays.

Actor: **Plays**—in *Hang Down Your Head and Die,* Oxford and London, 1964; Geoff Manham in *A Spring Song* by Ray Mathew, Edinburgh and London, 1964; Wagner in *Dr. Faustus* by Christopher Marlowe, Oxford, 1966; in Worcester, Watford, Edinburgh, Windsor, and Salisbury repertory companies, 1966-69; Roger in *After Haggerty* by David Mercer, London, 1970, 1971; The Son in *A Voyage round My Father* by John Mortimer, London, 1970, Toronto, 1972; James in *Me Times Me,* toured 1971; Frank in *Mrs. Warren's Profession* by G.B. Shaw, Leatherhead, Surrey, 1972; *Just the Ticket* (revue), Leatherhead, Surrey, 1972; Constant in *The Provok'd Wife* by Vanbrugh, London, 1973; Bingo Little in *Jeeves* by Alan Ayckbourn, London, 1975; *Three to One On* (revue), Peterborough, 1975; Lt. Bowers in *Terra Nova* by Ted Tally, Chichester, 1980; *Magic and Music Show,* London, 1983. **Films**—*If...,* 1968; *Aces High,* 1975; *Sweet William,* 1978; *North Sea Hijack,* 1979. **Radio**—*Semi-Circles* series by Simon Brett, 1982. **Television**—*Mad Jack*; *Fathers and Sons*; *The Vamp*; *Cheri*; *Disraeli*; *The Avengers*; *Van der Valk*; *Danger UXB*; *Huntingtower*; *Enemy at the Door*; *Jim'll Fix It*; *The Brack Report*; *Bureaucracy of Love*; *Jackanory 3000,* 1979; *Trouble with Gregory,* 1980; *When the Boat Comes In,* 1981; and other plays, since 1964.

David Wood comments:
Children's theatre in Great Britain has for too long been regarded within and without the profession as second or even third division theatre. I hope I may be making a small contribution towards its elevation to a higher division! After all, if live theatre is to survive it is up to those of us who work in it to interest our *potential* audiences as early as possible. I try to combine a strong story-line with hummable songs and imaginative characters. I try never to patronize the children and never to "play to the adults." Although fantasy often plays a strong part, I hope the plays have enough substance to evoke discussion and a continuation of the experience after the curtain has fallen. And I hope they make people laugh too.

My foray into the world of children's books began in 1984. I particularly enjoy my partnership with Richard Fowler, with whom I work on early-learning books, toy theatres, and other novelty ideas. The disciplines of playwriting and book writing are clearly related, and I have adapted many books for the stage. Yet I find it annoyingly difficult to adapt my own plays into books!

* * *

Just as a specialist literature for children has had to define its particular status, so children's theatre still seeks out new modes and appropriate forms for a demanding audience. David Wood's work is of importance in setting the standards by which we now judge an art form too often hampered by an English pantomime tradition increasingly aimed at the adults and by an often earnest, over-serious "educational drama."

His musical plays appeal to children's love of action, movement, colour, and spectacle. They all have an actor's instinct for their impact, as well as a gifted storyteller's feel for character, plot, and theme. The plays often build upon tales that his audiences know (or half know), so making them feel at home in the theatre and giving significance to the re-enactment of stories that children do themselves. *The Owl and the Pussycat Went to See...* conveys the essentially exotic and mysterious nature of the original and extends the musical potentiality of the poem. *Robin Hood* and *Old Mother Hubbard* have imaginative and convoluted fun with their sources—and celebrate minor characters. *Meg and Mog Show* successfully transfers contemporary story characters from the shared texts for today's children and skilfully uses a treasure hunt to get the ingredients for a spell and involve the audience.

The original plays are vital and unflagging. Wood responds to children's love of stock literary characters, but his inventions are always well-rounded: the pompous; the brainy but scatterbrained; the well-intentioned but muddled; good-natured dragons. His villains are particularly effective, especially Krafty Kingfisher in *Flibberty and the Penguin* and Dr. Spickenspan in *Hijack over Hygenia.* They are usually overcome by endeavour and action which incorporates the audience. The "Big Ones" are the enemies in *The Gingerbread Man* and *The Plotters of Cabbage Patch Cor-*

ner, and, though there is no didactic pushing of the point, Wood's audiences always sympathise with the plight of little people at the beck and call of others. In *The Selfish Shellfish,* he touches on ecological themes in a way that still foregrounds the imaginative enterprise but gets even the youngest playgoer *thinking* about issues as well as enjoying the action. Even with relatively uninspiring material like *The Old Man of Lochnagar* he manages to create a world on the stage—and poke some fun at the high-minded bits. He is a superb creator of names that capitalise upon children's love of word play: Blotch and Carbon, Kernal Walnut, Herr Von Cuckoo. In his dialogue and songs, he exploits the fun to be had from the topsy-turvy and the illogical—*Old Father Time* has some gloriously funny time-shifting when Big Ben stops.

Two recent novels (*The Operats of Rodent Garden* and *The Discorats*) have a tangy, contemporary feel to them and transfer the vigour, pace, and style to narrative prose. In all his work, a child's view of the world is centre stage. Wood's audiences (and readers) enjoy themselves, but, whereas they are passive in much of their television watching, and, sadly, still unchallenged in much of their fiction reading, they are *engaged* in the songs and the action so that theatre can be seen as proper way of looking at and reflecting upon the world.

—Colin Mills

WORTH, Valerie

Nationality: American. **Born:** Philadelphia, Pennsylvania, 29 October 1933. **Education:** Swarthmore College, Pennsylvania, 1951-55, B.A. in English 1955. **Family:** Married George W. Bahlke in 1955; one son and two daughters. **Career:** Secretary to the promotion manager, Yale University Press, New Haven, Connecticut, 1956-58. **Award:** Bread Loaf Writers Conference scholarship, 1965. **Died:** 31 July 1994.

Publications for Children

Fiction

Curlicues: The Fortunes of Two Pug Dogs, illustrated by Natalie Babbitt. New York, Farrar Straus, 1980; as *Imp and Biscuit,* London, Chatto and Windus, 1981.
Gypsy Gold. New York, Farrar Straus, 1983.
Fox Hill. New York, Farrar Straus, 1986.

Verse

Small Poems, illustrated by Natalie Babbitt. New York, Farrar Straus, 1972.
More Small Poems, illustrated by Natalie Babbitt. New York, Farrar Straus, 1976.
Still More Small Poems, illustrated by Natalie Babbitt. New York, Farrar Straus, 1978.
Small Poems Again, illustrated by Natalie Babbitt. New York, Farrar Straus, 1986.
All the Small Poems, illustrated by Natalie Babbitt. New York, Farrar Straus, 1987.
At Christmastime, illustrated by Antonio Frasconi. New York, HarperCollins, 1992.
All the Small Poems and Fourteen More, illustrated by Natalie Babbitt. New York, Farrar Straus, 1994.

Publications for Adults

Verse

The Crone's Book of Words. Minneapolis, Llewellyn, 1971.
The Crone's Book of Wisdom. Minneapolis, Llewellyn, 1988.

*

Valerie Worth commented:

(1989) Although I began as a writer of poetry and fiction for adults, I later found that writing for children made the best use of my particular abilities and perceptions. Children's poetry, especially, has provided me with a way to embody the essential qualities of things in brief, simple lyrics, while still using many of the techniques of "adult" poetry. In doing so, I have tried to create poems that go beyond the mere light verses or humorous jingles so frequently offered to children; my feeling is that many children themselves perceive the world in an essentially poetic way, and my work has been an attempt to translate some of these poetic experiences into words—for my own pleasure, as well as others'.

* * *

There are few poets writing for children today whose metaphoric eye is keener than that of Valerie Worth. Her four books of verse, *Small Poems, More Small Poems, Still More Small Poems* and *Small Poems Again,* published between 1972 and 1986, are testament to the excellence which poetry for the young offers. Hers is the gift not only of heightened consciousness but of an ability to make comparisons between objects which immediately awaken readers to new perspectives. A closed safety pin "sleeps/On its side/Quietly,/The silver/Image/Of some/Small fish"; whereas "Opened, it snaps/Its tail out/Like a thin/Shrimp, and looks/At the sharp/Point with a/Surprised eye." What reader can ever again look at a safety pin as a mere utilitarian object?

While many others seek to entertain children with instant laughter, Worth invites children to observe the world about them, to value the commonplace articles that make up their everyday world, from clocks, hollyhocks, and chairs to creatures at the zoo. Like haiku, Worth's poems are written in the present tense, of one thing keenly observed, inviting readers to complete the picture. Unlike haiku, they are not limited by subject matter or syllable pattern. Each word is carefully chosen, arranged in rhythms which emphasize the power of onomatopoeia. She writes of "Hard leather heels,/Their blocks carved/Thick, like rocks,/Clacked down/Waxed wood stairs," and of the "pale,/Soles/Of sneakers."

Worth's treasures do not lie in some distant, golden land but in the everyday world. She shows us earthworms who "Glisten in the sun/As fresh/As new rubies/Dug out of/Deepest earth." Her "...round jewels,/Slithering gold" are marbles poured into their bag. A hose "Can rain/Chill diamond/Chains/Across the yard" or "...hang/A silk/Rainbow/Halo/Over soft/fog." In the garbage she finds "Hammered-gold/Orange rind,/Eggshell ivory./Garnet coffee/Grounds, pearl/Wand of bared/Chicken bone." Riches to her are "satin sea lions," the "sleek velvets" on the back of a mosquito and the lions' "plush-covered clay."

Eschewing singsong meter and incessant end-rhyme, Worth brilliantly employs other aspects of the poet's craft. Through personification she notes the "soft skull" and "frail ribs" of a mushroom, a lawnmower that "Grinds its teeth/Over the grass/ Spitting out a thick/Green spray"; with a head "too full/Of iron and oil/To know/What it/Throws/Away." Telephone poles sweat "Black creosote," and coat hangers "Clash and cling/And fling them-/Selves to the/Floor in an/Inextricable tangle." She invites children, through simile and metaphor, to notice asparagus "Like a nest/Of snakes/Awakened, craning/Long-necked/Out of the/ Ground to stand/With sharp/Scaly heads/Alert, tasting/The air,/ Taking the sun,/Looking around." The frog's "gold-circles eyes/ stare hard/Like bright metal rings." Porch chairs "Wait, arranged/Strange and polite" whereas field grass "Whistles, slides" and "Tangles itself/With leaves..."

Her rhythms mesh with subject. "This clock/Has stopped,/ Some gear/Or spring/Gone wrong." Fireworks follow their accustomed ascent: "First/A far thud,/Then the rocket/Climbs the air,/ A dull red flare,/To hang, a moment,/Invisible, before/Its shut black shell cracks..." Alliteratively, she observes the beetle's "lacquered/ Coffer of/Curious/Compartments" or how "the slug/Slides sly." Rhyme is used judiciously, often internally or as slant rhyme. A masterful use of synesthesia occurs in "The harsh gold/Smell of lions." Worth's pragmatism is evident in several lyrical forays. She believes that a sparrow "is as good a bird/As anyone needs." A magnet, she writes, "is/Sold for a toy..." and "picks up pins" but "...later/It lies about/Getting its red/Paint chipped, being/Offered pins less/Often, until at/Last we leave it/Alone."

This pragmatism and a touch of quiet underlying humor is most evident in her fictional works *Gypsy Gold* and *Curlicues.* Here she employs a simple, yet elegant prose style. As storyteller she weaves into beautifully cadenced prose the same artful and judicious use of metaphor, simile, and personification that characterizes her poetry.

—Myra Cohn Livingston

WRIGHT, Kit

Nationality: British. **Born:** Kent in 1944. **Education:** Berkhamsted School, Hertfordshire; New College, Oxford. **Career:** Teacher in a comprehensive school, London; Lecturer in English, Brock University, St. Catharines, Ontario, three years. Education secretary, Poetry Society, London, 1970-75; Fellow-Commoner in Creative Arts, Trinity College, Cambridge, 1977-79. **Awards:** Geoffrey Faber Memorial prize, 1978; Poetry Society Alice Hunt Bartlett prize, 1978; Arts Council bursary, 1985. **Address:** c/o Viking Kestrel, 27 Wrights Lane, London W8 5TZ, England.

Publications for Children

Verse

Arthur's Father [*Granny, Sister, Uncle*], illustrated by Eileen Browne. London, Methuen, 4 vols., 1978.

Rabbiting On and Other Poems, illustrated by Posy Simmonds. London, Fontana, 1978.

Hot Dog and Other Poems, illustrated by Posy Simmonds. London, Kestrel, 1981.

Professor Potts Meets the Animals of Africa, illustrated by Gillian Chapman. London, Watts, 1981.

Cat among the Pigeons, illustrated by Posy Simmonds. London, Viking Kestrel, 1987.

Short Afternoons. London, Hutchinson, 1989.

Funnybunch. London, Viking, 1993.

Tigerella, illustrated by Peter Bailey. New York, Scholastic, 1994.

Great Snakes!, illustrated by Posy Simmonds. London, Puffin, 1994.

Dolphinella, illustrated by Peter Bailey. London, Deutsch Children's Books, 1995.

Other

Editor, *Soundings: A Selection of Poems for Speaking Aloud.* London, Heinemann, 1975.

Editor, *Poems for 9-Year-Olds and Under,* illustrated by Michael Foreman. London, Kestrel, 1984.

Editor, *Poems for Over 10-Year-Olds,* illustrated by Michael Foreman. London, Viking Kestrel, 1984.

Publications for Adults

Verse

Treble Poets 1, with Stephen Miller and Elizabeth Maslen. London, Chatto and Windus, 1974.

The Bear Looked over the Mountain. London, Salamander Imprint, 1977.

Bump-Starting the Hearse. London, Hutchinson, 1983.

From the Day Room. Liverpool, Windows Press, 1983.

Real Rags and Red. London, Hutchinson, 1988.

Poems 1974-1983. London, Hutchinson, 1988.

* * *

Kit Wright's poetry for children has an exuberance, a vitality, and a technical virtuosity that works equally well on the page or when read aloud. He is well known for his lively public readings to audiences of children and adults and there is an infectiously joyful quality about his attitude to his subject matter that is likely to serve as an inspiration to all aspiring writers, whether they be young or old. The manic exuberance reminds one at times of the work of Lewis Carroll—as if the desire to crack yet another joke in the poem, to add one more crowning pun to the puns that are already there, simply cannot be resisted. There is also a use of cumulative repetition that is somewhat reminiscent of his great predecessor. In what is probably his best collection of poems for children, *Hot Dog and Other Poems,* there is a poem entitled "Hugger Mugger" which beautifully captures the miseries of a little boy who is always being kissed against his will by his Auntie Jean. It has what amounts to a wonderful chant at its climax:

For as things are
I really would far,

Far sooner be
Jumped and thumped and dumped,

I'd sooner be
Slugged and mugged...than *hugged...*

And clobbered with a slobbering
Kiss by my Auntie

Jean!

Of course, the danger of revelling in word play to this extent might be an inability—or a reluctance—on the part of the poet to climb down from these heights of hilarity to deal with more sombre and serious matters—death, disfigurement, human tragedy of any kind. But there is sufficient evidence in this collection that Wright is perfectly capable of striking the right tone when dealing with such issues. And nowhere is this better illustrated than in a long narrative poem set in Liverpool station, "Useful Person." The plot is simple enough: a family—mum, dad, and child—has missed the train. There are two hours to wait, two hours of gloom and boredom—but the situation is miraculously transformed by the sudden appearance of a little Mongol girl who teaches the whole family a timely lesson in making the best of things. The poet achieves a finely tuned balance of sensitivity and humour—a most difficult thing to do. The refrain illustrates very well how the poet's tone has enabled him to steer well clear of mawkishness: "Mongol child,/ Funny-faced,/Something in your body wrong,/Something in your mind/Misplaced,/Something in your eyes, strange:/What, or why, I cannot tell:/I thought you were beautiful:/Useful, as well." Another little poem in this collection, "Cathedral Gardens," is a simple yet moving evocation of a place at sunset, and the poem again contrasts sharply with the dominant hilarity of most of the rest of the book and, consequently, comes as a refreshing reminder of the range of this poet's talents: "In the Cathedral Gardens/Underneath the trees/In the chilly evening/The sun is on its knees,/Dying by the gravestones/While their shadows freeze/And the dead are walking/Underneath the trees."

—Michael Glover

WYMARK, Olwen (Margaret)

Nationality: American. **Born:** Olwen Margaret Buck, Oakland, California, 14 February 1932. **Education:** Pomona College, Claremont, California, 1949-51; University College, London, 1951-52. **Family:** Married the actor Patrick Wymark in 1950 (died 1970); two daughters and two sons. **Career:** Writer-in-residence, Unicorn Theatre for Young People, London, 1974-75, and Kingston Polytechnic, Surrey, 1977; script consultant, Tricycle Theatre, London; Lecturer in Playwriting, New York University. Member, Arts Council of Great Britain Drama Panel, 1980-84. Lives in London. **Awards:** Zagreb Drama Festival prize, 1967. **Agent:** Harvey Unna and Stephen Durbridge Ltd., 24-32 Pottery Lane, London W11 4LZ, England.

Publications for Children

Plays

No Talking (produced London, 1970).
Daniel's Epic, with Daniel Henry (produced London, 1972).
Chinigchinich (produced London, 1973).
The Bolting Sisters (produced London, 1974).
Southwark Originals (collaborative work; produced London, 1975).
Starters (collaborative work; includes *The Giant and the Dancing Fairies, The Time Loop, The Spellbound Jellybaby, The Robbing of Elvis Parsley, I Spy*; produced London, 1975; Wausau, Wisconsin, 1976).
Three For All (collaborative work; includes *Box Play, Family Business, Extended Play*; produced London, 1976).
The Winners, and Missing Persons (produced London, 1978).

Publications for Adults

Plays

Lunchtime Concert (produced Glasgow, 1966). Included in *Three Plays,* 1967; in *The Best Short Plays 1975,* edited by Stanley Richards, Radnor, Pennsylvania, Chilton, 1975.
Three Plays (as *Triple Image: Coda, Lunchtime Concert, The Inhabitants,* produced Glasgow, 1967; *The Inhabitants,* produced London, 1974). London, Calder and Boyars, 1967.
The Gymnasium (produced Edinburgh, 1967; London, 1971). New York, Riverrun Press, 1988. Included in *The Gymnasium and Other Plays,* 1971.
The Technicians (produced Leicester, 1969; London, 1971). Included in *The Gymnasium and Other Plays,* 1971.
Stay Where You Are (produced Edinburgh, 1969; London, 1973). Included in *The Gymnasium and Other Plays,* 1971; in *The Best Short Plays 1972,* edited by Stanley Richards, Philadelphia, Chilton, 1972.
Neither Here nor There (produced London, 1971). Included in *The Gymnasium and Other Plays,* 1971.
Speak Now (produced Edinburgh, 1971; revised version produced Leicester, 1975).
The Committee (produced London, 1971). Included in *Best Friends, The Committee, The Twenty-Second Day,* 1984.
The Gymnasium and Other Plays. London, Calder and Boyars, 1971.
Jack the Giant Killer (produced Sheffield, 1972). Included in *The Gymnasium and Other Plays,* 1971.
Tales from Whitechapel (produced London, 1972).
Watch the Woman, with Brian Phelan (produced London, 1973).
The Twenty-Second Day (broadcast 1975; produced London, 1975). Included in *Best Friends, The Committee, The Twenty-Second Day,* 1984.
We Three, and After Nature, Art (produced London, 1977). Published in *Play Ten,* edited by Robin Rook, London, Arnold, 1977.
Find Me (produced Richmond, Surrey, 1977; Louisville, 1979). London, French, 1980.
Loved (produced London, 1978; Syracuse, New York, 1979). London, French, 1980.
The Child (broadcast 1979). London, BBC Publications, 1979.
Please Shine Down on Me (produced London, 1980).

Female Parts: One Woman Plays (includes *Waking Up, A Woman Alone, The Same Old Story, Medea*), adaptations of plays by Dario Fo and Franca Rame, translated by Margaret Kunzle and Stuart Hood (produced London, 1981). London, Pluto Press, 1981.
Best Friends (produced Richmond, Surrey, 1981). Included in *Best Friends, The Committee, The Twenty-Second Day,* 1984.
Buried Treasure (produced London, 1983).
Best Friends, The Committee, The Twenty-Second Day. London, Calder, and New York, Riverrun Press, 1984.
Lessons and Lovers: D.H. Lawrence in New Mexico (produced York, 1985). London, French, 1986.
Nana, adaptation of the novel by Zola (produced London, 1987).
Strike Up the Banns (produced Mold, Clwyd, 1988). London and New York, French, 1990.
Brezhnev's Children, adaptation of *The Women's Decameron* by Julia Voznesenskaya. London and New York, French, 1992.

Radio Plays: *The Ransom,* 1957; *The Unexpected Country,* 1957; *California Here We Come,* 1958; *The Twenty-Second Day,* 1975; *You Come Too,* 1977; *The Child,* 1979; *Vivien the Blockbuster,* 1980; *Mothering Sunday,* 1980; *Sea Changes,* 1984; *A Wreath of Roses,* from the novel by Elizabeth Taylor, 1985; *Mothers and Shadows,* from a novel by Marta Traba, 1987; *Out of the Woods,* BBC RAdio 4, 1997; *Stories by W.W. Jacobs,* 1997.

Television Plays: *Mrs. Moresby's Scrapbook,* 1973, *Vermin,* 1974, *Marathon,* 1975, *Mother Love,* 1975, *Dead Drunk,* 1975, and *Her Father's Daughter,* 1984 (all in *Crown Court* series); *Oceans Apart,* 1984; *Not That Kind of People,* 1984; *British Slaves,* BBC TV, 1995; *In Suspicious Circumstances* (two episodes), Granada TV, 1996-97; *The Things You Do for Love,* Granada TV, 1997.

Screen Plays: *All Men Are Mortal,* 1996; *Left Luggage,* 1997.

*

Olwen Wymark comments:

In 1966 I was commissioned by the late Caryl Jenner, founder of the Unicorn Theatre, to write my first children's play *No Talking.* I'd had no experience of plays specially written for children and had no idea if you did it differently; I think you don't. Under the tireless protective encouragement from script editor and playwright/actor Christopher Guinnee I managed to finish this play in about 11 months. *Chinigchinich* I wrote in a day to enter in a contest with *No Talking* (both one-acters) which I didn't win. In 1974 Chattie Salaman and Frank Whitton of the Common Stock Company asked me to work with them and a horde of kids (aged 2 to 15) in Whitechapel on a kid's play which was to be evolved in collaboration. It was absolute agony and the most exciting time I'd had in the theatre for years. The result was *Daniel's Epic,* an hour-long piece. My collaborator was a 9-year-old genius called Daniel Henry.

In 1974 and 1975 at the Unicorn Theatre I had another go at collaborating with children in playwriting. The first time was with 104 kids from four Southwark schools. Each class wrote a play with me which they performed themselves with me doing what might have been called directing but was more like sustained frenzy. We called the show *Southwark Originals* and we all had a very good time. The 1975 project was *Starters* in which I collaborated with eight kids between six and nine on five plays which were then performed at the Unicorn by professional actors and in 1976 in Wisconsin by children. In 1976 I worked with actress Janet Henfrey and directors Lucy Parker and Greville Hallam with a kids' workshop that was run by the Sidney Webb Teacher Training College in London and with this group of 40 kids we wrote together *Three For All* (which was performed by children). In 1978 I wrote a very black comedy about a holiday camp for the Old Vic Youth Theatre, again with Lucy Parker as director, and this was the last play I've written specifically for children though I hope I may write more in the future.

* * *

In the recent and rapid development of theatre for children, Olwen Wymark's *No Talking* is an important landmark. Written at a time when plays for under-12s inclined to be, at best, well-dramatised fairytales, at worst, a kind of kiddy-kit, Petrushka with words, Wymark's script made a tremendous impact. The play gave children a taut exploration of the appalling consequences to its hero of his somewhat flippant resolve to stop talking in protest against the triteness of other people's conversation. It did so in a frame of reference within the child's often conservative expectation of its own culture. There are witch-like ladies, clowns, changelings, spies, and so on, but, contrary to expectation, these characters happened to run electrical supply shops, land up in concentration camps, get shot, go blind, and fall in love, not prettily either but with a great deal of effort, pain, and joy. At the time, this theme and its treatment were revolutionary, and perhaps Wymark was applauded too much for daring and innovation and not enough for her craftsmanship and the kind of grip this gaudy, poetic, and shamelessly theatrical play has on young audiences. Similarly, its partner play, *Chinigchinich,* uses a familiar context—this time a Red Indian tribe—to examine the nature of authority, but likewise makes a few illuminating departures from the audience preconception of "Injun" behaviour that lightheartedly invites them to apply a little scepticism in their own dealings with power and those who administer it.

Her first two plays were written at the request of the Unicorn Theatre for Young People; her next, a collaboration with a small West Indian called Daniel, came about through her work with Common Stock. They produced *Daniel's Epic* after Wymark had done what she modestly calls an editing job, on the astonishing, cast-of-thousands fantasy he recorded at the company's workshop. This led to another collaboration with one hundred 9-year-old Southwark school children who performed their *Southwark Originals* at the Unicorn, under Wymark's direction. The plays proved an extraordinary mixture of adventure and surrealism and gave the bemused audience of parents and educationalists the heartening bonus of a totally unselfconscious culture cross. This occurred in a play that combined a London dockside family with Anansi, the West Indian folk hero. Further collaboration with children resulted in *Starters,* a five-play programme intended for performance by adult actors although they are equally suitable for children to act.

Written after much of her work with child authors, *The Bolting Sisters* shows a tendency in Wymark to dismiss her own maturity as playwright for kids, and to write for young audiences with the belief that a child is only capable of responding to that which it could express or articulate itself. If this were true, art would long since have festered to death at toddler level. However, it is a common error and Wymark makes it rarely. Certainly she remains one of the richest talents working for children's theatre.

—Ursula M. Jones

WYNNE, May

Pseudonym for Mabel Winifred Knowles. **Other Pseudonym:** Lester Lurgan. **Nationality:** British. **Born:** Streatham, London, in January 1875. **Education:** At home. **Career:** Worked in an East End Church of England mission. **Died:** 29 November 1949.

Publications for Children

Fiction

Mollie's Adventures. London, Russell, 1903.
Jimmy: The Tales of a Little Black Bear, illustrated by George Soper. London, Partridge, 1910.
Phil's Cousins, illustrated by Paul Hardy. London, Blackie, 1911.
Crackers: The Tale of a Mischievous Monkey. London, Partridge, 1911.
The Story of Heather. London, Nelson, 1912; New York, Sully, 1913.
Tony's Chums, illustrated by A.A. Dixon. London, Blackie, 1914.
Murray Finds a Chum. London, Stanley Paul, 1914.
When Auntie Lil Took Charge, illustrated by A.A. Dixon. London, Blackie, 1915.
An English Girl in Serbia. London, Collins, 1916.
Three's Company. London, Blackie, 1917.
Stranded in Belgium. London, Blackie, 1918.
A Cousin from Canada. London, Blackie, 1918.
The Honour of the School. London, Nisbet, 1918.
Dick. London, Religious Tract Society, 1919.
Phyllis in France, illustrated by Frank Gillett. London, Blackie, 1919.
The Little Girl Beautiful, illustrated by Gordon Browne. London, Religious Tract Society, 1919.
Nan and Ken. London, Nelson, 1919.
Nipper & Co. London, Stanley Paul, 1919.
Scouts for Serbia, illustrated by Archibald Webb. London, Nelson, 1919.
Comrades from Canada, illustrated by John Campbell. London, Blackie, 1919.
The Adventures of Dolly Dingle: A Fairy Story, illustrated by Florence Anderson. London, Jarrolds, 1920.
Adventures of Two, illustrated by Henry Coller. London, Blackie, 1920.
The Heroine of Chelton School. London, Stanley Paul, 1920.
The Girls of Beechcroft School, illustrated by C.E. Rhodes. London, Religious Tract Society, 1920.
Roseleen at School. London, Cassell, 1920.
Three Bears and Gwen, illustrated by John Campbell. London, Blackie, 1920.
Little Ladyship, illustrated by Gordon Browne. London, Religious Tract Society, 1921.
Lost in the Jungle. London, Stanley Paul, 1921.
Mervyn, Jock, or Joe, illustrated by Thomas Somerfield. London, Blackie, 1921.
Peggy's First Term. London, Ward Lock, 1922.
Angela Goes to School. London, Jarrolds, 1922; Cleveland, World, 1929.
The Girls of the Veldt Farm, illustrated by A.J. Shackel. London, Pearson, 1922.
The Red Boy's Gratitude. Exeter, Wheaton, 1922.
Christmas at Holford, illustrated by Thomas Somerfield. London, Blackie, 1922.
Two Girls in the Wild. London, Blackie, 1923; abridged edition, as *Sisters Out West,* 1930.
The Best of Chums. London, Ward Lock, 1923.
A Heather Holiday, illustrated by Thomas Somerfield. London, Blackie, 1923; as *Wendy's Adventure in Scotland,* 1933; *An Adventurous Holiday* (reader), 1933.
Blundering Bettina. London, Religious Tract Society, 1924.
The Girl Who Played the Game. London, Ward Lock, 1924.
Bertie, Bobby, and Belle, illustrated by Norman Sutcliffe. London, Blackie, 1924.
The Girls of Clanways Farm, illustrated by Archibald Webb. London, Cassell, 1924.
Kits at Clynton Court School. London, Warne, 1924.
The Sunshine Children. London, Nelson, 1924.
Three and One Over, illustrated by E.P. Kinsella. London, Cassell, 1924.
A Rebel at School. London, Jarrolds, 1924.
Two and a Chum, illustrated by D.C. Eyles. London, Pearson, 1924.
Hootie Toots of Hollow Tree. Philadelphia, Altemus, 1925.
The Girls of Old Grange School. London, Ward Lock, 1925.
Over the Hills and Far Away, illustrated by G.W. Goss. London, Religious Tract Society, 1925.
Dare-All Jack and the Cousins, illustrated by G.W. Goss. London, Religious Tract Society, 1925.
Hazel Asks Why. London, Ward Lock, 1926.
Carol of Hollydene School. London, Sampson Low, 1926.
The Secret of Carrock School. London, Jarrolds, 1926.
Diccon the Impossible. London, Religious Tract Society, 1926.
The Girl over the Wall, illustrated by G.W. Goss. London, Religious Tract Society, 1926.
Jean Plays Her Part, illustrated by Louise Parker. London, Religious Tract Society, 1926.
Dinah's Secret, illustrated by M.L. Parker. London, Religious Tract Society, 1927.
Jean of the Lumber Camp. London, Ward Lock, 1927.
Robin Hood to the Rescue. Exeter, Wheaton, 1927.
Terry the Black Sheep, illustrated by R.B. Ogle. London, Pearson, 1928.
The Girls of Mackland Court. London, Ward Lock, 1928.
Little Sally Mandy's Christmas Present, illustrated by Bess Goe Willis. Philadelphia, Altemus, 1929.
The House of Whispers. London, Ward Lock, 1929.
The Guide's Honour. London, Warne, 1929.
A Term to Remember. London, Aldine, 1930.
Two Girls in the Hawk's Den, illustrated by R.B. Ogle. London, Pearson, 1930.
Bobbety the Brownie. London, Warne, 1930.

The Masked Rider, illustrated by Peggy Beck. Chicago, Laidlaw, 1931.
Patient Pat Joins the Circus, illustrated by Bess Goe Willis. Philadelphia, Altemus, 1931.
Peter Rabbit and the Big Black Crows, illustrated by Bess Goe Willis. Philadelphia, Altemus, 1931.
Juliet of the Mill. London, Ward Lock, 1931.
Girls of the Pansy Patrol. London, Aldine, 1931.
Patsy from the Wilds. London, Warne, 1931.
Belle and Her Dragons. London, Jarrolds, 1931.
The Secret of Marigold Marnell. London, Religious Tract Society, 1931.
The Old Brigade. London, Religious Tract Society, 1932.
Who Was Wendy? London, Newnes, 1932.
The Heart of Glenayrt. London, Nelson, 1932.
The School Mystery. London, Readers' Library, 1933.
The Camping of the Marigolds. London, Marshall Morgan and Scott, 1933.
The Greater Covenant. London, Marshall Morgan and Scott, 1933.
Pixie's Mysterious Mission. London, Newnes, 1933.
Enter Jenny Wren. London, Ward Lock, 1933.
Comrades to Robin Hood. London, Religious Tract Society, 1934.
Malys Rockell. London, Ward Lock, 1934.
The Smugglers of Penreen. London, Religious Tract Society, 1934.
The Mysterious Island. London, Mellifont Press, 1935.
Their Girl Chum. London, Religious Tract Society, 1935.
Under Cap'n Drake. London, Religious Tract Society, 1935.
Up to Val. London, Newnes, 1935.
"Peter," The New Girl. London, Queensway Press, 1936.
The Daring of Star. London, Religious Tract Society, 1936.
Bunny and the Aunt. London, Religious Tract Society, 1936.
The Haunted Ranch. London, Dean, 1936.
Thirteen for Luck. London, Ward Lock, 1936.
Vivette on Trial. London, Queensway Press, 1936.
The Secret of Brick House. London, Ward Lock, 1937.
Two Maids of Rosemarkie. London, Epworth Press, 1937.
The Luck of Penrayne. London, Religious Tract Society, 1937.
Audrey on Approval. London, Ward Lock, 1937.
The Girl Sandy. London, Ward Lock, 1938.
The Lend-a-Hand Holiday. London, Epworth Press, 1938.
Heather the Second. London, Nelson, 1938.
The Term of Many Adventures. London, Nelson, 1939.
The Unexpected Adventure. London, Ward Lock, 1939.
The Coming of Verity. London, Ward Lock, 1940.
Sadie Comes to School. London, Epworth Press, 1942; as *Sally Comes to School,* London, Ward Lock, 1949.
Little Brown Tala. London, Mellifont Press, 1944.
Brown Tala Finds Little Tulsi. London, Mellifont Press, 1945.
Little Brown Tala Stories, illustrated by Stanley Jackson. London, Harrap, 1947.
Patch the Piebald. Croydon, Surrey, Blue Book, 1947.
Playing the Game. Croydon, Surrey, Blue Book, 1947.
Snow Fairies. London, Mellifont Press, 1947.
Ginger Ellen, illustrated by Doreen Debenham. London, Nelson, 1947.
The Great Adventure. London, Ward Lock, 1948.
The Furry Fairies. London, Mellifont Press, 1949.
Merion Plays the Game. London, Readers' Library, 1951.
Secrets of the Rockies. London, Ward Lock, 1954.

Other

Life's Object; or, Some Thoughts for Young Girls. London, Nisbet, 1899.
The Seven Champions of Christendom: A Legendary Chronicle, illustrated by Charles Folkard. London, Jarrolds, 1919.

Publications for Adults

Novels

For Faith and Navarre. London, Long, 1904.
Ronald Lindsay. London, Long, 1904.
A King's Tragedy. London, Digby Long, 1905.
The Temptation of Philip Carr. London, Sonnenschein, 1905.
Maid of Brittany. London, Greening, 1906.
The Goal. London, Digby Long, 1907.
When Terror Ruled. London, Greening, 1907.
Henry of Navarre: A Romance of August, 1572 (as Mabel W. Knowles). New York, Putnam, 1908; as May Wynne, London, Greening, 1909.
Let Erin Remember. London, Greening, 1908.
The Tailor of Vitré. London, Gay and Hancock, 1908.
For Church and Chieftain. London, Mills and Boon, 1909.
For Charles the Rover. London, Greening, 1909; New York, Fenno, 1910.
The Gipsy Count. New York, McBride, 1909.
A Blot on the Scutcheon. London, Mills and Boon, 1910; New York, Fenno, 1912.
A King's Masquerade. London, Greening, 1910.
Mistress Cynthia. London, Greening, 1910.
The Gallant Graham. London, Greening, 1911.
Honour's Fetters. London, Stanley Paul, 1911.
The Master Wit. London, Greening, 1911.
The Claim That Won. London, Everett, 1912.
Hey for Cavaliers! London, Greening, 1912.
The Red Fleur-de-Lys. London, Stanley Paul, 1912.
The Brave Brigands. London, Stanley Paul, 1913.
The Destiny of Claude. London, Stanley Paul, 1913.
The Secret of the Zenana. London, Greening, 1913.
A Run for His Money. London, Aldine, 1913.
The Curse of Gold. London, Aldine, 1914.
Goring's Girl. London, Mascot, 1914.
The Hero of Urbino. London, Stanley Paul, 1914.
The Silent Captain. London, Stanley Paul, 1914.
The Regent's Gift. London, Chapman and Hall, 1915.
Foes of Freedom. London, Chapman and Hall, 1916.
Marcel of the "Zephyrs." London, Jarrolds, 1916.
The Gipsy King. London, Chapman and Hall, 1917.
The Lyons Mail. London, Jarrolds, 1917.
Penance. London, Mascot, 1917.
A Spy for Napoleon. London, Jarrolds, 1917.
The Taint of Tragedy. London, Mascot, 1917.
The "Veiled Lady," with Draycot M. Dell. London, Jarrolds, 1918.
The King of a Day. London, Jarrolds, 1918.
Queen Jennie. London, Chapman and Hall, 1918.
The Red Whirlwind, with Draycot M. Dell. London, Jarrolds, 1919.
Robin the Prodigal. London, Jarrolds, 1919.
Love Finds a Way. London, Greening, 1920.
A Prince of Intrigue: A Romance of Mazeppa. London, Jarrolds, 1920.
A Gallant of Spain. London, Stanley Paul, 1920.
Janie's Great Mistake. London, Odhams Press, 1920.
The Spendthrift Duke. London, Holden and Hardingham, 1920.

The Ambitions of Jill. London, Long, 1920.
Mog Megone. London, Jarrolds, 1921.
My Lady's Honour. London, Lloyds, 1921.
The Red Rose of Lancaster. London, Holden and Hardingham, 1921.
A Trap for Navarre. London, Holden, 1922.
A King in the Lists. London, Stanley Paul, 1922.
The Witch-Finder. London, Jarrolds, 1923.
Jill the Hostage. London, Pearson, 1925.
Rachel Lee. London, Leng, 1925.
Theodore. London, Rivers, 1926.
Gwennola. London, Rivers, 1926.
The Fires of Youth. London, Rivers, 1927.
Plotted in Darkness. London, Stanley Paul, 1927.
King Mandrin's Challenge. London, Stanley Paul, 1927.
A Royal Traitor. London, Stanley Paul, 1927.
Love's Penalty. London, Stanley Paul, 1927.
The Terror of the Moor. London, Rivers, 1928.
Gipsy-Spelled. London, Rivers, 1929.
Red Fruit. London, Rivers, 1929.
Hamlet: A Romance from Shakespeare's Play. London, Rivers, 1930.
The Girl Upstairs. London, Thomson, 1932.
The Unseen Witness. London, Leng, 1932.
Stella Maris. London, Leng, 1932.
The Tempter's Power. London, Leng, 1932.
Tangled Fates. London, Mellifont Press, 1935.
Flower o' the Moor. London, Houghton and Scott-Snell, 1935.
The Choice of Mavis. London, Mellifont Press, 1935.
Temptation. London, Mellifont Press, 1937.
Whither? London, Heath Cranton, 1938.
Love Dismayed. London, Mellifont Press, 1942.
Echoed from the Past. London, Mellifont Press, 1944.
The Pursuing Shadow. London, Mellifont Press, 1944.
The Unsuspected Witness. London, Mellifont Press, 1945.
The Secret of the Caves. London, Mellifont Press, 1945.

Novels as Lester Lurgan

Bohemian Blood. London, Greening, 1910.
The Mill-Owner. London, Greening, 1910.
The League of the Triangle. London, Greening, 1911.
A Message from Mars. London, Greening, 1912.
The Ban. London, Stanley Paul, 1912.
The Wrestler on the Shore. London, Everett, 1913.

Other

In the Shadows; or, Thoughts for Mourners. London, Marshall, 1900.
Sympathy. London, Skeffington, 1901.
The Life and Reign of Victoria the Good. London, Stanley Paul, 1913.

* * *

May Wynne's output for children was prodigious, and her style altered noticeably after the first decade of the 20th century when the more extroverted girls' school story had largely supplanted the domestic tale. Her first stories were more appropriate in mood and setting for mid-Victorian readers. In *Life's Object; or, Some Thoughts for Young Girls* she reprovingly insists on the girl's place being firmly in the home, and deplores the influence of sport which she considers destructive of "the tender womanly woman"; in *Mollie's Adventures* some of her child characters are engaged in making matchboxes in a London basement, in conditions of employment that were grisly even for Edwardian times. She was then writing moral tales in which pace and characterization were sacrificed to narrative sermonizing and admonition. Yet soon afterwards, in a spate of lively stories, she was plunging her adolescent heroines into hectic adventures on school hockey-fields, and in Girl Guide camps in remote and surprisingly hazardous areas of the English countryside.

She carried into her stories for girls many of the elements which also proved successful in her adult romantic novels (kidnappings, strange encounters with gypsies, ancient houses, crumbling clock-towers, abundances of secret passages, and so on). In complete contrast to her turgid early stories, pace became all important in her books during the 1920s and 1930s. Many of her heroines went abroad, to get the better of Balkan brigands or jungle "savages." Her foreign adventures followed the tradition set by Bessie Marchant, in which no corner of the globe seemed too remote or dangerous to attract the British schoolgirl. And, also like Marchant, Wynne was especially partial to Canadian settings (*A Cousin from Canada, Comrades from Canada,* etc.).

In addition to her numerous full-length books, Wynne wrote short stories for periodicals like the *Girl's Own Paper* and *Little Folks,* and for several annuals.

—Mary Cadogan

WYNNE-JONES, Tim(othy)

Nationality: Canadian. **Born:** Bromborough, Cheshire, England, 12 August 1948. **Education:** University of Waterloo, Ontario, B.F.A. 1974; York University, Downsview, Ontario, M.A. in art 1978. **Family:** Married Amanda West Lewis in 1980; two sons and one daughter. **Career:** Book designer, PMA Books, Toronto, 1974-76; Instructor in Visual Arts, University of Waterloo, 1976-78, and York University, 1978-80; graphic designer, Solomon and Wynne-Jones, Toronto, 1976-79. Founding member and secretary, Crime Writers of Canada, Toronto, 1981-84; children's books critic, Toronto *Globe and Mail,* 1985-88. **Awards:** Ruth Schwartz award, 1984; Actra award, for radio play, 1987; Governor General's Award, 1993, 1995; Canadian Library Association Children's Book of the Year award, 1993. **Address:** DK Publishing, Inc., 95 Madison Ave., New York, New York 10016, U.S.A.; 142 Winona Dr., Toronto, Ontario M6G 3S9, Canada.

PUBLICATIONS FOR CHILDREN

Fiction

Madelaine and Ermadello, illustrated by Lindsey Hallam. Toronto, Before We Are Six, 1977.
Zoom at Sea, illustrated by Ken Nutt. Vancouver, Douglas and McIntyre, 1983; illustrated by Eric Beddows, New York, HarperCollins, 1993.

Zoom Away, illustrated by Ken Nutt. Vancouver, Douglas and McIntyre, 1985; illustrated by Eric Beddows, New York, HarperCollins, 1993.
I'll Make You Small, illustrated by Maryann Kovalski. Vancouver, Douglas and McIntyre, 1986.
Architect of the Moon, illustrated by Ian Wallace. Toronto, Groundwood, 1988; as *Builder of the Moon,* New York, McElderry, 1989.
The Hour of the Frog, illustrated by Katherine Oneal. Toronto, Groundwood, and Boston, Little Brown, 1989.
Mouse in the Manger, illustrated by Elaine Blier. Toronto, Penguin, 1993.
The Last Piece of Sky, illustrated by Marie-Louise Gray. Toronto, Groundwood, 1993.
Some of the Kinder Planets (short stories). Toronto, Groundwood, 1993; New York, Orchard Books, 1995.
Rosie Backstage, with Amanda Lewis. Toronto, Kids Can Press, 1994.
The Book of Changes (short stories). Toronto, Groundwood, 1994; New York, Orchard Books, 1995.
Zoom Upstream, illustrated by Eric Beddows. New York, HarperCollins, 1994.
The Maestro. Vancouver, Douglas & McIntyre, 1995; New York, Orchard Books, 1996.
Reteller, *The Hunchback of Notre Dame* by Victor Hugo, illustrated by Bill Slavin. New York, Orchard Books, 1996.
Stephen Fair: A Novel. New York, DK Ink, 1998.

Verse

Mischief City, illustrated by Victor Gad. Toronto, Groundwood, 1986.

Publications for Adults

Novels

Odd's End. Toronto, McClelland and Stewart, Boston, Little Brown, and London, Deutsch, 1980.
The Knot. Toronto, McClelland and Stewart, 1982.
Fastyngange. Toronto, Lester and Orpen Dennys, 1988; London, Hodder and Stoughton, 1989.
Voices. London, Hodder and Stoughton, 1990.

Plays

Radio Plays: *The Thinking Room,* 1981; *The Road Ends at the Sea,* 1982; *The Strange Odyssey of Lennis Freed,* 1983; *The Testing of Stanley Teagarden,* 1985; *The Enormous Radio,* from the story by John Cheever, 1986; *St. Anthony's Man,* from his own story, 1987; *Mr. Gendelman Crashes a Party,* 1987; *Dust Is the Only Secret,* 1988; *We Now Return You to Your Regularly Scheduled Universe,* 1992.

*

Bibliography: By Dave Jenkinson, in *Emergency Librarian* (Vancouver), January-February 1988.

Tim Wynne-Jones comments:

While I work diligently on novel writing; submit outlines and stick to them; write radio plays; and whip songs off at the drop of a hat—picture book stories come to me unbidden, usually in early morning or dead of night. I cannot decide to write a picture book, only make myself ready. Each storybook seems to grow from two ideas which have occurred to me at quite different times, sometimes years apart, and which "marry" across the ethers. The actual writing down takes very little time, but then, like poetry, there is the worrying over every word and syllable, for the rhythm of the thing is its heartbeat.

I write for children out of the child I was and am. I cannot write for an audience—where children's books are concerned, I am the Selfish Giant, shooing my audience away in order to reclaim the garden for myself!

* * *

Lyricist, playwright, novelist, and critic Tim Wynne-Jones brings to his poetry and fiction for children a relish for language, a quirky sense of humour, and a deep belief in the powers of imagination and creativity. At his best, in his picture books about the adventures of the little cat, Zoom, and in some of his short stories for older children, he combines great sophistication with a sure intuition of the childlike to produce works in which meaning can not be simply paraphrased but reverberates beneath the simple surface of image and dialogue.

Wynne-Jones' picture books often involve mysterious journeys, in which the context is not really explained but still draws the reader immediately into the fantasy. Zoom, a little white cat who loves water, is guided by messages from his sailor uncle Roy to undertake sea voyages, with the assistance of an enigmatic and beautiful woman, Maria. While each of Zoom's three journeys is by water, each also takes place—in dream-like fashion—within Maria's house, where the rooms transform themselves into a sea shore with crabs and waves, the frozen Arctic Ocean, and ancient Egypt. The idea of a house where rooms become landscapes, opening up before the adventurer, is a wonderful touch. From book to book, Zoom becomes progressively a little more independent: in *Zoom at Sea* he simply plays in the sea Maria has created for him, but in each of the two later books he undertakes a quest for the missing Uncle Roy. Zoom resembles a preschool child exploring the wonders and sensory pleasures of the world, under the loving and watchful eye of Maria; his individuality—as expressed in his un-catlike fondness for water—is celebrated and his courage in venturing into new worlds is rewarded by delightful experiences and a safe return to security at the end. The delicate, matter-of-fact quality of Wynne-Jones' accounts of these miraculous journeys is admirably matched by the softly detailed black and white pencil illustrations of Ken Nutt (Eric Beddows).

The Last Piece of Sky also involves a magical journey by water, although in this picture book the journey is undertaken by a boy rather than a cat, and has a motive other than the desire for adventure. In a fit of temper Colin has scattered the pieces of Olivia's jigsaw puzzle, and he is led by a duck and a snake to find at the bottom of the pond both the missing piece of sky from the puzzle and, by implication, his own good humour again. In *Architect of the Moon* a little boy flies through the night with his toy blocks to repair the moon. The journey in *I'll Make You Small* is a much shorter one but the dangers seem greater, as the ill-natured old man next door who delivers the threat made explicit in the title is as frightening as any fairy-tale ogre or witch. As in a fairy tale, he is eventually defeated by the courage and kindness of the little boy, and in this case is won over to good behavior rather than destroyed.

Zany charm and an engaging sense of connection with the interests and frustrations of children's everyday life characterize Wynne-Jones' books of verse. *The Hour of the Frog* builds a camp-fire ghost story atmosphere of mock horror up to a very funny moment of revelation: it is a miniature comic masterpiece, skillfully using words and rhythms to create suspense and then deflate it into bathos. The shorter poems of *Mischief City* are in the tradition of Dennis Lee's *Alligator Pie,* humorously exaggerating the complaints and tribulations of modern urban children's lives in brief, catchy verses with strongly marked end rhymes. Imagination and artistic creativity, the poems suggest, are good means by which to handle the frustrations of ordinary family life.

The conjunction of familiar and the strange is the basis for many of the stories for older children in *Some of the Kinder Planets.* One ingenious story about a technological-sophisticated family living in a geodesic dome in the woods amusingly relates how "alien abduction" accounts might get started, as an unsophisticated and suspicious boy who comes to the house in a snowstorm is alarmed by a FAX machine, Japanese food, and an accent and vocabulary that differs from his. Always on the side of his child characters in their conflicts with bossy, hypercritical, or uncomprehending adults, Wynne-Jones is also hopeful about the possibility of encounters with adults who are understanding and appreciative. The title story celebrates what one of these adults calls "every child's right to live without fear," replacing fear with wonder; the capacity to find the strange and wonderful in the familiar, ordinary world—like the rooms of Maria's house—underlies all of Wynne-Jones' work for children.

In *Some of the Kinder Planets, The Book of Changes,* and *The Maestro,* Tim Wynne-Jones addresses an audience of children slightly older than the ones for whom the picture books were marketed. The central figures in these stories are often at the end of childhood or in early adolescence. Poised at a moment of profound change, these child/adults are emblematic of our millennial anxieties. Two simultaneous pulls are in play: one a desire for a secure, familiar past; the other, a desire for an independent unsullied future. Wynne-Jones address both desires in his fiction. His criticism then serves as a gloss on how he sees the world in which he writes.

In *Onceuponatime@here.now: or Can Rumpelstiltskin Surf(viv)e the Net?,* the 1996 Stubbs Lecture for the Osborne Collection, Wynne-Jones returns to the fairy tale in an internet world as a way of negotiating the change. He writes that the "fairy tale is a hard little nub of a decoder ring. But it, itself, is also a code. Narrative information on which a story can be spun." That is what happens in *The Maestro* (1995), for which Wynne-Jones won the Governor General's Award. The story looks like a typical fairy tale quest, into the woods—though the Canadian woods are not quite like the Germanic woods of the Grimm stories. The protagonist, Burl Crow, finds the fairy tale house of a saviour/ogre, a reclusive pianist modeled on Glen Gould. As in all good fairy tales, Burl must "knock three times" to enter. Unlike the fairy tale—though like the world of the recording studio—Burl gets a "second take" at sorting out his destiny.

The strength of the novel is in the tension between the genuine anger of the adolescent and the inhospitable world in which he finds himself. As in the traditional fairy tale, the resourcefulness of the hero wins out, the adult aid provided not by the fairy tale ogre, but from an unlikely source, in a manner reminiscent of *Great Expectations.*

—Gwyneth Evans, updated by Lissa Paul

Y-Z

YAFFE, Alan. See **YORINKS, Arthur.**

YASHIMA, Taro

Pseudonym for Jun Atsushi Iwamatsu. **Nationality:** American (originally Japanese; emigrated to the United States, 1939). **Born:** Kagoshima, Japan, 21 September 1908. **Education:** Provincial High School, Kagoshima; Imperial Art Academy, Tokyo, 1927-30; Art Students' League, New York, 1939-41. **Military Service:** United States Army Office of War Information and Office of Strategic Services during World War II. **Family:** Married to Tomoe Iwamatsu (pseudonym: Mitsu Yashima); one son and one daughter. **Career:** Freelance artist, illustrator, and writer: several individual shows; collections include Phillips Memorial Museum, Washington, D.C. Director, Yashima Art Institute, Los Angeles, 1950s. **Awards:** Huntington Hartford Foundation grant, 1954; Child Study Committee award, 1956; Caldecott Honor Book (*Crow Boy*), 1956; Caldecott Honor Book (*Momo's Umbrella*), 1959; Award for Distinguished Contribution to the Fields of Illustration and Writing from Southern California Council on Literature for Young People, 1964; Caldecott Honor Book (*Seashore Story*) 1967; University of Mississippi de Grummond Collection Medallion, 1974. **Died:** 30 June 1994.

PUBLICATIONS FOR CHILDREN (ILLUSTRATED BY THE AUTHOR)

Fiction

The New Sun. New York, Holt, 1943.
Horizon Is Calling. New York, Holt, 1947.
The Village Tree. New York, Viking Press, 1953.
With Mitsu Yashima, *Plenty to Watch.* New York, Viking Press, 1954.
Crow Boy. New York, Viking Press, 1955; London, Penguin, 1976.
Umbrella. New York, Viking Press, 1958.
The Golden Footprints, with Hatoju Juku. Cleveland, World Publishing, 1960
With Mitsu Yashima, *Momo's Kitten.* New York, Viking Press, 1961.
The Youngest One. New York, Viking Press, 1962.
Seashore Story. New York, Viking Press, 1967.
One-Inch Fellow. New York, Harcourt Brace, 1995.

Other

Translator, *The Golden Footprints,* by Hatoju Muku. Cleveland, World, 1960.

*

Illustrator: *Which Was Witch* by Eleanore M. Jewett, 1953; *The Sugar Pear Tree* by Clyde Robert Bulla, 1961; *Soo Ling Finds a Way* by June Behrens, 1965; *The Fisherman and the Goblet* by Mark Taylor , 1971.

Media Adaptations: *Plenty to Watch* (recording), Bowmar Records, 1963; *Crow Boy* (audiovisual), Weston Woods, 1992; *Umbrella* (audiovisual) Learning Connection, 1993.

Manuscript Collection: The de Grummond Collection, University of Southern Mississippi, Hattisburg.

Bibliography: *Hurrah for Crow Boy!* by Naomi Wakan, Vancouver, Canada, Pacific-Rim, 1992.

Taro Yashima comments:

Let children enjoy living on this earth, let children be strong enough to be beaten or twisted by evil on this earth.

* * *

The picture books of Taro Yashima, including two written with his wife Mitsu, draw children into the Yashimas' world—to the Japan they knew as children and to their family life in this country with their daughter Momo. Readers now are quick to recognize the Taro Yashima pictures, which fill the pages with glowing crayon-like colors and textures, while figures and objects are rarely shown in clear detail. Instead, movement and rhythm and use of space suggestively convey story action and feeling. Because of this lack of specificity—which varies a little from book to book—some of the stories are less suitable than others for very young children, who generally need to see the details of a picture in order to understand it.

Plenty to Watch records in lively text and abundant pictures the fascinating sights children could see on their way home from the village school in Japan. It was *Crow Boy,* the next book, however, that really called the world's attention to the name Taro Yashima. This large, flat picture book, suitable for children in the lower elementary grades, tells the universal story of a schoolboy in Japan who was "different" and was called "stupid," but in the end was discovered to have a talent entirely his own. Readers identify with both the boy and his tormentors, and they ponder his elusive appeal. The suggestive pictures demand participation, and the story invites exploration of its layers of meaning.

In one of the three books about Momo, *The Youngest One,* she is a big girl finding ways to help a two-year-old neighbor boy overcome his shyness. But in *Umbrella* and *Momo's Kitten* she is a very little girl loving her first umbrella and her kitten. Yashima's prose depicts the fleeting moments that capture Momo's character and his illustrations reveal the small things that so engross a child. Large, bright, fairly detailed pictures in these two books have helped to make them great favorites.

Also popular with young children is *The Village Tree,* the author's recall of boyhood summer fun, similar in its intent to *Plenty to Watch.* Suitable for older children is *Seashore Story,* one of Yashima's most beautiful works, in which he tells the old legend of Urashima, the fisherman who stayed too long in the land beneath the sea. The story itself could appeal to a wide age range, but here Yashima's pictures require sophisticated ability to appreciate the abstraction of the illustrations and the philosophical questions presented for children to ponder. A departure from Yashima's usual picture book format is *The Golden Footprints,* an illustrated storybook translated and adapted from a story by an old friend, Hatoju Muku, that tells of the loyalty of some parent foxes to their captured baby fox and to the boy who befriended it.

Yashima was chosen by other writers as illustrator for their picture books, and his own *Seashore Story, Umbrella,* and *Crow Boy* have been runners-up for the Caldecott Medal, awarded annually to the illustrator of the most distinguished picture book published in the United States during the preceding year. Most of his books remain in print; many are included in educational curriculum materials, especially in units emphasizing multicultural literature and ethics, and several have been adapted to audiovisual mediums. Yashima's simple stories and evocative illustrations charm young readers as well as adults who read to them.

—Claudia Lewis, updated by Linda Benson

YEE, Paul (R.)

Nationality: Canadian. **Born:** Spalding, Saskatchewan, 1 October 1956. **Education:** University of British Columbia, B.A. 1978; M.A. 1983. **Career:** Assistant city archivist, City of Vancouver Archives, Vancouver, British Columbia, 1980-1988; portfolio manager, Archives of Ontario, Toronto, 1988-91; policy analyst, Ontario Ministry of Citizenship, since 1991. Writer since 1983. Teacher in British Columbia schools, and at Simon Fraser University, University of Victoria, University of British Columbia, Vancouver Museum, and Chinese Community Library Services Society of Vancouver. Prepared *Saltwater City* exhibition, Chinese Cultural Centre (CCC), Vancouver Centennial, 1986. **Awards:** Canada Council Literature Prizes, Honorable Mention, 1986; Vancouver Book Prize, 1989; Sheila A Egoff Book Prize for Children's Literature, 1990, for *Tales from Gold Mountain*; I.O.D.E. Violet Downey Children's Book Award, 1990, for *Tales from Gold Mountain*; Parents' Choice Honor, 1990 for *Tales from Gold Mountain*; Canadian Booksellers Association Ruth Schwartz Award, 1992 for *Roses Sing on New Snow* Governor General's Children's Literature Award, 1996 for *Ghost Train,* Ruth Schwarz Children's Book Award, 1997 for *Ghost Train.*

PUBLICATIONS FOR CHILDREN

Fiction

Teach Me to Fly, Skyfighter! and Other Stories, illustrated by Sky Lee. Toronto, James Lorimer & Co., 1983.

The Curses of Third Uncle (novel). Toronto, James Lorimer & Co., 1986.

Tales from Gold Mountain: Stories of the Chinese in the New World, illustrated by Simon Ng. Toronto, Groundwood Books, 1989; New York, Macmillan, 1990.

Roses Sing on New Snow: A Delicious Tale, illustrated by Harvey Chan. New York, Macmillan, 1992.

Breakaway (novel). Toronto, Groundwood Books, 1994.

Ghost Train, illustrated by Harvey Chan. Toronto, Groundwood Books, 1996.

Other

Saltwater City: An Illustrated History of the Chinese in Vancouver. Vancouver, Douglas & McIntyre, 1988; Seattle, University of Washington, Toronto, Douglas & McIntyre 1989.

Contributor, *The Unseen: Scary Stories,* selected by Janet Lunn. Toronto, Lester, 1994.

Struggle and Hope: The Story of Chinese Canadians. Toronto, Umbrella Press, 1996.

* * *

Paul Yee is a member of Canada's most promising new generation of children's writers. To date he has completed three books for young children, all of which are inspired by his Chinese Canadian roots: *Tales from Gold Mountain: Stories of the Chinese in the New World, Roses Sing on New Snow: A Delicious Story,* and *Ghost Train.*

Tales from Gold Mountain is a collection of eight original stories which, according to Yee's own afterword to the volume, are "all firmly rooted in real places and events, in things such as the work world of the Chinese, the folk traditions they brought from China, and the frontier society of this continent." The collection opens with "Spirits of the Railway," a ghost story about a man who learns the circumstances of his father's death from his dead father himself. In following the instructions of his father's spirit, the son eventually finds peace. "Sons and Daughters" is the rather bizarre story of a Chinese Canadian merchant who is determined that his family name continue. When his wife gives birth to twin daughters, he conceals their gender from everyone, whisking them off to China where they are exchanged for male infants who are raised as his sons. When the young men are ready to marry, they are sent to China to find brides; but as fate would have it, they wed the daughters sold so many years before. The merchant is punished for his selfish folly when both couples are cursed by the gods with barrenness.

In "The Friends of Kwan Ming," a gluttonous, selfish businessman receives just recompense for his lifestyle when he overeats and explodes. "Ginger for the Heart" tells how two lovers overcome adversity and repressive traditions, eventually marrying and finding true happiness. "Gambler's Eyes" is a haunting story about the burdens of racism and the stigma of miscegenation. In some ways, "Forbidden Fruit" is the mirror image of "Ginger for the Heart": it depicts a proud, tradition-bound father who destroys his daughter when he refuses to permit her to marry the man she has chosen. "Rider Chan and the Night River," another ghost story, tells how a young man escapes the clutches of a river spirit because of his courage and his loyalty to his mother. The final tale, "The Revenge of the Iron Chink," tells how, after having been replaced by a machine, a faithful employee takes revenge on his hard and greedy employer. Striking, emblematic illustrations by Simon Ng are the ideal complement to the text. The collection can be read and enjoyed by fourth graders, although older children and adolescents will better appreciate its ironies and political/social implications.

Roses Sing on New Snow describes how Maylin, a young woman who cooked for a restaurant famous "throughout the New World for its fine food," creates a new dish of "delectable flavors and aromas, which she named Roses Sing on New Snow." When the visiting governor of South China requests the recipe so that he may present it to the Emperor, Maylin's father and brothers claim to have invented the dish. Eventually, however, its true creator is revealed; and she explains that because the dish has been created in the New World, one "cannot recreate it in the Old." Although some words and phrases will be unfamiliar to young readers, most second graders will enjoy the text and Harvey Chan's wonderfully detailed watercolor illustrations—and will value Yee's portrait of Maylin as a woman of talent and wisdom.

Ghost Train tells the story of Choon-Yi, who grows up without her father. Because her father was killed while building the railway in North America, Choon-Yi uses her magic to paint the "fire car". This is the ghost train which will transport home the souls of the railway labourers who, like her father, were killed while constructing the North American railways. Like Maylin, Choon-Yi is both wise and talented and uses her gifts to help others.

Although they are intended for slightly older readers, three other books by Yee are sometimes read by third and fourth grade children: *The Curses of Third Uncle, Breakaway,* and *Teach Me to Fly, Skyfighter!* These two novels and one collection of short stories feature teenage protagonists and are set early in the twentieth century. As with his picture books, these works reflect Yee's interest in the experience of Chinese-Canadian children and the conflicts that arise out of their Chinese and Anglo-Canadian roots.

In addition, Yee has written two non-fiction works. *Saltwater City* combines Yee's text with photographs to present a history of Vancouver's Chinese community. And *Struggle and Hope,* which is part of the "People of Canada" series, examines Chinese Canadian history in a broader sense.

—Keith Lawrence, updated by Alexandra MacLennan

YERXA, Leo

Nationality: Canadian and Ojibwa. **Born:** Little Eagle Reserve, Ontario, Canada, 1947. **Education:** Algonquin College, Ottawa, University of Waterloo. **Career:** Artist/designer for Royal Ontario Museum, Canadian Museum of Civilization, Royal Canadian Mint. **Awards:** Amelia Frances Howard-Gibbon Award, 1994; Mr. Christie Book Award, 1994; Elizabeth Mrazik Cleaver Award, 1994, all for *Last Leaf First Snowflake to Fall.*

PUBLICATIONS FOR CHILDREN

Fiction

Last Leaf First Snowflake to Fall. Toronto and Vancouver, Douglas and McIntyre, 1993.

A Fish Tale, or The Little One that Got Away. Toronto and Vancouver, Douglas and McIntyre, 1995.

* * *

The remembrance of a childhood experience with his father and his desire to share the memory with his son led Ojibwa artist Leo Yerxa to create *Last Leaf First Snowflake to Fall,* his first picture book. The free verse account of a late autumn day and night spent by a parent and child in the northern forests presents a sequence of simple events and subtly emphasizes the unity among all elements of the created world. As day breaks, the two *nishnawbe* (human beings) leave their cabin, explore the countryside, set up camp, and fall asleep as the season's first snow blankets the carpet of leaves they had walked on during the day. The next morning, the child narrator expresses a sense of new life for himself and the land: "I arose from the earth / and walked into the light / of a new season."

Both words and pictures suggest continuity and interrelationship: the cycles of the season and of day and night and the harmony that exists among all created beings. The written text begins with a reverential hymn to creation, including the first snowfall. The father and child become part of the nonhuman world into which they enter. The clouds reflected in the water give a sense of "our canoe ... drifting across the sky." The ripples made by a falling leaf become a circle that embraces the entire pond on which they paddle. In his play, the child becomes a leaf, and the pair "mingled" their footprints with those of "the other animals." Yerxa's illustrations, created from dyed pieces of tissue paper, along with ink sketches and water colors, reinforce the sense of a unified, harmonious world. The human figures do not dominate the scenes through which they travel; in fact, they are often the smallest objects in the pictures. Their buckskin clothing links them to the brown autumn landscape. Circles, Native emblems of harmony and unity, are found in many illustrations, some of which are themselves shaped as circles or ovals. In words and pictures, the book embodies traditional Native themes. It also reveals such universal themes as the relationship between a parent and child and a child's sense of wonder at a marvelous natural event: the season's first snowfall.

For *A Fish Tale or, The Little One that Got Away,* Yerxa moved away from both the artistic techniques and overly autobiographical subject matter of his first book. The autobiography of a small walleye who becomes discouraged with his life at "darting school" and searches for answers to the large questions that trouble him, the story resembles moralistic animal fables frequently told to children. However, Yerxa's narrator, now an old fish who retells his youthful adventure to young fish, doesn't provide simple answers to the questions he once raised. In examining the importance of telling a story about his past, the narrator may, in fact, be presenting some of the author's own thoughts about narratives. A lover of the "fantastic tales" told by the old fish, the young hero wonders if they were true or if they were lies told as warnings. "One school of thought was that the stories could come true if you believed." Guided to the surface by a malicious, deceitful pike, the hero is caught and then released by a fisherman and returns to his home a wiser, more mature fish who understands the value and meaning of story. Yerxa;s water color washes, in various hues, reflect not only the shifting light patterns of the underwater world, but also the changing emotions of the little fish, a tiny often solitary figure in many of the book's double-spreads.

Although Yerxa's native Ojibwa heritage may be seen as an influence in both his artistic style and use of the journey as a major narrative pattern, his work is not specifically within the tradition of Native children's literature. His central characters are on travels of discovery that lead them to new awareness of themselves and the worlds around, as is the case in many Native spirit quest. The stylized landscapes of *Last Leaf First Snowflake* evoke the northern Ontario forests of Yerxa's childhood. However, the use of collage is similar to that of Elizabeth Cleaver, and the narrator's experience of the season's first snow recalls the experiences of the boy in Ezra Jack Keats's *The Snowy Day.* The water color washes of *A Fish Tale* are more reminiscent of the art of Michael Foreman or Ann Blades than that of Ojibwa vision painting, while the story is similar to Leo Lionni's *Swimmy.* Yerxa's works thus speak to the interests and concerns of children from many cultures.

—Jon C. Stott

YOLEN, Jane (Hyatt)

Nationality: American. **Born:** New York City, 11 February 1939. **Education:** Staples High School, Westport, Connecticut, graduated 1956; Smith College, Northampton, Massachusetts, B.A. 1960; New School for Social Research, New York; University of Massachusetts, Amherst, 1975-78, M.Ed. 1976. **Family:** Married David W. Stemple in 1962; one daughter and two sons. **Career:** Staff member, *This Week* magazine and *Saturday Review,* New York, 1960-61; assistant editor, Gold Medal Books, New York, 1961-62; associate editor, Rutledge Books, New York, 1962-63; assistant editor, Alfred A. Knopf Juvenile Books, New York, 1963-65; Lecturer in Education, Smith College, 1979-84. Columnist ("Children's Bookfare"), *Daily Hampshire Gazette,* Northampton, Massachusetts, 1972-80. Massachusetts delegate, Democratic National Convention, Miami, 1972. **Member:** Member of the Board of Directors, Society of Children's Book Writers since 1974, and Children's Literature Association, 1977-79; President, Science-Fiction Writers of America, 1986-88. **Awards:** Boys' Club of America Junior Book award, 1968, for *The Minstrel and the Mountain*; Lewis Carroll Shelf award, 1968, for *The Emperor and the Kite,* and 1973, for *The Girl Who Loved the Wind*; *The Emperor and the Kite* was selected one of the *New York Times*' Best Books of the Year and as a Caldecott Honor Book, both 1968; *World on a String: The Story of Kites* was named an ALA Notable Book, 1968; Chandler Book Talk Reward of Merit, 1970; *The Girl Who Loved the Wind* was selected for the Children's Book Showcase of the Children's Book Council, 1973, and *The Little Spotted Fish,* 1976; Society of Children's Book Writers Golden Kite award, 1974, ALA Notable Book and National Book award nomination, both 1975, all for *The Girl Who Cried Flowers and Other Tales*; Golden Kite Honor Book, 1975, for *The Transfigured Hart,* and 1976, for *The Moon Ribbon and Other Tales*; Christopher Medal, 1978, for *The Seeing Stick*; Children's Choice from the International Reading Association and the Children's Book Council, 1980, for *Mice on Ice,* and 1983, for *Dragon's Blood*; Parents' Choice award from the Parents' Choice Foundation, 1982, for *Dragon's Blood,* 1984, for *The Stone Silenus,* and 1989 for *Piggins and The Three Bears Rhyme Book*; *The Gift of Sarah Barker* was selected one of *School Library Journal*'s Best Books for Young Adults, 1982, and *Heart's Blood,* 1985; Garden State Children's Book award from the New Jersey Library Association, 1983, for *Commander Toad in Space*; CRABerry award from Acton Public Library, Maryland, 1983, for *Dragon's Blood*; *Heart's Blood* was selected one of ALA's Best Books for Young Adults, 1984; Daedelus award, 1986, for "body of work—fantasy and short fiction"; *The Lullaby Songbook* and *The Sleeping Beauty* were each selected one of Child Study Association of America's Children's Books of the Year, 1987; Caldecott Medal, 1988, for *Owl Moon*; World Fantasy award, 1988, for *Favorite Folktales from around the World*; Kerlan award for "singular achievements in the creation of children's literature," 1988; Parents' Choice Silver Seal award, Jewish Book Council award, and Association of Jewish Libraries award, all 1988, Judy Lopez Honor Book and Nebula award finalist, both 1989, all for *The Devil's Arithmetic*; Golden Sower award from the Nebraska Library Association, 1989, for *Piggins*; thirteen of Yolen's books have been selected by the Junior Literary Guild; Charlotte award, New York State Reading Council, for *Piggins,* 1991; Regina Medal, Catholic Library Association, 1992, for body of work; Smith College Medal, 1992, Distinguished Alumna; Mythopoeic Society award, 1993, for *Briar Rose*; Rhysling award for best science fiction/fantasy poem, for *Will,* 1993; Young Adult Best Books, American Library Association, for *Briar Rose,* 1993. L.L.D.: College of Our Lady of the Elms, Chicopee, Massachusetts, 1980. **Agent:** Marilyn Marlow, Curtis Brown, 10 Astor Place, New York, New York 10003. **Address:** 31 School Street, Box 27, Hatfield, Massachusetts 01038, U.S.A.

Publications for Children

Fiction

The Witch Who Wasn't, illustrated by Arnold Roth. New York, Macmillan, and London, Collier Macmillan, 1964.

Gwinellen, The Princess Who Could Not Sleep, illustrated by Ed Renfro. New York, Macmillan, 1965.

With Anne Huston, *Trust a City Kid,* illustrated by J.C. Kocsis. New York, Lothrop, 1966; London, Dent, 1967.

Isabel's Noel, illustrated by Arnold Roth. New York, Funk and Wagnalls, 1967.

The Emperor and the Kite, illustrated by Ed Young. Cleveland, World, 1967; London, Macdonald, 1969.

The Minstrel and the Mountain, illustrated by Anne Rockwell. Cleveland, World, and Edinburgh, Oliver and Boyd, 1968.

Greyling, illustrated by William Stobbs. Cleveland, World, 1968; London, Bodley Head, 1969.

The Longest Name on the Block, illustrated by Peter Madden. New York, Funk and Wagnalls, 1968.

The Wizard of Washington Square, illustrated by Ray Cruz. New York, World, 1969.

The Inway Investigators, or, The Mystery at McCracken's Place, illustrated by Allan Eitzen. New York, Seabury Press, 1969.

The Seventh Mandarin, illustrated by Ed Young. New York, Seabury Press, and London, Macmillan, 1970.

Hobo Toad and the Motorcycle Gang, illustrated by Emily McCully. New York, World, 1970.

The Bird of Time, illustrated by Mercer Mayer. New York, Crowell, 1971.

The Girl Who Loved the Wind, illustrated by Ed Young. New York, Crowell, 1972; London, Collins, 1973.

The Girl Who Cried Flowers and Other Tales, illustrated by David Palladini. New York, Crowell, 1974.

Rainbow Rider, illustrated by Michael Foreman. New York, Crowell, 1974; London, Collins, 1975.

The Adventures of Eeka Mouse, illustrated by Myra Gibson McKee. Middletown, Connecticut, Xerox, 1974.
The Boy Who Had Wings, illustrated by Helga Aichinger. New York, Crowell, 1974.
The Magic Three of Solatia, illustrated by Julia Noonan. New York, Crowell, 1974.
The Little Spotted Fish, illustrated by Friso Henstra. New York, Seabury Press, 1975.
The Transfigured Hart, illustrated by Donna Diamond. New York, Crowell, 1975.
The Moon Ribbon and Other Tales, illustrated by David Palladini. New York, Crowell, 1976; London, Dent, 1977.
Milkweed Days, photographs by Gabriel Amadeus Cooney. New York, Crowell, 1976.
The Sultan's Perfect Tree, illustrated by Barbara Garrison. New York, Parents' Magazine Press, 1977.
The Seeing Stick, illustrated by Remy Charlip and Demetra Marsalis. New York, Crowell, 1977.
The Lady and the Merman, illustrated by Barry Moser. Easthampton, Massachusetts, Pennyroyal Press, 1977.
The Hundredth Dove and Other Tales, illustrated by David Palladini. New York, Crowell, 1977; London, Dent, 1979.
The Giants' Farm, illustrated by Tomie de Paola. New York, Seabury Press, 1977.
Hannah Dreaming, photographs by Alan Epstein. Springfield, Massachusetts, Springfield Museum of Fine Arts, 1977.
The Mermaid's Three Wisdoms, illustrated by Laura Rader. New York, Collins World, 1978.
No Bath Tonight, illustrated by Nancy Winslow Parker. New York, Crowell, 1978.
The Simple Prince, illustrated by Jack Kent. New York, Parents' Magazine Press, 1978.
Spider Jane, illustrated by Stefen Bernath. New York, Coward McCann, 1978.
Dream Weaver, illustrated by Michael Hague. New York, Collins, 1979.
The Giants Go Camping, illustrated by Tomie de Paola. New York, Seabury Press, 1979.
Spider Jane on the Move, illustrated by Stefen Bernath. New York, Coward McCann, 1980.
Mice on Ice, illustrated by Lawrence Di Fiori. New York, Dutton, 1980.
Commander Toad in Space, illustrated by Bruce Degen. New York, Coward McCann, 1980.
The Robot and Rebecca, illustrated by Catherine Deeter. New York, Random House, 1980.
Shirlick Holmes and the Case of the Wandering Wardrobe, illustrated by Anthony Rao. New York, Coward McCann, 1981.
Uncle Lemon's Spring, illustrated by Glen Rounds. New York, Dutton, 1981.
The Boy Who Spoke Chimp, illustrated by David Wiesner. New York, Knopf, 1981.
Brothers of the Wind, illustrated by Barbara Berger. New York, Philomel, 1981.
The Gift of Sarah Barker. New York, Viking Press, 1981.
The Acorn Quest, illustrated by Susanna Natti. New York, Crowell, 1981.
The Robot and Rebecca and the Missing Owser, illustrated by Lady McCrady. New York, Knopf, 1981.
Sleeping Ugly, illustrated by Diane Stanley. New York, Coward McCann, 1981.
Dragon's Blood. New York, Delacorte Press, 1982; London, MacRae, 1983.
Commander Toad and the Planet of the Grapes, illustrated by Bruce Degen. New York, Coward McCann, 1982.
Neptune Rising: Songs and Tales of the Undersea Folk, illustrated by David Wiesner. New York, Philomel, 1982.
Commander Toad and the Big Black Hole, illustrated by Bruce Degen. New York, Coward McCann, 1983.
Heart's Blood. New York, Delacorte Press, and London, MacRae, 1984.
Children of the Wolf. New York, Viking Kestrel, 1984.
The Stone Silenus. New York, Philomel, 1984.
Commander Toad and the Dis-Asteroid, illustrated by Bruce Degen. New York, Coward McCann, 1985.
Commander Toad and the Intergalactic Spy, illustrated by Bruce Degen. New York, Coward McCann, 1986.
A Sending of Dragons, illustrated by Tom McKeveny. New York, Delacorte Press, and London, MacRae, 1987.
Piggins, illustrated by Jane Dyer. San Diego, Harcourt Brace, 1987; London, Piccadilly Press, 1988.
Owl Moon, illustrated by John Schoenherr. New York, Philomel, 1987.
Commander Toad and the Space Pirates, illustrated by Bruce Degen. New York, Putnam, 1987.
Picnic with Piggins, illustrated by Jane Dyer. San Diego, Harcourt Brace, 1988.
The Devil's Arithmetic. New York, Viking Kestrel, 1988.
Piggins and the Royal Wedding. San Diego, Harcourt Brace, 1989.
Dove Isabeau. San Diego, Harcourt Brace, 1989.
Baby Bear's Bedtime Book, illustrated by Jane Dyer. San Diego, Harcourt Brace, 1990.
Sky Dogs, illustrated by Barry Moser. San Diego, Harcourt Brace, 1990.
Tam Lin, illustrated by Charles Mikolaycak. San Diego, Harcourt Brace, 1990.
Elfabet: An ABC of Elves. N.p., Little, 1990.
Letting Swift River Go. N.p., Little, 1990.
Wizard's Hall. San Diego, Harcourt Brace, 1991.
Eeeny, Meeny, Miney Mole, illustrated by K. Brown. San Diego, Harcourt Brace, 1992.
Encounter, illustrated by David Shannon. San Diego, Harcourt Brace, 1992.
Beneath the Ghost Moon, illustrated by Laurel Molk. Boston, Little Brown, 1993.
Honkers, illustrated by Leslie Balker. Boston, Little Brown, 1993.
Little Mouse and Elephant: A Tale from Turkey, illustrated by John Segal. New York, HarperCollins, 1994.
The Musicians of Bremen: A Tale from Germany, illustrated by John Segal. New York, HarperCollins, 1994.
The Ballad of the Pirate Queens, illustrated by David Shannon. San Diego, Harcourt Brace, 1995.
Before the Storm, illustrated by Georgia Pugh. Honesdale, Pennsylvania, Boyds Mill Press, 1995.
Merlin and the Dragons, illustrated by Li Ming. New York, Cobblehill Books, 1995.
A Sip of Aesop, illustrated by Karen Barbour. New York, Blue Sky Press, 1995.
With Heidi E. Y. Stemple, *Meet the Monsters,* illustrated by Patricia Ludlow. New York, Walker, 1996.
Passager. San Diego, Harcourt Brace, 1996.
Hobby. San Diego, Harcourt Brace, 1996.

Child of Faerie, Child of Earth, illustrated by Jane Dyer. New York, Little, Brown, 1997.
Merlin. San Diego, Harcourt Brace, 1997.
Nocturne, illustrated by Anne Hunter. San Diego, Harcourt Brace, 1997.
Once Upon a Bedtime Story (retelling), illustrated by Ruth Tietjen Councell. Honesdale, Pennsylvania, Boyds Mills Press, 1997.
Miz Berlin Walks, illustrated by Floyd Cooper. New York, Philomel, 1997.
A Sending of Dragons. San Diego, Harcourt Brace, 1997.
Twelve Impossible Things Before Breakfast: Stories. San Diego, Harcourt Brace, 1997.
The Wild Hunt, illustrated by Francisco Mora. New York, Scholastic, 1997.

Plays

Robin Hood, music by Barbara Green (produced Boston, 1967).

Poetry

See This Little Line?, illustrated by Kathleen Elgin. New York, McKay, 1963.
It All Depends, illustrated by Don Bolognese. New York, Funk and Wagnalls, 1969.
An Invitation to the Butterfly Ball: A Counting Rhyme, illustrated by Jane Breskin Zalben. New York, Parents' Magazine Press, 1976; Kingswood, Surrey, World's Work, 1978.
All in the Woodland Early: An ABC Book, music by the author, illustrated by Jane Breskin Zalben. Cleveland, Collins, 1979.
How Beastly! A Menagerie of Nonsense Poems, illustrated by James Marshall. New York, Collins, 1980.
Dragon Night and Other Lullabies, illustrated by Demi. New York, Methuen, 1980; London, Methuen, 1981.
Ring of Earth: A Child's Book of Seasons, illustrated by John Wallner. San Diego, Harcourt Brace, 1986.
The Three Bear Rhyme Book, illustrated by Jane Dyer. San Diego, Harcourt Brace, 1987.
Best Witches: Poems for Halloween. New York, Putnam, 1989.
Bird Watch, illustrated by Ted Lewin. New York, Philomel, 1990.
Dinosaur Dances. New York, Putnam, 1990.
Jane Yolen's Mother Goose Song Book, musical arrangements by Adam Stemple, illustrated by Rosecrans Hoffman. Honesdale, New Jersey, Boyds Mill Press, 1992.
Mouse's Birthday, illustrated by Bruce Degen. New York, Putnam, 1993.
Raining Cats and Dogs, illustrated by Janet Street. San Diego, Harcourt Brace, 1993.
What Rhymes with Moon?, illustrated by Ruth Councell. New York, Philomel, 1993.
Grandad Bill's Song, illustrated by Melissa B. Mathis. New York, Putnam, 1993.
The Girl in the Golden Bower, illustrated by Jane Dyer. Boston, Little Brown, 1994.
Sacred Places, illustrated David Shannon. San Diego, Harcourt Brace, 1994.
The Three Bears Holiday Rhyme Book. San Diego, Harcourt Brace, 1995.
O Jerusalem, illustrated by John Thompson. New York, Scholastic, 1996.
Sea Watch, illustrated by Ted Lewin. New York, Philomel, 1996.

Other

Pirates in Petticoats, illustrated by Leonard Vosburgh. New York, McKay, 1963.
World on a String: The Story of Kites. Cleveland, World, 1968.
Friend: The Story of George Fox and the Quakers. New York, Seabury Press, 1972.
The Wizard Islands, illustrated by Robert Quackenbush. New York, Crowell, 1973.
Ring Out! A Book of Bells, illustrated by Richard Cuffari. New York, Seabury Press, 1974; London, Evans, 1978.
Simple Gifts: The Story of the Shakers, illustrated by Betty Fraser. New York, Viking Press, 1976.
The Sleeping Beauty (retelling), illustrated by Ruth Sanderson. New York, Knopf, 1986.
The Faery Flag: Stories and Poems of Fantasy and the Supernatural. New York, Orchard, 1989.
The Lap-Time Song and Play Book, musical arrangements by Adam Stemple, illustrated by Margot Tomes. San Diego, Harcourt Brace, 1989.
The Dragon's Boy. New York, Harper, 1992.
A Letter from Phoenix Farm, illustrated with photographs by Jason Stemple. Katonah, New York, Owen, 1992.
Storyteller. Framingham, Massachusetts, New England Science Fiction Association, 1992.
All Those Secrets of the World. Boston, Little Brown, 1993.
Welcome to the Greenhouse: A Story of the Tropical Rainforest, illustrated by Laura Regan. New York, Putnam, 1993.
Here There Be Dragons, illustrated by David Wilgus. San Diego, Harcourt Brace, 1993.
Jane Yolen's Songs of Summer, music arranged by Adam Stemple, illustrated by Cyd Moore. Honesdale, Pennsylvania, Boyd Mills Press, 1993.
Here There Be Unicorns, illustrated by David Wilgus. San Diego, Harcourt Brace, 1994.
Here There Be Witches, illustrated by David Wilgus. San Diego, Harcourt Brace, 1995.
Water Music, photographs by Jason Stemple. Honesdale, Pennsylvania, Boyds Mills Press, 1995.
Here There Be Angels, illustrated by David Wilgus. San Diego, Harcourt Brace, 1996.
Milk and Honey: A Year of Jewish Holidays, music arranged by Adam Stemple, illustrated by Louise August. New York, Putnam, 1996.
Welcome to the Sea of Sand, illustrated by Laura Regan. New York, Putnam, 1996.

Editor, *The Fireside Song Book of Birds and Beasts,* music by Barbara Green, illustrated by Peter Parnall. New York, Simon and Schuster, 1972.
Editor, *Zoo 2000: Twelve Stories of Science Fiction and Fantasy Beasts.* New York, Seabury Press, 1973; London, Gollancz, 1975.
Editor, *Rounds about Rounds,* music by Barbara Green, illustrated by Gail Gibbons. New York, Watts, 1977; London, Watts, 1978.
Editor, *Shape Shifters: Fantasy and Science Fiction Tales about Humans Who Can Change Their Shapes.* New York, Seabury Press, 1978.
Editor, *The Lullaby Songbook,* music arranged by Adam Stemple, illustrated by Charles Mikolaycak. San Diego, Harcourt Brace, 1986.

Editor, with Martin H. Greenberg and Charles G. Waugh, *Dragons and Dreams: A Collection of New Fantasy and Science Fiction Stories.* New York, Harper, 1986.
Editor, *Favorite Folktales from Around the World.* New York, Pantheon, 1986.
Editor, with Martin H. Greenberg and Charles G. Waugh, *Spaceships and Spells.* New York, Harper, 1987.
Editor, with Martin H. Greenberg, *Werewolves.* New York, Harper, 1988.
Editor, with Martin H. Greenberg, *Things That Go Bump in the Night.* New York, Harper, 1989.
Editor, *2041 AD.* New York, Delacorte, 1990.
Editor, with Martin H. Greenberg. *Vampires,* illustrated by Martin H. Greenberg. New York, Harper, 1991.
Editor, *Street Rhymes Around the World.* Honesdale, Pennsylvania, Boyds Mill Press, 1992.
Editor, *Weather Report,* illustrated by Annie Gusman. Honesdale, Pennsylvania, Boyds Mill Press, 1993.
Editor, *Jane Yolen's Songs of Summer,* illustrated by Cyd Moore. Honesdale, Pennsylvania, Boyds Mill Press, 1993.
Editor, *Sleep Rhymes Around the World.* Honesdale, Pennsylvania, Woodsong, 1994.
Editor, *Alphabestiary: Animal Poems From A to Z,* illustrated by Allen Eitzen. Honesdale, Pennsylvania, Wordsong, 1995.
Editor, *Camelot: A Collection of Original Arthurian Stories,* illustrated by Winslow Pels. New York, Philomel, 1995.
Editor, with Martin H. Greenberg, *The Haunted House,* illustrated by Doran Ben-Ami. New York, HarperCollins, 1995.
Editor, *Sky Scrape/City Scape: Poems of City Life,* illustrated by Ken Condon. Honesdale, Pennsylvania, Wordsong, 1996.
Editor, *Mother Earth, Father Sky: Poems of Our Planet,* illustrated by Jennifer Hewitson. Honesdale, Pennsylvania, Wordsong, 1996.
Editor, *Once Upon Ice and Other Frozen Poems,* illustrated with photographs by Jason Stemple. Honesdale, Pennsylvania, Wordsong/Boyds Mills Press, 1997.

PUBLICATIONS FOR ADULTS

Novels

Cards of Grief. New York, Ace, 1984; London, Futura, 1986.
Sister Light, Sister Dark. New York, Tor, 1988.
White Jenna. New York, Tor, 1989.
Briar Rose. New York, Tor, 1992.
The Books of Great Alta. New York, Tor, 1996.

Short Stories

Tales of Wonder. New York, Schocken, 1983; London, Futura, 1987.
Dragonfield and Other Stories. New York, Ace, 1985.
Merlin's Booke. New York, Steeldragon Press, 1986.

Other

Writing Books for Children. Boston, The Writer, 1973; revised edition, 1983.
Touch Magic: Fantasy, Faerie, and Folklore in the Literature of Childhood. New York, Philomel, 1981.
Guide to Writing for Children. Boston, Writer, 1989.
With Nancy Willard, *Among Angels,* illustrated by S. Saelig Gallagher. San Diego, Harcourt Brace, 1995.

Editor, with Martin H. Greenberg. *Xanadu.* New York, Tor, 1993.
Editor, with Martin H. Greenberg. *Xanadu Two.* New York, Tor, 1994.
Editor, with Martin H. Greenberg. *Xanadu Three.* New York, Tor, 1995.

*

Bibliography: Entry in *Children's Literature Review,* Vol. 4. Detroit, Gale, 1982; "An Empress of Thieves" by Jane Yolen, in *Horn Book* (Boston), November/December 1994, 702-6; entry in The Internet Public Library, http://www.ipl.org (updated 5 July 1995); "An Interview With...Jane Yolen" by John Koch, in *The Writer* (Boston), 1 March 1997, 20-21; "All in the Family" by Jane Yolen, in *Book Links* (New York), September 1997, 47-50.

Manuscript Collections: Kerlan Collection, University of Minnesota, Minneapolis.

Jane Yolen comments:
"Prolific" is a word often used to describe me, but I would rather say that I have a very low threshold of boredom. And so I have tried many different kinds of writing: picture books, fantasy, fairytales, straight fiction, verse, and non-fiction. Perhaps I am best known as a writer of Literary or Art Fairy Tales, stories that use the elements of old stories—the cadences, the characters, the magical settings of objects—but concern themselves with modern themes. Because of this, my stories are better known to more sophisticated and romantically inclined young people, and college students. I am a folk singer as well as a storyteller, and I hope my tales sound as if they could be sung.

* * *

The list of Jane Yolen's writings is long and varied: picture books, easy-readers, fairytales, fantasy novels and non-fiction for young adults, and books for adults about children's literature. Yet it is Yolen's "faerie and fantasy" stories that place her in the tradition of the Brothers Grimm and Hans Christian Andersen—tales which live on for future generations. *Touch Magic* is not only a commentary on the importance of faerie and fantasy tales, but also a celebration of storytelling ("Listen, touch magic, and pass it on"):

> I believe that culture begins in the cradle. Literature is a continuous process from childhood onward.... The continuum of literature is best maintained by these tales of fantasy, fancy, faerie, and the supra-natural, those crafted visions and bits and pieces of dream-remembering that link our past and our future. To do without tales and stories and books is to lose humanity's past, is to have no star map for our future.

Yolen's finely crafted fairytales are "visions and bits and pieces of dream-remembering" to be read aloud, listened to, shared, and remembered. Illustrations embellish the text in that "subtle play of text and type, illustrations and design" which Yolen has described and which mark her style. "Once in the East, where the wind blows gently on the bells of the temple, there lived a king of the highest degree": so begins *The Seventh Mandarin.* As in all classic fairytales, there is, of course, a quest: the string to the king's soul—transubstantiated every evening into a kite flown "high above the terrors of the night"—slips from the hand of the youngest mandarin, and the kite flies away. Knowing that it must be returned before dawn, he sets out to find it. At last, on a faraway mountain top, he discovers it, all tattered and torn. He carries it back to the castle through the poorest section of the surrounding town. Ramshackle hovels and huts, poverty-stricken people moaning and sighing shock the little mandarin—he'd never read of these in any of his books. He returns the king his tattered soul and courageously tells him the unpleasant truths of the world outside the castle. Together, they realize the folly of believing only what is written in books.

The title story of *The Girl Who Cried Flowers*—a collection of five fairytales beautifully illustrated in an art nouveau style by David Palladini—tells of gentle, generous Olivia, whose tears are flowers. Everyone wants Olivia's precious flowers—for weddings, funerals, all social occasions—and since Olivia is too tender-hearted to refuse them, she thinks sad thoughts and cries night and day until the storyteller Panos comes to her rescue by making her smile.

While there is gentle magic in Yolen's fairytales, there is also "tough magic," magic that has consequences. Aetos in *The Boy Who Had Wings* discovers that magic powers can have tragic consequences when his father, a horse herder, is stranded in a mountain snow storm and only he can soar above the mountains to save him. The price of his gift is heavy: his beautiful wings are frostbitten, they lose their feathers and drop off, leaving on his shoulders where his wings had been two large scars. But, no longer afraid of his wings, his family is now able to love him. "Saint Aetos" becomes the guardian angel of horse herders. (Flying and kites, in fact, are recurring motifs in Yolen's work—*The Emperor and the Kite, The Girl Who Loved the Wind, Rainbow Rider,* and *World on a String: The Story of Kites.* Yolen's father was a champion kite flyer, and ironically but most appropriately, *The Girl Who Cried Flowers* won the Golden Kite award.)

Jane Yolen loved horses as a child, and her *Sky Dogs* is a lyrically imaginative retelling of a native American legend about the coming of the horse to the Blackfeet, narrated by the elder He-who-loves-horses, who has painted on his tipi and recorded in his heart the tale of how he got his name and learned the magic of the fast-running Òsky dogs.

Yolen's more recent tales are sprinkled with a contemporary humor that is appealing to young children. Her retelling of Hans Christian Andersen's classic tale of "The Princess and the Pea" in *Once Upon a Bedtime Story* concludes: "So the prince married her. And the pea was exhibited for years in the royal museum. You can go and see it yourself—if it hasn't shriveled to nothing." The shoemaker's elves, in Yolen's retelling of the tale by the Brothers Grimm, work through the cold night "naked as newborns" to make the poor shoemaker a success. In "Talk," taken from an Ashanti folktale, dogs, fish, trees, stones—even humble yams—talk: "Go away, dirt man," the yam cries out to the farmer who has come to dig up the yam and take it to market, "You never bothered to weed me and never bothered to feed me, and now you come to dig me up."

Yolen's equally prolific production of non-faerie picture books has grown in sophistication and acclaim. To her intergalactic *Commander Toad* series, Yolen has added the delightful *Piggins,* featuring a portly porker butler who solves mysteries (of the non-murder kind) with the smoothest porcine logic. The *Piggins* books are set in the Upstairs, Downstairs Edwardian world of 47 The Meadows and environs, and feature—besides the series' namesake ("more than a butler," he was also "a hero in the Boar War")—Mr. and Mrs. Reynard and their children Rexy and Trixy (all foxes, of course), the world-famous explorer Pierre Lapin and his three unmarried sisters, Cook, Sara the scullery maid, and Jane, who polishes the silver and fixes the tea. Jane Dyer's large, colored-pencil and watercolor illustrations and her inspired use of small, illustrative silhouettes to decorate pages of text make the *Piggins* stories as charming to look at as they are to read.

"Have you ever met a monster? No—of course you haven't. There are no such things as monsters except in our imaginations." In *Meet the Monsters,* Yolen and her daughter Heidi E. Y. Stemple introduce young children to vampires, werewolves, mummies, the Abominable Snowman, and more. So, what do you do if you really meet one? "You tell yourself this is all for fun. This is just in your imagination. Then you get out your garlic, or the salty chips, or the mistletoe, or the weasel ... just in case."

Owl Moon, which won the 1989 Caldecott Medal, is illustrated with exquisite and dramatic watercolors by John Schoenherr. Dedicated to Yolen's husband David Stemple—"who took all of our children owling"—*Owl Moon* is the story of a magical winter night, long past the child-narrator's bedtime, when "Pa and I went owling":

> There was no wind.
> The trees stood still as giant statues.
> And the moon was so bright the sky seemed to shine.

After a long, cold, patient search, with Pa's call of "whoo-whoo-who-who-who-whooooooooo" resonating in the winter woods, child and father at last spot an owl's shadow. Pa's flashlight alights on the owl's face, and "for one minute, three minutes, maybe even a hundred minutes," child and owl stare at each other. Pumping its great wings, the owl finally flies off, leaving the child pondering a wonderful lesson:

> When you go owling
> you don't need words
> or warm
> or anything but hope.
> That's what Pa says.
> The kind of hope
> that flies
> on silent wings
> under a shining
> Owl Moon.

With its "brushstroked bluecoat velvet" illustrations by Anne Hunter, *Nocturne* is a gentle tribute to the "bluecoat velvet night," with the "big moon balloon" floating silent over trees, moths fluttering up and down "like wind-up toys," and owls with deep feathers writing "silent passages across the sky." Not a night to be afraid of, but a "starlit velvet night" where a child can nestle down "and drift through dark into dreams."

Yolen celebrates nature in two beautifully poetic non-fiction texts illustrated with luminous gouache paintings by Laura Regan—*Welcome to the Greenhouse: A Story of the Tropical Rainforest* and *Welcome to the Sea of Sand: The story of the Sonoran Desert.*

Faerie, fiction, or fact, Yolen's lyrical and magical tales are indeed tales to read and listen to, to share, remember, and pass on.

—Marcia G. Welsh

YORINKS, Arthur

Has also written as Alan Yaffe. **Nationality:** American. **Born:** 21 August 1953, Roslyn, Long Island, New York. **Education:** Attended New School for Social Research and Hofstra New College, 1971. **Family:** Married Adrienne Berg, 23 October 1983. **Career:** Author of children's books; writer for opera, ballet, film, and theater. Cornell University, Ithaca, New York, instructor in theater arts, 1972-79. Writer, teacher, and performer at American Mime Theatre, 1969-79. Associate director of New Works Project in New York City, from 1977; Moving Theatre, founder, artistic director, 1979; co-founder and associate artistic director of national children's theater The Night Kitchen, from 1990. **Awards:** *School Library Journal*'s Best Books of the Year citation, 1980, 1988, 1989, 1990; *Booklist* Children's Editor's Choice, 1984; Biennale of Illustrations plaque (Bratislava, Czechoslovakia), 1985; American Library Association (ALA) Notable Book citation, 1986, 1988; Caldecott Medal, 1987; Kentucky Bluegrass Award, 1988. **Agent:** Sheldon Fogelman, 10 East 40th St., New York, New York 10016. U.S.A. **Address:** Hilltop Dr., North Salem, New York 10560, U.S.A.

Publications for Children

Fiction

Sid and Sol, illustrated by Richard Egielski. New York, Farrar, Straus, 1977.
The Magic Meatballs (as Alan Yaffe), illustrated by Karen B. Anderson. New York, Dial, 1979.
Louis the Fish, illustrated by R. Egielski. New York, Farrar, Straus, 1980.
It Happened in Pinsk, illustrated by R. Egielski. New York, Farrar, Straus, 1983.
Hey, Al, illustrated by R. Egielski. New York, Farrar, Straus, 1986.
Bravo, Minski, illustrated by R. Egielski. New York, Farrar, Straus, 1988.
Company's Coming, illustrated by David Small. New York, Crown, 1988.
Rosalie, illustrated by David Palladini. Boston, Little, Brown, 1988.
Oh, Brother, illustrated by R. Egielski. New York, Farrar, Straus, 1989.
Ugh, illustrated by R. Egielski. New York, Farrar, Straus, 1990.
Christmas in July, illustrated by R. Egielski. New York, HarperCollins, 1991.
Whitefish Will Rides Again, illustrated by Mort Drucker, New York, HarperCollins, 1994.
The Miami Giant, illustrated by Maurice Sendak. New York, HarperCollins, 1995.
Frank and Joey Go to Work, photographs by Ky Chung. New York, HarperFestival, 1996.
Harry and Lulu, illustrated by Martin Matje. New York, Hyperion Books, 1998.

Plays

Six (one-act), first produced in New York City at Hunter College Playhouse, November 1973.
The Horse (one-act), first produced in New York City at Cornelia Street Cafe, November 1978.
Crackers (one-act), first produced in New York City at Theatre of the Open Eye, June 1979.
The King (one-act), first produced in New York City at South Street Theatre, July 1980.
Kissers (one-act), first produced at South Street Theatre, July 1980.
Piece for a Small Cafe (one-act), first produced at Cornelia Street Cafe, February 1981.
Piece for a Larger Cafe (one-act), first produced at Cornelia Street Cafe, April 1982.

Screenplay: *Sid and Sol,* adapted from the book of the same title, Four Penny Productions, 1982; *Making Scents,* developed by A & M Films; *Usher,* with film director Michael Powell.

Other

Opera Librettos: *Leipziger Kerzenspiel,* first produced at Mt. Holyoke College, 1984; *The Juniper Tree,* first produced at the American Repertory Theater, Boston, 1985, music by Philip Glass and Robert Moran, Dunvagen Music, 1985; adaptor, *The Fall of the House of Usher,* with P. Glass, first produced at American Repertory Theater, May, 1988.

Video: *Story by Arthur Yorinks, Pictures by Richard Egielski,* New York, Farrar, Straus, 1987.

Also author of a full-length story ballet commissioned by the Hartford Ballet.

*

Media Adaptations: *Louis the Fish* was produced as an episode of *Reading Rainbow,* PBS-TV, 1983. *Louis the Fish* and *Sid and Sol* have both been adapted into a cassette with hardcover book by Random House.

* * *

Since 1977, Arthur Yorinks has provided antic and mind-stretching texts for a dozen quirky picture books. The author credits his discovery of the picture book as an art form to his happening upon the works of Maurice Sendak when he was a high-school student. He describes the experience as being "like finding a suit of clothes that seemed to be made for me. They had drama, art, rhythm, music, all rolled into one. I devoured them." He went on to devour the works of William Steig, Tomi Ungerer, Wilhelm Basch, Randolph Caldecott, and William Nicholson as well. He finds the symbiotic relationship between words and pictures endlessly interesting and challenging. And as a writer, he has been uncannily lucky in the selections of illustrators for his stories, most notably in his first and chief collaborator (eight books together), Richard Egielski.

Not since the matching of Gilbert and Sullivan in 19th century England has a team worked so seamlessly and well. In their first joint effort, *Sid and Sol,* with dramatic illustrations in black and white, an uncommonly feisty little guy named Sid manages to best a fearful lummox of a giant, Sol. Seldom in children's books has brawn been so awesomely outclassed by brain.

It is difficult to convey the oddball zaniness of Yorinks's various tales without resorting liberally to quotation, for style is almost as central to their fantastic plots as content. In *Louis the Fish,* viewer/listeners learn to their amazement in the opening sentence: "One day last spring, Louis, a butcher, turned into a fish, a large salmon." And if they are inclined to doubt this incredible statement, there, on a full-color, absolutely convincing double-spread, is a large fish in striped pajamas just awakening in an ordinary, everyday bed. A total commitment by both author and artist is the key to the book's near-mesmerizing power. *It Happened in Pinsk* presents the reader with an equally startling premise: "One morning, March 19, at breakfast, Irv was just about to eat a roll when he realized his head was missing." What reader would not be instantaneously hooked?

Yorinks's fourth collaboration with Egielski, *Hey Al,* won the 1987 Caldecott medal. It is the affecting story of a loyal and loving dog named Eddie and his working-stiff master, the janitor Al. They live, eat, and watch TV together "in one room on the West Side," and, Yorinks comments with a characteristic ethnic shrug, "What could be bad?" We soon find out in a story that tugs genuinely at the heartstrings.

In *Company's Coming,* illustrated by David Small, a conventional middle-aged couple is surprised by a flying saucer that lands on their lawn. "Greetings," two small visitors from outer space proclaim on debarking, "We come in peace. Do you have a bathroom?" Yorinks's plot twists and turns of phrase are full of surprises. The resulting stories are eccentric, just a touch mad and, therefore, almost always irresistible.

In *Christmas in July,* the world is turned inside out when Santa Claus's trousers ("Size 67—with cuffs") are lost at the cleaners. And in yet another Egielski collaboration, *Ugh,* the young hero is a kind of cave-boy Cinderella, who is exploited by two mean-spirited older sisters and a pair of bullying big brothers. When Oy, the local scientist, invents the wheel, only Ugh appreciates its possibilities and ends up being proclaimed king. As Yorinks sums up the happy denouement, "Ugh be big-shot boy the rest of his happy life."

Whitefish Will Rides Again, is a wild western saga, a raucous comedy broadly illustrated by Mort Drucker. It chronicles the escapades of the rootin', tootin', "best danged sheriff that ever lived!" After the ungrateful citizens of Whitefish, Montana ("Pop. 61") put him out to pasture, he makes a spectacular comeback wielding not his six-shooter but an equally lethal harmonica that he's taught himself to play. The tale has its moments of high comedy but lacks the subtle magic of Yorinks at his oddball best. In addition to his children's books, Yorinks has in recent years become both a playwright for and co-director (with Maurice Sendak) of a projected national children's theater called The Night Kitchen.

—Selma G. Lanes

YOUNG, Ed (Tse-chun)

Nationality: American (immigrated to United States in 1951, naturalized citizen). **Born:** 28 November 1931, Tientsin, China. **Family:** Married 1) first wife in 1962 (divorced 1969); 2) Natasha Gorky in 1971 (marriage ended); 3) Filomena. **Education:** Attended City College of San Francisco, 1952, and University of Illinois at Urbana-Champaign, 1952-54; Art Center College of Design, Los Angeles, B.P.A. 1957; graduate study at Pratt Institute, Brooklyn, New York, 1958-59. **Career:** Illustrator and designer, Mel Richman Studio, New York City, 1957-62; instructor in visual communications, Pratt Institute, Brooklyn, New York, 1960-66; Children's book illustrator and author, from 1962. Shr Jung Tai Chi Chuan School, New York City, secretary and instructor, 1964-73, director, 1973; instructor, Sarah Lawrence College, Bronxville, New York, from 1975. **Awards:** American Institute of Graphic Arts award, 1962; Caldecott Medal runner-up, 1968; *Horn Book* Honor List, 1969; Child Study Association Book Award, 1969; Children's Book Showcase Title, 1973; *New York Times* Best Illustrated Children's Book Award, 1983 and 1988; Parents' Choice Award, 1983; *Horn Book* Honor List, 1986; Caldecott Medal, 1990; honor, 1993. **Address:** c/o Shr Jung Tai Chi Chuan School, 87 Bowery, New York, New York 10003, U.S.A.

PUBLICATIONS FOR CHILDREN (ILLUSTRATED BY THE AUTHOR)

Fiction

The Rooster's Horns: A Chinese Puppet Play to Make and Perform. with Hilary Beckett. New York, Collins, 1978.
The Terrible Nung Gwama: A Chinese Folktale. New York, Collins, 1978.
High on a Hill: A Book of Chinese Riddles. New York, Collins, 1980.
Up a Tree. New York, Harper, 1983.
The Other Bone. New York, Harper, 1984.
Seven Blind Mice. New York, Philomel, 1992.
Red Thread. New York, Philomel, 1993.
Little Plum. New York, Philomel Books, 1994.
Cat and Rat: The Legend of the Chinese Zodiac. New York, Holt, 1995.
Night Visitors. New York, Philomel Books, 1995.
Mouse Match, a Chinese Folktale. San Diego, Silver Whistle, 1997.
Voices of the Heart. New York, Scholastic Press, 1997.
The Lost Horse. San Diego, Silver Whistle/Harcourt Brace, 1998.

Other

Adapter, *Moon Mother.* New York, HarperCollins, 1993.
Adapter, *Pinocchio.* New York, Philomel Books, 1996.
Adapter, *Genesis.* New York, Laura Geringer Book, 1997.

Reteller, *Donkey Trouble.* New York, Atheneum Books for Young Readers, 1995.

Translator, *Lon Po Po: A Red Riding Hood Story from China.* New York, Putnam, 1989.

*

Illustrator: Janice M. Udry, *The Mean Mouse and Other Mean Stories,* Harper, 1962; Leland B. Jacobs and Sally Nohelty, editors, *Poetry for Young Scientists,* Holt, 1964; Margaret Hillert, *The Yellow Boat,* Follett, 1966; Jane Yolen, editor, *The Emperor and the Kite,* World Publishing, 1968; Robert Wyndham, editor, *Chi-*

nese Mother Goose Rhymes, World Publishing, 1968; Kermit Krueger, *The Golden Swans: A Picture Story from Thailand,* World Publishing, 1969; Mel Evans, *The Tiniest Sound,* Doubleday, 1969; Yolen, *The Seventh Mandarin,* Seabury, 1970; Renee K. Weiss, *The Bird from the Sea,* Crowell, 1970; Diane Wolkstein, *Eight Thousand Stones: A Chinese Folktale,* Doubleday, 1972; Yolen, *The Girl Who Loved the Wind,* Crowell, 1972; L. C. Hunt, editor, *The Horse from Nowhere,* Holt, 1973; Elizabeth F. Lewis, *Young Fu of the Upper Yangtze,* new edition, Holt, 1973; Wolkstein, *The Red Lion: A Tale of Ancient Persia,* Crowell, 1977; Feenie Ziner, *Cricket Boy: A Chinese Tale,* Doubleday, 1977; N. J. Dawood, *Tales from the Arabian Nights,* Doubleday, 1978; Wolkstein, *White Wave: A Chinese Tale,* Crowell, 1979; *The Lion and the Mouse: An Aesop Fable,* Doubleday, 1979; Priscilla Jaquith, *Bo Rabbit Smart for True: Folktales from the Gullah,* Philomel, 1981; Al-Ling Louie, *Yeh-Shen: A Cinderella Story from China,* Putnam, 1982; Mary Scioscia, *Bicycle Rider,* Harper, 1983; Rafe Martin, editor, *Foolish Rabbit's Big Mistake,* Putnam, 1985; Jean Fritz, *The Double Life of Pocahontas,* Putnam, 1985; Phyllis Root, *Moon Tiger,* Holt, 1985; Margaret Leaf, *Eyes of the Dragon,* Lothrop, 1987; James Howe, *I Wish I Were a Butterfly,* Harcourt, 1987; Tony Johnston, *Whale Song,* Putnam, 1987; Richard Lewis, *In the Night, Still Dark,* Atheneum, 1988; Nancy Larrick, editor, *Cats Are Cats,* Philomel, 1988; Robert Frost, *Birches,* Holt, 1988; Oscar Wilde, *The Happy Prince,* Simon & Schuster, 1989; Hearn, Lafcadio, *The Voice of the Great Bell,* retold by Margaret Hodges, Little, Brown, 1989; Ruth Y. Radin, *High in the Mountains,* Macmillan, 1989; Larrick, editor, *Mice Are Nice,* Putnam, 1990; R. Lewis, *All of You Was Singing,* Macmillan, 1991; Barbara Savadge Horton, What Comes in Spring, Knopf, 1992; Mary Calhoun, *While I Sleep,* Morrow, 1992; Audrey Osofsky, *Dreamcatcher,* Orchard, 1992; Laura Krauss Melmed, *The First Song Ever Sung,* Lothrop, 1993; Richard Lewis, *All of You Was Singing,* New York, Aladdin Books; Toronto, Maxwell Macmillan Canada; New York, Maxwell Macmillan International, 1994; Isaac Olaleye, *Bitter Bananas,* Honesdale, Pennsylvania, Caroline House/Boyds Mills Press, 1994; retold by Shulamith Levey Oppenheim, *Iblis,* San Diego, Harcourt Brace Jovanovich, 1994; Lisa Westberg Peters, *October Smiled Back,* Henry Holt, 1996; retold by Penny Pollock, *The Turkey Girl: A Zuni Cinderella Story,* Boston, Little, Brown, 1996; retold by Diane Wolkstein, *White Wave, a Chinese Tale,* San Diego, Harcourt Brace, 1996. Also illustrator of *The Child's First Books,* by Donnarae MacCann and Olga Richard, 1973, and of film *Sadako and the Thousand Paper Cranes,* based on the story by Eleanor Coerr.

* * *

Ed Young was born and raised in China, moved to the United States to go to college, and began his career in children's literature as an illustrator. Janice M. Udry's *The Mean Mouse and Other Mean Stories* was his first project, followed by a number of original tales by Jane Yolen (including the Caldecott Honor book, *The Emperor and the Kite*) and many other books of tales both folk and modern. As an illustrator, he developed a love for "telling stories through pictures" and, perhaps, a desire to tell the folktales he heard and read as a child in China as well as stories of his own imagining.

An authentic Chinese folktale is the basis of *The Terrible Nung Gwama,* Young's first book as both author/reteller and illustrator. In this tale, a poor young woman is on her way to deliver a basket of cakes to her venerable parents. She is confronted by a fierce monster—the legendary Nung Gwama, which has "the body of a bull and a head as big as an oven," gnashes its teeth, stretches out its claws in a horrible way, and "delights in eating people." Young's illustrations, set within fan-shaped album leaves, vividly contrast the huge fierceness of the monster, especially its eyes, teeth, and claws, with the timid smallness of the frightened young woman. With the helpful advice of the people she meets along the path, as well as her own wits and bravery, she is able to overcome the terrible monster, deliver the cakes, and live happily ever after. Young's retelling of another ancient Chinese tale won him the Caldecott medal in 1990; in *Lon Po Po: A Red-Riding Hood Story From China,* a cunning and monstrous wolf with devouring eyes and a looming shadow terrorizes three sisters who are home alone.

Up a Tree and *The Other Bone* are stories without words; in the former, a cat chasing a butterfly climbs up a tree and is too scared to come down until a man passes by with some fish, while in the latter, a dog loses the bone he has in his mouth by trying to get at its reflection in the water. *Seven Blind Mice* is a brilliantly colorful retelling of the fable of the Blind Men and the Elephant. A Native American creation story is the source of Young's most recent book, *Moon Mother.* And, all along, Young has continued to illustrate the work of other authors—Jean Fritz, James Howe, Robert Frost, and Oscar Wilde among them—with great creativity and versatility.

In the illustrated lecture he gave upon winning the *Boston Globe-Horn Book* award for *Lon Po Po,* Young stated his creative philosophy in eight points:

> Take time for repose
> it is the germ of creation
>
> Take time to read
> it is the foundation of wisdom
>
> Take time to think
> it is the source of strength
>
> Take time to work
> it is the path to patience and success
>
> Take time to play
> it is the secret of youth and constancy
>
> Take time to be cheerful
> it is the appreciation of life that brings happiness
>
> Take time to share
> it is in fellowship and sound relationships
> one finds meaning
>
> Take time to rejoice
> for joy is the music of the soul.

Readers young and old can rejoice that Ed Young has taken the time to share the music of his soul in his many unique and playful creations.

—Marcia Welsh

ZELINSKY, Paul

Nationality: American. **Born:** Paul Oser Zelinsky in Evanston, Illinois, 14 February 1953. **Education:** Yale University, B.A. 1974; Tyler School of Art, Philadelphia and Rome, M.F.A. 1976. **Family:** Married Deborah Hallen; two daughters. **Career:** Elementary school teacher, Brooklyn, New York; freelance illustrator. **Awards:** *New York Times* Best Illustrated Book, 1981, 1985, 1994; Bratislava Biennale Selection, 1982, 1984, 1986, 1988, 1990; Parents' Choice Award, 1984, 1985, 1986; American Library Association Caldecott Honor Book, 1985, 1987, 1995 and Medal Winner, 1998; *Redbook* Magazine Award, 1986, 1990; *Parenting Magazine* Reading Magic Award, 1990, 1994. **Address:** c/o Dutton Children's Books, 375 Hudson Street, New York, New York 10014, U.S.A.

PUBLICATIONS FOR CHILDREN (ILLUSTRATED BY THE AUTHOR)

The Maid and the Mouse and the Odd-Shaped House. New York, Dodd, Mead, 1981.
The Lion and the Stoat. New York, Greenwillow, 1984.
Rumpelstiltskin. New York, Dutton, 1986.
The Wheels on the Bus. New York, Dutton, 1990.
Rapunzel. New York, Dutton, 1997.

*

Illustrator: *Emily Upham's Revenge* by Avi, 1978; *How I Hunted the Little Fellows* by Boris Zhitkov, 1979; *The History of Helpless Harry* by Avi, 1980; *Three Romances* by Winifred Rosen, 1981; *What Amanda Saw* by Naomi Lazard, 1981; *Ralph S. Mouse* by Beverly Cleary, 1982; *The Song in the Walnut Grove* by David Kherdian, 1982; *The Sun's Asleep Behind the Hill* by Mirra Ginsburg, 1982; *Zoo Doings* by Jack Prelutsky, 1982; *Dear Mr. Henshaw* by Beverly Cleary, 1983; *Hansel and Gretel* by Rika Lesser, 1984; *The Story of Mrs. Lovewright and Purrless Her Cat* by Lore Segal, 1985; *The Random House Book of Humor for Children,* collected by Pamela Pollack, 1988; *Strider* by Beverly Cleary, 1991; *The Enchanted Castle* by E. Nesbit, 1992; *More Rootabagas* by Carl Sandburg, 1993; *Swamp Angel* by Anne Isaacs, 1994.

Paul Zelinsky comments:

Most of my illustrations for books look so different from each other that you might not recognize them—you probably wouldn't recognize them—as coming from the same hand. In this age of designer labels and brand names it isn't a good business decision to avoid having one instantly recognizable "look" but I get my satisfaction from trying to do justice to a good story, a good text, a good piece of writing. Good writing suggests its own look, to me, anyway, and I try to follow its suggestion, wherever it may lead me. It may be light and whimsical, as in *The Wheels on the Bus,* or primitive but tongue-in-cheek, as in *Swamp Angel*; it may evoke the antique, as in *Rapunzel,* or it may be very traditional storybook illustration that calls no attention to itself, as in my illustrations for Beverly Cleary's novels. I find it thrilling when I manage to succeed in a style I haven't tried before. And if the pictures do justice to the text, and if the text is something that children in a particular age range will appreciate, then it simply follows that my pictures will also be enjoyable to that particular audience.

I don't consider that I make pictures for children; I make pictures for stories, and the stories can be for children.

* * *

Versatility is the word that best defines the work of author and illustrator Paul Zelinsky. His choice of media, his various techniques, his application of color, and his use of line all fluctuate with each book he illustrates. He has not so much a Zelinsky style as he has the rare ability to superimpose his own vision onto a work, making it his own while maintaining the text's authenticity. "I want the pictures to speak in the same voice as the words, which often results in playing with different mediums on different kinds of surfaces," he has said in publicity fliers.

In his 1998 Caldecott Award-winning book *Rapunzel* this tactic is in high evidence. Having based the story on Italian, French, and Grimm Brothers sources (noted in a long Afterword), Zelinsky renders an Italian Renaissance setting in a painterly style. The luminescent colors, exacting lines, and full-bleed artwork, which seemingly extend the pictures beyond the page, all evoke the necessary magical landscape. Characterizations, while archetypal, are individualized through costumes, hairdos, and meaningful gestures and postures. A particularly interesting device is the repetition of upturned arms above the body, seen in the portrayals of Rapunzel, the sorceress, and the prince. Although used to evoke different emotions, the pattern makes an intriguing connection between the characters.

Among the many available renditions of Rapunzel, Zelinsky's tower is, undoubtedly, the most unusual edifice to house the longhaired maiden. Its aesthetic beauty, highly appropriate when considering the role of bell towers in Italian architecture, results from Zelinsky's intensive research.

Research has always been a component of the artist's pre-illustration work. In creating the black-and-white illustrations for his first picture book, *How I Hunted the Little Ones* by Russian author Boris Zhitkov, Zelinsky studied late-nineteenth-century Russian interiors, which figure as backgrounds in the story. He gave this somewhat bizarre tale the edge it required with lightning quick sketch lines, precise cross-hatching, and creative use of white space. The quirky perspectives and shapes are somewhat Sendakian, which probably occurred naturally as Zelinsky says that a college class he took from Maurice Sendak was influential in directing his art career into the field of children's book illustration.

The Maid the Mouse and the Odd-Shaped House was also situated in the late-nineteenth century, but this time in America, and patterned after "tell and draw" stories created on school room blackboards at the time. Clever use of space, line, and geometric designs bring the story into proper historical alignment and give the tale its full comic effect. This playfulness can also be seen in Zelinsky's rendition of Carl Sandburg's *More Rootabagas,* where a computer helped place his artwork in and around the text. Here he amusingly caricatures his characters and provides whimsical details that play off Sandburg's wry wit.

Colored pencil was the media of choice for illustrating Lore Segal's *The Story of Mrs. Lovewright and Purrless Her Cat.* The pencils supplied the needed sharp effect to juxtapose Mrs. Lovewright's chilly but determined efforts to cozy up to her pet with the cat's equally determined standoffishness. On the other hand, for Mirra Ginsburg's *The Sun's Asleep behind the Hill,*

Zelinsky wisely chose pastels and opaque watercolors to suggest the sounds and smells of a summer night. The resulting sense of quietness as night falls is altogether different from the energy he wanted for his adaptation of *The Wheels on the Bus*. This story needed a robust feeling, which he generated with thick oil paints creased with colored pencil lines; the deft paper engineering that allows doors to swing open, riders to bounce over bumps, and windshield wipers to swish back and forth further exhilarate the action.

Zelinsky's artwork for Avi's and Cleary's novels offers still another side to his illustrative talents. Line drawings throughout the texts are both expressive and individualized. The characters in Avi's *History of Helpless Harry* and *Emily Upham's Revenge,* both historical fiction, however, exude a different panache than the ones he fashioned for Cleary's contemporary stories, *Ralph S. Mouse* and the Newbery-winning *Dear Mr. Henshaw*. These novels, published in late in 1970s and early 1980s, provided good exposure for Zelinsky and set the stage for the welcome response he received when he created the artwork for Rika Lesser's retelling of *Hansel and Gretel*.

In this book, readers found the artist taking them on a different kind of artistic journey. The painterly illustrations with vivid colors and beautifully controlled line work, which suggest nuances of the European romantic painters, caught the attention of both children and adults. This approach can also be seen in *Rumpelstiltskin*. To effect a Northern European Renaissance ambience for his retelling, Zelinsky applied layers of oil paint to simulate the opulent, clear light reflective of the period. The illustrations have a sensuous effect—straw that seems to crinkle and gold that seemingly shines. Facial expressions are especially noteworthy and his use of sequential illustration further suggests the influence of such European masters as Patinir and Brueghel.

For Anne Isaac's *Swamp Angel,* which boisterously relates the story of Angelica Longrider, the "greatest woodswoman in Tennessee," the illustrator chose an early American primitive style, reflected in oil paints on cherry, maple, and birch veneers and in the use of large (sometimes double-page spreads) in oval frames. The characters, wildly exaggerated in size, play out the flamboyant tall tale against panoramic wilderness backgrounds.

If no one style emerges in Zelinsky's books, his ability to draw his readers into the narrative and compel them to turn each page may indicate a "Zelinsky style" after all. Sometimes, the emotional power is clearly in evidence (*Mrs. Lovewright* and *Swamp Angel*) while other times it is more subtle (*The Lion and the Stoat* and *Rapunzel*). The latter, in particular, is imbued with a creative force that mesmerizes, allowing the drama of this timeless tale to seep into children's minds and imaginations, while providing room for their own fanciful interpretations.

—Barbara Elleman

ZION, Gene

Nationality: American. **Born:** Eugene Zion, New York City, 5 October 1913. **Education:** At schools in Ridgefield and Fort Lee, New Jersey, 1919-27; Textile High School, New York, 1928-31; Pratt Institute, New York, 1932-36, diploma in pictorial illustration; New School for Social Research, New York, 1940-42. **Military Service:** Anti-Aircraft Artillery Visual Training Aids Section, United States Army, 1942-44. **Family:** Married Margaret Bloy Graham in 1948. **Career:** Designer, Esquire Publications, New York, 1940-42; designer and assistant art director, CBS, New York, 1944-46; graphic designer, Condé Nast Publications, New York, 1947-51. **Died:** 5 December 1975.

Publications for Children (illustrated by Margaret Bloy Graham)

Fiction

All Falling Down. New York, Harper, 1951; Kingswood, Surrey, World's Work, 1969.
Hide and Seek Day. New York, Harper, 1954.
The Summer Snowman. New York, Harper, 1955.
Harry, The Dirty Dog. New York, Harper, 1956; London, Bodley Head, 1960.
Really Spring. New York, Harper, 1956.
Jeffie's Party. New York, Harper, 1957.
Dear Garbage Man. New York, Harper, 1957; as *Dear Dustman,* London, Bodley Head, 1962.
No Roses for Harry! New York, Harper, 1958; London, Bodley Head, 1961.
The Plant Sitter. New York, Harper, 1959; London, Bodley Head, 1966.
Harry and the Lady Next Door. New York, Harper, 1960; Kingswood, Surrey, World's Work, 1962.
The Meanest Squirrel I Ever Met. New York, Scribner, 1962.
The Sugar Mouse Cake. New York, Scribner, 1964.
Harry by the Sea. New York, Harper, 1965; London, Bodley Head, 1966.

*

Manuscript Collections: Kerlan Collection, University of Minnesota, Minneapolis.

* * *

Gene Zion had an exceptional talent for envisioning a story through the eyes of a child. The characters, whether a dog, a squirrel, or a garbage collector, have a child's perspective on their world. Their predicaments and ensuing outcomes are frequently juxtaposed with an adult viewpoint of their dilemma. Thus, Zion enables a child to glimpse the feelings of others in a humorous and subtle way.

His early work represents an understanding of preliminary thought processes. *All Falling Down* and *Hide and Seek Day* explore a child's perception and fascination with things falling and hidden. Both books have become somewhat dated by their illustrations and choppy, stilted text.

The Summer Snowman explores the fun and enjoyment of a child's fantasy: preserving a snowman until summer. Zion's likable little boy uses the snowman to play a joke on his older brother. In *Really Spring* a boy ignites the town's interest in painting everything to look like spring. It climaxes with rain washing all the paint away to reveal the "real" spring. The effect is humorous but not as involving as *The Summer Snowman.*

Dear Garbage Man appeals to a child's fascination with rubbish. It cleverly dramatizes the concept of recycling trash. The climax, with the broken old junk reappearing on the street, is a realistic twist to an amusing story.

Harry, Zion's most successful character, is a dog embodying the excitement, curiosity, and mischief of a child. *Harry, The Dirty Dog* captivates his admirers by escaping from the bathtub to play in the dirtiest parts of town. As a final twist, Harry must beg for a bath to be recognized by his family. His problems are universal and his audience empathizes with his plight. In *No Roses for Harry!* he is given a sweater with roses on it. Feeling quite ridiculous, he loses it on purpose. This familiar situation immediately involves the reader in the solution. Grandma understands and helps create a happy satisfying climax. Bothersome behavior, in *Harry by the Sea,* makes him a nuisance at the beach. Harry inadvertently gets lost, reappearing as a sea weed monster. The monster effect is comical and blends an imaginative story with the trauma of being lost in a sea of umbrellas at the beach. Harry is a timeless personality inviting warmth, involvement, and understanding.

—Martha J. Fick

ZOLOTOW, Charlotte

Pseudonyms: Sarah Abbott; Charlotte Bookman. **Nationality:** American. **Born:** Charlotte Shapiro, Norfolk, Virginia, 26 June 1915. **Education:** University of Wisconsin, Madison, 1933-36. **Family:** Married the writer Maurice Zolotow in 1938 (divorced 1969); one son and one daughter. **Career:** Member of the children's book department, 1938-44, 1962-65, senior editor, 1965-76, editorial director, Harper Junior Books; associate publisher and vice-president, 1976-82, and, beginning in 1987, editorial consultant and editor of "Charlotte Zolotow Books", Harper Junior Books, New York; publisher emerita and editorial adviser, HarperCollins Children's Books. **Awards:** Caldecott Honor, for *The Storm Book,* 1953; Harper Gold Medal for Editorial Excellence, 1974; Christopher award, 1975; University of Minnesota Kerlan award, 1986; University of Southern Mississippi Silver Medallion, 1990, and American Library Association resolution, 1991, both for her contributions to children's literature. **Address:** 29 Elm Place, Hastings-on-Hudson, New York 10706, U.S.A.

Publications for Children

Fiction

The Park Book, illustrated by H.A. Rey. New York, Harper, 1944.

But Not Billy, illustrated by Lys Cassal. New York, Harper, 1947.

The Storm Book, illustrated by Margaret Bloy Graham. New York, Harper, 1952.

The Magic Word, illustrated by Eleanor Dart. New York, Wonder Books, 1952; as *Do You Know the Magic Word?,* n.d.

The City Boy and the Country Horse (as Charlotte Bookman), illustrated by William Moyers. New York, Treasure Books, 1952.

Indian, Indian, illustrated by Leonard Weisgard. New York, Simon and Schuster, 1952.

The Quiet Mother and the Noisy Little Boy, illustrated by Kurt Werth. New York, Lothrop, 1953.

One Step, Two..., illustrated by Roger Duvoisin. New York, Lothrop, 1955; London, Bodley Head, 1968; revised edition, Lothrop, 1981.

Not a Little Monkey, illustrated by Roger Duvoisin. New York, Lothrop, 1957.

Over and Over, illustrated by Garth Williams. New York, Harper, 1957.

Do You Know What I'll Do? illustrated by Garth Williams. New York, Harper, 1958.

Sleepy Book, illustrated by Vladmir Bobri. New York, Lothrop, 1958; Kingswood, Surrey, World's Work, 1960.

The Night When Mother Was Away, illustrated by Reisie Lonette. New York, Lothrop, 1958; as *The Summer Night,* New York, Harper, 1974; Kingswood, Surrey, World's Work, 1976.

The Bunny Who Found Easter, illustrated by Betty Peterson. Berkeley, California, Parnassus Press, 1959.

Aren't You Glad, illustrated by Elaine Kurty. New York, Golden Press, 1960.

The Little Black Puppy, illustrated by Lilian Obligado. New York, Golden Press, 1960.

Big Brother, illustrated by Mary Chalmers. New York, Harper, 1960.

The Three Funny Friends, illustrated by Mary Chalmers. New York, Harper, 1961.

The Man with the Purple Eyes, illustrated by Joe Lasker. New York, Abelard Schuman, 1961; London, Abelard Schuman, 1963.

Mr. Rabbit and the Lovely Present, illustrated by Maurice Sendak. New York, Harper, 1962; London, Bodley Head, 1968.

The Sky Was Blue, illustrated by Garth Williams. New York, Harper, 1963; Kingswood, Surrey, World's Work, 1976.

The Quarreling Book, illustrated by Arnold Lobel. New York, Harper, 1963.

The White Marble, illustrated by Lilian Obligado. New York and London, Abelard Schuman, 1963.

A Tiger Called Thomas, illustrated by Kurt Werth. New York, Lothrop, 1963.

I Have a Horse of My Own, illustrated by Yoko Mitsuhashi. New York and London, Abelard Schuman, 1964.

The Poodle Who Barked at the Wind, illustrated by Roger Duvoisin. New York, Lothrop, 1964; Kingswood, Surrey, World's Work, 1965.

A Rose, A Bridge, and a Wild Black Horse, illustrated by Uri Shulevitz. New York, Harper, 1964.

When I Have a Little Girl [*a Son*], illustrated by Hilary Knight. New York, Harper, 2 vols., 1965-67.

Someday, illustrated by Arnold Lobel. New York, Harper, 1965; Kingswood, Surrey, World's Work, 1966.

If It Weren't for You, illustrated by Ben Shecter. New York, Harper, 1966.

Big Sister and Little Sister, illustrated by Martha Alexander. New York, Harper, 1966; Kingswood, Surrey, World's Work, 1968.

Flocks of Birds, illustrated by Joan Berg. New York Abelard Schuman, 1965; London, Abelard Schuman, 1966.

I Want to Be Little, illustrated by Tony de Luna. New York and London, Abelard Schuman, 1967.

Summer Is..., illustrated by Janet Archer. New York and London, Abelard Schuman, 1967.

The New Friend, illustrated by Arvis Stewart. New York and London, Abelard Schuman, 1968.

My Friend John, illustrated by Ben Shecter. New York, Harper, 1968.

The Hating Book, illustrated by Ben Shecter. New York, Harper, 1969; Kingswood, Surrey, World's Work, 1971.
Where I Begin (as Sarah Abbott), illustrated by Rocco Negri. New York, Coward McCann, 1970.
You and Me, illustrated by Robert Quackenbush. New York, Macmillan, 1971.
A Father Like That, illustrated by Ben Shecter. New York, Harper, 1971; revised and newly illustrated edition, illustrated by Joanne Scribner, New York, HarperCollins, 1999.
William's Doll, illustrated by William Pène du Bois. New York, Harper, 1972.
Hold My Hand, illustrated by Thomas di Grazia. New York, Harper, 1972.
The Beautiful Christmas Tree, illustrated by Ruth Robbins. Berkeley, California, Parnassus Press, 1972.
The Old Dog (as Sarah Abbott), illustrated by George Mocniak. New York, Coward McCann, 1972.
Janey, illustrated by Ronald Himler. New York, Harper, 1973; Kingswood, Surrey, World's Work, 1974.
My Grandson Lew, illustrated by William Pène du Bois. New York, Harper, 1974; Kingswood, Surrey, World's Work, 1976.
The Unfriendly Book, illustrated by William Pène du Bois. New York, Harper, 1975.
It's Not Fair, illustrated by William Pène du Bois. New York, Harper, 1976; Kingswood, Surrey, World's Work, 1978.
May I Visit?, illustrated by Erik Blegvad. New York, Harper, 1976; Kingswood, Surrey, World's Work, 1977.
Someone New, illustrated by Erik Blegvad. New York, Harper, 1978; Kingswood, Surrey, World's Work, 1979.
Say It!, illustrated by James Stevenson. New York, Greenwillow, 1980.
If You Listen, illustrated by Marc Simont. New York, Harper, 1980.
The Song, illustrated by Nancy Tafuri. New York, Greenwillow, 1982.
I Know a Lady, illustrated by James Stevenson. New York, Greenwillow, 1984; London, Hutchinson, 1985.
Timothy Too!, illustrated by Ruth Robbins. Boston, Houghton Mifflin, 1986.
I Like to Be Little, illustrated by Erik Blegvad. New York, Harper, 1987.
Something Is Going to Happen, illustrated by Catherine Stock. New York, Harper, and London, Collins, 1988.
Wish You Were Here. London, BBC Books, 1990.
The Summer Night, illustrated by Ben Shecter. New York, Harper, 1991.
This Quiet Lady, illustrated by Anita Lobel. New York, Greenwillow, 1992.
The Seashore Book, illustrated by Wendell Minor. New York, Harper, 1992.
The Moon Was the Best, photographs by Tana Hoban. New York, Greenwillow, 1993.
Peter and the Pigeons, illustrated by Martine Gourbault. New York, Greenwillow, 1993.
Who Is Ben?, illustrated by Kathryn Jacobi. New York, HarperCollins Publishers, 1997.
The Bunny Who Found Easter, illustrated by Helen Craig. Boston, Houghton Mifflin, 1998.

Poetry

All That Sunlight, illustrated by Walter Stein. New York, Harper, 1967.
Some Things Go Together, illustrated by Sylvie Selig. New York, Abelard Schuman, 1969.
River Winding, illustrated by Regina Shekerjian. New York, Abelard Schuman, 1970; Kingswood, Surrey, World's Work, 1980.
Wake Up and Goodnight, illustrated by Leonard Weisgard. New York, Harper, 1971; Kingswood, Surrey, World's Work, 1972; illustrated by Pam Paparone, New York, HarperCollinsPublishers, 1997.
Everything Glistens and Everything Sings: New and Selected Poems, illustrated by Margot Tomes. San Diego, Harcourt Brace, 1987.
Snippets: A Gathering of Poems, Pictures, and Possibilities, illustrated by Melissa Sweet. New York, Harper, 1993.

Other

In My Garden, illustrated by Roger Duvoisin. New York, Lothrop, 1960; Kingswood, Surrey, World's Work, 1963.
When the Wind Stops, illustrated by Joe Lasker. New York, Abelard Schuman, 1962; London, Abelard Schuman, 1964; revised and newly illustrated edition, illustrated by Stefano Vitale, New York, HarperCollins, 1995.
A Week in Yani's World: Greece, photographs by Donald Getsug. New York, Crowell Collier, and London, Collier Macmillan, 1969.
A Week in Lateef's World: India, photographs by Ray Shaw. New York, Crowell Collier, 1970.

Editor, *An Overpraised Season: Ten Stories of Youth.* New York, Harper, 1973; London, Bodley Head, 1974.
Editor, *Early Sorrow: Ten Stories of Youth.* New York, Harper, 1986.

*

Film Adaptations: *My Grandason Lew,* 1976; *William's Doll,* 1981; "Someone New" (included in *The Wrong Way Kid*), 1983; *A Father Like That,* 1983; *The Hating Movie,* 1986.

Manuscript Collections: Kerlan Collection, University of Minnesota, Minneapolis.

* * *

In the more than 60 books which Charlotte Zolotow has written since her first, *The Park Book,* she has never raised her voice. This is true even when she constructs stories about quarreling or other extremes of emotion. Her hallmark is artful understatement; the bedrock of her success is her almost eerie sense of what matters to the young. For example, *Janey* describes the desolation of a little girl whose best friend moves far away. The touching tale is a comfort to readers in the same situation, particularly since Zolotow avoids the bathos of a phoney happy ending.

All the Zolotow titles are popular; several are award-winning classics. *William's Doll* argues the case of a perfectly virile boy who yearns for a doll to the disgust of his he-man pals and the dismay of his father. William's wise grandmother buys him a doll and tells his father the boy needs it "so that when he's a father like you, he'll know how to take care of his baby." Blessed by the woman's movement, the book is included automatically in all non-sexist anthologies and on all lists of such literature, and has been on television. Zolotow was also among the first to tackle the long-taboo subject of death in a picture book. *My Grandson Lew* tells of a boy whose mother avoids all mention of the death of his grandfather until she recognizes that children, like adults, need to mourn when they lose loved ones.

In other works, the author displays a talent for creating credible fantasies and quiet comedies. Widely enjoyed is *Mr. Rabbit and the Lovely Present,* in which a little girl matter-of-factly accepts the friendship of a tall bunny. As they wander companionably through the woods near her house, Mr. Rabbit helps the girl gather the makings of a birthday present for her mother. Equally appealing though decidedly different is *A Rose, A Bridge, and a Wild Black Horse.* Here we meet a feisty, young boy who promises that he'll deliver unimaginable wonders to his sister when he's grown up. In the finale, Zolotow scores a direct hit at male chauvinism and endears herself to underestimated females. Brother's oration concludes when he says he will not forget to bring his sister a friend to keep her company "while I explore the world."

On occasion, critics have complained that Zolotow's books are slight and/or plotless. That opinion is not shared by readers who always hear her, quiet though she is, because they know she is as close as children themselves to what is happening in their world.

—Jean F. Mercier

ZUROMSKIS, Diane Stanley. See **STANLEY, Diane.**

APPENDIX

ABBOTT, Jacob

Nationality: American. **Born:** Hallowell, Maine, 14 November 1803. **Education:** Hallowell Academy; Bowdin College, Brunswick, Maine, graduated 1820; Andover Theological Seminary, graduated 1825. **Family:** Married 1) Harriet Vaughan in 1828 (died 1843), six children; 2) Mary Woodbury in 1853 (died 1869). **Career:** Teacher, Portland Academy, Maine, 1820-21, and in Beverly, Massachusetts, 1823; Professor of Mathematics and Natural Philosophy, Amherst College, Massachusetts, 1825-27; founder and principal, Mount Vernon School, Boston, 1828-33; minister, Eliot Congregational Church, Roxbury, Massachusetts, 1834; co-founder, Abbott School for Girls, New York, 1843-51, and Mount Vernon School for Boys, 1845-48. **Died:** 31 October 1879. **Fiction:** *Lucy* series, from 1832; *Caleb in Town,* 1833; *Rollo* series, from 1835; *Hoaryhead, and The Valleys Below,* 1838; *Jonas* series, from 1839; *Caleb in the Country,* 1839; *Franconia* series, from 1850; *John True,* 1850; *Aunt Margaret,* 1854; *Bruno,* 1854; *Carl and Jocko,* 1854; *The Three Gold Dollars,* 1854; *Viola and Her Little Brother Arno,* 1854; *Willie and the Mortgage,* 1854; *Emma,* 1855; *The Harper Establishment,* 1855; *Hoaryhead and M'Donner,* 1855; *Prank,* 1855; *The Studio,* 1855; *Timboo and Joliba,* 1855; *Virginia,* 1855; *The Alcove,* 1856; *Elfred,* 1856; *The Engineer,* 1856; *The Gibraltar Gallery,* 1856; *The Great Elm,* 1856; *Vernon,* 1856; *Minigo,* 1857; *Jasper,* 1857; *Judge Justin,* 1857; *Lapstone,* 1857; *Little Paul,* 1857; *Madeleine,* 1857; *Orkney the Peacemaker,* 1857; *Congo,* 1857; *Rainbow and Lucky* series, from 1858; *Florence* series, from 1860; *Timboo and Fanny,* 1860; *Harlie* series, from 1863; *The Sea-Shore,* 1863; *John Gay* series, from 1864; *Mary Gay* series, from 1865; *William Gay* series, from 1869; *Juno* series, from 1870; *August Stories* series, from 1871(?); *Fergus,* 1874; *Gilbert and His Mother,* 1874; *The Museum,* 1884.

* * *

Jacob Abbott is among the earliest American writers of domestic tales for the young, and certainly the first to make the American scene familiar to English readers, who throughout the last century enjoyed his accounts of robust, self-reliant children seemingly delightfully independent of their parents. In all his books one senses the wise schoolmaster, patient, tolerant and good-humoured—but concerned to improve his pupils. His method of instructing the child through experience was a development of that of the Edgeworths (whose educational views, and Maria's stories to illustrate them, had always been far more popular in the United States than in England), and, realizing that children have great respect for the opinion and advice of a child a little older, he made a practice of introducing a youthful counsellor, very often a hired boy, who instructs and admonishes the impetuous and headstrong. This sage's word is invariably law; the children obey and accept his punishments which are reasonable and designed to fit the crime. In the Rollo series the authority is vested in Jonas; the Franconia series has "Beechnut" (the French hired boy Antoine Bianchinette); sometimes there is a little female preceptor like Mary Bell (also in the Franconia tales), or Juno "a nice and tidy-looking coloured girl" who has her own series and is the mentor of Georgie. There is always remarkably little adult presence.

The first two Rollo books in a series which came to number some 28 volumes were *The Little Scholar Learning to Talk* and *Rollo Learning to Read.* Rollo's childhood is more interesting than his adolescence when, with his character presumably formed, he is taken by his uncle on a 12-volume tour of Europe "with the satisfied consciousness of hailing from a land far superior to those inhabited by foreigners." Abbott had the same skill as Maria Edgeworth in portraying small children, and Rollo, aged five, is an engaging little boy with not much thought beyond his own concerns, unwilling to concentrate on anything for very long, loftily confident of being able to achieve anything he chooses, apt to cry when things go wrong. As the series progresses he learns about the world around him, and acquires various skills, and such virtues as self-control, restraint, and self-denial which Abbott presents not so much as moral law but reasonable and expedient if one is to live happily with others.

The Franconia books, set in a village in the mountains of New York State, are less overtly instructive than the Rollo series, though the author makes his intentions clear in the preface to each. The central characters are the little boy, Phonny (Alphonso), and his parents' hired boy, Beechnut; a neighbouring girl Ellen Linn; the good and gentle Mary Bell and her friend Caroline "a young lady thirteen years old"; and the visitors from New York Malleville and Wallace, most of these being the subject of individual titles in the series. What drama there is—such as the death of Ellen Linn's father in a snowstorm—is recounted in the same leisurely, unemotional style that is accorded to the descriptions of the blueberrying expeditions, the building of a diving pier, the maple sugaring; and when Beechnut is arrested on a false charge of arson the episode seems to be no more than an exercise to explain the processes of the law. Pace and drama were not characteristics of Abbott's writing. "Pleasing pictures of still life in the country," a contemporary reviewer said of the Franconia series, and the books are not less pleasing for their gentle goodness.

While not taking the same stern view of fairy stories as so many of his American contemporaries, Abbott thought children should be directed to more profitable matters. His one fairy story, *Minigo* (prefaced by a reminder that fairies were "fictitious and imaginary"), is about a firm and sensible fairy cast in much the same mould as Beechnut and Jonas, with ability to make an errant child feel instantly ashamed.

—Gillian Avery

ALCOTT, Louisa May

Nationality: American. **Born:** Germantown, Philadelphia, Pennsylvania, 29 November 1832; daughter of the philosopher Amos Bronson Alcott; grew up in Boston, and Concord, Massachusetts. **Education:** Educated at home by her father, with instruction from Thoreau, Emerson, and Theodore Parker. **Career:** Began to write for publication, 1848; also worked as a teacher, seamstress, and domestic servant; army nurse at the Union Hospital, Georgetown, Washington, D.C., during the Civil War, 1862-63; editor of the children's magazine *Merry's Museum,* 1867. **Died:** 6 March 1888. **Fiction:** *Flower Fables,* 1855; *The Rose Family,* 1864; *Morning-Glories and Other Stories,* 1867; *Three Proverb Stories,* 1868; *Kitty's Class Day,* 1868; *Aunt Kipp,* 1868; *Psyche's Art,* 1868; *Little Women (Little Women and Good Wives),* 1868-69; *An Old-Fashioned Girl,* 1870; *Will's Wonder Book,* 1870; *Little Men,* 1871; *Aunt Jo's Scrap-Bag,* 1872-82; *Eight Cousins,* 1875; *Rose in Bloom,* 1876; *A Modern Mephistopheles,* 1877; *Under the Lilacs,* 1877;

Meadow Blossoms, 1879; *Water Cresses,* 1879; *Jack and Jill,* 1880; *Proverb Stories,* 1882; *Spinning-Wheel Stories,* 1884; *Jo's Boys and How They Turned Out,* 1886; *Lulu's Library,* 1886-89; *A Garland for Girls,* 1888; *Louisa's Wonder Book,* 1975; *Behind a Mask,* 1975; *Plots and Counterplots,* 1976; *A Double Life,* 1988.

* * *

In 1868 when, at the request of Thomas Niles of Roberts Brothers, Lousia May Alcott sat down to write a household story for girls, the domestic novel as evolved by Susan Warner, Maria Cummins, Ann Stephens, and Mrs. E.D.E.N. Southworth consisted of commonplace episodes worked into a trite plot involving pious and insipid characters. Bronson Alcott's opinion of juvenile literature, recorded in his diary for 1839, had, in the generation that followed, been given no cause for alteration. In 1868 it was still true that the "literature of childhood" had not been written. If such extraodinary moral tales as *The Wide, Wide World,* the Rollo books, the Lucy books, and the first of the Elsie books became unbearable, there was compensation for a youthful reader only in grave-and-horror stories, Hawthorne's legendary tales, or "Peter Parley's" edifying descriptions of natural wonders.

The times were ripe for Alcott and she was well equipped to fill the gap in domestic literature. With the publication of *Little Women* (1868-69) she created a domestic novel for children destined to influence writers in that genre for generations to come. Responding to her publisher's request, she drew her characters from those of her own sisters, her scenes from the New England where she had grown up, and many of her episodes from those she and her family had experienced. In all this she was something of a pioneer, adapting her autobiography to the creation of a juvenile novel and achieving a realistic but wholesome picture of family life with which young readers could readily identify.

The literary influence of Bunyan and Dickens, Carlyle and Hawthorne, Emerson, Theodore Parker, and Thoreau can be traced in her work, but primarily she drew upon autobiographical sources for her plot and her characters, finding in her family and neighbors the groundwork for her three-dimensional characters. Her perceptively drawn adolescents, the Marches, modeled upon her sisters and herself, were not merely lifelike but alive. Her episodes, from the opening selection of a Christmas gift to the plays in the barn, from Jo March's literary career to Beth's death, were thoroughly believable for they had been lived. The Alcott humor which induced a chuckle at a homely phrase was appreciated by children. The Alcott poverty was sentimentalized; the eccentric Alcott father was an adumbrated shadow; yet, for all the glossing over, the core of the domestic drama was apparent. Reported simply and directly in a style that obeyed her injunction "Never use a long word, when a short one will do as well," the narrative embodied the simple facts and persons of a family and so filled a gap in the literature of childhood. Alcott had unlatched the door to one house, and "all find it is their own house which they enter." 20th-century writers for children who aim at credibility and verisimilitude in their reconstructions of contemporary family life are all, in one way or another, indebted to Alcott.

By the time she created *Little Women* she had served a long apprenticeship and was already a professional writer. She had edited a juvenile monthly, *Merry's Museum,* and produced several books aimed at a juvenile readership: her first published book, *Flower Fables,* "legends of faery land"; *The Rose Family: A Fairy Tale*; and *Morning-Glories and Other Stories,* readable short stories in which autobiographical details were combined with nature lore and moral tidbits.

Alcott had also written in a variety of genres for a wide range of adult readers, weaving stories of sweetness and light, dramatic narratives of strong-minded women and poor lost creatures, realistic episodes of the Civil War, and blood-and-thunder thrillers of revenge and passion whose leading character was usually a vindictive and manipulating heroine. From the exigencies of serialization for magazines she had developed the skills of the cliff-hanger and the page-turner. Her first full-length novel, *Moods* (1865), was a narrative of stormy passion and violence, death and intellectual love in which she attempted to apply Emerson's remark: "Life is a train of moods like a string of beads." Off and on, she had worked at her autobiographical and feminist novel *Success,* subsequently renamed *Work: A Story of Experience*. By 1868, Alcott had run a gamut of literary experimentation from stories of virtue rewarded to stories of vice unpunished. She had attempted tales of escape and realism and stirred her literary ingredients in a witch's cauldron before she kindled the fire in a family hearth.

With few exceptions—notably *A Modern Mephistopheles* (1877) in which she reverted to the sensational themes of her earlier blood-and-thunders—Alcott clung to that family hearth during the remainder of her career. Between 1868 when Part One of *Little Women* appeared and 1888 when she died, she produced in her so-called *Little Women Series* a string of wholesome domestic narratives more or less autobiographical in origin, simple and direct in style, perceptive in the characterization of adolescents. *An Old-Fashioned Girl, Little Men, Eight Cousins, Rose in Bloom, Under the Lilacs, Jack and Jill,* and *Jo's Boys* are all in a sense sequels to *Little Women* though none of them quite rises to its level. *An Old-Fashioned Girl* is a domestic dream in reverse, exposing the fashionable absurdities of the Shaw home by contrast with Polly, the wholesome representative of domesticity. The Campbell clan of *Eight Cousins* exalts the family hearth again. In *Jack and Jill* the author enlarges upon the domesticity, describing the home life of a New England village rather than of a single family.

Despite her experimentation with a diversity of literary techniques, despite the fact that she was a complex writer drawn to a variety of themes, Alcott has inevitably achieved fame as the "Children's Friend" and the author of a single masterpiece. Thanks to its psychological perceptions, its realistic characterizations, and its honest domesticity, *Little Women* has become an embodiment of the American home at its best. Consciously or unconsciously all subsequent writers who have attempted the domestic novel for children have felt its influence, for in *Little Women* the local has been transmuted into the universal and the incidents of family life have been translated to the domain of literature.

Today not only *Little Women* but the entire Alcott oeuvre are being subjected to critical re-evaluation. For this the reprinting of her previously unknown thrillers (written in secret during the 1860s and published anonymously or pseudonymously) is largely responsible. Their themes (mind control and madness, hashish experimentation and opium addiction, mesmerism, and a powerful feminism) are leading critics to re-examine the simplistic interpretation of "America's best-loved author of juveniles."

—Madeleine B. Stern

ALDRICH, Thomas Bailey

Nationality: American. **Born:** Portsmouth, New Hampshire, 11 November 1836. **Education:** Attended school in Portsmouth. **Family:** Married Lilian Woodman in 1865; twin sons. **Career:** Clerk in New York, 1852-55; staff member, *Evening Mirror,* 1855-56, editor, *Home Journal,* 1856-59, associate editor, *Saturday Press,* 1858-60, and editor, *Illustrated News,* 1863, all in New York; editor, *Every Saturday,* Boston, 1866-74, and *Atlantic Monthly,* Boston, 1881-90. **Awards:** M.A.: Yale University, New Haven, Connecticut, 1881; Harvard University, Cambridge, Massachusetts, 1896; LL.D.: University of Pennsylvania, Philadelphia, 1906. **Died:** 19 March 1907. **Fiction:** *The Story of a Bad Boy,* 1869.

* * *

Although Thomas Baily Aldrich first achieved literary renown as a poet in the mid-19th century, it is as a novelist and short story writer that he is chiefly remembered today.

His short stories, like his poems, many of which still retain their distinction, are impeccably crafted, disciplined, restrained, sparse, precise, and refined. Throughout Aldrich's works, there is artistic integrity, a subtle blending of sentiment and wit, and, ever present, a blithe young spirit that led Mark Twain to remark that he was tired of waiting for Aldrich to grow old. What does remain eternally, innocently childlike is his autobiographical novel, *The Story of a Bad Boy.* Aldrich wished to distinguish his young Tom, "an amiable, impulsive lad...and no hypocrite...from the faultless young gentleman who generally figure in narratives of this kind."

His somewhat idealized story parallels the actual events of his own boyhood: early years in New Orleans, schooling in New Hampshire in preparation for Harvard until the death of his father precluded college, completing his education in Portsmouth (Rivermouth in the book). Aldrich recalls these years affectionately, amusingly, nostalgically. On his arrival in Boston from the South, he was surprised to see no Indians on Long Wharf—either they "were early risers" or "they were away just then on the warpath." And, "speaking of the Pilgrim Fathers," why was there never any "mention of the Pilgrim Mothers." Gently, he satirized the "Old Puritan austerity" that cropped out on Sundays in the Nutter household where in the oppressive atmosphere of that one day a week, they ate "a dead cold dinner" that was "laid out yesterday." He vowed ever after to make Sundays cheerful days. The most haunting, poignant memory—a wholly fictitious happening—was the tragedy of poor little Binny Wallace who drifted out to sea in a gale and now sleeps in the Old South Burying Ground. One of the early regional novels, the story glows with local color, characteristic eccentricities, and traditions. In that old declining privateer port of Rivermouth, boys cruised down the river, island-hopping on excursions and learning about the sea and ships; they presented amateur theatricals in the barn, celebrated holidays properly, and not so properly burned an old stage coach, jumped jail, and waged frigid snow fights on Slater's Hill.

To Ferris Greenslet, Aldrich's official biographer and an editorial alumnus of the *Atlantic Monthly,* the book "marked an epoch in the history of juvenile literature." One of the first critics to discern that Aldrich had "done a new thing...in American literature" was William Dean Howells, then editor of the *Atlantic.* Howells's review appeared in the January 1870 issue: "No one else seems to have thought of telling the story of a boy's life with so great desire to show what a boy's life is, and with so little purpose of teaching what it should be; certainly no one has thought of doing this for the American boy!" Howells noted that the story of Aldrich's boyhood had suggested similar books, including his own *A Boy's Town,* Charles Dudley Warner's *Being a Boy,* Mark Twain's *Tom Sawyer* and *Huckleberry Finn.* Not so, declared Bernard DeVoto, one of Twain's fellow westerners and a historian ever alert to catch any misconceptions concerning Twain. DeVoto deemed it idle to speculate over the origins of *Tom Sawyer,* and whether Aldrich had any influence on it, for when Mark Twain had come around to writing *Tom Sawyer,* he had "at last arrived at the theme that was most harmonious with his interest, his experience, and his talents...Mark Twain was predestined to this work." Well, perhaps: but Howells was there! He was Twain's friend and editor. He read *Tom Sawyer* in manuscript, at Twain's request. By deleting some of the profanity and toning down the section where Becky tears a page of the teacher's book of anatomy, Howells may have slanted the story toward the juvenile market—Twain had intended it for adults. "It is not a boy's book at all," he had written to Howells. Also, by 1871, Twain and Aldrich had become friends. Twain must have been aware that what Aldrich had done for the waning years of New England Puritanism, he would do for the early years of western frontier life. While one is genteel and polite, the other is rugged and lusty, but both cover much the same kind of boyish pranks and activities: climbing out of windows in the dead of night, running away, camping out, falling miserably in love. Aunt Polly is to one what Grandfather Nutter is to the other: Injun Joe was starved "entirely to death in the cave" (incidentally, he ate candle wax in his struggle to survive just as, in Aldrich's story "A Struggle for Life," Philip Wentworth had in the tomb) for the same kind of heightened literary effect that Aldrich had used in letting Binny Wallace float helplessly out to sea. In his autobiography, Twain praised Aldrich's brilliance and wit, but referred blisteringly to Aldrich's prose as "diffuse, self-conscious, barren of distinction...," grudgingly conceding that "his fame as a writer...is based on half a dozen small poems which are not surpassed in our language for exquisite grace and beauty and finish."

The poem that Aldrich had written in honor of Longfellow's centennial—a poem that was read one month later at Aldrich's funeral—is also a fitting tribute to his boyhood story: "They do not die who leave their thoughts/Imprinted on some deathless page./Themselves may pass; the spell they wrought/Endures on earth from age to age." *The Story of a Bad Boy* wrought a spell that has wound its way down the years from Lucretia Peabody Hale to Sarah Orne Jewett, from Laura Ingalls Wilder to Maureen Daly, from Esther Forbes to Jack Schaefer, from J.D. Salinger to John Donovan.

—Mary Silva Cosgrave

ALGER, Horatio (Jr.)

Nationality: American. **Born:** Chelsea, Massachusetts, 13 January 1832. **Education:** Chelsea Grammar School; Gates Academy, Marlborough, Massachusetts, 1845-47; Harvard University, Cambridge, Massachusetts (Bowdoin prize, 1851), 1848-52, A.B. 1852 (Phi Beta Kappa); Harvard Divinity School, 1853, 1857-60, graduated 1860: ordained 1864. **Career:** Assistant editor, Boston *Daily Advertiser,* 1853-54; schoolteacher, East Greenwich, Rhode Island, 1854-55; principal, Deerfield Academy, Massachusetts, 1856; tutor, and editorial writer, *True Flag,* Boston, 1856-57; traveled in Europe, 1860-61; private tutor in Cambridge and Nahant, Massachusetts, 1861-64; minister, First Unitarian Church, Brewster, Massachusetts, 1864-66; lived in New York, 1866-96, and private tutor from 1869; lived in South Natick, Massachusetts, 1896-99. **Died:** 18 July 1899. **Fiction:** *Bertha's Christmas Vision* (includes verse), 1856; *Frank's Campaign,* 1864; *Paul Prescott's Charge (Paul Prescott the Runaway),* 1865; *Helen Ford,* 1866; *Timothy Crump's Ward (Jack's Ward),* 1866; *Charlie Codman's Cruise (Bill Sturdy),* 1866; *Fame and Fortune,* 1868; *Ragged Dick,* 1868; *Luck and Pluck,* 1869; *Mark, the Match Boy,* 1869; *Rough and Ready,* 1869; *Ben, the Luggage Boy,* 1870; *Rufus and Rose,* 1870; *Sink or Swim (Paddle Your Own Canoe),* 1870; *Paul the Peddler (Plucky Paul),* 1871; *Strong and Steady,* 1871; *Tattered Tom,* 1871; *Phil, the Fiddler,* 1872; *Slow and Sure,* 1872; *Strive and Succeed,* 1872; *Bound to Rise,* 1873; *Try and Trust (Trials and Adventures of Herbert Mason),* 1873; *Brave and Bold,* 1874; *Julius,* 1874; *Risen from the Ranks,* 1874; *Herbert Carter's Legacy (George Carter's Legacy),* 1875; *The Young Outlaw,* 1875; *Sam's Chance,* 1876; *Shifting for Himself (How His Ship Came Home),* 1876; *Wait and Hope,* 1877; *The Western Boy (Tom, the Bootblack),* 1878; *The Young Adventurer,* 1878; *The Young Miner,* 1879; *The Telegraph Boy (The District Telegraph Boy),* 1879; *The Young Explorer,* 1880; *Tony, The Hero (Tony, the Tramp),* 1880; *Ben's Nugget,* 1882; *The Train Boy,* 1883; *The Young Circus Rider,* 1883; *Dan, the Detective (Dan, the Newsboy; Dutiful Dan),* 1884; *Do and Dare,* 1884; *Hector's Inheritance (Never Despair!),* 1885; *Helping Himself,* 1886; *Joe's Luck,* 1887; *Frank Fowler, the Cash Boy,* 1887; *Number 91,* 1887; *The Store Boy* (*The Fortunes of Ben Barclay; Ben Barclay's Courage*), 1887; *Ben Stanton, the Explorer,* 1887; *Bob Burton* (*The Young Ranchman of the Missouri*), 1888; *The Errand Boy,* 1888; *The Merchant's Crime (Ralph Raymond's Heir),* 1888; *Tom Temple's Career,* 1888; *Tom Thatcher's Fortune,* 1888; *Tom Tracy,* 1888; *The Young Acrobat of the Great North American Circus (He Would Be a Mountebank),* 1888; *Luke Walton,* 1889; *Mark Stanton,* 1890; *Ned Newton,* 1890; *A New York Boy,* 1890; *The Odds Against Him (Driven from Home),* 1890; *Struggling Upward,* 1890; *Dean Dunham (Wait Till the Clouds Roll By),* 1890; *The Erie Train Boy (The Straight Ahead),* 1890; *The Erie Train Boy (The Straight Ahead),* 1890; *$500 (Uncle Jacob's Secret; The Five Hundred Dollar Check),* 1890; *Digging for Gold,* 1892; *The Young Boatman of Pine Point,* 1892; *Facing the World,* 1893; *In a New World (The Nugget Finders; Val Vane's Victory),* 1893; *Only an Irish Boy,* 1894; *Victor Vane,* 1894; *Adrift in the City,* 1895; Frank Hunter's Peril, 1896; *The Young Salesman,* 1896; *Walter Sherwood's Probation,* 1897; *Frank and Fearless,* 1897; *A Boy's Fortune,* 1898; *The Young Bank Messenger,* 1898; *Rupert's Ambition,* 1899; *Mark Mason's Victory,* 1899; *Jed, the Poorhouse Boy,* 1900; *A Debt of Honor,* 1900; *Ben Bruce,* 1901; *Lester's Luck,* 1901; *Making His Mark,* 1901; *Striving for Fortune (Walter Griffith),* 1901; *Tom Brace,* 1901; *Andy Grant's Pluck,* 1902; *A Rolling Stone (Wren Winter's Triumph),* 1902; *Tom Turner's Legacy,* 1902; *The World Before Him,* 1902; *Bernard Brook's Adventures,* 1903; *Chester Rand,* 1903; *Forging Ahead (Andy Gordon),* 1903; *Adrift in New York,* 1903; *Finding a Fortune (The Tin Box),* 1904; *Mark Manning's Mission,* 1905; *The Young Musician,* 1906; *In Search of Treasure,* 1907; *Wait and Win,* 1908; *Robert Coverdale's Struggle,* 1910; *Silas Snobden's Office Boy,* 1973; *Cast upon the Breakers,* 1974; *Hugo, the Deformed,* 1978; *Madeline, the Temptress,* 1981; *The Secret Drawer,* 1981; *The Cooper's Ward,* 1981; *Herbert Selden,* 1981; *Manson, the Miser,* 1981; *The Gipsy Nurse,* 1981; *The Discarded Son,* 1981; *The Mad Heiress,* 1981; *Marie Bertrand,* 1981; the following completed by Edward Stratemeyer—*Falling In with Fortune,* 1900; *Out for Business,* 1900; *Nelson the Newsboy,* 1901; *Young Captain Jack,* 1901; *Jerry, the Backwoods Boy,* 1904; *Lost at Sea,* 1904; *From Farm to Fortune,* 1905; *The Young Book Agent,* 1905; *Joe, the Hotel Boy,* 1906; *Randy of the River,* 1906; *Ben Logan's Triumph,* 1908.

* * *

Most of Horatio Alger's once popular juveniles are about young boys who achieve material success through their industry, thrift, and good character, aided by some happy coincidence. The stories have predictable plots, stilted dialogue, stock characters, and a banal use of language or device. Apologists say that Alger's works should be judged by the standards of the late 19th century, implying that his literary stock would rise. But would it? A lack of literary talent and imagination marks Alger as a second-rate formula writer.

Application of an earlier standard excuses the near plagiarism of Dicken's *Christmas Carol* as "The Veiled Mirror" in *Bertha's Christmas Vision.* It explains the errors resulting from careless editing and the speed or method of Alger's writing. *From Canal Boy to President,* a boy's life of President James A. Garfield, was available for sale within seven weeks of Garfield's death. Writing without revision, Alger worked on several stories at one time. On occasion, his characters—never very dissimilar in type or type of name—mistakenly slipped from one book to another. Luke Larkin suddenly appears in *Luke Walton.*

Both books are vintage Alger. In *Struggling Upward; or, Luke Larkin's Luck,* Luke, the son of a carpenter's widow, "had a pleasant expression, and a bright, resolute look, a warm heart, and a clear intellect, and was probably, in spite of his poverty, the most popular boy in Groveton." In contrast, Randolph, son of Groveton's unscrupulous banker, buys his popularity and, at the book's end, is "an office boy...no longer able to swagger and boast." Luke's benefactor, a stranger who sent Luke on a mission west for information about missing government bonds, turns out to be a lost, rich relative. There are the usual discussions about money; Luke returns to New York "with only three dollars and seventy-five cents," but is urged to take "a hundred dollars on account" with "fifty dollars more...for your thoughtfulness." Typically, Alger closes with a brief summary. Luke "has struggled upward from a boyhood of privation and self-denial into a youth and manhood of prosperity and honor. There has been some luck about it...but after all he is indebted for most of his good fortune to his own good qualities." The message was plain; the recipe simple. The books were unfailingly moral but did not preach. Identification with characters was easy; dialogue and action followed in quick succession. An Alger story entertains.

Ragged Dick established Alger. His best-known but not his best book, it is too long and too slow to get the action underway. Too many pages are a New York itinerary. Possibly readers in more rural times found the big city references exciting. To the book's credit, Dick's character has some dimension; he sprang from Alger's first enthusiastic acquaintance with actual poor boys who stayed at the Newsboys' Lodging House where Alger visited constantly.

Alger should be defended by shifting from literary criticism to literary history, and, better, to his place in the emotional history of a nation. For his readers, Alger interpreted democracy as a simple "rags to riches" dream; fortuitous luck might come to anyone and, most of all, to clean-living, hard-working boys. All was possible in Alger's America; that is the well-spring of his appeal. In 1982, the United States issued a Horatio Alger stamp showing the decorative title-page of *Ragged Dick*. Probably few people can identify the picture, and fewer still have cause to seek out the book. But, many would have an intuition that here is a symbol of America, and expression from the past reaffirming a faith in the future.

—Claire England

ANSTEY, F.

Pseudonym for Thomas Anstey Guthrie. **Nationality:** British. **Born:** London, 8 August 1856. **Education:** King's College School, London; Trinity Hall, Cambridge. **Career:** Called to the bar, 1880; worked briefly as a barrister. Regular contributor to *Punch*, London. **Died:** 10 March 1934. **Fiction:** *Vice-Versâ,* 1882; *Paleface and Redskin and Other Stories,* 1898; *Only Toys!,* 1903; *In Brief Authority,* 1915.

* * *

F. Anstey was not by design a writer for children, but one of those many late Victorian and Edwardian novelists who could create characters, plots, settings, immediately popular with readers of all ages. These include Richard Jefferies, with *Bevis,* and Rider Haggard, Kipling, Buchan, P.C. Wren, A.E.W. Mason, Anthony Hope, Conan Doyle, Marjorie Bowen, Jules Verne, Alexandre Dumas, and early H.G. Wells. For some years a regular contributor to *Punch,* Anstey is now really celebrated for only one book, *Vice-Versâ,* although *The Black Poodle* can occasionally be found and might still appeal, as could the lively *The Brass Bottle,* an adroit variation on the perennial, indestructible Aladdin theme. Magic and fantasy are seldom absent, notably in *Only Toys!* and books with such revealing titles as *Tourmalin's Time Cheques* and *The Talking Horse*.

The magic, however, is not a facile escape into mere make-believ. "I like the fantastic only inside the real," wrote Alain-Fournier, and Anstey succeeds by always obeying this. An inventive storyteller, he mixes a modicum of fantasy with direct, un-bizarre observation, human understanding, sly comedy. These combine most fully in *Vice-Versâ,* where the magic, a single involuntary trick in the beginning reversed at the end, supplies the catalyst for the plot, which develops as complete realism, in turn painful, comic, sardonic. Its target is the harsh world of the private school, run for personal profit and with unchallenged despotism by the headmaster for the benefit less of the pupils than of the complacent, prosperous parents. These are usually remote from their children, whom they continually assure, with the advantage of inadequate memory, that schooldays are life's happiest period. This fulsome belief is tested and shattered when the accidental manipulation of a magic charm transforms lordly, unimaginative Mr. Bultitude into his own son, Dick, on the last morning of the holidays, while Dick becomes his own father. Dazed, incredulous, Mr. Bultitude is thereupon packed off to school and, while Dick casually starts ruining the family business, endures a term wracked with misery. Anstey's picture of the school is no caricature: it seems a fair enough assessment of an average private school, still existing at least until 1939. The gap between parents and children, teachers and taught, headmaster and staff, is sharply exposed, though Mr. Bultitude's tribulations are extremely funny. Both Saki and P.G. Wodehouse must have relished the description of the hapless Victorian father, in pupil's uniform, in the school train surrounded by small, giggling boys, attempting to engage the formidable, increasingly irritated and suspicious Headmaster with informed remarks about market conditions in the City. The book must have had some useful effect on the adult world. It has been successfully filmed by Peter Ustinov, and, in present conditions, is unlikely to lack appreciation in many schools and homes today.

—Peter Vansittart

BALLANTYNE, R(obert) M(ichael)

Pseudonym: Comus. **Nationality:** British. **Born:** Edinburgh, 24 April 1825. **Education:** Edinburgh Academy, 1835-37, and privately. **Family:** Married Jane Dickson Grant in 1866; four sons and two daughters. **Career:** Apprentice clerk, Hudson's Bay Company, in Canada, 1841-47; clerk, North British Railway Company, Edinburgh, 1847-49; staff member, Alexander Cowan and Company, paper-makers, Edinburgh, 1849; junior partner, Thomas Constable and Company, printers, Edinburgh, 1849-55. Lecturer and free-lance writer after 1855. Member, 1858, Ensign, 1859, and Captain, 1860, Edinburgh Volunteers. Lived in Harrow, Middlesex, after 1883. **Died:** 8 February 1894. **Fiction:** *Snowflakes and Sunbeams,* 1856; *Three Little Kittens* (as Comus), 1856; *Mister Fox* (as Comus), 1857; *My Mother (Chit-Chat)* (as Comus), 1857; *The Butterfly's Ball and the Grasshopper's Feast* (as Comus), 1857; *The Life of a Ship from the Launch to the Wreck,* 1857; *Ungava,* 1858; *The Coral Island,* 1858; *The Robber Kitten* (as Comus), 1858; *Martin Rattler,* 1858; *Mee-a-ow!,* 1859; *The World of Ice,* 1860; *The Dog Crusoe,* 1861; *The Gorilla Hunters,* 1861; *The Golden Dream,* 1861; *The Red Eric,* 1861; *The Wild Man of the West,* 1863; *Fighting the Whales,* 1863; *Away in the Wilderness,* 1863; *Fast in the Ice,* 1863; *Gascoyne,* 1864; *The Lifeboat,* 1864; *Chasing the Sun,* 1864; *Freaks on the Fells,* 1864; *The Lighthouse,* 1865; *Shifting Winds,* 1866; *Fighting the Flames,* 1867; *Silver Lake,* 1867; *Deep Down,* 1868; *Erling the Bold,* 1869; Sunk at Sea, 1869; *Lost in the Forest,* 1869; *Over the Rocky Mountains,* 1869; *Saved by the Lifeboat,* 1869; *The Cannibal Islands,* 1869; *Hunting the Lions,* 1869; *Digging for Gold,* 1869; *Up in the Clouds,* 1869; *The Battle and the Breeze,* 1869; *The Floating Light of the Goodwin Sands,* 1870; *The Iron Horse,* 1871; *The Pioneers,* 1872; *The Norsemen in the West,* 1872; *Life in the Red Brigade,* 1873; *Black Ivory,* 1873; *The Pirate City,* 1874; *Rivers of Ice,* 1875; *The Story of the Rock,* 1875; *Under the Waves,* 1876; *The Settler and the Savage,* 1877; *In the Track of the Troops,* 1878; *Jarwin and Cuffy,* 1878; *Philosopher Jack,* 1880; *The Lonely Island,* 1880; *Post Haste,* 1880; *The Red Man's Revenge,* 1880; *My Doggie and I,* 1881; *The Giant of the North,* 1882; *The Kitten Pilgrims,* 1882; *The Battery and the Boiler,* 1883; *Battles with the Sea,* 1883; *The Thorogood Family,* 1883; *The Madman and the Pirate,* 1883; *Dusty Diamonds Cut and Polished,* 1884; *The Young Trawler,* 1884;

Twice Bought, 1885; *The Rover of the Andes,* 1885; *The Island Queen,* 1885; *Red Rooney,* 1886; *The Prairie Chief,* 1886; *The Lively Poll,* 1886; *The Big Otter,* 1887; *The Fugitives,* 1887; *Blue Lights,* 1888; *The Middy and the Moors (Slave of the Moors),* 1888; *The Crew of the Water Wagtail,* 1889; *The Eagle Cliff,* 1889; *Blown to Bits,* 1889; *The Garret and the Garden,* 1890; *Charlie to the Rescue,* 1890; *The Buffalo Runners,* 1891; *The Coxswain's Bride,* 1891; *The Hot Swamp,* 1892; *Hunted and Harried,* 1892; *The Walrus Hunters,* 1893; *Reuben's Luck,* 1896.

* * *

In his own lifetime R.M. Ballantyne gained the distinction of being identified in the minds of his young readers with the bravest of the deeds performed by the manly characters in the fictional tales he wrote. His photographs, which showed him as a handsome, bearded figure with the shoulder-length hair of a typical North American trapper, complete with long-barreled gun and powder-horn across his knees, went far to confirm this impression. His autobiographical experiences as a youth employed by the Hudson's Bay Company were related in his first book, *Hudson's Bay; or, Every-Day Like in the Wilds of North America,* and his early life in Rupert's Land formed the background to many of his tales.

His first fictional work for the young appeared in 1856 as *Snowflakes and Sunbeams; or, The Young Fur Trader;* but it was *The Coral Island* (1858) that made his name as a juvenile novelist. This was the book which Robert Louis Stevenson acknowledged as the formative influence of his own love of the South Seas, a work which later led to his writing the immortal *Treasure Island,* with its dedicatory allusion to "Ballantyne the Brave."

Ballantyne was one of the first writers of fictional adventure tales for the young to apply himself seriously to the background research so necessary to render the stories realistic. Unlike G.A. Henty, who wrote fictional tales set against historical backgrounds in the manner of Sir Walter Scott, Ballantyne almost without exception set himself the task of living and often working for weeks or months in the geographical location where he meant to set his story. Thus for *The Lifeboat* he lived at Deal with the lifeboat crew; for *The Lighthouse* he spent several weeks on the Bell Rock Lighthouse; for *Fighting the Flames* he was with the London Fire Brigade waiting for days on end for the bells to signal a fire; for *Deep Down: A Tale of the Cornish Mines* he lived with the tin-miners of St. Just for over three months. The same could be said for *The Floating Light of the Goodwin Sands,* for which he endured weeks of seasickness on the Gull Lightship, and for *The Iron Horse; or, Life on the Line,* for which he acted as fireman on board the tender of the London-to-Edinburgh express. The result of all these and countless other expeditions both at home and abroad was a series of well over 80 full-length juvenile novels embodying a realism never before seen in works for teenage boys.

He was the hero of Victorian youth; but his weakness lay in his being straitjacketed by his puritanism. Unlike Stevenson, he was unable to write a romantic and exciting story of adventure that was unmoralised and unashamed. Too often the action in Ballantyne's tales was braked by the gum of piety and evangelistic soliloquising of the often bloodthirsty young characters he made his heroes. They lightheartedly slaughtered the fauna and the natives of the islands and jungles where they found themselves marooned with an impartial vigour, before falling on their knees to thank God for his infinite mercy and a successful day's sport. *The Gorilla Hunters* is a typical example of unrelenting cruelty by young teenagers that passed without comment in the mid-19th century. He wrote, as we all do, for the age in which he lived.

Nevertheless, Ballantyne opened for the sons of the rapidly expanding *literati* of middle- and working-class families an exciting new vista of a world spiced with romance and danger which lay waiting for the young men of Britain to grow up and explore. He projected into lives which were often drab and humdrum a realistically coloured image, mirroring his readers in the figures of his heroes, and leaving them tantalized with the knowledge that they, too, could equally well have overcome the fearful odds against which Ralph, Jack, and Peterkin grappled so bravely. He employed what was soon a well-tried formula, by giving full rein to youthful emotions within the strict bounds of what then passed as Christian morality, while leading his readers through dramatically bloody chapters of shipwreck, slaughter, capture and escape, to the inevitable happy ending of a wealthy and pious old age.

He portrayed a world where the good were terribly good, and the bad were terribly bad, and the British were terribly British—and worth 10 of any foreigners alive, by Jingo! For any writer of his time to dare to suggest otherwise would have been considered the blackest heresy by the young men of Victoria's England. For these were the boys who, in their turn, were to become the soldiers and sailors, the explorers, and trail-blazers, the missionaries and merchant adventures, the exploiters, the Word-spreaders, the successes and failures of the great British Empire on which the sun would never set.

—Eric Quayle

CARROLL, Lewis

Pseudonym for Charles Lutwidge Dodgson. **Nationality:** British. **Born:** Daresbury, Cheshire, 27 January 1832. **Education:** Attended school in Richmond, Surrey, 1844-46; Rugby School, Warwickshire, 1846-49; Christ Church, Oxford (Boultor scholar, 1851), B.A. (honours) in mathematics 1854, M.A. 1857. **Career:** Fellow, and Master of the House, 1855, sub-librarian, 1855, Bostock Scholar, 1855, lecturer in mathematics, 1856-81, and curator of the Common Room, 1882-92, Christ Church, Oxford. Ordained, 1861. **Died:** 14 January 1898. **Fiction:** *Alice's Adventures in Wonderland,* 1865, revised edition, 1886, 1897; *Through the Looking-Glass, and What Alice Found There,* 1871, revised edition, 1897; *Alice's Adventures Underground,* 1886; *The Nursery Alice,* 1889; *Sylvie and Bruno,* 2 vols., 1889-93; *The "Wonderland" Postage-Stamp-Case,* 1890; *The Wasp in a Wig,* 1978. **Verse:** *Phantasmagoria and Other Poems,* 1869; *The Hunting of the Snark,* 1876; *Rhyme? and Reason?,* 1883; *Three Sunsets and Other Poems,* 1898; *Collected Verse,* 1929; *For the Train,* 1932; *The Poems,* 1973.

* * *

Little that is not general knowledge can be said about the Rev. Charles Lutwidge Dodgson whose books for children were published over the pseudonym of Lewis Carroll. After the Bible and Shakespeare, he is probably the most quoted author in the English language, and nearly every character from *Alice's Adventures in Wonderland, Through the Looking-Glass,* and *What Alice Found*

There is known and recognized almost universally. At the time of his death Andrew Lang wrote that Carroll was, "With the possible exception of Thackeray and Hans Andersen, the most successful writer of stories for children that the world has ever seen. *Alice's Adventures* and *Through the Looking-Glass* are books of which a child with an active mind never tires. They are equally full of imagination and humour. They suggest so much more than they say, that those who have grown up with them have found more in them every year."

The appearance and popularity of *Alice* (we may consider it as a single unity of two volumes, like *Sylvie and Bruno* towards the end of his life) brought about the greatest revolution so far in the literature of childhood. Apart from a few volumes of fairytales—Perrault, Grimm, Andersen, in various forms—and *The Rose and the Ring,* which appeared 10 years before *Wonderland*—the books a child might read (other than adult works like the Waverly novels) were still of an improving or moralistic kind, however well writers like Charlotte Yonge or Mrs. Craik might manage to transcend their limitations. But, in spite of Thackeray and Ruskin, whose inspiration overcame the moral and indeed turned it to their own use, *Alice* was something completely new. It was, as Harvey Darton wrote in 1932, "the coming to the surface, powerfully and permanently, the first unapologetic, undocumented appearance in print, for readers who sorely needed it, of liberty of thought in children's books. Henceforth fear had gone, and with it shy disquiet. There was to be in hours of pleasure no more dread about the moral value, the ponderable, measured qualtiy and extent, of pleasure itself. It was to be enjoyed and even promoted with neither forethought nor remorse."

It is possible to a certain extent to understand how the circumstances of his life and character made Dodgson the author of *Alice.* He grew up as an elder brother in a large family with girls predominating, and living in parsonages remote and self-contained. From an early age he was accustomed to the society of children younger than himself, and to entertaining them in various ways, the writing (and probably telling) of stories and verses being one of the chief ways in which he did this. While still an undergraduate at Christ Church, Oxford, he was telling stories to children whom he met during "reading holidays" and writing nonsense letters to his youngest sister and brother, who were still children. The fact that instead of growing out of these pastimes with children he pursued them more and more eagerly was due in a considerable extent to the fact that he suffered all his life from a stammer—which left him in the company of children, and of little girls in particular. Consequently he spent more and more time with his child-friends and achieved an understanding of them and their outlook which has probably never been equalled by any other author.

Chance—and a particularly good story out of many—caused him to write out *Alice's Adventures Underground* for Alice Liddell and another chance caused the movelist Henry Kingsley to pick up and read Alice's manuscript copy, and urge Mrs. Liddell and to persuade the author to publish it. Chance again made Dodgson, doubtful of the story's appeal to the children other than those for whom it was written, lend his own copy to George MacDonald, himself an outstanding writer for the young, to be read to his children—whose response was so enthusiastic that Dodgson at once began revising the story and adding other incidents from his retentive memory—from which rich source came also most of the incidents in *Through the Looking-Glass* a few years later.

All this might have produced only some glorified variant in *The Rose and the Ring* genre, had not Dodgson been a professional mathematician and logician—and already an accomplished manipulator of the English language. The exact logician making use lightheartedly of the illogicalities of daily speech—and occasionally making "portmanteau" words by weaving together two other words in an exactly balanced synthesis—was able to follow where fancy led, but always in strict obedience to the discipline which he seems to have evolved spontaneously. In fact Lewis Carroll, the adult writer who was able to look at life through a child's eyes, and C.L. Dodgson, the academic lecturer on mathematics and logic, formed the perfect union from which *Alice* could be born. They were still in harmony when *The Hunting of the Snark*—the only real nonsense-epic in existence—came into being; but the marriage of two minds was falling apart when *Sylvie and Bruno* was being forced into existence: the don was imposing his will consciously upon the dreamer—and the result was what Derek Hudson has so aptly called "the most interesting failure in English literature."

Though not itself numimous, *Alice* once and for all flung wide the "magic casement opening on the foam of perilous seas in faery lands forlorn": she was the ancestor of all the great children's books that were to follow her, however different in kind they may seem—of *The Midnight Folk* and *The Lion, the Witch and the Wardrobe* as well as more obvious descendants such as *The Just So Stories* and *Winnie-the-Pooh.* But unlike most progenitors, *Alice* is in no danger of growing old or being forgotten: she is as fresh and vivid today as she was a hundred years ago, and an everlasting delight to readers of all ages.

—Roger Lancelyn Green

COOLIDGE, Susan

Pseudonym for Sarah Chauncy Woolsey. **Nationality:** American. **Born:** Cleveland, Ohio, 29 January 1835. **Education:** Attended private schools in Cleveland; Mrs. Hubbard's Select Family School for Young Ladies, Hanover, New Hampshire. **Career:** Did hospital work and helped organize nursing service during the Civil War. Consulting reader for Roberts Brothers, publishers, Boston. **Died:** 9 April 1905. **Fiction:** *The New Year's Bargain,* 1872; *What Katy Did* series, from 1872; *Little Miss Mischief and Other Stories,* 1874; *Mischief's Thanksgiving and Other Stories,* 1874; *Nine Little Goslings,* 1875; *For Summer Afternoons,* 1876; *Eyebright,* 1879; *A Guersney Lily,* 1881; *A Round Dozen,* 1883; *A Little Country Girl,* 1885; *Clover,* 1888; *Just Sixteen,* 1889; *In the High Valley,* 1891; *The Barberry Bush and Eight Other Stories,* 1892; *Not Quite Eighteen,* 1894; *An Old Convent School in Paris and Other Papers,* 1895; *Curly Locks,* 1899; *A Little Knight of Labor,* 1899; *Little Tommy Tucker,* 1900; *Two Girls,* 1900; *Uncle and Aunt,* 1900; *The Rule of Three,* 1904; *A Sheaf of Stories,* 1906. **Verse:** *Rhymes and Ballads,* 1892.

* * *

Susan Coolidge gained her reputation from the *Katy* books, although she had some contemporary success as a critic. At first reading *What Katy Did* appears to be in the mainstream of Victorian children's fiction—the motherless family "mothered" by the heroine, the general religious ambiance and the moral retribution for wrong-doing—but a closer inspection reveals that Coolidge was in fact the forerunner of the 20th-century genre of British girl's school stories, her literary influence being greater in the United Kingdom than in her native United States. Figuratively speaking, she may be placed midway between the piety of L.T. Meade's *A World of Girls* with its sanctomonious principal dispensing sweetness and light to the pupils of Lavender House, and the feuds and frolics in the works of Angela Barzil.

Very probably Coolidge took her inspiration from Louisa May Alcott. Certainly Katy embodies some of the foibles of the outspoken Jo March. Like Jo, Katy endeared herself to her readers by her very human faults and spontaneous behaviour; like Jo, she was immediately popular, with her followers demanding a sequel; like Jo's, her popularity was not confined to her compatriots, and English girls readily identified with her. Coolidge received (in *The Independent*) the curious and confusing accolade that she was on her way to becoming a second "Aunt Jo." That Jo was a recognizable self-portrait of Louisa Alcott has to account for the mixed reference to the real and the fictional ladies.

Coolidge seems to have "written out" her Victorianism in *What Katy Did*. Her own upbringing and the expectations of teachers, ministers, and parents demanded a stereotyped "good angel" figure, and it is significant that the author did not select her heroine for the role but a somewhat peripheral character, crippled Cousin Helen. Katy had disobeyed authority and used the garden swing. In the Victorian tradition she had to be "punished" and became bedridden from the consequent fall. Instead of saintly suffering, Katy demonstrated untidiness, irritable temper, and general misery. It was left to the visiting cousin to fulfil the moral function.

"God is going to let you go to his school," Cousin Helen explained to Katy when she complained.

> "But what is the school?" asked Katy. "It is called The School of Pain," replied Cousin Helen, with her sweetest smile. "There's the lesson of Patience. That's one of the hardest studies...and there's the lesson of Cheerfulness. And the lesson of Making the Best of Things...."

Cousin Helen helped Katy to see her condition in a new light, and thus motivated the plot, but her formal utterances give a note of unreality to an otherwise natural and lively account. This must have occurred to Coolidge, for Cousin Helen made no other real contribution, and by the end of the sequel volume, *What Katy Did at School,* she does not even appear, merely sending two illuminated religious texts for Katy and her sister Clover on their homecoming: "The girls thought they had never seen anything so pretty." So much for Cousin Helen, the symbol of perfect behaviour, the model for the aspiring Victorian child.

What Katy Did at School is the most significant book in the series (*What Katy Did Next, Clover,* and *In the High Valley* followed) since it predates the entire output of girl's school stories which virtually dominated the reading of British middle-class girls until the 1940s. Adult books (such as *Jane Eyre*) might cast aspersions on the teaching profession, but for the youthful reader authority was irreproachable. There is a chasm between the approach of L.T. Meade to the pious principal Mrs. Willis and Coolidge's ironic appraisal of Mrs. Florence, who lost interest in her pupils once she had decided to leave the school, and made no real effort to mete out justice. Coolidge's own experiences at Mrs. Hubbard's Boarding School in Hanover, New Hampshire, had given her insight into both staff-room and dormitory and the economic strategy behind the school meals. Rebellion among the pupils at "The Nunnery," the nickname given to Hillsover by Katy's companions, was seen from the point of view of the girls, and the character of Rose Red (real name Rosamund Redding) reappeared in various guises in almost every 20th-century school story from Angela Brazil's American Gipsey Latimer in *The Leader of the Lower School* to Enid Blyton's heroine of *The Naughtiest Girl in the School*. Always defiant, ultimately likable, struggling against the system which may or may not be just, these girls form a continuous thread throughout girl's fiction, together with a casual use of slang which gives a sparkling spontaneity to the dialogue. Coolidge's schoolgirls were as iconoclastic over "correct" speech as they were over behaviour. With Katy as president of the *Society for the Suppression of Unladylike Conduct,* a title bestowed with conscious mockery, established precepts were overthrown. One of the main aims was to have a good time combined with the pursuit of virtue. Victorian writers for children would have considered that a contradiction in terms.

—Gillian Freeman

COX, Palmer

Nationality: Canadian. **Born:** Granby, Quebec, 28 April 1840. **Education:** Attended Granby Academy. **Career:** Railroad worker and ship carpenter in San Francisco, 1863-75; writer in New York from 1875. **Died:** 24 July 1924. **Play:** *The Brownies in Fairyland,* music and lyrics by Malcolm Douglas, 1925. **Verse:** *Brownies* series, 13 vols., from 1887.

* * *

Palmer Cox found success with his short stories in verse about the Brownies, whose first adventure, "The Brownies' Ride," appeared in *St. Nicholas Magazine* in 1883. This story, in which the Brownies borrow a farmer's horse and cart for a night-long ride, is reprinted in the collection of 24 episodes that form the first Brownie book (1887).

"The Brownies' Ride" is a good example of Cox's rhyming couplets illustrated with his own line drawings. While Cox derived his notion of brownies from a Scots background, he was not a folklorist, and his whimsical creation is an artistic invention.

Early pictures show Brownies, some with antennae or wings, in vaguely defined clothes and the occasional funny hat. Cox soon evolved his Brownies into spindle-legged rotund imps with wide eyes in their round amusing faces. Individual Brownies could be identified by costume as a monacled man-about-town, a policeman, a Dutchman or Chinaman, etc. Children could gleefully search for their particular Brownie.

The rhymes also provide evidence that Cox built his own group characterization of Brownies. A preface normally explains that they are "like fairies and goblins...imaginary little sprites who...delight in harmless pranks and helpful deeds. They work and sport while weary households sleep, and never allow themselves to be seen by mortal eyes."

Keightley's *Fairy Mythology* (1880) records brownies as "of small stature, wrinkled visage, covered with short brown hair and wearing a brown mantle and hood." Often attached to families, they could be repaid for work by small gifts, preferably food. K.M. Brigg's *A Dictionary of Fairies* (1976) adds more information and confirms the reticent and easily offended nature of brownies. At their most mischievous and wicked, brownies become boggarts who act like poltergeists. Cox's Brownies always retain their better nature; the Brownies' mischief is that of curious boys who investigate closed places or try some adult activity.

Each Brownie episode , if similar, is not the same. Cox is credited with purposely excluding crime and pain, and children are not made anxious about these confident little fellows. Moreover, children are often given a model for behaviour since Brownies do good deeds without thought of reward. For many reasons, it is not surprising that a *Palmer Cox Brownie Primer* appeared in 1906.

The Brownies were deservedly and tremendously popular for 40 and more years around the turn of the century. Cox can be judged a better cartoonist than versifier for neither his poems nor his stories were remarkable or memorable without his lively sketches. To read Cox generations later and to see his merry rogues scamper across the page is to experience some sentiment for a sweet, vanished, perhaps illusory, childhood past.

—Claire England

DODGE, Mary Mapes

Nationality: American. **Born:** New York City, 26 January 1831. **Education:** Educated privately. **Family:** Married William Dodge in 1851 (died 1858); two sons. **Career:** Helped her father edit the *Working Farmer* magazine, 1847; homemaking editor, *Hearth and Home* magazine, New York, 1870-73; founding editor, *St. Nicholas* magazine, New York, 1873-1905. **Awards:** French Academy Montyon prize. **Died:** 21 August 1905. **Fiction:** *The Irvington Stories,* 1865; *Hans Brinker*; or, *The Silver Skates,* 1865; *Donald and Dorothy,* 1883; *The Land of Pluck,* 1894; *The Golden Gate,* 1903; *Po-no-kah,* 1903. **Verse:** *When Life Is Young,* 1894; *Mary Anne,* 1983.

* * *

With the publication of *The Irvington Stories,* Mary Mapes Dodge was widely recognized in the United States as a promising new writer of literature for children. Reviewers and readers praised the eight tales, which derived from American colonial history and from stories told in the author's family, for their blend of realistic detail, engaging humor, and appropriate moral tone. Encouraged by the book's success, Dodge's publisher, James O'Kane, urged her to begin a second work and, with the Civil War approaching an end, suggested a timely theme—a boy leaving his family to enlist in the Union Army. Unenthusiastic about the idea, Dodge turned instead to notes she had retained from her reading of Motley's *Story of the Dutch Republic* years before as well as to stories she had heard from Dutch immigrant neighbors and began work on a story set in Holland.

Reluctantly, O'Kane agreed to publish the completed manuscript, *Hans Brinker.* An outstanding commercial success from the start, *Hans Brinker* quickly established itself as a classic children's book. As in *The Irvington Stories* there is an abundance of closely observed detail, abstracted from her sources (Dodge did not visit Holland until years after the book was written) and combined with a clear moral purpose. Not notably inventive or original, Dodge drew heavily on familiar popular conventions for the structure of the story. Hans Brinker and his sister Gretel are the impoverished but virtuous children of a dike engineer, a mute, uncomprehending invalid since he was injured 10 years before the events of the story take place. This premise, the incapacitation of a family's father and breadwinner and the subsequent suffering, however salutary, of his dependents, was one of the stock conventions of late 19th-century children's literature. For good measure, the plot involves a missing sum of money, a mysterious watch, and a father estranged from his son, as well as the ice skating race that gives the book its title—all familiar devices to create suspense in what is essentially a static book—a series of set pieces, detailing the characteristic and distinctive scenes, social types, customs, dress, and culture of Holland: the festival of St. Nicholas, the windmills and canals, the cities of Haarlem, Leyden, and the Hague.

The central chapters of *Hans Brinker*—and much the longest narrative sequence—detail a skating expedition undertaken by five of Hans's friends, boys from wealthier families who can afford the diversion. As a consequence, Hans and sister disappear from the story entirely. In order to get the necessary Anglo-American perspective on Dutch culture, Dodge makes one of the five boys an English visitor, and it is through his eyes that the reader sees the charming peculiarities of the Dutch. Enlivened somewhat by differences in temperament among the boys and by an occasional adventure—they capture a robber at one point—the expedition provides Dodge with the means and justification for a close, sympathetic, sometimes condescending description of Dutch life.

In the final third of the book, the focus returns to the Brinker family. The father is restored to health by the leading surgeon in Holland, whom Hans had chanced to meet early in the story. With his reason restored, Hans's father recalls hiding the family savings as well as the circumstances surrounding his possession of the mysterious watch. The young man from whom he received it turns out to be the estranged son of the eminent surgeon. The Brinker family, tested by 10 years of poverty, is restored to comfortable affluence, and the surgeon is reconciled with his son—and to his son's legitimate desire to have a vocation different from his father's. A conventional final chapter describes the fate of the several children introduced in this story, apportioning happiness and success to the virtuous, especially Hans and Gretel whose fortitude, perseverance, faith, and selfless devotion through years of poverty and care exemplify character at its best.

In its affectionate and detailed description of foreign peoples and places, *Hans Brinker* was a distinct improvement over the earlier travelogues of "Peter Parley" and a harbinger of greater attention to realistic detail in American fiction for children in the late 19th century. Its moral values, however, are quite representative of much children's literature written from the 1830s to the end of the century and beyond. Although Dodge was the pre-eminent children's periodical editor of her generation, she cannot be said to have made a very notable contribution to children's literature, *Hans Brinker* excepted. *The Irvington Stories* are deservedly forgotten, except by a few specialists, and *The Land of Pluck,* while testifying to her affection for Holland, represents no improvement on the similar sketches in *Hans Brinker,* many of her stories are simply cautionary tales of a kind indistinguishable in style or sentiment from the mass of homiletic narrative to be found in many a late 19th-century children's periodical—even the justly praised *St. Nicholas*.

—R. Gordon Kelly

EVERETT-GREEN, Evelyn

Pseudonyms: Also wrote as Cecil Adair; Evelyn Dare; H.F.E. British. **Born:** London, 17 November 1856. **Education:** Attended Gower Street Preparatory School; Bedford College, University of London (Reid scholar, 1872-73); Royal Academy, London. Worked as a nurse in a London hospital. **Died:** 27 April 1932. **Fiction:** *Tom Tempest's Victory* (as H.F.E.), 1880; *Carry's Christmas Gift* (as H.F.E.), 1881; *Fast Friends* (as H.F.E.), 1882; *Little Freddie* (as H.F.E.), 1882; *His Mother's Book* (as H.F.E.), 1883; *Fighting the Good Fight* (as H.F.E.), 1883; *Her Husband's Home,* 1885; *Mr. Hatherley's Boys,* 1885; *Uncle Roger,* 1885; *True to Himself (True to the Last),* 1885; *The Head of the House,* 1886; *Dulcie series,* from 1887; *Our Winnie,* 1887; *The Last of the Dacres,* 1887; *A Child Without a Name (Drifted Ashore),* 1887; *Barbara's Brothers,* 1887; *All or Nothing,* 1888; *Little Lady Clare,* 1888; *Dodo,* 1888; *The Little Midshipman and Other Stories,* 1889; *My Boynie,* 1889; *Miriam's Ambition,* 1889; *Monica,* 1889; *My Black Sheep,* 1889; *The Percevals,* 1890; *Little Ruth's Lady,* 1890; *Bertie Clifton,* 1890; *Birdie's Resolve and How It Was Accomplished,* 1890; *Clive's Conquest,* 1890; *Daring Dot,* 1890; *Marcus Stratford's Charge,* 1890; *Mischievous Moncton,* 1890; *Oliver Langton's Ward,* 1890; *The Stronger Will,* 1890; *A Summer Holiday,* 1890; *Dorothy's Vocation,* 1890; *The Secret of the Old House,* 1890; *Sir Aylmer's Heir,* 1890; *Syd's New Pony,* 1890; *The Witch of the Quarry Hut,* 1890; *Fir-Tree Farm,* 1891; Loyal Hearts, 1891; *Miss Meyrick's Niece,* 1891; *Mrs. Romaine's Household,* 1891; *Shadow-Land,* 1891; *Syney's Secret,* 1891; *Let's Toss for It,* 1891; *Fresh from the Fens,* 1891; *Dare Lorimer's Heritage,* 1891; *Duckworth's Diamonds,* n.d.; *Dick Whistler's Tramp,* 1891; *A Pair of Originals* (as Evelyn Dare), 1892; *Don Carlos,* 1892; *In the Wars of the Roses,* 1892; *The Church and the King,* 1892; *The Doctor's Dozen,* 1892; *Falconer of Falconhurst,* 1892; *A Holiday in a Manor House,* 1892; *In the Days of Chivalry,* 1892; *The Lord of Dynevor,* 1892; *Old Miss Audrey,* 1892; *A Pair of Pickles,* 1892; *Everybody's Friend,* 1893; *St. Dunstan's Clock* (as Evelyn Dare), 1893; *Evil May Day,* 1893; *Friends or Foes?,* 1893; *The Great Show,* 1893; *Little Miss Vixen,* 1893; *St. Wynfrith and Its Inmates,* 1893; *Tom Heron of Sax,* 1893; *The Wilful Willoughbys,* 1893; *Golden Gwendolyn,* 1893; *The Lost Treasure of Trevlyn,* 1893; *Maud Melville's Marriage,* 1893; *Namesakes,* 1893; *Over the Sea Wall,* 1893; *Ronald Kennedy,* 1893; *Afterthought House,* 1894; *Eustace Marchmont,* 1894; *The Family,* 1894; *Flats,* 1894; *Keith's Trial and Victory,* 1894; *Miss Uraca,* 1894; *The Secret Chamber at Chad,* 1894; *A Difficult Daughter,* 1894; *Pat the Lighthouse Boy,* 1894; *Two Bright Shillings,* 1894; *Shut In,* 1894; *Arnold Inglehurst the Preacher,* 1895; *Judith,* 1895; *Ralph Roxburgh's Revenge* (Ralph Roxburgh's Triumph), 1895; *A Soldier's Son and the Battle He Fought,* 1895; *A Stepmother's Strategy,* 1895; *The Sunny Side of the Street,* 1895; *His Choice—and Hers,* 1895; *Duff Darlington,* 1895; *Dominique's Vengeance,* 1896; *Squib and His Friends,* 1896; *Enid's Ugly Duckling,* with H. Louisa Bedford, 1896; *In Taunton Town,* 1896; *Olive Roscoe,* 1896; *The Sign of the Red Cross,* 1897; *The Young Pioneers,* 1897; *A Clerk of Oxford,* 1897; *Molly Melville,* 1897; *Battledown Boys,* 1898; *Esther's Charge,* 1898; *Gladys or Gwenyth,* 1898; *Sister,* 1898; *Tom Tufton's Toll* [and *Travels*], 2 vols., 1898; *For the Queen's Sake,* 1898; *Little Lois,* 1898; *Joy's Jubilee,* 1898; *French and English,* 1899; *Miss Marjorie of Silvermead,* 1899; *Sir Reginald's Ward,* 1899; *The Probation of Mervyn Castleton,* 1899; *Cross Purposes,* 1899; *The Heir of Hascombe Hall,* 1899; *The Mystery of Alton Grange,* 1899; *Priscilla,* with H. Louisa Bedford, 1899; *Bruno and Bimba,* 1900; *Eleanor's Hero,* 1900; *The Little Match-Girl,* 1900; *A Fiery Chariot,* 1900; *In Cloister and Court,* 1900; *The King's Butterfly,* 1900; *The Master of Fernhurst,* 1900; *Odeyne's Marriage,* 1900; *The Silver Axe,* 1900; *The Wooing of Val,* 1900; *Paul Harvard's Campaign,* 1901; *A Gordon Highlander,* 1901; *Princess Fairstar,* 1901; *The Secret of Maxshelling,* 1901; *Tregg's Triumph,* 1901; *Holidays at the Farm,* with others, 1901; *Bob and Bill,* 1901; *After Worcester,* 1901; *True Stories of Girl Heroines,* 1901; *Alwyn Ravendale,* 1902; *The Boys of the Red House,* 1902; *Gabriel Garth, Chartist,* 1902; *In Fair Granada,* 1902; *A Princess's Token,* 1902; *White Wyvill and Red Ruthven,* 1902; *For the Faith,* 1902; *Short Tales from Storyland,* 1902; *Fallen Fortunes,* 1902; *My Lady Joanna,* 1902; *Tiny and Her Grandfather,* 1902; *To the Rescue,* 1902; *Audrey Marsh,* 1903; *Cambria's Chieftan,* 1903; *The Castle of the White Flag,* 1903; *The Conscience of Roger Trehern (Roger Trehern),* 1903; *The Squire's Heir,* 1903; *Under Two Queens,* 1903; *A Hero of the Highlands,* 1903; *The Children's Crusade,* 1904; *The Faith of Hilary Lovel,* 1904; *The Jilting of Bruce Heriot,* 1904; *Ringed by Fire,* 1904; *The Three Graces,* 1904; *The Sisters of Silver Sands,* 1904; *Little Lady Val,* 1904; *Miss Greyshott's Girls,* 1905; *Uncle Boo,* 1905; *In Northern Seas,* 1905; *Jim Trelawny,* 1905; *Madam of Clyst Peveril,* 1905; *Smouldering Fires,* 1905; *Treasure Trove,* 1905; *The Defence of the Rock,* 1906; *In a Land of Beasts,* 1906; *The Master of Marshlands,* 1906; *Perry Vere,* 1906; *Dickie and Dorrie* series, from 1906; *A Motherless Maid,* 1906; *Our Great Undertaking,* 1906; *Clanrickard Court,* 1907; *Miss Lorimer of Chard,* 1907; *Carol Carew* (*The Imprudence of Carol Carew*), 1907; *Knights of the Road,* 1907; *Ruth Ravelstan the Puritan's Daughter,* 1907; *Gowries's Vengeance,* 1908; *Hilary Quest,* 1908; *The Cossart Cousins,* 1908; *Greyfriars,* 1908; *The Family Next Door,* 1908; *Stepsister Stella,* 1908; *Half-a-Dozen Sisters,* 1909; *A Wilful Maid,* 1909; *The City of the Golden Gate,* 1909; *A Lad of London Town,* 1909; *In Grandfather's Garden,* 1910; *Ursula Tempest,* 1910; *The Dean's Daughter* (as Cecil Adair), 1910; *General John,* 1910; *Patricia Pendragon* (as Evelyn Dare), 1911; *Cantacute Towers* (as Cecil Adair), 1911; *A Disputed Heritage,* 1911; *Aunt Patience,* 1912; *Miss Mallory of Mote,* 1912; *Tommy and the Owl,* 1912; *The Yellow Pup,* 1912; *Francesca* (as Cecil Adair), 1912; *Inchfallen,* 1913; *Dora's Doll's House,* 1914; *The House on the Cliff,* 1914; *The Heronstoke Mystery,* 1915; *Adventurous Anne,* 1916; *Sweepie,* 1918; *Daddy's Duckings,* 1921; *Crystal's Victory* (as Cecil Adair), 1921; *Queen's Manor School,* 1921; *The Tyrant of Tylecourt,* 1922; *Twins at Tachbury,* 1924; *The Squire's Daughters,* 1932.

* * *

Evelyn Everett-Green provided for some 50 years popular books for the young, and the style of her writing is representative of the trends of juvenile publishing of the late 19th and early 20th centuries. Her output (an average of six or seven volumes, rising to 11 in peak years), though large by present-day standards, was not considered unduly excessive then (her older contemporary, L.T. Meade, wrote even more). She ranged over most genres of fiction : historical novels, school stories, street arab tales, family adventures, romantic but safe tales for the girl on the brink of leaving the schoolroom ("Yet young maidens will have their dreams, and a maiden's dream requires a man to make it interesting"); she even attempted a story in 1910 for the newly emerging Boy Scout Movement.

Like most lady writers of her type, she extolled the virtues of the thoroughbred gentleman—whose children did not need to be taught the meaning of honour—and denounced the parvenu and nouveau riche—who could not learn it. Like them, too, her favorite scene was the grey-walled mansion with its tumble of roses and terraces descending to rolling parkland, and her favorite child characters the rosy-cheeked maiden with eyes of speedwell blue, the merry rogue, the scamp, the innocent pickle who leaves a trail of devastation but has a warm and loving heart. Occasionally, as in *My Boynie,* she succeeds in creating credible children, Though the plot of this is a familiar one of the period and turns on the gradual decline and ultimate death of a little boy from spinal injury—in this case through being led into mischief by a tomboy elder sister—the character of the latter is sympathetically observed, and the knowledgeable enthusiasm for gardens and for flowers is reminiscent of Mrs. Ewing's *Mary's Meadow* (which indeed the author may have had in mind). She did not, however, usually allow herself time to produce books of this quality, but was content to supply giftbooks for all occasions. These were in general well-received by reviewers who praised their "excellent tone," and described them as "wholesome fiction" and "simple, attractive, healthy stories."

—Gillian Avery

EWING, Juliana Horatia

Nationality: British. **Born:** Ecclesfield, Yorkshire, 3 August 1841; daughter of the children's writer Margaret Gatty. **Family:** Married Alexander Ewing in 1867. **Career:** Associated with her mother and sister in editing *Aunt Judy's* Magazine, London, 1866-85. **Died:** 13 May 1885. **Fiction:** *Melchior's Dream and Other Tales,* 1862; *Mrs. Overtheway's Remembrances,* 1869; *The Brownies and Other Tales,* 1870; *A Flat Iron for a Farthing,* 1872; *Lob Lie-by-the Fire,* 1874; *Six to Sixteen* 1875; *Jan of the Windmill,* 1876; *A Great Emergency and Other Tales,* 1877; *We and the World,* 1880; *Old Fashioned Fairy Tales,* 1882; *Brothers of Pity and Other Tales of Beasts and Men,* 1882; *The Story of a Short Life,* 1882; *Jackanapes,* 1883; *Daddy Darwin's Dovecot,* 1884; *Grandmother's Spring,* 1885; *Mary's Meadow and Letters from a Little Garden,* 1886; *Dandelion Clocks and Other Tales,* 1887; *The Peace Egg, and A Christmas Mumming Play,* 1887; *Snapdragon, and Old Father Christmas,* 1888; *Last Words,* 1891. **Verse:** *Blue and Red,* 1883; *A Soldier's Children,* 1883; *The Blue Bells on the Lea,* 1884; *Mother's Birthday Reviews,* 1888.

* * *

Juliana Horatia Ewing succeeded, better than any other Victorian writer for the young, in conveying the high spirits of childhood, and remembering its laughter and sheer enjoyment of life. She did not fall into the trap of presenting children's happiness as undiluted. She herself pointed out that "it is probably from an imperfect remembrance of their nursery lives that some people believe that the griefs of one's childhood are light, its joys uncomplicated, and its tastes simple." But she recorded light and shadow, rough and smooth, without moral reflections on their implication to the child that experienced them. It was a style very different from her mother, Mrs. Gatty, who, in the manner of her generation, had felt obliged to improve the occasion whenever she could. The early Victorian writers for the young could never forget their role as governess. Ewing, though no conscious innovator, did forget. She used much of the same material as her mother—large, happy families; she was fundamentally just as serious-minded, but she was fortunate in being born into a generation that saw no harm in *enjoying* writing for children.

No one could ever doubt the seriousness of her religious faith, but, perhaps because it was so strong, it was rarely directly stated, though one senses its influence in all she wrote. She could allow herself the occasional frivolous comment, poking gentle fun at the child who had morbid notions about sickbed piety; she could even be flippant about that sacred cow of the Victorians, Sabbath observance. She criticized the way that parents and teachers treated children; once she even so far forgot herself as to introduce an elopement into the beginning of a story. (Charlotte Yonge advised those reading *Jackanapes* aloud to omit this incident.) She sympathized with the boisterous rough ways of boys, even defended them, and, in *We and the World,* could take their side against their father—a unique occasion in Victorian children's literature. She was equally convincing when she presented a very different type of boy in *A Flat Iron for a Farthing,* a motherless only child, quaint but never muffish, who takes himself rather too seriously (though the author never does).

Perhaps she was at her best when writing of the Yorkshire scenes from which it was such anguish for her to be parted (none of the Gatty children ever wanted to live anywhere else in the world but the vicarage at Ecclesfield where they had been brought up) and of the exuberant life that young Victorians lived when families were large enough to mount private theatricals, to run their own journals and societies; when houses had space to accommodate a mass of different hobbies, and everybody could have his separate plot in the garden and a pet of his own.

Her forgetfulness of her readers sometimes transformed books for a specific class—such as Victorian publishers then produced—into books beyond their reach. *Lob Lie-by-the-Fire* and *Daddy Darwin's Dovecot,* which set out to be the sort of book about the poor boy who became a steady, decent artisan (a type produced by the ton by Anglican wives and daughters for the consumption of children in church schools), finished as exquisitely worked miniatures of Victorian social life.

Some of her longer works tend to sprawl and suffer from a plethora of sub-plot and too many ideas (the result of their being originally written in serial form for her mother's magazine, *Aunt Judy's*) but all of them are beautifully and fastidiously written. She was possibly the most literary of all the Victorian writers of the juvenile domestic tale, and the only one whose works were gathered into a complete edition. Many writers have testified to their affection for her, Kipling and Arthur Ransome among them; authors as various as Frances Hodgson Burnett and Angela Brazil have lifted (perhaps unconsciously) whole episodes from her books; *A Great Emergency* is the precursor of E. Nesbit's Bastable stories.

If one had to remember her by a single work then one might choose the short story "Our Field," so much admired by Ruskin. The plot turns on the efforts of a family of children to save enough for a dog license, but though their anxiety about this is the shadow, during the day the children forget it because they have found a field where nobody goes, where they can play undisturbed. The field has everything, a stream with freshwater shrimps, a hollow oak, bluebells, cowslips, blackberries. The fact that there are holly berries on the bushes and daisies in the grass at the same season does not matter; Mrs. Ewing is describing an earthly paradise that only a child could know.

— Gillian Avery

FARRAR, F(rederic) W(illiam)

Nationality: British. **Born:** Bombay, India, 7 August 1831. **Education:** Latin School, Aylesbury, Buckinghamshire; King William's College, Isle of Man; London University, B.A. 1852; Trinity College, Cambridge, B.A. 1854, M.A. 1857, D.D. 1874. **Family:** Married Lucy Cardew in 1860; five sons and five daughters. **Career:** Master, Marlborough College, 1854-55, and Harrow, 1855-70; headmaster, Marlborough College, 1871-76. Deacon, 1854; ordained priest, 1857; chaplain to Queen Victoria, 1869; Canon, 1875, and Archdeacon, 1883, Westminster; Dean of Canterbury, 1895. **Died:** 22 March 1903. **Fiction:** *Eric; or, Little by Little,* 1858; *Julian Home,* 1859; *St. Winifred's,* 1862; *Darkness and Dawn,* 1891; *Gathering Clouds,* 1895; *Allegories,* 1895; *The Three Homes,* 1896.

* * *

F.W. Farrar wrote several kinds of books for the young, but his seriousness of intention is recognisable in all of them. An historical tale like *Darkness and Dawn* was devised to illustrate the "supreme and deeply interesting problem" of the source of the strength of Christianity, by employing a fiction which "even for the minutest allusions" has "contemporary authority." His allegorical tales are learned, Biblical as well as moral; even the popular romance *The Three Homes,* published anonymously to detach it from his more serious studies, is a fable of the soul's formation. When he wrote stories about school boys, with whom he was professionally concerned, his passionate earnestness transformed his stories into dramas of emotional and spiritual struggle.

Of these, *Eric; or, Little by Little* is still known, at least by repute, but *St. Winifred's* and *Julian Home* are scarcely less extraordinary productions. *Eric* is a very dark tale. Eric is a perfectly brought-up and noble-natured boy until he is sent away to school, and yet is ruined morally and physically by his failure to resist the temptations he meets there. His own turpitude, reinforced by the deaths of his beloved little brother and his mother, brings him to an early grave. The plot is a combination of the trivial incidents really making up school life, and lurid misadventures, culminating in Eric's running away to sea and being starved and flogged into a state that leads to his death. The most remarkable aspect of the book is not the religiose melodrama that made it a favourite Sunday School prize, but its concentration upon the emotional and sexual lives of schoolboys. It was for the open avowal and display of feeling, the fervent prayer and the exchange of embraces and kisses between friends, that it was hated by Kipling's Stalky and Co. and other such believers in the stiff upper lip. The whole movement of late Victorian social behaviour, crushing men and boys into ever greater restraint and rejecting any sort of expression of feeling as unmanly, was against Farrar, and his readership was chiefly female or working-class Christians—groups to whom emotion did not appear embarrassing, and the struggle of good and evil within personal relationships was not a taboo subject. Farrar writes about the primitive life of the schools he knew, and grows hysterical and grandiloquent in the attempt to discriminate between the good he perceives in passionate friendship, and the corruption of casual and often enforced sex, without being able to mention any of these things explicitly. The laughter that he raised was partly a just response to the flamboyance and confusion of his style, partly the inevitable consequence of changing taste, but also partly a nervous reaction of shocked self-defence from readers who were not prepared to countenance his insistence that the educator's moral obligation to his pupils extended to their emotional and sexual lives, and that these required guidance rather than denial, concealment, and repression.

—J.S. Bratton

FENN, George Manville

Nationality: British. **Born:** Pimlico, London, 3 January 1831. **Education:** Battersea Training College for Teachers, 1851-54. **Family:** Married Susanna Leake in 1855; two sons and six daughters. **Career:** Schoolmaster in Lincolnshire, then a printer: produced his own magazine, *Modern Metre,* 1862; part-owner of *Herfordshire and Essex Observer,* Bishop's Stortford, 1864; then a writer: editor, *Cassell's Magazine,* London, 1870; publisher, *Once a Week,* London, 1873-79; drama critic, the *Echo,* and theatre producer, 1887-88. **Died:** 26 August 1909. **Fiction:** *Hollowdell Grange,* 1866; *Off to the Wilds,* 1881; *The Golden Magnet,* 1883; *Dutch the Diver,* 1883; *Middy and Ensign,* 1883; *The Silver Cañon,* 1884; *Menhardoc (The Boys of Menhardoc),* 1884; *Bunyip Land,* 1884; *Brownsmith's Boy,* 1885; *The Dark House,* 1885; *Patience Wins,* 1885; *A Terrible Coward, and Son Philip,* 1885; *Yussuf the Guide,* 1886; *Devon Boys,* 1886; *The Chaplain's Craze,* 1886; *The Bag of Diamonds,* 1887; *Dick o' the Fens,* 1887; *Mother Carey's Chicken,* 1887; *The Story of Antony Grace,* 1888; *Quicksilver,* 1888; *Commodore Junk,* 1888; *In Jeopardy,* 1889; *Three Boys,* 1889; *Burr Junior,* 1891; *The Raja of Dah,* 1891; *Syd Belton, the Boy Who Would Not Go to Sea,* 1891; *To the West,* 1891; *The Weathercock,* 1892; *The Crystal Hunters,* 1892; *Gil the Gunner,* 1892; *The Grand Chaco (Rob Harlow's Adventure),* 1892; *The Dingo Boys,* 1892; *The Black Bar,* 1893; *Real Gold,* 1893; *Blue Jackets,* 1893; *Steve Young,* 1893; *Sail-Ho!,* 1893; *The Vast Abyss,* 1894; *Mass' George,* 1894; *Fire Island,* 1894; *First in the Field,* 1894; *Cormorant Crag,* 1895; *Painter Jack,* 1895; *The Queen's Scarlet,* 1895; *Roy Royland,* 1895; *In Battle and Breeze,* with G.A. Henty and W. Clark Russell, 1896; *Smith's Weakness,* 1896; *In Honour's Cause,* 1896; *The Black Tor,* 1896; *Sappers and Miners,* 1896; *The Adventures of Don Lavington,* 1896; *Franks and Saxons,* 1897; *The Little Skipper,* 1897; *Vince the Rebel,* 1897; *The Silver Salvors,* 1898; *Nic Revel,* 1898; *Our Soldier Boy,* 1898; *Jungle and Stream,* 1898; *Draw Swords!,* 1898; *Fix Bay'nets!,* 1899; *In the Mahdi's Grasp,* 1899; *King o' the Beach,* 1899; *Nat the Naturalist,* 1899; *Ned Leger,* 1899; *Young Robin Hood,* 1899; *The Bag of Diamonds, and Three Bits of Paste,* 1900; *Charge,* 1900; *King Robert's Page,* 1900; *Old Gold,* 1900; *Uncle Bart,* 1900; *Running Amok,* 1901; *Something Like a Snake,* 1901; *The King's Sons,* 1901; *The Kopje Garrison,* 1901; *Pulabad,* 1901; *A Dash for Diamond City,* 1901; *Ching, the Chinaman and His Middy Friends,* 1901; *Coastguard Jack,* 1902; *The Lost Middy,* 1902; *A Meeting of Creeks, and the Tug of War,* 1902; *The Peril Finders,*

1902; *Stan Lynn,* 1902; *Two Rough Stones, and A Bad Day's Fishing,* 1902; *Walsh the Wonder-Worker,* 1903; *The King's Esquires,* 1903; *Fitz the Filibuster,* 1903; *Glyn Severn's Schooldays,* 1904; *The Khedive's Country,* 1904; *Marcus, the Young Centurion,* 1904; *The Ocean Cat's Paw,* 1904; *The Powder Monkey,* 1904; *To Win or Die,* 1904; *Trapper Dan,* 1905; *Shoulder Arms!,* 1905; *Nephew Jack,* 1905; *Dead Man's Land,* 1906; *Hunting the Skipper,* 1906; *'Tention!,* 1906; *The Traitor's Gate and Other Stories,* 1906; *Trapped by the Malays,* 1907; *Jack, the Rascal,* 1909; *Cutlass and Cudgel,* 1910; *In Mid-Air,* 1924; *In Marine Armour,* 1927; *Staunch as Steel,* 1927.

* * *

George Manville Fenn was a popular author whose eminently readable books were without the customary wordy descriptions or pious philosophy found in many of the earlier tales of adventure. In his first book, *Hollowdell Grange,* he showed his love of the "wonders of animal and vegetable life," while in *The Raja of Dah* he expressed his belief that "there was no grander education for a man than the study of the endless beauties of nature." He further developed this theme in *Nat the Naturalist,* one of his most successful books, which is set in Borneo and New Guinea. Fenn, unlike W.H.G. Kingston, R.M. Ballantyne, and G.A. Henty, did not permit his boy adventurers to kill for the love of sport, but only from necessity or for scientific investigation.

Fenn's ability to effect swift scene changes gives an uninterrupted pace to his stories, and he achieves immediacy through his skilful use of a natural dialogue that is also responsible for the success of many of his minor characters. At times he sacrifices clarity for supposed verisimilitude in an attempt to reproduce the colour and flavour of an unfamiliar idiom, such as the broken English spoken by the Australian Aborigines in *The Dingo Boys* and *Bunyip Land.* Fenn above all was a storyteller, and underlying even his most improbable adventures is his firm belief that a young man could gain more knowledge of himself and the things around him through contact with the world than through book learning. The major in *Mother Carey's Chicken* sums up Fenn's philosophy, "there is no such a fine bit of Latin anywhere as *nil desperandum.* You never know what course a battle may take."

A kindly, sometimes quietly humorous, acceptance of human frailty can be seen in Fenn's attitude towards his boy characters, who often lack confidence, manliness, and experience and have an all-consuming fear of cowardice. In *Bunyip Land* Fenn shows the absurdity of this, particularly when Master Jack Penny has his foot caught in a crocodile's mouth and feels foolish because he hollers "like a great girl." Later Jack talks of "those wonderful chaps" in books and papers, "who kill three or four men every day and think nothing of it...." "'I say, ain't it jolly nonsense, Joe Carstairs?'" "'I suppose it is,' I said sadly, for I had believed in some of these heroes too."

These are not the idealized brave heroes of Ballantyne's and Henty's world, but Fenn had his own way of encouraging British youth to do its duty, act like a man, and never be beaten. He had confidence in the civilizing influence of the "true Englishman," a man of honour and true to his word. In *The Dingo Boys* and in *First in the Field* he explores this theme showing the effect that friendship can have on an Australian Aborigine and on a convict both of whom respond by being faithful and brave. Braver still is the boy in *First in the Field,* who trusts in his own judgment of people despite opposition from his father and from the Governor of the Colony.

Fenn was a highly competent writer of his time who understood his audience and catered, mainly from the 1880s until his death in 1909, for the ever-increasing market for adventure. His books finally went out of print during the middle 1930s and were superseded in the popular field by those of W.E. Johns, who was by then promoting an updated image of British manhood. Later, more serious authors revealed the inner life of their characters with far greater complexity and perception than Fenn, who stood at the cross roads between upholding the individual's social nature and exploring his individuality.

—Juliana Bayfield

FINLEY, Martha (née Brown)

Pseudonym: Martha Farquharson. **Nationality:** American. **Born:** Martha Brown in Chillicothe, Ohio, 26 April 1828. **Education:** Educated at private schools in Philadelphia and South Bend, Indiana. **Career:** Taught at schools in Indiana, 1851-53, and Phoenixville, Pennsylvania, 1853; writer for Presbyterian Publications Committee, Philadelphia. **Died:** 30 January 1909. **Fiction:** *Ella Clinton,* 1856; *Aunt Ruth,* 1857; *Annandale,* 1858; *Lame Letty,* 1859; *Try,* 1863; *Willie Elton,* 1864; *Mysie's Work,* 1864; *Little Joe Carter, the Cripple,* 1864; *Black Steve,* 1865; *Brookside Farm-House, from January to December,* 1865; *Robert and Daisy,* 1865; *Hugo and Franz,* 1965; *Elsie Dinsmore* series, from 1868; *Casella,* 1868; *Anna Hand,* 1868; *Stupid Sally,* 1868; *Maud's Two Homes,* 1868; *Loitering Linus,* 1868; *Little Dick Positive,* 1868; *Little Patience,* 1868; *Grandma Foster's Sunbeam,* 1868; *The Shannon,* 1868; *Milly,* 1868; *The White Dress,* 1870; *Rufus the Unready,* 1870; *Jamie by the Lake,* 1870; *The Broken Basket,* 1870; *Betty Page,* 1870; *Lillian,* 1871; *An Old Fashioned Boy,* 1871; *The Twin Babies,* 1872; *Jim* series, from 1872; *Noll* series, from 1872; *Our Fred,* 1874; *The Peddler of La Grave,* 1875; *The Pewit's Nest,* 1876; *Rosa and Robbie,* 1876; *Aunt Hetty's Fowls,* 1876; *Harry* series, from 1876; *Mildred* series, from 1878; *Twiddledetwit,* 1898.

* * *

Martha Finley is remembered for her family saga, the 28-volume *Elsie Dinsmore* series, one of the first American series for girls, fabulously popular in the United States and England. The series was unintentionally launched when the publisher arbitrarily divided the too-lengthy first manuscript into *Elsie Dinsmore* and *Holiday at Roselands.* With their combination of morally tough, neurotic realism and pietistically morbid, sentimental melodrama, the books whetted and insatiable public appetite. The first six volumes have a thematic and structural unity revolving about the conflict of wills between the sad-eyed, humble, but resolute Elsie and her arrogant, authoritarian father, whom, until she was eight, she had not met. Born to be a sacrificed lamb and savior, Elsie longs for the approbation, the love, and the Christian conversion of Horace Dinsmore. Their first meetings are cold and tense, complicated by anxieties and misunderstandings. When finally they penetrate the barriers between them, the affection they lavish upon one another, continually, through volumes, creates an intense ambience, more suggestive of amorous than filial love. That relationship predominates though Elsie and Horace both marry and have large families. However, the Freudian assertions that the books' great appeal depended upon readers' unconscious attraction to the theme of veiled incest is an exaggerated response to only one dimension of the books. Reflecting the author's literal response to the Bible's dual image of God as the stern but merciful father and as tender bridegroom, *Elsie* is a conscious effort to make concrete for children the concepts of God as father-protector and as heart's love. In the literary tradition of pious children with an innate instinct for Puritanical good and evil, Elsie does have "clear and correct views on almost every subject connected with her duty to God and her neighbor," and despite her priggishness, her refusal to knuckle under to adults who lack the perspicacity to understand that she is right inspires emulation of her courage to stand up to wrongheaded authority. In *Elsie's Widowhood,* as the protagonist grows into grandmotherhood, the benevolent, eternally youthful matriarch of a manifold clan, Finley introduced new characters apparently looking ahead to sequels without any foreseeable end. The next several volumes are loosely linked by the finally successful attempt of Captain Levis Raymond, a son-in-law of Elsie, to subjugate through loving discipline his intractable daughter Lulu, which story echoes the Horace-Elsie father-daughter love-struggle. The last 14 volumes are virtually plotless. New characters are introduced, frequently to marry into the family and perpetuate it.

The world of the Elsie books is a soap-opera-like composite of fantasy and realism, an imitation fairytale world peopled by wealthy white folks and contented, servile blacks. The setting for the stories was based on exaggerated tales returning Union soldiers told of the sumptuous elegance of the pre-Civil War South. Finley's experience and imagination were limited. She was incapable of particularizing her worlds through local color and specific detail unless she was writing from actual experience as she occasionally did, for example, in the autobiographical *Mildred Keith.* Through repetition with slight variation of the same generalized scenes she does, however, evoke an intensely felt, powerfully enveloping, almost surrealistic world. Although in her later books she introduces heavily derivative, encyclopedic accounts of historic events, these serve as space fillers and are not integrated into what little plot the book might have.

Skillful at sketching memorable vignettes of recognizable character types fleshed out with original idiosyncracies, Finley lacked the insight into human nature which would have enabled her to create authentic protagonists. She neither explores nor analyzes motives. Her major characters, interpreted as attempts at realism, appear flat and irritatingly self-satisfied. However, as ideal types in a quasi-romance, in keeping with the quasi-fairytale world in which they live, they achieve a credibility through almost ritual repetition of predictable gestures and utterances. The cumulative impact induces a kind of fascination-aversion for what, conceivably, people like ourselves might do if situations were slightly altered, if there were no moral ambiguities, and if we acted with commitment to fundamental principles.

Dialogue is Finley's principal vehicle of narration. The style in which she records speech is labored and lugubrious. With few intrusions by the author either to inform or to interpret, characters deliver themselves of uncommonly articulate, formal set pieces spilling over with paraphrases of Biblical counsels and declamations of narcissistic emotions. Finley's attempts to reproduce baby talk, the speech of the uneducated, or black dialects—all offensively similar—make it obvious that she had no ear for distinctive idioms, much less nuances.

Making the male protagonist of her Elsie stories a father, rather than a lover or husband, provided Finley not only her dominant motif but also a more credible vehicle for her dominant theme: woman is by nature fragile, subservient, and ornamental, and ought to be elevated to a pedestal. Interknit with that theme is a cognate repeatedly endorsed: the primacy of unselfishness. To sacrifice one's needs and happiness to the welfare of others effects the highest felicity. Finley's fiction is imbued with vulgar and pernicious attitudes: the subordination of woman; the equation of blacks with servile, simpleminded, pious "chilluns"; the snobbish conviction that wealth breeds gentility and refined spirituality, which augment personal and social worth; religious bigotry. Her bombast, her exaggeration of situation, and her excessive sentimentality evoke both censure and satire. Still the Elsie books have too much substance to be dismissed as merely silly or stupid. Witness such reputable champions as G.B. Stern, who when she "crave[d] really tough stuff" returned to Elsie who faced trials with unquenchable conviction and unflagging fortitude.

Finley's enormous popularity, which like any cult remains in part inexplicable, resulted largely from a workable formula of sensational, artistically flawed storytelling whose chemistry appealed to a particular people at a favorable time. For more than three generations *Elsie Dinsmore* outsold every juvenile book in America except *Little Women,* and Elsie attained more "widespread interest and affection" than any character in juvenile fiction but Huckleberry Finn. The influence upon millions of impressionable readers of the beautiful, lachrymose, righteous paragon is staggering to contemplate. While *Elsie* is no longer sold at book counters, she is available in expensive reprints in two series, whose titles offer their own comment: "Popular Culture in America" and "Classics of Children's Literature."

—M. Sarah Smedman

HALE, Lucretia P(eabody)

Nationality: American. **Born:** Boston, Massachusetts, 2 September 1820; sister of the writer Edward Everett Hale. **Education:** Educated at Susan Whitney's, Miss Peabody's, and George G. Emerson's schools. **Career:** Taught for a correspondence school, and private history tutor. Member, Boston School Committee, 1874; **Died:** 12 June 1900. **Fiction:** *The Peterkin Papers,* 1880; *Alone in Rome,* 1883; *The Last of the Peterkins,* 1886; *Sunday School Stories,* with Mrs. Bernard Whitman, 1889; *Stories for Children,* 1892; *The Queen of the Red Chessmen,* n.d.

* * *

As a children's writer, Lucretia P. Hale is known principally for *The Peterkin Papers,* a collection of humorous sketches that had previously appeared in the children's periodical *Our Young Folks* and its distinguished successor *St. Nicholas.* A sequel, *The Last of the Peterkins,* was far less popular than the *Papers,* which made the Peterkins a household word.

The Peterkin Papers consists of 22 sketches of the ludicrous and improbable misadventures of the Peterkins, an astonishingly inept family consisting of *père* and *mère,* together with their six children: Agamemnon ("who had been to college"), Elizabeth Eliza, Solomon John, and three unnamed little boys, chiefly notable for the Indian rubber boots which they seem incessantly to be putting on and taking off. The sketches, which tend to be repetitive in form, begin with a problem that grows more formidable the more the family's collective wisdom is invoked to solve it: what to do with a cup of coffee into which Mrs. Peterkin has stirred salt instead of sugar; how to make the family wise; what to do about a piano placed with its keyboard against a window so that it can only be played by standing on the porch and reaching through the window; what to do with a Christmas tree that is too tall for the back parlor.

Once the premise is established, the rest of the sketch recounts the efforts of the family, attempting to work in concert and sometimes with the advice of neighbors, to remedy the situation. In the case of the salted coffee, the local chemist is consulted and tries to counter the presence of the salt with an array of chemicals. Hale is at her comic best cataloguing his inspired—but, alas, futile—efforts: "Then he tried, each in turn, some oxalic, cyanic, acetic, phosphoric, chloric, hyperchloric, sulphuric, boracic, silicic, nitric, formic, nitrous nitric, and carbonic acids. Mrs. Peterkin tasted each and said the flavor was pleasant, but not precisely that of coffee." In this instance, as in most of the sketches, the Petekins's comic fixation with a futile strategem is broken finally by the cool common sense of their friend Mrs. Leslie, "the lady from Philadelphia," who sensibly suggests throwing out the offending coffee and making a new cup—or moving the piano so that its keyboard faces into the room. Although she is not present to suggest sawing a foot or two from the overly large Christmas tree, and Mr. Peterkin will not accept the carpenter's advice to do so but has him raise a portion of the ceiling instead, the thoughtful lady does provide the Petekins with a box of Christmas ornaments, for which, with characteristic improvidence, they had neglected to plan.

The sequel, *The Last of the Peterkins,* seems, in retrospect, to be distinctly inferior to the earlier sketches. Convinced, perhaps, that she had explored most of the domestic difficulties likely to beset even a family as impractical as the Peterkins, Hale shifts her focus from the family as a whole to its several members and from the narrowly local setting to one that, in the end, is international. In the first episode of *The Last of the Peterkins,* Elizabeth Eliza prepares and delivers a paper on "The Sun" to the local women's cultural society, the Circumambient Club. Such a setting provides ample scope for Hale's gentle satire. In successive episodes, the family undertakes travel—first to grandfather's for maple syrup but eventually to Europe and the Middle East. Increasingly, the sketches describe the fragmentation of the family as, not surprisingly, travel connections are missed, baggage goes astray, and messages are misunderstood. In the final chapter, the family are briefly reunited, but with the exception of the three little boys, each has seen enough of the world to have a different dream. Elizabeth Eliza marries a Russian; Agamemnon is last heard of bound for Madagascar; and Mr. and Mrs. Peterkin are headed for Yakoutsk. Their misadventures as a family are over, and even the lady from Philadelphia could not retrieve them from the far ends of the earth, to which Hale consigns them.

The Peterkin Papers and its sequel enjoyed a considerable popularity with children and a measure of critical approval as well. Most of the sketches proceed from such obvious premise that children doubtless relished the absurd antics of the Peterkins, secure in knowing precisely what the lady from Philadelphia would prescribe when she should eventually appear on the scene. Despite the labored quality of the humor, on occasion, and the repetitious form of the episodes, Hale is often a clever and acute observer of human foibles. In contrast to much of the earnest moralizing characteristic of late 19th-century American children's literature, *The Peterkin Papers* is delightful nonsense—virtually the first example that we have. Moreover, it is humor, however gentle and affectionate, at the expense of the family, the institution then widely regarded as the fundamental social unit. Hale's mildly satirical view of the claustrophobic togetherness that was one aspect of Victorian family life marked a refreshing and popular alternative to the solemnity with which her contemporaries treated the family in books for children.

—R. Gordon Kelly

HARRIS, Joel Chandler

Nationality: American. **Born:** Near Eatonton, Georgia, 9 December 1848. **Education:** Educated at Eatonton Academy for Boys. **Family:** Married Esther LaRose in 1873; nine children. **Career:** Printer's devil and typesetter, *Countryman* weekly, published at the Turnwold Plantation, 1862-66; staff member, Macon *Telegraph,* Georgia, 1866, *Crescent Monthly,* New Orleans, 1866-67, *Monroe Advertiser,* Forsyth, Georgia, 1867-70, Savannah *Morning News,* Georgia, 1870-76, and Atlanta *Constitution,* 1876-1900; founder, with his son Julian, *Uncle Remus's* magazine, Atlanta, 1907-08. L.H.D.: Emory College, Oxford, Georgia, 1902. Member, American Academy, 1905. **Died:** 2 July 1908. **Fiction:** *Uncle Remus* series, from 1880; *Daddy Jake the Runaway and Short Stories Told after Dark,* 1889; *Little Mr. Thimblefinger and His Queer Country,* 1894; *Mr. Rabbit at Home,* 1895; *The Story of Aaron,* 1896; *Aaron in the Wildwoods,* 1897; *The Chronicles of Aunt Minervy Ann,* 1899; *Wally Wanderoon and His Story-Telling Machine,* 1903; *The Bishop and the Boogerman (The Bishop and the Bogie-Man),* 1909; *The Shadow Between His Shoulder-Blades,* 1909. **Verse:** *The Tar-Baby,* 1904.

* * *

Joel Chandler Harris labeled himself a "cornfield journalist" whose success as a writer of folktales of the American south was "a lucky accident." Nevertheless, in the last half of the 19th century and the first decade of the 20th, he was along with Mark Twain the best-loved author of his time. Twain even asked Harris to join him on a lecture tour which the latter declined, unfortunately for posterity. Harris's fame in mid-20th century America, however, rested largely on Walt Disney's skillful treatment of Uncle Remus and his animal stories in the feature film *Song of the South* (1947), and a nationally syndicated Disney newspaper cartoon series featuring Brer Rabbit in the 1950s and 1960s. In the waning decades of the 20th century, interest in Harris's negro tales, novels, and journalism is largely academic.

Born out of wedlock in the vicinity of Eatonton, Georgia, an upcountry summer resort town that is still filled today with well-preserved antebellum mansions, Harris was reared by the newspaperman, lawyer, and planter Joseph Addison Turner at Turnwold Plantation. From Turner young Harris learned typesetting and newspaper writing. He read the English classics in

Turnwold's well-stocked library. On the plantation he also learned from slaves many of the folktales of Brer Rabbit, Brer Fox, Brer Wolf that were to make him famous as a folklorist and humorist in the decades after the Civil War. Indeed, Harris wrote that Uncle Remus, the teller of so many of the tales, was a composite character "of three or four old darkies I had known" at Turnwold and in Eatonton. Significantly, too, it was among the deracinated blacks that the fatherless white boy found ready acceptance, and subtle empathy.

Having served his apprenticeship and made his mental notes of the blacks and their tales, Harris went to Atlanta, where he became a journalist with the South's most progressive newspaper, the Atlanta *Constitution.* It was in the pages of the *Constitution* that he started publishing his character sketches and Uncle Remus dialect tales in 1878. The most famous of these, "The Tar Baby," appeared in the newspaper in 1879. Harris's first book, *Uncle Remus: His Songs and His Sayings,* was published in 1880. And so began the dissemination of the Uncle Remus stories that eventually ran into six volumes. These are works, the literary critic and historian Jay B. Hubbell writes, that are American classics in children's literature.

In the aggregate, Harris was primarily a writer of character sketches and episodes rather than an author of well-constructed short stories and novels. He was too busy with journalism to master his storytelling craft; he himself felt his literary work had no great merit, but was merely an act of preservation of folk myth and experience of the South. To northern magazines Harris sent stories in which the chief characters were white. But Harris is best when he sticks to the short tale or episode, the recollection or anecdote as told by an illiterate black such as Uncle Remus, who speaks the dialect of the cotton plantations, or from a poor white such as Teague Poteet in *Mingo* (1884), who uses the dialect of the Georgia mountains. Furthermore, a careful reading of his writings, fiction or journalism, a knowledge of his life and aspirations, and even a cursory awareness of the mores of his time should allay any accusations of racism cast on Harris and his work. He believed not only in the progressive, industrial idealism of the New South creed posited by Henry W. Grady, managing editor of the *Constitution,* but also in constructive cooperation, harmony, and social equality between blacks and whites in the south and in the nation.

In the Uncle Remus tales, whose sources lie in dim recollections of Africa, there occurs the consistent triumph of Brer Rabbit, the most helpless of the wild animals Harris characterizes. Some scholars see a subtle parallel between the rabbit and the slave in their capacity to survive and, ironically, to triumph. Uncle Remus, too, makes his quiet digs at the white man's busyness and after questionable ways of making money. And on the plantations of the Old South that Harris's stories glorify, black slaves and not white masters are the romantic element. Primarily a writer of sketches, as were the antebellum Georgia humorists Augustus Baldwin Longstreet and Joseph Glover Baldwin, Harris is never sharply critical, however, of the human race and its institutions. His best qualities are humour, characterization, and respect for the poor and distressed. In his use of dialect, common people, and simple scenes from everyday life, Harris was a pioneer in moving southern literature from its 19th-century romanticism to its 20th-century realism. Uncle Remus and Brer Rabbit are his monument.

—Jan Bakker

HENTY, G(eorge) A(lfred)

Nationality: British. **Born:** Trumpington, Cambridgeshire, 8 December 1832. **Education:** Westminster School, London, 1847-52; Caius College, Cambridge, 1852. **Military Service:** Served in the Hospital Commissariat and the Purveyor's Department during the Crimean War; helped organize Italian hospitals, 1859; served in Belfast and Portsmouth: Turkish Order of the Medjidie. **Family:** Married 1) Elizabeth Finucane in 1858, two sons and two daughters; 2) Bessie Keylock. **Career:** Crimean War correspondent, *Morning Advertiser,* London; staff correspondent, in Europe, Africa, Asia, and North America, the *Standard,* London, 1865-76; editor, *Union Jack* magazine, London, 1880-83, *Beeton's Boy's Own Magazine,* London, 1888-90, and later annuals, 1890-93. **Died:** 16 November 1902. **Fiction:** *Out on the Pampas,* 1871; *The Young Franc-Tireurs,* 1872; *The Young Buglers,* 1879; *Seaside Maidens,* 1880; *In Times of Peril,* 1881; *The Cornet of Horse,* 1881; *Winning His Spurs (The Boy Knight; Fighting the Saracens),* 1882; *Facing Death,* 1882; *Under Drake's Flag,* 1882; *With Clive in India,* 1883; *By Sheer Pluck,* 1883; *Jack Archer (The Fall of Sebastopol),* 1883; *Friends, Though Divided,* 1883; *True to the Old Flag,* 1884; *In Freedom's Cause,* 1884; *St. George for England,* 1884; *The Lion of the North,* 1885; *The Young Colonists,* 1885; *The Dragon and the Raven,* 1885; *For Name and Fame,* 1885; *Through the Fray,* 1885; *Yarns on the Beach,* 1885; *With Wolfe in Canada,* 1886; *The Bravest of the Brave,* 1886; *A Final Reckoning,* 1986; *The Young Carthaginian,* 1886; *Bonnie Prince Charlie,* 1887; *For the Temple,* 1887; *In the Reign of Terror,* 1887; *Sturdy and Strong,* 1887; *The Cat of Bubastes,* 1888; *The Lion of St. Mark,* 1888; *Captain Bayley's Heir,* 1888; *Orange and Green,* 1888; *One of the 28th,* 1889; *By Pike and Dyke,* 1889; *Camps and Quarters,* 1889; *Tales of Daring and Danger,* 1889; *The Plague Ship,* 1889; *With Lee in Virginia,* 1889; *By Right of Conquest,* 1890; *By England's Aid,* 1890; *A Chapter of Adventures (The Young Midshipman),* 1890; *Maori and Settler,* 1890; *Redskin and Cowboy,* 1891; *The Dash for Khartoum,* 1891; *Held Fast for England,* 1891; *In Greek Waters,* 1892; *Beric the Briton,* 1892; *Condemned as a Nihilist,* 1892; *The Ranche in the Valley,* 1892; *A Jacobite Exile,* 1893; *St. Bartholomew's Eve,* 1893; *Through the Sikh War,* 1893; *In the Heart of the Rockies,* 1894; *When London Burned,* 1894; *Wulf the Saxon,* 1894; *The Tiger of Mysore,* 1895; *A Woman of the Commune (Cuthbert Hartington; A Girl of the Commune; Two Sieges of Paris),* 1895; *A Knight of the White Cross,* 1895; *Through Russian Snows,* 1895; *On the Irrawaddy,* 1896; *At Agincourt,* 1896; *Bears and Decoits and Other Stories,* 1896; *With Cochrane the Dauntless,* 1896; *In Battle and Breeze,* with George Manville Fenn and W. Clark Russell, 1896; *With Moore at Corunna,* 1897; *A March on London,* 1897; *With Frederick the Great,* 1897; *Among Malay Pirates (Among the Malays),* 1897; *At Aboukir and Acre,* 1898; *Both Sides the Border,* 1898; *Under Wellington's Command,* 1898; *The Golden Cañon,* 1899; *No Surrender!,* 1899; *On the Spanish Main,* 1899; *Won by the Sword,* 1899; *In the Irish Brigade,* 1900; *In the Hands of the Cave-Dwellers,* 1900; *With Buller in Natal,* 1900; *Out with Garibaldi,* 1900; *A Roving Commission,* 1900; *The Sole Survivors,* 1901; *With Roberts to Pretoria,* 1901; *At the Point of the Bayonet,* 1901; *John Hawke's Fortune,* 1901; *To Herat and Cabul,* 1901; *With Kitchener in the Soudan,* 1902; *With the British Legion,* 1902; *The Treasure of the Incas,* 1902; *With the Allies to Pekin,* 1903; *Through Three Campaigns,* 1903; *By Conduct and*

Courage, 1904; *Gallant Deeds,* 1905; *In the Hands of the Malays and Other Stories,* 1905; *Redskins and Colonists, Burton and Son, The Ranche in the Valley, Sole Survivors,* 1905; *A Soldier's Daughter and Other Stories,* 1906.

* * *

G.A. Henty belongs to that class of authors whose influence has far outstripped their literary achievement. His biographer and contemporary, George Manville Fenn, claimed that he "taught more lasting history to boys than to all the schoolmasters of his generation." It was a limited conception of history, but Henty's enthusiasm certainly infected his young readers and brought the past to life for them. His influence was in fact three-fold: besides making history palatable to boys, he inspired numerous imitators and set the adventure-story in a mould that was not broken until long after his death, while the ideology he propounded—the cult of "manliness" and the British Empire—had a far-reaching effect which rates consideration in a more than purely literary context. It has been argued that Henty and his followers helped to produce the type of adventurous young man who (wrote Edgar Osborne) "went overseas and did much towards building up our present Commonwealth of Nations." Less friendly critics have expressed this differently. Nearly 40 years after Henty's death, George Orwell complained: "Boys' fiction is sodden in the worst illusions of 1910."

Henty was of course the epitome of Victorianism, being born just five years before the queen's accession and outliving her by little more than a year. A delicate child, bullied at public school, he took lessons in "the noble art of self-defence" and had good reason thereafter to believe in the efficacy of Christian manliness, expressed in a straight left to the jaw. As a war correspondent on innumerable campaigns, he found it easy to identify himself with the conquering Empire-builders. In later life, as a popular London clubman, he had little cause to question the current assumptions of his class.

His success sprang from his ability to take a colourful theme, whether from recent or from remote history, and then, helping out the facts with invented incident and character, spin what approving parents and pedagogues called "a rattling good yarn." He worked to a formula, as his titles show—*With Clive in India, With Wolfe in Canada, With Kitchener in the Soudan,* or for variation, *Facing Death, True to the Old Flag,* and *Held Fast for England.* His young heroes ran similarly to type, manly, middle-class, and intellectually unremarkable. The great adventurers of real history, Ralegh and Burton and T.E. Lawrence, would have fitted less comfortably into his stock-size frame.

Many of his books were based on first-hand observation. He walked the field of Inkerman among the unburied Russian dead, and the Crimean story he eventually wrote, *Jack Archer,* is one of his most vivid. He reported the Franco-Prussian War; within a year he had written *The Young Franc-Tireurs.* He accompanied Garibaldi in Italy, the Turks in their savage Balkan wars, and British expeditions into West Africa and Abyssinia. None of the slaughter he witnessed dimmed his vision of military glory. Even in his posthumously published story of the Boxer rising, *With the Allies to Pekin,* there is undiminished gusto in his account of two intrepid lads who, caught in a confined space with a dozen murderous Chinese, use their magazine-loading rifles to wipe out their adversaries in a few moments.

Henty was a methodical worker. He would lie on a sofa in his weapon-festooned study, dictating to a male secretary—and then never look at the story again until he corrected the proofs. In a six-hour day he could produce over 6000 words. In the last 33 years of his life he packed something like 14 million words into about 90 fat volumes. It would be optimistic to seek, in such a mass, either striking originality of ideas or fastidious use of language. He at least achieved English which, if not quite as "good" as admiring schoolmasters declared it, never fell below a certain level. It was the prose of the period, rather too wordy for our own taste, and betraying his habit of unrevised dictation. Characters, after being "for a minute or two speechless with indignation," would then immediately plunge into paragraph-long speeches of advice or explanation.

Even when handling themes outside his own experience, Henty could invest his narrative with a good deal of verisimilitude, thanks to the analogous events in which he had participated. Occasionally he was lazy. His Cortez story, *By Right of Conquest,* reads like paraphrased Prescott. He makes only a feeble attempt to create his own characters and plot inside the historical framework. His conventional English boy hero, Roger—so implausibly present at the conquest of Mexico—is often forgotten for several pages at a time.

Henty set a pattern which many lesser writers adapted to the 1914 war and other themes, but by the mid-20th century his values were unfashionable, and, as the general quality of historical fiction improved, it became less heretical to criticise his literary weaknesses. Today his books are rather "collected" as Victorian than read by boys. They have not won a place upon the shelf with the children's classics that are loved from generation to generation.

—Geoffrey Trease

HUGHES, Thomas

Nationality: British. **Born:** Uffington, Berkshire, 20 October 1822. **Education:** Rugby School, 1834-42; Oriel College, Oxford, 1842-45 (played cricket for Oxford, 1842), B.A. 1845; entered Lincoln's Inn, London, 1845, then entered the Inner Temple, and called to the bar, 1848. **Family:** Married Frances Ford in 1848; three sons and three daughters. **Career:** Lawyer in London from 1848; Queen's Counsel, 1869; associated with F.D. Maurice and the Christian Socialists who subsequently helped to create the cooperative movement; contributed to the *Christian Socialist* and *Tracts on Christian Socialism* and acted as editor of the *Journal of Association;* chairman of the first Cooperative Congress, 1869; helped to pass the Industrial and Provident Societies Act, 1893; involved in the founding of the Working Men's College, Great Ormond Street, London, 1854, and served as its principal, 1872-83; Liberal Member of Parliament for Lambeth, 1865-68, and Frome, Somerset, 1868-74; founding member, Church Reform Union, 1870; established model community in Tennessee which proved unsuccessful, 1879; county court judge, Chester, Cheshire, 1882-96. **Died:** 22 March 1896. **Fiction:** *Tom Brown's School Days,* 1857; *Tom Brown at Oxford,* 1861.

* * *

Thomas Hughes did not invent the school story; it existed for a century or so before *Tom Brown's School Days,* and by the 1850s it had reached a degree of some sophistication (see, for example,

The Cherry-Stones by the Rev. William Adams, published in 1851). What Hughes did was to inject into the genre that species of ethic which has generally been labelled Muscular Christianity. Hughes himself disliked that term, but it is hard to think of a better way of describing, for example, his exhortation to his readers on the subject of fist-fighting: "Don't say 'no' [when challenged to a fight] because you fear a licking, and say or think it's because you fear God, for that's neither Christian nor honest. And if you do fight, fight it out; and don't give in while you can stand and see."

It has often been pointed out that this ethic has nothing whatever to do with liberal intellectual values cultivated by Thomas Arnold, Hughes's headmaster at Rugby and "the Doctor" of the novel. Hughes is generally accused of having completely failed to understand Arnold—and of having undone much of Arnold's good work by publishing a novel which equated Arnoldian educational policy with manly fist-fights, love of sport, and a despising of the intellect (Old Brooke, Tom's house captain in the novel, says he would rather win a football match than get a Balliol scholarship). The truth is surely that Hughes himself cannot be held personally to blame: somebody else would have written *Tom Brown's School Days* if he had not, so much does it typify the mid-Victorian enthusiasm for manliness with Christian overtones.

Hughes wrote it because he said he had "often thought that good might be done by a real novel for boys—not didactic...written in a right spirit, but distinctly aimed at being interesting." Charles Kingsley, like Hughes a member of F.D. Maurice's Christain Socialist movement, saw the finished book shortly before publication and forecast that "it will be a very great hit," which it was, immediately. The surprise is that a quarter of a century passed before its literary influence really began to be felt. Not until Talbot Baines Reed's *The Fifth Form at St. Dominic's,* which began to be serialised in 1881 in the *Boy's Own Paper,* did another writer begin to make methodical use of Hughes's format. After Reed, the floodgates opened, and one may find a thousand *Tom Browns* by different authors published between the 1880s and the 1930s—though none of them has the freshness and zest of the Hughes original. Reed and his successors retained the "jam" of the school story while eliminating the "powder" of Hughes's preaching; but it is the preaching that drives Hughes's story along. Without it, the book would soon have been forgotten.

—Humphrey Carpenter

INGELOW, Jean

Nationality: British. **Born:** Boston, Lincolnshire, 17 March 1820. **Education:** Educated at home. Lived in London after 1850. **Career:** Editor, *Youth Magazine,* 1855. **Died:** 20 July 1897. **Fiction:** *Tales of Orris (Stories Told to a Child),* 1860; *Studies for Stories,* 1864; *A Sister's Bye-Hours,* 1868; *Mopsa the Fairy,* 1869; *The Little Wonder-Horn,* 1872; *The Little Wonder Box,* 6 vols., 1887; *Very Young, and Quite Another Story,* 1890; *The Black Polyanthus, and Widow MacLean,* 1903.

* * *

One novel and a handful of anthology poems keep Jean Ingelow's name alive today; but these works are not negligible. They can suggest why, in her time, she was something of a celebrity, both as adult novelist and poet; why her work was admired by such fellow writers as Tennyson, Edward FitzGerald, the Rossettis. She was even thought a possible Laureate when the post fell vacant in 1892, but admittedly this was a very thin time. More pointed is the fact that, 16 years after her death, she rated an Oxford edition of her poems. They tend to be ballad-like and reverberating, with sharp and haunting cadences and a mysterious thread of narrative; their appeal is not hard to understand. *High Tide on the Coast of Lincolnshire,* where the energy of the theme absorbs the sentiment, is one of the best examples.

Still, most of her poetry is for the private discoverer or devotee; so too are her shorter mildly didactic tales for the young, written in a good brisk readable style but lacking the power of flight to travel far. Very few, indeed, are accessible now, though one charming tale, "My Grandmother's Shoe," has been revived in one of Gillian Avery's collections.

Ingelow's one long work for the young, her remarkable novel *Mopsa the Fairy,* is a different matter. Written within that short and dazzling period when so many leading Victorian authors experimented in children's fantasy, it remains, in its genre, a major achievement, one of those single, odd yet memorable works that make up so much of English literature. Influences? Certainly. Take the most Carollian passage in *Mopsa,* when a ballad sung by Jack includes the lines:

> And the lark said, give us glory!
> And the dove said, give us peace!
>
> "A very good song indeed," said the dame at the other end of the table, "only you made a mistake in the first verse. What the dove really said was, no doubt, 'Give us peas.'"
>
> "It isn't peas, though," said Jack. However, the court historian was sent for to write down the song...as the dame said it ought to be.

Flamingoes stand on military guard; there is an oddly macabre episode in which a gypsy's baby turns out to be a bundle of clothes with a turnip head. A further Carrollian echo surely sounds in Jack's disputation with the ravens:

> "Why," said Jack, "I see a full moon lying down there among the water-flags, and just going to set, and there is a half-moon overhead plunging among those great grey clouds, and just this moment I saw a thin crescent moon peeping out between the branches of that tree."
>
> "Well," said all the ravens at once, "did the young master never see a crescent moon in the men and women's world?"
>
> "Yes, of course," said Jack, "but they are all the same moon. I could never see all three of them at the same time."
>
> The ravens were very much surprised at this.

But the voice and the detail are essentially Ingelow's. Even the book's opening, which has been likened to the opening of *Alice,* sheers off at once in its own direction. A boy, Jack, is going through a meadow of buttercups. He leans against a hollow tree while eating a slice of plum cake, hears a twittering and climbs inside. Up above is a nest of white wool and moss. It is a nest of very young fairies; one is "creeping about rather like an old baby, and had on a little frock and pinafore." An albatross arrives, and off they fly to Fairyland, the fairies in Jack's pocket. "We are going the back way," says the albatross. "You could go in two minutes by the usual route; but these young fairies want to go before they are summoned, and therefore you and I are taking them." Does this flight echo George MacDonald? *At the Back of the North Wind* was being serialized when *Mopsa* was published, though it would not appear as a book until the following year.

Another episode, where they come to a great bay of becalmed ships, where the wind never blows, recalls another contemporary. How did the ships come to be there? asks Jack.

> Some of them had captains who abused their cabinboys, some were pirate ships and others were going out on evil errands....Many ships which are supposed by men to have foundered lie becalmed in this quiet sea. Look at these five grand ones with the high poops...they were part of the Spanish Armada; and the open boats with blue sails belonged to the Romans, they sailed with Caesar when he invaded Britain.

Kingsley, certainly. *Westward Ho!* had been published in 1855, *The Water-Babies* in 1863. Yet even this probable debt has its own sea-change in *Mopsa*. A visit made to a very different writer, Anna Sewell, at Shanklin in March 1868 illuminates a further episode. Jack and Mopsa land at a border country where horses, cruelly used in the human world, cab horses, race horses, are allowed to grow back to their youth, carefully tended by clockwork people. Why *clockwork*? It is not the only occasion in the book where one feels that the author's unconscious symbolism is rather more interesting than she could have known. But the voice that speaks on the ill-used horses is so remarkably like the voice of *Black Beauty*'s author that the episode could have been written almost immediately after the meeting. *Black Beauty* itself was not published until 19 years later. And nowhere in Ingelow's writing does the subject recur.

But the real originality of the tale is increasingly evident. Whatever you *can* do in this fairyland, you *may* do, Jack is told. But *can* has also its rules. It is a place that even holds the occasional human, like the apple-woman, who stays, still keeping a little stall with cherries on sticks and a few dry nuts. She could wish herself back into the world but has not the courage. "It would come into my head that I should be poor or that my boys would have forgotten me, or that my neighbours would look down on me, and so I always put off wishing for another day." Invention does not flag. Jack and Mopsa, in flight from certain primitive beasts, reach their boat and are offered the protection of a Craken's coils, arch after arch, endlessly reaching away. The water drips about them; the boat trembles "either because of its great age, or because it felt the grasp of the coil underneath." Then, as they sail on, they perceive the arches closing in; soon they have to crouch down in the boat. C.S. Lewis must have recalled this scene in *The Voyage of the "Dawn Treader."* The next arch almost touches the water. "No! that I cannot bear," cries Jack. "Somebody else may do the rest of the dream!" "Why don't you wake!" says Mopsa, as if amused.

But Mopsa is no ordinary fairy. She and Jack escape by night, crossing over the purple mountain, so that she need not rule over the unknown deer-people; so that she need not rule at all, only stay with Jack. And yet, their journey takes them to where they were fleeing from; it is her kingdom after all; there is even a shadow Jack to keep her company. But the real Jack, a human boy, must go home.

And here the book presents the basic difference between the real folk fairytale and the invented kind, the Victorian sort especially. Jack remains a boy, delightfully so, throughout. But Mopsa, through human contact, gradually changes from child and girl, first pet, then playmate, ally in danger, to a mystical Pre-Raphaelite adult queen. From a child's view, this should not be. Morals work well enough, of the straight pragmatic kind, but emotion, no. Goosegirl and prince may turn, in time, into ageing Queen and King but essentially they are children still, playing at kingdoms. Perhaps a really good illustrator (which *Mopsa* has so far lacked) could solve the problem of Mopsa's transformation. Indeed, older readers may find the end a necessary part of the whole experience. For experience it is. Victorian fantasy, rich as it is, offers few more remarkable journeys to any fairytale reader.

—Naomi Lewis

JEFFERIES, Richard

Nationality: British. **Born:** Near Swindon, Wiltshire, 6 November 1848. **Education:** Educated at schools in Sydenham, Kent, and Swindon, to age 15. **Family:** Married in 1874. **Career:** Wrote for the *North Wilts Herald,* 1866-70: became its regular reporter and local correspondent for a Gloucestershire paper; freelance writer from 1870; moved to London, 1876, and wrote for the *Pall Mall Gazette*; in later life lived in Sussex. **Died:** 14 August 1887. **Fiction:** *Wood Magic,* 1880; *Bevis,* 1882.

* * *

Bevis ("The Story of a Boy") is both a minor prestige classic and a literary oddity. A century after publication it remains in print not widely but sufficiently. Like Richard Jeffries himself, as "nature" writer—and for reasons which might be worth exploring—it has always had a few intense devotees. And yet, I suspect, it is not very closely read, or even read at all, by most of those today who republish or purchase the work as an item for the young. It is one of the author's very few works of fiction and the only one whose content relates to children. Yet no other single Jeffries book unites so well the author's best and worst. He was an excellent writer, with a meticulous eye and ear for the country matters—human, plant and animal—that were his usual theme. But something arrogant, self-absorbed, at times sadistic even, flaws his work for readers outside the cult. John Clare, for instance, perhaps our greatest writer in this field and the most understanding, makes a salutary contrast.

Long and substantial though *Bevis* is, the plot is simple enough. Two boys, Bevis and Mark, spend an ideal summer in the woods and on the waters of the family grounds. For the final fortnight they live wild (with parent's permission, and supplies) on a "Secret Island" in the lake. The book is full of seductive passages and splendid practical detail; but as a work of nature-magic (such is its reputation) the final effect is curious. And the hero-boy himself, in whom Jefferies seems to see no fault at all? Readers might think otherwise. Almost at once we see him ordering the servants.

> "Stop," said Bevis, "stop directly and hitch the chain on my raft."
>
> The boy hesitated; he dared not disobey the carter, and he had been in trouble for pleasing Bevis before.
>
> "This instant," said Bevis, stamping his foot. "I'm your master."

Animals fare worse. The boys' gear for the camping trip includes gun, spear, harpoon, darts, snares, bow and arrows—and all are lethally used. (To the end of his life Jefferies never lost his passion for the kill.) They shoot a heron for the plume. They get a moorcock with an arrow, pinning its wing to a tree. "Hurrah!" They thrash a working pony round and round a field "making him leap a broad furrow and gallop his hardest." They plan a pit with stakes as an animal trap. They beat, kick, and hurl stones at their loyal dog when it fails to do the impossible. If only there were a bird of paradise, thinks Bevis. It would do for Mark's sister's hat. In one of the nastiest episodes (there is no lack of choice) they tie a donkey to a tree and proceed to "break their sticks upon his back. They thrashed, thwacked, banged, thumped, poked, prodded, kicked, belaboured,...working themselves into a frenzy of rage." They continue with heavy logs that they can hardly lift. "No one came to help the donkey." Finally they lock it up without food or water.

And what is the peak achievement of their holiday? The killing of an otter, a special prize because so rare in those parts. Even mother and sister are summoned to witness the corpse and praise the deed. The womenfolk (knowing their place in the Jefferies hierarchy) humbly look and admire. They gaze at the noble boy: "Bevis was too fair to brown well. The sun and the wind had purified his skin almost to transparency, with a rosy olive behind the whiteness (etc., etc.)...Frances played with his golden ringlets, but did not kiss him as she used to. He looked too much a man." Ah yes, but all this could make up a picture of boy-life anywhere, even today, especially in countries where such views persist, and in high places everywhere. It is the uncritical adulation that rings so oddly, from Jefferies most of all.

But the book is not so much a story aimed at the young as a recapturing of memory—and there lies much of its strength. To see it as simple autobiography would be wrong. The golden Bevis, imperious, ruthless, admired and obeyed by all, was scarcely Jefferies himself (though wish-fantasy also tells us much). Socially, too, the boy Bevis seems on a higher rung of the ladder. As a small farmer's son, Jefferies would have been well above the peasants and labourers (some employed by his father), but below the landed gentry, with their body of servants, bailiffs, keepers, and obsequious tenants (who scrape and curtsy to Bevis and Mark). But what is certainly true to memory is the intense sensation of being a boy of 12 or less, acting out his reading of Homer and the bloodier fighting ballads, making rafts, mapping the stars, learning to swim, taking part in war-games against the village lads, roaming the woods, and never far from his cherished rod and gun.

No, it is not only for its beguiling prose that *Bevis* can still be read. As an (unintentional) view of social history, social attitudes: as an all-too-revealing glance at the hard-eyed cruelty of real child-nature, it has a decided place. But that place is not, it could be said, on the children's shelf.

—Naomi Lewis

KINGSLEY, Charles

Nationality: British. **Born:** Holne, Devon, 12 June 1819; brother of the writer Henry Kingsley. **Education:** Educated at a preparatory school in Clifton, Bristol, 1831-33; Helston Grammar School, Cornwall, 1833-35; King's College School, London, 1835-38; Magdalene College, Cambridge, 1838-42, B.A. (honours) in classics 1842, M.A. 1860. **Family:** Married Fanny Grenfell in 1844; two daughters and two sons. **Career:** Took holy orders: Curate, 1842-44, and Rector, 1844-75, Eversley, Hampshire; lecturer, Queen's College, London, 1848; Regius Professor of Modern History, Cambridge University, 1860-69; history tutor to the Prince of Wales, 1861; toured the West Indies, 1869-70; Canon of Chester Cathedral, 1869-73; made a lecture tour of the United States, 1873-74; Canon of Westminster Abbey, London, and chaplain to the Queen, 1873-75. **Died:** 23 January 1875. **Fiction:** *Westward Ho!*, 1855; *The Water-Babies*, 1863; *Hereward the Wake*, 1866.

* * *

It is a curious and perhaps significant fact that the most famous classics of childhood—*Alice, The Wind in the Willows, Peter Pan, The Water-Babies, The Hobbit*—are the works of men who did not ordinarily write for children. The place of *The Water-Babies* in this pantheon is also odd, in that to the vast majority of its readers it is only fragmentarily known; few of those who remember little Tom's adventures as a chimney-sweep could recount what became of him when he shed his human shell and turned into a water baby.

Charles Kingsley, in fact, wrote more for children that did Carroll, Grahame, Barrie, or Tolkien. *Westward Ho!* and *Hereward the Wake*, though not originally designed for young readers, have in their time pleased boys who, in spite of the inordinate length of both and the burden of the historical detail, have enjoyed the plethora of violence and killings, and perhaps the fierceness of the prejudices. (Children always enjoy taking sides, and Kingsley in this respect, and perhaps in others, remained a child to the end of his life.) *Madam How and Lady Why* (1870), an exposition of various natural phenomena, enjoyed a certain popularity with Victorian children. *The Heroes* (1855) has never been displaced from its position as one of the finest retellings of the Greek myths. It was written as a counter-blast to the versions that had appeared a few years earlier in Hawthorne's *Wonder-Book* (1851) and *Tanglewood Tales* (1853), which had given an incongruously cosy Victorian domestic background to these savage epics, and which Kingsley considered "distressingly vulgar." Only in this book did Kingsley restrain his urge to preach and expound and invove his readers in his views and prejudices; he might invest his Greek heroes with Christian virtues, but he delivers no lectures in so doing, and it is a marvellously realized, compellingly told piece of narration.

The Water-Babies in contrast is seriously flawed by the author's obtrusion of himself. He felt passionately on many topics, from the undesirable racial characteristics of everybody except the English and the Scots to the employment of child chimney-sweeps; from the erroneous views of the scientists of his day to the right hour that a gentleman should eat his dinner, and his lectures on all these make four-fifths of the book almost unreadable. But this only proves the amazing potency of the opening chapters, which have passed into the mythology of English childhood. "Once upon a time," the book begins, "there was a little chimney-sweep, and his name was Tom." Kinglsey takes no sentimental view of him; he is a cheerful, godless little pagan who "cried when he had to climb the dark flues, rubbing his poor knees and elbows raw" and laughed "the other half of the day when he was tossing half-pennies with the other boys, or playing leap-frog over the posts, or bowling stones at the horses' legs as they trotted by." Nor is Tom potentially any better than his master, the brutish Mr. Grimes, to emulate whom is his greatest ambition.

In a beautiful evocation of a midsummer early morning, Tom and Mr. Grimes leave the town, fringed with its coal-mines, and set out through the sleeping countryside to sweep the chimneys at Harthover Place. The Place is a vast and sprawling mansion of many styles and many flues, and Tom loses his way and comes down in "a room the like of which he had never seen before....He had never been in gentlefolks' rooms but when the carpets were all up, and the curtains down, and the furniture huddled together under a cloth." This room is all furnished and hung in white, and in the bed there sleeps a little girl. Almost the same moment that he sees her he sees himself in the glass, "a little ugly, black, ragged figure with bleared eyes and grinning white teeth....And Tom, for the first time in his life, found out that he was dirty." Ashamed and angry he tries to escape up the chimney, but wakes the little girl. The hue and cry that follows is powerfully drawn; the chase over the fells, shimmering with heat, Tom's thirst, the sound of the water twinkling many hundreds of feet below, his perilous descent, his arrival at the schoolhouse, and then submersion in the stream.

It is at this point that the impetus of the narrative falters and never again picks up strength. Tom is now a water baby and, in the remaining chapters to which the foregoing was only a prelude, undergoes a form of purgation (though Kingsley, stout Protestant that he was, would have been appalled if this had been interpreted as a belief in the "Romish doctrine of purgatory"). He meets water creatures and learns not to tease them, he is taught valuable lessons by Mrs. Bedonebyasyoudid and Mrs. Doasyouwouldbedoneby, he swims to far-off places and generally proves himself, but the text is now so choked with asides and theorizing and moral reflections that it is very difficult to disentangle what is in fact happening to him. Kingsley believed passionately that a knowledge of and a love for the wonders of nature could redeem man. He had said this in *Glaucus* (1855), subtitled "The Wonders of the Shore," and again in *Madam How and Lady Why*. To him the glory of God was made manifest in, say, the marvellous way the caddis worm pupates, and he wanted every child to know facts like these. What does not seem to have occurred to him was that young readers have not the knowledge nor the experience to sift fact from fantasy. He roundly denounces the Cousin Cramchilds of his time who would say there could not be water babies and exhorts his readers not to believe them; he avers that porpoises are shiny because the fairies French polish them; he produces a preposterous and elaborately worked out anti-Darwin theory that gorillas evolved from lotus-eating humans. Might not then a child suppose the life cycle of the dragonfly to be similar flight of fancy? Kingsley seems to have been too absorbed in his own oratory to care. *The Water-Babies* is thus an extraordinary combination, a timeless, compelling opening followed by a mishmash of personal fads, written by a warm-hearted but essentially muddled man.

—Gillian Avery

LANG, Andrew

Nationality: British. **Born:** Born in Selkirk, Scotland, 31 March 1844. **Family:** Attended Selkirk High School; Edinburgh Academy, 1854-61; University of St. Andrews (editor, *St. Leonard's Magazine*), 1861-63; University of Glasgow, 1863-64; Loretto School, Musselburgh, 1864; Balliol College, Oxford (Snell exhibitioner), 1864-68, B.A. 1866. **Family:** Married Leonora Blanche Alleyne in 1875. **Career:** Fellow, Merton College, Oxford, 1868-75; freelance writer after 1875; general editor, English Worthies series, Longmans, 1885-87, and Bibliothèque de Corabas series, Nutt, 1887-96. Gifford Lecturer, University of St. Andrews, 1888; Ford Lecturer, Oxford University, 1904. LL.D.: University of St. Andrews, 1885; Oxford University, 1904. **Died:** 20 July 1912.

Fiction: *The Princess Nobody,* 1884; *The Gold of Fairnilee,* 1888; *Prince Prigion,* 1889; *Prince Ricardo of Pantouflia,* 1893; *Tales of a Fairy Court,* 1907; *The Gold of Fairnilee and Other Stories,* 1967.

* * *

Writing in 1889 in *The Child and His Book,* Mrs. E.M. Field stated that "At the present moment the fairy-tale seems to have given way entirely in popularity to the child's story of real life, the novel of childhood, in which no effort is spared to make children appear as they are." But just before the publication of the book early in 1891, she added a note: "Since the above was written eighteen months ago, the tide of popularity seems to have set strongly in the direction of the old fairy stories."

These two quotations epitomise Andrew Lang's most important contribution in the development of the literature of childhood: and this came about largely because of the scholarly interest in folklore which made him one of the most important of the folklorists and anthropologists of his age. From the point of view of the folklorists, Lang first became notable for his essay "Mythology and Fairy Tales" in 1873, his introduction to Mrs. Hunt's complete translation of the Grimm's *Märchen* in 1884, and his two books, *Custom and Myth* (1884) and *Myth, Ritual, and Religion* (1887), the second of which contained a long section on folktales and fairy lore generally.

His writings for children began rather tentatively in 1884 with the short fairy story *The Princess Nobody* which he constructed most ingeniously to fit a large number of illustrations by Richard ("Dicky") Doyle which had appeared in 1869 to accompany (but not illustrate) poems by William Allingham. This charming tale was constructed on the lines of a traditional fairytale: issued in an edition of 10,000 copies it did not, however, reach a second edition, and was buried in oblivion until 1955 when it was included in *Modern Fairy Stories,* edited by Roger Lancelyn Green.

He followed this with *The Gold of Fairnilee,* a tale based on the Scottish Ballads and the fairy lore of the Border Country which was his home from his birth in 1844 until 1868. As a boy he and his brother and several others from his hometown of Selkirk were accustomed to meet every Saturday evening in a barn to hear local folktales and legends told by an old shepherd. Lang wrote that people in the Border Country believed in fairies "even when my father was a boy," and it is to the Fairyland, "which paid a fiend to Hell," that Randal of Fairnilee is carried by the Fairy Queen, even as Thomas the Rhymer had been, and from which Jean rescues him as Janet had rescued Tamlin in the ballad—in time to find the legendary Gold of Fairnilee for which Lang and his brother John had so often searched in vain.

The Fairyland of traditional belief did not prove popular, though of the few literary expeditions thither Lang's is outstanding the best. Perhaps for this reason his next venture was into the realm explored by the ladies of the *Cabinet des Fées* and so brilliantly exploited by Thackeray in *The Rose and the Ring.*

Prince Prigio and its slightly less successful sequel, *Prince Ricardo,* make an outstanding contribution to the literary fairy story as opposed to the traditional type, and seems to be accepted now as a classic in its own particular genre. In both these books Lang's knowledge of the Märchen of the world is given brilliant play, accepting the "rules" of the typical literary Fairyland with absolute gravity and following them to their logical conclusions. The humour and a tang of underlying irony make them two books which can be enjoyed by adults as well as children. *Prince Prigio* certainly illustrated C.S. Lewis's dictum that "a children's book which is enjoyed by children only is a bad children's book: the good ones last."

Lang turned back once more Prigio's Kingdom of Pantouflia in *Tales of a Fairy Court,* but with little of his earlier success, though in one or two of the stories the magic touch is still visible.

But good though the best of his original stories are, their excellencies have, from the start, tended to be eclipsed by the series of traditional tales which he chose, edited and occasionally retold, of which the first volume, *The Blue Fairy Book,* appeared in time for the same Christmas of 1889 as *Prince Prigio;* and it was on account of the unexpected popularity of this and its first sequel, *The Red Fairy Book,* the following year that Mrs. Field felt herself obliged to add the footnote quoted above.

The Blue Fairy Book was a complete gamble which Lang must have persuaded his friend and publisher, Charles Longman, to undertake—and which Longman probably risked on the strength of Lang's name, which was still very high in the literary world of the day. It appeared in an edition of 5,000 copies, and its success was instantaneous. By the time *The Yellow Fairy Book* (the fourth) appeared in 1894, the first edition was of 15,000.

The series finally consisted of 25 annual volumes, 12 of which were Fairy Books. But several others such as *The Arabian Nights,* two *Romance* books and the final *Strange Story Book* come almost within the category of Fairy Stories. And a volume outside the series, *Tales of Troy and Greece,* presents the greatest of the ancient Greek stories entirely in Lang's own retelling, and is still rivalled only by Kingsley's *The Heroes* (1855).

In the preface to the last of the actual Fairy Books (the *Lilac*) Lang wrote: "My part has been that of Adam, according to Mark Twain, in the Garden of Eden. Eve worked, Adam superintended; I find out where the stories are, and advise, and, in short, superintend. *I do not write the stories out of my own head.* The reputation of having written all the fairy books (a European reputation in nurseries and the United States of America) is 'the burden of an honour unto which I was not born....'"

But Lang's vast knowledge of the wide world's folklore and his magic touch in preparing the work of others for publication (and helped by the superbly complementary accompaniment of H.J. Ford's illustrations) make classics of these unrivalled collections, and, even more than his outstanding contribution to the history of Fairyland, ensure him a high place in the history of children's literature.

—Roger Lancelyn Green

LEAR, Edward

Nationality: British. **Born:** London, 12 May 1812. **Education:** Studied at Sass's School of Art, London, 1835, 1849; Royal Academy, London, 1850-52; studied painting with Holman Hunt. **Career:** Freelance artist after 1827, and teacher after 1830; assistant to the artists Prideaux Selby and John Gould; illustrated the animals at the home of the Earl of Derby, 1832-37; lived in Rome, 1837-45; gave drawing lessons to Queen Victoria, 1846. Exhibited at the Royal Academy, London, 1850-73. Lived in Italy and the Mediterranean, 1846-49, and in San Remo, Italy, 1868-88. **Died:** 29 January 1888. **Verse:** *A Book of Nonsense,* 1846, revised edition, 1861; *Nonsense Songs, Stories, Botany, and Alphabets,* 1870; *More Nonsense,* 1871; *Laughable Lyrics,* 1876; *Nonsense Songs and Stories,* 1894; *Queery Leary Nonsense,* 1911; *The Complete Nonsense Book,* 1912; *The Lear Omnibus (A Book of Lear),* 1938; *The Complete Nonsense,* 1947; *Teapots and Quails and Other New Nonsenses,* 1953; *For Lovers of Birds [Cats, Gardens and Flowers, Food and Drink],* 4 vols., 1978; *Gromboolian Poems,* 1983; *A Book of Learned Nonsense,* 1987.

* * *

When Edward Lear was a young man, he went to live at Knowsley Hall, the home of the Earls of Derby. At this time he was a natural history illustrator, and he had been commissioned to paint the birds and animals in Lord Derby's menagerie. At Knowsley he met "half the fine people of the day," but did not altogether like them. He wrote to a friend: "The uniform apathetic tone assumed by lofty society irks me *dreadfully,* nothing I long for half so much as to giggle heartily and to hop on one leg down the great gallery—but I dare not." Instead, he began to write his limericks. As apathy denied life, so also did the improving tale, for it disclaimed children as they were in favour of children as they ought to be:

There was an old man of Hong Kong,
Who never did anything wrong;
He lay on his back, with his head in a sack,
That innocuous old man of Hong Kong.

With the decorous and perfectly innocuous safely hidden away, Lear's real people could indulge in amiable excess:

There was a Young Girl of Majorca,
Whose aunt was a very fast walker;
She walked seventy miles, and leaped fifteen stiles,
Which astonished that Girl of Majorca.

Beyond the restraints of propriety where those imposed by life itself. "There's something in the world amiss will be unravelled by and by," Lear would quote in his diary. In his own case, epilepsy imposed an isolating barrier which he never broke down.

In his writing such anomalies might cause embarrassment: they could also be the source of real suffering. In the Pelican Chorus, the apparent affliction suffered by the King of the Cranes is politely ignored. With the Daddy Long-legs and the Fly, however, it is all far more serious and distressing. Each to the other seems fine and composed, and yet.... "Why," asks Mr. Daddy Long-Legs, "do you never come to court?"

"O Mr. Daddy Long-legs,"
Said Mr. Floppy Fly,
"It's true I never go to court,
And I will tell you why.
If I had six long legs like yours,
At once I'd go to court!
But oh! I can't, because *my* legs
Are so extremely short."

Mr. Daddy Long-legs also has his secret sadness. He, who once sang so beautifully, can no longer do so. But there is a remedy: they can escape to a land where none of this will matter any more:

Then Mr. Daddy Long-legs
And Mr. Floppy Fly
Rushed downward to the foamy sea
With one sponge-taneous cry;
And there they found a little boat,
Whose sails were pink and gray;
And off they sailed among the waves,
Far, and far away.
They sailed across the silent main
And reached the great Gromboolian plain;
And there they play for evermore
At battlecock and shuttledoor.

This is where Lear takes the children. Together they set out on their long and difficult journey. You must have courage to go to sea in a sieve, or indeed to sail away for a year and a day, but this courage is rewarded. There is no chance of the fainthearted following you. Critical, unimaginative adults are left behind. When the Jumblies returned home,

...every one said, "If we only live,
We too will go to sea in a Sieve,—
To the hills of the Chankly Bore!"

but we know perfectly well that they will not.

Of course, you may discover when you reach the sunset isles of Boshen, that you have moved from loneliness into loneliness; neither the Yonghy Bonghy Bò nor the Dong could redeem their isolation. There is sadness even here. But, in the end, it is all a game, perhaps of battlecock and shuttledoor, certainly of words and of the imagination. This is what gives it its safety. "There only remains a general, but very strong, pervading sense of well-being and innate rectitude from the standpoint of eight years," a child friend said of Lear. "I knew he was 'safe' and that I was safe and that we were all safe together, and that suspicions might at once be put aside." In a potentially alien world, Lear made children feel secure:

How pleasant to know Mr. Lear!
Who has written such volumes of stuff!
Some think him ill-tempered and queer,
But a few think him pleasant enough.

His mind is concrete and fastidious,
His nose is remarkable big;
His visage is more or less hideous,
His beard it resembles a wig.

As a child you may feel yourself to be strange and different, you know you can never be perfect; but there is no need to worry, for in an imaginary world where people have unlikely noses and legs and weird modes of expression, where they seek out oddities with whom they can identify themselves, and where they find kindness and spontaneity, you are never likely to feel alone. It is in this that we find Lear's influence on the children's writers who came after him.

—Vivien Noakes

MacDONALD, George

Nationality: British. **Born:** Near Huntly, Aberdeenshire, 10 December 1824. **Education:** King's College, University of Aberdeen, 1840-45, M.A. 1845; Congregationalist Theological College, Highbury, London, 1848-50. **Family:** Married Louisa Powell in 1850 (died 1902); 11 children. **Career:** Private tutor in London, 1845-48; minister, Trinity Congregational Church, Arundel, Sussex, 1850-53; lecturer and preacher in Manchester, 1855-56, Hastings, Sussex, 1857-59, and London, from 1859; editor, with Norman MacLeod, *Good Words for the Young* magazine, London, 1870-72; lived in Bordighera, Italy, in later life. LL.D.: University of Aberdeen, 1868. Granted Civil List pension, 1877. **Died:** 18 September 1905. **Fiction:** *Dealings with the Fairies,* 1867; *At the Back of the North Wind,* 1870; *Ranald Bannerman's Boyhood,* 1871; *The Princess and the Goblin,* 1871; *Gutta-Percha Willie, the Working Genius,* 1873; *The Wise Woman (A Double Story; The Lost Princess),* 1875; *Sir Gibbie,* 1879; *The Princess and Curdie,* 1882; *A Rough Shaking,* 1890; *The Light Princess and Other Fairy Tales,* 1893; *The Fairy Tales,* 5 vols., 1904; *The Gifts of the Child Christ,* 2 vols., 1973.

* * *

George MacDonald was a singular 19th-century writer whose outstanding talent for crossing literary types and age barriers makes critical discussion of his writings difficult. More than any writer of his time, he understood the symbolic richness of the traditional fairytale and worked to expand its dimensions. As a teller of fanciful tales, he is unequalled. It is his unusual mastery of the parable form, converting it, as he did, into a sort of allegorical fantasy, called a *fairytale,* which continues to attract modern writers of children's books to his stories. He possessed a fully integrated genius, whereby the creations of faerie lore and the realities of his own childhood were one; and it is this feature that characterizes him best.

Typical of his lifelong experimentation with the parable-fairytale form, or as he later designated it, " the double story," is his first and quite successful prose narrative, *Phantastes* (1858). Into it, he put a multifarious assortment of lyrics, chivalric Spenserian ballads, frame-stories, and imaginative beings related to his reading of Hoffmann's *Golden Pot,* Novalis, and Fouqué's *Undine,* his favorite fairytale. In type, *Phantastes* defies strict classification; it is in subject-matter most like the *volksmärchen*: an episode string of nature-parables focusing around the youthful hero Anodos and his lessons of self-renunciation. What the plot lacks in consistency of design, it compensates for by its symbolic depth. Contained in this story and its later companion, *Lilith,* are passages of double parable writing—for example the tale of Cosmo—which place MacDonald, unrivalled in this form, with Bunyan and Spenser.

During the 1870s MacDonald did most of his best writing for children. He edited *Good Words for the Young* and seralized *At the Back of the North Wind* in it, following with a story of his boyhood reminiscences, *Ranald Bannerman's Boyhood.* And in 1872 he published his second classic, *The Princess and the Goblin,* and *The Wise Woman: A Parable,* three years later. In these books—not originally limited to any certain age—MacDonald fully demonstrated his craft as a writer of children's books.

All of his stories have in them the moral fabric of parables. Educational in thrust, each tale contains a basic plot—Diamond, the coachman's son, takes up with Mistress North Wind who becomes his flying tutoress (*At the Back of the North Wind*); Princess Irene and Curdie, the miner's son, rid the royal city of Gwyntystorm of its corruptors (The Princess and Curdie books); and in *The Wise Woman,* his most lucid and long parable, Princess Rosamond and a shepherd's daughter are taught by a beatific old woman in a cottage in the woods. Simple contrasts are readily made between rich and poor, greed and charity, beauty and ugliness, youth and age, selfishness and true obedience—popular lessons of fairyland. Cannily the reader learns that appearances are not everything ("Little Daylight"), that true knowledge comes by acceptance of self-sacrifice and dependency on another ("The History of Photogen and Nycteris"), and, finally, in the best symbolic tale, "The Golden Key," that the source of all desire (imagination?) itself is found in a cosmic search up into the rainbow. But in spite of the teasing enchantment and obvious didacticism at work in the stories, there is always—most critics contend—something more than allegorical meaning in them.

As writer MacDonald claimed that his "aim" was to bring about "logical conviction" in his readers by creating a "mood-engendering" sensation: "The best thing you can do for your fellow, next to rousing his conscience, is—not to give him things to think about, but to wake things up that are in him; or say, to make him think things for himself." Transparency of thought and feeling is what one reacts to most in his stories. Like the Princess and Curdie, as they stand before the youthful but wise grandmother, the reader continually asks:

> "What does it all mean, Grandmother?" she sobbed and burst into fresh tears.
>
> "It means, my love, that I did not mean to show myself. Curdie is not yet able to believe some things. Seeing is not believing—it is only seeing."

Meaning in all his stories is linked up, at one point, with an attitude of childlikeness, his lifelong theme and concern.

There is throughout his writings a philosophical preoccupation with the conversion of evil into goodness and death into life. Graphically he sketches—in his best works—*Phantastes, At the Back of the North Wind,* The Princess books, "The Golden Key," *The Wise Woman, Sir Gibbie,* and *Lilith*—his own reformed picture of Scottish Calvinism transposed into fairytale language and scenes. This he does by placing the child in the center; predestination, for instance, becomes the prodding voice of North Wind, who explains to Diamond that he is limited only by what he *really* wants to do, which is the best way home. Good and Evil are no longer absolutes in his parables, as they are in most fairytales, but take part in the living process of getting better, of recovering from the illness of self. One mounts repeatedly in his fantasies the narrow stairs of submission that lead to the grandmother's garret room of rebirth and instruction.

All of this is to say that MacDonald's strong beliefs and cosmic vision of the role of the child in the universe quite naturally led him to select the fairytale-parable as the ideal form: in it he found poetic liberty of expression, symbolic regularity, and a disregard for age levels which allowed him to retell many of his childhood dreams and discoveries in Huntly, where he had known the art of castle-building as well as harsh discipline. As he grew older, he used the ordinary fairytale to convey, through his own sacramental symbolism in *Lilith,* his visionary romance of growing old, what C.S. Lewis defined as "good Death": the happy ending.

The word "homesickness" can be applied to all of MacDonald's books. His children's classics have in them crystal, descriptive and cosy passages of interlacing filial relationships which are in their beauty and provocative strength unsurpassed by any other author of the period. And with the recent return to the family unit in many modern children's books and revival of interest in the fairytale, it can safely be predicted that MacDonald will go on being rediscovered as the patriarch of the child and of the Victorian household.

—Glenn Edward Sadler

MARRYAT, Frederick

Nationality: British. **Born:** Westminster, London, 10 July 1792. **Education:** Educated privately. **Family:** Married Catherine Shairp in 1819; four sons and seven daughters, including the novelist Florence Marryat. **Military Service:** Joined the Royal Navy, 1806; sailed as a midshipman on the *Impérieuse,* under Lord Cochrane, 1806-09, in the flagship *Centaur,* in the Mediterranean, 1810, and on the *Aeolus* and *Spartan* in the West Indies and off the coast of North America, 1811-12; sailed to the West Indies on the *Espiègle,* 1813; Lieutenant of the *Newcastle,* off the coast of North America, 1814 until invalided home, 1815; appointed Commander, 1815; commanded the sloop *Beaver* cruising off St. Helena to guard against the escape of Napoleon, 1820-22; involved in suppression of Channel smuggling, on the *Rosario,* 1822; sailed in the *Larne* to the East Indies, 1823, and served in the Burmese war: Senior Naval Officer at Rangoon, 1824; commanded expedition up the Bassein River, 1825; appointed Captain of the *Tees,* 1825, and returned in her to England, 1826: C.B. (Companion, Order of the Bath), for services in Burma, 1826; commanded the *Ariadne* in the Atlantic service, 1828 until he retired to become full-time writer, 1830; editor, *Metropolitan Magazine,* London, 1832-35; lived in Brussels, 1836, Canada and the United States, 1837-39, and London, 1839-43; settled on a farm, Langham Manor, in Norfolk, 1843. **Awards:** Royal Humane Society Gold Medal, 1818. Fellow of the Royal Society, 1819. Member, Legion of Honour, 1833. **Died:** 9 August 1848. **Fiction:** *Masterman Ready,* 1841-42; *Narrative of the Travels and Adventures of Monsieur Violet in California, Sonora, and Western Texas,* 1843; *The Settlers in Canada,* 1844; *The Mission,* 1845; *The Children of the New Forest,* 1847; *The Little Savage,* completed by Frank S. Marryat, 1848-49.

* * *

Frederick Marryat is remarkably good, and not matched as an adventure story writer until the time of Stevenson. His impressive naval career is the clue to his writings, for Marryat, like many of his successors, learned to write adventure stories by living a life which sounded like one. As Conrad said, "his novels are not the outcome of his art, but of his character, like the deeds that make up his record of naval service."

Marryat's storytelling is not entirely artless, however, for, by the time he turned to writing children's books in the 1840s, he was able to draw not only upon a decade of writing sea stories such as *Mr. Midshipman Easy* (1836) in the manner of a Regency Smollett (and mixing with Dickens and other leading writers of the day), but also on the tradition of adventure stories established by Defoe's *Robinson Crusoe* and extended especially by the historical novels of Scott and the *Leatherstocking* tales of Cooper.

Marryat's children's books, then, *Masterman Ready, Settlers in Canada, The Mission, The Little Savage,* and *The Children of the New Forest,* belong to the line associated with the great writers of adventure stories for adults, especially the tradition of the Robinsonnades, but modified by Marryat in ways he thought appropriate for younger readers. His naval experiences brought to his tales of battles, storms, and shipwrecks a racy realism, while his Tory radicalism and warm humanity often combine to temper a deliberate didacticism, in ways which can be disconcerting and refreshing.

Masterman Ready, Marryat's first children's book, is a good example. Writing for his own children who had asked for a story like *The Swiss Family Robinson,* Marryat set out to produce a much more accurate tale of shipwreck and life on a desert island than Wyss had done. The ship carrying the Seagrave family to Australia is deserted after a gale, and the family have to fend for themselves on a small island, helped by kind old Masterman Ready. Marryat's account of hurricanes and seamanship, and of the wild life on the island, achieves real authenticity. At the same time Marryat's moral didacticism leads him to show the practical man's response in Mr. Seagrave's religious philosophy. But the dangers of an excessively rigid approach are avoided to a large degree, not only by Marryat's powers to surprise one didactically, as when Mr. Seagrave foresees the end of British imperialism in chapter 27, but also through the ways Marryat dramatises and humanises his story. Tommy, the Seagraves' six-year-old son, is a naughty boy who not only gets into silly scrapes through eating too many castor oil beans, for example, but is actually responsible for the book's tragic ending. Savages attack the Seagraves' stockade quite unsuccessfully until the supply of water is exhausted unexpectedly because of Tommy's laziness. Ready is seriously wounded in the attempt to get more water, and though the Seagraves are rescued, the old mariner dies of his wounds. "What a lesson it will be to Tommy when he is old enough to comprehend fully the consequences of his conduct," says his overpious father, but the dying man's last words are that the little boy shall never know the cause of Ready's death. So the story ends on a note, not of triumph, but of relief mingled with gravity.

Settlers in Canada initially seems to owe more to Cooper's stories of North American Indians than to Defoe, and Marryat also knew Canada at first hand, so his account of the Campbell family's settling near Lake Ontario carries real authority. The story of how the immigrants deal with wolves, survive a forest fire, and eventually rescue two prisoners from hostile Indians provides a lively narrative, and we are meant to feel that the prosperity Dr. Campbell achieves in the last chapter is more that the conventional happy ending, but represents genuine reward for the decorum maintained in a variety of testing circumstances. What gives the book its distinctive flavour, however, is the manner Marryat, in ways which are his distinctive modification of Defoe, vividly describes the more domestic adventures of the Campbells, the way they build a house, learn to shoot and fish, sow crops and begin to trade furs. This is a Robinsonnade with a difference, and it is one that writers such as Ballantyne and Henty were to learn from.

Marryat use foreign settings for three other children's books, *Narrative of the Travels and Adventures of Monsieur Violet, The Mission,* and *The Little Savage.* Of these the least successful is *Monsieur Violet,* for though the tale of how the French hero and his nine-year-old son emigrated and settled among the Snake Indians of Western America is potentially exciting, the story is told in such a halting fashion, with lengthy historical and topographical digressions and an inconsequential ending, as to make it almost unreadable. *The Mission* opens promisingly with an account of how Alexander Wilmot, one of Marryat's most "manly" heroes, sets out for South Africa to search for an aunt shipwrecked off the coast some years before. But after some early encounters with wild animals and the threat of hostile natives, the narrative peters out when the hero discovers his aunt is quite definitely dead barely half way through the book. *The Little Savage* is even more disjointed, though here we know that Marrayat's failing health was responsible. The book plunges straight into a sharp and ugly account given by a nameless boy of his desperate plight on a desert island where he is completely alone except for the company of a morose and cruel sailor who treats him as a slave. Only when the older man is blinded in a storm, and the young boy is able to turn on him with a knife, does the sailor begin to treat him as a human being. The drama of the opening is gradually dissipated by the theatricality of the subsequent plot, and the work of an inferior hand is clear in the final chapters, but the power of that opening is not easily forgotten.

Happily Marryat's last completed children's book, *The Children of the New Forest,* has few such lapses, and not only established the popularity of the historical tale for children but set standards which later writers have not found it easy to emulate. Scott's *Waverley* novels had produced a host of successors, but Marryat was the first writer to produce a historical novel for children, in his depiction of the adventures of the Beverley family, who, when their Royalist father is killed at Naseby, are protected from possible Cromwellian persecution by an old forester, Jacob Armitage, who hides them in his cottage in the New Forest. Marryat refuses to over-simplify the issues which lay behind the Civil War, and, though his central characters are Royalists, the Parliamentary superintendent of the New Forest and his daughter Patience are portrayed with equal sympathy. This is no case of the Wrong but Romantic versus the Right but Repulsive. Marryat also deliberately avoids romantic "tushery," and though Prince Charles does appear briefly, there are no interviews with Cromwell or overhead asides from John Milton.

Marryat was no great stylist, but is a master at describing the details of particular scenes or episodes in clear and simple language, and in describing the way in which Jacob trains the Beverley children to support themselves in the New Forest, farming, cooking, looking after the animals, he painted a series of scenes which have fascinated children in every generation. In a sense the Beverleys are as shipwrecked in the New Forest as the Seagraves were on their island. But though the acquisition and exploitation of land can perhaps be related to British imperialism, it would be a mistake to interpret Marryat purely in those terms. Playing at home-making is an activity which absorbs many children, of course, offering a symbolic form of growth and creativity in a world of insecurity and stress. This is perhaps why children have enjoyed Marryat's books for so long.

By the time Marryat died, the foundations of the 19th-century adventure story for children were firmly laid. Whether in stories of shipwreck, of history, or of contemporary adventure, he had pointed the way and produced exciting examples where previously only adult or unsatisfactory works existed. His influence on writers about the sea has stretched from Kingston to Masefield and Peter Dawlish, and as a writer of contemporary adventure tales from Ballantyne to Ivan Southall, but, most of all perhaps, he has been an indirect but potent force in the development of the historical novel from Henty to the present day.

—Dennis Butts

MEADE, L.T.

Nationality: Irish. **Born:** Elizabeth Thomasina Meade in Brandon, County Cork, in 1854. **Family:** Married Alfred Toulmin Smith in 1879; one son and two daughters. **Career:** Worked in the British Museum, London; editor, with A.A. Leith, *Atalanta* girls' magazine, London, for six years. **Died:** 26 October 1914.

Fiction: *Lotty's Last Home,* 1875; *A Knight of Today,* 1877; *Scamp and I,* 1877; *Bel Marjory,* 1878; *The Children's Kingdom,* 1878; *Your Brother and Mine (Outcast Robin),* 1878; *Water Lilies and Other Tales,* 1878; *Dot and Her Treasures,* 1879; *Water Gipsies,* 1879; *A Dweller in Tents,* 1880; *Mou-Setsé,* with *The Orphan's Pilgrimage* by T. von Gumpert, 1880; *The Floating Light of Ringfinnan, and Guardian Angels,* 1880; *Mother Herring's Chicken,* 1881; *A London Baby,* 1882; *The Children's Pilgrimage,* 1883; *Hermie's Rose-Buds and Other Stories,* 1883; *The Autocrat of the Nursery,* 1884; *A Band of Three,* 1884; *Scarlet Anemones,* 1884; *The Two Sisters,* 1884; *The Angel of Love,* 1885; *A Little Silver Trumpet,* 1885; *A World of Girls,* 1886; *Daddy's Boy,* 1887; *The O'Donnells of Inchfawn,* 1887; *The Palace Beautiful,* 1887; *Sweet Nancy,* 1887; *Deb and the Duchess,* 1888; *Nobody's Neighbors,* 1888; *A Farthingful,* 1889; *The Golden Lady,* 1889; *The Lady of the Forest,* 1889; *The Little Princess of Tower Hill,* 1889; *Polly, A New-Fashioned Girl,* 1889; *Poor Miss Carolina,* 1889; *The Beresford Prize,* 1890; *Dickory Dock,* 1890; *Engaged to Be Married,* 1890; *Heart of Gold,* 1890; *Just a Love Story,* 1890; *Marigold,* 1890; *Hepsy Gipsy,* 1891; *The Children of Wilton Chase,* 1891; *A Sweet Girl-Graduate,* 1891; *Little Mary and Other Stories,* 1891; *Bashful Fifteen,* 1892; *Four on an Island,* 1892; *Out of the Fashion,* 1892; *A Ring of Rubies,* 1892; *Beyond the Blue Mountains,* 1893; *A Young Mutineer,* 1893; *Betty,* 1894; *In an Iron Grip,* 1894; *Red Rose and Tiger Lily,* 1894; *Girls, New and Old,* 1895; *The Least of These and Other Stories,* 1895; *Catalina, Art Student,* 1896; *A Girl in Ten Thousand,* 1896; *Good Luck,* 1896; *A Little Mother to the Others,* 1896; *Merry Girls of England,* 1896; *Playmates,* 1896; *The White Tzar,* 1896; *The House of Surprises,* 1896; *Bad Little Hannah,* 1897; *A Handful of Silver,* 1897; *Wild Kitty,* 1897; *Cave Perilous,* 1898; *A Bunch of Cherries,* 1898; *The Cleverest Woman in England,* 1898; *The Girls of St. Wode's,* 1898; *Mary Gifford, M.B.,* 1898; *The Rebellion of Lil Carrington,* 1898; *The Siren,* 1898; *Adventuress,* 1899; *All Sorts,* 1899; *The Odds and the Evens,* 1899; *Light o' the Morning,* 1899; *Wages,* 1900; *A Plucky Girl,* 1900; *The Beauforts,* 1900; *A Brave Poor Thing,* 1900; *Daddy's Girl,* 1900; *Miss Nonentity,* 1900; *Seven Maids,* 1900; *A Sister of the Red Cross,* 1900; *The Time of Roses,* 1900; *Wheels of Iron,* 1901; *The Blue Diamond,* 1901; *Cosey Corner,* 1901; *Girls of the True Blue,* 1901; *The New Mrs. Lascelles,* 1901; *A Stumble by the Way,* 1901; *A Very Naughty Girl,* 1901; *Drift,* 1902; *Girls of the Forest,* 1902; *Margaret,* 1902; *The Pursuit of Penelope,* 1902; *Queen Rose,* 1902; *The Rebel of the School,* 1902; *The Princess Who Gave All Away, and The Naughty One of the Family,* 1902; *The Squire's Little Girl,* 1902; *Through Peril for a Wife,* 1902; *The Witch Maid,* 1903; *The Burden of Her Youth,* 1903; *By Mutual Consent,* 1903; *A Gay Charmer,* 1903; *The Manor School,* 1903; *Peter the Pilgrim,* 1903; *Resurgam,* 1903; *Rosebury,* 1903; *That Brilliant Peggy,* 1903; *A Maid of Mystery,* 1904; *The Adventures of Miranda,* 1904; *At the Back of the World,* 1904; *The Lady Cake-Maker,* 1904; *Castle Poverty,* 1904; *The Girls of Mrs. Pritchard's School,* 1904; *Love Triumphant,* 1904; *A Madcap,* 1904; *A Modern Tomboy,* 1904; *Nurse Charlotte,* 1904; *Petronella, and the Coming of Polly,* 1904; *Wilful Cousin Kate,* 1905; *Bess of Delaney's,* 1905; *A Bevy of Girls,* 1905; *Dumps,* 1905; *His Mascot,* 1905; *Little Wife Hester,* 1905; *Loveday,* 1905; *Old Readmoney's Daughter,* 1905; *Virginia,* 1905; *The Colonel and the Boy,* 1906; *The Face of Juliet,* 1906; *The Girl and Her Fortune,* 1906; *The Heart of Helen,* 1906; *The Hill-Top Girl,* 1906; *The Home of Sweet Content,* 1906; *In the Flower of Her Youth,* 1906; *The Maid with the Goggles,* 1906; *Sue,* 1906; *Turquoise and Ruby,* 1906; *Victory,* 1906; *The Colonel's Conquest,* 1907; *The Curse of the Feverals,* 1907; *A Girl from America,* 1907; *The Home of Silence,* 1907; *Kindred Spirits,* 1907; *The Lady of Delight,* 1907; *Little Josephine,* 1907; *The Little School-Mothers,* 1907; *The Love of Susan Cardigan,* 1907; *The Red Cap of Liberty,* 1907; *The Red Ruth,* 1907; *The Scamp Family,* 1907; *Three Girls from School,* 1907; *The Aim of Her Life,* 1908; *A Lovely Fiend and Other Stories,* 1908; *The Court-Harman Girls,* 1908; *The Courtship of Sybil,* 1908; *Hetty Beresford,* 1908; *Sarah's Mother,* 1908; *The School Favourite,* 1908; *The School Queens,* 1908; *Aylwyn's Friends,* 1909; *Betty Vivian,* 1909; *Blue of the Sea,* 1909; *Brother or Husband,* 1909; *The Fountain of Beauty,* 1909; *I Will Sing a New Song,* 1909; *The Princess of the Revels,* 1909; *The Stormy Petrel,* 1909; *The A.B.C. Girl,* 1910; *Belinda Treherne,* 1910; *A Girl of Today,* 1910; *Lady Anne,* 1910; *Miss Gwendoline,* 1910; *Nance Kennedy,* 1910; *Pretty-Girl and the Others,* 1910; *Rose Regina,* 1910; *A Bunch of Cousins and the Barn "Boys,"* 1911; *Desborough's Wife,* 1911; *The Doctor's Children,* 1911; *For Dear Dad,* 1911; *The Girl from Spain,* 1911; *The Girls of Merton College,* 1911; *Mother and Son,* 1911; *Ruffles,* 1911; *The Soul of Margaret Rand,* 1911; *Daddy's Girl, and Consuelo's Quest of Happiness,* 1911; *Corporal Violet,* 1912; *A Girl of the People,* 1912; *Kitty O'Donovan,* 1912; *Lord and Lady Kitty,* 1912; *Love's Cross Roads,* 1912; *Peggy from Kerry,* 1912; *The Chesterton Girl Graduates,* 1913; *The Girls of Abinger Close,* 1913; *The Girls of King's Royal,* 1913; *The Passion of Kathleen Duveen,* 1913; *A Band of Mirth,* 1914; *Col. Tracy's Wife,* 1914; *Elizabeth's Prisoner,* 1914; *A Girl of High Adventure,* 1914; *Her Happy Face,* 1914; *The Queen of Joy,* 1914; *The Wooing of Monica,* 1914; *The Darling of the School,* 1915; *Greater Than Gold,* 1915; *Jill the Irresistible,* 1915; *Hollyhock,* 1916; *Madge Mostyn's Nieces,* 1916; *The Maid Indomitable,* 1916; *Mother Mary,* 1916; *Daughters of Today,* 1916; *Better Than Riches,* 1917; *The*

Fairy Godmother, 1917; *Miss Patricia,* 1925; *Roses and Thorns,* 1928; *In Time of Roses,* n.d.

* * *

L.T. Meade was a prolific and highly professional writer of fiction for the middle-class child. Her prodigious output was all designed, one might almost say packaged, to please particular sections of this readership, and for each group she drew upon the appropriate conventions of storytelling as they had been developed by her predecessors. Her personal touch was certain emotional intensity of tone, which might be sentimental, or wild and romantic, but always tended to highly coloured extremes.

During the 1870s she tried her hand at the street-arab stories which were a mainstay of "Sunday" writing for children, developed by Evangelical and humanitarian writers. They had a strengthening earnestness; but Meade took up the convention chiefly for its emotional appeal. Such a story is *Scamp and I,* in which little orphan Flo is attacked by ruffians and dies in a children's hospital, murmuring blessings upon the Queen; her mongrel Scamp perishes defending her. One cannot help feeling that its pathetic thrill is an indulgence, and lacks any sense of the real sufferings of others. In writing about middle-class children Meade adopts the convention of the "pickle," the small child who is innocently naughty, whose scrapes are either evidence of a sturdy independent spirit or the result of parental misunderstanding; these stories are vivid with the writer's own sentimental view of children, no more challenging than the emotionalism of the arab tales, but drawn perhaps from more personal feeling.

Many other kinds of story proved adaptable to Meade's purposes of exciting pleasurable emotion for her readers. *Four on an Island* is a Crusoe story; *Cave Perilous* an historical romance about Chartism; *A Sister of the Red Cross* a tale of love and marriage against an exotic background of nursing in the South African war, highly charged with patriotic and militaristic excitement; *Beyond the Blue Mountains* an allegory derived from *Pilgrim's Progress* but set in a flower-fairy children's world. In all of these the spirit of brave, upright, British childhood triumphs over all troubles, from laziness to storms at sea and hunger-maddened mobs.

It was in school stories for girls that Meade found the story patterns and setting which best suited her emotional romanticism. In them she stressed adolescent passions, especially in the relationships between the girls and their feelings towards their teachers. In *A World of Girls,* one of her most popular books, the headmistress, Miss Willis, is an adored mother-substitute intimately involved with her pupils' lives, and the emotional storms between the girls are at least as important as the improbable plot in which a baby sister is carried off by gypsies and rescued by a wild tomboy who has a magic way with fierce dogs. It was for her ability to manipulate a tale excitingly, and fill it unashamedly with intended emotion, that Meade won her enormous popularity; and in the school story she had a hand herself in the shaping of a convention which later writers like Angela Brazil were to take up.

—J.S. Bratton

MOLESWORTH, Mary Louisa (née Stewart)

Pseudonym: Ennis Graham. **Nationality:** British. **Born:** Rotterdam, Netherlands, 29 May 1839; grew up in Manchester, England. **Education:** Attended school in Lausanne, Switzerland; attended classes given by William Gaskell. **Family:** Married Richard Molesworth in 1861 (separated 1879); seven children. Lived in France and Germany, and in London after 1884. **Died:** 20 July 1921. **Fiction:** *Tell Me a Story* (as Ennis Graham), 1875; *Carrots* (as Ennis Graham), 1876; *The Cuckoo Clock* (as Ennis Graham), 1877; *Grandmother Dear,* 1878; *The Tapestry Room,* 1879; *A Christmas Child,* 1880; *Hermy,* 1880; *The Adventures of Herr Baby,* 1881; *Hoodie,* 1882; *Rosy,* 1882; *The Boys and I,* 1882; *Summer Stories for Boys and Girls,* 1882; *Two Little Waifs,* 1883; *Christmas-Tree Land,* 1883; *The Little Old Portrait (Edmee),* 1884; *Lettice,* 1884; *Us,* 1885; *A Charge Fulfilled,* 1886; *Silverthorns,* 1886; *Four Winds Farm,* 1886; *The Palace in the Garden,* 1887; *Little Miss Peggy,* 1887; *The Abbey by the Sea,* 1887; *A Christmas Posy,* 1888; *Five Minutes' Stories,* 1888; *The Third Miss St. Quentin,* 1888; *Neighbours,* 1889; *A House to Let,* 1889; *The Old Pincushion,* 1889; *The Rectory Children,* 1889; *Nesta,* 1889; *Great Uncle Hoot-Toot,* 1889; *Twelve Tiny Tales,* 1890; *Family Troubles,* 1890; *The Children of the Castle,* 1890; *Little Mother Bunch,* 1890; *The Green Casket and Other Stories,* 1890; *The Story of a Spring Morning and Other Tales,* 1890; *The Red Grange,* 1891; *The Bewitched Lamp,* 1891; *The Lucky Ducks and Other Stories,* 1891; *Nurse Heatherdale's Story,* 1891; *Sweet Content,* 1891; *Imogen,* 1892; *An Enchanted Garden,* 1892; *The Girls and I,* 1892; *Farthings,* 1892; *The Man with the Pan-Pipes and Other Stories,* 1892; *Robin Redbreast,* 1892; *The Next-Door House,* 1892; *Studies and Stories,* 1893; *The Thirteen Little Black Pigs and Other Stories,* 1893; *Mary,* 1893; *Blanche,* 1893; *Olivia,* 1894; *My New House,* 1894; *The Carved Lions,* 1895; *Opposite Neighbours and Other Stories,* 1895; *Sheila's Mystery,* 1895; *White Turrets,* 1895; *Friendly Joey and Other Stories,* 1896; *The Oriel Window,* 1896; *Philippa,* 1896; *Stories for Children in Illustration of the Lord's Prayer,* 1897; *Meg Langholme,* 1897; *Miss Mouse and Her Boys,* 1897; *Greyling Towers,* 1898; *The Magic Nuts,* 1898; *The Grim House,* 1899; *This and That,* 1899; *The Children's Hour,* 1899; *The Three Witches,* 1900; *The House That Grew,* 1900; *The Wood-Pigeons and Mary,* 1901; *"My Pretty" and Her Little Brother "Too,"* 1901; *The Blue Baby and Other Stories,* 1901; *Peterkin,* 1902; *The Mystery of the Pinewood, and Hollow Tree House,* 1903; *The Ruby Ring,* 1904; *The Bolted Door and Other Stories,* 1906; *Jasper,* 1906; *The Little Guest,* 1907; *Fairies—of Sorts,* 1908; *The February Boys,* 1909; *The Story of a Year,* 1910; *Fairies Afield,* 1911.

* * *

On re-reading Mary Louisa Molesworth's stories after a long interval—or perhaps reading some of them for the first time—one is immediately struck by the fact that they are indeed very readable. She was above all else a good teller of tales. Yet when we come to analyse the content of the stories themselves, there is little in the way of dramatic events to account for this. The drama, and thereby the interest of the story, comes from the life of the characters in what is largely an everyday setting. Her stories—the best ones at any rate, for she was uneven in the quality of her writing—pick up the characters at a particular period in their lives usually between about 5 and 12 years old. But we feel that each one had a life of his own before the story started and will continue to develop after the book has closed, whereas the events in so many children's books appear to exist in their own world, without a past or a future.

Perhaps one of the most noticeable characteristics of Molesworth's books is their ordinariness. Her children are all very "genteel," and even if they are poor they tend to have a middle-class background. For the most part the stories are set in the comfortably solid world of nurseries and nannies, of brothers and sisters in plenty, and loving mothers (who may alas often have to go to India, or, as in *Carrots,* to Algeria). The daily routine is firmly sketched and indeed provides a useful social study of the upper-middle-class child-world of the latter 19th century. Even the names given to the children are redolent of class and period: Hermione, Rosalys, Mavis. In the case of *Four Winds Farm,* where she is dealing with a boy from a *farm,* she gives him the improbable name of Gratian, to show his "difference."

Magic comes into a number of her stories, especially the more successful ones like *The Cuckoo Clock* and *The Tapestry Room,* but for the most part even here it is everyday life which provides the frame of the story, though some at least of the magic comes from the twilight world between reality and fantasy. It is the insight into the child's mind, with its inability to distinguish between actuality and imagination, which sets Molesworth apart from so many of her contemporaries. Behind many of her characters are careful observations of real children, their speech, their behaviour, and, even more important, their minds. There is poor Carrots, who genuinely believes he has found a "yellow sixpenny piece," and in no way connects it with the missing half-sovereign—"sovereigns" is a game about kings and queens! And Hermy, in the book of the same name, has great problems as to what is meant by truth, as far as the adults in her life are concerned. Molesworth is aware that such little things assume enormous proportions in the life of the very young. But there is one big difference at that age, in that time for the young is so relative. If you are only five, last week can be as far away as yesterday, and next year, when you will be *six,* is a lifetime away.

In her descriptions of school life, Molesworth is fair and understanding. Her school teachers, who cause so much trouble to the young (in *The Carved Lions* and *Hermy,* for example), are given their due, as if *we* should not find them so bad. For here, too, much of the trouble lies once more with the child's limited understanding of the grown-up world, and his own ability to explain a situation in everyday terms. We have all known the child for whom a toy, or even an invisible companion, were as real, if not more so, than the people around him, and the "untruths" arising from this state of affairs cannot be dealt with as with older children. It is to Molesworth's credit that in the days before there was so much talk of child psychology, she saw and understood this aspect of child behaviour, and wrote about it as a normal part of growing up, with all its fears and confidences, and in a way that small children would understand and accept. Her world of magic, too, is gentle and charming, of the sort to banish fear, coming in the wind or with dreams. But she can also give her fairy characters a personality of their own: the North and East Winds in *Four Winds Farm,* the Raven in *The Tapestry Room,* and the Cuckoo in *The Cuckoo Clock* are not always sweet and obliging, but can be cross and need humouring every bit as much as the kindliest adult in the real world.

Perhaps Molesworth's real fault lies in the amount she wrote, for some of her later books (and she lived until 1921) were repetitive, thin, and with a tendency to the sentimental, which the best of her books avoid. But her best is very good indeed. The merit of *The Cuckoo Clock, The Carved Lions, The Tapestry Room, Us,* and many others is manifest in the fact that they can still be read and enjoyed by young children of today, because they are good straightforward stories still, even if the world of nannies has passed away with the Indian Empire to which parents were so conveniently banished.

—Joyce Irene Whalley

OTIS, James

Nationality: American. **Born:** James Otis Kaler in Frankfort (now Winterport), Maine, 19 March 1848. **Education:** Attended at public schools in Maine. **Family:** Married Amy L. Scammon in 1898; two sons. **Career:** Journalist: worked for Boston *Journal* and New York papers; staff member, *Boys and Girls;* also a publicity man for a circus. Superintendent, South Portland schools, c. 1898. **Died:** 11 December 1912. **Fiction:** *Toby Tyler,* 1881; *Tim and Tip,* 1883; *Mr. Stubbs's Brother,* 1883; *Raiding the "Pearl,"* 1884; *Left Behind,* 1885; *Silent Pete,* 1886; *A Runaway Brig,* 1888; *The Castaways,* 1888; *Little Joe,* 1888; *The Braganza Diamond,* 1891; *Jack the Hunchback,* 1892; *Jenny Wren's Boarding House,* 1893; *Josiah in New York,* 1893; *The Search for the Silver City,* 1893; *The Boys' Revolt,* 1894; *Chasing a Yacht,* 1894; *Jerry's Family,* 1895; *Andy's Ward,* 1895; *How Tommy Saved the Barn,* 1895; *The Boys of 1745 at the Capture of Louisbourg,* 1895; *Ezra Jordan's Escape from the Massacre at Fort Loyall,* 1895; *An Island Refuge,* 1895; *Neal, the Miller,* 1895; *With Lafayette at Yorktown,* 1895; *Under the Liberty Tree,* 1896; *Teddy and Carrots,* 1896; *Admiral J. of Spurwick,* 1896; *The Boy Captain,* 1896; *On Schedule Time,* 1896; *A Short Cruise,* 1896; *At the Siege of Quebec,* 1897; *The Wreck of the Circus,* 1897; *The Signal Boys of '75,* 1897; *With Washington at Monmouth,* 1897; *When Israel Putnam Served the King,* 1898; *The Capture of the Laughing Mary,* 1898; *With Warren at Bunker Hill,* 1898; *A Cruise with Paul Jones,* 1898; *A Traitor's Escape,* 1898; *Corporal Lige's Recruit,* 1898; *Morgan, the Jersey Spy,* 1898; *Sarah Dillard's Ride,* 1898; *An Amateur Fireman,* 1898; A *District Messenger Boy, and A Necktie Party,* 1898; *Dick in the Desert,* 1898; *Joel Harford,* 1898; *The Princess and Joe Potter,* 1898; *The Boys of '98,* 1898; *The Charming Sally,* 1898; *Captain Tom,* 1899; *With Perry on Lake Erie,* 1899; *Chased Through Norway,* 1899; *Christmas at Deacon Hackett's,* 1899; *Down the Slope,* 1899; *Messenger No. 48,* 1899; *Wheeling for Fortune,* 1899; *A Tory Plot,* 1899; *With the Swamp Fox,* 1899; *Off Santiago with Sampson,* 1899; *When Dewey Came to Manila,* 1899; *At the Siege of Havana,* 1899; *Boston Boys of 1775,* 1900; *The Defense of Fort Henry,* 1900; *On the Kentucky Frontier,* 1900; *Aunt Hannah and Seth,* 1900; *Lobster Catchers,* 1900; *The Armed Ship America,* 1900; *Fighting for the Empire,* 1900; *With Prebble at Tripoli,* 1900; *Our Uncle, the Major,* 1901; *With Porter in the Essex,* 1901; *The Story of Old Falmouth,* 1901; *Inland Waterways,* 1901; *Larry Hudson's Ambition,* 1901; *With the Regulators,* 1901; *When We Destroyed the Gaspee,* 1901; *Amos Dunkel, Oarsman (A Struggle for Freedom),* 1901; *Reuben Green's Adventure at Yale,* 1902; *The Treasure of Cocos Island,* 1902; *Wan Lun and Dandy,* 1902; *The Cruise of the Enterprise,* 1902; *How the Twins Captured a Hessian,* 1902; *The Story of Pemaquid,* 1902; *With the Tresure-Hunters,* 1903; *With Rodgers on the President,* 1903; *Across the Delaware,* 1903; *Defending the Island,* 1904; *At the Siege of Detroit,* 1904; *Minute Boys* series, from 1904; *Dorothy's Spy,* 1904; *When Washington Served the King,* 1905; *Among the Fur Traders,* 1906; *The Light Keepers,* 1906; *Commodore Barney's Young Spies,* 1907; *The Wreck of* *the Ocean Queen,* 1907; *Aboard the Hylow on Sable Island Bank,* 1907; *Afloat in Freedom's Cause,* 1908; *The Cruise of the Phoebe,* 1908; *Two Stowaways Aboard the Ellen Maria,* 1908; *The Cruise of the Pickering,* 1909; *Found by the Circus,* 1909; *The Sarah Jane, Dicky Dalton, Captain,* 1909; *The Cruise of the Sally D.,* 1910; *Silver Fox Farm* series, 1910; *With Grant at Vicksburg,* 1910; *Calvert of Maryland,* 1910; *Mary of Plymouth,* 1910; *Peter of New Amsterdam* 1910; *Richard of Jamestown,* 1910; *Ruth of Boston,* 1910; *Stephen of Philadelphia,* 1910; *With Sherman to the Sea,* 1911; *The Camp on Indian Island,* 1911; *Old Ben,* 1911; *Boy Scouts* series, 1911; *Wanted and Other Stories,* 1912; *The Wreck of the Princess,* 1912; *Antoine of Oregon,* 1912; *Benjamin of Ohio,* 1912; *Hannah of Kentucky,* 1912; *Seth of Colorado,* 1912; *Martha of California,* 1913; *Philip of Texas,* 1913; *The Roaring Lions,* 1913; *Across the Range and Other Stories,* 1914.

* * *

Of James Otis's 150 books, only *Toby Tyler* can still be found on the library shelf. Otis's army of ragged newsboys, Revolutionary War Minute Boys, silver fox farmers, Boy Scouts, and wreck survivors have marched into oblivion. Today, they are more likely to be found housed in a special collection or at the historical society.

Toby Tyler, Otis's first novel, was his best and most successful. The story, about a red-headed, freckle-faced 10-year-old orphan who ran away with the circus, tugged at the hearts of his readers a hundred years ago and still has the power to affect us. In his first job with the circus as a candy butcher, Toby is brutalized by his employers, Job Lord and Jacobs. Later, when he is trained to ride, Mr. Castle educates him with the whip. He is befriended by Old Ben, the monkey wagon driver, little Ella, the equestrienne, Sam Treat, the human skeleton, and Lilly, the fat lady. Toby finds comfort, as well, from his pet monkey. Mr. Stubbs, who is killed in Toby's escape from the circus. Toby learns that behind the circus spangles and spectacle is a soiled world of sordid reality.

Often Otis wrote lovingly about the circus, but he always inveighed against it as a hard, demanding, and unprofitable way of life. He tried to rekindle the spark of *Toby* in *Mr. Stubbs's Brother* and *Old Ben* but failed. These are far less circusy and far more moralizing and sentimental than *Toby.* A baby sitter loses his ward in a circus blowdown in *Found by the Circus.* In a gem of a short story entitled "The Acrobat," Otis tells of a young mill worker who joins a circus as an acrobat only to find that his notions of the glamour of circus life were mistaken. He returns to the mill in a lesser position, wiser and happier. Otis's best depiction of the 19th-century circus can be found in "The Clown's Protege," in which the orphaned hero, Jim Barker, is the virtual prisoner in the Great and Only Circus of Joe Maginly, a villain in clown white.

Abandonment and child abuse are recurrent themes in the works of this Maine writer. These elements help to make *Toby Tyler* more than just another story about a runaway. The themes emerge later in *Wan Lun and Dundy,* the story of a four-year-old Chinese orphan in a small New England coastal town. He becomes the ward of Faith Spaulding, a 12-year-old hunchback. Together Faith, her dog Dundy, and Wan Lun survive the cruel tricks of two nasty boys, a carriage accident in the woods, a forest fire, and a storm. The story is original, unique, and formulaic.

In effect, Otis learned his storytelling craft too well. He knew what worked with his young audience. He knew how to generate excitement, win sympathy, and how to milk a story for a moral. Often his dialogue is stilted and melodramatic. Nowhere in his later work does he exceed the character delineation, the descriptive force, and the emotional impact of *Toby Tyler.*

—Nels Juleus

PYLE, Howard

Nationality: American. **Born:** Wilmington, Delaware, 5 March 1853. **Education:** Friends' School and Clark and Taylor's School, Wilmington; Mr. van der Weilen's School, Philadelphia, 1868-72. **Family:** Married Anne Poole in 1881. **Career:** Freelance illustrator, for *St. Nicholas* magazine, *Harper's,* and *Harper's Young People.* Taught at Drexel Institute, Philadelphia, 1894-1900, and at his own art school in Wilmington, 1900-10. Muralist. **Died:** 9 November 1911. **Fiction:** *Pepper and Salt,* 1886; *The Wonder Clock,* with Katherine Pyle, 1888; *Otto of the Silver Hand,* 1888; *Men of Iron,* 1892; *The Story of Jack Ballister's Fortunes,* 1895; *The Garden Behind the Moon,* 1895; *Twilight Land,* 1895; Stolen Treasure, 1907.

* * *

Howard Pyle must be considered a giant in American literature for children. An innovative, vastly productive artist-writer-teacher, he was a modest man totally concerned with inspiring good artists and creating good books. But the term giant just might have appealed to him as a description, for his imagination was tuned in to the days of good knights and evil villains, heroes and dragons, magic stools and clever magicians, beautiful maidens and wicked queens, good boys, foolish men, and surely among them, giants. And of course, King Arthur and Robin Hood.

In his 58 years he accomplished an amazing amount of enduring work. His importance as an artist as well as writer must be mentioned here for several reasons. First, his work spanned a period of vital change in children's books. It began in an era when moralistic stories had themes of illness, suffering, and death, and were usually illustrated by inept saccharine pictures; standards for writing and illustrating were low. It ended with his work, both words and pictures, having produced the highest standards for others to follow. The author-artist Robert Lawson, writing in *Illustrators of Children's Books 1744-1945,* stated, "It is small wonder that the clean-cut, healthy, joyous work of Howard Pyle came to...children...like a fresh breeze flooding a fetid sickroom." Second, his illustration and stories intertwined and enhanced each other, growing equally from his concept of the subject undertaken, even though, to an extent rarely equalled by any other author-artist, each element is strong enough to stand alone. Third, any peice of artwork takes a great deal of time to produce. Thus to research, absorb, recreate, and retell the Robin Hood ballads and the vast lore of King Arthur was a gigantic, time-consuming task. He was a truly prodigious worker.

Although he could easily "see things in image-terms or in the continuity of words," as Henry C. Pitz describes his dual abilities, he was a deliberate craftsman. He actually experimented with various writing styles to achieve the effect of the archaic speech of Robin Hood's days and yet have it understandable to children. Reading it aloud today, now that we are even used to *you* taking the place of *thee-and-thou* in versions of the Bible, it sounds more unreal than ever to hear, "Now will I go too, for fain would I draw a string for the bright eyes of my lass, for so goodly a prize as that," or hear Pauline ask poor little Otto about his mother, "And didst thou never see her?" Such is his thoroughness in setting scene, delineating character, and sweeping all action forward in a dynamic plot—particularly in his own stories such as *Otto of the Silver Hand, Men of Iron* and his pirate tales—that one quickly accepts the language as another rich element of his writing skill.

Although *The Merry Adventures of Robin Hood* (1883) was his first book to be published, *Pepper and Salt* and *The Wonder Clock* contained stories and fables Pyle had written and illustrated for children's magazines. *Twilight Land* was more influenced by Eastern folktales. While at first he borrowed and retold old tales in different guises ("The Salt of Life" is the well-known Catskin motif of universal folklore), so steeped was he in folk and fairy lore that eventually he could turn his own rich imagination out into these forms to perfection, just as Andersen did. *The Garden Behind the Moon,* a long allegorical fantasy, is less derivative than his short stories and it contains such strong beautiful prose that it makes him a classic writer of fantasy.

With the grim sad story of medieval revenge, *Otto of the Silver Hand,* and that of 15th-century adventure, *Men of Iron,* and in his tales of Robin Hood and King Arthur, Pyle achieved new heights in literature for children; he gave them an immediate sense of their past, complete with authentic convincing details, replete with drama and pageantry, and taut with adventure.

Elizabeth Nesbitt, commenting on Pyle in *A Critical History of Children's Literature,* mentioned that the era in which Pyle developed his work had been called the Golden Age of children's literature and that "It is difficult to do justice to his contribution to the shining quality of that era. The magnitude and diversity of his work elude definition."

—Lee Kingman

REED, Talbot Baines

Nationality: British. **Born:** Hackney, London, 3 April 1852. **Education:** Attended Priory House School, London; City of London School, 1864-68. **Family:** Married Elizabeth Greer in 1876; two daughters and one son. **Career:** Joined his father's London type-founding firm, 1868, managing director after 1881. Regular contributor to *Boy's Own Paper,* London, and *Leeds Mercury.* Cofounder, and secretary, 1892-93, Bibliographical Society. Fellow of the Society of Antiquaries, 1893. **Died:** 28 November 1893.

Fiction: *The Adventures of a Three-Guinea Watch,* 1883; *Follow My Leader,* 1885; *The Fifth Form at St. Dominic's,* 1887; *The Willoughby Captains,* 1887; *Parkhurst Sketches and Other Stories,* 1889; *My Friend Smith,* 1889; *Sir Ludar,* 1889; *Roger Ingleton, Minor,* 1891; *The Cockhouse at Fellsgarth (The House at Fellsgarth),* 1893; *Reginald Cruden,* 1894; *A Dog with a Bad Name,* 1894; *The Master of the Shell,* 1894; *Tom, Dick, and Harry,* 1894; *Kilgorman,* 1894; *A Book of Short Stories,* 1897.

* * *

It was perhaps appropriate that Talbot Baines Reed's first fictional published words were: "It was a proud moment in my existence when Wright, captain of our football club, came up to me in school one Friday and said, 'Adams, your name is down to play in the match against Craven tomorrow.'" This comprised the opening of the first of his series of sketches of sporting life at Parkhurst School, tiled "My First Football Match" and appeared on the first page of the first issue of the famous *Boy's Own Paper* on 18 January 1879. It set the style, tone, and content for his many tales of public school life to come, most of which first ran as extremely popular serials in the *Boy's Own Paper.* His earliest and shorter contributors to the magazine appeared anonymously. Then, in 1880, came his first full-scale serial, *The Adventures of a Three-Guinea Watch,* followed by a further 10 serials, mainly about public schools, though some described life in the offices of the City of London. They included some of the most famous school stories ever written: *The Fifth Form at St. Dominic's, The Willoughby Captains, The Master of the Shell,* and *The Cockhouse at Fellsgarth.* Although, ironically, Reed himself attended a day-school, his fine descriptions of public boarding-school life are generally agreed to be extremely accurate for their period.

Although Thomas Hughes's *Tom Brown's School Days* (1857) and F.W. Farrar's *Eric; or, Little by Little* (1858) had virtually established the English public school story as a genre, it was undoubtedly Reed who shaped and developed this popular type of tale as readers later came to know and love it. Hughes and (especially) Farrar had dominated their stories with the dark side of Victorian boarding school life (death, disgrace, bullying, sin, and tears), allied with perhaps over-generous lashings of religion and prayer. Reed's boys tended to be much more extrovert, healthy, mischievous, and authentic—more "boy-like," in fact. He created superbly the essentially self-contained world of school, its rules and its traditions. But, if he was apt to concentrate upon the brighter side of the scholastic life, he by no means ignored the darker. There were, for instance, the bullies, cheats, and scoundrels. There was a certain amount of religion—conversions of would-be or actual sinners. George Hutchinson, editor of the *Boy's Own Paper* during Reed's time, once referred to his personal background of "simple, cheerful Puritanism," and this is the quality that often comes to the foreground in Reed's writings. And it's none the worse for that. The *Boy's Own Paper* was, after all, published by the highly respectable Religious Tract Society, and everything published in it was supposed to instil, in as entertaining and painless a way as possible, the right thoughts into its healthy manly young Christian readers.

It was Reed who really created and established many of the situations and character-types later to be copied by numerous succeeding boys' school story writers. There were the fine, upstanding heroes, the weak, easily led boys, the "bounders" who broke out after lights-out to frequent gambling-dens or (dare it be said?) music-halls, the "swots," the sportsmen, the bullies, and the jokers. There were the inter-house rivalries, the school magazines, the sporting contests, the "town-versus-gown" feuds, the different types of masters (both sympathetic and unsympathetic), the "fagging" and the dormitory midnight feasts. It was generally a cozy world, later to become something of a formula and to be written about, in a variety of ways, by such successful story writers as Harold Avery, R.S. Warren-Bell, Richard Bird, Hylton Cleaver, Gunby Hadath, Edwy Searles Brooks, and (most prolific of them all) Charles Hamilton. In his writing, Reed was an excellent storyteller, wrote good, realistic dialogue, had a fine descriptive flair, and, most of all, made his characters come vividly to life.

—Brian Doyle

SEWELL, Anna

Nationality: British. **Born:** Great Yarmouth, Norfolk, 30 March 1820; daughter of the poet Mary Sewell. **Education:** Educated privately, and at a school in Stoke Newington, London. Semi-invalid from youth. Lived in Brighton, 1836-45, and later in Sussex, Gloucestershire, Bath, and Norwich. **Career:** Teacher at the Working Man's Evening Institute, Wick, Gloucestershire, in early 1860s. **Died:** 25 April 1878. **Fiction:** *Black Beauty, His Grooms and Companions,* 1877.

* * *

Black Beauty is the imaginary autobiography of a horse. We follow his career from its gentle beginning in the care of a farmer, up through society via the squirearchy to the nobility, and thence sadly downwards, finally pulling a cab for a sordid villain called Skinner.

It is an unashamedly didactic book. Anna Sewell wrote that "its special aim" was "to induce kindness, sympathy, and an understanding treatment of horses." This, she believed, would "bring the thoughts of men more in harmony with the purposes of God on this subject." The model owner, Squire Gordon, upbraids a neighbour who is beating a pony with the words "By giving way to such passions you injure your own character as much, nay more, than you injure your horse, and remember, we shall all be judged according to our works, whether they be towards man or towards beast."

The book's moral influence was enormous. It was adopted and distributed by The Royal Society for the Prevention of Cruelty to Animals, and by its American counterpart. Within a short time, the fashionable but cruel habit of pulling the horse's head up high with bearing-reins was abandoned and the treatment of cab horses came under far closer scrutiny. Ignorance about the care and needs of horses is condemned as bitterly as plain brutality.

The didacticism at some points goes further than the care of animals. Like many 18th- and 19th-century fictitious autobiographies, it surveys critically a variety of social strata and finds as much to abhor in the life of the aristocracy as in the baser world of the East End. One of the best chapters consists of a well-argued debate about the rights of cab drivers to have a day off on Sunday rather than drive the gentry off to church. And the supreme villainy of Skinner is that he not only abuses his own cab horses but that he rents his cabs out to other drivers at appallingly high rates. One of the drivers, known as Seedy Sam, has to pay Skinner eighteen shillings a week for the use of the vehicle and also maintains and feeds the two horses, before he can earn a penny for himself and his hungry family. Small wonder that his horses are broken with exhaustion and he himself suddenly dies of the strain. The phrase "economic exploitation" had not entered Sewell's vocabulary, but that is what she meant.

What makes *Black Beauty* unique among Victorian children's books is the breadth of its appeal after a century. A major national survey of British children's reading preferences published in 1977 recorded it as the clear number one favourite book for 10-year-olds. The explanation may be two-fold: it is superbly written, and horses are extremely appealing characters.

Sewell's simple narrative style matches the straightforwardness of her moral intentions—as monosyllabic and as undecorated as the English language will allow. Plain but not naive. The technique of allowing the horse to tell its own tale in the first person, though absurd if one pauses to reflect on it, seems the most natural—in fact the only possible—way in which to convey the range of experiences that Black Beauty goes through. The horse describes what happens and how he feels with the articulate understanding of a human being—because it is a human view of his suffering that Sewell is trying to promote. She is not concerned with the inner realities of a horse's mind—its natural instincts and stages of development. She merely explains evident emotional behaviour in response to various forms of human treatment. And a great strength of the book is the precise and detailed technical account of the processes of breaking in, harnessing, maintaining, and riding horses, the means by which the horse's nature is changed by human beings for better or for worse.

It is hard to imagine a horsey book of such emotional interest being written in a contemporary setting of Pony Club or racing stable. In Black Beauty's day, horses worked alongside humans to earn their keep, and their careers had close affinities with those of working men in terms of exploitation and reward. This close resemblance between the life of man and beast in society may partly account for the intense concern that the reader had for Black Beauty. And we react with deep emotion to the revelation of human callousness and ingratitude. The end of the story is pleasing but improbable: the hero rediscovered by chance and restored to his former country background—a just reward for long-suffering service to man.

—Aidan Warlow

SIDNEY, Margaret

Pseudonym: Pseudonym for Harriet Mulford Lothrop. **Nationality:** American. **Born:** Harriet Mulford Stone, New Haven, Connecticut, 22 June 1844. **Education:** Attended Grove Hall School, New Haven. **Family:** Married Daniel Lothrop in 1881. **Career:** Founder, and national president, 1895-1901, and honorary president from 1901, National Society of Children of the American Revolution. **Died:** 2 August 1924. **Fiction:** *Five Little Peppers* series, from 1880; *So As by Fire,* 1881; *Half Year at Bronckton,* 1881; *What the Seven Did,* 1882; *How They Went to Europe,* 1884; *A New Departure for Girls,* 1886; *Two Modern Little Princes and Other Stories,* 1889; *St. George and the Dragon,* 1888; *The Little Red Shop,* 1889; *Our Town,* 1889; *An Adirondack Cabin,* 1890; *Rob,* 1891; *The Kaleidoscope,* 1892; *Little Paul and the Frisbie School,* 1893; *The Old Town Pump,* 1895; *A Little Maid of Concord Town,* 1896; *The Gingham Bag,* 1896; *Dilly and the Captain,* 1897; *Two Little Friends in Norway,* 1906; **Verse:** Ballad of the Lost Hare, 1882.

* * *

Margaret Sidney, author of many domestic stories for children, is now remembered only for *Five Little Peppers and How They Grew.* This has been described as the poor child's version of *Little Women,* but it lacks Louisa May Alcott's feeling for nuances of character and its mood is one of sustained euphoria. The family is undoubtedly poor and fatherless, but they are never allowed to experience real distress, and from the opening pages the young reader is aware that good fortune will always prevail. "[Mrs. Pepper] had met life too bravely to be beaten down....So with a stout heart and a cheery face, she had worked away day after day at making coats, and tailoring, and mending of all descriptions; and she had seen with pride that couldn't be concealed, her noisy, happy brood growing up around her, and filling her heart with comfort, and making the Little Brown House fairly ring with jollity and fun." It is the jollity and fun of being poor that is stressed, and when Polly is carried off to be the little light and guardian angel of a rich household she captivates the children with "accounts of Ben's skill, of Phronsie's cunning ways, of the boys who made fun for all, and above everything else, of the dear mother whom they all longed to help, and of all the sayings and doings in the Little Brown House."

The difference between this and contemporary English stories of poor households is very marked; there is a refreshing lack of didactic approach, and the Pepper family are allowed to attain material good fortune and prosperity in a way that no Victorian author in England, conscious of the need to discourage worldly ambition in the working class, would have dreamt of countenancing. They are even allowed tastes of luxury and high-living; the presents that their rich little benefactor showers upon them are not just blankets and coals, but hot-house flowers, singing birds, and wax dolls, and the whole Pepper family by the end of the book has been happily absorbed into his father's house—a fairytale conclusion deeply satisfying to children, who crave optimism in their books.

—Gillian Avery

STEVENSON, Robert Louis

Nationality: British. **Born:** Robert Lewis Balfour Stevenson, Edinburgh, 13 November 1850. **Education:** Edinburgh University, 1866-71; studied law in the office of Skene Edwards and Gordon, Edinburgh: called to the Scottish bar, 1875. **Family:** Married Fanny Osbourne in 1880; two stepchildren, including the writer Lloyd Osbourne. **Career:** Contributor, *Cornhill Magazine,* London, 1876-82. Tubercular: lived in California, 1879-80, Davos, Switzerland, 1880-81, 1881-82, Hyères, France, 1882-84, Bournemouth, England, 1884-87, and the South Seas from 1888, settling in Samoa, 1889. **Died:** 3 December 1894. **Fiction:** *Treasure Island,* 1883; *Kidnapped,* 1886; *The Black Arrow,* 1888; *Catriona (David Balfour),* 1893. **Verse:** *Penny Whistles,* 1883; *A Child's Garden of Verses,* 1885.

* * *

Nearly all Robert Louis Stevenson's mature fiction, with the exception of *Dr. Jekyll,* takes the form of the historical romance. *Treasure Island, Kidnapped, Catriona, The Master of Ballantrae, St. Ives,* and *Weir of Hermiston* all fall into this category, with the action mainly taking place in 18th-century Scotland. The two exceptions are *The Black Arrow,* which is set in the Middle Ages, and *Treasure Island,* which has an England and exotic background.

The plots are nearly always concerned with long journeys, the search for treasure, or flight from capture, and they are usually fraught with great hazards—piracy, murder, intrigue—against which the hero, normally a young person of some resourcefulness, struggles to survive. But Stevenson does not merely use the ingredients of the historical romance for dramatic effects; he also tries to integrate them into a design by which they throw light on various aspects of the human situation as he saw it.

Many of the stories have not a single hero at the centre, but a pair. David and Alan in *Kidnapped,* Jim and Long John in *Treasure Island,* Dr. Jekyll and Mr. Hyde are the best known examples, and they seem to achieve a kind of complementarity as if each partner compensates for the defects of the other. Many of the books also deal with conflicts between clearly defined sides, such as pirates versus honest sailors, English versus Scots, or York versus Lancaster. But there is usually a good deal of changing sides between these antagonists. Long John Silver, for example, begins as an apparently honest sea-cook, reveals himself as leader of the mutiny, then deserts the pirates, and finishes up by even jumping Captain Smollet's ship. Dick Shelton in *The Black Arrow* switches his allegiance from Lancaster to York, while Alan Breck actually deserts King George at the Battle of Prestonpans. James in *The Master of Ballantrae* seems to have the best of both worlds, fighting for Bonnie Prince Charlie but spying for the other side. Finally, there is a good deal of intrigue and duplicity in the way Stevenson's characters behave, and physical disguises are frequently adopted. In *Catriona* the heroine pretends to be David's sister, in *The Black Arrow* Joanna passes herself off as a boy; and Dr. Jekyll's disguise is even more fundamental.

Stevenson's use of the dual-hero, the changing of sides, and the adoption of disguises is not only appropriate to the kinds of stories he wrote, and adds to their dramatic effectiveness, but reveals his passionate concern with the problems of identity and morality. From Stevenson's biographers we know of the ambiguities of his own life, his troubled relations with his parents, whom he adored, with Scotland, which he worshipped from afar. It may be that his literary interests developed there, but, from the evidence of the fiction, it is clear that Stevenson saw man's nature as constantly shifting, and therefore all the more difficult to define and come to terms with. Dr. Jekyll, who can transform himself physically into a murderous villain, and Deacon Brodie, the clergyman who becomes a housebreaker at night-time, are simply extreme examples of such shifts. Long John Silver and Alan Breck are much more equivocal as their personalities and virtues fluctuate.

Long John, for example, is a pirate, thief, and murderer, and, as such, quite ruthless in pursuit of the gold. But he is also cheerful, brave, witty, and above all kind to Jim, who has no father. In this way Stevenson is constantly challenging our responses. Who is good or bad?, he seems to be saying. In your final judgement, do you find Long John sympathetic or not? Are these sorts of questions even relevant? David Balfour operates as a kind of moral censor of Alan Breck's behaviour in *Kidnapped,* but in the end, though he may be "right" in his quarrel with Alan in "The Flight in the Heather," he comes to see that their love complicates the whole matter of knowing who is right or wrong.

Stevenson's influence on later writers is less specific, more pervasive. The historical romance, first established by Scott at the beginning of the 19th century, and then adapted for children by such authors as Marryat and Henty, went from strength to strength, until it reached its Victorian peak with Stevenson himself. Though the quality of many early 20th-century historical novels deteriorated, honourable exceptions can be found in the work of John Masefield and Geoffrey Trease, and from the 1950s the emergence of such writers as Leon Garfield, Cynthia Harnett, and Rosemary Sutcliff has sparked a renaissance of the form.

Though the influence of Stevenson on the specific narrative techniques of the adventure story is doubtful, the influence of his moral values issuing into literary attitudes is everywhere absolutely pervasive, even among those authors who would say they had never read him, and this for two reasons. First, he showed it was possible to write books for children that were both thrilling in the most fundamental sense, and yet at the same time deeply serious. The loss of innocence—for example, by Jim Hawkins—is as prevalent in Stevenson's work as in that of Henry James, and the friendship of the two writers was, of course, very significant. And second, in his treatment of the complexities of human behaviour, in his refusal to compartmentalise characters as either "good" or "bad," his writing revealed a maturity which the best children's writers of today can only hope to emulate but not excel. It is significant that a novelist like Leon Garfield, whose stories of the 18th century differ so much from Stevenson's, should return time and again to the equivocal nature of human relationships, and the difficulties of distinguishing appearance from reality in exciting books such as *Smith* and *Jack Holborn.* Without the achievement of Stevenson so much of today's best writing would never have appeared.

—Dennis Butts

STOCKTON, Frank R.

Nationality: American. **Born:** Francis Richard Stockton, Philadelphia, Pennsylvania, 5 April 1834. **Education:** Attended Zane Street School, 1840-48, and Central High School, 1848-52, both in Philadelphia. **Family:** Married Marian Edwards Tuttle in 1860. **Career:** Apprenticed as a wood-engraver, 1852, and worked as an engraver until 1870. Assistant editor, *Hearth and Home,* 1868-73, and *St. Nicholas* magazine, 1873-78, both New York. Regular contributor to *Scribner's Magazine.* **Died:** 20 April 1902. **Fiction:** *Ting-a-Ling,* 1870; *What Might Have Been Expected,* 1874; *A Jolly Friendship,* 1880; *The Floating Prince and Other Fairy Tales,* 1881; *Ting-a-Ling Tales,* 1882; *The Story of Viteau,* 1884; *The Bee-Man of Orn and Other Fanciful Tales,* 1887; *The Queen's Museum,* 1887; *The Clocks of Rondaine and Other Stories,* 1892; *Fanciful Tales,* 1894; *Captain Chap (The Young Master of Hyson Hall),* 1896; *Kate Bonnet,* 1902; *Stories of the Spanish Main,* 1913; *The Poor Count's Christmas,* 1927.

* * *

One of the most prolific contributors to children's literature in the last third of the 19th century, Frank R. Stockton is perhaps best remembered for such modern fairytales as "Ting-a-Ling," "The Griffin and the Minor Canon," "Old Pipes and the Dryad," and "The Queen's Museum." But taken as a whole, his work is richly varied. During his long association with the quality children's periodical *St. Nicholas,* first as assistant editor and later as a regular contributor, he wrote such realistic tales of adventure as *What Might Have Been Expected,* in which a brother and sister manage to provide economic security for their aged and feeble aunt. *Personally Conducted* (1889) is a collection of travel sketches originally written for *St. Nicholas.* Stockton also produced two juvenile histories: *New Jersey, From the Discovery of the Scheyichbi to Recent Times* (1896), an anecdotal account of some dramatic occasions in the state's history, and *The Buccaneers and Pirates of Our Coasts* (1898). *Tales Out of School* (1875), like its predecessor *Roundabout Rambles* (1872), consists of informative stories, mostly dealing with natural history. In *The Story of Viteau* Stockton attempted a tale of medieval life that reveals his general inability to realize in his fiction a vivid sense of place. The same difficulty can be seen in *What Might Have Been Expected,* set in the American south. Unlike many northerners, Stockton was familiar with life in the south (his wife was from South Carolina) and his Negro characters have a substantiality not often found in children's literature of the period; but he was less successful in rendering the south as a locale. His principal interest throughout his career as a writer was in delineating character and situation. As assistant editor of *St. Nicholas,* Stockton adopted two pseudonyms, Paul Fort and John Lewees, under which he wrote numerous informative articles and such slight moralistic sketches as "Tommy Hooper's Choice," which describes the mildly humorous difficulties encountered by the young Tommy when he tries to decide how to spend 25 cents—a magnificent sum to a child in the 1870s.

Stockton's best work for children, and the most interesting, consists of his fairytales, or "fanciful tales" as he liked to call them, beginning with the adventures of Ting-a-Ling, a diminutive elf, who first appeared in *The Riverside Magazine* in 1867. Even as a student, Stockton had wanted to write fairytales of a particular sort. Of his approach, he later commented: "I wanted the fanciful creatures who inhabited the world of fairy-land to act, as far as possible for them to do so, as if they were inhabitants of the real world. I did not dispense with monsters and enchanters, or talking beasts and birds, but I obliged these creatures to infuse into their extraordinary actions a certain leaven of common sense." Stockton's efforts to infuse "realism" into the traditional elements of the fairytale had both a formal and psychological dimension. He made no attempt to render the world of faery through archaic language, for example, but told his tales simply, directly, and matter-of-factly, without archness. He was neither patronizing nor condescending to his audience, and his tales are remarkably free of the overt moralizing that often crept into the period's literature for children. Throughout the tales runs a strongly individualistic psychology—a contempt for dependence, authoritarianism, and timid conformity; a celebration of independence, sturdy self-reliance, and personal courage—that fits well with the ethic of individualism prominent in 19th-century American thought and evident in much post-Civil War literature for children. In his "fanciful tales," Stockton expressed a deft, sure touch, a gentle humor, a sweetness of temper that he rarely achieved in his other children's fiction.

The publication in the 1880s of "The Bee-Man of Orn," "The Griffin and the Minor Canon," and similar tales, as well as a series of yearly Christmas stories for *St. Nicholas,* marked the high point of Stockton's juvenile writing. By 1885, he was writing increasingly for an adult audience, who had acclaimed his short story "The Lady or the Tiger?" and in that year he undertook the writing of his first novel. Stockton produced little of note for children after the appearance in 1887 of "The Clocks of Rondaine" in *St. Nicholas*.

—R. Gordon Kelly

STRETTON, Hesba

Pseudonym for Sarah Smith. **Nationality:** British. **Born:** Wellington, Shropshire, 27 July 1832. **Education:** Attended Old Hall School, near Shrewsbury, Shropshire. **Career:** Worked in her father's post office, Wellington, until 1863; lived in Manchester, 1963-66, in London, 1867-92, and Ham Common, Surrey, from 1892. Co-founder, London Society for the Prevention of Cruelty to Children. **Died:** 8 October 1911. **Fiction:** *Fern's Hollow,* 1864; *The Children of Cloverley,* 1865; *Enoch Roden's Training,* 1866; *The Fishers of Derby Haven (Peter Killip's King),* 1866; *Pilgrim Street,* 1867; *Jessica's First Prayer,* 1867; *Little Meg's Children,* 1868; *Alone in London,* 1869; *Max Krömer,* 1871; *Bede's Charity,* 1872; *The King's Servants,* 1873; *Lost Grip,* 1873; *Cassy,* 1874; *No Work No Bread,* 1875; *Two Christmas Stories,* 1875; *Brought Home,* 1875; *Friends till Death and Other Stories,* 1875; *The Crew of the "Dolphin,"* 1876; *A Night and a Day,* 1876; *Left Alone, and Michel Lorio's Cross,* 1876; *Old Transome,* 1876; *The Storm of Life,* 1876; *The World of a Baby, and How Apple-Tree Court Was Won,* 1876; *A Man of His Word,* 1878; *Mrs. Burton's Best Bedroom and Other Stories,* 1878; *A Thorny Patch,* 1879; *In Prison and Out,* 1879; *Cobwebs and Cables,* 1881; *No Place Like Home,* 1881; *Under the Old Roof,* 1882; *Two Secrets, and A Man of His Word,* 1882; *The Lord's Purse-Bearers,* 1882; *Carola,* 1884; *Her Only Son,* 1887; *A Green Bay Tree,* 1887; *Only a Dog,* 1888; *A Miserable Christmas and a Happy New Year,* 1888; *Sam Franklin's Savings Bank,* 1888; *The Christmas Child,* 1888; *An Acrobat's Girlhood,* 1889; *Half Brothers,* 1892; *Jessica's Mother,* 1893; *The Highway of Sorrows at the Close of the Nineteenth Century,* with Stepniak, 1894; *Paul Rodents,* with Stepniak, 1894; *In the Hollow of His Hand,* 1897; *The Soul of Honour,* 1898.

* * *

Jessica's First Prayer is one of those books known by its title to thousands who have never seen a copy. This simply told story of a destitute child, daughter of a gin-sodden actress, who hears the Christmas message and by her simple faith brings a new light into the lives of her elders was to initiate a new genre of evangelical writing, the street arab story, and to remain perhaps the best of them. It is not, however, the very first example. Mary Howitt, in *The Story of Little Cristal* (1863), probably inspired by Hans Andersen's *The Little Match Girl,* had described how a street waif's last hours had been comforted by the memory of a stained glass window depicting Christ blessing the children.

Jessica's First Prayer, originally published in *Sunday at Home* in 1866, was the first of Hesba Stretton's works to attract attention, and its success was phenomenal, not only in England but all over the world. Written no doubt as "family" reading rather than directly for children, it and its legion of imitations soon became adopted as standard Sunday reading for the young, replacing the Calvinistic tracts of Mrs. Sherwood and Mrs. Cameron that the early Victorians had been reared on, and the compilations of holy deaths of young people that had gone before these. The idea of the child evangelist unconsciously melting the cold and stubborn heart of an adult was to have a compelling effect on young readers, and for once children of their own age were the centre of the amazed attention of their elders. The result was a deluge of mawkish novelettes which did not subside until well on in the next century. But *Jessica's First Prayer* cannot be blamed for this. It is finely observed, economically told, and the child Jessica's awakening faith—very difficult to convey, as Stretton's imitators were to find—is moving and convincing.

Stretton followed it up with some 50 stories sometimes on the theme of the suffering poor, sometimes on the evil brought about by love of money. Unlike Charlotte Yonge and others in the squarson tradition, who wrote with rural church schools in mind, she could not agree that the existing social order was right. She had first-hand knowledge of slum conditions in London and Manchester; she knew all about grasping landlords, the heavy hand of officialdom, how unjust justice could be. In *In Prison and Out* she spoke with warm indignation of the deplorable difference in society's attitude towards a slum boy who had knocked down a man for insulting his mother, and a public schoolboy such as Tom Brown who did the same sort of thing. One would be sent to prison, the other commended. She was frequently to take the side of the employee against the employer, as in *Fern's Hollow,* and always to attack the folly of laying up treasures on earth.

Her accounts of the poor and destitute were always moving: the bare-footed crossing sweepers shivering in their rags, the feverish child gasping for fresh air in the mid-summer furnace of a stifling London courtyard, the street arab's search for a lost baby sister whom nobody cared about but himself, the shame and degradation of having at last to take refuge in the "House," the terror of being buried as a pauper. But they were to be repeated so often that they lost their first impact: "It is possible to have too many of them," as Charlotte Yonge wrote. It was in any case a time when journalists and philanthropists were working hard to open the public's eyes to the atrocious conditions in which the poor lived, and there was much literature on this theme.

Nevertheless, at her best, in books such as *Alone in London, Little Meg's Children, Lost Gip, Pilgrim Street* (all written in the earlier part of her career), she rose far above the level of the ordinary Sunday School reward book. Her successors could harrow the reader with their accounts of the mirk and misery and vice of the slums, but Hesba Stretton could also enter into the small pleasures of the poor: a feast of bloaters, a mug of hot coffee, the sight of a garden, a baby to love.

—Gillian Avery

TWAIN, Mark

Pseudonym for Samuel Langhorne Clemens. **Nationality:** American. **Born:** Florida, Missouri, 30 November 1835; moved to Hannibal, Missouri, 1839. **Family:** Married Olivia Langdon in 1870 (died 1904); one son and three daughters. **Career:** Printer's apprentice and typesetter for Hannibal newspapers, 1847-50; helped brother with Hannibal *Journal,* 1850-52; typesetter and printer in St. Louis, New York, Philadelphia, for Keokuk *Saturday Post,* Iowa, 1853-56, and in Cincinnati, 1857; apprentice river pilot, on the Mississippi, 1857-58; licensed as pilot, 1859-60; went to Nevada as secretary to his brother, then on the staff of the Governor, and also worked as goldminer, 1861; staff member, Virginia City *Territorial Enterprise,* Nevada, 1862-64 (first used pseudonym Mark Twain, 1863); reporter, San Francisco *Morning Call,* 1864; correspondent, Sacramento *Union,* 1866, and San Francisco *Alta California,* 1866-69; visited Sandwich (i.e., Hawaiian) Islands, 1866, and France, Italy, and Palestine, 1867; lecturer from 1867; editor, *Express,* Buffalo, New York, 1869-71; moved to Hartford, Connecticut and became associated with Charles L. Webster Publishing Company, 1884; invested in unsuccessful Paige typesetter and went bankrupt, 1894 (last debts paid, 1898); lived mainly in Europe, 1896-1900, New York, 1900-07, and Redding, Connecticut, 1907-10. M.A.: Yale University, New Haven, Connecticut, 1888; Litt.D.: Yale University, 1901; Oxford University, 1907; LL.D.: University of Missouri, Columbia, 1902. Member, American Academy, 1904. **Died:** 21 April 1910. **Fiction:** *The Adventures of Tom Sawyer,* 1876; *The Prince and the Pauper,* 1881; *The Adventures of Huckleberry Finn,* 1884; *Tom Sawyer Abroad,* 1894; *Tom Sawyer Abroad; Tom Sawyer, Detective; and Other Stories,* 1896; *A Boy's Adventure,* 1928.

* * *

Ernest Hemingway wrote, in *Green Hills of Africa,* "All modern American literature comes from one book by Mark Twain called *Huckleberry Finn*...it's the best book we've had. All American writing comes from that. There was nothing before. There has been nothing as good since."

As criticism Hemingway's statement is admittedly overstated. Samuel Clemens, or Mark Twain, has always been an enigma for critics, many of whom have had great difficulty in analyzing his works, and others in psychoanalyzing him. Hemingway, however, was not speaking as a critic, but rather as a reader, as a devotee, as a writer who recognized his debt to one who came before him. In that role he is an apt and accurate spokesman for all of us who rejoice in listening to the voice of Mark Twain. Just as Lincoln remains the folk symbol of the American spirit, for many Twain remains the folk symbol of the American writer.

It is significant that Hemingway specifically referred to *The Adventures of Huckleberry Finn,* for it is in that work, along with *The Adventures of Tom Sawyer* and *Life on the Mississippi,* that Twain's narrative genius is self-evident. Today *Tom Sawyer* is usually categorized as a book for children, while *Huck Finn* is considered adult fiction. Nevertheless, in any discussion of Twain's influence on American authors of children's books, both must be considered.

Oddly enough, when Twain wrote *Tom Sawyer* he did not have a child audience in mind. It wasn't until his friend William Dean Howells suggested that it was a story most appropriate for children that Twain "cleaned up" the manuscript and added a preface in which he said: "Although my book is intended mainly for the entertainment of boys and girls, I hope it will not be shunned by men and women on that account, for part of my plan has been to try to pleasantly remind adults of what they once were themselves, and of how they felt and thought and talked, and what queer enterprises they sometimes engaged in." That he did not consciously write it for children is perhaps the book's strongest attribute, though occasionally Twain as narrator speaks directly to the adult readers he originally had in mind. This is overwhelmingly outweighed by the absence of any condescension or moralizing. In fact at the time of its publication (1876) it came under attack as a children's book. The *New York Times Book Review* concluded: "In the books to be placed into children's hands for purposes of recreation, we have a preference for those of a milder type than *Tom Sawyer*."

Tom Sawyer is much more than a grown man's reminiscences about the idyllic joys and pains of childhood. Twain stands high on the list of eminent writers like Stevenson, Dickens, and Saroyan who successfully depicted how children "felt and thought and talked." Though they did not write specifically for children, they demonstrated for those who would know how necessary it is to retain the heart of a child if your work is to have the ring of truth. Twain above all else sets out to entertain. One should not overlook the word "Adventures" in the titles of his "boy" books. He takes the blood and thunder stuff of the old-fashioned dime novels and the serial boy romances and makes it literature.

In *Huck Finn,* intended as a sequel to *Tom Sawyer,* Twain gets into the skin of Huck and tells the story through him, and by so doing he happens upon the narrative mode that is explicitly suited for his special talents. Huck, who could not possibly *write* a story, *tells* us the story. And that is how Twain himself would have it; as he says in his *Autobiography*: " With the pen in one's hand, narrative is a difficult art; narrative should flow as flows the brook down through the hills and leafy woodlands." This also was one of the reasons for Hemingway's acclaim, for he too, like many storytellers, was at heart a raconteur and a minstrel rather than a scribbler.

But there was even more important reason. Hemingway recognized the straightforward honesty in *Huck Finn.* Twain possessed, as H.L. Mencken put it, "a truly amazing instinct for the truth." Today many writers of books for children and young adults have turned to first-person narrative, with only a meager few of them handling it successfully. They would do well to look closely at *Huckleberry Finn,* for there they will find Mark Twain's greatest legacy to them—his integrity. He doesn't use the first-person point of view as a literary device for simulating a peer relationship with young readers; but rather he turns over the complete narrative to Huck, allowing him to tell the story as only he can do it. Huck's understated and innocent "telling" is the primary reason that this story of a boy's adventure is, at the same time, a devastating denunciation of the society in which the tale takes place.

A final word of caution. Too often *Huck Finn* appears on children's reading book lists as a companion piece to *Tom Sawyer,* when in fact it is a work best suited for a more mature audience. Indeed, anyone who recommends *The Adventures of Huckleberry Finn* to a young reader must first consider whether that reader is capable or not of handling the intricacies of its ironic thrust.

—James E. Higgins

WALTON, Mrs. O.F

Nationality: British. **Born:** Amy Catherine Deck in 1850. **Family:** Married Reverend Octavius Frank Walton in 1875 (died 1933). Lived in Cally, Kirkcudbright, 1876-83, York, 1883-93, Wolverhampton, 1893-1906, and Leigh, Kent (with a short period in Shamley Green, Surrey, after World War I), 1906-39. **Died:** July 1939. **Fiction:** *My Little Corner, and Wandering May,* 1872; *Little Dot,* 1873; *My Mates and I,* 1873; *Home, Sweet Home (Christie's Old Organ*), 1874; *A Peep Behind the Scenes,* 1877; *Angel's Christmas,* 1877; *Saved at Sea,* 1879; *Was I Right?,* 1879; *Little Faith,* 1880; *Olive's Story,* 1881; *Nobody Loves Me,* 1883; *Shadows,* 1884; *Taken or Left,* 1885; *Launch the Life-Boat,* 1886; *Poppy's Presents,* 1886; *The Mysterious House,* 1890; *Nemo (The Wonderful Door),* 1893; *Christie, the King's Servant,* 1896; *Whiter Than Snow, and Little Dot,* 1896; *Audrey,* 1897; *The Lost Clue,* 1907; *Strange Diana,* 1919.

* * *

Mrs. O.F. Walton was one of the best-known and longest-remembered of the ladies who wrote little books for Victorian Sunday reading. Countless children in chapel or church-going families spent Sunday afternoons over her touching and improving tales. Her work is distinguished from the mass of such stories by characteristics which appealed to the pious adults who bought it, but also by some features which we might pick out today to account for its undoubted attraction for the children themselves.

It was the centrality of the Christian message in all her writing that made her a favourite with the religious publishers. The sermons are lengthy and repeated; many of her stories dwell upon the deaths of small children, old folk, or suffering mothers in the most lachrymose way. In her writing the minatory insistence of early Evangelical writers upon infant death lived on, in a sentimentalised but no less extreme form. *Christie's Old Organ,* for example, tells of a homeless orphan and an old organ-grinder who find salvation together, by means of a chance-heard mission sermon (which readers are given in full, twice over). The old man dies, gloriously and at length, and the boy becomes a missionary himself. The book plucks remorselessly at the heartstrings, especially by the device of the organ, which plays "Home, Sweet Home."

The modern sense of the unhealthiness of such manipulation of the child's emotions was shared by many adults of her own time, but Walton's books had a hold on child readers for quite a different reason. The narrative patterns she used were often compelling versions of the basic stuff of storytelling, the romance. They offered young readers powerful imaginative satisfactions quite apart from any response to their preaching. This is clearly seen in her most popular story, *A Peep Behind the Scenes*. The beautiful child Rosalie shines like a jewel in the evil (but fascinating) setting of her father's fairground theatre. Her mother's romantic fancies have brought her to these depths, and she now lies dying. Rosalie's beauty and noble nature preserve her, bringing her the love of all she meets, and she is helped in her escape from the depths by dwarves and other fairground folk, who are like the miraculous helpers in a fairy-tale. She returns their kindnesses by converting them, and leaves a trail of blessed lives, and of course deaths, behind her, as she makes her journey through the underworld back to her rightful place in her aunt's idyllic home. It makes little essential difference to the effect of the romance that the talisman that brings aid to the heroine throughout is a picture of the Good Shepherd. The fairground setting and the perils of her journey are only made more exciting by the commentary telling the reader how wicked such things are, and converting an absorbing fantasy into a "Sunday" book.

—J.S. Bratton

WARNER, Susan (Bogert)

Pseudonym: Elizabeth Wetherell. **Nationality:** American. **Born:** New York City, 11 July 1819. **Education:** Educated privately. **Died:** 17 March 1885. **Fiction:** *The Wide, Wide World* (as Elizabeth Wetherell), 1851; *Queechy* (as Elizabeth Wetherell), 1852; *The Glen-Luna Family,* with Anna Bartlett Warner, 1852; *Carl Krinken: His Christmas Stocking (The Christmas Stocking),* with Anna Bartlett Warner, 1853; *Mr. Rutherford's Children,* 1853; *Sybil and Chrissa,* with Anna Bartlett Warner, 1854; *Casper,* with Anna Bartlett Warner, 1855; *The Birthday Visit to Holly Farm,* with Anna Bartlett Warner, 1860; *The Little Nurse of Cape Cod,* 1863; *The Carpenter's Daughter,* with Anna Bartlett Warner, 1864; *Melbourne House,* 1864; *Martha and Her Kind Friend Rachel,* with Anna Bartlett Warner, 1864; *The Prince in Disguise,* with Anna Bartlett Warner, 1864; *The Widow and Her Daughter,* with Anna Bartlett Warner, 1864; *The Rose in the Desert,* with Anna Bartlett Warner, 1864; *Martha's Hymn,* with Anna Bartlett Warner, 1865; *Walks from Eden,* 1866; *What She Could,* 1871; *Opportunities,* 1871; *The House in Town,* 1871; *Edith and Mary,* with Anna Bartlett Warner, 1871; *Hard Maple,* with Anna Bartlett Warner, 1871; *Trading,* 1872; *The Little Camp on Eagle Hill,* 1873; *Sceptres and Crowns,* 1874; *Willow Brook,* 1874; *The Flag of Truce,* 1875; *The Rapids of Niagara,* 1875; *Little Nettie; or Home Sunshine,* with Anna Bartlett Warner, 1878; *Stephen, M.D.,* 1883.

* * *

Susan Warner's brand of sentimental fiction exerted a powerful influence on later 19th-century American writers for girls. 1980s feminist attempts to establish her as a pioneer of women's writing, however, ignore her antecedents. Her accounts of female orphans buffeted by the world and rising above adversity with virtue intact are in a tradition much favoured from the mid-18th century onwards. There are Richardson's *Pamela,* of course; *Fatherless Fanny* by an unidentified writer of 1811 and popular through much of the last century; *Jane Eyre,* and, a work surprisingly little remembered by historians of women's fiction, *Redwood* (1842) by the Massachusetts author Catharine Maria Sedgwick. This has a heroine of the sort that Warner was to make so familiar—meek, grave, and a potent force for good, but also blessed with graceful manners as well as many accomplishments and housewifely virtues.

Much of the self-indulgent emotion in Warner's books arose out of a dreamy urge to escape from her own cramped background. The daughter of an improvident and litigious father, whose reckless investments and expensive disputes with his neighbours reduced the family to abject poverty, she wrote from the direst financial need. After Mr. Warner's New York business losses the family went to live on Constitution Island in the Hudson River, opposite West Point; here she and her sister Anna at times could not even find clothes fit to go to church. Her first and most famous book, *The Wide, Wide World,* was written, her sister said in her biography, "on her knees," which can be interpreted as much as a despairing plea for success as a prayer for divine guidance. Though the manuscript was returned by the first publishers to whom she submitted it (the Harpers reader indeed scribbled "Fudge" on one of the pages), Putnam took it on, and it was an instant success. In spite of the popularity of her earlier works she was never, however, to achieve the material prosperity for which she yearned.

The Wide, Wide World is the story of Ellen Montgomery, the child of an invalid mother who soon dies, and an uncaring, selfish father who also dies, unlamented. She is sent to live with her granite-hewn spinster aunt Fortune in upstate New York, and with the help of a neighbouring female guardian angel learns to accept adversity in a meek and Christian spirit. From her aunt she learns to be competent little housekeeper. The guardian angel has a brother, "Mr. John" who by virtue of his role as an adoptive brother to Ellen is allowed to kiss and caress her, at the same time giving her much moral teaching. In the course of some 220,000 words Warner only succeeded in covering four years of Ellen's life, from 10 to 14, and thus never succeeded (much to her chagrin, one senses) in bringing her to a nubile age. (She was always to have this difficulty in manipulating plot and characters.) The saga ends abruptly with Ellen taken over by her aristocratic Scottish relations, and the implication that Mr. John will come back in a few years to claim her as his bride. The storyline is minimal; the book's strength lies in the descriptions of Hudson River scenery and of rural life. There is also much about food, which endeared the book to the more austerely raised occupants of English schoolrooms.

Awkward and ungainly herself as an adolescent, "rude when in fact I do not mean to be," "her head in a rosy dream of fiction most of the time," self-willed, "a bit of a sybarite by nature," Warner loved in adult life to write about girls who fascinate the most worldly by their innate good breeding and poise. Ellen Montgomery's critical Scottish relations describe her as "the best-bred child in the world"; in her second book, *Queechy* (the name of the village where the book is set), the aristocratic Englishman who first meets Elfleda as a child and later crosses the Atlantic to claim her as his bride, describes her appearance as of "the highest—that degree of mould and finish which belongs only to the highest material." Little Daisy Randolph in *Melbourne House*, another popular work, is altogether of finer grain than her horrible family. Pale, grave, meek, sweet-faced and artless, she is admired and adored by everyone except her own kin. In all these works there are quantities of tears (Warner was herself a tempestuous weeper) and also much fondling and kissing by male protectors who are assiduous and caring, tender but strict—the sort of presence that Warner must have longed for in a life where masculine company was limited to her father and the West Point cadets who used to be invited for bible-reading and gingerbread. The erotic element is so marked in most of her work that the modern reader is amazed at her innocent unawareness that she was giving herself away. Nor had she apparently any idea that she was writing anything but the most chaste religious tales. Thousands of Sunday schools also took this view and her works were much in favour as prizes and Sunday reading, though Charlotte Yonge, the doyenne of children's books, disapproved and said they would lead little girls to see a lover in anybody who was kind to them. However, English girls, accustomed to much more ascetic fare from their own writers, loved them dearly. Warner was to influence writers like Martha Finley; the famous incident in *Elsie Dinsmore* where Elsie's brutal father tries to force her to play secular music on a Sunday is in fact based on an even more violent scene in *Melbourne House*. The religious teaching of her books is nebulous and vaguely attached to the Bible, which the child heroines invariably are confident of interpreting correctly without any guidance, and the abiding impression is of an author totally without humour, who dearly loved her comforts, and longed for wealth and male admiration.

—Gillian Avery

YONGE, Charlotte (Mary)

Nationality: British. **Born:** Otterbourne, Hampshire, 13 August 1823. **Career:** Editor, 1851-90, and assistant editor, 1891-95, the *Monthly Packet*, London; editor, the *Monthly Paper of Sunday Teaching*, 1860-75, and *Mothers in Council*, 1890-1900, both London. **Died:** 24 March 1901. **Fiction:** *Le Château de Melville*, 1838; *Abbey Church*, 1844; *Scenes and Characters (Beechcroft)*, 1847; *Henrietta's Wish*, 1850; *Kenneth*, 1850; *Langley School*, 1850; *The Two Guardians*, 1852; *The Heir of Redclyffe*, 1853; *The Herb of the Field*, 1853; *The Castle Builders*, 1854; *Heartsease*, 1854; *The Little Duke (Richard the Fearless)*, 1854; *The History of Sir Thomas Thumb*, 1855; *The Lances of Lynwood*, 1855; *The Railroad Children*, 1855; *Ben Sylvester's Word*, 1856; *The Daisy Chain*, 1856; *Harriet and Her Sister*, 1856; *Leonard the Lion-Heart*, 1856; *Dynevor Terrace*, 1857; *The Christmas Mummers*, 1858; *Friarswood Post Office*, 1860; *Hopes and Fears*, 1860; *The Mice at Play*, 1860; *The Strayed Falcon*, 1860; *The Pigeon Pie*, 1860; *The Stokesley Secret*, 1861; *The Young Stepmother*, 1861; *Countess Kate*, 1862; *Sea Spleenwort and Other Stories*, 1862; *Last Heartsease Leaves*, 1862(?); *The Trial*, 1864; *The Wars of Wapsburgh*, 1864; *The Clever Woman of the Family*, 1865; *The Dove in the Eagle's Nest*, 1866; *The Prince and the Page*, 1866; *The Danvers Papers*, 1867; *The Six Cushions*, 1867; *The Chaplet of Pearls*, 1868; *Kaffir Land*, 1868; *The Caged Lion*, 1870; *Little Lucy's Wonderful Globe*, 1871; *P's and Q's*, 1872; *The Pillars of the House*, 1873; *Lady Hester*, 1874; *My Young Alcides*, 1875; *The Three Brides*, 1876; *The Disturbing Element*, 1878; *Burnt Out*, 1879; *Magnus Bonum*, 1879; *Bye-Words*, 1880; *Love and Life*, 1880; *Mary and Norah; Nelly and Margaret*, 1880(?); *Cheap Jack*, 1881; *Frank's Debt*, 1881; *Lads and Lasses of Langley*, 1881; *Wolf*, 1881; *Given to Hospitality*, 1882; *Langley Little Ones*, 1882; *Pickle and His Page Boy*, 1882; *Sowing and Sewing*, 1882; *Unknown to History*, 1882; *Stray Pearls*, 1883; *Langley Adventures*, 1884; *The Armourer's 'prentices*, 1884; *Nuttie's Father*, 1885; *The Two Sides of the Shield*, 1885; *Astray*, with others, 1886; *Chantry House*, 1886; *The Little Rick-Burners*, 1886; *A Modern Telemachus*, 1886; *Under the Storm*, 1887; *Beechcroft at Rockstone*, 1888; *Nurse's Memories*, 1888; *Our New Mistress*, 1888; *The Cunning Woman's Grandson*, 1889; *A Reputed Changeling*, 1889; *The Slaves of Sabinus*, 1890; *More Bywords*, 1890; *The Constable's Tower*, 1891; *Two Penniless Princesses*, 1891; *The Cross Roads*, 1892; *That Stick*, 1892; *Grisly Grisell*, 1893; *Strolling Players*, 1893; *The Treasures in the Marshes*, 1893; *The Cook and the Captive*, 1894; *The Rubies of St. Lô*, 1894; *The Carbonels*, 1895; *The Long Vacation*, 1895; *The Release*, 1896; *The Wardship of Steepcombe*, 1896; *The Pilgrimage of Ben Beriah*, 1897; *Founded on Paper*, 1897; *The Patriots of Palestine*, 1898; *The Herd Boy and His Hermit*, 1899; *The Making of a Missionary*, 1900; *Modern Broods*, 1900. **Plays:** *The Apple of Discord*, 1864; *Historical Dramas*, 1864. **Verse:** *Verses on the Gospel*, 1880.

* * *

Charlotte Yonge's was the voice of the early Victorian daughter of the squirearchy, earnest in her fervor to do duty in that state of life to which God had called her, eager to help others to do the same. Her first book was published in 1838, her last in 1901. Between those dates she wrote over 150 works—domestic stories for cottage and drawing room, historical tales, books of instruction both religious and secular, lengthy sagas of family life. But her outlook scarcely changed at all in over 60 years of authorship.

She never wrote for purely literary ends, but always directly or indirectly for the promotion of Christian truth, and the truth as it had been taught to her by John Keble when he prepared her for confirmation. Her duty as she had been taught by her parents remained her touchstone of excellence; she desired no other guide. To the early and mid-Victorian girl she herself was a guide, providing them with chronicles of large and life-like upper-class families whose characters are so real that a devoted coterie still discusses and analyses them today. Nor was it only the school-room who read her; in the 1850s *The Heir of Redclyffe* was received with enthusiasm by bishops and statesmen, undergraduates and Guards officers; it was one of the most popular Tractarian novels of its day.

The fascination of works such as *The Daisy Chain* and *The Pillars of the House* and their successors lies in the way they are interwoven, that one can walk in them as in Barsetshire, viewing characters from all aspects, in youth and middle life; as central figures in one book, as peripheral ones in another. The creation of personalities, in whom she believed as well as the reader, was her particular gift; plots were a secondary matter and she had no great skill in manipulating them. In her rather solitary childhood, cut off from all contemporaries except during rare and ecstatic visits to cousins, she had paced the gravel walks of her father's small Hampshire estate, inventing large families.

Within the framework of her family sagas is contained Yonge's teaching on the girl and young woman's role in life. It was, in fact, her own role of ardent submission to those in authority, be it clergyman, teacher, or parent. On the duty of those who achieved the status of authority she had nothing to say. "For her the newest, *youngest* thing was to do home and family duties more perfectly. What greater happiness can be given to youth?" wrote Christabel Coleridge in her memoir of 1903, and two generations of girls loved the chronicles of the Mays and the Underwoods, the Mohuns and the Merrifields. Their lofty ideals, their intellectual pursuits and conversation, their happy family relationship presented a way of life that they themselves yearned to imitate.

To a privileged few who named themselves her "goslings," she was Mother Goose and guided their strivings to educate and improve themselves. Some of these, like Christabel Coleridge, Florence Wilford, Frances Peard, subsequently themselves wrote for children. But, although she had thousands of admirers all over the world, as the century went on her message had increasingly little appeal to a generation of girls very different from her own, with whom she found it difficult to sympathise. Her implacable hostility to the idea of girls being educated outside the home circle—at the new high schools and at universities, for instance—did at last modify a little, and a little uneasily in her last novels she allowed the daughters of some of her original characters to enter Oxford or Cambridge. But she made it clear that she felt rather wary of such girls.

Her outlook was narrow, parochial even, since during the whole of her long life she barely moved beyond the Hampshire village where she had been born. Her literary work came second in her mind to her parish duties there, her attendance at Otterbourne church and her devotion to its school whose girls she had known and lovingly taught from her own childhood. For them she wrote many tales of cottage life as it should be lived, with decency, order, and deference towards the "great house," and above all stressing their duty to the church into which they had been baptized. Even in these didactic stories her gift for characterization, for sketching a social background, shines out and makes them charming evocations of a vanished way of life.

—Gillian Avery

FOREIGN-LANGUAGE WRITERS

Throughout this century, children's books of high quality translated from other languages have been published in the English-speaking countries, although not, it is generally acknowledged, to such an extent as the other way around: the children's literature of other world languages includes a far greater proportion of translations. The importance of making good foreign books available was stressed by Jella Lepman, founder of the Munich International Youth Library. Her vision of a world in which children of different countries grow up knowing more of each other through what they read is expressed in the title of her own *A Bridge of Children's Books* (1969). Mildred L. Batchelder in the United States formulated the same ideal in saying that "Interchange of children's books between countries, through translation, influences communication between the people of those countries."

As the 20th century draws towards its close, it becomes possible to see which foreign children's books published in English-language versions are likely to remain established classics in the same way as such 19th-century works as *Heidi, Pinocchio,* or *The Swiss Family Robinson,* which have been assimilated into a common international heritage. It is perhaps fitting that one of the major translated works of this century, Selma Lagerlöf's *The Wonderful Adventures of Nils,* stands with one foot, as it were, in the previous century. Its leisurely pace and strong moral tone look back to the 19th century in the tale of little Nils Holgersson, transformed to elf size because of his own selfish naughtiness, who learns from experience as he travels with wild geese, while the book's deep feeling for nature also looks forward to later works by 20th-century writers.

Some of the best-remembered titles published in the years between World Wars I and II were animal stories. There is great understanding of the natural world in the books of Felix Salten (the pseudonym of Sigmund Salzmann), whose delicacy of touch inevitably became rather blurred in the famous Walt Disney film of *Bambi.* The fine Père Castor series of animal picture books from France were favourites over a long period. Other books which first appeared in English at this time have attained the status of modern classics. Notable among them are Erich Kästner's *Emil and the Detectives,* prototype of the urban adventure story in which a gang of children outwit villainous adults (and still much livelier and more realistic than many of its followers), and Jean de Brunhoff's *The Story of Babar.* The stories of Babar the elephant, his family and companions were continued by de Brunhoff's son, Laurent, after their original creator's death.

It is in publishing of the latter part of this century, however, that one finds real expansion of the market for translated books. Lepman's ideal of complete internationalism in children's literature cannot quite be said to have been achieved. Not surprisingly, publishers find it easier to make a commercial success of books from European countries with cultural similarities. However, the 1980s show some welcome trends towards further internationalism: a novel by the Brazilian Lygia Bojunga-Nunes, winner of the 1982 Hans Christian Andersen award for outstanding achievement in children's literature (and the first Third World writer to be honoured in this way), is to be published in both the United Kingdom and the U.S.A. under the title *The Companions.* Another novel, *A Handful of Stars,* is by Syrian-born writer, Rafik Schami, who emigrated to Germany and writes in German, but on subjects from his own childhood background.

Obviously the picture-book field is one of the easiest in which to achieve internationalism, the pictures mattering as much as, or more than, the words. Distinguished artists such as Katrin Brandt, Ruth Hürlimann, Svend Otto S., and Lisbeth Zwerger will often illustrate a traditional text from Grimm, or some other familiar source. Lisbeth Zwerger, in illustrating some of the tales of E.T.A. Hoffmann (*The Nutcracker, The Strange Child)* and of Clemens Brentano (*The Legend of Rosepetal*), offers a very accessible introduction to the classics of European Romanticism, and the richly detailed pictures of the Russian artist Gennady Spirin, in *The Enchanter's Spell,* do the same for a selection of five authors including Cervantes. Japanese picture-book artists turned towards the western market quite early; some, such as Mitsumasa Anno, and Chihiro Iwasaki in the *Momoko* books, have contributed an Eastern delicacy of line and colour, although in the case of the latter's illustrations of such western tales as *Swan Lake* and *The Little Mermaid* the style is extremely westernized.

Mitsumasa Anno is the "deviser" of an extremely international picture book, *All in a Day,* with illustrations by different artists depicting a day in the lives of children all over the world. Some picture books may be planned to have international appeal, as in the anti-factory-farming theme of Jörg Muller and Jörg Steiner's *Rabbit Island,* or they may appeal through local colour, as in Mario Soldati's *The Octopus and the Pirates,* whose illustrations by Alberto Longoni give an attractive picture of north Italian life. The bucolic humour of Helme Heine's picture books strikes a particularly German note, while the *Ernest and Celestine* books by Gabrielle Vincent, from Belgium, appeal to the English liking for stories of charmingly drawn animals in an anthropomorphized domestic setting. The German author/illustrator Janosch uses his cheerful little animal characters in the manner of the fable, commenting with offbeat humour on human failings, especially in the series of stories about Little Bear and Little Tiger (*The Trip to Panama,* etc.). The Dutch artist Dick Bruna's brightly illustrated little books for very young children have long been popular.

Moving to books for an older age group, one finds a number of titles which resemble their English-language counterparts in the fields of fantasy, the historical novel, or the modern adventure story—and yet which are often slightly and interestingly different. The Hans Anderson award winner Astrid Lindgren, in *Pippi Longstocking,* first published shortly after World War II, wrote an undisputed modern classics: nine-year-old Pippi, immensely strong and kind-hearted, who breaks all the rules of "good behavior," appeals to the anarchic streak in her readers while coming down on the side of genuine goodness. In a similar iconoclastic vein Lindgren wrote *Emil in the Soup Tureen* and *Karlson on the Roof,* and branched out into other fields as well. *The Brothers Lionheart* is a fantasy raising moral questions, while the prize-winning *Ronia, The Robber's Daughter* treats themes of friendship, conflict, and death with great depth beneath its entertaining surface.

Another fine Swedish fantasy is *The Glassblower's Children* by Maria Gripe, who has also written stories of everyday life about children who do not quite fit into an everyday background, such as the attractive heroine of *Pappa Pellerin's Daughter.* Fantasy in Holland is well represented by Paul Biegel, with his *The King of the Copper Mountains* and other works. Biegel strikes a vein of sometimes humorous magic, employing traditional themes from European folklore. So does the German writer Otfried Preussler, in his comic fantasies about the exploits of traditional figures (*The Little Witch, The Little Ghost*), and his powerful tales for older readers (*The Adventures of Strong Vanya, The Satanic Mill*). James Krüss, also of Germany, has written stories such as *My Great-Grandfather and I,* with elements of the poetic and the marvellous, while the comic, the poetic, and the magical are all intertwined in the deservedly popular *Moomintroll* series by Tove

Jansson of Finland. For younger readers, Alf Proysen of Norway created a popular character of comic fantasy in *Little Old Mrs. Pepperpot,* and Angela Sommer-Bodenburg's *Little Vampire* stories, like Preussler's, draw comedy from ancient traditional themes. Reiner Zimnik's *The Crane* is a book hard to classify under any heading: a fine fable which is bleak, haunting, and humorous by turns. Comic verse from Russia, Kornei Chukovsky's *Dr. Concocter,* comes to English readers in a rollicking translation by Richard N. Coe. Christoph Hen's *Jamie and His Friends,* from East Germany, the tale of a little boy's adventures with his friends (toys come to life) exists in a magic childhood world previously thought of as peculiarly English, the world of A.A. Milne and Kenneth Grahame.

Runer Jonsson's *Viki Viking,* from Denmark, shows the historical Viking in a comic light, but serious historical novels of high quality have also been published in English translation: among them are works by Hans Baumann (*Sons of the Steppe, Dimitri and the False Tsars*), Barbara Bartos-Höppner (*Storm over the Caucasus, The Conquering Ships*), and Willi Fährmann, whose *The Long Journey of Lukas B.* describes a company of carpenters emigrating from Germany to America in the last century. Adventure stories include books by Leif Hamre of Norway (*Otter Three Two Calling!*), and An Rutgers van der Loeff of Holland (*Avalanche!* and *Children on the Oregon Trail*). The more modest, domestic type of adventure story is well represented in France by the books of Paul Berna (*A Hundred Million Francs*).

A particular feature of French children's literature as it is seen in translation is the number of eminent French writers who have written one or two works for children, without actually making a habit of it: they include André Maurois with *Fattypuffs and Thinifers,* Marcel Aymé with *The Wonderful Farm,* Maurice Druon with *Tistou of the Green Fingers,* Antoine de Saint-Exupéry with *The Little Prince* and Michel Tournier with *Friday and Robinson,* a junior version of his famous novel *Vendredi* in which the Crusoe/Man Friday situation is turned upside down. Another French-language phenomenon is the popularity of the strip-cartoon format: the many titles of Hergé's *Tintin* series, and the *Asterix the Gaul* series by Goscinny and Uderzo, have proved to be extremely popular in translation too, and in the late 1980s were among the most-borrowed books from the children's sections of British public libraries.

A particularly important area of translated literature from Europe is that of the war story: not the hearty adventures of characters such as the British Biggles, but novels from countries which actually underwent German occupation during World War II. The true classic is not, of course, a novel at all, but Anne Frank's *The Diary of a Young Girl.* From Holland, where the Frank family themselves were in hiding from the Nazis, comes a novel by Evert Hartman, *War Without Friends,* its central figure a boy with collaborating parents; from Norway, Aimée Sommerfelt's *Miriam,* with an account of a friendship between Jew and Gentile; from Greece, Alki Zei's *Petros' War;* from Italy, Carlo Picchio's *Freedom Fighter.* From Germany itself we have a stark, semi-autobiographical trilogy by Hans Peter Richter (*Friedrich, I Was There, The Time of the Young Soldiers*), and from Austria, Christine Nöstlinger's account of the Russian occupation of Vienna at the end of the war. A World War I story by Rudolf Frank, *No Hero for the Kaiser,* a kind of young people's parallel to Remarque's *All Quiet on the Western Front,* also had the distinction of being burned by the Nazis in the 1930s, and enjoyed a revival in Germany in the 1970s. Finally, the category of war stories should perhaps include a novel about a war which, it is to be hoped, never happens at all: Gudrun Pausewang, a German writer who works consistently for the spirit of international understanding, has written *The Last Children of Schevenborn,* a story of the harrowing aftermath of a nuclear strike.

The actual political setting of Anne Holm's *I Am David,* from Denmark, is purposely left vague, but the story tellingly evokes the horror inspired in its young hero by the idea of the labour camp from which he has escaped. However, the background to the Greek author Alki Zei's *Wildcat Under Glass* is clear enough, the story being set at the time of the Fascist seizure of power in 1936.

Books from Spain in English translation are few and far between, but do include the books of José María Sánchez-Silva, and more recently José Luis Olaizola's *Uncle Ambrosio's Helper,* in which an enterprising boy tries various ways to make money against the urban background of Madrid. An English translation exists of the Portuguese writer Miguel Torga's *Farrusco the Blackbird,* a book of animal fables. From Italy come several works by the Hans Anderson award winner, Gianni Rodari.

Over recent decades, several books from Russia and Eastern Europe have reached the English-language market, including titles by the Czech writers Václav Ctvrtek (*The Little Chalk Man*), Ota Hofman (*Escape*), and Jan Prochazka (*Long Live the Republic* and *Lenka*). Soviet books include Yuri Korinetz's *There, Far Beyond the River* and several other titles, almost pastoral in their timelessly Russian atmosphere, and Chingiz Aitmatov's *The White Ship* (originally published under an adult imprint in the United Kingdom).

In the 1970s and thereafter, what might loosely be called the social problem novel emerged as a notable phenomenon in most of the European countries as well as in the English-speaking world. These books may be directed at quite young children, as in Monica Gydal and Thomas Danielsson's series *Olly Sees It Through,* where little Olly has to face death, birth, and divorce in his family, and his own hospitalization. Such a catalogue of disasters is not, of course, meant to be gulped down by the child reader in one go; taken separately, the titles are probably helpful. For rather older readers, the Austrian Elfie Donnely has written movingly on the subjects of death (*So Long, Grandpa*) and mental disturbance in old age (*Old Stockings*). Death also features in a story from Denmark, Bjarne Reuter's *Buster's World.* Feminist subjects occur as well: in AnneCath. Vestly's *Hallo Aurora!,* from Norway, for instance, the central character's parents have reversed their roles.

Naturally enough, the "social problem" tends to figure most prominently in books for older children. Sexual problems, divorce, drugs, death, alcoholism, racism all appear, as well as that staple theme of the young adult novel, the difficulties of adjusting to growing up. A good deal of mediocre stuff is written in this genre, but on the whole only the best examples come through to English-language readers: those books where the author puts the individual character or predicament first, and the generalized social problem comes second. Among such works are the books for older readers of Gunnel Beckman (*Mia, Admission to the Feast*), and Christine Nöstlinger, who combines radical social views with comedy.

Far more could be said about the relationship between children's literature originally written in English and that translated from other languages than the scope of this brief survey allows, and many more authors could have been named. It is a tenable theory that translations have a particularly important part to play in children's literature, because apart from a tiny minority of the genuinely bilingual, the young reader will simply be unable to read a good children's book in a foreign language while he or she is still a child. Considerable responsibility, therefore, lies with the publishers and translators who make such books available.

—Anthea Bell

Selected books in translation (dates are of first English-language editions):

AITMATOV, Chingiz. Russian. *Farewell, Gul'sary,* 1970; *The White Ship (The White Steamship),* 1972; *The Cranes Fly Early,* 1983.

ANNO, Mitsumasa. Japanese. *Topsy-Turvies,* 1970; *Upside-Downers,* 1971; *Dr. Anno's Magical Midnight Circus,* 1972; *Anno's Alphabet,* 1975; *Anno's Counting Book,* 1977; *Anno's Journey,* 1978; *Anno's Animals,* 1979; *Anno's Italy,* 1979; *The King's Flower,* 1979; *The Unique World of Mitsumasa Anno,* edited by Samuel Crowell Morse, 1980; *Anno's Medieval World,* 1980; *Anno's Magical ABC,* with Masaichiro Anno, 1981; *Anno's Counting House,* 1982; *Anno's Britain,* 1982; *Anno's Mysterious Multiplying Jar,* with Masaichiro Anno, 1983; *Anno's U.S.A.,* 1983; *Anno's Flea Market,* 1984; *Anno's Hat Tricks,* with Akihiro Nozaki, 1985; *All in a Day,* 1986; *Anno's Peekaboo,* 1987; *In Shadowland,* 1988.

AYMÉ, Marcel. French. *The Wonderful Farm,* 1951; *The Magic Pictures,* 1954.

BARTOS-HÖPPNER, Barbara. German. *The Cossacks,* 1962; *Save the Khan,* 1963; *Avalanche Dog,* 1966; *Storm over the Caucasus,* 1968; *Hunters of Siberia,* 1969; *Hallowe'en Lanterns,* 1971; *The Conquering Ships,* 1978; *My Favourite Trees,* 1980; *My Favourite Animals,* 1981.

BAUMANN, Hans. German. *Sons of the Steppe,* 1958; *The Barque of the Brothers,* 1958; *Jackie the Pit Pony,* 1958; *Angelina and the Birds,* 1959; *The Lion and the Unicorn,* 1959; *The Dragon Next Door,* 1960; *The Crotchety Crocodile,* 1960; *I Marched with Hannibal,* 1961; *The Bear and His Brothers,* 1962; *Caspar and His Friends,* 1967; *The Circus Is Here,* 1967; *Fenny,* 1970; *Dimitri and the False Tsars,* 1972; *The Hare's Race,* 1976; *The Three in the Blue Balloon,* 1976; *Katzimir the Greatest,* 1977; *Dragon Mountain,* 1979; *Wings for Icarus,* 1980; *Animal Babies,* 1984; *Barnabus the Dancing Bear,* 1984; *My Friends on the Farm,* 1985; *Chip Has Many Bothers,* 1985; *Mischa and His Brothers,* 1985.

BECKMAN, Gunnel. Swedish. *The Girl Without a Name,* 1970; *Admission to the Feast (19 Is Too Young to Die),* 1971; *A Room of His Own,* 1973; *Mia* series, from 1974; *That Early Spring,* 1977.

BERNA, Paul. French. *A Hundred Million Francs (The Horse Without a Head),* 1957; *Continent in the Sky,* 1959; *The Street Musician,* 1960; *Flood Warning,* 1962; *The Mystery of Saint-Salgue,* 1963; *The Clue of the Black Cat,* 1964; *The Mystery of the Crossed-Eyed Man,* 1965; *The Secret of the Missing Boat,* 1966; *The Mule of the Motorway (The Mule of the Expressway),* 1967; *A Truckload of Rice,* 1968; *They Didn't Come Back,* 1969; *The Myna Bird Mystery,* 1970; *Gaby and the New Money Fraud,* 1971; *Vagabonds of the Pacific,* 1973; *The Last Dawn,* 1977.

BIEGEL, Paul. Dutch. *The King of the Copper Mountains,* 1969; *The Little Captain* series, from 1971; *The Seven-Times Search,* 1971; *The Twelve Robbers,* 1974; *The Gardens of Dorr,* 1975; *The Elephant Party and Other Stories,* 1977; *Far Beyond and Back Again,* 1977; *Robber Hopsika,* 1978; *The Dwarfs of Nosegay* series, from 1978; *Letters from the General,* 1979; *The Looking-Glass Castle,* 1979; *The Clock Struck Twelve,* 1979; *The Tincan Beast,* 1980; *The Curse of the Werewolf,* 1981; *Virgil Nosegay* series, from 1981; *Crocodile Man,* 1982.

BOJUNGA-NUNES, Lygia. Brazilian. *The Companions,* 1990.

BRUNA, Dick. Dutch. *The Happy Apple,* 1959; *Tilly and Tessa (Tilly and Tess),* 1962; *The Little Bird,* 1962; *The Apple,* 1963; *The Circus,* 1963; *The Fish,* 1963; *Kitten Nell,* 1963; *Miffy* series, from 1964; *The Egg,* 1964; *The King,* 1964; *Hop-o'-My-Thumb,* 1966; *The School,* 1966; *The Sailor,* 1966; *A Story to Tell* series, from 1968; *I Can Read More,* 1969; *Snuffy* series, from 1970; *My Vest Is White (My Shirt Is White),* 1973; *Animal Book,* 1974; *Animal Frieze,* 1975; *Lisa and Lynn,* 1975; *My Meals,* 1975; *The Christmas Book,* 1976; *I Can Dress Myself,* 1977; *Poppy Pig* series, from 1978; *I Can Read,* 1979; *I Can Count,* 1979; *My Toys,* 1980; *Out and About,* 1980; *When I'm Big,* 1981; *I Know About Numbers,* 1981; *Word Book,* 1982; *The Lifeboat,* 1984; *I Can Make Music,* 1984; *Blue Boat,* with Peter Jones, 1984; *Farmer John,* 1984; *The Orchestra,* 1984; *The Rescue,* 1984; *I Know About Shapes,* 1984; *My House,* 1984; *Playing in Winter,* 1984; *My Playtime,* 1985; *Back to Front,* 1986; *Find My Hat,* 1986; *My Sport Book,* 1986; *Through the Year with Boris Bear,* 1987.

BRUNHOFF, Jean de. French. *The Story of Babar, The Little Elephant,* 1933; *The Travels of Babar,* 1934; *Babar the King,* 1935; *Babar and His Children,* 1938; *Babar and Father Christmas,* 1940; *Babar and Zephir,* 1942.

BRUNHOFF, Laurent de. French. Continuation of Jean de Brunhoff's *Babar* series, from 1948; *Serafina* series, from 1961; *Anatole and His Donkey,* 1963; *Bonhomme* series, from 1965; *Gregory and the Lady Turtle in the Valley of the Music Trees,* 1971; *The One Pig with Horns,* 1979.

PÈRE CASTOR (pseudonym for Lida). French. *Wild Animal Books: Bourru, Frou, Mischief, Plouf, Scaf, Quipic, Martin, Cuckoo,* 1937-42.

CHUKOVSKY, Kornei. Russian. *Crocodile,* 1931; *The Telephone,* 1961; *Wash 'em Clean,* 1962; *Dr. Concocter,* 1967; *The Muddle,* 1976; *The Silver Crest,* 1977; *Good Morning Chick,* 1980; *Cock the Roach,* 1981; *Stolen Sun,* 1983; *Little Chick,* 1985.

CTRTEK, Václav. Czechoslovakian. *The Little Chalk Man,* 1970.

DONNELLY, Elfie. Austrian. *So Long, Grandpa,* 1980; *Odd Stockings,* 1982; *Offbeat Friends,* 982; *Tina into Two Won't Go,* 1983; *A Package for Miss Marshwater,* 1987.
DRUON, Maurice. French. *Tistou of the Green Fingers (Tistou of the Green Thumbs),* 1958.

FÄHRMANN, Willi. German. *The Long Journey of Lukas B.,* 1985.

FRANK, Rudolf. German. *The Boy Who Forgot His Birthday (No Hero for the Kaiser),* 1985.

FROLOV, Vadim. Russian. *What It's All About,* 1968.

GRIPE, Maria. Swedish. *Pappa Pellerin's Daughter,* 1966; *Hugo and Josephine* series, from 1969; *The Night Daddy,* 1971; *The*

Glassblower's Children, 1974; *The Land Beyond,* 1974; *Julia's House,* 1975; *Elvis* series, from 1976; *In the Time of the Bells,* 1976; *The Green Coat,* 1977.

GUILLOT, René. French. *Companions of Fortune,* 1952; *Sirga,* 1953; *The 397th White Elephant,* 1954; *The King's Corsair,* 1954; *Kpo the Leopard,* 1955; *The Wind of Chance,* 1955; *A Boy and Five Huskies,* 1957; *Prince of the Jungle,* 1958; *Elephant Road,* 1959; *Grishka and the Bear,* 1959; *Nicolette and the Mill,* 1960; *The Fantastic Brother,* 1961; *The Wild White Stallion,* 1961; *Sama,* 1961; *The Troubadour,* 1965; *The Champion of Olympia,* 1968; *Little Dog Lost,* 1969; *Castle in Spain,* 1970.

GYDAL, Monica. Swedish. *Olly Sees It Through* series (with Thomas Danielsson), from 1976.

HAMRE, Leif. Norwegian. *Otter Three Two Calling! (Leap into Danger),* 1959; *Edge of Disaster,* 1960; *Perilous Wings,* 1961; *Blue Two-Bale Out!,* 1961; *Ready for Take-Off,* 1962; *Contact Lost,* 1967; *Operation Arctic,* 1973.

HARTMAN, Evert. Dutch. *War Without Friends,* 1982.

HEIN, Christoph. German. *Jamie and His Friends,* 1988.

HEINE, Helme. German. *The Pigs' Wedding,* 1978; *Superhare,* 1979; *Imagine If,* 1979; *Merry-Go-Round,* 1980; *Mr. Miller the Dog,* 1980; *King Bounce the First,* 1982; *Friends,* 1982; *The Most Wonderful Egg in the World,* 1983; *The Friends' Racing Cart (The Racing Cart),* 1984; *The Pearl,* 1985; *The Friends Have a Visitor (The Visitor),* 1985; *The Alarm Clock,* 1985; *Saturday in Paradise (One Day in Paradise),* 1986; *Seven Wild Pigs,* 1986.

HOFMAN, Ota. Czechoslovakian. *Escape,* 1970.

HOLM, Anne. Danish. *I Am David (North to Freedom),* 1965; *The Hostage,* 1980.

IWASAKI, Chihiro. Japanese. *Staying at Home on a Rainy Day,* 1969; *Momoko* series, from 1972; *The Birthday Wish,* 1974; *Will You Be My Friend?,* 1974; *What's Fun Without a Friend?,* 1975; *Onito's Hat,* 1978; *The Day I Got Better,* 1980; *The Wise Queen,* 1986.

JANOSCH. German. *Just One Apple,* 1966; *Joshua and the Magic Fiddle,* 1968; *Bollerbam,* 1969; *Dear Snowman,* 1970; *The Thieves and the Raven,* 1970; *The Magic Auto,* 1971; *The Yellow Auto Named Ferdinand,* 1973; *Zampano's Performing Bear,* 1976; *Hey Presto, You're a Bear!,* 1977; *Luke Caraway, Master Magician or Indian Chief,* 1977; *The Rain Car,* 1978; *The Trip to Panama,* 1978; *Crafty Caspar and His Good Old Granny,* 1979; *The Big Janosch Book of Fun and Verse,* 1980; *The Treasure-Hunting Trip,* 1980; *A Letter for Tiger,* 1981; *Animal Antics,* 1982; *See You in the Morning!,* 1983; *The Cricket and the Mole,* 1983; *The Higher and Higher House,* 1984; *I'll Make You Well, Tiger, Said the Bear (Little Tiger, Get Well Soon!),* 1985; *The Curious Tale of Hare and Hedgehog,* 1985; *The Old Man and the Bear,* 1987; *Hello, Little Pig,* 1988; *The Little Hare Book,* 1988.

JANSSON, Tove. Finnish. *Moomintroll* series, from 1950; *Who Will Comfort Toffle?,* 1960; *The Summer Book,* 1975; *Sun City,* 1976; *The Dangerous Journey,* 1978.

JONSSON, Runer. Danish. *Viki Viking (Vicke the Viking),* 1968.

KÄSTNER, Erich. German. *Emil and the Detectives,* 1930; *Annaluise and Anton,* 1932; *The 35th of May,* 1933; *The Flying Classroom,* 1934; *Emil and the Three Twins,* 1935; *The Animals' Conference,* 1949; *Lottie and Lisa (Lisa and Lottie),* 1950; *The Little Man,* 1966.

KORINETZ, Yuri. Russian. *There, Far Beyond the River,* 1973; *In the Middle of the World,* 1976; *The River and the Forest,* 1978.

KRÜSS, James. German. *My Great-Grandfather and I,* 1964; *Eagle and Dove,* 1965; *3 x 3,* 1965; *The Happy Islands Behind the Winds,* 1966; *Florentine,* 1967; *The Animal Parade,* 1968; *The Lighthouse on the Lobster Cliffs,* 1969; *The Proud Wooden Drummer,* 1969; *Letters to Pauline,* 1971; *My Great-Grandfather, the Heroes, and I,* 1973.

KUIJER, Guus. Dutch. *Daisy's New Head,* 1980.

KURATOMI, Chizuko (illustrator: Kozo Kakimoto). Japanese. *Barnabas Ball at the Circus,* 1967; *Mr. Bear* series, from 1968; *Runaway James and the Night Owl,* 1968; *Run, Chase the Sun,* 1969; *Pim and the Fisherboy,* 1975.

LAGERLÖF, Selma. Swedish. *The Wonderful Adventures of Nils,* 1907; *The Further Adventures of Nils,* 1911.

LINDGREN, Astrid. Swedish. *Pippi Longstocking* series, from 1950; *Bill Bergson* series, from 1952; *Mio, My Son,* 1956; *Kati* series, from 1961; *The Tomten* series, from 1961; *Rasmus and the Tramp (Rasmus and the Vagabond),* 1961; *Noisy Village (Bullerby)* series, from 1962; *The Children on Troublemaker Street,* 1962; *Christmas in the Stable,* 1962; *Lotta* series, from 1963; *The Mischievous Martens,* 1964; *Seacrow Island,* 1968; *Emil* series, from 1970; *Karlson (Karlsson)* series, from 1971; *The Brothers Lionheart,* 1975; *Mardie* series, from 1979; *I Want to Go to School Too,* 1980; *Ronia, The Robber's Daughter,* 1983; *The Runaway Sleigh Ride,* 1984; *My Nightingale Is Singing,* 1985; *The Dragon with Red Eyes,* 1986; *The Ghost of Skinny Jack,* 1988; *I Want a Brother or Sister,* 1988; *I Don't Want to Go to Bed,* 1988.

LOEFF, An Rutgers van der. Dutch. *Avalanche!,* 1954; *They're Drowning Our Village,* 1959; *Children on the Oregon Trail (Oregon at Last!),* 1961; *Rossie,* 1964; *Great Day in Holland,* 1965; *Vassilis on the Run,* 1965; *Flight from the Polar Night,* 1968; *Steffos and His Easter Lamb,* 1969.

MAUROIS, André. French. *Fattypuffs and Thinifers,* 1941.

MÜLLER, Jörg, and STEINER, Jörg. Germans. *Rabbit Island,* 1977; *The Bear Who Wanted to Stay a Bear (The Bear Who Wanted to Be a Bear),* 1977; *The Sea People,* 1982.

NAKATANI, Chiyoko. Japanese. *The Day Chiro Was Lost,* 1968; *Fumio and the Dolphins,* 1970; *The Zoo in My Garden,* 1973; *My Animal Friends,* 1975; *My Teddy Bear,* 1975; *My Day on the Farm,* 1976; *My Treasures,* 1979; *Feeding Babies,* 1981.

NÖSTLINGER, Christine. Austrian. *Fly Away Home,* 1975; *The Cucumber King,* 1975; *The Disappearing Cellar,* 1975; *Fiery*

Frederica, 1975; *Conrad (Conrad, The Factory-Made Boy; Konrad),* 1976; *Girl Missing,* 1976; *Four Days in the Life of Lisa,* 1977; *Mr. Bat's Great Invention,* 1978; *Marrying Off Mother,* 1978; *Luke and Angela,* 1979; *Lollipop,* 1982; *But Jasper Came Instead,* 1983; *Brainbox Sorts It Out (Brainbox Cracks the Case),* 1985; *Guardian Ghost,* 1986.

OLAIZOLA, José Luis. Spanish. *Uncle Ambrosio's Helper,* 1989.

PAUSEWANG, Gudrun. German. *The Last Children of Schevenborn,* 1989.

PICCHIO, Carlo. Italian. *Freedom Fighter,* 1980.

PREUSSLER, Otfried. German. *The Little Witch,* 1961; *Thomas Scarecrow,* 1963; *The Robber Hotzenplotz* series, from 1964; *The Little Ghost,* 1967; *The Adventures of Strong Vanya,* 1970; *The Satanic Mill,* 1972; *The Wise Men of Schilda,* 1974; *The Green Bronze Bell,* 1977; *Herbie's Magical Hat,* 1985; *The Tale of the Unicorn,* 1989.

PROCHAZKA, Jan. Czechoslovakian. *Long Live the Republic,* 1973; *The Carp,* 1977; Lenka, 1979.

PROYSEN, Alf. Norwegian. *Little Old Mrs. Pepperpot* series, from 1959; *Stories for Christmas,* 1987; *Stories for Summer,* 1989.

REUTER, Bjarne. Danish. *The Princess and the Sun, Moon and Stars,* 1986; *Buster's World,* 1988.

RICHTER, Hans Peter. German. *Friedrich,* 1970; *I Was There,* 1972; *The Time of the Young Soldiers,* 1976.

RODARI, Gianni. Italian. *Telephone Tales,* 1965; *The Befana's Toyshop,* 1970; *A Pie in the Sky,* 1971; *Mr. Cat in Business,* 1975; *Tales Told by a Machine,* 1976.

SAINT-EXUPÉRY, Antoine de. French. *The Little Prince,* 1943.

SALTEN, Felix. German. *Bambi: A Life in the Woods,* 1928; *Fifteen Rabbits,* 1930; *The Hound of Florence,* 1930; *Florian,* 1934; *Perri,* 1938; *Bambi's Children,* 1939; *Renni the Rescuer,* 1940.

SÁNCHEZ-SILVA, José María. Spanish. *Marcelino (The Miracle of Marcelino),* 1954; *The Boy and the Whale,* 1964; *Ladis* series, from 1968.

SANDMAN LILIUS, Irmelin. Swedish. *The Maharajah Adventure,* 1966; *Gold Crown Lane,* 1976; *The Goldmaker's House,* 1978; *Horses of the Night,* 1979; *King Tulle,* 1980.

SCHAMI, Rafik. German. *A Handful of Stars,* 1989.

SOLDATI, Mario. Italian. *The Octopus and the Pirates,* 1974.

SOMMER-BONDENBURG, Angela. German. *Little Vampire (Vampire)* series, from 1982; *Coco's Birthday Surprise,* 1987.

SOMMERFELT, Aimée. Norwegian. *The Road to Agra,* 1961; *Miriam,* 1963; *The White Bungalow,* 1963; *My Name Is Pablo,* 1966; *No Easy Way,* 1967.

TORGA, Miguel. Portuguese. *Farrusco the Blackbird,* 1950.

TOURNIER, Michel. French. *Friday and Robinson,* 1972.

UNNERSTAD, Edith. Swedish. *The Saucepan Journey,* 1951; *Pysen,* 1955; *Little O,* 1957; *The Spettecake Holiday,* 1958; *The Journey with Grandmother (Grandmother's Journey),* 1960; *A Journey to England,* 1961; *The Cats from Summer Island,* 1963; *The Picnic,* 1964; *The Urchin,* 1964; *The Pip-Larssons Go Sailing,* 1966; *Toppen and I at the Croft,* 1966; *Larry Makes Music,* 1967; *Two Little Gigglers,* 1967; *A House for Spinner's Grandmother,* 1970; *Mickie,* 1971; *The Cherry Tree Party,* 1978.

VESTLY, Anne-Cath. Norwegian. *Aurora* series, from 1973; *Eight Children* series, from 1973.

VINCENT, Gabrielle. Belgian. *Ernest and Celestine* series, from 1982.

WATANBE, Shigeo (illustrator: Yasuo Ohtomo). Japanese. *How Do I Put It On?,* 1979; *Hallo! How Are You? (Where's My Daddy?),* 1980; *How Do I Eat It? (What a Good Lunch!),* 1980; *Ready, Steady, Go! (Get Set! Go!),* 1981; *I Can Do It! (I Can Ride It!),* 1982; *I'm the King of the Castle,* 1982; *I Can Build a House!,* 1983; *I'm Going for a Walk! (I Can Take a Walk!),* 1984; *I'm Playing with Papa (Daddy, Play with Me!),* 1985; *I'm Having a Bath with Papa! (I Can Take a Bath!),* 1986; *It's My Birthday!,* 1988.

ZEI, Alki. Greek. *Wildcat under Glass,* 1968; *Petros' War,* 1972; *The Sound of Dragon's Feet,* 1979.

ZIMNIK, Reiner. German. *Jonah and the Fisherman,* 1956; *The Proud White Circus Horse,* 1957; *Little Owl,* 1960; *The Bear on the Motorcycle,* 1963; *The Crane,* 1969; *The Bear and the People,* 1971; *Bill's Balloon Ride,* 1973.

NATIONALITY INDEX

Below is the list of entrants that appear in the main body of the book and the appendix of 19th-century writers divided by nationality. It should be noted that "British" was used for all English entrants and for any other British entrant who chose that designation over a more specific one, such as "Scottish."

American
Verna Aardema
Chester Aaron
Arnold Adoff
Sue Ann Alderson
Lloyd Alexander
Aliki
George Ancona
C. W. Anderson
Frank Asch
Richard Atwater
Esther Averill
Jim Aylesworth
Natalie Babbitt
Martha Bacon
Carolyn Sherwin Bailey
Betty Baker
Molly Garrett Bang
Leonard Baskin
L. Frank Baum
John and Patricia Beatty
Shonto Begay
Harry Behn
Ludwig Bemelmans
Rex Benedict
Jan and Stan Berenstain
Claire Huchet Bishop
Joan W. Blos
Crosby Bonsall
Arna Bontemps
Helen Dore Boylston
Jan Brett
Norman Bridwell
Robert Bright
Carol Ryrie Brink
Bill Brittain
William J. Brooke
Walter R. Brooks
Marc Brown
Marcia Brown
Margaret Wise Brown
Joseph Bruchac III
Ashley Bryan
Clyde Robert Bulla
Thornton Waldo Burgess
Ben Lucien Burman
Frances Hodgson Burnett
Virginia Lee Burton
Oliver Butterworth
Eric Carle
Natalie Savage Carlson
Sylvia Cassedy
Mary Chalmers
Charlotte Chorpenning
John Ciardi
Ann Nolan Clark
Beverly Cleary
Lucille Clifton
Shirley Climo
Eleanor Clymer
Elizabeth Coatsworth
Eleanor Coerr
Barbara Cohen
Barbara Cooney
Scott Corbett
Donald Crews
Pat Cummings
Julia Cunningham
Jane Louise Curry
Alice Dalgliesh
James Daugherty
Edgar and Ingri Parin d'Aulaire
Marguerite de Angeli
Meindert De Jong
Demi
Tomie dePaola
Beatrice Schenk de Regniers
Elizabeth Borton de Treviño
William Pène du Bois
Roger Duvoisin
Edward Eager
Walter D. Edmonds
Lois Ehlert
Elizabeth Enright
Eleanor Estes
Marie Hall Ets
Louise Fatio
Edward Fenton
Rachel Field
Aileen Fisher
Dorothy Canfield Fisher
Leonard Everett Fisher
John D. Fitzgerald
Louise Fitzhugh
Marjorie Flack
Sid Fleischman
James Flora
Dennis Foon
Don Freeman
Jean Fritz
Gyo Fujikawa
Wanda Gág
Ruth Stiles Gannett
Patricia Lee Gauch
Gail Gibbons
Phoebe Gilman
Nikki Giovanni
Edward Gorey
Hardie Gramatky
Bette Greene
Constance C. Greene
Eloise Greenfield
Helen V. Griffith
Nikki Grimes
Johnny Gruelle
Berta and Elmer Hader

Australian

British

TITLE INDEX

The following list includes the titles of all fiction, drama, poetry, picture books, and selected non-fiction for children cited in the main entries and the appendix of 19th-century writers. The name in parentheses is meant to direct the reader to the appropriate entry where full publication information is given. Works of poetry, plays, and collections of short stories are indicated with the following abbreviations: p (poetry), pl (play), s (short stories). The term "series" indicates a recurring word or phrase in the titles of an entrant's books; the date listed is that of the earliest title in which the word or phrase occurs. Titles beginning with "The Adventure(s) of," "Case of," "Mystery of," "Story of ," "Tales from," and "Tale(s) of " are alphabetized according to the first key word.

123456789 Benn (McKee), 1970
3 Jelliplays (pl Jellicoe), 1975
4-Way Stop and Other Poems (p Livingston), 1976
9 Lives of Balthazar (Fienberg), 1989
13 Clocks (Thurber), 1950
13th Floor: A Ghost Story (Fleischman), 1995
18 Washington Square, South (pl L'Engle), 1940
26 Fairmount Avenue (dePaola), 1999
50 Below Zero (Munsch), 1985
50 Odd Jobs: A Wild and Wacky Rhyming Guide to One-of-a-Kind Careers (p Rosen, Michael J.), 1988
51 Sycamore Lane (Sharmat), 1971
59 Cats (Seed), 1983
69th Grandchild (Hunt, M.), 1951
121 Pudding Street (Fritz), 1955
264-Pound Burglar, Case of the (Fleischman), 1982
329th Friend (Sharmat), 1979
$500 (Alger, appendix) 1890
500 Hats of Bartholomew Cubbins (p Seuss), 1938
729 Animal Allsorts (Oxenbury), 1980
729 Curious Creatures (Oxenbury), 1980
729 Merry Mix-ups (Oxenbury), 1980
729 Puzzle People (Oxenbury), 1980
2095 (Scieszka), 1995

A.B.C. Girl (Meade, appendix), 1910
A.B.C. of Every-Day People (p Farrow), 1902
A.N.T.I.D.O.T.E (Blackman), 1996
"A" Stands for Angel (p Robinson), 1939
Aardvarks, Disembark! (Jonas), 1990
Aaron and Gayla's Alphabet Book (Greenfield), 1993
Aaron and Gayla's Counting Book (Greenfield), 1993
Aaron and the Green Mountain Boys (Gauch), 1972
Aaron in the Wildwoods (Harris, J., appendix), 1897
Aaron, Story of (Harris, J., appendix), 1896
Abandoned (Griffiths, G.), 1973
Abbey by the Sea (Molesworth, appendix), 1887
Abbey Church (Yonge, appendix), 1844
Abbie's God Book (Holland), 1982
Abbotsbury Ring (Greaves), 1979
ABC (Beck), 1995
ABC (Burningham), 1964
ABC (p Seuss), 1963
ABC (Szekeres), 1983
ABC Bunny (Gág), 1933
ABC Exhibit (Fisher, L.), 1991
ABC of Things (Oxenbury), 1972
ABCDEFGHIJKLMNOPQRSTUVWXYZ (p Kuskin), 1963
Abdul (Wells), 1975
Abdul the Awful (Hough), 1970
Abe Lincoln's Beard (Wahl), 1971
Abe Lincoln—New Salem Days (pl Chorpenning), 1941
Abel's Island (Steig), 1976
Abena and the Python (Appiah), 1991
Aboard the Hylow on Sable Island Bank (Otis, appendix), 1907
About Bellamy (de Treviño), 1940
About the B'nai Bagels (Konigsburg), 1969
About Us (Gibbs), 1912
Above Suspicion (Gordon, G.), 1990
Abraham Lincoln: A Man for All the People (p Livingston), 1993
Abraham Lincoln, Rail Splitter (pl Mackay, Constance D'Arcy), 1912
Abram, Abram, Where Are We Going? (McKissack), 1984
Absent Author, Case of the (Hildick), 1995
Absolute Zero (Cresswell), 1978
Absurd Ditties (p Farrow), 1903
Acacia Terrace (Wilson, B.), 1988
Acceptable Time (L'Engle), 1989
Accidental Twins (Bull), 1982
Ace Dragon Ltd. (Hoban), 1980
Ace: The Very Important Pig (King-Smith), 1990
Acorn Quest (Yolen), 1981
Acrobat Hamster (Cockett), 1965
Acrobat's Girlhood (Stretton, appendix), 1889
Across America on an Emigrant Train (Murphy, Jim), 1993
Across the Blue Mountains (Clark, E.), 1993
Across the Delaware (Otis, appendix), 1903
Across the Frontier (Pullein-Thompson, C.), 1990
Across the Range and Other Stories (Otis, appendix), 1914
Across the Roman Wall (Breslin), 1997
Action at Paradise Marsh (Wier), 1968
Active-Enzyme Lemon-Freshened Junior High School Witch (Hildick), 1973
Adam and the Golden Cock (Dalgliesh), 1959
Adam Troy, Astroman (Patchett), 1954
Adam's Key (Lattimore, E.), 1976
Adelaide (Ungerer), 1959
Adirondack Cabin (Sidney, appendix), 1890
Admiral J. of Spurwick (Otis, appendix), 1896
Admiral's Walk (Barne), 1953
Adolphus; or, The Adopted Dolphin and the Pirate's Daughter (p Flack), 1941
Adopted by the Eagles (Goble), 1994
Adopted Daughter (Clewes), 1968
Adopting of Mickie (Chaundler), 1925
Adrienne (Le Feuvre), 1928
Adrienne and the Chalet School (Brent-Dyer), 1965
Adrift in New York (Alger, appendix), 1903
Adrift in the City (Alger, appendix), 1895
Advantage Miss Jackson (Hardcastle), 1991

Ball Bounced (Tafuri), 1989
Ball, The Lollipop Man, The Nest (Tate, J.), 1969
Ballad of Aucassin and Nicolette (pl Causley), 1978
Ballad of Belle Dorcas (Hooks), 1990
Ballad of Benny Perhaps (Brinsmead), 1977
Ballad of Cactus Jack (Benedict), 1975
Ballad of the Lost Hare (p Sidney, appendix), 1882
Ballad of the Pirate Queens (Yolen), 1995
Ballet Family (Allan), 1963
Ballet Family Again (Allan), 1964
Ballet Shoes (Streatfeild), 1936
Ballet Shoes for Anna (Streatfeild), 1972
Balloon That Brought Luck (Cockett), 1978
Balloon Tree (Gilman), 1984
Ballooning Boy (Carter, B.), 1960
Ballot Box Battle (McCully), 1996
Bamboo Hats and a Rice Cake (Demi), 1993
Bamboo, The Grass Tree (Sperry), 1942
Banana Bird and the Snakemen (Roughsey; Trezise), 1980
Banana Blitz (Heide), 1983
Banana Twist (Heide), 1978
Bananas (Ancona), 1990
Bananas: From Manolo to Margie (Ancona), 1982
Bananas Gorilla: Richard Scarry's Smallest Pop-up Book Ever! (Scarry), 1992
Band in School (Berg), 1975
Band of Mirth (Meade, appendix), 1914
Band of Three (Meade, appendix), 1884
Bandaberry (Meynell), 1960
Bandit of Mok Hill (Lampman), 1969
Bandits in the Hills (Pullein-Thompson, C.), 1962
Bandit's Moon (Fleischman), 1998
Bang, Bang, You're Dead (Fitzhugh), 1969
Bank House Twins (Fidler), 1955
Banner, The Pacing White Stallion (Chipperfield), 1972
Bannister Twins (Marchant), 1929
Banshee Towers, Mystery of (Blyton), 1961
Barbara's Birthday (Stevenson, J.), 1983
Barbara's Brothers (Everett-Green, appendix), 1887
Barberry Bush and Eight Other Stories (Coolidge, appendix), 1892
Barbie (Barne), 1952
Barcha the Tiger (Bisset), 1971
Barclay of the Guides (Strang), 1908
Bard of Avon: The Story of William Shakespeare (Stanley), 1992
Bargain Bride (Lampman), 1977
Bargain for Frances (Hoban), 1970
Barge Children (Cresswell), 1968
Barkley (Hoff), 1975
Barn Party (Tafuri), forthcoming
Barnaby and Bell and the Birthday Cake (Oldfield), 1985
Barnaby and Bell and the Lost Button (Oldfield), 1985
Barney the Hedgehog (Mullen), 1988
Barney's Horse (Hoff), 1987
Barnyard Lullaby (Asch), 1998
Baron's Booty (p Kahl), 1963
Barracuda Mystery (Catherall), 1971
Barrel (Wier), 1966
Barrier Reef Bandits (Catherall, as Hallard), 1960
Barriers (Corlett), 1981
Barrow Lane Gang (Streatfeild), 1968
Barry Gets His Wish (Meynell, as Tring), 1952
Barry's Exciting Year (Meynell, as Tring), 1951
Barry's Great Day (Meynell, as Tring), 1954
Bartholomew and the Oobleck (p Seuss), 1949
Bartholomew the Bossy (Sharmat), 1984
Bartle Bequest (Bruce, D.), 1955
Barty Crusoe and His Man Saturday (Burnett), 1909
Baseball Bargain (Corbett, S.), 1970
Baseball Bats for Christmas (Kusugak), 1990
Baseball Crazy (Godfrey), 1987
Baseball Fever (Hurwitz), 1981
Baseball Mouse (Hoff), 1969
Baseball's All-time All-stars (Murphy, Jim), 1984
Bashful Bank Robber, Case of the (Hildick), 1981
Bashful Fifteen (Meade, appendix), 1892
Basil and the Lost Colony (Titus), 1964
Basil and the Pygmy Cats (Titus), 1971
Basil Brush of the Yard (Cole), 1977
Basil Chimpy Isn't Bright (Judah), 1959
Basil Chimpy's Comic Light (Judah), 1960
Basil in Mexico (Titus), 1976
Basil in the Wild West (Titus), 1981
Basil of Baker Street (Titus), 1958
Basil Ratski (Ungerer), 1967
Basket of Surprises (Blyton), 1970
Basketball Toss Up (Heide, as Allen), 1972
Bassumtyte Treasure (Curry), 1978
Bastable Cove (Strang), 1922
Bat Child's Haunted House (Mayer), 1983
Bat Is Born (p Jarrell), 1978
Bat-Poet (Jarrell), 1964
Bat, The Story of a Bull Terrier (Meader), 1939
Bath Time for John (Graham, B.), 1985
Bathtime (p Rosen, Michael), 1979
Bathtime for Garth Pig (Rayner), 1989
Batman: Exploring the World of Bats (Pringle), 1991
Bats about Baseball (Little, J.; Mackay, Claire), 1995
Bats' Nest (de Roo), 1986
Battery and the Boiler (Ballantyne, appendix), 1883
Battle and the Breeze (Ballantyne, appendix), 1869
Battle of Bubble and Squeak (Pearce), 1978
Battle of Clapham Common (Pullein-Thompson, D.), 1962
Battle of Pook Island (Lasenby), 1996
Battle of St. George Without (McNeill), 1966
Battle of Saint Street (Brown, R.), 1971
Battle of the Galah Trees (Mattingley), 1973
Battle of Zormla (Hoban), 1982
Battledown Boys (Everett-Green, appendix), 1898
Battles with the Sea (Ballantyne, appendix), 1883
Bayou Boy (Lattimore, E.), 1946
Bayou Suzette (Lenski), 1943
Be Brave, Little Noddy! (Blyton), 1956
Be Careful, Mr. Frumble (Scarry), 1990
Be Ever Hopeful, Hannalee (Beatty), 1988
Be Good, Harry (Chalmers), 1967
Be Ready at Eight (Parish), 1979
Beach Day (Oxenbury), 1982
Beach Party (Ryder), 1982
Beach: Year-Round Poems for Young People (Kennedy, X.J.), 1991
Beachcomber Boy (Lattimore, E.), 1960
Beachcombers (Cresswell), 1972
Beacon for the Romans (Rees, D.), 1981

Behind the Ranges (Meader), 1947
Behind the Waterfall (Kyle), 1943
Being a Plant (Pringle), 1983
Being Danny's Dog (Naylor), 1995
Bel Marjory (Meade, appendix), 1878
Bel the Giant and Other Stories (Clarke, P., as Clare), 1956
Believing Sophie (Hutchins, H.), 1995
Belinda (Allen, P.), 1992
Belinda Beats the Band (Awdry), 1961
Belinda the Beetle (Awdry), 1958
Belinda the Mouse (Sewell, H.), 1944
Belinda Treherne (Meade, appendix), 1910
Belinda's New Spring Hat (Clymer), 1969
Bell Family (Streatfeild), 1954
Bell of Nendrum (Andrews), 1969
Bell of the Four Evangelists (Needham), 1947
Bell Ringer and the Pirates (Coerr), 1983
Bellabelinda and the No-Good Angel (Moray Williams), 1982
Bella's Dragon (Powling), 1988
Belle and Her Dragons (Wynne), 1931
Bells and Grass: A Book of Rhymes (p de la Mare), 1941
Bells for a Chinese Donkey (Lattimore, E.), 1951
Bells of Rome (Allan), 1975
Bells of Rye (Church), 1960
Bells of the Harbor (De Jong), 1941
Belly Flop (Gleitzman), 1996
Belonging Place (Little, J.), 1997
Beloved Belindy (Gruelle), 1926
Beloved of the Gods (Wilson, B.), 1965
Ben and Annie (Tate, J.), 1973
Ben and Me (Lawson), 1939
Ben Bruce (Alger, appendix), 1901
Ben Logan's Triumph (Alger, appendix), 1908
Ben of the Barrier (Syme), 1949
Ben Stanton, the Explorer (Alger, appendix), 1887
Ben Sylvester's Word (Yonge, appendix), 1856
Ben the Bullfinch (Watkins-Pitchford), 1957
Ben, the Luggage Boy (Alger, appendix), 1870
Beneath a Blue Umbrella (p Prelutsky), 1990
Beneath the Ghost Moon (Yolen), 1993
Beneath the Hill (Curry), 1967
Benito (Bulla), 1961
Benjamin and Tulip (Wells), 1973
Benjamin Budge and Barnaby Ball (Heide), 1967
Benjamin Dickinson Carr and His (George) (Konigsburg), 1974
Benjamin Franklin, Journeyman (pl Mackay, Constance D'Arcy), 1912
Benjamin in the Woods (Clymer), 1962
Benjamin of Ohio (Otis, appendix), 1912
Benjamin Pig and the Apple Thieves (McKee), 1990
Benjie (Lexau), 1964
Benjie on His Own (Lexau), 1970
Benjie the Circus Dog (Bisset), 1969
Benjie's Hat (Hunt, M.), 1938
Benjy and the Others (Blyton), 1955
Benjy Comes (Heward), 1931
Bennie and the New Baby (Van Stockum), 1964
Benny (Cohen), 1977
Benny and His Penny (Lenski), 1931
Benny and the Princess and Other Stories (Blyton), 1951
Benny's Bazaar (Cockett), 1964
Benny's Flag (Krasilovsky), 1960
Bentley Beaver, Story of (Sharmat), 1984
Bently & Egg (Joyce), 1992
Ben's Baby (Foreman), 1987
Ben's Box (Foreman), 1986
Ben's Dream (Van Allsburg), 1982
Ben's Fish (Prince), 1972
Ben's Gingerbread Man (Daly), 1985
Ben's Nugget (Alger, appendix), 1882
Ben's Snow Song: A Winter Picnic (Hutchins, H.), 1987
Ben's Trumpet (Isadora), 1979
Beorn the Proud (Polland), 1961
Beppo Tate and Roy Penner; The Runaway Marriage Brokers: Two Stories (Palmer), 1980
Berenstain Bears series (Berenstain), from 1973
Beresford Prize (Meade, appendix), 1890
Beric the Briton (Henty, appendix), 1892
Berlioz the Bear (Brett), 1991
Bernard (Waber), 1982
Bernard and His Dogs (Bishop), 1952
Bernard Brook's Adventures (Alger, appendix), 1903
Bernard into Battle (Sharp), 1979
Bernard on His Own (Hoff), 1993
Bernard the Brave (Sharp), 1976
Bernie and the Bessledorf Ghost (Naylor), 1990
Berries in the Scoop (Lenski), 1956
Bert Breen's Barn (Edmonds), 1975
Bertha's Christmas Vision (Alger, appendix) 1856
Bertie and the Bear (Allen, P.), 1983
Bertie, Bobby, and Belle (Wynne), 1924
Bertie Boggin and the Ghost Again! (Waddell, as Sefton), 1988
Bertie Clifton (Everett-Green, appendix), 1890
Bertram (Streatfeild), 1959
Bertrams of Ladywell (Marchant), 1902
Bess and the Sphinx (Coatsworth), 1967
Bess of Delaney's (Meade, appendix), 1905
Bessie Bunter of Cliff House School (Richards, F.), 1949
Best Bad Thing (Uchida), 1983
Best Bat in the School (Bruce, D.), 1931
Best Bedtime Book Ever (Scarry), 1988
Best Bumper Book Ever (Scarry), 1984
Best Christmas (Kingman), 1949
Best Christmas Book Ever (Scarry), 1981
Best Fairytales Ever (Scarry), 1992
Best First Book Ever (Scarry), 1979
Best Friend Ever (Scarry), 1989
Best Friends (Kellogg), 1986
Best Friends for Frances (Hoban), 1969
Best Friends Together Again (Aliki), 1995
Best House in the School (Bruce, D.), 1930
Best Little House (p Fisher, A.), 1966
Best Little Word Book Ever! (Scarry), 1992
Best Loved Bear (Noonan), 1994
Best-Loved Dog Stories (Terhune), 1954
Best Mistake Ever! and Other Stories (Scarry), 1984
Best Music Book Ever (Scarry), 1987
Best of All Schools (Talbot), 1924
Best of Arlie Zack (Hutchins, H.), 1993
Best of Branestawm (Hunter, N.), 1980
Best of Chums (Wynne), 1923
Best of Friends (Bradman), 1988

Blanket Word (Arundel), 1973
Blaze and the Forest Fire (Anderson), 1938
Blaze and the Gray Spotted Pony (Anderson), 1968
Blaze and the Gypsies (Anderson), 1937
Blaze and the Indian Cave (Anderson), 1964
Blaze and the Lost Quarry (Anderson), 1966
Blaze and the Mountain Lion (Anderson), 1959
Blaze and Thunderbolt (Anderson), 1955
Blaze Finds Forgotten Roads (Anderson), 1970
Blaze Finds the Trail (Anderson), 1950
Blaze of Broadfurrow Farm (Severn), 1955
Blaze Shows the Way (Anderson), 1969
Bless Us All: A Child's Yearbook of Blessings (Rylant), 1998
Blessing in Disguise (Tate, E.), 1995
Blessu and Dumpling (King-Smith), 1992
Blind Colt (Rounds), 1941
Blind Connemara (Anderson), 1971
Blind Outlaw (Rounds), 1980
Blink (p O Huigin), 1984
Blinky Bill and Nutsy: Two Little Australians (Wall), 1937
Blinky Bill Connection (Wall), 1988
Blinky Bill Grows Up (Wall), 1934
Blinky Bill Joins the Army (Wall), 1940
Blinky Bill, The Quaint Little Australian (Wall), 1933
Blood and Thunder Adventure on Hurricane Peak (Mahy), 1989
Blood Brothers (Gordon, J.), 1989
Blood Money (Hardcastle), 1971
Blood of the Brave (Baker, B.), 1966
Blood Royal (Weir), 1973
Bloodhound Gang's Secret Code Book (Fleischman), 1983
Blooding (Wheatley), 1987
Blow a Wild Bugle for Catfish Bend (Burman), 1967
Blow for Liberty (Meader), 1965
Blow the Man Down (Vipont), 1939
Blown to Bits (Ballantyne, appendix), 1889
Bloxworth Blue (Corlett), 1984
Blue above the Trees (Clark, M.), 1967
Blue Admiral, Mystery of the (Clewes), 1954
Blue and Red (p Ewing, appendix), 1883
Blue Aunt (White), 1918
Blue Baby and Other Stories (Molesworth, appendix), 1901
Blue Balloon (Asch), 1971
Blue Barns (Sewell, H.), 1933
Blue Bells on the Lea (p Ewing, appendix), 1884
Blue Bird (French), 1972
Blue Canyon Horse (Clark, A.), 1954
Blue Castle (Montgomery), 1926
Blue Diamond (Meade, appendix), 1901
Blue Door Venture (Brown, P.), 1949
Blue Dragon Days (Allan), 1958
Blue Hill Meadows (Rylant), 1997
Blue Hill Meadows and the Much-loved Dog (Rylant), 1997
Blue Hills (Goudge), 1942
Blue Horse (Conlon-McKenna), 1993
Blue Jackal (Brown, Marcia), 1977
Blue Jackets (Fenn, appendix), 1893
Blue Lake (Cummings), 1997
Blue Lawn (Taylor, W.), 1994
Blue Lights (Ballantyne, appendix), 1888
Blue Misty Monsters (Waddell, as Sefton), 1985
Blue Moon Day (Prince), 1988
Blue Murder, Case of (McBratney), 1993
Blue of the Sea (Meade, appendix), 1909
Blue Rabbit (Kaye), 1967
Blue Raider (Strang), 1919
Blue Rhyme Book (p Fyleman), 1933
Blue Ribbon Puppies (Johnson, C.), 1958
Blue Ridge Billy (Lenski), 1946
Blue Shoes (Bull), 1996
Blue Spring Farm (Bishop), 1948
Blue Stars Watching (Beatty), 1969
Blue Story Book (Blyton), 1945
Blue Taps (p Sweeney), 1994
Blue Teapot: Sandy Cove Stories (Dalgliesh), 1931
Blue Umbrella (Bond, R.), 1974
Blue Veil and Black Gold (Catherall, as Maine), 1961
Bluebeard: A Musical Fantasy (pl Wiggin), 1914
Bluebeards series (Bradman), from 1988
Blueberries for Sal (McCloskey), 1948
Blueberry Corners (Lenski), 1940
Blueberry Mountain (Meader), 1941
Bluebirds over Pit Row (Cresswell), 1972
Bluecap and Bimbi, The Blue Wrens (Rees, L.), 1948
Bluegate Girl (Allan), 1961
Blue's Broken Heart (Merrill), 1960
Blunderbus (McGinley), 1951
Blundering Bettina (Wynne), 1924
Boastful Rabbit (Manning-Sanders), 1978
Boasting Monsters (Biro), 1994
Boat Book (Gibbons), 1983
Boat Girl (Cockett), 1972
Boat in the Reeds (Stewart), 1960
Boat Seekers (Pardoe), 1953
Boatride with Lillian Two Blossom (Polacco), 1988
Boats Finds a House (Chalmers), 1958
Boats on the River (Flack), 1946
Bob-a-Job (Cooper), 1963
Bob and Bill (Everett-Green, appendix), 1901
Bob Bodden and the Good Ship "Rover" (Coatsworth), 1968
Bob Bodden and the Seagoing Farm (Coatsworth), 1970
Bob Burton (Alger, appendix, appendix), 1888
Bob Strickland's Log (Westerman), 1953
Bob White, Adventures of (Burgess), 1919
Bobbety the Brownie (Wynne), 1930
Bobbin Girl (McCully), 1996
Bobby Budge from Nowhere (Heward), 1950
Bobby Coon, Adventures of (Burgess), 1918
Bobby Coon's Mistake (Burgess), 1940
Bobby Coon's Surprise (Burgess), 1961
Bobby the Bad (King-Smith), 1994
Bobcat (Anderson), 1949
Bobo the Troublemaker (Schlein), 1976
Bobs (Blyton), 1955
Bodies in the Bessledorf Hotel (Naylor), 1986
Body in the Brillstone Garage (Heide), 1980
Body Parts (Breslin), 1998
Boggart in the Barrel (Waddell, as Sefton), 1991
Boggarts and Dreams (Vipont), 1969
Bogwoppit (Moray Williams), 1978
Bolivar (Gramatky), 1961
Bolt Hole (Brown, R.), 1973
Bolted Door and Other Stories (Molesworth, appendix), 1906

Elaine of La Signe (Moray Williams), 1937
Elaine of the Mountains (Moray Williams), 1939
Elder Brother (Lampman), 1951
Eleanor, Elizabeth (Gleeson), 1984
Eleanor's Hero (Everett-Green, appendix), 1900
Elegant Patty (Treadgold), 1967
Elephant (Hoffman), 1983
Elephant (Manning-Sanders), 1938
Elephant Adventure (Price, W.), 1964
Elephant and the Bad Baby (Vipont), 1969
Elephant and the Flower: Almost-Fables (Patten), 1970
Elephant Big and Elephant Little, and Other Stories (Hewett), 1955
Elephant Book (Demi), 1981
Elephant Herd (Schlein), 1954
Elephant in a Well (Ets), 1972
Elephant in the House (Mahy), 1986
Elephant Is Not a Cat (Tresselt), 1962
Elephant Rhymes (Cowley), 1997
Elephant Rock (Macdonald, C.), 1984
Elephant Tree (Dale), 1991
Elephant War (Avery), 1960
Elephant Who Liked to Smash Small Cars (Merrill), 1967
Elephant Woman: Cynthia Moss Explores the World of Elephants (Pringle), 1997
Elephants Have Right of Way (Sherry), 1995
Eleventh Hour: A Curious Mystery (Base), 1988
ELF 61 (Powling), 1990
Elfabet: An ABC of Elves (Yolen), 1990
Elfen Hill (pl Mitchison), 1928
Elfgift (Price, S.), 1995
Elfred (Abbott, appendix), 1856
Elfrida and the Pig (Symonds), 1959
Elf's New House (Judah), 1962
Elfsong (Turner, A.), 1995
Elfwyn's Saga (Wisniewski), 1990
Eli (Peet), 1978
Elijah's Angel: A Story for Chanukah and Christmas (Rosen, Michael J.), 1992
Elin's Amerika (de Angeli), 1941
Elisa in the Middle (Hurwitz), 1995
Elisabeth, The Cow Ghost (du Bois), 1936
Eliza and the Elves (Field), 1926
Elizabeth: Young Policewoman (Meynell, as Baxter), 1955
Elizabeth's Angel and Other Stories (Moore), 1907
Elizabeth's Prisoner (Meade, appendix), 1914
Elizabeth's Tower (Stewart), 1972
Elizabite: The Adventures of a Carnivorous Plant (Rey), 1942
Ella (p Peet), 1964
Ella at the Wells (Hill, L.), 1954
Ella Clinton (Finley, appendix), 1856
Ella of All-of-a-Kind Family (Taylor, S.), 1978
Ella the Bad Speller (Kraus, R.), 1989
Ellen and the Queen (Avery), 1972
Ellen Tebbits (Cleary), 1951
Ellen's Birthday (Avery), 1971
Ellen's Lion: Twelve Stories (Johnson, C.), 1959
Elli of the Northland (Catherall, as Ruthin), 1968
Ellie and the Hagwitch (Cresswell), 1984
Ellie Bagg's Account (pl Prince), 1984
Elliott and the Cats Eating Out (Mahy), 1987
Elm Street Lot (Pearce), 1969
Elmer Again (McKee), 1991
Elmer Again and Again (McKee), 1975
Elmer and the Dragon (Gannett), 1950
Elmer and Wilbur (McKee), 1994
Elmer in the Snow (McKee), 1995
Elmer on Stilts (McKee), 1993
Elmer Takes Off (McKee), 1998
Elmer: The Story of a Patchwork Elephant (McKee), 1968
Elmer's Colors (McKee), 1994
Elmer's Day (McKee), 1994
Elmer's Friends (McKee), 1994
Elmer's Weather (McKee), 1994
Elsie Dinsmore series (Finley, appendix), from 1868
Elves and the Shoemaker (pl Chorpenning), 1946
Elvira Everything (Asch), 1970
Elworthy Children (Hewett), 1963
Emeka, Driver's Guard (Nwapa), 1972
Emer's Ghost (Waddell, as Sefton), 1981
Emerald City of Oz (Baum), 1910
Emerald Crown (Needham), 1940
Emergency! (Gibbons), 1994
Emile (Ungerer), 1960
Emily (Bedard), 1992
Emily and the Enchanted Frog (Griffith), 1989
Emily and the Golden Acorn (Beck), 1992
Emily and the Haunted Castle (Beresford), 1987
Emily and the Headmistress (Harris, M.), 1958
Emily and the Klunky Baby and the Next-Door Dog (Lexau), 1972
Emily and the Snowflake (Wahl), 1995
Emily Climbs (Montgomery), 1925
Emily Emerson's Moon (p Merrill), 1960
Emily of Deep Valley (Lovelace), 1950
Emily of New Moon (Montgomery), 1923
Emily's Legs (King-Smith), 1988
Emily's Own Elephant (Pearce), 1987
Emily's Quest (Montgomery), 1927
Emily's Runaway Imagination (Cleary), 1961
Emlyn's Moon (Nimmo), 1987
Emma (Abbott, appendix), 1855
Emma (Stevenson, J.), 1985
Emma at the Beach (Stevenson, J.), 1990
Emma Dilemma (Waddell, as Sefton), 1982
Emma in Love (Arundel), 1970
Emma's Doll (Patten), 1976
Emma's Island (Arundel), 1968
Emma's Magic Winter (Little, J.), 1998
Emma's Monster (Darke), 1992
Emma's Rug (Say), 1996
Emmet Otter's Jug-Band Christmas (Hoban), 1971
Emmie and the Purple Paint (Edwards, D.), 1984
Emperor and the Kite (Yolen), 1967
Emperor's Dan-Dan (p Agard), 1992
Emperor's Gifts (Johnson, C.), 1965
Emperor's New Clothes (Blegvad), 1959
Emperor's New Clothes (pl Chorpenning), 1935
Empty Field (Pullein-Thompson, C.), 1961
Empty House (Holland), 1983
Empty Pot (Demi), 1990
Empty Saddle (Meynell), 1965
Empty Schoolhouse (Carlson), 1965

Francis Fry Private Eye (McBratney), 1995
Franconia series (Abbott, appendix), from 1850
Frangipani Summer (Kaye), 1983
Frank and Fearless (Alger, appendix), 1897
Frank and Francesca (Martin), 1972
Frank and Joey Go to Work (Yorinks), 1996
Frank Forester (Strang), 1916
Frank Fowler, the Cash Boy (Alger, appendix), 1887
Frank Hunter's Peril (Alger, appendix), 1896
Frankenstein Moved in on the Fourth Floor (Levy), 1979
Frankenstein Teacher (Bradman), 1998
Frankenstein's Dog (Wahl), 1977
Frankie and the Green Umbrella (Meynell, as Tring), 1957
Frankie Makes a Friend (Bradman), 1992
Frankie's Story (Waddell, as Sefton), 1988
Franklin (pl Mackay, Constance D'Arcy), 1921
Franks and Saxons (Fenn, appendix), 1897
Frank's Campaign (Alger, appendix), 1864
Frank's Debt (Yonge, appendix), 1881
Frank's Fire (Parker), 1972
Frantic Phantom and Other Incredible Stories (Hunter, N.), 1973
Franzi and Gizi (Bianco), 1941
Freaks on the Fells (Ballantyne, appendix), 1864
Freaky Friday (Rodgers), 1972
Freaky Friday (pl Rodgers), 1992
Freckles (Porter, G.), 1904
Freckly Feet and Itchy Knees (Rosen, Michael), 1990
Fred Cat Board Books series (Allen, J.), from 1997
Fred the Angel (Waddell), 1989
Freddie's Feet (Avery), 1976
Freddy (Pearce), 1988
Freddy and Freginald (Brooks), 1952
Freddy and Mr. Camphor (Brooks), 1944
Freddy and Simon the Dictator (Brooks), 1956
Freddy and the Baseball Team from Mars (Brooks), 1955
Freddy and the Bean Home News (Brooks), 1943
Freddy and the Dragon (Brooks), 1958
Freddy and the Flying Saucer Plans (Brooks), 1957
Freddy and the Ignoramus (Brooks), 1941
Freddy and the Men from Mars (Brooks), 1954
Freddy and the Perilous Adventure (Brooks), 1942
Freddy and the Popinjay (Brooks), 1945
Freddy and the Space Ship (Brooks), 1953
Freddy Goes Camping (Brooks), 1948
Freddy Goes to Florida (Brooks), 1949
Freddy Goes to the North Pole (Brooks), 1951
Freddy Plays Football (Brooks), 1949
Freddy Rides Again (Brooks), 1951
Freddy the Cowboy (Brooks), 1950
Freddy the Detective (Brooks), 1932
Freddy the Explorer (Brooks), 1949
Freddy the Fire Engine (Kraus, R.), 1985
Freddy the Magician (Brooks), 1947
Freddy the Pied Piper (Brooks), 1946
Freddy the Pilot (Brooks), 1952
Freddy the Politician (Brooks), 1948
Freddy's Cousin Weedly (Brooks), 1940
Freddy's First Adventure (Brooks), 1949
Freddy's Teddy (Wilson, J.), 1994
Frederick (Lionni), 1967
Frederick Douglass: A Biography (McKissack), 1986
Frederick Douglass: Leader Against Slavery (McKissack), 1991
Frederick Douglass: The Black Lion (McKissack), 1987
Frederick's Fables: A Leo Lionni Treasury (Lionni), 1985
Frederick's Tales (Lionni), 1986
Free Fall (Wiesner), 1988
Free Kick (Hardcastle), 1974
Free Parking and Other Stories (McNeill), 1978
Freedom for a Cheetah (Catherall), 1971
Freedom of the Seas (Storr), 1965
Freedom Tree (Watson, J.), 1976
Freedom's Fruit (Hooks), 1996
Freewheeling of Joshua Cobb (Hodges, M.), 1974
Freeze a Crowd (Greenwood), 1996
Freginald, Story of (Brooks), 1936
Freight Train (Crews), 1978
Freighters: Cargo Ships and the People Who Work Them (Ancona), 1985
French and English (Everett-Green, appendix), 1899
French Lieutenant: A Ghost Story (Church), 1971
French Roundabout (Bishop), 1960
Frenchman's Secret (Edwards, M.), 1956
Fresh Brats (Kennedy, X.J.), 1990
Fresh from the Fens (Everett-Green, appendix), 1891
Freya's Fantastic Surprise (Hathorn), 1988
Friarswood Post Office (Yonge, appendix), 1860
Frida Maria: A Story of the Old Southwest (Lattimore, D.), 1994
Friday Parcel (Pilling), 1986
Friday's Tunnel (Verney), 1959
Fried Feathers for Thanksgiving (Stevenson, J.), 1986
Friend Dog (p Adoff), 1980
Friend Fire and the Dark Wings (Fyson), 1983
Friend for Kate (Bradman), 1996
Friend Like That (Slote), 1988
Friend Monkey (Travers), 1971
Friend Troll, Friend Taniwha (de Roo), 1986
Friend with a Secret (Bull), 1965
Friendly Animals (Burgess), 1925
Friendly Animals (Slobodkin), 1944
Friendly Bear (Bright), 1957
Friendly Beasts: An Old English Christmas Carol (dePaola), 1981
Friendly Book (Brown, Margaret Wise), 1954
Friendly Fairies (Gruelle), 1919
Friendly Gables (Van Stockum), 1960
Friendly Joey and Other Stories (Molesworth, appendix), 1896
Friendly Stories (Arthur), 1932
Friendly Story Book (Blyton), 1954
Friendly Tales: A Community Story Book (Bailey), 1923
Friendly Wolf (Goble), 1974
Friends (Isadora), 1990
Friends (Oxenbury), 1981
Friends and Brothers (King-Smith), 1987
Friends and Enemies (Mitchison), 1966
Friends and Neighbours (Rees, D.), 1986
Friends at Pine Street (Allan), 1984
Friends in the Fourth (Chaundler), 1929
Friends of the Road (Sorensen), 1978
Friends or Foes? (Everett-Green, appendix), 1893
Friends, Though Divided (Henty, appendix), 1883
Friends till Death and Other Stories (Stretton, appendix), 1875
Friendship and Other Poems (de Angeli), 1981
Friendship of Equals (Wilson, G.), 1981

Happy Birthday, Mouse!: A First Counting Book (Wood), 1990
Happy Birthday, Mrs. Felonius (Cowley), 1992
Happy Birthday, Sam (Hutchins, P.), 1978
Happy Birthday to Me (Rockwell), 1981
Happy Birthday to You! (p Seuss), 1959
Happy Birthday with Ant and Bee (Banner), 1964
Happy Christmas: Tales for Boys and Girls (Bishop), 1956
Happy City (Kraus, R.), 1987
Happy Cottage (Todd), 1930
Happy Day (Krauss), 1949
Happy Day Stories (Blyton), 1960
Happy Easter, Little Critter (Mayer), 1988
Happy Egg (Krauss), 1967
Happy Ever After (Travers), 1940
Happy Families: A Comic Opera (pl Fyleman), 1933
Happy Families: A Story for the Young of All Ages (Graham, H.), 1934
Happy Farm (Kraus, R.), 1987
Happy Ghost (Beresford), 1979
Happy Hedgehog Band (Waddell), 1991
Happy Holiday, Clicky (Blyton), 1961
Happy Horse (Bisset), 1974
Happy Hours Story Book (Blyton), 1964
Happy House Children Again (Blyton), 1947
Happy Hunter (Duvoisin), 1961
Happy Jack (Burgess), 1918
Happy Jack Squirrel Helps Unc' Billy (Burgess), 1924
Happy Lion (Fatio), 1954
Happy Lion and the Bear (Fatio), 1964
Happy Lion in Africa (Fatio), 1955
Happy Lion Roars (Fatio), 1957
Happy Lioness (Fatio), 1980
Happy Lion's Holiday (Fatio), 1968
Happy Lion's Quest (Fatio), 1961
Happy Lion's Rabbits (Fatio), 1974
Happy Lion's Treasure (Fatio), 1971
Happy Lion's Vacation (Fatio), 1967
Happy Little Time (Richards, L.), 1910
Happy Mouseday (King-Smith), 1994
Happy Orpheline (Carlson), 1957
Happy Place (Bemelmans), 1952
Happy Rag (Ross), 1990
Happy Story Book (Blyton), 1942
Happy Times Storybook (Krasilovsky), 1987
Happy Traveller (Bruce, M.), 1929
Happy Valentine's Day, Emma! (Stevenson, J.), 1987
Happy Woman (Le Feuvre), 1918
Happy Year (p Robinson), 1953
Happy's Christmas (Gramatky), 1970
Harbor (Crews), 1982
Harbour Thieves (Freeman, Bill), 1984
Hard Man (Hardcastle), 1974
Hard Maple (Warner, appendix), 1871
Hard to Be Six (p Adoff), 1991
Harding's Luck (Nesbit), 1909
Hare at Dark Hollow (Stranger), 1973
Hare series (Uttley), from 1942
Harebell's Friend (Le Feuvre), 1914
Hari the Jungle Lad (Mukerji), 1924
Hari's Pigeon (Griffiths, H.), 1982
Harlequin Corner (Brown, P.), 1953
Harlequinade (Streatfeild), 1943
Harlie series (Abbott, appendix), from 1863
Harmattan Man (de Graft-Hanson), 1995
Harold and the Purple Crayon (Johnson, C.), 1955
Harold at the North Pole: A Christmas Journey with the Purple Crayon (Johnson, C.), 1958
Harold Thinks Big (Murphy, Jim), 1980
Harold Was My King (Lewis, H.), 1968
Harold: The Story of a Friendship (Symonds), 1973
Harold's ABC (Johnson, C.), 1963
Harold's Circus (Johnson, C.), 1959
Harold's Fairy Tale: Further Adventures with the Purple Crayon (Johnson, C.), 1956
Harold's Trip to the Sky (Johnson, C.), 1957
Harper Establishment (Abbott, appendix), 1855
Harpoon of the Hunter (Markoosie), 1970
Harquin, The Fox Who Went Down to the Valley (Burningham), 1967
Harriet and Her Sister (Yonge, appendix), 1856
Harriet Goes a-Roaming (Marchant), 1922
Harriet series (Waddell), from 1982
Harriet the Spy (Fitzhugh), 1964
Harriet's Hare (King-Smith), 1994
Harry and Larry the Fishermen (Scarry), 1988
Harry and Lulu (Yorinks), 1998
Harry and the Lady Next Door (Zion), 1960
Harry by the Sea (Zion), 1965
Harry Cat's Pet Puppy (Selden), 1974
Harry Hates Shopping (Armitage), 1993
Harry in England (Richards, L.), 1937
Harry Kitten and Tucker Mouse (Selden), 1986
Harry Moves House (Powling), 1993
Harry on Holiday (Powling), 1997
Harry Pay the Pirate (Nye), 1981
Harry Rochester, Adventures of (Strang), 1905
Harry series (Finley, appendix), from 1876
Harry, The Dirty Dog (Zion), 1956
Harry the Superhero (Powling), 1996
Harry, The Wild West Horse (Clymer), 1963
Harry Wakatipu (Lasenby), 1993
Harry with Spots on (Powling), 1990
Harry's Mad (King-Smith), 1984
Harry's Party (Powling), 1989
Harum-Scarum Schoolgirl (Brazil), 1919
Harvey Slumfenburger's Christmas Present (Burningham), 1993
Harvey's Hideout (Hoban), 1969
Has Anyone Here Seen William? (Graham, B.), 1988
Has Anyone Seen Jack? (Bradman), 1992
Hat (Brett), 1997
Hat (Ungerer), 1970
Hat for Amy Jean (Chalmers), 1956
Hat for Emily (Bull), 1986
Hat for Rhinoceros and Other Stories (Hewett), 1959
Hatching of Joshua Cobb (Hodges, M.), 1967
Hatherly's First Fifteen (Clark, M.), 1930
Hating Book (Zolotow), 1969
Hats Off! (Hill, D.), 1995
Hattie and the Fox (Fox), 1986
Hattie and the Wild Waves (Cooney), 1990
Hattie the Backstage Bat (Freeman, D.), 1970
Haunt Fox (Kjelgaard), 1954

History of the Civil Rights Movement (McKissack), 1990
Hitchhike (Holland), 1977
Hitchhikers: Stories from Joy Cowley (Cowley), 1997
Hither and Thither (p Todd), 1927
Hitty, Her First Hundred Years (Field), 1929
Hitty: The Life and Adventures of a Wooden Doll (Field), 1932
Ho for a Hat! (p Smith), 1964
Hoaryhead and M'Donner (Abbott, appendix), 1855
Hoaryhead, and The Valleys Below (Abbott, appendix), 1838
Hob and Bob: A Tale of Two Goblins (Fyleman), 1944
Hobberdy Dick (Briggs, K.), 1955
Hobbie (Moray Williams), 1958
Hobbit; or, There and Back Again (Tolkien), 1937
Hobby (Yolen), 1996
Hobo Dog (Hurd), 1980
Hobo Dog in the Ghost Town (Hurd), 1985
Hobo Dog's Christmas Tree (Hurd), 1983
Hobo Toad and the Motorcycle Gang (Yolen), 1970
Hobyah! Hobyah! (pl Mitchison), 1928
Hockey Girls (Corbett, S.), 1976
Hodgeheg (King-Smith), 1987
Hogsel and Gruntel (King-Smith), 1996
Hokey Pokey Did It! (Cresswell), 1989
Hold My Hand (Zolotow), 1972
Holdfast (Beatty), 1972
Hole Is to Dig: A First Book of First Definitions (Krauss), 1952
Holes (Sachar), 1998
Holes and Peeks (Jonas), 1984
Holiday (Clewes), 1964
Holiday (Tate, J.), 1966
Holiday Annual Stories (Blyton), 1967
Holiday at Arnriggs (Allan), 1949
Holiday at Rosquin (Lynch), 1964
Holiday Book (Scarry), 1979
Holiday Chums (Talbot), 1923
Holiday Exchange (Pye), 1953
Holiday for Mister Muster (Lobel, Arnold), 1963
Holiday for Slippy (Beresford), 1964
Holiday House (Blyton), 1955
Holiday House (Hardcastle), 1977
Holiday in a Manor House (Everett-Green, appendix), 1892
Holiday Map (Thwaite), 1969
Holiday of Endurance (Allan), 1961
Holiday Programs for Boys and Girls (pl Fisher, A.), 1953
Holiday Story Book (Hough), 1976
Holiday Time in the Bush (Dallas), 1983
Holidays at the Farm (Everett-Green, appendix), 1901
Holidays! Holidays! (p Heide), 1971
Hollow Tree (Lunn), 1997
Hollow Tree House (Blyton), 1945
Hollowdell Grange (Fenn, appendix), 1866
Holly and Ivy, Story of (Godden), 1958
Holly Hotel (Kyle), 1945
Holly in the Snow (Lattimore, E.), 1954
Holly Lane, Mystery of (Blyton), 1953
Holly, Mud and Whisky (Rees, D.), 1981
Hollyberrys (Dalgliesh), 1939
Hollyhock (Meade, appendix), 1916
Home Again at Timber Creek (Clark, M.), 1950
Home and Away (Thwaite), 1967
Home Before Dark (Beck), 1997
Home Boy (Hansen), 1982
Home for a Bunny (Brown, Margaret Wise), 1956
Home for Jessie (Pullein-Thompson, C.), 1986
Home from Far (Little, J.), 1965
Home from Home (Price, S.), 1977
Home: How Animals Find Comfort and Safety (Pringle), 1987
Home in the Sky (Baker, J.), 1983
Home Is the North (Morey), 1967
Home Is the Sailor (Godden), 1964
Home-Made Dragon and Other Incredible Stories (Hunter, N.), 1971
Home-Makers (Hough), 1957
Home of Silence (Meade, appendix), 1907
Home of Sweet Content (Meade, appendix), 1906
Home on the Range: Jeremiah Jones and His Friend Little Bear in the Far West (Hader), 1955
Home, Sweet Home (Walton, Christie's Old Organ (Walton), appendix), 1874
Home, The Tale of a Mouse (Schlein), 1958
Home to the Island (Allan), 1962
Homecoming for Kezzie (Breslin), 1995
Homeless Katie (Pullein-Thompson, C.), 1964
Homer and the Circus Train (Gramatky), 1957
Homer Price (McCloskey), 1943
Homestead of the Free: The Kansas Story (Fisher, A.), 1953
Homesteader Girl (Marchant), 1932
Homework Caper (Lexau), 1966
Honey Forest (Brinsmead), 1978
Honey, I Love and Other Love Poems (p Greenfield), 1978
Honey Makers (Gibbons), 1997
Honey Mouse and Other Stories (Hewett), 1957
Honey River (Odaga), 1994
Honeybee and the Robber (Carle), 1981
Honeysuckle Line (Weir), 1959
Honeywell Badger (Stranger), 1972
Honk Honk! (Rockwell), 1980
Honkers (Yolen), 1993
Honor Bound (Downie), 1971
Honor Bright (Richards, L.), 1920
Honor Bright's New Adventure (Richards, L.), 1925
Honour First (Strang), 1923
Honour of the School (Wynne), 1918
Hoo-Ming's Discovery (Cockett), 1982
Hoodie (Molesworth, appendix), 1882
Hoodwinkers (Edwards, M.), 1962
Hoodwinking of Mrs. Elmo (Kraus, R.), 1987
Hoof and Claw (Roberts, C.), 1913
Hoofprint on the Wind (Clark, A.), 1972
Hooked! (Hardcastle), 1984
Hooligan's Shampoo (Ridley), 1996
Hoop Snakes, Hide-Behinds and Sidehill Winders (Bruchac), 1991
Hooper Humperdink...? Not Him! (p Seuss), 1976
Hooray for Diffendoofer Day! (p Prelutsky), 1998
Hooray for Father's Day! (Sharmat), 1986-87
Hooray for Me (Clewes), 1973
Hooray for Mother's Day! (Sharmat), 1986-87
Hootie Toots of Hollow Tree (Wynne), 1925
Hop on Pop (p Seuss), 1963
Hopeful Trout and Other Limericks (p Ciardi), 1989
Hopes and Fears (Yonge, appendix), 1860
Hope's Tryst (Marchant), 1904

Hopkins of the Mayflower: Portrait of a Dissenter (Hodges, M.), 1972
Hoppity-Gap (Powling), 1988
Horace and Maurice (King-Smith), 1991
Horace and Morris But Mostly Dolores (Howe), 1997
Horace the Ghost (Waddell, as Sefton), 1991
Horatio (Clymer), 1968
Horatio (Foreman), 1970
Horatio Goes to the Country (Clymer), 1978
Horatio Solves a Mystery (Clymer), 1980
Horatio's Birthday (Clymer), 1976
Horizon Is Calling (Yashima), 1947
Horn of Merlyns (Needham), 1943
Horns of Danger (Allan), 1981
Horrakopotchin (Mahy), 1985
Horrendous Hullabaloo (Mahy), 1992
Horrible Boy (Thwaite), 1975
Horrible Hilda and Henry, Story of (Clark, E.), 1988
Horrible Story and Others (s Mahy), 1987
Horribles (Rosen, Michael), 1988
Horribly Haunted School (Mahy), 1997
Horrie Kiwi and the Kids (Wall), 1984
Horrorscopes Sagittarius: Missing (Breslin), 1995
Horse (pl Yorinks), 1978
Horse and His Boy (Lewis, C.S.), 1954
Horse at Hilly Fields (Thwaite), 1995
Horse Came Running (De Jong), 1970
Horse for the Island (Bettina), 1952
Horse in Harry's Room (Hoff), 1970
Horse in the Attic (Clymer), 1983
Horse in the Camel Suit (du Bois), 1967
Horse in the Clouds (Griffiths, H.), 1957
Horse Named Peaceable (Holland), 1982
Horse of Hurricane Hill (Anderson), 1956
Horse of the Year (Oram), 1997
Horse on Wheels (Ainsworth), 1966
Horse Pie (King-Smith), 1993
Horse Sale (Pullein-Thompson, C.), 1960
Horse Stories (Coatsworth), 1954
Horse Who Had His Picture in the Paper (McGinley), 1951
Horse Who Lived Upstairs (McGinley), 1944
Horse with High-Heeled Shoes (Slobodkin), 1954
Horsehaven (Pullein-Thompson, C.), 1996
Horses (Brown, Margaret Wise, as White), 1944
Horses at Home, and Friends Must Part (Pullein-Thompson, D.), 1954
Horses I've Known (James), 1940
Horseshoe Reef (Armstrong), 1960
Horsey and Co. and the Bank Robbers (Daniell, as Bowood), 1965
Hortense, The Cow for a Queen (Carlson), 1957
Horton Hatches the Egg (p Seuss), 1940
Horton Hears a Who! (p Seuss), 1954
Hosea's Girl (Marchant), 1934
Hosie's Alphabet (Baskin), 1972
Hosie's Aviary (Baskin), 1979
Hosie's Zoo (Baskin), 1981
Hospital (Porter, S.), 1973
Hospital Day (Berg), 1972
Hostages and Other Stories for Boys and Girls (Mitchison), 1930
Hostilities: Nine Bizarre Stories (Macdonald, C.), 1991
Hot and Cold Summer (Hurwitz), 1984
Hot Dog and Other Poems (p Wright), 1981
Hot Fudge (Howe), 1990
Hot Shot (Slote), 1977
Hot Swamp (Ballantyne, appendix), 1892
Hot Thirsty Day (Sharmat), 1971
Hot Wheels (Hardcastle), 1980
Hotel Cat (Averill), 1969
Hottest Boy Who Ever Lived (Fienberg), 1993
Hotu-Puku (Bacon, R.), 1985
Houdini, Come Home (Palmer), 1981
Hound Dog and Other Yarns (Kjelgaard), 1958
Hound Dog Moses and the Promised Land (Edmonds), 1954
Hound Dog Zip to the Rescue (Steele, W.), 1970
Hound of Darkness (Stranger), 1983
Hounds of the Morrigan (O'Shea), 1985
Hour of the Frog (Wynne-Jones), 1989
Hours in Many Lands: Stories and Poems (Nesbit), 1894
House Across the Way (White), 1940
House at Brambling Minster (Marchant), 1902
House at Pooh Corner (Milne), 1928
House at Spaniard's Bay (Reid), 1967
House at the Corner (Blyton), 1947
House Beyond the Meadow (p Behn), 1955
House by Lough Neagh (Lynch), 1963
House by the Marsh (Allan), 1958
House by the Sea (Ryder), 1994
House for Hermit Crab (Carle), 1987
House for Jones (Cresswell), 1969
House in Cornwall (Streatfeild), 1940
House in Norham Gardens (Lively), 1974
House in the Middle of the Road (Weir), 1961
House in the Square (Robinson), 1972
House in the Water: A Book of Animal Life (Roberts, C.), 1908
House in the Wood (Sudbery), 1968
House in the Woods (Holland), 1991
House in Town (Warner, appendix), 1871
House in Turner Square (Thwaite), 1960
House Inside Out (Lively), 1987
House Is a House for Me (p Hoberman), 1978
House Like a Lotus (L'Engle), 1984
House Next Door: Utah 1896 (Sorensen), 1954
House of a Hundred Windows (Brown, Margaret Wise), 1945
House of a Mouse (p Fisher, A.), 1988
House of Arden (Nesbit), 1908
House of Four Seasons (Duvoisin), 1956
House of Good Spirits (Kushner), 1990
House of Happiness (Moray Williams), 1946
House of Happiness (pl Moray Williams), 1951
House of Secrets Trilogy (Stranger), 1994
House of Sixty Fathers (De Jong), 1956
House of Surprises (Meade, appendix), 1896
House of the Blue Horse (Kingman), 1960
House of the Heart and Other Plays (pl Mackay, Constance D'Arcy), 1909
House of the Paladin (Needham), 1945
House of the Pelican (Kyle), 1954
House of the Swan (Coatsworth), 1948
House of Whispers (Wynne), 1929
House of Wisdom (Heide), 1999
House on East 88th Street (Waber), 1962
House on Stink Alley (Monjo), 1977

House on the Brink (Gordon, J.), 1970
House on the Cliff (Everett-Green, appendix), 1914
House on the Cliffs (Dallas), 1975
House on the Common (Prince), 1969
House on the Edge of the Moor (Heward), 1968
House on the Green (Brown, R.), 1967
House on the Hill (Kyle), 1949
House on the Mountain (Clymer), 1971
House on the Rock (Butterworth, N.), 1986
House So Big (Lexau), 1968
House That Grew (Boston), 1969
House That Grew (Molesworth, appendix), 1900
House That Grew Smaller (Bianco), 1931
House That Guilda Drew (Parker), 1963
House That Jack Built (Tate, J.), 1976
House That Moved (Rees, D.), 1978
House That Ran Behind (Todd), 1943
House That Sailed Away (Hutchins, P.), 1975
House That Was Eureka (Wheatley), 1984
House to Let (Molesworth, appendix), 1889
House under the Stairs (Waddell), 1983
Houseboat Girl (Lenski), 1957
Houseboat Summer (Coatsworth), 1942
Housenapper (Curry), 1971
Houses for the Dead (p Turner, A.), 1976
Houses of the Eagle (Bruce, M.), 1925
How a Book Is Made (Aliki), 1986
How a House Is Built (Gibbons), 1990
How Beastly! A Menagerie of Nonsense Poems (p Yolen), 1980
How Big Am I? (Heide), 1968
How Brown Mouse Kept Christmas (p Watson, C.), 1992
How Brown Mouse Kept Christmas (Watson, C.), 1980
How Do I Go? (p Hoberman), 1958
How Do You Do, Mary Mouse (Blyton), 1948
How Do You Get from Here to There? (p Kuskin, as Charles), 1962
How Do You Get There? (Rey), 1941
How Do You Hide a Monster? (p Kahl), 1971
How Do You Make a Bubble? (Hooks), 1992
How Droofus the Dragon Lost His Head (Peet), 1971
How Funny You Are, Noddy (Blyton), 1954
How Giraffe Got Such a Long Neck—And Why Rhino is So Grumpy (Rosen, Michael), 1993
How Green Was My Mouse (King-Smith), 1998
How, Hippo! (Brown, Marcia), 1969
How I Went Shopping and What I Got (Clymer), 1972
How Jan Klaassen Cured the King (pl Ridge), 1969
How Joe the Bear and Sam the Mouse Got Together (de Regniers), 1965
How John Caught the Sea-Horse and Other Stories (Berg), 1966-67
How Lazy Can You Get? (Naylor), 1979
How Little Grey Rabbit Got Back Her Tail (Uttley), 1930
How Many Days to My Birthday (Clarke, G.), 1992
How Many Dragons Are Behind the Door? (p Kahl), 1977
How Many Kids Are Hiding on My Block? (Merrill), 1970
How Many Miles to Babylon? (Needham), 1953
How Many Miles to Cyprus (Allen, E.), 1955
How Many Miles to Sundown (Beatty), 1974
How Many Trucks Can a Tow Truck Tow? (Pomerantz), 1987
How Mrs. Monkey Missed the Ark (Kerr), 1992
How Mrs. Santa Claus Saved Christmas (p McGinley), 1963
How Mr. Rooster Didn't Get Married (Mahy), 1986
How My Garden Grew (Rockwell), 1982
How Nell Scored (Marchant), 1929
How Now Brown Cow (pl L'Engle), 1949
How Pizza Came to Our Town (Khalsa), 1989
How Pizza Came to Queens (Khalsa), 1989
How Six Found Christmas (Hyman), 1969
How Spider Saved series (Kraus, R.), from 1970
How the Animals Got Their Colours: Animal Myths from Around the World (Rosen, Michael), 1991
How the Brothers Joined the Cat Club (Averill), 1953
How the Children Stopped the Wars (Wahl), 1969
How the Ewoks Saved the Trees (Howe), 1984
How the Flowers Grow and Other Musical Plays (pl Blyton), 1939
How the Flying Fishes Came into Being (Rey), 1938
How the Grinch Stole Christmas (p Seuss), 1957
How the Leopard Got His Claws (Achebe), 1972
How the Ostrich Got a Long Neck: A Tale from the Akamba of Kenya (Aardema), 1995
How the Reindeer Saved Santa (Haywood), 1986
How the Rooster Saved the Day (Lobel, Arnold), 1977
How the Trollusk Got His Hat (Mayer), 1979
How the Twins Captured a Hessian (Otis, appendix), 1902
How the Weatherman Came (Ish-Kishor), 1938
How They Went to Europe (Sidney, appendix), 1884
How to Care for Your Monster (Bridwell), 1970
How to Go About Laying an Egg (Waber), 1963
How to Have a Gorgeous Wedding (Sharmat), 1985
How to Make an Earthquake (Krauss), 1954
How to Meet a Gorgeous Girl (Sharmat), 1984
How to Meet a Gorgeous Guy (Sharmat), 1983
How to Read a Rabbit (Fritz), 1959
How to Survive Summer Camp (Wilson, J.), 1985
How to Write Really Badly (Fine), 1996
How Tom Beat Captain Najork and His Hired Sportsmen (Hoban), 1974
How Tommy Saved the Barn (Otis, appendix), 1895
Howard (Stevenson, J.), 1980
Howards Go Sledding (Wahl), 1964
Howliday Inn (Howe), 1982
How's Business (Prince), 1987
Hubert's Hair-Raising Adventure (p Peet), 1959
Huck and Her Time Machine (Avery), 1977
Huck Finn's Story (pl Harris, A.), 1987
Huckle Cat's Busiest Day Ever (Scarry), 1992
Huckleberry Finn, Adventures of (Twain, appendix), 1884
Huckle's Book (Scarry), 1979
Huge Harold (p Peet), 1961
Hugh Stanford's Luck (Bruce, M.), 1925
Hughie (Martin), 1971
Hugh's Zoo (MacIntyre), 1964
Hugo and Franz (Finley, appendix), 1965
Hugo and His Grandma (Storr), 1977
Hugo and His Grandma's Washing Day (Storr), 1978
Hugo and the Sunshine Girl (Ní Dhuibhne), 1991
Hugo at the Window (Rockwell), 1988
Hugo series (Ross), from 1977
Hugo Takes Off (Parker), 1976
Hugo, the Deformed (Alger, appendix), 1978

Joking Man (Flora), 1968
Jolliest School of All (Brazil), 1923
Jolliest Term on Record (Brazil), 1915
Jolly Christmas Postman (Ahlberg), 1991
Jolly Farm Book (Berg), 1960
Jolly Friendship (Stockton, appendix), 1880
Jolly Jingles (p Richards, L.), 1912
Jolly Koala Bear (Demi), 1989
Jolly Little Jumbo (Blyton), 1944
Jolly Pocket Postman (Ahlberg), 1995
Jolly Postman (Ahlberg), 1986
Jolly Story Book (Blyton), 1944
Jolly Witch (King-Smith), 1990
Jon, Flora, and the Odd-Eyed Cat (Pevsner), 1994
Jon the Unlucky (Coatsworth), 1964
Jonas series (Abbott, appendix), from 1839
Jonathan Allen Board Books series (Allen, J.), from 1992
Jonathan Allen Picture Book (Allen, J.), 1997
Jonathan and Felicity (Cockett), 1955
Jonathan Cleaned Up, Then He Heard a Sound (Munsch), 1981
Jonathan Down Under (Beatty), 1982
Jonathan Frederick Aloysius Brown (p Ormondroyd), 1964
Jonathan Goes West (Meader), 1946
Jonathan on the Farm (Cockett), 1954
Jonathan's Children (Heward), 1963
Jonny (Lattimore, E.), 1939
Joppy Stories (Cockett), 1972
Jo's Boys and How They Turned Out (Alcott, appendix), 1886
Josefina February (Ness), 1963
Josefina Story Quilt (Coerr), 1986
Joseph and Koza; or, The Sacrifice to the Vistula (Singer), 1970
Joseph and Lulu and the Prindiville House Pigeons (Greenwood), 1972
Joseph's Boat (Macdonald, C.), 1988
Joseph's Other Red Sock (Daly), 1982
Joseph's Yard (Keeping), 1969
José's Christmas Secret (Lexau), 1963
Joshua by the Sea (Johnson, A.), 1994
Joshua's Night Whispers (Johnson, A.), 1994
Josiah in New York (Otis, appendix), 1893
Josie, Click, and Bun Again (Blyton), 1946
Josie, Click, and Bun and the Little Tree House (Blyton), 1951
Josie's Troubles (Naylor), 1992
Journal for One (Tate, J.), 1973
Journal of a Teenage Genius (Griffith), 1987
Journey (MacLachlan), 1991
Journey by First Class Camel (Konigsburg), 1983
Journey for Three (Holland), 1974
Journey from Peppermint Street (De Jong), 1968
Journey from the Heron (Treadgold), 1981
Journey Home (Holland), 1990
Journey Home (Uchida), 1978
Journey of Ching Lai (Lattimore, E.), 1957
Journey of the Eldest Son (Fyson), 1965
Journey of the Great Lake (Trezise), 1996
Journey of the Kiss (dePaola), 1970
Journey Outside (Steele, M.), 1969
Journey to an 800 Number (Konigsburg), 1982
Journey to Jorsala (Finkel), 1969
Journey to Space (Nwapa), 1980
Journey to Terezor (Asch), 1989
Journey to the Jungle (Bisset), 1977
Journey to Topaz (Uchida), 1971
Journey under Warning (Locke), 1983
Journey with Jonah (pl L'Engle), 1970
Joy Cometh in the Morning (Le Feuvre), 1917
Joy Cowley Answers Kids' Questions (Cowley), 1995
Joy Street Poems (p Fyleman), 1927
Joyce and the Rambler (Le Feuvre), 1910
Joyce Harrington's Trust (Marchant), 1915
Joyce Lankester Brisley Book (Brisley), 1981
Joyce Stranger's Book of Hanák's Animals (p Stranger), 1976
Joyous Adventures of Snakey Boo (Bisset), 1982
Joyous Story of Toto (Richards, L.), 1885
Joy's Jubilee (Everett-Green, appendix), 1898
Judge Justin (Abbott, appendix), 1857
Judith (Everett-Green, appendix), 1895
Judith in Hanover (Finlay), 1955
Judith Teachers (Allan), 1955
Judy and Lakshmi (Mitchison), 1959
Judy and the Martian (Lively), 1992
Judy, Patrol Leader series (Moore), from 1930
Judy the Bad Fairy (Waddell), 1989
Judy the Guide (Brent-Dyer), 1928
Judy the Tramp (Chaundler), 1924
Judy's Journey (Lenski), 1947
Ju-Ju Hand (Westerman), 1954
Juju Rock (Ekwensi), 1966
Julian (Khalsa), 1989
Julian and the Vacuum Cleaner (Cunliffe), 1991
Julian Home (Farrar, appendix), 1859
Julian's River War (Syme), 1949
Julie (Taylor, C.), 1985
Julie News (Wallace), 1974
Julie's Secret (Taylor, C.), 1991
Julie's Story (Berg), 1970
Juliet in Publishing (Carter, B., as Churchill), 1956
Juliet of the Mill (Wynne), 1931
Juliette, The Mail Carrier (Marchant), 1907
Julius (Alger, appendix), 1874
Julius (Hoff), 1959
Julius the Pig (Johnson, A.), 1993
July (Stevenson, J.), 1990
Jumanji (Van Allsburg), 1981
Jumble Sale (Berg), 1968
Jumbo (Smucker), 1989
Jumbo Afloat (Cresswell), 1966
Jumbo and the Big Dig (Cresswell), 1968
Jumbo Back to Nature (Cresswell), 1965
Jumbo Spencer (Cresswell), 1963
Jumper Goes to School (Parish), 1969
Jumping Jo the Joker (Tate, J.), 1984
June 7! (Aliki), 1972
June 29, 1999 (Wiesner), 1992
Jungle and Stream (Fenn, appendix), 1898
Jungle Beasts and Men (Mukerji), 1923
Jungle Book (Kipling), 1894
Jungle Jingles (King-Smith), 1992
Jungle Nurse (Catherall, as Ruthin), 1960
Jungle Rescue (Catherall, as Channel), 1967
Jungle River (Pease), 1938
Jungle Sale (Pilling), 1989

Keep Ms. Sugarman in the Fourth Grade (Levy), 1992
Keep Running (Storey), 1974
Keep Running, Allen! (Bulla), 1978
Keep Stompin' till the Music Stops (Pevsner), 1977
Keep the Pot Boiling (Clarke, P.), 1961
Keep Your Mouth Closed, Dear (Aliki), 1966
Keepers of Life: Discovering Plants through Native American Stories and Earth Activities for Children (Bruchac), 1994
Keepers of the Animals: Native American Stories and Wildlife Activities for Children (Bruchac), 1990
Keepers of the Cattle (Catherall), 1970
Keepers of the Earth: Native American Stories and Environmental Activities for Children (Bruchac), 1988
Keepers of the Khyber (Catherall), 1940
Keepers of the Narrow Seas (Westerman), 1931
Keepers of the Night: Native American Stories and Nocturnal Activities for Children (Bruchac), 1994
Keeping a Christmas Secret (Naylor), 1989
Keeping House (Mahy), 1991
Keeping Quilt (Polacco), 1988
Keeping Up with Teddy Robinson (Robinson), 1964
Keeping-Room (Levin), 1981
Keith's Trial and Victory (Everett-Green, appendix), 1894
Kele's Secret (Mollel), 1997
Kelly the Sleepy Koala (Wilson, B.), 1983
Kellyburn Braes (Nic Leodhas), 1969
Kellyhorns (Cooney), 1942
Kelpie, The Gipsies' Pony (Moray Williams), 1934
Kelso's Carnival (Kaye), 1994
Kenealy's Ride (Marchant), 1906
Kennelmaid Nan (Brent-Dyer), 1954
Kenneth (Yonge, appendix), 1850
Kenneth Grahame: An Innocent in the Wild Wood (Prince), 1994
Kenny's Window (Sendak), 1956
Kermit the Hermit (p Peet), 1965
Kermit's Garden of Verses (p Prelutsky), 1982
Kerry Caravan (Lynch), 1967
Kershaw Dogs (Griffiths, H.), 1978
Kersivay Kraken (MacVicar), 1966
Kersti and Saint Nicholas (Van Stockum), 1940
Kestrel (Alexander), 1982
Ketse and the Chief (Mitchison), 1965
Kevin (Chalmers), 1957
Kevin the Kookaburra (Wilson, B.), 1983
Kevin's Hat (Holland), 1984
Key (Heide), 1971
Key (p Smith), 1982
Key, Mystery of the (Westerman), 1948
Key of the Castle (Kyle), 1976
Key to the Treasure (Parish), 1966
Kezzie (Breslin), 1993
Khaki Boys and Other Stories (Brazil), 1923
Khedive's Country (Fenn, appendix), 1904
Kia Tanisha (Greenfield), 1997
Kia Tanisha Drives Her Car (Greenfield), 1997
Kick Back (Hill, D.), 1995
Kickback (Hardcastle), 1989
Kid's Guide to the Secret Knowledge of Grown-ups (Wisniewski), 1998
Kidnap of Jessie Parker (Taylor, W.), 1989
Kidnapped (Stevenson, R., appendix), 1886
Kidnapped by Accident (Catherall), 1968
Kidnapped by Blackbirders (Sutton), 1984
Kidnapped in Kandy (Catherall, as Ruthin), 1951
Kidnapped on Stromboli (Catherall, as Ruthin), 1966
Kidnapped Santa Claus (Baum), 1961
Kidnappers of Space (Patchett), 1953
Kidnapping of Kensington (Carter, B.), 1958
Kidnapping of My Grandmother (Moray Williams), 1972
Kidnapping of Suzie Q (Waddell), 1994
Kids Commune (Hildick), 1973
Kilgorman (Reed, appendix), 1894
Killer Dog (Edwards, M.), 1959
Killer Tadpole (Wilson, J.), 1984
Killer-of-Death (Baker, B.), 1963
Kilmeny of the Orchard (Montgomery), 1910
Kilpatrick, Special Reporter (MacVicar), 1963
Kim (Kipling), 1901
Kimchi Kid (pl Kraus, J.), 1986
Kind Dog on Monday (Banner), 1972
Kind Dog Up and Down the Hill (Banner), 1972
Kinderdike (Fisher, L.), 1994
Kindle of Kittens (Godden), 1978
Kindred of the Wild: A Book of Animal Life (Roberts, C.), 1902
Kindred Spirits (Meade, appendix), 1907
King (pl Yorinks), 1980
King Abbie's Adventure (MacVicar), 1950
King and the Tortoise (Mollel), 1993
King Change-a-Lot (Cole), 1988
King Dicky Bird and the Bossy Princess (Edwards, D.), 1987
King for a Month (Westerman), 1933
King George's Head Was Made of Lead (Monjo), 1974
King Henry's Palace (Hutchins, P.), 1983
King Hilary and the Beggarman (pl Milne), 1926
King Kong (Browne), 1994
King Max the Last: A Second Hodgeheg Story (King-Smith), 1995
King Midas and His Gold (McKissack), 1986
King Midas and the Golden Touch (pl Chorpenning), 1950
King o' the Beach (Fenn, appendix), 1899
King Oberon's Forest (Van Stockum), 1957
King of Another Country (French), 1992
King of Beasts and Other Stories (Roberts, C.), 1967
King of Kilba (Westerman), 1926
King of the Air (Strang), 1907
King of the Birds (Climo), 1988
King of the Birds (p O Huigin), 1991
King of the Castle (Hoffman), 1986
King of the Castle (Rush), 1956
King of the Castle (Trevor), 1966
King of the Cats (O'Faolain), 1941
King of the Commandos (Johns), 1943
King of the Hills (Meader), 1933
King of the Knock-Down Gingers (Kaye), 1979
King of the Mountain (Wier), 1975
King of the Playground (Naylor), 1991
King of the Seventh Grade (Cohen), 1982
King of the Tinkers (Lynch), 1938
King of the Wind (Henry), 1948
King of Wreck Island (Cooney), 1941
King Robert's Page (Fenn, appendix), 1900
King Rollo series (McKee), from 1979
King Tree (French), 1973

King Who Saved Himself from Being Saved (p Ciardi), 1965
King Who Took Sunshine (pl Reeves), 1954
Kingdom of Carbonel (Sleigh), 1959
Kingfisher Feather (Mitchell), 1962
Kings and Queens (p Farjeon), 1932
King's Barn; or, Joan's Tale (Farjeon), 1927
King's Birthday Cake (Cunliffe), 1973
King's Butterfly (Everett-Green, appendix), 1900
King's Curate (Bruce, D.), 1930
King's Daughter Cries for the Moon (Farjeon), 1929
Kings' Day (Bishop), 1940
King's Day: Louis XIV of France (Aliki), 1989
King's Equal (Paterson), 1992
King's Esquires (Fenn, appendix), 1903
King's Fountain (Alexander), 1971
King's Gardens: An Allegory (Farrow), 1896
Kings in Exile (Roberts, C.), 1909
King's Knight's Pawn (Beatty), 1971
King's Loon (Downie), 1979
King's Monster (Haywood), 1980
King's New Clothes (McKissack), 1987
Kings of Space (Johns), 1954
King's Servants (Stretton, appendix), 1873
King's Sons (Fenn, appendix), 1901
King's Stilts (p Seuss), 1939
King's Toothache (pl Fisher, A.), 1965
King's Treasure (Mahy), 1986
King's Trousers (Kraus, R.), 1981
King's White Elephant (Harris, R.), 1973
Kintu: A Congo Adventure (Enright), 1935
Kip series (Odaga), from 1972
Kip Van Wrinkle (Hoff), 1974
Kipling Stories and Poems Every Child Should Know (Kipling), 1909
Kipper Skips (Darke), 1979
Kipper's Turn (Darke), 1976
Kippy the Koala (Bonsall, as Newell), 1960
Kiss for Little Bear (Minarik), 1968
Kiss Hello, Kiss Goodbye (Brown, Marc), 1997
Kiss on the Nose (p Bradman), 1984
Kissers (pl Yorinks), 1980
Kisses (Szekeres), 1993
Kisses from Rosa (Mathers), 1995
Kitchen Knight (Hodges, M.), 1990
Kitchen Madonna (Godden), 1967
Kitchen People (Wayne), 1963
Kitchenmaid (Bull), 1994
Kite, Adventures of a (Mahy), 1985
Kite and Caitlin (McGough), 1996
Kite Man (Meynell, as Tring), 1955
Kite over Tenth Avenue (Lexau), 1967
Kite that Braved Old Orchard 1, 2, 3, to the Zoo (Carle), 1968
Kitoto the Mighty (Mollel), 1998
Kits at Clynton Court School (Wynne), 1924
Kit's Castle (Powling), 1996
Kitten for a Day (Keats), 1974
Kitten Pilgrims (Ballantyne, appendix), 1882
Kitten Stand (Coatsworth), 1945
Kitten Who Wouldn't Purr (p Martin), 1987
Kittens (Jordan), 1989
Kittens, Cubs, and Babies (Schlein), 1959
Kittens for Nothing (Kraus, R.), 1976
Kitty O'Donovan (Meade, appendix), 1912
Kitty Wilkinson (pl Vipont), 1956
Kitty's Class Day (Alcott, appendix), 1868
Kitty's Tea Party (Heward), 1926
Ki-yu: A Story of Panthers (Haig-Brown), 1934
Klunky Monkey, New Kid in Class (Kraus, R.), 1990
Knee-High to a Grasshopper (Parrish), 1923
Kneeknock Rise (Babbitt), 1970
Knight and the Dragon (dePaola), 1980
Knight Crusader (Welch), 1954
Knight of the Lion (McDermott), 1978
Knight of the White Cross (Henty, appendix), 1895
Knight of Today (Meade, appendix), 1877
Knight Prisoner: The Tale of Sir Thomas Malory and His King (Hodges, M.), 1989
Knight's Castle (Eager), 1956
Knights in Shining Armor (Gibbons), 1995
Knights of the Cardboard Castle (Beresford), 1965
Knights of the Red Cross (Moore), 1907
Knights of the Road (Everett-Green, appendix), 1907
Knitting (Berg), 1972
Knitwits (Taylor, W.), 1992
Knock at the Door (Coatsworth), 1931
Knockers (Porter, S.), 1965
Knot Squirrel Tied (Uttley), 1937
Know, Sow and Grow Kids Book of Plants (Noonan), 1997
Knoxville, Tennessee (p Giovanni), 1994
Koala Bear's Walkabout (Hewett), 1959
Koala Lou (Fox), 1987
Kobo (Strang), 1904
Kofi and the Crow (Appiah), 1991
Kofi and the Eagle (Kaye), 1963
Kookanoo and Kangaroo (p Durack), 1963
Koonaworra the Black Swan, Story of (Rees, L.), 1957
Kopje Garrison (Fenn, appendix), 1901
Korean Cinderella (Climo), 1993
Koto and the Lagoon (Kaye), 1967
Koya Delaney and the Good Girl Blues (Greenfield), 1995
Kraymer Mystery (Allan), 1969
Krindlekrax (Ridley), 1991
Kung Fu Nun (McCully), 1998
Kung-Hsi Fa-Ts'Ai!: Happy New Year Kung-Hsi (Demi), 1998
Kurri Kurri the Kookaburra, Story of (Rees, L.), 1950
Kwasi and the Parrot and Other Stories (Kaye), 1961
Kwasi Goes to Town (Kaye), 1962
Kweeks of Kookatumdee (p Peet), 1985
Kyekyekulee: Grandmother's Tales (Appiah), 1992

Lachlan's Walk (Hathorn), 1980
Lackawanna (Aaron), 1986
Lacy Makes a Match (Beatty), 1979
Lad, A Dog (Terhune), 1919
Lad of Grit (Westerman), 1908
Lad of London Town (Everett-Green, appendix), 1909
Lad of Sunnybank (Terhune), 1929
Lad with a Whistle (Brink), 1941
Laddie's Choice (Le Feuvre), 1912
Ladies of the White House (pl Mackay, Constance D'Arcy), 1948
Lads and Lasses of Langley (Yonge, appendix), 1881
Lads and Lassies (Nesbit), 1894

Loitering Linus (Finley, appendix), 1868
Lo-Jack & Pirates (Hooks), 1991
Lollipop Princess: A Play for Paper Dolls (pl Estes), 1967
Lollipops: Stories and Poems (Berg), 1957
Lollygag of Limericks (p Livingston), 1978
London Baby (Meade, appendix), 1882
London Bridge Is Falling Down! (Spier), 1967
London Men and English Men (Hoban), 1962
London Pride (Cannan), 1939
London Windows (p Talbot), 1912
Lone Bull's Horse Raid (Goble), 1973
Lone Hunt (Steele, W.), 1956
Lone Muskrat (Rounds), 1953
Lone Seal Pup (Catherall), 1964
Lone Stands the Glen (Chipperfield), 1966
Lone Texan (Richards, F.), 1954
Lonely Game (Scannell), 1979
Lonely Garden, and Ronald's Burglar (Chaundler), 1934
Lonely Island (Ballantyne, appendix), 1880
Lonely Lantern, Mystery of the (Heide), 1976
Lonely Lioness and the Ostrich Chicks: a Masai Tale (Aardema), 1996
Lonely Little Mole (Bradman), 1986
Lonely Maria (Coatsworth), 1960
Lonely Veronica (Duvoisin), 1963
Loner (Wier), 1963
Lonesome Boy (Bontemps), 1955
Lonesome End (Meader), 1968
Lonesome Little Colt (Anderson), 1961
Lonesome Sorrel (Robertson), 1952
Long Ago (Szekeres), 1977
Long Bow (Welch), 1957
Long Day (Cresswell), 1972
Long Drop (Hardcastle), 1974
Long Ears: The Story of a Little Grey Donkey (Lynch), 1943
Long Grass of Tumbledown Road (Mahy), 1986
Long Hard Journey: The Story of the Pullman Porter (McKissack), 1990
Long Island Ducklings (Slobodkina), 1961
Long Lost Coelacanth and Other Living Fossils (Aliki), 1973
Long March (Mullen), 1990
Long Pilgrimage (Finkel), 1967
Long Ride (Patchett), 1970
Long River (Bruchac), 1995
Long Road Home (Tate, J.), 1971
Long Road to Gettysburg (Murphy, Jim), 1992
Long Search (Pullein-Thompson, C.), 1991
Long Secret (Fitzhugh), 1965
Long Trail (Strang), 1918
Long Trains Roll (Meader), 1944
Long Vacation (Yonge, appendix), 1895
Long Walk (Mattingley), 1976
Long Way Home (Cohen), 1990
Long Way Round (Sudbery), 1977
Long Way to Go (Darke), 1978
Long Way to Whiskey Creek (Beatty), 1971
Long Wharf (Pease), 1939
Long Winter (Wilder), 1940
Long Year (Wier), 1969
Longbeard the Wizard (Fleischman), 1970
Longest Name on the Block (Yolen), 1968
Longest Way Round (Lynch), 1961
Longest Weekend (Arundel), 1969
Longlegs the Heron (Burgess), 1927
Longshanks (Meader), 1928
Longtime Dreaming (Brinsmead), 1982
Longtime Passing (Brinsmead), 1971
Look and Find A B C (Biro), 1990
Look Around: A Book About Shapes (Fisher, L.), 1987
Look at Me! (Daly), 1986
Look at the Little One (Cockett), 1974
Look Back, Moss (Levin), 1998
Look, Do and Listen (Ainsworth), 1969
Look! Look! (Foreman), 1997
Look! Look! A Story Book (Heide), 1971
Look Out, He's Behind You! (Bradman), 1988
Look Out Secret Seven (Blyton), 1962
Look under V (Mahy), 1977
Look What I've Got! (Browne), 1980
Look What You've Done Now, Moses (McKissack), 1984
Look Who's Talking (Bonsall), 1962
Looking After Chocolates (Armitage), 1992
Looking after Libby (Brown, P.), 1974
Looking Book (p Hoberman), 1973
Looking for a Friend (Beresford), 1967
Looking for Juliette (Lisle), 1994
Looking-for-Something: The Story of a Stray Burro of Ecuador (Clark, A.), 1952
Looking Out for Sampson (Hathorn), 1987
Look-See with Uncle Bill (James), 1938
Loopy (Gramatky), 1941
Loot! (Terhune), 1940
Lorax (p Seuss), 1971
Lord and Lady Kitty (Meade, appendix), 1912
Lord Fish and Other Tales (de la Mare), 1933
Lord Fox and Other Spine-Chilling Tales (Nye), 1997
Lord of Dynevor (Everett-Green, appendix), 1892
Lord of the Animals (French), 1997
Lord of the Castle (Clarke, P.), 1960
Lord of the Forest (Watkins-Pitchford), 1975
Lord of the Rushie River (Barker), 1938
Lord of the Seas (Strang), 1908
Lord Pip, Adventures of (Cunliffe), 1970
Lord Rex, The Lion Who Wished (McKee), 1973
Lord's Purse-Bearers (Stretton, appendix), 1882
Lore and Language of Schoolchildren (Opie), 1959
Lorenzo (Waber), 1961
Lorenzo Bear & Company (Wahl), 1971
Lorenzo the Magnificent, Story of (Allen, E.), 1961
Lorna at Wynyards (Brent-Dyer), 1947
Losers Weepers (Jukes), 1997
Losing Joe's Place (Korman), 1990
Loss of the "Night Wind" (Sherry), 1970
Lost and Found (Little, J.), 1985
Lost at Sea (Alger, appendix), 1904
Lost at the Fair (Sharp), 1965
Lost Birthday (Bisset), 1976
Lost Birthday (pl Barne), n.d.
Lost Cave (Fidler), 1978
Lost Children (Goble), 1993
Lost Clue (Walton, appendix), 1907
Lost Cow (Pullein-Thompson, C.), 1966

Magic in My Pocket: A Selection of Tales (Uttley), 1957
Magic in the Mirror (McKay), 1996
Magic Island (Talbot), 1926
Magic Jacket and Other Stories (de la Mare), 1943
Magic Kiss (Bradman), 1987
Magic Kiss (Chaundler), 1916
Magic Knitting Needles and Other Stories (Blyton), 1950
Magic Lollipop (McNeill), 1975
Magic Meadow (d'Aulaire), 1958
Magic Meatballs (Yorinks, as Yaffe), 1979
Magic Michael (p Slobodkin), 1944
Magic Money (Clark, A.), 1950
Magic Mysteries series (Levy), from 1988
Magic Nuts (Molesworth, appendix), 1898
Magic of Millicent Musgrave (Turkle), 1967
Magic of Oz (Baum), 1919
Magic or Not? (Eager), 1959
Magic Paintbrush (Muller), 1989
Magic Party (Hardcastle), 1988
Magic Pawnshop: A New Year's Eve Fantasy (Field), 1927
Magic Pencil and Other Plays from My Tales (pl Fyleman), 1938
Magic Pudding, Being the Adventures of Bunyip Bluegum and His Friends Bill Barnacle and Sam Sawnoff (Lindsay), 1918
Magic Purse (Uchida), 1993
Magic Rug (d'Aulaire), 1931
Magic Saddle (Mattingley), 1983
Magic Show (Fujikawa), 1981
Magic Show (Wood), 1995
Magic Snow-Bird and Other Stories (Blyton), 1951
Magic Squid (Manning-Sanders), 1968
Magic Summer (Streatfeild), 1967
Magic Three of Solatia (Yolen), 1974
Magic to Burn (Fritz), 1964
Magic Tree: A Tale from the Congo (McDermott), 1973
Magic Trumpet (p Durack), 1946
Magic Vase (French), 1991
Magic Word (Zolotow), 1952
Magic World (Beresford), 1965
Magic World (Nesbit), 1912
Magical Changes (Oakley), 1979
Magical Cockatoo (Sharp), 1974
Magical Cupboard (Curry), 1976
Magical Land of Noom (Gruelle), 1922
Magical Melons: More Stories about Caddie Woodlawn (Brink), 1944
Magician (Shulevitz), 1973
Magician and Double Trouble (McKee), 1981
Magician and the Balloon (McKee), 1978
Magician and the Dragon (McKee), 1979
Magician and the King's Crown (McKee), 1988
Magician and the Petnapping (McKee), 1976
Magician and the Sorcerer (McKee), 1974
Magician Who Kept a Pub and Other Stories (Edwards, D.), 1975
Magician Who Lost His Magic (McKee), 1970
Magician's Apprentice (McKee), 1987
Magician's Heart (pl Nesbit), 1907
Magician's Nephew (Lewis, C.S.), 1955
Magician's Nephew (pl Harris, A.), 1983
Magie d'un jour de pluie (Gay), 1986
Magnificent Morris Mouse Clubhouse (Gibbons), 1981
Magnificent Mummies (Bradman), 1997
Magnificent Nose, and Other Marvels (Fienberg), 1991
Magnus Bonum (Yonge, appendix), 1879
Magnus Powermouse (King-Smith), 1982
Magpie's Tale: Jesus and Zacchaeus (Butterworth, N.), 1988
Magus the Lollipop Man (Mullen), 1981
Mahatma (Hoff), 1969
Maid and the Mouse and the Odd-Shaped House (Zelinsky), 1981
Maid Indomitable (Meade, appendix), 1916
Maid of Mystery (Meade, appendix), 1904
Maid of the Wood (French), 1985
Maid with the Goggles (Meade, appendix), 1906
Maids of La Rochelle (Brent-Dyer), 1924
Maids' Ribbons (Treadgold), 1965
Mail Critter (Mayer), 1987
Main Line Engines (Awdry), 1966
Mainly in Moonlight (Gray), 1965
Maisie's Discovery (Marchant), 1906
Maitlands: All Change at Cuckly Place (Streatfeild), 1979
Make a Circle, Keep Us In: Poems for a Good Day (p Adoff), 1975
Make a Wish, Molly (Cohen), 1994
Make-Believe (Fujikawa), 1981
Make-Believe (Goudge), 1949
Make-Believe (pl Milne), 1921
Make-Believe Ballplayer (Slote), 1989
Make-Believe Twins (McGinley), 1953
Make Room for Elisa (Hurwitz), 1993
Make Way for Ducklings (McCloskey), 1941
Make Your Move (Watson, J.), 1988
Making a Difference: The Story of an American Family (Hodges, M.), 1989
Making Big Bucks (Taylor, W.), 1987
Making Faces (Butterworth, N.), 1993
Making Friends (Mahy), 1990
Making His Mark (Alger, appendix), 1901
Making Music Your Own (Ehlert), 1962
Making of a Missionary (Yonge, appendix), 1900
Making of a Woman (Le Feuvre), 1903
Making of Joshua Cobb (Hodges, M.), 1971
Making of Ursula (Moore), 1910
Makoto, The Smallest Boy (Uchida), 1970
Malcom's Race (Mayer), 1983
Malibu and Other Poems (p Livingston), 1974
Malkin's Mountain (Moray Williams), 1948
Malys Rockell (Wynne), 1934
Mama Bird, Baby Birds (Johnson, A.), 1994
Mama Don't Allow (Hurd), 1984
Mama Hattie's Girl (Lenski), 1953
"Mama, I Wish I Was Snow" "Child, You'd Be Very Cold" (Krauss), 1962
Mama One, Mama Two (MacLachlan), 1982
Mama, Papa and Baby Joe (Daly), 1991
Mammoth Mix-Up (Levy), 1995
Mammywater (Nwapa), 1979
Man (Briggs, R.), 1992
Man & Mustang (Ancona), 1992
Man-Eater (Catherall, as Corby), 1963
Man from the Sea (Andrews), 1970
Man in the Bowler Hat: A Terribly Exciting Affair (pl Milne), 1924
Man in the Hut (Meynell), 1967

Man in the Manhole and the Fix-It Men (Brown, Margaret Wise, as Sage), 1946
Man in the Red Turban (Martin), 1978
Man Mountain (Waddell), 1991
Man of His Word (Stretton, appendix), 1878
Man of the House (McLean), 1956
Man on a Steeple (Moray Williams), 1971
Man on the Moon-Eyed Horse (Fleischman), 1980
Man Who Came Back (Hope-Simpson), 1962
Man Who Cooked for Himself (Krasilovsky), 1982
Man Who Didn't Wash His Dishes (Krasilovsky), 1950
Man Who Enjoyed Grumbling (Mahy), 1986
Man Who Entered a Contest (Krasilovsky), 1980
Man Who Lost His Head (Bishop), 1942
Man Who Rang the Bell (Tate, J.), 1973
Man Who Sang the Sillies (p Ciardi), 1961
Man Who Stopped to Help (Blyton), 1965
Man Who Took the Indoors Out (p Lobel, Arnold), 1974
Man Who Tried to Fly (McBratney), 1980
Man Who Tried to Save Time (Krasilovsky), 1979
Man Who Vanished into Space (Johns), 1963
Man Who Walked on His Hands (Mahy), 1987
Man Who Was Too Lazy to Fix Things (Krasilovsky), 1992
Man Whose Mother Was a Pirate (Mahy), 1972
Man with Eyes like Windows (Owen), 1987
Man with No Shadow (Rosen, Michael), 1994
Man with the Pan-Pipes and Other Stories (Molesworth, appendix), 1892
Man with the Purple Eyes (Zolotow), 1961
Man with the Sack (Meynell, as Tring), 1963
Man with the Silver Eyes (Steele, W.), 1976
Man with the Yellow Eyes (Clark, C.), 1963
Man with Your Advantages (Andrew), 1970
Man Without a Face (Holland), 1972
Manchild (Patten), 1973
Manda (Hale, K.), 1952
Mandarin's Kite (Farrow), 1900
Mandog (Lamplugh), 1972
Mandy Duck, Adventures of (Bisset), 1974
Mandy Makes Cubby a Hat (Blyton), 1953
Mandy, Mops, and Cubby Again (Blyton), 1952
Mandy, Mops, and Cubby and the Whitewash (Blyton), 1955
Mandy, Mops, and Cubby Find a House (Blyton), 1952
Mangaboom (Pomerantz), 1997
Mango Tooth (Pomerantz), 1977
Mangrove Summer (Lasenby), 1989
Manhattan Is Missing (Hildick), 1969
Manka, The Sky Gipsy (Watkins-Pitchford), 1939
Manners (Aliki), 1990
Manor House School (Brazil), 1910
Manor, Mystery of the (Talbot), 1930
Manor School (Meade, appendix), 1903
Mansa Helps at Home (Asare), 1972
Manson, the Miser (Alger, appendix), 1981
Mantis and the Moon: Stories for the Children of Africa (Poland), 1979
Many Kinds of Magic: Tales of Mystery, Myth and Enchantment (Scott), 1988
Many Lives of Benjamin Franklin (Aliki), 1977
Many Lives of Chio and Goro (Lifton), 1966
Many Mice of Mr. Brice (p Seuss, as Le Sieg), 1973
Many Moons (pl Chorpenning), 1947
Many Moons (Thurber), 1943
Many Waters (L'Engle), 1986
Maori and Settler (Henty, appendix), 1890
Mapper Mundy's Treasure Hunt (Hildick), 1963
Maps of Time (Hunt, P.), 1983
Marathon and Steve (Rayner), 1989
Marc and Pixie and the Walls in Mrs. Jones's Garden (Fatio), 1975
Marcella Stories (Gruelle), 1929
Marcella's Guardian Angel (Ness), 1979
March on London (Henty, appendix), 1897
Marchers for the Dream (Carlson), 1969
Marcia (Steptoe), 1976
Marco Moonlight (Bulla), 1976
Marco Polo, Adventures of (Demi), 1981
Marcus series (Poland), 1984-88
Marcus Stratford's Charge (Everett-Green, appendix), 1890
Marcus the School Mouse (Mullen), 1993
Marcus, the Young Centurion (Fenn, appendix), 1904
Margaret (Meade, appendix), 1902
Margaret Finds a Future (Allan), 1954
Margaret in the Middle (Hunter, B.), 1986
Margaret Montfort (Richards, L.), 1898
Margaret on Her Way (Hunter, B.), 1988
Margaret's Birthday (Wahl), 1971
Marge's Diner (Gibbons), 1989
Marguerite Henry's Horseshoe Library: Stormy, Misty's Foal; Sea Star, Orphan of Chincoteague; Misty of Chincoteague (Henry), 1992
Maria (Lexau), 1964
Maria Escapes (Avery), 1992
Maria Theresa (Mathers), 1985
Maria's Cave (Hooks), 1977
Maria's House (Merrill), 1974
Maria's Italian Spring (Avery), 1993
Marian Anderson: A Great Singer (McKissack), 1991
Marianna May and Nursey (dePaola), 1983
Marianne and Mark (Storr), 1960
Marianne Dreams (Storr), 1958
Marianne Dreams (Storr), 1964
Marianthe's Story: Painted Words & Spoken Memories (Aliki), 1998
Marie (Richards, L.), 1894
Marie Alone (Kaye), 1973
Marie Bertrand (Alger, appendix), 1981
Marie Curie (Fisher, L.), 1994
Marie Louise and Christophe (Carlson), 1974
Marie Louise and Christophe at the Carnival (Carlson), 1981
Marie Louise's Heydey (Carlson), 1975
Marie-Eve et le piege a genies (Hutchins, H.), 1989
Marigold (Meade, appendix), 1890
Marigold in Godmother's House (Brisley), 1934
Marina (p Bemelmans), 1962
Marjorie & Co. (Hill, L.), 1948
Marjorie's Best Year (Brazil), 1923
Mark and the Monocycle (McKee), 1968
Mark England's Cap (Hardcastle), 1990
Mark Fox series (Hardcastle), from 1976
Mark Manning's Mission (Alger, appendix), 1905
Mark Mason's Victory (Alger, appendix), 1899
Mark Spark (Wilson, J.), 1992

Mouse God (Kennedy, R.), 1979
Mouse House (Godden), 1957
Mouse in the Manger (Wynne-Jones), 1993
Mouse Manor (Eager), 1952
Mouse Match, a Chinese Folktale (Young), 1997
Mouse Mess (Szekeres), 1990
Mouse Mischief (Greaves), 1989
Mouse Soup (Lobel, Arnold), 1977
Mouse Tales (Lobel, Arnold), 1972
Mouse Talk (de Roo), 1989
Mouse that Jack Built (Szekeres), 1997
Mouse, The Rabbit, and the Little White Hen (Uttley), 1966
Mouse Wedding (Mahy), 1986
Mouse Work (Kraus, R.), 1980
Mouse's Birthday (p Yolen), 1993
Mouse's Tale: Jesus and the Storm (Butterworth, N.), 1988
Mousewife (Godden), 1951
Mouthful of Magic (Morgan, H.), 1963
Movie Shoes (Streatfeild), 1949
Moving (Rosen, Michael), 1993
Moving Day (Szekeres), 1989
Moving Day for the Middlemans (Slobodkina), 1960
Moving Finger (Grice), 1962
Moving In (Slote), 1988
Moving Molly (Hughes, S.), 1978
Mozart: Music Magician (Bishop), 1968
Mpotse—Mpotse—Eguamba—Na—Feow (de Graft-Hanson), 1995
Much Ado about Aldo (Hurwitz), 1978
Much Bigger Than Martin (Kellogg), 1976
Much Too Much Magic (McNeill), 1971
Mucky Moose (Allen, J.), 1990
Mud Flat April Fool (Stevenson, J.), 1998
Mud Flat Mystery (Stevenson, J.), 1997
Mud Flat Olympics (Stevenson, J.), 1994
Mud Puddle (Munsch), 1979
Mud Snail Son (Lifton), 1971
Muddy Road to Glory (Meader), 1963
Muffletump Storybook (Wahl), 1975
Muffletumps: The Story of Four Dolls (Wahl), 1966
Muffletumps' Christmas Party (Wahl), 1975
Muffletumps' Halloween Scare (Wahl), 1977
Muggie Maggie (Cleary), 1990
Mulberry Bush (p Farjeon), 1945
Mulberry Street Team (Beresford), 1963
Mulberry Tree (Wahl), 1970
Mulbridge Manor (Reeves), 1958
Mulcaster Market: Three Plays for Young People (pl Reeves), 1951
Mule Who Struck It Rich (Hoff), 1971
Muley-Ears, Nobody's Dog (Henry), 1959
Mullion (Allan), 1949
Mum Goes to Work (Gleeson), 1992
Mum-Minder (Wilson, J.), 1993
Mumfie Marches On (Tozer), 1942
Mumfie the Admiral (Tozer), 1937
Mumfie's Magic Box (Tozer), 1938
Mumfie's Picture Book (Tozer), 1947
Mumfie's Uncle Samuel (Tozer), 1939
Mumford Ghosts series (Barry), 1971-74
Mummies Made in Egypt (Aliki), 1979
Mummy Dearest Creepy Hollow Whooooooooodunnit series (Kraus, R.), 1988
Mummy's Mask, Mystery of the (Heide), 1979
Munde and His Friends (Odaga), 1987
Munde Goes to the Market (Odaga), 1987
Mungo the Monkey (Ainsworth), 1968
Mungoon-Gali the Giant Goanna (Trezise), 1991
Muppy's Ball (Mahy), 1986
Murdered Players, Case of the (Newman), 1985
Murmel, Murmel, Murmel (Munsch), 1982
Murray Finds a Chum (Wynne), 1914
Muscles and Brains (Hoff), 1940
Museum (Abbott, appendix), 1884
Mushroom Center Disaster (Bodecker), 1974
Music Maker (Gibbons), 1996
Musical Honours (Barne), 1947
Musical Max (Kraus, R.), 1990
Musicians of Bremen: A Tale from Germany (Yolen), 1994
Musicians of the Sun: An Aztec Myth (McDermott), 1991
Mustang Machine (Powling), 1981
Mustang, Wild Spirit of the West (Henry), 1966
Mustard, Pepper, and Salt (Uttley), 1938
Mutineers (Armstrong), 1968
Mutineers (Hawes), 1920
Muttering Mummy, Case of the (Hildick), 1986
My Ain Sel' (pl Mitchison), 1928
My Animal Friends (Fujikawa), 1981
My Apron (Carle), 1994
My Aunt Came Back (Cummings), 1998
My Aunt Polly by the Sea (Cresswell), 1980
My Aunt Rosie (Hoff), 1972
My Auntie Sal and the Mega-Sized Moose (Waddell), 1996
My Babysitter (Rockwell), 1985
My Backyard (Rockwell), 1984
My Ballet Class (Isadora), 1980
My Ballet Diary (Isadora), 1995
My Barber (Rockwell), 1981
My Best Friend (Hutchins, P.), 1993
My Bible ABC Book (McKissack), 1987
My Big-Ears Picture Book (Blyton), 1958
My Black Sheep (Everett-Green, appendix), 1889
My Book about Christmas (Robinson, as thomas), 1946
My Boynie (Everett-Green, appendix), 1889
My Brother (Berg), 1972
My Brother Bernadette (Wilson, J.), 1995
My Brother Fine with Me (Clifton), 1975
My Brother Lambert (Rush), 1957
My Brother Stevie (Clymer), 1967
My Buddy, The King (Brittain), 1989
My Camera (Ancona), 1992
My Castle (Heide), 1972
My Cat (Allen, J.), 1986
My Cat Ginger (Wahl), 1992
My Cat Has Eyes of Sapphire Blue (p Fisher, A.), 1973
My Cat Likes to Hide in Boxes (p Sutton), 1973
My Cat Maisie (Allen, P.), 1990
My Cousin Abe (Fisher, A.), 1962
My Dad Is Brilliant (Butterworth, N.), 1989
My Dad: Story and Pictures (Daly), 1995
My Dad's a Fire-eater (p McGough), 1992
My Daughter Nicola (Arthur), 1965

My Dog (Allen, J.), 1987
My Dog and I (Titus, as Lord), 1958
My Dog Is Lost (Keats), 1960
My Dog Rinty (Ets), 1946
My Dog Sunday (Berg), 1968
My Doggie and I (Ballantyne, appendix), 1881
My Doll Keisha (Greenfield), 1991
My Dream of Martin Luther King (Ringgold), 1995
My Enid Blyton Story Book (Blyton), 1953
My Family (Bradman), 1992
My Family Vacation (Khalsa), 1988
My Family's Not Forever (Allan), 1977
My Famous Father (Hildick), 1990
My Father, Sun-Sun Johnson (Palmer), 1974
My Father, The Coach (Slote), 1972
My Father's Collie (Kjelgaard), 1961
My Father's Dragon (Gannett), 1948
My Father's Dragon, Elmer and the Dragon, and The Dragons of Blueland (Gannett), 1997
My Father's Hands (Ryder), 1994
My Favorite Thing (Fujikawa), 1978
My Feet (Aliki), 1990
My First Halloween (dePaola), 1991
My First Holy Communion (Conlon-McKenna), 1990
My First Horse (James), 1940
My First Passover (dePaola), 1991
My First Thanksgiving (dePaola), 1992
My First Word Book (Scarry), 1986
My Five Senses (Aliki), 1962
My Friend Charlie (Flora), 1964
My Friend Flicka (O'Hara), 1941
My Friend Jacob (Clifton), 1980
My Friend John (Zolotow), 1968
My Friend Mr. Leakey (Haldane), 1937
My Friend Smith (Reed, appendix), 1889
My Friend Specs McCann (McNeill), 1955
My Friend the Dog (Terhune), 1926
My Friend the Monster (Bulla), 1980
My Friend's a Gris-Quock! (Blackman), 1994
My Friends (Tafuri), 1987
My Gang (Waddell, as Sefton), 1984
My Garden Book (Robinson, as Thomas), 1947
My Grandma Has Black Hair (Hoffman), 1988
My Grandma Lived in Gooligulch (Base), 1983
My Grandpa Is Amazing (Butterworth, N.), 1991
My Grandson Lew (Zolotow), 1974
My Granma Is Wonderful (Butterworth, N.), 1991
My Granny Is a Sumo Wrestler (p Owen), 1994
My Great Grandpa (Waddell), 1990
My Hands (Aliki), 1962
My Head Is Red, and other Riddle Rhymes (p Livingston), 1990
My Heart's in the Highlands (Le Feuvre), 1924
My Hopping Bunny (p Bright, as Douglas), 1960
My House (Schlein), 1971
My Kid Sister (Hildick), 1971
My Kingdom for a Grave (Plowman), 1970
My Lady Joanna (Everett-Green, appendix), 1902
My Lady Venturesome (Moore), 1926
My Life as a Fifth-Grade Comedian (Levy), 1997
My Little Baby Brother (Bradman), 1992
My Little Book of Big and Little (p Smith), 1963
My Little Corner, and Wandering May (Walton, appendix), 1872
My Little Golden Book about Cats (Ryder), 1988
My Mama Needs Me (Walter), 1983
My Mama Says There Aren't Any Zombies... (Viorst), 1973
My Mates and I (Walton, appendix), 1873
My Mother (Chit-Chat) (Ballantyne, as Comus, appendix), 1857
My Mother and I (p Fisher, A.), 1967
My Mother Is the Smartest Woman in the World (Clymer), 1982
My Mother Never Listens to Me (Sharmat), 1984
My Mother's Ghost (Buffie), 1992
My Mum Is Fantastic (Butterworth, N.), 1989
My Name is Amelia (Sobol), 1994
My Naughty Little Sister (Edwards, D.), 1982
My Naughty Little Sister and Bad Harry (Edwards, D.), 1974
My Naughty Little Sister and Bad Harry's Rabbit (Edwards, D.), 1977
My Naughty Little Sister and Some Others (Edwards, D.), 1957
My Naughty Little Sister at the Fair (Edwards, D.), 1979
My Naughty Little Sister Goes Fishing (Edwards, D.), 1976
My Naughty Little Sister: Stories from "Listen with Mother" (Edwards, D.), 1952
My Naughty Little Sister's Friends (Edwards, D.), 1962
My New House (Molesworth, appendix), 1894
My Noddy Picture Book (Blyton), 1958
My Noisy Toys (Allen, J.), 1997
My Ol' Man (Polacco), 1995
My Old Tree (Gauch), 1970
My Pal Spadger (Naughton), 1977
My Parents Think I'm Sleeping (p Prelutsky), 1985
My Pet the Rock (Bridwell), 1975
My Place (Wheatley), 1987
"My Pretty" and Her Little Brother "Too (Molesworth)" 1901
My Real Family (McCully), 1994
My Red Umbrella (Bright), 1959
My Robot Buddy (Slote), 1975
My Rotten, Redheaded, Older Brother (Polacco), 1994
My School (Spier), 1981
My Second Best Friend (Kaye), 1998
My Simple Little Brother (Norman), 1979
My Sister Says (Baker, B.), 1984
My Sister's Rusty Bike (Aylesworth), 1996
My Son John (Aylesworth), 1994
My Son, The Mouse (Kraus, R.), 1966
My Special Best Words (Steptoe), 1974
My Spring Robin (Rockwell), 1989
My Summer of the Lions (Taylor, W.), 1986
My Tiger (Cowley), 1986
My Trip to Alpha I (Slote), 1978
My Uncle Charlie (Darke), 1977
My Very First Book (Petersham), 1948
My Very First Library (Carle), 1974
My Very Own Fairy Book (Gruelle), 1923
My Very Own Fairy Stories (Gruelle), 1917
My Visit to the Aquarium (Aliki), 1993
My Visit to the Dinosaurs (Aliki), 1969
My Visit to the Zoo (Aliki), 1997
My War with Goggle Eyes (Fine), 1989
My Wonderful Aunt (Mahy), 1986
My World (Brown, Margaret Wise), 1949
My Young Alcides (Yonge, appendix), 1875
Myrtle, Tertle, and Gertle (Clark, E.), 1989

Myrtle the Turtle, Tales of (Robertson), 1974
Mysie's Work (Finley, appendix), 1864
Mysteries of Harris Burdick (Van Allsburg), 1984
Mysteries of Zigomar (Ahlberg), 1997
Mysterious "Mr. Punch" (Farrow), 1905
Mysterious Appearance of Agnes (Griffiths, H.), 1975
Mysterious Baba and Her Magic Caravan: Two Stories (Ainsworth), 1980
Mysterious City (Marchant), 1905
Mysterious House (Walton, appendix), 1890
Mysterious Inheritance (Marchant), 1914
Mysterious Island (Beresford), 1984
Mysterious Island (Wynne), 1935
Mysterious Mr. Simister (Fidler), 1947
Mysterious Pool (Patchett), 1958
Mysterious Rattle (Rees, D.), 1982
Mysterious Shin Shira (Farrow), 1913
Mysterious Tadpole (Kellogg), 1977
Mysterious Voyage (Farrow), 1910
Mysterious Zetabet (Corbett, S.), 1979
Mysteriously Yours, Maggie Marmelstein (Sharmat), 1982
Mystery at Black Pony Inn (Pullein-Thompson, C.), 1976
Mystery at Keyhole Carnival (Heide), 1977
Mystery at MacAdoo Zoo (Heide), 1973
Mystery at Musket Bay (Bradman), 1989
Mystery at Mycenae: An Adventure Story of Ancient Greece (Green), 1957
Mystery at Penmarth (Manning-Sanders), 1940
Mystery at Southport Cinema (Heide), 1978
Mystery at the Meet (Levy), 1990
Mystery at Winklesea (Cresswell), 1995
Mystery Beast of Ostergeest (Kellogg), 1971
Mystery Began in Madeira (Allan), 1967
Mystery in Arles (Allan), 1964
Mystery in Florence (Fenton), 1959
Mystery in Manhattan (Allan), 1968
Mystery in Rome (Allan), 1974
Mystery in Spindle Bottom (Allan), 1986
Mystery in the Middle Marches (Finlay), 1964
Mystery in Wales (Allan), 1971
Mystery Island (Blyton), 1945
Mystery Island (Westerman), 1927
Mystery Man (Corbett, S.), 1970
Mystery on Bleecker Street (Hooks), 1980
Mystery on Danger Road (Heide), 1983
Mystery on Liberty Street (Hooks), 1982
Mystery on Rainbow Island (Clewes), 1957
Mystery on Telegraph Hill (Pease), 1961
Mystery on the Docks (Hurd), 1983
Mystery on the Farm (Cockett), 1988
Mystery on the Fourteenth Floor (Allan), 1965
Mystery on the Moor (Pullein-Thompson, J.), 1984
Mystery Ship (Westerman), 1920
Mystery Stories (Blyton), 1960
Mystery That Never Was (Blyton), 1961
Mystery Tour (Ahlberg), 1991
Mystery Train (Todd), 1937
Myth of Our Own (Highwater), 1996

Na of Wa (Aardema), 1960
Na Saoithe Anoir (Mullen), 1993
Nacar, the White Deer (de Treviño), 1963
Nadia to the Rescue (Moore), 1912
Naftali the Storyteller and His Horse, Sus, and Other Stories (Singer), 1976
Nag Called Wednesday (Brown, R.), 1977
Nail, A Stick, and a Lid (Kaye), 1975
Nailing the Shadow (p McGough), 1987
Naira Power (Emecheta), 1982
Name for Kitty (McGinley), 1948
Name Games (Breslin), 1997
Name on the Glass (Freeman, Barbara), 1964
Nameless Boat (Pardoe), 1957
Nameless Island (Westerman), 1915
Namesake (Hodges, C.), 1964
Namesake for Nathan (Monjo), 1977
Namesakes (Everett-Green, appendix), 1893
Naming (Greaves), 1992
Naming the Cat (Pringle), 1997
Naming the Dark (Dalton), 1992
Nan and Ken (Wynne), 1919
Nana Upstairs and Nana Downstairs (dePaola), 1973
Nance Kennedy (Meade, appendix), 1910
Nancekuke (Branfield), 1972
Nancy Afloat (Marchant), 1936
Nancy Alden (White), 1936
Nancy at St. Bride's (Bruce, D.), 1933
Nancy Calls the Tune (Bruce, D.), 1944
Nancy in the Sixth (Bruce, D.), 1935
Nancy, New Girl, and The Girl Who Was Different (Talbot), 1930
Nancy No-Size (Hoffman), 1987
Nancy Returns to St. Bride's (Bruce, D.), 1938
Nancy to the Rescue (Bruce, D.), 1927
Nanny Goat and the Fierce Dog (Keeping), 1973
Napper Goes for Goal (Waddell), 1981
Napper Super-Sub (Waddell), 1993
Napper's Big Match (Waddell), 1993
Napper's Golden Goals (Waddell), 1984
Napper's Luck (Waddell), 1993
Narcissa; or, The Road to Rome, and In Verona: Two Tales (Richards, L.), 1894
Narrative of the Travels and Adventures of Monsieur Violet (Marryat), 1843
Narrow Passage (Butterworth, O.), 1973
Narrow Squeak and Other Animal Stories (King-Smith), 1993
Nasty! (Rosen, Michael), 1982
Nasty Competition (Levy), 1991
Nat the Naturalist (Fenn, appendix), 1899
Nata (Griffith), 1985
Nate the Great series (Sharmat), from 1972
Nathaniel Talking (p Greenfield), 1988
Nation Builders (Hayes), 1968
National Velvet (Bagnold), 1935
National Velvet (pl Bagnold), 1946
National Worm Day (Stevenson, J.), 1990
Native American Animal Stories (Bruchac), 1992
Native American Plant Stories (Bruchac), 1995
Native American Stories (Bruchac), 1991
Native American Sweat Lodge, History and Legends (Bruchac), 1993
Native Wisdom (Bruchac), 1995
Nativity Play (Butterworth, N.), 1986

On Your Cycle, Michael (p Scannell), 1992
Once and Forever Christmas (p Corlett), 1975
Once at KwaFubesi (Poland), 1981
Once I Was a Plum Tree (Hurwitz), 1980
Once on a Time (Milne), 1917
Once There Was a King Who Promised He Would Never Chop Anyone's Head Off (Rosen, Michael), 1976
Once There Was a Swagman (Brinsmead), 1979
Once There Were Giants (Waddell), 1989
Once under the Cherry Blossom Tree: An Old Japanese Tale (Say), 1974
Once upon a Clothesline (pl Harris, A.), 1944
Once upon a Saturday (Fenton), 1958
Once upon a Time in a Pigpen and Three Other Stories (Brown, Margaret Wise), 1980
Once upon a Time Stories (Beresford), 1987
Once upon Little Big Horn (Lampman), 1971
Once Upon a Bedtime Story (Yolen), 1997
Once Upon a Dinkelsbuhl (Gauch), 1977
Once Upon a Golden Apple (Little, J.), 1991
Once Upon a Time: A Prince's Fantastic Journey (Oakley), 1990
Once Upon a Time Animal Stories (Bailey), 1918
Once We Had a Horse (Rounds), 1971
Once We Went on a Picnic (p Fisher, A.), 1975
Once When the World Was Green (Wahl), 1996
One and Only Two Heads (Ahlberg), 1979
One at a Time: His Collected Poems for the Young (p McCord), 1977
One Bad Thing about Father (Monjo), 1970
One Brave Summer (Turner, A.), 1995
One by One, Garth Pig's Rain Song (Rayner), 1994
One by Sea (Corbett, S.), 1965
One Crow: A Counting Rhyme (Aylesworth), 1988
One Day Event (Pullein-Thompson, J.), 1954
One Day with Jambi in Sumatra (Sperry), 1934
One Day with Manu (Sperry), 1933
One Day with Tuktu, An Eskimo Boy (Sperry), 1935
One Duck, Another Duck (Pomerantz), 1984
One Earth, Many People: The Challenge of Human Population Growth (Pringle), 1971
One-Eyed Jake (Hutchins, P.), 1979
One Fall Day (Bang), 1994
One Fine Day (Quinn), 1995
One Fish, Two Fish, Red Fish, Blue Fish (p Seuss), 1960
One Foot in Fairyland: Sixteen Tales (Farjeon), 1938
One Frog Too Many (Mayer), 1975
One Good Horse (Hardcastle), 1993
One Grain of Rice: A Mathematical Folktale (Demi), 1997
One Green Bottle (Parker), 1973
One Hundred Shining Candles (Lunn), 1989
One Hungry Spider (Baker, J.), 1982
One Hunter (Hutchins, P.), 1982
One Is Good but Two Are Better (p Slobodkin), 1956
One Is One (Picard), 1965
One Kick (Hardcastle), 1986
One-Legged Ghost (Lifton), 1968
One Little Baby (p Robinson), 1950
One Little Drum (Hodges, M.), 1958
One Monday Morning (Shulevitz), 1967
One Monster After Another (Mayer), 1974
One Moonlit Night (Armitage), 1983
One Morning in Maine (McCloskey), 1952
One Nil (Bradman), 1985
One of Clive's Heroes (Strang), 1906
One of Each (p Hoberman), 1997
One of the 28th (Henty, appendix), 1889
One of the Family (Beresford), 1985
One of the Many (Westerman), 1945
One of the Third Grade Thonkers (Naylor), 1988
One of Three (Johnson, A.), 1991
One Proud Summer (Mackay, Claire), 1981
One-Ring Circus (pl Fisher, A.), 1965
One Room School (Pringle), 1998
One Round Moon and a Star for Me (Daly), 1994
One Small Fish (Ryder), 1993
One Snowy Night (Butterworth, N.), 1989
One Step, Two... (Zolotow), 1955
One Sunday (Gleeson), 1988
One Terrific Thanksgiving (Sharmat), 1985
One Thousand Christmas Beards, See Smith Toy Shop, Eat at Joe's (Duvoisin), 1955
One, Two, Three, A Counting Book (Fujikawa), 1981
One, Two, Three with Ant and Bee: A Counting Story (Banner), 1958
One, Two, Where's My Shoe? (p Ungerer), 1964
One Very Best Valentine's Day (Blos), 1989
One Warm Fox (Butterworth, N.), 1997
One Week One Trouble (Okoro), 1973
One Wet Jacket (Tafuri), 1988
One White Mouse (Parker), 1966
One-Winged Dragon (Clark, C.), 1955
One Winter Night in August and Other Nonsense Jingles (Kennedy, X.J.), 1975
One with a Bun (Allen, J.), 1997
One World (Foreman), 1990
One-Inch Fellow (Yashima), 1995
Onion Journey (Cunningham), 1967
Only a Dog (Stretton, appendix), 1888
Only a Girl! (Moore), 1913
Only a Pony (Pullein-Thompson, D.), 1980
Only A Show (Fine), 1990
Only an Irish Boy (Alger, appendix), 1894
Only Child (White), 1905
Only Day-Girl (Moore), 1923
Only Earth We Have (Pringle), 1969
Only Toys! (Anstey, appendix), 1903
Only Treasure (Thwaite), 1970
Only You Can Save Mankind (Pratchett), 1992
Oomi, The New Hunter (Schlein), 1955
Oops (Mayer), 1977
Ootah's Lucky Day (Parish), 1970
Open Gate (Pullein-Thompson, C.), 1962
Open Gate (Seredy), 1943
Open Grave (Poole), 1979
Open House for Butterflies (Krauss), 1960
Open the Door and See All the People (Bulla), 1972
Open Wide (Rayner), 1990
Opening Night (Isadora), 1984
Operation Aladdin (Finkel), 1976
Operation Gadgetman (Blackman), 1993
Operation Seabird (Edwards, M.), 1957
Operation Sippacik (Godden), 1969

Outside over There (Sendak), 1981
OUTside INside Poems (p Adoff), 1981
Outsider (Edwards, M.), 1961
Over and Over (Zolotow), 1957
Over-Mountain Boy (Steele, W.), 1952
Over the Big Hill (Lovelace), 1942
Over the Garden Wall (p Farjeon), 1933
Over the Green Hills (Isadora), 1992
Over the Hills and Far Away (Wynne), 1925
Over the Hills to Fabylon (Gray), 1954
Over the Hills to Nugget (Fisher, A.), 1949
Over the Rocky Mountains (Ballantyne, appendix), 1869
Over the Sea to School (Allan), 1950
Over the Sea Wall (Everett-Green, appendix), 1893
Over the Sea's Edge (Curry), 1971
Overland Launch (Hodges, C.), 1969
Overnight at Mary Bloom's (Aliki), 1987
Owen John Owen—blwlch-y-gwyntyn hwyr unwaith eto (Burningham), 1990
Owl and Billy Stories (Waddell), 1994
Owl and the Pussycat Went to See (pl Wood), 1968
Owl at Home (Lobel, Arnold), 1975
Owl at School (Nicoll), 1984
Owl at the Vet (Nicoll), 1991
Owl Babies (Waddell), 1992
Owl Hoots Twice at Catfish Bend (Burman), 1961
Owl in the Barn (Hough), 1964
Owl Moon (Yolen), 1987
Owl People (Trezise), 1987
Owliver (Kraus, R.), 1974
Owliver the Actor Takes a Bow (Kraus, R.), 1981
Owl's Birthday Party (Wood), 1998
Owl's Kiss: Three Stories (Steele, M.), 1978
Owl's Lesson (Butterworth, N.), 1997
Owlstone Crown (Kennedy, X.J.), 1983
Owner of Rushcote (Marchant), 1903
Ox of the Wonderful Horns and Other African Folktales (Bryan), 1971
Ox-Team (Coatsworth), 1967
Oxfam: The Unloved Bear (Barry), 1995
Oxford Nursery Book (Beck), 1995
Oxford Nursery Story Book (Beck), 1998
Oxus in Summer (Hull and Whitlock), 1939
Oz-Man Tales (Baum), 1920
Ozma of Oz (Baum), 1907
Ozzie on His Own (Hurwitz), 1995

P's and Q's (Yonge, appendix), 1872
Pablo (Griffiths, H.), 1977
Pablo Remembers: The Fiesta of the Day of the Dead (Ancona), 1993
Pablos and the Bull (Fidler), 1979
Pack of Liars (Fine), 1988
Pack Rat's Day and Other Poems (p Prelutsky), 1974
Pack Up Pick Up and Off (Taylor, W.), 1981
Paco's Miracle (Clark, A.), 1962
Paddington series (Bond, M.), from 1958
Paddle-to-the-Sea (Holling), 1941
Paddock of Poems (p Fatchen), 1987
Paddock: A Story in Praise of the Earth (Norman), 1992
Paddy Joe (Stranger), 1973
Paddy Joe and Thomson's Folly (Stranger), 1979
Paddy Joe at Deep Hollow Farm (Stranger), 1975
Paddy on the Island (Moray Williams), 1987
Paddy the Beaver, Adventures of (Burgess), 1917
Paddy the Beaver's Visitor (Burgess), 1961
Paddy's Pot of Gold (King-Smith), 1990
Paddy's Surprise Visitor (Burgess), 1940
Pageant of Patriotism (pl Mackay, Constance D'Arcy), 1911
Pageant of Patriots (pl Mackay, Constance D'Arcy), 1912
Pageant of Schenectady (pl Mackay, Constance D'Arcy), 1912
Pageant of Sunshine and Shadow (pl Mackay, Constance D'Arcy), 1916
Pagoo (Holling), 1957
Painted Cave (Behn), 1957
Painted Devil (Bedard), 1994
Painted Garden (Streatfeild), 1949
Painter and the Fish (Storr), 1975
Painter Jack (Fenn, appendix), 1895
Painting Dreams: Minnie Evans, Visionary (Lyons), 1996
Paintings (Ross), 1994
Pair of Desert-Wellies (Sherry), 1985
Pair of Jesus-Boots (Sherry), 1969
Pair of Originals (Everett-Green, as Dare, appendix), 1892
Pair of Pickles (Everett-Green, appendix), 1892
Pair of Schoolgirls (Brazil), 1912
Palace Beautiful (Meade, appendix), 1887
Palace Bug (Hoff), 1970
Palace in the Garden (Molesworth, appendix), 1887
Palace of Eagles and Other Stories (Ish-Kishor), 1948
Paleface and Redskin and Other Stories (Anstey, appendix), 1898
Palio: The Wildest Horse Race in the World (Henry), 1976
Palm Tree Island (Strang), 1909
Pamela Camel (Peet), 1984
Pamela's Hero (Moore), 1907
Pancakes for Breakfast (dePaola), 1978
Pancakes, Pancakes! (Carle), 1970
Pancakes-Paris (Bishop), 1947
Pancho and the Bull with the Crooked Tail, Story of (Hader), 1942
Panda (Hoffman), 1983
Panda and the Bunyips (Foreman), 1984
Panda and the Bushfire (Foreman), 1986
Panda and the Odd Lion (Foreman), 1981
Panda's Puzzle, and His Voyage of Discovery (Foreman), 1977
Pandora of Parrham Royal (Needham), 1951
Panic at the Garage (Chauncy), 1965
Panic in the Cattle Country (Rees, L.), 1974
Pannychis (Farjeon), 1933
Pantaloni (Bettina), 1957
Panther (Haig-Brown), 1934
Panther's Moon (Bond, R.), 1969
Pantomime Cat, Mystery of the (Blyton), 1949
Paolo and Panetto (Bettina), 1960
Paolo's Secret (Hathorn), 1985
Papa and the Animals (de Graft-Hanson), 1973
Papa Ewusi and the Magic Marble (de Graft-Hanson), 1973
Papa Like Every One Else (Taylor, S.), 1966
Papa Lucky's Shadow (Daly), 1991
Papa, Please Get the Moon for Me (Carle), 1986
Papa Puss to the Rescue (Cowley), 1995-96
Papa Small (Lenski), 1951
Papagayo the Mischief Maker (McDermott), 1978

Puffin, Adventures of (Moray Williams), 1939
Puffins Are Back! (Gibbons), 1991
Pug Peter: King of Mouseland, Marquis of Barkshire, D.O.G., P.C. 1906, Knight of the Order of the Gold Dog Collar, Author of Doggerel Lays and Days... (Nesbit), 1905
Pulabad (Fenn, appendix), 1901
Pumpers, Boilers, Hooks, and Ladders (Fisher, L.), 1961
Pumpkin Man and the Crafty Creeper (Mahy), 1991
Pumpkin Pie (Arthur), 1938
Punch Back Gang (Parker), 1966
Punchbowl Harvest (Edwards, M.), 1954
Punchbowl Midnight (Edwards, M.), 1951
Punga, Goddess of Ugly (Lattimore, D.), 1993
Puppet Plays for Children (pl Ridge), 1953
Puppies Are Special Friends (Ryder), 1988
Puppies, Pussycats, and Other Friends (Fujikawa), 1975
Puppy Dear (Szekeres), 1993
Puppy Fat (Gleitzman), 1995
Puppy Learns to Share (Szekeres), 1990
Puppy Lost (Szekeres), 1986
Puppy Lost in Lapland (Catherall, as Hallard), 1971
Puppy Love (King-Smith), 1997
Puppy Summer (De Jong), 1966
Puppy Too Small (Szekeres), 1984
Puppy's House (Schlein), 1955
Puptents and Pebbles: A Nonsense ABC (p Smith), 1959
Pure Magic (Coatsworth), 1973
Purim (Schlein), 1983
Puritan Adventure (Lenski), 1944
Purl and Plain, Adventures of (Brisley), 1941
Purloined Corn Popper: A Felicity Snell Mystery (Hildick), 1997
Purloined Parrot, Case of the (Hildick), 1990
Purple Buttons (Bull), 1996
Purple Dragon and Other Fantasies (Baum), 1976
Purple, Green and Yellow (Munsch), 1992
Purple Mountain (Clewes), 1962
Purple Mouse (MacIntyre), 1975
Purple Sock, Pink Sock (Allen, J.), 1992
Pursuit of Penelope (Meade, appendix), 1902
Push Chair Polly (Bradman), 1996
Push Kitty (Wahl), 1968
Pushcart War (Merrill), 1964
Pushers, Spads, Jennies and Jets (Fisher, L.), 1961
Puss and Cat (Storr), 1969
Puss-in-Boots: A Peep-Show Book (Hale, K.), 1951
Pussy and Doggy Tales (Nesbit), 1899
Pussy Tales (Nesbit), 1895
Pussycat's Christmas (Brown, Margaret Wise), 1949
Put-em-Rights (Blyton), 1946
Put on My Crown (Levin), 1985
Put the Kettle On! (Berg), 1972
Puzzle (Hardcastle), 1995
Puzzle for Sherlock Holmes (Newman), 1979
Puzzle for the Secret Seven (Blyton), 1958
Puzzle People (Oxenbury), 1985
Puzzle Planet Adventures (Blackman), from 1996
Puzzling Pair (Le Feuvre), 1898
Pyewacket (Weir), 1967
Pyewacket & Son (Weir), 1980
Pyramid (Macaulay), 1975
Pyramid of the Sun, Pyramid of the Moon (Fisher, L.), 1988
Quack Quack (Hader), 1961
Quack! Said the Billy-Goat (p Causley), 1986
Quake (Hardcastle), 1988
Quantum Squeak (Hoffman), 1996
Quarantine Child (Symons), 1966
Quarrel of Koalas (Armitage), 1992
Quarrel of Witches (Storey), 1970
Quarreling Book (Zolotow), 1963
Quarry Adventure (Kingman), 1951
Quarry Line Mystery (Stewart), 1971
Quarter Boy (Parker), 1976
Quarter Horse Boy (Patchett), 1970
Quarterback Exchange: I Was John Elway (Korman), 1997
Quasar Quartz Quest (Blackman), 1996
Queechy (Warner, as Wetherell, appendix), 1852
Queen Always Wanted to Dance (Mayer), 1971
Queen and Rosie Randall (Oxenbury), 1979
"Queen Elizabeth" Family (Blyton), 1951
Queen for a Day (Cohen), 1981
Queen Hildegarde (Richards, L.), 1889
Queen of Eene (p Prelutsky), 1978
Queen of Hearts (pl Mackay, Constance D'Arcy), 1904
Queen of Joy (Meade, appendix), 1914
Queen of Shindy Flat (Marchant), 1905
Queen of the Dolls (pl Brink), 1928
Queen of the Dormitory and Other Stories (Brazil), 1926
Queen of the Red Chessmen (Hale, L.) n.d.
Queen of the Universe (Gleeson), 1997
Queen of the Wheat Castles (Mattingley), 1973
Queen Rita at the High School and Other School Stories (Allan), 1991
Queen Rose (Meade, appendix), 1902
Queen Silver-Bell (Burnett), 1906
Queen Without Crown (Polland), 1965
Queen Zixi of Ix (Baum), 1905
Queenie, One of the Family (Graham, B.), 1997
Queenie the Bantam (Graham, B.), 1997
Queen's Blessing (Polland), 1963
Queens for Choice (Moore), 1934
Queen's Goat (Mahy), 1991
Queen's Manor School (Everett-Green, appendix), 1921
Queen's Museum (Stockton, appendix), 1887
Queen's Nose (King-Smith), 1983
Queen's Own Grove (Beatty), 1966
Queen's Scarlet (Fenn, appendix), 1895
Queen's Treason (Rush), 1955
Queen's Wizard (Beatty), 1967
Queer Customer (Hough), 1972
Queer Mystery (Blyton), 1952
Queery Leary Nonsense (p Lear, appendix), 1911
Quelling Eye (Gordon, J.), 1986
Quest for Orion (Harris, R.), 1978
Quest for the Gloop: The Exploits of Murfy and PHIX (Nicoll), 1980
Quest for the Perfect Planet (Johns), 1961
Quest in the Cariboo (Hayes), 1960
Quest of Ati Manu (Patchett), 1960
Quest of the "Golden Hope" (Westerman), 1911
Questers (Hildick), 1966
Questers and the Whispering Spy (Hildick), 1967
Question of Courage (Darke), 1975

Round Trip (Jonas), 1983
Round Trip Space Ship (Slobodkin), 1968
Roundabout (Dalgliesh), 1934
Roundabout (Kemp), 1993
Rounding Up the Raider (Westerman), 1916
Rover of the Andes (Ballantyne, appendix), 1885
Roverandom (Tolkien), 1998
Roving Commission (Henty, appendix), 1900
Roy Royland (Fenn, appendix), 1895
Royal Dirk (Beatty), 1966
Royal Huddle (Rosen, Michael), 1990
Royal Kingdoms of Ghana, Mali, and Songhay: Life in Medieval Africa (McKissack), 1994
Royal Muddle (Rosen, Michael), 1990
Roz and Ozzie (Hurwitz), 1992
Rua and the Sea People (Bacon, R.), 1968
Rubadub Mystery (Blyton), 1952
Rubbalong Tales (Blyton), 1950
Rubberneck's Revenge (Waddell), 1993
Rubbish Heap (Appiah), forthcoming
Rubies of St. Lô (Yonge, appendix), 1894
Ruby and the Dragon (Owen), 1989
Ruby Ring (Molesworth, appendix), 1904
Ruby the Copycat (Rathmann), 1991
Rude Rowdy Rumors (Levy), 1994
Rudi and the Distelfink (Monjo), 1972
Ruey Richardson—Chaletian (Brent-Dyer), 1960
Ruff and Ready: The Fairy Guide (Farrow), 1905
Ruffles (Meade, appendix), 1911
Rufty Tufty series (Ainsworth), from 1952
Rufus (Storr), 1969
Rufus (Ungerer), 1961
Rufus and Rose (Alger, appendix), 1870
Rufus M. (Estes), 1943
Rufus, Red Rufus (Beatty), 1975
Rufus Round and Round (Van Stockum), 1973
Rufus the Unready (Finley, appendix), 1870
Rug (Rayner), 1989
Ruggles (Fine), 1998
Rule of Three (Coolidge, appendix), 1904
Rum Day of the Vanishing Pony (Treadgold), 1970
Rum-Tum-Tummy, The Elephant Who Ate (Holling), 1928
Rumble and Chuff (Blyton), 1958
Rumble Seat Pony (Anderson), 1971
Rummage (Mattingley), 1981
Rumpelstiltskin (Gay), 1997
Rumpelstiltskin (pl Chorpenning), 1947
Rumpelstiltskin (Zelinsky), 1986
Rumpelstiltskin's Daughter (Stanley), 1997
Rumple Nose-Dimple and the Three Horrible Snaps (Kraus, R.), 1969
Rumptydoolers (Wier), 1964
Run (Hardcastle, as Clark), 1973
Run-about's Holiday (Blyton), 1955
Run-Around Robins (McNeill), 1967
Run Away Home (Forest), 1982
Run Far, Run Fast (Morey), 1974
Run for the Money (Corbett, S.), 1973
Run for Your Life (Line), 1966
Run for Your Sweet Life (Benedict), 1986
Run, Run, White Hen (Seed), 1994
Run Swift, Run Free (McCaughren), 1986
Run to Earth (Kyle), 1957
Run to Earth (McCaughren), 1984
Run to the Ark (McCaughren), 1991
Run to the Wild Wood (McCaughren), 1996
Run Wild (McCaughren), 1993
Run with the Wind (McCaughren), 1983
Runabout Rhymes (p Fyleman), 1941
Runaway (Clewes), 1957
Runaway (Lampman, as Bronson), 1953
Runaway (Parker), 1977
Runaway (Stranger), 1992
Runaway Ben (Pullein-Thompson, C.), 1990
Runaway Boy (Kaye), 1971
Runaway Brig (Otis, appendix), 1888
Runaway Bunny (Brown, Margaret Wise), 1942
Runaway Jonah (Wahl), 1985
Runaway Kitten (Blyton), 1945
Runaway Marie Louise (Carlson), 1977
Runaway Princess (Moore), 1912
Runaway Ralph (Cleary), 1970
Runaway Settlers (Locke), 1965
Runaway Stallion (Morey), 1973
Runaway Teddy Bear and Other Stories (Blyton), 1951
Runaway to Freedom (Smucker), 1977
Runaways (Hader), 1956
Runaways (Kimenye), 1973
Runaways (Lynch), 1959
Runners (Tate, J.), 1974
Running Amok (Fenn, appendix), 1901
Running Back Conversion: I Was Barry Sanders (Korman), 1997
Running Out of Magic with Houdini (Levy), 1981
Running Out of Time (Levy), 1980
Running Wild (Griffiths, H.), 1977
Running with Rachel (Asch), 1979
Runny Days, Sunny Days: Merry Verses (p Fisher, A.), 1958
Rupert and the Dragon (pl Wood), 1993
Rupert's Ambition (Alger, appendix), 1899
Ruru and the Green Fairies (Bacon, R.), 1985
Russ the Australian Tree Kangaroo, Story of (Rees, L.), 1964
Russell and Elisa (Hurwitz), 1989
Russell Rides Again (Hurwitz), 1985
Russell Sprouts (Hurwitz), 1987
Russet and the Two Reds (Lipkind, as Will), 1962
Russian Blue (Griffiths, H.), 1973
Rustlers of Rattlesnake Valley (Johns), 1948
Rusty, Adventures of (Bond, R.), 1981
Rusty's Space Ship (Lampman), 1957
Ruth Crane (Morgan, A.), 1973
Ruth of Boston (Otis, appendix), 1910
Ruth of St. Roman's (Brazil), 1927
Ruth Ravelstan the Puritan's Daughter (Everett-Green, appendix), 1907
Ruthless Rhymes for Heartless Homes (p Graham, H., as Streamer), 1899
Ryan's Fort (Lynch), 1961

Sabarinda Island (Westerman), 1950
Sabotage! (Westerman), 1952
Sabotage at the Forge (Armstrong), 1946
Sabre of Storm Valley (Chipperfield), 1962

Snowman Sniffles and Other Verse (p Bodecker), 1983
Snowy and Woody (Duvoisin), 1979
Snowy Day (Keats), 1962
Snowy River Brumby (Mitchell), 1980
Snuff (Blake), 1973
Snuffle to the Rescue (Beresford), 1975
Snuffles for Short (Chaundler), 1921
Snug and Serena Count Twelve (Uttley), 1959
Snug and Serena Go to Town (Uttley), 1961
Snuggle Tales (Baum), 1916-17
Snugglepot and Cuddlepie: Their Adventures Wonderful (Gibbs), 1918
So As by Fire (Sidney, appendix), 1881
So Guy Came Too (Hill, L.), 1954
So Many Cats! (p de Regniers), 1985
So Many Raccoons (Wahl), 1985
So Soft Kitty (Demi), 1986
So Who Needs Lotto? (Hathorn), 1990
Soap Box Car (Tate, J.), 1967
Soap Box Derby (Weir), 1962
Soap Soup (p Kuskin), 1992
Soaring With the Wind: The Bald Eagle (Gibbons), 1998
Soccer Captain (Hardcastle), 1994
Soccer Comes First (Hardcastle), 1971
Soccer Is Also a Game (Hardcastle), 1966
Soccer Special (Hardcastle), 1978
Soccer Star (Hardcastle), 1993
Sociable Toby (Clymer), 1956
Socks (Cleary), 1973
Sod House (Coatsworth), 1954
Soeur de Robert (Gay), 1983
Soft Shoe (Clark, M.), 1988
Soft Skull Sam (Hoff), 1981
Sojourner Truth (McKissack), 1992
Soldier and Me (Line), 1965
Soldier's Children (p Ewing, appendix), 1883
Soldier's Daughter and Other Stories (Henty, appendix), 1906
Soldier's Son and the Battle He Fought (Everett-Green, appendix), 1895
Sole Survivors (Henty, appendix), 1901
Solo Girl (Pinkney, A.), 1997
Solomon the Rusty Nail (Steig), 1985
Solomon's Child (Clark, M.), 1981
Solve-It-Yourself Mysteries series (Waddell), from 1984
Some Birthday! (Polacco), 1991
Some Builders (Le Feuvre), 1913
Some Moonshine Tales (Uttley), 1945
Some of the Days of Everett Anderson (p Clifton), 1970
Some of the Kinder Planets (Wynne-Jones), 1993
"Some Say," and Neighbors in Cyrus (Richards, L.), 1896
Some Snow Said Hello (Hoban), 1963
Some Things Are Scary (Heide), 1971
Some Things Go Together (p Zolotow), 1969
Somebody Else's Nut Tree and Other Tales from Children (Krauss), 1958
Somebody Spilled the Sky (p Krauss), 1979
Someday (Zolotow), 1965
Someday Angeline (Sachar), 1983
Someone Could Win a Polar Bear (p Ciardi), 1970
Someone Else's Baby (Kaye), 1990
Someone Else's Ghost (Buffie), 1994
Someone in the Attic (Wayne), 1967
Someone New (Zolotow), 1978
Someone Saw a Spider (Climo), 1985
Someplace Beautiful (Brinsmead), 1986
Somerville Secret, Case of the (Newman), 1981
Something (Babbitt), 1970
Something Big (Cockett), 1968
Something Big (McBratney), 1992
Something Big Has Been Here (p Prelutsky), 1990
Something Fishy at MacDonald Hall (Korman), 1995
Something for Now, Something for Later (Schlein), 1956
Something from Nothing (Gilman), 1992
Something Good (Munsch), 1990
Something I Remember (p Farjeon), 1987
Something in the Barn (Wayne), 1971
Something in Thurlo Darby's House (Alderson), 1984
Something Is Going to Happen (Zolotow), 1988
Something Like a Snake (Fenn, appendix), 1901
Something Nasty in the Kitchen (Bond, M.), 1992
Something Old, Something New: Stories of People Who Are America (Fisher, D.), 1949
Something Queer Mystery series (Levy), from 1973
Something Sleeping in the Hall (p Kuskin), 1985
Something Special (p de Regniers), 1958
Something Special for Me (Williams), 1983
Something to Shout About (Beatty), 1976
Sometime Stories (Bisset), 1957
Sometimes Mama and Papa Fight (Sharmat), 1980
Somewhere Else (Sudbery), 1978
Somewhere in Africa (Daly), 1992
Son of a Gun (Ahlberg), 1979
Son of Billabong (Bruce, M.), 1939
Son of Interflux (Korman), 1986
Son of the Lamp-Maker: The Story of a Boy Who Knew Jesus (North), 1956
Son of the Salmon People (Evans), 1981
Son of the Slime that Ate Cleveland (Sharmat), 1985
Son of the Whirlwind (Mitchell), 1976
Song (Zolotow), 1982
Song for Gar (Merrill), 1957
Song-Garden for Children: A Collection of Children's Songs (p Graham, H.), 1906
Song I Sang to You (p Livingston), 1984
Song in My Drum (Hoban), 1962
Song of Pentecost (Corbett, W.J.), 1982
Song of St. Francis (Bulla), 1952
Song of the City (p Owen), 1985
Song of the Earth (Hoffman), 1995
Song of the Horse (Kennedy, R.), 1981
Song of the Lop-Eared Mule (Carlson), 1961
Song of the Nightingale (French), 1986
Song of the Pearl (Nichols), 1976
Song of the River (Cowley), 1994
Song of Thunder (Ray), 1978
Song under the Water (Morris), 1985
Songbird Story (Rosen, Michael), 1993
Songs for Music and Lyrical Poems (p Farjeon), 1922
Songs for My Dog and Other People (p Fatchen), 1980
Songs from "Punch" for Children (p Farjeon), 1925
Songs of Childhood (p de la Mare, as Ramal), 1902
Songs of Faith (Johnson, A.), 1998

Spirit Wind (Fatchen), 1973
Spiteful Letters, Mystery of the (Blyton), 1946
Spitfire Grave and Other Stories (Gordon, J.), 1979
Splash (Hardcastle, as Clark), 1972
Splash! (Jonas), 1995
Splendid Picnic (Todd), 1937
Splish Splash Sounds (Scarry), 1988
Spook at the Superstore (Powling), 1990
Spooky and the Bad Luck Raven (Carlson), 1988
Spooky and the Ghost Cat (Carlson), 1985
Spooky and the Witch's Goat (Carlson), 1989
Spooky and the Wizard's Bats (Carlson), 1986
Spooky Night (Carlson), 1982
Spooky Tail of Prewitt Peacock (Peet), 1972
Spooky Thing (Steele, W.), 1960
Spooner or Later (Greenwood), 1993
Sport (Fitzhugh), 1979
Sport of the School (Talbot), 1923
Sports Day! (Butterworth, N.), 1988
Sports Pages (p Adoff), 1986
Spots, Feathers, and Curly Tails (Tafuri), 1988
Spotty (Rey), 1945
Spotty Pig (King-Smith), 1997
Spring Break (Hurwitz), 1997
Spring Cleaning, as Told by Queen Crosspatch (Burnett), 1908
Spring Is Here (p Lenski), 1945
Spring Morning and Other Tales, Story of a (Molesworth, appendix), 1890
Spring of the Year (Vipont), 1957
Spring Snow (Duvoisin), 1963
Spring Tide (Ray), 1969
Springfellow (Kraus, R.), 1978
Springfellow's Parade (Kraus, R.), 1982
Sprout series (Wayne), from 1970
Spunky (Hader), 1933
Spy at Mill Green (Prince), 1983
Spy before Yesterday (Storr), 1990
Spy Hill (Seed), 1984
Spy in the Neighborhood (Sharmat), 1974
Spy, the No-Good Pup (Stranger), 1989
Squadron Leader (Westerman), 1946
Squanderbug's Christmas Carol (pl Fisher, A.), 1943
Squanderbug's Mother Goose (pl Fisher, A.), 1944
Squanto, Friend of the White Men (Bulla), 1954
Square as a House (p Kuskin), 1960
Square Pegs (Sharmat), 1982
Squash Pie (Steele, M., as Gage), 1976
Squaw Dog (Beatty), 1965
Squaw Man's Son (Lampman), 1978
Squeak-a-lot (Waddell), 1991
Squeak in the Gate (Mahy), 1986
Squeaky Books (Kraus, R., as Silly), 1982
Squib and His Friends (Everett-Green, appendix), 1896
Squire's Daughters (Everett-Green, appendix), 1932
Squire's Heir (Everett-Green, appendix), 1903
Squire's Little Girl (Meade, appendix), 1902
Squirmy's Big Secret (Kraus, R.), 1990
Squirrel Called Rufus (Church), 1941
Squirrel Goes Skating (Uttley), 1934
Squirrel Hotel (du Bois), 1952
Squirrel, The Hare, and the Little Grey Rabbit (Uttley), 1929
Squirrel Wife (Pearce), 1971
Squirrely of Willow Hill (Hader), 1950
Stack of Story Poems (Bradman), 1992
Staffordshire Terror (Beatty), 1979
Stage Fright (Howe), 1986
Stained Glass Window (Lively), 1976
Stalky & Co (Kipling), 1899
Stallion from the Sea (Fidler), 1953
Stallion of the Sands (Griffiths, H.), 1968
Stan (Pilling), 1988
Stan Lynn (Fenn, appendix), 1902
Stand in the Wind (Little, J.), 1975
Standing Lions (Ray), 1968
Standing on a Strawberry and Other Poems (p Cunliffe), 1987
Standish Gets His Man (Westerman), 1938
Standish Holds On (Westerman), 1941
Standish Loses His Man (Westerman), 1939
Standish of the Air Police (Westerman), 1935
Standish Pulls It Off (Westerman), 1940
Stanley (Hoff), 1962
Stanley and Rhoda (Wells), 1978
Staples for Amos (Morgan, A.), 1986
Star and the Flame (Weir), 1962
Star Boy (Goble), 1980
Star Bright: A Sequel to Captain January (Richards, L.), 1927
Star Horse (Greaves), 1992
Star in the Pail (p McCord), 1975
Star of Night (Paterson), 1980
Star of Wild Horse Canyon (Bulla), 1953
Star-Riders of the Moor (Pullein-Thompson, J.), 1976
Star Shine (Greene, C.), 1985
Star Signs (Fisher, L.), 1983
Star-Spangled Banner (Spier), 1973
Star-Spangled Salute (pl Harris, A.), 1975
Star Trap (Darke), 1974
Starbaby (Asch), 1980
Starbuck Valley Winter (Haig-Brown), 1943
Stargazers (Gibbons), 1992
Starlight Cloak (Nimmo), 1994
Starling and the Fox (Fyleman), 1951
Starlit Somersault Downhill (p Willard), 1992
Starring Mirette & Bellini (McCully), 1997
Starry Floor (p Farjeon), 1949
Starry Night (Waddell, as Sefton), 1986
Stars and Stripes (Fisher, L.), 1993
Stars for Cristy (Hunt, M.), 1956
Stars for Sarah (Turner, A.), 1991
Starshine and Sunglow (Levin), 1994
Starters series (pl Wymark), 1975
Starting Home: The Story of Horace Pippin (Lyons), 1993
Starting Out (pl Storr), 1973-78
Station Four (Beatty), 1969
Station-Master's Hen (Seed), 1987
Staunch as Steel (Fenn, appendix), 1927
Stay at Home Ben (Pullein-Thompson, C.), 1987
Steadfast Tin Soldier (Isadora), 1996
Steady, Boys, Steady (Strang), 1917
Steady, Freddie (Corbett, S.), 1970
Steal Away Home (pl Harris, A.), 1972
Steam on the Line (Turner, P.), 1968
Steamroller (Brown, Margaret Wise), 1974

Storyteller's House, Tales from the (Burgess), 1937
Storytime (Scarry), 1976
Storytime Book (Blyton), 1964
Stout Fellows: Chum, Angelina Wallaby, Um-Pig, and Flip (Wall), 1936
Stowaway (Stevenson, J.), 1990
Stowaway to Nowhere (Seed), 1990
Stowaways (McGough), 1986
Straggler (Wier), 1970
Straight Line Wonder (Fox), 1987
Stranded Duck (Finkel), 1973
Stranded in Belgium (Wynne), 1918
Strange Adventures of Captain Marwhopple (Fyleman), 1931
Strange and Exciting Adventures of Jeremiah Hush (Shulevitz), 1986
Strange Blackbird (Seed), 1986
Strange Bundle, Mystery of the (Blyton), 1952
Strange Courtship (Le Feuvre), 1931
Strange Diana (Walton, appendix), 1919
Strange Enchantment (Allan), 1981
Strange Hiding Place (Beresford), 1962
Strange Hill (Cockett), 1984
Strange House (Briggs, R.), 1961
Strange Intruder (Catherall), 1965
Strange Invader (Catherall), 1964
Strange Invasion of Catfish Bend (Burman), 1980
Strange Large Egg (Seed), 1996
Strange Light (Reeves), 1964
Strange Magic (Beresford), 1986
Strange Messages, Mystery of the (Blyton), 1957
Strange Riders at Black Pony Inn (Pullein-Thompson, C.), 1976
Strange Ruby, Adventure of the (Blyton), 1960
Strange Safari (Catherall, as Ruthin), 1955
Strange Secret (Richards, F., as Clifford), 1968
Strange Sunflower (Pearce), 1966
Strange Tale of the Marvelous Mouse Man (p Hoberman), 1999
Strange Umbrella and Other Stories (Blyton), 1949
Strange Valley (Cockett), 1967
Strange Year (White), 1920
Stranger (Van Allsburg), 1986
Stranger and Afraid (Baker, B.), 1972
Stranger at Green Knowe (Boston), 1961
Stranger Came to the Mine (Clark, M.), 1980
Stranger Danger? (Fine), 1989
Stranger from Somewhere in Time (McBratney), 1994
Stranger in Primrose Lane (Streatfeild), 1941
Stranger in the Herd (Patchett), 1964
Stranger in the Hills (Polland), 1968
Stranger in the Mirror (Say), 1995
Stranger in the Train (Hope-Simpson), 1960
Stranger in the Train and Other Stories (Talbot), 1925
Stranger on Big Hickory (Meader), 1964
Stranger on the Ball Club (Slote), 1970
Stranger on Wreck Buoy Sands (Catherall), 1975
Stranger Than Unicorns (p Clark, L.), 1979
Stranger Thing (Tomalin), 1975
Stranger Within the Gates and Other Stories (Ish-Kishor), 1948
Strangers at Brongwerne (Allan), 1953
Strangers at the Fair and Other Stories (Lynch), 1945
Strangers' Bread (Willard), 1977
Strangers in a Strange Land: A Migrant Play (pl Lenski), 1952
Strangers in Carrigmore (Reid), 1958
Strangers in Skye (Allan), 1956
Strangers in the Land (Seed), 1977
Strangers in Wood Street (Allan), 1981
Strangers to the Marsh (Edwards, M.), 1957
Strang's Penny Books (Strang), 1926-27
Strawberry Girl (Lenski), 1945
Strawberry Pop and Soda Crackers (Begay), 1996
Strawberry Shortcake and Sad Mr. Sun (Lexau), 1983
Stray (King-Smith), 1997
Stray Pearls (Yonge, appendix), 1883
Strayed Falcon (Yonge, appendix), 1860
Streamlined Pig (Brown, Margaret Wise), 1938
Street Music: City Poems (p Adoff), 1995
Street of Little Shops (Bianco), 1932
Street of the Small Night Market (Sherry), 1966
Street Talk (p Turner, A.), 1992
Strega Nona: Her Story (dePaola), 1996
Strider (Cleary), 1991
Strike! (Hardcastle), 1970
Stringbean's Trip to the Shining Sea (Williams), 1988
Striped Ice Cream! (Lexau), 1968
Strive and Succeed (Alger, appendix), 1872
Striving for Fortune (Walter Griffith) (Alger, appendix), 1901
Strolling Players (Yonge, appendix), 1893
Strong and Steady (Alger, appendix), 1871
Strong and Willing Girl (Edwards, D.), 1980
Strong Arm (Hardcastle), 1977
Stronger Will (Everett-Green, appendix), 1890
Strudwick: A Sheep in Wolf's Clothing (Kraus, R.), 1995
Struggling Upward (Alger, appendix), 1890
Stubborn Old Woman (Bulla), 1980
Stubby Pringle's Christmas (Schaefer), 1964
Stubby Sees It Through (MacVicar), 1950
Studies and Stories (Molesworth, appendix), 1893
Studies for Stories (Ingelow, appendix), 1864
Studio (Abbott, appendix), 1855
Stuff and Nonsense and So On (p de la Mare), 1927
Stuffed Dog (Symonds), 1967
Stumble by the Way (Meade, appendix), 1901
Stuntkid (Powling), 1985
Stuntumble Monday (Hathorn), 1989
Stupid Sally (Finley, appendix), 1868
Stupids Die (Marshall), 1981
Stupids Have a Ball (Marshall), 1978
Stupids Step Out (Marshall), 1974
Stupids Take Off (Marshall), 1989
Sturdy and Strong (Henty, appendix), 1887
Su Tung Po (Demi), 1996
Sub and a Submarine (Westerman), 1918
Sub. of the R.N.R (Westerman), 1915
Sub-Lieutenant John Cloche (Westerman), 1943
Submarine Hunters (Westerman), 1918
Such a Kind World (Hunt, M.), 1947
Sudden Glow of Gold (Fine), 1991
Sudden Puff of Glittering Smoke (Fine), 1989
Sudden Swirl of Icy Wind (Fine), 1990
Sue (Meade, appendix), 1906
Sue and the Honey Machine (Hunt, P.), 1989
Sue Barton series (Boylston), from 1936
Sugar and Spice: The ABC of Being a Girl (p McGinley), 1960

Teddy Bear Tears (Aylesworth), 1997
Teddy Bear's Party (Blyton), 1945
Teddy Bear's Scrapbook (Howe), 1980
Teddy Goes Swimming (Wilson, J.), 1994
Teddy Robber (Beck), 1989
Teddy Robinson (Robinson), 1953
Teddy Robinson Himself (Robinson), 1957
Teddy Robinson's Book (Robinson), 1955
Teddy's Button! (Le Feuvre), 1896
Teddy's Ear (Daly), 1985
Ted's Lucky Ball (Meynell, as Tring), 1961
Teeny Mouse Counts Herself (Szekeres), 1992
Teeny Tiny Tales (Scarry), 1965
Teeny, Tiny Witches (Wahl), 1979
Teep and Beep, Go to Sleep (Mayer), 1984
Telegraph Boy (The District Telegraph Boy) (Alger, appendix), 1879
Television Mystery (Beresford), 1957
Television Twins (Brown, P.), 1952
Tell-a-Story Books (Blyton), 1964
Tell about the Cowbarn, Daddy (Merrill), 1963
Tell Me a Real Adoption Story (Lifton), 1994
Tell Me a Story (Molesworth, as Graham, appendix), 1875
Tell Me a Story: A Book of Stories to Tell to Children (Fisher, D.), 1940
Tell Me a Story, Mama (Johnson, A.), 1989
Tell Me a Tale: A Book about Storytelling (Bruchac), 1997
Tell Me Some More (Bonsall), 1961
Tell-Tale from Hill and Dale (p Richards, L.), 1886
Tell-Tale-Tit (Marchant), 1899
Tell Tales (Rosen, Michael), 1989-90
Tell Us Your Secret (Cohen), 1989
Teller of Tales (Brooke, W.), 1994
Telling of the Tales: Five Stories (Brooke, W.), 1990
Temple of the Sun (Lampman), 1964
Ten Apples Up on Top! (p Seuss, as Le Sieg), 1961
Ten Black Dots (Crews), 1968
Ten Fathoms Deep (Catherall), 1954
Ten Frogs (Blake), 1997
Ten Green Monsters (Clarke, G.), 1993
Ten in a Bed (Ahlberg), 1983
Ten in the Bed (Dale), 1988
Ten Little Babies (Fujikawa), 1989
Ten Little Jappy Chaps (Farrow), 1905
Ten Minute Tales and Dialogue Stories (Power), 1943
Ten Minutes Tales: Twenty-Nine Varied Stories for Children (Blyton), 1934
Ten Minutes till Bed (Rathmann), 1998
Ten Mondays for Lots of Boxes (Alderson), 1995
Ten, Nine, Eight (Bang), 1983
Ten Out of Bed (Dale), 1993
Ten Oxherding Pictures (Clifton), 1988
Ten Pink Piglets, Garth Pig's Wall Song (Rayner), 1994
Ten Play Hide and Seek (Dale), 1998
Ten Silver Coins (Butterworth, N.), 1989
Ten Tales of Shellover (Ainsworth), 1963
Ten Tales of Tim Rabbit (Uttley), 1941
Ten Thousand Golden Cockerels (Hildick), 1970
Ten What? A Mystery Counting Book (Hoban), 1974
Tenderfoot Trapper (Catherall), 1958
Tenement Tree (Seredy), 1959
Tennis Menace (Heide, as Allen), 1975
Tennis Shoes (Streatfeild), 1937
Tent for the Sun (Ray), 1971
Tenth at Trinder's (Moore), 1927
Tenth Good Thing about Barney (Viorst), 1971
'Tention! (Fenn, appendix), 1906
Terhune Omnibus (Terhune), 1937
Term of Many Adventures (Wynne), 1939
Term to Remember (Wynne), 1930
Terrible Birthday Present (Bull), 1998
Terrible Coward, and Son Philip (Fenn, appendix), 1885
Terrible, Horrible Edie (Spykman), 1960
Terrible Nung Gwama: A Chinese Folktale (Young), 1978
Terrible Scar, Story of the (Storr), 1976
Terrible Taniwha of Timberditch (Cowley), 1982
Terrible Temptation (Arundel), 1971
Terrible, Terrifying Toby (Johnson, C.), 1957
Terrible Tiger (p Prelutsky), 1969
Terrible Tomboy (Brazil), 1904
Terrible Topsy-Turvy, Tissy-Tossy Tangle (Mahy), 1986
Terrible Trins (King-Smith), 1995
Terrible Troll (Mayer), 1968
Terribly Plain Princess and Other Stories (Oldfield), 1977
Terrie's Moorland Home (Le Feuvre), 1918
Terrific! I'm a Tarnatula (Bradman), 1997
Terror by Night: A Book of Strange Stories (Vipont), 1966
Terror of Manooka (Patchett), 1966
Terror of the Seas (Westerman), 1927
Terry Pratchett's Truckers (Pratchett), 1992
Terry the Black Sheep (Wynne), 1928
Terry the Girl-Guide (Moore), 1912
Terry's Brrrmmm GT (Greenwood), 1974
Terry's Only Term (Talbot), 1939
Tess (Hutchins, H.), 1996
Tessie (Jackson), 1968
Tested! (Le Feuvre), 1911
Testing of Tertius (Newman), 1973
Testing Year (Clewes), 1977
Texas Tomboy (Lenski), 1950
Thames in Story (Fidler), 1971
Thank You, Amelia Bedelia (Parish), 1964
Thank You, Dr. Martin Luther King, Jr! (Tate, E.), 1990
Thank You Henrietta (Daly), 1986
Thank You, Jackie Robinson (Cohen), 1974
Thank You, Mr. Falker (Polacco), 1998
Thanksgiving Day (Gibbons), 1983
Thanksgiving Day (Rockwell), 1999
That Baby (Berg), 1972
That Boarding School Girl (Bruce, D.), 1925
That Brilliant Peggy (Meade, appendix), 1903
That Dreadful Boy! (Marchant), 1901
That Dreadful Day (Stevenson, J.), 1985
That Fool of a Priest and Other Tales of Early Canterbury (Rush), 1970
That Must Be Julian (Syme), 1947
That New Dress (Blackman), 1991
That Scatterbrain Booky (Hunter, B.), 1981
That Spells Magic (Bradman), 1989
That Stick (Yonge, appendix), 1892
That Terrible Halloween Night (Stevenson, J.), 1980
That Wild Australian Schoolgirl (Talbot), 1925

Tumbleweed (King-Smith), 1987
Tumbling Ghosts (Levy), 1989
Tune Is in the Tree (Lovelace), 1950
Tunes of a Penny Piper (p Farjeon), 1922
Tunnel (Browne), 1989
Tunnel behind the Waterfall (Corlett), 1991
Tunnel Busters (Catherall, as Channel), 1960
Tunnel of Hugsy Goode (Estes), 1971
Tunnel with Problems (Sudbery), 1979
Tunnels (Gibbons), 1984
Tuppenny (Cunningham), 1978
Tuppenny Brown (Sutton), 1977
Turbulent Term of Tyke Tiler (Kemp), 1977
Turf-Cutter's Donkey (Lynch), 1934
Turf-Cutter's Donkey Goes Visiting (Lynch), 1935
Turf-Cutter's Donkey Kicks Up His Heels (Lynch), 1939
Turi's Poppa (de Treviño), 1968
Turk, The Border Collie (Fidler), 1975
Turkey Brother and Other Tales: Iroquois Folk Stories (Bruchac), 1975
Turkey for Christmas (de Angeli), 1944
Turkey Girl (Baker, B.), 1983
Turkey's Nest (Prince), 1979
Turn Again Whittington (Tate, J.), 1976
Turn Homeward, Hannalee (Beatty), 1984
Turnabout (Leaf), 1967
Turnaround Wind (p Lobel, Arnold), 1988
Turquoise and Ruby (Meade, appendix), 1906
Turramulli the Giant Quinkin (Roughsey; Trezise), 1982
Turret (Sharp), 1963
Turtle and the Dove (Freeman, D.), 1964
Turtle Knows Your Name (Bryan), 1989
Turtle Meat and Other Stories (Bruchac), 1992
Turtle Tale (Asch), 1978
Turtle Watch (Ancona), 1987
Tusk Tusk (McKee), 1978
Tut, Tut (Scieszka), 1996
Twelve and the Genii (Clarke, P.), 1962
Twelve Bells for Santa (Bonsall), 1977
Twelve Days of Christmas (p Briggs, K.), 1952
Twelve Gold Chairs (Cockett), 1967
Twelve Impossible Things Before Breakfast: Stories (Yolen), 1997
Twelve Minutes to Disaster and Other Stories (Catherall), 1977
Twelve Months: A Greek Folktale (Aliki), 1978
Twelve Months Make a Year (Coatsworth), 1943
Twelve Tales (Blegvad), 1994
Twelve Tiny Tales (Molesworth, appendix), 1890
Twenty and Ten (Bishop), 1952
Twenty-Elephant Restaurant (Hoban), 1978
Twenty-Five Dragons (Coerr), 1971
Twenty-Four Days Before Christmas (L'Engle), 1964
Twenty-One Balloons (du Bois), 1947
Twenty-Six Christine Chaundler School Stories for Girls (Chaundler), 1926
Twenty-Six Ethel Talbot Tales for Girls (Talbot), 1927
Twenty Tea-Time Tales (Fyleman), 1929
Twenty-Two Bears (Bishop), 1964
Twice Bought (Ballantyne, appendix), 1885
Twice Seven Tales (Picard), 1968
Twickham Tweer (p Prelutsky), 1991
Twiddledetwit (Finley, appendix), 1898
Twig of Cypress (Cooper), 1965
Twilight Land (Pyle, appendix), 1895
Twilight of Magic (Lofting), 1930
Twilight Province (Finkel), 1967
Twin Babies (Finley, appendix), 1872
Twin Engines (Awdry), 1960
Twin Spell (Lunn), 1969
Twin Trouble (Wilson, J.), 1994
Twinkie Squad (Korman), 1992
Twinkle and Chubbins (Baum), 1911
Twinkle Tales (Baum, as Bancroft), 1906
Twins Again (Cleary), 1989
Twins and Tabiffa (Heward), 1923
Twins and the Tree Spirits (Segun), 1991
Twins and Their Ponies (Moray Williams), 1936
Twins at St. Clare's (Blyton), 1941
Twins at Tachbury (Everett-Green, appendix), 1924
Twins from Timber Creek (Clark, M.), 1949
Twins Go to Nursery-Rhyme Land (Blyton), 1945
Twins of Emu Plains (Bruce, M.), 1923
Twins, Tales of the (Blyton), 1948
Twins Who Flew round the World (Holling), 1931
Twist in the Tail (Hoffman), 1998
Twist of Eight (Morris), 1981
Twist, Wiggle, and Squirm: A Book about Earthworms (Pringle), 1973
Twisted Key and Other Stories (Lynch), 1964
Twitchell the Wishful (Sharmat), 1981
Two Admirals (McKee), 1977
Two, Adventures of (Wynne), 1920
Two and a Chum (Wynne), 1924
Two and Too Much (Walter), 1990
Two and Two Are Four (Haywood), 1940
Two Are Better Than One (Brink), 1968
Two Bad Ants (Van Allsburg), 1988
Two Bad Boys (Clewes), 1971
Two Bear Cubs (Jonas), 1982
Two Bright Shillings (Everett-Green, appendix), 1894
Two Brothers and Their Animal Friends (Lenski), 1929
Two Brothers and Their Baby Sister (Lenski), 1930
Two Bunnykins Out for Tea (Pearce, as Warrener), 1984
Two by Two by Two (Allen, J.), 1994
Two Can Toucan (McKee), 1964
Two Cars (d'Aulaire), 1955
Two Christmas Stories (Stretton, appendix), 1875
Two Dartmoor Interludes (Chipperfield), 1935
Two Dog Biscuits (Cleary), 1961
Two Dogs and a Horse (Kjelgaard), 1964
Two Faces of Silenus (Clarke, P.), 1972
Two Fugitives (Chipperfield), 1966
Two Funny Clowns (Hader), 1929
Two Gentlemen Sharing (Corlett), 1997
Two Ghosts on a Beach (Sharmat), 1982
Two Giants (Foreman), 1967
Two Girls (Coolidge, appendix), 1900
Two Girls in the Hawk's Den (Wynne), 1930
Two Girls in the Wild (Wynne), 1923
Two Gold Dolphins (Beresford), 1961
Two Guardians (Yonge, appendix), 1852
Two Guys Noticed Me...And Other Miracles (Sharmat), 1985
Two Head Girls and Other School Stories (Allan), 1992

War and Peas (Foreman), 1974
War Boy (Foreman), 1989
War Cargo (Westerman), 1941
War Game (Foreman), 1993
War of the Wireless Waves (Westerman), 1923
War of Wizards (Storey), 1976
War on the Darnel (Turner, P.), 1969
War Party (Steele, W.), 1978
War Stories (pl Prince), 1970
War with Mr. Wizzle (Korman), 1982
Warden's Niece (Avery), 1957
Wardens of the Weir (Gray), 1978
Wardship of Steepcombe (Yonge, appendix), 1896
Warlock Watson (King-Smith), 1995
Warnings (Buffie), 1991
Warrimoo (Patchett), 1961
Warringtons in War-Time (Talbot), 1940
Warrior and the Wise Man (Wisniewski), 1989
Warriors on the Hills (Seed), 1975
Wars of Wapsburgh (Yonge, appendix), 1864
Warts and All (Sudbery), 1972
Was I Right? (Walton, appendix), 1879
Was It a Good Trade? (p de Regniers), 1956
Washday on Noah's Ark (Rounds), 1985
Washerwoman's Child (pl Uttley), 1946
Wasp in a Wig (Carroll, appendix), 1978
Wasteground Circus (Keeping), 1975
Watch-Dog of the North Sea (Westerman), 1916
Watch Fires to the North (Finkel), 1967
Watch for a Pony (Robertson), 1949
Watch Harry Grow! (Demi), 1984
Watch Me (Allen, P.), 1985
Watch Me Dance (Pinkney, A.), 1997
Watch Me Now (Allen, P.), 1988
Watch Out! A Giant! (Carle), 1978
Watch Out for the Chicken Feet in Your Soup (dePaola), 1974
Watch Out, Fred's About (Waddell, as Sefton), 1996
Watch William Walk (Jonas), 1997
Watch Your Step, Mr. Rabbit! (Scarry), 1991
Watcher (Howe), 1997
Watcher at the Window (Storr), 1995
Watcher Bee (Melwood), 1982
Watcher on the Hills (Chipperfield), 1968
Watchers (Curry), 1975
Watchers: A Mystery at Alton Towers (Cresswell), 1993
Watchers of the Trails: A Book of Animal Life (Roberts, C.), 1904
Watching Boy, Case of the (Newman), 1987
Water (Asch), 1995
Water-Babies (Kingsley, appendix), 1863
Water Breaks Its Neck (Grice), 1986
Water Cresses (Alcott, appendix), 1879
Water Gipsies (Meade, appendix), 1879
Water Horse (King-Smith), 1990
Water Lilies and Other Tales (Meade, appendix), 1878
Water Plants (Pringle), 1975
Water-Rat's Picnic (Uttley), 1943
Water Wings (Gleitzman), 1996
Water: The Next Great Resource Battle (Pringle), 1982
Waterfall (Lasenby), 1995
Waterfall Box (Gordon, J.), 1978
Waters Between (Bruchac), 1998
Watson, The Smartest Dog in the U.S.A (Kuskin), 1968
Wattle Babies (Gibbs), 1918
Wave (Hodges, M.), 1964
Wave of the Sea-Wolf (Wisniewski), 1994
Waves (Rees, D.), 1983
Way for a Soldier (Dawlish), 1955
Way Home (Hathorn), 1993
Way Home (Turner, A.), 1982
Way I Feel...Sometimes (p de Regniers), 1988
Way Mothers Are (Schlein), 1963
Way of a Dog (Terhune), 1932
Way of the Whirlwind (Durack), 1941
Way of the Whirlwind (pl Durack), 1970
Way over Windle (Allan), 1966
Way Things Are and Other Poems (p Livingston), 1974
Way Things Work (Macaulay), 1988
Way to Captain Yankee's (Rockwell), 1994
Way to Glen Bradan and Other Scottish, Welsh, and Irish Stories (Allan), 1993
Way to Sattin Shore (Pearce), 1983
Way to the House of Santa Claus: A Christmas Story (Burnett), 1916
Wayah of the Real People (Steele, W.), 1964
Wayland's Keep (Bull), 1966
Wayside School Is Falling Down (Sachar), 1989
Waza Wins at Windy Gulch (Coerr), 1977
We and the World (Ewing, appendix), 1880
We Are All in the Dumps with Jack & Guy (Sendak), 1993
We Are Best Friends (Aliki), 1982
We Are Thy Children (p Lenski), 1952
We Can't Sleep (Stevenson, J.), 1982
We Couldn't Leave Dinah (Treadgold), 1941
We Didn't Mean to Go to Sea (Ransome), 1937
We Didn't Think of Ostriches (Storr), 1990
We Do Love Mary Mouse (Blyton), 1950
We Hate Rain! (Stevenson, J.), 1988
We Hunted Hounds (Pullein-Thompson, C.), 1949
We Live by the River (Lenski), 1956
We Live in the City (Lenski), 1954
We Live in the Country (Lenski), 1960
We Live in the North (Lenski), 1965
We Live in the South (Lenski), 1952
We Live in the Southwest (Lenski), 1962
We Lived in the Almont (Clymer), 1970
We Love Them (Waddell), 1990
We Met Our Cousins (Cannan), 1937
We Read: A to Z (Crews), 1967
We Rode to the Sea (Pullein-Thompson, C.), 1948
We Shall Have Snow (Cooper), 1966
We the People: The Story of the U.S. Constitution (Spier), 1987
We Three Kings (McNeill), 1974
We Too Were There: More Stories from History (Power), 1956
We Want a Story (Blyton), 1948
We Went Looking (p Fisher, A.), 1968
We Were There (Power), 1955
We Were There at the Oklahoma Land Run (Kjelgaard), 1957
We Were There on the Oregon Trail (Steele, W.), 1955
We Were There with the Pony Express (Steele, W.), 1956
We Were Young That Year (pl Harris, A.), 1954
We Wonder What Will Walter Be When He Grows Up? (Johnson, C.), 1964

Weasel Tim (Marchant), 1897
Weather (Ross), 1994
Weather and Me (Allen, J.), 1997
Weather Boy (Treadgold), 1964
Weather Cat (Cresswell), 1971
Weather Cock and Other Stories (Uttley), 1945
Weather Forecasting (Gibbons), 1987
Weather Words and What They Mean (Gibbons), 1990
Weathercock (Fenn, appendix), 1892
Web of Time (Harding), 1979
Wednesday Wizard (Jordan), 1991
Wee Gillis (Leaf), 1938
Wee Little Books (Burgess), 1929-33
Weed Is a Flower: The Life of George Washington Carver (Aliki), 1965
Week in the Life of Best Friends and Other Poems of Friendship (p de Regniers), 1986
Weeping Sky (Harding), 1977
Weeping Witch, Case of the (Hildick), 1992
Weird and Wacky Inventions (Murphy, Jim), 1978
Welcome Home! (p Bemelmans), 1960
Welcome Is a Wonderful Word (Fujikawa), 1980
Welcome Josie, Click, and Bun (Blyton), 1952
Welcome, Little Baby (Aliki), 1987
Welcome, Lyle (Waber), 1969
Welcome Mary Mouse (Blyton), 1950
Welcome to Babytown (Kraus, R.), 1987
Welcome to Danger (Brand), 1950
Welcome to the Club (Godfrey), 1998
Well (Kemp), 1984
Well Done, Noddy (Blyton), 1952
Well Done, Sam! (Bradman), 1996
Well Done, Secret Seven (Blyton), 1951
Well, I Never! (Berg), 1972
Well-Mannered Balloon (Willard), 1976
We'll Meet in England (Barne), 1942
Well Met by Witchlight (Beachcroft), 1972
Well of the Star (Goudge), 1941
Well Really Mr. Twiddle! (Blyton), 1953
Well-Wishers (Eager), 1960
Well, You Can Imagine (p O Huigin), 1983
Wellington and the Blue Balloon (Beresford), 1975
Wendy Puzzle (Heide), 1982
Wendy's Adventure in Scotland (Wynne), 1933
Were-fox (Coatsworth), 1975
We're Going on a Bear Hunt (p Rosen, Michael), 1989
Werepuppy (Wilson, J.), 1991
Werepuppy on Holiday (Wilson, J.), 1994
Werewolf Knight (Wagner), 1972
Wesley at the Water Park (Powling), 1992
West Indian Play Days (Dalgliesh), 1926
West of Boston (p Daugherty), 1956
West of Widdershins: A Gallimaufry of Stories Brewed in Her Own Cauldron (Sleigh), 1971
West to a Land of Plenty (Murphy, Jim), 1998
West Wind (Kyle), 1948
Western Boy (Tom, the Bootblack) (Alger, appendix), 1878
Western Scout (Marchant), 1912
Westmark Trilogy (Alexander), from 1981
Westow Talisman (Westerman), 1934
Westward Ho! (Kingsley, appendix), 1855
Westwoods (Farjeon), 1930
Wet and Sandy Day (Ryder), 1977
Wet Magic (Nesbit), 1913
Wet Monday (Edwards, D.), 1975
Whale Adventure (Price, W.), 1960
Whale People (Haig-Brown), 1962
Whaler 'round the Horn (Meader), 1950
Whalers' Garden (Noonan), 1994
Whales (Gibbons), 1991
Whales (Rylant), 1996
Whales and Sharks (Hoffman), 1986
What a Beautiful Noise (p Behn), 1970
What a Fine Day for... (p Krauss), 1967
What a Lark (Weir), 1961
What a Little Moonlight Can Do (pl Watson, J.), 1982
What a Star (Hathorn), 1994
What a Surprise! (Blyton), 1954
What a Wonderful Day (Bradman), 1988
What an Adventure (Blyton), 1950
What Are We Going to Do about Andrew? (Sharmat), 1980
What Are You Looking At? (Bonsall, as Newell), 1954
What Bunny Loves (Szekeres), 1990
What Cabrillo Found (Lovelace), 1958
What Can I Do? (Darke), 1975
What Can You Do with a Shoe? (p de Regniers), 1955
What Did I See? (p Smith), 1962
What Did You Bring Me? (Kuskin), 1973
What Did You Leave Behind? (Tresselt), 1978
What Do They Do When It Rains? (Bridwell), 1969
What Do We Do with Dawson? (Greenwood), 1996
What Do You Do with a Kangaroo? (Mayer), 1974
What Do You Think I Saw? (Ehlert), 1975
What Does It Do and How Does It Work? (p Hoban), 1959
What Eric Knew (Howe), 1985
What Game Shall We Play? (Hutchins, P.), 1990
What Happened to Toyland (pl Fisher, A.), 1945
What Happened When Jack and Daisy Tried to Fool the Tooth Fairies (Hoban), 1965
What Happens Next: Adventures of a Hero (de Regniers), 1959
What I Did Last Summer (p Prelutsky), 1984
What If? (Minarik), 1987
What Is Right for Tulip (Duvoisin), 1969
What Is that Sound? (Ehlert), 1967
What Jim Knew (p Hoberman), 1963
What Katy Did series (Coolidge, appendix), from 1872
What Might Have Been Expected (Stockton, appendix), 1874
What My Friends Say (Allen, J.), 1997
What Next, Baby Bear! (Murphy, Jill), 1984
What Rhymes with Moon? (p Yolen), 1993
What Sadie Saw (King-Smith), 1997
What Shall We Do with the Land? Choices for America (Pringle), 1981
What She Could (Warner, appendix), 1871
What Spot? (Bonsall), 1963
What Stanley Knew (Oram), 1983
What the Dickens! (Curry), 1991
What the Gulls Were Singing (Naylor), 1967
What the Neighbours Did and Other Stories (Pearce), 1972
What the Seven Did (Sidney, appendix), 1882
What the Sun Sees, What the Moon Sees (Tafuri), 1997
What the Wind Did (Le Feuvre), 1899

Which Horse Is William? (Kuskin), 1959
Which Is Willy? (Bright), 1962
Which One Is Whitney? (Stevenson, J.), 1990
Which Two Will Meet? (Banner), 1972
Which Way, Black Cat? (Lattimore, E.), 1980
Which Way Freedom? (Hansen), 1986
Which Witch Is Which? (Hutchins, P.), 1989
Whiff, Sniff, Nibble, and Chew: The Gingerbread Boy Retold (Pomerantz), 1984
Whiffy McMann (Hader), 1933
While Mother Was Away (Talbot), 1924
While the Story-Log Burns (Burgess), 1938
Whingdingdilly (Peet), 1970
Whinnie the Lovesick Dragon (Mayer), 1986
Whinstone Drift (Armstrong), 1951
Whipping Boy (Fleischman), 1986
Whiskers and Rhymes (p Lobel, Arnold), 1985
Whisper (Wilson, G.), 1982
Whispering Knights (Lively), 1971
Whispering Rabbit (Brown, Margaret Wise), 1965
Whispering Voice, Mystery of the (Heide), 1974
Whispers: An Experiment in Lino Cuts (p Briggs, K.), 1940
Whispers and Other Poems (p Livingston), 1958
Whispers in the Graveyard (Breslin), 1994
Whistle for the Crossing (de Angeli), 1977
Whistle for the Train (p Brown, Margaret Wise), 1956
Whistle for Willie (Keats), 1964
Whistle Punk of Camp 15 (Rounds), 1959
Whistling Boy (Arthur), 1969
Whistling Piglet (King-Smith), 1990
White Arab (Westerman), 1933
White Bear, Ice Bear (Ryder), 1989
White Bird (Bulla), 1966
White Boots (Streatfeild), 1951
White Captives (Lampman), 1975
White Cockade Passes (Fidler), 1947
White Cranes Castle (Harris, G.), 1979
White Deer (Thurber), 1945
White Dingo (Patchett), 1965
White Doe (Church), 1968
White Dress (Finley, appendix), 1870
White Elephant (Clarke, P.), 1952
White Flower (Fyleman), 1953
White Horse (Coatsworth), 1942
White Horse of Hungary (Catherall, as Ruthin), 1954
White Horse of Morocco (Coatsworth), 1973
White Magic (Hoffman), 1975
White Marble (Zolotow), 1963
White Mist (Smucker), 1985
White Oak (Wier), 1971
White Rabbit's Road (O'Faolain), 1950
White Riders (Edwards, M.), 1950
White Sails to China (Bulla), 1955
White Sea Horse (Cresswell), 1964
White Snow Bright Snow (Tresselt), 1947
White Sparrow (Brown, R.), 1974
White Sparrow (Colum), 1933
White Stallion of Lipizza (Henry), 1964
White-Starred Hare and Other Stories (Fidler), 1951
White Turrets (Molesworth, appendix), 1895
White Twilight (Polland), 1962
White Tzar (Meade, appendix), 1896
White Wyvill and Red Ruthven (Everett-Green, appendix), 1902
Whitefish Will Rides Again (Yorinks), 1994
Whitefoot the Wood Mouse (Burgess), 1922
Whiter Than Snow, and Little Dot (Walton, appendix), 1896
Whitey and Jinglebob (Rounds), 1946
Whitey and the Blizzard (Rounds), 1952
Whitey and the Colt-Killer (Rounds), 1962
Whitey and the Rustlers (Rounds), 1951
Whitey and the Wild Horse (Rounds), 1958
Whitey Looks for a Job (Rounds), 1944
Whitey Ropes and Rides (Rounds), 1956
Whitey Takes a Trip (Rounds), 1954
Whitey's First Round-Up (Rounds), 1942
Whitey's New Saddle (Rounds), 1963
Whitey's Sunday Horse (Rounds), 1943
Whizz Kid (Tate, J.), 1969
Whizziwig (Blackman), 1995
Who? (Schlein), 1963
Who Calls from Afar? (Brinsmead), 1971
Who Comes to King's Mountain? (Beatty), 1975
Who Comes with Cannons? (Beatty), 1992
Who Drew on the Baby's Head (p Rosen, Michael), 1991
Who Has Stolen the Sky? (de Graft-Hanson), 1995
Who Is Ben? (Zolotow), 1997
Who Is Bugs Potter? (Korman), 1980
Who Is Coming? (McKissack), 1986
Who Is Frances Rain? (Buffie), 1987
Who Is Who? (McKissack), 1983
Who Knew There'd Be Ghosts? (Brittain), 1985
Who Likes the Sun? (de Regniers), 1961
Who Needs Me? (Heide), 1971
Who Rides in the Dark? (Meader), 1937
Who Sank the Boat? (Allen, P.), 1982
Who Took the Farmer's Hat? (Lexau, as Nodset), 1963
Who Wants a Cheap Rhinoceros? (Silverstein, as Uncle Shelby), 1964
Who Was Wendy? (Wynne), 1932
Who? What? Where? When? (Lionni), 1983
Who Will Be My Friends? (Hoff), 1960
Who Will Believe Tim Kitten? (Wahl), 1978
Who Will Hold the Giant? (pl Blyton), 1955
Whodunnit? (Cresswell), 1986
Whoever You Are (Fox), 1997
Whopper (Watkins-Pitchford), 1967
Who's a Clever Baby, Then? (McKee), 1988
Who's a Pest? (Bonsall), 1962
Who's Afraid and Other Strange Stories (Pearce), 1986
Who's Afraid of Ernestine? (Sharmat), 1986
Who's Afraid of the Big Bad Wolf? (Bradman), 1989
Who's Afraid of the Dark? (Bonsall), 1980
Who's at the Door? (Allen, J.), 1992
Who's Bill? (Storr), 1976
Who's Counting (Tafuri), 1986
Who's in Rabbit's House?: A Masai Tale (Aardema), 1977
Who's Upside Down? (Johnson, C.), 1952
Whose Cat Is That? (Kahl), 1979
Whose Eye Am I? (Bonsall), 1968
Whose Mouse Are You? (Kraus, R.), 1970
Why Did the Underwear Cross the Road? (Korman), 1994
Why Didn't You Tell Me? (McKay), 1996

Wrestle the Mountain (Naylor), 1971
Wrestling Match (Emecheta), 1980
Wretched Stone (Van Allsburg), 1991
Wrinkle in Time (L'Engle), 1962
Write On!: Joy Cowley's Guide for Young Authors (Cowley), 1994
Wrong Chalet School (Brent-Dyer), 1952
Wrong Gear (Storey), 1973
Wrong Overcoat (Oram), 1999
Wrong Side of the Bed (Ardizzone), 1970
Wrong Side of the Moon (pl Gray), 1966
Wry Rhymes for Troublesome Times (p Fatchen), 1983
Wu, The Gatekeeper's Son (Lattimore, E.), 1953
Wuggly Ump (Gorey), 1963
Wulf the Saxon (Henty, appendix), 1894
Wump Day (Tate, J.), 1972
Wump World (Peet), 1970
Wy-Lah the Cockatoo, Story of (Rees, L.), 1960
Wyndhams Went to Wales (Allan), 1948

X Marks the Spot (de Hamel), 1973

Yaba Roundabout Murder (Ekwensi), 1962
Yak, Adventures of (Bisset), 1978
Yak and the Buried Treasure (Bisset), 1972
Yak and the Ice Cream (Bisset), 1972
Yak and the Painted Cave (Bisset), 1971
Yak and the Sea Shell (Bisset), 1971
Yak Goes Home (Bisset), 1973
Yancy and Bear (Hutchins, H.), 1996
Yankee Doodle (pl Harris, A.), 1975
Yard for John (Clymer), 1943
Yard Sale (Stevenson, J.), 1996
Yarns on the Beach (Henty, appendix), 1885
Yarooh! A Feast of Frank Richards (Richards, F.), 1976
Yasu and the Strangers (Slobodkin), 1965
Year in Percy's Park (Butterworth, N.), 1995
Year In, Year Out (Fujikawa), 1981
Year of Jubilo (Sawyer), 1940
Year of the Black Pony (Morey), 1976
Year of the Bloody Sevens (Steele, W.), 1963
Year of the Christmas Dragon (Sawyer), 1960
Year of the Jeep (Robertson), 1968
Year of the Panda (Schlein), 1990
Year of the Raccoon (Kingman), 1966
Year of the Shining Cuckoo (West), 1961
Year of the Small Shadow (Lampman), 1971
Year of the Stranger (McLean), 1971
Year of the Worm (Pilling), 1984
Year One (Seed), 1981
Year Round: A Second Book of Poems (p Clark, L.), 1966
Year-Round Programs for Young Players (pl Fisher, A.), 1985
Year, Story of a (Molesworth, appendix), 1910
Year Walk (Clark, A.), 1975
Year Without a Santa Claus (p McGinley), 1957
Yeck Eck (Ness), 1974
Yellow and Pink (Steig), 1984
Yellow Ball (Bang), 1991
Yellow Blue Jay (Hurwitz), 1986
Yellow Boarding House (Macdonald, C.), 1985
Yellow Butter, Purple Jelly, Red Jam, Black Bread: Poems (p Hoberman), 1981
Yellow Coach (Kyle), 1976
Yellow Fairy Book (Blyton), 1936
Yellow Pom-Pom Hat (Kaye), 1974
Yellow Pup (Everett-Green, appendix), 1912
Yellow Shop (Field), 1931
Yellow Story Book (Blyton), 1950
Yellow Wellies (Bull), 1994
Yellow, Yellow (Asch), 1971
Yellowbird and Me (Hansen), 1986
Yertle the Turtle and Other Stories (p Seuss), 1958
Yeshu, Called Jesus (Bishop), 1966
Yew Tree Farm (Marchant), 1904
Yippee-Yay!: A Book About Cowboys & Cowgirls (Gibbons), 1998
Yob (King-Smith), 1986
Yoko (Wells), 1998
Yonie Wondernose (de Angeli), 1944
You and Me (Zolotow), 1971
You and Me, Little Bear (Waddell), 1996
You Can't Catch Me! (p Rosen, Michael), 1981
You Can't Explain Everything (Tate, J.), 1976
You Can't Pet a Possum (Bontemps), 1934
You Funny Little Noddy! (Blyton), 1955
You Know Who (p Ciardi), 1964
"You Look Ridiculous," Said the Rhinoceros to the Hippopotamus (Waber), 1966
You Lucky Duck! (McCully), 1988
You Read to Me, I'll Read to You (p Ciardi), 1962
You Say You Saw a Camel! (Coatsworth), 1958
You Shall Have a Carriage (Coatsworth), 1941
You Tell Me (p McGough; Rosen, Michael), 1979
You Wait Till I'm Older Than You (p Rosen, Michael), 1996
You Won't Catch Me (Hardcastle), 1994
You'll Never Guess (pl Jellicoe), 1973
You'll Soon Grow into Them, Titch (Hutchins, P.), 1983
Young Abe Lincoln (pl Fisher, A.), 1969
Young Acadian (Roberts, C.), 1907
Young Acrobat of the Great North American Circus (Alger, appendix) 1888
Young Adventurer (Alger, appendix), 1878
Young Adventurers (Barne), 1936
Young Architect (Meynell), 1958
Young Aunts (Dalgliesh), 1939
Young Bank Messenger (Alger, appendix), 1898
Young, Black, and Determined: A Biography of Lorraine Hansberry (McKissack), 1998
Young Black Beauty (pl Harris, A.), 1995
Young Boatman of Pine Point (Alger, appendix), 1892
Young Book Agent (Alger, appendix), 1905
Young Buglers (Henty, appendix), 1879
Young Captain Jack (Alger, appendix), 1901
Young Carthaginian (Henty, appendix), 1886
Young Cavalier (Westerman), 1911
Young Circus Rider (Alger, appendix), 1883
Young Colonists (Henty, appendix), 1885
Young Cowboy (James), 1935
Young Explorer (Alger, appendix), 1880
Young Flash, The Deer (Burgess), 1940
Young Folk and Old (p Farjeon), 1925

READING LIST

The following selected list includes critical works dealing in whole or in part with English-language creative writing for children in the 20th century. Studies of individual writers are cited in the appropriate entries.

Adams, Bes Porter. *About Books and Children: Historical Survey of Children's Literature.* New York, Holt, 1953.

Allen, Marjorie N. *One Hundred Years of Children's Books in America: Decade by Decade.* New York, Facts On File, 1996.

Anderson, Celia Catlett, and Marilyn Fain Apseloff. *Nonsense Literature for Children, Aesop to Seuss.* Hamden, Connecticut, Library Professional Publications, 1989.

Anderson, William D., and Patrick Groff. *A New Look at Children's Literature.* Belmont, California, Wadsworth, 1972.

Andrews, Siri, editor. *The Hewins Lectures 1947-1962.* Boston, Horn Book, 1963.

Arbuthnot, May Hill. *Children and Books.* Chicago, Scott Foresman, 1947; 7th edition, with Zena Sutherland, 1986.

Avery, Gillian. *Childhood's Pattern: A Study of the Heroes and Heroines of Children's Fiction 1770-1950.* London, Hodder and Stoughton, 1975.

Bader, Barbara. *American Picturebooks from Noah's Ark to the Beast Within.* New York, Macmillan, and London, Collier Macmillan, 1976.

Bechtel, Louise Seaman. *Books in Search of Children: Speeches and Essays,* edited by Virginia Haviland. New York, Macmillan, 1969; London, Hamish Hamilton, 1970.

Beckett, Sandra L., editor. *Reflections of Change: Children's Literature since 1945.* Westport, Connecticut, Greenwood Press, 1997.

Blishen, Edward, editor. *The Thorny Paradise: Writers on Writing for Children.* London, Kestrel, 1975.

Blount, Margaret. *Animal Land: The Creatures of Children's Fiction.* London, Hutchinson, 1974; New York, Morrow, 1975.

Broderick, Dorothy M. *Image of the Black in Children's Fiction.* New York, Bowker, 1973.

Brown, Marcia. *Lotus Seeds: Children, Pictures, and Books.* New York, Scribner, 1982.

Butler, Francelia, and Richard Rotert, editors. *Reflections on Literature for Children.* Hamden, Connecticut, Library Professional Publications, 1984.

———. *Triumphs of the Spirit in Children's Literature.* Hamden, Connecticut, Library Professional Publications, 1986.

Butts, Dennis, editor. *Good Writers for Young Readers: Critical Essays.* London, Hart Davis, 1977.

Cadogan, Mary, and Patricia Craig. *You're a Brick, Angela! A New Look at Girls' Fiction from 1839-1975.* London, Gollancz, 1976; revised edition, 1986.

Cameron, Eleanor. *The Green and Burning Tree: On the Writing and Enjoyment of Children's Books.* Boston, Little Brown, 1969.

———. *The Seed and the Vision: On the Writing and Appreciation of Children's Books.* New York, Dutton Children's Books, 1993.

Carlson, Ruth Kearney. *Emerging Humanity: Multi-Ethnic Literature for Children and Adolescents.* Dubuque, Iowa, Brown, 1972.

Carpenter, Humphrey. *Secret Gardens: The Golden Age of Children's Literature.* London, Allen and Unwin, 1985.

Carruth, Gorton. *The Young Reader's Companion.* New Providence, New Jersey, R.R. Bowker, 1993.

Cass, Joan E. *Literature and the Young Child.* London, Longman, 1967; revised edition, 1984.

Chambers, Aidan. *Introducing Books to Children.* London, Heinemann, 1973; revised edition, Boston, Horn Book, 1983.

———. *The Reluctant Reader.* Oxford, Pergamon Press, 1969.

———, editor. *Booktalk: Occasional Writing on Literature and Children.* London, Bodley Head, and New York, Harper, 1985.

Chambers, Nancy, editor. *The Signal Approach to Children's Books.* London, Kestrel, 1980; Metuchen, New Jersey, Scarecrow Press, 1981.

Christelow, Eileen. *What Do Authors Do?* New York, Clarion Books, 1995.

Cott, Jonathan. *Pipers at the Gates of Dawn: The Wisdom of Children's Literature.* New York, Random House, 1983; London, Viking, 1984.

Crewe, Judy. *Children's Literature for Multicultural Australia.* Ultimo, Library Association of Australia, School Libraries Section N.S.W. Group, 1986.

Crouch, Marcus. *The Nesbit Tradition: The Children's Novel in England 1945-1970.* London, Benn, 1972; Totowa, New Jersey, Rowman and Littlefield, 1973.

———. *Treasure Seekers and Borrowers: Children's Books in Britain 1900-1960.* London, Library Association, 1962.

Crouch, Marcus, and Alec Ellis, editors. *Chosen for Children: An Account of the Books Which Have Been Awarded the Library Association Carnegie Medal 1936-1975.* London, Library Association, 1977.

Cullinan, Bernice E., and Lee Galda. *Literature and the Child.* 4th edition, Fort Worth, Harcourt Brace College Publishers, 1998.

Culpan, Norman, and Clifford Waite, editors. *Variety Is King: Aspects of Fiction for Children.* Oxford School Library Association, 1977.

Darton, F. J. Harvey. *Children's Books in England: Five Centuries of Social Life.* Cambridge, University Press, 1932; 3rd edition, edited by Brian Alderson, London and New York, Cambridge University Press, 1982.

Dear Author: Students Write about the Books that Changed Their Lives. Berkeley, California, Conari Press, 1995.

Dixon, Bob. *Catching Them Young: Sex, Race and Class in Children's Fiction* and *Political Ideas in Children's Fiction.* London, Pluto Press, 2 vols., 1977.

Dolvers, Horst. *Fables Less and Less Fabulous: English Fables and Parables of the Nineteenth Century and Their Illustrations.* Newark, University of Delaware Press, and London, Associated University Presses, 1997.

Donelson, Kenneth L., and Alleen Pace Nilsen. *Literature for Today's Young Adults.* Chicago, Scott Foresman, 1980.

Egoff, Sheila. *The Republic of Childhood: A Critical Guide to Canadian Children's Literature in English.* Toronto, Oxford University Press, 1967.

———. *Thursday's Child: Trends and Patterns in Contemporary Children's Literature.* Chicago, American Library Association, 1981.

———. *Worlds Within: Children's Fantasy from the Middle Ages to Today.* Chicago, American Library Association, 1988.

Egoff, Sheila, and Judith Saltman. *The New Republic of Childhood: A Critical Guide to Canadian Children's Literature in English.* Toronto, New York, Oxford University Press, 1990.

Egoff, Sheila, G. T. Stubbs, and L. F. Ashley, editors. *Only Connect: Readings on Children's Literature.* Toronto and New York, Oxford University Press, 1969.

Ellis, Alec. *A History of Children's Reading and Literature.* Oxford, Pergamon Press, 1968.

Ellis, Anne W. *The Family Story in the 1960's.* London, Bingley, 1970.

Eyre, Frank. *20th Century Children's Books.* London, Longman, 1952; Boston, Bentley, 1953; revised edition, as *British Children's Books in the Twentieth Century,* Longman, 1971; New York, Dutton, 1973.

Fasick, Adele M., Margaret Johnston, and Ruth Osler, editors. *Lands of Pleasure: Essays on Lillian H. Smith and the Development of Children's Libraries.* Metuchen, New Jersey, Scarecrow Press, 1990.

Fenwick, Sara Innis, editor. *A Critical Approach to Children's Literature.* Chicago, University of Chicago Press, 1967.

Field, Elinor Whitney. *Horn Book Reflections on Children's Books and Reading: Selected from ... Horn Book Magazine 1949-1966.* Boston, Horn Book, 1969.

Fisher, Margery. *The Bright Face of Danger: An Exploration of the Adventure Story.* London, Hodder and Stoughton, 1986.

———. *Intent upon Reading: A Critical Appraisal of Modern Fiction for Children.* Leicester, Brockhampton Press, 1961; New York, Watts, 1962; revised edition, Brockhampton Press, 1964.

———. *Who's Who in Children's Books: A Treasury of the Familiar Characters of Childhood.* London, Weidenfeld and Nicolson, and New York, Holt Rinehart, 1975.

Fox, Geoff, and others, editors. *Writers, Critics and Children: Articles from Children's Literature in Education.* New York, Agathon Press, and London, Heinemann, 1976.

Fraser, James H., editor. *Society and Children's Literature.* Boston, Godine, 1978.

Fredericks, Anthony D. *Social Studies through Children's Literature: An Integrated Approach.* Englewood, Colorado, Teacher Ideas Press, 1991.

Fryatt, Norma R., editor. *A Horn Book Sampler on Children's Books and Reading, 1924-1948.* Boston, Horn Book, 1959.

Gilderdale, Betty. *A Sea Change: 145 Years of New Zealand Junior Fiction.* Auckland, Longman Paul, 1982.

Gillespie, Margaret C. *Literature for Children: History and Trends.* Dubuque, Iowa, Brown, 1970.

Givens, Archie, editor. *Strong Souls Singing: African American Books for Our Daughters and Our Sisters.* New York, Norton, 1998.

Glazer, Joan I., and Gurney Williams III. *Introduction to Children's Literature.* New York, McGraw Hill, 1979; 2nd edition, Upper Saddle River, Merrill, 1997.

Gose, Elliott. *Mere Creatures: A Study of Modern Fantasy Tales for Children.* Toronto, University of Toronto Press, 1988.

Green, Roger Lancelyn. *Tellers of Tales.* Leicester, Ward, 1946; revised edition, 1953; revised edition, London, Ward, and New York, Watts, 1965; revised edition, London, Kaye and Ward, 1969.

Greenwood, Barbara, general editor. *Behind the Story: The Creators of Our Best Children's Books and How They Do It.* Markham, Ontario, Pembroke, 1995.

Harrison, Barbara, and Gregory Maguire, editors. *Innocence and Experience: Essays and Conversations on Children's Literature.* New York, Lothrop, 1987.

Haviland, Virginia, editor. *Children and Literature: Views and Reviews.* Chicago, Scott Foresman, 1973; London, Bodley Head, 1974.

———. *The Openhearted Audience: Ten Authors Talk about Writing for Children.* Washington, D.C., Library of Congress, 1980.

Hazard, Paul. *Books, Children, and Men,* translated by Marguerite Mitchell. Boston, Horn Book, 1944; 5th edition, 1983.

Hearne, Betsy, editor. *The Zena Sutherland lectures, 1983-1992.* New York, Clarion Books, 1993.

Hearne, Betsy, and Marilyn Kaye, editors. *Celebrating Children's Books: Essays on Children's Literature in Honor of Zena Sutherland.* New York, Lothrop, 1981.

Heins, Paul, editor. *Crosscurrents of Criticism: Horn Book Essays 1968-1977.* Boston, Horn Book, 1977.

Hendrickson, Linnea. *Children's Literature: A Guide to the Criticism.* Boston, Massachusetts, G.K. Hall, 1987.

Higgins, James E. *Beyond Words: Mystical Fancy in Children's Literature.* New York, Teachers College Press, 1970.

Hildick, Wallace. *Children and Fiction: A Critical Study in Depth of the Artistic and Psychological Factors Involved in Writing Fiction for and about Children.* London, Evans, 1970; New York, World, 1971; revised edition, Evans, 1974.

Hilton, Mary, Morag Styles, and Victor Watson, editors. *Opening the Nursery Door: Reading, Writing, and Childhood, 1600-1900.* London and New York, Routledge, 1997.

Hollindale, Peter. *Choosing Books for Children.* London, Elek, 1974.

Huck, Charlotte S., and Doris A. Young. *Children's Literature in the Elementary School.* New York, Holt Rinehart, 1961; 3rd edition, 1976.

Human (and Anti-Human) Values in Children's Books. New York, Council on Interracial Books for Children, 1976.

Hunt, Peter. *Children's Book Research in Britain.* Cardiff, University of Wales, 1977; revised edition, with Beth Humphries and Sarah Wilkinson, 1982.

———. *Children's Literature: The Development of Criticism.* London and New York, Routledge, 1990.

———. *An Introduction to Children's Literature.* Oxford and New York, Oxford University Press, 1994.

———, editor. *Children's Literature: An Illustrated History.* Oxford and New York, Oxford University Press, 1995.

———. *Further Approaches to Research in Children's Literature.* Cardiff, University of Wales, 1982.

Hunter, Mollie. *The Pied Piper Syndrome, and Other Essays.* New York, HarperCollins, 1992.

Hürlimann, Bettina. *Picture-Book World,* edited and translated by Brian W. Alderson. London, Oxford University Press, 1968; Cleveland, World, 1969.

———. *Three Centuries of Children's Books in Europe,* edited and translated by Brian W. Alderson. London, Oxford University Press, 1967; Cleveland, World, 1968.

Inglis, Fred. *The Promise of Happiness: Value and Meaning in Children's Fiction.* London, Cambridge University Press, 1981; New York, Cambridge University Press, 1982.

Jackson, Mary V. *Engines of Instruction, Mischief, and Magic: Children's Literature in England from its Beginnings to 1839.* Lincoln, University of Nebraska Press, 1989.

Jagusch, Sybille A., editor. *Stepping Away from Tradition: Children's Books of the Twenties and Thirties; Papers from a Symposium.* Washington, D.C., Library of Congress, 1988.

Jan, Isabelle. *On Children's Literature,* edited by Catherine Storr. London, Allen Lane, 1973; New York, Schocken, 1974.

Johnson-Feelings, Dianne. *Telling Tales: The Pedagogy and Promise of African American Literature for Youth.* New York, Greenwood Press, 1990.

Jones, Anthony, and June Buttrey. *Children and Stories.* Oxford, Blackwell, 1970.

Jones, Raymond E. *Characters in Children's Literature.* Detroit, Gale Research, 1997.

Karl, Jean. *From Childhood to Childhood: Children's Books and Their Creators.* New York, Day, 1970.

Kingman, Lee, editor. *Newbery and Caldecott Medal Books 1956-1965* and *1966-1975.* Boston, Horn Book, 2 vols., 1965-75.

Kingston, Carolyn T. *The Tragic Mode in Children's Literature.* New York, Teachers College Press, 1974.

Lanes, Selma G. *Down the Rabbit Hole: Adventures and Misadventures in the Realm of Children's Literature.* New York, Atheneum, 1971; revised edition, 1976.

Lees, Stella, and Pam Macintyre. *The Oxford Companion to Australian Children's Literature.* Melbourne and New York, Oxford University Press, 1993.

Leeson, Robert. *Children's Books and Class Society: Past and Present.* London, Writers and Readers, 1977.

———. *Reading and Righting: The Past, Present and Future of Fiction for the Young.* London, Collins, 1985.

L'Engle, Madeleine. *Trailing Clouds of Glory: Spiritual Values in Children's Books.* Philadelphia, Westminster Press, 1985.

Lewis, Naomi. *Fantasy Books for Children.* London, National Book League, 1975; revised edition, 1977.

Lickteig, Mary J. *An Introduction to Children's Literature.* Columbus, Ohio, Merrill, 1975.

Litowinsky, Olga. *Writing and Publishing Books for Children in the 1990s: The Inside Story from the Editor's Desk.* New York, Walker, 1992.

Lochhead, Marion. *The Renaissance of Wonder in Children's Literature.* Edinburgh, Canongate, 1977.

Luecke, Fritz J., editor. *Children's Books: Views and Values.* Middletown, Connecticut, Xerox, 1973.

Lukens, Rebecca J. *A Critical Handbook of Children's Literature.* Chicago, Scott Foresman, 1976; revised edition, 1982; 3rd edition, 1986.

Lurie, Alison. *Don't Tell the Grown-ups: Subversive Children's Literature.* Boston, Little, Brown, 1990.

Lystad, Mary. *At Home in America, as Seen through Its Books for Children.* Cambridge, Massachusetts, Schenkman, 1984.

———. *From Dr. Mather to Dr. Seuss: 200 Years of American Books for Children.* Boston, Hall, 1980.

MacCann, Donnarae. *White Supremacy in Children's Literature: Characterizations of African Americans, 1830-1900.* New York, Garland, 1998.

MacCann, Donnarae, and Gloria Woodard, editors. *The Black American in Books for Children: Readings in Racism* and *Cultural Conformity in Books for Children; Further Readings in Racism.* Metuchen, New Jersey, Scarecrow Press, 2 vols., 1972-77; revised edition, 1 vol., 1985.

MacCann, Donnarae, and Olga Richard. *The Child's First Books: A Critical Study of Pictures and Texts.* New York, Wilson, 1973.

Mackey, Margaret. *The Case of Peter Rabbit: Changing Conditions of Literature for Children.* New York and London, Garland, 1998.

MacLeod, Anne Scott. *American Childhood: Essays on Children's Literature of the Nineteenth and Twentieth Centuries.* Athens, University of Georgia Press, 1994.

Magaliff, Cecile. *The Junior Novel: Its Relationship to Adolescent Reading.* Port Washington, New York, Kennikat Press, 1964.

Manna, Anthony L., and Carolyn S. Brodie, editors. *Many Faces, Many Voices: Multicultural Literary Experiences for Youth; The Virginia Hamilton Conference.* Fort Atkinson, Wisconsin, Highsmith Press, 1992.

Marshall, Margaret R. *An Introduction to the World of Children's Books.* Aldershot, Hampshire, Gower, 1982; revised edition, 1988.

Mason, Bobbie Ann. *The Girl Sleuth: A Feminist Guide.* Old Westbury, New York, Feminist Press, 1975.

McCaslin, Nellie. *Theatre for Children in the United States: A History.* Norman, University of Oklahoma Press, 1971.

———, editor. *Children and Drama: A Collection of Essays.* New York, McKay, 1975; revised edition, New York, Longman, 1981.

———. *Theatre for Young Audiences.* New York, Longman, 1978.

McClure, Amy A., and Janice V. Kristo, editors. *Books that Invite Talk, Wonder, and Play.* Urbana, Illinois, National Council of Teachers of English, 1996.

McVitty, Walter. *Innocence and Experience: Essays on Contemporary Australian Children's Writers.* Melbourne, Nelson, 1982.

Meek, Margaret, Aidan Warlow, and Griselda Barton, editors. *The Cool Web: The Pattern of Children's Reading.* London, Bodley Head, 1977; New York, Atheneum, 1978.

Meigs, Cornelia, and others. *A Critical History of Children's Literature.* New York, Macmillan, 1953; revised edition, Macmillan, and London, Collier Macmillan, 1969.

Miller, Bertha Mahony, and Elinor Whitney Field, editors. *Newbery Medal Books 1922-1955* and *Caldecott Medal Books 1938-1957.* Boston, Horn Book, 2 vols., 1955-57.

Miller, Wanda J. *U.S. History through Children's Literature, from the Colonial Period to World War II.* Englewood, Colorado, Teacher Ideas Press, 1997.

Moore, Anne Carroll. *My Roads to Childhood.* New York, Doubleday, 1939.

Murray, Gail Schmunk. *American Children's Literature and the Construction of Childhood.* New York, Twayne Publishers, 1998.

Niall, Brenda, and Frances O'Neill. *Australia Through the Looking-Glass: Children's Fiction 1830-1980.* Melbourne, Melbourne University Press, 1984.

Nieuwenhuizen, Agnes, editor. *The Written World: Youth and Literature.* Port Melbourne, Victoria, Thorpe, 1994.

Nodelman, Perry. *Words about Pictures: The Narrative of Children's Picture Books.* Athens, University of Georgia Press, 1988.

Paterson, Katherine. *A Sense of Wonder: On Reading and Writing Books for Children.* New York, Plume, 1995.

Pickard, P. M. *I Could a Tale Unfold: Violence, Horror, and Sensationalism in Books for Children.* London, Tavistock, and New York, Humanities Press, 1961.

Prentice, Jeffrey, and Bronwen Bennett. *A Guide to Australian Children's Literature.* Port Melbourne, Victoria, Thorpe, and Providence, New Jersey, Bowker, 1992.

Price, Hugh. *School Books Published in New Zealand to 1960.* Palmerston North, New Zealand, Dunmore Press with Gondwanaland Press, 1992.

Purves, Alan C., and Dianne L. Monson. *Experiencing Children's Literature.* Chicago, Scott Foresman, 1984.

Quigly, Isabel. *The Heirs of Tom Brown: The English School Story.* London, Chatto and Windus, 1982.

Racist and Sexist Images in Children's Books. London, Writers and Readers, 1975.

Rahn, Suzanne. *Rediscoveries in Children's Literature.* New York, Garland, 1995.

Raines, Shirley C., and Rebecca T. Isbell. *Stories: Children's Literature in Early Education.* Albany, New York, Delmar Publishers, 1994.

Rand, Donna, Toni Parker, and Sheila Foster. *Black Books Galore: Guide to Great African American Children's Books.* New York, Wiley, 1998.

Ray, Sheila G. *Children's Fiction.* Leicester, Brockhampton Press, 1970; revised edition, 1972.

Rees, David. *The Marble in the Water: Essays on Contemporary Writers of Fiction for Children and Young People.* Boston, Horn Book, 1980.

Reynolds, Kimberley, and Nicholas Tucker, editors. *Children's Book Publishing in Britain since 1945.* Aldershot, England, and Brookfield, Vermont, Scolar Press, 1998.

Richards, Jeffrey, editor. *Imperialism and Juvenile Literature.* Manchester, Manchester University Press, 1989.

Ringer, J. B. *Young Emigrants: New Zealand Juvenile Fiction 1833-1919.* Hamilton, New Zealand, Thackeray Street, 1980.

Robinson, Evelyn Rose, editor. *Readings about Children's Literature.* New York, McKay, 1966.

Rollock, Barbara. *Black Authors and Illustrators of Children's Books: A Biographical Dictionary.* 2nd edition, New York, Garland, 1992.

Rosenblum, Robert. *The Romantic Child: From Runge to Sendak.* London, Thames and Hudson, 1989.

Rothlein, Liz. *The Literature Connection: Using Children's Books in the Classroom.* Glenview, Illinois, Scott, Foresman, 1991.

Rudman, Masha Kabakow. *Children's Literature: An Issues Approach.* Lexington, Massachusetts, Heath, 1976; revised edition, White Plains, New York, Longman, 1984.

Ryan, John S., editor. *Australian Fantasy and Folklore.* Armidale, New South Wales, University of New England Department of Continuing Education, 1981.

Sadker, Myra Pollack, and David Miller Sadker. *Now Upon a Time: A Contemporary View of Children's Literature.* New York, Harper, 1977.

Sale, Roger. *Fairy Tales and After: From Snow White to E. B. White.* Cambridge, Massachusetts, Harvard University Press, 1978.

Saltman, Judith. *Modern Canadian Children's Books.* Toronto, Oxford University Press, 1987.

Saxby, H. M. *A History of Australian Children's Literature 1841-1941* and *1941-1970.* Sydney, Wentworth, 2 vols., 1969-71.

———. *The Proof of the Puddin': Australian Children's Literature, 1970-1990.* Sydney and New York, Ashton Scholastic, 1993.

Sexism in Children's Books. London, Writers and Readers, 1976.

Shavit, Zohar. *Poetics of Children's Literature.* Athens, University of Georgia Press, 1986.

Short, Kathy G., editor. *Research and Professional Resources in Children's Literature: Piecing a Patchwork Quilt.* Newark, Delaware, International Reading Association, 1995.

Silvey, Anita, editor. *Children's Books and Their Creators.* Boston, Houghton Mifflin, 1995.

Smith, Dora V. *Fifty Years of Children's Books 1910-1960: Trends, Backgrounds, Influences.* Champaign, Illinois, National Council of Teachers of English, 1963.

Smith, Irene. *A History of the Newbery and Caldecott Medals.* New York, Viking Press, 1957.

Smith, James Steel. *A Critical Approach to Children's Literature.* New York, McGraw Hill, 1967.

Smith, Karen Patricia. *The Fabulous Realm: A Literary-historical Approach to British Fantasy, 1780-1990.* Metuchen, New Jersey, Scarecrow Press, 1993.

Smith, Lillian. *The Unreluctant Years: A Critical Approach to Children's Literature.* Chicago, American Library Association, 1953.

Sorfleet, John Robert, editor. *Canadian Children's Drama and Theatre.* Guelph, Ontario, Canadian Children's Press, 1978.

Spindler, Graham, editor. *Behind the Lines: Views from "Behind the Scenes" of Writing and Publishing for Young Readers.* West Deakin, ACT, Australian Library and Information Association, School Libraries Section, 1991.

Stott, Jon C. *Children's Literature from A to Z: A Guide for Parents and Teachers.* New York, McGraw-Hill, 1984.

———. *Native Americans in Children's Literature.* Phoenix, Arizona, Oryx Press, 1995.

Stott, Jon C., and Raymond E. Jones. *Canadian Books for Children: A Guide to Authors and Illustrators.* Toronto and Orlando, Harcourt Brace Jovanovich, 1988.

Styles, Morag, Eve Bearne, and Victor Watson, editors. *After Alice: Exploring Children's Literature.* London and New York, Cassell, 1992.

———. *The Prose and the Passion: Children and Their Reading.* London and New York, Cassell, 1994.

———. *Voices Off: Texts, Contexts, and Readers.* London and New York, Cassell, 1996.

Sutherland, Zena, editor. *The Arbuthnot Lectures 1970-1979.* Chicago, American Library Association, 1980.

———. *Children in Libraries.* Chicago, University of Chicago Press, 1981.

Thomison, Dennis, editor. *Readings about Adolescent Literature.* Metuchen, New Jersey, Scarecrow Press, 1970.

Thwaite, Mary F. *From Primer to Pleasure: An Introduction to the History of Children's Books in England.* London, Library Association, 1963; revised edition, as *From Primer to Pleasure in Reading.* Library Association, 1972; Boston, Horn Book, 1973.

Townsend, John Rowe. *A Sense of Story: Essays on Contemporary Writers for Children.* London, Longman, and Philadelphia, Lippincott, 1971; revised edition, as *A Sounding of Storytellers,* London, Kestrel, and New York, Lippincott, 1979.

———. *Written for Children: An Outline of English Children's Literature.* London, J. Garnet Miller, 1965; New York, Lothrop, 1967; revised edition, London, Kestrel, 1974; Philadelphia, Lippincott, 1975; revised edition, London, Kestrel, and New York, Harper, 1983; revised edition, London, Penguin, 1987; New York, Harper, 1988.

Trease, Geoffrey. *Tales Out of School: A Survey of Children's Fiction.* London, Heinemann, 1949; revised edition, 1964.

Tucker, Nicholas. *The Child and the Book: A Psychological and Literary Exploration.* London, Cambridge University Press, 1981; New York, Cambridge University Press, 1982.

———, editor. *Suitable for Children? Controversies in Children's Literature.* London, Chatto and Windus, and Berkeley, University of California Press, 1976.

Vandergrift, Kay E. *Child and Story: The Literary Connection.* New York, Neal Schuman, 1980.

———. *Children's Literature: Theory, Research and Teaching.* Littleton, Colorado, Libraries Unlimited, 1989.

———. *Ways of Knowing: Literature and the Intellectual Life of Children.* Lanham, Maryland, Scarecrow Press, 1996.

Varlejs, Jana, editor. *Young Adult Literature in the Seventies: A Selection of Readings.* Metuchen, New Jersey, Scarecrow Press, 1982.

Viguers, Ruth Hill. *Margin for Surprise: About Books, Children, and Librarians.* Boston, Little Brown, 1964; London, Constable, 1966.

Waggoner, Diana. *The Hills of Faraway: A Guide to Fantasy.* New York, Atheneum, 1978.

Waterston, Elizabeth. *Children's Literature in Canada.* Toronto and New York, Maxwell Macmillan, 1992.

White, Dorothy Mary Neal. *About Books for Children.* Wellington, New Zealand Council for Educational Research, 1946; New York, Oxford University Press, 1948.

White, Mary Lou. *Children's Literature: Criticism and Response.* Columbus, Ohio, Merrill, 1976.

Whitehead, Winifred. *Old Lies Revisited: Young Readers and the Literature of War and Violence.* London, Pluto Press.

Wilkin, Binnie Tate. *Survival Themes in Fiction for Children and Young People.* Metuchen, New Jersey, Scarecrow Press, 1978.

Wintle, Justin, and Emma Fisher. *The Pied Pipers: Interviews with the Influential Creators of Children's Literature.* New York and London, Paddington Press, 1975.

Wyatt, Flora, Margaret Coggins, and Jane Hunter Imber. *Popular Nonfiction Authors for Children: A Biographical and Thematic Guide.* Englewood, Colorado, Libraries Unlimited, 1998.

NOTES ON
ADVISERS AND CONTRIBUTORS

AGOSTA, Lucien L. Assistant professor of English, California State University, Sacramento. Author of *Howard Pyle,* 1987, and of articles on the Brownings, D.G. Rossetti, Richard Wright, Kurt Vonnegut, Thomas Hughes, and Thornton Waldo Burgess. **Essay:** Thornton Waldo Burgess.

ALBERGHENE, Janice M. Associate professor of English, Fitchburg State College, Massachusetts. Author of 18 articles on children's literature, the most recent being "Moralists, But with No Pretense," 1988, "Humor in Children's Literature," 1988, and "Artful Memory: Jean Fritz, Autobiography and the Child Reader," 1989. **Essays:** Lessie Jones Little; Faith Ringgold.

ANDERSON, William D. Professor of English, California State University, Northridge. Author of *A New Look at Children's Literature* (with Patrick Groff), 1972. **Essay:** Norton Juster.

APSELOFF, Marilyn F. Associate professor of English, Kent State University, Kent, Ohio. Author of *Virginia Hamilton: Ohio Explorer in the World of Imagination,* 1978, *Nonsense Literature for Children: From Aesop to Seuss* (with Celia Catlett Anderson), and 1989, *They Wrote for Children Too: An Annotated Bibliography of Children's Literature in Education.* **Essays:** Joan W. Blos; Walter D. Edmonds; Angela Johnson; Shel Silverstein; Brinton Turkle.

ASHDOWN, Fran. Children's librarian, North Vancouver District Public Library; reviewer, *Canadian Book Review Annual.* **Essays:** Esther Averill; Sheila Burnford; Markoosie; Richard Scarry.

ATKINSON, Judith. Head of English Department, Wolfreton School. Author of numerous articles on English teaching, including contributions to *Developing Response to Fiction,* 1983, and *Teaching Literature for Examinations,* 1986. **Essays:** Gene Kemp; Gareth Own; Philippa Pearce; Chris Powling.

AVERY, Gillian. See her own entry. **Essays:** Jacob Abbott (appendix); Evelyn Everett-Green (appendix); Juliana Horatia Ewing (appendix); G.E. Farrow; Charles Kingsley (appendix); Amy Le Feuvre; Mary Norton; Arthur Ransome; Alice Hegan Rice; Margaret Sidney (appendix); Hesba Stretton (appendix); Booth Tarkington; Susan Warner (appendix); Charlotte Yonge (appendix).

BAKER, Janet E. Associate professor of English, St. Mary's University, Halifax, Nova Scotia. **Essay:** Hubert Evans.

BAKKER, Jan. Associate professor of English, Utah State University, Logan; consulting editor, *Children's Literature.* Author of *Pastoral in Antebellum Southern Romance,* and *Marxism, Feminism and Free Love* (with Francelia Butler), 1981, and of articles on southern literature in *Early American Literature, Studies in American Fiction, Southern Literary Journal, Southern Studies,* and other periodicals, and of two bibliographies of 19th-century children's literature in *Children's Literature.* **Essay:** Joel Chandler Harris (appendix).

BARKER, Keith. Deputy librarian, Westhill College, Birmingham; editor, *Youth Library Review,* and review editor, *School Librarian.* Author of *In the Realms of Gold,* 1986. **Essays:** Graeme Base; Peter Hunt; Philip Ridley; James Watson; Rosemary Wells.

BARTHOLOMEW, Ann. Freelance writer. Author of *Reading for Enjoyment with 7-11 Year Olds,* 1981. **Essays:** Carol Ryrie Brink; Grace Hogarth; Kate Seredy.

BAYFIELD, Juliana. Librarian, Children's Literature Research Collection, State Library of South Australia, Adelaide. Author of "From Simon Black to Ash Road and Beyond" in *Bookbird,* 1968, and of articles on library services for young people. **Essay:** George Manville Fenn (appendix).

BELL, Anthea. Freelance translator, specializing in French and German children's books; has translated nearly 100 books. Author of *E. Nesbit,* 1960, and the novels *A London Season,* 1983, and *The Floral Companion,* 1988. **Essays:** Christianna Brand; Anne Fine; Norman Hunter; Ruth Manning-Sanders; Foreign-Language Writers.

BENSON, Linda. Instructor in English, Southwest Missouri State University. **Essays:** Rachel Isadora; Robert Munsch; Taro Yashima.

BIERMAN, Valerie. Organizer, Edinburgh Book Festival Children's Fair; children's book reviewer, the *Scotsman*; co-editor, *Bookmark* magazine. Recipient, Eleanor Farjeon award, 1987. Editor of *Streets Ahead* (stories), 1989. **Essays:** Mairi Hedderwick; Alison Prince.

BOEGEHOLD, Betty. Former senior associate editor, Bank Street College of Education Publications Division, New York. Author of several books for children, including the *Pippa Mouse* series, from 1973, and most recently, *What the Wind Told,* 1987, and of *Choosing Books for Children* (with Joanne Oppenheim and Barbara Brenner), 1986. Died 1985. **Essays:** Eleanor Clymer; Jean Merrill; Evaline Ness.

BOSTIAN, Freida. Essays: Betty Levin; Mary E. Lyons; Gregory Maguire; Mary Rayner.

BOYLE, Bill. Advisory teacher, Wirral Local Education Authority; deputy editor, *Junior Education*; reviewer for the *Guardian, Books for Keeps,* and *School Librarian.* Author of *What's in a Poem?,* 1983, *Your Geography,* 1984, *Local Directories,* 1987, *Evidence Through Maps,* and of "Words Joined Together," a Thames Television poetry documentary. **Essay:** Edward Fenton.

BRADLEY, Patricia. Instructor in English, Western Kentucky University, Bowling Green. **Essay:** Louis Sachar.

BRATTON, J. S. Reader in Theatre and Cultural Studies, Royal Holloway and Bedford New College, University of London. Author of *The Victorian Popular Ballad,* 1975, and *The Impact of Victorian Children's Fiction,* 1981. **Essays:** F.W. Farrar (appendix); L.T. Meade (appendix); Mrs. O.F. Walton (appendix).

BRIGGS, Julia. Fellow and tutor in English, Hertford College, Oxford. Author of *Night Visitors: The Rise and Fall of the English Ghost Story,* 1977, *This Stage-Play World: English Literature and Its Background 1580-1625,* 1983, and *A Woman of Passion: The Life of E. Nesbit,* 1987. **Essay:** Walter de la Mare.

BRINKLEY-WILLSHER, Valerie. Freelance writer and lecturer; reviewer of children's books for several periodicals. Former contributor to *Signal.* Author of *Across Time,* 1973. **Essays:** Pauline Clarke; E.W. Hildick; Katherine Hull and Pamela Whitlock; Elisabeth Kyle; Ann Lawrence; Bessie Marchant; Alison Morgan; Pamela Oldfield; Susan Price; Gwynedd Rae; Rodie Sudbery.

BULL, Angela. See her own entry. **Essays:** Joanna Cannan; Lorna Hill; Josephine Pullein-Thompson; Noel Streatfeild.

BURNS, Mary Mehlman. Coordinator, Curriculum Library, and children's literature specialist, Framington State College, Massachusetts; reviewer, *Horn Book.* Author of an essay on Robert Lawson in *Horn Book,* 1972. **Essay:** Robert Lawson.

BUTLER, Dorothy. Bookseller in Auckland and lecturer. Recipient, Eleanor Farjeon award, 1979. Author of *Cushla and Her Books,* 1979, *Reading Begins at Home* (with Marie Clay), 1979, *Babies Need Books,* 1980, *The Dorothy Butler Pre-Reading Kit,* 1980, *Reading for Enjoyment with 0-6 Year Olds,* 1981, *For Me, Me, Me,* 1983, *I Will Build You a House,* 1984, *Five to Eight,* 1985, and *My Brown Bear Barney,* 1989. Editor of *The Magpies Said* (for children), 1980. **Essays:** Maurice Duggan; E. M. Ellin; Eve Sutton.

BUTLER, Francelia. Professor of English, University of Connecticut, Storrs; founder and editor-in-chief, *Children's Literature.* Founder, seminar on children's literature and permanent Division of Children's Literature, Modern Language Association; member of the founding board, Children's Literature Association. Author of *Children's Literature: A Module,* 1975, *Sharing Literature with Children,* 1977, *Masterworks of Children's Literature 1550-1739,* 1977, *Marxism, Feminism and Free Love* (with Jan Bakker), 1981, *The Lucy Piece* (novel), 1984, *200 Selected Film Classics for Children of All Ages* (with Phillip J. Steeman and Bernard Queenan), 1984, *Indira Gandhi,* 1986, *Skipping Around the World: The Ritual Nature of Folk Rhymes,* 1988, and of books on Shakespeare and 17th-century drama. Editor, with Richard Rotert, of *Reflections on Literature for Children,* 1984, and *Triumphs of the Spirit in Children's Literature,* 1986, and, with Rotert and Anne Devereaux Jordan, of *The Wide World All Around,* 1987. **Essay:** Natalie Savage Carlson.

BUTTS, Dennis. Freelance writer and critic; editor, *Henty Society Bulletin.* Formerly principal lecturer in English, Bulmershe College of Higher Education, Reading, Berkshire. Author of *Living Words* (with John Merrick), 1966, and *R.L. Stevenson,* 1966. Editor of *Pergamon Poets 8,* 1970, *Good Writers for Young Readers: Critical Essays,* 1977, and *The Secret Garden,* 1987. **Essays:** Russell Hoban; W. E. Johns; Frederick Marryat (appendix); Robert Louis Stevenson (appendix); Herbert Strang.

CADOGAN, Mary. Secretary of an educational trust, governor of an international school, and freelance writer. Author of three books on popular literature with Patricia Craig, *You're a Brick, Angela!,* 1976, *Women and Children First,* 1978, *The Lady Investigates,* 1981; also author of three volumes of *The Charles Hamilton Companion* (with John Wernham), 1976-82, *The Morcove Companion* (with Tommy Keen), 1981, *From Wharton Lodge to Linton Hall: The Charles Hamilton Christmas Companion* (with Tommy Keen), 1984, *Richmal Crompton: The Woman Behind William,* 1986, *Frank Richards: The Chap Behind the Chums,* 1988. **Essays:** Gillian Avery; Elinor M. Brent-Dyer; Dorita Fairlie Bruce; Christine Chaundler; Richmal Crompton; Tim Kennemore; Dorothea Moore; Frank Richards; Ethel Talbot; P. L. Travers; May Wynne.

CAMPBELL, Alasdair K.D. Consultant tutor librarian, Education Library, University of Keele, Staffordshire; columnist, "Children, Books, and Reading," *School Librarian.* Author of *Novels with a Background of School,* 1970 (revised as *Novels and Plays with a Background of School,* 1979), and of articles on children's literature and school librarianship in *School Librarian* and other periodicals. **Essays:** John Branfield; Angela Bull; Elizabeth Goudge; Eric Knight; Sylvia Sherry; Katharine Tozer.

CAMPBELL, Margaret. Freelance writer. Author of *Lend a Hand: Social Work for the Young,* 1966, and of articles on Oxfordshire personalities for *Limited Edition,* and articles and reviews for *British Book News, Countryman,* and other periodicals. Editor of *The Countryman Book* series, 3 vols., 1973-75. **Essays:** Val Biro; James Reeves; John Symonds.

CARPENTER, Humphrey. Freelance writer. Author of *J. R. R. Tolkien: A Biography,* 1977, *The Inklings,* 1978, *Jesus,* 1980, *W. H. Auden: A Biography,* 1981, the *Mr. Majeika* series (for children), from 1984, *OUDS: A Centenary History of the Oxford University Dramatic Society,* 1985, *Secret Gardens: The Golden Age of Children's Literature,* 1985, and *A Serious Character: The Life of Ezra Pound,* 1988. Editor of *The Letters of J. R. R. Tolkien,* 1981, and *The Oxford Companion to Children's Literature* (with Mari Prichard), 1984. **Essay:** Thomas Hughes (appendix).

CART, Michael. Former director of California Public Library, Beverly Hills; currently full-time writer and critic of young adult literature. **Essay:** Deborah Nourse Lattimore.

CARTER, Anne. Freelance writer, editor, and translator. **Essays:** Charles Keeping; Graham Oakley; Josephine Poole; Mary Treadgold.

CHANG, Charity. Retired librarian. Author of the preface to the Mary De Morgan volume of *Classics of Children's Literature* and of the bibliography in *Masterworks of Children's Literature 1550-1739* by Francelia Butler, 1977. **Essays:** Carolyn Sherwin Bailey; Eric Kelly; Monica Shannon.

CHASTON, Joel. Associate professor of English, Southwest Missouri State University. Author of *Lois Lowry,* 1997, co-author of *Theme Exploration: A Voyage of Discovery,* 1993, and author of many articles on literature for the young. **Essays:** Mem Fox; David Macauley.

CHRISTIAN, Mary Blount. Instructor of creative writing, Rice University Continuing Studies, Houston; co-founder, Association of Authors of Children's Literature, Houston; creator and moderator, *Children's Bookshelf* television program, Houston; children's books reviewer for Houston *Chronicle* and Houston *Post.* Author of more than 70 fiction and non-fiction books for children, including the *Goosehill Gang, Sebastian,* and *Penrod* series, and most recently, *Singin' Somebody Else's Song,* 1986. **Essay:** Robert Kraus.

CHURCHER, John. Librarian, London Borough of Brent; editor of a NALGO magazine. Author of articles in *Junior Bookshelf.* **Essays:** W. V. Awdry; Padraic Colum; Helen Nicoll.

CLARK, Berna C. Former schools librarian, Bristol Public Libraries, and senior assistant to the County Education/Children's Librarian, Avon County Council. Former national chairman of the Library Association Youth Library Group. **Essays:** Jane Duncan; Antonia Ridge; Jenifer Wayne.

CLEAVER, Pamela. Freelance journalist; tutor, London School of Journalism. Author of *The Sparrow Book of Record Breakers* [and *Animal Records*], 2 vols., 1981-82, and of children's stories for anthologies, annuals, and magazines. **Essay:** Ronald Welch.

COOPER, Ilene L. Reviewer, American Library Association *Booklist,* Chicago; consultant for the American Broadcasting Company. Author of *Susan B. Anthony,* 1984, *The Winning of Miss Lynn Ryan,* 1987, and *Queen of the Sixth Grade,* 1988. Editor, with Denise Murcko Wilms, of *A Guide to Non-Sexist Children's Books 2: 1976-1984,* 1985. **Essay:** Maud Hart Lovelace.

CORBETT, Frank. Essay: Eloise Greenfield.

COSGRAVE, Mary Silva. Former children's librarian and children's books editor for Houghton Mifflin and Pantheon. Former editor of "The Outlook Tower" column in *Horn Book.* **Essays:** Thomas Bailey Aldrich (appendix); Arna Bontemps.

CRAIG, Patricia. Freelance writer. Author of three books on popular literature with Mary Cadogan, *You're a Brick, Angela!,* 1976, *Women and Children First,* 1978, and *The Lady Investigates,* 1981; also author of a biography of Elizabeth Bowen. **Essays:** Lucy Boston; Patricia Lynch; Meta Mayne Reid; Geraldine Symons.

CREANY, Anne Drolett. Associate professor of Education, Clarion University, Clarion, Pennsylvania. Author of articles on censorship, environmental children's literature and gender issues in picture books; storyteller, specializing in multicultural folktales. **Essays:** Allan and Janet Ahlberg; Margaret Hodges; Deborah Nourse Lattimore; Gennedy Spirin.

CREW, Hilary S. Ph.D. candidate, School of Communication, Information, and Library Studies, Rutgers University, New Brunswick, New Jersey. Author of "Blossom Culp and Her Ilk: The Independent Female in Richard Peck's Young Adult Fiction" in *Top of the News,* 1987, and "From Labyrinth to Celestial City: Setting and Portrayal of the Female Adolescent in Science Fiction" in *Youth Services in Libraries,* 1988. **Essays:** Robin McKinley; Richard Peck.

CROUCH, Marcus. Former deputy county librarian, Kent. Author of *Beatrix Potter,* 1960, *Treasure Seekers and Borrowers,* 1962, *The Nesbit Tradition,* 1972, *Kentish Books, Kentish Writers,* 1988, and of several collections of retold tales for children. Editor, with Alec Ellis, of *Chosen for Children* (on the Carnegie Medal), 3rd edition, 1977. **Essays:** Ruth Arthur; Hilaire Belloc; Elisabeth Beresford; Margery Williams Bianco; Quentin Blake; Helen Cresswell; J. G. Fyson; Eric Linklater; Leo Lionni; Jenny Nimmo; Stephanie Plowman; E. V. Rieu.

CROXSON, Mary. Senior lecturer in English, Tutor-in-Charge of Diploma in Professional Studies in Education, and director of the annual summer school in children's literature, Worcester College of Higher Education. Author of *Using the Library,* 1966, and "The Emancipated Child in the Novels of E. Nesbit" in *Signal,* 1974. **Essays:** Walt Morey; C. Everard Palmer.

CULPAN, Norman. Former head of English Department, St. Paul's College of Education, Cheltenham; former review editor, *School Librarian.* Author of *Modern Adult Fiction,* 1955, and *Contemporary Adult Fiction* (with W. J. Messer), 1966. Editor of *Dialogue and Drama* (with James Reeves), 1950, and *Variety Is King: Aspects of Fiction for Children* (with Clifford Waite), 1977. **Essay:** Barbara Euphan Todd.

DAY, Alan Edwin. Head of Department of Library and Information Studies, Manchester Polytechnic. Author of three reference handbooks, *History,* 1976, *Archaeology,* 1977, and *Discovery and Exploration,* 1980; also author of *J. B. Priestley: An Annotated Bibliography,* 1980, *Search for the Northwest Passage: An Annotated Bibliography,* 1986, *The British Library,* 1988, and of an essay on W. E. Johns' Biggles in *Children's Literature in Education,* 1974. **Essays:** Mabel Esther Allan; Richard Church; Samuel Rutherford Crockett; Peter Dawlish; Kathleen Fidler; Roy Fuller; Michael Hardcastle; Ronald Syme; John Verney.

DONAHUE, Rosanne Fraine. Assistant to the vice chancellor for Academic Affairs, University of Massachusetts, Boston. Author of "New Realism in the Twentieth Century," in *Masterworks of Children's Literature,* 1986, and "A Solitary Blue," in *Beacham's Guide to Literature and Biography for Young Adults,* 1989. **Essay:** Betsy Byars.

DONLON, Pat. Former director of the National Library of Ireland, Dublin; vice-president of the Royal Irish Academy; one time lecturer on children's literature at University College Dublin; founding member of Children's Literature Association of Ireland and Irish Children's Book Trust. Editor of *The Lucky Bag: Classic Irish Children's Stories,* 1984, *Children's Books of the Celtic World,* 1988, and *Moon Cradle: Lullabies and Dandling Songs,* 1991. Recipient of the Children's Books Ireland Award for distinguished services to Irish children's literature, 1997. **Essays:** Marita Conlon-McKenna; Margrit Cruickshank; Maeve Friel; Sam McBratney; Éilís Ní Dhuibhne; Eileen O'Faolain; Pat O'Shea; Siobhan Parkinson; John Quinn.

DOONAN, Jane. Freelance teacher, reviewer, and writer. Author of several articles on picture books and picture-book artists/writers. **Essays:** Anthony Browne; Tony Ross.

DOYLE, Brian. Freelance writer, contributor to the *Guardian, Books and Bookmen,* and *Collector's Digest.* Author of *The Who's Who of Boys' Writers and Illustrators,* 1964, and *The Who's Who of Children's Literature,* 1968. **Essay:** Talbot Baines Reed (appendix).

DUNBAR, Robert. Lecturer in English, Church of Ireland College of Education, Dublin; founding member, Children's Literature Association of Ireland; children's book reviewer for the *Times Educational Supplement, School Librarian,* and the *Irish Times.* **Essay:** J. S. Andrews.

du SAUTOY, Peter. Former chairman of Faber and Faber Ltd., London. Author of *Alison Uttley: The Life of a Country Child,* 1986. **Essay:** Alison Uttley.

EAGLEN, Audrey. Order Department manager, Cuyahoga County Public Library, Cleveland; assistant professor, Kent State University, Kent, Ohio; contributing editor, *Collection Building*; columnist, *School Library Journal*; reviewer, *New York Times Book Review* and other journals. Author of *Buying Books: A Practical Guide for Librarians,* 1989. **Essay:** Judy Blume.

ELKIN, Judith. Freelance writer, lecturer, and children's books reviewer. Former head of library services to children and young people, Birmingham Public Libraries. Recipient, Eleanor Farjeon award, 1986. Author of *Multi-Racial Books for the Classroom,* 1980, *Nowhere to Play* (English text), 1982, *The Hiroshima Story,* 1983, *Mighty Mountain and the Three Strong Women,* 1984, *The Books for Keeps Guide to Children's Books for a Multicultural Society 8-12,* 1985, and *Japanese Family* (A Family in Japan), 1986. Editor of *The New Golden Land Anthology,* 1983. **Essays:** John Cunliffe; Marjorie Darke.

ELLEMAN, Barbara. Distinguished scholar of children's books, Marquette University, Milwaukee; creator and editor-in-chief, *Book Links: Connecting Books, Libraries, and Classrooms*; former editor, Children's Books Section, American Library Association's *Booklist,* Chicago. Author of *Tomie dePaola, His Art and His Stories,* 1999. **Essays:** Tomie dePaola; Constance C. Greene; Paul Zelinsky.

ELLIS, Anne W. Assistant librarian, Liverpool Institute of Higher Education. Author of *The Family Story in the 1960's,* 1970. **Essays:** Eric Allen; Pamela Brown; Antonia Forest; Eleanor Graham; Laurence Meynell; Sheena Porter.

ELLIS, Sarah. Librarian, North Vancouver District Library; columnist for *Horn Book.* Author of a children's novel *The Baby Project (The Family Project),* 1986. **Essay:** Sue Ann Alderson.

ENGLAND, A. W. Former lecturer in drama, Division of Education, University of Sheffield. Author of *Scripted Drama: A Practical Guide to Teaching Techniques,* 1981, the forthcoming *Theatre for the Young,* and of two television plays for children, television and stage adaptations of works by Sylvia Sherry and Bernard Ashley, several radio plays, and an article on Walter Macken in *Use of English.* Editor of *Man and Superman* by Shaw, 1969, and of the anthologies *Looking at Scenes,* 1969, *Two Ages of Man,* 1971, *Caves,* 1973, and *Islands,* 1974. **Essay:** Walter Macken.

ENGLAND, Clarie. Associate professor of library and information science, University of Toronto. Author with Adele M. Fasick, *Children Using Media,* 1977, *ChildView: Evaluating and Reviewing Materials for Children,* 1987, and of articles on children's literature. **Essays:** Horatio Alger (appendix); Palmer Cox (appendix).

ERISMAN, Fred. Professor of literature, Texas Christian University, Fort Worth. Author of *Frederic Remington,* 1975, *Barnbroken i USA* (with Zena Sutherland), 1986, and of articles on L. Frank Baum, Ralph Henry Barbour, Kate Douglas Wiggin, Howard Garis, Laura Ingalls Wilder, and Robert A. Heinlein. Editor, with Richard Etulain, of *Fifty Western Writers: A Bio-Bibliographical Sourcebook,* 1982. **Essays:** Mary O'Hara; Jack Schaefer.

EVANS, Gwyneth. Instructor, Malaspina University College, Vancouver Island, British Columbia. Contributor to *Canadian Children's Literature, Canadian Children's Literature,* and *The Lion and the Unicorn.* **Essays:** Quentin Blake; Margaret Buffie; Emma Chichester Clark; Rumer Godden; Sheryl McFarlane; Tony Ross; Tim Wynne-Jones.

FADER, Ellen G. Head of children's services, Westport Public Library, Connecticut; reviewer for *School Library Journal* and *Horn Book.* **Essay:** Edward Ormondroyd.

FASICK, Adele M. Professor of library science, University of Toronto. Author, with Claire England, of *Children Using Media,* 1977, and *ChildView: Evaluating and Reviewing Materials for Children,* 1987; also author of *What Should Libraries Do for Children?* Contributor of articles on Anne Carroll Moore, film adaptations of books for children, and children's librarianship. **Essay:** Betty Levin.

FICK, Martha J. Employee of computer software company in Chadds Ford, Pennsylvania. **Essays:** Peggy Parish; Bernard Waber; Gene Zion.

FITZGIBBON, Tom. Principal lecturer and head of department of English, School of Primary and Early Childhood Education, Auckland College of Education. Founder, New Zealand Children's Literature Association. Author of various articles and reviews and co-editor of two books on New Zealand writers and illustrators. **Essays:** R. L. Bacon; Joy Cowley; Anne de Roo; William Taylor; Joyce West.

FLANAGAN, Sheila. Librarian, Carysfort College, Blackrock, County Dublin. Former lecturer in children's librarianship. **Essays:** Tom McCaughren; Michael Mullen; Matthew Sweeney.

FORDYCE, Rachel. Associate professor of English, Virginia Polytechnic and State University, Blacksburg; contributing editor, *Children's Literature.* Author of *Children's Literature and Creative Dramatics,* 1975, *Caroline Drama: A Biliographic History of Criticism,* 1978, and *Lewis Carroll: A Reference Guide,* 1988. **Essays:** Alice Dalgliesh; Rachel Field; Joanna Halpert Kraus; Bill Peet; Louis Slobodkin.

FOX, Geoff. Senior lecturer, Exeter University School of Education; joint editor, *Children's Literature in Education,* and Collins Cascades series; regular contributor, *Times Educational Supplement.* Author of *Teaching Literature: Nine to Fourteen* (with Michael Benton), 1985. Editor, with Graham Hammond, of *Writers, Critics and Children,* 1976, and *Responses to Children's Literature,* 1980. **Essay:** C. Day Lewis.

FREEMAN, Gillian. Novelist, screenwriter, and journalist. Author of 12 novels—the most recent being *Love Child,* 1984, and *Termination Rock,* 1989—and of *The Undergrowth of Literature,* 1967, and *The Schoolgirl Ethic: The Life and Work of Angela Brazil,* 1976. **Essays:** Angela Brazil; Susan Coolidge (appendix).

FRYATT, Norma R. Freelance writer and editor. Author of *Sarah Josepha Hale,* 1976. Editor of *A Horn Book Sampler,* 1959. **Essay:** Lucy Fitch Perkins.

FUCHS, Marcia G. See **WELSH, Marcia.**

GIBLIN, James Cross. Editor and publisher, Clarion Books, New York. Author of *The Scarecrow Book* (with Dale Ferguson), 1980, *The Skyscraper Book,* 1981, *Chimney Sweeps: Yesterday and Today,* 1982, *Fireworks, Picnics, and Flags: The Story of the Fourth of July Symbols,* 1983, *Walls: Defenses Throughout History,* 1984, *The Truth about Santa Claus,* 1985, *Milk: The Fight for Purity,* 1986, *From Hand to Mouth, or, How We Invented Knives, Forks, Spoons, and Chopsticks and the Table Manners to Go with Them,* 1987, *Let There Be Light: A Book about Windows,* 1988, *Writing Books for Young People,* 1989; also author of articles on children's book writing and publishing. **Essays:** Beatrice Schenk de Regniers; Alvin Tresselt; Jan Wahl.

GIBSON, Lois Rauch. Professor of English and chair of the Department of Language and Literature, Coker College, Hartsville, South Carolina; contributor to various anthologies, journals, and reference books, including *Children's Literature Association Quarterly, Dictionary of Literary Biography,* and *Twentieth Century Young Adult Writers.* **Essay:** Ann Jonas.

GILDERDALE, Betty. Former lecturer in English, and lecturer in Continuing Education Department, Auckland University; reviewer, *New Zealand Herald*; editor, Hodder and Stoughton Kotare series of New Zealand children's classics; New Zealand editor, *Phaedrus.* Founding member and past president of the New Zealand Children's Literature Association. Author of *A Sea Change: 145 Years of New Zealand Junior Fiction,* 1982, *Introducing Margaret Mahy,* 1987, and *The Seven Lives of Lady Barker,* 1996; contributor, *The Oxford History of New Zealand Literature,* 1991, *Children's Literature: An Illustrated History,* 1995, and *Encyclopedia of Children's Literature,* 1996; author of several books for children. **Essays:** Ruth Dallas; Joan de Hamel; David Hill; Lynley Dodd; Gaelyn Gordon; Edith Howes; Sherryl Jordan; Caroline Macdonald; Margaret Mahy; Diana Noonan; Lilith Norman; Phyl Wardell.

GLOVER, Michael. Freelance writer and editor; reviewer, *Books and Bookmen, British Book News, P.N. Review,* the *Melbourne Age,* the *Observer,* and *School Librarian.* **Essays:** Charles Causley; Vernon Scannell; Kit Wright.

GMUCA, Jacqueline L. Assistant professor of English, University of South Carolina-Coastal Carolina College, Conway. Author of entry on Arnold Lobel in *Dictionary of Literary Biography.* **Essays:** Anita Lobel; Arnold Lobel; Cynthia Rylant.

GORDON, Cecilia. Librarian in London schools for 10 years, and Inner London Education Authority library organizer, 1972-76. Former national chairwoman of School Library Association. Author of *Resource Organization,* 1978, and of an article in *Teenage Reading,* 1979, and reviews in *Times Educational Supplement, Times Literary Supplement, Children's Book Review,* and *School Librarian.* **Essays:** Joseph E. Chipperfield; Janet McNeill.

GOUGH, John. Lecturer in Mathematics Education, Victoria College, Malvern, Victoria. Author of several articles on children's literature, including "The Dark is Rising: An Assessment" in *English in Education,* 1985, and "Reconsidering Judy Blume's Young Adult Novel *Forever*" in *Use of English,* 1985. **Essays:** Crosby Bonsall; William Corlett; Russell Hoban; Christobel Mattingley; Martin Waddell.

GREAVES, Margaret. See her own entry. **Essays:** Joyce Gard; Nicholas Stuart Gray; Rosemary Harris; Margery Sharp; Rosemary Weir.

GREEN, Roger Lancelyn. See his own entry. **Essays:** Lewis Carroll (appendix); Rudyard Kipling; Andrew Lang (appendix).

GREGORY, Lucille. Freelance writer and consultant. **Essay:** Angela Johnson.

GROFF, Patrick. Professor of education, San Diego State University; contributing editor, Chircorel Library Publishing Corporation. Author of *A New Look at Children's Literature* (with William D. Anderson), 1972, *Private Sector Alternatives for Preventing Reading Failure,* 1987, *Word Recognition* (with Dorothy Z. Seymour), 1987; contributor of articles to *Elementary English, Horn Book, School Librarian,* and other periodicals. **Essays:** Robert Bright; Carolyn Haywood; William Lipkind; Helen Sewell; Esphyr Slobodkina; William Jay Smith.

HAAS, Irene. Freelance illustrator; has illustrated books by Sesyle Joslin, Elizabeth Enright, Myra Cohn Livingston, and others. Author of *The Maggie B,* 1975, and *The Little Moon Theatre,* 1981. **Essay:** Elizabeth Enright.

HADLEY, Eric. Lecturer in education, South Glamorgan Institute of Higher Education, Cardiff. Author, with Tessa Hadley, of *Legends of the Sun and Moon,* 1983, and *Legends of Earth, Air, Fire and Water,* 1985, and of *English in the Middle Years,* 1985, and *Ivan the Fool and Other Plays,* 1988. Editor of *Teaching Practice and the Probationary Year,* 1982. **Essay:** Allan Ahlberg.

HALL, Dennis. Freelance journalist. Former children's librarian, Public Library of South Australia, Adelaide, and assistant editor, *School Magazine.* **Essay:** Norman Lindsay.

HAMLEY, Dennis. University instructor, Hertfordshire; school librarian; reviewer, *School Librarian* and *Times Educational Supplement.* Author of children's books. **Essays:** John Gordon; Michael Rosen; Gina Wilson.

HAMMOND, Graham. Lecturer, Exeter University School of Education; joint editor, *Children's Literature in Education.* Editor, with Geoff Fox, of *Writers, Critics and Children,* 1976, and *Responses to Children's Literature,* 1980, and, with Andrew Wilkison, *Language for Learning,* 1977. **Essays:** Roger Lancelyn Green; Madeleine A. Polland.

HAMMOND, Nancy C. Freelance writer; guest reviewer, *Horn Book.* Co-author of *Helping Young Children Learn,* 1976. **Essays:** Mary Chalmers; James Flora.

HANNIGAN, Jane Anne. Professor emerita, Columbia University, New York; editor, *The Best of Library Literature.* Author and editor of numerous articles and books. **Essays:** Bill Brittain; Eleanor Coerr; James Howe.

HARVEY, Anne. Freelance writer, broadcaster, actress, and drama specialist. Author of *Jewels,* 1981, *A Present for Nellie,* 1982, and of radio programmes on Edward Thomas, Eleanor Farjeon, Noel Streatfeild, and World War I women's literature. Editor of *Scenes for Two,* 1968, *Solo,* 1973, *Take Two,* 1981, *Poets in Hand,* 1985, *Of Caterpillars, Cats and Cattle,* 1987, *In Time of War,* 1987, *Something I Remember* (poetry of Eleanor Farjeon), 1987, and *A Picnic of Poetry,* 1988. **Essay:** Eleanor Farjeon.

HAY, Ann G. Teacher and librarian. **Essays:** Enid Bagnold; Dorothy Clewes; Lettice Cooper; W. J. Corbett; Rose Fyleman; Robert Newman; Barbara Softly; Margaret Storey; D. J. Watkins-Pitchford.

HAYNES, Renée. Freelance writer and critic; vice-president, Society for Psychical Research. Author of three early novels, and of *Pan, Caesar, and God,* 1938, *Hilaire Belloc,* 1953, *The Hidden Springs,* 1961, *Philosopher King,* 1973, *The Seeing Eye, The Seeing I,* 1976, and *The Society for Psychical Research 1882-1982,* 1982; also author of postscript to *Roots of Coincidence* by Arthur Koestler. Contributor of articles to many current periodicals. **Essays:** J. B. S. Haldane; Naomi Mitchison.

HEBLEY, Diane. Freelance writer and part-time teacher. Regular columnist on children's books for *New Zealand Listener,* 1985-88. Author of bibliography *Off the Shelf: Twenty-One Years of New Zealand Books for Children,* 1980, and of the children's books *A Is for Albatross,* 1981, *High on a Hilltop,* 1984, *The Gully That Gabriel Found,* 1985, *Jack Mackenzie and His Dog,* 1986, and *The Ballad of Young Nick: How He Sailed with Captain Cook,* 1987. Contributor of articles to *Landfall* and other periodicals. **Essays:** Maurice Gee; Jack Lasenby; Elsie Locke.

HEEKS, Peggy. Library consultant. Author of *Choosing and Using Books in the First School,* 1981, *Library Adult Education,* 1982, *Ways of Knowing,* 1983, *Information Providers in the School Library Field,* 1988, and *School Libraries on the Move,* 1988. Editor, with Paul Turner, of *Public Library Aims and Objectives,* 1981. **Essays:** Roy Brown; Mary Cockett; Geraldine Kaye; Rosemary Manning.

HELSON, Ravenna. Research psychologist, Institute of Personality Assessment and Research, University of California, Berkeley. Author of 15 articles on authors and critics of children's literature, the most recent being "Challenger and Upholder Syndromes in Critics" in *Journal of Personality and Social Psychology,* 1980, "Critics and Their Texts: An Approach to Jung's Theory of Cognition and Personality" in *Journal of Personality and Social Psychology,* 1982, and "E. Nesbit's Forty-First Year: Her Life, Times, and Symbolizations of Personality Growth" in *Imagination, Personality, and Cognition,* 1984. **Essays:** Scott Corbett; Edward Eager.

HENDRICKSON, Linnea. Part-time teacher, College of Education, University of New Mexico. Author of *Children's Literature: A Guide to the Criticism,* 1987; also author of numerous articles on children's literature. **Essays:** Erik Blegvad; Lois Ehlert; Thatcher Hurd; Trina Schart Hyman; Petra Mathers; Laurence Pringle; Vera B. Williams.

HIGGINS, James E. Professor of education, Queens College, City University of New York. Author of *Beyond Words: Mystical Fancy in Children's Literature,* 1970. **Essays:** Ann Nolan Clark; Marie Hall Ets; Marguerite Henry; Robert McCloskey; H. A. and Margaret Rey; Mark Twain (appendix).

HILL, Elbert R. Professor of children's and adolescent literature, Southeastern Oklahoma State University, Durant. Contributor, *Beacham's Guide to Literature for Young Adults*; author of "A Hero for the Movies," in *Children's Novels and the Movies.* **Essay:** Allen Say.

HIXON, Martha. Ph.D. in English, University of Southwestern Louisiana, 1997. **Essay:** William Brooke.

HOLLINDALE, Peter. Senior lecturer in English and education, University of York; general editor of the Macmillan Shakespeare series. Author of *Choosing Books for Children,* 1974, and *Ideology and the Children's Book,* 1988. **Essays:** David Line; Jenny Overton; Ruth Tomalin; Philip Turner.

HORNE, Jackie. Freelance writer, Cambridge, Massachusetts. **Essays:** W. J. Corbett; Joy Cowley; Jean Little; David McKee; Josephine Poole; Jack Prelutsky; Martin Waddell; Nancy Willard.

HOYLE, Karen Nelson. Curator of the Kerlan Collection, Walter Library, University of Minnesota, Minneapolis. Author of *Girls Series Books 1900-1975* and *Danish Children's Literature in English: A Bibliography,* 1982. **Essays:** Helen Dore Boylston; Edgar and Ingri Parin d'Aulaire; Aileen Fisher; Jim Kjelgaard; Eleanor Lattimore; Mary Rodgers; Glen Rounds; Sydney Taylor; Eve Titus.

HUNT, Caroline C. Member of Department of English, College of Charleston, South Carolina. Contributor of numerous articles to various publications, including *Beacham's Guide to Literature for Young Adults* and *Dictionary of Literary Biography.* **Essays:** Helen Cresswell; Buchi Emecheta; Erik Haugaard; Shirley Hughes; Jim Murphy; Philippa Pearce; Christine Pullein-Thompson; Catherine Storr.

HUNT, Peter. See his own entry. **Essay:** David Rees.

INGLIS, Fred. Reader in education, University of Bristol. Author of *The Imagery of Power,* 1972, *Ideology and Imagination,* 1975, *The Name of the Game: Sport and Industrial Society,* 1977, *The Promise of Happiness: Value and Meaning in Children's Fiction,* 1981, *Radical Earnestness: English Social Theory 1880-1980,* 1982, *The Management of Ignorance: A Political Theory of the Curriculum,* 1985, and *Popular Culture and Political Power,* 1988. **Essay:** Catherine Storr.

JACKSON, Clara O. Former professor at Kent State University, Kent, Ohio. Died 1987. **Essays:** Holling C. Holling; Ruth Sawyer.

JENKINSON, David H. Associate dean, Faculty of Education, University of Manitoba, Winnipeg. Author of essays in *Profiles* and *Meeting the Challenge:* contributor to *The Junior Encyclopedia of Canada* and *Twentieth-Century Children's Writers*; editor of electronic reviewing journal *CM.* **Essays:** Michael Bedard; Dennis Foon; Bernice Thurman Hunter; Gordon Korman; Cora Taylor.

JENNINGS, Coleman A. Professor and chairman, Department of Drama, University of Texas, Austin. Author of the children's play *The Honorable Urashima Taro,* the handbook *Creative Dramatics K-Grade 6,* and a doctoral thesis on Aurand Harris. Editor of *Six Plays for Children* by Aurand Harris, 1977, and, with Harris, of *Plays Children Love,* 2 vols., 1981-88. **Essay:** Aurand Harris.

JONES, Patrick. Manager, Tecumseh Branch, Allen County Public Library, Fort Wayne Indiana. **Essays:** Elizabeth Levy; Jon Scieszka.

JONES, Raymond E. Assistant professor of English, University of Alberta, Edmonton. Author of *Characters in Children's Literature,* 1997, and co-author of *Canadian Books for Children,* 1988; author of many articles on children's writers. **Essays:** Martyn Godfrey; Jan Hudson; Tololwa M. Mollel; sean ohuigan.

JONES, Ursula M. Actress. Former resident director, Unicorn Theatre for Young People, London. Author of several plays for children. **Essays:** Mary Melwood; Olwen Wymark.

JULEUS, Nels. Professor of speech and drama, Allegheny College, Meadville, Pennsylvania. Author of *Perspectives on Public Speaking,* 1966, *Laughter on the Hill,* 1979; contributor of articles on James Otis's *Toby Tyler,* Noah Webster, the circus, and language to *Horn Book* and other periodicals. **Essay:** James Otis (appendix).

KAYE, Marilyn. Associate professor, Division of Library and Information Science, St. John's University, New York. Author of several children's books, including the *Sisters* series, 5 vols., 1987-89, *No Boys Allowed!,* 1989, and *Camp Sunnyside Friends,* 2 vols., 1989; contributor of articles and reviews to *New York Times Book Review, School Library Journal,* and *Top of the News.* Editor, with Betsy Hearne, of *Celebrating Children's Books,* 1981. **Essay:** Arnold Adoff.

KEENAN, Hugh T. Associate professor of English, Georgia State University, Atlanta. Author of articles on Old English, Middle English, children's literature, and Joel Chandler Harris. Editor of *Papers by Medievalists,* 1971, *Typology and Medieval Literature,* 1975, "Narrative Theory and Children's Literature" issue of *Studies in the Literary Imagination,* 1985, and *Joel Chandler Haris: The Writer in His Time and Ours,* 1986. **Essay:** James Marshall.

KELLY, R. Gordon. Chairman of the Department of American Studies, University of Maryland, College Park. Author of *Mother Was a Lady: Self and Society in Selected American Children's Periodicals 1865-1890,* 1974. Editor of *Children's Periodicals of the United States,* 1984. **Essays:** Mary Mapes Dodge (appendix); Lucretia P. Hale (appendix); Frank R. Stockton (appendix).

KEMP, Edward. Acquisitions librarian, University of Oregon, Eugene. Editor of a series of bio-bibliographies of children's writers and illustrators for *Imprint: Oregon,* and compiler of the bibliographies of James Daugherty and Berta and Elmer Hader. **Essays:** C. W. Anderson; James Daugherty.

KHORANA, Meena. Associate professor, Coppin State College, Baltimore. Author of *Children's Literature: An International Module,* 1984, "Apartheid in South African Children's Fiction," 1987, "Traditions and Modernity: A Re-Discovery of India," 1989, and a forthcoming annotated bibliography of children's literature of the Indian sub-continent. **Essay:** Ruskin Bond.

KIMMEL, Eric A. Professor of education, Portland State University, Oregon. Author of picture books and children's stories, the most recent being *Anansi and the Moss-Covered Rock,* 1988, *The Chanukkah Tree,* 1988, and *Charlie Drives the Stage,* 1989, and of articles and reviews for *Horn Book* and *Cricket.* **Essays:** Charles Boardman Hawes; Jamake Highwater; Steven Kellogg; Shel Silverstein; Isaac Bashevis Singer.

KINGMAN, Lee. See her own entry. **Essays:** Virginia Lee Burton; Howard Pyle (appendix).

KINGSTON, Carolyn T. Freelance writer. Author of *The Tragic Mode in Children's Literature,* 1974; contributor of several articles for the *Christian Science Monitor.* Died 1987. **Essays:** Claire Huchet Bishop; Meindert De Jong.

KLEIN, Gillian. Multicultural resources librarian, Inner London Education Authority; founder editor of *Multicultural Teaching.* Author of *Reading into Racism: Bias in Children's Literature and Learning Materials,* 1985, *School Libraries for Multicultural Awareness, Agenda for Multicultural Teaching,* 1986, and of books for children and numerous articles on literary criticism and education. **Essay:** David McKee.

KNIGHT, Judson. Freelance writer, Atlanta, Georgia. **Essays:** Sid Fleishman; Jean Fritz; Rosemary Harris; Karla Kuskin; Phyllis Reynolds Naylor; Faith Ringgold; Marjorie Weinman Sharmat; Barbara Softly; Hilda Van Stockum; Judith Viorst.

LAFFERTY, Fiona. Freelance editor and writer. Former editor of *British Book News Children's Books*; children's books editor of *The Daily Telegraph*; advisor to *Good Book Guide* and compiler of the annual *Good Book Guide to Children's Books.* **Essays:** Jonathan Allen; Ian Beck; Malorie Blackman; Tony Bradman; Teresa Breslin; Ruth Brown; John Burningham; Nick Butterworth; Gus Clarke; Babette Cole; Penny Dale; Morris Gleitzman; Mary Hoffman; Hilary McKay; Hiawyn Oram; Sylvia Waugh.

LANES, Selma G. Freelance writer. Author of *Down the Rabbit Hole: Adventures and Misadventures in the Realm of Children's Literature,* 1971 (revised 1976), *The Art of Maurice Sendak,* 1980, *Lillian Gish: An Actor's Life for Me!,* 1980, and of many articles in *New York Times Book Review, Atlantic, Harper's, Geo,* and other periodicals. Adapter of *A Child's First Book of Nursery Tales,* 1983. **Essays:** Gyo Fujikawa; Maurice Sendak; Cyndy Szekeres; Arthur Yorinks.

LAWRENCE, Keith. Associate professor, American Literature, Brigham Young University, Provo, Utah. Author of articles on early American narratives and contemporary Asian American literature. **Essays:** Anita Desai; Shizuye Takashima; Yoshiko Uchida; Paul Yee.

LAZIM, Anne. Librarian, Centre for Language in Primary Education, London. Chair of the British Section of the International Board on Books for Young People (IBBY). **Essays:** Anne Fine; Jacqueline Wilson.

LEESON, Robert. See his own entry. **Essay:** Jacqueline Wilson.

LEVSTIK, Linda S. Associate professor, University of Kentucky, Lexington. Author of articles on children's literature, including "Coming to Terms with History: Historical Narrativity and the Young Reader," 1989, and "A Gift of Time: Historical Fiction" in *Weaving Charlotte's Web: Essays on Children's Literature* edited by J. Hickman and B. Cullinan, 1989. **Essays:** John and Patricia Beatty; Mary Q. Steele.

LEWIS, Claudia. Teacher of children's literature and publication consultant, Bank Street College of Education. New York. Author of several children's books, including *When I Go to the Moon,* 1961, *Poems of Earth and Space,* 1967, *Up and Down the River: Boat Poems,* 1979, and *Long Ago in Oregon,* 1987, and of *Writing for Young Children,* 1954 (revised 1981), and *A Big Bite of the World: Children's Creative Writing,* 1979. **Essays:** Ludwig Bemelmans; Lucille Clifton; David McCord; John Steptoe; Taro Yashima.

LEWIS, Naomi. Writer, critic, and broadcaster. Recipient, Eleanor Farjeon award, 1974. Author of *A Visit To Mrs. Wilcox,* 1957, *Fantasy Books for Children,* 1975 (revised 1977), books for children, including *Once Upon a Rainbow,* 1981, *Come with Us,* 1982, *A Mouse's Tail,* 1983, *Wedding Birds,* 1986, and *The Stepsister,* 1987, several retellings of fairytales, including, most recently, *The Flying Trunk and Other Stories from Andersen,* 1986, *Stories from the Arabian Nights,* 1987, and *Cry Wolf and Other Aesop Fables,* 1988, and *Proud Knight, Fair Lady: The Twelve Lais of Marie de France,* 1989, and of introductory essays to works on or by Hans Christian Andersen, E. Nesbit, Christina Rossetti, Arthur Waley, and others; contributor to the *Observer, New Statesman, Times Literary Supplement, Listener,* and other periodicals. Editor of *A Peculiar Music: Poems for Young Readers* by Emily Brontë, 1971, *The Silent Playmate: A Collection of Doll Stories,* 1979, and the anthologies *A Footprint on the Air,* 1983, and *Messages,* 1985. **Essays:** Chester Aaron; J. M. Barrie; Kenneth Grahame; G.D. Griffiths; Helen Griffiths; Jean Ingelow (appendix); Richard Jefferies (appendix); C. S. Lewis; Jean Morris; William Nicholson; James Stevenson; Jean Webster; Laura Ingalls Wilder; Henry Williamson.

LICKTEIG, Mary J. Professor, Department of Teacher Education, University of Nebraska, Omaha. Author of *An Introduction to Children's Literature,* 1975. **Essays:** Berta and Elmer Hader; Alfred Slote.

LIVINGSTON, Myra Cohn. See her own entry. **Essays:** Harry Behn; John Ciardi; Randall Jarrell; X. J. Kennedy; Maud and Miska Pertersham; Jack Prelutsky; Valerie Worth.

LUKENS, Rebecca J. Professor of English, Miami University, Oxford, Ohio. Author of *A Critical Handbook of Children's Literature,* 1976 (revised 1982, 1986); contributor of articles and reviews to many periodicals. **Essays:** Will James; Gene Stratton Porter; Ester Wier.

LYSTAD, Mary. Former research sociologist, National Institute of Mental Health, Washington, D.C. Author of *A Child's World,* 1974, *From Dr. Mather to Dr. Seuss: 200 Years of American Booksfor Children,* 1980, *At Home in America,* 1982, and several books for children. **Essays:** Jim Aylesworth; Leonard Baskin; Norman Bridwell; Ashley Bryan; Ben Lucien Burman; Patricia Lee Gauch; Nikki Giovanni; Nikki Grimes; Mary Ann Hoberman; Jesse Jackson; Emily Arnold McCully; Gerald McDermott; Stephen W. Meader; Anne Parrish; Howard Pease; Brian Pinkney; Charlotte Pomerantz; Peggy Rathmann; Julia Sauer; Uri Shulevitz; Peter Spier; Hilda Van Stockum; David Wiesner; David Wisniewski.

MacCANN, Donnarae. Freelance consultant and writer of children's books. Former librarian in Los Angeles, and faculty member at University of California, Los Angeles, University of Kansas, Lawrence, Virginia Polytechnic and State University, Blacksburg, and University of Iowa, Iowa City. Author of *The Child's First Books: A Critical Study of Pictures and Texts* (with Olga Richard), 1973. Editor, with Gloria Woodard, of *The Black American in Books for Children: Readings in Racism,* 1972 (revised 1985), and *Cultural Conformity in Books for Children: Further Readings in Racism,* 1977. **Essays:** Joyce Hansen; Virginia Kahl; Richard Kennedy; Sterling North; Dr. Seuss.

MacLENNAN, Alexandra. Freelance writer, Toronto, Canada; former professor, Seneca College of A.A.&T. **Essays:** Michael Bedard; Margaret Buffie; Gordon Korman; Cheryl McFarlane; Cora Taylor; Paul Yee.

MacLEOD, Anne Scott. Professor, College of Library and Information Services, University of Maryland, College Park. President, International Research Society for Children's Literature, 1985-89. Author of *A Moral Tale: Children's Fiction and American Culture 1820-1869,* 1975; contributor of articles on 19th- and 20th-century children's literature to *Children's Literature in Education, Harvard Education Review, Library Quarterly, Phaedrus,* and other periodicals. **Essays:** Natalie Babbitt; Crockett Johnson; Lois Lenski; Laura E. Richards; William O. Steele; Albert Payson Terhune; Kate Douglas Wiggin.

MANDER, Gertrud. Freelance writer and translator; arts correspondent for several German-language newspapers and magazines. Author of books on Shaw, Shakespeare's contemporaries, Molière, and Giraudoux in a German series on dramatists, and of two biographies. Translator of fiction and books on film and psychiatry. **Essays:** Ezra Jack Keats; Judith Kerr.

MARSH, Gwen. Children's books editor for Harrap and Dent publishers, 1958-76. Author of the novels *French Greeting,* 1944, and *Land of No Strangers,* 1950, and of the children's play *The King of the Coast,* 1969. Translator of more than 20 books by René Guillot, from 1952, and many German picture books. **Essays:** Richard Armstrong; Arthur Catherall; Joyce Stranger; Lorna Wood.

MARSHALL, Margaret R. Freelance writer, lecturer, and consultant on children's books. Former senior lecturer in children's literature and librarianship, Leeds Polytechnic. Recipient, Eleanor Farjeon award, 1980. Author of *Libraries and Literature for Teenagers,* 1975, *Each According to His Ability: Books for the Mentally Handicapped Child,* 1976, *Seeing Clear,* 1977, (2nd edition, 1985), *Libraries and the Handicapped Child,* 1980, *Parents and the Handicapped Child,* 1982, *Public Library Service to Teenagers in Britain,* 1982, *An Introduction to the World of Children's Books,* 1982, (2nd edition, 1988), *Mike,* 1983, *Jane* series, 1985, *Towards Excellence,* 1985, *Handicapped Children and Books,* 1986, and *The Right Stuff: Books for the Young Adult Collection,* 1987. **Essays:** Eric Carle; Fiona French.

MATHIS, Janelle. Professor of English, University of North Texas, Denton. **Essays:** Aliki; George Ancona; Demi; Gail Gibbons; William Hooks; Andrea Pinkney; Michael Rosen; Ann Turner.

MAXWELL, Margaret F. Professor, Graduate Library School, University of Arizona, Tucson. Author of *Shaping a Library: William L. Clements as Collector,* 1973, *Handbook for AACR2: Explaining and Illustrating Anglo-American Cataloguing Rules,* 1980 (revised edition, 1989), and *A Passion for Freedom: The Life of Sharlot Hall,* 1982. Editor, with Donald C. Dickinson and W. David Laird, of *Voices from the Southwest,* 1976. **Essays:** Betty Baker; N. M. Bodecker; Mabel Leigh Hunt; Karla Kuskin; Marjorie Weinman Sharmat.

MAY, Jill P. Associate professor, Purdue University, West Lafayette, Indiana; president, 1989, and publications chair, 1983-89, Children's Literature Association; member of board of directors, Modern Language Association. Editor of *Children and Their Literature: A Readings Book,* 1983, and, with Perry Nodelman, *Festschrift: A Ten Year Retrospective,* 1983. **Essay:** Lloyd Alexander.

McCLURE, Amy. Professor of Education and director of Elementary Education at Ohio Wesleyan University. Author of *Sunrises and Songs, Reading and Writing Poetry in the Elementary Classroom, Books that Invite Talk, Wonder, and Play,* and *Inviting Children's Responses to Literature,* as well as numerous articles and book chapters. Past president of the Children's Literature Assembly and the Children's Literature and Reading SIG of the International Reading Association. Winner of several awards for both teaching and research.

McCORD, David. See his own entry. **Essays:** Charles G. D. Roberts; Elizabeth Madox Roberts; James Thurber; Eliza Orne White.

McDONNELL, Christine. Teacher in Brookline, Massachusetts. Author of five books for children—*Don't Be Mad, Ivy,* 1981, *Toad Food and Measle Soup,* 1982, *Lucky Charms and Birthday Wishes,* 1984, *Count Me In,* 1986, and *Just for the Summer,* 1987—and of articles in *Horn Book.* **Essays:** Else Miniarik; Donald J. Sobol.

McDOWELL, Myles. Deputy headmaster, Holmfield High School, Halifax, Yorkshire. Author of "Fiction for Children and Adults: Some Essential Differences" in *Writers, Critics and Children,* 1976. **Essays:** Margaret Greaves; Aaron Judah; A. C. Stewart.

McGRATH, Joan. Library consultant, Toronto Board of Education; book review editor, *Reviewing Librarian.* Columnist for *In Review* and *Emergency Librarian,* and reviewer for Toronto *Star, Quill and Quire, Canadian Materials, Reviewing Librarian,* and *Canadian Book Review Annual.* Contributor to *Twentieth-Century Romance and Historical Writers, Growing with Books,* and *Writers on Writing.* **Essays:** Oliver Butterworth; Marguerite de Angeli; Mary Alice Downie; Lee Kingman; E. L. Konigsburg; Munro Leaf; Keith Robertson; Miriam Schlein; Virginia Sorenson; Armstrong Sperry; Tomi Ungerer; David Walker; Jay Williams.

McVITTY, Walter. Managing director, Walter McVitty Books, Glebe, New South Wales. Author of *Innocence and Experience: Essays on Contemporary Australian Children's Writers,* 1982, *Australian Children's Authors,* 1986, *Australian Children's Illustrators and Authors,* 1986, *International Children's Authors,* 1988, *Classic Children's Authors,* 1988, *Dorothy Wall: The Creator of Blinky Bill,* 1988, and *Australian Poets,* 1989. **Essays:** Ronda Armitage; Bette Greene; Ted Greenwood; David Martin; Christobel Mattingley; Dick Roughsey.

MEEK, Margaret. Reader in education, University of London Institute of Education. Former reviews editor, *School Librarian.* Author of *Geoffrey Trease,* 1960, *Rosemary Sutcliff,* 1962, *Learning to Read,* 1982, *Achieving Literacy,* 1983, *On Being Literate,* 1989, and other books on literacy and education; contributor of articles to *Times Literary Supplement* and *Times Educational Supplement.* Editor, with Aidan Warlow and Griselda Barton, of *The Cool Web: The Pattern of Children's Reading,* 1977, with Jane Miller, *Changing English: Essays for Harold Rosen,* 1984, and, with Colin Mills, *Language and Literacy in the Primary School,* 1988. **Essays:** Honor Arundel; Shirley Hughes.

MENDELSOHN, Leonard R. Associate professor of English, Concordia University, Montreal. Former editor of *Children's Literature.* Author of "The Survival of the Spirit in Holocaust Children's Literature" in *Triumph of the Spirit in Children's Literature* edited by Francelia Butler, 1986; contributor of articles on Aeschylus, Milton, Kafka, Renaissance drama, speed reading, toys, utopian writing, and other subjects to journals including *Studies in English Literature, Comparative Drama, Studies in Short Fiction,* and *Language Arts.* **Essays:** Frank Asch; Rex Benedict; Ann Blades; William Pène du Bois; Wanda Gág; Phyllis Krasilovsky; Joan M. Lexau; George Selden.

MERCIER, Cathryn M. Assistant director, Center for the Study of Children's Literature, and instructor in children's literature, Simmons College, Boston; reviewer for *The Five Owls.* **Essays:** Molly Bang; Beverly Cleary; Helen V. Griffith; Mavis Jukes.

MERCIER, Jean F. Former children's books editor, *Publishers Weekly,* New York, and freelance editor. Author of novel *Whatever You Do, Don't Panic,* 1961; contributor of articles and fiction to periodicals. **Essays:** Roger Duvoisin; Jean Fritz; Hardie Gramatky; Ruth Krauss; Charlotte Zolotow.

MEYERS, Susan. Freelance writer; contributing editor, *Learning.* Author of the children's books *Melissa Finds a Mystery,* 1966, *The Cabin on the Fjord,* 1968, *The Mysterious Bender Bones,* 1970, *The Truth about Gorillas,* 1980, *Pearson, A Harbor Seal Pup,* 1980, *P.J. Clover, Private Eye,* 2 vols., 1981-85, and *The Case of the Borrowed Baby,* 1988. **Essay:** E. C. Spykman.

MILLER, Christine. Branch assistant, Tecumseh Branch, Allen County Public Library, Fort Wayne, Indiana. **Essays:** Elizabeth Levy; Jon Scieszka.

MILLS, Colin. Senior lecturer in teaching studies, Worcester College of Higher Education. Author of articles and reviews in *Times Literary Supplement, Guardian, School Librarian,* and books for Keeps. Contributor to *Fiction Six to Nine,* 1987. Editor, with Margaret Meek, of *Language and Literacy in the Primary School,* 1988. **Essays:** Ruth Ainsworth; Margaret Stuart Barry; Helen Morgan; Gareth Owen; Richard Parker; Mary Rayner; David Wood.

MILLS, Joan. Founding director, Common Knowledge Theatre Company; organiser of the Academi Gymreig Playwrights Group; freelance director in Wales. Former director of the Young People's Theatre Scheme, Royal Court Theatre, London. **Essay:** Ann Jellicoe.

MILNES, Irma McDonough. Freelance writer. Founding editor, *In Review: Canadian Books for Children,* Toronto, 1967-82. Author of articles and reviews in *Quill and Quire, Saturday Night, School Library Journal, Emergency Librarian,* and other periodicals. Editor of *Profiles 1-2,* 1975-82, and *Canadian Books for Children,* 1976. **Essay:** Ruth Nichols.

MITCHISON, Naomi. See her own entry. **Essays:** Peggy Appiah; Rhoda Power.

MOE, Christian H. Professor of theatre, Southern Illinois University, Carbondale; director of Playwrights' Program, Association for Theater in Higher Education. Author of *Creating Historical Drama* (with George McCalmon), 1965, and of an essay on D.H. Lawrence as playwright, and, with Cameron Garbutt, of several plays for children. Joint editor of *The William and Mary Theatre: A Chronicle,* 1968, "Bibliography of Theatrical Craftsmanship" (published annually in several journals), 1971-80, and *Six New Plays for Children,* 1971. **Essays:** Margaret Wise Brown; Charlotte Chorpenning; Joanna Halpert Kraus; Betty Jean Lifton; Constance D'Arcy Mackay; Stuart Walker.

MOLSON, Francis J. Professor of English, Central Michigan University, Mount Pleasant. Author of *Children's Fantasy,* 1988, and of the chapter on juvenile science fiction in *Anatomy of Wonder,* revised edition 1981; contributor of articles on Emily Dickinson, Louise Fitzhugh, Frances Hodgson Burnett, Francis Finn, Ursula K. LeGuin, and children's fantasy and science fiction. **Essay:** Madeleine L'Engle.

MOORE, Doris Langley. Writer and historian of costume. Founder and former adviser, Museum of Costume, Bath; designer of period clothes for films and ballet. Author of many books: novels include *A Winter's Passion,* 1932, *They Knew Her When,* 1938, *All Done by Kindness,* 1951, and *My Caravaggio Style,* 1959; nonfiction includes *E. Nesbit: A Biography,* 1933 (revised 1966), *Pleasure: A Discursive Guide Book,* 1953, *The Late Lord Byron,* 1961, *Lord Byron: Accounts Rendered,* 1974, *Ada, Countess of Lovelace,* 1977, and other biographies and books on the history of fashion and taste. Died 1989. **Essay:** E. Nesbit.

MOOREHEAD, Caroline. Freelance writer and journalist. Author of *Helping: A Guide to Voluntary Work,* 1975, *Fortune's Hostages: Kidnapping in the World Today,* 1980, *Sidney Bernstein: A Biography,* 1984, *Freya Stark,* 1985, *Troublesome People: Enemies of War 1916-1986,* 1987; contributor of reviews to the *Times, Times Literary Supplement and Educational Supplement,* and *London Review of Books.* Editor of *Myths and Legends of Britain,* 1968, *The Letters of Freya Stark,* 2 vols., 1982, and *Betrayal: Child Exploitation in Today's World,* 1989. **Essay:** Hugh Lofting.

MOSS, Anita. Associate professor of English, University of North Carolina, Charlotte; editor, *Children's Literature in Education.* Author of many articles and reviews in *Children's Literature, Lion and the Unicorn, Children's Literature Association Quarterly,* and other periodicals. Editor, with Jon C. Stott, of *The Family of Stories: A Children's Literature Anthology,* 1986. **Essays:** Julia Cunningham; Louise Fitzhugh; Isabelle Holland; William Steig.

MOSS, Elaine. Children's books adviser, *The Good Book Guide,* 1980-86. Recipient, Eleanor Farjeon award, 1976. Selected and annotated *Children's Books of the Year* for the National Book League, 1970-79; author of *Picture Books for Young People 9-13,* 1981, *A Tale Unfolds,* 1984, *The Peter Piper* series, 1984, and *Part of the Pattern: A Personal Journey Through the World of Children's Books 1960-1985,* 1986. **Essay:** Pat Hutchins.

MUIR, Marcie. Freelance writer and bibliographer. Author of *A Bibliography of Australian Children's Books,* 2 vols., 1970-76, *Australian Children's Book Illustrators,* 1977, *Charlotte Barton: Australia's First Children's Author,* 1980, *A History of Australian Children's Book Illustration,* 1982, and *The Fairy World of Ida Rentoul Outhwaite* (with Robert Holden), 1985. **Essays:** Mary Durack; May Gibbs; Dorothy Wall.

NETTELL, Stephanie. Children's books editor, *Guardian,* London. Former editor of *Books and Bookmen.* Editor of *Guardian Angels* (short story anthology), 1987. **Essays:** Donald Bisset; Andrew Davies; Dick King-Smith.

NETTLEFOLD, Mary. Assistant manager of library supplies, Blacklock Farries Library, Dumfries, Scotland. **Essay:** Monica Edwards.

NEUMEYER, Peter F. Professor emeritus of English and comparative literature, San Diego State University. Author of four children's books, *Homage to John Clare,* 1980, the entry on E. B. White in *Dictionary of Literary Biography;* also author of articles on the draft versions of each of White's children's books, 1982-88. Editor of *Twentieth-Century Interpretations of The Castle,* 1969, *Elements of Fiction* (with William C. Carpenter), 1974, and *The Phantom of the Opera* (children's version), 1988. **Essay:** E. B. White.

NOAKES, Vivien. Freelance writer. Author of *Edward Lear: The Life of a Wanderer,* 1968 (revised, 1979, 1985), and *Edward Lear 1812-1888* (exhibition catalogue), 1985. Editor of *For Lovers of Edward Lear,* 1978, *Scenes from Victorian Life,* 1979, and *Selected Letters of Edward Lear,* 1988. **Essay:** Edward Lear (appendix).

OSA, Osayimwense. Head of Department of Languages and Literature, Bendel State University, Ekpoma, Nigeria; editor, *Journal of Education, Ekpoma Journal of Languages and Literary Studies,* and *Journal of African Children's Literature.* Author of *Nigerian Youth Literature,* 1987; contributor of numerous articles to *Children's Literature and Youth Literature* and other journals. Editor of *Youth Literature International,* 1988. **Essays:** Buchi Emecheta; Anezi Okoro; Mabel D. Segun.

OSLER, Ruth. Boys and Girls coordinator, Toronto Public Library. **Essay:** Catherine Anthony Clark.

PATON WALSH, Jill. See her own entry. **Essays:** C. Walter Hodges; Gregory Maguire.

PAUL, Lissa. Professor of English, University of New Brunswick, Fredericton. Author of *Growing with Books,* 1988. **Essays:** Janet Lunn; Ann Thwaite; Tim Wynne-Jones.

PEARSON, Kit. Author of children's books; part-time reference librarian, Burnaby Public Library, British Columbia. Author of *The Daring Game,* 1986, and *A Handful of Time,* 1987. **Essay:** Sylvia Cassedy.

PFLIEGER, Pat. Assistant professor of English, West Chester University, Pennsylvania. Author of *A Reference Guide to Modern Fantasy for Children,* 1984, and a forthcoming book on Beverly Cleary. **Essay:** Jane Louise Curry.

PIEHL, Kathy. Assistant professor and reference librarian, Mankato State University, Minnesota. Contributor of articles on children's and young adult books in *Children's Literature in Education, New Advocate, Children's Literature Association Quarterly, English Journal, Journal of Youth Services in Libraries, Voice of Youth Advocates,* and other journals. **Essays:** Gloria Houston; Dayal Kaur Khalsa.

PINNEY, Reba. Professor of education, Ohio University, Athens. Author of various journal articles and reviews. **Essay:** Leonard Everett Fisher.

PROTHEROUGH, Robert. Formerly senior lecturer in English in Education, Hull University. Author of seven books for teachers and lecturers, numerous articles; editor, *English in Education*; reviewer for many journals, including *Times Educational Supplement* and *School Librarian.* **Essays:** John Agard; James Berry; Raymond Briggs; Aidan Chambers; Roger McGough; Iona and Peter Opie; Brian Patten; Ann Pilling.

QUAYLE, Eric. Freelance writer. Author of *Ballantyne the Brave,* 1967, and a bibliography of Ballantyne, *The Ruin of Sir Walter Scott,* 1968, *The Collector's Book* series, 4 vols., 1971-73, *Old Cook Books: An Illustrated History,* 1978, *Early Children's Books: A Collector's Guide,* 1983, *The Magic Ointment and Other Cornish Legends,* 1986, and *The Shining Princess and Other Japanese Legends,* 1989. **Essay:** R. M. Ballantyne (appendix).

RAY, Sheila G. Editor, *School Librarian.* Author of *Children's Fiction,* 1970 (revised 1972), *Children's Librarianship,* 1979, *The Blyton Phenomenon,* 1982, *Library Service to Schools,* 3rd edition 1982, and of contributions to *Children's Literature Abstracts.* **Essays:** Prudence Andrew; Enid Blyton; Virginia Pye.

RAYNOR, Mary. See her own entry. **Essays:** Joyce Lankester Brisley; Dhan Gopal Mukerji.

REES, David. See his own entry. **Essay:** Meriol Trevor.

REEVES, James. See his own entry. **Essay:** Edward Ardizzone.

RICHARDSON, Selma K. Associate professor, Graduate School of Library and Information Science, University of Illinois, Urbana. Author of *Periodicals for School Media Programs,* 1978, *Analytical Survey of Illinois Public Library Services to Children,* 1978, *Magazines for Children,* 1983, and *Magazines for Young Adults,* 1984. Editor for *Children's Services of Public Libraries,* 1978, *Research about Nineteenth-Century Children and Books,* 1979, and *Study and Collecting of Historical Children's Books,* 1979. **Essay:** Florence Parry Heide.

ROGER, Mae Durham. Senior lecturer, School of Library and Information Studies, University of California, Berkeley. Author of *Tit for Tat and Other Latvian Folk Tales,* 1967, *Tobei: A Japanese Folktale,* 1974, and of the proceedings of the *International Jerusalem Symposium on Encouraging Reading,* 1983, 1985, 1987; contributor of articles to periodicals. Editor of *Literature Sampler: Junior Edition,* 1964. **Essays:** Clyde Robert Bulla; Don Freeman; Ruth Stiles Gannett; Sulamith Ish-Kishor.

ROGINSKI, Jim. Freelance writer, seminar leader, and publisher. Author of *Newbery and Caldecott Medalists and Honor Book Winners: Bibliographies and Resource Material Through 1977,* 1982. Editor of *Behind the Covers: Interviews with Authors and Illustrators of Children's and Young Adult Books,* 1985, 1989, and other reference books about children's books. **Essays:** Walter R. Brooks; Judith Viorst.

ROMALOV, Nancy Tillman. Instructor in children's literature, University of Iowa, Iowa City. Contributor of articles and reviews to *Lion and the Unicorn* and *Children's Literature Association Quarterly.* **Essay:** Vera B. Williams.

RUBIO, Gerald J. Assistant professor of English Literature, University of Guelph, Ontario; editor, *Sidney Newsletter.* Contributor of articles and reviews to *Canadian Children's Literature* and other journals. **Essay:** Monica Hughes.

RUBIO, Mary. Co-editor, *CCL: Canadian Children's Literature/Littérature canadienne pour la jeunese,* Guelph, Ontario; associate professor of English, University of Guelph. Editor, with Elizabeth Waterston, of *The Selected Journals of L.M. Montgomery,* 2 vols., 1985-87. **Essays:** Norman Duncan; Jean Little; Robert Munsch; Barbara Claassen Smucker.

RUSSELL, Jean. Editor of *Books for Your Children,* Ashbourne, Derbyshire, and children's books consultant. Editor of *The Methuen Book of Strange Tales* [and *Sinister Stories*], 2 vols., 1980-82. Died 1983. **Essay:** Joan Tate.

SADLER, Glenn Edward. Professor of English, Bloomsburg University, Pennsylvania. Editor of *The Gifts of the Child Christ,* 2 vols., 1973, *The Portent,* 1979, and *The Flight of the Shadow,* 1979, all by George Macdonald, and of the forthcoming *The Letters of George MacDonald and His Wife* and an edition of MacDonald's poetry. **Essay:** George MacDonald (appendix).

SAGE, Alison. Freelance editor and writer. Author of several picture books for children, including the *Teddy Bears* series, from 1978, *Stay Indoors,* 1987, *A Way of Seeing,* an illustrated series of fiction and non-fiction, and *Play Beethoven* [and *Mozart*], 2 vols., 1988. Editor of *The Book of Art,* 1979. **Essays:** Bettina; Constance Heward; Lois Lamplugh.

SALWAY, Lance. Freelance writer and translator. Author of many books for children, including *Second to the Right and Straight On Till Morning,* 1979, *A Nasty Piece of Work,* 1983, *The Haunting of Hemlock Hall,* 1984, and *The Darkness under the Stairs,* 1988, and of books and articles about children's literature, including *A Peculiar Gift,* 1976, and *Reading about Children's Books: An Introductory Guide to Books about Children's Literature,* 1986. Editor of collections of stories for children and translator of 17 Dutch children's books. **Essays:** Violet Needham; M. Pardoe.

SAULSBURY, Rebecca. Graduate student in American studies, Purdue University. **Essay:** Robert Nye.

SAXBY, Maurice. Former head of English Department, Kuring-gai College of Advanced Education, New South Wales. Author of *A History of Australian Children's Literature 1841-1941* and *1941-1970,* 2 vols., 1969-71, *Dimensions* series (with G. Smith, 1977-78, *Through Folklore to Literature,* 1979, *Give Them Wings* (with G. Winch), 1987, and *Teaching Literature to Adolescents* (with V. Hoogstadt), 1988. **Essays:** Mary Grant Bruce; Nan Chauncy; Libby Gleeson; Libby Hathorn; Elyne Mitchell; Leslie Rees; Bill Scott; Nadia Wheatley.

SCHAFER, Elizabeth D. Independent scholar; Ph.D. in American history, Auburn University. Co-author of *Women Who Made a Difference in Alabama,* 1995; contributor of article to *African American Review.* **Essays:** Elizabeth Levy; Jenny Seed.

SCHMIDT, Nancy J. African Studies Area specialist, Indiana University Library, Bloomington; editor, *Africana Libraries Newsletter.* Author of *Children's Books on Africa and Their Authors: An Annotated Bibliography,* 1975 (supplement 1979), *Children's Literature and Audio-Visual Materials on Africa,* 1975; *Children's Fiction about Africa in English,* 1981; contributor of articles on children's literature, Nigerian fiction, folklore, and other topics in African literature to *Journal of the New African Literatures and the Arts, Africa Report,* and other periodicals, and frequent reviews of children's literature in *African Book Publishing Record* and *School Library Journal.* **Essays:** Chinua Achebe; Meshack Asare; J. O. de Graft-Hanson; Cyprian Ekwensi; Elijah Kariuki; Flora Nwapa; Asenath Odaga; Jenny Seed.

SEGUN, Mabel D. See her own entry. **Essay:** Barbara Kimenye.

SEITER, Richard D. Associate professor of English, Central Michigan University, Mount Pleasant. Author of articles on Eleanor Cameron, Roald Dahl, Ezra I. Keats, Robert C. O'Brien, and Henry Treece. **Essay:** Brock Cole.

SHEPHERDSON, Nancy. Freelance writer. **Essay:** Mary Elwyn Patchett.

SHUTE, Carolyn. Staff assistant, Center for the Study of Children's Literature, Simmons College, Boston. Author of "Stout as Jessie's Shadow in *The Slave Dancer*" in *The Bulletin* (Children's Literature Assembly), 1988. **Essays:** Eleanor Estes; Mildred Pitts Walter.

SILES, Dorothy D. Head of technical services, Lafayette College, Easton, Pennsylvania; reviewer for *Library Journal* and *Choice.* **Essay:** Dorothy Canfield Fisher.

SIRCAR, Sanjay. Member of Department of English, University of Queensland, Brisbane. Author, with Rani Sircar, of several children's books about India. **Essay:** Evadne Price.

SMEDMAN, M. Sarah. Associate professor of English, University of North Carolina, Charlotte. Author of the entries on Sarah Josepha Hale, Martha Finley, Peter Spier, and Katherine Paterson in *Dictionary of Literary Biography;* contributor of articles on the contemporary picture book and 17th- and 18th-century conduct books for girls. **Essays:** Martha Finley (appendix); Katherine Paterson.

SMITH, Karen Patricia. Assistant professor, Graduate School of Library and Information Studies, Queens College, Flushing, New York; board member, Children's Literature Association. Author of "The English Psychological Fantasy Novel: A Bequest of Time" in *School Library Journal,* 1985, and "Claiming a Place in the University: The Portrayal of Minorities in Seven Works by Andre Norton" in *Top of the News,* 1986. Editor, with Rod McGillis, of "Special Section on Black Children's Literature" in *Children's Literature Association Quarterly,* 1988. **Essays:** Jeannie Baker; Percy Trezise.

SORFLEET, John Robert. Associate professor of English and Canadian studies, Concordia University, Montreal; member of editorial board, *Canadian Children's Literature*; contributor to *The Canadian Encyclopedia.* Author of *The Poems of Bliss Carman,* 1976, *The Work of Margaret Laurence,* 1980, and other books. Editor of *L. M. Montgomery: An Assessment,* 1976, and *Canadian Children's Drama and Theatre,* 1978. **Essays:** John D. Fitzgerald; John F. Hayes; James A. Houston; Dennis Lee; L.M. Montgomery.

STAHL, John D. Associate professor of English, Virginia Tech, Blacksburg, Virginia. Author of *Mark Twain, Culture and Gender* (Georgia, 1994); contributor of articles about children's literature in *Children's Literature, The Lion and the Unicorn,* and other journals. **Essays:** Shonto Begay; Mercer Mayer; Phyllis Reynolds Naylor; Doris Orgel; Stella Pevsner.

STEFFEL, Susan B. Professor of English, Central Michigan University, Mount Pleasant. **Essay:** Madeleine L'Engle.

STERCK, Kenneth J. Former member of the editorial committee, *Children's Literature in Education.* Joint editor of *Writers, Critics and Children,* 1976. Died 1988. **Essays:** Jacynth Hope-Simpson; Percy Westerman.

STERN, Madeleine B. Freelance writer; partner in Leona Rostenberg and Madeleine Stern Rare Books, New York. Author of *Imprints on History; Book Publishers and American Frontiers,* 1956, *We the Women: Career Firsts of Nineteenth-Century America,* 1963, *Heads and Headlines: The Phrenological Fowlers,* 1971, *Books and Book People in 19th Century America,* 1978, *Between Boards: New Thoughts on Old Books* (with Leona Rostenberg), 1978, *Antiquarian Bookselling in the United States: A History from the Origins to the 1940's,* 1985, *Old and Rare: Forty Years in the Book Business* (with Leona Rostenberg), 1988, and of biographies of Margaret Fuller, Louisa May Alcott, Mrs. Frank Leslie, Isabel Barrows, and Stephen Pearl Andrews. Editor of *Women on the Move,* 1972, *The Victoria Woodhull Reader,* 1974, *Publishers for Mass Entertainment in the 19th-Century America,* 1980, *Phrenological Dictionary of 19th-Century Americans,* 1982, and *Critical Essays on Louisa May Alcott,* 1984, and of *Louisa's Wonder Book,* 1975, *Behind a Mask: The Unknown Thrillers of Louisa May Alcott,* 1975, *Plots and Counterplots: More Unknown Thrillers,* 1976, *A Modern Mephistopheles and Taming a Tartar,* 1987, and *A Double Life: Newly Discovered Thrillers of Louisa May Alcott,* 1988, all by Louisa May Alcott; associate editor of *Selected Letters of Louisa May Alcott,* 1988, and *The Journals of Louisa May Alcott,* 1989. **Essay:** Louisa May Alcott (appendix).

STONES, Rosemary. Senior editor, Collins publishers, London; children's books reviewer and critic; co-editor, *Children's Book Bulletin,* London. Author of *The Spare Rib List on Non-Sexist Children's Books,* 1979, *A Penguin Multi-Ethnic Booklist,* 1982, *"Pour Out the Cocoa, Janet": Sexism in Children's Books,* 1983, *Too Close Encounters and What to Do about Them,* 1987, and *Loving Encounters: A Book for Teenagers About Sex,* 1988. Editor of *More to Life than Mr. Right,* 1985, and *Someday My Prince Won't Come,* 1988. **Essays:** Leila Berg; Bill Naughton.

STOTT, Christine Doyle. Educational consultant; freelance writer. **Essays:** Marc Brown; Shirley Climo; Syd Hoff; Johanna Hurwitz; Wendell Minor; Anne Rockwell; Joanne Ryder.

STOTT, Jon C. Professor emeritus of English, University of Alberta, Edmonton. Founding director, Children's Literature Association. Author of *Children's Literature from A to Z,* 1984, and *A Guide to Authors and Illustrators* (with Raymond E. Jones), 1988. Editor with Anita Moss, of *The Family of Stories: A Children's Literature Anthology,* 1986. **Essays:** Sue Ann Alderson; Ann Blades; Bill Freeman; Maria Louise Gay; Phoebe Gilman; Paul Goble; Roderick Haig-Brown; Hazel Hutchins; William Kurelek; Don Kushner; Michael Kusugak; Claire Mackay; Robin Muller; Mordecai Richler; Ian Wallace; Leo Yerxa.

SUTHERLAND, Zena. Professor emerita, University of Chicago Graduate Library School; associate editor, *Bulletin of the Center for Children's Books.* Author of *History in Children's Books,* 1967, *The Best in Children's Books,* 1973 (revised 1980, 1986), *Burning Bright,* 1979, *Close to the Sun,* 1979, *Barnboken i USA* (with Fred Erisman, 1986, *Children and Books* (with May Hill Arbuthnot), 7th edition 1986, and with M. Cunningham, *Across the World, From Sea to Shining Sea, Over the Moon, Promises to Keep, Slide Down the Sky, Sound of the Sea,* and *Time for Dreams,* all 1989. Editor of *The Arbuthnot Anthology* (with May Hill Arbuthnot), 4th edition 1976, *The Arbuthnot Lectures 1970-1979,* 1980, *Children in Libraries,* 1981, and *The Scott Foresman Anthology of Children's Literature* (with Myra Cohn Livingston), 1984. **Essays:** Martha Bacon; Florence Hightower; Harold Keith; Evelyn Sibley Lampman.

TARBOX, Gwen Athene. Assistant professor of American literature, children's literature, and ethnic studies, California State University, Hayward. **Essays:** Verna Aardema; Stan and Jan Berenstain; Elizabeth Beresford; Lucille Clifton; Libby Gleason; Helen V. Griffith; Mavis Jukes; Michael Rosen.

TAYLOR, Jennifer. Freelance writer, reviewer, and editor; contributor to *Bookseller* and *School Librarian.* **Essays:** Michael Foreman; Helen Oxenbury.

THOMAS, Joyce. Associate professor of English, Castleton State College, Vermont. Author of *Inside the Wolf's Belly: Aspects of the Fairy Tale,* 1989, and of articles on and reviews of children's literature. **Essay:** Chris Van Allsburg.

THWAITE, Ann. See her own entry. **Essays:** Angela Banner; Frances Hodgson Burnett; V. H. Drummond; Mary K. Harris; Penelope Lively.

TOWNSEND, John Rowe. See his own entry. **Essays:** Peter Dickinson; John Gordon; A. A. Milne.

TREASE, Geoffrey. See his own entry. **Essays:** Kitty Barne; Frederick Grice; G. A. Henty (appendix); Charlotte Hough; Barbara Sleigh; Elfrida Vipont.

TROTMAN, Felicity. Freelance editor and writer; fiction editor, Puffin, 1971-79, and Macmillan, 1980-82; co-founder, Signpost Books; has written on animals in the movies. **Essays:** K. M. Briggs; Niki Daly; Barbara C. Freeman; Geraldine Harris; Jill Murphy.

TYE, Margaret M. Collage librarian, North Cheshire College, Warrington. **Essays:** Bruce Carter; Barbara Leonie Picard; Philip Rush; Barbara Ker Wilson.

VANDERGRIFT, Kay E. Associate professor, School of Communication, Information and Library Studies, Rutgers University, New Brunswick, New Jersey; children's book reviewer for *School Library Journal.* Author of *Child and Story: The Literary Connection,* 1980, and *Children's Literature: Theory, Research and Teaching,* 1989. **Essays:** Verna Aardema; Marcia Brown; Barbara Cohen; Barbara Cooney; Donald Crews; Nikki Giovanni; Janet Taylor Lisle; Mary E. Lyons; Patricia Polacco; Nancy Tafuri.

VANSITTART, Peter. Novelist, historian, and critic. Author of more than 30 books, including three books for children; most recent novels are *Three Six Seven,* 1983, *Aspects of Feeling,* 1986, and *Parsifal,* 1988. Editor of *Voices from the Great War,* 1981, *Voices 1870-1914,* 1984, *John Masefield's Letters from the Front 1915-1917,* 1984, *Aspects of Royalty, Happy and Glorious: A Collins Anthology of Royalty,* 1988, and *Voices of the French Revolution,* 1989. **Essays:** F. Anstey (appendix); Leonard Clark; Robert Nye; Joan G. Robinson.

WALKER, Margaret. Chairwoman, Scottish Children's Book Association, Glasgow; editor, *Book Window.* **Essays:** Michael Bond; Angus MacVicar; Iona McGregor; Allan Campbell McLean.

WARLOW, Aidan. Founder and director of a school in Cumbria. Author of *Reading Matters* (with Moira McKenzie), 1978, and *Starting with Rhymes,* 1982. Editor, with Margaret Meek and Griselda Barton, of *The Cool Web: The Pattern of Children's Reading,* 1977. **Essay:** Anna Sewell (appendix).

WATERS, Fiona. Editor, Bodley Head publishers. Editor of *Out of the Blue,* 1982, *The Cat King's Daughter,* 1984, and *Golden Apples,* 1985. **Essays:** Cicely Mary Barker; Dorothy Edwards; Hilda Lewis; Willard Price.

WELSH, Marcia. Reference librarian and cataloguer, Guilford Free Library, Connecticut. Reviewer for *Library Journal.* **Essays:** Jan Brett; Edward Gorey; William Joyce; Diane Stanley; Jane Yolen.

WHALLEY, Joyce Irene. Former assistant keeper, Victoria and Albert Museum Library, London. Organised Beatrix Potter exhibition at the Victoria and Albert Museum, 1972. Author of *English Handwriting 1540-1843,* 1969, *Writing Implements and Accessories,* 1975, *Cobwebs to Catch Flies: Illustrated Books for the Nursery and Schoolroom 1700-1900,* 1975, *The Pen's Excellence: Calligraphy in Western Europe and America,* 1980, *The*

Student's Guide to Western Calligraphy, 1984, *Beatrix Potter, The V & A Collection* (with Anne Hobbs), 1985, *Beatrix Potter 1866-1943: The Artist and Her World* (with Judy Taylor and others), 1987, *Beatrix Potter's Derwentwater* (with Wynne Bartlett), 1988, and *A History of Naturalis* by Pliny, 1982. **Essays:** Mary Louisa Molesworth (appendix); Beatrix Potter.

WHITBY, Joy. Independent television producer and writer, Grasshopper Productions, London. Credits for television series include *Play School, Jackanory, Catweazle, The Book Tower, The EBU Drama Exchange for Children, Emma and Grandpa,* and *East of the Moon.* Author of the children's novel *Grasshopper Island,* 1971. **Essay:** Anita Hewett.

WHITE, Kerry. Freelance writer and bibliographer. Author of *Australian Children's Books: A Bibliography,* 1992, *Australian Children's Fiction: The Subject Guide,* 1993; also author of numerous articles and reviews on Australian writing. **Essays:** Pamela Allen; Hesba Brinsmead; Anna Fienberg; Simon French; Bob Graham; Lee Harding; Jenny Wagner.

WHITEHEAD, Frank. Reader in English and education, University of Sheffield, 1973-81; editor, *Use of English,* 1969-1975. Author of *The Disappearing Dais,* 1966, *Creative Experiment,* 1970, and *Children and Their Books* (with others), 1977. **Essays:** Helen Bannerman; Hester Burton; Harry Graham; Kathleen Hale.

WHITEHEAD, Winifred. Former senior lecturer in English literature and Curriculum Studies, Sheffield City Polytechnic. Author of *Faces: Growing Up with Books in a Multicultural Society,* 1988; contributor of many articles on children's writers to *Use of English* and other periodicals; also author of seven bibliographies of fiction for schools. **Essays:** Lynne Reid Banks; Nina Beachcroft; L. Leslie Brooke; Peter Carter; Elizabeth Borton de Treviño; Marjorie Flack; Ursula Moray Williams; Marguerite Poland.

WIGAN, Angela. Freelance writer. Co-author of *A Short and Remarkable History of New York City*; has written for *Time* and the Museum of Modern Art, New York City. **Essay:** Joseph Bruchac.

WILLIAMS, Martin. Editor, special projects, Smithsonian Institution Press, Washington, D.C. Author of several on jazz, including *The Jazz Tradition,* 1970 (revised 1983), *Jazz Heritage,* 1985, and *Jazz in Its Time,* 1989, and of *Griffith: First Artist of the Movies,* 1981; contributor of articles on Johnny Gruelle to *Children's Literature,* 1974, and L. Frank Baum. Editor of *More Raggedy Ann and Andy Stories* by Gruelle, 1977, and *A Smithsonian Book of Comic-Book Comics* (with Michael Barrier), 1982. **Essays:** L. Frank Baum; Johnny Gruelle.

WILMS, Denise Murcko. Children's books reviewer, American Library Association *Booklist,* Chicago. Author of *Science Books for Children from Booklist 1976-1983,* 1985. Editor, with Ilene L. Cooper, of *A Guide to Non-Sexist Children's Books 2: 1976-1984,* 1987. **Essay:** Eloise Greenfield.

WILSON, Barbara Ker. See her own entry. **Essays:** Mavis Thorpe Clark; Max Fatchen; George Finkel; Elisabeth MacIntyre.

WROBLE, Lisa A. Freelance writer and author of fiction and nonfiction for children and nonfiction for adults. Contributor to *Dictionary of Literary Biography.* **Essays:** Natalie Babbitt; Judy Blume; Patricia MacLachlan; Patricia and Frederick McKissack; Terry Pratchett.

YATES, Jessica. Freelance writer; reviewer for *School Librarian, Times Educational Supplement,* British Science Fiction Association and the Tolkien Society. Former school librarian. Author of *Tudors and Stuarts: An Annotated Bibliography of Children's Fiction,* 1977, the text for *A Middle-earth Album,* 1979, *Teenager to Young Adult: Recent Paperback Fiction for 13 to 19 Years,* 1986, and of articles on children's literature and librarianship in *Children's Literature in Education, Children's Book Bulletin, Books for Keeps, Times Educational Supplement,* and *School Librarian.* **Essays:** Annie Dalton; Marjorie Darke; Winifred Finlay; Diana Wynne Jones; Terry Pratchett; Mary Ray; J. R. R. Tolkien.

YEATMAN, Linda. Editor of children's books, Lutterworth Press, Cambridge. Author of the children's books *Noah's Ark,* 1984, and *Pickles, Perkins, Buttons,* 3 vols., 1988. Editor of *Best Book of Outdoor Games* [and *Indoor Games*], 2 vols., 1976-77, and *A Treasury of Bedtime Stories* [and *Animal Stories*], 2 vols., 1981-82. **Essays:** Christine Pullein-Thompson; Diana Pullein-Thompson; David Severn.

YOLEN, Jane. See her own entry. **Essays:** Sid Fleischman; F. N. Monjo; Clyde Watson.

ZAIDMAN, Laura M. Professor of English, University of South Carolina, Sumter. Contributor to *Dictionary of Literary Biography,* and of articles in other journals. Editor of *British Children's Writers, 1880-1914,* Vol. 141 of the *Dictionary of Literary Biography.* Guest co-editor, with Lois Rauch Gibson, of *Children's Literature Association Quarterly,* winter 1991 issue. **Essay:** Lois Lowry.

ZOPPA, Linda. Freelance writer. **Essay:** Pat Cummings.